Y0-AQW-145

# Who's Who in America®

## Published by Marquis Who's Who®

**Titles in Print**

Who's Who in America®
Who Was Who in America®
  Historical Volume (1607–1896)
  Volume I (1897–1942)
  Volume II (1943–1950)
  Volume III (1951–1960)
  Volume IV (1961–1968)
  Volume V (1969–1973)
  Volume VI (1974–1976)
  Volume VII (1977–1981)
  Volume VIII (1982–1985)
  Volume IX (1985–1989)
  Volume X (1989–1993)
  Volume XI (1993–1996)
  Index Volume (1607–1996)
Who's Who in the World®
Who's Who in the East®
Who's Who in the Midwest®
Who's Who in the South and Southwest®
Who's Who in the West®
Who's Who in American Art™
Who's Who in American Education®
Who's Who in American Law®
Who's Who in American Nursing®
Who's Who in American Politics™
Who's Who in Entertainment®
Who's Who in Finance and Industry®
Who's Who in Medicine and Healthcare™
Who's Who in Religion™
Who's Who in Science and Engineering®
Who's Who in the Media and Communications™
Who's Who of American Women®
Who's Who of Emerging Leaders in America®
Index to Marquis Who's Who® Publications
The *Official* ABMS Directory of Board Certified Medical Specialists®

**Available on CD-ROM**

The Complete Marquis Who's Who® on CD-ROM
ABMS Medical Specialists *PLUS*™

# Who'sWho in America®

## *1998*

## 52nd Edition

## Volume 3
## Indexes

MARQUIS
Who'sWho®  121 Chanlon Road
New Providence, NJ 07974 U.S.A.

# Who's Who in America®

## Marquis Who's Who®

Published by Marquis Who's Who, a division of Reed Elsevier Inc.

Copyright ©1997 by Reed Elsevier Inc. All rights reserved.

No part of this publication may be reproduced, stored in a retrieval system, or transmitted, in any form or by any means—including, but not limited to, electronic, mechanical, photocopying, recording, or otherwise—or used for any commercial purpose whatsoever without the prior written permission of the publisher and, if publisher deems necessary, execution of a formal license agreement with publisher. For information, contact Marquis Who's Who, 121 Chanlon Road, New Providence, New Jersey 07974, 1-908-464-6800.

WHO'S WHO IN AMERICA is a registered trademark of Reed Publishing (Nederland) B.V., used under license.

Library of Congress Catalog Card Number 4-16934

International Standard Book Number   0-8379-0183-9 (set, Classic Edition)
0-8379-0186-3 (volume 3, Classic Edition)
0-8379-0187-1 (set, Deluxe Edition)
0-8379-0190-1 (volume 3, Deluxe Edition)

International Standard Serial Number   0083-9396

No payment is either solicited or accepted for the inclusion of entries in this publication. Marquis Who's Who has used its best efforts in collecting and preparing material for inclusion in this publication, but does not warrant that the information herein is complete or accurate, and does not assume, and hereby disclaims, any liability to any person for any loss or damage caused by errors or omissions in this publication, whether such errors or omissions result from negligence, accident, or any other cause.

Manufactured in the United States of America

# Table of Contents

# Introduction

The *Who's Who in America* Geographic and Professional Indexes provide access to biographical information in the 52nd Edition through two avenues in alphabetical form—geography and profession. Each Biographee entry contains name and occupational description. A dagger symbol (†) indicates a new name first appearing in the 52nd Edition.

The Geographic Index lists names in the United States under state and city designations, as well as Biographees in American territories. Canadian listings include provinces and cities. Names in Mexico and other countries appear by city. Biographees whose addresses are not published in their sketches are found under Address Unpublished.

The Professional Index includes thirty-eight categories ranging alphabetically from Agriculture to Social Science. Within each area, the names appear under geographic subheadings. Names without published addresses appear at the end of each professional area listing under Address Unpublished. If the

occupation does not fall within one of the specified areas, the name is listed under Unclassified.

Some Biographees have professions encompassing more than one area; each of these appears under the field best suited to the Biographee's occupation. Thus, while most bankers are listed under Finance: Banking Services, investment bankers are found in Finance: Investment Services. A Biographee with two or more diverse occupations is found under the area that best fits his or her professional profile.

The Retiree Index lists the names of those individuals whose biographical sketches last appeared in the 49th, 50th, or 51st Edition of *Who's Who in America.*

The Necrology lists Biographees of the 51st Edition whose deaths were reported to Marquis prior to the close of the compilation of this edition of *Who's Who in America.*

# Alphabetical Practices

Names are arranged alphabetically according to the surnames, and under identical surnames according to the first given name. If both surname and first given name are identical, names are arranged alphabetically according to the second given name.

Surnames beginning with De, Des, Du, however capitalized or spaced, are recorded with the prefix preceding the surname and arranged alphabetically under the letter D.

Surnames beginning with Mac and Mc are arranged alphabetically under M.

Surnames beginning with Saint or St. appear after names that begin Sains, and are arranged according to the second part of the name, e.g. St. Clair before Saint Dennis.

Surnames beginning with Van, Von, or von are arranged alphabetically under the letter V.

Compound surnames are arranged according to the first member of the compound.

Many hyphenated Arabic names begin Al-, El-, or al-. These names are alphabetized according to each Biographee's designation of last name. Thus Al-Bahar, Neta may be listed either under Al- or under Bahar, depending on the preference of the listee.

Also, Arabic names have a variety of possible spellings when transposed to English. Spelling of these names is always based on the practice of the Biographee. Some Biographees use a Western form of word order, while others prefer the Arabic word sequence.

Similarly, Asian names may have no comma between family and given names, but some Biographees have chosen to add the comma. In each case, punctuation follows the preference of the Biographee.

Parentheses used in connection with a name indicate which part of the full name is usually deleted in common usage. Hence Chambers, E(lizabeth) Anne indicates that the usual form of the given name is E. Anne. In such a case, the parentheses are ignored in alphabetizing and the name would be arranged as Chambers, Elizabeth Anne. However, if the name is recorded Chambers, (Elizabeth) Anne, signifying that the entire name Elizabeth is not commonly used, the alphabetizing would be arranged as though the name were Chambers, Anne. If an entire middle or last name is enclosed in parentheses, that portion of the name is used in the alphabetical arrangement. Hence Chambers, Elizabeth (Anne) would be arranged as Chambers, Elizabeth Anne.

Where more than one spelling, word order, or name of an individual is frequently encountered, the sketch has been entered under the form preferred by the Biographee, with cross-references under alternate forms.

# Geographic Index

†New name in *Who's Who in America*, 52nd Edition

Davis, Marian Bloodworth secondary school educator
Kuehnert, Harold Adolph retired petroleum geologist

### Demopolis
Dinning, Woodford Wyndham, Jr. lawyer
Lloyd, Hugh Adams lawyer

### Dothan
Cross, Steven Jasper dean, educator
Garner, Alto Luther retired education educator
Inscho, Jean Anderson social worker
Wright, Burton sociologist

### Elberta
Brennan, Lawrence Edward electronics engineer

### Enterprise
Parker, Ellis D. retired career officer, electronics executive
†Steinhoff, Raymond O(akley) consulting geologist

### Eufaula
Dixon, Giles company executive

### Fairfield
Hamrick, Leon Columbus surgeon, medical director

### Fairhope
Brumback Patterson, Cathy Jean psychologist
Kanter, L. Erick public relations executive

### Florence
Burford, Alexander Mitchell, Jr. physician, pathologist
Butler, Michael Ward economics educator
Foote, Avon Edward webmaster, communications educator
Gillaspie, Lynn Clara education educator, director clinical experience
Haltom, Elbert Bertram, Jr. federal judge
Howard, G. Daniel university administrator
Johnson, Johnny Ray mathematics educator
Mullins, Betty Johnson realtor
Potts, Robert Leslie academic administrator
Tease, James Edward judge
Wright, Mildred Anne (Milly Wright) conservator, researcher
Zarate, Ann Gairing academic administrator, lawyer

### Foley
St. John, Henry Sewell, Jr. utility company executive

### Fort Rucker
Caldwell, John Alvis, Jr. experimental psychologist
Glushko, Gail M. military officer, physician

### Fultondale
Moss, Betty Smith social worker

### Gadsden
Arnold, Don Carl pastor, religious organization executive
Bangham, Robert Arthur orthotist
Hanson, Ronald Windell cardiologist, lawyer, physicist
Lefelhocz, Irene Hanzak nurse, business owner
Sledge, James Scott judge

### Gulf Shores
Wallace, John Loys aviation services executive
Wingard, Raymond Randolph transportation products executive

### Guntersville
Lyons, Brian Wesley marketing professional
Patterson, Harold Dean superintendent of schools
Sparkman, Brandon Buster educator, writer, consultant

### Hanceville
Bailey, James Curtis college administrator
Galin, Jerry Dean college dean

### Hartselle
Penn, Hugh Franklin small business owner
Penn, Hugh Franklin, Jr. psychology educator
Slate, Joe Hutson psychologist, educator

### Harvest
Norman, Ralph Louis physicist, consultant

### Heflin
Brady, Jennie M. wholesale and retail sales professional

### Helena
Smith, John Lee, Jr. minister, former association administrator

### Homewood
Haddox, Jeffrey Lynn cell biologist, electron microscopist
Hart, Virginia Wade elementary education educator

### Hoover
Cole, Charles DuBose, II law educator
Parrish, Sherry Dye elementary school educator

### Hueytown
Gilbert, Melba Caldwell special education and early childhood educator

### Huntsville
Adams, Gary Lee engineering manager
Allan, Barry David research chemist, government official
Anderson, Elmer Ebert physicist, educator
Balint, David Lee engineering company executive
Barros-Smith, Deborah Lynne publishing executive, editor, journalist
Billings, Nancy Carter secondary education educator
Boykin, Betty Ruth Carroll mortgage loan officer, bank executive
Bramon, Christopher John aerospace engineer
Bridwell, G. Porter aerospace engineer
Buddington, Patricia Arrington engineer
Chappell, Charles Richard space scientist
Costes, Nicholas Constantine aerospace technologist, government official
Daussman, Grover Frederick electrical engineer, consultant
Dayton, Deane Kraybill computer company executive
Decher, Rudolf physicist
de Loach, Anthony Cortelyou solar physicist
Dembowski, Fannie Ruth real estate brokerage executive
Dimmock, John Oliver university research center director
Douillard, Paul Arthur engineering and financial executive, consultant
Elliott, Sally Ann special education educator
Emerson, William Kary engineering company executive
Franz, Frank Andrew university president, physics educator
Freas, George Wilson, II computer consultant
Fries, Helen Sergeant Haynes civic leader
Garriott, Owen Kay astronaut, scientist
Graves, Benjamin Barnes business administration educator
Gray, Ronald W. business executive
Helton, Norma Jean special education educator
Hollowell, Jan Bennett adult education educator
Huber, Donald Simon physician
Huckaby, Gary Carlton lawyer
Imtiaz, Kauser Syed aerospace engineer
Johnson, Charles Leslie aerospace physicist, consultant
Jones, Harvie Paul architect
Kim, Young Kil aerospace engineer
Kowel, Stephen Thomas electrical engineer, educator
Leslie, Lottie Lyle retired secondary education educator
Loux, Peter Charles anesthesiologist
Lundquist, Charles Arthur university official
†Malkemes, William Charles career military officer
McCollough, Michael Leon astronomer
Mc Donough, George Francis, Jr. retired aerospace engineer, consultant
McKnight, William Baldwin physics educator
Mc Manus, Samuel Plyler chemist, academic administrator
Mercieca, Charles history, philosophy and political science educator
Michelini, Sylvia Hamilton auditor
Miller, Carol Lynn librarian
Moore, Fletcher Brooks engineering company executive
Morgan, Beverly Hammersley middle school educator, artist
Morgan, Ethel Branman accountant, retired electronics engineer
Noble, Ronald Mark sports medicine facility administrator
Nuessle, William Raymond surgeon
O'Reilly, Patty Mollett psychometrist, consultant
Parnell, Thomas Alfred physicist
Pastrick, Harold Lee aeronautical engineer
Perkins, James Francis physicist
Pittman, William Claude electrical engineer
Polites, Michael Edward aerospace engineer
Potate, John Spencer, Sr. engineering company executive, consultant
Potter, Ernest Luther lawyer
Pruitt, Alice Fay mathematician, engineer
Quick, Jerry Ray academic administrator
Reddy, Thikkavarapu Ramachandra electrical engineer
Richter, William, Jr. technical management consulting executive
Ritter, Alfred aerospace consultant
Robb, David Metheny, Jr. art historian
Roberts, Frances Cabaniss history educator
Roberts, Thomas George retired physicist
Russell, Lynn Darnell engineering educator
Schonberg, William Peter aerospace, mechanical, civil engineering educator
Schroer, Bernard Jon industrial engineering educator
Smith, Philip Wayne writer, communications company executive
Smith, Robert Earl space scientist
Smith, Robert Sellers lawyer
Stuhlinger, Ernst physicist
Theisen, Russell Eugene electrical engineer
Traylor, Orba Forest economist, lawyer, educator
Vaughan, William Walton atmospheric scientist
Watson, Raymond Coke, Jr. engineering executive, academic administrator
White, John Charles historian
Wieland, Paul Otto environmental control systems engineer
Wilson, Allan Byron graphics company executive
Wright, John Collins chemistry educator

### Jacksonville
Boswell, Rupert Dean, Jr. retired academic administrator, math educator
Clarke, Mary Elizabeth retired army officer
Dunaway, Carolyn Bennett sociology educator
Dunaway, William Preston retired academic administration educator
Fairleigh, James Parkinson music educator
Hale, Judy Ann education educator
Hubbard, William James library director
McGee, Harold Johnston academic administrator
Merrill, Martha instructional media educator
Wilson, Barbara T. physical education educator

### Jasper
Rowland, David Jack academic administrator

### Kimberly
Howell, Pamela Ann federal agency professional

### Lanett
Fowler, Conrad Murphree retired manufacturing company executive

### Lillian
Burnette, Ollen Lawrence, Jr. historian
Moyer, Kenneth Evan psychologist, educator
Shory, Naseeb Lein dentist, retired state official

### Livingston
Green, Asa Norman university president

### Loachapoka
Schafer, Robert Louis agricultural engineer, researcher

### Madison
Brannan, Eulie Ross education consultant
Dannenberg, Konrad K. aeronautical engineer
Frakes, Lawrence Wright retired career officer, businessman
Hawk, Clark Wiliams mechanical engineering educator
Jellett, James Morgan retired army officer, aerospace defense consultant

### Maxwell AFB
Davis, Cindy Ann military officer, nursing educator
Henry, Gary Norman air force officer, astronautical engineer
Kline, John Alvin academic administrator
Pendley, William Tyler naval officer, international relations educator
Wendzel, Robert Leroy political science educator

### Mc Calla
Gentry, Vicki Paulette museum director

### Mentone
Herndon, Mark musician

### Meridianville
Hongsermeier, Martin Karl software and systems architect, consultant

### Mobile
Anderson, Lewis Daniel medical educator, orthopaedic surgeon
Armbrecht, William Henry, III lawyer
Atkinson, William James, Jr. retired cardiologist
Baker, Amanda Sirmon university dean, nursing educator
Barik, Sailen biomedical scientist, educator
Bobo, James Robert economics educator
Braswell, Louis Erskine lawyer
Brogdon, Byron Gilliam physician, radiology educator
Butler, Charles Randolph, Jr. federal judge
Byrd, Gwendolyn Pauline school system superintendent
Callahan, Sonny (H.L. Callahan) congressman
Clark, Jack retired hospital company executive, accountant
Coker, Donald William economic banker, valuation & healthcare consultant
Coley, F(ranklin) Luke, Jr. lawyer
Conrad, Marcel Edward hematologist, educator
Copeland, Lewis principal
Cox, Emmett Ripley federal judge
Crow, James Sylvester retired banker, railway executive
Delaney, Thomas Caldwell, Jr. city official
Durizch, Mary Lou radiology educator
Edwards, Jack former congressman, lawyer
Eichold, Samuel medical educator, medical museum curator
Fox, Sidney Walter chemist, educator
French, Elizabeth Irene biology educator, violinist
Gardner, William Albert, Jr. pathologist, medical foundation executive
Goodin, Julia C. medical investigator, state official, educator
Gottlieb, Sheldon Fred biologist, educator
Guarino, Anthony Michael pharmacologist, educator, consultant, counselor
Hamid, Michael electrical engineering educator, consultant
Hand, William Brevard federal judge
Harris, Benjamin Harte, Jr. lawyer
Hearin, William Jefferson newspaper publishing company executive
Helmsing, Frederick George lawyer
Holland, Lyman Faith, Jr. lawyer
Holmes, Broox Garrett lawyer
Howard, Alex T., Jr. federal judge
Jackson, Bo (Vincent Edward Jackson) professional baseball, former football player
Johnston, Neil Chunn lawyer
Kahn, Gordon Barry retired federal bankruptcy judge
Kimbrough, William Adams, Jr. lawyer
Lager, Robert John state agency administrator
Lipscomb, Oscar Hugh archbishop
Littleton, Jesse Talbot, III radiology educator
Lyons, Champ, Jr. lawyer
Lyons, George Sage lawyer, oil industry executive, former state legislator
McCall, Daniel Thompson, Jr. retired judge
McCann, Clarence David, Jr. special events coordinator, museum curator and director, artist
McElhaney, Richard Franklin quality assurance nursing coordinator
Milling, Bert William, Jr. federal judge
Murchison, David Roderick lawyer
Parmley, Loren Francis, Jr. medical educator
Perry, Nelson Allen radiation safety engineer, radiological consultant
Pitcock, James Kent head and neck surgical oncologist
Pittman, Virgil federal judge
Pruitt, Albert W. dean
Raider, Louis physician, radiologist
Reeves, William Boyd lawyer
Richelson, Paul William curator
Rodning, Charles Bernard surgeon
Roedder, William Chapman, Jr. lawyer
Schenk, Joseph Bernard museum director
Smith, Jesse Graham, Jr. dermatologist, educator
Strodl, Peter educational administrator, educator
Suess, James Francis clinical psychologist
Taylor, Aubrey Elmo physiologist, educator
Thomas, Daniel Holcombe federal judge
Thomas, Joseph Paul psychiatrist
Vacik, James Paul university administrator
Vulevich, Edward, Jr. prosecutor
Whiddon, Frederick Palmer university president
White, Lowell E., Jr. medical educator
Winter, Arch Reese architect
Yett, Fowler Redford mathematics educator

### Monroeville
Adkisson, Randall Lynn minister
Kniskern, Maynard editor, writer

### Montevallo
McChesney, Robert Michael, Sr. political science educator

### Montgomery
Albritton, William Harold, III federal judge
Almon, Reneau Pearson state supreme court justice
Bailey, Randall Charles religious studies educator, consultant
Bennett, James Ronald secretary of state
Bigham, Wanda Ruth college president
Black, Robert Coleman judge, lawyer
Blount, Winton Malcolm, Jr. manufacturing company executive
Blount, Winton Malcolm, III investment executive
Boston, Hollis Buford, Jr. retired military officer
Boyd, Billy Willard internist
Brown, William Blake newspaper editor
Butts, Terry Lucas state supreme court justice
Byars, Walter Ryland, Jr. lawyer
Carnes, Edward E. federal judge
Copeland, Jacqueline Turner music educator
Cornett, Lloyd Harvey, Jr. retired historian
Deaton, Cheryl Davis school system administrator
De Ment, Ira judge
Dillon, Jean Katherine executive secretary, small business owner
Dixon, Larry Dean state legislator
Dubina, Joel Fredrick federal judge
Eubanks, Ronald W. lawyer, broadcaster
Franco, Ralph Abraham lawyer
Frazer, David Hugh, Jr. allergist
Frazer, Nimrod Thompson financial services company executive
Futrell, Robert Frank military historian, consultant
Gainous, Fred Jerome state agency administrator
Godbold, John Cooper federal judge
Graddick, Charles Allen lawyer
Gribben, Alan English language educator, research consultant
Hamner, Reginald Turner lawyer
Harris, Patricia Lea librarian
Harris, William Hamilton academic administrator
Hawthorne, Frank Howard lawyer
Hayes, John Edward broadcasting executive
Hennies, Clyde Albert (Lou ) military officer, state official
Hester, Douglas Benjamin lawyer, federal official
Hill, Thomas Bowen, III lawyer
Hobbs, Truman McGill federal judge, lawyer
Hoffman, Richard William banker
Houston, James Gorman, Jr. state supreme court justice
Howell, Allen Windsor lawyer
Hunker, Fred Dominic internist, medical educator
James, Fob, Jr. (Forrest Hood James) governor
Johnson, Andrew Emerson, III educational administrator
Johnson, Frank Minis, Jr. federal judge
Jones, Charles William association executive
Keaton, Charles Howard health care administrator
Kloess, Lawrence Herman, Jr. lawyer
Kurth, Ronald James university president, retired naval officer
Langford, Charles Douglas state legislator, lawyer
Latham, Larry Lee state administrator, psychologist
Laurie, Robin Garrett lawyer
Leslie, Henry Arthur lawyer, retired banker
Lunt, Jennifer Lee lawyer
Maddox, Alva Hugh state supreme court justice
Maddox, Hugh state supreme court justice
McFadden, Frank Hampton lawyer, business executive, former judge
McPherson, Vanzetta Penn federal judge
Myers, Ira Lee physician
Nachman, Merton Roland, Jr. lawyer
Napier, Cameron Mayson Freeman historic preservationist
Oliver, John William Posegate minister
Owens, Doris Jerkins insurance underwriter
Paddock, Austin Joseph engineering executive
Patterson, John Malcolm judge
Pickett, George Bibb, Jr. retired military officer
Pitt, Redding lawyer
Prestwood, Alvin Tennyson lawyer
Richardson, Edward R. state agency administrator
Ritvo, Roger Alan university dean, health management-policy educator
Robinson, Peter Clark general management executive
Rowan, John Robert retired medical center director
Saigo, Roy Hirofumi university chancellor
Salmon, Joseph Thaddeus lawyer
Schloss, Samuel Leopold, Jr. retired food service executive, consultant
Schwarz, Joseph Edmund artist
Shores, Janie Ledlow state supreme court justice
Siegelman, Don Eugene state official
Smith, Maury Drane lawyer
Stanley, Janice Faye special education educator
Steele, Rodney Redfearn judge
Tan, Boen Hie analytical biochemist, biomedical scientist
Taylor, Watson Robbins, Jr. investment banker
Teague, Larry Gene editor
Thompson, Myron H. federal judge
Torbert, Clement Clay, Jr. state supreme court justice
Tracy, Patricia Ann Koop secondary school educator
Varner, Robert Edward federal judge
Volz, Charles Harvie, Jr. lawyer
Walker, Annette counseling administrator
Wallace, George Corley former governor
Whitt, Mary F. reading educator, consultant
Williamson, Donald E. state official
Wright, Cathy Hess secondary education educator

### Muscle Shoals
Smith, Harry Delano educational administrator

### Normal
Bishnoi, Udai Ram agronomy and seed technology educator
Caulfield, Henry John physics educator
Coleman, Tommy Lee soil science educator, researcher, laboratory director
Okezie, B. Onuma food scientist, nutritionist, educator

### Ohatchee
Ellis, Bernice Allred personnel executive

### Opelika
Brown, Robert Glenn plastic surgeon
Jenkins, Richard Lee manufacturing company executive
Knecht, Charles Daniel veterinarian
Samford, Yetta Glenn, Jr. lawyer

### Orange Beach
Adams, Daniel Fenton law educator
Bennett, James Jefferson higher education consultant

**Ozark**
DuBose, Elizabeth community health nurse

**Pelham**
Allen, James Madison family practice physician, lawyer, consultant
Lee, James A. health facility finance executive
Miller, Edmond Trowbridge civil engineer, educator, consultant
Turner, Malcolm Elijah biomathematician, educator
Wabler, Robert Charles, II retail and distribution executive

**Pell City**
Passey, George Edward psychology educator

**Phenix City**
Greene, Ernest Rinaldo, Jr. anesthesiologist, chemical engineer

**Piedmont**
Ulrich, Russell Dean osteopathic physician

**Point Clear**
Elmer, William Morris retired pipe line executive
Englund, Gage Bush dancer, educator
Ferguson, Joseph Gantt chemical engineer
Hart, Eric Mullins finance company executive
Salter, LaNora Jeanette corporate financial officer
Williams, Willie John, II marketing consultant

**Rainsville**
Reece, Marilyn King college dean

**Roanoke**
McCarley, George David management executive

**Scottsboro**
McGill, Judy Annell McGee early childhood and elementary educator

**Selma**
Collins, Eugene Boyd chemist, molecular pathologist, consultant
Datiri, Benjamin Chumang soil and environmental scientist
Jackson, Michael Wayne judge, lawyer
LeBeau, Hector Alton, Jr. confectionary company executive
Stewart, Edgar Allen lawyer

**Sheffield**
Badger, Phillip Charles engineer
Meagher, James Francis atmospheric research executive

**Shelby**
Jackson, Jimmy Lynn engineer, consulting spectroscopist

**Shoal Creek**
Ahearn, John Francis, Jr. retired oil and gas company executive

**Southside**
Hill, Anita Griffith principal

**Sylacauga**
Bledsoe, Mary Louise medical, surgical nurse
Moore, Penelope school librarian
Poole, William Lannon, Jr. dermatologist

**Talladega**
Anderson, Sharon Rice special education educator
Cooper, Suzane physician
Johnson, Joseph Benjamin university president
Lanier, Anita Suzanne musician, piano educator
Paris, Virginia Hall (Ginger Paris) elementary school educator

**Theodore**
Mc Coy, Lee Berard paint company executive

**Troy**
Adams, Ralph Wyatt, Sr. university chancellor emeritus
Hawkins, Jack, Jr. academic administrator
Long, John Maloy university dean
Marsicano, Hazel Elliott education educator
Moffett, Thomas Delano music educator
Thompson, Jean Tanner retired librarian

**Trussville**
Best, Frederick Napier artist, designer, educator

**Tuscaloosa**
Abdel-Ghany, Mohamed family economics educator
Baklanoff, Eric Nicholas economist, educator
Barban, Arnold Melvin advertising educator
Barfield, Robert F. retired mechanical engineer, educator, dean
Barrett, Nancy Smith university administrator
Bell, Robert Fred German language educator
Bills, Robert E(dgar) emeritus psychology educator
Blackburn, John Leslie small business owner
Bryan, Colgan Hobson aerospace engineering educator
Cava, Michael Patrick chemist, educator
Christopher, Thomas Weldon legal educator, administrator
Cole, George David physicist
Cook, Camille Wright law educator
Cooper, Eugene Bruce speech, language pathologist, educator
Coulter, Philip Wylie physicist, educator
Cramer, Dale Lewis economics educator
Darden, William Howard, Jr. biology educator
Davis, Anthony Michael John mathematics educator
Doerr, Robert Wayne nursing administrator
Dolly, John Patrick university dean, educational psychologist
Doughty, Julian Orus mechanical engineer, educator
Drake, Albert Estern retired statistics educator, farming administrator
Fish, Mary Martha economics educator
Frye, John H., Jr. metallurgical engineering educator
Gilliland, Terri Kirby accountant
Gourley, Paula Marie art educator, artist, designer bookbinder
Griffin, Marvin Anthony industrial engineer, educator
Gunther, William David university administrator, economics educator
Gup, Benton Eugene banking educator
Hocutt, Max Oliver philosophy educator
Izatt, Jerald Ray physics educator
Jackson, Cynthia Williford special education educator
LaMoreaux, Philip Elmer geologist, hydrogeologist, consultant
Lee, Thomas Alexander accountant, educator
Mac Donald, Malcolm Murdoch editor, publisher
Mancini, Ernest Anthony geologist, educator, researcher
Mayer, Morris Lehman marketing educator
McDonald, Forrest historian, educator
McFarland, James William real estate development company executive
Meredith, Thomas C. academic administrator
Mills, Gary Bernard history educator
Mitchell, Herbert Hall former university dean, educational consultant
†Moody, Rick collegiate basketball coach
Morley, Lloyd Albert mining engineering educator
Moynihan, Gary Peter industrial engineering educator
Mozley, Paul David obstetrics and gynecology educator
Penz, Anton Jacob retired accounting educator
†Phifer, J. Reese manufacturing executive
Pieroni, Robert Edward internist, educator
Reinhart, Kellee Connely journalist
Rice, Margaret Lucille computer technology educator
Shellhase, Leslie John social work educator
Sorensen, Andrew Aaron academic administrator
Summersell, Frances Sharpley organization worker
Taaffe, James Griffith university administrator, educator
Taber, Robert Clinton retired army officer
Thomas, Jerry pharmacist
Thomas, Joab Langston academic administrator, biology educator
Thomson, H. Bailey editor
Umakantha, Kaggal V. physiatrist
Van Artsdalen, Ervin Robert physical chemist, educator
Wetzel, Robert George botany educator
Williams, Ernest Going retired paper company executive

**Tuscumbia**
Heflin, Howell Thomas former senator, lawyer, former state supreme court chief justice

**Tuskegee**
Green, Elbert P. university official
Payton, Benjamin Franklin college president
Pryce, Edward Lyons landscape architect
Smith, Edward Jude biologist
Thomas, Elaine Freeman artist, educator

**Tuskegee Institute**
Hill, Walter A. agricultural sciences educator, researcher

**Valley**
Striblin, Lori Ann critical care nurse, medicare coordinator, nursing educator

**Vernon**
Newell, Harold Joe quality assurance engineer

**Vestavia Hills**
Jacobs, Delores Hamm secondary education educator

**Wetumpka**
Curlee, Robert Glen, Jr. special education educator

**Woodville**
Wells, Robin Denise nurse

## ALASKA

**Anchorage**
Archer, Gary William cardiologist
Atwood, Robert Bruce publisher
Behrend, Donald Fraser university administrator
Brady, Carl Franklin retired aircraft charter company executive
Branson, Albert Harold (Harry Branson) magistrate judge, educator
Brunstad, Michael Lewis elementary education educator
Butler, Rex Lamont lawyer
Byrd, Milton Bruce college president, former business executive
Cairns, John J(oseph) retail executive
Cantor, James Elliot lawyer
Chen, Barbara Marie anesthesiologist
Collins, Michael Paul secondary school educator, earth science educator, consultant
Cuddy, Daniel Hon bank executive
De Lisio, Stephen Scott lawyer
Devens, John Searle natural resources administrator
Easley, George Washington construction executive
Edwards, George Kent lawyer
Ennis, William Lee physics educator
Erickson, Merlyn K. anesthesia nurse
Faulkner, Sewell Ford real estate executive
Fitzgerald, James Martin federal judge
Gottstein, Barnard Jacob retail and wholesale food company executive, real estate executive
Groh, Clifford J., Sr. lawyer
Haines, John Meade poet, translator, writer
Harris, Roger J. mortgage company executive, entrepreneur
Henderson-Dixon, Karen Sue psychologist
Hickel, Walter Joseph investment firm executive, forum administrator
Hopkins, Stephen Davis mining company executive
Hughes, Mary Katherine lawyer
Hurley, Francis T. archbishop
Illk, Serena Pearl accountant
Jay, Christopher Edward stockbroker
Jones, Garth Nelson business and public administration educator
Jones, Mark Logan educational association executive, educator
Kuehnert, Deborah Anne medical center administrator
Leman, Loren Dwight civil engineer
Lindauer, John Howard, II newspaper publisher
Mala, Theodore Anthony physician, consultant
Mann, Lester Perry mathematics educator
Mason, Robert (Burt Mason) lawyer
Matsui, Dorothy Nobuko elementary education educator
Meddleton, Daniel Joseph health facility administrator
Mitchell, Michael Kiehl elementary and secondary education educator, minister
Moore, Faye Annette social services professional
O'Regan, Deborah association executive, lawyer
Parsons, Donald D. bishop
Pearson, Larry Lester journalism educator, internet presence provider
Perkins, Joseph John, Jr. lawyer
Porcaro, Michael Francis advertising agency executive
Rasmuson, Elmer Edwin banker, former mayor
Reed, Frank Metcalf bank executive
Rieger, Steven Arthur state legislator, business consultant
Risley, Todd Robert psychologist, educator
Roberts, John Derham lawyer
Rollins, Alden Milton documents librarian
Rose, David Allan investment manager
Schmitt, Nancy Cain public and corporate relations executive, writer
Schneibel, Vicki Darlene public relations administrator
Schnell, Roger Thomas retired military officer, state official
Sedwick, John W. judge
Shadrach, (Martha) Jean Hawkins artist
Singleton, James Keith federal judge
Strohmeyer, John writer, former editor
Sullivan, George Murray transportation consultant, former mayor
Swalling, John Christian accountant, president
Thomas, Howard Paul civil engineer, consultant
Thomas, Lowell, Jr. author, lecturer, former lieutenant governor, former state senator
Vandergriff, Jerry Dodson retired computer store executive
von der Heydt, James Arnold federal judge, lawyer
Welch-McKay, Dawn Renee legal assistant
Williams, Charles D. bishop
Wilson, Joseph Morris, III lawyer
Young, Bettye Jeanne retired secondary education educator

**Chiniak**
Griffin, Elaine B. educator

**Cordova**
Bugbee-Jackson, Joan sculptor

**Delta Junction**
Holland, Bernard George pipeline security officer

**Eagle River**
Cotten, Samuel Richard former state legislator, fisherman

**Elmendorf AFB**
†Boese, Lawrence E. air force officer

**Fairbanks**
Abels, Michael Alan university administrator
Alexander, Vera dean, marine science educator
Behlke, Charles Edward civil engineer, former university dean
Beistline, Earl Hoover mining consultant
Bennett, Fred Lawrence engineering educator
Davis, Charles Lee fire marshal
Doolittle, William Hotchkiss internist
Doran, Timothy Patrick educational administrator
Fathauer, Theodore Frederick meteorologist
Fischer, Robert Edward meteorologist
Hatch, Kelley Marie journalist, television news anchor, writer
Helfferich, Merritt Randolph technology transfer administrator
Helmericks, Harmon R. author, explorer
Hopkins, David Moody geologist
Jonaitis, Aldona Claire museum administrator, art historian
Kaniecki, Michael Joseph bishop
Kessel, Brina ornithologist, educator
Kleinfeld, Andrew Jay federal judge
Komisar, Jerome Bertram university administrator
Krauss, Michael Edward linguist
Kunz, Michael Lenney archaeologist
Lingle, Craig Stanley glaciologist, educator
McBeath, Gerald Alan political science educator
Reichardt, Paul Bernard dean, chemistry educator
Rice, Julian Casavant lawyer
Roederer, Juan Gualterio physics educator
Smith, Robert London commissioner, retired air force officer, political scientist, educator
Tilsworth, Timothy retired environmental/civil engineering educator
Wadlow, Joan Krueger academic administrator
Weller, Gunter Ernst geophysics educator
White, Robert Gordon research director, biology educator
Wilkniss, Peter E. foundation administrator, researcher
Wolting, Robert Roy city official
Wood, William Ransom retired university president, city official, corporate executive

**Indian**
Wright, Gordon Brooks musician, conductor, educator

**Juneau**
Botelho, Bruce Manuel state official, mayor
Bushre, Peter Alvin investment company executive
Cole, Charles Edward lawyer, former state attorney general
Hensley, William Lynn (Willie Hensley) state senator, corporate executive
Holloway, Shirley J. state agency administrator
Kelly, Timothy Donahue state senator
Knowles, Tony governor
Lind, Marshall L. academic administrator
May, Scott C. special education educator
Meacham, Charles P. president, capital consulting
Pearce, Drue state legislator
Ruotsala, James Alfred historian, writer
Schorr, Alan Edward librarian, publisher
Twomley, Bruce Clarke commissioner, lawyer
Ulmer, Frances Ann state official
Willson, Mary F. ecology researcher, educator

**Ketchikan**
Kraft, Richard Joe sales executive
Laurance, Leonard Clark marketing researcher, educator and consultant

**Kodiak**
Jamin, Matthew Daniel lawyer, magistrate judge
Selby, Jerome M. mayor

**Kotzebue**
Harris, Jan C. health care administrator

**Nikiski**
Bumbaugh, Robert Warren, Sr. oil industry executive

**Ninilchik**
Oskolkoff, Grassim Native American Indian tribal chief

**Nondalton**
Gay, Sarah Elizabeth lawyer

**North Pole**
Fleming, Carolyn Elizabeth religious organization administrator, interior designer
James, Jeannette Adeline state legislator, accountant

**Old Harbor**
O'Brien, Annmarie education educator

**Seward**
Kincheloe, Lawrence Ray state official

**Sitka**
Carlson, Susan Spevack hospital administrator, family physician

**Soldotna**
Franzmann, Albert Wilhelm wildlife veterinarian, consultant

**Tuntutuliak**
Daniel, Barbara Ann elementary and secondary education educator

**Tununak**
Bond, Ward Charles mathematics and computer educator

**Valdez**
Todd, Kathleen Gail physician

## ARIZONA

**Apache Junction**
Bracken, Harry McFarland philosophy educator
Ransom, Evelyn Naill language educator, linguist

**Arizona City**
Donovan, Willard Patrick retired elementary education educator

**Avondale**
Rosztoczy, Ferenc Erno business executive
Thompson, Bonnie Ransa secondary educator, chemistry educator

**Bisbee**
Behney, Charles Augustus, Jr. veterinarian
Eley, Lynn W. political science educator, former mayor
Eppele, David Louis columnist, author
Holland, Robert Dale retired magistrate, consultant

**Bullhead City**
Jones, Vernon Quentin surveyor

**Carefree**
Beadle, Alfred Newman architect
Bergstrom, Richard Norman civil engineer
Birkelbach, Albert Ottmar retired oil company executive
Byrom, Fletcher Lauman chemical manufacturing company executive
Craft, Robert Homan banker, corporate executive
Galda, Dwight William financial company executive
Giolito, Caesar Augustus public relations executive, consultant
Hutchison, Stanley Philip lawyer
Johnson, Charles Foreman architect, architectural photographer, planning architecture and system engineering consultant
Menk, Louis Wilson retired manufacturing company executive
Robbins, Conrad W. naval architect
Trimble, George Simpson industrial executive
Wise, Paul Schuyler insurance company executive

**Casa Grande**
Davies, Harriett Marie (Lolly Davies) educator
Hopple, Janet Lynette medical technologist
Kramer, Donovan Mershon, Sr. newspaper publisher
McGillicuddy, Joan Marie psychotherapist, consultant

**Cave Creek**
Gose, Celeste Marlene writer
LeNeau, Thomas Ervin gas company executive
O'Reilly, Thomas Eugene human resources consultant

**Chandler**
Barnard, Annette Williamson elementary school educator
Barrett, Craig R. computer company executive
Farley, James Newton manufacturing executive, engineer
Goyer, Robert Stanton communication educator
Graham, Anita Louise correctional and community health nurse
Miller, Robert Carl library director
Ratkowski, Donald J. mechanical engineer, consultant
Rowe, Ernest Ras education educator, academic administrator
Rudibaugh, Melinda Campbell mathematics educator

**Chinle**
Reed, Leonard Newton *secondary school educator*

**Cortaro**
Smith, Dwight Raymond *ecology and wildlife educator, writer*

**Dewey**
Beck, Doris Olson *library media director*
Burch, Mary Lou *organization consultant, housing advocate*

**Flagstaff**
Aurand, Charles Henry, Jr. *music educator*
†Bryant, Leland Marshal *rail transportation executive, hotel executive*
Chen, Jian Hua *medical physicist*
Cline, Platt Herrick *author*
Colbert, Edwin Harris *paleontologist, museum curator*
Hallowell, Robert Edward *French language educator*
Hammond, Howard David *retired botanist and editor*
Heitland, Ann Rae *lawyer*
Hooper, Henry Olcott *academic administrator, physicist*
Lovett, Clara Maria *university administrator, historian*
Marcus, Karen Melissa *foreign language educator*
Millis, Robert Lowell *astronomer*
Mullens, William Reese *retired insurance company executive*
Poen, Monte M. *history educator, researcher*
Price, Peter Wilfrid *ecology educator, researcher*
Putnam, William Lowell *science association administrator*
Ratzlaff, Vernon Paul *elementary education educator, consultant*
Reno, Joseph Harry *retired orthopedic surgeon*
Ririe, Craig Martin *periodontist*
Shoemaker, Carolyn Spellmann *planetary astronomer*
Shoemaker, Eugene Merle *geologist*
Somerville, Mason Harold *mechanical engineering educator, university dean*
Zoellner, Robert William *chemistry educator*

**Florence**
Griffis, Stanley Douglas *county manager*

**Fort Huachuca**
Adams, Frank *education specialist*
Kelly, Maureen Ann *management accountant*
Weeks, Robert Lee *electronic engineer, program manager*

**Fountain Hills**
Herzberger, Eugene E. *retired neurosurgeon*
Humes, Charles Warren *counselor educator*
Tyl, Noel Jan *baritone, astrologer*
†York, Tina *painter*

**Gilbert**
Carrico, Donald Jefferson *public transit system manager*
Earnhardt, Hal J., III *automotive executive*
Kenney, Thomas Frederick *broadcasting executive*

**Glendale**
Altersitz, Janet Kinahan *principal*
Boettcher, Nancy Biondolillo *nurse*
Bret, Donna Lee *elementary education educator*
Brewer, Janice Kay *state legislator, property and investment firm executive*
Cassidy, Barry Allen *physician assistant, clinical medical ethicist*
Chan, Michael Chiu-Hon *chiropractor*
Covington, B(athild) June *business owner, advocate*
Galletti, Marie Ann *English language and linguistics educator*
Harris, Warren Lynn *development engineer*
Joseph, Gregory Nelson *media critic*
Neff, John *recording engineer, producer*
Shuck, Lola Mae *retired elementary school educator*
Tuman, Walter Vladimir *Russian language educator, researcher*
Voris, William *academic administrator emeritus*

**Globe**
Lee, Joyce Ann *administrative assistant*

**Gold Canyon**
Nelson, William O. *pharmaceutical company executive*

**Grand Canyon**
Dodson, Richard Lee *music educator*

**Green Valley**
Barich, Dewey Frederick *emeritus educational administrator*
Bates, Charles Carpenter *oceanographer*
Blickwede, Donald Johnson *retired steel company executive*
Brissman, Bernard Gustave *insurance company executive*
Carpenter, John Everett *retired principal, educational consultant*
Crystall, Joseph N. *communications company executive*
Dmytryshyn, Basil *historian, educator*
Egger, Roscoe L., Jr. *consultant, former IRS commissioner*
Ehrenfeld, John Henry *grocery company executive*
Friedman, Edward David *lawyer, arbitrator*
Furman, Robert Howard *physician, educator*
Lasch, Robert *former journalist*
Miner, Earl Howard *retired trust banker*
Page, John Henry, Jr. *artist, educator*
Perry, Roger Lawrence *printing executive*
Ramette, Richard Wales *chemistry educator*
Shafer, Susan Wright *retired elementary school educator*
Smith, Raymond Lloyd *former university president, consultant*
Wasmuth, Carl Erwin *physician, lawyer*
White, Herbert Spencer *research library educator, university dean*

**Kayenta**
Parrott, Sharon Lee *elementary educator*

**Lake Havasu City**
Shervheim, Lloyd Oliver *insurance company executive, lawyer*

**Lake Montezuma**
Burkee, Irvin *artist*

**Mc Neal**
Smith, Clifford Neal *business educator, writer*

**Mesa**
Allen, Merle Maeser, Jr. *lawyer*
Anderson, Herschel Vincent *librarian*
Backus, Charles Edward *engineering educator, researcher*
Baxter, Gene Kenneth *mechanical engineer, company executive*
Beck, Jerome Joseph *health care administrator, biomedical technologist*
Bell, Daniel Carroll *realtor, community association, ranch and land manager*
Boren, Kenneth Ray *endocrinologist*
Boyd, Leona Potter *retired social worker*
Cameron, Janice Carol *legal regulatory administrator*
Carter, Sally Packlett *elementary education educator*
DeRosa, Francis Dominic *chemical company executive*
Evans, Don A. *healthcare company executive*
Fairbanks, Harold Vincent *metallurgical engineer, educator*
Garwood, John Delvert *former college administrator*
Gunderson, Brent Merrill *lawyer*
Hagen, Nicholas Stewart *medical educator, consultant*
Jackson, Andrew Edwin *engineering educator, researcher, aviator*
Joardar, Kuntal *electrical engineer*
Johnson, Doug *advertising and public relations executive*
Luth, William Clair *retired research manager*
Markey, Thomas Adam *financial officer*
Mason, Marshall W. *theater director*
McCollum, Alvin August *real estate company executive*
McDonald, Thomas Robert *materials technologist, consultant, business owner*
Murphy, Edward Francis *sales executive*
Ramirez, Janice L. *assistant school superintendent*
Rummel, Robert Wiland *aeronautical engineer, author*
Sanders, Aaron Perry *radiation biophysics educator*
Shelley, James LaMar *lawyer*
Stott, Brian *software company executive*
Thompson, Ronald MacKinnon *family physician, artist, writer*
Tidwell, Joseph Paul, Jr. *systems safety engineer*
Verschoor, John, IV *physician assistant*
Wong, Willie *former mayor, automotive executive*
Woods, Joe Eldon *general contractor*

**Naco**
Davies, Daniel R. *retired educator*

**New River**
Bruder, William Paul *architect*

**Nogales**
Castro, Raul Hector *lawyer, former ambassador, former governor*

**Oracle**
Rush, Andrew Wilson *artist*

**Oro Valley**
Haas-Oro, Debra Ann *dentist*
Loeh, Corinne Genevieve *artist*
Tinker, Robert Eugene *minister, educational consultant*

**Page**
Hart, Marian Griffith *retired reading educator*
Tsinigine, Allen *educator*

**Paradise Valley**
Bergamo, Ron *marketing executive*
Cussler, Clive Eric *author*
Day, Richard Putnam *marketing, strategic planning and employee benefits consultant*
De Shazor, Ashley Dunn *business consultant*
Grimm, James R. (Ronald Grimm) *multi-industry executive*
Hazard, Robert Culver, Jr. *hotel executive*
Heller, Jules *artist, writer, educator*
Russell, Paul Edgar *electrical engineering educator*
Sapp, Donald Gene *minister*

**Peoria**
Bergmann, Fredrick Louis *English language educator, theater historian*
Bernstein, Eugene Merle *physicist, retired educator*
†Burke, Charlene B. *civilian military employee*
Degnan, Thomas Leonard *lawyer*
Jesse, Sandra Elizabeth *special education educator*
Keesling, Karen Ruth *lawyer*
Molinsky, Bert *tax consultant*
Morrison, Manley Glenn *real estate investor, former army officer*
Moshier, Mary Baluk *patent lawyer*
Palmer, Alice Eugenia *retired physician, educator*
Schindler, William Stanley *retired public relations executive*

**Phoenix**
Adler, Eugene Victor *forensic toxicologist, consultant*
Allen, John Rybolt L. *chemist, biochemist*
Allen, Robert Eugene Barton *lawyer*
Alsentzer, William James, Jr. *lawyer*
Anderson, Edward Frederick *biology educator*
Armstrong, Nelson William, Jr. *gaming company executive*
Aschaffenburg, Walter Eugene *composer, music educator*
Aybar, Charles Anton *aviation executive*
Babinec, Gehl P. *convenience store company executive*
Bachus, Benson Floyd *mechanical engineer, consultant*
Bain, C. Randall *lawyer*
Baker, William Dunlap *lawyer*
Bakker, Thomas Gordon *lawyer*
Barbanell, Alexander Stanley *insurance marketing company executive*
Bauman, Frederick Carl *lawyer*
Begam, Robert George *lawyer*
Beggs, Harry Mark *lawyer*
Beltrán, Anthony Natalicio *military non-commissioned officer, deacon*
Benson, Stephen R. *editorial cartoonist*
Bergin, Daniel Timothy *lawyer, banker*
†Berkery, Dan *television station executive*
Bertholf, Neilson Allan, Jr. *aviation executive*
Bidwill, William V. *professional football executive*
Bishop, C. Diane *state agency administrator, educator*
Blanchard, Charles Alan *lawyer, former state senator*
Bodney, David Jeremy *lawyer*
Bolin, Vladimir Dustin *chemist*
Bouma, John Jacob *lawyer*
Bower, Willis Herman *retired psychiatrist, former medical administrator*
Bradley, Gilbert Francis *retired banker*
Brockelman, Kent *lawyer*
Broomfield, Robert Cameron *federal judge*
Brown, James Carrington, III (Bing Brown) *public relations and communications executive*
Brunacini, Alan Vincent *fire chief*
Burchard, John Kenneth *chemical engineer*
Burke, Timothy John *lawyer*
Butler, Byron Clinton *obstetrician, gynecologist*
Cabot, Howard Ross *lawyer*
Cain, Robert Joseph *elementary school educator*
Calkins, Jerry Milan *anesthesiologist, educator, administrator, biomedical engineer*
Canby, William Cameron, Jr. *federal judge*
Carroll, Earl Hamblin *federal judge*
Carter, Ronald Martin, Sr. *pharmaceutical company executive*
Case, David Leon *lawyer*
Charlton, John Kipp *pediatrician*
Cheifetz, Lorna Gale *psychologist*
Chisholm, Tom Shepherd *environmental engineer*
Chrisman, William Herring *property tax consultant*
Cohen, Jon Stephan *lawyer*
†Colangelo, Bryan *professional sports team executive*
Colangelo, Jerry John *professional basketball team executive*
Colburn, Donald D. *lawyer*
Cole, George Thomas *lawyer*
Condo, James Robert *lawyer*
Cook, Neil D. *publishing executive*
Cooledge, Richard Calvin *lawyer*
Coppersmith, Sam *lawyer*
Copple, William Perry *federal judge*
Cordova, Alexander M. *city clerk*
Corson, Kimball Jay *lawyer*
Cozzi, Hugo Louis *psychiatrist*
Craig, Stephen Wright *lawyer*
Crockett, Clyll Webb *lawyer*
Culnon, Sharon Darlene *reading specialist, special education educator*
Curcio, Christopher Frank *city official*
Daniel, James Richard *accountant, computer company financial executive*
Daughton, Donald *lawyer*
Davies, David George *lawyer*
Davis, Colleen Teresa *elementary education educator, reading educator*
DeBartolo, Jack, Jr. *architect*
Deeny, Robert Joseph *lawyer*
DeMenna, Kevin Bolton *lobbyist*
De Michele, O. Mark *utility company executive*
Depies, Lisa J. *physicist*
Derdenger, Patrick *lawyer*
Derouin, James G. *lawyer*
Desser, Kenneth Barry *cardiologist, educator*
Dew, William Waldo, Jr. *bishop*
Dewalt, Judith K. *elementary school principal*
Dewane, John Richard *manufacturing company executive*
Dignac, Geny (Eugenia M. Bermudez) *sculptor*
Dillenberg, Jack *public health officer*
Donaldson, Wilburn Lester *property management corporation executive*
Donnelly, Charles Robert *retired college president*
†Dozer, Richard H. *professional sports team executive*
Drain, Albert Sterling *business management consultant*
DuMoulin, Diana Cristaudo *marketing professional*
Dunipace, Ian Douglas *lawyer*
Durrant, Dan Martin *lawyer*
Eaton, Berrien Clark *retired lawyer, author*
Ebert, Richard J. *principal*
Edens, Gary Denton *broadcasting executive*
Ehmann, Anthony Valentine *lawyer*
Elien, Mona Marie *air transportation professional*
Ellison, Cyril Lee *literary agent, publisher*
Elmore, James Walter *architect, retired university dean*
Estes, Mark Wayne *corporate communications writer, editor*
Evans, Ronald Allen *lodging chain executive*
Everett, James Joseph *lawyer*
Everroad, John David *lawyer*
Feinstein, Allen Lewis *lawyer*
Feldman, Stanley George *state supreme court justice*
Fennelly, Jane Corey *lawyer*
Fenzl, Terry Earle *lawyer*
Fine, Charles Leon *lawyer*
Fink, Joel Charles *dermatologist*
Fitzgerald, Joan *principal*
Fitzgerald-Verbonitz, Dianne Elizabeth *nursing educator*
Fitzsimmons, (Lowell) Cotton *professional basketball executive, broadcaster, former coach*
Fitzsimmons, Robert James *finance company executive*
Flickinger, Don Jacob *patent agent*
Fournier, Donald Frederick *dentist*
Fox, Frances Juanice *retired librarian, educator*
Frank, John Paul *lawyer, author*
Franke, William Augustus *corporate executive*
Freyermuth, Clifford L. *structural engineering consultant*
Friesen, Oris Dewayne *software engineer, historian*
Fulk, Roscoe Neal *retired accountant*
Fullmer, Steven Mark *systems engineer*
Gaffney, Donald Lee *lawyer*
Gaines, Francis Pendleton, III *lawyer*
Galbut, Martin Richard *lawyer*
Gall, Donald Alan *data processing executive*
Garrett, Dennis Andrew *police official*
Gartner, Michael Alfred *professional hockey player*
Genrich, Mark L. *newspaper editorial writer, columnist*
Gerber, Rudolph Joseph *judge, educator*
Gibbs, William Harold *university administrator*
Giedt, Bruce Alan *paper company executive*
Gilbert, Donald R. *lawyer*
Gladner, Marc Stefan *lawyer*
Godwin, Mary Jo *editor, librarian consultant*
Goldenthal, Nathan David *physician*
Goldstein, Stuart Wolf *lawyer*
Grant, Merwin Darwin *lawyer*
Grier, James Edward *hotel company executive, lawyer*
Griller, Gordon Moore *court administrator*
Grinell, Sheila *museum director*
Gunty, Christopher James *newspaper editor*
Gwozdz, Kim Elizabeth *interior designer*
Hacker, Kenneth Russell *insurance executive*
Hagerdon, Kathy Ann (Kay Hagerdon) *electric power industry executive*
Halpern, Barry David *lawyer*
Ham, Stephanie Ann *interior architect*
Hamilton, Ronald Ray *minister*
Hanley, Fred William *librarian, educator*
Hardy, Charles Leach *federal judge*
Hardy, Gary Wayne *financial planner*
Harelson, Hugh *publishing and tourism consultant*
Harrison, Mark I. *lawyer*
Harte, John Joseph Meakins *bishop*
Hawkins, Jasper Stillwell, Jr. *architect*
Hay, John Leonard *lawyer*
Hayden, William Robert *lawyer*
Hendricks, Ed *lawyer*
Hicks, William Albert, III *lawyer*
Hill, Edward G. *food marketing executive*
Hoecker, Thomas Ralph *lawyer*
Holloway, Edgar Austin *retired diversified business executive*
Houseworth, Richard Court *banker*
Hoxie, Joel P. *lawyer*
Hoyt, Monty *car purchase consultant*
Hudson, Laura Lyn Whitaker *scientific researcher*
Huffman, Edgar Joseph *oil company executive*
Hull, Jane Dee *state official, former state legislator*
Huntwork, James R. *lawyer*
Hutchinson, Ann *development director*
Inman, William Peter *lawyer*
Jacobson, (Julian) Edward *lawyer*
James, Charles E., Jr. *lawyer*
Jansen, Donald William *lawyer, legislative administrator*
Jirauch, Charles W. *lawyer*
Johnson, Kevin Maurice *professional basketball player*
Johnston, Logan Truax, III *lawyer*
Jones, Lucia Jean *physical education educator*
Jorgensen, Gordon David *engineering company executive*
Joyner, Seth *professional football player*
Kail, Konrad *physician*
Kandell, Howard Noel *pediatrician*
Karpman, Robert Ronald *orthopedic surgeon*
Kaufman, Roger Wayne *state judge*
Khan, Ahmed Mohiuddin *finance, insurance executive*
Kidd, Jason *professional basketball player*
Kimball, Bruce Arnold *soil scientist*
King, Felton *bishop*
†King, Kris *professional hockey player*
Klausner, Jack Daniel *lawyer*
Koester, Berthold Karl *lawyer, retired honorary consul, educator*
Kolbe, John William *newspaper columnist*
Kreutzberg, David W. *lawyer*
Kurn, Neal *lawyer*
Kurtz, Joan Helene *pediatrician*
Kuzma, George Martin *bishop*
Lacey, Henry Bernard *lawyer*
Land, George A. *philosopher, writer, educator, consultant*
Landers, Teresa Price *librarian*
Laufer, Nathan *cardiologist*
Lawes, Patricia Jean *art educator*
Lawrence, William Doran *physician*
Leach, John F. *newspaper editor, journalism educator*
Lee, Gilbert Brooks *retired ophthalmology engineer*
Lemon, Leslie Gene *consumer services company executive*
Leonard, Jeffrey S. *lawyer*
Levin, Linda Rose *mental health counselor*
Lewis, Orme, Jr. *investment company executive, land use advisor*
Linxwiler, Louis Major, Jr. *retired finance company executive*
Lorenzen, Robert Frederick *ophthalmologist*
Love, Duval Lee *professional football player*
†Lovett, William Lee *physician*
Lowry, Edward Francis, Jr. *lawyer*
Madden, Paul Robert *lawyer*
Maguire, Alan Edward *economist, public policy consultant*
Mangum, John K. *lawyer*
Manning, Daniel Ricardo *professional basketball player*
Manning-Weber, Claudia Joy *medical radiography administrator, consultant*
Mardian, Daniel *construction company director*
Marker, Loretta Irene *medical/surgical cardiac nurse*
Marks, Merton Eleazer *lawyer*
Marshall, Margaret Elizabeth *psychologist-therapist*
Martone, Frederick J. *judge*
Martori, Joseph Peter *lawyer*
McClelland, Norman P. *food products executive*
Mc Clennen, Louis *lawyer, educator*
McDaniel, Joseph Chandler *lawyer*
McNamee, Stephen M. *federal judge*
McRae, Hamilton Eugene, III *lawyer*
McWhorter, Ruth Alice *counselor, marriage and family therapist*
Meddles, Sharon Diane Gunstream *school counselor*
Melner, Sinclair Lewis *insurance company executive, retired*
Merritt, Nancy-Jo *lawyer*
Meyerson, Bruce Elliot *lawyer*
Might, Thomas Owen *newspaper company executive*
Miller, Louis Rice *lawyer*
Miller, Michael Jon *survey engineer, local government manager*
†Mitchell, Don *professional sports team executive*
Mitchell, Wayne Lee *health care administrator*
Moeller, James *state supreme court justice*
Mounes, Janice Rose Moore *real estate broker*
Moya, Patrick Robert *lawyer*
Moyer, Alan Dean *retired newspaper editor*
Muecke, Charles Andrew (Carl Muecke) *federal judge*
Mullen, Daniel Robert *finance executive*
Murian, Richard Miller *book company executive*
Myers, Robert David *judge*
Napolitano, Janet Ann *prosecutor*
Naylor, Franklin Llewellyn, Jr. *financial advisor*
Nielson, Theo Gilbert *law enforcement official, university official*
North, Gerald David William *lawyer*

North, Warren James government official
Norton, Douglas Ray auditor general
O'Brien, Thomas Joseph bishop
Olsen, Alfred Jon lawyer
Olsen, Gordon retired lawyer
Olson, Robert Howard lawyer
Oppedahl, John Fredrick publisher
O'Steen, Van lawyer
Paddock, John professional hockey team head coach
Parrett, Sherman O. lawyer
Paul, Elias food company consultant
Peabody, Debbie Kay elementary school educator
Perry, Lee Rowan lawyer
†Piatt, Malcolm Keith, Jr. medical center administrator
Platt, Warren E. lawyer
Powers, Noyes Thompson lawyer
Preble, Lou-Ann M. state legislator
Price, Charles Steven lawyer
Pulaski, Charles Alexander, Jr. lawyer
Quinsler, William Thomson retired investment advisor
Rathwell, Peter John lawyer
Rau, David Edward real estate company executive
Reed, Wallace Allison physician
Refo, Patricia Lee lawyer
Richards, Charles Franklin, Jr. lawyer
Richardson, Mary Lou psychotherapist
Rimsza, Skip mayor
Roe, William Thomas psychology educator, researcher
Romley, Richard M. lawyer
Rose, David L. lawyer
Rosenblatt, Paul Gerhardt federal judge
Roth, Sanford Harold rheumatologist, health care administrator, educator
Rowley, Beverley Davies medical sociologist
Rudolph, Gilbert Lawrence lawyer
St. Clair, Thomas McBryar mining and manufacturing company executive
Salerno, Thomas James lawyer
Salmonson, Marty Lee stockbroker, consulting engineer
Savage, Stephen Michael lawyer
Schatt, Paul newspaper editor
Schiffner, Charles Robert architect
Schiller, William Richard surgeon
Schmieder, Carl jeweler
Schoenfeld, Jim professional hockey coach
Schroeder, Mary Murphy federal judge
Seiler, Steven Lawrence health facility administrator
†Selanne, Teemu hockey player
Shaw, Lillie Marie King vocalist
Shelby, Ronald Van Dorn information systems executive
Sherk, Kenneth John lawyer
Showalter, Buck (William Nathaniel Showalter, III) major league baseball team manager
Silverman, Alan H. lawyer
Simmons, Clyde professional football player
Simunich, Mary Elizabeth Hedrick (Mrs. William A. Simunich) public relations executive
Skinner, Nancy Jo municipal recreation executive
Smock, Timothy Robert lawyer
Snell, Richard holding company executive
Sochacki, Andrzej mechanical engineer, researcher
Socwell, Margaret Gertrude Osborn Harris reading and language arts educator, consultant
†Solheim, Karsten golf equipment company executive
Stahl, Louis A. lawyer
Stahl, Richard G. C. journalist, editor
Starks, Rosalyn June physical education and health educator
Steckler, Phyllis Betty publishing company executive
Stephenson, Frank Alex environmental engineer, consultant
Stern, Richard David investment company executive
Steward, Lester Howard psychiatrist, academic administrator, educator
Stewart, Sally public relations practitioner
Stine, George Harry consulting engineer, author
Storey, Norman C. lawyer
Strand, Roger Gordon federal judge
Sullivan, George Anerson orthodontist
Sullivan, Martin Edward museum director
Sutton, Samuel J. lawyer, educator, engineer
Swann, Eric Jerrod professional football player
Sweet, Cynthia Kay business administrator
Swensen, Mary Jean Hamilton graphic artist
Symington, J. Fife, III governor
Targovnik, Selma E. Kaplan physician
Teets, John William retired diversifed company executive
Terry, Peter Anthony lawyer
Thomas, Harold William avionics systems engineer, flight instructor
Thompson, Herbert Ernest tool and die company executive
†Tkachuk, Keith professional hockey player
†Tobin, Vincent Michael professional sports team executive
Tour, Robert Louis ophthalmologist
Tribble, Richard Walter brokerage executive
Turner, William Cochrane international management consultant
Udall, Calvin Hunt lawyer
†Ueberroth, Peter Victor former baseball commissioner
Ulrich, Paul Graham lawyer, author, publisher, editor
Uthoff, Michael dancer, choreographer, artistic director
Van Arsdale, Dick professional basketball team executive
Van Kilsdonk, Cecelia Ann retired nursing administrator, volunteer
Walker, Richard K. lawyer
Wall, Donald Arthur lawyer
Wallace, Kenneth Alan investor
Ward, Yvette Hennig advertising executive
Watson, Harold George engineering executive, mechanical engineer
Weil, Louis Arthur, III newspaper publishing executive
Weinstein, Allan M. medical device company executive
Welliver, Charles Harold hospital administrator
Welsh, John Richard state official
Wheeler, Steven M. lawyer
Whisler, James Steven lawyer, mining and manufacturing executive
White, Edward Allen electronics company executive
Whitman, Kathy Velma Rose (Elk Woman Whitman) artist, sculptor, jeweler, painter, educator
Williams, Aeneas Demetrius professional football player
Williams, Bill academic administrator
Williams, Quinn Patrick lawyer
Wilson, Carl Arthur real estate broker, contractor
Wilson, Lawrence Frank (Larry Wilson) professional football team executive
Wilson, Stephen Rip public policy consultant
Winslow, Paul David architect
Winthrop, Lawrence Fredrick lawyer
Witherspoon, James Donald biology educator
Wolf, G. Van Velsor, Jr. lawyer
Wood, Barbara Butler secondary language arts and television production educator
Woods, Bobby Joe transportation executive
Woods, Cyndy Jones junior high educator, researcher
Woods, Grant state attorney general
Woolf, Michael E. lawyer
Wright, Richard Oscar, III pathologist, educator
Yarnell, Michael Allan lawyer
Ybarra, Kathryn Watrous systems engineer
Yearley, Douglas Cain mining and manufacturing company executive
Zeilinger, Philip Thomas aeronautical engineer
Zerella, Joseph T. pediatric surgeon

### Portal
Zweifel, Richard George curator

### Prescott
Alegre, Jose Alberto family practice physician
Anderson, Arthur George laboratory director, former computer company executive, consultant
Bieniawski, Zdzislaw Tadeusz Richard engineering educator emeritus, writer, consultant
†Brown, James Isaac rhetoric educator
Casserly, John Joseph author, journalist
Chesson, Eugene, Jr. civil engineering educator, consultant
Daly, Paul Sylvester mayor, retired academic administrator
Halvorson, Mary Ellen education educator, writer
Harris, Earl Edward business educator
Hasbrook, A. Howard aviation safety engineer, consultant
Kahne, Stephen James systems engineer, educator, academic administrator, engineering executive
Kleindienst, Richard Gordon lawyer
Longfellow, Layne Allen psychologist, educator, author, musician
Mayol, Richard Thomas advertising executive, political consultant
Mc Cormack, Fred Allen state social services administrator
Moses, Elbert Raymond, Jr. speech and dramatic arts educator
Osborn, DeVerle Ross insurance company executive
Parkhurst, Charles Lloyd electronics company executive
Samples, Martina nursing home administrator
Stasack, Edward Armen artist

### Prescott Valley
Wynn, Robert Raymond retired engineer, consultant

### Rio Verde
Jordan, Richard Charles engineering executive
Ramsey, David Selmer retired hospital executive

### Roll
Jorajuria, Elsie Jean elementary education educator

### Safford
Riddlesworth, Judith Himes elementary education educator

### San Manuel
Hawk, Dawn Davah secondary education educator

### Scottsdale
Blackburn, Jack Bailey retired civil engineering educator
Blanchet, Jeanne Ellene Maxant artist, educator, performer
Blinder, Martin S. business consultant, art dealer
Blumer, Harry Maynard architect
Boat, Ronald Allen business executive
Bodensieck, Ernest Justus mechanical engineer
Brock, Lonnie Rex landscape and nature photographer
Budge, Hamer Harold mutual fund company executive
Burr, Edward Benjamin life insurance company executive, financial executive
Carney, Richard Edgar foundation executive
Carpenter, Peter Rockefeller bank executive
Cary, Boyd Balford, Jr. physicist
Chase, James Keller retired artist, museum director, educator
Cherney, Elaine Ethel education educator
Chryss, George consulting company executive
Cianfarano, Sam Anthony, Jr. principal, educator
Clement, Richard William plastic and reconstructive surgeon
Cohn, Michael Jay psychologist, consultant, educator
Cordingley, Mary Jeanette Bowles (Mrs. William Andrew Cordingley) social worker, psychologist, artist, writer
Cormie, Donald Mercer investment company executive
Cunningham, Gilbert Earl business owner
Curtis, Philip C. artist
DeHaven, Kenneth Le Moyne retired physician
Doglione, Arthur George data processing executive
Donaldson, Scott English language educator, writer
Donnelly, Charles Francis management consultant, lawyer
Douglas, John Clifton architect
Ellensohn, Karol Kaye psychotherapist
Esquer, Deborah Anne elementary education educator
Evans, Tommy Nicholas physician, educator
Farris, Martin Theodore economist, educator
Fisher, John Richard engineering consultant, former naval officer
Fratt, Dorothy artist
Freedman, Stanley Marvin manufacturing company executive
Friedman, Shelly Arnold cosmetic surgeon
Frischknecht, Lee Conrad retired broadcasting executive
Garelick, Martin transportation executive
Garfield, Ernest bank consultant
Gillis, William Freeman telecommunications executive
Golden, Libby artist
Gookin, Thomas Allen Jaudon civil engineer
Gray, Walter Franklin retired banker
Grenell, James Henry retired manufacturing company executive
Hansen, Donald W. insurance and financial services executive
Harrison, Harold Henry physician, scientist, educator
Hill, Louis Allen, Jr. former university dean, consultant
Hill, Robert Martin police detective, consultant, lecturer
Hockmuth, Joseph Frank physicist, psychotherapist
Holliger, Fred Lee oil company executive
Hooker, Jo interior designer
Howe, H(ugh) Philip banker
Huizingh, William former accounting educator
Jacobson, Frank Joel cultural organization administrator
Joaquim, Richard Ralph hotel executive
Kinsinger, Jack Burl chemist, educator
Kitchel, Denison retired lawyer, writer
Kizziar, Janet Wright psychologist, author, lecturer
Kline, Arthur Jonathan retired electronics engineer
Krupp, Clarence William lawyer, personnel and hospital administrator
Kübler-Ross, Elisabeth physician
Lang, Margo Terzian artist
Leeland, Steven Brian electronics engineer
Leeser, David O. materials engineer, metallurgist
Lillestol, Jane Brush career development company executive
Lillo, Joseph Leonard osteopath, family practice physician
Lisa, Isabelle O'Neill law firm administrator, mergers and acquisitions executive
Malsack, James Thomas retired manufacturing company executive
McPherson, Donald J. metallurgist
Moeck, Walter F. conductor, music director
Muller, H(enry) Nicholas, III foundation executive
Nadler, Henry Louis pediatrician, geneticist, medical educator
Nebgen, Stephen Wade stage producer
Newman, William Louis geologist
O'Berry, Carl Gerald air force officer, electrical engineer
Orford, Robert Raymond consulting physician
Pavlik, Nancy convention services executive
Peshkin, Samuel David lawyer
Peterson, Louis Robert retired consumer products company executive
Peyton, William Maupin financial services executive, educator
Prisbrey, Rex Prince retired insurance agent, underwriter, consultant
Quayle, James Danforth former vice president United States, entrepreneur
Quigley, Jerome Harold management consultant
Ralston, Joanne Smoot public relations counseling firm executive
Reidy, Richard Robert publishing company executive
Reznick, Richard Howard pediatrician
Richie, Sharon I. army nursing officer, retired
Roberts, Peter Christopher Tudor engineering executive
Rudd, Eldon retired congressman, political consultant
Ruhlman, Terrell Louis business executive
Rutes, Walter Alan architect
Sanderson, David R. physician
Scherzer, Joseph Martin dermatologist
Schleifer, Thomas C. management consultant, author, lecturer
Scholder, Fritz artist
Searight, Patricia Adelaide retired radio and television executive
Sears, Alan Edward lawyer
Smith, Leonard Bingley musician
Starr, Isidore law educator
Sullivan, George Edmund editorial and marketing company executive
Swanson, Robert Killen management consultant
Swetnam, Monte Newton petroleum exploration executive
Timmons, Evelyn Deering pharmacist
Tyner, Neal Edward retired insurance company executive
Vairo, Robert John insurance company executive
Walsh, Edward Joseph toiletries and food company executive
Walsh, Mason retired newspaperman
Wright, C. T. Enus former university president

### Sedona
Catterton, Marianne Rose occupational therapist
Chicorel, Marietta Eva publisher
Copeland, Suzanne Johnson real estate executive
Edwards, F(loyd) Kenneth journalist, educator, management consultant, marketing executive
Eggert, Robert John, Sr. economist
Gregory, James actor
Hawkins, David Ramon psychiatrist, writer, researcher
Hoffmann, Joan Carol retired academic dean
Iverson, Wayne Dahl landscape architect, consultant
Keane, Mark Edward public executive and educator
Otto, Klaus physicist, physical chemist
Richards, Wanda Jamie education educator
Sasmor, James Cecil publishing representative, educator
Shors, Clayton Marion cardiologist
Silvern, Leonard Charles retired engineering executive
Stoufer, Ruth Hendrix community volunteer
Ware, Peggy Jenkins photographer, writer, artist, dancer
Wolfe, Al marketing and advertising consultant
Young, Mary Sean actress

### Sells
Enas, Lena Mae research coordinator, consultant

### Shonto
Haviland, Marlita Christine elementary school educator

### Sierra Vista
Bowen, Harry Ernest management consultant
Hasney, Christopher William retired investment company executive, educator
Lowe, Robert Charles lawyer, banker
Sizemore, Nicky Lee computer scientist

### Snowflake
Freyermuth, Gundolf S. writer

### Sonoita
Cook, William Howard architect
Scott, William Coryell medical executive

### Springerville
Geisler, Sherry Lynn justice of the peace, city magistrate

### Sun City
Corcoran, Eileen Lynch special education educator emerita
Cortright, Inga Ann accountant
Dapples, Edward Charles geologist, educator
Farwell, Albert Edmond retired government official, consultant
Feldman, Allan Jay financial planner, stockbroker
Fitch, W. Chester industrial engineer
Hauer, James Albert lawyer
Jackson, Randy computer networking executive
Jones, Alexander Elvin retired foundation executive
Lapsley, James Norvell, Jr. minister, pastoral theology educator
Moore, William Cullen retired electronics company executive
Musgrave, Charles Edward retired music director, correctional official
Oppenheimer, Max, Jr. foreign language educator, consultant
Pallin, Irving M. anesthesiologist
Pallin, Samuel Lear ophthalmologist
Roberts, Anna Ruth financial consultant
Treece, James Lyle lawyer
Woodside, Robert Elmer lawyer, former judge

### Sun City West
Anderson, Ernest Washington manufacturing company executive
Becker, Wesley Clemence psychology educator emeritus
Berkenkamp, Fred Julius management consultant
Black, Robert Frederick former oil company executive
Burke, Richard Kitchens lawyer, educator
Cohen, Abraham J. (Al Cohen) educational administrator
Curtin, Richard Daniel management consultant, retired air force officer, space pioneer
De Layo, Leonard Joseph former state education official
Forbes, Kenneth Albert Faucher urological surgeon
Madson, John Andrew architect
Mariella, Raymond P. chemistry educator, consultant
Mc Cune, John Francis, III retired architect
O'Brien, Gerald James utilities executive
Person, Robert John financial management consultant
Randall, Claire church executive
Schmitz, Charles Edison evangelist
Schrag, Adele Frisbie business education educator
Stevens, George Richard business consultant, public policy commentator
Williams, William Harrison retired librarian
Woodruff, Neil Parker agricultural engineer

### Sun Lakes
Cunningham, Arthur Francis university dean, marketing educator
Houser, Harold Byron epidemiologist
Richardson, Robert Carleton engineering consultant
Thompson, Loring Moore retired college administrator, writer

### Surprise
Clark, Lloyd historian, educator

### Tempe
Abell, James Logan architect
Adelson, Roger Dean history educator, editor, historian
Akers, Lex A. engineering educator
Alisky, Marvin Howard political science educator
†Allen, Charles R. television station executive
Anand, Suresh Chandra physician
Anchie, Toby Levine health facility administrator
Arters, Linda Bromley public relations consultant, writer, lecturer
Baker, Roland Jerald trade association administrator
Balanis, Constantine Apostle electrical engineering educator
Bauer, Ernst Georg physicist, educator
Berg, Linda Thoms real estate broker
Berman, Neil Sheldon chemical engineering educator
Blankenship, Robert Eugene chemistry educator
Brack, O. M., Jr. English language educator
Burgoyne, Edward Eynon chemistry educator
Buseck, Peter Robert geochemistry educator
Carpenter, Ray Warren materials scientist and engineer, educator
Clevenger, Jeffrey Griswold mining company executive
Coor, Lattie Finch university president
Cowley, John Maxwell physics educator
Evans, Lawrence Jack, Jr. lawyer
Farber, Bernard sociologist, educator
Ferreira, Jay Michael mechanical engineer
Ferry, David Keane electrical engineering educator
Forsyth, Ben Ralph academic administrator, medical educator
Gerking, Shelby Delos, Jr. zoologist, educator
Glick, Milton Don chemist, university administrator
Gordon, Leonard sociology educator
Goronkin, Herbert physicist
Greeley, Ronald geology educator
Grigsby, Jefferson Eugene, Jr. artist, educator
Guzzetti, Barbara Jean education educator
Gwinner, Robert Fred, Jr. marketing educator
Haggerson, Nelson Lionel, Jr. education educator
Harris, Mark English educator, author
Herald, Cherry Lou research educator, research director
Hickson, Robin Julian mining company executive
Hoke, Judy Ann physical education educator
Hoppensteadt, Frank Charles mathematician, university administrator
Ihrig, Edwin Charles, Jr. mathematics educator
Iverson, Peter James historian, educator
Juvet, Richard Spalding, Jr. chemistry educator
Karady, George Gyorgy electrical engineering educator, consultant
Kaufman, Herbert Mark finance educator
Kaufman, Irving retired engineering educator

Klett, Mark C. photographer, educator
Laananen, David Horton mechanical engineer, educator
Levin, Hal Alan psychiatrist
Lombardi, Eugene Patsy orchestra conductor, violinist, educator, recording artist
Lounsbury, John Frederick geographer, educator
MacKinnon, Stephen R. Asian studies administrator, educator
Mahajan, Subhash electronic materials educator
Manz, Charles C. management educator
Marsh, Roberta Reynolds elementary education educator, consultant
Matheson, Alan Adams law educator
Matthews, Gertrude Ann Urch retired librarian, writer
McKeever, Jeffrey D. computer company executive
Mc Sheffrey, Gerald Rainey architect, educator, city planner
Mense, Allan Tate research and development engineering executive
Metcalf, Virgil Alonzo economics educator
Miller, Warren Edward political scientist
Montero, Darrel Martin sociologist, social worker, educator
Moore, Carleton Bryant geochemistry educator
Moore, Rob professional football player
Nagrin, Daniel dancer, educator, choreographer, lecturer, writer
Ney, James Walter Edward Colby English language educator
Nigam, Bishan Perkash physics educator
O'Neil, Michael Joseph opinion survey executive, marketing consultant
Overman, Glenn Delbert college dean emeritus
Oxford, Sharon M. insurance company executive
Page, John Boyd physics educator
Pany, Kurt Joseph accounting educator, consultant
Patten, Duncan Theunissen ecologist educator
Pettit, George Robert chemistry educator, cancer researcher
Péwé, Troy Lewis geologist, educator
Poe, Jerry B. financial educator
Quadt, Raymond Adolph metallurgist, cement company executive
Raby, William Louis author
Rankin, William Parkman communications educator, former publishing company executive
Rice, Ross R(ichard) political science educator
Richardson, Richard Colby, Jr. higher education educator, researcher
Rios, Alberto Alvaro English educator
Ruiz, Vicki Lynn history educator
Sabine, Gordon Arthur educator, writer
Sackton, Frank Joseph public affairs educator
Schneller, Eugene S. sociology educator
Schroder, Dieter Karl electrical engineering educator
Scott, Judith Myers elementary education educator
Shaw, Milton Clayton mechanical engineering educator
Simmons, Howard Lee education educator
Simon, Sheldon Weiss political science educator
Singhal, Avinash Chandra engineering administrator, educator
Smith, David John physicist, educator
Smith, Harvey Alvin mathematics educator, consultant
†Snyder, Lester M. sports association executive
Spritzer, Ralph Simon lawyer, educator
Starrfield, Sumner Grosby astrophysics educator, researcher
Tambs, Lewis Arthur diplomat, historian, educator
Thompson, Anna Blanche retired educator
Thor, Linda Maria college president
Turk, Rudy Henry artist, retired museum director
Upson, Donald V. financial executive
Uttal, William R(eichenstein) psychology and engineering educator, research scientist
Vandenberg, Edwin James chemist, educator
Vanderpoel, James Robert lawyer
Weigend, Guido Gustav geographer, educator
Wesbury, Stuart Arnold, Jr. health administration and policy educator
Williams, James Eugene management consultant
Wills, J. Robert academic administrator, drama educator, writer
Yau, Stephen Sik-sang computer science and engineering educator, computer scientist, researcher
Zeitlin, Marilyn Audrey museum director
Zhang, Yong-Hang electrical engineering educator

### Tonopah
Brittingham, James Calvin nuclear engineer

### Tubac
Fey, John Theodore retired insurance company executive
Miller, Frederick Robeson banker

### Tucson
Abrams, Herbert Kerman physician, educator
Acker, Robert Flint microbiologist
Ahern, Geoffrey Lawrence behavioral neurologist
Alberts, David Samuel physician, pharmacologist, educator
Albrecht, Edward Daniel metals manufacturing company executive
Alpert, Joseph Stephen physician, educator
Anderson, Rachael Keller library administrator
Angel, James Roger Prior astronomer
Arnell, Walter James William mechanical engineering educator, consultant
Austin, John Norman classics educator
Barrett, Bruce Richard physics educator
Bartlett, David Carson state legislator
Bartocha, Bodo scientist, educator
Barton, Stanley Faulkner management consultant
Beach, Lee Roy psychologist, educator
Beckers, Jacques Maurice astrophysicist
Ben-Asher, M. David physician
Best, Gary Thorman real estate broker
Betteridge, Frances Carpenter retired lawyer, mediator
Bilby, Richard Mansfield federal judge
Birkinbine, John, II philatelist
Block, Michael Kent economics and law educator, public policy association executive, former government official, consultant
Blue, James Guthrie veterinarian
Bowlan, Nancy Lynn elementary and secondary school educator
Boyse, Edward Arthur research physician
Brainerd, Charles J(on) experimental psychologist, applied mathematician, educator
Brasswel, Kerry tax accountant, horsewoman
Breckenridge, Klindt Duncan architect
Brewer, David L. sociologist
Briggs, Peter Stromme art historian, curator
Broadfoot, Albert Lyle physicist
Broce, Dorothy Diane real estate broker, interior designer
Brosin, Henry Walter psychiatrist, educator
Brousseau, Georgia Cole school principal
Browning, William Docker federal judge
Bryan, Gordon Redman, Jr. nuclear power engineering consultant
Buras, Nathan hydrology and water resources educator
Burg, Walter A. airport terminal executive
Burrows, Benjamin retired physician, educator
Butcher, Russell Devereux author, photographer
Capp, Michael Paul physician, educator
Carruthers, Peter Ambler physicist, educator
Carter, L. Philip neurosurgeon, consultant
Cate, Rodney Michael academic administrator
Chen, Chuan Fang mechanical engineering educator
Chidester, Otis Holden retired secondary education educator
Cisler, Theresa Ann osteopath, former nurse
Clarke, James Weston political science educator, writer
Clarke, Robert Francis nuclear physicist, consultant
Clement, Nicholas I. principal
Coffman, Roy Walter, III publishing company executive
Conant, Howard Somers artist, educator
Cook, Annis Jane customer service executive
Cook, Gary Dennis music educator, administrator
Cortner, Hanna Joan science administrator, research scientist, educator
Cox, Robert Gene management consultant
Crawford, David L. astronomer
Dalen, James Eugene physician, educator
David, Ronald Sigmund psychiatrist
Davies, Roger geoscience educator
Davis, James Luther retired utilities executive, lawyer
†Davis, Richard Calhoun dentist
Davis, Stanley Nelson hydrologist, educator
Deluca, Dominick medical educator, researcher
Denton, Michael John research economist, electric utility expert, consultant
Desai, Chandrakant S. civil engineering and engineering mechanics educator
Dessler, Alexander Jack space physics and astronomy educator, scientist
De Young, David Spencer astrophysicist, educator
Dickinson, Robert Earl atmospheric scientist, educator
Dinnerstein, Leonard historian, educator
Dinsmore, Philip Wade architect
Dobbs, Dan Byron lawyer, educator
Dodd, Charles Gardner physical chemist
Dolph, Wilbert Emery lawyer
Doren, Henry Julius Thaddeus artist, painter
Dresher, William Henry research association executive
Dufner, Max retired German language educator
Dyer-Raffler, Joy Ann special education diagnostician, educator
Eckdahl, Donald Edward manufacturing company executive
Eckhardt, August Gottlieb law educator
Eribes, Richard dean
Ewy, Gordon Allen cardiologist, educator
Fang, Li-Zhi physicist, educator
Feliciano, José entertainer
†Fernandez, Jose J. cardiologist
Flint, Willis Wolfschmidt (Willi Wolfschmidt) artist
Forster, Leslie Stewart chemistry educator
Fountain, Linda secondary education educator
Franklin, John Orland lawyer
Fritts, Harold Clark dendrochronology educator, researcher
Froman, Sandra Sue lawyer
Gallagher, Rosanna Bostick elementary educator, administrator
Ganapol, Barry Douglas nuclear engineering educator, consultant
Gantz, David Alfred lawyer, university official
Geistfeld, Ronald Elwood retired dental educator
Gerba, Charles Peter microbiologist, educator
Giesser, Barbara Susan neurologist, educator
Gissing, Bruce retired aerospace company executive
Golden, Judith Greene artist, educator
Gonzales, Richard Joseph lawyer
Goodall, Jane anthropologist
Goodman, Seymour Evan computer science and international studies educator, researcher, consultant
Gourley, Ronald Robert architect, educator
Graham, Anna Regina pathologist, educator
Grams, Theodore Carl William librarian, educator
Grand, Marcia civic worker
Grand, Richard D. lawyer
Green, Robert Scott biotechnology company executive
Griffen, Agnes Marthe library administrator
Gross, Joseph Francis retired bio-engineering educator
Gruhl, James energy scientist, artist
Guice, John Thompson retired air force officer
Hancocks, David Morgan museum director, architect
Harcleroad, Fred Farley education educator
Harrington, Roger Fuller electrical engineering educator, consultant
Harris, David Thomas immunology educator
Hartmann, William Kenneth astronomy scientist
Hawk, Floyd Russell secondary school educator
Hawke, Robert Francis dentist
Haynes, Caleb Vance, Jr. geology and archaeology educator
Hays, James Fred geologist, educator
Heins, Marilyn college dean, pediatrics educator, author
Heller, Frederick retired mining company executive
Henderson, Roger C. law educator, former dean
Herrnstadt, Richard Lawrence American literature educator
Hershberger, Robert Glen architect, educator
Hildebrand, John G(rant) neurobiologist, educator
Hill, Henry Allen physicist, educator
Hoffmann, William Frederick astronomer
Howard, Robert Franklin observatory administrator, astronomer
Hruby, Victor Joseph chemistry educator
Hubbard, William Bogel planetary sciences educator
Hull, Herbert Mitchell plant physiologist, researcher
Humphrey, John Julius university program director, historian, writer
Hunt, Bobby Ray electrical engineering educator, consultant
Hunten, Donald Mount planetary scientist, educator
Hurt, Charlie Deuel, III library school director, educator
Hutchinson, Charles Smith, Jr. book publisher
Hutchinson, Edward Paul city official
Hutter, John Joseph, Jr. pediatric hematologist and oncologist, educator
Ingalls, Jeremy poet, educator
Irvin, Mark Christopher real estate consultant, broker and developer
Isenhower, Eleanor Anne Hexamer state government administrator
Jackson, Kenneth Arthur physicist, researcher
Jeffay, Henry biochemistry educator
Jefferies, John Trevor astronomer, astrophysicist, observatory administrator
Jeter, Wayburn Stewart retired microbiology educator, microbiologist
Johnson, John Gray retired university chancellor
Jones, Frank Wyman management consultant, mechanical engineer
Jones, Roger Clyde retired electrical engineering educator
Kaltenbach, C(arl) Colin dean, educator
Karkoschka, Erich planetary science researcher, writer
Kaszniak, Alfred Wayne neuropsychologist
Kearney, Joseph Laurence retired athletic conference administrator
Kececioglu, Dimitri Basil reliability engineering educator, consultant
Kellogg, Frederick historian, educator
Kerwin, William James electrical engineering educator, consultant
Kessler, John Otto physicist, educator
Kiersch, George Alfred geological consultant, retired educator
Kimble, William Earl lawyer
King, Marcia management consultant
Kingery, William David ceramics and anthropology educator
†Kingsolver, Barbara Ellen writer
Kinney, Robert Bruce mechanical engineering educator
Kischer, Clayton Ward embryologist, educator
Kmet, Rebecca Eugenia Patterson pharmacist
Koons, Stephen Eugene accountant, real estate developer
Kotin, Paul pathologist
Krasner, Scott Allan physician, health facility administrator
Krider, E. Philip atmospheric scientist, educator
†Labelle, James William pediatrician
Lacagnina, Michael Anthony judge
Lamb, Willis Eugene, Jr. physicist, educator
Langendoen, Donald Terence linguistics educator
Lauver, Edith Barbour nonprofit organization administrator
Law, John Harold biochemistry educator
Leavitt, Jerome Edward childhood educator
Lebowitz, Michael David epidemiologist
Lesher, Robert Overton lawyer
Levenson, Alan Ira psychiatrist, physician, educator
Lewis, Wilbur H. educational management consultant
Leydet, François Guillaume writer
Livermore, Joseph McMaster judge
Longan, George Baker, III real estate executive
Lunine, Jonathan Irving planetary scientist, educator
Lusk, Harlan Gilbert national park superintendent
Madden, James A. gifted and talented educator
Maker, Carol June gifted and talented educator
Marchalonis, John Jacob immunologist, educator
Marcialis, Robert Louis planetary astronomer
Marcus, Frank Isadore physician, educator
†Marks, Sheldon Harris Feiler urologist
Marquez, Alfredo C. federal judge
Marshall, Robert Herman economics educator
Martin, June Johnson Caldwell journalist
Martin, Paul Edward retired insurance company executive
Martinez, Maria Dolores pediatrician
Masters, William Howell physician, educator
Maxon, Don Carlton construction company executive, mining company executive
McConnell, Robert Eastwood architect, educator
McCormick, Floyd Guy, Jr. agricultural educator, college administrator
McCuskey, Robert Scott anatomy and cell biology educator, researcher
Mc Donald, John Richard lawyer
McEwen, Alfred Sherman planetary geologist
McNeill, Frederick Wallace lawyer, educator, writer, federal government consultant, former military and commercial pilot
Meehan, Michael Joseph lawyer
Meeker, Robert Eldon retired manufacturing company executive
Metcalfe, Darrel Seymour agronomist, educator
Miller, George mayor
Milton, Corinne Holm art history educator
Mishler, William, II political science educator
Mitchell, Robert Campbell nuclear consultant
Moreno, Manuel D. bishop
Morrow, James Franklin lawyer
Mullikin, Vernon Eugene aerospace executive
Nadler, George L. orthodontist
Nation, James Edward retired speech pathologist
Neal, James Madison, Jr. retired editor and educator
Nelson, Edward Humphrey architect
Neuman, Shlomo P. hydrology educator
Ning, Cun-Zheng physicist
Nixon, Robert Obey, Sr. business educator
Nordby, Gene Milo engineering educator
Nugent, Charles Arter physician
Olson, Lute university athletic coach
Osborne, Thomas Cramer mineral industry consultant
Osterberg, Charles Lamar marine radioecologist, oceanographer
Pace, Thomas M. lawyer
Pacheco, Manuel Trinidad academic administrator
Padilla, Elsa Norma school system administrator
Paley, Alfred Irving value engineering and consulting company executive, lecturer
Parmenter, Robert Haley physics educator
Partridge, William Russell retired federal executive
Peeler, Stuart Thorne petroleum industry executive and independent oil operator
Peete, Russell Fitch, Jr. aircraft appraiser
Pepper, Ian L. environmental microbiologist, research scientist, educator
Peters, Charles William research and development company manager
Porreca, Betty Lou education educator
Post, Roy Grayson nuclear engineering educator
Powell, Richard C. physicist, educator, researcher
Prince, John Luther, III engineering educator
Puente, Tito Anthony orchestra leader, composer, arranger
Rabuck, Donna Fontanarose English educator
Reid, Charles Phillip Patrick academic administrator, researcher, educator
Reinmuth, Oscar MacNaughton physician, educator
Renard, Kenneth George civil engineer
Re Velle, Jack B(oyer) statistician, consultant
Riggs, Frank Lewis foundation executive
Robinson, Bernard Leo retired lawyer
Rodeffer, Stephanie Lynn Holschlag archaeologist, government official
Roemer, Elizabeth astronomer, educator
Roll, John McCarthy judge
Roos, Nestor Robert consultant
Root, Nile photographer, educator
Rose, Hugh management consultant
Ross, Glynn opera administrator
Ross, Robert health agency administrator
Rountree, Janet Caryl astrophysicist
Rumler, Diana Gale geriatrics nurse
Running, Nels air force officer
Russ, Joanna author
Salmon, Sydney Elias medical educator, director
Sampliner, Linda Hodes psychologist, consultant
Schaefer, John Paul chemist, corporate executive
Schannep, John Dwight brokerage firm executive
Schorr, S. L. lawyer
Scotti, James Vernon astronomer
Sears, William Rees engineering educator
Seligman, Joel law educator
Severinsen, Doc (Carl H. Severinsen) conductor, musician
Shannon, Robert Rennie optical sciences center administrator, educator
Shropshire, Donald Gray hospital executive
Shultz, Silas Harold lawyer
Sibley, William Austin neurologist, educator
Silva, John Philip Costa newspaper editor
Skorupski, Diane Christine school library media specialist
Slack, Donald Carl agricultural engineer, educator
Smarandache, Florentin mathematics researcher, writer
Smerdon, Ernest Thomas academic administrator
Smith, David Wayne psychologist, educator
Smith, Josef Riley internist
Smith, Vernon Lomax economist, researcher
Soren, David archaeology educator, administrator
Speas, Robert Dixon aeronautical engineer, aviation company executive
Sprague, Ann Louise space scientist
Starr, Melvin Lee counselor
Stearns, Elliott Edmund, Jr. retired surgeon
Stini, William Arthur anthropologist, educator
Stoffle, Carla Joy university library dean
Strausfeld, Nicholas James neurobiology and evolutionary biology researcher, educator
Strittmatter, Peter Albert astronomer, educator
Strong, John William lawyer, educator
Stubblefield, Thomas Mason agricultural economist, educator
Sundt, Harry Wilson construction company executive
Swalin, Richard Arthur scientist, company executive
Swanson, Cheryl Ann small business owner, nurse
Swihart, H. Gregg real estate company executive
Sypherd, Paul Starr microbiologist
Tang, Esther Don development consultant, retired social worker
Tao, Chia-lin Pao humanities educator
Taylor, William Malcolm environmentalist, educator
Tellington, Wentworth Jordan engineer
Thompson, Raymond Harris anthropologist, educator
Tifft, William Grant astronomer
Tindall, Robert Emmett lawyer, educator
Tirrell, John Albert organization executive, consultant
Toland, Florence Winifred printing company executive
Tomoeda, Cheryl Kuniko academic researcher
Underwood, Jane Hainline Hammons anthropologist, educator
Vanatta, Chester B. business executive, educator
Vicker, Ray writer
Volgy, Thomas John political science educator, organization official
Wahlke, John Charles political science educator
Wait, James Richard electrical engineering educator, scientist
Wallach, Leslie Rothaus architect
Weaver, Albert Bruce university administrator
Weber, Charles Walter nutrition educator
Weber, Samuel editor, retired
†Weil, Andrew Thomas physician
Weinstein, Ronald S. physician, pathologist, educator
White, Alvin Swauger aerospace scientist, consultant
Whiting, Allen Suess political science educator, writer, consultant
Wickham, John Adams, Jr. retired army officer
Williams, Ben Franklin, Jr. mayor, lawyer
Willis, Clifford Leon geologist
Willoughby, Stephen Schuyler mathematics educator
Wilson, John Lewis university official
Winfree, Arthur Taylor biologist, educator
Witte, Marlys Hearst internist, educator
Wolfe, William Jerome librarian, English language educator
Wolff, Sidney Carne astronomer, observatory administrator
Woods, Winton D. law educator
Woolfenden, James Manning nuclear medicine physician, educator
Yan, Chong Chao pharmacology, toxicology and nutrition researcher
Yassin, Robert Alan museum administrator, curator
Yocum, Harrison Gerald horticulturist, botanist, educator, researcher
Zeigler, Bernard Phillip electrical and computer engineering educator
Ziehler, Tony Joseph insurance agent
Zube, Ervin Herbert landscape architect, geographer, educator
Zukoski, Charles Frederick surgeon, educator

### Vail
Reichlin, Seymour physician, educator
Saul, Kenneth Louis retired utility company executive
Wallach-Levy, Wendee Esther retired secondary school educator

### Waddell
Turner, Warren Austin state legislator

Patty, Claibourne Watkins, Jr. lawyer

### Osceola
Wilson, Ralph Edwin lawyer, justice

### Paragould
Toomey, Kent Edward manufacturing company executive

### Pine Bluff
Bradford, Jay Turner insurance executive, state legislator
Burdick, David library director
Davis, Lawrence A. academic administrator
Jones, John Harris lawyer, banker
Lea, George A., Jr. retail food executive
Long, Edward Arlo business consultant, retired manufacturing company executive
Moon, Deborah Joan paralegal
Ramsay, Louis Lafayette, Jr. lawyer, banker
Scott, Vicki Sue school system administrator
Seawell, William Thomas former airline executive
Walker, Richard Brian chemistry educator

### Rogers
Searles, Anna Mae Howard educator, civic worker
Spainhower, James Ivan retired college president
Summerlin, William Talley allergist, immunologist, dermatologist

### Russellville
Chesnut, Franklin Gilmore clergyman
Inch, Morris Alton theology educator
Jones, James Rees retired oil company executive
Morris, Lois Lawson education educator
Thompson, Robert Jaye minister

### Scranton
Uzman, Betty Geren pathologist, retired educator

### Searcy
Beebe, Mike state senator, lawyer
Burks, David Basil academic administrator, educator
Miller, Ken Leroy religious studies educator, consultant, writer
Oldham, Bill W. mathematics educator

### Sherwood
Vogler, Diane Clark elementary school principal
Wood, Marion Douglas state legislator, lawyer

### Siloam Springs
Hill, James Robert accountant

### Springdale
Cordell, Beulah Faye special education educator
Cypert, Jimmy Dean lawyer
Hill, Peggy Sue principal
Martin, Becca Bacon editor, journalist
Rollins, Jimmy Don school system administrator
Tollett, Leland Edward food company executive
Tyson, Donald John food company executive

### Stamps
Moore-Berry, Norma Jean secondary school educator

### State University
Bednarz, James C. wildlife ecologist educator
Fowler, Gilbert L. dean, educator
Jones, Charlott Ann museum director, art educator
Lindquist, Evan artist, educator
Power, Mary Susan political science educator
Ruby, Ralph, Jr. vocational business educator
Schichler, Robert Lawrence English language educator
Whitis, Grace Ruth nursing educator
Wyatt, James Leslie, III university president
Wyatt, Leslie academic administrator

### Strong
Nunnally, Dolores Burns retired physical education educator

### Stuttgart
Bell, Richard Eugene grain and food company executive

### Van Buren
Breeden, Betty Loneta secondary school educator

### Walnut Ridge
Nodine, Loren L. critical care nurse, consultant

### Warren
Claycomb, Hugh Murray lawyer, author

### West Memphis
Fogleman, Julian Barton lawyer
Nance, Cecil Boone, Jr. lawyer

## CALIFORNIA

### Acampo
Eger, Marilyn Rae artist

### Agoura
Laney, Michael L. manufacturing executive

### Agoura Hills
Chagall, David journalist, author
deCiutiis, Alfred Charles Maria medical oncologist, television producer
Gressak, Anthony Raymond, Jr. sales executive
Koff, Robert Louis insurance executive
Merchant, Roland Samuel, Sr. hospital administrator, educator
Scardina, Frank Joseph real estate executive
Teresi, Joseph publishing executive

### Alameda
Bartalini, C. Richard judge
Billings, Thomas Neal computer and publishing executive, management consultant
Blatt, Beverly Faye biologist, consultant
Card, James Conrad coast guard officer
Gossett, Jeffrey Alan professional football player
Herrera, John professional football team executive
Herrick, Sylvia Anne health service administrator
Jaeger, Jeff Todd professional football player
Koenig, Gina Lee microbiologist
Mewhinney, Bruce Harrison Nicholas publisher
Paustenbach, Dennis James environmental toxicologist
Swilling, Pat professional football player
Taveggia, Thomas Charles management educator
Whorton, M. Donald occupational and environmental health physician, epidemiologist
Wisniewski, Stephen Adam professional football player
Yeaw, Marion Esther retired nurse

### Alamo
Burchell, Mary Cecilia surgeon
More, Vishwas engineering laboratory administrator
†Morgan, Joe Leonard investment company executive, former professional baseball player
Pritchett, Thomas Ronald retired metal and chemical company executive
Shiffer, James David retired utility executive
Whalen, John Sydney management consultant

### Albany
Boris, Ruthanna dancer, choreographer, dance therapist, educator
Chook, Edward Kongyen university official, disaster medicine educator
Daniels, Lydia M. health care administrator
Sikora, Stephen Theodore publisher

### Albion
Martin, Bill artist, art educator

### Alhambra
Duke, Donald Norman publisher
Harnsberger, Therese Coscarelli librarian
Obert, Jessie Craig nutritionist, consultant
Porché-Burke, Lisa Marie chancellor
Siler, Walter Orlando, Jr. retired business executive

### Aliso Viejo
Baumgartner, Anton Edward automotive sales professional
Davidson, Melody Kay critical care nurse, educator
Sanford, Sarah J. healthcare executive

### Alpine
Greenberg, Byron Stanley newspaper and business executive, consultant
Roberts, Dwight Loren engineering consultant
Sharits, Dean Paul motion picture company executive

### Alta Loma
Cooper, George Robert electrical engineer, educator
Currie, Madeline Ashburn business administration educator
Tolan, Vicki Irvena physical education educator
Wu, Seng-Chai financial planner, life insurance agency official

### Altadena
Burden, Jean (Prussing) poet, writer, editor
Coles, Donald Earl aeronautics educator, retired
Vaughan, Audrey Judd paralegal, musician
Willans, Jean Stone religious organization executive
†Willans, Richard James religious organization executive, human resources management consultant
Ziegler, Raymond Stewart retired architect

### Anaheim
Abramson, Norman retail executive
Alicea, Luis Rene professional baseball player
Barbas, Jeffrey Lawrence finance company executive
†Bavasi, William Joseph professional sports team executive
Bowman, Jeffrey R. protective services official
Brigham, Gerald Allen research physicist, consultant
Brofman, Woody astronautical engineer, educator
Brownhill, H. Bud small business owner, canine behavior therapist
Carvajal, Jorge Armando endocrinologist, internist
Daly, Tom mayor
DiSarcina, Gary Thomas professional baseball player
Edmonds, James Patrick (Jim Edmonds) professional baseball player
Faal, Edi M. O. lawyer
Finley, Chuck (Charles Edward Finley) professional baseball player
Grose, Elinor Ruth retired elementary education educator
Hollins, David Michael professional baseball player
Jackson, David Robert school system administrator
Jurczyk, Joanne Monica price analyst
Kallay, Michael Frank, II medical devices company official
†Kariya, Paul professional hockey player
Lachemann, Marcel professional baseball manager
Langston, Mark Edward professional baseball player
Lano, Charles Jack retired financial executive
Lee, Donna Jean retired hospice and respite nurse
Lefebvre, Peggy Anderson advertising executive
Loeblich, Helen Nina Tappan paleontologist, educator
Murray, Eddie Clarence professional baseball player
Nguyen, Tai Anh minister
Noorda, Raymond J. computer software company executive
Price, Richard Taft, Jr. manufacturing company executive
Salmon, Timothy James professional baseball player
Tavares, Tony professional hockey team executive
Uyehara, Otto Arthur mechanical engineering educator emeritus, consultant
Wilson, Ronald Lawrence professional hockey coach

### Angwin
Maxwell, Donald Malcolm college president, minister

### Antioch
Adams, Liliana Osses music performer, harpist
Chu, Valentin Yuan-ling author
Neimann, Albert Alexander mathematician, business owner

### Anza
Skelton, Red (Richard Skelton) comedian, artist

### Apple Valley
Beller, Gerald Stephen professional magician, former insurance company executive
Ledford, Gary Alan real estate developer
Mays, George Walter, Jr. educational technology educator, consultant, tutor
Tishner, Keri Lynn secondary education educator
Win, Khin Swe anesthesiologist
Yochem, Barbara June sales executive, lecturer

### Aptos
Bohn, Ralph Carl educational consultant, retired educator
Dobey, James Kenneth banker
Heron, David Winston librarian
Hirsch, Bette G(ross) college administrator, foreign language educator
Mechlin, George Francis electrical manufacturing company executive
Woods, Gurdon Grant sculptor

### Arcadia
Anderson, Holly Geis women's health facility administrator, commentator, educator
Baillie, Charles Douglas banker
Barney, Kline Porter, Jr. retired engineering company executive, consultant
Broderick, Donald Leland electronics engineer
Danziger, Louis graphic designer, educator
Gamboa, George Charles oral surgeon, educator
Kalm, Arne investment banker
Massier, Paul Ferdinand mechanical engineer
Mc Cormack, Francis Xavier lawyer, former oil company executive
Sloane, Beverly LeBov writer, consultant
Sloane, Robert Malcolm healthcare consultant
Stangeland, Roger Earl retail chain store executive

### Arcata
Barratt, Raymond William biologist, educator
Bowker, Lee Harrington academic administrator
Emenhiser, JeDon Allen political science educator, academic administrator
Geyer, Dennis Lynn university administrator and registrar
Hise, Mark Allen dentist
Janssen-Pellatz, Eunice Charlene healthcare facility administrator
McCrone, Alistair William university president
Wayne, Lowell Grant air pollution scientist, consultant

### Aromas
Nutzle, Futzie (Bruce John Kleinsmith) artist, author, cartoonist

### Arroyo Grande
Edwards, Patrick Michael sales consultant
Oseguera, Palma Marie marine corps officer, reservist

### Arvin
Pankey, Edgar Edward rancher

### Atascadero
†Knapp, Robert S. psychiatrist
Ogier, Walter Thomas retired physics educator

### Atherton
Alexander, Theron behavioral scientist, psychologist, writer
Bales, Royal Eugene philosophy educator
Barker, Robert Jeffery financial executive
Chetkovich, Michael N. accountant
Fisher, Leon Harold physicist, emeritus educator
Fried, John H. chemist
Goodman, Sam Richard electronics company executive
Hogan, Clarence Lester retired electronics executive
Holvick, Patricia Valerie Jean property manager, financial planner
King, Jane Cudlip Coblentz volunteer educator
Lane, Joan Fletcher educational administrator
Lowry, Larry Lorn management consulting company executive
Mc Intyre, Henry Langenberg former business executive, lawyer
Rosen, Charles Abraham electrical engineer, consultant
Scandling, William Fredric retired food service company executive
Starr, Chauncey research institute executive
Surbeck, Leighton Homer retired lawyer

### Atwater
DeVoe, Kenneth Nickolas food service executive, mayor

### Auburn
Henry, Karen Hawley lawyer
Hess, Patrick Henry chemist
Jeske, Howard Leigh retired life insurance company executive, lawyer

### Avalon
Burns, Denise Ruth artist

### Avila Beach
Kamm, Herbert journalist

### Azusa
Felix, Richard E. academic administrator
Gray, Paul Wesley university dean
Kimnach, Myron William botanist, horticulturist, consultant
Sambasivam, Ezhilarasan computer science and mathematics educator

### Bakersfield
Akers, Tom, Jr. cotton broker, consultant
Arciniega, Tomas Abel university president
Boyd, William Harland historian
Dorer, Fred Harold chemistry educator
Drake, Stanley Joseph association executive
Duquette, Diane Rhea library director
Enriquez, Carola Rupert museum director
Glynn, James A. sociology educator, author
Hart, Donald Milton automotive and ranching executive, former mayor
Hefner, John principal
Izenstark, Joseph Louis radiologist, physician, educator
Kegley, Jacquelyn Ann philosophy educator
Lundquist, Gene Alan cotton company executive
Martin, George Francis lawyer
McAlister, Michael Hillis architect
McMillan, Leonard David family life specialist, consultant, lecturer
Murillo, Velda Jean social worker, counselor
Osterkamp, Dalene May psychology educator, artist
Owens, Buck (Alvis Edgar, Jr.) singer, musician, songwriter
Rahal, Paramvir Singh physician
Reep, Edward Arnold artist
Rice, Frances Mae pediatrician
Thompson, Joyce Ann education consultant

### Baldwin Park
Swartz, Stephen Arthur banker, lawyer

### Banning
Holmes, John Richard physicist, educator

### Barstow
Jones, Nathaniel bishop
Lundstrom, Thomas John lawyer

### Bayside
Bank, Ron principal
Cocks, George Gosson retired chemical microscopy educator
Pierce, Lester Laurin aviation consultant

### Bel Air
Wexler, Robert university administrator

### Bellflower
Cook, Karla Joan elementary education educator
Martin, Melissa Carol radiological physicist

### Belmont
Carlson, Gary R. publishing executive
Hollis, Mary Frances aerospace educator
Morris, Bruce Dorian technical writer, literary historian, educator
Pava, Esther Shub artist, educator
Wang, Su Sun chemical company executive, chemist

### Belvedere
Crockett, Ethel Stacy librarian
Gale, Daniel Bailey architect
Lake, David S. publisher, lawyer

### Belvedere Tiburon
Behrman, Richard Elliot pediatrician, neonatologist, university dean
Caselli, Virgil P. real estate executive
Cook, Robert Donald financial service executive
Denton, Charles Mandaville corporate consultant
Hudnut, David Beecher retired leasing company executive, lawyer
Kramer, Lawrence Stephen journalist
Power, Jules television producer
Widman, Gary Lee lawyer, former government official

### Ben Lomond
Sikora, James Robert educational business consultant

### Benicia
Szabo, Peter John investment company executive, financial planner, mining engineer, lawyer
von Studnitz, Gilbert Alfred state official

### Berkeley
Abel, Carlos Alberto immunologist
Adelman, Irma Glicman economics educator
Alhadeff, David Albert economics educator
Alpen, Edward Lewis biophysicist, educator
Alpert, Norman Joseph merchandising executive
Alter, Robert B. comparative literature educator and critic
Ames, Bruce N(athan) biochemist, molecular biologist
Anderson, John Richard entomologist, educator
Anderson, William Scovil classics educator
Angelakos, Diogenes James electrical engineering educator
Arveson, William Barnes mathematics educator
Attwood, David Thomas physicist, educator
Auerbach, Alan Jeffrey economist
Baas, Jacquelynn art historian, museum administrator
Bagdikian, Ben Haig journalist, emeritus university educator
Baldwin, Bruce Gregg botany educator, researcher
Barish, Jonas Alexander English language educator
Barker, Horace Albert biochemist, microbiologist
Barnes, Thomas G. law educator
Barnett, R(alph) Michael theoretical physicist, educational agency administrator
Barrett, Reginald Haughton biology educator, wildlife management educator
Bartlett, Neil chemist, educator
Bartlett, Paul A. organic chemist
Barton, Babette B. lawyer, educator
Bellah, Robert Neelly sociologist, educator
Bender, Richard university dean, architect, educator
Benedict, Burton retired museum director, anthropology educator
Berger, Stanley Allan mechanical engineering educator
Bergman, George Mark mathematician, educator
Bergman, Robert George chemist, educator
Berkner, Klaus Hans laboratory administrator, physicist
Berlekamp, Elwyn Ralph mathematic educator, electronics company executive
Bern, Howard Alan science educator, research biologist
Berry, William Benjamin Newell geologist, educator, former museum administrator
Bickel, Peter John statistician, educator
Birdsall, Charles Kennedy electrical engineer
Blume, James Beryl financial advisor
Bogy, David B(eauregard) mechanical engineering educator
Bolt, Bruce Alan seismologist, educator
Bouwsma, William James history educator
Bowker, Albert Hosmer retired university chancellor
Bragg, Robert Henry physicist, educator
Brandes, Stanley Howard anthropology educator, writer
Breslauer, George William political science educator
Brewer, Leo physical chemist, educator
Brocchini, Ronald Gene architect

Carreras, José *tenor*
Carrey, Jim *actor*
†Carter, Chris *producer, director*
Casey, Joseph T. *corporate executive*
Cates, Phoebe *actress*
Catz, Boris *endocrinologist, educator*
Channing, Carol *actress*
Chapman, Michael *cinematographer, director*
Cher, (Cherilyn Sarkisian) *singer, actress*
Chernin, Peter *motion picture company executive*
Chong, Thomas *comedian, writer, director, musician*
Chritton, George A. *film producer*
Clooney, George *actor*
Close, Glenn *actress*
Coen, Ethan *film producer, writer*
Coen, Joel *film director, writer*
Coleman, Dabney W. *actor*
Columbus, Chris Joseph *film director, screenwriter*
Connery, Sean (Thomas Connery) *actor*
Coolidge, Martha *film director*
Corman, Eugene Harold *motion picture producer*
Corwin, Stanley Joel *book publisher*
Covitz, Carl D. *state official, real estate and investment executive*
Cox, Courteney *actress*
Crawford, Cindy *model*
Crichton, (John) Michael *author, film director*
Crowe, Christopher *director, screenwriter*
†Crowe, Russell *actor*
Cundey, Dean *cinematographer*
Curtis, Jamie Lee *actress*
Cusack, John *actor*
†D'Abo, Olivia *actress*
Daly, Timothy *actor*
D'Angelo, Beverly *actress*
Danson, Ted *actor*
Dante, Joe *film director*
Darabont, Frank *screenwriter, director*
David, Clive *event planning executive*
Davis, Andrew *film director, screenwriter*
Davis, Judy *actress*
Dawber, Pam *actress*
De Anda, Alicia *artist*
DeBont, Jan *cinematographer, director*
Delany, Dana *actress*
Demme, Jonathan *director, producer, writer*
De Niro, Robert *actor*
Depardieu, Gérard *actor*
Depp, Johnny *actor*
Dern, Bruce MacLeish *actor*
Deschanel, Caleb *cinematographer, director*
DeVito, Danny Michael *actor*
Dickerson, William Roy *lawyer*
†D'Onofrio, Vincent Philip *actor*
†Donovan, Tate *actor*
†Douglas, Ileana *actress*
Douglas, Kirk (Issur Danielovitch Demsky) *actor, motion picture producer*
Douglas, Michael Kirk *actor, film producer, director*
†Dutton, Charles S. *actor*
Duvall, Shelley *actress*
Eastwood, Clint *actor, director, former mayor*
Eikenberry, Jill *actress*
Eisenshtat, Sidney Herbert *architect*
Elliott, Chris *actor*
Elliott, Paul *cinematographer*
Elliott, Sam *actor*
Elwes, Cary *actor*
†Epps, Omar *actor*
Epstein, Julius J. *screenwriter, playwright, producer*
Essex, Harry J. *screenwriter, novelist*
Estevez, Emilio *actor, writer, director*
Evans, Louise *investor, retired psychologist, philanthropist*
†Evereett, Rupert *actor*
Evigan, Greg *actor, musician*
Fahey, Jeff *actor*
Fein, William *ophthalmologist*
Feldshuh, Tovah S. *actress*
Fenimore, George Wiley *management consultant*
Fickinger, Wayne Joseph *advertising executive*
Fiennes, Ralph Nathaniel *actor*
Filosa, Gary Fairmont Randolph V., II *multimedia executive, financier, columnist*
†Fincher, David *film director*
Finfer, David *film editor*
Fisher, Terry Louise *television writer*
Flanagan, Fionnula Manon *actress, writer, producer*
Flaum, Marshall Allen *television producer, writer, director*
Fleischer, Richard O. *film director*
Foch, Nina *actress, creative consultant, educator, director*
†Foley, James *film director*
Fonda, Bridget *actress*
†Forsythe, William *actor*
Foster, Lawrence *concert and opera conductor*
Foxworth, Robert Heath *actor, director*
Frank, Harriet, Jr. *screenwriter*
Friedkin, William *film director*
Friendly, Ed *television producer*
Gassner, Dennis *production designer*
Gelbart, Larry *writer, producer*
Getchell, Robert *screenwriter*
Gilberg, Arnold L. *psychiatrist and psychoanalyst*
Gillard, Stuart Thomas *film and television director, writer*
Giorgi, Elsie Agnes *physician*
Glazer, Guilford *real estate developer*
Glover, John *actor*
Goldman, Bo *screenwriter, director*
Goldman, William *writer*
Goldsmith, Bram *banker*
Graff, Todd *screenwriter*
Grant, Hugh *actor*
Grant, Michael Ernest *educational administrator, institutional management educator*
Graves, Peter *actor*
Graysmark, John *production designer*
Green, Guy Mervin Charles *film director*
Green, Jack N. *cinematographer*
Green, Walon *screenwriter*
Greenberg, Gerald B. *film editor*
†Grey, Brad *producer, agent*
Griffin, Merv Edward *former entertainer, television producer, entrepreneur*
Guttenberg, Steve *actor*
Hagar, Sammy *musician, vocalist, composer*
Hagman, Larry *actor*
Haile, Lawrence Barclay *lawyer*
Hall, Arsenio *television talk show host, comedian*
Hall, Roger *production designer*
Haller, Howard Edward *investment banker, real estate developer, film writer and producer*
Hallowell, Todd *art director, production designer*
Hamel, Veronica *actress*
Hamlin, Harry Robinson *actor*
Hanks, Tom *actor*
Hanley, Daniel *film editor*
Harlin, Renny (Renny Lauri Mauritz Harjola) *film director*
Harrelson, Woody *actor*
Harris, Ed(ward Allen) *actor*
Harris, Jordan *record company executive*
Harris, Julie (Ann) *actress*
Harris, Mel (Mary Ellen Harris) *actress*
Harrison, Gregory *actor*
Haskell, Peter Abraham *actor*
Hawn, Goldie *actress*
Headly, Glenne Aimée *actress*
Hefner, Hugh Marston *editor-in-chief*
Heller, Paul Michael *film company executive, producer*
Helmond, Katherine *actress*
Henderson, Florence (Florence Henderson Bernstein) *actress, singer*
Hepburn, Katharine Houghton *actress*
Hershey, Barbara (Barbara Herzstein) *actress*
Hill, David *broadcast executive*
Hill, Michael J. *film editor*
Hilton, Barron *hotel executive*
Hoch, Orion Lindel *corporate executive*
Hoenig, Dov *film editor*
Hogan, Steven L. *lawyer*
Hopkins, Sir Anthony (Philip) *actor*
Horwin, Leonard *lawyer*
Howard, Ron *director, actor*
Hudlin, Reginald Alan *director, writer, producer*
Hughes, John W. *film producer, screenwriter, film director*
Hunt, Helen *actress*
Hurd, Gale Anne *film producer*
Hutshing, Joe *film editor*
Isham, Mark *composer, jazz musician*
Israel, David *journalist, screenwriter, producer*
Israel, Richard Stanley *investment banker*
Jackson, Samuel L. *actor*
Jaffe, F. Filmore *judge, retired*
Jarre, Maurice Alexis *composer*
Jenner, Bruce *sportscaster, former Olympic athlete*
Jessup, W. Edgar, Jr. *lawyer*
Jones, David Hugh *theater, film and television director*
Jones, Robert C. *film editor*
Jones, Terry *film director, author*
Jordan, Glenn *director*
Kahn, Michael *film editor*
Karpman, Harold Lew *cardiologist, educator, author*
Kasdan, Lawrence Edward *film director, screenwriter*
Kaufman, Philip *film director*
Keaton, Diane *actress*
Keaton, Michael *actor, comedian*
Kemper, Victor J. *cinematographer*
Kilmer, Val *actor*
Kirkland, John C. *lawyer*
Klein, Arnold William *dermatologist*
Kravitz, Ellen King *musicologist, educator*
Kravitz, Lenny *singer, guitarist*
Kudrow, Lisa *actress*
Kuhn, Michael *motion picture company executive*
Lahti, Christine *actress*
Landis, John David *film director, writer*
Lane, Nathan (Joseph Lane) *actor*
Langella, Frank *actor*
Lee, Peggy (Norma Delores Egstrom) *singer, actress*
Lehmann, Michael Stephen *film director*
Leigh, Jennifer Jason (Jennifer Leigh Morrow) *actress*
Leonard, Elmore John *novelist, screenwriter*
Lesser, Gershon Melvin *physician, lawyer, medical and legal media commentator*
Lester, Richard *film director*
Levine, Alan J. *entertainment company executive*
Levine, Michael *public relations executive, author*
Levy, David *broadcasting executive*
Levy, Eugene *actor, director, screenwriter*
Levy, Peter *cinematographer*
Lewis, Juliette *actress*
Limato, Edward Frank *talent agent*
†Lindo, Delroy *actor*
Linkletter, Arthur Gordon *radio and television broadcaster*
Liotta, Ray *actor*
Litman, Brian David *communications executive*
Littleton, Carol *film editor*
Lloyd, Christopher *television writer and producer*
Lloyd, Emily (Emily Lloyd Pack) *actress*
Locklear, Heather *actress*
Loggia, Robert *actor*
Loggins, Kenny (Kenneth Clarke Loggins) *singer, songwriter*
Lombardo, Tony *film editor*
Lond, Harley Weldon *editor, publisher*
Long, Shelley *actress*
†Lopez, Jennifer *actress, dancer*
Lott, Ronnie (Ronald Mandel Lott) *professional football player*
Lottman, Evan *film editor*
Loughnane, Lee David *trumpeter*
Louis-Dreyfus, Julia *actress*
Lovejoy, Ray *film editor*
Lyne, Adrian *director*
MacMillan, Kenneth *cinematographer*
Madden, John *television sports commentator, former professional football coach*
Madsen, Michael *actor*
†Maffia, Roma *actress*
Mandel, Babaloo *scriptwriter*
Mann, Michael K. *producer, director, writer*
Mann, Ted *screenwriter*
Manoff, Dinah Beth *actress*
Manulis, Martin *film producer*
Mark, John *film company executive*
Marsh, Terence *production designer*
Martin, Steve *comedian, actor*
Mason, Marsha *actress, director, writer*
Masterson, Mary Stuart *actress*
Mastrantonio, Mary Elizabeth *actress*
†Masur, Richard *actor*
Matlin, Marlee *actress*
Mazursky, Paul *screenwriter, theatrical director and producer*
McAlpine, Andrew *production designer*
†McDermott, Dylan *actor*
McGagh, William Gilbert *financial consultant*
Mc Kenna, William Edward *business executive*
Mc Mahon, Ed *television personality*
Mc Tiernan, John *film director*
Mechanic, William M. *television and motion picture industry executive*
Menkes, John Hans *pediatric neurologist*
Meyer, Nicholas *screenwriter, director*
Miller, Dennis *comedian*
Mindell, Earl Lawrence *nutritionist, author*
Mirkin, David *television producer*
Mischer, Donald Leo *television director and producer*
Moore, Demi (Demi Guynes) *actress*
Moore, Dudley Stuart John *actor, musician*
Moore, Michael *film director*
Murphy, Eddie *comedian, actor*
Musky, Jane Michelle *film production designer*
Myers, Barton *architect*
†Nava, Gregory *film director*
Neeson, Liam *actor*
Neill, Sam *actor*
Nelligan, Kate (Patricia Colleen Nelligan) *actress*
Nesmith, Michael *film producer, video specialist*
Neuwirth, Bebe *dancer, actress*
Nicholas, Frederick M. *lawyer*
Nichols, Mike *stage and film director*
Nicita, Rick *agent*
Nitzsche, Jack *composer*
Noble, (Terry) Thom *film editor*
Norris, Chuck (Carlos Ray) *actor*
Novak, Kim (Marilyn Novak) *actress*
Noyce, Phillip *film director*
Nykvist, Sven Vilhem *cinematographer*
Oakley, Bill *television producer*
O'Donnell, Rosie *comedienne, actress*
Oldfield, A(rthur) Barney *writer, radio commentator*
Ondricek, Miroslav *cinematographer*
Orenstein, (Ian) Michael *philatelic dealer, columnist*
Pacino, Al (Alfredo James Pacino) *actor*
Palance, Jack *actor*
Palminteri, Chazz *actor*
Paquin, Anna *actress*
Parker, Alan William *film director, writer*
Parker, Sarah Jessica *actress*
†Patric, Jason *actor*
Paull, Lawrence G. *production designer*
†Paymer, David *actor*
Peck, Eldred Gregory *actor*
Pedersen, Ken *recording industry executive*
Penderecki, Krzysztof *composer, conductor*
Perez, Rosie *actress*
Perkins, Elizabeth Ann *actress*
Perry, Matthew *actor*
Pfeiffer, Michelle *actress*
†Pinkett, Jada *actress*
Pitt, Brad *actor*
Platt, Oliver *actor*
Plummer, (Arthur) Christopher (Orme) *actor*
Polanski, Roman *film director, writer, actor*
†Pollak, Kevin *actor*
Portman, Rachel Mary Berkeley *composer*
Presley, Priscilla *actress*
Pressman, Michael *film director*
Priestley, Jason *actor*
Ptak, John Anthony *talent agent*
Pullman, Bill *actor*
Quartararo, Phil *recording industry executive*
Rabe, David William *playwright*
Rafkin, Alan *television and film director*
Raimi, Samuel M. *film director*
Ramer, Bruce M. *lawyer*
Rapke, Jack *agent*
Reiner, Rob *actor, writer, director*
Reitman, Ivan *film director, producer*
Reynolds, William Henry *film editor*
†Rhames, Ving *actor*
†Ricci, Christina *actress*
Rickman, Tom *screenwriter, director*
Riess, Gordon Sanderson *management consultant*
Rifkin, Arnold *film company executive*
Ringwald, Lydia Elaine *artist, poet*
Rivers, Joan *entertainer*
Robbins, Richard *composer*
Roberts, Eric *actor*
†Roberts, Julia Fiona *actress*
†Rodriguez, Robert *filmmaker*
Roeg, Nicolas Jack *film director*
Rolf, Tom *film editor*
Romero, George A. *film director*
Rondeau, Charles Reinhardt *lawyer*
Rosenzweig, Richard Stuart *publishing company executive*
Rosky, Burton Seymour *lawyer*
Ross, Herbert David *film director*
Rossellini, Isabella *actress, model*
Roth, Eric *screenwriter*
Rotunno, Giuseppe *cinematographer*
Rowan, Keith Patterson *communications executive, consultant*
Rubeo, Bruno *production designer*
Rush, Herman E. *television executive*
Ryan, Meg *actress*
Ryder, Winona (Winona Laura Horowitz) *actress*
Sakamoto, Ryuichi *composer*
Schepisi, Fred *producer, director, screenwriter*
Schiff, Gunther Hans *lawyer*
Schlatter, George H. *producer, director, writer*
Schlesinger, John Richard *film, opera and theater director*
Schneider, Charles I. *newspaper executive*
†Schneider, Rob *actor*
Schulian, John (Nielsen Schulian) *screenwriter, author*
Schwarzenegger, Arnold Alois *actor, author*
Schwimmer, David *actor*
Scott, Ridley *film director*
Seagal, Steven *actor*
Seinfeld, Jerry *comedian*
Shacter, David Mervyn *lawyer*
†Shaham, Gil *violinist*
Shandling, Garry *comedian, scriptwriter, actor*
Shapell, Nathan *financial and real estate executive*
Sheinberg, Sidney Jay *producer, entertainment company executive*
Shepard, Kathryn Irene *public relations executive*
Shepard, Sam (Samuel Shepard Rogers) *playwright, actor*
Shoemaker, Bill (William Lee Shoemaker) *retired jockey, horse trainer*
Shue, Elisabeth *actress*
Silverman, David Alan *screenwriter, television story consultant*
Singleton, Henry Earl *industrialist*
Singleton, John *director, screenwriter*
Sinise, Gary *actor, director*
†Sizemore, Tom *actor*
Skerritt, Tom *actor*
†Smith, John N. *film director*
†Smith, Kevin *film director, writer*
Smith, Roy Forge *art director, production designer*
Smith, Will *actor, rapper*
Snyder, David L. *film production designer*
Sonnenfeld, Barry *cinematographer, film director*
Sorvino, Mira *actress*
Spacek, Sissy (Mary Elizabeth Spacek) *actress*
Spader, James *actor*
Spheeris, Penelope *film director*
Spielberg, Steven *motion picture director, producer*
Spikings, Barry Peter *film company executive, producer*
Stack, Robert Langford *actor*
Stallone, Sylvester Enzio *actor, writer, director*
Steenburgen, Mary *actress*
Stefano, Joseph William *film and television producer, author*
Stein, Myron *internist, educator*
Steinkamp, Fredric *film editor*
Stern, Gardner *television writer and producer*
Stevens, Gary *professional jockey*
Stewart, Patrick *actor*
Stoltz, Eric *actor*
Stowe, Madeleine *actress*
Strauss, Peter *actor*
Streep, Meryl (Mary Louise Streep) *actress*
Streisand, Barbra Joan *singer, actress, director*
Stringfield, Sherry *actress*
Suschitzky, Peter *cinematagrapher*
Sutherland, Kiefer *actor*
†Sweeney, A.B. *actor*
Tally, Ted *screenwriter*
Thompson, Caroline Warner *film director, screenwriter*
Thompson, Larry Angelo *producer, lawyer, personal manager*
Thorin, Donald E. *cinematographer*
†Thornton, Billy Bob *actor, director*
Thurman, Uma Karuna *actress*
Tilly, Jennifer *actress*
Toffel, Alvin Eugene *corporate executive, business and governmental consultant*
Tomei, Marisa *actress*
Towers, Bernard Leonard *medical educator*
Towne, Robert *screenwriter*
Travis, Nancy *actress*
Trumbull, Douglas *film director, writer, creator special effects*
†Tucci, Stanley *actor*
Turner, Tina (Anna Mae Bullock) *singer*
†Turteltaub, Jon *film director*
Turturro, John *actor*
Tyson, Cicely *actress*
Van Ark, Joan *actress*
Van Sant, Gus, Jr. *director, screenwriter*
Victor, Robert Eugene *real estate corporation executive, lawyer*
Virkler, Dennis M. *film editor*
Von Wright, Victor, Sr. *actor, film producer*
Wagner, Lindsay J. *actress*
Wainess, Marcia Watson *legal management consultant*
Walker, Lesley *film editor*
Walker, William Tidd, Jr. *investment banker*
Ward, David Schad *screenwriter, film director*
Washington, Denzel *actor*
Weaver, Sigourney (Susan Alexandra Weaver) *actress*
†Weber, Steven *actor*
Weir, Peter Lindsay *film director*
Whaley, Frank *actor*
White, Betty *actress, comedienne*
Wilder, Billy *motion picture director, writer, producer*
Wilder, Gene *actor, director, writer*
Willson, James Douglas *aerospace executive*
Wilson, Brian Douglas *recording artist, composer, record producer*
Wincer, Simon *film director*
Winfield, David Mark *former professional baseball player, commentator*
Winger, Debra *actress*
Winkler, Henry Franklin *actor*
Winkler, Irwin *motion picture producer*
Winningham, Mare *actress*
Winslet, Kate *actress*
Winthrop, John *business executive*
Wise, Robert *film producer, director*
Woods, James Howard *actor*
Wright, John *film editor*
Yaryan, Ruby Bell *psychologist*
Yorkin, Bud (Alan Yorkin) *producer, director*
†Zane, Billy *actor*
Zanuck, Richard Darryl *motion picture company executive*
Zarem, Abe Mordecai *management consulting executive*
Zimmerman, Don *film editor*
Zwick, Edward M. *director, producer, scriptwriter*

### Big Bear Lake
Essman, Robert Norvel *artist, graphic designer*

### Big Sur
Cross, Robert Louis *realtor, land use planner, writer*
Owings, Margaret Wentworth *conservationist, artist*

### Bishop
Buchanan, James Douglas *lawyer*
Haber, Ralph Norman *psychology consultant, researcher, educator*
Naso, Valerie Joan *automotive dealership executive, travel company operator*

### Bloomington
Llanusa, Steven Michael *elementary education educator*

### Bodega
Hedrick, Wally Bill *artist*

### Bodega Bay
Allard, Robert Wayne *geneticist, educator*
Clegg, James Standish *physiologist, biochemist, educator*
Hand, Cadet Hammond, Jr. *marine biologist, educator*
King, Leland W. *architect*

### Bolinas
Harris, Paul *sculptor*
Lerner, Michael Albers *educator*
Murch, Walter Scott *director, writer, film editor, sound designer*

### Bonita
Curtis, Richard Earl *former naval officer, former company executive, business consultant*
Wood, Fergus James *geophysicist, consultant*
Yokley, Richard Clarence *fire department administrator*

### Boonville
Hanes, John Ward *sculptor, civil engineer consultant*

**Borrego Springs**
Scannell, William Edward *aerospace company executive, consultant, psychologist*
Shinn, Allen Mayhew *retired naval officer, business executive*

**Brawley**
Jaquith, George Oakes *ophthalmologist*

**Brea**
Dyer, Alice Mildred *psychotherapist*
Georgino, Susan Martha *city redevelopment services administrator*
Herzing, Alfred Roy *computer executive*
Lounsbury, Steven Richard *lawyer*
Pearson, April Virginia *lawyer*
Shell, Billy Joe *retired university president*
Shen, Gene Giin-Yuan *organic chemist*
Stegemeier, Richard Joseph *oil company executive*
Tamura, Cary Kaoru *fundraiser*

**Brisbane**
Anargyros, Spero *sculptor*
England, Cheryl *editor-in-chief*
Mulligan, Martin Frederick *clothing executive, professional tennis player*
Orban, Kurt *foreign trade company executive*

**Buena Park**
Papin, Nancy Sue *educational computer coordinator*
Turkus-Workman, Carol Ann *educator*

**Burbank**
Ajalat, Sol Peter *lawyer*
Allen, Tim *actor, comedian*
Becker, Walter *guitarist, record producer*
Berman, Bruce *entertainment company executive*
Berry, Bill *popular musician*
†Black, Carole *broadcast executive*
Bower, Richard James *minister*
Brogliatti, Barbara Spencer *television and motion picture executive*
Buck, Peter *musician, guitarist*
Casey, William Carleton *physician, urologist*
Chaffee, James Albert *protective services official*
Chierighino, Brianne Siddall *voice-over, actress, assistant location manager*
Chiolis, Mark Joseph *television executive*
Clark, Dick *performer, producer*
Clark, Susan (Nora Goulding) *actress*
Clements, Ronald Francis *animation director*
Costello, Elvis (Declan Patrick McManus) *musician, songwriter*
Costner, Kevin *actor*
de Cordova, Frederick Timmins *television producer, director*
DeMieri, Joseph L. *bank executive*
†DiBonaventure, Lorenzo *film company executive*
Disney, Roy Edward *broadcasting company executive*
Dodd, Richard *sound recording engineer*
Donner, Richard *film director, producer*
Eisner, Michael Dammann *entertainment company executive*
Feldman, Edward S. *producer*
Ferry, Bryan *singer, songwriter*
Flanagan, Tommy (Lee) *jazz pianist*
†Gerber, William Norman *motion picture executive*
Gibson, Mel *actor, director*
Godwin, Annabelle Palkes *retired early childhood education educator*
Gold, Jeffrey Alan *record company executive*
Gold, Stanley P. *diversified investments executive*
Goldthwait, Bob *comedian, actor*
Greene, Shecky *entertainer*
Guy, Buddy *blues guitarist*
Hashe, Janis Helene *editor*
Hope, Bob *actor, comedian*
Ingersoll, John Gregory *physicist, energy specialist, educator*
Isaak, Chris *popular musician, singer, songwriter, actor*
Joseff, Joan Castle *manufacturing executive*
Karras, Alex *actor, former professional football player*
Kellman, Barnet Kramer *film, stage and television director*
Kellner, Jamie *broadcasting executive*
Kelly, Michael Joseph *academic administrator, consultant*
Ketchum, Hal Michael *country music singer, songwriter*
Kleiser, (John) Randal *motion picture director*
Lamas, Lorenzo *actor, race car driver*
Lanois, Daniel *record producer, musician, popular*
Leno, Jay (James Douglas Muir Leno) *television personality, comedian, writer*
Levin, Mark Jay *director of photography, lighting designer, cinematographer, writer*
Levinson, Barry L. *film director*
Littlefield, Warren *television executive*
Litvack, Sanford Martin *lawyer*
Lurie, Rod *film critic, writer, film director*
Marinace, Kenneth Anthony *financial advisor*
Mark, Laurence Maurice *film producer*
Mather, Ann *international entertainment company executive*
Mathis, Johnny *singer*
Mc Vie, Christine Perfect *musician*
Merrill, Thomas St. John *medical photographer*
Mestres, Ricardo A., III *motion picture company executive*
Michael, George (Gergios Kyriakou Panayiotou) *musician, singer, songwriter*
Milchan, Arnon *film producer*
Miller, Clifford Albert *merchant banker, business consultant*
Naidorf, Louis Murray *architect*
Newman, Randy *singer, songwriter, musician*
Nicks, Stevie (Stephanie Nicks) *singer, songwriter*
Nieto del Rio, Juan Carlos *marketing executive*
Noddings, Sarah Ellen *lawyer*
Ohlmeyer, Donald Winfred, Jr. *film and television producer*
Petty, Tom *rock guitarist, band leader, composer*
†Rauch, Paul David *television producer*
Raulinaitis, Pranas Algis *electronics executive*
†Renner, Andrew Ihor *surgeon*
Robinson, James G. *film production executive*
Roth, Joe *motion picture company executive*
Sanborn, David *alto saxophonist*
Sandell, William *production designer*
†Schneider, Peter *film company executive*
Schumacher, Joel *film writer, director*
†Schumacher, Thomas *film company executive*
Scott, Jim *sound recording engineer*
Seals, Dan Wayland *country music singer*
Seiden, Andy *lawyer*
Shuler Donner, Lauren *film producer*
Silver, Joel *producer*
Stipe, Michael *musician*
Thornton, Cameron Mitchell *financial planner*
†Thyret, Russ *recording industry executive*
Tritt, Travis *country music singer, songwriter*
Volk, Robert Harkins *aviations company executive*
Weintraub, Jerry *motion picture producer, executive*
Wolper, David Lloyd *motion picture and television executive*
Wonder, Stevie (Stevland Morris) *singer, musician, composer*
York, Michael (Michael York-Johnson) *actor*

**Burlingame**
Beattie, George Chapin *orthopedic surgeon*
Bell, Herbert Aubrey Frederick *life insurance company executive*
Berwick, Andrew Struthers, Jr. *real estate executive*
Cotchett, Joseph Winters *lawyer, author*
Donlon, William Christopher *maxillofacial surgeon, educator, author, editor*
Gradinger, Gilbert Paul *plastic surgeon*
Heath, Richard Raymond *investment executive*
Hotz, Henry Palmer *physicist*
Mendelson, Lee M. *film company executive, writer, producer, director*
Most, Nathan *mutual fund executive*
Narayan, Beverly Elaine *lawyer*
Ocheltree, Richard Lawrence *lawyer, retired forest products company executive*
Pemberton, Bobette Marie (Harman) *nursing administrator*
Raffo, Susan Henney *elementary education educator*
Riach, Douglas Alexander *marketing and sales executive, retired military officer*
Tanzi, Carol Anne *interior designer*
Truta, Marianne Patricia *oral and maxillofacial surgeon, educator, author*
Ward, William Reed *composer, educator*
Ziegler, R. W., Jr. *lawyer, consultant*

**Calabasas**
Bartizal, Robert George *computer systems company executive, business consultant*
Broderick, Marsha *interior designer, general contractor*
Caren, Robert Poston *aerospace company executive*
Chiang, Albert Chin-Liang *electrical engineer*
Dworkoski, Robert John *headmaster*
Iacobellis, Sam Frank *retired aerospace company executive*
Landau, Martin *actor*
Revell, Graeme *composer*

**Calexico**
Dixon, Michel L. *educational administrator*
Patterson, Melissa *elementary education educator*

**California City**
Friedl, Rick *lawyer, former academic administrator*

**Calistoga**
Dillon, James McNulty *retired banker*
Ogg, Robert Danforth *corporate executive*
Sassoon, Janet *ballerina, educator*
Spindler, George Dearborn *anthropologist, educator, author, editor*

**Camarillo**
Cleary, Thomas Charles *technology company executive*
Denmark, Bernhardt *manufacturing executive*
DePatie, David Hudson *motion picture company executive*
Derr, Jeannie Combs *bilingual educator, anthropology educator*
Doebler, Paul Dickerson *publishing management executive*
Dunlevy, William Sargent *lawyer*
El Shami, Patricia Ann *elementary school tutor*
Frayssinet, Daniel Fernand *software company executive*
Griffith Joyner, Florence DeLorez *track and field athlete*
Knapp-Philo, Joanne *school system administrator*
Lam, Cheung-Wei *electrical engineer*
Leerabhandh, Marjorie Bravo *chemist, educator*
MacAlister, Robert Stuart *oil company executive*
Sime, Donald Rae *retired business administration educator*
Street, Dana Morris *orthopedic surgeon*
Tarnow, Malva May Wescoe *post-anesthesia care nurse*
Weiss, Carl *aerospace company executive*

**Cambria**
Blundell, William Edward *journalist, consultant*
DuFresne, Armand Frederick *retired management and engineering consultant*
Harden, Marvin *artist, educator*
Morse, Richard Jay *human resources and organizational development consultant, manufacturers' representative company executive*
Salaverria, Helena Clara *educator*
Villeneuve, Donald Avila *biology educator*

**Cameron Park**
Buckles, Robert Edwin *chemistry educator*

**Camino**
Miller, Carole Ann Lyons *editor, publisher, marketing specialist*

**Camp Pendleton**
Edwards, Bruce George *ophthalmologist, naval officer*
†McKissock, Gary S. *non-commissioned officer*

**Campbell**
Nicholson, Joseph Bruce *real estate developer*
Ross, Hugh Courtney *electrical engineer*
Sack, Edgar Albert *electronics company executive*
Wu, William Lung-Shen (You-Ming Wu) *aerospace medical engineering design specialist, foreign intelligence analyst*

**Campo**
Charles, Blanche *retired elementary education educator*
Jermini, Ellen *educational administrator, philosopher*

**Canoga Park**
Lederer, Marion Irvine *cultural administrator*
Olson, Paul S. *nuclear engineer*
Rosenfeld, Sarena Margaret *artist*
Taylor, Edna Jane *employment program representative*

**Canyon Lake**
Knight, Vick, Jr. (Ralph Knight) *dean, education educator, counselor*
Schilling, Frederick Augustus, Jr. *geologist, consultant*

**Capitola**
Barna, Arpad Alex *electrical engineering consultant*
Crawford, George Truett *health facility executive, minister*

**Capo Beach**
Roemer, Edward Pier *neurologist*

**Carlsbad**
Anderson, Paul Irving *management executive*
Billingsley, William Scott *accountant, controller*
Brown, Jack *magazine editor*
Crooke, Stanley Thomas *pharmaceutical company executive*
Halberg, Charles John August, Jr. *mathematics educator*
Kauderer, Bernard Marvin *retired naval officer*
Lange, Clifford E. *librarian*
Liddicoat, Richard Thomas, Jr. *professional society administrator*
McCracken, Steven Carl *lawyer*
Moore, Terry Wayne *high technology venture management consultant*
Peasland, Bruce Randall *financial executive*
Randall, William B. *manufacturing company executive*
Smith, Warren James *optical scientist, consultant, lecturer*
Swoap, David Bruce *children's relief official, art gallery director*
Wilson, Donald Grey *management consultant*

**Carmel**
Alsberg, Dietrich Anselm *electrical engineer*
Andreason, Sharon Lee *sculptor*
Blackstone, George Arthur *retired lawyer*
Bohannon-Kaplan, Margaret Anne *publisher, lawyer*
Bullock, Edna Jeanette *photographer*
Chester, Lynne *foundation executive, artist*
Chung, Kyung Cho *Korean specialist, scholar, educator, author*
Creighton, John Wallis, Jr. *consultant, author, former management educator*
Epstein-Shepherd, Bee J. *professional speaker*
Faul, George Johnson *former college president*
Faul, June Patricia *education specialist*
Felch, William Campbell *internist, editor*
Jordan, Edward George *business investor, former college president, former railroad executive*
Kenna, Michael *photographer*
Kennedy, John Edward *art dealer, appraiser, curator*
Koeppel, Gary Merle *publisher, art dealer, writer, marketing consultant*
Krugman, Stanley Lee *international management consultant*
Longman, Anne Strickland *special education educator, consultant*
Loper, D. Roger *retired oil company executive*
McGlynn, Betty Hoag *art historian*
Merrill, William Dickey *architect*
Mollman, John Peter *book publisher, consultant electronic publishing*
Parker, Donald Henry *psychologist, author*
Pinkham, Frederick Oliver *foundation executive, consultant*
Reese, William Albert, III *psychologist*
Robinson, John Minor *lawyer, retired business executive*
Skidmore, Howard Franklyn *public relations counsel*
Smith, Gordon Paul *management consulting company executive*
Steele, Charles Glen *retired accountant*
Stratton, Thomas Oliver *investment banker*

**Carmel Valley**
Meckel, Peter Timothy *arts administrator, educator*
Sands, Sharon Louise *graphic design executive, art publisher, artist*
Wolfe, Maurice Raymond *retired museum director, educator*

**Carmichael**
Areen, Gordon E. *finance company executive*
Edgar, Marilyn Ruth *marriage and family therapist, counselor*
Givant, Philip Joachim *mathematics educator, real estate investment executive*
Hellmuth, William Frederick, Jr. *economics educator*
McHugh, James Joseph *retired naval officer, retired associate dean*
Probasco, Calvin Henry Charles *clergyman, college administrator*
Sahs, Majorie Jane *art educator*
Wagner, Carruth John *physician*
Zickel, John *mechanical engineering educator*

**Carpinteria**
Ehrlich, Grant C(onklin) *business consultant*
Hansen, Robert William *artist, educator*
Lipinski, Barbara Janina *psychotherapist, psychology educator*
Montgomery, Parker Gilbert *investment banker*
Rosas, Susan Jane *designer, graphic artist, illustrator, art director*
Schmidhauser, John Richard *political science educator*
Wheeler, John Harvey *political scientist*

**Carson**
Brownell, John Arnold *retired university president*
Davidson, Mark *writer, educator*
Detweiler, Robert Chester *university president, historian*
Hirsch, Gilah Yelin *artist, writer*
Karkia, Mohammad Reza *energy engineer, educator*
Kowalski, Kazimierz *computer science educator, researcher*
Quijada, Angélica María *elementary educator*
Suchenek, Marek Andrzej *computer science educator*

**Castro Valley**
Denning, Eileen Bonar *management consultant*
Kinee-Krohn, Patricia *special education educator*
Palmer, James Daniel *inspector*

**Castroville**
Guglielmo, Eugene Joseph *software engineer*

**Cathedral City**
Jackman, Robert Alan *retail executive*

**Cayucos**
Hedlund, James Lane *retired psychologist, educator*
Theurer, Byron W. *aerospace engineer, business owner*

**Cedar Ridge**
Bruno, Judyth Ann *chiropractor*

**Century City**
Feiman, Thomas E. *investment manager*
Harbert, Ted *broadcast executive*
O'Neal, Tatum *actress*
Thomas, Issac David Ellis *clergy member*

**Cerritos**
Bovitz, Carole Jones *psychotherapist*
Madden, James Cooper, V *management consultant*
Sarno, Maria Erlinda *lawyer, scientist*
Webb, Lewis M. *retail executive*

**Chatsworth**
Boswell, Dan Alan *health maintenance organization executive, health care consultant*
Chernof, David *internist*
Dart, John Seward *religion news writer*
Erikson, J. Lance *financial corporation executive*
Koerber, John Robert *computer programmer*
Levine, Arnold Milton *retired electrical engineer, documentary filmmaker*
Miller, Robert Steven *secondary school educator*
Montgomery, James Fischer *savings and loan association executive*
Schneider, Duane Bernard *English literature educator, publisher*
Sklar, Louise Margaret *service executive*
Stephenson, Irene Hamlen *biorhythm analyst, consultant, editor, educator*
Urmer, Diane Hedda *management firm executive, financial officer*
Woodruff, Tom, Jr. *special effects designer*

**Chico**
Allen, Charles William *mechanical engineering educator*
Ediger, Robert Ike *botanist, educator*
Esteban, Manuel Antonio *university administrator, educator*
Farrer, Claire Anne Rafferty *anthropologist, folklorist, educator*
Greb, Gordon Barry *writer, educator*
Keithley, George *writer*
Kistner, David Harold *biology educator*
Moore, Brooke Noel *philosophy educator*
Olsen, Robert Arthur *finance educator*
O'Neill, Michael Foy *business educator*
Ritter, Dale William *obstetrician, gynecologist*
Rodrigue, Christine M(ary) *geography educator, business consultant*
Ward, Chester Lawrence *physician, retired county health official, retired military officer*

**China Lake**
Bennett, Jean Louise McPherson *physicist, research scientist*
†Pendleton, Robert Leon *civilian military employee*

**Chino**
Determan, John David *lawyer*
Goodman, Lindsey Alan *furniture manufacturing executive, architect*
Hemenway, Stephen James *record producer, author*
Ofner, William Bernard *lawyer*

**Chowchilla**
Von Prince, Kilulu Magdalena *occupational therapist, sculptor, retired*

**Chula Vista**
Allen, David Russell *lawyer*
Allen, Henry Wesley *biomedical researcher*
Austin, Mary Jane *small business owner*
Cohen, Elaine Helena *pediatrician, pediatric cardiologist*
Hanson, Eileen *principal*
Kemery, William Elsworth *psychotherapist, hypnotherapist*
Pasqua, Thomas Mario, Jr. *journalism educator*
Santee, Dale William *lawyer, air force officer*
Schorr, Martin Mark *forensic psychologist, educator, writer*
Steele, Nancy Eden Rogers *educator*
Wolk, Martin *electronic engineer, physicist*

**Claremont**
Ackerman, Gerald Martin *art historian, consultant*
Alexander, John David, Jr. *college administrator*
Ansell, Edward Orin *lawyer, arbitrator/mediator*
Arndt, Sven William *economics educator*
Atlas, Jay David *philosopher, consultant, linguist*
Barnes, Richard Gordon *English literature educator, poet*
Beardslee, William Armitage *religious organization administrator, educator*
Beilby, Alvin Lester *chemistry educator*
Bekavac, Nancy Yavor *academic administrator, lawyer*
Benjamin, Karl Stanley *art educator*
Benson, George Charles Sumner *political science educator*
Bentley, Donald Lyon *mathematics and statistics educator*
Bjork, Gordon Carl *economist, educator*
Blizzard, Alan *artist*
Bond, Floyd Alden *economist, educator*
Burns, Richard Dean *history educator, publisher, author*
Casanova, Aldo John *sculptor*
Christian, Suzanne Hall *financial planner*
Coleman, Courtney Stafford *mathematician, educator*
Cooke, Kenneth Lloyd *mathematician, educator*
Davis, Nathaniel *humanities educator*
Dunbar, John Raine *retired English educator*

Dym, Clive Lionel *engineering educator*
Elsbree, Langdon *English language educator*
Faranda, John Paul *college administrator*
Fucaloro, Anthony Frank *academic dean*
Gabriel, Earl A. *osteopathic physician*
Gold, Bela *economist, educator*
Goodrich, Norma Lorre (Mrs. John H. Howard) *French and comparative literature educator*
Grabiner, Sandy *mathematics educator*
Gray, Paul Bryan *lawyer, historian, arbitrator*
Helliwell, Thomas McCaffree *physicist, educator*
Henriksen, Melvin *mathematician, educator*
Herschensohn, Bruce *film director, writer*
Hinshaw, Randall (Weston) *economist, educator*
†Jaffa, Harry Victor *political philosophy educator emeritus*
Kronenberg, Klaus J(ohannes) *physicist*
Kubota, Mitsuru *chemistry educator*
Kucheman, Clark Arthur *religion educator*
Liggett, Thomas Jackson *retired seminary president*
Likens, James Dean *economics educator*
Lofgren, Charles Augustin *legal and constitutional historian, history educator*
Long, Franklin Asbury *chemistry educator*
Macaulay, Ronald Kerr Steven *linguistics educator, former college dean*
Maguire, John David *academic administrator, educator, writer*
Martin, Jay Herbert *psychoanalysis and English educator*
McKirahan, Richard Duncan, Jr. *classics and philosophy educator*
Mezey, Robert *poet, educator*
Miles, Jack (John Russiano) *journalist, educator*
Molinder, John Irving *engineering educator, consultant*
Monson, James Edward *electrical engineer, educator*
Moss, Myra Ellen (Myra Moss Rolle) *philosophy educator*
Mullikin, Harry Copeland *mathematics educator*
Neumann, Harry *philosophy educator*
Pedersen, Richard Foote *diplomat and academic administrator*
Phelps, Orme Wheelock *economics educator emeritus*
Phillips, John Richard *engineering educator*
Pinney, Thomas Clive *English language educator*
Platt, Joseph Beaven *former college president*
Post, Gaines, Jr. *history educator, dean, administrator*
Purves, William Kirkwood *biologist, educator*
Rankin, Robert *retired educational foundation executive*
Riggs, Henry Earle *academic administrator, engineering management educator*
Roth, John King *philosopher, educator*
Sanders, James Alvin *minister, biblical studies educator*
Sellery, J'nan Morse *English, Canadian and American literature educator*
Smith, Steven Albert *philosophy educator*
Sontag, Frederick Earl *philosophy educator*
Stanley, Peter William *academic administrator*
Stark, Jack Lee *academic administrator*
Strauss, Jon Calvert *academic administrator*
Tanenbaum, Basil Samuel *engineering educator*
Taylor, Roy Lewis *botanist, educator*
Warder, Michael Young *think tank executive*
Watson, Helen Richter *educator, ceramic artist*
Wettack, F. Sheldon *academic administrator*
White, Alvin Murray *mathematics educator, consultant*
White, Kathleen Merritt *geologist*
Wykoff, Frank Champion *economics educator*
Young, Howard Thomas *foreign language educator*

### Clayton
Bower, Fay Louise *retired academic administrator, nursing educator*

### Cloverdale
Collins, John Wendler *consumer products company executive*

### Clovis
Driscoll, Glen Robert *former university president*
Ensminger, Marion Eugene *animal science educator, author*

### Coalinga
Frame, Ted Ronald *lawyer*
Harris, John Charles *agriculturalist*

### Coloma
Sugarman, Matthew S. *historic site adminstrator*

### Colton
Brown, Jack H. *supermarket company executive*
Dybowski, Douglas Eugene *education educator, economist*
Slider, Margaret Elizabeth *elementary education educator*

### Commerce
Conover, Robert Warren *librarian*

### Compton
Bogdan, Carolyn Louetta *financial specialist*
Drew, Sharon Lee *sociologist*
†Golleher, George *food company executive*

### Concord
Bellson, Louis Paul *drummer*
Burrell, Kenneth Earl *guitarist, composer*
Cassidy, John Joseph *hydraulic and hydrologic engineer*
Chiappone, Robert Carl *orthodontist*
Clooney, Rosemary *singer*
Davis, Robert Leach *retired government official, consultant*
Fuld, Fred, III *computer consultant, financial consultant*
Gregory, Leslie Finlayson *tax accountant, financial consultant, realtor*
Ivy, Edward Everett *entomologist, consultant*
Jackson, Milton (Bags Jackson) *jazz musician*
Jones, Gerald Edward *religion educator*
Lee, Low Kee *electronics engineer, consultant*
Lhotka, Sidney Bruno *tax accountant*
Lonnquist, George Eric *lawyer*
McConnell, Rob *jazz musician, composer*
Thall, Richard Vincent *school system administrator*
Thompson, Jeremiah Beiseker *international medical business executive*
Williscroft, Beverly Ruth *lawyer*

### Cool
Toren, Robert *photojournalist*

### Corcoran
Roberts, Alice Noreen *educational administrator*

### Corona
Callender, Lorna Ophelia *nurse administrator*
Garrett, Thomas Monroe *chemist*
Ohmert, Richard Allan *architect*
Tillman, Joseph Nathaniel *engineering executive*

### Corona Del Mar
Brandt, Rexford Elson *artist*
Britten, Roy John *biophysicist*
Brokaw, Charles Jacob *educator, cellular biologist*
Crump, Spencer *publisher, business executive*
Delap, Tony *artist*
Helphand, Ben J. *actuary*
Hill, Melvin James *oil company executive*
Hinderaker, Ivan *political science educator*
Hobbs, Linder Charlie *computer company executive*
Michaels, Patrick Francis *broadcasting company executive*
Richmond, Ronald LeRoy *aerospace engineer*
Ripper, Rita Jo (Jody Ripper) *strategic planner, researcher*
Tether, Anthony John *aerospace executive*
Yeo, Ron *architect*

### Coronado
Allen, Charles Richard *retired financial executive*
Axelson, Joseph Allen *professional athletics executive, publisher*
Brunton, Paul Edward *retired diversified industry executive*
Butcher, Bobby Gene *retired military officer*
Crilly, Eugene Richard *engineering consultant*
Grant, Alan J. *business executive, educator*
Heap, Suzanne Rundio *elementary school educator*
Hostler, Charles Warren *international affairs consultant*
Hubbard, Donald *marine artist, writer*
Mock, David Clinton, Jr. *internist*
Neblett, Carol *soprano*
Robinson, David Brooks *retired naval officer*
Stames, William Alexander *realtor, cost management executive*
Stockdale, James Bond *writer, research scholar, retired naval officer*
Straley, Ruth A. Stewart *federal agency administrator, small business owner*
Wagener, Hobart D. *retired architect*
Weiss-Cornwell, Amy *interior designer*
Worthington, George Rhodes *retired naval officer*

### Corte Madera
Epstein, William Louis *dermatologist, educator*
Fawcett, F(rank) Conger *lawyer*
Kratka-Schneider, Dorothy Maryjohanna *psychotherapist*

### Costa Mesa
Anderson, Jon David *lawyer*
Arismendi-Pardi, Eduardo J. *mathematics educator*
Billiter, William Overton, Jr. *journalist*
Botello, Troy James *arts administrator, counselor*
Buchtel, Michael Eugene *optical mechanical engineer*
Camacho, Dianne Lynne *mathematics educator, administrator*
Currie, Robert Emil *lawyer*
Damsky, Robert Philip *communications executive*
Daniels, James Walter *lawyer*
Dougherty, Betsey Olenick *architect*
Frieden, Clifford E. *lawyer*
Gale, Mary Ellen *law educator*
Gardin, John George, II *psychologist*
Guilford, Andrew John *lawyer*
Hamilton, James William *lawyer*
Hansen, Sally Jo *school system coordinator*
Hay, Howard Clinton *lawyer*
Hazewinkel, Van *manufacturing executive*
Hugo, Nancy *county official, alcohol and drug addiction professional*
Jansen, Allan W. *lawyer*
Jones, H(arold) Gilbert, Jr. *lawyer*
Kay, Kenneth Jeffrey *toy company executive*
Labbe, Armand Joseph *museum curator, anthropologist*
Lattanzio, Stephen Paul *astronomy educator*
Lindstrom, Gregory P. *lawyer*
Lorance, Elmer Donald *organic chemistry educator*
Muller, Jerome Kenneth *photographer, art director, editor*
Olson, Cal Oliver *golf architect*
†Paine, David M. *public relations executive*
Patterson, Joseph Cromwell *financial company executive*
Reveal, Ernest Ira, III *lawyer*
†Schooley, Otis Bryson, III *commercial airport executive*
Shallenberger, Garvin F. *lawyer*
Steed, Emmett D. *hotel executive*
Stone, Samuel Beckner *lawyer*
Tanner, R. Marshall *lawyer*
Tennyson, Peter Joseph *lawyer*
Thurston, Morris Ashcroft *lawyer*
Williams, William Corey *theology educator, consultant*

### Cotati
Carroll, Bonnie *publisher, editor*

### Coulterville
Henderson, Pamela Mason *elementary education educator*

### Covina
Fillius, Milton Franklin, Jr. *food products company executive*
Phillips, Jill Meta *novelist, critic, astrologer*
Schneider, Calvin *physician*
Takei, Toshihisa *otolaryngologist*

### Crescent City
Carter, Neville Louis *geophysicist, educator*
Swart, Bonnie Blount *artist*

### Cromberg
Kolb, Ken Lloyd *writer*

### Culver City
Bancroft, Anne (Mrs. Mel Brooks) *actress*
Berland, James Fred *software company executive*
†Besson, Luc *film director*
Boonshaft, Hope Judith *public relations executive*
Brooks, James L. *writer, director, producer*
Brooks, Mel *producer, director, writer, actor*
Buskirk, Bruce David *marketing educator*
Buyse, Emile Jules *film company executive*
†Calley, John *film producer*
Clodius, Albert Howard *history educator*
Copeland, Stewart *composer, musician*
Crowe, Cameron *screenwriter, film director*
Eckel, James Robert, Jr. *financial planner*
Edwards, Marie Babare *psychologist*
Fisher, Lucy J. *motion picture company executive*
Gregg, David Paul *information storage media specialist*
Guber, Peter *producer*
Hankins, Hesterly G., III *computer systems analyst, inventor, educator*
Jaffe, Stanley Richard *film producer, director*
Kamm, Jacqueline Ann *elementary reading specialist*
Leve, Alan Donald *electronic materials manufacturing company owner, executive*
Maltzman, Irving Myron *psychology educator*
Marshall, Garry *film producer, director, writer*
Martin, Gary O. *film company executive*
McNeill, Daniel Richard *writer*
Melnick, Daniel *film producer*
Moss, Eric Owen *architect*
Netzel, Paul Arthur *fundraising management executive, consultant*
†Pascal, Amy *film company executive*
Pittard, William Blackburn (Billy Pittard) *television graphic designer*
Rich, Lee *entertainment industry executive*
Richardson, John Edmon *marketing educator*
Rose, Margarete Erika *pathologist*
Sagansky, Jeff *broadcast executive*
Sensiper, Samuel *consulting electrical engineer*
Stark, Ray *motion picture producer*
Tarantino, Quentin *film director, screenwriter*
Tisch, Steven E. *movie producer*
Trebek, Alex *television game show host*
von Kalinowski, Julian Onesime *lawyer*
Williams, Kenneth Scott *entertainment company executive*
Zucker, David *director*
Zucker, Jerry *producer, director*

### Cupertino
Anderson, Charles Arthur *former research institute administrator*
Burg, John Parker *signal processing executive*
Cheeseman, Douglas Taylor, Jr. *wildlife tour executive, photographer, educator*
Compton, Dale Leonard *retired space agency executive, consultant*
Dunbar, Maurice Victor *English language educator*
Fenn, Raymond Wolcott, Jr. *retired metallurgical engineer*
Fletcher, Homer Lee *librarian*
Flynn, Ralph Melvin, Jr. *sales executive, marketing consultant*
Holmes, Richard Albert *software engineer, consultant*
Horn, Christian Friedrich *venture capital company executive*
Krambeck, Robert Harold *communications and computer executive, researcher*
Lindsay, Leslie *packaging engineer*
Maddux, Parker Ahrens *lawyer*
Mathias, Leslie Michael *electronic manufacturing company executive*
Mattathil, George Paul *communications specialist, consultant*
†Mishelevich, David Jacob *medical company executive, consultant*
Nelson, Richard Burton *physicist, engineer, former patent consultant*
Norman, Donald Arthur *cognitive scientist*
Peltzer, Douglas Lea *semiconductor device manufacturing company executive*
Perkins, Thomas James *venture capital company executive*
Simon, Nancy Ruth *lawyer*
Tesler, Lawrence Gordon *computer company executive*
Togasaki, Shinobu *computer scientist*
Winslow, David Allen *chaplain, naval officer*
Zobel, Louise Purwin *author, educator, lecturer, writing consultant*

### Cypress
Baugh, Coy Franklin *corporate executive*
Edmonds, Ivy Gordon *writer*
Freedman, Gail *financial analyst*
Hoops, Alan *health care company executive*
Olschwang, Alan Paul *lawyer*

### Daggett
Bailey, Katherine Christine *artist, writer*

### Daly City
Hargrave, Sarah Quesenberry *marketing, public relations company executive*
Leong, Lam-Po (Lanbo Liang) *artist, educator*
Shaw, Richard Eugene *cardiovascular researcher*

### Dana Point
Furst, Raymond Bruce *engineer, consultant*
Hodara, Eden *artist*
Jelinek, Robert *advertising executive, writer*
Kesselhaut, Arthur Melvyn *financial consultant*
Reed, David Andrew *foundation executive*

### Danville
Amon, William Frederick, Jr. *biotechnology company executive*
Baker, William P. (Bill Baker) *former congressman*
Behring, Kenneth E. *professional sports team owner*
Davis, Ron Lee *clergyman, author*
Frederickson, John Marcus *insurance executive*
Gorman, Russell William *marketing executive, consultant*
Liggett, Lawrence Melvin *vacuum equipment manufacturing company executive*
Manghirmalani, Ramesh *international trade corporation executive*
Maninger, R(alph) Carroll *engineering executive, consultant*
Mattoon, Henry Amasa, Jr. *advertising and marketing consultant, writer*
Nothern, Marjorie Carol *nursing administrator*
Penner-Sekera, Cynthia Dawn *secondary education educator*
Plummer, Marcie Stern *real estate broker*
Randolph, Kevin H. *marketing executive*
Reed, John Theodore *publisher, writer*
Trezek, George James *mechanical engineer*

### Davis
Addicott, Fredrick Taylor *retired botany educator*
Akesson, Norman Berndt *agricultural engineer, emeritus educator*
Ardans, Alexander Andrew *veterinarian, laboratory director, educator*
Axelrod, Daniel Isaac *geology and botany educator*
Barbour, Michael G(eorge) *botany educator, ecological consultant*
Bartosic, Florian *lawyer, arbitrator, educator*
Baskin, Ronald Joseph *cell biologist, physiologist, biophysicist educator, dean*
Beadle, Charles Wilson *retired mechanical engineering educator*
Beagle, Peter Soyer *writer*
Biberstein, Ernst Ludwig *veterinary medicine educator*
Black, Arthur Leo *biochemistry educator*
Brandt, Harry *mechanical engineering educator*
Bruch, Carol Sophie *lawyer, educator*
Bruening, George E. *virologist*
Butler, Edward Eugene *plant pathology educator*
Cahill, Thomas Andrew *physicist, educator*
Cardiff, Robert Darrell *pathology educator*
Carman, Hoy Fred *agricultural sciences educator*
Carter, Harold O. *agricultural economics educator*
Chancellor, William Joseph *agricultural engineering educator*
Cheney, James Addison *civil engineering educator*
Cliver, Dean Otis *microbiologist, educator*
Cohen, Lawrence Edward *sociology educator, criminologist*
Colvin, Harry Walter, Jr. *physiology educator*
Conn, Eric Edward *plant biochemist*
Crane, Julian Coburn *agriculturist,retired educator*
Crowley, Daniel John *anthropologist*
Day, Howard Wilman *geology educator*
DePaoli, Geri M. *artist, art historian*
Dorf, Richard Carl *electrical engineering and management educator*
Dykstra, Daniel James *lawyer, educator*
Elmendorf, William Welcome *anthropology educator*
Enders, Allen Coffin *anatomy educator*
Epstein, Emanuel *plant physiologist*
Feeney, Floyd Fulton *legal educator*
Feeney, Robert Earl *research biochemist*
Fowler, William Mayo, Jr. *rehabilitation medicine physician*
Freedland, Richard Allan *retired biologist, educator*
Fridley, Robert Bruce *agricultural engineering educator*
Gardner, Murray Briggs *pathologist, educator*
Gardner, William Allen *electrical engineering educator*
Gates, Bruce Clark *chemical engineer, educator*
Ghausi, Mohammed Shuaib *electrical engineering educator, university dean*
Gifford, Ernest Milton *biologist, educator*
Grey, Robert Dean *biology educator*
Grossman, George Stefan *library director, law eductor*
Groth, Alexander Jacob *political science educator*
Hackett, Nora Ann *patent agent*
Hakimi, S. Louis *electrical and computer engineering educator*
Hance, Anthony James *retired pharmacologist, educator*
Harper, Lawrence Vernon *human development educator*
Hawkes, Glenn Rogers *psychology educator*
Hayden, John Olin *English literature educator, author*
Hays, Peter L. *English language and literature educator*
Hedrick, Jerry Leo *biochemistry and biophysics educator*
Hendrickx, Andrew George *anatomy educator*
Hess, Charles Edward *environmental horticulture educator*
Higgins, Charles Graham *geology educator*
Hoffman, Michael Jerome *humanities educator*
Hollinger, Mannfred Alan *pharmacologist, educator, toxicologist*
Horwitz, Barbara Ann *physiologist, educator, consultant*
Hughes, John P. *equine research adminstrator*
Imwinkelried, Edward John *law educator*
Ives, John David (Jack Ives) *geography and environmental sciences educator*
Jackson, William Turrentine *history educator*
Jett, Stephen Clinton *geography educator, researcher*
Juenger, Friedrich Klaus *lawyer, educator*
Jungerman, John Albert *physics educator*
Kado, Clarence Isao *molecular biologist*
Keizer, Joel Edward *theoretical scientist, educator*
Kepner, Robert Allen *agricultural engineering researcher, educator*
Kester, Dale Emmert *pomologist, educator*
Klasing, Susan Allen *environmental toxicologist, consultant*
Kofranek, Anton Miles *floriculturist, educator*
Krener, Arthur J. *systems engineering educator*
Krone, Ray Beyers *civil and environmental engineering educator, consultant*
Kunkee, Ralph Edward *viticulture and enology educator*
Laidlaw, Harry Hyde, Jr. *entomology educator*
Larock, Bruce Edward *civil engineering educator*
Laub, Alan John *engineering educator*
Lazarus, Gerald Sylvan *physician, university dean*
Learn, Elmer Warner *agricultural economics educator, retired*
Levy, Bernard C. *electrical engineer, educator*
†Lewis, Jonathan *health care association administrator*
Lipscomb, Paul Rogers *orthopedic surgeon, educator*
Lofland, John Franklin *sociologist, educator*
Lofland, Lyn Hebert *sociology educator*
Major, Clarence Lee *novelist, poet, educator*
Manoliu, Maria *linguist*
Mason, William A(lvin) *psychologist, educator, researcher*
Mazelis, Mendel *plant biochemist, educator, reseacher*
McHenry, Henry Malcolm *anthropologist, educator*
McPherson, Sandra Jean *poet, educator*
Meyer, Margaret Eleanor *microbiologist, educator*
Moyle, Peter Briggs *fisheries and biology educator*
Mukherjee, Amiya K *metallurgy and materials science educator*
Mulase, Motohico *mathematics educator*
Murphy, Terence Martin *biology educator*
Musolf, Lloyd Daryl *political science educator, institute administrator*

Nash, Charles Presley *chemistry educator*
Oakley, John Bilyeu *law educator, lawyer, judicial consultant*
Owings, Donald Henry *psychology educator*
Painter, Ruth Robbins *retired environmental biochemist*
Palmer, Philip Edward Stephen *radiologist*
Pappagianis, Demosthenes *microbiology educator, physician*
Petersen, Roland *artist, printmaker*
Plopper, Charles George *anatomist, cell biologist*
Pritchard, William Roy *former university system administrator*
Qualset, Calvin O. *agronomy educator*
Rappaport, Lawrence *plant physiology and horticulture educator*
Redenbach, Sandra Irene *educational consultant*
Reed, Nancy Ellen *computer science educator*
Rhode, Edward Albert *veterinary medicine educator, veterinary cardiologist*
Richman, David Paul *neurologist, researcher*
Rick, Charles Madeira, Jr. *geneticist, educator*
Rocke, David Morton *statistician, educator*
Rost, Thomas Lowell *plant biology educator*
Rothstein, Morton *historian, retired educator*
Schenker, Marc Benet *preventive medicine educator*
Schneeman, Barbara Olds *agricultural studies educator*
Schoener, Thomas William *zoology educator, researcher*
Schwabe, Calvin Walter *veterinarian, medical historian, medical educator*
Sharrow, Marilyn Jane *library administrator*
Shelton, Robert Neal *physics educator, researcher*
Sillman, Arnold Joel *physiologist, educator*
Siverson, Randolph Martin *political science educator*
Skinner, G(eorge) William *anthropologist, educator*
Smiley, Robert Herschel *university dean*
Smith, Michael Peter *social science educator, researcher*
Steffey, Eugene Paul *veterinary medicine educator*
Stewart, James Ian *agricultural water scientist, cropping system developer, consultant*
Storm, Donald John *archaeologist, historian*
Stowell, Robert Eugene *pathologist, retired educator*
Stumpf, Paul Karl *biochemistry educator emeritus*
Sumner, Daniel Alan *economist, educator*
Swift, Richard G(ene) *composer, educator*
Tchobanoglous, George *civil engineering educator*
Theilen, Gordon Henry *veterinary surgery educator*
Troy, Frederic Arthur, II *medical biochemistry educator*
Tupper, Charles John *physician, educator*
Uyemoto, Jerry Kazumitsu *plant pathologist, educator*
Vanderhoef, Larry Neil *academic administrator*
Volman, David Herschel *chemistry educator*
Waddington, Raymond Bruce, Jr. *English language educator*
Wang, Shih-Ho *electrical engineer, educator*
Watt, Kenneth Edmund Ferguson *zoology educator*
Wegge, Leon Louis François *economics educator*
Williams, Hibbard Earl *medical educator, physician*
Williams, William Arnold *agronomy educator*
Williamson, Alan Bacher *English literature educator, poet, writer*
Willis, Frank Roy *history educator*
Wilson, Barry William *biology educator*
Wolk, Bruce Alan *law educator*
Woodress, James Leslie, Jr. *English language educator*
Wooten, Frederick (Oliver) *applied science educator*
Wydick, Richard Crews *lawyer, educator*
Youmans, Julian Ray *neurosurgeon, educator*

**Deer Park**
Hodgkin, John E. *pulmonologist*

**Del Mar**
Comrie, Sandra Melton *human resource executive*
Cooper, Martin *electronics company executive*
Faludi, Susan C. *journalist, scholarly writer*
Farquhar, Marilyn Gist *cell biology and pathology educator*
Jeub, Michael Leonard *financial executive*
Kaye, Peter Frederic *television editor*
Koehler, John Edget *venture capitalist*
Lesko, Ronald Michael *osteopathic physician*
Randall, Chandler Corydon *church rector*
Stevenson, Robert Everett *oceanography consultant*
Watkins, Carol Charles *hotel, timeshare, apartments and shopping center executive, fundraiser*
Wilkinson, Eugene Parks *nuclear engineer*

**Diablo**
Pelandini, Thomas Francis *marketing executive*

**Diamond Bar**
Domeño, Eugene Timothy *elementary education educator, principal*
Mirisola, Lisa Heinemann *air quality engineer*

**Dillon Beach**
Caddy, Edmund H.H., Jr. *architect*

**Dinuba**
Leps, Thomas MacMaster *civil engineer, consultant*

**Downey**
Baumann, Theodore Robert *aerospace engineer, consultant, army officer*
De Lorca, Luis E. *educational administrator, educator, speaker*
Demarchi, Ernest Nicholas *aerospace engineering executive*
Emerson, (Virgil) Leon *retired judge*
Gong, Henry, Jr. *physician, researcher*
Hackney, Jack Dean *physician*
Huff, Ricky Wayne *sales executive*
Magnes, Harry Alan *physician*
Orden, Ted *gasoline service stations executive*
Redeker, Allan Grant *physician, medical educator*
Ruecker, Martha Engels *retired special education educator*
Sapico, Francisco Lejano *internist, educator*
Schoettger, Theodore Leo *city official*
Shapiro, Richard Stanley *physician*
Tucker, Marcus Othello *judge*

**Duarte**
Balch, Charles M. *surgeon, educator*
Chou, Chung-Kwang *bio-engineer*
Comings, David Edward *physician, medical genetics scientist*
Greenstein, Jesse Leonard *astronomer, educator*
Kovach, John Stephen *oncologist, research center administrator*
Levine, Rachmiel *physician*
Lundblad, Roger Lauren *research director*
Ohno, Susumu *research scientist*
Smith, Steven Sidney *molecular biologist*
Sollenberger, Donna Kay Fitzpatrick *hospital and clinics executive*
Tse, Man-Chun Marina *special education educator*
Vaughn, James English, Jr. *neurobiologist*

**Dublin**
Cope, Kenneth Wayne *chain store executive*
Grady, Cheryl R. *telecommunications executive*
Whetten, John D. *food products executive*

**East Los Angeles**
Tuthill, Walter Warren *retail executive*

**Edwards**
Brand, Vance Devoe *astronaut, government official*
Deets, Dwain Aaron *aerospace technology executive*
Elkins, Thomas Arthur *computer engineer*
Engel, Richard L. *career officer*
Garcia, Andrew B. *chemical engineer*

**El Cajon**
Brown, Marilynne Joyce *emergency nurse*
Burnett, Lowell Jay *physicist, educator*
Fagot, Joseph Burdell *corporate executive*
McClure, Donald Edwin *electrical construction executive, consultant*
McInerney, Joseph Aloysius *hotel executive*
Palafox, Mari Lee *private school educator*
Schenk, Susan Kirkpatrick *geriatric psychiatry nurse, educator, consultant*
Thomas, Esther Merlene *elementary education educator*
Turk, Robert Louis *radiologist*

**El Centro**
Albertson, Jack Aaron Paul *prosecutor*
Flock, Robert Ashby *retired entomologist*
Gotti, Margaret Lynn *library administrator*
Kussman, Eleanor (Ellie Kussman) *retired educational superintendent*
Lokey, Frank Marion, Jr. *broadcast executive, consultant*
Steensgaard, Anthony Harvey *federal agent*

**El Cerrito**
Amoore, John Ernest *biochemist*
Conti, Isabella *psychologist, consultant*
Cooper, William Clark *physician*
Dillenberger, John *theology educator emeritus, minister*
Garbarino, Joseph William *labor arbitrator, economics and business educator*
Griffith, Ladd Ray *retired chemical research director*
Gwinn, William Dulaney *physical chemist, educator, executive, consultant*
Jiménez, Leonardo *popular accordionist*
Kao, Yasuko Watanabe *retired library administrator*
Komatsu, S. Richard *architect*
Kuo, Ping-chia *historian, educator*
Schilling, Janet Naomi *nutritionist, consultant*
Siri, William E. *physicist*
Smith, Eldred Reid *library educator*

**El Dorado Hills**
Huppert, Merle Cecil *mechanical engineer*

**El Granada**
Heere, Karen R. *astrophysicist*

**El Macero**
Raventos, Antolin *radiology educator*
Wheeler, Douglas Paul *conservationist, government official, lawyer*

**El Monte**
Glass, Jean Ann *special education services professional*
Wallach, Patricia *mayor*

**El Segundo**
Amerman, John W. *toy company executive*
Armstrong, Wallace Dowan, Jr. *data processor*
Autolitano, Astrid *consumer products executive*
Barad, Jill Elikann *toy company executive*
Beach, Roger C. *oil company executive*
Brown, Timothy Donell *professional football player*
Chang, I-Shih *aerospace engineer*
Conrad, Paul Francis *editorial cartoonist*
Criss, William Sotelo *electronics company executive*
Davis, Allen *professional football team executive*
Dekok, Roger Gregory *air force officer*
Lantz, Norman Foster *electrical engineer*
Lotrick, Joseph *aeronautical engineer*
Mackey, Wayne Allison *electrical engineer*
Mehlman, Lon Douglas *information systems specialist*
Mitchell, John Noyes, Jr. *electrical engineer*
Mo, Roger Shih-Yah *electronics engineering manager*
Nguyen, Tien Manh *communications systems engineer*
Olson, Jeanne Innis *technology/technical management*
Paulikas, George Algis *physicist*
Rock, Angela *volleyball player*
Willis, Judy Ann *lawyer*

**Elk Grove**
McDavid, Douglas Warren *systems consultant*
Talbert, Melvin George *bishop*
Vang, Timothy Teng *church executive*

**Elverta**
Betts, Barbara Lang (Mrs. Bert A. Betts) *lawyer, rancher, realtor*

**Emeryville**
Chason, Lloyd Ralph *corporate educator*
Edginton, John Arthur *lawyer*
Finney, Lee *negotiator, social worker*
Masri, Merle Sid *biochemist, consultant*
Penhoet, Edward *biochemicals company executive*
Smith, Christopher Allen *technology company executive, marketing professional*
Weaver, Velather Edwards *small business owner*

**Encinitas**
Bloomberg, Warner, Jr. *urban affairs educator emeritus*
Coler, Myron A(braham) *chemical engineer, educator*
Frank, Michael Victor *risk assessment engineer*
Geier, Susan Asid *interior designer*
Goldberg, Edward Davidow *geochemist, educator*
Moe, Chesney Rudolph *physics educator*
Morrow, Charles Tabor *aerospace consulting engineer*
†Motoyama, Hiroshi *science association administrator*
Satur, Nancy Marlene *dermatologist*

**Encino**
Acheson, Louis Kruzan, Jr. *aerospace engineer and systems analyst*
Bach, Cynthia *educational program director, writer*
Bekey, Shirley White *psychotherapist*
Broughton, Bruce Harold *composer*
Colombier, Michel *composer*
Conway, Tim *comedian*
Cooper, Leroy Gordon, Jr. *former astronaut, business consultant*
Costea, Nicolas Vincent *physician, researcher*
Dor, Yoram *accountant, firm executive*
Eves, Jeffrey Parvin *entertainment industry executive*
Franklin, Bonnie Gail *actress*
Friedman, George Jerry *aerospace company executive, engineer*
Fuld, Steven Alan *financial advisor, insurance specialist*
Gasich, Welko Elton *retired aerospace executive, management consultant*
Hawthorne, Marion Frederick *chemistry educator*
Holman, Harland Eugene *retired motion picture company executive*
House-Hendrick, Karen Sue *nursing consultant*
Hubbard, Frederick Dewayne *trumpeter*
Johnson, Patricia Diane *psychotherapist, consultant*
Kanter, Hal *television and film writer, producer, director*
Kaufman, Albert I. *lawyer*
Kazan, Lainie (Lainie Levine) *singer, actress*
Knuth, Eldon Luverne *engineering educator*
Kuklin, Jeffrey Peter *lawyer, talent agency executive*
Lombardini, Carol Ann *lawyer*
Nicholson, Jack *actor, director, producer*
O'Connor, Patricia Ranville *secondary and special education educator*
Pryor, Richard *actor, writer*
Rance, Quentin E. *interior designer*
Rawitch, Robert Joe *journalist, educator*
Roderick, Robert Lee *aerospace executive*
Smith, Selma Moidel *lawyer, composer*
Vigdor, James Scott *distribution executive*
Vogel, Susan Carol *nursing administrator*
Webster, David Arthur *life insurance company executive*
Westmore, Michael George *make-up artist*
Wood, Raymund Francis *retired librarian*
Zsigmond, Vilmos *cinematographer, director*

**Englewood**
Fiske, Terry Noble *lawyer*
†Kupchak, Mitchell *professional sports team executive*

**Escalon**
Barton, Gerald Lee *farming company executive*

**Escondido**
Allen, Donald Vail *investment executive, author, concert pianist*
Briggs, Edward Samuel *naval officer*
Damsbo, Ann Marie *psychologist*
Everton, Marta Ve *ophthalmologist*
Gentile, Robert Dale *optometrist, consultant*
Ghandhi, Sorab Khushro *electrical engineering educator*
Gorsline, Samuel Gilbert, Jr. *school administrator*
Grew, Raymond Edward *mechanical engineer*
Moore, Marc Anthony *university administrator, writer, retired military officer*
Newman, Barry Ingalls *retired banker, lawyer*
Packer, Russell Howard *business services company executive*
Pershing, Richard Wilson *communications company executive, consultant*
Rich, Elizabeth Marie *nursing educator*
Rockwell, Elizabeth Goode *dance company director, consultant, educator*
Shanor, Clarence Richard *clergyman*
Sternberg, Harry *artist*
Strong, James Thompson *management, security, human resources consultant*
Tomomatsu, Hideo *chemist*

**Etna**
Auxentios, (Bishop Auxentios) *clergyman*

**Eureka**
Harvey, Carol Sammons *educator*
Kriger, Peter Wilson *healthcare administrator*
Roberts, Robert Chadwick *ecologist, environmental scientist, consultant*
Van Fleet, William Mabry *retired architect*

**Fair Oaks**
Agerbek, Sven *mechanical engineer*
Branch, Robert Lee *retired educational administrator*
Chernev, Melvin *retired beverage company executive*
Doyel, Cindy M. *controller*
Inglis, Andrew Franklin *author, consultant*
Nolan, Mark Gregory *advertising executive*
Parker, Brian Prescott *forensic scientist*
Smiley, Robert William *industrial engineer*

**Fairfax**
Ackerman, Arlene Alice *accountant, business consultant, artist, writer*
Delaney, Marion Patricia *bank executive*
Gores, Joseph Nicholas *novelist, scriptwriter*
Neuharth, Daniel J., II *psychotherapist*
Novello, Don *writer, comedian, actor*
Toney, Anthony *artist*

**Fairfield**
Datta, Purna Chandra *clinical psychologist, educator*
Martin, Clyde Verne *psychiatrist*
Moore, Marianna Gay *law librarian, consultant*
Munn, William Charles, II *psychiatrist*

**Fall River Mills**
Reed, Eva Silver Star *chieftain*

**Fallbrook**
Burns, Louis Francis *retired history educator*
Cralley, Lester Vincent *retired industrial hygienist, editor*
Freeman, Harry Lynwood *accountant*
Ragland, Jack Whitney *artist*
†Shaver, Carl A. *government official*

**Felicity**
Istel, Jacques Andre *mayor*

**Felton**
Kulzick, Kenneth Edmund *retired lawyer, writer*

**Fillmore**
Guthrie, Harvey Henry, Jr. *clergyman*

**Fish Camp**
Schneider, Arthur Paul *retired videotape and film editor, author*

**Flintridge**
Clauser, Francis H. *applied science educator*
Dales, Richard Clark *history educator*
Fry, Donald Owen *broadcasting company executive*
Hess, Robert Pratt *lawyer*
Read, William McClain *retired oil company executive*

**Folsom**
Aldridge, Donald O'Neal *military officer*
Campbell, Ann Marie *artist*
Ettlich, William F. *electrical engineer*
Meigel, David Walter *military officer, retired musician*
Mine, Hilary Anne *telecommunications company executive, consultant*

**Fontana**
Atkinson, Donald D., Sr. *real estate broker*
Barry(-Branks), Diane Dolores *podiatrist*
Cory, Rolland Wayne *business administrator*
Donica, Cheryl Marie *elementary education educator*
Poulsen, Dennis Robert *environmentalist*
Rynearson, Patricia Heaviside *elementary school educator*

**Foothill Ranch**
Testa, Stephen Michael *geologist, consultant*

**Forestville**
Benyo, Richard Stephen *magazine editor, writer*

**Fortuna**
Fisher, Bruce David *elementary school educator*
Fullerton, Gail Jackson *university president emeritus*

**Foster City**
Alvarez, Robert Smyth *editor, publisher*
Ball, John Paul *publishing company executive*
Baselt, Randall Clint *toxicologist*
Berman, Daniel K(atzel) *educational consultant, university official*
Goldstein, Morris *publishing company executive*
Ham, Lee Edward *civil engineer*
Lutvak, Mark Allen *computer company executive*
MacNaughton, Angus Athole *finance company executive*
Miller, Jon Philip *research and development organization executive*
Nugent, Denise Smith *holistic nurse*
Paterson, Richard Denis *financial executive*
Thomlinson, Ralph *demographer, educator*
Turner, Ross James *investment corporation executive*
Zaidi, Iqbal Mehdi *biochemist, scientist*

**Fountain Valley**
Berman, Steven Richard *computer systems analyst, research engineer*
Einstein, Stephen Jan *rabbi*
Gittleman, Morris *metallurgist, consultant*
Jessup, R. Judd *managed care executive*
Lonegan, Thomas Lee *retired restaurant corporation executive*
Penderghast, Thomas Frederick *business educator*

**Frazier Park**
Nelson, Harry *journalist, medical writer*

**Fremont**
Barreto, Charlton Bodenberg *software engineer*
Brown, David Richard *school system administrator, minister*
Chan, Steven S. *electronics company executive*
Eastin, Delaine Andree *state agency administrator*
Gill, Stephen Paschall *physicist, mathematician*
Lahri, Rajeeva *electronics executive*
Lautzenheiser, Marvin Wendell *computer software engineer*
Le, Thuy Trong *research and development engineer, educator*
Loarie, Thomas Merritt *healthcare executive*
Rugge, Henry Ferdinand *medical products executive*
Sahatjian, Manik *nurse, psychologist*
Smith, Bernald Stephen *retired airline pilot, aviation consultant*
Steinmetz, Seymour *pediatrician*
Torian, Henry *automotive executive*
†Wilson, Judy *small business owner*
Wu, James Chen-Yuan *aerospace engineering educator*

**Fresno**
Andresen, Claudia *principal*
Beck, Dennis L. *magistrate judge*
Blum, Gerald Henry *department store executive*
Brahma, Chandra Sekhar *civil engineering educator*
Buzick, William Alonson, Jr. *investor, lawyer, educator*
Cohen, Moses Elias *mathematician, educator*
Coyle, Robert Everett *federal judge*
Crocker, Myron Donovan *federal judge*
Dackawich, S. John *sociology educator*
Dandoy, Maxima Antonio *education educator emeritus*
Darden, Edwin Speight, Sr. *architect*
Dauer, Donald Dean *investment executive*
Emrick, Terry Lamar *financial business consultant*
Ewell, A. Ben, Jr. *lawyer, businessman*

Falcone, Alfonso Benjamin *physician and biochemist*
Ganulin, Judy *public relations professional*
Genini, Ronald Walter *history educator, historian*
Gerster, Robert Gibson *composer*
Gorman, Michael Joseph *library director, educator*
Gump, Barry Hemphill *research institute director*
Haak, Harold Howard *university president*
Hart, Russ Allen *telecommunications educator*
Holmes, Albert William, Jr. *physician*
Howard, Katsuyo Kunugi *counselor, educator, consultant*
Huddleston, Forest Willis *mental healing counselor*
Jamison, Oliver Morton *retired lawyer*
Kallenberg, John Kenneth *librarian*
Kauffman, George Bernard *chemistry educator*
Klassen, Peter James *academic administrator, history educator*
Kouymjian, Dickran *art historian, Orientalist, educator*
Leigh, Hoyle *psychiatrist, educator, writer*
Levy, Joseph William *department stores executive*
O'Brien, John Conway *economist, educator, writer*
O'Connor, Kevin John *psychologist*
Orr, Jim (James D. Orr) *columnist, writer, publicist*
Palmer, Samuel Copeland, III *lawyer*
Patnaude, William E. *architect*
Patterson, James *mayor*
Patton, Jack Thomas *family practice physician*
Petrucelli, James Michael *lawyer*
Pings, Anthony Claude *architect*
Pinkerton, Richard LaDoyt *management educator*
Price, Edward Dean *federal judge*
Putman, Robert Dean *golf course architect*
Rank, Everett George *government official*
Rehart, Burton Schyler *journalism educator, freelance writer*
Ryan, Charlotte Muriel *oncology nurse*
Schofield, John-David Mercer *bishop*
Shanafelt, Nancy Sue *quality consultant, career consultant*
Shmavonian, Gerald S. *entertainment executive*
Smith, Richard Howard *banker*
Smith, V. Roy *neurosurgeon*
Sobey, Edwin J. C. *museum director, oceanographer, consultant*
Steinbock, John Thomas *bishop*
Stude, Everett Wilson, Jr. *rehabilitation counselor, educator*
Tellier, Richard Davis *management educator*
Thompson, Leonard Russell *pediatrician*
Wanger, Oliver Winston *federal judge*
Welty, John Donald *academic administrator*
Wilson, Warren Samuel *clergyman, bishop*

### Fullerton
Aston, Edward Ernest, IV *dermatologist*
Ayala, John *librarian, dean*
Barchi, Barbara Ann *education educator*
Beers, Susan Alice *dean*
Brattstrom, Bayard Holmes *biology educator*
Cole, Sherwood Orison *psychologist*
Curran, Darryl Joseph *photographer, educator*
Donoghue, Mildred Ransdorf *education educator*
Fearn, Heidi *physicist, educator*
Frizell, Samuel *law educator*
Goldstein, Edward David *lawyer, former glass company executive*
Gordon, Milton Andrew *academic administrator*
Griffin, Kirsten Bertelsen *nursing educator*
Hershey, Gerald Lee *psychologist*
Hollander, Gerhard Ludwig *computer company executive*
Hopping, Richard Lee *college president*
Hugstad, Paul Steven *college dean*
Jones, Claris Eugene, Jr. *botanist, educator*
Kaisch, Kenneth Burton *psychologist, priest*
Karson, Burton Lewis *musician*
Kim, Gil *minister*
Lieberman, Paul *aeronautical engineer, engineering research company executive*
Linahon, James Joseph *music educator, musician*
Miller, Arnold *electronics executive*
Moerbeek, Stanley Leonard *lawyer*
Natsuyama, Harriet Hatsune *mathematician*
Oh, Tai Keun *business educator*
Parsons, Rodney Hunter *lawyer*
Roberts, Mark Scott *lawyer*
Ruby, Charles Leroy *law educator, lawyer, civic leader*
Sa, Julie *restaurant chain owner, former mayor*
Sadruddin, Moe *oil company executive, consultant*
Shapiro, Mark Howard *physicist, educator, academic dean, consultant*
Smith, Ephraim Philip *university dean, educator*
†Sugarman, Michael *physician, rheumatologist*
Tehrani, Fleur Taher *electrical engineer, educator, researcher*
Tuazon, Jesus Ocampo *electrical engineer, educator, consultant*
Woodhull, Patricia Ann *artist*

### Garden Grove
Chacon, Michael Ernest *computer networking specialist*
Dornan, Robert Kenneth *former congressman*
Virgo, Muriel Agnes *swimming school owner*
Williams, J(ohn) Tilman *insurance executive, real estate broker, city official*
Wong, Michael Henry *anesthesiologist*

### Gardena
Crismond, Linda Fry *public relations executive*
Hu, Steve Seng-Chiu *scientific research company executive, academic administrator*
Kanner, Edwin Benjamin *electrical manufacturing company executive*
Kronenberg, Jacalyn (Jacki Kronenberg) *nurse administrator*
Winston, Morton Manuel *equipment executive*

### Georgetown
Lengyel, Cornel Adam (Cornel Adam) *author*

### Gilroy
Borton, George Robert *airline captain*

### Glen Ellen
Anderson, Catherine *artist*
Rockrise, George Thomas *architect*

### Glendale
Aaronson, Robert Jay *aviation executive*
Ball, James Herington *lawyer*
Boukidis, Constantine Michael *lawyer*
Colby, Barbara Diane *interior designer, consultant*
Courtney, Howard Perry *clergyman*
Cross, Richard John *banker*
Dent, Ernest DuBose, Jr. *pathologist*
Farmer, Crofton Bernard *atmospheric physicist*
Hadley, Paul Ervin *international relations educator*
Herzer, Richard Kimball *franchising company executive*
Hoffman, Donald M. *lawyer*
Kazanjian, Phillip Carl *lawyer, business executive*
Kernen, Jules Alfred *pathologist*
Knoop, Vern Thomas *civil engineer, consultant*
Marr, Luther Reese *communications executive, lawyer*
Martin, John Hugh *lawyer, retired*
Martinetti, Ronald Anthony *lawyer*
Misa, Kenneth Franklin *management consultant*
Moorhead, Carlos J. *former congressman*
Nelson, James Augustus, II *real estate executive, architect, banker*
Odier, Pierre Andre *educator, writer, photographer, artist*
O'Donnell, Scott Richard *aviation administrator*
O'Malley, Joseph James *lawyer*
Rabe, Elizabeth Rozina *hair stylist, horse breeder*
Russell, Newton Requa *retired state senator*
Simpson, Allyson Bilich *lawyer*
Tookey, Robert Clarence *consulting actuary*
Trafton, Stephen J. *bank executive*
Tripoli, Masumi Hiroyasu *financial consultant and diplomat*
Whalen, Lucille *academic administrator*
Yegian, Richard *real estate executive*

### Glendora
Ahern, John Edward *mechanical engineer, consultant*
Barrett, Thomas Joseph *sales executive, computer systems consultant*
Cahn, David Stephen *cement company executive*
Christofi, Andreas Charalambos *finance educator*
Lindly, Douglas Dean *elementary school educator, administrator*
Richey, Everett Eldon *religion educator*
Schiele, Paul Ellsworth, Jr. *educational business owner, writer*

### Gold River
Gray, Myles McClure *retired insurance company executive*

### Goleta
Bartlett, James Lowell, III *investment company executive*
Koart, Nellie Hart *real estate investor and executive*
Thom, Richard David *aerospace executive*

### Granada Hills
Aller, Wayne Kendall *psychology educator, researcher, computer education company executive, property manager*
O'Connor, Betty Lou *service executive*
Pappas, Maria Eleni *nurse*
Shoemaker, Harold Lloyd *infosystem specialist*

### Granite Bay
Manzo, Salvatore Edward *retired business developer*

### Grass Valley
Cartwright, Mary Lou *laboratory scientist*
Hutcherson, Christopher Alfred *marketing and recruiting and educational consultant*
Lawrence, Dean Grayson *retired lawyer*
Stewart-Finocchiaro, Penny Morris *secondary school educator*

### Greenbrae
Blatt, Morton Bernard *medical illustrator*
Elder, Rex Alfred *civil engineer*
Levy, S. William *dermatologist*
Parnell, Francis William, Jr. *physician*

### Gualala
Gaustad, Edwin Scott *historian*

### Hacienda Heights
Love, Daniel Joseph *consulting engineer*

### Half Moon Bay
Fennell, Diane Marie *marketing executive, process engineer*
Hinthorn, Micky Terzagian *volunteer, retired*
Robertson, Abel L., Jr. *pathologist*

### Hanford
Hall, Richard Dennis *agribusiness and international trade writer*

### Hawthorne
Burns, Brent Emil *electrical engineer*
Gruenwald, James Howard *association executive, consultant*
McRuer, Duane Torrance *aerospace engineering executive*

### Hayward
Flora, Edward Benjamin *research and development company executive, mechanical engineer*
Hammerback, John Clark *communications educator*
Hirschfeld, Sue Ellen *geological sciences educator*
Hunnicutt, Richard Pearce *metallurgical engineer*
Jordahl, Geir Arild *photographer, educator*
Jordahl, Kathleen Patricia (Kate Jordahl) *photographer, educator*
Kam, Vernon Tam Siu *accounting educator*
Mayers, Eugene David *philosopher, educator*
McCune, Ellis E. *retired university system chief administrator, higher education consultant*
Prada, Gloria Ines *mathematics and Spanish language educator*
Ramos, Melvin John *artist, educator*
Rees, Norma S. *academic administrator*
Sabharwal, Ranjit Singh *mathematician*
Smith, John Kerwin *lawyer*
Smith, J(ohn) Malcolm *political science educator*
Stern, Ralph David *lawyer*
Tribus, Myron *quality counselor, engineer, educator*
Warnke, Detlef Andreas *geologist, educator*
Whalen, Thomas Earl *psychology educator*

### Healdsburg
Canfield, Grant Wellington, Jr. *management consultant*
Eade, George James *retired air force officer, research executive, defense consultant*
Erdman, Paul Emil *author*
Kamm, Thomas Allen *air transportation company executive*

### Hemet
Berger, Lev Isaac *physicist, educator*
Bible, Frances Lillian *mezzo-soprano, educator*
Galletta, Joseph Leo *physician*
Kopiloff, George *psychiatrist*
Masters, Judith Anne *elementary school educator*
Minnie, Mary Virginia *social worker, educator*
Shea, Robert Stanton *retired academic administrator*

### Hercules
Emmanuel, Jorge Agustin *chemical engineer, environmental consultant*

### Hermosa Beach
Kokalj, James Edward *retired aerospace administrator*
McDowell, Edward R. H. *chemical engineer*
Wickwire, Patricia Joanne Nellor *psychologist, educator*

### Hesperia
Butcher, Jack Robert (Jack Risin) *manufacturing executive*

### Hillsborough
Evans, Bob Overton *electronics executive*
Keller, John Francis *retired wine company executive, mayor*
Kraft, Robert Arnold *retired medical educator, physician*
Souter, Robert Taylor *retired banker*
West, Hugh Sterling *aircraft leasing company executive*
Willoughby, Rodney Erwin *retired oil company executive*
Zimmerman, Bryant Kable *retired lawyer*

### Hollywood
Byrnes, James Bernard *museum director emeritus*
Cannell, Stephen Joseph *television writer, producer, director*
Crow, Sheryl *singer/songwriter, musician*
Gibbons, Leeza *television talk show host, entertainment reporter*
†Greene, Stanley H. *broadcasting executive*
Hall, Allen *special effects expert*
Harris, Susan *television producer*
†Heftel, Richard *radio station executive*
Hovsepian, Vatche *clergyman*
Jordan, Stanley *musician*
Lempert, Philip *advertising executive, author, consumerologist, syndicated columnist, broadcast journalist*
Lewis, Huey (Hugh Anthony Cregg, III) *singer, composer, bandleader*
Little Richard, (Richard Wayne Penniman) *recording artist, pianist, songwriter, minister*
Marshall, Conrad Joseph *entrepreneur*
†Miles, Joanna *actress, playwright*
Parks, Robert Myers *appliance manufacturing company executive*
Robertson, Robbie *musician, popular*
Safan, Craig Alan *film composer*
Salomon, Mikael *cinematographer, director*
Sarley, John G. *broadcast executive, writer*
Schaefer, Carl George Lewis *writer, public relations and advertising executive*
Secada, Jon *musician*

### Hopland
Jones, Milton Bennion *agronomist, educator*

### Huntington Beach
Carey, Shirley Anne *nursing consultant*
Carino, Linda Susan *business consultant*
Davidson-Shepard, Gay *secondary education educator*
Desai, Veena Balvantrai *obstetrician and gynecologist, educator*
Dolan, Vikki Aldrich *healthcare nurse executive*
Frye, Judith Eleen Minor *editor*
Goldberg, David Charles *computer company executive*
Gruner, George Richard *secondary education educator*
Halvorsen, Jan La Rayne *library services manager*
Hildebrant, Andy McClellan *retired electrical engineer*
Kanode, Carolyn Kerrigan *school nurse, pediatric nurse practitioner*
Licata, Paul James *health products executive*
MacCauley, Hugh Bournonville *banker*
Martin, Wilfred Wesley Finny *psychologist, property owner and manager*
Nowlan, Daniel Ralph *engineering executive*
Olsen, Greg Scott *chiropractor*
Watts, Judith-Ann White *academic administrator*

### Idyllwild
Acheson, Barbara *real estate broker, small business owner*

### Imperial
Montenegro, Jean Baker *English language educator*
O'Leary, Thomas Michael *lawyer*

### Imperial Beach
Merkin, William Leslie *lawyer*

### Indian Wells
Carter, Paul Richard *physician*
Harris, Milton M. *distributing company executive*
Kelley, John Paul *communications consultant*
Reed, A(lfred) Byron *retired apparel and textile manufacturing company*
Smith, Byron Owen *retired lawyer*
Trotter, F(rederick) Thomas *retired academic administrator*

### Indio
Fischer, Craig Leland *physician*
Hare, Paul DeHaven *public safety director*

### Inglewood
Alaniz, Miguel José Castañeda *library director*
†Buss, Jerry Hatten *real estate executive, sports team owner*
Dymally, Mervyn Malcolm *retired congressman, international business executive*
Epstein, Marsha Ann *public health administrator, physician*
†Ferraro, Ray *hockey player*
Guzy, Marguerita Linnes *secondary education educator*
†Harris, Del William *professional basketball coach*
Jobe, Frank Wilson *orthopedic surgeon*
Leiweke, Timothy *sales executive, marketing professional*
Lewis, Roy Roosevelt *physicist*
Logan, Lynda Dianne *elementary education educator*
Moghadam, Amir *consultant, educational administrator*
O'Neal, Shaquille Rashaun *professional basketball player*
Robinson, Larry Clark *professional hockey coach*
Rogers, James Curtis *publisher, psychologist, screenwriter*
†Roski, Edward P. *professional sports team executive*
Sharman, William *professional basketball team executive*
†Tocchet, Rick *professional hockey player*
Van Exel, Nickey Maxwell *professional basketball player*
West, Jerry Alan *professional basketball team executive*
Zemel, Norman Paul *orthopedic surgeon*

### Inverness
Welpott, Jack Warren *photographer, educator*

### Inyokern
Norris, Lois Ann *elementary school educator*
Stallknecht-Roberts, Clois Freda *publisher, publicist*

### Irvine
Aigner, Dennis John *economics educator, consultant*
Alspach, Philip Halliday *manufacturing company executive*
Ang, Alfredo Hua-Sing *civil engineering educator*
Ayala, Francisco José *geneticist, educator*
Bander, Myron *physics educator, university dean*
Bañuelos, Robert Alexander *insurance company executive*
Bartkus, Richard Anthony *magazine publisher*
Bastiaanse, Gerard C. *lawyer*
Bennett, Bruce Michael *mathematics educator, musician*
Bershad, Neil Jeremy *electrical engineering educator*
Botwinick, Michael *museum director*
Bradshaw, Ralph Alden *biochemistry educator*
Bron, Walter Ernest *physics educator*
Burton, Michael Ladd *anthropology educator*
Cho, Zang Hee *physics educator*
Chronley, James Andrew *real estate executive*
Clark, Bruce Robert *geology consultant*
Clark, Karen Heath *lawyer*
Clark, Michael Phillip *English educator*
Click, James H. *automotive executive*
Cohen, Robert Stephen *drama educator*
Colino, Richard Ralph *communications consultant*
Connolly, John Earle *surgeon, educator*
Cushman, Robert Fairchild *political science educator, author, editor*
Dandashi, Fayad Alexander *operations research scientist*
Danziger, James Norris *political science educator*
Demetrescu, Mihai Constantin *research scientist, educator, computer company executive*
Dzyaloshinskii, Igor Ekhielievich *physicist*
Euster, Joanne Reed *librarian*
Fan, Hung Y. *virology educator, consultant*
Feldstein, Paul Joseph *management educator*
Felton, Jean Spencer *physician*
Finestone, Sandra Agnes *accountant*
Fitch, Walter M(onroe) *molecular biologist, educator*
Fleischer, Everly Borah *academic administrator*
Fouste, Donna H. *association executive*
Freeman, Linton Clarke *sociology educator*
Friou, George Jacob *immunologist, physician, educator*
Garcia, Stephen Gregory *vice chancellor, finance administrator*
Geis, Gilbert Lawrence *sociology educator emeritus*
†Giannulli, Mossimo *designer, apparel business executive*
Gottschalk, Louis August *neuropsychiatrist, psychoanalyst*
Greenberger, Ellen *psychologist, educator*
Gupta, Sudhir *immunologist, educator*
Gutman, George Andre *molecular biologist, educator*
Guymon, Gary LeRoy *civil engineering educator, consultant*
Haggerty, Charles A. *electronics executive*
Hardie, Robert C. *newspaper publishing executive*
Hemminger, John Charles *chemist, educator*
Herbert, Gavin Shearer *health care products company executive*
Hess, Cecil Fernando *engineering executive*
Hilker, Walter Robert, Jr. *lawyer*
Hine, Robert Van Norden, Jr. *historian, educator*
Hoffman, Donald David *cognitive and computer science educator*
Hubbell, Floyd Allan *physician, educator*
Ingram, Helen Moyer *political science educator*
Jacobs, Donald Paul *architect*
Jamshidipour, Yousef *bank executive, economist, financial planner*
Jeffers, Michael Bogue *lawyer*
†Jones, Chuck *cartoonist, writer, director*
Jones, Edward George *anatomy and neurobiology professor, department chairman*
Jones, Joie Pierce *acoustician, educator, writer, scientist*
Key, Mary Ritchie (Mrs. Audley E. Patton) *linguist, author, educator*
Kinsman, Robert Preston *biomedical plastics engineer*
Kluger, Ruth *German language educator, editor*
Knight, Patricia Marie *optics researcher*
Korc, Murray *endocrinologist*
Kraemer, Kenneth Leo *architect, urban planner, educator*
Krieger, Murray *English language educator, author*
Laird, Wilbur David, Jr. *bookseller, editor*
Lambert, Robert Lowell *scientific investigator*
Lanyi, Janos Karoly *biochemist, educator*
Larson, Kirk David *pomologist and extension specialist*
Lave, Charles Arthur *economics educator*
Le Bon, Douglas Kent *investment manager*
Lee, Meredith *German literature and language educator*
Leets, Peter John *outplacement consulting firm executive*

Lehnert, Herbert Hermann *foreign language educator*
Lenhoff, Howard Maer *biological sciences educator, academic administrator, activist*
Lesonsky, Rieva *editor-in-chief*
Lillyman, William John *German language educator*
Lindquist, Raymond Irving *clergyman*
Luce, R(obert) Duncan *psychology educator*
Maddy, Penelope Jo *philosopher*
Maradudin, Alexei A. *physics educator*
Margolis, Julius *economist, educator*
Marshall, Ellen Ruth *lawyer*
Maybay, Duane Charles *recycling systems executive*
McCraw, Leslie G. *engineering and construction company executive*
Mc Culloch, Samuel Clyde *history educator*
Mc Gaugh, James Lafayette *psychobiologist*
McLaughlin, Calvin Sturgis *biochemistry educator*
Miledi, Ricardo *neurobiologist*
Muller, Edward Robert *lawyer*
Nalcioglu, Orhan *physics educator, radiological sciences educator*
Nomura, Masayasu *biological chemistry educator*
Olofson, Roy Leonard *retail executive*
Orme, Melissa Emily *mechanical engineering educator*
Overman, Larry Eugene *chemistry educator*
Peltason, Jack Walter *former university president, educator*
Penrod, James Wilford *choreographer, dancer*
Phalen, Robert Franklynn *environmental scientist*
Pluta, Stanley John *manufacturing project engineer*
Power, Francis William *newspaper publisher*
Puzder, Andrew F. *lawyer*
Reines, Frederick *physicist, educator*
Rentzepis, Peter M. *chemistry educator*
Ristau, Kenneth Eugene, Jr. *lawyer*
Rollans, James O. *service company executive*
Rosse, James N. *newspaper publishing executive*
Rowland, Frank Sherwood *chemistry educator*
Ruyter, Nancy Lee Chalfa *dance educator*
Ryan, Julie Mae *optometrist, educator, researcher*
Rynn, Nathan *physics educator, consultant*
Samueli, Henry *electrical engineering educator*
Schonfeld, William Rost *political science educator, researcher*
Shusterman, Neal Douglas *author, screenwriter*
Silverman, Paul Hyman *parasitologist, former university official*
Sirignano, William Alfonso *aerospace and mechanical engineer, educator*
Sklansky, Jack *electrical and computer engineering educator, researcher*
Small, Kenneth Alan *economics educator*
Sperling, George *cognitive scientist, educator*
Spindler, Paul *public relations executive*
Stack, Geoffrey Lawrence *real estate developer*
Stubberud, Allen Roger *electrical engineering educator*
Sutton, Dana Ferrin *classics educator*
Tobis, Jerome Sanford *physician*
Trolinger, James Davis *laser scientist*
van-den-Noort, Stanley *physician, educator*
Walen, James Robert *engineering specialist*
Wallis, Richard Fisher *physicist, educator*
Wan, Frederic Yui-Ming *mathematician, educator*
Webb, Louis *automotive company executive*
Weinstein, Gerald D. *dermatology educator*
White, Douglas R. *anthropology educator*
White, Stephen Halley *biophysicist, educator*
Wiener, Jon *history educator*
Wilkening, Laurel Lynn *academic administrator, planetary scientist*
Williams, James E. *food products manufacturing company executive*
Williams, S. Linn *lawyer*
Wintrode, Ralph Charles *lawyer*
Wolff, Geoffrey Ansell *novelist, critic, educator*
Young, Robert Anthony *association director*

## Irwindale
Hughes, Roger K. *dairy and grocery store company executive*
Rinehart, Charles R. *savings and loan association executive*
Timmer, Barbara *lawyer*

## Joshua Tree
Styles, Beverly *entertainer*

## Keene
Rodriguez, Arturo Salvador *labor union official*

## Kelseyville
Berry, John Joseph *educational administrator*
Fletcher, Leland Vernon *artist*
Sandmeyer, E. E. *toxicologist, consultant*

## Kensington
Connick, Robert Elwell *retired chemistry educator*
Loran, Erle *artist*
Malkiel, Yakov *linguistics educator*
Nathan, Leonard Edward *writer, educator*
Oppenheim, Antoni Kazimierz *mechanical engineer*
Stent, Gunther Siegmund *molecular biologist, educator*

## Kentfield
Blum, Joan Kurley *fundraising executive*
Halprin, Anna Schuman (Mrs. Lawrence Halprin) *dancer*

## Kingsburg
Garrigus, Charles Byford *retired literature educator*
Olson, Maxine Louise *artist, lecturer*

## La Canada
Paniccia, Patricia Lynn *television news reporter, lawyer*

## La Canada Flintridge
Byrne, George Melvin *physician*
Costello, Francis William *lawyer*
Drees, Elaine Hnath *artist and educator*
Lamson, Robert Woodrow *retired school system administrator*
Pickering, William Hayward *physics educator, scientist*
Wallace, James Wendell *lawyer*

## La Crescenta
Purcell, Lee *actress, producer*
Winter-Neighbors, Gwen Carole *special education educator, art educator*

## La Habra
Chase, Cochrane *advertising agency executive*
Maxwell, Donald Stanley *publishing executive*
Woyski, Margaret Skillman *retired geology educator*

## La Jolla
Alksne, John F. *dean*
Alvariño De Leira, Angeles (Angeles Alvariño) *biologist, oceanographer*
Anderson, Richard William *retired psychiatrist, educator*
Andre, Michael Paul *physicist, educator*
Angotti, Antonio Mario *international merchant, banker*
Anthony, Harry Antoniades *city planner, architect, educator*
Antin, David *poet, critic*
Antin, Eleanor *artist*
Arnold, James Richard *chemist, educator*
Asmus, John Fredrich *physicist*
Attiyeh, Richard Eugene *economics educator*
Backus, George Edward *theoretical geophysicist*
Baesel, Stuart Oliver *architect*
Bardwick, Judith Marcia *management consultant*
Barrett-Connor, Elizabeth Louise *epidemiologist, educator*
Bavasi, Peter Joseph *professional baseball team executive*
Beebe, Mary Livingstone *curator*
Benson, Andrew Alm *biochemistry educator*
Bergan, John Jerome *vascular surgeon*
Berger, Wolfgang H. *oceanographer, marine geologist*
Bernstein, Michael Alan *history educator, department chairman*
Beutler, Ernest *physician, research scientist*
Block, Melvin August *surgeon, educator*
Bloom, Floyd Elliott *physician, research scientist*
Boger, Dale L. *chemistry educator*
Brand, Larry Milton *biochemist*
Brooks, Charles Lee, III *computational biophysicist, educator*
Brown, Stuart I. *ophthalmologist, educator*
Buckingham, Michael John *oceanography educator*
Bukry, John David *geologist*
Burbidge, E. Margaret *astronomer, educator*
Burbidge, Geoffrey *astrophysicist, educator*
Cain, William Stanley *psychologist, educator*
Carmichael, David Burton *physician*
Case, Ted Joseph *biologist, educator*
Castleman, Breaux Ballard *health management company executive*
Chang, William Shen Chie *electrical engineering educator*
Chien, Shu *physiology and bioengineering educator*
Christensen, Halvor Niels *biochemist, educator*
Churg, Jacob *pathologist*
Coburn, Marjorie Foster *psychologist, educator*
Cohen, Barbara Ann *artist*
Conn, Robert William *engineering science educator*
Continetti, Robert E. *chemistry educator*
Copley, David C. *newspaper publishing company executive*
Copley, Helen Kinney *newspaper publisher*
Counts, Stanley Thomas *aerospace consultant, retired naval officer, retired electronics company executive*
Covell, Ruth Marie *medical educator, medical school administrator*
Cox, Charles Shipley *oceanography researcher, educator*
Cunningham, Bruce Arthur *biochemist*
Dalessio, Donald John *physician, neurologist, educator*
Dixon, Frank James *medical scientist, educator*
Doolittle, Russell Francis *biochemist, educator*
Dorsey, Dolores Florence *corporate treasurer, business executive*
Dreilinger, Charles Lewis (Chips Dreilinger) *dean*
Drell, William *chemical company executive*
Driscoll, Charles F. *physics educator*
Dulbecco, Renato *biologist, educator*
Edelman, Gerald Maurice *biochemist, educator*
Edwards, Charles Cornell *physician, research administrator*
Farson, Richard Evans *psychologist*
Feher, George *physics and biophysics scientist, educator*
Fishman, William Harold *cancer research foundation executive, biochemist*
Foley, L(ewis) Michael *real estate executive*
Fosburg, Richard Garrison *cardiothoracic surgeon*
Freedman, David Noel *religion educator*
Fricke, Martin Paul *science company executive*
Friedmann, Theodore *physician*
Frieman, Edward Allan *university administrator, educator*
Fung, Yuan-Cheng Bertram *bioengineering educator, author*
Garland, Cedric Frank *epidemiologist, educator*
Geckler, Richard Delph *metal products company executive*
Geiduschek, E(rnest) Peter *biophysics and molecular biology educator*
Gilbert, James Freeman *geophysics educator*
Gill, Gordon N. *medical educator*
Gittes, Ruben Foster *urological surgeon*
Goguen, Joseph Amadee *computer science educator*
Goodman, Murray *chemistry educator*
Greer, Howard Earl *former naval officer*
Grier, Herbert Earl *scientist, consultant*
Grine, Donald Reaville *retired geophysicist, research executive*
Guillemin, Roger C. L. *physiologist*
Halkin, Hubert *mathematics educator, research mathematician*
Hamburger, Robert N. *pediatrics educator, consultant*
Harkins, Edwin L. *music educator, performer*
Harris, Philip Robert *management and space psychologist*
Harris, T. George *magazine editor*
Havis, Allan Stuart *playwright, theatre educator*
Haxo, Francis Theodore *marine biologist*
Helinski, Donald Raymond *biologist, educator*
Helstrom, Carl Wilhelm *electrical engineering educator*
Hench, Philip Kahler *physician*
Hofmann, Alan Frederick *biomedical educator, researcher*
Hoston, Germaine Annette *political science educator*
Imana, Jorge Garron *artist*
Inverarity, Robert Bruce *artist*
Itano, Harvey Akio *biochemistry educator*
Jacobson, Gary Charles *political science educator*
Johnson, Allen Dress *cardiologist*
Jones, Galen Everts *microbiologist, educator*
Jorgensen, Judith Ann *psychiatrist*
Joyce, Gerald Francis *biochemist, educator*
Kadonaga, James Takuro *biochemist*
Karin, Sidney *research and development executive*
Katzman, Robert *medical educator, neurologist*
Keeling, Charles David *oceanography educator*
Keeney, Edmund Ludlow *physician*
Kent, Paula *public relations, marketing and management consultant, lecturer*
Kirchheimer, Arthur E(dward) *lawyer, business executive*
Kitada, Shinichi *biochemist*
Klein, David *foreign service officer*
Klinman, Norman Ralph *immunologist, medical educator*
Knauss, John Atkinson *federal agency administrator, oceanographer, educator, former university dean*
Knox, Elizabeth Louise *community volunteer, travel consultant*
Knox, Robert Arthur *oceanographer, academic administrator*
La Bonté, C(larence) Joseph *weight management and lifestyle company executive*
Lakier, Nancy S. *health care consultant*
Lal, Devendra *nuclear geophysics educator*
Langacker, Ronald Wayne *linguistics educator*
Lauer, James Lothar *physicist, educator*
Lee, Jerry Carlton *university administrator*
Lele, Padmakar Pratap *physician, educator*
Levy, Ralph *engineering executive, consultant*
Lewin, Ralph Arnold *biologist*
Low, Mary Louise (Molly Low) *documentary photographer*
MacDougall, John Douglas *earth science educator*
Mandler, George *psychologist*
Mandler, Jean Matter *psychologist, educator*
Marshall, Sharon Bowers *nursing educator, director clinical trials*
Martin, James John, Jr. *retired consulting research firm executive, systems analyst*
Masys, Daniel Richard *medical school director*
Mathews, Kenneth Pine *physician, educator*
McCammon, James Andrew *chemistry educator*
McDonald, Marianne *classicist*
McIlwain, Carl Edwin *physicist*
McNamara, Tom *scientific consulting corporation executive*
Merrim, Louise Meyerowitz *artist, actress*
Mestril, Ruben *biochemist, researcher*
Milstein, Laurence Bennett *electrical engineering educator, researcher*
Mirsky, Phyllis Simon *librarian*
Monaghan, Eileen *artist*
Moore, F. Richard *music educator*
Morse, Jack Hatton *management consultant*
Movius, Alison Whitney Burton (Alison Whitney) *writer, educator, publisher, speaker, poet, songwriter*
Mullin, Michael Mahlon *Biology and oceanography educator*
Mullis, Kary Banks *biochemist*
Muniain, Javier P. *computer company executive, physicist, researcher*
Munk, Walter Heinrich *geophysics educator*
Nakamura, Robert Motoharu *pathologist*
Newmark, Leonard Daniel *linguistics educator*
Nyhan, William Leo *pediatrician, educator*
Ogdon, Wilbur *composer, music educator*
Ohkawa, Tihiro *physicist*
Olafson, Frederick Arlan *philosophy educator*
O'Neil, Thomas Michael *physicist, educator*
Onuchic, Jóse Nelson *biophysics educator, electrical engineer*
†Palmer, Paul Edward *communications executive*
Patton, Stuart *biochemist, educator*
Penner, Stanford Solomon *engineering educator*
Peterson, Laurence E. *physics educator*
Pollard, Thomas Dean *cell biologist, educator*
Purdy, Kevin M. *estate planner*
Quinton, Paul Marquis *physiology educator*
Randolph, Harry Franklin, III *health facility administrator, physician assistant*
Rearden, Carole Ann *clinical pathologist, educator*
Reissner, Eric (Max Erich Reissner) *applied mechanics researcher*
Resnik, Robert *medical educator*
Reynolds, Roger Lee *composer*
Richey, Phil Horace *former manufacturing executive, consultant*
Rosenblatt, Murray *mathematics educator*
Rosenfeld, Michael G. *medical educator*
Rotenberg, Manuel *physics educator*
Rudee, Mervyn Lea *engineering educator, researcher*
Saier, Milton H. Jr. *biology educator*
Schiller, Herbert Irving *social scientist, author*
Schmid-Schoenbein, Geert Wilfried *biomedical engineer, educator*
Seegmiller, Jarvis Edwin *biochemist, educator*
Shakespeare, Frank *ambassador*
Sham, Lu Jeu *physics educator*
Shannahan, William Paul *lawyer*
Shor, George G., Jr. *geophysicist, oceanographic administrator, engineer*
Shuler, Kurt Egon *chemist, educator*
Siegan, Bernard Herbert *lawyer, educator*
Silva, Ernest R. *visual arts educator, artist*
Silverstone, Leon Martin *dental research cariologist, neuroscientist, educator, researcher*
Simnad, Massoud T. *engineering educator*
Skalak, Richard *engineering mechanics educator, researcher*
Somerville, Richard Chapin James *atmospheric scientist, educator*
Spiegelberg, Hans Leonhard *medical educator*
Spiess, Fred Noel *oceanographer, educator*
Spiro, Melford Elliot *anthropology educator*
Squire, Larry Ryan *neuroscientist, psychologist, educator*
Starr, Ross Marc *economist, educator*
Steinberg, Daniel *preventive medicine physician, educator*
Stevens, Paul Irving *manufacturing company executive*
Stewart, John Lincoln *university administrator*
Streichler, Jerry *industrial engineer, consultant company executive*
Suhl, Harry *physics educator*
Sung, Kuo-Li Paul *bioengineering educator*
†Tajima, George Kazuo *electronics company executive*
Talke, Frank Eberhard *education educator*
Tan, Eng Meng *immunologist, rheumatologist, biomedical scientist*
Teirstein, Paul Shepherd *physician, health facility administrator*
Terras, Audrey Anne *mathematics educator*
Terry, Robert Davis *neuropathologist, educator*
Thal, Leon Joel *neuroscientist*
Thrower, F. Mitchell, III *advertising executive*
Thueson, David Orel *pharmaceutical executive, researcher, educator, writer*
Tietz, Norbert Wolfgang *clinical chemistry educator, administrator*
Todd, Harry Williams *aircraft propulsion system company executive*
Vacquier, Victor Dimitri *biology educator*
Van Lint, Victor Anton Jacobus *physicist*
Walker, Joseph *retired research executive*
Wall, Frederick Theodore *retired chemistry educator*
Wallace, Robert George *retired construction company executive, civil engineer*
Watson, Kenneth Marshall *physics educator*
Weigle, William Oliver *immunologist, educator*
Wertheim, Robert Halley *security consultant*
Wesling, Donald Truman *English literature educator*
West, John Burnard *physiologist, educator*
Whitaker, Eileen Monaghan *artist*
White, Halbert Lynn, Jr. *economist, educator, consultant*
Wilkie, Donald Walter *biologist, aquarium museum director*
Wilkins, Floyd, Jr. *retired lawyer, consultant*
Williams, Forman Arthur *engineering science educator, combustion theorist*
Wright, Andrew *English literature educator*
Wulbert, Daniel Eliot *mathematician, educator*
Wyle, Ewart Herbert *clergyman*
Yang, Zhen *research scientist*
Yen, Samuel S(how)-C(hih) *obstetrics and gynecology educator, reproductive endocrinologist*
York, Herbert Frank *physics educator, government official*
Zwain, Ismail Hassan *molecular endocrinologist*
Zyroff, Ellen Slotoroff *information scientist, classicist, educator*

## La Mesa
Bailey, Brenda Marie *accountant*
Black, Eileen Mary *elementary school educator*
Hansen, Grant Lewis *retired aerospace and information systems executive*
Schmidt, James Craig *retired bank executive, bankruptcy examiner*
Tarson, Herbert Harvey *university administrator emeritus*
Wohl, Armand Jeffrey *cardiologist*

## La Mirada
Lingenfelter, Sherwood Galen *university provost, anthropology educator*
Pike, Patricia Louise *psychology educator*

## La Palma
Akubuilo, Francis Ekenechukwu *secondary school educator*

## La Puente
Churchill, James Allen *lawyer*
Hitchcock, Fritz *automotive company executive*
Sheridan, Christopher Frederick *human resources executive*
Thornburg, Lee Ellis *film executive, director*

## La Quinta
Barr, Roger Terry *sculptor*
Harbert, Edward Wesley, II *television producer, writer, director*
Hartley, Celia Love *nursing educator, nursing administrator*
Houze, William Cunningham *executive recruiter, management consultant*

## La Verne
Fleck, Raymond Anthony, Jr. *retired university administrator*
Huigens, Daniel Dean *dentist*
Morgan, Stephen Charles *academic administrator*

## Lafayette
Alexander, Kenneth Lewis *editorial cartoonist*
Beaumont, Mona *artist*
Cotton, Barbara Lynn *correctional health systems management consultant*
Dethero, J. Hambright *banker*
Kahn, Robert Irving *management consultant*
Kapp, Eleanor Jeanne *impressionistic artist, writer, researcher*
Lewis, Sheldon Noah *technology consultant*
Oliveira, Elmar *violinist*
Peirano, Lawrence Edward *civil engineer*
Yarlagadda, Rambabu Venkata *financial manager*

## Laguna Beach
Banuelos, Betty Lou *rehabilitation nurse*
Bent, Alan Edward *political science educator, administrator*
Bezar, Gilbert Edward *retired aerospace company executive, volunteer*
Calderwood, James Lee *former English literature educator, writer*
Dale, Leon Andrew *economist, educator*
Fagin, Henry *public administration consultant*
Fry, Edward Bernard *retired education educator*
Garfin, Louis *actuary*
Hanauer, Joe Franklin *real estate executive*
Indiek, Victor Henry *finance corporation executive*
Johnson, Roger W. *former federal official, computer manufacturing company executive*
Kramarsic, Roman Joseph *engineering consultant*
Lurie, Harold *engineer, lawyer*
Powers, Runa Skötte *artist*
Reinglass, Michelle Annette *lawyer*
†Segard, Hubert J. *international marketing company executive, consultant*
Simons, Barry Thomas *lawyer*
Taylor, James Walter *marketing consultant*
Taylor, Theodore Langhans *author*
Warner, Robert S. *company director, former accountant*
Wilson, James Newman *retired laboratory executive*
Wolf, Karl Everett *aerospace and communications corporation executive*

## Laguna Hills
Batdorf, Samuel B(urbridge) *physicist*
Faw, Duane Leslie *retired military officer, law educator, lay worker, author*
Green, Leon, Jr. *mechanical engineer*
Herold, Ralph Elliott *motion picture arts educator*
Howard, Hildegarde (Mrs. Henry Anson Wylde) *paleontologist*
Hussey, William Bertrand *retired foreign service officer*

Iberall, Arthur Saul *physicist, publisher*
Ierardi, Stephen John *physician*
James, Sidney Lorraine *television executive*
Kaplan, Sidney Joseph *sociologist, educator*
Larson, Harry Thomas *electronics engineer, executive, consultant*
Lederer, Jerome *aerospace safety engineer, educator*
Leydorf, Frederick Leroy *lawyer*
Lindsay, Helen Mills *psychotherapist*
Miller, Eldon Earl *corporate business publications consultant, retired manufacturing company executive*
Noble, Marion Ellen *retired home economist*
Ross, Mathew *psychiatry educator*
Rossiter, Bryant William *chemistry consultant*
Schulz, Raymond Alexander *medical marketing professional, consultant*
Wheatley, Melvin Ernest, Jr. *retired bishop*
Widyolar, Sheila Gayle *dermatologist*

### Laguna Niguel
Apt, Charles *artist*
Born, Robert Heywood *consulting civil engineer*
Carr, Bernard Francis *hospital administrator*
Freeland, Darryl Creighton *psychologist, educator*
Hanson, Larry Keith *plastics company executive*
Hough, J. Marie *real estate company official*
Kursewicz, Lee Z. *marketing consultant*
Milunas, J. Robert *health care organization executive*
Nelson, Alfred John *retired pharmaceutical company executive*
Pierce, Hilda (Hilda Herta Harmel) *painter*
Smith, Leslie Roper *hospital and healthcare administrator*
Sturdevant, Charles Oliver *physician, neuropsychiatrist*
Teitelbaum, Marilyn Leah *special education educator*
York, James Orison *real estate executive*

### Lagunitas
Holman, Arthur Stearns *artist*

### Lake Arrowhead
Asher, James Edward *forestry consultant, engineer, arborist, forensic expert*
Bauer, Ralph Leroy *business executive*

### Lake Elsinore
Corral, Jeanie Beleyn *journalist, school board administrator*

### Lake Forest
Sheehy, Jerome Joseph *electrical engineer*

### Lake Hughes
La Mont-Wells, Tawana Faye *camera operator, video director*

### Lake Isabella
Fraser, Eleanor Ruth *radiologist, administrator*
Mansbridge, Mark *art director, production designer*

### Lake Sherwood
Burke, Tamara Lynn *marketing professional*
Pollak, Norman L. *retired accountant*

### Lakewood
Bogdan, James Thomas *secondary education educator, electronics researcher and developer*

### Lancaster
Berg, Hans Fredrik *lawyer*
Crew, Aubrey Torquil *aerospace inspector*
Hodges, Vernon Wray *mechanical engineer*
Roths, Beverly Owen *organization executive*

### Landers
Landers, Vernette Trosper *writer, educator, association executive*

### Larkspur
Finkelstein, James Arthur *management consultant*
Greenberg, Myron Silver *lawyer*
Kirk, Gary Vincent *investment advisor*
Maier, Peter Klaus *law educator, investment adviser*
Marker, Marc Linthacum *lawyer, investor*
Napoles, Veronica Kleeman *graphic designer, consultant*
Roulac, Stephen E. *real estate consultant*
Saxton, Lloyd *psychologist, author*
Shepard, James Edward *physician*

### Lebec
Shelby, Tim Otto *secondary education educator*

### Lemon Grove
Whitehead, Marvin Delbert *plant pathologist*

### Lemoore
Krend, William John *secondary education educator*

### Livermore
Alder, Berni Julian *physicist*
Bennett, Alan Jerome *electronics executive, physicist*
Blattner, Meera McCuaig *computer science educator*
Carley, James French *chemical and plastics engineer*
Chung, Dae Hyun *retired geophysicist*
Cook, Robert Crossland *research chemist*
Ellsaesser, Hugh Walter *retired atmospheric scientist*
Haga, Enoch John *computer educator, author*
Hooper, Edwin Bickford *physicist*
Hulet, Ervin Kenneth *retired nuclear chemist*
Jarnagan, Harry William, Jr. *project control manager*
Johnson, Roy Ragnar *electrical engineer*
Kidder, Ray Edward *physicist, consultant*
King, Ray John *electrical engineer*
Kirkwood, Robert Keith *applied physicist*
Lau, Albert Man-Fai *physicist*
Leith, Cecil Eldon, Jr. *retired physicist*
Lucas, Linda Lucille *dean*
Max, Claire Ellen *physicist*
Nuckolls, John Hopkins *physicist, researcher*
Portway, Patrick Stephen *telecommunications consulting company executive, telecommunications educator*
Schock, Robert Norman *geophysicist*
Sebasco, Salvador Monastra *safety engineer*
Sheem, Sang Keun *fiber optics engineering professional*
Shotts, Wayne J. *nuclear scientist, federal agency administrator*
Tarter, Curtis Bruce *physicist, science administrator*
Wong, Joe *physical chemist*

### Livingston
Fox, Robert August *food company executive*

### Lodi
Albert, N. Erick *urologist*
Bernhoft, Franklin Otto *psychotherapist, psychologist*
Wyrick, Daniel John *science/health textbook editor, science specialist*

### Loma Linda
Adey, William Ross *physician*
Aloia, Roland Craig *scientist, administrator, educator*
Alvarez, Ofelia Amparo *medical educator*
Ashwal, Stephen *pediatrician, child neurologist, educator*
Behrens, Berel Lyn *physician, academic administrator*
Bell, Denise Louise *newspaper reporter, photographer, librarian*
Brandstater, Murray Everett *physiatrist*
Buchholz, John Nicholas *pharmacology educator*
Bull, Brian Stanley *pathology educator, medical consultant, business executive*
Chan, Philip J. *medical educator*
Chang, Janice May *lawyer, law educator, naturopath, psychologist*
Coggin, Charlotte Joan *cardiologist, educator*
Condon, Stanley Charles *gastroenterologist*
Feller, Ralph Paul *dentist, educator*
Hardesty, Robert Alan *plastic surgeon*
Hinshaw, David B., Jr. *radiologist*
Johns, Varner Jay, Jr. *medical educator*
Kirk, Gerald Arthur *nuclear radiologist*
Klooster, Judson *academic administrator, dentistry educator*
Kuhn, Irvin Nelson *hematologist, oncologist*
Llaurado, Josep G. *nuclear medicine physician, scientist*
Longo, Lawrence Daniel *physiologist, obstetrician-gynecologist*
Mace, John Weldon *pediatrician*
Maurice, Don *personal care industry executive*
Peterson, John Eric *physician, educator*
Rendell-Baker, Leslie *anesthesiologist, educator*
Roberts, Walter Herbert Beatty *anatomist*
Sewell, Robert Dalton *pediatrician*
Slater, James Munro *radiation oncologist*
Slattery, Charles Wilbur *biochemistry educator*
Strother, Allen *biochemical pharmacologist, researcher*
Taylor, Barry Llewellyn *microbiologist, educator*
Wilcox, Ronald Bruce *biochemistry educator, researcher*
Young, Lionel Wesley *radiologist*

### Lompoc
Maxwell, Marilyn Julia *elementary education educator*
Sabo, Ronald William *lawyer, financial consultant*

### Long Beach
Adler, Jeffrey D. *political consultant, public affairs consultant, crisis management expert*
Alkon, Ellen Skillen *physician*
Anatol, Karl W. E. *provost*
Anderson, Garry Michael *diagnostic radiologist*
Anderson, Gerald Verne *retired aerospace company executive*
Armstrong, Joanna *education educator*
Bauer, Roger Duane *chemistry educator, science consultant*
Beebe, Sandra E. *retired English language educator, artist, writer*
Beljan, John Richard *university administrator, medical educator*
Brent, Paul Leslie *mechanical engineering educator*
Brisco, Valerie *track and field athlete*
Brown, Lester B. *social work educator*
Brown, (Jerene) Roxanne *sales executive*
Carlton-Adams, Dana Georgia Marie Anne *psychotherapist*
Crutchfield, James N. *publishing executive*
Dean, Charles Thomas *industrial arts educator, academic administrator*
de Soto, Simon *mechanical engineer*
Dillon, Michael Earl *engineering executive, mechanical engineer, educator*
Donald, Eric Paul *aeronautical engineer, inventor*
Fagan, Frederic *neurosurgeon*
Feldman, Stephen *university president*
Ferreri, Michael Victor *optometrist*
Fornia, Dorothy Louise *physical education educator*
Gehring, George Joseph, Jr. *dentist*
Glenn, Constance White *art museum director, educator, consultant*
Hall, Phyllis Charlene *therapist, counselor*
Hancock, John Walker, III *banker*
Hext, Kathleen Florence *internal audit college administrator*
Higginson, John *retired military officer*
Hobgood, E(arl) Wade *college dean*
Hu, Chi Yu *physicist, educator*
Hulsey, Neven C. *metal products executive*
Iliff, Warren Jolidon *zoo administrator*
Jeffery, James Nels *protective services official*
Johnson, Philip Leslie *lawyer*
Keller, J(ames) Wesley *credit union executive*
Kohn, Gerhard *psychologist, educator*
Kokaska, Charles James *educational psychologist*
Kumar, Rajendra *electrical engineering educator*
†Kunze, Chris *airport manager, educator*
Kurnick, Nathaniel Bertrand *oncologist-hematologist, educator, researcher*
Kwaan, Jack Hau Ming *retired physician*
Lathrop, Ann *librarian, educator*
Lathrop, Irvin Tunis *retired academic dean, educator*
Lauda, Donald Paul *university dean*
Lee, Isaiah Chong-Pie *social worker, educator*
Lewis, Ralph Jay, III *management and human resources educator*
Lobdell, Robert Charles *retired newspaper executive*
Loganbill, G. Bruce *logopedic pathologist*
Looney, Gerald Lee *medical educator, administrator*
Lowentrout, Peter Murray *religious studies educator*
Macer, George Armen, Jr. *orthopedic hand surgeon*
Mandeville, Craig H. *aircraft company executive, retired military officer*
Martinez, Patricia Ann *middle school educator, administrator*
McDonough, Patrick Dennis *academic administrator*
McGaughey, Charles Gilbert *retired research biochemist*
McGuire, James Charles *aircraft company executive*
Metzger, Vernon Arthur *management educator, consultant*
Mills, Don Harper *pathology and psychiatry educator, lawyer*
†Moran, Edgar M. *physician, educator*
Muchmore, Don Moncrief *museum, foundation, educational, financial fund raising and public opinion consulting firm administrator, banker*
Mullins, Ruth Gladys *pediatrics nurse*
Munitz, Barry *university administrator, English literature educator, business consultant*
Myers, John Wescott *aviation executive*
Nelson, Harold Bernhard *museum director*
O'Neill, Beverly Lewis *mayor, former college president*
Palacios, Alana Sue *computer programmer*
Patino, Douglas Xavier *foundation and university administrator*
Pokras, Sheila Frances *judge*
Pugay, Jeffrey Ibanez *mechanical engineer*
Raiklen, Harold *aerospace engineering consultant*
Rethore, Bernard Gabriel *diversified manufacturing company executive*
Roberts, James Donzil *lawyer*
Rosenberg, Jill *realtor, civic leader*
Ruszkiewicz, Carolyn Mae *newspaper editor*
Sato, Eunice Noda *former mayor, consultant*
Schinnerer, Alan John *entrepreneur*
Schroeder, Arnold Leon *mathematics educator*
Small, Richard David *research scientist*
Sosoka, John Richard *consulting firm executive, engineer*
†Stemmer, Edward Alan *surgeon, educator*
Swatek, Frank Edward *microbiology educator*
Tang, Paul Chi Lung *philosophy educator*
Taylor, Reese Hale, Jr. *lawyer, former government administrator*
Thompson, William Ancker *intramural-recreational sports director, educator*
Thorn, James Douglas *safety engineer*
Todd, Malcolm Clifford *surgeon*
Valek, Bernard Michael *accounting executive*
Vejsicky, Cathleen Lynn *management executive, educator*
Viola, Bill *artist, writer*
Walker, Linda Ann *financial planner*
White, Katherine Elizabeth *retired pediatrician*
Wiberg, Donald Martin *electrical engineering educator, consultant*
Wise, George Edward *lawyer*
Zappe, John Paul *city editor, educator*

### Loomis
Hartmann, Frederick Howard *political science educator emeritus*

### Los Alamitos
Abrams, Lois Marcia *psychotherapist*
Ayling, Henry Faithful *writer, editor, consultant*
Booth, John Nicholls *minister, magician, writer, photographer*
Jones, Dorothy Joanne *social services professional*
Spiegel, Marilyn Harriet *real estate executive*
Weinberger, Frank *information management consultant*

### Los Altos
Abrams, Arthur Jay *physician*
Barker, William Alfred *physics educator*
Beer, Clara Louise Johnson *retired electronics executive*
Bell, Chester Gordon *computer engineering company executive*
Bergrun, Norman Riley *aerospace executive*
Bracken, Thomas Robert James *real estate investment executive*
Burkhart, Dorothy P. *art critic, catalog essayist*
Carsten, Jack Craig *venture capitalist*
Cranston, Alan *former senator*
Esber, Edward Michael, Jr. *software company executive*
Fondahl, John Walker *civil engineering educator*
Frey, Christian Miller *research center executive*
Getreu, Sanford *city planner*
Gray, Robert Donald *municipal government official*
Hahn, Harold Thomas *physical chemist, chemical engineer*
Hall, Charles Frederick *space scientist, government administrator*
Halverson, George Clarence *business administration educator*
Hecker, Michael Hanns Louis *electrical engineer, speech scientist*
Hinckley, Gregory Keith *financial executive*
Jones, Robert Thomas *aerospace scientist*
Kazan, Benjamin *research engineer*
Miller, Ronald Grant *journalist*
Moll, John Lewis *electronics engineer, retired*
Mullaley, Robert Charles *manufacturing company executive*
Orr, Susan Packard *foundation administrator*
Peterson, Victor Lowell *aerospace engineer, management consultant*
Puder, Janice *special education educator*
Sharpe, Roland Leonard *engineering company executive, earthquake and structural engineering consultant*
Twersky, Victor *mathematical physicist, educator*
van Tamelen, Eugene Earle *chemist, educator*
Weir, Robert H. *lawyer*
Wickham, Kenneth Gregory *retired institute official, army officer*
Wilbur, Colburn Sloan *foundation administrator, chief executive officer*

### Los Angeles
Aaron, Benjamin *law educator, arbitrator*
Abdou, Mohamed A. *mechanical, aerospace, and nuclear engineering educator*
Abeles, Kim Victoria *artist*
Abernethy, Robert John *real estate developer*
Abrams, Norman *law educator, university administrator*
Adamek, Charles Andrew *lawyer*
Adams, William Wesley, III *architect*
Adamson, Arthur Wilson *chemistry educator*
Adell, Hirsch *lawyer*
Adler, Erwin Ellery *lawyer*
Afifi, Abdelmonem A. *biostatistics educator, academic dean*
Ahn, Samuel Seunghae *vascular surgeon, researcher, consultant*
Aki, Keiiti *seismologist, educator*
Alarcon, Arthur Lawrence *federal judge*
Alexander, Herbert E. *political scientist*
Alkon, Paul Kent *English language educator*
Allen, Karen Jane *actress*
Allen, Michael John Bridgman *English educator*
Allen, William Richard *retired economist*
Aller, Lawrence Hugh *astronomy educator, researcher*
Allerton, Samuel Ellsworth *biochemist*
Alley, Kirstie *actress*
Alpers, Edward Alter *history educator*
Altfeld, Sheldon Isaac *communications executive*
Alvarez, Rodolfo *sociology educator, consultant*
Alwan, Abeer Abdul-Hussain *electrical engineering educator*
Amneus, D. A. *English language educator*
Amos, John *actor, producer, director*
Anastos, Rosemary Park *retired higher education educator*
Anawalt, Patricia Rieff *anthropologist*
Andersen, Henning *linguistics educator*
Andersen, Ronald Max *health services educator, researcher*
Anderson, Austin Gilman *economics research company consultant*
Anderson, Daryl *actor*
Anderson, Isabel *artist, educator*
Anderson, Jane A. *scriptwriter*
Anderson, Kathryn Duncan *surgeon*
Anderson, Richard Norman *actor, film producer*
Anderson, Robert Marshall *bishop*
†Anderson, Roy A. *aerospace company executive*
Anderson, W. French *biochemist, physician*
Angeloff, Dann Valentino *investment banking executive*
†Angotti, Mark Everett *broadcast executive*
Anka, Paul *singer, composer*
Ansley, Julia Ette *elementary school educator, consultant, poet, writer*
Antin, Michael *lawyer*
Apfel, Gary *lawyer*
Appleby, Joyce Oldham *historian*
April, Rand Scott *lawyer*
Apt, Leonard *physician*
Arbib, Michael Anthony *neuroscientist, educator, cybernetician*
Archerd, Army (Armand Archerd) *columnist, television commentator*
Archie, Carol Louise *obstetrician and gynecologist, educator*
Argue, John Clifford *lawyer*
Armstrong, C. Michael *computer business executive*
Armstrong, Orville *judge*
Arnold, Dennis B. *lawyer*
Arnold, Jeanne Eloise *anthropologist, educator*
Aroni, Samuel *architecture and urban planning educator*
Ash, Roy Lawrence *business executive*
Ashley, Sharon Anita *pediatric anesthesiologist*
Askanas-Engel, Valerie *neurologist, educator, researcher*
Avallone, Michael Angelo *author*
Avery, Robert Dean *lawyer*
Axon, Donald Carlton *architect*
Ayres, James Marx *mechanical engineer*
Badie, Ronald Peter *banker*
Bahr, Ehrhard *Germanic languages and literature educator*
Bain, Conrad Stafford *actor*
Baird, Lourdes G. *federal judge*
Bakeman, Carol Ann *administrative services manager, singer*
Baker, Lawrence Colby, Jr. *insurance company executive*
Baker, Robert Frank *molecular biologist, educator*
Ballard, Glen *composer*
Bangs, Cate (Cathryn Margaret Bangs) *film production designer, interior designer*
Banner, Bob *television producer, director*
Bao, Joseph Yue-Se *orthopaedist, microsurgeon, educator*
Barbera, Joseph *motion picture and television producer, cartoonist*
†Bardt, Harry M. *sports association administrator*
Barker, Robert William *television personality*
Barker, Wiley Franklin *surgeon, educator*
†Barnes, Priscilla *actress*
Baron, Melvin Farrell *pharmacy educator*
†Barrett, Cynthia Townsend *neonatologist*
Barretta-Keyser, Jolie *professional athletics coach, author*
Barry, Gene *actor*
Barry, Philip Semple *television and film producer*
Bart, Peter Benton *newspaper editor, film producer, novelist*
Bartel, Paul *film director*
Barton, Alan Joel *lawyer*
Barza, Harold A. *lawyer*
Basch, Darlene Chakin *clinical social worker*
Basil, Douglas Constantine *author, educator*
Basile, Paul Louis, Jr. *lawyer*
Bass, Barbara DeJong *film assistant director, free-lance writer*
Bassett, Angela *actress*
Bates, Marcia Jeanne *information scientist educator*
Baum, Michael Lin *lawyer*
Bauman, John Andrew *law educator*
Baumann, Richard Gordon *lawyer*
Baumgarten, Ronald Neal *lawyer*
Bauml, Franz Heinrich *German language educator*
Bayless, Raymond *writer, artist, parapsychologist*
Baylor, Elgin Gay *professional basketball team executive*
†Bean, Donna *television station executive*
†Beard, John Jackson, III *journalist*
Beard, Ronald Stratton *lawyer*
Beart, Robert W., Jr. *surgeon, educator*
Beatty, Ned *actor*
Beban, Gary Joseph *real estate corporation officer*
Beck, John Christian *physician, educator*
Becker, Donald Paul *surgeon, neurosurgeon*
Beerbohm, Elisa Newell *advertising professional*
Bekey, George Albert *computer scientist, educator, engineer*
Bell, Lee Phillip *television personality, television producer*
Bell, Wayne Steven *lawyer*
Belleville, Philip Frederick *lawyer*
Belnap, David Foster *journalist*
Belzer, Richard *comedian, TV show host, actor*
†Bender, Dean *public relations executive*
Bennett, Charles Franklin, Jr. *biogeographer, educator*
Bennett, Fred Gilbert *lawyer*
Bennis, Warren Gameliel *business administration educator, author, consultant*
Benson, Sidney William *chemistry researcher*
Berenbaum, Michael G. *foundation adminstrator, theology educator*

Berglund, Robin G. psychiatrist, former corporate executive
Berman, Myles Lee lawyer
Bernacchi, Richard Lloyd lawyer
Bernhard, Herbert Ashley lawyer
Bernstein, Arthur Harold venture capital executive
Bernstein, Sol cardiologist, educator
Bernstein, William film company executive
Berry, Richard Douglas architectural educator, urban planner and designer
Berry, Stephen Joseph reporter
Bessman, Samuel Paul pediatrician, biochemist
Bhaumik, Mani Lal physicist
Bice, Scott Haas lawyer, educator
Biederman, Donald Ellis lawyer
Bierstedt, Peter Richard lawyer, entertainment industry consultant
Biles, John Alexander pharmacology educator, chemistry educator
Billig, Franklin Anthony chemist
Bird, Peter geology educator
Birnbaum, Henrik Slavic languages and literature educator
Birren, James Emmett university research center executive
Bishop, Sidney Willard lawyer
Black, Donna Ruth lawyer
Black, Lisa Hartman (Lisa Hartman Black) actress, singer
Blackman, Lee L. lawyer
Blackwelder, Ron Forest engineering educator, consultant, researcher
Blahd, William Henry physician
Blakely, Edward James economics educator
Blankenship, Edward G. architect
Blencowe, Paul Sherwood lawyer
Blitz-Weisz, Sally speech pathologist
Bloch, Paul public relations executive
Blodgett, Julian Robert small business owner
Boland, Paul Anson psychology educator emeritus
Bloom, Alan lawyer
Bluestone, David Allan pediatrician
Blumberg, Grace Ganz law educator, lawyer
Boak, Ruth Alice physician, educator
Bobrow, Michael Lawrence architect
Bodey, Bela immunomorphologist
Bodkin, Henry Grattan, Jr. lawyer
Bogart, Paul film director
Bogdanovich, Peter film director, writer, producer, actor
Bogen, Andrew E. lawyer
Bohle, Sue public relations executive
Boime, Albert Isaac art history educator
Bok, Dean cell biologist, educator
Bomes, Stephen D. lawyer
Bondareff, William psychiatry educator
Bonner, Robert Cleve lawyer
Borenstein, Daniel Bernard physician, educator
Borenstein, Mark A. lawyer
Borko, Harold information scientist, psychologist, educator
Borsch, Frederick Houk bishop
Borsting, Jack Raymond business administration educator
Bortman, David lawyer
Bosl, Phillip L. lawyer
Bosley, Tom actor
Boswell, James Douglas medical research executive
Bothwell, Dorr artist
Bottjer, David John earth sciences educator
Bower, Allan Maxwell lawyer
Bowers, John William church official
Bowlin, Michael Ray oil company executive
Bowman, C. Michael physician
Boyarsky, Benjamin William journalist
Boyd, Malcolm minister, religious author
Boyett, Joan Reynolds arts administrator
Boyle, Barbara Dorman motion picture company executive
Bradley, Lawrence D., Jr. lawyer
Bradshaw, Carl John investor, lawyer, consultant
Bradshaw, Murray Charles musicologist
Braginsky, Stanislav Iosifovich physicist, geophysicist, researcher
Branca, John Gregory lawyer, consultant
Brandler, Jonathan M. lawyer
Brassell, Roselyn Strauss lawyer
Bratt, Bengt Erik academic administrator, consulting engineer
Braun, David A(dlai) lawyer
Braunstein, Glenn David physician, educator
Brecht, Albert Odell library and information technology administrator
Breidenbach, Francis Anthony lawyer
Breslow, Lester physician, educator
Bressan, Paul Louis lawyer
Brest, Martin film director
Breuer, Melvin Allen electrical engineering educator
Breuer, Stephen Ernest temple executive
†Brittenham, Skip lawyer
Broad, Eli financial services executive
†Brockman, Kevin Michael public relations executive
Broderick, Carlfred Bartholomew sociology educator
Brosnan, Peter Lawrence documentary filmmaker
Brotman, David Joel architectural firm executive
Broussard, Thomas Rollins lawyer
Brown, Gay West school psychologist
Brown, Kathleen state treasurer, lawyer
Brubaker, William Rogers sociology educator
Brunell, Philip A. physician
Buchman, Mark Edward banker
Buckley, Betty Lynn actress
Bucy, Richard Snowden aerospace engineering and mathematics educator, consultant
Bufford, Samuel Lawrence federal judge
Buichl, Anna Elizabeth city official
Burch, Robert Dale lawyer
Burg, Gerald William religious organization administrator
Burgess, J. Wesley neuropsychiatrist
Burns, Marvin Gerald lawyer
Burns, Robert Ignatius historian, educator, clergyman
Burrows, James television and motion picture director, producer
Burton, Ralph Joseph international development consultant
Burton, Tim film director
Byers, Nina physics educator
Bymel, Suzan Yvette talent manager, film producer
Byrd, Christine Waterman Swent lawyer
Byrne, Jerome Camillus lawyer
Byrne, William Matthew, Jr. federal judge
Caan, James actor, director
Cafaro, Albert recording industry executive
Campbell, Glen singer, entertainer
Campbell, Kenneth Eugene, Jr. vertebrate paleontologist
Campbell, Malcolm film editor
Campion, Robert Thomas manufacturing company executive
Capron, Alexander Morgan lawyer, educator
Cardone, Bonnie Jean photojournalist
Carlin, George Denis comedian
Carlson, Robert E. lawyer
†Carmen, Julie actress
Caroompas, Carole Jean artist, educator
Carr, Allan film and stage producer, celebrity representative
Carr, Willard Zeller, Jr. lawyer
Carroll, Raoul Lord lawyer, investment banker
Carter, Emily Ann physical chemist, educator
Carter, Richard production designer
Cartwright, Brian Grant lawyer
Casey, Peter William television producer, screenwriter
Castro, Leonard Edward lawyer
Cates, Gilbert film, theater, television producer and director
Cathcart, David Arthur lawyer
Cavanagh, John Edward lawyer
Cecchetti, Giovanni poet, Italian language educator, literary critic
†Cerrell, Joseph R. business executive
Chacko, George Kuttickal systems science educator, consultant
Chaffin, Cean producer
Chamberlain, Wilton Norman retired professional basketball player
Champagne, Duane Willard sociology educator
Champlin, Charles Davenport television host, book critic, writer
Chan, David Ronald tax specialist
Chandor, Stebbins Bryant pathologist
Chang, Henry Chung-Lien library administrator
Chapman, Orville Lamar chemist, educator
Chappel, Timothy Paul costume designer
Charen, Mona syndicated columnist
Charles, Glen television producer
Charles, Les television producer
Charwat, Andrew Franciszek engineering educator
Chase, Chevy (Cornelius Crane Chase) comedian, actor, author
Chassman, Leonard Fredric labor union administrator
Chavez, Albert Blas financial executive
Chavez, Victor Edwin judge
Chedid, John G. bishop
Chen, Edna Lau art educator, artist
Cheng, Hsien Kei aeronautics educator
Cheng, Tsen-Chung electrical engineering educator
Cherkin, Adina interpreter, translator
Chernesky, John Joseph, Jr. naval officer
Cherry, James Donald physician
Chester, Marvin physics educator
Chetwynd, Lionel screenwriter, producer, director
Chiate, Kenneth Reed lawyer
Chin, Kelvin Henry legal association executive, mediator, consultant
Chobotov, Vladimir Alexander aerospace engineer, educator
Christol, Carl Quimby lawyer, political science educator
Christopher, James Roy executive director
Christopher, Warren lawyer, former government official
Chu, Morgan lawyer
Cicciarelli, James Carl immunology educator
Ciccone, Amy Navratil art librarian
Cisneros, Henry G. former federal official, broadcast executive
Clark, Burton Robert sociologist, educator
Clark, Marcia Rachel prosecutor
Clark, R. Bradbury lawyer
Clarke, Peter communications and health educator
Cleary, William Joseph, Jr. lawyer
Clemente, Carmine Domenic anatomist, educator
Cobb, Jewel Plummer former college president, educator
Cochran, Johnnie L., Jr. lawyer
Cochran, Sachiko Tomie radiologist
Cocker, Joe popular musician
Coffey, C. Shelby, III newspaper editor
Cohan, John Robert retired lawyer
Cohen, Cynthia Marylyn lawyer
Cohen, Daniel Morris museum administrator, marine biology researcher
Cohen, Leonard (Norman Cohen) poet, novelist, musician, songwriter
Cohen, S(tephen) Marshall philosophy educator
Cohen, William Alan marketing educator, author, consultant
Cole, Jay N. magazine publisher
Cole, Natalie Maria singer
Coleman, Charles Clyde physicist, educator
Coleman, Paul Jerome, Jr. physicist, educator
Collias, Elsie Cole zoologist
Collier, Charles Arthur, Jr. lawyer
Collins, Audrey B. judge
Collins, Charles Roland lawyer
Conniff, Ray popular musician, conductor, composer, arranger
Cooder, Ry recording artist, guitarist
Cook, Ian Ainsworth psychiatrist, researcher, educator
Coolbaugh, Carrie Weaver librarian
Coombs, John Wendell financial service executive
Coombs, Robert Holman behavioral scientist, medical educator, therapist, author
Cooper, Edwin Lowell anatomy educator
Cooper, Leon Melvin lawyer
Corea, Chick (Armando Corea) pianist, composer
Corman, Marvin Leonard surgeon
Corman, Roger William motion picture producer, director
Cornwall, John Michael physics educator, consultant, researcher
Coroniti, Ferdinand Vincent physics educator, consultant
Cort, Robert W. film company executive
Cortinez, Veronica literature educator
Corwin, Norman writer, director, producer
Counts, James Curtis management consultant
Craft, Cheryl Mae neurobiologist, anatomist, researcher
Cram, Donald James chemistry educator
Cravens, Virginia Lee church official
Crippens, David Lee broadcast executive
Crockett, Donald Harold composer, university educator
Crombie, Douglass Darnill aerospace communications system engineer
Cromwell, James actor
Crosby, Peter Alan management consultant
Cross, Glenn Laban engineering executive, development planner
Crow, John Armstrong writer, educator
Cuadra, Carlos Albert information scientist, management executive
Currie, Malcolm Roderick aerospace and automotive executive, scientist
Curry, Daniel Arthur superior court judge
Curry, Daniel Francis Myles filmmaker
Curtiss, Thomas, Jr. lawyer, educator
D'Accone, Frank Anthony music educator
Dai, Jing Chu Ling medical writer, researcher
Dalton, James Edward aerospace executive, retired air force officer
Dalton, Larry Raymond chemistry educator, researcher, consultant
Daniels, Jeff actor
Daniels, John Peter lawyer
Dann, Francis Joseph dermatologist, educator
Danoff, Dudley Seth surgeon, urologist
†D'Arbanville, Patti actress
Darby, G. Harrison lawyer
Darby, Joanne Tyndale (Jaye Darby) arts and humanities educator
Darby, Michael Rucker economist, educator
Darling, Juanita Marie correspondent
†Dash, Hal business executive
†Dash, Stacey actress
Davidson, Ezra C., Jr. physician, educator
Davidson, Gordon theatrical producer, director
Davidson, Herbert Alan Near Eastern languages and cultures educator
Davidson, Robert C., Jr. manufacturing executive
Davies, John G. federal judge
Davies, Kelvin James Anthony research scientist, educator, consultant, author
Davis, Don composer
Davis, Edmond Ray lawyer
Davis, J. Alan lawyer, producer, writer
Davis, Ossie actor, author
Dawson, John Myrick plasma physics educator
Day, Anthony newspaper writer
Dearing, Vinton Adams retired English language educator
DeBard, Roger investment executive
De Brier, Donald Paul lawyer
Decaminada, Joseph Pio insurance company executive, educator
de Castro, Hugo Daniel lawyer
De Cherney, Alan Hersh obstetrics and gynecology educator
Decker, David R. lawyer
Dee, Ruby (Ruby Dee Davis) actress, writer, director
De Jong-Hawley, Cherie reading and language arts educator
Dekmejian, Richard Hrair political science educator
Delaney, Matthew Sylvester mathematics educator, academic administrator
Delnik, Alexander engineering executive, business consultant
Del Olmo, Frank newspaper editor
†Del Toro, Benicio actor
DeLuce, Richard David lawyer
Delugach, Albert Lawrence journalist
De Luise, Dom actor
Demsetz, Harold economist, educator
de Passe, Suzanne record company executive
Detels, Roger epidemiologist, physician, former university dean
Deukmejian, George lawyer, former governor
Dewey, Donald Odell university dean
Dhir, Vijay K. mechanical engineering educator
Diamond, Stanley Jay lawyer
DiCaprio, Leonardo actor
Dickerson, Ernest cinematographer, director
Dickerson, Jaffe Dean lawyer
Dignam, William Joseph obstetrician, gynecologist, educator
Dillard, Suzanne interior designer
Dolenz, Mickey (George Michael Dolenz) singer, actor, television producer
Dolgen, Jonathan L. motion picture company executive
Doll, Lynne Marie public relations agency executive
Domino, Fats (Antoine Domino) pianist, singer, songwriter
Donovan, John Arthur lawyer
†Dorman, Albert A. consulting engineer executive, architect
Dougherty, Elmer Lloyd, Jr. retired chemical engineering educator, consultant
Downey, William J., III lawyer
Dows, David Alan chemistry educator
Drake, Hudson Billings aerospace and electronics company executive
Dr. Dre, (Andre Young) rapper, record producer
Drew, Paul entrepreneur
Dreyfuss, John Alan journalist
Dummett, Clifton Orrin dentist, educator
Dunham, Scott H. lawyer
Dunn, Arnold Samuel biochemistry educator
Dunn, Bruce Sidney materials science educator
Dunnahoo, Terry (Mrs. Thomas William Dunnahoo) editor, author
Dworsky, Daniel Leonard architect
Dwyre, William Patrick journalist, public speaker
Dyck, Andrew Roy philologist, educator
Edelman, Randy composer
Edgerton, Bradford Wheatly plastic surgeon
Edwards, Blake film director
Edwards, Kenneth Neil chemist, consultant
Edwards, William H., Sr. retired hotel corporation executive
Einstein, Clifford Jay advertising executive
Ellickson, Bryan Carl economics educator
Elliott, John Ed economics educator
Ellsworth, Frank L. university administrator, non-profit executive
Emanuel, William Joseph lawyer
Emmeluth, Bruce Palmer investment banker, venture capitalist
Engel, William King neurologist, educator
Engler, George Nichols financial consultant, educator
English, Stephen Raymond lawyer
Enstrom, James Eugene cancer epidemiologist
Estrin, Gerald computer scientist, engineering educator, academic administrator
Etra, Donald lawyer
Ettenger, Robert Bruce physician, nephrologist
Eule, Julian Nathan law educator
Evans, Caswell Alves, Jr. dentist
Everhart, Angie model
Ewing, Edgar Louis artist, educator
Fairbank, Robert Harold lawyer
Faltermeyer, Harold composer
Farhat, Vince Lee lawyer
Farmer, Robert Lindsay lawyer
Farrell, Mike actor
Faulwell, Gerald Edward insurance company executive
Feidelson, Marc advertising executive
Feig, Stephen Arthur pediatrics educator, hematologist, oncologist
Fein, Irving Ashley television and motion picture executive
Fenning, Lisa Hill federal judge
Ferrell, Conchata Galen actress, acting teacher and coach
Ferry, Richard Michael executive search firm executive
Feshbach, Seymour psychology educator
Field, Richard Clark lawyer
Field, Ted (Frederick Field) film and record industry executive
Fields, Bertram Harris lawyer
Fifield, James G. recording industry executive
Finch, Caleb Ellicott neurobiologist, educator
Fine, Richard Isaac lawyer
Finegold, Sydney Martin microbiology and immunology educator
Finerman, Wendy film producer
Firstenberg, Jean Picker film institute executive
Fischer, Alfred George geology educator
Fish, Barbara psychiatrist, educator
Fisher, Raymond Corley lawyer
Fisher, Richard N. lawyer
Fitch, William C. professional basketball coach
Fitzgerald, Tikhon (Lee R. H. Fitzgerald) bishop
Flanigan, James J(oseph) journalist
Fleischmann, Ernest Martin music administrator
Fleming, Arthur Wallace physician, surgeon
Fodor, Eugene Nicholas concert violinist
Fogelman, Alan Marcus internist
Fohrman, Burton H. lawyer
Folk, Robert composer
Follick, Edwin Duane law educator, chiropractic physician
Fonkalsrud, Eric Walter pediatric surgeon, educator
Foote, Christopher Spencer chemist, educator
Ford, Donald Hainline lawyer
Forester, Bernard I. recreational equipment company executive
Forness, Steven Robert educational psychologist
Foster, David composer, record producer
Foster, Jodie (Alicia Christian Foster) actress
Foster, Mary Christine motion picture and television executive
Fowler, Vincent R. dermatologist
Fox, Saul Lourie physician, researcher
Frackman, Russell Jay lawyer
Fragner, Matthew Charles lawyer
Frame, John Fayette sculptor
†France, Richard Xavier playwright, educator, narrator
Francis, Merrill Richard lawyer
Franke, Christopher composer
Franz, Dennis actor
Fraser, Brad playwright, theatrical director, screenwriter
Frasier, S. Douglas medical educator
Fredman, Howard S lawyer
Freehling, Allen Isaac rabbi
Fricker, John Arthur pediatrician, educator
Fried, Burton David physicist, educator
Friedlander, Sheldon Kay chemical engineering educator
Friedman, Alan E. lawyer
Friedman, Arthur Meeker magazine editor, professional motorcycle racer
Friedman, Nathan Baruch physician
Friedman, Robert Lee film company executive
Friedmann, Peretz Peter aerospace engineer, educator
Frimmer, Paul Norman lawyer
Frisch, Robert A. financial planning company executive
Fromkin, Victoria Alexandra linguist, phonetician, educator
Fry, Michael Graham historian, educator
Fulco, Armand John biochemist
Fuller, Larry choreographer, director
Fuller, Samuel (Michael) scriptwriter, film director
Furlotti, Alexander Amato real estate development company executive
Furth, George actor, playwright
Fybel, Richard D. lawyer
Fyfe, Alistair Ian cardiologist, scientist, educator
Galanos, James fashion designer
Gale, Robert Peter physician, scientist, researcher
Gallo, Jon Joseph lawyer
Ganas, Perry Spiros physicist
Garcetti, Gilbert I. prosecutor
Garcia, Andy actor
Garland, G(arfield) Garrett sales executive, golf professional
Garry, William James magazine editor
Garza, Oscar newspaper editor
Gates, Susan Inez magazine publisher
Geary, Patrick Joseph history educator
Gebb, Sheldon Alexander lawyer
Gebhart, Carl Grant security broker
Geller, Stephen Arthur pathologist, educator
Gentile, Joseph F. lawyer, educator
Gest, Howard David lawyer
Getty, Estelle actress
Geuss, Gary George lawyer
Ghez, Andrea Mia astronomy and physics educator
Ghil, Michael atmospheric scientist, geophysicist
Giannotta, Steven Louis neurosurgery educator
Gibbs, Marla (Margaret Gibbs) actress
Gibbs, Richard composer
Gibson, Arthur Charles biologist, educator
Gilbert, Judith Arlene lawyer
Gilbert, Robert Wolfe lawyer
†Gilchrist, Richard Irwin real estate developer
Gilman, John Joseph research scientist
Gilman, Nelson Jay library director
Gilmore, Mikal George critic, journalist, author
Gimbel, Norman lyricist, music publisher, television producer
Gimble, Johnny country musician
Ginsburg, Seymour computer science educator
Glaser, Daniel sociologist
Glass, Herbert music critic, lecturer, editor
Glazer, Michael lawyer
Glick, Earl A. lawyer
Glitz, Dohn George biochemistry educator
Godbold, Wilford Darrington, Jr. enclosure manufacturing company executive, lawyer
Gold, Arnold Henry judge
Gold, Richard Horace radiologist
Goldberg, Herb psychologist, educator
Goldenthal, Elliot composer
Goldman, Allan Bailey lawyer
Goldman, Benjamin Edward lawyer
†Goldman, Larry public relations executive
Goldschmidt, Walter Rochs anthropologist, educator

Goldsmith, Jerry *composer*
Goldwyn, Samuel John, Jr. *motion picture producer*
Göllner, Marie Louise *musicologist, educator*
Gonick, Harvey Craig *nephrologist, educator*
Gooch, Lawrence Boyd *accounting executive*
Gooding, Cuba, Jr. *actor*
Goodman, David Bryan *musician, educator*
Goodman, Max A. *lawyer, educator*
Gordon, Basil *mathematics educator*
Gordon, David Eliot *lawyer*
Gordon, Malcolm Stephen *biology educator*
Gordon, Milton G. *real estate counselor, consultant*
Gordon, Rob *recording industry executive*
Gordy, Berry *entrepreneur, record company executive, motion picture executive*
Gore, Michael *composer*
Gorman, Cliff *actor*
Gorman, Joseph Gregory, Jr. *lawyer*
Gorman, Lillian R. *human resources executive*
Gorney, Roderic *psychiatry educator*
Gorski, Roger Anthony *neuroendocrinologist, educator*
Gothold, Stuart E. *school system administrator, educator*
Gottfried, Ira Sidney *management consulting executive*
Gottlieb, Leonard *foundation administrator*
Gould, Charles Perry *lawyer*
Gould, David *lawyer*
Gould, Harold *actor*
Grammer, Kelsey *actor*
Grant, David Browne *manufacturing executive*
Grant, Lee (Lyova Haskell Rosenthal) *actress, director*
Grausam, Jeffrey Leonard *lawyer*
Gray, Jan Charles *lawyer, business owner*
Gray, Thomas Stephen *newspaper editor*
Grazer, Brian *film company executive*
Greaves, John Allen *lawyer*
Green, William Porter *lawyer*
Greenberg, Ira Arthur *psychologist*
Greenberger, Martin *educator, technologist*
Greene, Alvin *service company executive, management consultant*
Greene, Donald Johnson *retired English language educator, author*
Greenstadt, Melvin *investor, retired educator*
Griffey, Linda Boyd *lawyer*
Grinnell, Alan Dale *neurobiologist, educator, researcher*
Groh, Rupert James, Jr. *judge*
Gross, Allen Jeffrey *lawyer*
Grosz, Philip J. *lawyer*
Groves, Martha *newspaper writer*
Gruska, Jay *composer*
Gudea, Darlene *publishing company executive*
Gunn, Karen Sue *psychologist, educator*
Gurash, John Thomas *insurance company executive*
Gurfein, Peter J. *lawyer*
Guze, Phyllis Arlene *internist, educator, academic administrator*
Hackman, Gene *actor*
Hadda, Janet Ruth *Yiddish language educator, lay psychoanalyst*
Haden, Charles *jazz bassist, composer*
Haglund, Thomas Roy *research biologist, consultant, educator*
Hahn, Harlan Dean *political science educator, consultant*
Hale, Kaycee *research marketing professional*
Halkett, Alan Neilson *lawyer*
Hall, Carlyle Washington, Jr. *lawyer*
Hall, Clarence Albert, Jr. *geologist, educator*
Hall, Jeffrey Stuart *newspaper executive*
Halsey, Richard *film editor*
Hamill, Dorothy Stuart *professional ice skater*
Hamilton, Beverly Lannquist *investment management professional*
Hammer, (Stanley Kirk Burrell) *musician*
Hancock, Herbert Jeffrey (Herbie Hancock) *composer, pianist, publisher*
Handschumacher, Albert Gustave *retired corporate executive*
Handy, Lyman Lee *petroleum engineer, chemist, educator*
Handzlik, Jan Lawrence *lawyer*
Hansell, Dean *lawyer*
Hanson, John J. *lawyer*
Harberger, Arnold Carl *economist, educator*
Harold, John Gordon *cardiologist, internist*
Harris, Barbara Hull (Mrs. F. Chandler Harris) *social agency administrator*
Harris, F. Chandler *retired university administrator*
Harris, Theodore Edward *mathematician, educator*
Hart, John Lewis (Johnny Hart) *cartoonist*
Hart, Larry Calvin *lawyer*
Hart, Mary *television talk show host*
Hartke, Stephen Paul *composer, educator*
Hartsough, Gayla Anne Kraetsch *management consultant*
Haskell, Charles Mortimer *medical oncologist, educator*
Hauk, A. Andrew *federal judge*
Havel, Richard W. *lawyer*
Hawley, Philip Metschan *retired retail executive, consultant*
Hayes, Byron Jackson, Jr. *lawyer*
Hayes, Robert Mayo *university dean, library and information science educator*
Hayes, Vertis Clemon *painter, sculptor, educator*
Hayutin, David Lionel *lawyer*
Haywood, L. Julian *physician, educator*
Headlee, Rolland Dockeray *professional society administrator*
Hedlund, Paul James *lawyer*
Heer, David Macalpine *sociology educator*
Hein, Leonard William *accounting educator*
Heinisch, Robert Craig *sales and marketing executive, consultant*
Heinke, Rex S. *lawyer*
Helgeson, Duane Marcellus *retired librarian*
Hellwarth, Robert Willis *physicist, educator*
Helms, Harold Edwin *minister*
†Helper, Lee *public relations executive*
Hemion, Dwight Arlington *television producer, director*
Hemminger, Pamela Lynn *lawyer*
Hemmings, Peter William *orchestra and opera administrator*
†Henriksen, Lance *actor*
Henriksen MacLean, Eva Hansine *former anesthesiology educator*
Henry, Richard Joseph, Jr. *nursing home management executive*
Hester, John W. *motion picture company executive*
Heyck, Theodore Daly *lawyer*
Heyler, Grover Ross *retired lawyer*
Hiatt, John *musician, country, popular*
Hicklin, Ronald Lee *music production company executive*
Hieronymus, Edward Whittlesey *lawyer*
Highberger, William Foster *lawyer*
Hight, B. Boyd *lawyer*
Highwater, Jamake *author, lecturer*
Hill, Irving *judge*
Hiller, Arthur *motion picture director*
Hinerfeld, Robert Elliot *lawyer*
†Hirsch, Barry L. *lawyer*
Hirsch, Werner Zvi *economist, educator*
Hirson, Estelle *retired school educator*
Hoang, Duc Van *theoretical pathologist, educator*
Hockney, David *artist*
†Hodal, Melanie *public relations executive*
Hoffenberg, Marvin *political science educator, consultant*
Hoffman, Neil James *academic administrator*
†Holdsworth, Ray W. *architectural firm executive*
Holland, Gary Norman *ophthalmologist, educator*
Holland, John Ray *minister*
Holliday, Thomas Edgar *lawyer*
Holman, Bill *composer*
Holman, Tomlinson *engineer, film educator*
Holo, Selma Reuben *museum director, educator*
Holt, James Franklin *retired numerical analyst, scientific programmer analyst*
Holt, Susan Lynne *mental health counselor*
Holtzman, Robert Arthur *lawyer*
Hopkins, Carl Edward *public health educator*
Hopkins, Henry Tyler *museum director, art educator*
Horner, James *composer*
Horning, Robert Alan *securities broker*
Horowitz, Ben *medical center executive*
Horowitz, David Charles *consumer commentator, newspaper columnist*
Horwitz, David A. *physician, scientist, educator*
Hospers, John *philosophy educator*
Hotchkiss, Vivian Evelyn *employment agency executive*
Hotz, Robert Lee *science writer, editor*
Houk, Kendall Newcomb *chemistry educator*
House, John W. *otologist*
Houser, Gerald Burnett *university administrator*
Houston, Ivan James *insurance company executive*
Hovanessian, Shahen Alexander *electrical engineer, educator*
Hovannisian, Richard G. *Armenian and Near East history educator*
Howard, James Newton *composer*
Howard, Murray *manufacturing, real estate property management executive, farmer, rancher*
Howard, Nancy E. *lawyer*
Howard, Sandy *motion picture producer*
Howe, John Thomas *film director, educator*
Hoy, William *film editor*
Hsiao, Chie-Fang *neuroscientist*
Hu, Sze-Tsen *mathematics educator*
Hubbard, John Randolph *university president emeritus, history educator, diplomat*
Hubbs, Donald Harvey *foundation executive*
Hudson, Christopher John *publisher*
Hudson, Jeffrey Reid *lawyer*
Hufstedler, Seth Martin *lawyer*
Hufstedler, Shirley Mount (Mrs. Seth M. Hufstedler) *lawyer, former federal judge*
Hughes, Everett Clark *otolaryngology educator*
Hummel, Joseph William *hospital administrator*
Humphreys, Robert Lee *advertising agency executive*
Hundley, Norris Cecil, Jr. *history educator*
Hunt, Peter Roger *film director, writer, editor*
Hunter, Larry Dean *lawyer*
Hupp, Harry L. *federal judge*
Hurt, William Holman *investment management company executive*
†Hurtado, Eduardo *soccer player*
Hurwitz, Lawrence Neal *investment banking company executive*
Hutchins, Joan Morthland *manufacturing executive, farmer*
Hwang, John Dzen *municipal official*
Hyman, Milton Bernard *lawyer*
Iamele, Richard Thomas *law librarian*
Ice Cube, (O'Shea Jackson) *rap singer, actor*
Ida, Shoichi *painter, printmaker*
Ideman, James M. *federal judge*
Iglesias, Julio (Julio Jose Iglesias De La Cueva) *singer, songwriter*
Igo, George Jerome *physics educator*
Ilanit, Tamar *psychologist*
Incaudo, Joseph August *engineering company executive*
Ingels, Marty *theatrical agent, television and motion picture production executive*
Intriligator, Michael David *economist, educator*
Iovine, Jimmy *recording industry executive*
Irani, Ray R. *oil and gas and chemical company executive*
Ireland, Kathy *actress*
Irell, Lawrence E(lliott) *lawyer*
Irving, Jack Howard *technical consultant*
Irwin, Philip Donnan *lawyer*
Isinger, William R. *newspaper publishing executive*
Ito, Lance Allan *judge*
Itoh, Tatsuo *engineering educator*
Jackson, Isaiah *conductor*
Jackson, Janet Damita *singer, dancer*
Jackson, Kingsbury Temple *educational contract consultant*
Jackson, Mary *actress*
Jackson, Michael (Joseph) *singer*
Jacobs, Marilyn Susan *clinical psychologist*
Jacobsen, Laren *mathematician, classical musician*
Jaffe, Sigmund *chemist, educator*
Jalali, Behnaz *psychiatrist, educator*
James, William J. *lawyer*
Jamison, Dean Tecumseh *economist*
Janofsky, Leonard S. *lawyer, association executive*
Jarc, Frank Robert *printing company executive*
Jarmon, Lawrence *developmental communications educator*
Jarrott, Charles *film and television director*
Jelliffe, Roger Woodham *cardiologist, clinical pharmacologist*
†Jentzsch, Heber C. *church administrator*
Johansen, David (Buster Poindexter) *popular musician, actor*
Johns, Karen Louise *nurse, psychotherapist*
Johnson, Cage Saul *hematologist, educator*
Johnson, E. Eric *insurance executive*
Johnson, Jonathan Edwin, II *lawyer*
Johnson, Michael Marion *lawyer*
Johnston, Roy G. *consulting structural engineer*
Johnston, Ynez *artist*
Jones, Henry *actor*
Jones, James Earl *actor*
Jones, Quincy *producer, composer, arranger, conductor, trumpeter*
Jones, Tom *singer*
Jordan, Michelle Henrietta *public relations company executive*
Jordan, Robert Leon *lawyer, educator*
Jorgensen, Paul Alfred *English language educator emeritus*
Kadison, Stuart L. *lawyer and educator*
Kalaba, Robert Edwin *applied mathematician*
Kambara, George Kiyoshi *retired ophthalmologist, educator*
Kamen, Michael *composer, musician, conductor*
Kamil, Elaine Scheiner *physician, educator*
Kamine, Bernard Samuel *lawyer*
Kaplan, Isaac Raymond *chemistry educator, corporate executive*
Kaplan, Jonathan Stewart *film director, writer*
Kaplan, Samuel *pediatric cardiologist*
Karatz, Bruce E. *business executive*
Karplus, Walter J. *engineering educator*
Karros, Eric Peter *professional baseball player*
Karst, Kenneth Leslie *legal educator*
Katchur, Marlene Martha *nursing administrator*
Katleman, Harris L. *television executive*
Katz, Roger *pediatrician, educator*
Katz, Ronald Lewis *physician, educator*
Kaula, William Mason *geophysicist, educator*
Kay, Kelly W. *lawyer*
Kaye, Barry *investment company executive*
Kaye, Jhani *radio station manager, director*
Kelleher, Robert Joseph *federal judge*
Keller, William D. *federal judge*
Kelley, Harold Harding *psychology educator*
Kelly, Arthur Paul *physician*
Kelly, Henry Ansgar *English language educator*
Kendig, Ellsworth Harold, Jr. *retired corporate lawyer*
Kennelly, Sister Karen Margaret *college administrator*
Kent, Susan Goldberg *library director, consultant*
Kenyon, David V. *federal judge*
Kerman, Barry Martin *ophthalmologist, educator*
Ketchum, Robert Glenn *photographer, print maker*
Kidman, Nicole *actress*
Kiekhofer, William Henry *lawyer*
Kienholz, Lyn Shearer *international arts projects coordinator*
Kilburn, Kaye Hatch *medical educator*
Kim, Ke Bom *stockbroker, financial planner*
Kindel, James Horace, Jr. *lawyer*
Kirkwood, Gene *motion picture producer*
Kirwan, Ralph DeWitt *lawyer*
Kivelson, Margaret Galland *physicist*
Klausen, Raymond *sculptor, television and theatre production designer*
Klee, Kenneth Nathan *lawyer*
Klein, Benjamin *economics educator, consultant*
Klein, Elaine *advertising executive*
Klein, Jeffrey S. *lawyer, newspaper executive*
Klein, Joan Dempsey *judge*
Klein, Raymond Maurice *lawyer*
Kleinberg, Marvin H. *lawyer*
Kleingartner, Archie *founding dean, educator*
Kleinrock, Leonard *computer scientist*
Kline, Lee B. *architect*
Kline, Richard Stephen *public relations executive*
Klinger, Allen *engineering and applied science educator*
Klowden, Michael Louis *lawyer*
Knapp, Cleon Talboys *business executive*
Knight, Christopher Allen *art critic*
Knittle, William Joseph, Jr. *media executive, psychologist, religious leader, management and marketing consultant*
Koch, Howard W., Jr. *film producer*
Koch, Howard Winchel *film and television producer*
Koch, Richard *pediatrician, educator*
Koelzer, George Joseph *lawyer*
Koffler, Stephen Alexander *investment banker*
Koga, Rokutaro *physicist*
Kolve, V. A. *English literature educator*
Kopelson, Arnold *film producer*
Korge, Paavo *cell physiologist*
Korman, Harvey Herschel *actor*
Korn, Lester Bernard *business executive, diplomat*
Korsch, Barbara M. *pediatrician*
Koshalek, Richard *museum director, consultant*
Kraft, Scott Corey *correspondent*
Kramer, Barry Alan *psychiatrist*
Kramer, Stanley E. *motion picture producer, director*
Kresa, Kent *aerospace executive*
Krieg, Dorothy Linden *soprano, performing artist, educator*
Kristof, Kathy M. *journalist*
Krueger, Robert William *management consultant*
Krupp, Edwin Charles *astronomer*
Kuechle, John Merrill *lawyer*
Kuehl, Hans Henry *electrical engineering educator*
Kumar, Anil *nuclear engineer*
Kupchick, Alan Charles *advertising executive*
Kupietzky, Moshe J. *lawyer*
Kupperman, Henry John *lawyer*
Kurtz, Swoosie *actress*
Kuwayama, George *curator*
Laaly, Heshmat Ollah *chemist, roofing materials executive, consultant*
Laba, Marvin *management consultant*
Lachman, Morton *writer, theatrical director and producer*
Ladd, Alan Walbridge, Jr. *motion picture company executive*
La Force, James Clayburn, Jr. *economist, educator*
Laird, David *humanities educator emeritus*
Laird, Jere Don *news reporter*
Lambro, Phillip *composer, conductor, pianist*
Lamont, Peter *production designer, art director*
Landing, Benjamin Harrison *pathologist, educator*
Lane, Robert Gerhart *lawyer*
Lansing, Sherry Lee *motion picture production executive*
Lappen, Chester I. *lawyer*
Lark, Raymond *artist, art scholar*
Larson, Karin Louise *financial analyst*
Lashley, Lenore Clarisse *lawyer*
Lasorda, Thomas Charles (Tommy Lasorda) *professional baseball team manager*
Lasswell, Marcia Lee *psychologist, educator*
Latham, Joseph Al, Jr. *lawyer*
Lauchengco, Jose Yujuico, Jr. *lawyer*
Laventhol, David Abram *newspaper editor*
Lawrence, Martin *actor, comedian*
Lawrence, Sanford Hull *physician, immunochemist*
Laybourne, Everett Broadstone *lawyer*
Layton, Harry Christopher *artist, lecturer, consultant, hypnotherapist, poet*
Lazarus, Mell *cartoonist*
Leal, George D. *engineering company executive*
Lear, Norman Milton *producer, writer, director*
Lee, Burns Wells *public relations executive*
Lee, David C. *screenwriter*
Lee, Stan (Stanley Martin Lieber) *cartoon publisher, writer*
Lehan, Richard D'Aubin *English language educator, writer*
Lehovec, Kurt *electrical engineering educator*
Leibert, Richard William *special events producer*
Leibow, Ronald Louis *lawyer*
Leider, Gerald J. *motion picture and television company executive*
Leigh, Janet (Jeanette Helen Morrison) *actress*
Leighton, Robert *film editor*
Leijonhufvud, Axel Stig Bengt *economics educator*
Lem, Richard Douglas *painter*
Lenard, Michael Barry *merchant banker, lawyer*
Lepine, Jean *cinematographer*
Lerner, Vladimir Semion *computer scientist, educator*
Lesser, Joan L. *lawyer*
Letts, J. Spencer *federal judge*
Letwin, Leon *legal educator*
Leung, Frankie Fook-Lun *lawyer*
Levey, Gerald Saul *physician, educator*
Levine, C. Bruce *lawyer*
Levine, Philip *classics educator*
Levine, Raphael David *chemistry educator*
Levine, Robert Arthur *economist, policy analyst*
Levy, Alan David *real estate executive*
Levy, Norman *motion picture company executive*
Lew, Joycelyne Mae *actress*
Lew, Ronald S. W. *federal judge*
Lewin, Klaus J. *pathologist, educator*
Lewis, Charles Edwin *physician, educator*
Lewis, Richard *actor, comedian*
Lewis, Shari *puppeteer, entertainer*
Lewitzky, Bella *choreographer*
Li, Gerald *architect, film producer and director*
Li, Victor On-Kwok *electrical engineering educator*
Liberman, Robert Paul *psychiatry educator, researcher, writer*
Liebeler, Wesley J. *law educator, lawyer*
Lieber, David Leo *university president*
Lien, Eric Jung-chi *pharmacist, educator*
Lim, David Jong-Jai *otolaryngology educator, researcher*
Lin, Tung Hua *civil engineering educator*
Linder, Stu *film editor*
Lindholm, Dwight Henry *lawyer*
Lindley, F(rancis) Haynes, Jr. *foundation president, lawyer*
Link, George Hamilton *lawyer*
Linsk, Michael Stephen *real estate executive*
Lipsig, Ethan *lawyer*
Lipstone, Howard Harold *television executive*
Liu, Don *ophthalmologist, medical researcher*
Loeb, Ronald Marvin *lawyer*
Loehwing, Rudi Charles, Jr. *publicist, marketing, advertising, internet, commerce, radio broadcasting executive, journalist, broadcast journalist*
Löfstedt, Bengt Torkel Magnus *classics educator*
Logan, Francis Dummer *lawyer*
Logan, Joseph Granville, Jr. *physicist*
London, Andrew Barry *film editor*
Long, Gregory Alan *lawyer*
Longmire, William Polk, Jr. *physician, surgeon*
Lopez-Navarro, Eduardo Luis *family therapist*
†Love, Courtney *singer, actress*
Lowenthal, Abraham Frederic *international relations educator*
Lowry-Johnson, Junie *casting director*
Lublinski, Michael *lawyer*
Lucente, Rosemary Dolores *educational administrator*
Lukasik, Stephen Joseph *information technology executive*
Lurvey, Ira Harold *lawyer*
Lyashenko, Nikolai Nikolaevich *mathematician, educator*
Lyman, John *psychology and engineering educator*
Lynch, Beverly Pfeifer *education and information studies educator*
Lynch, Patrick *lawyer*
Mabee, John Richard *physician assistant, educator*
Mack, J. Curtis, II *civic organization administrator*
MacKenzie, John Douglas *engineering educator*
MacLaughlin, Francis Joseph *lawyer*
Madonna, (Madonna Louise Veronica Ciccone) *singer, actress*
Mager, Artur *retired aerospace company executive, consultant*
Maher, Bill *talk show host, comedian, producer*
Mahony, Roger M. Cardinal *archbishop*
Maki, Kazumi *physicist, educator*
Makowka, Leonard *medical educator, surgeon*
Malcolm, Dawn Grace *family physician*
Malden, Karl (Malden Sekulovich) *actor*
Malecki, Edward Stanley, Jr. *political science educator*
Mall, William John, Jr. *aerospace executive, retired air force officer*
Maloney, Robert Keller *ophthalmologist, medical educator*
Maltin, Leonard *television commentator, writer*
Maltzan, Michael Thomas *architect*
Manatt, Charles Taylor *lawyer*
Mancino, Douglas Michael *lawyer*
Mandel, Joseph David *university official, lawyer*
Mann, Delbert *film, theater, television director and producer*
Mann, Nancy Louise (Nancy Louise Robbins) *entrepreneur*
Mann, Wesley F. *newspaper editor*
Manolakas, Stanton Peter *watercolor artist*
Maquet, Jacques Jerome Pierre *anthropologist, writer*
Marciano, Maurice *apparel executive*
Marcus, Stephen Howard *lawyer*
Margol, Irving *personnel consultant*
Margulies, Lee *newspaper editor*
Markland, Francis Swaby, Jr. *biochemist, educator*
Marmarelis, Vasilis Zissis *engineering educator, author, consultant*
Marmor, Judd *psychiatrist, educator*
Maronde, Robert Francis *internist, clinical pharmacologist, educator*
Marsalis, Branford *musician*
Marsh, Dave *writer, publisher, editor*
Marshall, Arthur K. *lawyer, judge, arbitrator, educator, writer*
Marshall, Consuelo Bland *federal judge*
Marshall, Mary Jones *civic worker*
Martin, Albert Carey *architect*
Martin, J(ohn) Edward *architectural engineer*
Martin, Walter Edwin *biology educator*
Martinez, Al *journalist, screenwriter*
Martinez, Ramon Jaime *professional baseball player*

Masket, Edward Seymour television executive
Masters, Lee broadcast executive
Masterson, William A. judge
Matoian, John broadcasting company executive
Matthau, Walter actor
Maxworthy, Tony mechanical and aerospace engineering educator
McAniff, Edward John lawyer
McAuley, Skeet artist
McBirney, Bruce Henry lawyer
†McCabe, Edward R. B. academic administrator, educator, physician
McClure, William Owen biologist
Mc Coy, Frank Milton concert pianist, educator, lecturer
McDermott, John E. lawyer
McDermott, Thomas John, Jr. lawyer
Mc Guire, Dorothy Hackett actress
McKinzie, Carl Wayne lawyer
McKnight, Frederick L. lawyer
McLane, Frederick Berg lawyer
McLarnan, Donald Edward banker, corporation executive
McLaughlin, Joseph Mailey lawyer
McLean, Ian Small astronomer, physics educator
McLurkin, Thomas Cornelius, Jr. lawyer
Mc Pherson, Rolf Kennedy clergyman, church official
McQueen, Justice Ellis (L. Q. Jones) actor, director
McRae, Marion Eleanor critical care nurse
Medak, Peter film director
Medearis, Miller lawyer
Meecham, William Coryell engineering educator
Mellinkoff, David lawyer, educator
Mellinkoff, Sherman Mussoff medical educator
Mellor, Ronald John history educator
Meloan, Taylor Wells marketing educator
Mendel, Jerry Marc electrical engineering educator
Merlis, George television producer
Merrifield, Donald Paul university chancellor
Metheny, Patrick Bruce musician
Metzger, Robert Streicher lawyer
Meyer, Catherine Dieffenbach lawyer
Meyer, Michael Edwin lawyer
Michael, William Burton psychologist, educator
Michel, Donald Charles editor
Mihan, Richard retired dermatologist
Miles, Richard Robert art historian, writer
Miles, Samuel Israel psychiatrist, educator
Millard, Neal Steven lawyer
Miller, Harriet Sanders art center director
Miller, Milton Allen lawyer
Miller, Norman Charles, Jr. newspaper editor
Miller, Victoria Loren marketing and communications design executive
Milligan, Sister Mary theology educator, religious consultant
Mintz, Marshall Gary lawyer
Mintz, Ronald Steven lawyer
Mirisch, Lawrence Alan motion picture agent
Mishell, Daniel R., Jr. physician, educator
Mitchell, Theodore R. academic administrator
Mock, Theodore Jaye accounting educator
Mockary, Peter Ernest clinical laboratory scientist, researcher
Moe, Stanley Allen architect, consultant
Mohr, John Luther biologist, environmental consultant
Moloney, Stephen Michael lawyer
Mondesi, Raul professional baseball player
Money, Ruth Rowntree child development specialist, consultant
Montgomery, Robin Vera realtor
Montoya, Velma federal agency administrator
Moonves, Leslie television company executive
Mooser, Stephen author
Morales, Cynthia Torres clinical psychologist, consultant
Moran, Thomas Harry academic administrator
Moreno, Rita actress
Morganstern, Myrna Dorothy lawyer
Morgenthaler, Alisa Marie lawyer
Morgner, Aurelius economist, educator
Mori, Allen Anthony university dean, consultant, researcher
Morissette, Alanis musician
Morris, Herbert lawyer, educator
Morrison, Donald Graham business educator, consultant
Morriss, Frank film editor
Morrow, Winston Vaughan financial executive
Mortensen, Richard Edgar engineering educator
Mosich, Anelis Nick accountant, author, educator, consultant
Mosk, Richard Mitchell lawyer
Moskowitz, Joel Steven lawyer
Mossman, Thomas Mellish, Jr. television manager
†Mottek, Frank broadcaster, journalist
Moxley, John Howard, III physician
Moy, Ronald Leonard dermatologist, surgeon
Mueller, Carl Richard theater arts educator, author
Muhlbach, Robert Arthur lawyer
Muldaur, Diana Charlton actress
Mulligan, Richard M. actor, writer
Mulligan, Robert Patrick film director, producer
Muntz, Eric Phillip aerospace engineering and radiology educator, consultant
Munzer, Stephen R. law educator
Murphy, Philip Edward broadcast executive
Myers, Katherine Donna writer, publisher
Nadler, Gerald engineering educator, management consultant
Naef, Weston John museum curator
Nakanishi, Don Toshiaki Asian American studies educator, writer
Nathwani, Bharat Narottam pathologist, consultant
Natzler, Otto ceramic artist
Neal, Joseph C., Jr. church administrator
Neely, Sally Schultz lawyer
Neiter, Gerald Irving lawyer
Nelson, Anna Masterton writer
Nelson, Grant Steel lawyer, educator
Nelson, Howard Joseph geographer, educator
Nelson, Mark Bruce interior designer
Neufeld, Elizabeth Fondal biochemist, educator
Neufeld, Mace film company executive
Neufeld, Naomi Das pediatric endocrinologist
Neutra, Dion architect
Neville, Aaron musician
Neville, Art musician
Neville, Charles musician
Neville, Cyril musician
Newhart, Bob entertainer
Newman, David Wheeler lawyer
Newman, Michael Rodney lawyer
Newman, Thomas composer
Nibley, Robert Ricks retired lawyer
Nicholas, William Richard lawyer
Niehaus, Lennie composer, jazz saxophonist
Niemeth, Charles Frederick lawyer
Niemiec, Peter Jude lawyer
Niles, John Gilbert lawyer
Nilles, John Mathias (Jack Nilles) futurist
Nimni, Marcel Ephraim biochemistry educator
Nixon, John Harmon economist
Nobe, Ken chemical engineering educator
Noble, Ernest Pascal physician, biochemist, educator
Noble, James Wilkes actor
Noble, Richard Lloyd lawyer
Nocas, Andrew James lawyer
Noce, Walter William, Jr. hospital administrator
Nochimson, David lawyer
Nogales, Luis Guerrero communications company executive
Noguchi, Thomas Tsunetomi author, forensic pathologist
Nomo, Hideo professional baseball player
Norris, William Albert federal judge
Nunis, Doyce Blackman, Jr. historian, educator
Nyman, Michael Lawrence composer
O'Brian, Bonnie Jean library services supervisor
O'Brien, John William, Jr. investment management company executive
Obst, Lynda Rosen film company executive, producer, screenwriter
O'Connell, Kevin lawyer
O'Connor, Carroll actor, writer, producer
O'Day, Anita Belle Colton entertainer, singer
O'Donnell, Pierce Henry lawyer
Ogle, Edward Proctor, Jr. investment counseling executive
Ohlgren, Joel R. lawyer
Okeh, Samson Ewruje psychiatric nurse
Okrent, David engineering educator
Olah, George Andrew chemist, educator
O'Leary, Dennis Patrick biophysicist
Olsen, Frances Elisabeth law educator, theorist
Olson, Dale C. public relations executive
O'Malley, Peter professional baseball club executive
Onak, Thomas Philip chemistry educator
Orchard, Henry John electrical engineer
Ordin, Andrea Sheridan lawyer
O'Reilly, Richard Brooks journalist
Orme, Antony Ronald geography educator
Orr, Ronald Stewart lawyer
Orsatti, Alfred Kendall organization executive
Osgood, Frank William urban and economic planner, writer
†Osiander, Lothar soccer coach
O'Steen, Sam film editor, director
Ourieff, Arthur Jacob psychiatrist
Ovitz, Michael S. communications executive
Owen, Michael Lee lawyer
Packard, Robert Charles lawyer
Palazzo, Robert P. lawyer, accountant
Palmer, Roger Cain information scientist
Papiano, Neil Leo lawyer
Pappe, Stuart H. film editor
Park, Sam-Koo transportation executive
Parker, John William pathology educator, investigator
Parker, Robert George radiation oncology educator, academic administrator
Parks, Michael Christopher journalist
Parmelee, Arthur Hawley, Jr. pediatric medical educator
Parsky, Gerald Lawrence lawyer
Pasich, Kirk Alan lawyer
†Passaro, Edward, Jr. surgeon, educator
Patel, Chandra Kumar Naranbhai communications company executive, educator, researcher
Patron, Susan Hall librarian, writer
Paulson, Donald Robert chemistry educator
Paxton, Bill actor, writer, director
Pearl, Judea computer scientist, educator
Peck, Austin H., Jr. lawyer
Pedersen, Norman A. lawyer
Pederson, Con animator
Perdigao, George Michael advertising executive
Perenchio, Andrew Jerrold film and television executive
Perkins, Gladys Patricia retired aerospace engineer
Perkins, William Clinton company executive
Perlis, Michael Fredrick lawyer
Perlmutter, Donna music and dance critic
Perloff, Joseph Kayle cardiologist
Perrine, Richard Leroy environmental engineering educator
Perry, Donald Lester, II venture capitalist
Perry, Joe guitarist
Perry, Luke (Coy Luther Perry, III) actor
Perry, Ralph Barton, III lawyer
Perry, Robert Michael consulting engineering company executive
Perry, William Joseph food processing company executive
Petak, William John systems management educator
Peters, Aulana Louise government agency commissioner, lawyer
Peters, Richard T. lawyer
Petersen, Robert E. publisher
Pfaelzer, Mariana R. federal judge
Phelps, Barton Chase architect, educator
Phillips, Geneva Ficker editor
Phillips, Julia Miller film producer
Phillips, Keith Wendall minister
Philpott, Lindsey civil engineer, researcher, educator
Phinney, Jean Swift psychology educator
Piazza, Michael Joseph professional baseball player
Pieper, Darold D. lawyer
Pierskalla, William Peter university dean, management-engineering educator
Pircher, Leo Joseph lawyer
Pitkin, Roy Macbeth retired medical educator
Plate, Thomas Gordon newspaper columnist, educator
Poindexter, William Mersereau lawyer
Polan, Morris librarian
Pollack, Daniel concert pianist
Pollack, Sydney film director
Pollock, David television writer and producer
Pollock, John Phleger lawyer
Ponty, Jean-Luc violinist, composer, producer
Pope, Alexander H. lawyer, former county official
Port, Sidney Charles mathematician, educator
Portenier, Walter James aerospace engineer
Porter, Verna Louise lawyer
Post, Mike composer
Power, John Bruce lawyer
Prager, Susan Westerberg dean, law educator
Preonas, George Elias lawyer
Presant, Sanford Calvin lawyer
Pugsley, Robert Adrian legal educator
Purcell, Patrick B. motion picture company executive
Puzo, Mario author
Rabinovitz, Jason film and television consultant
Rabinovitz, Joel lawyer, educator
Rachelefsky, Gary S. medical educator
Radloff, William Hamilton editor, writer
Rae, Matthew Sanderson, Jr. lawyer
Raeder, Myrna Sharon lawyer, educator
Rafeedie, Edward federal judge
Raitt, Bonnie Lynn blues singer, guitarist
Ramer, Lawrence Jerome corporation executive
Ramo, Simon engineering executive
Rangell, Leo psychiatrist, psychoanalyst
Rankaitis, Susan artist
†Rapaport, Michael actor
Rappeport, Ira J. lawyer
Rath, Howard Grant, Jr. lawyer
Rathbun, John Wilbert American studies educator
Rauch, Lawrence Lee aerospace and electrical engineer, educator
Raven, Bertram H(erbert) psychology educator
Ray, Gilbert T. lawyer
Raymond, Arthur Emmons aerospace engineer
Rea, William J. federal judge
Reagan, Nancy Davis (Anne Francis Robbins) volunteer, wife of former President of United States
Reagan, Ronald Wilson former President of United States
Real, Manuel Lawrence federal judge
Reaney, Gilbert musician, educator
Rector, Robert Wayman mathematics and engineering educator, former association executive
Reed, Donald Anthony executive
Reed, George Ford, Jr. investment executive
Reeves, Barbara Ann lawyer
Reeves, Keanu actor
Rehme, Robert G. film company executive
Reich, Kenneth Irvin journalist
Reichenthal, Jay Jeffrey health facility administrator
Reiss, Howard chemistry educator
Rense, Paige editor, publishing company executive
Renwick, Edward S. lawyer
Reynolds, Burt actor, director
Rice, Susan F. fundraising counsel executive
Rich, Alan music critic, editor, author
Richards, Michael actor, comedian
Richardson, Arthur Wilhelm lawyer
Richardson, Douglas Fielding lawyer
Richardson, John Vinson, Jr. library science educator
Richie, Lionel B., Jr. singer, songwriter, producer
Richman, Peter Mark actor, painter, writer
Richter, W. D. screenwriter, director, producer
Rickles, Donald Jay comedian, actor
†Riedl, John Joseph communications executive
Riley, Jack actor, writer
Riley, John Graham economics educator
Rimoin, David Lawrence physician, geneticist
Ring, Michael Wilson lawyer
Rinsch, Charles Emil insurance company executive
Riordan, George Nickerson investment banker
Riordan, Richard J. mayor
Ritvo, Edward Ross psychiatrist
Riva, J. Michael art director, production designer
Rive, Sarelle Roselyn manufacturing company executive
Robert, Patrick playwright
Roberts, Robert Winston social work educator, dean
Roberts, Sidney biological chemist
Robertson, Hugh Duff lawyer
Robinson, Martha Stewart retired legal educator
Robinson, Smokey singer, composer
Rodnick, Eliot Herman psychologist, educator
Roeder, Richard Kenneth business owner, lawyer
Roemer, Milton Irwin physician, educator
Rogers, James Wilson church official
Rogers, Kenneth Ray entertainer, recording artist
Rogger, Hans Jack history educator
Rollins, Henry musician, author, publisher
Roney, John Harvey lawyer, consultant
Rosen, Charles production designer
Rosenberg, Howard Anthony journalist
Rosendahl, Roger Wayne lawyer
Rosenthal, Laurence composer
Rosenthal, Sol lawyer
Rosett, Arthur Irwin lawyer, educator
Ross, Diana singer, actress, entertainer, fashion designer
Ross, Joseph Foster physician, educator
Ross, Stan accounting firm executive
Ross, Stanley Ralph writer, publisher, producer, software manufacturing executive
Rosser, James Milton academic administrator
Rosten, Irwin writer, producer, director
Rothenberg, Alan I. lawyer, professional sports association executive
Rothman, Frank lawyer, motion picture company executive
Rothman, Michael Judah lawyer
Rouse, Richard Hunter historian, educator
Roussey, Robert Stanley accountant, educator
Rubin, Bruce Joel screenwriter, director, producer
Rubin, Stanley Creamer producer
Rubinstein, Moshe Fajwel engineering educator
Rucker, Thomas Douglas purchasing executive
Rudin, Scott film and theatre producer
Rudolph, Jeffrey N. museum director
Rundgren, Todd musician, record producer
Ruskin, Joseph Richard actor, director
Russell, James Brian broadcast executive
Russell, Pamela Redford writer, film documentarian
Rutter, Marshall Anthony lawyer
Ryan, Stephen J. academic dean
Ryan, Stephen Joseph, Jr. ophthalmology educator, university dean
Saar, Alison sculptor
Sadun, Alfredo Arrigo neuro-ophthalmologist, scientist, educator
Safonov, Michael George electrical engineering educator, consultant
Sager, Philip Travis academic physician, cardiac electrophysiologist
Saito-Furukawa, Janet Chiyo primary school educator
Salhany, Lucille S. broadcast executive
Saltzman, Barry actor
Saltzman, Joseph journalist, producer, educator
Salzman, David Elliot entertainment industry executive
Samet, Jack I. lawyer
Sample, Steven Browning university executive
Samuels, Donald L. lawyer
†San Giacomo, Laura actress
Sarian, Jirair Nerses radiologist
Sarnat, Bernard George plastic surgeon, educator, researcher
Sarnoff, Thomas Warren television executive
Savage, Edward Warren, Jr. physician
Sawyer, Charles Henry anatomist, educator
Saxe, Deborah Crandall lawyer
Saylor, Mark Julian editor
Scanlon, Deralee Rose dietitian, educator, author
Schaefer, William David English language educator
Scheibel, Arnold Bernard psychiatrist, educator, research director
Scheifly, John Edward retired lawyer
Schelbert, Heinrich Ruediger nuclear medicine physician
Schiff, Martin physician, surgeon
Schifsky, Charles Mark magazine editor
Schipper, Merle art historian and critic, exhibition curator
†Schlosberg, Richard T., III newspaper publishing executive
Schmidt, Arthur film editor
Schmidt, Karl A. lawyer
Schnabel, Rockwell Anthony ambassador
Schneider, Edward Lewis medicine educator, research administrator
Scholtz, Robert Arno electrical engineering educator
Schulman, Tom screenwriter
Schumacher, Joseph Charles chemical engineer
Schutz, John Adolph historian, educator, former university dean
Schwabe, Arthur David physician, educator
Schwartz, Leon foreign language educator
Scott, A. Timothy lawyer
Scott, Allen John public policy and geography educator
Scott, Kelly newspaper editor
Scott, Robert Lane chemist, educator
Scoular, Robert Frank lawyer
Scully, Vincent Edward sports broadcaster
See, Carolyn English language educator, novelist, book critic
Seeman, Melvin sociologist, educator
Segil, Larraine Diane materials company executive
Seide, Paul civil engineering educator
Seidelman, Arthur Allan director
Selwood, Pierce Taylor lawyer
Setian, Nerses Mikail bishop, former apostolic exarchate
Settles, F. Stan, Jr. manufacturing executive, educator
Seymour, Michael production designer
Shaiman, Marc composer, arranger, orchestrator
Shames, Henry Joseph lawyer
Shank, Russell librarian, educator
Shanks, Patricia L. lawyer
Shapazian, Robert Michael publishing executive
Shapiro, Isadore materials scientist, consultant
Shapiro, Marvin Seymour lawyer
Shapiro, Mel playwright, director, drama educator
Shapiro, Robert Leslie lawyer
Shapley, Lloyd Stowell mathematics and economics educator
Shatner, William actor
Shaw, David Lyle journalist, author
Shearer, Derek N. international studies educator, diplomat, administrator
Sheehan, Lawrence James lawyer
Sherwood, Allen Joseph lawyer
Sherwood, Arthur Lawrence lawyer
†Shestock, Linda community foundation executive
Shideler, Ross Patrick foreign language and comparative literature educator, author, translator, poet
Shire, David Lee composer
Shneidman, Edwin S. psychologist, educator, thanatologist, suicidologist
Shonk, Albert Davenport, Jr. advertising executive
Shore, Herbert writer, poet, educator
Shore, Howard Leslie composer
Shortz, Richard Alan lawyer
Shultz, John David lawyer
Shuster, Alvin journalist, newspaper editor
Shutler, Mary Elizabeth academic administrator
Siegel, Michael Elliot nuclear medicine physician, educator
Siegel, Sheldon C. physician
Sigband, Norman Bruce management communication educator
Silbergeld, Arthur F. lawyer
Silberman, Irwin Alan public health physician
Silverman, Bruce Gary advertising executive
Silverman, Fred television producer
Silverman, Leonard M. university dean, electrical engineering educator
†Silverstone, Alicia actress
Sinay, Hershel David publisher
Sinay, Joseph retail executive
Sitrick, Michael Steven communications executive
Sklar, Richard Lawrence political science educator
Skotak, Robert F. film production company executive
Slash, (Saul Hudson) guitarist
Slaughter, John Brooks university administrator
Slavitt, Earl Benton lawyer
Smathers, James Burton medical physicist, educator
Smith, Alexis artist, educator
Smith, Emil L. biochemist, consultant
Smith, Howard film editor
Smith, Jean Webb (Mrs. William French Smith) civic worker
Smith, Lane Jeffrey automotive journalist, technical consultant
Smith, William Ray retired biophysicist, engineer
Smits, Jimmy actor
Sokolov, Jacque Jenning health care executive, nuclear cardiologist
Solomon, David Harris physician, educator
Solomon, George Freeman academic psychiatrist
Somers, Harold Milton economist, educator
Somerville, Virginia Pauline Winters executive assistant
Sonnenschein, Ralph Robert physiologist
Spelling, Aaron film and television producer, writer, actor
Sperling-Orseck, Irene publishing company executive
Spitzer, William George university dean, physicist, educator, researcher
Spofford, Robert Houston advertising agency executive
Sprague, Norman Frederick, Jr. surgeon, educator
Stamm, Alan lawyer
Stancill, James McNeill finance educator, consultant
Stapleton, Jean (Jeanne Murray) actress
Steckel, Richard J. radiologist, academic administrator
Steel, Dawn motion picture producer
Steel, Ronald Lewis author, historian, educator
Steele, Victoria Lee librarian
Steinberg, David comedian, author, actor
Steinberg, Warren Linnington principal
Steinkamp, William film editor
Stellwagen, Robert Harwood biochemistry educator
Stephens, George Edward, Jr. lawyer

Sterling, Donald T. professional basketball team executive
Stern, James Coper sales executive
Stern, Leonard Bernard television and motion picture production company executive
†Stern, Mitchell broadcast executive
Stern, Walter Eugene neurosurgeon, educator
Stevens, Connie actress, singer
Stevens, Gerald D. secondary education educator, consultant
Stevens, Roy W. sales and marketing executive
Stevenson, Robert Murrell music educator
Stockwell, Robert Paul linguist, educator
Stone, Lawrence Maurice lawyer, educator
Stone, Richard James lawyer
Stone, Sharon actress
Stormes, John Max instructional systems developer
Storms, Lester (C Storms) retired veterinarian
Straatsma, Bradley Ralph ophthalmologist, educator
Strack, Stephen Naylor psychologist
Strawn, Judy C. public relations professional
Strock, Herbert Leonard motion picture producer, director, editor, writer
Stromberg, Ross Ernest lawyer
Suhrstedt, Tim cinematographer
Sullivan, Stuart Francis anesthesiologist, educator
Summers, Andy (Andrew James Somers) popular musician
Sumner, James DuPre, Jr. lawyer, educator
Sutherland, Donald actor
Sutherland, Michael Cruise librarian
Swartz, Roslyn Holt real estate investment executive
Swit, Loretta actress
Symonds, Norman Leslie computer programming specialist
Szego, Clara Marian cell biologist, educator
Szwarc, Michael polymer scientist
†Tabachnick, Norman Donald psychiatrist, educator
Tackowiak, Bruce Joseph lawyer
Takasugi, Robert Mitsuhiro federal judge
Talton, Chester Lovelle bishop
Tamkin, S. Jerome business executive, consultant
Tan, William Lew lawyer
Tanzmann, Virginia Ward architect
Tardio, Thomas A. public relations executive
Tarr, Ralph William lawyer, former federal government official
Tartikoff, Brandon broadcast executive
†Taylor, Charles Ellett biologist
Taylor, Leigh Herbert college dean
†Taylor, Minna lawyer
Teele, Cynthia Lombard lawyer
Tellem, Susan Mary public relations executive
Tennant, John Randall management advisory company executive
Tennyson, G(eorg) B(ernhard) English educator
Territo, Mary C. health facility administrator, oncologist
Tevrizian, Dickran M., Jr. federal judge
Tewkesbury, Joan F. film director, writer
Thoman, John Everett architect, mediator
Thomas, Robert Joseph columnist, author
Thomas, Shirley author, educator, business executive
Thompson, Earl Albert economics educator
Thompson, Richard Frederick psychologist, neuroscientist, educator
Thorne, Richard Mansergh physicist
Thorpe, Douglas L. lawyer
Thrower, Norman Joseph William geographer, educator
Tinsley, Walton Eugene lawyer
Title, Gail Migdal lawyer
Titus, Edward Depue psychiatrist, administrator
Tobia, Stephen Francis, Jr. marketing professional, consultant
Tobisman, Stuart Paul lawyer
Toman, Mary Ann federal official
Tomash, Erwin retired computer equipment company executive
Tompkins, Ronald K. surgeon
Torme, Mel(vin) (Howard Torme) musician, jazz vocalist
Tornek, Terry E. real estate executive
Totten, George Oakley, III political science educator
Toulmin, Stephen Edelston humanities educator
Tourtellotte, Wallace William neurologist
Townsend, Robert film director
Tranquada, Robert Ernest medical educator, physician
Treister, George Marvin lawyer
Trembly, Cristy television executive
Trembly, Dennis Michael musician
Trimble, Phillip Richard law educator
Trimble, Stanley Wayne hydrology and geography educator
Troispoux, Christianne Valerie Ann psychologist
Troy, Joseph Freed lawyer
Trueblood, Kenneth Nyitray retired chemist, educator
Truman, Edward Crane real estate manager, consultant, composer
Trygstad, Lawrence Benson lawyer
Tuckson, Reed V. university president
Turner, Ralph Herbert sociologist, educator
Tyler, Richard fashion designer
Tyler, Steven singer
Ufimtsev, Pyotr Yakovlevich physicist, electrical engineer, educator
Ukropina, James R. lawyer
Ungar, Roselva May primary and elementary educator
Unterman, Thomas E. newspaper publishing company executie, lawyer
Urioste, Frank J. film editor
Urist, Marshall Raymond orthopedic surgeon, educator, researcher
Van Asperen, Morris Earl banker
Van Buren, Abigail (Pauline Friedman Phillips) columnist, author, writer, lecturer
van Dam, Heiman psychoanalyst
Van de Kamp, John Kalar lawyer
Vanderet, Robert Charles lawyer
Van Der Meulen, Joseph Pierre neurologist
Van Horne, R. Richard oil company executive
Vaughan, Joseph Robert lawyer
Vaughn, William Weaver lawyer
Venis, Linda Diane academic administrator, educator
Verdery, David Norwood broadcast programming executive
Verger, Morris David architect, planner
Ver Steeg, Donna Lorraine Frank nurse, sociologist, educator
Villablanca, Jaime Rolando medical scientist, educator
Volpert, Richard Sidney lawyer
Vredevoe, Donna Lou research immunologist, microbiologist, educator
Vuckovic, Gojko Milos public administration scholar
Wagner, Christian Nikolaus Johann materials engineering educator
Wagner, D. William lawyer
Wagner, William Gerard university dean, physicist, consultant, information scientist, investment manager
Waits, Thomas Alan composer, actor, singer
Walcher, Alan Ernest lawyer
Walsh, John Harley medical educator
Walton, Brian labor union executive
Ward, Leslie Allyson journalist, editor
Wasserman, Steve editor
Waterman, Michael Spencer mathematics educator, biology educator
Waters, Laughlin Edward federal judge
Waterston, Samuel Atkinson actor
Watkins, Sydney Lynn sports administrator
Watson, Sharon Gitin psychologist, executive
Watts, Quincy Dushawn track and field athlete
Wayte, (Paul) Alan lawyer
Wazzan, A(hmed) R(assem) Frank engineering educator, dean
Weber, Charles L. electrical engineering educator
Webster, Jeffery Norman technology policy analyst
Weiner, Leslie Philip neurology educator, researcher
Weinman, Glenn Alan lawyer
Weinstein, Irwin Marshall internist, hematologist
Weinstein, Josh television producer
Weinstock, Harold lawyer
Weiss, Martin Harvey neurosurgeon, educator
Weiss, Walter Stanley lawyer
Weissbard, Samuel Held lawyer
Weiswasser, Stephen Anthony lawyer, broadcast executive
Welch, Lloyd Richard electrical engineering educator, communications consultant
Welch, Robert W. production designer, art director
Wellburn, Timothy film editor
Welles, Melinda Fassett artist, educator
Werner, Gloria S. librarian
Wessling, Robert Bruce lawyer
Westheimer, David Kaplan novelist
Weston, John Frederick business educator, consultant
Wheat, Francis Millspaugh retired lawyer
White, Leonard motion picture company executive
White, Robert Joel lawyer
Whitten, Charles Alexander, Jr. physics educator
Whybrow, Peter Charles psychiatrist, educator
Wigmore, John Grant lawyer
Wilkinson, Alan Herbert nephrologist, medical educator
Willes, Mark Hinckley media industry executive
Williams, David Welford federal judge
Williams, Donald Clyde lawyer
Williams, Harold Marvin foundation official
Williams, John Towner composer, conductor
Williams, Julie Ford mutual fund officer
Williams, Richard Thomas lawyer
Williams, Robert Martin economist, consultant
Williams, Robin actor, comedian
Williams, Ronald Dean minister, religious organization executive
Williams, Theodore Earle industrial distribution company executive
Williams, Walter David aerospace executive, consultant
Williams, Willie protective services official
Willner, Alan Eli electrical engineer, educator
Wills, John Elliot, Jr. history educator, writer
Wilson, Charles Zachary, Jr. newspaper publisher
Wilson, James Quinn government, management educator
Wilson, M. Roy medical educator
Wilson, Miriam Geisendorfer retired physician, educator
Wilson, Nancy Linda church officer
Wilson, Stephen Victor federal judge
Wincor, Michael Z. psychopharmacology educator, clinician, researcher
Wine, Mark Philip lawyer
Winfield, Paul Edward actor
Winkler, Howard Leslie investment banker, business and financial consultant
Winterowd, Walter Ross English educator
Winters, Barbara Jo musician
Winters, Ralph E. film editor
With, Gerda Becker artist
Withers, Hubert Rodney radiotherapist, radiobiologist, educator
Wittmann, Otto art museum executive
Wittrock, Merlin Carl educational psychologist
Wittry, David Beryle physicist, educator
Woelffer, Emerson Seville artist
Woessner, Frederick T. composer, pianist
Wolas, Herbert lawyer
Wolf, Alfred rabbi
Wolfen, Werner F. lawyer
Wolinsky, Leo C. newspaper editor
Wong, James Bok economist, engineer, technologist
Wood, Nancy Elizabeth psychologist, educator
Wood, Willis Bowne, Jr. utility holding company executive
Woodruff, Fay paleoceanographer, geological researcher
Woolf, Nancy Jean neuroscientist, educator
Wooten, Cecil Aaron religious organization administrator
Wortham, Thomas Richard English language educator
Wright, Donald Franklin newspaper executive
Wright, Ernest Marshall physiologist, consultant
Wright, Kenneth Brooks lawyer
Wright, Kenneth Weston pediatric ophthalmologist
Wu, Li-Pei banker
Wurtele, Morton Gaither meteorologist, educator
Wycoff, Robert E. petroleum company executive
†Wyland, (Robert ) artist
Yagiela, John Allen dental educator
Yamamoto, Joe psychiatrist, educator
Yang, Yang research scientist
†Yared, Gabriel composer
Yates, Peter director, producer
Yee, Stephen airport executive
Yeh, William Wen-Gong civil engineering educator
Yen, Teh Fu civil and environmental engineering educator
York, Gary Alan lawyer
Yoshiki-Kovinick, Marian Tsugie author
Young, Caprice Yvonne municipal official
Young, Charles Edward university chancellor
Young, Joseph Louis artist
†Youpa, Donald G. broadcast executive
Zamir, Frances Roberta (Frances Roberta Weiss-Swede) principal
Zawacki, Bruce Edwin surgeon, ethicist
Zeitlin, Maurice sociology educator, author
Zelikow, Howard Monroe management and financial consultant
Zelon, Laurie Dee lawyer
Zemeckis, Robert L. film director
Zentner, Anne Diener flutist
Ziffren, Kenneth lawyer
Ziskin, Laura film producer
Zwick, Barry Stanley newspaper editor, speechwriter

### Los Gatos
Asher, James John psychology educator
Bortolussi, Michael Richard aerospace human factors engineer
Cohen, James Robert oncologist, hematologist
Hartinger, Patricia Bernardine elementary school educator
Heymann, Stephen marketing management consultant
Monday, Jon Ellis music publishing company executive
Naymark, Sherman consulting nuclear engineer
Rissanen, Jorma Johannes computer scientist
Rosenheim, Donald Edwin electrical engineer
Seligmann, William Robert lawyer, author
Simonson, Ted principal
Tinsley, Barbara Sher historian, educator, writer
Zacher, Valerie Irene interior designer

### Los Osos
Cloonan, Clifford B. electrical engineer, educator
Mehring, Margaret filmmaker, retired educator
Thomas, Robert Murray educational psychology educator

### Lucerne Valley
Johnson, Jane Oliver artist

### Lynwood
Dove, Donald Augustine city planner, educator

### Magalia
Joffre, Stephen Paul consulting chemist

### Malibu
Aiken, Lewis Roscoe, Jr. psychologist, educator
Almond, Paul film director, producer, writer
Baskin, Otis Wayne business educator
Chester, Arthur Noble physicist
Davenport, David university president, lawyer
Downey, Robert, Jr. actor
Ensign, Richard Papworth transportation executive
Greer, Cynthia Faye university administrator, legal educator, mediator
Jenden, Donald James pharmacologist, educator
Louganis, Greg E. former Olympic athlete, actor
MacLeod, Robert Fredric editor, publisher
Margerum, J(ohn) David chemist
Mataré, Herbert F. physicist, consultant
Morgenstern, Leon surgeon
Nolte, Nick actor
Palacio, June Rose Payne nutritional science educator
Pepper, David M. physicist, educator, author, inventor
Phillips, Ronald Frank legal educator, academic administrator, dean
Price, Frank motion picture and television company executive
Samuels, Cynthia Kalish communications executive
Smith, George Foster retired aerospace company executive
Vereen, Ben actor, singer, dancer
Wilkins, (Jacques) Dominique professional basketball player
Wilson, John Francis religion educator, educational institution administrator
Yates, Jere Eugene business educator, management consultant
Young, Matt Norvel, Jr. university chancellor emeritus

### Mammoth Lakes
Buchanan, Lee Ann public relations executive

### Manhattan Beach
Anderson, Charles Michael accountant
Blanton, John Arthur architect
Bradburn, David Denison engineer, retired air force officer
Brooks, Edward Howard college administrator
Chettle, A(lvin) B(asil), Jr. lawyer, educator
Dworetzky, Thomas Alan publishing executive
Krienke, Carol Belle Manikowske (Mrs. Oliver Kenneth Krienke) realtor
Ricardi, Leon Joseph electrical engineer
Scott, Michael Dennis lawyer
Stern, Daniel Alan business management consultant
Weinstock, Herbert Frank public relations executive

### Manteca
Tonn, Elverne Meryl pediatric dentist, dental benefits consultant

### Marina
Cornell, Annie Aiko nurse, administrator, retired army officer
Grenfell, Gloria Ross freelance journalist
Myers, James David municipal government official
Shane, William Whitney astronomer

### Marina Del Rey
Adams, Thomas Merritt lawyer
Brown, Anthony B. aerospace executive
Dankanyin, Robert John international business executive
Davis, Donald G(lenn) lawyer
Gold, Carol Sapin international management consultant, speaker
Grobe, Charles Stephen lawyer, accountant
Hovland, Tim (The Hov) (The Hov) volleyball player
Smolker, Gary Steven lawyer
Steffes, Kent volleyball player
Stoklos, Randy (Stokey Stoklos) volleyball player
Timmons, Steve (Red) volleyball player
Touch, Joseph Dean computer scientist, educator

### Mariposa
Bruce, John Anthony artist
Rogers, Earl Leslie artist, educator
Shields, Allan Edwin writer, photographer, retired educator

### Marshall
Evans, Robert James architect

### Martinez
Bray, Absalom Francis, Jr. lawyer
Efron, Robert neurology educator, research institute administrator
Love, Gordon Lee pathologist, researcher
McKnight, Lenore Ravin child psychiatrist
Thomas, Walter Dill, Jr. forest pathologist, consultant
Uilkema, Gayle Burns mayor, councilwoman, business educator

### Mcclellan AFB
†Borland, Carter Allen military career officer

### Mckinleyville
Kulstad, Guy Charles public works official

### Mendocino
Alexander, Joyce Mary illustrator
Rappaport, Stuart R. lawyer

### Menlo Park
Altman, Drew E. foundation executive
Bader, W(illiam) Reece lawyer
Baez, Joan Chandos folk singer
Borovoy, Roger Stuart lawyer
Bourne, Charles Percy information scientist, educator
Boyarski, Adam Michael physicist
Bremser, George, Jr. electronics company executive
Carlick, David communications executive
Clair, Theodore Nat educational psychologist
Cody, Frank Joseph secondary school administrator, teacher education educator
Cook, Paul M. technology company executive
Craig, Gordon Alexander historian, educator
Crane, Hewitt David science advisor
Davis, William Emrys religious organization official
Dyer, Charles Arnold lawyer
Edson, William Alden electrical engineer
Fergason, James L. optical company executive
Ferris, Robert Albert lawyer, venture capitalist
Frisco, Louis Joseph retired materials science company executive, electrical engineer
Fuhrman, Frederick Alexander physiology educator
Funkhouser, Lawrence William retired geologist
Glaser, Robert Joy physician, foundation executive
Gunderson, Robert Vernon, Jr. lawyer
Hoagland, Laurance Redington, Jr. investment executive
Hodgen, Laurie Dee geologist, editor
Hoffman, Thomas Edward dermatologist
Holzer, Thomas Lequear geologist
Honey, Richard Churchill retired electrical engineer
Jorgensen, Paul J. research company executive
Katz, Robert Lee business executive
†Kaufman, Robert J. investment company executive
Kirk, Cassius Lamb, Jr. lawyer, investor
Kohne, Richard Edward retired engineering executive
Kovachy, Edward Miklos, Jr. psychiatrist
Kurtzig, Sandra L. software company executive
Kuwabara, James Shigeru research hydrologist
Lane, Laurence William, Jr. retired ambassador, publisher
Love, Amy Dundon business executive, marketing and sales executive
Lucas, Donald Leo private investor
Luepke, Gretchen geologist
MacGregor, James Thomas toxicologist
Madison, James Raymond lawyer
McCarthy, Roger Lee mechanical engineer
McDonald, Warren George accountant, former savings and loan executive
Morrison, David Fred freight company executive
Nell, Janine Marie metallurgical and materials engineer
Neumann, Peter Gabriel computer scientist
Nichols, William Ford, Jr. foundation executive, business executive
O'Brien, Raymond Francis transportation executive
Pake, George Edward research executive, physicist
Pallotti, Marianne Marguerite foundation administrator
Parker, Donn Blanchard retired information security consultant
Phipps, Allen Mayhew management consultant
Pooley, James Henry Anderson lawyer, author
Prabhakar, Arati federal administration research director, electrical engineer
Roberts, George R. investment banking company executive
Ross, Bernard engineering consultant, educator
Saifer, Mark Gary Pierce pharmaceutical executive
Salmon, Vincent acoustical consultant
Schmidt, Chauncey Everett banker
Shows, Winnie M. speaker, author, consultant
Sommers, William Paul management consultant, think tank executive
Speidel, John Joseph physician, foundation officer
Taft, David Dakin chemical executive
Taylor, Robert P. lawyer
Tokheim, Robert Edward physicist
Vickers, Roger Spencer physicist, program director
Wallace, Robert Earl geologist
Walsh, William former football coach
Walsh, William Desmond investor
Westcott, Brian John manufacturing executive
Wolfson, Mark Alan investor, business educator
Woodward, Susan Ellen economist, federal official
Wright, Rosalie Muller magazine and newspaper editor

### Mentone
Halstead, Bruce Walter biotoxicologist
Stockton, David Knapp professional golfer

### Merced
LeCocq, Karen Elizabeth artist

### Mill Valley
Benezet, Louis Tomlinson retired psychology educator, former college president
Crews, William Odell, Jr. seminary administrator
D'Amico, Michael architect, urban planner
Dillon, Richard Hugh librarian, author
DuBose, Francis Marquis clergyman
Flynn, Thomas Charles banker
Hahner, Linda R. R. artist, creative director
Harner, Michael James anthropologist, educator, author
Isslieb, Lutz finance company executive
Jackson, Sharon Juanita management consultant

Leslie, Jacques Robert, Jr. *journalist*
McNamara, Stephen *newspaper executive*
Nemir, Donald Philip *lawyer*
Padula, Fred David *filmmaker*
Taylor, Rose Perrin *social worker*
Wallerstein, Robert Solomon *psychiatrist*
Winskill, Robert Wallace *manufacturing executive*

### Millbrae
Koleniak Gignoux, Barbara Donna *nurse*
Lande, James Avra *lawyer*
Mank, Edward Warren *marketing professional*

### Milpitas
Berkley, Stephen Mark *computer peripherals manufacturing company executive*
Chiu, Peter Yee-Chew *physician*
Corrigan, Wilfred J. *data processing and computer company executive*
Fenner, Peter David *communications executive, management consultant*
Granchelli, Ralph S. *company executive*
Hodson, Roy Goode, Jr. *retired logistician*
Le, Yvonne Diemvan *chemist*
Lee, Kenneth *physicist*
Lobig, Janie Howell *special education educator*
McDonald, Mark Douglas *electrical engineer*
Mian, Guo *electrical engineer*
Mittal, Manmohan *electronic design automation engineer*
Wang, Huai-Liang William *mechanical engineer*

### Mission Hills
Cramer, Frank Brown *engineering executive, combustion engineer, systems consultant*
Jones, John Harding *photographer*

### Mission Viejo
Dergarabedian, Paul *energy and environmental company executive*
Foulds, Donald Duane *aerospace executive*
Harder, Wendy Wetzel *communications executive*
Henderson, Marsha Roslyn Thaw *clinical social worker*
LaRosa, Gianni *aerospace industry administrator*
Linton, Frederick M. *strategic planning consultant*
McGinnis, Joán Adell *retired secondary school educator*
Pohl, John Henning *chemical engineer, consultant*
Rodrigues, Mark *financial executive, manpower consultant*
Ruben, Robert Joseph *lawyer*
Sabaroff, Rose Epstein *retired education educator*
Samuelson, Norma Graciela *architectural illustrator, artist*
Smith, William K. *real estate developer*
Stampfli, John Francis *logistics consultant*

### Modesto
Bairey, Marie *principal*
Berry, John Charles *psychologist*
Bucknam, Mary Olivia Caswell *artist*
Crawford, Charles McNeil *winery science executive*
Dunbar, Sharon Kay *controller, accountant*
Gallo, Ernest *vintner*
Goldberg, Robert Lewis *preventive and occupational medicine physician*
LaMont, Sanders Hickey *journalist*
Mayhew, William A. *judge*
Moe, Andrew Irving *veterinarian*
Morrison, Robert Lee *physical scientist*
Owens, Jack Byron *lawyer*
Piccinini, Robert M. *grocery store chain executive*
Reberg, Rosalie *vice principal*
Richardson, Ernest Ray (Rocky Richardson) *housing program supervisor*
Shastid, Jon Barton *wine company executive*

### Moffett Field
Baldwin, Betty Jo *computer specialist*
Bousquet, John Frederick *security firm executive, desktop publishing executive, locksmith*
Cohen, Malcolm Martin *psychologist, researcher*
Dean, William Evans *aerospace agency executive*
Greenleaf, John Edward *research physiologist*
Haines, Richard Foster *psychologist*
Kerr, Andrew W. *aerodynamics researcher*
Kittel, Peter *research scientist*
Lissauer, Jack Jonathan *astronomy educator*
McCroskey, William James *aeronautical engineer*
Morrison, David *science administrator*
Munechika, Ken Kenji *research center administrator*
Ragent, Boris *physicist*
Scott, Donald Michael *educational association administrator, educator*
Seiff, Alvin *planetary, atmospheric and aerodynamics scientist*
Statler, Irving Carl *aerospace engineer*

### Monrovia
Huffey, Vinton Earl *clergyman*
Salaman, Maureen Kennedy *nutritionist*

### Montclair
Haage, Robert Mitchell *retired history educator, organization leader*

### Monte Rio
Pemberton, John de Jarnette, Jr. *lawyer, educator*

### Monte Sereno
Allan, Lionel Manning *lawyer*
Jackson, Suzanne Elise *health education coordinator*

### Montebello
Dible, Rose Harpe McFee *special education educator*
Orr, Stanley Chi-Hung *financial executive*

### Montecito
Atkins, Stuart (Pratt) *German language and literature educator*
Bell, Donald William *experimental psychologist*
McShirley, Marjorie Stone *art director*
Meghreblian, Robert Vartan *manufacturing executive, physicist*
Rose, Mark Allen *humanities educator*
Wheelon, Albert Dewell *physicist*

### Monterey
Atchley, Anthony Armstrong *physicist, educator*
Black, Robert Lincoln *pediatrician*
Bomberger, Russell Branson *lawyer, educator*
Bowman, Dorothy Louise *artist*
Bradford, Howard *graphic artist, painter*
Britton, Eve Marchant *newspaper reporter*
Butler, Jon Terry *computer engineering educator, researcher*
Collins, Curtis Allan *oceanographer*
Cutino, Bert Paul *restaurant owner, chef*
Dedini, Eldon Lawrence *cartoonist*
Fenton, Lewis Lowry *lawyer*
Finnberg, Elaine Agnes *psychologist, editor*
Gaskell, Robert Eugene *mathematician, educator*
Haddad, Louis Nicholas *paralegal*
Hamming, Richard Wesley *computer scientist*
Hoivik, Thomas Harry *military educator, international consultant*
Kadushin, Karen D. *dean*
Kennedy-Minott, Rodney *international relations educator, former ambassador*
Ketcham, Henry King *cartoonist*
Marto, Paul James *retired mechanical engineering educator, consultant, researcher*
Matthews, David Fort *military weapon system acquisition specialist*
Miller, Susan Heilmann *publishing executive*
Newberry, Conrad Floyde *aerospace engineering educator*
Newton, Robert Eugene *mechanical engineering educator*
Oder, Broeck Newton *school emergency management consultant*
Peet, Phyllis Irene *women's studies educator*
Reneker, Maxine Hohman *librarian*
Ryan, Sylvester D. *bishop*
Schrady, David Alan *operations research educator*
Shimpfky, Richard Lester *bishop*
Shull, Harrison *chemist, educator*
Spitler, Lee William *banker*
Stern, Gerald Daniel *lawyer*

### Monterey Park
Chan, Daniel Siu-Kwong *psychologist*
Choyke, George Raymond *safety educator, consultant*
Crawford, Philip Stanley *bank executive*
Kwong, Daniel Wai-Kin *business consultant, educator, songwriter, poet*
Meysenburg, Mary Ann *principal*
Ramsey, Nancy Lockwood *nursing educator*
Smith, Betty Denny *county official, administrator, fashion executive*
Stapleton, Jean *journalism educator*
Tseng, Felix Hing-Fai *accountant*
Waiter, Serge-Albert *retired civil engineer*
Wilson, Linda *librarian*

### Moorpark
Bahn, Gilbert Schuyler *retired mechanical engineer, researcher*
Kavli, Fred *manufacturing executive*

### Moraga
Allen, Richard Garrett *health care and education consultant*
Anderson, Brother Mel *academic administrator*
Frey, William Rayburn *healthcare educator, consultant*
Hollingsworth, Robert Edgar *nuclear consultant*
Schmaltz, Roy Edgar, Jr. *artist, art educator*
Sonenshein, Nathan *marine consulting company executive, retired naval officer*

### Moreno Valley
Moran, Patricia Eileen *special education educator*
Moulthrop, Rebecca Lee Stilphen *elementary education educator*

### Morgan Hill
Desimone, Richard Louis *school assistant principal*
Freimark, Robert (Bob Freimark) *artist*
Johnson, Noel Lars *biomedical engineer*
Kuster, Robert Kenneth *scientist*

### Morro Bay
Eggertsen, Paul Fred *psychiatrist*

### Moss Landing
Brewer, Peter George *ocean geochemist*
Heath, George Ross *oceanographer*
Lange, Lester Henry *mathematics educator*

### Mount Shasta
Armstrong, Kenneth *lawyer*

### Mountain View
†Andreessen, Marc *communications company executive*
Barksdale, James Love *communications company executive*
†Boyd, Dean Weldon *management consultant*
Braun, Michael Alan *data processing executive*
Castor, Jon Stuart *management consultant*
Craig, Joan Carmen *secondary school educator, drama teacher*
Crowley, Jerome Joseph, Jr. *investment company executive*
Cusumano, James Anthony *chemical company executive, former recording artist*
de Urioste, George Adolfo, IV *software company executive*
Di Muccio, Mary Jo *retired librarian*
Dorsch, Jeffrey Peter *journalist*
Gelpi, Armand Philippe *internist*
Guldimann, Till Markus *financial company executive*
Hamilton, Judith Hall *computer company executive*
Heaney, Dorothy Phelps *nurse, nursing administrator*
Klein, Harold Paul *microbiologist*
Kobza, Dennis Jerome *architect*
Koo, George Ping Shan *business consultant*
Martin, Roger John *computer scientist*
McCormac, Billy Murray *physicist, research institution executive, former army officer*
Mc Nealy, Scott *computer company executive*
Michalko, James Paul *library association administrator*
North, Daniel Warner *consulting analyst*
Oki, Brian Masao *software engineer*
Qureishi, A. Salam *computer software and services company executive*
Rulifson, Johns Frederick *computer company executive, computer scientist*
Shah, Devang Kundanlal *software engineer*
Spencer, Carol Brown *association executive*
Warren, Richard Wayne *obstetrician, gynecologist*

### Murrieta
Spangler, Lorna Carrie *pharmacy technician*

### Napa
Battisti, Paul Oreste *county supervisor*
Buchanan, Teri Bailey *communications executive*
Chiarella, Peter Ralph *vintner*
Francis, Marc Baruch *pediatrician*
Garnett, William *photographer*
Harrison, E(rnest) Frank(lin) *management educator, consultant, author, former university president and chancellor*
Hill, Orion Alvah, Jr. *retired banker*
LaRocque, Marilyn Ross Onderdonk *public relations consultant, writer*
Miller, John Laurence *professional golfer*
Muedeking, George Herbert *editor*
Norman, Sheri Hanna *artist, educator, cartographer*
Rada, Alexander *university official*
Schunke, Hildegard Heidel *accountant*
Smith, Robert Bruce *former security consultant, retired army officer*
Strock, David Randolph *brokerage house executive*
†Trepp, Leo *rabbi*
Zimmermann, John Paul *plastic surgeon*

### National City
Morgan, Jacob Richard *cardiologist*
Potter, J(effrey) Stewart *property manager*

### Nevada City
Holtz, Sara *lawyer, consultant*

### Newark
Ferber, Norman Alan *retail executive*
Joyce, Stephen Francis *human resource executive*

### Newbury Park
Fredericks, Patricia Ann *real estate executive*
Guggenheim-Boucard, Alan Andre Albert Paul Edouard *business executive, international consultant*
Kocen, Lorraine Ayral *accountant*
†Marshall, Trevor Gordon *computer company executive, editor*

### Newcastle
Hill, Bonnie Guiton *dean*

### Newhall
Stone, Susan Foster *mental health services professional, psychologist*

### Newport Beach
Adams, William Gillette *lawyer*
Albright, Archie Earl, Jr. *investment banker*
Allen, Russell G. *lawyer*
Allumbaugh, Byron *retired grocery company executive*
Armstrong, Robert Arnold *petroleum company executive*
Baskin, Scott David *lawyer*
Bernauer, Thomas A. *lawyer*
Bissell, George Arthur *architect*
Bren, Donald L. *real estate company executive*
Brown, Giles Tyler *history educator, lecturer*
Bryant, Thomas Lee *magazine editor*
Caldwell, Courtney Lynn *lawyer, real estate consultant*
Cano, Kristin Maria *lawyer*
Chihorek, John Paul *electronics company executive*
Clark, Thomas P., Jr. *lawyer*
Cook, Marcy Lynn *mathematics educator, consultant*
Cox, Christopher *congressman*
Curtis, Jesse William, Jr. *retired federal judge*
Dean, Paul John *magazine editor*
Dillion, Gregory Lee *lawyer*
Dovring, Karin Elsa Ingeborg *author, poet, playwright, communication analyst*
Fletcher, Douglas Baden *investment company executive*
Frederick, Dolliver H. *merchant banker*
Fries, Arthur Lawrence *life health insurance broker, disability claim consultant*
Gellman, Gloria Gae Seeburger Schick *marketing professional*
Gerken, Walter Bland *insurance company executive*
Giannini, Valerio Louis *investment banker*
Grager, Steven Paul *insurance consultant*
Green, Melanie Jane *speech-language pathologist*
Hansen, Mark H. *retired speech pathologist, consultant*
Harris, Brent Richard *investment company executive*
Hinshaw, Ernest Theodore, Jr. *private investor, former Olympics executive, former financial executive*
Johnson, Thomas Webber, Jr. *lawyer*
Kahn, Douglas Gerard *psychiatrist*
Kallman, Burton Jay *foods association director*
Katayama, Arthur Shoji *lawyer*
Kaufman, Marcus Maurice *retired judge, lawyer*
Kenney, William John, Jr. *real estate development executive*
Kienitz, LaDonna Trapp *city librarian, city official*
Klein, Maurice J. *lawyer*
Lipson, Melvin Alan *technology and business management consultant*
Mallory, Frank Linus *lawyer*
Marcoux, Carl Henry *former insurance executive, writer, historian*
Masotti, Louis Henry *management educator, consultant*
Matteucci, Dominick Vincent *real estate developer*
McEvers, Duff Steven *lawyer*
Mc Guire, Joseph William *business educator*
Millar, Richard William, Jr. *lawyer*
Mortensen, Arvid LeGrande *lawyer*
Otero-Smart, Ingrid Amarillys *advertising executive*
Panetti, Ramon Stanley *investment company executive, consultant, lawyer*
Pepe, Stephen Phillip *lawyer*
Phillips, Layn R. *lawyer*
Plat, Richard Vertin *corporate finance executive*
Potocki, Joseph Edmund *marketing company executive*
Richardson, Walter John *architect*
Rooklidge, William Charles *lawyer*
Schnapp, Roger Herbert *lawyer*
Sheppard, William Vernon *engineering and construction executive*
Snow, Alan Albert *publisher*
Spitz, Barbara Salomon *artist*
Stephens, Michael Dean *hospital administrator*
Strock, Arthur Van Zandt *architect*
Swan, Peer Alden *scientific company executive, bank director*
Tracy, James Jared, Jr. *accountant, law firm administrator*
Trivelpiece, Craig Evan *computer electronics executive*
Van Mols, Brian *publishing executive*
Wentworth, Diana von Welanetz *author*
Wentworth, Theodore Sumner *lawyer*
Whittemore, Paul Baxter *psychologist*
Willard, Robert Edgar *lawyer*
Wood, George H. *investment executive*
Zalta, Edward *otorhinolaryngologist, physician*

### Norco
Kromka, James Thomas Michael *designer, illustrator*
Lu, Guiyang *electrical engineer*
Parmer, Dan Gerald *veterinarian*

### North Hollywood
Badalamenti, Angelo *composer, conductor*
Baker, Richard Eugene *controller, corporate executive*
Baker, Rick *make-up artist*
Boulanger, Donald Richard *financial services executive*
Bull, David *fine art conservator*
Chang, Wung *researcher, lecturer, business advisor*
Clarke, Stanley Marvin *musician, composer*
Costello, Richard Neumann *advertising agency executive*
Cramer, Douglas Schoolfield *broadcasting executive*
Diller, Phyllis *actress, author*
Duffield, Thomas Andrew *art director, production designer*
Grasso, Mary Ann *theater association executive*
Horowitz, Zachary I. *entertainment company executive*
Hulse, Jerry *journalist*
Kahn, Sheldon F. *film editor, producer*
Katzenberg, Jeffrey *motion picture studio executive*
Koran, Dennis Howard *publisher*
Kreger, Melvin Joseph *lawyer*
Kuter, Kay E. *writer, actor*
LaBelle, Patti *singer*
Lantieri, Michael *special effects expert*
Levin, Alvin Irving *composer*
Lindheim, Richard David *television company executive*
Loper, James Leaders *broadcasting executive*
Lynn, Loretta Webb (Mrs. Oliver Lynn, Jr.) *singer*
McMartin, John *actor*
Meat Loaf, (Marvin Lee Aday) *popular musician, actor*
Meyer, Ron *agent*
Milner, Howard M. *real estate developer, international real estate financier*
Mirisch, Marvin Elliot *motion picture producer*
Neill, Ve *make-up artist*
Newton-John, Olivia *singer, actress*
Omens, Sherwood *cinematographer*
Paul, Charles S. *motion picture and television company executive*
Peter, Arnold Philimon *lawyer*
Pike, (John) Kevin *special effects expert*
Prince, Donna Jean *artist*
Reynolds, Debbie (Mary Frances Reynolds) *actress*
Robinson, John Peter *film composer, keyboardist*
Runquist, Lisa A. *lawyer*
Schlosser, Anne Griffin *librarian*
Smothers, Dick *actor, singer*
Smothers, Tom *actor, singer*
Spencer, James H. *art director, production designer*
Walker, Mallory Elton *tenor*
Wasserman, Lew R. *film, recording and publishing company executive*
Yablans, Frank *film company executive, motion picture producer*
Yearwood, Trisha *country music singer, songwriter*
Zappa, Gail *record producer*
Zimring, Stuart David *lawyer*

### Northridge
Bassler, Robert Covey *artist, educator*
Bekir, Nagwa Esmat *electrical engineer, educator, consultant*
Berger, Peter E. *film editor*
Bradshaw, Richard Rotherwood *engineering executive*
Chen, Joseph Tao *historian, educator*
Court, Arnold *climatologist*
Curzon, Susan Carol *university administrator*
Davidson, Sheldon Jerome *hematologist*
dePaolis, Potito Umberto *food company executive*
Devol, Kenneth Stowe *journalism educator*
Ellner, Carolyn Lipton *university dean, consultant*
Flores, William Vincent *Latin American studies educator*
Harwick, Betty Corinne Burns *sociology educator*
Jakobsen, Jakob Knudsen *mechanical engineer*
Kiddoo, Robert James *engineering service company executive*
Lauter, James Donald *retired stockbroker*
Lehtihalme, Larry (Lauri) K. *financial planner*
Mouzon, Alphonse *actor, composer, record producer, instrumentalist*
Oppenheimer, Steven Bernard *biology educator*
Reagan, Janet Thompson *psychologist, educator*
Rengarajan, Sembiam Rajagopal *electrical engineering educator, researcher, consultant*
Stout, Thomas Melville *control systems engineer*
Tanis, Norman Earl *retired university dean, library expert*
Torgow, Eugene N. *electrical engineer*
Wilson, Blenda Jacqueline *academic administrator*

### Norwalk
Drant, Sandra Elizabeth *court reporter, educator*

### Novato
Franklin, Robert Blair *cardiologist*
†Goldstein, Kenneth F. *entertainment executive, software executive*
Grove, Douglas David *insurance company executive*
Obninsky, Victor Peter *lawyer*
Patterson, W. Morgan *college president*
Pfeiffer, Phyllis Kramer *newspaper company executive*
Reed, Dwayne Milton *medical epidemiologist, educator*
Simon, Lee Will *astronomer*
Womack, Thomas Houston *manufacturing company executive*

### Oak Park
Caldwell, Stratton Franklin *kinesiologist*

**Oakdale**
Thomas, William LeRoy *geography educator, cruise lecturer*

**Oakhurst**
Bonham, Clifford Vernon *retired social work educator*

**Oakland**
Alba, Benny *artist*
Alderson, Richard Lynn (Sandy Alderson) *professional baseball team executive*
Allen, Jeffrey Michael *lawyer*
Al Malek, Amir Isa *entrepreneur, business consultant, actor, musician*
Anthony, Elaine Margaret *real estate executive, interior designer*
Armstrong, Saundra Brown *federal judge*
Atkinson, Richard Chatham *university president*
Barlow, William Pusey, Jr. *accountant*
Barricks, Michael Eli *retinal surgeon*
Beasley, Bruce Miller *sculptor*
Benham, Priscilla Carla *religion educator, college president*
Bordick, Michael Todd *professional baseball player*
Bowen-Forbes, Jorge Courtney *artist, author, poet*
Brewster, Andrea B. *artist*
Brown, Stephen Lawrence *environmental consultant*
Brust, David *physicist*
Burnison, Boyd Edward *lawyer*
Burns, Catherine Elizabeth *art dealer*
Burt, Christopher Clinton *publisher*
Caldwell, Carey Teresa *museum curator*
Canseco, Jose *professional baseball player*
Carlesimo, P. J. (Peter J. Carlesimo) *former college basketball coach, professional basketball coach*
Caulfield, W. Harry *health care industry executive, physician*
Champlin, Malcolm McGregor *retired municipal judge*
Chilvers, Robert Merritt *lawyer*
Cline, Wilson Ettason *retired administrative law judge*
Cohan, Christopher *professional sports team executive*
Collen, Morris Frank *physician*
Conway, Nancy Ann *editor*
Crane, Robert Meredith *health care executive*
Crompton, Arnold *minister, educator*
Crowley, Thomas B., Jr. *water transportation executive*
Dailey, Garrett Clark *publisher, lawyer*
DeFazio, Lynette Stevens *dancer, choreographer, educator, chiropractor, author, actress, musician*
Deming, Willis Riley *lawyer*
Diaz, Sharon *education administrator*
Dibble, David Van Vlack *visually impaired educator, lawyer*
Dickinson, Eleanor Creekmore *artist, educator*
Dozier, Flora Grace *civil and human rights activist, entrepreneur*
Dunn, David Cameron *entrepreneur, business executive*
Earle, Sylvia Alice *research biologist, oceanographer*
Eckbo, Garrett *landscape architect, urban designer*
Farley, Thelma *principal*
Farrell, Kenneth Royden *economist*
Fischer, Michael Ludwig *environmental executive*
Fogel, Paul David *lawyer*
Foley, Jack (John Wayne Harold Foley) *poet, writer, editor*
Frey, Viola *sculptor, educator*
Friedman, Gary David *epidemiologist, research facility administrator*
Fries, Lita Linda *school system administrator*
Gardner, Robert Alexander *career counselor, career management consultant*
Gates, Brent Robert *professional baseball player*
Goldstine, Stephen Joseph *college administrator*
Gomes, Wayne Reginald *academic administrator*
Grzanka, Leonard Gerald *writer, consultant*
Haiman, Franklyn Saul *author, communications educator*
Harpster, Robert Eugene *engineering geologist*
Harris, Elihu Mason *mayor*
Haskell, Arthur Jacob *retired steamship company executive*
Helvey, Julius Louis, II *finance company executive*
Heydman, Abby Maria *dean*
Heywood, Robert Gilmour *lawyer*
Hoopes, Lorenzo Neville *former retailing executive*
†Howard, Desmond Kevin *professional football player*
†Howe, Art (Arthur Henry Howe, Jr.) *professional baseball manager*
Jensen, D. Lowell *federal judge, lawyer, government official*
Johnson, Kenneth F. *lawyer*
Johnson, Leonard Morris *pediatric surgeon*
Jukes, Thomas Hughes *biological chemist, educator*
Kaplan, Alvin Irving *lawyer, adjudicator, investigator*
King, Cary Judson, III *chemical engineer, educator, university official*
Kropschot, Richard H. *physicist, science laboratory administrator*
Lawrence, David M. *health facility administrator*
Lee, Jong Hyuk *accountant*
Leslie, Robert Lorne *lawyer*
Liang, Junxiang *aeronautics and astronautics engineer, educator*
Long, William Joseph *software engineer*
Lusby, Grace Irene *infection control nurse practitioner*
Macmeeken, John Peebles *foundation executive, educator*
Matsumoto, George *architect*
McGwire, Mark David *professional baseball player*
McKinney, Judson Thad *broadcast executive*
McLain, Christopher M. *lawyer*
Melchert, James Frederick *artist*
Mikalow, Alfred Alexander, II *deep sea diver, marine surveyor, marine diving consultant*
Miller, Barry *research administrator, psychologist*
Miller, Kirk Edward *lawyer, health foundation executive*
Miller, Thomas Robbins *lawyer, publisher*
Misner, Charlotte Blanche Ruckman *community organization administrator*
Mullin, Chris(topher) Paul *professional basketball player*
Nebelkopf, Ethan *psychologist*
Newsome, Randall Jackson *judge*
Ng, Lawrence Ming-Loy *pediatric cardiologist*
Nicol, Robert Duncan *architect*
O'Connor, Paul Daniel *lawyer*
O'Hare, Marilynn Ryan *artist*
Okamura, Arthur *artist, educator, writer*
Patten, Bebe Harrison *minister, chancellor*
Patton, Warren Andre *non-commissioned officer, journalist*
Potash, Jeremy Warner *public relations executive*
Potash, Stephen Jon *international public relations practitioner*
Power, Dennis Michael *museum director*
Price, (William) Mark *professional basketball player*
Quinby, William Albert *lawyer, mediator, arbitrator*
Rath, Alan T. *sculptor*
Reynolds, Kathleen Diane Foy (K.D.F. Reynolds) *transportation executive*
Rosen, Corey M. *professional association executive*
Sandler, Herbert M. *savings and loan association executive*
Sandler, Marion Osher *savings and loan association executive*
Saunders, Ward Bishop, Jr. *retired aluminum company executive*
Saxton, Ruth Olsen *educator, dean*
Schacht, Henry Mevis *writer, consultant*
Schomer, Howard *retired clergyman, educator, social policy consultant*
Schwyn, Charles Edward *accountant*
Serenbetz, Robert *manufacturing executive*
Sidney, William Wright *retired aerospace company executive*
Silverberg, Robert *author*
Skaff, Andrew Joseph *lawyer, public utilities, energy and transportation executive*
Sullivan, G. Craig *household products executive*
Taylor, William James (Zak Taylor) *lawyer*
Tomlinson-Keasey, Carol Ann *university administrator*
Torrez, Naomi Elizabeth *editor, librarian*
Tsztoo, David Fong *civil engineer*
Tyndall, David Gordon *business educator*
Wallis, Eric G. *lawyer*
Weinmann, Robert Lewis *neurologist*
†White, Mike *professional sports team executive*
Whitsel, Richard Harry *biologist, entomologist*
Wick, William David *lawyer*
Wilken, Claudia *judge*
Wood, James Michael *lawyer*
Wood, Larry (Mary Laird) *journalist, author, university educator, public relations executive, environmental consultant*
Zschau, Marilyn *singer*

**Occidental**
Rumsey, Victor Henry *electrical engineering educator emeritus*

**Oceanside**
Haley, Thomas John *retired pharmacologist*
Hertweck, Alma Louise *sociology and child development educator*
Hertweck, E. Romayne *psychology educator*
Howard, Robert Staples *newspaper publisher*
Humphrey, Phyllis A. *writer*
Lyon, Richard *mayor, retired naval officer*
McIntyre, Louise S. *income tax consultant*
Pena, Maria Geges *academic services administrator*
Roberts, James McGregor *retired professional association executive*
Robinson, William Franklin *retired legal consultant*

**Oildale**
Gallagher, Joseph Francis *marketing executive*

**Ojai**
Weill, Samuel, Jr. *automobile company executive*

**Ontario**
Hawley, Nanci Elizabeth *public relations and communications professional*
Johnson, Maurice Verner, Jr. *agricultural research and development executive*
Kahn, Mario Santamaria *international marketing executive*
Kennedy, Mark Alan *middle and secondary school educator*
Morton, Laurel Anne *elementary education educator*

**Orange**
Achauer, Bruce Michael *plastic surgeon*
Anzel, Sanford Harold *orthopedic surgeon*
Armentrout, Steven Alexander *oncologist*
Barr, Ronald Jeffrey *dermatologist, pathologist*
Batchelor, James Kent *lawyer*
Berk, Jack Edward *physician, educator*
Boynton, Donald Arthur *retired title insurance company executive*
Crumley, Roger Lee *surgeon, educator*
Dana, Edward Runkle *physician, educator*
Doti, James L. *academic administrator*
†Eagan, Robert T. *oncologist*
Fisk, Edward Ray *civil engineer, author, educator*
Floyd, Brett Alden *mortgage banker*
Furnas, David William *plastic surgeon*
Gardin, Julius Markus *cardiologist, educator*
Gerhard, Nancy Lucile Dege *school counselor, educator*
Hamilton, Harry Lemuel, Jr. *academic administrator*
Janssen, Stephen Howard *clergyman*
Kelley, Robert Paul, Jr. *management consultation executive*
Lott, Ira Totz *pediatric neurologist*
MacArthur, Carol Jeanne *pediatric otolaryngology educator*
Martin, Michael Lee *orthodontist*
Mc Farland, Norman Francis *bishop*
McNeil, David James *communications executive, marketing consultant*
Montgomery, Thom Mathew *health program administrator, counselor*
Morgan, Beverly Carver *physician, educator*
Mosier, Harry David, Jr. *physician, educator*
Peralta, Joseph Soriano *financial planner*
Price, Gail J. Goodman *marriage family, and child therapist, deaf and hearing impaired specialist*
Quilligan, Edward James *obstetrician, gynecologist, educator*
Rowen, Marshall *radiologist*
Sawdei, Milan A. *lawyer*
Schlose, William Timothy *health care executive*
Schrodi, Tom *instructional services director*
Skilling, David van Diest *manufacturing executive*
Skinner, Harry Bryant *orthopaedic surgery educator*
Starr, Richard William *retired bank executive*
Thompson, William Benbow, Jr. *obstetrician, gynecologist, educator*
Underwood, Vernon O., Jr. *grocery stores executive*
Vasudevan, Ramaswami *engineering consultant*
Vaziri, Nosratola Dabir *internist, nephrologist, educator*
Wilson, Archie Fredric *medical educator*
Yeager, Myron Dean *English language educator, business writing consultant*
Yu, Jen *medical educator*
Zweifel, Donald Edwin *civic affairs volunteer, consultant*

**Orinda**
Brookes, Valentine *retired lawyer*
Dorn, Virginia Alice *art gallery director*
Epperson, Stella Marie *artist*
Fisher, Robert M. *foundation administrator, university administrator*
Glasser, Charles Edward *university president*
Heftmann, Erich *biochemist*
Hendler, Rosemary Nielsen *business owner, computer artist*
Lesher, Margaret *newspaper publisher, songwriter*
Medak, Walter Hans *lawyer*
Somerset, Harold Richard *retired business executive*
Spraings, Violet Evelyn *psychologist*

**Oroville**
Chapman, Joyce Eileen *law educator, administrator*
Strawn, Susan Heathcote *medical administrator*
Tamori, David Isamu *secondary education educator*

**Oxnard**
Carroll, Carmal Edward *retired librarian, educator, clergyman*
Cathcart, Linda *art historian*
Dimitriadis, Andre C. *health care executive*
Frodsham, Olaf Milton *music educator*
Herlinger, Daniel Robert *hospital administrator*
Hill, Alice Lorraine *history, genealogy and social researcher, educator*
O'Connell, Hugh Mellen, Jr. *retired architect*
O'Hearn, Michael John *lawyer*
Parriott, James Deforis *retired oil company executive, consultant*
Steele, Julius Raynard *special education educator*
Walker, Lorenzo Giles *surgeon, educator*

**Pacific Grove**
Adams, Margaret Bernice *retired museum official*
Davis, Robert Edward *retired communication educator*
Elinson, Henry David *artist, language educator*
Epel, David *biologist, educator*
Fleischman, Paul *children's author*
O'Shaughnessy, Ellen Cassels *writer*
Voss, Ali Annelies *history of art educator, antique dealer*

**Pacific Palisades**
Abrams, Richard Lee *physicist*
Albert, Eddie (Edward Albert Heimberger) *actor*
Bernheimer, Martin *music critic*
Brown, Robert N. *film editor*
Burum, Stephen H. *cinematographer*
Cale, Charles Griffin *lawyer, investor*
Chesney, Lee Roy, Jr. *artist*
Claes, Daniel John *physician*
Csendes, Ernest *chemist, corporate and financial executive*
Diehl, Richard Kurth *retail business consultant*
Dignam, Robert Joseph *retired orthopaedic surgeon*
Fink, Robert Morgan *biological chemistry educator*
Flattery, Thomas Long *lawyer, legal administrator*
Francis-Bruce, Richard *film editor*
Garwood, Victor Paul *retired speech communication educator*
Georges, Robert Augustus *emeritus professor, researcher, writer*
Gosnell, Raja *film editor*
Gregor, Eduard *laser physicist, consultant*
Herman, Elvin E. *retired consulting electronic engineer*
Hirsch, Paul Frederick *film editor*
Klein, Joseph Mark *retired mining company executive*
Kovacs, Laszlo *cinematographer*
Lewis, Frank Harlan *botanist, educator*
Longaker, Richard Pancoast *political science educator emeritus*
Malley, William *production designer*
Middleton, James Arthur *oil and gas company executive*
Milsome, Douglas *cinematographer*
Mulryan, Henry Trist *mineral company executive, consultant*
Nash, Gary Baring *historian, educator*
Nothmann, Rudolf S. *legal researcher*
Primes, Robert *cinematographer*
Rothenberg, Leslie Steven *lawyer, ethicist*
Schwartz, Murray Louis *lawyer, educator, academic administrator*
Sevilla, Stanley *lawyer*
Smith, Sinjin *beach volleyball player*
Spinotti, Dante *cinematographer*
Verrone, Patric Miller *lawyer, writer*
Washington, Dennis *production designer*
Zamparelli, Elsa Maria Johanna Elisabeth *costume designer, art director*
Zivelonghi, Kurt Daniel *artist, painter*

**Palm Desert**
Brown, James Briggs *retired business forms company executive*
Chambers, Milton Warren *architect*
Hartman, Ashley Powell *publishing executive, journalist, educator*
Humphrey, Charles Edward, Jr. *lawyer*
Hunt, Barnabas John *priest, religious order administrator*
Krallinger, Joseph Charles *entrepreneur, business advisor, author*
McKissock, Paul Kendrick *plastic surgeon*
Moroles, Jesus Bautista *sculptor*
Ponder, Catherine *clergywoman*
Reinhardt, Benjamin Max *lawyer, arbitrator, mediator*
Sausman, Karen *zoological park administrator*
Singer, Gerald Michael *lawyer, educator, author, arbitrator and mediator*
Spirtos, Nicholas George *lawyer, financial company executive*
Wiedle, Gary Eugene *real estate management company executive*

**Palm Springs**
Aikens, Donald Thomas *educational administrator, consultant*
Arnold, Stanley Norman *manufacturing consultant*
Borders, Karen Lynn *police officer*
Boyajian, Timothy Edward *public health officer, educator, consultant*
Browning, Norma Lee (Mrs. Russell Joyner Ogg) *journalist*
Capps, Anthony Thomas (Capozzolo Capps) *international public relations executive*
Frey, Albert *architect*
Fromm, Erwin Frederick *retired insurance company executive, health facility executive*
Gill, Jo Anne Martha *middle school educator*
Hartman, Rosemary Jane *special education educator*
Hearst, Rosalie *philanthropist, foundation executive*
Jones, Milton Wakefield *publisher*
Jumonville, Felix Joseph, Jr. *physical education educator, realtor*
Kimberling, John Farrell *retired lawyer*
Lees, Benjamin *composer*
Minahan, John English *author*
Parrish, Jeanne Elaine *former mayor, city councilwoman, former health services administrator, nurse*
Weil, Max Harry *physician, medical educator, medical scientist*

**Palmdale**
Anderson, R(obert) Gregg *real estate company executive*
Bowen, Jimmie Carl *vocational education educator*
Kinzell, La Moyne B. *school health services administrator, educator*
Moule, William Nelson *electrical engineer*
Storsteen, Linda Lee *librarian*
Weiss, Richard Ronald *rocket propulsion technology executive*

**Palo Alto**
Adams, Marcia Howe *lawyer*
Adamson, Geoffrey David *reproductive endocrinologist, surgeon*
Allen, Louis Alexander *management consultant*
Amylon, Michael David *physician, educator*
Andersen, Torben Brender *optical researcher, astronomer, software engineer*
Antuna-Munoz, Mary Josephine *elementary education educator*
Attig, John Clare *secondary education educator, consultant*
Balzhiser, Richard Earl *research and development company executive*
Bell, Richard G. *lawyer*
Beretta, Giordano Bruno *computer scientist, researcher*
Bhatt, Kiran *physician, educator*
Bienenstock, Arthur Irwin *physicist, educator*
Blaschke, Terrence Francis *medicine and molecular pharmacology educator*
Bohrnstedt, George William *educational researcher*
Bradley, Donald Edward *lawyer*
Breiner, Sheldon *geophysics educator, business executive*
Briggs, Winslow Russell *plant biologist, educator*
Brigham, Samuel Townsend Jack, III *lawyer*
Britton, M(elvin) C(reed), Jr. *physician, rheumatologist*
Brown, David Randolph *electrical engineer*
Brown, Robert McAfee *minister, religion educator*
Burke, Edmund Charles *retired aerospace company executive*
Buss, Claude Albert *history educator*
Case, Robbie *education educator, author*
Charlton, Randolph Seville *psychiatrist, educator*
Chase, Robert Arthur *surgeon, educator*
Chen, Stephen Shi-hua *pathologist, biochemist*
Chow, Winston *engineering research executive*
Cirigliano, John J(oseph) *investment company executive*
Climan, Richard Elliot *lawyer*
Cohen, Karl Paley *nuclear energy consultant*
Culler, Floyd LeRoy, Jr. *chemical engineer*
Cunningham, Andrea Lee *public relations executive*
Curry, William Sims *procurement executive*
Cutler, Leonard Samuel *physicist*
Dallin, Alexander *history and political science educator*
Dance, Maurice Eugene *college administrator*
Date, Elaine Satomi *physician*
Datlowe, Dayton Wood *space scientist, physicist*
DeLustro, Frank Anthony *biomedical company executive, research immunologist*
Dement, William Charles *sleep researcher, medical educator*
Desai, Karvin Hirendra *pediatrician*
De Smedt, Philippe *research scientist, technologist*
Donaldson, Sarah Susan *radiologist*
Early, James Michael *electronics research consultant*
Eggers, Alfred John, Jr. *research corporation executive*
Eliassen, Rolf *environmental engineer, emeritus educator*
Eng, Lawrence Fook *biochemistry educator, neurochemist*
Ernst, Wallace Gary *geology educator*
Eulau, Heinz *political scientist, educator*
Farber, Eugene Mark *psoriasis research institute administrator*
Farquhar, John William *physician, educator*
Flanagan, Robert Joseph *economics educator*
Flory, Curt A. *research physicist*
Fries, James Franklin *internal medicine educator*
Furbush, David Malcolm *lawyer*
Garland, Harry Thomas *research administrator*
Gibbons, James Franklin *university dean, electrical engineering educator*
Gilbert, David *computer company executive*
Goff, Harry Russell *retired manufacturing company executive*
Goldstein, Avram *pharmacology educator*
Goldstein, Mary Kane *physician*
Gordon, Marc Stewart *pharmacist, scientist*
Gouraud, Jackson S. *energy company executive*
Haisch, Bernhard Michael *astronomer*
Halperin, Robert Milton *retired electrical machinery company executive*
Hammett, Benjamin Cowles *psychologist*
Harris, Edward D., Jr. *physician*
Haslam, Robert Thomas, III *lawyer*
Hays, Marguerite Thompson *physician*
Hecht, Lee Martin *software company executive*
Herrick, Tracy Grant *fiduciary*
Hewlett, William (Redington) *manufacturing company executive, electrical engineer*
Hinckley, Robert Craig *lawyer*
Hodge, Philip Gibson, Jr. *mechanical and aerospace engineering educator*
Holman, Halsted Reid *medical educator*
Holmes, Richard Brooks *mathematical physicist*

Hornak, Thomas electronics company executive
Houpt, James Edward lawyer
Ivester, (Richard) Gavin industrial designer
Ivy, Benjamin Franklin, III financial and real estate investment advisor
Jadvar, Hossein physician, biomedical engineer
Jamison, Rex Lindsay medical educator
Jamplis, Robert Warren surgeon, medical foundation executive
Johnson, Conor Deane mechanical engineer
Johnson, Noble Marshall research scientist
Kaufman, Michael David management executive
Kennedy, W(ilbert) Keith, Jr. electronics company executive
Kincaid, Judith Wells electronics company executive
Kino, Gordon Stanley electrical engineering educator
Klotsche, John Chester lawyer
Knoles, George Harmon history educator
Kohn, Jean Gatewood medical facility administrator, physician
Kundu, Smriti Kana biomedical scientist
Kung, Frank F. C. medical products executive
Lamport, Leslie B. computer scientist
Lane, Alfred Thomas medical educator
Lane, William Kenneth physician
Lau, John Hon Shing company executive
Lawrence-Forrest, Lori Louise restaurateur
Lender, Adam electrical engineer
Leong, Helen Vanessa systems programmer
Lindzey, Gardner psychologist, educator
Linn, Gary Dean golf course architect
Linna, Timo Juhani immunologist, researcher, educator
Litt, Iris Figarsky pediatrics educator
Loew, Gilda Harris research biophysicist, biology research executive
Loewenstein, Walter Bernard nuclear power technologist
Loveless, Edward Eugene education educator, musician
Mahmood, Aamer computer system architect
Maiden, Eva Wenkart psychotherapist, school psychologist
Mansour, Tag Eldin pharmacologist, educator
Mario, Ernest pharmaceutical company executive
Massey, Henry P., Jr. lawyer
Mendelson, Alan Charles lawyer
Merrin, Seymour computer marketing company executive
Michie, Sara H. pathologist, educator
Moffitt, Donald Eugene transportation company executive
Mommsen, Katharina retired German language and literature educator
Monroy, Gladys H. lawyer
Moretti, August Joseph lawyer
Morris, Arlene Myers marketing professional
Nau, Charles John lawyer
Neil, Gary Lawrence pharmaceutical company research executive, biochemical pharmacologist
Nicholson, Bradley James lawyer
Nordlund, Donald Craig corporate lawyer
Nycum, Susan Hubbell lawyer
Panofsky, Wolfgang Kurt Hermann physicist, educator
Partain, Larry Dean solar research engineer
Pasahow, Lynn H(arold) lawyer
Patterson, Robert Edward lawyer
Pauling, Linus Carl, Jr. health science administrator
Phair, Joseph Baschon lawyer
Platt, Lewis Emmett electronics company executive
Polan, Mary Lake obstetrics and gynecology educator
†Polese, Kim software company executive
Quraishi, Marghoob A. management consultant
Rinsky, Arthur C. lawyer
Roberts, Charles S. software engineer
Robinson, Thomas Nathaniel pediatrician, educator, researcher
Saksen, Louis Carl hospital administrator, architect
Saldich, Robert Joseph electronics company executive
Salvatierra, Oscar, Jr. physician
Sawyer, Wilbur Henderson pharmacologist, educator
Saxena, Arjun Nath physicist
Schreiber, Everett Charles, Jr. chemist, educator
Schrier, Stanley Leonard physician, educator
Schurman, David Jay orthopedic surgeon, educator
Scitovsky, Anne Aickelin economist
Shortliffe, Edward Hance internist, medical informatics educator
Shuer, Lawrence Mendel neurosurgery educator
Skeff, Kelley Michael health facility administrator
Small, Jonathan Andrew lawyer
Smith, Glenn A. lawyer
Spinrad, Robert Joseph computer scientist
Staprans, Armand electronics executive
Stringer, John materials scientist
Strober, Samuel immunologist, educator
Szczerba, Victor Bogdan electrical engineer, sales engineer
Taimuty, Samuel Isaac physicist
Taylor, John Joseph nuclear engineer
Theeuwes, Felix physical chemist
Thompson, David Alfred industrial engineer
Tsien, Richard Winyu biology educator
Tune, Bruce Malcolm pediatrics educator, renal toxicologist
Urquhart, John medical researcher, educator
Van Atta, David Murray lawyer
Walker, Ann Yvonne lawyer
Walker, Carolyn Peyton English language educator
Watkins, Dean Allen electronics executive, educator
Weakland, Anna Wu artist, art educator
Weiser, Mark David computer scientist, researcher
Wheeler, Raymond Louis lawyer
Willrich, Mason utilities executive, consultant
Wilson, Frank Henry electrical engineer
Wong, Nancy L. dermatologist
Wong, Patrick Seck Lai chemical engineer
Wunsch, Kathryn Sutherland lawyer
Zuckerkandl, Emile molecular evolutionary biologist, scientific institute executive

## Palo Cedro
Haggard, Merle Ronald songwriter, recording artist

## Palomar Mountain
Day, Richard Somers author, editorial consultant, video producer

## Palos Verdes Estates
Basnight, Arvin Odell public administrator, aviation consultant
Lazzaro, Anthony Derek university administrator
Mackenbach, Frederick W. welding products manufacturing company executive
Smith, Stephen Randolph aerospace executive

## Palos Verdes Peninsula
Christie, Hans Frederick retired utility company subsidiaries executive, consultant
Copeland, Phillips Jerome former university administrator, former air force officer
Giles, Allen pianist, composer, music educator
Grant, Robert Ulysses retired manufacturing company executive
Haynes, Moses Alfred physician
King, Nancy communications educator
Leone, William Charles retired manufacturing executive
Lima, Luis Eduardo tenor
Marlett, De Otis Loring retired management consultant
Mennis, Edmund Addi investment management consultant
Miller, Francie Loraditch college counselor
Mirels, Harold aerospace engineer
†Pfund, Edward Theodore, Jr. electronics company executive
Raue, Jorg Emil electrical engineer
Rechtin, Eberhardt retired aerospace executive, retired educator
Reynolds, Harry Lincoln physicist
Ryker, Charles Edwin former aerospace company executive
Slayden, James Bragdon retired department store executive
Spinks, John Lee retired engineering executive
Thomas, Claudewell Sidney psychiatry educator
Thomas, Pearl Elizabeth English educator
Waaland, Irving Theodore retired aerospace design executive
Weiss, Herbert Klemm retired aeronautical engineer
Wilson, Theodore Henry retired electronics company executive, aerospace engineer
Yeomans, Russell Allen lawyer, translator

## Panorama City
Bass, Harold Neal pediatrician, medical geneticist
Henrickson, Mark social worker, priest

## Paradise
Fulton, Len publisher
Learned, Vincent Roy electrical engineer , educator

## Paramount
Hall, Howard Harry lawyer

## Pasadena
Adler, Fred Peter electronics company executive
Ahrens, Thomas J. geophysicist
Albee, Arden Leroy geologist, educator
Almore-Randle, Allie Louise special education educator
Alschuler, Frederick Harold lawyer
Anderson, Don Lynn geophysicist, educator
Anderson, John David astronomer, researcher
Anson, Fred Colvig chemistry educator
Arnott, Robert Douglas investment company executive
Axelson, Charles Frederic retired accounting educator
Babcock, Horace W. astronomer
Baines, Kevin Hays planetary scientist, astronomer
Bakaly, Charles George, Jr. lawyer, mediator
Baldeschwieler, John Dickson chemist, educator
Barnes, Charles Andrew physicist, educator
Baum, Dwight Crouse investment banking executive
Bean, Maurice Darrow retired diplomat
Beaudet, Robert Arthur chemistry educator
Beer, Reinhard atmospheric scientist
Bejczy, Antal Károly research scientist, research facility administrator
Bercaw, John Edward chemistry educator, consultant
Bergholz, Richard Cady political writer
Blandford, Roger David astronomy educator
Boehm, Felix Hans physicist, educator
Boochever, Robert federal judge
Boulos, Paul Fares civil and environmental engineer
Breckinridge, James Bernard optical science engineer
Bridges, William Bruce electrical engineer, researcher, educator
Buck, Anne Marie library director, consultant
Butler, Octavia Estelle free-lance writer
Cahill, Richard Frederick lawyer
Caillouette, James Clyde physician
Caine, Stephen Howard data processing executive
Caldwell, William Mackay, III business executive
Calleton, Theodore Edward lawyer
Carroll, William Jerome civil engineer
Cass, Glen Rowan environmental engineer
Chahine, Moustafa Toufic atmospheric scientist
Chamberlain, Willard Thomas retired metals company executive
Chan, Sunney Ignatius chemist
Cohen, Marshall Harris astronomer, educator
Cole, Roberta Carley nursing educator
Crowley, John Crane real estate developer
Culick, Fred Ellsworth Clow physics and engineering educator
Dallas, Saterios (Sam ) aerospace engineer, researcher, consultant
D'Angelo, Robert William lawyer
Davis, Lance Edwin economics educator
Dervan, Peter Brendan chemistry educator
Diehl, Digby Robert journalist
Dougherty, Dennis A. chemistry educator
Doyle, John C. lawyer
Dressler, Alan Michael astronomer
Drutchas, Gerrick Gilbert investigator
Duxbury, Thomas Carl planetary scientist
Elliot, David Clephan historian, educator
Epstein, Bruce Howard lawyer, real estate broker
Epstein, Samuel geologist, educator
Everhart, Thomas Eugene academic administrator, engineering educator
Farr, Donald Eugene engineering scientist
Fay, Peter Ward history educator
Fernandez, Ferdinand Francis federal judge
Finnell, Michael Hartman corporate executive
Flagan, Richard Charles chemical engineering educator
Franklin, Joel Nicholas mathematician, educator
Frautschi, Steven Clark physicist, educator
Freise, Earl Jerome university administrator, materials engineering educator
Fu, Lee-Lueng oceanographer
Gabel, Katherine academic administrator
Gavalas, George R. chemical engineering educator
Gillam, Max Lee lawyer
Gilman, Richard Carleton retired college president
Goei, Bernard Thwan-Poo (Bert Goei) architectural and engineering firm executive
Golombek, Matthew Philip structural and planetary geologist
Goodstein, David Louis physics educator
Goodwin, Alfred Theodore federal judge
Gould, Roy Walter engineering educator
Gray, Harry Barkus chemistry educator
Griesche, Robert Price hospital purchasing executive
Grubbs, Robert Howard chemistry educator
Gurnis, Michael Christopher geological sciences educator
Haight, James Theron lawyer, corporate executive
Hale, Charles Russell lawyer
Hall, Cynthia Holcomb federal judge
Harmsen, Tyrus George librarian
Harvey, Joseph Paul, Jr. orthopedist, educator
Hatheway, Alson Earle mechanical engineer
Hecht, Harold Michael retail executive
Heindl, Clifford Joseph physicist
Helsper, James T. surgical oncologist, researcher, educator
Hemann, Raymond Glenn research company executive
Hilbert, Robert S(aul) optical engineer
Hirsch, Robert W. engineering and construction company executive
Hitlin, David George physicist, educator
Horner, Althea Jane psychologist
Hornung, Hans Georg aeronautical engineering educator, science facility administrator
Housner, George William civil engineering educator, consultant
Howe, Graham Lloyd photographer, curator
Hudson, Donald Ellis engineering educator
Hunt, Gordon lawyer
Ingersoll, Andrew Perry planetary science educator
Jacobs, Joseph John engineering company executive
Jastrow, Robert physicist
Jenkins, Royal Gregory manufacturing executive
Jennings, Paul Christian civil engineering educator, academic administrator
Kanamori, Hiroo geophysics educator
Kaplan, Gary executive recruiter
Kavanagh, Ralph William physics educator
Kevles, Daniel Jerome history educator, writer
Knauss, Wolfgang Gustav engineering educator
Knowles, James Kenyon applied mechanics educator
Koch, Albin Cooper lawyer
Koenig, Marie Harriet King public relations director, fund raising executive
Koonin, Steven Elliot physicist, professor
Kousser, J(oseph) Morgan history educator
Kozinski, Alex federal judge
Lake, Kevin Bruce medical association administrator
Lawler, Alice Bonzi (Mrs. Oscar T. Lawler) retired college administrator, civic worker
Ledyard, John Odell economics educator, consultant
Leonard, Nelson Jordan chemistry educator
Levy, David Steven college administrator
Lewis, Edward B. biology educator
Lewis, Nathan Saul chemistry educator
Liepmann, Hans Wolfgang physicist, educator
List, Ericson John environmental engineering science educator, engineering consultant
Losh, Samuel Johnston engineering administrator
Luxemburg, Wilhelmus Anthonius Josephus mathematics educator
Mandel, Oscar literature educator, writer
Marcus, Rudolph Arthur chemist, educator
Marlen, James S. chemical-plastics-building materials manufacturing company executive
Marsden, Jerrold Eldon mathematician, educator, engineer
Martin, Craig Lee engineering company executive
Mathies, Allen Wray, Jr. physician, hospital administrator
Mc Carthy, Frank Martin oral surgeon, surgical sciences educator
McClellan, Bennett Earl producer
Mc Duffie, Malcolm oil company executive
Mc Koy, Basil Vincent Charles theoretical chemist, educator
McLaughlin, William Irving aerospace engineer
†Medina-Puerta, Antonio scientist
Mercereau, James Edgar physicist, educator
Messenger, Ron J. health facility administrator
Meye, Robert Paul retired seminary administrator, writer
Meyerowitz, Elliot Martin biologist, educator
Miller, Charles Daly self-adhesive materials company executive
Mosher, Sally Ekenberg lawyer
Mueth, Joseph Edward lawyer
Munger, Edwin Stanton political geography educator
Myers, R(alph) Chandler lawyer
Nackel, John George health care consulting director
Neal, Philip Mark diversified manufacturing executive
Nelson, Dorothy Wright (Mrs. James F. Nelson) federal judge
Neugebauer, Marcia physicist, administrator
Newman, Joyce Kligerman sculptor
North, Wheeler James marine ecologist, educator
Oemler, Augustus, Jr. astronomy educator
Oliver, Robert Warner economics educator
Opel, William medical research administrator
Otoshi, Tom Yasuo electrical engineer, consultant
Ott, George William, Jr. management consulting executive
Owen, Ray David biology educator
Parker, Garry Otis mission executive, missiologist
Pashgian, Margaret Helen artist
Patterson, Mark Jerome computer software designer
Patton, Richard Weston retired mortgage company executive
Pianko, Theodore A. lawyer
Plott, Charles R. economics educator
Politzer, Hugh David physicist, educator
Poon, Peter Tin-Yau engineer, physicist
Presecan, Nicholas Lee environmental and civil engineer, consultant
Revel, Jean-Paul biology educator
Roberts, John D. chemist, educator
Rymer, Pamela Ann federal judge
Sabersky, Rolf Heinrich mechanical engineer
Saffman, Philip G. mathematician
Sano, Roy I. bishop
Sargent, Wallace Leslie William astronomer, educator
Schander, Mary Lea police official
Schlinger, Warren Gleason retired chemical engineer
Schmidt, Maarten astronomy educator
Schober, Robert Charles electrical engineer
Scudder, Thayer anthropologist, educator
Searle, Eleanor Millard history educator
Seinfeld, John Hersh chemical engineering educator
Sekanina, Zdenek astronomer
Sharp, Robert Phillip geology educator, researcher
Sharp, Sharon Lee gerontology nurse
Simon, Marvin Kenneth electrical engineer, consultant
Smith, Howard Russell manufacturing company executive
Spector, Phil record company executive
Staehle, Robert L. foundation executive
Stevenson, David John planetary scientist, educator
Stewart, Homer Joseph engineering educator
Stolper, Edward Manin secondary education educator
Stone, Edward Carroll physicist, educator
Sudarsky, Jerry M. industrialist
Tanner, Dee Boshard retired lawyer
Tashima, Atsushi Wallace federal judge
Thomas, Joseph Fleshman architect
Todd, John mathematician, educator
Tollenaere, Lawrence Robert retired industrial products company executive
Tombrello, Thomas Anthony, Jr. physics educator, consultant
Torres, Ralph Chon minister
Trussell, R(obert) Rhodes environmental engineer
Ulrich, Peter Henry banker
Van Amringe, John Howard retired oil industry executive, geologist
Vanoni, Vito August hydraulic engineer
Vaughn, John Vernon banker, industrialist
Vogt, Rochus Eugen physicist, educator
Wasserburg, Gerald Joseph geology and geophysics educator
Watkins, John Francis management consultant
Wayland, J(ames) Harold biomedical scientist, educator
Weisbin, Charles Richard nuclear engineer
Westphal, James Adolph planetary science educator
Whitham, Gerald Beresford mathematics educator
Wood, Lincoln Jackson aerospace engineer
Wood, Nathaniel Fay editor, writer, public relations consultant
Wyatt, Joseph Lucian, Jr. lawyer, author
Wyllie, Peter John geologist, educator
Yamarone, Charles Anthony, Jr. aerospace engineer, consultant
Yariv, Amnon electrical engineering educator, scientist
Yau, Kevin Kam-ching astronomer
Yeager, Caroline Hale radiologist, consultant
Yeh, Paul Pao electrical and electronics engineer, educator
Yeomans, Donald Keith astronomer
Yohalem, Harry Morton lawyer
Zachariasen, Fredrik physics educator
Zammitt, Norman artist
Zirin, Harold astronomer, educator
Zuetel, Kenneth Roy, Jr. lawyer

## Paso Robles
Boxer, Jerome Harvey computer and management consultant, vintner, accountant
Brown, Benjamin Andrew journalist
Knecht, James Herbert lawyer
Rocha, Marilyn Eva clinical psychologist
Smith, Helen Elizabeth retired military officer

## Pauma Valley
Dooley, George Elijah health facility administrator
Magee, Dennis cultural organization administrator

## Pebble Beach
Burkett, William Andrew banker
Cameron, JoAnna actress, director
Carns, Michael Patrick Chamberlain air force officer
Crossley, Randolph Allin retired corporate executive
Fergusson, Robert George retired army officer
Gianelli, William Reynolds foundation administrator, civil engineering consultant, former federal agency commissioner
Harvie, J. Jason administrative aide, private secretary
Keene, Clifford Henry medical administrator
Mauz, Henry Herrward, Jr. retired naval officer
Maxeiner, Clarence William lawyer, construction company executive
Mortensen, Gordon Louis artist, printmaker
Rivette, Gerard Bertram manufacturing company executive
Rossing, Catherine Barrett Schwab dental hygienist
Sullivan, James Francis university administrator

## Penn Valley
Throner, Guy Charles, Jr. engineering executive, scientist, engineer, inventor, consultant

## Perris
Gonzales, Richard Daniel manufacturing executive

## Petaluma
Belmares, Hector chemist
Carr, Les psychologist, educator
Cuggino, Michael Joseph financial executive
Eck, Robert Edwin physicist
Frederickson, Arman Frederick minerals company executive
Hill, Debora Elizabeth author, journalist, screenwriter
McChesney, Robert Pearson artist
O'Hare, Sandra Fernandez elementary education educator, adult education educator
Pronzini, Bill John (William Pronzini) author
Reichek, Jesse artist
Samuel, George healthcare information company executive

## Phillips Ranch
Koestel, Mark Alfred geologist, photographer, consultant

## Piedmont
Cole, Peter William financial executive
Cuttle, Tracy Donald physician, former naval officer
Hoover, Robert Cleary retired bank executive
Hughes, James Paul physician
Hurley, Morris Elmer, Jr. management consultant
McCormick, Timothy Brian Beer lawyer
Montgomery, Theodore Ashton physician
Putter, Irving French language educator
Sharpton, Thomas physician
Yep, Wallen Lai import/export company executive, author

## Pine Valley
Collins, Frank Charles, Jr. industrial and service quality specialist

### Pinole
Gerbracht, Robert Thomas (Bob Gerbracht) *painter, educator*
Grogan, Stanley Joseph *educational consultant*
Harvey, Elinor B. *child psychiatrist*
Naughton, James Lee *internist*

### Pismo Beach
Saveker, David Richard *naval and marine architectural engineering executive*

### Pittsburg
Schmalenberger, Jerry Lew *pastor, seminary educator*

### Placentia
Frank, Judith Ann (Jann Frank) *entrepreneur, small business owner*
Galvez, William *artist*
Gobar, Alfred Julian *economic consultant, educator*
Linnan, Judith Ann *psychologist*

### Placerville
Bonser, Quentin *retired surgeon*
Craib, Kenneth Bryden *resource development executive, physicist, economist*
Morrin, Thomas Harvey *engineering research company executive*

### Playa Del Rey
Blomquist, Carl Arthur *medical and trust company executive, insurance executive*
Hite, Janet Sue *elementary education educator*
Tai, Frank *aerospace engineering consultant*
Weir, Alexander, Jr. *utility consultant, inventor*

### Pleasant Hill
Ashby, Denise Stewart *speech educator, communication consultant*
Gomez, Edward Casimiro *physician, educator*
Hassid, Sami *architect, educator*
Marshall, Carol Sydney *labor market analyst, employment counselor*
Newkirk, Raymond Leslie *management consultant*
Stevenson, James D(onald), Jr. *psychologist, counselor*
Weiss, Lionel Edward *geology educator*

### Pleasanton
Aladeen, Lary Joe *secondary school educator*
Anderson-Imbert, Enrique *retired Hispanic literature educator, author*
Brooks, Stephen Volume *foundation executive*
Burd, Steve *food service executive*
Choy, Clement Kin-Man *research scientist*
Eby, Frank Shilling *retired research scientist*
Fehlberg, Robert Erick *architect*
Howard, Karen Lynn *marketing executive*
Murthy, Srinivasa K. *engineering corporation executive*
Petersen, Ann Nevin *computer systems administrator, consultant*
Ruppert, Paul Richard *telecommunications executive*
Shen, Mason Ming-Sun *medical center administrator*
Stager, Donald K. *construction company executive*
Staley, John Fredric *lawyer*
Stout-Pierce, Susan *clinical specialist*
Weiss, Robert Stephen *medical manufacturing and services company financial executive*
Whisnand, Rex James *housing association executive*

### Plymouth
Andreason, John Christian *lawyer*

### Pollock Pines
Johnson, Stanford Leland *marketing educator*

### Pomona
Amaya, Patricia Mojarro *elementary education educator*
Armstrong, Bruce Irving *mechanical engineer*
Bernau, Simon John *mathematics educator*
Bidlack, Wayne Ross *nutritional biochemist, toxicologist, food scienti*
Bowman, Dean Orlando *economist, educator*
Burrill, Melinda Jane *animal science educator*
Coombs, Walter Paul *retired educator*
Demery, Dorothy Jean *secondary school educator*
Eaves, Ronald Weldon *university administrator*
Keating, Eugene Kneeland *animal scientist, educator*
Lawrence, William, Jr. *elementary education educator*
Lyle, John Tillman *landscape architecture educator*
Markham, Reed B. *education educator, consultant*
Patten, Thomas Henry, Jr. *management, human resources educator*
Shieh, John Ting-chung *economics educator*
Suzuki, Bob H. *university president*
†Swartz, James Eugene *international business educator, army officer*
Teague, Lavette Cox, Jr. *systems educator, consultant*
Thompson, Earlene *civic volunteer*

### Porterville
Hayes, Shirley Ann *special education educator*

### Portola Valley
Berghold, Joseph Philip *marketing executive*
Cooper, John Joseph *lawyer*
Creevy, Donald Charles *obstetrician-gynecologist*
Fogarty, Thomas James *surgery educator*
Graham, William James *packaging company executive*
Kuo, Franklin F. *computer scientist, electrical engineer*
Millard, Stephens Fillmore *electronics company executive*
Moses, Franklin Maxwell *retired chemical marketing executive*
Oscarson, Kathleen Dale *writing assessment coordinator, educator*
Purl, O. Thomas *retired electronics company executive*
Ward, Robert Edward *retired political science educator and university administrator*

### Poway
Aschenbrenner, Frank Aloysious *former diversified manufacturing company executive*
Brose, Cathy *principal*
Dollen, Charles Joseph *clergyman, writer*
Remer, Vernon Ralph *travel consultant*
Shippey, Lyn *reading center director*

### Quartz Hill
McKain, Mary Margaret *musician*

### Ramona
Bennett, James Chester *computer consultant, real estate developer*
Cesinger, Joan *author*
Decker, George John *litigation photographer, videographer, journalist*
Hoffman, Wayne Melvin *retired airline official*
Jordan, David Francis, Jr. *retired judge*
Vaughn, Robert Lockard *aerospace and astronautics company executive*

### Rancho Cordova
Alenius, John Todd *insurance executive*
Crowley, Daniel D. *health insurance executive*
Ling, Robert Malcolm *banker, publishing executive*

### Rancho Cucamonga
Bucks, Charles Alan *airline industry consultant, former executive*
Horton, Michael L. *mortgage company executive, publishing executive*

### Rancho Mirage
Cone, Lawrence Arthur *research medicine educator*
Copperman, William H. *value engineer, consultant*
Deiter, Newton Elliott *clinical psychologist*
Ford, Betty Bloomer (Elizabeth Ford) *health facility executive, wife of former President of United States*
Ford, Gerald Rudolph, Jr. *former President of United States*
Gardner, Donald LaVere *development company executive*
Greenbaum, James Richard *liquor distributing company executive, real estate developer*
Hegarty, William Kevin *medical center executive*
Lacey, Beatrice Cates *psychophysiologist*
Lacey, John Irving *psychologist, physiologist, educator*
Overby, Monessa Mary *clinical supervisor, counselor*
Reuben, Don Harold *lawyer*
Rotman, Morris Bernard *public relations consultant*
Stenhouse, Everett Ray *clergy administrator*

### Rancho Palos Verdes
Fischer, Robert Blanchard *university administrator, researcher*
Keenan, Retha Ellen Vornholt *retired nursing educator*
McFadden, Thomas *academic administrator*
Rubenstein, Leonard Samuel *communications executive, ceramist, painter, sculptor, photographer*
Savage, Terry Richard *information systems executive*

### Rancho Santa Fe
Affeldt, John Ellsworth *physician*
Baker, Charles Lynn *management consultant*
Best, Jacob Hilmer (Jerry), Jr. *hotel chain executive*
Capen, Richard Goodwin, Jr. *ambassador*
Creutz, Edward Chester *physicist, museum consultant*
DeMarco, Ralph John *real estate developer*
Gruenwald, George Henry *new products development management consultant*
Gunness, Robert Charles *chemical engineer*
Jordan, Charles Morrell *retired automotive designer*
Matthews, Leonard Sarver *advertising executive, consultant*
Peterson, Nad A. *lawyer, retired corporate executive*
Rible, Morton *financial services and manufacturing executive*
Rockoff, S. David *radiologist, physician, educator*
Ruiz, Ramon Eduardo *history educator*
Schirra, Walter Marty, Jr. *business consultant, former astronaut*
Simon, William Leonard *film and television writer and producer, author*
Trout, Monroe Eugene *hospital systems executive*

### Redding
Becker, Stephen Arnold *museum executive*
Emmerson, Red *sawmill owner*
Nicholas, David Robert *minister, college president*
Ragland, Carroll Ann *law educator, judicial officer*
Streiff, Arlyne Bastunas *business owner, educator*
Wilson, David Lee *clinical psychologist*

### Redlands
Appleton, James Robert *university president, educator*
Barnes, A. Keith *management educator*
Burgess, Larry Eugene *library director, history educator*
Clopine, Gordon Alan *consulting geologist, educator, business and facilities manager*
Ely, Northcutt *lawyer*
Flores, John A. *internist*
Hanson, Gerald Warner *retired county official*
Hirsch, Charles Bronislaw *retired religion educator and administrator*
Proffitt, Lawrence Alan *secondary school educator*
Richardson, A(rthur) Leslie *former medical group consultant*
Skomal, Edward Nelson *aerospace company executive, consultant*
Skoog, William Arthur *retired oncologist*
Treece, Joseph Charles *insurance broker*

### Redondo Beach
Ball, William Paul *physicist, engineer*
Battles, Roxy Edith *novelist, consultant, educator*
Buchta, Edmund *engineering executive*
Burris, Harrison Robert *computer and software developer*
Cardin, Suzette *nurse manager*
Chazen, Melvin Leonard *chemical engineer*
Cohen, Clarence Budd *aerospace engineer*
Dockstader, Jack Lee *electronics executive*
Hughes, James Arthur *electrical engineer*
Kagiwada, Reynold Shigeru *advanced technology manager*
Krause, Kurth Werner *aerospace executive*
Mahrenholtz, Dayla Dianne *elementary school principal*
Marsee, Stuart (Earl) *educational consultant, retired*
McWilliams, Margaret Ann *home economics educator, author*
Naples, Caesar Joseph *public policy educator, lawyer, consultant*
Roth, Thomas J. *physicist*
Sackheim, Robert Lewis *aerospace engineer, educator*
Shellhorn, Ruth Patricia *landscape architect*
Wagemaker, David Isaac *human resources development executive*

### Redwood City
Bertram, Jack Renard *information systems company executive*
Eaton, Mark Rayner *financial executive*
Elkus, Richard J. *finance and industrial company executive*
Ellison, Lawrence J. *computer software company executive*
Foley, Patrick *air courier company executive*
Gagarin, Dennis Paul *advertising agency executive*
Harrington, Walter Howard, Jr. *judge*
Itnyre, Jacqueline Harriet *programmer*
Jurdana, Ernest J. *banker, accountant*
Larson, Mark Allan *financial executive*
Nacht, Sergio *biochemist*
Neville, Roy Gerald *scientist, chemical management and environmental consultant*
Seltzer, Ronald Anthony *radiologist, educator*
Silvestri, Philip Salvatore *lawyer*
Stone, Herbert Allen *management consultant*
Strauss, Judith Feigin *physician*
Swinerton, William Arthur *retired construction company executive*
Tight, Dexter Corwin *lawyer*
Waller, Stephen *air transportation executive*
Wang, Chen Chi *electronics company, real estate, finance company, investment services and international trade executive*
Wilhelm, Robert Oscar *lawyer, civil engineer, developer*

### Reedley
Carey, Ernestine Gilbreth (Mrs. Charles E. Carey) *writer, lecturer*
Dick, Henry Henry *minister*

### Reseda
Anstad, Neil *director*
Hoover, Pearl Rollings *nurse*
Leahy, T. Liam *marketing and management consultant*
Pearson, Susan Rose *psychotherapist, fine arts educator, artist*

### Rialto
Johnson, Ruth Floyd *university educator, consultant*

### Richmond
Beall, Frank Carroll *science director and educator*
Corbin, Rosemary Mac Gowan *mayor*
Doyle, William Thomas *retired newspaper editor*
Herron, Ellen Patricia *retired judge*
Kirk-Duggan, Michael Allan *retired law and computer sciences educator*
Quenneville, Kathleen *lawyer*
Rubanyi, Gabor Michael *medical research company executive*
Thomas, John Richard *chemist*
Ward, Carl Edward *research chemist*
Wessel, Henry *photographer*
Zavarin, Eugene *forestry science educator*

### Ridgecrest
Bennett, Harold Earl *physicist, optics researcher*
Lepie, Albert Helmut *chemist, reseacher*
Matulef, Gizelle Terese *secondary education educator*
Pearson, John *mechanical engineer*
St. Amand, Pierre *geophysicist*

### Rio Linda
Lebrato, Mary Theresa *lawyer, psychologist*

### Riverside
Aderton, Jane Reynolds *lawyer*
Adrian, Charles Raymond *political science educator*
Allan, David R. *safety engineer*
Andersen, Frances Elizabeth Gold *religious leadership educator*
Balow, Irving Henry *retired education educator*
Barnes, Martin McRae *entomologist*
Bartnicki-Garcia, Salomon *microbiologist, educator*
Beni, Gerardo *electrical and computer engineering educator, robotics scientist*
Bergh, Berthold Orphie (Bob Bergh) *plant research scientist, human genetics educator*
Bhanu, Bir *computer information scientist, educator, director university program*
Brandt, Blanch Marie *health care facility administrator*
Chang, Sylvia Tan *health facility administrator, educator*
Childs, Donald Richard *pediatric endocrinologist*
Chute, Phillip Bruce *management consultant*
Crean, John C. *housing and recreational vehicles manufacturing company executive*
Darling, Scott Edward *lawyer*
Davis, JoAn *business manager, general contractor, tax preparer, vocational business educator*
DeTemple, William Charles *technology executive*
Diamond, Richard *secondary education educator*
Elliott, Emory Bernard *English language educator, educational adminstrator*
Embleton, Tom William *horticultural science educator*
Erwin, Donald Carroll *plant pathology educator*
Eyman, Richard Kenneth *psychologist, educator*
Fagundo, Ana Maria *creative writing and Spanish literature educator*
Foreman, Thomas Elton *drama critic*
Fung, Sun-Yiu Samuel *physics educator*
Geraty, Lawrence Thomas *academic administrator, archaeologist*
Green, Harry Western, II *geology-geophysics educator, university official*
Green, Jonathan William *museum administrator and educator, artist, author*
Griffin, Keith Broadwell *economics educator*
Hall, Anthony Elmitt *crop ecologist*
Ham, Gary Martin *psychologist*
Harrison, Ethel Mae *financial executive*
Hays, Howard H. (Tim Hays) *editor, publisher*
Hendrick, Irving Guilford *dean, education educator*
Hodgen, Maurice Denzil *foundation executive*
Jukkola, George Duane *obstetrician, gynecologist*
Jung, Timothy Tae Kun *otolaryngologist*
Keen, Noel Thomas *plant pathology educator*
Kronenfeld, David Brian *anthropologist*
Kummer, Glenn F. *manufactured housing executive*
Lacy, Carolyn Jean *elementary education educator, secondary education educator*
Letey, John Joseph, Jr. *soil scientist, educator*
Linaweaver, Walter Ellsworth, Jr. *physician*
Locke, Francis Philbrick *retired editorial writer*
MacQueen, Cher *newscaster, sportscaster*
Mc Cormac, Weston Arthur *retired educator and army officer*
Mc Laughlin, Leighton Bates, II *journalism educator, former newspaperman*
McQuern, Marcia Alice *newspaper publishing executive*
Miskus, Michael Anthony *electrical engineer*
Mohanty, Binayak Prasad *environmental engineer, hydrologist*
Morris, Stephen Allen *elementary school educator*
Nieves, Carmen *emergency services coordinator*
Norman, Anthony Westcott *biochemistry educator*
Opotowsky, Maurice Leon *newspaper editor*
Orbach, Raymond Lee *physicist, educator*
Page, Albert Lee *soil science educator, researcher*
Petrinovich, Lewis F. *psychology educator*
Pick, Arthur Joseph, Jr. *chamber of commerce executive*
Prosser, Michael Joseph *community college staff member*
Rabenstein, Dallas Leroy *chemistry educator*
Ratliff, Louis Jackson, Jr. *mathematics educator*
Reardon, James Louis *education educator, consultant*
Reuther, Walter *horticulture educator*
Rosenzweig, Herbert Stephen *stockbroker*
Ross, Delmer Gerrard *historian, educator*
Shapiro, Victor Lenard *mathematics educator*
Sherman, Irwin William *biological sciences educator*
Smith, Dorothy Ottinger *jewelry designer, civic worker*
Smith, Jeffry Alan *health administrator, physician, consultant*
Snyder, Henry Leonard *history educator, bibliographer*
Sokolsky, Robert Lawrence *journalist, entertainment writer*
Spencer, William Franklin, Sr. *soil scientist, researcher*
Steckel, Barbara Jean *city financial officer*
Talbot, Prue *biology educator*
Turk, Austin Theodore *sociology educator*
Turner, Arthur Campbell *political science educator, author*
Van Gundy, Seymour Dean *nematologist, plant pathologist, educator*
Walker, Moira Kaye *sales executive*
Warren, David Hardy *psychology educator*
Weide, William Wolfe *housing and recreational vehicles manufacturer*
White, Robert Stephen *physics educator*
Wild, Robert Lee *physics educator*
Wilkins, Charles L. *chemistry educator*
Wright, John MacNair, Jr. *retired army officer*
Yacoub, Ignatius I. *university dean*
Zentmyer, George Aubrey *plant pathology educator*

### Rocklin
Ha, Chong Wan *state government executive*

### Rohnert Park
Arminana, Ruben *university president, educator*
Babula, William *university dean*
Byrne, Noel Thomas *sociologist, educator*
Criswell, Eleanor Camp *psychologist*
Gordon, Sharon J. *special education educator*
Johnston, Edward Elliott *insurance and management consultant*
Lord, Harold Wilbur *electrical engineer, electronics consultant*
Schafer, John Francis *retired plant pathologist*
Trowbridge, Dale Brian *educator*

### Rolling Hills
Rumbaugh, Charles Earl *lawyer, arbitrator/mediator*

### Rolling Hills Estates
Bellis, Carroll Joseph *surgeon*
Castor, Wilbur Wright *futurist, author, consultant*
Kline, Frank Menefee *psychiatrist*
Wong, Sun Yet *engineering consultant*

### Rosamond
Trippensee, Gary Alan *aerospace executive*

### Rosemead
Allen, Howard Pfeiffer *electric utility executive, lawyer*
Bennett, Brian O'Leary *utilities executive*
Bryson, John E. *utilities company executive*
Bushey, Richard Kenneth *utility executive*
Gibson, Frances *nurse*
Hattar, Michael Mizyed *mathematics educator*

### Roseville
Folsom, Richard Gilman *retired mechanical engineer and academic administrator, consultant*
Hinshaw, Lerner Brady *physiology educator*
Robbins, Stephen J. M. *lawyer*
Simms, Thomas Haskell *police chief*

### Ross
Godwin, Sara *writer, author*
Rosenbaum, Michael Francis *securities dealer*
Scott, John Walter *chemical engineer, research management executive*
Way, Walter Lee *anesthetist, pharmacologist, educator*

### Rowland Heights
Allen, Delmas James *anatomist, educator, university administrator*
Perfetti, Robert Nickolas *educational services administrator*

### Rutherford
Staglin, Garen Kent *finance and computer service company executive*

### Sacramento
Albert-Sheridan, Lenore LuAnn *legal research fellow, business owner*
Aldrich, Thomas Albert *former brewing executive, consultant*
Alpert, Deirdre Whittleton *state legislator*

Andrew, John Henry *lawyer, retail corporation executive*
†Atkins, Thomas N. *medical administrator*
Baccigaluppi, Roger John *agricultural company executive*
Baltake, Joe *film critic*
Benfield, John Richard *surgeon*
Benner, Rick *professional basketball team executive*
Bennett, Lawrence Allen *psychologist, criminal justice researcher*
Betts, Bert A. *former state treasurer, accountant*
Bezzone, Albert Paul *structural engineer*
Black, Barbara Crowder *educational consultant*
Blake, D. Steven *lawyer*
Blum, Deborah *reporter*
Bobrow, Susan Lukin *lawyer*
Boekhoudt-Cannon, Gloria Lydia *business education educator*
Bohnen, Mollyn Villareal *nurse, educator*
Bottel, Helen Alfea *columnist, writer*
Brookman, Anthony Raymond *lawyer*
Bruce, Thomas Edward *psychology educator, thanatologist*
Burger, John Barclay *systems architect, computer scientist*
Burns, John Francis *archivist, state official, museum director*
Burrell, Garland E., Jr. *federal judge*
Callahan, Ronald *federal investigator, historian*
Cavigli, Henry James *petroleum engineer*
Chapman, Loring *psychology educator, neuroscientist*
Chapman, Michael William *orthopedist, educator*
Childress, Dori Elizabeth *nursing consultant*
Chole, Richard Arthur *otolaryngologist, educator*
Cole, Glen David *minister*
Collings, Charles LeRoy *supermarket executive*
Collins, William Leroy *telecommunications engineer*
Couzens, Julia *artist*
Cox, Whitson William *architect*
Cozad, Lyman Howard *city manager*
Crabbe, John Crozier *telecommunications consultant*
Crimmins, Philip Patrick *metallurgical engineer, lawyer*
Cunningham, Mary Elizabeth *physician*
Dahl, Loren Silvester *retired federal judge*
Dahlin, Dennis John *landscape architect*
Dalkey, Fredric Dynan *artist*
Davis, Gray *lieutenant governor*
Day, James McAdam, Jr. *lawyer*
Deitch, Arline Douglis *cell biologist*
Dorn, Robert Murray *physician, psychiatrist, educator, psychoanalyst*
Drown, Eugene Ardent *federal agency administrator*
Endicott, William F. *journalist*
Evrigenis, John Basil *obstetrician-gynecologist*
Farrell, Francine Annette *psychotherapist, educator, author*
Fertig, Ted Brian O'Day *producer, public relations and association director*
Fong, Matthew Kipling *state official*
Forsyth, Raymond Arthur *civil engineer*
†Fox, Ned *professional sports team owner*
Franz, Jennifer Danton *public opinion and marketing researcher*
Frey, Charles Frederick *surgeon, educator*
Friedman, Morton Lee *lawyer*
Garcia, Edward J. *federal judge*
Garth-Lewis, Kimberley Anne *political science consultant*
Gentry, James William *retired state official*
Gerth, Donald Rogers *university president*
†Gibson, Daniel James *career military officer*
Glackin, William Charles *arts critic, editor*
Goodart, Nan L. *lawyer, educator*
Gottfredson, Don Martin *criminal justice educator*
Grant, Brian Wade (General Grant) *professional basketball player*
Gray, Walter P., III *museum director, consultant*
Greenfield, Carol Nathan *psychotherapist*
Grimes, Pamela Rae *elementary school educator*
Grissom, Lee Alan *state official*
Hallenbeck, Harry C. *architect*
Holmes, Robert Eugene *state legislative consultant, journalist*
Hughes, Teresa P. *state legislator*
Hunt, Dennis *public relations executive*
†James, Robert William *lawyer*
Janigian, Bruce Jasper *lawyer, educator*
Jones, William Leon *state legislator, rancher*
Karlton, Lawrence K. *federal judge*
Kelley, Lisa Stone *public guardian, conservator*
Knight, William J. (Pete Knight) *state senator, retired air force officer*
Knudson, Thomas Jeffery *journalist*
Kolkey, Daniel Miles *lawyer*
Lathi, Bhagawandas Pannalal *electrical engineering educator*
Leslie, (Robert) Tim *state legislator*
Levi, David F. *federal judge*
Lionakis, George *architect*
Lukenbill, Gregg *real estate developer, sports promoter*
Lundstrom, Marjie *newspaper editor*
Lungren, Daniel Edward *state attorney general*
Lynch, Peter John *dermatologist*
MacBride, Thomas Jamison *federal judge*
Mack, Edward Gibson *retired business executive*
Majesty, Melvin Sidney *psychologist, consultant*
McClatchy, James B. *editor, newspaper publisher*
McElroy, Leo Francis *communications consultant, journalist*
McKinley, Donald Robert *former school system administrator, education advisor*
Meier, George Karl, III *pastor, lawyer*
Meindl, Robert James *English language educator*
Merwin, Edwin Preston *health care consultant, educator*
Mette, Joe *museum director*
Meyer, Rachel Abijah *foundation director, artist, theorist, poet*
Miller, Suzanne Marie *law librarian, educator*
Moulds, John F. *federal judge*
Muehleisen, Gene Sylvester *retired law enforcement officer, state official*
Mujumdar, Vilas Sitaram *structural engineer, management executive*
Muller, David Webster *architectural designer*
Nacht, Daniel Joseph *architect*
Naglestad, Frederic Allen *legislative advocate*
Napolitano, Grace F. *state legislator*
Nelson, Alan Curtis *government official, lawyer*
Nesbitt, Paul Edward *historian, author, educator*
Newland, Chester Albert *public administration educator*
Nice, Carter *conductor, music director*
Nussenbaum, Siegfried Fred *chemistry educator*
O'Leary, Marion Hugh *university dean, chemist*
Peck, Ellie Enriquez *retired state administrator*
Petrie, Geoff *professional basketball team executive*
Pettite, William Clinton *public affairs consultant*
Phillips, Dana Wayne *lawyer*
Plant, Forrest Albert *lawyer*
Post, August Alan *economist, artist*
Potts, Erwin Rea *newspaper executive*
Presley, Robert Buel *state senator*
Quinn, Francis A. *bishop*
Reed, Nancy Boyd *English language and elementary education educator*
Richmond, Mitchell James *professional basketball player*
Riles, Wilson Camanza *educational consultant*
Roberts, Paul Dale *health services administrator*
Romero, Philip Joseph *economic and policy advisor*
Root, Gerald Edward *courts resource manager*
Rosenberg, Dan Yale *retired plant pathologist*
Rounds, Barbara Lynn *psychiatrist*
Russell, David E. *judge*
Sato-Viacrucis, Kiyo *nurse, inventor, entrepreneur, consultant*
Sawiris, Milad Youssef *statistician, educator*
Schaber, Gordon Duane *law educator, former judge*
Schmitz, Dennis Mathew *English language educator*
Schrag, Peter *editor, writer*
Schwartz, Milton Lewis *federal judge*
Serna, Joe, Jr. *mayor*
Shapero, Harris Joel *pediatrician*
Sharma, Arjun Dutta *cardiologist*
Shaw, Eleanor Jane *newspaper editor*
Sherwood, Robert Petersen *retired sociology educator*
Shirley, George Pfeiffer *lawyer, educational consultant*
Shubb, William Barnet *federal judge*
Simeroth, Dean Conrad *chemical engineer*
Solone, Raymond Joseph *advertising executive*
†Starr, Kevin *librarian, educator*
Stegenga, Preston Jay *international education consultant*
Stevenson, Thomas Ray *plastic surgeon*
Strock, James Martin *state agency administrator, lawyer, conservationist*
Styne, Dennis Michael *physician*
Sullivan, Robert Joseph *lawyer*
Swatt, Stephen Benton *communications executive, consultant*
Sydnor, Robert Hadley *state government geologist*
Takasugi, Nao *state official, business developer*
Taylor, Walter Wallace *lawyer*
Thomas, Jim *professional basketball team executive*
Twiss, Robert Manning *prosecutor*
Unde, Madhavji Anant (Mark Unde) *welding specialist*
Van Camp, Brian Ralph *lawyer*
van Loben Sels, James W. *transportation executive*
Venema, Jon Roger *educator, pastor*
von Friederichs-Fitzwater, Marlene Marie *health communication educator*
Walsh, Denny Jay *reporter*
Walston, Roderick Eugene *state government official*
Walters, Daniel Raymond *political columnist*
Wasserman, Barry L(ee) *architect*
Weigand, William Keith *bishop*
West, Linda Lea *administrator*
Whitaker, Cynthia Ellen *nurse*
Whiteside, Carol Gordon *state official, former mayor*
†Wickland, J. Al, Jr. *petroleum product executive, real estate executive*
Wightman, Thomas Valentine *rancher, researcher*
Wilkins, Philip Charles *judge*
Wilks-Owens, Dixie Rae *conference/meeting planner*
Williams, Arthur Cozad *broadcasting executive*
Wilson, Pete *governor*
Wolfman, Earl Frank, Jr. *surgeon, educator*
Zeff, Ophelia Hope *lawyer*

## Saint Helena
Kamman, Alan Bertram *communications consulting company executive*
Spann, Katharine Doyle *marketing and communications executive*

## Salinas
Duncan, James Richard *systems administrator*
Eifler, Carl Frederick *retired psychologist*
Francis, Alexandria Stephanie *psychologist*
Leighton, Henry Alexander *physician, consultant*
Martins, Evelyn Mae *theatre owner*
Phillips, John P(aul) *retired neurosurgeon*
Quick, Valerie Anne *sonographer*
Spinks, Paul *retired library director*
Stevens, Wilbur Hunt *accountant*
Taylor, Steven Bruce *agriculture company executive*

## San Andreas
Arkin, Michael Barry *lawyer, arbitrator*
Breed, Allen Forbes *correctional administrator*

## San Anselmo
Enfield, Susan Ann *secondary education educator*
Mudge, Lewis Seymour *theologian, educator, university dean*
Murphy, Barry Ames *lawyer*

## San Bernardino
Barnes, Gerald R. *bishop*
Bauer, Steven Michael *cost containment engineer*
Burgess, Mary Alice (Mary Alice Wickizer) *publisher*
Burgess, Michael *library science educator, publisher*
Butler, Arthur Maurice *university administrator*
De Haas, David Dana *emergency physician*
Evans, Anthony Howard *university president*
Ewing, Robert Stirling *retired library administrator*
Fairley Raney, Rebecca *journalist*
French, Kirby Allan *transportation engineer, computer programmer*
Holtz, Tobenette *aerospace engineer*
Kaisershot, Edward Joseph *elementary education educator, coach*
Lenz, Philip Joseph *municipal administrator*
Little, Thomas Warren *broadcast executive*
Nies, Boyd Arthur *hematologist, oncologist*
Norton, Ruth Ann *education educator*
Robertson, Stewart *conductor*
Sagmeister, Edward Frank *business owner, hospitality industry executive, civic official, retired consultant, fund raiser, career officer*
Stark, S. Daniel, Jr. *convention and visitors bureau executive*
Tacal, Jose Vega, Jr. *public health official, veterinarian*
Timmreck, Thomas C. *health sciences and health administration educator*
Turpin, Joseph Ovila *counselor, educator*
Weis, Edmund Bernard, Jr. *orthopaedist, educator, engineer, lawyer*
Willis, Harold Wendt, Sr. *real estate developer*

## San Bruno
Bradley, Charles William *podiatrist, educator*
Kell-Smith, Carla Sue *federal agency administrator*

## San Carlos
Barnard, William Calvert *retired news service executive*
Eby, Michael John *marketing research and technology consultant*
Gutow, Bernard Sidney *packaging manufacturing company executive*
Morrison, Ellen M. *writer, researcher*
Schumacher, Henry Jerold *former career officer, business executive*
Symons, Robert Spencer *electronics engineer*
True, Richard Brownell *electrical engineer*

## San Clemente
Clark, Earnest Hubert, Jr. *tool company executive*
Dinkel, John George *magazine editor*
Fall, John Robert *management and information technology consultant*
Lewis, Jack (Cecil Paul Lewis) *publishing executive, editor*
Singer, Kurt Deutsch *news commentator, author, publisher*
Stenzel, William A. *consulting services executive*
White, Stanley Archibald *research electrical engineer*

## San Diego
Aaron, Cynthia G. *judge*
Airst, Malcolm Jeffrey *electronics engineer*
Akeson, Wayne Henry *orthopedic surgeon, educator*
Alpert, Michael Edward *lawyer*
Anderson, Karl Richard *aerospace engineer, consultant*
Anderson, Paul Maurice *electrical engineering educator, researcher, consultant*
Andreos, George Phillip *lawyer*
Anjard, Ronald Paul, Sr. *business and industry executive, consultant, educator, technologist, importer, author*
Archibald, James David *biology educator, paleontologist*
Ashton, Tamarah M. *learning disabilities specialist, consultant*
Bailey, David Nelson *pathologist, educator*
Bakko, Orville Edwin *retired health care executive, consultant*
Ballinger, Charles Edwin *educational association administrator*
Barone, Angela Maria *artist, researcher*
Barr, Robert Edward *computer company executive*
Barsan, Richard Emil *oral and maxillofacial surgeon*
Bateman, Giles Hirst Litton *finance executive*
†Beathard, Bobby *professional football team executive*
Bell, Gene *newspaper publishing executive*
Benirschke, Kurt *pathologist, educator*
Bennett, Ronald Thomas *photojournalist*
Bennitt, Brent Martin *naval officer*
Berger, Bennett Maurice *sociology educator*
Bernstein, Sanford Irwin *biology educator*
Beyster, John Robert *engineering company executive*
Bieler, Charles Linford *development director, zoo executive director emeritus*
Blakemore, Claude Coulehan *banker*
Bliesner, James Douglas *municipal/county official, consultant*
Blum, John Alan *urologist, educator*
Blumenfeld, Alfred Morton *industrial design consultant, educator*
Boarman, Patrick Madigan *economics and business administration educator, public official*
†Bochy, Bruce *professional sports team executive*
†Bogner, Jo L. *airport executive*
Bohrer, Robert Arnold *law educator*
Bowie, Peter Wentworth *lawyer, educator*
Boyd, Robert Giddings, Jr. *continuing care facility administrator*
Brandes, Raymond Stewart *history educator*
Brewster, Rudi Milton *federal judge*
Brimble, Alan *business executive*
Broening, Elise Hedwig *writer*
Brom, Robert H. *bishop*
Brookler, Harry Aaron *retired physician*
Brooks, John White *lawyer*
†Brown, Alan J. *electrical engineer*
Bruggeman, Terrance John *financial corporate executive*
Buchbinder, Maurice *cardiologist*
Burge, David Russell *concert pianist, composer, piano educator*
Burgin, George Hans *computer scientist, educator*
Burke, Arthur Thomas *engineering consultant*
Burke, John *science technology company executive*
Butler, Geoffrey Scott *systems engineer, educator, consultant*
Callahan, LeeAnn Lucille *psychologist*
Campbell, Ian David *opera company director*
Campo, Catherine (Sauter) *computer programmer*
Carleson, Robert Bazil *public policy consultant, corporation executive*
Carney, John Michael *professional football player*
Carver, Juanita Ash *plastic company executive*
Caulder, Jerry Dale *weed scientist*
Chambers, Henry George *orthopedic surgeon*
†Chang, Daniel Haiming *engineering executive*
Charles, Carol Morgan *education educator*
Chatroo, Arthur Jay *lawyer*
Chen, Kao *consulting electrical engineer*
Christiansen, David K. *healthcare administrator*
Clement, Betty Waidlich *literacy educator, consultant*
Cobble, James Wikle *chemistry educator*
Colling, Kenneth Frank *hospital administrator*
Conly, John Franklin *engineering educator, researcher*
Convery, F. Richard *surgeon, orthopedist*
Cooper, James Melvin *healthcare executive, consultant*
Coox, Alvin David *history educator*
Copeland, Robert Glenn *lawyer*
Cornett, William Forrest, Jr. *local government management consultant*
Cota, John Francis *utility executive*
Crick, Francis Harry Compton *science educator, researcher*
Crumpler, Hugh Allan *author*
Crutchfield, Susan Ramsey *neurophysiologist*
Dabiri, Ali *mechanical engineer, researcher*
Daley, Arthur Stuart *retired humanities educator*
Damoose, George Lynn *lawyer*
Darmstandler, Harry Max *real estate executive, retired air force officer*
Da Rosa, Alison *travel editor*
Dean, Richard Anthony *mechanical engineer, engineering executive*
Delawie, Homer Torrence *architect*
DeMaria, Anthony Nicholas *cardiologist, educator*
Demeter, Steven *neurologist, publishing company executive*
Devine, Brian Kiernan *pet food and supplies company executive*
†Diaz, David *illustrator*
DiMattio, Terry *historic site administrator*
Dolan, James Michael, Jr. *zoological society executive*
Donnelly, Tracy Ann *biological researcher*
Downing, David Charles *minister*
Duddles, Charles Weller *food company executive*
Dunn, David Joseph *financial executive*
Dwyer, Lauraine Theresa *ambulatory care administrator, rehabilitation nurse*
Dziewanowska, Zofia Elizabeth *neuropsychiatrist, pharmaceutical executive, researcher, educator*
Early, Ames S. *healthcare system executive*
Eckhart, Walter *molecular biologist, educator*
Elliott, David Duncan, III *science research company executive*
Enright, William Benner *judge*
Estep, Arthur Lee *lawyer*
Fauchier, Dan R(ay) *construction management consultant*
Feinberg, Lawrence Bernard *university dean, psychologist*
Feinberg, Leonard *English language educator*
Fernandez, Fernando Lawrence *aeronautical engineer, research company executive*
Fike, Edward Lake *newspaper editor*
Fisher, Frederick Hendrick *oceanographer*
Fleischmann, Paul *youth minister*
Flettner, Marianne *opera administrator*
Freedman, Jonathan Borwick *journalist, author, lecturer*
Freeman, Myrna Faye *county schools official*
Friedenberg, Richard Myron *radiology educator, physician*
Friedman, Paul Jay *radiologist, chest radiologist, educator*
Fuller, William Henry, Jr. *professional football player*
Garrison, Betty Bernhardt *retired mathematics educator*
Gastil, Russell Gordon *geologist, educator*
Gastwirth, Donald Edward *lawyer, literary agent*
Gazell, James Albert *public administration educator*
Gee, Roger Allan *accounting educator, writer*
Getis, Arthur *geography educator*
Gilbertson, Oswald Irving *marketing executive*
Gilliam, Earl B. *federal judge*
†Glickenhaus, Mike *radio station executive*
Golding, Brage *former university president*
Golding, Susan *mayor*
Goltz, Robert William *physician, educator*
Gonzalez, Irma Elsa *federal judge*
Goodall, Jackson Wallace, Jr. *restaurant company executive*
Goode, John Martin *manufacturing company executive*
Gray, Gavin Campbell, II *computer information engineer, computer consultant*
Greene, John M. *physicist*
Greenspan, Ralph Jay *biologist*
Griffin, Herschel Emmett *retired epidemiology educator*
Gross, Jeffrey *software engineer*
Grosser, T.J. *administrator, developer, fundraiser*
Gu, Zu-Han *research scientist*
Guinn, Stanley Willis *lawyer*
Guinn, Susan Lee *lawyer*
Gwynn, Anthony Keith (Tony Gwynn) *professional baseball player*
Halasz, Nicholas Alexis *surgeon*
Hales, Alfred Washington *mathematics educator, consultant*
Hamburg, Marian Virginia *health science educator*
Hanson, Wendy Karen *chemical engineer*
Harmon, Harry William *architect, former university administrator*
Harriett, Judy Anne *medical equipment company executive*
Hartland, Nanci Jean *communications executive, educator*
Harwood, Ivan Richmond *pediatric pulmonologist*
Hayes, Alice Bourke *university official, biology educator*
Hayes, Robert Emmet *retired insurance company executive*
†Hayes, William Meredith *career officer*
Hays, Garry D. *academic administrator*
Hemmingsen, Barbara Bruff *microbiology educator*
Henderson, John Drews *architect*
Henderson, Rickey Henley *professional baseball player*
Hills, Linda Launey *advisory systems engineer*
Hinsvark, Don George *social services agency professional*
Hofflund, Paul *lawyer*
Holl, Walter John *architect, interior designer*
Hooper, Jere Mann *retired hotel executive, consultant*
Hope, Douglas Olerich *newspaper editor*
Hosker, Donald *materials research technician*
Hourani, Laurel Lockwood *epidemiologist*
Howell, Thomas Edwin *manufacturing company executive*
Hoyt, Jack Wallace *engineering educator*
Huang, Kun Lien *software engineer, scientist*
Huff, Marilyn L. *federal judge*
Hughes, Gethin B. *bishop*
Hunt, Robert Gary *medical consultant, oral and maxillofacial surgeon*
Huston, Kenneth Dale *lawyer*
Hutcheson, J(ames) Sterling *lawyer*
Inoue, Michael Shigeru *industrial engineer, electrical engineer*
Intriere, Anthony Donald *physician*
Ivans, William Stanley *electronics company executive*
Jacoby, Irving *physician*
Jamieson, Stuart William *surgeon, educator*
Jeffers, Donald E. *retired insurance executive, consultant*
Johnson, Kenneth Owen *retired audiologist*
Jones, Clyde William *anesthesiologist*
Jones, Welton H., Jr. *critic*
Kaback, Michael *medical educator*
Kaplan, George Willard *urologist*
Kaufman, Julian Mortimer *broadcasting company executive, consultant*
Keep, Judith N. *federal judge*

Kendrick, Ronald H. banker
Kennedy, Peter Smithson personnel consultant
Kennerson, Paul lawyer, author, educator
Kent, Theodore Charles psychologist
Kerr, Donald MacLean, Jr. physicist
King, Verna St. Clair retired school counselor
Klausmeier, Herbert John psychologist, educator
Klein, Herbert George newspaper editor
Kopp, Harriet Green communication specialist
Kraus, Pansy Daegling gemology consultant, editor, writer
Kripke, Kenneth Norman lawyer
Krulak, Victor Harold newspaper executive
Krull, Kathleen juvenile fiction and nonfiction writer
Kuc, Joseph A. education educator, consultant
Lane, Gloria Julian foundation administrator
Lao, Lang Li nuclear fusion research physicist
Lathrop, Mitchell Lee lawyer
Lauer, Jeanette Carol college dean, history educator, author
Lebadang artist
LeBeau, Charles Paul lawyer
Lederer, Richard Henry writer, educator, columnist
Lee, Marianna editor
Levy, Jerome dermatologist, retired naval officer
Lewis, Alan James pharmaceutical executive, pharmacologist
Lewis, Gerald Jorgensen judge
Lewis, Gregory Williams scientist
Lin, Yeou-Lin engineer, consultant
Lindh, Patricia Sullivan banker, former government official
Ling, David Chang international book dealer
Linn, Edward Allen writer
Linton, Roy Nathan graphic arts company executive
Litrownik, Alan Jay psychologist, educator
Livingston, Stanley C. architect
Lory, Loran Steven lawyer
MacCracken, Peter James marketing executive, communications executive
Magnuson, Harold Joseph physician
Maier, Paul Victor pharmaceutical executive
March, Marion D. writer, astrologer, consultant
Markowitz, Harry M. finance and economics educator
Marple, Stanley Lawrence, Jr. electrical engineer, signal processing researcher
Maurer, Lawrence Michael acting school administrator, educator
Mayer, James Hock mediator, lawyer
McBroom, Nancy Lee insurance executive
Mc Comic, Robert Barry real estate development company executive, lawyer
McGinnis, Robert E. lawyer
McGraw, Donald Jesse biologist, historian of science, writer
McGuigan, Frank Joseph psychologist, educator
McKee, Roger Curtis federal magistrate judge
McManus, Richard Philip lawyer, agricultural products company executive
Mendoza, Stanley Atran pediatric nephrologist, educator
Meyer, Paul I. lawyer
Meyers, James William federal judge
Mickelson, Sig broadcasting executive, educator
Miller, William Charles lawyer
Mitchell, Thomas Edward, Jr. communications cabling executive
Mittermiller, James Joseph lawyer
Mohan, Chandra research biochemistry educator
†Moores, John professional sports team executive
Moossa, A. R. surgery educator
Morgan, Neil author, newspaper editor, lecturer, columnist
Morris, Grant Harold law educator
Morris, Henry Madison, Jr. education educator
Morris, Sandra Joan lawyer
Moser, Kenneth Miles physician, educator
Mullane, John Francis pharmaceutical company executive
Mulvaney, James Francis lawyer
Munson, Lucille Marguerite (Mrs. Arthur E. Munson) real estate broker
Murray, Colette Morgan healthcare executive, fundraising consultant
Myers, Douglas George zoological society administrator
†Myrland, Doug broadcast executive
Nagao, Norris Sadato political science educator, consultant
Nassif, Thomas Anthony business executive, former ambassador
Nelson, Craig Alan management consultant
Nenner, Victoria Corich nurse, educator
Neuman, Tom S. emergency medical physician, educator
Nielsen, Leland C. federal judge
Noehren, Robert organist, organ builder
Nugent, Robert J., Jr. fast food company executive
Oldham, Maxine Jernigan real estate broker
Oliphant, Charles Romig physician
O'Malley, Edward physician, consultant
O'Malley, James Terence lawyer
O'Neal, Leslie Cornelius professional football player
†Osborne, Richard George naval officer, cardiologist, educator
Osby, Robert Edward protective services official
Owen-Towle, Carolyn Sheets clergywoman
Owsia, Nasrin Akbarnia pediatrician
Paderewski, Clarence Joseph architect
Paget, John Arthur mechanical engineer
Parthemore, Jacqueline G. physician, educator
Partida, Gilbert A. chamber of commerce executive
Patterson, Jamee Jordan lawyer
Pecsok, Robert Louis chemist, educator
Petersen, Martin Eugene museum curator
Pfeffer, Rubin Harry publishing executive
Pierson, Albert Chadwick business management educator
Pincus, Howard Jonah geologist, engineer, educator
Pincus, Robert Lawrence art critic, cultural historian
Pray, Ralph Marble, III lawyer
Price, Betty Jeanne choirchime soloist, writer
Prsha, Marie Alice administrator, educator
Pugh, Richard Crawford lawyer
Purcifull, Robert Otis insurance company executive
Pyatt, Kedar Davis, Jr. research and development company executive
†Quinn, Edward J. broadcasting company executive
Ranney, Helen Margaret physician, educator
Ray, Albert family physician
Ray, Gene Wells industrial executive
Rea, Amadeo Michael ethnobiologist, ornithologist
Reading, James Edward transportation executive
Reed, Jody Eric professional baseball player
Reinhard, Christopher John merchant banking, venture capital executive
Rezin, Joyce June pediatric nurse practitioner
Rhoades, John Skylstead, Sr. federal judge
Rice, Clare I. electronics company executive
Riedy, Mark Joseph finance educator
Risser, Arthur Crane, Jr. zoo administrator
Ristine, Jeffrey Alan reporter
Rodin, Alvin Eli retired pathologist, medical educator, author
Roeder, Stephen Bernhard Walter chemistry and physics educator
Ross, John, Jr. physician, educator
Ross, Terry D. lawyer
Ross, Vonia Pearl insurance agent, small business owner
Rotter, Paul Talbott retired insurance executive
Rowe, Peter A. newspaper columnist
Rudolph, Charles Herman computer software development executive
Rufeh, Firooz high technology company executive
Russel, Richard Allen telecommunications consultant, aerospace engineer, nuclear engineer, electrical engineer, retired naval officer
Sabatella, Elizabeth Maria clinical therapist, educator, mental health facility administrator
St. Clair, Hal Kay electrical engineer
St. George, William Ross lawyer, retired naval officer, consultant
Samuelson, Derrick William lawyer
Sannwald, William Walter librarian
Sasaki, Tatsuo musician
Schade, Charlene Joanne adult and early childhood education educator
Schaechter, Moselio microbiology educator
Schaefer, Michael Jude industrial control systems engineer
Scher, Valerie Jean music critic
Scherger, Joseph E. family physician, educator
Schmidt, Joseph David urologist
Schmidt, Patricia Fain nurse educator
Schmidt, Terry Lane health care executive
Schuck, Carl Joseph lawyer
Schwartz, Alfred university dean
Schwartz, Edward J. federal judge
Scorgie, Glen Given religious organization leader
Seagren, Stephen Linner oncologist
Seau, Junior (Tiana Seau, Jr.) professional football player
Seitman, John M. lawyer
Sell, Robert Emerson electrical engineer
Sesonske, Alexander nuclear and chemical engineer
Shaw, Lee Charles lawyer
Shaw, Richard Allan lawyer
Shearer, Rick Leland academic administrator
Shearer, William Kennedy lawyer, publisher
Shelton, Dorothy Diehl Rees lawyer
Shevel, Wilbert Lee information systems executive
Shippey, Sandra Lee lawyer
Shirer, Bruce Edward pathologist
Shneour, Elie Alexis biochemist
Silverberg, Lewis Henry management consultant
Simms, Maria Kay publishing and computer services executive
Slate, John Butler biomedical engineer
Smith, Benjamin Eric venture capitalist, executive
Smith, Steven Cole engineering process consultant
Smith, Steven Ray law educator
Snyder, David Richard lawyer
Sorrentino, Renate Maria illustrator
Spanos, Alexander Gus professional football team executive
Springer, Wayne Richard medical center safety director
Steen, Paul Joseph retired broadcasting executive
Sterrett, James Kelley, II lawyer
Stiska, John C. lawyer
Stoorza Gill, Gail corporate professional
Storer, Norman William sociology educator
Stowell, Larry Joseph agricultural consultant
Sullivan, William Francis lawyer
Sutowski, Thor Brian choreographer
Taylor, George Allen advertising agency executive
Taylor, Tony S. research scientist
Tedeschi, Ernest Francis, Jr. retired naval officer, naval company executive
Teguh, Collin osteopathic physician, educator
Tennent, Valentine Leslie accountant
Theis, James Edward pastry chef, interior designer
Thomas, Charles Allen, Jr. molecular biologist, educator
Thompson, David Renwick federal judge
Thompson, Gordon, Jr. federal judge
Till, Franklin L. school system administrator
Tillinghast, Charles Carpenter, III marketing company executive
Tricoles, Gus Peter electromagnetics engineer, physicist, consultant
Trybus, Raymond J. academic administrator, psychology educator, rehabilitation services professional
Turrentine, Howard Boyd federal judge
Vallbona, Marisa public relations counselor
Vanderbilt, Kermit English language educator
Vaughn, Gregory Lamont professional baseball player
Vause, Edwin Hamilton research foundation administrator
Velasquez, Ana Maria languages educator
Viterbi, Andrew James electrical engineering and computer science educator, business executive
Wachendorf, Miles Benton naval officer
Wagner, George Francis Adolf naval officer
Walker, Donald Ezzell retired academic administrator
Wallace, Helen Margaret physician, educator
Wallace, J. Clifford federal judge
Ward-Steinman, David composer, music educator, pianist
Warner, John Hilliard, Jr. technical services, military and commercial systems and software company executive
Wasserman, Stephen Ira physician, educator
Weaver, Michael James lawyer
Weber, Stephen Lewis university president
Weeks, John Robert geographer, sociology educator
Weisman, Irving social worker, educator
Welch, Arnold DeMerritt pharmacologist, biochemist
West, James Harold accounting company executive
Whitehill, Jules Leonard surgeon, educator
Whitmore, Sharp lawyer
Wiesler, James Ballard retired banker
Wight, Nancy Elizabeth neonatologist
Willerding, Margaret Frances mathematician
Wilson, Richard Allan landscape architect
Winner, Karin newspaper editor
Wong-Staal, Flossie geneticist, medical educator
Wright, Jon Alan physicist, researcher
Youngs, Jack Marvin cost engineer
Zedler, Joy Buswell ecological sciences educator
Ziegaus, Alan James public relations executive

## San Dimas
Flores, Frank Cortez health sciences administrator, public health educator
Lau, Henry mechanical engineer, consultant
Sawyer, Nelson Baldwin, Jr. credit union executive

## San Fernando
Boeckmann, H. F. automotive executive
Chiu, Dorothy pediatrician
Gosselin, Kenneth Stuart minister
Yuan, Sidney Wei Kwun cryogenic engineer, consultant

## San Francisco
Abbott, Barry Alexander lawyer
Adams, Lee Stephen lawyer, banker
Adams, Philip lawyer
Adcock, Muriel W. special education educator
Adler, Adrienne Edna-Lois art dealer, gallery owner, publisher
Adler, Nancy Elinor psychologist, educator
Aird, Robert Burns neurologist, educator
Albino, Judith E.N. university president
Aldrich, Michael Ray library curator, health educator
Alexander, Robert C. lawyer
Allan, William George painter, educator
Allemann, Sabina ballet dancer
Allen, Jose R. lawyer
Allman, Gregg musician
Alsup, William lawyer
Amend, William John Conrad, Jr. physician, educator
Amidei, L. Neal public relations counselor
Ammiano, Tom school system administrator
Anargyros, Nedra Harrison cytotechnologist
Anderson, Carl West judge
Andrews, David Ralph lawyer
Angell, James Browne electrical engineering educator
Anthony, of Sourozh (Anthony Emmanuel Gergiannakis) bishop
Apatoff, Michael John finance executive
Appelman, Evan Hugh retired chemist
Arbuthnot, Robert Murray lawyer
Archer, Richard Joseph lawyer
August-deWilde, Katherine banker
Autio, Rudy artist educator
Backus, John computer scientist
Bainton, Dorothy Ford pathology educator, researcher
Baker, Cameron lawyer
Baker, Dusty (Johnnie B. Baker, Jr.) professional baseball team manager
Baker, Kenneth art critic, writer
Balin, Marty (Martyn Jerel Buchwald) musician
Bancel, Marilyn fund raising management consultant
Bancroft, James Ramsey lawyer, business executive
Barbagelata, Robert Dominic lawyer
Barber, James P. lawyer
Bare, Joseph Edward, Jr. retired lawyer
Barondes, Samuel Herbert psychiatrist, educator
Bates, John Burnham lawyer
Bates, William, III lawyer
Batlin, Robert Alfred editor
Bauer, Michael newspaper editor
Baumhefner, Clarence Herman banker
Baxter, Marvin Ray state supreme court judge
Baxter, Ralph H., Jr. lawyer
Beall, Dennis Ray artist, educator
Bechtel, Riley Peart engineering company executive
Bechtel, Stephen Davison, Jr. engineering company executive
Beck, Edward William lawyer
Beck, Rodney Roy professional baseball player
Bedford, Daniel Ross lawyer
Bee, Robert Norman banker
Benet, Leslie Zachary pharmacokineticist
Bennett, William oboist
Bensinger, David August dentist, university dean
Benvenutti, Peter J. lawyer
Berggruen, John Henry art gallery executive
Berman, Joanna dancer
Berning, Paul Wilson lawyer
Berns, Philip Allan lawyer
Bertain, G(eorge) Joseph, Jr. lawyer
Bertelsen, Thomas Elwood, Jr. investment banker
Bibel, Debra Jan microbiologist, ecologist
Biglieri, Edward George physician
Bishop, John Michael biomedical research scientist, educator
Bitterman, Mary Gayle Foley broadcasting executive
Blackburn, Elizabeth Helen molecular biologist
Blakey, Scott Chaloner journalist, writer
†Blanc, Maureen public relations executive
Boles, Roger otolaryngologist
Bonapart, Alan David lawyer
Bonds, Barry Lamar professional baseball player
Bonetti, David art critic
Bookin, Daniel Henry lawyer
Booth, Forrest lawyer
Borowsky, Philip lawyer
Boucher, Harold Irving lawyer
Boutin, Peter Rucker lawyer
Bow, Stephen Tyler, Jr. insurance company executive
Bowers, Edgar poet, educator
Bowers, Jack (John Burton Bowers, Jr.) artist, graphics and digital color executive
Boyd, William Sprott lawyer
Boyle, Antonia Barnes audio producer, writer
Braasch, Barbara Lynn banker
Brandin, Alf Elvin retired mining and shipping company executive
Bray, Arthur Philip management science corporation executive
Breeden, David clarinetist
Bridges, Robert Lysle retired lawyer
Briggs, Susan Shadinger lawyer
Briscoe, John lawyer
Bromley, Dennis Karl lawyer
Brooks, William George aeronautical engineer
Broome, Burton Edward insurance company executive
Brower, David Ross conservationist
Brown, Donald Wesley lawyer
Brown, Kathan publisher of artists' etchings and woodcuts
Brown, Margaret deBeers lawyer
Brown, Willie Lewis, Jr. mayor, former state legislator, lawyer
Browning, James Robert federal judge
Brubeck, David Warren musician
Bruen, James A. lawyer
Bucherre, Veronique environmental company executive
Buck, John sculptor
Buck, John E. sculptor, print maker, educator
Buckner, John Knowles pension administrator
Budge, Hamilton Whithed lawyer
Buidang, George (Hada Buidang) educator, administrator, consultant, writer
Bull, Henrik Helkand architect
Burgess, Leonard Randolph business administration and economics educator, writer
Burkett, William Cleveland management consultant
Burlingame, Alma Lyman chemist, educator
Burns, Brian Patrick lawyer, business executive
Burri, Betty Jane research chemist
Butenhoff, Susan public relations executive
Butz, Otto William political science educator
Cain, Leo Francis retired special education educator
Callan, Terrence A. lawyer
Calvin, Allen David psychologist, educator
Campbell, Scott Robert lawyer, former food company executive
Caniparoli, Val William choreographer, dancer
Cape, Ronald Elliot biotechnology company executive
Caputo, Gary Richard radiology educator
Carlson, John Earl lawyer
Carniglia, Stephen Davis accountant, real estate consultant, lawyer
Carroll, Jon newspaper columnist
Carson, Jay Wilmer pathologist, educator
Carter, George Kent oil company executive
Carter, John Douglas lawyer
Cartmell, Nathaniel Madison, III lawyer
Casillas, Mark lawyer
Castilla, Antonio ballet dancer
Cavanagh, John Charles advertising agency executive
Chao, Cedric C. lawyer
Chapin, Dwight Allan columnist, writer
Cheatham, Robert William lawyer
Cheitlin, Melvin Donald physician, educator
Cheng, Kwong Man structural engineer
Cheng, Wan-Lee mechanical engineer, industrial technology educator
Cherny, Robert Wallace history educator
Chiaverini, John Edward construction company executive
Chimsky, Mark Evan editorial executive
Chin, Jennifer Young public health educator
Chin, Sue Soone Marian (Suchin Chin) conceptual artist, portraitist, photographer, community affairs activist
Chu, Kuang-Han structural engineer, educator
Cirese, Robert Charles economist, real estate investment counselor
Cisneros, Evelyn dancer
Clark, Edgar Sanderford insurance broker, consultant
Clarke, Richard Alan electric and gas utility company executive, lawyer
Clements, John Allen physiologist
Clever, Linda Hawes physician
Close, Sandy journalist
Cluff, Lloyd Sterling earthquake geologist
Coblentz, William Kraemer lawyer
Coffin, Judy Sue lawyer
†Cohen, Jeffrey Mark media company executive
Coleman, Thomas Young lawyer
Collas, Juan Garduño, Jr. lawyer
Collins, Dennis Arthur foundation executive
Collins, Fuji mental health professional
Colton, Roy Charles management consultant
Colwell, Kent Leigh venture capitalist
Conti, Samuel federal judge
Coombe, George William, Jr. lawyer, retired banker
Coppola, Francis Ford film director, producer, writer
Corcoran, Maureen Elizabeth lawyer
Corrigan, Robert Anthony academic administrator
Costa-Zalessow, Natalia foreign language educator
Costello, Marcelle Welling federal agency administrator, marketing consultant
Counelis, James Steve education educator
Crawford, Roy Edgington, III lawyer
Cruse, Allan Baird mathematician, computer scientist, educator
Curley, John Peter sports editor
Currier, Frederick Plumer market research company executive
Curtis, David Lambert rheumatologist, educator
Dachs, Alan Mark investment company executive
Daggett, Robert Sherman lawyer
Dail, Joseph Garner, Jr. judge
Dallman, Mary F. physiology educator
Danziger, Bruce Edward structural engineer
Davies, Paul Lewis, Jr. retired lawyer
Davis, Roger Lewis lawyer
Dawson, Chandler Robert ophthalmologist, educator
Debas, Haile T. gastrointestinal surgeon, physiologist, educator
De Benedictis, Dario arbitrator, mediator
De Coteau, Denis music director, conductor
Delacote, Goery museum director
Del Campo, Martin Bernardelli architect
Dellas, Robert Dennis investment banker
De Lutis, Donald Conse investment manager, consultant
Demarest, David Franklin, Jr. banker, former government official
Derr, Kenneth T. oil company executive
deWilde, David Michael executive search consultant, financial services executive, lawyer
Diamond, Philip Ernest lawyer
Dibble, Suzanne Louise nurse, researcher
Dickey, Glenn Ernest, Jr. sports columnist
Dickinson, Wade physicist, oil company executive, educator
Diekmann, Gilmore Frederick, Jr. lawyer
Djordjevich, Michael insurance company executive
Doan, Mary Frances advertising executive
Dolby, Ray Milton engineering company executive, electrical engineer
Donnally, Patricia Broderick newspaper editor
Donnici, Peter Joseph lawyer, law educator, consultant
Dowlin, Kenneth Everett librarian
Doyle, Morris McKnight lawyer
Draper, William Henry, III business executive
Drexler, Fred insurance executive
Drexler, Millard S. retail executive
Dryden, Robert Eugene lawyer
Du Bain, Myron foundation administrator
Duff, James George financial services executive
Dugoni, Arthur A. orthodontics educator, university dean
Dullea, Charles W. university chancellor emeritus, priest
Dunn, Richard Joseph investment counselor
†Dunn, Suzanne Lynne media company executive
Dunne, Kevin Joseph lawyer
Dupree, Stanley M. lawyer

Raciti, Cherie artist
Raeber, John Arthur architect, construction specifier consultant
Ragan, Charles Ransom lawyer
Ralston, Henry James, III neurobiologist, anatomist, educator
Ramey, Drucilla Stender legal association executive
Ramsey, Robert Lee judge, lawyer
Rascón, Armando artist
Ratner, David Louis legal educator
Raven, Robert Dunbar lawyer
Read, Gregory Charles lawyer
Ream, James Terrill architect, sculptor
Rector, Floyd Clinton, Jr. physiologist, physician
Reding, John A. lawyer
Redo, David Lucien investment company executive
Reed, Robert Daniel publisher
Reese, John Robert lawyer
Rembe, Toni lawyer
Renfrew, Charles Byron oil company executive, lawyer
Renne, Louise Hornbeck lawyer
†Riccardi, Robert advertising executive
Rice, Denis Timlin lawyer
Rice, Dorothy Pechman (Mrs. John Donald Rice) medical economist
Rice, Jonathan C. retired educational television executive
Richards, Norman Blanchard lawyer
Richardson, Daniel Ralph lawyer
Riney, Hal Patrick advertising executive
Rippel, Clarence W. academic administrator
Risse, Guenter Bernhard physician, historian, educator
Robertson, Armand James, II judge
Rock, Arthur venture capitalist
Rockwell, Alvin John lawyer
Rockwell, Burton Lowe architect
Roe, Benson Bertheau surgeon, educator
Roethe, James Norton lawyer
Roman, Stan G. lawyer
Rosales, Suzanne Marie hospital coordinator
Rosch, John Thomas lawyer
Rosen, Moishe religious organization administrator
Rosen, Sanford Jay lawyer
Rosenberg, Claude Newman, Jr. investment adviser
Rosenberg, Richard Morris banker
Rosenheim, Daniel Edward journalist, television news director
Rosenthal, Herbert Marshall legal association executive
Rosinski, Edwin Francis health sciences educator
Rosmini, Gary David financial marketing executive, consultant
Ross, Sue entrepreneur, author, fundraising executive
Rosston, Edward William lawyer
Rowland, John Arthur lawyer
Rubenstein, Steven Paul newspaper columnist
Rubin, Michael lawyer
Rudolph, Abraham Morris physician, educator
Runnicles, Donald conductor
Rusher, William Allen writer, commentator
Russell, Carol Ann personnel service company executive
Russoniello, Joseph Pascal lawyer
Ryland, David Ronald lawyer
Saavedra, Charles James banker
Sachs, Marilyn Stickle author, lecturer, editor
†Saenger, Theodore Jerome telephone company executive
Salomon, Darrell Joseph lawyer
Salzman, Richard William artists representative
Sano, Emily Joy museum director
Satin, Joseph language professional, university administrator
Saunders, Debra J. columnist
Savage, Michael John Kirkness oil company and arts management executive
Schaffer, Jeffrey L. lawyer
Schiller, Francis neurologist, medical historian
Schlegel, John Peter academic administrator
Schmid, Rudi (Rudolf Schmid) internist, educator, academic administrator, scientist
Schmidt, Robert Milton physician, scientist, educator
Scholten, Paul obstetrician, gynecologist, educator
†Schrock, Theodore R. surgeon
Schwab, Charles R. brokerage house executive
Schwartz, Louis Brown legal educator
Schwarz, Glenn Vernon editor
Schwarzer, William W federal judge
Seabolt, Richard L. lawyer
Sears, George Ames lawyer
†Seavey, William Arthur lawyer, vintner
Seebach, Lydia Marie physician
Seegal, John Franklin lawyer
Seelenfreund, Alan distribution company executive
Seibel, Erwin oceanographer, educator
Selman, Roland Wooten, III lawyer
Selover, William Charlton corporate communications and governmental affairs executive
Seneker, Carl James, II (Kim Seneker) lawyer
Sevier, Ernest Youle lawyer
Shapiro, Larry Jay pediatrician, scientist, educator
Sheinfeld, David composer
Shenk, George H. lawyer
Shepherd, John Michael lawyer
Sherry, Robert Joseph lawyer
Shinefield, Henry Robert pediatrician
Shor, Samuel Wendell Williston naval engineer
Shorenstein, Walter Herbert commercial real estate development company executive
Shulgasser, Barbara writer
Shumate, Charles Albert retired dermatologist
Shushkewich, Kenneth Wayne structural engineer
Sias, John B. multi-media company executive, newspaper publisher, publishing executive
Siegel, Louis Pendleton forest products executive
Siegel, Patricia Ann association management consultant
Silverman, Mervyn F. health science association administrator, consultant
Silverstein, Richard advertising agency executive
Simini, Joseph Peter accountant, financial consultant, author, former educator
Simon, Cathy Jensen architect
Singer, Allen Morris lawyer
Skinner, Stanley Thayer utility company executive, lawyer
Small, Marshall Lee lawyer
Smegal, Thomas Frank, Jr. lawyer
Smith, Bernard Joseph Connolly civil engineer
Smith, David Elvin physician
Smith, Kerry Clark lawyer
Smith, Lloyd Hollingsworth physician
Smith, Robert Michael lawyer
Smuin, Michael choreographer, director, dancer
Sneed, Joseph Tyree, III federal judge
Snow, Tower Charles, Jr. lawyer
Soh, Chunghee Sarah anthropology educator
Sokolow, Maurice physician, educator
Solomon, Neal Edward management consultant
Spander, Art sportswriter
Sparks, John Edward lawyer
Sparks, Robert Dean medical administrator, physician
Sparks, Thomas E., Jr. lawyer
Spiegel, Hart Hunter retired lawyer
Sproul, John Allan retired public utility executive
Stamper, Robert Lewis ophthalmologist, educator
Stanzler, Jordan lawyer
Staples, John Norman, III lawyer
Staring, Graydon Shaw lawyer
Stauffer, Thomas Michael university president
Steer, Reginald David lawyer
Steinberg, Michael music critic, educator
Stephens, Elisa art college president, lawyer
Stermer, Dugald Robert designer, illustrator, writer, consultant
Stotter, Lawrence Henry lawyer
Stowell, Christopher R. dancer
Strack, Alison Merwin neurobiologist
Stratton, Richard James lawyer
Stuppi, Craig lawyer
Sugarman, Myron George lawyer
Sullivan, James N. fuel company executive
Sullivan, Robert Edward lawyer
Susskind, Teresa Gabriel publisher
Sussman, Brian Jay meteorologist, weather broadcaster
Sutcliffe, Eric lawyer
Sutton, John Paul lawyer
†Swanson, Jack broadcast executive
Swing, William Edwin bishop
Szabo, Zoltan medical science educator, medical institute director
Taylor, John Lockhart city official
Terr, Abba Israel allergist, immunologist
Terr, Lenore Cagen psychiatrist, writer
Thacher, Carter Pomeroy diversified manufacturing company executive
Thistlethwaite, David Richard architect
Thomas, William Geraint museum administrator
Thompson, Charlotte Ellis pediatrician, educator, author
Thompson, Gary W. public relations executive
Thompson, Robert Charles lawyer
Thompson, Roderick M. lawyer
Thornton, D. Whitney, II lawyer
Tiano, Anthony Steven television producer, book publishing executive
Tiffany, Joseph Raymond, II lawyer
Tingle, James O'Malley lawyer
Tobin, Gary Allan cultural organization educator
Tobin, James Michael lawyer
Tomasson, Helgi dancer, choreographer, dance company executive
Torme, Margaret Anne public relations executive, communications consultant
Trautman, William Ellsworth lawyer
Traynor, J. Michael lawyer
Trejo, JoAnn medical researcher
Trigiano, Lucien Lewis physician
Trone, Donald Burnell investment company executive
Trowbridge, Thomas, Jr. mortgage banking company executive
Truett, Harold Joseph, III (Tim Truett) lawyer
Tulsky, Fredric Neal journalist
Turnbull, William, Jr. architect
Turner, Marshall Chittenden, Jr. venture capitalist, consultant
Turnlund, Judith Rae nutrition scientist
Tusher, Thomas William retired apparel company executive
Tuttle, George D. lawyer
Tyran, Garry Keith banker
Ullman, Myron Edward, III retail executive
Uri, George Wolfsohn accountant
Valentine, William Edson architect
Van Dyck, Wendy dancer
Van Dyke, Craig psychiatrist
Van Hoesen, Beth Marie artist, printmaker
Veaco, Kristina lawyer
Veitch, Stephen William investment counselor
Veith, Ilza historian of psychiatric and Oriental medicine
Venning, Robert Stanley lawyer
Vizcaino, Jose Luis Pimental professional baseball player
Vogt, Evon Zartman, III (Terry Vogt) merchant banker
†Volberding, Paul Arthur academic physician
Volpe, Peter Anthony surgeon
Vyas, Girish Narmadashankar virologist, immunohematologist
Walker, Ralph Clifford lawyer
Walker, Vaughn R. federal judge
Walker, Walter Herbert, III lawyer, writer
Walklet, Judith Kula printing company executive
Wall, Brian Arthur sculptor
Wall, James Edward telecommunications, petroleum and pharmaceutical executive
Wallace, Arthur, Jr. college dean
Wallerstein, Ralph Oliver physician
Walsh, Francis Richard law educator
Wang, William Kai-Sheng law educator
Warmer, Richard Craig lawyer
Warner, Harold Clay, Jr. banker, investment management executive
Watkins, Rufus Nathaniel newspaper professional
Watts, Malcolm S(tuart) M(cNeal) physician, medical educator
Way, E(dward) Leong pharmacologist, toxicologist, educator
Weaver, Sara Lee sales executive
Weigel, Stanley Alexander judge
Weihrich, Heinz management educator
Weiner, Peter H. lawyer
Welch, Thomas Andrew retire lawyer, arbitrator
Wentz, Jeffrey Lee information systems consultant
Werdegar, Kathryn Mickle judge
Werner, William Arno architect
Wernick, Sandie Margot advertising and public relations executive
Wertheimer, Robert E. paper company executive
Wescott, William Burnham oral pathologist, educator
Westerfield, Putney management consulting executive
Whalen, Philip Glenn poet, novelist
Wheater, Ashley dancer
Whelan, John William lawyer, law educator, consultant
Whitaker, Clem, Jr. advertising and public relations executive
Wilbur, Brayton, Jr. distribution company executive
Wilbur, Dwight Locke physician
Wilczek, John Franklin history educator
Wild, Nelson Hopkins lawyer
Wiley, Thomas Glen retired investment company executive
Williams, Morgan Lloyd retired investment banker
Willner, Jay R. consulting company executive
Willson, Prentiss, Jr. lawyer
Wilner, Paul Andrew journalist
Wilson, Charles B. neurosurgeon, educator
Wilson, Ian Robert food company executive
Wilson, John Oliver economist, educator, banker
Wilson, Matthew Frederick newspaper editor
Winchester, Kenneth James publisher
Wingate, C. Keith law educator
Winkler, Agnieszka M. advertising executive
Winn, Steven Jay critic
Wintroub, Bruce Urich dermatologist, educator, researcher
Wirthlin, Milton Robert, Jr. periodontist
Witherington, Jennifer Lee sales and marketing executive
Wolaner, Robin Peggy internet and magazine publisher
Wolfe, Cameron Withgot, Jr. lawyer
Wolff, Sheldon radiobiologist, educator
Wood, Donald Frank transportation educator, consultant
Woods, James Robert lawyer
Wrona, Peter Alexander structural engineer
Wyle, Frederick S. lawyer
Yamaguchi, Michael Joseph prosecutor
Yamakawa, David Kiyoshi, Jr. lawyer
Yamamoto, Keith Robert molecular biologist, educator
Yamamoto, Michael Toru journalist
Yao, Hilda Maria Hsiang banker, strategic planner
Yost, Nicholas Churchill lawyer
Young, Bryant Llewellyn lawyer, business executive
Young, Douglas Rea lawyer
†Yu, Jessica director, producer, writer, editor
Yuan, Shao Wen aerospace engineer, educator
Zellerbach, William Joseph retired paper company executive
Zhukov, Yuri ballet dancer
Ziering, William Mark lawyer
Zimmerman, Bernard judge
Zippin, Calvin epidemiologist, educator

## San Gabriel
Chen, John Calvin child and adolescent psychiatrist
Tadian, Luanne F. B. financial analyst, consultant, researcher
Terry, Roger pathologist, consultant

## San Jacinto
Jones, Marshall Edward, Jr. retired environmental educator

## San Jose
Adams, William John, Jr. mechanical engineer
Alexander, Richard lawyer
Anderson, Edward Virgil lawyer
Aylesworth, John Richard software professional
Baseman, Sandra Libbie editor
Bennett, Charles Turner social welfare administrator
Bentel, Dwight journalism educator emeritus
Berkland, James Omer geologist
Boldrey, Edwin Eastland retinal surgeon, educator
Burkhart, Sandra Marie art gallery director
Burnside, Mary software company executive
Cade, Jack Carlton marketing professional
Callan, Josi Irene museum director
Caret, Robert Laurent university president
Carey, Peter Kevin reporter
Castellano, Joseph Anthony chemist, management consulting firm executive
Cedoline, Anthony John psychologist
Ceppos, Jerome Merle newspaper editor
Collett, Jennie principal
Cruz, B. Robert academic administrator
Dafforn, Geoffrey Alan biochemist
Dalis, Irene mezzo-soprano, opera company administrator, music educator
D'Arrigo, Stephen, Jr. agricultural company executive
Dean, Burton Victor management educator
†DeGrande, Kenneth P. production company executive
Delucchi, George Paul accountant
Doctor, Kenneth Jay editor
Dougherty, John James computer software company executive, consultant
Edmonds, Charles Henry publisher
Eigler, Donald Mark physicist
Elder, Robert Laurie newspaper editor
Ellner, Michael William art educator
Elsorady, Alexa Marie secondary education educator
Estabrook, Reed artist, educator
Faggin, Federico electronics executive
Finnigan, Robert Emmet business owner
Forster, Julian physicist, consultant
Frymer, Murry columnist, theater critic, critic-at-large
Gonzales, Daniel S. lawyer
Granneman, Vernon Henry lawyer
Greenstein, Martin Richard lawyer
Gruber, John Balsbaugh physics educator, university administrator
Gunther, Barbara artist, educator
Hall, Robert Emmett, Jr. investment banker, realtor
Hammer, Susan W. mayor
Higgins, James Bradley dentist
Hodgson, Peter John music educator, musician
Houle, Frances Anne physical chemist
Huang, Francis Fu-Tse mechanical engineering educator
Ingle, Robert D. newspaper editor, newspaper executive
Ingram, William Austin federal judge
Israel, Paul Neal computer design engineer, author
Jackson, Patrick Joseph insurance executive
Jacobson, Albert Herman, Jr. industrial and systems engineer, educator
Jacobson, Raymond Earl electronics company entrepreneur and executive
Jarrat, Henri Aaron semiconductor company executive
Johnson, Allen Halbert surgeon
Jordan, Thomas Vincent advertising educator, consultant
Kennedy, George Wendell lawyer
Kertz, Marsha Helene accountant, educator
Kiggins, Mildred L. marketing executive
Kirk, Donald Evan electrical engineering educator, dean
Kramer, Richard Jay gastroenterologist
Kraw, George Martin lawyer, essayist
Laskin, Barbara Virginia legal association administrator
Lippe, Philipp Maria physician, surgeon, neurosurgeon, educator, administrator
Lovell, Glenn Michael film critic
Loventhal, Milton writer, playwright, lyricist
Malish, David Marc physician
Martin, Bernard Lee former college dean
Mc Connell, John Douglas retail corporation executive, owner
McDowell, Jennifer sociologist, composer, playwright, publisher
McEnery, Tom professional sports team executive
Meegan, Brother Gary Vincent school administrator, music educator
Merriam, Janet Pamela special education educator
Migielicz, Geralyn photojournalist
Mitchell, David Walker lawyer
Montgomery, Leslie David biomedical engineer, cardiovascular physiologist
Moody, Frederick Jerome mechanical engineer, consultant thermal hydraulics
Morawitz, Hans physicist
Morgan, Marilyn federal judge
†Morgridge, John P. computer business executive
Morimoto, Carl Noboru computer system engineer, crystallographer
Myer, Warren Hitesh mortgage broker, internet advertising executive
Neptune, John Addison chemistry educator, consultant
Nguyen, Thinh Van physician
†Nicholls, Bernard Irvine hockey player
†Nolan, Owen professional hockey player
Oak, Ronald Stuart health and safety administrator
Okerlund, Arlene Naylor university official
Okita, George Torao pharmacologist educator
Ostrom, Philip Gardner computer company executive
†Panelli, Edward Alexander retired state supreme court justice
Parkin, Stuart S. P. materials scientist
Parruck, Bidyut electrical engineer
Pulcrano, Dan Michael newspaper and online services executive
Ratzlaff, Ruben Menno religion educator, minister
Richards, Lisle Frederick architect
Ritzheimer, Robert Alan educational publishing executive
Rosendin, Raymond Joseph electrical contracting company executive
Rothblatt, Donald Noah urban and regional planner, educator
Sanders, Adrian Lionel educational consultant
Schindler, Keith William software engineer
Schmidt, Cyril James librarian
Schofield, John Trevor environmental management company executive
Schroeder, William John electronics executive
Scifres, Donald R. semiconductor laser, fiber optics and electronics company executive
Shaw, Charles Alden engineering executive
Smirni, Allan Desmond lawyer
Smith, David Eugene business administration educator
Smith, Joan Petersen nursing administrator, educator
Sollman, George Henry telecommunications company executive
Stacy, Richard A. administrative law judge
Steele, Shelby writer, educator
Stutzman, Thomas Chase, Sr. lawyer
Sumrall, Harry journalist
Supan, Richard Matthew health facility administrator
Tanaka, Richard Koichi, Jr. architect, planner
Taylor, Kendrick Jay microbiologist
Towery, James E. lawyer
Trounstine, Philip J. editor, journalist
Valentine, Ralph Schuyler chemical engineer, research director
Ware, James W. federal judge
Weeker, Ellis emergency physician
Whyte, Ronald M. federal judge
Williams, Spencer Mortimer federal judge
Winters, Harold Franklin physicist
Woolls, Esther Blanche library science educator
Woytowitz, Peter John mechanical engineer
Yoshizumi, Donald Tetsuro dentist
Zaro, Brad A. research company executive, biologist

## San Juan Capistrano
Black, William Rea lawyer
Botway, Lloyd Frederick computer scientist, consultant
Chang, Zhao Hua biomedical engineer
Curtis, John Joseph lawyer
Fisher, Delbert Arthur physician, educator
Horn, Deborah Sue organization administrator, writer, editor
Kleiner, Richard Arthur writer, editor
Paul, Courtland Price landscape architect, planner
Purdy, Alan MacGregor financial executive
Robinson, Daniel Thomas brokerage company executive
White, Beverly Jane cytogeneticist
Wong, Wallace medical supplies company executive, real estate investor

## San Leandro
Chilcoat, Dale Allen artist, visual and performing arts educator
Leighton, Joseph pathologist
Nehls, Robert Louis, Jr. school system administrator
Newacheck, David John lawyer
Stallings, Charles Henry physicist

## San Lorenzo
Glenn, Jerome T. secondary school principal
Morrison, Martin (Earl) computer systems analyst

## San Luis Obispo
Baker, Warren J(oseph) university president
Bunge, Russell Kenneth writer, poet, editor
Cummings, Russell Mark aerospace engineer, educator
Daly, John Paul lawyer
Deasy, Cornelius Michael architect
Dickerson, Colleen Bernice Patton artist, educator
Ericson, Jon Meyer academic administrator, rhetoric theory educator
Grimes, Joseph Edward computer science educator
Grismore, Roger physics educator, researcher
Hafemeister, David Walter physicist
Haile, Allen Cleveland educator and administrator
Hasslein, George Johann architectural educator
Hoffmann, Jon Arnold aeronautical engineer, educator
Jamieson, James Bradshaw foundation administrator

McCorkle, Robert Ellsworth agribusiness educator
Piirto, Douglas Donald forester, educator
Riedlsperger, Max Ernst history educator
Smith, Joey Spauls mental health nurse, biofeedback therapist, bodyworker, hypnotist
Zingg, Paul Joseph university provost

### San Luis Rey
Williams, Elizabeth Yahn author, lecturer, lawyer

### San Marcos
Andersen, Robert health products/business executive
Barnes, Howard G. film company executive, film and video producer
Billing, Ronald James immunologist, researcher
Christman, Albert Bernard historian
Ciurczak, Alexis librarian
Jeffredo, John Victor aerospace engineer, manufacturing company executive, inventor
Knight, Edward Howden retired hospital administrator
Liggins, George Lawson microbiologist, diagnostic company executive
Lilly, Martin Stephen university dean
Maggay, Isidore, III engineering executive, food processing engineer
Page, Leslie Andrew disinfectant manufacturing company executive
Sauer, David Andrew writer, computer consultant

### San Marino
Baldwin, James William lawyer
Benzer, Seymour neuroscience educator
Footman, Gordon Elliott educational administrator
Galbraith, James Marshall lawyer, business executive
Grantham, Richard Robert real estate company consultant
Hull, Suzanne White retired administrator, author
Karlstrom, Paul Johnson art historian
Lashley, Virginia Stephenson Hughes retired computer science educator
Man, Lawrence Kong architect
Medearis, Roger Norman artist
Meyer, William Danielson retired department store executive
Mortimer, Wendell Reed, Jr. superior court judge
Mothershead, J. Leland, III dean
Ridge, Martin historian, educator
Robertson, Mary Louise archivist, historian
Rolle, Andrew F. historian, educator, author
Skotheim, Robert Allen museum administrator
Smith, Apollo Milton Olin retired aerodynamics engineer
Steadman, John Marcellus, III English educator
Thorpe, James humanities researcher
Tomich, Lillian lawyer
Wark, Robert Rodger art curator
Zall, Paul Maxwell retired English language educator, consultant
Zimmerman, William Robert entrepreneur, engineering based manufacturing company executive

### San Mateo
Aadahl, Jorg business executive
Adams, Robert Monroe retired dermatologist, educator
Bell, Frank Ouray, Jr. lawyer
Berkowitz, Steve publishing company executive
Besse, Robert Gale food technologist
Dworkin, Michael Leonard lawyer
Everett, Michael Thomas lawyer
Fenton, Noel John venture capitalist
Golding, George Earl journalist
Graham, Howard Holmes manufacturing executive
Grill, Lawrence J. lawyer, accountant, corporate/banking executive
Helfert, Erich Anton management consultant, author, educator
Hopkins, Cecilia Ann business educator
Hospy, Patricia L. chiropractor
Johnson, Charles Bartlett mutual fund executive
†Johnson, Rupert Harris, Jr. finance company executive
Kidera, George Jerome physician
Korn, Walter writer
†Martin, Jim publishing executive
Potts, David Malcolm population specialist, administrator
Richens, Muriel Whittaker AIDS therapist, counselor and educator
Roberts, Lawrence Gilman telecommunications company executive
Rollo, F. David hospital management company executive, health care educator
Steiner, Mary Ann nursing administrator, consultant
Trabitz, Eugene Leonard aerospace company executive
Van Kirk, John Ellsworth cardiologist
Xiong, Jean Z. artist, consultant

### San Pablo
Bristow, Lonnie Robert physician
Colfack, Andrea Heckelman elementary education educator
Woodruff, Kay Herrin pathologist, educator

### San Pedro
Colman, Ronald William computer science educator
Crutchfield, William Richard artist, educator
Ellis, George Edwin, Jr. chemical engineer
Main, Betty Jo management analyst
Matich, Matthew P. secondary school English educator
McCarty, Frederick Briggs electrical engineer
Price, Harrison Alan business research company executive
Simmons, William physicist, aerospace research executive

### San Rafael
Badgley, John Roy architect
Bobb, Richard Allen non-profit executive
Brevig, Eric special effects expert, executive
Bruyn, Henry Bicker physician
Carson, Dave special effects expert, executive
Danse, Ilene Homnick Raisfeld physician, educator, toxicologist
Dewey, Edward Allen retired construction company executive
Eekman, Thomas Adam Slavic languages educator
Elliott, Edward Procter architect
Farrar, Scott special effects expert, executive
Fink, Joseph Richard college president
Friesecke, Raymond Francis health company executive
Goldman, Clint Paul producer
Gorman, Ned film producer
Gryson, Joseph Anthony orthodontist
Heller, H(einz) Robert financial executive
Hill, Nathan Scott educator, writer, cultural consultant
Hinshaw, Horton Corwin physician
Kennedy, James Waite management consultant, author
Kennedy, Thomas executive producer
Latno, Arthur Clement, Jr. telephone company executive
Lee, Robert association executive, former theological educator, consultant, author
Lesh, Philip Chapman musician, composer
Lucas, George W., Jr. film director, producer, screenwriter
March, Ralph Burton retired entomology educator
Meecham, William James ophthalmologist
Murphy, George special effects expert
Nelson, James Carmer, Jr. advertising executive, writer
Nicholson, Bruce graphics expert, executive
Purcell, Stuart McLeod, III financial planner
Roffman, Howard motion picture company executive
Roth, Hadden Wing lawyer
Sansweet, Stephen Jay journalist, author, marketing executive
Santana, Carlos guitarist
Sheldon, Gary conductor, music director
Squires, Scott William special effects expert, executive
Stout, Gregory Stansbury lawyer
Thompson, John William international management consultant
Thompson, Peter L. H. golf course architect
Tift, Mary Louise artist
Turner, William Weyand author
Wilson, Ian Holroyde management consultant, futurist

### San Ramon
Gardner, Nord Arling management consultant administrator
Kahane, Dennis Spencer lawyer
Litman, Robert Barry physician, author, television and radio commentator
Novales-Li, Philipp neuropharmacologist
Pagter, Carl Richard lawyer
Rose, Joan L. computer security specialist
Schlitt, William Joseph, III metallurgical engineer
Schofield, James Roy computer programmer

### Sanger
Haddix, Charles E. legislative and regulatory consultant

### Santa Ana
Abbruzzese, Carlo Enrico physician, writer, educator
Adams, John M. library director
Amoroso, Frank retired communication system engineer, consultant
Barr, James Norman federal judge
Bauer, Bruce F. aerospace engineer
Beasley, Oscar Homer lawyer, educator
Blaine, Dorothea Constance Ragetté lawyer
Boynton, William Lewis electronic manufacturing company official
Buster, Edmond Bate metal products company executive
Capizzi, Michael Robert lawyer
Cheverton, Richard E. newspaper editor
Fay-Schmidt, Patricia Ann paralegal
Ferguson, Warren John federal judge
Foster, Julian Francis Sherwood political science educator
Harley, Robison Dooling, Jr. lawyer, educator
Heckler, Gerard Vincent lawyer
Holtz, Joseph Norman marketing executive
Izac, Suzette Marie retired air force officer
Katz, Tonnie newspaper editor
Kelly, James Patrick, Jr. retired engineering and construction executive
Kenney, Patti Marlene sales exeuctive
Kinosian, Janet Marie journalist
Knox Rios, Delilah Jane lawyer
McKee, Kathryn Dian Grant human resources consultant
McLaughlin, Linda Lee Hodge federal judge
Myers, Marilyn Gladys pediatric hematologist and oncologist
Nowel, David John marketing professional
Oberstein, Marydale geriatric specialist
Pratt, Lawrence Arthur thoracic surgeon, foreign service officer
Pratt, Paul Bernard financial services executive
Rockoff, Sheila G. nursing and health facility administrator, nursing and health occupations educator
Ryan, John Edward federal judge
St. Clair, Carl conductor, music director
†Schueler, John R. newspaper executive
Schuller, Eddie engineering executive
Shahin, Thomas John dry cleaning wholesale supply company executive
Storer, Maryruth law librarian
Stotler, Alicemarie Huber judge
Taylor, Gary L. federal judge
†Treshie, R. David newspaper publishing executive
Tu, John engineering executive
Ware, James Edwin retired international company executive
Zabsky, John Mitchell engineering executive
Zaenglein, William George, Jr. lawyer

### Santa Barbara
Ackerman, Marshall publishing company executive
Ah-Tye, Kirk Thomas lawyer
Aldisert, Ruggero John federal judge
Alldredge, Alice Louise biological oceanography educator
Amory, Thomas Carhart management consultant
Anderson, Donald Meredith bank executive
Atwater, Tanya Maria marine geophysicist, educator
Badash, Lawrence science history educator
Barbakow, Jeffrey health facility administrator
Bauer, Marvin Agather lawyer
Beutler, Larry Edward psychology educator
Bischel, Margaret DeMeritt physician, managed care consultant
Blasingame, Benjamin Paul electronics company executive
Blum, Gerald Saul psychologist, educator
Bock, Russell Samuel author
Boehm, Eric Hartzell information management executive
Bongiorno, James William electronics company executive
Boxer, Rubin software company owner, former research and development company executive
Boyan, Norman J. retired education educator
Branch, Taylor writer
Brant, Henry composer
Brantingham, Barney journalist, writer
Breunig, Robert G. natural history museum director
Bridges, B. Ried lawyer
Brown, Baillie Russell health services administrator
Brownlee, Wilson Elliot, Jr. history educator
Byers, Horace Robert former meteorology educator
Cameron, Heather Anne publishing executive
Campbell, Robert Charles clergyman, religious organization administrator
Campbell, William Steen writer, magazine publisher
Carlson, Arthur W. lawyer
Chafe, Wallace LeSeur linguist, educator
Childress, James J. marine biologist, biological oceanographer
Chmelka, Bradley Floyd chemical engineering educator
Christman, Arthur Castner, Jr. scientific advisor
Clinard, Marshall Barron sociologist, educator
Coldren, Larry Allen engineering educator, consultant
Collins, Robert Oakley history educator
Comanor, William S. economist, educator
Conley, Philip James, Jr. retired air force officer
Crawford, Donald Wesley philosophy educator, university official
Crispin, James Hewes engineering and construction company executive
Crowell, John C(hambers) geology educator, researcher
Dauer, Francis Watanabe philosophy educator
Davidson, Eugene Arthur author
Davis, James Ivey company president, laboratory associate
Del Chiaro, Mario Aldo art historian, archeologist, etruscologist, educator
Donnerstein, Edward Irving communications and psychology educator, researcher, author
Dougan, Robert Ormes librarian
Doutt, Richard Leroy entomologist, lawyer, educator
Duarte, Ramon Gonzalez nurse, educator, researcher
Dudziak, Walter Francis physicist
Dunne, Thomas geology educator
Easton, Robert (Olney) author, environmentalist
Eguchi, Yasu artist
Eisberg, Robert Martin physics educator, computer software author and executive
Emmons, Robert John corporate executive
Enelow, Allen Jay psychiatrist, educator
Erasmus, Charles John anthropologist, educator
Fan, Ky mathematician, educator
Fingarette, Herbert philosopher, educator
Fisher, Steven Kay neurobiology eductor
Fleming, Brice Noel retired philosophy educator
Focht, Michael Harrison health care industry executive
Ford, Anabel research anthropologist, archaeologist
Ford, Peter C. chemistry educator
Fredrickson, Glenn Harold chemical engineering and materials educator
Frizzell, William Kenneth architect
Gaines, Howard Clarke retired lawyer
Gallagher, James Wes journalist
Gibney, Frank Bray publisher, editor, writer, foundation executive
Gilbert, Paul Thomas chemical development engineer
Gossard, Arthur Charles physicist
Grayson, Robert Allen marketing executive, educator
Gunn, Giles Buckingham English educator, religion educator
Gutsche, Steven Lyle physicist
Harris, James Dexter lawyer
Hedgepeth, John M(ills) aerospace engineer, mathematician, engineering executive
Heeger, Alan Jay physicist
Helgerson, Richard English literature educator
Higgins, Isabelle Jeanette librarian
Hollister, Charles Warren history educator, author
Hsu, Immanuel Chung Yueh history educator
Iselin, Donald Grote civil engineering and management consultant
Israel, Barry John lawyer
Jackson, Beverley Joy Jacobson columnist, lecturer
Jacobson, Saul P. consumer products company executive
Jochim, Michael Allan archaeologist
Johnsen, Eugene Carlyle mathematician and educator
Karpeles, David museum director
Keator, Carol Lynne library director
Kendler, Howard H(arvard) psychologist, educator
Kennedy, John Harvey chemistry educator
Kennett, James Peter geology and oceanography educator
Kohn, Roger Alan surgeon
Kohn, Walter educator, physicist
Kokotovic, Petar V. electrical and computer engineer, educator
Korenic, Lynette Marie librarian
Kramer, Edward John materials science and engineering educator
Krieger, David Malcolm peace foundation executive, lawyer
Kroemer, Herbert electrical engineer, educator, computer engineer, educator
Kruger, Kenneth Charles architect
Kryter, Karl David research scientist
Langer, James Stephen physicist, educator
Lawrance, Charles Holway civil and sanitary engineer
Leal, Leslie Gary chemical engineering educator
Lee, Hua electrical engineering educator
Levi, Ilan Mosche computer and communications company consultant
Lockett, Barbara Ann librarian
Louis, Barbra Schantz dean
Luyendyk, Bruce Peter geophysicist, educator, institution administrator
Macdonald, Ken Craig geophysicist
Mac Intyre, Donald John college president
Marcus, Marvin mathematician, educator
Martinez-López, Enrique Spanish educator
Mathews, Barbara Edith gynecologist
Mayer, Richard Edwin psychology educator
Mc Coy, Lois Clark emergency services executive, retired county official, magazine editor
McGee, James Sears historian
Mehra, Rajnish finance educator
Meinel, Aden Baker optics scientist
Metzinger, Timothy Edward lawyer
Minc, Henryk mathematics educator
Mitra, Sanjit Kumar electrical and computer engineering educator
Moholy, Noel Francis clergyman
Moir, Alfred Kummer art history educator
Moncharsh, Philip Isaac lawyer
Montgomery, Michael Davis hotelier, advanced technology consultant
Morgan, Alfred Vance management consulting company executive
Narayanamurti, Venkatesh research administrator
Newman, Morris mathematician
Norris, Robert Matheson geologist
O'Dowd, Donald Davy retired university president
Peale, Stanton Jerrold physics educator
Perloff, Jean Marcosson lawyer
Peterson, Charles Marquis medical educator
Philbrick, Ralph botanist
Pilgeram, Laurence Oscar biochemist
Potter, David Samuel former automotive company executive
Prager, Elliot David surgeon, educator
Prindle, William Roscoe consultant, retired glass company executive
Rasher, George Joseph entrepreneur, business owner
Reed, Frank Fremont, II retired lawyer
Reis, Edward Thomas, Jr. insurance executive, educator
Renehan, Robert Francis Xavier Greek and Latin educator
Riemenschneider, Paul Arthur physician, radiologist
Rockwell, Don Arthur psychiatrist
Rosenberg, Alex mathematician, educator
Russell, Charles Roberts chemical engineer
Russell, Jeffrey Burton historian, educator
Schneider, Edward Lee botanic garden administrator
Schultz, Arthur Warren communications company executive
Segal, Helene R. editor
Shackman, Daniel Robert psychiatrist
Shapiro, Perry economics educator
Sherman, Alan Robert psychologist, educator
Shobe, Nancy fundraising consultant, small business owner
Simons, Stephen mathematics educator, researcher
Simpson, Curtis Chapman, III lawyer
Sinsheimer, Robert Louis retired university chancellor and educator
Smith, Michael Townsend author, editor, stage director
Snyder, Allegra Fuller dance educator
Sprecher, David A. university administrator, mathematician
Tapper, Joan Judith magazine editor
Tettegah, Sharon Yvonne education educator
Tilton, David Lloyd savings and loan association executive
Tilton, George Robert geochemistry educator
Tucker, Shirley Lois Cotter botany educator, researcher
Turner, Henry A. retired political science educator, author
Vos, Hubert Daniel private investor
Wade, Glen electrical engineer, educator
Wayland, Newton Hart conductor
Weinberg, William Henry chemical engineer, chemical physicist, educator
Wiemann, John Moritz communications educator, executive, consultant
Wilkins, Burleigh Taylor philosophy educator
Wilson, Leslie biochemist, cell biologist, biology educator
Witherell, Michael S. physics educator
Wooldridge, Dean Everett engineering executive, scientist
Wudl, Fred chemistry educator
Yang, Henry T. university chancellor, educator
Zaleski, James Vincent electronics executive
Zelmanowitz, Julius Martin mathematics educator, university administrator
Zimmerman, Everett Lee English educator, academic administrator

### Santa Clara
Abdaljabbar, Abdalhameed A. educational administrator
Alexander, George Jonathon legal educator, former dean
Alexanderson, Gerald Lee mathematician, educator, writer
Anderson, Gary Allan professional football player
Baird, Mellon Campbell, Jr. electronics industry executive
Beebe, Naomi Marie financial consultant, accountant
Bjorkholm, John Ernst physicist
Chan, Shu-Park electrical engineering educator
Charles, Mary Louise newspaper columnist, photographer, editor
Chen, James Jen-Chuan electrical engineer
Cooper, Adrian football player
DiUlio, Albert Joseph university president, priest
DuMaine, R. Pierre bishop
Dunlap, F. Thomas, Jr. electronics company executive, engineer, lawyer
Elkus, Richard J., Jr. electronics company executive
Facione, Peter Arthur dean, philosophy and education educator
Falgiano, Victor Joseph electrical engineer, consultant
Fernbach, Stephen Alton pediatrician
Glancy, Dorothy Jean lawyer, educator
Gogan, Kevin professional football player
Grove, Andrew S. electronics company executive
Halmos, Paul Richard mathematician, educator
Hanks, Merton Edward professional football player
Hoagland, Albert Smiley electrical engineer
Hopkinson, Shirley Lois library science educator
House, David L. electronics components company executive
Jain, Jawahar computer scientist, engineer, researcher
Jones, Brent Michael professional football player
Kershaw, David Joseph process engineer
Klosinski, Leonard Frank mathematics educator
Kwock, Royal architect
Lane, Holly Diana artist
Locatelli, Paul Leo university administrator
Lynch, Charles Allen investment executive, corporate director
Marken, Gideon Andrew, III advertising and public relations executive
Martin, Joseph Robert financial executive
McDonald, Tim professional football player
McEachern, Alexander electronics company executive
Meier, Matthias S(ebastian) historian
Moore, Gordon E. electronics company executive
Norton, Kenneth Howard professional football player

Parden, Robert James *engineering educator, management consultant*
†Policy, Carmen A. *professional sports team executive*
Reavis, Liza Anne *semiconductor executive*
Rice, Jerry Lee *professional football player*
Rostoker, Michael David *micro-electronics company executive, lawyer*
Sapolu, Manase Jesse *professional football player*
Schapp, Rebecca Maria *museum director*
Sproule, Betty Ann *computer industry strategic planning manager*
Stockton, Anderson Berrian *electronics company executive, consultant, genealogist*
Stubblefield, Dana William *professional football player*
Vincent, David Ridgely *management consulting executive*
Warmenhoven, Daniel John *communications equipment executive*
Woodall, Lee *professional football player*
Yin, Gerald Zheyao *technology and business executive*
†Young, Bryant Colby *football player*
Young, Steven *professional football player*
Zhang, Xiao-Feng *power system engineer, researcher*

### Santa Clarita
Abbott, John Rodger *electrical engineer*
Gardner, Frederick Boyce *library director*
Granlund, Thomas Arthur *engineering executive, consultant*
Lavine, Steven David *academic administrator*
Powell, Mel *composer*
Senter, Jack *art director, production designer*
Volpe, Eileen Rae *special education educator*

### Santa Cruz
Atchison, Rodney Raymond *lawyer, arbitrator*
Beevers, Harry *biologist*
Brown, George Stephen *physics educator*
Bunnett, Joseph Frederick *chemist, educator*
Cecil, Robert Salisbury *telecommunications company executive*
Child, Frank Clayton *economist, educator*
Corrick, Ann Marjorie *communications executive*
Dasmann, Raymond Fredric *ecologist*
Dilbeck, Charles Stevens, Jr. *real estate company executive*
Drake, Frank Donald *radio astronomer, educator*
Dyson, Allan Judge *librarian*
Ellis, John Martin *German literature educator*
Faber, Sandra Moore *astronomer, educator*
Flatté, Stanley Martin *physicist, educator*
Flegal, A(rthur) Russell, Jr. *toxicologist, geochemist, educator*
Griggs, Gary Bruce *earth sciences educator, oceanographer, geologist, consultant*
Heusch, Clemens August *physicist, educator*
Hill, Terrell Leslie *chemist, biophysicist*
Huskey, Harry Douglas *information and computer science educator*
Keizer, Lewis Stewart *headmaster*
Kraft, Robert Paul *astronomer, educator*
Langdon, Glen George, Jr. *electrical engineer*
Langenheim, Jean Harmon *biology educator*
Laporte, Leo Frederic *earth sciences educator*
Lay, Thorne *geosciences educator*
Lieberman, Fredric *ethnomusicologist, educator*
Magid, Gail Avrum *neurosurgeon, neurosurgery educator*
Millhauser, Glenn Lawrence *biochemist, educator*
Mumma, Gordon *composer, educator, author*
Noller, Harry Francis, Jr. *biochemist, educator*
Osterbrock, Donald E(dward) *astronomy educator*
Pettigrew, Thomas Fraser *social psychologist, educator*
Rorer, Leonard George *psychologist, writer*
Rydell, Amnell Roy *artist, landscape architect*
Sands, Matthew Linzee *physicist, educator*
Schwartz, Arthur Alan *surgeon*
Sherman, Frieda Frances *writer*
Shorenstein, Rosalind Greenberg *physician*
Silver, Mary Wilcox *oceanography educator*
Smith, M(ahlon) Brewster *psychologist, educator*
Stevens, Stanley David *local history researcher, retired librarian*
Stilwill, Belle Jean *record company executive, printing company owner*
Suckiel, Ellen Kappy *philosophy educator*
Summers, Carol *artist*
Tharp, Roland George *psychology, education educator*
Tonay, Veronica Katherine *psychology educator*
Williams, Quentin Christopher *geophysicist, educator*
Winston, George *pianist, guitarist, harmonica player*
Wipke, W. Todd *chemistry educator*
Woosley, Stanford Earl *astrophysicist*

### Santa Fe Springs
Butterworth, Edward Livingston *retail company executive*
Ittner, Perry Martin *sales and marketing consultant*
Morgan, Ronald William *sales executive*

### Santa Maria
Dunn, Judith Louise *secondary school educator*
Ellis, Emory Leon *retired biochemist*
Grames-Lyra, Judith Ellen *building engineering inspector, artist, educator*

### Santa Monica
Abarbanel, Gail *social service administratior, educator*
Abdul, Paula (Julie) *singer, dancer, choreographer*
Ackerman, Helen Page *librarian, educator*
Alpert, Herb *musician, painter, recording artist, theatrical producer, philanthropist*
Anderson, Loni Kaye *actress*
Anderson, Robert Helms *information scientist*
Ansen, David B. *critic, writer*
Augenstein, Bruno W. *research scientist*
Baer, Walter S. *research executive*
Barry, Julian *playwright, screenwriter*
Bedrosian, Edward *electrical engineer*
Bergman, Alan *lyricist, writer*
Bergman, Marilyn Keith *lyricist, writer*
Black, Noel Anthony *television and film director*
Bohn, Paul Bradley *psychiatrist, psychoanalyst*
Boltz, Gerald Edmund *lawyer*
Bonesteel, Michael John *lawyer*
Brook, Robert Henry *physician, educator, health services researcher*
Bruckheimer, Jerry *producer*
Cameron, James *film director, screenwriter, producer*
Carder, Kathy Young *critical care nurse*
Chartoff, Robert Irwin *film producer*
Cooper, Jackie *actor, director, producer*
Crain, Cullen Malone *electrical engineer*
Davies, Merton Edward *planetary scientist*
Demond, Joan *marine biologist*
Diamond, Neil Leslie *singer, composer*
Dickerson, Joe Bernard *principal, educator*
Dickson, Robert Lee *lawyer*
†Dobson, Kevin James *film director*
Edwards, Sarah Anne *radio and cable television personality, clinical social worker*
Eizenberg, Julie *architect*
Elson, Peter Frederic Alan *manufacturing company executive*
†Friedrichs, Edward C. *architect*
Fukuhara, Henry *artist, educator*
Gehry, Frank Owen *architect*
Gilbert-Rolfe, Jeremy Denton *artist, art critic, educator*
Goldberg, Leonard *television and movie producer*
Greene, Michael C. *art association administrator*
Gritton, Eugene Charles *nuclear engineer*
Hammond, R. Philip *chemical engineer*
Hearn, Charles Virgil *minister*
Heimann-Hast, Sybil Dorothea *language arts and literature educator*
Hirsch, Richard G. *lawyer*
Ho, Alexander Kitman *producer*
Holzman, D. Keith *record company executive, producer, arts consultant*
Intriligator, Devrie Shapiro *physicist*
Jacobson, Sidney *editor*
Janulaitis, M. Victor *consulting company executive*
Jenkins, George *stage designer, film art director*
Jones, William Allen *lawyer, entertainment company executive*
Jones, William Bowdoin *political scientist, retired diplomat, lawyer*
Kahan, James Paul *psychologist*
Kalb, Benjamin Stuart *television producer, director*
Kaminski, Janusz Zygmuni *photographer*
Kanner, Gideon *lawyer*
Kayton, Myron *engineering company executive*
Kempster, Victor *art director, production designer*
Kennedy, Kathleen *film producer*
Kerkorian, Kirk *motion picture company executive, consultant*
Koning, Hendrik *architect*
Krakower, Bernard Hyman *management consultant*
Kummer, Wolfgang H. *electrical engineer*
Launer, Dale Mark *screenwriter*
Leaf, Paul *producer, director, writer*
Lebenzon, Chris *film editor*
Le Berthon, Adam *lawyer*
Levine, Peggy Aylsworth *psychotherapist, writer, poet*
Lindsley, Donald Benjamin *physiological psychologist, educator*
Loo, Thomas S. *lawyer*
Mancuso, Frank G. *entertainment company executive*
Markoff, Steven C. *finance company executive*
Marshall, Frank W. *film producer, director*
Martin, Linda Gaye *demographer, economist*
McGuire, Michael Francis *plastic and reconstructive surgeon*
Mc Guire, Michael John *environmental engineering executive*
McMillan, M. Sean *lawyer*
Miller, Leroy Benjamin *architect*
Mitchell, Thomas Soren *urologist*
Morgan, Monroe *retired savings and loan executive*
Mortensen, William S. *banking executive*
Nathanson, Michael *film company executive*
Nizze, Judith Anne *physician assistant*
Norris, David Randolph *recording artist, philanthropist*
O'Donnell, Lawrence Francis, Jr. *author*
Pettit, John W. *administrator*
Pisano, A. Robert *entertainment company executive, lawyer*
Pleskow, Eric Roy *motion picture company executive*
Prewoznik, Jerome Frank *lawyer*
†Price, David *recreational facilities executive*
Rand, Robert Wheeler *neurosurgeon, educator*
Random, Ida *production designer*
Redford, Robert (Charles Robert Redford) *actor, director*
Reynolds, Norman *production designer, art director*
Rice, Donald Blessing *business executive, former secretary of air force*
Rich, Michael David *research corporation executive, lawyer*
Richards, David Kimball *investor*
Ringler, Jerome Lawrence *lawyer*
Risman, Michael *lawyer, business executive, securities company executive*
Roberts, Kevin *recreational facility executive*
Roberts, Virgil Patrick *lawyer, business executive*
Roney, Robert Kenneth *retired aerospace company executive*
†Rubin, Gerrold Robert *advertising executive*
Rydell, Mark *film director, producer, actor*
Salzer, John Michael *technical and management consultant*
Schultz, Michael *stage and film director, film producer*
Schultz, Victor M. *physician*
Seymour, Jeffrey Alan *governmental relations consultant*
Sheller, John Willard *lawyer*
Shubert, Gustave Harry *research executive, consultant, social scientist*
Singer, Frederick Raphael *medical researcher, educator*
Smith, Anna Deavere *actress, playwright*
Smith, James Patrick *economist*
Snedaker, Catherine Raupagh (Kit Snedaker) *editor*
Sperling, George Elmer, Jr. *lawyer*
Stone, Oliver William *screenwriter, director*
Taylor, Nigel Brian *financial planner*
Thompson, Dennis Peters *plastic surgeon*
Thomson, James Alan *research company executive*
Vacano, Jost *cinematographer*
Vega, Benjamin Urbizo *retired judge*
Veit, Clairice Gene Tipton *measurement psychologist*
Walker, Charles Montgomery *lawyer*
Walsh, John *museum director*
Ware, Willis Howard *computer scientist*
Watrous, William Russell *trombonist, composer, conductor*
Watson, Doc (Arthel Lane Watson) *vocalist, guitarist, banjoist, recording artist*
Weber, Samuel Lloyd *tap dancer, choreographer*
Weil, Leonard *banker*
Wexler, Haskell *film producer, cameraman*
Wolf, Charles, Jr. *economist, educator*

### Santa Rosa
Aman, Reinhold Albert *philologist, publisher*
Andriano-Moore, Richard Graf *naval officer*
Apfel, Joseph H. *optical engineer, research scientist*
Bowen, James Thomas *military officer*
Bozdech, Marek Jiri *physician*
Brunner, Howard William *professional land surveyor*
Christiansen, Peggy *principal*
Farrell, Thomas Joseph *insurance company executive, consultant*
Frowick, Robert Holmes *retired diplomat*
Furen, Shirley Ann *small business owner, art dealer*
Gioia, (Michael) Dana *poet, literary critic*
Harris, David Joel *foundation executive*
Leuty, Gerald Johnston *osteopathic physician and surgeon*
Locher, Richard Earl *editorial cartoonist*
Mc Donald, David William *retired chemist, educator*
Monk, Diana Charla *artist, stable owner*
Nickens, Catherine Arlene *retired nurse, freelance writer*
Pearson, Roger Lee *library director*
Person, Evert Bertil *newspaper and radio executive*
Rancourt, James Daniel *optical engineer*
Resch, Joseph Anthony *neurologist*
Rider, Jane Louise *artist, educator*
Schudel, Hansjoerg *international business consultant*
Schulz, Charles Monroe *cartoonist*
Sibley, Charles Gald *biologist, educator*
Swofford, Robert Lee *newspaper editor, journalist*
Webb, Charles Richard *retired university president*
†Wells, Annie *photographer*
Ziemann, G. Patrick *bishop*

### Santa Ynez
Byrne, Joseph *retired oil company executive*
Ellion, M. Edmund *engineering executive*
Stern, Marvin *management consultant*

### Santee
Peters, Raymond Eugene *computer systems company executive*
Vanier, Kieran Francis *business forms printing company executive*

### Saratoga
Cooper, George Emery *aerospace consultant*
Grubb, William Francis X. *consumer software executive, marketing executive*
Henderson, William Darryl *army officer, writer*
†Houston, Joseph Brantley, Jr. *optical instrument company executive*
Lynch, Milton Terrence *retired advertising agency executive*
Park, Joseph Chul Hui *computer scientist*
Rawson, Eric Gordon *optical engineer*
Reagan, Joseph Bernard *retired aerospace executive, management consultant*
Sherwood, Patricia Waring *artist, educator*
Syvertson, Clarence Alfred *engineering and research management consultant*
Wenzel, James Gottlieb *ocean engineering executive, consultant*
Wood, Gladys Blanche *retired secondary education educator, journalist*

### Sausalito
Arieff, Allen Ives *physician*
Berkman, William Roger *lawyer, army reserve officer*
Brand, Stewart *editor, writer*
Casals, Rosemary *professional tennis player*
Elliott, James Heyer *retired university art museum curator, fine arts consultant*
Glaser, Edwin Victor *rare book dealer*
Green, Joanta Hermion *electrical engineer*
Klingensmith, Arthur Paul *business and personal development consultant*
Klotsche, Charles Martin *real estate development company executive, writer*
Kuhlman, Walter Egel *artist, educator*
Lamoreaux, Phillip Addison *investment management company executive*
Leefe, James Morrison *architect*
McCarthy, Brian Nelson *marketing and distribution company executive*
Seymour, Richard Burt *health educator*
Treat, John Elting *management consultant*
Trimmer, Harold Sharp, Jr. *lawyer, international telecommunications consultant*

### Scotts Valley
Brough, Bruce Alvin *public relations and communications executive*
Janssen, James Robert *consulting software engineer*
Shugart, Alan F. *electronic computing equipment company executive*
Snyder, Charles Theodore *geologist*

### Seal Beach
Beall, Donald Ray *multi-industry high-technology company executive*
Burge, Willard, Jr. *software company executive*
Caesar, Vance Roy *newspaper executive*
Calise, William Joseph, Jr. *lawyer*
Harsha, Philip Thomas *aerospace engineer*
Merrick, George Boesch *aerospace company executive*
Nesmith, Audrey Marie *military housing manager (retired), writer*
O'Shaughnessy, James Patrick *lawyer*
Robinson, Michael R. *aeronautical engineer*
Rossi, Mario Alexander *architect*
Stillwell, Kathleen Ann Swanger *healthcare consultant*
Thompson, Craig Snover *corporate communications executive*

### Seaside
Gales, Samuel Joel *retired civilian military employee, counselor*
Weingarten, Saul Myer *lawyer*

### Sebastopol
DeMartini, Rodney J. *executive director religious organization, priest*
Kherdian, David *author*
Norman, Arnold McCallum, Jr. *engineer*
Sabsay, David *library consultant*

### Selma
Jura, Debra Dowell *bilingual educator*

### Sepulveda
Wasterlain, Claude Guy *neurologist*

### Shell Beach
Barca, Kathleen *marketing executive*

### Sherman Oaks
Atwood, Colleen *costume designer*
Azpeitia, Lynne Marie *psychotherapist, educator, trainer, consultant*
Barron, Tiana Luisa *foundation developer, fundraiser, educator*
Buckingham, Lindsey *musician*
Conrad, Robert (Conrad Robert Falk) *actor, singer, producer, director*
Crump, Gerald Franklin *retired lawyer*
Easton, Sheena *rock vocalist*
Ellison, Harlan Jay *author, screenwriter*
Farnsworth, Richard *actor, former stuntman*
Fisher, Joel Marshall *political scientist, legal recruiter, educator*
Gibbs, Antony (Tony) *film editor*
Gilmore, Art *television performer*
Hagenbuch, Rodney Dale *stock brokerage house executive*
Hall, Deidre *actress*
Hamilton, Scott Scovell *professional figure skater, former Olympic athlete*
Harper, Valerie *actress*
Kennedy, Burt Raphael *film director*
King, Peter D. *psychiatrist, educator, real estate developer*
Lindgren, Timothy Joseph *supply company executive*
Luna, Barbara Carole *expert witness, accountant, appraiser*
MacMullen, Douglas Burgoyne *writer, editor, retired army officer, publisher*
Miller, Margaret Haigh *librarian*
O'Neill, Sallie Boyd *educator, business owner, sculptor*
Peplau, Hildegard Elizabeth *nursing educator*
Reiner, Thomas Karl *manufacturing company executive*
Strauss, John *public relations executive*
Tesh, John *television talk show host*
Tsiros, John Andreas *accountant*
Weiss, Julie *costume designer*
Winkler, Lee B. *business consultant*
Yasnyi, Allan David *media communications executive*
Zemplenyi, Tibor Karol *cardiologist*

### Sierra Madre
Converse, Elizabeth Sheets *artist, writer*
Dewey, Donald William *magazine publisher, editor, writer*
Nation, Earl F. *retired urologist, educator*
Whittingham, Charles Edward *thoroughbred race horse owner and trainer*

### Signal Hill
Jarman, Donald Ray *retired public relations professional, minister*

### Simi Valley
Brock, James Wilson *drama educator, playwright, researcher*
Bumgardner, Larry G. *foundation administrator, law and political science educator*
Glindeman, Henry Peter, Jr. *real estate developer*
Hoover, Richard *special effects expert, film director*
Hunt, Mark Alan *museum director*
Killion, Jack Charles *newspaper columnist*
Rehart, Margaret Lee *controller*
Shartle, Keith Robert *producer*
Stratton, Gregory Alexander *computer specialist, administrator, mayor*
Weiser, Paul David *manufacturing company executive*
Whitley, David Scott *archaeologist*
Witman, Frank McConnell *clergyman, educator*
Yeatman, Hoyt *special effects expert, executive*

### Solana Beach
Agnew, Harold Melvin *physicist*
Arledge, Charles Stone *former aerospace executive, entrepreneur*
Beare, Bruce Riley *trading company and sales executive*
Brody, Arthur *industrial executive*
Derbes, Daniel William *manufacturing executive*
Dieffenbach, AliceJean *artist*
Ernst, Roger Charles *former government official, natural resources consultant, association executive*
Friedman, Maurice Stanley *religious educator*
Gildred, Theodore Edmonds *ambassador*
Gilliam, Vincent Carver *religion educator, minister, writer*
Watson, Jack Crozier *retired state supreme court justice*

### Solvang
Chandler, E(dwin) Russell *clergyman, author*
Morrow, Richard Towson *lawyer*

### Somerset
Setzekorn, William David *retired architect, consultant, author*

### Somis
Kehoe, Vincent Jeffré-Roux *photographer, author, cosmetic company executive*
Woodruff, Donald B. *motion picture art director, production designer*

### Sonoma
Allen, Rex Whitaker *architect*
Beckmann, Jon Michael *publisher*
Jayme, William North *writer*
Kizer, Carolyn Ashley *poet, educator*
Markey, William Alan *health care administrator*
Muchmore, Robert Boyer *engineering consultant executive*
Pollack, Phyllis Addison *ballerina*
Stadtman, Verne August *former foundation executive, editor*
Woodbridge, John Marshall *architect, urban planner*

### Sonora
Coffill, Marjorie Louise *civic leader*
Efford, Michael Robert *police administrator, educator*
Erich, Louis Richard *physician*
Price, Joe (Allen) *artist, former educator*
Smith, Carlton Myles *military officer*

### Soquel
Murray, Barbara Olivia psychologist

### South Dos Palos
Hirohata, Derek Kazuyoshi air force reserve officer

### South Lake Tahoe
Nason, Rochelle conservation organization administrator
Null, Paul Bryan minister
Prescott, Barbara Lodwich educational administrator

### South Pasadena
Askin, Walter Miller artist, educator
Castellano, Pasquale Allen clergyman, marriage, family and child counselor
Girvigian, Raymond architect
Glad, Dain Sturgis retired aerospace engineer, consultant
Kopp, Eugene Howard electrical engineer
Lowe, Richard Gerald, Jr. computer programming manager
Mantell, Suzanne Ruth editor
Patterson, Dawn Marie dean, consultant, author, educator
Saeta, Philip Max judge
White-Thomson, Ian Leonard mining company executive
Zagon, Laurie artist, writer, color consultant

### South San Francisco
Blethen, Sandra Lee pediatric endocrinologist
Levinson, Arthur David molecular biologist
Leylegian, Jack H., II investment management company executive
Masover, Gerald Kenneth microbiologist
Shelton, Leslie Habecker adult literacy program director
Spitzer, Walter Oswald epidemiologist, educator
†Tawg, Manyin editor, periodical
Walsh, Gary L. consumer products company executive
Westerdahl, John Brian nutritionist, health educator

### Spring Valley
Long, David Michael, Jr. biomedical researcher, cardiothoracic surgeon
Peterson, Donald Curtis life care executive, consultant

### Stanford
Abrams, Herbert LeRoy radiologist, educator
Allen, Matthew Arnold physicist
Almond, Gabriel Abraham political science educator
Amemiya, Takeshi economist, statistician
Andersen, Hans Christian chemistry educator
Anderson, Annelise Graebner economist
Anderson, Martin Carl economist
Anderson, Theodore Wilbur statistics educator
Andreopoulos, Spyros George writer
Arrow, Kenneth Joseph economist, educator
Atkin, J. Myron science educator
Aziz, Khalid petroleum engineering educator
Babcock, Barbara Allen lawyer, educator
Bagley, Constance Elizabeth lawyer, educator
Baker, Keith Michael history educator
Baldwin, Robert Lesh biochemist, educator
Ballam, Joseph physicist, educator
Bandura, Albert psychologist
Barnes, Grant Alan book publisher
Baron, James Neal organizational behavior and human resources educator, researcher
Barton, John Hays law educator
Basch, Paul Frederick international health educator, parasitologist
Bauer, Eugene Andrew dermatologist, educator
Baxter, William Francis lawyer, educator
Baylor, Denis Aristide neurobiology educator
Beard, Rodney Rau physician, educator
Beaver, William Henry accounting educator
Beichman, Arnold political scientist, educator, writer
Bensch, Klaus George pathology educator
Berg, Paul biochemist, educator
Bjorkman, Olle Erik plant biologist, educator
Blumenkranz, Mark Scott surgeon, researcher, educator
Bonner, William Andrew chemistry educator
Boskin, Michael Jay economist, government official, university educator, consultant
Boudart, Michel chemical engineer, chemist, educator
Bracewell, Ronald Newbold electrical engineering educator
Bradshaw, Peter engineering educator
Brauman, John I. chemist, educator
Breitrose, Henry S. communications educator
Brest, Paul A. law educator
Bridges, Edwin Maxwell education educator
Brinegar, Claude Stout retired oil company executive
Brown, Byron William, Jr. biostatistician, educator
Bube, Richard Howard materials scientist
Bunzel, John Harvey political science educator, researcher
Calfee, Robert Chilton psychologist, educational researcher
Campbell, Allan McCulloch bacteriology educator
Cannon, Robert Hamilton, Jr. aerospace engineering educator
Carlsmith, James Merrill psychologist, educator
Carlson, Robert Codner industrial engineering educator
Carlson, Robert Wells physician, educator
Carnochan, Walter Bliss retired English educator
Carnoy, Martin economics educator
Chaffee, Steven Henry communication educator
Cohen, Albert musician, educator
Cohen, Harvey Joel pediatric hematology and oncology educator
Cohen, William law educator
Cole, Wendell Gordon speech and drama educator
Coleman, Robert Griffin geology educator
Collman, James Paddock chemistry educator
Conquest, (George) Robert (Acworth) writer, historian, poet, critic, journalist
Cover, Thomas M. statistician, electrical engineer, educator
Cox, Donald Clyde electrical engineering educator
Dafoe, Donald Cameron surgeon, educator
Dantzig, George Bernard applied mathematics educator
Deal, Bruce Elmer physical chemist, educator
Degler, Carl Neumann history educator
Dekker, George Gilbert literature educator, literary scholar, writer
Derksen, Charlotte Ruth Meynink librarian
Djerassi, Carl chemist, educator, writer
Donohue, John Joseph law educator
Drell, Sidney David physicist, educator
Dunlop, John Barrett foreign language educator, research institution scholar
Duus, Peter history educator
Efron, Bradley mathematics educator
Ehrlich, Anne Howland research biologist
Ehrlich, Paul Ralph biology educator
Eitner, Lorenz Edwin Alfred art historian, educator
Enthoven, Alain Charles economist, educator
Eustis, Robert Henry mechanical engineer
Fee, Willard Edward, Jr. otolaryngologist
Fehrenbacher, Don Edward retired history educator
Fernald, Russell Dawson biologist, researcher
Fetter, Alexander Lees theoretical physicist, educator
Flinn, Paul Anthony materials scientist
Francke, Uta medical geneticist, genetics researcher, educator
Frank, Joseph Nathaniel comparative literature educator
Franklin, Gene Farthing engineering educator, consultant
Franklin, Marc Adam law educator
Fredrickson, George Marsh history educator
Friedman, Lawrence M. law educator
Friedman, Milton economist, educator emeritus, author
Fuchs, Victor Robert economics educator
Gage, Nathaniel Lees psychologist, educator
Ganesan, Ann Katharine molecular biologist
Gardner, John William writer, educator
Gelpi, Albert Joseph English educator, literary critic
Gelpi, Barbara Charlesworth English literature and women's studies educator
George, Alexander Lawrence political scientist, educator
Gere, James Monroe civil engineering educator
Gibson, Count Dillon, Jr. physician, educator
Girard, René Noel author, educator
Giraud, Raymond Dorner retired language professional
Glazer, Gary Mark radiology educator
Goldstein, Dora Benedict pharmacologist, educator
Goldstein, Paul lawyer, educator
Goodman, Joseph Wilfred electrical engineering educator
Graham, Stephan Alan earth sciences educator
Gray, Robert M(olten) electrical engineering educator
Greenberg, Joseph H. anthropologist
Gross, Richard Edmund education educator
Guerard, Albert Joseph retired modern literature educator, author
Gunther, Gerald lawyer, educator
Hall, Robert Ernest economics educator
Hanawalt, Philip Courtland biology educator, researcher
Harbaugh, John Warvelle applied earth sciences educator
Harris, Donald J. economics educator
Harrison, Walter Ashley physicist, educator
Harvey, Van Austin religious studies educator
Hellyer, Constance Anne communications executive, writer
Henriksen, Thomas Hollinger university official
Hentz, Vincent R. surgeon
Herring, William Conyers physicist, emeritus educator
Hesselink, Lambertus electrical engineering and physics educator
Hewett, Thomas Avery petroleum engineer, educator
Hickman, Bert George, Jr. economist, educator
Hilgard, Ernest Ropiequet psychologist
Hlatky, Mark Andrew cardiologist, health services researcher
Holloway, Charles Arthur public and private management educator
Holloway, David James political science educator
Horngren, Charles Thomas accounting educator
Howell, James Edwin economist, educator
Hubert, Helen Betty epidemiologist
Hughes, Thomas J.R. mechanical engineering educator, consultant
Inkeles, Alex sociology educator
Jardetzky, Oleg medical educator, scientist
Johnson, John J. historian, educator
Johnston, Bruce Foster economics educator
Johnstone, Iain Murray statistician, educator, consultant
Kailath, Thomas electrical engineer, educator
Kane, Thomas Reif engineering educator
Karlin, Samuel mathematics educator, researcher
Kays, William Morrow university administrator, mechanical engineer
Keller, Joseph Bishop mathematician, educator
Keller, Michael Alan librarian, educator, musicologist
Kendig, Joan Johnston neurobiology educator
Kennedy, David Michael historian, educator
Kennedy, Donald environmental science educator, former academic administrator
Kirst, Michael Weile education educator, researcher
Kline, Stephen Jay mechanical engineer, educator
Knuth, Donald Ervin computer sciences educator
Kornberg, Arthur biochemist
Kornberg, Roger David biochemist, structural biologist
Kovach, Robert Louis geophysics educator
Krauskopf, Konrad Bates geology educator
Kreps, David Marc economist, educator
Kruger, Charles Herman, Jr. mechanical engineering educator
Krumboltz, John Dwight psychologist, educator
Kurz, Mordecai economics educator
Lau, Lawrence Juen-Yee economics educator, consultant
Lazear, Edward Paul economics and industrial relations educator, researcher
Leavitt, Harold Jack management educator
Lehman, (Israel) Robert biochemistry educator, consultant
Lepper, Mark Roger psychology educator
Levin, Henry Mordecai economist, educator
Levinthal, Elliott Charles physicist, educator
Levitt, Raymond Elliot civil engineering educator
Lewis, John Wilson political science educator
L'Heureux, John Clarke English language educator
Lieberman, Gerald J. statistics educator
Lindenberger, Herbert Samuel writer, literature educator
Linvill, John Grimes engineering educator
Little, William Arthur physicist, educator
Loftis, John (Clyde), Jr. English language educator
Lohnes, Walter F. W. German language and literature educator
Long, Sharon Rugel molecular biologist, plant biology educator
Lyman, Richard Wall foundation and university executive, historian
Lyons, Charles R. drama educator and critic
Maccoby, Eleanor Emmons psychology educator
Macovski, Albert electrical engineering educator
Madix, Robert James chemical engineer, educator
Maffly, Roy Herrick medical educator
Maharidge, Dale Dimitro journalist, educator
Manley, John Frederick political scientist, educator
Mann, J. Keith arbitrator, law educator
March, James Gardner social scientist, educator
Mark, James B. D. surgeon
Marmor, Michael Franklin ophthalmologist, educator
Martin, Joanne business educator
Massy, William Francis education educator, academic administrator
Matin, A. microbiology educator, consultant
Mc Bride, Thomas Frederick lawyer, former university dean, government official
McCarthy, John computer scientist, educator
Mc Carty, Perry Lee civil engineering educator, research director
McCluskey, Edward Joseph engineering educator
McConnell, Harden Marsden biophysical chemistry researcher, chemistry educator
McDevitt, Hugh O'Neill immunology educator, physician
McDonald, John Gregory financial investment educator
McDougall, Iain Ross nuclear medicine educator
Mc Lure, Charles E., Jr. economist
Mc Namara, Joseph Donald researcher, retired police chief, novelist
Meier, Gerald Marvin economics educator
Melmon, Kenneth Lloyd physician, biologist, pharmacologist, consultant
Merigan, Thomas Charles, Jr. physician, medical researcher, educator
Middlebrook, Diane Wood English language educator
Miller, James Rumrill, III finance educator
Miller, William Frederick research company executive, educator, business consultant
Montgomery, David Bruce marketing educator
Moore, Thomas Gale economist, educator
Moravcsik, Julius Matthew philosophy educator
Moses, Lincoln E. statistician, educator
Moss, Richard B. pediatrician
†Naimark, Norman M. academic administrator
Nelson, Drew Vernon mechanical engineering educator
Nelson, Lyle Morgan communications educator
Newman-Gordon, Pauline French language and literature educator
Niederhuber, John Edward surgical oncologist and molecular immunologist, university educator and administrator
Nivison, David Shepherd Chinese and philosophy educator
Noddings, Nel education educator, writer
Noll, Roger Gordon economist, educator
North, Robert Carver political science educator
Oberhelman, Harry Alvin, Jr. surgeon, educator
Olshen, Richard A. statistician, educator
Ornstein, Donald Samuel mathematician, educator
Orr, Franklin Mattes, Jr. petroleum engineering educator
Ortolano, Leonard civil engineering educator, water resources planner
Osheroff, Douglas Dean physicist, researcher
Ott, Wayne Robert environmental engineer
Paffenbarger, Ralph Seal, Jr. epidemiologist, educator
Palm, Charles Gilman university official
Parkinson, Bradford Wells astronautical engineer, educator
Paté-Cornell, Marie-Elisabeth Lucienne industrial engineering educator
Paul, Benjamin David anthropologist, educator
Payne, Anita Hart reproductive endocrinologist, researcher
Pearson, Scott Roberts economics educator
Pease, Roger Fabian Wedgwood electrical engineering educator
Pecora, Robert chemistry educator
Perl, Martin Lewis physicist, educator
Perloff, Marjorie Gabrielle English and comparative literature educator
Perry, John Richard philosophy educator
Perry, William James educator, former federal official
Petrosian, Vahé astrophysicist, educator
Pfeffer, Jeffrey business educator
Phillips, Ralph Saul mathematics educator
Pierce, John Robinson electrical engineer, educator
Porterfield, James Temple Starke business administration educator
Quate, Calvin Forrest engineering educator
Raffin, Thomas A. physician
Raisian, John university institute director, economist
†Rakove, Jack Norman history educator
Reitz, Bruce Arnold cardiac surgeon, educator
Reynolds, Clark Winton economist, educator
Reynolds, William Craig mechanical engineer, educator
Rhode, Deborah Lynn law educator
Ricardo-Campbell, Rita economist, educator
Richter, Burton physicist, educator
Risser, James Vaulx, Jr. journalist, educator
Roberts, Donald Frank, Jr. communications educator
Roberts, Donald John economics and business educator, consultant
Robinson, Paul Arnold historian, educator, author
Rosaldo, Renato Ignacio, Jr. cultural anthropology educator
Rosenberg, Saul Allen oncologist, educator
Rosenthal, Myer H. anesthesiologist
Ross, John physical chemist, educator
Roster, Michael lawyer
Roth, Bernard mechanical engineering educator, researcher
Rott, Nicholas fluid mechanics educator
Rubenstein, Edward physician, educator
Rubin, Karl Cooper mathematics educator
†Rudd, Peter physician, medical educator
Sa, Luiz Augusto Discher physicist
Saloner, Garth management educator
Sanders, William John research scientist
Schatzberg, Alan Frederic psychiatrist, researcher
Schawlow, Arthur Leonard physicist, educator
Schendel, Stephen Alfred plastic surgery educator, craniofacial surgeon
Schneider, Stephen Henry climatologist, environmental policy analyst, researcher
Scott, Kenneth Eugene lawyer, educator
Scott, W(illiam) Richard sociology educator
Seligman, Thomas Knowles museum administrator
Serbein, Oscar Nicholas business educator, consultant
Shah, Haresh C. civil engineering educator
Shapiro, Lucille molecular biology educator
Shaw, Herbert John physics educator emeritus
Sheehan, James John historian, educator
Shepard, Roger Newland psychologist, educator
Shooter, Eric Manvers neurobiology educator, consultant
Shultz, George Pratt former government executive, economics educator
Siegman, Anthony Edward electrical engineer, educator
Silverman, Frederic Noah physician
Smelser, Neil Joseph sociologist
Sofaer, Abraham David lawyer, legal advisor, federal judge, legal educator
Solomon, Ezra economist, educator
Sorrentino, Gilbert English language educator, novelist, poet
Spence, Andrew Michael dean, finance educator
Spicer, William Edward, III physicist, educator
Spitz, Lewis William historian, educator
Spreiter, John Robert engineering educator, space physics scientist
Springer, George Stephen mechanical engineering educator
Staar, Richard Felix political scientist
Stamey, Thomas Alexander physician, urology educator
Stansky, Peter David Lyman historian
Steele, Charles Richard biomedical and mechanical engineering educator
Stone, William Edward association executive
Street, Robert Lynnwood civil and mechanical engineer
Strena, Robert Victor retired university research laboratory manager
Strober, Myra Hoffenberg education educator, consultant
Sweeney, James Lee engineering and economic systems educator
Switzer, Paul statistics educator
Taube, Henry chemistry educator
Taylor, John Brian economist, educator
Taylor, Richard Edward physicist, educator
Teller, Edward physicist
Thompson, George Albert geophysics educator
Traugott, Elizabeth Closs linguistics educator and researcher
Triska, Jan Francis retired political science educator
Trost, Barry Martin chemist, educator
Tsai, Stephen Wei-Lun aeronautical educator
Ullman, Jeffrey David computer science educator
Van Derveer, Tara university athletic coach
Van Dyke, Milton Denman aeronautical engineering educator
Van Etten, Peter Walbridge hospital administrator
Van Horne, James Carter economist, educator
Vincenti, Walter Guido aeronautical engineer, emeritus educator
Wagoner, Robert Vernon astrophysicist, educator
Walt, Martin physicist, consulting educator
Warnke, Roger Allen pathology educator
Weissman, Irving L. medical scientist
Wender, Paul Anthony chemistry educator
White, Robert Lee electrical engineer, educator
Whitney, Rodger Franklin university housing director
Williams, Howard Russell lawyer, educator
Wojcicki, Stanley George physicist, educator
Wolff, Tobias (Jonathan Ansell Wolff) author
Yanofsky, Charles biology educator
Yearian, Mason Russell physicist
Zajonc, Robert B(oleslaw) psychology educator
Zare, Richard Neil chemistry educator
Zarins, Christopher Kristaps surgery educator, vascular surgeon
Zimbardo, Philip George psychologist, educator, writer

### Stanton
Polk, Benjamin Kauffman retired architect, composer, educator

### Stinson Beach
Metz, Mary Seawell university dean, retired college president

### Stockton
Biddle, Donald Ray aerospace company executive
Blewett, Robert Noall lawyer
Curtis, Orlie Lindsey, Jr. lawyer
DeRicco, Lawrence Albert college president emeritus
Dornbush, Vicky Jean medical billing systems executive
Jackson, Jewel state youth authority executive
Jacobs, Marian advertising agency owner
Jantzen, J(ohn) Marc retired education educator
Klinger, Wayne Julius secondary education educator
Limbaugh, Ronald Hadley history educator, history center director
Magness, Rhonda Ann microbiologist
Matuszak, Alice Jean Boyer pharmacy educator
McNeal, Dale William, Jr. biological sciences educator
Montrose, Donald W. bishop
Oak, Claire Morisset artist, educator
O'Brien, Sister Maureen school system administrator
Shao, Otis Hung-I retired political science educator
Sorby, Donald Lloyd university dean
Talley, Robert Boyd physician
Thompson, Thomas Sanford former college president
Tregle, Linda Marie dance educator
Vargo, Richard Joseph accounting educator, writer
Viscovich, Andrew John educational management consultant
Washburn, Harriet Caroline secondary education educator
Whiteker, Roy Archie retired chemistry educator
Whittington, Robert Bruce retired publishing company executive

### Studio City
Autry, Gene (Orvon Gene Autry) actor, entertainer, broadcasting executive, baseball team executive
Barrett, Dorothy performing arts administrator
Basinger, Kim actress
Bergen, Polly actress
Bloodworth-Thomason, Linda television producer, writer
Bumstead, Henry art director, production designer
Carradine, David actor, director
Carsey, Marcia Lee Peterson television producer
Cockrell, Frank Boyd, II film production company executive

Coolidge, Rita *singer*
English, Diane *television producer, writer, communications executive*
Frumkin, Simon *political activist and columnist*
Gautier, Dick *actor, writer*
Haber, David M. *art director, production designer*
Hasselhoff, David *actor*
Hole, Fred *art director*
Hutman, Jon *art director, production designer*
Jacobs, Ronald Nicholas *television and motion picture producer/director*
Kenney, H(arry) Wesley, Jr. *producer, director*
Kilvert, Lilly *film production designer*
Lasarow, William Julius *retired federal judge*
Malone, Nancy *actor, director, producer*
Manders, Susan Kay *artist*
Mansbridge, John B. *art director, production designer*
Miller, Charles Maurice *lawyer*
Needham, Hal *director, writer*
Parish, James Robert *author, cinema historian*
Peerce, Larry *film director*
Ribman, Ronald Burt *playwright*
Roseanne *actress, comedienne, producer, writer*
Rosenberg, Philip *production designer*
Scarfiotti, Ferdinando *production designer*
Sertner, Robert Mark *producer*
Shavelson, Melville *writer, theatrical producer and director*
Shekhar, Stephen S. *obstetrician, gynecologist*
Shepherd, Cybill *actress, singer*
†Sinbad *actor, comedian*
Smith, Peter Lansdown *art director*
Sylbert, Paul *production designer, art director*
Sylbert, Richard *production designer, art director*
Taylor, Jack G., Jr. *art director*
Thomas, Wynn P. *art director, production designer*
Tomkins, Alan *art director, production designer*
Tortorici, Peter Frank *television executive*
von Zerneck, Frank Ernest *television producer*
†Wardlow, Bill *record industry consultant, entertainer*
Wedgeworth, Ann *actress*
Weiner, Sandra Samuel *critical care nurse, nursing consultant*
Werner, Tom *television producer, professional baseball team executive*
Wissner, Gary Charles *motion picture art director, production designer*

### Sugarloaf
Kind, Anne Wilson *engineer*

### Summerland
Calamar, Gloria *artist*
Cannon, Louis Simeon *journalist, author*
Hall, Lee Boaz *publishing company consultant, author*

### Sun City
Fisher, Weston Joseph *economist*

### Sun Valley
Dergrigorian, Ronald *water microbiologist*
Mayhue, Richard Lee *dean, pastor, writer*

### Sunnyvale
Amdahl, Gene Myron *computer company executive*
Amelio, Gilbert Frank *electronics company executive*
Antweiler, Dennis Francis *mechanical engineer*
Armistead, Robert Ashby, Jr. *scientific research company executive*
Bills, Robert Howard *political party executive*
Byers, Charles Frederick *public relations executive, marketing executive*
Charlton, (James) Paul(ett Jr.) *information systems architect*
Cognata, Joseph Anthony *football commissioner*
Davis, Michael Chase *aerospace industry executive, consultant, retired naval officer*
DeMello, Austin Eastwood *astrophysicist, concert artist, poet, writer*
Drmanac, Radoje *molecular biologist*
Evans, Barton, Jr. *analytical instrument company executive*
Hind, Harry William *pharmaceutical company executive*
Karp, Nathan *political activist*
Kim, Wan Hee *electrical engineering educator, business executive*
Koomen, Cornelis Jan *telecommunication and micro electronics executive*
Laurance, Mark Rodney *applications engineer, entrepreneur*
Lewis, John Clark, Jr. *manufacturing company executive*
Ludgus, Nancy Lucke *lawyer*
Ma, Fengchow Clarence *agricultural engineering consultant*
Mansfield, Elaine Schultz *molecular geneticist, automation specialist*
Michals, Lee Marie *retired travel agency executive*
Saluja, Sundar S. *international engineering consultant*
Sanders, Walter Jeremiah, III *electronics company executive*
Schubert, Ronald Hayward *retired aerospace engineer*
Scott, Edward William, Jr. *computer software company executive*
Simon, Ralph E. *electronics executive*
Thissell, James Dennis *physicist*
Zebroski, Edwin Leopold *consulting engineer*

### Surfside
Sonne, Maggie Lee *travel company executive*

### Sylmar
Corry, Dalila Boudjellal *internist*
Foster, Dudley Edwards, Jr. *musician, educator*
Madni, Asad Mohamed *engineering executive*
Scheib, Gerald Paul *fine art educator, jeweler, metalsmith*
Shaw, Anthony *physician, pediatric surgeon*
Tully, Susan Balsley *pediatrician, educator*
Ziment, Irwin *medical educator*

### Taft
Smith, Lee L. *hotel executive*

### Tarzana
Abbott, Philip *actor*
Broadhurst, Norman Neil *foods company executive*
Hansen, Robert Clinton *electrical engineering consultant*

Krueger, Kenneth John *corporate executive, nutritionist, educator*
Macmillan, Robert Smith *electronics engineer*
Meyers, Robert Allen *physical chemist, publisher*
Michaelson, Richard Aaron *health science facility administrator*
Rinsch, Maryann Elizabeth *occupational therapist*
Shaw, Carole *editor, publisher*
Shaw-Cohen, Lori Eve *magazine editor*
Smith, Mark Lee *architect*
Smuckler, Harvey Glasgow *financial consultant*
Yablun, Ronn *secondary education educator, small business owner*

### Tehachapi
Badgley, Theodore McBride *psychiatrist, neurologist*
Smith-Thompson, Patricia Ann *public relations consultant, educator*

### Temecula
Coram, David James *marketing professional*
Minogue, Robert Brophy *retired nuclear engineer*
Randall, John Albert, III *elementary and secondary education educator*
Roemmele, Brian Karl *electronics, publishing, internet, financial and real estate executive*
Rosenstein, Robert Bryce *lawyer*
Thompson, James Avery, Jr. *legal intern*
Thompson, Susannah Elizabeth *lawyer*
Yankee, Marie *educator, publishing executive*

### Templeton
Gandsey, Louis John *petroleum and environmental consultant*

### The Sea Ranch
Hayflick, Leonard *microbiologist, cell biologist, gerontologist, educator, writer*

### Thousand Oaks
Binder, Gordon M. *health and medical products executive*
Deisenroth, Clinton Wilbur *electrical engineer*
Falk, EuGene L. *publishing executive*
Gregory, Calvin *insurance service executive*
Hale, William Bryan, Jr. *newspaper editor*
Klein, Jeffrey Howard *oncologist, internist*
Krumm, Charles Ferdinand *electrical engineer*
Lark, M. Ann *management consultant, strategic planner, naturalist*
Malmuth, Norman David *scientist, program manager*
McCune, David Franklin *publisher*
Miller, Jim *film editor*
Monis, Antonio, Jr. (Tony Monis) *electric industry executive*
Mulkey, Sharon Renee *gerontology nurse*
Richelson, Harvey *lawyer, educator*
Rooney, Mickey (Joe Yule, Jr.) *actor*
Sherman, Gerald *nuclear physicist, financial estate adviser, financial company executive*
†Shirilla, Robert M. *executive recruiter*
Sladek, Lyle Virgil *mathematician, educator*
Wang, I-Tung *atmospheric scientist*

### Thousand Palms
Smith, Charles Thomas *retired dentist, educator*

### Tiburon
Bauch, Thomas Jay *lawyer, educator, former apparel company executive*
Cook, Lyle Edwards *retired fund raising executive, consultant*
Drury, Allen Stuart *author*
Harary, Keith *psychologist*

### Toluca Lake
†Firestone, Roy *sportscaster*

### Topanga
Redgrave, Lynn *actress*
Warner, Mark Roy *film editor*

### Torrance
Adelsman, (Harriette) Jean *newspaper editor*
Alter, Gerald L. *real estate executive*
Brasel, Jo Anne *physician*
Brodsky, Robert Fox *aerospace engineer*
Buckley, James W. *librarian*
Cai, Khiem Van *research scientist, administrator*
Carey, Kathryn Ann *advertising and public relations executive, consultant*
Culton, Paul Melvin *retired counselor, educator, interpreter*
Emmanouilides, George Christos *physician, educator*
Everts, Connor *artist*
Goldberg, Mark Arthur *neurologist*
Greaser, Constance Udean *automotive industry executive*
Harmon Brown, Valarie Jean *hospital laboratory director, information systems executive*
Harness, William Edward *tenor*
Houston, Samuel Robert *statistics educator, consultant*
Itabashi, Hideo Henry *neuropathologist, neurologist*
Kaufman, Sanford Paul *lawyer*
Krout, Boyd Merrill *psychiatrist*
Kucij, Timothy Michael *engineer, musician, minister*
Leake, Donald Lewis *oral and maxillofacial surgeon, oboist*
Leake, Rosemary Dobson *physician*
Manasson, Vladimir Alexandrovich *physicist*
Mann, Michael Martin *electronics company executive*
McNamara, Brenda Norma *secondary education educator*
Mehringer, Charles Mark *medical educator*
Mende, Howard Shigeharu *mechanical engineer*
Myhre, Byron Arnold *pathologist, educator*
Narasimhan, Padma Mandyam *physician*
Parady, John Edward *information systems executive, consultant*
Perrish, Albert *steel company executive*
Petillon, Lee Ritchey *lawyer*
Prell, Joel James *medical group administrator*
Rogers, Howard H. *chemist*
Savitz, Maxine Lazarus *aerospace company executive*
Signorovitch, Dennis James *communications executive*
Smith, Michael Cordon *lawyer*
†Stabile, Bruce Edward *surgeon*
Tanaka, Kouichi Robert *physician, educator*
Todd, Frances Eileen *pediatrics nurse*
Trousdale, Stephen Richard *newspaper editor*

Woodhull, John Richard *electronics company executive*
Yoon, Sewang *engineering executive*
Young, Aline Patrice *controller*

### Trabuco Canyon
Addy, Jo Alison Phears *economist*

### Trinidad
Marshall, William Edward *historical association executive*
Schaaf, Miv *writer, graphic designer, composer*

### Trinity Center
Hartman, Ruth Gayle *rancher*

### Truckee
Johnston, Bernard Fox *foundation executive*

### Tulare
Vickrey, Herta Miller *microbiologist*

### Turlock
Ahlem, Lloyd Harold *psychologist*
Amrhein, John Kilian *dean*
Goedecke, David Stewart *music educator, band educator, trumpet player*
Hughes, Marvalene *academic administrator*
Klein, James Mikel *music educator*
Williams, Delwyn Charles *telephone company executive*

### Tustin
Bartlett, Arthur Eugene *franchise executive*
Crouch, Paul Franklin *minister, church official*
Dearborn, Edwin Whittier *religious organization administrator, clergyman*
Evans, Thomas Edgar, Jr. *title insurance agency executive*
Gray, Sandra Rae *retired secondary school educator*
Hester, Norman Eric *chemical company technical executive, chemist*
LeBow, Bennett S. *communications executive*
Parker, Kimberly Jane *nonprofit association executive, paralegal*
Sinnette, John Townsend, Jr. *research scientist, consultant*

### Tustin Ranch
Ortlieb, Robert Eugene *sculptor*

### Twain Harte
Kinsinger, Robert Earl *property company executive, educational consultant*

### Twentynine Palms
Clemente, Patrocinio Ablola *psychology educator*
Fultz, Philip Nathaniel *management analyst*

### Ukiah
Elberg, Sanford Samuel *retired university dean and bacteriology educator*
McAllister, (Ronald) Eric *pharmaceutical executive, physician*
McClintock, Richard Polson *dermatologist*
Nugent, Constance Marie Julie *health facility administrator*

### Union City
Funston, Gary Stephen *publishing and advertising executive*
Glueck, Mary A. *psychiatric and mental health nurse, administrator*
Lewis, Mark Earldon *city manager*
Lockhart, Patsy Marie *secondary education educator*

### Universal City
Biondi, Frank J., Jr. *entertainment company executive*
Bishop, Stephen *singer, songwriter*
Buffett, Jimmy *singer, songwriter, author*
Ely, Joe *singer and songwriter*
Frey, Glenn *songwriter, vocalist, guitarist*
Geffen, David *recording company executive, producer*
Judd, Wynonna *vocalist, musician*
Lansbury, Angela Brigid *actress*
Metheny, Pat *jazz musician*
Michelson, Lillian *motion picture researcher*
†Silver, Casey *broadcast executive*

### Upland
Goodman, John M. *construction executive*
Jones, Nancy Langdon *financial planning practitioner*
Lewis, Goldy Sarah *real estate developer, corporation executive*
Lewis, Ralph Milton *real estate developer*
Rice, Sharon Margaret *clinical psychologist*

### Upper Lake
Twitchell, Kent *mural artist*

### Vacaville
Castro, David Alexander *construction executive*
Dedeaux, Paul J. *orthodontist*
Martinez, Gayle Frances *protective services official*
Wisneski, Mary Jo Elizabeth *reading specialist, educator*
Zaleski, Brian William *chiropractor*

### Valencia
Fiskin, Judith Anne *artist, educator*
Hunter, Diana Lynn *real estate consultant*
Looney, Claudia Arlene *academic administrator*
Windsor, William Earl *consulting engineer, sales representative*

### Vallejo
Baker, Christine Marie *secondary education educator*
Hudak, Paul Alexander *retired engineer*
Kleinrock, Robert Allen *physician*
Marshall, Roberta Navarre *middle school educator*
McGowan, Thomas Randolph *religious organization executive*

### Valley Center
Harper, Lilah Marie *health science administrator, consultant*

### Van Nuys
Allen, Stephen Valentine Patrick William *television comedian, author, pianist, songwriter*
Altshiller, Arthur Leonard *secondary education educator*
Arabian, Armand *arbitrator, mediator, lawyer*
Boyd, Harry Dalton *lawyer, former insurance company executive*
Corinblit, Nita Green *artist, educator*
Ferguson, Jay A. *composer*
Fox, James Michael *orthopedic surgeon*
Freiberg, Robert Jerry *physicist, engineer, technology administrator*
Ghent, Peer *management consultant*
Ivey, Judith *actress*
Kagan, Stephen Bruce (Sandy Kagan) *network marketing executive*
Mikesell, Richard Lyon *lawyer, financial counselor*
Newborn, Ira *composer*
Rosen, Alexander Carl *psychologist, consultant*
Schwab, Howard Joel *judge*
Simon, David Harold *retired public relations executive*
Sludikoff, Stanley Robert *publisher, writer*
Zucker, Alfred John *English educator, academic administrator*

### Venice
Annotico, Richard Anthony *legal scholar*
Bengston, Billy Al *artist*
Bill, Tony *producer, director*
Chiat, Jay *advertising agency executive*
Chipman, Jack *artist*
Chomsky, Marvin J. *director*
Dixon, Neil Edward *elementary school educator, paleo-anthropologist*
Eliot, Alexander *author, mythologist*
Eversley, Frederick John *sculptor, engineer*
Ferry, April *costume designer*
Hartley, Corinne *painter, sculptor, educator*
Naga, Tarek A. *architect, educator*
Rosenthal, Richard Jay *real estate consultant, mediator, educator*
Seger, Linda Sue *script consultant, writer*
Smith, Yvonne Smart *advertising agency executive*
Young, Christopher *composer*

### Ventura
Abul-Haj, Suleiman Kahil *pathologist*
Arant, Eugene Wesley *lawyer*
Bircher, Andrea Ursula *psychiatric mental health nurse, educator, clinical nurse specialist*
Bride, Robert Fairbanks *lawyer*
Cammalleri, Joseph Anthony *financial planner, retired air force officer*
Clabaugh, Elmer Eugene, Jr. *lawyer*
Evans, James Handel *university administrator, architect, educator*
Field, A. J. *former oil drilling company executive, engineering consultant*
Gaynor, Joseph *chemical engineer, management consultant*
Greig, William Taber, Jr. *publishing company executive*
Keister, Jean Clare *lawyer*
Kirman, Charles Gary *photojournalist*
Lawson, William Harold *college dean, labor economist*
Matley, Benvenuto Gilbert (Ben Matley) *computer engineer, educator, consultant*
Okuma, Albert Akira, Jr. *architect*
Shultz, Emmet Lavel *marketing executive, commodities trader*
Villaveces, James Walter *allergist, immunologist*
Williamson, John Henry, III *school administrator*

### Vernon
Lynch, Martin Andrew *retail company executive*

### Victorville
Grogan, Suzann Jeanette-Wyman *artist*
Syed, Moinuddin *electrical engineer*

### Villa Park
Britton, Thomas Warren, Jr. *management consultant*
Hawe, David Lee *consultant*

### Visalia
Crowe, John T. *lawyer*
Dixon, Andrew Derart *retired academic administrator*
Madden, Wanda Lois *nurse*
Riegel, Byron William *ophthalmologist*
Sickels, William Loyd *secondary educator*

### Vista
Beversdorf, Anne Elizabeth *astrologer, author, educator*
Cavanaugh, Kenneth Clinton *retired housing consultant*
Ferguson, Margaret Ann *tax consultant*
Helmuth, Philip Alan *tax consultant*
Patrick, Wendy Lynn *lawyer*
Rader, Paul Alexander *minister, administrator*
Tiedeman, David Valentine *education educator*

### Volcano
Prout, Ralph Eugene *physician*

### Walnut
Lane, David Christopher *humanities educator, author, researcher*
Martin, George *psychologist, educator*
Shannon, Cynthia Jean *biology educator*
Spencer, Constance Marilyn *secondary education educator*
Tan, Colleen Woo *communications educator*

### Walnut Creek
Acosta, Julio Bernard *obstetrician, gynecologist*
Bardy, Sharon Davis *language educator*
Burgarino, Anthony Emanuel *environmental engineer, consultant*
Carver, Dorothy Lee Eskew (Mrs. John James Carver) *retired secondary education educator*
Conger, Harry Milton *mining company executive*
Crandall, Ira Carlton *consulting electrical engineer*
Curtin, Daniel Joseph, Jr. *lawyer*
Du Bois, Philip Hunter *psychologist, educator*
Farr, Lee Edward *nuclear medicine physician*
Garlough, William Glenn *marketing executive*
Garrett, James Joseph *lawyer, partner*
Gentry, James Frederick *chemical engineer, consultant*

Mc Intosh, J(ohn) Richard biologist, educator
Mehalchin, John Joseph entrepreneur, finance company executive
Meier, Mark F. research scientist, glaciologist, educator
Melicher, Ronald William finance educator
Metzger, H(owell) Peter writer
Middleton-Downing, Laura psychiatric social worker, artist, small business owner
Miller, Norman Richard diversified manufacturing company executive
Moses, Raphael Jacob lawyer
Mycielski, Jan mathematician, educator
Neinas, Charles Merrill athletic association executive
Norcross, David Warren physicist, researcher
O'Brien, Elmer John librarian, educator
Oesterle, Dale Arthur law educator
Ostrovsky, Lev Aronovich physicist, oceanographer, educator
Pankove, Jacques Isaac physicist
Park, Roderic Bruce academic administrator
Peterson, Courtland Harry law educator
Peterson, Roy Jerome physics educator
Phelps, Arthur Van Rensselaer physicist, consultant
Pollard, George Marvin economist
Porzak, Glenn E. lawyer
Purvis, John Anderson lawyer
Quint, Bert journalist
Reitsema, Harold James aerospace engineer
Richardson, Donn Charles business and marketing educator
Rieke, Elizabeth Ann legal association administrator
Rienner, Lynne Carol publisher
Robinson, Peter paleontology educator, consultant
Rodriguez, Juan Alfonso technology corporation executive
Roellig, Leonard Oscar physics educator
Rood, David S. linguistics educator
Sable, Barbara Kinsey former music educator
Sani, Robert LeRoy chemical engineering educator
Sarson, John Christopher television producer, director, writer
Schneider, Nicholas McCord planetary scientist, educator
Schwarz, Josephine Lindeman retired ballet company director, choreographer
Seebass, Alfred Richard, III aerospace engineer, educator, university dean
Shanahan, Eugene Miles flow measurement instrumentation company executive
Shang, Er-Chang acoustician
Sirotkin, Phillip Leonard educational administrator
Smith, Ernest Ketcham electrical engineer
Smythe, William Rodman physicist, educator
Snow, Theodore Peck astrophysics educator
Sodal, Ingvar Edmund electrical engineer, scientist
Speiser, Theodore Wesley astrophysics, planetary and atmospheric sciences educator
Staehelin, Lucas Andrew cell biology educator
Stanton, William John, Jr. marketing educator, author
Steuben, Norton Leslie lawyer, educator
Stone, John Helms, Jr. admiralty advisor
Symons, James Martin theater and dance educator
Tatarskii, Valerian Il'Ich physics researcher
Taylor, Allan Ross linguist, educator
Thomas, Daniel Foley telecommunications company executive
Thomas, Gary Edward science educator, researcher
Timmerhaus, Klaus Dieter chemical engineering educator
Tippit, John Harlow lawyer
Tolbert, Bert Mills biochemist, educator
Trenberth, Kevin Edward atmospheric scientist
Uberoi, Mahinder Singh aerospace engineering educator
Utlaut, William Frederick electrical engineer
Waldman, Anne Lesley poet, performer, editor, publisher, educational administrator
Walker, Deward Edgar, Jr. anthropologist, educator
Washington, Warren Morton meteorologist
Waters, M. Bruce engineering technician
Wheat, Joe Ben anthropologist
White, Gilbert F(owler) geographer, educator
Whiteside, Lowell Stanley seismologist
Wieman, Carl E. physics educator
Williams, James Franklin, II university dean, librarian
Williams, Pamela R. secondary school administrator
Wood, William Barry, III biologist, educator

### Broomfield
Kober, Carl Leopold exploration company executive
Livesay, Valorie Ann security analyst
Lybarger, John Steven business development consultant, trainer
Rodriguez, Linda Takahashi secondary school educator, administrator

### Brush
Gabriel, Donald Eugene science educator

### Canon City
Bendell, Donald Ray writer, director, poet
Cochran, Susan Mills librarian
Fair, Annie May geological computer specialist
McBride, John Alexander retired chemical engineer
Mohr, Gary Alan physician
Romano, Rebecca Kay counselor

### Carbondale
Cowgill, Ursula Moser biologist, educator, environmental consultant

### Castle Rock
Eppler, Jerome Cannon private financial advisor
Graf, Joseph Charles retired foundation executive
Henry, Frances Ann journalist, educator
Thornbury, John Rousseau radiologist, physician

### Cherry Hills Village
Meyer, Milton Edward, Jr. lawyer, artist
Stapleton, Katharine Hall (Katie Stapleton) food broadcaster, author

### Clark
Bartoe, Otto Edwin, Jr. aircraft company executive

### Colorado Springs
Adams, Bernard Schroder retired college president
Adams, Deborah Rowland lawyer
Adnet, Jacques Jim Pierre astronautical and electrical engineer, consultant
Anderson, Paul Nathaniel oncologist, educator
Ansorge, Iona Marie retired real estate agent, musician, high school and college instructor
Armstrong, Lance professional cyclist
Barrowman, Mike Olympic athlete, swimmer
Barry, William Patrick military officer
Barton, Gregory Mark Olympic athlete, kayak racer
Bates, Michael Olympic athlete, track and field
†Beard, Amanda swimmer, Olympic athlete
Berkoff, David Olympic athlete, swimmer
Biondi, Matt Olympic athlete, swimmer
Bishop, Leo Kenneth clergyman, educator
†Botsford, Beth swimmer, Olympic athlete
Bowen, Clotilde Dent retired army officer, psychiatrist
Bressan, Robert R. accountant
†Bridgewater, Brad Olympic athlete
Brooks, Glenn Ellis political science educator, educational administrator
Budd, Barbara Tews sculptor
Budington, William Stone retired librarian
Buell, Bruce Temple lawyer
Burgess, Greg Olympic athlete, swimming
Byrd, Chris Olympic athlete, boxer
Byrne, Catherine swimmer
Cameron, Paul Drummond research facility administrator
Campbell, Frederick Hollister lawyer, historian
Chen, Lynn Chia-Ling librarian
Cimino, Jay automotive company executive
Cole, Julian Wayne (Perry Cole) computer educator, consultant, programmer, analyst
Comes, Robert George research scientist
Conley, Mike track and field athlete
Couger, James Daniel computer scientist, writer
Cramer, Owen Carver classics educator
Dahlman, Simon Jacques magazine editor, minister
Dassanowsky, Robert von writer, editor, educator, producer
†Davis, Richard Shermer, Jr. aerospace defense consultant
Dees, Tony Olympic athlete, track and field
Dello Joio, Norman olympic athlete, equestrian
Diebel, Nelson Olympic athlete, swimmer
Dimas, Trent Olympic athlete, gymnast
Doehrin, James Olympic athlete, track and field
DuPee, Pamela Annette fisheries biologist, educator, consultant
Ehrhorn, Richard William electronics company executive
Eldredge, Todd figure skater
Evans, Janet Olympic swimmer
Evans, Paul Vernon lawyer
Fields, Robert Charles retired printing company executive
Forgan, David Waller retired air force officer
Foth, Bob Olympic athlete, riflery
Fox, Douglas Allan religion educator
Freeman, J.P. Ladyhawk underwater exploration, security and transportation executive, educator, fashion model
Goehring, Kenneth artist
Grady, Dolores Anne academic administrator, educator, consultant
Gray, Johnny Olympic athlete, track and field
Groebli, Werner Fritz (Mr. Frick) professional ice skater, realtor
Guthrie, David Neal marketing executive
Hallenbeck, Kenneth Luster numismatist
Halling, Leonard William retired pathologist, laboratory administrator
Hamilton, James Milton veterinarian
Hanifen, Richard Charles bishop
Heffron, Michael Edward software engineer, computer scientist
Hoffman, John Raleigh physicist
Hoge, Robert Wilson museum curator
Isaac, Robert Michael former mayor
Jacobi, Joe Olympic athlete, canoeist
Jager, Tom Olympic athlete, swimmer
Johnson, Dave Olympic athlete, track and field
Keen, Ronald Lee career officer
Kelsey, Floyd Lamar, Jr. architect
Kendall, Phillip Alan lawyer
Killian, George Ernest educational association administrator
King, Peter Joseph, Jr. retired gas company executive
Kohlman, David Leslie engineering executive, consultant
†Kwan, Michelle professional skater
LeMieux, Linda Dailey museum director
Lenzi, Mark Olympic athlete, springboard diver
Leonard, George Edmund real estate, bank, and consulting executive
Leuver, Robert Joseph former government official, association executive
Lewis, Sheila Muriel O'Neil retired communications management specialist
Lewis, Steve Olympic athlete, track and field
Libby, Lauren Dean foundation executive
Loux, Gordon Dale organization executive
†Lucia, Don head coach men's ice hockey
MacLeod, Richard Patrick foundation administrator
Macon, Jerry Lyn software company owner, software publisher
Mangham, R. Harold church administrator
Markert, Clement Lawrence biology educator
Marsh, Michael track and field athlete
May, Melvin Arthur computer software company executive
McIntyre, Elizabeth Geary Olympic athlete
Midkiff, Donald Wayne program manager
Miller, Zoya Dickins (Mrs. Hilliard Eve Miller, Jr.) civic worker
Milton, Richard Henry retired diplomat, children's advocate
Mitchell, Dennis A. Olympic athlete, track and field
Mitchell, John Henderson retired army officer, management consultant
Mohrman, Kathryn academic administrator
Morales, Pablo Olympic athlete, swimmer
Munro, Michael Donald hotel industry executive, retired military officer
Murray, Ty (The Kid Murray) professional rodeo cowboy
Nolan, Barry Hance publishing company executive
Nowosatko, Jerome Raymond software engineer
Noyes, Richard Hall bookseller
Ogrean, David William sports executive
Olin, Kent Oliver banker
O'Rourke, Dennis lawyer
O'Shields, Richard Lee retired natural gas company executive
†Payne, Kevin Joseph association executive
Peiser, Robert Alan financial executive
Perkins, Floyd Jerry retired theology educator
Peterson, Amy Olympic athlete
Phibbs, Harry Albert interior designer, professional speaker, lecturer
Pickle, Joseph Wesley, Jr. religion educator
Pierce, Jack Olympic athlete, track and field
Pool, Timothy Kevin facilities management consultant
Porter, David Bruce air force officer, behavioral scientist, educator
Pressman, Glenn Spencer lawyer
Ramsay, Robert Henry investment manager
Reddel, Carl Walter education adminstration
†Reid, David Olympic athlete
Rhodes, Eric Foster arbitrator, employee relations consultant, insurance executive
Robinson, Robert James retired manufacturing executive
Robinson, Ronald Alan manufacturing executive
Rochette, Edward Charles retired association executive
Rogers, Steven Ray physicist
Rouse, Jeff Olympic athlete, swimmer
Rouss, Ruth lawyer
Ruch, Marcella Joyce educator, biographer
Sanders, Summer Olympic athlete
Sawyer, Thomas William air force officer
Schaeffer, Reiner Horst air force officer, retired librarian, foreign language professional
†Scherr, James E. sports association executive
Schultz, Richard Dale national athletic organizations executive
Schwartz, Donald chemistry educator
Schwebach, Gerhard Hermann microbiologist
Simmons, George Finlay mathematics educator
Sinclair, William Donald church official, fundraising consultant, political activist, state legislator
Stavig, Mark Luther English language educator
Stewart, Melvin Olympic athlete, swimmer
Street, Picabo Olympic athlete
Stulce, Mike Olympic athlete, track and field
Thor, Paul Viets computer science educator, software engineer, consultant
Todd, Harold Wade association executive, retired air force officer
Turner, Cathy Olympic athlete
†Van Dyken, Amy swimmer, Olympic athlete
Watkins, Lois Irene English educator
Watts, Oliver Edward engineering consultancy company executive
†Watz, Hallet N. emergency physician
West, Ralph Leland veterinarian
Wheeland, D. A. church administrator
Wilcox, Rhoda Davis elementary education educator
Williams, Ruth Lee clinical social worker
Yaffe, James author
Young, Kevin track and field athlete
Zapel, Arthur L. book publishing executive
Ziemer, Rodger Edmund electrical engineering educator, consultant
Zimkas, Charles Patrick, Jr. space foundation director

### Columbine Valley
Wittbrodt, Edwin Stanley consultant, former bank executive, former air force officer

### Commerce City
Trujillo, Lorenzo A. lawyer, educator

### Cortez
Winterer-Schulz, Barbara Jean art designer, author

### Crawford
Mosher, Lawrence Forsyth journalist

### Creede
Carter, Shirley Raedelle retired elementary school educator

### Crestone
McNamara, William priest
Temple, Lee Brett architect

### Deer Trail
Malson, Verna Lee special education educator

### Delta
Vanderheyden, Mirna-Mar resort management and services executive

### Denver
Abo, Ronald Kent architect
Abram, Donald Eugene federal magistrate judge
Adler, Charles Spencer psychiatrist
Ahern, Arleen Fleming retired librarian
Aikawa, Jerry Kazuo physician, educator
Alfers, Stephen Douglas lawyer
Allen, Robert Edward, Jr. physician assistant
Anderson, John David architect
Anderson, Paula D.J. pharmacist
Antonoff, Gary L. real estate executive
Ashton, Rick James librarian
Atkins, Dale Morrell physician
Atlass, Theodore Bruce lawyer, educator
Austin, H(arry) Gregory lawyer
Avrit, Richard Calvin defense consultant
Axley, Hartman underwriter
Babcock, Lewis Thornton federal judge
Bain, Donald Knight lawyer
Bain, James William lawyer
Ballentine, Lee Kenney writer, publishing company executive
Barkin, Roger Michael pediatrician, emergency physician, educator
Barnes, William Anderson real estate investment manager
Barnewall, Gordon Gouverneur news analyst, marketing educator
Barry, Henry Ford chemical company executive
†Bartholomew, Charles R. advertising executive
Bates, James Robert newspaper editor
Battaglia, Frederick Camillo physician
Bautista, Michael Phillip school system administrator
Baylor, Don Edward professional baseball manager
Baysinger, Stephen Michael quality assurance professional
Bearden, Thomas Howard news program producer, correspondent
Belitz, Paul Edward lawyer
Benson, Robert Eugene lawyer
Benson, Thomas Quentin lawyer
Benton, Auburn Edgar lawyer
Berardini, Jacqueline Hernandez lawyer
Berger, John Milton state agency administrator
Berger, William Merriam Bart investment management company executive
Berland, Karen Ina psychologist
Bichette, Alphonse Dante professional baseball player
Bies, Roger David cardiologist
Bishop, Tilman Malcolm state senator, retired college administrator
Blair, Andrew Lane, Jr. lawyer, educator
Blatter, Frank Edward travel agency executive
Blitz, Stephen M. lawyer
Blunk, Forrest Stewart lawyer
Boudreau, Robert Donald meteorology educator
Boulware, Richard Stark airport administrator
Bradley, Jeff(rey) Mark arts critic
Brainard, Edward Axdal academic administrator
Brantigan, Charles Otto surgeon
Breck, Allen du Pont historian, educator
Breeskin, Michael Wayne lawyer
Brega, Charles Franklin lawyer
Brom, Libor journalist, educator
Brown, Hank former senator
Brown, Keith Lapham retired ambassador
Browne, Spencer I. mortgage company executive
Brownlee, Judith Marilyn Wiccan priestess, psychotherapist
Brownson, Jacques Calmon architect
Bryan, A(lonzo) J(ay) service club official
Buckley, Vikki state official
Bunn, Paul A., Jr. oncologist, educator
Burford, Anne McGill lawyer
Burgess, Larry Lee aerospace executive
Burke, Kenneth John lawyer
Burnett, Elizabeth (Betsy Burnett) counselor
Burrell, Calvin Archie minister
Burshtan, John Willis television producer
Bush, Marjorie Evelynn Tower-Tooker educator, media specialist, librarian
Butler, David lawyer
Butler, Owen Bradford securities advisor
Bye, James Edward lawyer
Cain, Douglas Mylchreest lawyer
Campbell, David Neil physician, educator
Campbell, Leonard Martin lawyer
Cantwell, William Patterson lawyer
Carr, James Francis lawyer
Carraher, John Bernard lawyer
Carrigan, Jim R. arbitrator, mediator, retired federal judge
Carver, Craig R. lawyer
Castilla, Vinivio Soria professional baseball player
Ceci, Jesse Arthur violinist
Chappell, Willard Ray physics educator, environmental scientist
Chaput, Charles J. archbishop
Cheroutes, Michael Louis lawyer
Childears, Linda banker
Clark, Suzanne accountant
Clayton, Mack Louis surgery professor, educator
Clinch, Nicholas Bayard, III business executive
Clough, Nadine Doerr school psychologist, psychotherapist
Cobban, William Aubrey paleontologist
Cochran, John Howard plastic and reconstructive surgeon
Collins, Martha Traudt lawyer
Colvis, John Paris aerospace engineer, mathematician, scientist
Commander, Eugene R. lawyer
Conger, John Janeway psychologist, educator
Conover, Frederic King lawyer
Conroy, Thomas Francis insurance company executive
Cook, Albert Thomas Thornton, Jr. financial advisor
Cooper, Paul Douglas lawyer
Cope, Thomas Field lawyer
Cowley, Gerald Dean architect
Cox, William Vaughan lawyer
Craine, Thomas Knowlton academic administrator
Crawford, Marc professional hockey coach
Cubbison, Christopher Allen editor
Cutter, Gary Raymond biostatistician
Dallas, Sandra correspondent, writer
Dance, Francis Esburn Xavier communication educator
Daniel, Wiley Y. lawyer
Dauer, Edward Arnold law educator
Davidson, John Robert (Jay) banking executive
Dean, James Benwell lawyer
Decker, David B. architect, educator
De Gette, Diana Louise lawyer, state legislator
Deitrich, Richard Adam pharmacology educator
DeLong, James Clifford air transportation executive
de Marino, Thomas John lawyer
Dempsey, Howard Stanley lawyer, mining executive, investment banker
DeMuth, Alan Cornelius lawyer
DePew, Marie Kathryn retired secondary school educator
Dobbs, Gregory Allan journalist
Dolan, Brian Thomas lawyer
Dolsen, David Horton mortician
Dominick, Peter Hoyt, Jr. architect
†Dowdy, Andrea Lee business development executive
Downey, Arthur Harold, Jr. lawyer, mediator
Drake, Sylvie (Jurras Drake) theater critic
Droullard, Steven Maurice jewelry company executive
Dubroff, Henry Allen newspaper editor
Ducker, Bruce novelist, lawyer
East, Donald Robert civil engineer
Eaton, Gareth Richard chemistry educator, university dean
Ebel, David M. federal judge
Edelman, Joel medical center executive
Ehret, Josephine Mary microbiologist, researcher
Ehrlich, Stephen Richard lawyer
Eiberger, Carl Frederick trial lawyer
Eickhoff, Theodore Carl physician
Eklund, Carl Andrew lawyer
Engdahl, Todd Philip newspaper editor
Enright, Cynthia Lee illustrator
Erisman, Frank lawyer
Faatz, Jeanne Ryan state legislator
Fagin, David Kyle natural resource company executive
Fancher, George H., Jr. oil company executive, petroleum engineer
Farley, John Michael lawyer
Faxon, Thomas Baker lawyer
Featherstone, Bruce Alan lawyer
Fennessey, Paul Vincent pediatrics and pharmacology, educator, research administrator
Ferguson, Lloyd Elbert manufacturing engineer
Fielden, C. Franklin, III early childhood education consultant
Filley, Christopher Mark neurologist
Flowers, William Harold, Jr. lawyer
Fognani, John Dennis lawyer

Forsberg, Peter *professional hockey player*
Foster, Norman Holland *geologist*
Fredmann, Martin *ballet artistic director, educator, choreographer*
Friedman, H. Harold *cardiologist, internist*
Fulginiti, Vincent *university dean*
Fulkerson, William Measey, Jr. *college president*
Fuller, Kenneth Roller *architect*
Galarraga, Andres Jose *professional baseball player*
Gallagher, Dennis Joseph *city councilman, former state senator, educator*
Gates, Charles Cassius *rubber company executive*
Gebhard, Bob *professional baseball team executive*
Gibbs, Ronald Steven *obstetrician-gynecologist*
Giesen, John William *advertising executive*
Giffin, Glenn Orlando, II *music critic, writer, newspaper editor*
Golitz, Loren Eugene *dermatologist, pathologist, clinical administrator, educator*
Goss, Patricia Elizabeth *secondary education educator*
Grant, Patrick Alexander *lawyer, association administrator*
Grant, William West, III *banker*
Green, Jersey Michael-Lee *lawyer*
Green, Larry Alton *physician, educator*
Greenberg, David Ethan *communications consultant*
Greenspahn, Barbara *university administrator, law educator, librarian*
Grissom, Garth Clyde *lawyer*
Groff, JoAnn *organization administrator*
Grounds, Vernon Carl *seminary administrator*
Hackworth, Theodore James, Jr. *city official*
Haddon, Timothy John *mining engineer*
Hafenstein, Norma Lu *education educator*
Halgren, Lee A. *academic administrator*
Halverson, Steven Thomas *lawyer, construction executive*
Hamblin, Kenneth Lorenzo *radio talk show host, columnist*
Harken, Alden Hood *surgeon, thoracic surgeon*
Harris, Dale Ray *lawyer*
Hartley, James Edward *lawyer*
Hatami, Marvin *architect, educator, urban designer*
Havekost, Daniel John *architect*
Hayes, Edward Lee *religious organization administrator*
Heifets, Leonid *microbiologist, researcher*
Hendrix, Lynn Parker *lawyer*
Herz, Leonard *financial consultant*
Hetzel, Fredrick William *biophysicist, educator*
Hilbert, Otto Karl, II *lawyer*
Hildebrand, Verna Lee *human ecology educator*
Hill, Diane Seldon *corporate psychologist*
Hill, Kathleen Lois *performing art school executive*
Hinch, William Harry *retired consulting engineer*
Hinkle, Betty Ruth *educational administator*
Hirschfeld, Arlene F. *civic worker, homemaker*
Hixon, Janet Kay Erickson *education specialist*
Hoagland, Donald Wright *lawyer*
Hobson, Harry Lee, Jr. *lawyer*
Hodges, Joseph Gilluly, Jr. *lawyer*
Hoffman, Daniel Steven *lawyer, legal educator*
Hogan, Curtis Jule *union executive, industrial relations consultant*
Holleman, Paul Douglas *lawyer*
Holme, Richard Phillips *lawyer*
Holmes, Randall Kent *microbiology educator, physician, university administrator*
Holte, Debra Leah *investment executive, financial analyst*
Hoover, George Schweke *architect*
Hopfenbeck, George Martin, Jr. *lawyer*
Hopkins, Donald J. *lawyer*
Howlett, John David *government relations*
Hughes, Bradley Richard *business executive*
Husband, John Michael *lawyer*
Imber, Richard Joseph *physician, dermatologist*
Imhoff, Walter Francis *investment banker*
Imig, William Graff *lawyer, lobbyist*
Iona, Mario *retired physics educator*
Irwin, R. Robert *lawyer*
†Isenberg, Walter L. *recreational facility executive*
†Issel, Daniel Paul *former professional basketball coach*
Jablonski, James Arthur *lawyer*
Jackson, Richard Brooke *lawyer*
Jacobs, Paul Alan *lawyer*
Jacobson, Eugene Donald *educator, administrator, researcher*
Jafek, Bruce William *otolaryngologist, educator*
Jennett, Shirley Shimmick *home care management executive, nurse*
Johnson, Candice Elaine Brown *pediatrics educator*
Johnson, Mary Bettina Black *physical education educator, athletic trainer*
Johnston, Gwinavere Adams *public relations consultant*
Jones, Jean Correy *organization administrator*
Jones, Melvin Douglas, Jr. *pediatrician, educator, academic administrator*
Jones, Richard Michael *lawyer*
Kane, John Lawrence, Jr. *federal judge*
Karsh, Philip Howard *advertising executive*
Kauvar, Abraham J. *gastroenterologist, medical administrator*
Keatinge, Robert Reed *lawyer*
Keats, Donald Howard *composer, educator*
Keller, Glen Elven, Jr. *lawyer*
Keppler, Peter *lawyer*
Kern, Fred, Jr. *physician, educator*
Kerwin, Mary Ann Collins *lawyer*
Kintzele, John Alfred *lawyer*
Kinzie, Jeannie Jones *radiation oncologist*
Kirkpatrick, Charles Harvey *physician, immunology researcher*
Kirshbaum, Howard M. *arbiter, judge*
Klipping, Robert Samuel *geophysicist*
Koto, Paul *multicultural educator*
Kourlis, Rebecca Love *judge*
Krane, Robert Alan *banker*
Krikos, George Alexander *pathologist, educator*
Krill, Arthur Melvin *engineering, architectural and planning company executive*
Krugman, Richard David *physician, university administrator, educator*
Kushner, Todd Roger *computer scientist, software engineer*
†Lacroix, Pierre *professional sports team professional*
Landon, Susan Melinda *petroleum geologist*
Larsen, Gary Loy *physician, researcher*
Larsen, Gwynne E. *computer information systems educator*
Larson, Dayl Andrew *architect*
Law, John Manning *retired lawyer*
Lazarus, Steven S. *management consultant, marketing consultant*
Lee, Kate Leary *financial adviser*
Lee, Richard Kenneth *building products company executive*
Lefly, Dianne Louise *research psychologist*
Lemieux, Claude *professional hockey player*
Lerman, Eileen R. *lawyer*
Levinson, Shauna T. *financial services executive*
Levy, Mark Ray *lawyer*
Lewis, Jerome A. *petroleum company executive, investment banker*
Lidstone, Herrick Kenley, Jr. *lawyer*
Livingston, Johnston R. *manufacturing executive*
Loeup, Kong *cultural organization administrator*
Logan, James Scott, Sr. *federal agency administrator, emergency analyst*
Long, Francis Mark *retired electrical engineer, educator*
Low, John Wayland *lawyer*
Lubeck, Marvin Jay *ophthalmologist*
Lucero, Carlos *federal judge*
Lutz, John Shafroth *lawyer*
Lyons, Charles *professional hockey team executive*
Macey, William Blackmore *oil company executive*
MacGregor, George Lescher, Jr. *freelance writer*
Mackinnon, Peggy Louise *public relations executive*
†Magnus, Kathy Jo *religious organization executive*
Malone, Robert Joseph *bank executive*
Marcum, Walter Phillip *manufacturing executive, heavy*
Markman, Howard J. *psychology educator*
Martin, Richard Jay *medical educator*
Martz, Clyde Ollen *lawyer, educator*
Matsch, Richard P. *judge*
Mauro, Richard Frank *lawyer, investment manager*
May, Clifford Daniel *newspaper editor, journalist*
May, Francis Hart, Jr. *retired building materials manufacturing executive*
Maytham, Thomas Northrup *art and museum consultant*
McAtee, Patricia Anne Rooney *medical educator*
McCabe, John L. *lawyer*
McCandless, Bruce, II *aerospace engineer, former astronaut*
Mc Clenney, Byron Nelson *community college administrator*
McDonnell, Barbara *health facility administrator*
McGowan, Joseph Anthony, Jr. *news executive*
McGraw, Jack Wilson *government official*
McGuire, Michael William *communications executive*
McKechnie, Margaret A. *public relations professional*
McKibben, Ryan Timothy *newspaper executive*
Mc Kinney, Alexis *public relations consultant*
McLain, William Allen *lawyer*
McMorris, Jerry *transportation company executive*
McWilliams, Robert Hugh *federal judge*
Mehring, Clinton Warren *engineering executive*
Meiklejohn, Alvin J., Jr. *state senator, lawyer, accountant*
Meldrum, Daniel Richard *general surgeon, physician*
Mendelsohn, Harold *sociologist, educator*
Mendez, Celestino Galo *mathematics educator*
Merker, Steven Joseph *lawyer*
Messer, Donald Edward *theological school president*
Miller, Gale Timothy *lawyer*
Miller, Robert Nolen *lawyer*
Miller, Stanley Custer, Jr. *physicist, retired educator*
Minger, Terrell John *public administration institute executive*
Moore, Ernest Eugene, Jr. *surgeon, educator*
Moore, George Eugene *surgeon*
Morgan, David Forbes *minister*
Mornes, Amber J. Bishop *consultant, computer software trainer, analyst*
Morrison, Marcy *state legislator*
Movshovitz, Howard Paul *film critic, educator*
Moye, John Edward *lawyer*
Muftic, Felicia Anne Boillot *consumer relations professional*
Muldoon, Brian *lawyer*
Mullarkey, Mary J. *state supreme court justice*
Muller, Nicholas Guthrie *lawyer, business executive*
Mullineaux, Donal Ray *geologist*
Murane, William Edward *lawyer*
Murdock, Pamela Ervilla *travel and advertising company executive*
Nakakuki, Masafumi *physician, psychiatry educator*
Nanda, Ved Prakash *law educator, university official*
Nash, Stella B. *government nutrition administrator*
Nathan, J(ay) Andrew *lawyer*
Nelson, Bernard William *foundation executive, educator, physician*
Nelson, Nancy Eleanor *pediatrician, educator*
Nelson, Sarah Milledge *archaeology educator*
Nemiro, Beverly Mirium Anderson *author, educator*
Nesheim, Dennis Warren *art educator, artist, writer, instructional materials producer*
Nett, Louise Mary *nursing educator, consultant*
Neu, Carl Herbert, Jr. *management consultant*
Neumann, Herschel *physics educator*
†Neumeyer, Zachary T. *hotel executive*
Neville, Margaret Cobb *physiologist, educator*
Newton, James Quigg, Jr. *lawyer*
Nicholson, Will Faust, Jr. *bank holding company executive*
Norman, John Barstow, Jr. *designer, educator*
Norman, John Edward *petroleum landman*
Norton, Gale A. *state attorney general*
Notari, Paul Celestin *communications executive*
Nottingham, Edward Willis, Jr. *federal judge*
Nutting, Paul A. *medical educator, medical science administrator*
O'Keefe, Edward Franklin *lawyer*
Otten, Arthur Edward, Jr. *lawyer, corporate executive*
Otto, Jean Hammond *journalist*
Owen, James Churchill, Jr. *lawyer*
Owens, Marvin Franklin, Jr. *oil company executive*
Pakiser, Louis Charles, Jr. *geophysicist*
Palmer, David Gilbert *lawyer*
Palmreuter, Kenneth Richard Louis *principal*
Peloquin, Louis Omer *lawyer*
Perez, Jean-Yves *engineering company executive*
Petros, Raymond Louis, Jr. *lawyer*
Petty, Thomas Lee *physician, educator*
Pfenninger, Karl H. *cell biology and neuroscience educator*
Pfnister, Allan Orel *humanities educator*
Plummer, Ora Beatrice *nursing educator, trainer*
Poirot, James Wesley *engineering company executive*
Pomerantz, Marvin *thoracic surgeon*
Porfilio, John Carbone *federal judge*
Poulson, Robert Dean *lawyer*
Price, Kathleen McCormick *book editor, writer*
Pringle, Edward E. *legal educator, former state supreme court chief justice*
Prochnow, James R. *lawyer*
Prosser, John Martin *architect, educator, urban design consultant*
Puck, Theodore Thomas *geneticist, biophysicist, educator*
Purcell, Kenneth *psychology educator, university dean*
Quail, Beverly J. *lawyer*
Quiat, Gerald M. *lawyer*
Quinn, John Michael *physicist, geophysicist*
Rael, Henry Sylvester *retired health administrator, financial and management consultant*
Rainer, William Gerald *cardiac surgeon*
Rawls, Eugenia *actress*
Rendu, Jean-Michel Marie *mining executive*
Repine, John E. *internist, educator*
Reynolds, Collins James, III *foundation administrator*
Rich, Ben Arthur *lawyer, educator*
Rich, Robert Stephen *lawyer*
Ris, William Krakow *lawyer*
Ritchie, Daniel Lee *academic administrator*
Ritsema, Fredric A. *lawyer*
Rizzi, Teresa Marie *bilingual speech and language pathologist*
Robinson-Petersen, Carole Ann *insurance executive, retired*
Rockwell, Bruce McKee *retired banker, retired foundation executive*
Romer, Roy R. *governor*
†Romero, Lynette Denise *news reporter, anchor*
Rose, Gregory Mancel *neurobiologist*
Rosenwasser, Lanny Jeffrey *allergist, immunologist*
Rovira, Luis Dario *state supreme court justice*
Roy, Patrick *professional hockey player*
Rubright, Royal Cushing *lawyer*
Ruge, Daniel August *retired neurosurgeon, educator*
Ruppert, John Lawrence *lawyer*
Ryman, Ruth (Stacie) Marie *primary education educator*
†Sakic, Joseph Steve *professional hockey player*
Salmon, Merlyn Leigh *laboratory executive*
Saltz, Howard Joel *newspaper editor*
Sandler, Thomas R. *accountant*
Sardella, Edward Joseph *television news anchor*
Sayre, John Marshall *lawyer, former government official*
Schanfield, Moses Samuel *geneticist, educator*
Schaubman, Averi Lyn *social worker*
Schiff, Donald Wilfred *pediatrician, educator*
Schmidt, L(ail) William, Jr. *lawyer*
Schrier, Robert William *physician, educator*
Scudder, Richard B. *newspaper executive*
Seaman, Peggy Jean *lawyer*
Selbin, Joel *chemistry educator*
Sharkey, Richard David *product designer, architect, musician*
Shea, Kevin Michael *lawyer*
Sheeran, Michael John Leo *priest, educational administrator*
Shepard, Thomas Akers *physician assistant*
Shepherd, John Frederic *lawyer*
Shore, James H(enry) *psychiatrist*
Silverman, Arnold *physician*
Simons, Lynn Osborn *federal education official*
Smith, Dwight Morrell *chemistry educator*
Smith, Rita Sue *administrator*
Smith, Waldo Gregorius *former government official*
Smyth, David Shannon *real estate investor, commercial and retail builder and developer*
Snyder, Charles Royce *sociologist, educator*
Sondheimer, Judith McConnell *pediatrician, educator*
Sparr, Daniel Beattie *federal judge*
Speed, Leslie Bokee *lawyer*
Spencer, Margaret Gilliam *lawyer*
Steenhagen, Robert Lewis *landscape architect, consultant*
Stephens, Phillip *screenwriter, producer*
Stephenson, Arthur Emmet, Jr. *investment company executive, banker*
Stockmar, Ted P. *lawyer*
Storey, Brit Allan *historian*
Struever, Stuart McKee *archaeologist*
Strutton, Larry D. *newspaper executive*
Sujansky, Eva Borska *physician, educator*
Sullivan, Claire Ferguson *marketing educator*
Sutton, Leonard von Bibra *lawyer*
Swenson, Mary Ann *bishop*
Swift, William Charles *professional baseball player, Olympic athlete*
Szefler, Stanley James *pediatrics and pharmacology educator*
Talbott, Richard David *retired physician*
Talmage, David Wilson *microbiology and medical educator, physician, former university administrator*
Taussig, Lynn Max *healthcare administrator, pulmonologist, pediatrician, educator*
Taylor, Edward Stewart *physician, educator*
Thomasch, Roger Paul *lawyer*
Thompson, Lohren Matthew *oil company executive*
Timothy, Robert Keller *telephone company executive*
Tisdale, Douglas Michael *lawyer*
Tomlinson, Warren Leon *lawyer*
Tracey, Jay Walter, Jr. *retired lawyer*
Trueblood, Harry Albert, Jr. *oil company executive*
Tucker, James Raymond *primary education educator*
Ulevich, Neal Hirsh *photojournalist*
Ulrich, Theodore Albert *lawyer*
Vigil, Charles S. *lawyer*
Wachtel, Thomas Lee *surgeon*
Wagner, Judith Buck *investment firm executive*
Walker, Larry Kenneth Robert *professional baseball player*
Walker, Timothy Blake *lawyer, educator*
Walshe, Brian Francis *management consultant*
Ward, Lester Lowe, Jr. *arts executive, lawyer*
Washington, Reginald Louis *pediatric cardiologist*
Watson, William D. *lawyer*
Weatherley-White, Roy Christopher Anthony *surgeon, consultant*
Webb, Wellington E. *mayor*
Weihaupt, John George *geosciences educator, scientist, university administrator*
Weinshienk, Zita Leeson *federal judge*
Welch, Carol Mae *lawyer*
Welchert, Steven Joseph *public affairs consultant*
Welton, Charles Ephraim *lawyer*
Wessler, Mary Hraha *marketing and management executive*
Weston, William Lee *dermatologist*
Wetzel, Jodi (Joy Lynn Wetzel) *history and women's studies educator*
Wham, Dorothy Stonecipher *state legislator*
Wheeler, Malcolm Edward *lawyer, law educator*
Wiggs, Eugene Overbey *ophthalmologist, educator*
Williams, John James, Jr. *architect*
Williams, Michael Anthony *lawyer*
Williams, Wayne De Armond *lawyer*
Winterrowd, William J. *bishop*
Winters, Richard Allen *mineral economist*
Wirkler, Norman Edward *architectural, engineering, construction management firm executive*
Witt, Catherine Lewis *neonatal nurse practitioner, writer*
Wohlgenant, Richard Glen *lawyer*
Woodward, Lester Ray *lawyer*
Wunnicke, Brooke *lawyer*
Yamamoto, Kaoru *psychology and education educator*
Yegge, Robert Bernard *lawyer, college dean emeritus, educator*
Young, Thomas Harlan *lawyer*
Zaranka, William F. *academic administrator, author*
Zeilig, Nancy Meeks *magazine editor*
Zimet, Carl Norman *psychologist, educator*
†Zimmer, Lawrence William, Jr. *sports announcer*
Zisman, Lawrence S. *internist*

### Dillon
Becker, Quinn Henderson *orthopedic surgeon, army officer*
Follett, Robert John Richard *publisher*

### Divide
Trench, William Frederick *mathematics educator*

### Dolores
Kreyche, Gerald Francis *retired philosophy educator*

### Durango
Ballantine, Morley Cowles (Mrs. Arthur Atwood Ballantine) *newspaper editor*
Burnham, Bryson Paine *retired lawyer*
Candelaria, Angie Mary *special education educator*
Hansen, Leonard Joseph *author, journalist, marketing consultant*
Jones, Joel Mackey *college president*
Moore, John George, Jr. *medical educator*
Spencer, Donald Clayton *mathematician*
Steinhoff, Harold William *retired research institute executive*

### Eagle
Sullivan, Selby William *lawyer, business executive*

### Eaton
Brown, Carl Mitchell *minister, engineer, geologist*

### Edwards
Chambers, Joan Louise *dean of libraries*

### Englewood
Aguirre, Vukoslav Eneas *environmental engineer*
Albrecht, Duane Taylor *veterinarian*
Ames, A. Gary *communications company executive*
Arenberg, Irving Kaufman *ear surgeon, educator*
Atwater, Stephen Dennis *professional football player*
Bardsley, Kay *historian, archivist, dance professional*
Beake, John *professional football team executive*
Bingham, Paris Edward, Jr. *electrical engineer, computer consultant*
Bondi, Bert Roger *accountant, financial planner*
Bonnet, Beatriz Alicia *interpreter, translator, flutist*
†Bowlen, Patrick Dennis *holding company executive, lawyer, professional sports team executive*
Brierley, James Alan *research administrator*
Brown, Steven Harry *corporation health physicist, consultant*
Burg, Michael S. *lawyer*
Busse, Lu Ann *audiologist*
Chavez, Lloyd G. *automotive executive*
Chesser, Al H. *union official*
Claussen, Bonnie Addison, II *aerospace company executive*
Craw, Nicholas Wesson *motor sports association executive*
Dawson, Eugene Ellsworth *university president emeritus*
DeMuth, Laurence Wheeler, Jr. *lawyer, utility company executive*
Devine, Sharon Jean *lawyer*
Eames, Wilmer Ballou *dental educator*
Eccles, Matthew Alan *golf course and landscape architect*
Elway, John Albert *professional football player*
†Engleberg, David *health insurance company executive*
Erickson, William Hurt *retired state supreme court justice*
Gordon, Darrien X. Jamal *professional football player*
Hall, Kurt *movie theatre executive*
Hardy, Wayne Russell *insurance broker*
Hateley, Lynnette Sue *telecommunications, cable and multimedia analyst*
Haupenthal, Laura Ann *clinical psychologist*
Hendrick, Hal Wilmans *human factors educator*
Joffe, Barbara Lynne *computer project manager*
Jones, Glenn Robert *cable systems executive*
Lamb, Darlis Carol *sculptor*
Larkin, Edward Colby *securities analyst, financial services company executive*
Le, Khanh Tuong *utility executive*
Leigh, Shari Greer *software consulting firm executive*
Mahoney, Gerald Francis *manufacturing company executive*
Malone, John C. *telecommunications executive*
Manley, Richard Walter *insurance executive*
McCormick, Richard *telecommunications company executive*
Neiser, Brent Allen *public affairs consultant*
Nixon, Scott Sherman *lawyer*
Nuce, Madonna Marie *military officer*
†O'Brian, James *broadcast executive*
O'Bryan, William Hall *insurance executive*
Pearlman, David Samuel *allergist*
Perry, Michael Dean *professional football player*
Poe, Robert Alan *lawyer*
Ramsey, John Arthur *lawyer*
Reese, Monte Nelson *agricultural association executive*
Reisinger, George Lambert *management consultant*
Rogols, Saul *food scientist*
Rosich, Rayner Karl *physicist*
Rosser, Edwin Michael *mortgage company executive*
Rounds, Donald Michael *public relations executive*
Rumack, Barry H. *physician, toxicologist, pediatrician*
Saliba, Jacob *manufacturing executive*
Shanahan, Mike *professional football coach*
Sharpe, Shannon *professional football player*
Sims, Douglas D. *bank executive*
Slater, Shelley *operations process manager*
Smead, Burton Armstrong, Jr. *lawyer, retired*

Smith, Neil *professional football player*
Sprincz, Keith Steven *financial services company professional*
Steele, Elizabeth Meyer *lawyer*
Van Loucks, Mark Louis *venture capitalist, business advisor*
Wagner, David James *lawyer*
Ward, Milton Hawkins *mining company executive*
Wynar, Bohdan Stephen *librarian, author, editor*
Zernial, Susan Carol *education educator*

### Estes Park
Hillway, Tyrus *author, educator*
Moore, Omar Khayyam *experimental sociologist*
Ojalvo, Morris *civil engineer, educator*
Webb, Richard C. *engineering company executive*

### Evergreen
Foret, Mickey Phillip *air transportation company executive*
Haun, John Daniel *petroleum geologist, educator*
Jackson, William Richard *entrepreneur*
Jesser, Roger Franklyn *former brewing company engineering executive, consultant*
Newkirk, John Burt *metallurgical engineer, administrator*
Phillips, Adran Abner (Abe Phillips) *geologist, oil and gas exploration consultant*
White, John David *composer, theorist, cellist*

### Fort Carson
Chomko, Stephen Alexander *archaeologist*
Lewey, Scot Michael *gastroenterologist, army officer*

### Fort Collins
Altman, Jack *plant pathologist, educator*
Anderson, B(enard) Harold *educational administrator*
Bamburg, James Robert *biochemistry educator*
Benjamin, Stephen Alfred *veterinary medicine educator, environmental pathologist, researcher*
Bennett, Thomas LeRoy, Jr. *clinical neuropsychology educator*
Bernstein, Elliot Roy *chemistry educator*
Boyd, Landis Lee *agricultural engineer, educator*
Burns, Denver P. *forestry research administrator*
Cermak, Jack Edward *engineer, educator*
Charney, Michael *science laboratory administrator*
Christiansen, Norman Juhl *retired newspaper publisher*
Criswell, Marvin Eugene *civil engineering educator, consultant*
Cummings, Sharon Sue *state extension service youth specialist*
Curthoys, Norman P. *biochemistry educator, consultant*
Driscoll, Richard Stark *land use planner*
Eitzen, David Stanley *sociologist, educator*
Elkind, Mortimer Murray *biophysicist, educator*
Emslie, William Arthur *electrical engineer*
Ewing, Jack Robert *accountant*
Fixman, Marshall *chemist, educator*
Follett, Ronald Francis *soil scientist*
Frink, Eugene Hudson, Jr. *business and real estate consultant*
Garvey, Daniel Cyril *mechanical engineer*
Gilderhus, Mark Theodore *historian, educator*
Gillette, Edward LeRoy *radiation oncology educator*
Grandin, Temple *livestock equipment designer, educator*
†Grigg, Neil S. *civil engineering educator*
Gubler, Duane J. *research scientist, administrator*
Guest, Richard Eugene *psychologist*
Hafford, Patricia Ann *electronic company executive*
Hanan, Joe John *horticulture educator*
Harper, Judson Morse *university administrator, consultant, educator*
Heermann, Dale Frank *agricultural engineer*
Heird, James C. *agricultural studies educator*
Holcomb, Edie L. *educational administrator, consultant*
Hu, Edna Gertrude Fenske *pediatrics nurse*
Jacobs, Harold Robert *mechanical engineering educator*
Jaros, Dean *university official*
Johnson, Robert Britten *geology educator*
Kaufman, Harold Richard *mechanical engineer and physics educator*
Keim, Wayne Franklin *retired agronomy educator, plant geneticist*
Kennedy, George Alexander *classicist, educator*
Koessel, Donald Ray *retired banker*
Ladanyi, Branka Maria *chemist, educator*
Lubick, Sonny *college football coach*
Lumb, William Valjean *veterinarian*
MacLauchlin, Robert Kerwin *communications artist, educator*
Maga, Joseph Andrew *food science educator*
McHugh, Helen Frances *research administrator, consumption economist*
Medearis, Kenneth Gordon *engineering research consultant, educator*
Mesloh, Warren Henry *civil and environmental engineer*
Meyers, Albert Irving *chemistry educator*
Mielke, Paul William, Jr. *statistician*
Mortvedt, John Jacob *soil scientist*
Mosier, Arvin Ray *chemist, researcher*
Niehaus, Merle H. *agricultural educator, international agriculture consultant*
Niswender, Gordon Dean *physiologist, educator*
Ogg, James Elvis *microbiologist, educator*
Patton, Carl Elliott *physics educator*
Peterson, Gary Andrew *agronomics researcher*
Richardson, Everett Vern *hydraulic engineer, educator, administrator, consultant*
Roberts, Archibald Edward *retired army officer, author*
Rock, Kenneth Willett *history educator*
Rogers, Garth Winfield *lawyer*
Rollin, Bernard Elliot *philosophy educator, consultant on animal ethics*
Rolston, Holmes, III *theologian, educator, philosopher*
Roos, Eric Eugene *plant physiologist*
Runnells, Donald DeMar *geochemist, consultant*
Saysette, Janice Elaine *vertebrate paleontologist, zoo archaeologist*
Schatz, Mona Claire Struhsaker *social worker, educator, consultant, researcher*
Schumm, Stanley Alfred *geologist, educator*
Seidel, George Elias, Jr. *animal scientist, educator*
Sheng, Tse Cheng (Ted C. Sheng) *natural resources educator*
Sons, Raymond William *journalist*
Suinn, Richard Michael *psychologist*
Thies, Margaret Diane *nurse*
Tweedie, Richard Lewis *statistics educator, consultant*
Walsh, Richard George *agricultural economist*
Watz, Martin Charles *brewery executive*
Wilber, Charles Grady *forensic science educator, consultant*
Winn, C(olman) Byron *mechanical engineering educator*
Woolhiser, David Arthur *hydraulic engineer*
Yates, Albert Carl *academic administrator, chemistry educator*

### Fort Garland
Leighninger, David Scott *cardiovascular surgeon*

### Fort Morgan
Gibbs, Denis Laurel *radiologist*
Perdue, James Everett *university vice chancellor emeritus*

### Frisco
Helmer, David Alan *lawyer*

### Georgetown
Stern, Mort(imer) P(hillip) *journalism and communications educator, academic administrator, consultant*

### Glenwood Springs
Musselman, Norman Burkey *retired editor*
Violette, Glenn Phillip *construction engineer*
Walker, Robert Harris *historian, author, editor*

### Golden
Ansell, George Stephen *metallurgical engineering educator, academic administrator*
Baron, Robert Charles *publishing executive*
Baumgart, Norbert K. *retired government official*
Cassidy, Samuel H. *lawyer, lieutenant governor, state legislator*
Christensen, Robert Wayne *oral maxillofacial surgeon, minister*
Coors, William K. *brewery executive*
Eckley, Wilton Earl, Jr. *humanities educator*
Ervin, Patrick Franklin *nuclear engineer*
Evans, David Lynn *management consultant, executive*
Friede, Heather Ellen *computer consultant*
†Frix, Robert Scott *career military officer*
Grose, Thomas Lucius Trowbridge *geologist, educator*
Hager, John Patrick *metallurgy engineering educator*
Hamilton, Warren Bell *research geologist, educator*
Hopper, Sally *state legislator*
Hutchinson, Richard William *geology educator, consultant*
Johnstone, James George *engineering educator*
Kennedy, George Hunt *chemistry educator*
Kotch, Alex *chemistry educator*
Krauss, George *metallurgist*
Lerud, Joanne Van Ornum *library administrator*
Lindsay, Nathan James *aerospace company executive, retired career officer*
Mathews, Anne Jones *consultant, library educator and administrator*
Morrison, Roger Barron *geologist*
Mueller, William Martin *former academic administrator, metallurgical engineering educator*
Murphy, Robin Roberson *computer science educator*
Olson, Marian Katherine *emergency management executive, consultant, publisher*
Patino, Hugo *food science research engineer*
Pegis, Anton George *English educator*
Petrick, Alfred, Jr. *mineral economics educator, consultant*
Rodgers, Frederic Barker *judge*
Sacks, Arthur Bruce *environmental and liberal arts educator*
Salamon, Miklos Dezso Gyorgy *mining engineer, educator*
Shimanski, Charles Stuart *organization executive*
Sims, Paul Kibler *geologist*
Sloan, Earle Dendy, Jr. *chemical engineering educator*
Sneed, Joseph Donald *philosophy educator, author*
Stewart, Frank Maurice, Jr. *federal agency administrator*
Tilton, John Elvin *mineral economics educator*
Weimer, Robert Jay *geology educator, energy consultant, civic leader*
Wellisch, William Jeremiah *social psychology educator*
White, James Edward *geophysicist*
Wilson, James Robert *lawyer*
Woods, Sandra Kay *manufacturing executive*
Woolsey, Robert Eugene Donald *mineral economics, mathematics and business administration educator*
Yarar, Baki *metallurgical engineering educator*

### Granby
Johnson, William Potter *newspaper publisher*
Rienhoff, Joanne Winkenwerder *artist*

### Grand Junction
Achen, Mark Kennedy *city manager*
Bacon, Phillip *geographer, author, consultant*
Bergen, Virginia Louise *principal, language arts educator*
Kribel, Robert Edward *academic administrator, physicist*
McCarthy, Mary Frances *hospital foundation administrator*
Moberly, Linden Emery *educational administrator*
Morris, Rusty Lee *architectural consulting firm executive*
Nelson, Paul William *real estate broker*
Pantenburg, Michel *hospital administrator, health educator, holistic health coordinator*
Rutz, Richard Frederick *physicist, researcher*
Rybak, James Patrick *engineering educator*
Sadler, Theodore R., Jr. *thoracic and cardiovascular surgeon*
Sewell, Ralph Byron *investment broker, financial planner, manager*
Young, Ralph Alden *soil scientist, educator*
Zumwalt, Roger Carl *hospital administrator*

### Greeley
Arnold, Leonard J. *construction executive*
Bond, Richard Randolph *foundation administrator, legislator*
Caffarella, Edward Philip *educational technology educator*
Cook, Donald E. *pediatrician*
Duff, William Leroy, Jr. *university dean emeritus, business educator*
Fry, Linda Sue *restaurant manager, hotel sales director, food products company executive*
Hart, Milford E. *psychotherapist, counselor*
Hause, Jesse Gilbert *retired college president*
Houtchens, Barnard *lawyer*
Kelsey, Michael Loyal *geography educator*
Linde, Lucille Mae (Jacobson) *motor-perceptual specialist*
Mader, Douglas Paul *quality engineering manager*
Miller, Diane Wilmarth *human resources director*
Morgensen, Jerry Lynn *construction company executive*
Murry, Francie Roberta *special education educator*
Roberts, David Lowell *journalist*
Seager, Daniel Albert *university librarian*
Smith, Jack Lee *bank executive*
Townsend, Susan Louise *elementary school administrator*
Willis, Connie (Constance E. Willis) *author*
Worley, Lloyd Douglas *English language educator*

### Green Mountain Falls
Faber, Michael Warren *lawyer*

### Greenwood Village
Barnard, Rollin Dwight *retired financial executive*
Dymond, Lewis Wandell *lawyer, mediator, educator*
Katz, Michael Jeffery *lawyer*
Peterson, Ralph R. *engineering executive*
Shaddock, Paul Franklin, Sr. *human resources director*
Walker, Eljana M. du Vall *civic worker*

### Guffey
Ward, Larry Thomas *social program administrator*

### Gunnison
Myers, Rex Charles *history educator, retired college dean*

### Highlands Ranch
Bublitz, Deborah Keirstead *pediatrician*
Massey, Leon R. *professional society administrator*
McLellon, Richard Steven *aerospace engineer, consultant*

### Hotchkiss
Perry, Jeanne Elyce *principal*

### Idledale
Brown, Gerri Ann *physical therapist*

### Iliff
Nichols, Lee Ann *library media specialist*

### Jefferson
Maatsch, Deborah Joan *former paralegal, tax specialist, tax advisor, controller*

### Kersey
Guttersen, Michael *ranching and investments professional*

### Lafayette
McNeill, William *environmental scientist*
Short, Ray Everett *minister, sociology educator emeritus, author, lecturer*

### Lakewood
Beckman, L. David *university chancellor*
Bettinghaus, Erwin Paul *cancer research center administrator*
Danzberger, Alexander Harris *chemical engineer, consultant*
Finnie, Doris Gould *investment company executive*
Foster, David Mark *retired bishop*
Guyton, Samuel Percy *retired lawyer*
Hall, Larry D. *energy company executive, lawyer*
Heath, Gary Brian *manufacturing firm executive, engineer*
Hosokawa, William K. *newspaper columnist, author*
Isely, Henry Philip *association executive, integrative engineer, writer, educator, businessman*
Joy, Carla Marie *history educator*
Karlin, Joel Marvin *allergist*
Keller, Shirley Inez *accountant*
Knott, William Alan *library director, library management and building consultant*
Lewis, Charles D. *insurance executive, rancher, consultant*
Lu, Paul Haihsing *mining engineer, geotechnical consultant*
Mc Bride, Guy Thornton, Jr. *college president emeritus*
McElwee, Dennis John *lawyer, former parmaceutical company executive*
Milan, Marjorie Lucille *early childhood education educator*
Morton, Linda *mayor*
Orullian, B. LaRae *bank executive*
Owen, Robert Roy *retired manufacturing company executive*
Parker, John Marchbank *consulting geologist*
Penwell, Jones Clark *real estate appraiser, consultant*
Porter, Lael Frances *communication consultant, educator*
Purdy, Sherry Marie *lawyer*
Reed, Joan-Marie *special education educator*
Rosa, Fredric David *construction company executive*
Spisak, John Francis *environmental company executive*
Swan, Henry *retired surgeon*
Thomson, Marjorie Belle Anderson *sociology educator, consultant*
Ulery, Shari Lee *lawyer*
Walton, Roger Alan *public relations executive, mediator, writer*
West, Marjorie Edith *elementary education educator*
Woodruff, Kathryn Elaine *English educator*

### Larkspur
Bierbaum, J. Armin *petroleum company executive, consultant*
Bierbaum, Janith Marie *artist*

### LaVeta
Zehring, Peggy Johnson *artist*

### Littleton
Allery, Kenneth Edward *air force officer*
Anderson, Darrell Edward *psychologist, educator*
Bachman, David Christian *orthopedic surgeon*
Ballard, Jack Stokes *engineering educator*
Barnes, Cloyd Ray *sculptor, retired engineer*
Bass, Charles Morris *financial and systems consultant*
Bush, Stanley Giltner *secondary school educator*
Cabell, Elizabeth Arlisse *psychologist*
Champney, Linda Lucas *reading educator*
Chapman, Richard LeRoy *public policy researcher*
Choquette, Philip Wheeler *geologist, educator*
Cismaru, Pat Klein *municipal official*
Elrick, Billy Lee *English language educator*
Fisher, Louis McLane, Jr. *management consultant*
Forstot, S. Lance *ophthalmologist*
Gertz, David Lee *homebuilding company executive*
Greenberg, Elinor Miller *college official, consultant*
Hadley, Marlin LeRoy *direct sales financial consultant*
Haley, John David *petroleum consulting company executive*
Hayes, Roger Matthew *deputy sheriff*
Hopping, William Russell *hospitality industry consultant and appraiser*
Kazemi, Hossein *petroleum engineer*
Keely, George Clayton *lawyer*
Kleinknecht, Kenneth Samuel *retired aerospace company executive, former federal space agency official*
Kullas, Albert John *management and systems engineering consultant*
Lening, Janice Allen *physical education educator*
Lucero, Scott Alan *special education educator*
Make, Isabel Rose *multicultural studies educator, small business owner*
Martinen, John A. *travel company executive*
Mercer, Margaret Teele *medical and film industry marketing executive*
Milliken, John Gordon *research economist*
Moore, Dan Sterling *insurance executive, sales trainer*
Palmer, Madelyn Stewart Silver *family practice physician*
Pearlman, Mitzi Ann *elementary education educator*
Plusk, Ronald Frank *manufacturing company executive*
Price, Gayl Baader *residential construction company administrator*
Rockwell, Kay Anne *elementary education educator*
Schmidt, Ronald R. *academic administrator*
Sjolander, Gary Walfred *physicist*
Smart, Marriott Wieckhoff *research librarian consultant*
Smith, Derrin Ray *information systems company executive*
Snyder, John Millard *recreation resources executive, educator*
Snyder, William Harry *financial advisor*
Spelts, Richard John *lawyer*
Strang, Sandra Lee *airline official*
Truhlar, Doris Broaddus *lawyer*
Udevitz, Norman *publishing executive*
Ulrich, John Ross Gerald *aerospace engineer*
Vail, Charles Daniel *veterinarian, consultant*
VanderLinden, Camilla Denice Dunn *telecommunications industry manager*

### Livermore
Evans, Howard Ensign *entomologist, educator*

### Longmont
Adams, Robert Hickman *photographer*
Davis, Donald Alan *author, news correspondent, lecturer*
Dierks, Richard Ernest *veterinarian, educational administrator*
Ford, Byron Milton *computer consultant*
Hahn, Yubong *electro-optics company executive*
Hall, Kathryn O'Neil *photographic company official*
Hibler, Jude Ann *photojournalist*
Jones, Beverly Ann Miller *nursing administrator, patient services administrator*
Kaminsky, Glenn Francis *deputy chief of police retired, business owner, teacher*
King, Jane Louise *artist*
Melendez, Joaquin *orthopedic assistant*
Rueckert, Ronald Frank *engineering executive*
Stewart, William Gene *broadcast executive*
Ulrich, John August *microbiology educator*

### Louisville
Billings, Becky Leigh *nurse*
Brault, James William *physicist*
Day, Robert Edgar *retired artist, educator*
Donze, Jerry Lynn *electrical engineer*
Qualley, Charles Albert *fine arts educator*
Raymond, Dorothy Gill *lawyer*
Shively, Merrick Lee *pharmaceutical scientist, consultant*
†Willette, Donald Corliss *reverend*
Williams, Marsha Kay *data processing executive*

### Loveland
Balsiger, David Wayne *television-video director, researcher, producer, writer*
Rodman, Alpine Clarence *arts and crafts company executive*
Rodman, Sue Arlene *wholesale Indian crafts company executive, artist, consultant*

### Manassa
Garcia, Castelar Medardo *lawyer*

### Mc Coy
Hastings, Merrill George, Jr. *publisher, marketing consultant*

### Monte Vista
Tillman, John Lee *principal*

### Monument
Ahlgren, Aleda Joan *nursing administrator, career officer*
Breckner, William John, Jr. *retired air force officer, corporate executive, consultant*
Henrickson, Eiler Leonard *retired geologist, educator*
†Hindmarsh, George Ronald *air force officer*
Karasa, Norman Lukas *home builder, developer, geologist*
Miele, Alfonse Ralph *former government official*

### Morrison
Graham, Pamela Smith *artist, distributing company executive*
Myers, Harry J., Jr. *retired publisher*

### Nathrop
Ebel, Marvin Emerson *physicist,educator*

### Niwot
Sliker, Todd Richard *accountant, lawyer*

### Northglenn
Shaeffer, Thelma Jean *primary school educator*
Straub, Kenneth Richard *educator*

### Olathe
Shriver, Allen Keith *electrical engineer, contractor, executive*

### Pagosa Springs
Kelly, Reid Browne *lawyer*

### Parker
Cummings, Roger David *powder coatings consultant, sales executive*
Jankura, Donald Eugene *hotel executive, educator*
Nelson, Marvin Ray *retired life insurance company executive*
Pastore, Thomas Michael *telecommunications sales executive*
Roberts, James Carl *communications executive, engineer*

### Peterson AFB
†Ashy, Joseph W. *career officer*
Caruana, Patrick Peter *career officer*
†Dinerstein, Marc J. *career military officer*

### Placerville
Kickert, Juliana Arlene *private investor*

### Pueblo
Altman, Leo Sidney *lawyer*
Bates, Charles Emerson *library administrator*
Casey, William Robert, Jr. *ambassador, mining engineer*
Farwell, Hermon Waldo, Jr. *parliamentarian, educator, former speech communication educator*
Giffin, Walter Charles *retired industrial engineer, educator, consultant*
Hawkins, Robert Lee *health facility administrator*
Kelly, William Bret *insurance executive*
Kogovsek, Daniel Charles *lawyer*
Kulkosky, Paul Joseph *psychology educator*
Lewallen, William M., Jr. *ophthalmologist*
Lightell, Kenneth Ray *education educator*
O'Callaghan, Robert Patrick *lawyer*
Occhiato, Michael Anthony *city official*
O'Conner, Loretta Rae *lawyer*
Rawlings, Robert Hoag *newspaper publisher*
Shirley, Robert Clark *retired university president, strategic planning consultant, educator*
Sisson, Ray L. *retired dean*
Tafoya, Arthur N. *bishop*
Vest, Rosemarie Lynn Torres *secondary school educator*

### Ridgway
Decker, Peter Randolph *rancher, former state official*
Lathrop, Kaye Don *nuclear scientist, educator*
Weaver, Dennis *actor*

### Rollinsville
Burandt, Gary Edward *advertising agency executive*

### Silverthorne
Ponder, Herman *geologist*
Rutherford, Robert Barry *surgeon*

### Snowmass
Lovins, Amory Bloch *physicist, energy consultant*
Lovins, L. Hunter *public policy institute executive*

### Snowmass Village
Bancroft, Paul, III *investment company executive, venture capitalist*
Le Buhn, Robert *investment executive*

### Springfield
Wessler, Melvin Dean *farmer, rancher*

### Steamboat Springs
Langstaff, Gary Lee *marketing executive*

### Sterling
Jones, Daniel Lee *software development company executive*
Jones, Laurie Ganong *sales and marketing executive*

### Telluride
Hadley, Paul Burrest, Jr. (Tabbit Hadley) *chef services manager, photographer*
Smith, Samuel David *artist, educator*

### Trinidad
Amari, Kathryn Jane *elementary education educator*
Palovich, Marilyn Lee *elementary education educator*
Potter, William Bartlett *business executive*

### U S A F Academy
Cubero, Ruben Anthony *dean, military officer*
Linehan, Allan Douglas *prosthodontist*
Morris, Steven Lynn *career officer, aeronautical engineering educator*
Wright, Cameron Harrold Greene *electrical engineer*

### Vail
Bevan, William Arnold, Jr. *emergency physician*
Kelton, Arthur Marvin, Jr. *real estate developer*
Knight, Constance Bracken *writer, realtor, corporate executive*
McGee, Michael Jay *fire marshal, educator*
Nelson, Nevin Mary *interior designer*
Vosbeck, Robert Randall *architect*

### Westminster
DiPasquale-Lehnerz, Pamela Ann *occupational therapist*
Eaves, Stephen Douglas *educator, vocational administrator*
Poteet, Mary Jane *computer scientist*
Reed, John Howard *school administrator*

### Wheat Ridge
Barrett, Michael Henry *civil engineer*
Gerlick, Helen J. *tax practitioner, accountant*
Hashimoto, Christine L. *physician*
Hubbard, Harold Mead *retired research executive*
LaMendola, Walter Franklin *human services, information technology consultant*
Larson, Kurt Paul *fire chief*
Scherich, Erwin Thomas *civil engineer, consultant*

### Woodland Park
Cockrille, Stephen *art director, business owner*
Stewart, Robert Lee *retired army officer, astronaut*
Stufano, Thomas Joseph *investigative firm executive*

### Yuma
Pfalmer, Charles Elden *secondary school educator*

## CONNECTICUT

### Andover
Domagala, Richard Edward *mail marketing analyst*

### Ansonia
Nichols, Russell James *manufacturing company executive*
Yale, Jeffrey Franklin *podiatrist*

### Avon
Goodson, Richard Carle, Jr. *chemist, hazardous waste management consultant*
Kling, Phradie (Phradie Kling Gold) *small business owner*
Mc Ilveen, Walter *mechanical engineer*
O'Malley, Marjorie Glaubach *health care executive*
von Kutzleben, Bernd Eberhard *nuclear engineer*
Wiechmann, Eric Watt *lawyer*

### Berlin
Fox, Bernard Michael *utilities company executive, electrical engineer*

### Bethany
Childs, Brevard Springs *religious educator*

### Bethel
Ajay, Abe *artist*
DeLugo, Ernest Mario, Jr. *electrical engineer*
Kurfehs, Harold Charles *real estate executive*
Webb, Theora Graves *public relations executive*

### Bloomfield
Day, John G. *lawyer*
Gangell, Bernadette Anne *librarian, writer, biologist*
Hammer, Alfred Emil *artist, educator*
Handel, Morton Emanuel *management consultation executive*
Hilsenrath, Baruch M. *principal*
Johnson, Linda Thelma *information specialist*
Kissa, Karl Martin *electrical engineer*
Leonberger, Frederick John *electrical engineer, photonics manager*
Less, Anthony Albert *retired naval officer*
Mackey, William Arthur Godfrey *computer software company executive*
Mark, Henry Allen *lawyer*
Messemer, Glenn Matthew *lawyer*
Reid, Hoch *lawyer*
Schenkelbach, Leon *retired career officer, safety consultant*

### Branford
Agassi, Andre Kirk *tennis player*
Blake, Peter Jost *architect*
Cohen, Myron Leslie *mechanical engineer, business executive*
De Gennaro, Richard *retired library director*
Hegyi, Albert Paul *association executive, lawyer*
Izenour, George Charles *mechanical, electrical engineering educator*
Krupp, James Arthur Gustave *manufacturing materials executive, consultant*
McCurdy, Larry Wayne *automotive parts company executive*
Milgram, Richard Myron *music school administrator*
Resnick, Idrian Navarre *foundation administrator*

### Bridgeport
Agee, Kevin Jerome *minister*
Allen, Richard Stanley (Dick Allen) *English language educator, author*
Brunale, Vito John *aerospace engineer*
Cederbaum, Eugene E. *lawyer*
Chih, Chung-Ying *physicist, consultant*
Dworkin, Irma-Theresa *school system administrator, researcher*
Egan, Edward M. *bishop*
Eginton, Warren William *federal judge*
Ettre, Leslie Stephen *chemist*
Freeman, Richard Francis *banker*
Fuller, Doris Elizabeth *nurse*
†Ganim, Joseph P. *mayor*
Henderson, Albert Kossack *publishing company executive, dairy executive, consultant*
Hendricks, Edward David *speaker, consultant*
Jiang, John Jianzhong *materials engineer*
Marcus, Norman *tax and financial consultant*
Pitzschler, Kathryn Van Duren *secondary school educator*
Reed, Charles Eli *retired chemist, chemical engineer*
Rubenstein, Richard Lowell *theologian, educator*
Semple, Cecil Snowdon *retired manufacturing company executive*
Sheridan, Eileen *librarian*
Shiff, Alan Howard William *federal judge*
Sobh, Tarek Mahmoud *computer science educator, researcher*
Stokes, Charles Junius *economist, educator*
Trefry, Robert J. *healthcare administrator*
van der Kroef, Justus Maria *political science educator*
Watson, David Scott *financial services executive*
Wetzel, Edward Thomas *investment company executive*
Zeldes, Jacob Dean *lawyer*

### Bristol
Abdul-Jabbar, Kareem (Lewis Ferdinand Alcindor) *retired professional basketball player, sports commentator*
†Adamle, Mike *sports commentator*
†Aldridge, David *sports announcer*
Barnes, Carlyle Fuller *manufacturing executive*
Barnes, Wallace *manufacturing executive*
†Beil, Larry *sports announcer*
†Berman, Chris *sports anchor*
†Bernstein, Al *sports commentator*
†Bernstein, Bonnie *reporter*
Bornstein, Steven M. *broadcast executive*
†Campbell, Dave *baseball analyst*
†Carter, Frederick James *professional basketball coach*
†Clement, Bill *hocket analyst*
†Conley, Larry *basketball analyst*
†Corso, Lee *former football coach, football analyst*
†Cyphers, Steve *reporter*
†Davis, Rece *anchor, reporter*
†Edwards, Jack *anchor, reporter*
†Eisen, Rich *reporter*
†Fowler, Chris *anchor, reporter*
†Franklin, Ron *anchor, reporter*
†Gammons, Peter *columnist*
†Goldberg, Hank *sports analyst*
†Gottfried, Mike *sports analyst*
†Griffin, Mimi *basketball analyst*
†Herbstreit, Kirk *sports analyst*
Jabs, Jennifer *financial planner*
†Jackson, Jason *anchor, reporter*
†Jackson, Tom *anchor, reporter*
†Jarrett, Ned *auto racing analyst*
†Jaworski, Ron *sports analyst*
†Jones, Mark *sports network host*
†Kellogg, Clark *basketball analyst*
†Kernan, John *auto racing reporter*
†Kiper, Mel *sports commentator*
†Kremer, Andrea *sports correspondent*
†Levy, Steve *sports anchor, studio host*
†Ley, Bob *sports network anchor, reporter*
†Malone, Mark *sports reporter*
†Mayne, Kenny *sports anchor*
Melrose, Barry James *sportscaster, former professional hockey team coach*
†Miller, Jon *sports commentator*
Moffitt, George, Jr. *retired foreign service officer*
†Morganti, Al *reporter*
†Mortensen, Chris *sports analyst, reporter*
†Myers, Chris *network host*
†Nessler, Brad Ray *sports commentator*
Olbermann, Keith *sportscaster*
†Pang, Darren *hockey analyst*
†Paolantonio, Sal *sports correspondent*
†Parsons, Benny *auto racing commentator*
†Patrick, Bill *sports network host*
Patrick, Dan *sportscaster*
†Patrick, Mike *sports commentator*
†Phelps, Richard Frederick *basketball coach*
†Pidto, Bill *sports network anchorman*
Pope, Preston Carleton *anesthetist, nurse*
†Punch, Jerry *sports reporter*
†Raftery, Bill *basketball analyst*
†Ramsay, John T. *professional basketball team coach*
†Ravech, Karl *sports anchor, reporter*
†Reynolds, Harold Craig *professional baseball player*
Roberts, Alida Jayne *elementary school educator*
†Roberts, Jimmy *sports correspondent*
Roberts, Robin *sportcaster*
†Saunders, John *broadcast network host*
†Schwarz, Mark *sports correspondent*
†Scott, Stuart *sports anchor*
Steiner, Charles Harris *sports broadcaster, journalist*
†Thorne, Gary *sports commentator*
Tirico, Mike *sportscaster*
†Varsha, Bob *sports commentator*
†Visser, Lesley *sports correspondent*
Wells, Arthur Stanton *retired manufacturing company executive*

### Broad Brook
Kement, Isabella Viniconis *retired construction company executive*

### Brookfield
Cohen, Mark Steven *dentist*
Gross, Kenneth Paul *management executive*
Petrusky, John W. *banker, consultant*
Reynolds, Jean Edwards *publishing executive*
Rowe, Edward Lawrence, Jr. *graphic designer*
Sartori, Bridget Ann *home health care nurse*
Schetky, Laurence McDonald *metallurgist, researcher*
Williamson, Brian David *information systems executive, consultant*

### Brooklyn
Dune, Steve Charles *lawyer*
Meigs, Joseph Carl, Jr. *retired English language educator*

### Canterbury
Brown, Philip Henry *psychiatric social worker*

### Canton
Humphrey, Samuel Stockwell *former town official, physicist*

### Cheshire
Bozzuto, Michael Adam *wholesale grocery company executive*
Fuller, Jack Glendon, Jr. *retired plastics engineer*
McKee, Margaret Jean *federal agency executive*
Rowland, Ralph Thomas *architect*
Wallace, Ralph *superintendent*

### Chester
Cobb, Hubbard Hanford *magazine editor, writer*
Harwood, Eleanor Cash *librarian*
Hays, David Arthur *theater producer, stage designer*
Plotnik, Arthur *author, editorial consultant*

### Clinton
Douglas, Hope M. *psychotherapist, forensic hypnotist*
Hershatter, Richard Lawrence *lawyer, author*

### Colebrook
Ash, Hiram Newton *graphic designer*
Mc Neill, William Hardy *retired history educator, writer*

### Collinsville
Ford, Dexter *retired insurance company executive*

### Cornwall Bridge
Pfeiffer, Werner Bernhard *artist, educator*

### Cos Cob
Duncalf, Deryck *retired anesthesiologist*
Fishman, Claire *media specialist*
Hauptman, Michael *broadcasting company executive*
Kane, Margaret Brassler *sculptor*
Neal, Irene Collins *artist, educator*
Senter, William Joseph *publishing company executive*
Woodman, Harry Andrews *retired life insurance company executive, consultant*

### Cromwell
Darius, Franklin Alexander, Jr. (Chip Darius) *health administrator, educator, consultant*

### Danbury
Anderson, Alan Reinold *real estate executive, communications consultant*
Arbitelle, Ronald Alan *elementary school educator*
Bailey, Robert Elliott *financial executive*
Baker, Leonard Morton *manufacturing company executive*
Baruch, Eduard *management consultant*
Burns, Jacqueline Mary *laboratory administrator*
Chaifetz, David Harvey *lawyer*
Edelstein, David Simeon *historian, educator*
Gogliettino, John Carmine *insurance broker*
Goldstein, Joel *management science educator, researcher*
Hawkes, Carol Ann *university dean*
Jennings, Alfred Higson, Jr. *music educator, actor, singer*
Joyce, William H. *chemist*
Keenan, Linda Lee *paralegal*
Kennedy, Robert Delmont *chemical company executive*
Leish, Kenneth William *publishing company executive*
Lichtenberger, H(orst) William *chemical company executive*
Malino, Jerome R. *rabbi*
Nelson, Willie *musician, songwriter*
Primm, Earl Russell, III *publishing executive*
Proctor, Richard Jerome, Jr. *business educator, accountant, expert witness*
Roach, James R. *university president*
Roach, James Richard *academic administrator*
Saghir, Adel Jamil *artist, painter, sculptor*
Skolan-Logue, Amanda Nicole *lawyer, consultant*
Soviero, Joseph C. *chemical company executive*
Stewart, Albert Clifton *college dean, marketing educator*
Toland, John Willard *historian, writer*
Tolor, Alexander *psychologist, educator*
Weiner, Jonathan David *writer*
Weinstein, Sidney *neuropsychologist*
Yamin, Dianne Elizabeth *judge*

### Darien
Alderman, Rhenus Hoffard, III *investment company executive*
Allen, Joseph Henry *retired publishing company executive*
Bays, John Theophanis *consulting engineering executive*
Becker, Ralph Edward *broadcast executive, consultant*
Bowling, James Chandler *retired executive, farmer, philanthropist*
Britton, Robert Austin *manufacturing company executive*
Brooke, Avery Rogers *publisher, writer*
Brown, James Shelly *lawyer*
Buchanan, Robert Edgar *retired advertising agency executive*
Cowherd, Edwin Russell *management consultant*
Forman, J(oseph) Charles *chemical engineer, consultant, writer*
Glenn, Roland Douglas *chemical engineer*
Grace, John Kenneth *communications and marketing executive*
Hartong, Hendrik J., Jr. *transportation company executive*
Hubner, Robert Wilmore *retired business machines company executive, consultant*
Kaynor, Sanford Bull *lawyer*
Kutz, Kenneth John *retired mining executive*
Mapel, William Marlen Raines *retired banking executive*
McCurdy, Richard Clark *engineering consultant*
Moltz, James Edward *brokerage company executive*
Morse, Edmond Northrop *investment management executive*
Mundt, Barry Maynard *management consultant*
Nava, Eloy Luis *financial consultant*
Owen, Robert Vaughan *financial company executive*
Schell, James Munson *financial executive*
Smith, Elwin Earl *mining and oil company executive*
Spilman, Raymond *industrial designer*
Sprole, Frank Arnott *retired pharmaceutical company executive, lawyer*
Swiggart, Carolyn Clay *lawyer*
Wood, Christopher L. J. *real estate consulting firm executive*
Ziegler, William, III *diversified industry executive*

### Deep River
Healy, William Kent *environmental services executive*
Hieatt, Allen Kent *language professional, educator*
Hieatt, Constance Bartlett *English language educator*
Zack, Steven Jeffrey *master automotive instructor*

### Derby
Brassil, Jean Ella *psychologist*
McEvoy, Sharlene Ann *business law educator*

### Durham
Russell, Thomas J. *critical care supervisor*

### East Glastonbury
Smith, David Clark *research scientist*

### East Granby
Pfeifer, Howard M(elford) *mechanical engineer*
Scanlon, Lawrence Eugene *English language educator*

### East Haddam
Borton, John Carter, Jr. (Terry Borton) *producer, theater*
Clarke, Cordelia Kay Knight Mazuy *managment executive*
Clarke, Logan, Jr. *management consultant*

### East Hartford
Ahlberg, John Harold *mathematician, educator*

Barredo, Rita M. *auditor*
Cassidy, John Francis, Jr. *industrial research center executive*
Chao, Yong-Sheng *physicist*
Coburn, Richard Joseph *company executive, electrical engineer*
Day, William Hudson *mechanical engineer, turbomachinery company executive*
Foyt, Arthur George *electronics research administrator*
Hanson, Donald Burnett *mechanical engineer, researcher*
Henry, Paul Eugene, Jr. *minister*
Pudlo, Frances Theresa *real estate company administrator*
Scholsky, Martin Joseph *priest*
Soppelsa, George Nicholas Angelo *artist*
Whiston, Richard Michael *lawyer*

## East Haven
Conn, Harold O. *physician, educator*
Scarf, Margaret (Maggie Scarf) *author*

## East Windsor
Kaufmann, Sylvia Nadeau *office equipment sales company executive*

## Easton
Maloney, John Joseph *writer*
Meyer, Alice Virginia *state official*

## Ellington
Setzer, Herbert John *chemical engineer*

## Enfield
Berger, Robert Bertram *lawyer*

## Essex
Burris, Harriet Louise *emergency physician*
Curtis, Alva Marsh *artist*
Goff, Christopher Wallick *pediatrician*
Grover, William Herbert *architect*
Harper, Robert Leslie *architect, educator*
Kenyon, Charles Moir *publishing company executive*
Keppel, John *writer, former diplomat*
Miller, Elliott Cairns *retired bank executive, lawyer*
Riley, Georgianne Marie *lawyer*
Rooney, Maria Dewing *photographer*
Simon, Mark *architect*
Soule, Gardner Bosworth *writer*
Winterer, Victoria Thompson *hospitality executive*

## Fairfield
Ambrosino, Ralph Thomas, Jr. *retired telecommunications executive*
Barone, Rose Marie Pace *writer, retired educator, entertainer*
Blackburn, David Wheeler *management consultant, fundraiser*
Booth, George Keefer *finanical service executive*
Brett, Arthur Cushman, Jr. *banker*
Bryan, Barbara Day *retired librarian*
Bunt, James Richard *electric company executive*
Burd, Robert Meyer *hematologist, oncologist, educator*
Caruso, Daniel F. *lawyer, judge, former state legislator*
Cernera, Anthony Joseph *academic administrator*
Cole, Richard John *marketing executive*
Cox, Richard Joseph *former broadcasting executive*
Daley, Pamela *lawyer*
Dean, George Alden *advertising executive*
DeCarlo, Deena M. *mortgage company executive*
Denniston, Brackett Badger, III *lawyer*
Eigel, Edwin George, Jr. *mathematics educator, retired university president*
Everett, Wendy Ann *toy designer*
Frantz, Robert Wesley *lawyer*
Golub, Stephen Bruce *accountant, consultant, educator*
Hergenhan, Joyce *public relations executive*
Hodgkinson, William James *marketing company executive*
Jewitt, David Willard Pennock *retired banker*
Kaff, Albert Ernest *journalist, author*
Kantrowitz, Jonathan Daniel *educational software company executive, lawyer*
Kelley, Aloysius Paul *university administrator, priest*
Kenney, James Francis *lawyer*
Kijanka, Dorothy M. *library administrator*
Krueger, Kurt Edward *appliance manufacturing company official*
Leask, John McPhearson, II *accountant*
Limpitlaw, John Donald *retired publishing executive, clergyman*
Lumbard, Joseph Edward, Jr. *federal judge*
McCain, Arthur Williamson, Jr. *retired pension investment consultant*
Mead, Philomena *mental health nurse*
Meyer, Goldye W. *psychologist, educator*
Michael, Mary Amelia Furtado *retired educator, freelance writer*
Newton, Lisa Haenlein *philosophy educator*
Oberg, Muriel Curnin *community health nurse, health facility manager*
Obrig, Alice Marie *nursing educator*
O'Connell, Robert John *insurance company executive*
Peirce, George Leighton *airport administrator*
Richard, Patricia Antoinette *physician, dentist*
Rilla, Donald Robert *social services administrator*
Rosenman, Stephen David *physician, obstetrics, gynecology*
Sealy, Albert Henry *lawyer*
Shaffer, Dorothy Browne *retired mathematician, educator*
Spence, Barbara E. *publishing company executive*
Sutphen, Harold Amerman, Jr. *retired paper company executive*
Trager, Philip *photographer, lawyer*
Urquhart, John Alexander *management consultant*
Welch, John Francis, Jr. (Jack Welch) *electrical manufacturing company executive*
Wolff, Steven Alexander *arts and entertainment consultant*

## Falls Village
Cronin, Robert Lawrence *sculptor, painter*
Purcell, Dale *college president, consultant*
Purcell, Mary Louise Gerlinger *retired educator*
Toomey, Jeanne Elizabeth *animal activist*

## Farmington
Anderson, Buist Murfee *lawyer*
Besdine, Richard William *medical educator, scientist*
Bigler, Harold Edwin, Jr. *investment company executive*
Bronner, Felix *physiologist, biophysicist, educator, painter*
Buncher, James Edward *healthcare management executive*
Cooperstein, Sherwin Jerome *medical educator*
Deckers, Peter John *dean*
Donaldson, James Oswell, III *neurology educator*
Flynn, Daniel Francis *investment company executive*
Gossling, Harry Robert *orthopaedic surgeon, educator*
Grunnet, Margaret Louise *pathology educator*
Halligan, Howard Ansel *investment management company executive*
Herbette, Leo Gerard *biophysics educator*
Hickey, Kevin Francis *healthcare executive*
Hinz, Carl Frederick, Jr. *physician, educator*
Jestin, Heimwarth B. *retired university administrator*
Katz, Arnold Martin *medical educator*
Kegeles, S. Stephen *behavioral science educator*
Liebowitz, Neil Robert *psychiatrist*
Löe, Harald *dentist, educator, researcher*
Massey, Robert Unruh *physician, university dean*
Maulik, Nilanjana *medical educator*
Miser, Hugh Jordan *systems analyst, operations researcher, consultant*
O'Connor, Mary Scranton *public relations executive*
Osborn, Mary Jane Merten *biochemist*
Rabuska, Michèle Joanne *valuation analyst*
Raisz, Lawrence Gideon *medical educator, consultant*
Rothfield, Lawrence I. *microbiology educator*
Rothfield, Naomi Fox *physician*
Schenkman, John Boris *pharmacologist, educator*
Smith, Cary Christopher *artist*
Spencer, Richard Paul *biochemist, educator, physician*
Thibodeau, Robin Ann *union official, mail carrier*
Walker, James Elliot Cabot *physician*

## Georgetown
Duvivier, Jean Fernand *management consultant*
Roberts, Priscilla Warren *artist*

## Glastonbury
Googins, Sonya Forbes *state legislator, retired banker*
Hatch, D. Patricia P. *principal*
Juchnicki, Jane Ellen *secondary education educator*
Randall, Gerald J. *insurance company executive*
Roy, Kenneth Russell *school system administrator, educator*
Schroth, Peter W(illiam) *lawyer, management and law educator*
Singer, Paul Richard *ophthalmologist*

## Greens Farms
Deford, Frank *sportswriter, television and radio commentator, author*
Johnson, Jamieson Dregallo *women's athletics director*
McManus, John Francis, III *advertising executive*
St. Marie, Satenig *writer*

## Greenwich
Allain, Emery Edgar *retired paper company executive*
Amen, Robert Anthony *investor and corporate relations consultant*
†Badman, John, III *real estate developer, architect*
Baker, Charles Ernest *stockbroker*
Ball, John Fleming *advertising and film production executive*
Bam, Foster *lawyer*
Barber, Charles Finch *retired metals company executive, financial services company executive*
Behren, Robert Alan *lawyer, accountant*
Bennett, Jack Franklin *oil company executive*
Bentley, Peter *lawyer*
Berk, Alan S. *law firm executive*
Berkley, William Robert *insurance holding company executive*
Birle, James Robb *investment banker*
Bollman, Mark Brooks, Jr. *retired communications executive*
Brennan, Edward Noel *psychiatrist, educator*
†Buckley, Rick *broadcast executive*
Burton, Robert Gene *printing and publishing executive*
Cantor, Samuel C. *lawyer*
Cantwell, Robert *lawyer*
Carmichael, William Daniel *consultant, educator*
Caruso, Victor Guy *investment banker*
Chisholm, William Hardenbergh *management consultant*
Clements, Robert *insurance executive*
Close, Michael John *lawyer*
Coleman, Joel Clifford *lawyer*
Collins, Richard Lawrence *magazine editor, publisher, author*
Coudert, Victor Raphael, Jr. *marketing and sales executive*
Czajkowski, Frank Henry *lawyer*
Damon, Edmund Holcombe *plastics company executive*
Davidson, Thomas Maxwell *international management company executive*
DeCrane, Alfred Charles, Jr. *petroleum company executive*
de Mar, Leoda Miller *fabric and wallcovering designer*
Dettmer, Robert Gerhart *beverage company executive*
Donley, James Walton *management consultant*
Dorme, Patrick John *electronic company executive*
Drummond, Gillian M. *home furnishing company executive*
Egbert, Richard Cook *retired banker*
Ewald, William Bragg, Jr. *author, consultant*
Fates, Joseph Gilbert *television producer*
Fisher, Everett *lawyer*
†Flinn, Lawrence, Jr. *communications executive*
Foraste, Roland *psychiatrist*
Forrow, Brian Derek *lawyer, corporation executive*
Fuller, Theodore *retired insurance executive*
Gagnon, John Harvey *psychotherapist, educator*
Glick, Steven Lawrence *financial consultant*
Goldmann, Peter D. *editor*
Gorin, Robert Seymour *lawyer, corporation executive*
Heath, Gloria Whitton *aerospace scientist, consultant*
Heer, Edwin LeRoy *insurance executive*
Herbert, Kathy Lynne *lawyer*
Hershaft, Elinor *space planner, interior designer*
Higgins, Jay Francis *financial service executive*
Hoberman, Mary Ann *author*
Horton, Jared Churchill *retired corporation executive*
Howard, John Arnold *marketing educator*
Ix, Robert Edward *food company executive*
Jones, Edwin Michael *lawyer, former insurance company executive*
Keegan, Richard John *advertising agency executive*
Keeshan, William Francis, Jr. *advertising executive*
Kelly, David Austin *investment counselor*
Keogh, James *journalist*
†Kerr, Ian *public relations executive*
Kestnbaum, Albert S. *advertising executive*
Kopenhaver, Patricia Ellsworth *podiatrist*
Kurtz, Melvin H. *lawyer, cosmetics company executive*
Langley, Patricia Coffroth *psychiatric social worker*
Laudone, Anita Helene *lawyer*
Lawi, David Steven *energy, agriservice and thermoplastic resins industries executive*
Lewis, Audrey Gersh *financial marketing/public relations consultant*
Lewis, Perry Joshua *investment banker*
Loh, Arthur Tsung Yuan *finance company executive*
Lowenstein, Peter David *lawyer*
Lozyniak, Andrew *manufacturing company executive*
Lurie, Ranan Raymond *political cartoonist, political analyst, artist, lecturer*
Lynch, William Redington *lawyer*
MacDonald, Gordon Chalmers *management consultant*
Maroni, Paul L. *finance executive*
McLaughlin, Michael John *financial executive*
Mead, Dana George *diversified industrial manufacturing company executive*
Mendenhall, John Ryan *retired lawyer, transportation executive*
Miles, Jesse Mc Lane *retired accounting company executive*
Miller, Donald Keith *venture capitalist, asset management executive*
Mock, Robert Claude *architect*
†Moffly, John Wesley, IV *magazine publishing executive*
Moonie, Clyde Wickliffe *financial consultant*
More, Douglas McLochlan *lawyer*
Moskowitz, Stanley Alan *financial executive*
Nadel, Norman Allen *civil engineer*
Nelson, Don Harris *gas and oil industry executive*
Nevin, Crocker *investment banker*
Niemeyer, Gerhart *political science educator*
Pappas, Alceste Thetis *consulting company executive, educator*
†Pascarella, Henry William *lawyer*
Paul, Roland Arthur *lawyer*
Paulson, Paul Joseph *advertising executive*
Perless, Robert L. *sculptor*
Pfeiffer, Jane Cahill *former broadcasting company executive, consultant*
Pivirotto, Richard Roy *former retail executive*
Pollak, Edward Barry *chemical manufacturing company executive*
Prouty, Norman R. *investment banker*
†Rizzo, Raymond S. *advertising executive*
Rodenbach, Edward Francis *lawyer*
Roitsch, Paul Albert *pilot*
Rukeyser, Louis Richard *economic commentator*
Rutgers, Katharine Phillips (Mrs. Frederik Lodewijk Rutgers) *dancer*
Schlafly, Hubert Joseph, Jr. *communications executive*
Schmidt, Herman J. *former oil company executive*
Schneider, John Arnold *business investor*
Schoonmaker, Samuel Vail, III *lawyer*
Schutz, Herbert Dietrich *publishing executive*
Scott, John Constante *marketing company executive*
Shanks, Eugene Baylis, Jr. *banker*
Shepard, Thomas Rockwell, Jr. *publishing consultant*
Sheppard, Posy (Mrs. Jeremiah Milbank) *social worker*
Smith, Rodger Field *financial executive*
Snowdon, Jane Louise *industrial engineer*
Spaeh, Winfried Heinrich *retired banker*
†Squier, David Louis *manufacturing executive*
Srere, Benson M. *communications company executive, consultant*
Steinmetz, Richard Bird, Jr. *lawyer*
Sturges, Hollister, III *museum director*
Sweeney, Michael Andrew *newspaper editor*
Tetzlaff, Theodore R. *lawyer*
Tiegs, Cheryl *model, designer*
Tournillon, Nicholas Brady *trade finance, international investments company executive*
Trotta, Frank Paul, Jr. *lawyer*
Urstadt, Charles J. *real estate executive*
Wallach, Philip C(harles) *financial, public relations consultant*
Wearly, William Levi *business executive*
Weyher, Harry Frederick, III *metals company executive*
Whitmore, George Merle, Jr. *management consulting company executive*
Wyman, Ralph Mark *corporate executive*
Yonkman, Fredrick Albers *lawyer, management consultant*

## Groton
Auerbach, Michael Howard *chemical company research executive*
Boissevain, Matthijs Gideon Jan *mechanical engineer*
English, James Fairfield, Jr. *former college president*
Hinman, Richard Leslie *pharmaceutical company executive*
Holt, Edward Thomas Robert *physician, retired*
Hostetler, Dean Bryan *maritime industry professional consultant, towing, salvage, marine transportation and emergency response specialist*
Kennedy, Evelyn Siefert *foundation executive, textile restoration specialist*
Lincoln, Walter Butler, Jr. *marine engineer, educator*
Martin, Jeffrey Allen *anesthesiologist*
Perotti, Beatrice Yee-wa Tam *pharmacokineticist, research scientist*
Pinson, Ellis Rex, Jr. *chemist, consultant*
Routien, John Broderick *mycologist*
Sheets, Herman Ernest *marine engineer*
Sinko, Christopher Michael *pharmaceutical scientist*
Swindell, Archie Calhoun, Jr. *research biochemist, statistician*
Tassinari, Melissa Sherman *toxicologist*

## Guilford
Baillie, Priscilla Woods *aquatic ecologist*
Eustice, David C. *pharmaceutical researcher*
Granbery, Edwin Carleton, Jr. *architect, consultant*
Hayes, Michael Ernest *psychotherapist, educator*
Hayes, Samuel Perkins *social scientist, educator*
Kelley, Richard Everett *management consultant*
Morgan, Leon Alford *retired utility executive*
Peters, William *author, producer, director*
Ragan, James Thomas *communications executive*
Rotnem, Diane Louise *clinical social worker, educator, researcher*
Schaffer, James Mason *foundation administrator*
Springgate, Clark Franklin *physician, researcher*
Whitaker, Thomas Russell *English literature educator*

## Haddam
Twachtman-Cullen, Diane *communication disorders and autism specialist*

## Hamden
Bennett, Harry Louis *college educator*
Forman, Charles William *religious studies educator*
Gay, Peter *history educator, author*
Gordon, Angus Neal, Jr. *retired electric company executive*
Loro, Lauren Marguerite *secondary education educator*
Margulies, Martin B. *lawyer, educator*
McClellan, Edwin *Japanese literature educator*
Nuland, Sherwin *surgeon, author*
Parker, William Nelson *economics educator*
Pelikan, Jaroslav Jan *history educator*
Peterson, George Emanuel, Jr. *lawyer, business executive*
Robinson, Toni *lawyer, educator*
Roche, (Eamonn) Kevin *architect*
Rosenthal, Franz *language educator*
Spodick, Pearl Blegen *counselor, medical psychotherapist*
†Theroux, Dennis Robert *engineering executive*
Tomasko, Edward A. *financial planner*
Walker, Charles Allen *chemical engineer, educator*
Williams, Edward Gilman *retired banker*
Woodward, C. Vann *historian*

## Hanover
†Cheney, Glenn Alan *writer, educator*

## Hartford
Abbot, Quincy Sewall *retired insurance executive*
Alfano, Charles Thomas, Sr. *lawyer*
Anderson, James Brent *venture capitalist*
Anthony, J(ulian) Danford, Jr. *lawyer*
Asmar, Mark Abdon *lawyer*
Berall, Frank Stewart *lawyer*
Berdon, Robert Irwin *state supreme court justice*
Bieluch, William Charles *judge*
Blumberg, Phillip Irvin *law educator*
Blumenthal, Jeffrey Michael *lawyer*
Blumenthal, Richard *state attorney general*
Bonee, John Leon, III *lawyer*
Borden, David M. *judge*
Brauer, Rima Lois *psychiatrist*
Bronzino, Joseph Daniel *electrical engineer*
Bruner, Robert B. *hospital consultant*
Buck, Gurdon Hall *lawyer, urban planner, real estate broker*
Buckingham, Harold Canute, Jr. *lawyer*
Budd, Edward Hey *retired insurance company executive*
Burnham, Christopher Bancroft *state treasurer, investment banker*
Bysiewicz, Susan *state legislator*
Cain, George Harvey *lawyer, business executive*
Callahan, Robert Jeremiah *state supreme court chief justice*
Cantor, Donald Jerome *lawyer*
Carpenter, Michael Alan *financial services executive*
Centofanti, Joseph *accountant*
Chiarenza, Frank John *English language educator*
Church, William Handy *chemistry educator*
Clear, Albert F., Jr. *retired hardware manufacturing company executive*
Cole, William Kaufman *lawyer*
Coleman, Winifred Ellen *administrator*
Compton, Ronald E. *insurance and financial services executive*
Conard, Frederick Underwood, Jr. *lawyer*
Cook, Cathy Welles *state senator*
Cornell, Robert Witherspoon *engineering consultant*
Covello, Alfred Vincent *federal judge*
Coyle, Michael Lee *lawyer*
Crawford, Richard Bradway *biologist, biochemist, educator*
Cronin, Daniel Anthony *archbishop*
Cross, Vivian Alicia *school system administrator, educator*
Cullina, William Michael *lawyer*
Curran, Ward Schenk *economist, educator*
Daniell, Robert F. *diversified manufacturing company executive*
David, George Alfred Lawrence *industrial company executive*
Decker, Robert Owen *history educator, clergyman*
Decko, Kenneth Owen *trade association administrator*
Del Negro, John Thomas *lawyer*
Dennis, Anthony James *lawyer*
De Rocco, Andrew Gabriel *state commissioner, scientist, educator*
†Dobelle, Evan Samuel *college administrator*
Donnelly, John *psychiatrist, educator*
Doran, James Martin *retired food products company executive*
†Dworkin, Paul Howard *pediatrician*
Elliot, Ralph Gregory *lawyer*
Endrst, James Bryan *television critic, columnist*
Englehart, Robert Wayne, Jr. *cartoonist*
Ergin, M.T. *physician and surgeon*
Fain, Joel Maurice *lawyer*
Faude, Wilson Hinsdale *museum director*
Fiondella, Robert William *insurance company executive*
Fiszel, Geoffrey Lynn *investment banker, investment adviser*
Flaherty, Patrick John *state legislator, economist*
Flynn, Barbara Lois *developer*
Francis, Paul Wilbur, Jr. *former professional society administrator*
Frost, James Arthur *former university president*
Gale, John Quentin *lawyer*
Garfield, Gerald *lawyer*
Generas, George Paul, Jr. *finance educator, lawyer*
Giannaros, Demetrios Spiros *economist, educator, politician*
Gibbons, John Martin, Jr. *physician, educator*
Gillam, Linda Dawn *cardiologist, researcher*
Gillmor, Rogene Godding *medical technologist*
Gingold, George Norman *insurance company executive, lawyer*
Glasson, Lloyd *sculptor, educator*

Godfrey, Robert Douglas lawyer
Golden, Louis Joseph former business news editor, newspaper executive
Goodwin, Rodney Keith Grove international bank and trade company executive
Grant, Stephen Scott journalist
Gunderson, Gerald Axel economics educator, administrator
Gunther, George Lackman state senator, natureopathic physician, retired
Hamilton, Thomas Stewart physician, hospital administrator
Harden, Jon Bixby publishing executive
Harriman, Stephen A. state public health commissioner
Harris, James George, Jr. social services administrator, consultant
Harrison, Thomas Flatley lawyer
Hart, Donald Purple bishop
Hedrick, Joan Doran writer
Heiman, Maxwell judge, lawyer
Herman, Joan Elizabeth insurance company executive
Hermann, Robert Jay manufacturing company engineering executive, consultant
Hershfield, Lotte Cassel writer, editor
Hertel, Suzanne Marie personnel administrator
Hess, Marilyn Ann state legislator
Hickcox, Curtiss Bronson anesthesiologist
Holt, Timothy Arthur insurance company executive
Horgan, Denis Edward journalist
Hudson, Jane Duclos management consultant, writer
Humphrey, Chester Bowden cardio-thoracic surgeon
Johnson, Dwight Alan lawyer
Jones, Thomas Chester insurance company executive
Jung, Betty Chin epidemiologist, educator
Kaimowitz, Jeffrey Hugh librarian
†Karmanos, Peter, Jr. professional sports team executive
Karpe, Brian Stanley lawyer
Kennedy, Jack S. lawyer
Killian, Robert Kenneth former lieutenant governor
Killian, Robert Kenneth, Jr. judge, lawyer
King, Richard Hood newspaper executive
Knickerbocker, Robert Platt, Jr. lawyer
Korzenik, Armand Alexander lawyer
Koupal, Raymond newspaper publishing executive
Kramer, Karen Lee Van Brunt business administration educator
Kraus, Eileen S. bank executive
Krauss, Eileen S. bank executive
Krieble, Robert H. corporation executive
Kung, Pang-Jen materials scientist, electrical engineer
Lamos, Mark artistic director, administrator, actor
Leibin, Harvey Bruce architect
Libassi, Frank Peter lawyer
Lovejoy, Ann Louise organizational development consultant
Lumsden, Lynne Ann publishing company executive
Lyman, Peggy dancer, choreographer, educator
Lyon, James Burroughs lawyer
Mahoney, Michael Robert Taylor art historian, educator
Martocchio, Louis Joseph lawyer, educator
Mason, George Henry business educator, consultant
McCarthy, Patrice Ann lawyer
McCawley, Austin psychiatrist, educator
McGrattan, Mary K. state legislator
Mc Lean, Jackie jazz saxophonist, educator, composer, community activist
McNally, Alexander Campbell wine authority, consultant
Menses, Jan artist, draftsman, etcher, lithographer, muralist
Merriam, Dwight Haines lawyer, land use planner
Metzler, Robert J., II lawyer
Middlebrook, Stephen Beach lawyer
Miller, Jeffrey Clark lawyer
Moy, Samuel Yew psychologist
Mullane, Denis Francis insurance executive
Murtha, John Stephen lawyer
Newell, Robert Lincoln retired banker
Newman, Jon O. federal judge
Noel, Don Obert, Jr. newspaper columnist
Nolan, John Blanchard lawyer
Noonan, John G(erard) state financial management specialist
O'Connor, Richard Dennis lawyer
O'Donnell, Edward Francis, Jr. lawyer
Osborne, George Delano performing arts company director
Owen, H. Martyn lawyer
Pach, Peter Barnard newspaper columnist and editor
†Painter, Robert Lowell surgeon, educator
Palmer, Richard N. judge
Pangilinan, Danilo Manalese internist
Pepe, Louis Robert lawyer
Perez-Silva, Glaisma special education teacher
Peters, Ellen Ash state supreme court senior justice
Pinney, Sidney Dillingham, Jr. lawyer
Piotrowski, Richard Francis state agency administrator, council chairman
Pirro, Alfred Anthony, Jr. physician
Posteraro, Catherine Hammond librarian, gerontology educator
Powers, Robert David physician
Quinn, Andrew Peter, Jr. lawyer, insurance executive
Raffay, Stephen Joseph manufacturing company executive
Rapoport, Miles S. state official
Recchia, Christopher state agency environmental administrator
Rell, M. Jodi state official
Renner, Gerald Anthony journalist
Reynolds, Scott Walton academic administrator
Richter, Donald Paul lawyer
Roberts, Melville Parker, Jr. neurosurgeon, educator
Roessner, Barbara journalist
Rome, Donald Lee lawyer
Rowland, John G. governor, former congressman
Rutherford, Jim professional sports team executive
Ryan, David Thomas lawyer
†Sanders, William Michael emergency physician
Sargent, Joseph Denny insurance executive
Schatzki, George law educator
Scully, John Carroll life insurance marketing research company executive
See, Edmund M. lawyer
Seidl, Jane Patricia lawyer
†Shanahan, Brendan Frederick professional hockey player
Shea, David Michael state supreme court justice
Silver, Herbert physician
Simmons, Robert Ruhl state legislator, educator
Smith, Donald Arthur mechanical engineer, researcher
Space, Theodore Maxwell lawyer
Speziale, John Albert lawyer
Stoker, Warren Cady university president
Stravalle-Schmidt, Ann Roberta lawyer
Swerdloff, Mark Harris lawyer
Tancredi, James J. lawyer
Taylor, Allan Bert lawyer
Thomas, Calvert lawyer
Tonkin, Humphrey Richard academic administrator
Trachsel, William Henry corporate lawyer
Trowbridge, Phillip Edmund surgeon, educator
Uccello, Vincenza Agatha artist, director, educator emerita
Upson, Thomas Fisher state legislator, lawyer
Van Leer, Jerilyn Mosher library media specialist
Vohra, Ranbir political scientist, educator
Voigt, Richard lawyer
Webster, Arthur Edward lawyer
Welna, Cecilia mathematics educator
Westervelt, James Joseph insurance company executive
White, David Oliver museum executive
Wilde, Wilson insurance company executive
Wilder, Michael Stephen insurance company executive
Wilkie, Everett Cleveland, Jr. librarian
Winter, Miriam Therese (Gloria Frances Winter) nun, religious education educator
Wolfson, Nicholas law educator
Wolman, Martin lawyer
Wright, Douglass Brownell judge, lawyer
Yoskowitz, Irving Benjamin lawyer, manufacturing company executive
Young, Roland Frederic, III lawyer
Zakarian, Albert lawyer
Zakarian, John J. journalist
Zikmund, Barbara Brown minister, seminary president, church history educator

### Ivoryton
Bendig, William Charles editor, artist, publisher
LeCompte, Roger Burton management consultant
Osborne, John Walter historian, educator, author

### Kensington
Bailey, Debra Sue psychologist, neuropsychologist

### Kent
Ober, Robert Fairchild, Jr. retired government official, school administrator

### Killingworth
Sampson, Edward Coolidge humanities educator

### Lakeville
Armstrong, John Kremer lawyer, artist
Bookman, George B. public relations consultant
Estabrook, Robert Harley journalist
Jones, Ronald David lawyer
White, Norval Crawford architect

### Litchfield
Booth, John Thomas investment banker
Cox, Robert Hames chemist, scientific consultant
Phillips, Kevin Price columnist, author
Sheldon, Michael Richard judge, law educator
Winter, Paul Theodore musician

### Lyme
Bessie, Simon Michael publisher
Bloom, Barry Malcolm pharmaceutical consultant
Friday, John Ernest, Jr. retired securities company executive
Greene, Joseph Nathaniel, Jr. former foundation executive, former diplomat
Hoyt, Charles King architect, editor

### Madison
Azarian, Martin Vartan publishing company executive
Cappetta, Anna Maria art educator
Carlson, Dale Bick writer
Egbert, Emerson Charles retired publisher
Golembeski, Jerome John wire and cable company executive
Houghton, Alan Nourse association executive, educator, consultant
Keim, Robert Phillip retired advertising executive, consultant
Langdon, Robert Colin dermatologist, educator
Peterkin, Albert Gordon retired education educator
Platt, Sherman Phelps, Jr. publishing consultant
Purcell, Bradford Moore publishing company executive
Ross, Michael Frederick magistrate, lawyer
Snell, Richard Saxon anatomist

### Manchester
Chung, Douglas Chu pharmacist, consultant
Galasso, Francis Salvatore materials scientist
Milewski, Stanislaw Antoni ophthalmologist, educator
Ogedegbe, Henry medical technologist, clinical laboratory scientist, chemist, consultant
Precourt, George Augustine government official
Richard, Ann Bertha nursing administrator
Slaiby, Theodore George aeronautical engineer, consultant
Tanaka, Richard I. computer products company executive

### Mansfield Center
Aldrich, Robert Adams agricultural engineer
Liberman, Alvin Meyer psychology educator
Petrus, Robert Thomas distribution executive, real estate executive

### Marion
Perkins, James Winslow international business consultant, builder, contractor

### Meriden
Bertolli, Eugene Emil sculptor, goldsmith, designer, consultant
Brandt, Irene Hildegard secondary education educator
Cardona, Hector Manuel police officer
Cassidy, LeAnn Murphy elementary educator
Gaj, Stanley Thomas pharmacist, computer business consultant
†Lee, Henry C. forensic scientist
Luby, Thomas Stewart lawyer
Muzyczka, Kathleen Ann home economics educator
Smits, Helen Lida physician, administrator, educator

### Middlebury
Cohen, Andrew Stuart architect, landscape architect
Davis, Joanne Fatse lawyer
Galie, Louis Michael electronics company executive

### Middletown
Arnold, Herbert Anton German language educator
Baker, Lucy artist
Balay, Robert Elmore editor, reference librarian
Bennet, Douglas Joseph, Jr. university president
Beveridge, David Lewis chemistry educator
Briggs, Morton Winfield Romance language educator
Buel, Richard Van Wyck, Jr. history educator, writer, editor
Comfort, William Wistar mathematics educator
Crites, Stephen Decatur religion educator
Cumming, Robert Emil editor
D'Oench, Russell Grace, Jr. publishing consultant
Fry, Albert Joseph chemistry educator
Gerber, Murray A. molding manufacturing company executive
Gillmor, Charles Stewart history and science educator, researcher
Gourevitch, Victor philosophy educator
Haake, Paul chemistry and biochemistry educator
Hager, Anthony Wood mathematics educator
Harris, Dale Benner psychologist, educator
Kerr, Clarence William retired university administrator
Maltese, George John mathematics educator
Manchester, William writer
Meyer, Priscilla Ann Russian language and literature educator
Meyers, Arthur Solomon library director
Miller, Richard Alan economist, educator
Pomper, Philip history educator
Reed, Joseph Wayne American studies educator, artist
Reid, James Dolan mathematics educator, researcher
Rose, Phyllis English language professional, author
Rosenbaum, Robert Abraham mathematics educator
Scheibe, Karl Edward psychology educator
Sease, John W(illiam) chemistry educator
Shapiro, Norman Richard Romance languages and literatures educator
Slotkin, Richard Sidney American studies educator, writer
Stevens, Robert Edwin bank executive, former insurance company executive
Upgren, Arthur Reinhold, Jr. astronomer, educator, outdoor lighting consultant
Wensinger, Arthur Stevens language and literature educator, author
Winston, Krishna Ricarda foreign language professional

### Milford
Calabrese, Anthony marine biologist
Fink, Howard David pediatrician
Frazier, Howard Thomas professional society administrator
Haigh, Charles criminal justice educator
Hanlon, James Allison confectionery company executive
Khoury, Robert John international leadership management consultant
Muth, Eric Peter ophthalmic optician, consultant
Palochko, Eleanor LaRivere retired secondary education educator
Taylor, Charles Henry psychoanalyst, educator
Wall, Robert Emmet educational administrator, novelist

### Monroe
Turko, Alexander Anthony biology educator
Verano, Anthony Frank retired banker
Wheatley, Sharman B. art educator, artist

### Mystic
Antipas, Constantine George lawyer, civil engineer
Carr, James Revell museum executive, curator
Chiang, Albert Chinfa polymer chemist
Connell, Hugh P. foundation executive
Johnston, Waldo Cory Melrose museum director
Smith, Norman Clark fund raising consultant
Starks, William Edward (Skip Starks) investment consultant
Townsend, Thomas Perkins former mining company executive

### Naugatuck
Flannery, Joseph Patrick manufacturing company executive

### New Britain
Adams, John Francis, Jr. real estate executive
Ayers, Richard H. manufacturing company executive
Baskerville, Charles Alexander geologist, educator
Cline, John Carroll clinical psychologist
Davidson, Phillip Thomas retail company executive
Dimmick, Charles William geology educator
Emeagwali, Gloria Thomas humanities educator
Gallo, Donald Robert English educator
Kot, Marta Violette artist, art educator
Meskill, Thomas J. federal judge
Pearl, Helen Zalkan lawyer
Polinsky, Janet Naboicheck state official, former state legislator
Rybczyk, Edward Joseph university director, consultant
Sohn, Jeanne librarian

### New Canaan
Bartlett, Dede Thompson company executive
Burns, Ivan Alfred grocery products and industrial company executive
Caesar, Henry A., II sculptor
Cohen, Richard Norman insurance executive
Coughlin, Francis Raymond, Jr. surgeon, educator, lawyer
Crossman, William Whittard retired wire cable and communications executive
Davis, Emma Laura social services specialist
Dean, Robert Bruce architect
Flaschen, Joyce Davies business consultant
Gilbert, Steven Jeffrey venture capitalist, screenwriter, lawyer
Grace, Julianne Alice investor relations firm executive
Halverstadt, Robert Dale mechanical engineer, metals manufacturing company executive
Hodgson, Richard electronics company executive
Johnston, Douglas Frederick industrial holding company executive
Keating, Cornelius Francis record company executive
Kennedy, John Raymond pulp and paper company executive
Kovatch, Jak Gene artist
MacEwan, Nigel Savage merchant banker
Marcus, Edward economist, educator
McClure, Grover Benjamin management consultant
McIvor, Donald Kenneth retired petroleum company executive
Mc Mennamin, George Barry advertising agency executive
Means, David Hammond retired advertising executive
Mountcastle, Katharine Babcock foundation executive
Norman, Christina Reimarsdotter secondary education language educator
Oakley, Gary William travel incentive executive
O'Neill, Patrick Henry consulting mining engineer
Pickering, William Todd minister
Pike, William Edward business executive
Prescott, Peter Sherwin writer
Rendl-Marcus, Mildred artist, economist
Richards, Walter DuBois artist, illustrator
Richardson, Dana Roland video producer
Risom, Jens furniture designer, manufacturing executive
Rutledge, John William former watch company executive
Sachs, John Peter carbon company executive
Snyder, Nathan entrepreneur
Stack, J. William, Jr. management consultant
Thomas, Marianne Gregory school psychologist
Thomsen, Donald Laurence, Jr. institute executive, mathematician
Toumey, Hubert John (Hugh Toumey) textile company executive
Wallace, Kenneth Donald lawyer
Ward, Richard Vance, Jr. management executive

### New Fairfield
Daukshus, A. Joseph systems engineer
Meyers, Abbey S. foundation administrator

### New Hartford
Hall, Newman A. retired mechanical engineer
Perry, Lansford Wilder manufacturing executive, consultant

### New Haven
Abdelsayed, Wafeek Hakim accounting educator
Abell, Millicent Demmin university library administrator, consultant
Abelson, Robert Paul psychologist, educator
Ackerman, Bruce Arnold lawyer, educator
Aghajanian, George Kevork medical educator
Alexandrov, Vladimir Eugene Russian literature educator
Altman, Sidney biology educator
Amar, Akhil Reed law educator
Anderson, John Frederick science administrator, entomologist, researcher
Andreopoulos, George J. history educator, lawyer, political science educator
Apfel, Robert Edmund mechanical engineering educator, applied physicist, research scientist
Apter, David Ernest political science and sociology educator
Aronson, Peter Samuel medical scientist, physiology educator
Askenase, Philip William medicine and pathology educator
Aylor, Donald Earl biophysicist, research meteorologist, plant pathology educator and reseacher
Bailey, William Harrison artist, educator
Baker, Robert Stevens organist, educator
Barash, Paul George anesthesiologist, educator
Beardsley, G(eorge) Peter pediatric oncologist, biochemical pharmacologist
Behrman, Harold Richard endocrinologist, physiologist, educator
Bell, Wendell sociologist, educator, futurist
Belt, David Levin lawyer
Bennett, William Ralph, Jr. physicist, educator
Berliner, Robert William physician, medical educator
Berner, Robert Arbuckle geochemist, educator
Bers, Victor classics educator
Berson, Jerome Abraham chemistry educator
Blatt, Sidney Jules psychology educator, psychoanalyst
Bloom, Harold humanities educator
Blum, John Morton historian
Bolognia, Jean Lynn academic dermatologist
Borroff, Marie English language educator
Boyer, James Lorenzen physician, educator
Bracken, Paul political science educator
Brainard, Paul Henry musicologist, music educator
Brainard, William Crittenden economist, educator, university official
Braverman, Irwin Merton dermatologist, educator
Brewer, Charles H., Jr. bishop
Brewster, Carroll Worcester fund administrator
Bromley, David Allan physicist, engineer, educator
Brooks, Peter (Preston) French and comparative literature educator, writer
Brown, Arvin Bragin theater director
Brown, Ralph Sharp law educator
Brown, Thomas Huntington neuroscientist
Brownell, Kelly David psychologist, educator
Brünger, Axel Thomas biophysicist, researcher, educator
Bunney, Benjamin Stephenson psychiatrist
Burns, Ellen Bree federal judge
Burrow, Gerard Noel physician, educator
Burt, Robert Amsterdam lawyer, educator
Buss, Leo William biologist, educator
Byck, Robert Samuel psychiatrist, educator
Cabranes, José Alberto federal judge
†Cadman, Edwin C. health facility administrator, medical educator
Calabresi, Guido federal judge, law educator
Caprioli, Joseph ophthalmologist
Carlson, Dale Lynn lawyer
Carty, Paul Vernon lawyer
Casten, Richard Francis physicist
Chandler, William Knox physiologist
Chang, Richard Kounai physics educator
Child, Irvin Long psychologist, educator
Chupka, William Andrew chemical physicist, educator
Clark, Elias law educator
Clark, Susan Atkinson clinical social worker, educator
Clarke, Fred W., III architect, architectural firm executive
Clendenen, William Herbert, Jr. lawyer

Clizbe, John Anthony *psychologist*
Coe, Michael Douglas *anthropologist, educator*
Cohen, Donald Jay *pediatrics, psychiatry and psychology educator, administrator*
Cohen, Jane A. *social worker*
Cohen, Lawrence Baruch *neurobiologist, educator*
Cohen, Lawrence Sorel *physician, educator*
Cohen, Morris Leo *retired law librarian and educator*
Coleman, Joseph Emory *biophysics and biochemistry educator*
Collins, William F., Jr. *neurosurgery educator*
Comer, James Pierpont *psychiatrist, educator*
Condon, Thomas Brian (Brian Condon) *hospital executive*
Cooney, Leo Mathias, Jr. *geriatrician, educator*
Cooper, Dennis Lawrence *oncologist, educator*
Cooper, Jack Ross *pharmacology educator, researcher*
Craig, William Emerson *lawyer*
Crothers, Donald Morris *biochemist, educator*
Crowder, Robert George *psychology educator*
Cunningham, Walter Jack *electrical engineering educator*
Damaska, Mirjan Radovan *law educator*
Davey, Lycurgus Michael *neurosurgeon*
Davis, David Brion *historian, educator*
Davis, Michael *medical educator*
Days, Drew S., III *lawyer, law educator*
Dearington, Michael *lawyer*
Dechant, Virgil C. *fraternal organization administrator*
Demos, John Putnam *history educator, writer, consultant*
Diers, Donna Kaye *nurse educator*
Dileone, Carmel Montano *dental hygienist*
Dittes, James Edward *psychology of religion educator*
Donaldson, Robert Macartney, Jr. *physician*
Doob, Leonard William *psychology educator, academic administrator*
Dorsey, Peter Collins *federal judge*
Droney, Christopher F. *prosecutor*
DuBois, Arthur Brooks *physiologist, educator*
Duke, Steven Barry *law educator*
Dupré, Louis *philosopher, educator*
Edelson, Marshall *psychiatry educator, psychoanalyst*
Ellickson, Robert Chester *law educator*
Ember, Melvin Lawrence *anthropologist, educator*
Erikson, Kai *sociologist, educator*
Erlich, Victor *Slavic languages educator*
Farquhar, Doris Irene Davis *academic administrator*
Feinstein, Alvan Richard *physician, educator*
Ferholt, J. Deborah Lott *pediatrician*
Fikrig, Erol *rheumatologist, medical educator*
Fischer, Michael John *computer science educator*
Fiss, Owen M. *law educator*
Fleck, Stephen *psychiatrist*
Freed, Daniel Josef *law educator*
Freedman, Gerald Stanley *radiologist, healthcare administrator*
French, Kenneth Ronald *finance educator*
French, Richard Frederic *retired music educator*
Fried, Charles A. *accountant, financial executive*
Friedlaender, Gary Elliott *orthopedist, educator*
Gaddis, John Lewis *history educator*
Gallup, Donald Clifford *bibliographer, educator*
Galston, Arthur William *biology educator*
Garner, Wendell Richard *psychology educator*
Genel, Myron *pediatrician, educator*
Gewirtz, Paul D. *lawyer, legal educator*
Gilbert, Creighton Eddy *art historian*
Gilman, Richard *drama educator, author*
Glaser, Gilbert Herbert *neuroscientist, physician, educator*
Glier, Ingeborg Johanna *German language and literature educator*
Goldman-Rakic, Patricia Shoer *neuroscience educator*
Goldstein, Abraham S. *lawyer, educator*
Goldstein, Joseph *law educator*
Goodrich, Isaac *neurosurgeon, educator*
Gordon, John Charles *forestry educator*
Gordon, Robert Boyd *geophysics educator*
Górniak-Kocikowska, Krystyna Stefania *philosopher, educator*
Graedel, Thomas Eldon *chemist, researcher*
Greene, Liliane *French educator, editor*
Greene, Thomas McLernon *language professional, educator*
Greenfield, James Robert *lawyer*
Griffith, Ezra Edward Holman *health facility administrator, educator*
Gross, Ian *academic pediatrician, neonatologist*
Grossi, Richard J. *electric utility company executive*
Haller, Gary Lee *chemical engineering educator*
Hallo, William Wolfgang *Assyriologist*
Handschumacher, Robert Edmund *biochemistry educator*
Hansmann, Henry Baethke *law educator*
Harries, Karsten *philosophy educator, researcher*
Harrison, Henry Starin *real estate educator, appraiser, entrepreneur*
Hartman, Geoffrey H. *language professional, educator*
Heninger, George Robert *psychiatry educator, researcher*
Herbert, Peter Noel *physician, medical educator*
Hersey, George Leonard *art history educator*
Herzenberg, Arvid *physicist, educator*
Hickey, Leo J(oseph) *museum curator, educator*
Hines, Roberta L. *medical educator*
Hoffer, Paul B. *nuclear medicine physician, educator*
Hoffleit, Ellen Dorrit *astronomer*
Hoffman, Joseph Frederick *physiology educator*
Hoge, Michael Alan *psychologist*
Hohenberg, Pierre Claude *research physicist*
Holder, Angela Roddey *lawyer, educator*
Holford, Theodore Richard *biostatistician, educator*
Hollander, John *humanities educator, poet*
Holmes, Frederic Lawrence *science historian*
Holquist, James Michael *Russian and comparative literature educator*
Horstmann, Dorothy Millicent *physician, educator*
Horváth, Csaba *chemical engineering educator, researcher*
Horwitz, Ralph Irving *internist, medical educator, epidemiologist*
Howe, Roger Evans *mathematician, educator*
Hull, John McAllister *educator, painter*
Hyman, Paula E(llen) *history educator*
Igarashi, Peter *nephrologist, educator, researcher*
Insler, Stanley *philologist, educator*
Jackson, Stanley Webber *psychiatrist, medical historian*
Jacob, Deirdre Ann Bradbury *manufacturing executive, business educator, consultant*
Jacoby, Robert Ottinger *comparative medicine educator*
Jatlow, Peter I. *pathologist, medical educator, researcher*
Jekel, James Franklin *physician, public health educator*
Johnson, Lester Fredrick *artist*
Johnstone, Quintin *law educator*
Jorgensen, William L. *chemistry educator*
Kagan, Donald *historian, educator*
Kashgarian, Michael *pathologist, physician*
Katz, Jay *psychiatry and law educator*
Kavanagh, Aidan Joseph *priest, university educator*
Keck, Leander Earl *theology educator*
Keiser, David Wharton *biotechnology executive*
Kennedy, Paul Michael *history educator*
Kessen, William *psychologist, educator*
Kirchner, John Albert *retired otolaryngology educator*
Klein, Martin Jesse *physicist, educator, science historian*
Kleiner, Diana Elizabeth Edelman *art history educator, administrator*
Komp, Diane Marilyn *pediatric oncologist, hematologist, writer*
Krauss, Judith Belliveau *nursing educator*
Kronman, Anthony Townsend *lawyer, educator*
Kushlan, Samuel Daniel *physician, educator, hospital administrator*
Laderman, Ezra *composer, educator, college dean*
Lamar, Howard Roberts *educational administrator, historian*
Langbein, John Harriss *lawyer, educator*
LaPalombara, Joseph *political science educator*
Leeney, Robert Joseph *newspaper editor*
Leffell, David Joel *surgeon, medical administrator, dermatologist, educator, researcher*
Lentz, Thomas Lawrence *biomedical educator, dean, researcher*
Levin, Richard Charles *academic administrator, economist*
Levine, Robert John *physician, educator*
Lewis, Melvin *psychiatrist, pediatrician, psychoanalyst*
Li, Jianming *molecular and cellular biologist*
Lindroth, Linda (Linda Hammer) *artist, curator, writer*
Logue, Frank *arbitrator, mediator, urban consultant, former mayor New Haven*
Lord, George deForest *English educator*
Lorimer, Linda Koch *university educator*
Ma, Tso-Ping *electrical engineering educator, researcher, consultant*
MacAvoy, Paul Webster *economics, management educator, university dean*
Mac Dowell, Samuel Wallace *physics educator*
MacMullen, Ramsay *retired history educator*
Malherbe, Abraham Johannes, VI *religion educator, writer*
Malkin, Moses Montefiore *employee benefits administration company executive*
Marchesi, Vincent T. *biochemist, educator*
Mark, Harry Horst *ophthalmologist, researcher*
Marks, Lawrence Edward *psychologist*
Marshall, Burke *law educator*
Martz, Louis Lohr *English literature educator*
Massey, William S. *mathematician, educator*
Mayhew, David Raymond *political educator*
McCarthy, Paul Louis *pediatrics educator*
McClatchy, J. D. *editor, writer, educator*
Mc Guire, William James *social psychology educator*
Meeks, Wayne A. *religious studies educator*
Mermann, Alan Cameron *pediatrics educator, chaplain*
Merrell, Ronald Clifton *surgeon, educator*
Merritt, John Augustus *geriatrician, educator*
Miller, Neal Elgar *psychologist, emeritus educator*
Moore, Peter Bartlett *biochemist, educator*
Morgan, Robert P. *music theorist, educator*
Mostow, George Daniel *mathematics educator*
Mullen, Frank Albert *university official, clergyman*
Murphy, William Robert *lawyer*
Musto, David Franklin *physician, educator, historian, consultant*
Nadel, Ethan Richard *epidemiology educator*
Naftolin, Frederick *physician, reproductive biologist educator*
Newick, Craig David *architect*
Newman, Harry Rudolph *urologist, educator*
Niederman, James Corson *physician, educator*
Nolan, Victoria *theater director*
Nwangwu, John Tochukwu *epidemiologist, public health educator*
Oliver-Warren, Mary Elizabeth *retired library science educator*
Ostfeld, Adrian Michael *physician*
Ostrom, John H. *vertebrate paleontologist, educator, museum curator*
Outka, Gene Harold *philosophy and Christian ethics educator*
Palisca, Claude Victor *musicologist, educator*
Papageorge, Tod *photographer, educator*
Parks, Stephen Robert *curator*
Pease, David Gordon *artist, educator*
Peck, Merton Joseph *economist, educator*
Pelli, Cesar *architect*
Peterson, Linda H. *English language and literature educator*
Phillips, Peter Charles Bonest *economist, educator, researcher*
Platner, Warren *architect*
Pollitt, Jerome Jordan *art history educator*
Pospisil, Leopold Jaroslav *anthropology and law educator*
Priest, George L. *law educator*
Prown, Jules David *art historian educator*
Pruett, Kyle Dean *psychiatrist, writer, educator*
Prusoff, William Herman *biochemical pharmacologist, educator*
Rakic, Pasko *neuroscientist, educator*
Ranis, Gustav *economist, educator*
Rawson, Claude Julien *English educator*
Redmond, Donald Eugene, Jr. *neuroscientist, educator*
Reifsnyder, William Edward *meteorologist*
Reiser, Morton Francis *psychiatrist, educator*
Reisman, William M. *lawyer, educator*
Reiss, Albert John, Jr. *sociology educator*
Reynolds, Lloyd George *economist, educator*
Ricard, Thomas Armand *electrical engineer*
Richard, Alison Fettes *anthropology educator*
Richards, Frederic Middlebrook *biochemist, educator*
Rickart, Charles Earl *mathematician, educator*
Ritchie, J. Murdoch *pharmacologist, educator*
Robinson, Dorothy K. *lawyer*
Robinson, Fred Colson *English language educator*
Rodgers, John *geologist, educator*
Rodriguez, Cesar *librarian*
Rose-Ackerman, Susan *law and political economy educator*
Roth, Harold *architect*
Rouse, Irving *anthropologist, emeritus educator*
Rush, William John *newspaper executive*
Russett, Bruce Martin *political science educator*
Ryden, John Graham *publishing executive*
Saltzman, Barry *meteorologist, educator*
Sammons, Jeffrey Leonard *foreign language educator*
Sanneh, Lamin *religion educator*
Sartorelli, Alan Clayton *pharmacology educator*
Sasaki, Clarence Takashi *surgeon, medical educator*
Savin, Abby Luria *social worker*
Scarf, Herbert Eli *economics educator*
Schenker, Alexander Marian *Slavic linguistics educator*
Schowalter, John Erwin *psychiatrist, educator*
†Schriver, John Allen *emergency medicine physician*
Schultz, T. Paul *economics educator*
Schwartz, Peter Edward *physician, gynecologic oncology educator*
Sears, Marvin *ophthalmologist, educator*
Seashore, Margretta Reed *physician*
Seligman, George Benham *mathematics educator*
Shubik, Martin *economics educator*
Shulman, Gerald I. *clinical investigator*
Shulman, Robert Gerson *biophysics educator*
Siegel, Norman Joseph *pediatrician, educator*
Sigler, Paul Benjamin *molecular biology educator, protein crystallographer*
Silver, George Albert *physician, educator*
Silverstone, David Edward *ophthalmologist*
Silvestri, Robert *electric company executive*
Simon, John Gerald *law educator*
Simone, Angela Paolino *elementary education educator*
Skinner, Helen Catherine Wild *biomineralogist*
Slayman, Clifford Leroy *biophysicist, educator*
Smith, David Martyn *forestry educator*
Smith, John Edwin *philosophy educator*
Smith, William Hulse *forestry and environmental studies educator*
Sofia, Sabatino *astronomy educator*
Solimena, Michele *endocrinologist, educator, researcher*
Solnit, Albert Jay *physician, commissioner, educator*
Spence, Jonathan Dermot *historian, educator*
Spiro, Howard Marget *physician, educator*
Steitz, Joan Argetsinger *biochemistry educator*
Sternberg, Robert Jeffrey *psychology educator*
Stevens, Joseph Charles *psychology educator*
Stith-Cabranes, Kate *law educator*
Stolberg, Irving J. *state legislator, international consultant*
Stolwijk, Jan Adrianus Jozef *physiologist, biophysicist*
Stowe, Bruce Bernot *biology educator*
Stuehrenberg, Paul Frederick *librarian*
Sullivan, Shaun S. *lawyer*
Summers, William Cofield *science educator*
Sutterlin, James S. *political science educator, researcher*
Szczarba, Robert Henry *mathematics educator, mathematician*
Tamborlane, William V., Jr. *physician, biomedical researcher, pediatrics educator*
Tanaka, Kay *genetics educator*
Taylor, Kenneth J. *diagnostic sonologist*
Theodore, Eustace D. *alumni association executive, management consultant*
Tilson, John Quillin *lawyer*
Tirro, Frank Pascale *music educator, author, composer*
Tobin, James *economics educator*
Todd, Erica Weyer *lawyer*
Totman, Conrad Davis *history educator*
Trinkaus, John Philip *cell and developmental biologist*
Tufte, Edward Rolf *statistics educator, publisher*
Tully, John Charles *research chemical physicist*
Turekian, Karl Karekin *geochemistry educator*
Turner, Frank Miller *historian, educator*
Underdown, David Edward *historian, educator*
van Altena, Alicia Mora *language educator*
Vicenzi, Angela Elizabeth *nursing educator*
Vroom, Victor Harold *management consultant, educator*
Waggoner, Paul Edward *agricultural scientist*
Wagner, Allan Ray *psychology educator, experimental psychologist*
Wagner, Günter Paul *biologist educator*
Walker-LaRose, Linda Waleska *elementary education educator*
Wandycz, Piotr Stefan *history educator*
Warshaw, Joseph Bennett *pediatrician, educator*
Waters, Donald Joseph *information services administrator*
Waxman, Stephen George *neurologist, neuroscientist*
†Wedgwood, Ruth *law educator, international affairs expert*
Wegener, Peter Paul *engineering educator, author*
Weinstein, Stanley *Buddhist studies educator*
Wenig, Mary Moers *law educator*
Westerfield, Holt Bradford *political scientist, educator*
Winks, Robin William *history educator*
Winter, Ralph Karl, Jr. *federal judge*
Wojewodski, Stan, Jr. *artistic director, dean*
Wolf, Werner Paul *physicist, educator*
Woody, Carol Clayman *data processing executive*
Wright, Hastings Kemper *surgeon, educator*
Yandle, Stephen Thomas *law school dean*
Yeazell, Ruth Bernard *English language educator*
Zaret, Barry Lewis *cardiologist, medical educator*
Zeller, Michael Edward *physicist, educator*
Zhang, Heping *biostatistician*
Zigler, Edward Frank *psychologist, educator*
Zinn, Robert James *astronomer, educator*

### New London
Bobruff, Jerome *physician*
Clark, R. Thomas *lawyer*
Daragan, Patricia Ann *librarian*
Doro, Marion Elizabeth *political scientist, educator*
Gaudiani, Claire Lynn *academic administrator*
Goodwin, Richard Hale *botany educator*
MacCluggage, Reid *newspaper editor, publisher*
McGinley, Morgan *newspaper editor*
Mulvey, Helen Frances *retired history educator*
Pinhey, Frances Louise *physical education educator*
Rice, Argyll Pryor *Hispanic studies and Spanish language educator*
Rogers, Brian Deane *librarian*
Santaniello, Angelo Gary *retired state supreme court justice*
Schoenberger, Steven Harris *physician, research consultant*
Taranow, Gerda *English language educator, researcher, author*
Urbanetti, John Sutherland *internist, consultant*

### New Milford
Edmondson, John Richard *lawyer, pharmaceutical manufacturing company executive*
Fabricand, Burton Paul *physicist, educator*
Friedman, John Maxwell, Jr. *lawyer*
Johnson, Robert Clyde *theology educator*
Pendagast, Edward Leslie Jr. *physician*

### Newington
Seddon, John Thomas, III *theologian, business consultant, educator*
†Sumner, David George *association executive*
Vassar, William Gerald *gifted and talented education educator*

### Newtown
Bockelman, Charles Kincaid *physics educator*
Cayne, Bernard Stanley *editor*
Coates, John Peter *technical marketing executive*
Kotecki, Joanna Krystyna Emerle *primary school educator*
Krauss, Steven James *clothing executive*

### Niantic
Ashley, Eleanor Tidaback *retired elementary educator*
Deakyne, William John *library director, musician*
Hunt, Francis Howard *retired navy laboratory official*

### Noank
Bates, Gladys Edgerly *sculptor*

### Norfolk
Lambros, Lambros John *lawyer, petroleum company executive*
Vagliano, Alexander Marino *banker*

### North Branford
Gregan, Edmund Robert *landscape architect*
Logan, John Arthur, Jr. *retired foundation executive*
Mead, Lawrence Myers, Jr. *retired aerospace executive*

### North Haven
†Bradow, Barbara G. *health care executive*
Bulyk, Spider J(ohn) C(onrad) (Romanyshyn) *corporate development executive*
Culler, Arthur Dwight *English language educator*
Dahl, Robert Alan *political science educator*
Fuggi, Gretchen Miller *education educator*
Mahl, George Franklin *psychoanalyst, psychologist, educator*
McCauley, Lisa Francine *secondary education educator*
Montagna, Bernice Donna *education educator*
Pearce, Herbert Henry *real estate company executive*
Phillips, Elizabeth Vellom *social worker, educator*
Seton, Fenmore Roger *manufacturing company executive, civic worker*
Walker, Fred Elmer *broadcasting executive*
Wohlert, Earl Ross *health care analyst*

### North Stonington
Keane, John Patrick *retired secondary education educator*
Nolf, David Manstan *financial executive*

### Northford
James, Virginia Stowell *retired elementary, secondary education educator*
James, William Hall *former state official, educator*

### Norwalk
Albanese, Licia *retired operatic soprano*
Babcock, Catherine Evans *artist, educator*
Baez, Manuel *health care executive*
Bennett, Carl *retired discount department store executive*
Bermas, Stephen *lawyer*
Boles, Lenore Utal *nurse psychotherapist, educator*
Brandt, Richard Paul *communications and entertainment company executive*
Britt, David Van Buren *educational communications executive*
Brod, Morton Shlevin *oral surgeon*
DeCesare, Donald E. *broadcasting executive*
Dolson, Patricia *publishing company executive*
Eagan, Sherman G. *producer, communications executive*
Feskoe, Gaffney Jon *investment banker, management consultant*
Floch, Martin Herbert *physician*
Foster, John McNeely *accounting standards executive*
Fulweiler, Patricia Platt *civic worker*
Glidden, Germain G. *artist*
Griffin, Donald Wayne *diversified chemical company executive*
Hackett, Linda Lepley *nurse psychotherapist, consultant*
†Harris, Holton Edwin *plastics machinery manufacturing executive*
Hathaway, Carl Emil *investment management company executive*
Howatson, Marianne *publisher*
†Huskins, Dennis G. *internist*
Irving, Michael Henry *architect*
Jacobs, Mark Randolph *lawyer*
Johnstone, John William, Jr. *chemical company executive*
Kam, Frederick Anthony *internist, physician*
Maarbjerg, Mary Penzold *office equipment company executive*
Manning, James Forrest *computer executive*
McDonell, Horace George, Jr. *instrument company executive*
Mueller, Gerhard G(ottlob) *financial accounting standard setter*
Neuman, Curtis William *computer systems company executive*
Partch, Kenneth Paul *editor, consultant*
Peltz, Alan Howard *manufacturing company executive*
Perry, Charles Owen *sculptor*
Perschino, Arthur J. *elementary school principal*
Potluri, Venkateswara Rao *medical facility administrator*
Quittell, Frederic Charles *personnel and labor relations executive*

Reder, Robert Frank physician
Schmalzried, Marvin Eugene financial consultant
Tracey, Edward John physician, surgeon
Vanderbilt, Hugh Bedford, Sr. mineral and chemical company executive
Wiggins, Charles secondary education educator

### Norwich
Gualtieri, Joseph Peter museum director
Hart, Daniel Anthony bishop
Heinrich, Carl Chester physical education educator
LeClair, Peter R. state agency supervisor, mental retardation services professional
Sharpe, Richard Samuel architectural company executive

### Old Greenwich
Baritz, Loren history educator
Bonner, Charles William, III community services executive, newspaper writer
Dixon, John Morris magazine editor
Fernous, Louis Ferdinand, Jr. consumer products company executive
Hittle, Richard Howard corporate executive, international affairs consultant
Islan, Gregory deFontaine cable television executive
Kelley, Wendy Thue fine art advisor, consultant
Mc Donough, Richard Doyle retired paper company executive
Mc Quinn, William P. corporation executive
Nelson, Norma Randy deKadt psychotherapist, consultant
Plancher, Robert Lawrence manufacturing company executive
Rukeyser, Robert James manufacturing executive
Scullion, Tsugiko Yamagami non-profit organization executive
Strait, Almuth Vandiveer dentist
Yoder, Patricia Doherty public relations executive

### Old Lyme
Bond, Niles Woodbridge cultural institute executive, former foreign service officer
Chandler, Elisabeth Gordon (Mrs. Laci De Gerenday) sculptor, harpist
Cook, Charles Davenport pediatrician, educator
Crawford, Homer retired lawyer, paper company executive
Dangremond, David W. museum administrator, educator
de Gerenday, Laci Anthony sculptor
Johnson, James Myron psychologist, educator
LeBoutillier, Janet Ela real estate investment asset manager, writer
Mangin, Charles-Henri electronics company executive
St. George, Judith Alexander author

### Old Saybrook
Elrod, Harold Glenn retired engineering science educator, consultant
Hamilton, Donald Bengtsson author
Jensen, Oliver Ormerod editor, writer
Kaplan, Bernard Joseph surgeon
Phillips, William E. advertising agency executive
Spencer, William Courtney foundation executive, international business executive

### Orange
Bowerman, Richard Henry utility company executive, lawyer
†Fasanella, Rocko Michael ophthalmologist
Miller, Henry Forster architect

### Plainfield
Baranowski, Paul Joseph instrumentation technician
O'Connell, Francis V(incent) textile printing company executive

### Plainville
Glassman, Gerald Seymour metal finishing company executive

### Preston
Gibson, Margaret Ferguson poet, educator
Makara, Carol Pattie education educator, consultant

### Prospect
Thornley, Wendy Ann educator, sculptor

### Putnam
Desaulniers, Rene Gerard Lesieur optometrist

### Redding
Benyei, Candace Reed psychotherapist
Foster, Edward John engineering physicist
Isley, Alexander Max graphic designer, lecturer
Russell, Allan David lawyer

### Ridgefield
Bye, Arthur Edwin, Jr. landscape architect
Byrne, Daniel William biomedical research consultant, biostatistician, computer specialist, educator
Farina, Peter R. biochemist
Forbes, James Wendell publishing consultant
Kelley, Edward Allen publisher
Knortz, Herbert Charles retired conglomerate company executive
Leonard, Sister Anne C. superintendent, education director
Levine, Paul Michael paper industry executive, consultant
Lewis, Gerri newspaper columnist
Lodewick, Philip Hughes equipment leasing company executive
Malhotra, Surin M. aerospace manufacturing executive
McGovern, R(ichard) Gordon food company executive
Norman, Richard Arthur humanities educator
Phelps, Judson Hewett therapist, counselor, marketing sales executive
Robertson, Suzanne Marie primary education educator
Sadow, Harvey S. health care company executive
Stoddard, William Bert, Jr. economist
Tomanic, Joseph P(aul) research scientist
Weese, Bruce Eric pharmaceutical industry lobbyist, human services manager
Wyton, Alec composer, organist

### Riverside
Battat, Emile A. management executive
Coulson, Robert retired association executive, arbitrator, author
Geismar, Richard Lee communications executive
Isaacson, Gerald Sidney publishing company executive
Lovejoy, Allen Fraser retired lawyer
Lupia, David Thomas corporate financial advisor, management consultant
McCullough, Robert Willis former textile executive
McSpadden, Peter Ford retired advertising agency executive
Otto, Charles Edward health care administrator
Pearson, Robert Greenlees writing services company executive
Powers, Claudia McKenna state government official

### Rocky Hill
Chu, Hsien-Kun chemist, researcher
Chuang, Frank Shiunn-Jea engineering executive, consultant
Griesé, John William, III astronomer

### Rogers
Boomer, Walter Eugene marine officer

### Rowayton
Raikes, Charles FitzGerald retired lawyer

### Roxbury
Anderson, Robert Woodruff playwright, novelist, screenwriter
Gurney, Albert Ramsdell playwright, novelist, educator
Miller, Arthur playwright, author

### Salem
Diamond, Sigmund editor, educator

### Salisbury
Block, Zenas management consultant, educator
Blum, Robert Edward business executive

### Sandy Hook
Karkut, Emil Joseph manufacturing company executive

### Sharon
Gordon, Nicholas broadcasting executive
Gottlieb, Richard Matthew psychiatrist, consultant

### Shelton
Asija, S(atya) Pal lawyer
Eichhorst, Gerda Irene geriatrics nurse
Forbes, Richard E. retired publishing company executive
Lobsenz, Herbert Munter data base company executive
Smith, Craig Richards manufacturing executive
Storck, Herbert Evan marketing professional
Wham, William Neil publisher
Zeller, Claude physicist, researcher

### Sherman
Cohn, Jane Shapiro public relations executive
Goodspeed, Barbara artist
Piel, William, Jr. lawyer, arbitrator
Valeriani, Richard Gerard news broadcaster

### Simsbury
Barnicle, Stephan Patrick secondary school educator
DiCosimo, Patricia Shields art educator
Hildebrandt, Frederick Dean, Jr. management consultant
Krisher, William K. former insurance company executive
Long, Michael Thomas lawyer, manufacturing company executive
Nolan, Robert management consulting company executive
Vander Putten, LeRoy Andrew insurance company executive

### Somers
Blake, Stewart Prestley retired ice cream company executive
Hooper, Donald Robert retired corporate executive

### South Norwalk
Rodriguez, Carmen Vila artist, art educator, art historian

### South Windsor
Coullard, Chad information systems specialist
Gentile, George Michael manufacturing company finance executive
Hobbs, David Ellis mechanical engineer

### Southbury
Atwood, Edward Charles economist, educator
Cassidy, James Joseph public relations counsel
Fabiani, Dante Carl industrialist
Leonard, John Harry advertising executive
Rorick, William Calvin librarian, educator, portrait artist
Sallani, Marion Davis (Mrs. Werner Sallani) social work administrator, therapist
Usher, Elizabeth Reuter (Mrs. William A. Scar) retired librarian
Wescott, Roger Williams anthropologist
Wilson, Geraldine O'Connor psychologist

### Southington
Barry, Richard William chemist, consultant

### Southport
Damson, Barrie Morton oil and gas exploration company executive
Hill, David Lawrence research corporation executive
Perry, Vincent Aloysius corporate executive
Roache, Edward Francis retired manufacturing company executive
Sanetti, Stephen Louis lawyer
Sheppard, William Stevens investment banker
Singer, Henry A. behavioral scientist, institute director
Taylor, James Blackstone aviation company executive
Walker, Charles Dodsley conductor, organist
Wheeler, Wilmot Fitch, Jr. diversified manufacturing company executive
Wilbur, E. Packer investment company executive

### Stamford
Allaire, Paul Arthur office equipment company executive
Anderson, Susan Stuebing business equipment company executive
Ast, Steven Todd executive search firm executive
Aveni, Beverly A. executive aide
Axelson, Linda Rae recreational facility manager
Barker, James Rex water transportation executive
Baylis, Robert Montague investment banker
†Benedict, Peter Behrends lawyer
Beyman, Jonathan Eric information officer
Birenbaum, Jonathan lawyer
Block, Ruth retired insurance company executive
Bonina, Sally Anne secondary school educator
Bowen, Patrick Harvey lawyer, consultant
Brakeley, George Archibald, Jr. fundraising consultant
Breakstone, Robert Albert consumer products/information technology/entertainment executive
Britt, Glenn Alan media company executive
Calarco, Vincent Anthony specialty chemicals company executive
Carlin, Gabriel S. corporate executive
Castrignano, Robert Anthony retired dean, retired broadcasting company executive
Cavallon, Betty Gabler interior designer
Chiddix, James Alan cable television engineering executive
Chisolm, Barbara Wille world affairs organization executive
Cochran, David MacDuffie management consultant
Coleman, Ernest Albert plastics and materials consultant
†Collins, Joseph J. television services company executive
Conover, Harvey retired publisher
Cook, Colin Burford psychiatrist
Czajkowski-Barrett, Karen Angela human resources management executive
Dederick, Ronald Osburn lawyer
Dell, Warren Frank, II management consultant
Della Rocco, Kenneth Anthony lawyer
Dolian, Robert Paul lawyer
Donahue, Donald Jordan mining company executive
†Doolittle, James H. cable television systems company executive
Ekernas, Sven Anders investment company executive
Elkes, Terrence Allen communications executive
Epstein, Simon Jules psychiatrist
Evans, Robert Sheldon manufacturing executive
Ferguson, Ronald Eugene reinsurance company executive
Fernandez, Nino Joseph manufacturing company executive
Fickenscher, Gerald H. chemicals company executive
Fillet, Mitchell Harris financial services executive
Filter, Eunice Margie business equipment manufacturing executive
Fortune, Philip Robert metal manufacturing company executive
Frank, Charles Raphael, Jr. financial executive
Frey, Dale Franklin financial investment company executive, manufacturing company executive
Friedmann, Paul Garson control engineer
Fuller, Cassandra Miller programmer analyst
Gagnon, Monique Francine pediatrician
Gardiner, Hobart Clive petroleum company executive
Ge, Wen-Zheng materials scientist
Gefter, William Irvin physician, educator
Gilman, Derek lawyer
Gladstone, Herbert Jack manufacturing company executive
Godfrey, Robert R. financial services executive
Gold, Steven Michael lawyer
Goldstein, Frederick Arya marketing executive
Goodhue, Peter Ames obstetrician and gynecologist, educator
†Gorman, Maureen foundation administrator
Gross, Ronald Martin forest products executive
Haber, Judith Ellen nursing educator
Hagner, Arthur Feodor geologist, educator
Hathaway, Lynn McDonald education advocate, administrator
Hawley, Frank Jordan, Jr. venture capital executive
Hedge, Arthur Joseph, Jr. corporate executive
Hollander, Milton Bernard corporate executive
Hood, Edward Exum, Jr. retired electrical manufacturing company executive
Hudson, Harold Jordon, Jr. retired insurance executive
Huth, William Edward lawyer
Jacobson, Ishier retired utility executive
James, John Whitaker, Sr. financial services executive
Jason, J. Julie money manager, author, lawyer
Joondeph, Marcia diplomat
Karp, Steve artistic director
Kaufman, John E. retired association executive
Kellogg, Tommy Nason reinsurance corporation executive
Kingsley, John McCall, Jr. manufacturing company executive
Kinnear, James Wesley, III retired petroleum company executive
Kinsman, Robert Donald art museum administrator, cartoonist
Kisseberth, Paul Barto retired publishing executive
Klein, Neil Charles physician
Klenk, Rosemary Ellen pediatrician
Knag, Paul Everett lawyer
Koch, Robert art educator
Krinsky, Mary McInerney lawyer
Kweskin, Edward Michael lawyer
Lee, Charles Robert telecommunications company executive
Loeffel, Bruce software company executive, consultant
Lowman, George Frederick lawyer
Lynch, John T. management consultant
Malloy, Dannel Patrick mayor
Margolis, Emanuel lawyer, educator
Marlowe, Edward research company executive
Marsden, Charles Joseph financial executive
Martin, Patrick business equipment company executive
Maruyama, Karl Satoru graphic designer
Masin, Michael Terry lawyer
McGrath, Richard Paul lawyer
Mc Kinley, John Key retired oil company executive
McNamara, Francis Joseph, Jr. foundation executive, lawyer
McNear, Barbara Baxter financial communications executive, consultant
Merritt, William Alfred, Jr. lawyer, telecommunications company executive
Miklovic, Daniel Thomas research director
Miller, Wilbur Hobart business diversification consultant
†Mitzner, Donald H. cable television executive
Morgan, William J. accounting company executive
Morse, Jonathan Kent religious organization administrator
Murphy, Robert Blair management consulting company executive
Nichols, Ralph Arthur lawyer
Nierenberg, Roger symphony conductor
Nightingale, William Joslyn management consultant
Norman, Geoffrey Robert financial executive
Oatway, Francis Carlyle corporate executive
Obernauer, Marne corporate executive
Ogden, Dayton executive search consultant
O'Malley, Thomas D. diversified company executive
Owen, Nathan Richard manufacturing company executive
Padilla, James Earl lawyer
Palumbo, Matthew Aloysius marketing executive
Pansini, Michael Samuel tax and financial consultant
Parker, Jack Steele retired manufacturing company executive
Paul, Richard Stanley lawyer
Paul, Thomas A. book publisher
Penachio, Anthony Joseph, Jr. psychotherapist, hypnotherapist, behavioral therapist
Perle, Eugene Gabriel lawyer
Peterson, Carl Eric metals company executive, banker
Philipps, Edward William banker, real estate appraiser
Pollack, Gerald J. financial executive
Popelyukhin, Aleksey actuary, researcher
Porosoff, Harold chemist, research and development director
Preiss-Harris, Patricia music educator, composer, pianist
Quest, James Howard marketing executive
Rapp, James Allen marketing executive
Rodriguez, J. Louis civil engineer, land surveyor
Rose, Richard Loomis lawyer
Rosenberg, Charles Harvey otorhinolaryngologist
Rossman, Janet Kay architectural interior designer
Rowe, William John newspaper publishing executive
Rudman, Joan Eleanor artist, educator
Ryan, Raymond D. retired steel company executive, insurance and marketing firm executive
Sadove, Stephen Irving consumer products company executive
Sarbin, Hershel Benjamin management consultant, business publisher, lawyer
Sayers, Richard James newspaper editor
Schechter, Audrey medical, surgical nurse
Schofield, Herbert Spencer, III insurance executive
Scribner, Barbara Colvin museum administrator
Sheftell, Fred David psychiatrist, educator, writer
Siegel, Arthur Herbert accounting company executive
Silver, Charles Morton communications company executive
Silver, R. Philip metal products executive
Sisley, G. William lawyer
Skidd, Thomas Patrick, Jr. lawyer
Spindler, John Frederick lawyer
Stapleton, James Francis lawyer
Strone, Michael Jonathan lawyer
Strosahl, William Austin artist, art director
Sveda, Michael management and research consultant
Taylor, Stephen Hosmer sports entertainment executive, photographer
Teeters, Nancy Hays economist
Teitell, Conrad Laurence lawyer, author
Tierney, Patrick John information services executive
Tregurtha, Paul Richard marine transportation and construction materials company executive
Trivisonno, Nicholas Louis communications company executive, accountant
Twardy, Stanley Albert, Jr. lawyer
Veronis, Peter publisher
Vos, Frank advertising and marketing executive
Wallfesh, Henry Maurice business communications company executive, editor, writer
Wallington, Patricia McDevitt computer company executive
Walsh, Thomas Joseph neuro-ophthalmologist
Weitzel, William Conrad, Jr. lawyer
Wendt, Gary Carl finance company executive
White, Richard Booth management consultant
Wilensky, Julius M. publishing company executive
Wilhelm, Gayle Brian lawyer
Williams, Ernest William, Jr. economist, educator
Wilson, Robert Albert communications consultant
Worcester, Anne Person sports association executive
Wunsch, Bonnie Rubenstein fraternal organization executive
Yardis, Pamela Hintz computer consulting company executive

### Stonington
Dupont, Ralph Paul lawyer, educator
Mantz, Arlan W. physics educator
Rees, Charles H. G. retired financial officer, investor, consultant
Van Rees, Cornelius S. lawyer

### Storrs
Nieforth, Karl Allen university dean, educator

### Storrs Mansfield
Abramson, Arthur Seymour linguistics educator, researcher
Allen, John Logan geographer
Anderson, Gregory Joseph botanical sciences educator
Anderson, Stephen Alan family psychology educator
Auriemma, Geno university athletic coach
Austin, Philip Edward university president
Azaroff, Leonid Vladimirovitch physics educator
Bartram, Ralph Herbert physicist
Birdman, Jerome Moseley drama educator, consultant
Bobbitt, James McCue chemist
Breen, John Joseph journalism educator
†Calhoun, Jim college basketball coach
Charters, Ann biographer, editor, educator
Chinn, Peggy Lois nursing educator, editor
Coons, Ronald Edward historian, educator
Dardick, Kenneth Regen physician, educator
De Maria, Anthony John electrical engineer
Denenberg, Victor Hugo psychology educator
Devereux, Owen Francis metallurgy educator
DiBenedetto, Anthony Thomas engineering educator
Glasser, Joseph manufacturing and marketing executive
Gray, Robert Hugh college dean

Greene, John Colton *retired history educator*
Guttay, Andrew John Robert *agronomy educator, researcher*
Gutteridge, Thomas G. *academic administrator, consultant and labor arbitrator*
Katz, Leonard *psychology educator*
Kerr, Kirklyn M. *veterinary pathologist, researcher*
Klemens, Paul Gustav *physicist, educator*
Koths, Jay Sanford *floriculture educator*
Laufer, Hans *developmental biologist, educator*
Long, Richard Paul *civil engineering educator, geotechnical engineering consultant*
Marcus, Harris Leon *mechanical engineering and materials science educator*
Marcus, Philip Irving *virology educator, researcher*
McFadden, Peter William *mechanical engineering educator*
Pitkin, Edward Thaddeus *aerospace engineer, consultant*
Redman, Barbara Klug *nursing educator*
Reed, Howard Alexander *historian, educator*
Rimland, Lisa Phillip *writer, composer, lyricist, artist*
Romano, Antonio *microbiologist*
Rosen, William *English language educator*
Schuster, Todd Mervyn *biophysics educator, biotechnology company executive*
Schwarz, J(ames) Conrad *psychology educator*
Shaffer, Jerome Arthur *philosophy educator*
Shaw, Montgomery Throop *chemical engineering educator*
Skauen, Donald Matthew *retired pharmaceutical educator*
Stevens, Norman Dennison *retired library director*
Stwalley, William Calvin *physics and chemistry educator*
Tucker, Edwin Wallace *law educator*
Walker, David Bradstreet *political science educator*
Wood, Wendy Deborah *filmmaker*
Zelanski, Paul John *art educator, author*
Zirakzadeh, Cyrus Ernesto *political science educator*

## Stratford
Chase, J. Vincent *state agency official, shopping center executive, justice of the peace*
DiCicco, Margaret C. *lawyer*
Feinberg, Dennis Lowell *dermatologist*
Hageman, Richard Philip, Jr. *educational administrator*
Kaufman, Jess *communication, financial and marketing executive*
O'Rourke, James Louis *lawyer*
Salzberg, Emmett Russell *new product developer*

## Suffield
Connelly, William Howard *retired foundation executive*
Hanzalek, Astrid Teicher *public policy consultant*
Savoie, Ronald E. *secondary educator*
Tobin, Joan Adele *writer*

## Tariffville
Johnson, Loering M. *design engineer, historian, consultant*

## Thomaston
Kirshner, Hal *cinematographer*
Mühlanger, Erich *ski manufacturing company executive*

## Thompson
Fisher, William Thomas *business administration educator*

## Tolland
Wilde, Daniel Underwood *computer engineering educator*

## Torrington
Adorno, Monica S. *taxpayer representative*
Kucharek, Wilma Samuella *minister*
Leard, David Carl *lawyer*
Wall, Robert Anthony, Jr. *lawyer*

## Trumbull
†Brown, Tom *publishing executive*
FitzGerald, James W. (Jay) *magazine publisher*
Garelick, Melvin Stewart *engineering educator*
Gladki, Hanna Zofia *civil engineer, hydraulic mixer specialist*
Nevins, Lyn (Carolyn A. Nevins) *educational supervisor, trainer, consultant*
Norcel, Jacqueline Joyce Casale *educational administrator*
Schmitt, William Howard *cosmetics company executive*
Seitz, Nicholas Joseph *magazine editor*
Tarde, Gerard *magazine editor*
Watson, Donald Ralph *architect, educator, author*

## Vernon Rockville
Herbst, Marie Antoinette *former state senator*
Marmer, Ellen Lucille *pediatrician*
McKeever, Brian Edward *general contractor*
Roden, Jon-Paul *computer science educator*

## Voluntown
Caddell, Foster *artist*
Thevenet, Patricia Confrey *social studies educator*

## Wallingford
Cohen, Gordon S. *health products executive*
De George, Lawrence Joseph *diversified company executive*
Fleming, James Stuart, Jr. *pharmaceutial company manager*
Hay, Leroy E. *school system administrator*
Molinoff, Perry Brown *biologist, science administrator*
Spero, Barry Melvin *medical center executive*

## Warren
Abrams, Herbert E. *artist*
Gray, Cleve *artist*

## Washington
Leab, Daniel Joseph *history educator*
Pendleton, Moses Robert Andrew *dancer, choreographer*

## Washington Depot
Chase, Alison Becker *modern dancer, choreographer, teacher*
Mandler, Susan Ruth *dance company administrator*
Tracy, Michael Cameron *choreographer, performer*

## Waterbury
Cable, Richard Charles *education administrator, educator, consultant*
Clary, Alexia Barbara *management company executive*
Dost, Mark W. *lawyer*
Dudrick, Stanley John *surgeon, scientist, educator*
Farrell, Brian E. *school psychologist*
Fischbein, Charles Alan *pediatrician*
Glass, Robert Davis *judge*
Goettel, Gerard Louis *federal judge*
Higgins, Dorothy Marie *academic dean*
Leever, Harold *chemical company executive*
Marano, Richard Michael *lawyer*
Meyer, Judith Chandler Pugh *history educator*
Oliver, Eugene Alex *speech and language pathologist*
Ostrov, Melvyn R. *physician*
Pape, William James, II *newspaper publisher*
Sherwood, James Alan *physician, scientist, educator*
Wolfe, Harriet Munrett *lawyer*
Zampiello, Richard Sidney *metals and trading company executive*

## Waterford
Commire, Anne *playwright*
Hinerfeld, Lee Ann *veterinarian*
Hinkle, Muriel Ruth Nelson *naval warfare analysis company executive*
Sillin, Lelan Flor, Jr. *retired utility executive*
White, George Cooke *theater director, foundation executive*

## Weatogue
Dumais, Arlene *psychiatric mental health and critical care nurse*

## West Cornwall
Klaw, Barbara Van Doren *author, editor*
Klaw, Spencer *writer, editor, educator*
Prentice, Tim *sculptor, architect*
Simont, Marc *artist*

## West Granby
Conland, Stephen *publishing company executive*

## West Hartland
Perkins, Bob(by) F(rank) *geologist, dean*

## West Haven
DeNardis, Lawrence J. *academic administrator*
Ellis, Lynn Webster *management educator, telecommunications consultant*
Emerson, Thomas Edward, Jr. *cardiovascular physiologist*
†Ezekowitz, Michael David *physician*
Farquharson, Patrice Ellen *primary school educator*
Fischer, Alice Edna Waltz *computer science educator*
Janis, Ronald Allen *pharmacologist*
Linemeyer, David Lee *molecular biologist*
Perlmutter, Lynn Susan *neuroscientist*
Yoshizumi, Terry Takatoshi *medical physicist*

## West Mystic
Hoagland, Porter, Jr. *electrical and mechanical engineer, consultant*

## West Redding
Kipnis, Igor *harpsichordist, fortepianist, pianist, critic*

## West Simsbury
Brinkerhoff, Peter John *manufacturing company executive*
Morest, Donald Kent *neuroscientist*

## Westbrook
Hall, Jane Anna *writer, model, artist*

## Weston
Bleifeld, Stanley *sculptor*
Cadmus, Paul *artist, etcher*
Daniel, James *curator, business executive, writer, former editor*
Diforio, Robert G. *literary agent*
Fredrik, Burry *theatrical producer, director*
Kilty, Jerome Timothy *playwright, stage director, actor*
Liberatore, Nicholas Alfred *business consultant*
Lindsay, Charles Joseph *banker*
Meinke, Alan Kurt *surgeon*
Murray, Thomas Joseph *advertising executive*
Offenhartz, Edward *aerospace executive*
Reinker, Nancy Clayton Cooke *artist*
Schnitzer, Robert C. *theater administrator*
Thompson, N(orman) David *insurance company executive*
Zimmerman, Bernard *investment banker*

## Westport
Aasen, Lawrence Obert *public relations executive*
Albani, Suzanne Beardsley *lawyer*
Allen, Robert Hugh *retired communications corporation executive*
Barton, James Miller *lawyer, international business consultant*
Brandt, Kathy A. *public relations and events management executive, secondary school educator*
Breitbarth, S. Robert *manufacturing company executive*
Bronson, Carole *publishing executive*
Brooks, Andrée Aelion *journalist, educator, author*
Brooks, Babert Vincent *publisher*
Burns, John Joseph *pharmacology educator*
Chernow, Ann Levy *artist, art educator*
Chernow, Burt *artist, educator, writer*
Clausman, Gilbert Joseph *medical librarian*
Dale, Erwin Randolph *lawyer, author*
Davis, Joel *publisher*
Daw, Harold John *lawyer*
Deese, James LaMotte *financial executive*
Dickson, Sally I. *retired public relations executive*
Enos, Randall *cartoonist, illustrator*
Ferris, Roger Patrick *architect*
Fisher, Leonard Everett *artist, writer, educator*
Freedman, Judith Greenberg *state senator, importer*
†Friedman, Ron *advertising executive*
Gallagher, Michael Robert *consumer products company executive*
Gans, Eugene Howard *cosmetic and pharmaceutical company executive*
Gold, Richard N. *management consultant*
Hagelstein, Robert Philip *publisher*
Hambleton, George Blow Elliott *management consultant*
Hersey, Marilyn Elaine *performing company executive*
Hotaling, Brock Elliot *software development leader*
Hotchner, Aaron Edward *author*
Joseloff, Gordon Frederic *journalist, editor*
Kelly, Paul Knox *investment banker*
Knopf, Alfred, Jr. *retired publisher*
Kramer, Sidney B. *publisher, lawyer, literary agent*
Kraus, Hilda *designer, artist*
Logue-Kinder, Joan *alcoholic beverages company executive*
Lopker, Anita Mae *psychiatrist*
Martin, Ralph Guy *writer*
McCormack, Donald Paul *newspaper consultant*
McCormack, Patricia Seger *independent press service editor, journalist*
McFarland, Richard M. *executive recruiting consultant*
McKane, David Bennett *business executive*
Meckler, Alan Marshall *publisher, author*
Milton, Catherine Higgs *public service entrepreneur*
Muller, Frank B. *advertising executive*
Murphy, Thomas John *publishing executive*
Nathan, Irwin *business systems company executive*
Nedom, H. Arthur *petroleum consultant*
Nolte, Richard Henry *political science researcher, consultant*
O'Keefe, John David *investment specialist*
O'Leary, James John *economist*
Poundstone, Sally *library director*
Radigan, Joseph Richard *human resources executive*
Razzano, Pasquale Angelo *lawyer*
Ready, Robert James *financial company executive*
Reilly, Anne Caulfield (Nancy Reilly) *painter*
Rose, Reginald *television writer, producer*
Ross, John Michael *editor, magazine publisher*
Sacks, Herbert Simeon *psychiatrist, educator, consultant*
Safran, Claire *writer, editor*
Satinover, Jeffrey B. *psychiatrist, health science facility administrator, lecturer, author*
Savage, Robert Heath *advertising executive*
Saxl, Richard Hildreth *lawyer*
Schriever, Fred Martin *energy, environmental and information technology, satellite systems executive*
Silk, George *photographer*
Stashower, Michael David *retired manufacturing company executive*
Stewart, Martha Kostyra *editor-in-chief, lecturer, author*
Walton, Alan George *venture capitalist*
Weissman, Robert Evan *information services company executive*
Wexler, Herbert Ira *retail company executive*

## Wethersfield
Edwards, Kenneth S. *principal*
Gaudreau, Gayle Glanert *computer resource educator*
Moran, John Joseph *retired food and beverage company executive*

## Willimantic
Carter, David George, Sr. *university administrator*
De Rose, Sandra Michele *psychotherapist, educator, supervisor, administrator*
Enggas, Grace Falcetta *university administrator*
Loin, E. Linnea *social work administrator*
Lombardo, Michael John *lawyer, educator*
Mann, Prem Singh *economics educator*
Peagler, Owen F. *college administrator*
Philips, David Evan *English language educator*

## Wilton
Adams, Thomas Tilley *lawyer*
Bescherer, Edwin A., Jr. *business information services company executive*
Billings, Edward Robert *accountant*
Bishop, William Wade *advertising executive*
Black, Rita Ann *communications executive*
Brown, James Thompson, Jr. *computer information scientist*
Campbell, Robert Ayerst *accounting company executive*
Caravatt, Paul Joseph, Jr. *communications company executive*
Cassidy, George Thomas *international business development consultant*
Cook, Jay Michael *accounting company executive*
Cutler, Theodore John *cable company executive*
Forger, Robert Durkin *retired professional association administrator*
Fricke, Richard John *lawyer*
Grunewald, Donald *former college president, educator*
Healy, James Casey *lawyer*
Hoefling, Rudolf Joachim *power generating company executive*
Jessep, Jane Nordli *elementary education educator*
Juran, Joseph Moses *engineer*
Kangas, Edward A. *accounting firm executive*
Kovak, Ellen B. *public relations firm executive*
Lamb, Frederic Davis *lawyer*
Lewis, Margaret M. *marketing professional*
McCreight, John A. *management consultant*
Mc Dannald, Clyde Elliott, Jr. *management consultation company executive*
Nickel, Albert George *advertising agency executive*
Paulson, Loretta Nancy *psychoanalyst*
Rogers, Mark Charles *physician, educator*
Scheinman, Stanley Bruce *venture capital executive, lawyer*
Sideroff, Barry *advertising executive*
Simpson, W(ilburn) Dwain *physicist, corporate executive, computer systems, telecommunications, and advanced fueling systems consultant*
Sullivan, Adèle Woodhouse *organization official*

## Windsor
Auten, Arthur Herbert *history educator*
Cowen, Bruce David *environmental services company executive*
Ferraro, John Francis *business executive, financier*
Goldman, Ethan Harris *retail executive*
Kamerschen, Robert Jerome *consumer products executive*
Mangold, John Frederic *manufacturing company executive, former naval officer*
Molitor, Karen Ann *lawyer*
Saltman, Stuart Ivan *lawyer*

## Windsor Locks
Coelho, Sandra Signorelli *secondary school educator*
Heisler, Elwood Douglas *hotel executive*

## Wolcott
Gerace, Robert F. *secondary school principal*

## Woodbridge
Alvine, Robert *industrialist, entrepreneur, international business leader*
Bondy, Philip Kramer *physician, educator*
Cousins, William Joseph *lawyer, litigation consultant*
Ecklund, Constance Cryer *French language educator*
Ostfeld, Alexander Marion *advertising agency executive*
Russell, Cynthia Pincus *social worker, educator*
Van Sinderen, Alfred White *former telephone company executive*
Womer, Charles Berry *retired hospital executive, management consultant*

## Woodbury
†Duffy, Henry J. *museum director, consultant*
Farrell, Edgar Henry *lawyer, building components manufacturing executive*
Marsching, Ronald Lionel *lawyer, former precision instrument company executive*
Skinner, Brian John *geologist, educator*

## Woodstock
Allaby, Stanley Reynolds *clergyman*
Boote, Alfred Shepard *marketing researcher, educator*

# DELAWARE

## Camden Wyoming
Porterfield, Craig Allen *psychologist, consultant*

## Claymont
Doto, Paul Jerome *accountant*

## Dagsboro
Lally, Richard Francis *aviation security consultant, former association executive, former government official*

## Delmar
Czernik, Joanne *elementary and secondary education educator*
Tasker, John Baker *veterinary medical educator, college dean*

## Dover
Angstadt, F. V. *language arts and theatre arts educator*
Barrett, Marihelen Eggert *public health administrator, pediatrics nurse*
Bookhammer, Eugene Donald *state government official*
Braverman, Ray Howard *secondary school educator*
Britt, Maisha Dorrah *protective services official*
Carey, V. George *farmer, state legislator*
Carper, Thomas Richard *governor*
Cohen, William John *urban and environmental planner, educator, photographer*
Delauder, William B. *academic administrator*
Ennis, Bruce Clifford *lawyer*
Freel, Edward J. *state official*
Hoff, Samuel Boyer *political science educator*
Jones, Jay Paul *professional environmental engineer*
Lowell, Howard Parsons *government records administrator*
Minner, Ruth Ann *state official*
Olagunju, Amos Omotayo *computer science educator, consultant*
Ornauer, Richard Lewis *retired educational association administrator*
Peiffer, Randel Aaron *agricultural sciences educator, researcher*
Richman, Joseph Herbert *public health services official*
Smyth, Joel Douglas *newspaper executive*
Sorenson, Liane Beth McDowell *women's affairs director, state legislator*
Streetman, Lee George *sociology educator, criminology educator*
Wasfi, Sadiq Hassan *chemistry educator*
Williams, Donna Lee H. *state agency adminstrator*
Wilson, Samuel Mayhew *surgeon*
Wisneski, Sharon M. *critical care nurse, educator*

## Georgetown
Bond, Gorman Morton *ornithologist, researcher*

## Greenville
Dewees, Donald Charles *securities company executive*
Dombeck, Harold Arthur *insurance company executive*
Hindes, Gary Eugene *securities executive*
Levitt, George *retired chemist*
Reynolds, Nancy Bradford duPont (Mrs. William Glasgow Reynolds) *sculptor*
Schroeder, Herman Elbert *scientific consultant*

## Hockessin
Bischoff, Joyce Arlene *information systems consultant, lecturer*
Bischoff, Kenneth Bruce *chemical engineer, educator*
Crippen, Raymond C. *chemist, consultant*
Keenan, William Francis, Jr. *information and communications executive*
Mills, George Alexander *retired science administrator*
Moyer, Calvin Lyle *adult educator*
Sawin, Nancy Churchman *art educator, artist, historian*

## Lewes
Adams, John Pletch *orthopaedic surgeon*
Chapman, Janet Carter Goodrich (Mrs. John William Chapman) *economist, educator*
Fried, Jeffrey Michael *health care administrator*
Lane, William Harry, Jr. *principal*

## Middletown
Jackson, Donald Richard *marketing professional*

## Milford
Konowitz, Herbert Henry *textile company executive*

### Millsboro
Derrickson, Shirley Jean Baldwin elementary school educator
Jones, Lowell Robert safety and industrial hygiene consultant
Townsend, P(reston) Coleman agricultural business executive

### Montchanin
Olney, Robert C. diversified products manufacturing executive

### New Castle
Almquist, Don illustrator, artist
Bellenger, George Collier, Jr. physics educator
Blackshear, L. T., Sr. bishop
Cansler, Leslie Ervin retired newspaper editor
Freytag, Richard Arthur banker
Olden, Anna Beatrice former educator
Rangan, Chakravarthi Ravi environmental engineer

### Newark
Adams, Joseph Brian operations research engineer, mathematics educator
Allen, Herbert Ellis environmental chemistry educator
Allmendinger, David Frederick, Jr. history educator
Amick, Steven Hammond senator, lawyer
Armour, Clifford Arnett, Jr. minister
Barteau, Mark Alan chemical engineering and chemistry educator
Beris, Antony Nicolas chemical engineer, educator
Bilinsky, Yaroslav political scientist
Böer, Karl Wolfgang physicist, educator
Borgaonkar, Digamber Shankarrao cytogeneticist, educator
Brams, Marvin Robert economist, mental health counselor, interfaith minister
†Brown, Hilton visual arts educator, artist
Burmeister, John Luther chemistry educator
Byrne, John Michael energy and environmental policy educator, researcher
Campbell, Linzy Leon molecular biology researcher, educator
Cheng, Alexander Hung-Darh engineering educator, consultant
Christy, Charles Wesley, III industrial engineering educator
Collins, George Edwin computer scientist, mathematician, educator
Colton, David Lem mathematician, educator
Cooper, Stuart Leonard chemical engineering educator, researcher, consultant
Corballis, Ben Charles health facility administrator
Curtis, James C. cultural organization administrator/ history educator
Daniels, William Burton physicist, educator
Day, Robert Androus English language educator, former library director, editor, publisher
DeCherney, George Stephen research scientist, research facility administrator
DiRenzo, Gordon James sociologist, psychologist, educator
Doberenz, Alexander R. nutrition educator, chemist
Evans, Dennis Hyde chemist, educator
Evenson, Paul Arthur physics educator
Fishman, Brian Scott environmental policy research associate
Giacco, Alexander Fortunatus chemical industry executive
Graff, Harold psychiatrist, psychoanalyst, medical administrator
Graham, Frances Keesler (Mrs. David Tredway Graham) psychologist, educator
Grimaldi, Polly Nan wellness consultant and educator
Gulick, Walter Lawrence psychologist, former college president
Halio, Jay Leon language professional, educator
Homer, William Innes art history educator, art expert, author
Hossain, Murshed physicist
Hurst, Christina Marie respiratory therapist
Hutton, David Glenn environmental scientist, consultant, chemical engineer
Ih, Charles Chung Sen electrical engineering educator, consultant
Jordan, Robert Reed geologist, educator
Kasprzak, Lucian Alexander physicist, researcher
Keene, William Blair state education official
Kennedy, Christopher Robin ceramist
Kessler, Betty Dean elementary school educator, reading resource educator
Klein, Michael Tully chemical engineering educator, consultant
Kleinman, R. E. computer engineering educator
Lemole, Gerald Michael surgeon
Lomax, Kenneth Mitchell agricultural engineering educator
Mangone, Gerard J. international and maritime law educator
Mather, John Russell climatologist, educator
McCullough, Roy Lynn chemical engineering educator
McLain, William Tome principal
McLaren, James Clark French educator
Mitchell, Peter Kenneth, Jr. educational consultant, association administrator
Molz, Robert Joseph manufacturing company executive
Moss, Joe Francis sculptor, painter
Murray, Richard Bennett physics educator
Neal, James Preston state senator, project engineer
Ness, Norman Frederick astrophysicist, educator, administrator
Nye, John Calvin agricultural engineer, educator
Raffel, Jeffrey Allen urban affairs educator
Reider, Martha Crawford industrial immunologist
Roselle, David Paul university president, mathematics educator
Rowe, Charles Alfred artist, designer, educator
Russell, Thomas William Fraser chemical engineering educator
Sandler, Stanley Irving chemical engineering educator
Scarpitti, Frank Roland sociology educator
Schiavelli, Melvyn David academic administrator, chemistry educator, researcher
Sheer, Barbara Lee nursing educator
Somers, George Fredrick biology educator
Sparks, Donald Lewis soil chemistry educator
Stark, Robert Martin mathematician, civil engineer, educator
Steiner, Roger Jacob linguistics educator, author, researcher
Szeri, Andras Z. engineering educator
Tolles, Bryant Franklin, Jr. history and art history educator
Urquhart, Andrew Willard engineering and business executive
Valbuena-Briones, Angel Julian language educator, author
Venezky, Richard Lawrence English educator
Wetlaufer, Donald Burton biochemist, educator
Wolters, Raymond historian, educator
Woo, S. B. (Shien-Biau Woo) former lieutenant governor, physics educator

### Newport
Kirkland, Joseph J. research chemist

### Ocean View
Parler, Anne Hemenway elementary education educator, horse trainer

### Rehoboth Beach
Warden, Richard Dana government labor union official

### Rockland
Levinson, John Milton obstetrician, gynecologist
Rubin, Alan A. pharmaceutical and biotechnology consultant

### Seaford
Cosgrove, Martin Joseph radiologist
Slater, Charles James construction company executive
Slater, Kristie construction company executive

### Smyrna
Pippin, Kathryn Ann state agency administrator

### Wilmington
Adams, Wayne Verdun pediatric psychologist, educator
Arrington, Charles Hammond, Jr. retired chemical company executive
Aungst, Bruce Jeffrey pharmaceutical company scientist
Bader, John Merwin lawyer
Balick, Helen Shaffer judge
Bartley, Brian James lawyer
Baumann, Julian Henry, Jr. lawyer
Benson, Barbara Ellen state agency administrator
Bounds-Seemans, Pamella J. artist
Brady, M. Jane state official
Bruni, Stephen Thomas art museum director
Burton, Robert Jones psychologist
Carey, John Patrick, III lawyer
Carpenter, Edmund Nelson, II retired lawyer
Caspersen, Finn Michael Westby diversified financial services company executive
Clark, Esther Frances law educator
Connelly, Donald Preston electric and gas utility company executive
Connolly, Arthur Guild lawyer, partner emeritus
Cornelison, Floyd Shovington, Jr. retired psychiatrist, former educator
Crittenden, Eugene Dwight, Jr. chemical company executive
Curran, Barbara Sanson lawyer
Del Pesco, Susan Marie Carr state judge
delTufo, Theresa Lallana Izon state official
Desien, Mary Donna principal
Devine, Donn lawyer, archivist, former city official
DiLiberto, Richard Anthony, Jr. lawyer
Drudy, Patrick psychologist, human relations consultant
†duPont, Edward B. aviation service and sales company executive
†Du Pont, Pierre Samuel, IV lawyer, former governor of Delaware
Eichler, Thomas P. state agency administrator
Eleuterio, Marianne Kingsbury genetics educator
Emanuel, Abraham Gabriel photo processing company executive, consultant
Farnan, Joseph James, Jr. federal judge
Fenton, Wendell lawyer
Frank, George Andrew lawyer
Frelick, Robert W. physician
Gadsby, Robin Edward chemical company executive
Gebelein, Richard Stephen judge, former state attorney general
Gewirtz, Leonard Benjamin rabbi
Gibson, Joseph Whitton, Jr. retired chemical company executive
Gilman, Marvin Stanley real estate developer, educator
Goldberg, Morton Edward pharmacologist
Graves, Thomas Ashley, Jr. educational administrator
Green, James Samuel lawyer
Grenz, Linda L. Episcopal priest
Gunzenhauser, Stephen Charles conductor
Hannon, Leo Francis retired lawyer, educator
Harley, Robison Dooling physician, educator
Harris, Robert Laird minister, theology educator emeritus
Heald, Debbie Ann special education educator, counselor
Herdeg, John Andrew lawyer
Holtzman, Arnold Harold chemical company executive
Holzman, James L(ouis) lawyer
Houseman, Ann Elizabeth Lord educational administrator, state official
Howard, Richard James mycology researcher
Huntley, Donald Wayne lawyer
Ianni, Francis Alphonse state official, former army officer
Ikeda, Satoshi thoracic and cardiovascular surgeon
Inselman, Laura Sue pediatrician
Jacobson, Howard W. chemist
Jaffe, Edward E(phraim) retired research and development executive
Jezl, Barbara Ann chemist, automation consultant
Joseph, Michael Brandes lawyer
Kalil, James, Sr. investment executive
Kane, Edward Rynex retired chemical company executive, corporate director
Karrh, Bruce Wakefield retired industrial company executive
Kassal, Robert James polymer research scientist
Kay, Jerome retired psychiatrist, educator
Kimmel, Morton Richard lawyer
Kirk, Richard Dillon lawyer
Kirkpatrick, Andrew Booth, Jr. lawyer
Kissa, Erik retired chemist, consultant
Kjellmark, Eric William, Jr. management consultant, opera company director
Kneavel, Ann Callanan humanities educator, communications consultant
Kneavel, Thomas Charles, Jr. psychologist, educator
Knight, Kenneth George retired aerospace and defense company executive
Kohler, Frederick William, Jr. pharmacist
†Krol, John A. diversified chemicals executive
Kutemeyer, Peter Martin industrial engineering executive
Kwolek, Stephanie Louise chemist
Lahvis, Sylvia Leistyna art historian, educator, curator
Laird, Walter Jones, Jr. investment professional
Lange, James Braxton chemical company executive
Latchum, James Levin federal judge
Linderman, Jeanne Herron priest
Longobardi, Joseph J. federal judge
Magee, Thomas Hugh lawyer
Maley, Patricia Ann preservation planner
Manz, Betty Ann nurse, consultant
McDonough, Kenneth Lee disease management company executive
McKelvie, Roderick R. federal judge
Meitner, Pamela lawyer, educator
Mekler, Arlen B. lawyer, chemist
Miller, Christine Talley physical education educator
Moore, Carl Gordon chemist, educator
Morris, Kenneth Donald lawyer
Morris, Ronald Anthony county official
Mullen, Regina Marie lawyer
Murphy, Arthur Thomas systems engineer
Nelson, Dewey Allen neurologist, educator
Nottingham, Robinson Kendall life insurance company executive
Olson, Leroy Calvin retired educational administration educator
Otey, Orlando music executive, educator, pianist, theorist
Pan, Henry Yue-Ming clinical pharmacologist
Parshall, George William research chemist
Patton, James Leeland, Jr. lawyer
Pell, Jane Eileen insurance executive
Pell, Sidney epidemiologist
Perse, Aria Leon international business advanced technologies executive
Peterson, Russell Wilbur former association executive, former state governor
Porter, Glenn museum and library administrator
Porter, John Francis, III banker
Reeder, Charles Benton economic consultant
Renshaw, John Hubert retired secondary education educator
Rich, Michael Joseph lawyer
Riegel, John Kent corporate lawyer
Robertson, David Wayne pharmaceutical company executive
Robinson, Sue L(ewis) federal judge
Rogoski, Patricia Diana financial executive
Rose, Selwyn H. chemical company executive
Roth, Jane Richards federal judge
Rothschild, Steven James lawyer
St. Clair, Jesse Walton, Jr. retired savings and loan executive
Salzstein, Richard Alan biomedical engineer, researcher
Sawyer, H(arold) Murray, Jr. lawyer
Schofield, Paul Michael finance company executive
Schwartz, Marshall Zane pediatric surgeon
Schwartz, Murray Merle federal judge
Seitz, Collins Jacques federal judge
Semple, James William lawyer
Sganga, John B. furniture holding company executive
Shapiro, Irving Saul lawyer
Shipley, Samuel Lynn advertising and public relations executive
Smith, S(tewart) Gregory ophthalmologist, inventor, product developer, consultant, author
Smook, Malcolm Andrew chemist, chemical company executive
Stakgold, Ivar mathematics educator
Stapleton, Walter King federal judge
Stein, Robert Benjamin biomedical researcher, physician
Steinberg, Marshall toxicologist
Stone, F. L. Peter lawyer
Sutton, Richard Lauder lawyer
Tennis, Calvin Cabell bishop
Tise, Mary Shackelford public librarian
Turk, S. Maynard lawyer
Veasey, Eugene Norman chief justice
Waisanen, Christine M. lawyer, writer
Wallace, Jesse Wyatt pharmaceutical company executive
Walsh, Joseph Thomas state supreme court justice
Ward, Rodman, Jr. lawyer
Webster, Owen Wright chemist
Wesler, Ken theater company manager
Wheeler, M. Catherine organization executive
Wier, Richard Royal, Jr. lawyer, inventor
Williams, Richmond Dean library appraiser, consultant
Woods, Robert A. chemical company executive
Woolard, Edgar S., Jr. chemical company executive
Wright, Caleb Merrill federal judge
Wright, Vernon Hugh Carroll bank executive

### Winterthur
Hummel, Charles Frederick museum official
Lanmon, Dwight Pierson museum director

## DISTRICT OF COLUMBIA

### Fort Mcnair
Krise, Thomas Warren military officer, English language educator
Marr, Phebe Ann historian, educator

### Washington
Aaron, Henry Jacob economics educator
Aaronson, David Ernest lawyer, educator
Abbott, Alden Francis lawyer, government official, educator
Abbott, Rebecca Phillips museum director
Abel, Elie reporter, broadcaster, educator
Abeles, Charles Calvert retired lawyer
Abelson, Philip Hauge physicist
Abercrombie, Neil congressman
Ablard, Charles David lawyer
Able, Edward H. association executive
Abler, Ronald Francis geography educator
Abraham, Katharine Gail economics educator
Abraham, Spencer senator
Abrahamson, James Alan transportation executive, retired military officer
Abramowitz, Morton I. former ambassador
Abrams, Elliott think-tank executive, writer, foreign affairs analyst
Abrecht, Mary Ellen Benson lawyer
Abshire, David Manker diplomat, research executive
Acheson, David Campion lawyer, author, policy analyst
Acheson, Eleanor Dean federal government official
Achtenberg, Roberta federal official
Acker, Lawrence G. lawyer
Ackerman, F. Kenneth, Jr. health facility administrator
Ackerman, Gary Leonard congressman
Ackerson, Nels J(ohn) lawyer
Adams, Arvil Van economist, educator
Adams, Gordon Merritt federal agency administrator
Adams, Linette M. principal
Adams, Lorraine reporter
†Adams, Noah broadcaster
†Adams, Patrick O. career officer
Adams, Robert Edward journalist
Adams, Ronald Emerson army officer
Adamson, Richard Henry pharmacologist
Adamson, Terrence Burdett lawyer
Adelman, Roger Mark lawyer, educator
Adler, Howard, Jr. lawyer
Adler, Howard Bruce lawyer
Adler, Robert Martin lawyer
Affronti, Lewis Francis, Sr. microbiologist, educator
Aggarwal, Satish Kumar electrical engineer, government official
Agres, Theodore Joel editor
Aguirre-Sacasa, Francisco Xavier international banker
Ahl, Alwynelle Self zoology, ecology and veterinary medical executive
Ahmann, Mathew Hall social action organization administrator, consultant
Aikens, Joan Deacon government official
Aisenberg, Irwin Morton lawyer
Akaka, Daniel Kahikina senator
Akey, Steven John federal agency administrator
Akhter, Mohammad Nasir physician, government public health administrator
Alatis, James Efstathios university dean emeritus
Alberger, William Relph lawyer, government official
Alberts, Bruce Michael federal agency administrator, foundation administrator, biochemist
Albertson, Terry L. lawyer
†Albright, Madeleine Korbel federal official, diplomat, political scientist
Alcorn, Wendell Bertram, Jr. lawyer
Alexander, Arthur Jacob economist
Alexander, Benjamin Harold professional services firm executive, past government official
Alexander, Clifford Joseph lawyer
Alexander, Dawn Alicia public relations executive
Alexander, Donald Crichton lawyer
Alexander, Jane federal agency administrator, actress, producer
Alexander, Joseph Kunkle, Jr. physicist
Allard, A. Wayne senator, veterinarian
†Allard, Nicholas W. lawyer
Allbritton, Joe Lewis diversified holding company executive
Allen, Frederick Warner federal agency executive
Allen, Richard Vincent international business consultant, bank executive
†Allen, Terry Thomas, Jr. football player
†Allen, Thomas H. congressman, lawyer
Allen, Toni K. lawyer
Allen, William Hayes lawyer
Allen, William Jere minister
Allen, William L. editor
Allnutt, Robert Frederick management consultant
†Alm, Alvin Arthur forestry educator
†Alm, Alvin Leroy technical services executive
†Almquist, Theodore C. career officer
Alperovitz, Gar author
Alton, Bruce Taylor educational consultant
Altschul, Alfred Samuel airline executive
Alvarez, Aida federal agency administrator
Alward, Ruth Rosendall nursing consultant
Ambach, Gordon Mac Kay educational association executive
Ambrose, Myles Joseph lawyer
Ames, Frank Anthony percussionist, film producer
Amling, Frederick economist, educator, investment manager
Amolsch, Arthur Lewis publishing executive
Anand, Rajen S. physiologist
Andersen, Robert Allen retired government official
Anderson, Carl Albert theology school dean, lawyer
Anderson, David Turpeau government official, judge
Anderson, Dean William educational administrator
Anderson, Donald Morgan entomologist
Anderson, Frederick Randolph, Jr. lawyer, law educator
Anderson, J. Brady ambassador
Anderson, John Bayard lawyer, educator, former congressman
Andewelt, Roger B. federal judge
Andrews, John Frank editor, author, educator
Andrews, Laureen E. foundation administrator
Andrews, Mark Joseph lawyer
Andrews, Robert E. congressman
Anfinson, Thomas Elmer government financial administrator
Angier, Natalie Marie science journalist
Angula, Helmut Kangulohi Namibian government official
Ansary, Cyrus A. investment company executive, lawyer
Anschuetz, Norbert Lee retired diplomat, banker
Ansley, Darlene H. communications executive
Anthony, David Vincent lawyer
Anthony, Sheila Foster government official
Anthony, Virginia Quinn Bausch medical association executive
Apfel, Kenneth S. federal government official
Apple, Martin Allen scientific federation executive, educator
Apple, Raymond Walter, Jr. journalist
Applebaum, Harvey Milton lawyer
Appleberry, James Bruce higher education association executive
Applegarth, Paul Vollmer investment and finance executive
Aquino, John Thomas publishing executive, lawyer
Arana-Ward, Marie editor, writer
Archer, Glenn LeRoy, Jr. federal circuit judge
Archer, William Reynolds, Jr. (Bill Reynolds) congressman
†Archeson, Richard editor
Arena, Kelli news correspondent
Arend, Anthony Clark international relations educator
Arent, Albert Ezra lawyer

Argrett, Loretta Collins assistant attorney general, educator
Arkilic, Galip Mehmet mechanical engineer, educator
Arling, Bryan Jeremy internist
Arling, Donna Dickson social worker
Arlook, Ira Arthur public interest association executive
†Armacost, Michael Hayden research institution executive, ambassador
Armaly, Mansour F(arid) ophthalmologist, educator
†Armstrong, Alexandra financial advisor
Armstrong, David Andrew federal agency official, retired army officer
Armstrong, Robert federal agency administrator
Arndt, Richard T. writer, consultant
Arnett, Peter journalist
Arnez, Nancy Levi educational leadership educator
Arnold, G. Dewey, Jr. accountant
Arnold, Gary Howard film critic
Arnold, William Edwin foundation administrator, consultant
Arnovitz, Benton Mayer editor
Arundel, John Howard financial consultant
Aschheim, Joseph economist, educator
Ashcroft, John David senator
Ashkenazi, Elliott Uriel historian, lawyer
Ashton, Richard M. federal lawyer
Åslund, Anders economist
Atherton, Alfred Leroy, Jr. foundation executive, former foreign service officer
Atherton, Charles Henry federal commission administrator
Attaway, David Henry retired federal research administrator, oceanographer
Attkisson, Sharyl T. newscaster, correspondent, writer
Atwood, James R. lawyer
Atwood, John Brian federal agency administrator
Aucutt, Ronald David lawyer
Auerbach, Stuart Charles journalist
August, Diane L. educational program consultant, policy researcher
Aukofer, Frank Alexander journalist
Aultman, William Robert career officer
Austin, Page Insley lawyer
Auten, John Harold government official
Avil, Richard D., Jr. lawyer
Axelrod, Jonathan Gans lawyer
Ayer, Donald Belton lawyer
Ayres, Mary Ellen government official
Ayres, Richard Edward lawyer
Azcuenaga, Mary Laurie government official
Babbitt, Bruce Edward federal official
Babby, Ellen Reisman education administrator
Babby, Lon S. lawyer
Bachman, Kenneth Leroy, Jr. lawyer
Bachman, Leonard physician, retired federal official
Bachrach, Eve Elizabeth lawyer
Bachula, Gary R. federal official
Bachus, Spencer T., III congressman, lawyer
Bacon, Kenneth H. federal agency administrator, editor, journalist
Bacon, Sylvia retired judge
Bader, Rochelle Linda (Shelley Bader) educational administrator
†Bader, William Banks historian, foundation executive, former corporate executive
Baer, Donald Aaron federal official
Baer, William J. lawyer
Baesler, Scotty congressman
Bagge, Carl Elmer association executive, lawyer, consultant
†Bailey, Betty L. federal agency administrator
Bailey, Charles Waldo, II journalist, author
Bailey, John E. federal agency administrator
Bailey, Vicky A. federal agency administrator
Bainum, Peter Montgomery aerospace engineer, consultant
Baird, Bruce Allen lawyer
†Baker, David E. career officer
Baker, David Harris lawyer
Baker, D(onald) James government official, oceanographer
Baker, Emily Lind digital library specialist, editorial consultant
Baldacci, John Elias congressman
Baldwin, Sheryl Denise chemist, writer, editor
Baldwin, Velma Neville Wilson personnel consultant
Baldyga, Leonard J. diplomat, international consultant, retired
Balfour, Ana Maria office manager
Ball, (Robert) Markham lawyer
Ballantyne, Robert Jadwin former foreign service officer, consultant
Ballard, Frederic Lyman, Jr. lawyer
Ballenger, Thomas Cass congressman
Ballentine, J. Gregory economist
Bancroft, Elizabeth Abercrombie publisher, analytical chemist
Bandow, Douglas Leighton editor, columnist, policy consultant
Banister, Judith demographer, educator
Banta, James Elmer physician, epidemiologist, university dean
Banzhaf, John F., III organization executive, lawyer
Baquet, Charles R., III federal agency administrator
Baran, Jan Witold lawyer, educator
Barbash, Fred journalist, author
Barber, Ben Bernard Andrew journalist
Barbour, Haley political organization administrator, lawyer
Barcia, James A. congressman
Bardin, David J. lawyer
Barnard, Robert C. lawyer
Barnes, Dennis Norman lawyer
Barnes, Donald Michael lawyer
Barnes, Frederic Wood, Jr. journalist
Barnes, Mark James lawyer
Barnes, Michael Darr lawyer, think tank executive
Barnes, Peter lawyer
Barnes, Shirley Elizabeth foreign service officer
Barnet, Richard Jackson author, educator
Barnett, Arthur Doak political scientist, educator
Barnett, Robert Bruce lawyer
Barnett, Robert Warren diplomat, author
Barnicle, Timothy federal agency administrator
†Barolo, Daniel M. government official
Barone, Michael D. journalist
Barr, Michael Blanton lawyer
Barr, Robert Laurence, Jr. congressman, lawyer
Barram, David J. federal agency administrator
Barrett, Archie Don federal official
Barrett, Laurence Irwin journalist
Barrett, Richard David university director, consultant, bank executive
Barrett, Thomas M. congressman
Barrett, William E. congressman
Barringer, Philip E. government official
Barr-Kumar, Raj architect
Barron, Jerome Aure law educator
Barrow, Robert Earl retired agricultural organization administrator
Barry, John J. labor union leader
Barry, Marion Shepilov, Jr. mayor
†Barshefsky, Charlene diplomat
Bartholomew, Reginald diplomat
Bartlett, Charles L. think-tank executive
Bartlett, Charles Leffingwell foundation executive, former newspaperman
Bartlett, John Laurence lawyer
Bartlett, Michael John lawyer
Bartlett, Roscoe G. congressman
Bartnoff, Judith judge
Barto, Cheryl educational association administrator, researcher
Barton, Jean Marie psychologist, educator
Barton, William Russell government official
Baruch, Jordan Jay management consultant
Bass, Charles F. congressman
Basseches, Robert Treinis lawyer
Bassin, Jules foreign service officer
Batdorf, Lynn Robert horticulturist
Bateman, Herbert Harvell congressman
Bateman, Paul William government official, business executive
Bates, Jared Lewis army officer
Bates, John Cecil, Jr. lawyer
Battle, Lucius Durham retired educational institution administrator, former diplomat
Baucus, Max S. senator
Bauer, Gary Lee government official
Bauer, Robert Albert public policy consultant
Bauerlein, Robert D. federal agency administrator
Baum, Ingeborg Ruth librarian
Baumgartner, Eileen Mary government official
Baxter, Nevins Dennis bank consultant
Baylor, Valoria E. educational administrator, school counselor
Bayly, John Henry, Jr. judge
Beach, Walter Eggert publishing organization executive
Beale, Betty (Mrs. George K. Graeber) columnist, writer
Beale, Susan Yates social worker
Beall, James Robert toxicologist
Beard, Lillian B. McLean physician, consultant
Beary, John Francis, III physician, pharmaceutical executive
Beatty, Richard Scrivener lawyer
Beauchamp, Tom L. philosophy educator
Beazley, Hamilton Scott volunteer health organization executive
Becerra, Xavier congressman, lawyer
Becker, Brandon lawyer
Becker, Mary Louise political scientist
Becker, William Watters lawyer
Beckett, William Wade lawyer
Beckwith, Edward Jay lawyer
Becton, Julius Wesley, Jr. army officer
Beddow, Richard Harold judge
Bedini, Silvio A. historian, author
Bednarek, Jana Maria biochemist
Beebe, Cora Prifold government official
Beecher, William Manuel government official
Beehler, Bruce McPherson research zoologist, ornithologist, conservationist
Beeton, Alfred Merle laboratory director, limnologist, educator
Beghe, Renato federal judge
Begleiter, Ralph J. correspondent
Beisner, John Herbert lawyer
Beizer, Richard L. lawyer
Beizer, Robert A. lawyer
Bell, James Frederick lawyer
Bell, Jeanne Viner public relations counselor
Bell, Robert G. federal agency official
Bell, Stephen Robert lawyer
Beller, Herbert N. lawyer
Bellinger, Edgar Thomson lawyer
Bellinger, John B., Jr. federal official
Bello, Judith Hippler lawyer
Bellows, Michael Donald foreign service officer
Belman, A. Barry pediatric urologist
Belman, Murray Joel lawyer
Belmar, Warren lawyer
Belson, James Anthony judge
Beltz, William Albert publisher
Bender, David Ray library association executive
Benedick, Richard Elliot diplomat
Benedict, Lawrence Neal foreign service officer
Beneke, Patricia Jane fedeal agency administrator
Benezra, Neal curator
†Benken, Eric W. career officer
Bennett, Alexander Elliot lawyer
Bennett, Betty T. English language educator, university dean, writer
Bennett, Carolyn L. journalist, writer
Bennett, Gary Lee physicist, consultant
Bennett, Joel P. lawyer
Bennett, Marion Tinsley federal circuit judge
Bennett, Robert F. senator
Bentley, Carl minister
Bentley, James Daniel medical association executive
Bentley, James Luther journalist
Benton, Marjorie Craig federal agency administrator
Bentsen, Kenneth E., Jr. congressman
Ben-Veniste, Richard lawyer
Bercovici, Martin William lawyer
Berendzen, Richard astronomer, educator, author
Bereuter, Douglas Kent congressman
Berg, Norman Alf conservation consultant
Berg, Olena federal official
Berger, Samuel R. federal official
Bergmann, Barbara Rose economics educator
Bergsten, C. Fred economist
Berl, Joseph M. lawyer
Berlack, Evan Raden lawyer
†Berman, Ellen foundation administrator
Berman, Howard Lawrence congressman
Berman, Marshall Fox lawyer
Berman, Sidney psychiatrist
Bern, Paula Ruth syndicated columnist
Bernabei, Lynne Ann lawyer
Berner, Frederic George, Jr. lawyer
Bernhard, Berl lawyer
Bernstein, Edwin S. judge
Bernstein, Harvey Michael research foundation executive, engineer
Bernstein, Mitchell Harris lawyer
Bernthal, Frederick Michael association executive
†Berry, Marion congressman
Berry, Mary Frances federal agency administrator, history and law educator
†Berry, Morrell John cultural organization administrator
Berryman, Richard Byron lawyer
Berube, Raymond P. federal agency administrator
Berz, David R. lawyer
Besen, Stanley Martin economist
Best, Judah lawyer
†Betsch, Keith Albert airforce officer
Bibby, Douglas Martin mortgage association executive
Biddle, Livingston Ludlow, Jr. former government official, author, consultant
Biddle, Timothy Maurice lawyer
Biden, Joseph Robinette, Jr. senator
Biechman, John Charles federal agency official
Bier, Carol Manson museum curator, writer
Bierbauer, Charles correspondent, news analyst
Bierly, Eugene Wendell meteorologist, science administrator
Bierman, James Norman lawyer
Bigelow, Donald Nevius educational administrator, historian, consultant
Bilbray, Brian P. congressman
Bilirakis, Michael congressman, lawyer, business executive
Biller, Morris (Moe Biller) union executive
Billington, James Hadley historian, librarian
Bingaman, Jeff senator
Bingman, Charles Franklin public administration educator
†Birdsall, Nancy banking administrator
Birnbaum, Norman author, humanities educator
Birnbaum, S. Elizabeth lawyer
Bishop, Sanford Dixon, Jr. congressman
Bishop, Wayne Staton lawyer
Bishop, William Peter research scientist
Bissell, Richard Etter international finance agency executive
Bittman, William Omar lawyer
Black, Charlie J. technical writer, author, educator, business consultant
Black, Stephen F. lawyer
Blackwelder, Brent Francis environmentalist
†Blagojevich, Rod R. state legislator, congressman
†Blair, Dennis Cutler career officer
Blair, James Pease photographer
†Blair, Margaret Mendenhall research economist, consultant
Blair, Patricia Wohlgemuth economics writer
Blair, Warren Emerson federal judge
Blair, William Draper, Jr. conservationist
Blair, William McCormick, Jr. lawyer
Blake, Jonathan Dewey lawyer
Blanchard, Bruce environmental engineer, government official
Blanchard, James Johnston ambassador, former governor of Michigan
Blanchette, Robert Wilfred business executive, lawyer
Blasier, Cole political scientist
Blaxall, Martha Ossoff economist
Blazek-White, Doris lawyer
Bleakley, Peter Kimberley lawyer
Bleicher, Samuel Abram lawyer
Bliss, Donald Tiffany, Jr. lawyer
Blitzer, Charles educational administrator
Bloch, Richard Isaac labor arbitrator
Bloch, Stuart Marshall lawyer
Bloch, Susan Low law educator
Block, Herbert Lawrence (Herblock) editorial cartoonist
Blodgett, Todd Alan publisher, marketing consultant
Bloomfield, Maxwell Herron, III history and law educator
†Blumenauer, Earl congressman
Blumenfeld, Jeffrey lawyer, educator
Blumenthal, Ronnie lawyer
Blumenthal, Susan Jane physician
†Blunt, Roy D. congressman
Bluth, B. J. (Elizabeth Jean Catherine Bluth) sociologist, aerospace educator
Boaz, David Douglas foundation executive
†Bobbitt, Jane federal agency administrator
Bode, Barbara foundation executive, consultant
Bodner, John, Jr. lawyer
Boehlert, Sherwood Louis congressman
Boehm, Steven Bruce lawyer
Boehner, John A. congressman
Bogard, Lawrence Joseph lawyer
Boggs, George Trenholm lawyer
Boggs, Thomas Hale, Jr. lawyer
Bohlke, Gary Lee lawyer
Boland, Christopher Thomas, II lawyer
Bolton, John Robert lawyer, former government official
Bond, Christopher Samuel (Kit Bond) senator, lawyer
Bond, Julian civil rights leader
Bonde, Count Peder Carlsson investment company executive
Bonilla, Henry congressman, broadcast executive
Bonior, David Edward congressman
Bonner, Walter Joseph lawyer
Bonosaro, Carol Alessandra professional association executive, former government official
Bonvillian, William Boone lawyer
Book, Edward R. consultant, retired association executive
Bookbinder, Hyman H(arry) public affairs counselor
Boone, Theodore Sebastian lawyer
Boorstin, Daniel Joseph historian, lecturer, educator, author, editor
Borgiotti, Giorgio Vittorio research scientist, engineering consultant
Born, Brooksley Elizabeth lawyer
Born, Gary Brian lawyer, educator
Borsari, George Robert, Jr. lawyer, broadcaster
Borski, Robert Anthony congressman
Borut, Donald J. professional society administrator
Boskey, Bennett lawyer
Boss, Alan Paul astrophysicist
†Boswell, Eric J. federal official
Boucher, Frederick C. congressman, lawyer
Boucher, Wayne Irving policy analyst
Boughton, James Murray economist
Bourne, Francis Stanley foundation administrator
Bourne, Peter Geoffrey physician, educator, author
Bowen, Jerry Wayne federal agency administrator, retired army officer
Bowen, Margareta Maria interpretation and translation educator
Bowie, Calvert S. architect
Bowles, Erskine White House staff member
Bowron, Eljay B. federal agency administrator
Bowsher, Charles Arthur government official
Boxer, Barbara senator
†Boyd, F. Allen, Jr. farmer, congressman
Boyd, Stephen Mather arbitrator, mediator, lawyer
Boyd, Thomas Marshall lawyer
Boyle, John Edward Whiteford cultural organization administrator
Boyle, Renée Kent cultural organization executive, translator, editor
Bradford, William Allen, Jr. lawyer
Bradford, William Hollis, Jr. lawyer
Bradlee, Benjamin Crowninshield executive editor
Bradley, Melvin LeRoy communications company executive
Bradley, Mitchell Hugh retired professional society administrator, retired career officer
Brady, Phillip Donley lawyer
Braestrup, Peter editor
Bragg, Lynn Munroe commissioner
Brahms, Thomas Walter engineering institute executive
Bramson, Leon social scientist, educator
Brandt, Carl David virologist
Branigin, William Joseph journalist
Brannan, Beverly Wood curator of photography
Brant, Donna Marie journalist
Braunstein, Diane Karen government relations professional
Braverman, Jordan columnist
Brazaitis, Thomas Joseph journalist
Brazeal, Aurelia Erskine ambassador
Breaux, John B. senator, former congressman
Bredemeier, Kenneth Herbert journalist
Brennan, William Joseph, Jr. retired United States supreme court justice
Brenner, Janet Maybin Walker lawyer
†Brenner, Robert David federal agency administrator
Bresee, James Collins federal agency administrator
Bresnahan, Pamela Anne lawyer
Bretzfelder, Deborah May museum exhibit designer, photographer
Brewster, Bill K. business executive, former congressman
Brewster, Robert Charles diplomat, consultant
Breyer, Stephen Gerald United States supreme court justice
Brickhouse, Eugene Avon federal agency administrator
Briggs, Alan Leonard lawyer
Briggs, Harold Melvin corporate executive
Briggs, Steven Russell naval officer
Brightup, Craig Steven lobbyist
Brinkley, David McClure news commentator
Briskman, Robert David engineering executive
Britton, Katherine Lela Quainton lawyer
Broas, Timothy Michael lawyer
Brobeck, Stephen James consumer advocate
Broches, Aron international lawyer, arbitrator
Brock, Gerald Wayne telecommunications educator
Brockway, David Hunt lawyer
Broder, David Salzer reporter
Brody, Kenneth David investment banker
Bromwich, Michael Ray federal official
Bronstein, Alvin J. lawyer
Brooke, Edward William lawyer, former senator
Brooks, Daniel Townley lawyer
Brosnan, Carol Raphael Sarah arts administrator, musician
Brotzman, Donald Glenn government official, lawyer
Broun, Elizabeth art historian, museum administrator
Browder, John Glen congressman, educator
Brown, Charles Freeman lawyer
Brown, Corrine congresswoman
Brown, Dale Susan government administrator, educational program director, writer
Brown, David Nelson lawyer
Brown, David R. think-tank executive
Brown, Donald Arthur lawyer
Brown, Elizabeth Ann foreign service officer
Brown, George Edward, Jr. congressman
Brown, George Leslie legislative affairs and business development consultant, former manufacturing company executive, former lieutenant governor
Brown, Harold former secretary of defense, corporate director
Brown, Janet Huidekoper foundation executive
Brown, Jesse federal official
Brown, John Carter art and education consultant, federal agency administrator
Brown, John Patrick newspaper executive, financial consultant
Brown, June Gibbs government official
Brown, Lawrence Clifton, Jr. foundation administrator
Brown, Lester Russell research institute executive
Brown, Louis physicist, researcher
Brown, Michael Arthur lawyer
Brown, Omer Forrest, II lawyer
Brown, Preston lawyer
Brown, Richard Laurence broadcast executive
Brown, Sherrod congressman, former state official
Brown, William Robert association executive, consultant
Brownback, Sam senator
Browne, Ray insurance broker
Browne, Richard Cullen lawyer
Browner, Carol federal agency administrator
†Browning, Charles publishing executive
†Browning, Charles M. publisher
Browning, Stephen Carroll government official
Brownlee, Paula Pimlott professional society administrator
Brownstein, Philip Nathan lawyer
Bruce, E(stel) Edward lawyer
Bruce, John Foster lawyer
Bruder, George Frederick lawyer
Bruggink, Eric G. federal judge
Bruno, Harold Robinson, Jr. journalist
Bruno, Marilyn Joan foreign service officer, management consultant, trade specialist
Brunsvold, Brian Garrett lawyer, educator
Bruton, James Asa, III lawyer
Bryan, Richard H. senator
Bryant, Arthur H. lawyer
Bryant, Edward congressman
Bryant, John Wiley former congressman
Bryant, Thomas Edward physician, lawyer
Bryant, William B. federal judge
Brynn, Edward Paul ambassador
Bryson, William Curtis federal judge
Brzezinski, Zbigniew political science educator, author
Buben, Jeffrey Alan restaurant owner, chef
Buc, Nancy Lillian lawyer
Buchanan, Michael John economist, researcher, educator
Bucholtz, Harold Ronald lawyer
Buchwald, Art columnist, writer
Buck, Jennifer Cooney government administrator
Buckley, James Lane federal judge
Buckley, Jeremiah Stephen lawyer
Buckley, John Joseph, Jr. lawyer
Buechner, Jack W(illiam) lawyer, government affairs consultant

Heintz, John Edward lawyer
†Heinz, Teresa F. foundation administrator
Heiss, Harry Glen archivist
Helfer, Michael Stevens lawyer
Helfer, Ricki Tigert federal agency administrator
Heller, Jack Isaac lawyer
Hellmuth, George William architect
Hellwig, Monika Konrad theology educator
Helms, Jesse senator
Helms, Richard McGarrah international consultant, former ambassador
Helms, Robert Brake economist, research director
Henderson, Douglas Boyd lawyer
Henderson, Karen LeCraft federal judge
Henderson, Thomas Henry, Jr. lawyer, legal association executive
Henke, Michael John lawyer, educator
Henkin, Robert Irwin neurobiologist, internal medicine, nutrition and neurology educator, scientific products company executive, taste and smell disease physician
Hennessy, Ellen Anne lawyer, educator
†Henry, Katherine L. government official
Henry, Walter Lester, Jr. physician, educator
Herberger, Albert J. federal agency administrator, retired naval officer
Herbers, Tod Arthur publisher
Herbert, James Charles education executive
Herbster, William Gibson university administrator, consultant
Herger, Wally W. congressman
Herman, Alexis M. federal official
Herman, Andrea Maxine newspaper editor
Herman, George Edward radio and television correspondent
Herman, Mary Margaret neuropathologist
Hermens, Ferdinand Aloys political science educator
Hershey, Robert Lewis mechanical engineer, management consultant
Hervey, Homer Vaughan federal agency administrator
Herzstein, Robert Erwin lawyer
Hess, Stephen political scientist, author
Heumann, Judith federal agency administrator
Hewitt, Frankie Lea theater producer
Hewitt, Paul Buck lawyer
Hey, Robert Pierpont editor association bulletin
Hibbert, Robert George lawyer, food company executive
Hickey, Edward Joseph, Jr. lawyer, diplomatic consultant
Hickey, James Aloysius Cardinal archbishop
Hickman, R(obert) Harrison political pollster, strategist
Hicks, Sherman Gregory pastor
Higbee, Joan Florence librarian
Higgins, James Henry, III marketing executive
Higgins, John Edward, Jr. lawyer
Higgins, Kathryn O'Leary government official
Higgins, Mark C. development banker
High, George Borman executive director, research organization
Hill, David Lamar lawyer
Hill, Jim Tom association executive
Hill, Jimmie Dale retired government official
†Hill, Rick Allan congressman
Hilleary, Van congressman
Hilliard, Earl Frederick congressman, lawyer
Hillman, Jennifer Anne ambassador, trade negotiator
Hills, Carla Anderson lawyer, former federal official
Hills, John Merrill public policy research center executive, former educational administrator
Hills, Roderick M. lawyer, business executive, former government official
Hinchey, Maurice D., Jr. congressman
Hinden, Stanley Jay newspaper editor
Hinson, David Russell airline company executive, federal agency administrator
Hinson, Diane Silberstein lawyer
Hirsch, Robert Louis energy research and development consultant
Hirschhorn, Eric Leonard lawyer
Hitz, Frederick Porter federal agency administrator, lawyer
Hoagland, Jimmie Lee newspaper editor
Hobbs, J. Timothy, Sr. lawyer
Hobbs, Vivian Lee lawyer
Hobelman, Carl Donald lawyer
Hobson, David Lee congressman, lawyer
Hobson, James Richmond lawyer
Hodges, Robert H., Jr. federal judge
Hodgson, Frederick Kimmel radio station executive
Hodgson, Morgan Day lawyer
Hoecker, James John lawyer
Hoekstra, Peter congressman, manufacturing executive
Hoffman, E. Leslie lawyer
Hoffman, Joel Elihu lawyer
Hoffmann, Martin Richard lawyer
Hoffmann, Melane Kinney marketing and public relations executive, writer
Hoffmann, Robert Shaw museum administrator, educator
Hogan, John P. federal agency official
Ho-Gonzalez, William lawyer
Hoi, Samuel Chuen-Tsung art school dean
Hoke, Martin Rossiter former congressman
Holbrook, Douglas Cowen labor union administrator
†Holbrooke, Richard Charles Albert former ambassador, government official
Holdaway, Ronald M. federal judge
Holden, John Bernard former college president, educator
Holden, Raymond Thomas physician, educator
Holden, Tim congressman, protective official
Holladay, Wilhelmina Cole interior design and museum executive
Holland, Christie Anna biochemist, virologist
Holland, James Ricks public relations executive, association executive
Hollander, Richard Edward real estate executive
Holliday, Carolyn Pamela government agency administrator
Hollings, Ernest Frederick senator
Hollinshead, Ariel Cahill research oncologist
Hollis, Sheila Slocum lawyer
Hollis, Walter Winslow government official
Holloway, James Lemuel, III foundation executive, retired naval officer
Holloway, John Thomas physicist
Holmer, Alan Freeman trade association executive, lawyer
Holmes, Bradley Paul information technology management consultant
Holmes, Henry Allen government official
Holmes, Norman Leonard lawyer
Holmstead, Jeffrey Ralph lawyer
Holtz, Edgar Wolfe lawyer
Holum, John D. federal agency administrator
†Honigman, Steven lawyer
Hope, William Duane zoologist, curator
Horahan, Edward Bernard, III lawyer
Horan, Harold Eugene university administrator, former diplomat
Horlick, Gary Norman lawyer, legal educator
Horn, Charles M. lawyer
Horn, Donald Herbert lawyer
Horn, Marian Blank federal judge
Horn, (John) Stephen congressman, political science educator
Horne, Michael Stewart lawyer
Horner, Constance J. federal agency administrator
Horowitz, Herbert Eugene educator, consultant, former ambassador
Horsky, Charles Antone lawyer
Hosie, Stanley William foundation executive, writer
Hostettler, John N. congressman
Hotchkin, John Francis church official, priest
Houdek, Robert G. diplomat
Hough, Lawrence A. financial organization executive
Houghton, Amory, Jr. congressman
Houlihan, David Paul lawyer
Hourcle, Laurent Romain law educator
House, W(illiam) Michael lawyer
Hove, Andrew Christian federal agency administrator
Hoving, John Hannes Forester consulting firm executive
Howard, Barbara Viventi research foundation executive
Howard, Glen Scott foundation executive, lawyer
Howard, Jack consultant
Howard, Jeffrey Hjalmar lawyer
Howe, Fisher management consultant, former government official
Howerton, Helen Veronica federal agency administrator
Howes, Theodore Clark claims examiner
†Howland, Richard Hubbard architectural historian
Hoyer, Steny Hamilton congressman
Hoyt, David Richard federal agency program analyst
Hoyt, John Arthur humane society executive
Hrinak, Donna Jean ambassador
Hsu, Ming Chen federal agency administrator
Huband, Frank Louis educational association executive
Huberman, Benjamin technology consultant
Huddle, Franklin Pierce, Jr. diplomat
Huddleston, Vicki Jean diplomat
Hudec, Mary Suzanne nursing and patient services administrator
Hudnut, William Herbert, III senior resident fellow, political scientist
Hudson, J. Clifford federal agency administrator
†Hudson, Joel B. civilian military employee
Hudson, Michael Craig political science educator
Huerta, Michael Peter government official
Hug, James Edward religious organization administrator
Huggett, Robert J. federal agency administrator
Huggins, James Bernard corporate executive
Hughes, Ann Hightower economist, international trade consultant
Hughes, Kent Higgon economist
Hughes, Marija Matich law librarian
Hughes, Thomas Lowe foundation executive
†Hulshof, Kenny congressman
Hume, Brit (Alexander Britton Hume) journalist
Hundt, Reed Eric federal agency administrator, lawyer
Hunger, Frank Watson federal official
Hunnicutt, Charles Alvin lawyer
Hunt, Albert R. newspaper executive
Hunt, Earl Stephen educational research analyst
Hunt, Robert Gayle government official
Huntoon, Carolyn Leach physiologist
Huntress, Wesley Theodore, Jr. government official
Huntsman, Lawrence Darrow lawyer
Hurd, Shirley Dyer health care administrator
Hussain, Syed Taseer biomedical educator, researcher
Huston, John Wilson air force officer, historian
Hutchinson, Tim senator
Hutt, Peter Barton lawyer
Hyde, Henry John congressman
Hyman, Lester Samuel lawyer
Hynes, Terence Michael lawyer
Ikenberry, Stanley Oliver education educator, former university president
Iklé, Fred Charles former federal agency administrator, policy advisor, defense expert
Imam, M. Ashraf materials scientist, educator
Imig, David Gregg educational association executive
Inglis, Robert D. (Bob Inglis) congressman, lawyer
Ingold, Catherine White academic administrator
Inhofe, James M. senator
Innerst, Preston Eugene newspaper editor, journalist
Innis, Pauline writer, publishing company executive
Inouye, Daniel Ken senator
Ireland, Patricia association executive
Irey, Nelson Sumner pathologist
Irish, Leon Eugene lawyer, educator, non-profit executive
Irizarry, Estelle Diane foreign language educator, author, editor
Irvine, Reed John media critic, corporation executive
Irving, Clarence L., Jr. (Larry Irving) federal official
Irwin, Paul Garfield former minister, humane society executive
Isaacs, Amy Fay political organization executive
Isbell, David Bradford lawyer, legal educator
Iscoe, Craig Steven lawyer
Isenbergh, Max lawyer, musician, educator
Istook, Ernest James, Jr. (Jim Istook) congressman, lawyer
Ivers, Donald Louis judge
†Jackson, Jesse, Jr. congressman
Jackson, Karl Dion government official business executive, scholar
Jackson, Neal A. lawyer
Jackson, Shirley Ann federal agency administrator, physicist
Jackson, Thomas Penfield federal judge
Jackson Lee, Sheila congresswoman
Jacobs, David E. federal agency administrator
Jacobs, Julian I. federal judge
Jacobsen, Hugh Newell architect
Jacobsen, Raymond Alfred, Jr. lawyer
Jacobson, David Edward lawyer
Jacobson, Michael Faraday consumer advocate, writer
Jamar, Steven Dwight law educator
James, Charles Clinton science education educator
James, Estelle economics educator
James, Julie Ann congressional staff member
Jamme, Albert Joseph archaeologist, educator
Janis, Michael B. federal official
Jansen, E. Harold bishop
Jaspersen, Frederick Zarr economist
Javits, Joshua Moses lawyer
Jeff, Gloria Jean federal government administrator
Jefferson, William L. (Jeff Jefferson) congressman
Jeffords, James Merrill senator
Jenkins, John Smith academic dean, lawyer
†Jenkins, William L. (Bill Jenkins) congressman
Jensen, Joseph (Norman) priest, educator
†Jenson, William G. federal agency administrator
Jessup, Philip Caryl, Jr. lawyer, museum executive
Jeter, Howard F. diplomat
Joelson, Mark Rene lawyer
†John, Chris congressman
Johnson, Arlene Lytle government agency official
Johnson, David Raymond lawyer
Johnson, Eddie Bernice congresswoman
Johnson, Haynes Bonner author, journalist, television commentator
Johnson, James A. financial organization executive
†Johnson, Jay L. career officer
†Johnson, Jay Withington congressman
Johnson, Manuel Holman, Jr. government official, economics educator, business executive
Johnson, Mark ambassador
Johnson, Nancy Lee congresswoman
Johnson, Norma Holloway federal judge
Johnson, Oliver Thomas, Jr. lawyer
Johnson, Omotunde Evan George economist
Johnson, Paul W. federal executive
Johnson, Philip McBride lawyer
Johnson, Richard Clark lawyer
Johnson, Richard Tenney lawyer
Johnson, Robert Henry political science educator
Johnson, Robert Louis media company executive
Johnson, Samuel (Sam Johnson) congressman
Johnson, Shirley Z. lawyer
Johnson, Tim professional football player
Johnson, Timothy Peter senator
Johnston, Gerald Samuel physician, educator
Johnston, John Bennett, Jr. former senator
Johnston, Kenneth John astronomer, scientific director naval observatory
Johnston, Laurance Scott foundation director
Jones, Aidan Drexel lawyer
Jones, Boisfeuillet, Jr. lawyer, newspaper executive
Jones, George Fleming foundation executive
Jones, Howard St. Claire, Jr. electronics engineering executive
Jones, Meredith J. federal government official
Jones, Philip Howard broadcast journalist
Jones, Stanley Boyd health policy analyst, priest
Jones, Walter Beaman, Jr. congressman
Jones-Wilson, Faustine Clarisse education educator emeritus
†Jordan, Anne E. Dollerschell journalist
Jordan, Emma Coleman law educator
Jordan, Mary Lucille commissioner
Jordan, Robert Elijah, III lawyer
Jordan, Vernon Eulion, Jr. lawyer, former association official
Joseph, Daniel Mordecai lawyer
Joseph, James Alfred ambassador
Joseph, Stephen C. health sciences administrator
Josephson, Diana Hayward government agency official
Jost, Peter Hafner lawyer
Journey, Drexel Dahlke lawyer
Joyce, Anne Raine editor, director of publications
†Joyner, Christopher C. international relations educator
Judd, Jacqueline Dee (Jackie Judd) journalist, reporter
Julian, Elizabeth K. federal agency administrator
Juliana, James Nicholas ordnance company executive
Jurado, Kathy Elena government agency administrator
Kabel, Robert James lawyer
Kafka, Gerald Andrew lawyer
Kahlow, Barbara Fenvessy statistician
Kahn, Edwin Leonard lawyer
Kahn, Michael stage director
Kahn, Walter Kurt engineering and applied science educator
Kaiser, Robert Greeley newspaper editor
Kaji, Gautam Subodh federal agency administrator
Kalick, Laura Joy lawyer, healthcare tax specialist
Kalnay, Eugenia government official, meteorologist
Kalnins, Ojars Eriks Latvian diplomat
Kamber, Victor Samuel political consultant
Kamikawa, Alden Tanemitsu trade association executive
Kaminski, Paul Garrett federal agency administrator, investment banker
Kammerer, Kelly Christian lawyer
Kane, Annette Pieslak religious organization executive
Kane, Michael Barry social science research executive
Kanjorski, Paul Edmund congressman, lawyer
Kant, Gloria Jean neuroscientist, researcher
Kanter, Arnold Lee policy analyst
Kapetanakos, Christos Anastasios science administrator, physics educator
Kapp, Robert Harris lawyer
Kappaz, Michael H. engineering company executive
Kaptur, Marcia Carolyn congresswoman
Karcher, Donald Steven medical educator
Karelis, Charles Howard government official
Karle, Jerome physicist, researcher
Karmin, Monroe William editor
Karpinski, Gene Brien non-profit group administrator, think tank executive
Kaseman, A. Carl, III lawyer
Kasich, John R. congressman
Kass, Benny Lee lawyer
Kassebaum, Nancy Landon former senator
Kasten, Robert W., Jr. former senator
Katz, John W. lawyer, state official
Katz, Sherman E. lawyer
Katz, Sol physician
Katzen, Sally lawyer
Katzmann, Robert Allen law educator, non-profit association executive, political scientist
Kaufman, Irving N. transportation executive
Kaufman, John Gilbert, Jr. materials engineer
Kaulkin, Donna Brookman editor, writer
Kautter, David John lawyer
Kauzlarich, Richard Dale ambassador, foreign service officer
Kavanaugh, Everett Edward, Jr. trade association executive
Kearney, Stephen Michael corporate treasurer
Kearns, Darien Lee marine officer
Keating, Robert B. ambassador
Keck, Lois T. anthropology educator
Keeley, Robert Vossler retired academic administrator, retired ambassador
†Keena, J. Bradley political commentator
Keener, Mary Lou lawyer
Keeney, John Christopher, Jr. lawyer
Keeny, Spurgeon Milton, Jr. association executive
Keiner, R(obert) Bruce, Jr. lawyer
†Keller, Brian David marine ecologist
Kelley, Edward Watson, Jr. federal agency administrator
Kelley, Wayne Plumbley, Jr. federal official
Kellison, James Bruce lawyer
Kelly, Charles J., Jr. investment company executive
Kelly, Eugene Walter, Jr. counseling educator
Kelly, Nancy Frieda Wolicki lawyer
Kelly, Sue W. congresswoman
Kelly, William Charles, Jr. lawyer
Kelman, Steven Jay government official
Kemp, Geoffrey Thomas Howard international affairs specialist
Kemp, John D. professional society administrator
Kempley, Rita A. film critic, editor
Kempner, Jonathan L. professional society administrator
Kempster, Norman Roy journalist
Kempthorne, Dirk Arthur senator
Kendall, David E. lawyer
Kendall, Peter Landis television news executive
Kendrick, John Whitefield economist, educator, consultant
Kennard, Mary Elizabeth lawyer
Kennedy, Anthony McLeod United States supreme court justice
Kennedy, Davis Lee newspaper editor, publisher
Kennedy, Edward Moore senator
Kennedy, Eugene Richard microbiologist, university dean
Kennedy, Joseph Patrick, II congressman
Kennedy, Patrick F. federal official
Kennedy, Patrick J. congressman
Kennedy, Richard Thomas government official
Kennedy, Robert Emmet, Jr. history educator
Kennelly, Barbara B. congresswoman
Kenney, Robert James, Jr. lawyer
Kent, Jill Elspeth academic administrator, lawyer, art dealer, former government official
Kent, M. Elizabeth lawyer
Kerber, Frank John diplomat
Kern, John Worth, III judge
Kerr, Stuart H. lawyer, think tank executive
Kerrey, Bob (J. Robert Kerrey) senator
Kerry, John Forbes senator
Kerxton, Alan Smith lawyer
Kessler, Gladys federal judge
Kessler, Judd Lewis lawyer
Kesterman, Frank Raymond investment banker
Ketchum, James Roe curator
Keune, Russell Victor architect, architectural association executive
Keyes, Arthur Hawkins, Jr. architect
Khadduri, Majid international studies educator
Kidd, Charles Vincent former civil servant, educator
Kier, Porter Martin paleontologist
Kies, Kenneth J. lawyer
Kiko, Philip George lawyer
Kilborn, Peter Thurston journalist
Kilburn, Edwin Allen lawyer
Kildee, Dale Edward congressman
Kilgore, Edwin Carroll retired government official, consultant
Kilian, Michael David journalist, columnist, writer
Killion, Ruth Ann statistical researcher
Kim, Jay congressman
Kim, John Chan Kyu electrical engineer
Kimmitt, Robert Michael banker, lawyer, diplomat
King, Larry (Larry Zeiger) broadcaster, radio personality
King, Llewellyn Willings publisher, lecturer, journalist
King, Nina Davis journalist
King, Peter T. congressman, lawyer
King, Rufus lawyer
Kingston, Jack congressman
Kiper, Ali Muhlis mechanical engineering educator, consultant
Kiplinger, Knight A. journalist, publisher
Kirk, Donald journalist
Kirkien-Rzeszotarski, Alicia Maria academic administrator, researcher, educator
Kirkpatrick, Jeane Duane Jordan political scientist, government official
Kirsch, Laurence Stephen lawyer
Kitchen, John Howard economist
Kitchens, Clarence Wesley, Jr. physical science administrator
Kittrell, Steven Dan lawyer
Kittrie, Nicholas N(orbert Nehemiah) law educator, international consultant, author
Kitzmiller, William Michael government official
Kizer, Kenneth Wayne physician, educator
Klarfeld, Peter James lawyer
Klass, Philip Julian technical journalist, electrical engineer
Klawiter, Donald Casimir lawyer
Kleczka, Gerald D. congressman
Kleiman, Devra Gail zoologist, zoological park research scientist
Klein, Michael Roger lawyer, business executive
Kleinknecht, Christian Frederick Masonic official
Klimp, Jack Wilbur armed forces officer
Kline, Jerry Robert government official, ecologist
Kline, Norman Douglas federal judge
Kling, William economist, retired foreign service officer
Klink, Ron congressman, reporter, newscaster
Klosson, Michael foreign service officer
Knapp, Charles Boynton economist, educator, academic administrator
Knapp, George M. lawyer
Knapp, Richard Maitland association executive
Knapp, Rosalind Ann lawyer
Knebel, John Albert lawyer, former government official
Knight, Athelia Wilhelmenia journalist
†Knight, Edward S. lawyer,federal official
Knippers, Diane LeMasters organization administrator
Knoll, Jerry former government official
Knollenberg, Joseph (Joe Knollenberg) congressman
Knopman, Debra Sara hydrologist, policy analyst
Koch, Barbara Louise foreign service family nurse
Koch, George William lawyer
Koch, Kathleen Day lawyer
Koenig, Harold Martin U.S. Navy surgeon general
Koering, Marilyn Jean anatomy educator, researcher
Kohl, Herbert senator, professional sports team owner
Kolasky, William Joseph, Jr. lawyer
Kolb, Charles Chester humanities administrator
Kolbe, James Thomas congressman

McCarroll, Jeanne Louise association executive
McCarthy, Abigail Quigley writer, columnist, educator
McCarthy, David Jerome, Jr. law educator
McCarthy, Karen P. congresswoman, former state representative
McCartney, James Harold retired newspaper columnist, educator, journalist
Mc Carty, Robert Lee lawyer
McClain, William Thomas lawyer
McClintic, Howard Gresson foundation executive
McCloskey, J(ohn) Michael association administrator
McClure, William Pendleton lawyer
McCollam, William, Jr. utility company executive
Mc Collum, Ira William, Jr. (Bill Mc Collum) congressman
McConnell, Addison Mitchell, Jr. (Mitch McConnell, Jr.) senator, lawyer
McCormally, Kevin Jay editor
McCoy, Jerry Jack lawyer
†McCreight, Robert Edwin federal agency administrator, educator
McCrery, James (Jim McCrery) congressman
Mc Curdy, Patrick Pierre editor, consultant
McCurry, Michael Demaree government spokesman, press secretary
McDade, Joseph Michael congressman
McDaniel, John Perry health care company executive
McDaniels, William E. lawyer
McDavid, Janet Louise lawyer
Mc Dermott, Albert Leo lawyer
McDermott, Edward Aloysious lawyer
McDermott, James A. congressman, psychiatrist
McDonald, Bryant Edward physicist, oceanographer
McDonald, Gail Clements government official
Mc Donald, John Warlick diplomat, global strategist
McDowell, Charles R. columnist, news analyst, lecturer
McElroy, Edward J. union officer
McElroy, Frederick William economics educator, consultant
McElveen, Joseph James, Jr. author, journalist, public broadcasting executive
McElveen, Junius Carlisle, Jr. lawyer
McEntee, Gerald W. labor union official
Mc Gaughan, Alexander Stanley architect
McGeein, Mary Martha health care organization executive
Mc Giffert, David Eliot lawyer, former government official
McGinnies, Elliott Morse psychologist, educator
McGinnis, James Michael physician
McGinty, Kathleen federal official
McGinty, Michael Dennis air force officer
†McGovern, James P. congressman
McGovern, Michael Barbot lawyer
McGrath, Kathryn Bradley lawyer
McGrath, Mary Helena plastic surgeon, educator
McGraw, Lavinia Morgan retired retail company executive
Mc Grory, Mary columnist
McGue, Christie federal official
McGuire, Patricia A. lawyer, academic administrator
McGuirl, Marlene Dana Callis law librarian, educator
McHugh, James Lenahan, Jr. lawyer
McHugh, John Michael congressman, former state senator
McInnis, Scott Steve congressman, lawyer
McIntosh, David M. congressman
Mc Kay, Emily Gantz civil and human rights professional
McKay, Jack Alexander electronics engineer, physicist
McKay, John lawyer
McKee, Alan Reel foreign service officer
McKeon, Howard P. (Buck McKeon) congressman, former mayor
McKinley, Brunson diplomat
McKinney, Cynthia Ann congresswoman
McLarty, Thomas F., III (Mack McLarty) federal official
McLaughlin, John broadcast executive, television producer, political commentator, journalist
McLaughlin, Maureen A. federal agency administrator
Mc Lean, George Francis philosophy of religion educator, clergyman
McLean, R. Bruce lawyer
McLellan, Joseph Duncan critic, journalist
McLennan, Barbara Nancy management consultant
McLoughlin, Merrill publishing executive
McMahon, Debra Brylawski management consultant
McMahon, Joseph Einar lawyer, consultant
McMahon, Neil Michael real estate executive
McMichael, Guy H., III federal official
McMiller, Anita Williams army officer, transportation professional, educator
Mc Namara, Robert Strange former banking executive, cabinet member
†McNamara, Thomas Edmund diplomat
McNicol, David Leon federal official
McNulty, Michael Robert congressman
McNulty, Robert Holmes non-profit executive
Mc Phee, Henry Roemer lawyer
Mc Pherson, Harry Cummings, Jr. lawyer
McPherson, Ronald P. federal agency administrator
McShane, Franklin John, III nurse anesthetist, army officer
McSteen, Martha Abernathy organization executive
Mead, Gilbert D(unbar) geophysicist, lawyer
Means, Marianne political columnist
Means, Thomas Cornell lawyer
Mears, Walter Robert journalist
Medalie, Richard James lawyer
Medalie, Susan Diane management consultant
Mederos, Carolina Luisa transportation policy consultant
Meehan, Martin Thomas congressman, lawyer
Meek, Carrie P. congresswoman
Meggers, Betty J(ane) anthropologist
Mehle, Roger W. federal agency administrator
Meijer, Paul Herman Ernst educator, physicist
Meissner, Doris federal commissioner
Melamed, Arthur Douglas lawyer
Melamed, Carol Drescher lawyer
Melendez, Sara E. non-profit organization executive
Melendy, David Russell broadcast journalist
Mellon, Paul retired art gallery executive
Mellor, John Williams economist, policy consultant firm executive
Melnick, Vijaya Lakshmi biology educator, research center director
Meloy, Sybil Piskur lawyer
Melton, Augustus Allen, Jr. airport executive
†Melton, Carol A. publishing executive
Menard, Edith English language educator, artist, poet, actress
Mencher, Bruce Stephan judge
Menendez, Adolfo engineering company executive
Menendez, Robert congressman, lawyer
Menkel-Meadow, Carrie Joan law educator
Menzer, Robert Everett toxicologist, educator
Mercer, Lee William lawyer, corporate executive, former government agency administrator
Merow, James F. federal judge
Merrell, Jesse Howard writer
†Merrill, Cook congressman
Merrill, David Nathan ambassador
Merry, Robert William publishing executive
Meserve, Richard Andrew lawyer
Messenger, Jon Carleton government project manager
Messner, Howard Myron professional association executive
Meszar, Frank publishing executive, former army officer
Metcalf, Jack congressman, retired state senator
Metz, Craig Huseman legislative administrator
Metz, Ronald Irwin retired priest, addictions counselor
Metzenbaum, Howard Morton former senator
Meyer, Alden Merrill environmental association executive
Meyer, Armin Henry retired diplomat, author, educator
Meyer, Cord columnist
Meyer, Dennis Irwin lawyer
Meyer, Lawrence Robert journalist
Meyerhoff, James Lester medical researcher
Meyers, Jan former congresswoman
Meyers, Tedson Jay lawyer
Meyers, Wayne Marvin microbiologist
Meyerson, Adam magazine editor, foundation executive
†Mezainis, Valdis E. federal agency administrator
Michaelson, Martin lawyer
Michaud, Michael Alan George diplomat, writer
Michel, Paul Redmond federal judge
Middendorf, J. William, II investment banker
Mielke, James Edward geochemist
Miklaszewski, James Alan television news correspondent
Milam, William Bryant diplomat, economist
Miles, David Michael lawyer
Miles, Ellen Gross art historian, museum curator
Miles, Richard diplomat
Millar, James Robert economist, educator, university official
†Millender-McDonald, Juanita congresswoman, former school system administrator
Miller, Alan Stanley ecology center administrator, law educator
Miller, Andrew Pickens lawyer
Miller, Carroll Lee Liverpool educational researcher
Miller, Charles A. lawyer
Miller, Christine Odell Cook judge
Miller, Dan congressman
Miller, Gay Davis lawyer
Miller, George congressman
Miller, G(eorge) William merchant banker, business executive
Miller, H. Todd lawyer
Miller, Herbert John, Jr. lawyer
Miller, Hope Ridings author
Miller, James Clifford, III economist
Miller, Jeanne-Marie Anderson (Mrs. Nathan J. Miller) English language educator, academic administrator
Miller, John Francis association executive, social scientist
Miller, John T., Jr. lawyer, educator
Miller, Kerry Lee lawyer
Miller, Loye Wheat, Jr. journalist, corporate communications specialist
Miller, Marcia E. federal government official
Miller, Margaret Alison education association administrator
Miller, Margery Silberman psychologist, speech and language pathologist
Miller, Mark Karl journalist
Miller, Marshall Lee lawyer
Miller, Mary Hotchkiss lay worker
Miller, Robert Allen hotel executive
Miller, Warren Lloyd lawyer
Millian, Kenneth Young public policy consultant
Millie, Harold Raymond editor
Millon, Henry Armand fine arts educator, architectural historian
Mills, Kevin Paul lawyer
Milstein, Elliott Steven legal educator, academic administrator
Min, Nancy-Ann federal agency administrator
Minarik, Joseph John economist, researcher
Mineta, Norman Yoshio aerospace transportation executive, former congressman
Minge, David congressman, lawyer, law educator
Mink, Patsy Takemoto congresswoman
Minkoff, Alice Sydney interior designer, showroom owner
Minnich, Nelson Hubert Joseph historian, educator
Mintz, Richard I. federal official
Mintz, Seymour Stanley lawyer
Missar, Charles Donald librarian
Mitchell, Andrea journalist
Mitchell, Graham Richard government engineering executive
Mitchell, John David ophthalmologist
Mitchell, Margery Hope lawyer
Mitchell, Roy Shaw lawyer
Mlay, Marian consultant, former government official
Moakley, John Joseph congressman
Moates, G. Paul lawyer
Mobbs, Michael Hall lawyer
Mode, Paul J., Jr. lawyer
Modiano, Albert Louis gas, oil industry executive
Moe, Richard Palmer lawyer
Moe, Ronald Chesney public administration researcher
Moffett, Charles Simonton museum director, curator, writer
Mogel, William Allen lawyer
Moler, Elizabeth Anne federal agency administrator, lawyer
Molinari, Susan congresswoman
Molitoris, Jolene M. federal agency administrator
Mollohan, Alan B. congressman, lawyer
Monroe, Robert Rawson engineering construction executive
Montelongo, Michael career officer
Montgomery, George Cranwell lawyer, former ambassador
Montgomery, William D. ambassador
Mooney, Marilyn lawyer
Moore, Amy Norwood lawyer
Moore, Bob Stahly communications executive
Moore, Jacquelyn Cornelia labor union official, editor
Moore, Jerry religious organization administrator
Moore, Marsha Lynn elementary education educator
Moore, Robert Madison food industry executive, lawyer
Moorer, Thomas Hinman retired naval officer
Moose, George E. government official
Moran, James Patrick, Jr. congressman, stockbroker
†Moran, Jerry congressman
More, John Herron lawyer, classicist
Morella, Constance Albanese congresswoman
Moreno, G(ilberto) Mario federal agency administrator
Morgan, Linda J. federal agency administrator
Morgan, Richard Greer lawyer
Moring, John Frederick lawyer
Moritsugu, Kenneth Paul physician, government official
†Morningstar, Richard L. diplomat
Morris, Daniel Kearns journalist
†Morris, Joann Sebastion federal agency adminstrator
Morris, Russell D. federal agency administrator
Morrison, Bruce Andrew government executive, former congressman
Morrison, James William, Jr. lobbyist, government relations consultant
Morrison, Joel Lynn cartographer, geographer
Morse, Richard McGee historian
Moseley-Braun, Carol senator
Moser, Donald Bruce magazine editor
Mosettig, Michael David television producer, writer
Moss, Madison Scott editor
Moss, Thomas Henry science association administrator
Mossel, Patricia L. opera executive
Mossinghoff, Gerald Joseph patent lawyer, engineer
Mosso, David accountant
Mostoff, Allan Samuel lawyer, consultant
Moulton, David Aubin library director
Moyer, Homer Edward, Jr. lawyer
Moynihan, Daniel Patrick senator, educator
Mrazek, David Allen pediatric psychiatrist
Mtewa, Mekki foundation administrator
Muckenfuss, Cantwell Faulkner, III lawyer
Muir, J. Dapray lawyer
Muir, Patricia Allen educational association administrator
Muldrow, Tressie Wright psychologist
Mulhollan, Daniel Patrick research director
Munoz, George federal agency administrator
Munsell, Elsie Louise lawyer
Munson, Richard Jay congressional policy analyst
Muntzing, L(ewis) Manning lawyer
Murashige, Allen defense analysis executive
Murchison, David Claudius lawyer
Murkowski, Frank Hughes senator
Murphy, Betty Jane Southard (Mrs. Cornelius F. Murphy) lawyer
Murphy, Frances Louise, II newspaper publisher
Murphy, Gerald government official
Murphy, James Paul lawyer
Murphy, John Condron, Jr. lawyer
Murphy, Kathryn Marguerite archivist
Murphy, Kenneth Ray non-governmental organization executive
Murphy, Reg publishing executive
Murphy, Shaun Edward bank executive
Murphy, Terence Roche lawyer
Murray, Alan Stewart publishing executive
Murray, Christopher Charles, III architect
Murray, James Joseph, III association executive
Murray, John Einar lawyer, retired army officer, federal official
Murray, Patty senator
Murray, Robert Fulton, Jr. physician
Murry, Harold David, Jr. lawyer
Murtha, John Patrick congressman
Myers, Elissa Matulis publisher, association executive
Myers, James R. lawyer
Myers, Margaret Jane (Dee Dee Myers) television personality, editor
Myers, Marjorie Lora elementary school principal
Myers, Robert Manson English educator, author
Myers, Stephanie E. publishing company executive
Myers, William Gerry, III advocate, lawyer
Myrick, Bismarck diplomat
Myrick, Sue congresswoman, former mayor
Nabholz, Joseph Vincent biologist, ecologist
Nace, Barry John lawyer
Nader, Ralph consumer advocate, lawyer, author
Nadler, Jerrold Lewis congressman, lawyer
Nagorski, Zygmunt political scientist
Nakhleh, Emile A. governmental sciences educator
Namorato, Cono R. lawyer
Nangle, John Francis federal judge
Napier, John Light lawyer
Nash, Bob J. (Bob Nash) federal agency administrator
Nason, Charles Tuckey financial services executive
Natalie, Ronald Bruce lawyer
Navarro, Bruce Charles lawyer
Navas, William Antonio, Jr. military officer, civil engineer
Naylor, Brian news correspondent
Neal, Darwina Lee government official
Neal, Richard Edmund congressman, former mayor
†Neale, Tracey D. news anchor
Nebeker, Frank Quill federal judge
Nef, Evelyn Stefansson psychotherapist, author, editor, specialist polar regions
Neff, William L. lawyer
Negron, Jaime performing arts center sales director
Negroponte, John Dimitri diplomat
Nehmer, Stanley economics consultant
Neimark, Sheridan lawyer
Nelson, Alan Ray internist, medical assocation executive
Nelson, Candice Jean political science educator
Nelson, Charles J. university administrator, international consultant, diplomat, consultant
Nelson, Gaylord Anton former senator, association executive
Nelson, George Driver astronomy and education educator, former astronaut
Nelson, John Howard (Jack Howard Nelson) journalist
Nelson, Larry Dean telecommunications and computer systems company executive, consultant
Nelson, Lars-Erik newspaperman
Nelson, Robert Louis lawyer
Nemeroff, Michael Alan lawyer
Nemfakos, Charles Panagiotis federal official
Ness, Andrew David lawyer
Nethercutt, George Rector, Jr. congressman, lawyer
Nethery, John Jay government official
Neufeld, Michael John curator, historian
Neuman, Robert Henry lawyer
Neumann, Mark W. congressman
Neumann, Ronald Eldredge diplomat
Neviaser, Robert Jon orthopaedic surgeon, educator
Newman, Barbara Pollock journalist, television writer, producer
Newman, Monroe retired economist, educator
Newman, Pauline federal judge
Newman, William Bernard, Jr. railroad executive
Newquist, Don federal agency administrator
Newsome, Sandra Singleton secondary education educator, principal
Newton, David George diplomat
Newton, Hugh C. public relations executive
Newton, Leilani L. bank executive
Newton, Virginia archivist, historian, librarian
Ney, Robert W. congressman
Nicely, Olza M. (Tony) insurance company executive
Nichols, Henry Eliot lawyer, savings and loan executive
Nichols, Kenneth David consulting engineer
Nicholson, Richard Selindh educational association administrator
Nickel, Henry V. lawyer
Nickles, Donald (Don Nickles) senator
Nightingale, Elena Ottolenghi geneticist, physician, administrator
Nikkel, Ronald Wilbert social services administrator
Nims, Arthur Lee, III federal judge
Nintemann, Terri legislative staff member
Niskanen, William Arthur, Jr. economist, think tank executive
Nitze, William Albert government official, lawyer
Nohe, Richard Edgar telecommunications executive
Nolan, John Edward lawyer
Noland, Marcus economist, educator
Norberg, Charles Robert lawyer
Norcross, David Frank Armstrong lawyer
Nordhaus, Robert Riggs lawyer
Norland, Donald Richard retired foreign service officer
Norman, William Stanley travel and tourism executive
Norris, Genie M. senior government official
†North, David Morgan editor
†Northup, Anne Meagher state legislator
Norton, Eleanor Holmes congresswoman, lawyer, educator
Norton, Floyd Ligon, IV lawyer
Norton, Gerald Patrick lawyer
Norton, James J. union official
Norwood, Charles W., Jr. congressman
Norwood, Janet Lippe economist
Novak, Michael (John) religion educator, author, editor
Novak, Robert David Sanders newspaper columnist, television commentator
Novitch, Mark physician, educator, retired pharmaceutical executive
Nowak, Judith Ann psychiatrist
Nuland, Anthony C. J. lawyer
Nutter, Franklin Winston lawyer
Nutting, Wallace Hall army officer
Oakley, Diane insurance executive, benefit consultant
Oakley, Phyllis Elliott diplomat
Oakley, Robert Louis law librarian, educator
Oberdorfer, Louis F. federal judge
Oberstar, James L. congressman
Obey, David Ross congressman
O'Brien, Margaret Hoffman educational administrator
O'Brien, Timothy Andrew writer, journalist, lawyer
O'Bryon, James Fredrick defense executive
Ochmanek, David Alan defense analyst
O'Connell, Daniel Craig psychology educator
O'Connor, Charles P. lawyer
O'Connor, Jennifer lawyer
O'Connor, John Dennis academic administrator
O'Connor, John Jay, III lawyer
O'Connor, Sandra Day United States supreme court justice
O'Connor, Thomas Edward petroleum geologist, world bank officer
O'Connor, Tom corporate executive, management consultant
O'Day, Paul Thomas trade association executive
Odle, Robert Charles, Jr. lawyer
Odom, William Eldridge army officer, educator
O'Donnell, Terrence lawyer
O'Donovan, Leo Jeremiah university president, theologian, priest
Oehme, Wolfgang Walter landscape architect
Oertel, Goetz K. H. physicist, professional association administrator
Oertel, Yolanda Castillo pathologist, educator, diagnostician
Offutt, Susan Elizabeth economist
†Oge, Margo Tsirigotis environmentalist
Ogilvie, Donald Gordon bankers association executive
Oh, John Kie-Chiang political science educator, university official
O'Hara, James Thomas lawyer
Olcott, John Whiting aviation executive
O'Leary, Kathleen A. financial advisor, legal assistant
Oleksiw, Daniel Philip consultant, former foreign service officer
Olender, Jack Harvey lawyer
Oliphant, Charles Frederick, III lawyer
Oliver, William Albert, Jr. paleontologist
Oliver-Simon, Gloria Craig human resources advisor, consultant, lawyer
Olmstead, Cecil Jay lawyer
Olson, Theodore Bevry lawyer
Olson, Walter Justus, Jr. management consultant
Olver, John Walter congressman
Oman, Ralph lawyer
O'Neil, Joseph Francis association executive
O'Neill, Brian Dennis lawyer
O'Neill, John H., Jr. lawyer
O'Neill, June Ellenoff economist
O'Neill, Richard Paul federal agency administrator
O'Neill, Timothy federal agency administrator
O'Neill, William Patrick lawyer
Onek, Joseph Nathan lawyer
Ongman, John Will lawyer
Ooms, Van Doorn economist
Oppenheimer, Franz Martin lawyer
Oran, Elaine Surick physicist
O'Reilly, Kenneth William military officer
Ornstein, Norman Jay political scientist
O'Rourke, C. Larry lawyer
Orr, J. Scott newspaper correspondent
Orsini, Eric Andrew army official
Orski, C. Kenneth consulting company executive, lawyer

Ross, Christopher Wade Stelyan *diplomat*
Ross, Douglas *lawyer, legal academic administrator*
Ross, Marlene *educator*
Ross, Robinette Davis *publisher*
Ross, Stanford G. *lawyer, former government official*
Ross, Wendy Clucas *newspaper editor, journalist*
Rossides, Eugene Telemachus *lawyer, writer*
Rossotti, Barbara Jill Margulies *lawyer*
Rostker, Bernard *federal official*
Rostow, Eugene Victor *lawyer, educator, economist*
Rotberg, Eugene Harvey *investment banker, lawyer*
Roth, Alan J. *lawyer*
Roth, Kathryn Gaie *government executive*
Roth, William V., Jr. *senator*
†Rothman, Steven R. *lawyer*
Rothstein, Paul Frederick *lawyer, educator*
Rottman, Ellis *public information officer*
Rotunda, Donald Theodore *public relations consultant*
Roukema, Margaret Scafati *congresswoman*
Rousselot, Peter Frese *lawyer*
Rouvelas, Emanuel Larry *lawyer*
Rovelstad, Mathilde Verner *library science educator*
Rowan, Carl Thomas *columnist*
Rowden, Marcus Aubrey *lawyer, former government official*
Rowe, Richard Holmes *lawyer*
Rowson, Richard Cavanagh *publisher*
Roybal-Allard, Lucille *congresswoman*
Royce, Edward R. (Ed Royce) *congressman*
Roycroft, Howard Francis *lawyer*
Royle, David Brian Layton *television producer, journalist*
Rubin, Kenneth Allen *lawyer*
Rubin, Robert E. *federal official*
Rubin, Seymour Jeffrey *lawyer, judge, educator*
Rubinoff, Roberta Wolff *government administrator*
Ruckman, Roger Norris *pediatric cardiologist*
Rudder, Catherine Estelle *political science association administrator*
Ruddy, Frank S. *lawyer, former ambassador*
Rudman, Warren Bruce *former senator, lawyer, think tank executive*
Rugh, William Arthur *diplomat*
Ruiz, Vanessa *judge*
Rule, Charles Frederick (Rick Rule) *lawyer*
Runyon, Marvin Travis *postmaster general*
Rush, Bobby L. *congressman*
Rushnell, Squire Derrick *television executive*
Russell, H. Diane *museum curator, educator*
Russell, Mark *comedian*
Russell, Michael James *lawyer*
Russell, William Joseph *educational association administrator*
Russert, Timothy John *broadcast journalist, executive*
Russin, Jonathan *lawyer, consultant*
Russo, Roy R. *lawyer*
Ruttenberg, Charles Byron *lawyer*
Ruttenberg, Stanley Harvey *economist*
Ruttinger, George David *lawyer*
Ruwe, Robert P. *federal judge*
Ryan, David Alan *computer specialist*
Ryan, Frederick Joseph, Jr. *lawyer, public official*
Ryan, Jerry William *lawyer*
Ryan, Joseph *lawyer*
Ryan, Mary A. *diplomat*
Ryerson, Paul Sommer *lawyer*
Ryn, Claes Gösta *political science educator, author, research institute administrator*
Sabo, Martin Olav *congressman*
Sabshin, Melvin *psychiatrist, educator, medical association administrator*
Sacher, Steven Jay *lawyer*
Sachs, Stephen Howard *lawyer*
Sacksteder, Frederick Henry *former foreign service officer*
Safire, William *journalist, author*
Sagalkin, Sanford *lawyer*
Sagawa, Shirley Sachi *lawyer*
St. John, Adrian, II *retired army officer*
Salamon, Linda Bradley *university administrator, English literature educator*
Salant, Walter S. *economist*
Salem, George Richard *lawyer*
Salhani, Claude *photojournalist*
†Salisbury, Dallas L. *research institute administrator*
Salmon, Matt *congressman*
Salmon, William Cooper *mechanical engineer, engineering academy executive*
Saloom, Joseph A., III *diplomat*
Salop, Steven Charles *economics educator*
Saltzburg, Stephen Allan *law educator, consultant*
Samaniego Breach, Norma *Mexican government official*
Samartini, James Rogers *retired appliance company executive*
Samet, Andrew *government official*
Samet, Kenneth Alan *hospital administrator*
Samman, George *obstetrician, gynecologist*
Sampas, Dorothy M. *government official*
Sampson, Daphne Rae *library director*
Samuel, Howard David *union official*
Samuelson, Kenneth Lee *lawyer*
†Sanchez, Loretta *congresswoman*
Sandefur, James Tandy *mathematics educator*
Sanders, Bernard (Bernie Sanders) *congressman*
Sanderson, Fred Hugo *economist*
Sanderson, Jerome Alan *survey statistician, accountant*
Sandler, Bernice Resnick *women's rights specialist*
Sandler, Sumner Gerald *medical educator*
†Sandlin, Max Allen, Jr. *congressman*
Sandstrom, Sven *federal agency administrator*
Sanford, Bruce William *lawyer*
Sanford, Marshall (Mark Sanford) *congressman*
San Martin, Robert L. *federal official*
Santa, Donald F., Jr. *federal agency administrator*
Santorum, Rick *senator*
Santos, Leonard Ernest *lawyer*
Saperstein, Marc Eli *religious history educator, rabbi*
Sapienza, John Thomas *lawyer*
Sarbanes, Paul Spyros *senator*
Sass, Neil Leslie *toxicologist*
Sattler, Stephen Charles *writer, editor, communications consultant*
Sauntry, Susan Schaefer *lawyer*
Savage, Phillip Hezekiah *federal agency administrator*
Sawhill, Isabel Van Devanter *economist*
Saworotnow, Parfeny Pavlovich *mathematician, educator*
Sawyer, Thomas C. *congressman*
Saxton, H. James *congressman*
Saxton, James *congressman*
Sayre, Robert Marion *ambassador*
Sazima, Henry John *oral and maxillofacial surgery educator*

Scalia, Antonin *United States supreme court justice*
Scanlon, Terrence Maurice *public policy foundation administrator*
Scarborough, Joe *congressman*
Scarbrough, Frank Edward *government official*
Schad, Theodore MacNeeve *science research administrator, consultant*
Schaefer, Dan L. *congressman*
†Schaefer, James Lee *television news producer*
Schaffer, Robert (Bob Schaffer) *congressman*
Schall, Alvin Anthony *federal judge*
Schaller, James Patrick *lawyer*
Schapiro, Mary *federal agency administrator, lawyer*
Schechter, Geraldine Poppa *hematologist*
Scheibel, James Allen *volunteer service executive*
Scheibel, Kenneth Maynard *journalist*
Schenker, Carl Richard, Jr. *lawyer*
Scheppach, Raymond Carl, Jr. *association executive, economist*
Scheraga, Joel Dov *economist*
Schick, Michael William *public relations consultant*
Schiff, Margaret Scott *newspaper publishing executive*
Schiff, Stefan Otto *zoologist, educator*
Schiff, Steven Harvey *congressman, lawyer*
Schiffer, Lois Jane *lawyer*
Schifter, Richard *lawyer, government official*
Schlagel, Richard H. *philosophy educator*
Schlesinger, B. Frank *architect, educator*
Schlesinger, James Rodney *economist*
Schley, Wayne Arthur *political consultant*
Schlickeisen, Rodger Oscar *non-profit environmental organization executive*
Schloss, Howard Monroe *federal agency administrator*
Schlossberg, Stephen I. *management consultant*
Schluter, Gerald Emil *economist*
Schmeltzer, Edward *lawyer*
Schmidt, Berlie Louis *agricultural research administrator*
Schmidt, Richard Marten, Jr. *lawyer*
Schmidt, William Arthur, Jr. *lawyer*
Schneider, Mark Lewis *government official*
Schneider, Matthew Roger *lawyer*
Schneiter, George Robert *government executive*
Schoenberg, Mark George *government agency administrator*
Schoenberger, James Edwin *federal agency administrator*
Schorr, Lisbeth Bamberger *child and family policy analyst, author, educator*
Schram, Martin Jay *journalist*
Schriever, Bernard Adolph *management consultant*
Schroeder, Fredric Kauffmann *federal commissioner*
Schroeder, Patricia Scott (Mrs. James White Schroeder) *former congresswoman*
Schroeder, Paul Herman *entomologist*
Schropp, James Howard *lawyer*
Schubert, Richard Francis *consultant*
Schultze, Charles Louis *economist, educator*
Schumaker, James Frederick *foreign service officer*
Schumer, Charles Ellis *congressman*
Schwaab, Richard Lewis *lawyer, educator*
Schwartz, Amy Elizabeth *editorial writer, columnist*
Schwartz, Daniel C. *lawyer*
Schwartz, Richard Brenton *English language educator, university dean, writer*
Schwartz, Victor Elliot *lawyer*
Schwartzman, Andrew Jay *lawyer*
Schwelb, Frank Ernest *federal judge*
†Sconyers, Ronald T. *career officer*
Scott, Edward Philip *lawyer*
Scott, Gary Thomas *historian*
Scott, Helen Kinard *corporate executive*
Scott, Irene Feagin *federal judge*
Scott, Joyce Alaine *university official*
Scott, Raymond Peter William *chemistry research educator, writer*
Scott, Robert Cortez *congressman, lawyer*
Scott, Thomas Jefferson, Jr. *lawyer, electrical engineer*
Scott-Finan, Nancy Isabella *government administrator*
†Scouten, Rex W. *curator*
Scowcroft, Brent *retired air force officer, government official*
Scully, Malcolm Griffin *editor, writer*
Sczudlo, Raymond Stanley *lawyer*
Seale, William Edward *finance educator*
Searing, Marjory Ellen *government official, economist*
Sears, John Patrick *lawyer*
Sears, Mary Helen *lawyer*
Seats, Peggy Chisolm *marketing executive*
Seck, Mamadou Mansour *ambassador, career officer*
Segal, Donald E. *lawyer*
Seidel, Milton Joseph *government administrator*
Seidman, Ellen Shapiro *lawyer, government official*
Seidman, L(ewis) William *television commentator*
Seitz, Patricia Ann *lawyer*
Seldman, Neil Norman *cultural organization administrator*
Selin, Ivan *entrepreneur*
Sellin, Theodore *foreign service officer, consultant*
Semler Strong, Margot *association administrator*
†Seneff, Michael Geren *anesthesiologist*
Sensenbrenner, Frank James, Jr. *congressman, lawyer*
Sentelle, David Bryan *federal judge*
Serafin, Barry D. *television news correspondent*
Serrano, Jose E. *congressman*
Sessions, Jefferson Beauregard, III *senator*
Sessions, Roy Brumby *otolaryngologist, educator*
Sethness, Charles Olin *international financial official*
Sever, Tom *labor union administrator*
Severino, Roberto *foreign language educator, academic administration executive*
Shadegg, John B. *congressman*
Shafer, Raymond Philip *lawyer, business executive*
Shaffer, David James *lawyer*
Shaffer, Jay Christopher *lawyer*
Shaheen, Michael Edmund, Jr. *lawyer, government official*
Shah-Jahan, M. M. *economist*
Shalala, Donna Edna *federal official, political scientist, educator, university chancellor*
Shales, Thomas William *writer, journalist, television and film critic*
Shalowitz, Erwin Emmanuel *civil engineer*
Shanahan, Sheila Ann *pediatrician, educator*
Shank, Fred Ross *federal agency administrator*
Shanks, Hershel *editor, writer*
Shanks, Judith Weil *editor*
Shannon, Donald Hawkins *retired newspaperman*
Shapiro, George Howard *lawyer*
Shapiro, Michael Henry *government executive*
Shapiro, Paul Sauveur *chemical engineer, researcher*
Shapiro, Walter Elliot *political columnist*

Sharma, Dharmendra K. *federal agency administrator, electrical engineer*
Sharpe, Rochelle Phyllis *journalist*
Shattuck, John *federal official*
Shaw, Anesther O(live) *university administrative staff member*
Shaw, Bernard *television journalist*
Shaw, E. Clay, Jr. (Clay Shaw) *congressman*
Shaw, Gaylord *newspaper executive*
Shaw, Russell Burnham *author, journalist*
Shaw, William Frederick *statistician*
Shays, Christopher *congressman*
Shea, Donald William *career officer*
Shearer, Paul Scott *government relations professional*
†Sheehan, John J. *career officer*
Sheehan, Michael Terrence *arts administrator, historian, consultant*
Sheehan, Neil *reporter, scholarly writer*
Shelby, Richard Craig *senator, former congressman*
Shelley, Herbert Carl *lawyer*
Shenefield, John Hale *lawyer*
Shepard, Julian Leigh *lawyer, humanitarian*
Shepherd, Alan J. *construction executive, management consultant*
Sherer, Samuel Ayers *lawyer, urban planning consultant*
†Sherman, Bradley James *congressman*
Sherman, Charles Edwin *broadcasting executive, educator*
Sherzer, Harvey Gerald *lawyer*
Shestack, Alan *museum administrator*
Shihata, Ibrahim Fahmy Ibrahim *development banker, lawyer*
†Shimkus, John Mondy *congressman*
Shine, Kenneth Irwin *cardiologist, educator*
Shinn, David Hamilton *diplomat*
Shinolt, Eileen Thelma *artist*
Shlaudeman, Harry Walter *retired ambassador*
Shniderman, Harry Louis *lawyer*
Shogan, Robert *news correspondent*
Shon, Frederick John *nuclear engineer*
Shosky, John Edwin *communications consultant, speechwriter*
Shribman, David Marks *editor*
Shrier, Adam Louis *investment firm executive*
Shrier, Diane Kesler *psychiatrist*
Shrinsky, Jason Lee *lawyer*
Shriver, Robert Sargent, Jr. *lawyer*
Shulman, Stephen Neal *lawyer*
†Shuman, Michael *think tank executive, attorney*
Shuman, Michael Harrison *lawyer, policy analyst*
Shumate, John Page *diplomat*
Shuster, Bud *congressman*
Sibolski, Elizabeth Hawley *academic administrator*
Siciliano, Rocco Carmine *institute executive*
Sidey, Hugh Swanson *correspondent*
Sidransky, Herschel *pathologist*
Siegel, Allen George *lawyer*
Siegel, Frederic Richard *geology educator*
Siegel, Lloyd Harvey *architect, real estate developer, consultant*
Siegel, Richard David *lawyer, former government official*
Siegel, Robert Charles *broadcast journalist*
Sierck, Alexander Wentworth *lawyer*
Sieverts, Frank Arne *association executive*
Siggins, Jack Arthur *librarian*
Silano, Robert Anthony *editor, defense analyst, educator*
Silberg, Jay Eliot *lawyer*
Silby, Donald Wayne *investment executive, entrepreneur*
Sills, Hilary H. *public relations executive*
Silver, Daniel B. *lawyer*
Silver, David *financial executive, lawyer*
Silver, Harry R. *lawyer*
Silver, Jonathan Moses *investment management executive*
Silverman, Alvin Michaels *public relations consultant*
Silverman, Marcia *public relations executive*
Simes, Dimitri Konstantin *international affairs expert and educator*
Simko, Jan *English and foreign language literature educator*
Simmons, Anne L. *federal official*
Simmons, Caroline Thompson *civic worker*
Simmons, Edwin Howard *marine corps officer, historian*
Simon, Gary Leonard *internist, educator*
Simon, Jeanne Hurley *federal commissioner*
Simon, Kenneth Mark *lawyer*
Simons, Barbara M. *lawyer*
Simons, Lawrence Brook *lawyer*
Simopoulos, Artemis Panageotis *physician, educator*
Simpson, Carole Estelle *broadcast journalist*
Simpson, Charles Reagan *retired judge*
Simpson, John M. *lawyer*
Simpson, Louis A. *insurance company executive*
Simpson, Michael Marcial *science specialist, consultant*
Sims, Joe *lawyer*
Sims, Robert Bell *professional society administrator, public affairs official, newspaper publisher*
Singer, Daniel Morris *lawyer*
Singer, Maxine Frank *biochemist, think tank executive*
Singer, Suzanne Fried *editor*
†Singerman, Phillip A. *federal agency administrator*
Singleton, Harry Michael *lawyer*
†Singley, George T., III *mechanical engineer, federal agency administrator*
Sinkford, Jeanne Craig *dentist, educator*
Sisco, Joseph John *management consultant, corporation director, educator, government official*
Sisisky, Norman *congressman, soft drink bottler*
Sivasubramanian, Kolinjavadi Nagarajan *neonatologist, educator*
Skaggs, David E. *congressman*
Skeen, Joseph Richard *congressman*
Skelton, Isaac Newton, IV (Ike Skelton) *congressman*
Skene, Neil *publishing executive*
Skidmore, Linda Carol *science and engineering program administrator, consultant*
Skinner, Robert Earle, Jr. *civil engineer, engineering executive*
Skol, Michael *management consultant*
Skolfield, Melissa T. *government official*
Skolnik, Merrill I. *electrical engineer*
Slagle, Larry B. *human resources specialist*
Slate, Martin Ira *pension benefit executive*
Slater, Cathryn Buford *federal agency administrator*
Slater, Doris Ernestine Wilke *business executive*
Slater, Rodney E. *federal official*
Slatkin, Leonard Edward *conductor, music director, pianist*
Slaughter, Louise McIntosh *congresswoman*

Slenker, Richard Dreyer, Jr. *broadcast executive*
Slocombe, Walter Becker *government official, lawyer*
Sloyan, Patrick Joseph *journalist*
Sly, Ridge Michael *physician, educator*
Small, Jennifer Jean *writer, journalist*
Smedley, Lawrence Thomas *retired organization executive*
Smith, Brian William *lawyer, former government official*
Smith, Bruce David *archaeologist*
Smith, Bruce R. *English language educator*
Smith, Christopher Henry *congressman*
†Smith, D. Adam *congressman*
Smith, Dallas R. *federal official*
Smith, Daniel Clifford *lawyer*
Smith, Dean *communications advisor, arbitrator*
Smith, Dwight Chichester, III *lawyer*
Smith, Elaine Diana *foreign service officer*
†Smith, Gordon Harold *senator*
Smith, Jack Carl *foreign trade consultant*
Smith, Jack Prescott *journalist*
Smith, Lamar Seeligson *congressman*
Smith, Lee Elton *surgery educator, retired military officer*
Smith, Linda A. *congresswoman, former state legislator*
Smith, Marshall Savidge *government official, academic dean, educator*
Smith, Nick *congressman, farmer*
Smith, Patricia Grace *government official*
Smith, Philip Meek *science policy consultant, writer*
Smith, Richard Melvyn *government official*
Smith, Robert Clinton *senator*
Smith, Roy Philip *judge*
Smith, Stephen Grant *journalist*
Smith, Stuart Seaborne *writer, government official, union official*
Smith, Wendy Haimes *federal agency administrator*
Smoot, Oliver Reed, Jr. *lawyer, trade association executive*
Smuckler, Ralph Herbert *university dean, political science educator*
Smyth, Nicholas Patrick D. *surgeon*
Smyth, Paul Burton *lawyer*
Smythe-Haith, Mabel Murphy *consultant on African economic development, speaker, writer*
Sneed, William R., III *lawyer*
Snow, Robert Anthony *journalist*
Snowbarger, Vincent Keith *congressman*
Snowden, Frank Martin, Jr. *classics educator*
Snowe, Olympia J. *senator*
†Snyder, Vic *physician, congressman*
Soderberg, David Lawrence *chemist*
Sohn, Louis Bruno *lawyer, educator*
Soldo, Beth Jean *demography educator, researcher*
†Soller, R. William *association executive, pharmacologist*
Solomon, Elinor Harris *economics educator*
Solomon, George M. *newspaper editor*
Solomon, Gerald Brooks Hunt *congressman*
Solomon, Henry *university dean*
Solomon, Richard Harvey *political scientist*
Solomon, Sean Carl *geophysicist, lab administrator*
Solomons, Mark Elliott *lawyer, art dealer*
Sombrotto, Vincent R. *postal union executive*
Somerville, Walter Raleigh, Jr. *government official*
Sommer, Alphonse Adam, Jr. *lawyer*
Sommerfelt, Soren Christian *foreign affairs, international trade consultant, former Norwegian diplomat, lawyer*
Sonde, Theodore Irwin *lawyer*
Sonnenfeldt, Helmut *former government official, educator, consultant, author*
Sonnenfeldt, Marjorie Hecht *public relations executive, consultant*
Sorensen, John Noble *mechanical and nuclear engineer*
Souder, Mark Edward *congressman*
Southwick, E. Michael *diplomat*
Spaeder, Roger Campbell *lawyer*
Spaeth, Steven Michael *lawyer*
Spagnolo, Samuel Vincent *internist, pulmonary specialist, educator*
Spangler, Scott Michael *private investor*
Specter, Arlen *senator*
Spector, Eleanor Ruth *government executive*
Spence, Floyd Davidson *congressman*
Spence, Sandra *professional administrator*
Spencer, Samuel *lawyer*
Sperling, Godfrey, Jr. *journalist*
†Spilhaus, Athelstan Frederick, Jr. *oceanographer, association executive*
SpillenKothen, Melissa J. *federal agency administrator*
Spink, Frank Henry, Jr. *association manager, publisher, urban planner*
Splete, Allen Peterjohn *association executive, educator*
Spoon, Alan Gary *communications and publishing executive*
Sporkin, Stanley *federal judge*
Spratt, John McKee, Jr. *congressman, lawyer*
Springer, Fred Everett *federal agency administrator*
Springer, James van Roden *lawyer*
Springer, Michael Louis *federal agency administrator*
Sprott, John T. *ambassador*
Staats, Elmer Boyd *foundation executive, former government official*
†Stabenow, Deborah Ann *congresswoman*
Stahr, Elvis J(acob), Jr. *lawyer, conservationist, educator*
Stamberg, Susan Levitt *radio broadcaster*
Stamm, Geoffrey Eaton *arts administrator*
Stanford, Dennis Joe *archaeologist, museum curator*
Stanley, Daniel Jean *geological oceanographer, senior scientist*
†Stanley, Elaine Gerber *government official*
Stanley, Timothy Wadsworth *economist*
Stansbury, Philip Roger *lawyer*
Stanwick, Tad *retired systems engineer*
Staples, Edward Taylor *reporter*
Stark, Fortney Hillman (Pete Stark) *congressman*
Stark, Nathan J. *medical administrator, consultant, lawyer*
Starr, Stephen Frederick *academic administrator, historian*
Starrs, James Edward *law and forensics educator, consultant*
Stauffer, Ronald Eugene *lawyer*
Stavrou, Nikolaos Athanasios *political science educator*
Stayin, Randolph John *lawyer*
Steadman, Charles Walters *lawyer, corporate executive, writer*
Steadman, John Montague *judge*
Stearn, Todd *federal government official*
Stearns, Clifford Bundy *congressman, business executive*

West, E. Joseph financial analyst, investment portfolio manager
West, Gail Berry lawyer
West, Marvin Leon managing editor
West, Robert MacLellan science education consultant
West, Togo Dennis, Jr. secretary of Army, former aerospace executive
West, W. Richard museum director
Westberg, John Augustin lawyer
Wetherill, George West geophysicist, planetary scientist
Wexler, Anne government relations and public affairs consultant
†Wexler, Robert congressman
Weyrich, Paul Michael political organizations executive
Whalen, Laurence J. federal judge
Wheeler, Thomas Edgar communications technology executive
Wheelock, Arthur Kingsland, Jr. art historian
Whelan, Roger Michael lawyer, educator
Whitaker, A(lbert) Duncan lawyer
†Whitcomb, Vanessa Lide editor
White, Byron R. former United States supreme court justice
White, Durie Neumann federal agency administrator
White, George government official, physical scientist
White, George Malcolm architect
†White, John federal agency administrator
White, John Arnold physics educator, research scientist
White, Lee Calvin lawyer
White, Margita Eklund television association executive
White, Martha Vetter allergy and immunology physician, researcher
White, Richard A. congressman
White, Robert M., II newspaper executive, editor, columnist
White, Robert Mayer meteorologist
White, Robert Roy chemical engineer
White, Roy Martin engineering manager
Whitfield, Edward (Wayne Whitfield) congressman
Whiting, Richard Albert lawyer
Whitmore, Frank Clifford, Jr. geologist
Whittlesey, Judith Holloway public relations executive
Wicker, Roger F. congressman
Wides, Burton V. lawyer
Widnall, Sheila Evans secreatry of the airforce, former aeronautical educator, former university official
Wiener, Jerry M. psychiatrist
Wiese, John Paul federal judge
Wilcher, Shirley J. lawyer
†Wilderotter, James Arthur lawyer
Wilensky, Gail Roggin economist
Wiley, Richard Emerson lawyer
Wilford, Bonnie Baird health policy specialist
Wilker, Lawrence J. performing arts association administrator
†Wilkerson, Thomas L. career military officer
Wilkinson, Ronald Sterne science administrator, environmentalist, historian
Will, George Frederick editor, political columnist, news commentator
Willard, Richard Kennon lawyer
Willauer, Whiting Russell consultant
Willging, Paul Raymond trade association executive
Williams, Anthony A. federal official
Williams, B. John, Jr. lawyer, former federal judge
Williams, Eddie Nathan research institution executive
Williams, John Edward lawyer
Williams, Karen Hastie lawyer, think tank executive
Williams, Kent Harlan coast guard officer
Williams, Lawrence Floyd conservation organization official
Williams, Margaret federal official
Williams, Maurice Jacoutot development organization executive
Williams, Neville international development organization executive
Williams, Paul retired federal agency administrator
Williams, Ronald L. pharmaceutical association executive
Williams, Stephen Fain federal judge
Williams, Thomas Raymond lawyer
Williams-Bridgers, Jacquelyn federal government official
Williamson, Richard Hall federal association executive
Williamson, Thomas Samuel, Jr. lawyer
Willis, Arnold Jay urologic surgeon, educator
Willis, Clayton broadcaster, author, corporation executive, former government official, educator, arts consultant, photojournalist, lecturer, author
Willmore, Robert Louis lawyer
Wilson, Carolyn Ross school administrator
Wilson, Charles (Charlie Wilson) former congressman
Wilson, Charles Haven lawyer
Wilson, Ewen Maclellan economist
Wilson, Gary Dean lawyer
Wilson, Glen Parten professional society administrator
Wilson, Norman Louis psychiatrist, educator
Wilson, William Stanley oceanographer
Wince-Smith, Deborah L. federal agency administrator
†Winch, Terence Patrick publications director, writer
Wine, L. Mark lawyer
Winneker, Craig Anthony journalist
Winokur, Robert S. federal agency administrator
Winslow, James David international trade analyst
Winston, Judith Ann lawyer
Winter, Douglas E. lawyer, writer
Winter, Harvey John government official
Winter, Roger Paul government official
Winter, Thomas Swanson editor, newspaper executive
†Winters, Sam federal agency administrator, lawyer
Wintrol, John Patrick lawyer
Wippel, John Francis philosophy educator
Wirth, Timothy Endicott federal official, former senator
Wirtz, William Willard lawyer
Wise, Robert Ellsworth, Jr. (Bob Ellsworth) congressman
Wise, Sandra Casber lawyer
Wiseman, Alan M(itchell) lawyer
Wiseman, Laurence Donald foundation executive
Wisner, Frank George ambassador
Wiss, Marcia A. lawyer
Witcover, Jules Joseph newspaper columnist, author
Withrow, Mary Ellen treasurer of United States
Withuhn, William Lawrence museum curator, railroad economics and management consultant
Witt, James Lee federal agency administrator
Wofford, Harris Llewellyn former senator, national service executive
Wogaman, John Philip minister, educator
Wolanin, Barbara Ann Boese art curator, art historian
Wolanin, Thomas Richard educator, researcher
Wolf, Frank R. congressman, lawyer
Wolfe, Leslie R. think-tank executive
Wolff, Alan William lawyer
Wolff, Elroy Harris lawyer
Wolff, Paul Martin lawyer
Wolin, Neal Steven lawyer
Wollenberg, J. Roger lawyer
Wolters, Curt Cornelis Frederik foreign service officer
Wood, John Martin lawyer
Woodall, Samuel Roy, Jr. trade association executive
Woodruff, Judy Carline broadcast journalist
Woodward, Robert Forbes retired government official, consultant
Woodward, Robert Upshur newspaper reporter, writer
Woodworth, Ramsey Lloyd lawyer
Woolsey, Lynn congresswoman
Woolsey, R. James lawyer
Woosley, Raymond pharmacology and medical educator
Work, Charles Robert lawyer
Work, Jane Magruder professional society administrator
Worsley, James Randolph, Jr. lawyer
Worthy, K(enneth) Martin lawyer
Worthy, Patricia Morris municipal official, lawyer
Wortley, George Cornelius government affairs consultant, investor
Wouk, Herman writer
Wraase, Dennis Richard utilities company executive, accountant
Wray, Robert lawyer
Wright, Lawrence A. federal judge
Wright, Thomas William Dunstan architect
Wright, Wiley Reed, Jr. lawyer, retired judge, mediator
Wruble, Bernhardt Karp lawyer
Wulf, William Allan computer information scientist, educator
Wurtzel, Alan Leon retail company executive
Wyatt, Richard Jed psychiatrist, educator
Wyden, Ron senator
Wynn, Albert Russell congressman
Wyss, John Benedict lawyer
Xue, Lan engineering educator
Yablon, Jeffery Lee lawyer
Yalowitz, Kenneth Spencer ambassador
Yardley, Jonathan journalist, columnist
Yarrow, Andrew Louis writer, journalist, educator, international relations consultant
Yates, John Melvin ambassador
Yates, Sidney Richard congressman, lawyer
Yatsevitch, Gratian Michael retired army officer, diplomat, engineer
Yellen, Janet Louise government official, economics educator
Yellen, John Edward archaeologist
Yerkes, David Norton architect
Yochelson, Ellis L(eon) paleontologist
Yock, Robert John federal judge
Yoder, Hatten Schuyler, Jr. petrologist
Yoder, Ronnie A. judge
Yost, Paul Alexander, Jr. foundation executive, retired coast guard officer
Young, C. W. (Bill Young) congressman
Young, Donald Alan physician
Young, Donald E. congressman
Young, Johnny foreign service officer
Young, Kenneth Evans educational consultant
Young, Peter Robert librarian
Young, Thomas Wade journalist
Youtcheff, John Sheldon physicist
Yulish, Charles Barry public affairs executive
Yurow, John Jesse lawyer
Yuspeh, Alan Ralph lawyer
Yzaguirre, Raul Humberto civil rights leader
Zaloznik, Arlene Joyce oncologist, army officer
Zausner, L. Andrew lawyer
Zax, Leonard A. lawyer
Zeifang, Donald P. lawyer
Zelnick, Carl Robert Congressional correspondent
Zenowitz, Allan Ralph government official
Zielinski, Paul Bernard grant program administrator, civil engineer
Ziglar, James W. former federal official, lawyer, investment banker
Zimmerman, Edwin Morton lawyer
Zimmerman, Hyman Joseph internist, educator
Zimmerman, Richard Gayford journalist
Zion, Roger H. consulting firm executive, former congressman
Zipp, Joel Frederick lawyer
Zirschky, John H. federal government official
Zobel, Rya Weickert federal judge
Zuckman, Harvey Lyle law educator
†Žužul, Miomir government official, psychologist, educator
Zweben, Murray lawyer, consultant

## FLORIDA

### Alachua
Dinculescu, Antonie chemical engineer, researcher
Gaines, Weaver Henderson lawyer
Gifford, George E. immunology and medical microbiology educator
Marston, Robert Quarles university president
Neubauer, Hugo Duane, Jr. software engineer
Schneider, Richard T(heodore) optics research executive, engineer
Thornton, J. Ronald technology center director

### Altamonte Springs
Dotts, Randall James physician associate
Harner, David Paul development administrator
Poland, Phyllis Elaine secondary school educator, consultant

### Amelia Island
Harman, John Robert, Jr. management consultant

### Anna Maria
Kaiser, Albert Farr diversified corporation executive

### Apopka
Brandner, John William publishing company executive, insurance company executive
Rufenacht, Roger Allen accounting educator
Webb, Erma Lee nurse educator

### Arcadia
Davis, Bruce Livingston, Jr. retired accountant
Kurtz, Myers Richard hospital administrator
Schmidt, Harold Eugene real estate company executive
Turnbull, David John (Chief Piercing Eyes-Penn) cultural association executive

### Archer
Lockwood, Rhonda J. mental health services professional

### Atlantic Beach
Buell, Victor Paul marketing educator, author, editor
Engelmann, Rudolph Herman electronics consultant
Hayward, John Tucker management consultant
Herge, Henry Curtis, Sr. education educator, dean emeritus
Walker, Richard Harold pathologist, educator

### Atlantis
Gough, Carolyn Harley library director
Minshall, Drexel David retired manufacturing company executive

### Aventura
Babson, Irving K. publishing company executive
Cerri, Robert Noel photographer
Fishman, Barry Stuart lawyer
Hyman, Milton dental educator
Kliger, Milton Richard financial services executive

### Avon Park
Cornelius, Catherine Petrey college president

### Babson Park
Cloud, Linda Beal retired secondary school educator
Morrison, Kenneth Douglas author, columnist

### Bal Harbour
Ash, Dorothy Matthews civic worker
Bernay, Betti artist
Hastings, Lawrence Vaeth lawyer, physician, educator
Horton, Jeanette municipal government official
Radford, Linda Robertson psychologist
Spiegel, Siegmund architect

### Bartow
Mercadante, Anthony Joseph special education educator
Wean, Karla Denise middle school educator, secondary education educator

### Bay Harbor Island
Rosenbluth, Morton periodontist, educator

### Bay Pines
Johnson, David Porter infectious diseases physician
Keskiner, Ali psychiatrist
Law, David Hillis physician
Robson, Martin Cecil surgery educator, plastic surgeon
Stewart, Jonathan Taylor psychiatrist, educator
Wasserman, Fred, III internist

### Belle Glade
Waddill, Van Hulen entomology educator

### Belleair
Lasley, Charles Haden cardiovascular surgeon, health and fitness consultant

### Belleair Beach
Fuentes, Martha Ayers playwright

### Beverly Hills
Larsen, Erik art history educator

### Boca Grande
Baldwin, William Howard lawyer, retired foundation executive
Brock, Mitchell lawyer
Dyche, David Bennett, Jr. management consultant
Geoghegan, John Joseph retired publisher
Nimitz, Chester William, Jr. manufacturing company executive
VanItallie, Theodore Bertus physician

### Boca Raton
Agler, Richard Dean rabbi
Albrecht, Arthur John advertising agency executive
Alvarado, Ricardo Raphael retired corporate executive, lawyer
Amen, Irving artist
Aranson, Michael J. lawyer
Arden, Eugene retired university provost
Arnold, Walter Martin vocational education educator
Arockiasamy, Madasamy engineering educator
Averett-Short, Geneva Evelyn college administrator
Bagdan, Gloria interior designer
Barker, Charles Thomas retired lawyer
Barnes, Donald Winfree financial services executive
Barton, William Blackburn retired lawyer
Beber, Robert H. lawyer, financial services executive
†Beck, Louis S. hotel executive
Blanton, Jeremy dance company director
Breslauer, Charles S. chemical company executive
Burns, Gerald Phillip higher education educator
Camilleri, Michael lawyer, educator
Cannon, Herbert Seth investment banker
Caputi, Marie Antoinette university official
Carraher, Charles Eugene, Jr. chemistry educator, university administrator
Catanese, Anthony James academic administrator
Cohn, Jess Victor psychiatrist
Collins, Robert Arnold English language educator
Costello, Albert Joseph chemicals executive
Deppe, Henry A. insurance company executive
Dorfman, Allen Bernard international management consultant
Dunhill, Robert W. advertising direct mail executive
Epstein, Barry R. public relations counselor
Erdman, Joseph lawyer
Evert, Christine Marie (Chris Evert) retired professional tennis player
†Faust, Charles hotel executive
Fels, Robert Alan psychotherapist
Fengler, John Peter television producer, director, advertising executive
Fetter, Richard Elwood retired industrial company executive
Feuerlein, Willy John Arthur economist, educator
Fey, Dorothy (Mrs. George Jay Fey) former association executive
Finegold, Ronald computer service executive
Finkl, Charles William, II geologist, educator
Frank, Stanley Donald publishing company executive
Friend, Harold Charles neurologist
Gold, Catherine Anne Dower music history educator
Goldman, Lisa Eachus health facility administrator
Gralla, Eugene natural gas company executive
Greenfield-Moore, Wilma Louise social worker, educator
Guglielmino, Lucy Margaret Madsen education educator, researcher, consultant
Guillama-Alvarez, Noel Jesus healthcare company executive
Han, Chingping Jim industrial engineer, educator
Hedrick, Frederic Cleveland, Jr. lawyer
Houraney, William George marketing and public relations executive
Ingwersen, Martin Lewis shipyard executive
Jaffe, Leonard Sigmund financial executive
Jessup, Jan Amis arts volunteer, writer
Jessup, Joe Lee business educator, management consultant
Johnson, James Robert ceramic engineer, educator
Johnson, Martin Allen publisher
Kassner, Herbert Seymore lawyer
†Keil, Charles Emanuel corporation executive
Kelley, Eugene John business educator
Keyes, Daniel author
Klein, Robert manufacturing company executive
Knudsen, Rudolph Edgar, Jr. insurance company executive
Kramer, Cecile E. retired medical librarian
Lagin, Neil property management executive, landscape designer, consultant
Landry, Michael Gerard investment company executive
Langbort, Polly retired advertising executive
Langfield, Helen Elion artist, radio commentator
Latané, Bibb social psychologist
Leahy, William F. insurance company executive, lawyer
Lerner, Theodore Raphael dentist
Levine, Irving Raskin news commentator, university dean, author, lecturer
Levitetz, Jeff food wholesaler
Lin, Y. K. engineer, educator
Lipsey, John C. (Jack Lipsey) insurance company executive
Lynn, Eugene Matthew insurance company executive
MacFarland, Richard B. lawyer
Martin, Alvin Charles lawyer
McLeod, John Wishart architect
McNulty, James Ergler finance educator
McQueen, Scott Robert broadcasting company executive
Miller, Eugene university official, business executive
Miller, Kenneth Roy management consultant
Miller, William library administrator
Mirkin, Abraham Jonathan surgeon
Monroe, William Lewis human resources executive
Murray, John Ralph former college president
Nanz, Robert Augustus biochemist
Natkin, Alvin Martin environmental company executive
Nolan, Lone Kirsten financial advisor
Ohlman, Douglas Ronald commodities and securities trader, investment consultant, lawyer
Ortlip, Mary Krueger artist
Ortlip, Paul Daniel artist
Perlick, Lillian counselor, therapist
Posner, Sidney advertising executive
Reid, George Kell biology educator, researcher, author
Reinstein, Joel lawyer
Resnick, Robert physicist, educator
Reynolds, George Anthony, Jr. engineering executive
Richardson, R(oss) Fred(erick) insurance executive
Rosner, M. Norton business systems and financial services company executive
Ross, Donald Edward university administrator
Ross, Fred Michael organic chemist
Rothbaum, Ira retired advertising and marketing executive
Rothberg, June Simmonds retired nursing educator, psychotherapist, psychoanalyst
Rukeyser, M. S., Jr. television consultant, writer
Russo, Kathleen Marie art educator
Saffir, Leonard public relations executive
Samuels, William Mason physiology association executive
Sarna, Nahum Mattathias biblical studies educator
Sena, John Michael insurance agent
Shane, Ronald financial company executive
Siegel, David Burton lawyer
Sigel, Marshall Elliot financial consultant
Silver, Samuel Manuel rabbi, author
Stein, Irvin orthopedic surgeon, educator
Tennies, Robert Hunter headmaster
Turano, Emanuel Nicolas architect
Turner, Lisa Phillips human resources executive
Wallis, John James (Jimmy Wallis) comedian, impressionist, ventriloquist, comedy writer, video production executive
Weissbach, Herbert biochemist
Weitzman, Allan Harvey lawyer
Wiesenfeld, John Richard chemistry educator
Williams, Charlotte Evelyn Forrester civic worker
Wolgin, David Lewis psychology educator
Wyatt, James Luther drapery hardware company executive
Zuckerman, Sidney retired allergist, immunologist

### Bonita Springs
Birky, John Edward banker, consultant, financial advisor
Dacey, George Clement retired laboratory administrator, consultant
Johnson, Franklyn Arthur academic administrator
McDonald, Jacquelyn Milligan parent and family studies educator
Olander, Ray Gunnar retired lawyer
Payne, Alma Jeanette English language educator, author
St. Mary, Edward Sylvester direct mail marketing company executive
Sargent, Charles Lee manufacturing company executive

Snedden, James Douglas *retired health service management consultant*
Trudnak, Stephen Joseph *landscape architect*

### Bowling Green
Klein, Philip Howard *park ranger*

### Boynton Beach
Allison, Dwight Leonard, Jr. *investor*
Armstrong, Jack Gilliland *lawyer*
Babler, Wayne E. *retired telephone company executive, lawyer*
Balis, Moses Earl *biochemist, educator*
Bartholomew, Arthur Peck, Jr. *accountant*
Beisel, Daniel Cunningham *former newspaper publisher*
Birkenstock, Joyce Ann *artist*
Bloede, Victor Gustav *retired advertising executive*
Bryant, Donald Loyd *insurance company executive*
Caras, Joseph Sheldon *life insurance company executive*
Farace, Virginia Kapes *librarian*
Fields, Theodore *consulting medical radiation physicist*
Ganz, Samuel *human resource and management professional*
Geltner, Sharon *communications executive*
Heckelmann, Charles Newman (Charles Lawton) *author, publishing consultant*
Jacobs, C. Bernard *banker*
Jensen, Reuben Rolland *former automotive company executive*
Johnson, Edward A. *manufacturing executive*
Klein, Bernard *publishing company executive*
Koteen, Jack *management consultant, writer*
Kronman, Joseph Henry *orthodontist*
Leonard, Edward Paul *naval officer, dentist, educator*
Miller, Emanuel *retired lawyer, banker*
Mirman, Irving R. *scientific adviser*
Mittel, John J. *economist, corporate executive*
Oliveti, Susan Gail *sales promotion and public relations executive*
Pataky, Paul Eric *ophthalmologist*
Peltzie, Kenneth Gerald *hospital administrator, educator*
Rogers, John S. *retired union official*
Saxbe, William Bart *lawyer, former government official*
Smith, Charles Henry, Jr. *industrial executive*
Spannuth, John Roy *aquatics association executive*
Stubbins, Hugh A(sher), Jr. *architect*
Zarwyn, Berthold *physical scientist*

### Bradenton
Barnebey, Mark Patrick *lawyer*
Beall, Robert Matthews, II *retail chain executive*
Blancett, Suzanne Smith *editor-in-chief*
Brown, David Edward *elementary and environmental education educator*
Crouthamel, Thomas Grover, Sr. *editor*
Doenecke, Carol Anne *artist*
Feeley, John Paul *retired paper company executive*
Friedrich, Robert Edmund *retired electrical engineer, corporate consultant*
Godfrey, Paul *publisher*
Hodgell, Robert Overman *artist, art educator*
Jones, Horace Charles *former sales company executive*
Keane, Gustave Robert *architect, consultant*
Lengyel, Alfonz *art history, archeology and museology educator*
Mandell, Marshall *physician, allergist, consultant*
Maynard, Donald Nelson *horticulturist, educator*
McFarland, Richard Macklin *retired journalist*
McGarry, Marcia Langston *community service coordinator*
Pedersen, Norman Arno, Jr. *retired headmaster, literary club director*
Phelan, John Densmore *insurance executive, consultant*
Powers, Dudley *musician*
Price, Edgar Hilleary, Jr. *business consultant*
Reagan, Larry Gay *dean*
Robinson, Hugh R. *retired marketing executive*
Thompson, Barbara Storck *state official*
White, Dale Andrew *journalist*
Woodson-Howard, Marlene Erdley *former state legislator*

### Brandon
Blomgren, David Kenneth *dean, pastor*
Curry, Clifton Conrad, Jr. *lawyer*
Lafferty, Beverly Lou Brookover *retired physician, consultant*
Mussenden, Gerald *psychologist*
Williamson, Robert Charles *marketing executive*

### Brooksville
Anderson, Richard Edmund *city manager, management consultant*
Hetrick, Charles Brady *county official*
Manieri-Harvey, Michele Dawn *musician, educator*
Warsick-Rinzivillo, Mary Katrina *counselor, educator*

### Bryceville
Tippins, Susan Smith *elementary school principal*

### Bushnell
Hagin, T. Richard *lawyer*

### Cape Canaveral
Bell, James Bacon *business executive*

### Cape Coral
Andert-Schmidt, Darlene *management consultant and trainer*
Lane, William C., Jr. *principal*
Mair, Bruce Logan *interior designer, company executive*
Martin, Benjamin Gaufman *ophthalmologist*
Peters, Donald Cameron *construction company executive*
Purdy, Alan Harris *biomedical engineer*
Smith, Bruce William *safety engineer*
West, John Merle *retired physicist, nuclear consultant*

### Captiva
Fadiman, Clifton *writer, editor, radio and television entertainer*
Ronald, Peter *utility executive*

### Casselberry
Medin, A. Louis *computer company executive*

### Cedar Key
Starnes, Earl Maxwell *urban and regional planner, architect*

### Chattahoochee
Ivory, Peter B. C. B. *medical administrator*

### Chuluota
Hatton, Thurman Timbrook, Jr. *retired horticulturist, consultant*
McClintic, Fred Frazier *simulation engineer*

### Clearwater
Bairstow, Frances Kanevsky *labor arbitrator, mediator, educator*
Benavente, Javier Edgar *engineering executive*
Bertram, Frederic Amos *architect*
Birmingham, Richard Gregory *lawyer*
Blakely, John T. *lawyer*
Bokor, Bruce H. *lawyer*
Bramante, Pietro Ottavio *physiology educator, retired pathology specialist*
Byrd, Mary Laager *animal scientist, researcher, consultant*
Campolettano, Thomas Alfred *government contract manager*
Caronis, George John *insurance executive*
Chamberlin, Terry McBride *sailing equipment company executive*
Conetta, Tami Foley *lawyer*
Darack, Arthur J. *editor*
Dexter, Helen Louise *dermatologist, consultant*
Donahue, Katherine Mary *sales executive*
Dukore, Bernard Frank *theatre arts and humanities educator, writer*
Eshenbaugh, William Arthur *sales executive*
Falkner, William Carroll *lawyer*
Fenderson, Caroline Houston *psychotherapist*
Free, E. LeBron *lawyer*
Fromhagen, Carl, Jr. *obstetrician, gynecologist*
Gassman, Alan Scott *lawyer*
Gibson, Barbara Arlene *nurse, writer*
Greengold, Julian Bart *physician*
Hallam, Arlita Warrick *library system administrator*
Hoel, Robert Fredrick, Jr. *construction executive, civil engineer*
Hoornstra, Edward H. *retail company executive*
Horowitz, Harry I. *podiatrist*
Houtz, Duane Talbott *hospital administrator*
Howes, James Guerdon *airport director*
Jacobs, Marilyn Arlene Potoker *gifted education educator, consultant, author*
Jenkins, Linda Diane *accountant*
Johnson, Timothy Augustin, Jr. *lawyer*
Klingbiel, Paul Herman *information science consultant*
Leeds, Robert Lewis, Jr. *marketing and management educator*
Lokys, Linda J. *dermatologist*
Loos, Randolph Meade *financial planner*
Mattice, Howard LeRoy *education educator*
Maxwell, Richard Anthony *retail executive*
McAllister, Charles John *nephrologist, medical administrator*
Pendleton, Sumner Alden *financial consultant*
Peterson, James Robert *retired engineering psychologist*
Pope, Fred Wallace, Jr. *lawyer*
Puckett, Stanley Allen *consultant, realtor, marketing-management educator*
Raymund, Steven A. *computer company executive*
Rose, Susan Carol *restaurant executive, chef, consultant*
Scarne, John *game company executive*
Smith, Marion Pafford *avionics company executive*
Soechtig, Jacqueline Elizabeth *telecommunications executive*
Sontag, Peter Michael *travel management company executive*
Stilwell, Charlotte Finn *vocational counselor*
Tragos, George Euripedes *lawyer*
Turley, Stewart *retired retail company executive*
Van Dine, Paul Edwin *clergyman*
VanMeer, Mary Ann *publisher, writer, researcher*
Weidemeyer, Carleton Lloyd *lawyer*
Werner, Elizabeth Helen *librarian, Spanish language educator*
Wheat, Myron William, Jr. *cardiothoracic surgeon*
Whedon, George Donald *medical administrator, researcher*
Youngberg, Robert Stanley *principal, consultant*

### Clermont
Dyson, Raymond Clegg *building contractor, construction consultant*

### Cocoa
Hutton, Michael Thomas *planetarium and observatory administrator*
Parker, Mary Patrice *management consultant*

### Cocoa Beach
Choromokos, James, Jr. *former government official, consultant*
Gunn, Kenneth David *explosives safety specialist, consultant*
Pearson, Patricia Kelley *marketing representative*

### Coconut Creek
Cazes, Jack *chemist, marketing consultant, editor*
Godofsky, Stanley *lawyer*

### Coconut Grove
Alschuler, Al *freelance writer, public relations counselor*
Arboleya, Carlos Joaquin *lawyer, broker*
Cotton, John Pierce *principal*
Denaro, Gregory *lawyer*
McAmis, Edwin Earl *lawyer*

### Coleman
Crenshaw, Tena Lula *librarian*

### Coral Gables
Arcos, Cresencio S. *ambassador*
Baddour, Raymond Frederick *chemical engineer, educator, entrepreneur*
Bannard, Walter Darby *artist, art critic*
Bishopric, Susan Ehrlich *public relations executive*
Blumberg, David *builder, developer*
Burini, Sonia Montes de Oca *apparel manufacturing and public relations executive*
Chabrow, Sheila Sue *English language educator*
Criss, Cecil M. *chemistry educator*
Davis, Mattie Belle Edwards *retired county judge*
Einspruch, Norman Gerald *physicist, educator*
Eisner, Peter Norman *journalist, author, news agency executive*
Ely, John Hart *lawyer, university dean*
Groover, Sandra Mae *retail executive*
Hammes, Therese Marie (Terry) *advertising, public relations and marketing executive*
Hertz, Arthur Herman *business executive*
Hertz, David Bendel *management consultant, educator, lawyer*
Higginbottom, Samuel Logan *retired aerospace company executive*
Hoffman, Carl H(enry) *lawyer*
Howard, Bernard Eufinger *mathematics and computer science educator*
Jury, Eliahu Ibraham *electrical engineer, research educator*
Kirsner, Robert *language educator*
Kline, Jacob *biomedical engineering educator*
Kniskern, Joseph Warren *lawyer*
Lampert, Wayne Morris *corporate financier*
Leblanc, Roger Maurice *chemistry educator*
Lemos, Ramon Marcelino *philosophy educator*
Lott, Leslie Jean *lawyer*
McCarthy, Patrick A. *English language educator*
Moss, Ambler Holmes, Jr. *academic administrator, educator, lawyer, former ambassador*
Nunez-Portuondo, Ricardo *investment company executive*
Parry, Barbara Drepperd *educational administrator*
Perez, Josephine *psychiatrist, educator*
Quillian, Warren Wilson, II *pediatrician, educator*
Ramsey, John Hansberry *executive search firm executive, investment banker*
Rodgers, Frank *librarian*
Rosenn, Keith Samuel *lawyer, educator*
Saffir, Herbert Seymour *structural engineer, consultant*
Shipley, Vergil Alan *political science educator*
Speiller-Morris, Joyce *English composition educator*
Sumanth, David Jonnakoty *industrial engineer, educator*
Warburton, Ralph Joseph *architect, engineer, planner, educator*
Yarger, Sam Jacob *dean, educator*
Young, Tzay Y. *electrical and computer engineering educator*

### Coral Springs
Andrews, George Andreas *cardiologist*
Bartolotti, Jossif Peter *nutritionist, psychoanalyst, research scientist, educator*
Burg, Ralph *art association executive*
Caserta, Jean Kilsheimer *elementary education educator, family counselor*
Elmore, Walter A. *electrical engineer, consultant*
Heydet, Nathalie Durbin *gifted and talented education educator*
Luing, Gary Alan *financial management educator*
Polin, Alan Jay *lawyer*
Sommerer, John *accountant*
Valasquez, Joseph Louis *industrial engineer*
Wilson, Arthur Jess *psychologist, educator*

### Crystal River
Black, Charles Alvin *consulting engineering executive*

### Dade City
Burdick, Glenn Arthur *physicist, engineering educator*
†Feld, Harvey Joel *pathologist*
McBath, Donald Linus *osteopathic physician*

### Dania
Abbott, Linda Joy *stained glass artisan, educator*
Dodge, Richard Eugene *oceanographer, educator, marine life administrator*
Vecci, Raymond Joseph *airline industry consultant*

### Davie
Emtman, Steven Charles *professional football player*
Johnson, Jimmy *professional football coach*
†Jones, Eddie J. *professional football team executive*
Shula, Don Francis *former professional football coach, team executive*
Wong, Antonio Ham *family physician*

### Daytona Beach
Alcott, Amy Strum *professional golfer*
Amick, William Walker *golf course architect*
†Benson, Johnny *professional race car driver*
†Bodine, Brett *professional race car driver*
†Bodine, Geoff *professional race car driver*
Bronson, Oswald Perry *religious organization administrator, clergyman*
†Burton, Brandie *professional golfer*
Cardwell, Harold Douglas, Sr. *rehabilitation specialist*
Carmona, José Antonio *Spanish language educator, English language educator*
Chesnut, Nondis Lorine *writer, consultant, reading educator*
Collyer, Robert B. *trade association administrator*
Cool, Mary L. *elementary education educator*
†Craven, Ricky *professional race car driver*
Davidson, Herbert M. (Tippen), Jr. *newspaper publisher*
Di Nicolo, Roberto *allergist*
Duma, Richard Joseph *microbiologist, physician, pathologist, researcher, educator*
Earnhardt, (Ralph) Dale *professional race car driver*
Elliott, Carol Harris *nutrition counselor, dietitian*
Furstman, Shirley Elsie Daddow *advertising executive*
Gardner, Joseph Lawrence *editor, writer*
Gauch, Eugene William, Jr. *former air force officer*
Geier, George *optical engineering consultant*
Goldberg, Paul Bernard *gastroenterologist, clinical researcher*
Gordon, Jeff *race car driver*
Inkster, Juli *professional golfer*
†Irvan, Ernie (Swervin' Irvan) *professional race car driver*
†Jarrett, Dale *professional race car driver*
Keene, Douglas Ralph *diplomat*
King, Betsy *professional golfer*
†Klein, Emilee *professional golfer*
†Labonte, Bobby *professional race car driver*
†Labonte, Terry *professional race car driver*
Libby, Gary Russell *museum director*
Locke, Edwin Allen, Jr. *investment banker*
Mallon, Meg *professional golfer*
Marlin, Sterling *professional race car driver*
†Martin, Mark *professional race car driver*
Mc Collister, John Charles *writer, clergyman, educator, executive producer*
McCoy, Edward Fitzgerald *social services facility administrator*
†McGann, Michelle *professional golfer*
Millar, Gordon Halstead *mechanical engineer, agricultural machinery manufacturing executive*
Mochrie, Dottie *professional golfer*
Neitzke, Eric Karl *lawyer*
†Neumann, Liselotte *professional golfer*
†O'Reilly, Don *reporter, writer, photographer*
Osterholm, J(ohn) Roger *humanities educator*
Petty, Kyle *professional stock car driver*
Reeves, Donna Andrews *golfer*
†Ritts, Jim *professional sports team executive*
†Rudd, Ricky *professional race car driver*
St. James, Lyn *business owner, professional race car driver*
Salter, Leo Guilford *mental health services professional*
†Schrader, Ken *professional race car driver*
Sheehan, Patty *professional golfer*
†Shepherd, Morgan *professional race car driver*
Simatos, Nicholas Jerry *aerospace company executive, consultant*
†Sorenstam, Annika *professional golfer*
†Speed, Lake *professional race car driver*
Stephenson, Jan Lynn *professional golfer*
Wallace, Rusty *race car driver*
†Webb, Karrie *professional golfer*
Wehner, Henry Otto, III *pharmacist, consultant*
Whitworth, Kathrynne Ann *professional golfer*
Yarborough, William Caleb *former professional stock car race driver*

### Deerfield Beach
Areskog, Donald Clinton *retired chiropractor*
Bettmann, Otto Ludwig *picture archivist, graphic historian*
Brown, Colin W(egand) *lawyer, diversified company executive*
Fosback, Norman George *stock market econometrician, researcher*
Hochberger, Simon *communications educator*
Moran, James M. *automotive sales executive*
Moran, Patricia Genevieve *corporate executive*
Rung, Richard Allen *lawyer, retired air force officer, retired educator*
Solomon, Barry Jason *healthcare administrator, consultant*
Treibl, Hans George *industrial chemist*
Van Arnem, Harold Louis *marketing professional*
Waldman, Alan I. (Alawana) *songwriter, composer, lyricist, computer programmer*

### Defuniak Springs
Karger, Delmar William *industrial engineering and management consultant*

### Deland
Brakeman, Louis Freeman *retired university administrator*
Coolidge, Edwin Channing *chemistry educator*
Dascher, Paul Edward *university dean, accounting educator*
Duncan, Pope Alexander *college administrator*
Fant, Clyde Edward, Jr. *religion educator*
Garcia, Mary Elizabeth *Spanish and English as second language educator*
Gill, Donald George *education educator*
Horton, Thomas R. *business advisor*
Langston, Paul T. *music educator, university dean, composer*
Lee, Howard Douglas *academic administrator*
MacMahon, Charles Hutchins, Jr. *architect*
Morland, Richard Boyd *retired educator*
Sorensen, Jacki Faye *choreographer, aerobic dance company executive*
Tedros, Theodore Zaki *educator, real estate broker, appraiser*

### Delray Beach
Barlow, Joel *retired lawyer*
Blankenheimer, Bernard *economics consultant*
Bottner, Irving Joseph *cosmetic company executive*
Bryan, Robert Fessler *former investment analyst*
Burbank, Kershaw *writer*
Cary, James Donald *journalist*
Chavin, Walter *biological science educator and researcher*
Cohen, Stephen M(artin) *judge*
Coyle, William *educator*
Erenstein, Alan *emergency room nurse, medical education consultant, aeromedical specialist*
Fuente, D. I. *office supply manufacturing executive*
Gaffey, Thomas Michael, Jr. *consumer products executive*
Gatewood, Robert Payne *financial planning executive*
Goldenberg, George *retired pharmaceutical company executive*
Groening, William Andrew, Jr. *lawyer, former chemical company executive*
Hegstrom, William Jean *mathematics educator*
Himmelright, Robert John, Jr. *rubber company executive*
Knapp, Janis Ann *elementary school educator*
Larry, R. Heath *lawyer*
Levinson, Harry *psychologist, educator*
Mills, Agnes Eunice Karlin *artist, printmaker, sculptor*
Peoples, Thomas Edward *publisher, executive, writer*
Randall, Priscilla Richmond *travel executive*
Reef, Arthur *industry business consultant*
Rippeteau, Darrel Downing *architect*
Robinson, Richard Francis *writer, author*
Rosenfeld, Steven Ira *ophthalmologist*
Ross, Beatrice Brook *artist*
Saffer, Alfred *retired chemical company executive*
Salsberg, Arthur Philip *publishing company executive*
Shang, Charles Yulin *medical physicist*
Shister, Joseph *arbitrator, educator*
Shute, Melodie Ann *museum director*
Smith, Charles Oliver *engineer*
Smith, John Joseph, Jr. *textile company executive, educator*
Stewart, Patricia Carry *foundation administrator*

### Deltona
Neal, Dennis Melton *middle school educator*
Venuti, Ruth Louise *secondary school educator, counselor*

Zagnoli, Roland Candiano management and marketing consultant, pharmacist

### Destin
Asher, Betty Turner academic administrator
Carlton, Paul Kendall retired air force officer, consultant
Cunningham, James Everett retired energy services company executive
De Revere, David Wilsen professional society administrator
Horne, Thomas Lee, III entrepreneur

### Dover
Pearson, Walter Donald editor, columnist

### Dundee
Johnson, Gordon Selby consulting electrical engineer

### Dunedin
Bradley, Robert Lee surgeon
Espy, Charles Clifford English language educator, author, consultant, lecturer, administrator
Gambone, Victor Emmanuel, Jr. physician
Geer, James Hamilton retired broadcasting company executive
McIntosh, Roberta Eads retired social worker
Rosa, Raymond Ulric retired banker
Tweedy, Robert Hugh retired equipment company executive
Weber, Ellen Schmoyer pediatric speech pathologist

### Dunnellon
Dixon, W(illiam) Robert retired educational psychology educator

### Eglin AFB
Franzen, Larry William aerospace electronics engineer
Gal, Richard John industrial engineer
Head, William Christopher military officer, health care administrator
Smith, Sheila Diane medical transcriptionist
Stewart, J. Daniel air force development and test center administrator

### Englewood
Defliese, Philip Leroy accountant, educator
Korbuly, Laszlo John architect
Lahiff, Marilyn J. nursing administrator
Marchand, Leslie Alexis language educator, writer
Morphew, Dorothy Richards-Bassett artist, real estate broker
Schultz, Arthur Joseph, Jr. retired trade association executive
Simis, Theodore Luckey investment banker, information technology executive
Sisson, Robert F. photographer, writer, lecturer, educator

### Estero
Brush, George W. college president

### Eustis
Chorosinski, Eugene Conrad writer, poet, author
Pope, Theodore Campbell, Jr. utilities executive, consultant

### Fernandina
Manson, Keith Alan Michael lawyer

### Fernandina Beach
Barlow, Anne Louise pediatrician, medical research administrator
Burns, Stephen Redding golf course architect
D'Agnese, Helen Jean artist
Fishbaugh, Carole Sue secondary school educator
Hildebrand, Richard Allen retired bishop
Lilly, Wesley Cooper marine engineer, ship surveyor
Rogers, Robert Burnett naval officer

### Florida City
Valdes, Rolando Hector library director, law librarian

### Fort Lauderdale
Adams, Alfred Hugh college president
Adams, Daniel Lee lawyer
Adams, Kelly Lynn emergency physician
Aleff, Andrea Lee (Andy Aleff) newspaper editor
Alpert, Martin Jeffrey chiropractic physician
Anastasiou, Van E. lawyer
Andrews, John Harold health care administrator
Appel, Antoinette Ruth neuropsychologist
Azrin, Nathan Harold psychologist
Bamberg, Louis Mark estate planning specialist
Bartelstone, Rona Sue gerontologist
Becker, Edward A. accounting educator, consultant
Berwig, Newton Urbano aerospace executive
Bimstein, Benjamin William caterer, chef
Bird, Linda W. realtor
Bishop, George Williams, III supply company executive
Bogenschutz, J. David lawyer
Buckstein, Mark Aaron lawyer, educator
Buell, Rodd Russell lawyer
Bunnell, George Eli lawyer
Bustamante, Nestor lawyer
Carney, Dennis Joseph former steel company executive, consulting company executive
Carter, James Thomas contractor
Cash, Ralph Eugene psychologist
Caulkins, Charles S. lawyer
Clark, Desmond Laverne immigration legal secretary, editor, minister
†Clark, Mary Ellen Olympic athlete
†Cobb, David Keith business executive
Colsky, Andrew Evan lawyer, mediator, arbitrator
Cooney, David Francis lawyer
Costa, Robin Leueen psychologist, counselor
Cumerford, William Richard fund raising and public relations executive
Cummings, Virginia (Jeanne) retired real estate company executive
Daniel, Gerard Lucian physician, pharmaceutical company executive
Davis-Wexler, Ginia singer, association executive
Devol, George Charles, Jr. manufacturing executive
Dickinson, Richard landscape architect
Donoho, Tim Mark insurance and publishing executive
Dorn, Samuel O. endodontist
Dressler, Robert A. lawyer
Eisner, Will publishing company executive
Eynon, Steven Scott minister
Feld, Joseph construction executive
Ferguson, Wilkie D., Jr. federal judge
Fershleiser, Steven Buckler secondary education educator
Fine, Howard Alan travel industry executive
Fischler, Abraham Saul education educator, retired university president
Fitzpatrick, Mark professional hockey player
Flynn, Donald F. entertainment company executive
Forsyth, George Lionel psychotherapist, author
Gardner, Russell Menese lawyer
Garvin, Glenn venture capitalist
Gerbino, John advertising executive
Gerstner, Jonathan Neil religious studies educator
Gill, Carl Carter cardiothoracic surgeon
Gill, Richard Thomas opera singer, economic analyst
Gillam, Paula Sample artist, educator
Ginn, Vera Walker educational administrator
Golnick, Leon Shaffer advertising and marketing executive
Gonzalez, Jose Alejandro, Jr. federal judge
Goodstein, Richard George sales and management consultant
Greenberger, Sheldon Lee newspaper advertising executive
Gude, Nancy Carlson computer consultant
Gunzburger, Suzanne Nathan county commissioner, social worker
Hanbury, George Lafayette, II city manager
Hargrove, John Russell lawyer
Hartz, Deborah Sophia editor, critic
Hershenson, Miriam Hannah librarian
Hirsch, Jeffrey Allan lawyer
Hoefling, John Alan corporation executive, former army officer
Hoines, David Alan lawyer
Holland, Beth actress
Holtzman, Gary Yale administrative and financial executive
Honahan, H(enry) Robert motion picture theatre executive
Howard, William Matthew lawyer, business executive, arbitrator, author
Huizenga, Harry Wayne entrepreneur, entertainment corporation executive, professional sports team executive
James, Gordon, III lawyer
Joseph, Paul R law educator
Jotcham, Thomas Denis marketing communications consultant
Katz, Thomas Owen lawyer
Keats, Harold Alan corporate executive
Kemper Littman, Marlyn information scientist, educator
Kobert, Norman Noah asset management consultant
Koch, Katherine Rose communications executive
Kontos, George computer science educator
Krathen, David Howard lawyer
Kubler, Frank Lawrence lawyer
Kurzenberger, Dick health services executive
Lataif, Lawrence P. lawyer
LeRoy, Miss Joy model, designer
Levi, Kurt retired banker
Levy, Marvin David composer
Lipkin, David Lawrence physician
Lister, Mark Wayne clinical laboratory scientist
Lodwick, Gwilym Savage radiologist, educator
MacLean, Doug hockey coach
Martínez-Solanas, Gerardo Enrique reporting service reviser, writer
Maucker, Earl Robert newspaper editor, newspaper executive
Maulion, Richard Peter psychiatrist
Maurer, Yolanda Tahar publisher
Maxwell, Sara Elizabeth psychologist, educator, speech pathologist, director
McAusland, Randolph M. N. arts administrator
McCan, James Lawton education educator
McGinnis, Patrick Bryan mental health counselor
McIntyre, Charles Earl insurance executive
Meditz, Walter Joseph engineering consultant
Meeks, William Herman, III lawyer
Morse, Edward J. automotive executive
Moss, Stephen B. lawyer
Motes, Joseph Mark cruise and convention promotion company executive
Murray, Bryan Clarence professional sports team executive
Niehaus, Robert James investment banking executive
Nussbaum, Howard Jay lawyer
O'Bryan, William Monteith lawyer
Olen, Milton William, Jr. marketing executive
Ornstein, Libbie Allene primary school educator
Palmer, Marcia Stibal food and wine retailer, interior designer, real estate investor
Paulauskas, Edmund Walter real estate broker, retired
Perkel, Robert Simon photojournalist, educator
Pettijohn, Fred Phillips retired newspaper executive, consultant
Pohlman, Randolph A. business administration educator, dean
Randi, James (Randall James Hamilton Zwinge) magician, writer, educator
Raybeck, Michael Joseph surgeon
Reigrod, Robert Hull manufacturing executive
Rendon-Pellerano, Marta Ines dermatologist
Rentoumis, Ann Mastroianni psychotherapist
Richmond, Gail Levin law educator
Rider, Diane Elizabeth librarian
Riggs, Donald Eugene librarian, academic administrator
Rodriguez, Carlos Augusto lawyer
Roselli, Richard Joseph lawyer
Russo, Thomas Joseph hospitality and consumer durables industry executive
Sanders, Howard investment company executive
Sands, Roberta Alyse real estate investor
Schrader, Robert George lawyer
Schreiber, Alan Hickman lawyer
Schulte, Frederick James newspaper editor
Shaw, Bryan P. H. retired investment company executive
Sherman, Richard Allen lawyer
Shoemaker, William Edward financial executive
Singer, Donald Ivan architect
Skiddell, Elliot Lewis rabbi
Sklar, Alexander electric company executive
Smith, James Edward newspaper company executive
Soeteber, Ellen journalist, newspaper editor
Sorensen, Allan Chresten service company executive
Stone, Edward Durell, Jr. landscape architect and planner
Swiller, Randolph Jacob internist
Thayer, Charles J. investment banker
†Torrey, William Arthur professional hockey team executive
Turner, Hugh Joseph, Jr. lawyer
Tyson, Mike G. professional boxer
Van Alstyne, Judith Sturges English language educator, writer
Vanbiesbrouck, John professional hockey player
Van Howe, Annette Evelyn retired real estate agent
Vasquez, William Leroy marketing professional, educator
Vladem, Paul Jay investment advisor, broker
Walton, Rodney Earl lawyer
White, Mary Lou fundraiser, writer, educator
†Whitmore, Douglas Michael physician
Wojcik, Cass decorative supply company executive, former city official
Wynne, Brian James former association executive, consultant
Young, William Benjamin special education educator
Zikakis, John P. consultant, educator, researcher, biochemist
Zloch, William J. federal judge

### Fort Myers
Aleo, Joseph John pathology scientist, educator, academic research administrator
Allen, Richard Chester retired lawyer, educator
Anthony, Susan Mae entrepreneur
†Arnall, Robert Esric physician, medical administrator
Barbour, Hugh Revell book publisher
Barbour, William Rinehart, Jr. retired book publisher
Brown, Earl Kent historian, clergyman
Callanan, Kathleen Joan retired electrical engineer
Colgate, Doris Eleanor retailer, sailing school owner and administrator
Cooke, Joan Ellen healthcare executive, consultant
Cyphert, Frederick Ralph academic administrator
Dean, Jean Beverly artist
Fernandez, Laura Bove retired language educator
Frank, Elizabeth Ahls art educator, artist
Fromm, Winfield Eric retired corporate executive, engineering consultant and investor
Garside, Marlene Elizabeth advertising executive
Golian, Linda Marie librarian
Grove, William Johnson physician, surgery educator
Harmer, Rose marriage and family therapist, mental health counselor
Hoffman, Nelson Miles, Jr. retired academic administrator, consultant
Hudson, Leonard Harlow contractor
Jacobi, Fredrick Thomas newspaper publisher
Kareh, Ahmad Ragheb civil engineer
Koehler, Robert Brien priest
Laboda, Gerald oral and maxillofacial surgeon
Massa, Conrad Harry religious studies educator
Mc Grath, William Restore transportation planner, traffic engineer
Medvecky, Robert Stephen lawyer
Mergler, Harry Winston engineering educator
Missimer, Thomas Michael geologist
Moeschl, Stanley Francis electrical engineer, management consultant
Morse, John Harleigh lawyer
Newland, Jane Lou nursing educator
Norton, Elizabeth Wychgel lawyer
O'Dell, William Francis retired business executive, author
Ölling, Edward Henry aerospace engineer, consulting firm executive
Powell, Richard Pitts writer
Rachman, Bradley Scott chiropractic physician
Ranney, Mary Elizabeth business executive
Rogliano, Aldo Thomas publishing executive
Ryan, William Joseph communications company executive
Schwartz, Carl Edward artist, printmaker
Scott, Kenneth Elsner mechanical engineering educator
Sechrist, Chalmers Franklin, Jr. electrical engineering educator
Shafer, Robert Tinsley, Jr. judge
Simmons, Vaughan Pippen medical consultant
Steier, Michael Edward cardiac surgeon
Tyrer, John Lloyd retired headmaster
Wendeborn, Richard Donald retired manufacturing company executive
Whittaker, Douglas Kirkland school system adminstrator
Zupko, Arthur George consultant to drug industry, retired college administrator

### Fort Myers Beach
Caracciolo, Francis Samuel management consultant
Cotter, Richard Timothy lawyer
Waetjen, Walter Bernhard academic administrator emeritus

### Fort Pierce
Bynum, Henri Sue education and French educator
Calvert, David Victor soil science educator
Cassens, Susan Forget artist
Dusanek, Linda Sue municipal housing official
Garment, Robert James clergyman
Herd, Charmian June singer, actress
Hurley, William Joseph retired information systems executive
Norton, Robert Howard entertainer, musical arranger, author
Rice, Mary Esther biologist
Solon, Leonard R(aymond) physicist, educator, consultant
Thoma, Richard William chemical safety and waste management consultant
Wohlford, James Gregory pharmacist

### Fort Walton Beach
Cooke, Fred Charles real estate broker
Culver, Dan Louis federal agency administrator
†Day, George Everette lawyer, retired military officer
Gates, Philip Don anesthesiologist
Sanders, Jimmy Devon public administration and health services educator
Villecco, Judy Diana substance abuse, mental health counselor, director
Wyatt, Russell Scott optician

### Gainesville
Abbaschian, Reza materials science and engineering educator
Abbott, Thomas Benjamin speech educator
Agrios, George Nicholas plant pathology educator
Anderson, Richard McLemore internist
Anderson, Timothy J. chemical engineering educator
Andrew, Edward Raymond physicist
Anghaie, Samim nuclear engineer, educator
App, James Leonard educator
Baker, Bonnie Barbara mental health and school counselor, educator
Balabanian, Norman electrical engineering educator
Barber, Charles Edward newspaper executive, journalist
Barton, Allen Hoisington sociologist
Baughman, George Fechtig foundation executive
Bedell, George Chester retired publisher, educator, priest
Bednarek, Alexander Robert mathematician, educator
Behnke, Marylou neonatologist, educator
Bernard, H. Russell anthropology educator, scientific editor
Besch, Emerson Louis physiology educator, past academic administrator
Bishop, Budd Harris museum administrator
Block, Seymour Stanton chemical engineering educator, consultant, writer
Bodine, Willis Ramsey, Jr. music educator, organist
Bodor, Nicholas Stephen medicinal chemistry researcher, educator, consultant
Boyes, Patrice Flinchbaugh lawyer, environmental executive
Brown, Myra Suzanne librarian
Brown, William Samuel, Jr. communication processes and disorders educator
Bryan, Robert Armistead university administrator, educator
Burridge, Michael John veterinarian, educator, research administrator
Bzoch, Kenneth Rudolph speech and language educator, department chairman
Cantliffe, Daniel James horticulture educator
Capaldi, Elizabeth Ann Deutsch psychological sciences educator
Capehart, Barney Lee industrial and systems engineer
Carr, Glenna Dodson economics educator
Carr, Thomas Deaderick astronomer/physics educator, science administrator
Catasus, Jose Magin Perez school psychologist
Chait, Andrea Melinda special education educator
Challoner, David Reynolds university official, physician
Chapin, Kenneth Lee middle school educator
Cheek, Jimmy Geary university administrator, agricultural education and communications educator
Childers, Norman Franklin horticulture educator
Christie, Richard Gary plant pathologist
Clark, Elmer J. education educator
Cluff, Leighton Eggertsen physician
Coleman, Mary Stallings retired chief justice
Cooper, James Ralph engineering executive
Cousins, Robert John nutritional biochemist, educator
Crane, Beverly Rose counselor
Creel, Austin Bowman religion educator
Cristescu, Nicolaie D. engineering educator
Davidson, James Melvin academic administrator, researcher, educator
Davis, George Kelso nutrition biochemist, educator
Davis, Horance Gibbs, Jr. retired educator, journalist
Delfino, Joseph John environmental engineering sciences educator
Der-Houssikian, Haig linguistics educator
DeSimone, Rory Jean small business owner
Dewar, Michael James Steuart chemistry educator
Dewsbury, Donald Allen historian of psychology, comparative psychologist
Dickinson, Joshua Clifton, Jr. museum director, educator
Dilcher, David Leonard paleobotany educator, research scholar
Dinculeanu, Nicolae mathematician
Drago, Russell Stephen chemist, educator
Drucker, Daniel Charles engineer, educator
Drury, Kenneth Clayton biological scientist
Eder, George Jackson lawyer, economist
Edwardson, John Richard agronomist
Eichhorn, Heinrich Karl astronomer, educator, consultant
Elzinga, Donald Jack industrial engineering researcher, educator
Emch, Gerard Gustav mathematics and physics educator
Emch-Dériaz, Antoinette Suzanne historian, educator
Ernsberger, Fred Martin retired materials scientist
Eyler, Fonda Davis developmental psychologist
Felton, John Walter public relations executive
Fossum, Jerry George electrical engineering educator
Fournier, Donald Joseph, Jr. mechanical engineer, consultant
Freeland, James M. Jackson lawyer, educator
Gander, John Edward biochemistry educator
Gelband, Craig Harris physiologist, pharmacologist
Gerberg, Eugene Jordan entomologist
Goggin, Margaret Knox librarian, educator
Goldhurst, William retired humanities and English educator, writer
Gordon, Richard M. Erik retailing executive, educator
Gravenstein, Joachim Stefan anesthesiologist, educator
Green, Eleanor Myers veterinarian, educator
Greer, Melvin medical educator
Gutekunst, Richard Ralph microbiology educator
Haldeman, Joe William novelist
Hale, James Pierce education educator
Hanrahan, Robert Joseph chemist, educator
Hanson, Harold Palmer physicist, government official, editor, academic administrator
Haring, Ellen Stone (Mrs. E. S. Haring) philosophy educator
Harrer, Gustave Adolphus librarian, educator
Harrison, Willard W. chemist, educator
Heflin, Martin Ganier foreign service officer, international political economist
Henson, (Betty) Ann media specialist, educator
Heuer, Marvin Arthur physician, research and industry consultant
Himes, James Albert veterinary medicine educator emeritus
Holland, Norman Norwood literary critic
Hollien, Harry Francis speech and communications scientist, educator
Holloway, Paul Howard materials science educator
Holloway, Wade Justin civil engineer
Hope, George Marion vision scientist
Hornberger, Robert Howard psychologist
†Humphrey, Stephen college dean

Isaacs, Gerald William agricultural engineer, educator
Israel, Jerold Harvey law educator
Issacs, Gerald William retired agricultural engineering educator, consultant
Jacobs, Alan Martin physicist, educator
Javid, Nikzad Sabet dentist, prosthodontist educator
Jones, Elizabeth Nordwall county government official
Jones, Richard Lamar entomology educator
Katritzky, Alan Roy chemistry educator, consultant
Keesling, James Edgar mathematics educator
Kerslake, Kenneth Alvin artist, printmaker, art educator
Ketts, Sharon Davis elementary education educator
Kirkland, Nancy Childs secondary education educator, consultant
Klauder, John Rider physics educator
Kurzweg, Ulrich Hermann engineering science educator
Kushner, David Zakeri musicologist, educator
Law, Mark Edward electrical engineer, educator
Limacher, Marian Cecile cardiologist
Lindholm, Fredrik Arthur electrical engineering educator
Locascio, Salvadore Joseph horticulturist
Lombardi, John V. university administrator, historian
Lopez, Andy university athletic coach
Lowenstein, Ralph Lynn university dean emeritus
Malasanos, Lois Julanne Fosse nursing educator
Malvern, Lawrence Earl engineering educator, researcher
Maples, William Ross anthropology educator, consultant
May, Jackson Campbell real estate developer, writer
Mead, Frank Waldreth taxonomic entomologist
Medina, Jose Enrique dentist, educator
Merdinger, Emanuel retired chemistry educator
Meyer, Harvey Kessler, II retired academic administrator
Micha, David Allan chemistry and physics educator
Milanich, Jerald Thomas archaeologist, museum curator
Moberly, Robert Blakely lawyer, educator
Modell, Jerome Herbert anesthesiologist, educator
Murray, Ernest Don artist, educator
Neiberger, Richard Eugene pediatrician, nephrologist, educator
Neims, Allen Howard univeristy dean, medical scientist
Neugroschel, Arnost electrical engineering educator
Nicoletti, Paul Lee veterinarian, educator
Oberlander, Herbert insect physiologist, educator
Ohanian, Mihran Jacob nuclear engineering educator, research dean
Ohrn, Nils Yngve chemistry and physics educator
Otis, Arthur Brooks physiologist, educator
Palovcik, Reinhard Anton research neurophysiologist
Park, Robert McIlwraith science and engineering educator
Parker, Harry Lee retired military officer, counselor
Paul, Maurice M. federal judge
†Pearce, Joseph Huske industrial engineer
Pearton, Stephen John materials science and engineering educator
Peebles, Peyton Zimmerman, Jr. electrical engineer, educator
Penland, Arnold Clifford, Jr. college dean, educator
Person, Willis Bagley chemistry educator
Pfaff, William Wallace medical educator
Phillips, Winfred Marshall dean, mechanical engineer
Popenoe, Hugh Llywelyn soils educator
Price, Donald Ray university official, agricultural engineer
Probert, Walter lawyer, educator
Proctor, Samuel history educator
Purcifull, Dan Elwood plant virologist, educator
Quarles, James Cliv law educator
Quesenberry, Kenneth Hays agronomy educator
Randall, Malcom health care administrator
Reynolds, Richard Clyde physician, educator
Rhoton, Albert Loren, Jr. neurological surgery educator
Rosenbloom, Arlan Lee physician, educator
Rubin, Melvin Lynne ophthalmologist, educator
Schaub, James Hamilton engineering educator
Schelske, Claire L. limnologist, educator
Schiebler, Gerold Ludwig physician, educator
Schmeling, Gareth classics educator
Schmertmann, John Henry civil engineer, educator, consultant
Schmidt-Nielsen, Bodil Mimi (Mrs. Roger G. Chagnon) physiologist
Schueller, Wolfgang Augustus architectural educator, writer
Severy, Lawrence James psychologist, educator
Sheng, Yea-Yi Peter oceanographic engineer, educator, researcher
Sherif, S. A. mechanical engineering educator
Shyy, Wei aerospace, mechanical engineering researcher, educator
Singer, Robert Norman motor behavior educator
Singley, John Edward, Jr. environmental scientist, consultant
Sisler, Harry Hall chemist, educator
Slattery, William Joseph school psychologist
Small, Natalie Settimelli pediatric mental health counselor
Small, Parker Adams, Jr. pediatrician, educator
Smith, Alexander Goudy physics and astronomy educator
Smith, David Thornton lawyer, educator
Smith, Jo Anne writer, retired educator
Smith, Stanley Kent economics and demographics educator
†Smith, Wayne H. forest resources and conservation educator
Spurrier, Steve university athletic coach, former professional football player
Stehli, Francis Greenough geologist, educator
Stein, Jay M. planning and design educator, consultant
Stephan, Alexander F. German language and literature educator
Stern, William Louis botanist, educator
Stone, Williard Everard accountant, educator
Sullivan, Neil Samuel physicist, researcher, educator
Sutton, Douglas Hoyt nurse
Suzuki, Howard Kazuro retired anatomist, educator
Talbert, James Lewis pediatric surgeon, educator
Taylor, Grace Elizabeth Woodall (Betty Taylor) lawyer, law educator, law library administrator
Taylor, William Jape physician
Teitelbaum, Philip psychologist
Teixeira, Arthur Alves food engineer, educator, consultant
Thompson, Neal Philip food science and nutrition educator
Uthman, Basim Mohammad neurologist, epileptologist, consultant
Van Alstyne, W. Scott, Jr. lawyer, educator
Vasil, Indra Kumar botanist
Vaughen, Justine L. rehabilitation hospital medical professional
Verink, Ellis Daniel, Jr. metallurgical engineering educator, consultant
Viessman, Warren, Jr. academic dean, civil engineering educator, researcher
von Mering, Otto Oswald anthropology educator
Walker, Robert Dixon, III surgeon, urologist, educator
Wass, Hannelore Lina educational psychology educator
Watson, Robert Joe hospital administrator, retired career officer
Wethington, John Abner, Jr. retired nuclear engineering educator
Weyrauch, Walter Otto law educator
White, Jill Carolyn lawyer
Widmer, Charles Glenn dentist, researcher
Wilcox, Charles Julian geneticist, educator
Williams, Hiram Draper artist, educator
Williams, Norris Hagan, Jr. biologist, educator, curator
Williams, Ralph Chester, Jr. physician, educator
Willocks, Robert Max retired librarian
Wing, Elizabeth Schwarz museum curator, educator
Wyatt-Brown, Bertram historian, educator
York, E. Travis academic administrator, former university chancellor, consultant
York, Vermelle Cardwell real estate broker and developer
Young, David Michael biochemistry and molecular biology educator, physician
Zabel, Edward economist, educator
Zerner, Michael Charles chemistry and physics educator, consultant, researcher

### Goldenrod
Carmichael, William Jerome publishing company executive

### Gonzalez
Plischke, Le Moyne Wilfred research chemist

### Gotha
Powell, Thomas Ervin consultant, accountant, small business owner

### Graceville
Collier, Evelyn Myrtle elementary school educator
Kinchen, Thomas Alexander college president

### Green Cove Springs
Norton, Joan Jennings English language educator
Watson, Thomas Campbell economic development consulting company executive
Yelton, Eleanor O'Dell retired reading specialist

### Grove City
Suiter, John William industrial engineer, consultant

### Gulf Breeze
Jenkins, Robert Berryman real estate developer
Lankton, Stephen Ryan family therapist, management consultant
Mayer, Foster Lee, Jr. toxicologist
Strength, Janis Grace management executive, educator
Strength, Robert Samuel manufacturing company executive

### Gulf Stream
Stone, Franz Theodore retired fabricated metal products manufacturing executive

### Gulfport
Marshall, Nathalie artist, writer, educator

### Haines City
Clement, Robert William air force officer

### Hallandale
Boyce, Henry Worth, III portfolio manager, financial consultant
Contney, John Joseph trade association administrator
Cornblatt, Max automotive batteries manufacturing company executive
Geller, Bunny Zelda poet, writer, publisher, sculptor, artist
Haspel, Arthur Carl podiatrist, surgeon
Solomon, Michael Bruce lawyer

### Havana
Beare, Muriel Anita Nikki public relations executive, author
Whitehead, Lucy Grace health facility administrator

### Hawthorne
Fackler, Martin L(uther) surgeon
Ross, James Elmer economist, administrator

### Heathrow
†Darbelnet, Robert Louis automobile association executive

### Hernando
Bell, Philip Wilkes accounting and economics educator

### Hialeah
Dominik, Jack Edward lawyer
Economides, Christopher George pathologist
Edelcup, Norman Scott management and financial consultant
Hernandez, Roland broadcast executive
Iribar, Manuel R. internist, health facility administrator
Koreman, Dorothy Goldstein physician, dermatologist
Martinez, Raul L. mayor, publisher
Shaw, Steven John retired marketing educator, academic administrator
Stewart, Burch Byron chemist, physicist

### Highland Beach
Frager, Albert S. retired retail food company executive
Karp, Richard M. advertising agency executive
Schor, Stanley Sidney mathematical sciences educator
Stimson, Frederick Sparks Hispanist, educator
Summers, James Irvin retired advertising executive
Wegman, Harold Hugh management consultant

### Hilliard
Clough, Lauren C. special education educator

### Hillsboro Beach
Case, Manning Eugene, Jr. food products executive
McGarry, Carmen Racine historian, artist

### Hobe Sound
Casey, Edward Paul manufacturing company executive
Craig, David Jeoffrey retired manufacturing company executive
Etherington, Edwin Deacon lawyer, business executive, educator
Fiske, Guy Wilbur investment company executive
Havens, Oliver Hershman lawyer, consultant
Hotchkiss, Winchester Fitch retired investment banker
Markoe, Frank, Jr. lawyer, business and hospital executive
Matheson, William Lyon lawyer, farmer
McChristian, Joseph Alexander international business executive
Norman, Gregory John professional golfer
Nuñez de, Maria Irene small business owner, consultant
Parker, H. Lawrence investor, rancher, retired investment banker
Simpson, Russell Gordon lawyer, mayor, counselor to not-for-profit organizations
Vanderbilt, Oliver Degray financier

### Holiday
Jones, Vaughn Paul healthcare administrator

### Hollywood
Anger, Paul newspaper editor
Angstrom, Wayne Raymond communications executive
Bergman, Harry urologist
Blate, Michael author, lecturer
Burton, John Jacob retired real estate company executive appraiser
Cohen, Ronald J. lawyer
Cowan, Irving real estate owner, developer
Di Maggio, Joseph Paul former professional baseball player
Duffner, Lee R. ophthalmologist
Fell, Frederick Victor publisher
Giulianti, Mara Selena mayor, civic worker
Goldberg, Icchok Ignacy retired special education educator
Graves, Walter Albert retired association executive, editor
Harkin, Daniel John controller
Harringer, Olaf Carl architect, museum consultant
King, Alma Jean former health and physical education educator
Korngold, Alvin Leonard broadcasting company executive
Ladin, Eugene communications company executive
Napsky, Martin Ben insurance executive
Nusim, Stanley Herbert chemical engineer, consultant
Polivnick, Paul conductor, music director
Sadowski, Carol Johnson artist
Sim, Robert Wilson accountant
Singer, Saul food industry execurive, retired surgeon
†Tucker, Nina Angella hospital administrator
Weinberg, Harry Bernard cardiologist

### Holmes Beach
Browning, Henry Prentice banker
Neustadt, Barbara Mae artist, illustrator, etcher

### Homestead
Bachmeyer, Steven Allan secondary education educator
Brammer, Barbara Allison secondary school educator, consultant
Crouse, John Oliver, II journalist, publisher
Reeder, Cecelia Painter English educator
Revuelta, René Sergio marine scientist, educator
†Ring, Richard G. national park service administrator
Risi, Louis J., Jr. business executive
Roberts, Larry Spurgeon biological sciences educator, zoologist

### Homosassa
Acton, Norman international organization executive

### Hudson
Miller, Mary Jeannette office management specialist

### Hurlburt Field
Hobbs, Roy Jerry military career officer, health services administrator

### Indialantic
Carroll, Charles Lemuel, Jr. mathematician
Davenport, Fountain St. Clair electronic engineer
Lewis, Richard Stanley author, former editor

### Indian Harbor Beach
Barr, Constance Ransick school system administrator
Traylor, Angelika stained glass artist

### Indian Rocks Beach
Mortensen, James E. management consultant
Rocheleau, James Romig academic administrator
Sullivan, Paul William communications specialist

### Inverness
Lewis, Christina Lynn human services administrator
Mavros, George S. clinical laboratory director
Nichols, Sally Jo geriatrics nurse

### Islamorada
Poons, Larry artist

### Jacksonville
Ade, James L. lawyer
Aftoora, Patricia Joan transportation executive
Akers, James Eric medical practice marketing executive
Amornmarn, Rumpa physician
Anderson, John Quentin rail transportation executive
Ansbacher, Lewis lawyer
Austin, T. Edward (Ed Austin) former mayor
Bartholomew, John Niles church administrator
Beattie, Donald A. energy scientist, consultant
Belin, Jacob Chapman paper company executive
Bennett, Charles Edward former congressman, educator
Beytagh, Francis Xavier, Jr. college dean, lawyer
Black, Susan Harrell federal judge
Blackburn, Robert McGrady retired bishop
Bodkin, Lawrence Edward research development company executive, gemologist, inventor
Bodkin, Ruby Pate corporate executive, real estate broker, educator
Boylan, Kevin Bernard neurologist
Boyles, Carol Ann Patterson career development educator
Braddock, Donald Layton, Sr. lawyer, accountant, investor
Brady, James Joseph economics educator
Brann, William Paul retired university official
Broward, Robert Charles architect
Brown, Lloyd Harcourt, Jr. newspaper editor
Bryan, Joseph Shepard, Jr. lawyer
Bullock, Bruce Stanley lawyer
Carithers, Hugh Alfred physician
Ceballos, M(ichael) Alan lawyer
Christian, Gary Irvin lawyer
Clarkson, Charles Andrew real estate investment executive
Colby, Lestina Larsen secondary education educator
Commander, Charles Edward lawyer, real estate consultant
Constantini, JoAnn M. information management consultant
Cook, Mary Shepard education educator
Coughlin, Tom professional football coach
Criser, Marshall M. lawyer, retired university president
Davis, A. Dano grocery store chain executive
Delaney, John Adrian mayor
†Delaney, Kevin Francis naval officer
Drew, Horace Rainsford, Jr. lawyer
Dundon, Margo Elaine museum director
Eden, F(lorence) Brown artist
Edwards, Marvin Raymond investment counselor, economic consultant
Ehrlich, Raymond lawyer
Ejimofor, Cornelius Ogu political scientist, educator
Enns, John Benjamin polymer scientist
Fahner, Harold Thomas marketing executive
Farkas, Andrew library director, educator, writer
Farmer, Guy Otto, II lawyer
Fawbush, Andrew Jackson lawyer
Febel, Joel William mergers and acquisitions intermediary executive, international consultant
Francis, James Delbert oil company executive
Fredrickson, Arthur Allan retired publishing company executive
Fruit, Melvyn Herschel lawyer, management consultant
Gabel, George DeSaussure, Jr. lawyer
Getman, Willard Etheridge lawyer, mediator
Glover, Richard Bernard foundation administrator
Godfrey, John Munro economics consultant
Graham, Cynthia Armstrong banker
Gregg, Andrea Marie nursing administrator, educator, researcher
Groom, Dale physician, educator
Gunning, John Thaddeus retired superintendent
Hamilton, William Berry, Jr. shipping company executive
Hartmann, Frederick William newspaper editor
Hartzell, Charles R. research administrator, biochemist, cell biologist
Haskell, Preston Hampton, III construction company executive
Hawkins, James Douglas, Jr. structural engineer, architect
Hecht, Frederick physician, researcher, author, educator, consultant
Helganz, Beverly Buzhardt counselor
Herbert, Adam William, Jr. university president
Hill, James Clinkscales federal judge
Hodges, William Terrell federal judge
Holmes, Ray Edward human resources specialist
Howell, John Floyd insurance company executive
Huebner, Jay Stanley physicist, engineer, forensics consultant
Humm, Charles Allen sales and marketing professional
Jackson, Julian Ellis food company executive
Jelsma, Denny Gene water company executive
†Johnson, Douglas William physician, radiologist-oncologist
Johnson, Leland "Lee" Harry social services administrator
Joos, Olga Martín-Ballestero de language educator
Joyce, Edward Rowen retired chemical engineer, educator
Keefe, Kenneth M., Jr. lawyer
Kelalis, Panayotis pediatric urologist
Kelly, Patrick Chastain sales executive
Kelso, Linda Yayoi lawyer
Kensey, Calvin D. bishop
Kespohl, Elizabeth Kiser lead radiology special procedures nurse
Kilbourne, Krystal Hewett rail transportation executive
Kinne, Frances Bartlett chancellor emeritus
Korn, Michael Jeffrey lawyer
Kress, Mary Elizabeth newspaper editor
Lane, Edward Wood, Jr. retired banker
Lawrence, Christopher engineering executive
Legler, Mitchell Wooten lawyer
Lestage, Daniel Barfield retired naval officer, physician
Lestinger, Alan company executive
Lewis, Richard Harlow urologist
Liebtag, Benford Gustav, III (Ben Liebtag) engineer, consultant
Lindner, Carl Henry, Jr. financial holding company executive
Link, Robert James lawyer, educator
Lloyd, Jacqueline English language educator
Loomis, Henry former broadcasting company executive, former government official

Lovett, Radford Dow *real estate and investment company executive*
Lyon, Wilford Charles, Jr. *insurance executive*
MacDonald, Carolyn Helms *gifted education educator*
Mandia, Stephen Ernest *urologist*
Mann, Timothy *corporate executive*
Marion, Gail Elaine *reference librarian*
Mason, William Cordell, III *hospital administrator*
Mass, M. F. *allergist, immunologist*
McCullough, Ray Daniel, Jr. *insurance company executive*
McGehee, Frank Sutton *paper company executive*
McGehee, Thomas Rives *paper company executive*
McWilliams, John Lawrence, III *lawyer*
Melton, Howell Webster, Sr. *federal judge*
Mikulas, Joseph Frank *graphic designer, educator, painter*
Milton, Joseph Payne *lawyer*
Mitchell, John Adam, III *banker*
Mizrahi, Edward Alan *allergist*
Monroe, Helen Leola *nurse, consultant, educator*
Monsky, John Bertrand *investment banking executive*
Moore, David Graham *sociologist, educator*
Morehead, Charles Richard *insurance company executive*
Morgan, William Newton *architect, educator*
Morris, Max King *foundation executive, former naval officer*
Moseley, James Francis *lawyer*
Motsett, Charles Bourke *sales and marketing executive*
Mueller, Edward Albert *retired transportation engineer executive*
O'Neal, Michael Scott, Sr. *lawyer*
Osborn, Marvin Griffing, Jr. *educational consultant*
Parker, David Forster *real estate development consultant*
Paryani, Shyam Bhojraj *radiologist*
Pillans, Charles Palmer, III *lawyer*
Pope, Shawn Hideyoshi *lawyer*
Prom, Stephen George *lawyer*
Reed, Loy Wayne *minister, ministry director*
Rice, Charles Edward *bank executive*
Rinaman, James Curtis, Jr. *lawyer*
Rishel, Richard Clinton *banker*
Roth, Robert Allen *systems consultant*
Rubens, Linda Marcia *home health services administrator*
Rumpel, Peter Loyd *architect, educator, artist*
Russell, David Emerson *mechanical engineer, consultant*
Sadler, Luther Fuller, Jr. *lawyer*
Saltzman, Irene Cameron *perfume manufacturing executive, art gallery owner*
Schlageter, Robert William *museum administrator*
Schlesinger, Harvey Erwin *judge*
Schramm, Bernard Charles, Jr. *advertising agency executive*
Schultz, Frederick Henry *investor, former government official*
Sederbaum, William *marketing executive*
Seroka, James Henry *social sciences educator, university administrator*
Shivler, James Fletcher, Jr. *retired civil engineer*
†Siegel, Steven Douglas *oncologist*
Slade, Thomas Bog, III *lawyer, investment banker*
Slaughter, Frank Gill *author, physician*
Smith, Ivan Huron *architect*
Stanton, Robert John, Jr. *English language educator*
†Stein, Jay *retail executive*
Stephenson, Samuel Edward, Jr. *physician*
Stone, Dennis J. *law educator, chief information officer, lawyer*
Swenson, Courtland Sevander *musician*
Thorsteinsson, Gudni *physiatrist*
Tjoflat, Gerald Bard *federal judge*
Toker, Karen Harkavy *physician*
Tomlinson, William Holmes *management educator, retired army officer*
Vane, Terence G., Jr. *finance and insurance company executive, lawyer*
Vincent, Norman Fuller *broadcasting executive*
Vines, Charles Jerry *minister*
Wallis, Donald Wills *lawyer*
Walters, John Sherwood *retired newspaperman*
†Weaver, Wayne *professional sports team executive*
Welch, Philip Burland *electronics and office products company executive*
White, Edward Alfred *lawyer*
Wilson, C. Nick *health educator, consultant, researcher, lecturer*
Yamane, Stanley Joel *optometrist*
Zima, Michael David *lawyer*

**Jasper**
McCormick, John Hoyle *lawyer*

**Jaxville Beach**
Garza, Nora *systems engineer*

**Jay**
Brecke, Barry John *weed scientist, researcher, educator*
Peacock, Hugh Anthony *agricultural research director*

**Jensen Beach**
Gamble, Raymond Wesley *marriage and family therapist, clergyman*
Kirjassoff, Gordon Louis *consulting civil engineer*
Lowrie, Jean Elizabeth *librarian, educator*
Stuart, Harold Cutliff *lawyer, business executive*

**Juno Beach**
Broadhead, James Lowell *electrical power industry executive*
Migliaro, Marco William *electrical engineer*
Robe, Lucy Barry *editor, educator*

**Jupiter**
Anderson, Thomas Jefferson *publisher, rancher, public speaker, syndicated columnist*
Barhyte, Donald James *retired newspaper executive*
Biebuyck, Daniel Prosper *retired anthropologist, educator*
Boykin, Lykes M. *lawyer, real estate company executive*
Buck-Moore, Joanne Rose *nursing administrator, mental health educator*
Callahan, Edward William *chemical engineer, retired manufacturing executive*
Cotter, Joseph Francis *retired bank officer*
Danforth, Arthur Edwards *finance executive*
del Russo, Alessandra Luini *law educator*

Fazio, Tom *design firm executive, golf course designer*
Jacobson, Jerry Irving *biophysicist, theoretical physicist*
Komarek, Thomas Charles *retired government official*
Kulok, William Allan *entrepreneur, venture capitalist*
Mc Call, Charles Barnard *health facility executive, educator*
McCall, Duke Kimbrough *clergyman*
Moseley, Karen Frances F. *retired school system administrator, educator*
Nahavandi, Amir Nezameddin *retired engineering firm executive*
Nessmith, H(erbert) Alva *dentist*
Sproull, Robert Lamb *retired university president, physicist*
Strom, Carla Castaldo *elementary education educator*
Taylor, Claude J. *sales executive, consultant*
Wrist, Peter Ellis *pulp and paper company executive*

**Kennedy Space Center**
Banks, Lisa Jean *government official*
Evenson, Michael Donald *software engineer*
Fussell, Ronald Moi *aerospace engineer*

**Key Biscayne**
Duffy, Earl Gavin *hotel executive*
Kraft, C. William, Jr. *federal judge*
Markell, Alan William *linguistic company executive*
Navarro, Antonio (Luis) *public relations executive*
Palmer, Roger Farley *pharmacology educator*
Wilson, Robert Gordon *investment banker*

**Key Largo**
Brown, David *retired petrochemical corporation executive*
Chevins, Anthony Charles *retired advertising agency executive*
Daenzer, Bernard John *insurance company executive, legal consultant*
Davidson, Thomas Noel *business executive*
Fundora, Thomas *artist, journalist, composer*
Manning, John Warren, III *retired surgeon, medical educator*
Mattson, James Stewart *lawyer, environmental scientist, educator*

**Key West**
Barnard, Scott *artist consultant*
Coudert, Ferdinand Wilmerding *lawyer*
Heuer, Kenneth John *publishing company executive*
Mitchell, John Dietrich *theatre arts institute executive*
Stein, Michael Alan *cardiologist*
Trammell, Herbert Eugene *physicist, laboratory executive*

**Kissimmee**
Boswell, Tommie C. *middle school educator*
Evans-O'Connor, Norma Lee *secondary school educator, consultant*
Toothe, Karen Lee *elementary and secondary school educator*

**LaBelle**
Lester, W(illiam) Bernard *agricultural economist, business executive*

**Lady Lake**
Belok, Michael Victor *education educator*
Dore, Stephen Edward, Jr. *retired civil engineer*
Hartzler, Genevieve Lucille *physical education educator*
Langevin, Thomas Harvey *higher education consultant*

**Lake Alfred**
Kender, Walter John *horticulturist, educator*
Nagy, Steven *biochemist*

**Lake Buena Vista**
Lomonosoff, James Marc *marketing executive*
Nunis, Richard A. *amusement parks executive*
Parke, Robert Leon *communications executive*

**Lake City**
Norman, Alline L. *health facility administrator*

**Lake Mary**
Scott, Gary LeRoy *photographic manufacturing executive, photographer*
Strang, Stephen Edward *magazine editor, publisher*

**Lake Park**
Anderson, Mark Stephen *recovery company executive*
Heaton, Janet Nichols *artist, art gallery director*
McBride, Nancy Allyson *child resource center administrator*
Totten, Gloria Jean (Dolly Totten) *real estate executive, financial consultant*

**Lake Placid**
Layne, James Nathaniel *vertebrate biologist*

**Lake Wales**
Adams, Paul Winfrey *lawyer, business executive*
Hodapp, Shirley Jeaniene *curriculum administrator*
Mumma, Albert G. *retired naval officer, retired manufacturing company executive, management consultant*
Rynear, Nina Cox *retired registered nurse, author, artist*

**Lake Worth**
Bell, Melvin *management consultant*
Calder, Iain Wilson *publishing company executive*
†Coz, Steve *editor*
Freund, Norman Lawrence *colon and rectal surgeon*
Gorman-Gordley, Marcie Sothern *personal care industry franchise executive*
Lineberry, Sandra Beech *accountant*
Moore, Alderine Bernice Jennings (Mrs. James F. Moore) *association and organization administrator*
Newmark, Emanuel *ophthalmologist*
Newton, Wayne *entertainer, actor, recording artist*
Policy, Joseph J. *publisher, television producer*
Stafford, Shane Ludwig *lawyer*
Stevens, William John *management consultant, former association executive*

Stone, Ross Gluck *orthopaedic surgeon*

**Lakeland**
Artigliere, Ralph *lawyer, educator*
Campbell, Doris Klein *retired psychology educator*
Dufoe, William Stewart *lawyer*
Fadley, Ann Miller *English language and literature educator, writer*
Hammond, Vernon Francis *school administrator*
Hatten, William Seward *manufacturing company executive*
Henry, William Oscar Eugene *lawyer*
Hollis, Mark D. *federal official*
Jenkins, Howard M. *supermarket executive*
Kibler, David Burke, III *lawyer*
Kittleson, Henry Marshall *lawyer*
Knowlton, Kevin Charles *lawyer*
Koren, Edward Franz *lawyer*
Luther, George Albert *truck brokerage executive*
McFarlin, Richard Francis *industrial chemist, researcher*
Meads, Walter Frederick *executive recruitment consultant*
Peeler, Scott Loomis, Jr. *foreign language educator*
Perez, Louis Michael *newspaper editor*
Reich, David Lee *library director*
Roberts, William Smithson *gynecologic oncologist*
Schoonover, Jack Ronald *judge*
Sheppard, Albert Parker, Jr. *mathematics educator*
Siedle, Robert Douglas *management consultant*
Smith, Levie David, Jr. *real estate appraiser, consultant*
Smith, Sherwood Draughon *retired hospital administrator*
Spencer, Mary Miller *civic worker*
Spoto, Angelo Peter, Jr. *internist, allergist*
Stark, Bruce Gunsten *artist*
Stetson, Daniel Everett *museum director*
Wade, Ben Frank *college administrator*
Zucco, Ronda Kay *health facility administrator*

**Lantana**
Shanahan, Robert B. *banker*

**Largo**
Beck, Donald James *veterinarian, educator*
Brown, Warren Joseph *physician*
Craft Davis, Audrey Ellen *writer, educator*
Gall, Keith M. *director*
Grove, Jeffrey Scott *family practice physician*
Guthrie, John Craver *insurance agency owner*
Hinesley, J. Howard *superintendent*
Loader, Jay Gordon *retired utility company executive*
Mandelker, Lester *veterinarian*
†Newman, Francis A. *medical device company executive*
Ray, Roger Buchanan *retired communications executive, lawyer*
Weatherby, Susan Moormann *elementary school educator*

**Lauderdale Lakes**
Gay, John Marion *federal agency administrator, organization-personnel analyst*

**Lauderhill**
†Schultz, Howard Michael *registered nurse*

**Lecanto**
Walker, Mary Diane *secondary school educator*

**Leesburg**
Austin, Robert Eugene, Jr. *lawyer*
Burns, Diane *gifted education educator*
Clement, Howard Wheeler *lawyer*
Entorf, Richard Carl *management consultant*
Fechtel, Vincent John *legal administrator*
Fletcher, Mary H. *English language educator*
Gaeng, Paul Ami *foreign language educator*
Houston, John Coates, Jr. *consultant*
Talley, William Giles, Jr. *manufacturing company executive*

**Lehigh Acres**
Moore, John Newton *retired natural science educator*

**Lighthouse Point**
Farho, James Henry, Jr. *mechanical engineer, consultant*
Shein, Jay Lesing *financial planner*

**Longboat Key**
Albee, George Wilson *psychology educator*
Atwell, Robert Herron *higher education executive*
Cook, James Winfield Clinton *sales and marketing company executive*
Freeman, Richard Merrell *lawyer, corporate director*
Goldsmith, Jack Landman *former retail company executive*
Heitler, George *lawyer*
Kabara, Jon Joseph *biochemical pharmacology educator*
Levitt, Irving Francis *investment company executive*
Maha, George Edward *research facility administrator, consultant*
Phillips, Howard William *investment banker*
Prizer, Charles John *chemical company executive*
Sandy, William Haskell *training and communications systems executive*
Schoenberg, Lawrence Joseph *computer services company executive*
Stapleton, Harvey James *physics educator*
Workman, George Henry *engineer, consultant*

**Longwood**
Argirion, Michael *editor*
Bernabei, Raymond *management consultant*
Blumberg, Herbert Kurt *corporate executive*
Brooker, Robert Elton *corporate executive*
Brown, Donald James, Jr. *insurance company executive*
Dalles, John Allan *minister*
Dunne, Nancy Anne *retired social services administrator*
Faller, Donald E. *marketing and operations executive*
Gasperoni, Emil, Sr. *realtor, developer*
Hunter, Joel Carl *clergyman, educator*
St. John, John *food company executive*
Scoates, Wesley Marvin *mining company executive*
Smith, Barry Merton *financial planner, consultant*
Smyth, Joseph Patrick *retired naval officer, physician*

Tiblier, Fernand Joseph, Jr. *municipal engineering administrator*
Tomasulo, Virginia Merrills *retired lawyer*
Walters, Philip Raymond *foundation executive*

**Lutz**
Bedke, Ernest Alford *retired air force officer*
Castle, Raymond Nielson *chemist, educator*
Hayes, Timothy George *lawyer, consultant*

**Lynn Haven**
Goebert, Kimberly Mae *information systems specialist*
Leonard, Venelda Hall *writer*

**Maitland**
Acito, Daniel Joseph *interior designer*
Blackburn, John Oliver *economist, consultant*
Fichthorn, Luke Eberly, III *investment banker*
Hall, Richard C. Winton *psychiatrist*
MacKenzie, Charles Sherrard *academic administrator*
Nash, Ronald Herman *philosophy educator*
†Radi, Dorinda Rudy *health facility administrator*
Roesner, Larry August *civil engineer*
Vallee, Judith Delaney *environmentalist, writer, fundraiser*
Von Hilsheimer, George Edwin, III *neuropsychologist*
Whitlock, Luder Gradick, Jr. *seminary president*

**Mango**
Spencer, Francis Montgomery James *pharmacist*

**Marathon**
Calvert, William Preston *radiologist*
Janicki, Robert Stephen *retired pharmaceutical company executive*
Mc Cormick, Edward Allen *foreign language educator*
Wiecha, Joseph Augustine *linguist, educator*

**Marco Island**
Butler, Frederick George *retired drug company executive*
Cooper, Thomas Astley *banking executive*
Figge, Frederick Henry, Jr. *retired publishing executive*
Genrich, Judith Ann *real estate executive*
Guerrant, David Edward *retired food company executive*
Lavin, John Halley *editor, author*
Lesser, Joseph M. *retired business executive, retail store executive*
Llewellyn, Leonard Frank *real estate broker*
Pettersen, Kjell Will *stockbroker, consultant*
Sundberg, R. Dorothy *physician, educator*
Thorson, Oswald Hagen *architect*
Wheeler, Warren G(age), Jr. *retired publishing executive*

**Margate**
Albert, Calvin *sculptor*
Chastain, David Lee, Jr. *organic chemist*
Glick, Brad Peter *dermatologist, family physician*

**Marianna**
Flowers, Virginia Anne *academic administrator emerita*

**Melbourne**
Arnold, Toni Lavalle *software engineer*
Babich, Michael Wayne *chemistry educator, educational administrator*
Baney, Richard Neil *physician, internist*
Baylis, William Thomas *senior systems logistics engineer*
Boyd, Joseph Aubrey *communications company executive*
Bush, Norman *research and development executive*
Button, Kenneth John *physicist*
Cacciatore, S. Sammy, Jr. *lawyer*
Canfield, Constance Dale *accountant, nurse*
Costa, Manuel Antone *recreational facility manager*
Dale, Cynthia Lynn Arpke *educational administrator*
Delisio, Sharon Kay *secondary school educator, school administrator*
Denaburg, Charles Robert *metallurgical engineer, retired government official*
Edwards, David Northrop *retired university administrator*
Evans, Arthur Forte *real estate developer*
Farmer, Phillip W. *company executive*
Gabriel, Roger Eugene *management consulting executive*
Hartley, John T., Jr. *electronic systems, semiconductor, communications and office equipment executive*
Helmstetter, Charles Edward *microbiologist*
Hollingsworth, Abner Thomas *university dean*
Hughes, Ann Nolen *psychotherapist*
Jarrell, Patricia Lynn *photojournalist*
Jones, Elaine Hancock *humanities educator*
Krieger, Robert Edward *publisher*
Lakshmikantham, Vangipuram *mathematics educator*
Lederer, William Julius *author*
Lewis, Bernard Leroy *electronic scientist, consultant*
Lucier, Gregory Thomas *manufacturing executive*
Lyon, Isolda Yvette *dietitian*
Michalski, Thomas Joseph *city planner, developer*
Minor, Mark William *allergist*
Nelson, Gordon Leigh *chemist, educator*
Noonan, Norine Elizabeth *academic administrator, researcher*
Ott, James Forgan *financial executive*
Pocoski, David John *cardiologist*
Regis, Nina *librarian, educator*
Roub, Bryan R(oger) *financial executive*
Spezzano, Vincent Edward *newspaper publisher*
Stone, Elaine Murray *author, composer, television producer*
Storrs, Eleanor Emerett *research institute consultant*
Suojanen, Waino W. *management educator*
Vilardebo, Angie Marie *management consultant, parochial school educator*
Weaver, Lynn Edward *academic administrator, consultant, editor*

**Melrose**
Burt, Alvin Victor, Jr. *journalist*
Harley, Ruth *artist, educator*

**Merritt Island**
Deardoff, R. Bruce *automotive executive*
Martin, Judson Phillips *retired education educator*

McClanahan, Leland *academic administrator*

## Miami

Albright, John D. *emergency room and telemetry nurse*
Alexenberg, Mel *artist, art educator*
Allen, Charles Norman *television, film and video producer*
Alonso, Antonio Enrique *lawyer*
Alvarez, Raul Alberto *physician*
Amber, Laurie Kaufman *lawyer*
Anderson, Douglas Richard *ophthalmologist, educator, scientist, researcher*
Anscher, Bernard *manufacturing executive, investor, management consultant*
Arango, Jorge Sanin *architect*
Argibay, Jorge Luis *information systems firm executive and founder*
Astigarraga, Jose I(gnacio) *lawyer*
Atkins, C(arl) Clyde *federal judge*
Atlas, Randall Ivan *architect, criminologist*
Averch, Harvey Allan *economist, educator, academic administrator*
Babun, Teo Abraham *venture capital executive*
Bahadue, George Paul *general, family physician*
Balmaseda, Liz *columnist*
Barkett, Rosemary *federal judge*
Barkley, Marlene A. Nyhuis *nursing administrator*
Barrett, John Richard *lawyer*
Barritt, Evelyn Ruth Berryman *nurse, educator, university dean*
Barry, Dave *columnist, author*
Bartel, Jeffrey Scott *lawyer*
Barthel, William Frederick, Jr. *engineer, electronics company executive*
Bastian, James Harold *air transport company executive, lawyer*
Bauer, Peter Alexander *clothing executive*
Beatty, Robert Clinton *religious studies educator*
Beck, Morris *allergist*
Beckham, Walter Hull, Jr. *lawyer, educator*
Beckley, Donald K. *fundraiser*
Berger, Arthur Seymour *cultural organization executive, vice-mayor, lawyer, author*
Berger, Joyce Muriel *foundation executive, author, editor*
Berkman, Harold William *marketing educator*
Berley, David Richard *lawyer*
Berman, Bruce Judson *lawyer*
Bishopric, Karl *investment banker, real estate executive, advertising executive*
Bitter, John *university dean emeritus, musician, businessman, diplomat*
Black, Creed Carter *newspaper executive*
Blackburn, James Ross, Jr. *business executive, retired airline pilot*
Blanco, Luciano-Nilo *physicist*
Blumberg, Edward Robert *lawyer*
Bolooki, Hooshang *cardiac surgeon*
Bonilla, Bobby (Roberto Martin Antonio Bonilla) *professional baseball player*
Boyle, Judith Pullen *clinical psychologist, educator*
Brady, Alexander Childs *dancer*
Breman, Joseph Eliot *school administrator, lawyer*
Brenner, Esther Hannah *elementary school educator*
Brinkman, Paul Del(bert) *foundation executive*
Brock, James Daniel *retired airline executive, consultant*
Brown, James Kevin *professional baseball player*
Brown, Stephen Thomas *magistrate judge*
Brownell, Edwin Rowland *banker, civil engineer, land surveyor and mapper*
Burkett, Marjorie Theresa *nursing educator, gerontology nurse*
Burnett, Henry *lawyer*
Burns, Mitchel Anthony *transportation services company executive*
Capraro, Franz *accountant*
Carter, James Harrison *chemist, research director*
Casariego, Jorge Isaac *psychiatrist, psychoanalyst, educator*
Cassel, John Michael *plastic surgeon*
Cassileth, Peter Anthony *internist*
Catanzaroedu, Tony *dancer*
Chabrow, Penn Benjamin *lawyer*
Chaplin, Harvey *wine and liquor wholesale executive*
Chapman, Alvah Herman, Jr. *newspaper executive*
Cherry, Andrew Lawrence, Jr. *social work educator, researcher*
Chirovsky, Nicholas Ludomir *economics educator, historian, author*
Clark, James Kendall *lawyer*
Clarke, Donald Duhaney *secondary education educator*
Clarke, Mercer Kaye *lawyer*
Clifton, Douglas C. *newspaper editor*
Cohen, Alex *retired publisher*
Cohen, Eugene Erwin *university health institute administrator, accounting educator emeritus*
Cohen, Jacob *bishop*
Cohen, Sanford Irwin *physician, educator*
Cole, Robert Bates *lawyer*
Cole, Todd Godwin *management consultant transportation*
Collins, Susan Ford *leadership consultant*
Colwin, Arthur Lentz *biologist, educator*
Comras, Rema *retired library director*
Conine, Jeffrey Guy *professional baseball player*
Corcoran, Eugene Francis *chemist, educator*
Cornelius, Vicki Lynn *middle school educator*
Correll, Helen Butts *botanist, researcher*
Cosgrove, John Francis *state legislator, lawyer*
Coton, Carlos David *finance manager*
Coulter, Wallace Henry *medical products executive*
Courshon, Carol Biel *civic worker*
Crabtree, John Granville *lawyer*
Cristol, A. Jay *federal judge*
Cubas, Jose M(anuel) *advertising agency executive*
Cullom, William Otis *trade association executive*
Dady, Robert Edward *lawyer*
Dahlfues, Donald Michael *accountant*
Dammann, William Paul *oceanographer*
Daoud, Abraham Joseph, IV *funeral director, former police officer*
Daughtry, DeWitt Cornell *surgeon, physician*
Davis, Edward Bertrand *federal judge*
Davis, Richard Edmund *facial plastic surgeon*
Deaktor, Darryl Barnett *lawyer*
Dean, Stanley Rochelle *psychiatrist*
de la Guardia, Mario Francisco *electrical engineer*
de Leon, John Louis *lawyer*
Dellapa, Gary J. *airport terminal executive*
Denison, Floyd Gene *insurance executive*
Dickason, John Hamilton *foundation executive*
Dickey, Arden *newspaper publishing executive*
Dolen, Christine Arnold *theater critic*
Donelan, Mark Anthony *physicist*
Dorion, Robert Charles *entrepreneur, investor*
Dottin, Erskine S. *education educator*
Dribin, Michael A. *lawyer*
DuFresne, Elizabeth Jamison *lawyer*
Dye, H. Michael *marketing executive*
Dyer, David William *federal judge*
Dyer, John Martin *lawyer, marketing educator*
Eaglstein, William Howard *dermatologist, educator*
Eftekhari, Nasser *physiatrist*
Ehrlich, Morton *international finance executive*
Ehrlich, Richard *electrical engineer, researcher*
Eisdorfer, Carl *psychiatrist, health care executive*
England, Arthur Jay, Jr. *lawyer, former state justice*
Engle, Howard A. *pediatrician*
Esslinger, Anna Mae Linthicum *realtor*
Esteves, Vernon Xavier *financial consultant, investment advisor*
Etling, Russell Hull *museum director, production company executive*
Evans, Peter Kenneth *advertising executive*
Fain, Richard David *cruise line executive*
Fairchild, Susan S. *nursing educator, consultant*
Fascell, Dante B. *congressman, lawyer*
Favalora, John Clement *bishop*
Fay, Peter Thorp *federal judge*
Feingold, Laurence *lawyer*
Feito, Jose *architect*
Fern, Emma E. *state agency administrator*
Ferrell, Milton Morgan, Jr. *lawyer*
Fichtner, Margaria *journalist*
Fine, Rana Arnold *chemical, physical oceanographer*
Fitzgerald, John Thomas, Jr. *religious studies educator*
Fitzgerald, Joseph Michael, Jr. *lawyer*
Fitzgerald, Lynne Marie Leslie *family therapist*
Fletcher, John Greenwood II *state judge*
Fontaine, John C. *newspaper company executive, corporate lawyer*
Foote, Edward Thaddeus, II *university president, lawyer*
Fort-Brescia, Bernardo *architect*
Foster, Kathryn Warner *newspaper editor*
Freshwater, Michael Felix *surgeon, educator*
Frigo, James Peter Paul *industrial hardware company executive*
Frost, Philip *company executive*
Ganz, William I. *radiology educator, researcher*
Garber, Barry L. *judge*
Garcia, Isa *accountant*
Garrett, Richard G. *lawyer*
Gelband, Henry *pediatric cardiologist*
George, Stephen Carl *insurance company executive, educator, consultant, author*
Gibb, Robin *vocalist, songwriter*
Giller, Norman Myer *banker, architect, author*
Ginsberg, Myron David *neurologist*
Gittelson, George *physician*
Gittess, Ronald Marvin *dentist*
Gittlin, Arthur Sam *industrialist, banker*
Glenn, Frances Bonde *dentist*
Godofsky, Lawrence *lawyer*
Gold, Alan Stephen *judge, lawyer, educator*
Goldberg, Bernard R. *news correspondent*
Goldstein, Burton Jack *psychiatrist*
Gong, Edmond Joseph *lawyer*
Gonzalez-Pita, J. Alberto *lawyer*
Goodnick, Paul Joel *psychiatrist*
Gordon, Jack David *senator, foundation executive*
Gragg, Karl Lawrence *lawyer*
Graham, Donald Lynn *federal judge*
Greer, Alan Graham *lawyer*
Grossman, Robert Louis *lawyer*
Haas, Charles David *dentist*
Halberg, F. David *principal*
Hall, Andrew Clifford *lawyer*
Hampton, John Lewis *newspaper editor*
Hampton, Mark Garrison *architect*
Hanna, Ronald Everette *art educator, consultant*
Hardaway, Timothy Duane *basketball player*
Harper, David Michael *architect*
Harris, Douglas Clay *newspaper executive*
Hartman, Douglas Cole *lawyer*
Hartz, Steven Edward Marshall *lawyer, educator*
Hayashi, Teru *zoologist, educator*
Hector, Louis Julius *lawyer*
Heggen, Arthur William *insurance company executive*
Henderson, William Eugene *education educator*
Hendrickson, Harvey Sigbert *accounting educator*
Heuer, Robert Maynard, II *opera company executive*
Hicks, Dorothy Jane *obstetrician and gynecologist, educator*
Highsmith, Shelby *federal judge*
Higley, Bruce Wadsworth *orthodontist*
Hills, Lee *foundation administrator, newspaper executive, consultant*
Hodgetts, Richard Michael *business management educator*
Hoeveler, William M. *federal judge*
Hoffman, Larry J. *lawyer*
Houlihan, Gerald John *lawyer*
Howell, Ralph Rodney *pediatrician, educator*
Hoy, William Ivan *minister, religion educator*
Hoyt, Clark Freeland *journalist, newspaper editor*
Hudson, Robert Franklin, Jr. *lawyer*
Huysman, Arlene Weiss *psychologist, educator*
Ibarguen, Alberto *newspaper executive*
Iver, Robert Drew *dentist*
Johnson, Glendon E. *insurance company executive*
Johnson, Lisa Ann *mental health counselor*
Johnson-Cousin, Danielle *French literature educator*
Jones y Diez Arguelles, Gastón Roberto *language educator*
Jude, James Roderick *cardiac surgeon*
Kanter, Joseph Hyman *banker, community developer*
Karl, Robert Harry *cardiologist*
Kehoe, James W. *federal judge*
Kenin, David S. *lawyer*
Ketcham, Alfred Schutt *surgeon, educator*
Kidder, Benjamin Roger *safety engineer, consultant, educator*
King, James Lawrence *federal judge*
Kirton, Orlando Cecilio *surgeon, educator*
Kleinfeld, Denis A. *lawyer*
Klock, Joseph Peter, Jr. *lawyer*
Knight, Charles Frasuer *architect*
Korchin, Judith Miriam *lawyer*
Kregg, Judith Lynne *accountant*
Kuehne, Benedict P. *lawyer*
Kunce, Avon Estes *vocational rehabilitation counselor*
Kunz, Margaret McCarthy *realtor*
Lampen, Richard Jay *lawyer, investment banker*
Landon, Robert Kirkwood *insurance company executive*
Landy, Burton Aaron *lawyer*
Lapidus, Morris *retired architect, interior designer*
Lasseter, Kenneth Carlyle *pharmacologist*
Lawrence, David, Jr. *newspaper editor, publisher*
Lawson, Eve Kennedy *ballet mistress*
Lazowick, Andrea Lee *pharmacist*
Le Duc, Albert Louis, Jr. *management consultant*
Lee, J. Patrick *academic administrator*
Leeder, Ellen Lismore *language and literature educator, literary critic*
Leeds, Robert *dentist*
†Lefton, Donald E. *hotel executive*
Lehrman, Irving *rabbi*
Lemberg, Louis *cardiologist, educator*
León, Eduardo A. *diplomat, business executive*
Lew, Salvador *radio station executive*
Lewis, John Milton *cable television company executive*
Leyland, James Richard *professional baseball team manager*
†Lichacz, Sheila Enit *diplomat, artist*
Liebes, Raquel *import/export company executive, educator*
Lindquist, Claude S. *electrical and computer engineering educator*
Lipcon, Charles Roy *lawyer*
Long, Maxine Master *lawyer*
Louis, Paul Adolph *lawyer*
Lynch, Catherine Gores *social work administrator*
Mahnk, Karen *law librarian, legal assistant*
Maidique, Modesto Alex *academic administrator*
Man, Eugene Herbert *chemist, educator, business executive*
Manniello, John Baptiste Louis *research scientist*
Marcus, Stanley *federal judge*
Martinez, Walter Baldomero *architect*
Marx, Richard Benjamin *lawyer*
McCabe, Robert Howard *college president*
Mc Kenzie, John Maxwell *physician*
Mehta, Eileen Rose *lawyer*
Mendez, Jesus *history educator, education administrator*
Merrill, George Vanderneth *lawyer, investment executive*
Mettinger, Karl Lennart *neurologist*
Meyer, Sylvan Hugh *editor, magazine executive, author*
Mezey, Judith Paul *social worker*
Miller, Gene Edward *newspaper reporter and editor*
Milne, Edward Lawrence *biomedical engineer*
Milstein, Richard Craig *lawyer*
Mintz, Daniel Harvey *diabetologist, educator, academic administrator*
Mooers, Christopher Northrup Kennard *physical oceanographer, educator*
Moore, Kevin Michael *federal judge*
Moorman, Rose Drunell *county administrator, systems analyst*
Morales, Carlota Eloisa *principal*
Moreno, Federico Antonio *federal judge*
Morgan, Andrew Wesley *artist, educator*
Morgan, Marabel *author*
Morin, James Corcoran *editorial cartoonist*
Mourning, Alonzo *professional basketball player*
Mozian, Gerard Paul *real estate company executive, business consultant*
Mudd, John Philip *lawyer*
Muench, Karl H. *clinical geneticist*
Muir, Helen *journalist, author*
Munn, Janet Teresa *lawyer*
Murai, Rene Vicente *lawyer*
Myers, Kenneth M. *lawyer*
Myrberg, Arthur August, Jr. *marine biological sciences educator*
Nachwalter, Michael *lawyer*
Nadeau, Joseph Eugene *health care management consultant, information systems consultant*
Natoli, Joe *newspaper publishing executive*
Nen, Robert Allen (Robb Nen) *professional baseball player*
Nesbitt, Lenore Carrero *federal judge*
Nestor Castellano, Brenda Diana *real estate executive*
Neuman, Susan Catherine *public relations and marketing consultant*
Newlin, Kimrey Dayton *international trade consultant, political consultant, personal computer analyst*
Nisonson, Ian *urologist*
Noriega, Rudy Jorge *hospital administrator*
Nuernberg, William R(ichard) *lawyer*
O'Bryon, Linda Elizabeth *television station executive*
O'Laughlin, Sister Jeanne *university administrator*
Osman, Edith Gabriella *lawyer*
Ostlund, H. Gote *atmospheric and marine scientist, educator*
Page, Larry Keith *neurosurgeon, educator*
Pallot, Joseph Wedeles *lawyer*
Papper, Emanuel Martin *anesthesiologist*
Patarca, Roberto *immunologist, molecular biologist, physician*
Paul, Robert *lawyer*
Payne, R.W., Jr. *lawyer*
Pearson, Daniel S. *lawyer*
Pearson, John Edward *lawyer*
Perry, E. Elizabeth *social worker, real estate manager*
Pfenniger, Richard Charles, Jr. *lawyer*
Plater-Zyberk, Elizabeth Maria *architectural educator*
Poblete, Rita Maria Bautista *physician, educator*
Polo, Richard Joseph *engineering executive*
Pomeranz, Felix *accounting educator*
Pope, John Edwin, III *newspaper sports editor*
Porter, Charles King *advertising executive*
Poston, Rebekah Jane *lawyer*
Potamkin, Robert *automotive executive*
Potter, James Douglas *pharmacology educator*
Precht, William Frederick *environmental specialist*
Prineas, Ronald James *epidemiologist, educator*
Pyles, Carol DeLong *dean, consultant, educator*
Quencer, Robert Moore *neuroradiologist, researcher*
Quigley, John Joseph *special education educator*
Quirantes, Albert M. *lawyer*
Raffel, Leroy B. *real estate development company executive*
Raines, Jeff *biomedical scientist, medical research director*
Ralis, Paraskevy *art educator, artist*
Randolph, Jennings, Jr. (Jay Randolph) *sportscaster*
Rashkind, Paul Michael *lawyer*
Redruello, Rosa Inchaustegui *municipal official*
Reed, Alfred *composer, conductor*
Reik, Rita Ann Fitzpatrick *pathologist*
Reisinger, Sandra Sue *journalist, lawyer*
Ricordi, Camillo *surgeon, transplant and diabetes researcher*
Riley, Patrick James *professional basketball coach*
Ripstein, Charles Benjamin *surgeon*
Robinson, David Bradford *poet, scientific writer*
Roddenberry, Stephen Keith *lawyer*
†Rodriguez, Ray *broadcast executive*
Roemer, Elaine Sloane *real estate broker*
Rosen, Howard Robert *lawyer*
Rosenberg, Mark B. *think-tank executive*
Rosenthal, Stanley Lawrence *meteorologist*
Rothchild, Howard Leslie *advertising executive*
Routh, Donald K(ent) *psychology educator*
Rubin, Bruce Stuart *public relations executive*
Ruffner, Charles Louis *lawyer*
Russell, Elbert Winslow *neuropsychologist*
Russell, James Webster, Jr. *newspaper editor, columnist*
Rust, Robert Warren *retired lawyer*
Ryce, Donald Theodore *lawyer*
Sacher, Barton Stuart *lawyer*
Sackner, Marvin Arthur *physician*
Salazar-Carrillo, Jorge *economics educator*
Salvaneschi, Luigi *real estate and development executive, business educator*
Sanchez, Javier Alberto *industrial engineer*
†Sanchez, Rick *newscaster*
Sanchez, Robert Francis *journalist*
Sarnoff, Marc David *lawyer*
Satuloff, Barth *accounting executive, dispute resolution professional*
Savage, James Francis *editor*
Scerpella, Ernesto Guillermo *physician researcher*
Scheinberg, Peritz *neurologist*
Schiff, Eugene Roger *medical educator, hepatologist*
Schofield, Calvin Onderdonk, Jr. *bishop*
Schuette, Charles A. *lawyer*
Schuetzenduebel, Wolfram Gerhard *engineering executive*
Schulman, Clifford A. *lawyer*
Schwartz, Gerald *public relations and fundraising agency executive*
Schwartz, Kessel *modern language educator*
Shapiro, Samuel Bernard *management consultant*
Sheffield, Gary Antonian *professional baseball player*
Shevin, Robert Lewis *judge*
Shroder, Tom *newspaper editor*
Silber, Norman Jules *lawyer*
Silva, Felipe *former tobacco company executive*
Simmons, Sherwin Palmer *lawyer*
Smathers, Frank, Jr. *banker, horticulturist*
Smiley, Logan Henry *journalist, public concern consultant*
Smith, Samuel Stuart *lawyer*
Smith, Stanley Bertram *clinical pathologist, allergist, immunologist, anatomic pathologist*
Somerville, Mary Robinson *library director*
†Sonenreich, Steven Douglas *hospital administrator*
Spear, Laurinda Hope *architect*
Spencer, Richard Thomas, III *healthcare industry executive*
Stein, Allan Mark *lawyer*
Steinback, Robert Lamont *newspaper columnist*
Steinberg, Alan Wolfe *investment company executive*
Steinberg, Marty *lawyer*
Stern, Joanne Thrasher *elementary school educator*
†Stiehm, Judith Hicks *university official, political science educator*
Stokes, Paul Mason *lawyer*
Stover, James Howard *real estate executive*
Strickland, Thomas Joseph *artist*
Strong, Charles Robert *waste management administrator*
Strul, Gene M. *communications executive*
Stuchins, Carol Mayberry *nursing executive*
Sturge, Karl *surgeon*
Suarez, Xavier Louis *lawyer, former mayor*
Sundel, Martin *social work educator, psychologist*
Sussex, James Neil *psychiatrist, educator*
Tarkoff, Michael Harris *lawyer*
Teicher, Morton Irving *social worker, anthropologist, educator*
Tejada, Francisco *physician, educator*
Telesca, Francis Eugene *architect*
Terilli, Samuel A., Jr. *newspaper publishing executive*
Thornburg, Frederick Fletcher *diversified business executive, lawyer*
Torres, Milton John *industrial engineering educator*
Touby, Kathleen Anita *lawyer*
Touby, Richard *lawyer*
Treyz, Joseph Henry *librarian*
Trippe, Kenneth Alvin Battershill *shipping industry executive*
Tumpson, Joan Berna *lawyer*
Tuttle, Toni Brodax *swimming pool company executive*
Ugwu, Martin Cornelius *pharmacist*
Ungaro-Benages, Ursula Mancusi *federal judge*
Ural, Oktay *civil engineering educator*
Valdes-Dapena, Marie Agnes *pediatric pathologist, educator*
Valle, Laurence Francis *lawyer*
VanBrode, Derrick Brent, IV *trade association administrator*
Van Vliet, Carolyne Marina *physicist, educator*
Van Wyck, George Richard *insurance company executive*
Venet, Claude Henry *architect, acoustic engineer*
Vento, M. Thérèse *lawyer*
Veziroglu, Turhan Nejat *mechanical engineering educator, energy researcher*
Walters, David McLean *lawyer*
Wax, William Edward *photojournalist*
Webb, Richmond Jewel *professional football player*
Weber, Nancy Walker *charitable trust administrator*
Weeks, Marta Joan *priest*
Weiner, Lawrence *lawyer*
Weiner, Morton David *banker, insurance agent*
Weinstein, Alan Edward *lawyer*
Weinstein, Andrew H. *lawyer*
Weiser, Ralph Raphael *business executive*
Weiser, Sherwood Manuel *hotel and corporation executive, lawyer*
Wells, Daniel Ruth *physics educator*
Wheeler, Steve Dereal *neurologist*
Whitlow, James Adams *lawyer*
Whittington, Robert Wallace *corporate professional, pianist*
Wickstrom, Karl Youngert *publishing company executive*
Williamson, William Paul, Jr. *journalist*
Wolfenson, Azi U. *electrical engineer*
Wolff, Grace Susan *pediatrician*
Wolfson, Aaron Howard *radiation oncologist, educator*
Wolper, Marshall *insurance and financial consultant*
Wright, Robert Thomas, Jr. *lawyer*
†Yaffa, Jack Ber *healthcare administrator, educator*
Zanakis, Steve H. *management science/information systems educator*
Zeiller, Warren *former aquarium executive, consultant*

**Miami Beach**
Angel-Junguito, Antonio *writer*
Gitlow, Abraham Leo *retired university dean*
†Krieger, Bruce Phillip *medical educator*
Marcus, Eileen *public relations and advertising executive*
†Nixon, Daniel David. *physician*
†Ratzan, Kenneth Roy *physician*

**Miami Lakes**
Getz, Morton Ernest *medical facility director, gastroenterologist*
Rodriguez, Manuel Alvarez *pathologist*
Sharett, Alan Richard *lawyer, environmental litigator, mediator and arbitrator, law educator*
Weldon, Norman Ross *financial company executive*

**Micanopy**
Cripe, Wyland Snyder *veterinary medicine educator, consultant*

**Milton**
McKinney, George Harris, Jr. *training systems analyst*
Tarvin, Albert Leon *writer*

**Montverde**
Harris, Martin Harvey *aerospace company executive*

**Mount Dora**
Adams, Carl Morgan, Jr. *real estate appraiser, mortgage banker*
Chandler, Robert Flint, Jr. *international agriculture consultant*
Edgerton, Richard *restaurant and hotel owner*
Goodwin, Harry Eugene *journalist, educator*
Hart, Valerie Gail *writer*
Hensinger, Margaret Elizabeth *horticultural and agricultural advertising and marketing executive*
Laux, James Michael *historian, educator*
Myren, Richard Albert *criminal justice consultant*
Santini, John Amedeo *educational consultant*
Trussell, Charles Tait *columnist*

**Mulberry**
Bowman, Hazel Lois *retired English language educator*

**Naples**
Abbott, John Sheldon *law school dean and chancellor emeritus*
Alpert, Hollis *writer*
Ancker-Johnson, Betsy *physicist, engineer, retired automotive company executive*
Arthur, William Bolling *retired editor*
Bageant, Martha Dyer *retired volunteer*
Baldwin, Ralph Belknap *retired manufacturing company executive, astronomer*
Barth-Wehrenalp, Gerhard *chemical company executive*
Beam, Robert Thompson *retired lawyer*
Benedict, Manson *chemical engineer, educator*
Berman, Robert S. *marketing consultant*
Biondo, Michael Thomas *retired paper company executive*
Borman, Earle Kirkpatrick, Jr. *chemical company executive*
Bornmann, Carl M(alcolm) *lawyer*
Brooks, Joae Graham *psychiatrist, educator*
Budd, David Glenn *lawyer*
Bush, John William *federal transportation official*
Cantelon, John Edward *academic administrator*
Card, Orson Scott (Byron Walley) *writer*
Censits, Richard John *business consultant*
Chartrand, Robert Lee *information scientist*
Ciano, James Francis *computer systems analyst*
Cimino, Richard Dennis *lawyer*
Clapp, Roger Howland *retired newspaper executive*
Clark, Kenneth Edwin *psychologist, former university dean*
Conrad, Kelley Allen *industrial and organizational psychologist*
Corkran, Virginia Bowman *real estate associate*
Craighead, Rodkey *banker*
Crehan, Joseph Edward *lawyer*
Davis, Sidney Fant *lawyer, author*
Dion, Nancy Logan *health care administrator, management consultant*
Doyle, Robert Eugene, Jr. *lawyer*
Duff, Daniel Vincent *former insurance company executive, former mayor*
Dutton, Clarence Benjamin *lawyer*
Eggland, Ellen Thomas *community health nurse, consultant*
Eldridge, David Carlton *art appraiser*
Elliott, Edward *investment executive, financial planner*
Emerson, John Williams, II *lawyer*
Evans, Elizabeth Ann West *realtor*
Fess, Philip Eugene *accountant, educator*
Frazer, John Howard *tennis association executive, retired manufacturing company executive*
Gahagan, Thomas Gail *obstetrician, gynecologist*
Gaskins, William Darrell *ophthalmologist*
Gilman, John Richard, Jr. *organization behavior consultant*
Gray, Seymour *medical educator, author*
Gresham, Robert Coleman *transportation consultant*
Griffin, Linda Louise *English language and speech educator*
Guarino, Roger Charles *consulting company executive*
Gushman, John Louis *former corporation executive, lawyer*
Handy, Charles Brooks *accountant, educator*
Harvey, Walter H(ayden) *hematologist, medical oncologist*
Hedberg, Paul Clifford *broadcasting executive*
Hochschwender, Herman Karl *international consultant*
Hooper, John Allen *retired banker*
Hughes, Laura Elizabeth *resort and recreational facility executive*
Ivancevic, Walter Charles *former gas distribution company executive*
Jaffe, Marvin Eugene *pharmaceutical company executive, neurologist*
Johnson, Sally A. *nursing educator*
Johnson, Walter L. *transportation company executive*
Johnson, Zane Quentin *retired petroleum company executive*
Jones, Richard Wallace *interior designer*
Kapnick, Harvey Edward, Jr. *retired corporate executive*
Kay, Herbert *retired natural resources company executive*
Kennedy, Donald Davidson, Jr. *retired insurance company executive*
Kleinrock, Virginia Barry *public relations executive*
Kley, John Arthur *banker*
Lange, George Willard, Jr. *trust banker, lawyer*
Leitner, Alfred *mathematical physicist, educator, educational film producer*
Leverenz, Humboldt Walter *retired chemical research engineer*
Levitt, LeRoy Paul *psychiatrist, psychoanalyst*
Lewis, Gordon Gilmer *golf course architect*
Lewis, Marianne H. *psychiatric nurse practitioner*
Loft, Bernard Irwin *education educator, consultant*
Mac'Kie, Pamela S. *lawyer*
Marshall, Charles *communications company executive*
Martinuzzi, Leo Sergio, Jr. *banker*
McCaffrey, Judith Elizabeth *lawyer*
Mc Queen, Robert Charles *retired insurance executive*
Megee, Geraldine Hess *social worker*
Montgomery, Ruth Shick *author*
Montone, Liber Joseph *engineering consultant*
Moore, Mechlin Dongan *communications executive, marketing consultant*
Mutz, Oscar Ulysses *manufacturing and distribution executive*
Norins, Leslie Carl *publisher*
Oliver, Robert Bruce *retired investment company executive*
Ordway, John Danton *retired pension administrator, lawyer, accountant*
Osias, Richard Allen *international financier, investor, real estate investment executive, corporate investor*
Parish, John Cook *insurance executive*
Peck, Bernard Sidney *lawyer*
Price, Thomas Benjamin *former textile company executive*
Putzell, Edwin Joseph, Jr. *lawyer, mayor*
Quigley, Jack Allen *service company executive*
Reed, John Franklin *instrument manufacturing company executive*
Rigor, Bradley Glenn *bank executive*
Roberts, William B. *lawyer, business executive*
Rowe, Herbert Joseph *retired trade association executive*
Rowe, Jack Field *retired electric utility executive*
Schauer, Wilbert Edward, Jr. *lawyer, manufacturing company executive*
Sekowski, Cynthia Jean *corporate executive, contact lens specialist*
Sharpe, Robert Francis *equipment manufacturing company executive*
Smarg, Richard Michael *insurance and employee benefits specialist*
Smith, Numa Lamar, Jr. *lawyer*
Snyder, Marion Gene *lawyer, former congressman*
Stevens, William Kenneth *lawyer*
Stewart, Harris Bates, Jr. *oceanographer*
Stratton, John Caryl *real estate executive*
Strauss, Jerome Manfred *lawyer, banker*
Suziedelis, Vytautas A. *engineering corporation executive*
Taishoff, Lawrence Bruce *publishing company executive*
Tanner, Robert Hugh *engineer, consultant*
Terenzio, Peter Bernard *hospital administrator*
Thomas, Gary Lynn *financial executive*
Thompson, Didi Castle (Mary Bennett) *writer, editor*
von Arx, Dolph William *food products executive*
Waller, George Macgregor *historian, educator*
Weeks, Richard Ralph *marketing educator*
Westman, Carl Edward *lawyer*
White, Roy Bernard *theater executive*
Widman, Richard Gustave *engineering and construction company executive*
Williams, Edson Poe *retired automotive company executive*
Williams, George Earnest *engineer, retired business executive*
Wodlinger, Mark Louis *broadcast executive*
Wyant, Corbin A. *newspaper publisher*

**Navarre**
Korn, Irene Elizabeth *retired elementary education educator, consultant*

**New Port Richey**
Charters, Karen Ann Elliott *critical care nurse, health facility administrator*
Focht, Theodore Harold *lawyer, educator*
Hauber, Frederick August *ophthalmologist*
Hu, Chen-Sien *surgeon*
McCabe, Sharon *humanities and art educator*
Miller-Chermely, Dorothy L. *sales executive*
Oliveto, Frank Louis *recreation consultant*
Richardson, Richard Lewis *lawyer*
Sorensen, John Frederick *retired minister*

**New Smyrna**
Henderson, Clay *lawyer*
Leeper, Doris Marie *sculptor, painter*
Little, W(illia)m A(lfred) *foreign language educator, researcher*

**New Smyrna Beach**
Hollis, Reginald *archbishop*
Howard, Stanley Louis *investment banker*
Makela, Benjamin R. *editor, research director*
Skove, Thomas Malcolm *retired manufacturing company financial executive*
Thomson, John Christian *financial analyst, portfolio manager*

**Niceville**
Litke, Donald Paul *business executive, retired military officer*
Phillips, Richard Wendell, Jr. *air force officer*

**Nokomis**
Cather, Donald Warren *civil engineer*
Halladay, Laurie Ann *public relations consultant, former franchise executive*
Meyerhoff, Jack Fulton *financial executive*
Myers, Virginia Lou *education educator*
Novak, Robert Louis *civil engineer, pavement management consultant*
Wendt, Lloyd *writer*

**North Lauderdale**
Hawn, Micaela (Micki Hawn) *mathematics educator*

**North Miami**
Henry, John Raymond *sculptor*
Moreno, Christine Margaret *lawyer*
Paul, Joseph B. *information technology executive*

**North Miami Beach**
Ballman, Donna Marie *lawyer*
Fishel, Peter Livingston *accounting business executive*
†Gare, Fran *nutritionist*
Shuster, Frederick *internist*

**North Palm Beach**
Boyden, Christopher Wayne *lawyer, divorce mediator*
Crawford, Roberta *association administrator*
Doede, John Henry *investment company executive*
Edwards, William James *broadcasting executive*
Fierer, Joshua Allan *pathology educator*
Frevert, James Wilmot *financial planner, investment advisor*
Gray, Harry Jack *investment executive*
Hayman, Richard Warren Joseph *conductor*
Hushing, William Collins *retired corporate executive*
Nicklaus, Jack William *professional golfer*
Staub, W. Arthur *health care products executive*
Stein, Mark Rodger *allergist*

**Ocala**
Altenburger, Karl Marion *allergist, immunologist*
Booth, Jane Schuele *real estate broker, executive*
Clayton, Robert Beville *insurance and financial services professional*
Corwin, William *psychiatrist*
Forgue, Stanley Vincent *physics educator*
Fredericks, William John *chemistry educator*
Grissom, Robert Jesse, Sr. *criminal justice educator*
Hatch, John D. *lawyer, consultant*
Hodges, Elizabeth Swanson *educational consultant, tutor*
Hunter, Oregon K., Jr. *physiatrist*
Kaplan, Judith Helene *company executive*
Lamon, Kathy Lynn *nursing administrator*
Lewis, Richard Knox *city official*
Lincoln, Larry W. *automotive executive*
Stock, Stephen Michael *broadcast journalist*
Tait, Patricia Ann *secondary education educator*

**Ocoee**
Mabie, Susan (Susse ) *secondary education educator*

**Odessa**
Broderick, Patrick Rodney *artist*
Lister, Thomas Mosie *composer, lyricist, publishing company executive, minister*

**Okeechobee**
Hedges, Bobette Lynn *business administrator*
Raulerson, Phoebe Hodges *school superintendent*
Selmi, William, Jr. *lawyer*

**Oldsmar**
Brunner, George Matthew *management consultant, former business executive*
Burrows, William Claude *aerospace executive, retired air force officer*
Fernandez, Joseph Anthony *educational administrator*
Hirschman, Sherman Joseph *lawyer, educator*
Thompson, Mack Eugene *history educator*

**Ona**
Rechcigl, Jack Edward *soil and environmental sciences educator*

**Opa Locka**
Conner, Laban Calvin *librarian*
†Dombrowski, David *baseball team executive*
Hopton, Janice *elementary school principal*
Light, Alfred Robert *lawyer, political scientist, educator*
Marino, Daniel Constantine, Jr. *professional football player*
Sample, Althea Merritt *secondary education educator, conductor*

**Orange Park**
Enney, James Crowe *former air force officer, business executive*
Oglesby, Beverly Clayton *kindergarten educator*
Ratzlaff, Judith L. *secondary school educator*
Rice, Ronald James *hospital administrator*
Rodgers, Billy Russell *chemical engineer, research scientist*
Walsh, Gregory Sheehan *optical systems professional*

**Orlando**
Abbott, Edward Leroy *finance executive*
Ady, Laurence Irvin *academic administrator*
Allen, William Riley *lawyer*
Allison, Anne Marie *librarian*
Arkin, J. Gordon *lawyer*
Armacost, Robert Leo *management educator*
Arnett, Warren Grant *interior designer*
Bailey, Michael Keith *lawyer*
Baker, David A. *federal judge*
Baker, Peter Mitchell *laser scientist and executive, educator*
Barlow, Nadine Gail *planetary geoscientist*
Bittle, Polly Ann *nephrology nurse, researcher*
Blackford, Robert Newton *lawyer*
Blackwell, Bruce Beuford *lawyer*
Blue, Joseph Edward *physicist*
†Brazell, Stanley Harold *information systems specialist, Navy officer*
Brownlee, Thomas Marshall *lighting manufacturing company executive*
Bussey, John W., III *lawyer*
Capouano, Albert D. *lawyer*
Cary, Freeman Hamilton *physician*
Chong, Stephen Chu Ling *lawyer*
Chotas, Elias Nicholas *lawyer*
Christiansen, Patrick T. *lawyer*
Cirello, John *utility and engineering company executive*
Clark, James Covington *journalist, historian*
Clinton, Stephen Michael *academic administrator*
Colbourn, Trevor *retired university president, historian*
Connolly, Joseph Francis, II *defense company executive, government consultant*
Conti, Louis Thomas Moore *lawyer*
Conway, Anne Callaghan *federal judge*
Davis, Gene *civil engineer*
Davis, William Albert *theme park director*
deBeaubien, Hugo H. *lawyer*
Denton, Carol Forsberg *training systems designer*
Deo, Narsingh *computer science educator*
Dietz, Robert Lee *lawyer*
Dorsey, Norbert M. *bishop*
Dunlap, Charles Leonard *lawyer*
Dunn, William Bruna, III *journalist*
Eidson, Frank M. *lawyer*
Fawsett, Patricia Combs *federal judge*
Feuvrel, Sidney Leo, Jr. *lawyer, educator*
Gokee, Donald LeRoy *clergyman, author*
Grady, Thomas J. *bishop*
Grant, Joanne Cummings *social service agency administrator*
Grant, Raymond Thomas *arts administrator*
Gray, Anthony Rollin *capital management company executive*
Guest, Larry Samuel *newspaper columnist*
Haile, L. John, Jr. *journalist, newspaper executive*
Hall-Kelly, Kathy B. *small business owner, columnist, speaker, consultant*
Handley, Leon Hunter *lawyer*
Hardaway, Anfernee Deon (Penny Hardaway) *professional basketball player*
Hartley, Carl William, Jr. *lawyer*
Haxton, David *computer graphics educator, computer animator, photographer*
Healy, Jane Elizabeth *newspaper editor*
Higgins, Robert Frederick *lawyer*
Hitt, John Charles *university president*
Hornick, Richard Bernard *physician*
Howe, John Wadsworth *bishop*
Hughes, David Henry *manufacturing company executive*
Hwang, Miriam *information technology specialist*
Hyslop, Gary Lee *librarian*
Ioppolo, Frank S., Jr. *lawyer*
Ispass, Alan Benjamin *utilities executive*
Ivey, James Burnett *political cartoonist*
Jones, Constance Irene *medical products executive*
Jones, Joseph Wayne *food and beverage company executive, entrepreneur*
Jontz, Jeffry Robert *lawyer*
Kindlund, Newton C. *retail executive*
Laning, Richard Boyer *naval officer, writer, retired*
Leonhardt, Frederick Wayne *lawyer*
Llewellyn, Ralph Alvin *physics educator*
Mallette, Phyllis Spencer Cooper *medical/surgical nurse*
Martin, William Robert *accountant*
Martindale, Carla Joy *librarian*
Maupin, Elizabeth Thatcher *theater critic*
Medin, Julia Adele *mathematics educator, researcher*
Mock, Frank Mackenzie *lawyer*
Moltzon, Richard Francis *manufacturing executive*
Morrisey, Marena Grant *art museum administrator*
Nadeau, Robert Bertrand, Jr. *lawyer*
Nants, Bruce Arlington *lawyer*
Neff, A. Guy *lawyer*
Neiman, Norman *aerospace business and marketing executive*
Norris, Franklin Gray *thoracic and cardiovascular surgeon*
O'Farrell, Mark Theodore *religious organization administrator*
Okun, Neil Jeffrey *vitreoretinal surgeon*
Osborne-Popp, Glenna Jean *health services administrator*
Palmer, William D. *lawyer*
Pantuso, Vincent Joseph *food service consultant*
Pearlman, Louis Jay *aviation and promotion company executive*
Pelton, Charles R. *financial institution executive*
Pierce, Jerry Earl *business executive*
Puerner, John *newspaper publishing executive*
Quinn, Jane *journalist*
Raffa, Jean Benedict *author, educator*
Rattman, William John *electronics and eletro-optic engineer*
Reed, John Alton *lawyer*
Reese, Charles Edgar *columnist*
Renee, Lisabeth Mary *art educator, artist, galley director*
Rolle, Christopher Davies *lawyer*
Rosenbach, Leopold *engineer, consultant*
Rudolph, Wallace Morton *law educator*
Rush, Fletcher Grey, Jr. *lawyer*
Sathre, Leroy *mathematics educator, consultant*
Schroeter, Dirk Joachim *mechanical engineer*
Sharkey, Colleen Mary *sports association administrator*
Sharp, George Kendall *federal judge*
Shub, Harvey Allen *surgeon*
Silfvast, William T. *laser physics educator, consultant*
Simmons, Cleatous J. *lawyer*
Simon, James Lowell *lawyer*
Sims, Roger W. *lawyer*
Skambis, Christopher Charles, Jr. *lawyer*
Smetheram, Herbert Edwin *government official*
Smith, Paul Frederick *plant physiologist, consultant*
Snively, Stephen Wayne *lawyer*
Soileau, Marion Joseph *engineering and physics educator*
Spoonhour, James Michael *lawyer*
Stewart, Harry A. *lawyer*
Swedberg, Robert Mitchell *opera company director*
Terwilliger, Julia Anne *art educator, artist*
Ting, Robert Yen-ying *physicist*
Turner, Thomas William *lawyer*
Urban, James Arthur *lawyer*
†Vander Weide, Bob *professional sports team executive*
Van Sickle, Paul Brunton *financial executive*
Vaughn, E(lbert) Hardy *insurance and financial company executive*
Vining, F(rancis) Stuart *architect, consultant*
Walsh, James Anthony (Tony Walsh) *theater and film educator*
Warren, Dean Stuart *artist*
Weiss, Christopher John *lawyer*
White, Susan Victoria *nursing administrator*
†Williams, Pat *professional basketball team executive*
Willis, William Harris *internist, cardiologist*
Wilson, William Berry *lawyer*
Woodard, Clara Veronica *nursing home official*
Wright, Martha Helen *elementary education educator*
Yates, Leighton Delevan, Jr. *lawyer*
Yesawich, Peter Charles *advertising executive*
Young, George Cressler *federal judge*

**Ormond Beach**
Barker, Robert Osborne (Bob Barker) *mediator, property management and public relations executive*
Burton, Alan Harvey *city official*

Coke, C(hauncey) Eugene consulting company executive, scientist, educator, author
Cromartie, Robert Samuel, III thoracic surgeon
Jacobson, Ira David aerospace engineer, educator, researcher
Raimondo, Louis John psychiatrist
Riley, Daniel Edward air force officer
Wendelstedt, Harry Hunter, Jr. umpire
Wild, Harry E. engineering company executive

### Osprey
Allen, George Howard publishing management consultant
Boldt, Heinz aerospace engineer
Coates, Clarence Leroy, Jr. research engineer, educator
Cort, Winifred Mitchell microbiologist, biochemist
Fleming, William Harrison retired lawyer
Gross, James Dehnert pathologist
Maddocks, Robert Allen lawyer, manufacturing company executive
Robinson, Sally Winston artist
Weathermon, Sidney Earl elementary school educator
Woodall, William Leon retired insurance executive

### Oviedo
Brethauer, William Russell, Jr. claim investigator
Ferguson, Carmela social services administrator
Linhart, Letty Lemon editor
Whitworth, Hall Baker forest products company executive

### Pace
Sumrall, Kenneth Irvin religious organization administrator

### Palatka
Baldwin, Allen Adail lawyer, writer
Ginn, John Arthur, Jr. insurance agent

### Palm Bay
Bellstedt, Olaf senior software engineer
Colman, Charles Kingsbury academic administrator, criminologist
Jones, Mary Ann geriatrics nurse
Jurgevich, Nancy J. retail executive, educator

### Palm Beach
Adduci, Vincent James investment company executive
Adler, Frederick Richard lawyer, financier
Alpert, Seymour anesthesiologist, educator
Artinian, Artine French literature scholar, collector
Bagby, Joseph Rigsby financial investor
Bagby, Martha L. Green real estate holding company, novelist, publisher
Bane, Charles Arthur lawyer
Barness, Amnon Shemaya financial service executive
Becker, John Lionel, Jr. insurance company executive, marketing company executive
Bishop, Warner Bader finance company executive
Black, Leonard Julius retail store consultant
Callaway, Trowbridge banker
Chittick, Elizabeth Lancaster association executive, women's rights activist
Chopin, L. Frank lawyer
Cook, Edward Willingham diversified industry executive
Crawford, Sandra Kay lawyer
Curry, Bernard Francis former banker, consultant
Dillard, Rodney Jefferson real estate executive
Donnell, John Randolph petroleum executive
Druck, Kalman Breschel public relations counselor
Fitilis, Theodore Nicholas portfolio manager
Fogelson, David retired lawyer
Ford, Thomas Patrick lawyer
Gowdy, Curtis sportscaster
Graubard, Seymour lawyer
Gundlach, Heinz Ludwig investment banker, lawyer
Habicht, Frank Henry industrial executive
Hall, Kathryn Evangeline writer, lecturer
Halmos, Peter investment company executive
Hopper, Arthur Frederick biological science educator
Isenberg, Abraham Charles shoe manufacturing company executive
Jackson, John Tillson corporate executive
Kaplan, Muriel Sheerr sculptor
Korn, David investment company executive
Krois, Audrey artist
Lede, Richard investment company executive
Levine, Laurence Brandt investment banker
Lickle, William Cauffiel banker
Mallardi, Vincent organization executive
Mandel, Carola Panerai (Mrs. Leon Mandel) foundation trustee
Miller, Richard Jackson lawyer
Myers, Eugene Ekander art consultant
Oder, Frederic Carl Emil retired aerospace company executive, consultant
†Pryor, Hubert editor, writer
Rauch, George Washington lawyer
Rinker, Ruby Stewart foundation administrator
Robb, David Buzby, Jr. financial services company executive, lawyer
Roberts, Margaret Harold editor, publisher
Roberts, Margot Markels business executive
Robertson, Sara Stewart portfolio manager
Rudolph, Malcolm Rome investment banker
Rumbough, Stanley Maddox, Jr. industrialist
Steere, Anne Bullivant retired student advisor
Tiecke, Richard William pathologist, educator, association executive
Tremain, Alan hotel executive
Turner, William Benjamin electrical engineer
Unger, Gere Nathan physician, lawyer
Wenzel, Joan Ellen artist
Wirtz, Willem Kindler garden and lighting designer, public relations consultant

### Palm Beach Gardens
Awtrey, Jim L. sports association executive
†Beck, Chip professional golfer
†Brooks, Mark David professional golfer
Calcavecchia, Mark professional golfer
Christian, Robert Henry architect
Couples, Fred professional golfer
Daly, John professional golfer
Desormier-Cartwright, Anné Maria lawyer
Falk, Bernard Henry trade association executive
Freeman, Donald Wilford real estate developer, horse breeder
†Haas, Jay professional golfer
Hannon, John Robert investment company executive
Harnett, Joseph Durham oil company executive
†Henninger, Brian professional golfer
Herrick, John Dennis financial consultant, former law firm executive, retired food products executive
†Hoch, Scott professional golfer
†Huston, John professional golfer
†Jacobsen, Peter Erling professional golfer
Janzen, Lee professional golfer
Keppler, William Edmund multinational company executive
Koff, Bernard Louis retired engineering executive
Lambert, George Robert lawyer, insurance company executive, legal consultant, realtor
†Langer, Bernhard professional golfer
†Lehman, Tom professional golfer
†Leonard, Justin professional golfer
Mendelson, Richard Donald former communications company executive
Mergler, H. Kent investment counselor
†Mickelson, Phil professional golfer
Mize, Larry professional golfer
†Montgomerie, Colin professional golfer
†Olazabal, Jose Maria professional golfer
†O'Meara, Mark professional golfer
†Perry, Kenny professional golfer
Price, Nick professional golfer
Rodriguez, Chi Chi (Juan Rodriguez) professional golfer
Shapiro, Steven David dermatologist
†Sigel, Jay insurance company executive
†Simpson, Scott professional golfer
Small, Melvin D. physician, educator
Snead, Samuel Jackson former professional golfer
Symons, J. Keith bishop
Wackenhut, Richard Russell security company executive
†Woods, Tiger (Eldrick Woods) professional golfer

### Palm City
Ammarell, John Samuel retired college president, former security services executive
Burton, John Routh lawyer
Derrickson, William Borden manufacturing executive
Henry, David Howe, II retired diplomat
Huntington, Earl Lloyd lawyer, retired natural resources company executive
†Mc Hale, John Joseph baseball club executive
Pepitone, Byron Vincent former government official
Senter, William Oscar retired air force officer
Sloan, Richard artist
Thompson, George Lee consulting company executive
Wirsig, Woodrow magazine editor, trade organization executive, business executive
Wishart, Ronald Sinclair retired chemical company executive

### Palm Coast
Brumback, Gary Bruce industrial and organizational psychologist
Dickson, David Watson Daly retired college president
Godfrey, Eutha Marek elementary school educator, consultant
Linnen, Thomas Francis international strategic management consulting firm executive
Myckaniuk, Maria Anna elementary and special education educator
Patz, Edward Frank retired lawyer

### Palm Harbor
Hoppenstead, Jon Kirk law librarian
McIlveen, Walter Ronald architectural engineer
Smith, W. James health facility administrator
Stettner, Jerald W. retail drugs stores executive
Wolfe, Elizabeth Anne elementary education educator

### Palmetto
Castleman, Tonya Kay journalist
Compton, Charles Daniel chemistry educator
Rains, Gloria Cann environmentalist company executive

### Panama City
Byrne, Robert William lawyer
Childers, Perry Robert psychology educator
D'Arcy, Gerald Paul engineering executive, consultant
Dykes, James Edgar advertising educator, consultant
Miller, Robert William personal property appraiser, writer
Nelson, Edith Ellen dietitian
Patterson, Christopher Nida lawyer
Smith, Larry Glenn retired state judge
†Wimberly, Mark Vincent utility executive

### Panama City Beach
Schafer, John Stephen foundation administrator
Shugart, Cecil Glenn retired physics educator

### Patrick A F B
Haggis, Arthur George, Jr. retired military officer, educator, publisher

### Pembroke Pines
Gordon, Lori Heyman therapist, writer, educator
Jones, Janet Louise health services administrator

### Penney Farms
Bronkema, Frederick Hollander retired minister and church official
Meyer, Marion M. editorial consultant

### Pensacola
Abercrombie, Charlotte Manning reading specialist, supervisor
Adams, Joseph Peter retired lawyer, consultant
Albrecht, Carol Heath artist, educator
Bowden, Jesse Earle newspaper editor, author, cartoonist, journalism educator
Bozeman, Frank Carmack lawyer
Bullock, Ellis Way, Jr. architect
Caton, Betty Ann health science administrator
Collier, Lacey Alexander federal judge
DeBardeleben, John Thomas, Jr. retired insurance company executive
Dillard, Robert Perkins pediatrician, educator
Dixon, James Andrew, Jr. protective services official
Duvall, Charles Farmer bishop
Furlong, George Morgan, Jr. museum foundation executive, retired naval officer
Geeker, Nicholas Peter lawyer, judge
George, Katie lawyer, former city manager
†Hanline, Manning Harold internist
Hooley, James Robert oral and maxillofacial surgeon, educator, dean
Hutto, Earl retired congressman
Johnson, Alfred Carl, Jr. former navy officer
Johnson, Rodney Marcum lawyer
Kelly, John Barry, II lawyer
Killian, Lewis Martin sociology educator
Klepper, Robert Kenneth writer, silent film historian, journalist
Loesch, Harold C. retired marine biologist, consultant
Loesch, Mabel Lorraine social worker
Long, H. Owen retired economics educator, fiction writer
Love, Robert William, Jr. retired physician, government administrator
Maddock, Lawrence Hill language educator, writer
Marsh, William Douglas lawyer
Marx, Morris Leon academic administrator
McLeod, Stephen Glenn education educator, language educator
McSwain, Richard Horace materials engineer, consultant
Moulton, Wilbur Wright, Jr. lawyer
Mountcastle, William Wallace, Jr. philosophy and religion educator
Nickelsen, Eric J. bank executive
Platz, Terrance Oscar utilities company executive
Ray, Donald Hensley biologist
Sargent, James O'Connor freelance writer
†Serangeli, Deborah S. health care facility administrator
Sharp, Elaine Cecile obstetrician, gynecologist
Soloway, Daniel Mark lawyer
Taggart, Linda Diane women's health nurse
Toifel, Ronald Charles librarian
Vinson, C. Roger federal judge
Vuksta, Michael Joseph surgeon
Watt, Stuart George engineering contracting company executive
Weisner, Maurice Franklin former naval officer
Woolf, Kenneth Howard architect
Wyss, Norma Rose Topping counselor, supervisor, educator, writer
Yoder, Ronda Elaine nursing educator

### Pineland
Donlon, Josephine A. diagnostic and evaluation counseling therapist, educator

### Pinellas Park
Athanson, Mary Catheryne elementary school principal
Hall, Charles Allen aerospace and energy company executive
Pellegrino, Nancy Davis middle school educator
Perry, Paul Alverson utility executive
West, Wallace Marion cultural organization administrator

### Placida
Grissom, Joseph Carol retired leasing and investments business executive

### Plant City
Buchman, Kenneth William lawyer
Holland, Gene Grigsby (Scottie Holland) artist
Patronelli, Raymond church administrator

### Plantation
Ballantyne, Maree Anne Canine artist
Buck, Thomas Randolph lawyer, financial services executive
Collins, Ronald William psychologist, educator
Ferris, Robert Edmund lawyer
Garrett, Linda Silverstein financial planner
Gewirtzman, Garry Bruce dermatologist
Koltnow, H. Robert lawyer
Lehman, Joan Alice real estate executive
Louck, Lori Ann speech-language pathologist
Oxell, Loie Gwendolyn fashion and beauty educator, consultant, columnist
Ramos, Manuel Antonio, Jr. pulmonologist
Tingley, Floyd Warren physician
Tobias, Benjamin Alan portfolio manager, financial planner

### Plymouth
Voelker, Charles Robert archbishop, academic dean

### Pompano Beach
Bliznakov, Emile George biomedical research scientist
Crandell, K(enneth) James management and strategic planning consultant, entrepreneur
Elder, Robert Lee professional golfer
Fritsch, Billy Dale, Jr. construction company executive
Heir, Kal M. financial executive
Hoffman, Lynn Renee elementary education educator
Hoffman, Susan E. Sladen medical nurse, case manager
Kester, Stewart Randolph banker
Kimberly, Ann Geyer nursing administrator, medical, surgical nurse
Legler, Bob publishing company executive
Mulvey, John Thomas, Jr. financial consultant
Presley, Brian investment company executive
Rifenburgh, Richard Philip investment company executive
Roen, Sheldon R. publisher, psychologist
Schwartz, Joseph retired container company executive
Szilassy, Sandor retired lawyer, library director, educator
Valdes, Jacqueline C. neuropsychologist, consultant, researcher
Wright, Joseph Robert, Jr. corporate executive
Zinman, Jacques former insurance agency executive

### Ponte Vedra
Garner, John Michael investment company executive
Love, Davis, III professional golfer
Moore, Philip Walsh appraisal company executive
Sampras, Pete tennis player
Watson, John Lawrence, III former trade association executive

### Ponte Vedra Beach
Azinger, Paul professional golfer
Berry, Clare Gebert real estate broker
Cook, John professional golfer
de Selding, Edward Bertrand retired banker
Edberg, Stefan former professional tennis player
†Elkington, Steve professional golfer
Elston, William Steger food products company executive
Faxon, Brad professional golfer
Fiorentino, Thomas Martin transportation executive, lawyer
Floyd, Raymond professional golfer
Forsman, Dan professional golfer
†Frost, David professional golfer
Green, Norman Kenneth retired oil industry executive, former naval officer
Hartzell, Karl Drew retired university dean, historian
Kite, Thomas O., Jr. professional golfer
Klacsmann, John Anthony retired chemical company executive
Kuhn, Bowie K. lawyer, former professional baseball commissioner, consultant
Milbrath, Robert Henry retired petroleum executive
Nadler, Sigmond Harold physician, surgeon
O'Brien, Raymond Vincent, Jr. banker
Pavin, Corey professional golfer
Phelan, Martin DuPont retired film company executive
ReMine, William Hervey, Jr. surgeon
Scheller, Sanford Gregory printing company executive
†Singh, Vijay professional golfer
Spence, Richard Dee paper products company executive, former railroad executive
Stewart, (William) Payne professional golfer
Thorndike, Richard King former brokerage company executive
†Tway, Bob professional golfer
Wadkins, Lanny professional golfer
Weinstein, George William ophthalmology educator
Wu, Hsiu Kwang economist, educator
Zoeller, Fuzzy professional golfer

### Port Charlotte
Clark, Keith Collar musician, educator
Gendzwill, Joyce Annette retired health officer
Gravelin, Janesy Swartz elementary education educator
Hennessy, Brother Paul Kevin religion school president
Kok, Hans Gebhard consulting engineer
Munger, Elmer Lewis civil engineer, educator
Norris, Dolores June elementary school educator
Reynolds, Helen Elizabeth management services consultant
Soben, Robert Sidney computer scientist
Spatz, Hugo David film producer

### Port Richey
Mueller, Lois M. psychologist

### Port Saint Lucie
Arnold, Roxanne post-anesthesia nurse
Centerbar, Alberta Elaine education educator, research specialist
Clark, Harold Steve architect
Huang, Denis Kuo Ying chemical engineer, consultant
McBride, Wanda Lee psychiatric nurse
Olson, Edward Charles entrepreneur, conservationist, film industry executive, writer, environmental consultant, business consultant
Rhodes, Alfred William former insurance company executive
Sommers, Robert Thomas editor, publisher, author
Wedzicha, Walter foreign language educator

### Punta Gorda
Beever, James William, III biologist
Beever, Lisa Britt-Dodd transportation and environmental planner, researcher
Brenner, Jane Segrest city council member
Bulzacchelli, John G. financial executive
Goodman, Donald C. university administrator
Harrington, John Vincent retired communications company executive, engineer, educator
Haswell, Carleton Radley banker
Hepfer, John William, Jr. retired air force officer, consultant
Herum, Jane Lentz psychology educator, consultant
Hill, Richard Earl academic administrator
Kavanaugh, Frank James film producer, educator
Olson, James Robert consulting engineer
Parvin, Philip E. retired agricultural researcher and educator
Piacitelli, John Joseph county official, educator, pediatrician
Smith, Charles Edwin computer science educator, consultant
Varney, Suzanne Glaab health facility administrator
Wood, Emma S. nurse practitioner

### Quincy
Laughlin, William Eugene electric power industry executive
Teare, Iwan Dale retired research scientist

### Ramrod Key
Clark, John Russell ecologist

### Reddick
Corwin, Joyce Elizabeth Stedman construction company executive

### Redington Beach
McConnell, Robert Chalmers former city official

### River Ranch
Swett, Albert Hersey retired lawyer, business executive, consultant

### Riverview
Till, Beatriz Maria international business consultant, translator

### Rockledge
Mitchell, Virginia Brinkman development associate

### Royal Palm Beach
Graham, Carl Francis consultant, former chemical products company executive, chemist

### Safety Harbor
Banks, Allan Richard artist, art historian, researcher
Dohnal, William Edward retired steel company executive, consultant, accountant

Fay, Carolyn M. education marketing business owner

### Saint Augustine
Adams, William Roger historian
Armstrong, John Alexander political scientist, educator
Baker, Norman Henderson professional association administrator
Borchardt, Duke federal labor relations professional
Edwards, Page Lawrence, Jr. author, archivist, historical society administrat
Gilliland, Thomas art gallery director
Greenberg, Michael John biologist, editor
Marsolais, Harold Raymond trade association administrator
Matzke, Frank J. architect, consultant
Nolan, Joseph Thomas journalism educator, communications consultant
Oliver, Elizabeth Kimball writer, historian
Portman, Nancy Ann artist, art educator
Proctor, William Lee college president
Quirke, Lillian Mary retired art educator
Rountree, John Griffin Richardson association and retail executive
Sullivan, Mary Jean elementary school educator
Theil, Henri economist, educator
Tuseo, Norbert Joseph John marketing executive, consultant

### Saint Cloud
Everett, Woodrow Wilson electrical engineer, educator

### Saint Marks
Labitzke, Dale Russell chemical processing engineer

### Saint Petersburg
Allen, John Thomas, Jr. lawyer
Allshouse, Merle Frederick higher education executive
Alpert, Barry Mark insurance company and banking executive
Armacost, Peter Hayden college president
Bailey, Robin Keith physician assistant, perfusionist
Barca, James Joseph fire department administrative services executive
Barnes, Andrew Earl newspaper editor
Battaglia, Anthony Sylvester lawyer
Belich, John Patrick, Sr. journalist
Benbow, Charles Clarence retired writer, critic
Bercu, Barry B. pediatric endocrinologist
Betzer, Susan Elizabeth Beers family physician, geriatrician
Blumenthal, Herman Bertram accountant
Brown, Jacqueline Ley White lawyer
Bryant, John author, publisher
Buchmann, Alan Paul lawyer
Byrd, Isaac Burlin fishery biologist, fisheries administrator
Callahan, James K. fire chief
Carlson, Jeannie Ann writer
Carroll, Charles Michael music educator
Clark, Carolyn Chambers nurse, author, educator
Clarke, Kit Hansen radiologist
Collins, Carl Russell, Jr. corporate services
Collins, Paul Steven vascular surgeon
Corty, Andrew P. publishing executive
Critchfield, Jack Barron utilities company executive
Davis, Ann Caldwell history educator
Dickson, Suzanne Elizabeth (Sue Dickson) educational administrator
Donaldson, Merle Richard electrical engineering educator, consultant
Donovan, Denis Miller psychiatrist, author, lecturer
Duval, Cynthia museum curator, adminstrator
Elson, Charles Myer law educator
Emerson, William Allen retired investment company executive
Escarraz, Enrique, III lawyer
Fassett, John D. retired utility executive, consultant
Foley, Michael Francis newspaper executive
Freeman, Corinne financial services, former mayor
Galbraith, John William securities company executive
Giffin, Barbara Haines education coordinator
Godbold, Francis Stanley investment banker, real estate executive
Good, Robert Alan physician, educator
Grube, Karl Bertram judge
Haiman, Robert James newspaper editor, journalism educator, media consultant
Hallock-Muller, Pamela oceanography educator, biogeologist, researcher
Hancock, John Allan utility company executive
Hansel, Paul George physicist, consultant
Hargrave, Victoria Elizabeth librarian
Harrell, Roy G., Jr. lawyer
Harris, Rogers S. bishop
Harris, Rogers Sanders bishop
Hines, Andrew Hampton, Jr. utilities executive
Hooker, Robert Wright journalist
Hull, Anne Victoria journalist
Jacob, Bruce Robert dean, academic administrator, law educator
Jenkins, Robert Norman newswriter, editor
Johnson, Edna Ruth editor
Joyce, Walter Joseph retired electronics company executive
Kazor, Walter Robert statistical process control and quality assurance consultant
Kent, Allen library and information sciences educator
Keyes, Benjamin B. therapist
Kruse, James Joseph merchant banker
Kubiet, Leo Lawrence newspaper advertising and marketing executive
Kuttler, Carl Martin, Jr. academic administrator
Lau, Michele Denise advertising consultant, sales trainer, television personality
Layton, William George computer company executive, management consultant, human resources executive
Mann, Sam Henry, Jr. lawyer
Marsalisi, Frank Bernard obstetrician-gynecologist
Martin, Susan Taylor newspaper editor
McIntyre, Deborah psychotherapist, author
†McMurray, Joseph Patrick Brendan financial consultant
Meinke, Peter writer, retired educator
Meisels, Gerhard George academic administrator, chemist, educator
Mills, William Harold, Jr. construction company executive
Moody, Lizabeth Ann law educator
†Moore, Mike baseball league executive
Mueller, O. Thomas molecular geneticist, pediatrics educator
Naimoli, Raymond Anthony infosystems specialist, financial consultant
Naughton, James Martin journalist
Nussbaum, Leo Lester retired college president, consultant
Pardoll, Peter Michael gastroenterologist
Patterson, Eugene Corbett retired editor, publisher
Peterson, Arthur Laverne former college president
†Pierce, Mary professional tennis player
Pittman, Robert Turner retired newspaper editor
Potter, Deborah Ann news correspondent, educator
Putnam, J. Stephen financial executive
Pyle, William Carmody human resource management educator, researcher
Ransom, Brian Charles artist, educator, musician, composer
Remke, Richard Edwin lumber company executive
Roney, Paul H(itch) federal judge
Root, Allen William pediatrician, educator
Rummel, Harold Edwin real estate development executive
Runge, De Lyle Paul retired library director, consultant
Rydstrom, Carlton Lionel chemist, paint and coating consultant
Sabatini, Gabriela retired tennis player
Schell, Joan Bruning information specialist, business science librarian
Scott, Lee Hansen retired holding company executive
Serrie, Hendrick anthropology and international business educator
Sheen, Robert Tilton manufacturing company executive
Sherburne, Donald Wynne philosopher, educator
Shi, Feng Sheng mathematician
Shuck, Robert F. financial executive
Silver, Lawrence Alan marketing executive
Söderberg, Bo Sigfrid business executive
Southworth, William Dixon retired education educator
Stevens, Edward Ira information systems educator
Tash, Paul C. editor-in-chief
Walker, Brigitte Maria translator, linguistic consultant
Wasserman, Susan Valesky accountant
Weaver, Thomas Harold health facility administrator
Wedding, Charles Randolph architect
Westall, Sandra Thornton special education educator
Williams, Larry Ross surgeon
Wilson, Darryl Cedric lawyer, law educator, consultant
Wisler, Willard Eugene health care management executive

### Saint Petersburg Beach
Hurley, Frank Thomas, Jr. realtor

### Sanford
Dickison, Alexander Kane physical science educator
Luna, Charaline superintendent of schools
San Miguel, Sandra Bonilla social worker

### Sanibel
Adair, Charles Valloyd retired physician
Allen, Patricia J. library director
Ball, Armand Baer former association executive, consultant
Brodbeck, William Jan marketing consultant, speaker
Courtney, James Edmond real estate development
Crown, David Allan criminologist, educator
Hasselman, Richard B. transportation company executive, retired
Herriott, Donald Richard optical physicist
Horecker, Bernard Leonard retired biochemistry educator
Keogh, Mary Cudahy artist
Kiernan, Edwin A., Jr. lawyer, corporation executive
Lautenbach, Terry Robert information systems and communications executive
Perkinson, Diana Agnes Zouzelka import company executive
Sheldon, Nancy Way environmental management consultant

### Santa Rosa Beach
Wright, John Peale retired banker

### Sarasota
Adams, Richard Towsley university president, educational consultant
Altabe, Joan Augusta Berg artist, writer, art and architecture critic
Arreola, John Bradley diversified financial service company executive, financial planner
Aull, Susan physician
Balter, Frances Sunstein civic worker
Beal, Winona Roark retired church administrator
Beck, George William retired industrial engineer
Beck, Robert Alfred hotel administration educator
Berkoff, Charles Edward pharmaceutical executive
Blazon-Popper, Denise G. sales executive
Borle, André Bernard physiologist
Borsos, Erika cardiac care, medical/surgical nurse
Burket, Harriet (Mrs. Francis B. Taussig) editor
Burkett, Helen artist
Byron, H. Thomas, Jr. veterinarian, educator
Campbell, Donna Marie telecommunications executive
Christ-Janer, Arland Frederick college president
Christopher, William Garth lawyer
Connor, Robert T. former government official
Covert, Michael Henri healthcare facility administrator
Cox, Houston Abraham, Jr. financial and futures markets consultant
Dearden, Robert James retired pharmacist
Dlesk, George retired pulp and paper industry executive
Downey, John Charles university dean, zoology educator
Eachus, Joseph J(ackson) computer scientist, consultant
Ebitz, David MacKinnon art historian, museum director
Estrin, Richard William newspaper editor
Fabrycy, Mark Zdzislaw retired economist
Feder, Allan Appel management executive, consultant
Fendrick, Alan Burton retired advertising executive
Friedberg, Harold David cardiologist
Gilbert, Perry Webster emeritus educator
Gittelson, Bernard public relations consultant, author, lecturer
Goldsmith, Stanley Alan lawyer
Gordon, Sanford Daniel economics educator
Gourley, Mary E. education educator
Graham, Otto Everett, Jr. retired athletic director
Greenfield, Robert Kauffman lawyer
Grubbs, Elven Judson retired newspaper publisher
Gurvitz, Milton Solomon psychologist
Hackl, Alphons J. publisher
Hagen, George Leon computer systems consultant
Hamberg, Daniel economist, educator
Harmon, (Loren) Foster art consultant
Hayes, Joseph author
Held, Philip artist
Hennemeyer, Robert Thomas diplomat
Herb, F(rank) Steven lawyer
Highland, Marilyn M. principal
Hoffman, Oscar Allen retired forest products company executive
Honner Sutherland, B. Joan advertising executive
Hoover, Dwight Wesley history educator
Hrones, John Anthony mechanical engineering educator
Hull, J(ames) Richard retired lawyer, business executive
Hummel, Dana D. Mallett librarian
Ives, George Skinner arbitrator, former government official
Jacobson, Melvin Joseph applied mathematician, acoustician, educator
Janney, Oliver James lawyer, plastics and chemical company executive
Jelks, Mary Larson retired pediatrician
Kerker, Milton chemistry educator
Kimbrough, Robert Averyt lawyer
Kiplinger, Glenn Francis pharmacologist, medical-legal consultant
Klutzow, Friedrich Wilhelm neuropathologist
Krate, Nat artist
Lambert, John Phillip financial executive, consultant
Lawrence, George Durwood, Jr. lawyer, corporate executive
Lewis, Brian Kreglow computer consultant
Lindsay, David Breed, Jr. aircraft company executive, former editor and publisher
Long, Robert Radcliffe fluid mechanics educator
Loomis, Wesley Horace, III former publishing company executive
Loving, George Gilmer, Jr. retired air force officer
Lund, Wendell Luther lawyer
MacDonald, Robert Taylor newspaper executive
Mackey, Leonard Bruce lawyer, former diversified manufacturing corporation executive
Magenheim, Mark Joseph physician, epidemiologist, educator
Mahadevan, Kumar marine laboratory director, researcher
Marino, Eugene Louis publishing company executive
Mattran, Donald Albert management consultant, educator
McCollum, John Morris tenor
Meyer, B. Fred small business executive, home designer and builder, product designer
Middleton, Norman Graham social worker, psychotherapist
Miles, Arthur J. financial planner, consultant
Miranda, Carlos Sa food products company executive
Myerson, Albert Leon physical chemist
Neeley, Delmar George human resources consultant
Noether, Emiliana Pasca historian, educator
North, Marjorie Mary columnist
O'Malley, Thomas Anthony gastroenterologist, internist
Page, George Keith banker
Pesut, Timothy S. investment advisor, professional speaker, consultant
Phillips, Elvin Willis lawyer
Pierce, Richard Harry research director for laboratory
Pillot, Gene Merrill retired school system administrator
Pollack, Joseph diversified company executive
Poppel, Harvey Lee management consultant
Proffitt, Waldo, Jr. newspaper editor
Putterman, Florence Grace artist, printmaker
Raimi, Burton Louis lawyer
Retzer, Mary Elizabeth Helm retired librarian
Roberts, Merrill Joseph economist, educator
Ross, Gerald Fred engineering executive, researcher
Roth, James Frank manufacturing company executive, chemist
Russell, Margaret Jones (Peg Russell) secondary school educator, retired writer
Savenor, Betty Carmell painter, printmaker
Schersten, H. Donald management consultant, realtor, mortgage broker
Schwartz, Norman L. lawyer
Seibert, Russell Jacob botanist, research associate
Shulman, Arthur communications executive
Silberman, Charles Eliot magazine editor, author
Simon, Joseph Patrick food services executive
Skelton, Howard Clifton advertising and public relations executive
Slocum, Donald Hillman product development executive
Smith, Mark Hallard architect
Spencer, Lonabelle (Kappie Spencer) political agency administrator, lobbyist
Stickler, Daniel Lee health care management consultant
Sturtevant, Ruthann Patterson anatomy educator
Tatum, Joan Glennalyn John secondary school educator
Tucci, Steven Michael health facility administrator, physician, recording industry executive
Twentyman, Lee foreign service officer, economist
Veinott, Cyril George electrical engineer, consultant
Vestal, Lucian LaRoe financier
Weeks, Albert Loren author, educator, journalist
Welch, John Dana urologist, performing arts association executive
White, Will Walter, III public relations consultant, writer
Wigton, Paul Norton steel company consultant, former executive
Wilson, Kenneth Jay writer
Winterhalter, Dolores August (Dee Winterhalter) art educator
Wise, Warren Roberts lawyer
Wysnewski, Roy Edward physicist
Yonker, Richard Aaron rheumatologist
Yordan, Carlos Manuel foreign service officer

### Satellite Beach
Clark, John F. aerospace research and engineering educator
Van Arsdall, Robert Armes engineer, retired air force officer

### Sebastian
Becker, Jim small business owner
Mauke, Otto Russell retired college president
Muller, Henry John real estate developer
Pieper, Patricia Rita artist, photographer

### Sebring
McCollum, James Fountain lawyer
Sherrick, Daniel Noah real estate broker
Vance, Elbridge Putnam mathematics educator

### Seminole
Christ, Philip William orthopaedic surgeon, osteopath
Dubel, Doris Geraldine Cottrell gerontology nurse
Hoche, Philip Anthony life insurance company executive
Nesbitt, Robert Edward Lee, Jr. physician, educator, scientific researcher, writer

### Shalimar
Kelly, Kathleen Suzanne marketing professional
Sublette, Julia Wright music educator, performer, adjudicator

### South Miami
†Zwerling, Leonard Joseph physician, educator

### Spring Hill
Burnim, Kalman Aaron theatre educator emeritus
Collins, Stephen Allen environmental consultant
Finney, Roy Pelham, Jr. urologist, surgeon, inventor
Martin, Gary J. retired business executive, mayor
Rojas, Victor Hugo Macedo retired vocational education educator
Slaattè, Howard Alexander minister, philosophy educator
Youngman, Henny comedian

### Starke
Loper, George Wilson, Jr. physical education educator

### Stuart
Ankrom, Charles Franklin golf course architect, consultant
Bourque, Anita Mary school principal, health facility administrator
Conklin, George Melville retired food company executive
Delagi, Edward Francis physician, retired educator
DeRubertis, Patricia Sandra software company executive
Harvin, Wesley Reid lawyer
Haserick, John Roger retired dermatologist
Hutchinson, Janet Lois historical society administrator
Leibson, Irving industrial executive
McKenna, Sidney F. technical company executive
Morena, John Joseph manufacturing engineer, executive
Murchake, John publishing executive
O'Connor, Francis X. financial executive
Patterson, Robert Arthur physician, health care consultant, retired health care company executive, retired air force officer
Petzold, Anita Marie psychotherapist
Pisani, Joseph Michael physician
Slade, Gerald Jack publishing company executive
Wasiele, Harry W., Jr. diversified electrical manufacturing company executive
Westlake, Robert Elmer, Sr. physician
White, Donald Francis financial planner, insurance agent

### Summerland Key
Thomas, Vincent Cox editor

### Sun City Center
Calviello, Joseph Anthony research electrophysicist, consultant
Darling, Frank Clayton former political science educator, educational institute administrator
Fleischman, Sol Joseph, Sr. retired television broadcasting executive
Hall, John Fry psychologist, educator
Jeffries, Robert Joseph retired engineering educator, business executive
McGrath, John Francis utility executive
Parsons, George Williams retired medical center administrator, cattle rancher
Stanton, Vivian Brennan (Mrs. Ernest Stanton) retired educator

### Sunrise
Epstein, Samuel D. electronics executive
Symon-Gutierrez, Patricia Paulette dietitian

### Surfside
Batcheller, Joseph Ann entrepreneur
Berman, Mona S. actress, playwright, theatrical director and producer
Polley, Richard Donald microbiologist, polymer chemist
Prystowsky, Harry physician, educator

### Tallahassee
Adams, Perry Ronald former college administrator
Anthony, William Philip management educator
Arce, Pedro Edgardo chemical engineering educator
Ashler, Philip Frederic international trade and development advisor
Aurell, John Karl lawyer
Avant, David Alonzo, Jr. realty company executive, photographer
Bagley, James Robert freelance writer
Barley, John Alvin lawyer
Barnett, Martha Walters lawyer
Bartlett, Richard Adams American historian, educator
Baum, Werner A. former academic administrator, meteorologist
Beach, Cecil Prentice librarian
Beck, Earl Ray historian, educator
Bert, Clara Virginia home economics educator, administrator
Bishop, Barney Tipton, III political consultant, lobbyist
Boutwell, Wallace Kenneth, Jr. management consultant, health care executive
Bowden, Bobby university athletic coach
Boyd, Joseph Arthur, Jr. lawyer
Braswell, Robert Neil scientist, engineer, educator

Brueckheimer, William Rogers *social science educator*
†Brunais, Andrea *newspaper editor*
Burkman, Ernest, Jr. *education educator*
Burnette, Ada M. Puryear *educational administrator*
Burroway, Janet G. *English language educator, novelist*
Butterworth, Robert A. *state attorney general*
Bye, Raymond Erwin, Jr. *academic administrator*
Campbell, Frances Harvell *foundation administrator*
Carson, Leonard Allen *lawyer*
Caspar, Donald Louis Dvorak *biophysics and structural biology educator*
Chen, Ching Jen *mechanical engineering educator, research scientist*
Chiles, Lawton Mainor *governor, former senator*
Choppin, Gregory Robert *chemistry educator*
Clarke, Allan J. *oceanography educator, consultant*
Clarkson, Julian Derieux *lawyer*
Colberg, Marshall Rudolph *economist*
Coloney, Wayne Herndon *civil engineer*
Crawford, Bob *state commissioner*
Crow, Jack E. *physics administrator*
Curtin, Lawrence N. *lawyer*
Dadisman, Joseph Carrol *newspaper executive*
D'Alemberte, Talbot (Sandy D'Alemberte) *academic administrator, lawyer*
Dariotis, Terrence Theodore *lawyer*
Davis, Bertram Hylton *retired English educator*
Davis, Larry Michael *military officer, health-care consultant*
De Forest, Sherwood Searle *agricultural engineer, agribusiness services executive*
Dillingham, Marjorie Carter *foreign language educator*
Dorn, Charles Meeker *art education educator*
Durrence, James Larry *state executive, history educator*
Dye, Thomas Roy *political science educator*
Ehlen, Martin Richard *state agency administrator, management analyst*
Ervin, Robert Marvin *lawyer*
Fonvielle, Charles David *lawyer*
Ford, Ann Suter *family nurse practitioner, health planner*
Foss, Donald John *university dean, research psychologist*
Frechette, Ernest Albert *foreign language educator emeritus*
Friedmann, E(merich) Imre *biologist, educator*
Friedmann, Roseli Ocampo *microbiologist, educator*
Gil, Lazier *university dean*
Gilmer, Robert *mathematics educator*
Golden, Leon *classicist, educator*
Gould, Bruce Allan *state agency administrator, educator, consultant*
Griffith, Elwin Jabez *lawyer, university administrator*
Grimes, Stephen Henry *state supreme court justice*
Gunter, William Dawson, Jr. (Bill Gunter) *insurance company executive*
Gupta, Madhu Sudan *electrical engineering educator*
Hafner, Lawrence Erhardt *education educator*
Hall, Houghton Alexander *electrical engineering*
Harding, Major Best *state supreme court justice*
Harper, George Mills *English language educator*
Harris, Natholyn Dalton *food science educator, researcher*
Harrison, Thomas James *electrical engineer, educator*
Harsanyi, Janice *soprano, educator*
Hatchett, Joseph Woodrow *federal judge*
Hedstrom, Susan Lynne *maternal women's health nurse*
Herndon, Roy Clifford *physicist*
Holcombe, Randall Gregory *economics educator*
Housewright, Wiley Lee *music educator*
Humphries, Frederick S. *university president*
Hunt, John Edwin *insurance company executive, consultant*
Hunt, Mary Alice *library science educator*
Hunter, Christopher *mathematics educator*
James, Frances Crews *zoology educator*
Johnsen, Russell Harold *chemist, educator*
Johnson, Benjamin F., VI *real estate developer, consulting economist*
Kaelin, Eugene Francis *philosophy educator*
Kemper, Kirby Wayne *physics educator*
Kenshalo, Daniel Ralph *psychologist, educator*
Kirk, Colleen Jean *conductor, educator*
Koontz, Christine Miller *research faculty*
Laird, William Everette, Jr. *economics educator, administrator*
Leavell, Michael Ray *computer programmer, analyst*
Lick, Dale Wesley *educator*
Lindner, William H. *state official*
Lipner, Harry *retired physiologist, educator*
Lisenby, Dorrece Edenfield *realtor*
Loper, David Eric *mathematics educator, geophysics educator*
Lynn, Gwendolyn Renaye *educator*
MacKay, Kenneth Hood, Jr. (Buddy MacKay) *state official, former congressman*
Maguire, Charlotte Edwards *retired physician*
Mandelkern, Leo *biophysics and chemistry educator*
Manley, Walter Wilson, II *lawyer*
Marshall, Alan George *chemistry and biochemistry educator*
Marshall, Stanley *former educator, business executive*
McBride, Donna Jannean *publisher*
McConnell, Michael *opera company director*
Mc Cord, Guyte Pierce, Jr. *retired judge*
McCrimmon, James McNab *language educator*
Meredith, Michael *science educator, researcher*
Miller, Gregory R. *prosecutor*
Miller, Morris Henry *lawyer*
Mills, Belen Collantes *early childhood education educator*
Moore, John Hebron *history educator*
Morgan, Lucy W. *journalist*
Morgan, Robert Marion *educational research educator*
Mortham, Sandra Barringer *state official*
Moulton, Grace Charbonnet *physics educator*
Mustian, Middleton Truett *hospital administrator*
Nam, Charles Benjamin *sociologist, demographer, educator*
Newell, Barbara Warne *economist, educator*
Nichols, Eugene Douglas *mathematics educator*
Oldson, William Orville *history educator*
Overton, Benjamin Frederick *state supreme court justice*
Owens, Joseph Francis, III *physics educator*
Palladino-Craig, Allys *museum director*
Paredes, James Anthony *anthropologist, educator*
Parker, Herbert Gerald *state official*
Pelham, Thomas Gerald *lawyer*
Penrod, Kenneth Earl *medical education consultant, retired*
Penson, Edward Martin *management consulting company executive*
Peterson, Rodney Delos *mediator, forensic economist*
Pfeffer, Richard Lawrence *geophysics educator*
Pugh, Thomas Doering *architecture educator*
Reed, Charles Bass *academic administrator*
Reid, Sue Titus *law educator*
Rhodes, Roberta Ann *dietitian*
Rice, Nancy Marie *nursing consultant*
Rittberg, Eric Dondaro *political consultant*
Robbins, Jane Borsch *library science educator, information science educator*
Robson, Donald *physics educator*
Rockwood, Ruth H. *former library science educator*
Roland, Raymond William *lawyer, mediator*
Ryll, Frank Maynard, Jr. *professional society administrator*
Saunders, Ron *lawyer, former state legislator*
Schrieffer, John Robert *physics educator, science administrator*
Schroeder, Edwin Maher *law educator*
Semion, A. Kay *editor*
Sengbusch, Howard George *biology, parasitology educator*
Serow, William John *economics educator*
Shaw, Leander Jerry, Jr. *state supreme court justice*
Stafford, William Henry, Jr. *federal judge*
Stino, Farid K.R. *biostatistician, educator, researcher, consultant*
Summers, Frank William *librarian*
Summers, Lorraine Dey Schaeffer *librarian*
Sundberg, Alan Carl *former state supreme court justice, lawyer*
Taylor, J(ames) Herbert *cell biology educator*
Thomas, James Bert, Jr. *government official*
Trezza, Alphonse Fiore *librarian, educator*
Tuckman, Bruce Wayne *educational psychologist, educator, researcher*
Voran, James F. *principal*
Walborsky, Harry M. *chemistry educator, consultant*
Wells, Charles Talley *judge*
Wilkins, (George) Barratt *librarian*
Zachert, Martha Jane *retired librarian*
Zaiser, Kent Ames *lawyer*

**Tamarac**
Bekoff, Oscar *psychotherapist*
Krause, John L. *optometrist*
Weinstein, Peter M. *lawyer, state senator*

**Tampa**
Abell, Jan Mary *architect*
Adkins, Edward Cleland *lawyer*
Afield, Walter Edward *psychiatrist, service executive*
Aguinaldo, Jorge Tansingco *chemical engineer, water treatment consultant*
Aitken, Thomas Dean *lawyer*
Alexander, William Olin *finance company executive*
Anderson, Robert Henry *education educator*
Anton, John Peter *philosopher, educator*
Ault, Jeffrey Michael *investment banker*
Aye, Walter Edwards *lawyer*
†Bailey, Maxwell C. *career officer*
Baldwin, Maryann Powell *school counselor, educator*
Barkin, Marvin E. *lawyer*
Barness, Lewis Abraham *physician*
Barton, Bernard Alan, Jr. *lawyer*
Battle, Jean Allen *writer, educator*
Baynes, Thomas Edward, Jr. *judge, lawyer, educator*
Bedford, Robert Forrest *anesthesiologist*
Behnke, Roy Herbert *physician, educator*
Benjamin, Robert Spiers *foreign correspondent, writer, publicist*
†Bergeron, Jean-Claude *professional hockey player*
Bierley, John Charles *lawyer*
Biles, (Lee) Thomas *religious organization executive, clergyman*
Binford, Jesse Stone, Jr. *chemistry educator*
Blomgren, Bruce Holmes *real estate developer, motivational speaker*
Bondi, Joseph Charles, Jr. *education educator, consultant*
Bowen, Thomas Edwin *cardiothoracic surgeon, retired army officer*
Branch, William Terrell *urologist, educator*
Brown, John Lott *educator*
Brown, Troy Anderson, Jr. *electrical distributing company executive*
Bucklew, Susan Cawthon *federal judge*
Bukantz, Samuel Charles *physician, educator*
Bunker-Soler, Antonio Luis *physician*
Burnette, Guy Ellington, Jr. *lawyer*
Butler, Paul Bascomb, Jr. *lawyer*
†Callen, David H. *hotel executive*
Campbell, David Ned *retired electric utility executive, business consultant*
Campbell, Margaret Georgeson *retired librarian*
Campbell, Richard Bruce *lawyer*
Cannella, Deborah Fabbri *elementary school educator*
Cardoso, Anthony Antonio *artist, educator*
Carnahan, Robert Paul *civil engineer, educator, researcher, consultant*
Cavanagh, Denis *physician, educator*
Christopher, Wilford Scott *public relations consultant*
Cohen, Frank Burton *wholesale novelty company executive*
Corbitt, Doris Orene *real estate agent, dietitian*
Corcoran, C. Timothy, III *judge*
Crisp, Terry Arthur *professional hockey coach*
Crowder, Bonnie Walton *small business owner, composer*
Cundiff, Paul Arthur *English language educator*
Daniel, Patricia Lynne *educator, consultant*
Davis, Helen Gordon *former state senator*
Davis, Richard Earl *lawyer*
Davis, W. E. *clergyman, bishop*
del Regato, Juan Angel *radiotherapeutist, oncologist, educator*
DeMontier, Paulette LaPointe *chemist*
Deutsch, Sid *bioengineer, educator*
DeVine, B. Mack *management consultant*
Dickinson, Wendy Buchanan *measurement and research educator, artist*
Dodds, Linda Carol *insurance company executive*
Doliner, Nathaniel Lee *lawyer*
Donelan, Peter Andrew *dermatologist*
†Dungy, Tony *professional sports team executive*
Dunn, Henry Hampton *writer, former television commentator, former editor*
Eddy, Colette Ann *aerial photography studio owner, photographer*
Ellwanger, Thomas John *lawyer*
England, Lynne Lipton *lawyer, speech pathologist, audiologist*
Fagan, Mildred B. (Mitzi Fagan) *occupational health nurse*
Falls, William Wayne *aquaculturist*
Ferlita, Theresa Ann *clinical social worker*
Flom, Edward Leonard *retired steel company executive*
†Flynn, Michael Patrick *radiologist*
Franzen, Lavern Gerhard *bishop*
Freedman, Sandra Warshaw *former mayor*
Frias, Jaime Luis *pediatrician, educator*
Friedlander, Edward Jay *journalism educator*
Gamble, Mary G(race) *marketing and quality professional*
Gassler, Frank Henry *lawyer*
Germany, John Fredrick *lawyer*
Gilbert, Leonard Harold *lawyer*
Gilbert-Barness, Enid F. *pathologist, pathology and pediatrics educator*
Gillen, William Albert *lawyer*
Givens, Paul Edward *industrial engineer, educator*
Givens, Paul Ronald *former university chancellor*
Glasser, Stephen Paul *cardiologist*
†Glazer, Malcolm *professional sports team executive*
Glickman, Ronnie Carl *state official, lawyer*
Greco, Dick A. *mayor, hardware company executive*
Greenfield, George B. *radiologist*
Hadden, John Winthrop *immunopharmacology educator*
†Hamrlik, Roman *professional hockey player*
Hanford, Agnes Rutledge *financial adviser*
Hanford, Grail Stevenson *writer*
Hankenson, E(dward) Craig, Jr. *performing arts executive*
Hapner, Elizabeth Lynn *lawyer, writer*
Harkness, Mary Lou *librarian*
Harriman, Malcolm Bruce *software developer, healthcare consultant*
Hartmann, William Herman *pathologist, educator*
Hedrick, Steve Brian *psychotherapist*
Hegarty, Thomas Joseph *academic administrator, history educator*
Henning, Rudolf Ernst *electrical engineer, educator, consultant*
Hernandez, Gilberto Juan *accountant, auditor, management consultant*
Heuer, Martin *temporary services executive*
Hickman, Hugh V. *science educator, researcher*
†Hillman, James V. *pediatrician*
Hinsch, Gertrude Wilma *biology educator*
Holder, Anna Maria *holding company executive*
Holder, Harold Douglas, Sr. *investor, industrialist*
Holfelder, Lawrence Andrew *pediatrician, allergist*
Holmes, Dwight Ellis *architect*
Howey, John Richard *architect*
Hoyt, Brooks Pettingill *lawyer*
Hulls, James Robert *emergency physician*
Humphries, J. Bob *lawyer*
Jacobs, Timothy Andrew *epidemiologist, international health consultant*
Jacobson, Howard Newman *obstetrics and gynecology educator, researcher*
Jennewein, James Joseph *architect*
Johnson, Anthony O'Leary (Andy Johnson) *meteorologist, consultant*
Johnson, Ewell Calvin *research and engineering executive*
Jones, John Arthur *lawyer*
Kase-Polisini, Judith Baker *theater educator, playwright*
Kaufman, Ronald Paul *physician, school official*
Kaw, Autar Krishen *mechanical engineer, educator*
Kelly, Thomas Paine, Jr. *lawyer*
Kessen, George William *employment agency manager*
Kiernan, William Joseph, Jr. *lawyer, real estate investor*
Kimmel, Ellen Bishop *psychologist, educator*
Koopmann, Reta Collene *sales executive*
Kovac, Michael G. *engineering educator*
†Kowalski, John *soccer coach*
Krzanowski, Joseph John, Jr. *pharmacology educator*
Lakdawala, Sharad R. *psychiatrist*
Lane, Robin *lawyer*
†Lassiter, Roy *soccer player*
Leavengood, Victor Price *telephone company executive*
LeFevre, David E. *lawyer, professional sports team executive*
Levine, Jack Anton *lawyer*
Lim, Daniel Van *microbiology educator*
†Lionetti, Donald Michael *career military officer*
Litschgi, A. Byrne *lawyer*
Locker, Raymond Duncan *editor*
Lockey, Richard Funk *allergist, educator*
Lowe, Peter Stephen *non-profit company executive*
Lozner, Eugene Leonard *internal medicine educator, consultant*
Luddington, Betty Walles *library media specialist*
Lykes, Joseph T., III *shipping company executive*
Lyman, Gary Herbert *epidemiologist, cancer researcher, educator*
MacDonald, Thomas Cook, Jr. *lawyer*
MacManus, Susan Ann *political science educator, researcher*
Mahan, Charles Samuel *public health service officer*
Mandelbaum, Samuel Robert *lawyer*
Mangiapane, Joseph Arthur *consulting company executive, applied mechanics consultant*
Martin, Gary Wayne *lawyer*
Martin, Robert Leslie *physician*
Matheny, Charles Woodburn, Jr. *retired army officer, retired civil engineer*
McAdams, John P. *lawyer*
Mc Alister, Linda Lopez *educator, philosopher*
McClurg, Douglas P. *lawyer*
McCook, Kathleen de la Peña *university educator*
McDevitt, Sheila Marie *lawyer, energy company executive*
McEnery, Janet Goldberg *lawyer*
McIntosh, Henry Deane *cardiologist*
†McKay, Richard James *lawyer*
McNeel, Van Louis *chemical company executive*
Melendez, Edwin Manuel *orthopaedic hand surgeon*
Menendez, Manuel, Jr. *judge*
Merryday, Steven D. *federal judge*
Miller, Charles Leslie *civil engineer, planner, consultant*
Muroff, Lawrence Ross *nuclear medicine physician*
Murtagh, Frederick Reed *neuroradiologist, educator*
Nagera, Humberto *psychiatrist, psychoanalyst, educator, author*
Naimoli, Vincent Joseph *diversified operating and holding company executive*
Neusner, Jacob *humanities and religious studies educator*
Nevins, Albert J. *publisher, editor, author*
†Nickerson, Hardy Otto *football player*
Nimmons, Ralph Wilson, Jr. *federal judge*
Nord, Walter Robert *business administration educator, researcher, consultant*
Olson, John Karl *lawyer*
Olson, Robert Eugene *physician, biochemist, educator*
O'Neill, Albert Clarence, Jr. *lawyer*
O'Sullivan, Brendan Patrick *lawyer*
Pacheco, Felipe Ramon *lawyer*
Parker, Carol Jean *psychotherapist, consultant*
†Peay, J.H. Binford, III *career officer*
Perry, James Frederic *philosophy educator, author*
Pfeiffer, Eric Armin *psychiatrist, gerontologist*
Platt, Jan Kaminis *county official*
Plawecki, Judith Ann *nursing educator*
Poe, William Frederick *insurance agency executive, former mayor*
Pollara, Bernard *immunologist, educator, pediatrician*
Pope, Jesse Curtis *theology and religious studies educator*
Powers, Pauline Smith *psychiatrist, educator, researcher*
Preto-Rodas, Richard A. *foreign language educator*
†Pupello, Dennis Frank *cardiac surgeon, educator*
Reading, Anthony John *physician*
Reeher, James Irwin *minister*
Reese-Brown, Brenda *primary education educator, mathematics specialist*
Reyes, Lillian Jenny *lawyer*
Richardson, Sylvia Onesti *physician*
Roberson, Bruce H. *lawyer*
Roberts, Edwin Albert, Jr. *newspaper editor, journalist*
Robinson, Charles E. *building materials executive*
Robinson, John William, IV *lawyer*
Rogal, Philip James *physician*
Rosenkranz, Stanley William *lawyer*
Rowlands, David Thomas *pathology educator*
Ruth, Daniel John *journalist*
†Sakiewicz, Nick *professional sports team executive*
Sanchez, Mary Anne *secondary school educator*
Schmidt, Paul Joseph *physician, educator*
Schnitzlein, Harold Norman *anatomy educator*
Schonwetter, Ronald Scott *physician, educator*
Schwenke, Roger Dean *lawyer*
Scott, Charles Francis *health facility administrator*
Shevy, Allen Earl, Jr. *publishing executive*
Shively, John Adrian *pathologist*
Shons, Alan Rance *plastic surgeon, educator*
Siegel, Richard Lawrence *allergist, immunologist, pediatrician*
Sigety, Charles Birge *investment company executive*
Silbiger, Martin L. *radiologist, medical educator, college dean*
Silver, Paul Robert *marketing executive, consultant*
†Sinnott, John Thomas *internist, educator*
Soble, James Barry *lawyer*
Solomon, Eldra Pearl Brod *psychologist, educator, biologist, author*
Sparkman, Steven Leonard *lawyer*
Spellacy, William Nelson *obstetrician, gynecologist, educator*
Stallings, (Charles) Norman *lawyer*
Stiles, Mary Ann *lawyer*
Streeter, Richard Barry *academic official*
Studer, William Allen *county official*
Sweet, Charles G. *paralegal school administrator, dean*
Tabor, Curtis Harold, Jr. *library director*
Tapp, Mamie Pearl *educational association administration*
Taub, Theodore Calvin *lawyer*
Thomas, Wayne Lee *lawyer*
Thompson, Denisse R. *mathematics educator*
Tully, Darrow *newspaper publisher*
Tutwiler, Charles Richard (Dick Tutwiler) *insurance company executive*
Van Matre, Joyce Dianne *rehabilitation nurse*
Vessel, Robert Leslie *lawyer*
Wade, Thomas Edward *electrical engineering educator, university research administrator*
Wagner, Frederick William (Bill Wagner) *lawyer*
Waller, Edward Martin, Jr. *lawyer*
Watkins, Joan Marie *osteopath, occupational medicine physician*
Weiner, Irving Bernard *university administrator, psychologist, educator*
White, Nancy G. *journalism educator*
Williams, Thomas Arthur *biomedical computing consultant, psychiatrist*
Williams, Yvonne G. *corporate trainer*
Wilson, Wallace *art educator, artist*
Young, Gwynne A. *lawyer*
Zelinski, Joseph John *engineering educator, consultant*
Zhou, Huanchun *chemist, administrator*

**Tarpon Springs**
Byrne, Richard Hill *counselor, educator*
Dempster, Richard Vreeland *environmental company executive*
Georgiou, Ruth Schwab *retired social worker*
Giavis, Theodore Demetrios *commercial illustrator, artist*
Gills, James Pitzer, Jr. *surgeon, educator, philanthropist*
Green, May Clayman *early childhood educator and administrator*
Hubbs, Arden Perry, II *financial services company executive, consultant*
Jackel, Simon Samuel *food products company executive, technical marketing and business consultant*
Padberg, Daniel Ivan *agricultural economics educator, researcher*
Scala, Sinclaire Maximilian *retired aerospace engineer*
Vajk, Hugo *manufacturing executive*
Wilson, Robert William *defense systems company executive*

**Tavernier**
Mabbs, Edward Carl *retired management consultant*

**Temple Terrace**
Rink, Wesley Winfred *banker*

**Tequesta**
Danly, Donald Robert *retired manufacturing company executive*
Holmes, Melvin Almont *insurance company executive*
Kraft, Otto Fritz *investment advisor, artist*
Luster, George Orchard *professional society administrator*
Milton, Robert Mitchell *chemical company executive*

Peterson, James Robert *retired writing instrument manufacturing executive*
Ragno, Nancy Nickell *educational writer*
Seaman, William Bernard *physician, radiology educator*
Turrell, Richard Horton, Sr. *retired banker*
Vollmer, James E. *consulting company executive*

### Tierra Verde
Gaffney, Thomas Francis *investment company executive*
Garnett, Stanley Iredale, II *lawyer, utility company executive*
Schmitz, Dolores Jean *primary education educator*

### Titusville
Cockriel, Russell George, Sr. *crime investigation official*
Hartung, Patricia McEntee *therapist*
Kirchman, Budagail Simms *realtor*
Linscott, Jacqueline C. *education consultant, retired educator*
Roath-Algera, Kathleen Marie *massage therapist*

### Treasure Island
Meisner, Judith Anne *clinical social worker, marital and sex therapist, psychotherapist*

### Umatilla
Lange, Billie Carola *aquatic exercise video creator and specialist*

### Valrico
Benjamin, Sheila Pauletta *secondary education educator*

### Venice
Appel, Wallace Henry *retired industrial designer*
Baga, Margaret Fitzpatrick *nurse, medical office manager*
Bluhm, Barbara Jean *communications agency executive*
Buckley, John William *financial company executive*
Christy, Audrey Meyer *public relations consultant*
Concordia, Charles *consulting engineer*
Corrigan, William Thomas *retired broadcast news executive*
Dodderidge, Richard William *retired marketing executive*
Hays, Herschel Martin *electrical engineer*
Hrachovina, Frederick Vincent *osteopathic physician and surgeon*
Jackel, Lawrence *publishing company executive*
Jamrich, John Xavier *retired university administrator*
Kinney, Michael James *physician*
Leidheiser, Henry, Jr. *retired chemistry educator, consultant*
McEntee, Robert Edward *management consultant*
Miller, Allan John *lawyer*
Nevins, John J. *bishop*
Ogan, Russell Griffith *business executive, retired air force officer*
O'Keefe, Robert James *retired banker*
Przemieniecki, Janusz Stanislaw *engineering executive, former government senior executive and college dean*
Shaw, Bryce Robert *author*
Thomas, David Ansell *retired university dean*
Torrey, Richard Frank *utility executive*
Ward, Jacqueline Ann Beas *nurse, healthcare administrator*

### Vero Beach
Ahrens, William Henry *architect*
Allik, Michael *diversified industry executive*
Anderson, Rudolph J., Jr. *lawyer*
Baker, Richard H. *geneticist, educator*
Burton, Arthur Henry, Jr. *insurance company executive*
Calevas, Harry Powell *management consultant*
Clawson, John Addison *financier, investor*
Cochrane, William Henry *municipal administration executive*
Conway, Earl Cranston *business educator, retired manufacturing company executive*
Daly, John Francis *engineering company executive*
Dragone, Allan R. *manufacturing company executive*
Feagles, Robert West *insurance company executive*
Fetter, Robert Barclay *retired administrative sciences educator*
Fisher, Andrew *management consultant*
Glassmeyer, Edward *investment banker*
Grobman, Arnold Brams *retired biology educator and academic administrator*
Grobman, Hulda Gross (Mrs. Arnold B. Grobman) *retired health sciences educator*
Halan, John Paul *human resources executive*
Haywood, Oliver Garfield *engineer*
Hungerford, Lugene Green *physicist*
Koontz, Alfred Joseph, Jr. *financial and operating management executive, consultant*
Lawrence, Merle *medical educator*
MacTaggart, Barry *retired corporate executive*
McCrystal, Ann Marie *community health nurse, administrator*
McGee, Humphrey Glenn *architect*
McNamara, John J(oseph) *advertising executive, writer*
Michelson, Edward J. *journalist*
Nichols, Carl Wheeler *retired advertising agency executive*
Parkyn, John William *editor, writer*
Polan, Nancy Moore *artist*
Reed, Sherman Kennedy *chemical consultant*
Riefler, Donald Brown *financial consultant*
Ritterhoff, C(harles) William *retired steel company executive*
Schulman, Harold *obstetrician, gynecologist, perinatologist*
Schwarz, Berthold Eric *psychiatrist*
Shadek, Arthur Joseph *radio station executive*
Thompson, William David *investment banking executive*

### Village Of Golf
Bates, Edward Brill *retired insurance company executive*
Boer, F. Peter *chemical company executive*

### Wellington
Jankus, Alfred Peter *international management and marketing consultant*
Knudsen, Raymond Barnett *clergyman, association executive, author*

Patterson, Lydia Ross *industrial relations specialist, consulting company executive*

### Wesley Chapel
Holloway, Marvin Lawrence *retired automobile club executive, rancher, vintager*
Mendelsohn, Louis Benjamin *financial analyst*

### West Palm Beach
Aaron, M. Robert *electrical engineer*
Alimanestianu, Calin *retired hotel consultant*
Aron, Jerry E. *lawyer*
Asencio, Diego C. *state agency administrator, former federal commission administrator, consultant, business executive*
Baker, Bernard Robert, II *lawyer*
Borchers, Karen Lily *child welfare administrator*
Brannon, Dave Lee *lawyer*
Brumback, Clarence Landen *physician*
Cano, Marta Mendendez *securities company executive, financial consultant*
Coar, Richard John *mechanical engineer, aerospace consultant*
Corley, Leslie M. *investment banker*
Corts, Paul Richard *college president*
Cox, Linda Susan *allergist, immunologist*
Craft, Jerome Walter *plastic surgeon, health facility administrator*
Darby, Bonnie Mae Hanson *anesthetist*
Davis, Robert Edwin *manufacturing executive*
Davis, Shirley Harriet *social worker, editor*
Diener, Bert *former food broker, artist*
Dunston, Leigh Everett *lawyer*
Elder, Stewart Taylor *dentist, retired naval officer*
Engh, Fredric Charles *educational association administrator*
Eppley, Roland Raymond, Jr. *retired financial services executive*
Eschbach, Jesse Ernest *federal judge*
Fairbanks, Richard Monroe *broadcasting company executive*
Flanagan, L. Martin *lawyer*
Gildan, Phillip Clarke *lawyer*
Gillette, Frank C., Jr. *mechanical engineer*
Glinski, Helen Elizabeth *operating room nurse*
Goetz, Cecelia Helen *lawyer, retired judge*
Green, Linda Gail *international healthcare and management consultant*
Hill, Thomas William, Jr. *lawyer, educator*
Holloway, Edward Olin *human services manager*
Holt, Richard Duane *lawyer*
Hudson, Alice Peterson *chemistry consulting laboratory executive*
Hudson, Lise Lyn *lawyer*
Hurley, Daniel T. K. *federal judge*
Johnston, Harry A., II *former congressman*
Kamen, Michael Andrew *lawyer*
Kapnick, S. Jason *oncologist*
Kaslow, Florence W. *psychologist*
Katz, William David *psychologist, psychoanalytic psychotherapist, educator, mental health consultant*
Khouri, George George *ophthalmologist*
Kiely, Dan Ray *lawyer, banking and real estate development executive*
Koch, William I. *energy company executive*
Lampert, Michael Allen *lawyer*
Lane, Matthew Jay *lawyer*
Lavine, Alan *columnist, writer*
Lewter, Billy Ray *psychology educator*
Lively, Edwin Lowe *sociology educator*
Livingstone, John Leslie *accountant, management consultant, business economist, educator*
Luckett, Paul Herbert, III *manufacturing executive*
Lynch, William Walker *savings and loan association executive*
McHale, Michael John *lawyer*
Montgomery, Robert Morel, Jr. *lawyer*
Moody, Cheryl Anne *social services administrator, social worker, educator*
Moore, George Crawford Jackson *lawyer*
Mrachek, Lorin Louis *lawyer*
Nelson, Richard Henry *manufacturing company executive*
Nolan, Richard Thomas *clergyman, educator*
Norton, William Alan *lawyer*
O'Brien, Robert Brownell, Jr. *investment banker, consultant, yacht broker, opera company executive*
O'Brien, Thomas George, III *lawyer*
O'Flarity, James P. *lawyer*
O'Hara, Thomas Patrick *managing editor*
Olsak, Ivan Karel *civil engineer*
Oppenheim, Justin Sable *business executive*
†Orlovsky, Donald Albert *lawyer*
Paine, James Carriger *federal judge*
Passy, Charles *arts critic*
Petersen, David L. *lawyer*
Player, Gary Jim *professional golfer, businessman, golf course designer*
Porter, Jack A. *lawyer*
Pottash, A. Carter *psychiatrist, hospital executive*
Price, William James, IV *investment banker*
Rivers, Marie Bie *broadcasting executive*
Roberts, Carol Antonia *county commissioner, real estate associate*
Roberts, Hyman Jacob *internist, researcher, author, historian, publisher*
Robinson, Raymond Edwin *musician, music educator, writer*
Ronan, William John *management consultant*
Royce, Raymond Watson *lawyer, rancher, citrus grower*
Russell, Joyce Weber *principal*
Ryskamp, Kenneth Lee *federal judge*
Sammond, John Stowell *lawyer*
Saraf, Shevach *company executive*
Scheckner, Sy *former greeting card company executive*
Sears, Edward Milner, Jr. *newspaper editor*
Sklar, William Paul *lawyer, educator*
Smith, David Shiverick *lawyer, former ambassador*
Spillias, Kenneth George *lawyer*
Stauderman, Bruce Ford *advertising executive, writer*
Sturrock, Thomas Tracy *botany educator, horticulturist*
Terwillegar, Jane Cusack *librarian, educator*
Thurber, James Cameron *law enforcement officer, consultant, author*
Turner, Arthur Edward *college administrator*
Upledger, John Edwin *osteopath, physician*
Vecellio, Leo Arthur, Jr. *construction company executive*
Wagner, Arthur Ward, Jr. *lawyer*
†Wisnicki, Jeffrey Leonard *plastic surgeon*
Wright, Donald Conway *editorial cartoonist*
Wroble, Arthur Gerard *lawyer*

### Weston
Broder, Gail Steinmetz *lawyer*
Durfey, Robert Walker *sea transportation consultant*
Seelin, Judith Lee *rehabilitation specialist*

### Windermere
Alexander, Judd Harris *retired paper company executive*
Hylton, Hannelore Menke *retired manufacturing executive*

### Winter Garden
Clifford, Margaret Louise *psychologist*

### Winter Haven
Burns, Arthur Lee *architect*
Chase, Lucius Peter *lawyer, retired corporate executive*
Cover, Norman Bernard *retired electronic data processing administrator*
Gobie, Henry Macaulay *philatelic researcher, retired postal executive*
Goodman, Karen Lacerte *financial services executive*
Grierson, William *retired agricultural educator*
Honer, Richard Joseph *surgeon*
O'Connor, R. D. *health care executive*
Peck, Maryly VanLeer *college president, chemical engineer*
West, Mary Elizabeth *psychiatric management professional*

### Winter Park
Armstrong, (Arthur) James *minister, religion educator, religious organization executive, consultant*
Blair, Mardian John *hospital management executive*
Bornstein, Rita *academic administrator*
Britton, Erwin Adelbert *clergyman, college administrator*
Brooten, Kenneth Edward, Jr. *lawyer*
Builder, J. Lindsay, Jr. *lawyer*
Cerbin, Carolyn McAtee *transportation executive, writer*
Conrad, Judy L. *insurance company executive*
Counts, Christine Gay *dental hygienist*
Crosby, Philip Bayard *consultant, author*
Dawson, Ray Fields *research scientist, educator, consultant, tropical agriculturist*
Edge, Findley Bartow *clergyman, religious education educator*
Fowler, Mark Stapleton *lawyer, corporation counsel*
Granzig, William Walker *clinical sexologist, educator*
Hadley, Ralph Vincent, III *lawyer*
Hawkins, Paula *federal official, former senator*
Hill, Elizabeth Starr *writer*
Johannes, Virgil Ivancich *electrical engineer*
Johnson, Constance Ann Trillich *minister, librarian, educator, internet service provider, small business owner, writer, researcher, lecturer*
Kerr, James Wilson *engineer*
Kost, Wayne L. *business executive*
Maher, William James *investment executive*
Mc Kean, Keith Ferguson *former education educator*
McKean, Thomas Wayne *dentist, retired naval officer*
Mica, John L. *congressman*
Olsson, Nils William *former association executive*
Pineless, Hal Steven *neurologist*
Plane, Donald Ray *management science educator*
Richards, Max De Voe *management educator, consultant, researcher, author*
Rogers, Donald Patrick *business administration educator*
Rogers, Rutherford David *librarian*
Ruggiero, Laurence Joseph *museum director*
Seymour, Thaddeus *English educator*
Spake, Ned Bernarr *energy company executive*
Starr, Martin Kenneth *management educator*
Strawn, Frances Freeland *real estate executive*
Swan, Richard Gordon *retired mathematics educator*

### Winter Springs
Diamond, James Thomas, Jr. *publishing executive*
Monopoli, Daniel Marco *computer company executive*
San Miguel, Manuel *painter, historian, composer, poet*
Tran, Toan Vu *electronics engineer*

### Zellwood
Wallcraft, Mary Jane Louise *religious organization executive, songwriter, author*

### Zephyrhills
Jernstrom, Joan *secondary education educator*

## GEORGIA

### Acworth
Meyer, Mary Coeli *management consultant*

### Adrian
McCord, James Richard, III *chemical engineer, mathematician*

### Ailey
Windsor, James Thomas, Jr. *printing company executive, newspaper publisher*

### Albany
Cox, Lynetta Frances *neonatal nurse practitioner*
Ezeamii, Hyacinth Chinedum *public administration educator*
Hart, Mary *educator*
Marbury, Ritchey McGuire, III *engineering executive, surveyor*
McManus, James William *chemist, researcher*
Sands, W. Louis *federal judge*
Stultz, Thomas Joseph *newspaper executive*

### Alpharetta
Balows, Albert *microbiologist, educator*
Barker, Michael Dean *nuclear engineer, internet engineer*
Barr, John Baldwin *chemist, research scientist*
Bobo, Genelle Tant (Nell Bobo) *office administrator*
Esher, Brian Richard *environmental company executive*
Feuss, Linda Anne Upsall *lawyer*
Hung, William Mo-Wei *chemist*
Miller, Robert Allen *software engineer, consultant*

Mock, Melinda Smith *orthopedic nurse specialist, consultant*
Rettig, Terry *veterinarian, wildlife consultant*
White, Carl Edward, Jr. *pharmaceutical adminstrator*
Woodson, Al Curtis *software company executive, software engineer*
Wu, Wayne Wen-Yau *artist*
Zimmermann, John *financial consultant*

### Alto
Mosavi, Reza Khonsari *laser physicist*

### Americus
Capitan, William Harry *university president emeritus*
Fuller, Millard Dean *charitable organization executive, lawyer*
Hooks, George Bardin *state senator, insurance and real estate company executive*
Isaacs, Harold *history educator*
McGrady, Clyde A. *secondary school principal*
Nichols, Harold James *theatre educator*
Stanford, Henry King *college president*
Thomas, Paul Louis *health services administrator*
Worrell, Billy Frank *health facility administrator*

### Andersonville
Boyles, Frederick Holdren *historian*

### Ashburn
Harvey, J. Ernest, Jr. *agricultural company executive*
Paulk, Anna Marie *office manager*

### Athens
Agee, Warren Kendall *journalism educator*
Agosin, Moises Kankolsky *zoology educator*
Albersheim, Peter *biology educator*
Allinger, Norman Louis *chemistry educator*
Allsbrook, Ogden Olmstead, Jr. *economics educator*
Andrews, Grover Jene *adult education educator, administrator*
Atwater, Mary Monroe *science educator*
Baile, Clifton A. *biologist, researcher*
Bamber, Linda Smith *accounting educator*
Barry, John Reagan *psychology educator*
Beaird, James Ralph *legal educator*
Black, Clanton Candler, Jr. *biochemistry educator, researcher*
Boyd, Louis Jefferson *agricultural scientist, educator*
Brackett, Colquitt Prater, Jr. *judge*
Bullock, Charles Spencer, III *political science educator, author, consultant*
Carlson, Ronald Lee *lawyer, educator*
Clute, Robert Eugene *political and social science educator*
Cole, David Akinola *academic administrator*
Crowley, John Francis, III *university dean*
Cutlip, Scott Munson *public relations educator, former university dean*
Darvill, Alan G. *biochemist, botanist, educator*
Davis, Claude-Leonard *lawyer, educational administrator*
DerVartanian, Daniel Vartan *biochemistry educator*
Dickie, Margaret McKenzie *English language educator*
Dooley, Vincent Joseph *college athletics administrator*
Douglas, Dwight Oliver *university administrator*
Dunn, Delmer Delano *political science educator*
Edison, Diane *artist, educator*
Elkins, Robert Neal *lawyer*
Ellington, Charles Ronald *lawyer, educator*
Eriksson, Karl-Erik Lennart *biochemist, educator*
Fallows, Noel *foreign language educator*
Feldman, Edmund Burke *art critic*
Fink, Conrad Charles *journalism educator, communications consultant*
Freer, Coburn *English language educator*
Garbin, Albeno Patrick *sociology educator*
Giles, Norman Henry *educator, geneticist*
Grayson, Richard Andrew *aerospace engineer*
Gregory, John Michael *urologist*
Herbert, James Arthur *artist, filmmaker*
Hildebrand, Don *science foundation executive*
Hillenbrand, Martin Joseph *diplomat, educator*
Hofer, Charles Warren *strategic management, entrepreneurship educator, consultant*
Holder, Howard Randolph, Sr. *broadcasting company executive*
Huszagh, Fredrick Wickett *lawyer, educator, information management company executive*
Johnson, Michael Kenneth *chemistry educator*
Kamerschen, David Roy *economist, educator*
King, Robert Bruce *chemistry educator, writer*
Kleiner, Heather Smith *academic administrator*
Koppes, Steven Nelson *public information officer, science writer*
Kraszewski, Andrzej Wojciech *electrical engineer, researcher*
Kretzschmar, William Addison, Jr. *English language educator*
Landau, David Paul *physics educator*
†Landers, Andy *head coach women's basketball*
Lane, Walter Ronald, Jr. *advertising executive, educator*
Langdale, George Wilfred *soil scientist, researcher*
Lynch, James Walter *mathematician, educator*
Mamatey, Victor Samuel *history educator*
McCutcheon, Steven Clifton *environmental engineer, hydrologist*
Meeks, Carol Jean *educator*
Melton, Charles Estel *retired physicist, educator*
Miller, Herbert Elmer *accountant*
Miller, Ronald Baxter *English language educator, author*
Mixon, Deborah Lynn Burton *elementary school educator*
Moore, Margaret Bear *American literature educator*
Moore, Rayburn Sabatzky *American literature educator*
Morrison, Darrel Gene *landscape architecture educator*
Nelson, Stuart Owen *agricultural engineer, researcher, educator*
Neter, John *statistician*
Newsome, George Lane, Jr. *education educator*
Nute, Donald E., Jr. *philosophy educator*
Paul, William Dewitt, Jr. *artist, educator, photographer, museum director*
Pavlik, William Bruce *psychologist, educator*
Payne, William Jackson *microbiologist, educator*
Peacock, Lelon James *psychologist, educator*
Pelletier, S. William *chemistry educator*
Phillips, Walter Ray *lawyer, educator*
Plummer, Gayther L(ynn) *climatologist, ecologist, researcher*

Posey, Loran Michael pharmacist, editor
Potter, William Gray, Jr. library director
Puckett, Elizabeth Ann law librarian, law educator
Schaefer, Henry Frederick, III chemistry educator
Shaw, James Scott astronomy research administrator
†Smith, (Tubby) Orlando Henry college basketball coach
Speering, Robin educator, computer specialist
Spurgeon, Edward Dutcher law educator
Staub, August William drama educator, theatrical producer, director
Steer, Alfred Gilbert, Jr. foreign language educator
Sumner, Malcom Edward agronomist, educator
Swayne, David Eugene avian pathologist, researcher
Tesser, Abraham social psychologist
Tolley, Edward Donald lawyer
Tollner, Ernest William agricultural engineering educator, agricultural radiology consultant
Tyler, David Earl veterinary medical educator
Van Eseltine, William Parker microbiologist, educator
Wall, Bennett Harrison history educator
Wellman, Richard Vance legal educator
West, Marsha elementary school educator
Yamaguchi, Yukio chemistry research scientist
Yen, William Mao-Shung physicist
Younts, Sanford Eugene university administrator
Zinkhan, George Martin, III marketing educator

**Atlanta**

Aaberg, Thomas M., Sr. academic administrator, ophthalmology educator
Aaron, Henry L. (Hank Aaron) professional baseball team executive
Abdel-Khalik, Said Ibrahim nuclear and mechanical engineering educator
Abrams, Bernard William construction manufacturing and property development executive
Abrams, Edward Marvin construction company executive
Abrams, Harold Eugene lawyer
Aldridge, John lawyer
Alexander, Cecil Abraham college official, retired architect, consultant
Alexander, Constance Joy (Connie Alexander) stone sculptor
Alexander, Miles Jordan lawyer
Alexander, Robert Wayne medical educator
Alexander, William Henry senior judge
Allan, Frank Kellog bishop
Allen, Ivan, Jr. office products company owner
Allen, Ronald W. retired airline company executive
Allio, Robert John management consultant, educator
Ambrose, Samuel Sheridan, Jr. urologist
Ames, William Francis mathematician, educator
†Anderson, Gail Victor health science association administrator, educator
Anderson, Peter Joseph lawyer
Andrews, Gary Blaylock state judge, lawyer
Arani, Ardy A. professional sports marketing executive, lawyer
Armanios, Erian Abdelmessih aerospace engineer, educator
Artemis, Maria sculptor, educator
Ashby, Eugene Christopher chemistry educator
Ashley, John Bryan software executive, management consultant
Assunto, Richard Anthony payroll executive
Atkinson, A. Kelley insurance company executive
Attridge, Richard Byron lawyer
Averitt, Richard Garland, III securities executive
†Avery, Byllye Yvonne health association administrator
Axon, Michael education association field representative
Babcock, Peter Heartz professional sports executive
Bacon, Louis Albert retired consulting civil engineer
Bahl, Roy Winford economist, educator, consultant
Bainbridge, Frederick Freeman, III architect
Bakay, Roy Arpad Earle neurosurgeon, educator
Baker, Edward L., Jr. physician, science facility executive
Baldwin, Daniel Flanagan mechanical engineer, researcher, educator
Bales, Virginia S. healthcare administration
Bankoff, Joseph R. lawyer
Banks, Bettie Sheppard psychologist
Baran, William Lee food company executive
Barker, William Daniel hospital administrator
Barkoff, Rupert Mitchell lawyer
Barksdale, Richard Dillon civil engineer, educator
Barnard, Susan Muller zookeeper
Barnes, Harry G., Jr. human rights activist, conflict resolution specialist, retired ambassador
Barnett, Crawford Fannin, Jr. internist, educator, cardiologist, travel medicine specialist
Barnett, Elizabeth Hale organizational consultant
Baron, Linda psychotherapist, consultant
Barron, Patrick Kenneth bank executive
Barrow, Daniel Louis neurosurgeon
Bassett, Peter Q. lawyer
Batson, Richard Neal lawyer
Baxter, Arthur Pearce financial services marketing company executive
Baxter, Robert Hampton, III insurance executive
Beard, Rick cultural organization administrator
Beattie, George artist
Beckham, Walter Hull, III lawyer
Beckman, Gail McKnight law educator
†Bedelian, Haro architectural firm executive
Bell, Griffin B. lawyer, former attorney general
Bell, Jack Atkins percussionist, educator
Bell, Ronald Mack university foundation administrator
Bellanca, Joseph Paul engineering/construction executive
Beller, Michael E. lawyer
Benario, Herbert William classics educator
Benario, Janice Martin classics educator
Benatar, Leo packaging company executive
Benham, Robert state supreme court justice
Bennett, Jay D. lawyer
Benson, Ronald Edward state humanities program executive, clergyman, educator
Benston, George James accountant, economist
Bevington, E(dmund) Milton electrical machinery manufacturing company executive
Bibb, Daniel Roland antique painting restorer and conservator
Bickerton, Jane Elizabeth university research coordinator
Biggers, William Joseph retired manufacturing company executive
Birch, Stanley Francis, Jr. federal judge
Bird, Francis Marion, Jr. lawyer
Bird, Wendell Raleigh lawyer
Birdsong, Alta Marie volunteer
Bisher, James Furman journalist, author
Black, Kenneth, Jr. insurance executive, educator, author
Blackburn, William Stanley lawyer
Blackstock, Jerry Byron lawyer
Blackwell, Michael Sidney broker, financial services executive
Blank, A(ndrew) Russell lawyer
Blauser, Jeffrey Michael professional baseball player
Block, Mitchell Stern lawyer
Bloodworth, A(lbert) W(illiam) Franklin lawyer
Bockwitz, Cynthia Lee psychologist, psychology/women's studies educator
Boeke, Eugene H., Jr. construction executive
Boisseau, Richard Robert lawyer
Bolch, Carl Edward, Jr. corporation executive, lawyer
Boman, John Harris, Jr. retired lawyer
Bonds, John Wilfred, Jr. lawyer
Bondurant, Emmet Jopling, II lawyer
Boone, J. William lawyer
Booth, Gordon Dean, Jr. lawyer
Born, Allen mining executive
Bosah, Francis N. molecular biochemist, educator
Bourne, Henry Clark, Jr. electrical engineering educator, former academic official
Bowden, Henry Lumpkin, Jr. lawyer
Bowers, Michael Joseph state attorney general
Bowman, Juliette Joseph interior decorator, gourmet food consultant
Boyle, Robert Daniel management consultant, business process reengineering
Boynton, Frederick George lawyer
Bradfield, Richard Harold architectural firm executive
Bradley, William Hampton lawyer
Brady, Kimberly Ann editorial director
Branch, Thomas Broughton, III lawyer
Brandenburg, David Saul gastroenterologist, educator
Brannon, Lester Travis, Jr. lawyer
Bratton, James Henry, Jr. lawyer
Brecher, Armin G. lawyer
Bridgewater, Herbert Jeremiah, Jr. radio host
Bright, David Forbes academic administrator, classics and comparative literature educator
Brinkley, Donald R. oil industry executive
Brooks, David William farmer cooperative executive
Broome, Claire Veronica epidemiologist, researcher
Brown, John Robert lawyer, priest, philanthropist
Brown, Lorene B(yron) library educator, educational administrator
Brown-Olmstead, Amanda public relations executive
Buck, Lee Albert retired insurance company executive, evangelist
Buoch, William Thomas corporate executive
Burge, William Lee retired business information executive
Burgess, Chester Francis, III journalist, television producer
Burns, Thomas Samuel history educator
Butte, Anthony Jeffrey healthcare executive
Byrd, Larry Donald behavioral pharmacologist
Byrne, Granville Bland, III lawyer
Cadenhead, Alfred Paul lawyer
Calhoun, Scott Douglas lawyer
Calise, Anthony John aerospace engineering educator
Callahan, Harry Morey photographer
Callison, James W. former airline executive, lawyer
Cameron, Rondo economic history educator
Camp, Jack Tarpley, Jr. federal judge
Campbell, Bill mayor, broadcasting executive
Campbell, Colin McLeod journalist
Candler, John Slaughter, II retired lawyer
Cann, Sharon Lee health science librarian
Cannon, William Ragsdale bishop
Capron, John M. lawyer
Carey, Gerald John, Jr. research institute director, former air force officer
Cargill, Robert Mason lawyer
Carley, George H. judge
†Carlisle, Patricia Kinley mortgage company executive, paralegal
Carlos, Michael C. wine, spirits and linen service wholesale executive
Carlson, Robert Lee engineering educator
Carnes, Julie E. federal judge
Carpenter, David Allan lawyer
Carson, Christopher Leonard lawyer
Carter, Dan T. history educator
Carter, Jimmy (James Earl Carter, Jr.) former President of United States
Casarella, William Joseph physician
Chace, William Murdough university administrator
Chaiet, Alan Howard advertising agency executive
Chambers, Anne Cox newspaper executive, former diplomat
Champion, Charles Howell, Jr. retired army officer
Chandler, Robert Charles healthcare consultant
Chapman, Hugh McMaster banker
Chapman, Paul H. author
Charania, Barkat real estate consultant
Chasen, Sylvan Herbert computer applications consultant, investment advisor
Cheatham, Richard Reed lawyer
Chilivis, Nickolas Peter lawyer
Chilton, Horace Thomas pipeline company executive
Choa, Walter Kong technical service professional
Chong, Bruce Simon broadcast executive
Circeo, Louis Joseph, Jr. research center director, civil engineer
Clark, Thomas Alonzo federal judge
Clarke, Thomas Hal lawyer
Clements, James David retired psychiatry educator, physician
Clendenin, John L. telecommunications company executive
Clifton, David Samuel, Jr. research executive, economist
Clough, Gerald Wayne academic administrator
Cohen, Ezra Harry lawyer
Cohen, George Leon lawyer
Cohen, N. Jerold lawyer
Cohn, Bob public relations executive
Cole, Johnnetta Betsch academic administrator
Cole, Thomas Winston, Jr. chancellor, college president, chemist
Collins, Steven M. lawyer
Compans, Richard W. microbiology educator
Cook, Philip C. lawyer
Cooper, Frederick Eansor lawyer
Cooper, Gerald Rice clinical pathologist
Cooper, Jerome Maurice architect
Cooper, Thomas Luther retired printing company executive
Copeland, John Alexander, III physicist
Corr, James Vanis furniture manufacturing executive, investor, lawyer, accountant
Correll, Alston Dayton, Jr. forest products company executive
Cox, Bobby (Robert Joe Cox) professional baseball manager
Coxe, Tench Charles lawyer
Cramer, Howard Ross geologist, environmental consultant
Creed, Thomas Wayne retired federal agency administrator, individual investor
†Cremins, Bobby college basketball coach
Crews, William Edwin lawyer
Croft, Terrence Lee lawyer
Cross, Joyce Annette Oscar newscaster
Crutchfield, Carolyn Ann physical therapy educator
Cunningham, Randall professional football player
Cupp, Robert Erhard golf course designer, land use planner
Curran, Christopher economics educator
Curran, James W. epidemiologist, educator
Curry, Toni Griffin counseling center executive, consultant
Curtis, Philip Kerry real estate developer
Cutshaw, Kenneth Andrew lawyer
Dalrymple, Gordon Bennett former engineering company executive
Dalton, John Joseph lawyer
Daly, Chuck (Charles Jerome Daly) sports commentator, former professional basketball coach
Darden, Claibourne Henry, Jr. marketing professional
Davis, Eleanor Kay museum administrator
Davis, Frank Tradewell, Jr. lawyer
Davis, Lawrence William radiation oncologist
Dean, Andrew Griswold epidemiologist
DeConcini, Barbara association executive, religious studies educator
Dees, Julian Worth academic/research administrator
Delahanty, Edward Lawrence management consultant
DeLashmet, Gordon Bartlett newsprint executive
Dennison, Daniel Bassel chemist
Dennison, Stanley Scott retired lumber company executive, consultant
Denny, Richard Alden, Jr. lawyer
Despriet, John G. lawyer
Diedrich, Richard Joseph architect
Dobes, William Lamar, Jr. dermatologist
Dobson, Bridget McColl Hursley television executive and writer
Dollar, Steve music critic
Donoghue, John Frances archbishop
Dotson, Robert Charles news correspondent
Dougherty, John Ernest judge
Douglas, John Lewis lawyer
Dowda, William F. internist
Dowden, Thomas Clark telecommunication executive
Dowling, Roderick Anthony investment banker
Doyle, Michael Anthony lawyer
Drake, Miriam Anna librarian, educator
Draper, Stephen Elliot engineer, lawyer
Drennen, Eileen Moira editor
†Drewry, Joe Samuel Jr. design engineer
Driver, Walter W., Jr. lawyer
DuBose, Charles Wilson lawyer
Duffey, William Simon, Jr. lawyer
Dunahoo, Charles religious publisher, religious organization administrator, consultant, human resource director
Dunn, John Clinton writer, editor
Duquette, Diana Marie company official
Durden, Robert J. state commissioner, lawyer
Durrett, James Frazer, Jr. lawyer
Dutt, Kamla medical educator
Dykes, John Henry, Jr. retired finance executive
Dysart, Benjamin Clay, III environmental consultant, conservationist, engineer
Eason, William Everette, Jr. lawyer
Easterly, David Eugene communications executive
Eber, Herbert Wolfgang psychologist
Eckert, Charles Alan chemical engineering educator
Eckert, Michael Joseph cable and broadcast television executive
Edelhauser, Henry F. physiologist, ophthalmic researcher, educator
Edmondson, James Larry federal judge
Edwards, Louis Ward, Jr. diversified manufacturing company executive
Egan, Michael Joseph lawyer
Ehrlich, Jeffrey data processing company executive
Ehrlich, Margaret Isabella Gorley systems engineer, mathematics educator, consultant
Ehrlichman, John Daniel lawyer, company executive, author, former assistant to President of United States
Ellis, Elmo Israel broadcast executive, consultant, columnist
Elsas, Louis Jacob, II medical educator
Elsner, Carlene W. reproductive endocrinologist
Elson, Suzanne Goodman community activist
Emerson, James Larry beverage company executive
Endicott, John Edgar international relations educator
Epstein, David Gustav lawyer
Etheridge, Jack Paul arbitrator, mediator, former judge
Evans, Edwin Curtis internist, educator, geriatrician
Evans, Gail Hirschorn television news executive
Evans, Orinda D. federal judge
Farley, Charles P. public relations executive
Farnham, Clayton Henson lawyer
Fash, William Leonard retired architecture educator, college dean
Feldman, Joel Martin magistrate judge
Fellows, Henry David, Jr. lawyer
Felton, Jule Wimberly, Jr. lawyer
Ferebee, John Spencer, Jr. corporate executive
Ferris, James Leonard academic administrator
Finkelstein, David Ritz physicist, educator, consultant
Finley, Sarah Maude Merritt social worker
Fitzgerald, David Patrick advertising agency executive
Fitzgerald, John Edmund civil engineering educator
Fleming, Julian Denver, Jr. lawyer
Fletcher, Norman S. state supreme court justice
Flinn, Michael Joseph marketing executive
Foerster, David Wendel, Jr. counselor, consultant, human resources specialist
Forbes, Theodore McCoy, Jr. retired lawyer, arbitrator, mediator
Ford, Edward Francis process engineer
Foreman, Edward Rawson lawyer
Forrestal, Robert Patrick banker, lawyer
Forrester, J. Owen federal judge
Foster, Andrew Nichols, Jr. professional society administrator
Foster, Roger Sherman, Jr. surgeon, educator, health facility administrator
Fowler, Andrea teachers academy administrator
Fowler, Vivian Delores insurance company executive
Fox, Ronald Forrest physics educator
Fox-Genovese, Elizabeth Ann Teresa humanities educator
Frank, Erica preventive medicine physician
Frank, Ronald Edward marketing educator
Franklin, Charles Scothern lawyer
Franks, Tommy Ray army officer
Freedman, Louis Martin dentist
Freeman, Richard Cameron federal judge
Frost, Norman Cooper retired telephone company executive
Frye, Billy Eugene university administrator, biologist
Fuqua, John Brooks retired consumer products and services company executive
Gable, Carl Irwin business consultant, private investor, lawyer
Galambos, John Thomas medical educator, internist
Galloway, Thomas D. dean
Gambrell, David Henry lawyer
Garner, Edwin Bruce government official
†Garner, Thomas Emory, Jr. health insurance executive
Garrow, David Jeffries historian, author
Gayles, Joseph Nathan, Jr. adminstrator, fund raising consultant
Gearon, John Michael professional basketball team executive
Geigerman, Clarice Furchgott writer, actress, consultant
Gelardi, Robert Charles trade association executive, consultant
Genberg, Ira lawyer
Genovese, Eugene Dominick historian, educator
Gertzman, Stephen F. lawyer
Gilchrist, Paul R. religious organization administrator
Gilmer, Harry Wesley publishing executive, educator
Girth, Marjorie Louisa lawyer, educator
Gittens, Angela airport executive
Glaser, Arthur Henry lawyer
Glassick, Charles Etzweiler academic foundation administrator
Glavine, Tom (Thomas Michael Glavine) professional baseball player
Glover, John Trapnell real estate executive
Goizueta, Roberto Crispulo food and beverage company executive
Goldman, John Abner rheumatologist, immunologist, educator
Goldstein, Burton Benjamin, Jr. communications executive
Goldstein, Elliott lawyer
Goldstein, Jacob Herman retired physical chemist
González, Carlos A. lawyer
Gonzalez, Emilio Bustamante rheumatologist, educator
Goodwin, George Evans public relations executive
Gordon, Frank Jeffrey medical educator
Gordon, Robert Dana transplant surgeon
Grady, Joseph Patrick real estate professional
Greer, Bernard Lewis, Jr. lawyer
Gregory, Mel Hyatt, Jr. retired insurance company executive
Griffin, Clayton Houstoun retired power company engineer, lecturer
Griffith, Linda Marie county government official
Grissom, Marquis Dean professional baseball player
Grogan, Paula Cataldi newspaper editor
Grove, Russell Sinclair, Jr. lawyer
Grumet, Priscilla Hecht fashion specialist, consultant, writer
Guberman, Sidney Thomas painter, writer
Guest, Rita Carson interior designer
Gunn, Robert Burns physiology educator
Haas, George Aaron lawyer
Hackett, Stanley Hailey lawyer
Haddad, Wassim Michael aerospace engineer, educator
Hagan, James Walter lawyer
Hale, Jack K. mathematics educator, research center administrator
Hall, Sarah E. magazine editor, educator
Hall, Wilbur Dallas, Jr. medical educator
Halwig, Nancy Diane banker
Hanna, Frank Joseph credit company executive
Hanson, Victor Arthur surgeon
Harkey, Robert Shelton lawyer
Harlin, Robert Ray lawyer
†Harmon, Mark Thomas sports anchor
Harney, Thomas C. lawyer
Harris, Econ Nigel rheumatologist, internist
Harris, Henry Wood cable television executive
Harrison, John Raymond foundation executive, retired newspaper executive
Hartle, Robert Wyman retired foreign language and literature educator
Harvey, Bryan Stanley professional baseball player
Hassett, Robert William lawyer
Hasson, James Keith, Jr. lawyer
Hatcher, Charles Ross, Jr. cardiothoracic surgeon, medical center executive
Haverty, John Rhodes physician, former university dean
Haverty, Rawson retail furniture company executive
Hawkins, Robert Garvin management educator, consultant
Henderson, Albert John federal judge
Henderson, Charles William health and medical publishing executive
Henry, Ronald James Whyte university official
Henry, William Ray business administration educator
Henson, Michele state legislator
Hershatter, Andrea Silver university official
Hess, Dennis William chemical engineering educator
Hickerson, Patricia Parsons military officer
Hicks, Heraline Elaine environmental health scientist, educator
Higgins, Richard J. educational administrator
Hill, Paul Drennen lawyer, banker
Hiller, George Mew financial advisor, investment manager, lawyer
Hites, Becky E. financial executive
Hodges, Dewey Harper aerospace engineer, educator
Hoff, Gerhardt Michael lawyer, insurance company executive
Hoffman, Fred L. human resources professional
Hogan, John Donald college dean, finance educator
Holder, Beth D. ballet company administrator
Holliday, Jennifer Yvette singer, actress
Holliman, John news broadcaster
Holzel, David Benjamin newspaper editor
Honaman, J. Craig health facility administrator
Hopkins, Donald Roswell public health physician
Hopkins, George Mathews Marks lawyer, business executive

Horsman, David A. Elliott writer, financial services executive, educator
Houpt, Jeffrey Lyle psychiatrist, educator
House, Donald Lee, Sr. software executive, private investor, management consultant
Howard, Harry Clay lawyer
Howard, Pierre state official
Hug, Carl Casimir, Jr. pharmacology and anesthesiology educator
Hughes, James Mitchell epidemiologist
Hulbert, Daniel J. theater critic, entertainment writer
Hull, Frank Mays federal judge
Humphrey, Charles Durham microbiologist, biomedical researcher
Hunt, Willis B., Jr. federal judge
Hunter, Douglas Lee religious organization administrator
Hunter, Forrest Walker lawyer
Hunter, Howard Owen law educator, dean
Huntley, William Thomas, III investor, consultant
Hurley, John Steven electrical engineering educator, research scientist
Iacobucci, Guillermo Arturo chemist
Ingram, Roland Harrison, Jr. physician, educator
Invester, M. Douglas consumer products company executive
Iodice, Joanna DiMeno (Jody Iodice) psychotherapist
Isaf, Fred Thomas lawyer
Israili, Zafar Hasan scientist, clinical pharmacologist, educator
Ivester, Melvin Douglas beverage company executive
Izard, John lawyer
Jackson, Richard Joseph epidemiologist, public health physician, educator
James, Rose Victoria sculptor, poet
Jann, Brigitte physiatrist, educator
Janney, Donald Wayne lawyer
Jarrett, William Hope ophthalmologist
Jeffery, Geoffrey Marron medical parasitologist
Jeffries, McChesney Hill retired lawyer
Jenkins, Albert Felton, Jr. lawyer
Jennings, Carol marketing executive
Jester, Carroll Gladstone lawyer
Johns, Michael Marieb Edward otolaryngologist, academic administrator
†Johnson, Ben editor, periodical
Johnson, Carl Frederick marriage and family therapist
Johnson, Ellis Lane mathematician
Johnson, J. J. trombonist
Johnson, Ronald Carl chemistry educator
Johnson, Weyman Thompson, Jr. lawyer
Johnson, Wyatt Thomas, Jr. (Tom Johnson) cable news executive
Johnston, John Philip social services executive
Johnston, Kevin Richard marketing and customer service executive, consultant
Johnston, Summerfield K., Jr. food products executive
Joiner, Ronald Luther toxicologist
Jolley, Samuel Delanor, Jr. academic administrator
Jones, Christine Massey furniture company executive
Jones, Dorothy Clement accountant
Jones, Frank Cater lawyer
Jones, Glower Whitehead lawyer
Jones, J. Kenley journalist
Jordan, Hilary Peter lawyer
Jorgensen, Alfred H. computer software and data communications executive
Jova, Henri Vatable architect
Joy, Edward Bennett electrical engineer, educator
Jurkiewicz, Maurice John surgeon, educator
Kafoglis, Milton Zachary economics educator
Kahn, Bernd radiochemist, educator
Kaiser, Fred computer leasing company executive
Kalafut, George Wendell distribution company executive, retired naval officer
Kamm, Laurence Richard television producer, director
Karp, Herbert Rubin neurologist, educator
Kasten, Stanley Harvey sports association executive
Katz, Joel Abraham lawyer, music consultant
Kaufman, Mark David lawyer
Kaufman, Mark Stuart lawyer
Kaufmann, James A. internist, educator
Keiller, James Bruce college dean, clergyman
Kelley, James Francis lawyer
Kelly, James Michael lawyer
Kelly, James P. delivery service executive
Kelly, James Patrick lawyer
Kelly, William Watkins educational association executive
Kennedy, James C. publishing and media executive
Kent, Philip communications executive
Keough, Donald Raymond investment company executive
Kerr, Nancy Helen psychology educator
Killorin, Edward Wylly lawyer, tree farmer
King, Coretta Scott (Mrs. Martin Luther King, Jr.) educational association administrator, lecturer, writer, concert singer
King, Frederick Alexander neuroscientist, educator
King, Jennie Louise research director
King, K(imberly) N(elson) computer science educator
Kinzer, William Luther lawyer
Kitchens, William H. lawyer
Klamon, Lawrence Paine lawyer
Klein, Luella Voogd obstetrics-gynecology educator
Kloer, Philip Baldwin television critic
Kneisel, Edmund M. lawyer
Knight, W. Donald, Jr. lawyer
Knowles, Marjorie Fine lawyer, educator, dean
Kokko, Juha Pekka physician, educator
Komerath, Narayanan Menon aerospace engineer
Koplan, Jeffrey Powell physician
Kravitch, Phyllis A. federal judge
Kuntz, Marion Lucile Leathers classicist, historian, educator
Kuse, James Russell chemical company executive
Lackland, Theodore Howard lawyer
Laettner, Christian Donald professional basketball player
La Farge, Timothy plant geneticist
Lamkin, William Pierce editor
Lamon, Harry Vincent, Jr. lawyer
Landess, Mike (Malcolm Lee Landess, III) television news anchorman
Landon, James Henry lawyer
Lane, Louis musician, conductor
Laney, James Thomas ambassador, educator
Langdale, Noah Noel, Jr. research educator, former university president
Lanier, George H. lawyer
Larche, James Clifford, II state agency administrator
Laubscher, Robert James consumer products company executive
Lawson, A(bram) Venable retired librarian
Leach, James Glover lawyer
Lebow, Jeffrey Albert manufacturing engineer
Lee, John Everett physician
Lee, R(aymond) William, Jr. apparel company executive
Leonard, David Morse lawyer
Lester, Charles Turner, Jr. lawyer
Levine, Susan Michelle social worker
Levy, Daniel economics educator
Levy, David lawyer
Liebmann, Seymour W. construction consultant
Lin, Ming-Chang physical chemistry educator, researcher
Linkous, William Joseph, Jr. lawyer
Lipman, Bernard internist, cardiologist
Lipshutz, Robert Jerome lawyer, former government official
Lissimore, Troy historic site director
Lobb, William Atkinson financial services executive
Loewy, Robert Gustav engineering educator, aeronautical engineering executive
Long, Leland Timothy geophysics educator, seismologist
Long, Maurice Wayne physicist, electrical engineer, radar consultant
Lopez, Antonio Vincent education educator
Love, William Jenkins sales and marketing executive
Lower, Robert Cassel lawyer, educator
Lubin, Michael Frederick physician, educator
Lucero, Michael sculptor
Lucido, Chester Charles, Jr. educational consultant
Ludovice, Peter John chemical engineer
Lunsford, Julius R(odgers), Jr. lawyer
Lurey, Alfred Saul lawyer
Lybarger, Jeffrey Allen epidemiology research administrator
Macey, Morris William lawyer
Maddux, Greg(ory Alan) professional baseball player
Malhotra, Naresh Kumar management educator
Malone, Perrillah Atkinson (Pat Malone) retired state official
Manley, Frank English language educator
Manners, George Emanuel business educator, emeritus dean
Marcus, Bernard retail executive
Margolis, Harold Stephen epidemiologist
Marks, James S. public health service administrator
Marshall, John Treutlen lawyer
Marshall, Thomas Oliver, Jr. lawyer
Martin, David Edward health sciences educator
Martin, James Francis state legislator, lawyer
Martin, Virve Paul licensed professional counselor
Massey, Charles Knox, Jr. advertising agency executive
Massey, Lewis state official
Massey, Walter Eugene physicist, science foundation administrator
McBee, Mary Louise state legislator, former academic administrator
McClellan, James Harold electrical engineering educator
McCormick, Donald Bruce biochemist, educator
McDavid, Sara June librarian
McDuffie, Frederic Clement physician
McGowan, John Edward, Jr. medical and public health educator, epidemiologist
McGriff, Fred (Frederick Stanley McGriff) baseball player
McGuinn, Michael Edward, III retired army officer
Mc Kenzie, Harold Cantrell, Jr. retired manufacturing executive
McKenzie, Kay Branch public relations executive
McLean, Ephraim Rankin information systems educator
McLean, James Albert artist, educator
McMahon, Donald Aylward investor, corporate director
McMaster, Belle Miller religious organization administrator
McNabb, Dianne Leigh investment banker, accountant
McNeill, Thomas Ray lawyer
McTier, Charles Harvey foundation administrator
Medlin, Charles McCall lawyer
Meehan, Patrick John public health officer
Melvin, Dorothy Mae retired microbiologist
Merdek, Andrew Austin publishing/media executive, lawyer
Meyer, George Wilbur internist, health facility administrator
Miles, John Karl marketing executive
Millar, John Donald occupational and environmental health consultant, educator
Miller, Janise Luevenia Monica lawyer
Miller, Zell Bryan governor
Millikan, James Rolens cleaning service executive, musician, composer
Mills, Stephen Nathaniel computer software company executive
Mirsky, Jeffrey science foundation administrator
Mitch, William Evans nephrologist
Mobley, John Homer, II lawyer
Moderow, Joseph Robert package distribution company executive
Moeling, Walter Goos, IV lawyer
Moore, Henry Rogers consulting engineer, retired railroad executive
Moore, Linda Kathleen personnel agency executive
Moran, Thomas Francis chemistry educator
Morris, Robert Renly minister, clinical pastoral education supervisor
Moses, Edwin former track and field athlete
Moultrop, Edward Allen architect, artist
Moye, Charles Allen, Jr. federal judge
†Moynihan, James J. architectural firm executive
Mull, Gale W. lawyer
Mullenix, Kathy Ann relocation company executive
Murphy, Margaret Hackett federal bankruptcy judge
Murphy, Patrick Gregory real estate executive
Murphy, Richard Patrick lawyer
Murphy, Thomas Bailey state legislator
†Murray, Sonia Yvette newswriter
Muth, Richard Ferris economics educator
Navalkar, Ramchandra Govindrao microbiologist, immunologist
Neagle, Dennis Edward (Denny Neagle) professional baseball player
Neiss, Edgar civic organization administrator
Nelson, Brian James broadcast journalist
Nelson, Kent C. delivery service executive
Nelson, Robert Earl, Jr. financial services company executive
Nemeroff, Charles Barnet neurobiology and psychiatry educator
Nemhauser, George L. industrial, systems engineer, operations research educator
Nerem, Robert Michael engineering educator, consultant
Nethercut, Philip Edwin honorary consul, retired
Newman, Stuart lawyer
Newton, Floyd Childs, III lawyer
Nichols, Horace Elmo state justice
Nichols, Joseph J., Sr. surgeon
Nichols, William Curtis psychologist, family therapist, consultant
Nie, Zenon Stanley manufacturing company executive
Nunn, Samuel (Sam Nunn) former senator
Nwagbara, Chibu Isaac industrial designer, consultant
Oakley, Godfrey Porter, Jr. health facility administrator, medical educator
Oakley, Mary Ann Bryant lawyer
O'Brien, Mark Stephen pediatric neurosurgeon
O'Day, Stephen Edward lawyer
O'Kelley, William Clark federal judge
Oliker, Vladimir mathematician, educator
Oppenlander, Robert retired airline executive
Orenstein, Walter A. health facility administrator
O'Shea, Patricia A. physician, educator
Overstreet, Jim public relations executive
Owen, Robert Hubert lawyer, real estate broker
Owings, Francis Barre surgeon
Pace, Wayne H. communications executive
Panlilio, Adelisa Lorna public health physician
Pannell, Robert D. lawyer
Paris, Demetrius Theodore electrical engineering educator
Parko, Edith Margaret special education educator
Parks, John Scott pediatric endocrinologist
Parks, R(obert) Keith missionary, religious organization administrator
Parr, Sandra Hardy government affairs administrator
Parsons, Leonard Jon marketing educator, consultant
Partain, Eugene Gartly lawyer
Patterson, William Robert lawyer
Pattillo, Manning Mason, Jr. academic administrator
Patton, Carl Vernon academic administrator, educator
Payne, Maxwell Carr, Jr. retired psychology educator
Peacock, George Rowatt retired life insurance company executive
Peacock, Lamar Batts retired physician
Pence, Ira Wilson, Jr. material handling research executive, engineer
Perkowitz, Sidney physicist, educator, author
Perry, Timothy Sewell lawyer
Persons, Oscar Newton lawyer
Petersen-Frey, Roland manufacturing executive
†Philipp, Alicia community foundation executive
Phillips, Barry lawyer
Phillips, John D. media company executive
Phillips, William Russell, Sr. lawyer
Piassick, Joel Bernard lawyer
Pike, Larry Samuel lawyer
Pless, Laurance Davidson lawyer
Poe, H. Sadler lawyer
Pontius, Priscilla Floyd nursing administrator
Porter, Alan Leslie industrial and systems engineering educator
Pound, E. Jeanne school psychologist, consultant
Powers, Esther Safir organizational consultant
Poythress, David Bryan state commissioner, lawyer
Pratt, Harry Davis retired entomologist
Pratt, John Sherman lawyer
Pratt, Michael Francis physician and surgeon, otolaryngologist
Price, Charles Eugene lawyer, legal educator
Prince, Larry L. automotive parts and supplies company executive
Pucket, Susan newspaper editor
Puckett, James Manuel, Jr. genealogist
Pulgram, William Leopold architect, space designer
Purcell, Ann Rushing state legislator, office manager medical business
Ramsey, Ira Clayton retired pipeline company executive
Raper, Charles Albert retired management consultant
Rauh, Richard Paul architect
Reed, Glen Alfred lawyer
Reed, Grant phamaceutical executive
Reed, James Whitfield physician, educator
Reedy, Edward K. research operations administrator
Regenstein, Lewis Graham conservationist, author, lecturer, speech writer
Reith, Carl Joseph apparel industry executive
Rex, Christopher Davis classical musician
Rhodes, Thomas Willard lawyer
Richards, Robert Wadsworth civil engineer, consultant
Richardson, Maurice M. manufacturing executive
Richey, Thomas S. lawyer
Riggs, Gregory Lynn lawyer
Ringel, Eleanor film critic
Rivera, Richard E. food products executive
Robbins, James O. advertising executive
Roberts, Cassandra Fendley investment company executive
Roberts, Edward Graham librarian
Robinson, Jeffery Herbert transportation company executive
Robison, Richard Eugene architect
Rock, John Aubrey gynecologist and obstetrician, educator
Rodenbeck, Sven E. environmental engineer, consultant
Rogers, C. B. lawyer
Rogers, Werner state superintendent schools
Rojas, Carlos Spanish literature educator
Roney, Shirley Fletcher retail company executive
Rosenberg, George A. public relations company executive
Rosenberg, Mark L. health facility administrator
Rosenfeld, Arnold Solomon newspaper editor
Rucker, Kenneth Lamar public administrator, educator
Russell, Harold Louis lawyer
Ryan, J. Bruce health care management consulting executive
Saidman, Gary K. lawyer
Salo, Ann Sexton Distler lawyer
Sands, Robert O. lawyer
Satcher, David public health service officer, federal official
Savell, Edward Lupo lawyer
Schafer, Ronald William electrical engineering educator
Schewe, Donald Bruce archivist, library director
Schimberg, Henry Aaron soft drink company executive
Schoborg, Thomas William urologist
Schroder, Jack Spalding, Jr. lawyer
†Schuerholz, John Boland, Jr. professional baseball executive
Schulte, Jeffrey Lewis lawyer
Schwartz, Arthur Jay lawyer
Schwartz, Dale Marvin lawyer
Schwartz, David Alan infectious diseases and placental pathologist, educator
Schwartz, Miriam Catherine biology educator
Schwartz, William A(llen) broadcasting and cable executive
Schwartz, William B., Jr. ambassador
Scott, William Fred cultural organization administrator
Scovil, Roger Morris engineering company executive
Sears, Curtis Thornton, Jr. educational administrator
Seffrin, John Reese health science association administrator, educator
†Seretean, Martin B. (Bud Seretean) carpet manufacturing company executive
Seto, William Roderick public accounting company executive
†Sexson, William R. pediatrician, educator
Shaw, Robert Lawson symphony orchestra conductor
Shelton, Robert Warren marketing executive
Sherman, Roger Talbot surgeon, educator
Sherry, Henry Ivan marketing consultant
Sheth, Jagdish Nanchand business administration educator
Shivers, Jane corporate communications executive, director
Shoob, Marvin H. federal judge
Sibley, Celestine (Mrs. John C. Strong) columnist, reporter
Sibley, Horace Holden lawyer
Sibley, James Malcolm retired lawyer
Simms, Arthur Benjamin management consultant, financier
Simpson, Allan Boyd real estate company executive
Sink, John Davis leadership consultant, scientist, minister
Sitter, John Edward English literature educator
Skal, Debra Lynn lawyer
Skillrud, Harold Clayton minister
Skube, Michael journalist, critic
Smith, Alexander Wyly, Jr. lawyer
Smith, Anderson Dodd psychologist
Smith, David Doyle international management consultant, consulting engineer
Smith, Dennis A. insurance company executive
Smith, Glenn Stanley electrical engineering educator
Smith, James Louis, III lawyer
Smith, Janet Marie professional sports team executive
Smith, Jeffrey Michael lawyer
Smith, Joseph Newton, III retired architect, educator
Smith, Michael Vincent surgeon
Smith, Robert Boulware, III vascular surgeon, educator
Smith, Sidney Oslin, Jr. lawyer
Smith, Steven Delano professional basketball player
Smith, Walton Napier lawyer
Smoltz, John Andrew professional baseball player
Spangler, Dennis Lee physician
Spiegel, John William banker
Spitznagel, John Keith microbiologist, immunologist
Spivey, Ted Ray English educator
Stacey, Weston Monroe, Jr. nuclear engineer, educator
Stafford, Patrick Morgan biophysicist
Stallings, Ronald Denis lawyer
Stamps, Thomas Paty lawyer, consultant
Stanton, Donald Sheldon academic administrator
Steinhaus, John Edward physician, medical educator
Stephenson, Mason Williams lawyer
Stewart, Jeffrey Bayrd lawyer, commodity trading advisor
Stimpert, Michael Alan agricultural products company executive
Stokes, James Sewell lawyer
Stokes, Mack (Marion) Boyd bishop
Stormont, Richard Mansfield hotel executive
Strauss, Robert David lawyer
Streeb, Gordon Lee diplomat, economist
Strekowski, Lucjan chemistry educator
Strong-Tidman, Virginia Adele marketing and advertising executive
Stubbs, Thomas Hubert company executive
Su, Kendall Ling-Chiao engineering educator
Sullivan, Louis Wade former secretary health and human services, physician
Summerlin, Glenn Wood advertising executive
Surber, Eugene Lynn architect
Sutherland, Raymond Carter clergyman, English educator emeritus
Suttles, William Maurrelle university administrator, clergyman
Sutton, Berrien Daniel beverage company executive
Swan, George Steven law educator
Swann, Jerre Bailey lawyer
Swanson, David H(enry) economist, educator
Swartz, Christopher John musician, instrument designer/builder
Swift, Frank Meador lawyer
Tamin, Azaibi molecular virologist, researcher
Tanner, W(alter) Rhett lawyer
Tarver, Jackson Williams newspaper executive
Taylor, George Kimbrough, Jr. lawyer
Tedder, Daniel William chemical engineering educator
Teepen, Thomas Henry newspaper editor, journalist
Teja, Amyn Sadrudin chemical engineering educator, consultant
Tennant, Thomas Michael lawyer
Thacker, Stephen Brady medical association administrator, epidemiologist
Tharpe, Frazier Eugene journalist
Thomas, Barbara Ann record company executive
Thomas, James Edward, Jr. brokerage house executive
Thomas, Kenneth Eastman cardiothoracic surgeon
Thomas, Mable communications company executive, former state legislator
Thompson, Hugh P justice
Thompson, Larry Dean lawyer
Thuesen, Gerald Jorgen industrial engineer, educator
Thumann, Albert association executive, engineer
Tidwell, George Ernest federal judge
Tierney, Michael Stewart newspaper editor, journalist
Tillman, Mary Norman urban affairs consultant
Tipping, William Malcolm social services administrator
Tkaczuk, Nancy Anne cardiovascular services administrator
Tomaszewski, Richard Paul market representation specialist

Tomeh, Amin Adnan *geotechnical engineer, consultant*
Toner, Michael F. *journalist*
Truly, Richard H. *academic administrator, former federal agency administrator*
Tucker, Cynthia Anne *journalist*
Tucker, Robert Arnold *electrical engineer*
Turner, Ed Sims *broadcast executive, writer*
Turner, John Sidney, Jr. *otolaryngologist, educator*
Turner, Michael Griswold *advertising executive, writer*
Turner, Ted (Robert Edward Turner) *television executive*
Tyler, Carl Walter, Jr. *physician, health research administrator*
Vaishnavi, Vijay Kumar *computer science educator, researcher*
Van Assendelft, Onno Willem *hematologist*
Vanegas, Jorge Alberto *civil engineering educator*
Varner, Chilton Davis *lawyer*
Veatch, J. William, III *lawyer*
Verrill, F. Glenn *advertising executive*
Vigtel, Gudmund *museum director emeritus*
Vining, Robert Luke, Jr. *federal judge*
Voss, William Charles *retired oil company executive*
†Waffenschmidt, Lori Ann *television executive producer*
Waggoner, Leland Tate *insurance company executive*
Wald, Michael Leonard *economist*
Walden, Philip Michael *recording company executive, publishing company executive*
Walker, Carolyn Smith *college services administrator, counselor*
Walker, David Michael *human capital consultant, accountant*
Wallace, Gladys Baldwin *librarian*
Waller, John Louis *anesthesiology educator*
Walsh, W. Terence *lawyer*
Walter, John *newspaper editor*
Walton, Carole Lorraine *clinical social worker*
Ward, Horace Taliaferro *federal judge*
Ward, Janet Lynn *magazine editor, sports wire reporter*
Wartell, Roger Martin *biophysics educator*
Waters, Lou *anchorman, correspondent*
Watne, Alvin L. *surgeon, educator*
Weathersby, James Roy *lawyer*
Webb, Brainard Troutman, Jr. *lawyer, distribution company executive*
Weed, Roger Oren *rehabilitation services professional, educator*
Weiss, Jay M(ichael) *psychologist, educator*
Wellon, Robert G. *lawyer*
Wells, Everett Clayton, Jr. *marketing professional*
Wertheim, Steven Blake *orthopedist*
Westerhoff, John Henry, III *clergyman, theologian, educator*
White, Ann Wells *community activist*
White, Annette Jones *early childhood education administrator*
White, Gayle Colquitt *religion writer, journalist*
White, John Austin, Jr. *engineering educator, dean, consultant*
White, Perry Merrill, Jr. *orthopedic surgeon*
White, Ronald Leon *financial management consultant*
Whitehead, John Jed *healthcare and biotech company executive*
Whitley, Joe Dally *lawyer*
Whitman, Homer William, Jr. *investment counseling company executive*
Whitt, Richard Ernest *reporter*
Whittington, Frederick Brown, Jr. *business administration educator*
Wiedeman, John Herman *civil engineer*
Wiesenfeld, Kurt Arn *physicist, educator*
Wilkins, J. Ernest, Jr. *mathematician*
Williams, Charles Murray *computer information systems educator, consultant*
Williams, David Howard *lawyer*
Williams, James Bryan *banker*
Williams, John Young *merchant banker*
Williams, Neil, Jr. *lawyer*
Williams, Ralph Watson, Jr. *retired securities company executive*
Williams, W. Clyde *religious organization administrator*
Willis, Isaac *dermatologist, educator*
Wilson, Frank Lyndall *surgeon*
Wilson, James Hargrove, Jr. *lawyer*
Winer, Ward Otis *mechanical engineer, educator*
Winship, Wadleigh Chichester *holding company executive*
Winter, Wilburn Jackson, Jr. *financial executive*
Withrow, William N., Jr. *lawyer*
Wittenstein, Michael David *marketing professional*
Wolbrink, James Francis *real estate investor*
Wolensky, Michael K. *lawyer*
Wong, Ching-Ping *chemist, materials scientist, engineer, educator*
Woodard, John Roger *urologist*
Woody, Mary Florence *nursing educator, university administrator*
Wright, Daniel *wine specialist, consultant*
Wright, Peter Meldrim *lawyer*
Wylly, Barbara Bentley *performing arts association administrator*
Wyvill, J. Craig *research engineer, program director*
Yancey, Asa Greenwood, Sr. *physician*
Yarnell, Jeffrey Alan *regional credit executive*
Yates, Ella Gaines *library consultant*
Yeargin-Allsopp, Marshalyn *epidemiologist, pediatrician*
Yoganathan, Ajit Prithiviraj *biomedical engineer, educator*
Yother, Michele *publisher*
Zink, Charles Talbott *lawyer*
Zinn, Ben T. *engineer, educator, consultant*
Zumpe, Doris *ethologist, researcher, educator*
Zunde, Pranas *information science educator, researcher*

**Auburn**
Clines, Cindy Collins *elementary school administrator, educator*

**Augusta**
Barab, Patsy Lee *nutritionist, consultant, realtor*
Barnard, Druie Douglas, Jr. *former congressman, former bank executive*
Bloodworth, William Andrew, Jr. *academic administrator*
Bowen, Dudley Hollingsworth, Jr. *federal judge*
Cashin, Edward Joseph *history educator*
Chandler, Arthur Bleakley *pathologist, educator*
Christensen, David William *mathematician, engineer*
Colborn, Gene Louis *anatomy educator, researcher*
Davison, Frederick Corbet *foundation executive*
Dolen, William Kennedy *allergist, immunologist, pediatrician, educator*
Feldman, Elaine Bossak *medical nutritionist, educator*
†Gadacz, Thomas Roman *surgery educator*
Gambrell, Richard Donald, Jr. *endocrinologist, educator*
Gillespie, Edward Malcolm *hospital administrator*
Given, Kenna Sidney *surgeon, educator*
Grier, Leamon Forest *social services administrator*
Guill, Margaret Frank *pediatrics educator, medical researcher*
Hammer, Wade Burke *oral and maxillofacial surgeon, educator*
Hill, Michael John *newspaper editor*
Hooks, Vendie Hudson, III *surgeon*
Kirch, Darrell G. *dean*
Lambert, Vickie Ann *dean*
Lee, Lansing Burrows, Jr. *lawyer, corporate executive*
Loomis, Earl Alfred, Jr. *psychiatrist*
Luxenberg, Malcolm Neuwahl *ophthalmologist, educator*
Mahesh, Virendra Bhushan *endocrinologist*
Mansberger, Arlie Roland, Jr. *surgeon*
Martin, Willie Pauline *elementary school educator, illustrator*
Mayberry, Julius Eugene *realty company owner, investor*
Merin, Robert Gillespie *anesthesiology educator*
Meyer, Carol Frances *pediatrician, allergist*
Miller, Jerry Allan, Jr. *pediatrician*
Morris, William Shivers, III *newspaper executive*
Parrish, Robert Alton *retired pediatric surgeon, educator*
Powell, James Kevin *financial planner*
Prisant, L(ouis) Michael *cardiologist*
Pryor, Carol Graham *obstetrician, gynecologist*
Puchtler, Holde *histochemist, pathologist, educator*
Puryear, James Burton *college administrator*
Puryear, Joan Copeland *English language educator*
Rasmussen, Howard *medical educator, medical institute executive*
Rausch, Jeffrey Lynn *psychiatrist, psychopharmacologist*
Rivner, Michael Harvey *neurologist*
Rosen, James Mahlon *artist, art historian, educator*
Rowland, Arthur Ray *librarian*
Ryan, James Walter *physician, medical researcher*
Solursh, Lionel Paul *psychiatrist*
Taylor, Janelle Diane Williams *writer*
Tedesco, Francis Joseph *university administrator*
Woodhurst, Robert Stanford, Jr. *architect*
Woods, Gerald Wayne *lawyer*
Wray, Betty Beasley *allergist, immunologist, pediatrician*
Yaworski, JoAnn *reading skills educator*
Zachert, Virginia *psychologist, educator*

**Austell**
Friedrich, Stephen Miro *credit bureau company executive*
Halwig, J. Michael *allergist*

**Ball Ground**
McGhee, Vicki Gunter *home health nurse, pediatrics psychiatry, alcohol and Drug rehabilitation*

**Barnesville**
Kennedy, Harvey John, Jr. *lawyer*

**Baxley**
Reddy, Yenamala Ramachandra *metal processing executive*
Reddy, Yenemala Jaysimha *mechanical engineer*

**Bogart**
Butts, David Phillip *science educator*

**Bowdon**
Henson, Diana Jean *county official*

**Bremen**
McBrayer, Laura Jean H. *school media specialist*

**Brunswick**
Alaimo, Anthony A. *federal judge*
Brubaker, Robert Paul *food products executive*
Crowe, Hal Scott *chiropractor*
Harper, Janet Sutherlin Lane *educational administrator, writer*
Holder, Kathleen *elementary education educator*
Iannicelli, Joseph *chemical company executive, consultant*
Shockley, Carol Frances *psychologist, psychotherapist*
Zbiegien, Andrea *religious education educator, consultant, educational administrator*

**Buford**
Carswell, Virginia Colby *primary school educator, special education educator*

**Canton**
Williams, Sally Broadrick *infection control nurse and consultant*

**Carrollton**
Barr, Mary Jeanette *art educator*
Barron, Purificacion Capulong *nursing administrator, educator*
Clark, Janet Eileen *political scientist, educator*
Driver, Judy Anne *home health consultant*
Goodson, Carol Faye *librarian*
Johnson, Harris Tucker *university administrator*
Morris, Robert Christian *education educator*
Richards, Roy, Jr. *wire and cable manufacturing company executive*
Romain, Bella Mary *graphic designer*
Sethna, Beheruz Nariman *university president, marketing, management educator*
Williams, Mary Eleanor Nicole *writer*
Willis, Roni May Lewis *library administrator*

**Cartersville**
Cleveland, Julia Lynn *elementary school educator*
Harris, Joe Frank *former governor*
Pope, Robert Daniel *lawyer*
Wheeler, Susie Weems *retired educator*

**Chatsworth**
Witherow, Jimmie David *secondary school educator*

**Clarkesville**
Melichar, Barbara Ehrlich *educational administrator*

**Clarkston**
Conway, Edward Gerald, Jr. *university educational technology administrator*
Downs, Jon Franklin *theater educator, director*
Foster, Dorothy Jean Peck *English for speakers of other languages educator*
Thatcher, Sharon Louise *medical educator*

**Clayton**
English, Cheryl Ann *medical technologist*

**Cleveland**
Lewis, Richard, Sr. *securities broker, consultant*

**Cochran**
Halaska, Thomas Edward *academic administrator, director, engineer*
Welch, Joe Ben *academic administrator*

**College Park**
Ferguson, Wendell *private school educator*
Hood, Ollie Ruth *health facilities executive*
Williams, Mattie Pearl *accounting educator*

**Columbus**
Amos, Daniel Paul *insurance executive*
Andrews, Gerald Bruce *textile executive*
Averill, Ellen Corbett *secondary education science educator, administrator*
Brabson, Max LaFayette *health care executive*
Brinkley, Jack Thomas *lawyer, former congressman*
Brown, Frank Douglas *academic administrator*
Cavezza, Carmen James *career officer, cultural organization administrator*
Cloninger, Kriss, III *insurance company executive*
Collins, Wayne Winford *protective services official*
Cook, Mary Gooch *elementary school educator*
Edmondson, Michael Herman *secondary school educator*
Elliott, James Robert *federal judge*
Gore, James Arnold *biology educator, aquatic ecologist, hydrologist*
Harp, John Anderson *lawyer*
Heard, William T. *automotive executive*
Johnson, Walter Frank, Jr. *lawyer*
Kerr, Allen Stewart *psychologist*
Laney, John Thomas, III *federal judge*
Lasseter, Earle Forrest *lawyer*
Leebern, Donald M. *distilled beverage executive*
McGlamry, Max Reginald *lawyer*
Montgomery, Anna Frances *elementary school educator*
Page, William Marion *lawyer*
Patrick, Carl Lloyd *theatre executive*
Patrick, James Duvall, Jr. *lawyer*
Patrick, Michael Wynn *theatre executive*
Riggsby, Dutchie Sellers *education educator*
Riggsby, Ernest Duward *science educator, educational development executive*
Robbins, Brenda Sue *early childhood educator*
Shelnutt, John Mark *lawyer*
Zallen, Harold *corporate executive, scientist, former university official*

**Conyers**
Kelly, John Hubert *diplomat, business executive*
Kemp, Gina Christine *social services provider*
Mc Clung, Jim Hill *light manufacturing company executive*
Morse, Richard Van Tuyl *manufacturing executive, consultant*
Polstra, Larry John *lawyer*
Smith, Michael Joseph *composer, pianist, lecturer*

**Cordele**
Wade, Benny Bernar *educational administrator*

**Cornelia**
Reabold, Anthony Maurice *school system administrator*

**Covington**
Griffey, Karen Rose *special education educator*
Penland, John Thomas *import and export and development companies executive*

**Crawford**
Bower, Douglas William *pastoral counselor, psychotherapist, clergyman*

**Cumming**
Benson, Betty Jones *school system administrator*
Pirkle, George Emory *television and film actor, director*

**Cuthbert**
Swinson, Sue Whitlow *secondary education educator*
Treible, Kirk *college president*

**Dacula**
Reid, Ginger Meredith *school counselor, educator*

**Dahlonega**
Frank, Mary Lou Bryant *psychologist, educator*
Friedman, Barry David *political scientist, educator*
Jones, William Benjamin, Jr. *electrical engineering educator*

**Dallas**
Calhoun, Patricia Hanson *secondary education educator*

**Dalton**
Ashworth, Robert Vincent *data processing executive*
Bouckaert, Carl *manufacturing executive*
Laughter, Bennie M. *corporate lawyer*
Orsee, Joe Brown *library director*
Saul, Julian *retail executive*
Shaw, Robert E. *carpeting company executive*
Winter, Larry Eugene *accountant*

**Danielsville**
Bond, Joan *elementary school educator*

**Decatur**
Bain, James Arthur *pharmacologist, educator*
Baker, Stephen M. *school system administrator*
Carey, John Jesse *academic administrator, religion educator*
Dame, Laureen Eva *nursing administrator*
Dillingham, William Byron *literature educator, author*
Fletcher, Regina Roberson *school system administrator*
Gay, Robert Derril *public agency director*
Gericke, Paul William *minister, educator*
Hale, Cynthia Lynette *religious organization administrator*
Hamilton, Frank S. *jazz musician, folksinger, composer and arranger, educator*
Hill, Thomas Glenn, III *dermatologist*
Hinman, Alan Richard *public health administrator, epidemiologist*
Hollis, Charles Eugene, Jr. *accountant, financial consultant*
Jones, Sherman J. *academic administrator, management educator, investment executive*
Keaton, Mollie M. *elementary school educator*
Knight, Walker Leigh *editor, publisher, clergyman*
Loehle, Betty Barnes *artist, painter*
Major, James Russell Richards *historian, educator*
Martinez-Maldonado, Manuel *medical service administrator, physician*
Middleton, James Boland *lawyer*
Mirra, Suzanne Samuels *neuropathologist, researcher*
Myers, Clark Everett *retired business administration educator*
Myers, Orie Eugene, Jr. *university official*
Pepperdene, Margaret Williams *English educator*
Rausher, David Benjamin *internist, gastroenterologist*
Rodgers, Richard Malcolm *management accountant*
Sadun, Alberto Carlo *astrophysicist, physics educator*
Shaw, Jeanne Osborne *editor, poet*
Shulman, Arnold *judge, lawyer*
Wilkinson, Ben *chancellor, evangelist, ministry organizer, writer*
Young, James Harvey *historian, educator*

**Demorest**
Vance, Cynthia Lynn *psychology educator*

**Dillard**
Wilkinson, Albert Mims, Jr. *lawyer*

**Doraville**
Wempner, Gerald Arthur *engineering educator*
Yancey, Eleanor Garrett *retired crisis intervention clinician*

**Douglas**
Hayes, Dewey Norman *lawyer*
Pugh, Joye Jeffries *educational administrator*

**Douglasville**
Henley, Lila Jo *school social worker, consultant, retired*
Hubbard, Charles Ronald *engineering executive*
Turnipseed, Barnwell Rhett, III *journalist, public relations consultant*

**Dublin**
Fatum, Delores Ruth *school counselor*
Greene, Jule Blounte *lawyer*
Joyner, Jo Ann *geriatrics nurse*
Watson, Mary Alice *academic administrator*

**Duluth**
Brody, Aaron Leo *food and packaging consultant*
Burns, Carroll Dean *insurance company executive*
Cooke, Steven John *chemical engineer, consultant, scientist*
Galfas, Timothy, II *franchising and turnaround administrator*
Gullickson, Nancy Ann *art association administrator*
Holutiak-Hallick, Stephen Peter, Jr. *businessman, educator*
Johnson, Barry Lee *public health research administrator*
Milaski, John Joseph *business transformation industry consultant*
Neuman, Ted R. *principal*
Rogers, William Brookins *financial consultant, business appraiser*

**Dunwoody**
Bartolo, Donna Marie *hospital administrator, nurse*
Clark, Faye Louise *drama and speech educator*
La Motte, Louis Cossitt, Jr. *medical scientist, consultant*

**East Point**
Pierre, Charles Bernard *mathematician, statistician, educator*

**Ellijay**
Davis, Janet Holmes *special education educator*

**Evans**
Beaudreau, David Eugene *dentist, educator*
Fournier, Joseph Andre Alphonse *nurse, social worker, psychotherapist*
Hartlage, Lawrence Clifton *neuropsychologist, educator*
Little, Robert Colby *physiologist, educator*
Shrader, Lynne Ann *secondary school educator, coach*

**Fayetteville**
Harris, Dorothy Clark *designer, design instructor, project manager*

**Flowery Branch**
Monroe, Melrose *retired banker*

**Folkston**
Crumbley, Esther Helen Kendrick *realtor, retired secondary education educator*

**Forest Park**
†Pulliam, James Michael *military career officer*

**Fort Benning**
Alles, Rodney Neal, Sr. *information management executive*
Chan, Philip *dermatologist, army officer*

**Fort Gordon**
Xenakis, Stephen Nicholas *psychiatrist, army officer*

**Fort Valley**
Porter, Douglas Taylor *athletic administrator*
Swartwout, Joseph Rodolph *obstetrics and gynecology educator, administrator*

**Gainesville**
Burd, John Stephen *academic administrator, music educator*
Embry, Karen Thompson *elementary education educator*
Hastings, Trish D. *clinical counselor, marriage counselor*
Kartzinel, Ronald *pharmaceutical company executive, neuroscientist*
Leet, Richard Hale *oil company executive*
Schuder, Raymond Francis *lawyer*

**Glynco**
Mihal, Sandra Powell *distance learning specialist*
†Rinkevich, Charles Francis *federal official*

**Gracewood**
Whittemore, Ronald P. *hospital administrator, retired army officer, nursing educator*

**Grayson**
Hollinger, Charlotte Elizabeth *medical technologist, tree farmer*
Wilson, Barbara Mitchell *nurse*

**Griffin**
Canup, Sherrie Margaret *foreign languages educator*
Carter, Edward Fenton, III *pathologist, medical examiner*
Doyle, Michael Patrick *food microbiologist, educator, administrator*
Duncan, Ronny Rush *agriculturist, turf researcher*
Shuman, Larry Myers *soil chemist*
Wilkinson, Robert Eugene *plant physiologist*

**Hazlehurst**
Welsh, Michael Louis *business executive*

**Jasper**
Parrish, Carmelita *secondary school educator*

**Jersey**
Batchelor, Joseph Brooklyn, Jr. *electronics engineer, consultant*

**Jonesboro**
Frey, Bob Henry *psychotherapist, sociologist, educator, poet*
King, Glynda B. *state legislator*
Pulliam, Brenda Jane *secondary school educator*
Sprayberry, Roslyn Raye *secondary school educator*
Ziegler, Robert Oliver *special education educator*

**Kennesaw**
Aronoff, Craig Ellis *management educator, consultant*
Corley, Florence Fleming *history educator*
Munoz, Steven Michael *physician associate*
Siegel, Betty Lentz *college president*
Whitworth, Elaine Atkins *counselor*

**La Fayette**
Hendrix, Bonnie Elizabeth Luellen *elementary school educator*

**La Grange**
Ault, Ethyl Lorita *special education educator, consultant*
Copeland, Robert Bodine *internist, cardiologist*
Gresham, James Thomas *foundation executive*
Morgan, Lewis Render *retired federal judge*
Naglee, Elfriede Kurz *retired medical nurse*
Rhodes, Eddie, Jr. *medical technologist, phlebotomy technician, educator*
West, John Thomas *surgeon*

**Lawrenceville**
Fetner, Robert Henry *radiation biologist*
Greene, William Joshua, III *investment executive and consultant*
Henson, Gene Ethridge *retired legal administrator*
Wall, Clarence Vinson *state legislator*

**Lilburn**
Bristow, Preston Abner, Jr. *civil engineer, environmental engineer*
Magill, Dodie Burns *early childhood education educator*
Neumann, Thomas William *archaeologist*

**Lithonia**
Flanagan, James Lee *educational administrator*
Keyes, David Taylor *telecommunications company administrator*

**Locust Grove**
Short, Betsy Ann *elementary education educator*

**Lookout Mountain**
Hitching, Harry James *retired lawyer*

**Lula**
Suggs, Josephine Greenway *controller*

**Lyons**
Cancer, Cathy Lynn *elementary education educator*

**Mableton**
Brannon, Winona Eileen *electrical contractor*
Rowe, Bonnie Gordon *music company executive*

**Macon**
Ackerman, Robert Kilgo *college president, historian*
Adkison, Linda Russell *geneticist, consultant*
Alexander, David Lee *clergyman*
Anderson, Robert Lanier, III *federal judge*
Bayliss, Sister Mary Rosina *principal*
Cole, John Prince *lawyer*
Dantzler, Deryl Daugherty *dean, law educator*
Dessem, R. Lawrence *dean, law educator*
Dunwody, Eugene Cox *architect*
Ennis, Edgar William, Jr. *lawyer*
Fickling, William Arthur, Jr. *health care manager*
Fitzpatrick, Duross *federal judge*
Gerson, Robert Walthall *judge, retired lawyer*
Godsey, R(aleigh) Kirby *university president*
Hails, Robert Emmet *aerospace consultant, business executive, former air force officer*
Hartman, Alan Frazier *estate planning specialist*
Hershner, Robert Franklin, Jr. *judge*
Innes, David Lyn *university official, educator*
Jones, John Ellis *real estate broker*
Looney, Richard Carl *bishop*
Marshall, Howard Lowen *music educator, musicologist*
Mills, Cynthia Spraker *association executive*
Mitchell, Carolyn Cochran *college official*
Murdoch, Bernard Constantine *psychology educator*
Owens, Wilbur Dawson, Jr. *federal judge*
Phillips, J(ohn) Taylor *judge*
Popper, Virginia Sowell *education educator*
Rich, Arthur Lowndes *music educator*
†Robinson, Joe Sam *neurosurgeon*
Robinson, W. Lee *lawyer*
Rutledge, Ivan Cate *retired legal educator, arbitrator*
Savage, Randall Ernest *journalist*
Sell, Edward Scott, Jr. *lawyer*
Skelton, William Douglas *physician*
Smith, Constance Lewis *secondary school educator*
Smith, Michael Charles *personnel director, human resources specialist*
Snow, Cubbedge, Jr. *lawyer*
Steeples, Douglas Wayne *university dean, consultant, researcher*
Volpe, Erminio Peter *biologist, educator*
Weaver, Jacquelyn Kunkel Ivey *artist, educator*
Young, Henry E. *medical educator*

**Manchester**
McIntyre, Richard Rawlings, II *elementary school educator*

**Marietta**
Bemis, Royce Edwin *publishing executive*
Bentley, Fred Douglas, Sr. *lawyer*
†Biggs, Barbara Conner *internist*
Bradshaw, Rod Eric *personnel consultant*
Bridges, Alan Lynn *physicist, computer scientist, systems software engineer*
Brown, Billy Charlie *secondary school educator*
Burkey, J(acob) Brent *lawyer, company executive*
Cheshier, Stephen Robert *university president, electrical engineer*
Daresta, Pamela Beagle *artist*
Diercks, Chester William, Jr. *capital goods manufacturing company executive*
Dunwoody, Kenneth Reed *magazine editor*
East, Nancy McKinley *private primary music educator*
Falk, John Robert *packaging company executive*
Hagood, M. Felton *surgeon*
Hammond, John William *lawyer*
Ingram, George Conley *lawyer*
Johnson, Herbert Frederick *sales executive, former university administrator, librarian*
Kagan, Jeffrey Allen *telecommunications analyst, consultant, author, columnist*
Kanter, Donald Richard *statistician, pharmaceutical and psychobiology researcher*
Kiger, Ronald Lee *price analyst*
Krug, Douglas Edward *emergency physician*
Laframboise, Joan Carol *middle school educator*
Lazenby, Gail R. *library director*
Lewis, William Headley, Jr. *manufacturing company executive*
Matias, Patricia Trejo *secondary education educator*
Miles, Thomas Caswell *aerospace engineer*
North, John Adna, Jr. *accountant, real estate appraiser*
O'Haren, Thomas Joseph *financial services executive*
Oliver, Ann Breeding *fine arts education curator*
Overton, Bruce *personnel executive, consultant*
Petit, Parker Holmes *health care corporation executive*
Pounds, Gerald Autry *aerospace engineer*
Rabon, William James, Jr. *architect*
Rainey, Kenneth Tyler *English language educator*
Ranu, Harcharan Singh *biomedical scientist, administrator, orthopaedic biomechanics educator*
Rutherfoord, Rebecca Hudson *computer science educator*
Smith, Baker Armstrong *management executive, lawyer*
Smith, Beverly Ann Evans *performance management consultant*
Smith, George Thornewell *retired state supreme court justice*
Spann, George William *management consultant*
Thomas, Pamella Delores *medical director, physician, educator*
Tissue, Mike *medical educator, respiratory therapist*
Veatch, Sheila Williamson *counselor*
Wells, Palmer Donald *performing arts executive*
Wheatley, Joseph Kevin *physician, urologist*
Wrege, Julia Bouchelle *tennis professional, physics educator*

**Martinez**
McKenzie, Harry James *surgeon, surgical researcher*

**Metter**
Doremus, Ogden *lawyer*
Guido, Michael Anthony *evangelist*

**Midland**
Hadden, Mayo Addison *chamber of commerce executive, military officer, educator*

**Midway**
Cobb, John Anthony *retired state veterinarian*

**Milledgeville**
Bouley, Eugene Edward, Jr. *criminal justice and sociology educator*
Engerrand, Doris Dieskow *business educator*
Peterson, Dave Leonard *psychologist*

**Millen**
Cremer, Thomas Gerhard *music educator*

**Millwood**
King, Mary Ann *secondary education educator*

**Monroe**
Adams, Lamar Taft *physician*
Felker, G(eorge) Stephen *textile company executive*

**Moody AFB**
Kennedy, Kimberly Kaye *history educator, bookkeeper*

**Morrow**
Becker, Robert Dean *academic administrator, educator, author, consultant*
Samson, Linda Forrest *nursing educator and administrator*

**Moultrie**
Vereen, William Jerome *uniform manufacturing company executive*

**Mount Berry**
Mathis, Luster Doyle *college administrator, political scientist*
Mew, Thomas Joseph, III (Tommy Mew) *artist, educator*
Shatto, Gloria McDermith *academic administrator*

**Newnan**
Andrews, Rowena *public relations executive*
Johnson, Hardwick Smith, Jr. *school psychologist*
McBroom, Thomas William, Sr. *utility manager*

**Norcross**
Adams, Belinda Jeanette Spain *nursing administrator*
Adams, Dee Briane *hydrologist, civil engineer*
Adams, Kenneth Francis *automobile executive*
Burnett, Cassie Wagnon *middle school educator*
Cole, David Winslow *personal care industry executive*
Conway, Hobart McKinley, Jr. *geo-economist*
Darst, Bobby Charles *soil chemist, administrator*
Dibb, David Walter *research association administrator*
Emanuele, R.M. *business executive*
Garwood, Robert Ashley, Jr. *network communications analyst*
Gifford, Anita Sheree *lawyer*
Harrison, Gordon Ray *engineering executive, consultant, research scientist*
Kyle, John Emery *mission executive*
LaFramboise, Patrick Joseph *trade association administrator*
Manoukian, Rita Chake *sales executive*
McDonald, James *science foundation executive*
Nardelli-Olkowska, Krystyna Maria *ophthalmologist, educator*
Nottay, Baldev Kaur *microbiologist*
Ramsay, Ernest Canaday *lawyer*
Rouse, William Bradford *systems engineering executive, researcher, educator*
Sherwood, Kenneth Wesley *information systems executive, consultant*
Storey, Bobby Eugene, Jr. *electrical engineer, engineering consultant*
van Reenen, Jane Smith *speech and language pathologist*
Wagner, Harvey Alan *finance executive*
Wagner, Robert Earl *agronomist*
Wingate, Thomas Marie Joseph *assistant headmaster*
Young, Andrea C. *communications executive*

**Ocilla**
Miller, Mavis Moss *school administrator, social worker*

**Oxford**
Cody, William Bermond *political science educator*
McNeill, Mary Kathryn Morgan *librarian*
Sitton, Claude Fox *newspaper editor*

**Peachtree City**
Ebneter, Stewart Dwight *utility industry management consultant*
Eichelberger, Charles Bell *retired career officer*
Robben, Mary Margaret *portrait artist*
Roobol, Norman Richard *industrial painting consultant, educator*
Yeosock, John John *army officer*

**Perry**
Hinnant, Tony *superintendent*

**Pine Mountain**
Callaway, Howard Hollis *business executive*

**Powder Springs**
Collins, Lisa Diane *art educator*

**Quitman**
Baum, Joseph Herman *retired biomedical educator*

**Richmond Hill**
McCormack, Dennis K. *clinical psychologist*

**Ringgold**
Hayes, Laura Joanna *psychologist*

**Riverdale**
Awachie, Peter Ifeacho Anazoba *chemistry educator, research chemist*
Lambert, Ethel Gibson Clark *secondary school educator*
Minter, Jimmie Ruth *accountant*
Waters, John W. *minister, educator*

**Robins AFB**
Christian, Thomas Franklin, Jr. *aerospace engineer, educator*
Corley, Rose Ann McAfee *customer service representative*
Head, William Pace *historian, educator*
Hedden, Kenneth Forsythe *chemical engineer*
Hunnicutt, Victoria Anne Wilson *school system administrator*
Lewis, Clinton *federal agency administrator*

**Rome**
Janowski, Thaddeus Marian *architect*
Mosley, Mary Mac *retired librarian*
Murphy, Harold Loyd *federal judge*
Papp, Leann Ilse Kline *respiratory therapy educator*
Wynn, Bruce *physician assistant*

**Roswell**
Brands, James Edwin *medical products executive*
Burgess, John Frank *management consultant, former utility executive, former army officer*
Causey, Susan Marie *health educator*
Dalia, Vesta Mayo *artist*
Forbes, John Ripley *museum executive, educator, naturalist*
Graham, Charles Passmore *retired army officer*
Huckeba, Karen Kaye *crafts designer, consultant*
Jordan, DuPree, Jr. *management consultant, educator, journalist, publisher, business executive*
King, Jack L. *electric power industry executive*
Peterson, Donald Robert *magazine editor, vintage automobile consultant*
Richkin, Barry Elliott *financial services executive*
Sanks, Charles Randolph, Jr. *minister, psychotherapist*
Sherman, Ron *photographer*
Siepi, Cesare *opera singer*
Smith, Sheryl Velting *elementary school executive director*
Tucker, Robert Dennard *health care products executive*
Udoff, Eric Joel *diagnostic radiologist*
Wang, Dehua *chemist*
Woon, Paul Sam *technical executive*

**Saint Simons Island**
Douglas, William Ernest *retired government official*
Edwards, Brenda Faye *rehabilitation services professional, counselor*
Hicks, Harold Eugene *chemical engineer*
King, Linda Orr *museum director*
Riedeburg, Theodore *management consultant*
Sullivan, Barbara Boyle *management consultant*
Tomberlin, William G. *principal*
Webb, Lamar Thaxter *architect*

**Sapelo Island**
Alberts, James Joseph *scientist, researcher*

**Saute Nacoche**
Warren, Edus Houston, Jr. *investment management executive*

**Sautee Nacoochee**
Hill, Ronald Guy *non-profit organization consultant*

**Savannah**
Albert, Theodore Merton *computer scientist*
Alley, James Pinckney, Jr. *computer art and graphic design educator*
Aquadro, Jeana Lauren *graphic designer, educator*
Ball, Ardella Patricia *library media educator*
Barnette, Candice Lewis *speech/language pathologist*
Beals, L(oren) Alan *association executive*
Bell, William Henry, Jr. *banker*
Belles, Martin Russel *manufacturing engineer*
Boland, John K. *bishop*
†Boone, James Latham *healthcare executive*
Burnett, Robert Adair *university administrator, history educator*
Cartledge, Raymond Eugene *retired paper company executive*
Coberly, Patricia Gail *elementary education educator, adult education educator*
Coffey, Thomas Francis, Jr. *editor*
†Davis, Chris *aerospace company executive*
Dickerson, Lon Richard *library administrator*
Dickey, David Herschel *lawyer, accountant*
DiClaudio, Janet Alberta *health information administrator*
Dodge, William Douglas *insurance company consultant*
Eaves, George Newton *lecturer, consultant, research administrator*
Edenfield, Berry Avant *federal judge*
Forbes, Morton Gerald *lawyer*
Gabeler-Brooks, Jo *artist*
Giblin, Patrick David *retired banker*
Gillespie, Daniel Curtis, Sr. *retired non-profit company executive, consultant*
Granger, Harvey, Jr. *manufacturing company executive, retired*
Haywood, John William, Jr. *engineering consultant*
Hemphill, John Michael *neurologist*
Highsmith, Anna Bizzell *executive secretary*
Horan, Leo Gallaspy *physician, educator*
Hsu, Ming-Yu *engineer, educator*
Innes, John Phythian, II *insurance company executive*
Kenrich, John Lewis *lawyer*
Krahl, Enzo *retired surgeon*
Lessard, Raymond William *bishop*
Moore, William Theodore, Jr. *judge*
Morrell, Diane Marie *lawyer*
Otter, John Martin, III *television advertising consultant, retired*
Painter, Paul Wain, Jr. *lawyer*
Peer, George Joseph *metals company executive*
Priester, Horace Richard, Jr. *quality assurance professional*
†Ramage, James Everett, Jr. *respiratory and critical care physician, educator*
Rawson, William Robert *lawyer, retired manufacturing company executive*
Rousakis, John Paul *former mayor*
Schafer, Thomas Wilson *advertising agency executive*
Scott, Walter Coke *retired sugar company executive, lawyer*
Seedlock, Robert Francis *engineering and construction company executive*
†Sheehy, Barry M. *management consultant*
Shields, Richard Owen, Jr. *emergency physician*
Sortor, Harold Edward *financial executive*
Spitz, Seymour James, Jr. *retired fragrance company executive*
Sprague, William Wallace, Jr. *retired food company executive*
Standbridge, Peter Thomas *retired insurance company executive*
Stillwell, Walter Brooks, III *lawyer*
Stonnington, Henry Herbert *physician, medical executive, educator*
Strauser, Beverly Ann *education educator*
Strauser, Edward B. *psychologist, educator*
Su, Helen Chien-fan *research chemist*
Theis, Francis William *business executive*
Thomas, Dwight Rembert *writer*
Tobey, Carl Wadsworth *retired publisher*
Walter, Paul Hermann Lawrence *chemistry educator*
Wheeler, Ed Ray *mathematics educator*
Whitaker, Von Best *nursing educator*
Windom, Herbert Lynn *oceanographer, environmental scientist*
Wirth, Fremont Philip *neurosurgeon, educator*
Wolfe, John Thomas, Jr. *university president*
Woodhouse, Bernard Lawrence *pharmacologist, educator*

Zoller, Michael *otolaryngologist, head and neck surgeon, educator*

**Scottdale**
Borochoff, Ida Sloan *real estate executive, artist*

**Sea Island**
Brown, Ann Catherine *investment company executive*
Brown, George Hay *investment counselor*
Carter, Don Earl *newspaper editor, publisher*
LaWare, John Patrick *retired banker, federal official*
Mattis, Louis Price *pharmaceutical and consumer products company executive*

**Smyrna**
Atkins, William Austin (Bill ) *state legislator*
Craig, Nadine Karamarkovich *pharmaceutical executive*
Cressey, Douglas B. *insurance company executive*
Head, John Francis, Jr. *distributing company executive*
Passantino, Richard J. *architect*
Waters, Cynthia Winfrey *media advertising specialist*
Wilding, Diane *marketing, financial and information systems executive*

**Snellville**
Brueckner, Lawrence Terence *orthopedic surgeon*
Carlson, Roy Perry Merritt *retired banker*

**Social Circle**
Malcom, Joseph Adams *retired military officer, project manager*

**Statesboro**
Black, Charlene Rushton *university official, sociology educator*
Henry, Nicholas Llewellyn *college president, political science educator*
Murkison, Eugene Cox *business educator*
Parrish, Benjamin Emmitt, II *insurance executive*
Ragans, Rosalind Dorothy *textbook author, retired art educator*

**Stockbridge**
Davis, Raymond Gilbert *retired career officer, real estate developer*
Grimes, Richard Allen *economics educator*

**Stone Mountain**
Boothe, Edward Milton *aeronautical engineer, pilot*
Brown, Jane Bowden *artist, educator*
Gotlieb, Jaquelin Smith *pediatrician*
Honea, Nance *artist, educator*
Nelson, Larry Keith *document investigation laboratory executive*
Speed, Billie Cheney (Mrs. Thomas S. Speed) *retired editor, journalist*
Weiman, Enrique Watson *lawyer*
Wingate, Henry Taylor, Jr. *foundation administrator, fundraiser*

**Suwanee**
Doleman, Christopher John *professional football player*
Harvey, Rebecca Suzanne *accountant, business analyst*
Hebert, Bobby Joseph, Jr. *professional football player*
Jones, June *professional football coach*
Mathis, Terance *professional football player*
Reeves, Daniel Edward *professional football coach*
Shell, Art *professional football team coach*
Shelley, Elbert Vernell *professional football player*
†Smith, Rankin M., Jr. *professional football team executive*
Smith, Taylor *professional football team executive*
Tucker, George Maxwell, Sr. *interactive distribution company executive, business and political consultant*
Tuggle, Jessie Lloyd *professional football player*

**Sylvania**
Johnson, Daniel McDonald (Dan Johnson) *newspaper editor*

**Thomaston**
Beohm, Richard Thomas *fire protection/safety and loss control consultant*
Hightower, Neil Hamilton *textile manufacturing company executive*
Zimmerman, James Robert *radiologist, engineer*

**Thomasville**
Flowers, Langdon Strong *foods company executive*
Flowers, William Howard, Jr. *food company executive*
Mc Mullian, Amos Ryals *food company executive*
Watt, William Vance *surgeon*

**Thomson**
English, John Rife *educational administrator*
Smith, Robert L. *principal*

**Tifton**
Austin, Max Eugene *horticulture educator*
Dorminey, Henry Clayton, Jr. *allergist*
Douglas, Charles Francis *agronomist*
Miller, John David *retired agronomist*
Rogers, Charlie Ellic *entomologist*
Thomas, Adrian Wesley *laboratory director*

**Toccoa**
Gardner, William Wayne *academic administrator*
Maypole, John Floyd *real estate holding company executive*
Scott, Louyse Hulsey *school social worker*

**Toccoa Falls**
Alford, Paul Legare *college and religious foundation administrator*

**Tucker**
Baker, Russ *executive search firm owner*
O'Neil, Daniel Joseph *science research executive, university consultant*
†Owens, W. Larry *hotel executive*
Twining, Henrietta Stover *retired English language educator*
Valk, Henry Snowden *physicist, educator*

**Tunnel Hill**
Martin, Teresa Ann Hilbert *special education educator*

**Union City**
Graham, John Hamilton, II *customer service specialist*

**Valdosta**
Adler, Brian Ungar *English language educator, program director*
Bailey, Hugh Coleman *university president*
Bass, Jay Michael *lawyer*
Beal, John M. *surgeon, medical educator*
Branan, John Maury *psychology educator, counselor*
Cripe, Juliann Woods *education educator*
Halter, H(enry) James, Jr. (Diamond Jim Halter) *retail executive*
McClain, Benjamin Richard *music educator, educational administrator*
McRae, John Henry *educational administrator*
Von Taaffe-Rossmann, Cosima T. *physician, writer, inventor*
Waldrop, Mary Louise *nursing educator*

**Vidalia**
Gres, Dusty Beverly Snipes *librarian*

**Warm Springs**
Barnes, Charles Gerald *historic site administrator*
Knowles, James Barron *rehabilitative medicine physician*
Peach, Paul E. *physician, medical facility administrator*

**Warner Robins**
DePriest, C(harles) David *engineer, retired air force officer*
Nugteren, Cornelius *air force officer*
Owens, Helen Dawn *elementary school educator, reading consultant*

**Washington**
Mansfield, Norman Connie *bookkeeper*
Wills, Olive Boline *elementary education educator*

**Watkinsville**
Johnson, Norman James *physician, lawyer*
Kennon, Pamela Canerday *secondary school educator*
Tate, Curtis E. *management educator*
Wright, Robert Joseph *lawyer*

**Waycross**
Losty, Barbara Paul *college official*
Stock, Maxine *sculptor, librarian, art therapist*

**West Point**
Glover, Clifford Clarke *retired construction company executive*

**Winder**
Allen, B. Janice *elementary educator*
Hutchins, Cynthia Barnes *special education educator*

**Winterville**
Anderson, David Prewitt *retired university dean*
Shockley, W. Ray *travel trade association executive*

**Woodstock**
Austin, John David *financial executive*
Collins, David Browning *religious institution administrator*
Webb, Edsel Philip *retired textile engineer*

**Young Harris**
Jones, Mary Emma B. *counselor, therapist, educator*
Yow, Thomas Sidney, III *college administrator*

**Zebulon**
Bizzell Yarbrough, Cindy Lee *school counselor*

## HAWAII

**Aiea**
Walker, Welmon, Jr. (Rusty Walker) *publisher, consultant*

**Camp Smith**
Teare, Richard Wallace *ambassador*

**Eleele**
Takanishi, Lillian K. *elementary school educator*

**Fort Shafter**
Maruoka, Jo Ann Elizabeth *information systems manager*

**Haiku**
Riecke, Hans Heinrich *architect*

**Haleiwa**
Woolliams, Keith Richard *arboretum and botanical garden director*

**Hanalei**
Vogel, Richard Wiedemann *business owner, ichthyodynamicist, educator*

**Hawaii National Park**
Swanson, Donald Alan *geologist*

**Hilo**
Best, Mary Lani *university program coordinator*
Dixon, Paul William *psychology educator*
Evans, Franklin Bachelder *marketing educator emeritus*
Gersting, Judith Lee *computer science educator, researcher*
Griep, David Michael *astronomical scientist, researcher*
Nagao, Mike Akira *horticulturist, county administrator*
Schnell, Russell Clifford *atmospheric scientist, researcher*
Taniguchi, Tokuso *surgeon*
Ushijima, John Takeji *state senator, lawyer*
Wang, James Chia-Fang *political science educator*
Werner, Marlin Spike *speech pathologist and audiologist*

**Honolulu**
Abbott, Isabella Aiona *biology educator*
Aizawa, Herman *state agency administrator*
Akinaka, Asa Masayoshi *lawyer*
Albano, Andres, Jr. *real estate developer, real estate broker*
Alm, Richard Sanford *education educator*
Amioka, Wallace Shuzo *retired petroleum company executive*
Amor, Simeon, Jr. *photographer*
Anderson, John Wynn *attorney general*
Andrasick, James Stephen *agribusiness company executive*
Ardolf, Deborah Ann *speech pathologist*
Ashford, Clinton Rutledge *judge*
Ashton, Geoffrey Cyril *geneticist, educator*
Aung-Thwin, Michael Arthur *history educator*
Ayer, David Clay *architect*
Baker, Kent Alfred *broadcasting company executive*
Baker, Rosalyn Hester *state legislator*
Bates, George E. *oil industry executive*
Behnke, Richard Frederick *investment banking executive*
Belknap, Jodi Parry *graphic designer, business owner, writer*
Bender, Byron Wilbur *linguistics educator*
Bess, Henry David *dean*
Betts, Barbara Stoke *artist, educator*
Betts, James William, Jr. *financial analyst*
Bitterman, Morton Edward *psychologist, educator*
Bloede, Victor Carl *lawyer, academic executive*
Boas, Frank *lawyer*
Bossert, Philip Joseph *information systems executive*
Botsai, Elmer Eugene *architect, educator, former university dean*
Brady, Stephen R.P.K. *physician*
Brantley, Lee Reed *chemistry educator*
†Bronster, Margery S *attorney general*
Buyers, John William Amerman *agribusiness and specialty foods company executive*
Cachola, Romy Munoz *state representative*
Cain, Raymond Frederick *landscape architect, planning company executive*
Callies, David Lee *lawyer, educator*
Case, James Hebard *lawyer*
Cassiday, Paul Richard *estate administrator*
Cayetano, Benjamin Jerome *governor, former state senator and representative*
Chambers, Kenneth Carter *astronomer*
Chang, Rodney Eiu Joon *artist, dentist*
Chaplin, George *newspaper editor*
Char, Vernon Fook Leong *lawyer*
Chee, Percival Hon Yin *ophthalmologist*
†Chesne, Edward Leonard *physician*
Ching, Chauncey Tai Kin *agricultural economics educator*
Ching, Larry Fong Chow *construction company executive*
Chiu, Arthur Nang Lick *engineering educator*
Chiu, Margaret Chi Yuan Liu *real estate broker*
Cho, Lee-Jay *social scientist, demographer*
Chock, Clifford Yet-Chong *family practice physician*
Choy, Herbert Young Cho *judge*
Chuck, Walter G(oonsun) *lawyer*
Chun Oakland, Suzanne Nyuk Jun *state legislator*
Clarke, Robert F. *utilities company executive*
Copi, Irving Marmer *philosophy educator*
Corsini, Raymond Joseph *psychologist*
Cotlar, Morton *organizational scientist, educator*
Couch, John Charles *diversified company executive*
Cox, Richard Horton *civil engineering executive*
Crumpton, Charles Whitmarsh *lawyer*
Dang, Marvin S. C. *lawyer*
Devenot, David Charles *human resource executive*
Devens, Paul *lawyer*
DiLorenzo, Francis X. *bishop*
Dods, Walter Arthur, Jr. *bank executive*
Dreher, Nicholas C. *lawyer*
Dyen, Isidore *linguistic scientist, educator*
Edel, (Joseph) Leon *biographer, educator*
Ellis, George Richard *museum administrator*
Ezra, David A. *federal judge*
Fasi, Frank Francis *state senator*
Feher, Steve Joseph Kent *design engineer, research developer*
Finney, John Edgar, III *food products executive*
Fischer, Joel *social work educator*
Flanagan, John Michael *editor, publisher*
Flannelly, Kevin J. *psychologist, research analyst*
Flannelly, Laura T. *mental health nurse, nursing educator, researcher*
Flynn, Joan Mayhew *librarian*
Fok, Agnes Kwan *cell biologist, educator*
Fong, Bernard W. D. *physician, educator*
Fong, Hiram Leong *former senator*
Fong, Peter C. K. *lawyer, judge*
†Fukunaga, Barry *airport executive*
Fuller, Lawrence Robert *newspaper publisher*
Fullmer, Daniel Warren *psychologist, educator, retired*
Gary, James Frederick *business and energy advising company executive*
Gay, E(mil) Laurence *lawyer*
Gaydos, Gregory George *political scientist, educator*
Gee, Chuck Yim *dean*
Gelber, Don Jeffrey *lawyer*
George, Peter T. *orthodontist*
Gerson, Mervyn Stuart *lawyer*
Gillmar, Jack Notley Scudder *real estate company executive*
Gillmor, Helen *federal judge*
Glogower, Michael Howard *public housing revitalization specialist*
Goldstein, Sir Norman *dermatologist*
Goodhue, William Walter, Jr. *pathologist, military officer, medical educator*
Greenberg, Marvin *retired music educator*
Greenfield, David W. *zoology educator*
Gulbrandsen, Christian L. *academic dean*
Guthrie, Edgar King *artist*
Haight, Warren Gazzam *investor*
Hale, Nathan Robert *architect*
Hall, Donald Norman Blake *astronomer*
Halloran, Richard Colby *writer, former research executive, former news correspondent*
Hamada, Duane Takumi *architect*
Hanson, Dennis Michael *medical imaging executive*
Harris, Jeremy *mayor*
Hatfield, Elaine Catherine *psychology educator*
Hawke, Bernard Ray *planetary scientist*
Hays, Ronald Jackson *naval officer*
Hee, Vivian Sanae Mitsuda *principal*
Heller, Ronald Ian *lawyer*
Herbig, George Howard *astronomer, educator*
Hertlein, Fred, III *industrial hygiene laboratory executive*
Hirono, Mazie Keiko *state official*
Ho, Donald Tai Loy *entertainer, singer*
Ho, Reginald Chi Shing *medical educator*
Ho, Stuart Tse Kong *investment company executive*
Hoag, John Arthur *retired bank executive*
Hoffmann, Kathryn Ann *humanities educator*
Hollison, Robert Victor, Jr. *physician, executive, army officer*
Hong, Norman G. Y. *architect*
Hook, Ralph Clifford, Jr. *business educator*
Hughes, Robert Harrison *former agricultural products executive*
Hundahl, Scott Alfred *oncologic surgeon*
Ihrig, Judson La Moure *chemist*
Inaba, Lawrence Akio *educational director*
Ingersoll, Richard King *lawyer*
Jackson, Miles Merrill *retired university dean*
Jellinek, Roger *editor*
Jenkins, Robert Gordon *air force officer*
Johnson, Lawrence M. *banker*
Jordan, Amos Azariah, Jr. *foreign affairs educator, retired army officer*
Joseph, Robert David *astronomer, educator*
Kaiser-Botsai, Sharon Kay *early chilhood educator*
Kamemoto, Fred Isamu *zoologist*
Kamemoto, Garett Hiroshi *reporter*
Kamemoto, Haruyuki *horticulture educator*
Kane, Bartholomew Aloysius *state librarian*
Kane, Thomas Jay, III *orthopaedic surgeon, educator*
Kanehiro, Kenneth Kenji *insurance educator, risk analyst, consultant*
Katayama, Robert Nobuichi *lawyer*
Katz, Alan Roy *public health educator*
Kawachika, James Akio *lawyer*
Kay, Alan Cooke *federal judge*
Kay, Elizabeth Alison *zoology educator*
Keil, Klaus *geology educator, consultant*
Keir, Gerald Janes *banker*
Keith, Kent Marsteller *academic administrator, corporate executive, government official, lawyer*
Kelley, Richard Roy *hotel executive*
Keogh, Richard John *firearms consultant*
Khan, Mohammad Asad *geophysicist, educator, former energy minister and senator of Pakistan*
Kim, Joung-Im *communication educator, consultant*
King, Arthur R., Jr. *education educator, researcher*
King, Samuel Pailthorpe *federal judge*
Klein, Robert Gordon *judge*
Klink, Paul Leo *business executive*
Klobe, Tom *art gallery director*
Knowlton, Edgar Colby, Jr. *linguist, educator*
Kohloss, Frederick Henry *consulting engineer*
Koide, Frank Takayuki *electrical engineering educator*
Kolonel, Laurence Norman *epidemiologist, public health educator*
Kong, Laura S. L. *geophysicist*
Krauss, Bob *newspaper columnist, author*
Kuroda, Yasumasa *political science educator, researcher*
Kwok, Reginald Yin-Wang *urban planning and development educator, architect*
Lamoureux, Charles Harrington *botanist, arboretum administrator*
Laney, Leroy Olan *economist, banker*
Langhans, Edward Allen *drama and theater educator*
Lau, Charles Kwok-Chiu *architect, architectural firm executive*
Laughlin, Charles William *agriculture educator, research administrator*
Learned, John Gregory *physicist*
Lee, Beverly Ing *educational administrator*
Lee, Marcia Ellen *insurance agent*
Lee, Yeu-Tsu Margaret *surgeon, educator*
Levinson, Steven Henry *judge*
Lewis, Mary Jane *communication educator, writer*
Lilly, Michael Alexander *lawyer, author*
Lin, Shu *electrical engineering educator*
Linman, James William *retired physician, educator*
Loeffler, Richard Harlan *retail and technology company executive*
Lombardi, Dennis M. *lawyer*
Lum, Jean Loui Jin *nurse educator*
Lum, Jody Mae Kam Quon *real property appraiser*
Ma, Alan Wai-Chuen *lawyer*
Mader, Charles Lavern *chemist*
Mandel, Morton *molecular biologist*
Mark, Shelley Muin *economist, educator, government official*
Marks, Michael J. *lawyer, corporate executive*
Marsella, Anthony Joseph *psychologist, educator*
Marvit, Robert Charles *psychiatrist*
Matayoshi, Coralie Chun *lawyer, bar association executive*
Mau, William Koon-Hee *financier*
†Mc Dermott, John Francis, Jr. *psychiatrist, physician*
Meagher, Michael *radiologist*
Meech, Karen Jean *astronomer*
Meyer, Robert Allen *human resource management educator*
Midkiff, Robert Richards *financial and trust company executive, consultant*
Miike, Lawrence Hiroshi *public health officer*
Miller, Clifford Joel *lawyer*
Miller, Richard Sherwin *legal educator*
Mirikitani, Andrew Kotaro *lawyer*
Mirikitani, John Masa *foundation administrator*
Miyasaki, Shuichi *lawyer*
Moccia, Mary Kathryn *social worker*
Moon, Ronald T. Y. *state supreme court chief justice*
Moore, Willis Henry Allphin *history and geography educator*
Moore, Willson Carr, Jr. *lawyer*
Moreno-Cabral, Carlos Eduardo *cardiac surgeon*
Morse, Richard *social scientist*
Nagtalon-Miller, Helen Rosete *humanities educator*
Naitoh, Yutaka *biology educator*
Nakamoto, Fay *public health officer*
Nakashima, Mitsugi *state agency administrator*
Nakayama, Paula Aiko *justice*
Nishimura, Pete Hideo *oral surgeon*
Nunn, G. Raymond *history educator*
Ogawa, Dennis Masaaki *American studies educator*
Ogburn, Hugh Bell *chemical engineer, consultant*
Okada, Ronald Masaki *insurance agent*
Okinaga, Lawrence Shoji *lawyer*
Olmsted, Ronald David *foundation executive, consultant*
Olsen, Harris Leland *real estate and international business executive, educator, diplomat*
O'Neill, Charles Kelly *marketing executive, former advertising agency executive*

Pagotto, Louise *English language educator*
Paige, Glenn Durland *political scientist, educator*
Palia, Aspy Phiroze *marketing educator, researcher, consultant*
Pang, Herbert George *ophthalmologist*
Pedesky, Geraldine Golick *design project professional*
Pence, Martin *federal judge*
Pfeiffer, Robert John *business executive*
Pickens, Alexander Legrand *education educator*
Pien, Francis D. *internist, microbiologist*
Quinn, William Francis *lawyer*
Raleigh, Cecil Baring *geophysicist*
Rambo, A. Terry *anthropologist, research program director*
Ramler, Siegfried *educator*
Rapson, Richard L. *history educator*
Rautenberg, Robert Frank *consulting research statistician*
Reber, David James *lawyer*
Rho, Edward *information systems professional*
Riggs, Fred Warren *political science educator*
Roberti, Mario Andrew *lawyer, former energy company executive*
Robinson, Robert Blacque *foundation administrator*
Ronsman, Wayne John *insurance company executive*
Russi, John Joseph *priest, educational administrator*
Sagawa, Yoneo *horticulturist, educator*
Saiki, Patricia (Mrs. Stanley Mitsuo Saiki) *former federal agency administrator, former congresswoman*
Sato, Glenn Kenji *lawyer*
Sato, Richard Michio *consulting engineering company executive*
Saxena, Narendra K. *marine research educator*
Schatz, Irwin Jacob *cardiologist*
Scheerer, Ernest William *dentist*
Scheuer, Paul Josef *chemistry educator*
Schnack, Gayle Hemingway Jepson (Mrs. Harold Clifford Schnack) *corporate executive*
Sekine, Deborah Keiko *systems analyst, programmer*
Sharma, Santosh Devraj *obstetrician, gynecologist, educator*
Sharma, Shiv Kumar *geophysicist*
Shen, Edward Nin-Da *cardiologist, educator*
Sherman, Martin *entomologist*
Shirai, Scott *communications executive*
Shoemaker, Forrest Hilton, Jr. *marketing and sales executive, consultant*
Shotwell, Cherrie Leigh *speech and language pathologist*
Simonds, John Edward *newspaper editor*
Simpson, Andrea Lynn *energy communications executive*
Smales, Fred Benson *corporate executive*
Smith, Albert Charles *biologist, educator*
Smith, Barbara Barnard *music educator*
Smith, Thomas Kent *radiologist*
Smyser, Adam Albert *newspaper editor*
Solheim, Wilhelm Gerhard, II *anthropologist, educator*
Solidum, James *finance and insurance executive*
†Sorenson, Perry *resort facility executive*
Sparks, Robert William *retired publishing executive*
Statler, Oliver Hadley *writer*
Stephan, John Jason *historian, educator*
Stephenson, Herman Howard *retired banker*
Sterrett, James Melville *accountant, business consultant*
Stevens, Robert David *librarian, educator*
Stevens, Stephen Edward *psychiatrist*
Sugiki, Shigemi *ophthalmologist, educator*
Suh, Dae-Sook *political science educator*
Sutton, Charles Richard *architect, designer*
Swanson, Richard William *statistician*
Takumi, Roy Mitsuo *state representative*
Tehranian, Majid *political economy and communications educator*
Terminella, Luigi *critical care physician, educator*
Thompson, Henry Nainoa *hospital administrator*
Topping, Donald M. *English language professional, educaor*
Turbin, Richard *lawyer*
Twigg-Smith, Thurston *newspaper publisher*
Umebayashi, Clyde Satoru *lawyer*
Uyehara, Harry Yoshimi *library educator*
Varley, Herbert Paul *Japanese language and cultural history educator*
Vidal, Alejandro Legaspi *architect*
Wageman, Lynette Mena *librarian*
Walker, Margaret Smith *real estate company executive*
†Wallach, Stephen Joseph *cardiologist*
Wang, Jaw-Kai *agricultural engineering educator*
Wataru, Weston Yasuo *civil engineer*
Weightman, Judy Mae *lawyer*
Weiner, Ferne *psychologist*
Wiley, Bonnie Jean *journalism educator*
Williams, Carl Harwell *utilities executive*
Wolff, Herbert Eric *banker, former army officer*
Wong, Henry Li-Nan *bank executive, economist*
Wright, Chatt Grandison *academic administrator*
Wright, Harold Stanley *lawyer*
Wyrtki, Klaus *oceanography educator*
Yamato, Kei C. *international business consultant*
Yee, Alfred Alphonse *structural engineer, consultant*
Yeh, Raymond Wei-Hwa *architect, educator*
Yount, David Eugene *physicist, educator*
Zabanal, Eduardo Olegario *lawyer*
†Zander, Glenn R. *airline company executive*

**Kahului**
Richardson, Robert Allen *lawyer, educator*
Shaw, Virginia Ruth *clinical psychologist*

**Kailua**
Amos, Wally *entrepreneur*
Bone, Robert William *writer, photojournalist*
Engelbardt, Robert Miles *telecommunications executive*
George, Mary Shannon *state senator*
Sullivan, Karen Lau *real estate company executive, campaign consultant, federal commissioner*
Tokumaru, Roberta *principal*
Young, Jacqueline Eurn Hai *state legislator*

**Kailua Kona**
Ashley, Darlene Joy *psychologist*
Causey, Gill Terry *recreation company executive*
Clewett, Kenneth Vaughn *college official*
Diama, Benjamin *retired educator, artist, composer, writer*
Feaver, Douglas David *university dean, classics educator*
Luizzi, Ronald *wholesale distribution executive*
Scarr, Sandra Wood *psychology educator, researcher*
Wageman, Virginia Farley *editor, writer*

**Kaneohe**
Baker, Paul Thornell *anthropology educator*
Fisette, Scott Michael *golf course designer*
Fukumoto, Geal S. *investment representative*
Ikeda, Moss Marcus Masanobu *retired state education official, lecturer, consultant*
McGlaughlin, Thomas Howard *publisher, retired naval officer*

**Kapaa**
Atkins, William Theodore *community volunteer, retired insurance executive*

**Kapaau**
Jankowski, Theodore Andrew *artist*
McFee, Richard *electrical engineer, physicist*

**Keaau**
Bailey, Charles-James Nice *linguistics educator*

**Kealakekua**
Patton, David Wayne *health care executive*

**Kihei**
Wright, Thomas Parker *computer science educator*

**Koloa**
Blair, Samuel Ray *lawyer*
Donohugh, Donald Lee *physician*

**Kula**
Miguel deSousa, Linda J. *critical care nurse, nursing educator*
Rohlfing, Frederick William *travel executive, consultant, retired judge*

**Lahaina**
Ard, James George *family physician*
Arnold, Joan Dean *publisher*
Killingsworth, Kathleen Nola *artist, photographer, company executive*
Sato, Tadashi *artist*

**Laie**
Bradshaw, James R. *business educator*

**Lihue**
Lai, Waihang *art educator*
Pironti, Lavonne De Laere *developer, fundraiser*
Shigemoto, April Fumie *English educator secondary school*

**Makawao**
Mascho, George Leroy *education educator emeritus*

**Mililani**
Gardner, Sheryl Paige *gynecologist*
Kiley, Thomas *rehabilitation counselor*
Kiyota, Heide Pauline *clinical psychologist*
Magee, Donald Edward *retired national park service administrator*

**Ocean View**
Gilliam, Jackson Earle *bishop*

**Paia**
Richman, Joel Eser *lawyer, mediator, arbitrator*

**Pearl City**
Duncan, John Wiley *mathematics and computer educator, retired air force officer*
Rhinelander, Esther Richard *secondary school educator*
Sue, Alan Kwai Keong *dentist*
Takemoto, Cory Noboru *mathematics educator*

**Tripler Army Medical Center**
Person, Donald Ames, Sr. *pediatrician, rheumatologist*
Uyehara, Catherine Fay Takako (Yamauchi) *physiologist, educator, pharmacologist*

**Waialua**
Singlehurst, Dona Geisenheyner *horse farm owner*

**Waianae**
Kakugawa, Terri Etsumi *osteopath*
Kunewa-Armitage, Carinthia Urbanette *realtor*
Pinckney, Neal Theodore *psychologist, educator*

**Waikoloa**
Copman, Louis *radiologist*

**Wailuku**
Kinaka, William Tatsuo *lawyer*
Savona, Michael Richard *physician*

**Waipahu**
Kuwabara, Dennis Matsuichi *optometrist*
Matsui, Jiro *importer, wholesaler, small business owner*

**IDAHO**

**Aberdeen**
Sparks, Walter Chappel *horticulturist, educator*

**Boise**
Andrus, Cecil Dale *academic administrator*
Appleton, Steven R. *electronics executive*
Barber, Phillip Mark *lawyer*
Barr, Robert Dale *university dean, educator*
Batt, Philip E. *governor*
Beaumont, Pamela Jo *marketing professional*
Beebe, Stephen A. *agricultural products company executive*
Black, Pete *state legislator, educator*
Blonshine, Sheena Kay *medical, surgical nurse*
Bolles, Charles Avery *librarian*
Boyle, Larry Monroe *federal judge*
Brown, Christopher Patrick *health care administrator, educator*
Brown, Tod David *bishop*
Brownfield, Shelby Harold *soil scientist*
Caufield, Marie Celine *religious organization administrator*
Cenarrusa, Pete T. *secretary of state*

Cleary, Edward William *retired diversified forest products company executive*
Cook, Sharon Evonne *university official*
DeVilbiss, Jonathan Frederick *aircraft sales engineer*
Edwards, Lydia Justice *state official*
Erickson, Robert Stanley *lawyer*
Graves, Ronald Norman *lawyer*
Griffin, Gloria Jean *elementary school educator*
Griffin, Sylvia Gail *reading specialist*
Hagan, Alfred Chris *federal judge*
Harad, George Jay *manufacturing company executive*
Hawkins, James Victor *state official*
Heitman, Gregory Erwin *state official*
Hendren, Merlyn Churchill *investment company executive*
Hennessey, Alice Elizabeth *community foundation executive*
Hunsucker, (Carl) Wayne *architectural firm executive, educator*
Ilett, Frank, Jr. *trucking company executive*
Johnson, Byron Jerald *state supreme court judge*
Kemp, J. Robert *beef industry consultant, food company executive*
†Killebrew, Harmon Clayton *retail automobile executive, former baseball player, former insurance company executive*
Klein, Edith Miller *lawyer, former state senator*
Lance, Alan George *lawyer, legislator, attorney general*
Langenfeld, Mary Lucille *healthcare facility administrator*
Lee, Roger Ruojia *semiconductor engineer*
Lemmon, Philip Douglas *publishing company executive*
Leroy, David Henry *lawyer, state and federal official*
Littman, Irving *forest products company executive*
Lodge, Edward James *federal judge*
Long, William D. *grocery store executive*
Luthy, John Frederick *management consultant*
Maloof, Giles Wilson *academic administrator, educator, author*
Manning, Darrell V. *national guard officer*
Marcus, Craig Brian *lawyer*
McClary, James Daly *retired contractor*
McDevitt, Charles Francis *state supreme court justice*
McKee, Joseph Fulton *engineering and construction executive*
Mc Quade, Henry Ford *state justice*
Michael, Gary G. *retail supermarket and drug chain executive*
Minnich, Diane Kay *state bar executive*
Mock, Stanley Clyde *financial planner, investment advisor*
Nelson, Thomas G. *federal judge*
Nelson, Willard Gregory *veterinarian, mayor*
Nguyen, King Xuan *language educator*
Nuttall, Michael Lee *engineer, educator*
Otter, Clement Leroy *lieutenant governor*
Overgaard, Willard Michele *retired political scientist, jurisprudent*
Peterson, Eileen M. *state agency administrator*
Pomeroy, Horace Burton, III *accountant, corporate executive*
Pon-Brown, Kay Migyoku *technical marketing engineer*
Poore, Ralph Ezra, Jr. *public relations professional*
Richardson, Betty H. *prosecutor*
Risch, James E. *lawyer*
Ruch, Charles P. *academic administrator*
Shurtliff, Marvin Karl *lawyer*
Silak, Cathy R. *judge*
Slavich, Denis Michael *engineering and construction company executive*
Smith, Marsha H. *state agency administrator, lawyer*
Speer, William Thomas, Jr. *banker, investor, consultant, rancher*
Steinfort, James Richard *university program director*
Stone, Ruby Rocker *state legislator*
Sullivan, James Kirk *forest products company executive*
Taylor, W. O. (Bill Taylor) *state legislator, business consultant*
Thornton, John S., IV *bishop*
Tinstman, Robert Allen *construction company executive*
Trott, Stephen Spangler *federal judge, musician*
Turner, Hal Wesley *state agency administrator*
VanHole, William Remi *lawyer*
Wang, Xiaodong *corporate executive, consultant*
Wells, Merle William *historian, state archivist*
Wilson, Barbara Louise *communications executive*
Wilson, Jack Fredrick *retired federal government official*
Wood, Jeannine Kay *state official*
Woodard, Larry L. *college official*
Young, Katherine Ann *education educator*

**Bonners Ferry**
McClintock, William Thomas *health care administrator*

**Buhl**
Ray, Leo Eldon *fish breeding and marketing company executive*

**Burley**
Westfall, Stephen Donald *accountant, small business owner*

**Calder**
Rechard, Ottis William *mathematics and computer science educator*

**Caldwell**
Allen, Edward Raymond *retired business educator, accountant*
Attebery, Louie Wayne *English language educator, folklorist*
Gipson, Gordon *publishing company executive*
Hendren, Robert Lee, Jr. *academic administrator*
Kerrick, David Ellsworth *lawyer*
Lonergan, Wallace Gunn *economics educator, management consultant*

**Coeur D Alene**
Chamberlain, Barbara Kaye *small business owner*
Griffith, William Alexander *former mining company executive*
Medved, Sandra Louise *elementary education educator*
Sanderson, Holladay Worth *domestic violence advocate*
Strimas, John Howard *allergist, immunologist, pediatrician*

West, Robert Sumner *surgeon*

**Driggs**
Nelson, Robert E. *public relations executive, political consultant*

**Emmett**
Farnham, Wallace Dean *historian*

**Harrison**
Carlson, George Arthur *artist*

**Hayden Lake**
Lehrer, William Peter, Jr. *animal scientist*
Wogsland, James Willard *retired heavy machinery manufacturing executive*

**Idaho Falls**
Harris, Darryl Wayne *publishing executive*
Newman, Stanley Ray *oil refining company executive*
Reich, Charles William *nuclear physicist*
Riemke, Richard Allan *mechanical engineer*
Thorsen, James Hugh *aviation director*
Thorsen, Nancy Dain *real estate broker*
Whittier, Monte Ray *lawyer*
Williams, Phyllis Cutforth *retired realtor*
Woodruff, Shirley *middle school educator*

**Inkom**
Ambrose, Tommy W. *chemical engineer, executive*

**Island Park**
Stratford, Ray Paul *electrical engineer, consultant*

**Ketchum**
Hogue, Terry Glynn *lawyer*
Ziebarth, Robert Charles *management consultant*

**Lewiston**
Duley, Charlotte Dudley *vocational counselor*
Peterson, Philip Everett *legal educator*
Tait, John Reid *lawyer*

**Mc Call**
Evans, Darrell J. *secondary education educator*

**Meridian**
Patterson, Beverly Ann Gross *fund raising consultant, grant writer, federal grants administrator, social services administrator, poet*

**Middleton**
Brown, Ilene De Lois *special education educator*

**Moscow**
Anderson, Clifton Einar *writer, communications consultant*
Bartlett, Robert Watkins *academic dean, metallurgist*
Bitterwolf, Thomas Edwin *chemistry educator*
Bobisud, Larry Eugene *mathematics educator*
Butterfield, Samuel Hale *former government official and educator*
Crawford, Don Lee *microbiologist*
DeShazer, James Arthur *agricultural engineer, educator, administrator*
Force, Ronald Wayne *librarian*
Greever, William St. Clair *educator, historian*
†Hatch, Charles R. *university dean*
Hendee, John Clare *university research educator*
Jackson, Melbourne Leslie *chemical engineering educator and administrator, consultant*
Jacobsen, Richard T. *mechanical engineering educator*
Johnson, Brian Keith *electrical engineering educator*
LeTourneau, Duane John *biochemist, educator*
Mahler, Robert Louis *soil scientist, educator*
Martin, Boyd Archer *political science educator emeritus*
Miller, Maynard Malcolm *geologist, educator, research institute director, explorer, state legislator*
Peterson, Charles Loren *agricultural engineer, educator*
Renfrew, Malcolm MacKenzie *chemist, educator*
Roberts, Lorin Watson *botanist, educator*
Samaniego, Pamela Susan *organization administrator*
Scott, James Michael *research biologist*
Shreeve, Jean'ne Marie *chemist, educator*
Stumpf, Bernhard Josef *physicist*
Vincenti, Sheldon Arnold *law educator, lawyer*
Woodall, David Monroe *research engineer, dean*

**Mountain Home**
Meyr, Shari Louise *webmaster*

**Nampa**
Botimer, Allen Ray *retired surgeon, retirement center owner*

**Payette**
Bragg, Darrell Brent *nutritionist, consultant*
Jones, Donna Marilyn *real estate broker, legislator*

**Pocatello**
Bennion, John Stradling *engineering educator, consultant*
Bowen, Richard Lee *academic administrator, political science educator*
Eichman, Charles Melvin *career assessment educator, school counselor*
Hillyard, Ira William *pharmacologist, educator*
Hofman, Elaine D. *state legislator*
Jackson, Allen Keith *museum administrator*
Lawson, Jonathan Nevin *academic administrator*
McCune, Mary Joan Huxley *microbiology educator*
Nye, W. Marcus W. *lawyer*
Sagness, Richard Lee *education educator, former academic dean*
Seeley, Rod Ralph *physiology educator*
Stanek, Alan Edward *music educator, performer, music administrator*

**Rigby**
Peterson, Erle Vidaillet *retired metallurgical engineer*

**Sandpoint**
Bowne, Martha Hoke *publishing consultant*
Glock, Charles Young *sociologist*

**Stanley**
Kimpton, David Raymond *natural resource consultant, writer*

Spodek, Bernard *early childhood educator*
Sprenkle, Case Middleton *economics educator*
Sprugel, George, Jr. *ecologist*
Sundy, George Joseph, Jr. *engineering executive*
Surles, Richard Hurlbut, Jr. *law librarian*
Taylor, James David *health care executive*
Triandis, Harry Charalambos *psychology educator*
Vedder, Byron Charles *newspaper executive*
Ward, James Gordon *education administration educator*
†Wentworth, Richard Leigh *editor*
Wolfram, Stephen *physicist, computer company executive*

### Charleston
Buckellew, William Franklin *retired education educator*
Jorns, David Lee *university president*
Price, Dalias Adolph *geography educator*
Rives, Stanley Gene *university president emeritus*
Smith, Betty Elaine *geography educator*

### Chatham
Chew, Keith Elvin *healthcare services administrator*
Powell, Carol Sue *pediatric special education educator, nursing consultant*

### Chester
Gross, Melissa Kay *elementary education educator*
Welge, Donald Edward *food manufacturing executive*

### Chicago
Abcarian, Herand *surgeon, educator*
Abelson, Herbert Traub *pediatrician, educator*
Abrams, Lee Norman *lawyer*
Acker, Ann *lawyer*
Acker, Frederick George *lawyer*
Acs, Joseph Steven *transportation engineering consultant*
Adair, Wendell Hinton, Jr. *lawyer*
Adelman, Stanley Joseph *lawyer*
Adelman, Steven Herbert *lawyer*
Adler, Mortimer Jerome *philosopher, author*
Agarwal, Gyan Chand *engineering educator*
Agema, Gerald Walton *broadcasting company executive*
Aggarwal, Suresh Kumar *mechanical and aerospace engineering educator*
Aguilera, Gloria Patricia *financial executive*
†Ahern, Joseph A. *television station executive*
Aitay, Victor *concert violinist, music educator*
†Akers, Michelle Anne *soccer player*
Akos, Francis *violinist*
Albrecht, Ronald Frank *anesthesiologist*
Aldrich, Thomas Lawrence *lawyer*
Alesia, James H(enry) *judge*
Alexander, William Henry *lawyer*
Alexis, Geraldine M. *lawyer*
Aliber, Robert Z. *economist, educator*
Allard, Jean *lawyer, urban planner*
Allen, Belle *management consulting firm executive, communications company executive*
Allen, Janice Mandabach *interior designer, nurse, office manager, actress, model*
Allen, Richard Blose *legal editor, lawyer*
Allen, Ronald Jay *law educator*
Allen, Thomas Draper *lawyer*
Almeida, Richard Joseph *finance company administrator*
Almen, Lowell Gordon *church official*
Alschuler, Albert W. *law educator*
Altman, Louis *lawyer, author, educator*
Altmann, Stuart Allen *biologist, educator*
Amato, Isabella Antonia *real estate executive*
Amberg, Thomas L. *public relations executive*
Amonte, Anthony Lewis *professional hockey player*
Amstadter, Laurence *retired architect*
Andersen, Burton Robert *physician, educator*
Andersen, Wayne R. *federal judge*
Anderson, David A. *lawyer*
†Anderson, Hugh George *bishop*
Anderson, J. Trent *lawyer*
Anderson, John Thomas *lawyer*
Anderson, Jon Stephen *newswriter*
Anderson, Karl Stephen *newspaper executive*
Anderson, Kimball Richard *lawyer*
Anderson, Louise Eleanor *biochemistry educator*
Anderson, William Cornelius, III *lawyer*
Andreoli, Kathleen Gainor *nurse, educator, administrator*
Angst, Gerald L. *lawyer*
Annable, James Edward *economist*
Anthony, Michael Francis *lawyer*
Anthony-Perez, Bobbie Cotton Murphy *psychology educator, researcher*
Antonio, Douglas John *lawyer*
Anvaripour, M. A. *lawyer*
Appel, Nina Schick *law educator, dean*
Applebaum, Edward Leon *otolaryngologist, educator*
Appleton, Arthur Ivar *retired electric products manufacturing company executive, horse breeder*
Arditti, Fred D. *economist, educator*
Arekapudi, Kumar Vijaya Vasantha *sanitarian, real estate agent*
Arekapudi, Vijayalakshmi *obstetrician-gynecologist*
Armstrong, Edwin Richard *lawyer, publisher, editor*
Aronson, Howard Isaac *linguist, educator*
Aronson, Virginia L. *lawyer*
Arpino, Gerald Peter *performing company executive*
Artner, Alan Gustav *art critic, journalist*
Ash, J. Marshall *mathematician, educator*
Aspen, Marvin Edward *federal judge*
Astrachan, Boris Morton *psychiatry educator, consultant*
Athas, Gus James *lawyer*
Auerbach, Marshall Jay *lawyer*
Axley, Frederick William *lawyer*
Ayman, Iraj *international education consultant*
Babcock, Lyndon Ross, Jr. *environmental engineer, educator*
Bacher, Robert Newell *church official*
Badel, Julie *lawyer*
Baer, John Richard Frederick *lawyer*
Baetz, W. Timothy *lawyer*
Baffes, Thomas Gus *cardiac surgeon, lawyer*
†Baglivo, Mary L. *client services administrator*
Bailar, Barbara Ann *statistician, researcher*
Bailar, John Christian, III *public health educator, physician, statistician*
Bailey, Orville Taylor *neuropathologist*
Bailey, Robert, Jr. *advertising executive*
Bailey, Robert Short *lawyer*
Baines, Harold Douglass *professional baseball player*
Baird, Douglas Gordon *law educator*
Baker, Bruce Jay *lawyer*
Baker, James Edward Sproul *retired lawyer*
Baker, Pamela *lawyer*
Baker, Robert J. *medical academic dean, surgeon*
Bakwin, Edward Morris *banker*
Baldwin, Shaun McParland *lawyer*
Balsam, Theodore *physician*
Balz, Douglas Charles *journalist*
Balzekas, Stanley, Jr. *museum director*
Ban, Stephen Dennis *natural gas industry research institute executive*
Banerjee, Prashant *industrial engineering educator*
Banks, Deirdre Margaret *church organization administrator*
†Banks, Lyle *television station executive*
Banoff, Sheldon Irwin *lawyer*
Baptist, Allwyn J. *health care consultant*
Barany, Kate *biophysics educator*
Barber, Edward Bruce *medical products executive*
Barbour, Claude Marie *minister*
Bard, John Franklin *consumer products executive*
Barker, Emmett Wilson, Jr. *trade association executive*
Barker, Walter Lee *thoracic surgeon*
Barker, William Thomas *lawyer*
Barnard, Robert N. *lawyer*
Barnes, James Garland, Jr. *lawyer*
Barnette, Dennis Arthur *management consultant*
Barney, Carol Ross *architect*
†Barr, David *actor, playwright*
Barr, John Robert *lawyer*
Barrett, Roger Watson *lawyer*
Barron, Howard Robert *lawyer*
Barrow, Charles Herbert *investment banker*
Barry, Norman J., Jr. *lawyer*
Bartholomay, William C. *insurance brokerage company executive, professional baseball team executive*
Bartoletti, Bruno *conductor*
†Barton, John Joseph *obstetrician-gynecologist, educator*
Bartter, Brit Jeffrey *investment banker*
Baruch, Hurd *lawyer*
Bashwiner, Steven Lacelle *lawyer*
Bassiouny, Hishan Salah *surgeon, educator*
Batlle, Daniel *nephrologist*
Batory, Ronald Louis *rail transportation executive*
Baudendistel, Daniel *dancer*
Bauer, William Joseph *federal judge*
Baugher, Peter V. *lawyer*
Baum, Bernard Helmut *sociologist, educator*
Baumhart, Raymond Charles *Roman Catholic church administrator*
Bayer, Gary Richard *advertising executive*
Beane, Marjorie Noterman *academic administrator*
Beattie, Janet Holtzman *accounting firm executive*
Beattie, Ted Arthur *zoological gardens and aquarium administrator*
Beaty, Harry Nelson *internist, educator, university dean*
Bechina, Melvin Jeremiah *leasing company executive*
Beck, Irene Clare *educational consultant, writer*
Beck, Joan Wagner *journalist*
Beck, John Matthew *education educator*
Beck, Philip S. *lawyer*
Beck, Robert N. *nuclear medicine educator*
Becker, Gary Stanley *economist, educator*
Becker, Michael Allen *physician, educator*
Beeby, Thomas H. *architect*
Beecher, William John *zoologist, museum director*
Beem, Jack Darrel *lawyer*
Beigl, William *physician, naturopath, hypnotist, acupuncturist, consultant*
Belfour, Ed *professional hockey player*
Bell, Clark Wayne *business editor, educator*
Bell, Jason Cameron *accountant*
Belle, Albert Jojuan *professional baseball player*
Belluschi, Anthony C. *architect*
Bender, Janet Pines *artist*
Bennett, Lerone, Jr. *magazine editor, author*
Bennett, Russell Odbert *lawyer*
Bensinger, Peter Benjamin *consulting firm executive*
Berendi, Erlinda Bayaua *surgeon*
Berens, Mark Harry *lawyer*
Berenzweig, Jack Charles *lawyer*
Berger, Miles Lee *land economist*
Berger, Robert Michael *lawyer*
Bergere, Carleton Mallory *contractor*
Bergonia, Raymond David *venture capitalist*
Bergstrom, Betty Howard *consulting executive, foundation administrator*
Berkery, Michael John *insurance company executive*
Berland, Abel Edward *lawyer, realtor*
Berman, Arthur Leonard *state senator*
Berman, Bennett I. *lawyer*
Bernard, Frank Charles *lawyer*
Bernatowicz, Frank Allen *management consultant, expert witness*
Berner, Robert Lee, Jr. *lawyer*
Berning, Larry D. *lawyer*
Bernstein, H. Bruce *lawyer*
Berolzheimer, Karl *lawyer*
Beser, Roberta Ruth (Bobbie Beser) *physical therapy company executive*
Betts, Henry Brognard *physician, health facility administrator, educator*
Betz, Hans Dieter *theology educator*
Beugen, Joan Beth *communications company executive*
Bevan, Norman Edward *religious organization executive*
Bevington, David Martin *English literature educator*
Bevington, Terry Paul *professional baseball manager*
Bidwell, Charles Edward *sociologist, educator*
Biebel, Paul Philip, Jr. *lawyer*
Biederman, Jerry H. *lawyer*
Bierig, Jack R. *lawyer, educator*
Biggles, Richard Robert *marketing executive*
Biggs, Robert Dale *Near Eastern studies educator*
Bilandic, Michael A. *state supreme court justice, former mayor*
Bishop, Oliver Richard *state official*
Bitner, John Howard *lawyer*
Bixby, Frank Lyman *lawyer*
†Black, James *advertising executive*
Blair, Bowen *investment banker*
Blair, Edward McCormick *investment banker*
Blanchard, James Arthur *engineer and computer systems specialist*
Blatt, Richard Lee *lawyer*
Bloch, Ralph Jay *professional association executive*
Block, Neal Jay *lawyer*
Block, Philip Dee, III *investment counselor*
Bloom, Benjamin S. *education educator*
Blount, Michael Eugene *lawyer*
Blumberg, Avrom Aaron *physical chemistry educator*
Blumenthal, Carlene Margaret *vocational-technical school educator*
Blust, Larry D. *lawyer*
Blutter, Joan Wernick *interior designer*
Bobins, Norman R. *banker*
Bockelman, John Richard *lawyer*
Bodi, Sonia Ellen *academic librarian*
Bodine, Laurence *lawyer, editor, marketer*
Boehnen, Daniel A. *lawyer*
Boers, Terry John *sportswriter, radio and television personality*
Bogert, John Alden, II *dental association executive*
Boggess, Thomas Phillip, III *graphic arts company executive*
Boggs, Joseph Dodridge *pediatric pathologist, educator*
Bolnick, Howard Jeffrey *insurance consultant, educator, private investor*
Bonham, Russell Aubrey *chemistry educator*
Bonow, Robert Ogden *medical educator*
Bookstein, Abraham *information science educator*
Booth, Wayne Clayson *English literature and rhetoric educator, author*
Borleis, Melvin William *management consultant*
Borling, John Lorin *military officer*
Bornholdt, Laura Anna *university administrator*
Boshes, Louis D. *physician, scientist, educator*
Bosselman, Fred Paul *law educator*
Bott, Harold Sheldon *accountant, management consultant*
Bourdon, Cathleen Jane *executive director*
Bowe, William John *lawyer*
Bowen, Stephen Stewart *lawyer*
Bowen, William Joseph *management consultant*
Bower, Glen Landis *lawyer*
Bowman, Barbara Taylor *institute president*
Bowman, George Arthur, Jr. *judge*
Bowman, James Edward *physician, educator*
Bowman, Leah *fashion designer, consultant, photographer, educator*
Boyce, David Edward *transportation and regional science educator*
Boyd, Karen Johnson *art dealer*
Boyd, Willard Lee *museum administrator, educator, lawyer*
†Boyda, Debora *advertising executive*
Boyer, John William *history educator, dean*
Bradburn, Norman M. *behavioral science educator*
Braddock, David Lawrence *health science educator*
Braidwood, Linda Schreiber *archaeologist*
Braidwood, Robert John *archaeologist, educator*
Brake, Cecil Clifford *diversified manufacturing executive*
Bramnik, Robert Paul *lawyer*
Brand, Mark Allen *lawyer*
Brandt, William Arthur, Jr. *consulting executive*
Bransfield, James Joseph *surgeon*
Bratton, Christopher Alan *video and art educator*
Brennan, Bernard Francis *retail chain store executive*
Brennan, James Joseph *lawyer, banking and financial services executive*
Bresnahan, James Francis *medical ethics educator*
Breyer, Norman Nathan *metallurgical engineering educator, consultant*
Brice, Roger Thomas *lawyer*
Brickhouse, John B. (Jack Brickhouse) *sports broadcaster*
Bridewell, David Alexander *lawyer*
Bridgman, Thomas Francis *lawyer*
Brinkman, John Anthony *historian, educator*
Bristol, Douglas *lawyer*
Brizzolara, Charles Anthony *lawyer*
Brodsky, Robert Jay *wholesale executive*
Brodsky, William J. *futures options exchange executive*
Brooker, Thomas Kimball *oil company executive*
Brooks, Gwendolyn *writer, poet*
Brookstone, Arnold F. *retired paper packaging company executive*
Brotman, Barbara Louise *columnist, writer*
Brown, Alan Crawford *lawyer*
Brown, Carlos *secondary education educator, psychology educator*
Brown, Charles Eric *biochemistry educator, analytical instrumentation consultant, petrochemical analytical researcher*
Brown, Donald James, Jr. *lawyer*
Brown, Faith A. *communications manager*
Brown, Gregory K. *lawyer*
Brown, Richard Holbrook *library administrator, historian*
Browning, Don Spencer *religion educator*
Brubaker, Charles William *architect*
Brueschke, Erich Edward *physician, researcher, educator*
Brumback, Charles Tiedtke *retired newpaper executive*
Brummel, Mark Joseph *magazine editor*
Bruner, Stephen C. *lawyer*
Bryan, John Henry *food and consumer products company executive*
Bryan, William Royal *finance educator*
Bua, Nicholas John *retired federal judge*
Buckle, Frederick Tarifero *international holding company executive, political and business intelligence analyst*
Buckley, Joseph Paul, III *polygraph specialist*
Bucklo, Elaine Edwards *federal judge*
Buckner, James Lowell *dentist*
Buehler, Evelyn Judy *poet*
Bueschel, David Alan *management consultant*
Bugielski, Robert Joseph *state legislator*
Bulger, Brian Wegg *lawyer*
Burack, Elmer Howard *management educator*
Burditt, George Miller, Jr. *lawyer*
Burgdoerfer, Jerry *lawyer*
Burger, Mary Louise *psychologist, educator*
Burhoe, Brian W. *automotive service executive*
Burke, Edmund Patrick, Sr. *lawyer*
Burke, Thomas Joseph, Jr. *lawyer*
Burkey, Lee Melville *lawyer*
Burns, Terrence Michael *lawyer*
Burt, Robert Norcross *diversified manufacturing company executive*
Burton, Raymond Charles, Jr. *transportation company executive*
Busey, Roxane C. *lawyer*
Bushman, Mary Laura Jones *developer, fundraiser*
Buss, Daniel Frank *environmental scientist*
Butler, Robert Allan *psychologist, educator*
Bynoe, Peter Charles Bernard *real estate developer, lawyer*
Byrne, Katharine Crane *lawyer*
Caccamo, Nicholas James *financial executive*
Calderón, Alberto Pedro *mathematician, educator*
Caldwell, Ethel Louise Lynch *academic administrator*
Calenoff, Leonid *radiologist*
Callahan, Michael J. *chemicals and manufacturing company executive*
Callaway, Karen A(lice) *journalist*
Campbell, Bruce Crichton *hospital administrator*
Campbell, Edward Fay, Jr. *religion educator*
Campbell, Gavin Elliott *real estate investor and developer*
Camper, John Jacob *writer, university administrator*
Cappo, Joseph C. *publisher*
Caray, Harry Christopher *sports announcer*
Carl, John L. *petroleum industry executive*
Carlin, Dennis J. *lawyer*
Carlson, Rolland S. *healthcare system administrator*
Carlson, Stephen Curtis *lawyer*
Carlson, Walter Carl *lawyer*
Carlton, Dennis William *economics educator*
Carney, Jean Kathryn *psychologist*
Caro, William Allan *physician*
Carpenter, Allan *author, editor, publisher*
Carpenter, David William *lawyer*
Carr, Robert Clifford *petroleum company executive*
Carren, Jeffrey P. *lawyer*
Carroll, James J. *lawyer*
Carroll, William Kenneth *law educator, psychologist, theologian*
Case, Clyde Willard, Jr. *sales and marketing executive*
†Case, Donni Marie *investment company executive*
†Cass, Edward Roberts (Peter) *hotel and travel marketing professional*
Castillo, Mario Enrique *artist, educator*
Castorino, Sue *communications executive*
Cederoth, Richard Alan *lawyer*
Chacko, Samuel *association official*
Chakrabarty, Ananda Mohan *microbiologist*
Chaleff, Carl Thomas *brokerage house executive*
Champagne, Ronald Oscar *academic administrator, mathematics educator*
Chandler, Kent, Jr. *lawyer*
Chang, Yi-Cheng *insurance agent*
Chapman, Alger Baldwin *finance executive, lawyer*
Chapman, Delores *elementary education educator*
Chapman, Howard Stuart *lawyer, educator*
Chapman, Stephen James *columnist*
Chappell, Sally *art historian*
Charles, Allan G. *physician, educator*
Charlier, Roger Henri *oceanographer, geographer, educator*
Chartier, Janellen Olsen *airline service coordinator*
Chatterton, Robert Treat, Jr. *reproductive endocrinology educator*
Cheely, Daniel Joseph *lawyer*
Chefitz, Joel Gerald *lawyer*
Chelios, Christos K *professional hockey player*
Chemers, Robert Marc *lawyer*
Chen, Wai-Kai *electrical engineering and computer science educator, consultant*
Cherney, James Alan *lawyer*
Cherry, Robert Steven, III *municipal agency administrator*
Chiles, Stephen Michael *lawyer*
Chin, Davis *lawyr*
Chlebowski, John Francis, Jr. *financial executive*
Cho, Wonhwa *biomedical researcher*
Chookaszian, Dennis Haig *financial executive*
Choyke, Phyllis May Ford (Mrs. Arthur Davis Choyke, Jr.) *management executive, editor, poet*
Christian, John M. *lawyer*
Christiansen, Richard Dean *newspaper editor*
Christianson, Stanley David *corporate executive*
Chudzinski, Mark Adam *lawyer*
Chun, Shinae *state official*
Chung, Paul Myungha *mechanical engineer, educator*
Ciccone, Richard *newspaper editor*
Cicero, Frank, Jr. *lawyer*
Cizza, John Anthony *insurance executive*
†Clark, Erin M. *advertising executive*
Clark, James Allen *lawyer, educator*
Clark, Jeanne (Barbara) *police deputy chief*
Clark, John Whitcomb *diagnostic radiologist*
Clarke, Philip Ream, Jr. *investment banker*
Clayton, Robert Norman *chemist, educator*
Clemens, Richard Glenn *lawyer*
Cloonan, James Brian *investment executive*
Closen, Michael Lee *law educator*
Coar, David H. *federal judge*
Coase, Ronald Harry *economics educator*
Coduti, Philip James *legal association admininstration*
Coe, Donald Kirk *university official*
Coe, Fredric L. *physician, educator, researcher*
Coffey, Raymond Richard *newspaper editor, journalist*
Coffey, Susanna Jean *artist, educator*
Cohen, Christopher B. *lawyer*
Cohen, Edward Philip *microbiology and immunology educator, physician*
Cohen, Jerome *psychology educator, electrophysiologist*
Cohen, Melanie Rovner *lawyer*
Cohen, Melvin R. *physician, educator*
Cohen, Ted *philosophy educator*
Cohler, Bertram Joseph *social sciences educator, clinical psychologist*
Cohodes, Eli Aaron *publisher*
Coleman, Roy Everett *secondary education educator, computer programmer*
Collen, Sheldon Orrin *lawyer*
Collens, Lewis Morton *university president, legal educator*
Colley, Karen J. *medical educator, medical researcher*
Colten, Harvey Radin *pediatrician, educator*
Comiskey, Michael Peter *lawyer*
Conant, Howard Rosset *steel company executive*
Congalton, Susan Tichenor *lawyer*
Conibear, Shirley Ann *occupational health consultant, physician*
Conklin, Michael L. *newspaper columnist*
Conklin, Thomas William *lawyer*
Conlon, Suzanne B. *federal judge*
Connelly, Kathleen Fitzgerald *public relations executive*
Connelly, Mary Jo *lawyer*
Connors, Dorsey *television and radio commentator, newspaper columnist*
Connors, Mary Eileen *psychologist*
Conrad, John R. *corporate executive*
Consey, Kevin Edward *museum administrator*
Constant, Anita Aurelia *publisher*
Conviser, Richard James *law educator, lawyer, publications company executive*
Conway, James Joseph *physician*
Conway, Michael Maurice *lawyer*
Cook, Catherine Coghlan *lawyer*
Cook, Richard Borreson *architect*
Coolley, Ronald B. *lawyer*
Cooper, Charles Gilbert *toiletries and cosmetics company executive*
Cooper, Ilene Linda *magazine editor, author*

Cooper, Jo Marie elementary school administrative assistant
Coopersmith, Bernard Ira obstetrician, gynecologist, educator
Copeland, Edward Jerome lawyer
Coppersmith, Susan Nan physicist
Corcoran, James Martin, Jr. lawyer, writer, lecturer
†Cornell, Rob hotel executive
Corwin, Sherman Phillip lawyer
Costa, Erminio pharmacologist, cell biology educator
Costello, John William lawyer
Costin, J(oseph) Laurence, Jr. information services executive
Cotter, Daniel A. diversified company executive
Cotton, Eugene lawyer
Coughlan, Kenneth Lewis lawyer
Coulson, William Roy lawyer
Covalt, Robert Byron chemicals executive
Cox, Allan James management consultant and sports executive
Cox, Charles C. economist
Coy, Patricia Ann special education director, consultant
Crane, Mark lawyer
Crane, Peter Robert botanist, geologist, paleontologist, educator
Craven, George W. lawyer
Crawford, Dewey Byers lawyer
Crawford, William F. corporate executive, consultant
Creighton, Neal foundation administrator, retired army officer
Cremin, Susan Elizabeth lawyer
Cressey, Bryan Charles lawyer
Crihfield, Philip J. lawyer
Crisham, Thomas Michael lawyer
Cronin, James Watson physicist, educator
Cropsey, Joseph political science educator
Cross, Dolores Evelyn university administrator, educator
Cross, Robert Clark journalist
Crossan, John Robert lawyer
Crown, James Schine investment executive
Crown, Lester manufacturing company executive
Csar, Michael F. lawyer
Csikszentmihalyi, Mihaly psychology educator
Cudahy, Richard D. federal judge
Cui, Ke-hui embryologist, obstetrician, gynecologist
Cullen, Charles Thomas historian, librarian
Culp, Kristine Ann dean, theology educator
Cummings, Maxine Gibson elementary school educator
Cummings, Walter J. federal judge
Cunningham, Robert James lawyer
Cunningham, Thomas Justin lawyer
Currie, David Park lawyer, educator
Curwen, Randall William journalist, editor
Cushman, Aaron D. public relations executive
Custer, Charles Francis lawyer
Cyr, Arthur I. institute executive
Daley, Michael Joseph lawyer
Daley, Richard Michael mayor
Daley, Susan Jean lawyer
Daly, Patrick F. real estate executive, architect
Dam, Kenneth W. lawyer, law educator
D'Amato, Anthony law educator
Dancewicz, John Edward investment banker
Daniels, Keith Byron, Jr. lawyer
Darby, Edwin Wheeler retired newspaper financial columnist
Darnall, Robert J. steel company executive
Darr, Milton Freeman, Jr. banker
Datta, Rathin chemical engineer
Datta, Syamal Kumar medical educator, researcher
†Davidson, Richard J. medical association administrator
Davidson, Richard Laurence geneticist, educator
Davidson, Stanley J. lawyer
†Davis, Danny K. healthcare consultant, educator
†Davis, DeForest P., Jr. architectural engineer
Davis, G(eorge) Gordon lawyer, international environmental policy consultant
Davis, Michael W. lawyer
Davis, Muller lawyer
Davis, Scott Jonathan lawyer
Davison, Richard physician, educator
†Daze, Eric professional hockey player
DeBat, Donald Joseph media consultant
†Debczek, Arnold pharmaceutical company executive
Debus, Allen George history educator
DeCarlo, William S. lawyer
Dechene, James Charles lawyer
Decker, Richard Knore lawyer
De Francesco, John Blaze, Jr. public relations company executive
Degroot, Leslie Jacob medical educator
Deitrick, William Edgar lawyer
De Leonardis, Nicholas John banker
Delp, Wilbur Charles, Jr. lawyer
Dembowski, Peter Florian foreign language educator
DeMoss, Jon W. insurance company executive, lawyer
Dempsey, James Randall academic administrator
Dempsey, Mary A. library commissioner, lawyer
Dent, Thomas G. lawyer
Deorio, Anthony Joseph surgeon
Derlacki, Eugene L(ubin) otolaryngologist, physician
Desch, Theodore Edward health insurance company executive, lawyer
Desjardins, Claude physiologist, dean, administrator
D'Esposito, Julian C., Jr. lawyer
Despres, Leon Mathis lawyer, former city official
Detmer, Lawrence McCormick professional society administrator
Detuno, Joseph Edward lawyer
Deutsch, Thomas Alan ophthalmologist, educator
DeWolfe, John Chauncey, Jr. lawyer
Diamond, Seymour physician
Diamond, Shari Seidman psychology educator, law researcher
Diaz-Franco, Carlos surgeon, anatomist, anesthesiologist
Diaz-Gemmati, Griselle Maritza secondary education educator
†DiCicco, Tony soccer coach
Diefenbach, Viron Leroy dental, public health educator, university dean
Dilling, Kirkpatrick Wallwick lawyer
Dimond, Robert Edward publisher
Di Spigno, Guy Joseph international management consultant, industrial psychologist
Dix, Rollin C(umming) mechanical engineering educator, consultant
Dixon, Stewart Strawn lawyer
Dockterman, Michael lawyer
Dodds, Claudette La Vonn radio executive and consultant
Dolan, Thomas Christopher professional society administrator
Dold, Robert Bruce journalist
Dondanville, John Wallace lawyer
Doniger, Wendy history of religions educator
Donlevy, John Dearden lawyer
Donnell, Harold Eugene, Jr. professional society administrator
Donnelley, James Russell printing company executive
Donner, Ted A. lawyer
Donohoe, Jerome Francis lawyer
Donovan, Dianne Francys journalist
Donovan, John Vincent consulting company executive
Donovan, Margaret educational association administrator
Doolittle, Sidney Newing retail executive
Dorman, Jeffrey Lawrence lawyer
Dowling, Doris Anderson business owner, educator, consultant
Downing, Robert Allan lawyer
Doyle, John Robert lawyer
Drabek, Doug (Douglas Dean Drabek) baseball player
†Draft, Howard advertising executive
Drexler, Richard Allan manufacturing company executive
Driskell, Claude Evans college director, educator, dentist
Dropkin, Allen Hodes lawyer
Drymalski, Raymond Hibner lawyer, banker
Duell, Daniel Paul artistic director, choreographer, lecturer
Duff, Brian Barnett federal judge
Duhl, Michael Foster lawyer
Duncan, John Patrick Cavanaugh lawyer
Dunea, George nephrologist, educator
Dunea, Mary Mills protocol consultant
Dunlap, Patricia Pearl elementary school educator
Dunston, Shawon Donnell professional baseball player
Dupont, Todd F. mathematics and computer science educator
Durchslag, Stephen P. lawyer
Dye, Carl Melvyn academic administrator, educational association executive, insurance consultant
Dykla, K.H.S. Edward George social services administrator
Dykstra, Paul Hopkins lawyer
Dyrud, Jarl Edvard psychiatrist
Early, Bert Hylton lawyer, legal search consultant
Easterbrook, Frank Hoover federal judge
†Eastham, Dennis Michael advertising executive
Eaton, John C. composer, educator
Ebert, Paul Allen surgeon, educator
Ebert, Roger Joseph film critic
Echols, M(ary) Evelyn travel consultant
Ecker, Lori D. lawyer
Eddy, David Latimer banker
Edelman, Alvin lawyer
Edelman, Daniel Joseph public relations executive
Edelsberg, Sally C. physical therapy educator and administrator
Edelstein, Teri J. museum administrator, educator
Egan, Kevin James lawyer
Eggert, Russell Raymond lawyer
Eimer, Nathan Philip lawyer
Einhorn, Edward Martin (Eddie Einhorn) professional baseball team executive
Eisenberg, James food company executive
Eisenman, Trudy Fox dermatologist
Eisenmann, Dale Richard dental educator
Ekdahl, Jon Nels lawyer, corporate secretary
Elbaz, Sohair Wastawy library director, consultant
Elden, Gary Michael lawyer
Ellwood, Scott lawyer
Elson, Alex lawyer, educator, arbitrator
Ender, Jon T. investment management executive, banker
Engel, Joel Stanley telecommunications executive
†Engel, Philip L. insurance company executive
English, John Dwight lawyer
Ephraim, Donald Morley lawyer
Eppen, Gary Dean business educator
Epstein, Raymond engineering and architectural executive
Epstein, Sidney architect and engineer
Epstein, Wolfgang biochemist, educator
Erber, Thomas physics educator
Erdös, Ervin George pharmacology and biochemistry educator
Erens, Jay Allan lawyer
Erlebacher, Albert history educator
Ernest, J. Terry ocular physiologist, educator
Espinosa, Gustavo Adolfo radiologist, educator
Esrick, Jerald Paul lawyer
Essex, Joseph Michael visual communication planner
Eubanks-Pope, Sharon G. real estate entrepreneur
Evans, Earl Alison, Jr. biochemist
†Evans, Mariwyn periodical editor
Evans, Thelma Jean Mathis internist
Even, Francis Alphonse lawyer
†Everhart, Bruce radio station executive
Fabian, Larry Louis bank executive
Fabisch, Gale Warren civil engineer
Fahner, Tyrone C. lawyer, former state attorney general
Fahnestock, Jean Howe retired civil engineer
Fairchild, Thomas E. federal judge
Falls, Robert Arthur artistic director
Fano, Ugo physicist, educator
Fanta, Paul Edward chemist, educator
Farber, Bernard John lawyer
†Farina, Dennis actor
Farley, William F. corporation executive
Farrakhan, Louis religious leader
Farrell, Thomas Dinan lawyer
Favors, Malachi jazz musician, bassist
Fazio, Peter Victor, Jr. lawyer
Feder, Robert television and radio columnist
Feeley, Henry Joseph, Jr. (Hank Feeley) artist, former advertising agency executive
Fein, Roger Gary lawyer
Feingold, Daniel Leon anesthesiologist
Feinstein, Fred Ira lawyer
Feldman, Burton Gordon printing company executive
Feldman, Edwin health care executive, internist, cardiologist
Feldman, Scott M. lawyer
Feldstein, Charles Robert fund raising consultant
Fellows, Jerry Kenneth lawyer
Felsenthal, Steven Altus lawyer
Felton, Cynthia principal
Fennessy, John James radiologist, educator
Fensin, Daniel diversified financial service company executive
Fenters, James Dean research institute administrator
Fenton, Clifton Lucien investment banker
Ferencz, Robert Arnold lawyer
Ferguson, Bradford Lee lawyer
Ferguson, Donald John surgeon, educator
Ferguson, Mark Kendric physician, educator, researcher
Ferrini, James Thomas lawyer
Fetridge, Bonnie-Jean Clark (Mrs. William Harrison Fetridge) civic volunteer
Fetridge, Clark Worthington publisher
Field, Henry Frederick lawyer
Field, Marshall business executive
Field, Robert Edward lawyer
Fina, Paul Joseph lawyer
Finch, Herman Manuel academic administrator
Finke, Robert Forge lawyer
Finley, Harold Marshall investment banker
Fiorentino, Leon Francis holding company executive
Fisher, Eugene marketing executive
Fisher, Herbert Hirsh lawyer
Fisher, Lawrence Edgar market research executive, anthropologist
Fisher, Lester Emil zoo administrator
Fisk, Carlton Ernest retired professional baseball player
Fitch, Frank Wesley pathologist educator, immunologist, educator, administrator
Fitch, Morgan Lewis, Jr. intellectual property lawyer
Fitzgerald, Robert Maurice financial executive
Fizdale, Richard advertising agency executive
Flagg, Michael James communications and graphics company executive
Flaherty, Emalee Gottbrath pediatrician
Flanagin, Neil lawyer
Flaum, Joel Martin federal judge
Fleischer, Cornell Hugh history educator
Fleming, Graham Richard chemistry educator
Fleming, Richard H. finance executive
Fligg, James Edward oil company executive
Flock, Jeffrey Charles news bureau chief
Flynn, John J. museum curator
Flynn, Peter Anthony lawyer
Fogel, Henry orchestra administrator
Fogel, Robert William economist, educator, historian
Foley, Joseph Lawrence sales executive
Forbes, John Edward financial consultant
Formeller, Daniel Richard lawyer
Fort, Jeffrey C. lawyer
Fortune, Michael Joseph religion educator
Foster, James Reuben investment company executive
Foster, Teree E. law educator, university dean
Foudree, Bruce William lawyer
Fournier, Maureen Mary physical education educator
Fowler, George Selton, Jr. architect
Fox, Elaine Saphier lawyer
Fox, Paul T. lawyer
Franch, Richard Thomas lawyer
Francois, William Armand packaging company executive, lawyer
Franke, Richard James investment banker
†Franklin, Cory Michael medical administrator, educator
Franklin, Richard Mark lawyer
Fraumann, Willard George lawyer
Frazen, Mitchell Hale lawyer
Frederiksen, Marilynn Elizabeth Conners physician
Freeborn, Michael D. lawyer
Freed, Karl Frederick chemistry educator
Freed, Mayer Goodman law educator
Freedman, Walter G. corporate services executive
Freehling, Paul Edward lawyer
Freehling, Stanley Maxwell investment banker
Freeman, Charles E. state supreme court chief justice
Freeman, Lee Allen, Jr. lawyer
Freeman, Leslie Gordon anthropologist, educator
Freeman, Louis S. lawyer
Freeman, Susan Tax anthropologist, educator
Freidheim, Cyrus F., Jr. management consultant
Fried, Josef chemist, educator
Friedland, Richard Stewart electronics company executive
Friedman, Lawrence Milton lawyer
Friedman, Roselyn L. lawyer
Friedrich, Paul anthropologist, linguist, poet
Frisch, Henry Jonathan physics educator
Frohman, Lawrence Asher endocrinology educator, scientist
Fromm, Erika (Mrs. Paul Fromm) clinical psychologist
Fross, Roger Raymond lawyer
Fruchter, Rosalie Klausner elementary school educator
Fuchs, Elaine V. molecular biologist, educator
Fukui, Yoshio biology educator
Fullagar, William Watts lawyer
Fuller, Harry Laurance oil company executive
Fuller, Jack William writer, publishing executive
Fuller, Perry Lucian lawyer
Fullmer, Paul public relations counselor
Fultz, Dave meteorology educator
Funk, Carla Jean library association executive
Furcon, John Edward management and organizational consultant
Furlane, Mark Elliott lawyer
Gaines, William Chester journalist
Gamwell, Franklin I. dean, educator
Gancer, Donald Charles lawyer
Gannon, Sister Ann Ida retired philosophy educator, former college administrator
Garber, Daniel Elliot philosophy educator
Garber, Samuel Baugh lawyer, retail company executive
Gardner, Howard Alan travel marketing executive, travel writer and editor
Garrigan, Richard Thomas finance educator, consultant, editor
Garth, Bryant Geoffrey law educator, foundation executive
Gartner, Lawrence Mitchel pediatrician, medical college educator
Gates, Stephen Frye lawyer
Gearen, John J. lawyer
Gecht, Martin Louis physician, bank executive
Gehr, Mary illustrator, painter, printmaker
Geiman, J. Robert lawyer
Gelman, Andrew Richard lawyer
Genetski, Robert James economist
George, Francis bishop
George, John Martin, Jr. lawyer
Geraldson, Raymond I. lawyer
Geraldson, Raymond I., Jr. lawyer
Gerbie, Albert Bernard obstetrician, gynecologist, educator
Gerdes, Neil Wayne library director
Gerlits, Francis Joseph lawyer
Gerst, C(ornelius) Gary real estate executive
Gerstman, George Henry lawyer
Gerstner, Robert William structural engineering educator, consultant
Gertz, Elmer lawyer, author, educator
Gettleman, Robert William judge
Getzels, Jacob Warren psychologist, educator
Getzendanner, Susan lawyer, former federal judge
Gewertz, Bruce Labe surgeon, educator
Giampietro, Wayne Bruce lawyer
Gibbons, William John lawyer
Gibson, McGuire archaeologist, educator
Gidwitz, Ronald J. personal care products company executive
Giesen, Richard Allyn business executive
Gilbert, Howard N(orman) lawyer
Gilford, Steven Ross lawyer
Gilman, Sander Lawrence German language educator
Gilson, Jerome lawyer, writer
Gin, Jackson architect
Gingiss, Benjamin Jack retired formal clothing stores executive
Ginley, Thomas J. banker
Ginsberg, Lewis Robbins lawyer
†Ginsburg, Dan marketing company executive
Ginsburg, Norton Sydney geography educator
Giovacchini, Peter Louis psychoanalyst
Gislason, Eric Arni chemistry educator
Gladden, James Walter, Jr. lawyer
Gladden, Robert Wiley corporate executive
Glasser, James J. leasing company executive, retired
Gleeson, Paul Francis lawyer
Glenner, Richard Allen dentist, dental historian
Glieberman, Herbert Allen lawyer
Goepp, Robert August dental educator, oral pathologist
Golan, Stephen Leonard lawyer
Goldberg, Arnold Irving psychoanalyst, educator
Goldberg, Stephanie Benson editor, magazine writer, lawyer
Goldblatt, Stanford Jay lawyer
Golden, Bruce Paul lawyer
Golden, William C. lawyer
Goldman, Louis Budwig lawyer
Goldman, Robert David cell biologist, educator
Goldmann, James Allen healthcare consultant
Goldring, Norman Max advertising executive
Goldsborough, Robert Gerald publishing executive, author
Goldschmidt, Lynn Harvey lawyer
Goldsmith, Ethel Frank medical social worker
Goldsmith, John Anton linguist, educator
Goldsmith, Julian Royce geochemist, educator
Goldwasser, Eugene biochemist, educator
Golomb, Harvey Morris oncologist, educator
Gomer, Robert chemistry educator
Goodman, Gary Alan lawyer
Gordon, Howard Lyon advertising and marketing executive
Gordon, William A. lawyer
Gorter, James Polk investment banker
Goss, Howard S(imon) manufacturing executive
Gossett, Philip musicologist
Gotfryd, William Ted lawyer
Gottlieb, Gidon Alain Guy law educator
Gould, John Philip economist, educator
Gould, Samuel Halpert pediatrics educator
Graber, Doris Appel political scientist, editor, author
Graber, Thomas M. orthodontist
Grabowski, Roger J. business, intangible assets, real estate appraiser
Grace, Mark Eugene professional baseball player
Gradowski, Stanley Joseph retired newspaper publishing company executive
Graham, David F. lawyer
Graham, Jarlath John publishing executive
Graham, Patricia Albjerg education educator, foundation executive
Gralen, Donald John lawyer
Grant, Dennis newspaper publishing executive
Grant, Paul Bernard industrial relations educator
Grant, Robert McQueen humanities educator
Grant, Robert Nathan lawyer
Graupe, Daniel electrical and computer engineering educator, systems and biomedical engineer
Graves, Robert Lawrence mathematician, educator
Gray, Dawn Plambeck public relations executive
Gray, Hanna Holborn history educator
Gray, Milton Hefter lawyer
Gray, Richard art dealer, consultant, holding company executive
Grayck, Marcus Daniel lawyer
Grayhack, John Thomas urologist, educator
Greenberg, Bernard entomologist, educator
Greenberger, Ernest lawyer
Greene, Robert Bernard, Jr. (Bob Greene) broadcast television correspondent, columnist, author
Greifenstein, Frederick John software company executive
Grenesko, Donald C. publishing company executive
Griffin, Jean Latz newspaper reporter
Griffith, Donald Kendall lawyer
Grimes, Hugh Gavin physician
Griswold, Frank Tracy, III bishop
Gross, Theodore Lawrence university administrator, author
Gross, Wendy S. public relations consultant
Grossi, Francis Xavier, Jr. lawyer, educator
Grossman, Robert Mayer lawyer
Grosso, James Alan sales executive
Gruber, William Paul journalist
Grunsfeld, Ernest Alton, III architect
Guastafeste, Roberta Harrison cellist
Gucker, Jane Gleason architect
Guillen, Oswaldo Jose Barrios (Ozzie Guillen) baseball player
Gupta, Krishna Chandra mechanical engineering educator
Guralnick, Sidney Aaron civil engineering educator
Gustman, David Charles lawyer
Guthman, Jack lawyer
Gutmann, David Leo psychology educator
Haas, Howard Green bedding manufacturing company executive
Haber, Meryl Harold physician, educator, author
Hablutzel, Margo Lynn lawyer
Hackl, Donald John architect
Haddix, Carol Ann Mighton journalist
Haderlein, Thomas M. lawyer
Haffner, Charles Christian, III retired printing company executive
Hahn, Frederic Louis lawyer
Haines, Martha Mahan lawyer
Hales, Daniel B. lawyer
Haley, George Romance languages educator
Hall, Joan M. lawyer
Hall, William King manufacturing company executive
Halloran, Michael J. lawyer

Halpern, Jack chemist, educator
Halprin, Rick lawyer
Hamada, Robert S(eiji) economist, educator
Hambrick, Ernestine colon and rectal surgeon
Hamister, Donald Bruce retired electronics company executive
†Hamm, Mariel Margaret soccer player
Hammesfahr, Robert Winter lawyer
Hamp, Eric Pratt linguist
Hand, Roger physician, educator
†Hanika, Stephen D. advertising executive
Hanna, James Leanord financial consultant
Hannah, Wayne Robertson, Jr. lawyer
Hannay, William Mouat, III lawyer
Hansen, Carl R. management consultant
Hansen, Claire V. financial executive
Hanson, Floyd Bliss applied mathematician, computational scientist, mathematical biologist
Hanson, Ronald William lawyer
Hardaway, Ernest, II oral and maxillofacial surgeon, public health official
Hardgrove, James Alan lawyer
Harding, James Warren finance company executive
Haring, Olga Munk medical educator, physician
Harkna, Eric advertising executive
Harmon, Robert Lon lawyer
Harrington, Carol A. lawyer
Harrington, James Timothy lawyer
Harris, Chauncy Dennison geographer, educator
Harris, Donald Ray lawyer
Harris, Irving Brooks cosmetics executive
Harris, Jules Eli medical educator, physician, clinical scientist, administrator
Harris, Neil history educator
Harris, Ronald William commodities trader
Harrold, Bernard lawyer
Hart, William Thomas federal judge
Hartman, David Elliott neuropsychologist
Hartnett, James Patrick engineering educator
Hartsburg, Craig William professional hockey coach
Hartz, Renee Semo cardiothoracic surgeon
Harvey, Katherine Abler civic worker
Harvey, Paul news commentator, author, columnist
Harvey, Ronald Gilbert research chemist
Haselkorn, Robert virology educator
Haskins, Charles Gregory, Jr. lawyer
Hassan, M. Zia management educator
Hast, Malcolm Howard medical educator, biomedical scientist
Haupt, Roger A. advertising executive
Havener, Scott Charles software engineer
Hawkins, Loretta Ann secondary school educator, playwright
Hawkinson, John former investment management company executive
Hayden, Harrold Harrison information company executive
Hayes, David John Arthur, Jr. legal association executive
Hayes, Richard Johnson association executive, lawyer
Hayes, William Aloysius economics educator
Hayward, Thomas Zander, Jr. lawyer
Head, Patrick James lawyer
Headrick, Daniel Richard history and social sciences educator
Heagy, Thomas Charles banker
Heatwole, Mark M. lawyer
Hebel, Doris A. astrologer
Hecht, Frank Thomas lawyer
Heckman, James Joseph economist, econometrician, educator
Hefner, Christie Ann publishing and marketing executive
Hefner, Philip James theologian
Heidrick, Gardner Wilson management consultant
Heidrick, Robert Lindsay management consultant
Heindl, Warren Anton law educator, retired
Heinecken, Robert Friedli art educator, artist
Heineman, Ben Walter corporation executive
Heineman, Natalie (Mrs. Ben W. Heineman) civic worker
Heinz, John Peter lawyer, educator
Heinz, William Denby lawyer
Heisler, Quentin George, Jr. lawyer
Heldrich, Gerard Charles, Jr. lawyer
Heller, Paul medical educator
Heller, Reinhold August art educator, consultant
Heller, Stanley J. lawyer, physician, educator
Hellie, Richard Russian history educator, researcher
Hellman, Samuel radiologist, physician, educator
Helman, Robert Alan lawyer
Helmbold, Nancy Pearce classical languages educator
Helmholz, R(ichard) H(enry) law educator
Helms, Byron Eldon associate director of research, biology and physiology administrator
Heltne, Paul Gregory museum executive
Hengstler, Gary Ardell publisher, editor, lawyer
Henikoff, Leo M., Jr. academic administrator, medical educator
Henning, Joel Frank lawyer, author, publisher, consultant
Henning, Lorne Edward professional hockey coach
Henry, Frederick Edward lawyer
Henry, Robert John lawyer
Herbert, Victor James foundation administrator
Herbert, William Carlisle lawyer
Herbolsheimer, Henrietta physician, consultant
Herbst, Arthur Lee obstetrician, gynecologist
Herguth, Robert John columnist
Herman, Sidney N. lawyer
Hermann, Donald Harold James lawyer, educator
Hermann, Edward Robert health engineer, educator, writer, consultant, hygieologist
Herpe, David A. lawyer
Herzel, Leo lawyer
Herzog, Fred F. law educator
Hess, Sidney J., Jr. lawyer
Hesse, Carolyn Sue lawyer
Hester, Thomas Patrick lawyer
Heuer, Michael Alexander dean, endodontist educator
Hewitt, Brian journalist
Hickey, Jerome Edward investment company executive
Hickey, John Thomas, Jr. lawyer
Hickman, Frederic W. lawyer
Hicks, Cadmus Metcalf, Jr. financial analyst
Hier, Daniel Barnet neurologist
Higgins, Jack editorial cartoonist
Hilborn, Michael G. lawyer, real estate development executive
Hildebrand, Roger Henry astrophysicist, physicist
Hilliard, David Craig lawyer
Hillis, Margaret conductor, musician
Hillman, Jordan Jay law educator
Himes, Laurence Austin professional baseball executive
Himmelfarb, John David artist
Hines, James Rodger surgeon
Hinkelman, Ruth Amidon insurance company executive
Hinojosa, Raul physician, ear pathology researcher
Hirshman, Harold Carl lawyer
Hoban, George Savre lawyer
Hobbs, Marvin engineering executive
Hodes, Scott lawyer
Hoey, Rita Marie public relations executive
Hofer, Roy Ellis lawyer
Hoff, John Scott lawyer
Hoffman, Richard Bruce lawyer
Hoffman, Valerie Jane lawyer
Hoffman, William August art educator
Hofrichter, David Alan management consultant
Hogarth, Robin Miles business educator, university official
Holabird, John Augur, Jr. retired architect
Holderman, James F., Jr. federal judge
Holland, Eugene, Jr. lumber company executive
Hollins, Mitchell Leslie lawyer
Hollis, Donald Roger banking consultant
Holmes, Colgate Frederick hotel executive
Holmes, Stephen T. political science and law educator
Holowinski, John Joseph state executive
Holt, Thomas Cleveland history educator, consultant, writer, lecturer
Holzer, Edwin advertising executive
Homans, Peter psychology and religious studies educator
Honig, George Raymond pediatrician
Hooks, William Henry lawyer
Hoover, Paul poet
Hopkins, Kevin L. law educator, consultant
Horne, John R. farm equipment company executive
Horowitz, Fred L. dentist, administrator, consultant
Horwath, Leslie Kathleen lawyer
Horwich, Allan lawyer
Horwitz, Irwin Daniel otolaryngologist, educator
Hoskins, Richard Jerold lawyer
Hotz, V. Joseph economics educator
Houk, James Charles physiologist, educator
†Howard, Will George advertising executive
Howe, Jonathan Thomas lawyer
Howell, R(obert) Thomas, Jr. lawyer, former food company executive
Huckman, Michael Saul neuroradiologist, educator
Huggins, Rollin Charles, Jr. lawyer
Hughes, John Russell physician, educator
Hughes, Sarah Gillette consulting company executive
Hummel, Gregory William lawyer
Hunt, Lawrence Halley, Jr. lawyer
Hunter, James Alexander surgeon, educator
Hunter, James Galbraith, Jr. lawyer
Hunter, J(ames) Paul English language educator, literary critic, historian
Huntley, Robert Stephen newspaper editor
†Hurley, Brian Xavier advertising executive
Husar, John Paul newspaper columnist, television panelist
Huston, DeVerille Anne lawyer
Huston, John Lewis chemistry educator
Huston, Steven Craig lawyer
Hyman, Michael Bruce lawyer
Iglauer, Bruce record company executive
Iltis, John Frederic advertising and public relations company executive
Inbau, Fred Edward lawyer, educator, author
Ingham, Norman William Russian literature educator, genealogist
Ingram, Donald insurance company executive
Inskeep, Kenneth W. church administrator
Iqbal, Zafar Mohd cancer researcher, biochemist, pharmacologist, toxicologist, consultant, molecular biologist
Isaacs, Roger David public relations executive
Istock, Verne George banker
Ivan, Thomas Nathaniel professional hockey team executive
Iwanski, Mary parochial school educator
Jachna, Joseph David photographer, educator
Jackson, Jesse Louis civic and political leader, clergyman
Jackson, Philip Douglas professional basketball coach
Jacobson, Harold LeLand lawyer
Jacobson, Marian Slutz lawyer
Jacobson, Richard Joseph lawyer
Jacoby, John Primm lawyer
Jacover, Jerold Alan lawyer
Jager, Melvin Francis lawyer
Jahn, Helmut architect
Jahns, Jeffrey lawyer
Jain, Nemi Chand chemist, coating scientist, educator
Jakstas, Alfred John museum conservator, consultant
Jambor, Robert Vernon lawyer
James, A. Lincoln, Sr. minister, religious organization executive
Jaramillo, Carlos Alberto civil engineer
Jast, Raymond Joseph lawyer
Jegen, Sister Carol Frances religion educator
Jerome, Jerrold V. insurance company executive
Jersild, Thomas Nielsen lawyer
Jester, Jack D. lawyer
Jezuit, Leslie James manufacturing company executive
Jhawar, Shiv Ratan computer and tax consultant, computer software writer
Jibben, Laura Ann state agency administrator
†Jirchman, Donna advertising executive
Jock, Paul F., II lawyer
Joehl, Raymond Joseph surgeon, educator
Johns, Catherine radio personality
Johnson, Barbara Elaine Spears education educator
Johnson, C. Richard lawyer
Johnson, Gary Thomas lawyer
Johnson, Glenn Thompson judge
Johnson, Janet Helen Egyptology educator
Johnson, Lael Frederic lawyer
Johnson, Richard Fred lawyer
Johnson, Robert Bruce public relations executive
Johnston, Alan Rogers lawyer
Jonas, Harry S. professional society administrator
Jonasson, Olga surgeon, educator
Jones, Dennis Paul food and consumer goods company executive
Jones, Richard Cyrus lawyer
Jones, Richard Jeffery physician, educator
†Jones, Zemira radio station executive
Jordan, Michael Jeffery professional basketball player, retired baseball player
Jordan, Michelle Denise lawyer
Joseph, Robert Thomas lawyer
Josephson, Kenneth Bradley artist, educator
Joslin, Rodney Dean lawyer
Judge, Bernard Martin law bulletin editor, publisher
Junewicz, James J. lawyer
Kadanoff, Leo Philip physicist
Kahn, Herta Hess (Mrs. Howard Kahn) retired stockbroker
Kahn, James Steven museum director
Kahrilas, Peter James medical educator, researcher
Kaiserlian, Penelope Jane publishing company executive
Kalina, Christine Marie occupational health nurse
Kallick, David A. lawyer
Kamin, Chester Thomas lawyer
Kamyszew, Christopher D. museum curator, executive educator, art consultant
Kanne, Michael Stephen federal judge
Kaplan, Jared lawyer
Kaplan, Morton A. political science educator
Kaplan, Sidney Mountbatten lawyer
Karanikas, Alexander English language educator, author, actor
Karl, Barry Dean historian, educator
Karnes, Evan Burton, II lawyer
Kass, Leon Richard educator
Kastel, Howard L. lawyer
Katz, Adrian Izhack physician, educator
Katz, Marilyn Faye communications consultant, political strategist
Katz, Robert Stephen rheumatologist, educator
Katz, Stuart Charles lawyer, concert jazz musician
Kaufman, Andrew Michael lawyer
Kazik, John Stanley newspaper executive
Kearney, John Walter sculptor, painter
Kearney, Michael John banker
Keenan, James George classics educator
Kelley, Michael John newspaper editor
Kelly, Arthur Lloyd management and investment company executive
Kelly, Charles Arthur lawyer
†Kelly, James radio station executive
Kelly, Robert Donald management consultant
Kempf, Donald G., Jr. lawyer
Kendrick, William Monroe insurance company executive
Kennedy, Eugene Cullen psychology educator, writer
Kennett, Robert L. publisher
Kenney, Frank Deming lawyer
Kenny, Edmund Joyce lawyer
Kerbis, Gertrude Lempp architect
Keroff, William B. advertising agency executive
Kidd, Lynden Louise healthcare consultant
Kikoler, Stephen Philip lawyer
Kim, H. J. (Shaun Kim) engineering company executive
Kim, Michael Charles lawyer
Kindzred, Diana communications company executive
King, Andre Richardson architectural graphic designer
King, Billie Jean Moffitt former professional tennis player
King, Clark Chapman, Jr. lawyer
King, David Edgar librarian, editor
King, Michael Howard lawyer
King, Sharon L. lawyer
Kins, Juris lawyer
Kinzie, Raymond Wyant banker, lawyer
Kipper, Barbara Levy corporate executive
Kirby, William Joseph corporation executive
Kirkland, John Leonard lawyer
Kirschner, Barbara Starrels pediatric gastroenterologist
Kirshner, Julius journal editor
Kirsner, Joseph Barnett physician, educator
Kisor, Henry Du Bois newspaper editor, critic, columnist
Kissel, Richard John lawyer
Kite, Steven B. lawyer
Kittle, Charles Frederick surgeon
Klapperich, Frank Lawrence, Jr. investment banker
Klarich, Nina Marie economic development executive
Klaviter, Helen Lothrop magazine editor
Kleckner, Robert A. accounting firm executive
Klein, Michael Sherman manufacturing executive
Klenk, James Andrew lawyer
Klenk, Timothy Carver lawyer
Kleppa, Ole J. chemistry educator
Kloc, Emily Alvina retired elementary school principal
Knapp, Donald Roy musician, educator
Knepper, Thomas M. lawyer
Knight, Christopher Nichols lawyer
Knoblauch, Mark George librarian, consultant
Knox, James Edwin lawyer
Knox, Lance Lethbridge venture capital executive
Kobs, James Fred advertising agency executive
Koenig, Bonnie non-profit organization consultant
Koester, Robert Gregg record company executive
Koga, Mary artist, photographer, social worker
Kohn, Shalom L. lawyer
Kohn, William Irwin lawyer
Kohrman, Arthur Fisher pediatric educator
Kolb, Gwin Jackson language professional, educator
Kolek, Robert Edward lawyer
Kolkey, Eric Samuel screenwriter
Kolkey, Gilda P. artist
Kopelman, Ian Stuart lawyer
Kotulak, Ronald newspaper science writer
Kouvel, James Spyros physicist, educator
Kozanecki, Robert Francis educator
Kraft, Sumner Charles physician, educator
Kramer, Ferdinand mortgage banker
†Kramer, Weezie Crawford broadcast executive
Kraus, Herbert Myron public relations executive
Krause, Jerry (Jerome Richard Krause) professional basketball team executive
Kravitt, Jason Harris Paperno lawyer
Krawetz, Arthur Altshuler chemist, science administrator
Kremin, David Keith lawyer
Kresse, William Joseph lawyer, educator, accountant
Kriss, Robert J. lawyer
Kroch, Carl Adolph retail executive
Kroll, Barry Lewis lawyer
Krueger, Bonnie Lee editor, writer
Krug, Judith Fingeret association administrator
Krupka, Robert George lawyer
Krupnik, Vee M. financial company executive
Kruskal, William Henry statistician, educator
Kubida, Judith Ann museum administrator
Kubistal, Patricia Bernice educational consultant
Kudish, David J. financial executive
Kudo, Irma Setsuko not-for-profit executive director
Kuhn, James Paul management consultant
Kullberg, Duane Reuben accounting firm executive
Kumar, Anand medical educator, researcher
Kunkle, William Joseph, Jr. lawyer
Kupcinet, Irv columnist
Kurtich, John William architect, film-maker, educator
Kuta, Jeffrey Theodore lawyer
Kyle, Robert Campbell, II publishing executive
Lach, Alma Elizabeth food and cooking writer, consultant
Laidlaw, Andrew R. lawyer
Laitin, David Dennis political science educator
Lampert, Steven A. lawyer
Landau, Richard L. physician, educator
Landers, Ann (Mrs. Esther P. Lederer) columnist
Landes, William M. law educator
Landow-Esser, Janine Marise lawyer
Landsberg, Jill Warren lawyer, consultant to government agencies
Lane, Kenneth Edwin retired advertising agency executive
Lane, Ronald Alan lawyer
Laner, Richard Warren lawyer
Langhenry, John Godfred, Jr. lawyer
Lannert, Robert Cornelius manufacturing company executive
Lanzl, Lawrence Herman medical physicist
LaPointe-Peterson, Kittie Vadis choreographer, ballet school director, educator
Lappin, Richard C. corporate executive
Larsen, Paul Emanuel religious organization administrator
Larson, Allan Louis political scientist, educator, lay church worker
Larson, Nancy Celeste computer systems manager
Larson, Paul William public relations executive
LaRue, Paul Hubert lawyer
Lassers, Willard J. judge
Latimer, Kenneth Alan lawyer
Lauderdale, Katherine Sue lawyer
Laumann, Anne Elizabeth dermatologist
Laumann, Edward Otto sociology educator
LaVelle, Arthur anatomy educator
Lawler, James Ronald French language educator
Lazar, Ludmila concert pianist, pedagogue
Lazar, Richard Beck physician, medical administrator
Lazarus, George Milton newspaper columnist
LeBaron, Charles Frederick, Jr. lawyer
Lecker, Abraham former banker
Lederman, Leon Max physicist, educator
Lee, Raphael Carl plastic surgeon, biomedical engineer
Lee, William Kendall, Jr. insurance industry executive
Lee, William Marshall lawyer
Lefco, Kathy Nan law librarian
LeFevre, Perry Deyo minister, theology educator
Leff, Alan Richard medical educator
†Leff, Deborah foundation executive
Lehman, Dennis Dale chemistry educator
Lehman, George Morgan food sales executive
Lehrman, Nat magazine editor
Leibowitz, David Perry lawyer
Leigh, Sherren communications executive, editor, publisher
Leighton, George Neves retired federal judge
Leinenweber, Harry D. federal judge
Leisten, Arthur Gaynor lawyer
Lemberis, Theodore Thomas international law and law educator
†Lemon, Jim radio station executive
LeMonnier, Daniel Brian small business owner, entertainer
Lennes, Gregory manufacturing and financing company executive
Lerner, Alexander Robert association executive
Lerner, Nathan Bernard artist
Lesly, Philip public relations counsel
Lester, Robin Dale educator, author, former headmaster
Levenfeld, Milton Arthur lawyer
Leventhal, Bennett Lee psychiatry and pediatrics educator, administrator
Levi, John G. lawyer
Levin, Arnold Murray social worker, psychotherapist
Levin, Charles Edward lawyer
Levin, Jack S. lawyer
Levine, Donald Nathan sociologist, educator
Levine, Laurence Harvey lawyer
†Levi-Setti, Riccardo physicist, director
Levy, Donald Harris chemistry educator
Levy, Richard Herbert lawyer
Levy, Robert Michael neurosurgeon, researcher
Lewert, Robert Murdoch microbiologist, educator
Lewis, Charles A. investment company executive
Lewis, Philip educational and technical consultant
Lewis, Phillip Harold museum curator
Lewis, Ramsey Emanuel, Jr. pianist, composer
Lewis, Sylvia Gail journalist
Lewy, Ralph I. hotel executive
Leyhane, Francis John, III lawyer
Liao, Shutsung biochemist, oncologist
Lichter, Edward Arthur physician, educator
Lieb, Michael English educator, humanities educator
Liggio, Carl Donald lawyer
Light, John Caldwell chemistry educator
Light, Kenneth B. manufacturing company executive
Lilly, Kristine Marie soccer player
Lin, Chin-Chu physician, educator, researcher
Lin, James Chih-I biomedical and electrical engineer, educator
Lincicome, Bernard Wesley journalist
Lind, Jon Robert lawyer
Lindberg, George W. federal judge
Linde, Ronald Keith corporate executive, private investor
Linden, Henry Robert chemical engineering research executive
Lindskog, Norbert F. business and health administration educator, consultant
Linklater, William Joseph lawyer
Lipinski, Ann Marie newspaper editor
Lippe, Melvin Karl lawyer
Lipton, Lois Jean lawyer
Lipton, Richard M. lawyer
Litweiler, John Berkey writer, editor
Litwin, Burton Howard lawyer
Liu, Ben-chieh economist
Liu, Khang-Lee dentist, educator
Lloyd, William F. lawyer
Lochbihler, Frederick Vincent lawyer
Lockwood, Frank James manufacturing company executive
Lockwood, Gary Lee lawyer
Loesch, Katharine Taylor (Mrs. John George Loesch) communication and theatre educator
Logemann, Jerilyn Ann speech pathologist, educator
Lohman, Gordon R. manufacturing executive
Long, Earline Davis elementary education educator
Longman, Gary Lee accountant

Longworth, Richard Cole journalist
Look, Dona Jean artist
Looman, James R. lawyer
Loomis, Salora Dale psychiatrist
Lopata, Helena Znaniecka sociologist, researcher, educator
Lopatka, Susana Beaird maternal, child health nurse consultant
Lorch, Kenneth F. lawyer
Lorenz, Hugo Albert retired insurance executive, consultant
Lorenz, Katherine Mary banker
Lorie, James Hirsch business administration educator
Lotocky, Innocent Hilarius bishop
Loucks, Ralph Bruce, Jr. investment company executive
Loughnane, David J. lawyer
Lowrie, William G. oil company executive
Lowry, Donald Michael lawyer
Lubawski, James Lawrence health care consultant
Lubin, Donald G. lawyer
Lucas, John Kenneth lawyer
Lundberg, George David, II medical editor, pathologist
Lundergan, Barbara Keough lawyer
Luning, Thomas P. lawyer
†Lurain, John Robert, III gynecologic oncologist
Lurie, Paul Michael lawyer
Lutter, Paul Allen lawyer
Lyman, Arthur Joseph financial executive
†Lynch, Edward Francis professional sports team executive
Lynch, John James lawyer
Lynch, John Peter lawyer
Lynch, William Thomas, Jr. advertising agency executive
Lynn, Laurence Edwin, Jr. university administrator, educator
Lynnes, R. Milton advertising executive
Lyon, Jeffrey journalist, author
Lythcott, Marcia A. newspaper editor
Ma, Tai-Loi library curator, Chinese studies specialist
Ma, Yuanxi Chinese and English language and literature educator, translator
MacCarthy, Terence Francis lawyer
MacDougal, Gary Edward corporate director, foundation trustee
†Mach, Kenneth advertising executive
MacLane, Saunders mathematician, educator
Mac Nelly, Jeffrey Kenneth cartoonist
Macsai, John architect
Madansky, Albert statistics educator
Madigan, John William publishing executive
Maggio, Michael John artistic director
Mahaffey, John Christopher association executive
Maher, David Willard lawyer
Maher, Francesca Marciniak air transportation executive, lawyer
Mahowald, Anthony Peter geneticist, cell biologist, educator
Makinen, Marvin William biophysicist, educator
Malik, Raymond Howard economist, scientist, corporate executive, inventor, educator
Malkin, Cary Jay lawyer
Mallory, Robert Mark controller, finance executive
Mancoff, Neal Alan lawyer
Manelli, Donald Dean screenwriter, film producer
Manning, Blanche M. federal judge
Manning, Frederick James insurance company executive
Manny, Carter Hugh, Jr. architect, foundation administrator
Mansfield, Karen Lee lawyer
Marco, Guy Anthony librarian, educator
Marcus, Joseph child psychiatrist
Marcuse, Manfred Joachim paper products executive
Maresh, Alice Marcella retired educational administrator
Margoliash, Emanuel biochemist, educator
Mariotti, Jay Anthony journalist
Marks, Jerome lawyer
Markus, Robert Michael journalist, retired
Marovich, George M. federal judge
Marovitz, Abraham Lincoln judge
Marovitz, James Lee lawyer
Marsh, Jeanne Cay social welfare educator, researcher
Marshall, Cody bishop
Marshall, Donald Glenn English language and literature educator
Marshall, John David lawyer
Marshall, Kerry James artist
Marston-Scott, Mary Vesta nurse, educator
Martin, Arthur Mead lawyer
Martin, Gary Joseph medical educator
†Martinez, Elizabeth professional association administrator
Marty, Martin Emil religion educator, editor
Marwedel, Warren John lawyer
Marx, David, Jr. lawyer
Masek, Barry Michael accountant
†Mason, Bruce advertising agency executive
Mason, Gregory Wesley, Jr. secondary education educator
Mason, Henry Lowell, III lawyer
Mason, Richard J. lawyer
Matasar, Ann B. former dean, business and political science educator
Mateles, Richard Isaac biotechnologist
Matthei, Edward Hodge architect
Mattson, Stephen Joseph lawyer
May, J. Peter mathematics educator
Mayer, Frank D., Jr. lawyer
Mayer, Raymond Richard business administration educator
Mayer, Robert Samuel physician
Mayes, Frank Gorr management consultant
McAuliffe, Richard L. church official
McCaleb, Malcolm, Jr. lawyer
McCarron, John Francis columnist
Mc Carter, John Wilbur, Jr. museum executive
†McCarter, William J., Jr. broadcasting executive
McCausland, Thomas James, Jr. brokerage house executive
McClain, Lee Bert corporate lawyer, insurance executive
McCloskey, Guy Corbett Buddhist religious leader
Mc Clure, James J., Jr. lawyer, former municipal executive
McConahey, Stephen George securities company executive
McConnell, E. Hoy, II advertising executive
McConnell, James Guy lawyer
McCormack, Robert Cornelius investment banker
McCracken, Thomas James, Jr. lawyer
McCrohon, Craig lawyer
McCrone, Walter Cox research institute executive
McCue, Judith W. lawyer
McCullagh, Grant Gibson architect
McCullough, Richard Lawrence advertising agency executive
McCurry, Margaret Irene architect, educator
McDaniel, Charles-Gene journalism educator, writer
McDermott, John H(enry) lawyer
McDermott, Robert B. lawyer
McDonald, Thomas Alexander lawyer
McDonough, John Michael lawyer
McDougal, Alfred Leroy publishing executive
Mc Dougall, Dugald Stewart retired lawyer
McGarr, Frank James retired federal judge, dispute resolution consultant
McGinn, Bernard John religious educator
McKay, Neil banker
McKee, Keith Earl manufacturing technology executive
McKenzie, Robert E. lawyer
McKinley, Vicky Lynn biology educator
McKinney, William T. psychiatrist, educator
McLaughlin, T. Mark lawyer
McLaughlin, William F. paper company executive
McLean, Robert David lawyer
McMenamin, John Robert lawyer
McMorrow, Mary Ann G. judge
McNeill, G. David psychology educator
McNeill, Thomas B. lawyer
McVisk, William Kilburn lawyer
McWhirter, Bruce J. lawyer
McWilliams, Dennis Michael lawyer
†Meade, Robin Michele news anchor, reporter
Mecklenburg, Gary Alan hospital executive
Meers, Henry W. investment banker
Mehlman, Mark Franklin lawyer
Melamed, Leo investment company executive
Melbinger, Michael S. lawyer
Melton, David Reuben lawyer
Meltzer, Bernard David legal educator
Menchin, Robert Stanley marketing executive
Mercer, David Robinson cultural organization administrator
Merrill, Thomas Wendell lawyer, law educator
Mets, Marilyn Baird pediatric ophthalmologist
Metz, Charles Edgar radiology educator
Meyer, Edward Paul advertising executive
Meyer, J. Theodore lawyer
Meyer, Michael Louis lawyer
Meyer, Raymond Joseph former college basketball coach
Meyers, Dorothy education consultant, writer
Michalak, Edward Francis lawyer
Migala, Lucyna Jozefa broadcast journalist, arts administrator, radio station executive
Mikesell, Marvin Wray geography educator
Mikva, Abner Joseph lawyer, retired federal judge
Millard, Richard Steven lawyer
Miller, Bernard Joseph, Jr. advertising executive
Miller, Charles S. clergy member, church administrator
Miller, Douglas Andrew lawyer
Miller, Edward Boone lawyer
Miller, James Edwin, Jr. English language educator
Miller, Jay Alan civil rights association executive
Miller, Maurice James lawyer
Miller, Patrick William research administrator, educator
Miller, Paul J. lawyer
Miller, Paul McGrath, Jr. executive search consulting company executive
Miller, Stephen Ralph lawyer
Millichap, Joseph Gordon neurologist, educator
Millner, Robert B. lawyer
Milnikel, Robert Saxon lawyer
Mindes, Gayle Dean education educator
Miner, Thomas Hawley international entrepreneur
Minichello, Dennis lawyer
Minkowycz, W. J. mechanical engineering educator
Minkus, Raymond David communications and public relations executive
Minnick, Malcolm L., Jr. clergy member, church administrator
Minogue, John P. academic administrator, priest, educator
Minow, Josephine Baskin civic worker
Mintzer, David physics educator
Mirkin, Bernard Leo clinical pharmacologist, pediatrician
Mirza, David Brown economist, educator
Mitchell, Lee Mark communications executive, investment fund manager, lawyer
Mittendorf, Robert physician, epidemiologist
Moawad, Atef obstetrician, gynecologist, educator
Moffatt, Joyce Anne performing arts executive
Molo, Steven Francis lawyer
Moltz, Marshall Jerome lawyer
Momeyer, Douglas H. lawyer
Montgomery, Charles Barry lawyer
Montgomery, Charles Howard retired bank executive
Moor, Roy Edward finance educator
Moore, John Ronald manufacturing executive
Moran, James Byron federal judge
Moran, John Thomas, Jr. lawyer
Morency, Paula J. lawyer
Morgan, James Evan lawyer
Morisato, Susan Cay actuary
Morris, Naomi Carolyn Minner medical educator, administrator, researcher, consultant
Morris, Norval criminologist, educator
Morris, Ralph William chronopharmacologist
Morrison, John Horton lawyer
Morrison, Portia Owen lawyer
Morrow, Richard Martin retired oil company executive
Morsch, Thomas Harvey lawyer
Moses, Irving Byron architect
Moss, Gerald S. dean, medical educator
Muchin, Allan B. lawyer
Mugnaini, Enrico neuroscience educator
Mukoyama, James Hidefumi, Jr. securities executive
Mulholland, Terence John (Terry Mulholland) professional baseball player
Mullan, John Francis (Sean Mullan) neurosurgeon, educator
Mullen, Charles Frederick health educator
Mullen, J. Thomas lawyer
Mulligan, Robert William university official, clergyman
Mullin, Leo Francis utility executive
Mulvihill, Terence Joseph investment banking executive
Mumford, Manly Whitman lawyer
Munoz, Mario Alejandro civil engineer, consultant
Murata, Tadao engineering and computer science educator
Murdock, Charles William lawyer, educator
Murphy, Ellis association management executive
Murphy, Michael Emmett food company executive
Murray, Daniel Richard lawyer
Murtaugh, Christopher David lawyer
Mustoe, Thomas Anthony physician, plastic surgeon
Muthuswamy, Petham Padayatchi pulmonary medicine and critical care specialist
Myers, Lonn William lawyer
Nachman, Frederick J. public relations executive
Nachman, Norman Harry lawyer
Naclerio, Robert Michael otolaryngologist, educator
Nagel, Sidney Robert physics educator
Nahrwold, David Lange surgeon, educator
Najita, Tetsuo history educator
Nakajima, Yasuko medical educator
Nambu, Yoichiro physics educator
Narahashi, Toshio pharmacology educator
Nash, Donald Gene commodities specialist
Nason, Robert E. accountant
Nault, William Henry publishing executive
Neal, Steven George journalist
Nebenzahl, Paul broadcast executive
Nechin, Herbert Benjamin lawyer
Nelson, H(arry) Donald communications executive
Nelson, Richard David lawyer
Nemickas, Rimgaudas cardiologist, educator
Neubauer, Charles Frederick investigative reporter
Neuhausen, Benjamin Simon auditor, accountant
Neumeier, Matthew Michael lawyer
Newell, Frank William ophthalmologist, educator
Newey, Paul Davis lawyer
Newlin, Charles Fremont lawyer
Newman, Ralph Geoffrey literary scholar historian
Newman, Wade Davis trade association executive
Nichol, Norman J. manufacturing executive
Nicholas, Arthur Soterios manufacturing company executive
Nicholas, Ralph Wallace anthropologist, educator
Nickel, Melvin Edwin metallurgical engineer
Nicolaides, Mary lawyer
Nims, John Frederick writer, educator
Nissen, William John lawyer
Nitikman, Franklin W. lawyer
Nord, Henry J. transportation executive
Nord, Robert Eamor lawyer
Nordberg, John Albert senior federal judge
Nordland, Gerald art museum administrator, historian, consultant
Norek, Joan I. lawyer
Norgle, Charles Ronald, Sr. federal judge
Notebaert, Richard C. telecommunications industry executive
Notz, John Kranz, Jr. arbitrator and mediator, retired lawyer
Novak, Marlena artist, educator, writer, curator
Nowacki, James Nelson lawyer
Nugent, Lori S. lawyer
Null, Michael Elliot lawyer
Nussbaum, Bernard J. lawyer
Nussbaum, Martha Craven philosophy and classics educator
Nyhus, Lloyd Milton surgeon, educator
Oates, James G. advertising executive
O'Brien, James Phillip lawyer
O'Brien, Patrick William lawyer
O'Connell, Edward Joseph, III financial executive, accountant
O'Connell, Harold Patrick, Jr. banker
O'Connor, James John utility company executive
O'Connor, William Michael executive search company executive
O'Dell, James E. newspaper publishing executive
Oehme, Reinhard physicist, educator
Oesterle, Eric Adam lawyer
Offer, Daniel psychiatrist
O'Flaherty, Paul Benedict lawyer
O'Hagan, James Joseph lawyer
Oka, Takeshi physicist, chemist, astronomer, educator
†O'Laughlin, Donna editor periodical
O'Leary, Daniel Vincent, Jr. lawyer
Olian, Robert Martin lawyer
Olins, Robert Abbot communications research executive
Oliver, Harry Maynard, Jr. retired brokerage house executive
Oliver, Roseann lawyer
Olsen, Edward John geologist, educator
Olsen, Rex Norman trade association executive
†Olson, Curtis D. advertising executive
Olson, Patricia Joanne artist, educator
O'Malley, John Daniel law educator, banker
Ong, Michael King mathematician, educator, banker
O'Reilly, Charles Terrance university dean
Orr, Richard Tuttle journalist
Oryshkevich, Roman Sviatoslav physician, physiatrist, dentist, educator
Osborn, William A. trust company executive
O'Shea, Lynne Edeen marketing executive, educator
Osiyoye, Adekunle obstetrician, attorney medical and legal consultant, gynecologist, educator
Osowiec, Darlene Ann clinical psychologist, educator, consultant
Ott, Gilbert Russell, Jr. lawyer
Overgaard, Mitchell Jersild lawyer
Overton, George Washington lawyer
Overton, Jane Vincent Harper biology educator
Oxtoby, David William chemistry educator
Pachman, Daniel J. physician, educator
Page, Dozzie Lyons vocational secondary school educator
Page, Ernest medical educator
†Palewicz, Richard Alfred judge
Pallasch, B. Michael lawyer
Pallasch, Magdalena Helena (Mrs. Bernhard Michael Pallasch) artist
Pallmeyer, Rebecca Ruth federal judge
Palm, Gary Howard lawyer, educator
Palmer, John Bernard, III lawyer
Palmer, Martha H. counseling educator
Palmer, Patrick Edward radio astronomer, educator
Palmer, Robert Towne lawyer
Panich, Danuta Bembenista lawyer
Panko, Jessie Symington education educator
Pappas, George Demetrios anatomy and cell biology educator, scientist
Pappas, Philip James real estate company executive
Paprocki, Thomas John lawyer, priest
Parcells, Frederick R. product management
Paretsky, Sara N. writer
Parish, Robert Lee (Chief Parish) professional basketball player
Parisi, Joseph (Anthony) magazine editor, writer-consultant, educator
Park, Chung Il librarian
Park, Thomas Joseph biology researcher, educator
Parrish, Overton Burgin, Jr. pharmaceutical corporation executive
Partridge, Mark Van Buren lawyer
Pascal, Roger lawyer
Pascale, Daniel Richard circuit judge
Patel, Homi Burjor apparel company executive
Patterson, Roy physician, educator
Pattishall, Beverly Wyckliffe lawyer
Paul, Arthur artist, graphic designer, illustrator, art and design consultant
Paul, Ronald Neale management consultant
Pavalon, Eugene Irving lawyer
Peck, Donald Vincent musician
Peerman, Dean Gordon magazine editor
Pell, Wilbur Frank, Jr. federal judge
Pelton, Russell Meredith, Jr. lawyer
Peltzman, Sam economics educator
Peres, Judith May journalist
Perlberg, Jules Martin lawyer
Perlstadt, Sidney Morris lawyer
Perry, Edna Burrell retired elementary school principal
Pestureau, Pierre Gilbert literature educator, literary critic, editor
Peters, Gordon Benes musician
Petersen, Donald Sondergaard lawyer
Petersen, William Otto lawyer
Peterson, Mildred Othmer (Mrs. Howard R. Peterson) civic leader, lecturer, writer, librarian
Peterson, Ronald Roger lawyer
Pezzella, Jerry James, Jr. investment and real estate corporation executive
†Philipson, Morris university press director
Phillips, Ethel C. (Mrs. Lloyd J. Phillips) writer
Phillips, Frederick Falley architect
Pick, Ruth research scientist, physician, educator
Piderit, John J. university educator
Piecewicz, Walter Michael lawyer
Piekarski, Victor J. lawyer
Pierson, Don sports columnist
Pigott, Richard J. food company executive
Pikler, Charles musician
Pilchen, Ira A. journal editor
Pillarella, Deborah Ann elementary education educator, consultant
Pincus, Theodore Henry public relations executive
Pinsky, Michael S. lawyer
Pinsky, Steven Michael radiologist, educator
Pippen, Scottie professional basketball player
Pisciotta, Vivian Virginia psychotherapist
Pitt, George lawyer
Pitt, Judson Hamilton publisher, author
Pizer, Howard Charles sports and entertainment executive
Plank, Betsy Ann (Mrs. Sherman V. Rosenfield) public relations counsel
Platzman, George William geophysicist, educator
Pless, Vera mathematics and computer science educator
Plotkin, Manuel D. management consultant, educator, former corporate executive and government official
Plotnick, Harvey Barry publishing executive
Plunkett, Paul Edward federal judge
Poe, Douglas Allan lawyer
Polaski, Anne Spencer lawyer
Pollak, Raymond general and transplant surgeon
Polley, Edward Herman anatomist, educator
Pollock, Alexander John banker
Pollock, Earl Edward lawyer
Pollock, George Howard psychiatrist, psychoanalyst
Pollock, Sheldon Ivan language professional, educator
Pope, Daniel James lawyer
Pope, Kerig Rodgers magazine executive
Pope, Michael Arthur lawyer
Pope, Richard M. rheumatologist
Porter, Stuart Williams investment company executive
Posner, Richard Allen federal judge
Poznanski, Andrew Karol pediatric radiologist
Pratt, Robert Windsor lawyer
Pratt, Susan G. architect
Preisler, Harvey D. medical facility administrator, medical educator
Presser, Stephen Bruce lawyer, educator
†Price, Henry Escoe broadcast executive
Price, Paul L. lawyer
Price, William S. lawyer
Priess, Howard K., II lawyer
Prince, Oliver Gilbert, Jr. human resources professional
Prinz, Richard Allen surgeon
Prior, Gary L. lawyer
Pritikin, James B. lawyer, employee benefits consultant
Pritzker, Jay travel company executive , lawyer
Pritzker, Robert Alan manufacturing company executive
Pritzker, Thomas Jay lawyer, business executive
Prochnow, Douglas Lee lawyer
Prochnow, Herbert Victor former government official, banker, author
Prochnow, Herbert Victor, Jr. lawyer
Proctor, Barbara Gardner advertising agency executive
Prosperi, David Philip public relations executive
Provus, Barbara Lee executive search consultant
Pugh, Roderick Wellington psychologist, educator
Pumper, Robert William microbiologist
Quaal, Ward Louis broadcast executive
Quade, Victoria Catherine editor, writer
Quebe, Jerry Lee architect
Rachwalski, Frank Joseph, Jr. financial executive
Rafelson, Max Emanuel, Jr. biochemist, medical school administrator
Rahe, Maribeth Sembach bank executive
Rajan, Fred E. N. clergy member, church administrator
Ramseyer, J. Mark law educator
Ramsey-Goldman, Rosalind physician
Ran, Shulamit composer
Rankin, James Winton lawyer
Raphaelson, Joel retired advertising agency executive
Rapoport, David E. lawyer
Rapoport, Ronald Jon journalist
Rasin, Rudolph Stephen corporate executive
Ratner, Gerald lawyer
Rattner, William Edward lawyer
Reda, Robert Salvatore lawyer
Reddy, Janardan K. medical educator
Redman, Clarence Owen lawyer
Reed, Charles Allen anthropologist
Reed, John Shedd former railway executive
Reed, Keith Allen lawyer
Reed, Vastina Kathryn (Tina Reed) child psychotherapist
Reedy, Jerry Edward editor, writer
Reeves, Michael Stanley public utility executive
Regensteiner, Else Friedsam (Mrs. Bertold Regensteiner) textile designer, educator
Reggio, Vito Anthony management consultant

Reich, Allan J. lawyer
Reicin, Ronald Ian lawyer
Reid, Daniel James public relations executive
Reiffel, Leonard physicist, scientific consultant
Reilly, Robert Frederick valuation consultant
Reingold, Haim mathematics educator
Reinke, John Henry educational administrator, clergyman
Reinsdorf, Jerry Michael professional sports teams executive, real estate executive, lawyer, accountant
Reiss, Dale Anne accounting executive
Reiter, Michael A. lawyer, educator
Reitman, Jerry Irving advertising agency executive
Relias, John Alexis lawyer
Renkar-Janda, Jarri J. paint manufacturing executive
Reschke, Michael W. real estate executive
Resnick, Donald Ira lawyer
Reum, James Michael lawyer
†Reyna, Claudio soccer player
Reynolds, Frank Everett religious studies educator
Reynolds, Ruth Carmen school administrator, secondary school educator
Rhind, James Thomas lawyer
Rhoads, Paul Kelly lawyer
Rhodes, Charles Harker, Jr. lawyer
Rhone, Douglas Pierce pathologist, educator
Rice, Charles Lane surgical educator
Rice, Linda Johnson publishing executive
Rice, William Edward newspaper columnist
Rich, S. Judith public relations executive
Richardson, John Thomas academic administrator, clergyman
Richardson, William F. lawyer
Richman, Harold Alan social welfare policy educator
Richman, John Marshall lawyer, business executive
Richmond, James G. lawyer
Richmond, William Patrick lawyer
Rieger, Mitchell Sheridan lawyer
Rielly, John Edward educational association administrator
Riggleman, James David professional baseball team manager
Rigsbee, Stephen Reese risk management executive
Rikoski, Richard Anthony engineering executive, electrical engineer
Riley, Jack T., Jr. lawyer
Rissman, Burton Richard lawyer
Ritchie, Albert lawyer
Rizzo, Ronald Stephen lawyer
Robbins, Henry Zane public relations and marketing executive
Roberts, Harry Vivian statistics educator
Roberts, John Charles law school educator
Roberts, Theodore Harris banker
Robin, Richard C. lawyer
Robinson, Gwendolyn Powell savings and loan executive, church executive
Robinson, June Kerswell dermatologist, educator
Robinson, Martin (Marty) television and radio broadcaster, media consultant
†Robinson, Michael R. advertising executive
Robinson, Theodore Curtis, Jr. lawyer
Roche, James McMillan lawyer
Rodenkirk, Robert Francis, Jr. journalist
Rodgers, James Foster association executive, economist
Rodman, Dennis Keith basketball player
Rodriguez, David G., Jr. art and religion educator, priest
Rodriguez, Matt L. protective services professional
Roenick, Jeremy professional hockey player
Roeper, Richard columnist
Rogalski, Carol Jean clinical psychologist, educator
Rogers, Desiree Glapion utilities executive
Rogers, John Washington, Jr. investment management company executive
Roizen, Nancy J. physician, educator
Roizman, Bernard virologist, educator
Rollhaus, Philip Edward, Jr. manufacturing company executive
Rooney, Matthew A. lawyer
Ropski, Gary Melchior lawyer
Rosemarin, Carey Stephen lawyer
Rosen, George economist, educator
Rosen, Sherwin economist, educator
Rosen, Steven Terry oncologist, hematologist
Rosenbaum, Michael A. investor relations consultant
Rosenberg, Gary Aron construction executive, lawyer
Rosenbloom, Lewis Stanley lawyer
Rosenbloom, Steve sportswriter
Rosenblum, Victor Gregory political science and law educator
Rosenbluth, Marion Helen educator, consultant, psychotherapist
Rosenfield, Robert Lee pediatric endocrinologist, educator
Rosenheim, Edward Weil English educator
Rosenheim, Margaret Keeney social welfare policy educator
Rosenthal, Albert Jay advertising agency executive
Rosenthal, Ira Maurice pediatrician, educator
Rosner, Jonathan Lincoln physicist, educator
Rosner, Robert astrophysicist
Roston, David Charles lawyer
Roth, Sanford Irwin pathologist, educator
Rothman-Denes, Lucia Beatriz biology educator
Rothstein, Ruth M. hospital adminstrator
Rotman, Carlotta J.H. Hill physician
Rovner, Ilana Kara Diamond federal judge
Rovner, Jack Alan lawyer
Rowder, William Louis lawyer
Rowe, Randall Keith real estate executive
Rowley, Janet Davison physician
Roy, David Tod Chinese literature educator
Rubenstein, Arthur Harold physician, educator
Rubin, E(rwin) Leonard lawyer
Rucker, Dennis Morton Arthur telecommunications executive
Ruder, David Sturtevant lawyer, educator, government official
Rudnick, Paul David lawyer
Rudstein, David Stewart law educator
Rudy, Lester Howard psychiatrist
Rumsfeld, Donald Henry former government official, corporate executive
Rundio, Louis Michael, Jr. lawyer
Runkle, Martin Davey library director
Rupert, Donald William lawyer
Russell, Lillian medical, surgical nurse
Russell, Paul Frederick lawyer
Russo, Gilberto engineering educator
Rutkoff, Alan Stuart lawyer
Ruxin, Paul Theodore lawyer
Ryan, Patrick G. insurance company executive
Ryan, Randel Edward, Jr. airline pilot
Ryan, Thomas F. lawyer
Rychlak, Joseph Frank psychology educator, theoretician
Rycroft, Donald Cahill insurance executive
Rydholm, Ralph Williams advertising agency executive
Rymer, Randal Eugene chemical engineer
Rymer, William Zev research scientist, administrator
Rynkiewicz, Stephen Michael journalist
Sabbagha, Rudy E. obstetrician, gynecologist, educator
Sabl, John J. lawyer
Sachs, Lloyd Robert entertainment critic, writer
Sachs, Robert Green physicist, educator, laboratory administrator
Sager, William F. retired chemistry educator
Sahler, Christy Lee real estate manager
Saller, Richard Paul classics educator
Sampson, Ronald A. advertising executive
Sampson, Steve professional soccer coach
Sandberg, Ryne professional baseball player
Sanders, David P. lawyer
Sanders, Jacquelyn Seevak psychologist, educator
Sanders, Richard Henry lawyer
Sandlow, Leslie Jordan physician, educator
Santangelo, Mario Vincent dentist
Saunders, David Alan lawyer
Saunders, George Lawton, Jr. lawyer
Saunders, Terry Rose lawyer
Savard, Denis Joseph professional hockey player
Sawdey, Richard Marshall lawyer
Sawinski, Vincent John chemistry educator
Sawyier, David R. lawyer
Scalish, Frank Anthony labor union administrator
Scanlan, Thomas Cleary publishing executive, editor
Scarse, Olivia Marie cardiologist, consultant
Schade, Stanley Greinert, Jr. hematologist, educator
Schafer, Michael Frederick orthopedic surgeon
Schar, Stephen L. lawyer
Scheinkman, José Alexandre economics educator
Scherer, Norbert Franz chemistry educator
Schieser, Hans Alois education educator
Schiller, Donald Charles lawyer
Schiller, Eric M. lawyer
Schillinger, Edwin Joseph physics educator
Schilsky, Richard Lewis oncologist, researcher
Schimberg, A(rmand) Bruce retired lawyer
Schimberg, Barbara Hodes organizational development consultant
Schindel, Donald Marvin lawyer
Schindler, Judi(th Kay) public relations executive, marketing consultant
Schink, James Harvey lawyer
Schippers, David Philip lawyer
Schirn, Janet Sugerman interior designer
Schlickman, J. Andrew lawyer
Schlitter, Stanley Allen lawyer
Schloss, Nathan economist
Schlossman, John Isaac architect
Schmetterer, Jack Baer federal judge
Schneider, Dan W. lawyer, consultant
Schneider, Robert Jerome lawyer
Schnell, Joseph dancer
Schommer, Carol Marie principal
Schoonhoven, Ray James retired lawyer
Schornack, John James accountant
Schoumacher, Bruce Herbert lawyer
Schramm, David Norman astrophysicist, educator
Schreck, Robert A., Jr. lawyer
Schriver, John T., III lawyer
Schroeder, Charles Edgar banker, investment management executive
Schroeder, W(illiam) Widick religion educator
Schubert, Helen Celia public relations executive
Schubert, William Henry curriculum studies educator
Schuerman, John Richard social work educator
Schuette, Michael lawyer
Schug, Kenneth Robert chemistry educator
Schuler, James Joseph vascular surgeon
Schulhofer, Stephen Joseph law educator
Schulman, Sidney neurologist, educator
Schulte, Bruce John lawyer
Schulte, David Michael investment banker
Schulte, Stephen Charles lawyer
Schultz, Paul Neal electronic publishing executive
Schultz, Theodore William retired economist, educator
Schulz, Keith Donald corporate lawyer
Schumer, William surgeon, educator
Schupp, Ronald Irving clergyman, civil rights leader
Schuyler, Daniel Merrick lawyer, educator
Schwab, James Charles urban planner
Schwartz, Alan Gifford sport company executive
Schwartz, Charles Phineas, Jr. replacement auto parts company executive, lawyer
Schwartz, Donald Lee lawyer
Schwartz, John Norman health care executive
Schwarzkopf, Gloria A. education educator, psychotherapist
Schweikert, Norman Carl musician
Sciarra, John J. physician, educator
Scogland, William Lee lawyer
Scommegna, Antonio physician, educator
Scott, Alice H. librarian
Scott, John Brooks research institute executive
Scott, Louis Edward advertising agency executive
Scott, Stephen Brinsley theater producer
Scott, Theodore R. lawyer
Scotti, Michael John, Jr. medical association executive
Scrimshaw, Susan dean
Scullion, Annette Murphy lawyer, educator
†Scurry, Briana Collette amateur soccer player
Seaman, Irving, Jr. public relations consultant
Sedelmaier, John Josef film director, cinematographer
Seeler, Ruth Andrea pediatrician, educator
Seemann, Rosalie Mary international business association executive
Selfridge, Calvin lawyer
Sen, Ashish Kumar urban planner, educator
Sennet, Charles Joseph lawyer
Serritella, James Anthony lawyer
Serritella, William David lawyer
Serwer, Alan Michael lawyer
Sfikas, Peter Michael lawyer, educator
Shadur, Robert H. lawyer
Shafer, Eric Christopher minister
Shah, Manu Hirachand civil and structural engineer
Shambaugh, George Elmer, III internist
Shank, William O. lawyer
Shannon, Peter Michael, Jr. lawyer
Shapey, Ralph composer, conductor, educator
Shapiro, Harold David lawyer, educator
Shapiro, Stephen Michael lawyer
Shapo, Marshall Schambelan lawyer, educator
Shaughnessy, Edward Louis Chinese language educator
Shedlock, James library director, consultant
Shepherd, Daniel Marston executive recruiter
Shepherd, Stewart Robert lawyer
Shepro, Richard W. lawyer
Shere, Dennis publishing executive
Sherwin, Byron Lee religion educator, college official
Shieh, Ching-Long structural engineering executive
Shields, Thomas Charles lawyer
Shields, Thomas William surgeon, educator
Shindler, Donald A. lawyer
Shirley, Virginia Lee advertising executive
Shoenberger, Allen Edward law educator
Short, Marion Priscilla neurology educator
Sido, Kevin Richard lawyer
Siegel, Arthur corporate executive
Siegel, Howard Jerome lawyer
Siegler, Mark internist, educator
Sigal, Michael Stephen lawyer
Sigler, Hollis artist, educator
Sigmon, Joyce Elizabeth professional society administrator
Silberman, Alan Harvey lawyer
Silets, Harvey Marvin lawyer
Silins, Ints M. ambassador
Simon, Bernece Kern social work educator
Simon, John Bern lawyer
Simon, Mordecai religious association administrator, clergyman
Simon, Seymour lawyer, former state supreme court justice
Simons, Helen school psychologist, psychotherapist
Simpson, John Alexander physicist
Singh, Manmohan orthopedic surgeon, educator
Siske, Roger Charles lawyer
Sive, Rebecca Anne public affairs company executive
Sizemore, Barbara Ann Black studies educator
Skilling, Thomas Ethelbert, III meteorologist, meteorology educator
Sklarsky, Charles B. lawyer
Skrebneski, Victor photographer
Slansky, Jerry William investment company executive
Small, Bruce W. sales and marketing executive
Smedinghoff, Thomas J. lawyer
Smith, Adrian Devaun architect
†Smith, Almon R. labor union administrator
Smith, Arthur B(everly), Jr. lawyer
Smith, David Waldo Edward pathology and gerontology educator, physician
Smith, Freddye L(ee) financial planner
Smith, Gordon Howell lawyer
Smith, James Barry lawyer
†Smith, James Stephen hockey player
Smith, Jeffrey Earl management consulting executive
Smith, John Gelston lawyer
Smith, Kenneth Bryant seminary administrator
Smith, Lawrence R. lawyer
Smith, Leo Emmet lawyer
Smith, Michele lawyer
Smith, Raymond Thomas anthropology educator
Smith, Sam Pritzker columnist, author
Smith, Scott Clybourn media company executive
Smith, Stan Vladimir economist, financial service company executive
Smith, Stephen Edward lawyer
Smith, Tefft Weldon lawyer
Smithburg, William Dean food manufacturing company executive
Sneed, Michael (Michele) columnist
Snider, Lawrence K. lawyer
Snyder, Jean Maclean lawyer
Sochen, June history educator
Socol, Michael Lee obstetrician, gynecologist, educator
Socolofsky, Jon Edward banker
Solaro, Ross John physiologist, biophysicist
Solomon, Jack Avrum lawyer, automotive distributor, art dealer
Solomon, Richard Jay architect
Solomonson, Charles D. corporate executive
Solovy, Jerold Sherwin lawyer
Solti, Sir Georg conductor
Sonderby, Susan Pierson federal bankruptcy judge
Sopranos, Orpheus Javaras manufacturing company executive
Sorensen, Leif Boge physician, educator
Sorensen, W. Robert clergy member, church administrator
Sosa, Samuel (Sammy Sosa) professional baseball player
Spain, Richard Colby lawyer
Sparberg, Marshall Stuart gastroenterologist, educator
Spargo, Benjamin H. educator, renal pathologist
Spearman, David Leroy elementary education educator, administrator
Spector, David M. lawyer
Spellmire, George W. lawyer
Spencer, Lewis Douglas lawyer
Spiotto, James Ernest lawyer
Spivey, Bruce E. integrated healthcare delivery systems management executive
Springer, David Edward lawyer
Sproger, Charles Edmund lawyer
Sprowl, Charles Riggs lawyer
Squires, John Henry judge
Staab, Michael Joseph lawyer
Stack, John Wallace lawyer
Stack, Paul Francis lawyer
Stack, Stephen S. manufacturing company executive
Standberry, Herman Lee school system administrator, consultant
Stanley, Robert Anthony artist, educator
Starkman, Gary Lee lawyer
Stassen, John Henry lawyer
Stead, James Joseph, Jr. securities company executive
Steck, Theodore Lyle biochemistry and molecular biology educator, physician
Steele, Glenn Daniel, Jr. surgical oncologist
Steffy, Marion Nancy state agency administrator
Stein, Paula Jean Anne Barton hotel real estate consultant
†Stein, Robert Allen legal association executive, law educator
Steinberg, Morton M. lawyer
Steiner, Donald Frederick biochemist, physician, educator
Steinfeld, Manfred furniture manufacturing executive
Steingraber, Frederick George management consultant
Stelzel, Walter Tell, Jr. accountant, financial company executive
Stephan, Edmund Anton lawyer
Stern, Carl William, Jr. management consultant
Stern, Richard Gustave author, educator
Sternberg, Paul retired ophthalmologist
Sternstein, Allan J. lawyer
Stetler, David J. lawyer
Steven, Donald Anstey dean, educator
Stevens, Mark banker
Stevenson, Adlai Ewing, III lawyer, former senator
Stewart, S. Jay chemical company executive
Stigler, Stephen Mack statistician, educator
Stillman, Nina Gidden lawyer
Stirling, James Paulman investment banker
Stocking, George Ward, Jr. anthropology educator
Stoll, John Robert lawyer, educator
Stoller, Patricia Sypher structural engineer
Stone, Alan container company executive
Stone, Geoffrey Richard law educator, lawyer
Stone, James Howard management consultant
Stone, Randolph Noel law educator
Stone, Roger Warren container company executive
Stone, Steven Michael sports announcer, former baseball player
Storb, Ursula Beate molecular genetics and cell biology educator
Stotler, Edith Ann grain company executive
Stotter, David W. marketing executive
Stover, Leon (Eugene) anthropology educator, writer, critic
Stowell, Joseph, III academic administrator
Strange, Gary R. medical educator
Strasburger, Joseph Julius retired lawyer
Strauch, Gerald Otto surgeon
Straus, Helen Lorna Puttkammer biologist, educator
Streeto, Joseph Michael catering company official
Streff, William Albert, Jr. lawyer
Streicker, James Richard lawyer
Strubel, Ella Doyle advertising executive
Strubel, Richard Perry manufacturing company executive
Struggles, John Edward management consultant
Stuart, Robert container manufacturing executive
Stukel, James Joseph academic administrator, mechanical engineering educator
Stumpf, David Allen pediatric neurologist
Sulkin, Howard Allen college president
Sullivan, Bernard James accountant
Sullivan, Marcia Waite lawyer
Sullivan, Thomas Patrick lawyer
Sumner, William Marvin anthropology and archaeology educator
Sussman, Arthur Melvin law educator
†Sutter, Brent Colin hockey player
Sutter, William Paul lawyer
Svanborg, Alvar geriatrics educator, researcher
Swaney, Thomas Edward lawyer
Swanson, Bernet Steven consulting engineer, former educator
Swanson, Don Richard university dean
Swanson, Patricia K. university official
Sween, Joyce Ann sociologist, psychologist, evaluation methodologist
Sweeney, James Raymond lawyer
Sweet, Charles Wheeler executive recruiter
Swerdlow, Martin Abraham physician, pathologist, educator
Swibel, Howard Jay lawyer, investment advisor
Swibel, Steven Warren lawyer
Swift, Edward Foster, III investment banker
Swiger, Elinor Porter lawyer
Szczepanski, Slawomir Zbigniew Steven lawyer
Tabin, Julius patent lawyer, physicist
Talbot, Earl Armour lawyer
Talbot, Pamela public relations executive
Tallchief, Maria ballerina
Tanner, Helen Hornbeck historian
Tardy, Medney Eugene, Jr. otolaryngologist, facial plastic surgeon
Tarun, Robert Walter lawyer
Taub, Richard Paul social sciences educator
Taylor, John Wilkinson education educator
Taylor, Roger Lee lawyer
Teichner, Lester management consulting executive
Telfer, Margaret Clare internist, hematologist
Telling, Edward Riggs former retail, insurance, real estate and financial services executive
Terkel, Studs (Louis Terkel) author, interviewer
Terp, Dana George architect
Tessing, Louise Scire graphic designer
Thaden, Edward Carl history educator
Theobald, Edward Robert lawyer
Theobald, Thomas Charles banker
Thies, Richard Brian lawyer
Thisted, Ronald Aaron statistician, educator, consultant
Thomas, Dale E. lawyer
Thomas, Frank Edward professional baseball player
Thomas, Frederick Bradley lawyer
Thomas, John Thieme management consultant
Thomas, Leona Marlene health information educator
Thomas, Richard Lee banker
Thomas, Stephen Paul lawyer
Thompson, James Robert, Jr. lawyer, former governor
Thomson, George Ronald lawyer, educator
Thorne-Thomsen, Thomas lawyer
Thornton, Theodore Kean investment advisor
Thurston, Stephen John pastor
Tigerman, Stanley architect, educator
Timbers, Stephen Bryan financial services company executive
Timmer, Stephen Blaine lawyer
Tipp, Karen Lynn Wagner school psychologist
Tobaccowala, Rishad marketing professional
Tobin, Calvin Jay architect
Tobin, Craig Daniel lawyer
Tobin, Thomas F. lawyer
Tocklin, Adrian Martha insurance company executive, lawyer
Todd, James S. surgeon, educator, medical association administrator
Todd Copley, Judith Ann materials and metallurgical engineering educator
Toll, Daniel Roger corporate executive, civic leader
Tomaino, Joseph Carmine retail executive, retired postal inspector
Tomek, Laura Lindemann marketing executive
Tone, Philip Willis lawyer, former federal judge
Toohey, James Kevin lawyer
Topinka, Judy Baar state official
Torgersen, Torwald Harold architect, designer
Torshen, Jerome Harold lawyer
Totlis, Gust John title insurance company executive
Tracy, David theology educator
Trapp, James McCreery lawyer
Travis, Dempsey Jerome real estate executive, mortgage banker
Trexler, Edgar Ray minister, editor
Trienens, Howard Joseph lawyer
Tripp, Marian Barlow Loofe retired public relations company executive
Trost, Eileen Bannon lawyer
Truran, James Wellington, Jr. astrophysicist
Truskowski, John Budd lawyer
Tsou, Tang political science educator, researcher

Tucker, Bowen Hayward lawyer
Tucker, Watson Billopp lawyer
Tulsky, Alex Sol physician
Turkevich, Anthony Leonid chemist, educator
Turner, Cristina Benitez advertising professional
Turner, Lynne Alison (Mrs. Paul H. Singer) harpist
Turner, Michael Stanley physics educator
Turow, Scott F. lawyer, author
Tyler, W(illiam) Ed printing company executive
Tyner, Howard A. publishing executive, newspaper editor, journalist
Ultmann, John Ernest physician, educator
Underwood, Robert Leigh venture capitalist
Ungaretti, Richard Anthony lawyer
Utigard, Philip Richard real estate executive
†Uukas, Ronald publishing executive
Valerio, Joseph M. architectural firm executive, educator
Valukas, Anton Ronald lawyer, former federal official
Van Cura, Joyce Bennett librarian
Van Demark, Ruth Elaine lawyer
Van Den Hende, Fred J(oseph) human resources executive
VanderBeke, Patricia K. architect
Vander Wilt, Carl Eugene banker
Vanecko, Robert Michael surgeon, educator
†Vanover, Neil advertising executive
Van Pelt, Robert Irving firefighter
Van Valen, Leigh Maiorana biologist, educator
Varchetta, Felix R. advertising agency executive
Varro, Barbara Joan editor
Veit, Fritz librarian
Velisaris, Chris Nicholas financial analyst
Ventura, Robin Mark professional baseball player
Verbockel Rogers, Jolene Mary auditor
Verdi, Robert William sports columnist
Verschoor, Curtis Carl business educator, consultant
Vie, Richard Carl insurance company executive
Vieregg, Robert Todd lawyer
Vilim, Nancy Catherine advertising agency executive
Vinci, John Nicholas architect, educator
Visotsky, Harold Meryle psychiatrist, educator
Voedisch, Lynn Andrea reporter
Vogelzang, Jeanne Marie professional association executive, attorney
Von Mandel, Michael Jacques lawyer
von Rhein, John Richard music critic, editor
Vrablik, Edward Robert import/export company executive
Vranicar, Michael Gregory lawyer
Vree, Roger Allen lawyer
Wackerle, Frederick William management consultant
Wadden, Richard Albert environmental engineer, educator, consultant, research director
Wade, Edwin Lee writer, lawyer
Wagner, Joseph M. church administrator
Wahlen, Edwin Alfred lawyer
Waintroob, Andrea Ruth lawyer
Waite, Dennis Vernon investor relations consultant
Waite, Ellen Jane vice president of academic services
Waite, Norman, Jr. lawyer
Walberg, Herbert John psychologist, educator, consultant
Waldstein, Sheldon Saul physician, educator
Walker, John Patrick theater producer, actor
Walker, Ronald Edward psychologist, educator
Wall, James McKendree minister, editor
Wall, Robert F. lawyer
Wallace, Helen Marie secondary school educator, coach
Walsh, Michael S. lawyer
Walter, Priscilla Anne lawyer
†Walters, Lawrence Charles advertising executive
Walton, Robert Lee, Jr. plastic surgeon
Waltz, Jon Richard lawyer, educator, author
Wander, Herbert Stanton lawyer
Wang, Albert James violinist, educator
Wang, Gung H. management consultant
Wanke, Ronald Lee lawyer
Ward, James Frank pension fund administrator
Wardropper, Ian Bruce museum curator, educator
Warfield, William Caesar singer, actor, educator
Warnecke, Michael O. lawyer
Wasan, Darsh Tilakchand university official, chemical engineer educator
Wasik, John Francis editor, writer, publisher
Wasiolek, Edward literary critic, language and literature educator
Watanabe, Mark David pharmacist, educator
Watson, Robert R. lawyer
Watts, John Ransford university administrator
Waxler, Beverly Jean anesthesiologist, physician
Weaver, Donna Rae company executive
Weaver, Timothy Allan lawyer
Webb, Dan K. lawyer
Weber, Donald B. advertising and marketing executive
Weber, Hanno architect
Webster, James Randolph, Jr. physician
Webster, Ronald D. communications company executive
Wechter, Clari Ann paint manufacturing company executive
Weclew, Robert George lawyer, educator
Weclew, Victor T. dentist
Weese, Benjamin Horace architect
Weil, Roman Lee accounting educator
Weiman, Heidi early childhood education educator
Weimer, Jean Elaine nursing educator
Weinberg, David B. lawyer, investor
Weinberg, Lila Shaffer writer, editor
Weinberg, Meyer humanities educator
Weinkopf, Friedrich J. lawyer
Weinsheimer, William Cyrus lawyer
Weintraub, Joseph Barton publishing executive
Weintraub, Karl Joachim history educator
Weir, Bryce Keith Alexander neurosurgeon, neurology educator
Weis, Mervyn J. physician, gastroenterologist
Weisberg, Lois arts administrator, city official
Weiss, Hedy theater critic
Weissman, Michael Lewis lawyer
Weitzman, Robert Harold investment company executive
Wellington, Robert Hall manufacturing company executive
Wells, Joel Freeman editor, author
Welsh, Kelly Raymond lawyer, telecommunications company executive
Wetzel, Franklin Todd spinal surgeon, educator, researcher
Wexler, Richard Lewis lawyer
Whalen, Wayne W. lawyer
White, Craig Mitchell lawyer
White, H. Blair lawyer
White, Linda Diane lawyer
White, R. Quincy lawyer
Wick, Lawrence Scott lawyer
Wiecek, Barbara Harriet advertising executive
Wied, George Ludwig physician
Wier, Patricia Ann publishing executive, consultant
Wiggins, Charles Henry, Jr. lawyer
Wilber, David James cardiologist
Wilbur, Andrew Clayton radiologist
Wilcox, Mark Dean lawyer
Wildman, Max Edward lawyer
Wilhelm, David C. political organization administrator
Williams, Ann Claire federal judge
Williams, Carl Chanson oil company executive
Williams, David Arthur marketing professional
Williams, Edward Joseph banker
Williams, George Howard lawyer, association executive
Williams, Mark H. marketing communications agency executive
Williams, Richard Lucas, III electronics company executive, lawyer
Williams-Ashman, Howard Guy biochemistry educator
Williamson, Richard Salisbury lawyer
Willoughby, William Franklin, II physician, researcher
Wilmouth, Robert K. commodities executive
Wilson, Anne Gawthrop artist, educator
Wilson, Clarence Sylvester, Jr. lawyer, educator
Wilson, Karen Lee museum director
Wilson, Richard Harold government official
Wilson, Roger Goodwin lawyer
Winfrey, Oprah television talk show host, actress, producer
Winkler, Charles Howard lawyer, investment management company executive
Winnie, Alon Palm anesthesiologist, educator
Winston, Roland physicist, educator
Winter, John Dawson, III blues guitarist, singer
Winton, Jeffrey Blake arbitrator
Wirszup, Izaak mathematician, educator
Wirtz, Arthur Michael, Jr. professional hockey team executive
Wirtz, William Wadsworth real estate and sports executive
Wise, William Jerrard lawyer
Wiser, James Louis political science educator
Wishner, Maynard Ira finance company executive, lawyer
Witcoff, Sheldon William lawyer
Witwer, Samuel Weiler, Jr. lawyer
Wiwchar, Michael bishop
Wolf, Charles Benno lawyer
Wolfe, David Louis lawyer
Wolfe, Sheila A. journalist
Wolfson, Larry M. lawyer
Wolpert, Edward Alan psychiatrist
Wood, Allison Lorraine lawyer
Wood, Arthur MacDougall retired retail executive
Wood, James Nowell museum director and executive
Woodle, E. Steve transplant surgeon
Woodley, David Timothy dermatology educator
Woods, Robert Archer investment counsel
Wooldridge, Patrice Marie marketing professional, martial arts and meditation educator
Wooten-Bryant, Helen Catherine academic administrator
Workman, Robert Peter artist, cartoonist
Wright, Helen Kennedy professional association administrator, publisher, editor, librarian
Wright, Judith Margaret law librarian, educator
Wycliff, Noel Don journalist, newspaper editor
Yacktman, Donald Arthur financial executive, investment counselor
Yale, Seymour Hershel dental radiologist, educator, university dean, gerontologist
Yamakawa, Allan Hitoshi academic administrator
Yao, Tito Go pediatrician
Yarkony, Gary Michael physician, researcher
York, Donald Gilbert astronomy educator, researcher
Young, Keith Lawrence lawyer
Young, Ronald Faris commodity trader
Youngman, Owen Ralph newspaper executive
Yu, Anthony C. religion and literature educator
Zabel, Sheldon Alter lawyer, law educator
Zagel, James Block federal judge
Zajicek, Jeronym music educator
Zaki, Abdelmoneim Emam dental educator
Zaremski, Miles Jay lawyer
Zaslow, Jeffrey Lloyd syndicated columnist
Zatuchni, Gerald Irving physician, educator
Zeffren, Eugene toiletries company executive
Zekman, Pamela Lois (Mrs. Fredric Soll) reporter
Zellner, Arnold economics and statistics educator
Zemm, Sandra Phyllis lawyer
Zenner, Sheldon Toby lawyer
Zhao, Meishan chemical physics educator, researcher
Zimmerman, Martin E. financial executive
Zlatoff-Mirsky, Everett Igor violinist
Zolno, Mark S. lawyer
Zoloto, Jerrold Albert psychologist, consultant
Zonis, Marvin political scientist, educator
Zorn, Eric John newspaper columnist
Zucaro, Aldo Charles insurance company executive
Zukowsky, John Robert curator
Zwecker, William Rene, Jr. (Bill Zwecker) newspaper columnist, television reporter

**Chicago Heights**
Carpenter, Kenneth Russell international trading executive
Cifelli, John Louis lawyer
Galloway, Sister Mary Blaise mathematics educator
Patton, Sharlene Darlage nurse

**Cicero**
Cichowicz, Wayne Richard health commissioner, dean

**Clarendon Hills**
Moritz, Donald Brooks mechanical engineer, consultant
Walton, Stanley Anthony, III lawyer

**Clinton**
Ramanuja, Teralandur Krishnaswamy structural engineer

**Coal City**
Major, Mary Jo dance school artistic director

**Collinsville**
Morris, Calvin Curtis architect

**Columbia**
Megahy, Diane Alaire physician

**Crestwood**
Cowie, Norman Edwin credit manager

**Crete**
Langer, Steven human resources management consultant and industrial psychologist

**Crystal Lake**
Althoff, J(ames) L. construction company executive
Anderson, Lyle Arthur manufacturing company executive
Chamberlain, Charles James railroad labor union executive
Dabkowski, John electrical engineering executive
Haas, Jonathan Stuart financial company executive
Keller, William Francis publishing consultant
Knox, Susan Marie paralegal
Linklater, Isabelle Stanislawa Yarosh-Galazka (Lee Linklater) foundation administrator
Smyth, Joseph Vincent manufacturing company executive
Thoms, Jeannine Aumond lawyer

**Danville**
Burnside, William Charles investment company executive
Evans, Austin James hospital administrator
Kettling, Virginia health facility administrator
Prabhudesai, Mukund M. pathology educator, laboratory director, researcher, administrator

**Darien**
Hanson, Martin Philip mechanical engineer, farmer
Meyer, James Philip secondary education social studies educator

**De Kalb**
Aufdenkamp, Jo Ann retired librarian
Bach, Jan Morris composer, educator
†Das, Man Singh sociology educator
Eineke, Alvina Marie public health nurse
Even, Robert Lawrence art educator
Hanna, Nessim marketing educator
Kevill, Dennis Neil chemistry educator
Kimball, Clyde William physicist, educator
King, Kenneth Paul secondary education educator
Kostic, Milivoje mechanical engineering educator
La Tourette, John Ernest academic administrator
McSpadden, Lettie political science educator
Monat, William Robert university official
Rollman, Charlotte artist, educator
Rossing, Thomas D. physics educator
Sons, Linda Ruth mathematics educator
Troyer, Alvah Forrest seed corn company executive, plant breeder
Vance Siebrasse, Kathy Ann newspaper publishing executive
Wit, Daniel international consultant
Witmer, John Harper, Jr. lawyer
Zar, Jerrold H(oward) academic administrator, biology educator, statistician

**Decatur**
Blake, William Henry credit and public relations consultant
Bluhm, Myron Dean sales professional
Braun, William Joseph life insurance underwriter
Decker, Charles Richard business educator
Dreyer, Alec Gilbert independent power producer
Dunn, John Francis lawyer, state representative
Graf, Karl Rockwell nuclear engineer
Koucky, John Richard metallurgical engineer, manufacturing executive
Kraft, Burnell D. agricultural products company executive
McCray, Curtis Lee university president
Moorman, John A. librarian
Morgan, E. A. church administrator
Perry, Anthony John retired hospital executive
Requarth, William Henry surgeon
Rockefeller, Margaretta Fitler Murphy (Happy Rockefeller) widow of former vice president of U.S.
Staley, Henry Mueller manufacturing company executive
Strong, John David insurance company executive
Womeldorff, Porter John utilities executive

**Deerfield**
Abbey, G(eorge) Marshall lawyer, former health care company executive, general counsel
Bartlett, Robert William lawyer, publishing executive
Batts, Warren Leighton diversified industry executive
Boyd, Joseph Don financial services executive
Chiozzi, Richard Emilio financial planner, investment advisor
Chromizky, William Rudolph accountant
Cruikshank, John W., III life insurance underwriter
Dawson, Suzanne Stockus lawyer
Fulrath, Andrew Wesley financial planner, charitable gift planner
Gaither, John F. lawyer
Gaples, Harry Seraphim computer service company executive
Graham, William B. pharmaceutical company executive
Hannafan, Kay H. Pierce lawyer
Heiman, Marvin Stewart financial services company executive
Howell, George Bedell equity investing and managing executive
Kessler, Paula Gail controller
Kingdon, Henry Shannon physician, biochemist, educator, executive
Kinzelberg, Harvey leasing company executive
Kushner, Jeffrey L. manufacturing company executive
Larrimore, Randall Walter manufacturing company executive
Larsen, Samuel Harry minister, educator
Leatham, John Tonkin business executive
Loucks, Vernon R., Jr. medical technologies executive
McCarthy, Gerald Michael electronics executive
Meyer, Mara Ellice special education educator, consultant
Miller, James A. wholesale grocery executive
Nelson, Richard Lawrence public relations executive
Oettinger, Julian Alan lawyer, pharmacy company executive
Pigozzi, Raymond Anthony architect
Plamondon, William N. rental company executive
Ringler, James M. cookware company executive
Russell, William Steven finance executive
Sanner, John Harper retired pharmacologist
Scheiber, Stephen Carl psychiatrist
Slavin, Craig Steven management and franchising consultant
Smith, Carole Dianne legal editor, writer, product developer
Staubitz, Arthur Frederick lawyer, healthcare products company executive
Vollen, Robert Jay lawyer
Walgreen, Charles Rudolph, III retail store executive
Weiss, Stanley C. electrical and electronics products wholesale distribution executive
Williams, Robert Jene lawyer, rail car company executive
Zywicki, Robert Albert electrical distribution company executive

**Des Plaines**
Banach, Art John graphic artist
Bartoo, Richard Keith chemical engineer, consultant
Brodl, Raymond Frank lawyer, former lumber company executive
Carper, James David magazine editor
Carroll, Barry Joseph manufacturing and real estate executive
Clapper, Marie Anne magazine publisher
Coburn, James LeRoy educational administrator
Cronin, Kathleen Anne executive search consultant
Cucco, Ulisse P. obstetrician, gynecologist
†Daniele, Dan hotel executive
Demouth, Robin Madison lawyer, corporate executive
Dlouhy, Phillip Edward engineering, construction executive
†Dolan, C. Michael hotel executive
Drezdzon, William Lawrence mathematics educator
Frank, James S. automotive executive
Grahn, Barbara Ascher publisher
Harrington, Richard J. newspaper publishing executive
Henrikson, Lois Elizabeth photojournalist
Hlavacek, Roy George publishing executive, magazine editor
†Holtz, Michael P. hotel executive
Jacobs, William Russell, II lawyer
Kelly, Timothy Michael magazine publisher
Krupa, John Henry English language educator
Lakier, Thelma child development specialist, librarian
Lee, Bernard Shing-Shu research company executive
Lee, Margaret Burke college administrator, English educator
Lyu, Seung Won metallurgical engineer, environmental scientist
May, Frank Brendan, Jr. lawyer
Meinert, John Raymond clothing manufacturing and retailing executive, investment banker
Mortimer, Lawrence Patrick sales executive
†Mueller, Kurt M. hotel executive
Munden, Robin Ghezzi lawyer
Neel, Judy Murphy association executive
Pannke, Peggy M. long term care insurance agency executive
Ripp, Bryan Jerome geological engineer
Small, Richard Donald travel company executive
†Torchia, H. Andrew hotel executive
Tory, John A. newspaper publishing executive
Winfield, Michael D. engineering company executive

**Dixon**
Belcher-Redebaugh-Levi, Caroline Louise nursing home administrator, nurse
Huber, Marianne Jeanne art dealer
Polascik, Mary Ann ophthalmologist
Shaw, Thomas Douglas newspaper executive

**Dolton**
Lucas, Patricia Lynn financial executive

**Dorsey**
Hinkle, Jo Ann English language educator

**Downers Grove**
Bielefeldt, Catherine C. sales executive
Colbert, Marvin Jay retired internist, educator
Feeney, Don Joseph, Jr. psychologist
Gioioso, Joseph Vincent psychologist
Gruen, Dolores Colen psychologist consultant
Hegenderfer, Jonita Susan public relations executive
Henkin, Robert Elliott nuclear medicine physician
Hubbard, Lincoln Beals retired medical physicist, consultant
Kirkegaard, R. Lawrence architectural acoustician
Pollard, Charles William diversified services company executive
Ruffolo, Paul Gregory police officer, educator
Saricks, Joyce Goering librarian
Schwemm, John Butler printing company executive, lawyer
Shea, John J. catalog and retail company executive
†Shen, Sin-Yan conductor, acoustics specialist, music director
Siedlecki, Nancy Therese lawyer, funeral director
Soder-Alderfer, Kay Christie counseling administrator

**Du Quoin**
Smith, Lucius Skinner, III educational foundation administrator

**Dundee**
Burger, George Vanderkarr wildlife ecologist, researcher

**Dunlap**
Bailey, John Maxwell retired mechanical engineer, consultant

**East Moline**
Adams, Stewart Lee special education educator
Silliman, Richard George retired lawyer, retired farm machinery company executive

**East Peoria**
Dries, Colleen Patricia adult education educator

**East Saint Louis**
Baltz, Richard Arthur chemical engineer
Beatty, William Louis federal judge
Martin, Betty J. speech, language pathologist
Stiehl, William D. federal judge
Wright, Katie Harper school system administrator

### Edinburg
Charlesworth, Brian *biologist, genetics and evolution educator*

### Edwardsville
Adkerson, Donya Lynn *clinical counselor*
Carlson, Jon Gordon *lawyer*
Going, William Thornbury *English educator*
Lazerson, Earl Edwin *academic administrator emeritus*
Malone, Robert Roy *artist, art educator*
May, Mary Louise *elementary education educator*
Ottwein, Merrill William George *real estate company executive, veterinarian*
Virgo, John Michael *economist, researcher, educator*
Wentz, Charles Alvin, Jr. *environmentalist, chemical engineer*

### Effingham
Shetler, Christopher David *chiropractor*

### Elburn
Hansen, H. Jack *management consultant*
Liechty, Eric *church administrator*
Willey, James Lee *dentist*

### Elgin
Deeter, Joan G. *church administrator*
Didier, James William *academic administrator, consultant*
Dodohara, Jean Noton *music educator*
Duffy, John Lewis *Latin, English and reading educator*
Freeman, Corwin Stuart, Jr. *investment adviser*
Hoeft, Elizabeth Bayless *speech and language pathologist*
†Johnson, John George, Jr. (Jack ) *industrial services executive*
Juergensmeyer, John Eli *lawyer*
Kelly, Matthew Edward *association executive, retired*
Kirkland, Alfred Younges, Sr. *federal judge*
Miller, Donald Eugene *minister, educator*
Minnich, Dale E. *religious administrator*
Myers, Anne M. *church administrator*
Nelson, John Thilgen *retired hospital administrator, physician*
Nolen, Wilfred E. *church administrator*
Patterson, Paul M. *school administrator*
Perry, Harold Tyner *dentist, educator*
Ratthahao, Sisouphanh *minister*
Weber, Harm Allen *college chancellor, former college president*
Wiese, Dorothy Jean *business educator*
Zack, Daniel Gerard *library director*
Ziegler, Earl Keller *minister*

### Elk Grove Village
Bandel, David Brian *accountant*
Epstein, Stephen Roger *financial executive*
Field, Larry *paper company executive*
Flaherty, John Joseph *quality assurance company executive*
Herrerias, Carla Trevette *epidemiologist, program manager*
Lombardo, Gaetano (Guy Lombardo) *venture capitalist*
McLain, Roger Sette *electronics company executive*
Nadig, Gerald George *manufacturing executive*
Yiannias, Nancy Magas *municipal official*

### Elmhurst
Baker, Robert I. *business executive*
Begando, Joseph Sheridan *retired university chancellor, educator*
Berry, James Frederick *lawyer, biology educator*
Blain, Charlotte Marie *physician, educator*
Burton, Darrell Irvin *engineering executive*
Chitwood, Lera Catherine *marketing information professional*
Cureton, Bryant Lewis *college president, educator*
Duchossois, Richard Louis *manufacturing executive, racetrack executive*
Ephland, John Russell *magazine editor*
Fornatto, Elio Joseph *otolaryngologist, educator*
Grisim, J. Terrence *safety consulting company executive*
Hildreth, R(oland) James *foundation executive, economist*
John, Richard C. *enterprise development organization executive*
Latzel, Lynn Marina *college administrator*
Mastandrea, Linda Lee *lawyer*
Pruter, Margaret Franson *editor*

### Elmwood Park
Spina, Anthony Ferdinand *lawyer*

### Erie
Latham, LaVonne Marlys *physical education educator*

### Eureka
Hearne, George Archer *academic administrator*
Steffer, Robert Wesley *clergyman*

### Evanston
Abnee, A. Victor *trade association executive*
Achenbach, Jan Drewes *engineering educator, scientist*
Adelson, Bernard Henry *physician*
Alak, Ala Mohammed *health facility administrator, pharmaceutical researcher*
Allred, Albert Louis *chemistry educator*
Bankoff, Seymour George *chemical engineer, educator*
Bareiss, Erwin Hans *computer scientist, mathematician, nuclear engineer, educator*
Barnett, Gary *football coach*
Bashook, Philip G. *medical association executive, educator*
Basolo, Fred *chemistry educator*
Bazant, Zdenek Pavel *structural engineering educator, scientist, consultant*
Beatty, William Kaye *medical bibliography educator*
Bellow, Alexandra *mathematician, educator*
Belytschko, Ted Bohdan *civil, mechanical engineering educator*
Bienen, Henry Samuel *political science educator, university executive*
Bishop, David Fulton *library administrator*
Bjorncrantz, Leslie Benton *librarian*
Borcover, Alfred Seymour *journalist*
Bordwell, Frederick George *chemistry educator*
Boye, Roger Carl *academic administrator, journalism educator, writer*
Braeutigam, Ronald Ray *economics educator*
Brazelton, William Thomas *chemical engineering educator*
Brown, Laurie Mark *physicist, educator*
Buchbinder-Green, Barbara Joyce *art and architectural historian*
Bufe, Noel Carl *program director*
†Buhrfeind, George Edward *marketing executive*
Burwell, Robert Lemmon, Jr. *chemist, educator*
Butt, John Baecher *chemical engineering educator*
Carr, Stephen Howard *materials engineer, educator*
Cassell, Frank Hyde *business educator*
Cates, Jo Ann *librarian, writer*
Catlett, George Roudebush *accountant*
Cheng, Herbert Su-Yuen *mechanical engineering educator*
Christian, Richard Carlton *university dean, former advertising agency executive*
Chung, Yip-Wah *engineering educator*
Citron, Michelle *filmmaker, educator*
Cohen, Jerome Bernard *materials science educator*
Cole, Douglas *English literature educator*
Conger, William Frame *artist, educator*
Corey, Gordon Richard *financial advisor, former utilities executive*
Crawford, James Weldon *psychiatrist, educator, administrator*
Crawford, Susan *library director, educator*
Dallos, Peter John *neurobiologist, educator*
Daniel, Isaac Mordochai *mechanical engineering educator*
Daskin, Mark Stephen *civil engineering educator*
Davis, Stephen Howard *applied mathematics educator*
De Coster, Cyrus Cole *Spanish language and literature educator*
Devinatz, Allen *mathematics educator*
Dockery, J. Lee *medical school administrator*
Domowitz, Ian *economics educator*
Downen, David Earl *investment banking executive*
Downing, Joan Forman *editor*
Duncan, Robert Bannerman *strategy and organizations educator*
Eagly, Alice Hendrickson *social psychology educator*
Eberley, Helen-Kay *opera singer, classical record company executive, poet*
Eisner, Robert *economics educator*
Enroth-Cugell, Christina Alma Elisabeth *neurophysiologist, educator*
Fessler, Raymond R. *metallurgical engineering consultant*
Fine, Arthur I. *philosopher*
Fine, Morris Eugene *materials engineer, educator*
Fisher, Neal Floyd *religious organization administrator*
Fourer, Robert H. *industrial engineering educator, consultant*
Fox, Edward Inman *education administrator and Spanish educator*
Freeman, Arthur J. *physics educator*
Frey, Donald Nelson *industrial engineer, educator, manufacturing company executive*
Friedman, Hans Adolf *architect*
Fryburger, Vernon Ray, Jr. *advertising and marketing educator*
Galati, Frank Joseph *stage and opera director, educator, screen writer, actor*
Galvin, Kathleen Malone *communications educator*
Gasper, George, Jr. *mathematics educator*
Gellman, Aaron Jacob *management educator, transportation center administrator*
Gibbons, William Reginald, Jr. *poet, novelist, editor*
Giordano, August Thomas (Gus Giordano) *choreographer, dancer*
Goldstick, Thomas Karl *biomedical engineering educator*
Goodyear, Julie Ann *marketing and fundraising specialist*
Gordon, Julie Peyton *foundation administrator*
Gordon, Robert James *economics educator*
Gormley, R(obert) James *retired lawyer*
Greenberg, Douglas Stuart *history educator*
Gross, Dorothy-Ellen *library director, dean*
Haberman, Shelby Joel *statistician, educator*
Haddad, Abraham Herzl *electrical engineering educator, researcher*
Handler, Douglas Perry *economist*
Hemke, Frederick L. *music educator, university administrator*
Herron, Orley R. *college president*
Howard, Kenneth Irwin *psychology educator*
Hughes, Edward *physician, educator*
Hurter, Arthur Patrick *economist, educator*
Ibers, James Arthur *chemist, educator*
Ihlanfeldt, William *university administrator, consultant*
Ingersoll, Robert Stephen *former diplomat, federal agency administrator*
Ionescu Tulcea, Cassius *research mathematician, educator*
Irons, William George *anthropology educator*
Jacobs, Donald P. *banking and finance educator*
Jacobs, Norman Joseph *publishing company executive*
Jerome, Joseph Walter *mathematics educator*
Johnson, David Lynn *materials scientist, educator*
Jones, Robert Russell *magazine editor*
Kalai, Ehud *decision sciences educator, researcher in economics and decision sciences*
Karlins, M(artin) William *composer, educator*
Keer, Leon Morris *engineering educator*
Keith, Thomas Warren, Jr. *marketing executive*
Kern, Charles William *university official, chemistry educator*
Ketterson, John Boyd *physics educator*
Khandekar, Janardan Dinkar *oncologist, educator*
King, Robert Charles *biologist, educator*
Kistler, Alan Lee *engineering educator*
Kliphardt, Raymond A. *engineering educator*
Klotz, Irving Myron *chemist, educator*
Kotler, Philip *marketing educator, consultant, writer*
Kreml, Franklin Martin *educational administrator, association executive*
Krizek, Raymond John *civil engineering educator, consultant*
Krulee, Gilbert Koreb *computer scientist, educator*
Kuenster, John Joseph *magazine editor*
Kujala, Walfrid Eugene *musician, educator*
Kung, Harold Hing-Chuen *engineering educator*
Lambert, Joseph Buckley *chemistry educator*
Langsley, Donald Gene *psychiatrist, medical board executive*
Langsley, Pauline Royal *psychiatrist*
Larson, Roy *journalist, publisher*
Lavengood, Lawrence Gene *management educator, historian*
Lavine, John M. *journalism educator, management educator*
Lee, Der-Tsai *electrical engineering and computer science educator, researcher, consultant*
Letsinger, Robert Lewis *chemistry educator*
Lewis, Dan Albert *education educator*
Lippincott, James Andrew *biochemistry and biological sciences educator*
Liu, Shu Qian *biomedical engineer, researcher, educator*
Liu, Wing Kam *mechanical and civil engineering educator*
Mah, Richard Sze Hao *chemical engineering educator*
Marhic, Michel Edmond *engineering educator, entrepreneur, consultant*
Matkowsky, Bernard Judah *applied mathematician, educator*
McCleary, Elliott Harold *magazine editor*
McCoy, Marilyn *university official*
Meshii, Masahiro *materials science educator*
Meyer, Stuart Lloyd *management educator*
Miller, Deborah Jean *computer training and document consultant*
Miller, Thomas Williams *former university dean*
Monroe, Kenneth Anthony *facility and project management consultant*
Moskos, Charles C. *sociology educator*
Murphy, Gordon John *engineering educator*
Myerson, Roger Bruce *economist, game theorist, educator*
Nakoneczny, Michael Martin *artist*
Neuschel, Robert Percy *management consultant, educator*
Novales, Ronald Richards *zoologist, educator*
Oakes, Robert James *physics educator*
Olmstead, William Edward *mathematics educator*
Olson, Gregory Bruce *materials science and engineering educator, academic director*
Ottino, Julio Mario *chemical engineering educator, scientist*
Otwell, Ralph Maurice *retired newspaper editor*
Pabst, Edmund G. *retired insurance company executive, lawyer*
Peck, Abraham *editor, writer, educator, magazine consultant*
Peponis, Harold Arthur *insurance agent, broker*
Plaut, Eric Alfred *retired psychiatrist, educator*
Poeppelmeier, Kenneth Reinhard *chemistry educator*
Polzin, John Theodore *lawyer*
Pople, John Anthony *chemistry educator*
Porter, Robert Hugh *economics educator*
Prince, Thomas Richard *accountant, educator*
Ratner, Mark Alan *chemistry educator*
Reimer, Bennett *music educator, writer*
Reiter, Stanley *economist, educator*
Revsine, Lawrence *accounting educator, consultant*
Robinson, R. Clark *mathematician, educator*
Rolfe, Michael N. *management consulting firm executive*
Rosenbaum, James Edward *psychologist, educator*
Rubenstein, Albert Harold *industrial engineering and management sciences educator*
Saari, Donald Gene *mathematician*
Sachtler, Wolfgang Max Hugo *chemistry educator*
Salzman, Arthur George *architect*
Samter, Max *physician, educator*
Schank, Roger Carl *computer science and psychology educator*
Schnaiberg, Allan *sociology educator*
Schneider-Criezis, Susan Marie *architect*
Scholten, Menno Nico *mortgage banker*
Schwartz, Neena Betty *endocrinologist, educator*
Schwartz, Theodore B. *physician, educator*
Schwarzlose, Richard Allen *journalism educator*
Scott, Walter Dill *management educator*
Seidman, David N(athaniel) *materials science and engineering educator*
Shah, Surendra Poonamchand *engineering educator, researcher*
Shanas, Ethel *sociology educator*
Sheridan, James Edward *history educator*
Shortell, Stephen M. *medical educator*
Shriver, Duward Felix *chemistry educator, researcher, consultant*
Silverman, Richard Bruce *chemist, biochemist, educator*
Sisk, Mark Sean *priest, seminary dean, religious educator*
Slaughter-Defoe, Diana Tresa *education educator*
Smith, Spencer Bailey *engineering and business educator*
Sobel, Alan *electrical engineer, physicist*
Spears, Kenneth George *chemistry educator*
Sprang, Milton LeRoy *obstetrician, gynecologist, educator*
Stern, Louis William *marketing educator, consultant*
Sundquist, Eric John *American studies educator*
Taam, Ronald Everett *physics and astronomy educator*
Taflove, Allen *electrical engineer, educator, researcher, consultant*
Takahashi, Joseph S. *neuroscientist*
Tankin, Richard Samuel *fluid dynamics engineer, educator*
Tanner, Martin Abba *statistics and human oncology educator*
Taronji, Jaime, Jr. *lawyer*
Thrash, Patricia Ann *educational association administrator*
Tornabene, Russell C. *communications executive*
Traisman, Howard Sevin *pediatrician*
Ulmer, Melville Paul *physics and astronomy educator*
Vanderstappen, Harrie Albert *Far Eastern art educator*
Van Duyne, Richard Palmer *analytical chemistry and chemical physics educator*
Vanneman, Edgar, Jr. *lawyer*
Van Ness, James Edward *electrical engineering educator*
Vaynman, Semyon *materials scientist*
Ver Steeg, Clarence Lester *historian, educator*
Vick, Nicholas A. *neurologist*
Villa-Komaroff, Lydia *molecular biologist, educator, university official*
Wagner, Durrett *former publisher, picture service executive*
Walker, Harold Blake *minister*
Warshaw, Roberta Sue *lawyer, financial specialist*
Weber, Arnold R. *academic administrator*
Weertman, Johannes *materials science educator*
Weertman, Julia Randall *materials science and engineering educator*
Weil, Irwin *Slavic languages and literature educator*
Well, Irwin *language educator*
Werckmeister, Otto Karl *art historian and educator*
Wessels, Bruce W. *materials scientist, educator*
Weston, Michael C. *lawyer*
Whitaker, Charles F. *journalism educator*
White, Sylvia Frances *gerontology home care nurse, consultant*
White, Willmon Lee *magazine editor*
Wills, Garry *journalist, educator*
Worthy, James Carson *management educator*
Wright, Donald Eugene *retired librarian*
Wright, John *classics educator*
Wu, Tai Te *biological sciences and engineering educator*
Yoder, Frederick Floyd *fraternity executive*
Yoder, John Clifford *producer, consultant*
Zarefsky, David Harris *academic administrator, communication studies educator*
Zelinsky, Daniel *mathematics educator*
Zhang, Jianping *electrical engineering educator, researcher*
Ziomek, Jonathan S. *journalist, educator*
Zolomij, Robert William *landscape architect, consultant*

### Evergreen Park
Bak, Diann Lee *accountant*
Ephraim, Max, Jr. *mechanical engineer*
Nelson, Mary Bertha *public relations executive*
Smith, Lawrence J. *bishop*
Sochacki, Tina Marie *secondary education educator*

### Fairview Heights
Grace, Walter Charles *lawyer*
Moses, Daniel David *civil engineer*

### Fithian
Ford, Richard Earl *plant virologist, educator*

### Flossmoor
Ferreira, Daniel Alves *secondary education Spanish language educator*
Lis, Edward Francis *pediatrician, consultant*
Schillings, Denny Lynn *history educator*
Walker, George W. *bishop*

### Forest Park
Hatch, Edward William (Ted Hatch) *health care executive*
Orland, Frank *oral microbiologist, educator*

### Fox Lake
Galitz, Laura Maria *secondary education educator*

### Fox River Grove
Abboud, Alfred Robert *banker, consultant, investor*

### Frankfort
Dennis, Peter Ray *environmental corporate executive*
Ruggles, Barbara Ann *elementary education educator*

### Franklin Park
Dean, Howard M., Jr. *food company executive*
Simpson, Michael *metals service center executive*
Watts, Ernest Francis *manufacturing company executive*
Wilson, Steven J. *metal products executive*

### Freeport
Hunter, Georgia L. *clergywoman*

### Galena
Crandall, John Lynn *insurance consultant, retired insurance company executive*
Hermann, Paul David *retired association executive*

### Galesburg
Hane, Mikiso *history educator*
Haywood, Bruce *retired college president*
Kowalski, Richard Sheldon *hospital administrator*
McCrery, David Neil, III *lawyer*
Tourlentes, Thomas Theodore *psychiatrist*

### Gays
Finley, Gary Roger *financial company executive*

### Geneseo
Cherry, Robert Earl Patrick *retired food company executive*
Simonich, Sandra Sue *elementary education educator*

### Geneva
Barney, Charles Richard *transportation company executive*
Goulet, Charles Ryan *retired insurance company executive*
Kallstrom, Charles Clark *dentist*
Kopec, John William *research scientist*
Pershing, Robert George *retired telecommunications company executive*
Shapiro, Joan Isabelle *laboratory administrator, nurse*
Young, Jack Allison *financial executive*

### Genoa
Cromley, Jon Lowell *lawyer*

### Gilman
Ireland, Herbert Orin *engineering educator*

### Glen Ellyn
Baloun, John Charles *wholesale grocery company executive, retired*
Beers, V(ictor) Gilbert *publishing executive*
Cvengros, Joseph Michael *manufacturing company executive*
Dieter, Raymond Andrew, Jr. *physician, surgeon*
Drafke, Michael Walter *business educator, consultant*
Egan, Richard Leo *retired medical educator*
Frateschi, Lawrence Jan *economist, statistician, educator*
Kaleba, Richard Joseph *healthcare consultant*
Kirkpatrick, Clayton *former newspaper executive*
Larson, Ward Jerome *lawyer, retired banker*
Lischer, Ludwig Frederick *retired consultant, former utility company executive*
Logan, Henry Vincent *transportation executive*
Mooring, F. Paul *physics editor*
Patten, Ronald James *university dean*
Temple, Donald *allergist, dermatologist*
Ulrich, Werner *patent lawyer*

### Glencoe
Baer, Joseph Winslow retired lawyer, mediator, arbitrator
Carr, Barbara Whitney foundation administrator
Cole, Kathleen Ann advertising agency executive, retired social worker
Fenninger, Leonard Davis medical educator, consultant
Grabow, Beverly learning disability therapist
Grossweiner, Leonard Irwin physicist, educator
Heise, Marilyn Beardsley public relations company executive
Hickey, John Thomas retired electronics company executive
Lifschultz, Phillip financial and tax consultant, accountant, lawyer
Milloy, Frank Joseph, Jr. surgeon
Nebenzahl, Kenneth rare book and map dealer, author
Niefeld, Jaye Sutter advertising executive
Silver, Ralph David distilling company director
Stewart, Charles Leslie lawyer
Webb, James Okrum, Jr. insurance company executive

### Glendale Heights
Pimental, Patricia Ann neuropsychologist, consulting company executive, author
Spearing, Karen Marie physical education educator, coach

### Glenview
Berkman, Michael G. lawyer, chemical consultant
Bible, Geoffrey Cyril tobacco company executive
Biedron, Theodore John newspaper executive
Bradtke, Philip Joseph architect
Corley, Jenny Lynd Wertheim elementary education educator
Coulson, Elizabeth Anne physical therapy educator
Cozad, James William retired oil company executive
Franklin, Lynne business communications consultant, writer
Freedman, Philip physician, educator
Gillis, Marvin Bob investor, consultant
Harris, Ronald David chemical engineer
Hudnut, Stewart Skinner manufacturing company executive, lawyer
Lacy, Herman Edgar management consultant
Levine, Edwin Burton retired classics educator
Mabley, Jack newspaper columnist, communications consultant
Mc Cormick, James Charles leasing and financial services company executive
Nichols, John Doane diversified manufacturing corporation executive
Panarese, William C. civil engineer
Ptak, Frank S. manufacturing executive
Rorig, Kurt Joachim chemist, research director
Russell, Henry George structural engineer
Savic, Stanley Dimitrius physicist
Sherman, Elaine C. gourmet foods company executive, educator
Smith, Harold B. manufacturing executive
Stern, Gerald Joseph advertising executive
Taylor, D(arl) Coder architect, engineer
Traudt, Mary B. elementary education educator
Van Zelst, Theodore William civil engineer, natural resource exploration company executive
Winett, Samuel Joseph manufacturing company executive
†Witting, Christian James, Jr. (Chris Witting) broadcast executive

### Godfrey
Harner, Linda Jeane allied health educator
King, Ordie Herbert, Jr. oral pathologist

### Golf
Fellingham, Warren Luther, Jr. retired banker

### Granite City
Humphrey, Owen Everett retired education administrator
Kaegel, Ray Martin real estate and insurance broker
Raczkiewicz, Paul Edward hospital administrator

### Grayslake
Devney, Anne Marie nursing educator

### Greenville
Junod, Daniel August podiatrist
Kelsey, John Walter lawyer, business owner
Stephens, William Richard college president emeritus

### Gurnee
Sommerlad, Robert Edward environmental research engineer
Southern, Robert Allen lawyer
Theis, Peter Frank engineering executive, inventor

### Hanover Park
Gale, Neil Jan finance company executive, computer consultant

### Harrisburg
Endsley, Jane Ruth nursing educator
Rushing, Philip Dale retired social worker

### Harvey
Dunn, Eraina Burke non-profit organization administrator, city official
Heilicser, Bernard Jay emergency physician
Jensen, Harold Leroy physician
Liem, Khian Kioe medical entomologist
Replogle, Robert L. cardiovascular and thoracic surgeon

### Hazel Crest
Roberts, Jo Ann Wooden school system administrator

### Hennepin
Bumgarner, James McNabb judge

### Highland Park
Axelrod, Leah Joy tour company executive
Bluefarb, Samuel Mitchell physician
Boruszak, James Martin insurance company executive
Charlson, David Harvey executive search company professional
Dolin, Albert Harry lawyer
Dubin, Arthur Detmers architect
Goldstein, Marsha Feder tour company executive
Grimmer, Margot dancer, choreographer, director
Haight, Edward Allen lawyer
Harris, Thomas L. public relations executive
Herbert, Edward Franklin public relations executive
Hirsch, Jay G. psychiatrist, educator
Hoffman, Sharon Lynn adult education educator
Johnson, Curtis Lee publisher, editor, writer
Karol, Nathaniel H. lawyer, consultant
Kravets, Barbara Zeitlin clinical nutritionist
Liebow, Phoebe Augusta Recht nursing educator, school nurse
Markman, Raymond Jerome marketing executive
Mehta, Zarin music festival administrator
Mordini, Marilyn Heuer physical education educator
Pattis, S. William publisher
Rudo, Milton retired manufacturing company executive, consultant
Rutenberg-Rosenberg, Sharon Leslie retired journalist
Saltzberg, Eugene Ernest physician, educator
Singer, Norman Sol food products executive, inventor
Slavick, Ann Lillian art educator, arts
Smith, Malcolm Norman manufacturing company executive
Uhlmann, Frederick Godfrey commodity and securities broker

### Highwood
Brown, Lawrence Haas banker

### Hillsboro
Herrmann, Jane Marie physical therapist
Mulch, Robert F., Jr. physician

### Hines
Best, William Robert physician, educator, university official
†Folk, Frank Anton surgeon, educator
Green, Joseph Barnet neurologist, educator
Nosek, Laura J. health facility administrator
Zvetina, James Raymond pulmonary physician

### Hinsdale
Ahmad, Essam Ali project manager
Anderson, Harry Frederick, Jr. architect
Beatty, Robert Alfred surgeon
Bennett, Margaret Airola lawyer
Bishop, Linda Dilene lawyer, small business owner
Bloom, Stephen Joel distribution company executive
Bottom, Dale Coyle management consultant
Brandt, John Ashworth fuel company executive
Burrows, Donald Albert college dean, artist, painter, writer
Butler, Margaret Kampschaefer retired computer scientist
Caron, Theresa Lynn White health facility administrator, medical educator
Cohen, Burton David franchising executive, lawyer
Dederick, Robert Gogan economist
Denton, Ray Douglas insurance company executive
Gallagher, John Pirie retired corporation executive
Kaminsky, Manfred Stephan physicist
Karplus, Henry Berthold physicist, research engineer
Kinney, Kenneth Parrish banker, retired
Lowenstine, Maurice Richard, Jr. retired steel executive
Paloyan, Edward physician, educator, researcher
Urbik, Jerome Anthony financial consultant
Whitney, William Elliot, Jr. advertising agency executive
Yastow, Shelby lawyer

### Hoffman Estates
Beitler, Stephen Seth retail company executive
Biggins, James J. fundraiser
Costello, John H., III business and marketing executive
Dennis, Steven Pellowe retail executive
Laubenstein, Vernon Alfred state agency administrator
Martinez, Arthur C. retail company executive
Pagonis, William Gus retired army general
Roach, William Russell training and education executive
Schulz, Michael John fire and explosion analyst, consultant
Starzynski, Christine Joy secondary educator
Weston, Roger Lance banker

### Homer
Gilhaus, Barbara Jean secondary education home economics educator

### Homewood
Bultema, Janice Kay mental health and skilled nursing administrator
Dietch, Henry Xerxes judge
MacMaster, Daniel Miller retired museum official
Parker, Eugene Newman retired physicist, educator
Reed, Michael A. agricultural products supplier
Schumacher, Gebhard Friederich Bernhard obstetrician-gynecologist

### Hudson
Mills, Frederick VanFleet art educator, watercolorist
Mills, Lois Jean company executive, former legislative aide, former education educator

### Huntley
Hollatz, Mike C. software engineer

### Indianhead Park
Frisque, Alvin Joseph retired chemical company executive

### Ingleside
Krentz, Eugene Leo university president, educator, minister
Propst, Catherine Lamb biotechnology company executive

### Island Lake
Benson, John Earl construction executive
O'Day, Kathleen Louise food products executive

### Itasca
Ayedun, Kehinde Peter information systems executive
Boler, John manufacturing executive
Bradshaw, Linda Jean English language educator
Floyd-Teniya, Kathleen business services executive
Garratt, Reginald George electronics executive
Kerr, Wayne Nelson data processing professional
Mockus, Joseph Frank electrical engineer

### Jacksonville
Findley, Paul former congressman, author, educator
Gallas, Martin Hans librarian
Pfau, Richard Anthony college president
Randall, Robert Quentin nursery executive
Scott, Fred Dacon surgeon
Welch, Rhea Jo special education educator

### Joliet
Barber, Andrew Bollons bank executive
Benfer, David William hospital administrator
Boyer, Andrew Ben lawyer
Caamano, Kathleen Ann Folz gifted education professional
Cochran, Mary Ann nurse educator
Gamble, Thomas Ellsworth academic administrator
Guzman, Matthew Lopez lawyer
Holmgren, Myron Roger social sciences educator
Imesch, Joseph Leopold bishop
Johnson, Mary Ann computer training vocational school owner
Johnston, James Robert library director
Kaffer, Roger Louis bishop
Layman, Dale Pierre medical educator, author, researcher
Lenard, George Dean lawyer
Lynch, Priscilla A. nursing educator, therapist
O'Connell, James Joseph port official
Ring, Alvin Manuel pathologist
Scott, Linda Ann assistant principal, elementary education educator
Starner, Barbara Kazmark marketing, advertising and export sales executive

### Kampsville
Schumann, Alice Melcher medical technologist, educator, sheep farmer

### Kankakee
Bowling, John C. academic administrator
Kanouse, Donald Lee wastewater treatment executive
Schroeder, David Harold health care facility executive
Van Fossan, Kathryn Ruth library director

### Kenilworth
Cook, Stanton R. media company executive
Corrigan, John Edward, Jr. banker, lawyer
Guelich, Robert Vernon retired management consultant
McKittrick, William Wood lawyer
Weiner, Joel David retired consumer packaged goods products executive

### Kildeer
Harrod, Scott consulting manufacturing executive
Muffoletto, Mary Lu retired school program director, consultant, editor

### La Grange
Kerr, Alexander Duncan, Jr. lawyer
Mehlenbacher, Dohn Harlow civil engineer, consultant
Norby, William Charles financial consultant

### La Grange Park
Brown, Helen Sauer fund raising executive
Carroll, Thomas John retired advertising executive
Stone, Gail Susan retired gifted, talented education educator

### Lafox
Seils, William George lawyer

### Lake Bluff
Anderson, Roger E. bank executive
Burns, Kenneth Jones, Jr. lawyer, consultant
Coutts, John Wallace chemist, educator
Felknor, Bruce Lester editorial consultant, writer
Fortuna, William Frank architectural engineer, architect
Fromm, Henry Gordon retired manufacturing and marketing executive
Hiestand, Sharon DiLorenzo real estate professional, architect
Kelly, Daniel John physician
Marino, William Francis telecommunications industry executive, consultant
Preschlack, John Edward management consultant
Schreiber, George Richard association executive, writer
Wacker, Frederick Glade, Jr. manufacturing company executive

### Lake Forest
Adelman, Pamela Bernice Kozoll education educator
Barney, Alan librarian
Bell, Charles Eugene, Jr. industrial engineer
Bermingham, John Scott associate dean
Bernthal, Harold George health care company executive
Bradley, Kim Alexandra sales and marketing specialist
Bransfield, Joan principal
Brown, Cameron insurance company consultant
Brown, Sharon Gail company executive, consultant
Carrier, Mark Anthony professional football player
Carter, Donald Patton advertising executive
Chieger, Kathryn Jean recreation company executive
Covington, George Morse lawyer
Cox, Bryan Keith professional football player
Deters, James Raymond retired manufacturing and services company executive
DuBose, Cornelius Bates educational director
Dur, Philip Alphonse automotive executive, retired naval officer
Eckert, Ralph John insurance company executive
Emerson, William Harry lawyer, retired, oil company executive
Everson, Leonard Charles lawyer
Ford, Donald James retired insurance company executive, consultant, lawyer
Frederick, Virginia Fiester state legislator
Goodrich, Maurice Keith retired business forms, systems and services company executive
Hamilton, Peter Bannerman lawyer, business executive
Hammar, Lester Everett health care manufacturing company executive
Hotchkiss, Eugene, III college president emeritus
Kenly, Granger Farwell marketing consultant, college official
Kozitka, Richard Eugene retired consumer products company executive
Krouse, Ann Wolk publishing executive
Lambert, John Boyd chemical engineer, consultant
Larsen, Peter N. leisure products manufacturing executive
Levy, Nelson Louis physician, scientist, corporate executive
McCaskey, Edward W. professional football team executive
McCaskey, Michael B. professional football team executive
Mc Cutcheon, John Tinney, Jr. journalist
Mohr, Roger John advertising agency executive
Murad, Ferid physician
O'Loughlin, John Kirby retired insurance executive
O'Mara, Thomas Patrick manufacturing company executive
Palmer, Ann Therese Darin lawyer
Peterson, Donald Matthew insurance company executive
Pope, John Charles airline company executive
Rand, Kathy Sue public relations executive
Reichert, Jack Frank manufacturing company executive
Reichert, Norman Vernon financial services consultant
Rentschler, William Henry publisher, editor, columnist, writer, corporate executive
Ross, Robert Evan bank executive
Salaam, Rashaan professional football player
Salter, Edwin Carroll physician
Schulze, Franz, Jr. art critic, educator
Sikorovsky, Eugene Frank retired lawyer
Smith, Wendy L. foundation executive
Strauss, Jeffrey Lewis healthcare executive
Swanton, Virginia Lee author, publisher, bookseller
Taylor, Barbara Ann educational consultant
Van Gorkom, Jerome William financial executive
Walter, Robert Irving chemistry educator, chemist
Wannstedt, David Raymond professional football team coach
Weston, Arthur Walter chemist, scientific and business executive
Wilbur, Richard Sloan physician, foundation executive
Woolford, Donnell professional football player

### Lake Villa
Anderson, Milton Andrew chemical executive

### Lake Zurich
Fachet, William F., Jr. insurance company executive
Schmitz, Shirley Gertrude marketing and sales executive
Schultz, Carl Herbert real estate management and development company executive
Teeters, Joseph Lee mathematician, consultant

### Lanark
Etter, David Pearson poet, editor

### Lansing
Guzak, Debra Ann special education educator
Hill, Philip retired lawyer

### Lemont
Chen, Shoei-Sheng mechanical engineer
Tomkins, Frank Sargent physicist
Urban, Patricia A. former elementary school educator
Williams, Jack Marvin research chemist

### Lewistown
Davis, William C., Jr. lawyer

### Libertyville
Beeler, Thomas Joseph lawyer, general management consultant
Burrows, Brian William research and development manufacturing executive
Kremkau, Paul principal
Krolopp, Rudolph William industrial designer, consultant
Price, Sandra Hoffman secondary school educator
Ranney, George Alfred lawyer, former steel company executive
Ransom, Margaret Palmquist public relations executive
Treanor, Helen June nursing administrator, geriatrics professional

### Lincoln
Wilson, Robert Allen religion educator

### Lincolnshire
Bayly, George V. manufacturing executive
Caballero, Mario Gustavo investment company executive
Carmichael, Leonard Lawrence manufacturing executive, accountant
Conklin, Mara Loraine public relations executive
DuFour, Richard P. school system administrator
Freund, Charles Gibson retired holding company executive
Giza, David Alan lawyer
Hughes, William Franklin, Jr. ophthalmologist, emeritus educator
Keyser, Richard Lee distribution company executive
Pappano, Robert Daniel financial company executive
Prasil, Linda Ann lawyer, writer
Rapp, Charles Warren computer scientist, researcher
Schauble, John Eugene physical education educator

### Lincolnwood
Astrin, Marvin H. retired broadcasting company executive
Lebedow, Aaron Louis consulting company executive
Whiteley, Sandra Marie librarian, editor

### Lisle
Birck, Michael John manufacturing company executive, electrical engineer
Davis, Gregory Thomas marine surveyor
Krehbiel, Frederick August, II electronics company executive
Myers, Daniel N. lawyer, association executive

Nykiel, Karen Ann *retirement facility administrator, religious studies instructor*
Psaltis, John Costas *retired manufacturing company executive*
Reum, W. Robert *manufacturing executive*
Sandrok, Richard William *lawyer*
Staab, Thomas Eugene *chemist*
Tyson, Kirk W. M. *management consultant*
Vora, Manu Kishandas *chemical engineer, quality consultant*

**Litchfield**
Deaton, Beverly Jean *nursing administrator, educator*
Jackson, David Alonzo *retired newspaper editor*
Talley, Brian Chandler *broadcasting executive*

**Lockport**
Musa, Mahmoud Nimir *psychiatry educator*

**Lombard**
Ahlstrom, Ronald Gustin *artist*
Bachop, William Earl, Jr. *retired anatomist, zoologist*
Beideman, Ronald Paul *chiropractor, college dean*
Branum, William Howell *engineering company executive*
Goodman, Elliott I(rvin) *lawyer*
Hudson, Samuel Campbell, Jr. *art educator, artist, sculptor*
Johnson, Dennis Lester *marketing consultant*
Kasprow, Barbara Anne *biomedical scientist, writer*
Sheehan, Dennis William, Sr. *lawyer*
Velardo, Joseph Thomas *molecular biology and endocrinology educator*
Williams, Ronald Boal, Jr. *financial consulting company executive, software designer, consultant*
Willis, Douglas Alan *lawyer*
Winterstein, James Fredrick *academic administrator*
Yeager, Phillip Charles *transportation company executive*

**London Mills**
McKinley Balfour, Stephanie Ann *learning resources director, librarian*

**Long Grove**
Ausman, Robert K. *surgeon, research executive*
Connor, James Richard *foundation administrator*
Conway, John K. *lawyer*
Liuzzi, Robert C. *chemical company executive*
Obert, Paul Richard *lawyer, manufacturing company executive*

**Loves Park**
Zaksheske, Mark Richard *treasurer*

**Lynwood**
Dyer-Dawson, Diane Faye *educational administrator*

**Macomb**
Anderson, Richard Vernon *ecology educator, researcher*
Brown, Spencer Hunter *historian*
Dexter, Donald Harvey *surgeon*
Goehner, Donna Marie *university dean*
Hallwas, John Edward *English language educator*
Hopper, Stephen Rodger *hospital administrator*
Maguire, Dave *real estate manager*
Spencer, Donald Spurgeon *historian, academic administrator*
Vos, Morris *foreign languages educator, language services consultant*
Walzer, Norman Charles *economics educator*
Witthuhn, Burton Orrin *university official*

**Madison**
Pope, Sarah Ann *elementary education educator*
Purdes, Alice Marie *adult education educator, retired*

**Marengo**
Franks, Herbert Hoover *lawyer*
Mrkvicka, Edward Francis, Jr. *financial writer, publisher, consultant*

**Marion**
†Crane, Hugh W. *railroad executive*
Livengood, Joanne Desler *healthcare administrator*

**Markham**
Ruffolo, Marilyn Claire *primary education educator*

**Marseilles**
Van Horn, John Kenneth *health physicist, consultant*

**Marshall**
Mitchell, George Trice *physician*

**Maryville**
Stark, Patricia Ann *psychologist, educator*

**Matteson**
Goyak, Elizabeth Fairbairn *public relations executive*

**Mattoon**
Horsley, Jack Everett *lawyer, author*
Phipps, John Randolph *retired army officer*
Sherline, Harold Albert *adult education professional*
Simonelli, Michael Tarquin *chemical engineer*

**Maywood**
Baldwin, Allan Oliver *information scientist, higher education executive*
Blumenthal, Harold Jay *microbiologist, educator*
Canning, John Rafton *urologist*
Celesia, Gastone Guglielmo *neurologist, neurophysiologist, researcher*
Cera, Lee Marie *veterinarian*
Ellington, Mildred L. *librarian*
Flores, Susan M. *health facility administrator*
Freeark, Robert James *surgeon, educator*
Greenlee, Herbert Breckenridge *surgeon, educator*
Hanin, Israel *pharmacologist, educator*
Hart, Cecil William Joseph *otolaryngologist, head and neck surgeon*
Light, Terry Richard *orthopedic hand surgeon*
Mason, George Robert *surgeon, educator*
Newman, Barry Marc *pediatric surgeon*
Picklemann, Jack R. *surgeon*
Slogoff, Stephen *anesthesiologist, educator*

**Mc Henry**
Duel, Ward Calvin *health care consultant*
Schultz, Richard Martin *electronics application engineering executive*

**Melrose Park**
Bernick, Howard Barry *manufacturing company executive*
Cernugel, William John *hair care and household products company financial executive*
Gass, Raymond William *lawyer, consumer products company executive*
Umans, Alvin Robert *manufacturing company executive*

**Mendota**
Hume, Horace Delbert *manufacturing company executive*

**Metamora**
Crow, Mary Jo Ann *elementary education educator*

**Midlothian**
Cagala, M. Therese *assistant principal*

**Milan**
Yeggy-Davis, Geraldine Marie *elementary reading and special education educator*

**Mokena**
Sangmeister, George Edward *lawyer, consultant, former congressman*

**Moline**
Arnell, Richard Anthony *radiologist*
Banas, John Stanley *obstetrician, gynecologist*
Becherer, Hans Walter *agricultural equipment manufacturing executive*
†Bradley, Walter James *emergency physician*
Carls, Judith Marie *physical education educator, golf coach*
Cottrell, Frank Stewart *lawyer, manufacturing executive*
Hanson, Robert Arthur *retired agricultural equipment executive*
Harrington, Roy Edwards *agricultural engineer, author*
Johnson, Mary Lou *lay worker*
Larson, Sandra Mae *nursing educator*
Malicki, Gregg Hillard *engineer*
Morrison, Deborah Jean *lawyer*
Schaeffer, Robert Ollie *elevator company executive*

**Monmouth**
Kirk, Sherwood *librarian*

**Montgomery**
Butcher, Ann Patrice *elementary school educator*

**Mooseheart**
Ross, Donald Hugh *fraternal organization executive*

**Morrison**
French, Raymond Douglas *insurance agent, realtor*

**Morton**
Corey, Judith Ann *educator*
Grisham, George Robert *mathematics educator*

**Morton Grove**
Farber, Isadore E. *psychologist, educator*
McKenna, Andrew James *paper distribution and printing company executive, baseball club executive*
Vega, Steve *poet*

**Mount Carmel**
Fornoff, Frank J(unior) *retired chemistry educator, consultant*
Rhine, John E. *lawyer*

**Mount Carroll**
Hayes, Randy Alan *family therapist*

**Mount Prospect**
Covey, Frank Michael, Jr. *lawyer, educator*
DeVol, Skip *entertainer*
Garvin, Paul Joseph, Jr. *toxicologist*
Kilian, Mark Kenneth *engineering executive*
Kuffel, Joan Elizabeth *school nurse*
Pulsifer, Edgar Darling *leasing service and sales executive*
Rogers, Richard F. *construction company executive, architect, engineer*
Scott, Norman Laurence *engineering consultant*
Smith, Ora Everett *corporate executive, lawyer*
Stamper, James M. *retired English language educator*
Zorko, Mark A. *financial executive*

**Mount Vernon**
Knight, Brenda Lee *quality engineer*
Withers, W. Russell, Jr. *broadcast executive*

**Mundelein**
Carr, Bonnie Jean *professional ice skater*
Meehan, Jean Marie Ross *occupational health and safety management consultant*
Mills, James Stephen *medical supply company executive*
Terris, William *publishing executive*

**Murphysboro**
Hall, James Robert *secondary education educator*
Miller, Donald Morton *physiology educator*

**Naperville**
Arzoumanidis, Gregory G. *chemist*
Balasi, Mark Geoffrey *architect*
Copley, Stephen Michael *materials science and engineering educator*
Cowlishaw, Mary Lou *state legislator*
Crawford, Raymond Maxwell, Jr. *nuclear engineer*
Florence, Ernest Estell, Jr. *special education educator*
Fritz, Roger Jay *management consultant*
Galvan, Mary Theresa *economics and business educator*
Grimley, Jeffrey Michael *dentist*
Hensley, Albert Lloyd, Jr. *research chemist, technical consultant*

Katai, Andrew Andras *chemical company executive*
L'Allier, James Joseph *educational multimedia company executive, instructional designer*
Landwehr, Arthur John *minister*
Larson, Mark Edward, Jr. *lawyer, educator, financial advisor*
Many, Robert Todd *telecommunications executive*
Modery, Richard Gillman *marketing and sales executive*
Pagano, Jon Alain *data processing consultant*
Penisten, Gary Dean *entrepreneur*
†Raccah, Dominique Marcelle *publisher*
Reuss, Robert Pershing *telecommunications executive, consultant*
Rosenmann, Daniel *physicist, educator*
Schaack, Philip Anthony *retired beverage company executive*
Schwab, Paul Josiah *psychiatrist, educator*
Sellers, Lucia Sunhee *marketing professional*
Shaw, Michael Allan *lawyer, mail order company executive*
Sherren, Anne Terry *chemistry educator*
Spiotta, Raymond Herman *editor*
Tan, Li-Su Lin *accountant, insurance executive*
Wake, Richard W. *food products executive*
Wake, Thomas G. *food products executive*
Wake, William S. *wholesale distribution executive*
Wellek, Richard Lee *business executive*
Wilde, Harold Richard *college president*

**Niles**
Bates, William Richie *electrical engineer*
Chertack, Melvin M. *internist*
†Herb, Marvin J. *food products executive*
Rastogi, Anil Kumar *medical device manufacturer executive*
Walker, A. Harris *lawyer, manufacturing executive, retired*

**Normal**
Bender, Paul Edward *lawyer*
Bolen, Charles Warren *university dean*
Brown, Francis Robert *mathematics educator*
Cooley, William Emory, Jr. *radiologist*
Edwards, Marianne *city clerk*
Hickrod, George Alan Karnes Wallis *educational administration educator*
Jelks, Edward Baker *archaeologist, educator*
Jones, Graham Alfred *mathematics educator*
Matsler, Franklin Giles *higher education educator*
Mc Knight, William Warren, Jr. *publisher*
Ohinouye, Tsuneo *automobile manufacturing executive*
Young, Robert Donald *physicist, educator*

**Norridge**
Karlin, Bernard Richard *retired educational administrator*

**North Aurora**
†Hillberg, Owen Eugene *pharmacist*

**North Chicago**
Beer, Alan Earl *physician, medical educator*
Chu, Alexander Hang-Torng *chemical engineer*
Ehrenpreis, Seymour *pharmacology educator*
Freese, Uwe Ernest *physician, educator*
Gall, Eric Papineau *physician, educator*
Hawkins, Richard Albert *medical educator, administrator*
Hui, Ho-Wah *pharmaceutical scientist*
Kim, Yoon Berm *immunologist, educator*
Kringel, John G. *health products company executive*
Kyncl, John Jaroslav *pharmacologist*
Loga, Sanda *physicist, educator*
Morris, Charles Elliot *neurologist*
Nair, Velayudhan *pharmacologist, medical educator*
Rogers, Eugene Jack *medical educator*
Rudy, David Robert *physician, educator*
Schlager, Seymour Irving *physician*
Schneider, Arthur Sanford *physician, educator*
Sierles, Frederick Stephen *psychiatrist, educator*
Taylor, Michael Alan *psychiatrist*

**North Riverside**
Sedlak, S(hirley) A(gnes) *freelance writer*

**Northbrook**
Afterman, Allan B. *accountant, educator, researcher, consultant*
Boyce, Donald Nelson *diversified industry executive*
Cerveny, Kathryn M. *educational administrator*
†Chappuie, Louis Edward *management consultant*
Choate, Jerry D. *insurance company executive*
Clarey, John Robert *executive search consultant*
Cohen, Seymour *lawyer*
Colton, Frank Benjamin *retired chemist*
Day, Emerson *physician*
Degen, Bernard John, II *association executive*
Demaree, David Harry *utilities executive*
Edelson, Ira J. *venture banker*
Elleman, Barbara *editor*
Harris, Neison *manufacturing company executive*
Hecker, Lawrence Harris *industrial hygienist*
Hill, Thomas Clarke, IX *accountant, systems specialist, entrepreneur*
Hirsch, Lawrence Leonard *physician, retired educator*
Kahn, Sandra S. *psychotherapist*
Kasperson, Richard Willet *retired pharmaceutical company executive*
Keehn, Silas *retired bank executive*
Klemens, Thomas Lloyd *editor*
Lapin, Harvey I. *lawyer*
Lenon, Richard Allen *chemical corporation executive*
Lever, Alvin *health science association administrator*
Levy, Arnold S(tuart) *real estate company executive*
Magad, Samuel *orchestra concertmaster, conductor*
Marshall, Irl Houston, Jr. *residential and commercial cleaning company executive*
McFadden, Joseph Patrick *insurance company executive*
McGinn, Mary Jovita *lawyer, insurance company executive*
Mc Laren, John Alexander *retired physician*
Michna, Andrea Stephanie *real estate agent and developer*
Moser, Larry Edward *marketing professional*
Newman, Lawrence William *financial executive*
Nordman, Richard Dennis *chemical company executive*
Pesmen, Sandra (Mrs. Harold William Pesmen) *editor*
Pike, Robert William *insurance company executive, lawyer*
Pinsof, Nathan *retired advertising executive*

Polsky, Michael Peter *mechanical engineer*
Rodriguez-Erdmann, Franz *physician*
Roehl, Kathleen Ann *financial executive*
Rudnick, Ellen Ava *health care executive*
Saunders, Kenneth D. *insurance company executive, consultant, arbitrator*
Sayatovic, Wayne Peter *manufacturing company executive*
Scanlon, Edward F. *surgeon, educator*
Sernett, Richard Patrick *lawyer*
Slattery, James Joseph (Joe Slattery) *actor*
Snader, Jack Ross *publishing company executive*
Stearns, Neele Edward, Jr. *diversified holding company executive*
Sudbrink, Jane Marie *sales and marketing executive*
Tucker, Frederick Thomas *electronics company executive*
Turner, Lee *travel company executive*
Wajer, Ronald Edward *management consultant*
Wallace, Harry Leland *lawyer*
Wasserman, Stephen Miles *communications manager*
Weber, Merrill Evan *lawyer, business executive*
Weil, John David *company executive*
Weinstein, Ira Phillip *advertising executive*
Wilson, Rita P. *insurance company executive*

**Northfield**
Adler, Robert *electronics engineer*
Bruns, Nicolaus, Jr. *retired agricultural chemicals company executive, lawyer*
Carlin, Donald Walter *retired food products executive, consultant*
Cartwright, Howard E(ugene) *retired association executive*
Cutler, Robert Porter *psychiatrist, psychoanalyst*
Fodrea, Carolyn Wrobel *educational researcher, publisher, consultant*
Giffin, Mary Elizabeth *psychiatrist, educator*
Glass, Henry Peter *industrial designer, interior architect, educator*
Hestad, Marsha Anne *educational administrator*
Hoopis, Harry Peter *insurance executive, entrepreneur*
Hotze, Charles Wayne *publisher, printer*
Hough, Richard T. *chemical company executive*
Otis, James, Jr. *architect*
Porter, Helen Viney (Mrs. Lewis M. Porter, Jr.) *lawyer*
Pratt, Murray Lester *information systems specialist*
Seaman, Jerome Francis *actuary*
Shabica, Charles Wright *geologist, earth science educator*
Smart, Jackson Wyman, Jr. *business executive*
Smeds, Edward William *retired food company executive*
Spear, Kathleen Kelly *lawyer*
Stepan, Frank Quinn *chemical company executive*
Tenuta, Jean Louise *sports reporter, medical technologist*

**Northlake**
Burkle, Ronald W. *food service executive*
Haack, Richard Wilson *retired police officer*
Jasper, Paul Tucker *food company executive*
Roti, Thomas David *lawyer, food service executive*

**O'Fallon**
Bjerkaas, Carlton Lee *technology services company executive*
Bradley, Thomas Michael *school system administrator*
Cecil, Dorcas Ann *property management executive*
Jenner, William Alexander *meteorologist, educator*

**Oak Brook**
Baar, John Greenfield, II *school educator*
Baker, Robert J(ohn) *hospital administrator*
Barnes, Karen Kay *lawyer*
Bower, Barbara Jean *nurse*
Cannon, Patrick Francis *public relations executive*
Christian, Joseph Ralph *physician*
DeLorey, John Alfred *printing company executive*
Dmowski, W. Paul *obstetrician, gynecologist*
Duerinck, Louis T. *retired railroad executive, attorney*
Goodwin, Daniel L. *real estate company executive*
Higgens, William John, III (Trey Higgens) *sales executive*
Holsinger, Wayne Townsend *apparel manufacturing executive*
Johnson, Grant Lester *lawyer, retired manufacturing company executive*
Kelly, Donald Philip *entrepreneur*
La Petina, Gary Michael *lawyer*
Morello, Josephine A. *microbiology and pathology educator*
Quinlan, Michael Robert *fast food franchise company executive*
Rensi, Edward Henry *restaurant chain executive*
Risk, Richard Robert *health care executive*
Schultz, Karen Rose *clinical social worker, author, publisher, speaker*
Stonich, Timothy Whitman *financial executive*
Wheeler, Paul James *real estate executive*

**Oak Brook Mall**
Buntrock, Dean Lewis *waste management company executive*
Getz, Herbert A. *lawyer*

**Oak Forest**
Hull, Charles William *special education educator*

**Oak Lawn**
†Earle, Richard H. *medical educator*
Gordon, Edward Earl *management consultant*
Laird, Jean Elouise Rydeski (Mrs. Jack E. Laird) *columnist, adult education educator*
Rathi, Manohar Lal *pediatrician, neonatologist*
Surma, Jane Ann *secondary education educator*

**Oak Park**
Adelman, William John *university labor and industrial relations educator*
Bowman, James Henry *writer*
Brackett, Edward Boone, III *orthopedic surgeon*
Cary, William Sterling *retired church executive*
Clark, John Peter, III *engineering consultant*
Davis, Christine Eurich *elementary education educator*
Devereux, Timothy Edward *advertising agency executive*
Douglas, Kenneth Jay *food products executive*
Edwards, Linda H. *public health professional*
Fiorella, Beverly Jean *medical technologist, educator*

Forst, Edmund Charles, Jr. communications educator, consultant
Goetz, Thomas systems engineer, consultant
Hallstrand, Sarah Laymon denomination executive
Koenig, Michael Edward Davison information science educator
Kotlowitz, Alex writer, journalist
Mason, Barbara E. Suggs educator
McNaney, Robert Trainor retired lawyer
Patricks, Edward J elementary education educator
Relwani, Nirmalkumar Murlidhar (Nick Relwani) mechanical engineer
Spartz, Alice Anne Lenore retired retail executive
Varchmin, Thomas Edward environmental health administrator
Venerable, Shirley Marie gifted education educator
Worley, Marvin George, Jr. architect

**Oakbrook Terrace**
Becker, Robert Jerome allergist, health care consultant
Brady, Catherine Rawson software company executive
Cason, Marilynn Jean technological institute official, lawyer
Ciccarone, Richard Anthony financial executive
Fenech, Joseph C. lawyer
Kohlstedt, James August lawyer
Rosenberg, Robert Brinkmann technology organization executive
Samet, Dean Henry safety engineer
Shalek, James Arthur, Jr. insurance agent, financial consultant
Tibble, Douglas Clair lawyer

**Oglesby**
Zeller, Francis Joseph dean

**Okawville**
Schmale, Allen Lee financial services company executive

**Olney**
Edwards, Ian Keith retired obstetrician, gynecologist

**Olympia Fields**
Haley, David Alan preferred provider organization executive
Kasimos, John Nicholas pathologist
Sprinkel, Beryl Wayne economist, consultant
Webster, Douglas Peter emergency physician

**Oregon**
Abbott, David Henry manufacturing company executive

**Orland Park**
Dyott, Richard Burnaby research engineering executive
English, Floyd Leroy telecommunications company executive
Gittelman, Marc Jeffrey manufacturing and financial executive
Knop, Charles Milton electrical engineer
Rasmason, Frederick C., III emergency nurse
Schultz, Barbara Marie insurance company executive

**Oswego**
Stephens, Steve Arnold real estate broker
Weilert, Ronald Lee data processing executive

**Palatine**
Benzies, Bonnie Jeanne clinical and industrial psychologist
Brod, Catherine Marie foundation administrator
Butler, John Musgrave business financial consultant
Claassen, W(alter) Marshall employment company executive
Fitzgerald, Gerald Francis retired banker
Fitzgerald, Peter Gosselin state senator, lawyer
Hetzel, William Gelal executive search consultant
Hull, Elizabeth Anne English language educator
Lindberg, Richard Carl editor, author, historian
Makowski, M. Paul electronics research executive
McMinn, Virginia Ann human resources consulting company executive
Medin, Lowell Ansgard management executive
Nagatoshi, Konrad R. anthropology educator, information systems specialist
Pohl, Frederik writer
Roe, Richard C. industry consultant, former home furnishings manufacturing executive

**Palos Heights**
Higgins, Francis Edward history educator
Matug, Alexander Peter lawyer
McInerney, John Vincent obstetrician and gynecologist
Nederhood, Joel H. church organization executive, minister, retired

**Palos Hills**
Crawley, Vernon Obadiah academic adminstrator

**Palos Park**
Lawler, Susan George elementary education educator
Nelson, Lawrence Evan business consultant
Nicholls, Richard Allen middle school social studies educator

**Paris**
Essinger, Susan Jane special education educator

**Park Forest**
Billig, Etel Jewel theater director, actress
Cribbs, Maureen Ann artist, educator
Goodrich, John Bernard lawyer, consultant
McDonald, Stanford Laurel clinical psychologist
McDonnell, Rosemary Cynthia social services administrator
Putnam, Robert E. writer, editor
Steinmetz, Jon David mental health executive, psychologist

**Park Ridge**
Bailey, Marianne Therese social service administrator
Bitran, Jacob David internist
Boe, Gerard Patrick health science association administrator, educator
Bridges, Jack Edgar electronics engineer
Carr, Gilbert Randle retired railroad executive
Curtis, Philip James lawyer
Fried, Walter hematologist, educator
Johnson, Kenneth Stuart publisher, printer
Kleckner, Dean Ralph trade association executive
Kukla, Robert John professional society administrator educator
Mangun, Clarke Wilson, Jr. public health physician, consultant
McCarthy, Michael Shawn health care company executive, lawyer
Peterson, Richard Elton publisher
Rojek, Kenneth J. health facility administrator, hospital
Rosenheim, Howard Harris management consultant
Tongue, William Walter economics and business consultant, educator emeritus
Weber, Philip Joseph retired manufacturing company executive
Weinberg, Milton, Jr. cardiovascular, thoracic surgeon

**Patoka**
Borgmann, Norma Lee school superintendent

**Pekin**
Bell, John Richard dentist
Frison, Rick agricultural company executive
Heiple, James Dee state supreme court chief justice
Herbstreith, Yvonne Mae primary education educator
Novak, Martha Lois elementary education educator

**Peoria**
Allen, Lyle Wallace lawyer
Atterbury, Robert Rennie, III lawyer
Ballowe, James English educator, author
Brazil, John Russell academic administrator
Browder, Charles Barclay sales executive
Bussone, Frank Joseph foundation executive, television broadcaster
Chamberlain, Joseph Miles retired astronomer, educator
Christison, William Henry, III lawyer
Cunningham, Raymond Leo research chemist
Dabney, Seth Mason, III lawyer
Dancey, Charles Lohman newspaper executive
Duncan, Royal Robert publisher
Eissfeldt, Theodore L. lawyer
Fites, Donald Vester tractor company executive
Francis, John Elbert university dean
Gross, Thomas Lester obstetrician, gynecologist, researcher
Hungate, Carolyn Wolf nursing administrator
Kenyon, Leslie Harrison architect
King, Jerry Wayne research chemist
Kroll, Dennis Edwards industrial engineering educator
Maloof, James A. mayor, real estate company executive
McCollum, Jean Hubble medical assistant
McConnell, John Thomas newspaper executive, publisher
McDade, Joe Billy federal judge
McMullen, David Wayne education educator
Meriden, Terry physician
Michael, Jonathan Edward insurance company executive
Mihm, Michael Martin federal judge
†Miller, Rick Frey emergency physician
Murphy, Sharon Margaret university official, educator
Myers, John Joseph bishop
Nielsen, Harald Christian retired chemist
Osborn, Terry Wayne biochemist, executive
Parsons, Donald James retired bishop
Polanin, W. Richard engineering educator
Ryan, Michael Beecher lawyer, former government official
†Saha, Badal Chandra biochemist
Slane, Henry Pindell retired broadcasting executive
Smith, Clyde R. counselor educator
Stine, Robert Howard pediatrician
Strodel, Robert Carl lawyer
Traina, Jeffrey Francis orthopedic surgeon
Viets, Robert O. utilities executive
Walker, Philip Chamberlain, II health care executive

**Peru**
Benning, Joseph Raymond principal
Kurtz, James Eugene freelance writer, minister
Lane, Patricia Peyton nursing consultant
Powell, Robert Charles marriage and family counselor

**Philo**
Martin, Earl Dean physical therapist

**Pinckneyville**
Cawvey, Clarence Eugene physician

**Plainfield**
Aldinger, Thomas Lee construction executive
Chakrabarti, Subrata Kumar marine research engineer
Chase, Maria Elaine Garoufalis publishing company executive
Glenn, Gerald Marvin marketing, engineering and construction executive
Schinderle, Robert Frank retired hospital administrator

**Pontiac**
Glennon, Charles Edward judge, lawyer

**Princeton**
Johnson, Watts Carey lawyer
Schultz, Robert Vernon entrepreneur

**Prospect Heights**
Byrne, Michael Joseph business executive
Clark, Donald Robert retired insurance company executive
Kosinski, Richard Andrew public relations executive
Leopold, Mark F. lawyer

**Quincy**
Adams, Beejay (Meredith Elisabeth Jane J. Adams) sales executive
Liebig, Richard Arthur retired manufacturing company executive
Points, Roy Wilson municipal official
Taylor, Judith Caroline entrepreneur
Toal, James Francis academic administrator
Tyer, Travis Earl library consultant

**River Forest**
Hamper, Robert Joseph marketing executive
Li, Tze-chung lawyer, educator
Lund, Sister Candida college chancellor
Notaro, Michael R. data processing and computer service executive
Puthenveetil, Jos Anthony laboratory executive
Rimbach, Evangeline Lois retired music educator
Sloan, Jeanette Pasin artist
Sullivan, Peggy (Anne) librarian
Wanamaker, Robert Joseph advertising company executive
White, Philip Butler artist
Wirsching, Charles Philipp, Jr. brokerage house executive, investor

**River Grove**
Gardner, Sandi J. biology educator
Hill-Hulslander, Jacquelyne L. nursing educator and consultant
Litzsinger, Paul Richard publishing company executive
Stein, Thomas Henry social science educator
ZeLeVas, Sharon Rose art history educator, lawyer

**Riverdale**
Hoekwater, James Warren treasurer
Szabo, Joseph Clark labor lobbyist

**Riverside**
Dengler, Robert Anthony professional association executive
Gwinn, Robert P. publishing executive
Howlett, Carolyn Svrluga art educator
Perkins, William H., Jr. finance company executive

**Riverwoods**
Douglas, Bruce Lee oral and maxillofacial surgeon, educator, health consultant, gerontology consultant
Kirby, Emily Baruch psychologist, writer
Wieseneck, Robert L. business executive

**Robinson**
Wolfe, Ellen Darlene school librarian, elementary school educator

**Rochelle**
Blomquist-Stanbery, Ruth Ellen computer services company owner, elementary education educator
†Stanbery, Ruth Blomquist computer company executive, educator

**Rochester**
Petterchak, Janice A. researcher, writer

**Rock Falls**
Bippus, David Paul manufacturing company executive

**Rock Island**
Bergendoff, Conrad John Immanuel clergyman
Brauch, Merry Ruth Moore gifted education consultant
Cheney, Thomas Ward insurance company executive
Forlini, Frank John, Jr. cardiologist
Hammer, William Roy paleontologist, educator
Horstmann, James Douglas college official
Kruse, Rosalee Evelyn accountant, auditor
Lardner, Henry Petersen (Peter Lardner) insurance company executive
Osborn, David Lee engineer
Sundelius, Harold W. geology educator
Telleen, John Martin retired judge
Thompson, Joyce Elizabeth arts management educator
Tredway, Thomas college president
Wallace, Franklin Sherwood lawyer
Whitmore, Charles Horace utility executive, lawyer, management consultant

**Rockford**
Albert, Christine Lynnette accountant
Anderson, LaVerne Eric lawyer
Barrick, William Henry lawyer
Cadigan, Elise social worker
Channick, Herbert S. lawyer, arbitrator, mediator
Chitwood, Julius Richard librarian
DeLuca, August Frank, Jr. financial executive
Doran, Thomas George bishop
Duck, Vaughn Michael software company executive
Eliason, Jon Tate electrical engineer
Frakes, James Terry physician, gastroenterologist, educator
Frang, Jerry Lee mathematics educator
Gann, Gregory Charles manufacturing company executive
Gloyd, Lawrence Eugene diversified manufacturing company executive
Gossell, Terry Rae advertising agency executive, small business owner
Gurnitz, Robert Ned steel industry company executive
Hasley, Ronald K. bishop
Heerens, Robert Edward physician
Hornby, Robert Ray mechanical engineer
Horst, Bruce Everett manufacturing company executive
Hoshaw, Lloyd historian, educator
Howard, John Addison former college president, institute executive
Johnson, Thomas Stuart lawyer
Kimball, Donald Robert food company executive
Larsen, Steven orchestra conductor
Liebovich, Samuel David warehouse executive
Lukac, George Joseph fundraising executive
Marelli, Sister M. Anthony secondary school principal
Maysent, Harold Wayne hospital administrator
O'Donnell, William David construction firm executive
Olson, Stanley William physician, educator, medical school dean
Rauch, Janet Melodie elementary school educator
Reinhard, Philip G. federal judge
Reno, Roger lawyer
Robinson, Donald Peter musician, retired electrical engineer
Rosenfeld, Joel Charles librarian
Schilling, Richard M. lawyer, corporate executive
Schmerse, Traci Jo financial services company executive
Steele, Carl Lavern academic administrator
Steffan, Wallace Allan entomologist, educator
Vincenti-Brown, Crispin Rufus William engineering executive
Walhout, Justine Simon chemistry educator
Weissbard, David Raymond minister
Whitsell, Doris Benner retired educator
Wilke, Duane Andrew educator

**Rolling Meadows**
Brennan, Charles Martin, III construction company executive
Cain, R. Wayne sales, finance and leasing company executive
Miles, Frank Charles retired newspaper executive
Moore, William B. lawyer
Saporta, Jack psychologist, educator

**Romeoville**
DePaul, John Phil construction company executive, firefighter
Houlihan, James William criminal justice educator
Lifka, Mary Lauranne history educator

**Roselle**
Fry, Evelyn Leona clinical social worker
Gomopoulos, Mary elementary school educator
Kiel, William Frederick architectural specifications consultant
Lueder, Dianne Carol library director

**Rosemont**
Bacevicius, John Anthony, V (John Bace) communications executive
Burkhardt, Edward Arnold transportation company executive
Currie, Earl James transportation company executive
Good, William Allen professional society executive
Isenberg, Howard Lee manufacturing company executive
Macioch, James Edward investment consultant, financial planner
Moster, Mary Clare public relations executive
Myers, Michael Charles marketing executive
Zorio, John William financial services executive

**Round Lake**
Breillatt, Julian Paul, Jr. biochemist, biomedical engineer
Johnston, William David health care company executive

**S Barrington**
Kissane, Sharon Florence writer, consultant

**Saint Charles**
Alfini, James Joseph dean, educator, lawyer
Felt, Jennifer Ruth elementary physical education educator
Libka, Robert John educational director, consultant
McCartney, Charles Price retired obstetrician-gynecologist
†McGuire, John W., Sr. advertising executive, marketing professional, author
Mc Kay, Thomas, Jr. lawyer
Stone, John McWilliams, Jr. electronics executive
Urhausen, James Nicholas real estate developer, construction executive
Zinn, Marcie Lynn music educator, pianist
Zito, James Anthony retired railroad company executive

**Saint Joseph**
McDade, Linna Springer retired academic program administrator

**Savoy**
Bosworth, Douglas LeRoy international company executive, educator
Ridgway, Marcella Davies veterinarian

**Scales Mound**
Lieberman, Archie photographer, writer

**Schaumburg**
Adrianopoli, Barbara Catherine librarian
Balasa, Mark Edward investment consultant
Boston, Leona organization executive
Buchanan, Richard Kent electronics company executive
Colvard, Michael David periodontist, oral medicine and laser surgery specialist
Edmunds, Jane Clara communications consultant
Fitzpatrick, John Henry insurance company executive
Gardner, Caryn Sue lawyer
Griffin, Sheila MB electronics marketing excutive
Hill, Raymond Joseph packaging company executive
Hlousek, Joyce B(ernadette) school system administrator
Kennedy, Patrick Michael fire analyst
Kitt, Walter psychiatrist
Meltzer, Brian lawyer
Pandak, Carol Ann fraternal organization administrator
Parker, Norman W. scientist
Piecuch, Pamela Gayle systems operator/coordinator
Roderick, William Rodney academic administrator
Smith-Pierce, Patricia A. speech professional
Stephens, Norval Blair, Jr. marketing consultant
Tompson, Marian Leonard professional society administrator
Tooker, Gary Lamarr electronics company executive
Weisz, William Julius electronics company executive
Wyslotsky, Ihor engineering company executive

**Schiller Park**
†Canella, Joseph M. preventive medicine physician
Ring, Alice Ruth Bishop physician

**Scott AFB**
†Andrews, James E. career officer

**Shelbyville**
Storm, Sandy Lamm secondary education educator

**Skokie**
Alexander, John Charles pharmaceutical company executive, physician
Bakalar, John Stephen printing and publishing company executive
Bellows, Randall Trueblood ophthalmologist, educator
Caldwell, Wiley North retired distribution company executive

Corley, William Gene *engineering research executive*
Filler, Robert *chemist educator*
Forman, Linda Helaine *accountant*
Gleason, John Patrick, Jr. *trade association executive*
Green, David *manufacturing company executive*
Hedien, Wayne Evans *retired insurance company executive*
Herting, Robert Leslie *pharmaceutical executive*
Manos, John *editor-in-chief*
McNally, Andrew, IV *publishing executive*
Olwin, John Hurst *surgeon*
Salit, Gary *lawyer*
Siegal, Burton Lee *product designer, consultant, inventor*
Siegal, Rita Goran *engineering company executive*
Steele, Kurt D. *publishing company executive*
Vandenbroucke, Russell James *theatre director*
White, William James *information management and services company executive*

## Smithfield
Corsaw, Ardith *geriatrics nurse, administrator*

## South Beloit
McDonald, Susan F. *business executive, county official*

## South Elgin
Burdett, George Craig *plastics industry executive*

## Springfield
Bergschneider, David Philip *defender*
Blackman, Jeanne A. *policy advisor*
Budinger, Charles Jude *state agency insurance analyst*
Campbell, Kathleen Charlotte Murphey *audiology educator and researcher*
Carroll, Howard William *state senator, lawyer*
Chen, Eden Hsien-chang *engineering consultant*
Cowles, Ernest Lee *academic administrator, educator, consultant, researcher*
Craig, John Charles *educational researcher, consultant*
Cullen, Mark Kenneth *lawyer*
Currie, Barbara Flynn *state legislator*
Davis, George Cullom *historian*
Dodd, Robert Bruce *physician, educator*
Dodge, James William *lawyer, educator*
Edgar, Jim *governor*
Ellis, Michael Eugene *documentary film producer, writer, director*
Feldman, Bruce Alan *psychiatrist*
Ferguson, Mark Harmon *banker, lawyer*
Fischoff, Ephraim *humanities educator, sociologist, social worker*
Fleck, Gabriel Alton *electrical engineer*
Frank, Stuart *cardiologist*
Gallina, Charles Onofrio *nuclear scientist*
Geo-Karis, Adeline Jay *state senator*
Hahin, Christopher *metallurgical engineer, corrosion engineer*
Hallmark, Donald Parker *museum director*
Hanley, William Stanford *lawyer*
Hanson, Walter Edmund *consulting civil engineer*
Herriford, Robert Levi, Sr. *army officer*
Hines, Daisy Marie *writer*
Holland, John Madison *family practice physician*
Hughes, Ann *state legislator*
Hulin, Frances C. *prosecutor*
Kerr, Gary Enrico *lawyer, educator*
Khardori, Nancy *infectious disease specialist*
Kustra, Robert W. (Bob Kustra) *state official, educator*
Kwon, Ojoung *computer scientist, educator, consultant*
Larison, Brenda Irene *law librarian*
Lessen, Larry Lee *federal judge*
Lohman, Walter Rearick *banker*
Lucore, Charles Lee *cardiologist*
Lynn, Naomi B. *academic administrator*
Lyons, J. Rolland *civil engineer*
Madigan, Michael Joseph *state legislator*
Mathewson, Mark Stuart *lawyer, editor*
Mc Millan, R(obert) Bruce *museum executive, anthropologist*
Miller, Benjamin K. *state supreme court justice*
Mills, Jon K. *psychologist, educator, philosopher*
Mills, Richard Henry *federal judge*
Mogerman, Susan *state agency administrator*
Moore, Andrea S. *state legislator*
Morse, Saul Julian *lawyer*
Moy, Richard Henry *academic dean, educator*
Mulligan, Rosemary Elizabeth *paralegal*
Munyer, Edward A. *zoologist, museum administrator*
Myers, Phillip Ward *otolaryngologist*
Nanavati, Grace Luttrell *dancer, choreographer, instructor*
Narmont, John Stephen *lawyer*
Newtson, Richard Evan *stockbroker*
Oxtoby, Robert Boynton *lawyer*
Penning, Patricia Jean *elementary education educator*
Philip, James (Pate Philip) *state senator*
Phillips, John Robert *college administrator, political scientist*
Poorman, Robert Lewis *education educator, consultant, academic administrator*
Puckett, Carlissa Roseann *non-profit association executive*
Rabinovich, Sergio *physician, educator*
Reed, Robert Phillip *lawyer*
Rockey, Paul Henry *physician, medical educator, university official*
Ronen, Carol *state legislator*
Rowe, Max L. *lawyer, corporate executive, management consultant, judge*
Ryan, Daniel Leo *bishop*
Ryan, James E. *attorney general*
Schmidt, Mark James *state public health official*
Schroeder, Joyce Katherine *state agency administrator, research analyst*
Severns, Penny L. *state legislator*
Shim, Sang Koo *state mental health official*
Stamp, Zachary Layne *state agency administrator*
Stroh, Raymond Eugene *personnel executive*
Sumner, David Spurgeon *surgery educator*
Temple, Wayne Calhoun *historian*
Travis, Lawrence Allan *accountant*
Van Meter, Abram DeBois *lawyer, retired banker*
Wehrle, Leroy Snyder *economist, educator*
Whitney, John Freeman, Jr. *political science educator*
Wood, Harlington, Jr. *federal judge*
Yaffe, Stuart Allen *physician*
Zaricznyj, Basilius *orthopedic surgeon*
Zook, Elvin Glenn *plastic surgeon, educator*

## Sterling
Albrecht, Beverly Jean *special education educator*
Durkin, Cheryl Jean *nurse*
Knight, Herbert Borwell *manufacturing company executive*
Moran, Joan Jensen *physical education and health educator*
von Bergen Wessels, Pennie Lea *state legislator*

## Streamwood
Samuelson, Rita Michelle *speech language pathologist*

## Streator
Harrison, Frank Joseph *lawyer*
Williams, Jeffry Cephas *business executive*

## Sullivan
Holder, Lonnie Edward *engineering administrator, design engineer*

## Summit Argo
Abramowicz, Alfred L. *retired bishop*

## Sutton
Babb, Michael Paul *engineering magazine editor*

## Sycamore
Grace, John Eugene *business forms company executive*
Johnson, Yvonne Amalia *elementary education educator, science consultant*
Young, Arthur Price *librarian, educator*

## Taylorville
Gardner, Jerry Dean *dentist, military officer*

## Thornton
Braico, Carmella Elizabeth Lofrano *clergy member*

## Tinley Park
Prouty, Jill *psychodramatist, psychotherapist*
Vogt, John Henry *corporate executive*

## Toledo
Icenogle, Evelyn Sue *emergency room nurse*
Prather, William C. III *lawyer, writer*

## Tonica
Ryan, Howard Chris *retired state supreme court justice*

## Tuscola
Kirchhoff, Michael Kent *economic development executive*

## Union
Perlick, Richard Allan *steel company executive*

## University Park
Leftwich, Robert Eugene *oncological nursing educator*
McClellan, Larry Allen *educator, writer*
Wentz, Walter John *health administration educator*

## Urbana
Addy, Alva Leroy *mechanical engineer*
Aiken, Michael Thomas *academic administrator*
Albrecht, Felix Robert *mathematics educator*
Aldridge, Alfred Owen *English language educator*
Alkire, Richard Collin *chemical engineering educator*
Andersen, Kenneth Eldon *speech communication educator, consultant*
Antonsen, Elmer Harold *Germanic languages and literature educator*
Aref, Hassan *fluid mechanics educator*
Arnstein, Walter Leonard *historian, educator*
Austin, Jean Philippe *medical educator, radiologist*
Axford, Roy Arthur *nuclear engineering educator*
Baer, Werner *economist, educator*
Baker, David Hiram *nutritionist, nutrition educator*
Baker, Harold Albert *federal judge*
Balbach, Stanley Byron *lawyer*
Banwart, Wayne Lee *agronomy, environmental science educator*
Basar, Tamer *electrical engineering educator*
Bateman, John Jay *classics educator*
Bateman, Paul Trevier *mathematician, educator*
Baym, Nina *English educator*
Beak, Peter Andrew *chemistry educator*
Beck, Paul Adams *metallurgist, educator*
Becker, Donald Eugene *animal science educator*
Bedford, Norton Moore *accounting educator*
Benekohal, Rahim Farahnak *civil engineering educator, researcher, consultant*
Berenbaum, May Roberta *entomology educator*
Bergeron, Clifton George *ceramic engineer, educator*
Birnbaum, Howard Kent *materials science educator*
Blahut, Richard Edward *electrical and computer engineering educator*
Blair, Lachlan Ferguson *urban planner, educator*
Bloomfield, Daniel Kermit *college dean, physician*
Boardman, Eunice *music educator*
Brichford, Maynard Jay *archivist*
Broudy, Harry Samuel *retired philosophy educator*
Brown, Theodore Lawrence *chemistry educator*
Brün, Herbert *composer*
Bruner, Edward M. *anthropology educator*
Bryant, Marvin Pierce *bacteriologist, microbiologist, educator*
Buetow, Dennis Edward *physiology educator*
Burger, Ambrose William *agronomy educator*
Burger, Robert Harold *librarian*
Burkholder, Donald Lyman *mathematician, educator*
Carmen, Ira Harris *political scientist, educator*
Carroll, Robert Wayne *mathematics educator*
Chao, Bei Tse *mechanical engineering educator*
Chato, John Clark *mechanical and bioengineering educator*
Cheng, Chin-Chuan *linguistics educator*
Cheryan, Munir *agricultural studies educator, biochemical engineering educator*
Choldin, Marianna Tax *librarian, educator*
Chow, Poo *wood technologist, scientist*
Churchill, Mair Elisa Annabelle *medical educator*
Clausing, Arthur M. *mechanical engineering educator*
Cole, Michael Allen *microbiologist, educator*
Coleman, Paul Dare *electrical engineering educator*
Conry, Thomas Francis *mechanical engineering educator, consultant*

Crang, Richard Francis Earl *plant and cell biologist, research center administrator*
Crofts, Antony Richard *biophysics educator*
Cunningham, Clark Edward *anthropology educator*
Cusano, Cristino *mechanical engineer, educator*
Davidson, Fred *education educator*
Davis, Elisabeth Bachman *librarian, library administration educator*
Davis, Wayne Joseph *engineering educator*
Dawn, Clarence Ernest *history educator*
Debrunner, Peter George *physics educator*
Dobrovolny, Jerry Stanley *engineering educator*
Doob, Joseph Leo *mathematician, educator*
Dovring, Folke *land economics educator, consultant*
Drickamer, Harry George *retired chemistry educator*
Due, Jean Margaret *agricultural economist, educator*
Dunn, Floyd *biophysicist, bioengineer, educator*
Dziuk, Philip John *animal scientist educator*
Eades, J. A. *electron microscopist, physicist, consultant*
Edelsbrunner, Herbert *computer scientist, mathematician*
Eden, James Gary *electrical engineering and physics educator, researcher*
Elyn, Mark *opera singer, educator*
Endress, Anton G. *horticulturist, educator*
Faulkner, Larry Ray *chemistry educator, academic officer*
Feng, Albert Shih-Hung *science educator, researcher*
Fitz-Gerald, Roger Miller *lawyer*
Forbes, Richard Mather *biochemistry educator*
Fossum, Robert Merle *mathematician, educator*
Frazzetta, Thomas H. *evolutionary biologist, functional morphologist, educator*
Friedman, Stanley *insect physiologist, educator*
Gabriel, Michael *psychology educator*
Gaddy, Oscar Lee *electrical engineering educator*
Garrigus, Upson Stanley *animal science and international agriculture educator*
Giertz, J. Fred *economics educator*
Giles, Eugene *anthropology educator*
Ginsberg, Donald Maurice *physicist, educator*
Goering, Carroll E. *agricultural engineering educator*
Goldberg, Samuel Irving *mathematics educator*
Goldwasser, Edwin Leo *physicist*
Gove, Samuel Kimball *political science educator*
Govindjee *biophysics and biology educator*
Gray, John Walker *mathematician, educator*
Greene, Laura Helen *physicist*
Greenwold, Warren Eldon *retired physician, medical educator*
Gruebele, Martin *chemistry educator*
Gutowsky, Herbert Sander *chemistry educator*
Hager, Lowell Paul *biochemistry educator*
Haile, H. G. *German language and literature educator*
Hall, William Joel *civil engineer, educator*
Hannon, Bruce Michael *engineer, educator*
Hanratty, Thomas Joseph *chemical engineer, educator*
Harper, James Eugene *plant physiologist*
Hay, Richard Le Roy *geology educator*
Hedlund, Ronald *baritone*
Heichel, Gary Harold *crop sciences educator*
Helle, Steven James *journalism educator, lawyer*
Hendrick, George *English language educator*
Henson, C. Ward *mathematician, educator*
Herrin, Moreland *civil engineering educator, consultant*
Hess, Karl *electrical and computer engineering educator*
Hill, Lowell Dean *agricultural marketing educator*
Hobgood, Burnet McLean *theater educator*
Hoeft, Robert Gene *agriculture educator*
Hoffmeister, Donald Frederick *zoology educator*
Holonyak, Nick, Jr. *electrical engineering educator*
Holt, Donald A. *university administrator, agronomist, consultant, researcher*
Horwitz, Alan Fredrick *cell and molecular biology educator and researcher*
Huang, Thomas Shi-Tao *electrical engineering educator, researcher*
Hurt, James Riggins *English language educator*
Hymowitz, Theodore *plant geneticist, educator*
Iben, Icko, Jr. *astrophysicist, educator*
Isaacson, Richard Evan *microbiologist*
Jackson, Edwin Atlee *physicist, educator*
Jacobson, Howard *classics educator*
Jakle, John Allais *geography educator*
Jenkins, William Kenneth *electrical engineering educator*
Jerrard, Richard Patterson *mathematics educator*
Jockusch, Carl Groos, Jr. *mathematics educator*
Jones, Benjamin Angus, Jr. *retired agricultural engineering educator, administrator*
Kachru, Braj Behari *linguist*
Kachru, Yamuna *linguist*
Kang, Sung-Mo (Steve Kang) *electrical engineering educator*
Kaufmann, Urlin Milo *English literature educator*
Kesler, Clyde Ervin *engineering educator*
Kirkpatrick, R(obert) James *geology educator*
Klein, Miles Vincent *physics educator*
Knake, Ellery Louis *weed science educator*
Knight, Frank Bardsley *mathematics educator*
Kocheril, Abraham George *physician, educator*
Kolodziej, Edward Albert *political scientist, educator*
Krock, Curtis Josselyn *pulmonologist*
Kumar, Panganamala Ramana *electrical and computer engineering educator*
Kushner, Mark Jay *physicist educator*
Langenheim, Ralph Louis, Jr. *geology educator*
Lauterbur, Paul C(hristian) *chemistry educator*
Lazarus, David *physicist, educator*
Leuthold, Raymond Martin *agricultural economics educator*
Lieberman, Laurence *poet, educator*
Linowes, David Francis *political economist, educator, corporate executive*
Littlewood, Thomas Benjamin *retired journalism educator*
Liu, Chung Laung *computer engineer, educator*
Lo, Kwok-Yung *astronomer*
Lodge, James Robert *dairy science educator*
Mainous, Bruce Hale *foreign language educator*
Makri, Nancy *chemistry educator*
Manning, Sylvia *English studies educator*
Mapother, Dillon Edward *physicist, university official*
Marcovich, Miroslav *classics educator*
Maxwell, William Hall Christie *civil engineering educator*
May, Walter Grant *chemical engineer*
Mayer, Robert Wallace *emeritus finance educator*
Mayes, Paul Eugene *engineering educator, technical consultant*
McColley, Robert McNair *history educator*

Mc Conkie, George Wilson *education educator*
Mc Glamery, Marshal Dean *agronomy, weed science educator*
McGlathery, James Melville *foreign language educator*
Melby, John B. *composer, educator*
Meyer, Richard Charles *microbiologist*
Mihalas, Dimitri Manuel *astronomer, educator*
Miley, George Hunter *nuclear engineering educator*
Miller, Robert Earl *engineer, educator*
Moore, David Robert *lawyer*
Myers, Miles A. *educational association administrator*
Nanney, David Ledbetter *genetics educator*
Nardulli, Peter F. *political science educator*
Nelson, Ralph Alfred *physician*
Nettl, Bruno *anthropology and musicology educator*
Newman, John Kevin *classics educator*
O'Brien, Nancy Patricia *librarian, educator*
O'Morchoe, Charles Christopher Creagh *administrator, anatomical sciences educator*
O'Morchoe, Patricia Jean *pathologist, educator*
Pai, Anantha Mangalore *electrical engineering educator, consultant*
Parker, Alan John *veterinary neurologist, educator, researcher*
Peterson, Theodore Bernard *retired journalism educator*
Poss, Jeffery Scott *architect, educator*
Prosser, C. Ladd *physiology educator, researcher*
Prussing, Laurel Lunt *state official, economist*
Rao, Nannapaneni Narayana *electrical engineer*
Rebeiz, Constantin A. *plant physiology educator*
Replinger, John Gordon *architect, retired educator*
Resek, Robert William *economist*
Rich, Robert F. *political sciences educator, academic administrator*
Ricketts, Gary Eugene *animal scientist*
Roberts, Glyn Caerwyn *psychology educator*
Rogers, Paula Ann *secondary school educator*
Rotzoll, Kim Brewer *advertising and communications educator*
Rowland, Theodore Justin *physicist, educator*
Salamon, Myron Ben *physicist, educator*
Satterthwaite, Cameron B. *physics educator*
Scanlan, Richard Thomas *classics educator*
Schacht, Richard Lawrence *philosopher, educator*
Schmidt, Stephen Christopher *agricultural economist, educator*
Schweizer, Kenneth Steven *physics educator*
Seigler, David Stanley *botanist, chemist, educator*
Shtohryn, Dmytro Michael *librarian, educator*
Shuman, R(obert) Baird *academic program director, writer, English language educator, educational consultant*
Shurtleff, Malcolm C. *plant pathologist, consultant, educator, extension specialist*
Siedler, Arthur James *nutrition and food science educator*
Siess, Chester Paul *civil engineering educator*
Simon, Jack Aaron *geologist, former state official*
Sinclair, James Burton *plant pathology educator, consultant*
Small, Erwin *veterinarian, educator*
Snyder, Lewis Emil *astrophysicist*
Socie, Darrell Frederick *mechanical engineering educator*
Solberg, Winton Udell *history educator*
Soo, Shao Lee *mechanical engineer, educator*
Spence, Mary Lee *historian*
Spitze, Robert George Frederick *agricultural economics educator*
Splittstoesser, Walter Emil *plant physiologist*
Stallmeyer, James Edward *engineer, educator*
Stillinger, Jack Clifford *English educator*
Stout, Glenn Emanuel *retired science administrator*
Sturtevant, William T. *fundraising executive, consultant*
Suslick, Kenneth Sanders *chemistry educator*
Suzuki, Michio *mathematics educator*
Swenson, George Warner, Jr. *electronics engineer, radio astronomer, educator*
Switzer, Robert Lee *biochemistry educator*
Talbot, Emile Joseph *French language educator*
Thompson, Margaret M. *physical education educator*
Tondeur, Philippe Maurice *mathematician, educator*
Trick, Timothy Noel *electrical and computer engineering educator, researcher*
Trigger, Kenneth James *manufacturing engineering educator*
Visek, Willard James *nutritionist, animal scientist, physician, educator*
Voss, Edward William, Jr. *immunologist, educator*
Waldbauer, Gilbert Peter *entomologist, educator*
Watson, Paula D. *library administrator*
Watts, Emily Stipes *English language educator*
Wedgeworth, Robert *dean, university librarian, former association executive*
Weir, Morton Webster *retired academic administrator, educator*
Welch, William Ben *emergency physician*
Wert, Charles Allen *metallurgical and mining engineering educator*
Westwater, James William *chemical engineering educator*
White, W(illiam) Arthur *geologist*
Whitt, Gregory Sidney *molecular phylogenetics, evolution educator*
Williams, Martha Ethelyn *information science educator*
Wirt, Frederick Marshall *political scientist*
Wisniewski, Thomas Joseph *music educator*
Wolfe, Ralph Stoner *microbiology educator*
Wolynes, Peter Guy *chemistry researcher, educator*
Yoerger, Roger Raymond *agricultural engineer, educator*
Yu, George Tzuchiao *political science educator*

## Vernon Hills
Ferkenhoff, Robert J. *retail executive*
Jensen, Rolf H. *fire protection engineer, company executive*
Michalik, John James *legal educational association executive*
Powers, Anthony Richard, Jr. *educational sales professional*
Strother, Jay D. *legal editor*

## Villa Grove
Moss Bower, Phylis Dawn *medical researcher*

## Villa Park
Miczuga, Mark Norbert *metal products executive*
Peterson, Elaine Grace *technology director*
Smith, Barbara Ann *gifted education coordinator*
Tang, George Chickchee *financial consultant*
Taylor, Ronald Lee *school administrator*

### Warrenville
McGurn, George William *lawyer*

### Washington
Hallinan, John Cornelius *mechanical engineering consultant*
McKinney-Keller, Margaret Frances *retired special education educator*

### Waukegan
Brady, Terrence Joseph *judge*
Cherry, Peter Ballard *electrical products corporation executive*
Drapalik, Betty Ruth *civic worker, artist*
Hall, Albert L. *lawyer, retired*
Henrick, Michael Francis *lawyer*
Marks, Martha Alford *author*
Schueppert, George Louis *financial executive*
Srinivasa, Venkataramaniah *engineer*
Walter, Melinda Kay *health department evaluator*

### Wayne
Evans, Charlotte Mortimer *communications consultant, writer*

### West Chicago
Franzen, Janice Marguerite Gosnell *magazine editor*
Kieft, Gerald Nelson *mechanical engineer*
Paulissen, James Peter *retired physician, county official*

### West Dundee
Woltz, Kenneth Allen *consulting executive*

### West Frankfort
Lindsey, Steven Frank *banker*

### Westchester
Barrett, Robert David *engineering executive*
Clarke, Richard Lewis *health science association administrator*
Masterson, John Patrick *retired English language educator*
Webb, Emily *retired plant morphologist*

### Western Springs
Carroll, Jeanne *public relations executive*
Frommelt, Jeffrey James *management consulting firm executive*
Hanson, Heidi Elizabeth *lawyer*
Lynn, Phyllis Jean *entrepreneur*
Tiefenthal, Marguerite Aurand *school social worker*
Zamora, Marjorie Dixon *retired political science educator*

### Westmont
Bajek, Frank Michael *career officer, retired, financial consultant*
Biggert, Judith Borg *lawyer, state representative*
Gottlander, Robert Jan Lars *dental company executive*

### Wheaton
Algeo, John Thomas *retired educator, association executive*
Bellock, Patricia Rigney *county government official*
Bogdonoff, Maurice Lambert *physician*
Butt, Edward Thomas, Jr. *lawyer*
Estep, John Hayes *religious denomination executive, clergyman*
Fawell, Beverly Jean *state legislator*
Flynn, James Rourke *retired insurance company executive*
Haenszel, William Manning *epidemiologist, educator*
†Hollingsworth, Pierce *publishing executive*
Holman, James Lewis *financial and management consultant*
Hughes, Tom D. *agronomist, consultant*
Jack, Nancy Rayford *supplemental resource company executive, consultant*
Jett, Charles Cranston *management consultant*
Koenigsmark, Joyce Elyn Sladek *geriatrics nurse*
Landan, Henry Sinclair *lawyer, business consultant*
Leston, Patrick John *judge*
Maibenco, Helen Craig *anatomist, educator*
Mayer, Donna Marie *management information systems manager*
Mellott, Robert Vernon *advertising executive*
Pappas, Barbara E. *Biblical studies educator, author*
Reszka, Alfons *computer systems architect*
Roberts, Keith Edward, Sr. *lawyer*
Roskam, Peter James *state legislator, lawyer*
Spedale, Vincent John *manufacturing executive*
Stein, Lawrence A. *lawyer*
Taylor, Mark Douglas *publishing executive*
Thomas, Joseph Erumappettical *psychologist*
Thompson, Bert Allen *retired librarian*
Votaw, John Frederick *educational foundation executive, educator*
Wolfram, Thomas *physicist*

### Wheeling
Hammer, Donald Price *librarian*
Keats, Glenn Arthur *manufacturing company executive*
Kuennen, Thomas Gerard *journalist*
Long, Sarah Ann *librarian*
Mc Clarren, Robert Royce *librarian*

### Willow Springs
Jashel, Larry Steven (L. Steven Rose) *entrepreneur, consultant*

### Wilmette
Albright, Townsend Shaul *investment banker, government benefits consultant*
Barnett, Ralph Lipsey *engineering educator*
Barth, David Keck *industrial distribution industry consultant*
Brink, Marion Francis *trade association administrator*
Bro, Kenneth Arthur *plastic manufacturing company executive*
Egloff, Fred Robert *manufacturers representative, writer, historian*
Ellis, Helene Rita *social worker*
Espenshade, Edward Bowman, Jr. *geographer, educator*
Fries, Robert Francis *historian, educator*
Hansen, Andrew Marius *retired library association executive*
Kohl, Dolores *educator, administrator*
Kurtzman, Allan Roger *advertising executive*
Mc Nitt, Willard Charles *business executive*
Merrier, Helen *actress, writer*
Miller, Frederick Staten *music educator, academic administrator*
Muhlenbruch, Carl W. *civil engineer*
Pearlman, Jerry Kent *electronics company executive*
Randolph, Lillian Larson *medical association executive*
Rocek, Jan *chemist, educator*
Rodgers, Ronald Carl *psychometrician*
Smutny, Joan Franklin *academic director, educator*
Williams, Emory *former retail company executive, banker*

### Wilmington
Anderson, Mary Jane *public library director*

### Winfield
McNutt, Kristen Wallwork *consumer affairs executive*

### Winnetka
Abell, David Robert *lawyer*
Andersen, Kenneth Benjamin *retired association executive*
Bartlett, William McGillivray *hospital and scientific products company executive*
Bohne, Carl John, Jr. *accountant*
Carrow, Leon Albert *physician*
Crowe, Robert William *lawyer, mediator*
Dailey, Mary *counselor, educator*
Davis, Britton Anthony *lawyer*
dePeyster, Frederic Augustus *surgeon*
Earle, David Prince, Jr. *physician, educator*
Folds, Charles Weston *merchandising consultant*
Fowle, Frank Fuller *retired lawyer*
Fraenkel, Stephen Joseph *engineering and research executive*
Gavin, James John, Jr. *diversified company executive*
Greenblatt, Ray Harris *lawyer*
Hartman, Robert S. *retired paper company executive*
Huff, Stanley Eugene *dermatologist*
Huggins, Charlotte Susan Harrison *secondary education educator, author, travel specialist*
Jones, Philip Newton *physician, medical educator*
Kahn, Paul Frederick *executive search company executive*
Kennedy, George Danner *chemical company executive*
Lang, Lenore Schulman *visual artist*
Mathers, Thomas Nesbit *financial consultant*
Mc Millen, Thomas Roberts *lawyer, arbitrator, mediator, retired judge*
Menke, Allen Carl *industrial corporation executive*
Piper, Robert Johnston *architect, urban planner*
Plowden, David *photographer*
Puth, John Wells *consulting company executive*
Radell, Nicholas John *management consultant*
Rossi, Ennio C. *physician, educator*
Sharboneau, Lorna Rosina *artist, educator, author, poet, illustrator*
Sick, William Norman, Jr. *investment company executive*
Weber, John Bertram *architect*
Weldon, Theodore Tefft, Jr. *retail company executive*

### Wood Dale
Kearns, Janet Catherine *corporate secretary*
Smith, Michael William *biomedical engineer, consultant*

### Woodhull
Lotspeich, Ellin Sue *art specialist, educator*

### Woodridge
Allen, Charles Joseph, II *advertising agency executive*
Conti, Lee Ann *lawyer*
Everett, C. Curtis *retired lawyer*
Krugly, Andrew *elementary school principal*

### Woodstock
Berry, Virgil Jennings, Jr. *management consultant*

### Worth
Ammeraal, Robert Neal *biochemist*
Bilder, James Gerard *marketing manager*

## INDIANA

### Alexandria
Irwin, Gerald Port *physician*

### Anderson
Conrad, Harold August *retired religious pension board executive*
Dale, Doris *religious organization executive*
Dye, Dwight Latimer *minister*
Grubbs, J. Perry *church administrator*
Hayes, Sherrill D. *religious organization administrator*
King, Charles Ross *physician*
Lawson, David Lewis *religious organization administrator, minister*
Massey, James Earl *clergyman, educator*
Miller, Linda J. *healthcare consultant*
Nicholson, Robert Arthur *college president*
Nuwer, Henry Joseph (Hank Nuwer) *journalist, educator*

### Angola
Lin, Ping-Wha *engineering educator, consultant*
McAlhany, Toni Anne *lawyer*

### Attica
Harrison, Joseph William *state senator*

### Auburn
Kempf, Jane Elmira *marketing executive*
Mountz, Louise Carson Smith *retired librarian*

### Batesville
Buettner, Michael Lewis *healthcare manufacturing executive*
Myers, Daniel Lee *manufacturing engineer*
Smith, Lonnie Max *diversified industries executive*
Volk, Cecilia Ann *elementary education educator*

### Beech Grove
Clapper, George Raymond *accountant, computer consultant*

### Bicknell
Risley, Gregory Byron *furniture company executive, interior designer*

### Bloomfield
Waymire, Bonnie Gladine *nursing administrator*

### Bloomington
Adams, William Richard *archaeologist, lecturer, curator*
Aman, Alfred Charles, Jr. *law educator*
Anderson, Judith Helena *English language educator*
Arnove, Robert Frederick *education educator*
Bain, Wilfred Conwell *former university dean, music educator, opera theater director*
Bair, Edward Jay *chemistry educator*
Barnes, A. James *academic dean*
Barnstone, Willis (Robert Barnstone) *language literature educator, poet, scholar*
Bauman, Richard *anthropologist, educator*
Baxter, Maurice Glen *historian, educator*
Belth, Joseph Morton *retired business educator*
Bent, Robert Demo *physicist, educator*
Bishop, Michael D. *emergency physician*
Boerner, Peter *language and literature educator*
Bonser, Charles Franklin *public administration educator*
Braden, Samuel Edward *economics educator*
Brand, Myles *academic administrator*
Brantlinger, Patrick *English educator*
Browar, Lisa Muriel *librarian*
Brown, Keith *musician, educator*
Buelow, George John *musicologist, educator*
Bundy, Wayne M. *retired geologist, consultant*
Burton, Philip Ward *advertising executive, educator*
Byrnes, Robert Francis *history educator*
Cagle, William Rea *librarian*
Caldwell, Lynton Keith *social scientist, educator*
Calinescu, Adriana Gabriela *museum curator, art historian*
Cameron, John M. *nuclear scientist, educator, science administrator*
Campaigne, Ernest Edward *chemistry educator*
Chisholm, Malcolm Harold *chemistry educator*
Clevenger, Sarah *botanist, computer consultant*
Cohen, William Benjamin *historian, educator*
Cole, Bruce Milan *art historian*
Conrad, Geoffrey Wentworth *archaeologist, educator*
Counsilman, James Edward *physical education educator*
Crowe, James Wilson *university administrator, educator*
Davidson, Ernest Roy *chemist, educator*
Davis, Charles Hargis *information scientist, educator*
Day, Harry Gilbert *nutritional biochemist, consultant*
DeHayes, Daniel Wesley *management executive, educator*
DeVoe, Robert Donald *visual physiologist*
Diamant, Alfred *political science educator*
Dieterle, Donald Lyle *accountant, educator*
Dinsmoor, James Arthur *psychology educator*
Dunn, Jon Michael *philosophy educator*
Edgerton, William B. *foreign language educator*
Edmondson, Frank Kelley *astronomer*
Ellis, Lucille Lorraine Laughlin (Mrs. Wallace Iverson Ellis) *realtor*
Ferrell, Robert Hugh *historian, educator*
Gealt, Adelheid Maria *museum director*
Gest, Howard *microbiologist, educator*
Goodman, Charles David *physicist, educator*
Gordon, Paul John *management educator*
Gough, Pauline Bjerke *magazine editor*
Grieco, Paul Anthony *chemistry educator*
Gros Louis, Kenneth Richard Russell *university chancellor*
Guth, Sherman Leon (S. Lee Guth) *psychologist, educator*
Hammel, Harold Theodore *physiology and biophysics educator, researcher*
Hanson, Karen *philosopher, educator*
Harder, John E. *electrical engineer*
Hattin, Donald Edward *geologist, educator*
Hegeman, George Downing *microbiology educator*
Heidt, Robert Harold *law educator, consultant*
Heiser, Charles Bixler, Jr. *botany educator*
Hites, Ronald Atlee *environmental science educator, chemist*
Hodge, Carleton Taylor *linguist, educator*
Hofstadter, Douglas Richard *cognitive scientist, educator, writer*
Hopkins, Jack Walker *former university administrator, environmental educator*
Jacobi, Peter Paul *journalism educator, author*
Johnson, Hollis Ralph *astronomy educator*
Johnson, Owen Verne *program director*
Johnson, Sidney Malcolm *foreign language educator*
Juergens, George Ivar *history educator*
Karkut, Richard Theodore *clinical psychologist*
Kibbey, Hal Stephen *science writer*
†Kitzmiller, Greg Louis *marketing educator, strategic consultant, conference speaker*
Klotman, Robert Howard *music educator*
Knight, Bob *college basketball coach*
Kohr, Roland Ellsworth *retired hospital administrator*
Komunyakaa, Yusef (James Willie Brown, Jr.) *poet*
Lebano, Edoardo Antonio *foreign language educator*
Lee, Don Yoon *publisher, academic researcher and writer*
Long, John D. *retired insurance educator*
Lowe, Marvin *artist*
Macfarlane, Malcolm Harris *physics educator*
Mac Watters, Virginia Elizabeth *singer, music educator, actress*
Markman, Ronald *artist, educator*
Martins, Heitor Miranda *foreign language educator*
Mc Clung, Leland Swint *microbiologist, educator*
Mehlinger, Howard Dean *education educator*
Mickel, Emanuel John *foreign language educator*
Mitchell, Bert Breon *literary translator*
Mobley, Tony Allen *university dean, recreation educator*
Moore, Ward Wilfred *medical educator*
Murray, Haydn Herbert *geology educator*
Muth, John Fraser *economics educator*
Nolan, Val, Jr. *biologist, lawyer*
O'Hearn, Robert Raymond *stage designer*
O'Meara, Patrick O. *political science educator*
Orrego-Salas, Juan Antonio *composer, retired music educator*
Ostrom, Vincent A(lfred) *political science educator*
Otteson, Schuyler Franklin *former university dean, educator*
Pagels, Jürgen Heinrich *balletmaster, dance educator, dancer, choreographer, author*
Parmenter, Charles Stedman *chemistry educator*
Patrick, John Joseph *social sciences educator*
Patterson, James Milton *marketing specialist, educator*
†Peebles, Christopher Spalding *anthropologist, dean, academic administrator*
Peters, Dennis Gail *chemist*
Phillips, Harvey *musician, soloist, music educator, arts consultant*
Pletcher, David Mitchell *history educator*
Pollock, Robert Elwood *nuclear physicist*
Preer, John Randolph, Jr. *biology educator*
Prosser, Franklin Pierce *computer scientist*
Purdom, Paul Walton, Jr. *computer scientist*
Puri, Madan Lal *mathematics educator*
Putnam, Frank William *biochemistry and immunology educator*
Rebec, George Vincent *neuroscience researcher, educator, administrator*
Rink, Lawrence Donald *cardiologist*
Risinger, C. Frederick *social studies educator*
Rosenberg, Samuel Nathan *French and Italian language educator*
Roush, William R. *chemistry educator*
Rousseau, Eugene Ellsworth *musician, music educator, consultant*
Rudolph, Lavere Christian *library director*
Ruesink, Albert William *biologist, plant sciences educator*
Ryan, John William *retired university president*
Samuelsen, Roy *bass-baritone*
Saunders, W(arren) Phillip, Jr. *economics educator, consultant, author*
Schaich, William L. *physics educator*
Schuessler, Karl Frederick *sociologist, educator*
Schurz, Scott Clark *journalist, publisher*
Sebeok, Thomas Albert *linguistics educator*
Sebok, Gyorgy *pianist, educator*
Sharrow, Leonard *musician, educator*
Simmons, Merle Edwin *foreign language educator*
Sinor, Denis *Orientalist, educator*
Smith, Carl Bernard *education educator*
Smith, Frederick Robert, Jr. *social studies educator*
Sperling, Elliot Harris *history educator*
Spulber, Nicolas *economics educator emeritus*
Stirratt, Betsy *artist, gallery director*
Stolnitz, George Joseph *economist, educator, demographer*
Stryker, Sheldon *sociologist, educator*
Sullivan, Michael Francis, III *executive*
Svetlova, Marina *ballerina, choreographer, educator*
Swanson, Robert Mclean *retired business educator*
Vincent, Jeffrey Robert *labor studies educator*
von Furstenberg, George Michael *economics educator, researcher*
Weaver, David Hugh *journalism educator, communications researcher*
Webb, Charles Haizlip, Jr. *university dean*
Weinberg, Eugene David *microbiologist, educator*
Wells, Herman B *university chancellor*
Wentworth, Jack Roberts *business educator, consultant*
Williams, Camilla *soprano, voice educator*
Williams, Edgar Gene *university administrator*
Wilson, John Douglas *economics educator*
Wilson, Kathy Kay *foundation executive*
Wittlich, Gary Eugene *music theory educator*
Wolin, Jeffrey Alan *artist*
Yeager, Janice Skinner *library director*

### Bluffton
Brockmann, William Frank *medical facility administrator*
Lawson, William Hogan, III *electrical motor manufacturing executive*

### Boggstown
Gray, Carlos Gibson *restaurateur, seedsman, entertainer, producer*

### Brownsburg
Weddell, Linda Anne *speech and language pathologist*

### Brownstown
Robertson, Joseph Edmond *grain processing company executive*

### Cambridge City
Schwartz, Susan Lynn Hill *principal*

### Carmel
Eden, Barbara Janiece *commercial and residential interior designer*
Hayashi, Tetsumaro *English and American literature educator, author*
Hilbert, Stephen C. *insurance company executive*
Mc Laughlin, Harry Roll *architect*
Monical, Robert Duane *consulting structural engineer*
Pickens, Robert Bruce *accountant*
Roche, James Richard *pediatric dentist, university dean*
Shoup, Charles Samuel, Jr. *chemicals and materials executive*
Stein, Richard Paul *lawyer*
Walsh, John Charles *metallurgical company executive*

### Centerville
Wendeln, Darlene Doris *English language educator*

### Charlestown
Schmidt, Jakob Edward *medical and medicolegal lexicographer, physician, author, inventor*

### Chesterfield
Fry, Meredith Warren *civil engineer, consultant*

### Chesterton
Blaschke, Lawrence Raymond *steel manufacturing executive, energy professional*
Brown, Gene W. *steel company executive*
Crewe, Albert Victor *physicist, artist, business executive*
Haines, Robert Earl *retired industrial construction executive*
Martino, Robert Salvatore *orthopedic surgeon*
Petrakis, Harry Mark *author*
Wilkes, Delano Angus *architect*

### Churubusco
Deck, Judith Therese *elementary school educator*

### Cicero
Poindexter, Beverly Kay *media and communications professional*

### Columbia City
Behrens, Diane R. *nursing educator*

### Columbus
Abts, Henry William *banker*
Arthur, Jewell Kathleen *dental hygienist*
Berman, Lewis Paul *financial executive*
Boll, Charles Raymond *engine company executive*
Draeger, Wayne Harold *manufacturing company executive*
Garton, Robert Dean *state senator*
Hackett, John Thomas *economist*
Harrison, Patrick Woods *lawyer*
Henderson, James Alan *engine company executive*
Hercamp, Richard Dean *chemical engineer*
Higgins, Harold Bailey *executive search company executive*
Hollansky, Bert Voyta *stock brokerage executive*
Kendall, James William *retired manufacturing company executive*
Kidwell, Mary F. *accountant*
Kubo, Isoroku *mechanical engineer*
Nash, John Arthur *bank executive*
Perkins Senn, Karon Elaine *lawyer*
Sales, A. R. *financial executive*
Stoner, R(ichard) B(urkett) *manufacturing company executive*
Tucker, Thomas Randall *public relations executive*

### Connersville
Kuntz, William Henry *lawyer, mediator*

### Corydon
Kelty, Paul David *physician educator*

### Crane
Waggoner, Susan Marie *electronics engineer*

### Crawfordsville
Barnes, James John *history educator*
Donaldson, Steven Bryan *lawyer*
Fisher, A. James *theater educator, director, actor*
Ford, Andrew Thomas *academic administrator*
Karg, Thelma Aileen *writer, retired educator*
Simmons, Emory G. *mycologist*

### Crown Point
Jones, Walter Dean *community program director*
Palmeri, Sharon Elizabeth *freelance writer, community educator*

### Culver
Holaday, Allan Gibson *English educator*
Manuel, Ralph Nixon *private school executive*

### Danville
Baldwin, Jeffrey Kenton *lawyer, educator*
Wean, Blanche McNeely *accountant*

### Dyer
Teuscher, George William *dental educator*

### East Chicago
Crum, James Francis *waste recycling company executive*
Platis, James G. *secondary school educator*

### Elkhart
Bowers, Richard Stewart, Jr. *lawyer*
Cascino, Lawrence Anthony *chemist*
Chism, James Arthur *information systems executive, business consultant*
Corson, Thomas Harold *manufacturing company executive*
Decio, Arthur Julius *manufacturing company executive*
Drexler, Rudy Matthew, Jr. *professional law enforcement dog trainer*
Free, Helen Mae *chemist, consultant*
Gassere, Eugene Arthur *lawyer, business executive*
Groom, Gary Lee *recreational vehicle manufacturing executive*
Harman, John Royden *lawyer*
Hill, Thomas Stewart *electronics executive, consultant, engineer*
Holtz, Glenn Edward *band instrument manufacturing executive*
Kloska, Ronald Frank *manufacturing company executive*
Martin, Rex *manufacturing executive*
McCarty, Richard Joseph *consulting engineer*
Meyer, Albert James *educational researcher*
Mischke, Frederick Charles *manufacturing company executive*
Oltz, Richard John *minister, publishing executive*
Rand, Phillip Gordon *chemist*
Speas, Charles Stuart *personnel director*
Tatum, Rita *communications executive*
Treckelo, Richard M. *lawyer*

### Elwood
Barnett, Marilyn Doan *secondary education business educator*
Dawson, James Buchanan *computer consulting firm executive*

### Evansville
Able, Warren Walter *natural resource company executive, physician*
Bennett, Paul Edmond *engineering educator*
Blesch, K(athy) Suzann *small business owner*
Brill, Alan Richard *entrepreneur*
Brooks, Gene Edward *federal judge*
Brown, Randall Keith *orthodontist*
Capshaw, Tommie Dean *judge*
Clouse, John Daniel *lawyer*
Denner, Melvin Walter *retired life sciences educator*
Early, Judith K. *social services director*
Faw, Melvin Lee *retired physician*
Fritz, Edward Lane *dentist*
Gaither, John Francis *accountant, consultant*
Gerhart, Philip Mark *engineering educator*
Guthrie, Catherine S. Nicholson (Catherine S. Nicholson-Guthrie) *research scientist*
Halterman, Martha Lee *social services administrator, counselor*
Harrison, Joseph Heavrin *lawyer*
Hartsaw, William O. *mechanical engineering educator*
Hoy, George Philip *clergyman, food bank executive*
Jackson, Bill D. *newspaper editor*
Justice, Phillip Howard *securities broker*
Kiechlin, Robert Jerome *retired coal company executive, financial consultant*
Kitch, Frederick David *advertising executive*
Koch, Robert Louis, II *manufacturing company executive, mechanical engineer*
Luckett, John Mills, III *construction company financial executive*
Mathews, Walter Garret *columnist*
Muehlbauer, James Herman *manufacturing executive*
Penkava, Robert Ray *radiologist, educator*
Powelson, Mary Voliva *golf course and banquet facility executive*
Ragsdale, Rex H. *health facility administrator, physician*
Roth, Carolyn Louise *art educator*
Rusche, Herman Frederick *gastroenterologist*
Ryder, Thomas Michael *newspaper editor*
Shaw, Margery Wayne Schlamp *geneticist, physician, lawyer*
Streetman, John William, III *museum official*
Thompson, Robin Jill *special education educator*
Vinson, James Spangler *academic administrator*
Will, Jane Anne *psychologist*
Young Lively, Sandra Lee *nurse*

### Fishers
Christie, Walter Scott *retired state official*
Gatto, Louis Constantine *educational authority executive*

### Fort Branch
Bertram, Michael Wayne *secondary education educator*

### Fort Wayne
Andorfer, Donald Joseph *university president*
Baker, Carl Leroy *lawyer*
Beineke, Lowell Wayne *mathematics educator*
Bender, Linda Arlene *bank officer*
Bunkowske, Eugene Walter *religious studies educator*
Burns, Thagrus Asher *manufacturing company executive, former life insurance company executive*
Clancy, Terrence Patrick *food service executive*
Clarke, Kenneth Stevens *insurance company executive*
Cole, Kenneth Duane *architect*
Collins, Linda Lou Powell *manager of contracts*
Cox, David Jackson *biochemistry educator*
Curtis, Douglas Homer *small business owner*
D'Arcy, John Michael *bishop*
Donesa, Antonio Braganza *neurosurgeon*
Dunsire, P(eter) Kenneth *insurance company executive*
Fairchild, David Lawrence *philosophy educator*
Fink, Thomas Michael *lawyer*
Flynn, Pauline T. *speech pathologist, educator*
Franklin, Al *artistic director*
Fry, Charles George *theologian, educator*
Gerberding, Miles Carston *lawyer*
Goeglein, Gloria J. *state legislator*
Graf, Robert Arlan *financial services executive*
Helmke, (Walter) Paul, Jr. *mayor, lawyer*
Hunter, Jack Duval *lawyer*
Hwang, Santai *electrical engineering educator*
Keefer, J(ames) Michael *lawyer*
Kern, Patricia Joan *media specialist*
Kerr, Frederick Hohmann *health care company executive*
Kirkwood, Maurice Richard *banker*
Klugman, Stephan Craig *newspaper editor*
Krull, Jeffrey Robert *library director*
Latz, G. Irving, II *manufacturing company executive*
Lawson, Jack Wayne *lawyer*
Lee, Shuishih Sage *pathologist*
Lee, Timothy Earl *international agency executive, paralegal*
Lee, William Charles *judge*
Lewark, Carol Ann *special education educator*
Lockwood, Robert Philip *publishing executive*
Lupke, Duane Eugene *insurance company executive*
Lyons, Harvey Isaac *mechanical engineering educator*
Lyons, Jerry Lee *mechanical engineer*
Mahmoud, Aly Ahmed *electrical engineering educator*
Mann, David William *minister*
Marine, Clyde Lockwood *agricultural business consultant*
Mather, George Ross *clergy member*
Molfenter, David P. *electronics executive*
Moran, John *religious organization administrator*
Moses, Winfield C., Jr. *state legislator, construction company executive*
Niewyk, Anthony *lawyer*
Pathak, Sunit Rawly *business owner, consultant, journalist*
Pease, Ella Louise *elementary education educator*
Peebles, Carter David *lawyer*
Pellegrene, Thomas James, Jr. *editor, researcher*
Richardson, Joseph Hill *physician, medical educator*
Rifkin, Leonard *metals company executive*
Robertson, Richard Stuart *insurance holding company executive*
Rolland, Ian McKenzie *insurance executive*
Sack, James McDonald, Jr. *radio and television producer, marketing executive*
Sandeson, William Seymour *cartoonist*
Scheetz, Sister Mary JoEllen *English language educator*
Shaffer, Paul E. *retired banker*
Shoaff, Thomas Mitchell *lawyer*
Sims, Debbie Deann *psychotherapist*
Stebbins, Vrina Grimes *elementary school educator, counselor*
Steinbronn, Richard Eugene *lawyer*
Steiner, Paul Andrew *retired insurance executive*
Stevenson, Kenneth Lee *chemist, educator*
Stucky, Ken *clergy member, church organization administrator, foundation executive*
Szuhaj, Bernard Francis *food research director*
Taritas, Karen Joyce *telemarketing executive*
Vachon, Marilyn Ann *retired insurance company executive*
Weatherford, George Edward *civil engineer*
Weicker, Jack Edward *educational administrator*
West, Thomas Meade *financial services strategic consultant*
Williams, Walter Jackson, Jr. *electrical engineer, consultant*
Wolf, Don Allen *hardware wholesale executive*

### Fowler
Kepner, Rex William *lawyer*

### Frankfort
Borland, Kathryn Kilby *author*
Stonehill, Lloyd Herschel *gas company executive, mechanical engineer*

### Franklin
Farrar, Susan Lee *special education educator, consultant*
Jacobs, Harvey Collins *newspaper editor, writer*
Janis, F. Timothy *technology company executive*
Launey, George Volney, III *economics educator*
Martin, William Bryan *chancellor, lawyer*

### Fremont
Elliott, Carl Hartley *former university president*

### Gary
Bosley, John Scott *editor*
Gaughan, Norbert F. *bishop*
Hall, James Rayford, III *adult education educator*
Iatridis, Panayotis George *medical educator*
Lewis, Robert Lee *lawyer*
Meyerson, Seymour *retired chemist*
Moran, Robert Francis, Jr. *library director*
Richards, Hilda *academic administrator*
Rosen, Kay *painter*
Smith, Vernon G. *education educator, state representative*
Thomas, Carolyn Harper *elementary educator*
Wells, Charles Robert *secondary education educator*
Williams, Mary Elizabeth *elementary school educator*
Zunich, Janice *pediatrician, geneticist, educator, administrator*

### Georgetown
Dailey, Donald Harry *adult education educator, volunteer*

### Goshen
Lehman, Karl Franklyn *accountant*
Loomis, Norma Irene *marriage and family therapist*
Morris, Robert Julian, Jr. *art gallery owner*
Schrock, Harold Arthur *manufacturing company executive*
Stoltzfus, Victor Ezra *retired university president, academic consultant*

### Granger
Brissey, Ruben Marion *retired container company executive*

### Greencastle
Anderson, John Robert *retired mathematics educator*
Bonifield, William Clarence *economist, educator*
Bottoms, Robert Garvin *academic administrator*
DiLillo, Leonard Michael *Spanish language educator, researcher, academic administrator*
Dittmer, John Avery *history educator*
Gass, Clinton Burke *mathematics educator*
Houck, Carolyn Marie Kumpf *special education educator*
Lamar, Martha Lee *chaplain*
Phillips, Clifton J. *history educator*
Weiss, Robert Orr *speech educator*

### Greenfield
Myerholtz, Ralph W., Jr. *retired chemical company executive, research chemist*

### Greensburg
Moore, Albert Lawrence *investment company executive, investment broker*
Ricke, David Louis *agricultural and environmental consultant*
Small, Ralph Milton *publisher, clergyman*

### Greenwood
Atkins, Clayton H. *family physician, epidemiologist, educator*
Daniel, Michael Edwin *insurance agency executive*
Means, George Robert *organization executive*

### Hammond
Adik, Stephen Peter *energy company executive*
Ash, Frederick Melvin *manufacturing company executive*
Ashbach, David Laurence *internist, nephrologist*
Delph, Donna Jean (Maroc) *education educator, consultant, university administrator*
Diamond, Eugene Christopher *lawyer, hospital administrator*
Kohl, Jacquelyn Marie *lawyer*
Lozano, Rudolpho *federal judge*
Moody, James T(yne) *federal judge*
Neff, Gregory Pall *manufacturing engineering educator, consultant*
Pierson, Edward Samuel *engineering educator, consultant*
Rodovich, Andrew Paul *lawyer, federal magistrate*
Schroer, Edmund Armin *utility company executive*
Steen, Lowell Harrison *physician*
Yackel, James William *mathematician, academic administrator*
Yovich, Daniel John *educator*

### Hanna
Stephenson, Dorothy Maxine *volunteer*

### Hartford City
Ford, David Clayton *lawyer, Indiana state senator*

### Highland
Forsythe, Randall Newman *paralegal, educator*
Goodman, Samuel J. *lawyer*
Purcell, James Francis *former utility executive, consultant*

### Hope
Golden, Eloise Elizabeth *community health nurse*

### Howe
Bowerman, Ann Louise *author, genealogist, educator*

### Huntingburg
Matthews, William Edmund *newspaper and travel magazine publisher*

### Huntington
Doermann, Paul Edmund *retired surgeon*
Seilhamer, Ray A. *bishop*

### Indianapolis
†Adkins, Derrick Ralph *Olympic athlete*
Albright, Terrill D. *lawyer*
Aliev, Eldar *artistic director, choreographer, educator*
Allan, Marc David *music critic*
Allen, David James *lawyer*
Allen, Stephen D(ean) *pathologist, microbiologist*
Altman, Joseph *author, neuroscientist*
Alvarez, Thomas *film and video producer, director*
Applegate, Malcolm W. *newspaper executive*
Aprison, Morris Herman *biochemist, experimental and theoretical neurobiologist, emeritus educator*
Aschleman, James Allan *lawyer*
Ashford, Evelyn *former track and field athlete*
†Austin, Charles *Olympic athlete*
Austin, Robert Brendon *civil engineer*
Austin, Spencer Peter *minister*
Avery, Dennis Teel *agricultural analyst*
Badger, David Harry *lawyer*
Baetzhold, Howard George *English language educator*
Baker, R. Kent *entrepreneur*
Bannister, Geoffrey *university president, geographer*
Barcus, Mary Evelyn *primary school educator*
Barcus, Robert Gene *educational association administrator*
Barker, Sarah Evans *judge*
†Barnes, Eric Randolph *Olympic athlete*
Bates, Gerald Earl *bishop*
Bauer, Dietrich Charles *medical educator*
Baxter, Carla Louise Chaney *insurance product specialist*
Bayh, Evan *former governor*
Beckwith, Lewis Daniel *lawyer*
Beeler, Virgil L. *lawyer*
Behar, Lucien E. *church administrator*
Bepko, Gerald Lewis *university administrator, law educator, lecturer, consultant, lawyer*
Bergstein, Jerry Michael *pediatric nephrology*
Besch, Henry Roland, Jr. *pharmacologist, educator*
Bessey, William Higgins *physicist, educator*
Biller, Jose *neurologist*
Bindley, William Edward *pharmaceutical executive*
Bird, Larry Joe *retired professional basketball player, coach*
Birky, Nathan Dale *publishing company executive*
Blackwell, Henry Barlow, II *lawyer*
†Blanchard, Cary *football player*
Block, Amanda Roth *artist*
Boldt, Michael Herbert *lawyer*
Bolin, Daniel Paul *music educator*
Born, Samuel Roydon, II *lawyer*
Borns, Robert Aaron *real estate developer*
Braddom, Randall L. *physician, medical educator*
Brady, Mary Sue *nutrition and dietetics educator*
Brandt, Ira Kive *pediatrician, medical geneticist*
Brannon, Ronald Roy *minister*
Brannon-Peppas, Lisa *chemical engineer, researcher*
Brash, Susan Kay *principal*
Brashear, Diane Lee *marital and sex therapist*
Braun, Robert Clare *retired association and advertising executive*
Braunstein, Ethan Malcolm *skeletal radiologist, paleopathologist*
Bray, Donald Lawrence *religious organization executive, minister*
Brickley, Richard Agar *retired surgeon*
Brinkerhoff, Tom J. *financial services executive*
†Broadie, Thomas Allen *surgeon, educator*
Brooks, Patricia Scott *principal*
Brown, Edwin Wilson, Jr. *physician, educator*
Broxmeyer, Hal Edward *medical educator*
Budniakiewicz, Therese *author*
Buechlein, Daniel Mark *archbishop*
Bundy, David Dale *librarian, educator*
Burnett, Judith Jane *foundation administrator, consultant*
Burr, David Bentley *anatomy educator*
Burrell, Leroy Russel *track and field athlete*
Buttrey, Donald Wayne *lawyer*
Campbell, Judith Lowe *child psychiatrist*
Campbell, Patti Susan *public relations professional*
Capehart, Harriet Jane Holmes *economics educator*
Caperton, Albert Franklin *newspaper editor*
Carey, Edward Marshel, Jr. *accounting company executive*
Carney, Joseph Buckingham *lawyer*
Carpenter, Susan Karen *lawyer*
Carr, William H(enry) A. *public relations executive, author*
†Carson, Julia M. *congresswoman*
Carter, Pamela Lynn *former state attorney general*
Cason, Andre Royal *track and field athlete*
Cassel, Herbert William *religion educator*
Castle, Howard Blaine *religious organization administrator*
Chernish, Stanley Michael *physician*
Chiki, Frank T. *printing company professional*
Choplin, John M., II *lawyer*
Christen, Arden Gale *dental educator, researcher, consultant*
Christenson, Le Roy Howard *insurance company officer*
Christian, Joe Clark *medical genetics researcher, educator*
Chuang, Tsu-Yi *dermatologist, epidemiologist, educator*
Clark, Charles M., Jr. *research institution adminstrator*
Clark, James Murray *state legislator*
Clary, Keith Uhl *retired industrial relations executive*
Cliff, Johnnie Marie *mathematics and chemistry educator*
Cohen, Gabriel Murrel *editor, publisher*
Comer, Jerome Edward *lawyer*
Cones, Van Buren *electronics engineer, consultant*
Conly, Michael Frederick *architect*
Conway, Hollis *track and field athletie, Olympic athlete*
Cramer, Betty F. *life insurance company executive*
Crow, Paul Abernathy, Jr. *clergyman, religious council executive, educator*
Dafoe, Christopher Randy *marketing, healthcare education professional, diplomat*
Daly, Walter Joseph *physician, educator*
Daniel, Melvin Randolph *lawyer*
Davis, Kenneth Wayne *English language educator, business communication consultant*
†Dawes, Dominique *gymnast, Olympic athlete*
Decker Slaney, Mary Teresa *Olympic athlete*
Deer, Richard Elliott *lawyer*
Dent, Richard Lamar *professional football player*
Dickeson, Robert Celmer *retired university president, corporation president, political science educator*

Dickinson, Richard Donald Nye clergyman, educator, theological seminary administrator
Dickson, Brent E. state supreme court justice
Dietz, William Ronald financial services executive
Dillin, S. Hugh federal judge
Dollens, Ronald W. pharmaceuticals company executive
†Donaldson, Raymond Canute professional football player
Donohue, John Patrick urologist
Dortch, Carl Raymond former association executive
Downs, Thomas K. lawyer
Dunn, Sidney N. fraternity administrator
Durbin, Robert Cain hotel executive
Dutton, Stephen James lawyer
Eigen, Howard pediatrician, educator
Ellerbrook, Niel Cochran gas company executive
Ellis, Carollyn religious organization administrator
Ellis, Raymond W. religious organization executive, consultant
Emerson, Andrew Craig retired lawyer, insurance executive
Evans, Daniel Fraley, Jr. lawyer
Evans, Richard James mechanical engineer
Ewbank, Thomas Peters lawyer, retired banker
Ewick, Charles Ray librarian
Fadely, James Philip admissions and financial aids director, educator, writer
Faulk, Marshall William professional football player
Favor-Hamilton, Suzanne Marie track and field athlete, Olympian
Feigenbaum, Harvey cardiologist, educator
Felicetti, Daniel A. academic administrator, educator
Feng, Gen-sheng medical educator, researcher
Fer, Ahmet F. electrical engineer, educator
Fife, Wilmer Krafft chemistry educator
Fisch, Charles physician, educator
Fisher, Gene Lawrence financial executive
Fisher, James R. lawyer
FitzGibbon, Daniel Harvey lawyer
Fleming, Marcella journalist
Fortune, William Lemcke journalist
Foulkes, John R. minister
Fox, Donald Lee mental health counselor, consultant
Fredrickson, William Robert trading company executive
Fritz, Cecil Morgan investment company executive
Fruehwald, Kristin G. lawyer
Fryer, Robert Samuel state agency administrator, consultant
Fuller, Samuel Ashby lawyer, mining company executive
Funk, David Albert retired law educator
Furlow, Mack Vernon, Jr. retired financial executive, treasurer
Gagel, Barbara Jean health insurance administrator
Galbraith, Bruce W. educational administrator
Galvin, Matthew Reppert psychiatry educator
Gantz, Richard Alan museum administrator
†Gardocki, Christopher football player
Garmel, Marion Bess Simon journalist
Gaunce, Michael Paul insurance company executive
Gehring, Perry James toxicologist, chemical company executive
Geisler, Hans Emanuel gynecologic oncologist
Gerdes, Ralph Donald fire safety consultant
Ghetti, Bernardino Francesco neuropathologist, neurobiology researcher
Gibson, David Mark biochemist, educator
Gilmore, H. William college dean, dentistry educator
Gilroy, Sue Anne state official
Givan, Richard Martin state supreme court justice, retired
Gnat, Raymond Earl librarian
Godich, John Paul federal magistrate judge
Goldsmith, Stephen mayor
Goodwin, William Maxwell financial executive
Gooldy, Patricia Alice elementary education educator
Gooldy, Walter Raymond genealogist
Grant, Claudia Ewing minister
Grayson, John Allan lawyer
Green, James Murney software products executive
Green, Morris physician, educator
Greene, Joe Olympic athlete, track and field
Greist, Mary Coffey dermatologist
Griffiths, David Neal utility executive
Griggs, Ruth Marie retired journalism educator, writer, publications consultant
Grosfeld, Jay Lazar pediatric surgeon, educator
Grossman, Elizabeth Korn nursing administrator, retired college dean
Haddad, Freddie Duke, Jr. hospital development administrator
Haines, Lee Mark, Jr. religious denomination administrator
Hamburger, Richard James physician, educator
Hamm, Richard L. church administrator
Hammack, Julia Dixon music educator
Handel, David Jonathan health care administrator
Hansell, Richard Stanley obstetrician, gynecologist, educator
Harbaugh, James Joseph professional football player
Harris, Robert Allison biochemistry educator
Haycox, Rolanda Moore lawyer, nurse
Hayes, John Robert health care executive, psychiatrist
Heard, William Robert retired insurance company executive
Hefler, William Louis elementary education educator
Hegel, Carolyn Marie farmer, farm bureau executive
Helveston, Eugene McGillis pediatric ophthalmologist, educator
Henderson, Bruce Wingrove insurance executive
Henderson, Eugene Leroy lawyer
Herman, Barbara F. psychologist
Hicks, Allen Morley hospital administrator
Hill, Beverly Ellen health sciences educator
Hillman, Charlene Hamilton public relations executive
Hingtgen, Joseph Nicholas psychologist, neuroscientist, educator
Ho, Thomas Inn Min computer scientist, educator
Hodes, Marion Edward genetics educator, physician
Holden, Robert Watson radiologist, educator, university dean
Holland, George Frank, II investment company executive
Honor, Noël Evans social services supervisor
Hovde, F. Boyd lawyer
Hubbard, Jesse Donald pathology educator
Huffman-Hine, Ruth Carson adult education administrator, educator
Hunt, Robert Chester construction company executive
Husman, Catherine Bigot insurance company executive, actuary
Husted, Ralph Waldo former utility executive
Huston, Michael Joe lawyer
Ilchman, Warren Frederick university administrator, political science educator
†Infante, Lindy professional football coach
Irsay, James Steven professional football team executive
Irwin, Glenn Ward, Jr. medical educator, physician, university official
Isaac, Stanley Eugene accountant
Israelov, Rhoda financial planner, writer, entrepreneur
Jackson, Valerie Pascuzzi radiologist, educator
Jacobs, Andrew, Jr. former congressman
Jegen, Lawrence A., III law educator
Jewett, John Rhodes real estate executive
†Johnson, Allen Olympic athlete
Johnson, David Allen singer, songwriter, investor, minister
Johnson, James P. religious organization executive
†Johnson, Michael Olympic athlete
Johnston, Cyrus Conrad, Jr. medical educator
Johnstone, Joyce Visintine education educator
Johnstone, Robert Philip lawyer
Jones, Robert Brooke microbiologist
Joyner, John Erwin medical educator, neurological surgeon
Justice, Brady Richmond, Jr. medical services executive
Kacek, Don J. management consultant, business owner
Kashani, Hamid Reza lawyer, computer consultant
Kaufman, Barton Lowell financial services company executive
Kemper, James Dee lawyer
Kemper, Walker Warder, Jr. dentist, educator
Kempski, Ralph Aloisius bishop
Kerr, William Andrew lawyer, educator
Kesler, Kenneth Allen thoracic surgeon, educator
Khalil, Michael O. actuary
King, J. B. medical device company executive, lawyer
King, Kay Sue investment company executive
King, Lucy Jane psychiatrist, health facility administrator
Kirk, Carol lawyer
Klaper, Martin Jay lawyer
Kleiman, David Harold lawyer
Klinker, Sheila Ann J. state legislator, middle school educator
Klug, Michael Gregory scientist
Knebel, Donald Earl lawyer
Knoebel, Suzanne Buckner cardiologist, medical educator
Knutson, Roger Craig marketing and sales professional, inventor
Krasean, Thomas Karl historian
Krauss, John Landers public policy and urban affairs consultant
Krueger, Alan Douglas communications company executive
Krueger, Betty Jane telecommunications company executive
La Crosse, James retail executive
Lacy, Andre Balz industrial executive
Lahiri, Debomoy Kumar molecular neurobiologist, educator
Lake, Carol Lee anesthesiologist, educator
Lamkin, E(ugene) Henry, Jr. internist, medical management executive
Landis, Larry Seabrook marketing and communications consultant
Lanford, Luke Dean electronics company executive
Lantz, George Benjamin, Jr. business executive, college executive, consultant
Lee, Stephen W. lawyer
Lefstein, Norman lawyer, educator
Lemberger, Louis pharmacologist, physician
lilman, Alan B. restaurant company executive
Lisher, John Leonard lawyer
Lobley, Alan Haigh retired lawyer
Lofton, Thomas Milton lawyer
Long, Clarence William accountant
Long, Timothy Scott chemist, consultant
Long, William Allan retired forest products company executive
Lumeng, Lawrence physician, educator
†Lynch, Jair Olympic athlete
Lytle, L(arry) Ben insurance company executive, lawyer
MacDougall, John Duncan surgeon
Madura, James Anthony surgical educator
Manders, Karl Lee neurosurgeon
Manworren, Donald B. church administrator
Mason, Thomas Alexander historian, educator, author
McCarthy, Harold Charles retired insurance company executive
McCarthy, Kevin Bart lawyer
McDonell, Edwin Douglas information systems executive, consultant, writer
McDonell, Katherine Mandusic professional society administrator
Mc Farland, H. Richard food company executive
McKeand, Patrick Joseph newspaper publisher, educator
McKinney, Dennis Keith lawyer
McKinney, E. Kirk, Jr. retired insurance company executive
McKinney, Larry J. federal judge
McTurnan, Lee Bowes lawyer
Merritt, Doris Honig pediatrics educator
Meyer, Fred William, Jr. memorial parks executive
Meyer, William Michael mortgage banking executive
Mihelich, Edward David chemist
†Mikelsons, J. George air aerospace transportation executive
Miller, David Anthony lawyer
Miller, David W. lawyer
Miniear, J. Dederick software company executive, consultant
Mirsky, Arthur geologist, educator
Miyamoto, Richard Takashi otolaryngologist
†Modisett, Jeffrey A. lawyer, consultant
Moffatt, Michael Alan lawyer
Molitoris, Bruce Albert nephrologist, educator
Morris, Greg James advertising executive
Mullen, Thomas Edgar real estate consultant
Neff, Robert Matthew lawyer, investment and insurance executive
Newton, Pynkerton Dion chiropractor
Nolan, Alan Tucker retired lawyer
Norins, Arthur Leonard physician, educator
Norman, LaLander Stadig insurance company executive
Nurnberger, John I., Jr. psychiatrist, educator
Nyhart, Eldon Howard, Jr. biopharmaceuticist, biomedical engineer
Nzeyimana, Noah bishop
O'Bannon, Frank Lewis governor, lawyer
O'Brien, Daniel Dion track and field athlete, Olympic athlete
Ochs, Sidney neurophysiology educator
Ott, Carl Neil environmental engineer
Padgett, Gregory Lee lawyer
Page, Curtis Matthewson minister
Patrick, William Bradshaw lawyer
Paul, Stephen Howard lawyer
Petersen, James L. lawyer
Pettinga, Cornelius Wesley pharmaceutical company executive
Phillippi, Wendell Crane editor
Pierce, Ricky Charles professional basketball player
Plaster, George Francis Roman Catholic priest
Plater, William Marmaduke English language educator, academic administrator
Poel, Robert Walter air force officer, physician
Polston, Mark Franklin minister
Ponder, Lester McConnico lawyer, educator
Poray, John Lawrence professional association executive
Powlen, David Michael lawyer
Pratt, Arthur D. printing company executive
Prible, Larry R. insurance company executive
Price, (John) Nelson journalist
Pulliam, Eugene Smith newspaper publisher
Quayle, Marilyn Tucker lawyer, wife of former vice president of United States
Ramer, Winnifred Robison school nurse
Rand, Leon academic administrator
Recker, Thomas Edward fraternal organization executive
Reed, Suellen Kinder state education administrator
Reeve, Ronald Cropper, Jr. manufacturing executive
Reid, William Hill mathematics educator
Reilly, Jeanette P. clinical psychologist
Reynolds, Robert Hugh lawyer
Rhoades, Rodney Allen physiologist, educator
Richmond, James Ellis restaurant company executive
Richter, Judith Anne pharmacology educator
Riegsecker, Marvin Dean pharmacist, state senator
Riemenschneider, Dan LaVerne religious organization administrator
Ritz, Stephen Mark financial advisor, lawyer
†Robbins, N. Clay foundation administrator
†Roberts, David airport executive
Roberts, William Everett lawyer
Robinson, Larry Robert insurance company executive
Rogers, Robert Ernest medical educator
†Roob, E. Mitchell healthcare admnistrator
Rose, Jalen professional basketball player
Ross, Edward cardiologist
Ross, Robert E. psychologist, clergyman, counselor
Roth, Lawrence Max pathologist, educator
Ruben, Gary A. marketing and communications consultant
Russell, David Williams lawyer
Russell, Frank Eli newspaper publishing executive
Ryder, Henry C(lay) lawyer
Salentine, Thomas James pharmaceutical company executive
Sarbinoff, James Adair periodontist, consultant
Scaletta, Phillip Ralph, III lawyer
†Scanlan, Kathy sports association administrator
Scanlon, Thomas Michael lawyer
Scannell, Dale Paul education educator
Schellen, Nando opera director
Schilling, Emily Born editor, association executive
Schlegel, Fred Eugene lawyer
Schmetzer, Alan David psychiatrist
Schmidt, William C. chemical company executive
Schneider, Robert E., II lawyer
Scholer, Sue Wyant state legislator
Scism, Daniel Reed lawyer
Seitz, Melvin Christian, Jr. distributing company executive
Seneff, Smiley Howard business owner
SerVaas, Beurt Richard corporate executive
Ser Vaas, Cory health sciences association administrator
Shaffer, Alfred Garfield (Terry) service organization executive
Shepard, Randall Terry judge
Sherman, Stuart physician
Shideler, Shirley Ann Williams lawyer
Shula, Robert Joseph lawyer
Silver, David Mayer former university official
Simmons, Roberta Johnson public relations firm executive
Simon, Herbert professional basketball team executive
Sindlinger, Verne E. bishop
Slaymaker, Gene Arthur public relations executive
Small, Joyce Graham psychiatrist, educator
Smith, Donald Eugene healthcare facility management administrator owner
Smith, James Warren pathologist, microbiologist, parasitologist
Smith, Keith protective services official
Smith, Stephen Kendall lawyer
Snyder, Jack Ralph lawyer
Solomon, Marilyn Kay educator, consultant
Soper, Quentin Francis chemist
Spanogle, Robert William marketing and advertising company executive, association administrator
Staff, Charles Bancroft, Jr. music and theater critic
Standish, Samuel Miles oral pathologist, college dean
Stayton, Thomas George lawyer
Steger, Evan Evans, III lawyer
Stehman, Frederick Bates gynecologic oncologist, educator
Step, Eugene Lee retired pharmaceutical company executive
Stieff, John Joseph legislative lawyer, educator
Stookey, George Kenneth research institute administrator, dental educator
Stout, William Jewell department store executive
Strain, Edward Richard psychologist
Sullivan, Frank, Jr. state supreme court justice
Sutherland, Donald Gray lawyer
Sutton, Gregory Paul obstetrician, gynecologist
Suzuki, Hidetaro violinist
Swanson, David Heath agricultural company executive
Sweezy, John William political party official
Swhier, Claudia Versfelt lawyer
Tabler, Bryan G. lawyer
Tabler, Norman Gardner, Jr. lawyer
Taylor, Doris Denice physician, entrepreneur
Thomas, John David musician, composer, arranger, photographer, recording engineer, producer
Throgmartin, Dianne educational foundation executive
Tobias, Randall L. pharmaceutical company executive
Todd, Zane Grey retired utilities executive
Tomlinson, Joseph Ernest manufacturing company executive
Torrence, Gwen Olympic athlete
Townsend, Earl C., Jr. lawyer, writer
†Turner, William W., Jr. surgeon, educator
Updegraff Spleth, Ann L. church executive, pastor
Usher, Phyllis Land state official
Vandivier, Blair Robert lawyer
Vereen, Robert Charles retired trade association executive
Walker, Frank Dilling market research executive
†Walker, Steven Frank management consultant
Walsh, Donnie sports club executive
Walther, Joseph Edward health facility administrator, retired physician
Wampler, Lloyd Charles retired lawyer
Wappner, Rebecca Sue pediatrics educator
Watanabe, August Masaru physician, scientist, medical educator, corporate executive
Watkins, Harold Robert minister
Watkins, Sherry Lynne elementary school educator
Weber, George oncology and pharmacology researcher, educator
Weinberger, Myron Hilmar medical educator
Wellnitz, Craig Otto lawyer, English language educator
Welsh, Robert K. relgious organization executive
Whale, Arthur Richard lawyer
Wheeler, Daniel Scott management executive, editor
White, Arthur Clinton physician
White, James Patrick law educator
Williams, Gloria Louise gifted and talented education educator
Wilson, Charles Vincent human resources executive
Wilson, Earle Lawrence church administrator
Wilson, Fred M., II ophthalmologist, educator
Wise, Rita J. writer, poet
Wishard, Gordon Davis lawyer
Wolsiffer, Patricia Rae insurance company executive
Wong, David T. biochemist
Wood, William Jerome lawyer
Woodard, Harold Raymond lawyer
Woodring, DeWayne Stanley religion association executive
Woody, John Frederick secondary education educator
Woollen, Evans architectural firm executive
Woolling, Kenneth Rau internist
Wright, David Burton retired newspaper publishing company executive
Wynn, Sherri Lorraine educational administrator
Yeager, Joseph Heizer, Jr. lawyer
Yee, Robert Donald ophthalmologist
Young, Philip Howard library director
Yovits, Marshall Clinton computer and information science educator, university dean
Yune, Heun Yung radiologist, educator
Zapapas, James Richard pharmaceutical company executive
Zeller, Kenneth J. state official
Zipes, Douglas Peter cardiologist, researcher

### Indianpolis
Abbott, Verlin Leroy military career officer

### Jamestown
Waymire, John Thomas principal

### Jasper
Fleck, Albert Henry, Jr. insurance agency executive
Kohler, Jeffrey Martin office furniture manufacturing executive

### Jeffersonville
Barthold, Clementine B. retired judge
Hoehn, Elmer Louis lawyer, state and federal agency administrator, educator, consultant
McMichael, Jeane Casey real estate corporation executive, educator
Reisert, Charles Edward, Jr. real estate executive
Rhodes, Betty Fleming rehabilitation services professional, nurse

### Knox
Weiss, Randall A. television producer, supermarket executive

### Kokomo
Coppock, Janet Elaine mental health nurse
Daniels, Doral Lee education educator
Hall, Milton L. bishop
Highlen, Larry Wade music educator, piano rebuilder, tuner
Hill, Emita Brady academic administrator
Miller, Robert Frank retired electronics engineer, educator
Ray, Tuhin computer engineer
Schraut, Kenneth Charles mathematician, educator
Ungerer, Walter John minister

### La Porte
Ake, Jeffrey James management consultant
Heiden, Susan Jane elementary education educator
Hiler, John Patrick former government official, former congressman, business executive
Madsen, Dorothy Louise (Meg Madsen) writer
Morris, Leigh Edward hospital executive officer
Shreve, Michael Gerald computer consultant

### Lafayette
Andrews, Frederick Newcomb emeritus university administrator
Bement, Arden Lee, Jr. engineering educator
Brewster, James Henry retired chemistry educator
Claflin, Robert Malden veterinary educator, university dean
de Branges de Bourcia, Louis mathematics educator
Etzel, James Edward environmental engineering educator
Feuer, Henry chemist, educator
Finch, Robert Jonathan communications engineering consultant
Fox, Robert William mechanical engineering educator
Gartenhaus, Solomon physicist
Gautschi, Walter mathematics educator
Geddes, LaNelle Evelyn nursing educator, physiologist
Geddes, Leslie Alexander bioengineer, physiologist, educator
Gordon, Irene Marlow radiology educator
Gustafson, Winthrop Adolph aeronautical and astronautical engineering educator
Hardin, Lowell Stewart retired economics educator
Harris, Donald Wayne research scientist

Higi, William L. bishop
Judd, William Robert engineering geologist, educator
Layden, Lynn McVey lawyer
Lindenlaub, J.C. electrical engineer, educator
Loeffler, Frank Joseph physicist, educator
McBride, Angela Barron nursing educator
Melhorn, Wilton Newton geosciences educator
Meyer, Brud Richard pharmaceutical company executive
Michaud, Howard Henry conservation educator
Nicholson, Ralph Lester botanist, educator
O'Callaghan, Patti Louise court program administrator
O'Connell, Lawrence B. lawyer
Ott, Karl Otto nuclear engineering educator, consultant
Porile, Norbert Thomas chemistry educator
Rubin, Jean Estelle mathematics educator
Sato, Hiroshi materials science educator
Schönemann, Peter Hans psychology educator
Sperandio, Glen Joseph pharmacy educator
Stob, Martin physiology educator
Truce, William Everett chemist, educator
VanHandel, Ralph Anthony librarian
Vaughn, Vicki Lynn education educator
Whitsel, Robert Malcolm retired insurance company executive

### Lagrange
Brown, George E. judge, educator
Young, Rebecca Lee special education educator

### Lanesville
Cleveland, Peggy Rose Richey cytotechnologist

### Lawrenceburg
Dautel, Charles Shreve retired mining company executive
Taylor, Donna Bloyd vocational rehabilitation consultant

### Leesburg
Pryor, Dixie Darlene elementary education educator

### Leo
Worman, Richard W. insurance company executive, state senator

### Linden
Lefebvre, Gren Gordon school superintendent

### Logansport
Brewer, Robert Allen physician
Parker, Camille Killian physician, surgeon

### Lynnville
Ellis, Joe Mike reclamation scientist

### Madison
Gunter, Frank Elliott artist
Snodgrass, Robert Eugene psychiatrist

### Marion
Barnes, James Byron university president
Fisher, Pierre James, Jr. physician
Hall, Charles Adams information systems specialist
Kucera, Keith Edward physician
McFarlane, Neil church administrator
McIntyre, Robert Walter church official
Philbert, Robert Earl secondary school educator

### Martinsville
Kendall, Robert Stanton newspaper editor, journalist
†Miller, John foundation administrator

### Merrillville
Brenman, Stephen Morris lawyer
Hale, Carl Stanley clinical psychologist, poet
Magry, Martha J. elementary education educator
Roberts, Samuel Alden secondary school educator
Wang, Josephine L. Fen physician
†White, Dean advertising executive

### Michigan City
Blake, George Alan, Jr. non-profit association executive
Brockway, Lee J. architect
Higgins, William Henry Clay, III retired telecommunications consultant
Mothkur, Sridhar Rao radiologist
Nasr, Suhayl Joseph psychiatrist

### Middlebury
Guequierre, John Phillip manufacturing company executive

### Milltown
Pesek, James Robert management consultant

### Mishawaka
Bella, Dantina Carmen Quartaroli human services consultant
Goebel, Richard Alan veterinarian
Kapson, Jordan automotive executive
Ponko, William Reuben architect
Scott, Darrel Joseph healthcare executive
Silver, Neil Marvin manufacturing executive
Troyer, LeRoy Seth architect

### Monroeville
Ray, Annette D. business executive
Sorgen, Elizabeth Ann retired educator

### Monrovia
Bennett, James Edward retired plastic surgeon, educator

### Monticello
Howarth, David H. retired bank executive
McTaggart, Patrick William principal

### Montpelier
Neff, Kenneth D. realtor

### Moores Hill
Ramsey, William Ray professional society administrator

### Morgantown
Boyce, Gerald G. artist, educator

### Mount Vernon
Bach, Steve Crawford lawyer

### Muncie
Anderson, Stefan Stolen bank executive
Barber, Earl Eugene consulting firm executive
Bell, Stephen Scott (Steve Bell) journalist, educator
Bennon, Saul electrical engineer, transformer consultant
Carmin, Robert Leighton retired geography educator
Cheng, Chu Yuan economics educator
Connally, Sandra Jane Oppy art educator
Eddy, Darlene Mathis poet, educator
Fisher, John Wesley manufacturing company executive
Freestone, Jeannette Warren nurse practitioner
Harris, Joseph McAllister chemist
Hendrix, Jon Richard biology educator
Henzlik, Raymond Eugene zoophysiologist, educator
Hoffman, Mary Catherine nurse anesthetist
Irvine, Phyllis Eleanor Kuhnle nursing educator, administrator
Joyaux, Alain Georges art museum director
Kelly, Eric Damian lawyer, educator
Kumbula, Tendayi Sengerwe journalism educator
Leitze, Annette Emily Ricks mathematics educator
Mertens, Thomas Robert biology educator
Radcliff, William Franklin lawyer
Rippy, Frances Marguerite Mayhew English language educator
Robold, Alice Ilene mathematician, educator
Sappenfield, Charles Madison architect, educator
Sargent, Thomas Andrew political science educator, university program director
Seymour, Richard Deming technology educator
Sissel, George Allen manufacturing executive
Smith, Van P. airplane engine company executive
Sursa, Charles David banker
Swartz, B(enjamin) K(insell), Jr. archaeologist, educator
Terrell, Pamela Sue pharmacist
Wagner, Joseph Crider retired academic administrator
Zemtsov, Alexander dermatology and biochemistry educator

### Munster
Corsiglia, Robert Joseph electrical construction company executive
Fies, James David elementary education educator
Luerssen, Frank Wonson retired steel company executive
Moore, Carolyn Lannin video specialist
†Platis, Chris Steven educator
Sherman, Mona Diane school system administrator

### Nappanee
Shea, James F. manufacturing executive

### Nashville
McDermott, James Alexander retired lawyer
McDermott, Renée R(assler) lawyer

### New Albany
Baker, Claude Douglas biology educator, researcher
Chowhan, Naveed Mahfooz oncologist
Conway, William Frederick, Sr. business founder
Crooks, Edwin William former academic administrator
Riehl, Jane Ellen education educator

### New Carlisle
Serpe-Schroeder, Patricia L. elementary education educator

### New Castle
Walburn, John Clifford mental health services professional

### New Haven
Chapman, Reid Gillis former broadcasting company executive

### Newburgh
McGavic, Judy L. coal company official
Reavis, Hubert Gray, Jr. metal products executive
Tierney, Gordon Paul real estate broker, genealogist

### Noblesville
Almquist, Donald John retired electronics company executive
Morrison, Joseph Young transportation consultant
Thacker, Jerry Lynn school administrator
Wilson, Norman Glenn church administrator, writer

### North Manchester
Harshbarger, Richard B. economics educator

### Notre Dame
Arnold, Peri Ethan political scientist
Bartell, Ernest economist, educator
Bass, Steven Craig computer science educator
Bella, Salvatore Joseph management educator
Blenkinsopp, Joseph biblical studies educator
Browne, Cornelius Payne physics educator
Bruns, Gerald L. English literature educator
Castellino, Francis Joseph university dean
Craypo, Charles labor economics educator
Crosson, Frederick James former university dean, humanities educator
Delaney, Cornelius Francis philosophy educator
De Santis, Vincent Paul historian, educator
Despres, Leo Arthur sociology and anthropology educator, academic administrator
Dowty, Alan Kent political scientist, educator
Feigl, Dorothy Marie chemistry educator, university official
Gabriel, Astrik Ladislas medieval studies educator, scholar
Goulet, Denis André political science educator, writer, development ethicist
Gray, William Guerin civil engineering educator
Grazin, Igor Nikolai law educator, state official
Gunn, Alan law educator
Gutting, Gary Michael philosophy educator
Haimo, Ethan T. music educator
Hatch, Nathan Orr university administrator
Hayes, Stephen Matthew librarian
Helquist, Paul M. chemistry educator, researcher
Hesburgh, Theodore Martin clergyman, former university president
Huber, Paul William biochemistry educator, researcher
Jemielity, Thomas John English educator
Jensen, Richard Jorg biology educator
Jerger, Edward William mechanical engineer, university dean
Kennedy, John Joseph political science educator
Kmiec, Douglas William government official, law educator, columnist
Kogge, Peter Michael computer scientist, educator
Kohn, James Paul engineering educator
Langford, James Rouleau university press administrator
Lanzinger, Klaus language educator
Lauck, Anthony Joseph artist, retired art educator, priest
Leege, David Calhoun political scientist, educator
Loescher, Gilburt Damian international relations educator
Malloy, Edward Aloysius priest, university administrator, educator
Marshalek, Eugene Richard physics educator
Matthias, John Edward English literature educator
McBrien, Richard Peter theology educator
McCormick, Richard Arthur priest, religion educator, writer
McInerny, Ralph Matthew philosophy educator, author
Mc Mullin, Ernan Vincent philosophy educator
Michel, Anthony Nikolaus electrical engineering educator, researcher
Mirowski, Philip Edward economics educator
Nugent, Walter Terry King historian
O'Meara, Onorato Timothy academic administrator, mathematician
O'Meara, Thomas Franklin priest, educator
Pollak, Barth mathematics educator
Pollard, Morris microbiologist, educator
Porter, Dean Allen art museum director, art historian, educator
†Poulin, David James hockey coach
Quinn, Philip Lawrence philosophy educator
Reilly, Frank Kelly business educator
Rice, (Ethel) Ann publishing executive, editor
Roche, Mark William German language educator
Rosenberg, Charles Michael art historian, educator
Sain, Michael Kent electrical engineering educator
Sayre, Kenneth Malcolm philosophy educator
Scheidt, W. Robert chemistry educator, researcher
Schmitz, Roger Anthony chemical engineering educator, academic administrator
Schuler, Robert Hugo chemist, educator
Shannon, William Norman, III marketing and international business educator, food service executive
Sommese, Andrew John mathematics educator
Stoll, Wilhelm mathematics educator
Stroik, Duncan Gregory architect, architectural design educator
Swartz, Thomas R. economist, educator
Szewczyk, Albin Anthony engineering educator
Thomas, John Kerry chemistry educator
Trozzolo, Anthony Marion chemistry educator
Truesdell, Timothy Lee research director, consultant, real estate investor
Varma, Arvind chemical engineering educator, researcher
Vecchio, Robert Peter business management educator
Wadsworth, Michael A. athletic director, former ambassador
Walicki, Andrzej Stanislaw history of ideas educator
Walshe, Aubrey Peter political science educator
Weigert, Andrew Joseph sociology educator
White, James Floyd theology educator
Wong, Warren James mathematics educator

### Oakland City
Kendrick, William David physician assistant

### Ogden Dunes
Gasser, Wilbert (Warner), Jr. retired banker
Mulvaney, Mary Jean physical education educator

### Owensville
Snow, Jeffrey Scott fuels engineer

### Pendleton
Kischuk, Richard Karl insurance company executive
Phenis, Nancy Sue educational administrator

### Peru
Davidson, John Robert dentist
Marburger, John Allen food manufacturing company executive
Stackhouse, John Wesley publishing executive

### Plymouth
Sherwood, Lillian Anna librarian, retired

### Portage
Cunningham, R. John retired financial consultant
Cuttill, Raymond Francis, Jr. psychologist
Henke, Robert John lawyer
Murphy, Newton Jerome steel company executive
Zuick, Diane Martina elementary education educator

### Portland
Martig, John Frederick anesthesiologist

### Princeton
Mullins, Richard Austin chemical engineer

### Purdue University
Bannatyne, Mark William McKenzie technical graphics educator
Liley, Peter Edward mechanical engineering educator

### Rensselaer
Ahler, Kenneth James physician
Shannon, Albert Joseph education educator

### Richmond
Bennett, Douglas Carleton academic administrator
Farber, Evan Ira librarian
Kirk, Thomas Garrett, Jr. librarian
Maurer, Johan Fredrik religious denomination administrator
Passmore, Jan William private investor
Porter, Patrick Kevin secondary education educator, administrator
Robinson, Dixie Faye school system administrator
Ronald, Pauline Carol art educator
Roop, Eugene Frederic religion educator
†Rubenstein, David H. media manufacturing executive

Talbot, Ardith Ann editor

### Rochester
Merrill, Arthur Lewis retired theology educator

### Rolling Prairie
Eggleston, Alan Edward musician, opera singer, Boy Scout executive

### Saint Mary Of The Woods
Doherty, Sister Barbara, S.P. (Ann Doherty) academic administrator

### Saint Meinrad
Daly, Simeon Philip John librarian

### Sandborn
Gregg, John Richard lawyer, state legislator

### Santa Claus
Platthy, Jeno cultural association executive

### Schererville
Griffin, Anita Jane elementary education educator

### Seymour
Bollinger, Don Mills grocery company executive
Gill, W(alter) Brent lawyer
Norrell, Mary Patricia nursing educator

### Shelby
Kurzeja, Richard Eugene professional society administrator

### Shelbyville
Lisher, James Richard lawyer
Short, Ann Marie Herold library director

### South Bend
Altman, Arnold David business executive
Black, Virginia Morrow writer
Carey, John Leo lawyer
Charles, Isabel university administrator
Cohen, Ronald S. accountant
Ecker, Carol Adele veterinarian
Fatum, Sandra Kaye nurse
Ford, George Burt lawyer
Grant, Robert Allen federal judge
Gray, Francis Campbell bishop
Gray, Frank C. bishop
†Greenberg, Bruce L. health facility adminstrator
Harriman, Gerald Eugene retired business administrator, economics educator
Horsbrugh, Patrick architect, educator
Jorgensen, Robert William product engineer
MacLeod, John college basketball coach
Manion, Daniel Anthony federal judge
McGill, Warren Everett lawyer, consultant
Miller, Robert L., Jr. federal judge
Mills, Nancy Anne elementary education educator
Moore-Riesbeck, Susan osteopathic physician
Murphy, Christopher Joseph, III financial executive
Murphy, William Host sales executive
Perrin, Kenneth Lynn university chancellor
Plunkett, Phyllis Jean nursing administrator
Raclin, Ernestine Morris banker
Reinke, William John lawyer
Ripple, Kenneth Francis federal judge
Rodibaugh, Robert Kurtz judge
Schurz, Franklin Dunn, Jr. media executive
Seall, Stephen Albert lawyer
Shaffer, Thomas Lindsay lawyer, educator
Sharp, Allen chief federal judge
Sopko, Thomas Clement lawyer
Szigeti, Michelle Marie critical care nurse
Thomas, Debi (Debra J. Thomas) ice skater
van Inwagen, Peter Jan philosophy educator
Vogel, Nelson J., Jr. lawyer
Wensits, James Emrich newspaper editor
White, Robert Dennis pediatrician
Yeh, Tsung orchestral conductor

### Speedway
Unser, Alfred, Jr. professional race car driver

### Tell City
Gebhard, Diane Kay county administrator, political advisor

### Terre Haute
Aldridge, Sandra civic volunteer
Baker, Ronald Lee English educator
Bopp, James, Jr. lawyer
Brennan, Matthew Cannon English literature educator, poet
Campbell, Judith May physical education educator
Carmony, Marvin Dale linguist, educator
Carraher, Shawn Michael management educator
Coe, Michual William physical therapist
De Marr, Mary Jean English language educator
Dusanic, Donald Gabriel parasitology educator, microbiologist
Gilman, David Alan education educator, editor
Grimley, Liam Kelly special education educator
Guthrie, Frank Albert chemistry educator
Hulbert, Samuel Foster college president
Hunt, Effie Neva former college dean, former English educator
Jerry, Robert Howard education educator
Kicklighter, Clois Earl academic administrator
Kunkler, Arnold William surgeon
Lamis, Leroy artist, retired educator
Landini, Richard George university president, emeritus English educator
Leach, Ronald George educational administration educator
Little, Robert David library science educator
Mausel, Paul Warner geography educator
Moore, John W. academic administrator
Moore, John William university president
Perry, Eston Lee real estate and equipment leasing company executive
Puckett, Robert Hugh political scientist, educator
Roshel, John Albert, Jr. orthodontist
Smith, Donald E. banker
Van Til, William education educator, writer
Wheelock, Larry Arthur engineer, consultant

### Unionville
Franklin, Frederick Russell retired legal association executive

Barta, James Omer *priest, psychology educator, church administrator*
Boettcher, Norbe Birosel *chemist*
Chapman, Kathleen Halloran *state legislator, lawyer*
Damrow, Richard G. *advertising executive*
Faches, William George *lawyer*
Feld, Thomas Robert *academic administrator*
Fick, E(arl) Dean *insurance executive*
Hansen, David Rasmussen *federal judge*
Healey, Edward Hopkins *architect*
Huber, Rita Norma *civic worker*
Kasparek, Ann Janine *health facility administrator*
Knapp, Barbara Allison *financial services, oncological nurse consultant*
Kucharski, Robert Joseph *power industry financial executive*
Lewis, Daniel Edward *systems engineer, computer company executive*
Lisio, Donald John *historian, educator*
Mc Manus, Edward Joseph *federal judge*
Melloy, Michael J. *federal judge*
Mitchell, Beverly Ann Bales *insurance agency owner, women's rights advocate*
Nazette, Richard Follett *lawyer*
Nebergall, Donald Charles *investment consultant*
Norris, Albert Stanley *psychiatrist, educator*
Novetzke, Sally Johnson *former ambassador*
Plagman, Ralph *principal*
Quarton, William Barlow *broadcasting company executive*
Reinertson, James Wayne *pediatrician*
Riley, Tom Joseph *lawyer*
Rosberg, Merilee Ann *education educator*
Stone, Herbert Marshall *architect*
Vanderpool, Ward Melvin *management and marketing consultant*
Wax, Nadine Virginia *retired banker*
Wilson, Robert Foster *lawyer*
Ziese, Nancylee Hanson *social worker*

## Center Point
Neenan, Thomas Francis *association executive, consultant*

## Chariton
Stuart, William Corwin *federal judge*
Vredenburg, Dwight Charles *retired supermarket chain executive*

## Charles City
Mc Cartney, Ralph Farnham *lawyer*
McCartney, Rhoda Huxsol *farm manager*

## Charter Oak
Kutschinski, Dorothy Irene *elementary education educator*

## Cherokee
Clark, Larry Dalton *civil engineer*

## City
Bjorndal, Arne Magne *endodontist*

## Clear Lake
Broshar, Robert Clare *architect*

## Clinton
Weil, Myron *retired banker*
Winkler, Joann Mary *secondary school educator*

## Clive
Miller, Kenneth Edward *sociologist, educator*

## Coon Rapids
Shirbroun, Richard Elmer *veterinarian, cattleman*

## Corydon
Olson, Diane Louise *secondary education educator*

## Council Bluffs
Boone, Dorothy Mae *county official*
Johnson, Michael Randy *insurance company executive*
Nelson, H. H. Red *insurance company executive*
Peterson, Richard William *magistrate judge, lawyer*
Roberts, Antonette *special education educator*

## Creston
Turner, Lula Mae Mansur *retail executive*

## Dallas Center
McDonald, John Cecil *lawyer*

## Davenport
Arnold, David Alan *surgeon*
Bhatti, Iftikhar Hamid *chiropractic educator*
Bradley, William Steven *art museum director*
Brocka, Bruce *editor, educator, software engineer*
Brocka, M. Suzanne *controller*
Campagna, Timothy Nicholas *institute executive*
Currence, Glennda Kay *elementary education educator*
DCamp, Charles Barton *musician, educator*
Fries, Peter Donald *ophthalmologist*
Gottlieb, Richard Douglas *media executive*
Jecklin, Lois Underwood *art corporation executive, consultant*
Juckem, Wilfred Philip *manufacturing company executive*
Le Grand, Clay *lawyer, former state justice*
Luzkow, Jack Lawrence *history educator, writer, consultant*
O'Keefe, Gerald Francis *bishop, retired*
Potter, Corinne Jean *librarian*
Rogalski, Edward J. *university administrator*
Runge, Kay Kretschmar *library director*
Shammas, Nicolas Wahib *internist, cardiologist*
Shaw, Donald Hardy *lawyer*
Vorbrich, Lynn Karl *lawyer, utility executive*
Weinberg, Marylin Lynn *foreign language educator*
Wilson, Frances Edna *protective services official*

## Davis City
Boswell, Leonard L. *congressman*

## Decorah
Belay, Stephen Joseph *lawyer*
Erdman, Lowell Paul *civil engineer, land surveyor*
Farwell, Elwin D. *minister, educational consultant*
Kalsow, Kathryn Ellen *library clerk*
Price, Lucile Brickner Brown *retired civic worker*

## Des Moines
Andreasen, James Hallis *state supreme court judge*
Begleiter, Martin David *law educator, consultant*
Boyle, Bruce James *publisher*
Branstad, Terry Edward *governor, lawyer*
Bremer, Celeste F. *judge*
Brickman, Kenneth Alan *state lottery executive*
Brooks, Roger Kay *insurance company executive*
Bucksbaum, Matthew *real estate investment trust company executive*
Burnett, Robert A. *publisher*
†Byal, Nancy Louise *food editor*
Campbell, Bruce Irving *lawyer*
Carrigan, Pamela Sue *family development specialist*
Carroll, Frank J. *lawyer, educator*
Charron, Joseph L. *bishop*
Clark, Beverly Ann *lawyer*
Claypool, David L. *lawyer*
Collins, Richard Francis *microbiologist, educator*
Conlin, Roxanne Barton *lawyer*
Corning, Joy Cole *state official*
Daggett, Horace Clinton *retired state legislator*
Davilla, Donna Elaine *school system administrator*
Davis, James Casey *lawyer*
DeAngelo, Anthony James *media specialist, architect*
Deluhery, Patrick John *state senator*
Demorest, Allan Frederick *retired psychologist*
Drake, Richard Francis *state senator*
Drury, David J. *insurance company executive*
Durrenberger, William John *retired army general, educator, investor*
Edwards, John Duncan *law educator, librarian*
Eichner, Kay Marie *mental health nurse*
Ellis, Mary Louise Helgeson *insurance company executive*
Elmets, Harry Barnard *osteopath, dermatologist*
Epting, C. Christopher *bishop*
Fagg, George Gardner *federal judge*
Ferrari, Michael Richard, Jr. *university administrator*
Fisher, Thomas George *lawyer, retired media company executive*
Fisher, Thomas George, Jr. *lawyer*
Fitzgerald, Michael Lee *state official*
Foster, James Franklin *professional sports management executive*
Giunta, Joseph *conductor, music director*
Glomset, Daniel Anders *physician*
Goldsmith, Janet Jane *pediatric nurse practitioner*
Gotsdiner, Murray Bennett *lawyer*
Graham, Diane E. *newspaper editor*
Grefe, Rolland Eugene *lawyer*
Gross, Mary Elizabeth *pharmacy manager, educator*
Hall, Donald Vincent *social worker*
Hansell, Edgar Frank *lawyer*
Harper, Patricia M. *state legislator*
Harris, Charles Elmer *lawyer*
Harris, K. David *justice*
Hill, Luther Lyons, Jr. *lawyer*
Hockenberg, Harlan David *lawyer*
Hutchison, Theodore Murtagh *insurance company executive*
Jensen, Dick Leroy *lawyer*
Jordan, Charles Wesley *bishop*
Kalainov, Sam Charles *insurance company executive*
Kaplan, Jerry *magazine publisher*
Kelley, Bruce Gunn *insurance company executive, lawyer*
Kelley, Robb Beardsley *retired insurance company executive*
Kerr, William T. *publishing and broadcasting executive*
Kramer, Mary Elizabeth *health services executive, state legislator*
Kruidenier, David *newspaper executive*
Langdon, Herschel Garrett *lawyer*
Larson, Jerry L. *state supreme court justice*
Lavorato, Louis A. *state supreme court justice*
Lawless, James L. *editor, columnist*
Leach, Dave Francis *editor, musician*
Lemmon, Jean Marie *editor-in-chief*
Lewis, Calvin Fred *architect, educator*
Longstaff, Ronald E. *federal judge*
Lund, Doris Hibbs *retired dietitian*
MacDonald, Kenneth *journalist, former editor*
Marker, David George *university president*
Mattern, David Bruce *elementary education educator*
McGiverin, Arthur A. *state supreme court justice*
McLane, Peter *broadcast executive*
Miller, Thomas J. *state attorney general*
Molden, A(nna) Jane *retired counselor*
Moulder, William H. *chief of police*
Murphy, Patrick Joseph *state representative*
Myers, Mary Kathleen *publishing executive*
Narber, Gregg Ross *lawyer*
Neis, Arthur Veral *healthcare and development company executive*
Nelson, Charlotte Bowers *public administrator*
†Pannier, Cheryl Jane *radio broadcast executive*
Pate, Paul Danny *state senator, business executive, entrepreneur*
Peddicord, Roland Dale *lawyer*
Peterson, David Charles *photojournalist*
Powell, Sharon Lee *social welfare organization administrator*
Power, Joseph Edward *lawyer*
Reece, Maynard Fred *artist, author*
Richards, Riley Harry *insurance company executive*
Rittmer, Elaine Heneke *library media specialist*
Rittmer, Sheldon *state senator, farmer*
Rodgers, Louis Dean *retired surgeon*
Rogers, Rodney Albert *biologist, educator*
Rosen, Matthew Stephen *botanist, consultant*
Rosenberg, Ralph *former state senator, lawyer, consultant, educator*
Schneider, William George *former life insurance company executive*
Shors, John D. *lawyer*
Slade, Llewellyn Eugene *lawyer, engineer*
Smith, Mary Louise *politics and public affairs consultant*
Smith, Sharman Bridges *state librarian*
Snell, Bruce M., Jr. *state supreme court justice*
Song, Joseph *pathologist, educator*
Speas, Raymond Aaron *retired insurance company executive*
Stauffer, William Albert *insurance company executive*
†Stubbs, David H. *vascular surgeon*
Szymoniak, Elaine Eisfelder *state senator*
Thoman, Mark Edward *pediatrician*
Vande Krol, Jerry Lee *architect*
Van Zante, Shirley M(ae) *magazine editor*
Vietor, Harold Duane *federal judge*
Webb-Groe, Mary Christine *special education educator*
Westphal, Deborah Louise *retail executive, choreographer*
Wine, Donald Arthur *lawyer*
Witke, David Rodney *newspaper editor*
Wolle, Charles Robert *federal judge*
Zagoren, Allen Jeffrey *surgeon*

## Dubuque
Agria, John Joseph *retired college official*
Bertsch, Frank Henry *furniture manufacturing company executive*
Crahan, Jack Bertsch *manufacturing company executive*
Drummond, Richard Henry *religion educator*
Dunn, M. Catherine *college administrator, educator*
Ernst, Daniel Pearson *lawyer*
Hammer, David Lindley *lawyer, author*
Hanus, Jerome George *archbishop*
Hemmer, Paul Edward *musician, composer, broadcasting executive*
Kolz, Beverly Anne *publishing executive*
McDonald, Robert Delos *manufacturing company executive*
Peterson, Walter Fritiof *academic administrator*
Pike, George Harold, Jr. *religious organization executive, clergyman*
Toale, Thomas Edward *school system administrator, priest*
Tully, Thomas Alois *building materials executive, consultant, educator*

## Dunkerton
Wede, Richard J. *school superintendent*

## Elliott
Hunt, Colleen A. *college administrator*

## Fairfield
Hawthorne, Timothy Robert *direct response advertising and communications company executive*
Schaefer, Jimmie Wayne, Jr. *agricultural company executive*
Wright, Max *information processing executive, consultant, youth leadership corporate training executive*

## Forest City
Beebe, Raymond Mark *lawyer*

## Fort Dodge
Pratt, Diane Adele *elementary education educator*

## Fort Madison
Carroll, Melody Jane *educator, writer*

## George
Symens, Maxine Brinkert Tanner *restaurant owner*

## Gilmore City
Worthington, Patricia *elementary education educator*

## Glenwood
Campbell, William Edward *state hospital school administrator*

## Greenfield
Wilson, Wendy Melgard *primary and elementary school educator*

## Grimes
Harper, Karen Beidelman *elementary school educator*

## Grinnell
Adelberg, Arnold Melvin *mathematics educator, researcher*
Campbell, David George *ecologist, researcher, author*
Cervene, Richard T. *art educator*
Christiansen, Kenneth Allen *biologist, educator*
Erickson, Luther Eugene *chemist, educator*
Ferguson, Pamela Anderson *mathematics educator, educational administrator*
Fitzgerald, Michael J. *secondary school principal*
Kaiser, Daniel Hugh *historian, educator*
Kintner, Philip L. *history educator*
Kissane, James Donald *English literature educator*
Leggett, Glenn *former English language educator, academic administrator*
McKee, Christopher Fulton *librarian, naval historian, educator*
Michaels, Jennifer Tonks *foreign language educator*
Mitchell, Orlen E. *clergyman, former college president*
Walker, Waldo Sylvester *academic administrator*

## Harlan
Ahrenholtz, Mary Mickelson *special education educator*

## Hiawatha
Ashbacher, Charles David *computer programmer, educator, mathematician*

## Indianola
Jennings, Stephen Grant *academic administrator*
Larsen, Robert LeRoy *artistic director*

## Iowa City
Abboud, Francois Mitry *physician, educator*
Addis, Laird Clark, Jr. *philosopher, educator, musician*
Afifi, Adel Kassim *physician*
Albrecht, William Price *economist, educator, government official*
Andreasen, Nancy Coover *psychiatrist, educator*
Apicella, Michael Allen *physician, educator*
Arora, Jasbir Singh *engineering educator*
Aydelotte, Myrtle Kitchell *nursing administrator, educator, consultant*
Baird, Robert Dahlen *religious educator*
Baker, Richard Graves *geology educator, palynologist*
Balukas, Jean *professional pocket billiard player*
Banker, Gilbert Stephen *industrial and physical pharmacy educator, administrator*
Barkan, Joel David *political science educator*
Baron, Jeffrey *pharmacologist, educator*
Bayne, David Cowan *priest, legal scholar, law educator*
Bedell, George Noble *physician, educator*
Bell, Marvin Hartley *poet, English language educator*
Bentz, Dale Monroe *librarian*
Berg, Mary Jaylene *pharmacy educator, researcher*
Bergman, Ronald Arly *anatomist, educator*
Bishara, Samir Edward *orthodontist*
Bonfield, Arthur Earl *lawyer, educator*
Brennan, Robert Lawrence *educational director, psychometrician*
Broffitt, James Drake *professor statistics and actuarial science*
Bruch, Delores Ruth *education educator, musician*
Buckwalter, Joseph Addison *orthopedic surgeon, educator*
Burns, C(harles) Patrick *hematologist-oncologist*
Burton, Donald Joseph *chemistry educator*
Butchvarov, Panayot Krustev *philosophy educator*
Carmichael, Gregory Richard *chemical engineering educator*
Clifton, James Albert *physician, educator*
Collins, Daniel W. *accountant, educator*
Colloton, John William *university health care executive*
Cooper, Reginald Rudyard *orthopedic surgeon, educator*
Cox, Jeffrey Lee *history educator*
Cruden, Robert William *botany educator*
Daniels, Lacy *microbiology educator*
Davis, Tom *university athletic coach*
Dettmer, Helena R. *classics educator*
Donelson, John Everett *biochemistry educator, molecular biologist*
Downer, Robert Nelson *lawyer*
Duck, Steve Weatherill *communications educator*
Dudziak, Mary Louise *law educator, lecturer*
Eckhardt, Richard Dale *physician, educator*
Eckstein, John William *physician, educator*
Ehrenhaft, Johann Leo *surgeon*
Erkonen, William E. *radiologist, medical educator*
Ertl, Wolfgang *German language and literature educator*
Eyman, Earl Duane *electrical science educator, consultant*
Feldt, Leonard Samuel *university educator and administrator*
Fellows, Robert Ellis *medical educator, medical scientist*
Ferguson, Richard L. *educational administrator*
Filer, Lloyd Jackson, Jr. *pediatric educator, clinical investigator*
Folsom, Lowell Edwin *English language educator*
Forell, George Wolfgang *religion educator*
Forsythe, Robert Elliott *economics educator*
Fry, Hayden *university athletic coach*
Fuller, John Williams *economics educator*
Fumerton, Richard Anthony *philosopher educator*
Galask, Rudolph Peter *obstetrician and gynecologist*
Galbraith, William Bruce *physician, educator*
Gantz, Bruce Jay *otolaryngologist, educator*
Gelfand, Lawrence Emerson *historian, educator*
Gerber, John Christian *English language educator*
Gergis, Samir Danial *anesthesiologist, educator*
Goldstein, Jonathan Amos *ancient history and classics educator*
Grabbe, Crockett Lane *physicist, researcher, writer*
Graham, Jorie *author*
Green, William *archaeologist*
Grose, Charles Frederick *pediatrician, infectious disease specialist*
Gurnett, Donald Alfred *physics educator*
Hammond, Harold Logan *pathology educator, oral and maxillofacial pathologist*
Hardt, Hanno Richard Eduard *communications educator*
Hardy, James Chester *speech pathologist, educator*
Haug, Edward Joseph, Jr. *mechanical engineering educator, simulation research engineer*
Hausler, William John, Jr. *microbiologist, educator, public health laboratory administrator*
Hawley, Ellis Wayne *historian, educator*
Heistad, Donald Dean *cardiologist*
Hering, Robert Gustave *mechanical engineer, educator, university administrator*
Hines, N. William *law educator, administrator*
Hoffmann, Louis Gerhard *immunologist, educator, sex therapist*
Hogg, Robert Vincent, Jr. *mathematical statistician, educator*
Holstein, Jay Allen *Judaic studies educator*
Hornsby, Roger Allen *classics educator*
Howell, Robert Edward *hospital administrator*
Husted, Russell Forest *research scientist*
Jacobs, Richard Matthew *dentist, orthodontics educator*
January, Lewis Edward *physician, educator*
Johnson, Eugene Walter *mathematics editor*
Johnson, Nicholas *writer, lawyer, lecturer*
Justice, Donald Rodney *poet, educator*
Kelch, Robert Paul *pediatric endocrinologist*
Keller, Eliot Aaron *broadcasting executive*
Kelley, Patricia Lou *social work educator*
Kerber, Linda Kaufman *historian, educator*
Kessel, Richard Glen *zoology educator*
Kim, Chong Lim *political science educator*
Kirchner, Peter Thomas *physician nuclear medicine, educator, consultant*
Kisker, Carl Thomas *physician*
Kleinfeld, Erwin *mathematician, educator*
Knapp, Howard Raymond *internist, clinical pharmacologist*
Knutson, John Franklin *psychology educator, clinical psychologist*
Koch, Donald LeRoy *geologist, state agency administrator*
Kottick, Edward Leon *music educator, harpsichord maker*
Krause, Walter *retired economics educator, consultant*
Kurtz, Sheldon Francis *lawyer, educator*
Kusiak, Andrew *manufacturing engineer, educator*
Lance, George Milward *mechanical engineering educator*
Lauer, Ronald Martin *pediatric cardiologist, researcher*
LeBlond, Richard Foard *internist, educator*
†Lee, Angie *basketball coach*
Levey, Samuel *health care administration educator*
Linhardt, Robert John *medicinal chemistry educator*
Loewenberg, Gerhard *political science educator*
Long, John Paul *pharmacologist, educator*
Longren, Karl Erik *electrical and computer engineering educator*
Marshall, Jeffrey Scott *mechanical engineer, educator*
Mason, Edward Eaton *surgeon*
Mather, Betty Bang *musician, educator*
Mather, Roger Frederick *music educator, writer*
McAndrew, Paul Joseph, Jr. *lawyer*

Medh, Jheem D. *medical educator, biochemistry researcher*
Milkman, Roger Dawson *genetics educator, molecular evolution researcher*
Miller, Richard Keith *engineering educator*
Montgomery, Rex *biochemist, educator*
Morriss, Frank Howard, Jr. *pediatrics educator*
Muir, Ruth Brooks *counselor, substance abuse service coordinator*
†Nair, Vasu *chemist, educator*
Nathan, Peter E. *psychologist, educator*
Nelson, Herbert Leroy *psychiatrist*
Nelson, Richard Philip *medical educator, dean*
Neumann, Roy Covert *architect*
Noyes, Russell, Jr. *psychiatrist*
Olin, William Harold *orthodontist, educator*
Osborne, James William *radiation biologist*
Patel, Virendra Chaturbhai *mechanical engineering educator*
Paulina, Diana *alternative school educator*
Payne, Gerald Lew *physics educator*
Percas de Ponseti, Helena *foreign language and literature educator*
Persons, Stow Spaulding *historian, educator*
Plapp, Bryce Vernon *biochemistry educator*
Ponseti, Ignacio Vives *orthopaedic surgery educator*
Potra, Florian Alexander *mathematics educator*
Prokopoff, Stephen Stephen *art museum director, educator*
Raeburn, John Hay *English language educator*
Randell, Richard C. *mathematics educator*
Richenbacher, Wayne Edward *cardiothoracic surgeon*
Richerson, Hal Bates *physician, internist, allergist, immunologist, educator*
Riesz, Peter Charles *marketing educator, consultant*
Ringen, Catherine Oleson *linguistics educator*
Robertson, Timothy Joel *statistician, educator*
Robinson, Robert George *psychiatry educator*
Ross, Russell Marion *political science educator*
Routh, Joseph Isaac *biochemist*
Saks, Michael Jay *law educator*
Sayre, Robert Freeman *English language educator*
Schmidt, Julius *sculptor*
Schoenbaum, David Leon *historian*
Schultz, Louis William *judge*
Schulz, Rudolph Walter *university dean emeritus*
Shannon, Lyle William *sociology educator*
Siebert, Calvin D. *economist, educator*
Skorton, David Jan *university official, physician, educator, researcher*
Smith, Wilbur Lazear *radiologist, educator*
Snyder, Peter M. *medical educator, medical researcher*
Solbrig, Ingeborg Hildegard *German literature educator, author*
Stay, Barbara *zoologist, educator*
Steele, Oliver *English educator*
†Stein, Robert A. *writer*
Stern, Gerald Daniel *poet*
Stratton, Margaret Mary *art educator*
Strauss, John Steinert *dermatologist, educator*
Tephly, Thomas Robert *pharmacologist, toxicologist, educator*
Thompson, Herbert Stanley *neuro-ophthalmologist*
Titze, Ingo Roland *physics educator*
Tomkovicz, James Joseph *law educator*
Trank, Douglas Monty *rhetoric and speech communications educator*
Tsalikian, Eva *physician, educator*
Van Allen, James Alfred *physicist, educator*
Van Gilder, John Corley *neurosurgeon, educator*
Vaughan, Emmett John *academic dean, insurance educator*
Vernon, David Harvey *lawyer, educator*
Wachal, Robert Stanley *linguistics educator, consultant*
Wasserman, Edward Arnold *psychology educator*
Weinberger, Miles M. *physician, pediatric educator*
Weingeist, Thomas Alan *ophthalmology educator*
Weinstock, Joel Vincent *immunologist*
Whitmore, Jon Scott *university official, play director*
Widiss, Alan I. *lawyer, educator*
Wing, Adrien Katherine *law educator*
Wunder, Charles C(ooper) *physiology and biophysics educator, gravitational biologist*
Wurster, Dale Erwin *pharmacy educator, university dean*
Ziegler, Ekhard Erich *pediatrics educator*
Zimmer, Paul Jerome *publisher, editor, poet*

**Johnston**
Churchill, Steven Wayne *state legislator, fund-raising consultant*
Duvick, Donald Nelson *plant breeder*
Leitner, David Larry *lawyer*
Odell, Mary Jane *former state official*

**Kellogg**
Anderson, Dale C. *state agency professional, travel consultant*

**Keokuk**
Atterberg, Douglas Keith *financial planner*
Mills, Sylvia Janet *secondary education educator*

**Knoxville**
Joslyn, Wallace Danforth *psychologist*
Taylor, Mary Kay *geriatrics nurse*

**Lamoni**
Wight, Darlene *retired speech educator*

**Lockridge**
Wolfe, Eva Agnes *retired educator*

**Madrid**
Handy, Richard Lincoln *civil engineer, educator*

**Marion**
McDonald, Carolyn Ann *dance educator, choreographer*

**Marshalltown**
Brennecke, Allen Eugene *lawyer*
Geffe, Kent Lyndon *lawyer, educator*
Shawstad, Raymond Vernon *business owner, retired computer specialist*

**Mason City**
Collison, Jim *business executive*
Kuhlman, James Weldon *county extension education director*
MacNider, Jack *retired cement company executive*

Rosenberg, Dale Norman *retired psychology educator*
Schumacher, Larry P. *health facility administrator*
Winston, Harold Ronald *lawyer*

**Mc Callsburg**
Lounsberry, Robert Horace *former state government administrator*

**Middle Amana**
Setzer, Kirk *religious leader*

**Mount Vernon**
Elliott, Candice K. *interior designer*
Ruppel, Howard James, Jr. *sociologist*

**Muscatine**
Coulter, Charles Roy *lawyer*
Dahl, Arthur Ernest *former manufacturing executive, consultant*
Dvorchak, Thomas Edward *financial executive*
Fosholt, Sanford Kenneth *consulting engineer*
Howe, Stanley Merrill *manufacturing company executive*
Johnson, Donald Lee *agricultural materials processing company executive*
Kautz, Richard Carl *chemical and feed company executive*
Koll, Richard Leroy *retired chemical company executive*
McMains, Melvin L(ee) *controller*
Nepple, James Anthony *lawyer*
Stanley, Richard Holt *consulting engineer*
Strand, Dean Paul *disc jockey, audio engineer*
Thomopulos, Gregs G. *consulting engineering company executive*
Yoder, Anna Mary *reading educator*

**Nevada**
Countryman, Dayton Wendell *lawyer*

**New Hampton**
Yared, Linda S. *mechanical engineer*

**New Sharon**
Sullivan, Mary Jane *elementary school educator*

**Newton**
Bennett, Edward James *lawyer*
Cooper, Janis Campbell *public relations executive*
Hadley, Leonard Anson *appliance manufacturing corporation executive*
Haines, Richard Joseph *appliance manufacturing executive*
†Ward, Lloyd D. *appliance company executive*

**North Liberty**
Glenister, Brian Frederick *geologist, educator*

**Oakdale**
Spriestersbach, Duane Caryl *university administrator, speech pathology educator*

**Oelwein**
McFarlane, Beth Lucetta Troester *former mayor*

**Orange City**
Hancock, Albert Sidney, Jr. *engineering executive*
Scorza, Sylvio Joseph *religion educator*

**Osceola**
Reynoldson, Walter Ward *state supreme court chief justice*

**Oskaloosa**
Gleason, Carol Ann *mental health nurse, educator*
Porter, David Lindsey *history and political science educator, author*
Steele, Betty Louise *retired banker*

**Ottumwa**
Krafka, Mary Baird *lawyer*

**Pacific Junction**
Krogstad, Jack Lynn *accounting educator*

**Pella**
Farver, Mary Joan *building products company executive*

**Plainfield**
Lynes, James William, Sr. *communications company executive*

**Remsen**
Hamil, Lynn Ray *secondary education educator*

**Saint Ansgar**
Koenigs, Deo Aloysius *state representative*

**Schaller**
Currie, James Morton *bank executive*

**Shenandoah**
Rose, Jennifer Joan *lawyer*

**Sioux Center**
Schut, Donna Sue *elementary education educator*

**Sioux City**
Andersen, Leonard Christian *former state legislator, real estate investor*
Deck, Paul Wayne, Jr. *federal judge*
Madsen, George Frank *lawyer*
Marks, Bernard Bailin *lawyer*
Mayne, Wiley Edward *lawyer*
Nichols, Roger Sabin *school counselor*
O'Brien, David A. *lawyer*
O'Brien, Donald Eugene *federal judge*
Rants, Carolyn Jean *college official*
Redwine, John Newland *physician*
Rooney, Gail Schields *college administrator*
Silverberg, David S. *financial consultant*
Soens, Lawrence D. *bishop*
Spellman, George Geneser, Sr. *internist*
Tommeraasen, Miles *college president*
Vaught, Richard Loren *urologist*
Walker, Jimmie Kent *mechanical engineer*
Wharton, Beverly Ann *utility company executive*

Wick, Sister Margaret *college administrator*

**Sloan**
Ullrich, Roxie Ann *special education educator*

**Spencer**
Lemke, Alan James *environmental specialist*
Pearson, Gerald Leon *food company executive*

**Spirit Lake**
Brett, George Wendell *retired geologist, philatelist*

**Springville**
Nyquist, John Davis *retired radio manufacturing company executive*

**Steamboat Rock**
Taylor, Ray *state senator*

**Storm Lake**
Crippin, Byron Miles, Jr. *lawyer, religious organization professional, consultant*
Hetzler, Susan Elizabeth Savage *educational administrator*
Miller, Curtis Herman *bishop*
Shafer, Everett Earl *business administration educator*

**Story City**
Kruger, Vicki Henry *elementary education educator*
Wattleworth, Roberta Ann *family practice physician, nursing home director*

**Stuart**
Bump, Wilbur Neil *retired lawyer*

**Urbandale**
Alumbaugh, JoAnn McCalla *magazine editor*

**Vinton**
Jorgensen, Ann *farmer*

**Walnut**
Myers, Gloria J. *elementary education educator*

**Washington**
Coffman, William Eugene *educational psychologist*

**Waterloo**
Kimm, Robert George *animal science educator*
Kober, Arletta Refshauge (Mrs. Kay L. Kober) *educational administrator*
Mast, Frederick William *construction company executive*
Rapp, Stephen John *United States attorney*
Taylor, Lyle Dewey *economic development company executive*
Wirth, David Eugene *software designer, consultant*

**Waverly**
Vogel, Robert Lee *college administrator, clergyman*

**West Branch**
Forsythe, Patricia Hays *development professional*
Mather, Mildred Eunice *retired archivist*
Sulg, Madis *corporation executive*
Walch, Timothy George *library administrator*

**West Des Moines**
Alberts, Marion Edward *physician*
Davis, Ronald Arthur *life insurance brokerage executive*
Dooley, Donald John *publishing executive*
Marshall, Russell Frank *consulting company executive*
Neiman, John Hammond *lawyer*
Pandeya, Nirmalendu Kumar *plastic surgeon, flight surgeon, military officer*
Pearson, Ronald Dale *retail food stores corporation executive*
Pomerantz, Marvin Alvin *container corporation executive*
Sather, Everett Norman *accountant*
Soth, Lauren Kephart *journalist, economist*
Westerbeck, Kenneth Edward *retired insurance company executive*
Zimmerman, Jo Ann *health services and educational consultant, former lieutenant governor*

**West Union**
Hansen, Ruth Lucille Hofer *business owner, consultant*

**Windsor Heights**
Belin, David William *lawyer*

**Zearing**
Britten, William Harry *editor, publisher*

# KANSAS

**Alta Vista**
Grimsley, Bessie Belle Gates *special education educator*

**Atchison**
Cray, Cloud Lanor, Jr. *grain products company executive*

**Atwood**
Gatlin, Fred *seed and feed business owner, state legislator*

**Baldwin City**
Lambert, Daniel Michael *academic administrator*

**Bonner Springs**
Elliott-Watson, Doris Jean *psychiatric, mental health and gerontological nurse educator*
Jarrett, Gracie Mae *junior high school guidance counselor*

**Chanute**
Dillard, Dean Innes *English language educator*

**Claflin**
Burmeister, Paul Frederick *farmer*

**Clay Center**
Braden, James Dale *former state legislator*

**Coffeyville**
Brittain, Sister Janelle Ann *parochial school educator*
Garner, Jim D. *state legislator, lawyer*
Seaton, Richard Melvin *newspaper and broadcasting executive*

**Colby**
Baldwin, Irene S. *corporate executive, real estate investor*
Finley, Philip Bruce *retired state adjutant general*
Morrison, James Frank *optometrist, state legislator*
Squibb, Sandra Hildyard *special education educator*

**Concordia**
Fowler, Wayne Lewis, Sr. *internist*

**Copeland**
Birney, Walter Leroy *religious administrator*

**Derby**
Champion, Michael Edward *physician assistant, clinical perfusionist*
Sandwell, Kristin Ann *special education educator*

**DeSoto**
Marcy, Charles Frederick *food packaging company executive*

**Dighton**
Stanley, Ellen May *historian, consultant*

**Dodge City**
Chaffin, Gary Roger *business executive*
Clifton-Smith, Rhonda Darleen *art center director*
Haviland, Camilla Klein *lawyer*
Schlarman, Stanley Gerard *bishop*

**El Dorado**
Edwards, Alisyn Arden *marriage and family therapist*
Edwards, James Lynn *college dean*

**Emporia**
Glennen, Robert Eugene, Jr. *university president*
Hashmi, Sajjad Ahmad *business educator, university dean*
O'Reilly, Hugh Joseph *restaurant executive*
Schallenkamp, Kay *academic administrator*
Sundberg, Marshall David *biology educator*
Torrens, Peggy Jean *technical school coordinator*

**Enterprise**
Wickman, John Edward *librarian, historian*

**Fairway**
Marquardt, Christel Elisabeth *lawyer*

**Fort Leavenworth**
Oliver, Thornal Goodloe *health care executive*
Schneider, James Joseph *military theory educator, consultant*

**Fort Riley**
Spurrier, Patricia Ann *executive director*

**Garden City**
Japp, Nyla F. *infection control services administrator*

**Goddard**
Peterman, Bruce Edgar *aircraft company executive, retired*

**Goodland**
Ross, Chester Wheeler *retired clergyman, consultant*
Sharp, Glenn (Skip Sharp) *technical education administrator*

**Great Bend**
Jones, Edward *physician, pathologist*
Rittenhouse, Nancy Carol *elementary education educator*
Straub, Larry Gene *business executive*

**Haven**
Schlickau, George Hans *cattle breeder, professional association executive*

**Hays**
Coyne, Patrick Ivan *physiological ecologist*
Hammond, Edward H. *university president*
Harman, Nancy June *elementary education educator*
Hassett, Mary Ruth *nursing educator*

**Hesston**
Yost, Lyle Edgar *farm equipment manufacturing company executive*

**Hiawatha**
Pennel, Marie Lucille Hunziger *elementary education educator*

**Horton**
Kirschner, Rod *secondary education educator*

**Hugoton**
Nordling, Bernard Erick *lawyer*

**Hutchinson**
Baumer, Beverly Belle *journalist*
Buzbee, Richard Edgar *newspaper editor*
Dick, Harold Latham *manufacturing executive*
Green, Theresa Ellen *elementary education educator*
Hayes, John Francis *lawyer*
Kerr, David Mills *state legislator*
O'Neal, Michael Ralph *state legislator, lawyer*
Schmidt, Gene Earl *hospital administrator*
Swearer, William Brooks *lawyer*
Wendelburg, Norma Ruth *composer*

**Iola**
Talkington, Robert Van *state senator*

## Junction City
Lochamy, Richard Edward *physician*
Werts, Merrill Harmon *management consultant*

## Kansas City
Anderson, Harrison Clarke *pathologist, educator, biomedical researcher*
Arakawa, Kasumi *physician, educator*
Ardinger, Robert Hall, Jr. *physician, educator*
Baker, Clarence Albert, Sr. *structural steel construction company executive*
Baska, James Louis *wholesale grocery company executive*
Behbehani, Abbas M. *clinical virologist, educator*
Besharse, Joseph Culp *cell biologist, researcher*
Boal, Marcia Anne Riley *clinical social worker, administrator*
Calkins, David Ross *physician, medical educator*
Campbell, Joseph Leonard *trade association executive*
Cantwell, Sandra Lee *legal assistant*
Carolan, Douglas *wholesale company executive*
Cho, Cheng Tsung *pediatrician, educator*
Clifton, Thomas E. *seminary president, minister*
Damjanov, Ivan *pathologist, educator*
Doull, John *toxicologist, pharmacologist*
Dunn, Marvin Irvin *physician*
Ebner, Kurt Ewald *biochemistry educator*
Forst, Marion Francis *bishop*
Freund, Ronald S. *management consultant, marketing company executive*
Gilliland, Marcia Ann *nurse clinician, infection control specialist*
Godfrey, Robert Gordon *physician*
Godwin, Harold Norman *pharmacist, educator*
Goldberg, Ivan D. *microbiologist, educator*
Goodwin, Donald William *psychiatrist, educator*
Grantham, Jared James *nephrologist, educator*
Greenberger, Norton Jerald *physician*
Greenwald, Gilbert Saul *physiologist*
†Hagen, Donald Floyd *university administrator, former military officer*
Hollenbeck, Marynell *municipal government official*
Holmes, Grace Elinor *pediatrician*
Hudson, Robert Paul *medical educator*
Jerome, Norge Winifred *nutritionist, anthropologist*
Johnson, Joy Ann *diagnostic radiologist*
Kenyon, Elinor Ann *social worker*
Koller, William Carl *neurology educator*
Krantz, Kermit Edward *physician, educator*
Lee, Kyo Rak *radiology educator*
Lungstrum, John W. *federal judge*
Mathews, Paul Joseph *allied health educator*
Mathewson, Hugh Spalding *anesthesiologist, educator*
McCallum, Richard Warwick *medical researcher, clinician, educator*
Mohn, Melvin Paul *anatomist, educator*
Morrison, David Campbell *immunology educator*
Noelken, Milton Edward *biochemistry educator, researcher*
O'Connor, Earl Eugene *federal judge*
Olofson, Tom William *electronics executive*
Robinson, David Weaver *surgeon, educator*
Rushfelt, Gerald Lloyd *magistrate judge*
Samson, Frederick Eugene, Jr. *neuroscientist, educator*
Schloerb, Paul Richard *surgeon, educator*
Sciolaro, Charles Michael *cardiac surgeon*
Spangler, Douglas Frank *state legislator*
Strecker, Ignatius J. *archbishop*
Suzuki, Tsuneo *molecular immunologist*
Thompson, Catherine Rush *physical therapist, educator*
Tröster, Alexander I. *neuropsychologist, educator*
Van Bebber, George Thomas *federal judge*
Voogt, James Leonard *medical educator*
Vratil, Kathryn Hoefer *federal judge*
Walaszek, Edward Joseph *pharmacology educator*
Waxman, David *physician, university consultant*
Whelan, Richard J. *director special education and pediatrics programs, academic administrator*
Ziegler, Dewey Kiper *neurologist*

## Kiowa
Conrad, Melvin Louis *biology educator*
Drewry, Marcia Ann *osteopath*

## Lake Quivira
Hall, R. Vance *psychology researcher, educator, administrator, consultant, business executive*

## Larned
Davis, Mary Elizabeth *speech pathologist, educator, counselor*
Hewson, Mary McDonald *civic volunteer*

## Lawrence
Alexander, John Thorndike *historian, educator*
Ammar, Raymond George *physicist, educator*
Angino, Ernest Edward *geology educator*
Armitage, Kenneth Barclay *biology educator, ecologist*
Augelli, John Pat *geography educator, author, consultant, rancher*
Beedles, William LeRoy *finance educator, financial consultant*
Benjamin, Bezaleel Solomon *architecture and architectural engineering educator*
Bovee, Eugene Cleveland *protozoologist, emeritus educator*
Bowman, Laird Price *retired foundation administrator*
Byers, George William *retired entomology educator*
Casad, Robert Clair *legal educator*
Craig, Susan Virginia *librarian*
Crowe, William Joseph *academic administrator, dean, educator*
Darwin, David *civil engineering educator, researcher, consultant*
Debicki, Andrew Peter *foreign language educator*
De George, Richard Thomas *philosophy educator*
Dickinson, William Boyd, Jr. *editorial consultant*
Dreschhoff, Gisela Auguste Marie *physicist, educator*
Duerksen, George Louis *music educator, music therapist*
Eldredge, Charles Child, III *art history educator*
Enos, Paul *geologist, educator*
Frederickson, Horace George *former college president, public administration educator*
Gay, Aleda Susan *mathematician, educator*
Gerhard, Lee Clarence *geologist, educator*
Gerry, Martin Hughes, IV *federal agency administrator, lawyer*
Ginn, John Charles *journalism educator, former newspaper publisher*

Grabow, Stephen Harris *architecture educator*
Green, Don Wesley *chemical and petroleum engineering educator*
Gunn, James E. *English language educator*
Harmony, Marlin Dale *chemistry educator*
Heller, Francis H(oward) *law and political science educator emeritus*
Heller, George Norman *music educator*
Hemenway, Robert E. *university administrator, language educator*
Hilding, Jerel Lee *music and dance educator, former dancer*
Himmelberg, Charles John, III *mathematics educator, researcher*
Hoeflich, Michael Harlan *law school dean*
Johnston, Richard Fourness *biologist*
Kleinberg, Jacob *chemist, educator*
Koepp, Donna Pauline Petersen *librarian*
Laird, Roy Dean *political science educator*
Landgrebe, John Allan *chemistry educator*
Leonard, Roy Junior *civil engineering educator*
Levine, Stuart George *editor, English literature educator, author*
Li, Chu-Tsing *art history educator*
Lichtwardt, Robert William *mycologist*
Locke, Carl Edwin, Jr. *academic administrator, engineering educator*
Loudon, Karen Lee *physical therapist*
Lucas, William Max, Jr. *structural engineer, university dean*
Mackenzie, Kenneth Donald *management consultant, educator*
McCabe, Steven Lee *structural engineer*
Michener, Charles Duncan *entomologist, researcher, educator*
Miller, Don Robert *surgeon*
Mitscher, Lester Allen *chemist, educator*
†Mona, Stephen Francis *golf association executive*
Moore, Richard Kerr *electrical engineering educator*
Morgan, Scott Ellingwood *publisher, lawyer*
Muirhead, Vincent Uriel *aerospace engineer*
Murray, Thomas Veatch *lawyer*
Norris, Andrea Spaulding *art museum director*
O'Brien, William John *ecology researcher*
Orel, Harold *literary critic, educator*
Papanek, Victor *designer, educator, writer*
Pickett, Calder Marcus *retired journalism educator*
Pinet, Frank Samuel *former university dean*
Pozdro, John Walter *music educator, composer*
Quinn, Dennis B. *English language and literature educator*
Robinson, Walter Stitt, Jr. *historian*
Rolfe, Stanley Theodore *civil engineer, educator*
Roskam, Jan *aerospace engineer*
Rowland, James Richard *electrical engineering educator*
Saul, Norman Eugene *history educator*
Schiefelbusch, Richard L. *research administrator*
Schilling, John Michael *golf course executive*
Schoeck, Richard J(oseph) *English and humanities scholar*
Seaver, James Everett *historian, educator*
Seibold, Ronald Lee *sociologist, writer*
Shankel, Delbert Merrill *microbiology and biology educator*
Sheridan, Richard Bert *economics educator*
Simons, Dolph Collins, Jr. *newspaper publisher*
Smith, Glee Sidney, Jr. *lawyer*
Spires, Robert Cecil *foreign language educator*
Tacha, Deanell Reece *federal judge*
Tsubaki, Andrew Takahisa *theater director, educator*
Turnbull, Ann Patterson *special education educator, consultant*
Turnbull, H. Rutherford, III *law educator, lawyer*
Tuttle, William McCullough, Jr. *history educator*
Vincent, Jon Stephen *foreign language educator*
Wiechert, Allen LeRoy *educational planning consultant, architect*
Williams, Roy *university athletic coach*
Willner, Ann Ruth *political scientist, educator*
Wilson, Paul Edwin *lawyer, educator*
Winter, Winton Allen, Jr. *state senator, lawyer*
Woelfel, James Warren *philosophy educator*
Woodward, Frederick Miller *publisher*
Worth, George John *English literature educator*

## Leavenworth
Hamilton, Mark Alan *electrical engineer*
McGilley, Sister Mary Janet *nun, educator, writer, academic administrator*
Mengel, Charles Edmund *physician, medical educator*
Stanley, Arthur Jehu, Jr. *federal judge*

## Leawood
Ballard, John William, Jr. *banker*
Briscoe, Keith G. *retired college president*
Carmody, Timothy James *lawyer, educator*
Karmeier, Delbert Fred *consulting engineer, realtor*
Snyder, Willard Breidenthal *lawyer*

## Lebanon
Colwell, John Edwin *retired aerospace scientist*

## Lecompton
Conard, John Joseph *financial official*

## Lenexa
Ascher, James John *pharmaceutical executive*
Crater, Timothy Andrews *medical student*
Dockhorn, Robert John *physician, educator*
Herbel, LeRoy Alec, Jr. *telecommunications engineer*
Loughman, Barbara Ellen *immunologist researcher*
Oldham, Dale Ralph *life insurance company executive, actuary*
Parkinson, Mark Vincent *state legislator, lawyer*
Pierson, John Theodore, Jr. *manufacturer*
Rayburn, George Marvin *business executive, investment executive*
Starr, Darlene R. *special education educator, education educator*
White, Dirk Bradford *printing company executive*

## Liberal
Rosel, Carol Ann *artist*
Wilkerson, Rita Lynn *special education educator, consultant*

## Manhattan
Appl, Fredric Carl *retired mechanical engineering educator*
Babcock, Michael Ward *economics educator*
Barkley, Theodore Mitchell *biology educator*
Coffman, James Richard *academic administrator, veterinarian*
Davis, Kenneth Sidney *writer*

Durkee, William Robert *retired physician*
Erickson, Howard Hugh *veterinarian, physiology educator*
Erickson, Larry Eugene *chemical engineering educator*
Fateley, William Gene *chemist, educator, inventor, administrator*
Flaherty, Roberta D. *university official*
Foerster, Bernd *architecture educator*
Hagen, Lawrence Jacob *agricultural engineer*
Hahn, Richard Ray *academic administrator*
Havlin, John Leroy *soil scientist, educator*
Higgins, James Jacob *statistics educator*
Higham, Robin *historian, editor, publisher*
Hoyt, Kenneth Boyd *educational psychology educator*
Johnson, Terry Charles *biologist, educator*
Johnson, William Howard *agricultural engineer, educator*
Kaufman, Donald Wayne *research ecologist*
Kirkham, M. B. *plant physiologist, educator*
Kirmser, Philip George *engineering educator*
Kremer, Eugene R. *architecture educator*
Kruh, Robert F. *university administrator*
Lee, E(ugene) Stanley *engineer, mathematician, educator*
Lee, William Franklin, III *association administrator*
Madanshetty, Sameer Ishwar *mechanical engineer*
McCulloh, John Marshall *historian*
McKee, Richard Miles *animal studies educator*
Muir, William Lloyd, III *academic administrator*
Murray, John Patrick *psychologist, educator, researcher*
Nafziger, Estel Wayne *economics educator*
Oehme, Frederick Wolfgang *medical researcher and educator*
Parish, Thomas Scanlan *human development educator*
Phares, E. Jerry *psychology educator*
Posler, Gerry Lynn *agronomist, educator*
Richard, Patrick *science research administrator, nuclear scientist*
Russell, Eugene Robert, Sr. *engineering educator, administrator*
Sears, Rollin George *wheat geneticist, small grains researcher*
Seaton, Edward Lee *newspaper editor and publisher*
Setser, Donald Wayne *chemistry educator*
Simons, Gale Gene *nuclear and electrical engineer, educator*
Spears, Marian Caddy *dietetics and institutional management educator*
Stolzer, Leo William *bank executive*
Streeter, John Willis *information systems manager*
Thomas, Lloyd Brewster *economics educator*
Twiss, Page Charles *geology educator*
Vetter, James Louis *food research association administrator*
Vorhies, Mahlon Wesley *veterinary pathologist, educator*
Walker, Kathrine L. *museum educational administrator, educator*
Watt, Willis Martin (Bill Watt) *academic administrator, communications educator*

## Marion
Meyer, Bill *newspaper publisher, editor*

## Mc Pherson
Hull, Robert Glenn *retired financial administrator*
Mason, Stephen Olin *academic administrator*
Nichols, Richard Dale *former congressman, banker*
Shriver, Garner Edward *lawyer, former congressman*
Steffes, Don Clarence *state senator*

## Mission
Novak, Alfred *retired biology educator*
Thomas, Christopher Yancey, III *surgeon, educator*

## Neosho Falls
Bader, Robert Smith *biology, zoology educator and researcher*

## Newton
Hymer, Martha Nell *elementary education educator*
Westerhaus, Catherine K. *social worker*

## North Newton
Fast, Darrell Wayne *minister*
Preheim, Vern Quincy *religious organization administrator, minister*
Quiring, Frank Stanley *chemist, educator*

## Oakley
Wolfe, Mindy René *early childhood education educator*

## Olathe
Branham, Melanie J. *lawyer*
Burke, Paul E., Jr. *state senator, business consultant, public government affairs*
Chipman, Marion Walter *judge*
Dennis, Patricia Lyon *librarian*
Goodwin, Becky K. *secondary education educator*
Hackler, Ruth Ann *retired educator*
Haskin, J. Michael *lawyer*
O'Connor, Kay *state legislator*
Shelton, Jody *educational executive director*
Stevens, Diana Lynn *elementary education educator*

## Ottawa
Howe, William Hugh *artist*
Tyler, Priscilla *retired English language and education educator*

## Overland Park
Bennett, Richard Douglas *electrical engineer*
Bronaugh, Deanne Rae *home health care administrator, consultant*
Burger, Henry G. *anthropologist, vocabulary scientist, publisher*
Cole, Elsa Kircher *lawyer*
Dempsey, Cedric W. *sports association administrator*
Dore, James Francis *financial services executive*
Eshelman, Enos Grant, Jr. *prosthodontist*
Gaar, Norman Edward *lawyer, former state senator*
Haas, Kelley Weyforth *marketing and communications company executive*
Jekel, Joseph Frank *government official*
Jones, Charles Calhoun *estate and business planning consultant*
Keim, Robert Bruce *lawyer*
Krauss, Carl F. *lawyer*
Kutscher, Thomas Alan *electrical engineer*

Landry, Mark Edward *podiatrist, researcher*
Linn, James Herbert *retired banker*
Loepp, Herman Albert *subrogation examiner*
Mealman, Glenn *corporate marketing executive*
Murdock, Stuart Laird *banker, investment adviser*
†Myers, A. Maurice *transportation executive*
Neal, Louise Kathleen *life insurance company executive, accountant*
Ostby, Frederick Paul, Jr. *meteorologist, retired government official*
Parker, Cheryl Jean *small business owner*
Randolph, Scott Howard *chemical company executive*
Sampson, William Roth *lawyer*
Semegen, Patrick William *lawyer*
Short, Joel Bradley *lawyer, consultant, software publisher*
Starrett, Frederick Kent *lawyer*
Steinkamp, Robert Theodore *lawyer*
Van Dyke, Thomas Wesley *lawyer*
Voska, Kathryn Caples *consultant, facilitator*
Waxse, David John *lawyer*
Webb, William Duncan *lawyer, investment executive*
Zhan, Steve Q. *optical engineer, researcher*

## Parsons
Lomas, Lyle Wayne *agricultural research administrator, educator*

## Pittsburg
Behlar, Patricia Ann *political science educator*
Darling, John Rothburn, Jr. *university administrator, educator*
Fish, David Carlton *architect*
Huddleston, Michael Ray *counseling administrator, consultant, educator*
Nettels, George Edward, Jr. *mining executive*
Smoot, Joseph Grady *university administrator*
Sullivan, F(rank) Victor *university administrator, retired educator*

## Pomona
Gentry, Alberta Elizabeth *elementary education educator*

## Prairie Village
Franking, Holly Mae *software publisher*
Jacobs, Vernon Kenneth *publisher*
Langworthy, Andrew Hansen *state legislator*
Pew, Kevin Dale *association executive*
Stanton, Roger D. *lawyer*

## Pratt
Loomis, Howard Krey *banker*

## Rose Hill
Chapman, Randell Barkley *family and emergency physician, medical educator*

## Saint John
Robinson, Alexander Jacob *clinical psychologist*

## Salina
Cosco, John Anthony *health care executive, educator, consultant*
Crawford, Lewis Cleaver *engineering executive*
Fitzsimons, George K. *bishop*
Horst, Deena Louise *state legislator*
Reh, John W. *engineer, consultant*
Richards, Jon Frederick *physician*
Ryan, Stephen Collister *funeral director*
Stanton, Marshall P. *academic administrator, minister*

## Satanta
Small, Sally Christine (Chris) *registered nurse*

## Shawnee
Cashman, William Elliott *investment manager, consultant*

## Shawnee Mission
Albright, Richard Scott *marketing executive*
Arneson, George Stephen *manufacturing company executive, management consultant*
Asher, Donna Thompson *psychiatric-mental health nurse*
Badgerow, John Nicholas *lawyer*
Barton, C. Robert *insurance company executive*
Bell, Deloris Wiley *physician*
Bennett, Robert Frederick *lawyer, former governor*
Biggs, J. O. *lawyer, general industry company executive*
Bond, Richard Lee *lawyer, state senator*
Breen, Katherine Anne *speech and language pathologist*
Byers, Walter *athletic association executive*
Cahal, Mac Fullerton *lawyer, publisher*
Callahan, Harry Leslie *civil engineer*
Cassidy, John Lemont *engineering executive*
Coleman, Timothy Stewart *middle school principal*
Deaver, Darwin Holloway *former utility executive*
Dougherty, Robert Anthony *manufacturing company executive*
Dyches, Kevin James *investment analyst*
Fairchild, Robert Charles *pediatrician*
Findlay, Theodore Bernard *management consultant, motivational speaker*
Gaar, Marilyn Audrey Wiegraffe *political science educator, property manager*
Gamet, Donald Max *appliance company executive*
Goetz, Kenneth Lee *cardiovascular physiologist, research consultant*
Grady, William Earl *marketing executive*
Green, John Lafayette, Jr. *education executive*
Hartzler, Geoffrey Oliver *retired cardiologist*
Hechler, Robert Lee *financial services company executive*
Henson, Paul Harry *transportation executive*
Herring, Raymond Mark *strategic planning and organizational development*
Hoffman, Alfred John *retired mutual fund executive*
Holliday, John Moffitt *insurance company executive*
Holter, Don Wendell *retired bishop*
Julien, Gail Leslie *model, public relations professional*
Kaplan, Marjorie Ann Pashkow *school district administrator*
Kemp, John Bernard *retired state secretary of transportation*
Landau, Mason Stephen *business broker, insurance professional*
McEachen, Richard Edward *banker, lawyer*

Diana, John Nicholas *physiologist*
Dorio, Martin Matthew *material handling company executive*
Drake, David Lee *electronics engineer*
Drake, Vaughn Paris, Jr. *electrical engineer*
Eberle, Todd Bailey *lawyer, educator*
Ehmann, William Donald *chemistry educator*
Elitzur, Moshe *physicist, educator*
Ettensohn, Frank Robert *geologist, educator*
Fleming, Juanita W. *academic administrator*
Foree, Edward Golden *environmental engineer, consultant*
Forester, Karl S. *federal judge*
Fowler, Harriet Whittemore *art museum director*
Friedell, Gilbert Hugo *pathologist, hospital administrator, educator, cancer center director*
Frye, Wilbur Wayne *soil science educator, researcher, administrator*
Fryman, Virgil Thomas, Jr. *lawyer*
Gable, Robert Elledy *real estate investment company executive*
Gilliam, M(elvin) Randolph *urologist, educator*
Girone, Vito Anthony *architect, city planner, educator emeritus, artist*
Glenn, James Francis *urologist, educator*
Glixon, David M(orris) *editor, writer*
Goldman, Alvin Lee *lawyer, educator*
Grabau, Larry J. *crop physiologist, educator*
Griffen, Ward O., Jr. *surgeon, educator, medical board executive*
Grimes, Craig Alan *electrical engineering educator*
Grimes, Dale Mills *physics and electrical engineering educator*
Hagan, Wallace Woodrow *geologist*
Hagen, Michael Dale *family physician educator*
Hamburg, Joseph *physician, educator*
Hamilton-Kemp, Thomas Rogers *organic chemist, educator*
Hanson, Mark Tod *engineering mechanics educator*
Henderson, Hubert Platt *fine arts association executive*
Hines-Martin, Vicki Patricia *nursing educator*
Hinkle, Buckner, Jr. *lawyer*
Hochstrasser, Donald Lee *cultural anthropologist, community health and public administration educator*
Holsinger, James Wilson, Jr. *physician*
Hultman, Charles William *economics educator*
Johnson, Lizabeth Lettie *insurance agent*
Kang, Bann C. *immunologist*
Kaplan, Martin P. *allergist, immunologist, pediatrician*
Kasperbauer, Michael John *plant physiology educator, researcher*
Keeling, Larry Dale *journalist*
Kelly, Timothy Michael *newspaper publisher*
Kern, Bernard Donald *retired educator, physicist*
Kissling, Fred Ralph, Jr. *publishing executive, insurance agency executive*
Krone, Julie *jockey*
Landon, John William *minister, social worker, educator*
Lawson, Frances Gordon *child guidance specialist*
Lee, Joe *federal judge*
Lewis, Robert Kay, Jr. *fundraising executive*
Lewis, Thomas Proctor *law educator*
Liu, Keh-Fei Frank *physicist, educator*
Lodder, Robert Andrew *chemistry and pharmaceutics educator*
Logan, Joyce Polley *education educator*
Loghry, Richard M. *architecture and engineering services executive*
Madden, Edward Harry *philosopher, educator*
Mann, Marvin L. *electronics executive*
Mason, Ellsworth Goodwin *librarian*
Matheny, Samuel Coleman *academic administrator*
Mayer, Lloyd D. *allergist, immunologist, physician, medical educator*
Mercer, Leonard Preston, II *biochemistry educator*
Miller, Pamela Gundersen *mayor*
Mink, John Robert *dental educator*
Mitchell, George Ernest, Jr. *animal scientist, educator*
Mitchell, John Charles *business executive*
Mostert, Paul Stallings *mathematician, educator*
Nasar, Syed Abu *electrical engineering educator*
Nathan, Richard Arnold *technology company executive*
Ng, Kwok-Wai *physics educator*
Noonan, Jacqueline Anne *pediatrics educator*
Nyere, Robert Alan *banker*
O'Connor, William Noel *pathologist*
Parks, Harold Francis *anatomist, educator*
Pass, Bobby Clifton *entomology educator*
Philpott, James Alvin, Jr. *lawyer*
Pirone, Thomas Pascal *plant pathology educator*
Reed, Michael Robert *agricultural economist*
Regan, David Michael *health care administrator*
Rodriguez, Juan Guadalupe *entomologist*
Rogers, Lon B(rown) *lawyer*
Romanowitz, Byron Foster *architect, engineer*
Sandoval, Arturo Alonzo *art educator, artist*
Sands, Donald Edgar *chemistry educator*
Schaeffer, Edwin Frank, Jr. *lawyer*
Schmitt, Frederick Adrian *gerontologist, neuropsychologist*
Schneider, George William *horticulturist, educator, researcher*
†Schwarcz, Thomas H. *surgeon*
Sendlein, Lyle V. A. *geology educator*
Sexton, Robert Fenimore *educational organization executive*
Shah, Ramesh Keshavlal *engineering educator, researcher*
Shipley, David Elliott *university dean, lawyer*
Sineath, Timothy Wayne *library educator, university dean*
Singletary, Otis Arnold, Jr. *university president emeritus*
Smith, Mikel Dwaine *physician, educator, researcher*
Snowden, Ruth O'Dell Gillespie *artist*
Steele, Earl Larsen *electrical engineering educator*
Steensland, Ronald Paul *librarian*
Straus, Robert *behavioral sciences educator*
Tauchert, Theodore Richmond *mechanical engineer, educator*
Thelin, John Robert *academic administrator, education educator, historian*
Timoney, Peter Joseph *veterinarian, virologist, educator, consultant*
†Tollison, Joseph W. *family practice physician*
Turner, H(arry) Spencer *preventive medicine physician, educator*
Tyson, Rosendo Felicito, Jr. *urban planner*
Ulmer, Shirley Sidney *political science educator, researcher, consultant*
Varellas, Sandra Motte *judge*
Vore, Mary Edith *pharmacology educator, researcher*
Wagner, Alan Burton *entrepreneur*
Walters-Parker, Kimberly Kay *secondary school educator*
Warth, Robert Douglas *history educator*
Wesley, Robert Cook *dental educator*
Wethington, Charles T., Jr. *academic administrator*
Williams, Jackson Jay *education consultant*
Williams, James Kendrick *bishop*
Willis, Paul Allen *librarian*
Wilson, Emery Allen *university dean, obstetrician-gynecologist, educator*
Worell, Judith P. *psychologist, educator*
Yates, Isabel McCants *city council member*
Young, Paul Ray *medical board executive, physician*
Zinser, Elisabeth Ann *academic administrator*

## London
Coffman, Jennifer B. *federal judge*
Early, Jack Jones *college administrator*
Keller, John Warren *lawyer*
Ridner, Kathleen Rader *elementary education educator*
Siler, Eugene Edward, Jr. *federal judge*
Unthank, G. Wix *federal judge*

## Louisa
Burton, John Lee, Sr. *banker*

## Louisville
Aberson, Leslie Donald *lawyer*
Adams, Christine Beate Lieber *psychiatrist, educator*
Adams, Robert Waugh *state agency administrator, economics educator*
Allen, Charles Ethelbert, III *lawyer*
Allen, Charles Mengel *federal judge*
Amin, Mohammad *urology educator*
Andrews, Billy Franklin *pediatrician, educator*
Ardery, Philip Pendleton *lawyer*
Aronoff, George Rodger *medicine and pharmacology educator*
Bailey, Irving Widmer, II *insurance holding company executive*
Ballantine, John Tilden *lawyer*
Baron, Martin Raymond *psychology educator*
Baxter, James William, III *insurance and investment executive*
Becker, Gail Roselyn *museum director*
Belanger, William Joseph *chemist, polymer applications consultant*
Bertolone, Salvatore J. *pediatric medicine educator*
Bishop, Robert Whitsitt *lawyer*
Boggs, Danny Julian *federal judge*
†Bramer, Kevin Lee *healthcare executive*
Brockwell, Charles Wilbur, Jr. *history educator*
Brown, Owsley, II *diversified consumer products company executive*
Bujake, John Edward, Jr. *beverage company executive*
Bullard, Claude Earl *newspaper, commercial printing and radio and television executive*
Callen, Jeffrey Phillip *dermatologist, educator*
Carden, Joy Cabbage *educational consultant*
Chauvin, Leonard Stanley, Jr. *lawyer*
Clark, John Hallett, III *consulting engineering executive*
Coggins, Homer Dale *retired hospital administrator*
Cohn, David V(alor) *biochemistry educator*
Collins, James Francis *lawyer, financial consultant*
Conner, Stewart Edmund *lawyer*
Cook, Howard Ruskin *construction company executive*
Copes, Marvin Lee *college president*
Cornelius, Wayne Anderson *electrical and computer engineering consultant*
Cowan, Frederic Joseph *lawyer*
Crim, Gary Allen *dental educator*
Crum, Denny (Denzel Edwin Crum) *collegiate basketball coach*
Cybulski, Joanne Karen *nutritionist, diabetes educator*
Dale, Judy Ries *religious organization administrator*
Danzl, Daniel Frank *emergency physician*
Daulton, David Coleman *actuary*
Davenport, Gwen (Mrs. John Davenport) *author*
Davidson, Gordon Byron *lawyer*
Deering, Ronald Franklin *librarian, minister*
DeVries, William Castle *surgeon, educator*
Dudley, George Ellsworth *lawyer*
Duffy, Martin Patrick *lawyer*
Edgell, Stephen Edward *psychology educator, statistical consultant*
Ekstrom, William Ferdinand *college administrator*
Ellison, Rebecca Linda Raymond *newspaper editor*
Ethridge, Larry Clayton *lawyer*
Ferguson, Duncan Sheldon *education administrator*
Ferguson, Jo McCown *lawyer*
Ford, Gordon Buell, Jr. *English language, linguistics, and medieval studies educator, author, retired hospital industry accounting financial management executive*
Freund, Adrian Paul *county official*
Fuchs, Olivia Anne Morris *lawyer*
Furka, Árpád *organic chemist, educator*
Galandiuk, Susan *colon and rectal surgeon, educator*
Gall, Stanley Adolph *physician, immunology researcher*
Garcia, Rafael Jorge *chemical engineer*
Garcia-Varela, Jesus *language educator, literature educator*
Garfinkel, Herbert *university official*
Garretson, Henry David *neurosurgeon*
Gleis, Linda Hood *physician*
Goff, Jim *religious organization administrator*
Gorman, Chris *construction company executive*
Gott, Marjorie Eda Crosby *conservationist, former educator*
Granady, Juanita H. *religious organization administrator*
Gray, Laman A., Jr. *thoracic surgeon, educator*
Guillaume, Raymond Kendrick *banker*
Haddaway, James David *retired insurance company official*
Hallenberg, Robert Lewis *lawyer*
Hampton, Martin Justus *financial planner*
Hanley, Thomas Richard *engineering educator*
Harris, Patrick Donald *physiology educator*
Hawpe, David Vaughn *newspaper editor, journalist*
Haynes, Douglas Martin *physician, educator*
Haynie, Hugh *editorial cartoonist*
Hazen, Elizabeth Frances *retired special education educator*
Heiden, Charles Kenneth *former army officer, metals company executive*
Heinicke, Ralph Martin *biotechnology company executive*
Henderson, Harriet *librarian*
Heyburn, John Gilpin, II *federal judge*
Hockenberger, Susan Jane *nurse educator*
Hopson, Edwin Sharp *lawyer*
Hower, Frank Beard, Jr. *retired banker*
Hoye, Robert Earl *systems science educator*
Huang, Kee Chang *pharmacology educator, physician*
Humphreys, Gene Lynn *lawyer*
Hunter, William Jay, Jr. *lawyer*
Jenkins, C(arle) Frederick *religious organization executive, minister, lawyer*
Jones, David Allen *health facility executive*
Karibo, John Michael *allergist, immunologist, pediatrician*
Kearney, Anna Rose *history educator*
Kelly, Thomas Cajetan *archbishop*
†King, William Bradley *emergency medicine physician*
Kinsey, William Charles *building materials company executive*
Kleinert, Harold Earl *plastic surgery educator*
Klotter, John Charles *retired legal educator*
Kmetz, Donald R. *academic administrator*
Lavelle, Charles Joseph *lawyer*
Lay, Norvie Lee *law educator*
Lewis, Ronald Chapman *record company executive*
Lomicka, William Henry *investor*
Luber, Thomas J(ulian) *lawyer*
Luvisi, Lee *concert pianist*
Lyndrup, Peggy B. *lawyer*
Macdonald, Lenna Ruth *lawyer*
Maddox, Robert Lytton *lawyer*
Maggiolo, Allison Joseph *lawyer*
Martin, Boyce Ficklen, Jr. *federal judge*
Marvin, Oscar McDowell *retired hospital administrator*
Mather, Elizabeth Vivian *health care executive*
McCormick, Steven Thomas *insurance company executive*
McKinney, Owen Michael *special education educator, training and security consultant*
Mellen, Francis Joseph, Jr. *lawyer*
Melnykovych, Andrew O. *journalist*
Meuter, Maria Coolman *lawyer*
Miller, John Ulman *minister, author*
Mohler, Richard Albert, Jr. *academic administrator, theologian*
Moll, Joseph Eugene *chemical engineer, chemical company executive*
Morrin, Peter Patrick *museum director*
Morris, Benjamin Hume *lawyer*
Mountz, Wade *retired health service management executive*
Mueller, Robert William *process and instrument engineer*
†Nash, Alanna Kay *critic, writer*
Netter, Virginia Thompson *produce company owner*
Neustadt, David Harold *physician*
Niblock, William Robert *manufacturing executive*
Nystrand, Raphael Owens *university dean, educator*
Oates, Thomas R. *university executive*
Olson, William Henry *neurology educator, administrator*
Osborn, John Simcoe, Jr. *lawyer*
Parker, Joseph Corbin, Jr. *pathologist*
Parkins, Frederick Milton *dental educator, university dean*
Peden, Katherine Graham *industrial consultant*
Pelfrey, D. Patton *lawyer*
Pence, Hobert Lee *physician*
Pepples, Ernest *tobacco company executive*
Pettyjohn, Shirley Ellis *lawyer, real estate executive*
Polk, Hiram Carey, Jr. *surgeon, educator*
Porter, Henry Homes, Jr. *investor*
Prough, Russell Allen *biochemistry educator*
Reed, David Benson *bishop*
Reed, John Squires, II *lawyer*
Reinbold, Darrel William *energy engineering specialist*
Roberts, J. Wendell *federal judge*
Roisen, Fred Jerrold *neurobiologist, educator, researcher, anatomy educator*
Rosky, Theodore Samuel *insurance company executive*
Rowe, Melinda Grace *public health service officer*
Royer, Robert Lewis *retired utility company executive*
Runyon, Keith Leslie *lawyer, newspaper editor*
Sanders, Russell Edward *protective services official*
Sanfilippo, Joseph Salvatore *physician, reproductive endocrinologist, educator*
Scheu, Lynn McLaughlin *scientific publication editor*
Schneider, Jayne B. *school librarian*
Schuster, Stephen Fowler *lawyer*
Schwab, John Joseph *psychiatrist, educator*
Scott, Ralph Mason *physician, radiation oncology educator*
Shoemaker, Gradus Lawrence *chemist, educator*
Shumaker, John William *academic administrator*
Skees, William Leonard, Jr. *lawyer*
Slater, Marilee Hebert *theatre administrator, producer, director, consultant*
Slung, Hilton B. *surgeon*
Smillie, Thomson John *opera producer*
Smith, Robert F., Jr. *civil engineer*
Snider, Ruth Atkinson *retired counselor*
Spinnato, Joseph Anthony, II *obstetrician*
Spratt, John Stricklin *surgeon, educator, researcher*
Stewart, Arthur Van *dental educator, geriatric health administrator*
Straus, R(obert) James *lawyer*
Street, William May *beverage company executive*
Swain, Donald Christie *retired university president, history educator*
Swann, Rande Nortof *public relations executive*
Talbott, Ben Johnson, Jr. *lawyer*
Tasman, Allan *psychiatry educator*
Taylor, Kenneth Grant *chemistry educator*
Taylor, Robert Lewis *academic administrator*
Tinsley, Tuck, III *book publishing executive*
Towles, Donald Blackburn *retired newspaper publishing executive*
Tran, Long Trieu *industrial engineer*
Tsai, Tsu-Min *surgeon*
Tyrrell, Gerald Gettys *banker*
Uhde, George Irvin *physician*
VanMeter, Vandelia L. *library director*
Waddell, William Joseph *pharmacologist, toxicologist*
Ward, Thomas Leon *engineering educator*
Watts, Beverly L. *civil rights executive*
Weinberg, Edward Brill *lawyer*
Weisskopf, Bernard *pediatrician, child behavior, development and genetics specialist, educator*
Welsh, Alfred John *lawyer, consultant*
Willenbrink, Rose Ann *lawyer*
Wingenbach, Gregory Charles *priest, religious-ecumenical agency director*
Woolsey, Frederick William *retired journalist, music critic*
Wren, Harold Gwyn *arbitrator, lawyer, legal educator*
Wright, Jesse Hartzell *psychiatrist, educator*
Zimmerman, Gideon K. *minister*
Zimmerman, Thom Jay *ophthalmologist, educator*
Zingman, Edgar Alan *lawyer*

## Madisonville
Monhollon, Leland *lawyer*
Stulc, Jaroslav Peter *surgeon, educator*

## Marrowbone
Clark, Betty Pace *banking executive*

## Mayfield
Harris, Isaac Henson *university dean*

## Midway
Minister, Kristina *speech communication educator*

## Morehead
Berry, Lemuel, Jr. *university dean*
Besant, Larry Xon *librarian, administrator, consultant*
Miller, Jon William *emergency physician*

## Munfordville
Lang, George Edward *lawyer*

## Murray
Boston, Betty Lee *investment broker, financial planner*
Bumgardner, Cloyd Jeffrey *school principal*
Herndon, Donna Ruth Grogan *educational administrator*
Hunt, Charles Brownlow, Jr. *university dean, musician*
†Keller, Randal Joseph *toxicology educator*
Thornton, Anna Vree *pediatrics and medical-surgical nurse*

## Nancy
Walters, Robert Ancil, II *protective services coordinator*

## Nazareth
Dundon, Mark Walden *hospital administrator*

## Newport
Seaver, Robert Leslie *law educator*
Siverd, Robert Joseph *lawyer*

## Nicholasville
Crouch, Dianne Kay *secondary school guidance counselor*

## Olive Hill
Rose, Melissa Eva Anderson *small business owner*

## Owensboro
Derstadt, Ronald Theodore *health care administrator*
Eaton, Clara Barbour *retired librarian*
Hood, Mary Bryan *museum director, painter*
Hooks, Vandalyn Lawrence *former elementary school educator*
Hulse, George Althouse *steel company executive*
Martin, Barbara Ann *secondary education educator*
McRaith, John Jeremiah *bishop*
Mong, Robert William, Jr. *publisher*
Poling, Wesley Henry *college president*
Vickery, Robert Bruce *oil industry executive, consultant*

## Paducah
Frankel, Andrew Joel *manufacturing company executive*
Johnstone, Edward Huggins *federal judge*
Walden, Robert Thomas *physicist educator, consultant*
Westberry, Billy Murry *lawyer*

## Partridge
Burton, Sharon Kay *primary education educator*

## Pewee Valley
Gill, George Norman *newspaper publishing company executive*

## Pineville
Whittaker, Bill Douglas *minister*

## Port Royal
Berry, Wendell *farmer, author*

## Prestonsburg
Mc Aninch, Robert Danford *philosophy and government affairs educator*
Pridham, Thomas Grenville *retired research microbiologist*

## Princeton
P'Pool, Gerald W. *retired manufacturing executive*

## Radcliff
Cranston, John Welch *historian, educator*

## Richmond
Beck, Joe Eugene *environmental health scientist, educator*
Branson, Branley Allan *biology educator*
Funderburk, H(enry) Hanly, Jr. *college president*
Morgan, Tim Dale *physical education educator*
Shearon, Forrest Bedford *humanities educator*
Witt, Robert Wayne *English educator*

## Russell
Crimmins, Sean T(homas) *oil company executive*
Gates, Deborah Wolin *petroleum company executive, lawyer*

## Russellville
Harper, Shirley Fay *nutritionist, educator, consultant*
Hattem, Albert Worth *physician*

## Salvisa
Lancaster, Clay *architecture/design educator, writer*

Costello, Joseph Mark, III broadcasting and motion picture executive
Del Rio, Jack professional football player
Derbes, Max Joseph, Jr. real estate appraiser
DiBenedetto, Robert Lawrence obstetrician, gynecologist, insurance company executive
Edisen, Clayton Byron physician
Evans, Carol Rockwell nursing administrator
Falco, Maria Josephine political scientist, academic administrator
Flake, Leone Elizabeth special education educator
Ford, Robert David lawyer
Gennaro, Glenn Joseph principal
Gereighty, Andrea Saunders polling company executive, poet
Grimm, John Lloyd business executive, marketing professional
Hartman, James Austin retired geologist
Janis, Donald Emil corporate controller
Johnson, Beth Michael principal
Lake, Wesley Wayne, Jr. internist, allergist, educator
Martin, Gerald Wayne professional football player
McShan, Clyde Griffin, II financial executive
Murphy, Alvin Leo educational administrator
Myers, Iona Raymer real estate and property manager
Newman, Claire Poe corporate executive
N'Vietson, Tung Thanh civil engineer
Ochsner, Seymour Fiske radiologist, editor
Ostendorf, Lance Stephen lawyer, investor, financial officer
Perlis, Sharon A. lawyer
Piper, Claudia Rosemary academic administrator
Roaf, William Layton professional football player
Sandmel, Ben journalist, musician
Spruiell, Vann psychoanalyst, educator, editor, researcher
Stansbury, Harry Case state commissioner
Thomas, Everette Earl federal judge
Turnbull, Renaldo professional football player
Young, Lucy Cleaver physician

### Minden
Doerge, Everett Gail retired school system administrator, state rep

### Monroe
Cage, Bobby Nyle research and statistics educator
†Cooksey, John Charles ophthalmic surgeon
Curry, Robert Lee, III lawyer
Khan, Khalid Saifullah engineering executive
Martin, Diane Caraway school librarian
Sartor, Daniel Ryan, Jr. lawyer

### Natchitoches
Alost, Robert Allen university executive
Egan, Shirley Anne nursing educator, retired
Wolfe, George Cropper retired private school educator, artist, author

### New Iberia
Henton, Willis Ryan bishop
Ledbetter, Deidre Leday special education educator

### New Llano
Boren, Lynda Sue gifted education educator

### New Orleans
Abaunza, Donald Richard lawyer
Abbott, Hirschel Theron, Jr. lawyer
Acomb, Robert Bailey, Jr. lawyer, educator
Agrawal, Krishna Chandra pharmacology educator
Album, Jerald Lewis lawyer
Allen, F(rank) C(linton), Jr. manufacturing executive, lawyer
Allerton, William, III public relations executive
Alsobrook, Henry Bernis, Jr. lawyer
Ambrose, Stephen Edward history educator, author
Amoss, W. James, Jr. shipping company executive
Amoss, Walter James, III editor
Andrews, Bethlehem Kottes research chemist
Andrus, Gerald Louis utilities holding company consultant
Angelides, Demosthenes Constantinos civil engineer
Arshad, M. Kaleem psychiatrist
Ates, J. Robert lawyer
Bachmann, Richard Arthur oil company executive
Backstrom, William M., Jr. lawyer
Bailey, Barry Stone sculptor, educator
Balée, William L. anthropology educator
Ball, Millie (Mildred Porteous Ball) editor, journalist
Barham, Mack Elwin lawyer, educator
Barker, Larry Lee communications educator
†Barnes, David Plank, Jr. meteorologist
Baron, John Herschel music educator, musicologist
Barone, Carol Parker director quality management
Barry, Francis Julian, Jr. lawyer
Bautista, Abraham Parana immunologist
Beard, Elizabeth Letitia physiologist, educator
Beck, David Edward surgeon
Beer, Peter Hill federal judge
Benerito, Ruth Rogan (Mrs. Frank H. Benerito) chemist
Benjamin, Edward Bernard, Jr. lawyer
Bernstein, Joseph lawyer
Berrigan, Helen Ginger federal judge
Bertoniere, Noelie Rita research chemist
Bertrand, William Ellis public health educator, academic administrator
Bieck, Robert Barton, Jr. lawyer
Birtel, Frank Thomas mathematician, philosopher, educator
Blitch, Ronald Buchanan architect
Bordelon, Alvin Joseph, Jr. lawyer
Boudreaux, J. Philip transplant surgeon, educator
Boudreaux, Kenneth Justin economics and finance educator, consultant
Bricker, Harvey Miller anthropology educator
Bricker, Victoria Reifler anthropology educator
Brody, Arnold Ralph research scientist, educator
Brown, James Barrow bishop
Bullard, Edgar John, III museum director
Burch, Robert Emmett physician, educator
Caldwell, Delmar Ray ophthalmologist, educator
Calogero, Pascal Frank, Jr. state supreme court chief justice
Carr, Patrick E. judge
Carter, James Clarence university administrator
Casellas, Joachim art gallery executive
Chambers, Thomas Edward college president, psychologist
Cheatwood, Roy Clifton lawyer
Chetta, Holly Ann transportation executive
Claverie, Philip deVilliers lawyer
Clement, Edith Brown federal judge
Cohen, Joseph English literature educator, writer, business owner
Cohn, Isidore, Jr. surgeon, educator
Coleman, James Julian, Jr. lawyer, industrialist, real estate executive
Collins, Harry David construction consultant, forensic engineering specialist, mechanical and nuclear engineer, retired army officer
Combe, John Clifford, Jr. lawyer
Connolly, Edward S. neurological surgeon
Cook, Samuel DuBois academic administrator, political scientist
Cook, Victor Joseph, Jr. marketing educator, consultant
Correro, Anthony James, III lawyer
Corrigan, James John, Jr. pediatrician, dean
Cosenza, Arthur George opera director
Cospolich, James Donald electrical engineering executive, consultant
Craft, Carol Ann librarian
Crumley, Martha Ann company executive
Crusto, Mitchell Ferdinand lawyer, educator
Cummings, Anthony Michael music historian, educator, academic administrator
Curry, Dale Blair journalist
Danahar, David C. academic administrator, history educator
Daniels, Robert Sanford psychiatrist, administrator
Davillier, Brenda Bozant university administrator
Deasy, William John construction, marine dredging, engineering and mining company executive
Defenbaugh, Richard Eugene marine ecologist
Denegre, George lawyer
Dennery, Moise Waldhorn lawyer, educator
Dickinson, Catherine Schatz retired microbiologist
Dodds, Richard Crofton theater critic
Domer, Floyd Ray pharmacologist, educator
Domingue, Gerald James medical scientist, microbiology, immunology and urology educator, researcher, clinical bacteriologist
Duffy, John Charles psychiatric educator
Duncan, Margaret Caroline physician
Duplantier, Adrian Guy federal judge
Easson, William McAlpine psychiatrist
Eichberg, Rodolfo David physician, educator
England, John David neurologist
Ensenat, Louis Albert surgeon
Epstein, Arthur William physician, educator
Espinoza, Luis Rolan rheumatologist
Ewin, Dabney Minor surgeon
Fagaly, William Arthur curator
Fallon, Eldon Edward lawyer, educator
Fantaci, James Michael lawyer
Feldman, Martin L. C. federal judge
Ferguson, Charles Austin retired newspaper editor
Fertel, Ruth U. restaurant owner
Fierke, Thomas Garner lawyer
Filson, Ronald Coulter architect, educator, college dean
Fingerman, Milton biologist, educator
Fisch, Bruce Jeffrey physician, educator
Fischer, Ashton John, Jr. investor
Fisher, James William medical educator, pharmacologist
Fishman, Louis Yarrut lawyer
Fisk, Raymond Paul marketing educator
Flower, Walter Chew, III investment counselor
Force, Robert law educator
Fountain, Peter Dewey, Jr. (Pete Fountain) clarinetist
Frantz, Phares Albert architect
Freeman, Montine McDaniel museum trustee
Freudenberger, Herman retired economics educator
Friedlander, Miles Herbert ophthalmologist
Friedman, Joel William law educator
Frohlich, Edward David medical educator
†Fuselier, Harold Anthony, Jr. physician, urologist
Garcia, Patricia A. lawyer
Garcia Oller, José Luis neurosurgeon
Gathright, John Byron, Jr. colon and rectal surgeon, educator
Gatipon, Betty Becker medical educator, consultant
Gelpi, C. James (Jim Gelpi) lawyer
Glasgow, Vaughn Leslie museum curator and administrator
Gonzales, Brother Alexis (Joseph M. Gonzales) theater and communications educator
Gordon, Joseph Elwell university official, educator
Gottlieb, A(braham) Arthur medical educator
Grace, Marcellus pharmacy educator, university dean
Grau, Shirley Ann (Mrs. James Kern Feibleman) writer
Greenleaf, Richard Edward Latin American history educator
Grundmeyer, Douglas Lanaux lawyer, editor
Hamlin, James Turner, III university dean, physician
†Handelsman, Walt cartoonist
Hansel, Stephen Arthur holding company executive
Harness, Francis William naval officer
Harper, Robert John, Jr. chemist, researcher
Hassenboehler, Donalyn principal
Haygood, Paul M. lawyer
Healy, George William, III lawyer, mediator
Henderson, Helena Naughton legal association administrator
Hewitt, Robert Lee surgeon, educator
Hicks, Terrell Cohlman surgeon
Hilbert, Peter Louis, Jr. lawyer
Howard, Richard Ralston, II medical health advisor, researcher, financier
Hudzinski, Leonard Gerard social worker
Hunter, Sue Persons former state official
Hyman, Albert Lewis cardiologist
Hyman, Edward Sidney physician, researcher
Hyslop, Newton Everett, Jr. infectious disease specialist
Imig, John David medical educator
Incaprera, Frank Philip internist, medical educator, health facility administrator
Ingraham, Joseph Edwin financial officer
Ivens, Mary Sue microbiologist, mycologist
Jacobsen, Thomas Warren archaeologist, educator
Jaffe, Bernard Michael surgeon
Jefferson, Patrick O'Neal university program director, administrative assistant
Johnson, Arnold Ray public relations executive
Johnson, Lee Harnie dean, educator
Johnson, Patrick, Jr. lawyer
Jones, John Anderson, Jr. school system administrator
Jones, Philip Kirkpatrick, Jr. lawyer
Jordan, John Patrick government agency executive, research scientist, educator
Jung, Rodney C. internist, academic administrator
Karam, Jim Daniel biochemistry educator
Keller, Thomas Clements lawyer
Kelly, Eamon Michael university president
†Kemp, James Bradley, Jr. lawyer
Kewalramani, Laxman Sunderdas surgeon, consultant
Kilanowski, Michael Charles, Jr. oil, natural gas, minerals exploration company executive, lawyer
†Kilroy, James Francis dean provost
Kline, David Gellinger neurosurgery educator
Klingman, John Philip architect, educator
Kolinsky, Michael Allen emergency physician
Krementz, Edward Thomas surgeon
Kukla, Jon (Keith) historian, museum director
Kupperman, Stephen Henry lawyer
Laborde, Alden James oil company executive
Lambert, Olaf Cecil hotel executive
Lang, Erich Karl physician, radiologist
Lannes, William Joseph, III electrical engineer
Latorre, Robert George naval architecture and engineering educator
LaValle, Irving Howard decision analysis educator
Lavelle, Paul Michael lawyer
Lee, Griff Calicutt civil engineer
Leinbach, Philip Eaton librarian
Le Jeune, Francis Ernest, Jr. otolaryngologist
Lemann, Thomas Berthelot lawyer
Levell, Edward, Jr. city official
Levert, John Bertels, Jr. investment executive
Levitt, Gregory Alan education educator
Lewy, John Edwin pediatric nephrologist
Lief, Thomas Parrish sociologist, educator
Lind, Thomas Otto barge transportation company executive
Litwin, Martin Stanley surgeon
Livaudais, Marcel, Jr. federal judge
Locke, William endocrinologist
Lopez, Manuel immunology and allergy educator
Lovejoy, Barbara Campbell sculptor, architectural designer
Lovett, William Anthony law and economics educator
Low, Frank Norman anatomist, educator
Lowe, Robert Charles lawyer
Lupo, Robert Edward Smith real estate developer and investor
Luza, Radomir Vaclav historian, educator
Mackin, Cooper Richerson university chancellor
Marcus, Bernard lawyer
Marks, Charles Dennery insurance salesman
Martin, David Hubert physician, educator
Mason, Henry Lloyd political science educator
Massare, John Steve medical association administrator, educator
McCall, John Patrick college president, educator
McDaniel, Donald Hamilton lawyer
McFarland, James W. academic administrator
McGlone, Michael Anthony lawyer
McMahon, Maeve middle school administrator
McMillan, Lee Richards, II lawyer
McNamara, A. J. federal judge
Mentz, Henry Alvan, Jr. federal judge
Miller, Robert Harold otolaryngologist, educator
Millikan, Larry Edward dermatologist
Mintz, Albert lawyer
Misiek, Dale Joseph oral and maxillofacial surgeon
Mitchell, Kenneth D. physiologist, medical educator
Mitchell, Lansing Leroy federal judge
Moely, Barbara E. psychology educator
Mogabgab, William Joseph epidemiologist, educator
Molony, Michael Janssens, Jr. lawyer
Monroe, James Walter organization executive
Morial, Marc Haydel mayor
Morrell, Arthur Anthony lawyer, state legislator
Murrish, Charles Howard oil and gas exploration company executive, geologist
Navar, Luis Gabriel physiology educator, researcher
Nehrbass, Seth Martin patent lawyer
Nelson, James Smith pathologist, educator
Nelson, Waldemar Stanley civil engineer, consultant
Nice, Charles Monroe, Jr. physician, educator
Nichols, Ronald Lee surgeon, educator
Norman, Edward Cobb retired psychiatrist, educator
Norwood, Colvin Gamble, Jr. lawyer
Novakov, George John, Jr. gifted and talented educator
Nuzum, Robert Weston lawyer
O'Brien, Gregory Michael St. Lawrence university official
Ochsner, John Lockwood thoracic-cardiovascular surgeon
Oliver, Ronald retired medical technologist
Olson, Richard David psychology educator
O'Meallie, Kitty artist
O'Neal, Edgar Carl psychology educator
O'Quinn, April Gale physician, educator
Orihel, Thomas Charles parasitology educator, research scientist
Ortique, Revius Oliver, Jr. city official
Paddison, Richard Milton neurologist, educator
Pankey, George Atkinson physician, educator
Paolini, Gilberto literature and science educator
Paradise, Louis Vincent educational psychology educator, university official
Pennington, Richard J. police chief
Perdew, John Paul physics educator, condensed matter and density functional theorist
Pfister, Richard Charles physician, radiology educator
Phelps, Ashton, Jr. newspaper publisher
Phelps, Carol Jo neuroendocrinologist
Phelps, Esmond, II lawyer
Pickett, Stephen Alan hospital executive
Pindle, Arthur Jackson, Jr. philosopher, researcher
Pizer, Donald author, educator
Plaeger, Frederick Joseph, II lawyer
Plavsic, Branko Milenko radiology educator
Poesch, Jessie Jean art historian
Poitevent, Edward Butts, II lawyer
Pope, John M. journalist
Pugh, William Whitmell Hill lawyer
Purvis, George Frank, Jr. life insurance company executive
Puschett, Jules B. medical educator, neprhrologist, researcher
Puyau, Francis Albert physician, radiology educator
Quirk, Peter Richard engineering company executive
Rathke, Dale Lawrence community organizer and financial analyst
Re, Richard Noel endocrinologist
Reck, Andrew Joseph philosophy educator
Regan, William Joseph, Jr. energy company executive
Reisin, Efrain nephrologist, researcher, educator
Remley, Theodore Phant, Jr. counseling educator, lawyer
Rice, Winston Edward lawyer
Riddick, Frank Adams, Jr. physician, health care facility administrator
Rietschel, Robert Louis dermatologist
Rigby, Perry Gardner medical center administrator, educator, former university dean, physician
Roberts, Louise Nisbet philosopher
Robins, Robert Sidwar political science educator, administrator
Rodriguez, Antonio Jose lawyer
Roesler, Robert Harry city official
Rosen, Charles, II lawyer
Rosen, William Warren lawyer
Rosensteel, George Thomas physics educator, nuclear physicist
Roskoski, Robert, Jr. biochemist, educator, author
Salatich, John Smyth cardiologist
Sarpy, Leon lawyer
Schally, Andrew Victor endocrinologist, researcher
Schneider, George T. obstetrician-gynecologist
Schoemann, Rudolph Robert lawyer
Schulte, Francis B. archbishop
Schwartz, Charles, Jr. federal judge
Seab, Charles Gregory astrophysicist
Sear, Morey Leonard federal judge, educator
Sellin, Eric linguist, poet, educator
Shapira, Emmanuel clinical geneticist, biochemical geneticist, educator
Shinn, Clinton Wesley lawyer
Shofstahl, Robert Maxwell savings and loan executive
Simms, Ellenese Brooks civic leader, retired school system administrator
Simon, H(uey) Paul lawyer
Simons, Dona artist
Sims, John William lawyer
Sinor, Howard Earl, Jr. lawyer
†Slater, Benjamin Richard, Jr. lawyer
Smith, John Webster retired energy industry executive
Snyder, Charles Aubrey lawyer
†Stabler, Rose Burch meteorologist
Stapp, Dan Ernest retired lawyer, utility executive
Steinmetz, Robert Charles architect
Stephens, Richard Bernard natural resource company executive
Stewart, Gregory Wallace physician
Stovall, Gerald Thomas religious organization administrator
Straumanis, John Janis, Jr. psychiatry educator
Sumrell, Gene research chemist
Superneau, Duane William geneticist, physician
Tarver, Michael Keith lawyer
Taylor, Kenneth Byron, Jr. librarian, minister, religion educator
Terrell, Suzanne Haik lawyer
Thomas, Robert Allen environmental communications educator
Thompson, Annie Laura foreign language educator
Thornell, Jack Randolph photographer
Timmcke, Alan Edward physician and surgeon
Title, Peter Stephen lawyer
Toussaint, Allen Richard recording studio executive, composer, pianist
Trapolin, Frank Winter retired insurance executive
Trostorff, Alexander Peter lawyer
Truehill, Marshall, Jr. minister
Turkish, Lance physician, ophthalmologist
Turner, Kathleen J. communication educator, consultant
Usdin, Gene Leonard physician, psychiatrist
Vance, Robert Patrick lawyer
Vance, Sarah S. federal judge
Vanselow, Neal Arthur university administrator, physician
Vaudry, J. William, Jr. lawyer
Ventura, Hector Osvaldo cardiologist
Villavaso, Stephen Donald urban planner, lawyer
Waechter, Arthur Joseph, Jr. lawyer
Wakefield, Benton McMillin, Jr. banker
Wakeman, Richard John psychologist, neuropsychologist
Walsh, John Joseph medical school administrator, physician
Waring, William Winburn pediatric pulmonologist, educator
Washington, Robert Orlanda educator, former university official
Wax, George Louis lawyer
Webb, Watts Rankin surgeon
Weigel, John J. lawyer
Weill, Hans physician, educator
Weinmann, John Giffen lawyer, diplomat
Weiss, Kenneth Andrew lawyer, law educator
Weiss, Susette Marie technical consultant, specialist in imaging
Weiss, Thomas Edward physician
Welden, Arthur Luna biology educator
Welsh, Ronald Arthur physician, educator
Wild, Dirk Jonathan accountant
Willems, Constance Charles lawyer
Williamson, Ernest Lavone petroleum company executive
Wilson, C. Daniel, Jr. library director
Winstead, Daniel Keith psychiatrist
Wisdom, John Minor federal judge
Womack, Edgar Allen, Jr. technology executive
Woodward, Ralph Lee, Jr. historian, educator
Wright, Clifford Sidney accounting educator
Yates, Robert Doyle anatomy educator
Zimny, Marilyn Lucile anatomist, educator

### New Roads
Haag, William George anthropologist, educator

### Oakdale
Johnson, Bess Orr retired librarian

### Opelousas
Pinac, André Louis, III obstetrician, gynecologist

### Pearl River
Pendarvis, Donna Kaye elementary secondary school educator, adminstrator

### Pineville
Beall, Grace Carter business educator
Boswell, Bill Reeser religious organization executive
Hirsch, Joe Elbe surgeon
Howell, Thomas history educator
Matthews, Betty Parker special education educator
Sennett, Henry Herbert, Jr. theatre arts educator and consultant
Swearingen, David Clarke physician, musician
Tapley, Philip Allen English language and literature educator

### Plaquemine
Goodwin, Billy Wayne chemical engineer

### Pride
Jones, LaCinda assistant principal

### Quitman
Davis, Ella Delores special education educator, elementary school educator
Maxwell, Patricia Anne writer

### Ragley
Magee, Thomas Eston, Jr. minister

### Reserve
Hanson, Clarence Francis home health nurse, retired firefighter

### Ruston
Barron, Randall Franklin mechanical engineer, educator, consultant
Benedict, Barry Arden dean
Freasier, Aileen W. special education educator
Hale, Paul Nolen, Jr. engineering administrator, educator
Halliburton, Lloyd Romance philology educator
Maxfield, John Edward retired university dean
Painter, Jack Timberlake civil engineer
Posey, Clyde Lee business administration and accounting educator
Reneau, Daniel D. university administrator
Sale, Tom S., III financial economist, educator
Sterling, Raymond Leslie civil engineering educator, researcher, consultant
Taylor, Foster Jay retired university president

### Saint Gabriel
Das, Dilip Kumar chemical engineer

### Saint Rose
Lennox, Edward Newman holding company executive

### Scott
Bergeron, Wilton Lee physician

### Shreveport
Achee, Roland Joseph lawyer
Angermeier, Ingo hospital administrator, educator
Beaird, Charles T. publishing executive
Becker, Roger Vern information science educator
Bradley, Ronald James neuroscientist
Breffeilh, Louis Andrew ophthalmologist, educator
Burch, Paul Michael financial consultant
Carmody, Arthur Roderick, Jr. lawyer
Conrad, Steven Allen physician, biomedical engineer, educator, researcher
Dilworth, Edwin Earle retired obstetrician, gynecologist
Fish, Howard Math aerospace industry executive
Fort, Arthur Tomlinson, III physician, educator
Freeman, Arthur Merrimon, III psychiatry educator, dean
Friend, William Benedict bishop
Ganley, James Powell ophthalmologist, educator
†George, Ronald Baylis physician, educator
Greene, Dallas Whorton, Jr. fire chief
Griffith, Robert Charles allergist, educator, planter
Haas, Lester Carl architect
Hall, John Whitling geography educator
Hall, Pike, Jr. lawyer
Heacock, Donald Dee social worker
Hetherwick, Gilbert Lewis lawyer
Hughes, Mary Sorrows artist
Huot, Rachel Irene biomedical educator, research scientist
Jamison, Richard Melvin virologist, educator
Jeter, Katherine Leslie Brash lawyer
Jones, Ernest Edward minister, religious organization administrator
Lazarus, Allan Matthew retired newspaper editor
Levy, Harold Bernard pediatrician
Linhart, Joseph Wayland cardiologist, educational administrator
Lloyd, Cecil Rhodes pediatric dentist
Mancini, Mary Catherine cardiothoracic surgeon, researcher
McDonald, John Clifton surgeon
Misra, Raghunath Prasad physician, educator
Nelson, Sydney B. state senator, lawyer
Payne, Roy Steven judge
Pederson, William David political scientist, educator
Pelton, James Rodger librarian
Politz, Henry Anthony federal judge
Preston, Loyce Elaine retired social work educator
Ramey, Cecil Edward, Jr. lawyer
Reddy, Pratap Chandupatla cardiologist, educator, researcher
Rush, Benjamin McGraw surgeon
St. Aubyn, Ronald Anthony pediatrics nurse
Schneider, Thomas Richard hospital administrator
Schwab, Kenneth Lynn college president
Shelby, James Stanford cardiovascular surgeon
Smith, Brian David lawyer, educator
Staats, Thomas Elwyn neuropsychologist
Stagg, Tom federal judge
Stewart, Carl E. federal judge
Thomas, Bessie primary education educator
Thurmon, Theodore Francis medical educator
Tullis, John Ledbetter retired wholesale distributing company executive
Vestal, Judith Carson occupational therapist
Walter, Donald Ellsworth federal judge
Webb, Donald Arthur minister
Whitehead, Barbara Ann secondary school educator
Wiener, Jacques Loeb, Jr. federal circuit judge
Witt, Elizabeth Nowlin (Beth Witt) special education educator, speech-language pathologist
Woodman, Walter James lawyer
Wray, Geraldine Smitherman (Jerry Wray) artist

### Slaughter
Gremillion, Curtis Lionel, Jr. psychologist, hospital administrator, musician

### Slidell
Bishop, Mary Lou artist
Breeding, J. Ernest, Jr. (Sunny Breeding) physicist, travel consultant, photographer
Faust, Marilyn B. elementary school principal
Grantham, Donald James engineer, educator, author
Hall, Ogden Henderson allied health educator
McBurney, Elizabeth Innes physician, educator
Muller, Robert Joseph gynecologist
O'Neal, Edwin A. geologist, geophysicist, petroleum engineer
Sullivan, Daniel Thomas electrical engineer, consultant
Tewell, Joseph Robert, Jr. electrical engineer

### Sulphur
Sumpter, Dennis Ray lawyer, construction company executive

### Sunset
Brinkhaus, Armand J. lawyer, former state senator

### Thibodaux
Delozier, Maynard Wayne marketing educator
Hebert, Leo Placide physician
Klaus, Kenneth Sheldon choral conductor, vocalist, music educator
Nunn, Thomas Calvin school supervisor, retired army officer
Swetman, Glenn Robert English language educator, poet
Worthington, Janet Evans academic director, English language educator

### Tioga
Tenney, Tom Fred bishop

### West Monroe
Costello, Elizabeth Ann home health nurse
Houchin, John Frederick, Sr. human services administrator

### Zachary
Blevins, Donna Caton writer

## MAINE

### Alfred
Benson, S. Patricia artist, educator

### Andover
Ellis, George Hathaway retired banker and utility company executive

### Auburn
Bastow, Richard Frederick civil engineer, educator, surveyor
Clifford, Robert William judge
Phillips, Charles Franklin economic consultant

### Augusta
Adelberg, Arthur William lawyer
Amero, Jane Adams state legislator
Barth, Alvin Ludwig, Jr. state legislator
Billings, Richard Whitten professional society administrator
Brown, Arnold health science facility administrator
Butland, Jeffrey H. president of senate, customer service representative
Cheng, Hsueh Ching physician
Cohen, Richard Stockman lawyer
Daggett, Beverly Clark state legislator
Davis, Virginia Estelle lawyer
Desmond, Mabel Jeannette state legislator, educator
Fiori, Michael J. pharmacist
Gervais, Paul Nelson foundation administrator, psychotherapist, public relations executive
Gwadosky, Dan A. secretary of state
Hussey, John Francis physician, geriatrician
Kany, Judy C(asperson) health policy analyst, former state senator
Ketterer, Andrew prosecutor
Kilkelly, Marjorie Lee state legislator
King, Angus S., Jr. governor of Maine
Lewis, Jacquelyn Rochelle quality administrator
Martin, John L. state legislator
Moody, Stanley Alton entrepreneur, financial consultant
Nickerson, John Mitchell political science educator
Phillips, Joseph Robert museum director
Scribner, Rodney Latham state official
Sotir, Thomas Alfred healthcare executive, retired shipbuilder
Trites, Donald George human service consultant

### Bangor
Albrecht, Ronald Lewis financial services executive
Ballesteros, Paula M. nurse
Brody, Morton Aaron federal judge
Bullock, William Clapp, Jr. banker
Ervin, Spencer lawyer
Haddow, Jon Andrew lawyer
Hsu, Yu Kao aerospace scientist, mathematician, educator
Johnson, Sharon Marguerite social worker, clinical hypnotherapist
Libbey, Robert David television producer
McGuigan, Charles James rehabilitation therapist
Rea, Ann W. librarian
Turner, Marta Dawn youth program specialist
Warren, Richard Jordan newspaper publisher
Warren, Richard Kearney newspaper publisher
Watt, Thomas Lorne dermatologist
Woodcock, John Alden lawyer

### Bar Harbor
Dworak, Marcia Lynn library director, library building consultant
Hoppe, Peter Christian biologist, geneticist
Leiter, Edward Henry scientist
Paigen, Kenneth geneticist, research director
Swazey, Judith Pound institute president, sociomedical science educator

### Bath
Stoudt, Howard Webster biological anthropologist, human factors specialist, consultant
Webb, Todd (Charles Clayton Webb) photographer, writer

### Belfast
Porter, Bernard Harden consulting physicist, author, publisher
Worth, Mary Page mayor

### Biddeford
Ally, Ahmmed neuroscientist, researcher, educator
Featherman, Sandra university president, political science educator
Ford, Charles Willard university administrator, educator

### Blue Hill
Mills, David Harlow psychologist, association executive
Minarik, Else Holmelund (Bigart Minarik) author

### Blue Hill Falls
Stookey, Noel Paul folksinger, composer

### Boothbay Harbor
Cavanaugh, Tom Richard artist, antiques dealer, retired art educator
Eames, John Heagan etcher
Grossman, Morton S. artist
Lenthall, Franklyn theatre historian

### Bowdoin
Watts, Helen Caswell civil engineer

### Bremen
Hauschka, Theodore Spaeth biologist, researcher, educator

### Bristol
Schmidt, Thomas Carson international development banker

### Brooklin
Schmidt, Klaus Dieter management consultant, university administrator, marketing and management educator
Yglesias, Helen Bassine author, educator

### Brownfield
Ellison, Thorleif consulting engineer
Kloskowski, Vincent John, Jr. educational consultant, writer, educator

### Brunswick
Edwards, Robert Hazard college president
Fuchs, Alfred Herman psychologist, college dean, educator
Geoghegan, William Davidson religion educator, minister
Greason, Arthur LeRoy, Jr. university administrator
Hodge, James Lee German language educator
Lowndes, Janine Marie Herbert journalist
Morgan, Richard Ernest political scientist, educator
Pfeiffer, Sophia Douglass state legislator, lawyer
Porter, Richard Sterling retired metal processing company executive, lawyer
Schwartz, Elliott Shelling composer, author, music educator
Tucker, Allen Brown, Jr. computer science educator
Watson, Katharine Johnson art museum director, art historian

### Bryant Pond
Conary, David Arlan investment company executive

### Camden
Anderson, George Harding broadcasting company executive
Barney, John Bradford legal counsel
Lavenson, James H. hotel industry executive
Lavenson, Susan Barker hotel corporate executive, consultant
Spock, Benjamin McLane physician, educator
Thomas, (Charles) Davis editor
Weidman, Hazel Hitson anthropologist, educator

### Canaan
Walker, Willard Brewer anthropology educator, linguist
Zikorus, Albert Michael golf course architect

### Cape Elizabeth
Dalbeck, Richard Bruce insurance executive
Emerson, Paul Carlton retired publishing executive
Simonds, Stephen Paige former state legislator

### Caribou
Swanson, Shirley June registered nurse, adult education educator

### Castine
Berleant, Arnold philosopher
Davis, Peter Frank filmmaker, author
Hall, David sound archivist, writer
Wiswall, Frank Lawrence, Jr. lawyer, educator

### Center Lovell
Adams, Herbert Ryan management consultant, retired clergyman, actor, director, educator, publishing executive

### Chebeague Island
Middleton, Elliott, Jr. physician
Traina, Albert Salvatore publishing executive

### Cumberland Center
Brewster, Linda Jean family nurse practitioner

### Cumberland Foreside
Dill, William Rankin college president
Harper, Ralph Champlin retired banker

### Cushing
Magee, A. Alan artist

### Damariscotta
Blake, Bud (Julian Watson) cartoonist
Emerson, William Stevenson retired chemist, consultant, writer
Haas, Warren James librarian, consultant
Johnson, Arthur Menzies retired college president, historian, educator
Robinson, Walter George arts management and funding consultant

### Dresden
Turco, Lewis Putnam English educator

### East Blue Hill
Taylor, Samuel A. playwright

### East Boothbay
Eldred, Kenneth McKechnie acoustical consultant
Peters, Andrea Jean artist
Smith, Merlin Gale engineering executive, researcher

### Eastport
Kennedy, Robert Spayde electrical engineering educator

### Edgecomb
Carlson, Suzanne Olive architect

### Ellsworth
Becker, Ray Everett management consultant
Dudman, Richard Beebe communications company executive, journalist
Eustice, Russell Clifford consulting company executive
Goodyear, Austin electronics and retail company executive
Wiggins, James Russell newspaper editor

### Fairfield
Douglas, Jeanne Masson academic administrator, education educator

### Falmouth
Cabot, Lewis Pickering manufacturing company executive, art consultant
Eno, Amos Stewart natural resource foundation administrator

### Farmington
Kalikow, Theodora June university president

### Fort Fairfield
Donnelly, James Owen state legislator, bank executive

### Freeport
Gorman, Leon A. mail order company executive

### Friendship
Du Bois, Clarence Hazel, Jr. clergy member
MacIlvaine, Chalmers Acheson retired financial executive, former association executive
Merrill, Mary Lee professional society administrator
Owen, Wadsworth oceanographer, consultant
Walker, Douglass Willey retired pediatrician, medical center administrator

### Gardiner
Nowell, Glenna Greely librarian, consultant, city manager

### Georgetown
Chapin, Maryan Fox civic worker
Ipcar, Dahlov illustrator, painter, author

### Gorham
Bearce, Jeana Dale artist, educator

### Gray
Durgin, Scott Benjamin radio frequency engineer

### Greenville
Pepin, John Nelson materials research and design engineer

### Hampden
Brown, Robert Horatio, Sr. retired orthopedic surgeon

### Hancock
Silvestro, Clement Mario museum director, historian
Truitt, Charlotte Frances clergywoman

### Hartland
Larochelle, Richard Clement tanning company executive

### Hebron
Farwell, Margaret Wheeler elementary education educator

### Jefferson
Fiore, Joseph Albert artist

### Jonesport
Radomski, Jack London toxicology consultant

### Kennebunk
Betts, Edward artist
Escalet, Frank Diaz art gallery owner, artist, educator
McConnell, David M. secondary school principal
Sholl, John Gurney, III physician

### Kittery
Clark, Sandra Ann clinical social worker

### Kittery Point
Howells, Muriel Gurdon Seabury (Mrs. William White Howells) volunteer
Howells, William White anthropology educator

### Leeds
Lynn, Robert Wood theologian, educator, dean

### Lewiston
Baxter, William MacNeil priest
Chute, Robert Maurice retired biologist, educator, poet
Harward, Donald academic official
Murray, Michael Peter economist, educator
Petersen, Dean Mitchell computer systems operator
Stauffer, Charles Henry retired chemistry educator

### Lincoln
Kneeland, Douglas Eugene retired newspaper editor

### Lincolnville
Nichols, David Arthur mediator, retired state justice
Pattison, Abbott Lawrence sculptor
Williams, Robert Luther city planning consultant

### Machias
Rosen, David Matthew education educator

### Madawaska
Vollmann, John Jacob, Jr. cosmetic packaging executive

### Milbridge
Enslin, Theodore Vernon poet
Heath, Douglas Hamilton educational consultant

### Millinocket
Mitchell, Charles Peter *library director*
Steeves, Eric William *school administrator*

### Monhegan Island
Hudson, Jacqueline *artist*

### Mount Desert
Straus, Donald Blun *retired company executive*

### New Harbor
Fradley, Frederick Macdonell *architect*
Fuller, Melvin Stuart *botany educator*
Lyford, Cabot *sculptor*

### New Vineyard
West, Arthur James, II *biologist*

### North Yarmouth
Fecteau, Rosemary Louise *educational administrator, educator, consultant*

### Oakland
Poulin, Thomas Edward *marine engineer, state legislator, retail business owner*

### Old Orchard Beach
Bartner, Jay B. *school system administrator*

### Oquossoc
Hughes, William Frank *mechanical and electrical engineering educator*

### Orient
Chenevert, Edward Valmore, Jr. *retired librarian, real estate broker*

### Orono
Bartel, Lavon Lee *university administrator, foods and nutrition scientist*
Borns, Harold William, Jr. *geologist, educator*
Butterfield, Stephen Alan *education educator*
Campana, Richard John *retired plant pathology educator, writer, consultant*
Cohn, Steven Frederick *sociology educator, consultant*
†Cronin, Greg *ice hockey coach*
Devino, William Stanley *economist, educator*
Goldstone, Sanford *psychology educator*
Hartgen, Vincent Andrew *museum director, educator, artist*
Hatlen, Burton Norval *English educator*
Ives, Edward Dawson *folklore educator*
Knight, Fred Barrows *forester, entomologist, educator*
Norton, Stephen Allen *geological sciences educator*
Perkins, Ralph Linwood *business executive, public health administration specialist*
Phippen, Sanford Edwin *secondary school educator, writer*
Rivard, William Charles *mechanical engineering educator*
Ruthven, Douglas Morris *chemical engineering educator*
Tarr, Charles Edwin *physicist, educator*
Weiss, Robert Jerome *psychiatrist, educator*
Wiersma, G. Bruce *dean, forest resources educator*
Wilson, Dorothy Clarke *author*

### Orrs Island
Porter, Maxiene Helen Greve *civic worker*

### Oxford
Bensen, Pamela Parke *emergency medicine physician, educator, researcher*

### Palermo
Robbins, Marjorie Jean Gilmartin *elementary education educator*

### Phippsburg
Mc Lanathan, Richard (Barton Kennedy) *author, consultant*
Schuman, Howard *sociologist, educator*

### Port Clyde
Thon, William *artist*

### Portland
Allen, Charles William *lawyer*
Bennett, Jeffrey *lawyer*
Bohan, Thomas Lynch *lawyer, physicist*
Bradford, Carl O. *judge*
Brigham, Christopher Roy *occupational medicine physician*
Carter, Gene *federal judge*
Clark, Gordon Hostetter, Jr. *physician*
Coffin, Frank Morey *federal judge*
Coggeshall, Bruce Amsden *lawyer*
Coughlan, Patrick Campbell *lawyer*
Culley, Peter William *lawyer*
Durgin, Frank Albert *economics educator*
End, William Thomas *business executive*
Freilinger, James Edward *insurance and investments company executive*
Gerry, Joseph John *bishop*
Gilmore, Roger *college president*
Glassman, Caroline Duby *state supreme court justice*
Goodman, Craig Stephen *musician*
Goodman, James A. *federal judge*
Graffam, Ward Irving *lawyer*
Grosset, Alexander Donald, Jr. *banker*
Hall, Christopher George Longden *management consultant*
Harte, Christopher McCutcheon *investment manager*
Harvey, Charles Albert, Jr. *lawyer*
Haynes, Peter Lancaster *utility holding company executive*
Hirshon, Robert Edward *lawyer*
Hornby, David Brock *federal judge*
Hull, William Floyd, Jr. *former museum director, ceramic consultant*
Kendrick, Peter Murray *communications executive, investor*
Lancaster, Ralph Ivan, Jr. *lawyer*
LeBlanc, Richard Philip *lawyer*
McCloskey, Jay P. *prosecutor*
McKusick, Vincent Lee *former state supreme judicial court chief justice, lawyer*
Melanson, Susan C. *property manager*
Monaghan, Matthew John *lawyer*
Moody, James L., Jr. *retail food distribution company executive*
Neavoll, George Franklin *newspaper editor*
Nixon, Philip Andrews *diversified company executive*
Nosanow, Barbara Shissler *art association administrator*
O'Leary, Edward Cornelius *former bishop*
Orr, James F., III *insurance company executive*
Parks, George Richard *librarian*
Pattenaude, Richard Louis *academic administrator*
Philbrick, Donald Lockey *lawyer*
Potter, Lillian Florence *business executive secretary*
Quinn, Thomas Joseph *lawyer*
Raisbeck, Gordon *systems engineer*
Roberts, David Glendenning *state supreme court justice*
Saufley, William Edward *banker, lawyer*
Schwanauer, Francis *philosopher, educator*
Schwartz, Stephen Jay *lawyer*
Shaffer, James Burgess *communications executive*
Shimada, Toshiyuki *orchestra conductor, music director*
Smith, William Charles *lawyer*
Stauffer, Eric P. *lawyer*
White, Jeffrey M. *lawyer*
Whiting, Stephen Clyde *lawyer*
Zarr, Melvyn *lawyer, law educator*

### Presque Isle
Huffman, Durward Roy *college president, electrical engineer, educator*
McGrath, Anna Fields *librarian*

### Prospect Harbor
Shipman, Charles William *chemical engineer*

### Rangeley
Conwill, Joseph Dillard *photographer*
Hunter, J(ohn) Robert *insurance consumer advocate*

### Rockland
Collins, Samuel W., Jr. *judge*

### Rockport
Duarte, Patricia M. *real estate and insurance broker*
Jackson, David Pingree *publishing executive*
Swenson, Orvar *surgeon*

### Scarborough
Farrington, Hugh G. *wholesale food and retail drug company executive*
Martin, Harold Clark *humanities educator*
Sadik, Marvin Sherwood *art consultant, former museum director*
Warg, Pauline *artist, educator*

### Sebago Lake
Murray, Wallace Shordon *publisher, educator*

### Sedgwick
Donnell, William Ray *small business owner, farmer, editor, author, lecturer*
Mc Millan, Brockway *former communications executive*
Schroth, Thomas Nolan *editor*

### South Berwick
Carroll, Gladys Hasty *author*

### South Bristol
Lasher, Esther Lu *minister*

### South Portland
Connell, Lawrence *lawyer*
Howard, Eric Sevan *conservationist, environmental manager*
Huntoon, Abby Elizabeth *artist, teacher*
Katz, Steven Edward *psychiatrist, state health official*
Rand, Peter W. *environmental health researcher*

### Springvale
Eastman, Harland Horace *former foreign service officer*

### Spruce Head
Bird, John Adams *educational consultant*

### Surry
Kilgore, John Edward, Jr. *former petroleum company executive*
Pickett, Betty Horenstein *psychologist*
Sopkin, George *cellist, music educator*

### Thorndike
Treleaven, Phillips Albert *retired publishing company executive*

### Topsham
Palesky, Carol East *tax accountant*
Skolnik, Barnet David *entrepreneur*
Tierney, James Edward *attorney general*

### Union
Buchan, Ronald Forbes *preventive medicine physician*
Taylor, Roger Conant *writer*

### Waterford
Cutler, Cassius Chapin *physicist, educator*

### Waterville
Bassett, Charles Walker *English language educator*
Bennett, Miriam Frances *biologist, educator*
Cotter, William Reckling *college president*
Gemery, Henry Albert *economics educator*
Hudson, Yeager *philosophy educator, minister*
Mavrinac, Albert Anthony *political scientist, educator, lawyer, international legal consultant*
Muehlner, Suanne Wilson *library director*
Sandy, Robert Edward, Jr. *lawyer*
Tormollan, Gary Gordon *health facility administrator, physical therapist*
Zukowski, Walter Henry *administrative science educator*

### Wells
Carleton, Joseph George, Jr. *lawyer, state legislator*
Hero, Barbara Ferrell *visual and sound artist, writer*
Neilson, Elizabeth Anastasia *health sciences educator, association executive, author, editor*

### West Baldwin
Simmonds, Rae Nichols *musician, composer, educator*

### Windham
Diamond, G. William *former secretary of state*
Mulvey, Mary C. *retired adult education director, gerontologist, senior citizen association administrator*

### Wiscasset
Leslie, Seaver *artist*

### Yarmouth
Bischoff, David Canby *retired university dean*
Bissonnette, Jean Marie *elementary school educator, polarity therapist*
Grover, Mark Donald *computer scientist*
Hart, Loring Edward *academic administrator*
Hopkins, Harold Anthony, Jr. *bishop*

### York
Hallam, Beverly (Beverly Linney) *artist*
Lauter, M. David *family physician*
Peterson, Karen Ida *marketing research company executive*
Smart, Mary-Leigh Call (Mrs. J. Scott Smart) *civic worker*

### York Beach
Davison, Nancy Reynolds *artist*

### York Harbor
Curtis, Edward Joseph, Jr. *gas industry executive, management consultant*

## MARYLAND

### Aberdeen
Bonsack, Rose Mary Hatem *state legislator, physician*
Engel, James Harry *computer company executive*
Russell, William Alexander, Jr. *environmental scientist*
Schueler, Betty Jane *writer, counselor*

### Aberdeen Proving Ground
Cozby, Richard Scott *electronics engineer, reserve army officer*
Steger, Ralph James *chemist*
Tobin, Aileen Webb *educational administrator*

### Abingdon
Bonsack, Karen Nancy *physical therapist*
Wolf, Martin Eugene *lawyer*

### Accokeek
Aguirre-Sacasa, Rafael Eugenio *marketing administrator*
Dorsch, Roberta Funk *association executive, volunteer coordinator*

### Adamstown
Ohlke, Clarence Carl *public affairs consultant*

### Adelphi
Langenberg, Donald Newton *academic administrator, physicist*
Lyons, John W(inship) *government official, chemist*

### Andrews AFB
Morris, Dorothea Louise *nurse midwife*
Wong, Ruth Ann *nursing administrator*

### Annapolis
Alderdice, Cynthia Lou *artist*
Arlow, Allan Joseph *lawyer*
Barber, James Alden *military officer*
Biddle, A.G.W., III (Jack Biddle) *computer industry executive*
Bontoyan, Warren Roberts *chemist, state laboratories administrator*
Brady, Frank Benton *retired technical society executive*
Brann, Eva Toni Helene *educator*
Brown-Christopher, Cheryl Denise *physician*
Brunk, William Edward *astronomer*
Calabrese, Anthony Joseph *gastroenterologist*
Carman, Anne *management consultant*
Casey, Edward Dennis *newspaper editor*
Chambers, Ronald D. *book publishing executive*
Clotworthy, John Harris *oceanographic consultant*
Colussy, Dan Alfred *aviation executive*
Core, Mary Carolyn W. Parsons *radiologic technologist*
Coulter, James Bennett *state official*
DiAiso, Robert Joseph *civil engineer*
Drury, Paul Eugene *life insurance manager*
Duncan, Charles Tignor *lawyer*
Elder, Samuel Adams *physics educator*
Eldridge, John Cole *judge*
Ellis, George Fitzallen, Jr. *energy services company executive*
†Erickson, Donald C. *executive*
Evans, William Davidson, Jr. *lawyer*
Forehand, Jennie Meador *state legislator*
Forkin, Sister Jean Louise *organization administrator*
Fowler, Terri (Marie Therese Fowler) *artist*
Glendening, Parris Nelson *governor, political science educator*
Goldstein, Louis Lazarus *state official*
Granger, Robert Alan *aerospace engineer*
Halpern, Joseph Alan *physician*
Hammer, Jacob Myer *physicist, consultant*
Heller, Austin Norman *chemical and environmental engineer*
Hixson, Sheila Ellis *state legislator*
Hollinger, Paula Colodny *state senator*
Holmberg, Lawrence Oscar, Jr. *documentary film producer, photographer, writer*
Holmes, David Charles *broadcasting company executive*
Holtgrewe, Henry Logan *urologist*
Hyde, Lawrence Henry, Jr. *industrial company executive*
Jansson, John Phillip *architect, consultant*
Jefferson, Ralph Harvey *international affairs consultant*
Johnson, Bruce *engineering educator*
Johnson, David Simonds *meteorologist*
Jones, Sylvanus Benson *adjudicator, consultant*
Kapland, Mitchell Arthur *engineering firm executive*
Karwacki, Robert Lee *judge*
Kelley, Delores Goodwin *state legislator*
Klima, Martha Scanlan *state legislator*
Koscianski, Leonard Joseph *artist*
Kozlowski, Ronald Stephan *librarian*
Larson, Charles Robert *naval officer*
Lee, T. Girard *church growth consultant*
Levin, David Alan *lawyer*
Levitan, Laurence *lawyer, former state senator*
Lillard, John Franklin, III *lawyer*
Long, Robert Lyman John *naval officer*
Madden, Martin Gerard *state legislator, insurance agent*
Marton, Michael *cinematographer*
McDonough, Joseph Corbett *former army officer, aviation consultant*
Menes, Pauline H. *state legislator*
Michaelson, Benjamin, Jr. *lawyer*
Miller, John Grider *magazine editor*
Miller, Richards Thorn *naval architect, engineer*
Moellering, John Henry *aviation maintenance company executive*
Montague, Brian John *consulting company executive*
Morgan, John Stephen *state legislator, materials science researcher*
Ness, Frederic William *former academic administrator, educator, consultant*
Nicholson, William Mac *naval architect, marine engineer, consultant*
Nuesse, Celestine Joseph *retired university official*
Papenfuse, Edward Carl, Jr. *archivist, state official*
Parham, Carol Sheffey *school system administrator*
Perkins, Roger Allan *lawyer*
Rapkin, Jerome *marine engineer, defense industry executive*
Roesser, Jean Wolberg *state legislator*
Rosenthal, Michael Ross *academic administrator, dean*
Rowell, Charles Frederick *chemistry educator*
Ruben, Ida Gass *state senator*
Schleicher, Nora Elizabeth *banker, treasurer, accountant*
Sheppard, John Wilbur *computer research scientist*
Stahl, David Edward *trade association administrator, retired*
Taussig, Joseph Knefler, Jr. *retired government official, lawyer*
Townsend, Kathleen Kennedy *state official*
Werking, Richard Hume *librarian, historian, academic administrator*
Whitford, Dennis James *naval officer, meteorologist, oceanographer*
Wilkes, Joseph Allen *architect*
Willis, John T. *state official*
†Wilson, Benjamin Franklin, Jr. *steamship agency executive*
Wyman, L. Pilar *indexer*

### Arnold
Barrett, John Anthony *publishing and printing company financial executive*
Green, John Cawley *lawyer*
Kellogg-Smith, Peter *educator, sculptor, inventor*

### Baldwin
Decker, James Ludlow *management consultant*

### Baltimore
Abeloff, Martin David *medical administrator, educator, researcher*
Abrams, Rosalie Silber *retired state agency administrator*
Achinstein, Peter Jacob *philosopher, educator*
Adams, Harold Lynn *architect*
Adkins, Edward James *lawyer*
Adkinson, N. Franklin, Jr. *clinical immunologist*
Albinak, Marvin Joseph *chemistry educator*
Albuquerque, Edson Xavier *pharmacology educator*
Allen, Ronald John *astrophysics educator, researcher*
Alomar, Roberto Velazquez *professional baseball player*
Ambler, Bruce Melville *finance company executive*
Anderson, Gary Dean *architect, planner, educator*
Anderson, Gerard Fenton *economist, university program administrator*
Anderson, John William *protective services official*
Andres, Reubin *gerontologist*
Applebaum, Gary E. *medical director, executive*
Archibald, James Kenway *lawyer*
Arnick, John Stephen *lawyer, legislator*
Arsham, Hossein *operations research analyst*
Ayres, Jeffrey Peabody *lawyer*
Bachur, Nicholas Robert, Sr. *research physician*
Bacigalupo, Charles Anthony *brokerage company executive*
Backas, James Jacob *foundation administrator*
Bair, Robert Rippel *lawyer*
Baker, Barry *broadcast executive*
Baker, R. Robinson *surgeon*
Baker, Susan P. *public health educator*
Baker, Timothy Danforth *physician, educator*
Baker, William Parr *lawyer*
Baldwin, Henry Furlong *banker*
Baldwin, John Chandler *lawyer*
Baldwin, John Wesley *history educator*
Barker, Stephen Francis *philosophy educator*
Barnhouse, Robert Bolon *lawyer*
Barth, John Simmons *writer, educator*
Bartlett, James Wilson, III *lawyer*
Bartlett, John Gill *infectious disease physician*
Battaglia, Lynne Ann *prosecutor*
Batterden, James Edward *business executive*
Baughman, Kenneth Lee *cardiologist, educator*
Baumgartner, William Anthony *cardiac surgeon*
Bausell, R. Barker, Jr. *research methodology educator*
Bayless, Theodore M(orris) *gastroenterologist, educator, researcher*
Beall, George *lawyer*
Beasley, Robert Scott *financial executive*
Beckenstein, Myron *journalist*
Beer, Alice Stewart (Mrs. Jack Engeman) *retired musician, educator*
Behm, Mark Edward *university administrator, consultant*
Bell, Robert M. *judge*
Bellack, Alan Scott *clinical psychologist*
Benton, George Stock *meteorologist, educator*
Benz, Edward J., Jr. *physician, educator*
Bereston, Eugene Sydney *retired dermatologist*
Berlin, Fred Saul *psychiatrist, educator*

GEOGRAPHIC INDEX 4893 MARYLAND


Berman, Barnett internist, educator
Bernhardt, Herbert Nelson law educator
Bhardwaj, Anish neuroscientist, medical educator
Bianco, Frederick Anthony dean
Bigelow, George E. psychology and pharmacology scientist
Black, Walter Evan, Jr. federal judge
Blake, Catherine C. judge
Blake, Norman Perkins, Jr. finance company executive
Blanton, Edward Lee, Jr. lawyer
Boardman, John Michael mathematician, educator
Boone, Harold Thomas retired lawyer
Bor, Jonathan Steven journalist
Boughman, Joann Ashley dean
Bowe, Peter Armistead manufacturing executive
Bowen, Kit Hansel, Jr. chemistry educator
Bowen, Lowell Reed lawyer
Bradley, Sterling Gaylen microbiology and pharmacology educator
Bradley, Thomas Andrew insurance company executive
Brady, Joseph Vincent behavioral biologist, educator
Bready, James Hall reporter
Breitenecker, Rudiger pathologist
Brewster, Gerry Leiper lawyer
Brieger, Gert Henry medical historian, educator
Bright, Margaret sociologist
Brinkley, James Wellons investment company executive
Briscoe, Marian Denise real estate agent, lyricist
Broadbent, J. Streett engineering executive
Brodie, M. J. (Jay Brodie) architect, city planner, government executive
Brody, Eugene B. psychiatrist, educator
Brody, William R. radiologist, educator
Brotman, Phyllis Block advertising and public relations executive
Brown, Donald David biology educator
Brown, Gerald Curtis retired army officer, engineering executive
Brumbaugh, John Maynard lawyer, educator
Brunson, Dorothy Edwards broadcasting executive
Brusilow, Saul pediatrics researcher
Bryan, Sukey artist
Bryan, Thelma Jane dean, English educator
Bucher, Richard David sociology educator
Bundick, William Ross retired dermatologist
Burch, Francis Boucher, Jr. lawyer
Buser, Carolyn Elizabeth correctional education administrator
Cacossa, Anthony Alexander Romance languages educator
Cain, Marcena Jean Beesley retail store executive
Cameron, Duke Edward cardiac surgeon, educator
Campazzi, Earl James physician
Carbine, James Edmond lawyer
Carey, Anthony Morris lawyer
Carey, Jana Howard lawyer
Carlin, Paul Victor legal association executive
Carmi, Shlomo mechanical engineering educator, scientist
Carper, Gertrude Esther artist, marina owner
Carroll, John Sawyer newspaper editor
†Carson, Benjamin Solomon neurosurgeon
Cashman, Edmund Joseph, Jr. investment banker
Castro-Klaren, Sara Latin American literature educator
Catania, A(nthony) Charles psychology educator
Chaplin, Peggy Fannon lawyer
Chernow, Bart critical care physician
Chiarello, Donald Frederick lawyer
Chien, Chia-Ling physics educator
Childs, Barton retired, physician, educator
Chiu, Hungdah lawyer, legal educator
Chriss, Timothy D. A. lawyer
Cohen, June Laura state agency administrator
Cohen, Warren I. history educator
Colhoun, Howard Post financial executive
Collins, George Joseph investment counselor
Conley, Carroll Lockard physician, emeritus educator
Connaughton, James Patrick psychiatrist
Cook, Bryson Leitch lawyer
Cook, Joseph Daniel finance executive, accountant
Cooper, Jerrold Stephen historian, educator
Cooper, Joseph political scientist, educator
Corn, Morton environmental engineer, educator
Cornblath, Marvin pediatrician, educator
Couper, William banker
Crawford, Edward E. psychologist
Cropper, M. Elizabeth art history educator
Cummings, Charles William physician, educator
Cunningham, M(urray) Hunt, Jr. aerospace company executive, mechanical engineer, author
Cunningham, Terence Thomas, III hospital administrator
Curley, John Francis, Jr. securities company executive
Curran, J. Joseph, Jr. state attorney general
Dagdigian, Paul Joseph chemistry educator
Dang, Chi Van hematology and oncology educator
Daniels, Worth B., Jr. retired internist
Dannenberg, Arthur Milton, Jr. experimental pathologist, immunologist, educator
Davis, Ada Romaine nursing educator
Davis, Eric Keith former professional baseball player
DeAngelis, Catherine D. pediatrics educator
Degenford, James Edward electrical engineer, educator
DeGroff, Ralph Lynn, Jr. investment banker
DeLateur, Barbara Jane medical educator
DeLuna, D.N. literary educator
Dembo, Donald Howard cardiologist, medical administrator, educator
Dempsey, Charles Gates art historian, educator
Deoul, Neal electronics company executive
†D'Erasmo, Martha Jean health company executive
Derby, Ernest Stephen federal judge
DeRouchey, Beverly Jean investment company executive
DeTolla, Louis James veterinarian, researcher
Devan, Deborah Hunt lawyer
DeVito, Mathias Joseph retired real estate executive
Dicello, John Francis, Jr. physicist, educator
Dietze, Gottfried political science educator
Digges, Dudley Perkins retired editor
Dilloff, Neil Joel lawyer
Dishon, Cramer Steven sales executive
Djordjevic, Borislav Boro materials scientist, researcher
Dodge, Calvert Renaul education and training executive, author, educator
Donaldson, Sue Karen dean, nursing educator
Donkervoet, Richard Cornelius architect
Donovan, Sharon Ann educator
Doory, Robert Leonard, Jr. lawyer
Dorsey, John Russell journalist
Dorst, John Phillips physician, radiology and pediatrics educator
Drachman, Daniel Bruce neurologist
Dubner, Ronald neurobiologist, educator
Dunne, Richard Edwin, III lawyer
Eanes, Joseph Cabel, Jr. surety company executive
Ebinger, Mary Ritzman pastoral counselor
Eichhorn, Gunther Louis chemist
Eisenberg, Gerson G. author, historian
Eisenberg, Howard Michael neurosurgeon
Eisner, Henry Wolfgang advertising executive
Eldefrawi, Amira Toppozada medical educator
Ellingwood, Bruce Russell structural engineering researcher, educator
Engel, Paul Bernard lawyer
Englund, Paul Theodore biochemist, educator
Entwisle, Doris Roberts sociology educator
Epstein, Daniel Mark poet, dramatist
Eveleth, Janet Stidman law association administrator
Evers-Williams, Myrlie cultural organization administrator
Faden, Ruth R. medical educator, ethicist, researcher
Feldman, Deborah Karpoff nursing education consultant
Feldman, Gordon physics educator
Felsenthal, Gerald physiatrist, educator
Fenselau, Catherine Clarke chemistry educator
Ferencz, Charlotte pediatrician, epidemiology and preventive medicine educator
†Fergenson, Arthur Friend lawyer
Ferrara, Steven educational administrator, researcher, consultant
Finch, Walter Goss Gilchrist lawyer, engineer, accountant, retired army officer
Finnerty, Joseph Gregory, Jr. lawyer
Fishbein, Estelle Ackerman lawyer
Fisher, Jack Carrington environmental engineering educator
Fisher, Morton Poe, Jr. lawyer
Fishman, Bernard Philip museum director
Fishman, Jacob Robert psychiatrist, administrator, educator, corporate executive, investor
Fitzgerald, Thomas Rollins university administrator
Fleishman, Avrom Hirsch English educator
Fletcher, Sherryl Ann higher education administrator
Fontanazza, Franklin Joseph accountant
Ford, John Gilmore interior designer
Forster, Robert history educator
†Foss, Joseph E. professional sports team executive
Fowler, Bruce Andrew toxicologist, marine biologist
Fox, Harold Edward obstetrician, gynecologist, educator, researcher
Fox, Madeline Joan speech and language pathologist
Fraser, Joan Catherine lawyer
Frazier, Thomas C. protective services official
Freeman, John Mark pediatric neurologist
Freeze, James Donald administrator, clergyman
Freire, Ernesto biophysicist, educator
Fried, Herbert Daniel advertising executive
Friedman, Louis Frank lawyer
Friedman, Maria Andre public relations executive
Friedman, Marion internist, family physician, medical administrator, medical editor
Fuentealba, Victor William professional society administrator
Fulton, Thomas theoretical physicist, educator
Gaber, Robert psychologist
Gall, Joseph Grafton biologist, researcher, educator
Garbis, Marvin Joseph federal judge
Gately, Mark Donohue lawyer
Gauvey, Susan K. judge
Giddens, Don Peyton engineering educator, researcher
Gifford, Donald George academic dean
Gillece, James Patrick, Jr. lawyer
Gillick, Patrick professional baseball team executive
Gimbel, Michael Marc alcohol and drug abuse services professional
Gimenez, Luis Fernando physician, educator
Ginsberg, Benjamin political science educator
Glasgow, Jesse Edward newspaper editor
Glassgold, Israel Leon construction company executive, engineer, consultant
Gleichmann, Frances Evangeline retired elementary educator
Godenne, Ghislaine Dudley physician, psychoanalyst, educator
Goedicke, Hans archeology educator
Goetz, Clarence Edward magistrate, judge, retired
Goetze, Marian Engle business executive
Goldberg, Alan Marvin toxicologist, educator
Goldberg, Morton Falk ophthalmologist, educator
Goldman, Brian Arthur lawyer, accountant
Goldscheider, Sidney lawyer
Gordis, Leon physician
Graham, George Gordon physician
Graham, Jerry Fisher bank executive, accountant
Graham, John Stuart, III lawyer
Grasmick, Nancy S. superintendent of schools
Gray, Dahli accounting educator and administrator
Gray, Frank Truan lawyer
Gray, Oscar Shalom lawyer
Green, Bert Franklin, Jr. psychologist
Green, Robert Edward, Jr. physicist, educator
Greene, Jack Phillip historian, educator
Greenough, William Bates, III medical educator
Greenspan, Arnold Michael computer company executive
Griffin, Diane Edmund research physician, virologist, educator
Griffith, Lawrence Stacey Cameron cardiologist
Groenheim, Henri Arnold psychologist, consultant
Grossman, Joel B(arry) political science educator
Grossman, Lawrence biochemist, educator
Guest, James Alfred public service official
Habermann, Helen Margaret plant physiologist, educator
Hafets, Richard Jay lawyer
Haig, Frank Rawle physics educator, clergyman
Haines, Thomas W. W. lawyer
Hale, Danny Lyman financial executive
Hall, Merrill Souel, III head master
Handelsman, Jacob Charles surgeon
Hanks, James Judge, Jr. lawyer
Hansen, Barbara Caleen physiology educator, scientist
Hansen, Jeanne Bodine retired counselor
Hardiman, Joseph Raymond securities industry executive
Hargrove, John R. federal judge
†Harp, Solomon, III airport executive
Harrison, Michael opera company executive
Hart, John, Jr. behavioral neurologist, neuroscientist, educator
Hart, Robert Gordon federal agency administrator
Hartigan, Grace artist
Hartman, Charles Henry association executive, educator
Harvey, Abner McGehee physician, educator
Harvey, Alexander, II federal judge
Harvey, Curran Whitthorne, Jr. investment management executive
Hauser, Michael George astrophysicist
Haysbert, Raymond Victor food company executive
Hecht, Alan Dannenberg insurance executive
Heldrich, Eleanor Maar publisher
Hellmann, David Bruce medical educator
Helm, Donald Cairney hydrogeologist, engineer, educator
Helrich, Martin anesthesiologist, educator
Henderson, Donald Ainslie public health educator
Henderson, Lenneal Joseph, Jr. political science educator
Henry, Richard Conn astrophysicist, educator
Herschman, Jeffrey D. lawyer
Herstein, Louis Arthur, III physicist
Heyssel, Robert Morris physician, retired hospital executive
Higham, John history educator
Hill, Barbara Benton healthcare executive
Hillers, Delbert Roy Near East language educator
Himelfarb, Richard Jay securities firm executive
Hirsch, Richard Arthur retired mechanical engineer
Hirsh, Allan Thurman, Jr. publishing executive
Hirsh, Theodore William lawyer
Hobish, Mitchell Kent consulting synthesist, biochemist
Hochberg, Bayard Zabdial lawyer
Hoffberger, Jerold Charles corporation executive
Hofkin, Gerald Alan gastroenterologist
Hoiles, Christopher Allen professional baseball player
Honemann, Daniel Henry lawyer
Hopkins, Samuel retired investment banker
Hopps, Raymond, Jr. film producer
Houck, John Roland clergyman
Howard, Bettie Jean surgical nurse
Howard, J. Woodford, Jr. political science educator
Howell, Harley Thomas lawyer
Huang, Pien Chien biochemistry educator, scientist
Hubbard, Herbert Hendrix lawyer
Hug, Richard Ernest environmental company executive
Hughes, Harry Roe lawyer
Hulse, Stewart Harding, Jr. educator, experimental psychologist
Hungerford, David Samuel orthopedic surgeon, educator
Hutchins, Grover MacGregor pathologist, educator
Igusa, Jun-Ichi mathematician, educator
Ihrie, Robert oil, gas and real estate company executive
Imboden, John Baskerville psychiatry educator
Immelt, Stephen J. lawyer
Irwin, John Thomas humanities educator
Jackson, Harold journalist
Jackson, Stanley Edward retired special education educator
Jacobs, Richard James banker, educator
Jancuk, Kathleen Frances principal
Jani, Sushma Niranjan pediatrics and child and adolescent psychiatrist
Jastreboff, Pawel Jerzy neuroscientist, educator
Jelinek, Frederick electrical engineer, educator
Jenkins, Louise Sherman nursing researcher
Jernigan, Kenneth social services administrator
Johns, Carol Johnson physician, educator
Johns, Richard James physician, educator
Johnson, Davey (David Allen Johnson) baseball team manager
Johnson, Elaine McDowell retired federal government administrator
Johnson, Kenneth Peter neurologist, medical researcher
Johnson, Michael Paul history educator
Johnston, Edward Allan lawyer
Johnston, George W. lawyer
Jones, John Martin, Jr. lawyer
Jones, Raymond Moylan strategy and public policy educator
Judd, Brian Raymond physicist, educator
Judson, Horace Freeland history of science, writer, educator
Junck, Mary newspaper publishing executive
Kagan, Richard Lauren history educator
Kallina, Emanuel John, II lawyer
Kandel, Nelson Robert lawyer
Kandel, Peter Thomas lawyer
Karni, Edi economics educator
Kastor, John Alfred cardiologist, educator
Katz, Joseph Louis chemical engineer, educator
Katz, Richard Stephen political science educator
Kaufman, Frank Albert federal judge
Keller, George Charles higher education consultant, editor
Kelly, Thomas Jesse, Jr. molecular biologist
Kelman, Gary F. environmental engineer
Kent, Edgar Robert, Jr. investment banker
Kern, David Evans physician
Kessler, Herbert Leon art historian, educator
Key, Jimmy (James Edward Key) professional baseball player
Killebrew, Robert Sterling, Jr. investment manager
Kim, Chung Wook physics educator, researcher
King, David Paul lawyer
King, Ora Sterling education educator
Kinnard, William James, Jr. retired pharmacy educator
Klarman, Herbert Elias economist, educator
†Kleiner, Arnold Joel television executive
Klitzke, Theodore Elmer former college dean, arts consultant
Knapp, David Allan pharmaceutical educator, researcher
Knight, Franklin W. history educator
Knoedler, Elmer L. retired chemical engineer
Kohn, Melvin L. sociologist
Kosaraju, S. Rao computer science educator, researcher
Koski, Walter S. chemistry educator, scientist
Kowarski, Allen Avinoam endocrinologist, educator
Kramer, Morton biostatistician, epidemiologist
Kramer, Paul R. lawyer
Krolik, Julian Henry astrophysicist, educator
Krongard, Alvin B. corporation executive
Kruger, Jerome materials science educator, consultant
Kues, Irvin William health care financial executive
Kumar, Martha Joynt political science educator
Kumin, Libby Barbara speech language pathologist, educator
Kuppusamy, Periannan medical educator, medical researcher
Kurth, Lieselotte foreign language educator
Kwiterovich, Peter Oscar, Jr. medical science educator, researcher, physician
Lafferty, Joyce G. Zvonar retired middle school educator
Lakatta, Edward Gerard biomedical researcher
Lamp, Frederick John museum curator
Lanier, Jacqueline Ruth curator, artist
Larch, Sara Margaret medical administrator
Laric, Michael Victor academic administrator
Larrabee, Martin Glover biophysics educator
Lawrence, Robert Swan physician, educator, academic administrator
Lazarus, Fred, IV college president
Lee, Carlton K. K. clinical pharmacist, consultant, educator
Lee, Yung-Keun physicist, educator
Lefko, Jeffrey Jay hospital administrator
Legg, Benson Everett federal judge
Legum, Jeffrey Alfred automobile company executive
Lemer, Andrew Charles engineer, economist
Leonard, John Wirth English educator, retailer
Lerch, Richard Heaphy retired lawyer
Levin, Edward Jesse lawyer
Levin, Marshall Abbott judge, educator
Levine, Richard E. lawyer
Levine, Robert Joseph secondary school administrator
Lewis, Alexander Ingersoll, III lawyer
Lewison, Edward Frederick surgeon
Liberto, Joseph Salvatore banker
Lichtenstein, Lawrence Mark allergy, immunology educator, physician
Lidtke, Doris Keefe computer science educator
Lidtke, Vernon LeRoy history educator
Liebmann, George W(illiam) lawyer
Litrenta, Frances Marie psychiatrist
Littlefield, John Walley geneticist, cell biologist, pediatrician
Liu, Rhonda Louise librarian
Livingstone, Harrison Edward writer
Lohr, Walter George, Jr. lawyer
Long, Donlin Martin surgeon, educator
Lowenthal, Henry retired greeting card company executive
Luck, Georg Hans Bhawani classics educator
Lundy, Audie Lee, Jr. lawyer
Maccini, Louis John economic educator
Macleod, Donald clergyman, educator
Madansky, Leon particle physicist, educator
Magnuson, Nancy librarian
Maletz, Herbert Naaman federal judge
Manson, Paul Nellis plastic surgeon
Marimow, William Kalmon journalist
Markowska, Alicja Lidia neuroscientist, researcher
Marriot, Salima Siler state legislator, social work educator
Marsh, Bruce David geologist, educator
Marvel, L. Paige lawyer
Massof, Robert William neuroscientist, educator
Matheson, Nina W. medical researcher
Matjasko, M. Jane anesthesiologist, educator
Maumenee Hussels, Irene E. ophthalmology educator
Maurer, Marc Morgan federation administrator, lawyer
McCarter, P(ete) Kyle, Jr. Near Eastern studies educator
McCarty, Harry Downman tool manufacturing company executive
McCarty, Richard Earl biochemist, biochemistry educator
McClung, A(lexander) Keith, Jr. lawyer
Mc Cord, Kenneth Armstrong consulting engineer
McDowell, Elizabeth Mary retired pathology educator
McGowan, George Vincent public utility executive
McGuirk, Ronald Charles banker
Mc Hugh, Paul R. psychiatrist, neurologist, educator
McKhann, Guy Mead physician, educator
McKinney, Richard Ishmael philosophy educator
McKusick, Victor Almon geneticist, educator, physician
McManus, Walter Leonard investment executive
McPartland, James Michael university official
McPherson, Donald Paxton, III lawyer
McWilliams, John Michael lawyer
Melvin, Norman Cecil lawyer
Meny, Robert medical research administrator
Mericle, Sally Diane graphic artist
Messinger, Scott James advertising executive
Meyer, Jean-Pierre Gustave mathematician, educator
Mfume, Kweisi former congressman
Mierzwicki, Anthony Joseph real estate executive
Migeon, Barbara Ruben pediatrician, geneticist
Migeon, Claude Jean pediatrics educator
Miller, Carl Frank business appraiser
Miller, Decatur Howard lawyer
Miller, Donald LeSessne publishing executive
Miller, Edward Doring, Jr. anesthesiologist
†Miller, Jayne Ellen journalist, educator
Milnor, William Robert physician
Mintz, Sidney Wilfred anthropologist
Mizel, Mark Stuart orthopedic surgeon
Mocko, George Paul minister
Mohraz, Judy Jolley college president
Money, John William psychologist
Monroe, Russell Ronald psychiatrist, educator
Montgomery, Paula Kay publisher
Moos, H. Warren physicist, astronomer, educator, administrator
Morrel, William Griffin, Jr. banker
Moser, Hugo Wolfgang physician
Moser, M(artin) Peter lawyer
†Mosley, W. Henry medical educator
Moszkowski, Lena Iggers secondary school educator
Motz, Diana Gribbon federal judge
Motz, John Frederick federal judge
Mulligan, Joseph Francis physicist, educator
Munster, Andrew Michael surgery educator
Murnaghan, Francis Dominic, Jr. federal judge
Murphy, Philip Francis bishop
Murray, Joseph William banker
Mussina, Michael Cole professional baseball player
Myers, Randall Kirk (Randy Myers) professional baseball player
Mysko, William Keifer emergency physician, educator
Nagey, David Augustus physician, researcher
Nathans, Daniel molecular biology and genetics educator
Nelson, Randy J. psychology educator
Newman, William C. bishop
Nichols, Stephen George Romance languages educator
Nickerson, William Milnor federal judge
Nickon, Alex chemist, educator
Niemeyer, Paul Victor federal judge
Nilson, George Albert lawyer
Norman, Colin Arthur astrophysics educator
Norman, Philip Sidney physician

North, Richard Boydston *neurological surgery educator*
Northrop, Edward Skottowe *federal judge*
Nwofor, Ambrose Onyegbule *vocational assessment evaluator*
O'Leary, David Michael *priest, educator*
O'Melia, Charles Richard *environmental engineering educator*
Orman, Leonard Arnold *lawyer*
Ott, John Harlow *museum administrator*
Ourednik, Patricia Ann *accountant*
Owen, Stephen Lee *lawyer*
†Paine, Ruth M. *medical insurance company administrator*
Palmeiro, Rafael Corrales *professional baseball player*
Palumbo, Francis Xavier Bernard *pharmacy educator*
Pappas, George Frank *lawyer*
Park, Mary Woodfill *information consultant*
Passano, E. Magruder, Jr. *publishing executive*
Passano, Edward Magruder *printing company executive*
Patz, Arnall *physician*
Paulson, Ronald Howard *English and humanities educator*
Peacock, James Daniel *lawyer*
Peirce, Carol Marshall *English educator*
Permutt, Solbert *physiologist, physician*
Peters, Douglas Alan *neurology nurse*
Pettijohn, Francis John *geology educator*
Phillips, Carla *county official*
Phillips, Owen Martin *oceanographer, geophysicist, educator*
Pigott, Karen Gray *community health nurse, geriatrics nurse*
Piotrow, Phyllis Tilson *public health educator, international development specialist*
Plant, Albin MacDonough *lawyer*
Platt, William Rady *pathology educator*
Plummer, Risque Wilson *lawyer*
Poindexter, Christian Herndon *utility company executive*
Pokempner, Joseph Kres *lawyer*
Pollak, Joanne E. *lawyer*
†Pollak, Lisa *columnist*
Pollak, Mark *lawyer*
Pollard, Shirley *employment training director, consultant*
Popel, Aleksander S. *engineering educator*
Posner, Gary Herbert *chemist, educator*
Potts, Bernard *lawyer*
Preston, Mark I. *investment company executive*
Priest, Troy Alfred-Wiley *lawyer*
Prince, Jerry Ladd *engineering educator*
Proctor, Donald Frederick *otolaryngology educator, physician*
Provost, Thomas Taylor *dermatology educator, researcher*
Putzel, Constance Kellner *lawyer*
Quinn, Michael Desmond *diversified financial services executive*
Radding, Andrew *lawyer*
Rafferty, William Bernard *lawyer*
Randall, Lilian Maria Charlotte *museum curator*
Ranney, Richard Raymond *dental educator, researcher*
Ranum, Orest Allen *historian, educator*
Rayson, Glendon Ennes *internist, preventive medicine specialist, writer*
Redden, Roger Duffey *lawyer*
Reed, Gregory *lawyer*
Reeder, Ellen Dryden *museum curator*
Reeder, Oliver Howard *paint products manufacturing executive*
Rennels, Marshall Leigh *neuroanatomist, biomedical scientist, educator*
Reno, Russell Ronald, Jr. *lawyer*
ReVelle, Charles S. *environmental engineer, geophysicist, systems analysis and economics educator*
Reynolds, William Leroy *lawyer, educator*
Ricard, John H. *bishop, educator*
Ripken, Calvin Edwin, Jr. (Cal Ripken) *professional baseball player*
Ritzenthaler, Patty Parsons *lawyer*
Roberts, Randolph Wilson *health and science educator*
†Robinson, Brooks Calbert, Jr. *former professional baseball player, TV commentator, business consultant*
Robinson, Zelig *lawyer*
Rodowsky, Lawrence Francis *state judge*
Rodricks, Daniel John *columnist, television commentator*
Roland, Donald Edward *advertising executive*
Rolland, Donald F. *printing company executive*
Rose, Hugh *retired economics educator*
Rose, Noel Richard *immunologist, microbiologist, educator*
Rose, Rudolph L. *lawyer*
Rose, Sara Margaret *English as a second language educator*
Roseman, Saul *biochemist, educator*
Rosenberg, Henry A., Jr. *petroleum executive*
Rosenstein, Beryl Joel *physician*
Rosenthal, William J. *lawyer*
Ross, Dorothy Rabin *history educator*
Ross, Richard Starr *medical school dean emeritus, cardiologist*
Roth, George Stanley *research biochemist, physiologist*
Rothschild, Amalie Rosenfeld *artist*
Roupe, James Paul *accountant*
Rousuck, J. Wynn *theater critic*
†Runk, Carl *head coach men's lacrosse*
Russell-Wood, Anthony John R. *history educator*
Sachs, Murray B. *audiologist, educator*
Sack, George Henry, Jr. *molecular geneticist*
Sack, Sylvan Hanan *lawyer*
Safran, Linda Jacqueline *fundraising consultant*
Sagett, Jan Jeffrey *lawyer, former government official*
Salamon, Lester Milton *political science educator*
Samet, Jonathan Michael *epidemiologist, educator*
Sampson, Richard Thomas *lawyer*
Sanfilippo, Alfred Paul *pathologist, educator*
Schaefer, Robert Wayne *banker*
Schaefer, William G. *lawyer*
Scheeler, Charles *construction company executive*
Schimpff, Stephen Callender *internist, oncologist*
Schmoke, Kurt L. *mayor*
Schneewind, Jerome Borges *philosophy educator*
Schneider, James Frederick *federal judge*
Schochor, Jonathan *lawyer*
Schoenfeld, Henry F. *insurance executive*
Schoenrich, Edyth Hull *academic administrator, physician*
Schuster, Marvin Meier *physician, educator*

Scott, Frederick Isadore, Jr. *editor, business executive*
Scott, Robert Edward, Jr. *lawyer*
Scriggins, Larry Palmer *lawyer*
Seaman, Tony *university athletic coach*
Sedlak, Valerie Frances *English language educator, university administrator*
Semans, Truman Thomas *investment company executive*
Sfekas, Stephen James *lawyer*
Shaeffer, Charles Wayne *investment counselor*
Shah, Shirish Kalyanbhai *computer science, chemistry and environmental science educator*
Shamoo, Adil Elias *biochemist, biophysicist, educator*
Shapiro, Harry Dean *lawyer*
Shapiro, Sam *health care analyst, biostatistician*
Sharfstein, Steven Samuel *health care executive, medical director*
Sharkey, Robert Emmett *lawyer*
Sharpe, Donald Edward *lawyer*
Sharpe, William Norman, Jr. *mechanical engineer, educator*
Shattuck, Mayo Adams, III *investment bank executive*
Shiffman, Bernard *mathematician, educator*
Short, Alexander Campbell *lawyer*
Shortridge, Deborah Green *lawyer*
Shriver, Pamela Howard *professional tennis player*
Shuldiner, Alan Rodney *physician, endocrinologist, educator*
Silbergeld, Ellen Kovner *environmental epidemiologist and toxicologist*
Silver, Michael Joel *lawyer*
Silverstein, Arthur Matthew *ophthalmic immunologist, educator, historian*
Silverstone, Harris J. *chemistry educator*
Simpson, Thomas William *physician*
Slatkin, Murray *paint sundry distribution executive*
Slavin, Robert Edward *research scientist, educator*
Slepian, Paul *mathematician, educator*
Smalkin, Frederic N. *federal judge*
Smith, Gardner Watkins *physician*
Smith, Hoke LaFollette *university president*
Smith, Julian Payne *gynecological oncologist, educator*
Smith, Robert G. *lawyer*
Smith, Robert Luther *management educator*
Smouse, H(ervey) Russell *lawyer*
Snead, James Arrington *architect*
Snyder, Solomon Halbert *psychiatrist, pharmacologist*
Somerville, Romaine Stec *arts administrator*
Sommer, Alfred *medical educator, scientist, ophthalmologist*
Sorkin, Alan Lowell *economist, educator*
Southern, Hugh *performing arts consultant*
Stair, Thomas Osborne *physician, educator*
Stalfort, John Arthur *lawyer*
Stanley, Julian Cecil, Jr. *psychology educator*
Stanley, Steven Mitchell *paleobiologist, educator*
Starfield, Barbara Helen *physician, educator*
Stein, Bernard Alvin *business consultant*
Steinbach, Alice *journalist*
Steiner, Robert Frank *biochemist*
Steinwachs, Donald Michael *public health educator*
Stenberg, Carl W(aldamer), III *academic program director, educator*
Sterne, Joseph Robert Livingston *newspaper editor, educator*
Stevens, Elisabeth Goss (Mrs. Robert Schleussner, Jr.) *writer, journalist*
Stewart, C(ornelius) Van Leuven *lawyer*
Stewart, Doris Mae *biology educator*
Stiller, Shale David *lawyer, educator*
Stobo, John David *physician, educator*
Stolley, Paul David *medical educator, researcher*
Storrs, Alexander David *astronomer*
Strickland, George Thomas, Jr. *physician, researcher, educator*
Strickland, Marshall Hayward *bishop*
Strull, Gene *technology consultant, retired electrical manufacturing company executive*
Suchkov, Anatoly *astronomer*
Summers, Thomas Carey *lawyer*
Sunshine, Eugene Samuel *university and public administrator*
Suskind, Sigmund Richard *microbiology educator*
Sweeting, Linda Marie *chemist*
Sykes, Melvin Julius *lawyer*
Tabatznik, Bernard *physician, educator*
Talalay, Paul *pharmacologist, physician*
Talbot, Donald Roy *consulting services executive*
Tamminga, Carol Ann *neuroscientist*
Taylor, Carl Ernest *physician, educator*
Taylor, Janet Winona Mills *secondary school educator*
Tepper, Michael Howard *publishing company executive*
Thomas, Daniel French *lawyer*
Thompson-Cager, Chezia Brenda *literature educator, writer, performance artist*
Trimble, William Cattell, Jr. *lawyer*
Tringali, Joseph *financial planner, accountant*
Trostel, Michael Frederick *architect*
Trpis, Milan *vector biologist, scientist, educator*
Tyler, Anne (Mrs. Taghi M. Modarressi) *author*
Udvarhelyi, George Bela *neurosurgery educator emeritus, cultural affairs administrator*
Uhl, Scott Mark *state agency administrator*
Vasile, Gennaro James *health care executive*
Viall, J(ohn) Thomas *non-profit organization executive, fundraiser*
Vice, LaVonna Lee *lawyer*
Vogelstein, Bert *oncology educator*
Waalkes, T. Phillip *physician, educator*
Wagner, Henry Nicholas, Jr. *physician*
Wagner, James Warren *engineering educator*
Walker, Irving Edward *lawyer*
Walker, Mack *historian, educator*
Wallace, Paul Edward, Jr. *health services management*
Wallach, Edward Eliot *physician, educator*
Walser, Mackenzie *physician, educator*
Walsh, Patrick Craig *urologist*
Washington, Vivian Edwards *social worker, former government official*
Wasserman, Martin P. *human health administrator*
Wasserman, Richard Leo *lawyer*
†Waterbury, Larry *physician, educator*
Weaver, Kenneth Newcomer *geologist, state official*
Weiss, James Lloyd *cardiology educator*
Welch, Robert Bond *ophthalmologist, educator*
Weller, Jane Kathleen *emergency nurse*
Westerhout, Gart *retired astronomer*
Wheeler, Peter Martin *federal agency administrator*
White, Pamela Janice *lawyer*
White, William Nelson *lawyer*

Wierman, John Charles *mathematician, educator*
Wilgis, Herbert E., Jr. *corporate executive*
Williams, G(eorge) Melville *surgeon, medical educator*
Williams, Harold Anthony *retired newspaper editor*
Williams, Herman, Jr. *protective services offical*
Williams, Richard Francis *insurance executive*
Williams, Robert Eugene *astronomer*
Wilmot, Louise C. *retired naval commander, charitable organization executive*
Wilson, Donald Edward *physician, educator*
Wilson, Peter Mason *computer programmer*
Wilson, W. Stephen *mathematics educator, researcher*
Winn, James Julius, Jr. *lawyer*
Wolman, M. Gordon *geography educator*
Wood, Howard Graham *banker*
Woodward, Theodore Englar *medical educator, internist*
Wortham, Deborah Lynne *school system director, principal*
Yannuzzi, William A(nthony) *conductor*
Yarmolinsky, Adam *law educator*
Young, Barbara *psychiatrist, psychoanalyst, psychiatry educator, photographer*
Young, Grace May-En *pediatrician*
Young, Joseph H. *federal judge*
Yuan, Xiao-Jian *medical researcher, educator*
Zaiman, Joel Hirsh *rabbi*
Zassenhaus, Hiltgunt Margret *physician*
Ziff, Larzer *English language educator*
Zimmerly, James Gregory *lawyer, physician*
Zinkham, W. Robert *lawyer*
Zinman, David Joel *conductor*
Zizic, Thomas Michael *physician, educator*

## Bel Air

Crocker, Michael Pue *lawyer*
Eichelberger, Robert John *retired government research and development administrator, consultant*
Hagenbuch, Stephen Lee *principal*
Klett, Shirley Louise *columnist, writer, critic, researcher*
Lu, David John *history educator, writer*
Miller, Dorothy Eloise *education educator*
Miller, Max Dunham, Jr. *lawyer*
Nye, Daniel William *elementary school educator*
Phillips, Bernice Cecile Golden *retired vocational education educator*
Powers, Doris Hurt *retired engineering company executive*
Riley, Catherine Irene *university official, cosultant, former state senator*

## Beltsville

Adams, Jean Ruth *entomologist, researcher*
Andre, Pamela Q. J. *library director*
Collins, Anita Marguerite *research geneticist*
Hoberg, Eric Paul *parasitologist*
Johnson, Phyllis Elaine *chemist*
Kasprick, Lyle Clinton *volunteer, financial executive*
Levin, Gilbert Victor *health information, services and products*
Norris, Karl Howard *optics scientist, agricultural engineer*
Pachepsky, Ludmila Baudinovna *ecologist*
Palm, Mary Egdahl *mycologist*
Quirk, Frank Joseph *management consulting company executive*
Schenkel, Suzanne Chance *natural resource specialist*
Shands, Henry Lee *plant geneticist, administrator*
Tallent, William Hugh *chemist, research administrator*
Terrill, Clair Elman *animal scientist, geneticist, consultant*
Tso, Tien Chioh *federal agency official, plant physiologist*
Zehner, Lee Randall *biotechnologist, research director*

## Berlin

Crawford, Norman Crane, Jr. *academic administrator, consultant*
Horner, William Harry *biochemist*
Howarth, Thomas *tax consultant*
Passwater, Barbara Gayhart *real estate broker*
Passwater, Richard Albert *biochemist, writer*

## Bethesda

Abbrecht, Peter Herman *medical educator*
Abrams, Samuel K. *lawyer*
Ahmed, S. Basheer *research company executive, educator*
Alexander, Duane Frederick *pediatrician, research administrator*
Alper, Jerome Milton *lawyer*
Asbell, Fred Thomas *telecommunications company executive*
Atlas, David *meteorologist, research scientist*
Atwell, Constance Woodruff *health services executive, researcher*
Auerbach, Seymour *architect*
Augustine, Norman Ralph *industrial executive, educator*
Axelrod, Julius *pharmacologist, biochemist*
Azaryan, Anahit Vazgenovna *biochemist, researcher*
Backus, Robert Coburn *biophysical chemist*
Ballhaus, William Francis, Jr. *aerospace industry executive, research scientist*
Banik, Sambhu Nath *psychologist*
Barber, Arthur Whiting *communications company executive*
Barquín, Ramón Carlos *consulting company executive*
Barrick, Joan Lizbeth *genetics researcher*
Barter, Robert Henry *physician, retired educator*
Bauersfeld, Carl Frederick *lawyer*
Beall, Robert Joseph *foundation executive*
Becerra, Sofia Patricia *biomedical research scientist*
Becker, Edwin Demuth *chemist, laboratory director*
Bennink, Jack Richard *microbiologist, researcher*
Benson, Elizabeth Polk *Pre-Columbian art specialist*
Berendes, Heinz Werner *medical epidemiologist, pediatrician*
Berger, Robert Lewis *biophysicist, researcher*
Bernardini, Isa *biochemist*
Berns, Walter Fred *political scientist, educator*
Bloomfield, Arthur Irving *economics educator*
Boshart, Edgar David *editor, journalist, photographer*
Bowles, Walter Donald *economist, educator*
Brady, Roscoe Owen *neurogeneticist, educator*
Breggin, Peter Roger *psychiatrist, author*
Bregman, Jacob Israel *environmental consulting company executive*

Brickfield, Cyril Francis *lawyer, retired association executive*
Briend-Walker, Monique Marie *French and Spanish language educator*
Briggs, Shirley Ann *retired organization executive, writer*
Brodine, Charles Edward *physician*
Brouha, Paul *association executive, fishery-wildlife biologist*
Brown, Ann *federal agency administrator*
Brown, Dudley Earl, Jr. *psychiatrist, educator, health executive, former federal agency administrator, former naval officer*
Brown, Earle Palmer *advertising agency executive*
Brown, Thomas Philip, III *lawyer*
Bryan, Billie Marie (Mrs. James A. Mackey) *biologist*
Bryngelson, Joseph Donald *molecular biophysicist*
Buccino, Alphonse *university dean emeritus, consultant*
Buhler, Leslie Lynn *institute administrator*
Bunger, Rolf *physiology educator*
Burdeshaw, William Brooksbank *engineering executive*
Burg, Maurice Benjamin *renal physiologist, physician*
Burton, Charles Henning *lawyer*
Calvert, Gordon Lee *retired legal association executive*
Carney, William Patrick *medical educator*
Cass, Millard *lawyer, arbitrator*
Cassman, Marvin *biochemist*
Castelli, Alexander Gerard *accountant*
Cath, Stanley Howard *psychiatrist, psychoanalyst*
Chang, Kai *molecular biologist, geneticist*
Chanock, Robert Merritt *pediatrician*
Chase, Thomas Newell *neurologist, researcher, educator*
Cheever, Allen Williams *pathologist*
Chretien, Jane Henkel *internist*
Clark, A. James *real estate company executive*
Clark, William Doran *former government official*
Cleary, Timothy Finbar *professional society administrator*
Clema, Joe Kotouc *computer scientist*
Cody, Thomas Gerald *management consultant, writer*
Coelho, Anthony Mendes, Jr. *health science administrator*
Cohen, Max Harry *surgeon*
Cohen, Robert Abraham *retired physician*
Cohen, Sheldon Gilbert *physician, historian, immunology educator*
Collins, Francis S. *medical research scientist*
Comings, William Daniel, Jr. *mortgage banker, housing development executive*
†Contreras, Thomas J., Jr. *naval officer*
Cooper, Merri-Ann *psychologist*
Cooper, William Ewing, Jr. *retired army officer*
Corbett, Jack Elliott *clergyman, retired foundation administrator, author*
Corn, Milton *academic dean, physician*
Cornette, William Magnus *scientist, technical advisor*
Cornish, Edward Seymour *magazine editor*
Cowie, Catherine Christine *epidemiologist*
Crout, J(ohn) Richard *physician, pharmaceutical researcher*
Cutting, Mary Dorothea *audio and audio-visual communications company executive*
Danforth, David Newton, Jr. *physician, scientist*
Daniel, Charles Dwelle, Jr. *consultant, retired army officer*
Datiles, Manuel Bernaldes, III *ophthalmologist, scientist*
Dawson, John Frederick *retired architect*
Day, Marylouise Muldoon (Mrs. Richard Dayton Day) *appraiser*
Day, Robert Dwain, Jr. *foundation executive, lawyer*
Dean, Jurrien *biomedical researcher, physician*
Deane, Leon *retired company executive*
Decker, John Laws *physician*
de Vries, Margaret Garritsen *economist*
Didisheim, Paul *internist, hematologist*
Dietrich, Robert Anthony *pathologist, medical administrator, consultant*
Di Marzo, Marino *engineering researcher, educator*
Di Marzo Veronese, Fulvia *research scientist*
Di Paolo, Joseph Amedeo *geneticist*
Dogoloff, Lee Israel *clinical social worker, psychotherapist, consultant*
Dommen, Arthur John *agricultural economist*
Drucker, William Richard *surgeon*
Duncan, Constance Catharine *psychologist, researcher*
Duncan, Francis *historian, government official*
Dunning, Herbert Neal *government official, physical chemist*
Dyer, Frederick Charles *writer, consultant*
Dykstra, Vergil Homer *retired academic administrator*
Eden, Murray *electrical engineer, emeritus educator*
Egan, John Frederick *electronics executive*
Ehrenstein, Gerald *biophysicist*
Elin, Ronald John *pathologist*
Elman, Philip *lawyer*
English, William deShay *lawyer*
Epps, Roselyn Elizabeth Payne *pediatrician, educator*
Ernst, Roger *international studies educator, consultant*
Estrin, Melvyn J. *computer products company executive*
Eule, Norman L. *lawyer*
Evans, Charles Hawes, Jr. *immunologist, medical researcher*
Fales, Henry Marshall *chemist*
Farmer, Richard Gilbert *physician, foundation administrator, medical advisor, health care consultant*
Fauci, Anthony Stephen *health facility administrator, physician*
Feingold, S. Norman *psychologist*
Feldman, Valerie Michele *marketing professional*
Feller, William Frank *surgery educator*
Felsenfeld, Gary *government official, scientist*
Ferris, Frederick Joseph *gerontologist, social worker*
Fleisher, Thomas Arthur *physician*
Fowler, James D., Jr. *marketing and human resources consultant*
Frank, Martin *physiology educator, health scientist, association executive*
Fraumeni, Joseph F., Jr. *scientific researcher, medical educator, physician, military officer*
Free, Ann Cottrell *writer*
Freedman, Joseph *sanitary and public health engineering consultant*
Freedman, Laurence Stuart *statistician*

### Chester
Dabich, Eli, Jr. *insurance company executive*
Pelczar, Michael Joseph, Jr. *microbiologist, educator*

### Chestertown
Clarke, Garry Evans *composer, educator, musician, administrator*
Gordon, James Braund *management consultant*
Schreiber, Harry, Jr. *management consultant*
Sener, Joseph Ward, Jr. *securities company executive*
Trout, Charles Hathaway *historian, educator*
Van Houten, Elizabeth Ann *corporate communications executive*
Wendel, Richard Frederick *economist, educator, consultant*
Williams, Henry Thomas *retired banker, real estate agent*

### Chevy Chase
Adler, James Barron *publisher*
Albright, Raymond Jacob *government official*
Anderson, Owen Raymond *scientific and educational organization executive*
Asher, Lila Oliver *artist*
Bacon, Donald Conrad *author, editor*
Beilenson, Anthony Charles *former congressman*
Bissinger, Frederick Lewis *retired manufacturing executive, consultant*
Bodman, Richard Stockwell *telecommunications executive*
Bush, Frederick Morris *federal official*
Carey, Stephen Clayton *foundation administrator*
Causey, G(eorge) Donald *medical educator*
Chase, Nicholas Joseph *lawyer, educator*
Chaseman, Joel *media executive*
Choppin, Purnell Whittington *research administrator, virology researcher, educator*
Coleman, Joseph Michael *truck lease and logistics consultant*
Corrigan, Robert Foster *business consultant, retired diplomat*
Cowan, William Maxwell *neurobiologist*
Crawford, Meredith Pullen *research psychologist*
Cron, Theodore Oscar *writer, editor, educator*
Cross, Christopher T. *professional society administrator*
Delano, Victor *retired naval officer*
Dulin, Maurine Stuart *volunteer*
Durant, Frederick Clark, III *aerospace history and space art consultant*
Duvall, Bernice Bettum *artist, exhibit coordinator, jewelry designer*
Dyer, Robert Francis, Jr. *internist, educator*
Edelson, Burton Irving *electrical engineer*
Elliott, R Lance *lawyer*
Ellis, Sydney *pharmacological scientist, former pharmacology educator*
Emery, Robert Firestone *economist, educator*
Felton, Gordon H. *retired publishing executive*
Ferguson, James Joseph, Jr. *academic administrator, researcher*
Freeman, Harry Louis *investment executive*
Freeman, Raymond Lee *landscape architect, planning consultant*
Geber, Anthony *economist, retired foreign service officer*
Goodwin, Ralph Roger *historian, editor*
Greenberg, Robert Milton *retired psychiatrist*
Groner, Beverly Anne *lawyer*
Harlan, William Robert, Jr. *physician, educator, researcher*
Harris, Judith Linda *lawyer*
Harter, Donald Harry *research administrator, medical educator*
Holloway, William Jimmerson *retired educator*
Hudson, Anthony Webster *retired federal agency administrator, minister*
Hudson, Ralph P. *physicist*
Ikenberry, Henry Cephas, Jr. *lawyer*
Kainen, Jacob *artist, former museum curator*
Ketcham, Orman Weston *lawyer, former judge*
Klain, Ronald Alan *lawyer*
Lee, Edward Brooke, Jr. *real estate executive, fund raiser*
Lukens, Alan Wood *retired ambassador and foreign service officer*
Lyons, Ellis *retired lawyer*
Mackall, Laidler Bowie *lawyer*
Mayers, Jean *aeronautical engineering educator*
McNamara, Francis John *writer*
Meltzer, Jack *consultant, retired college dean*
Michaelis, Michael *management and technical consultant*
Mulligan, James Kenneth *government official*
Nance, William Bennett *economic development specialist*
Nelson, John Marshall *medical information services company executive*
Norwood, Bernard *economist*
Oler, Wesley Marion, III *physician, educator*
Oudens, Gerald Francis *architect, architectural firm executive*
Pancoast, Edwin C. *retired senior foreign service officer, writer, researcher*
Paul, Carl Frederick *lawyer*
Pogue, John Marshall *physician, editor, researcher*
Promisel, Nathan E. *materials scientist, metallurgical engineer*
Quinn, Eugene Frederick *government official, clergyman*
Richards, Merlon Foss *retired diversified technical services company executive*
Riley, John Winchell, Jr. *consulting sociologist*
Roberts, Clyde Francis *business executive*
Rockwell, Theodore *nuclear engineer*
Romansky, Monroe James *physician, educator*
Rose, John Charles *physician, educator*
Sauer, Richard John *developer fundraiser*
Saul, B. Francis, II *bank executive*
Scammon, Richard Montgomery *retired political scientist, retired editor*
Schlegel, John Frederick *management consultant, speaker, trainer*
Schneider, John Hoke *health science administrator*
Shipler, David Karr *journalist, correspondent, author*
Teitel, Simon *economist, educator*
Walk, Richard David *retired psychology educator*
Weiss, Ernest *federal agency administrator*
Williams, Charles Laval, Jr. *physician, international organization official*
Zurkowski, Paul George *information company executive*

### Childs
Perkins, Esther Roberta *literary agent*

### Claiborne
Moorhead, Paul Sidney *geneticist*

### Clarksville
Brancato, Emanuel Leonard *electrical engineering consultant*

### Clinton
Cruz, Wilhelmina Mangahas *nephrologist, educator, critical care specialist*
Harrison, Virginia M. *federal government agency employee*
Jones, Sandra LaVern *day care administrator, small business owner*
Kennedy, G. Alfred *retired federal agency administrator*
Sizemore, Carolyn Lee *nuclear medicine technologist*

### Cobb Island
Rudy, Linda Mae *secondary school educator*
Vanderslice, Joseph Thomas *chemist*

### Cockeysville Hunt Valley
Barr, Irwin Robert *retired aeronautical engineer*
Dans, Peter Emanuel *medical educator*
Edgett, William Maloy *lawyer, labor arbitrator*
Elkin, Lois Shanman *business systems company executive*
Futcher, Palmer Howard *physician, educator*
Kinstlinger, Jack *engineering executive, consultant*
Mather, Dennis Bryan *wholesale insurance company executive*
Peirce, Brooke *English language educator*
Schnering, Philip Blessed *investment banker*
Simms, Charles Averill *environmental management company executive*
Spinella, J(oseph) John *insurance company executive*
Whitehurst, William Wilfred, Jr. *management consultant*

### Colesville
Peterson, William Frank *retired physician*

### College Park
Antman, Stuart Sheldon *mathematician, educator*
Armstrong, William Francis *purchasing professional*
†Ayyub, Bilal Mohammed *civil engineering educator, researcher, executive*
Barbe, David Franklin *electrical engineer, educator*
Benesch, William Milton *molecular physicist, atmospheric researcher, educator*
Berman, Louise Marguerite *education educator*
Blankenship, Gilmer Leroy *electrical engineering educator, engineering company executive*
Broadnax, Walter D. *public policy educator*
Brodsky, Marc Herbert *physicist, research and publishing executive*
Brown, Peter Gilbert *philosopher, educator, tree farmer*
Burke, Frank Gerard *archivist*
Clark, Eugenie *zoologist, educator*
Cleghorn, Reese *journalist, educator*
Collinson, Vivienne Ruth *education educator, researcher*
Colwell, Rita Rossi *microbiologist, molecular biologist, educator*
Cunniff, Patrick Francis *mechanical engineer*
Davidson, Roger H(arry) *political scientist, educator*
DeMonte, Claudia Ann *artist, educator*
DeSilva, Alan W. *physics educator, researcher*
Diener, Theodor Otto *plant pathologist*
Dieter, George Elwood, Jr. *university official*
Dorsey, John Wesley, Jr. *university administrator, economist*
Dragt, Alexander James *physicist*
Ehrlich, Gertrude *retired mathematics educator*
Ephremides, Anthony *electrical engineering educator*
Fanning, Delvin Seymour *soil science educator*
Feinstein, Martin *performing arts educator*
Finkelstein, Barbara *education educator*
Fisher, Michael Ellis *mathematical physicist, chemist*
Franz, Judy R. *physics educator*
Fretz, Thomas A. *agricultural studies educator*
Fuegi, John *comparative literature educator, author, filmmaker*
Gantt, Elisabeth *botany educator and researcher*
Gaylin, Ned L. *psychology educator*
Gentry, James Walter *chemical engineer, educator*
Geoffroy, Gregory L. *academic administrator*
Gessow, Alfred *aerospace engineer, educator*
Gluckstern, Robert Leonard *physics educator*
Gomery, Douglas *communications educator, writer*
Gordon, Lawrence Allan *accounting educator*
Gouin, Francis Romeo *physiologist*
Granatstein, Victor Lawrence *electrical engineer, educator*
Greenberg, Jerrold Selig *health education educator*
Greenberg, Oscar Wallace *physicist, educator*
Greer, Thomas Vernon *business consultant and educator*
Griem, Hans Rudolf *physicist, educator*
Grim, Samuel Oram *chemistry educator*
Grunig, James Elmer *communications educator, researcher, public relations consultant*
Gupta, Ashwani Kumar *mechanical engineering educator*
Harlan, Louis Rudolph *history educator, writer*
Heath, James Lee *food science educator, researcher*
Helz, George Rudolph *chemistry educator, research center director*
Hey, Nancy Henson *educational administrator*
Hiebert, Ray Eldon *journalism educator, author, consultant*
Hill, Clara Edith *psychology educator*
Holder, Sallie Lou *training and meeting management consultant*
Holton, William Milne *English language and literature educator*
Irwin, George Rankin *physicist, mechanical engineering educator*
Jackson, Vivian Michele *school administrator*
Just, Richard Eugene *agricultural and resource economics educator consultant*
Kearney, Philip Charles *biochemist*
Keller, Samuel William *aerospace administrator*
Kellogg, Betty L. *librarian*
Kerr, Frank John *astronomer, educator*
Kirk, James Allen *mechanical engineering educator*
Kirwan, William English, II *mathematics educator, university official*
Kolodny, Richard *finance educator*
Kotz, Samuel *statistician, educator, translator, editor*
Kundu, Mukul Ranjan *physics and astronomy educator*
Lamone, Rudolph Philip *business educator*
Lapinski, Tadeusz Andrew *artist, educator*
Lea-Cox, John Derek *plant physiologist*
Lee, Chi Hsiang *electrical engineer, educator*
Levine, William Silver *electrical engineering educator*
Lewis, Roger Kutnow *architect, educator, author*
Lightfoot, David William *linguistics educator*
Lin, Hung C. *electrical engineer educator*
Locke, Edwin Allen, III *psychologist, educator*
Lubkin, Gloria Becker *physicist*
Lyon, Andrew Bennet *economics educator*
Marcus, Steven Irl *electrical engineering educator*
Massey, Thomas Benjamin *educator*
Mayer, William Emilio *investor*
Mikulski, Piotr Witold *mathematics educator*
Miller, Raymond Edward *computer science educator*
Miller, Raymond Jarvis *agronomy educator*
Minker, Jack *computer scientist, educator*
Misner, Charles William *physics educator*
Moss, Lawrence Kenneth *composer, educator*
Nakayama, Wataru *engineering educator*
Nerlove, Marc Leon *economics educator*
Newcomb, Robert Wayne *electrical engineer*
Nusinovich, Gregory Semeon *physicist, researcher*
Olson, Keith Waldemar *history educator*
Oster, Rose Marie Gunhild *foreign language professional, educator*
Panichas, George Andrew *English language educator, critic, editor*
Pasch, Alan *philosopher, educator*
Patterson, Glenn Wayne *botany educator*
Peterson, David Frederick *government agency executive*
Piper, Don Courtney *political science educator*
Polakoff, Murray Emanuel *university dean, economics and finance educator*
Popper, Arthur N. *zoology educator*
Prentice, Ann Ethelynd *academic adminstrator*
Presser, Harriet Betty *sociology educator*
Presser, Stanley *sociology educator*
Quebedeaux, Bruno *horticulture and plant physiology educator*
Quester, George Herman *political science educator*
Rabin, Herbert *physics educator, university official*
Redish, Edward Frederick *physicist, educator*
Rosenfeld, Azriel *computer science educator, consultant*
Schelling, Thomas Crombie *economist, educator*
Schneider, Benjamin *psychology educator*
Schwab, Susan Carroll *university dean*
Seefeldt, Carol *education educator*
Sigall, Harold Fred *psychology educator*
Silverman, Joseph *chemistry educator, scientist*
Sims, Henry P., Jr. *management educator*
Snow, George Abraham *physicist*
Stark, Francis C., Jr. *horticulturist, educator*
Stover, Carl Frederick *foundation executive*
Stumpff, Robert Thomas *academic administrator*
Taylor, Leonard Stuart *engineering educator, consultant*
Thirumalai, Devarajan *physical sciences researcher, educator*
Toll, John Sampson *university administrator, physics educator*
Ulmer, Melville Jack *economist, educator*
Vandersall, John Henry *dairy science educator*
Wasserman, Paul *library and information science educator*
Weart, Spencer Richard *historian*
Webb, Richard Alan *physicist*
Weil, Raymond Richard *soil scientist*
White, Marilyn Domas *information science educator*
Whittemore, Edward Reed, II *poet, retired educator*
Williams, Aubrey Willis *anthropology educator*
Williams, Gary *collegiate basketball team coach*
Winik, Jay B. *writer, political scientist, consultant*
Yaney, George *history educator*
Yorke, James Alan *chaos mathematician*
Zen, E-an *research geologist*

### Columbia
Alexander, Bruce Donald *real estate executive*
Alexander, Nancy J. *psychotherapist, educator*
Askew, Laurin Barker, Jr. *architect*
Bailey, John Martin *retired transportation planner, educator*
Bareis, Donna Lynn *biochemist, pharmacologist*
Barrow, Lionel Ceon, Jr. *communications and marketing consultant*
Blackwell, Camellia Ann *art educator*
Bremerman, Michael Vance *reliability engineer*
Bretz, Thurman Wilbur *corporate professional*
Bruley, Duane Frederick *academic administrator, consultant, engineer*
Butcher, (Charles) Philip *English language educator, author*
Carr, Charles Jelleff *pharmacologist, educator, toxicology consultant*
Clark, Billy Pat *physicist*
Collins, Grace Elizabeth *English educator, writer*
Cook, Stephen Bernard *homebuilding company executive*
Crowe, Thomas Leonard *lawyer*
Deutsch, Robert William *physicist*
Driggs, Margaret *educator*
Fisher, Dale John *chemist, instrumentation and medical diagnostic device investigator*
Freeman, Joel Arthur *behavioral consultant*
Gray, Kirk Lamond *social investment firm executive, anthropologist*
Gregorie, Corazon Arzalem *operations supervisor*
Grewal, Parwinder S. *biologist, researcher*
Hall, Wiley A. *columnist, journalist*
Harrison, Elza Stanley *medical association executive*
Hartman, Lee Ann Walraff *educator*
Hayes, Charles Lawton *insurance company executive, holding company executive*
Hilderbrandt, Donald Franklin, II *urban designer, landscape architect, artist*
Hotchkies, Barry *financial executive*
Keeton, Morris Teuton *research institute director*
Khare, Mohan *chemist*
Kime, J. William *career officer, engineer, ship management executiv*
Letaw, Harry, Jr. *technology corporation executive*
Lijinsky, William *biochemist*
Maier, William Otto *martial arts school administrator, educator, consultant*
Margolis, Vivienne O. *psychotherapist*
May, John Raymond *clinical psychologist*
McCuan, William Patrick *real estate company executive*
Meima, Ralph Chester, Jr. *corporate execuitve, former foreign service officer*
Millspaugh, Martin Laurence *real estate developer, urban development consultant*
Moore, Sheryl Stansil *medical nurse*
Peck, Charles Edward *retired construction and mortgage executive*
Queen, Sandy (Sandra Jane Queen) *psychologist, trainer, small business owner*
Radinsky, Allan Michael *human services adminstrator, behavior consultant, mental health services professional*
Riddle, Mark Alan *child psychiatrist*
Slater, John Blackwell *landscape architect*
Steele, Richard J. *management consultant*
Ulman, Louis Jay *lawyer*
van Remoortere, Francois Petrus *chemical company research and development executive*
Welty, Gail Ann Harper *physical education educator*
Whiting, Albert Nathaniel *former university chancellor*
Wolter, John Amadeus *librarian, government official*

### Crofton
Eastman, John Robert *educator*
Ross, E(dwin) Clarke *association executive, educator*
Watson, Robert Tanner *physical scientist*

### Crownsville
Hanna, James Curtis *state official*
Wright, Harry Forrest, Jr. *retired banker*

### Cumberland
Heckert, Paul Charles *sociologist, educator*
Mazzocco, Gail O'Sullivan *nursing educator*
Shelton, Bessie Elizabeth *school system administrator*
Wolford, Nancy Lou *medical and surgical nurse*

### Damascus
Cockrell, Diane Elyse *librarian*

### Darnestown
Knox, Bernard MacGregor Walker *retired classics educator*

### Davidsonville
Mahaffey, Redge Allan *movie producer, director, writer, actor, scientist*

### Dayton
Fischell, Robert Ellentuch *physicist*

### Delmar
Cugler, Carol Marie Miller *retired mental health services professional*

### Derwood
Stadtman, Thressa Campbell *biochemist*

### Dunkirk
Ewing, Richard Tucker *diplomat, educator, publisher*

### Easton
Boutte, David Gray *oil industry executive, lawyer*
Buescher, Adolph Ernst (Dolph Buescher) *aerospace company executive*
Burns, Michael Joseph *operations and sales-marketing executive*
Engle, Mary Allen English *physician*
Engle, Ralph Landis, Jr. *internist, educator*
Gipe, Albert Bondsfield *electrical engineering consultant*
Jacobs, Michael Joseph *lawyer*
Maffitt, James Strawbridge *lawyer*
Peterson, James Kenneth *manufacturing company executive*
Rever, George Wright *psychiatrist, health facility administrator*
Woods, William Ellis *lawyer, pharmacist, association executive*

### Edgewater
Malley, Kenneth Cornelius *retired military officer, corporation executive*

### Edgewood
Matthews, Jeffrey Alan *physicist*

### Eldersburg
Bastress, Robert Lewis *principal*

### Elkridge
Calton, Gary Jim *chemical company executive, medical educator*
Calton, Sandra Jeane *accountant*
Szilagyi, Sherry Ann *psychotherapist, lawyer*

### Elkton
Chen, Oliver Tsung-Yu *chemical engineer, researcher*
Harrington, Benjamin Franklin, III *business consultant*
Jasinski-Caldwell, Mary L. *company executive*
Scherf, Christopher N. *foundation administrator*
Smith, James Morton *museum administrator, historian*

### Ellicott City
Becker, Shawn Coniff *community health professional*
Faulstich, Albert Joseph *banking consultant*
Gagnon, Robert Michael *engineering executive, educator*
Galinsky, Deborah Jean *county official*
Gleaves, Leon Rogers *marketing and sales executive*
Neil, Fred Applestein *public relations executive*
Robison, Susan Miller *psychologist, educator, consultant*
Scott, Richard Kevin *army officer*
Shatto, John Frederick *court administrator*
Tillman, Elizabeth Carlotta *nurse, educator*
Veasel, Walter *minister, educator*
Wehland, Granville Warren Pearson *lawyer, consultant*
Weingarten, Murray *manufacturing executive*

### Emmitsburg
Houston, George R. *college president*
Obloy, Leonard Gerard *priest*

### Fallston
Lewis, Howard Franklin *chiropractor*

### Finksburg
Konigsberg, Robert Lee *electrical engineer*

Hagans, Robert Reginald, Jr. *financial executive*
Kendall, Katherine Anne *social worker*
Lauer, Michael Thomas *software company executive*
Manvel, Allen Dailey *fiscal economist*
Phelps, Flora L(ouise) Lewis *editor, anthropologist, photographer*
Simpich, William Morris *public affairs consultant*

**Monkton**
Mountcastle, Vernon Benjamin *neurophysiologist*
O'Neill, Catherine R. *emergency nurse, nurse manager*

**Monrovia**
Cooney, William Joseph, Jr. *transportation company owner*

**Mount Airy**
Collins, Henry James, III *insurance company executive*

**Mountain Lake Park**
Forrester, Donald Dean *university administrator, educator, consultant*

**Myersville**
Blake, John Ballard *retired historian*

**New Market**
Billig, Frederick Stucky *mechanical engineer*
Gabriel, Eberhard John *lawyer*

**North East**
Marie, Linda *artist, photographer*

**North Potomac**
Kehoe, Patrick Emmett *law librarian, educator*
Lide, David Reynolds *handbook and database editor*

**Oakland**
Ferren, Emily Holchin *public library director, consultant*
McClintock, Donna Mae *social worker*

**Ocean City**
Wimbrow, Peter Ayers, III *lawyer*

**Odenton**
Mucha, John Frank *information systems professional*

**Olney**
Brady, Anita Kelley *training and organizational development executive*
Delmar, Eugene Anthony *architect*
Graham, William Howard *theatre producer, consultant*
Kimble, Seruch Titus, Jr. *retired internist*
Michael, Jerrold Mark *public health specialist, former university dean, educator*
Terry, Glenn A. *retired nuclear chemist*

**Owings**
Oring, Stuart August *visual information specialist, writer, photographer*

**Owings Mills**
Berg, Barbara Kirsner *health education specialist*
Burnett, Robert Barry *professional football player*
Casper, Mary Lee *speech and language pathologist*
Disharoon, Leslie Benjamin *retired insurance executive*
Green, Bernard Eric *professional football player*
Holdridge, Barbara *book publisher*
Kissel, William Thorn, Jr. *sculptor*
Leibtag, Bernard *accountant*
Marchibroda, Ted (Theodore Joseph Marchibroda) *professional football coach*
Modell, Arthur B. *professional football team executive*
Mulholland, John Henry *physician, educator*
Siegel, Bernard *foundation administrator*
Thompson, Bennie *professional football player*
Turner, Eric Ray *professional football player*
Walsh, Semmes Guest *retired insurance company executive*
†Yen, Sherman *applied behavior analyst, educator, substance abuse treatment specialist*

**Oxford**
Radcliffe, George Grove *retired life insurance company executive*

**Oxon Hill**
Boerrigter, Glenn Charles *educational administrator*
Christian, Mary Jo Dinan *educator, real estate professional*
McLean, Edgar Alexander *physicist*
Shaffer, Sheila Weekes *mathematics educator*

**Parkton**
Fitzgerald, Edwin Roger *physicist, educator*

**Parkville**
Jensen, Arthur Seigfried *consulting engineering physicist*
Munson, Paul Lewis *pharmacologist*
Payne, Winfield Scott *national security policy research executive*

**Parsonsburg**
Feeney, Edward Charles Patrick *minister, psychologist, writer, composer*

**Pasadena**
Young, Russell Dawson *physics consultant*

**Patuxent River**
Watkiss, Eric John *naval flight officer*

**Perry Point**
Peszke, Michael Alfred *psychiatrist, educator*
Yackley, Luke Eugene *head nurse, mental health nurse*

**Phoenix**
Byrd, Harvey Clifford, III *information management company executive*

**Pikesville**
Davis, Esther Yvonne Butler *religious studies educator*

**Poolesville**
Blush, Steven Michael *nuclear scientist, safety consultant*

**Port Republic**
Hanke, Byron Reidt *residential land planning and community associations consultant*
Miller, Ewing Harry *architect*

**Potomac**
Ahmad, Sharmin *elementary education educator*
Baer, Ledolph *oceanographer, meteorologist*
Bollum, Frederick James *biotechnology executive*
Bradley, Mark Edmund *physician, consultant*
Brewer, Nathan Ronald *veterinarian, consultant*
Broderick, John Caruthers *retired librarian, educator*
Casella, Russell Carl *physicist*
Christian, John Kenton *organization executive, publisher, writer, marketing consultant*
Conner, Troy Blaine, Jr. *lawyer, writer*
Cotton, William Robert *dentist*
Crowley, Mary Elizabeth (Mary Elizabeth Crowley-Farrell) *journalist, editor*
DeVaney, Carol Susan *management consultant*
DiPentima, Renato Anthony *systems executive*
DiSibio, Carol Lynn Kridler *lawyer*
Eaves, Maria Perry *realtor*
Elisburg, Donald Earl *lawyer*
Engelmann, Rudolf Jacob *meteorologist*
Epstein, Edward S. *meteorologist*
Evans, Christine Burnett *healthcare management executive*
Fink, Daniel Julien *management consultant*
Fischetti, Michael *public administration educator, arbitrator*
Fox, Arthur Joseph, Jr. *editor*
Frey, James McKnight *government official*
Gowda, Narasimhan Ramaiah *financial consultant*
Haddy, Francis John *physician, educator*
Heller, Peggy Osna *psychotherapist*
Higgins, Dr. Nancy Branscome *management and counseling educator*
Jones, Sidney Lewis *economist, government official*
Jung, Richard Kieth *headmaster*
Karch, Karen Brooke *principal*
Karson, Emile *international business executive*
Keil, Marilyn Martin *artist*
Kessler, Ronald Borek *author*
Latham, Patricia Horan *lawyer*
Leva, Neil Irwin *psychotherapist, hypnotherapist*
Meyer, Lawrence George *lawyer*
Munroe, Pat *retired newsman*
Newhouse, Alan Russell *retired federal government executive*
Noonan, Patrick Francis *conservation executive*
Pastan, Linda Olenik *poet*
Peter, Phillips Smith *lawyer*
Peters, Carol Beattie Taylor (Mrs. Frank Albert Peters) *mathematician*
Peters, Frank Albert *retired chemical engineer*
Reichart, Stuart Richard *lawyer*
Reynolds, Frank Miller *retired government administrator*
Rhode, Alfred Shimon *business consultant, educator*
Rotberg, Iris Comens *social scientist*
Schonholtz, Joan Sondra Hirsch *banker, civic worker*
Shapiro, Richard Gerald *retired department store executive, consultant*
Shepard, William Seth *government official, diplomat, writer*
Sowalsky, Patti Lurie *author*
Terragno, Paul James *information industry executive*
Tomlinson, John Edward *secret service agent*
Vadus, Gloria A. *scientific document examiner*
†Ventry, Paul Guerin *physician*
Walker, Charls Edward *economist, consultant*
Whang, Yun Chow *space science educator*

**Prince Frederick**
Karol, Victoria Diane *educational administrator*

**Queenstown**
Mc Laughlin, David Thomas *academic administrator, business executive*
Ryans, Reginald Vernon *music education educator*

**Randallstown**
Myers, Debra Taylor *elementary school educator, writer*
Torgerson, Richard Warren *investment broker*

**Riva**
Barto, Bradley Edward *small business owner, educator*

**Riverdale**
Gonzalez Arias, Victor Hugo *management executive*
Guetzkow, Daniel Steere *technology company entrepreneur*
Ruderman, Robert *internist, hematologist*

**Rockville**
Aamodt, Roger Louis *federal agency administrator*
Adams, Mark David *molecular biologist*
Anderson, George Kenneth *physician, retired air force officer*
Anderson, Walter Dixon *trade association management consultant*
Barkley, Brian Evan *lawyer, political consultant*
Barr, Solomon Efrem *allergist, educator*
Belak, Michael James *information systems executive*
Birns, Mark Theodore *physician*
Boice, John Dunning, Jr. *epidemiologist, science administrator*
Brown, David Harry *speech educator*
Buchanan, John Donald *health physicist, radiochemist*
Burdick, William MacDonald *biomedical engineer*
Byrne, Olivia Sherrill *lawyer*
Cain, Karen Mirinda *musician, educator*
Cannon, Grace Bert *immunologist*
Cantelon, Philip Louis *historian*
Carlton, Patricia Paletsky *marketing and business professional*
Carter, Kenneth Charles *geneticist*
Chakravarty, Dipto *computer performance engineer*
Chang, Kung-Li (Charlie) *engineering consulting firm executive*
Chavez, Nelba *federal agency administrator*
Chiogioji, Melvin Hiroaki *government official*
Cosmides, George James *medical scientist, consultant*
Cox, David Leon *telecommunications company executive*
Cypess, Raymond Hardd *think tank executive*
Davies-Venn, Christian *environmental engineer*
Day, LeRoy Edward *aerospace scientist, consultant*
De Jong, David Samuel *lawyer, educator*
Drzewiecki, Tadeusz Maria *corporate executive, defense consultant*
Dunn, Bonnie Brill *chemist*
Eisenberg, John Meyer *physician, educator*
Elliott, Benjamin Paul *architect*
Epstein, Jay Stuart *medical researcher*
Finch, Frank Robert *environmental engineer*
Finlayson, John Sylvester *biochemist*
Fischer, Irene Kaminka *retired research geodesist, mathematician*
Forbes, Allan Louis *physician, foods and nutrition consultant*
Fouchard, Joseph James *retired government agency administrator*
Fratantoni, Joseph Charles *medical researcher, hematologist, medical and regulatory consultant*
†Friedman, Michael A. *federal agency adminstrator*
Frye, Roland Mushat, Jr. *lawyer*
Fthenakis, Emanuel John *diversified aerospace company executive*
Gabelnick, Henry Lewis *medical research director*
Galaty, Carol Popper *health policy administrator*
Garotta, Gianni *research scientist*
Gaus, Clifton R. *federal agency administrator*
Geier, Mark Robin *obstetrical genetics and infertility physician*
Generlette, Bertram B. *elementary school educator*
Ginsberg, Harold Samuel *virologist, educator*
Gleich, Carol S. *health professions education executive*
Gluckstein, Fritz Paul *veterinarian, biomedical information specialist*
Goldenberg, Melvyn Joel *information management services company executive*
Goodwin, Frederick King *psychiatrist*
Gordon, Joan Irma *lawyer*
Grady, Lee Timothy *pharmaceutical chemist*
Graff, Stuart Leslie *accounting executive*
Griffith, Jerry Dice *energy consultant*
Gulya, Aina Julianna *neurotologist, surgeon, educator*
Haffner, Marlene Elisabeth *internist, public health administrator*
Halperin, Jerome Arthur *pharmaceutical executive*
Hanna, Michael George, Jr. *immunologist, institute administrator*
Harvey, Donald Phillips *retired naval officer*
Haudenschild, Christian Charles *pathologist, educator, inventor*
Hawkins, James Alexander, II *mental health fund executive*
Hewlett, Richard Greening *historian*
Holston, Sharon Smith *government official*
Hoobler, James Ferguson *federal executive*
Horowitz, Harold *architect*
Howard, Lee Milton *international health consultant*
Hoyer, Leon William *physician, educator*
Hubbard, William Keith *government executive*
Huber, John Michael *director non-profit organization*
Ink, Dwight A. *government agency administrator*
Isbister, James David *pharmaceutical business executive*
Jamieson, Graham A. *biochemist, organization official*
Johnson, Emery Allen *physician*
Johnston, Linda Louise Hanna *public health analyst*
Kadish, Richard L. *lawyer*
Kafka, Marian Stern *neuroscientist*
Kalton, Graham *survey statistician*
Karnow, Stanley *journalist, writer*
Kawazoe, Robin Inada *federal official*
Keillor, Sharon Ann *computer company executive*
Kelsey, Frances Oldham (Mrs. Fremont Ellis Kelsey) *government official*
Kessler, David A. *health services commissioner*
Keston, Joan Balboul *government agency administrator*
Kline, Raymond Adam *professional organization executive*
Knox, C. Neal *political and governmental affairs consultant, writer*
Kohlhorst, Gail Lewis *librarian*
Koslow, Stephen Hugh *science administrator, pharmacologist*
Krahnke, Betty Ann *county official*
Krear, Gail Richardson *elementary education educator, consultant*
Kusterer, Thomas *environmental planner*
Landon, John Campbell *medical research company executive*
Lee, Fred Steven *telecommunications engineer*
Lee, James Jieh *environmental educator, computer specialist*
Leef, James Lewis *biology educator, immunology research executive*
Leshner, Alan Irvin *science foundation administrator*
Leslie, John Walter *development consultant*
Leventhal, Carl M. *neurologist, consultant, retired government official*
Levine, Barbara Gershkoff *early childhood education educator, consultant*
Lewis, Andrew Morris, Jr. *virologist*
Ley, Herbert Leonard, Jr. *retired epidemiologist*
Li, Chaoying *biomedical researcher*
Liau, Gene *medical educator*
Lightfoote, Marilyn Madry *molecular immunologist*
Lin, Jonathan Chung-Shih *computer scientist*
Lloyd, Douglas Seward *physician, public health administrator*
Long, Cedric William *health research facility executive*
Macafee, Susan Diane *reporter*
Manley, Audrey Forbes *medical administrator, physician*
Margulies, Laura Jacobs *lawyer*
Marsik, Frederic John *microbiologist*
McAuliffe, John F. *retired judge*
McCormick, Kathleen Ann Krym *geriatrics nurse, computer information specialist, federal agency administrator*
McDonald, Capers Walter *biomedical engineer, corporate executive*
McMahon, Edward Peter *systems engineer, consultant*
Meade, Kenneth Albert *minister*
Mealy, J. Burke () *psychological services administrator*
Megan, Thomas Ignatius *retired judge*
Menkello, Frederick Vincent *computer scientist*
Mertz, Walter *retired government research executive*
Meyer, F. Weller *bank executive*
Milan, Thomas Lawrence *accountant*
Miller, Kenneth Michael *electronics executive*
Milner, Max *food and nutrition consultant*
Mitchell, Charles F. *lawyer*
Molitor, Graham Thomas Tate *lawyer*
Morrison, Howard Irwin *computer services executive*
Motayed, Asok K. *engineering company executive*
Murphy, Gerard Norris *trade association executive*
Murray, Peter *metallurgist, manufacturing company executive*
Nash, Jonathon Michael *program manager, mechanical engineer*
Naunton, Ralph Frederick *surgeon, educator*
Nevin, Joseph Francis *computer systems engineer*
Niewiaroski, Trudi Osmers (Gertrude Niewiaroski) *social studies educator*
Nightingale, Stuart Lester *physician, public health officer*
Nilsson, Nancy Mitchell *playwright*
Nora, Audrey Hart *physician*
Pagan Martinez, Juan *administrative corps officer*
Petzold, Carol Stoker *state legislator*
Poljak, Roberto J(uan) *research director, biotechnology educator*
Pollack, Louis *telecommunications company executive*
Porter, John Robert, Jr. *space technology company executive, geochemist*
Proffitt, John Richard *business executive, educator*
Rachanow, Gerald Marvin *lawyer, pharmacist*
Rafajko, Robert Richard *medical research company executive*
Ramsey, William Edward *retired naval officer, space systems executive*
Rechcigl, Miloslav, Jr. *government official*
Regeimbal, Neil Robert, Sr. *retired journalist*
Rheinstein, Peter Howard *government official, physician, lawyer*
Rinkenberger, Richard Krug *physical scientist, geologist*
Robinson, William Andrew *health service executive, physician*
Rohr, Karolyn Kanavas *school system administrator*
Rosenberg, Judith Lynne *middle school educator*
Sacchet, Edward M. *foreign service officer*
Saljinska-Markovic, Olivera T. *oncology researcher, educator*
Schindler, Albert Isadore *physicist, educator*
Schweickart, Russell Louis *communications executive, astronaut*
Scully, Martha Seebach *speech and language pathologist*
Seagle, Edgar Franklin *environmental engineer, consultant*
Selby, Clark Linwood, Jr. *sales executive*
Seltser, Raymond *epidemiologist, educator*
Shadoan, George Woodson *lawyer*
Shah, Vinod Purushottam *research scientist*
Shaw, Robert William, Jr. *management consultant, venture capitalist*
Shelton, Wayne Vernon *professional services and systems integration company executive*
Simpson, Lisa Ann *government agency administrator, physician*
†Snyder, Robert M. *communication company executive*
†Spahr, Frederick Thomas *association executive*
Sparks, David Stanley *university administrator*
Standing, Kimberly Anna *educational researcher*
Stansfield, Charles W. *educational administrator*
Stenger, Judith Antoinette *middle school educator*
Stewart, Harold Leroy *pathologist, educator, cancer investigator*
Stoiber, Carlton Ray *government agency official*
Stover, Ellen Simon *health scientist, psychologist*
Sumaya, Ciro Valent *pediatrician, educator*
Sumberg, Alfred Donald *professional association executive*
Szabo, Daniel *government official*
Tabor, Edward *physician, researcher*
Tangoren, Gulen F. *retired anesthesiologist, pain management specialist*
Titus, Roger Warren *lawyer*
Tripp, Frederick Gerald *investment advisor*
Trost, Carlisle Albert Herman *retired naval officer*
Ulbrecht, Jaromir Josef *chemical engineer*
Uppoor, Rajendra *pharmaceutical scientist, educator, researcher*
†Vogel, Linda Ann *federal agency administrator*
Waksberg, Joseph *statistical company executive, researcher*
Waugaman, Richard Merle *psychiatrist, psychoanalyst, educator*
Woodcock, Janet *federal official*
Yao, Andy Shunchi *computer science educator*
Zoon, Kathryn Egloff *biochemist*

**Royal Oak**
Israel, Lesley Lowe *political consultant*

**Saint Inigoes**
Swanson, Norma Frances *federal agency administrator*

**Saint Leonard**
Sanders, James Grady *biogeochemist*

**Saint Marys City**
Matelic, Candace Tangorra *museum studies educator, consultant, museum director*

**Saint Michaels**
Jones, Raymond Edward, Jr. *brewing executive*
Marshall, Robert Gerald *language educator*
Meendsen, Fred Charles *retired food company executive*

**Salisbury**
Houlihan, Hilda Imelio *physician*
Kleiman, Gary Howard *broadcast, advertising and cellular communications consultant*
Lin, Frank Chiwen *computer science educator*
Madden, Heather Ann *aluminum company executive*
Moultrie, Fred *geneticist*
Perdue, Franklin P. *poultry products company executive*
Perdue, James *food products executive*

**Sandy Spring**
Cope, Harold Cary *former university president, higher education association executive*
Gibian, Thomas George *chemical company executive*
Kanarowski, Stanley Martin *chemist, chemical engineer, government official*

Moulton, Phillips Prentice *religion and philosophy educator*

### Savage
Filby, Percy William *library consultant*

### Severna Park
Davis, Clayton *writer, pilot*
Davis, John Adams, Jr. *electrical engineer, roboticist, corporate research executive*
Ebersberger, Arthur Darryl *insurance company executive, consultant*
Greulich, Richard Curtice *anatomist, gerontologist*
Kumm, William Howard *energy products company executive*
Moore, John Leo, Jr. *journalist, writer, editor*
Pumphrey, Janet Kay *editor*
Retterer, Bernard Lee *electronic engineering consultant*
Schick, Edgar Brehob *German literature educator*

### Silver Spring
Abdelrahman, Talaat Ahmad Mohammad *financial executive*
Adams, Andrew Joseph *army officer*
Adams, Diane Loretta *physician*
Barkin, Robert Allan *graphic designer, newspaper executive, consultant*
Beach, Bert Beverly *clergyman*
Beckmann, David Milton *minister, economist, social activist*
Bennett, Carol(ine) Elise *reporter, actress*
Benz, Carl Arvell *nuclear engineer, physics educator*
Berger, Allan Sidney *psychiatrist, educator*
Blake, Lamont Vincent *electronics consultant*
Borkovec, Vera Z. *Russian studies educator*
Brodie, Norman *retired financial actuary*
Brog, David *consultant, former air force officer*
Bundukamara, Moses Abram *pharmacologist*
Burke, Gerard Patrick *business executive, lawyer*
Calabrese, Diane Marie *entomologist, writer*
Calinger, Ronald Steve *historian*
Camphor, James Winky, Jr. *educational administrator*
Carnell, Paul Herbert *federal education official*
Cheek, King Virgil, Jr. *educational administrator, lawyer*
Coates, Robert Jay *retired electronic scientist*
Cole, Wayne Stanley *historian, educator*
Coles, Anna Louise Bailey *university official, nurse*
Colyer, Sheryl Lynn *psychologist*
Compton, Mary Beatrice Brown (Mrs. Ralph Theodore Compton) *public relations executive, writer*
Craig, Paul Max, Jr. *lawyer*
Crawford-Mason, Clare Wootten *television producer, journalist*
Day, Daniel Edgar *government information officer*
Doerr, Edd *religious liberty organization administrator*
Doherty, William Thomas, Jr. *historian, retired educator*
Douglass, Carl Dean *biochemistry consultant, former government official*
Dowd, Mary-Jane Martin *historian*
Eades, James Beverly, Jr. *aeronautical engineer*
Eiserer, Leonard Albert Carl *publishing executive*
Fanelli, Joseph James *retired public affairs executive, consultant*
Flieger, Howard Wentworth *editor*
Fockler, Herbert Hill *foundation executive*
Foresti, Roy, Jr. *chemical engineer*
Friday, Elbert Walter, Jr. *federal agency administrator, meteorologist*
Gilbert, Arthur Charles Francis *psychologist*
Golden, Joseph Hilary *meteorologist*
Goldstein, Laurence Alan *trade association executive*
Goott, Daniel *government official, consultant*
Grossberg, David Burton *cardiologist*
Grubbs, Donald Shaw, Jr. *retired actuary*
Hall, J. Michael *federal agency administrator, oceanographer*
Hannan, Myles *lawyer, banker*
Hayman, Harry *association executive, electrical engineer*
Haynes, Leonard L., III *former government official, consultant, educator*
Hedgepeth, Leroy J. *retired park director*
Hegstad, Roland Rex *magazine editor*
Hermach, Francis Lewis *consulting engineer*
Hermanson Ogilvie, Judith *foundation executive*
Hersey, David Floyd *information resources management consultant, retired government official*
Hoar, William Patrick *editor, author*
Hoch, Peggy Marie *computer scientist*
Howze, Karen Aileen *newspaper editor, lawyer, multi-cultural communications consultant*
Hsueh, Chun-tu *political scientist, historian, foundation executive*
Humphries, Weldon R. *real estate/hotel executive*
Hunt, Mary Elizabeth *association executive*
Husemann, Robert William *retired mechanical engineer*
Jacobs, George *broadcast engineering consulting company executive*
Jaskot, John Joseph *insurance company executive*
Kendrick, James Earl *business consultant*
Kirkland, (Joseph) Lane *labor union official*
Kohler, Max Adam *consulting hydrologist, weather service administrator*
Kolodny, Debra Ruth *labor management consultant*
Kronstadt, Arnold Mayo *regional and architectual planner*
LaSala, Kenneth Paul *engineer, consultant*
Leedy, Daniel Loney *ecologist*
Lett, Cynthia Ellen Wein *marketing executive*
Luo, Jessica Chaoying *actuary*
Maas, Joe (Melvin Joseph Maas) *retired federal agency administrator*
Manheimer, Bernard Henry *federal agency administrator, consultant*
Mashin, Jacqueline Ann Cook *medical sciences adminstrator*
McGinn, Cherie M. *secondary education educator*
McLurkin-Harris, Kimberly Elana *secondary education educator*
McQueen, Jeffery Thomas *meteorologist*
Mitchell, Milton *lawyer*
Mok, Carson Kwok-Chi *structural engineer*
Mooney, James Hugh *newspaper editor*
Moore, Shirley Throckmorton (Mrs. Elmer Lee Moore) *accountant*
Moseley, Theresa *guidance counselor, actress*
Munson, John Christian *acoustician*
Myers, Evelyn Stephenson *editor, writer*
Oliver, Wilbert Henry *religious organization administrator*
Oswald, Rudolph A. *economist*
Pacuska, Alison Brandi *Russian studies professional*
Papas, Irene Kalandros *English language educator, writer, poet*
Peiperl, Adam *kinetic sculptor, photographer*
Pellerzi, Leo Maurice *lawyer*
Perlmutter, Jerome Herbert *communications specialist*
Poinsett-White, Sadie Ruth *elementary education educator*
Porter, Dwight Johnson *former electric company executive, foreign affairs consultant*
Raphael, Coleman *business consultant*
Rasi, Humberto Mario *educational administrator, editor, minister*
Rayburn, Carole (Mary Aida) Ann *psychologist, researcher, writer*
Rueger, Lauren John *retired physicist, consultant*
Ryan, Miles Francis, III *lawyer*
Ryan, Patrick Andrew *educator*
Sahli, Nancy Ann *retired federal agency administrator, consultant*
Scheer, Milton David *chemical physicist*
Schick, Irvin Henry *academic administrator, educator*
Schmitten, Rolland Arthur *government official*
Schneider, William Charles *aerospace consultant*
Senseman, Ronald Sylvester *architect*
Shames, Irving Herman *engineering educator*
Shelton, William Chastain *retired statistician*
Shih-Carducci, Joan Chia-mo *cooking educator, biochemist, medical technologist*
Shira, Robert Bruce *university administrator, oral surgery educator*
Short, Steve Eugene *engineer*
Simon, Donald John *financial planner, insurance and investment broker*
Sirken, Monroe Gilbert *statistician*
Telesetsky, Walter *government official*
Thompson, George Ralph *church administrator*
Tokar, John Michael *oceanographer, ocean engineer*
Ventre, Francis Thomas *environmental design and policy educator*
Vernon, Weston, III (Wes Vernon) *freelance journalist*
Waldrop, Francis Neil *physician*
Ware, Thomas Earle *building consultant*
Weger, William John *public relations executive*
Whalen, John Philip *retired educational administrator*
White, Edmund William *chemical engineer*
White, Herbert Laverne *meterologist, federal agency administrator*
Whitten, Leslie Hunter, Jr. *author, newspaper reporter, poet*
Winston, Michael Russell *foundation executive, historian*
Wright, Mary Doris *physician*
Yasher, Michael *accountant*
Young, Jay Alfred *chemical safety and health consultant, writer, editor*
Zwerdling, David Mark *psychiatrist*

### Solomons
Whitaker, Mary Fernan *lawyer*

### Sparks
Single, Richard Wayne, Sr. *lawyer*
Suarez-Murias, Marguerite C. *retired language and literature educator*

### Sparks Glencoe
Swackhamer, Gene L. *bank executive*

### Stevenson
Hendler, Nelson Howard *physician, medical clinic director*

### Stevensville
Deen, Thomas Blackburn *retired transportation research executive*
Kepley, Thomas Alvin *management consultant*
Trescott, Sara Lou *water resources engineer*

### Street
Spangler, Ronald Leroy *retired television executive, aircraft executive, automobile collector*

### Suitland
McKinney-Ludd, Sarah Lydelle *middle school education, librarian*
Rao, Desiraju Bhavanarayana *meteorologist, oceanographer, educator*

### Sykesville
Buck, John Bonner *retired biologist*
Enoff, Louis D. *international consultant*
Gubernatis, Thomas Frank, Sr. *electrical buyer*
Weyandt, Daniel Scott *naval officer, engineer*

### Takoma Park
Lancaster, Alden *educational consultant*
Porter, Clarence A. *academic dean*
von Hake, Margaret Joan *librarian*

### Tall Timbers
Jensen, Paul Erik *marketing executive*

### Temple Hills
Day, Mary Jane Thomas *cartographer*
Strauss, Simon Wolf *chemist, materials scientist*
Whidden, Stanley John *physiologist, physician*

### Timonium
Orlando, Alexander Mariano *international marketing and trade consultant*

### Towson
Baker, Jean Harvey *history educator*
Barton, Meta Packard *business executive, financial planner*
Carney, Bradford George Yost *lawyer, educator*
Chappell, Annette M. *university dean*
Eyler, James R. *judge*
Fish, James Henry *library director*
Fitzpatrick, Vincent de Paul, Jr. *gynecologist*
Hildebrand, Joan Martin *education educator*
Levasseur, William Ryan *lawyer*
Mark, Michael Laurence *music educator*
Mc Indoe, Darrell Winfred *nuclear medicine physician, former air force officer*
Morris, Edwin Thaddeus *construction consultant*
Proctor, Kenneth Donald *lawyer*
Ryker, Norman J., Jr. *retired manufacturing company executive*
Spodak, Michael Kenneth *forensic psychiatrist*
Wilmot-Weidman, Kimberly Jo *journalist*
Wubah, Daniel Asua *microbiologist*
Wurmser, Leon *psychiatry educator*

### Trappe
Anderson, Andrew Herbert *retired army officer*

### Union Bridge
Laughlin, Henry Prather *physician, psychiatrist, educator, author, editor*

### Upper Fairmount
Dougherty, Barbara Lee *artist, writer*

### Upper Marlboro
Beasley, Diana Lee *educational administrator*
Bowles, Liza K. *construction executive*
Carroll, Cyril James *speech communication and theatre educator*
Chasanow, Howard Stuart *judge, lecturer*
Clark, Jerome *educational administrator*
Dortch, Susan Madeline *elementary education educator*
Elwood, Patricia Cowan *school hearing therapist, political consultant*
Hechinger, John W., Jr. *home improvement company executive*
Lilly, John Richard, II *lawyer*
McClelland, W. Clark *retail company financial executive*
Reed, Jacqueline K(emp) *educational researcher*
Smith, Ralph Lee *author, musician*
Street, Patricia Lynn *secondary education educator*
Uzzell-Baggett, Karon Lynette *career officer*

### Waldorf
Robey, Sherie Gay Southall Gordon *secondary education educator, consultant*
Wiggins, Stephen Edward *family practice physician, medical administrator*

### West Bethesda
Gaunaurd, Guillermo C. *physicist, engineer, researcher*
Spurling, Everett Gordon, Jr. *architect, construction specifications consultant*

### West River
Bower, Catherine Downes *communications and public relations executive*
Patermaster, John Joseph *inventor, consultant*

### Westminster
Bryson, Brady Oliver *lawyer*
Chambers, Robert Hunter, III *college president, American studies educator*
Cronin, Susan Gayle *county official*
Cueman, Edmund Robert *county official*
Dulany, William Bevard *lawyer*
LeGates, Gary A. *secondary education educator*
McAdam, Paul Edward *library administrator*

### Wheaton
Goode, Margaret Nighan *nurse*
Kirchman, Eric Hans *lawyer*

### White Hall
Radigan, Frank Xavier *pharmaceutical company executive*

### White Sands
Andrea, Elma Williams *retail executive*

### Woodbine
Brush, Peter Norman *federal agency administrator, lawyer*

### Woodstock
Price, John Roy, Jr. *financial executive*

### Wye Mills
Lednum, Florence Nash *biological sciences educator*
Schnaitman, William Kenneth *finance company executive*

## MASSACHUSETTS

### Abington
Auton, Linda May Eisenschmidt *lawyer, nurse*

### Acton
Aldwinckle, Joseph George *electronic engineer*
Brody, Leslie Gary *social worker, sociologist*
Hoopes, Walter Ronald *chemical company executive, retired*
Kittross, John Michael *retired communications educator*
Leighton, Charles Milton *specialty consumer products company executive*
Tamaren, Michele Carol *special education educator*
Wade, Samuel David *medical products company executive*
Webber, Howard Rodney *computer company executive*

### Agawam
Ashley, Cynthia Elizabeth *psychotherapist, human service administrator*
Schilling-Nordal, Geraldine Ann *secondary school educator*

### Allston
Becton, Henry Prentiss, Jr. *broadcasting company executive*
Mills, Daniel Quinn *business educator, consultant, author*

### Amesbury
DeLucia, Gene Anthony *government administrator, computer company executive*
Dowd, Frances Connelly *librarian*
Labaree, Benjamin Woods *history educator*

### Amherst
Abbott, Douglas Eugene *engineering educator*
Adrion, William Richards *academic administrator, computer and information sciences educator, author*
Alfange, Dean, Jr. *political science educator*
Anderson, Ronald Trent *art educator*
Archer, Ronald Dean *chemist, educator*
Averill, James Reed *psychology educator*
Bagg, Robert Ely *poet*
Baker, Lynne Rudder *philosophy educator*
Beals, Ralph Everett *economist, educator*
Belt, Edward Scudder *sedimentologist, educator*
Benson, Lucy Peters Wilson *political and diplomatic consultant*
Bentley, Richard Norcross *regional planner, educator*
Berger, Bernard Ben *environmental and civil engineer, former educator and public health officer*
Berger, Seymour Maurice *social psychologist*
Bestor, Charles Lemon *composer, educator*
Bezucha, Robert Joseph *history educator*
Brandon, Liane *filmmaker, educator*
Bridegam, Willis Edward, Jr. *librarian*
Byron, Frederick William, Jr. *physicist, educator, university vice chancellor*
Carpino, Louis A. *chemist, educator*
Chappell, Vere Claiborne *philosophy educator*
Commager, Henry Steele *retired writer, history educator*
Coppinger, Raymond Parke *biologist, educator*
Cornish, Geoffrey St. John *golf course architect*
Creed, Robert Payson, Sr. *literature educator*
Demerath, Nicholas Jay, III *sociology educator*
Ehrlich, Paul *chemist, educator*
Fink, Richard David *chemist, educator*
Fleischman, Paul R. *psychiatrist, writer*
†Flint, James *university head basketball coach*
Fox, Thomas Walton *veterinary science educator*
Franks, Lewis E. *electrical and computer engineering educator, researcher*
Gerety, Tom *college administrator, educator*
Gibson, Walker *retired English language educator, poet, writer*
Godfrey, Paul Joseph *science foundation director*
Goldman, Sheldon *political science educator*
Goldstein, Joseph Irwin *materials scientist, educator*
Grose, Robert Freeman *psychology educator*
Haensel, Vladimir *chemical engineering educator*
Hendricks, James Powell *artist*
Hernon, Joseph Martin, Jr. *history educator*
Hewlett, Horace Wilson *former educational administrator, association executive*
Holmes, Francis William *plant pathologist*
Holmes, Helen Bequaert *association administrator*
Jenkins, Paul Randall *poet, editor*
Kantor, Simon William *chemistry educator*
Kinney, Arthur Frederick *literary history educator, author, editor*
Klare, Michael Thomas *social science educator, program director*
Koren, Israel *electrical and computer engineering educator*
Langland, Joseph Thomas *author, emeritus educator*
Larson, Joseph Stanley *environmentalist, educator, researcher*
Lasch, Pat *artist, educator*
Laurence, Robert Lionel *chemical engineering educator*
Lenz, Robert William *polymer chemistry educator*
Lester, Julius B. *author*
Liebling, Jerome *photographer, educator*
Litsky, Bertha Yanis *microbiologist, artist*
MacKnight, William John *chemist, educator*
Mc Donagh, Edward Charles *sociologist, university administrator*
McIntosh, Robert Edward, Jr. *electrical engineering educator, consultant, electronics executive*
Mills, Patricia Jagentowicz *political philosophy educator, writer*
Nash, William Arthur *civil engineer, educator*
Oates, Stephen Baery *history educator*
Palser, Barbara F. *botany researcher, retired educator*
Parkhurst, Charles *retired museum director, art historian*
Partee, Barbara Hall *linguist, educator*
Peterson, Gerald Alvin *physics educator*
Ponte, Jay Michael *research associate in information retrieval*
Porter, Roger Stephen *chemistry educator*
Prince, Gregory Smith, Jr. *academic administrator*
Rabin, Monroe Stephen Zane *physicist*
Ratner, James Henry *dermatologist*
Romer, Robert Horton *physicist, educator*
Rosbottom, Ronald Carlisle *French, arts and humanities educator*
Rossi, Alice S. *sociology educator, author*
Rupp, William John *architect*
Sandweiss, Martha A. *author, American studies and history educator*
Scott, David Knight *physicist, university administrator*
Slakey, Linda Louise *biochemistry educator*
Stein, Otto Ludwig *botany educator*
Stein, Richard Stephen *chemistry educator*
Strickland, Bonnie Ruth *psychologist, educator*
Swift, Calvin Thomas *electrical and computer engineering educator*
Tager, Jack *historian, educator*
Tate, James Vincent *poet, English educator*
Taubman, Jane Andelman *Russian literature educator*
Taubman, William Chase *political science educator*
Temeles, Margaret Stewart *psychiatrist*
Tenenbaum, Jeffrey Mark *academic librarian*
Tippo, Oswald *botanist, educator, university administrator*
Tirrell, David A. *research scientist, educator*
Torras, Joseph Hill *pulp and paper company executive*
Vogl, Otto *polymer science and engineering educator*
Wideman, John Edgar *English literature educator, novelist*
Wilcox, Bruce Gordon *publisher*
Wills, David Wood *minister, educator*
Wolff, Robert Paul *philosophy educator*
Woodbury, Richard Benjamin *anthropologist, educator*
Wyman, David Sword *historian, educator*
Yarde, Richard Foster *art educator*

### Andover
Anderson, Amelia E. *nursing administrator, geriatrics nurse*
Bucci, Kathleen Elizabeth *lawyer, nurse*

Butler, Fred Jay, Jr. manufacturing company executive
Chase, Barbara Landis school administrator
Fitzgerald, Michael Anthony insurance company executive
Gaut, Norman Eugene electronics firm executive
Jakes, William Chester electrical engineer
Lakin, John Francis lawyer
Lloyd, Robert Andrew art educator
Mac Neish, Richard Stockton archaeologist, educator
Maguire, Robert Edward retired public utility executive
Marsh, Robert Buford chemical engineer, consultant
Pedini, Kenneth radiologist
Schlecker, James Henry sales and engineering executive
Schmidt-Nelson, Martha Alice communications and training executive, ergonomist
Sintros, James Lee management consultant, arbitrator
Thorn, Andrea Papp lawyer
Whidden, Robert Lee, Jr. health care consultant
Wise, Kelly private school educator, photographer, critic

### Arlington
Braithwaite, John Michael title company executive
Casagrande, Dirk Rainer civil engineer
Freeland, Richard Middleton academic affairs administrator, historian
Fulmer, Vincent Anthony retired college president
Gumpertz, Werner Herbert structural engineering company executive
Hefferon, Lauren Jeanine tour operator, business owner
Horn, Roberta Claire psychotherapist, photographer
O'Connell, Paul Edmund publisher
†Samuelson, Joan professional runner
Whitehead, George William retired mathematician

### Ashburnham
Timms, Peter Rowland art museum administrator

### Ashfield
Nye, Edwin Packard mechanical engineering educator
Pepyne, Edward Walter lawyer, psychologist, former educator

### Ashland
Gohlke, Frank William photographer

### Attleboro
DeWerth, Gordon Henry management consultant
Hammerle, Fredric Joseph metal processing executive
King, Melvin James internist

### Auburn
Bachelder, Robert Stephen minister
Baker, David Arthur small business owner, manufacturer
McQuarrie, Bruce Cale mathematics educator

### Auburndale
Gulotta, Victor public relations executive, writer

### Babson Park
Genovese, Francis Charles (Frank Genovese) economist, consultant, editor
Glavin, William Francis academic administrator

### Barnstable
Brown, Robert G. lawyer

### Bedford
Alarcon, Rogelio Alfonso physician, researcher
Carr, Paul Henry physicist
Cronson, Harry Marvin electronics engineer
Elkinton, Joseph Russell medical educator
Fante, Ronald Louis engineering scientist
Ferrandino, Vincent L. stage agency administrator
Frederickson, Arthur Robb physicist
Goodman, William Beehler editor, literary agent
Griffin, Donald R(edfield) zoology educator
Hicks, Walter Joseph electrical engineer
Jelalian, Albert V. electrical engineer
Kennedy, X. J. (Joseph Kennedy) writer
Klobuchar, John A. research engineer
Kouyoumjian, Charles H. diversified financial services company executive
Nunes, Geoffrey lawyer, corporate executive
Sizer, Irwin Whiting biochemistry educator
†Steinberg, James Jonah medical administrator, educator
Volicer, Ladislav physician, educator
Winter, David Louis systems engineer, human factors scientist, retired

### Belchertown
Russell, Joseph William regional planner, emergency planner

### Belmont
Benyo, Joanne critical care nurse
Bergson, Abram economist, educator
Bloch, Herbert retired foreign language and literature and history educator
Buckley, Jerome Hamilton English language educator
Cavarnos, Constantine Peter writer, philosopher
Cohen, Bruce Michael psychiatrist, educator, scientist
Coyle, Joseph Thomas psychiatrist
de Marneffe, Francis psychiatrist, hospital administrator
Glines, Stephen Ramey software industry executive
Haralampu, George Stelios electric power engineer, former engineering executive electric utility company
Haselkorn, David educator, recruiting executive
Hauser, George biochemist, educator
Klein, Martin Samuel management consulting executive
Lange, Nicholas Theodore biostatistician
Levendusky, Philip George clinical psychologist, administrator
Lewis, Henry Rafalsky manufacturing company executive
Luick, Robert Burns lawyer
Merrill, Edward Wilson chemical engineering educator
Nixon, Ralph Angus psychiatrist, educator, research neuroscientist
Ognibene, Edward John research and development mechanical engineer
Onesti, Silvio Joseph psychiatrist
Ottenstein, Donald psychiatrist
Pollack, William Shelley psychologist, organizational consultant
Pope, Harrison Graham, Jr. psychiatrist, educator
Rich, Sharon Lee financial planner
Ronningstam, Elsa Frideborg psychologist
Sifneos, Peter Emanuel psychiatrist
Washburn, Barbara Polk cartographer, researcher, explorer
Youngberg, Robert Lovett psychologist

### Beverly
Barger, Richard Wilson hotel executive
Carlson, Sandra Anne nursing educator, consultant
Ghen, Edythe Solberg artist
Golin, Joyce Arlene public information officer
Harris, Miles Fitzgerald meteorologist
Marion, John Martin academic administrator
McReynolds, Larry Austin molecular biologist
Murray, Mary early childhood, elementary and secondary educator
Roberts, Richard John molecular biologist, consultant, research director

### Billerica
Ahern, Barbara Ann nursing educator, vocational school educator
Gray, Charles Agustus chemical company research executive
Kolb, Charles Eugene research corporation executive
Kronick, Barry lumber company executive
McCaffrey, Robert Henry, Jr. retired manufacturing company executive

### Bolton
Dyer-Cole, Pauline school psychologist, educator

### Boston
Ablow, Joseph artist, educator
Aborn, Foster Litchfield insurance company executive
Abraham, Nicholas Albert lawyer, real estate developer
Achatz, John lawyer
Ackerman, Jerome Leonard radiology educator
Adams, Douglass Franklin radiologist, educator, medical ethicist
Adams, John Quincy economist, educator
Adams, Phoebe-Lou journalist
Adelstein, S(tanley) James physician, educator
Adler, David Avram psychiatrist
Ahima, Rexford Sefah neuroendocrinologist, internist
Aisenberg, Alan C. physician, educator, researcher
Akin, Steven Paul financial company executive
Alden, Vernon Roger corporate director, trustee
Aldrich, Bailey federal judge
Alexander, James Garth architect
Alie, Alleyn A. construction and engineering company executive
Allard, David Henry judge
Allukian, Myron, Jr. government administrator, public health educator, dental educator
Alpert, Joel Jacobs medical educator, pediatrician
Ames, James Barr lawyer
Amirault, Richard B. retired career officer, financial planner
Ampola, Mary G. pediatrician, geneticist
Amy-Moreno de Toro, Angel Alberto social sciences educator, writer, oral historian
Anastasi, Gaspar Walter plastic surgeon
Andre, Rae writer, organizational behavior educator
Andrews, Kenneth Richmond business administration educator
Angelou, Maya author
Annas, George J. health law educator
Anselme, Jean-Pierre Louis Marie chemist
Anthony, Ethan architect
Aresty, Jeffrey M. lawyer
Argyris, Chris organizational behavior educator
Arias, Irwin Monroe physician, educator
Arky, Ronald Alfred medical educator
Armand, Patrick dancer
Armstrong, Rodney librarian
Arnold, John David management counselor, catalyst
Aronow, Saul physicist
Auchincloss, Hugh, Jr. transplant surgeon
Auerbach, Arnold (Red Auerbach) professional basketball team executive
Auerbach, Joseph lawyer, educator
Austen, K(arl) Frank physician, educator
Austen, W(illiam) Gerald surgeon, educator
Avery, Mary Ellen pediatrician, educator
Avery, Steven Thomas professional baseball player
Avison, David photographer
Bacigalupe, Gonzalo Manuel family therapist, educator
Backus, Ann Swift Newell education educator, consultant
Bacon, A(delaide) Smoki public relations consultant, radio and television host
Bae, Frank S. H. law educator, law librarian
Bailey, Richard Briggs investment company executive
Baker, Charles Duane business administration educator, former management executive
Ballas, Nadia S. writer, poet
Bangs, Will Johnston lawyer
Banks, Henry H. academic dean, physician
Bargmann, Joel David architect
Barnett, Guy Octo physician, educator
Barry, Patricia Pound physician, educator
Barry, William Anthony priest, writer
Batchelder, Samuel Lawrence, Jr. corporate lawyer
Bauer, Elaine Louise ballet dancer
Baughman, James Carroll information and communication educator
Beal, Robert Lawrence real estate executive
Beard, Charles Julian lawyer
Beck, William Samson physician, educator, biochemist
Becker, Fred Ronald lawyer
Becker, James Murdoch surgeon, educator
Beinfeld, Margery Cohen neurobiology educator
Beinhocker, Gilbert David investment banker
Belin, Gaspard d'Andelot lawyer
Benacerraf, Baruj pathologist, educator
Benjamin, William Chase lawyer
Bennett, George Frederick investment manager
Berenberg, William physician, educator
Berenson, Paul Stewart advertising executive
Berg, Norman Asplund management educator
Bergelson, Jeffrey Michael pediatrician , educator
Bergen, Kenneth William lawyer
Berger, Francine Ellis radio station executive, communications executive
Berlew, Frank Kingston lawyer
Bern, Murray Morris hematologist, oncologist
Bernfield, Merton Ronald pediatrician, scientist, educator
Bernhard, Alexander Alfred lawyer
Bernhard, William Francis thoracic and cardiovascular surgeon
Berson, Eliot Lawrence ophthalmologist, medical educator
Bertonazzi, Louis Peter state agency administrator
Berube, Margery Stanwood publishing executive
Bieber, Frederick Robert medical educator
Bines, Harvey Ernest lawyer, educator, writer
Black, Paul Henry medical educator, researcher
Blau, Monte radiology educator
Blendon, Robert Jay health policy educator
Bloch, Kurt Julius physician
Blodgett, Mark Stephen lawyer, legal studies educator, author
Blout, Elkan Rogers biological chemistry educator, university dean
Blute, Peter I. transportation executive, former congressman
Bodman, Samuel Wright, III specialty chemicals and materials company
Bohnen, Michael J. lawyer
Bok, Joan Toland utility executive
Bok, John Fairfield lawyer
Bondoc, Conrado Cervania surgeon, educator
Borenstein, Milton Conrad lawyer, manufacturing company executive
Bornheimer, Allen Millard lawyer
Borod, Ronald Sam lawyer
Boudin, Michael federal judge
Bougas, James Andrew physician, surgeon
Bouloukos, Don P. broadcast company executive
Bourne, Katherine Day journalist, educator
Bourque, Ray professional hockey player
Bower, Joseph Lyon business administration educator
Bowler, Marianne Bianca judge
Bownes, Hugh Henry federal judge
Boyd, David Preston business educator
Brain, Joseph David biomedical scientist
Brandt, Allan M. medical history educator
Braunwald, Eugene physician, educator
Brazelton, Thomas Berry pediatrician, educator
Brecher, Kenneth astrophysicist
Brenner, Barry Morton physician
Brody, Richard Eric lawyer
Broitman, Selwyn Arthur microbiologist, educator
Bromsen, Maury Austin historian, bibliographer, antiquarian bookseller
†Bronner, Michael advertising executive
Brountas, Paul Peter lawyer
Brown, Judith Olans lawyer, educator
Brown, Matthew lawyer
Brown, Michael information technology executive
Brown, Michael Robert lawyer
Brown, Stephen Lee insurance company executive
Brown, William L. banker
Browne, Kingsbury lawyer
Browne, Thomas Reed neurologist, researcher, educator
Brownell, Gordon Lee physicist, educator
Bruns, William John, Jr. business administration educator
Buchanan, Robert McLeod lawyer
Buchin, Stanley Ira management consultant, educator
Buckley, Joseph W. insurance company executive
Buckley, Mortimer Joseph physician
Burack, Sylvia Kamerman editor, publisher
Burakoff, Steven James immunologist, educator
Burgess, John Allen lawyer
Burleigh, Lewis Albert lawyer
Burnes, Kennett Farrar chemical company executive
Burns, Padraic physician, psychiatrist, psychoanalyst, educator
Burns, Richard Michael public utility company executive
Burns, Thomas David lawyer
Burr, Francis Hardon lawyer
Bursma, Albert, Jr. publishing company executive
Bustin, Edouard Jean political scientist, educator
Buxbaum, Robert C(ourtney) internist
Cabot, Charles Codman, Jr. lawyer
Cabot, Louis Wellington foundation trustee
Caisse, Thomas Louis safety engineer
Calderwood, Stanford Matson investment management executive
Caldwell, Gail book critic
Callow, Allan Dana surgeon
Campbell, Levin Hicks federal judge
Campbell, Richard P. lawyer
Canavan, Christine Estelle state legislator
Caner, George Colket, Jr. lawyer
Cantella, Vincent Michele stockbroker
Cantor, Charles Robert biochemistry educator
Cantor, Stefanie Dara lawyer
Caplan, Louis Robert neurology educator
Cardona, Rodolfo Spanish language and literature educator
Carfora, John Michael university administrator, economics and political science educator
Carr, Daniel Barry anesthesiologist, endocrinologist, medical researcher
Carr, Jay Phillip critic
Carr, Michael Leon professional sports team executive, former professional basketball player
Carr, Stephen W. lawyer
Carradini, Lawrence comparative biologist, science administrator
Carroll, James author
Carroll, James Edward lawyer
Carroll, Matthew Shaun reporter
Carter, T(homas) Barton law educator
Carton, Lonnie Caming educational psychologist
Casner, Truman Snell lawyer
Cass, Ronald Andrew lawyer, educator
Cassilly, Richard tenor, voice educator
Cekala, Chester lawyer
Cellucci, Argeo Paul state official
Chabner, Bruce A. oncologist, researcher
Chandler, Harriette Levy management consultant, educator, legislator
Chapin, Melville lawyer
Chaplin, Ansel Burt lawyer
Chen, Ching-chih information science educator, consultant
Chilvers, Derek insurance company executive
Chinlund, Christine newspaper editor
Chobanian, Aram Van medical school dean, cardiologist
Christensen, Carl Roland business administration educator
Christenson, Charles John business educator
Christopher, Irene librarian, consultant
Clarke, Terence Michael public relations and advertising executive
Clarkson, Cheryl Lee surgical products executive
Cleven, Carol Chapman state legislator
Clouse, Melvin E. radiologist
Coffey, James Francis lawyer
Coffey, Joanne Christine dietitian
Coffin, John Miller molecular biologist, educator
Coffman, Jay Denton physician, educator
Cogan, John Francis, Jr. lawyer
Cogan, Robert David composer, school official
Coggins, Cecil Hammond physician, educator
Cohen, Alan Seymour internist
Cohen, Daniel Booth financial executive
Cohen, Jonathan Brewer molecular neurobiologist, biochemist
Cohen, Rachelle Sharon journalist
Cohen, Robert Sonné physicist, philosopher, educator
Cohn, Andrew Howard lawyer
Cole, Carolyn Jo brokerage company executive
Collings, Robert Biddlecombe judge
Collins, Martha English language educator, writer
Collins, Monica Ann journalist
Collins, Tucker pathologist, molecular biologist
Comeau, Susan bank executive
Comegys, Walker Brockton lawyer
Connell, William Francis diversified company executive
Connolly, Michael Joseph state official
Connolly, Thomas Edward judge
Conrad, Jeffrey Alan investment company executive
Cook, David editor
Copeland, Anne Pitcairn psychologist
Corcoran, Paul John physician
Cordero, Wilfredo Nieva professional baseball player
Cornwall, Deborah Joyce consulting firm executive, management consultant
Costellese, Linda E. Grace banker
Cotran, Ramzi S. pathologist, educator
Countryman, Gary Lee insurance company executive
Cox, Howard Ellis, Jr. venture capitalist
Craig, Clifford Lindley orthopaedic pediatric surgery educator
Crocker, Allen Carrol pediatrician
Cronin, Bonnie Kathryn Lamb legislative staff executive
Cronin, Philip Mark lawyer
Crook, Robert Wayne mutual funds executive
Crossen, Gary Charles lawyer
Crotty, William political science educator
†Crowder, Bruce collegiate ice hockey coach
Crowley, William Francis, Jr. medical educator
Crozier, William Marshall, Jr. bank holding company executive
Curley, Arthur library director
Curran, Emily Katherine museum director
Curry, John Anthony, Jr. university educator
Curtin, John Joseph, Jr. lawyer
Curtin, Phyllis music educator, former dean, operatic singer
Cushing, George Littleton lawyer
Cutler, Arnold Robert lawyer
Dacey, Kathleen Ryan judge
D'Agostino, Ralph Benedict mathematician, statistician, educator, consultant
D'Alessandro, David Francis financial services company executive
Daley, Paul Patrick lawyer
Darehshori, Nader Farhang publishing sales executive
David, John R. internist, educator
Davies, Don education educator
Davis, David William transportation consultant
Davis, William Arthur writer, editor
Davison, Peter Hubert editor, poet
Daynard, Richard Alan law educator
DeAmicis, Susan McNair small business owner
de Burlo, Comegys Russell, Jr. investment advisor, educator
Dederer, William Bowne music educator, administrator
Deissler, Mary A. foundation executive
Delaney, John White lawyer
Delbanco, Thomas Lewis medical educator, researcher
De Luca, Carlo John biomedical engineer
Dentler, Robert Arnold sociologist, educator
de Rham, Casimir, Jr. lawyer
DeSanctis, Roman William cardiologist
Desforges, Jane Fay medical educator, physician
Desnoyers, Megan Floyd archivist, educator
Deuel, Thomas Franklin physician
Deutsch, Thomas Frederick physicist
Di Domenica, Robert Anthony musician, composer
Diener, Betty Jane trade association administrator
Dignan, Thomas Gregory, Jr. lawyer
Dillin, John Woodward, Jr. newspaper editor, correspondent
Dillon, James Joseph lawyer
Dineen, John K. lawyer
DiStasio, James Shannon accountant
Dluhy, Deborah Haigh college dean
Dluhy, Robert George physician
Doebler, James Carl naval officer, engineering executive
Doherty, Robert Francis, Jr. aerospace industry professional
Donahue, Douglas Aidan, Jr. bank executive
Donovan, Helen W. newspaper editor
Dooley, Arch Richard retired business administration educator
Douglas, Pamela Susan physician, researcher, educator
Dowd, Peter Jerome public relations executive
Dreben, Raya Spiegel judge
Driver, William Raymond, Jr. banker
Drought, James Henry healthcare business owner, exercise physiologist
Duffy, James Francis, III lawyer
Dunning, Thomas E. newspaper editor
†Duquette, Daniel F. professional baseball team executive
Durand, Robert Alan state senator
Dusseault, C. Dean lawyer
Dvorak, Harold F. pathologist, educator, scientist
Eastman, Thomas George investment management executive
Eckstein, Marlene R. vascular radiologist
Eder, Richard Gray newspaper critic
Edmonds, Dean Stockett, Jr. physicist, educator, director
Edwards, Edward Allen retired vascular surgeon, anatomist
Egdahl, Richard Harrison surgeon, medical educator, health science administrator

Ehrlich, M. Gordon lawyer
Eisenberg, Leon psychiatrist, educator
Eisner, Sister Janet Margaret college president
El-Baz, Farouk research director, educator
Elfers, William retired investment company director
Elfman, Eric Michael lawyer
Elfner, Albert Henry, III mutual fund management company executive
Elkus, Howard Felix architect
Ellis, David Wertz museum director
Ellis, Franklin Henry, Jr. surgeon, educator
Engel, David Lewis lawyer
Epstein, Franklin Harold physician, educator
Eraklis, Angelo John surgeon
Erickson, Kenneth W. lawyer
Eskandarian, Edward advertising agency executive
Essex, Myron Elmer microbiology educator
Estes, Nathan Anthony Mark, III cardiologist, medical educator
Estin, Hans Howard investment executive
Eurich, Richard Rex lawyer
Evans, Paul F. protective services official
Everett, Jonathan Jubal lawyer
Fairbanks, Jonathan Leo museum curator
Falb, Peter Lawrence mathematician, educator, investment company executive
Faller, Douglas V. cancer research scientist, physician
Fanning, Katherine Woodruff editor, journalism educator
Farkas, Charles Michael management consultant
Farrar, Constance Mosher marketing executive
Farrer, Lindsay Ames genetic epidemiologist
Fausch, David Arthur public relations executive
Fay, Michael Leo lawyer
Feder, Donald Albert syndicated columnist
Federman, Daniel David medical educator, educational administrator, endocrinologist
Feeney, Mark newspaper editor
Fein, Rashi health sciences educator
Feldman, Robert George neurologist, medical educator
Felter, John Kenneth lawyer
Field, James Bernard internist, educator
Fieleke, Norman Siegfried economist
Fine, Samuel biomedical engineering educator, consultant
Fineberg, Harvey Vernon physician, educator
Finegold, Maurice Nathan architect
Fink, Aaron artist
Finn, Terrence M. lawyer
Finnegan, Neal Francis banker
Fischbach, Gerald D. neurobiology educator
Fischer, Eric Robert lawyer, educator
Fischer, Thomas Covell law educator, consultant, writer, lawyer
Fisher, Champe Andrews lawyer
Fitzgerald, Daniel Louis securities dealer
Fitzpatrick, Thomas Bernard dermatologist, educator
Flanders, Jefferson publishing executive
Flansburgh, Earl Robert architect
Flax, Martin Howard pathologist, educator
Fletcher, Norman Collings architect
Fletcher, Robert Hillman medical educator
Fletcher, Suzanne Wright physician, educator
Flint, Anthony Evans journalist
Floor, Richard Earl lawyer
Folkman, Moses Judah surgeon
Fonvielle, William Harold management consultant
Forbes, Peter architect
Foss, Clive Frank Wilson history educator
Fox, Bernard Hayman cancer epidemiologist, educator
Fox, Francis Haney lawyer
Frankenheim, Samuel lawyer
Frankl, Spencer Nelson dentist, university dean
Franks, Peter John educational administrator
†Frantz, Ivan D., III pediatrician
Fraser, Robert Burchmore lawyer
Frazier, Howard Stanley physician
Freed, Rita Evelyn curator, Egyptologist, educator
Freedberg, A. Stone physician
Freehling, Daniel Joseph law educator, law library director
Freeman, Robert Schofield musicologist, educator, pianist
Frei, Emil, III physician, medical researcher, educator
Freiman, David Galland pathologist, educator
Fremont-Smith, Marion R. lawyer
Fried, Charles judge, educator
Fried, Marvin Peter physician
Gad, Robert K., III lawyer
Galvani, Paul B. lawyer
Galvin, William Francis secretary of state, lawyer
Gamst, Frederick Charles anthropology educator
Garcia, Adolfo Ramon lawyer
†Garcia, Frieda community foundation executive
Gaston, Paul E. professional basketball team executive
Gaudreau, Russell A., Jr. lawyer
Gault, Robert Mellor lawyer
Gelfand, Jeffrey Alan physician, educator
Gellis, Sydney Saul physician
Gendron, George magazine editor
Gerratt, Bradley Scott presidential library director
Gerrity, Daniel Wallace real estate developer
Gerstmayr, John Wolfgang lawyer
Gertner, Nancy federal judge, legal educator
Gesmer, Henry lawyer
Gibran, Kahlil sculptor
Gibson, Barry Joseph magazine editor
Gifford, Nelson Sage financial company executive
Gilchrest, Barbara A. D. dermatologist
Gill, Robert Tucker lawyer
Gilmore, Maurice Eugene mathematics educator
Gimbrone, Michael Anthony, Jr. research scientist, pathologist, educator
Girouard, Donald Joseph, Jr. marine ecologist, bacteriologist
Giso, Frank, III lawyer
Givelber, Daniel James law educator
Glass, Milton Louis retired manufacturing company executive
Glass, Renée educational health foundation executive
Glassman, Herbert Haskel architect
Gleason, Jean Berko psychology educator
Glickman, Robert Morris physician, educator
Glimcher, Melvin Jacob orthopedic surgeon
Glosband, Daniel Martin lawyer
Goldberg, Irving Hyman molecular pharmacology and biochemistry educator
Goldhaber, Paul dental educator
Goldman, Peter nutrition and clinical pharmacology educator
Goodman, Bruce Gerald lawyer
Goodman, Louis Allan lawyer
Goody, Joan E. architect
Gottlieb, Leonard Solomon pathology educator
Gould, James Spencer financial consultant
Gould, John Joseph communications executive
Grabauskas, Patricia Anne nurse midwife
Graceffa, John Philip lawyer
Grassl, Anton Maria artist
Green, Gareth Montraville physician, educator, scientist
Greenblatt, David J. pharmacologist, educator
Greene, Leonard J. newspaper columnist
Greene, Robert Allan former university administrator
Greenwald, Sheila Ellen writer, illustrator
Greer, Gordon Bruce lawyer
Greiner, Jack Volker ophthalmologist, physician, surgeon, research scientist
Grimes, Heilan Yvette publishing executive
Grossfeld, Stan newspaper photography executive, author
Grossman, Frances Kaplan psychologist
Grossman, Jerome Harvey medical educator, administrator
Guild, Richard Samuel trade association management company executive
Gulley, Joan Long banker
Gupta, Paul R. lawyer
Haber, Edgar physician, educator
Haddad, Ernest Mudarri lawyer
Hagler, Jon Lewis investment executive
Hailey, Arthur author
Hale, Martin de Mora investor
Haley, Paul Richard lawyer, state legislator
Hall, David dean, law educator
Hall, Henry Lyon, Jr. lawyer
Hall, John Emmett orthopedic surgeon, educator
Hamel, Louis H., Jr. lawyer
Hamill, John P. bank executive
Hammond, Norman David Curle archaeology educator, researcher
Hampton, Henry Eugene film and television producer
Hand, John lawyer
Handford, Martin John illustrator, author
Harkness, John Cheesman architect
Harrington, Edward F. federal judge
Harrington, John Leo baseball company executive
Harrington, John Michael, Jr. lawyer
Harrington, Joseph John environmental engineering educator
Harris, Barbara C(lementine) bishop
Harris, Jay Robert radiation oncologist
Harris, Virginia Sydness publisher, educator
Harris, William Hamilton orthopedic surgeon
Harshbarger, Scott state attorney general
Hart, Douglas Edward investment company executive
Harvey, Les composer, producer
Haussermann, Oscar William, Jr. lawyer
Hawke, Robert Douglas state legislator
Hawkey, G. Michael lawyer
Hay, Elizabeth Dexter embryology researcher, educator
Hayes, Andrew Wallace, II consumer products company executive
Hayes, Robert Francis lawyer
Hayes, Robert Herrick technology management educator
Hayes, Samuel Linton, III business educator
Headding, Lillian Susan (Sally Headding) writer, forensic clairvoyant
Hedley-Whyte, Elizabeth Tessa neuropathologist
Heigham, James Crichton lawyer
Heimann, David Isidore software quality/reliability engineer, mathematical analyst
Hemperly, Rebecca Sue publishing manager
Henry, DeWitt Pawling, II creative writing educator, writer, arts administrator
Henry, Joseph Louis university dean
Hester, Patrick Joseph lawyer
Hiatt, Howard H. physician, educator
Hickey, Paul Robert anesthesiologist , educator
Higgins, George Vincent journalist, lawyer, author, educator
Hillman, Carol Barbara communications executive
Hillman, William Chernick federal bankruptcy judge
Hills, Patricia Gorton Schulze curator
Hilts, Philip James correspondent
Hines, Edward Francis, Jr. lawyer
Hines, Marion Ernest electronic engineering consultant
Hingson, Ralph W. medical educator
Hintikka, Jaakko philosopher, educator
Hjerpe, Edward Alfred, III finance and banking executive
Hobbs, Matthew Hallock investment banker
Hobson, John Allan psychiatrist, researcher, educator
Hoffman, Christian Matthew lawyer
Hoffman, David Alan lawyer
Hoffman, S. Joseph advertising agency executive
Holland, Hubert Brian lawyer
Holloway, Bruce Keener former air force officer
Holman, Bruce Leonard radiology educator, researcher
Hoort, Steven Thomas lawyer
Hopkins, Esther Arvilla Harrison chemist, patent lawyer
Hornig, Donald Frederick scientist
Hostetter, Amos Barr, Jr. cable television executive
Hotchkiss, Andra Ruth lawyer
Howard, Samson computer consultant, middle school educator
Howe, Jas. Murray lawyer
Howlett, D(onald) Roger art gallery executive, art historian
Howley, Peter Maxwell pathology educator
Hoyt, Herbert Austin Aikins television producer
Hubel, David Hunter physiologist, educator
Hunter, Durant Adams executive search company executive
Hurd, J. Nicholas executive recruiting consultant, former banker
Hutchinson, Bernard Thomas ophthalmologist
Hutter, Adolph Matthew, Jr. cardiologist, educator
Huvos, Andrew internist, cardiologist, educator
Hyatt, Raymond Russell, Jr. educator
Imperato, Robert Edward real estate company executive
Jackson, Earl, Jr. medical technologist
Jandl, James Harriman physician, educator
Jellinek, Michael Steven psychiatrist, pediatrician
Jha, Prakash Kumar molecular biologist, researcher
Jochum, Veronica pianist
Johnson, Edward Crosby, III financial company executive
†Johnson, Willard Chapin surgeon, researcher
Johnston, Richard Alan lawyer
Jones, Jeffrey Foster lawyer
Jones, Robert Emmet French language educator
Jones, Sheldon Atwell lawyer
Jordan, Alexander Joseph, Jr. lawyer
Joseph, J. Jonathan interior designer
Judson, Arnold Sidney management consultant
Kahn, Carl Ronald research laboratory administrator
Kamarck, Martin Alexander federal agency administrator, lawyer
Kamer, Joel Victor insurance company executive, actuary
Kames, Kenneth F. manufacturing company executive
Kaminer, Benjamin physician, educator
Kandarian, Susan Christine medical educator
Kane, Louis Isaac merchant
Kanin, Dennis Roy lawyer
Kanter, Rosabeth Moss management educator, consultant, writer
Kapioltas, John hotel company executive
Kaplan, Lawrence Edward lawyer
Kaplan, Marshall Myles gastroenterologist, researcher, educator
Kaplan, Michael Daniel physics and chemistry researcher, educator
Karelitz, Richard Alan financial executive, lawyer
Karelitz, Robert N(elson) lawyer
Karnovsky, Manfred L. biochemistry educator
Karnovsky, Morris John pathologist, biologist
Kasper, Stephen Neil professional hockey coach
Kassirer, Jerome Paul medical educator, editor-in-chief
Katz, Larry writer
Katz, Steven Theodore religious studies educator
Katzmann, Gary Stephen lawyer
Kauffman, Godfrey newspaper publishing executive
Kaufman, Jonathan Reed journalist
†Kaufman, Kasey television news anchor, reporter
Kavanaugh, James Francis, Jr. lawyer
Kazemi, Homayoun physician, medical educator
Keating, Michael Burns lawyer
Keeton, Robert Ernest federal judge
Kehoe, William Francis lawyer
Keller, Stanley lawyer
Kelley, Kevin H. insurance company executive
Kelly, Thomas J. lawyer
Kennedy, Eugene Patrick biochemist, educator
Kenney, Raymond Joseph, Jr. lawyer
Kerry, Cameron F. lawyer
Kessler, Diane Cooksey religious organization administrator, minister
Kety, Seymour S(olomon) physiologist, neuroscientist
Kieff, Elliott Dan medical educator
Kim, Ducksoo radiologist, inventor and educator
Kimball, George Edward, III sports columnist
Kindl, Patrice writer
King, Diane Marie creative services national manager
King, Nick newspaper editor
King, Robert David insurance company executive
King, William Bruce lawyer
Kingman, William Lockwood financial consultant
Kirchick, William Dean lawyer
Kirk, Paul Grattan, Jr. lawyer, former political organization official
Kirkpatrick, Edward Thomson college administrator, mechanical engineer
Kitz, Richard John anesthesiologist, educator
Klarfeld, Jonathan Michael journalism educator
Klein, Jerome Osias pediatrician, educator
Kleiner, Fred Scott art history and archaeology educator, editor
Klempner, Mark Steven Joel physician, research scientist, educator
Klingenstein, R. James physician
Klotz, Charles Rodger shipping company executive
Knight, Norman broadcast executive
Knight, Peter Carter lawyer
Knox, Richard Albert journalist
Koffel, William Barry lawyer
Kolodner, Richard David biochemist, educator
Kopelman, Leonard lawyer
Korb, Kenneth Allan lawyer
Korff, Yitzchok Aharon rabbi
Kornberg, Sir Hans Leo biochemist
Kowal, Ruth Elizabeth library administrator
Krakoff, Robert Leonard publishing executive
Krane, Stephen Martin physician, educator
Krasnow, Jordan Philip lawyer
Kravitz, Edward Arthur biochemist
Kressel, Herbert Yehude medical educator
Kubzansky, Philip Eugene environmental and organizational psychologist
Kunkel, Louis Martens research scientist, educator
Kurzweil, Edith sociology educator, editor
Kwasnick, Paul Jack retail executive
Lagarde, Jacques Yves metal products company executive
Lambert, Gary Ervery lawyer
Lane, Newton Alexander retired lawyer
Langer, Lawrence Lee English educator, writer
Langer, Robert Martin retired chemical engineering company executive, consultant
Langermann, John W. R. institutional equity salesperson
Lanner, Michael research administrator, consultant
Larkin, Alfred Sinnott, Jr. newspaper editor
Larkin, Michael John newspaper editor, journalist
Lasagna, Louis Cesare medical educator
Lasker, Morris E. judge
Last, Michael P. lawyer
Latham, James David lawyer
†Lawner, Ron advertising executive
Lawrence, Mary Josephine (Josie Lawrence) library official, artist
Lawrence, Merloyd Ludington editor
Lawrence, Paul Roger retired organizational behavior educator
†Lawson, Thomas Elsworth advertising agency executive
Leaf, Alexander physician, educator
Leaman, J. Richard, Jr. paper company executive
Lee, Donald Young (Don Lee) publishing executive, editor, writer
Lee, Jonathan Owen financial services company executive, lawyer
Leeman, Susan Epstein neuroscientist, educator
Lees, Sidney research facility administrator, bioengineering educator
Le Quesne, Philip William chemistry educator, researcher
Lerner, Richard Martin academic administrator, educator
Lesser, Laurence musician, educator
Levine, Robert A. cardiologist
Levine, Ruth Rothenberg biomedical science educator
Levinsky, Norman George physician, educator
Levitin, Lev Berovich engineering educator
Lewis, Anthony newspaper columnist
Lewis, Scott P. lawyer
Liang, Matthew H. medical director
Libby, Peter cardiologist, medical researcher
Licata, Arthur Frank lawyer
Lichtin, Norman Nahum chemistry educator
Lieberman, Gail Forman investment company executive
†Linsky, Martin Alan state official
Lipton, Stuart Arthur neuroscientist
Little, Arthur Dehon investment banker
Little, John Bertram physician, radiobiology educator, researcher
Livingston, David Morse biomedical scientist, physician, internist
Lockhart, Keith Alan conductor
Lockwood, Rhodes Greene retired lawyer
Lodge, George C(abot) business administration educator
Loeser, Hans Ferdinand lawyer
Logan, Lox Albert, Jr. museum director
Looney, William Francis, Jr. lawyer
Loring, Arthur lawyer, financial services company executive
Loring, Caleb, Jr. investment company executive
Loscalzo, Joseph cardiologist, biochemist
Lovejoy, George Montgomery, Jr. real estate executive
Lovell, Francis Joseph investment company executive
Lovett, Miller Currier management educator, clergyman
Lowry, Bates art historian, museum director
Lowry, Lois (Hammersberg) author
Lucker, Jay K. library education educator
Lukey, Joan A. lawyer
Luongo, C. Paul public relations executive
Lykins, Marshall Herbert insurance company executive
Lyman, Henry retired publisher, marine fisheries consultant
Lynch, Francis Charles lawyer
Lynch, Sandra Lea federal judge
Lyons, David Barry philosophy and law educator
Lyons, Paul Vincent lawyer
MacCombie, Bruce Franklin composer, college administrator
MacDougall, Peter lawyer
Macera, Salvatore industrial executive
MacFarlane, Maureen Anne lawyer
Macomber, John D. construction executive
Madara, James L. epitheliologist, pathologist, educator
Maher, Timothy John pharmacologist, educator
Malamy, Michael H(oward) molecular biology and microbiology educator
Malenka, Bertram Julian physicist, educator
Malone, Joseph D. state treasurer
Malt, Ronald A. surgeon, educator
Mandel, David Michael lawyer
Manfredi, David Peter architect
Mankin, Henry Jay physician, educator
Mannick, John Anthony surgeon
Manning, Robert Joseph editor
Manning, William Frederick wire service photographer
Mansfield, Christopher Charles insurance company legal executive
Margolis, Bernard Allen library administrator, antique book appraiser
Markel, Robert Thomas mayor
Markham, Jesse William economist
Marks, Bruce artistic director, choreographer
Marshall, Martin Vivan business administration educator, business consultant
Martin, Stanley A. lawyer
Maso, Michael Harvey managing director
Mason, Charles Ellis, III magazine editor
Mason, Herbert Warren, Jr. religion and history educator, author
Mason, Nancy Tolman state agency director
Matthews, Roger Hardin lawyer
Maxwell, J.B. financial and marketing consultant
Maynard, Kenneth Irwin medical educator, researcher
Mazzone, A. David federal judge
Mc Arthur, Janet Ward endocrinologist, educator
McArthur, John Hector business educator
McCann, Edward investment banker
Mc Carthy, Joseph Michael historian
McChesney, S. Elaine lawyer
McCluskey, Jean Louise civil and consulting engineer
McCormick, Marie Clare pediatrician, educator
McCraw, Thomas Kincaid business history educator, editor, author
McCullen, Joseph T., Jr. venture capitalist
Mc Dermott, William Vincent, Jr. physician, educator
McDougal, William Scott urology educator
McFarlan, Franklin Warren business administration educator
McGivney, John Joseph lawyer
McGovern, Patrick J. communications executive
McIntyre, Mildred Jean clinical psychologist, writer, neuroscientist
McKinley, William Thomas composer, performer, educator
McLennan, Bernice Claire human resources professional
McLinden, James Hugh molecular biologist
McMullin, Ruth Roney publishing company executive, management fellow
Mc Neice, John Ambrose, Jr. retired investment company executive
McNeil, Barbara Joyce radiologist, educator
McPhee, Jonathan music director, conductor, composer, arranger
Meacham, Brian Jay professional society administrator
Medearis, Donald Norman, Jr. physician, educator
Meister, Doris Powers investment management executive
Meister, Mark Jay museum director, professional society administrator
Melconian, Linda Jean state senator, lawyer
Mellins, Harry Zachary radiologist, educator
Menino, Thomas M. mayor
Menyuk, Paula developmental psycholinguistics educator
Menzies, Ian Stuart newspaper editor
Mercer, Douglas lawyer
Merk, Frederick Bannister biomedical educator, medical researcher
Merrill, Stephen former governor
Merton, Robert C. economist, educator
Meserve, William George lawyer

Messerle, Judith Rose *medical librarian, public relations director*
Metcalf, Arthur George Bradford *electronics company executive*
Metzer, Patricia Ann *lawyer*
Michel, Thomas Mark *internal medicine educator, scientist, physician*
Mikels, Richard Eliot *lawyer*
Miliora, Maria Teresa *chemist, psychotherapist, psychoanalyst, educator*
Millar, Sally Gray *nurse*
Miller, Alan Gershon *lawyer*
Miller, J. Philip *television producer, director, educator*
Miller, Naomi *art historian*
Minkel, Herbert Philip, Jr. *lawyer*
Moellering, Robert Charles, Jr. *internist, educator*
Mokriski, J. Charles *lawyer*
Monaco, Anthony Peter *surgery educator, medical institute administrator*
Monaghan, William Edward, II *financial services company executive*
Moncreiff, Robert P. *lawyer*
Mone, Michael Edward *lawyer*
Mongan, James John *physician, hospital administrator*
Monrad, Ernest Ejner *trust company executive*
Montgomery, William Wayne *surgeon*
Mooney, Michael Edward *lawyer*
Moore, Richard Lawrence *structural engineer, consultant*
Moore, Richard Thomas *state legislator*
Moran, James J., Jr. *lawyer*
Morby, Jacqueline *venture capitalist*
Morgan, James Philip *pharmacologist, cardiologist, educator*
Morgentaler, Abraham *urologist, researcher*
Moriarty, George Marshall *lawyer*
Moriarty, John *opera administrator, artistic director*
Morris, Gerald Douglas *newspaper editor*
Morrison, Gordon Mackay, Jr. *investment company executive*
†Morrissey, Peter A. *public relations executive*
Morton, Edward James *insurance company executive*
Morton, William Gilbert, Jr. *stock exchange executive*
Moseby, LeBaron Clarence, Jr. *mathematics and computer science educator*
Muldoon, Robert Joseph, Jr. *lawyer*
Mullaney, Joseph E. *lawyer*
Murphy, Evelyn Frances *healthcare administrator, former lieutenant governor*
Mygatt, Susan Hall *lawyer*
Nadas, Alexander Sandor *pediatric cardiologist, educator*
Naeser, Margaret Ann *linguist, medical researcher*
Naimi, Shapur *cardiologist, educator*
Nashe, Carol *association executive, public relations consultant*
Nathan, David Gordon *physician, educator*
Neely, Cameron Michael *professional hockey player*
Neely, Thomas Emerson *lawyer*
Nesmith, Richard Duey *clergyman, theology educator*
Neumeier, Richard L. *lawyer*
Newbrander, William Carl *health economist, management consultant*
Newhouse, Joseph Paul *economics educator*
Newman, Richard Alan *publisher, editor and consultant*
Nichols, David Harry *gynecologic surgeon, obstetrics and gynecology educator, author*
Nichols, Guy Warren *retired institute executive, utilities executive*
Norman, Dennis Keith *psychologist, educator*
Norment, Eric Stuart *newspaper editor*
Norton, Augustus Richard *political science educator*
Notopoulos, Alexander Anastasios, Jr. *lawyer*
Nutt, Robert L. *lawyer*
Nyberg, Stanley Eric *cognitive scientist*
Nylander, Jane Louise *museum director*
Oates, Adam R. *professional hockey player*
Oates, William Armstrong, Jr. *investment company executive*
O'Block, Robert Paul *management consultant*
O'Connor, Francis Patrick *state supreme court justice*
O'Dell, Edward Thomas, Jr. *lawyer*
O'Donnell, Thomas Francis *vascular surgeon, health facility administrator*
O'Donnell, Thomas Lawrence Patrick *lawyer*
O'Hern, Jane Susan *psychologist, educator*
O'Neil, William Francis *academic administrator*
O'Neill, Philip Daniel, Jr. *lawyer, educator*
O'Neill, Timothy P. *lawyer*
Orr, Bobby (Robert Gordon Orr) *former hockey player*
Osteen, Carolyn McCue *lawyer*
O'Sullivan, Chris *collegiate hockey player*
Otten, Jeffrey *health facility administrator*
Oxenkrug, Gregory Fayva *psychopharmacologist*
Packenham, Richard Daniel *lawyer*
Packer, Rekha Desai *lawyer*
Palmer, David Scott *political scientist, educator*
Papageorgiou, Panagiotis *medical educator*
Pardee, Arthur Beck *biochemist, educator*
Pardus, Donald Gene *utility executive*
Park, James Theodore *microbiologist, educator*
Park, William H(erron) *financial executive*
Park, William Wynnewood *law educator*
Parker, Christopher William *lawyer*
Parker, Jack *collegiate athletic coach*
Parker, Olivia *photographer*
Parks, Paul *corporate executive*
Partan, Daniel Gordon *lawyer, educator*
Patterson, John de la Roche, Jr. *lawyer*
Paul, Oglesby *cardiologist*
Payne, Douglas DeFrees *cardiothoracic surgeon, educator*
Pechilis, William John *lawyer*
Peckham, John Munroe, III *investment executive, author, lecturer*
Pedersen, Karen Sue *electrical engineer*
†Peek, Robin Patricia *library and information science educator*
Penney, Sherry Hood *university president, educator*
Pereira, Julio Cesar *middle school educator*
Perera, Lawrence Thacher *lawyer*
Perkins, James Wood *lawyer*
Perkins, John Allen *lawyer*
Perkins, Samuel *lawyer*
Petersen, Robert Allen *pediatric ophthalmologist*
Phillips, Daniel Anthony *trust company executive*
Phillips, William *English language educator, editor, author*
Pierce, Allan Dale *engineering educator, researcher*
Pierce, Martin E., Jr. *fire commissioner*
Pinsky, Robert Neal *poet, educator*
Piret, Marguerite Alice *investment banker*
Pitino, Richard *college basketball coach*
Pitts, James Atwater *financial executive*
Pochi, Peter Ernest *physician*
Pomeroy, Robert Corttis *lawyer*
Poser, Charles Marcel *neurology educator*
Potts, John Thomas, Jr. *physician, educator*
Poussaint, Alvin Francis *psychiatrist, educator*
Pratt, Albert *financial consultant, trustee*
Pratt, John Winsor *statistics educator*
Prescott, John Hernage *aquarium executive*
Preston, Malcolm *artist, art critic*
Prout, Curtis *physician*
Psathas, George *sociologist, educator*
Puliafito, Carmen Anthony *ophthalmologist, laser researcher*
Purcell, Patrick Joseph *newspaper publisher*
Pynchon, Thomas Ruggles, Jr. *author*
Quelle, Frederick William, Jr. *physicist*
Rabkin, Mitchell Thornton *physician, hospital administrator, educator*
Radloff, Robert Albert *real estate executive*
Raemer, Harold Roy *electrical engineering educator*
Raish, David Langdon *lawyer*
Ramsden, Linda Gisele *lawyer*
Rand, William Medden *biostatistics educator*
Ransil, Bernard J(erome) *research physician, methodologist, consultant, educator*
†Ratner, Steven A. *television broadcast executive*
Rawn, William Leete, III *architect*
Ray, William F. *banker*
Reardon, Frank Emond *lawyer*
Reid, Lynne McArthur *pathologist*
Reiling, Henry Bernard *business educator*
Reinherz, Helen Zarsky *social services educator*
Relman, Arnold Seymour *physician, educator, editor*
Remis, Shepard M. *lawyer*
Reppert, Steven Marion *scientist, educator, pediatrician*
Rhinesmith, Stephen Headley *international management consultant*
Riccelli, Richard Joseph *advertising agency executive*
Rice, William Phipps *investment counselor*
Richie, Jerome Paul *surgeon, educator*
Richmond, Alice Elenor *lawyer*
Righter, Anne Robinson *clinical social worker, psychotherapist*
Riley, Stephen Thomas *historian, librarian*
Rines, S. Melvin *investment banker*
Ritt, Roger Merrill *lawyer*
Rittner, Carl Frederick *educational administrator*
Rittner, Stephen Lee *academic administrator*
Rivlin, Rachel *lawyer*
Rizzo, William Ober *lawyer*
Robinson, William J. *health facility administrator*
Rockoff, Mark Alan *pediatric anesthesiologist*
Rogeness, Mary Speer *state legislator*
Rogers, Malcolm Austin *museum director, art historian*
Rohrer, Richard Jeffrey *surgeon, educator*
Ronayne, Michael Richard, Jr. *academic dean*
Rose, Alan Douglas *lawyer*
Rosen, Fred Saul *pediatrics educator*
Rosen, Stanley Howard *humanities educator*
Rosenberg, Manuel *retail company executive*
Rosenblatt, Michael *medical researcher, educator*
Rosensteel, John William *insurance company executive*
Rossell, Christine Hamilton *political science educator*
Rostow, Charles Nicholas *lawyer, educator*
Rotenberg, Sheldon *violinist*
Row, Peter Lyman *musician, educator*
Rush, David *medical investigator, epidemiologist*
Russell, Paul Snowden *surgeon, educator*
Rutstein, Stanley Harold *apparel retailing company executive*
Ryan, Kenneth John *physician, educator*
Ryser, Hugues Jean-Paul *pharmacologist, medical educator, cell biologist*
Saberhagen, Bret William *professional baseball player*
Sadeghi-Nejad, Abdollah *pediatrician, educator*
Safe, Kenneth Shaw, Jr. *fiduciary firm executive*
St. Clair, James Draper *lawyer*
Saleh, Bahaa E. A. *electrical engineering educator*
Sallan, Stephen E. *pediatrician*
Salzman, Edwin William *surgery educator*
Sanborn, George Freeman, Jr. *genealogist*
Sanders, Irwin Taylor *sociology educator*
Sandson, John I. *physician, educator, retired university dean*
†Santos, Gilbert Antonio (Gil Santos) *radio and television sportscaster*
Saparoff, Peter M. *lawyer*
Saper, Clifford Baird *neurobiology and neurology educator*
Sapers, Carl Martin *lawyer*
Sargeant, Ernest James *lawyer*
Sargent, David Jasper *university executive, lawyer*
Saris, Patti B. *federal judge*
Sastry, Kedarnath Nanjund *microbiologist, educator*
Saunders, Roger Alfred *hotel group executive*
Savrann, Richard Allen *lawyer*
Say, Allen *children's writer, illustrator*
Scanlon, Dorothy Therese *history educator*
Schaller, Jane Green *pediatrician*
Schlossman, Stuart Franklin *physician, educator, researcher*
Schmelzer, Henry Louis Phillip *lawyer, financial company executive*
Schneider, Robert Edward *insurance company executive, actuary*
Schnitzer, Iris Taymore *financial management executive, lawyer*
Schnitzer, Jan Eugeniusz *medical educator, scientist*
Schorr, Marvin G. *technology company executive*
Schrager, Mindy Rae *business professional*
Schram, Ronald Byard *lawyer*
Schram, Stephen C. *professional basketball team executive*
Schubel, Jerry Robert *marine science educator, scientist, university dean*
Schubert, Fred Eric *electrical engineer, educator*
Schulz, John Joseph *communications educator*
Schwartz, Bernard *physician*
Schwartz, Carl Robert Emden *psychiatrist and educator*
Schwartz, Lloyd *music critic, poet*
Scipione, Richard Stephen *insurance company executive, lawyer*
Scofield, John *jazz guitarist*
Scott, A. Hugh *lawyer*
Scott, James Arthur *radiologist, educator*
Scrimshaw, Nevin Stewart *physician, nutrition and health educator*
Seddon, Johanna Margaret *ophthalmologist, epidemiologist*
Seely, Ellen Wells *endocrinologist*
Segal, Robert Mandal *lawyer*
Selkoe, Dennis Jesse *neurologist, researcher, educator*
Shader, Richard Irwin *psychiatrist, educator*
Shafto, Robert Austin *insurance company executive*
Shapiro, Eli *business consultant, educator, economist*
Shapiro, Jerome Herbert *radiologist, educator*
Shapiro, Sandra *lawyer*
Sharp, William Leslie *performing arts educator*
Shattuck, Lawrence William *admissions director*
Sheehan, Monica Mary *banker*
Shemin, Barry L. *insurance company executive*
Shepard, Henry Bradbury, Jr. *lawyer*
Shepley, Hugh *architect*
Shields, Lawrence Thornton *orthopedic surgeon, educator*
Shklar, Gerald *oral pathologist, periodontist, educator*
Silber, John Robert *academic administrator*
Silberman, Robert A. S. *lawyer*
Silen, William *physician, surgery educator*
Silk, Alvin John *business educator*
Silvey, Anita Lynne *editor*
Simmons, Jean Elizabeth Margaret (Mrs. Glen R. Simmons) *chemistry educator*
Simmons, Sylvia Jeanne Quarles (Mrs. Herbert G. Simmons, Jr.) *university administrator, educator, senior manager*
Sinai, Allen Leo *economist, educator*
Sinden, Harry *professional hockey team executive*
Singer, Thomas Eric *industrial company executive*
Sirkin, Joel H. *lawyer*
Skelly, Thomas Francis *manufacturing company executive*
Skinger, Kenneth Robert *communications executive, engineer, lawyer*
Skinner, Walter Jay *federal judge*
Skinner, Wickham *business administration educator*
Sklar, Holly L(yn) *nonfiction writer*
Slechta, Robert Frank *biologist, educator*
Sledge, Clement Blount *orthopedic surgeon, educator*
Sloane, Carl Stuart *business educator, management consultant*
Slocumb, Heathcliff *professional baseball player*
Slosberg, Mike *advertising executive*
Smith, Anders Downey *financial services company executive*
Smith, Edwin Eric *lawyer*
Smith, Philip Jones *lawyer*
Smith, Thomas Woodward *cardiologist, educator*
Smyth, Peter Hayes *radio executive*
Snyder, John Gorvers *lawyer*
Snydman, David Richard *infectious diseases specialist, educator*
Sobin, Julian Melvin *international consultant*
Soden, Richard Allan *lawyer*
Solet, Maxwell David *lawyer*
Solomon, Arthur Kaskel *biophysics educator*
Solomon, Caren Grossbard *internist*
Sommerfeld, Nicholas Ulrich *lawyer*
Sonenshein, Abraham Lincoln *microbiology educator*
Sonnabend, Roger Philip *hotel company executive*
Sonnenschein, Adam *lawyer*
Southard, William G. *lawyer*
Spilhaus, Karl Henry *textiles executive, lawyer*
Sprague, Jo Ann *state legislator*
Stanley, H(arry) Eugene *physicist, educator*
Stanley, Robert Michael *professional baseball player*
Stare, Fredrick John *nutritionist, biochemist, physician*
Stearns, Richard Gaylore *judge*
Stebbins, Theodore Ellis, Jr. *museum curator*
Steere, Allen Caruthers, Jr. *physician, educator*
Stein, Marshall David *lawyer*
Steinberg, Laura *lawyer*
Steinhauer, Gillian *lawyer*
Stepanian, Ira *banking executive*
†Stern, Diane *broadcaster*
Stevens, Marilyn Ruth *editor*
Stevenson, Howard Higginbotham *business educator*
Stevenson, Philip Davis *lawyer*
Stobaugh, Robert Blair *business educator, business executive*
Stokes, James Christopher *lawyer*
Stollar, Bernard David *biochemist, educator*
Stone, Arthur Harold *mathematics educator*
Stone, David Barnes *investment advisor*
Stone, James J. *photographer*
Stoneman, Samuel Sidney *cinema company executive*
Storer, Jeffrey B. *lawyer*
Storer, Thomas Perry *lawyer*
Storey, James Moorfield *lawyer*
Storin, Matthew Victor *newspaper editor*
Strange, Donald Ernest *health care company executive*
Streeter, Henry Schofield *lawyer*
Streilein, J. Wayne *research scientist*
Strothman, Wendy Jo *book publisher*
Stull, Donald LeRoy *architect*
Sugarman, Paul Ronald *lawyer, educator, academic administrator*
Sullivan, James Leo *organization executive*
Sullivan, John Louis, Jr. *retired search company executive*
Surkin, Elliot Mark *lawyer*
Swain, Charles Hall *lawyer*
Swartz, Morton Norman *medical educator*
Swift, Humphrey Hathaway *manufacturing executive*
Swift, Jane Maria *former state senator*
Swope, Jeffrey Peyton *lawyer*
Sykes, Tracy Allan *lawyer*
Szep, Paul Michael *editorial cartoonist*
Tappé, Albert Anthony *architect*
Taqqu, Murad Salman *mathematics educator*
Tarlov, Alvin Richard *former philanthropic foundation administrator, physician, educator, researcher*
Tauber, Alfred Imre *hematologist, immunologist, philosopher of science*
Taubman, Martin Arnold *immunologist*
Tauro, Joseph Louis *federal judge*
Taveras, Juan Manuel *physician, educator*
Taylor, Benjamin B. *newspaper publishing executive*
Taylor, Edward Michael *insurance and risk management consultant*
Taylor, Stephen Emlyn *publishing executive*
Taylor, Thomas William *lawyer*
Taylor, William Osgood *newspaper executive*
Teich, Malvin Carl *electrical engineering educator*
Teixeira, Joseph *advertising executive*
Temkin, Robert Harvey *accountant*
Tempel, Jean Curtin *venture capitalist*
Terrill, Ross Gladwin *author, educator*
Testa, Richard Joseph *lawyer*
Theoharides, Theoharis Constantin *pharmacologist, physician, educator*
Thibeault, George Walter *lawyer*
Thibedeau, Richard Herbert *environmental planner, administrator*
Thorn, George Widmer *physician, educator*
Thorndike, John Lowell *investment executive*
Tilney, Nicholas Lechmere *surgery educator*
Toomey, Paula Kathleen *financial analyst, consultant*
Tosteson, Daniel Charles *physiologist, medical school dean*
Totenberg, Roman *violinist, music educator*
Trichopoulos, Dimitrios Vassilios *epidemiologist, educator*
Trier, Jerry Steven *gastroenterologist, educator*
Trimmier, Roscoe, Jr. *lawyer*
Tsuang, Ming Tso *psychiatrist, educator*
Tuchmann, Robert *lawyer*
Tucker, Louis Leonard *historical society administrator*
Tucker, Richard Lee *financial executive*
Turek, Sonia Fay *journalist*
Turillo, Michael Joseph, Jr. *management consultant*
Turner, Raymond Edward *science educator, researcher, administrator*
Upshur, Carole Christofk *psychologist, educator*
Utiger, Robert David *medical editor*
Uyterhoeven, Hugo Emil Robert *business educator and consultant*
Vachon, Louis *psychiatrist, educator*
Vaillant, George Eman *psychiatrist*
Valentin, John William *professional baseball player*
Van, Peter *lawyer*
Van Allsburg, Chris *author, artist*
Vance, Verne Widney, Jr. *lawyer*
Vanderslice, Thomas Aquinas *electronics executive*
Van Domelen, John Francis *academic administrator*
Vatter, Paul August *business administration educator, dean*
Vaughan, Herbert Wiley *lawyer*
Vaughn, Maurice Samuel (Mo Vaughn) *professional baseball player*
Vermeule, Cornelius Clarkson, III *museum curator*
Vermilye, Peter Hoagland *banker*
Vestner, Eliot N., Jr. *bank executive*
Vick, James Albert *publishing executive, consultant*
Villee, Claude Alvin, Jr. *biochemistry educator*
Vineburgh, James Hollander *banking executive*
Volk, Jan *professional sports team executive*
Volk, Kristin *advertising agency executive*
von Fettweis, Yvonne Caché *archivist, historian*
†Wahlberg, Mark *actor*
Walker, Gordon T. *lawyer*
Wallace, David Dunsmore *architect*
Wallraff, Barbara Jean *magazine editor, writer*
†Walls, Ron M. *emergency medicine physician, educator, health facility administrator*
Walrath, Patricia A. *state legislator*
Walton, Richard Eugene *business educator*
Warga, Jack *mathematician, educator*
Warren, Rosanna *poet*
Warshaw, Andrew Louis *surgeon, researcher*
Washburn, Bradford (Henry B. Washburn, Jr.) *museum administrator, cartographer, photographer*
Watts, Charles Henry, II *university administrator*
Webb, Alexander, III *investment company executive*
Weber, Georg Franz *immunologist*
Webster, Edward William *medical physicist*
Wechsler, Henry *research psychologist*
Weiner, Stephen Mark *lawyer*
Weinstein, David Carl *investment company executive, lawyer*
Weinstein, Milton Charles *health policy educator*
Weiss, Earle Burton *physician*
Weiss, James Michael *financial analyst, portfolio manager*
Weitzel, John Patterson *lawyer*
Weitzman, Arthur Joshua *English educator*
Weld, William Floyd *governor, lawyer*
Wellington, Carol Strong *law librarian*
Weltman, David Lee *lawyer*
Wendorf, Richard Harold *library director, educator*
Wentworth, Michael Justin *curator*
Wermuth, Paul Charles *retired English educator*
Westling, Jon *university administrator*
Wheatland, Richard, II *fiduciary services executive, museum executive*
Wheeler, W(illiam) Scott *composer, conductor, music educator*
White, Barry Bennett *lawyer*
White, George Edward *pedodontist, educator*
Whitlock, John L. *lawyer*
Whitters, James Payton, III *lawyer, university administrator*
Whitworth, William A. *magazine editor*
Wiesel, Elie *writer, educator*
†Wiesner, David *illustrator, children's writer*
Wilkes, Brent Ames *management consultant*
Wilkins, Herbert Putnam *judge*
Willens, Alan Rush *management consultant*
Williams, Charles Marvin *commercial banking educator*
Williams, Gordon Harold *internist, medical educator, researcher*
Williams, John Taylor *lawyer*
Williams, Rhys *minister*
Williams, Robert Dana *lawyer*
Wilson, Robert Gould *management consultant*
Wind, Herbert Warren *writer*
Winkelman, James Warren *hospital administrator, pathology educator*
Winter, Donald Francis *lawyer*
Wirth, Dyann Fergus *public health educator, microbiologist*
Wiseman, James Richard *classicist, archaeologist, educator*
†Woerner, Frederick Frank *international relations educator*
Wolf, David *lawyer*
Wolf, Gary Herbert *architect*
Wolf, Mark Lawrence *federal judge*
Wood, Henry Austin *architect*
Wood, Lawrence Crane *medical association administrator, educator*
Woodburn, Ralph Robert, Jr. *lawyer*
Woodlock, Douglas Preston *judge*
Woog, John J. *eye plastic surgeon*
Woolsey, John Munro, Jr. *lawyer*
Worthley, Harold Field *minister, educator*
Wright, Walter Augustine, III *business and corporate lawyer*
Wu, Tung *curator, art historian, art educator, artist*
Yanoff, Arthur Samuel *artist, art therapist*
Yastrzemski, Carl Michael *former baseball player, public relations executive*
Yemma, John *newspaper editor*
Young, David William *accounting educator*
Young, Laura *dance educator, choreographer*
Young, Raymond Henry *lawyer*
Young, William Glover *federal judge*

Yuan, Junying *medical educator, researcher*
Yurko, Richard John *lawyer*
Zack, Arnold Marshall *lawyer, mediator, arbitrator*
Zaldastani, Guivy *business consultant*
Zaldastani, Othar *consulting engineer*
Zaleznik, Abraham *psychoanalyst, management specialist, educator*
Zannieri, Nina *museum director*
Zarins, Bertram *orthopaedic surgeon*
Zeien, Alfred M. *consumer products company executive*
Zelen, Marvin *statistics educator*
Zellman, Ande *editor*
Zervas, Nicholas Themistocles *neurosurgeon*
Zimmerman, George Ogurek *physicist, educator*
Zinner, Michael Jeffrey *surgeon, educator*
Zobel, Hiller Bellin *judge*
Zupcofska, Peter F. *lawyer*

### Boston College
Helmick, Raymond G. *priest, educator*

### Bourne
Roper, Burns Worthington *retired opinion research company executive*

### Boxboro
Lee, Shih-Ying *mechanical engineering educator*

### Boxford
Schubert, Glendon *political scientist, educator*
Siegert, Barbara (Marie) *health care administrator*

### Braintree
Conlon, Eugene *artist, administrator*
Davis, Robert Jocelyn *engineering executive*
Fantozzi, Peggy Ryone *environmental planner*
Foster, Arthur Rowe *mechanical engineering educator*
Gittleman, Sol *university official, humanities educator*
Harris, Jeffrey Sherman *direct marketing company executive*
Lane, Barbara Ann *environmental company official, systems analyst*
Latham, Allen, Jr. *manufacturing company consultant*
Segersten, Robert Hagy *lawyer, investment banker*

### Brewster
Coburn, John Bowen *retired bishop*
Fowle, Arthur Adams *mechanical engineer*
Gumpright, Herbert Lawrence, Jr. *dentist*

### Bridgewater
Barry, Marilyn White *dean, educator*
Cost, Richard Willard *university administrator, educator*
Farrar, Ruth Doris *reading and literacy educator*
Fitzpatrick, Ruth Ann *education educator*
Tinsley, Adrian *college president*
Troupe, Bonnie Lee *college program coordinator, teacher*

### Brighton
Law, Bernard Francis Cardinal *archbishop*
Megherbi, Dalila *electrical and computer engineer, researcher*

### Brockton
Carlson, Desiree Anice *pathologist*
Clark, Carleton Earl *tax consultant*
Droukas, Ann Hantis *management executive*
Hodge-Spencer, Cheryl Ann *orthodontist*
Holland, David Vernon *minister*
†Kligler, Roger Michael *physician*
Wiegner, Allen Walter *biomedical engineering educator, researcher*

### Brookfield
Couture, Ronald David *art administrator, design consultant*
Kring, Walter Donald *minister*

### Brookline
Alvino, Gloria *charitable organization administrator, speaker*
Barron, Ros *artist*
Blom, Gaston Eugene *psychiatrist*
Buchin, Jacqueline Chase *clinical psychologist*
Burnstein, Daniel *lawyer*
Cromwell, Adelaide M. *sociology educator*
Epstein, Alvin *actor, director, singer, mime*
Finkelstein, Norman Henry *librarian*
Frankel, Ernst Gabriel *shipping and aviation business executive, educator*
Gewirtz, Mindy L. *organizational and human relations consultant*
Jakab, Irene *psychiatrist*
Jordan, Ruth Ann *physician*
Katz, Israel *retired engineering educator*
Kibrick, Anne *nursing educator, university dean*
Kraut, Joel Arthur *ophthalmologist*
Lown, Bernard *cardiologist, educator*
Lynton, Ernest Albert *physicist, educator, former university official*
Mc Cormick, Thomas Julian *art history educator*
Nadelson, Carol Cooperman *psychiatrist, educator*
Nayor, Charles Francis *lawyer*
Newman, Thomas Daniel *minister, school administrator*
Perry, Frederick Sayward, Jr. *electronics company executive*
Rachlin, William Selig *surgeon*
Saini, Gulshan Rai *soil physicist, agricultural hydrologist*
Sarfaty, Suzanne *internist and educator*
Schiller, Sophie *artist, graphic designer*
Shaw, Samuel Ervine, II *retired insurance company executive, consultant*
Spellman, Mitchell Wright *surgeon, academic administrator*
Swan, Barbara *artist*
Sweet, William Herbert *neurosurgeon*
Tuchman, Avraham *physicist, researcher*
Tuchman, Maurice Simon *library director*
Tyler, H. Richard *physician*
Vallee, Bert Lester *biochemist, physician, educator*
Walter, Helen Joy *executive director, teacher*
Wax, Bernard *research and development consultant, lecturer*
Weinstein, Rhonda Kruger *elementary mathematics educator, administrator*
Wertsman, Vladimir Filip *librarian, information specialist, author, translator*
West, Doe *bioethicist, social justice activist*
Wilson, John *artist*

### Brookline Village
Zoll, Miriam Hannah *activist, writer, communication specialist*

### Burlington
Africk, Steven Allen *physicist*
Anaebonam, Aloysius Onyeabo *pharmacist*
Bright, Willard Mead *manufacturing company executive*
Clerkin, Eugene Patrick *physician*
DeCrosta, Susan Elyse *graphic designer*
Dubois, Cindy A. *guidance counselor*
Fager, Charles Anthony *physician, neurosurgeon*
Hall, John Reginald, II *electronics company executive, retired army officer*
Harding, Wayne Michael *sociologist, researcher*
McAlpine, Frederick Sennett *anesthesiologist*
Moschella, Samuel L. *dermatology educator*
Pettinella, Nicholas Anthony *financial executive*
Reno, John F. *communications equipment company executive*
Schoetz, David John, Jr. *colon and rectal surgeon*
Scogno, Stacie Joy *financial services company executive*
Shaikh, Naimuddin *medical physicist*
Skene, G(eorge) Neil *publisher, lawyer*
Wise, Robert Edward *radiologist*

### Byfield
Bragdon, Peter Wilkinson *headmaster*
Kozol, Jonathan *writer*

### Cambridge
Abelson, Harold *electrical engineer, educator*
Abernathy, Frederick Henry *mechanical engineering educator*
Abt, Clark C. *social scientist, executive, engineer, publisher, educator*
Ackerman, James Sloss *fine arts educator*
Akylas, Triantaphyllos R. *mechanical engineering educator*
Alberty, Robert Arnold *chemistry educator*
Alcalay, Albert S. *artist, design educator*
Alevizos, Susan Bamberger *lawyer, santouri player, author*
Alevizos, Theodore G. *lawyer, singer, author*
Alfred, William *author, educator*
Alt, James Edward *political science educator*
†Alters, Brian Josiah *science educator*
†Altshuler, David T. *software company executive*
†Ancona, Henry *camera equipment company executive*
Anderson, Donald Gordon Marcus *mathematics educator*
Anderson, James Gilbert *chemistry educator*
Anderson, Stanford Owen *architect, architectural historian, educator*
Anderson, William Henry *psychobiologist, educator*
Andrews, William Dorey *lawyer, educator*
Appiah, Kwame Anthony *philosophy educator*
Appley, Mortimer Herbert *psychologist, university president emeritus*
Argon, Ali Suphi *mechanical engineering educator*
Arnesen, Deborah Arnie *educator*
Aronson, Michael Andrew *editor*
Ashton, Peter Shaw *tropical forest science educator*
Aspinall, Mara Glickman *marketing and general management professional*
Athans, Michael *electrical engineering educator, consultant*
Babson, David Leveau *retired investment counsel*
Badian, Ernst *history educator*
Baggeroer, Arthur B. *electrical engineering educator*
Bailyn, Bernard *historian, educator*
Bailyn, Lotte *psychology and management educator*
Bakanowsky, Louis Joseph *visual arts educator, architect, artist*
Baltimore, David *microbiologist, educator*
Bane, Mary Jo *federal agency administrator*
Bapst, Sarah *artist, educator*
Barger, James Edwin *physicist*
Barnet, Sylvan *English literature educator*
Baron, Judson Richard *aerospace educator*
Baron, Sheldon *research and development company executive*
Bartee, Thomas Creson *computer scientist, educator*
Bartholet, Elizabeth *law educator*
Bartus, Raymond Thomas *neuroscientist, pharmaceutical executive, writer*
Bate, Walter Jackson *English literature educator*
Bator, Francis Michel *economist, educator*
Battin, Richard Horace *astronautical engineer*
Bazzaz, Fakhri A. *plant biology educator, administrator*
Bedrosian, Edward Robert *investment management company executive*
Beér, János Miklós *engineering educator*
Ben-Akiva, Moshe Emanuel *civil engineering educator*
Beranek, Leo Leroy *acoustical consultant*
Berg, Howard C. *biology educator*
Berger, Harvey James *pharmaceutical company executive, physician, educator*
Berliner, Joseph Scholom *economics educator*
Bernays, Anne Fleischman *writer, educator*
Berndt, Ernst Rudolf *economist, educator*
Berwick, Robert Cregar *computer science educator*
Biemann, Klaus *chemistry educator*
Birgeneau, Robert Joseph *physicist, educator*
Bishop, Robert Lyle *economist, educator*
Bizzi, Emilio *neurophysiologist, educator*
Blackmer, Donald Laurence Morton *political scientist*
Bloch, Konrad Emil *biochemist*
Bloembergen, Nicolaas *physicist, educator*
Bloom, Kathryn Ruth *public relations executive*
Bloomfield, Lincoln Palmer *political scientist*
Bluestone, Hugh Lawrence *architect*
Boghani, Ashok Balvantrai *consulting firm executive*
Bogorad, Lawrence *biologist, educator*
Bok, Derek *law educator, former university president*
Bolnick, Bruce Robert *economist, professor*
Bolster, Arthur Stanley, Jr. *history educator*
Bond, William Henry *librarian, educator*
Borjas, George J(esus) *economics educator*
Bott, Raoul *mathematician, educator*
Boyden, W(alter) Lincoln *lawyer*
Boyle, Edward Allen *oceanography educator*
Bradt, Hale Van Dorn *physicist, x-ray astronomer, educator*
Branscomb, Anne Wells *communications consultant*
Branscomb, Lewis McAdory *physicist*
Bras, Rafael Luis *engineering educator*
Brown, Edgar Cary *retired economics educator*
Brown, Robert Arthur *chemical engineering educator*
Brown, Roger William *psychologist, educator*
Bruce, James Donald *academic administrator*
Bruck, Ferdinand Frederick *architect*
Bruck, Phoebe Ann Mason *landscape architect*
Brusch, John Lynch *physician*
Brustein, Robert Sanford *English language educator, theatre director, author*
Buchanan, John Robert *physician, educator*
Buchwald, Jed Zachary *environmental health researcher, science history educator*
Buckler, Sheldon A. *energy company executive*
Budiansky, Bernard *engineering educator*
Bullock, Francis Jeremiah *pharmaceutical research executive*
Burchfiel, Burrell Clark *geology educator*
Burke, Bernard Flood *physicist, educator*
Burlage, Dorothy Dawson *clinical psychologist*
Burnham, Charles Wilson *mineralogy educator*
Burns, Carol J. *architect, educator*
Butler, James Newton *chemist, educator*
Cameron, Alastair Graham Walter *astrophysicist, educator*
Campbell, Robert *architect, writer*
Canizares, Claude Roger *astrophysicist, educator*
Carmichael, Alexander Douglas *engineering educator*
Carrier, George Francis *applied mathematics educator*
Carter, Ashton Baldwin *physicist, educator, government agency executive*
Chall, Jeanne Sternlicht *psychologist, educator*
Champion, (Charles) Hale *political science educator, former public official*
Chapin, Richard *arbitrator, consultant*
Chayes, Abram *law educator, lawyer*
Cheatham, Thomas Edward, Jr. *computer scientist, educator*
†Chen, Martha Alter *international development, gender and poverty specialist*
Chen, Sow-Hsin *nuclear engineering educator, researcher*
Chernoff, Herman *statistics educator*
Chomsky, Avram Noam *linguistics and philosophy educator*
Chvany, Catherine Vakar *foreign language educator*
Clausen, Wendell Vernon *classics educator*
Cleary, David Michael *composer, library assistant*
Clendenning, Bonnie Ryon *college administrator*
†Clifton, Anne Rutenber *psychotherapist*
Cohen, Morris *engineering educator*
Cohen, Robert Edward *chemical engineering educator, consultant*
Cohn, Marjorie Benedict *curator, art historian, educator*
Colby, Anne *psychologist*
Cole, Heather Ellen *librarian*
Coleman, Sidney Richard *physicist, educator*
Coles, Robert *child psychiatrist, educator, author*
Collins, Allan Meakin *cognitive scientist, psychologist, educator*
Collins, John William, III *librarian*
†Collins, Susan Margaret *economics educator*
Colton, Clark Kenneth *chemical engineering educator*
Conley, Tom Clark *literature educator*
Conrades, George Henry *information systems company executive*
Cook, Robert Edward *plant ecology educator, research director*
†Cooney, James Allen *international educator*
Cooper, Richard Newell *economist, educator*
Corbato, Fernando Jose *electrical engineer and computer science educator*
Corey, Elias James *chemistry educator*
Coser, Lewis Alfred *sociology educator*
Counselman, Charles Claude, III *electrical engineering educator*
Covert, Eugene Edzards *aerophysics educator*
Cox, Archibald *lawyer, educator*
Crandall, Stephen Harry *engineering educator*
Crawley, Edward Francis *aerospace engineering educator*
Cross, Frank Moore, Jr. *foreign language educator*
Cummings-Saxton, James *chemical engineer, consultant, educator*
Cuno, James *art museum director*
Cushing, Steven *linguist, educator, researcher, consultant*
Dalgarno, Alexander *astronomy educator*
Danheiser, Rick Lane *organic chemistry educator*
Davidson, Charles Sprecher *physician*
Davidson, Frank Paul *macroengineer, lawyer*
Davie, Joseph Myrten *physician, pathology and immunology educator, science administrator*
Davis, Edgar Glenn *science and health policy executive*
Davis, James Spencer *temporary service executive*
Della-Terza, Dante Michele *comparative literature educator*
Demain, Arnold Lester *microbiologist, educator*
de Marneffe, Barbara Rowe *volunteer*
de Neufville, Richard Lawrence *engineering educator*
Dennis, Jack Bonnell *computer consultant*
Dershowitz, Alan Morton *lawyer, educator*
Desai, Anita *writer*
Deshpandé, Rohit *marketing educator*
Deutch, John Mark *federal agency administrator, chemist, academic administrator*
de Varon, Lorna Cooke *choral conductor*
Dewart, Christopher *architectural educator, furniture maker*
Dewey, Clarence Forbes, Jr. *engineering educator*
DiCamillo, Gary Thomas *manufacturing executive*
Dickson, William Robert *academic administrator*
Dominguez, Jorge Ignacio *government educator*
Donahue, John David *public official, educator*
Donnelly, Thomas William *physicist*
Dorfman, Robert *economics educator*
Dornbusch, Rudiger *economics educator*
†Dorwart, Robert Alan *psychiatrist*
Dowling, John Elliott *biology educator*
Drago-Severson, Eleanor Elizabeth *developmental psychologist, educator, researcher*
Drake, Elisabeth Mertz *chemical engineer*
Dresselhaus, Mildred Spiewak *physics and engineering educator*
Driscoll, Kimberlee Marie *lawyer*
Dubowsky, Steven *mechanical engineering educator*
Dudley, Richard Mansfield *mathematician, educator*
Duffy, Robert Aloysius *aeronautical engineer*
Dugundji, John *aeronautical engineer*
Dunlop, John Thomas *economics educator, former secretary of labor*
Dunn, Charles William *Celtic languages and literature educator, author*
Dunn, Mary Maples *library director*
Dupree, Anderson Hunter *historian, educator*
Durant, Graham John *medicinal chemist, drug researcher*
Dyck, Arthur James *ethicist, educator*
Dyck, Martin *literary theorist, mathematics historian*
Eagar, Thomas Waddy *metallurgist, educator*
Eagleson, Peter Sturges *hydrologist, educator*
Eckaus, Richard Samuel *economist, educator*
Edgerly, William Skelton *banker*
Edsall, John Tileston *biological chemistry educator*
Ehrenreich, Henry *physicist, educator*
Eisen, Herman Nathaniel *immunology researcher, medical educator*
Eisenberg, Carola *psychiatry educator*
Eldridge, Larry (William Lawrence Eldridge) *journalist*
Elias, Peter *electrical engineering educator*
†Elkies, Noam D. *mathematics educator*
Ellwood, David T. *public policy educator, university administrator*
Emanuel, Kerry Andrew *earth sciences educator*
Emerson, Anne Devereux *university administrator*
Emmons, Howard Wilson *engineer, educator, consultant, researcher*
Engell, James Theodore *English educator*
Epstein, David Mayer *composer, conductor, educator*
Epstein, Henry David *electronics company executive*
Erdely, Stephen Lajos *music educator*
Estes, William Kaye *psychologist, educator*
Eurich, Nell P. *educator, author*
Fagans, Karl Preston *real estate facilities administration executive*
Fallon, Richard H., Jr. *law educator*
Fanger, Donald Lee *Slavic language and literature educator*
Fano, Robert Mario *electrical engineering educator*
Fay, James Alan *mechanical engineering educator*
Feininger, Theodore Lux *artist*
Feld, Michael Stephen *physics educator*
Feldman, Gary Jay *physicist, educator*
Feldstein, Martin Stuart *economist, educator*
Feshbach, Herman *physicist, educator*
Field, Robert Warren *chemistry educator*
Fiorenza, Francis P. *religion educator*
Fischer, Kurt Walter *education educator*
Fisher, Franklin Marvin *economist*
Fisher, Philip J. *English language and literature educator*
Fisher, Roger Dummer *lawyer, educator, negotiation expert*
Flannery, Susan Marie *library administrator*
Fleming, Donald Harnish *historian, educator*
Flemings, Merton Corson *engineering educator, materials scientist*
Flier, Michael Stephen *Slavic languages educator*
Foley, James David *computer science educator, consultant*
Foner, Simon *research physicist*
Ford, Franklin Lewis *history educator, historian*
Ford, Patrick Kildea *Celtic studies educator*
Forman, Richard T. T. *ecology educator*
Forrester, Jay Wright *management specialist, educator*
Fortmann, Thomas Edward *research and development company executive*
†Fountain, Jane Ellen *public policy educator*
Fox, Ellen *academic administrator*
Fox, John Bayley, Jr. *university dean*
Fox, Maurice Sanford *molecular biologist, educator*
French, Anthony Philip *physicist, educator*
Frenkel, Edward Vladimir *mathematician, educator*
Frey, Frederick August *geochemistry researcher, educator*
Friedman, Benjamin Morton *economics educator*
Friedman, Orrie Max *biotechnology company executive*
Frisch, Rose Epstein *population sciences researcher*
Frug, Gerald E. *law educator*
Frye, Richard Nelson *historian, educator*
Fujimoto, James G. *electrical engineering educator*
Furlong, Charles Richard *broadcasting executive*
Furman, Thomas D., Jr. *engineering company executive*
Gage, (Leonard) Patrick *research company executive*
Gagliardi, Ugo Oscar *systems software architect, educator*
Galizzi, Monica *economics researcher*
Gallager, Robert Gray *electrical engineering educator*
Gardner, Howard Earl *psychologist, author*
Garland, Carl Wesley *chemist, educator*
Gaskell, Ivan George Alexander De Wend *art museum curator*
Gates, Henry Louis, Jr. *English language educator*
Gatos, Harry Constantine *engineering educator*
Gaulin, Kenneth *writer, designer*
Geller, Margaret Joan *astrophysicist, educator*
Georgi, Howard *physics educator*
Gerrish, Catherine Ruggles *food company executive*
Gerrish, Hollis G. *confectionery company executive*
Gienapp, William Eugene *history educator*
Gilbert, Walter *molecular biologist, educator*
†Gilligan, Carol F. *psychologist, writer*
Gingerich, Owen Jay *astronomer, educator*
Glaser, Peter Edward *mechanical engineer, consultant*
Glauber, Roy Jay *theoretical physics educator*
Glauner, Alfred William *lawyer, engineering company executive*
Gleason, Andrew Mattei *mathematician, educator*
Glendon, Mary Ann *law educator*
Golay, Michael Warren *nuclear engineering educator*
Goldberg, Ray Allan *agribusiness educator*
Goldblith, Samuel Abraham *food science educator*
Goldfarb, Warren (David) *philosophy educator*
Goldin, Claudia Dale *economics educator*
Goldman, Ralph Frederick *research physiologist, educator*
Goldstone, Jeffrey *physicist*
Gomes, Peter John *clergyman, educator*
Gonson, S. Donald *lawyer*
Goodwin, Neva R. *economist*
Gordon, Roy Gerald *chemistry educator*
Gould, Stephen Jay *paleontologist, educator*
Graham, Loren Raymond *historian, educator*
Graham, William Albert *religion educator, history educator*
Graubard, Stephen Richards *history educator, editor*
Gray, Paul Edward *academic official*
Green, Richard John *architect*
Greene, Frederick D., II *chemistry educator*
Greeno, J(ohn) Ladd *consulting company executive*
Greenspan, Harvey Philip *applied mathematician, educator*
Greitzer, Edward Marc *aeronautical engineering educator, consultant*

Griffith, Peter *mechanical engineering educator, researcher*
Griliches, Zvi *economist, educator*
Grindlay, Jonathan Ellis *astrophysics educator*
Grosz, Barbara Jean *computer science educator*
Grove, Timothy Lynn *geology educator*
Guerra, John Michael *optical engineer*
Guthke, Karl Siegfried *foreign language educator*
Gyftopoulos, Elias Panayiotis *mechanical and nuclear engineering educator*
Gyger, Terrell Lee *minister*
Hadzi, Dimitri *sculptor, educator*
Halle, Morris *linguist, educator*
Halperin, Bertrand Israel *physics educator*
Hamilton, Malcolm Cowan *librarian, editor, indexer, personnel professional*
Hamner, W. Easley *architect*
Hanan, Patrick Dewes *foreign language professional, educator*
Handlin, Oscar *historian, educator*
Hansen, Kent Forrest *nuclear engineering educator*
Hansman, Robert John, Jr. *aeronautics and astronautics educator*
Harbison, John *composer*
Harleman, Donald Robert Fergusson *environmental engineering educator*
Harris, Wesley L. *aeronautics engineering educator*
Harris, William Wolpert *treasurer political action committee*
Hart, Oliver D'Arcy *economics educator*
Hartl, Daniel Lee *genetics educator*
Hass, Michael Shepherdson *architect*
Hastings, John Woodland *biologist, educator*
Haus, Hermann Anton *electrical engineering educator*
Hauser, John Richard *marketing and management science educator*
Hausman, Jerry Allen *economics educator, consultant*
Hausman, Leonard J. *university official, educator*
Havens, Leston Laycock *psychiatrist, educator*
Hax, Arnoldo Cubillos *management educator, industrial engineer*
Heaney, Seamus Justin *poet, educator*
Heimert, Alan Edward *humanities educator*
Helgason, Sigurdur *mathematician, educator*
Heney, Joseph Edward *environmental engineer*
Henninger, Polly *neuropsychologist, researcher and clinician*
Henrichs, Albert Maximinus *classicist, educator*
Herschbach, Dudley Robert *chemistry educator*
Heywood, John Benjamin *mechanical engineering educator*
Ho, Yu-Chi *electrical engineering educator*
Hodges, Kip Vernon *geologist, educator*
Hoffman, Paul Felix *geologist, educator*
†Hogan, William Walter *public policy educator, administrator, consultant*
Holbik, Karel *economics educator*
Holton, Gerald *physicist, science historian*
Holzman, Philip Seidman *psychologist, educator*
Homburger, Freddy *physician, scientist, artist*
Horowitz, Morris A. *economist*
Horrell, Jeffrey Lanier *library administrator*
Horvitz, Howard Robert *biology educator, researcher*
Horwitz, Paul *physicist*
Houtchens, Robert Austin, Jr. *biochemist*
Howard, Jack Benny *chemical engineer, educator, researcher*
Howard, Susanne C. *lawyer*
†Howitt, Arnold Martin *university researcher, administrator, educator*
Hsiao, William C. *economist, actuary, educator*
Huang, Kerson *physics educator*
Hubbard, Ruth *biology educator*
Huchra, John Peter *astronomer, educator*
Huntington, Samuel Phillips *political science educator*
Huppe, Alex *public relations executive*
Hynes, Richard Olding *biology researcher and educator*
Iriye, Akira *historian, educator*
Irwin, William Edward, III *health physicist*
Jackiw, Roman *physicist, educator*
Jackson, Francis Joseph *research and development company executive*
Jacobson, Ralph Henry *laboratory executive, former air force officer*
Jacoby, Henry Donnan *economist, educator*
Jencks, Christopher Sandys *public policy educator*
Jensen, Klavs Flemming *chemical engineering educator*
John, Richard Rodda *transportation executive*
Johnson, Howard Wesley *former university president, business executive*
Johnson, Michael Lewis *psychiatrist*
Johnson, Willard Raymond *political science educator, consultant*
Jones, Christopher Prestige *classicist, historian, educator, consultant*
Jordan, Thomas Hillman *geophysicist, educator*
Jorgenson, Dale Weldeau *economist, educator*
Joskow, Paul Lewis *economist, educator*
Joss, Paul Christopher *astrophysicist, atmospheric physicist, educator*
Kac, Victor G. *mathematician, educator*
Kagan, Jerome *psychologist, educator*
†Kahin, Brian *lawyer, computer industry professional, consultant*
†Kalb, Marvin *public policy and government educator*
Kalelkar, Ashok Satish *consulting company executive*
Kamentsky, Louis Aaron *biophysicist*
Kamm, Roger Dale *biomedical engineer, educator*
Kaplan, Benjamin *judge*
Kaplan, Justin *author*
Kaplow, Louis *law educator*
Kassakian, John Gabriel *research electrical engineer, engineering director*
Kassman, Herbert Seymour *lawyer, management consultant*
Kaufman, Andrew Lee *law educator*
Kaufman, Gordon Dester *theology educator*
Kaysen, Carl *economics educator*
Kazimi, Mujid Suliman *nuclear engineer, educator*
Keck, James Collyer *physicist, educator*
Keenan, Edward Louis *history educator*
Kelley, Albert Joseph *global management strategy consultant*
Kendall, Henry Way *physicist*
Keniston, Kenneth *psychologist, educator*
Kennedy, David W. *law educator*
Kennedy, Stephen Dandridge *economist, researcher*
Kerman, Arthur Kent *physicist, educator*
Kerpelman, Larry Cyril *consulting firm executive*
Kerrebrock, Jack Leo *aeronautics and astronautics engineering educator*
Keyfitz, Nathan *sociologist, demographer, educator*
Keyser, Samuel Jay *linguistics educator, university official*
Khorana, Har Gobind *chemist, educator*
Khoury, Philip S. *social sciences educator, historian*
Kilson, Martin Luther, Jr. *government educator*
Kim, Peter Sungbai *biochemistry educator*
King, Ronold Wyeth Percival *physics educator*
Kirby, Kate Page *physicist*
Kistiakowsky, Vera *physics researcher, educator*
Klemperer, William *chemistry educator*
Klibanov, Alexander Maxim *chemistry educator*
Knickrehm, Glenn Allen *management executive*
Knoll, Andrew Herbert *biology educator*
Knowles, Jeremy Randall *chemist, educator*
Kobus, Richard Lawrence *architect, designer, executive*
Koester, Helmut Heinrich *theologian, educator*
Kong, Jin Au *electrical engineering educator*
Kosslyn, Stephen M. *psychologist educator*
Kovach, Bill *educational foundation administrator*
Krieger, Alex *architecture and design educator*
Kruger, Kenneth *architect*
Kung, H. T. *computer science and engineering educator, consultant*
Kuttner, Robert Louis *editor, columnist*
Kyhl, Robert Louis *electrical engineering educator*
Ladd, Charles Cushing, III *civil engineering educator*
Ladjevardi, Habib *historian*
Laibinis, Paul Edward *chemical engineering educator*
Lala, Jaynarayan Hotchand *computer engineer*
LaMantia, Charles Robert *management consulting company executive*
Lamberg-Karlovsky, Clifford Charles *anthropologist, archaeologist*
Lamport, Felicia (Mrs. Benjamin Kaplan) *writer*
Landry, John Marsdale *university fundraiser, consultant*
Langer, Ellen Jane *psychologist, educator, writer*
Langer, Robert Samuel *chemical, biomedical engineering educator*
Langstaff, John Meredith *musician*
Latanision, Ronald Michael *materials science and engineering educator, consultant*
Layton, Billy Jim *composer*
Lazarus, Maurice *retired retail executive*
Leehey, Patrick *mechanical and ocean engineering educator*
Lehner, Mark *archaeologist, educator*
Leonard, Herman Beukema (Dutch Leonard) *public finance and management educator*
Lerman, Leonard Solomon *science educator, scientist*
Levi, Herbert Walter *biologist, educator*
Levins, Richard *science educator*
Levy, Stephen Raymond *high technology company executive*
Lieberson, Stanley *sociologist, educator*
Light, Richard Jay *statistician, education educator*
Lightman, Alan Paige *physicist, writer, educator*
Lim, Jae Soo *engineering educator, information systems*
Lindzen, Richard Siegmund *meteorologist, educator*
Lippard, Stephen James *chemist, educator*
Lipscomb, William Nunn, Jr. *retired physical chemistry educator*
Litster, James David *physics educator, dean*
Little, John Dutton Conant *management scientist, educator*
Littlefield, Paul Damon *management consultant*
Liu, Guosong *neurobiologist*
Livingston, James Duane *physicist, educator*
Lodish, Harvey Franklin *biologist, educator*
Loew, Franklin Martin *medical and biological scientist, business entrepreneur*
Lomon, Earle Leonard *physicist, educator, consultant*
London, Irving Myer *physician, educator*
Longwell, John Ploeger *chemical engineering educator*
Loss, Louis *lawyer, retired educator*
Low, Francis Eugene *physics educator*
Lunt, Horace Gray *linguist, educator*
Luu, Jane *astronomer*
Lynch, Harry James *biologist*
Lynch, Nancy Ann *computer scientist, educator*
Lyon, Richard Harold *physicist educator,*
Maass, Arthur *political science and environmental studies educator*
Mack, Robert Whiting *computer consultant*
MacMaster, Robert Ellsworth *historian, educator*
Magee, John Francis *research company executive*
Maher, Brendan Arnold *psychology educator, editor*
Mahoney, Thomas Henry Donald *historian, educator, government official*
Maier, Charles Steven *history educator*
Maier, Pauline *history educator*
Makhoul, John Ibrahim *electrical engineer, researcher*
Malme, Jane Hamlett *lawyer, educator, researcher*
Malmstad, John Earl *Slavic languages and literatures, educator*
Mann, Robert Wellesley *biomedical engineer, educator*
†Mansbridge, Jane Jebb *political scientist, educator*
Mansfield, John H. *lawyer, educator*
Marini, Robert Charles *environmental engineering executive*
Markey, Winston Roscoe *aeronautical engineering educator*
Marolda, Anthony Joseph *management consulting company executive*
Marsden, Brian Geoffrey *astronomer*
Martin, Paul Cecil *physicist, educator*
Martin, Roger Lloyd *management consultant*
Martino, Donald James *composer, educator*
Marvin, Ursula Bailey *geologist*
Masubuchi, Koichi *marine engineer, educator*
Mathews, Joan Helene *pediatrician*
May, Ernest Richard *historian, educator*
Mayr, Ernst *retired zoologist, philosopher*
Mazlish, Bruce *historian, educator*
Mazur, Eric *physicist, educator*
Mazur, Michael *artist*
McCormick, Michael *history educator*
McCue, Gerald Mallon *architect*
Mc Cune, William James, Jr. *manufacturing company executive*
McGarry, Frederick Jerome *civil engineering educator*
McKenna, Margaret Anne *college president*
Mc Kie, Todd Stoddard *artist*
McMahon, Thomas Arthur *biology and applied mechanics educator*
Meltzer, Daniel J. *law educator*
Meselson, Matthew Stanley *biochemist, educator*
Meyer, John Edward *nuclear engineering educator*
Meyer, John Robert *economist, educator*
Meyers, Harold Vernon *chemist*
Michelman, Frank I. *lawyer, educator*
Milgram, Jerome H. *marine and ocean engineer, educator*
Miller, Arthur Raphael *legal educator*
Miller, Rene Harcourt *aerospace engineer, educator*
Mitchell, William J. *dean, architecture educator*
Mitten, David Gordon *classical archaeologist*
Mitter, Sanjoy K. *electrical engineering educator*
Mnookin, Robert Harris *lawyer, educator*
Molina, Mario Jose *physical chemist, educator*
Moneo, José Rafael *architecture educator*
Moniz, Ernest Jeffrey *physics educator*
Montgomery, John Dickey *political science educator*
Moore, Mark Harrison *criminal justice and public policy educator*
Moran, James Michael, Jr. *astronomer*
Moses, Joel *computer scientist, educator*
Mosteller, Frederick *mathematical statistician, educator*
Mowry, Robert Dean *art museum curator, educator*
Mueller, Robert Kirk *management consulting company executive*
Narayan, Ramesh *astronomy educator*
Negele, John William *physics educator, consultant*
Nelson, Keith Adam *chemistry educator*
Neustadt, Richard Elliott *political scientist, educator*
Newell, Reginald Edward *physics educator*
Newman, John Nicholas *naval architect educator*
Nichols, Albert L. *economics consultant*
Nordell, Hans Roderick *journalist, retired editor*
Nozick, Robert *philosophy educator, author*
†Nye, Joseph S(amuel), Jr. *government studies educator, administrator*
Nykrog, Per *French literature educator*
Oettinger, Anthony Gervin *mathematician, educator*
Ogilvie, T(homas) Francis *engineer, educator*
O'Neil, Wayne *linguist, educator*
Oppenheim, Alan Victor *electrical engineering educator*
Oppenheim, Irwin *chemical physicist, educator*
Orchard, Robert John *theater producer, educator*
Orlen, Joel *professional society administrator*
Orlin, James Berger *mathematician, management scientist, educator*
Orme-Johnson, William Henry, III *chemist, educator*
Oye, Kenneth A. *political scientist, educator*
Ozment, Steven *historian, educator*
Papaliolios, Costas Demetrios *physics educator*
Paradis, James Gardiner *historian*
Pardue, Mary Lou *biology educator*
Parker, Harry Lambert *university rowing coach*
Parthum, Charles Albert *civil engineer*
Patterson, Orlando *sociologist*
Paul, William *physicist, educator*
Peattie, Lisa Redfield *urban anthropology educator*
Penfield, Paul Livingstone, Jr. *electrical engineering educator*
Perkins, David *English language educator*
Perkins, Dwight Heald *economics educator*
Pershan, Peter Silas *physicist, educator*
Petersen, Ulrich *geology educator*
Pettengill, Gordon H(emenway) *physicist, educator*
Pfaltzgraff, Robert Louis, Jr. *political scientist, educator*
Pian, Rulan Chao *musicologist, scholar*
Pian, Theodore Hsueh-Huang *engineering educator, consultant*
Piene, Otto *artist, educator*
Pierce, Naomi Ellen *biology educator, researcher*
Pinker, Steven A. *cognitive science educator*
Pinkham, Daniel *composer*
Piore, Michael Joseph *educator*
Pipes, Richard *historian, educator*
Platika, Doros *neurologist*
Plotkin, Irving H(erman) *economist, consultant*
Polenske, Karen Rosel *economics educator*
Pollock, Wilson F. *architectural firm executive*
Porter, Roger Blaine *government official, educator*
Porter, William Lyman *architect, educator*
Poterba, James Michael *economist, educator*
Potter, Ralph Benajah, Jr. *theology and social ethics educator*
Pounds, William Frank *management educator*
Powers, Michael Kevin *architectural and engineering executive*
Press, William Henry *astrophysicist, computer scientist*
Preyer, Robert Otto *English literature educator*
Probstein, Ronald Filmore *mechanical engineering educator*
Ptashne, Mark Steven *biochemistry educator*
Pye, Lucian Wilmot *political science educator*
Quine, Willard Van Orman *philosophy educator*
Ragone, David Vincent *former university president*
Rajur, Sharanabasava Basappa *chemistry educator, researcher*
Ramsey, Norman F. *physicist, educator*
Rands, Bernard *composer, educator*
Rathbone, Perry Townsend *art museum director*
Rathjens, George William *political scientist, educator*
Rediker, Robert Harmon *physicist*
Redwine, Robert Page *physicist, educator*
Reid, Robert Clark *chemical engineering educator*
Reimann, William Page *artist, educator*
Remington, Paul James *mechanical engineer, educator*
Rice, James Robert *engineering scientist, geophysicist*
Rich, Alexander *molecular biologist, educator*
Roberts, Edward Baer *technology management educator*
Roberts, Nancy *computer educator*
Robinson, Marguerite Stern *anthropologist, educator, consultant*
Roche, John Jefferson *lawyer*
Rockart, John Fralick *information systems reseacher*
†Rodrik, Dani *economics and international affairs educator*
Roedder, Edwin Woods *geologist*
Rogers, Peter Philips *environmental engineering educator, city planner*
Rohsenow, Warren Max *retired mechanical engineer, educator*
Roos, Daniel *civil engineering educator*
Rose, Robert Michael *materials science and engineering educator*
Rosenblith, Walter Alter *scientist, educator*
Rosenfeld, Walter David, Jr. *architect, writer*
Rosenof, Howard Paul *electrical engineer*
Rosenthal, Robert *psychology educator*
Rosovsky, Henry *economist, educator*
Rotemberg, Julio Jacobo *economist, educator, consultant*
Rowe, Mary P. *academic administrator, management educator*
Rowe, Peter Grimmond *architecture educator, researcher*
Rowley, Geoffrey Herbert *management consultant*
Rubin, Donald Bruce *statistician, educator, research company executive*
Rubin, Lawrence Gilbert *physicist, laboratory manager*
Rudenstine, Neil Leon *academic administrator, educator*
Ruina, Jack Philip *electrical engineer, educator*
Russell, George Allen *composer, theoritician, author, conductor*
Russell, Kenneth Calvin *metallurgical engineer, educator*
Ryan, Allan Andrew, Jr. *lawyer, author, lecturer*
Ryan, Judith Lyndal *German language and literature educator*
Sadoway, Donald Robert *materials science educator*
Safran, Edward Myron *financial service company executive*
Saltzer, Jerome Howard *computer science educator*
Samuels, Richard Joel *political science educator*
Samuelson, Paul Anthony *economics educator*
Sander, Frank Ernest Arnold *law educator*
Sapolsky, Harvey Morton *political scientist, educator*
Satterfield, Charles Nelson *chemical engineer, educator*
Schauer, Frederick Franklin *legal educator*
Scheffler, Israel *philosopher, educator*
Schein, Edgar Henry *management educator*
Scherer, Frederic Michael *economics educator*
Schimmel, Paul Reinhard *biochemist, biophysicist, educator*
Schmalensee, Richard Lee *economist, former government official, educator*
Schmid, Wilfried *mathematician*
Schreiber, William Francis *electrical engineer*
Schuessler Fiorenza, Elisabeth *theology educator*
Schultes, Richard Evans *retired botanist, biology educator*
Scott, Hal S. *law educator*
Scott Morton, Michael Stewart *business management educator*
Seaman, Jeffrey Richard *academic administrator*
Seamans, Warren Arthur *museum director*
Segal, Charles Paul *classics educator, author*
Segal, Irving Ezra *mathematics educator*
Sekler, Eduard Franz *architect, educator*
Sevcenko, Ihor *history and literature educator*
Seyferth, Dietmar *chemist, educator*
Shapiro, David Louis *lawyer, educator*
Shapiro, Irwin Ira *physicist, educator*
Sharp, Phillip Allen *academic administrator, biologist, educator*
Shaw, M. Thomas, III *bishop*
Sheridan, Thomas Brown *mechanical engineering and applied psychology educator, researcher, consultant*
Shinagel, Michael *English literature educator*
Shore, Miles Frederick *psychiatrist, educator*
Shultz, Leila McReynolds *botanist, educator*
Siebert, William McConway *electrical engineering educator*
Siegel, Abraham J. *economics educator, academic administrator*
Silbey, Robert James *chemistry educator, researcher, consultant*
Simon, Eckehard (Peter) *foreign language educator*
Sims, Ezra *composer*
Singer, Irving *philosophy educator*
Sisler, William Philip *publishing executive*
Skolnikoff, Eugene B. *political science educator*
Slive, Seymour *museum director, fine arts educator*
Smith, David Julian *educational consultant*
Smith, Kenneth Alan *chemical engineer, educator*
Smith, Merritt Roe *history educator*
Snider, Eliot I. *lumber company executive*
Sollors, Werner *English language, literature and American studies educator*
Solow, Robert Merton *economist, educator*
Sonin, Ain A. *mechanical engineering educator, consultant*
Southern, Eileen (Mrs. Joseph Southern) *music educator*
Spaepen, Frans August *applied physics researcher, educator*
Spunt, Shepard Armin *real estate executive, management and financial consultant*
Squire, James Robert *retired publisher, consultant*
Staelin, David Hudson *electrical engineering educator, consultant*
Stager, Lawrence E. *archaeologist, educator*
Steiner, Henry Jacob *law and human rights educator*
Steinfeld, Jeffrey Irwin *chemistry educator, consultant, writer*
Steinmetz, Michael *biochemist*
Stephanopoulos, Gregory *chemical engineering educator, consultant, researcher*
Stevens, Kenneth Noble *electrical engineering educator*
Stoddard, Roger Eliot *librarian*
Stone, Alan A. *law educator, psychiatry educator*
Strandberg, Malcom Woodrow Pershing *physicist*
Strang, William Gilbert *mathematician, educator*
Strauch, Karl *physicist, educator*
Striker, Gisela *philosophy educator*
Stroock, Daniel Wyler *mathematician, educator*
Sulloway, Frank Jones *historian*
Susskind, Lawrence Elliott *urban and environmental planner, educator, mediator*
Swets, John Arthur *psychologist, researcher*
Szabo, Albert *architect, educator*
Ta, Tai Van *lawyer, researcher*
Tambiah, Stanley Jeyarajah *anthropologist*
Tannenbaum, Steven Robert *toxicologist, chemist*
Tarrant, R(ichard) J(ohn) *classicist, educator*
Tayler, Irene *English literature educator*
Teeter, Karl van Duyn *retired linguistic scientist, educator*
Temin, Peter *economics educator*
Termeer, Henricus Adrianus *biotechnology company executive*
Thaddeus, Patrick *physicist, educator*
Thernstrom, Stephan Albert *historian, educator*
Thiemann, Ronald Frank *dean, religion educator*
Thomas, Harold Allen, Jr. *civil engineer, educator*
Thompson, Dennis Frank *political science and ethics educator, consultant*
Thorburn, David *literature educator*
Timmer, Charles Peter *agricultural economist*
Ting, Samuel Chao Chung *physicist, educator*
Tinkham, Michael *physicist, educator*
Tobin, James Robert *biotechnology company executive*
Todreas, Neil Emmanuel *nuclear engineering educator*
Tofias, Allan *accountant*
†Tomassoni, Ronn *men's ice hockey coach*

Tonegawa, Susumu biology educator
Toomre, Alar applied mathematician, theoretical astronomer
Torriani-Gorini, Annamaria microbiologist
Trainor, Bernard Edmund retired military officer
Triantafyllou, Michael Stefanos ocean engineering educator
Trilling, Leon aeronautical engineering educator
Tritter, Richard Paul strategic planning consulting executive
Troxel, Donald Eugene electrical engineering educator
Tsoi, Edward Tze Ming architect, interior designer, urban planner
Tu, Wei-Ming historian, philosopher, writer
Tuller, Harry Louis materials science and engineering educator
Ulam, Adam B. history and political science educator
Ulrich, Laurel Thatcher historian, educator
Ungar, Eric Edward mechanical engineer
Urban, Glen L. management educator
Urbanowski, Frank publishing company executive
Vagts, Detlev Frederick lawyer, educator
Valiant, Leslie Gabriel computer scientist
van der Merwe, Nikolaas Johannes archaeologist
Vander Velde, Wallace Earl aeronautical and astronautical educator
Vanger, Milton Isadore history educator
Vendler, Helen Hennessy literature educator, poetry critic
Vér, István László noise control consultant
Verba, Sidney political scientist, educator
Verdine, Gregory Lawrence chemist, educator
Vernon, Raymond economist, educator
Vessot, Robert Frederick Charles physicist
Vest, Charles Marstiller academic administrator
Vigier, François Claude Denis city planning educator
Villars, Felix Marc Hermann physicist, educator
Vincent, James Louis biotechnology company executive
Vogel, Ezra F. sociology educator
Vogt, Evon Zartman, Jr. anthropologist
von Mehren, Arthur Taylor lawyer, educator
Vorenberg, James lawyer, educator, university dean
Wacker, Warren Ernest Clyde physician, educator
Wang, Daniel I-Chyau biochemical engineering educator
Ward, John Milton music educator
Ward, Robertson, Jr. architect
Warren, Alvin Clifford, Jr. lawyer
Waugh, John Stewart chemist, educator
†Weber, Larry public relations executive
Wechsler, Alfred Elliot engineering executive, consultant, chemical engineer
Weiner, Myron political science educator
Weinreb, Lloyd Lobell law educator
Weiss, Thomas Fischer electrical engineering educator, biophysicist
Welsch, Roy Elmer statistician
Wenger, Luke Huber educational association executive, editor
Westfall, David lawyer, educator
Westheimer, Frank Henry chemist, educator
Whipple, Fred Lawrence astronomer
White, David Calvin electrical engineer, energy educator, consultant
Whitesides, George McClelland chemistry educator
Whitlock, Charles Preston former university dean
Whitman, Robert Van Duyne civil engineer, educator
Wilcox, Maud editor
Wiley, Don Craig biochemistry and biophysics educator
Willard, Louis Charles librarian
Williams, George Huntston church historian, educator
Williams, James Henry, Jr. mechanical engineer, educator, consultant
Williams, Preston Noah theology educator
Willie, Charles Vert sociology educator
Wilson, David Gordon mechanical engineering educator
Wilson, Edward Osborne biologist, educator, author
Wilson, Linda Smith academic administrator
Wilson, Mary Elizabeth physician, educator
Wilson, Robert Woodrow radio astronomer
Wilson, William Julius sociologist, educator
Winkler, Gunther biotechnology executive, drug development expert
Winner, Thomas Gustav foreign literature educator
Wirth, Peter lawyer
Wiseman, Frederick filmmaker
Wogan, Gerald Norman toxicology educator
Wolff, Christoph Johannes music historian, educator
Wolff, Cynthia Griffin humanities educator, author
Wolfman, Bernard lawyer, educator
Wood, John Armstead planetary scientist, geological sciences educator
Wu, Tai Tsun physicist, educator
Wuensch, Bernhardt John ceramic engineering educator
Wunderlich, Renner film producer, cinematographer
Wunsch, Carl Isaac oceanographer, educator
Wurtman, Judith Joy research scientist
Wurtman, Richard Jay physician, educator, inventor
Yannas, Ioannis Vassilios polymer science and engineering educator
Yergin, Daniel Howard writer, consultant
Young, Laurence Retman biomedical engineer, educator
Young, Vernon Robert nutrition, biochemistry educator
Zeckhauser, Richard Jay economist, educator
Zeidenstein, George population educator
Zinberg, Dorothy Shore science policy educator
Ziolkowski, Jan Michael medievalist educator

### Canton
Bentas, Lily H. retail executive
Bihldorff, John Pearson hospital director
Ferrera, Arthur Rocco food distribution company executive
Ferrera, Kenneth Grant food distribution company executive
Friend, William Kagay lawyer
Lyman, Charles Peirson comparative physiologist
Pitts, Virginia M. human resources executive
Raven, Gregory Kurt retail executive
Sawtelle, Carl S. psychiatric social worker
Tockman, Ronald Chester accountant

### Carlisle
Fohl, Timothy consulting and investment company executive
Tema-Lyn, Laurie management consultant

### Carver
Neubauer, Richard A. library science educator, consultant

### Centerville
Anderson, Gerald Edwin utilities executive
Embree, Ainslie Thomas history educator
Kiernan, Owen Burns educational consultant
Scherer, Harold Nicholas, Jr. electric utility company executive, engineer

### Charlestown
Armstrong, Nancy L. soprano, voice coach
Bonventre, Joseph Vincent physician, scientist, medical educator
Dickerson, Frank Secor, III computer company executive
Gusella, James F. geneticist, educator
Isselbacher, Kurt Julius physician, educator
Lamont-Havers, Ronald William physician, research administrator
Moskowitz, Michael Arthur neuroscientist, neurologist
Murphy-Lind, Karen Marie health educator, dermatology nurse
Waldfogel, Morton Sumner prefabricated housing/plywood company executive
Wong, Po Kee research company executive, educator

### Chatham
Anderson, Barbara Graham philanthropic resources development consultant
Bianchi-Bigelow, Cheryl Ann mental health facility director
Leighten, Edward Henry publisher, consultant
Miles, Robert Henry management consultant, educator
Pacun, Norman lawyer

### Chelmsford
Fulks, Robert Grady engineering computer executive
Grossman, Debra A. lawyer, real estate manager, radio talk show host
Howard, Terry Thomas obstetrician/gynecologist
Lerer, Neal M. lawyer
Sheldon, Eric retired physics educator

### Chelsea
Ablow, Keith Russell psychiatrist, journalist, author
Danckert, Stephen Christopher retail executive
Dunn, Norman Samuel plastics and textiles company executive
Kaneb, Gary oil industry executive

### Cheshire
Frye-Moquin, Marsha Marie social worker

### Chestnut Hill
Altbach, Philip higher education director, educator
Barth, John Robert English educator, priest
Baum, Jules Leonard ophthalmologist, educator
Belsley, David Alan economics educator, consultant
Bender, Harold beverage company consultant
Blanchette, Oliva philosophy educator
Bursley, Kathleen A. lawyer
Casper, Leonard Ralph American literature educator
Cohen, David Joel medical educator
Collins, Arthur Worth, Jr. (Bud Collins) sports columnist and commentator
Cook, John Rowland publishing and retail company executive
Courtiss, Eugene Howard plastic surgeon, educator
Daniel-Dreyfus, Susan B. Russe civic worker
Duhamel, Pierre Albert English language professional
Fouraker, Lawrence Edward retired business administration educator
Fourkas, John T. chemistry educator
Franklin, Morton Jerome emergency physician
Glynn, Arthur Lawrence business administration and accounting educator
Hawkins, Joellen Margaret Beck nursing educator
Hunt-Clerici, Carol Elizabeth academic administrator
Knapp, Robert Charles retired obstetrics and gynecology educator
Kosasky, Harold Jack gynecologic researcher
†Leahy, William P. academic administrator, educator
Mahoney, John L. English literature educator
McAleer, John Joseph English literature educator
Mc Innes, William Charles priest, campus ministry director
Meissner, William Walter psychiatrist, clergyman
Mellins, Judith Weiss retired archivist
Monan, James Donald university administrator
Munro, Barbara Hazard nursing educator, college dean, researcher
Norris, Melvin lawyer
Reed, James Eldin historian, educator
Simon, Harold radiologist
Smith, Richard Alan publishing and speciality retailing executive
Stanbury, John Bruton physician, educator
Thier, Samuel Osiah physician, educator
Valette, Rebecca Marianne Romance languages educator
Wysocki, Boleslaw A(ntoni) psychologist, educator

### Chicopee
Collins, Donald Francis electrical contractor
Czerwiec, Irene Theresa gifted education educator
Dame, Catherine Elaine acupuncturist

### Chilmark
Geyer, Harold Carl artist, writer
Low, Joseph artist

### Cohasset
Campbell, John Coert political scientist, author
Lyne, Austin Francis sporting goods business executive
Porter, John Stephen television executive
Rabstejnek, George John executive

### Concord
Berger, Raoul law educator, violinist
Bloom, Edwin John, Jr. human resources consultant
Brown, Linda Weaver academic administrator
Codere, Helen Frances anthropologist, educator, university dean
Cutting, Heyward designer, planner
Daley, Royston Tuttle architect
Daltas, Arthur John management consultant
Drew, Philip Garfield consultant engineering company executive
Eberle, William Denman international management consultant
Edmonds, Walter Dumaux author
Hogan, Daniel Bolten management consultant
Huxley, Hugh Esmor molecular biologist, educator
Ihara, Michio sculptor
Lilien, Elliot Stephen secondary education educator
Meistas, Mary Therese endocrinologist, diabetes researcher
Moore, Robert Lowell, Jr. (Robin Moore) author
Osepchuk, John Moses engineering physicist, consultant
Palay, Sanford Louis retired scientist, educator
Rarich, Anne Lippitt management and organizational development consultant
Rathore, Naeem Gul retired United Nations official
Schiller, Pieter Jon venture capital executive
Smith, Eric Parkman retired railroad executive
Smith, Peter Walker finance executive
Valley, George Edward, Jr. physicist, educator
Villers, Philippe mechanical engineer
White, James Barr lawyer, real estate investor, consultant
Wickfield, Eric Nelson investment company executive
Woll, Harry J. electrical engineer

### Cotuit
Miller, Robert Charles retired physicist

### Cummington
Smith, William Jay author
Wilbur, Richard Purdy writer, educator

### Danvers
Baures, Mary Margaret psychotherapist, author
Dolan, John Ralph retired corporation executive
Langford, Dean Ted lighting and precision materials company executive
Manganello, James Angelo psychologist
Rubinstein, Sidney Jacob orthopedic technologist
Traicoff, George college president
Waite, Charles Morrison food company executive

### Dartmouth
Kahalas, Harvey business educator
Leclair, Susan Jean hematologist, clinical laboratory scientist, educator

### Dedham
Firth, Everett Joseph timpanist
Ghosh, Asish control engineer
Janson, Barbara Jean publisher
Magner, Jerome Allen entertainment company executive
Redstone, Sumner Murray entertainment company executive
Spoolstra, Linda Carol minister, educator, religious organization administrator
Winder, Alvin Eliot public health educator, clinical psychologist

### Deerfield
Friary, Donald Richard museum administrator

### Dennis
Weilbacher, William Manning advertising and marketing consultant

### Dorchester
Brelis, Matthew Dean Burns journalist
Bruzelius, Nils Johan Axel journalist
Daly, Charles Ulick foundation executive
Garrison, Althea government official
Goodman, Ellen Holtz journalist
Greenway, Hugh Davids Scott journalist
Hatfield, Julie Stockwell journalist, newspaper editor
Lee, June Warren dentist
Leland, Timothy newspaper executive

### Dover
Aldrich, Frank Nathan bank executive
Bonis, Laszlo Joseph business executive, scientist
Borel, Richard Wilson communications executive, consultant
Buyse, Marylou pediatrician, clinical geneticist, medical administrator
Craver, James Bernard lawyer
Crittenden, Gazaway Lamar retired banker
Kovaly, John Joseph consulting engineering executive, educator
Smith, William Henry Preston writer, editor, former corporate executive
Stockwell, Ernest Farnham, Jr. banker

### Dudley
Carney, Roger Francis Xavier retired army officer

### Duxbury
Albritton, William Hoyle training and consulting executive, lecturer, writer
Bowes, Frederick, III publishing consultant
Erickson, Phyllis Traver marketing executive
McAuliffe, Eugene Vincent retired diplomat and business executive
Mc Carthy, D. Justin emeritus college president
Phipps, Lynne Bryan interior architect, clergywoman, parent educator
Thrasher, Dianne Elizabeth mathematics educator, computer consultant
Vose, Robert Churchill, Jr. former art gallery executive
Wangler, William Clarence retired insurance company executive

### East Falmouth
Selman, Jan Collins artist
Weisberg, Leonard R. retired research and engineering executive

### East Longmeadow
Green, Frank Walter industrial engineer
Skutnik, Bolesh optics scientist, lay worker, lawyer
Upton, Larry Dewayne refrigeration engineer

### East Orleans
Hallowell, Burton Crosby economist, educator
Nenneman, Richard Arthur retired publishing executive

### East Walpole
Oh, Se-Kyung immunochemist

### Eastham
McLaughlin, Richard Warren retired insurance company executive
Miller, Gabriel Lorimer physicist, researcher
Thompson, Cheryl Ann special education educator

### Easthampton
Grubbs, Dennis H. secondary school principal
Perkins, Homer Guy manufacturing company executive

### Edgartown
Treat, Lawrence author

### Essex
Broome, Roger Greville Brooke, IV fundraiser
McMillen, Louis Albert architect

### Everett
Jenkins, Alexander, III financial business executive
Shedden, Kenneth Charles fire department official, business owner
Wright, Franz poet, writer, translator

### Fairhaven
Hotchkiss, Henry Washington real estate broker and financial consultant

### Fall River
Correia, Robert state legislator
Ingles, James H. dean
O'Malley, Sean bishop
Sullivan, Ruth Anne librarian

### Falmouth
Bonn, Theodore Hertz computer scientist, consultant
Brewer, William Dodd former ambassador, political science educator emeritus
Goody, Richard Mead geophysicist
Hollister, Charles Davis oceanographer
Litschgi, Richard John computer manufacturing company executive
Litterer, William Edward, III physician
Mitchell, Charles Archie financial planning consultant, engineer
Nolan, Edmund Francis management consultant
Sato, Kazuyoshi pathologist
Schlesinger, Robert Walter microbiologist, microbiology educator emeritus

### Feeding Hills
Bianchi, Maria critical care nurse, adult nurse practitioner

### Fitchburg
Bogdasarian, John Robert otolaryngologist
Mara, Vincent Joseph college president
Niemi, Beatrice Neal social services professional
Price, Malcolm Ivan podiatrist
Riccards, Michael Patrick academic administrator
Wiegersma, Nan economics educator

### Florence
Park, Beverly Goodman public relations professional

### Foxboro
Bush, Raymond T. accountant, corporate professional
Coates, Ben Terrence professional football player
†Kraft, Robert K. professional sports team executive
Lalas, Alexi professional soccer player
Martin, Curtis professional football player
Martin, Peter Gerard infosystems specialist, consultant, teacher
Pierce, Francis Casimir civil engineer

### Framingham
Ballou, Kenneth Walter retired transportation executive, university dean
Bogard, Carole Christine lyric soprano
Bose, Amar Gopal electrical engineering educator
Cammarata, Bernard retail company executive
Crossley, Frank Alphonso former metallurgical engineer
Dawicki, Doloretta Diane research biochemist, educator
Dube, Beatrice Dorothy psychologist
Feldberg, Sumner Lee retired retail company executive
Gillin, Paul Donald magazine editor
Hunt, Samuel Pancoast, III lawyer, corporate executive
Lavin, Philip Todd biostatistician executive
Levy, Joseph Louis publishing company executive
Lipton, Leah art historian, educator, museum curator
Meador, Charles Lawrence management and systems consultant, educator
Meltzer, Jay H. lawyer, retail company executive
†Merrell, Therese Elizabeth trade show production executive
Merser, Francis Gerard manufacturing company executive, consultant
Munro, Meredith Vance lawyer
Oleskiewicz, Francis Stanley retired insurance executive
Paul, Nancy Elizabeth psychiatric-mental health nurse
Reiss, Martin Harold engineering executive
Scherr, Allan Lee computer scientist, executive
Silverman, Harold Irving pharmaceutical executive
Stuart, Anne Elizabeth journalist, freelance writer, educator
Vermette, Raymond Edward clinical laboratories administrator
Waters, James Logan analytical instrument manufacturing executive
Wishner, Steven R. retail executive

### Franklin
Bonin, Paul Joseph real estate and banking executive

### Gardner
Coulter, Sherry Parks secondary education educator
McCarthy, Albert Henry human resources executive
Wagenknecht, Edward author

### Gloucester
Baird, Gordon Prentiss publisher
Birchfield, John Kermit, Jr. lawyer
Braver, Barbara Leix religious organization communications administrator

Curtis, Roger William *artist, educator*
Duca, Alfred Milton *artist*
Erkkila, Barbara Howell Louise *writer, photographer*
Hancock, Walker Kirtland *sculptor*
Hausman, William Ray *fund raising and management consultant*
Lanzkron, Rolf Wolfgang *manufacturing company executive*
Lauenstein, Milton Charles *management consultant*
Means, Elizabeth Rose Thayer *financial consultant, lawyer*
Sallah, Majeed (Jim Sallah) *real estate developer*
Socolow, Arthur Abraham *geologist*
White, Harold Jack *pathologist*
Zawinul, Josef *bandleader, composer, keyboardist, synthesist*

**Grafton**
Haggerty, John Edward *research center administrator, former army officer*
Tite, John Gregory *secondary school educator*

**Great Barrington**
Berryhill, Mary Finley *emergency nurse*
Gilmour, Robert Arthur *foundation executive, educator*
Lewis, Karen Marie *writer, editor*
Rodgers, Bernard F., Jr. *academic administrator, dean*
Schenck, Benjamin Robinson *insurance consultant*
Stonier, Tom *theoretical biologist, educator*

**Greenfield**
Curtiss, Carol Perry *nursing consultant*
Lee, Marilyn (Irma) Modarelli *law librarian*
Moylan, Jay Richard *medical products executive*
Robinson, John Alan *logic and computer science educator*

**Hanover**
Lonborg, James Reynold *dentist, former professional baseball player*

**Hanscom AFB**
Herrlinger, Stephen Paul *flight test engineer, air force officer, educator*
Lemieux, Jerome Anthony, Jr. *electrical and computer engineer*
Mailloux, Robert Joseph *physicist*
Manning, Thomas Edwin, II *aeronautical engineer*
Rollins, James Gregory *air force officer*

**Hanson**
Norris, John Anthony *health sciences executive, lawyer, educator*

**Harvard**
Larson, Roland Elmer *health care executive*
Sutherland, Malcolm Read, Jr. *clergyman, educator*

**Harwich**
Bush, Richard James *engineering executive, lay worker*
Randolph, Robert Lee *economist, educator*
Rigg, Charles Andrew *pediatrician*
Thorndike, Joseph Jacobs, Jr. *editor*

**Harwich Port**
Staszesky, Francis Myron *electric company consultant*

**Hatfield**
Yolen, Jane *author*

**Haverhill**
Charlesworth, Marion Hoyen *secondary school educator*
DeSchuytner, Edward Alphonse *biochemist, educator*
Dimitry, John Randolph *academic administrator*
Ehrig, Ulrich *physician*
MacMillan, Francis Philip *physician*
Niccolini, Drew George *gastroenterologist*
Ruiz, Eduardo Antonio *psychology and sociology educator*

**Hingham**
Cooke, Gordon Richard *retail executive*
Ford, Joseph *retired superior court judge*
Hart, Richard Nevel, Jr. *financial exective, consultant*
Lane, Frederick Stanley *lawyer*
Malme, Charles Irving *acoustical engineer*
Replogle, David Robert *publishing company executive*

**Holbrook**
Crandlemere, Robert Wayne *engineering executive*

**Holden**
Botty, Kenneth John *editor, newspaper executive*

**Holliston**
O'Connor, Jude *special education educator, consultant*

**Holyoke**
Chapdelaine, Lorraine Elder *gerontology nurse*
Dwight, William, Jr. *former newspaper executive, restaurateur*
Hedrick, Janet Lee *fundraising executive*
Radner, Sidney Hollis *retired rug company executive*

**Hopkinton**
Main, Martha Lane Hughes *medical/surgical nurse*
McGuire, Frank Joseph *accountant*
Nickerson, Richard Gorham *research company executive*
Preston, William Hubbard *consultant to specialty businesses*

**Hull**
Anderson, Timothy Christopher *consulting company executive*
Burgess, David Lowry *artist*
Chase, David Marion *applied physicist, mathematical modeler*

**Hyannis**
Makkay, Maureen Ann *broadcast executive*
Paquin, Thomas Christopher *lawyer*
White, Allen Jordan *nursing home adminstrator, consultant*
White, Timothy Oliver *newspaper editor*

**Hyannis Port**
Ludtke, James Buren *business and finance educator*

**Hyde Park**
Harris, Emily Louise *special education educator*
Riley, Lawrence Joseph *bishop*

**Ipswich**
Barth, Elmer Ernest *wire and cable company executive*
Bryant, Edward Curtis *education consultant*
Getchell, Charles Willard, Jr. *lawyer, publisher*
Jennings, Frederic Beach, Jr. *economist, consultant, saltwater flyfishing guide*

**Jamaica Plain**
Arbeit, Robert David *physician*
Manzo, David William *human services administrator*
Pierce, Chester Middlebrook *psychiatrist, educator*
Shapiro, Ascher Herman *mechanical engineer, educator, consultant*
Snider, Gordon Lloyd *physician*
Tirella, Theresa Mary *special education educator*
Zahn, Carl Frederick *museum publications director, designer, photographer*

**Kingston**
Hybertson, Beverly Blaisdell *elementary education educator*
Squarcia, Paul Andrew *school superintendent*
Stair, Gobin *publishing executive, painter, graphic designer*

**Lakeville**
Chase, Karen Humphrey *middle school education educator*

**Lancaster**
McDowell, David Jamison *clinical psychologist*

**Lawrence**
Devaney, Robert James, Jr. *environmental engineer*
McBride, Thomas Dwayne *manufacturing executive*

**Lee**
Rich, Philip Dewey *publishing executive*

**Leeds**
Baskin, Leonard *sculptor, graphic artist*

**Lenox**
Coffin, Louis Fussell, Jr. *mechanical engineer*
Curtis, William Edgar *conductor, composer*
Krofta, Milos *engineering company executive*
LiMarzi, Joseph *artist*
Pierson, John Herman Groesbeck *economist, writer*
Shammas, Nazih Kheirallah *environmental engineering educator, consultant*
Slavin, Simon *social administration educator*
Smith, Elske Van Panhuys *retired university administrator*

**Leominster**
Cormier, Robert Edmund *writer*
Lambert, Lyn Dee *library media specialist, law librarian*
Libby, Sandra Chiavaras *special education educator*

**Leverett**
Barkin, Solomon *economist*

**Lexington**
Baddour, Anne Bridge *aviatrix*
Baer, Michael Alan *political scientist, educator*
Bailey, Fred Coolidge *retired engineering consulting company executive*
Barton, David Knox *engineering executive, radar engineer*
Bell, Carolyn Shaw *economist, educator*
Berstein, Irving Aaron *biotechnology and medical technology executive*
Bishop, Robert Calvin *pharmaceutical company executive*
Bombardieri, Merle Ann *psychotherapist*
Brick, Donald Bernard *consulting company executive*
Brookner, Eli *electrical engineer*
Buchanan, John Machlin *biochemistry educator*
Caslavska, Vera Barbara *chemist, researcher*
Cathou, Renata Egone *chemist, consultant*
Chaskelson, Marsha Ina *neuropsychologist*
Colburn, Kenneth Hersey *financial executive*
Cooper, William Eugene *consulting engineer*
D'Avignon, Roy Joseph *lawyer*
Deitcher, Herbert *financial executive*
Dionne, Gerald Francis *research physicist, consultant*
Drouilhet, Paul Raymond, Jr. *science laboratory director, electrical engineer*
Duboff, Robert Samuel *marketing professional*
Eaton, Allen Ober *lawyer*
Farb, Thomas Forest *financial executive*
Fillios, Louis Charles *retired science educator*
France-Litchfield, Ruth A. *reading and literacy specialist*
Fray, Lionel Louis *management consultant*
Freed, Charles *engineering consultant, researcher*
Freitag, Wolfgang Martin *librarian, educator*
Frey, John Ward *landscape architect*
Garing, John Seymour *retired physicist, research executive*
Gibbs, Martin *biologist, educator*
Golden, John Joseph, Jr. *information systems executive*
Guertin, Robert Powell *physics educator, university dean*
Guivens, Norman Roy, Jr. *mathematician, engineer*
Hedlund, Ronald David *academic administrator, researcher, educator*
Hoffmann, Christoph Ludwig *lawyer*
Holzman, Franklyn Dunn *economics educator*
Kanter, Irving *mathematical physicist*
Kerr, Thomas Henderson, III *electrical engineer, researcher*
Kindleberger, Charles P., II *economist, educator*
Kingston, Robert Hildreth *engineering educator*
Kirkpatrick, Francis H(ubbard), Jr. *biophysicist, intellectual property practitioner, consultant*
Melngailis, Ivars *solid state research executive*
Miller, Charles Q. *engineering company executive*
Mollo-Christensen, Erik Leonard *oceanographer*
Morrow, Walter Edwin, Jr. *electrical engineer, university laboratory administrator*
Nash, Leonard Kollender *chemistry educator*
O'Donnell, Robert Michael *electrical engineering executive*
Papanek, Gustav Fritz *economist, educator*
Paul, Norman Leo *psychiatrist, educator*
Picard, Dennis J. *electronics company executive*
Powers, Martha Mary *nursing consultant, education specialist*
Risch, Martin Donald *marketing-management consulting company executive*
Ross, Douglas Taylor *retired software company executive*
Samour, Carlos Miguel *chemist*
Schultz, Samuel Jacob *clergyman, educator*
Shapiro, Marian Kaplun *psychologist*
Shull, Clifford G. *physicist, educator*
Smith, Edgar Eugene *biochemist, university administrator*
Smith, Robert Louis *construction company executive*
Wainberg, Alan *footwear company executive*
Ward, William Weaver *electrical engineer*
Williamson, Richard Cardinal *physicist*
Wyss, David Alen *financial service executive*

**Lincoln**
Adams, Thomas Boylston *journalist*
Barrett, Beatrice Helene *psychologist*
Cannon, Bradford *surgeon*
Donald, David Herbert *author, history educator*
Eschenroeder, Alan Quade *environmental scientist*
Gnichtel, William Van Orden *lawyer*
Godine, David Richard *publishing company executive*
Green, David Henry *manufacturing company executive*
Holberton, Philip Vaughan *entrepreneur, educator, professional speaker*
Kulka, J(ohannes) Peter *retired physician, pathologist*
LeGates, John Crews Boulton *information scientist*
Master-Karnik, Paul Joseph *art museum director*
Merrill, Vincent Nichols *landscape architect*
Payne, Harry Morse, Jr. *architect*
Payne, Roger S. *conservation organization executive*
Schwann, William Joseph *publisher, musician, discographer*
Schwartz, Edward Arthur *lawyer, foundation executive*

**Littleton**
Ibe, Oliver Chukwudi *electrical engineer, researcher*
Reinschmidt, Kenneth Frank *engineering and construction executive*

**Longmeadow**
Cobbs, Russell L(ewis) *English language educator*
Donoghue, Linda *nursing administrator, community health nurse*
Ferris, Theodore Vincent *chemical engineer, consulting technologist*
Hasty, Richard Spencer *minister*
Hopfe, Harold Herbert *chemical engineer*
Keady, George Cregan, Jr. *judge*
Leary, Carol Ann *academic administrator*
Lo Bello, Joseph David *bank executive*
Locklin, Wilbert Edwin *management consultant*
Louargand, Marc Andrew *real estate executive, financial consultant*
Skelton, Don Richard *consulting actuary, retired insurance company executive*
Stewart, Alexander Doig *bishop*

**Lowell**
Carr, George Leroy *physicist, educator*
†Clark, Richard Paul *electronics company executive*
Coleman, Robert Marshall *biology educator*
Curtis, James Theodore *lawyer*
Dubner, Daniel William *pediatrician*
Greenwald, John Edward *newspaper and magazine executive*
Hayes, Donald Paul, Jr. *elementary and secondary education educator*
Korkin, Steven Arthur *research and development company executive, industrial engineer*
Natsios, Nicholas Andrew *retired foreign service officer*
Reinisch, Bodo Walter *atmospheric science educator*
Ruskai, Mary Beth *mathematics researcher, educator*
Sakellarios, Gertrude Edith *retired office nurse*
Salamone, Joseph Charles *polymer chemistry educator*
Sullivan, Anne Dorothy Hevner *artist*
Sutter, Linda Diane *health services administrator*
Tripathy, Sukant Kishore *chemistry educator*
Wakim, Fahd George *physicist, educator*

**Ludlow**
Budnick, Thomas Peter *social worker*
Koeninger, Edward Calvin *chemical engineer*

**Lynn**
Astuccio, Sheila Margaret *educational administrator*
Chow, Humphrey Wai *mechanical engineer*
Denzler, Nancy J. *artist*
Kercher, David Max *mechanical engineer*
Loftis, Rebecca Hope *psychotherapist*
McManus, Patrick J. *mayor, lawyer, accountant*

**Lynnfield**
Gianino, John Joseph *former insurance executive*
Paradis, Richard Robert *engineering executive*

**Malden**
Antonucci, Robert V. *state agency administrator*

**Manchester**
Arntsen, Arnt Peter *engineer, consultant*
Lothrop, Kristin Curtis *sculptor*

**Mansfield**
Forney, G(eorge) David, Jr. *electronics company executive*

**Marblehead**
Ehrich, Fredric F. *aeronautical engineer*
Heins, Esther *botanical artist, painter*
Plakans, Shelley Swift *social worker, psychotherapist*
Pruyn, William J. *energy industry executive*
Zeo, Frank James *health products company professional*

**Marion**
Cederholm, Theresa Miriam Dickason *museum director*
McPartland, Patricia Ann *health educator*
Walsh, William Egan, Jr. *electronics executive*

**Marlborough**
Bennett, C. Leonard *consulting engineer*
Bethel, Tamara Ann *psychiatric nurse, consultant*
Birk, Lee (Carl Birk) *psychiatrist, educator*
Birstein, Seymour Joseph *aerospace company executive*
Lohr, Harold Russell *bishop*
Monia, Joan *management consultant*
Palihnich, Nicholas Joseph, Jr. *retail chain executive*
Petrin, John Donald *town administrator*
Ryan, John William *association executive*
Stiffler, Jack Justin *electrical engineer*

**Marshfield**
French, Frederic Rawson, Jr. *psychotherapist*
Mc Carthy, Thomas Patrick *magazine publisher*
Sostilio, Robert Francis *office equipment marketing executive*

**Marshfield Hills**
Johnson, Margaret Hill *retired educational administrator, consultant*

**Marstons Mills**
Martin, Vincent George *management consultant*
Vila, Robert Joseph *television host, designer, real estate developer*
Wheeler, Richard Warren *banker*

**Mashpee**
LeBaron, Francis Newton *biochemistry educator*

**Mattapan**
Deen, Alusaine *foundation administrator*

**Mattapoisett**
Andersen, Laird Bryce *retired university administrator*
Busher, Penelope Chace-Squire *school psychologist*

**Maynard**
Fuller, Samuel Henry, III *computer engineer*
Palmer, Robert B. *computer company executive*
Siekman, Thomas Clement *lawyer*

**Medfield**
Heffernan, Peter John *state official*
Hein, John William *dentist, educator*
Woolston-Catlin, Marian *psychiatrist*

**Medford**
Anderson, Thomas Jefferson, Jr. *composer, educator*
†Arnold, Stuart *publishing executive*
Astill, Kenneth Norman *mechanical engineering educator*
Bedau, Hugo Adam *philosophy educator*
Berman, David *lawyer, poet*
Brooke, John L. *history educator*
Burke, Edward Newell *radiologist*
Byrnes, Don *publishing executive*
Conklin, John Evan *sociology educator*
Cormack, Allan MacLeod *physicist, educator*
DeBold, Joseph Francis *psychology educator*
Dennett, Daniel Clement *philosopher, author, educator*
DiBiaggio, John A. *university administrator*
Elkind, David *psychology educator*
Fyler, John Morgan *English language educator*
Galvin, John Rogers *educator, retired army officer*
Garrelick, Joel Marc *acoustical scientist, consultant*
Greif, Robert *mechanical engineering educator*
Gunther, Leon *physicist*
Harrison, Bettina Hall *retired biology educator*
Howell, Alvin Harold *engineer, company executive, educator*
Junger, Miguel Chapero *acoustics researcher*
Klema, Ernest Donald *nuclear physicist, educator*
Laurent, Pierre-Henri *history educator*
Luria, Zella Hurwitz *psychology educator*
Manno, Vincent Paul *mechanical engineer*
Marcopoulos, George John *history educator*
Mc Carthy, Kathryn A. *physicist*
Miczek, Klaus Alexander *psychology educator*
Milburn, Richard Henry *physics educator*
Mumford, George Saltonstall, Jr. *former university dean, astronomy educator*
Nelson, Frederick Carl *mechanical engineering educator*
Nitecki, Zbigniew Henry *mathematician, educator*
O'Connell, Brian *community organizer, public administrator, writer, educator*
Reynolds, William Francis *mathematics educator*
Salacuse, Jeswald William *lawyer, educator*
Schneps, Jack *physics educator*
Siegal, Kenneth Harvey *editor*
Simches, Seymour Oliver *language educator*
Sloane, Marshall M. *banker*
Sung, Nak-Ho *science educator*
Sussman, Martin Victor *chemical engineering educator, inventor, consultant*
Swap, Walter Charles *academic dean, psychology educator*
Tilger, Justine Tharp *research director*
Uhlir, Arthur, Jr. *electrical engineer, university administrator*
Urry, Grant Wayne *chemistry educator*

**Medway**
Hoag, David Garratt *aerospace engineer*
Yonda, Alfred William *mathematician*

**Melrose**
Brown, Ronald Osborne *telecommunications and computer systems consultant*
Henken, Bernard Samuel *clinical psychologist, speech pathologist*

**Methuen**
Bonanno, A. Richard *weed management scientist, educator*
Conran, Lisa Ann *educational administrator*
Pollack, Herbert William *electronics executive*

**Middleboro**
Beeby, Kenneth Jack *lawyer, food products executive*
Castaldi, David Lawrence *health care company executive*

Llewellyn, John Schofield, Jr. *food company executive*

### Middleton
Stover, Matthew Joseph *communications executive*

### Milford
Carson, Charles Henry *electronics engineer*
Gliksberg, Alexander David *engineering executive*
Murray, Brian William *lawyer*

### Mill River
Haworth, Donald Robert *educator, retired association executive*

### Millbury
Noonan, Stephen Joseph *accounting firm executive*
Pan, Coda H. T. *mechanical engineering educator, consultant, researcher*

### Millis
Masterson, Patricia O'Malley *publications editor, writer*

### Milton
Berzon, Faye Clark *retired nursing educator*
Cooperstein, Paul Andrew *lawyer, business consultant*
Desmond, Patricia Lorraine *psychotherapist, writer, publisher*
Frazier, Marie Dunn *speech educator, public relations and human resources specialist*
Gaffey, Virginia Anne *anesthetist*
Gerring, Clifton, III *corporate executive*
Kennedy, Thomas Leo *investment management company executive*
Lucek, Donald Walter *surgeon*
Mills, Elizabeth Ann *librarian*
Sgarlat, Mary Anne E. A. *public relations professional, entrepreneur*
Warren, John Coolidge *private school dean, history educator*

### Monson
Krach, Mitchell Peter *retired financial services executive*
St. Louis, Paul Michael *foreign language educator*

### Montague
Andersen, Richard Arnold *writer, consultant*
Coughlin, Jack *printmaker, sculptor, art educator*

### Nantucket
Baldwin, John Ashby, Jr. *retired naval officer*
Jesser, Benn Wainwright *chemical engineering and construction company executive*
Lethbridge, Francis Donald *architect*
Lobl, Herbert Max *lawyer*
Mercer, Richard Joseph *retired advertising executive, freelance writer*
Murray, Caroline Fish *psychologist*
Rorem, Ned *composer, author*

### Natick
Bensel, Carolyn Kirkbride *psychologist*
Bower, Kathleen Anne *nurse consultant*
Cukor, Peter *chemical research and development executive, educator, consultant*
DeCosta, Peter F. *chemical engineer*
Deutsch, Marshall E(manuel) *medical products company executive, inventor*
Donovan, R. Michael *management consultant*
Geller, Esther (Bailey Geller) *artist*
Gomberg, Sydelle *dancer educator*
Grassia, Thomas Charles *lawyer*
†Kushner, Harold Samuel *rabbi*
Lachica, R(eynato) Victor *microbiologist*
Lebowitz, Marshall *retired publishing company executive*
Milius, Richard A. *organic chemist*
Morgan, Betty Mitchell *artist, educator*
Narayan, K(rishnamurthi) Ananth *biochemist*
†Rendell, Kenneth William *rare and historical documents dealer, consultant*
Sahatjian, Ronald Alexander *science foundation executive*
Savage, James Cathey, III *lawyer*
Strauss, Harlee Sue *environmental consultant*
Strayton, Robert Gerard *public communications executive*
Sutcliffe, Marion Shea *writer*
Swanson, Karin *hospital administrator, consultant*
Wang, Chia Ping *physicist, educator*
Zarkin, Herbert *retail company executive*

### Needham
Bottiglia, William Filbert *humanities educator*
Bullard, Robert Oliver, Jr. *lawyer*
Cantor, Pamela Corliss *psychologist*
Carey, Robert Williams *retired insurance company executive*
Carr, Iris Constantine *artist, writer*
Cogswell, John Heyland *retired telecommunications executive, financial consultant*
Cohen, Lewis Cobrain *security products firm executive*
Kaplan, Steven F. *business management executive*
Kung, Patrick Chung-Shu *biotechnology executive*
MacMahon, Brian *epidemiologist, educator*
Pucel, Robert Albin *electronics research engineer*
Reichman, Joel H. *retail executive*
Tarsky, Eugene Stanley *accountant, management and systems consultant*
Walworth, Arthur *author*
Weller, Thomas Huckle *physician, former educator*

### New Bedford
Anderson, James Linwood *pharmaceutical sales official*
Bennett, Michelle Swann *quality control chemist, scientist*
Benoit, Richard Armand *retired police chief, lawyer*
Chang, Robin *engineering executive*
Merolla, Michele Edward *chiropractor, broadcaster*
Shapiro, Gilbert Lawrence *orthopedist*
Soares, Carl Lionel *metrologist, quality control engineer*

### New Salem
Lenherr, Frederick Keith *neurophysiologist, computer scientist*

### Newbury
Jones, Christopher Edward *manufacturing systems consultant*

### Newburyport
Berggren, Dick *editor*
MacWilliams, Kenneth Edward *investment banker*

### Newton
Balsamo, Salvatore Anthony *technical and temporary employment companies executive*
Barnet, Bruce *publishing executive*
Baron, Charles Hillel *lawyer, educator*
Bassuk, Ellen Linda *psychiatrist*
Bernard, Michael Mark *city planning consultant, lawyer*
Bettes, Richard S., III *publishing company executive*
Blacher, Richard Stanley *psychiatrist*
Brilliant, Barbara *television host, producer, columnist, consultant, journalist*
Capon, Edwin Gould *church organization administrator, clergyman*
Chlamtac, Imrich *computer company executive, educator*
Chubb, Stephen Darrow *medical corporation executive*
Cleary, Paul David *sociomedical educator*
Coquillette, Daniel Robert *lawyer, educator*
Daya, Jackie *publishing company executive*
Deats, Paul Kindred, Jr. *religion educator, clergyman*
Dunlap, William Crawford *physicist*
Gerrity, J(ames) Frank, II *building materials company executive*
Gill, Benjamin Franklin *physician*
Glazer, Donald Wayne *business executive, lawyer, educator*
Glick-Weil, Kathy *library director*
Hauser, Harry Raymond *lawyer*
Henderson, Kenneth Atwood *investment counseling executive*
Heyn, Arno Harry Albert *retired chemistry educator*
Hogan, Brian Joseph *editor*
Horbaczewski, Henry Zygmunt *lawyer, publishing executive*
Huber, Richard Gregory *lawyer, educator*
Hughes, George Michael *lawyer*
Kardon, Brian *publishing company executive*
Knupp, Ralph *publishing company executive*
Kosowsky, David I. *retired biotechnical company executive*
Levine, Barry William *internist*
Lisman, Eric *publishing executive, lawyer*
McEvoy, Michael Joseph *economist*
Messing, Arnold Philip *lawyer*
Neth, Jerry *publishing company executive*
Oles, Paul Stevenson (Steve Oles) *architect, perspectivist, educator*
Ravnikar, Veronika A. *medical educator*
Rodman, Sumner *insurance executive*
Rogoff, Jerome Howard *psychiatrist, psychoanalyst, forensic expert*
Saffran, Kalman *engineering consulting company executive, entrepreneur*
Sheehy, Joan Mary *nurse*
Stein, Seymour *electronics executive, scientist*
Stundza, Thomas John *journalist*
Thompson, Stephen Arthur *publishing executive*
White, Burton Leonard *educational psychologist, author*
Zohn, Harry *author, educator*

### Newton Center
Adams, F. Gerard *economist, educator*
Mark, Melvin *consulting mechanical engineer, educator*
Sandman, Peter M. *risk communication consultant*
Schuller, Gunther Alexander *composer*

### Newton Highlands
Porter, Jack Nusan *writer, sociologist, educator*

### Newtonville
Polonsky, Arthur *artist, educator*

### North Adams
Thurston, Donald Allen *broadcasting executive*

### North Andover
Goldstein, Charles Henry *architect, consultant*
Jannini, Ralph Humbert, III *electronics executive*
Longsworth, Ellen Louise *art historian, consultant*
McGovern, Barbara Elizabeth Ann *elementary education educator*
Scully, Stephen J. *plastic surgeon*

### North Attleboro
Bordeleau, Lisa Marie *human services professional, consultant*
Cote, Louise Roseann *creative director, designer*
Friend, Dale Gilbert *retired medical educator*
Williams, Ruth L. *rehabilitation counselor, consultant*

### North Billerica
Mellon, Timothy *transportation executive*
Witover, Stephen Barry *pediatrician*

### North Brookfield
Neal, Avon *artist, author*
Parker, Ann (Ann Parker Neal) *photographer, graphic artist*

### North Chatham
McCarthy, Joseph Harold *consultant, former retail food company executive*
Rowlands, Marvin Lloyd, Jr. *publishing and communications consultant*

### North Chelmsford
Osenton, Thomas George *publisher*

### North Dartmouth
Barrow, Clyde Wayne *political scientist, educator*
Cressy, Peter Hollon *naval officer, academic administrator*
Dace, Tish *drama educator*
Hodgson, James Stanley *antiquarian bookseller*
Law, Frederick Masom *engineering educator, structural engineering firm executive*
Tuttle, Clifford Horace, Jr. *electronics manufacturing company executive*

Yoken, Mel B(arton) *French language educator, author*

### North Dighton
Cserr, Robert *psychiatrist, physician, hospital administrator*
Silvia, David Alan *insurance broker*

### North Eastham
DeMuth, Vivienne Blake McCandless *artist, illustrator*
Simmel, Marianne Lenore *graphic designer*
York, Elizabeth Jane *innkeeper*

### North Easton
Paul, Donald W. *therapist, audiologist*

### North Egremont
Le Comte, Edward Semple *author, educator*

### North Falmouth
Bass, Norman Herbert *physician, scientist, university and hospital administrator, health care executive*
Morse, Robert Warren *research administrator*

### North Grafton
Nelson, John Martin *corporate executive*
Ross, James Neil, Jr. *veterinary educator*
Schwartz, Anthony *veterinary surgeon, educator*

### North Quincy
Segelman, Allyn Evan *dentist, researcher*

### North Reading
Day, Ronald Elwin *management consultant*
Dolan, Edward Corcoran *real estate developer and investor*
Green, Jack Allen *lawyer*
O'Neil, John P(atrick) *athletic footwear company executive*

### Northampton
Anderson, Margaret Ellen (Margaret Ellen Anderson) *physiologist, educator*
Burk, Carl John *biological sciences educator*
Dashef, Stephen Sewell *psychiatrist*
Derr, Thomas Sieger *religion educator*
Donfried, Karl Paul *minister, theology educator*
Elkins, Stanley Maurice *historian, educator*
Ellis, Frank Hale *English literature educator*
Fleck, George Morrison *chemistry educator*
Flesher, Hubert Louis *religion educator*
Heartt, Charlotte Beebe *university official*
Hoyt, Nelly Schargo (Mrs. N. Deming Hoyt) *history educator*
Lehmann, Phyllis Williams *archaeologist, educator*
Lightburn, Anita Louise *dean, social work educator*
Little, Lester Knox *historian, educator*
Naegele, Philipp Otto *violinist, violist, music educator*
Piccinino, Rocco Michael *librarian*
Pickrel, Paul *English educator*
Robinson, Donald Leonard *social scientist, educator*
Rose, Peter Isaac *sociologist, writer*
Rupp, Sheron Adeline *photographer, educator*
†Simmons, Ruth J. *academic administrator*
Smith, Malcolm Barry Estes *philosophy educator, lawyer*
Unsworth, Richard Preston *minister, school administrator*
Vaget, Hans Rudolf *language professional, educator*
Vesely, Alexander *civil engineer*
Volkmann, Frances Cooper *psychologist, educator*
von Klemperer, Klemens *historian, educator*

### Northborough
Fulmer, Hugh Scott *physician, educator*
Jeas, William C. *aerospace engineering executive, consultant*

### Norton
Dahl, Curtis *English literature educator*
Deekle, Peter Van *library director*
Marshall, Dale Rogers *college president, political scientist, educator*
Norris, Curtis Bird *writer, journalist*
Olson, Roberta Jeanne Marie *art historian, author, educator*
Taylor, Robert Sundling *English educator, art critic*

### Norwell
Brett, Jan Churchill *illustrator, author*
Case, David Knowlton *management consultant*
Mullare, T(homas) Kenwood, Jr. *lawyer*
Rolnik, Zachary Jacob *publishing company executive*
Smith, Jeffrey Koestlin *publishing executive*
Wentworth, Murray Jackson *artist, educator*

### Norwood
Berliner, Allen Irwin *dermatologist*
Carpenter, Pamela Prisco *bank officer, foreign language educator*
Florian, Agustin Max *thoracic and cardiovascular surgeon*
Imbault, James Joseph *engineering executive*
Pence, Robert Dudley *biomedical research administrator, hospital administrator*
Sheingold, Daniel H. *electrical engineer*
Smith, William Bridges *diversified company executive*

### Nutting Lake
Furman, John Rockwell *wholesale lumber company executive*

### Oakham
Poirier, Helen Virginia Leonard *elementary education educator*

### Onset
Kish, Grace Edna *mechanical engineer*

### Orange
Bate, Judith Ellen *artist*

### Orleans
Hiscock, Richard Carson *marine safety investigator*
Hughes, Libby *author*
Lawton, Nancy *artist*

### Osterville
El-Fayoumy, J.P.G. *writer, poet*
Malayery, Nasrin *educator, consultant*
Schwarztrauber, Sayre Archie *former naval officer, maritime consultant*
Weber, Adelheid Lisa *former nurse, chemist*

### Otis
Wampler, Barbara Bedford *entrepreneur*

### Palmer
Dupuis, Robert Simeon *sales executive*

### Paxton
Kuklinski, Joan Lindsey *librarian*

### Peabody
Bernstein, Emil S. *financial executive*
Dee, Pauline Marie *artist*
Goldberg, Harold Seymour *electrical engineer, academic administrator*
Peters, Leo Francis *environmental engineer*
Stahl, William Martin *professional training director*
Torkildsen, Peter G. *congressman*
Wood, Richard Robinson *real estate executive*

### Pembroke
Freitas, Jeffrey Anthony *textile design agency executive*

### Pepperell
Holmes, Reed M. *clergyman, historian, photographer*
Scholefield, Adeline Peggy *therapist*

### Petersham
Chivian, Eric Seth *psychiatrist, educator*
Kenney, Joseph Edmund *special education educator*

### Pittsfield
Cornelio, Albert Carmen *insurance executive*
Fanelli, Robert Drew *surgeon*
Feigenbaum, Armand Vallin *systems engineer, systems equipment executive*
Liveright, Betty Fouch *actress, director, writer*
Murray, David *journalist, author*

### Plymouth
Barreira, Brian Ernest *lawyer*
Forman, Peter *sheriff, former state legislator*
Freyermuth, Virginia Karen *secondary art educator*
Gregory, Dick *comedian, civil rights activist*
Joseph, Rodney Randy *artist, arts society executive*
Taylor, Maryann Courtney *elementary education educator*

### Provincetown
Doty, Mark *poet*
Harmon, Lily *artist, author*
Oliver, Mary *poet*
Wolfman, Brunetta Reid *education educator*

### Quincy
Bierman, George William *technical consulting executive, food technologist*
Colgan, Sumner *manufacturing engineer, chemical engineer*
Edelman, Raymond Howard *investment company executive*
Gorfinkle, Constance Sue *journalist*
Hagar, William Gardner, III *photobiology educator*
Hall, John Raymond, Jr. *fire protection executive*
Harold, Paul Dennis *state senator*
Hayes, Bernardine Frances *computer systems analyst*
Hill, Kent Richmond *college president*
Kelley, James Francis *civil engineer*
Levin, Robert Joseph *retail grocery chain store executive*
Lippincott, Joseph P. *photojournalist, educator*
McGlinchey, Joseph Dennis *retail corporation executive*
Miller, George David *retired air force officer, marketing consultant*
O'Brien, John Steininger *clinical psychologist*
Spangler, Arthur Stephenson, Jr. *psychologist*
Tobin, Robert G. *supermarket chain executive*
Young, Richard William *corporate director*

### Randolph
Cammarata, Richard John *financial advisor*
Morrissey, Edmond Joseph *classical philologist*

### Raynham
Kaplan, Kenneth Barry *psychologist*

### Reading
Burbank, Nelson Stone *investment banker*
Donald, John Hepburn, II *quality assurance professional, consultant*
Neville, Elisabeth *computer applications specialist*
Smith, Derek Armand *publishing company executive*
Terilli, Joseph Anthony *secondary education educator*
White, Karen Ruth Jones *information systems executive*

### Revere
Chesna-Serino, Edna Mae *nurse*
Herron, Carolivia *novelist, English educator*
Pennacchio, Linda Marie *secondary school educator*

### Rockport
Bakrow, William John *college president emeritus*
Bissell, Phil (Charles P. Bissell) *cartoonist*
Deedy, John Gerard, Jr. *writer*
Delakas, Daniel Liudviko *retired foreign language educator*
Nicholas, Thomas Andrew *artist*
Strisik, Paul *artist*
Walen, Harry Leonard *historian, lecturer, author*
Wiberg, Lars-Erik *human resources consultant*

### Roslindale
Blomquist, Cecile La Chance *quality assurance professional, technologist*

### Rowe
Foshay, Arthur Wellesley *retired educator*

### Roxbury
Berman, Marlene Oscar *neuropsychologist, educator*

Franzblau, Carl *biochemist, consultant, researcher*
Gamer, Frances *elementary educator*
Kelley, Ruth M. *nurse, alcohol, drug abuse services professional*
MacNichol, Edward Ford, Jr. *biophysicist, educator*
McLaughlin, Garland Eutreé *librarian*
Meenan, Robert Francis *academician, rheumatologist, researcher*
Peters, Alan *anatomy educator*
Resnick, Oscar *neuroscientist*
Short, Janet Marie *principal*
Simons, Elizabeth R(eiman) *biochemist, educator*
Small, Donald MacFarland *biophysics educator, gastroenterologist*

### Sagamore Beach
Martin, Dale *vocational rehabilitation executive*

### Salem
Del Vecchio, Debra Anne *lawyer*
Ettinger, Mort *marketing educator*
Finamore, Daniel Robert *museum curator*
Goddard, Joseph (Iain Goddard) *medical imaging engineer*
Gozemba, Patrica Andrea *women's studies and English language educator, writer*
Griffin, Thomas McLean *retired lawyer*
Harrington, Nancy D. *college president*
Moran, Philip David *lawyer*
O'Brien, Robert Kenneth *insurance company executive*
Piro, Anthony John *radiologist*
Wathne, Carl Norman *hospital administrator*

### Salisbury
Camacho, Henry Francis *accountant*

### Sandwich
Pearson, Paul Holding *insurance company executive*
Terrill, Robert Carl *hospital administrator*

### Saugus
Austill, Allen *dean emeritus*

### Scituate
Keating, Margaret Mary *entrepreneur, business consultant*

### Sharon
Honikman, Larry Howard *pediatrician*
Kahn, Marilyn Zeldin *artist, art educator*
Paolino, Richard Francis *manufacturing company executive*
Wisotsky, Serge Sidorovich, Sr. *engineering executive*

### Sheffield
Velmans, Loet Abraham *retired public relations executive*

### Sherborn
Borgeson, Earl Charles *law librarian, educator*
Kasser, James R. *medical educator*
Kennedy, Chester Ralph, Jr. *former state official, art director*
Pickhardt, Carl Emile, Jr. *artist*

### Shirley
Field, Hermann Haviland *architect, educator, author*

### Shrewsbury
Forde, Mary Margaret *foundation executive*
Lanza, Robert Paul *medical scientist*
Magee, Bernard Dale *obstetrician, gynecologist*
Poteete, Robert Arthur *editor*
Zamecnik, Paul Charles *oncologist, medical research scientist*

### Siasconset
Kreitler, Richard Rogers *company executive*

### Somerset
Sabra, Steven Peter *lawyer*

### Somerville
Halevi, Marcus *photographer*
Korobkin, Barry Jay *architect*
Safdie, Moshe *architect*
Verderber, Joseph Anthony *capital equipment company executive*
Wheeler, Katherine Frazier (Kate Wheeler) *writer*

### South Dartmouth
Backes, Joan *artist*
Stern, T. Noel *political scientist, educator*
Ward, Richard Joseph *university official, educator, author*

### South Dennis
Stiefvater, Pamela Jean *chiropractor*

### South Easton
Clarke, Cornelius Wilder *religious organization administrator, minister*

### South Hadley
Berek, Peter *English educator*
Brownlow, Frank Walsh *English language educator*
Campbell, Mary Kathryn *chemistry educator*
Ciruti, Joan Estelle *Spanish language and literature educator*
Creighton, Joanne Vanish *academic administrator*
Doezema, Marianne *art historian*
Farnham, Anthony Edward *English language educator*
Harrison, Anna Jane *chemist, educator*
Herbert, Robert Louis *art history educator*
Johnson, Richard August *English language educator*
Mazzocco, Angelo *language educator*
Quinn, Betty Nye *former classics educator*
Robin, Richard Shale *philosophy educator*
Sheridan, Daniel Joseph *lawyer*
Todorovic, John *chemical engineer*
Townsend, Jane Kaltenbach *zoologist, educator*
Viereck, Peter *poet, historian, educator*
Williamson, Kenneth Lee *chemistry educator*

### South Hamilton
Kalland, Lloyd Austin *minister*
Patton, George Smith *military officer*

### South Harwich
Micciche, Salvatore Joseph *retired journalist, lawyer*

### South Orleans
Burton, Robert William *retired office products executive*
Hickok, Richard Sanford *accountant*
Parker, Douglas Martin *writer, retired lawyer*

### South Wellfleet
Bargellini, Pier Luigi *electrical engineer*

### South Weymouth
Greineder, Juergen Kurt *surgeon*
Milley, Jane Elizabeth *academic administrator*
Young, Michael C. *allergist, immunologist, pediatrician*

### South Yarmouth
Arthur, George Roland *accountant, engineer, mathematician*
Benoit, Leroy James *language educator*

### Southborough
Astill, Robert Michael *credit manager*
Dews, P(eter) B(ooth) *medical scientist, educator*
Sidman, Richard Leon *neuroscientist*

### Southbridge
Anderson, Ross Barrett *healthcare environmental services manager*
Mangion, Richard Michael *health care executive*

### Southfield
Melvin, Ronald McKnight *retired museum director*

### Southwick
MacEwan, Barbara Ann *middle school educator*

### Springfield
Albano, Michael J. *mayor*
†Archibald, Nathaniel *retired basketball player*
†Bellamy, Walter Jones *retired basketball player*
Bixby, Allan Barton *retired insurance company executive*
†Blazejowski, Carol *retired basketball player*
Caprio, Anthony S. *university president*
Ciak, Brenda Susan *nurse*
Clark, William James *retired insurance company executive*
Cleland, Thomas Edward, Jr. *secondary school educator*
D'Amour, Donald H. *supermarket chain executive*
Dastgeer, Ghulam Mohammad *surgeon*
Dunn, Donald Jack *law librarian, law educator, lawyer*
†Dupre, Thomas L. *bishop*
Farkas, Paul Stephen *gastroenterologist*
Finnegan, Thomas Joseph, Jr. *insurance executive, lawyer*
Frankel, Kenneth Mark *thoracic surgeon*
Freedman, Frank Harlan *federal judge*
Frey, Mary Elizabeth *artist*
Friedmann, Paul *surgeon, educator*
†Gallatin, Harry Junior *retired basketball player*
Gallup, John Gardiner *retired paper company executive*
Garvey, Richard Conrad *journalist*
†Gates, William *retired baseball player*
†Gola, Tom *retired basketball player*
†Goodrich, Gail Charles, Jr. *retired basketball player*
Gordon, Ronni Anne *journalist*
†Greer, Harold Everett *retired basketball player*
†Hagan, Clifford *retired basketball player*
Haggerty, Thomas Francis *newspaper editor*
†Harris-Stewart, Lusia *retired basketball player*
†Hawkins, Cornelius L. (Connie) *retired basketball player*
†Hayes, Elvin Ernest *retired basketball player*
†Holzman, William *retired basketball player*
†Houbregs, Bob *retired basketball player*
Johnson, Robert Allison *life insurance company executive*
†Jones, Samuel *retired basketball player*
†Kundla, John *coach, retired*
†Lieberman-Cline, Nancy *retired basketball player*
Liptzin, Benjamin *psychiatrist*
†Lovellette, Clyde *retired basketball player*
†Lucas, Jerry *retired basketball player*
Maidman, Stephen Paul *lawyer*
†Martin, Slater Nelson, Jr. *retired basketball player*
McGee, William Tobin *intensive care physician*
†McGuire, Richard Joseph *retired basketball player*
†Mikan, George *retired basketball player*
†Mikkelsen, Arlid Verner Agerskov *retired basketball player*
Miller, J(ohn) Wesley, III *lawyer, author*
Miller, Leroy Paul, Jr. *secondary English educator*
†Miller, Ralph *coach, retired*
Milstein, Richard Sherman *lawyer*
Miranda, Michele Renee *optometrist*
Mish, Frederick Crittenden *editor*
Morse, John M. *book publishing executive*
Muhlberger, Richard Charles *former museum administrator, writer, educator*
Navab, Farhad *medical educator*
†Newell, Peter *retired basketball coach*
Oldershaw, Louis Frederick *lawyer*
†Pettit, Robert *retired basketball player*
Ponsor, Michael Adrian *federal judge*
Porter, Burton Frederick *philosophy educator, author, dean*
†Ramsey, Frank *retired basketball player*
Rivest, Anne-Marie Therese *post-anesthesia nurse*
†Schayes, Adolf *retired basketball player*
Smith, James Almer, Jr. *psychiatrist*
Stack, May Elizabeth *library director*
Susse, Sandra Slone *lawyer*
†Taylor, Fred *retired basketball coach*
†Thompson, David O'Neal *retired basketball player*
†Thurmond, Nathaniel *retired basketball player*
Utley, F. Knowlton *library director, educator*
Vella, Sandra Rachael *principal*
†Wanzer, Robert *retired basketball player*
Wheeler, Thomas Beardsley *insurance company executive*
†White, Nera *retired basketball player*

### Stockbridge
Shapiro, Edward Robert *psychiatrist, educator, psychoanalyst*
Storch, Arthur *theater director*

### Stoneham
Dalimonte, Josephine Ann (Jo-Ann Dalimonte) *school nurse practitioner*
Igou, Raymond Alvin, Jr. *orthopedic surgeon*
Mc Donald, Andrew Jewett *securities firm executive*

### Stoughton
Bestgen, William Henry, Jr. *financial planner*
Douglas, John Breed, III *lawyer*
Fireman, Paul B. *footwear and apparel company executive*
Ross, Edward Joseph *architect*
Schepps, Victoria Hayward *lawyer*
Snyder, Mark Irwin *marketing and public relations executive*

### Stow
Becherer, Richard Joseph *scientific consulting firm executive, physicist*
Champine, George A. *computer scientist*
Kulas, Frederick John *computer company executive*
Langenwalter, Gary Allan *manufacturing and management consulting company executive*
Shrader, William Whitney *radar consulting scientist*
Vrablik, Edward A. *computer company executive, management consultant*

### Sturbridge
Belforte, David Arthur *company president*
Flynn, Richard Jerome *manufacturing company executive*
McMahon, Maribeth Lovette *physicist*

### Sudbury
Aronson, David *artist, retired art educator*
Blackey, Edwin Arthur, Jr. *geologist*
Fowler, Charles Albert *electronics engineer*
Freund, Mitchell David *cable television executive, producer, consultant*
Hillery, Mary Jane Larato *columnist, producer, television host, reserve army officer*
McCree, Paul William, Jr. *systems design and engineering company executive*
Meltzer, Donald Richard *treasurer*
Nyman, Georgianna Beatrice *painter*
Richards, James Carlton *microbiologist, business executive*

### Swampscott
Neumann, Gerhard *mechanical engineer*
Smith, Carl Dean, Jr. *counselor, child advocate, business broker*
Truog, Dean-Daniel Wesley *educator, consultant*

### Swansea
Holmes, Henry (Hank Holmes) *advertising and marketing executive, editor*

### Taunton
Bornstein, Myer Sidney *obstetrician, gynecologist*
Buote, Rosemarie Boschen *special education educator*
Donly, Michael J. *headmaster*
Lopes, Maria Fernandina *commissioner*
Mosher, Wendy Jean *retail chain official*
Ricciardi, Louis Michael *brokerage house executive*
Tenney, Patricia Ann *psychotherapist, nurse*
White, Christine *physical education educator*

### Tewksbury
DeAngelis, Michele F. *school system administrator*
DeMoulas, Telemachus A. *retail grocery company executive*
Dulchinos, Peter *lawyer*
Hantman, Barry G. *software engineer*
Wilson, Daniel Donald *engineering executive*

### Topsfield
Brady, James Robert, Jr. *real estate developer*
Fubini, Eugene Ghiron *business consultant*
Peirce, John Wentworth *architect*
Webster, Larry Russell *artist*

### Truro
Cassill, Ronald Verlin *author*
Falk, Lee Harrison *performing arts executive, cartoonist*
Woolley, Catherine (Jane Thayer) *writer*

### Vineyard Haven
Billingham, Rupert Everett *zoologist, educator*
Hough, George Anthony, III *journalism educator*
Jacobs, Gretchen Huntley *psychiatrist*
McIntosh, Jon Charles *illustrator*
Porter, James H. *chemical engineering executive*

### Waban
Aisner, Mark *internist*
Rossolimo, Alexander Nicholas *management consultant*

### Wakefield
Hatch, Mark Bruce *software engineer*
Irons, Diane Havelick *small business owner*
Kerrigan, Nancy *professional figure skater, former Olympic athlete*
Spaulding, William Rowe *investment consultant*

### Walpole
Coleman, John Joseph *telephone company executive*
Hunter, Elizabeth Ives-Valsam *fashion consultant*
Marshall, Virginia Mary *technology educator*
Morton, Robert Allen *small business owner*
Warthin, Thomas Angell *physician, educator*

### Waltham
Abeles, Robert Heinz *biochemistry educator*
Adamian, Gregory Harry *academic administrator*
Arena, Albert A. *museum director*
Barnes-Brown, Peter Newton *lawyer*
Bernstein, Stanley Joseph *manufacturing executive*
Black, Eugene Charlton *historian, educator*
Bohlen, Nina *artist*
Boykan, Martin *composer, music educator*
Brown, Edgar Henry, Jr. *mathematician, educator*
Brown, Seyom *international relations educator, government consultant*
Cohen, Saul G. *chemist, educator*
Conrad, Peter *sociology educator*
Cotter, Douglas Adrian *healthcare executive*
Delaney, Mary Anne *pastoral educator*
De Rosier, David John *biophysicist, educator*
Deser, Stanley *physicist, educator*
Ellenbogen, George *poet, educator*
Ellenbogen, S. David *electronics company executive*
Epstein, Irving Robert *chemistry educator*
Evans, Robert, Jr. *economics educator*
Fallon, John Golden *banker*
Fasman, Gerald David *biochemistry educator*
Fleming, Samuel Crozier, Jr. *health care publishing and consulting firm executive*
Floyd, John Taylor *electronics executive*
Foxman, Bruce Mayer *chemist, educator*
Fuchs, Lawrence Howard *government official, educator*
Galinat, Walton C. *research scientist*
Gibbons, Patrice Ellen *critical care nurse*
Hahn, Bessie King *library administrator, lecturer*
Harth, Erica *French language and comparative literature educator*
Hatsopoulos, George Nicholas *mechanical engineer, thermodynamicist, educator*
Hayes, Sherman Lee *library director*
Hindus, Milton *writer, literature educator*
Jackendoff, Ray Saul *linguistics educator*
Jeanloz, Roger William *biochemist, educator*
Jencks, William Platt *biochemist, educator*
Johnson, William Alexander *clergyman, philosophy educator*
Kalba, Kas *international communications consultant*
Kasputys, Joseph Edward *corporate executive, economist*
Kern, Fred Robert, Jr. *engineer*
Kustin, Kenneth *chemist*
Lackner, James Robert *aerospace medicine educator*
Large, G. Gordon M. *computer software company executive*
Leach, Robert Ellis *physician, educator*
Lees, Marjorie Berman *biochemist, neuroscientist*
Levitan, Irwin Barry *neuroscience educator, academic administrator*
Marshall, Robert Lewis *musicologist, educator*
McCulloch, Rachel *economics researcher, educator*
Mc Feeley, John Jay *chemical engineer*
Mitchell, Janet Brew *health services researcher*
Morant, Ricardo Bernardino *psychology educator*
Murray, Pius Charles William *priest, educator*
Nahigian, Alma Louise *technical documentation administrator*
Nelson, Arthur Hunt *real estate management development company executive*
Nisonoff, Alfred *biochemist, educator*
Nogelo, Anthony Miles *retired health care company executive*
Notkin, Leonard Sheldon *architect*
O'Donnell, Teresa Hohol *software development engineer, antennas engineer*
Pantazelos, Peter George *financial executive*
Paris, Steven Mark *software engineer*
Petsko, Gregory Anthony *chemistry and biochemistry educator*
Poduska, John William, Sr. *computer company executive*
Reilly, Philip Raymond *medical research administrator*
Reinharz, Jehuda *academic administrator, history educator*
Reisman, Bernard *theology educator*
Riley, Henry Charles *banker*
Rodiger, William King *telecommunications and media industry consultant*
Ross, George William *social scientist, educator*
Schweber, Silvan Samuel *physics and history educator*
Sekuler, Robert William *psychology educator, scientist*
Slifka, Alfred A. *oil corporation executive*
Snider, Barry B. *organic chemist*
Staves, Susan *English educator*
†Tamasanis, Douglas Thomas *physicist*
Titcomb, Caldwell *music and theatre historian*
Touster, Saul *law educator*
Weinert, Henry M. *biomedical company executive*
Wyner, Yehudi *composer, pianist, conductor, educator*
Yancey, Wallace Glenn *retired insurance company executive*
Young, Dwight Wayne *ancient civilization educator*
Zebrowitz, Leslie Ann *psychology educator*

### Watertown
Dawson, Stuart Owen *landscape architect, urban designer*
Goodheart, Eugene *English language educator*
Katz, William Emanuel *chemical engineer*
Lin, Alice Lee Lan *physicist, researcher, educator*
Pellegrom, Daniel Earl *international health and development executive*
Rivers, Wilga Marie *foreign language educator*
True, Edward Keene *architectural engineer*

### Wayland
Blair, John *consulting scientist*
Boulding, Elise Marie *sociologist, educator*
Clark, Melville, Jr. *physicist, electrical engineer, consultant*
Clogan, Paul Maurice *English language and literature educator*
Dergalis, George *artist, educator*
Hagenstein, Perry Reginald *economist*
Huygens, Remmert William *architect*
Neumeyer, John Leopold *research company administrator, chemistry educator*
Wolf, Irving *clinical psychologist*

### Webster
Siddall, Patricia Ann *English language educator*

### Wellesley
Aldrich, Richard Orth *lawyer*
Anthony, Edward Lovell, II *retired investments executive*
Auerbach, Jerold S. *university educator*
Bidart, Frank *English educator, poet*
Carlson, Christopher Tapley *lawyer*
Coyne, Mary Downey *biologist, endocrinologist, educator*
Doku, Hristo Chris *dental educator*
Eilts, Hermann Frederick *international relations educator, former diplomat*
Freeman, Judi H. *curator, art historian*
Gailius, Gilbert Keistutis *manufacturing company executive*
Gerety, Robert John *microbiologist, pharmaceutical company executive, pediatrician, vaccinologist*
Giddon, Donald B(ernard) *psychologist, educator*
Gladstone, Richard Bennett *retired publishing company executive*
Goglia, Charles A., Jr. *lawyer*

Goldberg, Pamela Winer *strategic consultant*
Hildebrand, Francis Begnaud *mathematics educator*
Hornig, Lilli Schwenk *educational administrator, researcher*
Jacobs, Ruth Harriet *poet, playwright, sociologist, gerontologist*
Jovanovic, Miodrag Stevana *surgeon, educator*
Klein, Lawrence Allen *accounting educator*
Kobayashi, Yutaka *biochemist, consultant*
Kucharski, John Michael *scientific instruments manufacturing company executive*
Lefkowitz, Mary Rosenthal *Greek literature educator*
Marcus, William Michael *rubber and vinyl products manufacturing company executive*
Miller, Linda B. *political scientist*
Mistacco, Vicki E. *foreign language educator*
Myers, Arthur B. *journalist, author*
Nagler, Leon Gregory *management consultant, business executive*
O'Gorman, James Francis *art educator, writer*
Papageorgiou, John Constantine *management science educator*
Parker, William H., III *federal official*
Piper, Adrian Margaret Smith *philosopher, artist, educator*
Putnam, Ruth Anna *philosopher, educator*
Ritt, Paul Edward *communications and electronics company executive*
Rowe, Stephen Cooper *venture capitalist, entrepreneur*
Shea, Robert McConnell *lawyer*
Stannard, Jan Gregory *academic administrator*
Tagge, Anne Katherine *not-for-profit organization administrator*
Tarr, Robert Joseph, Jr. *publishing executive, retail executive*
Tierney, Thomas J. *business management consultant*
Walsh, Diana Chapman *academic administrator, social and behavioral sciences educator*
Weil, Thomas Alexander *electronics engineer, retired*
Weiss, Andrew Richard *lawyer*

### Wellesley Hills
Coco, Samuel Barbin *venture consultant*
Spierings, Egilius Leonardus Hendricus *neurologist, headache specialist, pharmacologist*

### Wellfleet
Mc Feely, William Shield *historian, writer*
Piercy, Marge *poet, novelist, essayist*

### Wenham
Herrmann, Robert Lawrence *biochemistry, science, religion educator*
Whittemore, Frank Bowen *environmental, energy and management consultant*

### West Barnstable
Corsa, Helen Storm *language professional*

### West Bridgewater
Gulvin, David Horner *electric company executive*
Worrell, Cynthia Lee *bank executive*
Wyner, Justin L. *laminating company executive*

### West Brookfield
Higgins, Brian Alton *art gallery executive*

### West Chatham
Rowley, Glenn Harry *lawyer*

### West Dennis
Toner, Walter Joseph, Jr. *transportation engineer, financial consultant*

### West Falmouth
Carlson, David Bret *lawyer, consultant*
Holz, George G., IV *research scientist, medicine educator*
Vaccaro, Ralph Francis *marine biologist*

### West Newbury
Dooley, Ann Elizabeth *freelance writers cooperative executive, editor*

### West Newton
Elya, John Adel *bishop*
Frieden, Bernard Joel *urban studies educator*
Sasahara, Arthur Asao *cardiologist, educator, researcher*

### West Roxbury
Goyal, Raj Kumar *medical educator*
Hedley-Whyte, John *anesthesiologist, educator*

### West Springfield
Engebretson, Douglas Kenneth *architect*

### West Stockbridge
Stokes, Allison *pastor, researcher, religion educator*

### West Tisbury
Logue, Edward Joseph *development company executive*
Méras, Phyllis Leslie *journalist*
Smith, Henry Clay *retired psychology educator*

### Westborough
Atsumi, Ikuko *management school administrator, educator*
Drees, Stephen Daniel *financial services executive, strategy, marketing and product development consultant*
Frank, Jacob *lawyer*
Gionfriddo, Maurice Paul *aeronautical engineer, research and development manager*
Houston, Alfred Dearborn *energy company executive*
Jackson, Frederick Herbert *educational administrator*
Rowe, John William *utility executive*
Skates, Ronald Louis *computer manufacturing executive*
Staffier, Pamela Moorman *psychologist*
Tobias, Lester Lee *psychological consultant*
Young, Roger Austin *natural gas distribution company executive*

### Westfield
Buckmore, Alvah Clarence, Jr. *computer scientist, ballistician*
Ettman, Philip *business law educator*
Tower, Horace Linwood, III *consumer products company executive*

### Westford
Dennison, Byron Lee *electrical engineering educator, consultant*
Salah, Joseph Elias *research scientist, educator*
Selesky, Donald Bryant *software developer*
Stansberry, James Wesley *air force officer*
Tuttle, David Bauman *data processing executive*
Weston, Joan Spencer *production director, communications executive*

### Weston
Aquilino, Daniel *banker*
Bales, Robert Freed *social psychologist, educator*
Chu, Jeffrey Chuan *business executive, consultant*
Clayton, Richard Reese *holding company executive*
Conners, John Brendan *insurance company executive*
Fine, Bernard J. *retired psychologist, consultant*
Fish, David Earl *insurance company executive*
Haas, Jacqueline Crawford *lawyer*
Higgins, Sister Therese *English educator, former college president*
Ives, J. Atwood *financial executive*
Kendall, Julius *consulting engineer*
Kraft, Gerald *economist*
Landis, John William *engineering and construction executive, government advisor*
Mc Elwee, John Gerard *retired life insurance company executive*
Oelgeschlager, Guenther Karl *publisher*
Paresky, David S. *travel company executive*
Resden, Ronald Everett *medical devices product development engineer*
Rockwell, George Barcus *financial consultant*
Saad, Theodore Shafick *retired microwave company executive*
Safiol, George E. *electronics company executive*
Sanzone, Donna S. *publishing executive*
Schloemann, Ernst Fritz (Rudolf August) *physicist, engineer*
Stambaugh, Armstrong A., Jr. *restaurant and hotel executive*
Sturgis, Robert Shaw *architect*
Thomas, Roger Meriwether *lawyer*
Valente, Louis Patrick (Dan Valente) *business and financial consultant*
Wells, Lionelle Dudley *psychiatrist*
Whitehouse, David Rempfer *physicist*
Zraket, Charles Anthony *systems research and engineering company executive*

### Westport
Howard, James Merriam, Jr. *education writer*
Somerson, Rosanne *artist*

### Westport Point
Fanning, William Henry, Jr. *computer scientist*

### Westwood
Bernfeld, Peter Harry William *biochemist*
Borgman, George Allan *journalist*
Brooks, John Robinson *surgeon, educator*
Burrell, Sidney Alexander *history educator*
Galston, Clarence Elkus *lawyer*
Gillette, Hyde *investment banker*
Old, Bruce Scott *chemical and metallurgical engineer*
Philbrick, Margaret Elder *artist*

### Weymouth
Boers, Celia Ann *public relations executive*

### Whitman
Delaney, Matthew Michael *school administrator, fine arts educator*

### Wilbraham
Anderson, Eric William *retired food service company executive*
Gaudreau, Jules Oscar, Jr. *insurance and financial services company executive*
O'Shaughnessy, Joseph A. *restaurant company executive*
Woloshchuk, Candace Dixon *secondary school educator, artist, consultant*

### Williamsburg
Healy, Robert Danforth *manufacturing executive*

### Williamstown
Bahlman, Dudley Ward Rhodes *history educator*
Bell-Villada, Gene H. *literature educator, writer*
Bleezarde, Thomas Warren *magazine editor*
Bolton, Roger Edwin *economist, educator*
Burns, James MacGregor *political scientist, historian*
Conforti, Michael Peter *museum director, art historian*
Conklin, Susan Joan *psychotherapist, educator, corporate staff development*
Cramer, Phebe *psychologist*
Crampton, Stuart Jessup Bigelow *physicist, educator*
Crider, Andrew Blake *psychologist*
Dalzell, Robert Fenton, Jr. *historian*
Dew, Charles Burgess *historian, educator*
Dickerson, Dennis Clark *history educator*
Edgerton, Samuel Youngs, Jr. *art historian, educator*
Erickson, Peter Brown *librarian, scholar, writer*
Eusden, John Dykstra *theology educator, minister*
Filipczak, Zirka Zaremba *art historian, educator*
Fuqua, Charles John *classics educator*
Graver, Lawrence Stanley *English language professional*
Hamilton, George Heard *curator*
Hastings, Philip Kay *psychology educator*
Hill, Victor Ernst, IV *mathematics educator, musician*
Hyde, John Michael *history educator*
Lee, Arthur Virgil, III *biotechnology company executive*
Markgraf, J(ohn) Hodge *chemist, educator*
McGill, Robert Ernest, III *retired manufacturing company executive*
McGill, Thomas Emerson *psychology educator*
Morgan, Frank *mathematics educator*
Norton, Glyn Peter *French literature educator*
Oakley, Francis Christopher *history educator, former college president*
Park, David Allen *physicist, educator*
Pasachoff, Jay Myron *astronomer, educator*
Payne, Harry Charles *historian, educator*
Payne, Michael Clarence *gastroenterologist*
Pistorius, George *language educator*
Raab, Lawrence Edward *English educator*
Rudolph, Frederick *history educator*
Sabot, Richard Henry *economics educator, researcher, consultant*
Shainman, Irwin *music educator, musician*
Sheahan, John Bernard *economist, educator*
Solomon, Paul Robert *neuropsychologist, educator*
Sprague, John Louis *management consultant*
Stamelman, Richard Howard *French and humanities educator*
Waite, Robert George Leeson *history educator*
Wikander, Lawrence Einar *librarian*
Wilkins, Earle Wayne, Jr. *surgery educator emeritus*
Wobus, Reinhard Arthur *geologist, educator*

### Wilmington
Altschuler, Samuel *electronics company executive*
Bartlett, John Bruen *financial executive*
Buckley, Robert Paul *aerospace company executive*
Freeman, Donald Chester, Jr. *health care company executive*
Hartford, Ann Marie *accountant, controller*
Hayes, Carol Jeanne *physical education educator*

### Winchester
Blackham, Ann Rosemary (Mrs. J. W. Blackham) *realtor*
Brennan, Francis Patrick *banker*
Brown, David A.B. *strategy consultant*
Casey, Norine Therese *school principal*
Cecich, Donald Edward *business executive*
Cowgill, F(rank) Brooks *retired insurance company executive*
Ewing, David Walkley *magazine editor*
Hansen, Robert Joseph *civil engineer*
Hirschfeld, Ronald Colman *retired consulting engineering executive*
Hottel, Hoyt Clarke *consulting chemical engineer*
Jabre, Eddy-Marco *architect*
Neuman, Robert Sterling *art educator, artist*
Ockerbloom, Richard C. *newspaper executive*
Smith, Robert Moors *anesthesiologist*
Taggart, Ganson Powers *management consultant*

### Winthrop
Costantino, Frank Mathew *architectural illustrator*
Lutze, Ruth Louise *retired textbook editor, public relations executive*
Moses, Ronald Elliot *retired toiletries products executive*
O'Connell, Henry Francis *lawyer*

### Woburn
Caplitz, Gregg D. *financial planner*
Eddison, Elizabeth Bole *entrepreneur, information specialist*
Gelb, Arthur *science association executive, electrical and systems engineer*
Goela, Jitendra Singh *researcher, consultant*
Mehra, Raman Kumar *data processing executive, automation and control engineering researcher*
†Tramonte, Michael Robert *school psychologist*

### Woods Hole
Berggren, William Alfred *geologist, research micropaleontologist, educator*
Butman, Bradford *oceanographer*
Cohen, Seymour Stanley *biochemist, educator*
Copeland, Donald Eugene *research marine biologist*
Ebert, James David *research biologist, educator*
Emery, Kenneth Orris *marine geologist*
Fofonoff, Nicholas Paul *oceanographer, educator*
Gagosian, Robert B. *chemist, educator*
Grice, George Daniel *marine biologist, science administrator*
Hart, Stanley Robert *geochemist, educator*
Inoué, Shinya *microscopy and cell biology scientist, educator*
Jannasch, Holger Windekilde *microbiologist*
Loewenstein, Werner Randolph *physiologist, biophysicist, educator*
Rafferty, Nancy Schwarz *anatomy educator*
Steele, John Hyslop *marine scientist, oceanographic institute administrator*
Uchupi, Elazar *geologist, researcher*
Von Herzen, Richard Pierre *research scientist, consultant*
Woodwell, George Masters *ecology research director, lecturer*

### Worcester
Appelbaum, Paul Stuart *psychiatrist, educator*
Bagshaw, Joseph Charles *molecular biologist, educator*
Barnhill, Georgia Brady *print curator*
Bernhard, Jeffrey David *dermatologist, educator*
Berth, Donald Frank *university official, consultant*
Billias, George Athan *history educator*
Brill, A. Bertrand *nuclear medicine educator*
Britt, Margaret Mary *financial services educator*
Brooks, John Edward *college president emeritus*
Camougis, George *health, safety and environmental protection consultant*
Candib, Murray A. *business executive, retail management consultant*
Charney, Evan *pediatrician, educator*
Clarke, Edward Nielsen *engineering science educator*
Cowan, Fairman Chaffee *lawyer*
Curran, Louis Jerome, Jr. *choral master*
Davidson, Lee David *insurance executive*
DeFalco, Frank Damian *civil engineering educator*
Drachman, David Alexander *neurologist*
Dunlap, Ellen S. *library administrator*
Dunlop, George Rodgers *retired surgeon*
Erskine, Matthew Forbes *lawyer*
Escott, Shoolah Hope *microbiologist*
Gorton, Nathaniel M. *federal judge, lawyer*
Greenberg, Nathan *accountant*
Grogan, William Robert *university dean*
Hagan, Joseph Henry *college president*
Hanshaw, James Barry *physician, educator*
Hanson, Susan Easton *geography educator*
Herman, Barbara Rose *interior decorator*
Hohenemser, Christoph *physics educator, researcher*
Hunt, John David *retired banker*
Hunter, Richard Edward *physician*
Isaksen, Robert L. *bishop*
Jareckie, Stephen Barlow *museum curator*
Johnson, Penelope B. *librarian*
Johnston, Robert Everett *information management administrator*
Joshi, Harihar S. *medical laboratory executive*
Kaplan, Melvin Hyman *immunology, rheumatology, medical educator*
Katz, Robert Nathan *ceramic engineer, educator*
King, Anthony Gabriel *museum administrator*
Kotilainen, Helen Jean Rosen *infection control epidemiologist, researcher*
Langevin, Edgar Louis *retired humanities educator*
Laster, Leonard *physician, consultant, author*
Latham, Eleanor Ruth Earthrowl *neuropsychology therapist*
Lawrence, Walter Thomas *plastic surgeon*
LeDoux, William John *lawyer*
Levine, Peter Hughes *physician, health facility administrator*
Lidz, Charles Wilmanns *sociologist*
Ludlum, David Blodgett *pharmacologist, educator*
Magiera, Frank Edward *journalist, critic*
Maini, Baltej S. *surgeon*
Malone, Joseph James *mathematics educator, researcher*
McCorison, Marcus Allen *librarian, cultural organization administrator*
Menon, Mani *urological surgeon, educator*
Micklitsch, Christine Nocchi *health care administrator*
Mirza, Shaukat *engineering educator, researcher, consultant*
Norton, Robert Leo, Sr. *mechanical engineering educator, researcher*
O'Brien, John F. *insurance company executive*
Och, Mohamad Rachid *psychiatrist, consultant*
Olson, Robert Leonard *retired insurance company executive*
Onorato, Nicholas Louis *program director, economist*
Parrish, Edward Alton, Jr. *electrical and computer engineering educator, academic administrator*
Parsons, Edwin Spencer *clergyman, educator*
Pavlik, James William *chemistry educator*
Peura, Robert Allan *electrical and biomedical engineering educator*
Plummer, Edward Bruce *college librarian*
Reilly, Daniel Patrick *bishop*
Rencis, Joseph John *engineering educator, mechanical/civil engineer*
Sinkis, Deborah Mary *principal*
Sioui, Richard Henry *chemical engineer*
Smith, Edward Herbert *radiologist, educator*
Spencer, Harry Irving, Jr. *retired banker*
Szaban, Marilyn C. *small business owner*
Townes, Philip Leonard *pediatrician, educator*
Traina, Richard Paul *academic administrator*
Turner, Billie Lee, II *geography educator*
Ullrich, Robert Albert *business management educator*
Vaughan, Alden True *history educator*
Vick, Susan *playwright, educator*
Von Laue, Theodore Herman *historian, educator*
Wapner, Seymour *psychologist, educator, administrator*
Weiss, Alvin Harvey *chemical engineering educator, catalysis researcher and consultant*
Welu, James A. *art museum director*
Wheeler, Hewitt Brownell *surgeon, educator*
Wilbur, Leslie Clifford *mechanical engineering educator*
Wilkinson, Harold Arthur *neurosurgeon*
Yankauer, Alfred *physician, educator*
Zeugner, John Finn *history educator, writer*
Zurier, Robert Burton *medical educator, clinical investigator*
Zwiep, Donald Nelson *mechanical engineering educator, administrator*

### Worthington
Hastings, Wilmot Reed *lawyer*

### Wrentham
Teplow, Theodore Herzl *valve company executive*

### Yarmouth Port
Gordon, Benjamin Dichter *medical executive, pediatrician*
Gorey, Edward St. John *author, artist*
Hall, James Frederick *retired college president*
Stauffer, Robert Allen *former research company executive*
Stott, Thomas Edward, Jr. *engineering executive*

## MICHIGAN

### Ada
Bandemer, Norman John *healthcare consulting executive*
†De Vos, Daniel G. *sports team executive, marketing professional*
†DeVos, Douglas Lee *sales company executive*
Engel, Albert Joseph *federal judge*
Mc Callum, Charles Edward *lawyer*
Van Andel, Jay *direct selling company executive*
Van Andel, Steve Alan *business executive*
†Vander Weide, Cheri DeVos *sports team executive, marketing professional*

### Addison
Durant, Charles Edward, Jr. *medical facility administrator*
Knight, V. C. *manufacturing executive*

### Adrian
Caine, Stanley Paul *college administrator*
Dombrowski, Mark Anthony *librarian*
Henricks, Roger Lee *social services administrator*
Kralick, Richard Louis *lawyer*
Weathers, Milledge Wright *retired economics educator*

### Albion
Vulgamore, Melvin L. *college president*

### Allegan
Krause, Liz Young *community health nurse*

### Allen Park
Victor, Jay *dermatologist*

### Allendale
Haller, Kathleen *nursing educator, family nurse practitioner*
Lubbers, Arend Donselaar *academic administrator*
Murray, Diane Elizabeth *librarian*
Niemeyer, Glenn Alan *academic administrator, history educator*

### Alma
Moerdyk, Charles Conrad *school system administrator*
Sanders, Jack Ford *physician*
Stone, Alan Jay *college administrator*
Swanson, Robert Draper *college president*

### Alpena

Fraleigh, John Walter *psychotherapist, social worker*

### Ann Arbor

Abrams, Gerald David *physician, educator*
Adamson, Thomas Charles, Jr. *aerospace engineering educator, consultant*
Agno, John G. *management consultant*
Agranoff, Bernard William *biochemist, educator*
Akcasu, Ahmet Ziyaeddin *nuclear engineer, educator*
Akerlof, Carl William *physics educator*
Akil, Huda *neuroscientist, educator, researcher*
Aldridge, John Watson *English language educator, author*
Allen, Layman Edward *law educator, research scientist*
Allen, Sally Lyman *biologist*
Aller, Margo Friedel *astronomer*
Anderson, Austin Gothard *university administrator, lawyer*
Anderson, William R. *botanist, educator, curator, director*
Ansbacher, Rudi *physician*
Apperson, Jean *psychologist*
Arlinghaus, Sandra Judith Lach *mathematical geographer, educator*
Arthos, John *English language educator*
Asgar, Kamal *dentistry educator*
Ash, Major McKinley, Jr. *dentist, educator*
Ashe, Arthur James, III *chemistry educator*
Atreya, Sushil Kumar *space science educator, astrophysicist, researcher*
Avery, James Knuckey *dental educator*
Bacon, George Edgar *pediatrician, educator*
Bailey, David Roy Shackleton *classics educator*
Bailey, Reeve Maclaren *museum curator*
Bailey, Richard Weld *English language educator*
Baker, Sheridan *English educator, author*
Banks, Peter Morgan *enviromental research business executive*
Barbarin, Oscar Anthony *psychologist*
Bartell, Lawrence Sims *chemist, educator*
Bartle, Robert Gardner *mathematics educator*
Bassett, Leslie Raymond *composer, educator*
Beaubien, Anne Kathleen *librarian*
Beaulieu, Carol Marie *special education educator*
Beaver, Frank Eugene *communication educator, film critic and historian*
Becher, William Don *electrical engineering educator, engineering consultant*
Becker, Marvin Burton *historian*
Beckley, Robert Mark *architect, educator*
Bedard, Patrick Joseph *editor, writer, consultant*
Behling, Charles Frederick *psychology educator*
Behmer, Kevin Shea *mathematics educator*
Belcher, Louis David *marketing and operations executive, former mayor*
Benford, Harry Bell *naval architect*
†Berenson, Gordon *head coach men's ice hockey*
Bernstein, Isadore Abraham *biochemistry educator, researcher*
Beutler, Frederick Joseph *information scientist*
Bidlack, Russell Eugene *librarian, educator, former dean*
Bilello, John Charles *materials science and engineering educator*
Bitondo, Domenic *engineering executive*
Blinder, Seymour Michael *chemistry educator*
Bloom, David Alan *pediatric urology educator*
Bloom, Jane Maginnis *emergency physician*
Blouin, Francis Xavier, Jr. *history educator*
Bogaard, William Joseph *lawyer*
Bolcom, William Elden *musician, composer, educator, pianist*
Bole, Giles G. *physician, researcher, medical educator*
Bollinger, Lee Carroll *law educator*
Bornstein, George Jay *literary educator*
Bornstein, Morris *economist, educator*
Boylan, Paul Charles *music educator, academic administrator*
Brandt, Richard Booker *former philosophy educator*
Brewer, Garry Dwight *social scientist, educator*
Britton, Clarold Lawrence *lawyer, consultant*
Browder, Olin Lorraine *legal educator*
Brown, Deming Bronson *Slavic languages and literature educator*
Brown, Donald Robert *psychology educator*
Brown, Morton B. *biostatistics educator*
Bryant, Barbara Everitt *academic researcher, market research consultant, former federal agency administrator*
Burbank, Jane Richardson *Russian and European studies educator*
Burdi, Alphonse Rocco *anatomist*
Burke, Robert Harry *surgeon, educator*
Cain, Albert Clifford *psychology educator*
Calahan, Donald Albert *electrical engineering educator*
Cameron, Oliver Gene *psychiatrist, educator psychobiology reseacher*
Campbell, John Creighton *political science educator, association administrator*
Cannell, Charles Frederick *psychologist, educator*
Carlen, Sister Claudia *librarian*
Carlson, Bruce Martin *anatomist*
Carnahan, Brice *chemical engineer, educator*
Casey, Kenneth Lyman *neurologist*
Cassara, Frank *artist, printmaker*
Chen, Michael Ming *mechanical engineering educator*
Christensen, A(lbert) Kent *anatomy educator*
Christiansen, Richard Louis *orthodontics educator, research director, former dean*
Chupp, Timothy Edward *physicist, educator, nuclear scientist, academic administrator*
Clark, John Alden *mechanical engineering educator*
Clark, Noreen Morrison *behavioral science educator, researcher*
Clark, Thomas B., Sr. *real estate broker*
Clarke, John Terrel *astrophysicist*
Cochran, Kenneth William *toxicologist*
Cohen, Malcolm Stuart *economist, research institute director*
Cole, David Edward *university administrator*
Cole, Juan R.I. *history educator*
Cole, Roland Jay *lawyer*
Converse, Philip Ernest *social science educator*
Cooper, Edward Hayes *lawyer, educator*
Copeland, Carolyn Abigail *retired university dean*
Coran, Arnold Gerald *pediatric surgeon*
Cordes, Eugene Harold *pharmacy and chemistry educator*
Cornelius, Kenneth Cremer, Jr. *finance executive*
Counsell, Raymond Ernest *pharmacology educator*
Courant, Paul Noah *economist, educator*
Cowen, Roy Chadwell, Jr. *German language educator*
Craig, Robert George *dental science educator*
Crane, Horace Richard *physicist, educator*
Crawford, Charles Merle *business administration educator*
Csere, Csaba *magazine editor*
Curley, Edwin Munson *philosophy educator*
Curtis, George Clifton *psychiatry educator, clinical research investigator*
Danly, Robert Lyons *Japanese studies educator, author, translator*
Daub, Peggy Ellen *library administrator*
Davis, Wayne Kay *university dean, educator*
Dawson, William Ryan *zoology educator*
Day, Colin Leslie *publisher*
Decker, Raymond Frank *scientist, technology transfer executive*
Dekker, Eugene Earl *biochemistry educator*
De La Iglesia, Felix Alberto *pathologist, toxicologist*
DeVine, Edmond Francis *lawyer*
DeWeese, Marion Spencer *educator, surgeon*
Diana, Joseph A. *retired foundation executive*
Director, Stephen William *electrical and computer engineering educator, academic administrator*
Dirks, Nicholas B. *cultural research organization administrator/history educator*
Dixon, Jack E. *biological chemistry educator, consultant*
†Dominguez, Kathryn Mary *educator*
Domino, Edward Felix *clinical pharmacologist, educator*
Donabedian, Avedis *physician*
Donahue, Thomas Michael *physics educator*
Dougherty, Richard Martin *library and information science educator*
Douvan, Elizabeth *social psychologist, educator*
Dow, William Gould *electrical engineer, educator*
Drach, John Charles *scientist, educator*
Drake, Richard Paul *physicist, educator*
Dubin, Howard Victor *dermatologist*
Duderstadt, James Johnson *academic administrator, engineering educator*
Duke, Richard De La Barre *urban planner, educator*
Dumas, Rhetaugh Etheldra Graves *university official*
Dunlap, Connie *librarian*
Dunnigan, Brian Leigh *military historian, curator*
Duquette, Donald Norman *law educator*
Duren, Peter Larkin *mathematician, educator*
Easter, Stephen Sherman, Jr. *biology educator*
Eberbach, Steven John *consumer electronics company executive*
Eisenberg, Marvin Julius *art history educator*
Eisendrath, Charles Rice *journalism educator, manufacturer, farmer, consultant*
Eisenstein, Elizabeth Lewisohn *historian, educator*
Elger, William Robert, Jr. *accountant*
Ellmann, Douglas Stanley *lawyer*
Ellmann, William Marshall *lawyer, mediator, arbitrator, researcher*
England, Anthony Wayne *electrical engineering and computer science educator, astronaut, geophysicist*
Enns, Mark Kynaston *electrical engineer*
Eron, Leonard David *psychology educator*
Evans, Francis Cope *ecologist*
Fader, Daniel Nelson *English language educator*
Faeth, Gerard Michael *aerospace engineering educator, researcher*
Fajans, Stefan Stanislaus *internist, retired educator*
Farrand, William Richard *geology educator*
Faulkner, John Arthur *physiologist, educator*
Fekety, Robert *physician, educator*
Feldman, Eva Lucille *neurology educator*
Feuerwerker, Albert *history educator*
Fifield, Russell Hunt *political science educator*
Filisko, Frank Edward *physicist, educator*
Fisher, Stephen Louis *collegiate basketball team coach*
Fisk, Lennard Ayres *physicist, educator*
Fitzsimmons, Joseph John *publishing executive*
Fleming, Suzanne Marie *university official, chemistry educator*
Flowers, Damon Bryant *architect, facility planner*
Foley, Daniel Ronald *business and personnel executive*
Forsyth, Ilene Haering *art historian*
Foster, Alan Herbert *financial consultant*
Fox, David Alan *rheumatologist, immunologist*
Fraser, Russell Alfred *author, educator*
Freedman, Ronald *sociology educator*
Freese, Katherine *physicist, educator*
†French, David A. *lawyer*
Frier, Bruce W. *law educator*
Frueh, Bartley Richard *surgeon*
Fry, Richard E. *architectural firm executive*
Fusfeld, Daniel Roland *economist*
Garn, Stanley Marion *physical anthropologist, educator*
Gaston, Hugh Philip *marriage counselor, educator*
Gehring, Frederick William *mathematician, educator*
Gelehrter, Thomas David *medical and genetics educator, physician*
Gibala, Ronald *metallurgical engineering educator*
Gikas, Paul William *medical educator*
Gilbert, Elmer Grant *aerospace engineering educator, control theorist*
Gilbert, Robert Edward *lawyer*
Gilman, Sid *neurologist*
Gingerich, Philip Derstine *paleontologist, evolutionary biologist, educator*
Ginsburg, David *human genetics educator, researcher*
Goldstein, Irwin Joseph *medical research executive*
Goldstein, Steven Alan *medical and engineering educator*
Gomberg, Edith S. Lisansky *psychologist, educator*
Gomez, Luis Oscar *Asian and religious studies educator*
Gooch, Nancy Jane *realtor, mortgage executive*
Gordinier, Terri Klein *speech-language pathologist*
Gray, Michael William *osteopathic, general and aesthetic plastic and bariatric surgeon*
Greden, John Francis *psychiatrist, educator*
Greene, Douglas A. *internist, educator*
Griffith, John Randall *health services administrator, educator*
Guy, Ralph B., Jr. *federal judge*
Hackett, Barbara (Kloka) *federal judge*
Hackett, Roger Fleming *history educator*
Haddad, George Ilyas *engineering educator, research scientist*
Haddock, Fred T. *astronomer, educator*
Hagen, John William *psychology educator*
Halter, Jeffrey B. *internal medicine educator, geriatrician*
Hanson, Robert Duane *civil engineering educator*
Hartung, Rolf *environmental toxicology educator, researcher, consultant*
Hawkins, Joseph Elmer, Jr. *retired acoustic physiologist, educator*
Hawthorne, Victor Morrison *epidemiologist, educator*
Hayes, John Patrick *electrical engineering and computer science educator, consultant*
Heidelberger, Kathleen Patricia *physician*
Henderson, John Woodworth *ophthalmologist, educator*
Herzig, David Jacob *pharmaceutical company executive, immunopharmacologist*
Hessler, David William *information and multimedia systems educator*
Hill, Bruce Marvin *statistician, scientist, educator*
Hiss, Roland Graham *physician, medical educator*
Hochster, Melvin *mathematician, educator*
Hodel, Mary Anne *library director*
Hoff, Julian Theodore *physician, educator*
Holbrook, Robert Sumner *economist, educator*
Hollenberg, Paul Frederick *pharmacology educator*
Horowitz, Samuel Boris *biomedical researcher, educational consultant*
Horton, William David, Jr. *scientist*
House, James Stephen *social psychologist, educator*
Howrey, Eugene Philip *economics educator, consultant*
Humes, H(arvey) David *nephrologist, educator*
Huntington, Curtis Edward *actuary*
Iadipaolo, Donna Marie *secondary school educator, writer, director, artist*
Jackson, James Sidney *psychology educator*
Jackson, John Howard *lawyer, educator*
Jacobson, Harold Karan *political science educator, researcher*
Jeanes, William *publishing executive*
Johnston, Lloyd Douglas *social scientist*
Joiner, Charles Wycliffe *judge*
Jones, Lawrence William *educator, physicist*
Jones, Phillip Sanford *mathematics educator emeritus*
Joscelyn, Kent Buckley *lawyer, research scientist*
Kahn, Douglas Allen *legal educator*
Kalisch, Beatrice Jean *nursing educator, consultant*
Kamisar, Yale *lawyer, educator*
Kamrowski, Gerome *artist*
Kapteyn, Henry Cornelius *physics educator*
Kauffman, Charles William *aerospace engineer*
Kaufman, Peter Bishop *biological sciences educator*
Kelly, Raymond Case *anthropology educator*
Kennedy, David Boyd *foundation executive, lawyer*
Kennedy, Frank Robert *lawyer*
Keppelman, Nancy *lawyer*
Kerr, William *nuclear engineering educator*
Kesler, Stephen Edward *economic geology educator*
Ketefian, Shaké *nursing educator*
Kim, E. Han *finance and business administration educator*
Kimbrough, William Walter, III *psychiatrist*
Kingdon, John Wells *political science educator*
Kister, James Milton *mathematician, educator*
Kleinsmith, Lewis Joel *cell biologist, educator*
Kmenta, Jan *economics educator*
Knoll, Glenn Frederick *nuclear engineering educator*
Knott, John Ray, Jr. *language professional, educator*
Konigsberg, Ira *film and literature educator, writer*
Kostyo, Jack Lawrence *physiology educator*
Kozma, Adam *electrical engineer*
Kramer, Charles Henry *psychiatrist*
Krause, Charles Joseph *otolaryngologist*
Krier, James Edward *law educator, author*
Krimm, Samuel *physicist, educator*
Krisch, Alan David *physics educator*
Kronfol, Ziad Anis *psychiatrist, educator, researcher*
Kuhl, David Edmund *physician, nuclear medicine educator*
La Du, Bert Nichols, Jr. *pharmacology educator, physician*
Lehman, Jeffrey Sean *law educator*
Leith, Emmett Norman *electrical engineer, educator*
Lempert, Richard Owen *lawyer, educator*
Leong, Sue *retired community health and pediatrics nurse*
Lewis, David Lanier *business history educator*
Lewis, Donald John *mathematics educator*
Lewis, Robert Enzer *lexicographer, educator*
Lichter, Paul Richard *ophthalmology educator*
Lindsay, June Campbell McKee *communications executive*
Liu, Vi-Cheng *aerospace engineering educator*
Lockwood, Dean H. *physician, pharmaceutical executive*
Longone, Daniel Thomas *chemistry educator*
Lopatin, Dennis Edward *immunologist, educator*
Lowe, John Burton *molecular biology educator, pathologist*
Lozoff, Betsy *pediatrician*
MacKinnon, Catharine A. *lawyer, law educator, legal scholar, writer*
Macnee, Alan Breck *electrical engineer, educator*
Malkawi, Ali Mahmoud *architecture educator, researcher*
Mangouni, Norman *publisher*
Manis, Melvin *psychologist, educator*
Marans, Robert Warren *architect, planner*
Margolis, Philip Marcus *psychiatrist, educator*
Marletta, Michael *biochemistry educator, researcher, pharmacologist*
Martel, William *radiologist, educator*
Martin, Bruce James *newspaper editor*
Martin, Claude Raymond, Jr. *marketing consultant, educator*
Martin, William Russell *nuclear engineering educator*
Massey, Vincent *biochemist, educator*
Matthews, Rowena Green *biological chemistry educator*
Mazumder, Jyotirmoy *mechanical and industrial engineering educator*
McCarus, Ernest Nasseph *retired language educator*
McClamroch, N. Harris *aerospace engineering educator, consultant, researcher*
Mc Cracken, Paul Winston *retired economist, business educator*
McDougal, Stuart Yeatman *comparative literature educator, author*
McHugh, Richard Walker *lawyer*
McKeachie, Wilbert James *psychologist, educator*
†McMahon, Brian *publishing executive*
Meitzler, Allen Henry *electrical engineering educator, automotive scientist*
Mersereau, John, Jr. *Slavic languages and literatures educator*
Metcalf, Robert Clarence *architect, educator*
Midgley, A(lvin) Rees, Jr. *reproductive endocrinology educator, researcher*
Mitchell, Edward John *economist, retired educator*
Monaghan, Thomas Stephen *restaurant chain executive*
Monto, Arnold Simon *epidemiology educator*
Moore, Thomas E. *biology educator, museum director*
Morgan, James Newton *research economist, educator*
Morley, George William *gynecologist*
Morris, Phyllis Sutton *philosophy educator*
†Morton, Harrison Leon *forestry educator*
Moss, Cruse Watson *automobile company executive*
Munro, Donald Jacques *philosopher, educator*
Murphey, Rhoads *history educator*
Musa, Samuel Albert *technology and manufacturing executive director*
Nagy, Andrew Francis *engineering educator*
Neal, Homer Alfred *physics educator, researcher, university administrator*
Neidhardt, Frederick Carl *microbiologist*
Nelson, Virginia Simson *pediatrician, physiatrist, educator*
Nisbett, Richard Eugene *psychology educator*
Nordman, Christer Eric *chemistry educator*
Nriagu, Jerome Okon *environmental geochemist*
Nugent, Theodore Anthony *musician*
Oakley, Deborah Jane *researcher, educator*
O'Brien, William Joseph *materials engineer, educator, consultant*
Oliver, William John *pediatrician, educator*
Organski, Abramo Fimo Kenneth *political scientist, educator*
Orringer, Mark Burton *surgeon, educator*
Owyang, Chung *gastroenterologist, researcher*
Paige, Jeffery Mayland *sociologist, educator*
Parkinson, William Charles *physicist, educator*
Parsons, Jeffrey Robinson *anthropologist, educator*
Paul, Ara Garo *university dean*
Paulsen, Serenus Glen *architect, educator*
Pedley, John Griffiths *archaeologist, educator*
Pehlke, Robert Donald *materials and metallurgical engineering educator*
Pepe, Steven Douglas *federal magistrate judge*
Petrick, Ernest Nicholas *mechanical engineer*
Phillips, Daniel Miller *lawyer*
Pierce, Roy *political science educator*
Pierce, William James *law educator*
Pierpont, Wilbur K. *retired administrator, accounting educator*
Pitt, Bertram *cardiologist, educator, consultant*
Ploger, Robert Riis *retired military officer, engineer*
Pollack, Henry Nathan *geophysics educator*
Pollock, Stephen Michael *industrial engineering educator, consultant*
Powell, Linda Rae *educational healthcare consultant*
Powers, William Francis *automobile manufacturing company executive*
Pritts, Bradley Arthur, Jr. *management systems consultant*
Pulgram, Ernst *linguist, philologist, Romance and classical linguistics educator, writer*
Quinnell, Bruce Andrew *retail book chain executive*
Radock, Michael *foundation executive*
Rea, David K. *geology and oceanography educator*
Reed, John Wesley *lawyer, educator*
Reese, James W. *orthodontist*
Richardson, Rudy James *toxicology and neurosciences educator*
Riley-Davis, Shirley Merle *advertising agency executive, marketing consultant, writer*
Roach, Thomas Adair *lawyer*
Robbins, Jerry Hal *educational administration educator*
Robertson, Richard Earl *physical chemist, educator*
Roe, Byron Paul *physics educator*
Romani, John Henry *health administration educator*
Root, William Lucas *electrical engineering educator*
Rosenthal, Amnon *pediatric cardiologist*
Rosseels, Gustave Alois *music educator*
Rumman, Wadi (Saliba Rumman) *civil engineer*
Rupp, Ralph Russell *audiologist, educator, author*
Rycus, Mitchell Julian *urban planning educator, urban security and energy planning consultant*
St. Antoine, Theodore Joseph *law educator, arbitrator*
Samson, Perry J. *environmental scientist, educator*
Sandalow, Terrance *law educator*
Saussele, Charles William *marking systems company executive*
Savageau, Michael Antonio *microbiology and immunology educator*
Sawyer, Charles Henry *art educator, art museum director emeritus*
Schacht, Jochen Heinrich *biochemistry educator*
Scharp-Radovic, Carol Ann *choreographer, classical ballet educator, artistic director*
Schenk, John Erwin *environmental engineer*
Schmitt, Mary Elizabeth *postal supervisor*
Schneider, Carl Edward *law educator*
Schnitzer, Bertram *hematopathologist*
Schottenfeld, David *epidemiologist, educator*
Schriber, Thomas Jude *computer and information systems educator, researcher*
Schteingart, David Eduardo *internist*
Schultz, Albert Barry *engineering educator*
Schwank, Johannes Walter *chemical engineering educator*
Scott, Norman Ross *electrical engineering educator*
Senior, Thomas Bryan A. *electrical engineering educator, researcher, consultant*
Shapiro, Matthew David *economist*
Shappirio, David Gordon *biologist, educator*
Shaw, Jiajiu *chemist*
Shayman, James Alan *nephrologist, educator*
Sheldon, Ingrid Kristina *mayor*
Silverman, Albert Jack *psychiatrist, educator*
Simms, Lillian Miller *nursing educator*
Simpson, A. W. B. *law educator*
Singer, Eleanor *sociologist, editor*
Singer, Joel David *political science educator*
Slavens, Thomas Paul *library science educator*
Sloan, Herbert Elias *physician, surgeon*
Smith, David John, Jr. *plastic surgeon*
Smith, Dean Gordon *economist, educator*
Smith, Donald Cameron *physician, educator*
Smith, Donald Norbert *engineering executive*
Smith, J(ames) E(verett) Keith *psychologist, educator*
Solomon, David Eugene *engineering company executive*
Soslowsky, Louis Jeffrey *bioengineering educator, researcher*
Southwick, Arthur Frederick *legal educator*
Sparling, Peter David *dancer, dance educator*
Stafford, Frank Peter, Jr. *economics educator, consultant*
Stark, Joan Scism *education educator*
Starr, Chester G. *history educator*
Steel, Duncan Gregory *physics educator*
Stein, Eric *retired law educator*
Steiner, Erich Ernst *botany educator*
Steiner, Peter Otto *economics educator, dean*

Steinhoff, William Richard English literature educator
Steiss, Alan Walter research administrator, educator
Stevenson, Harold William psychology educator
Stoermer, Eugene Filmore biologist, educator
Stolper, Wolfgang Friedrich retired economist, educator
Stolz, Benjamin Armond foreign language educator
Strang, Ruth Hancock pediatric educator, pediatric cardiologist, priest
Stross, Jeoffrey Knight physician, educator
Surovell, Edward David real estate company executive
Tai, Chen-To electrical engineering educator
Tamres, Milton chemistry educator
Tandon, Rajiv psychiatrist, educator
Taren, James Arthur neurosurgeon, educator
Terpstra, Vern marketing educator
Thompson, Norman Winslow surgeon, educator
Tice, Carol Hoff middle school educator, consultant
Todd, Robert Franklin, III oncologist, educator
Townsend, LeRoy B. chemistry educator, university administrator, researcher
Trautmann, Thomas Roger history and anthropology educator
Turcotte, Jeremiah George physician, surgery educator
Turner, Hazel M. educator
Ulaby, Fawwaz Tayssir electrical engineering and computer science educator, research center administrator
Upatnieks, Juris optical engineer, researcher, educator
Vakalo, Emmanuel-George architecture and planning educator, researcher
Van der Voo, Rob geophysicist
Van Houweling, Douglas Edward university administrator, educator
Vinh, Nguyen Xuan aerospace engineering educator
Vining, (George) Joseph law educator
Waggoner, Lawrence William law educator
Wagner, Warren Herbert, Jr. botanist, educator
Waller, Patricia Fossum transportation executive, researcher, psychologist
Ward, Peter Allan pathologist, educator
Ware, Richard Anderson foundation executive
Warner, Kenneth E. public health educator, consultant
Warner, Robert Mark university dean, archivist, historian
Warshaw, Martin Richard marketing educator
Watkins, Paul B. academic research center administrator, medical educator
Watson, Andrew Samuel psychiatry and law educator
Weber, Walter Jacob, Jr. engineering educator
Weber, Wendell William pharmacologist
Weddige, Emil Albert lithographer, art educator
Weg, John Gerard physician
Wegman, Myron Ezra physician, educator
Weinreich, Gabriel physicist, minister, educator
Wharton, John James, Jr. research physicist
White, James Boyd law educator
White, Michelle Jo economics educator
Whitman, Marina Von Neumann economist
Wiggins, Roger C. internist, educator, researcher
Williams, John Andrew physiology educator, consultant
Williams, John Troy librarian, educator
Willmarth, William Walter aerospace engineering educator
Wilson, Richard Christian engineering firm executive
Winbury, Martin Maurice pharmaceutical executive, educator
Wong, Victor Kenneth physics educator, academic administrator
Woo, Peter Wing Kee organic chemist
Woodcock, Leonard humanities educator, former ambassador
Wylie, Evan Benjamin civil engineering educator, consultant, researcher
Yang, Ralph Tzu-Bow chemical engineer
Yeh, Chai electrical engineer, educator
Yeh, Gregory Soh-Yu physicist, educator
Yih, Chia-Shun fluid mechanics educator
Yocum, Charles Fredrick biology educator
Young, Edwin Harold chemical and metallurgical engineering educator
Zhang, Youxue geology educator
Zucker, Robert A(lpert) psychologist
Zuidema, George Dale surgeon

### Auburn Hills
Beeckmans, Johan Jan automotive company executive
Corace, Joseph Russell automotive parts company executive
Davidson, William M. diversified company executive, professional basketball executive
Dumars, Joe, III professional basketball player
Eaton, Robert James automotive company executive
Etefia, Florence Victoria academic and behavior specialist
Farrar, Stephen Prescott glass products manufacturing executive
Hill, Grant professional basketball player
Lutz, Robert Anthony automotive company executive
Meier, Robert Joseph, Jr. software engineer
Neumann, Charles Henry mathematics educator
Thorpe, Otis Henry professional basketball player
Trebing, David Martin corporate finance manager
Wagner, Bruce Stanley marketing communications executive

### Bad Axe
Sullivan, James Gerald business owner, postal letter carrier

### Battle Creek
Bruce, Thomas Allen physician, philanthropic administrator, educator
Cline, Charles William poet, pianist, rhetoric and literature educator
Davis, Laura Arlene foundation administrator
DeVries, Robert Allen foundation administrator
Dillard, Joan Helen financial executive
Grace, Helen Kennedy foundation administrator
Hollenbeck, Karen Fern foundation executive
Knowlton, Thomas A. food products executive
Langbo, Arnold Gordon food company executive
Matthews, Wyhomme S. music educator, college administrator
Mawby, Russell George retired foundation executive
McKay, Eugene Henry, Jr. food company executive
Richardson, William Chase foundation executive
Wendt, Linda M. educational association administrator

### Bay City
Greve, Guy Robert lawyer
McDermott, Larry Arnold newspaper publisher, newspaper editor
Spector, Arthur Jay federal judge
Van Dyke, Clifford Craig retired banker

### Beaverton
Glenn, James sales executive

### Benton Harbor
Goldin, Sol marketing consultant
Hopp, Daniel Frederick manufacturing company executive, lawyer
LeBlanc, James E. financial services company executive
Rasmussen, Alice Call nursing educator
Whitwam, David Ray appliance manufacturing company executive

### Berkley
Arroyo, Rodney Lee city planning and transportation executive
Linkner, Monica Farris lawyer

### Berrien Springs
Ali, Muhammad (Cassius Marcellus Clay) retired professional boxer
Andreasen, Niels-Erik Albinus religious educator
Lesher, William Richard retired academic administrator
Waller, John Oscar English language educator

### Beulah
Auch, Walter Edward securities company executive
Edwards, Wallace Winfield retired automotive company executive

### Big Rapids
Barnes, Isabel Janet microbiology educator, college dean
Curtis, Mark Allen engineering educator, author, consultant
Mathison, Ian William chemistry educator, academic dean
Mehler, Barry Alan humanities educator, journalist, consultant
Santer, Richard Arthur geography educator
Weinlander, Max Martin retired psychologist

### Bingham Farms
Gratch, Serge mechanical engineering educator
McKeen, Alexander C. engineering consulting company owner
Moffitt, David Louis lawyer, county and state official

### Birch Run
Radwick, Melissa Jane elementary counselor

### Birmingham
Ashleigh, Caroline art and antiques appraiser
Bromberg, Stephen Aaron lawyer
Bublys, Algimantas Vladas architect
Buesser, Anthony Carpenter lawyer
Denes, Michel Janet physical therapist, consultant in rehabilitation
Elsman, James Leonard, Jr. lawyer
Gold, Edward David lawyer
La Plata, George federal judge
McDonald, Alonzo Lowry, Jr. business and financial executive
McIntyre, Bruce Herbert media and marketing consultant
Morganroth, Fred lawyer
Ortman, George Earl artist
VanDeusen, Bruce Dudley company executive
Van Dine, Harold Forster, Jr. architect
Van Dyke-Cooper, Anny Marion retired financial company executive

### Bloomfield
Brown, Lynette Ralya journalist, publicist

### Bloomfield Hills
Adams, Charles Francis advertising and real estate executive
Adams, Thomas Brooks advertising consultant
Allen, Maurice Bartelle, Jr. architect
Andrews, Frank Lewis lawyer
Baker, Robert Edward lawyer, retired financial corporation executive
Ball, Patricia Ann physician
Benton, Robert Austin, Jr. investment banker, broker
Benton, William Pettigrew advertising agency executive
Berline, James H. advertising executive, public relations agency executive
Berlow, Robert Alan lawyer
Bianco, Joseph Paul, Jr. foundation and art museum executive
Birkerts, Gunnar architect
Bissell, John Howard marketing executive
Bonner, Thomas Neville history and higher education educator
Brodhead, William McNulty lawyer, former congressman
Brown, Jack Wyman architect
Bruegel, David Robert lawyer
Caldwell, Will M. former automobile company executive
Caplan, John David retired automotive company executive, research director
Casey, John Patrick (Jack Casey) public relations executive, political analyst
Chason, Jacob (Leon Chason) retired neuropathologist
Clippert, Charles Frederick lawyer
Colladay, Robert S. trust company executive, consultant
Cumbey, Constance Elizabeth lawyer, author, lecturer
Cunningham, Gary H. lawyer
Davis-Cartey, Catherine Bernice bank executive
Dawson, Stephen Everette lawyer
Doyle, Jill J. elementary school principal
Fauver, John William mayor, retired business executive
Frey, Stuart Macklin automobile manufacturing company executive
Gelder, John William lawyer
Googasian, George Ara lawyer
Gornick, Alan Lewis lawyer
Greenwood, Frank information scientist
Gulati, Vipin accountant
Haidostian, Alice Berberian concert pianist, civic volunteer and fundraiser
Houston, E. James, Jr. bank officer
Hurlbert, Robert P. lawyer
James, William Ramsay cable television executive
Jeffe, Sidney David automotive engineer
Jones, John Paul probation officer, psychologist
Kasischke, Louis Walter lawyer
Kaufman, Ira Gladstone judge
Klingler, Eugene Herman consulting engineer, educator
Knudsen, Semon Emil manufacturing company executive
Lauer, Clinton Dillman automotive executive
Leonard, Michael A. automotive executive
LoPrete, James Hugh lawyer
Lower, Joyce Q. lawyer
Marko, Harold Meyron diversified industry executive
Marks, Craig management educator, consultant, engineer
Maxwell, Jack Erwin manufacturing company executive
McDonald, Patrick Allen lawyer, arbitrator, educator
Meyer, George Herbert lawyer
†Mills, Peter Richard advertising executive
Nolte, Henry R., Jr. lawyer, former automobile company executive
Norris, John Hart lawyer
Nuss, Shirley Ann computer coordinator, educator
Pappas, Edward Harvey lawyer
Paul, Richard Wright lawyer
Pero, Joseph John retired insurance company executive
Pingel, John Spencer advertising executive
Poth, Stefan Michael retired sales financing company executive
Rader, Ralph Terrance lawyer
Robinson, Jack Albert retail drug stores executive
Rom, (Melvin) Martin securities executive
Rosenfeld, Joel ophthalmologist, lawyer
Snyder, George Edward lawyer
Solomon, Mark Raymond lawyer, educator
Stivender, Donald Lewis mechanical engineering consultant
Thurber, John Alexander lawyer
Weil, John William technology management consultant
Weinstein, William Joseph lawyer
Williams, Walter Joseph lawyer
Wydra, Frank Thomas healthcare executive

### Brethren
Crandell, Deborah Lynne Kaskinen art educator

### Brighton
Bitten, Mary Josephine quality consultant, municipal official
Chrysler, Richard R. former congressman
Darlington, Judith Mabel clinical social worker, Christian counselor
Jensen, Baiba principal
Lamson, Evonne Viola counselor, computer software company executive, consultant, pastor, Christian education administrator

### Buchanan
French, Robert Warren economics educator emeritus, writer, consultant
Paustian, Bonita Joyce school health administrator

### Cadillac
McKay, Laurie Marie special education educator

### Capac
Wagner, Dorothy Marie retired senior creative designer, artist

### Carsonville
Kummerow, Arnold A. superintendent of schools

### Cass City
Althaver, Lambert Ewing manufacturing company executive
Walpole, Robert heavy manufacturing executive

### Cedar
Kunkel, Dorothy Ann music educator

### Center Line
Johnson, John Jay automotive company administrator

### Charlevoix
Lobenherz, Richard Ernest real estate developer

### Charlotte
LeDoux, Chris Lee country musician
Young, Everett J. management consultant, agricultural economist

### Clarkston
Erkfritz, Donald Spencer mechanical engineer

### Clinton Township
Brown, Ronald Delano endocrinologist
Darby, Lewis Randal special education educator
Waldmann, Robert hematologist

### Coloma
Tallman, Clifford Wayne school system administrator, consultant

### Commerce Township
Wager, Paula Jean artist

### Conklin
Kelly, Josephine Kaye social worker

### Copemish
Wells, Herschel James physician, former hospital administrator

### Cross Village
Stowe, Robert Allen catalytic and chemical technology consultant

### Dearborn
Bixby, Harold Glenn manufacturing company executive
Boulanger, Rodney Edmund energy company executive
Brennan, Leo Joseph, Jr. foundation executive
Brown, James Ward mathematician, educator, author
Cairns, James Robert mechanical engineering educator
Cape, James Odies E. fashion designer
Cassady, Kenneth Edward creative and marketing analyst, public relations specialist, graphic artist
Coady, Reginald Patrick library director
Coburn, Ronald Murray ophthalmic surgeon, researcher
Fair, Jean Everhard education educator
Ford, William Clay automotive company executive
Fordyce, James George physician
Gardner, Gary Edward lawyer
Good, Cheryl Denise veterinarian
Hagenlocker, Edward E. automobile company executive
Hirsch, Lore psychiatrist
Jeffries Ashford, Alecia accounting analyst
Jelinek, John Joseph public relations executive
Katz, Sidney Franklin obstetrician, gynecologist
LeVasseur, Susan Lee Salisbury secondary education educator
Little, Robert Eugene mechanical engineering educator, materials behavior researcher, consultant
Lundy, J(oseph) Edward retired automobile company executive
Marquis, Rollin Park retired librarian
Martin, John William, Jr. lawyer, automotive industry executive
Mc Cammon, David Noel retired automobile company executive
McTague, John Paul automobile manufacturing company executive, chemist
Montgomery, Martha M. nursing educator
Myers, Woodrow Augustus, Jr. physician, health care management director
Orlowska-Warren, Lenore Alexandria art educator
Presley, John Woodrow academic administrator
Sagan, John former automobile company executive
Schneider, Michael Joseph biologist
Schulz, Karen Alice medical and vocational case manager
Simon, Evelyn lawyer
Skramstad, Harold Kenneth, Jr. museum administrator, consultant
Suchy, Susanne N. nursing educator
Tai, Julia Chow chemistry educator
Taub, Robert Allan lawyer
Trotman, Alexander J. automobile manufacturing company executive
Werling, Donn Paul environmental educator

### Dearborn Heights
Darin, Frank Victor John management consultant

### Detroit
Abramson, Hanley Norman pharmacy educator
Abt, Jeffrey art and art history educator, artist, writer
†Adamany, David Walter law and political science educator
Adams, Charles Gilchrist pastor
Adams, William Johnston financial and tax consultant
Albom, Mitch David sports columnist
Alford, Sandra Elaine university official
Alpert, Daniel television executive
Amsden, Ted Thomas lawyer
Anderson, John Albert physician
Anderson, Moses B. bishop
Anderson, Sparky (George Lee Anderson) former professional baseball team manager
Andreoff, Christopher Andon lawyer
Anstett, Pat newspaper editor
†Antoniotti, Steve broadcast executive
Archer, Dennis Wayne mayor, lawyer
Ashenfelter, David Louis reporter, former newspaper editor
Baba, Marietta Lynn business anthropologist
Babb, Ralph Wheeler, Jr. banker
Babcock, Charles Witten, Jr. lawyer
Bainbridge, Leesa newspaper editor
†Baker, Elaine R. radio station executive
Balon, Richard psychiatrist, educator
Banas, C. Leslie lawyer
Banks, Lois Michelle nurse
Bassett, Tina communications executive
Beaufait, Frederick W(illiam) civil engineering educator
†Behrmann, Joan Gail newspaper editor
†Bell, David Gus (Buddy Bell) professional baseball manager
Bennett, Margaret Ethel Booker psychotherapist
Berkelhamer, Jay Ellis pediatrician
Berman, Laura journalist
†Bing, David retired basketball player, metal products executive
Birdsong, Emil Ardell psychologist
Blain, Alexander, III surgeon, educator
Bohm, Henry Victor physicist
Bowman, Scotty professional hockey coach
Boykin, Nancy Merritt former academic administrator
Bradford, Christina newspaper editor
Brady, Edmund Matthew, Jr. lawyer
Brammer, Forest Evert electrical engineering educator
Brand, George Edward, Jr. lawyer
Braun, Richard Lane, II lawyer
Braun, Robert C. airport executive
Bray, Thomas Joseph journalist, editor
Brill, Lesley literature and film studies educator
Brown, Eli Matthew anesthesiologist
Brown, Ray Kent biochemist, physician, educator
Brown, Stratton Shartel lawyer
Brown, William Paul investment executive
Brustad, Orin Daniel lawyer
Bryfonski, Dedria Anne publishing company executive
Brynski, Christina Halina school system administrator, consultant, educator
Bullard, George newspaper editor
Burstein, Richard Joel lawyer
Burzynski, Susan Marie newspaper editor
Buselmeier, Bernard Joseph insurance company executive
Bushnell, George Edward, Jr. lawyer
Caldwell, John Thomas, Jr. communications executive
Callahan, John William (Bill) judge
Camp, Kimberly N. museum administrator, artist

Candler, James Nall, Jr. lawyer
Cantoni, Louis Joseph psychologist, poet, sculptor
Cantor, George Nathan journalist
Cerny, Joseph Charles urologist, educator
Chapin, Roy Dikeman, Jr. automobile company executive
Charfoos, Lawrence Selig lawyer
Charla, Leonard Francis lawyer
Choate, Robert Alden lawyer
†Ciccarelli, Dino professional hockey player
Coffey, Paul professional hockey player
Cohan, Leon Sumner lawyer, retired electric company executive
Cohen, Sanford Ned pediatrics educator, academic administrator
Colby, Joy Hakanson art critic
Collier, James Warren lawyer
Connor, Laurence Davis lawyer
Corrigan, Maura Denise lawyer, state judge
Cothorn, John Arthur lawyer
Cox, Clifford Ernest deputy superintendent, chief information officer
Cox, John William architect, educator
Czarnecki, Walter P. truck rental company executive
Darlow, Julia Donovan lawyer
Darr, Alan Phipps curator, historian
Dauch, Richard E. automobile manufacturing company executive
Devellano, James Charles professional hockey manager
DeVine, (Joseph) Lawrence drama critic
Di Chiera, David performing arts impresario
Dickerson, Brian editor, periodical
Diebolt, Judith newspaper editor
Dixson, J. B. communications executive
Dombrowski, Mitchell Paul physician, inventor, researcher
Draper, James Wilson lawyer
Driker, Eugene lawyer
Dudley, John Henry, Jr. lawyer
Duggan, Patrick James federal judge
Dunn, William Bradley lawyer
Dziuba, Henry Frank dental school administrator
Edelstein, Tilden Gerald academic administrator, history educator
Edmunds, Nancy Garlock federal judge
Edwards, Esther G. museum administrator, former record, film and entertainment company executive
Eggertsen, John Hale lawyer
Elsila, David August editor
Enam, Syed Ather neurosurgeon, researcher
Ernst, Calvin Bradley vascular surgeon, surgery educator
Ettinger, David A. lawyer
Evans, Mark Ira obstetrician, geneticist
Faison, W. Mack lawyer
Falls, Joseph Francis sportswriter, editor
Fay, Sister Maureen A. university president
†Fedotov, Sergei professional hockey player
Feikens, John federal judge
Ferguson, James Peter distilling company executive
Ferguson, Tamara clinical sociologist
†Fetisov, Slava professional hockey player
†Fezzey, Mike radio station executive
Finkenbine, Roy Eugene history educator
Forbes-Richardson, Helen Hilda state agency administrator
Frade, Peter Daniel chemist, educator
Francis, Edward D. architect
†Frank, Alan W. television station executive
Friedman, Bernard Alvin federal judge
Fromm, David surgeon
Fromm, Frederick Andrew, Jr. lawyer
Fryman, David Travis professional baseball player
Garberding, Larry Gilbert utilities companies executive
Garriott, Lois Jean clinical social worker, educator
Garzia, Samuel Angelo lawyer
Getz, Ernest John lawyer
†Gilchrist, Grace television station executive
Gilmore, Horace Weldon federal judge
†Ginsburg, Scott radio station executive
Glancy, Alfred Robinson, III public utility company executive
Go, Robert A. management consultant
Gonzalez, Ricardo surgeon, educator
Goodman, Allen Charles economics educator
Gould, Wesley Larson political science educator
Graves, Ray Reynolds judge
Gumbleton, Thomas J. bishop
Gupta, Suraj Narayan physicist, educator
Gushee, Richard Bordley lawyer
Hagman, Harlan Lawrence education educator
Hamilton, Jonnie Mae pediatric nurse practitioner, educator
Hampton, Verne Churchill, II lawyer
Hanson, David Bigelow construction company executive, engineer
Hardon, John Anthony priest, research educator
Hashimoto, Ken dermatology educator
Hatie, George Daniel lawyer
Hayashi, Hajime immunologist
Heaphy, John Merrill lawyer
Hearns, Thomas professional boxer
Henry, William Lockwood sales and marketing executive
Heppner, Gloria Hill medical science administrator, educator
Herstein, Carl William lawyer
Hill, Draper editorial cartoonist
Holness, Gordon Victor Rix engineering executive, mechanical engineer
Hood, Denise Page federal judge
Hough, Leslie Seldon educational administrator
Howbert, Edgar Charles lawyer
Ilitch, Marian professional hockey team executive
Ilitch, Michael professional hockey team executive
Jacox, Ada Kathryn nurse, educator
Jarvi, Neeme conductor
Jeffs, Thomas Hamilton, II banker
Johnson, Carl Randolph chemist, educator
Johnson, Mark Paul obstetrics and gynecology educator, geneticist
Kachadoorian, Zubel artist, educator
Kahn, Mark Leo arbitrator, educator
Kalman, Andrew manufacturing company executive
Kantrowitz, Adrian surgeon, educator
Kantrowitz, Jean Rosensaft research program administrator medical products
Kaplan, Bernice Antoville anthropologist, educator
Kaplan, Joseph pediatrician
Keith, Damon Jerome federal judge
Kelleher, Timothy John publishing company executive
Kennedy, Cornelia Groefsema federal judge
Kessler, Philip Joel lawyer
Kessler, William Henry architect
Kirschner, Stanley chemist
Kiska, Timothy Olin newspaper columnist
Kline, Kenneth Alan mechanical engineering educator
Klosinski, Deanna Dupree medical laboratory sciences educator
Kowalczyk, Richard Leon English language educator, technical writing consultant
Kramer, Mary Louise journalist
Krawetz, Stephen Andrew molecular biology and genetics educator
Krsul, John Aloysius, Jr. lawyer
Krull, Edward Alexander dermatologist
Kuehn, George E. lawyer, beverage company executive
Kummler, Ralph H. chemical engineering educator
Kushma, David William journalist
Kyle, Gene Margerl merchandise presentation artist
Lamborn, LeRoy Leslie legal educator
†Lamka, Philip Charles broadcasting company executive
Lasker, Gabriel Ward anthropologist, educator
Laughlin, Nancy newspaper editor
Lawrence, John Kidder lawyer
Ledwidge, Patrick Joseph lawyer
Lee, André Lafayette hospital administrator
Lee, James Edward, Jr. educational administrator
Lenga, J. Thomas lawyer
Lerner, Stephen Alexander microbiologist, physician, educator
Lesch, Michael cardiologist
Levin, Charles Leonard state supreme court justice
Levy, Edward Charles, Jr. manufacturing company executive
Lewand, F. Thomas lawyer
†Lewis, Frank R., Jr. surgeon, hospital administrator
Li, Yi staff investigator
†Lim, Henry Wan-Peng physician
Livingood, Clarence S. dermatologist
Lobbia, John E. utility company executive
Lockman, Stuart M. lawyer
Lombard, Arthur J. judge
Longhofer, Ronald Stephen lawyer
Lucow, Milton lawyer
Lupulescu, Aurel Peter medical educator, researcher, physician
Lusher, Jeanne Marie pediatric hematologist, educator
Mack, Robert Emmet hospital administrator
Madgett, Naomi Long poet, editor, educator
Maida, Adam Joseph Cardinal cardinal
Maiese, Kenneth neurologist
Majzoub, Mona Kathryne lawyer
Mallett, Conrad LeRoy, Jr. state chief supreme court justice
Malone, Daniel Patrick lawyer
Mamat, Frank Trustick lawyer
Martin, Fred retired municipal official
Marx, Thomas George economist
Massura, Edward Anthony accountant
Maurer, David L. lawyer
Maycock, Joseph Farwell, Jr. lawyer
Mayes, Maureen Davidica physician, educator
McCarroll, Kathleen Ann radiologist, educator
McCracken, Caron Francis computer company executive, consultant
McCracken, Ina business executive
Mc Gehee, H(arry) Coleman, Jr. bishop
McGruder, Robert newspaper publishing executive
McKim, Samuel John, III lawyer
McKinnon, Isaiah police chief
Mc Millan, James manufacturing executive
McNair, Russell Arthur, Jr. lawyer
McNamara, Edward Howard county official, former mayor
McNish, Susan Kirk lawyer
McWhorter, Sharon Louise business executive, inventor, consultant
McWilliams, Michael G. writer, television critic
Meilgaard, Morten Christian food products specialist, international educator
Meisel, Jerome electrical engineer
Mengel, Christopher Emile lawyer, educator
Meriwether, Heath J. newspaper publisher
Mika, Joseph John library director, consultant
Miller, Dorothy Anne Smith retired cytogenetics educator
Miller, Eugene Albert bank executive
Miller, George DeWitt, Jr. lawyer
Miller, Orlando Jack physician, educator
Miller Davis, Mary-Agnes social worker
Mitseff, Carl lawyer
Moghissi, Kamran S. obstetrician/gynecologist, educator
Moldenhauer, Judith A. graphic design educator
Morgan, Virginia magistrate judge
Moss, Leslie Otha criminal justice administrator, philanthropist
Murphy, Thomas Aquinas former automobile manufacturing company executive
Nadeau, Steven C. lawyer
†Newman, Jay broadcast executive
Nix, Robert Royal, II lawyer
Noland, Mariam Charl foundation executive
Novak, Raymond Francis research institute director, pharmacology educator
Oliver, John Preston chemistry educator, academic administrator
O'Meara, John Corbett federal judge
Openshaw, Helena Marie investment company executive, portfolio manager
Orton, Colin George medical physicist
†Osgood, Chris professional hockey player
Ownby, Dennis Randall pediatrician, allergist, educator, researcher
Parker, George Edward, III lawyer
Parrish, Maurice Drue museum executive
Parry, Dale D. newspaper editor
Paul, Rhonda Elizabeth university program director, career development counselor
Pearce, Harry Jonathan lawyer
Peck, William Henry museum curator, art historian, archaeologist, author, lecturer
Pepper, Jonathon L. newspaper columnist
Perry, Burton Lars pediatrician
Peters, William P. oncologist, science administrator, educator
Phillips, Eduardo surgeon, educator
Phillips, Elliott Hunter lawyer
Phillis, John Whitfield physiologist, educator
†Piper, William Howard banker
†Pobinson, Suzette E. airport executive
Porter, Arthur T. oncologist, educator
Prasad, Ananda Shiva medical educator
Putchakayala, Hari Babu engineering company executive
Rajlich, Vaclav Thomas computer science educator, researcher, consultant
Rakolta, John construction company executive
Ransom, Kevin Renard Dortch investment banker
Rashid, Harun Ur philosopher, educational administrator
Reide, Jerome L. humanities educator, lawyer
Richardson, Ralph Herman lawyer
Riley, Dorothy Comstock judge
Rines, John Randolph automotive company executive
Roberts, Seymour M. (Skip Roberts) advertising agency executive
Robinson, James Kenneth lawyer, educator
Roche, Douglas David lawyer, bar examiner
Roehling, Carl David architect
Rogers, Richard Lee educator
Rosen, Gerald Ellis federal judge
Ross, Mary O. religious organization administrator
Rossen, Jordan lawyer
Rossman, Richard Alan lawyer
Rozof, Phyllis Claire lawyer
Ruffner, Frederick G., Jr. book publisher
Russell, Robert Gilmore lawyer
Ryan, James Leo federal judge
Sachs, Samuel, II museum director
Salter, Linda Lee security officer
Sax, Stanley Paul manufacturing company executive
Saxton, William Marvin lawyer
Saylor, Larry James lawyer
Schaffler, Mitchell Barry research scientist, anatomist, educator
Scherer, Karla foundation executive, venture capitalist
Schiffer, Daniel L. gas company executive
Schindler, Marvin Samuel foreign language educator
Schreiber, Bertram Manuel mathematics educator
Schultz, Dennis Bernard lawyer
Schuster, Elaine civil rights professional, state official
Schwartz, Alan E. lawyer
Schwartz, Jerome Merrill lawyer
Scott, John Edward Smith lawyer
Sedler, Robert Allen law educator
Semanik, Anthony James university program administrator
Semple, Lloyd Ashby lawyer
Sengupta, Dipak Lal electrical engineering and physics educator, researcher
Shaevsky, Mark lawyer
Shannon, Margaret Anne lawyer
Shapiro, Michael B. lawyer
Shaw, Nancy Rivard museum curator, art historian, educator
Shay, John E., Jr. academic administrator
Silverman, Norman Alan cardiac surgeon
Skoney, Sophie Essa educational administrator
Small, Melvin history educator
Smith, James Albert lawyer
Smith, John Francis, Jr. automobile company executive
Smyntek, John Eugene, Jr. newspaper editor
Snead, David L. superintendent
Sokol, Robert James obstetrician, gynecologist, educator
Sott, Herbert lawyer
Sparrow, Herbert George, III lawyer
Spyers-Duran, Peter librarian, educator
Stanalajczo, Greg C. computer services executive
Stark, Susan R. film critic
Stein, Paul David cardiologist
Stella, Frank Dante food service and dining equipment executive
Stewart, Melbourne George, Jr. physicist, educator
Stroud, Joe Hinton newspaper editor
Stynes, Stanley Kenneth retired chemical engineer, educator
Sullivan, Joseph B. retired judge
Sutton, Lynn Sorensen librarian
Syropoulos, Mike school system director
Szilagyi, D(esiderius) Emerick surgeon, researcher, educator
Talbert, Bob newspaper columnist
Tallet, Margaret Anne theatre executive
Taylor, Anna Diggs federal judge
Teagan, John Gerard newspaper executive
Thelen, Bruce Cyril lawyer
Thoms, David Moore lawyer
Thurber, Peter Palms lawyer
Timm, Roger K. lawyer
Tolia, Vasundhara K. pediatric gastroenterologist, educator
Toll, Sheldon Samuel lawyer
Topey, Ishmael Aloysius urban planner
Trim, Donald Roy consulting engineer
Tsai, Bor-sheng educator
Tse, Harley Y. immunologist, educator
Turnley, David Carl photojournalist
Tushman, J. Lawrence wholesale distribution executive
Uhde, Thomas Whitley psychiatry educator, psychiatrist
Uicker, Joseph Bernard engineering company executive
Ursache, Victorin (His Eminence The Most Reverend Archbishop Victorin) archbishop
Vaitkevicius, Vainutis Kazys foundation administrator, medical educator
van der Marck, Jan art historian
Vega, Frank J. newspaper publishing executive
†Vernon, Mike professional hockey player
Vigneron, Allen Henry theology educator, rector, auxiliary bishop
Vincent, Charles Eagar, Jr. sports columnist
Visci, Joseph Michael newspaper editor
Volz, William Harry law educator, administrator
Waldmeir, Peter Nielsen journalist
Warden, Gail Lee health care executive
Weiss, Mark Lawrence anthropology educator
Weiss, Robert Benjamin lawyer
Werba, Gabriel public relations consultant
White, Joseph B. reporter
Whitehouse, Fred Waite endocrinologist, researcher
Wiener, Joseph pathologist
Wierzbicki, Jacek Gabriel physicist, researcher
Wilkes, James E. telecommunications industry executive
Williams, J. Bryan lawyer
Williamson, Marilyn Lammert English educator, university administrator
Willingham, Edward Bacon, Jr. ecumenical minister, administrator
Wise, John Augustus lawyer
Wittlinger, Timothy David lawyer
Wittrup, Richard Derald health care executive
Wood, R. Stewart bishop
Woods, George Edward judge
Worden, William Michael city agency administrator, preservation consultant
Wyse, Roy labor union administrator
Young, Gordon Ellsworth composer, organist
Yzerman, Steve professional hockey player
Zaremba, Thomas Edmund Michael Barry biology educator
Zatkoff, Lawrence P. federal judge
Ziegler, John Augustus, Jr. lawyer
Zuckerman, Richard Engle lawyer, law educator

### Dowagiac

Mulder, Patricia Marie education educator

### Dundee

Yhouse, Paul Alan manufacturing executive

### East Lansing

Abbett, William S. dean
Abeles, Norman psychologist, educator
Abolins, Maris Arvids physics researcher and educator
Abramson, Paul Robert political scientist, educator
Allen, Bruce Templeton economics educator
Andersland, Orlando Baldwin civil engineering educator
Anderson, David Daniel retired humanities educator, writer, editor
Anderson, Donald Keith chemical engineering educator
Appel, John J. history educator
Arens, Alvin Armond accountant, educator
Asmussen, Jes, Jr. electrical engineer, educator, consultant
Austin, Sam M. physics educator
Axinn, George Harold rural sociology educator
Bandes, Susan Jane museum director, educator
Beckmeyer, Henry Ernest anesthesiologist, medical educator
Benenson, Walter nuclear physics educator
Berding, Thomas George art educator
Bickart, Theodore Albert electrical and computer engineering educator, university dean
Blosser, Henry Gabriel physicist
Brody, Theodore Meyer pharmacologist, educator
Brophy, Jere Edward education educator, researcher
Brown, Boyd Alex physicist, educator
Bukovac, Martin John horticulturist, educator
Burnett, Jean Bullard (Mrs. James R. Burnett) biochemist
Byerrum, Richard Uglow college dean
Cantlon, John E. environmental scientist, consultant
Case, Eldon Darrel materials science educator
Chapin, Richard Earl librarian
Chen, Kun-Mu electrical engineering educator
Chimoskey, John Edward physiologist, medical educator
Cross, Aureal Theophilus geology and botany educator
Cutts, Charles Eugene civil engineering educator
De Benko, Eugene librarian, consultant
Dennis, Frank George, Jr. retired horticulture educator
D'Itri, Frank Michael environmental research chemist
Dye, James Louis chemistry educator
Eadie, John William history educator
Falk, Julia S. linguist, educator
Fischer, Lawrence Joseph toxicologist, educator
Fisher, Alan Washburn historian, educator
Fisher, Ronald C. economics educator
Fluck, Michele M(arguerite) biology educator
Foss, John Frank mechanical engineering educator
Freedman, Eric journalist
Fromm, Paul Oliver physiology educator
Gast, Robert Gale agriculture educator, experiment station administrator
Gelbke, Claus-Konrad nuclear physics educator
Gerhardt, Philipp microbiologist, educator
Goodman, Erik David engineering educator
Gottschalk, Alexander radiologist, diagnostic radiology educator
Greenberg, Bradley Sander communications educator
Hackel, Emanuel science educator
Hackett, Wesley Phelps, Jr. lawyer
Harrison, Jeremy Thomas dean
Harrison, Michael Jay physicist, educator
Hocking, John Gilbert mathematics educator
Hoffman, Gwendolyn Leah emergency medicine physician, educator
Hollander, Stanley Charles marketing educator
Hollingworth, Robert Michael toxicology researcher
Honhart, Frederick Lewis, III academic director
Hull, Jerome, Jr. horticultural extension specialist
Huzar, Eleanor Goltz history educator
Ilgen, Daniel Richard psychology educator
Isleib, Donald R. agricultural researcher
Johnson, J. David communication educator
Johnson, John Irwin, Jr. neuroscientist
Johnson, Theodore Oliver, Jr. musician, educator
Jones, Kensinger advertising executive
Kamrin, Michael Arnold toxicology educator
Kaplan, Thomas Abraham physics educator
Kende, Hans Janos plant physiology educator
Kirk, Edgar Lee musician, educator
Knobloch, Irving William retired biology educator, author
†Koelling, Melvin R. forestry educator
Kreinin, Mordechai Eliahu economics educator
Kronegger, Maria Elisabeth French and comparative literature educator
Lang, Marvel urban affairs educator
Leepa, Allen artist, educator
Lloyd, John Raymond mechanical engineering educator
Lockwood, John LeBaron plant pathologist
Lucas, Robert Elmer soil scientist
Luecke, Richard William biochemist
Lund, Lois A. retired food science and human nutrition educator
Mackey, Maurice Cecil university president, economist, lawyer
Macrakis, Kristie Irene history of science educator
Majors, Richard George psychology educator
Manderscheid, Lester Vincent agricultural economics educator
Manning, Peter Kirby sociology educator
Mansour, George P. Spanish language and literature educator
McMeekin, Dorothy botany, plant pathology educator
McPherson, Melville Peter academic administrator, former government official
Mead, Carl David educator
Melnyk, Steven Alexander business management educator
Menchik, Paul Leonard economist, educator
Miracle, Gordon Eldon advertising educator
Mitstifer, Dorothy Irwin honor society administrator
Montgomery, James Huey state government administrator, consultant
Moore, Kathryn McDaniel education educator

Moore, Kenneth Edwin pharmacology educator
Moran, Daniel Austin mathematician
Mukherjee, Kalinath materials science and engineering educator, researcher
Munger, Benson Scott professional society administrator
Murray, Raymond Harold physician
Nelson, Ronald Harvey animal science educator, researcher
Netzloff, Michael Lawrence pediatric educator, endocrinologist, geneticist
Olson, Judy Mae geography, cartography educator
Overton, Sarita Rosa psychologist
Paananen, Victor Niles English educator
Papsidero, Joseph Anthony social scientist, educator
Patterson, Maria Jevitz microbiology-pediatric infectious disease educator
Paul, Eldor Alvin agriculture, ecology educator
Perrin, Robert federal agency consultant, writer
Petrides, George Athan ecologist, educator
Pierre, Percy Anthony university president
Platt, Franklin Dewitt history educator
Poland, Robert Paul business educator, consultant
Pollack, Gerald Leslie physicist, educator
Pollack, Norman history educator
Preiss, Jack biochemistry educator
Press, Charles retired political science educator
Ralph, David Clinton communications educator
Rasche, Robert Harold economics educator
Reinhart, Mary Ann medical board executive
Ricks, Donald Jay agricultural economist
Ristow, George Edward neurologist, educator
Robbins, Lawrence Harry anthropologist
Robinson, Lawrence Phillip television engineer, inventor, consultant
Root-Bernstein, Robert Scott biologist, educator
Rosenman, Kenneth D. medical educator
Rovner, David Richard endocrinology educator
Rudman, Herbert Charles education educator
Sato, Paul Hisashi pharmacologist
Saul, William Edward civil engineering educator
Schlesinger, Joseph Abraham political scientist
Shaw, Robert Eugene minister, administrator
Silverman, Henry Jacob history educator
Snell, John Raymond civil engineer
Snoddy, James Ernest education educator
Sommers, Lawrence Melvin geographer, educator
Soutas-Little, Robert William mechanical engineer, educator
Sparks, Harvey Vise, Jr. physiologist
Spence, Robert Dean physics educator
Stapleton, James Hall statistician, educator
Strassmann, W. Paul economics educator
Suits, Daniel Burbidge economist
Summitt, (William) Robert chemist, educator
Tesar, Milo Benjamin agricultural researcher, educator, and administrator
Tien, H. Ti biophysics and physiology educator, scientist
Useem, John Hearld sociologist, anthropologist
Useem, Ruth Hill sociology educator
van der Smissen, M. E. Betty physical education educator
von Bernuth, Robert Dean agricultural engineering educator, consultant
Von Tersch, Lawrence Wayne electrical engineering educator, university dean
Waite, Donald Eugene medical educator, consultant
Wakoski, Diane poet, educator
Walker, Bruce Edward anatomy educator
Weng, John Juyang computer science educator, researcher
Whallon, William literature educator
Wilkinson, William Sherwood lawyer
Wilson, R. Dale marketing educator, consultant
Winder, Clarence Leland psychologist, educator
Witter, Richard Lawrence veterinarian, educator
Wojcik, Anthony Stephen computer science educator
Wolterink, Lester Floyd biophysicist, educator
Woodbury, Stephen Abbott economics educator
Wronski, Stanley Paul education educator
Yussouff, Mohammed physicist, educator

### Eastpointe
Andrzejewski, Darryl Lee clergyman

### Eastport
Tomlinson, James Lawrence mechanical engineer

### Eaton Rapids
Hall, Rebecca Ann executive secretary

### Edwardsburg
Floyd, Alton David cell biologist, consultant
Stuck, Wanda Marie special education educator

### Elk Rapids
Briggs, Robert Peter banker

### Escanaba
Cooper, Janelle Lunette neurologist, educator
Ling, Robert William, Jr. academic director

### Fair Haven
Wittbrodt, Frederick Joseph, Jr. automotive designer

### Farmington
Baker, Edward Martin engineering and industrial psychologist
Burns, Sister Elizabeth Mary hospital administrator
Chou, Clifford Chi Fong research engineering executive
Ginsberg, Myron computer scientist
Neyer, Jerome Charles consulting civil engineer
Pittelko, Roger Dean clergyman
Wine, Sherwin Theodore rabbi

### Farmington Hills
Allen, Janet Louise school system administrator
Bahr, Sheila Kay physician
Birnkrant, Sherwin Maurice lawyer
Blum, Jon H. dermatologist
Dolan, Jan Clark former state legislator
Donald, Edward Milton, Jr. graphic designer
Dragun, James soil chemist
Ellmann, Sheila Frenkel investment company executive
Ethridge, James Merritt editor, former publishing company executive, writer
Faxon, Jack headmaster
Fox, Dean Frederick coporate executive
Frederick, Raymond Joseph sales engineering executive
Gladchun, Lawrence L. banker, lawyer
Gordon, Craig Jeffrey oncologist, educator
Haliw, Andrew Jerome, III lawyer, engineer
Hartman-Abramson, Ilene adult education educator
Harwell, William Earnest (Ernie Harwell) broadcaster
Heiss, Richard Walter former bank executive, consultant, lawyer
Helppie, Charles Everett, III financial consultant
Karniotis, Stephen Paul computer scientist
Kussy, Frank Werner electrical engineer, consultant
Landry, Thomas Henry construction executive
Leyh, George Francis association executive
Mackey, Robert Joseph business executive
McNamara, Ann Dowd medical technologist
Michlin, Arnold Sidney finance executive
Nathanson, Leonard Mark lawyer
Papai, Beverly Daffern library director
Plaut, Jonathan Victor rabbi
Ryan, Earl M. public affairs analyst
Sobczak, Judy Marie clinical psychologist

### Ferndale
Cole, Gretchen Bornor distribution and service executive
Dunn, Elwood minister
Gienapp, Helen Fischer jewelry company owner

### Flint
Alarie, Peggy Sue physician assistant
Belcher, Max social services administrator
Cawood, Thomas Fred music therapist
Cooley, Richard Eugene lawyer
Farrehi, Cyrus cardiologist, educator
Germann, Steven James museum director
Green, Allison Anne retired secondary education educator
Hayes, Joyce Merriweather secondary education educator
Heymoss, Jennifer Marie librarian
Jayabalan, Vemblaserry nuclear medicine physician, radiologist
Lehman, Richard Leroy lawyer
Lorenz, John Douglas college official
Marx, Sharon Rose health facility administrator
McClanahan, Connie Dea pastoral minister
Meissner, Suzanne Banks pastoral associate
Nelms, Charlie academic administrator
Newblatt, Stewart Albert federal judge
Palinsky, Constance Genevieve hypnotherapist, educator
Pelavin, Michael Allen lawyer
Piper, Mark Harry retired banker
Rappleye, Richard Kent financial executive, consultant, educator
Soderstrom, Robert Merriner dermatologist
Stanley, Woodrow mayor
Taeckens, Pamela Webb bank executive
Tauscher, John Walter retired pediatrician, emeritus educator
Tomblinson, James Edmond architect
White, William Samuel foundation executive

### Flushing
Barnes, Robert Vincent elementary and secondary school art educator
Himes, George Elliott pathologist

### Fort Gratiot
Stevens, Brenda Joy educator

### Fowlerville
Edwards, Nelson Grey optometrist

### Frankfort
Acker, Nathaniel Hull retired educational administrator
Foster, Robert Carmichael banker

### Franklin
Adler, Philip osteopathic physician
Roy, Ranjit Kumar mechanical engineer
Vanderlaan, Richard B. marketing company executive

### Fraser
Cannon, Christopher Perry human resource development executive

### Fremont
Melonakos, Christine Marie educational administrator

### Fruitport
Anderson, Frances Swem nuclear medical technologist

### Gaylord
Cooney, Patrick Ronald bishop
Magsig, Judith Anne early childhood education educator

### Glenn
Rizzolo, Louis B. M. artist, educator

### Grand Blanc
Hicks, Susan Lynn Bowman small business owner
Lemke, Laura Ann foreign language educator, assistant principal
Wasfie, Tarik Jawad surgeon, educator

### Grand Haven
Anderson, Cynthia Finkbeiner Sjoberg speech and language pathologist

### Grand Ledge
Evert, Sandra Florence medical/surgical nurse

### Grand Rapids
Anderson, Roger Gordon minister
Arthur Estner, Charthel artistic director
Auwers, Stanley John motor carrier executive
Babcock, Wendell Keith religion educator
Baker, Hollis MacLure furniture manufacturing company executive
Baker, Richard Lee book publishing company executive
Barnes, Thomas John lawyer
Bartek, Gordon Luke radiologist
Beeke, Joel Robert minister, theology educator, writer
Bell, Robert Holmes federal judge
Bissell, Mark consumer products company executive
Blackwell, Thomas Francis lawyer
Blovits, Larry John retired art educator
Bolt, Eunice Mildred DeVries artist
Borgdorff, Peter church adminstrator
Boyden, Joel Michael lawyer
Bradshaw, Conrad Allan lawyer
Bransdorfer, Stephen Christie lawyer
Brenneman, Hugh Warren, Jr. judge
Brent, Helen Teressa health planner/evaluator
Brink, William P. clergyman
Canepa, John Charles banking consultant
Comet, Catherine conductor
Curtin, Timothy John lawyer
Daniels, Joseph neuropsychiatrist
Davis, Henry Barnard, Jr. lawyer
Deems, Nyal David lawyer, mayor
DeHaan, John religious organization administrator
DeLapa, Judith Anne business owner
DeVries, Robert K. religious book publisher
Dickerson, Allen Bruce interior designer, consultant
Diekema, Anthony J. college president, educational consultant
Dykstra, William Dwight business executive, consultant
Ehlers, Vernon James congressman
Frankforter, Weldon DeLoss retired museum administrator
Gemmell-Akalis, Bonni Jean psychotherapist
Gibson, Benjamin F. federal judge
Hackett, James P. manufacturing executive
Hakala, Judyth Ann data processing executive
Hardy, Michael C. performing arts administrator
Hillman, Douglas Woodruff federal judge
Hofman, Leonard John minister
Hollies, Linda Hall pastor, educator, author, publisher
Hooker, Robert automotive executive
Jacobsen, Arnold archivist
Jennette, Noble Stevenson, III lawyer
Kaczmarczyk, Jeffrey Allen journalist, classical music critic
Kramer, Carol Gertrude marriage and family counselor
Lloyd, Michael Stuart newspaper editor
Logie, John Hoult mayor, lawyer
MacDonald, David Richard industrial psychologist
†Maurer, John Raymond internist, educator
McGarry, John Everett lawyer
McNeil, John W. lawyer
Mears, Patrick Edward lawyer
Meijer, Douglas retail company executive
Meijer, Frederik retail company executive
Meijer, Hendrik retail company executive
Miles, Wendell A. federal judge
Monsma, Marvin Eugene library director
Pestle, John William lawyer
Petkus, Alan Francis microbiologist
Pew, Robert Cunningham, II office equipment manufacturing company executive
Quinn, Patrick Michael wholesale food executive
Quist, Gordon Jay federal judge
Rougier-Chapman, Alwyn Spencer Douglas furniture manufacturing company executive
Rozeboom, John A. religious organization administrator
Ryskamp, Bruce E. publishing executive
Sadler, David Gary management executive
Sadler, Robert Livingston banker
Schwanda, Tom religious studies educator
Schwartz, Garry Albert advertising executive
Smith, H(arold) Lawrence lawyer
Smith, Peter Wilson symphony orchestra administrator
Sytsma, Fredric A. lawyer
Titley, Larry J. lawyer
Van Haren, W(illiam) Michael lawyer
VanHarn, Gordon Lee college administrator and provost
Van't Hof, William Keith lawyer
Vrancken, Robert Danloy facilities planner, designer and educator
Wilt, Jeffrey Lynn pulmonary and critical care physician
Wold, Robert Lee architect, engineer
Woodrick, Robert food products executive
Zuidervaart, Lambert Paul philosophy educator

### Grass Lake
Popp, Nathaniel bishop

### Greenbush
Paulson, James Marvin engineering educator

### Gregory
Frank, Richard Calhoun architect

### Grosse Ile
Frisch, Kurt Charles polymer engineering educator, administrator
Smith, Veronica Latta real estate corporation officer

### Grosse Pointe
Allen, Lee Harrison wholesale company executive, industrial consultant
Avant, Grady, Jr. lawyer
Axe, John Randolph lawyer, financial executive
Beierwaltes, William Henry physician, educator
Beltz, Charles Robert engineering executive
Blevins, William Edward management consultant
Brucker, Wilber Marion lawyer
Canfield, Francis Xavier priest, English language educator
Cartmill, George Edwin, Jr. retired hospital administrator
Christian, Edward Kieren broadcasting station executive
Cross, Ralph Emerson mechanical engineer
Fromm, Joseph L. financial consultant
Gilbride, William Donald lawyer
Goss, James William lawyer
Hudson, Marlene Mary speech and language pathologist
King, John Lane lawyer
Krebs, William Hoyt company executive, industrial hygienist
Lane, James McConkey investment executive
McIntyre, Anita Grace Jordan lawyer
McWhirter, Glenna Suzanne (Nickie McWhirter) retired newspaper columnist
Mecke, Theodore Hart McCalla, Jr. management consultant
Mengden, Joseph Michael investment banker
Mogk, John Edward law educator, association executive, consultant
Nicholson, George Albert, Jr. financial analyst
Obolensky, Marilyn Wall (Mrs. Serge Obolensky) metals company executive
Perez-Borja, Carlos M. neurologist, hospital executive
Peters, Thomas Robert English language educator, writer
Powsner, Edward Raphael physician
Pytell, Robert Henry lawyer, former judge
Richardson, Dean Eugene retired banker
Robie, Joan elementary school principal
Sphire, Raymond Daniel anesthesiologist
Surdam, Robert McClellan retired banker
Thurber, Cleveland, Jr. trust banker
Thurber, Donald MacDonald Dickinson public relations counsel
Valk, Robert Earl corporate executive
Whittaker, Jeanne Evans former newspaper columnist
Wilkinson, Warren Scripps manufacturing company executive
Wilson, Henry Arthur, Jr. management consultant

### Grosse Pointe Shores
Smith, Frank Earl retired association executive

### Grosse Pointe Woods
Wagner, Harvey Arthur nuclear engineer

### Gwinn
Lasich, Vivian Esther Layne secondary education educator

### Hancock
Dresch, Stephen Paul economist, state legislator
Puotinen, Arthur Edwin college president, clergyman

### Harbert
Morrissette, Bruce Archer Romance languages educator

### Harper Woods
DeGiusti, Dominic Lawrence medical science educator, academic administrator
Havrilcsak, Gregory Michael historian, educator

### Harrison Township
Cobb, Cecelia Annette counselor
Kennard, Margaret Anne middle school educator
Suchecki, Lucy Anne elementary education educator

### Harsens Island
Slade, Roy artist, college president, museum director

### Haslett
Hotaling, Robert Bachman community planner, educator

### Hastings
Adrounie, V. Harry public health administrator, scientist, educator, environmentalist

### Hickory Corners
Bristol, Norman lawyer, arbitrator, former food company executive
Brown, Norman A. consultant, educator
Hubbard, William Neill, Jr. pharmaceutical company executive
Klug, Michael J. microbiology educator, ecology educator
Lauff, George Howard biologist

### Highland Park
Crittenden, Mary Lynne science educator

### Hillsdale
Castel, Albert Edward history educator
Kline, Faith Elizabeth college administrator
Roche, George Charles, III college administrator
Trowbridge, Ronald Lee college admininstrator

### Holland
Brooks, James W. beverage manufacturing executive
Cook, James Ivan clergyman, religion educator
Haworth, Gerrard Wendell office systems manufacturing company executive
Haworth, Richard G. office furniture manufacturer
Hesselink, I(ra) John, Jr. theology educator
Hill, JoAnne Francis elementary education educator
Hountras, Peter Timothy psychologist, educator
Inghram, Mark Gordon physicist, educator
Jacobson, John Howard, Jr. college president
Johanneson, Gerald Benedict office products company executive
Moritz, John Reid lawyer
Nelson, David Leonard process management systems company executive
Nelson, Helaine Queen lawyer
Nyenhuis, Jacob Eugene college official
Quimby, Robert Sherman retired humanities educator
Spoelhof, John consumer products company executive
Van Wylen, Gordon John former college president
Zick, Leonard Otto accountant, manufacturing executive, financial consultant

### Holt
Ribby, Alice Marie nurse

### Hopkins
Ludlam, Heather Jo veterinarian

### Houghton
Goel, Ashok Kumar electrical engineering educator
Heckel, Richard Wayne metallurgical engineering educator
Huang, Eugene Yuching civil engineer, educator
Krenitsky, Michael V. librarian
McGinnis, Gary David chemist, science educator
Pelc, Karol I. engineering management educator, researcher
Tompkins, Curtis Johnston university president

### Howell
Cattani, Luis Carlos manufacturing engineer
Korsgren, Mary Louise home care nurse
Watkins, Curtis Winthrop artist

### Huntington Woods
Gutmann, Joseph art history educator

### Indian River
Knecht, Richard Arden family practitioner

### Interlochen
Stolley, Alexander *advertising executive*

### Ishpeming
Steward, James Brian *lawyer, pharmacist*

### Ithaca
Craig, Zane Grant *obstetrician, gynecologist*

### Jackson
Curtis, Philip James *lawyer*
Feldmann, Judith Gail *language professional, educator*
Genyk, Ruth Bel *psychotherapist*
Haglund, Bernice Marion *elementary school educator*
Kelly, Robert Vincent, Jr. *metal company executive*
Kendall, Kay Lynn *interior designer*
Marcoux, William Joseph *lawyer*
McCormick, William Thomas, Jr. *electric and gas company executive*
Nathaniel *bishop*
Patrick, Ueal Eugene *oil company executive*
Raduazo, Anthony F. *lawyer*
Vischer, Harold Harry *manufacturing company executive*
Weaver, Franklin Thomas *newspaper executive*

### Jenison
Roberts Harvey, Bonita *secondary school educator*

### Kalamazoo
Aladjem, Silvio *obstetrician, gynecologist, educator*
Amdursky, Saul Jack *library director*
Arnold Hubert, Nancy Kay *writer*
Bennett, Arlie Joyce *clinical social worker emeritus*
Breisach, Ernst A. *historian, educator*
Brown, Eric Vandyke, Jr. *lawyer*
Burns, James W. *education educator*
Calloway, Jean Mitchener *mathematician, educator*
Campbell, Raymond William *surgical nurse*
Carlson, Andrew Raymond *archivist*
Carver, Norman Francis, Jr. *architect, photographer*
Cheney, Brigham Vernon *physical chemist*
Chodos, Dale David Jerome *physician, consumer advocate*
Clarke, Allen Bruce *mathematics educator, retired academic administrator*
Cline, Sandra Williamson *elementary education educator*
Cogswell, Kenneth Mark *newspaper executive*
Connable, Alfred Barnes *retired business executive*
Dietz, Alma *microbiologist*
Dybek, Stuart *English educator, writer*
Edmondson, Keith Henry *chemical company executive, retired*
Engelmann, Paul Victor *plastics engineering educator*
Enslen, Richard Alan *federal judge*
Fredericks, Sharon Kay *nurses aide*
Freed, Karl Francis *professional planner*
Gilmore, James Stanley, Jr. *broadcast executive*
Gladstone, William Sheldon, Jr. *radiologist*
Gordon, Edgar George *lawyer, business executive*
Gordon, Jaimy *English educator, writer*
Greenfield, John Charles *bio-organic chemist*
Gregory, Ross *history educator, author*
Grotzinger, Laurel Ann *university librarian*
Halpert, Richard L. *lawyer*
Hamilton, Diane Bronkema *nursing educator*
Hilboldt, James Sonnemann *lawyer, investment advisor*
Holland, Harold Herbert *banker*
Hooker, Richard Alfred *lawyer*
Hudson, Roy Davage *retired pharmaceutical company executive*
Inselberg, Rachel *retired educator, researcher*
Jamison, Frank Raymond *communications educator*
Johnson, Tom Milroy *academic dean, medical educator, physician*
Jones, James Fleming, Jr. *college president, Roman language and literature educator*
Lander, Joyce Ann *nursing educator, medical/surgical nurse*
Lawrence, William Joseph, Jr. *retired corporate executive*
Lee, Edward L. *bishop*
Lennon, Elizabeth M. *retired educator*
Light, Christopher Upjohn *freelance writer, computer musician*
Maier, Paul Luther *history educator, author, chaplain*
Markin, David Robert *motor company executive*
Marshall, Vincent de Paul *industrial microbiologist, researcher*
McCarthy, Catherine Therese *elementary educator*
Moritz, Edward *historian, educator*
Norris, Richard Patrick *museum director, history educator*
O'Boyle, Robert L. *landscape architect*
Pinkham, Eleanor Humphrey *retired university librarian*
Ritter, Charles Edward *lawyer*
Rowland, Doyle Alfred *federal judge*
Ruoff, Cynthia Osowiec *foreign language educator*
Shah, Shirish Anantlal *pharmacist*
Slager, Joan K. *nurse midwife*
Slatter, John Gregory *research scientist*
Stufflebeam, Daniel LeRoy *education educator*
Taborn, Jeannette Ann *real estate investor*
Taylor, Duncan Paul *research neuropharmacologist*
Tracy, Joel Dean *marketing researcher*
Van Vlack, Lawrence Hall *engineering educator*
Vescovi, Selvi *pharmaceutical company executive*
Walcott, Delores Deborah *psychologist, educator*
Waring, Walter Weyler *English language educator*
Welborn, John Alva *former state senator, small business owner*
Zupko, Ramon *composer, music professor*

### Kalkaska
Batsakis, John George *pathology educator*

### Kentwood
Kelly, William Garrett *judge*

### Kincheloe
Light, Kenneth Freeman *college administrator*

### Laingsburg
Scripter, Frank C. *manufacturing company executive*

### Lake Angelus
Kresge, Bruce Anderson *retired physician*

### Lake Ann
Monteith, Clifton James *artist*

### Lake Leelanau
Shannahan, John Henry Kelly *energy consultant*

### Lambertville
Korthuis, Kathleen E. *dean*

### Lansing
Anderton, James Franklin, IV *holdings company executive*
Baker, Frederick Milton, Jr. *lawyer*
Ballbach, Philip Thornton *political consultant*
Beardmore, Dorothy *state education official*
Bell Wilson, Carlotta A. *state official, consultant*
Binsfeld, Connie Berube *state official*
Boyle, Patricia Jean *judge*
Brennan, Thomas Emmett *law school president*
Brown, Nancy Field *editor*
Bullard, Willis Clare, Jr. *state legislator*
Carlotti, Ronald John *food scientist*
Carter, Pamela Lee *school system administrator*
Cavanagh, Michael Francis *state supreme court justice*
Cisky, Jon Ayres *state senator*
Croxford, Lynne Louise *social services administrator*
DeHaven, Clark Edwin *business educator*
Demlow, Daniel J. *lawyer*
Dobronski, Agnes Marie *state legislator*
Doty, Brant Lee *academic administrator*
Emmons, Joanne *state senator*
Feight, Theodore J. *financial planner*
Fink, Joseph Allen *lawyer*
Fitzgerald, John Warner *law educator*
Foster, Joe C., Jr. *lawyer*
Gallagher, Byron Patrick, Jr. *lawyer*
Geake, Raymond Robert *state senator*
Geiger, Terry *state legislator*
Hammerstrom, Beverly Swoish *state legislator*
Harrison, Michael Gregory *judge*
Harvey, Joanne H. *genealogist*
†Herman, James George *radiation oncologist*
Hilbert, Virginia Lois *computer consultant and training executive*
Hines, Marshall *construction engineering company executive*
Hoffman, Philip Edward *state senator*
Houston, David John *lawyer*
Hull, Christopher Neil *state agency biologist*
Jellema, Jon *state legislator*
Kaza, Greg John *state representative, economist*
Kelley, Frank Joseph *state attorney general*
Kluge, Len H. *director, actor, theater educator*
Kritselis, William Nicholas *lawyer*
LaForge, Edward *state legislator*
LaHaine, Gilbert Eugene *retail lumber company executive*
Liebler, Edward Charles *veterinarian, construction company executive*
Lindemer, Lawrence Boyd *lawyer, former utility executive, former state justice*
Lobenherz, William Ernest *association executive, legislative counsel, lawyer*
Lowe, William Daniel *automotive company research executive, consultant*
McCoy, Bernard Rogers *television anchor*
McKeague, David William *district judge*
McManus, George Alvin, Jr. *state senator, cherry farmer*
Miller, Candice S. *state official*
Mitzelfeld, Jim *commentor, legal assistant*
Muchmore, Dennis C. *governmental affairs consultant*
Muneio, Patricia Anne *public health nurse*
Perricone, Charles *state legislator*
Posthumus, Richard Earl *state senator, farmer*
Roberts, Calvin *materials engineer*
Rooney, John Philip *law educator*
Saltzman, Robert Paul *insurance company executive*
†Schmidt, Thomas Walter *airport executive*
Schuette, Bill *state senator*
Schwarz, John J.H. *state senator, surgeon*
Shirtum, Earl Edward *retired civil engineer*
Sikkema, Kenneth R. *state legislator*
Stackable, Frederick Lawrence *lawyer*
Stanaway, Loretta Susan *small business owner*
Stockmeyer, Norman Otto, Jr. *law educator, consultant*
Suhrheinrich, Richard Fred *federal judge*
Valade, Alan Michael *lawyer*
Vaughn, Jackie, III *state legislator*
Vincent, Frederick Michael, Sr. *neurologist, electromyographer, educational administrator*
Warrington, Willard Glade *former university official*
Weaver, Elizabeth A *judge*
Wiegenstein, John Gerald *physician*
Winder, Richard Earnest *legal foundation administrator, writer, consultant*

### Leland
Small, Hamish *chemist*

### Lewiston
Ruehle, Dianne Marie *retired elementary education educator*

### Lincoln Park
Russell, Harriet Shaw *social worker*

### Litchfield
Edwards, E. Dean *banking, building and real estate executive*

### Livonia
Campbell, Barbara Ann *editor*
Davis, Lawrence Edward *church official*
Hess, Bartlett Leonard *clergyman*
Hess, Margaret Johnston *religious writer, educator*
Hoffman, Barry Paul *lawyer*
Holtzman, Roberta Lee *French and Spanish language educator*
McCuen, John Francis, Jr. *lawyer*
McCuen, John Joachim *building company and financial company executive*
Needham, Kathleen Ann *gerontology educator, consultant*
Sobel, Howard Bernard *osteopath*
Swift, Jonathan *television personality, education educator, tenor*
Van de Vyver, Sister Mary Francilene *academic administrator*

### Ludington
Puffer, Richard Judson *retired college chancellor*

### Mackinac Island
Mc Cabe, John Charles, III *writer*

### Macomb
Farmakis, George Leonard *education educator*

### Madison Heights
Chapman, Gilbert Bryant *physicist*
Kafarski, Mitchell I. *chemical processing company executive*
O'Hara, Thomas Edwin *professional administrator executive*
Pricer, Wayne Francis *counseling administrator*

### Mancelona
Whelan, Joseph L. *neurologist*

### Manistee
Behring, Daniel William *educational and business professional*

### Maple City
Morris, Donald Arthur Adams *college president*

### Marquette
Burt, John Harris *bishop*
Camerius, James Walter *marketing educator, corporate researcher*
Garland, James H. *bishop*
Geiger, David Scott *mathematician, researcher*
Harrington, Lucia Marie *elementary education educator*
Heldreth, Leonard Guy *English educator, university official*
Hill, Betty Jean *nursing educator, academic administrator*
Jajich, James Gary *elementary and middle school educator*
Manning, Robert Hendrick *media consultant*
Poindexter, Kathleen A. Krause *nursing educator, critical care nurse*
Ray, Thomas Kreider *bishop*
Skogman, Dale R. *bishop*
Suomi, Paul Neil *alumni association director*
Vandament, William Eugene *academic administrator, educator*

### Mattawan
Lough, Rick Leo *sales and marketing professional*

### Mears
Binder, Leonard James *magazine editor, retired*

### Menominee
Anuta, Michael Joseph *lawyer*

### Middleville
Miller, Stephen Bryan *social worker, marriage counselor*

### Midland
Barker, Nancy Lepard *university official*
Bus, James Stanley *toxicologist*
Carson, Gordon Bloom *engineering executive*
Chao, Marshall *chemist*
Chen, Catherine Wang *provost*
Crummett, Warren Berlin *analytical chemistry consultant*
Cuthbert, Robert Lowell *product specialist*
Dorman, Linneaus Cuthbert *retired chemist*
Hall, David McKenzie *marketing and management educator*
Hampton, Leroy *retired chemical company executive*
Hanes, James Henry *consulting business executive, lawyer*
Hazleton, Richard A. *chemicals executive*
Hyde, Geraldine Veola *retired secondary education educator*
Maneri, Remo R. *management consultant*
McCarty, Leslie Paul *pharmacologist, chemist*
McCarty, Roger Leland *chemical company official*
McDaniels, Peggy Ellen *special education educator*
Meister, Bernard John *chemical engineer*
Nowak, Robert Michael *chemist*
Popoff, Frank Peter *chemical company executive*
Powell, Rebecca Ann *secondary school educator*
Robbins, Lanny Arnold *chemical engineer*
Shastri, Ranganath Krishna *materials scientist*
Stavropoulos, William S. *chemical executive*
Stenger, Vernon Arthur *analytical chemist, consultant*
Stull, Daniel Richard *retired research thermochemist, educator, consultant*
Weiler, Scott Michael *machine tool manufacturing company executive*
Weyenberg, Donald Richard *chemist*
Wright, Antony Pope *research chemist*

### Monroe
Knezevich, Janice A. *critical care nurse*
Lipford, Rocque Edward *lawyer, corporate executive*
Mlocek, Sister Frances Angeline *financial executive*
Sewell, Robert Terrell, Jr. *executive search company owner*
Siciliano, Elizabeth Marie *secondary education educator*

### Montague
Gundy-Reed, Frances Darnell *librarian, healthcare manager*

### Mount Clemens
Kolakowski, Diana Jean *county commissioner*
Robinson, Earl, Jr. *marketing and economic research executive, transportation executive, business educator, retired air force officer*

### Mount Pleasant
Croll, Robert Frederick *economist, educator*
Dietrich, Richard Vincent *geologist, educator*
Grabinski, C. Joanne *gerontologist, educator*
Lippert, Robert J. *administrator and culinary arts educator, consultant*
Lovinger, Sophie Lehner *child psychologist*
McBryde, James Edward *state legislator*
Meltzer, Bernard N(athan) *sociologist, educator*
Novitski, Charles Edward *biology educator*
Orlik, Peter Blythe *media educator, author, musician*
Rubin, Stuart Harvey *computer science educator, researcher*
Steffel, Susan Elizabeth *English language and literature educator*

Thompson, Clifton C. *chemistry educator, university administrator*
Zimmerman, Helene Loretta *business educator*

### Muskegon
Anderson, Harvey Gregg *pattern company executive*
Delong, Donald R. *accountant*
Hadiaris, Marie Ellen *special education educator*
McKendry, John H., Jr. *lawyer, educator*
Nehra, Gerald Peter *lawyer*
Roy, Paul Emile, Jr. *county official*
Van Leuven, Robert Joseph *lawyer*

### Naubinway
Smith, Richard Ernest *retired insurance company executive*

### Negaunee
Friggens, Thomas George *state official, historian*

### New Haven
Shaw, Charles Rusanda *government investigator*

### Newport
Riches, Kenneth William *nuclear regulatory engineer*

### North Branch
Stevenson, James Laraway *communications engineer, consulting*

### Northport
Schultz, Richard Carlton *plastic surgeon*
Thomas, Philip Stanley *economics educator*

### Northville
Abbasi, Tariq Afzal *psychiatrist, educator*
Hariri, V. M. *arbitrator, mediator, lawyer, educator*
Leavitt, Martin Jack *lawyer*
Liegl, Joseph Leslie *lawyer*

### Novi
Crane, Patricia Sue *probation services administrator, social worker*
Kinsey, Charles John *industrial auctioneer, consultant, cattle breeder, farmer*
Simpkin, Lawrence James *utilities executive*

### Oak Park
Borovoy, Marc Allen *podiatrist*
Moilanen, Thomas Alfred *construction equipment distributor*
Novick, Marvin *investment company executive, former automotive supplier executive, accountant*

### Okemos
Giacoletto, Lawrence Joseph *electronics engineering educator, researcher, consultant*
Hickey, Howard Wesley *retired education educator*
Huddleston, Eugene Lee *retired American studies educator*
Janicki, Gregory John *writer, consultant*
Luecke, Eleanor Virginia Rohrbacher *civic volunteer*
Monson, Carol Lynn *osteopath, psychotherapist*
Oberg, Roger Winston *management educator*
Ochberg, Frank Martin *psychiatrist, foundation administrator*
Solo, Robert Alexander *economist, educator*
Velicer, Janet Schafbuch *elementary school educator*

### Olivet
Bassis, Michael Steven *academic administrator*
Fuller, Judith Kay Altenhein *special education educator*
Mahmoudi, Hoda *academic administrator, sociology educator*
Walker, Donald Edwin *history educator*

### Ortonville
Coffel, Patricia K. *retired clinical social worker*

### Owosso
Bentley, Margaret Ann *librarian*
Hoddy, George Warren *electric company executive, electrical engineer*
Moorhead, Thomas Edward *lawyer*

### Petoskey
Smith, Wayne Richard *lawyer*

### Pinckney
Duquet, Suzanne Frances *special education educator*
Hernandez, Ramon Robert *clergyman, librarian*

### Plainwell
Flower, Jean Frances *art educator*
Ortiz-Button, Olga *social worker*

### Pleasant Ridge
Krabbenhoft, Kenneth Lester *radiologist, educator*

### Plymouth
Belobraidich, Sharon Lynn Goul *elementary education educator*
Berry, Charlene Helen *librarian, musician*
Brown, Bruce Harding *naval officer*
deBear, Richard Stephen *library planning consultant*
Garpow, James Edward *financial executive*
Grannan, William Stephen *safety engineer, consultant*
Massey, Donald E. *automotive executiv*
McClendon, Edwin James *health science educator*
Merrill, Kenneth Coleman *retired automobile company executive*
Moore, Joan Elizabeth *human resources executive, lawyer*
Morgan, Donald Crane *lawyer*
Scott, George Ernest *publisher, writer*
Vlcek, Donald Joseph, Jr. *food distribution company executive, consultant*

### Pontiac
Carter, Anthony *football player*
Decker, Peter William *academic administrator*
†Glover, Kevin *football player*
Grant, Barry M(arvin) *judge*
Love, Sharon Irene *elementary education educator*
Mahone, Barbara Jean *automotive company executive*
Sanders, Barry *football player*
Schmidt, Chuck *professional football team executive*

**Williamston**
Landis, Elwood Winton *retired newspaper editor*

**Wixom**
Boynton, Irvin Parker *educational administrator*

**Wyandotte**
Dunn, Gloria Jean *artist*

**Ypsilanti**
Barnes, James Milton *physics and astronomy educator*
Boone, Morell Douglas *academic administrator, information and instructional technology educator*
Cantrell, Linda Maxine *counselor*
Caswell, Herbert Hall, Jr. *retired biology educator*
Corriveau, Arlene Josephine *educational specialist*
deSouza, Joan Melanie *psychologist*
Duncan, Charles Howard *business education educator*
Evans, Gary Lee *communications educator and consultant*
Gledhill, Roger Clayton *statistician, engineer, mathematician, educator*
Gwaltney, Thomas Marion *education educator, researcher*
Holland, Joy *health care facility executive*
Lewis-White, Linda Beth *elementary school educator*
Lou, Zheng (David) *mechanical engineer, biomedical engineer*
Norton, Jody (John Douglas Norton) *English language educator*
Olmsted, Patricia Palmer *education educator, researcher*
Perkins, Bradford *history educator*
Porter, John Wilson *education executive*
Ritter, Frank Nicholas *otolaryngologist, educator*
Shelton, William Everett *university president*
Sullivan, Thomas Patrick *academic administrator*
Tobias, Tom, Jr. *elementary school educator*
Ullman, Nelly Szabo *statistician, educator*
Walker, Michael Leon *education educator*
Washington, Adrienne Marie *elementary school educator*
Weinstein, Jay A. *social science educator, researcher*
Wilson, Lorraine M. *medical and surgical nurse, nursing educator*

**Zeeland**
Guarr, Thomas Frederick *research chemist*

## MINNESOTA

**Aitkin**
Prickett, Gordon Odin *mining, mineral and energy engineer*

**Albert Lea**
Jensen, Annette M. *mental health nurse, administrator*
Rechtzigel, Sue Marie (Suzanne Rechtzigel) *child care center executive*

**Alexandria**
Hultstrand, Donald Maynard *bishop*
Templin, Kenneth Elwood *paper company executive*

**Annandale**
Johnson, Jon E. *magazine editor and publisher*
Schilplin, Yvonne Winter *educational administrator*

**Anoka**
Hicken, Jeffrey Price *lawyer*

**Apple Valley**
Doyle, O'Brien John, Jr. *emergency medical services consultant, lobbyist, writer*

**Arden Hills**
Lindmark, Ronald Dorance *retired federal agency administrator*
Van Houten, James Forester *insurance company executive*

**Austin**
Hodapp, Don Joseph *food company executive*
Holman, Ralph Theodore *biochemistry and nutrition educator*
Johnson, Joel W. *food products executive*
Knowlton, Richard L. *retired food and meat processing company executive*
Leighton, Robert Joseph *state legislator*
Schmid, Harald Heinrich Otto *biochemistry educator, academic director*

**Bayport**
Wulf, Jerold W. *manufacturing executive*

**Bemidji**
Bonner, Helen Ward *English language and literature educator*
Bridston, Paul Joseph *strategic consultant*
Kief, Paul Allan *lawyer*
Martel, Petra Jean Hegstad *elementary school educator*

**Bertha**
Peterson, Myra M. *special education educator*

**Bloomington**
Allen, Mary Louise Hook *physical education educator*
Beckwith, Larry Edward *mechanical engineer*
Dahlberg, Burton Francis *real estate corporation executive*
Jodsaas, Larry Elvin *computer components company executive*
Lakin, James Dennis *allergist, immunologist, director*
McDill, Thomas Allison *minister*
Miller, Alan M. *editor*
Smith, Henry Charles, III *symphony orchestra conductor*
Thomas, Margaret Jean *clergywoman, religious research consultant*
Wilson, Rebecca Lynn *lawyer*

**Brooklyn Center**
Brosnahan, Roger Paul *lawyer*

**Brooklyn Park**
Frank, Paul Wilbur *social worker*
Rogers, David *apparel executive*

**Burnsville**
Knutson, David Lee *lawyer, state senator*
Lai, Juey Hong *chemical engineer*
Larson, Doyle Eugene *retired air force officer, consultant*

**Chanhassen**
Severson, Roger Allan *bank executive*
Thorson, John Martin, Jr. *electrical engineer, consultant*

**Chisago City**
Bergstrand, Wilton Everet *minister*

**Cloquet**
Ellison, David Charles *special education educator*

**Cokato**
Thomas, Paul S. *principal*

**Collegeville**
Haile, Getatchew *archivist, educator*
Powers, James Farl *author*
Reinhart, Dietrich Thomas *university president, history educator*

**Coon Rapids**
Carlson, Linda Marie *language arts educator, consultant*

**Cottage Grove**
Glazebrook, Rita Susan *nursing educator*
Hudnut, Robert Kilborne *clergyman, author*

**Crookston**
Balke, Victor H. *bishop*

**Crosslake**
Kettleson, David Noel *retired orthopaedic surgeon, timber manager*

**Dassel**
Kay, Craig *principal*

**Detroit Lakes**
Eginton, Charles Theodore *surgeon, educator*

**Duluth**
Aadland, Thomas Vernon *minister*
Aufderheide, Arthur Carl *pathologist*
Balmer, James Walter *lawyer*
Billig, Thomas Clifford *publishing and marketing executive*
Bowman, Roger Manwaring *real estate executive*
Burns, Richard Ramsey *lawyer*
Chee, Cheng-Khee *artist*
Coffman, Phillip Hudson *music educator, arts administrator*
Eisenberg, Richard Martin *pharmacology educator*
Fischer, Roger Adrian *history educator*
Franks, Ronald Dwyer *university dean, psychiatrist, educator*
Fryberger, Elizabeth Ann *financial consultant*
Gallinger, Lois Mae *medical technologist*
Heaney, Gerald William *federal judge*
Heller, Lois Jane *physiologist, educator, researcher*
Jankofsky, Klaus Peter *medieval studies educator*
Johnson, Arthur Gilbert *microbiology educator*
Johnson, Joseph Bernard *lawyer*
Latto, Lewis M., Jr. *broadcasting company executive*
Lease, Martin Harry, Jr. *retired political science educator*
Pearce, Donald Joslin *retired librarian*
Rapp, George Robert, Jr. (Rip Rapp) *geology and archeology educator*
Salmela, David Daniel *architect*
Schroeder, Fred Erich Harald *humanities educator*
Schwietz, Roger L. *bishop*
Whiteman, Richard Frank *architect*

**Eagan**
Angle, Margaret Susan *lawyer*

**East Grand Forks**
Schmitz, Daniel Dean *mechanical engineer*

**Eden Prairie**
Carter, Cris *professional football player*
Cervilla, Constance Marlene *marketing consultant*
Emison, James W. *petroleum company executive*
Grant, Bud (Harry Peter Grant) *retired professional football coach*
Green, Dennis *professional football coach*
Hanson, Dale S. *banker*
Headrick, Roger Lewis *professional sports executive*
Higgins, Robert Arthur *electrical engineer, educator, consultant*
Knotek, Robert Frank *management consultant, educator*
McCoy, Gerald Leo *superintendent of schools*
Nilles, John Michael *lawyer*
Randle, John *professional football player*
Reveiz, Fuad *professional football player*
Roth, Thomas *marketing executive*
Schulze, Richard M. *consumer products executive*
Skoglund, John C. *former professional football team executive*
Talley, Darryl Victor *professional football player*
Verdoorn, Sid *food service executive*

**Eden Valley**
Stringer, Patricia Anne *retired secondary educator*

**Edina**
Brown, Charles Eugene *retired electronics company executive*
Burdick, Lou Brum *public relations executive*
Burk, Robert S. *lawyer*
Emmerich, Karol Denise *former retail company executive, consultant*
Hunt, David Claude *sales and marketing executive*
Prince, Robb Lincoln *manufacturing company executive*
Putnam, Frederick Warren, Jr. *bishop*
Ryan, Allan James *publishing executive, editor*
Saltzman, William *painter, sculptor, designer*
Sampson, John Eugene *consulting company executive*
Schwarzrock, Shirley Pratt *author, lecturer, educator*
Slocum, Rosemarie R. *physician management search consultant*

**Elysian**
Nickerson, James Findley *retired educator*
Thayer, Edna Louise *medical facility administrator, nurse*

**Excelsior**
Bilka, Paul Joseph *physician*
French, Lyle Albert *surgeon*
Hoyt, Richard Comstock *economics consulting company executive*
Kaufman, Jeffrey Allen *publisher*
Rich, Willis Frank, Jr. *banker*

**Fairmont**
Hillestad, Donna Dawn *nurse*
Rosen, Thomas J. *food and agricultural products executive*

**Fergus Falls**
Egge, Joel *clergy member, academic administrator*
Jahr, Armin *clergy member, church administrator*
MacFarlane, John Charles *utility company executive*
Overgaard, Robert Milton *religious organization administrator*
Rinden, David Lee *editor*

**Forest Lake**
Marchese, Ronald Thomas *ancient history and archaeology educator*

**Fridley**
Savelkoul, Donald Charles *lawyer*

**Golden Valley**
Hagglund, Clarance Edward *lawyer, publishing company owner*
Savitt, Steven Lee *computer scientist*
Van Hauer, Robert *former health care company executive*

**Grand Marais**
Kreitlow, Burton William *retired adult education educator*

**Grand Rapids**
King, Sheryl Jayne *secondary education educator, counselor*

**Hastings**
Blackie, Spencer David *physical therapist, administrator*

**Hermantown**
Leland, Paula Susan *educational administrator, educator*

**Hopkins**
Hedberg, Laurentius Arthur *educator*
Hunter, Donald Forrest *lawyer*
Johnson, James Erling *insurance executive*
Karls, Nicholas James *engineering executive*
Passi, Beth *school administrator*
Rappaport, Gary Burton *defense equipment and software company executive*

**Hutchinson**
Graf, Laurance James *communications executive*

**International Falls**
Stevens, Linda Louise Halbur *addiction counselor*

**Lakeland**
Helstedt, Gladys Mardell *vocational education educator*

**Lakeville**
Krueger, Richard Arnold *state legislator*
Phinney, William Charles *retired geologist*

**Le Roy**
Erickson, Larry Alvin *electronics sales and marketing executive*

**Lindstrom**
Messin, Marlene Ann *plastics company executive*

**Litchfield**
Snelling, Norma June *retired music educator, English educator*

**Little Falls**
Zirbes, Mary Kenneth *social justice ministry coordinator*

**Long Lake**
Tomhave, Beverly Korstad *corporate executive*

**Lutsen**
Napadensky, Hyla Sarane *engineering consultant*

**Madison**
Husby, Donald Evans *engineering company executive*

**Mankato**
Descy, Don Edmond *library media technology educator, writer, editor*
Dumke, Melvin Philip *dentist*
Erickson-Weerts, Sally Annette *dietetics educator*
Frink, Brian Lee *artist, educator*
Gage, Fred Kelton *lawyer*
Hopkins, Layne Victor *computer science educator*
Hottinger, John Creighton *state legislator, lawyer*
Hustoles, Paul John *theater educator*
Janavaras, Basil John *university business educator, consultant*
Lee, Chan H. *finance educator*
Orvick, George Myron *church denomination executive, minister*
Rush, Richard R. *academic administrator*
Taylor, Glen *professional sports team executive, printing and graphics company executive*
Zeller, Michael James *psychologist, educator*

**Maple Lake**
Andrus, Theresa Kester *photojournalist, communications specialist*

**Mapleton**
John, Hugo Herman *natural resources educator*

**Marcell**
Aldrich, Richard John *agronomist, educator*

**Marshall**
Rice, Stanley Arthur *biology educator*
Schwan, Alfred *food products executive*
Skramstad, Robert Allen *retired oceanographer*

**Mendota Heights**
Dennis, Clarence *surgeon, educator*
Frechette, Peter Loren *dental products executive*

**Minneapolis**
Ackerman, Eugene *biophysics educator*
Ackman, Lauress V. *lawyer*
Adams, John Stephen *geography educator*
Adamson, Oscar Charles, II *lawyer*
Aguilera, Richard Warren (Rick Aguilera) *professional baseball player*
Albertson, Vernon Duane *electrical engineering educator*
Alcott, James Arthur *communications executive*
Amdahl, Douglas Kenneth *retired state supreme court justice*
Anderson, Albert Esten *publisher*
Anderson, Charles S. *college president, clergyman*
Anderson, Chester Grant *English educator*
Anderson, Eric Scott *lawyer*
Anderson, Geraldine Louise *medical researcher*
Anderson, John Edward *mechanical engineering educator*
Anderson, Laurence Alexis *lawyer*
Anderson, Ron *advertising executive*
Anderson, Thomas Willman *lawyer*
Anderson, Tim *airport terminal executive*
Andreas, David Lowell *banker*
Appel, William Frank *pharmacist*
Argento, Dominick *composer*
Aris, Rutherford *applied mathematician, educator*
Arthur, Lindsay Grier *retired judge, author, editor*
Asp, William George *librarian*
Asplin, Edward William *retired packaging company executive*
†Atwater, Horace Brewster, Jr. *retired food company executive*
Baker, John Stevenson (Michael Dyregrov) *writer*
Baker, Michael Harry *chemical engineer*
Bales, Kent Roslyn *English language educator*
Balfour, Henry Hallowell, Jr. *medical educator, researcher, physician, writer*
Bashiri, Iraj *Central Asian studies educator*
Bazany, Le Roy Francis *manufacturing company executive, controller*
Beardsley, John Ray *public relations firm executive*
Bearmon, Lee *lawyer*
Bell, Jerry *professional sports team executive*
Belton, Sharon Sayles *mayor*
Benson, Donald Erick *holding company executive*
Berens, William Joseph *lawyer*
Berg, Stanton Oneal *firearms and ballistics consultant*
Berg, Thomas Kenneth *lawyer*
Berry, David J. *financial services company executive*
Berryman, Robert Glen *accounting educator, consultant*
Bileydi, Sumer *advertising agency executive*
Bisping, Bruce Henry *photojournalist*
Blackburn, Henry Webster, Jr. *retired physician*
Blanton, W. C. *lawyer*
Bleck, Michael John *lawyer*
Blomquist, Robert Oscar *insurance company executive*
Bly, Robert *poet*
Boelter, Philip Floyd *lawyer*
Bolan, Richard Stuart *urban planner, educator, researcher*
†Bolman, Ralph Morton (Chip), III *cardiac surgeon*
Bonsignore, Michael Robert *electronics company executive*
Bonvino, Frank W. *lawyer*
Borger, John Philip *lawyer*
Bouassida, Hafed *director, producer*
Bouchard, Thomas Joseph, Jr. *psychology educator, researcher*
Boudreau, Robert James *nuclear medicine physician, researcher*
Bowie, Norman Ernest *university official, educator*
Boyd, Belvel James *newspaper editor*
Boylan, Brian Richard *author, producer, photographer, director, literary agent*
Brand, Steve Aaron *lawyer*
Brasket, Curt Justin *systems analyst, chess player*
Breimayer, Joseph Frederick *patent lawyer*
Bress, Michael E. *lawyer*
Brink, David Ryrie *lawyer*
Brooks, Phillip *advertising executive*
Brown, David M. *physician, educator, dean*
Brown, Laurence David *retired bishop*
Browne, Donald Roger *speech communication educator*
Bruner, Philip Lane *lawyer*
Buchwald, Henry *surgeon, educator, researcher*
Bullock, Norma Kathryn Rice *chemical development and engineering professional*
Buoen, Roger *newspaper editor*
Buratti, Dennis P. *lawyer*
Burke, Martin Nicholas *lawyer*
Burns, Neal Murray *advertising agency executive*
Burns, Robert Arthur *lawyer*
Burton, Charles Victor *physician, surgeon, inventor*
Busdicker, Gordon G. *lawyer*
Campbell, James Robert *banker*
Campbell, Karlyn Kohrs *speech and communication educator*
Cardozo, Richard Nunez *marketing, entrepreneurship and business educator*
Carlson, Curtis LeRoy *corporate executive*
Carlson, Norman A. *government official*
Carlson, Thomas David *lawyer*
Carlton, Steven Norman *retired professional baseball player*
Carpenter, Norman Roblee *lawyer*
Carr, Charles William *biochemist, emeritus educator*
Carr, Robert Wilson, Jr. *chemistry educator*
Carter, Roy Ernest, Jr. *journalist, educator*
Cavert, Henry Mead *physician, retired educator*
Cedar, Paul Arnold *church executive, minister*
Cerra, Frank Bernard *dean*
Champlin, Steven Kirk *lawyer*

Sanger, Stephen W. *consumer products company executive*
Sanner, Royce Norman *lawyer*
Saunders, Philip D. *professional basketball team executive*
Sawchuk, Ronald John *pharmaceutical sciences educator*
Sawicki, Zbigniew Peter *lawyer*
Scallen, Thomas Kaine *broadcasting executive*
Schanfield, Fannie Schwartz *community volunteer*
Schermer, Judith Kahn *lawyer*
Schnell, Robert Lee, Jr. *lawyer*
Schnobrich, Roger William *lawyer*
Schoettle, Ferdinand P. *lawyer, educator*
Schreiner, John Christian *economics consultant, software publisher*
Schuh, G(eorge) Edward *university dean, agricultural economist*
Schultz, Alvin Leroy *retired internist, retired endocrinologist, retired university health science facility administrator*
Schultz, Louis Edwin *management consultant*
Schwartz, Howard Wyn *health facility administrator*
Scott, Andrew *retired corporate executive*
Scott, Rebecca Andrews *biology educator*
Scott, Robert Lee *speech educator*
Scoville, James Griffin *economics educator*
Scriven, L. E.(dward), II *chemical engineering educator, scientist*
Seaman, William Casper *retired news photographer*
Seidel, Robert Wayne *science historian, educator, institute administrator*
Serrin, James Burton *mathematics educator*
Shapiro, Burton Leonard *oral pathologist, geneticist, educator*
Shapiro, Fred Louis *physician, educator*
Shaughnessy, Thomas William *librarian, consultant*
Sheikh, Suneel Ismail *aerospace engineer, researcher*
Shively, William Phillips *political scientist, educator*
Shnider, Bruce Jay *lawyer*
Shulman, Daniel Rees *lawyer*
Shulman, Yechiel *engineering educator*
Sidders, Patrick Michael *financial executive*
Siepmann, Joern Ilja *chemistry educator*
Silver, Alan Irving *lawyer*
Silverman, Robert Joseph *lawyer*
Simonett, John E. *state supreme court justice*
†Sjoblad, Steven A. *architectural firm executive*
Skillingstad, Constance Yvonne *social services administrator, educator*
Skrowaczewski, Stanislaw *conductor, composer*
Slagle, James Robert *computer science educator*
Slorp, John S. *academic administrator*
Slovut, Gordon *reporter*
Smith, Michael Lawrence *computer company executive, consultant*
Smyrl, William Hiram *chemical engineering educator*
Soland, Norman R. *corporate lawyer*
Sonkowsky, Robert Paul *classicist, educator, actor*
Sortland, Paul Allan *lawyer*
Sparrow, Ephraim Maurice *mechanical engineering scientist, educator*
Speer, Nancy Girouard *educational administrator*
Spoor, William Howard *food company executive*
Staba, Emil John *pharmacognosy and medicinal chemistry educator*
Stageberg, Roger V. *lawyer*
Stark, Matthew *higher education and civil rights administrator*
Stauff, William James *commitment systems manager*
Steilen, James R. *lawyer*
Steinbach, Terry Lee *professional baseball player*
Steinberg, Paul *allergist, immunologist*
Stenwick, Michael William *internist, geriatric medicine consultant*
Stern, Leo G. *lawyer*
Strickler, Jeff *newspaper movie critic*
Stroup, Stanley Stephenson *lawyer, educator*
Struthers, Margo S. *lawyer*
Struyk, Robert John *lawyer*
Stubbs, Jan Didra *retired travel industry executive, travel writer*
Stuebner, James Cloyd *real estate developer, contractor*
Sullivan, Austin Padraic, Jr. *diversified food company executive*
Sullivan, Michael Patrick *food service executive*
Suryanarayanan, Raj Gopalan *researcher, consultant, educator*
Susanka, Sarah Hills *architect*
Swanson, Lloyd Oscar *former savings and loan association executive*
Swartz, Donald Everett *television executive*
Swatsky, Ben *church administrator*
Swenson, Faye Lorene *executive and management development firm administrator*
Symosek, Peter Frank *research scientist*
Tagatz, George Elmo *obstetrician, gynecologist, educator*
Tanick, Marshall Howard *lawyer, law educator*
Thompson, Roby Calvin, Jr. *orthopedic surgeon, educator*
Thompson, Theodore Robert *pediatric educator*
Thompson, William Moreau *radiologist, educator*
Tirrell, Matthew *chemical engineering/materials science educator*
Todd, John Joseph *lawyer*
Toscano, James Vincent *medical institute administration*
Toupin, Harold Ovid *chemical company executive*
Tracy, James Donald *historian*
Travis, Marlene O. *healthcare management executive*
Tree, David L. *advertising agency executive*
Trestman, Frank D. *distribution company executive*
Trucano, Michael *lawyer*
Truhlar, Donald Gene *chemist, educator*
Ueland, Sigurd, Jr. *lawyer*
Ulrich, Robert J. *retail discount chain stores executive*
Vander Molen, Thomas Dale *lawyer*
Van Dyke, William Grant *manufacturing company executive*
Van Housen, Thomas Corwin, III *architect, designer, builder*
Vaughan, Peter Hugh *theater critic*
Vecoli, Rudolph John *history educator*
Viera, James Joseph *financial executive*
Wahoske, Michael James *lawyer*
Walsh, Paul S. *food products executive*
Walters, Glen Robert *banker*
Walton, Gloria Jean *secretary*
Wang, L. Edwin *church official*
Ward, David Allen *sociology educator*
Ware, D. Clifton *singer, educator*
Warner, William Hamer *applied mathematician*
Watson, Catherine Elaine *journalist*
Watson, Dennis Wallace *microbiology educator, scientist*
Wehrwein-Hunt, Jeri Lynn *elementary education educator*
Weinberg, Richard Alan *psychologist*
Weinberger, Adrienne *artist*
Weir, Edward Kenneth *cardiologist*
Weiss, Gerhard Hans *German language educator*
†Westbrook, Bill *advertising executive*
Whelpley, Dennis Porter *lawyer*
White, Robert James *newspaper columnist*
Wickesberg, Albert Klumb *retired management educator*
Wiener, Daniel Norman *psychologist*
Wild, John Julian *surgeon, director medical research institute*
Wille, Karin L. *lawyer*
Wilson, Leonard Gilchrist *history of medicine educator*
Windhorst, John William, Jr. *lawyer*
Wirtschafter, Jonathan Dine *neuro-ophthalmology educator, scientist*
Wolff, Larry F. *dental educator, researcher*
Wood, Wellington Gibson, III *biochemistry educator*
Woods, Robert Edward *lawyer*
†Woog, Doug *collegiate ice hockey coach*
Wright, Frank Gardner *newspaper editor*
Wright, Herbert E(dgar), Jr. *geologist*
Wright, Michael William *wholesale distribution, retailing executive*
Wurtele, Christopher Angus *paint and coatings company executive*
Wyman, James Thomas *petroleum company executive*
Youngblood, Richard Neil *columnist*
Younger, Judith Tess *lawyer, educator*
Yourzak, Robert Joseph *management consultant, engineer, educator*
Ysseldyke, James Edward *psychology educator, research center administrator*
Zalk, Robert H. *lawyer*
Ziebarth, E. William *news analyst, educator*
Ziegenhagen, David Mackenzie *healthcare company executive*
Zotaley, Byron Leo *lawyer*

### Minnetonka
Boubelik, Henry Fredrick, Jr. *travel company executive*
Ehlert, John Ambrose *publisher*
Fogelberg, Paul Alan *continuing education company executive*
Gillies, Donald Richard *advertising agency and marketing consultant*
Gottier, Richard Chalmers *retired computer company executive*
Henningsen, Peter, Jr. *diversified industry executive*
Kostka, Ronald Wayne *marketing consultant*
Macfarlane, Alastair Iain Robert *business executive*
Mc Guire, William W. *health service organization executive*
Robbins, Orem Olford *insurance company executive*
Rogers, James Devitt *judge*
Vanstrom, Marilyn June *retired elementary education educator*

### Minnetonka Mills
Hoard, Heidi Marie *lawyer*

### Moorhead
Anderson, Jerry Maynard *speech educator*
Barden, Roland Eugene *university administrator*
Dille, Roland Paul *college president*
Gee, Robert LeRoy *agriculturist, dairy farmer*
Heuer, Gerald Arthur *mathematician, educator*
Noblitt, Harding Coolidge *political scientist, educator*
Revzen, Joel *conductor*
Rothlisberger, Rodney John *music educator*
Trainor, John Felix *retired economics educator*
Treumann, William Borgen *university dean*

### Morris
Dee, Scott Allen *veterinarian*
Johnson, David Chester *university chancellor, sociology educator*
Kahng, Sun Myong *economics educator*

### New Brighton
Grieman, John Joseph *communications executive*
Pellow, Richard Maurice *state legislator*
Shier, Gloria Bulan *mathematics educator*

### New Ulm
Lucker, Raymond Alphonse *bishop*

### Nisswa
Marmas, James Gust *retired businees educator, retired college dean*

### North Saint Paul
O'Brien, Daniel William *lawyer, corporation executive*

### Northfield
Appleyard, David Frank *mathematics and computer science educator*
Berwald, Helen Dorothy *education educator*
Casper, Barry Michael *physics educator*
Cederberg, James *physics educator*
Clark, Clifford Edward, Jr. *history educator*
Clark, William Hartley *political science educator*
Crouter, Richard Earl *religion educator*
Edwards, Mark U., Jr. *college president, history educator, author*
Flaten, Robert Arnold *retired ambassador*
Hong, Howard Vincent *library administrator, philosophy educator, editor, translator*
Hvistendahl, Joyce Kilmer *journalism and communications educator*
Iseminger, Gary H. *philosophy educator*
Jorgensen, Daniel Fred *academic director*
Knutson, Gerhard I. *retired bishop*
Lamson, George Herbert *economics educator*
Levin, Burton *diplomat*
Lewis, Stephen Richmond, Jr. *economist, academic administrator*
Lloyd, Timothy L. *art educator*
Mason, Perry Carter *philosophy educator*
McKinsey, Elizabeth *college dean*
Metz, T(heodore) John *librarian, consultant*
Noer, Richard J. *physics educator, researcher*
Schuster, Seymour *mathematician, educator*
Sipfle, David Arthur *philosophy educator*
Soule, George Alan *literature educator*
Sovik, Edward Anders *architect, consultant*
Steen, Lynn Arthur *mathematician, educator*
Will, Robert Erwin *economics educator*
Yandell, Cathy Marleen *foreign language educator*
Zelliot, Eleanor Mae *history educator*

### Olivia
Cosgriff, James Arthur *physician*

### Osseo
Haun, James William *retired food company executive, consultant, chemical engineer*

### Ottertail
Hanson, Al *financial newsletter editor and publisher*

### Palisade
Kilde, Sandra Jean *nurse anesthetist, educator, consultant*

### Park Rapids
Tonn, Robert James *entomologist*

### Perham
Kingsbury, Rex Alan *elementary education educator, administrator*

### Pipestone
Scott, William Paul *lawyer*

### Plainview
Reincke, Rhonda *nursing educator*

### Plymouth
†Barden, Robert Christopher *psychologist, educator, lawyer, public policy consultant*
Bergerson, David Raymond *lawyer*
Checker, Chubby (Ernest Evans) *musician*
Friswold, Fred Ravndahl *manufacturing executive*
Froemming, Herbert Dean *retail executive*
Groves, Franklin Nelson *construction company executive*
Kahler, Herbert Frederick *diversified business executive*
Peterson, Donn Neal *forensic engineer*
Quinn, Richard Kendall *environmental engineer*
Rusch, Thomas William *manufacturing executive*
Setterholm, Jeffrey Miles *systems engineer*

### Preston
Hokenson, David Leonard *secondary school educator*
Schommer, Trudy Marie *pastoral minister, religion education*

### Princeton
Maas, Duane Harris *distilling company executive*

### Prior Lake
Tufte, Obert Norman *retired research executive*

### Red Wing
Sorensen, Peter Alan *employee benefits consultant*

### Redlake
Ceterski, Dorothy *nutritionist*

### Remer
McNulty-Majors, Susan Rose *special education administrator*

### Richfield
Devlin, Barbara Jo *school district administrator*
Thompson, Steve Allan *writer*

### Robbinsdale
Anderson, Scott Robbins *hospital administrator*
Be Vier, William A. *religious studies educator*

### Rochester
Bajzer, Željko *scientist, educator*
Bartholomew, Lloyd Gibson *physician*
Beahrs, Oliver Howard *surgeon, educator*
Beckett, Victoria Ling *physician*
Berge, Kenneth George *retired internist, educator*
Brimijoin, William Stephen *pharmacology educator, neuroscience researcher*
Butt, Hugh Roland *gastroenterologist, educator*
Carlson, Roger Allan *manufacturing company executive, accountant*
†Cascino, Terrence *neurologist*
Corbin, Kendall Brooks *physician, scientist*
Danielson, Gordon Kenneth, Jr. *cardiovascular surgeon, educator*
DeRemee, Richard Arthur *physician, educator, researcher*
Dickson, Edgar Rolland *gastroenterologist*
Douglass, Bruce E. *physician*
Du Shane, James William *physician, educator*
Engel, Andrew George *neurologist*
Feldt, Robert Hewitt *pediatric cardiologist, educator*
Gervais, Sister Generose *hospital consultant*
Gilbertson, Steven E(dward) Satyaki *real estate broker, guidance counselor*
Gilchrist, Gerald Seymour *pediatric hematologist, oncologist, educator*
Gleich, Gerald Joseph *immunologist, medical scientist*
Gomez, Manuel Rodriguez *physician*
Goodman, Julie *nurse midwife*
Gracey, Douglas Robert *physician, physiologist, educator*
Hattery, Robert R. *radiologist, educator*
Hudson, Winthrop Still *minister, history educator*
Huffine, Coy Lee *retired chemical engineer, consultant*
Hunder, Gene Gerald *physician, educator*
Kao, Pai Chih *clinical chemist*
Kempers, Roger Dyke *obstetrics and gynecology educator*
Key, Jack Dayton *librarian*
Krom, Ruud Arne Finco *surgeon*
Kurland, Leonard Terry *epidemiologist educator*
Kyle, Robert Arthur *medical educator, oncologist*
LaRusso, Nicholas F. *gastroenterologist, educator, scientist*
Leachman, Roger Mack *librarian*
Lofgren, Karl Adolph *surgeon*
Lucas, Alexander Ralph *child psychiatrist, educator*
Mackenzie, Ronald Alexander *anesthesiologist*
Maher, L. James, III *molecular biologist*
Malkasian, George Durand, Jr. *physician, educator*
Martin, Maurice John *psychiatrist*
Marttila, James Konstantin *pharmacy administrator*
Mc Conahey, William McConnell, Jr. *physician, educator*
Mc Goon, Dwight Charles *retired surgeon, educator*
Michenfelder, John Donahue *anesthesiology educator*
Milner, Harold William *hotel executive*
Morlock, Carl Grismore *physician, medical educator*
Mulder, Donald William *physician, educator*
Neel, Harry Bryan, III *surgeon, scientist, educator*
Nichols, Donald Richardson *medical educator*
Nycklemoe, Glenn Winston *bishop*
Oesterling, Joseph Edwin *urologic surgeon*
Olsen, Arthur Martin *physician, educator*
Orwoll, Gregg S. K. *lawyer*
Payne, W(illiam) Spencer *retired surgeon*
Perry, Harold Otto *dermatologist*
Phillips, Sidney Frederick *gastroenterologist*
Pittelkow, Mark Robert *physician, dermatology educator, researcher*
Pratt, Joseph Hyde, Jr. *surgeon*
Reitemeier, Richard Joseph *physician*
Rogers, Roy Steele, III *dermatology educator, dean*
Rosenow, Edward Carl, III *medical educator*
Seeger, Ronald L. *lawyer*
Shepherd, John Thompson *physiologist*
Sherman, Thomas Francis *education educator*
Shulman, Carole Karen *professional society administrator*
Siekert, Robert George *neurologist*
Stewart, Karen Meyer *pediatrics nurse, nursing manager*
Stillwell, G(eorge) Keith *physician*
Symmonds, Richard Earl *gynecologist*
Unni, Chandra Sheila *psychiatrist*
Van Norman, Willis Roger *computer systems researcher*
Verbout, James Paul *recreational therapist*
Waller, Robert Rex *ophthalmologist, educator, foundation executive*
Whisnant, Jack Page *neurologist*
Wicks, John R. *lawyer*
Wojcik, Martin Henry *foundation development official*
Wood, Earl Howard *physiologist, educator*
Woods, John Elmer *plastic surgeon*

### Roseville
Berry, James Frederick *biochemistry educator*
Hughes, Jerome Michael *education foundation executive*
Marten, Gordon Cornelius *research agronomist, educator, federal agency administrator*

### Saginaw
Stauber, Marilyn Jean *secondary and elementary school*

### Saint Cloud
Bates, Margaret Helena *special education educator*
Berling, John George *academic dean*
Braun, Janice Larson *language arts educator*
Frank, Stephen Ira *political science educator*
Gruys, Robert Irving *physician, surgeon*
Henry, Edward LeRoy *former foundation executive, consultant, college president, public official*
Hofsommer, Donovan Lowell *history educator*
Hughes, Kevin John *lawyer*
Kirick, Daniel John *agronomist*
Lalor, Edward David Darrell *labor and employment arbitrator, lawyer*
Musah, Al-Hassan Issah *reproductive physiologist*
Olson, Barbara Ford *physician*
Seifert, Luke Michael *lawyer*
Tripp, Luke Samuel *educator*
Wertz, John Alan *secondary school educator*

### Saint Joseph
Bye, Lynn Ellen *social work educator*
Rowland, Howard Ray *mass communications educator*

### Saint Louis Park
Dooley, David J. *elementary school principal*
Frestedt, Joy Louise *scientist, educator, consultant*
Galbraith, Richard Frederick *physician, neurologist*
Gerike, Ann Elizabeth *psychologist*
Knighton, David Reed *vascular surgeon, educator*
Porter, Jeannette Upton *elementary education educator*
Rothenberg, Elliot Calvin *lawyer, writer*
Svendsbye, Lloyd August *college president, clergyman, educator*

### Saint Paul
Allison, John Robert *lawyer*
Alsop, Donald Douglas *federal judge*
Althof, Jay Allen *marketing executive*
Andersen, Elmer Lee *manufacturing and publishing executive, former governor of Minnesota*
Anderson, Clyde Bailey *musician, educator*
Anderson, Gordon Louis *foundation administrator*
Anderson, Paul Holden *justice*
Archabal, Nina M(archetti) *historical society director*
Ashton, Sister Mary Madonna *healthcare administrator*
Aune, Benjamin *health association administrator*
Baker, Donald Gardner *retired soil science educator*
Barnwell, Franklin Hershel *zoology educator*
Baukol, Ronald Oliver *manufacturing company executive*
Benson, Joanne E. *lieutenant governor of Minnesota*
Best, Eugene Crawford, Jr. *musician*
Bingham, Christopher *statistics educator*
Bloch, Ricardo Adrian *visual artist*
Bloomfield, Victor Alfred *biochemistry educator*
Boehnen, David Leo *grocery company executive, lawyer*
Boudreau, James Lawton *insurance company executive*
Brehl, James William *lawyer*
Brozek, Josef *psychology educator, scientist*
Brudvig, Glenn Lowell *retired library director*
Brushaber, George Karl *academic president, minister*
Burchell, Howard Bertram *retired physician, educator*
Burnside, Orvin Charles *agronomy educator, researcher*
Caldwell, Elwood Fleming *food scientist*
Carlson, Arne Helge *governor*
Carlson, Lyndon Richard Selvig *state legislator, educator*
Carruthers, Philip Charles *public official, lawyer*
Charmoli, Margaret Charity *psychologist*
Checchi, Alfred A. *airline company executive*
Cheng, H(wei) H(sien) *soil scientist, agriculture and environmental science educator*
Chiang, Huai Chang *entomologist, educator*

Christiano, Mary Helen *systems analyst*
Clapp, C(harles) Edward *research chemist, soil biochemistry educator*
Clark, Ronald Dean *newspaper editor*
Close, Elizabeth Scheu *architect*
Close, Winston Arthur *retired architect*
Coleman, Norm *mayor*
Crabb, Kenneth Wayne *obstetrician, gynecologist*
Crookston, Robert Kent *agronomy educator*
Czarnecki, Caroline MaryAnne *veterinary anatomy educator*
Dahl, Reynold Paul *applied economics educator*
Dalton, Howard Edward *accounting executive*
Daly, Joseph Leo *law educator*
Davis, Margaret Bryan *paleoecology researcher, educator*
D'Cruz, Osmond Jerome *research scientist, educator*
Denn, James N. *commissioner*
Desimone, Livio Diego *diversified manufacturing company executive*
Devoy, Kimball John *lawyer*
Diesch, Stanley La Verne *veterinarian, educator*
Dietz, Charlton Henry *lawyer*
Doermann, Humphrey *foundation administrator*
Dykstra, Robert *retired education educator*
Eames, Earl Ward, Jr. *management educator, development specialist*
Ebert, Robert Alvin *retired lawyer, retired airline executive*
Edwards, Jesse Efrem *physician, educator*
Ek, Alan Ryan *forestry educator*
Elliott, Jack *folk musician*
Engle, Donald Edward *retired railway executive, lawyer*
Esposito, Bonnie Lou *marketing professional*
Estenson, Noel K. *refining and fertilizer company executive*
Failinger, Marie Anita *law educator, editor*
Faricy, Richard Thomas *architect*
Farnum, Sylvia Arlyce *physical chemist*
Feinberg, David Erwin *publishing company executive*
†Feldman, Nancy Jane *health organization executive*
Fesler, David Richard *foundation director*
Fingerson, Leroy Malvin *engineering executive, mechanical engineer*
Fisk, Martin H. *lawyer*
Flynn, Harry Joseph *bishop*
Frame, Clarence George *retired oil and gas refining company executive*
Frederickson, Dennis Russel *senator, farmer*
Friel, Bernard Preston *lawyer*
Fryxell, David Allen *publishing executive, newspaper editor*
Fuller, Benjamin Franklin *physician, educator*
Galvin, Michael John, Jr. *lawyer*
Gardebring, Sandra S. *judge*
Garretson, Donald Everett *retired manufacturing company executive*
Gehrz, Robert Gustave *retired railroad executive*
Geis, Jerome Arthur *lawyer, legal educator*
Goff, Lila Johnson *historical society administrator*
Goodman, Lawrence Eugene *structural analyst, educator*
Goodrich, Leon Raymond *lawyer*
Graham, Charles John *university educator, former university president*
Greenfield, Lee *state legislator*
Growe, Joan Anderson *state official*
Hall, Beverly Joy *police officer*
Halva, Allen Keith *legal publications consultant*
Halverson, Richard Paul *investment management company executive*
Hammond, Frank Joseph *lawyer*
Hansen, Robyn L. *lawyer*
Hart, Myrna Jean *art gallery and gift shop owner*
Hasling, Robert J. *retired lawyer*
Haukoos, Melvin Robert *state representative*
Haynsworth, Harry Jay, IV *lawyer, educator*
Hays, Thomas S. *medical educator, medical researcher*
Heidenreich, Douglas Robert *lawyer*
Henry, John Thomas *retired newspaper executive*
Hill, James Stanley *computer consulting company executive*
Hirst, Richard B. *lawyer*
Hodgson, Jane Elizabeth *obstetrician and gynecologist, consultant*
Holbert, Sue Elisabeth *archivist, writer, consultant*
Hopper, David Henry *religion educator*
Hubbard, Stanley Stub *broadcast executive*
Huber, Sister Alberta *college president*
Humphrey, Hubert Horatio, III *state attorney general*
Jacob, Rosamond Tryon *librarian*
Jensen, James Robert *dentist, educator*
Jessup, Paul Frederick *financial economist, educator*
Johnson, Janet B. *state legislator*
Johnson, Kenneth Harvey *veterinary pathologist*
Johnson, Paul Oren *lawyer*
Jones, C. Paul *lawyer, educator*
Jones, Thomas Neal *manufacturing executive, mechanical engineer*
Kane, Lucile Marie *archivist, historian*
Kane, Stanley Phillip *insurance company executive*
Kane, Thomas Patrick *lawyer*
Kaner, Harvey Sheldon *lawyer, executive*
Keffer, Charles Joseph *academic administrator*
Keillor, Garrison Edward *writer, radio host, storyteller*
Keith, Alexander Macdonald *state supreme court chief justice*
Kerr, Sylvia Joann *educator*
Kirwin, Kenneth Francis *law educator*
Kiscaden, Sheila M. *state legislator*
Kishel, Gregory Francis *federal judge*
Kling, William Hugh *broadcasting executive*
Kommedahl, Thor *plant pathology educator*
Kuhrmeyer, Carl Albert *manufacturing company executive*
Kyle, Richard House *federal judge*
Lanegran, David Andrew *geography educator*
Lay, Donald Pomeroy *federal judge*
Leatherdale, Douglas West *insurance company executive*
Lehr, Lewis Wylie *diversified manufacturing company executive*
Lein, Malcolm Emil *architect*
Leonard, Kurt John *plant pathologist, university program director*
Leppik, Margaret White *state legislator*
Lillehei, C. Walton *surgeon*
Loken, James Burton *federal judge*
Lund, Bert Oscar, Jr. *publisher*
Lundy, Walker *newspaper editor*
Luther, Darlene *state legislator*
Maclin, Alan Hall *lawyer*
Magee, Paul Terry *geneticist and molecular biologist, college dean*
Magnuson, Norris Alden *librarian, history educator*
Magnuson, Paul Arthur *federal judge*
Martin, David George *lawyer*
Martin, Frank Burke *statistics consultant*
Mason, John Milton (Jack Mason) *judge*
Mather, Richard Burroughs *retired Chinese language and literature educator*
Matteson, Clarice Chris *artist, educator*
McCollum, Betty *state legislator*
McGrath, Michael Alan *state government officer*
McGuire, Mary Jo *state legislator*
McKinnell, Robert Gilmore *zoology, genetics and cell biology educator*
McMillan, Mary Bigelow *retired minister, volunteer*
McNamee, Sister Catherine *educational association executive*
McNeely, John J. *lawyer*
Mitchell, Pamela Ann *airline pilot*
Molnau, Carol *state legislator*
Morgan, Carol Miró *marketing executive*
Murray, Peter Bryant *English language educator*
Nash, Nicholas David *retailing executive*
Nelson-Mayson, Linda Ruth *art museum curator*
Newman, Margaret Ann *nursing educator*
Nicholson, Morris Emmons, Jr. *metallurgist, educator*
Orfield, Myron Willard, Jr. *state legislator, educator*
Osman, Stephen Eugene *historic site administrator*
Osnes, Larry G. *academic administrator*
Ostby, Ronald *dairy and food products company executive*
Oswald, Eva Sue Aden *insurance executive*
Page, Alan Cedric *judge*
Palmer, Roger Raymond *accounting educator*
Pampusch, Anita Marie *academic administrator*
Parsons, Mark Frederick *college development officer*
Paulus, Stephen Harrison *composer*
Perry, James Alfred *environmental scientist, consultant, educator, administrator*
Peterson, James Lincoln *museum executive*
Peterson, Willis Lester *economics educator*
Phillips, Ronald Lewis *plant geneticist, educator*
Pomeroy, Benjamin Sherwood *veterinary medicine educator*
Preus, David Walter *bishop, minister*
Ridder, Bernard Herman, Jr. *newspaper publisher*
Roach, John Robert *retired archbishop*
Robertson, Jerry Earl *retired manufacturing company executive*
†Rockstroh, Robert John *broadcast television executive*
Rogosheske, Walter Frederick *lawyer, former state justice*
Rossmann, Jack Eugene *psychology educator*
Rothmeier, Steven George *merchant banker, investment manager*
Roy, Robert Russell *toxicologist*
Ruttan, Vernon Wesley *agricultural economist*
Schlentz, Robert Joseph *reliability engineer*
Seagren, Alice *state legislator*
Seymour, Mary Frances *lawyer*
Seymour, McNeil Vernam *lawyer*
Shannon, Michael Edward *specialty chemical company executive*
Sher, Phyllis Kammerman *pediatric neurology educator*
Sinklar, Robert *insurance company executive*
Sippel, William Leroy *lawyer*
Solberg, Loren Albin *state legislator, secondary education educator*
Southwick, David Leroy *geology researcher*
Spear, Allan Henry *state senator, historian, educator*
Stadelmann, Eduard Joseph *plant physiologist, educator*
Stewart, James Brewer *historian, author, college administrator*
Sullivan, Alfred Dewitt *academic administrator*
Swaiman, Kenneth Fred *pediatric neurologist, educator*
Swanson-Schones, Kris Margit *developmental adapted physical education educator*
Tecco, Romuald Gilbert Louis Joseph *violinist, concertmaster*
Thompson, Mary Eileen *chemistry educator*
Titus, Jack L. *pathologist, educator*
Tomljanovich, Esther M. *judge*
Tordoff, Harrison Bruce *retired zoologist, educator*
Ursu, John Joseph *lawyer*
Vaughn, John Rolland *auditor*
Vellenga, Kathleen Osborne *former state legislator*
Victor, Lorraine Carol *critical care nurse*
Wagner, Mary Margaret *library and information science educator*
Walker, Charles Thomas *physicist, educator*
Walton, Matt Savage *retired geologist, educator*
Wang, Zeng-Yu *neurologist, immunologist*
Washburn, Donald Arthur *transportation executive*
Wehrwein, Austin Carl *newspaper reporter, editor, writer*
Weiner, Carl Dorian *historian*
Wendt, Hans W(erner) *life scientist*
Williams, Chester Arthur, Jr. *insurance educator*
Willis, Wesley Robert *college administrator*
Wollner, Thomas Edward *manufacturing company executive*
Yeh, John *reproductive endocrinologist*
Zander, Janet Adele *psychiatrist*
Zeyen, Richard John *plant pathology educator*
†Zietlow, Ruth Ann *reference librarian*
Zylstra, Stanley James *farmer, food company executive*

### Saint Peter
Haeuser, Michael John *library administrator*
Mc Rostie, Clair Neil *economics educator*
Nelsen, William Cameron *foundation president, former college president*
Ostrom, Don *political science educator*
Turnbull, Charles Vincent *real estate broker*

### Savage
Bean, Glen Atherton *entrepreneur*

### Scandia
Borchert, John Robert *geography educator*
Speer, David James *retired public relations executive*

### Shoreview
Bertelsen, Michael William *lawyer*

### South Saint Paul
Koenig, Robert August *clergyman, educator*
Pugh, Thomas Wilfred *lawyer*

### Spicer
Wescoe, W(illiam) Clarke *physician*

### Spring Grove
Hellyer, Clement David *writer*
Roverud, Eleanor *pathologist, neuropathologist*

### Spring Park
Nelson, Craig Wayne *academy administrator*
Porter, William L. *electrical engineer*

### Stillwater
Asch, Susan McClellan *pediatrician*
Francis, D. Max *healthcare management executive*
Sowman, Harold Gene *ceramic engineer, researcher*

### Sunfish Lake
Corn, Joseph Edward, Jr. *arts management consultant*

### Thief River Falls
Gouin, Warner Peter *project engineer*

### Vadnais Heights
Polakiewicz, Leonard Anthony *foreign language and literature educator*

### Victoria
Courtney, Eugene Whitmal *computer company executive*

### Virginia
Knabe, George William, Jr. *pathologist, educator*

### Walker
Doughty, Anthony Rutgers *small business owner*

### Waseca
Frederick, Edward Charles *university official*

### Waubun
Christensen, Marvin Nelson *venture capitalist*

### Wayzata
Alton, Howard Robert, Jr. *lawyer, real estate and food company executive*
Blodgett, Frank Caleb *retired food company executive*
Fish, James Stuart *college dean, advertising consultant*
Hoffman, Gene D. *food company executive, consultant*
Mithun, Raymond O. *advertising agency executive, banker, real estate and insurance executive*
Reutiman, Robert William, Jr. *lawyer*
Shannon, James Patrick *foundation consultant, retired food company executive*
Swanson, Donald Frederick *retired food company executive*
Waldera, Wayne Eugene *crisis management specialist*

### West Saint Paul
Bremer, Victor John *broadcasting executive*
Cento, William Francis *retired newspaper editor*
Markwardt, Kenneth Marvin *former chemical company executive*

### White Bear Lake
Gabrick, Robert William *secondary education educator*
Gutchë, Gene *composer*
Holmen, Reynold Emanuel *chemist*
Williams, Julie Belle *psychiatric social worker*

### Willmar
Vander Aarde, Stanley Bernard *retired otolaryngologist*

### Winona
Adickes, Sandra Elaine *English language educator, writer*
Beyer, Mary Edel *primary education educator*
DeThomasis, Brother Louis *college president*
Holm, Joy Alice *psychology educator, art educator, artist, goldsmith*
Krueger, Darrell William *university president*
Preska, Margaret Louise Robinson *education educator, district service professional*
Towers, James Mc *education educator*

### Woodbury
Benforado, David M. *environmental engineer*
Bretz, Kelly Jean Rydel *actuary*

## MISSISSIPPI

### Aberdeen
Davis, Jerry Arnold *judge*
Senter, Lyonel Thomas, Jr. *federal judge*

### Ackerman
Coleman, Frances McLean *secondary school educator*

### Amory
Bryan, Hob *state senator, lawyer*

### Batesville
Neal, Joseph Lee *vocational school educator*

### Bay Saint Louis
Corbin, James H. *executive engineer, meteorologist, oceanographer*
Gaffney, Paul Golden, II *military officer*
Sprouse, Susan Rae Moore *human resources specialist*
Zeile, Fred Carl *oceanographer, meteorologist*

### Belzoni
Halbrook, Rita Robertshaw *artist, sculptor*

### Biloxi
Bramlette, David C., III *federal judge*
Brown, Sheba Ann *elementary education educator*
Cox, Albert Harrington, Jr. *economist*
Gex, Walter Joseph, III *federal judge*
Hagood, Annabel Dunham *speech communication educator, consultant*
Howze, Joseph Lawson Edward *bishop*
Manners, Pamela Jeanne *middle school educator*
Ozolek, John Anthony *pediatrician, neonatologist*
Ransom, Perry Sylvester *civil engineer*
Roper, John Marlin *federal magistrate judge*
Weeks, Roland, Jr. *newspaper publisher*

### Brandon
Buckley, Frank Wilson *newspaper executive*
Mitchell, Roy Devoy *industrial engineer*
Read, Virginia Hall *biochemistry educator*
Stampley, Norris Lochlen *former electric utility executive*

### Brookhaven
Perkins, Thomas Hayes, III *furniture company executive*

### Calhoun City
Macon, Myra Faye *retired library director*

### Carriere
Wilson, Raymond Clark *former hospital executive*
Woodmansee, Glenn Edward *employee relations executive*

### Carrollton
McConnell, David Stuart *insurance agent, retired federal executive*

### Clarksdale
Curtis, Chester Harris *lawyer, retired bank executive*
Walters, William Lee *accountant*
Williams, Kenneth Ogden *farmer*

### Cleveland
Alexander, William Brooks *lawyer, former state senator*
Baker-Branton, Camille B. *counselor, educator*
Cash, William McKinley *history educator*
Thornton, Larry Lee *psychotherapist, author, educator*
Wyatt, Forest Kent *university president*

### Clinton
Bigelow, Martha Mitchell *retired historian*
Hensley, John Clark *religious organization administrator, minister*
Montgomery, Keith Norris, Sr. *insurance executive, state legislator*
Sanders, Barbara Boyles *health services director*

### Columbia
Simmons, Miriam Quinn *state legislator*

### Columbus
Gholson, Hunter Maurice *lawyer*
Holt, Robert Ezel *data processing executive*
Hudnall, Jarrett, Jr. *management and marketing educator*
Kaye, Samuel Harvey *architect, educator*
Pounds, Billy Dean *law educator*
Rent, Clyda Stokes *academic administrator*

### Diamondhead
Jaumot, Frank Edward, Jr. *automobile parts manufacturing company executive*

### Fayette
La Salle, Arthur Edward *historic foundation executive*

### Gautier
Egerton, Charles Pickford *anatomy and physiology educator*

### Greenville
Martin, Andrew Ayers *lawyer, physician, educator*

### Gulfport
Allen, Harry Roger *lawyer*
Freret, René Joseph *minister*
Harral, John Menteith *lawyer*
Hash, John Frank *broadcasting executive*
Hewes, William Gardner, III *insurance executive, real estate agent, legislator*
Hopkins, Alben Norris *lawyer*
Kaufman-Derbes, Linda Ruth *physician*
Russell, Dan M., Jr. *federal judge*
Thatcher, George Robert *banker*

### Hattiesburg
Bedenbaugh, Angela Lea Owen *chemistry educator, researcher*
Boyd, William Douglas, Jr. *library science educator, clergyman*
Brinson, Ralph Alan *physician, pediatrician, neonatologist*
Burrus, John N(ewell) *sociology educator*
Fleming, Horace Weldon, Jr. *higher education administrator, educator*
Gonzales, John Edmond *history educator*
Lucas, Aubrey Keith *university president*
Miller, James Edward *computer scientist, educator*
Moore, Henderson Alfred, Jr. *retired savings and loan executive*
Noblin, Charles Donald *clinical psychologist, educator*
Noonkester, James Ralph *retired college president*
Pickering, Charles W. *federal judge*
Saucier, Gene Duane *state legislator, import/export company executive*
Saucier Lundy, Karen *college dean, educator*
Sims, James Hylbert *English educator, former university administrator*
Traylor, Joan Sadler *interior design educator*
Watkins, Cathy Collins *corporate purchasing agent*
Wood, Vivian Poates *mezzo soprano, voice educator*

### Holly Springs
Beckley, David Lenard *academic administrator*

### Horn Lake
Golliver, Cheryl Rena *nurse*

### Indianola
Crigler, Sammie Mae *secondary school English language educator*

Gary, Toni Berryhill *school counselor, psychotherapist*
Matthews, David *clergyman*

## Itta Bena
Thomas, William Eric *biochemistry educator*
Ware, William Levi *physical education educator, researcher*

## Jackson
Achord, James Lee *gastroenterologist, educator*
Allin, John Maury *bishop*
Ball, Carroll Raybourne *anatomist, medical educator, researcher*
Baltz, Richard Jay *health care company executive*
Barbour, William H., Jr. *federal judge*
Barksdale, Rhesa Hawkins *federal judge*
Barnett, Robert Glenn *lawyer*
Bates, Lura Wheeler *trade association executive*
Biggs, Thomas Jones *architect*
Bloom, Sherman *pathologist, educator*
Brooks, Thomas Joseph, Jr. *preventive medicine educator*
Burnham, Tom *state school system administrator*
Burns, Robert, Jr. *architect, freelance writer, artist*
Burrow, William Hollis, II *dermatologist*
Butler, George Harrison *lawyer*
Chambers-Mangum, Fransenna Ethel *special education educator*
Chinn, Mark Allan *lawyer*
Clark, David Wright *lawyer*
Clark, Eric C. *state official*
Conerly, Albert Wallace *academic administrator, dean*
Conwill, David E. *preventive medicine educator, emergency physician*
Corlew, John Gordon *lawyer*
Cruse, Julius Major, Jr. *pathologist, educator*
Currier, Robert David *neurologist*
Curtis, Verna P. *reading educator*
Das, Suman Kumar *plastic surgeon, researcher*
Dean, Jack Pearce *retired insurance company executive*
Ditto, (John) Kane *mayor*
Downing, Margaret Mary *newspaper editor*
Draper, Edgar *psychiatrist*
Dubbert, Patricia Marie *psychologist, educator*
Eigenbrodt, Edwin Hixson *physician, pathologist, educator*
Eigenbrodt, Marsha Lillian *internal medicine educator, epidemiologist*
Fordice, Kirk (Daniel Kirkwood Fordice, Jr.) *governor, construction company executive, engineer*
Freeland, Alan Edward *orthopedic surgery educator, physician*
Furrh, James Brooke, Jr. *oil company executive*
Fuselier, Louis Alfred *lawyer*
Galloway, Patricia Kay *systems analyst, ethnohistorian*
Gray, Duncan Montgomery, Jr. *retired bishop*
Guyton, Arthur Clifton *physician, educator*
Halaris, Angelos *psychiatrist, educator*
Hammond, Frank Jefferson, III *lawyer*
Harmon, George Marion *college president*
Henegan, John C(lark) *lawyer*
Hosemann, C. Delbert, Jr. *lawyer*
Houck, William Russell *bishop*
Houston, Gerry Ann *oncologist*
Howard, William Percy *physician*
Hurt, Joseph Richard *law educator*
Irby, Stuart Charles, Jr. *construction company executive*
Johnson, Joyce Thedford *state agency administrator*
Jolly, E. Grady *federal judge*
Julian, Michael *grocery company executive*
Kermode, John Cotterill *pharmacology educator, researcher*
Langford, James Jerry *lawyer*
Lee, Tom Stewart *judge*
Leszczynski, Jerzy Ryszard *chemistry educator, researcher*
LeTourneau, Richard Howard *retired college president*
Lewis, Larry Lisle *human resources specialist company executive*
Lewis, Robert Edwin, Jr. *pathology immunology educator, researcher*
Lilly, Thomas Gerald *lawyer*
Malloy, James Matthew *managed care executive, health care consultant*
McKnight, William Edwin *minister*
McLin, Hattie Rogers *school system administrator*
Mitchell, Jackie Williams *state agency administrator, consultant*
Moize, Jerry Dee *lawyer, government official*
Moore, Mike *state attorney general*
Musgrove, Ronnie *state official*
Palmer, Dora Deen Pope *English and French language educator*
†Palmer, John N. *communications executive*
Patterson, Helen Crosby *clinical psychologist*
Payne, Mary Libby *judge*
Pearce, Colman Cormac *conductor, pianist, composer*
Pearce, David Harry *biomedical engineer*
Penick, George Dial, Jr. *foundation executive*
Phillips, George Landon *prosecutor*
Poole, Galen Vincent *surgeon, educator, researcher*
Prather, Lenore Loving *state supreme court presiding justice*
Pyle, Luther Arnold *lawyer*
Ray, H. M. *lawyer*
Risley, Rod Alan *education association executive*
Roehm, MacDonell, Jr. *retail executive*
Rogers, Oscar Allan, Jr. *academic administrator*
Sewell, Charles Haslett *banker*
Shirley, Aaron *pediatrician*
Skelton, Gordon William *data processing executive, educator*
Smith, James W., Jr. *judge*
Sneed, Raphael Corcoran *physiatrist, pediatrician*
Stovall, Jerry (Coleman Stovall) *insurance company executive*
Stubbs, James Carlton *retired hospital administrator*
Suess, James Francis *retired psychiatry educator*
Sugg, Robert Perkins *former state supreme court justice*
Sullivan, John Magruder, II *government affairs administrator*
Sullivan, Michael David *state supreme court justice*
Summers, Tracy Yvonne *assistant principal*
Tchounwou, Paul Bernard *environmental health specialist, educator*
Thrash, Edsel E. *educational administrator*
Timmer, Wayne Francis *architectural firm executive*
Tourney, Garfield *psychiatrist, educator*

Tullos, John Baxter *banker*
Vance, Ralph Brooks *oncologist and educator*
Walcott, Dexter Winn *allergist*
Welty, Eudora *author*
Wingate, Henry Travillion *federal judge*
Winter, William Forrest *former governor, lawyer*

## Keesler AFB
Rigdon, David Tedrick *air force officer, geneticist, director*

## Kosciusko
Kearley, F. Furman *minister, religious educator, magazine editor*
May, Cecil Richard, Jr. *academic adminstrator*

## Long Beach
Horton, Jerry Smith *minister*
Kanagy, Steven Albert *foundation administrator*

## Lorman
Ezekwe, Michael Obi *reseach scientist*
Hylander, Walter Raymond, Jr. *retired civil engineer*
Waters, Rudolph Earl *university administrator*

## Madison
Hays, Donald Osborne *retired government official*
Hiatt, Jane Crater *arts agency administrator*
Robinson, John David *retired army officer*

## Magnolia
Coney, Elaine Marie *English and foreign languages educator*

## Mendenhall
Rotenberry, Clinton Grice *state representative, real estate broker*

## Meridian
Blackwell, Cecil *science association executive*
Church, George Millord *real estate executive*
Eppes, Walter W., Jr. *lawyer*
Lindstrom, Donald Fredrick, Jr. *priest*
Marshall, John Steven *artist, educator, museum administrator*
Phillips, Patricia Jeanne *retired school administrator, consultant*
Reed, Vanessa Regina *secondary education educator*

## Mississippi State
Alley, Earl Gifford *chemist*
Arnizaut de Mattos, Ana Beatriz *veterinarian*
Bishop, Calvin Thomas *landscape architect, educator*
Chatham, James Ray *foreign language educator*
Cliett, Charles Buren *aeronautical engineer, educator, academic administrator*
Clynch, Edward John *political science educator, researcher*
Crowell, Lorenzo Mayo *historian, educator*
Donaghy, Henry James *English literature educator, academic administrator*
Dorough, H. Wyman *toxicologist, educator, consultant*
†Gunter, John E. *dean*
Hawkins, Merrill Morris, Sr. *college administrator*
Howell, Everette Irl *physicist, educator*
Hughes, Patricia Newman *academic administrator*
Hurt, Verner Gene *forestry researcher*
Jacob, Paul Bernard, Jr. *electrical engineering educator*
Jenkins, Johnie Norton *research geneticist, research administrator*
Lowery, Charles Douglas *history educator, academic administrator*
Mabry, Donald Joseph *university administrator, history educator*
Martin, Edward Curtis, Jr. *landscape architect, educator*
McGilberry, Joe Herman, Sr. *university administrator*
Nash, Henry Warren *marketing educator*
Parrish, William Earl *history educator*
Reddy, Kambham Raja *plant physiology educator*
Taylor, Clayborne Dudley *engineering educator*
Thompson, Joe Floyd *aerospace engineer, educator*
Wall, Diane Eve *political science educator*
Watson, James Ray, Jr. *education educator*
White, Charles H. *food science and technology educator*
Wiltrout, Ann Elizabeth *foreign language educator*
Zacharias, Donald Wayne *academic administrator*

## Monticello
Allen, Frank Carroll *retired banker*

## Myrtle
Pirkle, Estus Washington *minister*

## Natchez
Parker, Mary Evelyn *former state treasurer*
Profice, Rosena Mayberry *elementary school educator*

## Nesbit
Berti, Phyllis Mae *health information management specialist*

## Newton
Hagan, Lynn Purnell *social worker, recreation therapist*

## Ocean Springs
Gunter, Gordon *zoologist*
Lawson-Jowett, M. Juliet *lawyer*
Luckey, Alwyn Hall *lawyer*
McNulty, Matthew Francis, Jr. *health sciences and health services administrator, educator, university administrator, consultant, horse and cattle breeder*
Morrison, Mable Johnson *business technology educator*

## Oxford
Biggers, Neal Brooks, Jr. *federal judge*
Duke, Stephen Oscar *physiologist, researcher*
Foster, George Rainey *soil erosion research scientist*
Knight, Aubrey Kevin *vocational education educator*
Moorhead, Sylvester Andrew *education educator retired*
Rayburn, S. T. *lawyer*

## Pascagoula
Chapel, Theron Theodore *quality assurance engineer*

Corben, Herbert Charles *physicist, educator*
Krebs, Robert Preston *lawyer*
McIlwain, Thomas David *fishery administrator, marine biologist, educator*
McKee, Ronald Gene *vocational education educator*
Roberts, David Ambrose *lawyer*

## Pass Christian
Clark, John Walter, Jr. *shipping company executive*
McCardell, James Elton *retired naval officer*

## Philadelphia
Molpus, Dick H. *resource management company executive*

## Picayune
Pardue, Larry G. *botanical garden administrator, educator*

## Pontotoc
Roberts, Rose Harrison *social services administrator, consultant*

## Purvis
Young, Raymond Guinn *music educator*

## Ridgeland
Brady, Michael Jay *environmental engineer, geologist*
Dye, Bradford Johnson, Jr. *lawyer, former state official*
Lee, Daniel Kuhn *economist*
Morrison, Francis Secrest *physician*
O'Neill, Paul John *retired psychology educator*

## Robinsville
Buxton, Glenn *marketing professional, public relations executive*

## Southaven
Utroska, William Robert *veterinarian*

## Starkville
Carley, Charles Team, Jr. *mechanical engineer*
Emerich, Donald Warren *retired chemistry educator*
Ford, Robert MacDonald, III *architect, educator*
George, Ernest Thornton, III *financial consultant*
Gregg, Billy Ray *seed industry executive, consultant*
Hunt, Pamela Stafford *secondary school educator*
Loftin, Marion Theo *sociologist, educator*
MacLeod, John Daniel, Jr. *religious organization administrator*
Martin, Theodore Krinn *former university administrator (deceased)*
Priest, Melville Stanton *retired consulting hydraulic engineer*
Wolverton, Robert Earl *classics educator*

## Stennis Space Center
Baker, Robert Andrew *environmental research scientist*
Hurlburt, Harley Ernest *oceanographer*
Mc Call, Jerry Chalmers *government official*

## Stoneville
Hardee, D. D. *laboratory director, research program leader*
Ranney, Carleton David *plant pathology researcher, administrator*
Wilson, Alphus Dan *plant pathologist, researcher*

## Stringer
Gordon, Granville Hollis *church official*

## Summit
Jones, Lawrence David *insurance and medical consultant*

## Tupelo
Brown, Betty Harrison *mental health counselor*
Bullard, Rickey Howard *podiatric physician, surgeon*
Bush, Fred Marshall, Jr. *lawyer*
Lukas, Joseph Frank *paralegal*
Patterson, Aubrey Burns, Jr. *banker*
Radojcsics, Anne Parsons *librarian*
Ramage, Martis Donald, Jr. *banker*
Rupert, Daniel Leo *elementary education consultant*
Zurawski, Jeanette *rehabilitation services professional*

## University
Bomba, Anne Killingsworth *family relations and child development educator*
Ferris, William Reynolds *folklore educator*
Horton, Thomas Edward, Jr. *mechanical engineering educator*
Jordan, Winthrop Donaldson *historian, educator*
Keiser, Edmund Davis, Jr. *biologist, educator*
Khayat, Robert C. *chancellor*
Kiger, Joseph Charles *history educator*
Landon, Michael de Laval *historian, educator*
Leary, William James *educational administrator*
Meador, John Milward, Jr. *university dean*
Sam, Joseph *retired university dean*
Smith, Allie Maitland *university dean*
Uddin, Waheed *civil engineer, educator*
Walton, Gerald Wayne *English educator, university officiala*

## Vicksburg
Aarons, Cecilia *retired secondary school educator*
Bagby, Rose Mary *pollution control administrator, chemist*
Howard, Bruce Kenneth *army officer, environmental engineer*
Mather, Bryant *research administrator*

## Walls
Jones, Yvonne Dolores *social worker*

## Waveland
Jackson, Judith Ann *elementary education educator*

## Waynesboro
Brashier, Edward Martin *environmental consultant*
Dickerson, Marie Harvison *nurse anesthetist*

## Whitfield
Morton, James Irwin *hospital administrator*

## Yazoo City
Arnold, David Walker *chemical company executive, engineer*
Brown, Marion Lipscomb, Jr. *publisher, retired chemical company executive*
Cartlidge, Shriley Ann Bell *school administrator*

# MISSOURI

## Arrow Rock
Bollinger, Michael *artistic director*

## Aurora
Goodman, Nancy Jane *small business owner*

## Ballwin
Altman, Jeannette Mehr *pharmaceutical sales specialist*
Banton, Stephen Chandler *lawyer*
Cornell, William Daniel *mechanical engineer*
Kern, Gary L. *golf course architect*
Meiner, Sue Ellen Thompson *gerontologist, nursing educator and researcher*
Stevens, Julie Ann *peri-operative nurse*
Waskow, Joyce Ann *school administrator*

## Belton
Shymanski, Catherine Mary *health facility administrator, nursing education administrator*

## Benton
Heckemeyer, Anthony Joseph *circuit court judge*

## Berkeley
Stonecipher, Harry Curtis *manufacturing company executive*

## Bloomfield
Ferrell, Paul Cleveland *author*

## Blue Springs
Foudree, Charles M. *financial executive*
Hatley, Patricia Ruth *school system administrator*
Olsson, Björn Eskil *railroad supply company executive*
Reed, Tony Norman *aviation company executive*
Shover, Joan *secondary school educator*

## Bois D Arc
Westphal, Leonard Wyrick *health care executive, consultant*

## Bolivar
Jackson, James Larry *recreation educator*

## Boonville
Cline, Dorothy May Stammerjohn (Mrs. Edward Wilburn Cline) *educator*

## Bowling Green
Galloway, Daniel Lee *investment executive*

## Branson
Hamon, Christopher Lloyd *electrical engineer*
Tillis, Mel(vin) *musician, songwriter*
Williams, Andy *entertainer*

## Bridgeton
Asma, Lawrence Francis *priest*
Brauer, Stephen Franklin *manufacturing company executive*
Campbell, Anita Joyce *computer company executive*
Delaney, Robert Vernon *logistics and transportation executive*
Hemming, Bruce Clark *microbiologist*
†Henderson, Gene M. *marketing executive*
†Johnson, Kevin Todd *physician*
Joyner Kersee, Jacqueline *track and field athlete*
Lohmiller, John M. (Chip Lohmiller) *professional football player*
McSweeney, Michael Terrence *manufacturing executive*

## Bucklin
Payne, Flora Fern *retired social service administrator*

## Buffalo
Louderback, Kevin Wayne *business owner*

## Camdenton
Clark, Mark Jeffrey *paralegal, researcher*
DeShazo, Marjorie White *occupational therapist*

## Canton
Glover, Albert Downing *retired veterinarian*

## Cape Girardeau
Blackwelder, Richard E(liot) *entomologist, zoology educator, archivist*
Farrington, Thomas Richard *financial executive, investment advisor*
Haugland, Susan Warrell *education educator*
McManaman, Kenneth Charles *lawyer*
Nicholson, Gerald Lee *medical facilities administrator*
Smallwood, Glenn Walter, Jr. *utility marketing management executive*
Southard-Ritter, Marcia *nursing administrator*

## Carthage
Coffield, Mary Eleanor *speech clinician, educator*
Glauber, Michael A. *manufacturing company executive*
Jefferies, Robert Aaron, Jr. *diversified manufacturing executive, lawyer*

## Cassville
Melton, Emory Leon *lawyer, state legislator, publisher*

## Centralia
Harmon, Robert Wayne *electrical engineering executive*

## Chesterfield
Armstrong, Theodore Morelock *financial executive*
Berland, David I. *psychiatrist, educator*

Biggerstaff, Randy Lee *medical products executive, sports medicine rehabilitation consultant*
Carpenter, Will Dockery *chemical company executive*
Cornelsen, Paul Frederick *manufacturing and engineering company executive*
Frawley, Thomas Francis *physician*
Goodwin, Leslie Diane *elementary education educator*
Hale, David Clovis *former state representative*
Henry, Roy Monroe *financial planner*
Hier, Marshall David *lawyer*
Hunter, Harlen Charles *orthopedic surgeon*
Kelly, James Joseph *printing company executive*
Levin, Marvin Edgar *physician*
Liggett, Hiram Shaw, Jr. *retired diversified industry financial executive*
Malvern, Donald *retired aircraft manufacturing company executive*
Matros, Larisa Grigoryevna *medical philosophy researcher*
McCarthy, Paul Fenton *aerospace executive, former naval officer*
Palazzi, Joseph L(azarro) *manufacturing executive*
Payne, Meredith Jorstad *physician*
Pollihan, Thomas Henry *lawyer*
Pylipow, Stanley Ross *retired manufacturing company executive*
Robinson, Patricia Elaine *women's health nurse practitioner*
Schierholz, William Francis, Jr. *real estate developer*
Smith, Ronald Earl *aircraft design engineer*
Welshans, Merle Talmadge *management consultant*
Williams, John Franklin *real estate broker*
Willis, Frank Edward *retired air force officer*
Yardley, John Finley *aerospace engineer*

**Chula**
Murphy, Jenny Lewis *special education educator*

**Clayton**
Belz, Mark *lawyer*
Beracha, Barry Harris *food company executive*
Buechler, Bradley Bruce *plastic processing company executive, accountant*
Christner, Theodore Carroll *architect*
Hall, Carl Loren *electrical distribution executive*
Heininger, S(amuel) Allen *retired chemical company executive*
Keyes, Marion Alvah, IV *manufacturing company executive*
Klarich, David John *lawyer, state senator*
Kohm, Barbara *principal*
Livergood, Robert Frank *prosecutor*
Marcus, Larry David *broadcasting executive*
McCann-Turner, Robin Lee *child, adolescent analyst*
Richmond, Richard Thomas *journalist*
Ross, E. Earl *small business owner*
Turner, Terry Madison *architect*
Vecchiotti, Robert Anthony *management and organizational consultant*

**Columbia**
Adams, Algalee Pool *college dean, art educator*
Alexander, Martha Sue *librarian*
Alexander, Thomas Benjamin *history educator*
Allen, William Cecil *physician, educator*
Almony, Robert Allen, Jr. *librarian, businessman*
Anderson, Donald Kennedy, Jr. *English educator*
Archer, Stephen Murphy *theater educator*
Barbero, Giulio John *physician, educator*
Basu, Asit Prakas *statistician*
Bauman, John E., Jr. *chemistry educator*
Bay, Marjorie Seaman *secondary school educator*
Beem, John Kelly *mathematician, educator*
Biddle, Bruce Jesse *social psychologist, educator*
Bien, Joseph Julius *philosophy educator*
Blaine, Edward H. *health science administrator, educator*
Blevins, Dale Glenn *agronomy educator*
Blount, Don H. *physiology educator*
Boedeker, Ben Harold *anesthesiologist, educator*
Breimyer, Harold Frederick *agricultural economist*
Brooks, Brian Shedd *journalist, educator*
Brouder, Gerald T. *academic administrator*
Brown, Olen Ray *medical microbiology research educator*
Bryant, Lester R. *surgeon, educator*
Bunn, Ronald Freeze *political science educator, lawyer*
Burdick, Allan Bernard *geneticist*
Colwill, Jack Marshall *physician, educator*
Cunningham, Billie M. *accounting educator*
Cunningham, Milamari Antoinella *anesthesiologist*
Darrah, Larry Lynn *plant breeder*
Davis, James O(thello) *physician, educator*
Day, Cecil LeRoy *agricultural engineering educator*
Decker, Wayne Leroy *meteorologist, educator*
Denney, Arthur Hugh *management consultant*
Dolliver, Robert Henry *psychology educator*
Duncan, Donald Pendleton *retired forestry educator*
Dyrenfurth, Michael John *vocational technical and industrial arts educator, consultant*
Eaton, Gary David *physician*
Eggers, George William Nordholtz, Jr. *anesthesiologist, educator*
Ethington, Raymond Lindsay *geology educator, researcher*
Finkelstein, Richard Alan *microbiologist*
Fisch, William Bales *lawyer, educator*
Fluharty, Charles William *policy research institute director, consultant, researcher*
Francis, Lee, III *trade association administrator*
Frisby, James Curtis *agricultural engineering educator*
Fulweiler, Howard Wells *language professional*
Gehrke, Charles William *biochemistry educator*
Geiger, Louis George *historian*
George, Melvin Douglas *retired university president*
Goodrich, James William *historian, association executive*
Griffing, George Thomas *medical educator, endocrinologist*
Gysbers, Norman Charles *education educator*
Hardin, Christopher D. *medical educator*
Hatley, Richard V(on) *education educator*
Heimburger, Elizabeth Morgan *psychiatrist*
Heldman, Dennis Ray *engineering educator*
Hensley, Elizabeth Catherine *nutritionist, educator*
Hess, Darla Bakersmith *cardiologist, educator*
Hess, Leonard Wayne *obstetrician gynecologist, perinatologist*
Hillman, Richard Ephraim *pediatrician, educator*
Horner, Winifred Bryan *humanities educator, researcher, consultant, writer*
Ignoffo, Carlo Michael *insect pathologist-virologist*
James, Elizabeth Joan Plogsted *pediatrician, educator*
Johns, Williams Davis, Jr. *geologist, educator*
Jones, William McKendrey *language professional, educator*
Kashani, Javad Hassan-Nejad *physician*
Kausler, Donald Harvey *psychology educator*
Keith, Everett Earnest *educator, education administrator*
Khojasteh, Ali *medical oncologist, hematologist*
Kierscht, Marcia Selland *academic administrator, psychologist*
Kiesler, Charles Adolphus *psychologist, academic administrator*
Kilgore, Randall Freeman *health information services administrator*
Lago, Mary McClelland *English language educator, author*
Lambeth, Victor Neal *horticulturist, researcher*
Larson, Sidney *art educator, artist, writer, painting conservator*
Longo, Daniel Robert *health services researcher, medical educator*
Loory, Stuart Hugh *journalist*
LoPiccolo, Joseph *psychologist, educator, author*
Lubensky, Earl Henry *diplomat, anthropologist*
Mayer, Dennis Thomas *biochemist, educator*
McCollum, Clifford Glenn *college dean emeritus*
McFate, Kenneth Leverne *trade association administrator*
Mc Ginnes, Edgar Allen, Jr. *forestry educator*
Miller, Paul Ausborn *adult education educator*
Mitchell, Roger Lowry *agronomy educator*
Morehouse, Georgia Lewis *microbiologist, researcher*
Morehouse, Lawrence Glen *veterinarian, emeritus professor*
Mullen, Edward John, Jr. *Spanish language educator*
Nikolai, Loren Alfred *accounting educator, author*
Northup, Beverly A. Baker *principal chief*
Novacky, Anton Jan *plant pathologist, educator*
Overby, Osmund Rudolf *art historian, educator*
Palo, Nicholas Edwin *professional society administrator*
Parrigin, Elizabeth Ellington *lawyer*
Perkoff, Gerald Thomas *physician, educator*
Perry, Michael Clinton *physician, medical educator, academic administrator*
Pfeifer, Peter Martin *physics educator*
Plummer, Patricia Lynne Moore *chemistry and physics educator*
Poehlmann, Carl John *agronomist, researcher*
Pringle, Oran Allan *mechanical and aerospace engineering educator*
Puckett, C. Lin *plastic surgeon, educator*
Rabjohn, Norman *chemistry educator emeritus*
Ratti, Ronald Andrew *economics educator*
Reid, Loren Dudley *speech educator*
Rhyne, James Jennings *condensed matter physicist*
Rothwell, Robert Clark *agricultural products executive*
Rowlett, Ralph Morgan *archaeologist, educator*
Rutter, Elizabeth Jane *consulting firm executive*
Sanders, Keith Page *journalism educator*
Schrader, Keith William *mathematician*
Shelton, Kevin L. *geology educator*
Silver, Donald *surgeon, educator*
Silvoso, Joseph Anton *accounting educator*
Staley, Marsha Lynn *elementary school educator*
Stockglausner, William George *accountant*
Strickland, Arvarh Eunice *history educator*
Taft, William Howard *journalism educator*
Timberlake, Charles Edward *history educator*
Twaddle, Andrew Christian *sociology educator*
Unklesbay, Athel Glyde *geologist, educator*
Viswanath, Dabir Srikantiah *chemical engineer*
†Vogt, Albert R. *forester, educator, program director*
Wagner, Joseph Edward *veterinarian, educator*
Wagner, William Burdette *business educator*
Weisman, Gary Andrew *biochemist*
Weiss, James Moses Aaron *psychiatrist, educator*
Welliver, Warren Dee *lawyer, retired state supreme court justice*
Westbrook, James Edwin *lawyer, educator*
Wheeler, Otis V., Jr. *public school principal*
Williams, Frederick *statistics educator*
Windsor, Margaret Eden *writer*
Witten, David Melvin *radiology educator*
Yanders, Armon Frederick *biological sciences educator, research administrator*
Yarwood, Dean Lesley *political science educator*
Yasuda, Hirotsugu Koge *chemical engineering professor*
Yesilada, Birol Ali *political science educator*
Zemmer, Joseph Lawrence, Jr. *mathematics educator*

**Cottleville**
Shepperd, Susan Abbott *special education educator*

**Creve Coeur**
Bockserman, Robert Julian *chemist*

**Cuba**
Work, Bruce Van Syoc *business consultant*

**Delta**
Burton, Drenna Lee O'Reilly *kindergarten educator*

**Des Peres**
Smith, Barbara Martin *art educator*

**Dexter**
Owens, Debra Ann *chiropractor*

**Earth City**
Anderhalter, Oliver Frank *educational organization executive*
Frontiere, Georgia *professional football team executive*
Landeta, Sean *professional football player*

**Eldon**
†Pelan, Alan D. *manufacturing company executive*

**Eureka**
Lindsey, Susan Lyndaker *zoologist*

**Excelsior Springs**
Mitchell, Earl Wesley *clergyman*

**Fair Grove**
Pickering, Becky Ruth Thompson *special education educator*

**Fayette**
Inman, Marianne Elizabeth *college administrator*
Keeling, Joe Keith *religion educator, college vice president and dean*
Stewart, Bobby Gene *laboratory director*

**Fenton**
Bubash, James Edward *engineering executive, entrepreneur, inventor*
Greenblatt, Maurice Theodore *transportation executive*
Maritz, William E. *communications company executive*
Stolar, Henry Samuel *lawyer*

**Florissant**
Barnes, Rebecca Marie *assistant principal*
Bartlett, Robert James *principal*
Basler, Theodore Eugene *poet*
Betts, Warren Romeo *retired health facility administrator*
Hicks, Ritchie B. *physical education educator*
Johnson, Mary Elizabeth *retired elementary education educator*
Martin, Edward Brian *electrical engineer*
Ordinachev, Joann Lee *special education counselor and administrator*
Payuk, Edward William *elementary education educator*
Reese, Alferd George *retired army civilian logistics specialist*
Tanphaichitr, Kongsak *rheumatologist, allergist, immunologist, internist*

**Fort Leonard Wood**
Combs, Robert Kimbal *museum director*

**Fortuna**
Ramer, James LeRoy *civil engineer*

**Fulton**
Backer, William Earnest *food products executive*
Barnett, Jahnae Harper *academic administrator*
Davidson, Robert Laurenson Dashiell *college president emeritus, philatelist*
Gish, Edward Rutledge *surgeon*

**Gallatin**
Wilsted, Joy *elementary education educator, reading specialist, parenting consultant*

**Golden City**
Howard, Joanne Frances *marketing executive, funeral director, extended care coordinator*

**Grandview**
Dietrich, William Gale *lawyer, real estate developer, consultant*
Justesen, Don Robert *psychologist*

**Half Way**
Graves, Jerrell Loren *demographic studies researcher*

**Hamilton**
Esry, Cordelia Cochran *community health nurse, emeritus educator*

**Hannibal**
Dothager, Julie Ann *librarian*
Sweets, Henry Hayes, III *museum director*
Terrell, James Daniel *lawyer*
Welch, Joseph Daniel *lawyer*
Wilhoit, Carol Diane *special education educator*

**Harrisonville**
Hartzler, Vicky J. *state legislator*
James, William Edward *publishing executive*

**Hayti**
Skelton, Diann Clevenger *elementary education educator*

**Hazelwood**
Martin, Barbara Jean *elementary education educator*
Rose, Joseph Hugh *clergyman*
Urshan, Nathaniel Andrew *minister, church administrator*

**Hermann**
Mahoney, Catherine Ann *artist, educator*

**Highlandville**
Pruter, Karl Hugo *bishop*

**Hillsboro**
Adkins, Gregory D. *higher education administrator*

**Hollister**
Head, Mary Mae *elementary education educator*

**Houston**
Ruckert, Rita E. *elementary education educator*

**Imperial**
Hughes, Barbara Bradford *nurse*

**Independence**
Booth, Paul Wayne *retired minister*
Cady, Elwyn Loomis, Jr. *medicolegal consultant, educator*
Ferguson, John Wayne, Sr. *librarian*
Fraker, Barbara J. *elementary education educator, school system administrator, middle school education educator*
Hansen, Francis Eugene *minister*
Henley, Robert Lee *school system administrator*
Lashley, Curtis Dale *lawyer*
Lindgren, A(lan) Bruce *church administrator*
Muñoz, Margaret Ellen *reading specialist*
Potts, Barbara Joyce *historical society executive*
Scott, Helen Cecile *critical care nurse*
Sheehy, Howard Sherman, Jr. *minister*
Smith, Wallace Bunnell *physician, church official*
Swails, Norman E. *church officer*
Tyree, Alan Dean *clergyman*
Vigen, Kathryn L. Voss *nursing administrator, educator*
Walsh, Rodger John *lawyer*

**Ironton**
Douma, Harry Hein *social service agency administrator*

**Jefferson City**
Bartlett, Alex *lawyer*
Bartman, Robert E. *state education official*
Beatty, Grover Douglas *stockbroker*
Benton, W. Duane *judge*
Bray, Joan *state legislator*
Carnahan, Mel *governor, lawyer*
Clay, William Lacy, Jr. *state legislator*
Cook, Rebecca McDowell *state official*
Covington, Ann K. *judge, lawyer*
Decker, Malcolm Doyle *insurance executive*
Deutsch, James Bernard *lawyer*
Dey, Charlotte Jane *retired community health nurse*
Donnelly, Robert True *retired state supreme court justice*
Forks, Thomas Paul *osteopathic physician*
Gaw, Robert Steven *lawyer, state representative*
Giffen, Lawrence Everett, Sr. *family physician, anesthesiologist, historian*
Holden, Bob *state official*
Holstein, John Charles *state supreme court chief justice*
Karll, Jo Ann *state agency administrator, lawyer*
Kelley, Patrick Michael *minister, state legislator*
King, Robert Henry *minister, church denomination executive, former educator*
Limbaugh, Stephen Nathaniel, Jr. *judge*
Lumpe, Sheila *state legislator*
Mahfood, Stephen Michael *governmental agency executive*
Maxwell, Joe *state senator*
Mc Auliffe, Michael F. *bishop*
McClelland, Emma L. *state legislator*
McDaniel, Sue Powell *cultural organization administrator*
Nixon, Jeremiah W. (Jay Nixon) *state attorney general*
Parker, Sara Ann *librarian*
Parr, Lloyd Byron *state official*
Peeno, Larry Noyle *state agency administrator, consultant*
Pouche, Fredrick *state legislator*
Price, William Ray, Jr. *state supreme court judge*
Reidinger, Russell Frederick, Jr. *fish and wildlife scientist*
Richardson, Mark *state legislator*
Robertson, Edward D., Jr. *state supreme court chief justice*
Scott, Gary Kuper *retired academic administrator*
Stroup, Kala Mays *state higher education commissioner*
Tettlebaum, Harvey M. *lawyer*
Westfall, Morris *state legislator*
Wilks, R(alph) Kenneth, Jr. *state official*
Wilson, Roger Byron *lieutenant governor, school administrator*
Winn, Kenneth Hugh *archivist, historian*

**Jennings**
Robards, Bourne Rogers *elementary education educator*

**Joplin**
Allman, Margaret Ann Lowrance *counselor*
Daus, Arthur Steven *neurological surgeon*
Gee, James David *minister*
Guillory, Jeffery Michael *lawyer*
Hadley, Debra Sue *electric company executive*
Lamb, Robert Lewis *electric utility executive*
Malzahn, Ray Andrew *chemistry educator, university dean*
Minor, Ronald Ray *minister*
Pulliam, Frederick Cameron *educational administrator*
Scott, Robert Haywood, Jr. *lawyer*
Singleton, Marvin Ayers *otolaryngologist, senator*
Wilson, Aaron Martin *religious studies educator, college executive*

**Kansas City**
Abdou, Nabih I. *physician, educator*
Acheson, Allen Morrow *retired engineering executive*
Adam, Paul James *engineering company executive, mechanical engineer*
Allen, Marcus *professional football player*
Alt, John *football player*
Anderson, Christopher James *lawyer*
Anderson, Edgar R., Jr. *career officer, hospital administrator, physician*
Anderson, James Keith *retired magazine editor*
Andrews, Kathleen W. *book publishing executive*
Appier, (Robert) Kevin *professional baseball player*
Ayers, Jeffrey David *lawyer*
Baker, John Russell *utilities executive*
Baker, Robert Thomas *interior designer*
Baker, Ronald Phillip *service company executive*
Ball, Owen Keith, Jr. *lawyer*
Barnes, Donald Gayle *management consultant*
Bartlett, Paul Dana, Jr. *agribusiness executive*
†Bass, Lee Marshall *food products company executive*
Bates, William Hubert *lawyer*
Batiuk, Thomas Martin *cartoonist*
Becker, Thomas Bain *lawyer*
Beckett, Theodore Charles *lawyer*
Beckett, Theodore Cornwall *lawyer*
Beihl, Frederick *lawyer*
Bell, Jay Stuart *professional baseball player*
Benner, Richard Edward, Jr. *management and marketing consultant, investor*
Berkley, Eugene Bertram (Bert Berkley) *envelope company executive*
Berkowitz, Lawrence M. *lawyer*
Berrey, Robert Wilson, III *judge, lawyer*
Bevan, Robert Lewis *lawyer*
Bixby, Walter E. *insurance company executive*
Black, John Sheldon *lawyer*
Blackwell, Menefee Davis *lawyer*
Blim, Richard Don *pediatrician*
Bloch, Henry Wollman *tax preparation company executive*
Bodinson, Nancy Sue *art educator*
Boland, Raymond James *bishop*
Bolender, Todd *choreographer*
Bonci, Andrew S. *chiropractor*
Boone, Robert Raymond *professional baseball coach*
Borel, Steven James *lawyer*
Bowers, Curtis Ray, Jr. *chaplain*
Bowman, Pasco Middleton, II *federal judge*
Boyd, John Addison, Jr. *civil engineer*
Boysen, Melicent Pearl *finance company executive*
Bradbury, Daniel Joseph *library administrator*

Bradshaw, Jean Paul, II *lawyer*
Brannon, Wilbur *church administrator*
Bransby, Eric James *muralist, educator*
Braude, Michael *commodity exchange executive*
Brett, George Howard *baseball executive, former professional baseball player*
Brisbane, Arthur Seward *newspaper editor*
Brous, Thomas Richard *lawyer*
Brown, John O. *banker*
Bruening, Richard P(atrick) *lawyer*
Bryant, Richard Todd *lawyer*
Buchanan, Carla Williams *data processing consultant*
Bugher, Robert Dean *professional society administrator*
Burk, Norman *oral surgeon*
Busby, Marjorie Jean (Marjean Busby) *journalist*
Callo, Joseph Francis *writer*
Canfield, Robert Cleo *lawyer*
Cantrell, (Thomas) Scott *newspaper music critic*
Carr, Jack Richard *candy company executive*
Carter, Dale Lavelle *professional football player*
Cavitt, Bruce Edward *lawyer*
Chisholm, Donald Herbert *lawyer*
Clark, Charles Edward *arbitrator*
Clarke, Milton Charles *lawyer*
Cleaver, Emanuel, II *mayor, minister*
Cleberg, Harry C. *food products company executive*
Click, Marianne Jane *credit manager*
Cloud, Randall R. *church administrator*
Colaizzi, Joseph John *homeless services professional, clergyman*
Collins, Mark *professional football player*
Conrad, William Merrill *architect*
Cook, Mary Rozella *psychophysiologist*
Cooper, Scott Kendrick *professional baseball player*
Costin, James D. *performing arts company executive*
Couch, Daniel Michael *healthcare executive*
Courson, Marna B.P. *public relations executive*
Cozad, John Condon *lawyer*
Crawford, Howard Allen *lawyer*
Cronkleton, Thomas Eugene *physician*
Cross, William Dennis *lawyer*
†Cunningham, Paul George *minister*
Dahl, Andrew Wilbur *health services executive*
Danner, Kathleen Frances Steele *federal official*
Davidson, Ian Edwards *pharmaceutical research and development director*
Davis, Charles Theodore *professional baseball player*
Davis, Florea Jean *social worker*
Davis, F(rancis) Keith *civil engineer*
Davis, James Robert *cartoonist*
Davis, John Charles *lawyer*
Davis, Richard Francis *city government official*
Deacy, Thomas Edward, Jr. *lawyer*
Dees, Stephen Phillip *petroleum, farm and food products company executive, lawyer*
Dickenson, H. H. *professional society administrator*
†Diehl, James Harvey *church administrator*
Dillingham, John Allen *marketing professional*
Dimond, Edmunds Grey *medical educator*
Diuguid, Lewis Walter *editor, columnist*
Doyle, Wendell E. *retired band director, educator*
Dumovich, Loretta *real estate and transportation company executive*
Durig, James Robert *college dean*
Eddy, William Bahret *psychology educator, university dean*
Edgar, John M. *lawyer*
Edwards, Horace Burton *former state official, former oil pipeline company executive, management consultant*
Egan, Charles Joseph, Jr. *greeting card company executive, lawyer*
Eldridge, Truman Kermit, Jr. *lawyer*
Ellfeldt, Howard James *orthopedic surgeon*
English, R(obert) Bradford *marshal*
Estep, Michael R. *church administrator*
Eubanks, Eugene Emerson *education educator, consultant*
Evans, Margaret Ann *human resources administrator, business owner*
Field, Lyman *lawyer*
Flora, Jairus Dale, Jr. *statistician*
Foster, Mark Stephen *lawyer*
Fox, Thomas Charles *editor, publisher, writer*
Frank, Eugene Maxwell *bishop*
Fremont, Ernest Hoar, Jr. *lawyer*
French, Linda Jean *lawyer*
Fries, James Lawrence *trade association executive*
Fullerton, Fred *church administrator*
Gaitan, Fernando J., Jr. *federal judge*
Gardner, Brian E. *lawyer*
Gibson, Floyd Robert *federal judge*
Gibson, John Robert *federal judge*
Gier, Audra May Calhoon *environmental chemist*
Giffin, Reggie Craig *lawyer*
Gilbert, John R. *advertising and public relations agency executive*
Graham, Charles *psychologist*
Graham, Harold Steven *lawyer*
Graham, Robert *medical association executive*
Gray, Helen Theresa Gott *religion editor*
Green, Jerry Howard *investment banker*
Greer, Norris E. *lawyer*
Grosskreutz, Joseph Charles *physicist, engineering researcher, educator*
Grossman, Jerome Barnett *retired service firm executive*
Gusewelle, Charles Wesley *journalist*
Hagan, John Charles, III *ophthalmologist*
Hagans, Robert Frank *industrial clothing cleaning company executive*
Hagsten, Ib *animal scientist, educator*
Hall, Donald Joyce *greeting card company executive*
Hall, Miriam *church administrator*
Hall, Rochelle Denise *elementary school educator*
Hazlett, James Arthur *insurance administrator*
Hebenstreit, James Bryant *agricultural products executive, bank and venture capital executive*
Helder, Jan Pleasant, Jr. *lawyer*
†Herman, Michael Edward *pharmaceutical company executive*
Hockaday, Irvine O., Jr. *greeting card company executive*
Hoffmann, Donald *architectural historian*
Hopkins, William Carlisle, II *lawyer*
Hoskins, William Keller *pharmaceutical company executive, lawyer*
Hubbell, Ernest *lawyer*
Hunt, Lamar *professional football team executive*
Hunter, Elmo Bolton *federal judge*
Hunzicker, Warren John *research consultant, physician, cardiologist*
Huston, Kent Allen *rheumatologist*
Ingram, Robert Palmer *magazine publisher*
Irvine, Robert Keith *librarian*
James, Claudia Ann *business educator and trainer, motivational speaker*
Jenkins, Orville Wesley *retired religious administrator*
Jennings, A. Drue *utility company executive*
Johnson, Jerald D. *religious organization administrator*
Johnson, Leonard James *lawyer*
Johnson, Mark Eugene *lawyer*
Johnson, Vincent Gregory *anesthesiologist*
Joyce, Michael Patrick *lawyer*
Juarez, Martin *priest*
Kagan, Stuart Michael *pediatrician*
Kanaby, Robert F. *sports association administrator*
Kaplan, Harvey L. *lawyer*
†Kauffman, Larry *professional sports team executive*
Kaufman, Michelle Stark *lawyer*
Kelley, Clarence Marion *retired lawyer*
Kemper, David Woods, II *banker*
Kilroy, John Muir *lawyer*
Kilroy, William Terrence *lawyer*
King, Richard Allen *lawyer*
Kingsley, James Gordon *healthcare executive*
Kipp, Robert Almy *greeting card company executive*
Knight, John Allan *clergyman, philosophy and religion educator*
Koelling, Thomas Winsor *lawyer*
Koger, Frank Williams *federal judge*
Kramer, Lawrence John *college president*
†Kreamer, Janice C. *sports association executive*
Kroenert, Robert Morgan *lawyer*
Kronschnabel, Robert James *manufacturing company executive*
La Budde, Kenneth James *librarian*
Lancaster, Ruth Vysoky *tax training manager*
Langworthy, Robert Burton *lawyer*
Larsen, Robert Emmett *federal judge*
Larson, Gary *cartoonist*
Latza, Beverly Ann *accountant*
Lee, Margaret Norma *artist*
Levi, Peter Steven *chamber of commerce executive, lawyer*
Levings, Theresa Lawrence *lawyer*
Lindsey, David Hosford *lawyer*
Lofland, Gary Kenneth *cardiac surgeon*
Lombardi, Cornelius Ennis, Jr. *lawyer*
Londré, Felicia Mae Hardison *theater educator*
Long, Edwin Tutt *surgeon*
Loudon, Donald Hoover *lawyer*
Lubin, Bernard *psychologist, educator*
Malacarne, C. John *insurance company executive, lawyer*
Manka, Ronald Eugene *lawyer*
Martin, Deanna Coleman *university director*
Martin, Donna Lee *publishing company executive*
Martin-Bowen, (Carole) Lindsey *freelance writer*
Martinez-Carrion, Marino *biochemist, educator*
Massey, Vickie Lea *radiologist*
Mast, Kande White *artist*
Matheny, Edward Taylor, Jr. *lawyer*
Matzeder, Jean Marie Znidarsic *lawyer*
Maxwell, Delores Young *elementary school principal*
Mc Coy, Frederick John *retired plastic surgeon*
Mc Gee, Joseph John, Jr. *former insurance company executive*
†McGuff, Joseph Thomas *professional sports team executive*
Mc Kelvey, John Clifford *research institute executive*
McKenna, George LaVerne *art museum curator*
McManus, James William *lawyer*
Mc Meel, John Paul *newspaper syndicate and publishing executive*
†McPhee, Mark Steven *medical educator, physician, gastroenterologist*
McSweeney, William Lincoln, Jr. *retired publishing executive*
Mebust, Winston Keith *surgeon, educator*
Mick, Howard Harold *lawyer*
Miller, Patricia Elizabeth Cleary *American and British literature educator*
Milton, Chad Earl *lawyer*
Molzen, Christopher John *lawyer*
Montgomery, Jeffrey Thomas *professional baseball player*
Moore, David Lowell *dentist*
Moore, Dorsey Jerome *dentistry educator, maxillofacial prosthetist*
Moore, Stephen James *lawyer*
Mordy, James Calvin *lawyer*
Mustard, Mary Carolyn *financial executive*
Nelson, Carlon Justine *engineering and operations executive*
Newcom, Jennings Jay *lawyer*
Newsom, James Thomas *lawyer*
Noback, Richardson Kilbourne *medical educator*
Nofsinger, William Morris *engineering executive*
Northrip, Robert Earl *lawyer*
Offerman, Jose Antonio Dono *professional baseball player*
Oliphant, Patrick *cartoonist*
Owen, Loyd Eugene, Jr. *lawyer*
Owens, Donald D. *church officer*
Owens, Stephen J. *lawyer*
Palmer, Cruise *newspaper editor*
Palmer, Dennis Dale *lawyer*
Parizek, Eldon Joseph *geologist, college dean*
Parker, Dennis Gene *former sheriff, karate instructor*
Patterson, Russell *conductor, opera executive*
Patty, R. Bruce *architect*
Pearce, Margaret Tranne *law librarian*
Pedram, Marilyn Beth *reference librarian*
Pelofsky, Joel *lawyer*
Peterson, Carl *professional football team executive*
Petosa, Jason Joseph *publisher*
Piepho, Robert Walter *pharmacy educator, researcher*
Popper, Robert *law educator, former dean*
Price, Charles H., II *former ambassador*
Price, James Tucker *lawyer*
Prince, William J. *church officer*
Prugh, William Byron *lawyer*
Ralston, Richard H. *lawyer*
Reiter, Robert Edward *banker*
Rethemeyer, Robert John *social studies educator*
Robertson, Leon H. *management consultant, educator*
Robinson, Spencer T. (Herk Robinson) *professional baseball team executive*
Rodenhuis, David Roy *meteorologist, educator*
Rost, William Joseph *chemist*
Sachs, Howard F(rederic) *federal judge*
Samuel, Robert Thompson *optometrist*
Sanders, William Huggins *lawyer, rancher*
Satterlee, Terry Jean *lawyer*
Sauer, Gordon Chenoweth *physician, educator*
Schoolman, Arnold *neurological surgeon*
Schottenheimer, Martin Edward *professional football coach*
Schult, Thomas Peter *lawyer*
Scott, Deborah Emont *curator*
Scott, Ruth Lois *dental hygiene educator*
Seligson, Theodore H. *architect, interior designer, art consultant*
Setzler, Edward Allan *lawyer*
Sexton, Donald Lee *business administration educator*
Shaw, John W. *lawyer*
Shaw, Richard David *marketing and management educator*
Shay, David E. *lawyer*
Sheldon, Ted Preston *library director*
Sherwood, Joan Karolyn Sargent *career counselor*
†Shields, Will Herthie *football player*
Shutz, Byron Christopher *real estate executive*
Slater, William Adcock *retired social services organization executive*
†Smith, Louis *sports association administrator*
Smith, Richard Conrad, Jr. *telecommunications company executive*
Smith, R(onald) Scott *lawyer*
Smithson, Lowell Lee *lawyer*
Spalty, Edward Robert *lawyer*
Sparks, Donald Eugene *interscholastic activities association executive*
Spencer, Richard Henry *lawyer*
Stanley, David *retail company executive*
Steadman, Jack W. *professional football team executive*
Stephens, Joe Alan *investigative reporter*
Stevens, James Hervey, Jr. *retired financial advisor*
Stevens, Joseph Edward, Jr. *federal judge*
Stewart, Albert Elisha *safety engineer, industrial hygienist*
Stites, C. Thomas *journalist, publisher*
Stolov, Jerry Franklin *healthcare executive*
Stone, Jack *religious organization administrator*
Stoup, Arthur Harry *lawyer*
Stowers, James Evans, Jr. *investment company executive*
Stubbs, Marilyn Kay *education administrator*
Stueck, William Noble *small business owner*
Sullivan, Bill *church administrator*
Svadlenak, Jean Hayden *museum administrator, consultant*
Switzer, Samuel Thomas *non-profit administrator*
Tammeus, William David *journalist, columnist*
Tansey, Robert Paul, Sr. *pharmaceutical chemist*
Thomas, Derrick Vincent *professional football player*
Thornton, Thomas Noel *publishing executive*
Toll, Perry Mark *lawyer*
Townsend, Harold Guyon, Jr. *publishing company executive*
Tunley, Naomi Louise *retired nurse administrator*
Ucko, David Alan *museum director*
Ulrich, Robert Gene *judge*
Van Ackeren, Maurice Edward *college administrator*
Vandever, William Dirk *lawyer*
Varner, Barton Douglas *lawyer*
Vaughan, Kirk William *banker*
Vering, John Albert *lawyer*
Viani, James L. *lawyer*
Vogel, Arthur Anton *clergyman*
Wade, Robert Glenn *engineering executive*
Walker, Thomas H. *federal agency administrator*
Whipple, Dean *federal judge*
Whitener, William Garnett *dancer, choreographer*
Whittaker, Judith Ann Cameron *lawyer*
Wiegner, Edward Alex *multi-industry executive*
Wilkinson, Ralph Russell *biochemistry educator, toxicologist*
Williams, Thelma Jean *social worker*
Williams, Wade Hampton, III *motion picture producer, director, distributor*
Wilson, Eugene Rolland *foundation executive*
Wilson, Marc Fraser *art museum administrator and curator*
Wilson, Tom *cartoonist, greeting card company executive*
Wirken, James Charles *lawyer*
Woods, Richard Dale *lawyer*
Wright, Scott Olin *federal judge*
Wrobley, Ralph Gene *lawyer*
Wyrsch, James Robert *lawyer, educator, author*
Yates, Dan Charles *insurance company official*
†Zechman, David Mark *hospital administrator, educator*

**Kirksville**
Ediger, Marlow *education educator*
French, Michael Francis *non-profit education agency administrator*
Schnucker, Robert Victor *history and religion educator*
Smith, Dwyane *university administrator*

**Kirkwood**
Gibbons, Michael Randolph *lawyer*
Holsen, James Noble, Jr. *retired chemical engineer*
Warner, Alvina (Vinnie Warner) *principal*

**Laddonia**
Scheffler, Lewis Francis *pastor, educator, research scientist*

**Lake Lotawana**
Heineman, Paul Lowe *consulting civil engineer*
Zobrist, Benedict Karl *library director, historian*

**Lake Saint Louis**
Czarnik, Marvin Ray *retired aerospace engineer*
Dommermuth, William P. *marketing consultant, educator*
German, John George *transportation consultant*

**Lamar**
Geddie, Rowland Hill, III *lawyer*

**Lambert Airport**
Griggs, Leonard LeRoy, Jr. *federal agency administrator*

**Lebanon**
Beavers, Roy L. *retired utility executive, essayist, activist*
Caplinger, Patricia E. *family nurse practitioner*
Hutson, Don *lawyer*

**Lees Summit**
Boehm, Toni Georgene *seminary dean, nurse*
Ferguson, Julie Ann *physical education educator*
Griffith-Thompson, Sara Lynn *resource reading educator*
Kahwaji, George Antoine *computer and mathematics educator*
Korschot, Benjamin Calvin *investment executive*
Letterman, Ernest Eugene *manufacturers representative company executive*
Waite, Daniel Elmer *retired oral surgeon*

**Lexington**
Terrill, Julia Ann *elementary education educator*

**Liberty**
Harriman, Richard Lee *performing arts administrator, educator*
Orth-Aikmus, Gail Marie *police chief*
Tanner, Jimmie Eugene *college dean*

**Linn**
Gove, Peter Charles *special education educator*

**Marionville**
Estep, Mark Randall *secondary education educator*

**Marshall**
Gruber, Loren Charles *English language educator, writer*
Wymore, Luann Courtney *education educator*

**Maryland Heights**
Beumer, Richard Eugene *engineer, architect, construction firm executive*
Dokoudovsky, Nina Ludmila *dance educator*
Hampton, Margaret Josephine *secondary education educator, decorating consultant*
†Marcus, John *wholesale distribution executive*
Schultz, Daniel Joseph *manufacturing executive, writer*
Sobol, Lawrence Raymond *lawyer*
Uselton, James Clayton *engineering executive*

**Maryville**
Heusel, Barbara Stevens *English scholar and educator*
Hubbard, Dean Leon *university president*

**Mexico**
Hummer, Paul F., II *manufacturing company executive*
Stover, Harry M. *corporate executive*

**Moberly**
Blackmar, Charles Blakey *state supreme court justice*
Noel, Larry Kenneth *family physician*

**Mountain Grove**
Smith, Martha Virginia Barnes *elementary school educator*

**Neosho**
Hargis, Billy James *minister*
Mailes, Kim(ber Dean) *automotive executive*

**Nevada**
Ewing, Lynn Moore, Jr. *lawyer*
Hizer, Marlene Brown *library director*
Hornback, Joseph Hope *mathematics educator*
Studer, Patricia S. *psychologist*

**New Florence**
Francis, Albert W. *elementary education educator*

**O'Fallon**
Lottes, Patricia Joette Hicks *foundation administrator, retired nurse*

**Osage Beach**
East, Mark David *physician*

**Perryville**
Fischer, James Adrian *clergyman*

**Pilot Grove**
Betteridge, Elizabeth Ann *elementary education educator*

**Plato**
Wood, Joetta Kay *special education educator*

**Pleasant Valley**
Nelson, Freda Nell Hein *librarian*

**Poplar Bluff**
Black, Ronnie Delane *religious organization administrator, mayor*
Carr, Charles Louis *retired religious organization administrator*
Duncan, Leland Ray *mission administrator*
Piland, Donald Spencer *internist*

**Raytown**
Smith, Robert Francis *psychologist, consultant, investment advisor*

**Richmond**
Nordsieck, Karen Ann *custom design company owner*

**Richmond Heights**
Chandler, James Barton *international education consultant*

**Rogersville**
Davis, Evelyn Marguerite Bailey *artist, organist, pianist*

**Rolla**
Adawi, Ibrahim Hasan *physics educator*
Alexander, Ralph William, Jr. *physics educator*
Allison, Sandy *genealogist, appraiser, political consultant*
Armstrong, Daniel Wayne *chemist, educator*
Babcock, Daniel Lawrence *chemical engineer, educator*
Barr, David John *civil, geological engineering educator*
Crosbie, Alfred Linden *mechanical engineering educator*
Dagli, Cihan Hayreddin *engineering educator*
Datz, Israel Mortimer *information systems specialist*
Day, Delbert Edwin *ceramic engineering educator*
Finaish, Fathi Ali *aeronautical engineering educator*
Grayson, Robert Larry *educator mining engineering educator*

Grimm, Louis John *mathematician, educator*
Hagni, Richard Davis *geology and geophysics educator*
Ingram, William Thomas, III *mathematics educator*
Irion, Arthur Lloyd *psychologist, educator*
James, William Joseph *chemistry educator*
Johnson, James Winston *chemical engineering educator*
Leventis, Nicholas *chemistry educator, consultant*
Mc Farland, Robert Harold *physicist, educator*
Munger, Paul R. *civil engineering educator*
Numbere, Daopu Thompson *petroleum engineer, educator*
O'Keefe, Thomas Joseph *metallurgical engineer*
Rueppel, Melvin Leslie *environmental research director and educator*
Saperstein, Lee Waldo *mining engineering educator*
Sarchet, Bernard Reginald *retired chemical engineering educator*
Sauer, Harry John, Jr. *mechanical engineering educator, university administrator*
Scott, James J. *retired mining engineer*
Shrestha, Bijaya *nuclear scientist*
Tsoulfanidis, Nicholas *nuclear engineering educator, university official*
Warner, Don Lee *dean emeritus*
Zobrist, George Winston *computer scientist, educator*

## Rothville

Ginn, M. Stanly *retail executive, lawyer, bank executive*

## Saint Charles

Barnett, Howard Albert *English language educator*
Brahmbhatt, Sudhirkumar *chemical company executive*
Cassy, Catherine Mary *elementary school educator*
Castro, Jan Garden *author, arts consultant, educator*
Dauphinais, George Arthur *import company executive*
Gross, Charles Robert *personnel executive, legislator, appraiser*
Huckshold, Wayne William *elementary education educator*
McClintock, Eugene Jerome *minister*
Radke, Rodney Owen *agricultural research executive*
Schneider, Thomas Aquinas *surgeon, educator*
Woods, Marvin *project controls engineer*

## Saint Clair

Gullet, Leon Estle *retired cartographer*

## Saint Joseph

Boor, Myron Vernon *psychologist, educator*
Chilcote, Gary M. *museum director, reporter*
Heizer, David Eugene *health information management educator*
†Johnson, Robert Charles *medical administrator*
Kelly, Glenda Marie *state legislator*
Kranitz, Theodore Mitchell *lawyer*
Miller, Lloyd Daniel *real estate agent*
Murphy, Janet Gorman *college president*
†Nassar, Ahmed Hassan *engineering educator, department head*
Rachow, Sharon Dianne *realtor*
Taylor, Michael Leslie *lawyer*

## Saint Louis

Abelov, Stephen Lawrence *uniform clothing company executive, consultant*
Abrahamson, Barry *chemical company executive*
Ackerman, Joseph J. H. *chemistry educator*
Adams, Albert Willie, Jr. *lubrication company executive*
Agrawal, Harish Chandra *neurobiologist, researcher, educator*
Allen, Garland Edward *biology educator, science historian*
Allen, Renee *principal*
Alpers, David Hershel *physician, educator*
Anderhub, Beth Marie *medical educator*
Anderson, James Donald *mining company executive*
Anderson, Vinton Randolph *bishop*
Appleton, R. O., Jr. *lawyer*
Arnold, John Fox *lawyer*
Arrington, Barbara *public health educator*
Asa, Cheryl Suzanne *biologist*
Attanasio, John Baptist *law educator*
Atwood, Hollye Stolz *lawyer*
Avis, Robert Grier *investment company executive, civil engineer*
Aylward, Ronald Lee *lawyer*
Babington, Charles Martin, III *lawyer*
Bachmann, John William *securities firm executive*
Backer, Matthias, Jr. *obstetrician-gynecologist*
Bacon, Bruce Raymond *physician*
Baernstein, Albert, II *mathematician*
Bagley, Mary Carol *literature educator, writer, broadcaster*
Baker, Shirley Kistler *university library administrator*
Baldwin, Edwin Steedman *lawyer*
Ball, Kenneth Leon *manufacturing company executive, organizational development consultant*
Ballinger, Walter Francis *surgeon, educator*
Baloff, Nicholas *business educator, consultant*
Barken, Bernard Allen *lawyer*
Barksdale, Clarence Caulfield *banker*
Barmann, Lawrence Francis *history educator*
Barnes, Harper Henderson *movie critic, editor*
Barnett, William Arnold *economics educator*
Barney, Steven Matthew *human resources executive*
Barry, A. L. *church official*
Barta, James Joseph *judge*
Bascom, C. Perry *foundation administrator*
Bateman, Sharon Louise *public relations executive*
Battram, Richard L. *retail executive*
Baue, Arthur Edward *surgeon, educator, administrator*
Baum, Gordon Lee *lawyer, non-profit organization administrator*
Bauman, George Duncan *former newspaper publisher*
Bealke, Linn Hemingway *bank executive*
Bean, Bourne *lawyer*
Beare, Gene Kerwin *electric company executive*
Beck, Lois Grant *anthropologist, educator*
Becker, David Mandel *legal educator, author, consultant*
Becker, Rex Louis *architect*
Bender, Carl Martin *physics educator, consultant*
Benes, Andrew Charles *professional baseball player*
Berendt, Robert Tryon *lawyer*
Berg, Leonard *neurologist, educator, researcher*
Berger, John Torrey, Jr. *lawyer*
Bernstein, Donald Chester *brokerage company executive, lawyer*
Bernstein, Merton Clay *lawyer, educator, arbitrator*
Berthoff, Rowland Tappan *historian, educator*
Bickel, Floyd Gilbert, III *investment counselor*
Biondi, Lawrence *university administrator, priest*
Bloomberg, Terry *early childhood education administrator*
Blumenthal, Herman Theodore *physician, educator*
Bock, Edward John *retired chemical manufacturing company executive*
Bohle, Bruce William *editor*
Bohne, Jeanette Kathryn *mathematics and science educator*
Boldt, H. James *church administrator*
Bonacorsi, Mary Catherine *lawyer*
Boothby, William Munger *mathematics educator*
Bosley, Freeman Robertson, Jr. *former mayor*
Bourke, Vernon Joseph *philosophy educator*
Bourne, Carol Elizabeth Mulligan *biology educator, phycologist*
Bowen, Stephen Francis, Jr. *ophthalmic surgeon*
Boyarsky, Saul *lawyer, forensic urologist, physiologist, educator*
Boyd, Robert Cotton *English language educator*
Brasunas, Anton de Sales *metallurgical engineering educator*
Breece, Robert William, Jr. *lawyer*
Breihan, Erwin Robert *civil engineer, consultant*
Brennan, Donald George *university dean, research administrator*
Briccetti, Joan Therese *theater manager, arts management consultant*
Brickey, Kathleen Fitzgerald *law educator*
Brickler, John Weise *lawyer*
Brickson, Richard Alan *lawyer*
Bridgewater, Bernard Adolphus, Jr. *footwear company executive*
Briggs, John James *nuclear pharmacist, clinical specialist*
Briggs, William Benajah *aeronautical engineer*
†Brock, Louis Clark *business executive, former professional baseball player*
Brockhaus, Robert Herold, Sr. *business educator, consultant*
Brodeur, Armand Edward *pediatric radiologist*
Brodsky, Philip Hyman *chemical executive, research director*
Brody, Lawrence *lawyer, educator*
Broeg, Bob (Robert William Broeg) *writer*
Browde, Anatole *electronics company executive, consultant*
Browman, David L(udvig) *archaeologist*
Brown, Eric Joel *biomedical researcher*
Brown, JoBeth Goode *food products executive, lawyer*
Brown, Melvin F. *corporate executive*
Brown, Paul Sherman *lawyer*
Brown, Wendy Weinstock *nephrologist*
Brownlee, Robert Hammel *lawyer*
Bryan, Henry C(lark), Jr. *lawyer*
Bryant, Ruth Alyne *banker*
Buck, Jack *sportscaster, broadcast executive*
Burgess, James Harland *physics educator, researcher*
Burke, James Donald *museum administrator*
Burkett, Randy James *lighting designer*
Burks, Verner Irwin *architect*
Busch, August Adolphus, III *brewery executive*
Butler, James Lawrence *financial planner*
Byrnes, Christopher Ian *academic dean, researcher*
Cabbabe, Edmond Bechir *plastic and hand surgeon*
Cain, James Nelson *arts school and concert administrator*
Cairns, Donald Fredrick *engineering educator, management consultant*
Callis, Clayton Fowler *research chemist*
Cameron, Paul Scott *architect*
†Carberry, John J. Cardinal *archbishop*
Carlson, Arthur Eugene *accounting educator*
Caron, Ronald Jacques *professional sports team executive*
Carp, Richard Lawrence (Larry Carp) *lawyer*
Carr, Gary Thomas *lawyer*
Chaplin, David Dunbar *medical research specialist, medical educator*
Chaplin, Hugh, Jr. *physician, educator*
Chestnut, Kathi Lynne *lawyer*
Chivetta, Anthony Joseph *architect*
Clear, John Michael *lawyer*
Cleary, Thomas John *aluminum products company executive*
Clement, Richard Francis *retired investment company executive*
Cloninger, Claude Robert *psychiatric researcher, educator, genetic epidemiologist*
Coe, Rodney Michael *medical educator*
Cole, Barbara Ruth *pediatrician, nephrologist*
Collins, James Slade, II *lawyer*
Conaway, Mary Ann *dean*
Conerly, Richard Pugh *retired corporation executive*
Conran, Joseph Palmer *lawyer*
Contis, John Chris *surgeon, educator*
Cornfeld, Dave Louis *lawyer*
†Corson, Shayne *professional hockey player*
Costigan, Edward John *investment banker*
Cotton, W(illiam) Philip, Jr. *architect*
Cox, Jerome Rockhold, Jr. *electrical engineer*
Craig, Andrew Billings, III *bank holding company executive*
Craig, Jerry Walker *engineering graphics educator*
Crandell, Dwight Samuel *museum executive*
Crebs, P(aul) Terence *lawyer*
Crider, Robert Agustine *international financier, law enforcement official*
Cryer, Philip Eugene *medical educator, scientist, endocrinologist*
Cummings, James M. *urology educator*
Cunningham, Charles Baker, III *manufacturing company executive*
Curran, Michael Walter *management scientist*
Curtiss, Roy, III *biology educator*
Dames, Joan Foster (Mrs. Urban L. Dames) *magazine editor, columnist*
Danforth, John Claggett *senator, lawyer, clergyman*
Danforth, William Henry *retired academic administrator, physician*
Davis, Christopher Kevin *equipment company executive*
Davis, Irvin *advertising, public relations, broadcast executive*
Deal, Joseph Maurice *university dean, art educator, photographer*
Denneen, John Paul *lawyer*
Devantier, Paul W. *communications executive, broadcaster*
Dewald, Paul Adolph *psychiatrist*
DeWoskin, Alan Ellis *lawyer*
Dill, Charles Anthony *manufacturing and computer company executive*
Dill, John Francis *retired publishing company executive*
Dill, Virginia S. *accountant*
Dodge, Paul Cecil *academic administrator*
Dodge, Philip Rogers *physician, educator*
Doggett, John Nelson, Jr. *clergyman*
Domjan, Laszlo Karoly *newspaper editor*
Donohue, Carroll John *lawyer*
Dorsey, Gray Lankford *law educator emeritus*
Dorwart, Donald Bruce *lawyer*
Dougherty, Charles Hamilton *pediatrician*
Dougherty, Charles Joseph *retired utility executive*
Dowd, Edward L., Jr. *prosecutor*
Dreifke, Gerald Edmond *electrical engineering educator*
Drews, Robert Carrel *physician*
Dudukovic, Milorad P. *chemical engineering educator, consultant*
Duesenberg, Richard William *lawyer*
Duhme, Carol McCarthy *civic worker*
Duhme, H(erman) Richard, Jr. *sculptor, educator*
DuMaine, Daniel Jerome *musician, composer, musical director*
Dunivent, John Thomas *artist, educator*
Earle, James A. *educational administrator*
Early, Gerald *writer*
Eckersley, Dennis Lee *professional baseball player*
Edison, Bernard Alan *retired retail apparel company executive*
Ehrlich, Ava *television executive producer*
†Eisenberg, Paul Richard *cardiologist, consultant, educator*
Elkins, Ken Joe *broadcasting executive*
Elliott, Howard, Jr. *gas distribution company executive*
Ellis, Dorsey Daniel, Jr. *dean, lawyer*
Engelhardt, Thomas Alexander *editorial cartoonist*
Epner, Steven Arthur *computer consultant*
Erickson, Robert Anders *optical engineer, physicist*
Erwin, James Walter *lawyer*
Etzkorn, K. Peter *sociology educator, author*
Evens, Ronald Gene *radiologist, medical center administrator*
Falk, William James *lawyer*
Farnam, Thomas Campbell *lawyer, educator*
Farrell, David Coakley *department store executive*
Farrell, John Timothy *hospital administrator*
Farris, Clyde C. *lawyer*
Faught, Harold Franklin *electrical equipment manufacturing company executive*
Feir, Dorothy Jean *entomologist, physiologist, educator*
Ferguson, Gary Warren *editorial consultant*
Filippine, Edward Louis *federal judge*
Finkel, Donald *poet*
Finnigan, Joseph Townsend *public relations executive*
Fitch, Coy Dean *physician, educator*
Fitch, Rachel Farr *health policy analyst*
Flanagan, Fidelma Louise *radiologist*
Fletcher, James Warren *physician*
Flye, M. Wayne *surgeon, immunologist, educator*
Fogarty, William Martin, Jr. *physician*
Fogle, James Lee *lawyer*
Folk, Roger Maurice *laboratory director*
Foster, Scarlett Lee *public relations executive*
Fowler, Marti *secondary education educator*
Fox, Richard Gabriel *anthropologist, educator*
Frederick, William Sherrad *manufacturing and retailing company executive*
Frieden, Carl *biochemist, educator*
Friedlander, Michael Wulf *physicist, educator*
Friedman, William Hersh *otolaryngologist, educator*
Fryer, Edwin Samuel *lawyer*
Fuhr, Grant *professional hockey player*
Gaertner, Donell J. *library director*
Gant, Ron (Ronald Edwin Gant) *professional baseball player*
Gass, William H. *author, educator*
Gauen, Patrick Emil *newspaper correspondent*
Gay, William Arthur, Jr. *thoracic surgeon, educator*
Gerard, Jules Bernard *law educator*
Gerdine, Leigh *retired academic administrator*
Gershenson, Harry *lawyer*
Gianoulakis, John Louis *lawyer*
Gibbons, Patrick Chandler *physicist, educator*
Gilbert, Allan Arthur *manufacturing executive*
Gilligan, Sandra Kaye *private school director*
Gillis, John L., Jr. *lawyer*
Gladding, Nicholas C. *lawyer*
Godiner, Donald Leonard *lawyer*
Godsey, C. Wayne *broadcasting executive*
Goebel, John J. *lawyer*
Goldberg, Anne Carol *physician, educator*
Goldberg, Norman Albert *music publisher, writer*
Goldstein, Michael Gerald *lawyer*
Goldstein, Steven *lawyer*
Gomes, Edward Clayton, Jr. *construction company executive*
Goodenberger, Daniel Marvin *medical educator*
Goodman, Harold S. *lawyer*
Gould, Phillip Louis *civil engineering educator, consultant*
Graff, George Stephen *aerospace company executive*
Graham, Colin *stage director*
Graham, John Dalby *public relations executive*
Graham, Lester Lynn *radio executive*
Gray, Charles Elmer *lawyer, rancher, investor*
Green, Dennis Joseph *lawyer*
Green, Maurice *molecular biologist, virologist, educator*
Greenbaum, Stuart I. *economist, educator*
Greenfield, Milton, Jr. *lawyer*
Griffin, W(illiam) L(ester) Hadley *shoe company executive*
Groennert, Charles Willis *electric company executive*
Gross, Michael Lawrence *chemistry educator*
Grossberg, George Thomas *psychiatrist, educator*
Grubb, Robert L., Jr. *neurosurgeon*
Guenther, Charles John *librarian, writer*
Guerri, William Grant *lawyer*
Gunn, George F., Jr. *federal judge*
Gupta, Surendra Kumar *chemical firm executive*
Guze, Samuel Barry *psychiatrist, educator, university official*
Haake, Arthur C. *church administrator*
Haberstroh, Richard David *insurance agent*
Haley, Johnetta Randolph *musician, educator, university administrator*
Hall, Mary Taussig *volunteer*
Hamburger, Viktor *retired biology educator*
Hamilton, Jean Constance *judge*
Hammerman, Marc Randall *nephrologist, educator*
Handel, Peter H. *physics educator*
Hanley, Thomas Patrick *obstetrician, gynecologist*
Hansen, Charles *lawyer*
Harris, Whitney Robson *lawyer*
Haskins, James Leslie *mathematics educator*
Hays, Ruth *lawyer*
Heath, Peter *foreign language educator*
Heck, Debra Upchurch *information technology professional*
Hecker, George Sprake *lawyer*
Heinrich, Ross Raymond *geophysicist, educator*
Hellmuth, George Francis *architect*
Hellmuth, Theodore Henning *lawyer*
Herbert, Kevin Barry John *classics educator*
Hermann, Robert Ringen *conglomerate company executive*
Herzfeld-Kimbrough, Ciby *mental health educator*
Hetlage, Robert Owen *lawyer*
Hewitt, Thomas Edward *financial executive*
Higgins, Edward Aloysius *retired newspaper editor*
Hiles, Bradley Stephen *lawyer*
Hilgert, Raymond Lewis *management and industrial relations educator, consultant, arbitrator*
Hillard, Robert Ellsworth *public relations consultant*
Hirsch, Raymond Robert *chemical company executive, lawyer*
Hirsh, Ira Jean *pyschology educator, researcher*
Hoblitzelle, George Knapp *former state legislator*
Hoessle, Charles Herman *zoo director*
Hofstatter, Leopold *psychiatrist, researcher*
Holmes, Nancy Elizabeth *pediatrician*
Holt, Glen Edward *library administrator*
Holt, Leslie Edmonds *librarian*
Holtzer, Alfred Melvin *chemistry educator*
Horwitt, Max Kenneth *biochemist, educator*
Howard, Walter Burke *chemical engineer*
Hsu, Chung Yi *neurologist*
†Hudgens, Richard Watts *psychiatry educator*
Hull, Brett A. *professional hockey player*
Hunter, Earle Leslie, III *professional association executive*
Hunter, Thom Hugh *seminary administrator*
Hyers, Thomas Morgan *physician*
Ihde, Daniel Carlyle *health science executive*
Ihde, Mary Katherine *mathematics educator*
Immel, Vincent Clare *retired law educator*
Inkley, John James, Jr. *lawyer*
Irwin, Hale S. *professional golfer*
Israel, Martin Henry *astrophysicist, educator, academic administrator*
Isselhard, Donald Edward *dentist*
Ittner, H. Curtis *architect*
Jackson, Carol E. *federal judge*
Jackson, Gayle Pendleton White *venture capitalist, international energy specialist*
Jackson, Paul Howard *librarian, educator*
Jacobsen, Thomas H(erbert) *banker*
James, William W. *banker*
Jaudes, Richard Edward *lawyer*
Jenkins, James Allister *mathematician, educator*
†Jocketty, Walt *professional sports team executive*
Johnson, Gloria Jean *counseling professional*
Johnson, Kennett Conrad *advertising agency executive*
Johnston, Marilyn Frances-Meyers *physician, medical educator*
Jones, Wilbur Boardman, Jr. *trust company executive*
Kagan, Sioma *economics educator*
Kaiser, George Charles *surgeon*
Kaminski, Donald Leon *medical educator, surgeon, gastrointestinal physiologist*
Kang, Juan *pathologist*
Kanne, Marvin George *newspaper publishing executive*
Kaplan, Henry Jerrold *ophthalmologist, educator*
Kauffman, William Ray *lawyer*
Keller, Juan Dane *lawyer*
Kelly, Ann Terese *elementary education educator*
Kelly, Daniel P. *cardiologist, molecular biologist*
Keltner, Raymond Marion, Jr. *surgeon, educator*
Kessler, Nathan *technology consultant*
Ketner, Joseph Dale *museum director, art historian*
Khoury, George Gilbert *printing company executive, baseball association executive*
Killenberg, George Andrew *newspaper consultant, former newspaper editor*
Kimmey, James Richard, Jr. *medical educator, consultant*
Kincaid, Marilyn Coburn *medical educator*
King, William Terry *manufacturing company executive*
Kinsella, Ralph Aloysius, Jr. *physician*
Kipnis, David Morris *physician, educator*
Kirsch, Jeffrey Philip *otolaryngologist*
Kiser, Karen Maureen *medical technologist, educator*
Klahr, Saulo *physician, educator*
Kling, Merle *political scientist, university official*
Kling, S(tephen) Lee *banker*
Klobasa, John Anthony *lawyer*
Kniffen, Jan Rogers *finance executive*
Knight, Charles Field *electrical equipment manufacturing company executive*
Knutsen, Alan Paul *pediatrician, allergist, immunologist*
Koehler, Harry George *real estate executive*
Koesterer, Larry J. *pharmacist*
Koff, Robert Hess *program director*
Kolker, Allan Erwin *ophthalmologist*
Korando, Donna Kay *journalist*
Kornblet, Donald Ross *communications company executive*
Kornfeld, Rosalind Hauk *research biochemist*
Kornfeld, Stuart A. *hematology educator*
Kouchoukos, Nicholas Thomas *surgeon*
Krehbiel, Robert J. *lawyer*
Krenzke, Richard L. *church administrator, clergy member, social worker*
†Kroenke, Stan *sports association administrator*
Krukowski, Lucian *philosophy educator, artist*
LaBruyere, Thomas Edward *health facility administrator*
Lacy, Paul Eston *pathologist*
Lagunoff, David *physician, educator*
†Lamping, Mark *professional sports team executive*
Lander, David Allan *lawyer*
Lane, Frank Joseph, Jr. *lawyer*
†Lankford, Raymond Lewis *professional baseball player*
La Russa, Tony, Jr. (Anthony La Russa, Jr.) *professional baseball manager*
Laskowski, Leonard Francis, Jr. *microbiologist*
Lause, Michael Francis *lawyer*
Lebowitz, Albert *lawyer, author*
Leguey-Feilleux, Jean-Robert *political scientist, educator*
Lents, Don Glaude *lawyer*
Leonard, Eugene Albert *banker*
Leven, Charles Louis *economics educator*
Levin, Ronald Mark *law educator*

Le Vine, Victor Theodore *political science educator*
Lewis, Robert David *ophthalmologist, educator*
Lickhalter, Merlin Eugene *architect*
Lieberman, Edward Jay *lawyer*
Lilly, Peter Byron *coal company executive*
Limbaugh, Stephen Nathaniel *federal judge*
Lipeles, Maxine Ina *lawyer*
Lipkin, David *chemist*
Lipman, David *multimedia consultant for publishing company*
Loeb, Jerome Thomas *retail executive*
Loeb, Virgil, Jr. *oncologist, hematologist*
Logan, Joseph Prescott *lawyer*
Loomstein, Arthur *real estate company executive*
Lovelace, Eldridge Hirst *retired landscape architect, city planner*
Lovin, Keith Harold *university administrator, philosophy educator*
Lowenhaupt, Charles Abraham *lawyer*
Loynd, Richard Birkett *consumer products company executive*
Luberda, George Joseph *lawyer, educator*
Lucking, Peter Stephen *marketing consultant, industrial engineering consultant*
Lucy, Robert Meredith *lawyer*
Lustman, Patrick J. *psychiatrist*
Luther, George Aubrey *orthopedic surgeon*
†MacArthur, Robert S. *foundation administrator, Episcopalian priest*
†Macauley, Edward C. *company executive*
Macias, Edward S. *chemistry educator, university official and dean*
†MacInnis, Al *professional hockey player*
†MacTavish, Craig *hockey player*
Maguire, John Patrick *investment company executive*
Mahan, David James *school superintendent*
Mahsman, David Lawrence *religious publications editor*
Majerus, Philip Warren *physician*
Mandelker, Daniel Robert *law educator*
Mandelstamm, Jerome Robert *lawyer*
Mangelsdorf, Thomas Kelly *psychiatrist, consultant*
Manske, Paul Robert *orthopedic hand surgeon, educator*
Mantovani, John Francis *neurologist, educator*
Marsh, James C., Jr. *secondary school principal*
Marshall, Garland Ross *biochemist, biophysicist, medical educator*
Martin, Kevin John *nephrologist, educator*
Maupin, Stephanie Zeller *French language educator*
McCarter, Charles Chase *lawyer*
Mc Daniel, James Edwin *lawyer*
McDonnell, John Finney *aerospace and aircraft manufacturing company executive*
McFarland, Mary A. *elementary and secondary school educator, administrator*
McGannon, John Barry *university chancellor*
McKelvey, James Morgan *chemical engineering educator*
McKenna, William John *textile products executive*
McKinnis, Michael B. *lawyer*
†McKissack, Patricia Carwell *children's book author*
McMillian, Theodore *federal judge*
McMullin, Kimball Ray *lawyer*
Meiners, Ginny *clinical psychologist, nurse consultant*
Meisel, George Vincent *lawyer*
Meissner, Edwin Benjamin, Jr. *real estate broker*
Merbaum, Michael *psychology educator, clinical psychologist*
Merrell, James Lee *religious editor, clergyman*
Merrill, Charles Eugene *lawyer*
Mertz, Stuart Moulton *landscape architect*
Metcalfe, Walter Lee, Jr. *lawyer*
Michaelides, Constantine Evangelos *architect, educator*
Middelkamp, John Neal *pediatrician, educator*
†Middleton, Leslie Lyles *journalist*
Miller, Gary J. *political economist*
Miller, James Gegan *research scientist, physics educator*
Miller, Michael Everett *chemical company executive*
Mills, Linda S. *public relations executive*
Mohan, John J. *lawyer*
Molloff, Florence Jeanine *speech and language therapist*
Monroe, Thomas Edward *industrial corporation executive*
Monteleone, Patricia *academic dean*
Mooradian, Arshag Dertad *physician, educator*
Moore, McPherson Dorsett *lawyer*
Morales-Galarreta, Julio *psychiatrist, child psychoanalyst*
Morgan, Lawrence Allison *headmaster, educational administrator*
Morgan, Robert Peter *engineering educator*
Morley, Harry Thomas, Jr. *real estate executive*
Morley, John Edward *physician*
Moseley, Marc Robards *sales executive*
Mueller, Charles William *electric utility executive*
Muller, Lyle Dean *religious organization administrator*
Muller, Marcel W(ettstein) *electrical engineering educator*
Mulligan, Michael Dennis *lawyer*
Murphy, George Earl *psychiatrist, educator*
Murray, Robert Wallace *chemistry educator*
†Musial, Stan(ley) (Frank Musial) *hotel and restaurant executive, former baseball team executive, former baseball player*
Myers, Raymond Irvin *optometrist, researcher*
Myerson, Robert J. *radiation oncologist, educator*
Neufeeind, Wilhelm *economics educator, university administrator*
Neville, James Morton *food company executive, lawyer*
Newman, Andrew Edison *restaurant executive*
Newman, Charles A. *lawyer*
Newman, Joan Meskiel *lawyer*
Newton, George Addison *investment banker, lawyer*
Noel, Edwin Lawrence *lawyer*
Norberg, Richard Edwin *physicist, educator*
Norman, Charles Henry *broadcasting executive*
North, Douglass Cecil *economist, educator*
Nussbaum, A(dolf) Edward *mathematician, educator*
O'Keefe, Michael Daniel *lawyer*
Olshwanger, Ron *photojournalist*
Olson, Clarence Elmer, Jr. *newspaper editor*
Olson, Robert Grant *lawyer*
O'Malley, Kevin Francis *lawyer, writer, educator*
O'Neill, Eugene Milton *mergers and acquisitions consultant*
O'Neill, John Robert *airline executive*
O'Neill, Sheila *principal*
Ong, Walter Jackson *priest, English educator, author*
Orton, George Frederick *aerospace engineer*
O'Shoney, Glenn *church administrator*
Owens, William Don *anesthesiology educator*
Owyoung, Steven David *curator*
Ozawa, Martha Naoko *social work educator*
Palans, Lloyd Alex *lawyer*
Parks, Beatrice Griffin *elementary school educator*
Patton, Thomas F. *academic administrator, pharmaceutical chemist*
Peck, William Arno *physician, educator, university official and dean*
Penniman, Nicholas Griffith, IV *newspaper publisher*
Peper, Christian Baird *lawyer*
Perez, Carlos A. *radiation oncologist, educator*
Perlmutter, David H. *physician, educator*
Perry, Catherine D. *judge*
Peters, David Allen *mechanical engineering educator, consultant*
Petru, Suzanne Mitton *health care finance executive*
Pfautch, Roy *minister, public affairs consultant*
Pfefferkorn, Michael Gene, Sr. *secondary school educator, writer*
Pfefferkorn, Sandra Jo *secondary school educator*
Pickle, Robert Douglas *lawyer, footwear industry executive*
Pittman, David Joshua *sociologist, educator, researcher, consultant*
Pollack, Joe *retired newspaper critic and columnist, writer*
Pollack, Seymour Victor *computer science educator*
Pon-Salazar, Francisco Demetrio *diplomat, educator, deacon, counselor*
Pope, Robert E(ugene) *fraternal organization administrator*
Poscover, Maury B. *lawyer*
Prensky, Arthur Lawrence *pediatric neurologist, educator*
Prenzlow, Elmer John-Charles, Jr. *minister*
Preuss, Ronald Stephen *lawyer, educator*
Priestley, G. T. Eric *manufacturing company executive*
Profeta, Salvatore, Jr. *chemist*
Proscino, Steven Vincent *food products company executive*
Pulitzer, Emily S. Rauh (Mrs. Joseph Pulitzer, Jr.) *art consultant*
Pulitzer, Michael Edgar *publishing executive*
Purkerson, Mabel Louise *physician, physiologist, educator*
Quenon, Robert Hagerty *retired mining consultant and holding company executive*
Quinn, Jack J. *professional hockey team executive*
Radford, Diane Mary *surgeon, surgical oncologist*
Raeuchle, John Steven *computer analyst*
Ramming, Michael Alexander *school system administrator*
Rao, Dabeeru C. *genetic epidemiologist*
Rasmussen, David Tab *physical anthropology educator*
Rataj, Edward William *lawyer*
Reinert, Paul Clare *university chancellor emeritus*
Reinhard, James Richard *judge*
Rhodes, Marlene Rutherford *counseling educator, educational consultant*
Rich, Harry E. *financial executive*
Richardson, Thomas Hampton *design consulting engineer*
Rigali, Justin F. *archbishop*
Ring, Lucile Wiley *lawyer*
Ritter, Robert Forcier *lawyer*
Ritterskamp, Douglas Dolvin *lawyer*
Roberts, Hugh Evan *business investment services company executive*
Robins, Lee Nelken *medical educator*
Rockwell, Hays Hamilton *bishop*
Rosenthal, Harold Leslie *biochemistry educator*
Rosenzweig, Saul *psychologist, educator, administrator*
Rosin, Walter L. *religious organization administrator*
Ross, Donald Kenneth *consulting engineering executive*
Ross, Monte *electrical engineer*
Royal, Henry Duval *nuclear medicine physician*
Rubenstein, Jerome Max *lawyer*
Ruland, Richard Eugene *English and American literature educator, critic, literary historian*
Ryall, Jo-Ellyn M. *psychiatrist*
Ryckman, DeVere Wellington *consulting environmental engineer*
Sachs, Alan Arthur *lawyer, corporate executive*
Sale, Llewellyn, III *lawyer*
Sale, Merritt *classicist, comparatist, educator*
Saligman, Harvey *consumer products and services company executive*
Salisbury, Robert Holt *political science educator*
Sandberg, John Steven *lawyer*
Sanders, Fred Joseph *aerospace company executive*
Sant, John Talbot *lawyer*
Santiago, Julio Victor *medical educator, researcher, administrator*
Sathe, Sharad Somnath *chemical company executive*
Schlafly, Phyllis Stewart *author*
Schlesinger, Milton J. *virology educator, researcher*
Schmidt, Clarence Anton *financial consultant*
Schmidt, Robert Charles, Jr. *finance executive*
†Schmidt, Wayne William *museum director, curator*
Schnuck, Craig D. *grocery stores company executive*
Schoendienst, Albert Fred (Red Schoendienst) *professional baseball coach, former baseball player*
Schoene, Kathleen Snyder *lawyer*
Schoenhard, William Charles, Jr. *health care executive*
Schonfeld, Gustav *medical educator, researcher*
Schreiber, James Ralph *obstetrics, gynecology researcher*
Schulte, Stephen Thomas *employee benefits director*
Schwabe, John Bennett, II *lawyer*
Schwartz, Alan Leigh *pediatrician, educator*
Schwartz, Henry Gerard *surgeon, educator*
Schwarz, Egon *humanities and German language educator, author, literary critic*
Searls, Eileen Haughey *lawyer, librarian, educator*
Seiler, James Elmer *judge*
Self, Larry Douglas *architectural firm executive*
Selfridge, George Dever *dentist, retired naval officer*
Sestric, Anthony James *lawyer*
Sexton, Owen James *vertebrate ecology educator, conservationist*
Shands, Courtney, Jr. *lawyer*
Shank, Robert Ely *physician, preventive medicine educator emeritus*
Shapiro, Robert B. *manufacturing executive*
Sharkey, Kathleen *accountant*
Shaw, Charles Alexander *judge*
†Shaw, John *sports association administrator*
Shaw, John Arthur *lawyer*
Shea, Daniel Bartholomew, Jr. *English language educator, actor*
Shehadi, Sameer Ibrahim *plastic surgeon*
Shell, Owen G., Jr. *banker*
Shepperd, Thomas Eugene *accountant*
Sherby, Kathleen Reilly *lawyer*
Shrauner, Barbara Wayne Abraham *electrical engineering educator*
Sibbald, John Ristow *management consultant*
Siegel, Barry Alan *nuclear radiologist*
Siegel, Sarah Ann *lawyer*
Siemer, Paul Jennings *public relations executive*
Sikorski, James Alan *research chemist*
†Sincoff, Jerome J. *architect*
Slavin, Raymond Granam *allergist, immunologist*
Sly, William S. *biochemist, educator*
Smith, Arthur Lee *lawyer*
Smith, Jeffrey E. *historian, educator*
Smith, Ozzie (Osborne Earl Smith) *professional baseball player*
Snyder, Peter Larsen *public relations executive*
Sonnino, Carlo Benvenuto *electrical manufacturing company executive*
Spector, Gershon Jerry *physician, educator, researcher*
Spector, Stanley *historian, foreign language educator*
Stann, John Anthony *investment banker*
Stauder, William Vincent *geophysics educator*
Stearley, Robert Jay *retired packaging company executive*
Steigman, Carmen Kay *pathologist*
Stewart, John Harger *music educator*
Stiritz, William P. *food company executive*
Stodghill, Ronald *school system administrator*
Stoecker, David Thomas *banker*
Stohr, Donald J. *federal judge*
Stoneman, William, III *physician, educator*
Storandt, Martha *psychologist*
Stork, Donald Arthur *advertising executive*
Stretch, John Joseph *social work educator, management and evaluation consultant*
Strevey, Tracy Elmer, Jr. *army officer, surgeon, physician executive*
Strunk, Robert Charles *physician*
Suba, Antonio Ronquillo *retired surgeon*
Suhre, Walter Anthony, Jr. *retired lawyer and brewery executive*
Suter, Albert Edward *manufacturing company executive*
Sutera, Salvatore Philip *mechanical engineering educator*
Sutter, Richard Anthony *physician*
Swiener, Rita Rochelle *psychologist, educator*
Szabo, Barna Aladar *mechanical engineering educator, mining engineer*
Takano, Masaharu *physical chemist*
Taylor, Andrew C. *rental leasing company executive*
Taylor, Dennis Del *marketing executive*
Taylor, Jack C. *rental and leasing company executive*
Taylor, Morris Anthony *chemistry educator*
Teasdale, Kenneth Fulbright *lawyer*
Teitelbaum, Steven Lazarus *pathology educator*
Templeton, Alan Robert *biology educator*
Ternberg, Jessie Lamoin *pediatric surgeon*
Thalden, Barry R. *architect*
Thomas, James Lewis *biomedical research scientist*
Thomas, Pamela Adrienne *special education educator*
Thomas, Rhonda Churchill *lawyer*
Thompson, James Clark *utilities executive*
Thompson, Vetta Lynn Sanders *psychologist, educator*
Throdahl, Monte Corden *former chemical company executive*
Tierney, Michael Edward *lawyer*
Tober, Lester Victor *shoe company executive*
Tolan, Robert Warren *pediatric infectious disease specialist*
Touhill, Blanche Marie *university chancellor, history-education educator*
Truitt, William Harvey *private school educator*
Turley, Michael Roy *lawyer*
Turner, Harold Edward *education educator*
Tyler, William Howard, Jr. *advertising executive, educator*
Ulett, George Andrew *psychiatrist*
Ullian, Joseph Silbert *philosophy educator*
Ungacta, Malissa Sumagaysay *software engineer*
Upbin, Hal Jay *consumer products executive*
Van Cleve, William Moore *lawyer*
Virtel, James John *lawyer*
Vonk, Hans *conductor*
Waddington, Bette Hope (Elizabeth Crowder) *violinist, educator*
Wagner, Raymond Thomas, Jr. *lawyer*
Walentik, Corinne Anne *pediatrician*
Walker, Robert Mowbray *physicist, educator*
Wallis, Michael Van *financial consultant, insurance agent*
Walsh, John E., Jr. *business educator, consultant*
Walsh, Joseph Leo, III *lawyer*
Walsh, Thomas Charles *lawyer*
Wang, Hengtao (Hank T. Wang) *lawyer*
Ward, R. J. *bishop*
Waters, Richard *retired publishing company executive*
Watkins, Hortense Catherine *middle school educator*
Watson, Patty Jo *anthropology educator*
Watson, Richard Allan *philosophy educator, writer*
Watters, Richard Donald *lawyer*
Weaver, Charles Lyndell, Jr. *educational facilities administrator*
Weaver, William Clair, Jr. (Mike Weaver) *human resources development executive*
Weber, Gloria Richie *minister, retired state representative*
Weber, Morton M. *microbial biochemist, educator*
Weese, Cynthia Rogers *architect, educator*
Weidenbaum, Murray Lew *economics educator*
Weiss, Charles Andrew *lawyer*
Weiss, Robert Francis *former academic administrator, religious organization administrator, consultant*
Welch, Michael John *chemistry educator, researcher*
Weldon, Virginia V. *corporate executive, physician*
Wellman, Carl Pierce *philosophy educator*
Wells, Samuel Alonzo, Jr. *surgeon, educator*
Whyte, Michael Peter *medicine and pediatrics educator, research director*
Wickline, Samuel Alan *cardiologist, educator*
Wildhaber, Michael Rene *accountant*
Wiley, Gregory Robert *publisher*
Wilke, LeRoy *church administrator*
Will, Clifford Martin *physicist, educator*
Willard, Gregory Dale *lawyer*
Williams, Frank James, Jr. *department store chain executive, lawyer*
Williams, Theodore Joseph, Jr. *lawyer*
Williamson, Donald Ray *retired career Army officer*
Willman, John Norman *management consultant*
Willman, Vallee Louis *physician, surgery educator*
Willnow, Ronald Dale *editor*
Wilson, Edward Nathan *mathematician, educator*
Wilson, Harry B. *retired public relations company executive*
Wilson, Margaret Bush *lawyer, civil rights leader*
Wilson, Michael E. *lawyer*
Winer, Warren James *insurance executive*
Winning, John Patrick *lawyer*
Winter, David Ferdinand *electrical engineering educator, consultant*
Winter, Richard Lawrence *financial and health care consulting company executive*
Winter, William Earl *mayor, retired beverage company executive*
Witherspoon, William *investment economist*
Wold, William Sydney *molecular biology educator*
Wolfe, Charles Morgan *electrical engineering educator*
Wolff, Frank Pierce, Jr. *lawyer*
Wood, Samuel Eugene *college administrator, psychology educator*
Woodruff, Bruce Emery *lawyer*
Worseck, Raymond Adams *economist*
Wrighton, Mark Stephen *chemistry educator*
Wu, Nelson Ikon *art history educator, author, artist*
Young, Marvin Oscar *lawyer*
Young, Paul Andrew *anatomist*
Zhuo, Min *neurobiology educator*
Zienty, Ferdinand Benjamin *chemical company research executive, consultant*
Zurheide, Charles Henry *consulting electrical engineer*

### Saint Peters
Greene, Christopher William *marketing professional*
Lynch, Mark Bradley *electrical engineer, biomechanical researcher*

### Sainte Genevieve
Cantu, Dino Antonio *secondary education history educator*

### Salem
Dent, Catherine Gale *secondary education educator*
Pace, Karen Yvonne *mathematics and computer science educator*

### Sedalia
Noland, Gary Lloyd *vocation educational administrator*

### Seymour
Wallace, Dorothy Alene *special education administrator*

### Sibley
Morrow, Elizabeth Hostetter *business owner, sculptress, museum association administrator, educator*

### Sparta
Madore, Joyce Louise *gerontology nurse*

### Springfield
Abraham, Yohannan *management educator*
Ames, Jimmy Ray *education educator*
Archibald, Charles Arnold *holding company executive*
Baird, Robert Dean *mission director*
Berger, Jerry Allen *museum director*
Boehm, Robert Kenneth *telecommunications consultant*
Bohnenkamper, Katherine Elizabeth *library science educator*
Booze, Joyce Wells *retired publishing executive*
Burgess, Ruth Lenora Vassar *speech and language educator*
Busch, Annie *library director*
Carlson, Thomas Joseph *lawyer, real estate developer, former mayor*
Champion, Norma Jean *communications educator, state legislator*
Clark, Russell Gentry *federal judge*
Condellone, Trent Peter *real estate developer*
Coscia, Robert Lingua *surgeon, educator*
Cunningham, Robert Cyril *clergyman, editor*
Dearmore, Thomas Lee *retired journalist*
Delaney, Jean Marie *art educator*
Denton, D. Keith *management educator*
FitzGerald, Kevin Michael *lawyer*
Geter, Rodney Keith *plastic surgeon*
Glazier, Robert Carl *publishing executive*
Good, Stephen Hanscom *academic administrator*
Grams, Betty Jane *minister, educator, writer*
Groves, Sharon Sue *elementary education educator*
Gruhn, Robert Stephen *parole officer*
Hackett, Earl Randolph *neurologist*
Hancock, Mel *former congressman*
Hansen, John Paul *metallurgical engineer*
H'Doubler, Francis Todd, Jr. *surgeon*
Hignite, Michael Anthony *computer information systems educator, researcher, writer*
Himstedt, Ronald Eugene *union official*
Hulston, John Kenton *lawyer*
Jones, Sheryl Leanne *paralegal*
Jura, James J. *electric utility executive*
King, (Jack) Weldon *photographer*
Liu, Yuan Hsiung *drafting and design educator*
Lowther, Gerald Halbert *lawyer*
Luttrull, Shirley JoAnn *protective services official*
McCartney, N. L. *investment banker*
McCullough, V. Beth *pharmacist, educator*
McDonald, William Henry *lawyer*
Montgomery, Linda Stroupe *county official*
Moore, John Edwin, Jr. *college president*
Morris, Ann Haseltine Jones *social welfare administrator*
Moulder, T. Earline *musician*
Ostergren, Gregory Victor *insurance company executive*
Ownby, Jerry Steve *landscape architect, educator*
Penninger, William Holt, Jr. *lawyer*
Petersen, George James *educational administration educator*
Roberts, Patrick Kent *lawyer*
Robertson, Ruth Ann *systems analyst, engineer*
Rogers, Roddy *civil and geotechnical engineer*
Rowan, Gerald Burdette *insurance company executive, lawyer*
Shealy, Clyde Norman *neurosurgeon*
Smith, Donald L. *social sciences educator*
Spicer, Holt Vandercook *speech and theater educator*
Starnes, James Wright *lawyer*
Stone, Allan David *economics educator*
Strickler, Ivan K. *dairy farmer*
Sylvester, Ronald Charles *newspaper writer*

Fisher, Calvin David *food manufacturing company executive*
Fleharty, Mary Sue *secretary, receptionist*
Foy, Edward Donald *financial planner*
Gardner, Charles Olda *plant geneticist and breeder, design consultant, analyst*
Genoways, Hugh Howard *systematic biologist, educator*
Grew, Priscilla Croswell *university official, geology educator*
Hamilton, David Wendell *medical services executive*
Hanway, Donald Grant *retired agronomist, educator*
Harding, William Alan *lawyer*
Hastings, William Charles *retired state supreme court chief justice*
Hendrickson, Kent Herman *university administrator*
Heng, Stanley Mark *national guard officer*
Hermance, Lyle Herbert *college official*
Hewitt, James Watt *lawyer*
†Hillegass, Clifton Keith *publisher*
Hirai, Denitsu *surgeon*
Hubbard, Kenneth Gene *climatologist*
Janzow, Walter Theophilus *retired college administrator*
Johnson, Cindy Coble *councilwoman, marketing executive*
Johnson, Margaret Kathleen *business educator*
Johnson, Virgil Allen *retired agronomist*
Jolliff, Carl R. *clinical biochemist, immunologist, laboratory administrator*
Jones, Lee Bennett *chemist, educator*
Knox, Arthur Lloyd *investor*
Kopf, Richard G. *federal judge*
Koszewski, Bohdan Julius *internist, medical educator*
Landis, David Morrison *state legislator*
Laursen, Paul Herbert *retired university educator*
Leinieks, Valdis *classicist, educator*
Lienemann, Delmar Arthur, Sr. *accountant, real estate developer*
Liggett, Twila Marie Christensen *college official, public television executive*
Lingle, Muriel Ellen *elementary education educator*
Luedtke, Roland Alfred *lawyer*
Lundstrom, Gilbert Gene *banker, lawyer*
MacPhee, Craig Robert *economist, educator*
Marsh, Frank (Irving) *former state official*
Massengale, Martin Andrew *agronomist, university president*
McClurg, James Edward *research laboratory executive*
Mignon, Paul Killian *laboratory executive*
Miller, Tice Lewis *theatre educator*
Minahan, John C., Jr. *federal judge*
Montag, John Joseph, II *librarian*
Moore, Scott *state official*
Morris, M(ary) Rosalind *cytogeneticist, educator*
Morrow, Andrew Nesbit *interior designer, business owner*
Moul, Maxine Burnett *state official*
Nelson, Darrell Wayne *university administrator, scientist*
Nelson, Don Jerome *electrical engineering and computer science educator*
Nelson, E. Benjamin *governor*
Ogle, Robbin Sue *criminal justice educator*
Oldfather, Charles Eugene *lawyer*
Osborne, Tom *college football coach*
Ottoson, Howard Warren *agricultural economist, former university administrator*
Perry, Edwin Charles *lawyer*
Peterson, Wallace Carroll, Sr. *economics educator*
Piester, David L(ee) *magistrate judge*
Pirsch, Carol McBride *county official, community relations manager*
Powers, David Richard *educational administrator*
Preister, Donald George *greeting card manufacturer, state senator*
Rawley, Ann Keyser *small business owner, picture framer*
Rawley, James Albert *history educator*
Raz, Hilda *editor-in-chief periodical, educator*
Robak, Kim M. *state official*
Robson, John Merritt *library and media administrator*
Rogers, Vance Donald *former university president*
Rohren, Brenda Marie Anderson *therapist, educator*
Rosenow, John Edward *foundation executive*
Sander, Donald Henry *soil scientist, researcher*
Sawyer, Robert McLaran *history educator*
Schimek, DiAnna Ruth Rebman *state legislator*
Sellmyer, David Julian *physicist, educator*
Sheffield, Leslie Floyd *retired agricultural educator*
Smith, Lewis Dennis *academic administrator*
Splinter, William Eldon *agricultural engineering educator*
Stange, James Henry *architect*
Stenberg, Donald B. *state attorney general*
Steward, Weldon Cecil *architecture educator, architect, consultant*
Stover, John Ford *railroad historian, educator*
Stuart, James *banker, broadcaster*
Stuhr, Elaine Ruth *state legislator*
Swartz, Jack *chamber of commerce executive*
Swartzendruber, Dale *soil physicist, educator*
Tavlin, Michael John *telecommunications company executive*
Taylor, Stephen Lloyd *food toxicologist, educator, food scientist*
Tinstman, Dale Clinton *food products company consultant*
Travis, Shirley Louise *nursing administrator*
Treves, Samuel Blain *geologist, educator*
Ullman, Frank Gordon *electrical engineering educator*
Urbom, Warren Keith *federal judge*
Wagner, Rod *library director*
Wesely, Donald Raymond *state senator*
White, C. Thomas *state supreme court justice*
White, John Wesley, Jr. *university president*
Wiegand, Sylvia Margaret *mathematician, educator*
Wiersbe, Warren Wendell *clergyman, author, lecturer*
Will, Eric John *state senator*
Woollam, John Arthur *electrical engineering educator*
Yoder, Bruce Alan *chemist*
Young, Dale Lee *banker*

### Madison
Wozniak, Richard Michael, Sr. *retired city and regional planner*

### Mc Cook
Creasman, Virena Welborn (Rene Creasman) *retired elementary and secondary school educator, genealogist, researcher*
Koetter, Leila Lynette *college administrator*

### Morrill
Steele, Sarah Jane *elementary school educator*

### Nehawka
Schlichtemeier-Nutzman, Sue Evelyn *training consultant*

### Newcastle
Myers, Kenneth L(eRoy) *secondary education educator*

### Norfolk
Mortensen-Say, Marlys (Mrs. John Theodore Say) *school system administrator*
Stites, Ray Dean *minister, college president*
Wehrer, Charles Siecke *business and education educator*

### North Bend
Johnson, Lowell C. *state commissioner*

### North Platte
Hawks, James Wade *county highway superintendent, county surveyor*

### O'Neill
Hedren, Paul Leslie *national park administrator, historian*

### Offutt AFB
Luckett, Byron Edward, Jr. *air force chaplain*

### Omaha
Ames, George Ronald *insurance executive*
Andersen, Harold Wayne *contributing editor, newspaper executive*
Andreski, Raymond John *financial planner*
Andrews, Richard Vincent *physiologist, educator*
Ansorge, Luella M. *retired association administrator*
Badeer, Henry Sarkis *physiology educator*
Barmettler, Joseph John *lawyer*
Barrett, Frank Joseph *insurance company executive*
Batchelder, Anne Stuart *former publisher, political party official*
Bauer, Otto Frank *university official, communication educator*
Bell, C(lyde) R(oberts) (Bob Bell) *foundation administrator*
Bookout, John G. *insurance company executive*
Bowen, Gary Roger *architect*
Brody, Alfred Walter *pulmonologist*
Brown, Bob Oliver *retired manufacturing company executive*
Brownrigg, John Clinton *lawyer*
Buffett, Warren Edward *entrepreneur*
Cady, Mary Margaret *advertising agency executive*
Cambridge, William G. *federal judge*
Chen, Zhengxin *computer scientist*
Cinque, Thomas J. *dean*
Conley, Eugene Allen *retired insurance company executive*
Coy, William Raymond *civil engineer*
Cross, W. Thomas *investment company executive*
Cunningham, Glenn Clarence *government official*
Curtiss, Elden F. *bishop*
Dash, Alekha K. *pharmaceutical scientist, educator*
Daub, Hal *mayor of Omaha, former congressman*
Davis, Chip *record producer, arranger*
Davis, Jerry Ray *railroad company executive*
Davis, John Byron *surgeon*
Dolan, James Vincent *lawyer*
Donaldson, William L. *newspaper publishing company executive*
Dougherty, Charles John *philosophy and medical ethics educator*
Drummer, Donald Raymond *financial services executive*
Eggers, James Wesley *executive search consultant*
Erickson, James Paul *retired financial service company executive*
Evans, G. Anne *lawyer*
Faith, Marshall E. *grain company executive*
Fitzgerald, James Patrick *lawyer*
Fjell, Mick *principal*
Fletcher, Philip B. *food products company executive*
Flickinger, Thomas Leslie *hospital alliance executive*
Forbes, Franklin Sim *lawyer, educator*
Fowler, Stephen Eugene *retired military officer, human resources executive*
Frazier, Chet June *advertising agency executive*
Frederickson, Keith Alvin *advertising agency executive*
Fusaro, Ramon Michael *dermatologist, researcher*
Gallagher, Paula Marie *real estate appraiser*
Gambal, David *biochemistry educator*
Gessaman, Margaret Palmer *mathematics educator, college dean*
Girouard, Gail Patricia *family practice physician*
Grant, John Thomas *retired state supreme court justice*
Greer, Randall Dewey *investment company executive*
Hachten, Richard Arthur, II *health system administrator*
Hamann, Deryl Frederick *lawyer, bank executive*
Haney, J. Terrence *insurance consultant*
Harned, Roger Kent *radiology educator*
Harr, Lawrence Francis *lawyer*
Haselwood, Eldon LaVerne *education educator*
Heaney, Robert Proulx *physician, educator*
Hill, John Wallace *special education educator*
Hodgson, Paul Edmund *surgeon*
Horning, Ross Charles, Jr. *historian, educator*
Howard, Thomas Clement *surgeon*
Howe, G(ary) Woodson (Woody Howe) *newspaper editor, newspaper executive*
Hultquist, Paul Fredrick *electrical engineer, educator*
Humphries, Roger Lee *postal service administrator*
Imray, Thomas John *radiologist, educator*
Inatome, Rick *retail computer company executive*
Jackson, Mary Teresa *critical care nurse*
Jacobs, Henrietta Marie *early childhood educator, consultant*
Jay, Burton Dean *insurance actuary*
Jensen, Sam *lawyer*
Jetter, Arthur Carl, Jr. *insurance company executive*
Johnson, James David *concert pianist, organist, educator*
Johnson, Richard Walter *investment executive*
Jugel, Richard Dennis *corporate executive, management consultant*
Kaspar, Victoria Ann *educator English*
Kessinger, Margaret Anne *medical educator*
Korbitz, Bernard Carl *retired oncologist, hematologist, educator, consultant*
Krotz, James Edward *bishop*
Lackner, Rudy Paul *cardiothoracic surgeon*
Lee, Carla Ann Bouska *nursing educator*
Leininger, Madeleine Monica *nurse, anthropologist, administrator, consultant, editor, author*
Lemon, Henry Martyn *physician, educator*
Lenz, Charles Eldon *electrical engineering consultant, author*
Lietzen, John Hervy *human resources executive, health agency volunteer*
Lindsay, James Wiley *agricultural company executive*
Lovas, Sándor *chemist, researcher, educator*
Lynch, Benjamin Leo *oral surgeon educator*
Mardis, Hal Kennedy *urological surgeon, educator, researcher*
Matthies, Frederick John *architectural engineer*
Maurer, Harold Maurice *pediatrician*
McDaniels, B. T. *bishop*
McEniry, Robert Francis *education educator*
Meyers, Louisa Ann *business and communications consultant*
Mohiuddin, Syed Maqdoom *cardiologist, educator*
Monaghan, Michael Sean *pharmacist*
Monaghan, Thomas Justin *prosecutor*
Monasee, Charles Arthur *retired healthcare foundation executive*
Morrison, Michael Gordon *university president, clergyman, history educator*
†Munger, Charles T. *diversified company executive*
Murphy-Barstow, Holly Ann *financial consultant*
Nettles, Toni Olesco *non-commissioned officer*
Newton, John Milton *acadmeic administrator, psychology educator*
North, John E., Jr. *lawyer*
Norton, Robert R., Jr. *food products executive*
O'Brien, Richard L(ee) *academic administrator, physician, cell biologist*
O'Donohue, Walter John, Jr. *medical educator*
Okhamafe, Imafedia *English literature and philosophy educator*
Omer, Robert Wendell *hospital administrator*
Parker, Carol Tommie *psychotherapist, educator*
Pearson, Paul Hammond *physician*
Peck, Ernest James, Jr. *academic administrator*
Phares, Lynn Levisay *public relations communications executive*
Pitts, Robert Eugene, Jr. *marketing educator, consultant*
Polsky, Donald Perry *architect*
Prince, Frances Anne Kiely *civic worker*
Puglisi, Philip James *electrical engineer*
Rakowicz-Szulczynska, Eva Maria *molecular oncologist*
Regan, Timothy James *grain company executive*
Riley, William Jay *lawyer*
Rock, Harold L. *lawyer*
Rogan, Eleanor Groeniger *cancer researcher, educator*
Roskens, Ronald William *international business consultant*
Rosse, Therese Marie *reading and special education educator, curriculum and instruction specialist*
Runge, Patrick Richard *lawyer*
Rupp, Mark Edmund *medical educator*
Ryan, Mark Anthony *architect*
Sanders, W(illiam) Eugene, Jr. *physician, educator*
Sawtell, Stephen M. *private investor, lawyer*
Schlessinger, Bernard S. *retired university dean*
Schmidman, Jo Ann *artistic director*
Schmidt, Kathleen Marie *lawyer*
Schuerman, Norbert Joel *school superintendent*
Scott, David Michael *pharmacy educator*
Scott, Walter, Jr. *construction company executive*
Shanahan, Thomas M. *judge*
Sheehan, Daniel Eugene *bishop*
Sheehan, John Francis *cytopathologist, educator*
Skoog, Donald Paul *retired physician, educator*
Skutt, Thomas James *insurance company executive*
Smithey, Donald Leon *airport authority director*
Sokolof, Phil *industrialist, consumer advocate*
Soshnik, Joseph *investment banking consultant*
Spencer, Jeffrey Paul *art educator*
Strom, Lyle Elmer *federal judge*
Tinker, John Heath *anesthesiologist, educator*
Tollman, Thomas Andrew *librarian*
Townley, Robert Gordon *medical educator*
Truhlsen, Stanley Marshall *physician, educator*
Tucker, Michael *elementary school principal*
Tunnicliff, David George *civil engineer*
Vallery, Janet Alane *industrial hygienist*
Velde, John Ernest, Jr. *business executive*
Vosburg, Bruce David *lawyer*
Waggener, Ronald Edgar *radiologist*
Ward, Vernon Graves *internist*
Watt, Dean Day *retired biochemistry educator*
Weber, Delbert Dean *academic administrator*
Weekly, John William *insurance company executive*
Wright, Norman Harold *lawyer*
Wunsch, James Stevenson *political science educator*
Zaiman, K. Robert *dentist*
Zepf, Thomas Herman *physics educator, researcher*
Zerbs, Stephen Taylor *telecommunications development engineer*
Zuerlein, Damian Joseph *priest*

### Papillion
Casale, Thomas Bruce *medical educator*
Dvorak, Allen Dale *radiologist*
Rees, Patricia Glines *occupational health nurse, consultant, educator*

### Plainview
Mauch, Jeannine Ann *elementary education educator*

### Rushville
Plantz, Christine Marie *librarian, union officer*

### Scottsbluff
Fisher, J. R. *marketing executive*
Scovil, Larry Emery *minister*
Weichenthal, Burton A. *beef cattle specialist*

### Seward
Vrana, Verlon Kenneth *retired professional society administrator, conservationist*

### South Sioux City
Graves, Maureen Ann *counselor*
Wilson, Esther Elinore *technical college educator*

### Superior
Drullinger, Leona Pearl *obstetrics nurse*

### Wayne
Mash, Donald J. *college president*

### West Point
Paschang, John Linus *retired bishop*

### Wood River
Bish, Milan David *former ambassador, consultant*

### York
Givens, Randal Jack *communications educator*

## NEVADA

### Boulder City
Heinlein, Oscar Allen *former air force officer*
Holmes, BarbaraAnn Krajkoski *secondary education educator*
Kidd, Hillery Gene *educational publisher*
Shrader, Thomas Henry *biologist*
Wyman, Richard Vaughn *engineering educator, exploration company executive*

### Carson City
Alcorn, Karen Zefting Hogan *artist, art educator, analyst*
Ayres, Janice Ruth *social service executive*
Burns, Dan W. *manufacturing company executive*
Crawford, John Edward *geologist, scientist*
Del Papa, Frankie Sue *state attorney general*
Fischer, Michael John *ophthalmologist, physician*
Gunderson, Elmer Millard *state supreme court justice, law educator*
Heller, Dean *state official*
James, Daryl Norman *environmental engineer*
Kwalick, Donald S. *human services manager*
Larson, Gerald Lee *auditor*
Marangi, Vito Anthony, Sr. *claim administrator*
McLain, John Lowell *resource specialist, consultant*
Miller, Robert Joseph *governor, lawyer*
Noland, Robert LeRoy *retired manufacturing company executive*
O'Connell, Mary Ann *state senator, business owner*
Patrie, Peter Hugo *gaming control board investigator*
Peterson, Mary L. *state agency official*
Rankin, Teresa P. Froncek *insurance educator, consultant, former state agency administrator*
Reid, Belmont Mervyn *brokerage house executive*
Rocha, Guy Louis *archivist, historian*
Rodefer, Jeffrey Robert *lawyer, prosecutor*
Rose, Robert E(dgar) *state supreme court justice*
Seale, Robert L. *state treasurer*
Springer, Charles Edward *state supreme court justice*
Tiffany, Sandra L. *state legislator*
Titus, Alice Cestandina (Dina Titus) *state legislator*
Wadman, William Wood, III *educational director, technical research executive, consulting company executive*
Yoder, Marianne Eloise *software developer, consultant*
Young, C. Clifton *judge*
Zetter, Lois C. *personal manager*

### East Ely
Alderman, Minnis Amelia *psychologist, educator, small business owner*

### Elko
Lovell, Walter Benjamin *secondary education educator*

### Fallon
Plants, Walter Dale *elementary education educator, minister*
Sanwick, James Arthur *mining executive*

### Gardnerville
Jackson, Mark Bryan *lawyer*

### Glenbrook
Buscaglia, (Felice) Leo(nardo) *special education educator, author*
Goldsmith, Harry Sawyer *surgeon, educator*
Jabara, Michael Dean *investment banker*

### Hawthorne
Graham, Lois Charlotte *retired educator*
Sortland, Trudith Ann *speech and language therapist, educator*

### Henderson
Benson, James DeWayne *university administrator*
Bentley, Kenton Earl *aerospace scientist, researcher*
Byleckie, Scott Andrew, Sr. *health facility coordinator*
Campbell, David Martin *bank executive*
Cohan, George Sheldon *advertising and public relations executive*
Creech, Wilbur Lyman *retired military officer*
Fehr, Gregory Paris *marketing and distribution company executive*
Freyd, William Pattinson *fund raising executive, consultant*
Knight, Gladys (Maria) *singer*
Martin, Donald Walter *author, publisher*
McKinney, Sally Vitkus *state official*
Perel, Michael Joseph *dermatologist, inventor*
Riske, William Kenneth *producer, cultural services consultant*
Turner, Florence Frances *ceramist*

### Incline Village
Dale, Martin Albert *investment banking executive*
Diederich, J(ohn) William *internet publisher*
DuBois, L(uther) Carl *development company executive*
Henderson, Paul Bargas, Jr. *economic development consultant*
Hiatt, Robert Worth *former university president*
Johnson, James Arnold *business consultant, venture capitalist*
Jones, Robert Alonzo *economist*
Merdinger, Charles John *civil engineer, naval officer, academic administrator*
Strack, Harold Arthur *retired electronics company executive, retired air force officer, planner, analyst, author, musician*
Wahl, Howard Wayne *retired construction company executive, engineer*
Yount, George Stuart *paper company executive*

### Las Vegas
Abramson, Albert *television historian, consultant*
Adams, Charles Lynford *English language educator*

**Gilmanton**
Daigle, Candace Jean *municipal services provider*
Osler, Howard Lloyd *controller*

**Glen**
Zager, Ronald I. *chemist, consultant*

**Goffstown**
Gillmore, Robert *landscape designer, author, editor, publisher*
Glines, Jon Malcolm *secondary education educator*

**Grantham**
Behrle, Franklin Charles *retired pediatrician and educator*
Boothroyd, Herbert J. *insurance company executive*
Feldman, Roger Bruce *government official*
Hansen, Herbert W. *management consultant*
Knights, Edwin Munroe *pathologist*
MacNeill, Arthur Edson *physician, science consultant*
Smith, Dudley Renwick *retired insurance company executive*
Springsteen, David Folger *retired financial consultant*
Wells, Edward Phillips *radiologist*

**Greenfield**
Wheelock, Major William, Jr. *health care adminstrator*

**Groveton**
Kegeles, Gerson *chemistry educator*

**Hampstead**
Sewitch, Deborah E. *health science association administrator, educator, sleep researcher*

**Hampton**
Morton, Donald John *librarian*
Rice, Frederick Colton *environmental management consultant*
Russell, Richard R. *chemicals executive*

**Hancock**
Brown, David Warfield *management educator*
Carney, David Mitchel *political party official*
Pollaro, Paul Philip *artist*

**Hanover**
Almy, Thomas Pattison *physician, educator*
Anthony, Robert Newton *management educator emeritus*
Arndt, Walter W. *Slavic scholar, linguist, writer, translator*
Baumgartner, James Earl *mathematics educator*
Bien, Peter Adolph *English language educator, author*
Bogart, Kenneth Paul *mathematics educator, consultant*
Boghosian, Varujan Yegan *sculptor*
Braun, Charles Louis *chemistry educator, researcher*
Brooks, H. Allen *architectural educator, author, lecturer*
Browning, James Alexander *engineering company executive,inventor*
Byrne, Patrick Michael *writer, educator, entrepreneur*
Campbell, Colin Dearborn *economist, educator*
Clement, Meredith Owen *economist, educator*
Crory, Elizabeth L. *state legislator*
Crowell, Richard Henry *mathematician, educator*
Daniell, Jere Rogers, II *history educator, consultant, public lecturer*
Dean, Robert Charles, Jr. *mechanical engineer, entrepreneur, innovator*
Demko, George Joseph *geographer*
Dodge, Charles Malcolm *composer, music educator*
Doenges, Norman Arthur *retired classics educator*
Doney, Willis Frederick *philosophy educator*
Doyle, William Thomas *physicist, educator*
Drake, Charles Lum *geology educator*
Ehrlich, David Gordon *film director, educator*
Ermenc, Joseph John *mechanical engineering educator*
Fischel, William Alan *economics educator*
Freedman, James Oliver *university president, lawyer*
Garmire, Elsa Meints *electrical engineering educator, consultant*
Garthwaite, Gene Ralph *historian, educator*
Gert, Bernard *philosopher, educator*
Gilbert, John Jouett *aquatic ecologist, educator*
Green, Mary Jean Matthews *foreign language educator*
Green, Ronald Michael *ethics and religious studies educator*
Guest, Robert Henry *state legislator, management educator*
Gustman, Alan Leslie *economics educator*
Hall, Raymond *sociology educator*
Heffernan, James Anthony Walsh *English language and literature educator*
Hennessey, John William, Jr. *academic administrator*
Howe, Harold, II *academic administrator, former foundation executive, educator*
Hutchinson, Charles Edgar *engineering educator, dean emeritus*
Kantrowitz, Arthur *physicist, educator*
Kemp, Karl Thomas *insurance company executive*
Kleck, Robert Eldon *psychology educator*
Koop, Charles Everett *surgeon, educator, former surgeon general*
Kritzman, Lawrence David *humanities educator*
Kurtz, Thomas Eugene *mathematics educator*
Lamperti, John Williams *mathematician, educator*
Logue, Dennis Emhardt *financial economics educator, consultant*
Long, Carl Ferdinand *engineering educator*
Lubin, Martin *cell physiologist educator*
Lyons, Gene Martin *political scientist, educator*
Mansell, Darrel Lee, Jr. *English educator*
Masters, Roger Davis *government educator*
Mc Farland, Thomas L. *book publishing executive*
Moeschler, John Boyer *physician, educator*
Montgomery, David Campbell *physicist, educator*
Moss, Ben Frank, III *art educator, painter*
Olcott, William Alfred *magazine editor*
Otto, Margaret Amelia *librarian*
Oxenhandler, Neal *language educator, writer*
Paganucci, Paul Donnelly *banker, lawyer, former college official*
Parton, James *historian*
Penner, Hans Henry *historian*
Perrin, Noel *environmental studies educator*
Rawnsley, Howard Melody *physician, educator*

Rieser, Leonard Moos *college administrator, physics educator*
Riggs, Lorrin Andrews *psychologist, educator*
Roos, Thomas Bloom *biological scientist, educator*
Rueckert, Frederic *plastic surgeon*
Russell, Robert Hilton *Romance languages and literature educator*
Rutter, Jeremy Bentham *archaeologist, educator*
Sabinson, Mara Beth *theatre educator, director, actress*
Scher, Steven Paul *literature educator*
Scherr, Barry Paul *foreign language educator*
Sheldon, Richard Robert *Russian language and literature educator*
Shewmaker, Kenneth Earl *history educator*
Slesnick, William Ellis *mathematician, educator*
Snell, James Laurie *mathematician, educator*
Spiegel, Evelyn Sclufer *biology educator, researcher*
Spiegel, Melvin *retired biology educator*
Sporn, Michael Benjamin *cancer researcher*
Staples, O. Sherwin *orthopedic surgeon*
Starzinger, Vincent Evans *political science educator*
Stearns, Stephen Russell *civil engineer, forensic engineer, educator*
Stockmayer, Walter H(ugo) *retired chemistry educator*
Sturge, Michael Dudley *physicist*
Wallace, Andrew Grover *physician, educator, medical school dean*
Wallis, Graham Blair *engineer, educator*
Wegner, Gary Alan *astronomer*
Wetterhahn, Karen Elizabeth *chemistry educator*
Wood, Charles Tuttle *history educator*
Wright, James Edward *dean, history educator*
Young, Oran Reed *political scientist, educator*
Zubkoff, Michael *medical educator*

**Henniker**
Braiterman, Thea Gilda *economics educator, state legislator*

**Hill**
Thierry, John Adams *heavy machinery manufacturing company executive, lawyer*

**Hillsboro**
Gibson, Raymond Eugene *clergyman*
Pearson, William Rowland *retired nuclear engineer*

**Holderness**
Cutler, Laurence Stephan *architect, urban designer, advertising executive, educator*

**Hollis**
Lerner, Arnold Stanley *radio station executive*
Lumbard, Eliot Howland *lawyer, educator*
Merritt, Thomas Butler *lawyer*

**Hooksett**
Bagan, Merwyn *neurological surgeon*
Gustafson, Richard Alrick *college president*

**Hudson**
Rice, Annie L. Kempton *medical, surgical and rehabilitation nurse*

**Jackson**
Johnson, Ned (Edward Christopher Johnson) *publishing company executive*
Synnott, William Raymond *retired management consultant*
Zeliff, William H., Jr. *former congressman*

**Jaffrey**
Alderman, Bissell *architect*
Coffin, Lori Ann *police officer*
Schott, John (Robert) *international consultant, educator*
Schulte, Henry Frank *journalism educator*
Van Ness, Patricia Wood *religious studies educator, consultant*
Walling, Cheves Thomson *chemistry educator*

**Keene**
Baldwin, Peter Arthur *psychologist, educator, author, minister*
Bell, Ernest Lorne, III *lawyer*
Blacketor, Paul Garber *minister*
Burkart, Walter Mark *manufacturing company executive*
Fachada, Ederito Paul *podiatrist, surgeon*
Fuld, Gilbert Lloyd *pediatrician*
Gardner, Eric Raymond *lawyer*
Hickey, Delina Rose *education educator*
Lyon, Ronald Edward *management consultant, computer consultant*
Martin, Vernon Emil *librarian*
Stearns, Lloyd Worthington *investment adviser, Oriental artifact consultant*
Yarosewick, Stanley J. *academic administrator, physicist*

**Laconia**
Grow, Philip William *accountant*
Shoup, Carl Sumner *retired economist*

**Lancaster**
Drapeau, Phillip David *banking executive*
Pratt, Leighton Calvin *state legislator*

**Lebanon**
Barney, Christine Anne *psychiatrist, educator*
Clendenning, William Edmund *dermatologist*
Cornwell, Gibbons Gray, III *physician, medical educator*
Cronenwett, Jack LeMoyne *vascular surgeon educator*
Emery, Virginia Olga Beattie *psychologist, researcher*
Fanger, Michael W. *medical educator*
Foote, Robert Stephens *physician*
Galton, Valerie Anne *endocrinology educator*
Jillette, Arthur George, Jr. *school system administrator*
Kelley, Maurice Leslie, Jr. *gastroenterologist, educator*
Mc Cann, Frances Veronica *physiologist, educator*
McCollum, Robert Wayne *physician, educator*
Munck, Allan Ulf *physiologist, educator*
Rolett, Ellis Lawrence *medical educator, cardiologist*
Rous, Stephen Norman *urologist, educator*
Shorter, Nicholas Andrew *pediatric surgeon*
Silberfarb, Peter Michael *psychiatrist, educator*

Smith, Barry David *obstetrician-gynecologist, educator*
Sox, Harold Carleton, Jr. *physician, educator*
Varnum, James William *hospital administrator*
von Reyn, C. Fordham *infectious disease physician*

**Lee**
Blidberg, D. Richard *marine engineer*
Young, James Morningstar *physician, naval officer*

**Lisbon**
Trelfa, Richard Thomas *paper company executive*

**Littleton**
McGruder-Houlihan, Ruby Lee *special education educator*

**Londonderry**
Kennedy, Ellen Woodman *elementary and home economics educator*
Michaud, Norman Paul *association administrator, logistics consultant*
Nelson, Lloyd Steadman *statistics consultant*

**Loudon**
Heath, Roger Charles *state senator, writer*
Moore, Beatrice *religious organization administrator*

**Lyman**
Kaplan, Frada M. *retired principal, special education educator*

**Lyme**
Darion, Joe *librettist, lyricist*
Demarest, Chris Lynn *writer, illustrator*
Dwight, Donald Rathbun *newspaper publisher, corporate communications executive*
McIntyre, Oswald Ross *physician*
Swan, Henry *forester, consultant*

**Madbury**
Bruce, Robert Vance *historian, educator*

**Manchester**
Angoff, Gerald Harvey *cardiologist*
Arnold, Barbara Eileen *state legislator*
Coolidge, Daniel Scott *lawyer*
DesRochers, Gerard Camille *surgeon*
Ehlers, Eileen Spratt *family therapist*
Emery, Paul Emile *psychiatrist*
Gallagher, Nancy Anne *college official*
Loeb, Nackey Scripps *publisher*
Mailloux, Raymond Victor *health services administrator*
Mc Lane, John Roy, Jr. *lawyer*
McQuaid, Joseph Woodbury *newspaper executive*
Middleton, Jack Baer *lawyer*
Millimet, Joseph Allen *retired lawyer*
Monson, John Rudolph *lawyer*
Nardi, Theodora P. *former state legislator*
O'Neil, Leo E. *bishop*
Perkins, Charles, III *newspaper editor*
Richards, Thomas H. *lawyer, arbitrator*
Roth, Pamela Jeanne *strategic marketing professional, web site developer and publisher*
Scotch, Barry Martin *lawyer*
Stefanik, Jean Marianne *secondary school educator, naturalist*
Sullivan, Robert Martin *educational fundraiser*
Wieczorek, Raymond J. *mayor*
Zachos, Kimon Stephen *lawyer*

**Marlborough**
Walton, Russell Sparey *foundation administrator*

**Meredith**
Hamlin, Robert Henry *public health educator, management consultant*
Hatch, Frederick Tasker *chemicals consultant*

**Merrimack**
Drobny, Jiri George *chemical engineer*
Hower, Philip Leland *semiconductor device engineer*
Kotelly, George Vincent *editor, writer*
Malley, James Henry Michael *industrial engineer*
Vogt, Sharon Madonna *author, educator*

**Milford**
Morison, John Hopkins *casting manufacturing company executive*

**Nashua**
Barry, William Henry, Jr. *federal judge*
Barton, Carl P. *retired insurance company executive*
Flynn, William Berchman, Jr. *psychology educator, clinical psychologist*
Garbacz, Gerald George *information services company executive*
Gregg, Hugh *former cabinet manufacturing company executive, former governor New Hampshire*
Hanson, Arnold Philip *retired lawyer*
Hargreaves, David William *communications company executive*
Hemming, Walter William *business financial consultant*
Light, James Forest *English educator*
Mitsakos, Charles Leonidas *education educator, consultant*
Perkins, George William, II *financial services executive, film producer*
Rotithor, Hemant Govind *electrical engineer*
Smith, Thomas Raymond, III *software engineer*
Weinstein, Jeffrey Allen *consumer products company executive, lawyer*
Woodruff, Thomas Ellis *electronics consulting executive*

**New Castle**
Friese, George Ralph *retail executive*
Silva, Joseph Donald *English language educator*

**New Hampton**
Lockwood, Joanne Smith *mathematician educator*

**New London**
Condict, Edgar Rhodes *medical electronics, aviation instrument manufacturing and medical health care executive, inventor, mediator, pastor*
Hurley, Patrick Mason *geology educator*
Nye, Thomas Russell *retired drafting, reproduction and surveying company executive*

Sheerr, Deirdre McCrystal *architectural firm executive*
Wheaton, Perry Lee *management consultant*
York, Michael Charest *librarian*
Zuehlke, Richard William *technical communications consultant, writer*

**Newmarket**
Getchell, Sylvia Fitts *librarian*

**Newport**
Hickey, William Francis *retired surgeon, medical consultant*
Ruger, William Batterman *firearms manufacturing company executive*
Stamatakis, Carol Marie *state legislator, lawyer*

**North Hampton**
White, Ralph Paul *automotive executive, consultant*

**North Haverhill**
Charpentier, Keith Lionel *school system administrator*

**Pelham**
Holmes, Richard Dale *secondary education educator, historical consultant*

**Penacook**
Denham, Robin Richardson *secondary school educator*

**Peterborough**
Farnham, Sherman Brett *retired electrical engineer*
Wolfe, Albert Blakeslee *lawyer*

**Plaistow**
Senter, Merilyn P(atricia) *former state legislator and freelance reporter*

**Plymouth**
Swift, Robert Frederic *music educator*
Wiseman, Douglas Carl *education educator*

**Portsmouth**
†Akridge, William David *hotel management company executive*
Barr, Jane Kay *investment advisor*
Brage, Carl Willis *genealogist*
Doleac, Charles Bartholomew *lawyer*
†Greene, Douglas E. *hotel executive*
Hopkins, Jeannette Ethel *book publisher, editor*
Levin, Harvey Jay *financial institution design and construction specialist, developer, auctioneer*
Lyman, William Welles, Jr. *retired architect*
Morin, Carlton Paul *private investments executive*
O'Toole, Dennis Allen *museum director*
Powers, Henry Martin, Jr. *oil company executive*
Silverman, George Alan *broadcasting executive*
Thornhill, Arthur Horace, Jr. *retired book publisher*
Tober, Stephen Lloyd *lawyer*
Volk, Kenneth Hohne *lawyer*

**Randolph**
Bradley, William Lee *retired foundation executive, educator*

**Rindge**
Emerson, Susan *oil company executive*
Palmer, Bruce Harrison *college director*
White, Jean Tillinghast *former state senator*

**Rochester**
Coviello, Robert Frank *retail executive*
Dworkin, Gary Steven *insurance company executive*

**Rumney**
King, Wayne Douglas *state senator*
Smith, F(rederick) Dow(swell) *physicist, retired college president*

**Rye**
MacRury, King *management counselor*

**Salem**
Flanagan, Anne Patricia *art educator, artist*
Simmons, Marvin Gene *geophysics educator*
Snierson, Lynne Wendy *communications executive*

**Sanbornton**
Andrews, Henry Nathaniel, Jr. *botanist, scientist, educator*

**Sanbornville**
Berg, Warren Stanley *retired banker*

**Sandown**
Densen, Paul Maximillian *former health administrator, educator*

**Seabrook**
Ganz, Mary Keohan *lawyer*

**Silver Lake**
Pallone, Adrian Joseph *research scientist*

**Spofford**
Szmit, Frederick Andrew *paper manufacturing company executive*

**Strafford**
Simic, Charles *English language educator, poet*

**Sunapee**
Cary, Charles Oswald *aviation executive*
Chait, Lawrence G. *marketing consultant*
Rauh, John David *manufacturing company executive*

**Suncook**
Weiss, Joanne Marion *writer*

**Tilton**
Wolf, Sharon Ann *psychotherapist*

**Walpole**
Burns, Kenneth Lauren *filmmaker, historian*
Gooding, Judson *writer*
Harris, Grant Warren *principal*

**Warner**
Hunt, Everett Clair *engineering educator, researcher, consultant*

**Washington**
Halverson, Wendell Quelprud *former educational association executive, clergyman, educator*

**Waterville Valley**
Grimes, Howard Ray *management consultant*

**West Chesterfield**
Garinger, Louis Daniel *religion educator*

**West Lebanon**
Bower, Richard Stuart *economist, educator*
MacAdam, Walter Kavanagh *consulting engineering executive*

**Winchester**
MacKay, Neil Duncan *plastics company executive*

**Windham**
Arvai, Ernest Stephen *consulting executive*
Hurst, Michael William *psychologist*

**Wolfeboro**
Mancke, Richard Bell *economics writer, investor*
Murray, Roger Franklin *economist, educator*
Pierce, Edward Franklin *retired academic administrator*
Varnerin, Lawrence John *physicist, retired educator*

## NEW JERSEY

**Aberdeen**
Smith, Marvin Frederick, Jr. *chemical engineer, consultant*

**Absecon**
Byrne, Shaun Patrick *law enforcement officer*
Steinruck, Charles Francis, Jr. *management consultant, lawyer*

**Allendale**
Birdsall, Blair *consulting engineering executive*
Castor, William Stuart, Jr. *chemist, consultant, laboratory executive, educator*
Hampton, Lionel Leo *composer, conductor, entertainer*
Hollands, John Henry *electronics consultant*

**Allenhurst**
Hinson, Robert William *advertising executive, consultant*

**Alloway**
Tackett, William Edward *school system administrator*

**Alpine**
Yuelys, Alexander *former cosmetics company executive*

**Andover**
Gioseffi, (Dorothy) Daniela *poet, performer, author, educator*

**Annandale**
Appelbaum, Michael Arthur *finance company executive*
Cohen, Morrel Herman *physicist, biologist, educator*
Drakeman, Donald Lee *biotechnology company executive, lawyer*
Drakeman, Lisa N. *biotechnology company executive*
Gorbaty, Martin Leo *chemist, researcher*
Sinfelt, John Henry *chemist*

**Asbury**
Konrad, Adolf Ferdinand *artist*

**Atlantic City**
Geary, William John *entreprenuer, researcher*
Harris, Paul Smith *human resources professional*
Jacobson, Carole Renee *lawyer, educator*
Knight, Edward R. *judge, lawyer, educator, psychologist*
McKee, Mary Elizabeth *producer*
Targan, Donald Gilmore *lawyer*
Tucci, Mark A. *state agency administrator*

**Atlantic Highlands**
Crowley, Cynthia Johnson *secondary school educator*
Royce, Paul Chadwick *medical administrator*

**Avalon**
Beatrice, Ruth Hadfield *hypnotherapist, retired educator*
Emmert, Richard Eugene *professional association executive, retired*
Yochum, Philip Theodore *retired motel and cafeteria chain executive*

**Avenel**
Berg, Louis Leslie *investment executive*
Heller, Patricia Ann *container company executive*
Sansone, Paul J. *automotive executive*

**Avon By The Sea**
Bruno, Grace Angelia *accountant, educator*
Potter, Emma Josephine Hill *language educator*

**Barnegat**
Berroa, David Allen *environmental services director*
Hawk, Frank Carkhuff, Sr. *industrial engineer*
Lowe, Angela Maria *small business owner*

**Barnegat Light**
Gibbs, Frederick Winfield *lawyer, communications company executive*
Sparano, Vincent Thomas *editor*

**Barrington**
Fanelle, Carmella *dentist*
Florio, Maryanne J. *state health research scientist*

**Basking Ridge**
Abeles, James David *manufacturing company executive*
Allen, Katherine Spicer *writer, former chemist*
Bodden, M. David *computer professional*
Collis, Sidney Robert *retired telephone company executive*
Conklin, Donald Ransford *retired pharmaceutical company executive*
Darrow, William Richard *pharmaceutical company executive, consultant*
Frediani, Diane Marie *graphic designer, interior designer*
Heckendorf, Glenn *sales and marketing executive*
Kastner, Cynthia *lawyer*
Kurkjian, Charles R(obert) *ceramic engineer, researcher*
†Laurie, Marilyn *communications company executive*
Manda, Joseph Alexander, III *veterinary consulting executive*
Munch, Douglas Francis *pharmaceutical and health industry consultant*
Perry, Matthew Edward, Jr. *telecommunications professional*
Schneider, Donald Frederic *banker*

**Bay Head**
Benning, Joseph Francis, Jr. *portfolio manager, financial analyst*

**Bayonne**
Gorman, William David *artist, graphic artist*
Searle, Ronald *artist*

**Bedminster**
David, Edward Emil, Jr. *electrical engineer, business executive*
Hart, Terry Jonathan *communications executive*

**Belford**
Bauer, Linda P. *nurse*

**Belle Mead**
Carroll, David Joseph *actor*
Hansen, Ralph Holm *chemist*
Sarle, Charles Richard *health facility executive*
Singley, Mark Eldridge *agricultural engineering educator*
Wilson, Nancy Jeanne *laboratory director, medical technologist*

**Belleville**
Caputo, Wayne James *surgeon, podiatrist*
Goldenberg, David Milton *experimental pathologist, oncologist*
Weyland, Deborah Ann *learning disabilities teacher consultant*

**Bellmawr**
Wilke, Constance Regina *elementary education educator*

**Belmar**
De Santo, Donald James *psychologist*

**Belvidere**
Aaroe, Paul *superior court judge*

**Bergenfield**
Alfieri, John Charles, Jr. *educational administrator*
Knowles, John *author*
Mango-Hurdman, Christina Rose *psychiatric art therapist*

**Berkeley Heights**
Geusic, Joseph Edward *physicist*
Gottheimer, George Malcolm, Jr. *insurance executive, educator*
Klüver, Johan Wilhelm (Billy Klüver) *electrical engineer, writer*
Mac Rae, Alfred Urquhart *physicist, electrical engineer*
Older, Richard Samuel *elementary school music educator*
Rabiner, Lawrence Richard *electrical engineer*
Shaffer, Gail Dorothy *secondary education educator*

**Bernardsville**
Coheleach, Guy Joseph *artist*
Cooperman, Saul *foundation administrator*
DiDomenico, Mauro, Jr. *communication executive*
Dixon, Richard Wayne *retired communications company executive*
Dixon, Rosina Berry *physician, pharmaceutical development consultant*
Lazor, Patricia Ann *interior designer*
Spofford, Sally Hyslop *artist*
Wiedenmayer, Christopher M. *writing instrument manufacturer, distributor*

**Blackwood**
Sperduto, Leonard Anthony *mathematics eductor*

**Blairstown**
Bean, Bennett *artist*
Horn-Alsberge, Michele Maryann *school psychologist*

**Bloomfield**
Becker, Robert Clarence *clergyman*
Chagnon, Joseph V. *school system administrator*
Dohr, Donald R. *metallurgical engineer, researcher*
Hutcheon, Forbes Clifford Robert *engineer, company executive*

**Bloomingdale**
Wanamaker, Ellen Ponce *tax specialist*

**Bloomsbury**
Clymer, Jerry Alan *educational administrator*
Danjczek, William Emil *engineering supplies manufacturing executive*

**Bogota**
Condon, Francis Edward *retired chemistry educator*

**Boonton**
Bridges, Beryl Clarke *marketing executive*
DiGiovachino, John *special education educator*
Fuller, Ross Kennedy *chemist*

**Bordentown**
Blackson, Benjamin F(ranklin) *clinical social worker*

**Bound Brook**
Borah, Kripanath *pharmacist*
Gould, Donald Everett *retired chemical company executive*
Karol, Frederick John *industrial chemist*
Kish, Elissa Anne *educational administrator*
Marchishin, Daniel *construction executive*

**Branchville**
Johanson, Gregory John *psychotherapy trainer, minister*

**Brick**
Abel, Mark *dermatologist*
Rusoff, Irving Isadore *industrial food scientist, consultant*
Shortess, Edwin Steevin *marketing consultant*
Tivenan, Charles Patrick *lawyer*
Zalinsky, Sandra H. Orlofsky *school counselor*

**Bridgewater**
Albrethsen, Adrian Edysel *metallurgist, consultant*
Baldwin, Dorothy Leila *secondary school educator*
Bernson, Marcella Shelley *psychiatrist*
Colline, Marguerite Richnavsky *maternal, women's health and pediatrics nurse*
Conroy, Robert John *lawyer*
Cucco, Judith Elene *international marketing professional*
Freeman, Henry McCall *newspaper publisher*
Glesmann, Sylvia-Maria *artist*
Grey, Ruthann E. *pharmaceutical company executive*
Healey, Lynne Kover *editor, writer, broadcaster, educator*
Hillegass, Christine Ann *psychologist*
Hirsch, Paul J. *orthopedic surgeon, educator*
Hulse, Robert Douglas *high technology executive*
Iovine, Carmine P. *chemicals executive*
Kennedy, James Andrew *chemical company executive*
Mack, Robert William *secondary school educator*
Patton, Diana Lee Wilkoc *artist*
Pickett, Doyle Clay *employment and training counselor, consultant*
Schoppmann, Michael Joseph *lawyer*
Skidmore, James Albert, Jr. *management, computer technology and engineering services company executive*
Torrey, Henry Cutler *physicist*
Weingast, Marvin *laboratory executive*
Wieschenberg, Klaus *chemical company executive*

**Brigantine**
Carlson, Marsha George *performing company executive*
Kickish, Margaret Elizabeth *elementary education educator*

**Browns Mills**
Cha, Se Do *internist*
Lumia, Francis James *internist*
McNabb, Talmadge Ford *religious organization administrator, retired military chaplain*

**Budd Lake**
Cornish, Jeannette Carter *lawyer*
Havens, Edwin Wallace *manufacturing executive*
Lustig, Joanne *librarian*
Peck, Mira Paszko *lawyer*
Pollack, Jordan Ellis *pharmaceutical company executive*

**Burlington**
†Denbo, Alexander *retired bank executive*
Holmes-Baxter, Maureen Olivia *language arts educator*
Rowlette, Henry Allen, Jr. *social worker*

**Butler**
Klaas, Nicholas Paul *management and technical consultant*
Ward, Robert Allen, Jr. *advertising executive*
Wingert, Hannelore Christiane *real estate sales executive, chemical company executive*

**Caldwell**
Bentley, Alfred Young, Jr. *information technology and education consultant*
Chatlos, William Edward *management consultant*
Friedman, Richard I(rwin) *lawyer*
Jennings, Sister Vivien Ann *English language educator*
Kapusinski, Albert Thomas *economist, educator*
Simplicio, Joseph S.C. *education educator*
Stanton, George Basil, Jr. *engineering executive, chemical engineer*
Stevens, William Dollard *consulting mechanical engineer*
Werner, Patrice (Patricia Ann Werner) *college president*

**Califon**
Hannigan, Frank *sportswriter, television writer and commentator, golf course design consultant*
Rosen, Carol Mendes *artist*

**Camden**
Abbott, Ann Augustine *social worker, educator*
Ances, I. G(eorge) *obstetrician, gynecologist, educator*
Beck, David Paul *biochemist*
Brotman, Stanley Seymour *federal judge*
Camishion, Rudolph Carmen *physician*
Citron, Richard Ira *management consultant*
Coney, Stephné Reniá *education educator*
Edgerton, Brenda Evans *soup company executive*
Fairbanks, Russell Norman *law educator, university dean*
Gans, Samuel Myer *temporary employment service executive*
†Goldberg, Jack *hematologist*
Gordon, Walter Kelly *retired provost, English language educator*
Irenas, Joseph Eron *judge*
Johnson, David Willis *food products executive*
Kirk, James Robert *research development and quality assurance executive*
Lashman, Shelley Bortin *judge*
Laskin, Lee B. *judge, laywer, former state senator*
McHugh, James T. *bishop*
Pomorski, Stanislaw *lawyer, educator*
Rodriguez, Joseph H. *federal judge*
Showalter, English, Jr. *French language educator*
Sigler, Jay Adrian *political scientist, educator*
Simandle, Jerome B. *federal judge*
Stahl, Gary Edward *neonatologist*
Weeks, Sandra Kenney *healthcare facilitator*
Wellington, Judith Lynn *cultural organization administrator*

**Cape May**
Cadge, William Fleming *gallery owner, photographer*
Janosik, Edward Gabriel *retired political science educator*
Lassner, Franz George *educator*
Wilson, H(arold) Fred(erick) *chemist, research scientist*

**Cape May Court House**
Cohen, Daniel Edward *writer*
Cohen, Susan Lois *author*
Gronka, M(artin) Steven *educational association executive, film and television producer*

**Carlstadt**
Cooke, Edward Francis, Jr. *accountant*

**Carteret**
Goldberg, Arthur M. *gaming and fitness company executive, food products executive, lawyer*
Jemal, Lawrence *retail executive*

**Cedar Grove**
Brownstein, Alan P. *health foundation executive, consultant*
Carlozzi, Catherine Laurel *public relations, communications consultant, writer*
Martini, William J. *former congressman*

**Cedar Knolls**
†Dixon, Gerald Authur *aerospace manufacturing company executive*

**Chatham**
Bast, Ray Roger *retired utility company executive*
Glatt, Mitchell Steven *consumer products company executive*
Glover, Janet Briggs *artist*
Hurley, Allyson Kingsley *dentist*
Lax, Philip *land developer, space planner*
Lenz, Henry Paul *management consultant*
Manning, Frederick William *retired retail executive*
Merianos, John James *medicinal chemist*
Murphy, Joseph James *chiropractic physician*
Rockwood, Thomas Julian *management services executive, information technolgy consultant*

**Cherry Hill**
Adler, John Herbert *lawyer, state legislator*
Amsterdam, Jay D. *psychiatrist, educator*
Belin, Henry A., Jr. *bishop*
Brenner, Lynnette Mary *reading specialist, educator*
Bryan, Richard Arthur *special education educator*
Callaway, Ben Anderson *journalist*
Carter, Catherine Louise *elementary school educator*
Dunfee, Thomas Wylie *law educator*
Erving, Julius Winfield, II (Dr. J. Erving) *business executive, retired professional basketball player*
Gardner, Joel Robert *writer, historian*
Grado-Wolynies, Evelyn (Evelyn Wolynies) *clinical nurse specialist, educator*
Hayasi, Nisiki *physicist, business executive, inventor*
Holfeld, Donald Rae *railroad consultant*
Iglewicz, Raja *state agency administrator, researcher, industrial hygienist*
Israelsky, Roberta Schwartz *speech pathologist, audiologist*
Kahn, Sigmund Benham *retired internist and dean*
Keele, Lyndon Alan *electronic company executive*
Levin, Susan Bass *lawyer*
Marsh, Robert Harry *chemical company executive*
Melick, George Fleury *mechanical engineer, educator*
Myers, Daniel William, II *lawyer*
Newell, Eric James *financial planner, tax consultant, former insurance executive*
Olearchyk, Andrew *cardiothoracic surgeon, educator*
Rabil, Mitchell Joseph *lawyer*
Robinson, Mary Jo *pathologist*
Rose, Joel Alan *legal consultant*
Rudman, Solomon Kal *magazine publisher*
Sax, Robert Edward *food service equipment company executive*
Schelm, Roger Leonard *information systems specialist*
Teare, Bernice Adeline *elementary school educator, reading specialist*
Weinstein, Steven David *lawyer*
Werbitt, Warren *gastroenterologist, educator*

**Chester**
Gurian, Mal *telecommunications executive*
Maddalena, Lucille Ann *management executive*

**Cinnaminson**
Johnson, Victor Lawrence *banker*

**Clark**
Burtnick, Ronald *sales executive*
Kinley, David *physical therapist, acupuncturist*
Orlando, Joseph Michael *sales executive*

**Cliffside Park**
Ginos, James Zissis *retired research chemist*
Goldstein, Howard Bernard *investment banker, advertising and marketing executive*
Perhacs, Marylouise Helen *musician, educator*
Pushkarev, Boris S. *research foundation director, writer*

**Clifton**
Adelsberg, Harvey *hospital administrator*
Charsky, Thomas Robert *elementary education educator*
Epstein, William Eric *health care executive*
Feinstein, Miles Roger *lawyer*
Held, George Anthony *architect*
Kessler, Carolyn Joan *industrial and commercial real estate developer*
Kirrer, Ernest Douglas *physician*
Magnus, Frederick Samuel *investment banker*
McCoy, Linda Korteweg *media specialist*
Rigolo, Arthur Emil *architect*
Rodimer, Frank Joseph *bishop*

Silber, Judy G. dermatologist
Srinivasachari, Samavedam chemical engineer

### Clinton
Acerra, Michele (Mike Acerra) engineering and construction company executive
DeGhetto, Kenneth Anselm engineering and construction company executive
Hansen, Arthur Magne engineering and manufacturing executive
Kennedy, Harold Edward lawyer
Swift, Richard J. engineering company executive

### Closter
Hillman, Leon electrical engineer
Soroka, Cynthia Anne photographer, writer

### Collingswood
Mohrfeld, Richard Gentel heating oil distributing company executive

### Cologne
Hoffman, Maryhelen H. Paulick communications company executive

### Colts Neck
French, Charles Ferris, Jr. banker
Rode, Leif real estate personal computer consultant

### Columbus
Litman, Bernard electrical engineer, consultant

### Convent Station
Healy, Gwendoline Frances controller
Weber, Joseph H. communications company executive

### Cranbury
Bodin, Jerome I. pharmaceutical company executive, pharmaceutical chemist
Burke, Peter Arthur microbiologist, chemist
Copleman, Rosalyn Rosenberg volunteer
Cuthbert, Robert Allen pet products company executive
Daoust, Donald Roger pharmaceutical and toiletries company executive, microbiologist
Greenwald-Ward, Alice Marian museum consultant
Hochreiter, Joseph Christian, Jr. engineering company executive
Kemmerer, Peter Ream financial executive
Perhach, James Lawrence pharmaceutical company executive
Rector, Milton Gage social work educator, former association executive
Reichek, Morton Arthur retired magazine editor, writer
Schoenfeld, Theodore Mark industrial engineer
Sofia, R. D. pharmacologist
Sorensen, Henrik Vittrup electrical engineering educator
Yoseloff, Julien David publishing company executive
Yoseloff, Thomas publisher

### Cranford
Bardwil, Joseph Anthony investments consultant
Bodian, Nat G. publishing, marketing consultant, author, lecturer, lexicographer
Cleaver, William Pennington retired sugar refining company executive, consultant
Herz, Sylvia Beatrice clinical and community psychologist
Mullen, Edward K. paper company executive
Nasta, Marilyn Jean speech and language pathologist, consultant
Schink, Frank Edward electrical engineer

### Cresskill
Gardner, Richard Alan psychiatrist, writer
Smyth, Craig Hugh fine arts educator

### Dayton
Mencher, Stuart Alan sales and marketing executive

### Deal
Becker, Richard Stanley music publisher

### Delaware
Hill-Rosato, Jane Elizabeth elementary education educator

### Delran
Hartman, Mary Louise information services librarian

### Demarest
Ahr, Ernest Stephan business archive executive

### Denville
Breed, Ria anthropologist
Coes, Kent Day artist
Fisher, Sharon Mary musician
Greer, Robert Bruce, III orthopedic surgeon, educator
Kirna, Hans Christian lawyer, consultant
Minter, Jerry Burnett electronic component company executive, engineer
Price, Robert Edmunds civil engineer

### Dover
†Kassell, Paula Sally editor, publisher
Lichtig, Leo Kenneth health economist
Mc Donald, John Joseph electronics executive

### Dumont
Davidson, Grace Evelyn nursing educator, retired administrator

### Dunellen
Richmond, Ernest Leon research engineer, consultant

### East Brunswick
Burns, Barbara lawyer
Elias, Harry medical educator
Fisher, Lucille principal
Haupin, Elizabeth Carol retired secondary school educator
Johnson, Edward Elemuel psychologist, educator
Kabela, Frank, Jr. broadcast executive
Karmazin, Sharon Elyse library director
Marshall, Keith pharmaceutical consultant
Mooney, William Piatt actor

Muro, Roy Alfred retired media service corporation executive
Rosenberg, Norman surgeon
Wagman, Gerald Howard retired biochemist
Wheeler, Valerie A. Syslo credit analyst
Yttrehus, Rolv Berger composer, educator

### East Hanover
Davidson, Anne Stowell lawyer
Elam, Karen Morgan food company executive, consultant
Finkel, Marion Judith physician
Knight, Frank James pharmaceutical marketing professional
Nemecek, Georgina Marie molecular pharmacologist
Reiley, T. Phillip systems analyst, consultant
Salans, Lester Barry physician, scientist, educator
Tamburro, Peter James, Jr. social studies secondary school educator
Traina, Vincent Michael pharmaceutical company executive

### East Orange
†Carbajal, Michael boxer
Cunningham, Robert Marcus ophthalmologist
Fielo, Muriel Bryant interior designer, space engineer
†Gatti, Arturo professional boxer
Gibson, Althea retired professional tennis player, golfer, state official
†Hopkins, Bernard professional boxer
Howe, James Everett investment company executive
Husar, Walter Gene neurologist, neuroscientist, educator
†Johnson, Tom boxer
Jones Gregory, Patricia secondary art educator
Moese, Mark Douglas environmental consultant
†Norris, Terry professional boxer
†Pazienza, Vinny professional boxer
†Romero, Danny, Jr. boxer
Shea, Gerald Patrick engineering executive
†Trinidad, Felix professional boxer
Wolff, Derish Michael economist, company executive
Yoo, James H. radiation oncologist, nuclear medicine physician

### East Rutherford
Aufzien, Alan L. professional sports team executive
†Brodeur, Martin professional hockey player
Calipari, John collegiate basketball team coach
†Cohen, Jerry L. professional sports team executive
Gerstein, David Brown hardware manufacturing company executive, professional basketball team executive
Gilmour, Doug professional hockey player
Hampton, Rodney professional football player
Kempner, Michael W. public relations executive
Kluge, John Werner broadcasting and advertising executive
Lamoriello, Louis Anthony professional hockey team executive
Lemaire, Jacques professional hockey coach
†MacLean, John professional hockey player
Mann, Bernard (Bernie Mann) professional basketball team executive
Mara, Wellington T. professional football team executive
McMullen, John J. professional hockey team executive
Montross, Eric Scott professional basketball player
Nash, John N. professional basketball team executive
O'Bannon, Ed professional basketball player
Reed, Willis professional basketball team executive, former head coach
†Stevens, Scott professional hockey player
†Subotnick, Stuart food service executive
Wadler, Arnold L. lawyer
Young, George Bernard, Jr. professional football team executive

### Eastampton
Holloway, William Raymond, Jr. state official

### Eatontown
Dalton, John Joseph healthcare financial consultant
Furman, Samuel Elliott dentist
Granet, Kenneth M. internist
Orlando, Carl medical research and development executive
Van Winkle, William certified financial planner

### Edgewater
Lape, Robert Cable broadcast journalist

### Edison
Applebaum, Charles lawyer
Austad, Vigdis computer software company executive
Avery, James Stephen oil company executive
Behr, Marion Ray artist, author
Cangemi, Michael Paul accountant, financial executive, author
Carretta, Richard Louis beverage company executive
Cavanaugh, James Henry medical corporate executive, former government official
Comstock, Robert Ray journalism educator, newspaper editor
D'Agostino, Matthew Paul bakery executive
Ensor, Richard Joseph athletic conference commissioner, lawyer
Francis, Peter T. gas and oil industry executive
Hecht, William David accountant
Hunter, Michael publishing executive
Jacobey, John Arthur, III surgeon, educator
Johnson, Dewey, Jr. biochemist
Jones, James Thomas, Jr. tobacco company executive
Lavigne, Lawrence Neil lawyer
Levy, Joseph lawyer
Lijoi, Peter Bruno lawyer
Lo Surdo, Antonio physical chemist, educator
Maeroff, Gene I. academic administrator, journalist
Marash, Stanley Albert consulting company executive
Pruden, Ann Lorette chemical engineer, researcher
Rothenberg, Adam Leigh lawyer
Torchia, Karin G. sports association administrator

### Egg Harbor Township
Blee, Francis J. municipal official

### Elizabeth
Beglin, Edward W., Jr. judge
Berger, Harold Richard physician
Blecher, Carol Stein oncology clinical nurse specialist
Gellert, George Geza food importing company executive

Gutfreund, Donald E. internist, hematologist, oncologist
Leonett, Anthony Arthur banker
Rocha, Pedro, Jr. academic administrator
†Rosenstein, Neil surgeon, genealogical researcher
Willis, Ben writer, artist

### Elmwood Park
Mangano, Louis lawyer
Nadzick, Judith Ann accountant
Semeraro, Michael Archangel, Jr. civil engineer
Wygod, Martin J. pharmaceuticals executive

### Emerson
Cheslik, Francis Edward management consultant

### Englewood
Anuszkiewicz, Richard Joseph artist
Beer, Jeanette Mary Scott foreign language educator
Casarella, Edmond sculptor, printmaker
Deresiewicz, Herbert mechanical engineering educator
Downes, John writer, editor
Farrell, Patricia Ann psychologist, educator
Friedman, Emanuel publishing company executive
Grom, Bogdan sculptor, painter, illustrator
Hertzberg, Arthur rabbi, educator
Khouri, Antoun church administrator
Lapidus, Arnold mathematician
Mc Mullan, Dorothy nurse educator
Miles, Virginia (Mrs. Fred C. Miles) marketing consultant
Neis, Arnold Hayward pharmaceutical company executive
Orlando, George (Joseph) union executive
Rawl, Arthur Julian (Lord of Cursons) retail executive, accountant, consultant, author
Saliba, Philip E. archbishop
Schmidt, Ronald Hans architect
Schwartz, Howard Alan periodontist
Wuhl, Charles Michael psychiatrist
Zwilich, Ellen Taaffe composer

### Englewood Cliffs
Brandreth, John Breckenridge, II chemical importer
Guiher, James Morford, Jr. publisher
Haltiwanger, Robert Sidney, Jr. book publishing executive
Saible, Stephanie magazine editor
Scott, John William food processing executive
Shoemate, Charles Richard food company executive
Shrem, Charles Joseph metals corporation executive
Solomon, Edward David chain store executive
Storms, Clifford Beekman lawyer
Vane, Dena magazine editor-in-chief

### Englishtown
Rudins, Leonids (Lee Rudins) retired chemical company executive, financial executive

### Essex Fells
Boardman, Harold Frederick, Jr. lawyer, corporate executive

### Ewing
D'Antonio, Cynthia Maria sales executive
Jenson, Pauline Marie speech and hearing educator

### Fair Haven
Labrecque, Theodore Joseph lawyer
McKissock, David Lee retired manufacturing company executive

### Fair Lawn
Aitchison, Suann elementary school educator
Hayden, Neil Steven communications company executive
Infantino, Salvatore physician
Mazel, Joseph Lucas publications consultant
Parker, Adrienne Natalie art educator, art historian
Wallace, Mary Monahan elementary and secondary schools educator

### Fairfield
Byer, Theodore Scott accountant
Edwards, William Pearson retail company executive
Finn, James Francis consulting engineering executive
Giambalvo, Vincent manufacturing company executive
†Hower, Paul H. hotel executive
Meilan, Celia food products executive
Stein, Robert Alan electronics company executive

### Fairview
Anton, Harvey textile company executive
Ciccone, Joseph Lee criminal justice educator

### Fanwood
Whitaker, Joel publisher

### Far Hills
Barnum, William Douglas communications company executive
Fay, David B. sports association executive
Holt, Jonathan Turner public relations executive
Laing, Beverly Ann sports administrator
McCall, David Warren retired chemistry research director, consultant

### Farmingdale
Martin, Robert Francis roof maintenance systems executive
Schluter, Peter Mueller electronics company executive
Smith, Sibley Judson, Jr. historic site administrator

### Flanders
Huang, Jacob Chen-ya physician

### Flemington
Bieri, Barbara Normile systems analyst, consultant
Katcher, Avrum L. pediatrician
Kettler, Carl Frederick airline executive
Lance, Leonard assemblyman
Miller, Louis H. lawyer
Nielsen, Lynn Carol lawyer, educational consultant
Roth, Lee B(ritton) lawyer
Salamon, Renay real estate broker
Slovikowski, Gerald Jude manufacturing company executive

### Florham Park
Atkins, Richard Bart film, television producer
Bhagat, Phiroz Maneck mechanical engineer
Bossen, Wendell John insurance company executive
Chase, Eric Lewis lawyer
Clayton, William L. investment banking executive
Eidt, Clarence Martin, Jr. research and development executive
Erickson, Charles Edward insurance company executive
Hardin, William Downer retired lawyer
Kovach, Andrew Louis human resources executive
Laulicht, Murray Jack lawyer
Lovell, Robert Marlow, Jr. retired investment company executive
Marshall, Philips Williamson insurance agency executive
Mott, Vincent Valmon publisher, author
Naimark, George Modell marketing and management consultant
Oths, Richard Philip health systems administrator
Sloane, Neil James Alexander mathematician, researcher
Smith, Robert William former insurance company executive, lawyer
Sniffen, Michael Joseph hospital administrator
Sperber, Martin pharmaceutical company executive, pharmacist
Stanton, Patrick Michael lawyer
Whitley, Arthur Francis retired international consulting company executive, engineer, lawyer

### Fords
Blond, Stuart Richard newsletter editor
Kaufman, Alex chemicals executive

### Forked River
Novak, Dennis E. family practice physician

### Fort Lee
Abut, Charles C. lawyer
Chessler, Richard Kenneth gastroenterologist, endoscopist
Cohen, Judith Lynne healthcare administrator
Cox, Melvin Monroe lawyer
Fischel, Daniel Norman publishing consultant
Forson, Norman Ray controller
Gharib, Susie television newscaster
Houston, Whitney vocalist, recording artist
Kadish, Lori Gail clinical psychologist
Kiriakopoulos, George Constantine dentist
Lippman, William Jennings investment company executive
Locke, Virginia Otis freelance writer, editor
McCullough, Kevin news anchor, correspondent
Schiessler, Robert Walter retired chemical and oil company executive
Screpetis, Dennis nuclear engineer, consultant
Seitel, Fraser Paul public relations executive
Sugarman, Alan William educational administrator
Vignolo, Biagio Nickolas, Jr. chemical company executive
Weitzer, Bernard telecommunications executive
Welfeld, Joseph Alan healthcare consultant
Winkler, Joseph Conrad former recreational products manufacturing executive

### Fort Monmouth
Ignoffo, Matthew Frederick English language educator, writer, counselor
Kalwinsky, Charles Knowlton government official
Leciston, David John computer scientist
Perlman, Barry Stuart electrical engineering executive, researcher
Schwering, Felix Karl electronics engineer, researcher
Thornton, Clarence Gould electronics engineering executive

### Franklin Lakes
Castellini, Clateo medical products manufacturing executive
Friedman, Martin Burton chemical company executive
Galiardo, John William lawyer
Ginsberg, Barry Howard physician, researcher
Hegelmann, Julius retired pharmacy educator
Howe, Wesley Jackson medical supplies company executive
Neglia, John Peter chemical engineer, environmental scientist
Throdahl, Mark Crandall medical technology company executive

### Franklin Park
Perry, Arthur William plastic surgeon

### Franklinville
DiGregory, Nicholas A. secondary educator, coach

### Freehold
Fisher, Clarkson Sherman, Jr. judge
Flynn, Pamela artist, educator
Foster, Eric H., Jr. retail executive
Hooper, John David career military officer
Laden, Karl toiletries company executive
Schockaert, Barbara Ann operations executive
Schwartz, Perry Lester information systems engineer, consultant
Shapiro, Michael supermarket corporate officer
Stirrat, William Albert electronics engineer
Topham, Sally Jane ballet educator

### Garfield
Nickles, I. MacArthur librarian

### Gladstone
Detwiler, Peter Mead investment banker
†Standish, Robert C. professional sports team executive

### Glassboro
Fails, Donna Gail mental health services professional
Gephardt, Donald Louis university official
James, Herman Delano college administrator
Letki, Arleen secondary school educator
Marcus, Laurence Richard education leadership and policy educator
Martin, Marilyn Joan library director
Stone, Don Charles computer science educator

### Glen Gardner
Yates, Michael Francis management consultant

GEOGRAPHIC INDEX 4931 NEW JERSEY


**Glen Ridge**
Agnew, Peter Tomlin *employee benefit consultant*
Bracken, Eddie (Edward Vincent) *actor, director, writer, singer, artist*
Clemente, Celestino *physician, surgeon*
McGovern, Thomas Aquinas *retired utility executive*
Pendley, Donald Lee *association executive*
Szamek, Pierre Ervin *anthropologist, researcher*

**Glen Rock**
Fine, Seymour Howard *marketing educator, lecturer, author, consultant*
Harper, Pamela Solvith *management consultant*
Lewis, Donald Emerson *banker*
Mc Elrath, Richard Elsworth *retired insurance company executive*
Riggs, Gina Ginsberg *educational association administrator*

**Green Brook**
Elias, Donald Francis *environmental consultant*

**Green Village**
Castenschiold, René *engineering company executive, author, consultant*
Roper, William Lee *physician, health care executive*

**Guttenberg**
Pesin, Ella Michele *journalist, public relations professional*
Pozniakoff, Rita Oppenheim *education software consultant*

**Hackensack**
Ahearn, James *newspaper columnist*
Baker, Andrew Hartill *clinical laboratory executive*
Blomquist, David Wels *journalist*
Borg, Malcolm Austin *communications company executive*
Carra, Andrew Joseph *advertising executive*
Cicchelli, Joseph Vincent *secondary education educator*
Daut, Eleanor Gilmore *vocational education educator*
De Groote, Robert David *general and vascular surgeon*
Duques, Ric *information services executive*
Duus, Gordon Cochran *lawyer*
Ferguson, John Patrick *medical center executive*
Gross, Peter Alan *epidemiologist, researcher*
Haworth, Gregory Robert *lawyer*
Kestin, Howard H. *judge*
Margulies, James Howard *editorial cartoonist*
Mavrovic, Ivo *chemical engineer*
Mehta, Jay *financial executive*
Michel, Robert Charles *retired engineering company executive*
Nemets, Boris Lvovich *programmer*
Pennington, William Mark *sportswriter*
Pollinger, William Joshua *lawyer*
Riegel, Norman *physician*
Spackman, Thomas James *radiologist*
Stein, Gary S. *state supreme court associate justice*
Timmins, Michael Joseph *communications services company executive*
Waixel, Vivian *journalist*
Yagoda, Harry Nathan *system engineering executive*
Zimmerman, Marlin U., Jr. *chemical engineer*

**Hackettstown**
DeAngelis, Margaret Scalza *publishing executive*
Kobert, Joel A. *lawyer*
Mulligan, Elinor Patterson *lawyer*
Passantino, Benjamin Arthur *marketing executive*

**Haddon Heights**
Gwiazda, Stanley John *university dean*
Luste, Joseph Francis, Jr. *land use, environmental transportation and planning specialist*

**Haddonfield**
Bauer, Raymond Gale *sales professional*
Capelli, John Placido *nephrologist*
Carter, Joan Pauline *investment company executive*
Cheney, Daniel Lavern *retired magazine publisher*
Cheney, Eleanora Louise *retired secondary education educator*
Henry, Ragan A. *lawyer, broadcaster*
Heuisler, Charles William *lawyer*
Iavicoli, Mario Anthony *lawyer*
Lee, Young Bin *psychiatrist, neurologist*
Siskin, Edward Joseph *engineering and construction company executive*
Suflas, Steven William *lawyer*
White, Warren Wurtele *retired retailing executive*

**Hainesport**
Sylk, Leonard Allen *housing company executive, real estate developer*

**Hamburg**
Buist, Richardson *corporate executive, retired banker*

**Hamilton**
Kane, Michael Joel *physician*

**Hammonton**
Levitt, Gerald Steven *natural gas company executive*
Pellegrino, Peter *surgeon*
Proll, George Simon *psychologist*
Stephanick, Carol Ann *dentist, consultant*

**Harrington Park**
Rizzi, Deborah L. *public relations professional*

**Haworth**
Biesel, Diane Jane *librarian*
Stokvis, Jack Raphael *urban planner, entrepreneur computer consultnt and developer, government agency administrator*

**Hawthorne**
Cole, Leonard Aaron *political scientist, dentist*
Lozito, Deborah Ann *osteopathic internist*

**Hazlet**
Miller, Duane King *health and beauty care company executive*
Morrison, James Frederick *management consultant*

**Hewitt**
Selwyn, Donald *engineering administrator, researcher, inventor, educator*

**Highland Park**
Alman, Emily Arnow *lawyer, sociologist*
Broggi, Barbara Ann *elementary education educator, staff developer*
Brudner, Harvey Jerome *physicist*
Collier, Albert, III *school system administrator*
Coughlin, Caroline Mary *library consultant, educator*
Feigenbaum, Abraham Samuel *nutritional biochemist*
Michaels, Jennifer Alman *lawyer*
Pane, Remigio Ugo *Romance languages educator*

**Highlands**
Hansen, Christian Andreas, Jr. *plastics and chemical company executive*

**Hightstown**
Brodman, Estelle *librarian, retired educator*
Bronner, William Roche *lawyer*
Di Carlo, Lawrence *analytical research chemist, manager*
Fitch, Lyle Craig *economist, administrator*
Frank, Betty Pope *editor*
Hart, Patricia A. *public health officer*
Howard, Barbara Sue Mesner *artist*
Jagow, Charles Herman *lawyer, finance consultant*
Raichle, Elaine Lucas *retired art educator*

**Hillsdale**
Copeland, Lois Jacqueline (Mrs. Richard A. Sperling) *physician*

**Hillside**
Fox, Sheldon *retired radiologist, medical educator*

**Ho Ho Kus**
Van Slooten, Ronald Henry Joseph *dentist*

**Hoboken**
Abel, Robert Berger *science administrator*
Biesenberger, Joseph A. *chemical engineer*
Boesch, Francis Theodore *electrical engineer, educator*
Bonsal, Richard Irving *textile marketing executive*
Bose, Ajay Kumar *chemistry educator*
Bruno, Michael Stephen *ocean engineering educator, researcher*
Buckman, Thomas Richard *foundation executive, educator*
Donskoy, Dimitri Michailovitch *physicist, researcher, educator*
Fajans, Jack *physics educator*
Griskey, Richard George *chemical engineering educator*
Jurkat, Martin Peter *management educator*
Mankin, Robert Stephen *financial executive*
Mintz, Kenneth Andrew *librarian*
Regazzi, John James, III *publishing executive*
Rose, Roslyn *artist*
Savitsky, Daniel *engineer, educator*
Schmidt, George *physicist*
Sgaramella, Peter *chemical products executive, technical consultant*
Sisto, Fernando *mechanical engineering educator*
Swern, Frederic Lee *engineering educator*
Talimcioglu, Nazmi Mete *civil and environmental engineer, educator*
Widdicombe, Richard Palmer *librarian*

**Holmdel**
Abate, John E. *electrical and electronic engineer, communications consultant*
Ayub, Yacub *financial consultant*
Boyd, Gary Delane *electro-optical engineer, researcher*
Burrus, Charles Andrew, Jr. *research physicist*
Erfani, Shervin *electrical engineer, educator, scientist*
Gordon, James Power *optics scientist*
Haskell, Barry Geoffry *communications company research administrator*
Heirman, Donald Nestor *telecommunications engineering company manager*
Hudson, Wendy Joy *software manager*
Kogelnik, Herwig Werner *electronics company executive*
Lang, Howard Lawrence *electrical engineer*
Linker, Kerrie Lynn *systems engineer*
Lundgren, Carl William, Jr. *physicist*
Meadors, Howard Clarence, Jr. *electrical engineer*
Meyer, Robert Alan *insurance company executive*
Mollenauer, Linn Frederick *physicist*
Opie, William Robert *retired metallurgical engineer*
Orost, Joseph Martin *internet applications architect*
Ross, Ian Munro *electrical engineer*
Schmidt, Barnet Michael *communications and electronic engineer*
Slovik, Sandra Lee *art educator*
Stolen, Rogers Hall *optics scientist*
Tambaro, Marie Grace *health specialist, nursing educator*
Tien, Ping King *electronics engineer*
Wyndrum, Ralph W., Jr. *communications company executive*

**Hopatcong**
Cullen, Lawrence David *elementary education educator*
Reese, Harry Edwin, Jr. *electronics executive*
Wolahan, Caryle Goldsack *nursing educator*

**Hopewell**
Halpern, Daniel *poet, editor, educator*

**Irvington**
McConnell, Lorelei Catherine *library director*
Paden, Harry *municipal official*

**Iselin**
Clarke, David H. *industrial products executive*
Cruz, Nelson Xavier *healthcare executive*
Dornbusch, Arthur A., II *lawyer*
Garfinkel, Harmon Mark *specialty chemicals company executive*
Hempstead, George H., III *lawyer, diversified company executive*
Krebs, Gary Michael *editor, author*
LaTorre, L. Donald *chemical company executive*
Smith, Orin Robert *chemical company executive*
Tice, George A(ndrew) *photographer*
Wolynic, Edward Thomas *specialty chemicals technology executive*

**Jackson**
Hagberg, Carl Thomas *financial executive*
Hunter, Lynn *publications company executive*

**Jamesburg**
Chase, Aurin Moody, Jr. *biology educator*
Denton, John Joseph *retired pharmaceutical company executive*
Finch, Jeremiah Stanton *English language educator*
Karol, Reuben Hirsh *civil engineer, sculptor*
Maxwell, Bryce *engineer,educator*
Miller, Theodore Robert *surgeon, educator*
Penny, Josephine B. *retired banker*
Zeigen, Spencer Steven *architect*

**Jersey City**
Alfano, Michael Charles *pharmaceutical company executive*
Callum, Myles *magazine editor, writer*
Chatterjee, Amit *structural engineer*
Christensen, Walter Frederick, Jr. *information, telecommunications and financial systems specialist*
Connors, Richard F. *judge*
D'Amico, Thomas F. *economist, educator*
Degatano, Anthony Thomas *educational association administrator*
Demos, Nicholas John *physician, surgeon, researcher*
Dubin, Michael *financial services executive*
Feder, Arthur A. *lawyer*
Fields, Walter Lee, Jr. *public affairs executive, journalist*
Fortune, Robert Russell *financial consultant*
Foster, Delores Jackson *elementary school principal*
Gibson, William Francis *investment banking executive*
Giuffra, Lawrence John *hospital administrator, medical educator*
Goldberg, Arthur Abba *merchant banker, financial advisor*
Gurevich, Grigory *visual artist, educator*
Hakeem, Muhammad Abdul *artist, educator*
Ingrassia, Paul Joseph *publishing executive*
Jackson, Jimmy Joe *litigation consultant*
Katz, Colleen *editor in chief*
Koster, Emlyn Howard *geologist, educator*
Lane, Ted *literacy education educator*
Levine, Richard James *publishing executive*
Makar, Boshra Halim *mathematics educator*
Moore-Szepesy, Mariann Lydia *health care executive*
Mortensen, Eugene Phillips *hospital administrator*
Nakhla, Atif Mounir *scientist, biochemist*
Nash, Lee J. *banker*
Niemiec, Edward Walter *professional association executive*
Patterson, Grace Limerick *library director*
Pietrini, Andrew Gabriel *automotive aftermarket executive*
Pietruska, Stanley Robert *lawyer, jury consultant*
Poiani, Eileen Louise *mathematics educator, college administrator, higher education planner*
Sanders, Franklin D. *insurance company executive*
Signorile, Vincent Anthony *lawyer*
Smith, James Frederick *securities executive*
Stencer, Mark Joseph *academic administrator, consultant*
Wagner, Douglas Walker Ellyson *journal editor*
Williams, Alan Davison *publishing company executive*
Zuckerberg, David Alan *pharmaceutical company executive*

**Johnsonburg**
Cioffi, Eugene Edward, III *educational administrator*

**Kearny**
Meissner, Dorothy Theresa *reading specialist*

**Keasbey**
Hari, Kenneth Stephen *painter, sculptor, writer*

**Kendall Park**
Berger, Richard Stanton *dermatologist*
Goldberg, Bertram J. *social agency administrator*
Hershenov, Bernard Zion *electronics research and development company executive*

**Kenilworth**
Cayen, Mitchell Ness *biochemist*
Ganguly, Ashit Kumar *organic chemist*
Hoffman, John Fletcher *lawyer*
Scott, Mary Celine *pharmacologist*

**Keyport**
Graupe-Pillard, Grace *artist, educator*
Warren, Craig Bishop *flavor and fragrance company executive, researcher*

**Kinnelon**
Haller, Charles Edward *engineering consultant*
Kossl, Thomas Leonard *lawyer*
Preston, Andrew Joseph *pharmacist, drug company executive*
Richardson, Irene M. *health facility administrator*
Richardson, Joseph Blancet *former biology educator, educational facilities planning consultant*

**Lafayette**
Mitchell, Peter William *addictions counselor*

**Lake Hiawatha**
Falconer, Thomas Robert *paralegal*

**Lake Hopatcong**
Dowling, Robert Murray *oil company executive*

**Lakewood**
Bowers, John Zimmerman *physician, educator*
Houle, Joseph E. *mathematics educator*
Hurlbut, Terry Allison *pathologist*
Levovitz, Pesach Zechariah *rabbi*
Rodgers, Dianna Sue *private school educator*
Shawl, S. Nicole *hypnobehavioral scientist*
Sloyan, Sister Stephanie *mathematics educator*
Taylor, Robert M. *minister*
Williams, Barbara Anne *college president*

**Laurel Springs**
Cleveland, Susan Elizabeth *library administrator, researcher*
Ferreri, Vito Richard *lawyer*

**Lawrenceville**
Coleman, Wade Hampton, III *management consultant, mechanical engineer, former banker*
Cox, Teri P. *public relations executive*
Farrar, Donald Keith *financial executive*
Gideon, Richard Walter *broadcasting management consultant*
Griffith, Barbara E. *social worker, political activist*
Hunt, Wayne Robert, Sr. *state government official*
Kihn, Harry *electronics engineer, manufacturing company executive*
Leonard, Patricia Louise *education educator, consultant*
Megna, Jerome Francis *university dean*
Moser, Rosemarie Scolaro *psychologist*
O'Brien, James Jerome *construction management consultant*
Pouleur, Hubert Gustave *cardiologist*
Rudy, James Francis Xavier *lawyer*
Stehle, Edward Raymond *secondary education educator, school system administrator*
Wiater, Teresa Veronica *writer*

**Lebanon**
Goulazian, Peter Robert *retired broadcasting executive*
O'Neill, Elizabeth Sterling *trade association administrator*
Suchodolski, Ronald Eugene *publishing company executive*

**Ledgewood**
Smith, Sally Elaine Beckley *veterinary technician*

**Leonia**
Armstrong, Edward Bradford, Jr. *oral and maxillofacial surgeon, educator*
Deutsch, Nina *pianist*
Fjordbotten, Alf Lee *minister*
Penin, Linda Margaret *elementary education educator*

**Liberty Corner**
Apruzzese, Vincent John *lawyer*
Bergeron, Robert Francis, Jr. (Terry Bergeron) *software engineer*
Edwards, Robert Nelson *lawyer*
Rothenberger, Jack Renninger *clergyman*

**Lincroft**
Jones, Floresta D. *English educator*
Keenan, Robert Anthony *financial services company executive, educator, consultant*
Pollock, William John *secondary school administrator*
Sullivan, Brother Jeremiah Stephen *former college president*

**Linden**
Banda, Geraldine Marie *chiropractic physician*
Bedrick, Bernice *retired science educator, consultant*
Covino, Charles Peter *metal products company executive*
Foege, Rose Ann Scudiero *human resources professional*
Tamarelli, Alan Wayne *chemical company executive*

**Linwood**
Cohen, Diana Louise *mental health administrator, psychology, educator, psychotherapist*
McCormick, Robert Matthew, III *newspaper executive*

**Little Falls**
Armellino, Michael Ralph *retired asset management executive*
Draper, Daniel Clay *lawyer*
Glasser, Lynn Schreiber *publisher*
Glasser, Stephen Andrew *publishing executive, lawyer*
†Maurer, Theodore A. *advertising executive*
Regan-Geraci, Theresa Elizabeth *learning disability educator, consultant*

**Little Silver**
Finch, Rogers Burton *association management consultant*
Gagnebin, Albert Paul *retired mining executive*
Sizer, Rebecca Rudd *performing arts educator, arts coordinator*
Turbidy, John Berry *investor, management consultant*

**Livingston**
Batshaw, Marilyn Seidner *educational administrator*
Bertenshaw, Bobbi Cherrelle *producer*
Brenner, Betty Esther Bilgray *social worker*
Caballes, Romeo Lopez *pathologist, bone tumor researcher*
Cohn, Joseph David *surgeon*
Daman, Ernest Ludwig *mechanical engineer*
Eisenstein, Theodore Donald *pediatrician*
Francavilla, Barbara Jean *human services administrator*
Friedman, Merton Hirsch *retired psychologist, educator*
Grant, Daniel Gordon *information services company executive*
Klein, Peter Martin *lawyer, retired transportation company executive*
Krieger, Abbott Joel *neurosurgeon*
Lieberman, Lester Zane *engineering company executive*
Machlin, Lawrence J. *nutritionist, biochemist, educator*
Mandelbaum, Howard Arnold *marketing and management consultant*
Maron, Arthur *pediatrician, medical administrator*
Pantages, Louis James *lawyer*
Rickert, Robert Richard *pathologist, educator*
Rinsky, Joel Charles *lawyer*
Rommer, James Andrew *physician*
Saffer, Amy Beth *foreign language educator*
Samojlik, Eugeniusz *medical educator, retired researcher*
Schlesinger, Stephen Lyons *horticulturist*
Sikora, Barbara Jean *library director*
Watson, Stephen Allison, III *lawyer*

**Locust**
Freeman, David Forgan *retired foundation executive*

**Lodi**
Force, Herman Edgar *psychologist*
Karetzky, Joanne Louise *librarian*
Karetzky, Stephen *library director, educator, researcher*

**Long Branch**
Barnett, Lester Alfred *surgeon*
Fox, Howard Alan *physician, medical educator*
Kristan, Ronald Wayne *physician, consultant*
Lagowski, Barbara Jean *writer, book editor*
Makhija, Mohan *nuclear medicine physician*
Pachman, Frederic Charles *library director*
Poch, Herbert Edward *pediatrician, educator*
Stamaty, Clara Gee Kastner *artist*

**Long Valley**
Collins, Kathleen *writer*

**Lyndhurst**
Bunda, Stephen Myron *political advisor, consultant, lawyer, classical philosopher*
DeBellis, Francine Darnel *elementary education educator*
Lasky, David *lawyer, corporate executive*
Ridenour, James Franklin *fund raising consultant*
Sieger, Charles *librarian*

**Lyons**
Zimering, Mark Bernard *endocrinologist, researcher*

**Madison**
Byrd, Stephen Fred *human resource consultant*
Calligan, William Dennis *retired life insurance company executive*
Campbell, William Cecil *biologist*
Connors, Joseph Conlin *lawyer*
Ellenbogen, Leon *nutritionist, pharmaceutical company executive*
Fogarty, John Thomas *lawyer*
George, David J. *toxicologist, pharmacologist*
Gibson, William Ford *author*
Goodman, Michael B(arry) *communications educator*
Hassan, Frederich *pharmaceutical executive*
Johnson, William Joseph *stockbroker*
Knox, John, Jr. *philosopher, educator*
†Kogan, Richard Jay *pharmaceutical company executive*
Leak, Margaret Elizabeth *insurance company executive*
Luciano, Robert Peter *pharmaceutical company executive*
Markowski, John Joseph *human resources executive*
Marquis, Harriet Hill *social worker*
McCulloch, James Callahan *manufacturing company executive*
Mc Mullen, Edwin Wallace, Jr. *English language educator*
Mitsis, George *English language and literature educator*
Monte, Bonnie J. *performing company executive, director, educator*
O'Brien, Mary Devon *communications executive, consultant*
Shelby, Bryan Rohrer *information systems consultant*
Siegel, George Henry *international business development consultant*
Stafford, John Rogers *pharmaceutical and household products company executive*
Tramutola, Joseph Louis *lawyer, educator*
Udenfriend, Sidney *biochemist*
Yrigoyen, Charles, Jr. *church denomination executive*

**Magnolia**
Holt, James Theodore *nursing educator*

**Mahwah**
Borowitz, Grace Burchman *chemistry educator, researcher*
Bram, Leon Leonard *publishing company executive*
Bryan, Thomas Lynn *lawyer, educator*
Eiger, Richard William *publisher*
Inserra, Lawrence R. *retail executive*
King, Lis Sonder *public relations executive, writer*
Korb, Miriam Meyers *computer analyst*
Padovano, Anthony Thomas *theologian, educator*
Scott, Robert Allyn *academic administrator*
Weinberg, Sydney Stahl *historian*

**Manahawkin**
Aurner, Robert Ray, II *oil company, auto diagnostic, restaurant franchise and company development executive*
Logan, Ralph Andre *physicist*
Privetera, Lora Marie *lawyer*
Scully, Paula Constance *journalist*

**Manalapan**
Harrison-Johnson, Yvonne Elois *pharmacologist*
Hurley, Anne Irène *medical illustrator*
Stone, Fred Michael *lawyer*

**Manasquan**
Topilow, Arthur Alan *internist*

**Mantoloking**
Mehta, Narinder Kumar *marketing executive*

**Maple Shade**
Martin, Darris Lee *quality assurance executive*

**Maplewood**
Dennis, Anita Anna *journalist*
Joseph, Susan B. *lawyer*
Kusnetz, Hyman *investment advisor*
Leeds, Norma S. *chemistry educator*
Lev, Alexander Shulim *mechanical engineer*
MacWhorter, Robert Bruce *retired lawyer*
Newmark, Harold Leon *biochemist*
Safian, Gail Robyn *public relations executive*
Shuttleworth, Anne Margaret *psychiatrist*
Tatyrek, Alfred Frank *consultant, materials/environmental engineer, analytical/research chemist*
Weston, Randy (Randolph Edward Weston) *pianist, composer*

**Margate City**
Kennedy, Berenice Connor (Mrs. Jefferson Kennedy, Jr.) *magazine executive, writer, consultant*
Videll, Jared Steven *cardiologist*

**Marlboro**
Friedman, Howard Martin *financial executive*
Leveson, Irving Frederick *economist*

**Marlton**
Cullen, Mary Lynne *artist*
Farwell, Nancy Larraine *public relations executive*
Forbes, Gordon Maxwell *sports journalist, commentator*
Hayes, Michele Thelma *insurance professional*
Klein, Anne Sceia *public relations executive*
Klein, Gerhart Leopold *public relations executive*
Mann, Louis Eugene *financial planner*
Misiorek, Mary Madelyn *social worker*
Singh, Krishna Pal *mechanical engineer*
Zurick, Jack *electrical engineer*

**Marmora**
Camp, Barbara Ann *municipal government official*

**Matawan**
Klein, George D. *geologist, executive*
Rodgers, John Joseph, III *school administrator*

**Mays Landing**
Pizzuto, Debra Kay *secondary school mathematics educator*

**Mc Afee**
Fogel, Richard *lawyer*

**Medford**
Andres, Kenneth G., Jr. *lawyer*
Cerulli, Patricia Ann *secondary school educator*
Dunn, Roy J. *landscape architect*
Galbraith, Frances Lynn *educational administrator*
Hogan, Thomas Harlan *publisher*
Katzell, Raymond A. *psychologist, educator*
Kesty, Robert Edward *chemical manufacturing company executive*
Wallis, Robert Ray *psychologist, entrepreneur*

**Mendham**
Chatfield, Mary Van Abshoven *librarian*
Desjardins, Raoul *medical association administrator, financial consultant*
Kaprelian, Edward K. *mechanical engineer, physicist*
Kirby, Allan Price, Jr. *investment company executive*
Lunt, Harry Edward *metallurgist, consultant*
Posunko, Barbara *retired elementary education educator*
Posunko, Linda Mary *retired elementary education educator*
Shrader, William Keating *clinical psychologist, consultant*
Winters, Robert W. *medical educator, pediatrician*

**Mercerville**
Pitynski, Andrzej Piotr *sculptor*

**Metuchen**
Brause, Fred S., Jr. *lawyer*
Daub, Albert Walter *publishing executive*
Hughes, Edward T. *bishop*
Rakov, Barbara Streem *marketing executive*

**Middlesex**
Colanduoni, Bernadette Louise *school nurse*

**Middletown**
Anania, William Christian *podiatrist*
Meyler, William Anthony *financial executive*
O'Neill, Eugene Francis *communications engineer*
Roesner, Peter Lowell *manufacturing company executive*
Shields, Patricia Lynn *educational broker, consultant*

**Midland Park**
Koster, John Peter, Jr. *journalist, author*
Rosin, Henry David *physician*

**Milford**
Carter, Clarence Holbrook *artist*

**Millburn**
Corwin, Andrew David *physician*
Diamond, Richard Scott *lawyer*
Kuttner, Bernard A. *lawyer*
Schiavello, Bruno *mechanical engineer*
Tinning, Herbert Peter *association executive*

**Millington**
Donaldson, John Cecil, Jr. *consumer products company executive*

**Milltown**
Bradley, Edward William *sports foundation executive*
Holland, Joseph John *financial manager*

**Millville**
De Bevoise, Lee Raymond *editor, nurse, writer, photographer*

**Mine Hill**
Nadeau, Michael Joseph *college service assistant*

**Monmouth Beach**
Herbert, LeRoy James *retired accounting firm executive*

**Monmouth Junction**
Ellerbusch, Fred *environmental engineer*
Lawton, Deborah Simmons *educational media specialist*
Yun, Samuel *minister, educator*

**Montclair**
Alexander, Fernande Gardner *writer, photographer*
Aronson, David *chemical and mechanical engineer*
Beerman, Miriam *artist, educator*
Bolden, Theodore Edward *denist, educator, dental research consultant*
Brown, Geraldine Reed *lawyer, consulting executive*
Brownrigg, Walter Grant *cartoonist, corporate executive*
Campbell, Stewart Fred *foundation executive*
Clech, Jean Paul Marie *mechanical engineer*
Dubrow, Marsha Ann *high technology company executive, composer*
Eager, George Sidney, Jr. *electrical engineer, business executive*
Egan, Patricia Jane *former university director of development, writer*
Fannin, Caroline Mather *library consultant*
Fleming, Thomas Crawley *physician, medical director, former editor*
Gogick, Kathleen Christine *magazine editor, publisher*
Hutchins, Carleen Maley *acoustical engineer, violin maker, consultant*
Jacoby, Tamar *journalist, author*
Jones, Rees Lee *golf course architect*
Kidde, John Lyon *investment manager*
Lucenko, Leonard Konstantyn *sport, recreation management, and safety educator, coach, consultant*
Mason, Lucile Gertrude *fundraiser, consultant*
Mayo, Joan Bradley *microbiologist, healthcare administrator*
Mc Carthy, Daniel Christopher, Jr. *manufacturing company executive*
Pierson, Robert David *banker*
Sabin, William Albert *editor*
Sierra, Roberto *composer, music educator*
Tonges, Mary Crabtree *patient care executive*
Walker, George Theophilus, Jr. *composer, pianist, music educator*

**Montvale**
Beattie, James Raymond *lawyer*
Brecht, Warren Frederick *business executive*
Corrado, Fred *food company executive*
Friis, Erik Johan *editor, publisher*
Kanter, Carl Irwin *lawyer*
Mackerodt, Fred *public relations specialist*
O'Gorman, Peter Joseph *retail company executive*
Roob, Richard *manufacturing executive*
Sbarbaro, Robert Arthur *banker*
Schindler, Donald Warren *biopharmaceutical engineer, consultant*
Scopes, Gary Martin *professional association executive*
Sifton, David Whittier *magazine editor*
Smith, Kenneth David *performance technologist, musician*
Steinberg, Charles Allan *electronics manufacturing company executive*
Ulrich, Robert Gardner *retail food chain executive, lawyer*
Wood, James *supermarket executive*

**Montville**
Bizub, Johanna Catherine *library director*
Buzak, Edward Joseph *lawyer*
Klapper, Byron D. *financial company executive*
Leeson, Lewis Joseph *research pharmacist, scientist*
Teubner, Ferdinand Cary, Jr. *retired publishing company executive*

**Moonachie**
Malley, Raymond Charles *retired foreign service officer, industrial executive*

**Moorestown**
Begley, Thomas D., Jr. *lawyer*
Bennington, William Jay *public relations executive*
†Cassidy, Richard Michael, Jr. *retired officer, defense company executive*
Cervantes, Luis Augusto *neurosurgeon*
Margolis, Gerald Joseph *psychiatrist, educator*
Schwerin, Horace S. *marketing research executive*
Springer, Douglas Hyde *retired food company executive, lawyer*

**Morganville**
Karp, Stefanie *special education educator*
Sternfeld, Marc Howard *investment banker*

**Morris Plains**
Fielding, Stuart *psychopharmacologist*
Goodes, Melvin Russell *manufacturing company executive*
†Goodman, Steve Edward *public relations executive*
Guarino, Walter Francis *advertising executive*
O'Neill, Robert Edward *business journal editor*
Picozzi, Anthony *dentistry educator, educational administrator*
Pluciennik, Thomas Casimir *lawyer, former assistant county prosecutor*
Townsend, Palmer Wilson *chemical engineer, consultant*
Williams, Joseph Dalton *pharmaceutical company executive*

**Morristown**
Ahl, David Howard *writer, editor*
Arnow, Leslie Earle *scientist*
Aspero, Benedict Vincent *lawyer*
Azzato, Louis Enrico *manufacturing company executive*
Baughman, Ray Henry *materials scientist*
Berkley, Peter Lee *lawyer*
Bickerton, John Thorburn *retired pharmaceutical executive*
Booth, Albert Edward, II *investment executive*
Bossidy, Lawrence Arthur *industrial manufacturing executive*
Bromberg, Myron James *lawyer*
Burton, Valerie Diane *elementary school educator*
Cameron, Nicholas Allen *diversified corporation executive*
Campion, Thomas Francis *lawyer*
Casale, Alfred Stanley *thoracic and cardiovascular surgeon*
Clemen, John Douglas *lawyer*
Cregan, Frank Robert *financial executive, consultant*
Everhart, Rodney Lee *telecommunications industry executive*
Flynn, Marie Cosgrove *portfolio manager*
Fredericks, Robert Joseph *language company executive*
Gearhart, Marguerite Theresa *school nurse, health educator, nurse, counselor*
Golecki, Ilan *physicist, researcher, educator*
Granet, Roger B. *psychiatrist, educator*
Greenman, Jane Friedlieb *lawyer*
Hager, Mary Hastings *nutritionist, educator, consultant*
Handler, Lauren E. *lawyer*
Heilmeier, George Harry *electrical engineer, researcher*
Herman, Robert Lewis *cork company executive*
Herzberg, Peter Jay *lawyer*
Hesselink, Ann Patrice *financial executive, lawyer*
Hittinger, William Charles *electronics company executive*
Huck, John Lloyd *pharmaceutical company executive*
Humick, Thomas Charles Campbell *lawyer*
Hyland, William Francis *lawyer*
Isko, Irving David *corporate executive*
Janis, Ronald H. *lawyer*
Kandravy, John *lawyer*
Kearns, William Michael, Jr. *investment banker*
Kirby, Fred Morgan, II *corporation executive*
Klindt, Steven *art museum director*
Korf, Gene Robert *lawyer*
Kreindler, Peter Michael *lawyer*
Krumholz, Dennis Jonathan *lawyer*
Kubas, Christine *retired law enforcement officer*
Lavey, Stewart Evan *lawyer*
Lunin, Joseph *lawyer*
McClung, Kenneth Austin, Jr. *training executive, performance consultant*
McDonough, Joseph Richard *lawyer*
Mc Elroy, William Theodore *lawyer*
Miller, Hasbrouck Bailey *financial and travel services company executive*
Moore, Milo Anderson *banker*
Munson, William Leslie *insurance company executive*
Musa, John Davis *computer and infosystems executive, software reliability engineering researcher and expert, independent consultant*
Nadaskay, Raymond *architect*
Newman, John Merle *lawyer*
Nittoly, Paul Gerard *lawyer*
O'Connell, Daniel F. *lawyer*
O'Grady, Dennis Joseph *lawyer*
Orlowsky, Martin L. *executive manager*
Pantel, Glenn Steven *lawyer*
Parr, Grant Van Siclen *surgeon*
Personick, Stewart David *electrical engineer*
Pollock, Stewart Glasson *state supreme court justice*
Prince, Leah Fanchon *art educator and research institute administrator*
Reid, Charles Adams, III *lawyer*
Rogers, Alan Victor *former career officer*
Rose, Robert Gordon *lawyer*
Rosenthal, Meyer L(ouis) *lawyer*
Sangiuliano, Barbara Ann *tax manager*
Scher, Allan Joseph *oncologist, consultant*
Scott, Susan *lawyer*
Sharkey, Vincent Joseph *lawyer*
Silberman, H. Lee *public relations executive*
Simon, William Edward *investment banker, former secretary of treasury*
†Smith, Thomas J. *surgeon, educator*
Sweeney, John Lawrence *lawyer*
Szuch, Clyde Andrew *lawyer*
Thornton, Yvonne Shirley *physician, author, musician*
Tierney, Raymond Moran, Jr. *lawyer*
Tokar, Edward Thomas *manufacturing company executive*
Urban, John S. *engineering company executive*
Whitmer, Frederick Lee *lawyer*

**Mount Arlington**
Cohen, Irving David *science administrator*
Jacobs, Richard Moss *consulting engineer*
Krosser, Howard S. *aerospace company executive*

**Mount Ephraim**
Nusbaum, Geoffrey Dean *psychotherapist*

**Mount Holly**
Brown, Hershel M. *retired newspaper publisher*
Losse, Catherine Ann *pediatric nurse, critical care nurse, educator, clinical nurse specialist, family nurse practitioner*
Mintz, Jeffry Alan *lawyer*

**Mount Laurel**
Buchan, Alan Bradley *land planner, consultant, civil engineer*
Gorenberg, Charles Lloyd *financial services executive*
Hart, Larry Edward *communications company executive*
Instone, John Clifford *manufacturing company executive*
Laubach, Roger Alvin *accountant*
Li, Pearl Nei-Chien Chu *information specialist, executive*
†Sabol, Steve *film company executive*
Schmoll, Harry F., Jr. *lawyer, educator*
Shapiro, Cheryl Beth *lawyer*
Stallings, Viola Patricia Elizabeth *systems engineer, educational systems specialist*
Taylor, Henry Roth *sales and marketing executive*
Torres, Robert Alvin *dancer, singer, actor, sign language interpreter*
Vidas, Vincent George *engineering executive*

**Mountain Lakes**
Cook, Charles Francis *insurance executive*
LaForce, William Leonard, Jr. *photojournalist*
Mazur, Leonard L. *pharmaceutical company executive*
Turnheim, Palmer *banker*
Williams, Edward David *consulting executive*

**Mountainside**
Cardoni, Horace Robert *retired lawyer*
DiPietro, Ralph Anthony *marketing and management consultant, educator*
Horner, Shirley Jaye *columnist, writing and publishing consultant*
Kozberg, Donna Walters *rehabilitation administration executive*
Kozberg, Ronald Paul *health and human services administrator*
Lipton, Bronna Jane *marketing communications executive*
Lissenden, Carolkay *pediatrician*
Ricciardi, Antonio *prosthodontist, implantologist, educator*
Stefanile, Lawrence Vincent *management counsulting company executive*
Weigele, Richard Sayre *police officer*

**Mullica Hill**
Demola, James, Sr. *church administrator*

**Murray Hill**
Buchanan, William Hobart, Jr. *lawyer, publishing company executive*
Laskowski, Edward John *chemist*

### Neptune
Aguiar, Adam Martin chemist, educator
Boak, Joseph Gordon cardiologist
Clurfeld, Andrea editor, food critic
Harrigan, John Thomas, Jr. physician, obstetrician-gynecologist
Ollwerther, William Raymond newspaper editor
Plangere, Jules L., III newspaper company executive
Rice, Stephen Gary medical educator

### Neshanic Station
Muckenhoupt, Benjamin retired mathematics educator

### Netcong
Davis, Dorinne Sue Taylor Lovas audiologist
Sekula, Edward Joseph, Jr. financial executive

### New Brunswick
Aisner, Joseph oncologist, physician
Akinlabi, Akinbiyi linguistics educator
Alexander, Robert Jackson economist, educator
Amarel, Saul computer scientist, educator
Ballou, Janice Marie research director
Becker, Ronald Leonard archivist
Bern, Ronald Lawrence consulting company executive
Bernstein, Adriana Bennett library and information consultant
Boehm, Werner William social work educator
Boocock, Sarane Spence sociologist
Bowden, Henry Warner religion educator
Budd, Richard Wade communications scientist, educator, lecturer, consultant, university dean
Burke, James Edward consumer products company executive
Cate, Phillip Dennis art museum director
Cheiten, Marvin Harold writer, hardware manufacturing company executive
Chelius, James Robert economics educator
Chiapperini, Patricia Bignoli real estate appraiser, consultant
Day, Peter Rodney geneticist, educator
Day-Salvatore, Debra Lynn medical geneticist
Derbyshire, William Wadleigh language educator, translator
Dill, Ellis Harold university dean
Dinerman, Miriam social work educator
Domm, Alice lawyer
Dougherty, Neil Joseph physical education educator, safety consultant
Durnin, Richard Gerry education educator
Edelman, Hendrik library and information science educator
Ehrenfeld, David William biology educator, author
Eisenreich, Steven John chemistry educator, environmental scientist
Eisinger, Robert Peter nephrologist, educator
Elinson, Jack sociology educator
Ettinger, Lawrence Jay pediatric hematologist and oncologist, educator
Fisher, Hans nutritional biochemistry educator
Funk, Cyril Reed, Jr. agronomist, educator
Gale, Paula Jane chemist
Gardner, Lloyd Calvin, Jr. history educator
Garner, Charles William educational administration educator, consultant
Gillette, William historian, educator
Glasser, Paul Harold sociologist, educator, university administrator, social worker
Glickman, Norman Jay economist, urban policy analyst
Gocke, David Joseph immunology educator, physician, medical scientist
Goffen, Rona art educator
Goodyear, John Lake artist, educator
Graham, Alan Morrison surgeon
Grassle, John Frederick oceanographer, marine sciences educator
Greco, Ralph Steven surgeon, researcher, medical educator
Greenberg, Michael Richard urban studies and community health educator
Grob, Gerald N. historian, educator
Gupta, Ayodhya Prasad entomologist, immunologist, cell biologist
Hartman, Mary S. historian
Hayakawa, Kan-Ichi food science educator
Ho, Chi-Tang food chemistry educator
Horowitz, Irving Louis publisher, educator
Hurst, Gregory Squire artistic director, director, producer
Jacob, Charles Elmer political scientist, educator
Jaluria, Yogesh mechanical engineering educator
Kansfield, Norman J. seminary president
Katz, Carlos electrical engineer
Kelley, Donald Reed historian
Kovach, Barbara Ellen management and psychology educator
Kulikowski, Casimir Alexander computer science educator
Lachance, Paul Albert food science educator, clergyman
Laraya-Cuasay, Lourdes Redublo pediatric pulmonologist, educator
Larsen, Ralph S(tanley) health care company executive
Lawrence, Francis Leo language educator, educational administrator
Lebowitz, Joel Louis mathematical physicist, educator
Lee, Barbara Anne academic administrator, lawyer
Leggett, John Carl sociology educator
Lettvin, Theodore concert pianist
Levine, George Lewis English language educator, literature critic
Lewis, David Levering history educator
Liao, Mei-June biopharmaceutical company executive
Lynch, John A. state senator, lawyer
Maramorosch, Karl virologist, educator
McGuire, John Lawrence pharmaceuticals research executive
Mechanic, David social sciences educator
Midlarsky, Manus Issachar political scientist, educator
Mills, Dorothy Allen investor
Mills, George Marshall insurance and financial consultant
Momah, Ethel Chukwuekwe women's health nurse
Mondschein, Lawrence Geoffrey medical products executive
Nawy, Edward George civil engineer, educator
Nelson, Jack Lee education educator
Nosko, Michael Gerrik neurosurgeon
O'Neill, William Lawrence history educator
Ortiz, Raphael Montañez performance artist, educator
Ostriker, Alicia Suskin poet
†Pallone, Nathaniel John psychologist, educator
Pandey, Ramesh Chandra chemist, executive
Paz, Harold Louis internist and educator
Peterson, Donald Robert psychologist, educator, university administrator
Poirier, Richard English educator, literary critic
Psuty, Norbert Phillip marine sciences educator
Reed, James Wesley social historian, educator
Reeling, Patricia Glueck library educator, educational consultant
Reock, Ernest C., Jr. retired government services educator, academic director
Rosen, Robert Thomas analytical and food chemist
Rosenberg, Seymour psychologist, educator
Ruben, Brent David communication educator
Russell, Louise Bennett economist, educator
Scanlon, Jane Cronin mathematics educator
Scott, David Rodick lawyer, legal educator
Scully, John Thomas obstetrician, gynecologist, educator
Seibold, James Richard physician, researcher
Smith, Fredric Charles electronic technician, consultant
Solberg, Myron food scientist, educator
Stewart, Joseph Turner, Jr. retired pharmaceutical company executive
Stewart, Ruth Ann public policy analyst, library adminstrator
Stich, Stephen Peter philosophy educator
Stimpson, Catharine Roslyn English language educator, writer
Strauss, Ulrich Paul chemist, educator
Strawderman, William E. statistics educator
Stuart, Robert Crampton economics educator
Szarka, Laslo Joseph pharmaceutical company executive
Tanner, Daniel curriculum theory educator
Tedrow, John Charles Fremont soils educator
Terrill, Thomas Edward health facility administrator
Tiger, Lionel social scientist, anthropology consultant
Toby, Jackson sociologist, educator
Turock, Betty Jane library and information science educator
Uchrin, Christopher George environmental scientist
Vieth, Wolf Randolph chemical engineering educator
Walters, Arthur Scott neurologist, educator, clinical research scientist
Webre, Septime ballet company artistic director, choreographer
Wilkinson, Louise Cherry psychology educator, dean
Wilson, Donald Malcolm publishing executive
Wilson, Robert Nathan health care company executive
Wolfe, Robert Richard bioresource engineer, educator
Yorke, Marianne lawyer, real estate executive

### New Milford
Walsh, Joseph Michael magazine distribution executive

### New Monmouth
Donnelly, Gerard Kevin retail executive

### New Providence
†Andreozzi, Louis Joseph lawyer
Atal, Bishnu Saroop speech research executive
Baker, William Oliver research chemist, educator
Barnes, Sandra Henley publishing company executive
Bartels, Joachim Conrad marketing and publishing corporation executive
Bishop, David John physicist
Bopp, William Clarence financial executive
Brinkman, William Frank physicist, research executive
Capasso, Federico physicist, research administrator
Chatterji, Debajyoti manufacturing company executive
Cho, Alfred Yi electrical engineer
Cohen, Melvin Irwin communications systems and technology executive
Dodabalapur, Ananth electrical engineer
Faist, Jerome physicist
Fishburn, Peter Clingerman research mathematician, economist
Fisher, Darryl information services company executive
Garavaglia, Susan Berger decision systems designer
Gaylord, Norman Grant chemical and polymer consultant
Glass, Alastair Malcolm physicist, research director
†Goff, Neal publishing company executive
Graham, Ronald Lewis mathematician
Helfand, Eugene chemist
Hollister, Dean publishing company executive
Johnson, David Wilfred, Jr. ceramic scientist, researcher
Krishnamurthy, Ramachandran (Krish) chemical engineer, researcher
Lanzerotti, Louis John physicist
Laudise, Robert Alfred research chemist
Longfield, William Herman health care company executive
Manthei, Richard Dale lawyer, health care company executive
Meyer, Andrew W. publishing executive
Miskiewicz, Susanne Piatek elementary education educator
Morgan, Samuel P(ope) physicist, applied mathematician
Mostello, Robert Anthony chemical engineer
Murray, Cherry Ann physicist, researcher
Mysel, Randy Howard publishing company executive
Pinczuk, Aron physicist
Roycroft, Edward J. publishing company executive
Schacht, Henry Brewer manufacturing executive
Sivco, Deborah Lee research materials scientist
Stepanski, Anthony Francis, Jr. computer company executive
Stillinger, Frank Henry chemist, educator
Stormer, Horst Ludwig physicist
Sullivan, Barbara publishing company executive
Sundberg, Carl-Erik Wilhelm telecommunications executive, researcher
Symanski, Robert Anthony treasurer
Taylor, Volney information company executive
van Dover, Robert Bruce physicist
Walker, Stanley P. publishing executive
Wernick, Jack Harry chemist
White, Alice Elizabeth physicist, researcher
Williams, Alun Gwyn publishing company executive
Wyner, Aaron Daniel mathematician

### New Vernon
Dugan, John Leslie, Jr. foundation executive

### Newark
Abrams, Roger Ian university dean, law educator, arbitrator
Ackerman, Harold A. federal judge
Alito, Samuel Anthony, Jr. federal judge
Arabie, Phipps marketing educator, researcher
Aregood, Richard Lloyd editor
Askin, Frank law educator
Baker, Herman vitaminologist
Bar-Ness, Yeheskel electrical engineer, educator
Barry, Maryanne Trump federal judge
Bartner, Martin newspaper executive
Bassler, William G. federal judge
Bergen, Stanley Silvers, Jr. university president, physician
Bigley, William Joseph, Jr. control engineer
Bissell, John W. federal judge
Bradley, Bill former senator
Brescher, John B., Jr. lawyer
Carroll, John Douglas mathematical and statistical psychologist
Cheng, Mei-Fang psychobiology educator, neuroethology researcher
Cherniack, Neil Stanley physician, medical educator
Chesler, Stanley Richard federal judge
Chinard, Francis Pierre physiologist, physician
Christodoulou, Aris Peter pharmaceutical executive, investment banker
Cinotti, Alfonse Anthony ophthalmologist, educator
Cohen, Stanley pathologist, educator
Colli, Bart Joseph lawyer
Contractor, Farok business and management educator
Cook, Stuart Donald physician, educator
Cummis, Clive Sanford lawyer
Dauth, Frances Kutcher journalist, newspaper editor
Day, Edward Francis, Jr. lawyer
Debevoise, Dickinson Richards federal judge
Dee, Francis X. lawyer
Defeis, Elizabeth Frances law educator, lawyer
Deitch, Edwin Alan surgeon
Del Tufo, Robert J. lawyer, former US attorney, former state attorney general
Dickson, Jim playwright, stage director, arts consultant
Donahoo, James Saunders cardiothoracic surgeon
Dreyfuss, Stephen Lawrence lawyer
Eittreim, Richard MacNutt lawyer
English, Nicholas Conover lawyer
Eslami, Hossein Hojatol surgeon, educator
Estrin, Herman Albert English language educator
Evans, Hugh E. pediatrician
Everett, Richard G. newspaper editor
Feldman, Susan Carol neurobiologist, anatomy educator
Fenster, Saul K. university president
Ferland, E. James electric utility executive
Fink, Aaron Herman box manufacturing executive
Friedland, Bernard engineer, educator
Gambert, Steven Ross geriatrician
Gardner, Bernard surgeon, educator
Garth, Leonard I. federal judge
Gerathy, E. Carroll former insurance executive, real estate developer
Gillen, James Robert insurance company executive, lawyer
Goldman, Glenn architecture educator, architect
Gouraige, Hervé lawyer
Greenfield, Sanford Raymond architect
Griffinger, Michael R. lawyer
Guenzel, Frank Bernhard chemical engineer
Hadas, Rachel poet, educator
Hallard, Wayne Bruce economist
Hanesian, Deran chemical engineer, chemistry and environmental science educator, consultant
Haring, Eugene Miller lawyer
Harrison, Charles R. retired newspaper editor
Harrison, Roslyn Siman lawyer
Healy, Phyllis M. Cordasco school social worker
Herman, Steven Douglas cardiothoracic surgeon, educator
Hermann, Steven Istvan textile executive
Hernon, Richard Francis civil engineer
Hiltz, Starr Roxanne sociologist, educator, computer scientist, writer, lecturer, consultant
Hobson, Robert Wayne, II surgeon
Hollander, Toby Edward education educator
Holzer, Marc public administrator educator
Hooper-Perkins, Marlene technical editor, educator
Hrycak, Peter mechanical engineer, educator
Hsu, Cheng-Tzu Thomas civil engineering educator
Huhn, Darlene Marie county official, poet
Hutcheon, Duncan Elliot physician, educator
Iffy, Leslie medical educator
James, Sharpe mayor
Jonakait, Gene Miller developmental neurobiologist
Jones, Etta singer
Kaltenbacher, Philip D(avid) industrialist, former public official
Kantor, Mel Lewis dental educator, researcher
Kanzler, George journalist, critic
Karp, Donald Mathew lawyer, banker
Kelleher, Kathleen financial services marketing specialist
Knee, Stephen H. lawyer
Kott, David Russell lawyer
Latini, Anthony A. financial services company executive
Laura, Anthony Joseph lawyer
Lawatsch, Frank Emil, Jr. lawyer
Layman, William Arthur psychiatrist, educator
Lechner, Alfred James, Jr. judge
Ledeen, Robert Wagner neurochemist, educator
Lederman, Peter (Bernd) environmental services executive, consultant, educator
Leevy, Carroll Moton medical educator, hepatology researcher
Lenehan, Art newspaper editor
Leu, Ming Chuan engineering educator
Levin, Simon lawyer
Lieberman, Leonard retired supermarket executive
Lifland, John C. federal judge
†Light, Dorothy Kaplan insurance executive, lawyer
Linken, Dennis C. lawyer
Lourenco, Ruy Valentim physician, educator
Martin, James Hanley deputy state attorney general
Martinez, Arturo newspaper editor
Materna, Thomas Walter ophthalmologist
Mc Carrick, Theodore Edgar archbishop
McGuire, William B(enedict) lawyer
McKelvey, Jack M. bishop
McKinney, John Adams, Jr. lawyer
Misra, Raj Pratap engineering educator, electrical engineer
Morgenstern, Dan Michael jazz historian, educator, editor
Moskowitz, Sam (Sam Martin) author, editor, publisher
Mullin, Mary Ann career counselor
Murnick, Daniel Ely physicist, educator
Muscato, Andrew lawyer
Nathan, Edward Singer lawyer
Neuer, Philip David lawyer, real estate consultant
Newhouse, Donald E. newspaper publishing executive
Newhouse, Mark William publishing executive
Norwood, Carolyn Virginia business educator
Oberdorf, John J. lawyer
O'Leary, Paul Gerard investment executive
Pagán, Gilberto, Jr. clinical psychologist
Paul, James Caverly Newlin law educator, former university dean
Pedone, Joseph Lawrence advertising executive
Pfeffer, Edward Israel educational administrator
Pfeffer, Robert chemical engineer, academic administrator, educator
Pignataro, Louis James engineering educator
Pisano, Joel A. federal judge
Politan, Nicholas H. federal judge
Reichman, Lee Brodersohn physician
Reilly, William Thomas lawyer
Reynolds, Valrae museum curator
Riggs, Benjamin Clapp, Jr. building products manufacturing company executive
Robertson, William Withers lawyer
Rosato, Anthony Dominick mechanical engineer, educator
Rosenberg, Jerry Martin business administration educator
Roth, Allan Robert lawyer, educator
Ryan, Arthur Frederick insurance company executive
Salvador, Richard Anthony pharmaceutical company executive
Schweizer, Karl Wolfgang historian, writer
Shain-Alvaro, Judith Carol physician assistant
Shoup, Michael C. newspaper reporter, editor
Silipigni, Alfredo opera conductor
Simmons, Peter law and urban planning educator
Spillers, William Russell civil engineering educator
Spong, John Shelby bishop
Steinbaum, Robert S. publisher, lawyer
Storrer, William Allin consultant
Thomas, Gary L. academic administrator
Tischman, Michael Bernard lawyer
Vajtay, Stephen Michael, Jr. lawyer
Vecchione, Frank Joseph lawyer
Wachenfeld, William Thomas lawyer, foundation executive
Waelde, Lawrence Richard chemist
Walls, William Hamilton judge
Weis, Judith Shulman biology educator
Weiss, Gerson physician, educator
Willse, James Patrick newspaper editor
Wolfe, Lilyan special education clinical educator
Wolin, Alfred M. federal judge
Wyer, James Ingersoll lawyer
Yamner, Morris lawyer
Yu, Yi-Yuan mechanical engineering educator
Ziavras, Sotirios George computer and electrical engineer, educator

### Newfoundland
Van Winkle, Edgar Walling electrical engineer, computer consultant

### Newton
Ancona, Francesco Aristide humanities and mythology educator, writer
Carstens, Harold Henry publisher
Cox, William Martin lawyer, educator
MacMurren, Margaret Patricia secondary education educator, consultant
Worman, Linda Kay nursing administrator

### North Bergen
Karp, Roberta S. wholesale apparel and accessories executive
Lanier, Thomas chemical and export company executive
Marth, Fritz Ludwig sports association executive
Miller, Samuel Martin apparel company finance executive
Zondler, Joyce Evelyn kindergarten educator

### North Branch
Gartlan, Philip M. secondary school director

### North Brunswick
Awan, Ahmad Noor civil engineer
Barcus, Gilbert Martin medical products executive, business educator
Coslow, Richard David electronics company executive
Kahrmann, Linda Irene child care supervisor

### North Haledon
Anstatt, Peter Jan marketing services executive
Brown, James Joseph manufacturing company executive
Harrington, Kevin Paul lawyer

### North Plainfield
Steiner, Ulrich Alfred chemist

### Northvale
Aronson, Jason publisher
Barna, Richard Allen lighting company executive, broadcasting executive
Goodman, Stanley Leonard advertising executive
Kurzweil, Arthur publisher, writer, educator

### Norwood
Barbini, Richard John chemical engineer, marketing manager

### Nutley
Bess, Alan L. pharmaceutical executive, physician
Dennin, Robert Aloysius, Jr. pharmaceutical research scientist
Drews, Jürgen pharmaceutical researcher
English, Robert Joseph electronic corporation executive
Mallard, Stephen Anthony retired utility company executive
Mostillo, Ralph medical association executive
Seyffarth, Linda Jean Wilcox corporate executive
Smith, Susan Elizabeth guidance director

Weber, Paul Frederick *physician, pharmacist, educator*

**Oakhurst**
Konvitz, Milton Ridbaz *law educator*
Seltzer, Ronald *retail company executive*

**Oakland**
Bacaloglu, Radu *chemical engineer*
Bloom, Arnold Sanford *lawyer*

**Ocean**
Kreider, Clement Horst, Jr. *neurosurgeon*
Weisberg, Adam Jon *lawyer*

**Ocean City**
Dittenhafer, Brian Douglas *banker, economist*
Gross, Kathleen Frances *parochial school mathematics educator*
Speitel, Gerald Eugene *consulting environmental engineer*

**Ocean Gate**
Campbell, Edward Wallace *nutritionist*

**Old Bridge**
Engel, John Jacob *communications executive*
Kesselman, Bruce Alan *marketing executive, consultant, composer, writer*
Mount, Karl A. *manufacturing executive*
Swett, Stephen Frederick, Jr. *principal*

**Old Tappan**
Dubnick, Bernard *retired pharmaceutical company administrator*
Gaffin, Joan Valerie *secondary school educator*

**Oldwick**
Griggs, Stephen Layng *management consultant*
Hitchcock, Ethan Allen *lawyer*
Purcell, Richard Fick *lawyer, food companies advisor and counsel*
Snyder, Arthur *publishing company executive*

**Oradell**
Dinsmore, Gordon Griffith *writer*

**Palmyra**
Overholt, Miles Harvard, III *management consultant, family therapist*

**Paramus**
Adams, Eda Ann Fischer *nursing educator*
Aronson, Miriam Klausner *gerontologist, consultant, researcher, educator*
Ascher, David Mark *lawyer*
Bagli, Vincent Joseph *plastic surgeon*
Balter, Leslie Marvin *business communications educator*
Brissie, Eugene Field, Jr. *publisher*
DeVita, Marie N. *physician*
DiGeronimo, Suzanne Kay *architect*
Fader, Shirley Sloan *writer*
Forman, Beth Rosalyne *entertainment industry professional*
Giantonio, Clifford John *lawyer*
Gilbert, Stephen Alan *lawyer*
Gingras, Paul Joseph *real estate management company executive*
Goldstein, Michael *retail executive*
Greenberg, William Michael *psychiatrist*
Liva, Edward Louis *eye surgeon*
Maclin, Ernest *biomedical diagnostics company executive*
Nakasone, Robert C. *retail toy and game company executive*
Plucinsky, Constance Marie *school counselor, supervisor*
Samuels, Reuben *engineering consultant*

**Park Ridge**
De Pol, John *artist*
Kaplan, Daniel I. *leasing company executive*
Kennedy, Brian James *marketing executive*
Maurer, C(harles) F(rederick) William, III *museum curator*
Olson, Frank Albert *car rental company executive*

**Parlin**
Flick, Ferdinand Herman *surgeon, prevention medicine physician*

**Parsippany**
Adams, Christine Hanson *advertising executive*
Belmonte, Steven Joseph *hotel chain executive*
Bridwell, Robert Kennedy *lawyer*
Deones, Jack E. *corporate executive*
Derr, Debra Hulse *advertising executive, publisher, editor*
Dixon, E. A., Jr. *lawyer*
†Ferguson, Thomas George *health care advertising agency executive*
Fleisher, Seymour *manufacturing company executive*
Gallagher, Jerome Francis, Jr. *lawyer*
Geyer, Thomas Powick *newspaper publisher*
†Gokal, Ramesh B. *hotel executive*
Graham, John Gourlay *utility company executive*
Hafer, Frederick Douglass *utility executive*
Harab, Elliot Peter *lawyer*
Harris, Margaret Elizabeth *writer*
Haselmann, John Philip *marketing executive*
Jolles, Ira Hervey *lawyer*
Kallmann, Stanley Walter *lawyer*
Karpf, Ilene Phyllis *lawyer*
Leva, James Robert *electric utility company executive*
Manfredi, John Frederick *food products executive*
McGirr, David William John *investment banker*
McNicholas, David Paul *automobile rental company executive*
Nalewako, Mary Anne *corporate secretary*
Ostroff, Allen J. *insurance company executive*
Ross, Thomas J., Jr. *personal finanical adviser*
†Seymour, Jeffrey L. *hotel executive*
Shaw, Alan *lawyer, corporate executive*
Singleterry, Gary Lee *investment banker*
Visocki, Nancy Gayle *data processing consultant*
Wechter, Ira Martin *tax specialist, financial planner*
Weller, Robert N(orman) *hotel executive*
Wernick, Edward Raymond *company executive, computer consultant*
Winograd, Bernard *financial adviser*

**Passaic**
Haddad, Jamil Raouf *physician*
Lindholm, Clifford Falstrom, II *engineering executive, mayor*
Pino, Robert Salvatore *radiologist*

**Paterson**
Danziger, Glenn Norman *chemical sales company executive*
DeBari, Vincent Anthony *medical researcher, educator*
Deffaa, Chip *jazz critic*
Dicovsky, Carlos Jose *physician*
†McEvoy, Lorraine K. *oncology nurse*
Pulhamus, Marlene Louise *retired elementary school educator*
Welles, Ernest I. *chemical company executive*

**Paulsboro**
Banks, Theresa Ann *elementary education educator*
Domingue, Raymond Pierre *chemist, consultant, educator*
Wise, John James *oil company executive*

**Peapack**
Walsh, Philip Cornelius *retired mining executive*
Weiss, Allan Joseph *transport company executive, lawyer*

**Pemberton**
Witkin, Isaac *sculptor*

**Pennington**
Calvo, Roque John *professional society administrator*
Halasi-Kun, George Joseph *hydrologist, educator*
Harris, Frederick George *publishing company executive*
Widmer, Kemble *geologist*

**Penns Grove**
Reilley, James Clark *artist, cartoonist, small business owner*

**Pennsauken**
Alday, Paul Stackhouse, Jr. *mechanical engineer*
Bareford, William John *chemical engineer*
Daly, Charles Arthur *health services administrator*
Holman, Joseph S. *automotive sales executive*

**Pequannock**
MacMurren, Harold Henry, Jr. *psychologist, lawyer*

**Perth Amboy**
Gemmell, Joseph Paul *banker*
Richardson-Melech, Joyce Suzanne *secondary school educator, singer*

**Philadelphia**
Hextall, Ron *professional hockey player*

**Phillipsburg**
Burkhart, Glenn Randall *corporate internal auditor*
Cooper, Paul *mechanical engineer, research director*
Richards, Jay Claude *commercial photographer, news service executive, historian*
Rosenthal, Marvin Bernard *pediatrician, educator*
Stull, Frank Walter *elementary school educator*
Testa, Douglas *biotechnology company executive*

**Picatinny Arsenal**
Janow, Chris *mechanical engineer*

**Piscataway**
Alderfer, Clayton Paul *organizational psychologist, educator, author, consultant, administrator*
Bretschneider, Ann Margery *histotechnologist*
Burke, Jacqueline Yvonne *telecommunications executive*
Colaizzi, John Louis *college dean*
Conney, Allan Howard *pharmacologist*
Coppola, Sarah Jane *special education educator*
Denhardt, David Tilton *molecular and cell biology educator*
Devlin, Thomas Joseph *physicist*
Escobar, Javier Ignacio *psychiatrist*
Flanagan, James Loton *electrical engineer, educator*
Florio, Jim *lawyer, former governor*
Fogiel, Max *publishing executive*
Freeman, Herbert *computer engineering educator*
Frenkiel, Richard Henry *systems engineer, consultant*
Goldstein, Bernard David *physician, educator*
Goodwin, Douglas Ira *steel distribution company executive*
Gotsch, Audrey Rose *environmental health sciences educator, researcher*
Idol, James Daniel, Jr. *chemist, educator, inventor, consultant*
Julesz, Bela *experimental psychologist, educator, electrical engineer*
Kampouris, Emmanuel Andrew *corporate executive*
Kear, Bernard Henry *materials scientist*
Lazarus, Arnold Allan *psychologist, educator*
Lewis, Peter A. *energy consultant*
Lindenfeld, Peter *physics educator*
Lioy, Paul James *environmental health scientist*
Liu, Alice Yee-Chang *biology educator*
Madey, Theodore Eugene *physics educator*
Manowitz, Paul *biochemist, researcher, educator*
Mc Cormick, Richard Patrick *history educator*
Mehlman, Myron A. *environmental and occupational medicine educator, environmental toxicologist*
Murphree, Henry Bernard Scott *psychiatry and pharmacology educator, consultant*
Pandina, Robert John *neuropsychologist*
Passmore, Howard Clinton, Jr. *geneticist, biological sciences educator*
Pollack, Irwin William *psychiatrist, educator*
Pond, Thomas Alexander *physics educator*
Pramer, David *microbiologist, educator, research administrator*
Rhoads, George Grant *medical epidemiologist*
Riss, Richard Michael *research economist, church history educator*
Robbins, Allen Bishop *physics educator*
Rudczynski, Andrew B. *academic administrator, medical researcher*
Salkind, Alvin J. *electrochemical engineer, educator*
Sannuti, Peddapullaiah *electrical engineering educator*
Schwebel, Milton *psychologist, educator*
Shanefield, Daniel Jay *ceramics engineering educator*
Shatkin, Aaron Jeffrey *biochemistry educator*
Shea, Stephen Michael *physician, educator*
Smith, Robert G. (Bob Smith) *lawyer, assemblyman, educator*
Snitzer, Elias *physicist*
Stedge-Fowler, Joyce *retired clergywoman*
Upton, Arthur Canfield *experimental pathologist, educator*
Welkowitz, Walter *biomedical engineer, educator*
Witkin, Evelyn Maisel *geneticist*
Witz, Gisela *chemist, educator*
Yacowitz, Harold *biochemist, nutritionist*
Young, James Earl *ceramics educator, educational administrator*
Zaleski, Jan Franciszek *biochemist*
Zhao, Jian Hui *electrical and computer engineering educator*

**Pitman**
Beebe, Leo Clair *industrial equipment executive, former educator*
Powell, J. R. *lawyer, judge*

**Plainfield**
Eisenstat, Theodore Ellis *colon and rectal surgeon, educator*
Granstrom, Marvin Leroy *civil and sanitary engineering educator*
Limpert, John H., Jr. *fundraising executive*
Montford, Claudian Hammond *gifted and talented education educator*
Stella, John Anthony *investment company executive*
Winell, Marvin *orthopaedic surgeon*
Yood, Harold Stanley *internist*

**Plainsboro**
Norback, Craig Thomas *writer*
Royds, Robert Bruce *physician*
Schreyer, William Allen *retired investment firm executive*
Spiegel, Phyllis *public relations consultant, journalist*
Urciuoli, J. Arthur *investment executive*

**Pleasantville**
Bennett, Eileen Patricia *copy editor, reporter*
Briant, Maryjane *newspaper editor*
London, Charlotte Isabella *secondary education educator, reading specialist*
Pollock, Michael Jeffrey *periodical editor*

**Point Pleasant**
Albano, Pasquale Charles *management educator, management and organization development consultant*
Feeks, J. Michael *bank executive*
Monaco, Robert Anthony *radiologist*

**Point Pleasant Beach**
Motley, John Paul *psychiatrist, consultant*

**Pomona**
Bukowski, Elaine Louise *physical therapist*
Colijn, Geert Jan *academic administrator, political scientist*
Farris, Vera King *college president*
Jahangir, Z(ulfiquar) M(uhammed) G(olam) Sarwar *molecular biology educator*
Sharon, Yitzhak Yaakov *physicist, educator*

**Pompton Lakes**
Wildebush, Joseph Frederick *economist*

**Pompton Plains**
Costello, Gerald Michael *editor*

**Port Liberte**
Frank, William Fielding *computer systems design executive, consultant*

**Port Monmouth**
Lechtanski, Cheryl Lee *chiropractor*

**Port Murray**
Kunzler, John Eugene *physicist*

**Port Norris**
Canzonier, Walter Jude *shellfish aquaculturist*

**Pottersville**
Mellberg, James Richard *dental research chemist*

**Princeton**
Aarsleff, Hans *linguistics educator*
Ackourey, Peter Paul *lawyer*
Adler, Stephen Louis *physicist*
Aizenman, Michael *mathematics and physics educator, researcher*
Allen, Diogenes *clergyman, philosophy educator*
Anderson, Ellis Bernard *retired lawyer, pharmaceutical company executive*
Armstrong, Richard Stoll *minister, educator, writer, poet*
Ashenfelter, Orley Clark *economics educator*
Autera, Michael Edward *health care products company executive*
Ayers, William McLean *electrochemical engineering company executive*
Bahcall, John Norris *astrophysicist*
Bahcall, Neta Assaf *astrophysicist*
Baker, Richard Wheeler, Jr. *real estate executive*
Balch, Stephen Howard *professional society administrator*
Barker, Richard Gordon *corporate research and development executive*
Barlow, Walter Greenwood *public opinion analyst, management consultant*
Bartolini, Robert Alfred *electrical engineer, researcher*
Beeners, Wilbert John *speech professional, minister*
Beidler, Marsha Wolf *lawyer*
Belshaw, George Phelps Mellick *bishop*
Bergman, Edward Jonathan *lawyer*
Bergman, Richard Isaac *engineering executive, consultant*
Berry, Charles Horace *economist, educator*
Billington, David Perkins *civil engineering educator*
Bogan, Elizabeth Chapin *economist, educator*
Bogdonoff, Seymour Moses *aeronautical engineer*
Bonini, William Emory *geophysics educator*
Borel, Armand *mathematics educator*
Bowersock, Glen Warren *historian*
Boyd, John Howard *corporate location consultant*
Bradford, David Frantz *economist*
Brennan, William Joseph, III *lawyer*
Brief, Henry *trade association consultant*
Brombert, Victor Henri *literature educator, author*
Brown, Leon Carl *history educator*
Bryan, Kirk, Jr. *research meteorologist, research oceanographer*
Bunn, William Bernice, III *physician, lawyer, epidemiologist*
Bunnell, Peter Curtis *photography and art educator, museum curator*
Burns, Patrick Owen *venture capital company executive*
Buttenheim, Edgar Marion *publishing executive*
Cakmak, Ahmet Sefik *civil engineering educator*
Carnes, James Edward *electronics executive*
Carter, Jeanne Wilmot *lawyer, publisher*
Carver, David Harold *physician, educator*
Chamberlin, John Stephen *investor, former cosmetics company executive*
Champlin, Edward James *classics educator*
Chandler, James John *surgeon*
Chang, Clarence Dayton *chemist*
Chlopak, Donna Gayle *marketing and management consultant*
Chow, Gregory Chi-Chong *economist, educator*
Church, Martha Eleanor *retired academic administrator, scholar*
Cinlar, Erhan *engineering educator*
Coffey, Joseph Irving *international affairs educator*
Coffin, David Robbins *art historian, educator*
Cole, Nancy Stooksberry *educational research executive*
Conn, Hadley Lewis, Jr. *physician, educator*
Connor, Geoffrey Michael *lawyer*
Cook, Michael Allan *social sciences educator*
Cooper, Joel *psychology educator*
Cooper, John Madison *philosophy educator*
Corbett, Siobhan Aiden *surgeon*
Corngold, Stanley Alan *German and comparative literature educator, writer*
Crandall, David LeRoy *research scientist*
Crespi, Irving *public opinion and market research consultant*
Cryer, Dennis Robert *pharmaceutical company executive, researcher*
Curschmann, Michael Johann Hendrik *German language and literature educator*
Curtiss, Howard Crosby, Jr. *mechanical engineer, educator*
†Cushmore, Carole Lee *publisher*
Darnton, Robert Choate *history educator*
Darr, Walter Robert *financial analyst*
Davidson, Ronald Crosby *physicist, educator*
Davies, Horton Marlais *clergyman, religion educator*
Debenedetti, Pablo Gaston *chemical engineering educator*
Deligné, Pierre R. *mathematician*
Denlinger, Edgar Jacob *electronics engineering research executive*
Denne-Hinnov, Gerd Boël *physicist*
Devine, Hugh James, Jr. *marketing executive, consultant*
Dickinson, Bradley William *electrical engineering educator*
Dilworth, Joseph Richardson *investment banker*
Doherty, Leonard Edward *financial publishing company executive*
Doig, Jameson Wallace *political science educator*
Douglass, Jane Dempsey *theology educator*
Dovey, Brian Hugh *health care products company executive, venture capitalist*
Durbin, Enoch Job *aeronautical engineering educator*
Durst, Robert Joseph, II *lawyer*
Dyson, Freeman John *physicist*
Ehrenberg, Edward *executive, consultant*
Ekstrom, Ruth Burt *psychologist*
Elliott-Moskwa, Elaine Sally *psychologist, researcher*
Emmerich, Walter *psychologist*
Ermolaev, Herman Sergei *Slavic languages educator*
Estey, Audree Phipps *artistic director*
Farley, Edward Raymond, Jr. *mining and manufacturing company executive*
Feeney, John Robert *banker*
File, Joseph *research physics engineer*
Fisch, Nathaniel Joseph *physicist*
Fitch, Val Logsdon *physics educator*
Florey, Klaus Georg *chemist, pharmaceutical consultant*
Ford, Jeremiah, III *architect*
Fouss, James H. *marketing executive*
Fox, Mary Ann Williams *librarian*
Fresco, Jacques Robert *biochemist, educator*
Fried, Eleanor Reingold *psychologist, educator*
Ganoe, Charles Stratford *banker*
Gear, Charles William *computer scientist*
Geertz, Clifford James *anthropology educator*
Geertz, Hildred Storey *anthropology educator*
George, Thomas *artist*
Gibson, James John *electronics engineer, consultant*
Gillespie, Thomas William *theological seminary administrator, religion educator*
Gillham, John Kinsey *chemical engineering educator*
Gilpin, Robert George, Jr. *political science educator*
Girgus, Joan Stern *psychologist, university administrator*
Glassman, Irvin *mechanical and aeronautical engineering educator, consultant*
Glucksberg, Sam *psychology educator*
Goheen, Robert Francis *classicist, educator, former ambassador*
Goldfarb, Irene Dale *financial planner*
Goldman, Clifford Alan *financial advisor*
Gomoll, Allen Warren *cardiovascular pharmacologist*
Gordenker, Leon *political sciences educator*
Gordon, Ernest *clergyman*
Gott, J. Richard, III *astrophysicist*
Gould, James L. *biology educator*
Grabar, Oleg *art educator*
Graessley, William Walter *chemical engineering educator*
Grafton, Anthony Thomas *history educator*
Grant, Peter Raymond *biologist, researcher, educator*
Green, Joseph *chemist*
Greenberg, Joel S. *management consultant, engineer*
Greenstein, Fred Irwin *political science educator*
Griffiths, Phillip A. *mathematician, academic administrator*
Grisham, Larry Richard *physicist*
Gross, Charles Gordon *psychology educator, neuroscientist*
Grossman, Allen Neil *publishing executive*
Groves, John Taylor, III *chemist, educator*
Gunning, Robert Clifford *mathematician, educator*
Habicht, Christian Herbert *history educator*
Haggerty, John Richard *banker*

### Rutherford
Aberman, Harold Mark veterinarian
†Donahue, Timothy M. communications executive
Gerety, Peter Leo archbishop
†McAuley, Brian D. communications executive
Petrie, Ferdinand Ralph illustrator, artist

### Saddle River
Buckler, Beatrice editor
Dowden, Carroll Vincent publishing company executive
Giovannoli, Joseph Louis entrepreneur
Gorham, David L. newspaper executive
Lehmann, Doris Elizabeth elementary education educator
McClelland, William Craig paper company executive
Peters, Eleanor White retired mental health nurse
Ross, Martin Harris advertising executive

### Saddlebrook
Donahoe, Maureen Alice accounting consultant

### Salem
Petrin, Helen Fite lawyer, consultant
Seabrook, John Martin retired food products executive, chemical engineer

### Sayreville
Corman, Randy lawyer

### Scotch Plains
Abramson, Clarence Allen pharmaceutical company executive, lawyer
Barnard, Kurt retail marketing forecaster, publisher
Bishop, Robert Milton former stock exchange official
Edwards, Thomas Robert, Jr. language professional, investment company executive
Ehmann, Carl William consumer products executive, researcher
Gross, Ruth Chaiken educational administrator
Klock, John Henry lawyer
Sweeney, Lucy Graham psychologist
Ungar, Manya Shayon volunteer, education consultant

### Sea Bright
Plummer, Dirk Arnold professional engineer

### Sea Isle City
Tull, Theresa Anne retired ambassador

### Secaucus
Bailey, Steven Frederick publishing executive
Bender, Bruce F. book publishing executive
Black, Hillel Moses publisher
†Donaldoni, Roberto soccer player
Endyke, Mary Beth lawyer
Fahy, John J. lawyer
†Fredericks, Alan editor-in-chief
Gomes, Celeste Regina writer, editor
Highet, Mac publishing company executive
Marcus, Alan C. public relations consultant
Meola, Tony professional soccer player, actor
Nathan, Martin publishing company executive
Newton, V. Miller medical psychotherapist, neuropsychologist, writer
†Parreira, Carlos Alberto soccer coach
Povich, Lynn journalist, magazine editor
Rachlin, Stephen Leonard psychiatrist
Rosenblum, Edward G. lawyer
Rothman, Martin finance company executive, accountant
Schenck, Frederick A. business executive
Thomas, Ian Leslie Maurice publisher
Unanue, Joseph food products executive
Verdi, David Joseph broadcast news executive

### Sewell
Wright, William Cook archivist, historian, researcher

### Shamong
Knight, Margaret Elizabeth music educator

### Ship Bottom
Turkot, Dorothy Regester Felton writer, illustrator

### Short Hills
Aviado, Domingo M. pharmacologist, toxicologist
Broder, Patricia Janis art historian, writer
Brous, Philip retail consultant
Chaiken, Bernard Henry internist, gastroenterologist
Danzis, Rose Marie emeritus college president
Furst, E(rrol) Kenneth transportation executive, accountant
Good, Allen Hovey acquisitions broker, real estate broker, business consultant
Good, Joan Duffey artist
Greenberg, Carl lawyer
Harwood, Jerry market research executive
Hazlehurst, Robert Purviance, Jr. lawyer
Jackson, William Ward chemical company executive
Kaye, Jerome R. retired engineering and construction company executive
King, Charles Thomas retired school superintendent, educator
Klemme, Carl William banker
Lohse, Austin Webb banker
MacKinnon, Malcolm D(avid) retired insurance company executive
Mebane, William Black controller, financial consultant
Middleton, Timothy George writer
Moore, Robert Condit civil engineer
Ogden, Maureen Black retired state legislator
Parks, Robert Henry consulting economist, educator
Pilchik, Ely Emanuel rabbi, writer
†Price, Michael F. money management executive
Rinsky, Judith Lynn foundation administrator, educator consultant
Robbins-Wilf, Marcia educational consultant
Schaefer, Charles James, III advertising agency executive, consultant
Schaffer, Edmund John management consultant, retired engineering executive
Siegfried, David Charles lawyer
Soderlind, Sterling Eugene newspaper industry consultant
Wharton, Lennard engineering company executive
Winter, Ruth Grosman (Mrs. Arthur Winter) journalist

### Shrewsbury
Abel, Mary Elizabeth art educator, artist
Alburtus, Mary Jo social worker, consultant, trainer
Gilbert, Liane Marie research scientist executive
Hopkins, Charles Peter, II lawyer
Jones, Charles Hill, Jr. banker
Reich, Bernard telecommunications engineer
†Shagan, Bernard Pellman endocrinologist, educator

### Skillman
Brill, Yvonne Claeys engineer, consultant
Goldblatt, Barry Lance manufacturing executive
†Kluger, Richard author, editor
Rhett, Haskell Emery Smith educator
Schoen, Alvin E., Jr. environmental engineer, consultant
Wang, Jonas Chia-Tsung pharmaceutical executive
Wheelock, Keith Ward retired consulting company executive, educator

### Somerset
Aronson, Dana Lynne program/public relations executive
Aronson, Louis Vincent, II manufacturing executive
Bieber, Mark Allan nutrition scientist, researcher
Brophy, Joseph Thomas information company executive
Chaitman, Helen Davis lawyer
De Salva, Salvatore Joseph pharmacologist, toxicologist
DeVaris, Jeannette Mary psychologist
Greenberg, Lenore public relations professional
Hall, Edwin Huddleston, Jr. investment company executive
Kozlowski, Thomas Joseph, Jr. lawyer, trust company executive
Kwetkauskie, John A. medical technologist
Plenty, Royal Homer writer
Robinson, Patricia Snyder lawyer
Wasson, Richard Howard English language educator

### Somerville
Cohen, Walter Stanley accountant, financial consultant
Dammel, Ralph Rainer chemist, researcher
Dixon, Joanne Elaine music educator
Dobrinsky, Susan Elizabeth human resources director
Grant, Robert James animal nutritional research manager
Hutcheon, Peter David lawyer
McCoy, Eileen Carey academic dean
Palmer, Stuart Michael microbiologist
Peterson, John Douglas museum administrator
Plant, Maretta Moore public relations and marketing executive
Shive, Richard Byron architect
Weidenfeller, Geraldine Carney speech and language pathologist
Yuster-Freeman, Leigh Carol publishing company executive

### South Amboy
Kosmoski, Mary Lou Teresa special education educator
Moskal, Anthony John former dean, professor, management and education consultant

### South Hackensack
Cohen, Brett I. health products executive

### South Orange
Babu, Addagatla John Gabrial decision sciences educator
DeVaris, Panayotis Eric architect
Fleming, Edward J. priest, educator
Goldman, Harvey S. therapist, rabbi
Green, Donald Webb economist
Gruenwald, Renee special education educator
Lapinski, Frances Constance data processing systems executive
Long, Philip Lee information systems executive

### South Plainfield
Hunsinger, Doyle J. electronics executive
Janiak, Cathy Lynn sales consultant
Kennedy, John William engineering company executive
Munger, Janet Anne education administrator
Saltz, Ralph corporate lawyer

### Southampton
Knortz, Walter Robert accountant, former insurance company executive

### Sparta
Alberto, Pamela Louise oral and maxillofacial surgeon, educator
Buist, Jean Mackerley veterinarian
Harrison, Alice Kathleen retired elementary educator
Saxe, Thelma Richards secondary school educator, consultant
Seaman, Emma Lucy artist, poet
Spence, Robert Leroy publishing executive
Truran, William Richard electrical engineer

### Spring Lake
Anderson, James Francis lawyer
Connor, Frances Partridge education educator
D'Luhy, John James investment banker
Ernst, John Louis management consultant
Perkowski, Paul James accountant

### Springfield
Adams, James Mills chemicals executive
Coleman, James H., Jr. state supreme court justice
DeVone, Denise artist, educator
Duberstein, Joel Lawrence physician
Goldstein, Irving Robert mechanical and industrial engineer, educator, consultant
Grayson, Bette Rita lawyer
Merachnik, Donald superintendent of schools
Panish, Morton B. physical chemist, consultant
Perilstein, Fred Michael electrical engineer, consultant
Shilling, A. Gary economic consultant, investment advisor
Stoller, Mitchell Robert non-profit organization administrator
Toresco, Donald automotive executive

### Stanhope
Scala, John Charles secondary education educator, astronomer

### Stanton
Clayton, Raymond Arthur purchasing executive
Jagel, Kenneth Irwin, Jr. chemical engineer, consultant

### Stillwater
Finkelstein, Louis retired art educator

### Stirling
Walsh, Peter Joseph physics educator

### Stockholm
dePaolo, Ronald Francis editor, publisher

### Stockton
Griffin, Bryant Wade retired judge
Kent, George Cantine, Jr. zoology educator
Mahon, Robert photographer
Schoenherr, John (Carl) artist, illustrator
Taylor, Rosemary artist
Tunley, Roul author

### Stone Harbor
Koss, Rosabel Steinhauer retired education educator

### Stratford
Mendels, Joseph psychiatrist, educator
Rollins, Sandra L. academic administrator

### Summit
Avery, Christine Ann pediatrician
Batzer, R. Kirk accountant
Bostwick, Randell A. retired retail food company executive
Bottelli, Richard retired architect
Carniol, Paul J. plastic and reconstructive surgeon, otolaryngologist
Fuess, Billings Sibley, Jr. advertising executive
Fukui, Hatsuaki electrical engineer, art historian
Hall, Pamela Elizabeth psychologist
Keith, Garnett Lee, Jr. insurance company investment executive
Kenyon, Edward Tipton lawyer
Malin, Robert Abernethy investment management executive
May, Ernest Max charitable organization official
McDonough, Patrick Joseph, Jr. lawyer
Mueller, Paul Henry retired banker
Mulreany, Robert Henry retired lawyer
Nessen, Ward Henry typographer, lawyer
O'Byrne, Elizabeth Milikin pharmacologist, researcher, endocrinologist
Pace, Leonard retired management consultant
Panzarino, Saverio Joseph physician
Parsons, Judson Aspinwall, Jr. lawyer
Pawelec, William John retired electronics company executive
Phillips, James Charles physicist, educator
Pollak, Henry Otto retired utility research executive, educator
Rosensweig, Ronald Ellis scientist consultant
Rossey, Paul William school superintendent, university president
Rousseau, Irene Victoria artist, sculptor
Sayles, Thomas Dyke, Jr. banker
Scudder, Edward Wallace, Jr. newspaper and broadcasting executive
Slepian, David mathematician, communications engineer
Starks, Florence Elizabeth retired special education educator
Terracciano, Anthony Patrick banker
Thompson, Robert L., Jr. lawyer
Vogel, Julius consulting actuary, former insurance company executive
Williams, Sandra Castaldo elementary school educator
Wissbrun, Kurt Falke chemist, consultant
Woller, James Alan lawyer
Ziegler, John Benjamin chemist, lepidopterist

### Surf City
Sommer, Joseph William retired middle school educator

### Swedesboro
Lovell, Theodore electrical engineer, consultant

### Teaneck
Allen, Brenda Joyce management consultant, editor in chief
Alperin, Richard Martin clinical social worker, psychoanalyst
Borg, Sidney Fred mechanical engineer, educator
Browne, Robert Span economist
Brudner, Helen Gross social sciences educator
Bukovec, Joseph Aloysius special education educator
Bullough, John Frank organist, music educator
Cassimatis, Peter John economics educator
Ehrlich, Ira Robert mechanical engineering consultant
Fairfield, Betty Elaine Smith psychologist
Fanshel, David social worker
Fatemi, Faramarz Saifpour history and political science educator, consultant
Feinberg, Robert S. plastics manufacturing company executive, marketing consultant
Gordon, Jonathan David psychologist
Gordon, Lois Goldfein English language educator
Gordon, Maxwell pharmaceutical company executive
Hollman, Barbara Carol psychoanalyst, psychotherapist, consultant
Huang, Theresa C. librarian
Koszarski, Richard film historian, writer
Kramer, Bernard physicist, educator
Meno, John Peter chorepiscopus
Mertz, Francis James academic administrator
Nagy, Christa Fiedler biochemist
Ngai, Shih Hsun physician
Palitz, Clarence Yale, Jr. commercial finance executive
Pischl, Adolph John school administrator
†Reid, Rufus Lamar jazz bassist, educator
Rizio, Ronald R. writer, information specialist
Rudy, Willis historian
Scotti, Dennis Joseph educator, researcher, consultant
Tamir, Theodor electrophysics researcher, educator
Williams, John Alfred educator, author
Wiseman, Gloria Diana medical educator, physician
Zwass, Vladimir computer scientist, educator

### Tenafly
Badr, Gamal Moursi Arab laws consultant
Blank, Marion Sue psychologist
Cosgriff, Stuart Worcester internist, consultant, medical educator
Gibbons, Robert Philip management consultant
Heghinian, Elizabeth Alban Trumbower artist, educator
Katzman, Merle Hershel orthopaedic surgeon
Koons, Irvin Louis design and marketing executive, graphic artist, consultant
Kronenwett, Frederick Rudolph microbiologist
Lang, Hans Joachim engineering company executive
Levy, Norman Jay investment banker, financial consultant
Lilley, Theodore Robert financial executive
Stowe, David Metz clergyman
Vinocur, M. Richard publisher

### Teterboro
Ficalora, Joseph Paul aeronautical engineering supervisor
Gambino, S(alvatore) Raymond medical laboratory executive, educator

### Three Bridges
Lawrence, Gerald Graham management consultant

### Tinton Falls
Canfield, William Newton retired editorial cartoonist
Priesand, Sally Jane rabbi

### Titusville
Conway, Paul Gary neuropharmacologist
Godly, Gordon Thomas retired chemist, consultant
Hassell, Alan Edward pharmaceutical administrator, researcher
Marden, Kenneth Allen advertising executive

### Toms River
Adamo, Joseph Albert biologist, educator, researcher
Chambers, Elizabeth Donan neonatal nurse, administrator
†Clancy, Kevin F. cardiologist
Donaldson, Marcia Jean lay worker
Fanuele, Michael Anthony electronics engineer, research engineer
Gottesman, Roy Tully chemical company executive
Gross, Leroy sugar company executive
Kanarkowski, Edward Joseph data processing company executive
Marchese, Michael James, Jr. radiation oncologist
Okusanya, Olubukanla Tejumola ecologist
Tweed, John Louis consultant, association executive, lecturer, small business owner
Wagner, Edward Kurt publishing company executive
Whitman, Russell Wilson lawyer

### Totowa
Holyfield, Evander boxer
Jelliffe, Charles Gordon banker
Moorer, Michael professional boxer

### Trenton
Bigham, William J. lawyer
Binder, Elaine Kotell consultant to associations
Brandinger, Jay Jerome electronics executive, state official
Brearley, Candice fashion designer
Brown, Garrett Edward, Jr. federal judge
Brown, Richard Alexander chemist
Butorac, Frank George librarian, educator
Caldwell, Wesley Stuart, III lawyer, lobbyist
†Case, Richard W. professional sports team executive
Chavooshian, Marge artist, educator
Christopherson, Elizabeth Good broadcast executive
Clymer, Brian William state official
Courtney, Esau bishop
Cowen, Robert E. federal judge
Cushman, David Wayne research biochemist
DeMontigney, James Morgan health services administrator
DiFrancesco, Donald T. state senator
Dimasi, Linda Grace epidemiologist
Donahue, Donald Francis secondary education educator
Eickhoff, Harold Walter college president, humanities educator
Fisher, Clarkson Sherman federal judge
Fishman, Len state commissioner
George, Emery Edward foreign language and studies educator
Gindin, William Howard judge
Glass, Michael George college administrator
Greenberg, Morton Ira federal judge
Handler, Alan B. state supreme court justice
Hill, Robyn Marcella lawyer
Himm, Emilie Gina records and information manager, consultant
Hooks, Lonna R. state official
Joseph, Edith Hoffman retired editor
Losi, Maxim John medical communications and regulatory executive
†Manahan, Kent newscaster
Medley, Alex Roy executive minister
Old, Hughes Oliphant research theologian, clergyman
Parell, Mary Little federal judge, former banking commissioner
Peroni, Peter A., II psychologist, educator
Poritz, Deborah T. former state attorney general, state judge
Pruitt, George Albert academic administrator
Ranck, Edna Runnels academic administrator, researcher
Reiss, John C. bishop
Robinson, Susan Mittleman data processing executive
Roshon, George Kenneth manufacturing company executive
Rubin, Bernard pharmacologist, biomedical writer, consultant
Russell, Joyce Anne Rogers librarian
Saraf, Komal C. psychologist
Schirber, Annamarie Riddering speech and language pathologist, educator
Shindledecker, J. Gregory programmer, analyst
Stefane, Clara Joan business education secondary educator
Stein, Sandra Lou educational psychologist, educator
Sterns, Joel Henry lawyer
Thompson, Anne Elise federal judge
Verniero, Peter state attorney general
Weinberg, Martin Herbert retired psychiatrist
Whitman, Christine Todd governor
Wolfe, Albert J. state agency researcher

Wolfe, Deborah Cannon Partridge *government education consultant*
Zanna, Martin Thomas *physician*

### Tuckerton
DeCicco, James Joseph *media specialist*
Dinges, Richard Allen *entrepreneur*
Egan, Roger Edward *publishing executive*

### Turnersville
Cammarota, Marie Elizabeth *health services administration/nursing educator*
DePace, Nicholas Louis *physician*

### Union
Applbaum, Ronald Lee *academic administrator*
Darden-Simpson, Barbara L. *library director*
Franks, Robert D. (Bob Franks) *congressman*
French, Kathleen Patricia *educational evaluator, consultant*
Hennings, Dorothy Grant (Mrs. George Hennings) *education educator*
Kaplan, Doris Weiler *social worker*
Lapidus, Norman Israel *food broker*
†Lederman, Susan Sturc *public administration educator*
Lewandowski, Andrew Anthony *utilities executive, consultant*
Muller, Gregory Alan *health facilities administrator, mayor*
Pasvolsky, Richard Lloyd *parks, recreation, and environment educator*
Rokosz, Gregory Joseph *emergency medicine physician, educator*
Schiffman, Robert Stanley *environmental test equipment manufacturing executive*
Soni, Maria Habib *controller, treasurer*
White, Robert L. G., Jr. *aerospace company executive*
Williams, Carol Jorgensen *social work educator*
Zois, Constantine Nicholas Athanasios *meteorology educator*

### Union City
Bull, Inez Stewart *special education and gifted music educator, coloratura soprano, pianist, editor, author*
Feingold, Janice Ann *elementary education educator*
Makar, Nadia Eissa *secondary education educator, educational administrator*
Ortizio, Debra Louise *elementary education educator*

### Upper Montclair
Cordasco, Francesco *sociologist, educator, author*
Kowalski, Stephen Wesley *chemistry educator*
Morris, John Lunden *global logistics and communications executive*

### Upper Saddle River
Butterfield, Bruce Scott *publishing company executive*
Dojny, Richard Francis *publishing company executive*
Oolie, Sam *manufacturing and investment company executive*
Wallace, William, III *engineering executive*

### Ventnor City
Bolton, Kenneth Albert *management consultant*
Robbins, Hulda Dornblatt *artist, printmaker*
Zuckerman, Stuart *psychiatrist, educator*

### Verona
Ayaso, Manuel *artist*
Brightman, Robert Lloyd *importer, textile company executive, consultant*
Greenwald, Robert *public relations executive*
Meyer, Helen (Mrs. Abraham J. Meyer) *retired editorial consultant*
Ward, Roger Coursen *lawyer*

### Vineland
DeVivo, Sal J. *newspaper executive*
Howell, James Burt, III *agricultural products company sales consultant*
Hunt, Howard F(rancis) *psychologist, educator*
Popp, Charlotte Louise *health development center administrator, nurse*

### Voorhees
Barone, Donald Anthony *neurologist, educator*
Schmid, Patricia Jean *personnel professional*
Swiecicki, Martin *neurosurgeon*

### Waldwick
Samuelson, Billie Margaret *artist*
Surdoval, Donald James *accounting and management consulting company executive*

### Wall
Cobb, Lorene Pozyc *physical therapist*
Colford, Francis Xavier *gas industry executive*

### Wanaque
Jordan, Leo John *lawyer*

### Warren
Blass, Walter Paul *consultant, management educator*
Chubb, Percy, III *insurance company executive*
Cohen, Bertram David *psychologist, educator*
Earle, Jean Buist *computer company executive*
Hartman, David Gardiner *actuary*
Jackson, John Wyant *medical products executive*
Kasper, Horst Manfred *lawyer*
Massler, Howard Arnold *lawyer, corporate executive*
Maull, George Marriner *music director, conductor*
O'Hare, Dean Raymond *insurance company executive*
Sartor, Anthony Joseph *environmental engineer*
Wightman, Glenn Charles *environmental, health and safety administrator*

### Washington
De Sanctis, Vincent *college president*
Drago, Joseph Rosario *urologist, educator*

### Watchung
Knudson, Harry Edward, Jr. *retired electrical manufacturing company executive*
Nadeau, Earl Raymond *electronics executive*
Reeves, Patricia Ruth *heavy machinery manufacturing company executive*
Schaefer, Jacob Wernli *military systems consultant*
Tornqvist, Erik Gustav Markus *chemical engineer, research scientist*

### Wayne
Benjamin, James Anthony *electrical engineer, educator*
Cheng, David Hong *mechanical engineering educator*
Cordover, Ronald Harvey *business executive, venture capitalist*
Donald, Robert Graham *retail food chain human resources executive*
†Dougherty, Mildred Swanson *English educator*
Freimark, Jeffrey Philip *retail supermarket executive*
Friedman, Michael Lazar *chemical engineer*
†Goldstein, Marjorie Tunick *special education educator*
Gollance, Robert Barnett *ophthalmologist*
Hamill, A(llen) William *finance executive*
Heyman, Samuel J. *chemicals and building materials manufacturing company executive*
Jeffrey, Robert George, Jr. *industrial company executive*
Katz, Leandro *artist, filmmaker*
Lang, William Charles *retail executive*
Law, Janet Mary *music educator*
Nicastro, Francis Efisio *defense electronics and retailing executive*
O'Connor, John Morris, III *philosophy educator*
Siepser, Stuart Lewis *cardiologist, internist*
†Silverman-Dresner, Toby Roslyn *psychologist*
Speert, Arnold *college president, chemistry educator*
Tanzman-Bock, Maxine M. *psychotherapist, hypnotherapist, consultant*
†Wallace, Edith *biology educator*
†Wepner, Shelley Beth *education educator, software developer*
†Werth, Jean Marie *biology educator*
White, Doris Gnauck *science educator, biochemical and biophysics researcher*
†Younie, William John *special education educator, researcher*

### Weehawken
Hayden, Joseph A., Jr. *lawyer*
Hess, Dennis John *investment banker*
Murphy, Barbara Ann *protective services official*

### West Caldwell
Page, Frederick West *business consultant*
Schiff, Robert *health care consultancy company executive*
Vachher, Sheila Ann *information systems analyst*

### West Long Branch
Herman, Martin Neal *neurologist, educator*
Lutz, Francis Charles *university dean, civil engineering educator*
Rouse, Robert Sumner *former college official*
Stafford, Rebecca *academic administrator, sociologist*

### West Milford
Ferguson, Harley Robert *service company executive*
Kinney, Dorothy Jean *retired elementary educator*
Stelpstra, William John *minister*

### West New York
Arias, David *bishop*
Gruenberg, Elliot Lewis *electronics engineer and company executive*
Kelly, Lucie Stirm Young *nursing educator*

### West Orange
Askin, Marilyn *lawyer*
Bornstein, Lester Milton *retired medical center executive*
Brodkin, Roger Harrison *dermatologist, educator*
De Lisa, Joel Alan *rehabilitation physician, rehabilitation facility executive*
Eisenberg, R. Neal *restoration company executive*
Ghali, Anwar Youssef *psychiatrist, educator*
Haney, James Kevin *lawyer*
Johnson, Clarice P. *materials procurement executive*
Kushen, Allan Stanford *retired lawyer*
Kyle, Corinne Silverman *management consultant*
Langsner, Alan Michael *pediatrician*
Nessel, Edward Harry *swimming coach*
Panagides, John *pharmacologist*
Rayfield, Gordon Elliott *playwright, political risk consultant*
Richmond, Harold Nicholas *lawyer*
Schreiber, Eileen Sher *artist*

### West Paterson
Seiffer, Neil Mark *photographer*

### West Trenton
D'Anna, Vincent P. *federal commissioner*
Woods, Howard James, Jr. *civil engineer*

### Westfield
Bartok, William *environmental technologies consultant*
Besch, Lorraine W. *special education educator*
Boutillier, Robert John *accountant*
Connell, Grover *food company executive*
Cushman, Helen Merle Baker *retired management consultant*
†Decker, Mark Richard *lawyer*
Devlin, Wende Dorothy *writer, artist*
Feret, Adam Edward, Jr. *dentist*
Fitts, Leonard Donald *educational administrator*
Ganz, Felix *marketing professional*
Gutman, Sharon Weissman *Holocaust educator, poet*
Jacobson, Gary Steven *lawyer*
Keyko, George John *electronics company executive*
Lipkin, William Joel *controller, history educator*
Mazzarese, Michael Louis *executive coach, consultant*
McDevitt, Brian Peter *history educator, educational consultant*
Mc Fadden, G. Bruce *hospital administrator*
McLean, Vincent Ronald *former manufacturing company financial executive*
Simon, Martin Stanley *commodity marketing company executive, economist*
Smith, Joan Lowell *writer, public relations consultant*
Specht, Gordon Dean *retired petroleum executive*

### Westville
Doughty, A. Glenn *minister*

### Westwood
Black, Theodore Halsey *retired manufacturing company executive*
Cullen, Ruth Enck *reading specialist, elementary education educator*
Nachtigal, Patricia *equipment manufacturing company executive, general counsel*
Noyes, Robert Edwin *publisher, writer*
Schutz, Donald Frank *geochemist, healthcare corporate executive*

### Wharton
Loughlin, William Joseph *priest, religious organization administrator*
Rodzianko, Paul *energy and environmental company executive*

### Whippany
Golden, John F. *packaging company executive*
Maggiore, Susan *geophysical oceanographer*
Michaelis, Paul Charles *engineering physicist executive*
Morris, Patricia Smith *media specialist, author, educator*
Nwosu, Kingsley Chukwudum *research and development scientist, educator*
Petitto, Barbara Buschell *artist*
Scroggs, Debbie Lee *communications professional*

### Whitehouse Station
Atieh, Michael Gerard *accountant*
Douglas, Robert Gordon, Jr. *physician*
Gilmartin, Raymond V. *health care products company executive*
Lewent, Judy Carol *pharmaceutical executive*

### Whiting
Case, Elizabeth *artist, writer*
Williams, Roger Wright *public health educator*

### Willingboro
Bass, Joseph Oscar *minister*
Greene, Natalie Constance *protective services official*
Ingerman, Peter Zilahy *infosystems consultant*
Schnapf, Abraham *aerospace engineer, consultant*

### Windsor
Phelan, Richard Paul *bank executive*

### Woodbridge
Amato, Vincent Vito *business executive*
Becker, Frederic Kenneth *lawyer*
Brauth, Marvin Jeffrey *lawyer*
Brown, Morris *lawyer*
Buchsbaum, Peter A. *lawyer*
Chesky, Pamela Bosze *school system administrator, curriculum specialist*
Cirafesi, Robert J. *lawyer*
Constantinou, Clay *lawyer*
Galkin, Samuel Bernard *orthodontist*
Hoberman, Stuart A. *lawyer*
Jaffe, Sheldon Eugene *lawyer*
Kull, Bryan Paul *food products executive, real estate investor*
Lepelstat, Martin L. *lawyer*
McCarthy, G. Daniel *lawyer*
Moran, Jeffrey William *safety engineer*
Morris, David *retired electrical engineer*

### Woodbury
Gehring, David Austin *physician, adminstrator, cardiologist*
Stambaugh, John Edgar *oncologist, hematologist, pharmacologist, educator*
White, John Lindsey *lawyer*
Zane, Raymond J. *state senator, lawyer*

### Woodcliff Lake
Morath, Max Edward *entertainer, composer, writer*
Morrione, Melchior S. *management consultant, accountant*
Perrella, James Elbert *manufacturing company executive*
Pollak, Cathy Jane *lawyer*
Sneirson, Marilyn *lawyer*
Travis, J(ames) Frank *manufacturing company executive*

### Wrightstown
Drechsel, Edward Russell, Jr. *retired utility company executive*

### Wyckoff
Bauer, Theodore James *physician*
Bucko, John Joseph *investment corporation executive*
Cropper, Susan Peggy *veterinarian*
Lavery, Daniel P. *marketing management consultant*
Marcus, Linda Susan *dermatologist*
Miller, Walter Neal *insurance company consultant*
Mirza, Muhammad Zubair *product development company executive, researcher, engineering consultant, inventor*
Rice, Richard Charles *academic administrator, educator, consultant*
Stahl, Alice Slater *psychiatrist*

### Yardville
Telencio, Gloria Jean *elementary education educator*

## NEW MEXICO

### Alamogordo
Dewey, David Lawrence *banker, business consultant, author*
Green, Francis William *investment consultant, former missile scientist*
Lee, Joli Fay Eaton *elementary education educator*
Lindley, Norman Dale *physician*
McFadin, Helen Lozetta *retired elementary education educator*
Stapp, John Paul *flight surgeon, retired air force officer*

### Albuquerque
Adams, Clinton *artist, historian*
Addis, Richard Barton *lawyer*
Anaya, Rudolfo *educator, writer*
Anderson, Lawrence Keith *electrical engineer*
Antreasian, Garo Zareh *artist, lithographer, art educator*
Arvizu, Dan Eliab *mechanical engineer*
Aubin, Barbara Jean *artist*
†Auger, Tamara M. *psychotherapist*
Austin, Edward Marvin *retired mechanical engineer, researcher*
Ballard, David Eugene *anesthesiologist*
Barbo, Dorothy Marie *obstetrician, gynecologist, educator*
Bardacke, Paul Gregory *lawyer, former attorney general*
Barrow, Thomas Francis *artist, educator*
Basso, Keith Hamilton *cultural anthropologist, linguist, educator*
Beach, Arthur O'Neal *lawyer*
Beckel, Charles Leroy *physics educator*
Bell, Stoughton *computer scientist, mathematician, educator*
Bencke, Ronald *financial executive*
Benson, Sharon Stovall *primary school educator*
Black, Craig Call *retired museum administrator*
Bolie, Victor Wayne *science and engineering consultant*
Bova, Vincent Arthur, Jr. *lawyer, consultant, photographer*
Bretton, Henry L. *political scientist, educator*
Brown, James Randall *mechanical engineer*
Campbell, C(harles) Robert *architect*
Caplan, Edwin Harvey *university dean, accounting educator*
Cargo, David Francis *lawyer*
Caruso, Mark John *lawyer*
Chavez, Martin Joseph *mayor, attorney*
Clark, Alan Barthwell *city administrator*
Clark, Arthur Joseph, Jr. *retired mechanical and electrical engineer*
Clark, Teresa Watkins *psychotherapist, clinical counselor*
Coes, Donald Vinton *economics educator*
Cofer, Charles Norval *psychologist, educator*
Cole, Terri Lynn *organization administrator*
Coleman, Barbara McReynolds *artist*
Condie, Carol Joy *anthropologist, research facility administrator*
Conway, John E. *federal judge*
Culpepper, Mabel Claire *artist*
D'Anza, Lawrence Martin *marketing educator*
Danziger, Jerry *broadcasting executive*
Dasgupta, Amitava *chemist, educator*
Davidson, Juli *creativity consultant*
Dixon, George Lane, Jr. *orthopedic surgeon*
Dorato, Peter *electrical and computer engineering educator*
Drummond, Harold Dean *education educator*
Easley, Mack *retired state supreme court chief justice*
Eaton, George Wesley, Jr. *petroleum engineer, oil company executive*
Edwards, William Sterling, III *cardiovascular surgeon*
Ehrhorn, Thomas Frederick *software quality assurance engineer*
Elliott, Charles Harold *clinical psychologist*
Ellis, Willis Hill *lawyer, educator*
Evans, Bill (James William Evans) *dancer, choreographer, educator, arts administrator*
Evans, Max Allen *writer, artist*
Evans, Pauline D. *physicist, educator*
Exner, Jane Frances *nursing administrator*
Fleury, Paul Aimé *university dean, physicist*
Flournoy, John Charles, Sr. *training specialist, retired military officer*
Friberg, George Joseph *electronics company executive*
Friedenberg, Walter Drew *journalist*
Frings, Manfred Servatius *philosophy educator*
Frost, W. Gregory *mortgage company executive*
Frumkin, Gene *writer, educator*
Fuller, Anne Elizabeth Havens *English language and literature educator, consultant*
Garcia, F. Chris *academic administrator, political science educator, public opinion researcher*
Garland, James Wilson, Jr. *retired physics educator*
Geary, David Leslie *communications executive, educator, consultant*
Gensler, Thomas Daniel *military officer, medical services executive*
Golden, Julius *advertising and public relations executive, lobbyist, investor*
Goldston, Barbara M. Harral *editor*
Goodman, Phyllis L. *public relations executive*
Gordon, Larry Jean *public health administrator and educator*
Gorham, Frank DeVore, Jr. *petroleum company executive*
Griffin, W. C. *bishop*
Guthrie, Patricia Sue *newspaper reporter, free-lance writer*
Hadas, Elizabeth Chamberlayne *publisher*
Haddad, Edward Raouf *civil engineer, consultant*
Hadley, William Melvin *college dean*
Hahn, Betty *artist, photographer, educator*
Hakim, Besim Selim *architecture and urban design educator, researcher*
Hale, Bruce Donald *retired marketing professional*
Hall, Jerome William *research engineering educator*
Hall, Lois Riggs *former state senator, former symphony orchestra administrator*
Haltom, B(illy) Reid *lawyer*
Hancock, Don Ray *researcher*
Hansen, Curtis LeRoy *federal judge*
Harman, Wallace Patrick *lawyer*
Harris, Fred R. *political science educator, former senator*
Harrison, Charles Wagner, Jr. *applied physicist*
Hart, Frederick Michael *law educator*
Hayo, George Edward *management consultant*
Heady, Ferrel *retired political science educator*
Henderson, Rogene Faulkner *toxicologist, researcher*
Hooker, Van Dorn *architect, artist*
Hovel, Esther Harrison *art educator*
Howard, William Jack *mechanical engineer, retired*
Hsi, David Ching Heng *plant pathologist and geneticist, educator*
Hull, McAllister Hobart, Jr. *retired university administrator*
Hutton, Paul Andrew *history educator, writer*
Hylko, James Mark *health physicist, certified quality auditor*
Ivester, Vicky Jo *sales professional*
Jaramillo, Mari-Luci *federal agency administrator*
Johnson, Daniel Leon *aeronautical engineer*
Johnson, Robert Hersel *journalist*
Johnson, William Hugh, Jr. *hospital administrator*
Kaehele, Bettie Louise *accountant*
Karni, Shlomo *engineering and religious studies educator*
Kelley, Robert Otis *medical science educator*
Kelshaw, Terence *bishop*

King, James Nedwed construction company executive, lawyer
Knospe, William Herbert medical educator
Knowles, Richard John judge
Koffler, Herbert health facility administrator, educator
Korman, Nathaniel Irving research and development company executive
Kroken, Patricia Ann health science association administrator
Kutvirt, Duda Chytilova (Ruzena) scientific translator
Land, Cecil E. electrical engineer
Lang, Thompson Hughes publishing company executive
Lattman, Laurence Harold retired academic administrator
Lawit, John Walter lawyer
Lee-Smith, Hughie artist, educator
Lind, Levi Robert classics educator, author
Loftfield, Robert Berner biochemistry educator
Loubet, Jeffrey W. lawyer
Lucchetti, Lynn L. career officer
Lynch, Paul Vincent safety engineer, consultant
MacCurdy, Raymond Ralph, Jr. modern language educator
Mateju, Joseph Frank hospital administrator
Mauderly, Joe Lloyd pulmonary toxicologist
May, Gerald William university administrator, educator, civil engineering consultant
May, Philip Alan sociology educator
McCarty, W(illard) Duane obstetrician, gynecologist, physician executive
McCue, Stephen Patrick lawyer
McKiernan, John William mechanical engineer
Mc Million, John Macon retired newspaper publisher
Meiering, Mark C. lawyer
Miller, Mickey Lester retired school administrator
Minahan, Daniel Francis manufacturing company executive, lawyer
Molzen, Dayton Frank consulting engineering executive
Moody, Patricia Ann psychiatric nurse, artist
Mora, Federico neurosurgeon
Multhaup, Merrel Keyes artist
Nagatani, Patrick Allan Ryoichi artist, art educator
Napolitano, Leonard Michael anatomist, university administrator
Narath, Albert laboratory administrator
Nash, Gerald David historian
Ofte, Donald retired environmental executive, consultant
Omer, George Elbert, Jr. orthopaedic surgeon, hand surgeon, educator
Oppedahl, Phillip Edward computer company executive
Ortiz, Kathleen Lucille travel consultant
O'Toole, Robert John, II telemarketing consultant
Ottensmeyer, David Joseph healthcare consultant, retired neurosurgeon
Papike, James Joseph geology educator, science institute director
Parker, James Aubrey federal judge
Paster, Janice D. lawyer, former state legislator
Peck, Ralph Brazelton civil engineering educator, consultant
Peck, Richard Earl academic administrator, playwright, novelist
Peña, Juan José interpreter
Picraux, Samuel Thomas applied science and physics researcher
Plough, Charles Tobias, Jr. retired electronics engineering executive
Prinja, Anil Kant nuclear engineering educator
Ransom, Richard Edward retired state supreme court justice
Reyes, Edward pharmacology educator
Riley, Ann J. former state legislator, technology specialist
Roberts, Dennis William trade association administrator
Robinett, Rush Daleth, III robotics research manager
Robinson, Charles Paul nuclear physicist, diplomat, business executive
Roehl, Jerrald J(oseph) lawyer
Romero, Jeff lawyer
Romig, Alton Dale, Jr. metallurgist, educator
Rosenberg, Arthur James company executive
Rotherham, Larry Charles insurance executive
Rust, John Laurence heavy equipment sales/service company executive
Rutherford, Thomas Truxtun, II state senator, lawyer
Sabatini, William Quinn architect
Saland, Linda Carol anatomy educator
Sanchez, Victoria Wagner science educator
Sanderlin, Terry Keith counselor
Schoen, Stevan Jay lawyer
Schwerin, Karl Henry anthropology educator, researcher
Scott, Hanson Lee airport executive
Seiler, Fritz Arnold physicist
Sheehan, Michael Jarboe archbishop
Sickels, Robert Judd political science educator
Sisk, Daniel Arthur lawyer
Skipp, Tracy John academic advisor, counselor
Slade, Lynn Heyer lawyer
Snell, Patricia Poldervaart librarian, consultant
Sobolewski, John Stephen computer information scientist, consultant
Solomon, Arthur Charles pharmacist
Sparks, Morgan physicist
Stahl, Jack Leland real estate company executive
Stamm, Robert Jenne building contractor, construction company executive
Stephenson, Barbera Wertz lawyer
Stevenson, James Richard radiologist, lawyer
Stuart, David Edward anthropologist, author, educator
†Sullivan, Terry Brian semiconductor plant executive
Summers, William Koopmans neuropsychiatrist, researcher
Swenka, Arthur John food products executive
Tatum, Ronald Winston physician, endocrinologist
Thompson, Rufus E. lawyer
Thorson, James Llewellyn English language educator
Tope, Dwight Harold retired management consultant
Travelstead, Chester Coleman former educational administrator
Uhlenhuth, Eberhard Henry psychiatrist, educator
Unser, Al professional auto racer
Van Devender, J. Pace physical scientist, management consultant
Vianco, Paul Thomas metallurgist
Waitzkin, Howard Bruce physician, sociologist, educator
Ward, Charles Richard extension and research entomologist, educator
Wellborn, Charles Ivey science and technology licensing company executive
Westwood, Albert Ronald Clifton engineer
Whiddon, Carol Price writer, editor, consultant
Wilde, David publisher, writer, biographer
Wildin, Maurice Wilbert mechanical engineering educator
Winslow, Walter William psychiatrist
Witkin, Joel-Peter photographer
Wolf, Cynthia Tribelhorn librarian, library educator
Wollman, Nathaniel economist, educator
Wong, Phillip Allen osteopathic physician
Worrell, Richard Vernon orthopedic surgeon, educator, academic administrator
Young, Joan Crawford advertising executive
Youngdahl, James Edward lawyer
Zink, Lee B. academic administrator, economist, educator
Zumwalt, Ross Eugene forensic pathologist, educator

### Alto
Thrasher, Jack D. toxicologist, researcher, consultant

### Arroyo Hondo
Davis, Ronald artist, printmaker

### Artesia
Sarwar, Barbara Duce school system administrator

### Aztec
Moore, Roger Albert, Jr. archaeologist

### Belen
Gutjahr, Allan Leo mathematics educator, researcher
Toliver, Lee mechanical engineer

### Carlsbad
Byers, Matthew T(odd) lawyer, educator
Markle, George Bushar, IV surgeon
Moore, Bobbie Fay geriatrics nurse practitioner, nurse administrator
Regan, Muriel librarian
Watts, Marvin Lee minerals company executive, chemist, educator
Wayman, Cooper Harry environmental legal counsel

### Cedar Crest
Sheppard, Jack W. retired air force officer

### Cerrillos
Goodwin, Samuel McClure officer

### Chama
Moser, Robert Harlan physician, educator, writer

### Clovis
Goodwin, Martin Brune radiologist
Rehorn, Lois M(arie) nursing administrator

### Cordova
Kazmierski, Susan Hedwig family nurse practitioner, nurse midwife

### Corona
Steen, Nancy artist

### Corrales
Adams, James Frederick psychologist, educational administrator
Cobb, John Candler medical educator
Eaton, Pauline artist
Eisenstadt, Pauline Doreen Bauman investment company executive
Page, Jake (James K. Page, Jr.) writer, editor

### Edgewood
Hamilton, Jerald musician

### Espanola
Abeyta, Santiago Audoro (Jim Abeyta) human services administrator

### Farmington
Caldwell, John Winston, III petroleum engineer
Garretson, Owen Loren petroleum engineer
Hagan, Richard Francies computer system educator
Macaluso, Frank Augustus oil company executive
Morgan, Jack M. lawyer
Neidhart, James Allen physician, educator
Plummer, Steven Tsosie bishop
Titus, Victor Allen lawyer

### Galisteo
Holt, Nancy Louise artist
Lippard, Lucy Rowland writer, lecturer

### Gallup
Fellin, Octavia Antoinette retired librarian
Lindenmeyer, Mary Kathryn secondary education educator
Swain, Melinda Susan elementary education educator

### Glenwood
Tackman, Arthur Lester newspaper publisher, management consultant

### Glorieta
Mc Coy, Robert Baker publisher

### Grants
Ward, Katherine Marie school system administrator

### Hobbs
Garey, Donald Lee pipeline and oil company executive
Martin, Thomas Howard pastor
Reagan, Gary Don state legislator, lawyer
Stout, Lowell lawyer

### Holloman Air Force Base
†Klause, Klaus J. aircraft company executive

### Kirtland AFB
Anderson, Christine Marlene software engineer
Baum, Carl Edward electromagnetic theorist
Degnan, James Henry physicist
Harrison, George Brooks career officer
Heckathorn, William Gary military officer
Voelz, David George electrical engineer

### Las Cruces
Bell, M. Joy Miller financial planner, real estate broker
Bloom, John Porter historian, editor, administrator, archivist
Borman, Frank former astronaut, laser patent company executive
Bratton, Howard Calvin federal judge
Coburn, Horace Hunter retired physics educator
Cochrun, John Wesley chartered financial consultant
Colbaugh, Richard Donald mechanical engineer, educator, researcher
Cowden, Louis Fredrick electronics executive, engineer
Dudenhoeffer, Frances Tomlin physical education educator
Easterling, Kathy school system administrator
Eriksson, Anne-Marie social services executive, educator
Ford, Clarence Quentin mechanical engineer, educator
Gale, Thomas Martin university dean
Jacobs, Kent Frederick dermatologist
Kemp, John Daniel biochemist, educator
Kilmer, Neal Harold software engineer
Lease, Jane Etta environmental science consultant
Lease, Richard Jay police science educator, former police officer
Lutz, William Lan lawyer
Matthews, Larryl Kent mechanical engineering educator
McElyea, Ulysses, Jr. veterinarian
Medoff, Mark Howard playwright, screenwriter, novelist
Merrick, Beverly Childers journalism, communications educator
Morgan, John Derald electrical engineer
Myers, R. David library director, dean
Newman, Edgar Leon historian, educator
Peterson, Robin Tucker marketing educator
Ramirez, Ricardo bishop
Reinfelds, Juris computer science educator
Ritter, Sallie painter, sculptor
Roscoe, Stanley Nelson psychologist, aeronautical engineer
Sandenaw, Thomas Arthur, Jr. lawyer
Schemnitz, Sanford David wildlife biology educator
Shepard, Earl Alden retired government official
Sims, James Larry hospital administrator, healthcare consultant
Southward, Glen Morris statistician, educator
Talamantes, Roberto developmental pediatrician
Thode, Edward Frederick chemical engineer, educator
Way, Jacob Edson, III museum director

### Las Vegas
Riley, Carroll Lavern anthropology educator

### Loco Hills
Sánchez, Frank Perez elementary education educator

### Los Alamos
Andrews, Andrew Edward nuclear engineer
Baker, George Allen, Jr. physicist
Bame, Samuel Jarvis, Jr. research scientist
Becker, Stephen A. physicist, designer
Bell, George Irving biophysics researcher
Bradbury, Norris Edwin physicist
Campbell, Mary Stinecipher research chemist, educator
Colgate, Stirling Auchincloss physicist
Cucchiara, Alfred Louis health physicist
Engel, Emily Flachmeier school administrator, educator
Engelhardt, Albert George physicist
Friar, James Lewis physicist
Gibson, Benjamin Franklin physicist
Gregg, Charles Thornton research company executive
Grilly, Edward Rogers physicist
Gupta, Goutam biologist, biophysicist
Jackson, James F. nuclear engineer
Jarmie, Nelson physicist
Johnson, Mikkel Borlaug physicist
Judd, O'Dean P. physicist
Keepin, George Robert, Jr. physicist
Kelly, Robert Emmett physicist, educator
Kubas, Gregory Joseph research chemist
Linford, Rulon Kesler physicist, engineer
Matlack, George Miller radiochemist
McComas, David John science administrator, space physicist
McNally, James Henry physicist, defense consultant
Mendius, Patricia Dodd Winter editor, educator, writer
Michaudon, André Francisque physicist
Mitchell, Terence Edward materials scientist
†Moore, Tom O. program administrator
Nix, James Rayford nuclear physicist, consultant
Nunz, Gregory Joseph aerospace engineer, program manager, educator, entrepreneur
Pack, Russell T. theoretical chemist
Penneman, Robert Allen retired chemist
Petschek, Albert George physicist, consultant
Ramsay, John Barada research chemist, educator
Rosen, Louis physicist
Selden, Robert Wentworth physicist, science advisor
Simon-Gillo, Jehanne E. physicist
Smith, Fredrica Emrich rheumatologist, internist
Smith, James Lawrence research physicist
Stoddard, Stephen Davidson ceramic engineer, former state senator
Terrell, (Nelson) James physicist
Thompson, Lois Jean Heidke Ore psychologist
Tingley, Walter Watson computer systems manager
Wahl, Arthur Charles retired chemistry educator
Wallace, Jeannette Owens state legislator
Wallace, Terry Charles, Sr. technical administrator, researcher, consultant
Whetten, John Theodore geologist
Williams, Joel Mann polymer material scientist
WoldeGabriel, Giday research geologist
Zweig, George physicist, neurobiologist

### Los Lunas
Graham, Robert Albert research physicist

### Mayhill
Carter, Joy Eaton electrical engineer, consultant

### Mesilla
Harrison, Edward Robert physicist, educator

### Mesilla Park
Shutt, Frances Barton special education educator

### Milan
Kanesta, Nellie Rose chemical dependency counselor

### Montezuma
Geier, Philip Otto, III college president

### Mora
Hanks, Eugene Ralph land developer, cattle rancher, retired naval officer
Mossavar-Rahmani, Bijan oil and gas company executive

### Placitas
Dunmire, William Werden author, photographer
Forrest, Suzanne Sims research historian
Pirkl, James Joseph industrial designer, educator, writer
Reade, Lewis Pollock retired diplomat, engineer
Smith, Richard Bowen retired national park superintendent

### Portales
Agogino, George Allen anthropologist, educator
Byrnes, Lawrence William dean
Morris, Donald tax specialist
Paschke, Donald Vernon music educator
Williamson, Jack (John Stewart ) writer

### Ranchos De Taos
Dickey, Robert Preston author, educator, poet
Marx, Nicki Diane sculptor, painter

### Raton
Carter, Kathryn Ann home health nurse, mental health counselor
Robinson, Janie Monette education educator

### Rio Rancho
Meyerson, Barbara Tobias elementary school educator

### Roswell
Anderson, Donald Bernard oil company executive
Armstrong, Billie Bert retired highway contractor
Avery, Keith Willette artist, educator
Baldock, Bobby Ray federal judge
Casey, Barbara A. Perea state representative, school superintendent
Ebie, William D. museum director
Jennings, Emmit M. surgeon
Jennings, Timothy Zeph state senator, rancher
Johnston, Mary Ellen nursing educator
Lewis, George Raymond state agency administrator, clinical social worker
MacKellar, Keith Robert hospital administrator
Olson, Richard Earl lawyer, state legislator
Pretti, Bradford Joseph lay worker, insurance company executive
Wiggins, Kim Douglas artist, art dealer

### Ruidoso
Coe, Elizabeth Ann elementary education educator
Stover, Carolyn Nadine middle school educator
Wade, Pamela Sue women's health nurse

### Ruidoso Downs
Eldredge, Bruce Beard museum director

### Sandia Park
Greenwell, Ronald Everett communications executive

### Santa Fe
Agresto, John college president
†Allen, Ethan Edward internet specialist, webmaster
Allen, Terry artist
Anderson, Denice Anna editor
Atkinson, John Christopher magazine editor, critic, writer
Baca, Joseph Francis state supreme court justice
Ballard, Louis Wayne composer
Barrett, Bill sculptor
Baustian, Robert Frederick conductor
Bergé, Carol author
Besing, Ray Gilbert lawyer
Bradley, Walter D. lieutenant governor, real estate broker
Brockway, Merrill LaMonte television producer and director
Burk, Yvonne Turner artist, educator
Burton, John Paul (Jack Burton) lawyer
Calloway, Larry columnist
Campos, Santiago E. federal judge
Casey, Patrick Anthony lawyer
Citrin, Phillip Marshall retired lawyer
Clift, William Brooks, III photographer
Coffield, Conrad Eugene lawyer
Connell, Evan Shelby, Jr. author
Conron, John Phelan architect
Cowan, George Arthur chemist, bank executive, director
Crosby, John O'Hea conductor, opera manager
Cuming, George Scott retired lawyer, retired gas company official
Davis, Shelby Moore Cullom investment executive, consultant
Dechert, Peter photographer, writer, foundation adminstrator
DiMaio, Virginia Sue gallery owner
Dirks, Lee Edward newspaper executive
Dodds, Robert James, III lawyer
Dreisbach, John Gustave investment banker
Enyeart, James L. museum director
Erdman, Barbara visual artist
Fisher, Philip Chapin physicist
Fisher, Robert Alan laser physicist
Forsdale, (Chalmers) Louis education and communication educator
Fox, Jack Rex military professional
Franchini, Gene Edward state supreme court chief justice
Frost, Stanley retired judge
Gaddes, Richard performing arts administrator
†Garcia, Alex R. career military officer
Gell-Mann, Murray theoretical physicist, educator
Gilmour, Edward Ellis psychiatrist
Giovanielli, Damon Vincent physicist, consulting company executive
Gonzales, Stephanie state official
Graybeal, Sidney Norman national security executive, former government official

Harding, Marie ecological executive, artist
Hassrick, Peter Heyl museum director
Hickey, John Miller lawyer
Johnson, Gary Earl governor
Jones, Walter Harrison chemist
Kasbeer, Stephen Frederick retired university official
Kelly, Paul Joseph, Jr. federal judge
Knapp, Edward Alan government administrator, scientist
Leon, Bruno architect, educator
Lichtenberg, Margaret Klee publishing company executive
Livesay, Thomas Andrew museum administrator, lecturer
Longley, Bernique artist, painter, sculptor
Loriaux, Maurice Lucien artist, ecclesiologist
Maehl, William Henry historian, university administrator, educational consultant
Mc Kinney, Robert Moody newspaper editor and publisher
Miller, Edmund Kenneth retired electrical engineer, educator
Morgan, Alan Douglas state education official
Myers, Charlotte Will biology educator
Nava, Cynthia D. state legislator
Noble, Merrill Emmett retired psychology educator, psychologist
Noland, Charles Donald lawyer, educator
Nuckolls, Leonard Arnold retired hospital administrator
Nurock, Robert Jay investment analysis company executive
Odell, John H. construction company executive
Pearson, Margit Linnea development company executive
Perkins, Van L. university administrator, educator, conservationist
Phipps, Claude Raymond research scientist
Phister, Montgomery, Jr. computer engineering consultant, writer
Pickrell, Thomas Richard retired oil company executive
Pound, John Bennett lawyer
Price, Thomas Munro computer consultant
Quintana, Sammy J. lawyer
Ratliff, Floyd biophysics educator, scientist
Reggio, Godfrey film director
Reichman, Nanci Satin oil company owner
Robinson, Charles Wesley energy company executive
Roesler, John Bruce lawyer
Rogers, Jerry L. federal agency administrator
Rubenstein, Bernard orchestra conductor
Scheinbaum, David photography educator
Schuyler, Robert Len investment company executive
Schwarz, Michael lawyer
Shubart, Dorothy Louise Tepfer artist, educator
Stefanics, Elizabeth T. (Liz Stefanics) state legislator
Steinke, Bettina artist
Stephenson, Donnan lawyer, former state supreme court justice
Stevens, Ron A. lawyer, public interest organization administrator
Stieber, Tamar journalist
Sturgen, Winston photographer, printmaker, artist
Sumner, Gordon, Jr. retired military officer
Swartz, William John transportation resources company executive/retired
Tarn, Nathaniel poet, translator, educator
Taylor, Beverly Lacy stringed instrument restorer, classical guitarist
Udall, Thomas state attorney general
Vazquez, Martha Alicia judge
Watkins, Stephen Edward accountant
White, David Hywel physics educator
Whiteford, Andrew Hunter anthropologist
Williams, Stephen anthropologist, educator
Wilson, Tish children's services administrator
Yalman, Ann magistrate, lawyer

### Santa Teresa
Leffler, Stacy Brent retired government employee

### Seneca
Monroe, Kendyl Kurth retired lawyer

### Silver City
Bettison, Cynthia Ann museum director, archaeologist
Foy, Thomas Paul lawyer, state legislator, banker
French, Laurence Armand social science educator, psychology educator
Moses-Foley, Judith Ann special education educator
Snedeker, John Haggner university president

### Socorro
Kottlowski, Frank Edward geologist
Lyons, William Claypool engineering educator and consultant

### Sunspot
Altrock, Richard Charles astrophysicist

### Taos
Bacon, Wallace Alger speech communications educator, author
Bell, Larry Stuart artist
Lipscomb, Anna Rose Feeny entrepreneur, arts organizer, fundraiser
Martin, Agnes artist
McFadden, David Revere museum director
Murphey, Michael Martin country western singer, songwriter
Pasternack, Robert Harry school psychologist
Witt, David L. curator, writer
Young, Jon Nathan archeologist

### Tijeras
Berry, Dawn Bradley lawyer, writer
Van Arsdel, Eugene Parr tree pathologist, consultant meteorologist

### Tohatchi
Hansen, Harold B., Jr. elementary school educator

### Truth Or Consequences
Rush, Domenica Marie health facilities administrator

### Wagon Mound
Abeyta, Jose Reynato retired pharmacist, state legislator, cattle rancher

### White Sands Missile Range
Arthur, Paul Keith electronic engineer

## NEW YORK

### Adams Center
Hood, Thomas Gregory minister

### Afton
Church, Richard Dwight electrical engineer, scientist
Schwartz, Aubrey Earl artist

### Akron
Greatbatch, Wilson biomedical engineer

### Albany
Able, Kenneth Paul biology educator
Aceto, Vincent John librarian, educator
Alexander, Clark Everts accountant
Ambros, Robert Andrew pathologist, educator
Arseneau, James Charles physician
Beach, John Arthur lawyer
Beebe, Richard Townsend physician
Behariell, Frederick John German and comparative literature educator
Bellacosa, Joseph W. judge
Bellizzi, John J. law enforcement association administrator, educator, pharmacist
Bennett, Edward Virdell, Jr. surgeon
Berman, Carol commissioner
Blount, Stanley Freeman marketing educator
Bowen, Mary Lu ecumenical developer, community organizer
Bradley, Wesley Holmes physician
Brown, Albert Joseph, Jr. banker
Brown, Judith Anne law librarian
Bruno, Cathy Eileen state official
Bruno, Joseph L. state legislator
†Burkart, Peter Thomas hematologist
Calhoun, Nancy state legislator
†Capone, Robert Joseph physician, educator
Carovano, John Martin not-for-profit adminstrator, conservationist
Case, Forrest N., Jr. lawyer
Catalano, Jane Donna lawyer
Chonski, Denise Theresa primary school educator, artist
Clarey, Donald Alexander government affairs consultant
Clark, Janet retired health services executive
Cole, John Adam insurance executive
Couch, Mark Woodworth lawyer
Creegan, Robert Francis philosophy educator
Cross, Robert Francis city official
Csiza, Charles Karoly veterinarian, microbiologist
Culp, Margaret Geralyn tax administrator
Danziger, Peter lawyer
Davis, Paul Joseph endocrinologist
DeFelice, Eugene Anthony physician, medical educator, consultant, magician
Demerjian, Kenneth Leo atmospheric science educator, research center director
DeNuzzo, Rinaldo Vincent pharmacy educator
Donovan, Robert Alan English educator
Dougherty, James orthopedic surgeon, educator
Doyle, Joseph Theobald physician, educator
Durovic, Jerry John psychologist, state official
Eckstein, Jerome philosopher, educator
Edmonds, Richard dean
Farley, Hugh T. state senator, law educator
Ferris, Walter V. retired lawyer
Frost, Robert Edwin chemistry educator
Galvin, Thomas John information science policy educator, librarian, information scientist
Genshaft, Judy Lynn psychologist, educator
Giblin, Mary Ellen mental health professional
Han, Jaok cardiologist, researcher, educator
Hancox, David Robert audit administrator, educator
Happ, Harvey Heinz electrical engineer, educator
Harenberg, Paul E. state legislator
Harris, Eric R. policy analyst, county official
Herman, Robert S. former state official, economist, educator
Hill, Earlene Hooper state legislator
Hill, Valerie Charlotte nurse
Hitchcock, Karen Ruth biology educator, university dean, academic administrator
Hof, Liselotte Bertha biochemist
Hoffmeister, Jana Marie cardiologist
Holstein, William Kurt business administration educator
Holt-Harris, John Evan, Jr. lawyer
Howard, Lyn Jennifer medical educator
Hubbard, Howard James bishop
Hyde, Carol Ann lawyer
Kadamus, James Alexander educational administrator
Katz, William Armstrong library science educator
Kaye, Gordon Israel pathologist, anatomist, educator
Kaye, Judith Smith judge
Kelley, Sister Helen hospital executive
Kennedy, William Joseph novelist, educator
Kim, Jai Soo physics educator
†Kim, Paul David emergency medical administrator
Kinney, Thomas J. adult education educator
Koff, Howard Michael lawyer
Kristofferson, Kris singer, songwriter, actor
Lack, James J. state senator, lawyer
Lenardon, Robert Joseph classics educator
Levine, Louis David museum director, archaeologist
Lewis, Kirk McArthur lawyer
Ley, Ronald psychologist, educator
Lobosco, Anna Frances state development disabilities program planner
Lumpkin, Lee Roy dermatologist, educator
Macario, Alberto Juan Lorenzo physician
Martland, T(homas) R(odolphe) philosophy educator
Matusow, Naomi C. state legislator
Matuszek, John Michael, Jr. environmental scientist, educator, consultant
McCaughey Ross, Elizabeth P. (Betsy McCaughey) state official
Meader, John Daniel state agency administrator, judge
Mehtabdin, Khalid Rauf economist, educator
Mills, Richard P. state agency administrator
Miner, Roger Jeffrey federal judge
Mitchell, Mark-Allen Bryant state government administrator
Moelleken, Wolfgang Wilfried Germanic languages and literature educator
Morga Bellizzi, Celeste editor
Murphy, Thomas Joseph strategic communications consultant
Murray, Neil Vincent computer science educator
Murray, Terrence banker
Nathan, Richard P(erle) political scientist, educator
Naumann, Hans Juergen manufacturing company executive
O'Neil, Chloe Ann state legislator
Ortloff, George Christian, Sr. (Chris Ortloff) journalist, state legislator
Pataki, George E. governor
Patterson, Rodney Lee foreign language and literature educator, translator
Paulson, Peter John librarian, publishing company executive
Pohlsander, Hans Achim classics educator
Proskin, Arnold W. state assemblyman, lawyer
Quackenbush, Roger E. retired secondary school educator
Quellmalz, Henry printing company executive
Reese, William Lewis philosophy educator
Reichert, Leo Edmund, Jr. biochemist, endocrinologist
Reid, William James social work educator
Robbins, Cornelius (Van Vorse) education administration educator
Robinson, John Bowers, Jr. bank holding company executive
Rohan, Brian Patrick lawyer
Rosenfeld, Harry Morris editor
Rosenkrantz, Daniel J. computer science educator
Roth, Laura Maurer physics educator, researcher
Roy, Rob J. biomedical engineer, anesthesiologist
Salkin, Patricia E. law educator
Sbuttoni, Karen Ryan reading specialist
Schmidt, John Thomas neurobiologist
Schneider, Allan Stanford biochemistry neurosience and pharmacology educator, biomedical research scientist
Shubert, Joseph Francis librarian
Siegel, David Donald law educator
Smith, Ada L. state legislator
Smith, Ralph Wesley, Jr. federal judge
Smith, Rex William journalist
Spooner, Eric Warbasse pediatric cardiologist
Sprow, Howard Thomas lawyer, educator
Stachowski, William T. state senator
Standish, John Spencer textile manufacturing company executive
Stevens, Roy White microbiologist
Stewart, Margaret McBride biology educator, researcher
Stone, James Lester mental health administrator
Sturman, Lawrence Stuart health research administrator
Swartz, Donald Percy physician
Teevan, Richard Collier psychology educator
Teitelbaum, Steven Usher lawyer
Thompson, Frank Joseph political science educator
Thornberry, Terence Patrick criminologist, educator
Thornton, Maurice academic administrator
Tieman, Suzannah Bliss neurobiologist
Titone, Vito Joseph judge
Toombs, Russ William laboratory director
Treadwell, Alexander F. state official
Vaccaro, Louis Charles college president
Vacco, Dennis C. state attorney general
Vitaliano, Eric Nicholas state legislator, lawyer
Volker, Dale Martin state senator, lawyer
Wright, Theodore Paul, Jr. political science educator
Yunich, Albert Mansfeld physician
Zacek, Joseph Frederick history educator, international studies consultant, East European culture and affairs specialist
Zimmerman, Joseph Francis political scientist, educator

### Albertson
Ferber, Samuel publishing executive
Goodstein, Daniel Bela oral and maxillofacial surgeon, educator, consultant
Michaels, Craig Adam psychologist

### Alfred
Billeci, Andre George art educator, sculptor
Coll, Edward Girard, Jr. university president
Frechette, Van Derck ceramic engineer
Higby, (Donald) Wayne artist, educator
Keith, Timothy Zook psychology educator
Ott, Walter Richard academic administrator
Potter, Barrett George historian, educator
Pye, Lenwood David materials science educator, researcher, consultant
Rand, Joella Mae nursing educator, counselor
Rossington, David Ralph physical chemistry educator
Spriggs, Richard Moore ceramic engineer, research center administrator

### Alfred Station
Love, Robert Lyman educational consulting company executive

### Amagansett
†Frankl, Jeanne Silver educational association administrator
Frankl, Kenneth Richard retired lawyer

### Amherst
Anisman, Martin Jay academic administrator
Ashgriz, Nasser mechanical and aerospace engineer, educator
Beahan, Susan Nancy video producer
Brown, Stephen Ira mathematics educator
Clark, Donald Malin professional society administrator
Cohen, Herman Nathan private investigator
Coover, James Burrell music educator
Cramer, Stanley Howard psychology educator, author
Eberlein, Patricia James mathematician, computer scientist, educator
Jen, Frank Chifeng finance and management educator
Katz, Leonard Allen medical director, educator
Kibby, Michael William reading educator
Kurtz, Paul publisher, philosopher, educator
Levy, Gerhard pharmacologist
Reinhorn, Andrei M. civil engineering educator, consultant
Vanderwerf, Mary Ann elementary school educator, consultant
Wiesenberg, Jacqueline Leonardi medical lecturer

### Amityville
Banks, Marilyn Kellogg sculptor
Brennan, Patrick Thomas meteorology company executive
Degrassi, David John physical therapist
Gicola, Paul middle school science educator, administrator
Hughes, Spencer Edward, Jr. retired financial executive, consultant
Linehan, Patrick Francis, Jr. financial planner
Upadhyay, Yogendra Nath physician, educator

### Ancramdale
Weinstein, Joyce artist

### Angola
Meno, Lionel R. state agency administrator

### Annandale On Hudson
Achebe, Chinua writer, humanities educator
Ashbery, John Lawrence language educator, poet, playwright
Botstein, Leon college president, historian, conductor, music critic
Chace, James Clarke editor
Ferguson, John Barclay biology educator
Kelly, Robert poet, novelist, educator
Kiviat, Erik ecologist, administrator, educator
Manea, Norman writer, educator
Mullen, William Cocke classics educator
Papadimitriou, Dimitri Basil economist, college administrator
Sullivan, Jim artist

### Appleton
Singer, Thomas Kenyon international business consultant, farmer

### Ardsley
Barton, Joan Chi-Hung Lo sales executive
Kuntzman, Ronald pharmacology research executive
Mohl, Allan S. social worker
Sokolow, Isobel Folb sculptor

### Ardsley On Hudson
Stein, Milton Michael lawyer

### Argyle
Bruce, David Lionel retired anesthesiologist, educator

### Armonk
Behr, Richard Henry architect, educator
Bergson, Henry Paul professional association administrator
Bolduc, Ernest Joseph association management consultant
Cannella, Nancy Anne educational administrator
Chin, Carolyn Sue business executive
Elliott, David H. insurance company executive
Elson, Charles stage designer, educator
Gerstner, Louis Vincent, Jr. diversified company executive
Grove, David Lawrence economist
Harreld, James Bruce computer company executive
Levy, Kenneth James advertising executive
Lynett, Lawrence Wilson electronics company executive
Mc Groddy, James Cleary retired computer company executive, consultant
Mellors, Robert Charles physician, scientist
Quinn, James W. lawyer
Sharpe, Myron Emanuel publisher, editor, writer
Thoman, G. Richard computer company executive
Weill, Richard L. lawyer

### Astoria
Chan, See Fong retired linguist, composer
Davidson, Rex L. association executive
Frazier, Walter, Jr. (Clyde Frazier) radio announcer, television analyst, retired professional basketball player
Morrow, Scott Douglas choreographer, educator
Parascos, Edward Themistocles utilities executive

### Athens
Lew, Roger Alan manufacturing company executive

### Auburn
Eldred, Thomas Gilbert secondary education educator, historian
Sayles, Edward Thomas theatrical producer
Wolczyk, Joseph Michael lawyer

### Aurora
Slocum, George Sigman energy company executive

### Averill Park
Haines, Walter Wells retired economics educator
Traver, Robert William, Sr. management consultant, author, lecturer, engineer

### Babylon
Collis, Charles aircraft company executive
Haley, Priscilla Jane artist, printmaker
Hennelly, Edmund Paul lawyer, oil company executive
Keane, Daniel J. banker
Lopez, Joseph Jack oil company executive, consultant
Meirowitz, Claire Cecile public relations executive
Wilkes, David Ross therapist, social worker

### Baldwin Place
Kurian, George Thomas publisher

### Baldwinsville
Kline, Carole June special education educator

### Ballston Lake
Cotter, William Donald state commissioner, former newspaper editor
Fiedler, Harold Joseph electrical engineer, consultant
Silverman, Gerald Bernard journalist

### Ballston Spa
Barba, Harry author, educator, publisher

### Barrytown
Higgins, Dick (Richard Carter Higgins) writer, publisher, composer, artist
Shimmyo, Theodore Tadaaki seminary president
Tsirpanlis, Constantine N. theology, philosophy, classic and history educator

### Batavia
Litteer, Harold Hunter, Jr. lawyer
Rigerman, Ruth Underhill mathematics educator

Steiner, Stuart *college president*

### Bay Shore
Killian, Edward James *pediatrician*
Pinsker, Walter *allergist, immunologist*
Williams, Tonda *entrepreneur, consultant*

### Bayport
Courant, Ernest David *physicist*
Poli, Kenneth Joseph *editor*

### Bayside
Gavencak, John Richard *pediatrician, allergist*
Helfat, Lucille Podell *social services professional*
Lewkowitz, Karen Helene *orthodontist*
Zinn, William *violinist, composer, business executive*

### Beacon
Flagello, Ezio Domenico *basso*
Garell, Paul Charles *physician, family practice*
Moreno, Zerka Toeman *psychodrama educator*

### Bear Mountain
Smith, Andrew Josef *historian, publishing executive, naturalist, writer*

### Bedford
Atkins, Ronald Raymond *lawyer*
Barth, Richard *pharmaceutical executive*
Benedek, Armand *landscape architect*
Bowman, James Kinsey *publishing company executive, rare book specialist*
Chia, Pei-Yuan *banker*
Damora, Robert Matthew *architect*
Lord, Jere Williams, Jr. *retired surgeon*
Philip, Peter Van Ness *former trust company executive*
Weinman, Robert Alexander *sculptor*

### Bedford Corners
Singer, Craig *broker, consultant, investor*

### Bedford Hills
Fissell, William Henry *investment advisor*
Jensen-Carter, Philip Scott *advertising and architectural photographer, medical photographer*
Ludlum, Robert *author*
Waller, Wilhelmine Kirby (Mrs. Thomas Mercer Waller) *civic worker, organization official*

### Bellerose
Paramekanthi, Srinivasan Mandayam *software services executive*

### Bellmore
Andrews, Charles Rolland *library administrator*
Crouch, Howard Earle *health service organization executive*

### Bellport
Hendrie, Elaine *public relations executive*
Hughes, Elinor Lambert *drama and film critic*

### Berlin
Stephens, Donald Joseph *retired architect*

### Berne
Lounsbury, Helen Marie *education educator, consultant*

### Bethpage
Barnathan, Jack Martin *chiropractor*
Brodie, Sheldon J. *physician*
Budoff, Penny Wise *physician, author, researcher*
De Santis, Mark *osteopathic physician*
Marrone, Daniel Scott *business, production and quality management educator*
Melnik, Robert Edward *aeronautical engineer*
Rockensies, John William *mechanical engineer*
Sanna, Richard Jeffrey *lawyer*

### Big Flats
Orsillo, James Edward *computer systems engineer, company executive*

### Binghamton
Anderson, Warren Mattice *lawyer*
Babb, Harold *psychology educator*
Banks, Arthur Sparrow *political scientist, educator*
Beach, Beth *elementary educator*
Bearsch, Lee Palmer *architect, city planner*
Best, Robert Mulvane *insurance company executive*
Bethje, Robert *general surgeon, retired*
Block, Haskell Mayer *humanities educator*
Carrigg, James A. *retired utility company executive*
Coates, Donald Robert *geology educator, scientist*
Cornacchio, Joseph Vincent *engineering educator, computer researcher, consultant*
DeFleur, Lois B. *university president, sociology educator*
Eisch, John Joseph *chemist, educator*
Farley, Daniel W. *lawyer, utility company executive*
Fay, Rowan Hamilton *minister*
Feisel, Lyle Dean *university dean, electrical engineering educator*
Gaddis Rose, Marilyn *comparative literature educator, translator*
Gerhart, Eugene Clifton *lawyer*
Hilton, Peter John *mathematician, educator*
Isaacson, Robert Lee *psychology educator, researcher*
Jennings, Frank Louis *engineering company executive, engineer*
Kessler, Milton *English language educator, poet*
Klir, George Jiri *systems science educator*
Kunjukunju, Pappy *insurance company financial executive*
Levis, Donald James *psychologist, educator*
Libous, Thomas William *state senator*
Lowen, Walter *mechanical engineering educator*
Mazrui, Ali Al'Amin *political science educator, researcher*
McAvoy, Thomas James *federal judge*
Michael, Sandra Dale *reproductive endocrinology educator, researcher*
O'Neil, Patrick Michael *political scientist, educator*
Peterson, Alfred Edward *family physician*
Regenbogen, Adam *lawyer*
Schecter, Arnold Joel *preventive medicine educator*
Schwartz, Richard Frederick *electrical engineering educator*

Shillestad, John Gardner *financial services company executive*
Sklar, Kathryn Kish *historian, educator*
Stein, George Henry *historian, educator, administrator*
Surgent, Susan Pearl *human resources specialist*
von Schack, Wesley W. *energy services company executive*
Whittingham, M(ichael) Stanley *chemist*

### Blauvelt
Citardi, Mattio H. *business analyst, project manager, researcher*
Gillespie, John Fagan *mining executive*

### Bloomington
Ruffing, Anne Elizabeth *artist*

### Blue Point
O'Hare, John Dignan *library director*

### Bohemia
Hausman, Howard *electronics executive*
Manley, Gertrude Ella *librarian, media specialist*
Ortiz, Germaine Laura De Feo *secondary education educator, counselor*

### Brewster
Barnhart, Robert Knox *writer, editor*
Shepard, Jean Heck *author, publishing company consultant, agent*

### Briarcliff
Hopkins, Lee Bennett *writer, educator*

### Briarcliff Manor
Bates, Barbara J. Neuner *retired municipal official*
Bhargava, Rameshwar Nath *physicist*
Bingham, J. Peter *electronics research executive*
Callahan, Daniel John *biomedical researcher*
Carey, James Henry *banker*
Cugnini, Aldo Godfrey *electrical engineer*
Dolmatch, Theodore Bieley *management consultant*
Driver, Sharon Humphreys *marketing executive*
Glassman, Jerome Martin *clinical pharmacologist, educator*
Haddad, Jerrier Abdo *engineering management consultant*
Leiser, Burton Myron *philosophy and law educator*
Luck, Edward Carmichael *professional society administrator*
Pasquarelli, Joseph J. *real estate, engineering and construction executive*
Weintraub, Michael Ira *neurologist*
Zimmar, George Peter *publishing executive, psychology educator*

### Briarwood
Danna, Jo J. *publisher, author, anthropologist*

### Bridgehampton
Baird, Charles Fitz *retired mining and metals company executive*
Enstine, Raymond Wilton, Jr. *propane gas company executive*
Jackson, Lee *artist*
McMenamin, Joan Stitt *headmistress*
Needham, James Joseph *retired financial services executive*
Phillips, Warren Henry *publisher*

### Bridgeport
Sheldon, Thomas Donald *academic administrator*

### Brockport
Bucholz, Arden Kingsbury *historian, educator*
Fisher, Robert Joseph *marketing and corporate executive*
Herrmann, Kenneth John, Jr. *social work educator*
Leslie, William Bruce *history educator*
Marcus, Robert D. *historian, educator*
Stier, William Frederick, Jr. *academic administrator*
Van de Wetering, John E(dward) *academic administrator*

### Bronx
Adams, Alice *sculptor*
Adler, Nadia C. *lawyer*
Aiken, William *accountant*
Andreen, Aviva Louise *dentist, researcher, academic administrator, educator*
Asare, Karen Michelle Gilliam *reading and English educator*
Balka, Sigmund Ronell *lawyer*
†Balsano, Nicholas A. *surgeon, educator*
Bamberger, Phylis Skloot *judge*
Barton, Lewis *food manufacturing company executive*
Battista, Leon Joseph, Jr. *economics educator*
Berger, Frederick Jerome *electrical engineer, educator*
Bhalodkar, Narendra Chandrakant *cardiologist*
Blaufox, Morton Donald *physician, educator*
Boggs, Wade Anthony *professional baseball player*
Bowers, Francis Robert *literature educator*
Burde, Ronald Marshall *neuro-ophthalmologist*
Buschke, Herman *neurologist*
Caffin, Louise Anne *library media educator*
Cannizzaro, Linda Ann *geneticist, researcher*
Capodilupo, Jeanne Hatton *public relations executive*
Cherkasky, Martin *physician*
†Chiaramida, Salvatore *cardiologist, educator, health facility adminstrator*
Cimino, James Ernest *physician*
Cohen, Herbert Jesse *physician, educator*
Cohen, Michael I. *pediatrician*
Connor, Paul Eugene *social worker*
Constantine, Gus *physical education educator, coach*
†Conway, William Gaylord *zoologist, zoo director, conservationist*
Cornfield, Melvin *lawyer, university institute director*
Coupey, Susan McGuire *pediatrician, educator*
DeMartino, Anthony Gabriel *cardiologist, internist*
Diamond, Betty Ann *internist, educator*
Dickens, Joan Wright *hospital administrator*
Dulles, Avery *priest, theologian*
Duncan, Mariano *professional baseball player*
Dutcher, Janice Jean Phillips *oncologist*
Edelmann, Chester Monroe, Jr. *pediatrician, medical school dean*
Eder, Howard Abram *physician*
Eliasoph, Joan *radiologist, educator*
Elkin, Milton *radiologist, physician, educator*
†Eng, Calvin *cardiologist, researcher*

Fahey, Charles Joseph *priest, gerontology educator*
Fernandez, Ricardo R. *university administrator*
Fielder, Cecil Grant *professional baseball player*
Fishman, Glenn I. *medical educator*
Fishman, Joshua Aaron *sociolinguist, educator*
Flam, Bernard Vincent *secondary education educator*
Fleischer, Norman *director of endocrinology, medical educator*
Foreman, Spencer *pulmonary specialist, hospital executive*
Freeman, Leonard Murray *radiologist, nuclear medicine physician, educator*
Frenz, Dorothy Ann *cell and developmental biologist*
Friedman, Joel Matthew *oral and maxillofacial surgeon, educator*
Frishman, William Howard *cardiology educator, cardiovasular pharmacologist, gerontologist*
Fulop, Milford *physician*
Garance, Dominick (D. G. Garan) *lawyer, author*
Gerst, Paul Howard *physician*
Gillman, Arthur Emanuel *psychiatrist*
†Girardi, Joseph Elliott *professional baseball player*
Gliedman, Marvin L. *surgeon, educator*
Goldberg, Marcia B. *medical educator*
Gootzeit, Jack Michael *rehabilitation institute executive*
Greenberg, Blu *author*
Greene, Aurelia *state legislator*
Gross, Ludwik *physician*
Hallett, Charles Arthur, Jr. *English and humanities educator*
Hamilton, John Ross *financial consultant, educator*
Hayes, Charles Dewayne *professional baseball player*
Heilbrun, James *economist, educator*
Hennessy, Thomas Christopher *clergyman, educator, retired university dean*
Herbert, Victor Daniel *medical educator*
Hilfstein, Erna *science historian, educator*
Hilliard, John Mauk *university official*
Himmelberg, Robert Franklin *historian, educator*
Hirano, Asao *neuropathologist*
Hirschy, James Conrad *radiologist*
Holland, Darryl Boyd *foundation executive*
Hooker, Olivia J. *psychologist, educator*
Hovnanian, H. Philip *biomedical engineer, physicist*
Humphry, James, III *librarian, publishing executive*
Hurwitz, Ted H. *sports conference administrator*
Ianniello, Peter Louis *school system administrator*
Ignat, Ana *chemical engineer*
Jacobson, Harold Gordon *radiologist, educator*
Jaffé, Ernst Richard *medical educator and administrator*
†Jeter, Derek *professional baseball player*
Joseph, Stephen *nephrology, dialysis nurse*
Kadish, Anna Stein *pathologist, educator, researcher*
Kahn, Thomas *medical educator*
Karasu, T(oksoz) Byram *psychiatry educator*
Karkanias, George B. *neurologist, educator*
Karp, Abraham Joseph *historian, rabbi, educator*
Kassoy, Hortense (Honey Kassoy) *artist*
Kelly, Patrick Franklin *professional baseball player*
Kitt, Olga *artist*
Koranyi, Adam *mathematics educator*
Koss, Leopold G. *physician, pathologist, educator*
Lattis, Richard Lynn *zoo director*
Lewis, Harold Alexander *insurance company executive*
Lieber, Charles Saul *physician, educator*
Macklin, Ruth *bioethics educator*
†Martinez, Constantino *professional baseball player*
Martinez-Tabone, Raquel *school psychologist supervisor*
Marx, Gertie Florentine *anesthesiologist*
McCabe, James Patrick *library director*
McShane, Joseph Michael *priest, dean, theology educator*
Michelsen, W(olfgang) Jost *neurosurgeon, educator*
Mittler, Diana (Diana Mittler-Battipaglia) *music educator and administrator, pianist*
Moldovan, Leonard Michael *chemist*
†Molloy, Joseph A. *professional sports team executive*
Moritz, Charles Fredric *book editor*
†Mullender, Barton *insurance company executive*
Murray, Phyllis Cynthia *educator*
Muschel, Louis Henry *immunologist, educator*
Nagler, Arnold Leon *pathologist, scientist, educator*
Nanna, Michele *cardiologist, educator*
Nathanson, Melvyn Bernard *university provost, mathematician*
Nitowsky, Harold Martin *physician, educator*
O'Neill, Paul Andrew *professional baseball player*
Orkin, Louis Richard *physician, educator*
Ottenberg, James Simon *hospital executive*
Parker, Everett Carlton *clergyman*
Pearlman, Barbara *artist, educator*
Pitchumoni, Capecomorin Sankar *gastroenterologist, educator*
Plimpton, Calvin Hastings *physician, university president*
Purpura, Dominick P. *neuroscientist, university dean*
Radel, Eva *pediatrician, hematologist*
Raines, Timothy *professional baseball player*
Rapin, Isabelle *physician*
Reichert, Marlene Joy *secondary school educator*
Revelle, Donald Gene *manufacturing and health care company executive, consultant*
Reynolds, Benedict Michael *surgeon*
Riba, Netta Eileen *secondary school educator*
Richman, Arthur Sherman *sports association executive*
†Rivera, Mariano *professional baseball player*
Rizzuto, Philip Francis (Scooter ) *sports broadcaster, former professional baseball player*
Roberts, Burton Bennett *administrative judge*
Robinson, John Gwilym *conservationist*
Romney, Seymour Leonard *physician, educator*
Rose, Israel Harold *mathematics educator*
Ruben, Robert Joel *physician, educator*
Rubinstein, Arye *pediatrician, microbiology and immunology educator*
Sable, Robert Allen *gastroenterologist*
Scanlan, Thomas Joseph *college president, educator*
Scharff, Matthew Daniel *immunologist, cell biologist, educator*
Schaumburg, Herbert Howard *neurology educator*
†Scheuer, James *physician, educator, researcher*
Schwam, Marvin Albert *graphic design company executive*
Sedacca, Angelo Anthony *financial executive*
Seltzer, William *statistician, social researcher, former international organization director*
Senturia, Yvonne Dreyfus *pediatrician, epidemiologist*
Shafritz, David Andrew *physician, research scientist*
Shamos, Morris Herbert *physicist educator*
Shapiro, Nella Irene *surgeon*

Shatin, Harry *medical educator, dermatologist*
Sherman, Judith Dorothy *producer, recording company owner, recording engineer*
Sherman, Susan Jean *English language educator*
†Shine, Daniel I. *hospital administrator*
Shinnar, Shlomo *child neurologist, educator*
Siddons, Sarah Mae *chemist*
Singer, Jeffrey Michael *organic analytical chemist*
Skurdenis, Juliann Veronica *librarian, educator, writer, editor*
Smith, Sharon Patricia *university dean*
Spitzer, Adrian *pediatrician, medical educator*
Sprecher, Baron William Gunther *pianist, composer, conductor, diplomat*
Stein, Ruth Elizabeth Klein *physician*
Steinbrenner, George Michael, III *professional baseball team executive, shipbuilding company executive*
Stuhr, David Paul *business educator, consultant*
Surks, Martin I. *medical educator, endocrinologist*
Sylvester, John Edward *social worker*
Thysen, Benjamin *biochemist, health science facility administrator, researcher*
Tong, Hing *mathematician, educator*
Ultan, Lloyd *historian*
Vassel, Lee Hylton *urbanist, social services administrator, writer*
Waelsch, Salome Gluecksohn *geneticist, educator*
†Watson, Robert *professional sports team executive*
Wells, David Lee *professional baseball player*
Wertheim, Mary Danielle *elementary education coordinator*
Wiernik, Peter Harris *oncologist, educator*
Williams, Bernabe Figueroa *professional baseball player*
Williams, Lovie Jean *elementary education educator*
Williams, Marshall Henry, Jr. *physician, educator*
Yalow, Rosalyn Sussman *medical physicist*
Zalaznick, Sheldon *editor, journalist*
Zeichner, Oscar *historian, educator*
Zimmer, Donald William *coach professional athletics, former professional baseball manager*

### Bronxville
Arndt, Kenneth Eugene *banker*
Biscardi, Chester *composer, educator*
Broas, Donald Sanford *hospital executive*
Cook, Charles David *international lawyer, arbitrator, consultant*
Dvorak, Roger Gran *health facility executive*
Ellinghaus, William Maurice *communications executive*
Falvey, Patrick Joseph *lawyer*
Farber, Viola Anna *dancer, choreographer, educator*
Forester, Erica Simms *decorative arts historian, consultant, educator*
Franklin, Margery Bodansky *psychology educator, researcher*
Greenwald, Martin *publishing company executive*
Hutchison, Dorris Jeannette *retired microbiologist, educator*
Ilchman, Alice Stone *college president, former government official*
Kaplan, Sanford Allen *internist, allergist*
Keller, LeRoy *journalist, consultant*
Kirk, Grayson Louis *retired political science educator, retired universtiy president, trustee*
Knapp, George Griff Prather *insurance consultant, arbitrator*
Leonard, Edward F. *chemical engineer, educator*
Levitt, Miriam *pediatrician*
L'Huillier, Peter (Peter) *archbishop*
Lombardo, Philip Joseph *broadcasting company executive*
Martin, R. Keith *business and information systems educator, consultant*
Perez, Louis Anthony *radiologist*
Peters, Sarah Whitaker *art historian, writer, lecturer*
Randall, Francis Ballard *historian, educator, writer*
Recabo, Jaime Miguel *lawyer*
Rizzo, Thomas Dignan *orthopedic surgeon*
Sharp, Donald Eugene *bank consultant*
Shuker, Gregory Brown *publishing and production company executive*
Wilson, John Donald *banker, economist*

### Brookhaven
Reeves, John Drummond *English language professional, writer*

### Brooklyn
Abrams, Roni *business education educator, communications consultant, trainer*
Adasko, Mary Hardy *speech pathologist*
Agard, Emma Estornel *psychotherapist*
Ahrens, Thomas H. *production company executive*
Alfano, Edward Charles, Jr. *elementary education educator*
Alfonso, Antonio Escolar *surgeon*
Al-Hafeez, Humza *minister, editor*
Allen, George Desmond *epidemiology nurse, surgical nurse*
Allman, Avis Louise *artist, Turkish and Islamic culture educator*
Altura, Bella T. *physiologist, educator*
Altura, Burton Myron *physiologist, educator*
Amendola, Sal John *artist, educator, writer*
Amon, Carol Bagley *federal judge*
Armenakas, Anthony Emmanuel *aerospace educator*
Ashley, Leonard Raymond Nelligan *English language educator*
Bachman, George *mathematics educator*
Balbi, Kenneth Emilio *environmental lead specialist, researcher*
Baltakis, Paul Antanas *bishop*
Bartels, John Ries *federal judge*
Barth, Robert Henry *nephrologist, educator*
Battle, Turner Charles, III *art educator, educational association administrator*
Baumgarten, Stephen Robert *physician, urologist*
Bergeron, R. Thomas *radiologist, educator*
Berman, David Hirsh *physician*
Bertoni, Henry Louis *electrical engineering educator*
Bianco, Anthony Joseph, III *newswriter*
Birenbaum, William M. *former university president*
Biro, Laszlo *dermatologist*
Bisbee, Joyce Evelyn *utility company manager*
Blackman, Robert Irwin *real estate developer and investor, lawyer, accountant*
Blasi, Alberto *Romance languages educator, writer*
Block, Frederic *judge*
Bode, Walter Albert *editor*
Boloker, Rose L. *school psychologist*
Borel, Ludmila Ivanovna *ballerina, educator*
Bosman, Richard *painter, printmaker*
Bostic, Mary Jones *librarian*
Bowers, Patricia Eleanor Fritz *economist*

Bramwell, Henry federal judge
Breen, Vincent de Paul vicar, school system administrator
Brillhart, Susan J. pediatric nurse, nursing educator
Brownstone, Paul Lotan retired speech communications and drama educator
Bugliarello, George university chancellor
Carlile, Janet Louise artist, educator
Carswell, Lois Malakoff botanical gardens executive, consultant
Castleman, Louis Samuel metallurgist, educator
Catell, Robert Barry gas utility executive
Charton, Marvin chemist, educator
Chernow, Ron writer, columnist
Choudhury, Deo Chand physicist, educator
Ciolli, Antoinette librarian, retired educator
Clark, Luther Theopolis physician, educator, researcher
Colker, Edward artist, educator
Cornell, Thomas Browne artist, educator
Corry, Emmett Brother librarian, educator, researcher, archivist
Cracco, Roger Quinlan medical educator, neurologist
Cranin, Abraham Norman oral and maxillofacial surgeon, researcher
Crawford, Patricia Alexis healthcare and social justice advocate, writer
†Crawford, Robert Roy rail company executive
Cunningham, Julia Woolfolk author
Curry, David guidance staff developer
Daily, Thomas V. bishop
Daley, Sandra Dakota retired artist, filmmaker, photographer
Davidson, Steven J. emergency physician
Dearie, Raymond Joseph federal judge
DeBock, Florent Alphonse controller
De Lisi, Joanne communications executive, educator
Delson, Elizabeth artist
Delson, Sidney Leon architect
DeLustro, Frank Joseph financial executive, consultant
Dinnerstein, Harvey artist
Dinnerstein, Simon Abraham artist, educator
Duffoo, Frantz Michel nephrologist, director of medicine
Ebanks, Marlon Udel health paraprofessional
Edemeka, Udo Edemeka surgeon
Eirich, Frederick Roland chemist, educator
Eisenberg, Karen Sue Byer nurse
El-Choum, Mohammed Kassem civil engineer, educator
El Kodsi, Baroukh gastroenterologist, educator
Erber, William Franklin gastroenterologist
Everdell, William Romeyn humanities educator
Faison, Seth Shepard retired insurance broker
Fallek, Andrew Michael lawyer
Faunce, Sarah Cushing museum curator
Feit, Alan cardiologist, internist, medical educator
Ferber, Linda S. museum curator
Flam, Jack Donald art historian, educator
Fodstad, Harald neurosurgeon
Franco, Victor theoretical physics educator
Fratianni, Margaret Moroney critical care nurse
Friedman, Eli Arnold nephrologist
Friedman, Gerald Manfred geologist, educator
Friedman, Paul chemistry educator
Frisch, Ivan Thomas computer and communications company executive
Furchgott, Robert Francis pharmacologist, educator
Gabriel, Mordecai Lionel biologist, educator
Garibaldi, Louis E. aquarium administrator
Gintautas, Jonas physician, scientist, administrator
Glasser, Israel Leo federal judge
Goldsmith, Clifford Henry former tobacco company executive
Goodman, Alvin S. engineering educator, consultant
Gootman, Phyllis Myrna physiology, biophysics, educator
Gordon, Conrad J. financial executive
Gordon, Edward Harrison choral conductor, educator
Gotta, Alexander Walter anesthesiologist, educator
Grado, Angelo John artist
Graham, Arnold Harold lawyer, educator
Grayson, D. W. bishop
Gresser, Carol A. school system administrator
Gross, Stephen Mark pharmacist, academic dean
Gustin, Mark Douglas hospital administrator
Hamm, Charles John banker
Harris, Fred orthotist, prosthetist
Hechtman, Howard financial analyst
Helly, Walter Sigmund engineering educator
Hendra, Barbara Jane public relations executive
Hochstadt, Harry mathematician, educator
Hohenrath, William Edward retired banker
Holden, David Morgan medical educator
Hood, Ernest Alva, Sr. pharmaceutical company executive
Hoogenboom, Ari Arthur historian, educator
Hopkins, Karen Brooks performing arts executive
Ivanhoe, Herman dentist
Jacobson, Leslie Sari biologist, educator
Jarman, Joseph jazz musician
Jenkins, Leroy violinist, composer
Jimenez, Kathryn Fisher nurse, patient educator
Jofen, Jean foreign language educator
Johnson, Sterling, Jr. federal judge
Jones, Susan Emily fashion educator, administrator, educator
Kamholz, Stephan L. physician
Kaplan, Mitchell Alan sociologist, researcher
Karmel, Roberta Segal lawyer, educator
Kazan, Basil Gibran religious music composer
Kempner, Joseph aerospace engineering educator
†Kiepper, Alan Frederick rapid transit executive, educator
Kimmich, Christoph Martin academic administrator, educator
King, Margaret Leah history educator
Kippel, Gary M. psychologist
Kjeldaas, Terje, Jr. physics educator emeritus
Klainberg, Marilyn Blau community health educator
Koppel, Audrey Feiler electrologist, educator
Korman, Edward R. federal judge
Kramer, Allan Franklin, II botanical garden official, researcher
Kravath, Richard Elliot pediatrician, educator
†LaCosta, Cosmo Joseph medical center executive
Landron, Michel John lawyer
Lawrence, Deirdre Elizabeth librarian, coordinator research services
Lebouitz, Martin Frederick financial services industry executive, consultant
Lederman, Stephanie Brody artist
†Leff, Sanford Erwin cardiologist
Lehman, Arnold Lester museum official, art historian
Levendoglu, Hulya gastroenterologist
Levere, Richard David physician, academic administrator, educator
†Levowitz, Bernard Samuel surgeon, administrator
Levy, Norman B. psychiatrist, educator
Lewin, Ted Bert writer, illustrator
Lewis, Felice Flanery lawyer, educator
Leyh, Richard Edmund, Sr. retired investment executive
Lichtenstein, Harvey performing arts executive
Lindo, J. Trevor psychiatrist, consultant
Lizt, Sara Enid Vanefsky lawyer, educator
Lobron, Barbara L. speech educator, writer, editor, photographer
Madigan, Richard Allen museum director
Magliocco, John wholesale distribution executive
Malach, Monte physician
Marcus, Harold physician, health facility administrator
Mark, Richard Kushakow internist
Marsala-Cervasio, Kathleen Ann medical/surgical nurse
Martinez-Pons, Manuel psychology educator
Masterson, Charles Francis retired social scientist
Matthews, Craig Gerard gas company executive
Mayer, Ira Edward gastroenterologist
McLean, William Ronald electrical engineer, consultant
Mendez, Hermann Armando pediatrician, educator
Milhorat, Thomas Herrick neurosurgeon
Milman, Doris Hope pediatrics educator, psychiatrist
Minkoff, Jack economics educator
Moehring, Fred Adolf fastener distribution company executive
Mohaideen, A. Hassan surgeon, healthcare executive
Moore, Martin educator
Morawetz, Herbert chemistry educator
Mulvihill, Maureen Esther writer, educator, scholar
Murillo-Rohde, Ildaura Maria marriage and family therapist, consultant, educator, dean
Mydlo, Jack Henry surgeon, researcher
Namba, Tatsuji physician, medical researcher
Naqvi, Shehla Hasnain pediatric infectious disease specialist, pediatrician
Newbauer, John Arthur editor
Norstrand, Iris Fletcher psychiatrist, neurologist, educator
O'Connor, Sister George Aquin (Margaret M. O'Connor) college president, sociology educator
Ogden, Peggy A. personnel director
Olson, Harry Andrew, Jr. communications consultant
Olson, Robert Goodwin philosophy educator
Onken, George Marcellus lawyer
Oussani, James John stapling company executive
Pagala, Murali Krishna physiologist
Pan, Huo-Hsi mechanical engineer, educator
Pearce, Eli M. chemistry educator, administrator
Pearlstein, Seymour artist
Peker, Elya Abel artist
Pennisten, John William computer scientist, linguist, actuary
Pertschuk, Louis Philip pathologist
Peter, Sebastian Augustine endocrinologist
Peters, Mercedes psychoanalyst
Phillips, Gretchen clinical social worker
Pinczower, Kenneth Ephraim lawyer
Plotz, Charles Mindell physician
Pollack, Bruce banker, real estate consultant
Poser, Norman Stanley law educator
Poster, June performing company executive
Price, Ely dermatologist
Prince, Leslie Francis lobbyist, activist
Purdy, James writer
Pustilnik, Seymour W. mathematics educator, education educator
Qiao, Liang physician
Raggi, Reena federal judge
Raskind, Leo Joseph law educator
Ravitz, Leonard, Jr. physician, scientist, consultant
Reich, Nathaniel Edwin physician, poet, author, artist, educator
Reinisch, June Machover psychologist, educator
Reynolds, Nancy Remick editor, writer
Ricca, Joseph John internist, gastroenterologist
Rice, John Thomas architecture educator
Rike, Susan public relations executive
Rocco, Ron artist
Roess, Roger Peter engineering educator
Ross, Allyne R. federal judge
Roth, Pamela Susan lawyer
Rothenberg, Mira Kowarski clinical psychologist and psychotherapist
Ryan, Leonard Eames administrative law judge
Sainer, Arthur writer, theater educator
Salzman, Eric composer, writer
Sands, Edith Sylvia Abeloff (Mrs. Abraham M. Sands) retired finance educator, author
Sanford, David Boyer writer, editor
†Savits, Barry Sorrel surgeon
Sawyer, Philip Nicholas surgeon, educator, health science facility administrator
Schaefer, Marilyn Louise artist, writer, educator
Scherer, Suzanne Marie artist, educator
Schiffman, Gerald microbiologist, educator
Schmidt, Fred (Orval Frederick Schmidt) editor
Schussler, Theodore lawyer, physician, educator
Schwarz, Richard Howard obstetrician, gynecologist, educator
Shalita, Alan Remi dermatologist
†Sharify, Nasser educator, librarian, author
Shaw, Leonard Glazer electrical engineering educator, consultant
Shechter, Ben-Zion artist, illustrator
Shechter, Laura Judith artist
Shubert, Gabrielle S. museum executive director
Sifton, Charles Proctor federal judge
Silverstein, Louis art director, designer, editor
†Skolnik, Miriam lawyer
Solomon, Martin M. judge, state senator
Sonenberg, Jack artist
Spector, Robert Donald language professional, educator
Spivack, Frieda Kugler psychologist, administrator, educator, researcher
Steiner, Robert S. psychologist
Stracher, Alfred biochemistry educator
Strauss, Dorothy Brandfon marital, family, and sex therapist
Sullivan, Colleen Anne physician, educator
Sullivan, Joseph M. bishop
Sultzer, Barnet Martin microbiology and immunology researcher
Szenberg, Michael economics educator, editor, consultant
Tesoro, Giuliana Cavaglieri chemistry research educator, consultant
Trager, David G. federal judge
Twining, Lynne Dianne psychotherapist, writer
Verma, Ram Sagar geneticist, educator, author, administrator
Vidal, Maureen Eris English educator, actress
von Rydingsvard, Ursula Karoliszyn sculptor
Walsh, George William publishing company executive, editor
Weil, Edward David chemistry researcher, consultant, inventor
Weill, Georges Gustave mathematics educator
Weiner, Irwin M. medical educator, college dean, researcher
Weinstein, Jack Bertrand federal judge
Weston, I. Donald architect
Williams, Carl E., Sr. bishop
Williams, Vida Veronica guidance counselor
Williams, William Magavern headmaster
Wolf, Edward Lincoln physics educator
Wolfe, Ethyle Renee (Mrs. Coleman Hamilton Benedict) college administrator
Wolintz, Arthur Harry physician, neuro-ophthalmologist
Wollman, Leo physician
Woolley, Margaret Anne (Margot Woolley) architect
Yeaton, Cecelia E(mma) healthcare administration executive
Youngblood, Johnny Ray pastor
Zakanitch, Robert Rahway artist
Zelin, Jerome retail executive
Zivari, Bashir architect, industrial designer
Zuk, Judith botanic garden administrator
Zukowski, Barbara Wanda clinical social work psychotherapist

**Brookville**
Abdolali, Nasrin political scientist, educator, consultant
Araoz, Daniel Leon psychologist, educator

**Buchanan**
Somerstein, Aurora Abrera preschool administrator, educator

**Buffalo**
Abrahams, Athol Denis geography researcher, educator
Ackerman, Philip Charles utility executive, lawyer
Allen, William Sheridan history educator
Amborski, Leonard Edward chemist
Ambrus, Clara Maria physician
Ambrus, Julian L. physician, medical educator
Anbar, Michael biophysics educator
Anderson, Wayne Arthur electrical engineering educator
Aquilina, Alan T. physician
Arcara, Richard Joseph federal judge
Aurbach, Herbert Alexander sociology educator
Bakay, Louis neurosurgeon
Bardos, Thomas Joseph chemist, educator
Barney, Thomas McNamee lawyer
Basu, Rajat Subhra physicist, researcher
Bayles, Jennifer Lucene museum education curator
Bean, Edwin Temple, Jr. lawyer
Benenson, David Maurice engineering educator
Berner, Robert Frank statistics educator
Bishop, Beverly Petterson physiologist
Blaine, Charles Gillespie retired lawyer
Blane, Howard Thomas research institute administrator
Bobinski, George Sylvan librarian, educator
Borst, Lyle Benjamin physicist, educator
Brady-Borland, Karen reporter
Brock, David George lawyer
Brody, Harold neuroanatomist, gerontologist
Bross, Irwin Dudley Jackson biostatistician
Brown, John M. gas company executive
Brydges, Thomas Eugene lawyer
Calkins, Evan physician, educator
Carmichael, Donald Scott lawyer, business executive
Chapman, Frederick John manufacturing executive
Chiaravalloti, Mary Frances nurse, educator
Chrisman, Diane J. librarian
Chu, Tsann Ming immunochemist, educator
Chutkow, Jerry Grant neurologist, educator
Ciancio, Sebastian Gene periodontist, educator
Clarkson, Elisabeth Ann Hudnut civic worker
Clemens, David Allen lawyer
Coburn, Lewis Alan mathematics educator
Coles, Robert Traynham architect
Coles, William Henry ophthalmologist, educator
Collins, J. Michael public broadcasting executive
Coppens, Philip chemist
Cordes, Alexander Charles lawyer
Creaven, Patrick Joseph physician, research oncologist
Creeley, Robert White author, English educator
Curtin, John T. federal judge
Day, Donald Sheldon lawyer
Deasy, Jacqueline Hildegard insurance consultant
Dewald, Jonathan Stewart history educator
Draper, Verden Rolland accountant
Drew, Fraser Bragg Robert English language educator
Drinnan, Alan John oral pathologist
Drury, Colin Gordon engineering consultant, educator
Duax, William Leo biological researcher
Duke, Emanuel lawyer
Elfvin, John Thomas federal judge
Enhorning, Goran obstetrician, gynecologist, educator
Fallavollita, James A. cardiologist, educator, researcher
Federman, Raymond novelist, English and comparative literature educator
Feldman, Irving poet
Feuerstein, Alan Ricky lawyer, consultant
Fiedler, Leslie Aaron English educator, actor, author
Floyd, David Kenneth lawyer, judge
Freedman, Maryann Saccomando lawyer
Freschi, Bruno Basilio architect, educator
Fryer, Appleton publisher, sales executive, lecturer, diplomat
Fuzak, Victor Thaddeus lawyer
Gardner, Arnold Burton lawyer
Garver, Newton philosophy educator
Garvey, James Anthony lawyer
Gemmett, Robert James university dean, English language educator
Genco, Robert Joseph scientist, immunologist, periodontist, educator
Gephart, Michele Marie elementary education educator
Gerstman, Sharon Stern lawyer
Glanville, Robert Edward lawyer
Glasauer, Franz Ernst neurosurgeon
Glickman, Marlene non-profit organization administrator
Goldberg, Neil A. lawyer
Goldhaber, Gerald Martin communication educator, author, consultant
Goodberry, Diane Jean (Oberkircher) mathematics educator, tax accountant
Goodell, Joseph Edward manufacturing executive
Gort, Michael economics educator
Gracia, Jorge Jesus Emiliano philosopher, educator
Graham, (Lloyd) Saxon epidemiology educator
Grasser, George Robert lawyer
Gray, F(rederick) William, III lawyer
Green, Martin Lincoln medical instrumentation executive
Greiner, William Robert university administrator, educator, lawyer
Gresham, Glen Edward physician
Gress, Edward J(ules) academic program director, consultant
Gruen, David Henry financial executive, consultant
Halbreich, Uriel Morav psychiatrist, educator
Hall, David Edward lawyer
Hall, Linda McIntyre biochemical pharmacology educator, consultant
Halpern, Ralph Lawrence lawyer
Halpert, Leonard Walter retired editor
Halt, James George advertising executive, graphic designer
Hare, Peter Hewitt philosophy educator
Hasek, Dominik professional hockey player
Hauptman, Herbert Aaron mathematician, educator, researcher
Hayes, J. Michael lawyer
Hazlewood, Olga Alicia lawyer, educator
He, Guang Sheng research scientist
Head, Christopher Alan lawyer
Headrick, Thomas Edward lawyer, educator
Heckman, Carol E. judge
Heilman, Pamela Davis lawyer
Henderson, Edward Shelton oncologist
Hershey, Linda Ann neurology and pharmacology educator
Hetzner, Donald Raymund social studies educator, forensic social scientist
Hida, George T. chemical and ceramic engineer
Ho, Alex Wing-keung statistician
Hohn, David physician
Holzinger, Brian professional hockey player
Hoover, Eddie Lee cardiothoracic surgeon, educator
Horoszewicz, Juliusz Stanislaw oncologist, cancer researcher, laboratory administrator
Hudson, Stanton Harold, Jr. public relations executive, educator
Huntington, Richard (John) art critic
Iggers, Georg Gerson history educator
Ireland, Barbara Hennig newspaper editor
Irwin, Robert James Armstrong investment company executive
Jacobs, Jeremy M. diversified holding company executive, hockey team owner
Jain, Piyare Lal physics educator
Jasen, Matthew Joseph state justice
Jerge, Marie Charlotte minister
Joslin, Norman Earl judge
Karwan, Mark Henry engineering educator, dean
Katz, Jack audiology educator
Keem, Michael Dennis veterinarian
Kennedy, Bernard Joseph utility executive
Kieffer, James Marshall lawyer
Kinzly, Robert Edward engineering company executive
Kiser, Kenneth M(aynard) chemical engineering educator
Kite, Joseph Hiram, Jr. microbiologist, educator
Knox, Northrup Rand banker
Koontz, Eldon Ray management and financial consultant
Krackow, Kenneth Alan orthopaedic surgeon, educator, inventor
Krims, Leslie Robert photographer, art educator
Kristoff, Karl W. lawyer
Kurlan, Marvin Zeft surgeon, educator
Lafontaine, Pat professional hockey player
LaHood, Marvin John English educator
Lamb, Charles F. minister
Landi, Dale Michael industrial engineer, academic administrator
Larson, Wilfred Joseph chemical company executive
Layton, Rodney Eugene controller, newspaper executive
Lee, George C. civil engineer, university administrator
Lele, Amol Shashikant obstetrician and gynecologist
Levine, George Richard English language educator
Levine, Murray psychology educator
Levy, Harold James physician, psychiatrist
Levy, Kenneth Jay psychology educator, academic administrator
Light, Murray Benjamin newspaper editor
Lippes, Gerald Sanford lawyer, business executive
Littlewood, Douglas Burden business brokerage executive
†Logue, Gerald L. hematologist
Machtei, Eli E. periodontist
MacLeod, Gordon Albert retired lawyer
Manes, Stephen Gabriel concert pianist, educator
Manning, Kenneth Alan lawyer
†Mansell, Henry J. bishop
Marinelli, Lynn M. county official
Masiello, Anthony M. (Tony Masiello) mayor
Mates, Robert Edward mechanical engineering educator
McElvein, Thomas I., Jr. lawyer
Menasco, William Wyatt mathematics educator
Mendelow, Gary N. physician, emergency consultant
Meredith, Dale Dean civil engineering educator
Merini, Rafika foreign language and literature and women's studies educator
Metzger, Ernest Hugh aerospace engineer, scientist
Mihich, Enrico medical researcher
Milgrom, Felix immunologist, educator
Milligan, John Drane historian, educator
Mindell, Eugene Robert surgeon, educator
Mirand, Edwin Albert medical scientist
Morgan, James Durward computer company executive
Moss, Douglas G. professional hockey team executive
Mucci, Gary Louis lawyer
Muckler, John professional hockey coach, professional team executive
Murray, William Michael lawyer
Naughton, John Patrick cardiologist
Newman, Stephen Michael lawyer
Nolan, James Paul medical educator, scientist
Nolan, Theodore John professional hockey coach
Oak, H. Lorraine academic administrator, geography educator
Odza, Randall M. lawyer

O'Loughlin, Sandra S. *lawyer*
Pajak, David Joseph *lawyer, consultant*
Panaro, Victor Anthony *radiologist*
Patel, Mulchand Shambhubhai *biochemist*
Payne, Frances Anne *literature educator, researcher*
Pearson, Paul David *lawyer, mediator*
Pegels, C. Carl *management science and systems educator*
Pentney, Roberta Jean *neuroanatomist, educator*
Peradotto, John Joseph *classics educator, editor*
Perry, J. Warren *health sciences educator, administrator*
Petrie, Hugh Gilbert *university dean, philosophy of education educator*
Piccillo, Joseph *artist*
Piech, Margaret Ann *mathematics educator*
Pincus, Stephanie Hoyer *dermatologist, educator*
Pitegoff, Peter Robert *lawyer, educator*
Piver, M. Steven *gynecologic oncologist*
Priore, Roger L. *biostatistics educator, consultant*
Pruitt, Dean Garner *psychologist, educator*
Rachlin, Lauren David *lawyer*
Raghavan, Derek *oncology and medical educator*
Reece-Porter, Sharon Ann *global education educator*
Regan, Peter Francis, III *physician, psychiatry educator*
Reismann, Herbert *engineer, educator*
Reitan, Paul Hartman *geologist, educator*
Rekate, Albert C. *physician*
Rice, Victor Albert *manufacturing executive, heavy*
Rich, Robert E., Jr. *food products company executive*
Richards, David Gleyre *German language educator*
Richmond, Allen Martin *speech pathologist, educator*
Riepe, Dale Maurice *philosopher, writer, illustrator, educator, Asian art dealer*
Ritchie, Stafford Duff, II *lawyer*
Robinson, David Clinton *reporter*
Rochwarger, Leonard *former ambassador*
Rogovin, Milton *photographer, retired optometrist*
Rooney, Paul Monroe *former library administrator*
Rosenthal, Donald B. *political scientist, educator*
Ruckenstein, Eli *chemical engineering educator*
Rumer, Ralph Raymond, Jr. *civil engineer, educator*
St. Pierre, Cheryl Ann *art educator*
Salisbury, Eugene W. *lawyer, justice*
Sampson, John David *lawyer*
Sarjeant, Walter James *electrical and computer engineering educator*
Saveth, Edward Norman *history educator*
Schatz, Lillian Lee *playwright, molecular biologist, educator*
Schroeder, Harold Kenneth, Jr. *lawyer*
Schultz, Douglas George *art museum director*
Segarra, Tyrone Marcus *pharmacist, medicinal chemist*
Seidl, Fredrick William *dean, social work educator*
Seitz, Mary Lee *mathematics educator*
Seller, Robert Herman *cardiologist, family physician*
Selman, Alan Louis *computer science educator*
Shapiro, Stuart Charles *computer scientist, educator*
Shaw, David Tai-Ko *electrical and computer engineering educator, university administrator*
Shedd, Donald Pomroy *surgeon*
Sherwood, Arthur Morley *lawyer*
Siedlecki, Peter Anthony *English language and literature educator*
Simpson, George True *surgeon, educator*
Singletary, James, Jr. *principal*
Skretny, William Marion *federal judge*
†Smith, Bennett Walker *minister*
Solo, Alan Jere *medicinal chemistry educator, consultant*
Southwick, Lawrence, Jr. *management educator*
Spencer, Foster Lewis *newspaper editor*
Stachowski, Michael Joseph *lawyer*
Stainrook, Harry Richard *banker*
Starks, Fred William *chemical company executive*
Stoll, Howard Lester, Jr. *dermatologist*
Swanson, Austin Delain *educational administration educator*
Tedlock, Barbara Helen *anthropologist, educator*
Tedlock, Dennis *anthropology and literature educator*
Thurston, John Thomas *university advancement official*
Toles, Thomas Gregory *editorial cartoonist*
Tomasi, Thomas B. *cell biologist, administrator*
Toohey, Philip S. *lawyer*
Treanor, Charles Edward *physicist*
Trevisan, Maurizio *epidemiologist, researcher*
Triggle, David John *university dean, consultant*
Trotter, Herman Eager, Jr. (Herman Trotter) *music critic*
Urban, Henry Zeller *newspaperman*
Valdes, Maximiano *conductor*
Vitagliano, Kathleen Alyce Fuller *secondary education educator*
Vogel, Michael N. *journalist, writer, historian*
Voorhess, Mary Louise *pediatric endocrinologist*
Wang, Jui Hsin *biochemistry educator*
Weber, Thomas William *chemical engineering educator*
Weller, Sol William *chemical engineering educator*
Wickser, John Philip *lawyer*
Wiesenberg, Russel John *statistician*
Wilbur, Barbara Marie *elementary education educator*
Wilmers, Robert George *banker*
Wisbaum, Wayne David *lawyer*
Woelfel, Joseph Donald *communications educator*
Wolck, Wolfgang Hans-Joachim *linguist, educator*
Wright, John Robert *pathologist*
Zagare, Frank Cosmo *political science educator*
Zarembka, Paul *economics educator*
Zatko, Patricia Ann *nursing administrator, geriatrics nurse*
Zimmerman, Nancy Picciano *library science educator*

### Buskirk
Johanson, Patricia Maureen *artist, architect, park designer*

### Camillus
Caryl, William R., Jr. *orthodontist*

### Campbell Hall
Greenly, Colin *artist*
Ottaway, James Haller, Jr. *newspaper publisher*
Stone, Peter George *lawyer, publishing company executive*

### Canaan
Pennell, William Brooke *lawyer*
Rothenberg, Albert *psychiatrist, educator*
Walker, William Bond *painter, retired librarian*

### Canandaigua
Clark, Louis Morris, Jr. *investment manager, antique dealer, innkeeper*
Malinowski, Patricia A. *community college educator*
Read, Eleanor May *financial analyst*
Sands, Marvin *wine company executive*
Williams, Carolyn Woodworth *retired elementary education educator, consultant*

### Canton
Fleming, Barbara Joan *university official*
Goldberg, Rita Maria *foreign language educator*
O'Connor, Daniel William *retired religious studies and classical languages educator*
Pollard, Fred Don *finance company executive*
Romey, William Dowden *geologist, educator*

### Carle Place
Linchitz, Richard Michael *psychiatrist, pain medicine specialist, physician*
Matturro, Anthony *lawyer*
Smolev, Terence Elliot *lawyer, educator*

### Carmel
Caporino, Grace Connolly *secondary education educator, consultant*
Carruth, David Barrow *landscape architect*
Huckabee, Carol Brooks *psychologist*
Laporte, Cloyd, Jr. *retired manufacturing executive, lawyer*
Lowe, E(dwin) Nobles *lawyer*
Shen, Chia Theng *former steamship company executive, religious institute official*

### Castle Point
Laubscher, Leeann *medical and surgical nurse*

### Castleton On Hudson
Lanford, Oscar Erasmus, Jr. *retired university vice chancellor*

### Catskill
Markou, Peter John *economic developer*

### Cazenovia
Durgin, Patricia Harte *college administrator, chemistry educator, counselor*

### Cedarhurst
Cohen, David B. *optical company executive*
Cohen, Harris L. *diagnostic radiologist, consultant*
Cohen, Philip Herman *accountant*
Solymosy, Hattie May *writer, publisher, storyteller, educator*
Taubenfeld, Harry Samuel *lawyer*

### Centereach
Buggé, Brian Keith *police supervisor, educator*
Cutrone, Dee T(heresa) *elementary education educator*

### Centerport
Fischel, Edward Elliot *physician*
Mallett, Helene Gettler *elementary education educator*
Stevens, Martin Brian *publisher*

### Central Islip
Cordle, Kevin Gerard *electronic engineer*
Griffith, Philip Arthur *elementary school educator*
McCrain, Michael William *accountant, consultant*
McGowan, Harold *real estate developer, investor, scientist, author, philanthropist*
Piemontese, David Stefano *pharmaceutical scientist*
Rodriguez, Teresa Ida *elementary education educator, educational consultant*

### Chappaqua
Boal, Lyndall Elizabeth *social worker*
Brennan, Terrence Michael *publisher*
Brockway, George Pond *economist*
de Janosi, Peter Engel *research manager*
George, Jean Craighead *author, illustrator*
Gstalder, Herbert William *publisher*
Howard, John Brigham *lawyer, foundation executive*
Kingsley, Emily Perl *writer*
Laun, Louis Frederick *government official*
O'Neill, Robert Charles *inventor, consultant*
Pomerene, James Herbert *retired computer engineer*
Whittingham, Charles Arthur *library administrator, publisher*

### Charlton
Kekes, John *philosopher, educator*

### Chateaugay
Kanzler, Kathleen Patricia *kennel owner*

### Cheektowaga
Freedman, Anne Maureen *nurse, consultant*
LaForest, Lana Jean *lawyer, real estate broker*
Woldman, Sherman *pediatrician*

### Chestnut Ridge
Day, Stacey Biswas *physician, educator*

### Chittenango
Cassell, William Walter *retired accounting operations consultant*

### Cicero
Webster, Michael Lee *academic administrator*

### Circleville
Hazan, Marcella Maddalena *author, educator, consultant*

### Clarence
Hubler, Julius *artist*
Mehaffy, Thomas N. *retired tire company executive*
Muffoletto, Barry Charles *engineering executive*
Trinkus, Laima Mary *special education educator*

### Clifton Park
Farley, John Joseph *library science educator emeritus*
Favreau, Donald Francis *corporate executive*
Fell, Samuel Kennedy (Ken Fell) *infosystems executive*
Hughes, Edward Thomas *English educator*

Murphy, Mary Patricia *elementary education educator*
Orsini, Paul Vincent *music educator*
Panek, Jan *electrical power engineer, consultant*
Scher, Robert Sander *instrument design company executive*

### Climax
Adler, Lee *artist, educator, marketing executive*

### Clinton
Anthony, Donald Charles *librarian, educator*
Blackwood, Russell Thorn, III *philosophy educator*
Couper, Richard Watrous *foundation executive, educator*
Fuller, Ruthann *principal*
Pagani, Albert Louis *aerospace system engineer*
Ring, James Walter *physics educator*
Rupprecht, Carol Schreier *comparative literature educator, dream researcher*
Stowens, Daniel *pathologist*
Wagner, Frederick Reese *language professional*

### Cobleskill
Ingels, Jack Edward *horticulture educator*

### Cohocton
Frame, Paul Sutherland *medical educator, physician*
Sarfaty, Wayne Allen *insurance agent, financial planner*

### Cohoes
Kennedy, Kathleen Ann *faculty/nursing consultant*
Tabner, Mary Frances *secondary school educator*

### Cold Spring
Brill, Ralph David *architect, real estate developer, venture capitalist*
Powell, Carol Ann *accountant*
Pugh, Emerson William *electrical engineer*

### Cold Spring Harbor
Freeman, Ira Henry *author, journalist*
Hargraves, Gordon Sellers *banker*
Ma, Hong *plant molecular biologist, educator*
Watson, James Dewey *molecular biologist, educator*

### Colton
Bulger, Dennis Bernard *military officer, engineer*

### Commack
Cohen, Judith W. *academic administrator*
Landau, Dorothy *psychotherapist, consultant*
Nelson, Marvin Bernard *financial executive*
Nilson, Patricia *clinical psychologist*
Rakower, Joel A. *business appraiser, litigation consultant*

### Conesus
Dadrian, Vahakn Norair *sociology educator*

### Congers
Nelson, Marguerite Hansen *special education educator*

### Cooperstown
†Aparicio, Luis Ernesto *retired baseball player*
†Ashburn, Don Richard *retired baseball player, broadcaster*
†Barlick, Al *retired baseball umpire*
Bordley, James, IV *surgeon*
Carew, Rodney Cline *batting coach, former professional baseball player*
†Doerr, Robert Pershing *retired baseball player*
†Early, Wynn *retired baseball player*
†Ferrell, Rick *retired baseball player*
†Fingers, Roland Glen *retired baseball player*
†Ford, Edward Charles (Whitey Ford) *retired baseball player*
Franck, Walter Alfred *rheumatologist, medical administrator, educator*
Gibson, Robert *broadcaster, former baseball player*
Harman, Willard Nelson *malacologist, educator*
†Hunter, James Augustus *retired baseball player*
†Irvin, Monte *retired baseball player*
†Kaline, Albert William *retired baseball player*
†Koufax, Sandy *retired baseball player*
†Lemon, Robert Granville *retired baseball player*
†Leonard, Buck *retired baseball player*
†Lopez, Alfonso Ramon *retired baseball player*
MacLeish, Archibald Bruce *museum director*
†Mathews, Edwin Lee *retired baseball player*
†Newhouser, Hal *retired baseball player*
Peters, Theodore, Jr. *research biochemist, consultant*
†Reese, Harold Henry *retired baseball player*
Reynolds, Jack Mason *manufacturing company executive*
Schmidt, Michael Jack *former professional baseball player*
†Slaughter, Enos *retired baseball player*
†Snider, Edwin D. *retired baseball player*
†Spahn, Warren *retired baseball player*
Tilton, Webster, Jr. *contractor*
†Wilhelm, James Hoyt *retired baseball player*
Williams, Ted (Theodore Samuel Williams) *former baseball player, former manager, consultant*

### Copake Falls
Chalk, Howard Wolfe *marketing company executive*

### Coram
Helmer, Carol A. *psychologist, school psychologist*

### Corning
†Ackerman, Roger G. *ceramic engineer*
Becraft, Charles D., Jr. *lawyer*
Behm, Forrest Edwin *glass manufacturing company executive*
Booth, C(hesley) Peter Washburn *manufacturing company executive*
Buechner, Thomas Scharman *artist, retired glass manufacturing company executive, museum director*
Dulude, Richard *glass manufacturing company executive*
Hauselt, Denise Ann *lawyer*
Houghton, James Richardson *retired glass manufacturing company executive*
Josbeno, Larry Joseph *physics educator*
Keck, Donald Bruce *physicist*
Lin, Min-Chung *obstetrician-gynecologist*
†Luther, David Byron *glass company executive*
Maurer, Robert Distler *retired industrial physicist*

Nary, John Henry *interior designer*
Peck, Arthur John, Jr. *diversified manufacturing executive, lawyer*
Spillman, Jane Shadel *curator, researcher, writer*
Ughetta, William Casper *lawyer, manufacturing company executive*
Whitehouse, David Bryn *museum director*

### Cornwall
Gentile, Melanie Marie *record producer, marketing and public relations consultant, writer*

### Cornwall On Hudson
Abrams-Collens, Vivien *artist*
Grant, Joanne Catherine *auctioneer, fine art appraiser*
Holstein, David *psychotherapist, management consultant*
Weiss, Egon Arthur *retired library administrator*

### Corona
Cole, Donald H. *middle school educator*
Jackson, Andrew Preston *library director*
Miele, Joel Arthur, Sr. *civil engineer*
Saunders, Adah Wilson *physical education educator*

### Cortland
Anderson, Donna Kay *musicologist, educator*
Kaminsky, Alice Richkin *English language educator*
Miller, John David *manufacturing company executive*

### Cortlandt Manor
Rath, Bernard Emil *trade association executive*

### Coxsackie
Amado, Lisa *elementary education educator*

### Cranberry Lake
Glavin, James Edward *landscape architect*

### Craryville
Payson, Ronald Sears *biology educator*

### Cross River
Larsen, Lawrence Bernard, Jr. *priest, pastoral psychotherapist*

### Croton On Hudson
Adelson, Alexander Michael *physicist*
Coleman, Earl Maxwell *publishing company executive*
Henderson, Harry Brinton, Jr. *author, editor*
Kahn, Roger *author*
Miranda, Robert Nicholas *publishing company executive*
Needham, Richard Lee *magazine editor*
Nelson, Charles Arthur *publisher, consultant*
Plotch, Walter *management consultant, fund raising counselor*
Rubinfien, Leo H. *photographer, filmmaker*
Shatzkin, Leonard *publishing consultant*
Straka, Laszlo Richard *publishing consultant*
Turner, David Reuben *publisher, author*

### Crown Point
Dajany, Innam *academic administrator*

### Crugers
Norman, Jessye *soprano*

### Cutchogue
Dank, Leonard Dewey *medical illustrator, audio-visual consultant*
O'Connell, Francis Joseph *lawyer, arbitrator*

### Deer Park
Gorme, Eydie *singer*
Lawrence, Steve *entertainer*
Martone, Jeanette Rachele *artist*
Taub, Jesse J. *electrical engineering researcher*

### Delhi
Needham, Nancy Jean *management consultant*

### Delmar
Button, Rena Pritsker *public affairs executive*
Collins, Sandra Dee *physical education educator*
Houghton, Raymond Carl, Jr. *computer science educator*
Nitecki, Joseph Zbigniew *librarian*
Pember, John Bartlett *social worker, educator*
Shen, Thomas To *environmental engineer*
Ting, Joseph K. *mechanical engineer*

### Dix Hills
Blumstein, Reneé J. *research and statistical consultant*
Fisher, Fenimore *business development consultant*
Meyers, George Edward *plastics company executive*
Sampino, Anthony F. *physician, obstetrician and gynecologist*
Schultheis, Edwin Milford *dean, business educator*

### Dobbs Ferry
Grunebaum, Ernest Michael *investment banker*
Holtz, Sidney *publishing company executive*
Juettner, Diana D'Amico *lawyer, educator*
Kapp, Richard P. *conductor, arts administrator*
Kraetzer, Mary C. *sociologist, educator, consultant*
Maiocchi, Christine *lawyer*
Miss, Robert Edward *fundraiser*
Pap, Beatriz Díaz *secondary education educator*
Perelle, Ira B. *psychologist, educator*
Sanders, Robert Martin *commodity trader*
Simon, Lothar *publishing company executive*
Sutton, Francis Xavier *social scientist, consultant*
Triplett, Kelly B. *chemist*
Williams, Ross Edward *physicist*

### Douglaston
Costa, Ernest Fiorenzo *graphic designer*
Valero, René Arnold *clergyman*

### Dryden
Baxter, Robert Banning *insurance company executive*

**Dundee**
Pfendt, Henry George *retired information systems executive, management consultant*

**Dunkirk**
Huels, Steven Mark *laboratory analyst*

**East Amherst**
Soong, Tsu-Teh *engineering science educator*

**East Aurora**
Brott, Irving Deerin, Jr. *lawyer, judge*
Hawk, George Wayne *retired electronics company executive*
Hayes, Bonaventure Francis *priest*
Spahn, Mary Attea *retired educator*
Weidemann, Julia Clark *principal, educator*
Woodard, Carol Jane *educational consultant*

**East Berne**
Grenander, M. E. *English language educator, critic*

**East Greenbush**
Mucci, Patrick John *financial consultant, realtor, commercial loan broker*

**East Hampton**
Dalzell, Fred Briggs *financial consultant*
Damaz, Paul F. *architect*
De Bruhl, Marshall *writer, editor, publishing consultant*
Dello Joio, Norman *composer*
Fulbright, Harriet Mayor *foundation administrator*
Gaddis, William *writer*
Garrett, Charles Geoffrey Blythe *physicist*
Harmon, Marian Sanders *writer, sculptor*
Ignatow, David *poet*
Jaudon, Valerie *artist*
Karp, Harvey Lawrence *metal products manufacturing company executive*
Munson, Lawrence Shipley *management consultant*
Praetorius, William Albert, Sr. *artist, former advertising and real estate executive*
Richenburg, Robert Bartlett *artist, retired art educator*
Scott, Rosa Mae *artist, educator*
Stein, Ronald Jay *artist, airline transport pilot*
Vered, Ruth *art gallery director*

**East Islip**
Chassman, Karen Moss *educational administrator*
Delman, Michael Robert *physician*
Fleishman, Philip Robert *internist*
Rogers, Jeanne Valerie *art educator, artist*
Somerville, Daphine Holmes *elementary education educator*

**East Meadow**
Adler, Ira Jay *lawyer*
Albert, Gerald *clinical psychologist*
Beyer, Norma Warren *secondary education educator*
Fuchs, Jerome Herbert *management consultant*

**East Northport**
Reed, Robert Monroe *publishing executive*

**East Patchogue**
Metz, Donald Joseph *retired science educator*

**East Quogue**
Weiss, Elaine Landsberg *community development management official*

**East Rochester**
Clendenin, Johann Alfred (John Clendenin) *office products company executive*
Murray, James Doyle *accountant*

**East Setauket**
Barcel, Ellen Nora *secondary school educator, free-lance writer, indexer*
Briggs, Philip Terry *biologist*
Thom, Joseph M. *librarian*

**East Syracuse**
Duffy, Nancy Keogh *television broadcast professional*
Wiley, Richard Gordon *electrical engineer*

**East Williston**
Abernethy, Ann Lawson *retired elementary education educator*
Berman, Sara Jane *library director*

**Eastchester**
Katz, Kenneth Arthur *lawyer, accountant*
Keeffe, John Arthur *lawyer, director*
Liebert, Peter S. *pediatric surgeon, consultant*

**Eatons Neck**
Altner, Peter Christian *orthopedic surgeon, medical educator*

**Edmeston**
Price, James Melford *physician*

**Elizabethtown**
Davis, George Donald *executive land use policy specialist*
Lawrence, Richard Wesley, Jr. *foundation executive*

**Ellenville**
Baer, Albert Max *metal products executive*

**Elmhurst**
Barron, Charles Thomas *psychiatrist*
Cheng, Alexander Lim *internist*
Lester, Lance Gary *education educator, researcher*
Masci, Joseph Richard *medical educator, physician*
Matsa, Loula Zacharoula *social services administrator*
Shanies, Harvey Michael *pulmonologist, medical educator*
Wachsteter, George *illustrator*

**Elmira**
Bellohusen, Ronald Michael *orthodontist, educator*
Graham, David Richard *orthopedic surgeon*
Hall, Geraldine Cristofaro *biology educator*
Meier, Thomas Keith *college president, English educator*
Quintos, Elias Rilloraza *cardiac surgeon, thoracic surgeon*
Wavle, Elizabeth Margaret *music educator, college official*

**Elmont**
Cusack, Thomas Joseph *banker*
Stephens, Woodford Cefis (Woody Stephens) *horse trainer, breeder*

**Elmsford**
Kroner, Arnold Friedrich *financial consultant, economist*
Kucic, Joseph *management consultant, industrial engineer*
Shaviv, Eddie *marketing and sales executive*
Sklarew, Robert Jay *biomedical research educator, consultant*
Turk, Stanley Martin *advertising agency executive*
Urbanas, Alban William *financial planner*

**Endicott**
Goodwin, Charles Hugh *technology education educator*

**Endwell**
Del Bianco, Kenneth Louis *civil engineer, house designer*

**Erieville**
Snodgrass, W. D. *writer, educator*

**Esopus**
Tetlow, Edwin *author*

**Fairport**
Badenhop, Sharon Lynn *psychologist, educator, entrepreneur*
Bolt, Richard Henry *science educator, business executive, author*
Gorzka, Margaret Rose *elementary education educator*
Halpern, David Rodion *special education administrator, principal*
Kelly, Francis W. *retired psychiatrist*
Lavoie, Dennis James *secondary education educator*
Nastasi, Kathleen Patricia *systems analyst*
Oldshue, James Y. *chemical engineering consultant*
Tomaino, Michael Thomas *lawyer*

**Falconer**
Ruhlman, Herman C(loyd), Jr. *manufacturing company executive*

**Fallsburg**
Carey, Janet L. *physical education educator*

**Far Rockaway**
Epstein, Samuel Abraham *stock and bond broker, petroleum consultant*
Kelly, George Anthony *clergyman, author, educator*
Madhusoodanan, Subramoniam *psychiatrist, educator*
†Re, Edward Domenic, Jr. *construction executive*

**Farmingdale**
Austin, William James *humanities educator, poet, literary critic*
Blum, Melvin *chemical company executive, researcher*
Bolle, Donald Martin *engineering educator*
Bongiorno, Joseph John, Jr. *electrical engineering educator*
Cipriani, Frank Anthony *college president*
Dordelman, William Forsyth *food company executive*
Doucette, David Robert *computer systems company executive*
Firetog, Theodore Warren *lawyer*
Klosner, Jerome Martin *mechanical engineer, educator*
Kostanoski, John Ivan *criminal justice educator*
LaTourrette, James Thomas *retired electrical engineering and computer science educator*
Marcuvitz, Nathan *electrophysics educator*
Smith, Joseph Seton *electronics company executive, consultant*
Steckler, Larry *publisher, editor, author*

**Fayetteville**
Cantwell, John Dalzell, Jr. *management consultant*
Dall, Jane Vollbrecht *psychotherapist*
Dosanjh, Darshan S(ingh) *aeronautical engineer, educator*
Evans, Nolly Seymour *lawyer*
Hiemstra, Roger *adult education educator, writer, networker*
Pachter, Irwin Jacob *pharmaceutical consultant*
Paul, Linda Baum *geriatrics nurse, toy business owner*
Pirodsky, Donald Max *psychiatrist, educator*
Sager, Roderick Cooper *retired life insurance company executive*
Sears, Bradford George *landscape architect*
Wallace, Spencer Miller, Jr. *hotel executive*

**Fishkill**
Brocks, Eric Randy *ophthalmologist, surgeon*
Dixon, Linda *child, adolescent and adult therapist*
Stein, Paula Nancy *psychologist, educator*

**Floral Park**
Brancaleone, Laurie Ann *social worker*
Chatoff, Michael Alan *lawyer*
Corbett, William John *government and public relations consultant, lawyer*
Heyderman, Mark Baron *sales and marketing company executive*
Scricca, Diane Bernadette *principal*
Weinrib, Sidney *retired optometric and optical products and services executive*

**Florida**
Fisher, Joseph V. *retail executive*

**Flushing**
Allen, Ralph Gilmore *dramatist, producer, drama educator*
Bird, Thomas Edward *foreign language and literature educator*
Birnstiel, Charles *consulting engineer*
Bohner, Robert Joseph *lawyer*
Bruder, Harold Jacob *artist, educator*
Carlson, Cynthia Joanne *artist, educator*
Cathcart, Robert Stephen *mass media consultant*
Chako, Nicholas *mathematician, physicist, educator*
Chook, Paul Howard *publishing executive*
Commoner, Barry *biologist, educator*
Cooke, Constance Blandy *librarian*
Doubleday, Nelson *professional baseball team executive*
Dubov, Spencer Floyd *podiatrist, educator*
Eden, Alvin Noam *pediatrician, author*
Ellis, John Taylor *pathologist, retired educator*
Erickson, Raymond *academic dean*
Fauntleroy, Carma Cecil *arts administration executive*
Fichtel, Rudolph Robert *retired association executive*
Finks, Robert Melvin *paleontologist, educator*
Gafney, Harry D. *chemistry educator*
Goldman, Norman Lewis *chemistry educator*
Goldsmith, Howard *writer, consultant*
Goldstein, Milton *art educator, printmaker, painter*
Grossman, Julius *conductor*
Hacker, Andrew *political science educator*
Hatcher, Robert Douglas *physicist, educator*
Henshel, Harry Bulova *watch manufacturer*
Hirshson, Stanley Philip *history educator*
Hon, John Wingsun *physician*
Hsu, Charles Jui-cheng *manufacturing company executive, advertising agent*
†Hundley, Todd Randolph *professional baseball player*
Kaplan, Barry Hubert *physician*
†Katz, Saul B. *professional sports team executive*
Kaufman, Michele Beth *clinical pharmacist, educator*
Kiner, Ralph McPherran *sports commentator, former baseball player*
Kornhauser, Stanley Henry *medical administrator, educator, consultant*
Kresic, Eva *pediatrician*
Laderman, Gabriel *artist*
Lamont, Rosette Clementine *Romance languages educator, theatre journalist, translator*
Lee, Paul Ching-Lai *banker, real estate developer*
Madden, Joseph Daniel *trade association executive*
Mendelson, Elliott *mathematician, educator*
Milone, James Michael *occupational health-safety engineering executive, evironmental engineer*
Nicotra, Joseph Charles *artist*
Nussbaum, Michel Ernest *physician*
Olerud, John Garrett *professional baseball player*
Psomiades, Harry John *political science educator*
Rabassa, Gregory *Romance languages educator, translator, poet*
Ranald, Margaret Loftus *English literature educator, author*
Rathbone, Susan Wu *social services administrator*
Safadi-Psyllos, Gina Moni *administrative assistant, business owner*
Sanborn, Anna Lucille *pension and insurance consultant*
Schnall, Edith Lea (Mrs. Herbert Schnall) *microbiologist, educator*
Schwartz, Estar Alma *lawyer*
Shirvani, Hamid *architect, educator, author, administrator*
Smaldone, Edward Michael *composer*
Smith, Charles William *social sciences educator, sociologist*
Speidel, David Harold *geology educator*
Stahl, Frank Ludwig *civil engineer*
Stark, Joel *speech language pathologist*
†Tepper, Marvin B. *professional sports team executive*
Tytell, John *humanities educator, writer*
†Wilpon, Fred *real estate developer, baseball team executive*

**Fly Creek**
Dusenbery, Walter Condit *sculptor*

**Forest Hills**
Baral, Lillian *artist, retired educator*
Crystal, Boris *artist*
Dessylas, Ann Atsaves *human resources and office management executive*
Flowers, Cynthia *investment company executive*
Immerman, Mia Fendler *artist*
Janson, Patrick *singer, actor, conductor, educator*
Kane, Sydell *elementary school principal*
Kra, Pauline Skornicki *French language educator*
Miller, Donald Ross *management consultant*
O'Brien, Margaret Josephine *retired community health nurse*
Pinto, Rosalind *retired educator, civic volunteer*
Polakoff, Abe *baritone*
Prager, Alice Heinecke *music company executive*
Silver, Sheila Jane *composer, music educator*
Tewi, Thea *sculptor*
Van Westering, James Francis *management consultant, educator*

**Fort Covington**
Dunwich, Gerina *author, magazine editor, astrologer*

**Fort Drum**
Ebbels, Bruce Jeffery *physician, health facility administrator*
†Juskowiak, Terry Eugene *career military officer*

**Franklin Square**
Indiviglia, Salvatore Joseph *artist, retired naval officer*

**Fredonia**
Barnard, Walther M. *geosciences educator*
Benton, Allen Haydon *biology educator*
Dowd, Morgan Daniel *political science educator*
Jordan, Robert *concert pianist, educator*
Mac Vittie, Robert William *retired college administrator*
Sonnenfeld, Marion *linguist, educator*
Strauser, Jeffrey Arthur *public safety official*

**Freeport**
Landsberg, Jerry *management and investment consultant, optical laboratory executive*
Martorana, Barbara Joan *secondary education educator*
Pullman, Maynard Edward *biochemist*
Terris, Albert *metal sculptor*

**Fresh Meadows**
Watson, Joseph Gartrell *medical facility administrator*

**Friendship**
Kingdon, Mary Oneida Grace *elementary education educator*

**Fulton**
Long, Robert Emmet *author*

**Gainesville**
MacWilliams, Debra Lynne *secondary reading specialist, consultant*

**Garden City**
Accordino, Frank Joseph *architect, car rental company executive*
Baker, J. A., II *monetary architect, financial engineer, coordination consultant*
Balkan, Kenneth J. *lawyer*
Brooks, Helene Margaret *editor-in-chief*
Campbell, James R. *transportation executive*
Caputo, Kathryn Mary *paralegal*
Conlon, Thomas James *marketing executive*
Cook, George Valentine *lawyer*
Corsi, Philip Donald *lawyer*
Crom, James Oliver *professional training company executive*
Deane, Leland Marc *plastic surgeon*
DeMille, Nelson Richard *writer*
Desch, Carl William *banker, consultant*
Diamandopoulos, Peter *philosopher, educator*
Doucette, Mary-Alyce *computer company executive*
Egan, Frank T. *writer, editor*
Feingold, Ronald Sherwin *physical education educator*
Fishberg, Gerard *lawyer*
Fleisig, Ross *aeronautical engineer, engineering manager*
Friedman, Sari Martin *lawyer*
Good, Larry Irwin *physician, consultant*
Gordon, Barry Joel *investment advisor*
Gordon, Jay F(isher) *lawyer*
Hand, Stephen Block *lawyer*
Harwood, Stanley *retired judge, lawyer*
Jenkins, Kenneth Vincent *literature educator, writer*
Korshak, Yvonne *art historian*
Kreger-Grella, Cheryl Leslie *lawyer*
Kurlander, Neale *accounting and law educator, lawyer*
Lioz, Lawrence Stephen *lawyer, accountant*
Louis-Cotton d'Englesqueville, Francois Pierre *automobile company executive*
Lovely, Thomas Dixon *banker*
Minicucci, Richard Francis *lawyer, former hospital administrator*
Nicklin, George Leslie, Jr. *psychoanalyst, educator, physician*
Ohrenstein, Roman Abraham *economics educator, economist, rabbi*
Okulski, John Allen *principal*
Podwall, Kathryn Stanley *biology educator*
Posch, Robert John, Jr. *lawyer*
Shneidman, J. Lee *historian, educator*
Smith, Paul Thomas *financial services company executive*
Tucker, William P. *lawyer, writer*
Vitale, Paul *accountant*
Webb, Igor Michael *academic administrator*
Weinrich, Gloria Joan Castoria *retired elementary education educator*
Zirkel, Gene *computer science and mathematics educator*

**Gardiner**
Mabee, Carleton *historian, educator*

**Garrison**
Duncan, Thomas Webb *magazine publishing executive*
Egan, Daniel Francis *priest*
Grossman, Allen, III *educational administrator*
Pierpont, Robert *fund raising executive, consultant*

**Geneseo**
Battersby, Harold Ronald *anthropologist, archaeologist, linguist*
Edgar, William John *philosophy educator*
Fausold, Martin Luther *history educator*
Hickman, John Hampton, III *entrepreneurial investment banker, industrialist, educator*
Moore, Gary Alan *academic administrator, educator*
Small, William Andrew *mathematics educator*

**Geneva**
Berta, Joseph Michel *music educator, musician*
Caponegro, Mary *English language educator*
Hersh, Richard H. *academic administrator*
Howard, Rustin Ray *corporate executive*
Roelofs, Wendell Lee *biochemistry educator, consultant*
Siebert, Karl Joseph *food science educator*

**Germantown**
Geistfeld, James Gordon *veterinarian*
Rollins, (Theodore) Sonny *composer, musician*

**Gilbertsville**
Roos, Casper *actor*

**Glen Cove**
Burnham, Harold Arthur *pharmaceutical company executive, physician*
Conti, James Joseph *chemical engineer, educator*
Dehn, Joseph William, Jr. *chemist*
Greenberg, Allan *advertising and marketing research consultant*
Maxwell, J. Douglas, Jr. *chemical service company executive*
Mills, Charles Gardner *lawyer*

**Glen Head**
Boyrer, Elaine M. *principal*
Cohen, Lawrence N. *health care management consultant*
Huber, Don Lawrence *publisher*
Savinetti, Louis Gerard *town councilperson*
Sutherland, Denise Jackson (Denise Suzanne Jackson) *ballerina*
Sutherland, Donald James *investment company executive*

Vizza, Robert Francis *hospital executive, former university administrator, marketing educator*

**Glendale**
Maltese, Serphin Ralph *state senator, lawyer*
Pipia, Rosaria Anna *publishing executive, consultant*

**Glenham**
Douglas, Fred Robert *cost engineering consultant*

**Glenmont**
Block, Murray Harold *educational consultant*
Kolb, Lawrence Coleman *psychiatrist*

**Glens Falls**
Bacas, William Augustus *judge, lawyer*
Bartlett, Richard James *lawyer, former university dean*
Fawcett, Christopher Babcock *civil engineer, construction and water resources company executive*
McMillen, Robert Stewart *lawyer*
Tenne, Donald Paul *financial planner*
Wright, Stephen Charles *financial planner*
Wurzberger, Bezalel *psychiatrist*

**Glenville**
Anderson, Roy Everett *electrical engineering consultant*

**Glenwood Landing**
Hahn, Joan Marjorie *public relations consultant, marketing consultant*
Tane, Susan Jaffe *retired manufacturing company executive*

**Golden's Bridge**
Ambrose, Daniel Michael *publishing executive*

**Goshen**
Goodreds, John Stanton *newspaper publisher*
Hall, Wanda Jean *mental health professional, consultant*
Hawkins, Barry Tyler *author, mental health services professional*
Ward, William Francis, Jr. *real estate investment banker*

**Grand Island**
White, Ralph David *retired editor and writer*

**Great Neck**
Appel, Gerald *investment advisor*
Arlow, Jacob A. *psychiatrist, educator*
Blumberg, Barbara Salmanson (Mrs. Arnold G. Blumberg) *retired state housing official, housing consultant*
Brand, Oscar *folksinger, author, educator*
Busner, Philip H. *lawyer*
Christie, George Nicholas *economist, consultant*
Donenfeld, Kenneth Jay *management consultant*
Elkowitz, Lloyd Kent *dental anesthesiologist, dentist, pharmacist*
Feiler Goldstein, Paulette *secondary education educator, researcher*
Fialkov, Herman *investment banker*
Fiel, Maxine Lucille *journalist, behavioral analyst, lecturer*
Friedland, Louis N. *retired communications executive*
Gellman, Yale H. *lawyer*
Gillin, John F. *quality engineer*
Glushien, Morris P. *lawyer, arbitrator*
Goldberg, Melvin Arthur *communications executive*
Gross, Lillian *psychiatrist*
Haber, Diane Lois *psychotherapist, clinical specialist*
Hamovitch, William *economist, educator, university official*
Hampton, Benjamin Bertram *brokerage house executive*
Harris, Rosalie *psychotherapist, clinical counselor, Spanish language professional and multi-linguist, English as second language educator*
Hurwitz, Johanna (Frank) *author, librarian*
Joskow, Jules *economic research company executive*
Katz, Edward Morris *banker*
Kechijian, Paul *dermatologist, educator*
Kodsi, Sylvia Rose *ophthalmologist*
Kraft, Leo Abraham *composer*
Machiz, Leon *electronic equipment manufacturing executive*
Panes, Jack Samuel *publishing company executive*
Pohl, Gunther Erich *retired library administrator*
Pollack, Paul Robert *airline service company executive*
Ratner, Harold *pediatrician, educator*
Rosenberg, Richard F. *physician, radiologist*
Roth, Harvey Paul *publisher*
Rubin, Irving *pharmaceutical editor*
Samanowitz, Ronald Arthur *lawyer*
Satinskas, Henry Anthony *airline services company executive*
Seidler, Doris *artist*
Shaffer, Bernard William *mechanical and aerospace engineering educator*
Simon, Arthur *pharmacologist, research laboratory executive*
Turofsky, Charles Sheldon *landscape architect*
Wachsman, Harvey Frederick *lawyer, neurosurgeon*
Wank, Gerald Sidney *periodontist*
Weisgall, Hugo David *composer, conductor*
Wolff, Edward *physician*
Zirinsky, Daniel *real estate investor and photographer*

**Greene**
Sternberg, Paul J. *lawyer*

**Greenfield Center**
Conant, Robert Scott *harpsichordist, music educator*
Fonseca, John dos Reis *writer, former law educator*
Templin, John Leon, Jr. *healthcare consulting executive*

**Greenlawn**
Bachman, Henry Lee *electrical engineer, engineering executive*
Newman, Edward Morris *engineering executive*
Stevens, John Richard *architectural historian*

**Greenvale**
Cook, Edward Joseph *college president*

Halper, Emanuel B(arry) *real estate lawyer, developer, consultant, author*
Leipzig, Arthur *photographer, educator emeritus*
Shenker, Joseph *academic administrator*
Steinberg, David Joel *academic administrator, historian, educator*
Woodsworth, Anne *university dean, librarian*

**Greenwood**
Rollins, June Elizabeth *elementary education educator*

**Guilderland**
Byrne, Donn Erwin *psychologist, educator*
Gordon, Leonard Victor *psychologist, educator emeritus*
Persico, Joseph Edward *author*
Sills, Nancy Mintz *lawyer*

**Hague**
Cartwright, Alton Stuart *electrical manufacturing company executive*
Jones, Tracey Kirk, Jr. *minister, educator*

**Hamburg**
Gaughan, Dennis Charles *lawyer*
Green, Gerard Leo *priest, educator*
†Markulis, Henryk John *career military officer*

**Hamilton**
Berlind, Bruce Peter *poet, educator*
Blackton, Charles S(tuart) *history educator*
Busch, Briton Cooper *historian, educator*
Busch, Frederick Matthew *writer, literature educator*
Cappeto, Michael Arnold *dean*
Carter, John Ross *philosophy and religion educator*
Edmonston, William Edward, Jr. *publisher, educator*
Farnsworth, Frank Albert *retired economics educator*
Garland, Robert Sandford John *classical studies educator*
Grabois, Neil Robert *college president*
Hathaway, Robert Lawton *Romance languages educator*
Holbrow, Charles Howard *physicist, educator*
Johnston, (William) Michael *political science educator, university administrator*
Jones, Frank William *language educator*
Jones, Howard Langworthy *educational administrator, consultant*
Kessler, Dietrich *biology educator*
Levy, Jacques *educator, theater director, lyricist, writer*
Noyes, Judith Gibson *library director*
Pownall, Malcolm Wilmor *mathematics educator*
Staley, Lynn *English educator*
Tucker, Thomas William *mathematics professor*
Van Schaack, Eric *art historian, educator*

**Hammond**
Deno, Lawrence M. *academic administrator*
Musselman, Francis Haas *lawyer*

**Hampton Bays**
Allmen, Robert Joseph *psychotherapist, priest*
Yavitz, Boris *business educator and dean emeritus*

**Hancock**
DeLuca, Ronald *former advertising agency executive, consultant*

**Harrison**
Fuchs, Hanno *communications consultant, lawyer*
Herrick, Doris Eileen Schlesinger *sports association administrator*
Krantz, Melissa Marianne *public relations company executive*
†Schulz, Helmut Wilhelm *chemical engineer, environmental executive*
Serenbetz, Warren Lewis *financial management company executive*
Wadsworth, Frank Whittemore *foundation executive, literature educator*

**Hartsdale**
Brozak-McMann, Edith May *performing and visual artist*
Chait, Maxwell Mani *physician*
Gillingham, Stephen Thomas *financial planner*
Jones, Donald Kelly *state agency executive*
Katz, John *investment banker*

**Hastings On Hudson**
Barth, Katrine *chemical company executive*
Cooney, Patrick Louis *writer*
Reich, Herb *editor*
Rosch, Paul John *physician, educator*
Shillinglaw, Gordon *accounting educator, consultant, writer*
Thornlow, Carolyn *law firm administrator, consultant*
Weinstein, Edward Michael *architect, consultant*
Wolfe, Stanley *composer, educator*

**Hauppauge**
Arams, Frank Robert *electronics company executive*
Costa, Pat Vincent *automation sciences executive*
Finke, Douglas Lane *electronics company executive*
Graham, David Gregory *preventive medicine physician, psychiatrist*
Harrington, Carolyn Marie *accountant, artist*
Hurley, Denis R. *federal judge*
Malaga, Stanley *accounting educator*
Miller, Ronald M. *manufacturing executive*
Reich, William Michael *advertising executive*
Reis, Don *publishing executive*
Stemple, Joel Gilbert *computer company executive*
Uy, Philip M. *aeronautical engineer*
Wexler, Leonard D. *federal judge*

**Haverstraw**
Motin, Revell Judith *retired data processing executive*

**Hawthorne**
Batstone, Joanna L. *physicist*

Green, Paul Eliot, Jr. *communications scientist*
Karnaugh, Maurice *computer scientist, educator*
Kiamie, Don Albert Najeeb *accountant*
McConnell, John Edward *electrical engineer, company executive*
Sandbank, Henry *photographer, film director*
Traub, Richard Kenneth *lawyer*

**Hempstead**
Agata, Burton C. *lawyer, educator*
Berliner, Herman Albert *university provost and dean, economics educator*
Block, Jules Richard *psychologist, educator, university official*
Chapman, Ronald Thomas *musician, educator*
Conway-Gervais, Kathleen Marie *reading specialist, educational consultant*
Evans, Joel Raymond *marketing educator*
Freedman, Monroe Henry *lawyer, educator, columnist*
Freese, Melanie Louise *librarian, professor*
Goldstein, Stanley Philip *engineering educator*
Graffeo, Mary Thérèse *music educator, performer*
Gutman, Steve *professional football team executive*
Haynes, Ulric St. Clair, Jr. *university dean*
Laano, Archie Bienvenido Maaño *cardiologist*
Lally, Laura Holloway *computer information systems educator*
Lee, Keun Sok *business educator, consultant*
Lewis, Mo *professional football player*
Mahon, Malachy Thomas *lawyer, educator*
Maier, Henry B. *environmental engineer*
Masheck, Joseph Daniel *art critic, educator*
Montana, Patrick Joseph *management educator*
Parcells, Bill (Duane Charles Parcells) *professional football coach*
Pell, Arthur Robert *human resources development consultant, author*
Rabinowitz, Stuart *law educator, dean*
Shuart, James Martin *academic administrator*
Smith, June Ann *counseling educator*
Sparberg, Esther B. *chemist, educator*
Turgeon, Edgar Lynn *economics educator*
Wattel, Harold Louis *economics educator*

**Henrietta**
Carmel, Simon J(acob) *anthropologist*
Snyder, Donald Edward *corporate executive*

**Herkimer**
Martin, Lorraine B. *humanities educator*
Mitchell, Donald J. *former congressman*

**Hewlett**
Cohen, David Leon *physician*
Flomenhaft, Eleanor *art curator*
Kislik, Louis A. *marketing company executive*
Steinfeld, Philip S. *pediatrician*
Wolff, Eleanor Blunk *actress*

**Hicksville**
Calabrese, Alphonse Francis Xavier *psychotherapist*
Giuffré, John Joseph *lawyer*
Horowitz, Barry Allan *music company executive*
Kneitel, Thomas Stephen *writer, consultant, editor*
Kremin, Daniel Paul *educational administrator*
Reedy, Catherine Irene *library and media specialist*
Rubano, Richard Frank *civil engineer*
Tucci, Gerald Frank *manufacturing company executive*
Walsh, Charles Richard *banker*
Yen, Henry Chin-Yuan *computer systems programmer, engineer, consulting company executive*

**Highland**
Brady, Christine Ellen *language arts educator*
Rosenberger, David A. *research scientist, cooperative extension specialist*
Siemer, Fred Harold *securities analyst*

**Hillsdale**
Lunde, Asbjorn Rudolph *lawyer*
Parmet, Herbert Samuel *historian, educator*
Richards, Joseph Edward *artist*

**Hilton**
Ratigan, Hugh Lewis *middle school and elementary school educator*

**Holbrook**
Lissman, Barry Alan *veterinarian*
Senholzi, Gregory Bruce *secondary school educator*

**Holland**
Blair, Robert Noel *artist*

**Hollis**
Malis, Leonard Irving *neurosurgeon*

**Holtsville**
†Musteric, Peter *engineering manager*

**Homer**
Gustafson, John Alfred *biology educator*

**Honeoye**
Stone, Alan John *manufacturing company executive, real estate executive*

**Honeoye Falls**
Hillabrandt, Larry Lee *service industry executive*

**Hoosick Falls**
Dodge, Cleveland Earl, Jr. *manufacturing executive*
Hatfield, David Underhill *artist*
Morris, Margretta Elizabeth *government official*

**Hopewell Junction**
Coppola, Patricia L. (Scheffel) *elementary school educator*
Walden, Stanley Eugene *composer, clarinetist*

**Horseheads**
Huffman, Patricia Joan *retired accounting coordinator*
Tanner, David Harold *professional roof consultant*

**Houghton**
Chamberlain, Daniel Robert *college president*

Luckey, Robert Reuel Raphael *retired academic administrator*

**Howard Beach**
Berliner, Patricia Mary *psychologist*
Krein, Catherine Cecilia *public relations professional*
Livingston, Barbara *special education educator*

**Hudson**
Avedisian, Edward *artist*
Miner, Jacqueline *political consultant*
Mustapha, Tamton *gastroenterologist*

**Hudson Falls**
Bronk, William *writer, retail businessman*
Leary, Daniel *artist*

**Hunter**
Jaeckel, Christopher Carol *memorabilia company executive, antiquarian*

**Huntington**
Augello, William Joseph *lawyer*
Christiansen, Donald David *electrical engineer, editor, publishing consultant*
Connor, Joseph Robert *editor*
D'Addario, Alice Marie *school administrator*
German, June Resnick *lawyer*
Glickstein, Howard Alan *law educator*
Holahan, Richard Vincent *former magazine and book publisher*
Jackson, Richard Montgomery *former airline executive*
Joseph, Richard Saul *cardiologist*
Maglione, Lili *fine artist, art consultant*
Munson, Nancy Kay *lawyer*
Myers, Robert Jay *retired aerospace company executive*
Pettersen, Kevin Will *investment company executive*
Pratt, George Cheney *law educator, retired federal judge*
Rosar, Virginia Wiley *librarian*
Ruppert, Mary Frances *management consultant, school counselor*
Schulz, William Frederick *human rights association executive*
Twardowicz, Stanley Jan *artist, photographer*
Vale, Margo Rose *physician*

**Huntington Station**
Agosta, Vito *mechanical/aerospace engineering educator*
Boxwill, Helen Ann *primary and secondary education educator*
Braun, Ludwig *educational technology consultant*
Lanzano, Ralph Eugene *civil engineer*
Liguori, Frank Nickolas *temporary personnel company executive*
Pierce, Charles R. *electric company consultant*
Schoenfeld, Michael P. *lawyer*
Williams, Una Joyce *psychiatric social worker*
Zingale, Robert G. *surgeon*

**Hurley**
Bedford, Brian *actor*

**Hyde Park**
Metz, Ferdinand *chef, educator, academic administrator*
Newton, Verne Wester *library director*
Pastrana, Ronald Ray *Christian ministry counselor, theology and biblical studies educator, former school system administrator*

**Interlaken**
Bleiler, Everett Franklin *writer, publishing company executive*
Taylor, Richard *philosopher, educator*

**Irvington**
Angelakis, Manos G(eorge) *filmmaker, communications executive*
Bonomi, John Gurnee *retired lawyer*
Devons, Samuel *educator, physicist*
Harris, Maria Loscutoff *special education educator, consultant*
Holden, Donald *artist, author*
Lugenbeel, Edward Elmer *publisher*
Massie, Robert Kinloch *author*
Peyser, Peter A. *former congressman, investment management company executive*
Sexter, Deborah Rae *lawyer*
Steinberg, James Ian *marketing executive*
Wolf, Eric Robert *anthropologist, educator*

**Island Park**
Feir-Stillitano, Elisabeth *gifted/talented education educator*

**Islandia**
Wang, Charles B. *computer software company executive*

**Islip**
DeCillis, Michael Arthur *hydrogeologist*
Muuss, John *public safety and emergency management director*

**Ithaca**
Abrams, Meyer Howard *English language educator*
Adler, Kraig (Kerr) *biology educator*
Alexander, Gregory Stewart *law educator*
Alexander, Martin *microbiology educator, consultant*
Ammons, Archie Randolph *poet, English educator*
Arntzen, Charles Joel *bioscience educator*
Ascher, Robert *anthropologist, archaeologist, educator, filmmaker*
Ashcroft, Neil William *physics educator, researcher*
Bail, Joe Paul *agricultural educator emeritus*
Barcelo, John James, III *law educator*
Barney, John Charles *lawyer*
Bassett, William Akers *geologist, educator*
Batterman, Boris William *physicist, educator, academic director*
Bauer, Simon Harvey *chemistry educator*
Bauman, Dale Elton *nutritional biochemistry educator*
Becherer, Richard John *architecture educator*
Ben Daniel, David Jacob *entrepreneurship educator, consultant*
Beneria, Lourdes *economist, educator*
Berger, Toby *electrical engineer*
Berkelman, Karl *physics educator*

Bethe, Hans Albrecht *physicist, educator*
Billera, Louis J(oseph) *mathematics educator*
Blackler, Antonie William Charles *biologist*
Blau, Francine Dee *economics educator*
Booker, John Franklin *mechanical engineer, educator*
Bourne, Russell *publisher, author*
Briggs, Vernon Mason, Jr. *economics educator*
Brown, Theodore Morey *art history educator*
Burns, Joseph Arthur *planetary science educator*
Calnek, Bruce Wixson *virologist, zoologist*
Carlin, Herbert J. *electrical engineering educator, researcher*
Carpenter, Barry Keith *chemistry educator, researcher*
Caughey, David Alan *engineering educator, researcher*
Clardy, Jon Christel *chemistry educator, consultant*
Clark, David Delano *physicist, educator*
Clermont, Kevin Michael *law educator*
Colby-Hall, Alice Mary *Romance studies educator*
Conway, Richard Walter *computer scientist, educator*
Cooke, William Donald *university administrator, chemistry educator*
Corson, Dale Raymond *retired university president, physicist*
Cotton, Dorothy Foreman *former director student activities, consultant*
Court, Patricia Grace *law librarian*
Craft, Harold Dumont, Jr. *university official, radio astronomer*
Craighead, Harold G. *physics educator*
Cramton, Roger Conant *lawyer, legal educator*
Culler, Jonathan Dwight *English language educator*
Dalman, Gisli Conrad *electrical engineering educator*
Darlington, Richard Benjamin *psychology educator*
Davies, Peter John *plant physiology educator, researcher*
De Boer, Pieter Cornelis Tobias *mechanical and aerospace engineering educator*
Dick, Richard Irwin *environmental engineer, educator*
Dietert, Rodney Reynolds *immunology and toxicology educator*
Dobson, Alan *veterinary physiology educator*
Dodd, Jack Gordon, Jr. *physicist, educator*
Dyckman, Thomas Richard *accounting educator*
Earle, Clifford John, Jr. *mathematician*
Earle, Elizabeth Deutsch *biology educator*
Easley, David *economics educator*
Eastman, Lester Fuess *electrical engineer, educator*
Eddy, Donald Davis *English language educator*
Ehrenberg, Ronald Gordon *economist, educator*
Eisenberg, Theodore *law educator*
Eisner, Thomas *biologist, educator*
Elledge, Scott Bowen *language professional, educator*
Elliott, John *accountant, educator*
Ewing, Elmer Ellis *agricultural science educator*
Farley, Jennie Tiffany Towle *industrial and labor relations educator*
Fay, Robert Clinton *chemist, educator*
Fick, Gary Warren *agronomy educator, forage crops researcher*
Finch, C. Herbert *retired archivist, library administrator, historia*
Firebaugh, Francille Maloch *university official*
Fireside, Harvey Francis *political scientist, educator*
Fitchen, Douglas Beach *physicist, educator*
Foote, Robert Hutchinson *animal physiology educator*
Forker, Olan Dean *agricultural economics educator*
Fox, Francis Henry *veterinarian*
Freed, Jack Herschel *chemist, educator*
Germain, Claire Madeleine *law librarian, educator*
Gibian, George *Russian and comparative literature educator*
Gillespie, James Howard *veterinary microbiologist, educator*
Gillett, James Warren *toxicologist, educator*
Glock, Marvin David *retired psychology educator*
Gold, Thomas *astronomer, educator*
Goldsmith, Paul Felix *physics and astronomy educator*
Goldsmith, William Woodbridge *city and regional planning educator*
Gottfried, Kurt *physicist, educator*
Green, Nancy Elizabeth *curator, writer*
Greisen, Kenneth Ingvard *physicist, emeritus educator*
Grippi, Salvatore William *artist*
Groos, Arthur Bernhard, Jr. *German literature educator*
Grunes, David Leon *research soil scientist, educator, editor*
Haas, Jere Douglas *nutritional sciences educator, researcher*
Hairston, Nelson George, Jr. *ecologist, educator*
Halpern, Bruce Peter *academic administrator*
Haltom, Cristen Eddy *psychologist*
Hart, Edward Walter *physicist*
Hay, George Alan *law and economics educator*
Hess, George Paul *biochemist, educator*
Hillman, Robert Andrew *law educator, former university dean*
Hockett, Charles Francis *anthropology educator*
Hoffmann, Roald *chemist, educator*
Hohendahl, Peter Uwe *German language and literature educator*
Holcomb, Donald Frank *physicist, academic administrator*
Hopcroft, John Edward *dean, computer science educator*
Hsu, John Tseng Hsin *music educator, cellist, gambist, barytonist, conductor*
Husa, Karel Jaroslav *composer, conductor, educator*
Isard, Walter *economics educator*
Jagendorf, Andre Tridon *plant physiologist*
Jarrow, Robert Alan *economics and finance educator, consultant*
Jenkins, James Thomas *mechanical engineering researcher*
Kahin, George McTurnan *political science and history educator*
Kahn, Alfred Edward *economist, educator, government official*
Kallfelz, Francis A. *veterinary medicine educator*
Kammen, Michael *historian, educator*
Kendler, Bernhard *editor*
Kennedy, Kenneth Adrian Raine *biological anthropologist, forensic anthropologist*
Kennedy, Wilbert Keith, Sr. *agronomy educator, retired university official*
Kent, Robert Brydon *law educator*
Kingsbury, John Merriam *botanist, educator*
Kinoshita, Toichiro *physicist*
Kirsch, A(nthony) Thomas *anthropology and Asian studies educator, researcher*
Korf, Richard Paul *mycology educator*
Koschmann, J. Victor *history educator, academic program director*
Kramer, John Paul *entomologist, educator*
Kramnick, Isaac *government educator*
Kronik, John William *Romance studies educator*
LaCapra, Dominick Charles *historian*
LaFeber, Walter Frederick *history educator, author*
Law, Gordon Theodore, Jr. *library director*
Lee, David Morris *physics educator*
Leibovich, Sidney *engineering educator*
Lengemann, Frederick William *physiology educator, scientist*
Lesser, William Henri *marketing educator*
Liboff, Richard Lawrence *physicist, educator*
Little, George Daniel *clergyman*
Loucks, Daniel Peter *environmental systems engineer*
Lowi, Theodore J(ay) *political science educator*
Lumley, John Leask *physicist, educator*
Lund, Daryl Bert *food science educator*
Lurie, Alison *author*
Lust, Barbara C. *psychology and linguistics educator*
Lynn, Walter Royal *civil engineering educator, university administrator*
Lyons, Thomas Patrick *economics educator*
Macey, Jonathan R. *law educator*
Mai, William Frederick *plant nematologist, educator*
Martin, Peter William *lawyer, educator*
Maxwell, William Laughlin *industrial engineering educator*
McConkey, James Rodney *English educator, writer*
McDaniel, Boyce Dawkins *physicist, educator*
Mc Guire, William *civil engineer, educator*
McIsaac, Paul Rowley *electrical engineer, educator*
McLafferty, Fred Warren *chemist, educator*
McMurry, John Edward *chemistry educator*
Meinwald, Jerrold *chemist, educator*
Meyburg, Arnim Hans *transportation engineer, educator, consultant*
Mikus, Eleanore Ann *artist*
Moore, Charles Hewes, Jr. *industrial and engineered products executive*
Morrison, George Harold *chemist, educator*
Mortlock, Robert Paul *microbiologist, educator*
Mueller, Betty Jeanne *social work educator*
Murphy, Eugene Francis *retired government official, consultant*
Nation, John Arthur *electrical engineering educator, researcher*
Naylor, Harry Brooks *microbiologist*
Neisser, Ulric *psychology educator*
Nerode, Anil *mathematician, educator*
Nesheim, Malden C. *academic administrator, nutrition educator*
Norton, Mary Beth *history educator, author*
Novak, Joseph Donald *science educator, knowlege studies specialist*
Obendorf, Sharon Kay *fiber science educator*
Oliver, Jack Ertle *geophysicist*
Orear, Jay *physics educator, researcher*
O'Rourke, Thomas Denis *civil engineer, educator*
Pagliarulo, Michael Anthony *physical therapy educator*
Palmer, Larry Isaac *lawyer, educator*
Park, Roy Hampton, Jr. *advertising media executive*
Payne, Lawrence Edward *mathematics educator*
Peterson, Patti McGill *academic administrator*
Phelan, Richard Magruder *mechanical engineer*
Phemister, Robert David *veterinary medical educator*
Pickett, Lawrence Kimball *physician, educator*
Pimentel, David *entomologist, educator*
Plaisted, Robert Leroy *plant breeder, educator*
Pohl, Robert Otto *physics educator*
Poleskie, Stephen Francis *artist, educator, writer*
Pope, Stephen Bailey *engineering educator*
Poppensiek, George Charles *veterinary scientist, educator*
Porte, Joel Miles *English educator*
Quimby, Fred William *pathology educator, veterinarian*
Radzinowicz, Mary Ann *language educator*
Rasmussen, Kathleen Maher *nutritional sciences educator*
Rawlings, Hunter Ripley, III *university president*
Rhodes, Frank Harold Trevor *university president emeritus, geologist*
Rhodin, Thor Nathaniel *educational administrator*
Richardson, Robert Coleman *physics educator, researcher*
Robinson, Franklin Westcott *museum director, art historian*
Rodríguez, Ferdinand *chemical engineer, educator*
Rossi, Faust F. *lawyer, educator*
Ruoff, Arthur Louis *physicist, educator*
Salpeter, Edwin Ernest *physical sciences educator*
Scheraga, Harold Abraham *physical chemistry educator*
Schlafer, Donald Hughes *veterinary pathologist*
Schwartz, Donald Franklin *communication educator*
Scott, Fredric Winthrop *veterinarian*
Scott, Norman Roy *academic administrator, agricultural engineering educator*
Seeley, Harry Wilbur, Jr. *microbiology educator*
Seeley, John George *horticulture educator*
Shell, Karl *economics educator*
Shoemaker, Sydney S. *philosophy educator*
Shore, Richard Arnold *mathematics educator*
Shuler, Michael Louis *biochemical engineering educator, consultant*
Sievers, Albert John, III *physics educator*
Silbey, Joel Henry *history educator*
Sims, William Riley *design and facility management educator, consultant*
Simson, Gary Joseph *law educator*
Slate, Floyd Owen *chemist, materials scientist, civil engineer, educator, researcher*
Smith, Julian Cleveland, Jr. *chemical engineering educator*
Smith, Robert John *anthropology educator*
Smith, Robert Samuel *banker, former agricultural finance educator*
Squier, Jack Leslie *sculptor, educator*
Stamp, Neal Roger *lawyer*
Streett, William Bernard *university dean, engineering educator*
Stycos, Joseph Mayone *demographer, educator*
Sudan, Ravindra Nath *electrical engineer, physicist, educator*
Summers, Robert Samuel *lawyer, author, educator*
Terzian, Yervant *astronomy and astrophysics educator*
Thomas, J. Earl *physicist*
Thorbecke, Erik *economics educator*
Thoron, Gray *lawyer, educator*
Thorp, James Shelby *electrical engineering educator*
Tomek, William Goodrich *agricultural economist*
Trotter, Leslie Earl *operations research educator, consultant*
Turcotte, Donald Lawson *geophysical sciences educator*
Vandenberg, John Donald *entomologist*
Van Houtte, Raymond A. *financial executive*
Viands, Donald Rex *plant breeder and educator*
Walcott, Charles *neurobiology and behvior educator*
Wang, Kuo-King *manufacturing engineer, educator*
Ward, William Binnington *agricultural communicator*
Wasserman, Robert Harold *biology educator*
Webb, Watt Wetmore *physicist, educator*
Weinstein, Leonard Harlan *institute program director*
Welch, Ross Maynard *plant physiologist, researcher, educator*
Whalen, James Joseph *college president*
Whitaker, Susanne Kanis *veterinary medical librarian*
White, Richard Norman *civil and environmental engineering educator*
Whyte, William Foote *industrial relations educator, author*
Widom, Benjamin *chemistry educator*
Williams, David Vandergrift *organizational psychologist*
Williams, Leslie Pearce *history educator*
Wilson, Robert Rathbun *retired physicist*
Windmuller, John Philip *industrial relations educator, consultant*
Wootton, John Francis *physiology educator*
Wu, Ray Jui *biochemistry educator*
Zall, Robert Rouben *food scientist, educator*
Zilversmit, Donald Berthold *nutritional biochemist, educator*

### Jackson Heights
Fischbarg, Zulema F. *pediatrician, educator*
Schiavina, Laura Margaret *artist*
Schuyler, Jane *fine arts educator*
Sklar, Morty E. *publisher, editor*

### Jamaica
Angerville, Edwin Duvanel *accountant, educator*
Angione, Howard Francis *lawyer, editor*
Bartilucci, Andrew Joseph *university administrator*
Berman, Richard Miles *lawyer*
Boal, Bernard Harvey *cardiologist, educator, author*
Carrington, Betty Watts *nurse midwife, educator*
Clemmons, Ithiel *bishop*
Cline, Janice Claire *education educator*
Crivelli, Joseph Louis *security specialist*
Davis-Jerome, Eileen George *principal*
Desser, Maxwell Milton *artist, art director, filmstrip producer*
Dircks, Richard Joseph *English educator, writer*
Etzel, Joseph Vincent *pharmacy educator*
Faust, Naomi Flowe *education educator, poet*
Fay, Thomas A. *philosopher, educator*
Feldman, Arlene Butler *aviation industry executive*
Geffner, Donna Sue *speech pathologist, audiologist*
Greenberg, Jacob *biochemist, educator, consultant*
Hammer, Deborah Marie *librarian*
Harmond, Richard Peter *historian, educator*
Harrington, Donald James *university president*
Jones, Cynthia Teresa Clarke *artist*
Kahn, Faith-Hope *nurse, administrator, writer*
Kelly, Robert *airport executive*
Lassiter, Katrina Ann *medical/surgical nurse*
Lengyel, István *chemist, educator*
Lin, Shu-Fang Hsia *librarian*
Mangru, Basdeo *secondary school educator*
McGuire, William Dennis *health care system executive*
McKenzie, André *academic administrator, educator*
Mc Kinnon, Clinton Dan *aerospace transportation executive*
Paolucci, Anne Attura *playwright, poet, English and comparative literature educator*
Prendergast, Thomas Francis *railroad executive*
Reams, Bernard Dinsmore, Jr. *lawyer, educator*
Rosner, Fred *physician, educator*
Scheich, John F. *lawyer*
Sciame, Joseph *university administrator*
†Sossi, Anthony *medical administrator*
Strong, Gary Eugene *librarian*
Taylor, Joyce *religious organization executive*
Tschinkel, Andrew Joseph, Jr. *law librarian*
Walker, Sonia Evadne *osteopath*
Wetherington, Roger Vincent *journalism educator, newspaper copy editor*
Wintergerst, Ann Charlotte *language educator*
Zambito, Raymond Francis *oral surgeon, educator*
Zenbopwe, (Walter Cade), III *artist, musician, singer, actor*

### Jamaica Estates
Morrill, Joyce Marie *social worker*
Rose, Jodi *opera company founder and artistic director*

### Jamestown
Anderson, R. Quintus *diversified company executive*
Bargar, Robert Sellstrom *investor*
Benke, Paul Arthur *college president*
David, Christine A. *artist, marketing consultant*
DeAngelo, Charles Salvatore *lawyer*
Goldman, Simon *broadcasting executive*
Idzik, Martin Francis *lawyer*
Leising, Mary Kathleen *manufacturing executive*
Seguin, David Gerard *community college official*
Wellman, Barclay Ormes *furniture company executive*

### Jamesville
DeCrow, Karen *lawyer, author, lecturer*
Mazer, Norma Fox *writer*
Nuckols, William Marshall *electrical goods manufacturing executive*

### Jeffersonville
Craft, Douglas Durwood *artist*
Finn, David Thurman *artist, sculptor*
Harms, Elizabeth Louise *artist*
Wooddell, Philo Glenn *fine arts educator, radio broadcaster and producer*

### Jericho
Astuto, Philip Louis *retired Spanish educator*
Axinn, Donald Everett *real estate investor, developer*
Berger, Charles Martin *food company executive*
Blau, Harvey Ronald *lawyer*
†Faletra, Robert *editor*
Fitteron, John Joseph *petroleum products company executive*
Friedman, David Samuel *lawyer, law review executive*
Mandery, Mathew M. *principal*
†Mannion, Kevin *publishing executive*
Martin, David S. *educator, administrator*
Schell, Norman Barnett *physician, consultant*
Shinners, Stanley Marvin *electrical engineer*
Spivack, Henry Archer *life insurance company executive*

### Johnson City
McGovern, Thomas Boardman *physician, pediatrician*

### Katonah
Baker, John Milnes *architect*
Bashkow, Theodore Robert *electrical engineering consultant, former educator*
Fry, John *magazine editor*
Giobbi, Edward Giacchino *artist*
Krefting, Robert J(ohn) *publishing company executive*
Levine, Pamela Gail *business owner*
Mooney, Robert Michael *ophthalmologist*
Raymond, Jack *journalist, public relations executive, foundation executive*
Simpson, William Kelly *curator, Egyptologist, educator*
White, Harold Tredway, III *management consultant*

### Keene Valley
Neville, Emily Cheney *author*

### Kenmore
Bates Stoklosa, Evelynne (Eve Bates Stoklosa) *educational consultant, educator*

### Kew Gardens
Adler, David Neil *lawyer*
Levine, Gerald Richard *mortgage investment and merchant banker, financial advisor*

### Kinderhook
Benamati, Dennis Charles *law librarian, editor, consultant*
Lankhof, Frederik Jan *publishing executive*

### Kings Park
Greene, Robert William *journalism educator, media consultant*
Smith, Norma Jane *elementary education educator*

### Kings Point
Billy, George John *library director*
Bloom, Murray Teigh *author*
Matteson, Thomas T. *academic administrator*
Mazek, Warren F(elix) *academic administrator, economics educator*

### Kingston
Bruck, Arlene Lorraine *secondary education educator*
Johnson, Marie-Louise Tully *dermatologist, educator*
Lanitis, Tony Andrew *market researcher*
Petruski, Jennifer Andrea *speech and language pathologist*
Soltanoff, Jack *nutritionist, chiropractor*
Steller, Arthur Wayne *educational administrator*

### Lagrangeville
Sedlak, James William *organization administrator*

### Lake Grove
Braff, Howard *brokerage house executive, financial analyst*

### Lake Luzerne
Goldstein, Manfred *retired consultant*

### Lake Placid
Caguiat, Carlos Jose *health care administrator, episcopal priest*
Fava, Donald Anthony *clinical psychologist*
Reiss, Paul Jacob *college president*
†Rossi, Ronald Aldo *sports association administrator, Olympic athlete*

### Lake Ronkonkoma
Halper, Evelyn Ann *occupational therapist*

### Lakewood
Brown, Melvin Henry *retired chemical engineer*

### Lancaster
Neumaier, Gerhard John *environment consulting company executive*
Walsh, J(ohn) B(ronson) *lawyer*
Weinberg, Norman Louis *electrochemist*

### Lansing
Thomas, John Melvin *retired surgeon*

### Larchmont
Aburdene, Odeh Felix *banker*
Bellak, Leopold *psychiatrist, psychoanalyst, psychologist*
Berridge, George Bradford *retired lawyer*
Bloom, Lee Hurley *lawyer, public affairs consultant, retired household products manufacturing executive*
Engel, Ralph Manuel *lawyer*
Greenwald, Carol Schiro *professional services marketing research executive*
Guttenplan, Joseph B. *biochemist*
Halket, Thomas D(aniel) *lawyer*
Hinerfeld, Ruth J. *civic organization executive*
Holleb, Arthur Irving *surgeon*
Kaufmann, Henry Mark *mortgage banker*
Levi, James Harry *real estate executive, investment banker*
Levy, Walter Kahn *management consultant executive*
Lurie, Alvin David *lawyer*
Margolin, Harold *metallurgical educator*
Murphy, James Gilmartin *lawyer*
Pelton, Russell Gilbert *lawyer*
Plumez, Jean Paul *advertising agency executive, consultant*
Rainier, Robert Paul *publisher*
Rosenberg, Paul *physicist, consultant*
Seton, Charles B. *lawyer*
Silverstone, David *advertising executive*
Swire, Edith Wypler *music educator, musician, violist, violinist*
Tobey, Alton Stanley *artist*

Vitt, Samuel Bradshaw communications media services executive
White, Thomas Edward lawyer
Wielgus, Charles Joseph information services company executive
Wolfson, Harold public relations consultant

### Latham
Agard, Nancey Patricia nursing administrator
Conway, Robert George, Jr. lawyer
Garner, Doris Traganza educator
Stallman, Donald Lee corporate executive
Standfast, Susan J(ane) state official, research, consultant, educator
Tepper, Clifford allergist, immunologist, educator

### Lawrence
Sklarin, Ann H. artist
Sklarin, Burton S. endocrinologist
Wurzburger, Walter Samuel rabbi, philosophy educator

### Le Roy
Harner, Timothy R. lawyer

### Levittown
Cohen, Max retired government official
Dwyer, Mary Elizabeth nursery school director
Rode, Helen Jane special education educator
Rubin, Arnold Jesse aeronautical engineer

### Lewiston
Dexter, Theodore Henry chemist
†Domzella, Janet library director
Newlin, Lyman Wilbur bookseller, consultant
O'Neil, Mary Agnes health science facility administrator
Zavon, Mitchell Ralph physician

### Lido Beach
Billauer, Barbara Pfeffer lawyer, educator

### Lily Dale
Merrill, Joseph Hartwell religious association executive
Wittich, Brenda June religious organization executive, minister

### Lima
Spencer, Ivan Carlton clergyman

### Lindenhurst
Boltz, Mary Ann aerospace materials company executive, travel agency executive
Hamilton, Daniel Stephen clergyman
Levy, (Alexandra) Susan construction company executive

### Little Falls
Feeney, Mary Katherine O'Shea retired public health nurse

### Liverpool
Emmert, Roberta Rita health facility administrator
Green, Edward Francis manufacturing executive
Greenway, William Charles electronics executive, design engineer
Harris, Dana Bound software company executive
Mann, Linda Marie elementary school educator
Miller, Eileen Renee counselor
Mitchell, John David journalism educator
Morabito, Bruno Paul machinery manufacturing executive
Stefano, Ross William business executive
Williams, John Alan secondary education educator, coach

### Livingston Manor
Zagoren, Joy Carroll health facility director, researcher

### Lloyd Harbor
Deavers, Karl Alan investment banker

### Lockport
Carr, Edward Albert, Jr. medical educator, physician
Cull, John Joseph novelist, playwright
Godshall, Barbara Marie special education educator
Hoyme, Chad Earl packaging company executive
Penney, Charles Rand lawyer, civic worker

### Lockwood
McMahon, Maria Driscoll artist

### Locust Valley
Benson, Robert Elliott investment banker, consultant
Bentel, Frederick Richard architect, educator
Bentel, Maria-Luise Ramona Azzarone (Mrs. Frederick R. Bentel) architect, educator
DeRegibus, William artist
Devendorf, Barbara Lancaster (Bonnie Lancaster Devendorf) real estate broker
Lippold, Richard sculptor
McGee, Dorothy Horton writer, historian
Schaffner, Charles Etzel consulting engineering executive
Schor, Joseph Martin pharmaceutical executive, biochemist
Sunderland, Ray, Jr. retired insurance company executive
Webel, Richard Karl landscape architect
Zulch, Joan Carolyn retired medical publishing company executive, consultant

### Long Beach
Bernstein, Lester editorial consultant
Robbins, Jeffrey Howard media consultant, research writer, educator
Sherman, Zachary civil and aerospace engineer, consultant
Siegel, Herbert Bernard certified professional management consultant
Thompson, Dorothy Barnard elementary school educator

### Long Eddy
Hoiby, Lee composer, concert pianist
Van Swol, Noel Warren secondary education educator

### Long Island City
Barbanel, Sidney William engineering consulting firm executive
Barnholdt, Terry Joseph, Jr. lawyer, real estate executive
Bowen, Raymond Cobb academic administrator
Craig, Elizabeth Coyne marketing executive
Cushing, Robert Hunter lawyer, real estate investment executive
Donneson, Seena Sand artist
Gussow, Roy sculptor, educator
Kane Hittner, Marcia Susan bank executive
Rothman, Barbara Schaeffer education director
Sadao, Shoji architect
Theodoru, Stefan Gheorghe civil engineer, writer
Trent, James Alfred city official
Villinski, Paul Stephen artist
Walker, Linda Lee lawyer

### Loudonville
Ferguson, Henry international management consultant

### Lowville
Becker, Robert Otto orthopedic surgery educator

### Lynbrook
Amorosi, Teresa artist
Pagillo, Carl Robert elementary school educator
Yee, David chemist, pharmaceutical company executive

### Mahopac
Richards, Edgar Lester psychologist, educator
Silbert, Linda Bress educational counselor, therapist

### Malverne
Freund, Richard L. communications company executive, consultant, lawyer
Knight, John Francis insurance company executive
Pollio, Ralph Thomas editor, writer, magazine consultant
Ryan, Suzanne Irene nursing educator

### Mamaroneck
Drexler, Michael David advertising agency executive
Flagg, Jeanne Bodin editor
Fletcher, Denise Koen strategic and financial consultant
Halpern, Abraham Leon psychiatrist
Holz, Harold A. chemical and plastics manufacturing company executive
Mazzola, Claude Joseph physicist, small business owner
Meadow, Susan Ellen publisher
Mizrahi, Abraham Mordechay retired cosmetics and health care company executive, physician
New, Anne Latrobe public relations, fund raising executive
Nolletti, James Joseph lawyer
Pugh, Grace Huntley artist
Rosenthal, Elizabeth Robbins physician
Topol, Robert Martin retired financial services executive

### Manchester
Wells, Robert Alfred lawyer

### Manhasset
Anderson, Arthur N. retired utility company executive
Bialer, Martin George geneticist
Brackett, Ronald E. investment company executive, lawyer
Bukrinsky, Michael Ilya virologist
Callaway, David James Edward physicist/bioinformaticist, expedition mountaineer
Carucci, Samuel Anthony lawyer
Cavill, Karen A. publishing executive
Chesney, Robert Henry communications executive, consultant
Corva, Angelo Francis architect
Enquist, Irving Fridtjof surgeon
Fendt, John W. minister, religious organization administrator
Fenton, Arnold N. obstetrician, gynecologist, educator
Frankum, James Edward airlines company executive
Grossi, Olindo architect, educator
Hayes, Arthur Michael lawyer
Hinds, Glester Samuel financier, program specialist, tax consultant
Keen, Constantine retired manufacturing company executive
Kreis, Willi physician
Lipson, Steven Mark cliniical virologist, educator
McGreal, Joseph A., Jr. publishing company executive
Moran, Timothy newspaper editor
Mullin, Gerard Emmanuel physician, educator, researcher
Nelson, Roy Leslie cardiac surgeon, researcher, educator
Pogo, Gustave Javier cardiothoracic surgeon
Rostky, George Harold editor
Samuel, Paul cardiologist, consultant
Scala, Marilyn Campbell special education educator, writer, consultant
Scherr, Lawrence physician, educator
Schiller, Arthur A. architect, educator
Spitz, Charles Thomas, Jr. clergyman
Wachtler, Sol retired judge, arbitration corporation executive, writer
Wallace, Richard editor, writer

### Manlius
Harriff, Suzanna Elizabeth Bahner advertising consultant
Prior, John Thompson pathology educator

### Marcellus
Baker, Bruce Roy retired art educator, artist
Lafferty, Richard Thomas architect

### Margaretville
Barabash, Claire lawyer, special education administrator, psychologist
Brockway-Henson, Amie producing artistic director
Matalon, Vivian theatrical director

### Marietta
Goyette, Geoffrey Robert sales executive

### Maryknoll
Gormley, Robert John book publisher
†LaVerdiere, Claudette Marie sister, head religious order

### Massapequa
Margulies, Andrew Michael chiropractor
McCann, Susan Lynn elementary education educator
Molitor, Michael A. entrepreneur, consultant
Zwanger, Jerome physician

### Massapequa Park
Johnson, Jeanne Marie nurse psychotherapist, clinical nurse specialist
Plotkin, Martin retired electrical engineer
Zizzo, Alicia concert pianist

### Massena
Schroll, Edwin John theater educator, stage director
Vazquez, Sue Ellen elementary education educator

### Mastic Beach
Casciano, Paul school system administrator
Pagano, Alicia I. education educator

### Mattituck
Gazouleas, Panagiotis J. journalist
Marquardt, Ann Marie small business administrator

### Medford
Brower, Robert Charles rehabilitation counselor, small business owner

### Melville
Bass, Elizabeth Ruth editor
Brandt, Robert Frederic, III newspaper editor, journalist
Carter, Sylvia journalist
†Cole, Kirstin Elizabeth television news anchor
Cooke, Robert William science journalist
Donovan, Brian reporter, journalist
Dooley, James C. newspaper editor, director of photography
Drewry, Elizabeth newspaper publishing executive
†Garrett, Laurie science correspondent
Graziani, Jeanne Patricia health facility administrator
Grebow, Edward television company executive
Green, Carol H. lawyer, educator, journalist
Hall, Charlotte Hauch newspaper editor
Hildebrand, John Frederick newspaper columnist
Jagoda, Donald Robert sales promotion agency executive
Jansen, Raymond A., Jr. newspaper publishing executive
†Kahn, David editor, author
Kaufman, Stephen P. electronics company executive
Kett, Herbert Joseph retail executive
Kissinger, Walter Bernhard automotive test and service equipment manufacturing executive
Klatell, Robert Edward lawyer, electronics company executive
Klurfeld, James Michael journalist
Krusos, Denis Angelo communications company executive
LaRocco, Elizabeth Anne management information systems professional
Lynn, James Dougal newspaper editor, journalist
Marchesano, John Edward electro-optical engineer
Marro, Anthony James newspaper editor
McCusker, John financial executive
McMillan, Robert Ralph lawyer
Moran, Paul James journalist, columnist
Olivero, Gary insurance company executive, financial planner
Olson, Gary Robert banker
Payne, Leslie newspaper editor, columnist, journalist, author
Phelps, Timothy Miller reporter
Reich, Paula Judy nursing educator
Richards, Carol Ann Rubright editor, columnist
Robins, Marjorie Kaplan newspaper editor
Roel, Ron newspaper editor
Saul, Stephanie journalist
Scire, Frank Jackson retired radar scientist

### Merrick
Baron, Theodore public relations executive
Beckman, Judith Kalb financial counselor and planner, educator, writer
Cariola, Robert Joseph artist
Cherry, Harold insurance company executive
Copperman, Stuart Morton pediatrician
Doyle, James Aloysius retired association executive
Kaplan, Steven Mark accountant
O'Brien, Kenneth Robert life insurance company executive
Poppel, Seth Raphael entrepreneur

### Mexico
Sade, Donald Stone anthropology educator

### Middle Island
Ferrara, Frank Gregory middle school educator
Linick, Andrew S. direct marketing executive
Mastrion, Guy secondary school principal

### Middle Village
Chang, Lydia Liang-Hwa school social worker, educator
Farb, Edith Himel chemist
Kolatch, Alfred Jacob publisher
Meyers, Edward photographer, writer, publisher

### Middleport
Massaro, Joseph James secondary school educator

### Middletown
Bedell, Barbara Lee journalist
Blumenthal, Fritz printmaker, painter
Isseks, Evelyn retired educational administrator
McCord, Jean Ellen secondary art educator, coach
Shaw, Roslyn Lee elementary education educator
Sprick, Dennis Michael critic, copy editor

### Mill Neck
Grieve, William Roy psychologist, educator, researcher, consultant
von Briesen, Edward Fuller builder, real estate developer

### Millbrook
Johnston, Robert Cossin consulting engineer executive
Likens, Gene Elden biology and ecology educator, administrator
Turndorf, Jamie clinical psychologist

### Miller Place
Mahoney, Lisa Reeves dermatologist

### Millerton
Burgee, John Henry architect
Hastings, Donald Francis actor, writer

### Millwood
Doyle, John McCormick actuary, pension plan consultant

### Mineola
Abraham, Carl Joel executive, safety specialist, inventor, consultant
Bartlett, Clifford Adams, Jr. lawyer
Bartol, Ernest Thomas lawyer
Braid, Frederick Donald lawyer
Cirker, Hayward publisher
Feinsilver, Steven Henry physician, educator
Feinstein, Robert P. dermatologist
Hines, George Lawrence surgeon
Hinson, Gale Mitchell social worker
Jones, Lawrence Tunnicliffe lawyer
Klein, Arnold Spencer lawyer
Kral, William George lawyer
Lynn, Robert Patrick, Jr. lawyer
McGonigle, James Gregory financial consultant
Meyer, Bernard Stern lawyer, former judge
Millman, Bruce Russell lawyer
Mofenson, Howard C. pediatrician, toxicologist
Murphy, George Austin justice
Newman, Malcolm civil engineering consultant
Paterson, Basil Alexander lawyer
Rosen, Meyer Robert chemical engineer
Rubine, Robert Samuel lawyer
Salten, David George county agency administrator, academic administrator
Schaffer, David Irving lawyer
Shperling, Irena internist
Stanisci, Thomas William lawyer
Tankoos, Sandra Maxine court reporting services executive

### Mohegan Lake
Galleno, Anthony Massimo retired bank executive, consultant

### Monroe
Karen, Linda Tricarico fashion designer
Werzberger, Alan pediatrician

### Monsey
Schore, Robert social worker, educator
Zeisel, Gloria real estate company executive

### Montauk
Butler, Thomas William retired health and social services administrator
First, Wesley publishing company executive
Lavenas, Suzanne writer, editor, consultant

### Monticello
Cooke, Lawrence Henry lawyer, former state chief judge
Lauterstein, Joseph cardiologist
Lubrecht, Heinz D. publishing company executive, antiquarian book expert, appraiser

### Montour Falls
Stillman, Joyce L. artist, educator, writer, illustrator, consultant

### Montrose
Lee, Edna Pritchard education educator

### Morrisville
Rouse, Robert Moorefield mathematician, educator

### Mount Kisco
Dangler, Richard Reiss corporate service companies executive, entrepreneur
Goodhue, Mary Brier lawyer, former state senator
Gudanek, Lois Bassolino clinical social worker
Keesee, Patricia Hartford volunteer
Keesee, Thomas Woodfin, Jr. financial consultant
Laster, Richard biotechnology executive
Moore, J. Scott materials engineer
Pastorelle, Peter John film company executive, radiological services and waste management company executive
Schneider, Robert Jay oncologist
Schwarz, Wolfgang psychologist
Stillman, Michael Allen dermatologist
Wood, James broker

### Mount Sinai
Feinberg, Sheldon Norman pediatrician

### Mount Vernon
Ben-Dak, Joseph David United Nations official, educator
Fitch, Nancy Elizabeth historian
Mc Neill, Charles James publishing executive
Richardson, W. Franklyn minister
Rossini, Joseph contracting and development corporate executive
Stern, Harold Peter business executive
Zucker, Arnold Harris psychiatrist

### Munnsville
Carruth, Hayden poet

### Nanuet
Savitz, Martin Harold neurosurgeon
Vamvaketis, Carole health services administrator

### Naples
Beal, Myron Clarence osteopathic physician

### Narrowsburg
Kunkel, Barbara psychotherapist, consultant, educator

### Neponsit
Re, Edward Domenic law educator, retired federal judge

### Nesconset
Feldman, Gary Marc nutritionist, consultant

### New City
Elberg, Darryl Gerald publisher, educator
Esser, Aristide Henri psychiatrist
Gromack, Alexander Joseph state legislator
Schaefer, Rhoda Pesner elementary school educator
†Wechman, Robert Joseph economist, educator

### New Hartford
Benzo-Bonacci, Rosemary Anne health facility administrator
Jones, Hugh Richard lawyer
Kelley, Sharon Lee physical education educator
Maurer, Gernant Elmer metallurgical executive, consultant
Muzyka, Donald Richard specialty metals executive, metallurgist

### New Hyde Park
Anderson, Ronald Howard consumer packaged goods company marketing executive
Cohen, Maurice gynecologist, educator
Cooper, Milton real estate investment trust executive
Dalal, Mayur Thakorbhai estate planner
Daley, John Terence priest
Dantzker, David Roy health facility administrator
Elkowitz, Sheryl Sue radiologist
Eviatar, Lydia pediatric neurologist
Frankel, Arnold J. chemical company executive
Gagnon, Bruce Alan child psychiatry nurse
Hyman, Abraham electrical engineer
Isenberg, Henry David microbiology educator
Lee, Brian Edward lawyer
Lee, Won Jay radiologist
Mealie, Carl A. physician, educator
Offner, Eric Delmonte lawyer
Reddan, Harold Jerome sociologist, educator
Richards, Bernard investment company executive
Seltzer, Vicki Lynn obstetrician, gynecologist
Shenker, Ira Ronald pediatrician
Wolf, Julius medical educator
Wolf-Klein, Gisele Patricia geriatrician

### New Paltz
Emanuel-Smith, Robin Lesley special education educator
Fleisher, Harold computer scientist
Franco, Carole Ann international consultant
Hathaway, Richard Dean language professional, educator
Nyquist, Thomas Eugene consulting business executive, mayor
Richbart, Carolyn Mae mathematics educator
Ryan, Marleigh Grayer Japanese language educator
Schneemann, Carolee painter, performing artist, filmmaker, writer
Schnell, George Adam geographer, educator
Whittington-Couse, Maryellen Frances education administrator

### New Rochelle
Beardsley, Robert Eugene microbiologist, educator
Berlage, Gai Ingham sociologist, educator
Black, Page Morton civic worker
Blotner, Norman David lawyer, real estate broker, corporate executive
Branch, William Blackwell playwright, producer
Capasso, Frank Louis secondary school educator
Cleary, James Charles, Jr. audio-visual producer
Donahue, Richard James secondary school educator
Frenkel, Michael lawyer
Gallagher, John Francis education educator
Glassman, George Morton dermatologist
Golub, James Robert internist, allergist
Golub, Sharon Bramson psychologist, educator
Gunning, Francis Patrick lawyer, insurance association executive
Hayes, Arthur Hull, Jr. physician, clinical pharmacology educator, medical school dean, business executive, consultant
Hoxter, Allegra Branson radio news and freelance writer
Iarocci, Kent Alexander newswriter, home improvement contractor
Kelly, Sister Dorothy Ann college president
Kelly, James Anthony priest
Klein, Arthur Luce theatrical company executive
Maher, Vincent F. academic administrator, educator, lawyer
Mallary, Robert sculptor
Menzies, Henry Hardinge architect
Merrill, Robert baritone
Miller, Rita retired diecasting company personnel executive, consultant
Nienburg, George Frank photographer
Rovinsky, Joseph Judah obstetrician, gynecologist
Saperstein, David novelist, screenwriter, film director
Saunders, Rubie Agnes former magazine editor, author
Slotnick, Mortimer H. artist
Tassone, Gelsomina (Gessie Tassone) metal processing executive
Thornton, Elaine Seretha oncology nurse
Veith, Mary Roth assistant dean
Vernon, Lillian mail order company executive
Wolf, Robert Irwin psychoanalyst, art and art therapy educator
Wolotsky, Hyman retired college dean

### New York
Aaron, Betsy journalist
Abatemarco, Fred editor in chief
Abberley, John J. lawyer
Abboud, Joseph M. fashion designer
Abel, Reuben humanities educator
Abeles, Sigmund M. artist, printmaker
Abelson, Alan columnist
Abernathy, James Logan public relations executive
Abish, Cecile artist
Ablow, Ronald Charles radiology director, pediatric radiologist
Abrahams, William Miller editor, author
Abramovitz, Max architect
Abrams, Floyd lawyer
Abrams, Muhal Richard pianist, composer
Abrams, Pamela Nadine magazine editor
Abrams, Robert lawyer, former state attorney general
Abramson, Sara Jane radiologist, educator
Abularach, Rodolfo Marco Antonio artist
Abu-Lughod, Janet Lippman sociologist, educator
Acampora, Ralph Joseph brokerage firm executive
Achenbaum, Alvin Allen marketing and management consultant
Acrivos, Andreas chemical engineering educator
Adam, Ken production designer
Adams, Alice writer
Adams, Dennis Paul artist
Adams, Edward A. legal journalist
Adams, Edward Thomas (Eddie Adams) photographer
Adams, George Bell lawyer
Adams, Joey comedian, author
Adams, John Hamilton lawyer
Adams, Roy M. lawyer, writer
†Adams, Scott cartoonist
Adamson, John William hematologist
Addison, Herbert John publishing executive
Adler, Freda Schaffer (Mrs. G. O. W. Mueller) criminologist, educator
Adler, Karl Paul medical educator, academic administrator
Adler, Margot Susanna journalist, radio producer
Adler, Richard composer, lyricist
Adri, (Adrienne Steckling) fashion designer
Adrian, Barbara (Mrs. Franklin C. Tramutola) artist
Agisim, Philip advertising and marketing company executive
Agosta, William Carleton chemist, educator
Ahmad, Jameel civil engineer, researcher, educator
Ahrens, Edward Hamblin, Jr. physician
Aibel, Howard J. lawyer
Aidinoff, M(erton) Bernard lawyer
Aisenbrey, Stuart Keith trust company official
Aksen, Gerald lawyer, educator
Alabiso, Vincent photojournalist
†Alarcon, Raul, Jr. broadcast executive
Alazraki, Jaime Romance languages educator
Albee, Edward Franklin author, playwright
Albers, Charles Edgar investment manager, insurance executive
†Albert, Garett J. lawyer
Albert, Marv sportscaster, program director
Albert, Neale Malcolm lawyer
Alcantara, Theo conductor
Aldea, Patricia architect
Alden, Steven Michael lawyer
Alderson, Philip Otis radiologist, educator
Alessandroni, Venan Joseph lawyer
Alexander, Barbara Toll investment banker
Alexander, Roy public relations executive, editor, author
Alexander, Shana journalist, author, lecturer
Alexopoulos, Helene ballet dancer
Alford, Robert Ross sociologist
Allard, Linda Marie fashion designer
Allen, Alice communications, public relations and marketing executive
Allen, Alice Catherine Towsley public relations professional, writer, consultant
Allen, Betty (Mrs. Ritten Edward Lee, III) mezzo-soprano
Allen, Herbert investment banker
Allen, Jay Presson writer, producer
Allen, Leon Arthur, Jr. lawyer
Allen, Nancy musician, educator
Allen, Robert Eugene communications company executive
Allen, Roberta L. fiction and nonfiction writer, conceptual artist
Allen, Woody (Allen Stewart Konigsberg) actor, filmmaker, author
Allfrey, Vincent George cell biologist
Allison, David Bradley psychologist
Allison, Michael David space scientist, astronomy educator
Allmendinger, Paul Florin retired engineering association executive
Allner, Walter Heinz designer, painter, art director
Alonzo, Martin Vincent mining and aluminum company executive, investor, financial consultant
Alper, Merlin Lionel financial executive
Alpern, David Mark magazine editor, broadcast journalist and producer
Alpern, Mildred history educator, consultant
Alpert, Warren oil company executive, philanthropist
Alpert, William Harold artist
Al-Sawwaf, Monqidh Mohammed surgeon
Alschuler, Steven public relations executive, communications consultant, writer, political consultant
Alten, Jerry art director
Alter, David lawyer
Alter, Eleanor Breitel lawyer
Alter, Jonathan Hammerman journalist
Altfest, Karen Caplan financial planning executive
Altfest, Lewis Jay financial and investment advisor
Altman, Harold artist educator
Altman, Lawrence Kimball physician, journalist
Altman, Roy Peter pediatric surgeon
Altschul, Arthur Goodhart investment banker
Alvarez, Paul Hubert communications and public relations consultant
Alvary, Lorenzo bass
Amabile, John Louis lawyer
Amara, Lucine opera and concert singer
Amdur, Martin Bennett lawyer
Amdur, Neil Lester sports editor, writer
Ames, George Joseph investment banker
Ames, Richard Pollard physician, educator, lecturer
Amhowitz, Harris J. lawyer, educator
Amory, Cleveland writer
Amos, Tori singer, musician
Amster, Gerald Stanley electrical engineer
Amster, Linda Evelyn newspaper executive, consultant
Amsterdam, Anthony Guy law educator
Anagnostopoulos, Constantine Efthymios cardiac surgeon
Ancona, Barry publishing and marketing consultant
Andersen, Kurt Byars writer
Anderson, Arthur Allan management consultant
Anderson, Bradley Jay cartoonist
Anderson, Cherine Esperanza television and film production manager, special events planner
Anderson, David Poole sportswriter
Anderson, Eugene Robert lawyer
Anderson, Gavin public relations consultant
Anderson, Gloria Faye editor
Anderson, O(rvil) Roger biology educator, marine biology and protozoology, researcher
Anderson, Poul William author
Anderson, Quentin English language educator, critic
Anderson, Sydney biologist, museum curator
Anderson, Theodore Wellington portfolio strategist
Anderson, Walter Herman magazine editor
Andolsen, Alan Anthony management consultant
Andre, Carl sculptor
Andrews, Frederick Franck newspaper editor
Andrews, Gordon Clark lawyer
Andrus, Roger Douglas lawyer
Angell, Roger writer, magazine editor
Angell, Wayne D. economist, banker
Angland, Joseph lawyer
Angle, Richard Warner, Jr. not-for-profit administrator, publishing executive
Ankerson, Robert William management consultant
†Annan, Kofi A. diplomat
Anspach, Ernst economist, lawyer
Anthoine, Robert lawyer, educator
Anthony, William Graham artist
Antilla, Susan journalist
Antonakos, Stephen sculptor
Antonuccio, Joseph Albert hospitality industry executive
Antupit, Samuel Nathaniel art director
Apostolakis, James John shipping company executive
Appel, Albert M. lawyer
Appel, Marsha Ceil association executive
Appelbaum, Ann Harriet lawyer
Applebaum, Stuart S. public relations executive
Applebroog, Ida artist
Appleton, Myra magazine editor, writer
Aptekar, Ken painter
Apter, Arthur William mathematician
Aquilino, Thomas Joseph, Jr. federal judge, law educator
Araiza, Francisco (José Francisco Araiza Andrade) opera singer
Araiza, Joseph Phillip physician
Araskog, Rand Vincent diversified telecommunications multinational company executive
Arcara, James Amadeus retired broadcasting company executive
Archibald, Reginald Mac Gregor physician, chemist, educator
Arcilesi, Vincent Jasper artist
Arenson, Gregory K. lawyer
Arkin, Alan Wolf actor
Arkin, Stanley S. lawyer
Arledge, Roone television executive
Arlow, Arnold Jack advertising agency executive
Armstrong, James Sinclair foundation director, retired lawyer
Armstrong, Jane Botsford sculptor
Arnold, Audrey Jayne communications company executive
Arnold, C. Stuart publishing executive
Arnold, Charles Burle, Jr. psychiatrist, writer
Arnold, Kenneth Lloyd publisher, playwright
Arnold, Martin journalist
Arnot, Andrew H. art gallery director
Arnot-Heaney, Susan Eileen cosmetics executive
Aron, Alan Milford pediatric neurology educator
Aron, Roberto lawyer, writer, educator
Aronoff, Michael Stephen psychiatrist
Aronson, Donald Eric professional services firms consultant, value added tax consultant
Aronson, Edgar David venture capitalist
Aronson, Esther Leah association administrator, psychotherapist
Arouh, Jeffrey Alan lawyer
Arquit, Kevin James lawyer
Arther, Richard Oberlin polygraphist, educator
Arvystas, Michael Geciauskas orthodontist, educator
Asahina, Robert James editor, publishing company executive
Asakawa, Takako dancer, dance teacher, director
Asanuma, Hiroshi physician, educator
Asch, Arthur Louis apparel company executive
Ascher, Michael Charles transportation executive
Asensi, Gustavo advertising executive
Ashdown, Marie Matranga (Mrs. Cecil Spanton Ashdown, Jr.) writer, lecturer
Asher, Aaron editor, publisher
Ashjian, Mesrob archbishop
Ashley, Elizabeth actress
Ashley, Merrill ballerina
Ashton, Dore author, educator
Ashton, Jean Willoughby library director
Ashton, Robert W. lawyer, foundation administrator
Asperilla, Purita Falgui retired nursing administrator
Assael, Henry marketing educator
Aston, Sherrell Jerone plastic surgeon, educator
Astor, David Warren journalist
Athanassiades, Ted insurance company executive
Atkins, Peter Allan lawyer
Atkinson, Holly Gail physician, journalist, author, lecturer, human rights activist
Atlas, James Robert magazine editor, writer
Atwater, Verne Stafford finance educator
Auchincloss, Kenneth magazine editor
Auchincloss, Louis Stanton writer
Aucoin, Kevyn J. make-up artist
Auel, Jean Marie author
Auerbach, William lawyer
Aufses, Arthur H(arold), Jr. surgeon, medical educator
Auriemmo, Frank Joseph, Jr. financial holding company executive
Auster, Paul writer
Austin, Danforth Whitley newspaper executive
Austin, Gabriel Christopher publisher
Austrian, Neil R. football league executive
Avedon, Richard photographer
Avrett, John Glenn advertising executive
Ax, Emanuel pianist
Axelrod, Norman N(athan) technical planning and technology application consultant
Axinn, Stephen Mark lawyer
†Azzoli, Val music company executive
Babyface, (Kenny Edmonds) popular musician
Bacall, Lauren actress
Bach, Arthur James investment banker
Bache, Theodore Stephen recording company executive
Bachelder, Joseph Elmer, III lawyer
Bacher, Judith St. George executive search consultant
Bachrach, Nancy advertising executive
Backman, Gerald Stephen lawyer
Bacot, John Carter banking executive
Badertscher, David Glen law librarian, consultant
Baechler, Donald painter
Baer, Andrew Rudolf public relations consultant
Baer, Harold, Jr. judge
Bagger, Richard Hartvig lawyer
Bagnoli, Vincent James, Jr. construction company executive, engineer
Bahr, Lauren S. publishing company executive
Bailey, Janet Dee publishing company executive
Bains, Harrison MacKellar, Jr. financial executive
Bains, Leslie Elizabeth banker
Bainton, J(ohn) Joseph lawyer
Baird, Dugald Euan oil field service company executive
Baity, John Cooley lawyer
Bakal, Carl writer, public affairs consultant, photojournalist
Baker, David Remember lawyer
Baker, Elizabeth Calhoun magazine editor
Baker, Elmer Elias, Jr. speech pathology and communication educator
Baker, James Barnes architect
Baker, James Estes foreign service officer
Baker, Martin S. lawyer
Baker, Paul Raymond history educator
Baker, Russell Wayne columnist, author
Baker, Stephen advertising executive, author
Baker, Stuart David lawyer
Baker, William Franklin public broadcasting company executive
Baker-Riker, Margery television executive
Balakian, Anna foreign language educator, scholar, critic, writer
Baldassano, Corinne Leslie radio executive
†Baldwin, Beth advertising executive
Baldwin, David Allen political science educator
Baldwin, David Shepard physician
Baldwin, Stephen actor
Balick, Kenneth D. international real estate finance executive
Ball, John H(anstein) lawyer
Ballard, Charles Alan investment banker
Balliett, Whitney writer, critic
Bamberger, Michael Albert lawyer
Bancroft, Alexander Clerihew lawyer
Bancroft, Margaret Armstrong lawyer
Bandy, Mary Lea museum official
Banks, Helen Augusta singer, actress
Banks, Russell financial planner, consultant
Bankston, Archie Moore, Jr. lawyer
Bansinath, Mylarrao pharmacologist, educator
Baquet, Dean Paul newspaper editor
Bara, Jean Marc finance and communications executive
Baragwanath, Albert Kingsmill curator
Barandes, Robert lawyer
Baranik, Rudolf artist
Baranski, Joan Sullivan publisher
Barasch, Clarence Sylvan lawyer
Barasch, Mal Livingston lawyer
Barbee, Victor ballet dancer
Barbeosch, William Peter banker, lawyer
Barber, Ann McDonald internist, physician
Barber, Russell Brooks Butler television producer
Barbera, Jose Eduardo international trade diplomat
Bardach, Joan Lucile clinical psychologist
Barie, Philip Steven surgeon, educator
Barist, Jeffrey A. lawyer
Barkann, Jeremy automotive advertising and marketing professional
Barker, Charles conductor
Barker, Edwin Bogue musician
Barkhorn, Henry Charles, III investment banker
Bar-Levav, Doron Mordecai lawyer
Barnes, Clive Alexander drama and dance critic
Barnes, Duncan magazine editor, writer
Barnes, Edward Larrabee architect
Barnes, Jack Whittier political party official
Barnes, Jhane Elizabeth fashion design company executive, designer
Barnet, Will artist, educator
Barnett, Bernard accountant
Barnett, Henry Lewis pediatrician, medical educator
Barnett, Jonathan architect, city planner
Barnett, Vivian Endicott curator
Barnum, Barbara Stevens nursing educator
Barolini, Teodolinda literary critic
Baron, Carolyn editor, author, publishing executive
Baron, Melvin Leon civil engineer, consultant
Baron, Sheri Colonel advertising agency executive
Barondess, Jeremiah Abraham physician
Barr, Michael Charles securities analyst, investment banker
Barr, Thomas D. lawyer
Barrasi, Susan artist
Barratt, Michael Scott architect
Barrett, Celia Elizabeth interior designer
Barrett, Herbert artists management executive
Barrett, Loretta Anne publishing executive
Barrett, Martin Jay financial executive
Barrett, Paulette Singer public relations executive
Barrett, William Gary advertising executive
Barron, Francis Patrick lawyer
Barron, James Turman journalist
Barry, David Earl lawyer
Barry, Desmond Thomas, Jr. lawyer
Barry, Edward William publisher
Barry, Thomas Corcoran investment counsellor
Barsalona, Frank Samuel theatrical agent
Barsamian, Khajag Sarkis primate
Barth, Mark Harold lawyer
Bartle, Annette Gruber (Mrs. Thomas R. Bartle) artist, writer, photographer
Bartlett, Jennifer Losch artist
Bartlett, Joseph Warren lawyer
Bartlett, Thomas Foster international management consultant
Bartley, Robert LeRoy newspaper editor
Barton, John Murray artist, appraiser, consultant, lecturer
Bartow, Diane Grace marketing and sales executive
Bartucci, Janet Evelyn marketing communications executive
Baruch, Ralph M. communications executive
Baryshnikov, Mikhail ballet dancer
Basden, Cameron ballet mistress, dancer
Basilico, Claudio geneticist, educator
Bason, George R., Jr. lawyer
Bass, Hyman mathematician, educator
Bassen, Ned Henry lawyer
Bates, Don public relations and marketing executive
Bates, Michael Lawrence curator
Batscha, Robert Michael museum executive
Batts, Deborah A. judge
Bauer, Douglas F. lawyer
Bauer, Frances Brand research mathematician
Bauer, Marion Dane writer
Bauer, Ralph Glenn lawyer, maritime arbitrator
Baum, Richard Theodore engineering executive
Bauman, Martin Harold executive search firm executive
†Bauman, Steve television station executive
Baumanis, Aivars Latvian diplomat
Baumann, Gary Joseph accountant
Baumgardner, John Ellwood, Jr. lawyer
Baumgardner, Matthew Clay artist
Baumgarten, Paul Anthony lawyer
Baumrin, Bernard Stefan Herbert lawyer, educator
Bausch, James John foundation executive
Bazell, Robert Joseph science correspondent

Bazerman, Steven Howard lawyer
Beal, Jack artist
Beale, Christopher William banker
Bear, Larry Alan lawyer, educator
Beard, Eugene P. advertising agency executive
Beardsley, Charles William engineering publisher, editor, writer
Bearn, Alexander Gordon physician scientist, former pharmaceutical company executive
Beatie, Russel Harrison, Jr. lawyer
Beattie, Ann author
Beatty, Prudence Carter federal judge
Beaumont, Richard Austin management consultant
Beausoleil, Doris Mae federal agency administrator, housing specialist
Beck, Adrian Robert surgeon, educator
Beck, Andrew James lawyer
Beck, Rosemarie artist, educator
Becker, Don Crandall newspaper executive
Becker, Isidore A. business executive
Becker, Ivan advertising executive
Becker, Robert A. advertising executive
Becker-Roukas, Helane Renée securities analyst, financial executive
Beckham, Edgar Frederick foundation administrator
Beckhard, Herbert architect
Beckmann, John architect, industrial designer
Beckwith, Rodney Fisk management consulting firm executive
Becofsky, Arthur Luke arts administrator, writer
Bederson, Benjamin physicist, educator
Bedi, Rahul import and distribution company executive
Bedrij, Orest investment banker, scientist
Beer, David Wells architect
Beerbower, Cynthia Gibson lawyer
Beerbower, John Edwin lawyer
Beers, Charlotte Lenore advertising agency executive
Beeson, Jack Hamilton composer, educator, writer
†Beeston, Paul professional baseball executive
Begell, William publisher
Beha, James Joseph lawyer
Behr, Alan Andrew lawyer
Behrens, Hildegard soprano
Beim, David Odell investment banker, educator
Beim, Norman playwright, actor, director
Beinecke, Candace Krugman lawyer
Beinecke, Frederick William investment company executive
Beinecke, William Sperry corporate executive
Belden, David Leigh professional association executive, engineering educator
Bel Geddes, Joan writer
Belkin, Boris David violinist
Belknap, Norton petroleum company consultant
Belknap, Robert Lamont Slavic language educator
Bell, David Arthur advertising agency executive
Bell, Derrick Albert legal educator, author, lecturer
Bell, James Halsey lawyer
Bell, Jonathan Robert lawyer
Bell, Martin Allen investment company executive
Bell, Theodore Augustus advertising executive
Bell, Thomas Devereaux, Jr. public relations company executive
Bellamy, Carol international organization executive
Bellamy, Richard art gallery owner, director
Bellanger, Serge René banker
Bellas, Albert Constantine investment banker, advisor
Beller, Daniel J. lawyer
Bellin, Howard Theodore plastic surgeon
Bellin, Milton Rockwell artist
Belliveau, Gerard Joseph, Jr. librarian
Bellows, Howard Arthur, Jr. marketing research executive
Belnick, Mark Alan lawyer
Bemis, Mary Ferguson magazine editor
Benchley, Peter Bradford author
Bendelius, Arthur George engineering firm executive
Bender, John Charles lawyer
Bender, Thomas history and humanities educator, writer
Benderly, Beryl Lieff journalist, author
Benedetto, M. William investment banker
Benedict, James Nelson lawyer
Benedikt, Michael poet, educator, author, editor, free-lance consultant
Benenson, Edward Hartley realty company executive
Benenson, Mark Keith lawyer
Benglis, Lynda artist, sculptor
Ben-Haim, Zigi artist
Ben-Hur, Ehud research scientist
Benjamin, George David retired insurance company executive, risk consultant
Benkard, James W. B. lawyer
Benn, T(heodore) Alexander (Alec Benn) writer
Bennack, Frank Anthony, Jr. publishing company executive
Benner, Mary Wright lobbyist
Bennett, Georgette communications and planning consultant
Bennett, Joel Herbert construction company executive
Bennett, Scott Lawrence lawyer
Bennett, Tony (Anthony Dominick Benedetto) entertainer
Benson, Constance Louise religious educator
Benton, Nicholas theater producer
Ben-Zvi, Jeffrey Stuart gastroenterologist, internist
Berendt, John Lawrence writer, editor
Berg, Alan lawyer, government official
Berg, David author, artist
Berg, Jonathan Albert investment company executive
Berg, Wayne architect, educator
Bergan, Edmund Paul, Jr. lawyer
Bergan, Philip James lawyer
Bergen, Jack public relations company executive
Berger, Curtis Jay law educator
Berger, Frank Milan biomedical researcher, scientist, former pharmaceutical company executive
Berger, George lawyer
Berger, Michael Gary lawyer
Berger, Miriam Roskin creative arts therapy director, educator, therapist
Berger, Pearl library director
Berger, Stephen financial services company executive
Bergeret, Albert Hamilton artistic director, conductor, singer
Bergonzi, Carlo tenor, voice educator
Bergreen, Morris Harvey lawyer, business executive, private investor
Bergstein, Daniel Gerard lawyer
Beringer, Stuart Marshall investment banker
Berk, Paul David physician, scientist, educator
Berkman, Lillian foundation executive, corporation executive, art collector
Berkow, Ira Harvey author, journalist
Berlin, Howard Richard investment advisory company executive
Berlind, Robert Elliot artist
Berlind, Roger Stuart stage and film producer
Berliner, Barbara librarian, consultant
Berliner, Ruth Shirley real estate company executive
Berlowe, Phyllis Harriette public relations counselor
Berman, Ariane R. artist
Berman, Joshua Mordecai lawyer, manufacturing company executive
Berman, Keith solicitor, lawyer
Berman, Lazar pianist
Berman, Philip Averill journalist, consultant
Berman, Simeon Moses mathematician, educator
Bermudez, Jorge Alberto bank executive
Bernard, David George management consultant
Bernard, Kenneth (Otis Bernard) poet, author, playwright
Bernard, Richard Phillip lawyer
Bernard, Viola Wertheim psychiatrist
Bernard, Walter art director
Bernardi, Mario conductor
Bernbach, John Lincoln consultant
Berne, Bruce J. chemistry educator
Berner, Andrew Jay library director, writer
Berner, Mary publisher
Berns, Kenneth Ira physician
Bernstein, Alan Arthur oil company executive
Bernstein, Anne Elayne psychoanalyst
Bernstein, Bernard lawyer, corporate executive
Bernstein, Daniel Lewis lawyer
Bernstein, Donald Scott lawyer
Bernstein, Elliot Louis television executive
Bernstein, Laurel publishing executive
Bernstein, Robert Louis publishing company executive
Bernstein, Theresa artist
Bernstein, William Robert banker
Bernstein, Zalman C. research and money management executive
Berresford, Susan Vail philanthropic foundation executive
Berry, Edna Janet patent lawyer, chemist
Berry, John Nichols, III publishing executive, editor
Berry, Joseph John brokerage house executive
Berry, Joyce Charlotte university press editor
Berry, Nancy Michaels philanthropy consultant
Berry, Walter baritone
Bertelle, Jeanne T. publishing company executive, human resources director
Berthot, Jake artist
Bertino, Joseph Rocco physician, educator
Bertuccioli, Bruno petrochemical company executive
Beshar, Robert Peter lawyer
Betcher, Albert Maxwell anesthesiologist
Bettman, Gary Bruce lawyer
Betts, Dicky (Richard Forrest Betts) guitarist, songwriter, vocalist
Betts, Richard Kevin political science educator
Beuchert, Edward William lawyer
Bewkes, Eugene Garrett, Jr. investment company executive, consultant
Bewkes, Jeff television broadcasting company executive
Beyer, Charlotte Bishop investment management marketing executive, consultant
Bezanson, Thomas Edward lawyer
Bhavsar, Natvar Prahladji artist
Bialkin, Kenneth Jules lawyer
Bialo, Kenneth Marc lawyer
Bickers, David Rinsey physician, educator, hospital administrator
Bickford, Jewelle Wooten investment banker
Bicks, David Peter lawyer
Bicks, Peter Andrews lawyer
Biddle, Flora Miller art museum administrator
Biderman, Mark Charles investment banker
Bidwell, James Truman, Jr. lawyer
Biederman, Barron Zachary (Barry Biederman) advertising agency executive
Biel, Leonard, Jr. urologist
Biggs, Barton Michael investment company executive
Biggs, Jeremy Hunt trust company executive
Biggs, John Herron insurance company executive
Bikel, Theodore actor, singer
Biller, Hugh Frederick medical educator
†Billington, Ken lighting designer
Binger, Wilson Valentine civil engineer
Binkert, Alvin John hospital administrator
Binkowski, Edward Stephan research analysis director, lawyer, educator
Bird, Mary Lynne Miller professional society administrator
Bird, Sharlene clinical psychologist
Birkelund, John Peter investment banking executive
Birkenhead, Thomas Bruce theatrical producer and manager, educator
Birman, Joseph Leon physics educator
Birnbaum, Edward Lester lawyer
Birnbaum, Henry librarian
Birnbaum, Irwin Morton lawyer
Birsh, Arthur Thomas publisher
Birstein, Ann writer, educator
Bishop, André artistic director, producer
Bishop, Susan Katharine executive search company executive
Bishop, Thomas Walter French language and literature educator
Bisno, Alison Peck investment banker
Bizar, Irving lawyer
Bjornson, Edith Cameron foundation executive, communications consultant
Black, Barbara Aronstein legal history educator
Black, Cathleen Prunty publishing executive
Black, James Isaac, III lawyer
Black, Jerry Bernard lawyer
Black, Rosemary newspaper editor
Black, Shawn Morgado dancer
Black, Susan public relations executive
†Blackford, John magazine editor
Blackman, Kenneth Robert lawyer
Blackwell, John Wesley securities industry executive, consultant
Blades, Carol Brady public relations executive
Blair, William Granger retired newspaperman
Blakeslee, Edward Eaton lawyer, insurance executive
Blakney, Larry Alonzo investment company executive, consultant
Blalock, Sherrill investment advisor
Blanc, Peter (William Peters Blanc) sculptor, painter
Blanc, Roger David lawyer
Bland, Frederick Aves architect
Blattmachr, Jonathan George lawyer
Blechman, R. O. artist, filmmaker
Bleiberg, Robert Marvin retired financial editor
Blind, William Charles lawyer
Blinder, Richard Lewis architect
Blinken, Robert James manufacturing and communications company executive
Blitzer, Andrew otolaryngologist, educator
Bliven, Bruce, Jr. writer
Bliven, Naomi book reviewer
Bliwise, Lester Martin lawyer
Blobel, Günter cell biologist, educator
Bloch, Julia Chang foundation administrator, former government official
Bloch, Peter editor
Block, Dennis Jeffrey lawyer
Block, Francesca Lia writer
Block, John Douglas auction house executive
Block, Lawrence author
Block, Ned philosophy educator
Block, William Kenneth lawyer
Bloom, Jack Sandler investment banker
Bloom, Robert Avrum lawyer
†Bloom, Robert H. advertising executive
Bloomberg, R. Michael finance and information services company executive
Bloomer, Harold Franklin, Jr. lawyer
†Bloomfield, Louise Anne editor
Bloomfield, Peter statistics educator
Bloomgarden, Kathy Finn public relations executive
Bluestone, Andrew Lavoott lawyer
Blumberg, Gerald lawyer
Blume, Judy Sussman author
Blume, Lawrence Dayton lawyer
Blumkin, Linda Ruth lawyer
Blyth, Myrna Greenstein publishing executive, editor, author
Blythe, William LeGette, II editor, writer
Boal, Peter Cadbury dancer
Boardman, Seymour artist
Boccardi, Louis Donald news agency executive
Bocchino, Lisa magazine editor
Bock, Walter Joseph zoology educator
Bockstein, Herbert lawyer
Bodovitz, James Philip lawyer
†Bodow, Warren G. radio station executive
Boehm, David Alfred publisher, producer
Boelzner, Gordon orchestral conductor
Boes, Lawrence William lawyer
Bogdonoff, Morton David physician, educator
Boggs, Gil principal ballet dancer
Bohnen, Blythe artist
Bohrman, David Ellis television news producer
Boice, Craig Kendall management consultant
Bolan, Thomas Anthony lawyer
Boley, Bruno Adrian engineering educator
Bolt, Thomas writer, artist
Bolter, Eugene P. investment counselor
Bolton, Michael singer, songwriter
Bona, Frederick Emil public relations executive
Bonazzi, Elaine Claire mezzo-soprano
Bond, George Clement anthropologist, educator
Bond, J. Max, Jr. architect, educational administrator
Bonfante, Larissa classics educator
Bonino, Fernanda art dealer
Bon Jovi, Jon rock singer, composer
Boodey, Cecil Webster, Jr. political science educator
Bookhardt, Fred Barringer, Jr. architect
Boorstein, Laurence economist
Booth, Edgar Hirsch lawyer
Booth, Margaret A(nn) communications company executive
Booth, Mitchell B. lawyer
Boothby, Willard Sands, III bank executive
Borchard, William Marshall lawyer
Borders, William Alexander journalist
Bordiga, Benno automotive parts manufacturing company executive
Borer, Jeffrey Stephen cardiologist
Borge, Victor entertainer, comedian, pianist
Borisoff, Richard Stuart lawyer
Boros, Jerome S. lawyer
Borowitz, Sidney retired physics educator
Borrelli, John Francis architect
Borsody, Robert Peter lawyer
Bosco, Philip Michael actor
Boshkov, Stefan Hristov mining engineer, educator
Boshkov, Stefan Robert lawyer
Bostock, Roy Jackson advertising agency executive
Bothmer, Dietrich Felix von museum curator, archaeologist
Bottiglia, Frank Robert bank executive
Botvin, Gilbert Joseph psychologist, educator
Boultinghouse, Marion Craig Bettinger editor
Bourdon, David art critic, writer
Bourjaily, Vance novelist
Bourke, Thomas Anthony librarian, writer
Boutis, Tom artist, painter, print maker
Bouton, Marshall Melvin academic administrator
Bove, John Louis chemistry and environmental engineering educator, researcher
Boves, Joaquin Lorenzo marketing consultant
Bowden, Sally Ann choreographer, teacher, dancer
Bowden, William P., Jr. lawyer, banker
Bowen, Jean librarian, consultant
Bowen, William Gordon economist, educator, foundation administrator
Bower, Marvin management consultant
Boxer, Leonard lawyer
Boyce, Joseph Nelson journalist
Boyd, Michael Alan investment banking company executive, lawyer
Boylan, Elizabeth Shippee academic administrator, biology educator
Bozorth, Squire Newland lawyer
Brach, Paul Henry artist
Brack, Reginald Kufeld, Jr. publisher
†Bradbury, Ray Douglas author
Brademas, John retired university president, former congressman
Bradford, Barbara Taylor writer, journalist, novelist
Bradford, John Carroll retired magazine executive
Bradford, Richard Roark writer
Bradford, Robert Ernest motion picture producer
Bradley, E. Michael lawyer
Bradley, Edward R. news correspondent
Bradley, Lisa M. artist
Brady, Adelaide Burks public relations agency executive, giftware catalog executive
Braham, Randolph Lewis political science educator
Brams, Steven John political scientist, educator, game theorist
Brancato, Carolyn Kay economist, consultant
Brand, Leonard physician, educator
Brandrup, Douglas Warren lawyer
Brandt, Warren artist
Brant, Sandra J. magazine publisher
Braude, Robert Michael medical library administrator
Braudy, Susan Orr writer
Braun, Craig Allen producer
Braun, Jeffrey Louis lawyer
Braun, Neil S. communications execuitve
Braverman, Robert Jay international consultant, public policy educator
Bravo, Rose Marie retail executive
Braxton, Toni popular musician
Braz, Evandro Freitas management consultant
Brazinsky, Irv(ing) chemical engineering educator
Brecher, John newspaper editor
Brechner, Stanley artistic director
Brecker, Jeffrey Ross lawyer, educator
Brecker, Manfred retail company executive
Brecker, Michael saxophonist
Breglio, John F. lawyer
Bregman, Martin film producer
Breindel, Eric Marc communications executive, television moderator, columnist
Breines, Simon architect
Breinin, Goodwin M. physician
Brendel, Alfred concert pianist
Brennan, Donald P. merchant banker
Brennan, Henry Higginson architect
Brenner, Beth Fuchs publishing executive
Brenner, Egon university official, education consultant
Brenner, Erma author
Brenner, Frank lawyer, venture capitalist
Brenner, Howard Martin banker
Bresani, Federico Fernando business executive
Bresler, Martin Isidore lawyer
Breslow, Esther May Greenberg biochemistry educator, researcher
Breslow, Ronald Charles chemist, educator
Bressler, Bernard lawyer
Brett, Nancy Heléne artist
Breuer, Lee playwright, theatrical director, producer, actor
Brewer, John Charles journalist
Brewer, Karen librarian
Brewster, Robert Gene concert singer, educator
Brickman, Marshall screenwriter, director
Bridges, Linda Kay journalist
Briess, Roger Charles brewing and food industry executive
Briggs, Jean Audrey publishing company executive
Briggs, Philip insurance company executive
Briggs, Taylor Rastrick lawyer
Brightman, Sarah singer, actress
Brill, Steven magazine editor
Brilliant, Richard art history educator
Brimelow, Peter journalist
Bring, Murray H. lawyer
Brinkley, Christie model
Bristah, Pamela Jean librarian
Brittenham, Raymond Lee investment company executive
Broadwater, Douglas Dwight lawyer
Broches, Paul Elias architect
Brock, Charles Lawrence lawyer, business executive
Brock, Kerry Lynn broadcast executive
Broder, Douglas Fisher lawyer
Brodsky, Edward lawyer
Brodsky, Samuel lawyer
Brody, Alan Jeffry investment company executive
Brody, Eugene David investment company executive
Brody, Jacqueline editor
Brody, Jane Ellen journalist
Brody, Saul Nathaniel English literature educator
Brofman, Lance Mark portfolio manager, mutual fund executive
Broisman, Emma Ray economist, retired international official
Brome, Thomas Reed lawyer
Bronfman, Edgar M., Jr. food products executive
Bronfman, Edgar Miles beverage company executive
Bronkesh, Annette Cylia public relations executive
Bronstein, Richard J. lawyer
Brook, Barry S. musicologist, foundation administrator
Brook, David William psychiatrist, researcher
Brook, Judith Suzanne psychiatry and psychology researcher and educator
Brooke, Paul Alan finance company executive
Brooks, Anita Helen public relations executive
Brooks, Diana B. auction house executive
Brooks, Jerome Bernard English and Afro-American literature educator
Brooks, Lorimer Page patent lawyer
Brooks, Timothy H. media executive
Brooks, Tyrone dancer
Bross, Steward Richard, Jr. lawyer
Brosterman, Melvin A. lawyer
Brothers, Joyce Diane television personality, psychologist
Broude, Richard Frederick lawyer, educator
Broughton, Phillip Charles lawyer
Browdy, Joseph Eugene lawyer
†Brown, Andreas Le book store and art gallery executive
Brown, Arthur Edward physician
Brown, Carroll diplomat, association executive
Brown, Charles Dodgson lawyer
Brown, Christopher artist
Brown, Darrell James publishing executive
Brown, David motion picture producer, writer
Brown, Edward James, Sr. utility executive
Brown, Eric Lucasen art gallery director, art dealer
Brown, Fred Elmore investment executive
Brown, G(lenn) William, Jr. financial services executive
Brown, Helen Gurley editor, writer
Brown, Hobson, Jr. executive recruiting consultant
Brown, James Nelson, Jr. accountant
Brown, Jason Walter neurologist, educator, researcher
Brown, Jeffrey Wisner publishing company executive
Brown, Jonathan art historian, fine arts educator
Brown, Kevin writer
Brown, Les (Lester Louis) journalist
Brown, Linda psychotherapist, psychoanalyst
Brown, Meredith M. lawyer
Brown, Milton Wolf art historian, educator
Brown, Paul M. lawyer
Brown, Peter Megargee lawyer, writer, lecturer
Brown, Ralph Sawyer, Jr. lawyer, business executive
Brown, Raymond Edward educator, priest
Brown, Robert Mott, III investment banker
Brown, Ronald stockbroker
Brown, Ronald Erik lawyer
Brown, Terrence Charles art association executive, researcher, lecturer
Brown, Tina magazine editor
Brown, Trisha dancer
†Brown, William Anthony (Tony) broadcast executive
Brown, William Michael scientific consultant, writer, editor
Browne, Arthur newspaper editor
Browne, Jeffrey Francis lawyer

Cook, Robert S., Jr. *lawyer*
†Cook, Robin *author*
Cooke, Alfred Alistair *correspondent, broadcaster*
Coolio *popular musician*
Cooney, Joan Ganz *broadcasting executive*
Cooney, John Patrick, Jr. *lawyer*
Cooney, Lenore *public relations executivechairman*
Cooper, Alice (Vincent Furnier) *popular musician*
Cooper, Arthur Martin *magazine editor*
Cooper, Gloria *editor, press critic*
Cooper, Michael Anthony *lawyer*
Cooper, Norman Streich *pathologist, medical educator*
Cooper, Paula *art dealer*
Cooper, Paulette Marcia *writer*
Cooper, R. John, III *lawyer*
Cooper, Stephen Herbert *lawyer*
†Corbin, Herbert Leonard *public relations executive*
Corbin, Sol Neil *lawyer*
Corcoran, David *newspaper editor*
Corigliano, John Paul *composer*
Corliss, Richard Nelson *critic, magazine editor*
Corn, Alfred DeWitt *poet, educator*
Cornell, Thomas Charles *peace activist, writer*
†Cornwell, Patricia Daniels *author*
Corporon, John Robert *broadcasting executive*
Corrigan, E. Gerald *investment banker*
Corry, John Adams *lawyer*
Corsaro, Frank Andrew *theater, musical and opera director*
Cortez, Ricardo Lee *investment management executive*
Cortor, Eldzier *artist, printmaker*
Cory, Jeffrey *television, film, stage, event and creative director*
†Coryat, Sonja Heinze *journalist, freelance writer*
Corzine, Jon Stevens *investment banker*
Cose, Ellis *journalist, author*
Costa, Max *health facility administrator, pharmacology educator, environmental medicine educator*
Costa, Rosann *sociologist, educator*
Costa, Victor Charles *fashion designer*
Costello, John Robert *linguistics educator*
Costikyan, Edward N. *lawyer*
Cote, Denise Louise *federal judge*
Cotter, James Michael *lawyer*
Cotton, Richard *lawyer*
Couric, Katherine *broadcast journalist*
Couture, Josie Balaban *foundation director, insurance executive*
Cowan, Wallace Edgar *lawyer*
Cowen, Edward S. *lawyer*
Cowen, Robert Nathan *lawyer*
Cowin, Stephen Corteen *biomedical engineering educator, consultant*
Cowles, Charles *art dealer*
Cowles, Frederick Oliver *lawyer*
Cowley, Robert William *editor, writer*
Cox, Archibald, Jr. *investment banker*
Cox, Marshall *lawyer*
Coyne, Nancy Carol *advertising executive*
Craft, Randal Robert, Jr. *lawyer*
Craig, Charles Samuel *marketing educator*
Craig, Sandra Kay *sales executive*
Cramer, Edward Morton *lawyer, music company executive*
Cramer, Marjorie *plastic surgeon*
Crandell, Susan *magazine editor*
Crane, Benjamin Field *lawyer*
Crane, Stephen Andrew *insurance company executive*
Cranefield, Paul Frederic *physiology educator, physician, scientist*
Cranney, Marilyn Kanrek *lawyer*
Crary, Miner Dunham, Jr. *lawyer*
Crawford, Bruce Edgar *advertising executive*
Crawford, Harold Bernard *publisher*
Creech, Sharon *children's author*
Creedon, John J. *insurance company executive*
Creel, Thomas Leonard *lawyer*
†Crews, Harry Eugene *author*
†Cripps, Kathy Hickey *public relations company official*
Crisci, Mathew G. *marketing executive*
Crisona, James Joseph *lawyer*
Crist, Judith *film and drama critic*
Critchlow, Charles Howard *lawyer*
Croce, Arlene Louise *critic*
†Crocker, Frankie *radio broadcast executive*
Cromwell, Oliver Dean *investment banker*
Cronholm, Lois S. *biology educator*
Cronkite, Walter *radio and television news correspondent*
Crosby, Gordon Eugene, Jr. *insurance company executive*
Cross, George Alan Martin *biochemistry educator, researcher*
Cross, Theodore Lamont *publisher, author*
Crow, Elizabeth Smith *publishing company executive*
Crowdus, Gary Alan *film company executive*
Cruz, Celia *vocalist*
Cryer, Gretchen *playwright, lyricist, actress*
Crystal, James William *insurance company executive*
Cubitto, Robert J. *lawyer*
Cudd, Robert A. N. *lawyer*
Cuiffo, Frank Wayne *lawyer*
Culhane, John William *journalist, author, film historian*
Cullen, Patrick Colborn *English educator*
Culligan, John William *retired corporate executive*
Culp, Michael *securities company executive, research director*
Cuming, Pamela *marketing professional, author*
Cummings, Josephine Anna *writer*
Cummins, Herman Zachary *physicist*
Cuneo, Donald Lane *lawyer, educator*
Cuneo, Jack Alfred *real estate investment executive*
Cunha, Mark Geoffrey *lawyer*
Cunningham, Jeffrey Milton *publishing executive*
Cunningham, Merce *dancer*
Cuozzo, Steven David *newspaper editor*
Curie, Eve *writer, lecturer*
Curley, Walter Joseph Patrick *diplomat, investment banker*
Curry, Ann *correspondent, anchor*
Curry, Jack *magazine editor*
Curry, Jane Louise *writer*
Curtin, Brian Joseph *ophthalmologist*
Curtin, Jane Therese *actress, writer*
Curtis, Frank R. *lawyer*
Curtis, Paul James *mime*
Curtis, Susan Grace *lawyer*
Cushing, Harry Cooke, IV *investment banker*
Cushman, Karen Lipski *writer*
Cutler, Kenneth Burnett *lawyer, investment company executive*
Cutler, Laurel *advertising agency executive*
Cutler, Rhoda *psychologist*
Cutler, Ronnie *artist*
Czarnecki, Selina Michelle Snyder *sales and marketing executive, artist*
Czerwinski, Edward Joseph *foreign language educator*
Dacey, Eileen M. *lawyer*
Dailey, Benjamin Peter *chemistry educator*
Dailey, Thomas Hammond *surgeon*
Daily, John Charles *executive recruiting company executive*
Dakin, Christine Whitney *dancer, educator*
Dale, Jim *actor*
Dales, Samuel *microbiologist, virologist, educator*
Dallas, William Moffit, Jr. *lawyer*
Dallmann, Daniel F. *artist, educator*
Dalrymple, Jean Van Kirk *theatrical producer, publicist, author*
Dalton, Dennis Gilmore *political science educator*
Daltrey, Roger *musician*
Daly, Charles Patrick *publishing company executive*
Daly, Cheryl *broadcast executive*
Daly, George Garman *college dean, educator*
Daly, Joe Ann Godown *publishing company executive*
Daly, John Neal *investment company executive*
Daly, Robert Anthony *film executive*
Daly, Tyne *actress*
d'Amboise, Jacques Joseph *dancer, choreographer*
Dana, F(rank) Mitchell *theatrical lighting designer*
Danaher, Frank Erwin *transportation technologist*
Dane, Maxwell *former advertising executive*
D'Angelo, Joseph Francis *publishing company executive*
Daniel, David Ronald *management consultant*
Daniel, Richard Nicholas *fabricated metals manufacturing company executive*
Danitz, Marilynn Patricia *choreographer, videographer*
Dankner, Jay Warren *lawyer*
Danto, Arthur Coleman *author, philosopher, art critic*
Danzig, Frederick Paul *newspaper editor*
Danziger, Jeff *political cartoonist, writer*
Danziger, Paula *author*
Daphnis, Nassos *artist*
Darling, Robert Edward *designer, stage director*
Darlington, Henry, Jr. *investment broker*
Darnell, James Edwin, Jr. *molecular biologist, educator*
Darnton, John Townsend *journalist*
Darrell, Norris, Jr. *lawyer*
Darrow, Jill E(llen) *lawyer*
Darst, David Martin *investment banking company executive, writer, educator*
Darvarova, Elmira *violinist, concertmaster*
Das, T. K. *management educator, consultant*
Dattner, Richard *architect, educator*
Dauben, Joseph Warren *history educator*
Dauten, Dale Alan *newspaper columnist*
David, Hal *lyricist*
David, Miles *association and marketing executive*
David, Theoharis Lambros *architect, educator*
Davidovich, Bella *pianist*
Davidovich, Jaime *video artist, researcher*
Davidson, Clifford Marc *lawyer*
Davidson, Daniel P. *transportation executive*
Davidson, Donald William *advertising executive*
Davidson, George Allan *lawyer*
Davidson, Joy Elaine *mezzo-soprano*
Davidson, Mark Edward *lawyer*
Davidson, Nancy Brachman *artist, educator*
Davidson, Robert Bruce *lawyer*
David-Weill, Michel Alexandre *investment banker*
Davies, Dennis Russell *conductor, music director, pianist*
Davies, Jane B(adger) (Mrs. Lyn Davies) *architectural historian*
Davila, Jaime *broadcast executive*
Davis, Anthony *composer, pianist, educator*
Davis, Clive Jay *record company executive*
Davis, Evan Anderson *lawyer*
Davis, Frederick Townsend *lawyer*
Davis, J. Steve *advertising agency executive*
Davis, Karen Padgett *fund executive*
Davis, Kathryn Wasserman *foundation executive, writer, lecturer*
Davis, Kenneth Leon *psychiatrist, pharmacologist, medical educator*
Davis, Leonard *violist*
Davis, Lorraine Jensen *writer, editor*
Davis, Martin S. *investment company executive*
Davis, Richard Bruce *investment banker*
Davis, Richard Joel *lawyer, former government official*
Davis, Samuel *hospital administrator, educator, consultant*
Davis, Stephen Arnold *artist, educator*
Davis, Stephen Edward Folwell *banker*
Davis, Susan Lynn *public relations executive*
Davis, Wendell, Jr. *lawyer*
Davison, Daniel Pomeroy *retired banker*
Dawson, Thomas Cleland, II *financial executive*
Dayson, Diane Harris *superintendent, park ranger*
Deak, Istvan *historian, educator*
Dean, Diane D. *youth service agency executive, fund development consultant*
Dean, Jay Douglas *lawyer*
De Angelis, Judy *anchorwoman*
De Blasio, Michael Peter *satellite company executive*
Debo, Vincent Joseph *lawyer, manufacturing company executive*
DeBow, Jay Howard Camden *public relations executive*
DeBow, Thomas Joseph, Jr. *advertising executive*
Debs, Richard A. *investment banker, government official*
†DeBusschere, David Albert *brokerage executive, retired professional basketball player and team executive*
de Champlain, Vera Chopak *artist, painter*
Decker, Dennis Dale *industrial designer*
DeCotis, Deborah Anne *investment company executive*
Decter, Midge *writer*
De Deo, Joseph E. *advertising executive*
de Duve, Christian René *chemist, educator*
Deem, George *artist*
Defendi, Vittorio *medical research administrator, pathologist*
De Ferrari, Gabriella *curator, writer*
Deffenbaugh, Ralston H., Jr. *immigration agency executive, lawyer*
De Forest, Roy Dean *artist, sculptor*
DeFranco, Elizabeth Carol *editor*
De Gaster, Zachary *engineering company executive*
Degener, Carol Marie-Laure *lawyer*
†De Gregorio, Anthony *advertising executive*
De Gregorio, Jorge Eduardo *psychoanalyst, educator*
de Hartog, Jan *writer*
Deitz, Paula *magazine editor*
De Johnette, Jack *musician*
Dekker, Marcel *publishing company executive*
de la Falaise, Lucie *model*
Delaney, Robert Vincent *former gas company executive, economic development consultant*
Delano, Lester Almy, Jr. *advertising executive*
de la Renta, Oscar *fashion designer*
DeLay, Dorothy (Mrs. Edward Newhouse) *violinist, educator*
Delbourgo, Joëlle Lily *publishing executive*
Dell, Ralph Bishop *pediatrician, researcher*
Delson, Robert *lawyer*
Delz, William Ronald *petroleum company executive*
Demarest, Daniel Anthony *retired lawyer*
de Margitay, Gedeon *acquisitions and management consultant*
†Demaria, Walter *sculptor*
deMause, Lloyd *psychohistorian*
De Medeiros, Melissa Brown *librarian, art researcher*
de Montebello, Philippe Lannes *museum administrator*
De Natale, Andrew Peter *lawyer*
Denham, Robert Edwin *lawyer, investment company executive*
Denhof, Miki *graphic designer*
Denker, Henry *playwright, author, director*
Dennis, Donna Frances *sculptor, art educator*
Dennis, Walter Decoster *suffragan bishop*
Denoon, David Baugh Holden *economist, educator, consultant*
Dent, V. Edward *former advertising and communications company executive*
DeNunzio, Ralph Dwight *investment banker*
Denver, John (Henry John Deutschendorf, Jr.) *singer, songwriter*
DeOrchis, Vincent Moore *lawyer*
Derman, Cyrus *mathematical statistician*
DeRoma, Leonard James *securities firm executive*
Derow, Peter Alfred *publishing company executive*
Derzaw, Richard Lawrence *lawyer*
Desai, Vishakha N. *gallery executive, society administrator*
de St. Paer, Jerry Michael *insurance executive*
de Saint Phalle, Pierre Claude *lawyer*
De Sear, Edward Marshall *lawyer*
†Desiato, Michael *editor-in-chief, periodical*
†DeSimone, Glenn J. *advertising executive*
Desnick, Robert John *human geneticist*
Despommier, Dickson Donald *microbiology educator, parasitologist, researcher*
des Rioux, Deena Victoria Coty *artist, graphics designer*
Dessi, Adrian Frank *marketing, communications executive*
Deupree, Marvin Mattox *accountant, business consultant*
Deuschle, Kurt Walter *physician, educator*
†Deutsch, Donny *advertising executive*
Deutsch, Martin Bernard Joseph *editor, publisher*
De Vido, Alfredo Eduardo *architect*
DeVita, M. Christine *foundation administrator*
De Vivo, Darryl Claude *pediatric neurologist*
DeWeil, Dawn Susan *lawyer*
Dewing, Merlin Eugene *diversified financial services company executive*
DeWitt, Eula *accountant*
Dhrymes, Phoebus James *economist, educator*
Diamond, Bernard Robin *lawyer*
Diamond, David Howard *lawyer*
Diamond, Edwin *journalism educator, editor, columnist*
Diamond, Harris *corporate communications executive, lawyer*
Diamond, Irene *foundation administrator*
Diamondstone, Lawrence *paper company executive*
Diamonstein-Spielvogel, Barbaralee *writer, television interviewer/ producer*
Diaz, Justino *bass-baritone*
DiBlasi, Gandolfo Vincent *lawyer*
DiCarlo, Dominick L. *federal judge*
Dichter, Barry Joel *lawyer*
Dichter, Misha *concert pianist*
Dick, Harold Michael *orthopedic surgeon*
Dickie, Brian Norman *management consultant*
Dicterow, Glenn Eugene *violinist*
Didion, Joan *author*
Diehl, Stephen Anthony *human resources consultant*
Dienstag, Eleanor Foa *corporate communications consultant*
Dierdorf, Daniel Lee (Dan Dierdorf) *football analyst, sports commentator, former professional football player*
Dieterich, Douglas Thomas *gastroenterologist, researcher*
Di Franco, Loretta Elizabeth *lyric coloratura soprano*
Diggins, Peter Sheehan *arts administrator*
DiGuido, Al *publishing executive*
Dill, Lesley *sculptor*
Dillard, Annie *author*
Dillingham, Robert Bulger *publishing executive*
Dillon, Clarence Douglas *retired investment company executive*
Dillon, Matt *actor*
DiMaggio, Frank Louis *civil engineering educator*
Dimen, Muriel Vera *psychoanalyst*
Di Meo, Dominick *artist, sculptor, painter*
Dimling, John Arthur *marketing executive*
Dinaburg, Mary Ellen *art education and curatorial consultant*
Dintenfass, Terry *art dealer*
Dionne, Joseph Lewis *publishing company executive*
Di Salvo, Nicholas Armand *dental educator, orthodontist*
Diskant, Gregory L. *lawyer*
Disney, Anthea *publishing executive*
Dispeker, Thea *artists' representative*
Dissette, Alyce Marie *television and multimedia producer, non-profit foundation executive*
Djeddah, Richard Nissim *investment banker*
D'Lower, Del *manufacturing executive*
Dlugoszewski, Lucia *artistic director*
Dobbs, John Barnes *artist, educator*
Dobelis, Inge Nachman *editor*
Dobell, Byron Maxwell *magazine consultant*
Dobrof, Rose Wiesman *geriatrics services professional*
Doctorow, Edgar Lawrence *novelist, English educator*
Dodd, Lois *artist, art professor*
Dodge, Geoffrey A. *magazine publisher*
Dodson, Daryl Theodore *ballet administrator, arts consultant*
Doerr, Harriet *writer*
Doherty, Thomas *publisher*
Dohrenwend, Bruce Philip *psychiatric epidemiologist, social psychologist, educator*
Dolan, Raymond Bernard *insurance executive*
Dole, Vincent Paul *medical research executive, educator*
Dolger, Jonathan *editor, literary agent*
Dolgin, Martin *cardiologist*
Dolice, Joseph Leo *multimedia publisher, exhibition director*
†Doman, Nicholas R. *lawyer*
Domingo, Placido *tenor*
Donahue, Phil *television personality*
Donald, Norman Henderson, III *lawyer*
Donald, Roger Thomas *publishing executive*
Donaldson, Stephen Reeder *author*
Donaldson, William Henry *financial executive*
Donati, Enrico *artist*
Doner, Frederick Nathan *advertising and communications executive*
Donnellan, Andrew B., Jr. *lawyer*
Donohue, William Anthony *religious organization administrator*
Doorish, John Francis *physicist, mathematician, educator*
Dore, Anita Wilkes *English language educator*
Dorfman, Howard David *pathologist*
Dormann, Henry O. *magazine publisher*
Dorn, Sue Bricker *hospital and medical school administrator*
Dornemann, Michael *book publishing executive*
Dorsen, Norman *lawyer, educator*
Dorsett, Burt *investment company executive*
Douchkess, George *lawyer*
Douglas, Andra Christine *entertainment company executive*
Douglas, Paul Wolff *retired mining executive*
Douglass, Robert Royal *banker, lawyer*
Dowling, Edward Thomas *economics educator*
Downes, Edward Olin Davenport *musicologist, critic, radio broadcaster*
Downey, John Alexander *physician, educator*
Downs, Hugh Malcolm *radio and television broadcaster*
Doyle, Eugenie Fleri *pediatric cardiologist, educator*
Doyle, Joseph Anthony *lawyer*
Doyle, L. F. Boker *trust company executive*
Doyle, Paul Francis *lawyer*
Doyle, William Stowell *venture capitalist*
†Drake, Owen Burtch Winters *association administrator*
Draper, James David *art museum curator*
Drasler, Gregory John *artist*
Drasner, Fred *newspaper publishing executive*
Drawbaugh, Kevin Alan *journalist*
Drebsky, Dennis Jay *lawyer*
Dreizen, Alison M. *lawyer*
Drescher, Jack *psychoanalyst, psychiatrist*
Dressner, Howard Roy *foundation executive, lawyer*
Drexler, Joanne Lee *art appraiser*
†Driver, Bruce *professional hockey player*
Driver, Martha Westcott *English language educator, writer, researcher*
Driver, Tom Faw *theologian, writer, justice/peace advocate*
Drobis, David R. *public relations company executive*
Druck, Mark *director, producer, writer*
Drucker, Jacquelin F. *lawyer, arbitrator, author*
Drucker, Mort *commercial artist*
Druker, Henry Leo *investment banker*
Drusin, Lewis Martin *physician, educator*
Duberman, Martin *historian*
Dubin, James Michael *lawyer*
Dubin, Morton Donald *management consultant, film producer*
Duchin, Peter Oelrichs *musician*
Duddy, Joan Frances *performing arts administrator, dancer*
Duff, John Ewing *sculptor*
Duffy, James Henry *writer, former lawyer*
Duffy, Kevin Thomas *federal judge*
Dufour, Val (Albert Valery Dufour) *actor*
Dugan, Edward Francis *investment banker*
Dugan, Michael J. *former air force officer, health agency executive*
Duggan, Dennis Michael *newspaper editor*
Dukakis, Olympia *actress*
Duke, Anthony Drexel *sociologist, educator, philanthropist*
Duke, Robert Dominick *mining executive, lawyer*
Duke, Robin Chandler Tippett *public relations executive*
Dulaine, Pierre *ballroom dancer*
Du Mont, Nicolas *psychiatrist, educator*
Duncan, Sandy *actress*
Dundas, Philip Blair, Jr. *lawyer*
Dunham, Christine *dancer*
Dunham, Corydon Busnell *lawyer, broadcasting executive*
Dunham, Donald Carl *diplomat*
Dunham, Wolcott Balestier, Jr. *lawyer*
Dunkelman, Loretta *artist*
Dunleavy, Rosemary *ballet dancer*
Dunn, James Joseph *magazine publisher*
Dunn, Mignon *mezzo-soprano*
Dunn, M(orris) Douglas *lawyer*
Dunn, Susan *singer*
Dunne, John Gregory *author*
Dunst, Laurence David *advertising executive*
Duquesnay, Ann *actress, singer*
Durst, Carol Goldsmith *educator*
Dwek, Cyril S. *banker*
Dworetzky, Murray *physician, educator*
Dworkin, Ronald Myles *legal educator*
Dwyer, Jim *reporter, columnist*
Dykhouse, David Wayne *lawyer*
Dylan, Bob (Robert Allen Zimmerman) *singer, composer*
Dystel, Jane Dee *literary agent*
Dyyon, Frazier (LeRoy Frazier) *artist*
Dzodin, Harvey Cary *communications executive*
Eagan, Marie T. (Ria Eagan) *chiropractor*
Eaker, Sherry Ellen *entertainment newspaper editor*
Earle, Victor Montagne, III *lawyer*
Earls, Kevin Gerard *insurance company executive*
Easum, Donald Boyd *consultant, educator, former institute executive, diplomat*
Eaton, Richard Gillette *surgeon, educator*
Ebersol, Dick *television broadcasting executive*
Ebin, Leonard Ned *radiologist, educator, consultant*
Eckman, Fern Marja *journalist*
Eckstut, Michael Kauder *management consultant*
Edelman, Harold *architect*
Edelman, Judith H. *architect*
Edelman, Paul Sterling *lawyer*
Edelman, Richard Winston *public relations executive*
Edelson, Gilbert Seymour *lawyer*
Edelson, Mary Beth *artist, educator*
Edelstein, David Northon *federal judge*

Edelstein, Joan Erback physical therapy educator
†Edelstein, Robert Glenn magazine editor
Edgar, Harold Simmons Hull legal educator
Edinger, Lewis Joachim political science educator
Edlow, Kenneth Lewis securities brokerage official
Edmiston, Mark Morton publishing company executive
Edmunds, Robert Thomas retired surgeon
Edson, Andrew Stephen public relations executive
Edwards, Adrian L. medical educator
Edwards, Franklin R. economist, educator, consultant
Edwards, Harold Mortimer mathematics educator
Edwards, James D. accounting company executive
Effel, Laura lawyer
Efrat, Isaac financial analyst, mathematician
Eger, Joseph conductor, music director
Egielski, Richard illustrator
Ehinger, Albert Louis, Jr. securities trader
Ehlers, Kathryn Hawes (Mrs. James D. Gabler) physician
Ehrenkranz, Joel S. lawyer
Eidsvold, Gary Mason physician, public health officer, medical educator
Eig, Norman investment company executive
Eimicke, William Brewster management and finance educator, consultant
Einhorn, Harold lawyer, writer
Einiger, Carol Blum university administrator
Eins, Stefan painter, conceptual artist, arts curator, sculptor
Eisenberg, Alan professional society administrator
Eisenberg, Sonja Miriam artist
Eisenman, Peter David architect, educator
Eisenstadt, G. Michael diplomat, author, lecturer, research scholar
Eisenthal, Kenneth B. physical chemistry educator
Eisert, Edward Gaver lawyer
Eisler, Colin Tobias art historian, curator
Eisler, Susan Krawetz advertising executive
Eisner, Richard Alan accountant
Ekman, Richard foundation executive, educator
Elam, Leslie Albert museum administrator
Elder, Eldon stage designer, theatre consultant
Elias, Rosalind mezzo-soprano
Elicker, Gordon Leonard lawyer
Eliot, Lucy artist
Elkin, Jeffrey H. lawyer
Elkman, Steven Munro stockbroker
Ellenbogen, Rudolph Solomon library curator
Ellerbee, Linda broadcast journalist
Ellig, Bruce Robert personnel executive
†Elliman, Donald M., Jr. magazine publisher and executive
Ellins, Howard A. lawyer
Elliott, Donald Harrison lawyer
Elliott, Eleanor Thomas foundation executive, civic leader
Elliott, Inger McCabe designer, textile company executive, consultant
Elliott, John, Jr. advertising agency executive
Elliott, Osborn journalist, educator, urban activist, former dean
Elliott, Tim advertising agency executive
Elliott-Smith, Paul Henry marketing and economics consultant
Ellis, Albert clinical psychologist, educator, author
Ellis, Carolyn Terry lawyer
Ellis, Charles Richard publishing executive
Elman, Naomi Geist artist, producer
Elsen, Sheldon Howard lawyer
Elster, Samuel Kase college dean, medical educator, physician
Emerson, Alice Frey political scientist, educator emerita
Emerson, Andi (Mrs. Andi Emerson Weeks) sales and advertising executive
Emil, Arthur D. lawyer
Emmerich, Andre art gallery executive, author
Emmerman, Michael N financial analyst
Emmons, Delia McQuade investment industry executive
Enders, Anthony Talcott banker
Enders, Elizabeth McGuire artist
Engelhardt, Sara Lawrence organization executive
Englander, Roger Leslie television producer, director
Engler, Robert political science educator, author
English, Joseph Thomas physician, medical administrator
Engstrom, Erik publishing company executive
Entremont, Philippe conductor, pianist
Ephron, Nora writer, director
Epling, Richard Louis lawyer
Eppes, William David civic worker, writer
Epstein, Barbara editor
Epstein, Cynthia Fuchs sociology educator, writer
Epstein, Harriet Pike public relations executive
Epstein, Jason publishing company executive
Epstein, Jeremy G. lawyer
Epstein, Matthew performing company director
Epstein, Melvin lawyer
Epstein, Michael Alan lawyer
Epstein, Seth Paul immunologist, researcher
Erbsen, Claude Ernest journalist
Ercklentz, Alexander Tonio investment executive
Ercklentz, Enno Wilhelm, Jr. lawyer
Ergas, Enrique orthopedic surgeon
Ericson, Robert Walter lawyer
Erlanger, Bernard Ferdinand biochemist, educator
Erosh, William Daniel financial services company executive
Ertegun, Ahmet Munir record company executive
Ertur, Omer Selcukhan United Nations official, educator
Eschenbach, Christoph conductor, pianist
Escobar, Marisol sculptor
Esman, Aaron H. physician, psychiatrist
Esman, Rosa Mencher art gallery executive
Esposito, Richard Joseph journalist, executive
Espy, Willard Richardson author
Estabrook, Alison breast surgeon, surgical oncologist, educator
Estefan, Gloria Maria singer, songwriter
Esterow, Milton magazine editor, publisher
Estes, Richard artist
Estreicher, Samuel lawyer, educator
Eswein, Bruce James, II human resources executive
Ethan, Carol Baehr psychotherapist
Etheridge, Melissa Lou singer, songwriter
Etra, Aaron lawyer
Eustice, James Samuel lawyer, educator
Evangelista, Linda model
Evans, Alfred Lee, Jr. advertising executive
Evans, James Bremond (Jim Evans) major league baseball umpire
Evans, James Hurlburt retired transportation and natural resources executive
Evans, Jerry Norman television director
Evans, Linda Kay publishing company executive
Evans, Martin Frederic lawyer
Evans, Mary Johnston transportation company director
Evans, Thomas Chives Newton communications executive
Evans, Thomas R. magazine publisher
Evans, Thomas William lawyer
Evans, Van Michael advertising agency executive, consultant
†Evarts, William Maxwell, Jr. lawyer
Eveillard, Jean-Marie financial company executive
Everett, James William, Jr. lawyer
Everly, Jack conductor
Evnin, Anthony Basil venture capital investor
Ewers, Patricia O'Donnell university administrator
Ewing, Maria Louise soprano
Ewing, Patrick Aloysius professional basketball player
Fabbri, Brian John economist, investment strategist
Faber, Neil advertising executive
Faber, Peter Lewis lawyer
Fahey, James Edward financial executive
Fahn, Stanley neurologist, educator
Fair, William Robert physician
Fairbairn, Ursula Farrell human resources executive
Fairbanks, Douglas Elton, Jr. actor, producer, writer, corporation director
Fairchild, John Burr publisher
Fales, Haliburton, II lawyer
Falk, Edgar Alan public relations consulting executive, author
Fallaci, Oriana writer, journalist
Falletta, Jo Ann musician
Fan, Linda C. investment company executive
Farah, Roger retail company executive
Faraone, Ted public relations executive, consultant
Farber, Jackie editor
Farber, John J. chemical company executive
Farber, Saul Joseph physician, educator
Farberman, Harold conductor, composer
Fargis, Paul McKenna publishing consultant, book developer, editor
Farinelli, Jean L. public relations firm executive
Farkas, Carol Garner nurse, administrator
Farkas, Robin Lewis retail company executive
Farley, Carole soprano
Farley, Peggy Ann finance company executive
Farley, Robert Donald lawyer, business executive
Farley, Terrence Michael banker
Farney, Dennis journalist
Farnsworth, E(dward) Allan lawyer, educator
Farr, Charles Sims lawyer
Fass, Peter Michael lawyer, educator
Fast, Howard Melvin author
Fast, Julius author, editor
Faulkner, Walter Thomas lawyer
Faurer, Louis photographer
Fay, Toni Georgette communications executive
Feder, Harry Simon bank executive
Feder, Saul E. lawyer
Feders, Sid journalist, television producer
Feeney, Maryann McHugh fundraiser
Feigelson, Philip biochemist, educator
Feigen, Richard L. art dealer
Fein, Bernard investments executive
Feinberg, Mortimer Robert psychologist, educator
Feinberg, Robert Edward advertising agency executive, writer
Feinberg, Wilfred federal judge
Feingold, Michael E. critic, translator, stage director
Feininger, Andreas Bernhard Lyonel photographer
†Feintuch, Henry P. public relations executive
Feist, Gene theater director
Feit, Glenn M. lawyer
Feld, Eliot dancer, choreographer
Feld, Katherine Phoebe lawyer
Feldberg, Chester Ben banker, lawyer
Feldberg, Meyer university dean
Feldberg, Michael Svetkey lawyer
Felder, Raoul Lionel lawyer
Feldkamp, John Calvin lawyer, educational administrator
Feldman, Franklin lawyer, printmaker
Feldman, Jerome Ira lawyer, patent development executive
Feldman, Ronald art gallery director
Feldman, Ronald Arthur social work educator, researcher
Feldman, Samuel Mitchell neuroscientist, educator
Feldmann, Shirley Clark psychology educator
Fellner, Michael Josef dermatologist
Fenchel, Gerd H(erman) psychoanalyst
Feniger, Jerome Roland, Jr. broadcasting executive
Fennell, John magazine publisher
Fensterstock, Blair Courtney lawyer
Fenton, Thomas Trail journalist
Ferber, Laurence Robert television producer
Ferguson, Milton Carr, Jr. lawyer
Ferguson, Robert Harry Munro lawyer
Ferm, David G. magazine publisher
Fernandez, Jose Walfredo lawyer
Ferrante, Joan Marguerite English and comparative literature educator
Ferrell, John Frederick advertising executive
Ferri, Alessandra Maria ballet dancer
Fertig, Howard publisher, editor
Fetscher, Paul George William brokerage house executive
Feuer, Cy motion picture and theatrical producer, director
Feurey, Claudia Packer not-for-profit executive
Fewell, Christine Huff psychoanalyst, alchohol counselor
Fidanza, Giovanni securities broker, dealer, executive
Fields, Jennie advertising executive, writer
Fier, Elihu lawyer
Fierstein, Harvey Forbes playwright, actor
Filimonov, Mikhail Anatolyevitch investment company executive
Filler, Ronald Howard lawyer
Finberg, Barbara Denning foundation executive
Finch, Edward Ridley, Jr. lawyer, diplomat, author, lecturer
Findlay, Michael Alistair auction house executive, poet
†Findlen, Barbara J. magazine editor
Fine, Donald Irving editor, publisher, writer
Fine, Michael Joseph publishing company executive
Fineman, Martha Albertson law educator
Finger, Seymour Maxwell political science educator, former ambassador
Fink, Robert Steven lawyer, writer, educator
Finkelstein, Allen Lewis lawyer
Finkelstein, Bernard lawyer
Finkelstein, Edward Sydney department store executive
Finlay, Thomas Hiram biochemist, researcher
Finn, David public relations company executive, artist
Finn, Edwin, Jr. publishing executive
Finn, Peter public relations executive
Fiorato, Hugo conductor
Fiori, Pamela publishing executive, magazine editor
Fiorillo, John A(nthony) health care executive
First, Harry legal educator
Fischer, Carl graphic designer, photographer
Fischler, Stan sportswriter, sportscaster
Fischman, Bernard D. lawyer
Fishbein, Peter Melvin lawyer
Fisher, Ann Bailen lawyer
Fisher, Arthur magazine editor
Fisher, Bennett Lawson investment executive
†Fisher, Edward Abraham cardiologist, educator
Fisher, Florence Anna association executive, author, lecturer
Fisher, Gary Alan publishing executive
Fisher, Jules Edward producer, lighting designer, theatre consultant
Fisher, Richard B. investment banker
Fisher, Robert Abel advertising executive
Fisher, Robert I. lawyer
Fishman, Fred Norman lawyer
Fishman, Mitchell Steven lawyer
Fiske, Robert Bishop, Jr. lawyer
Fitch, James Marston architectural preservationist, architectural historian, critic
FitzGerald, Gerald P. state agency executive
Fitzpatrick, Joseph Mark lawyer
†Fitzsimmons, Sophie Sonia interior designer
Fiumefreddo, Charles A. investment management company executive
Flack, Roberta singer
Flaherty, Tina Santi corporate communications executive
Flaherty, William E. chemicals and metals company executive
Flanagan, Dennis journalist
Flanagan, William Francis writer and editor
Flanigan, Peter Magnus investment banker
Fleder, Robert Charles lawyer
Fleischer, Arthur, Jr. lawyer
Fleischer, Joseph Linden architect
Fleischman, Albert Sidney (Sid Fleischman) writer
Fleischman, Edward Hirsh lawyer
Fleischman, Lawrence Arthur art dealer, publisher, consultant
Fleming, Alice Carew Mulcahey (Mrs. Thomas J. Fleming) author
Fleming, Peter Emmet, Jr. lawyer
Fleming, Renée L. opera singer
Fleming, Thomas James writer
Fletcher, Anthony L. lawyer
Fletcher, George P. law educator
Fletcher, Harry George, III curator
Fletcher, Mary Lee business executive
Fletcher, Raymond Russwald, Jr. lawyer
Fleur, Mary Louise legal administrator
Flexner, James Thomas author
†Flicker, John foundation executive
Flint, George Squire lawyer
Flom, Joseph Harold lawyer
Florio, Steven T. magazine executive
Florio, Thomas magazine publisher
Flugger, Penelope Ann banker
Flumenbaum, Martin lawyer
Flynn, George William chemistry educator, researcher
†Flynn-Connors, Elizabeth Kathryn editor
Fodor, Susanna Serena lawyer
Foerst, John George, Jr. fundraising executive
Fogel, Irving Martin consulting engineer
Fogg, Blaine Viles lawyer
Fogge, Len advertising executive
Foley, Kathleen M. neurologist, educator, researcher
Fondiller, David Stewart journalist
Foner, Eric historian, educator
Fontana, John Arthur employee benefits specialist
Fontana, Thomas Michael producer, scriptwriter
Fontana, Vincent Robert lawyer
Foote, Horton playwright, scriptwriter
Forbes, Christopher (Kip Forbes) publisher
Forbes, Colin Ames graphic design consultant
Forbes, John Francis federal government executive
Forbes, Steve (Malcolm Stevenson Forbes, Jr.) publishing executive
Forbes, Timothy Carter publisher
Ford, Eileen Otte (Mrs. Gerard W. Ford) modeling agency executive
Ford, John Charles communications executive
Forden, Diane Claire magazine editor
Foreman, Laura dancer, choreographer, conceptual artist, writer, educator
Foreman, Richard theater director, playwright
Fornes, Maria Irene playwright, director
Forst, Judith Doris mezzo-soprano
Forstadt, Joseph Lawrence lawyer
Forster, Arnold lawyer, author
Fort, Randall Martin investment banking executive
Forte, Wesley Elbert insurance company executive, lawyer
Fortenbaugh, Samuel Byrod, III lawyer
Fortgang, Charles wholesale distribution executive
Fortner, Joseph Gerald surgeon, educator
Foscarinis, Rosa pediatrician, allergist
Foster, David Lee lawyer
Foster, James Henry advertising and public relations executive
Foster, Kim art dealer, gallery owner
Foulke, William Green, Jr. business executive
Fountain, Karen Schueler physician
Fowler, Henry Hamill investment banker
Fowler, Robert Ramsay Canadian government official
Fox, Arthur Charles physician, educator
Fox, Daniel Michael foundation administrator, author
Fox, Donald Thomas lawyer
Fox, Eleanor Mae Cohen lawyer, educator, writer
Fox, Jack Jay chemist, educator
Fox, Jeanne Marie lawyer
Fox, Mitchell magazine publisher
Fox, Paula (Mrs. Martin Greenberg) author
Fox, Sylvan journalist
Fox-Freund, Barbara Susan real estate executive
Foxman, Abraham H. advocacy organization administrator
Foxworth, Jo advertising agency executive
Frackman, Richard Benoit investment banker
Fraenkel, George Kessler chemistry educator
†Fragola, Joseph Ralph executive
Fraidin, Stephen lawyer
Fraiman, Genevieve Lam lawyer
France, Joseph David securities analyst
Francis, Charles K. medical educator
Francis, Dick (Richard Stanley Francis) novelist
Franck, Thomas Martin law educator
Frangopoulos, Zissimos A. banker
Frank, Elizabeth English literature, author
Frank, Frederick investment banker
Frank, James Aaron magazine editor, author
Frank, Lloyd lawyer, retired chemical company executive
Frank, Robert Allen advertising executive
Frankel, Benjamin Harrison lawyer
Frankel, Gene theater director, author, producer, educator
Frankel, Martin Richard statistician, educator, consultant
Frankel, Marvin E. lawyer
Frankel, Max journalist
Franken, Martin public relations company executive
Franklin, Blake Timothy lawyer
Franklin, Edward Ward international investment consultant, lawyer, actor
Franklin, Julius Harold political science educator
Franklin, Phyllis professional association administrator
Franks, Lucinda Laura journalist
Frantz, Andrew Gibson physician, educator
Frantz, Jack Thomas advertising executive
Frantzen, Henry Arthur investment company executive
Franz, Donald Eugene, Jr. merchant banker, security analyst
Franzen, Ulrich J. architect
Frassetto, Floriana Domina performer, choreographer, costume designer
Frawley, Sean Paul publishing executive
†Frazier, Ian writer
Frazza, George S. lawyer, business executive
Fredericks, Wendy Ann graphic designer
Fredericks, Wesley Charles, Jr. lawyer
Freed, James Ingo architect
Freed, Stanley Arthur museum curator
Freedberg, David Adrian art educator, historian
Freedberg, Irwin Mark dermatologist
Freedman, Albert Z. publishing company executive
Freedman, Alfred Mordecai psychiatrist, educator
Freedman, Audrey Willock economist
Freedman, Gerald M. lawyer
Freedman, Helen Edelstein justice
Freedman, Michael Leonard geriatrician, educator
Freeman, David John lawyer
Freeman, Elaine Lavalle sculptor
Freeman, Mark artist
Freiberg, Lowell Carl financial executive
Freid, Jacob association executive, educator
Freilicher, Morton lawyer
Freitas, Elizabeth Frances lawyer
Freizer, Louis A. radio news producer
French, Harold Stanley food company executive
French, John, III lawyer
French, Stephanie Taylor arts administrator
Freudenberger, Herbert Justin psychoanalyst
Freudenheim, Milton B. journalist
Freudenheim, Tom Lippmann museum administrator
Freudenstein, Ferdinand mechanical engineering educator
Freund, Fred A. lawyer
Freund, Gerald foundation administrator
Freund, William Curt economist
Frey, Andrew Lewis lawyer
Fribourg, Michel international agribusiness executive
Fricklas, Michael David lawyer
Fried, Albert, Jr. investment banker
Fried, Burton Theodore lawyer
Fried, Donald David lawyer
Fried, Walter Jay lawyer
Friedberg, Barry Sewell investment banker
Friedberg, Marvin Paul landscape architect
Friedenberg, Daniel Meyer financial investor
Friedewald, William Thomas physician
Friedheim, Eric Arthur publisher, editor
Friedhoff, Arnold J. psychiatrist, medical scientist
Friedlander, Ralph thoracic and vascular surgeon
†Friedman, Adam Issac public relations consultant
Friedman, Alan Herbert ophthalmologist
Friedman, Alan Roy lawyer
Friedman, Alvin Edward investment executive
Friedman, Bart lawyer
Friedman, B(ernard) H(arper) writer
Friedman, Elaine Florence lawyer
Friedman, Emanuel A. medical educator
Friedman, Frances public relations executive
Friedman, Ira Hugh surgeon
Friedman, J. Roger publisher
Friedman, Robert Laurence lawyer
Friedman, Samuel Selig lawyer
Friedman, Stephen James lawyer
Friedman, Victor Stanley lawyer
Friedman, Wilbur Harvey lawyer
Friend, David publishing executive
Friesner, Richard A. chemistry educator
Frimerman, Leslie financial services company executive
Frischling, Carl lawyer
Frisell-Schröder, Sonja Bettie opera producer, stage director
Fritz, Maura Kathleen magazine editor
Froewiss, Kenneth Clark corporate finance executive
Frommer, Henry financial executive
Frost, Ellen Elizabeth psychologist
Frost, William Lee lawyer
Fruitman, Frederick Howard investment banker
Frumkin, Allan art dealer
Fry, Morton Harrison, II lawyer
Frye, Clayton Wesley, Jr. financial executive
Fryer, Judith Dorothy lawyer
Fryer, Robert Sherwood theatrical producer
Fuchs, Anna-Riitta medical educator, scientist
Fuchs, Anne Sutherland magazine publisher
Fugate, Judith ballet dancer
Fugate-Wilcox, Tery artist
Fuhrer, Arthur K. lawyer
Fuks, Zvi Y. medical educator
Fuld, James Jeffrey lawyer
Fuld, Stanley Howells lawyer
Fulghum, Robert L. author, lecturer
†Fuller, Bonnie editor
Fuller, Charles playwright
Fulrath, Irene corporate sales and marketing executive
Furman, Anthony Michael public relations executive
Furman, Roy L. investment banker
Furmanski, Philip cancer research scientist
Fursland, Richard Curtis international business executive
Fuster, Valentin cardiologist, educator
Fuzesi, Stephen, Jr. lawyer, communications executive
Gabay, Donald David lawyer
Gable, Carol Brignoli health economics researcher
Gabrilove, Jacques Lester physician

Gainsburg, Roy Ellis publishing executive
Galanopoulos, Kelly biomedical engineer
Galant, Herbert Lewis lawyer
Galanter, Eugene psychologist, educator
Galanter, Marc psychiatrist, educator
Galassi, Jonathan White book publishing company executive
Galazka, Jacek Michal publishing company executive
Galbraith, Evan Griffith investment banker
Galin, Miles A. ophthalmologist, educator
Gallagher, Edward Peter foundation administrator
Gallagher, Terence Joseph lawyer
Gallagher, Thomas Joseph banker
Gallantz, George Gerald lawyer
Gallick, Sarah Patricia editor, writer
Gallo, Pia art historian
Gallo, William Victor cartoonist
Galotti, Ronald A. magazine publisher
Galway, James flutist
Gambee, Robert Rankin investment banker
Gamble, Harry T. professional football team executive
Gamble, Theodore Robert, Jr. investment banker
Gamboni, Ciro Anthony lawyer
Gambro, Michael S. lawyer
Gammill, Lee Morgan, Jr. insurance company executive
Gamson, Annabelle dancer
Gandolf, Raymond L. media correspondent
Gans, Herbert J. sociologist, educator
Gans, Walter Gideon lawyer
Gant, Donald Ross investment banker
Gantman, Geraldine Ann marketing executive, consultant
Ganz, Howard Laurence lawyer
Ganzi, Victor Frederick lawyer
Garabedian, Paul Roesel mathematics educator
Garagiola, Joe sports broadcaster
Garba, Edward Aloysius financial executive
Garber, Robert Edward lawyer, insurance company executive
Garcia, Josefina Margarita dancer, nurse, educator
Gardiner, E. Nicholas P. executive search executive
Gardino, Vincent Anthony broadcast executive
†Gardner, Andre V. broadcast executive
Gardner, James Richard pharmaceutical company executive
Gardner, Janet Paxton journalist, video producer
Gardner, Ralph David advertising executive
Gardner, Richard Newton diplomat, lawyer, educator
Garfinkel, Barry Herbert lawyer
†Garfinkel, Lee advertising agency executive
Garland, Sylvia Dillof lawyer
Garner, Albert Headden investment banker
Garratt, Graham publishing executive
Garrett, Robert financial advisory executive
Garrison, John Raymond organization executive
Gartner, Alan P. university official, author
Gartner, Murray lawyer
Garvey, Michael Steven veterinarian, educator
Garvey, Richard Anthony lawyer
Garvin, Andrew Paul information company executive, author, consultant
Gassel, Philip Michael lawyer
Gatch, Milton McCormick, Jr. library administrator, clergyman, educator
Gatje, Robert Frederick architect
Gatting, Carlene J. lawyer
Gatto, John Taylor educational consultant, writer
Gaudieri, Alexander V. J. museum director
Gaudieri, Millicent Hall association executive
Gaughan, Eugene Francis accountant
Gavrity, John Decker insurance company executive
Gayle, Crystal singer
Gaylin, Willard physician, educator
Gazzara, Ben actor
Gebbie, Kristine Moore health science educator, health official
Gechtoff, Sonia artist
Geer, John Farr religious organization administrator
Geeslin, Bailey M. telecommunications company executive
Gehringer, Richard George publishing executive
Geier, Philip Henry, Jr. advertising executive
Geiger, H. Jack medical educator
Geiser, Elizabeth Able publishing company executive
Geismar, Thomas H. graphic designer
Geissbuhler, Stephan graphic designer
Gelb, Arthur newspaper editor
Gelb, Bruce S. city commissioner
Gelb, Harold Seymour industrial company executive, investor
Gelb, Judith Anne lawyer
Gelb, Leslie Howard organization president, lecturer
Gelber, Jack playwright, director
Gelfand, Neal oil company executive
Gelfman, Robert William lawyer
Geller, Jeffrey Lawrence financier
Geller, Robert James advertising agency executive
Gellert, Michael Erwin investment banker
Gellhorn, Alfred physician, educator
Geltzer, Sheila Simon public relations executive
Genaro, Donald Michael industrial designer
Genkins, Gabriel physician
Genova, Joseph Steven lawyer
Geoghegan, Patricia lawyer
Georgantas, Aristides William banking executive
George, Beauford James, Jr. lawyer, educator
Georges, Paul Gordon artist
Georgescu, Peter Andrew advertising executive
Georgopoulos, Maria architect
Geraghty, Kenneth George financial services company executive
Gerard, Whitney Ian lawyer
Gerard-Sharp, Monica Fleur communications executive
Gerber, Robert Evan lawyer
Gerdts, William Henry art history educator
Germano, William Paul publisher
Gershengorn, Marvin Carl physician, scientist, educator
†Gershon, Bernard broadcast executive
Gerson, Irwin Conrad advertising executive
Gerson, Robert Elisha periodical editor-in-chief
Gersony, Welton Mark physician, pediatric cardiologist, educator
Gersten, Bernard theatrical producer
Gertler, Menard M. physician, educator
Gessner, Charles Herman apparel company executive
Getnick, Neil Victor lawyer
Gewirtz, Gerry editor
Ghiaurov, Nicolai opera singer
Giannetti, Thomas Leonard lawyer
Gibbs, Jamie landscape architect, interior designer
Gibbs, Joe Jackson former professional football coach, broadcaster, professional sports team executive
Gibbs, L(ippman) Martin lawyer
Giblin, James Cross author, editor
Gibson, Charles DeWolf broadcast journalist
Gibson, Ralph H(olmes) photographer
Gibson, William Shepard insurance executive
Giddins, Gary Mitchell music critic, columnist
Gifford, Frank Newton sportscaster, commentator, former professional football player
Gifford, Kathie Lee television personality, singer
Gifford, William C. lawyer
Gilbert, Phil Edward, Jr. lawyer
Giles, Robert Hartmann foundation executive
Gilinsky, Stanley Ellis department store executive
Gill, Ardian C. actuary, photographer
Gill, Brendan writer
Gill, E. Ann lawyer
Gillers, Stephen law educator
Gillespie, George Joseph, III lawyer
Gillespie, John Thomas university administrator
Gilliatt, Neal advertising executive, consultant
Gilman, Richard H. newspaper publishing executive
Gilmore, Jennifer A. computer systems analyst
Gilmore, Louise Jacobson labor union director
Gilmore, Robert Gordon retired insurance company executive
Giniger, Kenneth Seeman publisher
Ginsberg, David Lawrence architect
Ginsberg, Ernest lawyer, banker
Ginsberg, Frank Charles advertising executive
Ginsberg, Hersh Meier rabbi, religious organization executive
†Ginsberg, Robert Jason thoracic surgeon
Ginsberg-Fellner, Fredda pediatric endocrinologist, researcher
Ginsburg, Sigmund G. museum administrator
Ginter, Valerian Alexius urban historian, educator
Ginzberg, Eli economist, emeritus educator, government consultant, author
Giraldi, Robert Nicholas film director
Girden, Eugene Lawrence lawyer
Giroux, Robert editor, book publisher, author
Gisondi, John Theodore theater and television design
Gissler, Sigvard Gunnar, Jr. journalism educator, former newspaper editor
Gitelson, Susan Aurelia business executive, civic leader
Gitner, Gerald L. aviation and investment banking executive
Gitter, Max lawyer
Gitterman, Alex social work educator
Gittler, Wendy artist, art historian, writer
Giuliani, Rudolph W. mayor, former lawyer
Gladstone, William Louis accountant
Glaser, Milton graphic designer and illustrator
Glass, David Carter psychology educator
Glass, Philip composer, musician
Glasser, Ira Saul civil liberties organization executive
Glassgold, Alfred Emanuel physicist, educator
Glassman, Alexander Howard psychiatrist, researcher
Glassman, Urania Ernest social worker, educator
Glazer, Esther violinist
Glekel, Jeffrey Ives lawyer
Glicksman, Eugene Jay lawyer
Glickstein, Steven lawyer
Glissant, Edouard Mathieu French language educator, writer
Globus, Dorothy Twining museum director
Glos, Margaret Beach real estate company executive, developer
Glover, Savion actor, dancer
Gluck, Carol history educator
Glynn, Gary Allen pension fund executive
Glynn, Robert lawyer, foundation chairman
Gnehm, Edward W., Jr. ambassador
Gochberg, Thomas real estate investor, financial executive
Goddess, Lynn Barbara commercial real estate broker
Godman, Gabriel Charles pathology educator
Goelet, Robert G. corporate executive
Goertz, Augustus Frederick, III artist
Goetz, Maurice Harold lawyer
Gold, Albert artist
Gold, Christina A. cosmetics company executive
Gold, Jay D. broadcasting company executive
Gold, Jeffrey Mark investment banker, financial adviser
Gold, Leonard Singer librarian, translator
Gold, Mari S. public relations executive
Gold, Martin Elliot lawyer, educator
Gold, Simeon lawyer
Gold, William Elliott health care management consultant
Goldberg, David lawyer, law educator
Goldberg, David Alan investment banker, lawyer
Goldberg, Edward L. financial services executive
Goldberg, Gary David producer, writer
Goldberg, Harold Howard psychologist, educator
Goldberg, Jane G. psychoanalyst
Goldberg, Sidney editor
Goldberg, Victor Paul law educator
Goldberger, Paul Jesse architecture critic, writer, educator, editor
Goldblatt, David Ira lawyer
Goldblatt, Eileen Witzman arts administrator, executive director
Golde, David William physician, educator
Golden, Arthur F. lawyer
Golden, Robert Charles brokerage executive
Golden, Soma newspaper editor
Golden, William Theodore trustee, corporate director
Goldenberg, Charles Lawrence real estate company executive
Goldenberg, Marvin Manus pharmacologist, pharmaceutical developer
Goldfarb, Donald industrial engineering educator
Goldin, Leon artist, educator
Goldman, Donald Howard lawyer
Goldman, James playwright, screenwriter, novelist
Goldman, Lawrence Saul lawyer
Goldman, Leo psychologist, educator
Goldman, Marvin Gerald lawyer
Goldman, Robert Irving financial services company executive
Goldmark, Peter Carl, Jr. foundation executive
Goldmark, Peter Francis banker
Goldrich, Stanley Gilbert optometrist
Goldschmid, Harvey Jerome law educator
Goldschmidt, Charles advertising agency executive
Goldschmidt, Robert Alphonse financial executive
Goldsmith, Caroline L. arts executive
Goldsmith, Gerald P. lawyer
Goldsmith, Lee Selig lawyer, physician
Goldsmith, Merwin actor, theater director
Goldsmith, Robert Lewis youth association magazine executive
Goldsmith, Stanley Joseph nuclear medicine physician, educator
Goldstein, Alvin lawyer
Goldstein, Bernard Herbert lawyer
Goldstein, Charles Arthur lawyer
Goldstein, Fred accountant
Goldstein, Gary S. executive recruiter
Goldstein, Howard Warren lawyer
Goldstein, Lisa Joy writer
Goldstein, Marc microsurgeon, urology educator, academic administrator
Goldstein, Marcia Landweber lawyer
Goldstein, Menek neurochemistry educator
Goldstein, Norm editor, writer
Goldstone, Steven F. consumer products company executive
Gollin, Albert Edwin media research executive, sociologist
Gollob, Herman Cohen retired publishing company, editor
Golomb, Frederick Martin surgeon, educator
Golson, George Barry editor
Golub, Gerald Leonard accounting company executive
Golub, Harvey financial services company executive
Golub, Leon Albert artist
Gomez, Francis D(ean) corporate executive, former foreign service officer
Gomory, Ralph Edward mathematician, manufacturing company executive, foundation executive
†Gong, Li actress
Gonzalez, Eugene Robert investment banker
Gooch, Anthony Cushing lawyer
Goodacre, Jill model
Goodale, James Campbell lawyer, media executive, television producer/host
Goodale, Toni Krissel development consultant
Goode, Richard Stephen pianist, educator
Goodfriend, Herbert Jay lawyer
Goodhartz, Gerald law librarian
Goodkind, Louis William lawyer
Goodman, Gary A. lawyer
Goodman, George Jerome Waldo (Adam Smith) author, television journalist, editor
Goodman, Jordan Elliot journalist
Goodman, Roger Mark television director
Goodrich, James Tait neuroscientist, pediatric neurosurgeon
Goodridge, Allan D. lawyer
Goodstein, Les newspaper publishing executive
Goodstone, Edward Harold retired insurance company executive
†Goodwill, George Walton hospital administrator
Goodwin, Bernard lawyer, executive, educator
Goodwin, Todd banker
Goott, Alan F(ranklin) lawyer
Gordevitch, Igor publishing company executive
Gordimer, Nadine author
Gordon, David playwright, director, choreographer
Gordon, David Jamieson tenor
Gordon, Janine M. advertising agency executive
Gordon, Jeffrey Neil law educator
Gordon, Mary Catherine author
Gordon, Michael Mackin lawyer
Gordon, Nicole Ann lawyer
Goren, Arnold Louis educator, former university official
Gorewitz, Rubin Leon accountant, financial consultant
Gorlin, Richard physician, educator
Gorup, Gregory James marketing executive
Goss, Mary E. Weber sociology educator
Gossage, Wayne library director, management consultant, entrepreneur, executive recruiter
Gossett, Oscar Milton advertising executive
Gossett, Robert Francis, Jr. merchant banker
Gotschlich, Emil Claus physician, educator
Gottesman, David Sanford investment executive
Gotthoffer, Lance lawyer
Gottlieb, Jerrold Howard advertising executive
Gottlieb, Morton Edgar theatrical and film producer
Gottlieb, Paul publishing company executive
Gottlieb, Paul Mitchel lawyer
Gottlieb, Robert Adams publisher
Gotto, Antonio Marion, Jr. internist, educator
Gotts, Ilene Knable lawyer
Gottschall, Edward Maurice graphic arts company executive
Gould, Eleanor Lois (Eleanor Gould Packard) editor, grammarian
Gould, Harry Edward, Jr. industrialist
Gould, Jay Martin economist, consultant
Gould, Milton Samuel lawyer, business executive
Goulden, Joseph Chesley author
Goulianos, Konstantin physics educator
Gourdine, Simon Peter professional basketball executive
Gowens, Walter, II financial and business services executive
Graber, Edward Alex obstetrician, gynecologist, educator
Grace, Jason Roy advertising agency executive
Grad, Frank Paul lawyer
Graf, Peter Gustav accountant, lawyer
Graff, George Leonard lawyer
Graff, Randy actress
Graffeo, John Jude musician, actor
Graffin, Guillaume ballet dancer
Grafstein, Bernice physiology and neuroscience educator, researcher
Graham, Alma Eleanor religious magazine editor, writer, educational consultant
Graham, Jesse Japhet, II lawyer
Graham, Robert sculptor
Graifman, Brian Dale lawyer
Gralla, Lawrence publishing company executive
Gramatte, Joan Helen graphic designer, art director, photographer
Granik, Russell T. sports association executive
†Grann, Phyllis publisher, editor
Granoff, Gary Charles lawyer, investment company executive
Grant, Alfred David orthopaedic surgeon, educator
Grant, Cynthia D. writer
Grant, James Deneale health care company executive
Grant, Merrill Theodore producer
Grant, Stephen Allen lawyer
Grant, Virginia Annette newspaper editor, journalist
Grant, William Packer, Jr. banker
Grant, William Robert investment banker
Grashof, August Edward lawyer
Grasso, Richard A. stock exchange executive
Graves, Adam professional hockey player
Graves, Earl Gilbert publisher
Graves, Fred Hill librarian
Graves, Morris Cole artist
Gray, Ann Maynard broadcasting company executive
Gray, Arthur, Jr. investment counselor
Gray, Bradford Hitch health policy researcher
Gray, Diane dancer, choreographer
Gray, George mural painter
Gray, Robert Loren professional society administrator
Greaney, Patrick Joseph electronics industry executive
Greco, Jose choreographer
Green, Adolph playwright, lyricist
Green, Al soul and gospel singer
Green, Alvin lawyer, consultant
Green, Ashbel publishing executive, book editor
Green, Dan publishing company executive
Green, David Edward librarian, priest, translator
Green, David O. accounting educator, educational administrator
Green, George Joseph publishing executive
Green, Jack Peter pharmacology educator, medical scientist
Green, Maurice Richard neuropsychiatrist
Green, Miriam Blau psychologist
Green, Robert S. lawyer
†Green, Rosario United Nations official
Greenawalt, Peggy Freed Tomarkin advertising executive
Greenawalt, Robert Kent lawyer, law educator
Greenawalt, William Sloan lawyer
Greenbaum, Maurice Coleman lawyer
Greenberg, Alan Courtney (Ace Greenberg) stockbroker
Greenberg, Carolyn Phyllis anesthesiologist, educator
Greenberg, Daniel Herbert lawyer
Greenberg, Gary Howard lawyer
Greenberg, Ira George lawyer
Greenberg, Jack lawyer, law educator
Greenberg, Jerome advertising executive
Greenberg, Joshua F. lawyer, educator
Greenberg, Maurice Raymond insurance company executive
Greenberg, Ronald David lawyer, law educator
Greenberger, Howard Leroy lawyer, educator
Greene, Adele S. management consultant
Greene, Bernard Harold lawyer
Greene, Ira S. lawyer
Greene, Kay C. psychologist, author
Greene, Richard H. journalist
Greenfield, Bruce Paul investment analyst, biology researcher
Greenfield, Gordon Kraus software company executive
Greenfield, (Henry) Jeff news analyst
Greenfield, Seymour Stephen mechanical engineer
Greengard, Paul neuroscientist
Greenland, Leo advertising executive
Greenstein, Abraham Jacob mortgage company executive, accountant
Greer, Allen Curtis, II lawyer
Greer, James Alexander, II lawyer
Grefé, Richard graphic design executive
Gregg, Donald Phinney federal agency administrator, lecturer
Gregg, Robert Thomson lawyer
Greilsheimer, James Gans lawyer
Grein, Richard Frank bishop, pastoral theology educator
Greiner, Stephen W. lawyer
Grenquist, Peter Carl publishing executive
Gretzky, Wayne Douglas professional hockey player
Grey, Linda publishing company executive
Griefen, John Adams artist, educator
Griesa, Thomas Poole federal judge
†Griffin, Dan radio station executive
Griffin, Kelly Ann public relations executive, consultant
Griffith, Alan Richard banker
Griffith, Katherine Scott communications executive
Griffiths, Sylvia Preston physician
Grigsby, Henry Jefferson, Jr. editor
Grillo, Joann Danielle mezzo-soprano
Grimaldi, Nicholas Lawrence social services administrator
Grinnell, Helen Dunn musicologist, arts administrator
Grisham, John writer
Grisi, Jeanmarie Conte finance executive
Grizzard, George actor
Groban, Robert Sidney, Jr. lawyer
Groberg, James Jay information sciences company executive
Gromada, Thaddeus V. historian, administrator
†Grooms, Red artist
Gropp, Louis Oliver editor in chief
Gropper, Allan Louis lawyer
Grose, William Rush publishing executive
Groseclose, Everett Harrison editor
Gross, Abraham rabbi, educator
Gross, Amy publishing executive
Gross, Ernest Arnold lawyer
Gross, Jonathan Light computer scientist, mathematician, educator
Gross, Lawrence Robert manufacturing executive
Gross, Richard Benjamin lawyer
Gross, Steven Ross lawyer
Grossman, Dan Steven lawyer
Grossman, Jack advertising agency executive
Grossman, Janice publisher
Grossman, Nancy artist
Grossman, Sanford lawyer
Grove, Barry theater executive
Groves, Ray John accountant
Grumbach, Doris novelist, editor, critic, educator, bookseller
Grunberger, Dezider biochemist, researcher
Grune, George Vincent publishing company executive
Grunes, Robert Lewis consulting engineer company executive
Grunewald, Raymond Bernhard lawyer
†Grunfeld, Ernie professional sports team executive
Grunstein, Leonard lawyer
Gruson, Michael lawyer
Gruss, Martin David private investor
Gruver, William Rolfe investment banker
Guare, John playwright
Guccione, Robert Charles Joseph Edward Sabatini publisher
Gudas, Lorraine Jean biochemist, molecular biologist, educator
Guenther, Jack Donald banker
Guenther, Paul Bernard volunteer
Guettel, Henry Arthur retired arts executive
Gugel, Craig Thomas advertising and new media executive
Guggenheim, Martin Franklin law educator
Guida, Peter Matthew surgeon, educator

Hunter-Bone, Maureen Claire magazine editor
Hunter-Stiebel, Penelope art historian, art dealer
Huntington, Lawrence Smith investment banker
Hupp, Robert Martin artistic director, educator
Hupper, John Roscoe lawyer
Hurewitz, J(acob) C(oleman) retired international relations educator, author, consultant
Hurley, Cheryl Joyce book publishing executive
Hurlock, James Bickford lawyer
Hurst, Robert Jay securities company executive
Hurwitz, Sol business policy organization executive
Hutchings, Peter Lounsbery insurance company executive
Hutner, Seymour Herbert microbiologist, protozoologist
Hutsaliuk, Liuboslav artist
Hutter, Rudolf Gustav Emil physics educator
Hutton, Ernest Watson, Jr. urban designer, city planner
Huxtable, Ada Louise architecture critic
Hwang, David Henry playwright, screenwriter
Hyde, David Rowley lawyer
Hyman, Allen Irwin physician
Hyman, Bruce Malcolm ophthalmologist
Hyman, Jerome Elliot lawyer
Hyman, Morton Peter shipping company executive
Hyman, Seymour capital and product development company executive
Hymes, Norma internist
Iakovos, (Demetrios A. Coucouzis) archbishop
Ianni, Francis Anthony James anthropologist, psychoanalyst, educator
Iannuzzi, John Nicholas lawyer, author, educator
Ichel, David W. lawyer
Idzik, Daniel Ronald lawyer
†Ienner, Don music company executive
Iger, Robert A. broadcast executive
Ilacqua, Rosario S. securities analyst
Ilson, Bernard public relations executive
Imparato, Anthony Michael vascular surgeon, medical educator, researcher
Impellizzeri, Anne Elmendorf insurance company executive, social services executive
Imperato-McGinley, Julianne Leone endocrinologist, educator
†Imus, Don radio host
Incandela, Gerald Jean-Marie artist
Inez, Colette poet
Ingraham, John Wright banker
Ingram, Samuel William, Jr. lawyer
Innis, Roy Emile Alfredo organization executive
Insardi, Nina Elizabeth benefits administrator
Insel, Michael S. lawyer
Intriligator, Marc Steven lawyer
Iovenko, Michael lawyer
Ireland, Patrick artist
Isaacson, Allen Ira lawyer
Isaacson, Melvin Stuart library director
Isaacson, Walter Seff editor
Isay, Jane Franzblau publisher
Isay, Richard Alexander psychiatrist
Iselin, John Jay university president
Iselin, Sally Cary writer
Iseman, Joseph Seeman lawyer
Isenberg, Steven Lawrence law educator
Isogai, Masaharu women's apparel executive
Isquith, Fred Taylor lawyer
Issler, Harry lawyer
Istomin, Marta Casals performing arts administrator, former educator
Ivanick, Carol W. Trencher lawyer
Ivanov, Lyuben Dimitrov naval architecture researcher, educator
Ives, Colta Feller museum curator, educator
Ivory, James Francis film director
Ivy, Robert Adams, Jr. architect, editor-in-chief
Jacey, Charles Frederick, Jr. accounting company executive, consultant
Jacker, Corinne Litvin playwright
Jackson, Anne (Anne Jackson Wallach) actress
Jackson, Joe musician, singer, composer, songwriter
Jackson, Kate Morgan children's book editor
Jackson, Keith MacKenzie television commentator, writer, producer
Jackson, Kenneth Terry historian, educator
Jackson, Raymond Sidney, Jr. lawyer
Jackson, Reginald Martinez former professional baseball player
Jackson, Richard George advertising agency executive
Jackson, Thomas Gene lawyer
Jackson, Ward artist
Jackson, William Eldred lawyer
Jacob, Edwin J. lawyer
Jacob, Marvin Eugene lawyer
Jacobowitz, Harold Saul lawyer
Jacobs, Allan Joel gynecologist, administrator
Jacobs, Arnold Stephen lawyer
Jacobs, Dennis federal judge
Jacobs, Jane Brand lawyer
Jacobs, Jim playwright, composer, lyricist, actor
Jacobs, Marisa Frances lawyer
Jacobs, Mark Neil financial services corporation executive, lawyer
Jacobs, Robert Alan lawyer
Jacobsen, Theodore H. (Ted H. Jacobsen) labor union official, educator
Jacobson, Gaynor I. retired association executive
Jacobson, Jerold Dennis lawyer
Jacobson, Sandra W. lawyer
Jacoby, A. James securities brokerage firm executive
Jacoby, Jacob consumer psychology educator
Jacoby, Robert Harold management consulting executive
Jacqueney, Stephanie A(lice) lawyer
Jacquette, Yvonne Helene artist
Jaffe, Alan Steven lawyer
Jaffe, Fredrick F. surgeon
Jaffe, Susan ballerina
Jaffe, William J(ulian) industrial engineer, educator
Jaffin, Charles Leonard lawyer
Jagger, Mick (Michael Philip Jagger) singer, musician
Jahiel, Rene Ino physician
Jakes, John author
James, Gary Douglas biological anthropologist, educator, researcher
James, Hamilton Evans investment banking firm executive
James, Robert Leo advertising agency executive
Jameson, Richard magazine editor, film critic
Jamieson, Edward Leo magazine editor
Jamison, Jayne magazine publisher
Jamison, Judith dancer
Jander, Klaus Heinrich lawyer
Janeway, Elizabeth Hall author
Janiak, Anthony Richard, Jr. investment banker
Janney, Stuart Symington, III investment company executive
Janowitz, Henry David physician, researcher, medical educator
Janssen, Peter Anton magazine editor and publisher
Jarecki, Henry George physician, financial executive
Jarmusch, Jim director
Jaroff, Leon Morton magazine editor
Jarriel, Thomas Edwin correspondent
Jasper, Seymour lawyer
Jassy, Everett Lewis lawyer
Javits, Eric Moses lawyer
Javitt, Norman B. medical educator, researcher
Jefferies, Jack P. lawyer
Jefferson, Denise dance school director
Jefferson, Margo L. theater critic
Jelinek, Josef Emil dermatologist
Jelinek, Vera university director
Jellinek, George broadcast executive, writer, music educator
Jenkins, Paul artist
Jennings, Frank Gerard editor
Jennings, Peter Charles television anchorman
Jensen, Michael Charles journalist, lecturer, author
Jepson, Hans Godfrey investment company executive
Jerome, Fred Louis science organization executive
Jervis, Robert political science educator
Jessup, John Baker lawyer
Jewler, Sarah magazine editor
Jeydel, Richard K. lawyer
Jeynes, Mary Kay college dean
Jhabvala, Ruth Prawer author
Jibaja, Gilbert insurance company executive
Jinnett, Robert Jefferson lawyer
Joffe, Robert David lawyer
Johanos, Donald orchestra conductor
Johansen, John MacLane architect
Johns, Jasper artist
Johns, William Potter non-profit organization administrator
Johnsen, Niels Winchester ocean shipping company executive
Johnson, Barbara L. publishing executive
Johnson, Betsey Lee fashion designer
Johnson, Christian Carl equity analyst
Johnson, Clarke Courtney finance educator
Johnson, Douglas Wayne church organization official, minister
Johnson, Freda S. public finance consultant
Johnson, Harold Earl human resources specialist
Johnson, Horton Anton pathologist
Johnson, J. Chester financial executive, poet
Johnson, James M. orchestra executive
Johnson, John broadcast journalist
Johnson, John H. publisher, consumer products executive
Johnson, John William, Jr. executive recruiter
Johnson, Samuel Frederick English and literature educator emeritus
Johnson, Thomas Stephen banker
Johnson, Virginia Alma Fairfax ballerina
Johnston, Catherine V. magazine publisher
Jonas, Gilbert public relations and fund raising executive
Jonas, Ruth Haber psychologist
Jonas, Saran neurologist, educator
Jones, Abbott C. investment banking executive
Jones, Alex S. journalist, writer, broadcaster
Jones, Anne librarian
Jones, Barclay Gibbs, III investment banker
Jones, Bill T. dancer, choreographer
Jones, Caroline Robinson advertising executive
Jones, Cherry actress
Jones, David Milton economist, educator
Jones, David Rhodes newspaper editor
Jones, Diana Wynne writer
Jones, Douglas W. lawyer
Jones, Edward Powis artist
Jones, George country music singer, songwriter
Jones, Gwenyth Ellen director information systems
Jones, Gwyneth soprano
†Jones, K. C. professional basketball coach
Jones, Laurie Lynn magazine editor
Jones, Rickie Lee singer, songwriter
Jones, Roy professional boxer
Jones, Sally Daviess Pickrell writer
Jones, Thomas Owen computer industry executive
Jong, Erica Mann writer, poet
Jordan, John W., II holding company executive
Joseph, Ellen R. lawyer
Joseph, Frederick Harold investment banker
Joseph, Gregory Paul lawyer
Joseph, L. Anthony, Jr. lawyer
Joseph, Leonard lawyer
Joseph, Michael Sarkies accountant
Josephs, Ray public relations and advertising executive, writer, international relations consultant
Josephson, Marvin talent and literary agency executive
Josephson, William Howard lawyer
Joskow, Renee W. dentist, educator
Juceam, Robert E. lawyer
†Judge, Mike animator
Judson, Jeannette Alexander artist
Juliber, Lois manufacturing executive
Jung, Doris dramatic soprano
Juran, Sylvia Louise editor
Jurka, Edith Mila psychiatrist, researcher
Jurman, Elisabeth Antonie economist
Just, Gemma Rivoli retired advertising executive
Juszczyk, James Joseph artist
Kadar, Avraham immunologist
Kaden, Ellen Oran lawyer, broadcasting corporation executive
Kaden, Lewis B. law educator
Kael, Pauline film critic, author
Kagan, Julia Lee magazine editor
Kaggen, Lois Sheila non-profit organization executive
Kahan, Marlene professional association executive
Kahen, Harold I. lawyer
Kahn, Alan Edwin lawyer
Kahn, Alfred Joseph social worker and policy scholar, educator
Kahn, Anthony F. lawyer
Kahn, Jenette Sarah publishing company executive
Kahn, Laurence communications executive
Kahn, Leonard Richard communications and electronics company executive
Kahn, Norman pharmacology and dentistry educator
†Kahn, Peter R. publishing executive
Kahn, Richard Dreyfus lawyer
Kahn, Robert Theodore author, photographer
Kahn, Susan Beth artist
Kahn, Walter steel company executive
Kahn, Wolf artist
Kailas, Leo George lawyer
Kaish, Luise Clayborn sculptor, former educator
Kaish, Morton artist, educator
Kaku, Michio theoretical nuclear physicist
Kalajian, Donna publishing executive
Kalikow, Peter Stephen real estate developer, former newspaper owner, publisher
Kalish, Arthur lawyer
Kalish, Myron lawyer
Kallir, Jane Katherine art gallery director, author
Kalmanoff, Martin composer
Kalsner, Stanley pharmacologist, physiologist, educator
Kamali, Norma fashion designer
Kamen, Harry Paul life insurance company executive, lawyer
Kamerman, Sheila Brody social worker, educator
Kamin, Sherwin lawyer
Kaminer, Peter H. lawyer
Kaminsky, Arthur Charles lawyer
Kamlot, Robert performing arts executive
Kamm, Linda Heller lawyer
Kamsky, Leonard economist, retired manufacturing executive, financial advisor
Kan, Diana Artemis Mann Shu artist
Kander, John Harold composer
Kane, Daniel Hipwell lawyer
Kane, Herman William research company executive, political scientist
Kane, Jay Brassler banker
†Kane, Thomas Patrick broadcast executive
Kanick, Virginia radiologist
Kann, Peter Robert journalist, newspaper publishing executive
Kanner, Frederick W. lawyer
Kanof, Norman B. dermatologist
Kanovitz, Howard artist
Kanuk, Leslie Lazar management consultant, educator
Kapelman, Barbara Ann physician, educator
Kaplan, Carl Eliot lawyer
Kaplan, Harold Irwin psychiatrist, psychoanalyst, educator
Kaplan, Helene Lois lawyer
Kaplan, Joseph Solte lawyer
Kaplan, Keith Eugene insurance company executive, lawyer
Kaplan, Larry public relations executive
Kaplan, Leo Sylvan social scientist, former college administrator
Kaplan, Lewis A. judge
Kaplan, Madeline legal administrator
Kaplan, Mark Norman lawyer
Kaplan, Peter James lawyer
Kaplan, Phyllis computer artist, painter
Kaplan, Richard James producer, director, writer, educator, consultant
Kaplan, Robert Arthur trade association executive
†Kaplan, Roger F.S. writer, editor
Kappas, Attallah physician, medical scientist
†Kara, Gerald B. ophthalmologist
Karalekas, George Steven advertising agency executive, political consultant
Karan, Donna (Donna Faske) fashion designer
Karatz, William Warren lawyer
Karchin, Louis Samuel composer
Kardon, Janet museum director, curator
Kardon, Peter Franklin foundation administrator
Karls, John Spencer lawyer, accountant
Karmali, Rashida Alimahomed lawyer
Karol, Michael Alan editor
Karp, Marshall Warren creative director, writer
Karp, Martin Everett management consultant
Karpel, Craig S. journalist, editor
Karr, Norman trade association executive
Karsen, Sonja Petra retired Spanish educator
Kasinec, Edward Joseph library administrator
Kaskell, Peter Howard association executive, lawyer
Kaslick, Ralph Sidney dentist, educator
Kasowitz, Marc Elliot lawyer
Kassebaum, John Philip lawyer
Kassel, Catherine M. community and maternal-women's health nurse
Kassel, Virginia Weltmer television producer, writer
†Kastan, David S. university professor, writer
Katalinich, Peggy magazine editor
Katsh, Abraham Isaac university president emeritus, educator
Katsh, Salem Michael lawyer
Katsoyannis, Panayotis George biochemist, educator
Katz, Abraham retired foreign service officer
Katz, Alex artist
Katz, Daniel Roger conservation executive
Katz, Gregory lawyer
Katz, Hilda (Hulda Weber) artist, poet
Katz, Jerome Charles lawyer
Katz, Jose cardiologist, theoretical physicist, educator
Katz, Lois Anne internist, nephrologist
Katz, Marcia public relations company executive
Katz, Morris artist, entertainer
Katz, Ronald S. lawyer
Katz, Thomas J. chemistry educator
Katz, William Loren author
Katzman, Herbert Henry artist
Kauffmann, Stanley Jules author
Kaufman, Arthur Stephen lawyer
Kaufman, Bel author, educator
Kaufman, David Marc pediatric neurologist
Kaufman, Robert Max lawyer
Kaufman, Victor A. film company executive
Kaufmann, Ed lawyer
Kaufmann, Jack lawyer
Kaufmann, Mark Steiner banker
Kauth, Benjamin podiatric consultant
Kautz, James Charles investment banker
Kavaler, Thomas J. lawyer
Kavalerchik, Boris Yakovlevich computer systems developer, researcher
Kavee, Robert Charles insurance company executive
Kavesh, Robert A. economist, educator
Kavoukjian, Michael Edward lawyer
Kaye, Stephen Rackow lawyer
Kaye, Walter financial executive
Kazanjian, John Harold lawyer
Kazanjian, Shant religious organization administrator
Kazemi, Farhad political science educator
Kazin, Alfred writer
Keagy, Dorothy (Dotti Keagy) copywriter
Kean, Hamilton Fish lawyer
Keane, Bil cartoonist
Keany, Sutton lawyer
Kearse, Amalya Lyle federal judge
Keating, Charles actor
Keenan, John Fontaine federal judge
Keenan, Michael Edgar advertising executive
Keene, Donald writer, translator, language educator
Keeshan, Bob television producer, actor
Keevil, Philip Clement investment banker
Kehr, David film critic
Kehret, Peg writer
Keilin, Eugene Jacob investment banker, lawyer
Keill, Stuart Langdon psychiatrist
Keith, John Pirie urban planner
Keller, Bill journalist
Keller, Martha Ann artist, painter
Kelley, Sheila Seymour public relations executive, crisis consultant
Kellogg, Cal Stewart, II conductor, composer
Kellogg, David publisher
Kellogg, Herbert Humphrey metallurgist, educator
Kelly, Brian commodities trader
Kelly, Daniel Grady, Jr. lawyer
Kelly, James artist
Kelly, William Michael investment executive
Kelm, Linda opera singer
Kelman, Charles D. ophthalmologist, educator
Kelmenson, Leo-Arthur advertising executive
Kelne, Nathan editorial and public relations consultant, retired
Kempa, Gerald manufacturing company executive
Kempton, James Murray journalist
Kendall, Dolores Diane Pisapia artist, author, marketing executive
Kende, Christopher Burgess lawyer
Kenin, David broadcast executive
Kennedy, Daniel John national and international public relations consultant, communications executive
†Kennedy, John Fitzgerald, Jr. lawyer, magazine editor
Kennedy, John Joseph trade association executive
Kennedy, Michael John lawyer
Kennedy, Moorhead foundation administrator
Kenney, John Joseph lawyer
Kenny, Roger Michael executive search consultant
Kent, Deborah Warren hypnotherapist, consultant, lecturer
Kent, Julie ballet dancer, actress, model
Kent, Linda Gail dancer
Keogh, Kevin lawyer
Kepets, Hugh Michael artist
Keppler, Herbert publishing company executive
Kern, George Calvin, Jr. lawyer
Kern, Jerome H. lawyer
Kernis, Aaron Jay composer
Kernochan, John Marshall lawyer, educator
Kerz, Louise historian
Kess, Sidney lawyer, educator, accountant, author
Kessel, Mark lawyer
Kesselman, Mark Jonathan political science educator, writer
Kessler, Jeffrey L. lawyer
Kessler, Ralph Kenneth lawyer, manufacturing company executive
Kesting, Theodore magazine editor
Kevlin, Mary Louise lawyer
Khan, Chaka (Yvette Marie Stevens) singer
Khanzadian, Vahan tenor
Kheel, Theodore Woodrow arbitrator and mediator
Khuri, Nicola Najib physicist, educator
Kiam, Victor Kermit, II consumer products company executive
Kidd, John Edward lawyer, corporate executive
Kidd, Michael (Milton Greenwald) choreographer, director
Kiechel, Walter, III editor
Kiel, Catherine Ann public relations executive
†Kientz, Steven J. advertising executive
Kieren, Thomas Henry management consultant
Kies, David M. lawyer
Kifner, John William journalist, newspaper correspondent
Kilburn, H(enry) T(homas), Jr. investment banker
Kiley, Bruce Edward real estate financing executive
Kill, Lawrence lawyer
Killeffer, Louis MacMillan advertising executive
Kim, Se Jung civil engineer
Kimball, Richard Arthur, Jr. lawyer
Kimm, Michael S. lawyer
Kinberg, Judy television producer, director
Kind, Phyllis art gallery owner
King, B. B. (Riley B. King) singer, guitarist
King, Carole songwriter, singer
King, Edward Joseph clinical chemist, laboratory administrator
King, Henry Lawrence lawyer
King, Lawrence Philip lawyer, educator
King, Marvin research executive
King, Sheldon Selig medical center administrator, educator
King, Thomas physician, physiology educator
King, Thomas Creighton thoracic surgeon, educator
King, Woodie, Jr. producer, actor, director
Kingman, Dong artist, educator
Kingsley, April art critic, curator, historian, art educator
Kinnear, John Kenyon, Jr. architect
Kinnell, Galway poet, translator
Kinney, Stephen Hoyt, Jr. lawyer
Kinser, Richard Edward management consultant
Kinsman, Sarah Markham investment company executive
Kinsolving, Augustus Blagden lawyer
Kinsolving, Charles McIlvaine, Jr. marketing executive
Kinstler, Everett Raymond artist
Kinzler, Thomas Benjamin lawyer
Kirby, John Joseph, Jr. lawyer
Kirchner, Jake publishing executive
Kirk, Alexis Vemian designer
Kirk, Donald James accounting educator, consultant
Kirk, Susanne Smith editor
Kirsch, Arthur William investment consultant
Kirsch, Donald financial consultant, author
Kirschbaum, Myron lawyer
Kirschenbaum, Lisa L. portfolio manager, financial advisor
Kirshenbaum, Jerry editor, journalist
Kirshenbaum, Richard Irving public health physician
Kish, Joseph Laurence, Jr. management consultant
Kismaric, Carole Lee editor, writer, book packaging company executive
Kisner, Jacob poet, editor
Kissel, Howard William drama critic
Kissiloff, William industrial designer
Kistler, Darci Anna ballet dancer
Kito, Teruo former international trading company executive
Kivette, Ruth Montgomery English language educator
Klapper, Molly lawyer, educator
Klatell, Jack dentist
Kleckner, Robert George, Jr. lawyer
Klein, Calvin Richard fashion designer
Klein, Donald Franklin psychiatrist, scientist, educator

Li, David Wan-Cheng cell biologist
Libby, John Kelway financial services company executive
Libin, Paul theatre executive, producer
Lichtblau, John H. economist
Lichtenstein, Roy artist
Liddell, Donald Macy, Jr. retired investment counsellor
Lieberman, Charles economist
Lieberman, Harvey Michael hepatologist, gastroenterologist, educator
Lieberman, Seymour biochemistry educator emeritus
Liebermann, Lowell composer, pianist, conductor
Liebman, Lance Malcolm law educator, lawyer
Liebman, Theodore architect
Liebmann, Martha psychotherapist
Lifland, Burton R. federal judge
Lifland, William Thomas lawyer
Lifton, Robert Jay psychiatrist, author
Lifton, Robert Kenneth diversified companies executive
Lightman, Harold Allen marketing executive
Lilien, Mark Ira publishing, retailing and systems executive
Liman, Arthur Lawrence lawyer
Limbaugh, Rush Hudson radio and talk show host
Lin, Joseph Pen-Tze neuroradiologist, clinical administrator, educator
Lin, Maria C. H. lawyer
Lincoln, Edmond Lynch investment banker
Lindenbaum, Sandford Richard lawyer
Linder, Bertram Norman foundation administrator, horse-breeder, actor
Lindheim, James Bruce public relations executive
Lindquist, Richard James portfolio manager
Lindsay, George Peter lawyer
Lindskog, David Richard lawyer
Lingeman, Richard Roberts editor, writer
Linn, Judy NMN photographer
Linney, Romulus author, educator
Linsenmeyer, John Michael lawyer
Lipkin, Martin physician, scientist
†Lipper, Kenneth investment banker, author, producer
Lipscomb, Thomas Heber, III information technology executive
Lipsey, Robert Edward economist, educator
Lipton, Charles public relations executive
Lipton, Charles Jules lawyer
Lipton, Joan Elaine advertising executive
Lipton, Lester ophthalmologist, entrepreneur
Lipton, Martin lawyer
Lipton, Robert Steven lawyer
†Liss, Walter C., Jr. television station executive
Liu, Brian Cheong-Seng urology and oncology educator, researcher
Liu, Hung-Ching medical educator
Livengood, Victoria Ann opera singer
Livingston, Jay Harold composer, lyricist
LL Cool J, (James Todd Smith) rap singer, actor
Llinás, Rodolfo Riascos medical educator, researcher
†Lobo, Rebecca basketball player
Localio, S. Arthur retired surgeon, educator
Lochner, Philip Raymond, Jr. lawyer
Lockshin, Michael Dan rheumatologist
Loeb, John Langeloth, Jr. investment counselor
Loeb, Marshall Robert journalist
Loeb, Peter Kenneth money manager
Loengard, John Borg photographer, editor
Loengard, Richard Otto, Jr. lawyer
†Logan, Douglas George service company executive
Logan, J. Murray investment manager
Logan, Vicki advertising executive
Lohf, Kenneth A. librarian, writer
Lois, George advertising agency executive
Lomas, Eric James investment banker
London, Herbert Ira humanities educator
Loney, Glenn Meredith drama educator
Long, David L. magazine publisher
Long, Elizabeth Valk magazine publisher
Longley, Marjorie Watters newspaper executive
Longstreth, Bevis lawyer
Loo, Marcus H. physician, educator
Loomis, Carol J. journalist
Loomis, Philip Clark investment executive
Loomis, Robert Duane publishing company executive, author
Lopez, Lourdes ballerina
Lopez, Ramon recording industry executive
Lorber, Barbara Heyman communications executive
Lorch, Ernest Henry lawyer
Lorch, Maristella De Panizza (Mrs. Inama von Brunnenwald) Romance languages educator, writer, lecturer
Lord, M. G. writer
Lord, Marvin apparel company executive
Lord Rosenthal, Shirley cosmetics magazine executive, novelist
Lore, Martin Maxwell lawyer
Lorenz, Lee Sharp cartoonist
Loring, John Robbins artist
Lortel, Lucille theatrical producer
LoSchiavo, Linda Bosco library director
Losee, Thomas Penny, Jr. publisher
Loss, Margaret Ruth lawyer
Loss, Stuart Harold financial executive
Lotas, Judith Patton advertising executive
Lotwin, Stanford Gerald lawyer
Loudon, Dorothy actress
Louis, Murray dancer, choreographer, dance teacher
Loveless, Patty (Patty Ramey) country music singer
Low, Anthony English language educator
Low, Barbara Wharton biochemist, biophysicist
Low, Richard H. broadcasting executive, producer
†Lowe, Kevin Hugh professional hockey player
Lowe, Mary Johnson federal judge
Lowen, Gerard Gunther mechanical engineering educator
Lowenfeld, Andreas Frank law educator, arbitrator
Lowenfels, Fred M. lawyer
Lowenfels, Lewis David lawyer
Lowenstein, Louis legal educator
Lowenthal, Constance art historian
Lowenthal, Jacob finance executive
Lowry, Glenn David art museum director
Lowry, William Ketchin, Jr. insurance company executive
Lowy, George Theodore lawyer
Lubetski, Edith Esther librarian
Lubkin, Virginia Leila ophthalmologist
Lubovitch, Lar dancer, choreographer
Lucander, Henry investment banker
Lucas, Christopher artist
Lucas, Henry Cameron, Jr. information systems educator, writer, consultant
Lucas, James E(vans) operatic director
†Lucca, Maria advertising executive
Luce, Charles Franklin former utilities executive, lawyer
Luce, Henry, III foundation executive
Lucht, John Charles management consultant, executive recruiter, writer
Luck, David Jonathan Lewis biologist, educator
Luders, Adam ballet dancer
Ludgin, Chester Hall baritone, actor
Luers, William Henry art museum administrator
Luftglass, Murray Arnold manufacturing company executive
Luke, John A., Jr. paper, packaging and chemical company executive
Luks, Allan Barry executive director
Lund, Peter Anthony broadcast executive
Lunden, Joan television personality
Lunding, Christopher Hanna lawyer
Lundquist, John Milton librarian, author, travel writer, photographer
Luntz, Maurice Harold ophthalmologist
Lupert, Leslie Allan lawyer
Lupkin, Stanley Neil lawyer
LuPone, Patti actress
Luria, Mary Mercer lawyer
Lusky, Louis legal educator
Lust, Herbert Cohnfeldt, II finance executive
Lustenberger, Louis Charles, Jr. lawyer
Lustgarten, Ira Howard lawyer
Lutringer, Richard Emil lawyer
Lynch, Gerald Weldon academic administrator, psychologist
Lynch, Gerard E. law educator
Lynch, William Dennis, Jr. broadcast journalist
Lynn, Theodore Stanley lawyer
Lynton, Harold Stephen lawyer
Lyon, Carl Francis, Jr. lawyer
†Lyon, Patty advertising executive
Lyons, John Matthew telecommunications executive, broadcasting executive
Lyons, Laurence securities executive
Ma, Yo-Yo cellist
Maas, Peter writer
Maas, Werner Karl microbiology educator
Macais, Tello Manuel diplomat
Macan, William Alexander, IV lawyer
Macchiarola, Frank Joseph academic administrator
Macdonald, Robert Rigg, Jr. museum director
Macero, Teo composer, conductor
Macer-Story, Eugenia Ann writer, artist
MacGowan, Sandra Firelli publishing executive, publishing educator
Machlin, Eugene Solomon metallurgy educator, consultant
Machlin, Milton Robert magazine editor, writer
Macioce, Frank Michael lawyer, financial services company executive
MacIver, Loren artist
Mack, Dennis Wayne lawyer
†Mack, John J. investment company executive
MacKay, Malcolm executive search consultant
MacKenzie, John Pettibone journalist
Mackey, Patricia Elaine librarian
Mackie, Robert Gordon costume and fashion designer
MacKinnon, John Alexander lawyer
MacKinnon, Roger Alan psychiatrist, educator
Mackler, Tina artist
Mac Namara, Donal Eoin Joseph criminologist
Macpherson, Elle model
MacRae, Cameron Farquhar, III lawyer
Macri, Theodore William book publisher
Macris, Michael lawyer
Macro, Lucia Ann editor
Macurdy, John Edward basso
Madden, Donald Paul lawyer
Madden, John Patrick lawyer
Madden, Michael Daniel finance company executive
Mader, Bryn John vertebrate paleontologist
Madonna, Jon C. accounting firm executive
Madsen, Loren Wakefield sculptor
Madsen, Stephen Stewart lawyer
Magdol, Michael Orin bank executive
Mager, Ezra Pascal automobile dealership executive
Maguire, Robert Alan Slavic languages and literatures educator
Mahon, Arthur J. lawyer
Mahoney, Margaret Ellerbe foundation executive
†Maiale, Nicholas F. healthcare communications executive
Maidman, Richard Harvey Mortimer lawyer
Mailer, Norman author
Mailer-Howat, Patrick Lindsay Macalpine investment banker
Majda, Andrew J. mathematician, educator
†Makovsky, Kenneth Dale public relations executive
Makrianes, James Konstantin, Jr. management consultant
Malamed, Seymour H. motion picture company executive
Maldonado-Bear, Rita Marinita economist, educator
Malefakis, Edward E. history educator
Maleska, Martin Edmund publishing executive
Malgieri, Nick chef, author, educator
Malin, Irving English literature educator, literary critic
Malina, Michael lawyer
Malino, John Gray real estate executive
Malitz, Sidney psychiatrist, educator, researcher
Malkin, Barry film editor, consultant
Malkin, Peter Laurence lawyer
Malkin, Stanley Lee neurologist
Malloy, William Michael book editor, reviewer, writer
Mallozzi, Cos M. public relations executive
Malone, Joseph Lawrence linguistics educator
Maloney, Michael Patrick lawyer, corporate executive
Malozemoff, Plato mining executive
Maltby, Richard Eldridge, Jr. theater director, lyricist
Mamlok, Ursula composer, educator
Mandel, Irwin Daniel dentist
Mandelstam, Charles Lawrence lawyer
Mandracchia, Violet Ann Palermo psychotherapist, educator
Maneker, Morton M. lawyer
Maney, Michael Mason lawyer
Mangan, Mona association executive, lawyer
Manger, William Muir internist
Manges, James Horace investment banker
Mango, Wilfred Gilbert, Jr. construction company executive
Manilow, Barry singer, composer, arranger
Mann, Philip Roy lawyer
Mann, Sally photographer
Mann, Theodore theatrical producer and artistic director
Manning, Burt advertising executive
Manning, Jack photographer, columnist, author
Manning, William Joseph lawyer
Manoff, Richard Kalman advertising executive, public health consultant, author
Mansi, Joseph Anneillo public relations company executive
Manski, Wladyslaw Julian microbiology educator, medical scientist
Mantle, Raymond Allan lawyer
Manton, Edwin Alfred Grenville insurance company executive
Manz, Johannes Jakob Swiss diplomat
Mapes, Glynn Dempsey newspaper editor
Maraynes, Allan Lawrence filmmaker, television producer
Marceau, Yvonne ballroom dancer
Marchi, Lorraine June social services executive
†Marchioni, Allen publishing company executive
Marcosson, Thomas I. service company executive
Marcus, Eric Peter lawyer
Marcus, Eric Robert psychiatrist
Marcus, Hyman business executive
Marcus, Maria Lenhoff lawyer, law educator
Marcus, Norman lawyer
Marcus, Steven dean, English educator
Marcusa, Fred Haye lawyer
Marcuse, Adrian Gregory academic administrator
Marder, John G. real estate investor, marketing consultant, corporate director
Marder, Michael Zachary dentist, researcher, educator
Mardin, Arif musician
Marella, Philip Daniel broadcasting company executive
Margaritis, John Paul public relations executive
Margolin, Arthur Stanley distillery company executive
Margolis, David I(srael) corporate executive
Marion, John Louis fine arts auctioneer and appraiser
Marisol, (Marisol Escobar) sculptor
Mark, Reuben consumer products company executive
Marke, Julius Jay law librarian, educator
Markle, Cheri Virginia Cummins nurse
Marks, Edward B. international social service administrator
Marks, Edwin S. investment company executive
Marks, Paul Alan oncologist, cell biologist, educator
Marlas, James Constantine holding company executive
Marlette, Douglas Nigel editorial cartoonist, comic strip creator
Marlin, Alice Tepper research organization administrator
Marlin, John Tepper economist, writer, consultant
Marlin, Kenneth Brian information and software company executive
Marlin, Richard lawyer
Marmer, Nancy editor
Marron, Donald Baird investment banker
Marron-Corwin, Mary-Joan neonatologist
Marsh, Cheryl Leppert marketing professional
Marsh, Jean Lyndsey Torren actress, writer
Marsh, William Laurence retired research pathology executive
Marshak, Hilary Wallach psychotherapist, owner
Marshall, Alton Garwood real estate counselor
Marshall, Daniel Stuart advertising executive
Marshall, Geoffrey university official
Marshall, John Patrick lawyer
Marshall, Sheila Hermes lawyer
Marshall, Susan choreographer
Marshall, Thomas Carlisle applied physics educator
Marston, Robert Andrew public relations executive
Martin, Elliot Edwards theatrical producer
Martin, George J., Jr. lawyer
Martin, John S., Jr. federal judge
Martin, Joseph Paul university department director
Martin, Judith Sylvia journalist, author
Martin, Malcolm Elliot lawyer
Martin, Mary-Anne art gallery owner
Martin, Michael Townsend racing horse stable executive, sports marketing executive
Martin, Paul Ross editor
Martin, Richard Harrison curator, art historian
Martin, Richard L. insurance executive
Martinez, Roman, IV investment banker
Martini, Richard K. theatrical producer
Martins, Nilas dancer
Martins, Peter ballet master, choreographer, dancer
Martone, Patricia Ann lawyer
Martz, Lawrence Stannard periodical editor
Marx, Owen Cox lawyer
Marzulli, John Anthony, Jr. lawyer
Masey, Jack exhibition designer
Masinter, Edgar Martin investment banker
Maslin, Janet film critic
Maslow, Melanie Jane physician
Maslow, Will lawyer, association executive
Mason, Bobbie Ann novelist, short story writer
Mason, Jackie comedian, actor
Massey, Stephen Charles auctioneer
Massis, Bruce Edward library director, media executive, consultant
Masters, Jon Joseph lawyer
Masterson, James Francis psychiatrist
Masur, Kurt conductor
Materna, Joseph Anthony lawyer
Mathers, William Harris lawyer
Mathews, Jack Wayne journalist, film critic
Mathews, Linda McVeigh newspaper editor
Mathews, Michael Stone investment banker
Matteson, William Bleecker lawyer
Matthews, Edward E. insurance company executive
Matthews, Edwin Spencer, Jr. lawyer
Matthews, Norman Stuart department store executive
Matthews, Westina Lomax finance and banking executive
Matthews, William Procter English educator
Mattson, Francis Oscar retired librarian and rare books curator
Mattson, Joy Louise oncological nurse
Matus, Wayne Charles lawyer
Matz, Robert internist, educator
Matzner, Chester Michael writer
Maubert, Jacques Claude headmaster
Maughan, Deryck C. investment banker
Maulsby, Allen Farish lawyer
Maupin, Armistead Jones, Jr. writer
Maurer, Gilbert Charles media company executive
Maurer, Jeffrey Stuart finance executive
Maxfield, Guy Budd lawyer, educator
Maxwell, Anders John investment banker
Maxwell, Carla Lena dancer, choreographer, educator
May, Elaine actress, theatre and film director
May, Gita French language and literature educator
May, William Frederick manufacturing executive
Mayer, Carl Joseph lawyer, town official
Mayerson, Philip classics educator
Mayerson, Sandra Elaine lawyer
Mayesh, Jay Philip lawyer
Maynard, John Rogers English educator
Maynard, Parrish ballet dancer
Maynard, Virginia Madden charitable organization executive
Mayor, Alfred Hyatt editor
Mazur, Jay J. trade union official
Mazza, Thomas Carmen lawyer
Mazzia, Valentino Don Bosco physician, educator, lawyer
Mazzilli, Paul John investment banker
Mazzo, Kay ballet dancer, educator
Mazzola, Anthony Thomas editor, art consultant, designer, writer
Mazzola, John William former performing arts center executive, consultant
McAniff, Nora P. publishing executive
McBride, Rodney Lester investment counselor
McBryde, Thomas Henry lawyer
McCabe, John Charles oral surgeon
McCaffrey, William Thomas financial services company executive
Mc Cann, John Joseph lawyer
McCarrick, Edward R. magazine publisher
Mc Carter, Thomas N., III investment counseling company executive
McCarthy, Denis artist, educator
McCarthy, Patrick magazine publishing executive
McCarthy, Robert Emmett lawyer
McCartin, Thomas Joseph advertising executive
McCarty, Maclyn medical scientist
McCaslin, Teresa Eve human resources executive
McCleary, Benjamin Ward investment banker
McClelland, Timothy Reid baseball umpire
McClimon, Timothy John lawyer
McClung, Richard Goehring lawyer
McCollum, Allan Lloyd artist
McCormack, Elizabeth J. foundation administrator
McCormack, John Joseph, Jr. insurance executive
McCormack, Thomas Joseph retired publishing company executive
McCormick, Donald E. librarian, archivist
McCormick, Hugh Thomas lawyer
Mc Cormick, Kenneth Dale retired editor
McCoy, Larry journalist
McCoy, Millington F. management recruitment company executive
McCrary, Eugenia Lester (Mrs. Dennis Daughtry McCrary) civic worker, writer
McCredie, James Robert fine arts educator
McCree, Donald Hanna, Jr. banker
Mc Crie, Robert Delbert editor, publisher, educator
Mc Crory, Wallace Willard pediatrician, educator
McCullough, David author
Mc Cullough, J. Lee industrial psychologist
McDarrah, Fred William photographer, editor, writer, photography reviewer
McDavid, William Henry lawyer
McDermott, Richard T. lawyer, educator
Mcdonald, Gregory Christopher author
McDonald, Thomas Paul controller
McDonell, Robert Terry magazine editor, novelist
McDonough, Mamie public relations executive
McDonough, William J. banker
McDormand, Frances actress
McEnroe, John Patrick, Jr. retired professional tennis player, commentator
McEwen, James publishing executive
McFadden, Mary Josephine fashion industry executive
Mc Fadden, Robert Dennis reporter
McFeely, William Drake publishing company executive
McFerrin, Bobby singer, musician, composer and conductor
McGanney, Thomas lawyer
McGarry, John Patrick, Jr. advertising agency executive
McGeady, Sister Mary Rose religious organization administrator, psychologist
McGill, Jay magazine publisher
Mc Gillicuddy, John Francis retired banker
Mc Ginnis, Arthur Joseph publisher
McGinnis, John Oldham lawyer, educator
McGivern, Diane nursing educator
Mc Goldrick, John Gardiner lawyer
McGovern, John Hugh urologist, educator
Mc Gowin, William Edward artist
McGrath, Eugene R. utility company executive
McGrath, Judith broadcast executive
†McGrath, Patrick J. advertising agency executive
McGrath, Thomas J. lawyer, writer, film producer
McGraw, Harold Whittlesey, Jr. publisher
†McGraw, Harold Whittlesey, III (Terry McGraw) financial services company executive
McGraw, Robert Pierce publishing executive
Mc Gruder, Stephen Jones portfolio manager
McHenry, Barnabas lawyer
McHugh, Caril Dreyfuss art dealer, gallery director, consultant
Mc Inerney, Denis lawyer
McIntyre, Thomas recording industry executive
McKay, Craig film editor
Mc Kay, Jim television sports commentator
†McKelvey, Andrew J. advertising executive
McKenna, Lawrence M. federal judge
Mc Kenna, Malcolm Carnegie vertebrate paleontologist, curator, educator
McKenna, Peter Dennis lawyer
McKenna, William Michael advertising executive
McKenzie, Kevin Patrick artistic director
McKenzie, Mary Beth artist
Mc Keown, William Taylor magazine editor, author
McKerrow, Amanda ballet dancer
McKesson, John Alexander, III international relations educator
McKinnon, Floyd Wingfield textile executive
Mc Kitrick, Eric Louis historian, educator
McLaughlin, Joseph lawyer
McLaughlin, Joseph Michael federal judge, law educator
McLaughlin, Mary Rittling magazine editor
McLaughlin, Michael John insurance company executive
Mc Lean, Don singer, instrumentalist, composer
Mc Lendon, Heath Brian securities investment company executive
McMahon, Colleen judge
McMeen, Albert Ralph, III writer, lecturer
McMeen, Elmer Ellsworth, III lawyer, guitarist
†McMorrow, Eileen editor periodical
McMullan, William Patrick, III investment banker
Mc Murtry, James Gilmer, III neurosurgeon

McMurtry, Larry Jeff author
McNally, John Joseph lawyer
McNally, Terrence playwright
Mc Namara, J(ohn) Donald retired lawyer, business executive
McNamara, John Jeffrey advertising executive
McNamara, Mary E. nonprofit executive, asset manager, minister
McNamee, Louise advertising agency executive
Mc Nicol, Donald Edward lawyer
McNutt, Charlie Fuller, Jr. bishop
Mc Pherson, Paul Francis publishing and investment banking executive
McQueeney, Henry Martin, Sr. publisher
McQuown, Judith Hershkowitz author, financial advisor
McSherry, William John, Jr. lawyer, consultant
McWilliam, Joanne Elizabeth religion educator
Meachin, David James Percy investment banker
Meadow, Lynne (Carolyn Meadow) theatrical producer and director
Meagher, James Proctor editor
Medenica, Gordon publisher
Medina, Standish Forde, Jr. lawyer
Mee, Charles L. playwright, historian, editor
Meek, Phillip Joseph communications executive
Meeks, Kenneth magazine editor
Mehta, A. Sonny publishing company executive
Mehta, Ved (Parkash) writer, literature and history educator
Meier, August historian, educator
Meier, Richard Alan architect
Meigher, S. Christopher, III communications and media investor
Meikle, Thomas Harry, Jr. retired neuroscientist, foundation administrator, educator
Meiklejohn, Donald Stuart lawyer
†Meiner, Howard advertising executive
Meisel, Louis Koenig art dealer, art historian, writer
Meisel, Martin English and comparative literature educator
Meisel, Perry English educator
Meisel, Steven advertising photographer
Meiselas, Susan Clay photographer
Meislich, Herbert chemistry educator emeritus
Mellencamp, John (John Cougar) singer, songwriter
Mellins, Robert B. pediatrician, educator
Melone, Joseph James insurance company executive
Meltzer, Milton author
Melvin, Russell Johnston magazine publishing consultant
Menack, Steven Boyd lawyer, mediator
Menaker, Ronald Herbert bank executive
Mencher, Melvin journalist, retired educator
Mendell, Oliver M. banking executive
Mendelson, Haim artist, educator, art gallery director
Menges, Carl Braun investment banker
Menk, Carl William executive search company executive
Menken, Alan composer
Menninger, Edward Joseph public relations executive
Menotti, Gian Carlo composer
Menschel, Richard Lee investment banker
Menschel, Robert Benjamin investment banker
Menuhin, Yehudi violinist
Meranus, Arthur Richard advertising agency executive
Merchant, Ismail Noormohamed film producer and director
Mercorella, Anthony J. lawyer, former state supreme court justice
Meron, Theodor law educator, researcher
Merow, John Edward lawyer
Merrifield, Robert Bruce biochemist, educator
Merriss, Philip Ramsay, Jr. banker
Merritt, Bruce Gordon lawyer
Mertens, Joan R. museum curator, art historian
Merton, Robert K. sociologist, educator
Mesches, Arnold artist
Meserve, Mollie Ann publisher
Mesnikoff, Alvin Murray psychiatry educator
Messer, Thomas Maria museum director
Messier, Mark Douglas professional hockey player
Messmore, Thomas Ellison asset management company executive
Messner, Thomas G. advertising executive, copywriter
Mestres, Ricardo Angelo, Jr. lawyer
Mesznik, Joel R. investment banker
Metcalf, Karen foundation executive
Metcalf, William Edwards museum curator
Metz, Emmanuel Michael investment company executive, lawyer
Metz, Robert Roy publisher, editor
Meyaart, Paul Jan distilling company executive
Meyer, Edward Henry advertising agency executive
Meyer, Fred Josef advertising executive
Meyer, Jackie Merri publishing executive
Meyer, Karl Ernest journalist
Meyer, Pearl executive compensation consultant
Meyer, Pucci newspaper editor
Meyer, Sandra W(asserstein) bank executive, management consultant
Meyer, Sheldon publisher
Meyer-Bahlburg, Heino F. L. psychologist, educator
Meyerhoff, Erich librarian, administrator
Meyers, John Allen magazine publisher
Meyers, Nancy Jane screenwriter, producer
Miano, Louis Stephen advertising executive
Michaels, Alan Richard sports commentator
Michaels, James Walker magazine editor
Michaels, Lorne television writer, producer
Michaelson, Arthur M. lawyer
Michel, Clifford Lloyd lawyer, investment executive
Michel, Henry Ludwig civil engineer
Michels, Robert psychiatrist, educator
Michelsen, Christopher Bruce Hermann surgeon
Michelson, Gertrude Geraldine retired retail company executive
Michenfelder, Joseph Francis public relations executive
Middendorf, John Harlan English literature educator
Middleton, David physicist, applied mathematician, educator
Midler, Bette singer, entertainer, actress
Midori, (Midori Goto) classical violinist
Mikita, Joseph Karl broadcasting executive
Milbank, Jeremiah foundation executive
Mildvan, Donna infectious diseases physician
Miles, Randall David investment company executive
Milgrim, Roger Michael lawyer
Miller, Arthur Madden investment banker, lawyer
Miller, B. Jack investment company executive
Miller, Caroline editor-in-chief
Miller, Charles Hampton lawyer
Miller, Darcy M. publishing executive
Miller, David lawyer, advertising executive
Miller, Douglas L. stockbroker, money manager
Miller, Edward Daniel banker
Miller, Ernest Charles management consultant
Miller, Harry Brill scenic designer, director, acting instructor, lyricist, interior designer
Miller, Harvey R. lawyer, bankruptcy reorganization specialist
Miller, Harvey S. Shipley foundation trustee
Miller, Israel rabbi, university administrator
Miller, John R. accountant
Miller, Lenore labor union official
Miller, Michael Jeffrey publishing executive
Miller, Morgan Lincoln textile manufacturing company executive
Miller, Neil Stuart financial officer, advertising executive
Miller, Paul Lukens investment banker
Miller, Paul S(amuel) lawyer
Miller, Philip Efrem librarian
Miller, Richard Jerome bank executive
Miller, Richard Kidwell artist, actor, educator
Miller, Richard McDermott sculptor
Miller, Richard Steven lawyer
Miller, Robert advertising executive
Miller, Roberta Davis editor
Miller, Sam Scott lawyer
Miller, Steven Scott lawyer
Miller, Walter James English and humanities educator, writer
Millett, Kate (Katherine Murray Millett) political activist, sculptor, artist, writer
Milligan, Michael Edward insurance services company executive
Millson, Rory Oliver lawyer
Millstein, Ira M. lawyer, lecturer
Milnes, Sherrill E. baritone
Milonas, Minos artist, designer, poet
Milton, Christian Michel insurance executive
Minard, Everett Lawrence, III journalist, magazine editor
Minasi, Anthony software company executive
Mincer, Jacob economics educator
Mines, Herbert Thomas executive recruiter
Minicucci, Robert A. business executive
Minkowitz, Martin lawyer, former state government official
Minsky, Bruce William lawyer
Mintz, Dale Leibson health education executive
Mintz, Donald Edward psychologist, educator
Mintz, Norman Nelson investment banker, educator
Mintz, Shlomo conductor, violist, violinist
Mintz, Walter investment company executive
Mirante, Arthur J., II real estate company executive
Mirenburg, Barry Leonard publisher, company executive, educator
†Mironovich, Alex publisher
Mirsky, Sonya Wohl librarian, curator
Misthal, Howard Joseph accountant, lawyer
Mitchell, Arthur dancer, choreographer, educator
Mitchell, Martin Morgan, Jr. advertising executive, educator
Mitchell, Richard Boyle advertising executive
Mitgang, Herbert author, journalist
Model, Peter molecular biologist
Modlin, Howard S. lawyer
Moeller, Achim Ferdinand Gerd art dealer, curator, consultant, publisher
Moerdler, Charles Gerard lawyer
Mohler, Mary Gail magazine editor
Mohr, Jay Preston neurologist
Moise, Edwin Evariste mathematician, educator
Molho, Emanuel publisher
Molholt, Pat academic administrator, associate dean
Molinaro, Valerie Ann lawyer
Moloney, Thomas Joseph lawyer
Molz, Redmond Kathleen public administration educator
Mondlin, Marvin retail executive, antiquarian book dealer
Monegro, Francisco psychology educator, alternative medicine consultant
Monge, Jay Parry lawyer
Monk, Debra actress
Monk, Meredith Jane artistic director, composer, choreographer, film maker, director
Montgomery, Robert Humphrey, Jr. lawyer
Montorio, John Angelo magazine editor
Mooney, Richard Emerson writer
Moore, Andrew Given Tobias, II investment banker, educator
Moore, Ann S. magazine publisher
†Moore, Anne physician
Moore, Brian writer
Moore, Donald Francis lawyer
Moore, Franklin Hall, Jr. lawyer
Moore, Geoffrey Hoyt economist
Moore, Jane Ross librarian
Moore, John Joseph lawyer
Moore, Kathleen dancer
Moore, Michael Watson musician, string bass, educator
Moore, Nicholas G. finance company executive
Moore, Paul, Jr. bishop
Moore, Thomas Ronald (Lord Bridestowe ) lawyer
Moore Hutton, Anne museum consultant
Moorhead, Thomas Burch lawyer, pharmaceutical company executive
Morales, Armando artist
Moran, Edward Kevin lawyer, consultant
Moran, Martin Joseph fundraising company executive
Morath, Inge photographer
Morawetz, Cathleen Synge mathematics educator
Moreira, Marcio Martins advertising executive
Morfopoulos, V. metallurgical engineer, materials engineer
Morgan, Frank Edward, II lawyer
Morgan, (George) Frederick poet, editor
Morgan, Jacqui illustrator, painter, educator
Morgan, Robin Evonne poet, author, journalist, activist, editor
Morgan, Thomas Bruce author, editor, public affairs executive
Morgen, Lynn public relations executive
Morgenthau, Robert Morris lawyer
Morley, Michael B. public relations executive
Moroz, Pavel Emanuel research scientist
Morphy, James Calvin lawyer
Morris, Clayton Leslie priest
Morris, Douglas Peter recording company executive
Morris, Eugene Jerome lawyer
Morris, James Peppler bass
Morris, John composer, conductor, arranger
Morris, Mark William choreographer
Morris, Stephen Burritt marketing information executive
Morris, Thomas Quinlan hospital administrator, physician
Morris, William Charles investor
Morris, Wright novelist, critic
Morrisett, Lloyd N. foundation executive
Morrison, Patricia Kennealy author
†Morrison, Stacy Lynne magazine editor
Morrissey, Dolores Josephine investment executive
Morrissey, Thomas Jerome investment banker
Morse, Edward Lewis periodical publishing executive
Morse, Stephen Scott virologist, immunologist
Mortimer, Peter Michael lawyer
Morton, Brian writer, editor, educator
Morton, Frederic author
†Morton, James Parks priest
Mosbacher, Martin Bruce public relations executive
Moseley, Carlos DuPre former music executive, musician
Moskin, John Robert editor, writer
Moskin, Morton lawyer
Moskovitz, Stuart Jeffrey lawyer
Moskowitz, Arnold X. economist, strategist, educator
Moss, Charles advertising agency executive
Moss, Kate model
Moss, Melvin Lionel anatomist, educator
Moss, William John lawyer
Mosse, Peter John Charles financial services executive
Moss-Salentijn, Letty (Aleida Moss-Salentijn) anatomist
Most, Jack Lawrence lawyer, consultant
Motley, Constance Baker (Mrs. Joel Wilson Motley) federal judge, former city official
†Mottola, Thomas entertainment company executive
Mouchly-Weiss, Harriet business executive
Mountcastle, Kenneth Franklin, Jr. retired stockbroker
Mow, Van C. engineering educator, researcher
Moyers, Bill D. journalist
Moyers, Judith Davidson television producer
Moyne, John Abel computer scientist, linguist, educator
†Mroz, John Edwin political scientist
Muchnick, Richard Stuart ophthalmologist, educator
Mukasey, Michael B. federal judge
Mullen, Peter P. lawyer
Muller, Alexandra Lida real estate management director
Muller, Charlotte Feldman economist, educator
Muller, Frank mediator, arbitrator
Muller, Henry James journalist, magazine editor
Muller, Jennifer choreographer, dancer
Muller, Priscilla Elkow art historian
Mulligan, David Keith consulting company executive
Mulligan, Hugh Augustine journalist
Mulligan, Jeremiah T. lawyer
Mullman, Michael S. lawyer
Mulroy, Richard E., Jr. lawyer
Mulvihill, James Edward periodontist
Mundell, Robert Alexander economics educator
Mundheim, Robert Harry law educator
Mundy, John Hine history educator
Munhall, Edgar curator, art history educator
Munro, Alice author
Munroe, George Barber former metals company executive
Munzer, Cynthia Brown mezzo-soprano
Munzer, Stephen Ira lawyer
Murase, Jiro lawyer
Murdock, Robert Mead art consultant, curator
Murdolo, Frank Joseph pharmaceutical company executive
Murphy, Ann Pleshette magazine editor-in-chief
Murphy, Arthur William lawyer, educator
Murphy, Austin de la Salle economist, educator, banker
Murphy, Charles Joseph investment banker
Murphy, Donna Jeanne actress
Murphy, Helen recording industry executive
Murphy, James E. public relations and marketing executive
Murphy, John Arthur tobacco, food and brewing company executive
Murphy, John Cullen illustrator
Murphy, Joseph Samson political science educator
Murphy, Ramon J.C. physician, pediatrician
Murphy, Richard William retired foreign service officer, Middle East specialist, consultant
Murphy, Rosemary actress
Murphy, Russell Stephen theater company executive
Murray, Allen Edward retired oil company executive
Murray, Archibald R. lawyer
Murray, Richard Maximilian insurance executive
Musgrave, R. Kenton federal judge
Musser, Tharon theatrical lighting designer, theatre consultant
Mustalish, Anthony Charles physician, educator
Muth, John Francis newspaper editor, columnist
Myerberg, Marcia investment banker
Myers, Gerald E. humanities educator
Myers, Wayne Alan psychiatrist, educator
Myerson, Toby Salter lawyer
Nabatoff, Robert Allan vascular surgeon, educator
Nabi, Stanley Andrew investment executive
Nachman, Ralph Louis physician, educator
Nachtwey, James Alan photojournalist
Nadel, Elliott investment firm executive
Nadelberg, Eric Paul brokerage house executive
Nadich, Judah rabbi
Nadiri, M. Ishaq economics educator, researcher, lecturer, consultant
Nadler, Allan Lawrence institute director
Naftalis, Gary Philip lawyer, educator
Nagano, Kent George conductor
Nagle, Arthur Joseph investment banker
Nagler, Stewart Gordon insurance company executive
Nagourney, Herbert publishing company executive
Nahas, Gabriel Georges pharmacologist, educator
Nakamura, James I. economics educator
Nakanishi, Koji chemistry educator, research institute administrator
Nance, Allan Taylor lawyer
Nash, Edward L. advertising agency executive
Nash, Graham William singer, composer
Nash, Paul LeNoir lawyer
Nassau, Michael Jay lawyer
Nathan, Andrew James political science educator
Nathan, Frederic Solis lawyer
Nathan, Paul S. editor, writer
Natori, Josie Cruz apparel executive
†Naumann, Michael publishing executive
Navasky, Victor Saul magazine editor, publisher
Nazem, Fereydoun F. venture capitalist, financier
†Ndour, Youssou musician
Neal, Leora Louise Haskett social services administrator
Neal, Philip dancer
Necarsulmer, Henry investment banker
Nederlander, James Morton theater executive
Nederlander, Robert E. entertainment and television executive, lawyer
Needham, George Austin investment banker
Neff, Robert Arthur business and financial executive
Neff, Thomas Joseph executive search firm executive
Neft, David Samuel marketing professional
Neidell, Martin H. lawyer
†Neier, Aryeh author, human rights organization administrator
Neiman, LeRoy artist
Nelkin, Dorothy sociology and science policy educator
Nelson, Bruce Sherman advertising agency executive
Nelson, Iris Dorothy retired guidance and rehabilitation counselor
Nelson, Merlin Edward international business consultant, company director
Nelson, Richard John playwright
Nemser, Earl Harold lawyer
Nentwich, Michael Andreas Erhart educator, consultant
Nesbit, Robert Grover management consultant
Netzer, Dick economics educator
Neubauer, Peter Bela psychoanalyst
Neuberger, Roy R. investment counselor
Neuhaus, Richard John priest, research institute president
Neuwirth, Alan James lawyer
Neuwirth, Robert Samuel obstetrician, gynecologist
Neveloff, Jay A. lawyer
New, Maria Iandolo physician, educator
Newcomb, Danforth lawyer
Newcombe, George Michael lawyer
Newell, Norman Dennis paleontologist, geologist, museum curator, educator
Newhouse, Nancy Riley newspaper editor
Newhouse, Samuel I., Jr. publishing executive
Newman, Bernard federal judge
Newman, Bruce Murray antiques dealer
Newman, Elias artist
Newman, Frank Neil bank executive
Newman, Fredric Samuel lawyer, business executive
Newman, Geraldine Anne advertising executive, inventor
Newman, Howard Neal lawyer, educator
Newman, J. Kevin broadcast journalist
Newman, Kenneth E. lawyer
Newman, Lawrence Walker lawyer
†Newman, Nancy publishing executive
Newman, Rachel magazine editor
Newman, Robert Gabriel physician
Ney, Edward N. ambassador, advertising and public relations company executive
Nibley, Andrew Mathews editorial executive
Nicholls, Richard H. lawyer
Nichols, Carol D. real estate professional, association executive
Nichols, Edie Diane executive recruiter
Nichols, Kyra ballerina
Nicola, James B. stage director, composer, playwright, lyricist
Nied, Thomas H. publishing company executive
Niemiec, David Wallace investment company executive
Niesen, James Louis theater director
Niles, Nicholas Hemelright publisher
Nimetz, Matthew lawyer
Nimkin, Bernard William retired lawyer
Nirenberg, Louis mathematician, educator
Nisenholtz, Martin Abram telecommunications executive, educator
†Nivarthi, Raju Naga anesthesiology educator
Noback, Charles Robert anatomist, educator
Noble, Ronald Kenneth government official, lawyer
Nonna, John Michael lawyer
Noonan, Susan Abert public relations counselor
Norcia, Stephen William advertising executive
Norell, Mark Allen paleontology educator
Noren-Iacovino, Mary-Jo Patricia insurance company executive
Norfolk, William Ray lawyer
Norgren, William Andrew religious denomination administrator
Norman, Marsha playwright
Norman, Stephen Peckham financial services company executive
Norris, Floyd Hamilton financial journalist
North, Steven Edward lawyer
Norvell, Patsy artist
Norville, Deborah news correspondent
Notarbartolo, Albert artist
Novak, Barbara art history educator
†Novak, Christine Allison advertising agency executive
Novick, Nelson Lee dermatologist, internist, writer
Novick, Robert physicist, educator
Novikoff, Harold Stephen lawyer
Novitz, Charles Richard television executive
Novogrod, Nancy Ellen editor
Nowick, Arthur Stanley metallurgy and materials science educator
Nugent, Nelle theater, film and television producer
Nusbacher, Gloria Weinberg lawyer
Nussbaum, Jeffrey Joseph musician
Nussbaumer, Gerhard Karl metals company executive
Nuzum, John M., Jr. banker
Nyren, Neil Sebastian publisher, editor
Oakes, John Bertram writer, editor
Oates, Joyce Carol author
Oberly, Kathryn Anne lawyer
Oberman, Michael Stewart lawyer
Obernauer, Marne, Jr. business executive
Obolensky, Ivan investment banker, foundation consultant, writer, publisher
O'Brien, Conan writer, performer, talk show host
O'Brien, Donal Clare, Jr. lawyer
O'Brien, Geoffrey Paul editor
O'Brien, Kevin J. lawyer
O'Brien, Richard Francis advertising agency executive
O'Brien, Thomas Ignatius lawyer
O'Brien, Timothy James lawyer
Ochman, B. L. public relations executive
Ochoa, Manuel, Jr. oncologist
Ochs, Michael editor, librarian, music educator
O'Connell, Margaret Ellen editor, writer
O'Connor, John Joseph Cardinal archbishop, former naval officer
O'Connor, Sinead singer, songwriter
O'Dair, Barbara editor
O'Dea, Dennis Michael lawyer
O'Dell, Charlene Anne Audrey lawyer
Odenweller, Robert Paul philatelist, association executive, airline pilot
O'Doherty, Brian playwright, filmmaker
O'Donnell, John Logan lawyer

Oechler, Henry John, Jr. lawyer
Oettgen, Herbert Friedrich physician
Offit, Morris Wolf investment management executive
Offit, Sidney writer, educator
Ogden, Alfred lawyer
O'Grady, Beverly Troxler investment executive, counselor
O'Grady, John Joseph, III lawyer
Ohannessian, Griselda Jackson publishing executive
O'Hara, Alfred Peck lawyer
O'Hare, Joseph Aloysius academic administrator, priest
Ohira, Kazuto theatre company executive, writer
Ohlson, Douglas Dean artist
O'Horgan, Thomas Foster composer, director
O'Keefe, Vincent Thomas clergyman, educational administrator
Okrent, Daniel magazine editor, writer
Okun, Herbert Stuart ambassador, international executive
olan, William Joseph, III banker
Old, Lloyd John cancer biologist
Oldenburg, Claes Thure artist
Oldenburg, Richard Erik auction house executive
Oldfield, Barney entertainment executive
Oldham, Joe editor
Oldham, John Michael physician, psychiatrist, educator
Oldham, Todd fashion designer
Olds, John Theodore banker
Olick, Arthur Seymour lawyer
Olick, Philip Stewart lawyer
Oliensis, Sheldon lawyer
Olinger, Carla D(ragan) medical advertising executive
Olitski, Jules artist
Oliva, Lawrence Jay academic administrator, history educator
Olivares, Rene Eugenio translator
Oliver, Stephanie Stokes magazine editor
Oliver, Steven Wiles banker
Olsen, David Alexander insurance executive
†Olshan, Kenneth S. business executive, advisor
Olson, Renée Alicia magazine editor
Olson, Thomas Francis, II communications company executive
Olsson, Carl Alfred urologist
Olyphant, David cultural, educational association executive
Omura, Yoshiaki physician, educator
O'Neal, Hank entertainment producer, business owner
O'Neil, James Peter financial printing company executive
O'Neil, John Joseph lawyer
O'Neil Bidwell, Katharine Thomas fine arts association executive, performing arts executive
O'Neill, Francis Xavier, III marketing executive
O'Neill, George Dorr business executive
O'Neill, Harry William survey research company executive
O'Neill, Mary Jane health agency executive
Opel, John R. business machines company executive
Oppenheimer, Martin J. lawyer
Oppenheimer, Michael physicist
Oppenheimer, Paul Eugene English comparative literature educator, poet, author
Oppenheimer-Nicolau, Siobhan think tank executive
Orben, Jack Richard investment company executive
Ordorica, Steven Anthony obstetrician, gynecologist, educator
Oreskes, Irwin biochemistry educator
Oreskes, Naomi earth sciences educator, historian
Oreskes, Susan private school educator
Ornitz, Richard Martin lawyer, business executive
O'Rorke, James Francis, Jr. lawyer
O'Rourke, P. J. (Patrick Jake O'Rourke) writer, humorist
Orr, Terrence S. dancer
Orwoll, Mark Peter magazine editor
Osborn, Donald Robert lawyer
Osborn, Frederick Henry, III church foundation executive
Osborn, June Elaine pediatrician, microbiologist, educator
Osborne, Mary Pope writer
Osborne, Michael Piers surgeon, researcher, health facility administrator
Osborne, Richard de Jongh mining and metals company executive
Osborne, Stanley de Jongh investment banker
Osbourne, Ozzy (John Osbourne) vocalist
Osgood, Richard Magee, Jr. applied physics and electrical engineering educator, research administrator
Oshima, Michael W. lawyer
Osnos, Gilbert Charles management consultant
Osnos, Peter Lionel Winston publishing executive
Ostberg, Henry Dean corporate executive
Osten, Margaret Esther librarian
Ostergard, Paul Michael bank executive
Ostling, Richard Neil journalist, author, broadcaster
Ostrager, Barry Robert lawyer
Ostrander, Thomas William investment banker
Ostrow, Joseph W. advertising executive
Ostrow, Rona Lynn librarian, educator
Ostrum, Dean Gardner actor, writer, calligrapher
O'Sullivan, Eugene Henry retired advertising executive
O'Sullivan, John editor
O'Sullivan, Thomas J. lawyer
Oursler, Fulton, Jr. editor-in-chief, writer
Ovadiah, Janice cultural institute administrator
Overweg, Norbert Ido Albert physician
Owen, Michael ballet dancer
Owen, Richard federal judge
Owen, Robert Dewit lawyer
Owen, Thomas Llewellyn investment executive
Owens, Alexandra Cantor professional society administrator
Owsley, David Thomas art consultant, appraiser, lecturer, author
Oxman, David Craig lawyer
Oz, Frank (Frank Richard Oznowicz) puppeteer, film director
Ozawa, Seiji conductor, music director
Ozero, Brian John chemical engineer
Ozick, Cynthia author
Paalz, Anthony L. beverage company executive
Paaswell, Robert Emil civil engineer, educator
Pace, Eric Dwight journalist
Pace, Stephen Shell artist, educator
Pacella, Bernard Leonardo psychiatrist
Pack, Leonard Brecher lawyer
Padberg, Manfred Wilhelm mathematics educator
Paddock, Anthony Conaway financial consultant
Pados, Frank John, Jr. investment company executive
†Pagan, Hargot Owens public relations executive
Page, Jonathan Roy investment analyst
Painter, Mary E. (Mary Painter Yarbrough) editor
Pais, Abraham physicist, educator
Pakter, Jean medical consultant
Pakula, Alan J. producer, director
Paladino, Daniel R. lawyer, beverage corporation executive
Palermo, Robert James architect, consultant, inventor
Palermo, Steve sportscaster, color analyst, former umpire
Paley, Alan H. lawyer
†Paley, Norman advertising executive
Palitz, Bernard G. finance company executive
Palladino, Vincent Neil lawyer
Palmer, Edward Lewis banker
Palmer, Paul Richard librarian, archivist
Palmer, Robert Baylis librarian
Palmieri, Victor Henry lawyer, business executive
Pan, Loretta Ren-Qiu retired educator
Paneth, Donald Joseph editor, writer
Panken, Peter Michael lawyer
Papa, Vincent T. insurance company executive
Papadakos, Dorothy Jean composer, organist
Papalia, Diane Ellen human development educator
Papernik, Joel Ira lawyer
Papi, Liza artist, writer, educator
†Pappas, Michael financial services company executive
Paradise, Robert Richard publishing executive
Pardee, Margaret Ross violinist, violist, educator
Pardee, Scott Edward securities dealer
Pardes, Herbert psychiatrist, educator
Pardo, Marian Ursula investment management company executive
†Paret, Dominique petroleum company executive
Parish, J. Michael lawyer, writer
Parker, Alice composer, conductor
Parker, James retired curator
Parker, Maceo jazz musician, alto saxophone
Parker, Maynard Michael journalist, magazine executive
Parker, Mel editor
Parker, Nancy Winslow artist, writer
Parker, Susan Brooks healthcare executive
Parkin, Gerard Francis Ralph chemistry educator, researcher
Parkinson, Georgina ballet mistress
Parkinson, James Thomas, III investment consultant
Parks, Gordon Roger Alexander Buchanan film director, author, photographer, composer
Parrish, Thomas Kirkpatrick, III marketing consultant
Parseghian, Gene talent agent
Parsons, Andrew John management consultant
Parsons, David artistic director, choreographer
Parsons, Estelle actress
Parton, Dolly Rebecca singer, composer, actress
Parver, Jane W. lawyer
Pasanella, Giovanni architect, architectural educator
Pascal, David artist
†Paseornek, Helene public relations executive
Passage, Stephen Scott energy company executive
Paster, Howard G. public relations, public affairs company executive
†Pasternack, Fred L. cardiologist
Pastores, Gregory McCarthy physician, researcher
Paterson, Katherine Womeldorf writer
Paton, Leland B. investment banker
Patrick, Hugh Talbot economist, educator
Patrikis, Ernest T. lawyer
Patterson, Ellmore Clark banker
Patterson, Jerry Eugene author
Patterson, Perry William economist, publishing company executive
Patterson, Robert Porter, Jr. federal judge
Patton, Joanna advertising executive
Paul, Andrew Mitchell venture capitalist
Paul, Douglas Allan insurance executive
Paul, Eve W. lawyer
Paul, James William lawyer
Paul, Les entertainer, inventor
Paul, Robert Carey lawyer
Paul, Robert David management consultant
Pauley, Jane television journalist
Paulus, Eleanor Bock professional speaker, author
Pavarotti, Luciano lyric tenor
Pawliczko, George Ihor academic administrator
Paxton, Robert Owen historian, educator
Pazicky, Edward Paul human resources executive
Peacock, Molly poet
Pearlstine, Norman editor
Pearson, Clarence Edward management consultant
Pearson, Henry Charles artist
Peasback, David R. recruiting company executive
Peaslee, James M. lawyer
Pechukas, Philip chemistry educator
Peck, Fred Neil economist, educator
Peck, Richard Wayne novelist
Peck, Thomas newspaper publishing executive
Pecker, David J. magazine publishing company executive
Peckolick, Alan graphic designer
Pedley, Timothy Asbury, IV neurologist, educator, researcher
Pedraza, Pedro research director
Peebler, Charles David, Jr. advertising executive
Peet, Charles D., Jr. lawyer
Pei, Ieoh Ming architect
Pelé, (Edson Arantes do Nascimento) professional soccer player
Pellegrini, Anna Maria soprano
Pelli, Denis Guillermo visual perception, psychology educator
Peloso, John Francis Xavier lawyer
Pelster, William Charles lawyer
Pelz, Robert Leon lawyer
Penn, Arthur Hiller film and theatre producer
Penn, Stanley William journalist
Pennoyer, Paul Geddes, Jr. lawyer
Pennoyer, Robert M. lawyer
Pepe, Michael publishing executive
Peper, George Frederick editor
Pepper, Allan Michael lawyer
Pepper, Beverly artist, sculptor
Peppers, Jerry P. lawyer
Peppet, Russell Frederick accountant
Perahia, Murray pianist
Percus, Jerome Kenneth physicist, educator
Perelman, Ronald Owen diversified holding company executive
Peress, Maurice symphony conductor, musicologist
Peretz, Eileen interior designer
Pérez-Rivera, Francisco writer
Peritz, Abraham Daniel business executive
Perkiel, Mitchel H. lawyer
Perkins, Lawrence Bradford, Jr. architect
Perkins, Leeman Lloyd music educator, musicologist
Perkins, Roswell Burchard lawyer
Perless, Ellen advertising executive
Perlis, Donald M. artist
Perlman, Itzhak violinist
Perlmuth, William Alan lawyer
Perlmutter, Alvin Howard television and film producer
Perlmutter, Diane F. communications executive
Perlmutter, Louis investment banker, lawyer
Perney, Linda newspaper editor
Perraud, Pamela Brooks human resources professional
Perry, David priest
Perry, Douglas opera singer
Perry-Widney, Marilyn (Marilyn Perry) international finance and real estate executive, television producer
Perschetz, Martin L. lawyer
Persell, Caroline Hodges sociologist, educator, author, researcher, consultant
Pershan, Richard Henry lawyer
Pesce, Gaetano architectural, interior, industrial and graphic designer
Pesner, Carole Manishin art gallery owner
Petchesky, Rosalind Pollack political science and women's studies educator
Peters, Alton Emil lawyer
Peters, Robert Wayne organization executive, lawyer
Peters, Roberta soprano
Peterson, Charles Gordon retired lawyer
Peterson, M. Roger international banker, retired manufacturing executive, retired air force officer
Peterson, Peter G. banker
Petkanics, Bryan G. lawyer
Petrie, Donald Joseph banker
Petrocelli, Anthony Joseph management executive, consultant
Pettibone, Peter John lawyer
Pettus, Barbara Wyper bank executive
Petz, Edwin V. real estate executive, lawyer
Petzal, David Elias editor, writer
Pfaff, Donald W. neurobiology and behavior educator
Pfeffer, David H. lawyer
Pfeffer, Philip Maurice book publishing executive
Pfenning, Arthur George social scientist
Phelps, Edmund Strother economics educator
Philbin, Regis television personality
Philipp, Elizabeth R. manufacturing company executive, lawyer
Phillips, Anthony Francis lawyer
Phillips, Barnet, IV lawyer
Phillips, Charles Gorham lawyer
Phillips, Elizabeth Joan marketing executive
Phillips, Gerald Baer internal medicine educator, scientist
Phillips, John David management consultant
Phillips, Joyce Martha human resources executive
Phillips, Pamela Kim lawyer
Phillips, Reneé magazine editor, writer, public speaker
Phillips, Russell Alexander, Jr. foundation executive
Phillips, Thomas H. writer, journalism educator, editor
Pickholz, Jerome Walter advertising agency executive
Picower, Warren Michael editor
Pidot, Whitney Dean lawyer
Piel, Gerard science editor, publisher
Piemonte, Robert Victor association executive
Pierce, Charles Eliot, Jr. library director, educator
Pierce, Marianne Louise pharmaceutical and healthcare companies executive, consultant
Pierce, Morton Allen lawyer
Pierpoint, Powell lawyer
Pierri, Mary Kathryn Madeline cardiologist, critical care physician, educator
Pietruski, John Michael, Jr. biotechnology company executive, pharmaceuticals executive
Pietrzak, Alfred Robert lawyer
Pigott, Irina Vsevolodovna educational administrator
Pike, Laurence Bruce retired lawyer
Pilcz, Maleta psychotherapist
Pilgrim, Dianne Hauserman art museum director
Pincus, Lionel I. venture banker
Pines, Burton Yale broadcasting executive
Piombino, Nicholas psychotherapist
Piore, Emanuel Ruben physicist
Piper, Thomas Laurence, III investment banker
Pirani, Conrad Levi pathologist, educator
Pirsig, Robert Maynard author
Pisano, Ronald George art consultant
Pi-Sunyer, F. Xavier medical educator, medical investigator
Pitt, Jane medical educator
Pittaway, David Bruce investment banker, lawyer
Pittman, Preston Lawrence executive assistant
Piven, Frances Fox political scientist, educator
Placzek, Adolf Kurt librarian
Plain, Belva writer
Plant, David William lawyer
Platnick, Norman I. curator, arachnologist
Platt, Charles Adams architect, planner
Platt, Nicholas Asian affairs specialist, retired ambassador
Plavinskaya, Anna Dmitrievna artist
Plevan, Bettina B. lawyer
Plimpton, George Ames writer, editor, television host
Plottel, Jeanine Parisier foreign language educator
Plum, Bernard Mark lawyer
Plum, Fred neurologist
Podd, Ann newspaper editor
Pogo, Beatriz Teresa Garcia-Tunon cell biologist, virologist, educator
Pogrebin, Letty Cottin writer, lecturer
Polacco, Patricia children's author, illustrator
Polak, Werner L. lawyer
Polenz, Joanna Magda psychiatrist
Polevoy, Nancy Tally lawyer, social worker, genealogist
Polisi, Joseph W(illiam) academic administrator
Poll, Robert Eugene, Jr. bank executive
Pollack, Milton federal judge
Pollack, Robert Elliot biologist, educator
Pollack, Stanley P. lawyer
Pollack, Stephen J. stockbroker
Pollak, Martin Marshall lawyer, patent development company executive
Pollak, Richard writer, editor
Pollak, Tim advertising agency executive
Pollitt, Katha writer, poet, educator
Pollock-O'Brien, Louise Mary public relations executive
Pomerantz, Charlotte writer
Pomerantz, John J. manufacturing executive
Pomeroy, Lee Harris architect
Pompadur, I. Martin communications executive
Pool, Mary Jane design consultant, writer
Poor, Peter Varnum producer, director
Popchristov, Damyan Christov theater director and educator
Pope, Liston, Jr. writer, journalist
Poppen, Alvin J. religious organization administrator
Porizkova, Paulina model, actress
Portale, Carl publishing executive
Porter, Karl Hampton orchestra musical director, conductor
Porter, Liliana Alicia artist, printmaker, photographer
Porter, Stephen Winthrop stage director
Porterfield, Christopher magazine editor, writer
Posamentier, Alfred Steven mathematics educator, university administrator
Posen, Susan Orzack lawyer
Posin, Kathryn Olive choreographer
Posner, Donald art historian
Posner, Jerome Beebe neurologist, educator
Posner, Louis Joseph lawyer, accountant
Posner, Roy Edward finance executive
Post, David Alan broadcast executive, producer
Potter, Delcour S. finance company executive
Potter, Elizabeth Stone academic administrator
Potter, William James investment banker
Povich, (Maurice) Maury Richard broadcast journalist, talk show host, television producer
Powell, James Henry lawyer
Powell, Mike olympic athlete, track and field
Powell, Richard Gordon retired lawyer
Powers, Edward Alton minister, educator
Powers, Elizabeth Whitmel lawyer
†Pran, Dith photographer, social activist
Pratt, Michael Theodore book publishing company executive, marketing, sales and publishing specialist
Pratt, Richardson, Jr. retired college president
Preble, Laurence George lawyer
Prehle, Tricia A. accountant
Preiskel, Barbara Scott lawyer, association executive
Prem, F. Herbert, Jr. lawyer
Prentice, Eugene Miles, III lawyer
Presby, J. Thomas financial advisor
Preska, Loretta A. federal judge
Press, Michelle editor
Pressman, Robert retail executive
Prestbo, John Andrew newspaper editor, journalist, author
Prestia, Michael Anthony accounting executive
Preston, Frances Williams performing rights organization executive
Preston, James E. cosmetics company executive
Previn, Andre composer, conductor
Prewitt, Kenneth political science educator, foundation executive
†Price, Hugh B. foundation executive, lawyer
Price, Leontyne concert and opera singer, soprano
Price, Reynolds novelist, poet, playwright, essayist, educator
Price, Robert lawyer, media executive, investment banker
Prince, (Prince Rogers Nelson) musician, actor
Prince, Harold theatrical producer
Prince, Kenneth Stephen lawyer
Princz, Judith publishing executive
Prizzi, Jack Anthony investment banking executive
Protas, Ron dance company executive
Proulx, Edna Annie writer
Pulanco, Tonya Beth special education educator
Puleo, Frank Charles lawyer
Pulitzer, Roslyn K. social worker, psychotherapist
Pulling, Thomas Leffingwell investment advisor
Purcell, Philip James financial services company executive
Purse, Charles Roe real estate investment company executive
Puschel, Philip P. textiles executive
Putney, John Alden, Jr. insurance company executive
Pye, Gordon Bruce economist
Pyle, Robert Milner, Jr. financial services company executive
Qian, Jin law librarian
Quackenbush, Margery Clouser psychoanalyst, administrator
Quackenbush, Robert Mead artist, author, psychoanalyst
Quain, Mitchell I. investment executive
Quaytman, Harvey painter
Queler, Eve conductor
Queller, Fred lawyer
Quennell, Nicholas landscape architect, educator
Questel, Mae actress
Quick, Thomas Clarkson brokerage house executive
Quigley, Martin Schofield publishing company executive, educator
Quilico, Louis baritone
Quinlan, Guy Christian lawyer
Quinlan, Mary Lou advertising executive
Quinn, Jane Bryant journalist, writer
Quinn, Timothy Charles, Jr. lawyer
Quinn, Yvonne Susan lawyer
Quinson, Bruno Andre publishing executive
Quint, Ira retail executive
Quintero, Jose theatrical director
Quintero, Ronald Gary management consultant
Quirk, John James investment company executive
Quraishi, Nisar Ali internist
Raab, Selwyn journalist
Raab, Sheldon lawyer
Raasch, Ernest Martin company executive
Rabb, Bruce lawyer
Rabb, Maxwell M. lawyer, former ambassador
Rabin, Jack lawyer
Rabinowitch, David George sculptor
Rabinowitz, Jack Grant radiologist, educator
Rabinowitz, Mayer Elya librarian, educator
Rabunski, Alan E. lawyer
Rachleff, Owen Spencer (Owen Spencer Rackleff) actor, author
Rachow, Louis A(ugust) librarian
Radner, Roy economist, educator, researcher
†Rafferty, Brian Joseph investor relations consultant
Ragan, David publishing company executive
Rahl, Leslie Lynn risk advisor, entrepreneur
Rahm, David Alan lawyer
Rahm, Susan Berkman lawyer
Rainer, John David psychiatrist, educator
Raines, Howell Hiram newspaper editor, journalist
Rainess, Alan Edward psychiatrist
Rainis, Eugene Charles brokerage house executive
Raisler, Kenneth Mark lawyer
Rajkumar, Ajay computer scientist, consultant
Rakoff, Jed Saul federal judge, author
Ralli, Constantine Pandia lawyer
Ramey, Samuel Edward bass soloist
Ramirez, Carlos David publisher
Ramirez, Gloria Maria physician

Sanseverino, Raymond Anthony *lawyer*
Santana, Robert Rafael *lawyer*
Santiago-Hudson, Ruben *actor*
Santlofer, Jonathan *artist, educator*
Santoro, Charles William *investment banker*
Santos, Eileen *management consultant*
Santulli, Thomas Vincent *surgeon*
Saphir, Richard Louis *pediatrician*
Sapinsky, Joseph Charles *magazine executive, photographer*
Sarachik, Myriam Paula *physics educator*
Sarazen, Richard Allen *media company executive*
Sargent, James Cunningham *lawyer*
Sargent, Joseph Dudley *insurance executive*
Sargent, Pamela *writer*
Sarkis, J. Ziad *management consultant*
Sarnelle, Joseph R. *electronic publishing specialist, magazine and newspaper editor*
Sartori, Giovanni *political scientist*
Satine, Barry Roy *lawyer*
Sauerhaft, Stan *public relations executive, consultant*
Saufer, Isaac Aaron *lawyer*
Saul, John Woodruff, III *writer*
Saunders, Arlene *opera singer*
Saunders, Dero Ames *writer, editor*
Saunders, Mark A. *lawyer*
Saunders, Paul Christopher *lawyer*
Savas, Emanuel S. *public management educator*
Savich, René *broadway theater executive, producer*
Savitt, Susan Schenkel *lawyer*
Savory, Mark *management consultant, insurance company executive*
Savrin, Louis *lawyer*
Sawyer, (L.) Diane *television journalist*
Sawyer, William Dale *physician, educator, university dean, foundation administrator*
Saxe, Leonard *social psychologist, educator*
Saxena, Brij B. *biochemist, endocrinologist, educator*
Saylor, Steven Warren *writer prose, fiction*
Sayre, Linda Damaris *human resources professional*
Scaffidi, Judith Ann *school volunteer program administrator*
Scaglione, Aldo Domenico *literature educator*
Scammell, Michael *writer, translator*
Scanlon, Peter Redmond *accountant*
Scanlon, Rosemary *economist*
Scarborough, Charles Bishop, III *broadcast journalist, writer*
Scarola, John Michael *dentist, educator*
Scaturro, Philip David *investment banker*
Scelsa, Joseph Vincent *sociologist*
Schaab, Arnold J. *lawyer*
Schaap, Richard Jay *journalist*
Schacht, Ronald Stuart *lawyer*
Schachter, Barry *economist*
Schachter, Oscar *lawyer, educator, arbitrator*
Schade, Malcolm Robert *lawyer*
Schaffer, Kenneth B. *communications executive, satellite engineer, inventor, consultant*
Schaffer, Seth Andrew *lawyer*
Schaffner, Bertram Henry *psychiatrist*
Schaffner, Cynthia Van Allen *writer, researcher*
Schallert, Edwin Glenn *lawyer*
Schama, Simon *historian, educator, author*
Schapiro, Donald *lawyer*
Schapiro, Miriam *artist*
Scharfman, Scott Phillip *investment banker*
Schaub, Sherwood Anhder, Jr. *management consultant*
Schechner, Richard *theater director, author, educator*
Scheeder, Louis *theater producer, director, educator*
Scheiman, Eugene R. *lawyer*
†Schein, Gerald D. *publishing executive*
Scheindlin, Raymond Paul *Hebrew literature educator, translator*
Scheindlin, Shira A. *federal judge*
Scheler, Brad Eric *lawyer*
Scher, Irving *lawyer*
Schick, Harry Leon *investment company executive*
Schickele, Peter *composer*
Schieffer, Bob *broadcast journalist*
†Schiekofer, Susan *advertising executive*
Schiff, Andrew Newman *physician, venture capitalist*
Schiff, David Tevele *investment banker*
Schiffer, Claudia *model*
Schiffrin, Andre *publisher*
Schilling, Warner Roller *political scientist, educator*
Schindler, Alexander Moshe *rabbi, organization executive*
Schirmeister, Charles F. *lawyer*
Schiro, James J. *brokerage house executive*
Schisgal, Murray Joseph *playwright*
Schizer, Zevie Baruch *lawyer*
Schlaifer, Charles *advertising executive*
Schlain, Barbara Ellen *lawyer*
Schlein, Miriam *author*
Schlesinger, Arthur (Meier), Jr. *writer, educator*
Schlesinger, Edward Bruce *neurological surgeon*
Schlesinger, Sanford Joel *lawyer*
Schless, Phyllis Ross *investment banker*
Schley, William Shain *otorhinolaryngologist*
Schlittler, Gilberto Bueno *former United Nations official, lecturer*
Schlosser, Herbert S. *broadcasting company executive*
Schmemann, Serge *journalist*
Schmertz, Eric Joseph *lawyer, educator*
Schmertz, Herbert *public relations and advertising executive*
Schmertz, Mildred Floyd *editor, writer*
Schmidt, Daniel Edward, IV *lawyer*
Schmidt, Joseph W. *lawyer*
Schmidt, Stanley Albert *editor, writer*
Schmitter, Charles Harry *electronics manufacturing company executive, lawyer*
Schmitz, Robert Allen *publishing executive, investor*
Schmolka, Leo Louis *law educator*
Schnall, David Jay *management and administration educator*
Schneck, Jerome M. *psychiatrist, medical historian, educator*
Schneider, Greta Sara *economist, financial consultant*
Schneider, Howard *lawyer*
Schneider, Jane Harris *sculptor*
Schneider, JoAnne *artist*
Schneider, Martin Aaron *photojournalist, ecologist, engineer, writer, artist, television director, public intervenor, educator, university instructor, lecturer*
Schneider, Norman M. *business executive*
Schneider, Willys Hope *lawyer*
Schneiderman, David Abbott *publisher, journalist*
Schneiderman, Irwin *lawyer*
Schoenfeld, Robert Louis *biomedical engineer*
Schonberg, Harold Charles *music critic, columnist*
Schoonmaker Powell, Thelma *film editor*
Schoonover, Jean Way *public relations consultant*
Schor, Laura Strumingher *academic administrator, historian*
Schorer, Suki *ballet teacher*
Schorr, Brian Lewis *lawyer, business executive*
Schorsch, Ismar *clergyman, Jewish history educator*
Schotter, Andrew Roye *economics educator, consultant*
Schrade, Rolande Maxwell Young *composer, pianist, educator*
Schrader, Michael Eugene *columnist, editor*
Schrader, Paul Joseph *film writer, director*
Schreiber, Paul Solomon *lawyer*
Schroeder, Aaron Harold *songwriter*
Schroeder, Edmund R. *lawyer*
Schubart, Mark Allen *arts and education executive*
Schueller, Thomas George *lawyer*
Schulhof, Michael Peter *entertainment, electronics company executive*
Schulman, Grace *poet, English language educator*
Schulman, Mark Allen *market research company executive*
Schulte, Stephen John *lawyer, educator*
Schulz, Ralph Richard *publishing consultant*
Schumacher, Hans H. *steel company executive*
Schumacher, Robert Denison *banker*
Schuman, Patricia Glass *publishing company executive, educator*
Schupak, Leslie Allen *public relations company executive*
Schur, Jeffrey *advertising executive*
Schuster, Carlotta Lief *psychiatrist*
Schuster, Karen Sutton *administrator*
Schuur, Robert George *lawyer*
Schwab, Frank, Jr. *management consultant*
Schwab, George David *social science educator*
Schwab, Harold Lee *lawyer*
Schwab, Terrance Walter *lawyer*
Schwalbe, Mary Anne *nonprofit committee executive*
Schwartz, Alan Victor *advertising executive*
Schwartz, Allen G. *federal judge*
Schwartz, Anna Jacobson *economic historian*
Schwartz, Arthur Robert *food writer, critic, consultant*
Schwartz, Barry Fredric *lawyer, diversified holding company executive*
Schwartz, Barry Steven *lawyer*
Schwartz, Bernard L. *electronics company executive*
Schwartz, Daniel Bennett *artist*
Schwartz, Herbert Frederick *lawyer*
Schwartz, Hilda G. *retired judge*
Schwartz, Irving Leon *physician, scientist, educator*
Schwartz, Lyle Victor *advertising executive*
Schwartz, Marvin *lawyer*
Schwartz, Melvin *physics educator, laboratory administrator*
Schwartz, Miles Joseph *cardiologist*
Schwartz, Mischa *electrical engineering educator*
Schwartz, Renee Gerstler *lawyer*
Schwartz, Robert George *retired insurance company executive*
Schwartz, Roselind Shirley Grant *podiatrist*
Schwartz, Stephen Lawrence *composer, lyricist*
Schwartz, William *lawyer, educator*
Schwartzman, David *economist, educator*
Schwarz, Ralph Jacques *engineering educator*
Schwed, Peter *author, retired editor and publisher*
Schweitzer, George *communications executive*
Schweitzer, Melvin L. *commissioner, lawyer*
Schwind, Michael Angelo *law educator*
Scorsese, Martin *film director, writer*
Scott, Adrienne *social worker, psychotherapist*
Scott, Dale Allan *major league umpire*
Scott, Mimi Koblenz *psychotherapist, actress, publicist, journalist*
Scott, Stanley DeForest *real estate executive, former lithography company executive*
Scott, Tom *musician*
Scott, Willard Herman *radio and television performer*
Scott, William Clement, III *entertainment industry executive*
Scotto, Renata *soprano*
Scribner, Charles, III *publisher, art historian, lecturer*
Scurry, Richardson Gano, Jr. *investment management company financial executive*
Seadler, Stephen Edward *business and computer consultant, social scientist*
Seal *popular musician*
Seaman, Alfred Barrett *journalist*
Seaman, Alfred Jarvis *retired advertising agency executive*
Seaman, Barbara (Ann Rosner) *author*
Seaver, Tom (George Thomas Seaver) *former professional baseball player*
Secunda, Eugene *marketing communications executive, educator*
Sedaka, Neil *singer, songwriter*
Sedares, James L. *conductor*
Sederbaum, Arthur David *lawyer*
Sedlin, Elias David *physician, orthopedic researcher, educator*
See, Saw-Teen *structural engineer*
Seegal, Herbert Leonard *department store executive*
Seeger, Pete *folk singer, songwriter*
Seely, Robert Daniel *physician, medical educator*
Seessel, Thomas Vining *nonprofit organization executive*
Seff, Leslie S. *securities trader*
Segal, George *sculptor*
Segal, Joel Michael *advertising executive*
Segal, Jonathan Bruce *editor*
Segal, Lore *writer*
Segal, Martin Eli *retired actuarial and consulting company executive*
Segal, Sheldon Jerome *biologist, educator, foundation administrator*
Segalas, Hercules Anthony *investment banker*
Segall, Harold Abraham *lawyer*
Segesváry, Victor Gyözö *retired diplomat*
Seidel, Selvyn *lawyer, educator*
Seidelman, Susan *film director*
Seiden, Henry (Hank Seiden) *advertising executive*
Seiden, Steven Arnold *executive search consultant*
Seidenberg, Rita Nagler *education educator*
Seidman, Samuel Nathan *investment banker, economist*
Seifert, Thomas Lloyd *lawyer*
Seiff, Eric A. *lawyer*
Seigel, Jerrold Edward *historian, writer*
Seigel, Stuart Evan *lawyer*
Seitelman, Mark Elias *lawyer*
Seitz, Frederick *former university administrator*
Selby, Cecily Cannan *dean, educator, scientist*
Seldes, Marian *actress*
Selig, Karl-Ludwig *language and literature educator*
Seliger, Mark Alan *photographer*
Seligman, Daniel *editor*
Seligman, Frederick *lawyer*
Seligson, Carl Harold *management consultant*
Selkowitz, Arthur *advertising agency executive*
Sellers, Peter Hoadley *mathematician*
Seltzer, Leo *documentary filmmaker, educator, lecturer*
Seltzer, Richard C. *lawyer*
Selver, Paul Darryl *lawyer*
Semaya, Francine L. *lawyer*
Semel, Terry *entertainment company executive*
Semmel, Joan *artist, educator*
Semple, Robert Baylor, Jr. *newspaper editor, journalist*
Sendak, Maurice Bernard *writer, illustrator*
Sendax, Victor Irven *dentist, educator, dental implant researcher*
Senior, Enrique Francisco *investment banker*
Sennett, Richard *sociologist, writer*
Senzel, Martin Lee *lawyer*
Sepahpur, Hayedeh C(hristine) *investment executive*
Serbaroli, Francis J. *lawyer, educator, writer*
Serebrier, José *musician, conductor, composer*
Serkin, Peter *pianist*
Serota, Susan Perlstadt *lawyer*
Servodidio, Pat Anthony *broadcast executive*
Sesser, Gary Douglas *lawyer*
Setrakian, Berge *lawyer*
Settipani, Frank G. *news correspondent*
Severs, Charles A., III *lawyer*
Severs, William *actor*
Seward, George Chester *lawyer*
Seymore, James W., Jr. *magazine editor*
Shadwell, Wendy Joan *curator, writer*
Shafer, Jeffrey Richard *federal official, investment banker*
Shaffer, Paul *musician, bandleader*
Shaffer, Peter Levin *playwright*
Shaffer, Russell K. *advertising agency executive*
Shainess, Natalie *psychiatrist, educator*
Shair, David Ira *human resources executive*
Shane, Rita *opera singer, educator*
Shange, Ntozake (Paulette Williams) *playwright, poet*
Shanks, David *publishing executive*
Shanman, James Alan *lawyer*
Shapiro, Ellen Marie *graphic designer, writer*
Shapiro, George M. *lawyer*
Shapiro, Harvey *poet*
Shapiro, Howard Alan *lawyer*
Shapiro, Jerome Gerson *lawyer*
Shapiro, Joel Elias *artist*
Shapiro, Judith R. *anthropology educator, academic administrator*
†Shapiro, Marvin Lincoln *communications company executive*
Shapiro, Murray *structural engineer*
Shapiro, Robert Frank *investment banking company executive*
Shapiro, Theodore *psychiatrist, educator*
Shapoff, Stephen H. *financial executive*
Sharp, Anne Catherine *artist, educator*
Sharp, Daniel Asher *foundation executive*
Sharp, J(ames) Franklin *finance educator, academic administrator*
Sharpton, Alfred Charles *minister, political activist*
Shatan, Chaim Felix *psychiatrist, medical educator, expert on Vietnam veterans, traumatic stress pioneer*
Shaw, Alan Roger *financial executive, educator*
Shaw, (Francis) Harold *performing arts administrator*
Shaw, (George) Kendall *artist, educator*
Shaw, L. Edward, Jr. *lawyer*
Shawn, Wallace *playwright, actor*
Shaykin, Leonard P. *investor*
Shays, Rona Joyce *lawyer*
Shea, Dion Warren Joseph *university official, fund raiser*
Shea, Edward Emmett *lawyer, educator, author*
Shea, James William *lawyer*
Shechtman, Ronald H. *lawyer*
Sheehan, Robert C. *lawyer*
Sheehan, Susan *writer*
Sheinkman, Jack *union official, lawyer*
Sheinman, Morton Maxwell *editor, consultant, writer, photographer*
Shelby, Jerome *lawyer*
Sheldon, Eleanor Harriet Bernert *sociologist*
Sheldon, Sidney *author, producer*
Shelley, Carole *actress*
Shellman, Eddie J. *ballet dancer, teacher, choreographer*
Shen, Michael *lawyer*
Shen, Theodore Ping *investment banker*
Shepard, Elaine Elizabeth *writer, lecturer*
Shepard, Robert M. *lawyer, investment banker, engineer*
Shepard, Stephen Benjamin *journalist, magazine editor*
Shepard, Thomas Rockwell, III *magazine executive*
Shepherd, Gillian Mary *physician*
Shepherd, Kathleen Shearen Maynard *television executive*
Sherak, Thomas Mitchell *motion picture company executive*
Sheresky, Norman M. *lawyer*
Sherman, Arthur *theater educator, writer, actor, composer*
Sherman, Cindy *artist*
Sherman, Eugene Jay *marketing executive, economist, retired*
Sherman, Jonathan Henry *lawyer*
Sherman, Norman Mark *advertising agency executive*
Sherman, Randolph S. *lawyer*
Sherrill, H. Virgil *securities company executive*
Sherrod, Lonnie Ray *foundation administrator, researcher, psychologist*
Sherry, George Leon *political science educator*
Sherva, Dennis G. *investment company executive*
Shestack, Melvin Bernard *editor, author, filmmaker, television producer*
Sheward, David John *newspaper editor and critic*
Shields, James Joseph *educational administrator, educator, author*
Shientag, Florence Perlow *lawyer*
Shier, Shelley M. *production company executive*
Shih, Wei *astrophysicist*
Shimer, Zachary *lawyer*
Shineman, Edward William, Jr. *retired pharmaceutical executive*
Shinn, George Latimer *investment banker, consultant, educator*
Shinn, Richard Randolph *former insurance executive, former stock exchange executive*
Shinnar, Reuel *chemical engineering educator, industrial consultant*
Shipley, L. Parks, Jr. *banker*
Shipley, Walter Vincent *banker*
Shnayerson, Robert Beahan *editor*
Shohen, Saundra Anne *health care communications and public relations executive*
Short, George William *financial executive*
Short, Robert Waltrip (Bobby Short) *entertainer, author*
Shorter, James Russell, Jr. *lawyer*
Shortz, Will *puzzle editor*
Shoss, Cynthia Renée *lawyer*
Shostakovich, Maxim Dmitriyevich *symphonic conductor*
Shriver, Donald Woods, Jr. *theology educator*
Shulevitz, Uri *author, illustrator*
Shull, Richard Bruce *actor*
Shulman, Max Rees *lawyer*
Shuman, Stanley S. *investment banker*
Shupack, Paul Martin *law educator*
Shyer, John D. *lawyer*
Sidamon-Eristoff, Anne Phipps *museum official*
Sidamon-Eristoff, Catherine Baxter *securities broker*
Sidamon-Eristoff, Constantine *lawyer*
Sidney, Sylvia (Sophia Kossow) *actress*
Sidran, Miriam *retired physics educator, researcher*
Siebert, Muriel *brokerage house executive, former state banking official*
Siefert-Kazanjian, Donna *corporate librarian*
Siegal, Allan Marshall *newspaper editor*
Siegel, Herbert Jay *communications executive*
Siegel, Jeffrey Norton *lawyer*
Siegel, Joel Steven *television news correspondent*
Siegel, Lucy Boswell *public relations executive*
Siegel, Marc Monroe *television and film producer, writer, director*
Siegel, Martin Jay *lawyer, investment advisor*
Siegel, Marvin *newspaper editor*
Siegel, Stanley *lawyer, educator*
Siegel, Sylvia *law librarian*
Siegler, Thomas Edmund *investment banking executive*
Siegman, Henry *association executive, foreign policy analyst*
Siek, Rainer *broadcast executive*
Siffert, Robert Spencer *orthopedic surgeon*
†Sigety, Cornelius Edward *office manager*
Siguler, George William *financial services executive*
Sikes, Alfred Calvin *communications executive*
†Sikorsky, Robert Bellarmine *syndicated columnist*
Silber, William Leo *finance educator*
Silberberg, Michael Cousins *lawyer*
Silberberg, Richard Howard *lawyer*
Silberman, James Henry *editor, publisher*
Silberman, John Alan *lawyer*
Silberstein, Alan Mark *financial services executive*
Silberstein, Diane *publishing executive*
Silkenat, James Robert *lawyer*
Silleck, Harry Garrison *lawyer*
Silver, Morris *economist, educator*
Silver, Richard Tobias *physician, educator*
Silver, Sheldon *state legislator, lawyer*
Silver, Shelly Andrea *media artist*
Silverberg, Michael Joel *lawyer*
Silverman, Al *editor*
Silverman, Arthur Charles *lawyer*
Silverman, Burton Philip *artist*
Silverman, Henry Richard *diversified business executive, lawyer*
Silverman, Herbert R. *corporate financial executive*
Silverman, Ira Norton *news producer*
Silverman, Jeffrey Stuart *manufacturing executive*
Silverman, Kenneth Eugene *English educator, writer*
Silverman, Martin Morris Bernard *secondary education educator*
Silverman, Marylin A. *advertising agency executive*
Silverman, Moses *lawyer*
Silverman, Samuel Joshua *lawyer*
Silverman, Stephen Meredith *journalist, screenwriter, producer*
Silverman, Sydel Finfer *anthropologist*
Silvers, Eileen S. *lawyer*
Silvers, Robert Benjamin *editor*
Silvers, Sally *choreographer, performing company executive*
Silverstein, Samuel Charles *cellular biology and physiology educator, researcher*
Silverstein, Shelby (Shel Silverstein) *author, cartoonist, composer, folksinger*
Sim, Craig Stephen *investment banker*
Simkhovich, Semen Lasarevich *cryogenic engineer, researcher, educator*
Simmons, Charles *author*
Simmons, Gene *musician*
Simmons, J(ames) Gerald *management consultant*
Simmons, John Derek *investment banker*
Simmons, Russell *recording industry executive*
Simon, Carly *singer, composer, author*
Simon, Eric Jacob *neurochemist, educator*
Simon, Jacqueline Albert *political scientist, writer*
Simon, John Ivan *film and drama critic*
Simon, Neil *playwright, television writer*
Simon, Norma Plavnick *psychologist*
Simon, Ronald Charles *curator*
Simonds, Charles Frederick *artist*
Simone, Joseph R. *lawyer*
Simons, Albert, III *lawyer*
Simonson, Lee Stuart *broadcast company executive*
Simpson, Mary Michael *priest, psychotherapist*
Sinclair, Daisy *advertising executive, casting director*
Singer, Arthur Louis, Jr. *foundation executive*
Singer, Barbara Helen *photographer*
Singer, Eric T. *investment banker*
Singer, Niki *publishing executive, public relations executive*
†Singerman, Martin *newspaper publishing executive*
Singh, Jyoti Shankar *political organization director*
Singleton, Donald Edward *journalist*
Sinnott, John Patrick *lawyer, educator*
Siris, Ethel Silverman *endocrinologist*
Sirkin, Michael S. *lawyer*
Sis, Peter *illustrator, children's book author, artist, filmmaker*
Sischy, Ingrid Barbara *magazine editor, art critic*
Siskind, Arthur *lawyer, director*
Siskind, Donald Henry *lawyer*
Sisman, Elaine Rochelle *musicology educator*
Sitarz, Anneliese Lotte *pediatrics educator, physician*
Sitomer, Sheila Marie *television producer, director*
Sitrick, James Baker *lawyer*
Skigen, Patricia Sue *lawyer*
Skillin, Edward Simeon *magazine publisher*
Skinner, David Bernt *surgeon, educator, administrator*
Skirnick, Robert Andrew *lawyer*
Sklaren, Cary Stewart *lawyer*
Skolnick, Jerome H. *law educator*
Skomorowsky, Peter P. *accounting company executive, lawyer*
Skupinski, Bogdan Kazimierz *artist*
Skwiersky, Paul *accountant*
Slade, Bernard *playwright*

Todd, David Fenton Michie *architect*
Todd, Ronald Gary *lawyer*
Toepfer, Susan Jill *editor*
Tofel, Richard Jeffrey *communication executive*
Toff, Nancy Ellen *book editor*
Tognino, John Nicholas *financial services executive*
Tolchin, Joan Gubin *psychiatrist, educator*
Toledo, Francisco *painter, printmaker*
Tomashefsky, Philip *biophysicis*
Tomasz, Alexander *cell biologist*
Tomka, Peter *diplomat*
Tomkins, Calvin *writer*
Tomlinson, James Francis *retired news agency executive*
Tondel, Lawrence Chapman *lawyer*
Tooker, George *artist*
Toote, Gloria E. A. *developer, lawyer, columnist*
Torffield, Marvin *artist*
Torrenzano, Richard *public affairs executive*
Torres, Edwin *state judge, writer*
Tortorello, Nicholas John *public opinion and market research company executive*
Touborg, Margaret Earley Bowers *non-profit executive*
Tourlitsas, John Constantine *radiologist*
Towbin, A(braham) Robert *investment banker*
Townsend, Alair Ane *municipal official*
Townsend, Charles H. *publishing executive*
Townshend, Peter *musician, composer, singer*
Tozer, W. James, Jr. *investment company executive*
Tracey, Margaret *dancer*
Trachtenberg, Matthew J. *bank holding company executive*
Tract, Marc Mitchell *lawyer*
Tracy, Janet Ruth *legal educator, librarian*
Trager, William *biology educator*
Train, John *investment counselor, writer, government official*
†Trakas, George *sculptor*
Tramontine, John Orlando *lawyer*
Traub, J(oseph) F(rederick) *computer scientist, educator*
Traum, Jerome S. *lawyer*
Treadway, James Curran *investment company executive, lawyer, former government official*
Treaster, Joseph B. (Bland) *journalist*
Tree, Michael *violinist, violist, educator*
Tregellas, Patricia *musical director, composer*
Treitel, David Henry *financial consultant*
Treuhold, Charles Richard *retired investment banker*
Tricarico, Joseph Archangelo *lawyer*
Trigere, Pauline *fashion designer*
Trillin, Calvin Marshall *writer, columnist*
Tripodi, Louis Anthony *advertising agency executive*
Trost, J. Ronald *lawyer*
Trubin, John *lawyer*
Truesdell, Walter George *minister, librarian*
Truesdell, Wesley Edwin *public relations and investor relations consultant*
Tscherny, George *graphic designer*
Tschumi, Bernard *dean*
Tsividis, Yannis P. *electrical engineering educator*
Tsoucalas, Nicholas *federal judge*
Tsui, Soo Hing *educational research consultant*
Tuchman, Gary Robert *television news correspondent*
Tuchman, Phyllis *critic*
Tuck, Edward Hallam *lawyer*
Tucker, Alan David *publisher*
Tudryn, Joyce Marie *professional society administrator*
Tulchin, David Bruce *lawyer*
Tully, Daniel Patrick *financial services executive*
Tumminello, Stephen Charles *consumer electronics manufacturing executive*
Tumpowsky, Ira Bruce *advertising agency executive*
Tune, Tommy (Thomas James Tune) *musical theater director, dancer, choreographer, actor*
Tung, Ko-Yung *lawyer*
Turino, Gerard Michael *physician, medical scientist, educator*
Turk, Patricia Avedon *dance company executive*
Turkel, Stanley *hotel consultant, management executive*
Turndorf, Herman *anesthesiologist, educator*
Turner, Almon Richard *art historian, educator*
Turner, Craig *journalist*
Turner, E. Deane *lawyer*
Turner, Hester Hill *management consultant*
Turo, Joann K. *psychoanalyst, psychotherapist, consultant*
Turrentine, Stanley William *musician*
Turro, Nicholas John *chemistry educator*
Turso, Vito Anthony *public relations executive*
Tusiani, Joseph *foreign language educator, author*
Tuttleton, James Wesley *English educator*
Tutun, Edward H. *retired retail executive*
Twiname, John Dean *minister, health care executive*
Tyler, Harold Russell, Jr. *lawyer, former government official*
Tyner, McCoy *jazz pianist, composer*
Tyson, Harry James *investment banker*
Tzimas, Nicholas Achilles *orthopedic surgeon, educator*
Ubell, Robert Neil *editor, publisher, consultant, literary agent*
Uchitelle, Louis *journalist*
Udell, Richard *lawyer*
†Udell Turshen, Rochelle Marcia *publishing executive*
Ufford, Charles Wilbur, Jr. *lawyer*
Uhry, Alfred Fox *playwright*
Ule, Guy Maxwell, Jr. *stockbroker*
Ullman, Leo Solomon *lawyer*
Ulrich, Lars *drummer*
Ulrich, Max Marsh *executive search consultant*
Underberg, Mark Alan *lawyer*
Underhill, Jacob Berry, III *retired insurance company executive*
Underweiser, Irwin Philip *mining company executive, lawyer*
Underwood, Joanna DeHaven *environmental research and education organizations president*
Ungaro, Susan Kelliher *magazine editor*
Unger, Irwin *historian, educator*
Unger, Peter Kenneth *philosophy educator*
Unger, Stephen Herbert *electrical engineer, computer scientist*
Upbin, Shari *theatrical producer, director, agent, educator*
Updike, Helen Hill *economist, investment manager, financial planner*
Uppman, Theodor *concert and opera singer, voice educator*
Upright, Diane Warner *art dealer*
Upshaw, Dawn *soprano*
Upson, Stuart Barnard *advertising agency executive*
Uram, Gerald Robert *lawyer*
Urdang, Alexandra *book publishing executive*
Uris, Leon Marcus *author*
Urkowitz, Michael *banker*
Urowsky, Richard J. *lawyer*
Vaadia, Boaz *sculptor*
Vai, Steve *guitarist*
Valente, Peter Charles *lawyer*
Valenti, Carl M. *newspaper publisher*
Valles, Jean-Paul *finance company executive*
Van Brunt, Albert Daniel *advertising agency executive*
Vance, Andrew Peter *lawyer*
Vance, Cyrus Roberts *lawyer, former government official*
Vanden Heuvel, Katrina *magazine editor*
Van Dine, Vance *investment banker*
Vandross, Luther *singer*
Van Gundy, Gregory Frank *lawyer*
Van Gundy, Jeff *coach*
Van Halen, Eddie *guitarist, rock musician*
van Hengel, Maarten *banker*
Van Sant, Peter Richard *news correspondent*
Varet, Michael A. *lawyer*
Varnedoe, John Kirk Train *museum curator*
Varney, Carleton Bates, Jr. *interior designer, columnist, educator*
Vass, Joan *fashion designer*
Vassallo, Edward E. *lawyer*
Vaughan, Edwin Darracott, Jr. *urologist, surgeon*
Vaughan, Samuel Snell *editor, author, publisher*
Vecsey, George Spencer *sports columnist*
Vedder, Eddie *singer*
Vega, Marylois Purdy *journalist*
Vega, Matias Alfonso *lawyer*
Verdon, Gwen (Gwyneth Evelyn) *actress, dancer, choreographer*
VerDorn, Jerry *actor*
Vergilis, Joseph Semyon *mechanical engineering educator*
Vermeer, Maureen Dorothy *sales executive*
Vernon, Arthur *educational administrator*
Versfelt, David Scott *lawyer*
Vicente, Esteban *artist*
Vickrey, William Spencer *economist, educator*
Vidal, David Jonathan *insurance company executive, journalist*
Viemeister, Tucker L. *industrial designer*
Viener, John D. *lawyer*
Viertel, Jack *theatrical producer, writer*
Vig, Vernon Edward *lawyer*
Vignelli, Massimo *architecture and design executive*
Vilcek, Jan Tomas *medical educator*
Violenus, Agnes A. *retired school system administrator*
Vitale, Alberto Aldo *publishing company executive*
Vitale, Dick *commentator, sports writer*
Vitkowsky, Vincent Joseph *lawyer*
Vittorini, Carlo *publishing company executive*
Vitz, Paul Clayton *psychologist, educator*
Viviano, Sam Joseph *illustrator*
Vizard, Frank Joseph *journalist*
Vogel, Eugene L. *lawyer*
Vogelman, Joseph Herbert *scientific engineering company executive*
Volckhausen, William Alexander *lawyer, banker*
Volk, Stephen Richard *lawyer*
Volpe, Joseph *opera company administrator*
Volpe, Thomas J. *advertising executive*
Von Brandenstein, Patrizia *production designer*
Von Fraunhofer-Kosinski, Katherina *bank executive*
von Furstenberg, Betsy *actress, writer*
Von Furstenberg, Diane Simone Michelle *fashion designer, writer, entrepreneur*
von Mehren, Jane *editor, publisher*
von Mehren, Robert Brandt *lawyer, retired*
Vonnegut, Kurt, Jr. *writer*
Von Ringelheim, Paul Helmut *sculptor*
Von Stade, Frederica *mezzo-soprano*
Voorhees, David William *editor, historian*
Voorsanger, Bartholomew *architect*
Vora, Ashok *financial economist*
Vuilleumier, François *curator*
Wachner, Linda Joy *apparel marketing and manufacturing executive*
Wachtel, Norman Jay *lawyer*
Wacker, Susan Regina *cosmetic design director*
Wadsworth, Charles William *pianist*
Wadsworth, Dyer Seymour *lawyer*
Wadsworth, Robert David *advertising agency executive*
Wager, Walter Herman *author, communications director*
Wages, Robert Coleman *equity investor*
Wagner, Alan Cyril *television and film producer*
Wagner, Donald Arthur *securities group executive*
Wagner, Robin Samuel Anton *stage and set designer*
Wailand, George *lawyer*
Wainwright, Carroll Livingston, Jr. *lawyer*
Wainwright, Cynthia Crawford *banker*
Wakefield, Dan *author, screenwriter*
†Wakeham, Matthew S. *electronics marketing manager*
Wakeman, Rick *musician, composer*
Waks, Jay Warren *lawyer*
Waksman, Byron Halsted *neuroimmunologist, experimental pathologist, educator, medical association administrator*
Waksman, Ted Stewart *lawyer*
Wald, Bernard Joseph *lawyer*
Wald, Richard Charles *broadcasting executive*
Wald, Sylvia *artist*
Wales, Gwynne Huntington *lawyer*
Walke, David Michael *public relations executive*
Walker, Alice Malsenior *author*
Walker, Dale Rush *financial company executive*
Walker, Jeffrey Clemens *venture capitalist*
Walker, John Mercer, Jr. *federal judge*
Walker, Kenneth Henry *architect*
Walker, Mort *cartoonist*
Walker, Sally Barbara *retired glass company executive*
Walker, Sandra *mezzo-soprano*
Walkowitz, Daniel J. *historian, filmmaker, educator*
Wallace, G. David *magazine editor*
Wallace, Joyce Irene Malakoff *internist*
Wallace, Ken *magazine publisher*
Wallace, Mike *television interviewer and reporter*
Wallace, Nora Ann *lawyer*
Wallace, Thomas C(hristopher) *editor, literary agent*
Wallace, Walter C. *lawyer, government official*
Wallach, Eric Jean *lawyer*
Wallach, Stanley *medical educator, consultant, administrator*
Wallance, Gregory J. *lawyer*
Waller, Robert James *writer*
Walman, Jerome *psychotherapist, publisher, consultant, critic*
Walpin, Gerald *lawyer*
Walsh, Annmarie Hauck *research firm executive*
Walsh, Joseph Brennan *ophthalmologist*
Walsh, Thomas Gerard *actuary*
Walter, Ingo *economics educator*
Walters, Barbara *television journalist*
Walters, Milton James *investment banker*
Walters, Raymond, Jr. *newspaper editor, author*
Walton, Anthony John (Tony Walton) *theater and film designer, book illustrator*
Walton, Bill (William Theodore Walton, III) *sportscaster, former professional basketball player*
Waltz, Joseph McKendree *neurosurgeon, educator*
Walzer, Judith Borodovko *academic administrator, educator*
Walzog, Nancy Lee *film and television executive*
Wanek, William Charles *public relations executive*
Wang, Arthur Woods *publisher*
Wang, Frederick Mark *pediatric ophthalmologist, medical educator*
Wanner, Eric *foundation executive*
Ward, Geoffrey Champion *author, editor*
Ward, Robert Joseph *federal judge*
Warden, John L. *lawyer*
Wardwell, Allen *art historian*
Wareham, Raymond Noble *investment banker*
Waren, Stanley A. *university administrator, theatre and arts center administrator, director*
Warfield, Gerald Alexander *composer, writer*
Warner, Douglas Alexander, III *banker*
Warner, Edward Waide, Jr. *lawyer*
Warner, John Edward *advertising executive*
†Warner, Miner Hill *investment banker*
Warner, Peter David *publishing executive*
Warner, Rawleigh, Jr. *oil company executive*
Warner, Scott Dennis *investment banker*
Warren, Irwin Howard *lawyer*
Warren, William Bradford *lawyer*
Warren, William Clements *law educator*
Warsawer, Harold Newton *real estate appraiser and consultant*
Warshauer, Irene Conrad *lawyer*
Warshaw, Leon J(oseph) *physician*
Warwick, Dionne *singer*
Washburn, David Thacher *lawyer*
Washington, Clarence Edward, Jr. *insurance company executive*
Washington, Shelley Lynne *dancer*
Wasser, Henry *retired English educator*
Wasserman, Albert *writer, director*
Wasserman, Charles *banker*
Wasserman, Dale *playwright*
Wasserman, Louis Robert *physician, educator*
Waters, Roger *rock musician*
Waters, Sylvia *dance company artistic director*
Waters, Willie Anthony *opera and orchestra conductor*
Watkins, Charles Booker, Jr. *mechanical engineering educator*
Watson, James Lopez *federal judge*
Watson, Solomon Brown, IV *lawyer, business executive*
Watt, Douglas (Benjamin Watt) *writer, critic*
Wattman, Malcolm Peter *lawyer*
Watts, André *concert pianist*
Watts, David Eide *lawyer*
Watts, Harold Wesley *economist, educator*
Waugh, Theodore Rogers *orthopedic surgeon*
Waxenberg, Alan M. *publisher*
Weathersby, George Byron *investment management executive*
Webb, Patrick McIvor *artist, educator*
Webb, Veronica *fashion model, journalist*
Weber, Carol Martinez *physician*
Weber, Robert Maxwell *cartoonist*
Webster, John Kimball *investment executive*
Wechsler, Gil *lighting designer*
Wechsler, Herbert *retired legal educator*
Wecker, William A. *preventive medicine physician, neuropsychiatrist*
Weeks, David Frank *foundation administrator*
Wegman, William George *artist*
Weida, Lewis Dixon *marketing analyst, consultant*
Weidlinger, Paul *civil engineer*
Weidman, Jerome *author*
Weiksner, Sandra S. *lawyer*
Weil, Frank A. *investment banker, lawyer*
Weil, Gilbert Harry *lawyer*
Weil, Leon Jerome *diplomat*
Weil-Garris Brandt, Kathleen (Kathleen Brandt) *art historian*
Weill, Sanford I. *bank executive*
Weinbach, Lawrence Allen *financial executive*
Weinbaum, Sheldon *biomedical engineer*
Weinberg, H. Barbara *art historian, educator, curator paintings and sculpture*
Weinberg, Herschel Mayer *lawyer*
Weinberg, John Livingston *investment banker*
Weinberger, Harold Paul *lawyer*
Weiner, Andrew Jay *lawyer*
Weiner, Annette Barbara *university dean, anthropology educator*
Weiner, Earl David *lawyer*
Weiner, Lawrence Charles *sculptor*
Weiner, Max *educational psychology educator*
Weiner, Richard *public relations executive*
Weiner, Ronald Gary *accounting firm executive*
Weiner, Stephen Arthur *lawyer*
Weiner, Stephen L. *lawyer*
Weiner, Walter Herman *banker, lawyer*
Weingrow, Howard L. *financial executive, investor*
Weins, Leo Matthew *retired publishing executive*
Weinschel, Alan Jay *lawyer*
Weinstein, Harvey *film company executive*
Weinstein, Herbert *chemical engineer, educator*
Weinstein, I. Bernard *oncologist, geneticist, research administrator*
Weinstein, Mark Michael *lawyer*
†Weinstein, Mark S. *finance company executive*
Weinstein, Martin *aerospace manufacturing executive, materials scientist*
Weinstein, Robert *film company executive*
Weinstein, Ruth Joseph *lawyer*
Weinstein, Sharon Schlein *public relations executive, educator*
Weinstein, Sidney *university program director*
Weinstock, Leonard *lawyer*
Weintraub, Daniel Ralph *social welfare administrator*
Weintz, Jacob Frederick, Jr. *retired investment banker*
Weintz, Walter Louis *book publishing company executive*
Weir, John Keeley *lawyer*
Weir, Peter Frank *lawyer*
Weisberg, Jonathan Mark *public relations executive*
Weisbrod, Carl Barry *lawyer, public official*
Weisburd, Steven I. *lawyer*
Weisenburger, Randall *company executive*
Weisfeldt, Myron Lee *physician, educator*
Weisl, Edwin Louis, Jr. *foundation executive, lawyer*
Weiss, David *religion educator*
Weiss, Donald L(ogan) *retired sports association executive*
Weiss, Lawrence N. *lawyer*
Weiss, Mark *public relations executive*
Weiss, Myrna Grace *business consultant*
Weissman, Norman *public relations executive*
Weissmann, Gerald *medical educator, researcher, writer, editor*
Weitz, John *fashion designer, writer*
Weitzner, Harold *mathematics educator*
Weksler, Marc Edward *physician, educator*
Welch, (William) Roger *artist*
Weld, Jonathan Minot *lawyer*
Welikson, Jeffrey Alan *lawyer*
Welles, James Bell, Jr. *lawyer*
Wellin, Keith Sears *investment banker*
Welling, Kathryn Marie *editor*
Wellington, Harry Hillel *lawyer, educator*
Wellington, Sheila Wacks *foundation administrator, psychiatry educator*
Wells, Linda Ann *editor-in-chief*
Wells, Victor Hugh, Jr. *advertising agency executive*
Welsh, Donald Emory *publisher*
Welt, Philip Stanley *lawyer, consultant*
Welts, Rick *sports association executive*
Wemple, William *lawyer*
Wendel, Martin *lawyer*
Wender, Ira Tensard *lawyer*
Wender, Phyllis Bellows *literary agent*
Wenegrat, Saul S. *arts administrator, art educator, consultant*
Wenglowski, Gary Martin *economist*
Wenner, Jann Simon *editor, publisher*
Werner, Robert L. *lawyer*
Werthamer, N. Richard *physicist*
Werthein, Jorge R. *diplomat*
Weschler, Anita *sculptor, painter*
Weschler, Lawrence Michael *writer, journalist*
Wesely, Edwin Joseph *lawyer*
Wesley, John Mercer *artist*
Wessinger, W. David *management consultant*
Wessler, Sheenah Hankin *psychotherapist, consultant*
†West, Dorothy *writer*
West, Paul Noden *author*
Westin, Alan Furman *political science educator*
Westin, David *broadcast executive*
Westin, David Lawrence *lawyer*
Weston, M. Moran, II *real estate developer, banker, clergyman, educator*
†Westover, Becke Karl *advertising executive*
†Wetschler, Ed *editor*
Wetzler, James Warren *economist*
Wetzler, Monte Edwin *lawyer*
Wexelbaum, Michael *lawyer*
Wexler, Peter John *producer, director, set designer*
Weyher, Harry Frederick *lawyer*
Wham, George Sims *publishing executive*
Wharton, Danny Carroll *zoo biologist*
Wheeler, Kenneth William *history educator*
Whelan, Elizabeth Ann Murphy *epidemiologist*
Whelan, Stephen Thomas *lawyer*
Whelan, Wendy *ballet dancer*
Whelchel, Betty Anne *lawyer*
Whitcraft, Edward C. R. *investment banker*
White, Faith *sculptor*
White, Harry Edward, Jr. *lawyer*
White, John Patrick *lawyer*
White, Kate *editor-in-chief*
White, Lawrence J. *economics educator*
White, Timothy Thomas Anthony *writer, editor, broadcaster*
Whitehead, E. Douglas *urology educator*
Whitehead, John Cunningham *investment executive*
Whitehead, Robert *theatrical producer*
Whiteman, Douglas E. *publisher*
Whitman, Martin J. *investment banker*
Whitney, Edward Bonner *investment banker*
Whitney, Phyllis Ayame *author*
Whitney, Ruth Reinke *magazine editor*
Whitsell, John Crawford, II *general surgeon*
Whittell, Polly (Mary) Kaye *editor, writer*
Whittemore, Laurence Frederick *private banker*
Whoriskey, Robert Donald *lawyer*
Wickes, R(ichard) Paul *lawyer*
Widlund, Olof Bertil *computer science educator*
Wiener, Harry *pharmaceutical company executive, physician*
Wiener, Hesh (Harold Frederic Wiener) *publisher, editor, consultant*
Wiener, Malcolm Hewitt *foundation executive*
Wiener, Marvin S. *rabbi, editor, executive*
Wiener, Robert Alvin *accountant*
Wiener, Solomon *writer, consultant, former city official*
Wiesel, Torsten Nils *neurobiologist, educator*
Wiggers, Charlotte Suzanne Ward *magazine editor*
Wigmore, Barrie Atherton *investment banker*
Wilby, William Langfitt *global mutual fund manager, economist*
Wilcox, John Caven *lawyer, corporate consultant*
Wilder, Charles Willoughby *lawyer, consultant*
Wildes, Leon *lawyer, educator*
Wilds, Bonnie *author, community volunteer*
Wilensky, Saul *lawyer*
Wilford, John Noble, Jr. *news correspondent*
Wilkin, Miles Clifford *theatrical group executive*
Wilkinson, Donald McLean *investment counsel*
Wilkinson, John Hart *lawyer*
Willett, Roslyn Leonore *public relations executive, food service consultant*
Williams, Charles Linwood (Buck Williams) *professional basketball player*
Williams, Dave Harrell *investment executive*
Williams, Donald Maxey *dancer, singer, actor*
Williams, Harriet Clarke *retired academic administrator, artist*
Williams, Lowell Craig *lawyer, employee relations executive*
Williams, Omer S. J. *lawyer*
Williams, Stanley *ballet dancer and teacher*
Williams, Thomas Allison *lawyer*
Williams, Vanessa *recording artist, actress*
Williams, William Thomas *artist, educator*
Williamson, Douglas Franklin, Jr. *lawyer*
Williamson, Robert Webster *brokerage house executive*
Willis, Beverly Ann *architect*
Willis, Everett Irving *lawyer*
Willis, John Alvin *editor*
Willis, Thornton Wilson *painter*
Willis, William Ervin *lawyer*
Willkie, Wendell Lewis, II *lawyer*
Wilson, August *playwright*
Wilson, F(rancis) Paul *novelist, screenwriter*
Wilson, Paul Holliday, Jr. *lawyer*

Wilson, Philip Duncan, Jr. *orthopedic surgeon*
Wilson, Robert M. *theatre artist*
Wilson, Thomas William *lawyer*
Winawer, Sidney Jerome *physician, clinical investigator, educator*
Wincenc, Carol *concertizing flutist, educator*
Windels, Paul, Jr. *lawyer*
Windhager, Erich Ernst *physiologist, educator*
Windsor, Laurence Charles, Jr. *publishing executive*
Windsor, Patricia (Katonah Summertree) *author, educator, lecturer*
Winfrey, Carey Wells *journalist, magazine editor*
Wing, John Russell *lawyer*
Winger, Ralph O. *lawyer*
Winship, Frederick Moery *journalist*
Winsor, Kathleen *writer*
Winstead, Clint *financial publisher*
†Winston, Stanley S. *advertising executive*
Winterer, Philip Steele *lawyer*
Wintour, Anna *editor*
Wirz, Pascal Francois *trust company executive*
Wise, David *author, journalist*
†Wishner, Howard E. *public relations executive*
Wishnick, Marcia Margolis *pediatrician, geneticist, educator*
Wit, David Edmund *software and test preparation company executive*
Wit, Harold Maurice *investment banker, lawyer, investor*
Witkin, Eric Douglas *lawyer*
Witkin, Mildred Hope Fisher *psychotherapist, educator*
Witmeyer, John Jacob, III *lawyer*
†Wittenberg, Kate *editor*
Wittstein, Edwin Frank *stage and film production designer*
Wixom, William David *art historian, museum administrator, educator*
Woetzel, Damian Abdo *ballet dancer, educator*
Wogan, Robert *broadcasting company executive*
Woglom, Eric Cooke *lawyer*
Wohlgelernter, Beth *organization executive*
Woit, Erik Peter *corporate executive, lawyer*
Woiwode, Larry (Alfred Woiwode) *writer, poet*
Wojnilower, Albert Martin *economist*
Wolcott, Samuel H., III *investment banker*
Wolf, Gary Wickert *lawyer*
Wolf, James Anthony *insurance company executive*
Wolf, Peter Michael *investment management and land planning consultant, educator, author*
Wolfe, George C. *theater director, producer, playwright*
Wolfe, James Ronald *lawyer*
Wolfe, Thomas Kennerly, Jr. *writer, journalist*
Wolfert, Ruth *Gestalt therapist*
Wolff, Jesse David *lawyer*
Wolff, Kurt Jakob *lawyer*
Wolff, Richard Joseph *public relations executive, consultant, historian*
Wolff, Sanford Irving *lawyer*
Wolff, Virginia Euwer *writer, secondary education educator*
Wolff, William F., III *investment banker*
Wolfson, Michael George *lawyer*
Wolins, Joseph *artist*
Wolitzer, Steven Barry *investment banker*
Wolkoff, Eugene Arnold *lawyer*
Wolmer, Bruce Richard *magazine editor*
Wolper, Allan L. *journalist, educator*
Wolson, Craig Alan *lawyer*
Wood, Kimba M. *judge*
Wood, Paul F. *national health agency executive*
Wood, Ronald *musician*
Woodbury, Marion A. *insurance company executive*
Woodrum, Robert Lee *executive search consultant*
Woods, Ward Wilson, Jr. *investment company executive*
Wood-Smith, Donald *plastic surgeon*
Woolsey, David Arthur *finance company executive*
Wordsman, Elizabeth Schmitt *senior manager print production*
Worenklein, Jacob Joshua *lawyer*
Worley, Robert William, Jr. *lawyer*
Worman, Howard Jay *physician, educator*
Worner, Theresa Marie *physician*
Worth, Irene *actress*
Wortman, Richard S. *historian, educator*
Wray, Cecil, Jr. *lawyer*
Wray, Gilda Gates *foundation administrator*
Wright, Bob *broadcasting executive*
Wright, Faith-dorian *artist*
Wright, Gwendolyn *art center director, writer, educator*
Wright, Hugh Elliott, Jr. *association executive, writer*
Wright, Irving Sherwood *physician, retired educator*
Wright, Jane Cooke *physician, educator, consultant*
Wright, Laurali R. (Bunny Wright) *writer*
Wright, Michael Kearney *public relations executive*
Wright, Richard John *business executive*
Wright, Robert *broadcast executive*
Wriston, Walter Bigelow *retired banker*
Wrong, Dennis Hume *sociologist, educator*
Wruble, Brian Frederick *investment firm executive*
Wulf, Melvin Lawrence *lawyer*
Wunderman, Jan Darcourt *artist*
Wuorinen, Charles Peter *composer*
Wurmfeld, Sanford *artist, educator*
Wurtzel, Alan Henry *television executive*
Wyckoff, E. Lisk, Jr. *lawyer*
Wyeth, James Browning *artist*
Wyn-Jones, Alun (William Wyn-Jones) *software developer, mathematician*
Wyse, Lois *advertising executive, author*
Wyser-Pratte, John Michael *lawyer*
Wysocki, Annette B. *nurse scientist, educator*
Yablon, Leonard Harold *publishing company executive*
Yahr, Melvin David *physician*
Yalen, Gary N. *insurance company executive*
Yamaguchi, Kristi Tsuya *ice skater*
Yamin, Michael Geoffrey *lawyer*
Yancey, Richard Charles *investment banker*
Yang, Edward S. *electrical engineering educator*
Yao, David Da-Wei *engineering educator*
Yeager, George Michael *investment counsel executive*
Yegulalp, Tuncel M. *mining engineer, educator*
Yelenick, Mary Therese *lawyer*
Yellin, Victor Fell *composer, music educator*
Yerman, Fredric Warren *lawyer*
Yerushalmi, Yosef Hayim *historian, educator*
Yeston, Maury *composer, lyricist, educator*
Yetman, Leith Eleanor *academic administrator*
Yin, Beatrice Wei-Tze *medical researcher*
Yodowitz, Edward J. *lawyer*
Yorburg, Betty (Mrs. Leon Yorburg) *sociology educator*
Yorinks, Arthur *children's author, writer, director*
York, Richard Travis *art dealer*
Young, Alice *lawyer*
Young, Genevieve Leman *publishing executive, editor*
Young, George H., III *investment banker*
Young, John Edward *lawyer*
Young, Michael Warren *geneticist, educator*
Young, Nancy *lawyer*
Young, Neil *musician, songwriter*
Young, William F. *legal educator*
Youngerman, Jack *artist, sculptor*
Youngwood, Alfred Donald *lawyer*
Yousef, Mona Lee *psychotherapist*
Yurchenco, Henrietta Weiss *ethnomusicologist, writer*
†Yuriko, (Yuriko Kikuchi) *dancer, choreographer*
Yurt, Roger William *surgeon, educator*
Zackheim, Adrian Walter *editor*
Zahn, Timothy *writer*
Zahnd, Richard Hugo *professional sports executive, lawyer*
Zaitzeff, Roger Michael *lawyer*
Zakim, David *biochemist*
Zakkay, Victor *aeronautical engineering educator, scientist*
Zammit, Joseph Paul *lawyer*
Zand, Dale Ezra *business management educator*
Zanetti, Richard Joseph *editorial director*
Zara, Louis *author, editor*
Zatlin, Gabriel Stanley *physician*
Zawistowski, Stephen Louis *psychologist, educator*
Zazula, Bernard Meyer *physician administrator*
Zedrosser, Joseph John *lawyer*
Zeisler, Richard Spiro *investor*
Zeldin, Richard Packer *publisher*
Zelnick, Strauss *entertainment company executive*
Zerin, Steven David *lawyer*
Zeuschner, Erwin Arnold *investment advisory company executive*
Zevon, Susan Jane *editor*
Zevon, Warren *singer, songwriter*
Zhu, Ai-Lan *opera singer*
Ziegler, William Alexander *lawyer*
Zifchak, William C. *lawyer*
Ziff, William Bernard, Jr. *retired publishing executive*
Zimand, Harvey Folks *lawyer*
Zimbalist, Efrem, III *publishing company executive*
Zimmerman, Jean *lawyer*
Zimmerman, Kathleen Marie *artist*
Zimmerman, Sol Shea *pediatrician*
Zimmerman, William Edwin *newspaper editor, publisher, writer*
Zimmett, Mark Paul *lawyer*
Zinder, Norton David *genetics educator, university dean*
Zinsser, William Knowlton *editor, writer, educator*
Zipprodt, Patricia *costume designer*
Zirin, James David *lawyer*
Zirinsky, Bruce R. *lawyer*
Zitrin, Arthur *physician*
Zlowe, Florence Markowitz *artist*
Zoeller, Donald J. *lawyer*
Zollar, Jawole Willa Jo *art association administrator*
Zolotow, Charlotte Shapiro *author, editor*
Zonana, Victor *lawyer, educator*
Zonszein, Joel *endocrinologist*
Zoogman, Nicholas Jay *lawyer*
Zornow, David M. *lawyer*
Zosike, Joanie Fritz *theater director, actor*
Zoss, Abraham Oscar *chemical company executive*
Zuck, Alfred Christian *consulting mechanical engineer*
Zucker, Howard Alan *pediatric cardiologist, intensivist, anesthesiologist*
Zucker, Stefan *tenor, writer, radio broadcaster*
Zuckerberg, Roy J. *investment banking executive*
Zucker-Franklin, Dorothea *medical scientist, educator*
Zuckerman, Mortimer Benjamin *publisher, editor, real estate developer*
Zuckert, Donald Mack *marketing executive*
Zukerman, Michael *lawyer*
Zukerman, Pinchas *concert violinist, violist, conductor*
Zuniga, Francisco *sculptor, graphic artist*
Zweibel, Joel Burton *lawyer*
†Zweigenthal, Gail *magazine editor*
Zwerling, Gary Leslie *investment bank executive*
Zychick, Joel David *lawyer*

## Newark
Hughes, Owen Willard *artist*

## Newburgh
Apuzzo, Gloria Isabel *retired accountant*
Fallon, Rae Mary *psychology educator, early childhood consultant*
Joyce, Mary Ann *principal*
Koskella, Lucretia C. *real estate broker, appraiser*
Liberth, Richard Francis *lawyer*
Orbacz, Linda Ann *physical education educator*
Saturnelli, Annette Miele *school system administrator*
Severo, Richard *writer*
Weiss, Barry Ronald *education administrator*
Wilcox, David Eric *electrical engineer, educational consultant*

## Newton Falls
Hunter, William Schmidt *engineering executive, environmental engineer*

## Newtonville
Apostle, Christos Nicholas *social psychologist*
Weber, Barbara M. *sales executive, consultant*

## Niagara Falls
Anton, Ronald David *lawyer*
Bundy-Iannarelli, Barbara Ann *educational administrator*
Collins, Christopher Carl *manufacturing executive*
Dojka, Edwin Sigmund *civil engineer*
Gromosiak, Paul *author, historian, science & mathematics educator*
Grove, Jeffery Lynn *minister*
Jessiman, Marilynn R. *library media specialist*
King, George Gerard *chemical company executive*
Knowles, Richard Norris *chemist*
Kuciewski, Patrick Michael *music educator*
May, David A. *protective services official, public official*
Powers, Bruce Raymond *author, English language educator, consultant*
Shaghoian, Cynthia Lynne *accountant*
Sheeran, Thomas Joseph *education educator, writer, consultant, judge*
Smeal, Carolyn A. *community health nurse, educator*
Stirling, Michelle Dianne *tax specialist, accountant*

## Niagara University
O'Leary, Daniel Francis *university dean*
Osberg, Timothy M. *psychologist, educator, researcher*

## Niskayuna
De Jesus-McCarthy, Fe Teresa *physician*
Edelheit, Lewis S. *research physicist*
Fitzroy, Nancy deLoye *technology executive, engineer*
Huening, Walter Carl, Jr. *retired consulting application engineer*
Johnson, Ingolf Birger *retired electrical engineer*
Katz, Samuel *geophysics educator*
Lafferty, James Martin *physicist*
Mangan, John Leo *retired electrical manufacturing company executive, international trade and trade policy specialist*
Mihran, Theodore Gregory *retired physicist*
Sacklow, Stewart Irwin *advertising executive*
Whittingham, Harry Edward, Jr. *retired banker*

## North Bellmore
Chun, Arlene Donnelly *special education educator*

## North Boston
Herbert, James Alan *writer*

## North Hartford
Fellone, Christina Kates *oncology nurse*

## North Rose
Anderson, Nancy Marie Greenwood *special education educator*

## North Salem
Burlingame, Edward Livermore *book publisher*
Gruber, Alan Richard *insurance company executive*
Larsen, Jonathan Zerbe *journalist*
†Sloves, Marvin *advertising agency executive*

## North Syracuse
Brophy, Mary O'Reilly *industrial hygienist*
Williamson, Donna Maria *pastoral counselor*

## North Tarrytown
Otten, Michael *data processing executive*

## Northport
Brown, John Edward *textile company executive*
Gelfand, Andrew *software developer, consultant*
Hohenberger, Patricia Julie *fine arts and antique appraiser, consultant*
Litchford, George B. *aeronautical engineer*
Reinertsen, Norman *retired aircraft systems company executive*
Weber, Ray Everett *engineering executive, consultant*

## Norwich
Berman, Ethel Wargotz *artist, educator*
Garzione, John Edward *physical therapist*
Hanna, Eduardo Zacarias *pharmaceutical company executive*

## Nyack
Degenshein, Jan *architect, planner*
Flood, (Hulda) Gay *editor, consultant*
Hendin, David Bruce *literary agent, author, consultant, numismatist*
Karp, Peter Simon *marketing executive*
Keil, John Mullan *advertising agency executive*
Leiser, Ernest Stern *journalist*
Mann, Kenneth Walker *retired minister, psychologist*
Ortiz, Angel Vicente *church administrator*
Rodwell-Bell, Regina *museum director*
Rossi, Harald Hermann *retired radiation biophysicist, educator, administrator*
Seidler, B(ernard) Alan *lawyer*

## Oakdale
Bragdon, Clifford Richardson *city planner, educator*
Meskill, Victor Peter *college president, educator*
Sherman, Jeffrey Alan *dentist*

## Oceanside
Mills, James Spencer *author*

## Ogdensburg
Loverde, Paul S. *bishop*
Rusaw, Sally Ellen *librarian*

## Old Bethpage
Buzzelli, Dennis Kevin *mechanical engineer*
Dryce, H. David *accountant, consultant*

## Old Brookville
Fairman, Joel Martin *broadcasting executive*
Feinberg, Irwin L. *retired manufacturing company executive*

## Old Chatham
Teng, Juliet *artist*

## Old Westbury
Dibble, Richard Edward *academic administrator*
Katz, Roger Martin *infosystems engineer*
Kurlander, Honey Wachtel *artist, educator*
Ozelli, Tunch *economics educator, consultant*
Pettigrew, L. Eudora *academic administrator*
Rabil, Albert, Jr. *humanities educator*
Saueracker, Edward *academic administrator*
Schure, Matthew *college president*

## Olean
Catalano, Robert Anthony *ophthalmologist, physician, hospital administrator, writer*
Godfrey, John *internist*
Rauhut, Horst Wilfried *research scientist*

## Olmstedville
Frost, David *former biology educator, medical editor, consultant*

## Oneida
Matthews, William D(oty) *lawyer, consumer products manufacturing company executive*
Muschenheim, Frederick *pathologist*

## Oneonta
Bergstein, Harry Benjamin *psychology educator*
Detweller, Richard Allen *college president*
Diehl, Lesley Ann *psychologist*
Donovan, Alan Barton *college president*
Freckelton, Sondra *artist*
Grappone, William Eugene *clinical social worker, gerontologist, consultant*
Hickey, Francis Roger *physicist, educator*
Johnson, Richard David *retired librarian*
Knudson, Richard Lewis *editor*
Malhotra, Ashok Kumar *philsophy educator*
Merilan, Michael Preston *astrophysicist, dean, educator*
Smith, Geoffrey Adams *special purpose mobile unit manufacturing executive*
Zachmeyer, Richard Frederick *administrator*

## Orangeburg
Frommelt, John Banta *financial executive*
Furlong, Patrick Louis *health science association administrator*
Hennessy, James Ernest *academic administrator, telecommunications executive, retired*
Levine, Jerome *psychiatrist, educator*
Rivet, Diana Wittmer *lawyer, developer*
Siegel, Carole Ethel *mathematician*
Squires, Richard Felt *research scientist*

## Orchard Park
†Brown, Ruben Pernell *football player*
†Butler, John *professional sports team executive*
Franklin, Murray Joseph *retired steel foundry executive*
Hull, Kent *professional football player*
Lee, Richard Vaille *physician, educator*
Levy, Marvin Daniel *professional football coach, sports team executive*
Noll, John F. *sales and marketing executive, investment banker*
Paup, Bryce Eric *professional football player*
Reed, Andre Darnell *professional football player*
Reid, Thomas Fenton *minister*
Schulz, Lawrence A. *lawyer*
Smith, Bruce *professional football player*
Spielman, Chris *professional football player*
Sullivan, Mortimer Allen, Jr. *lawyer*
Tasker, Steven Jay *professional football player*
Thomas, Thurman *professional football player*

## Orient
Hanson, Thor *retired health agency executive and naval officer*

## Ossining
Beard, Janet Marie *health care administrator*
Carter, Richard *publisher, writer*
Chervokas, John Vincent *chamber of commerce executive*
Daly, William Joseph *lawyer*
Eurell, Joseph Michael *marketing professional, municipal official*
Finnegan, George Bernard, III *financial advisor*
Gilbert, Joan Stulman *public relations executive*
Ravis, Howard Shepard *conference planner and publishing consultant*
Reynolds, Calvin *management consultant, business educator*
Stein, Sol *publisher, writer, editor in chief*
Weintz, Caroline Giles *non-profit association consultant, travel writer*
Wolfe, Mary Joan *physician*

## Oswego
Fox, Michael David *art educator, visual imagist artist*
Gerber, Barbara Ann Witter *university dean, educator*
Gooding, Charles Thomas *psychology educator, college provost*
Gordon, Norman Botnick *psychology educator*
Kumar, Alok *physics educator*
Moody, Florence Elizabeth *education educator, retired college dean*
Nesbitt, Rosemary Sinnett *theatre educator*
Silveira, Augustine, Jr. *chemistry educator*
Smiley, Marilynn Jean *musicologist*

## Owego
McCann, Jean Friedrichs *artist, educator*
Smoral, Vincent J. *electrical engineer*

## Oyster Bay
Gable, John Allen *historian, association executive, educator*
Mooney, James David, Jr. *security consultant*
Prey, Barbara Ernst *artist*
Prey, Jeffrey Drew *minister*
Robinson, Edward T., III *lawyer*
Russell, Mary Wendell Vander Poel *non-profit organization executive, interior*
Schwab, Hermann Caspar *banker*
Trevor, Bronson *economist*
Urdea, John *electromechanical engineer*

## Painted Post
Hammond, George Simms *chemist, consultant*
Ogden, Anita Bushey *nursing educator*

## Palenville
Coletti, Louis Roland *financial planner, realtor*

## Palisades
Anderson, Margaret Tayler *real estate broker, career consultant*
Berger, Thomas Louis *author*
Cane, Mark Alan *oceanography and climate researcher*
Cavett, Dick *entertainer*
Davis, Dorothy Salisbury *author*
Hayes, Dennis Edward *geophysicist, educator*
Kent, Dennis Vladimir *geophysicist, researcher*
Knowlton, Grace Farrar *sculptor, photographer*
Krainin, Julian Arthur *film director, producer, writer, cinematographer*
Langmuir, Charles Herbert *geology educator*
Richards, Paul Granston *geophysics educator, seismologist*
Scholz, Christopher Henry *geophysicist, writer*

Sykes, Lynn Ray *geologist, educator*

### Patchogue
Fogarty, James Vincent, Jr. *special education administrator, educator*
Gibbard, Judith R. *library director*
Gibbons, Edward Francis *psychobiologist*
Orlowski, Karel Ann *elementary education educator*

### Patterson
Winby, Mary Bernadette *marketing executive*

### Pawling
Peale, Ruth Stafford (Mrs. Norman Vincent Peale) *religious leader*

### Pearl River
Barik, Sudhakar *microbiologist, research scientist*
Caliendo, G. D. (Jerry Caliendo) *public utility executive*
Colman, Samuel *assemblyman*
Galante, Joseph Anthony, Jr. *computer programmer*
Jackson, Phillip Ellis *cause-related marketing executive, writer*
Meyer, Irwin Stephan *lawyer, accountant*
Rasch, Stuart Gary *emergency physician*

### Peconic
Mitchell, Robert Everitt *lawyer*

### Peekskill
Harte, Andrew Dennis *transportation company executive, travel agent*
Rosenberg, Marilyn Rosenthal *artist, visual poet*

### Pelham
Bornand, Ruth Chaloux *small business owner*
Conroy, Tamara Boks *artist, special education educator, former nurse*
Decker, Carol Arne *magazine publishing consultant*
Fayon, Abram Miko *chemical engineer*
Minick, Michael *publishing executive*
Moore, Ellis Oglesby *retired public affairs consultant*
Ralston, Lucy Virginia Gordon *artist*
Simon, Robert G. *lawyer*

### Phillipsport
Hengesbach, Alice Ann *public relations consultant*

### Piermont
Berkon, Martin *artist*
Fox, Matthew Ignatius *publishing company executive*
Gussow, Alan *artist, sculptor*

### Pine City
Searle, Robert Ferguson *minister*

### Pittsford
Benson, Warren Frank *composer, educator*
Biklen, Stephen Clinton *student loan company executive*
Dorsey, Eugene Carroll *former foundation and communications executive*
Faloon, William Wassell *physician, educator*
Herge, Henry Curtis, Jr. *consulting firm executive*
Hollingsworth, Jack Waring *mathematics and computer science educator*
Kieffer, James Milton *lawyer*
Lyttle, Douglas Alfred *photographer, educator*
Marshall, Joseph Frank *electronic engineer*
Palermo, Peter M., Jr. *photography equipment company executive*
Schubert, John Edward *former banker*
Schwartz, Ruth Wainer *physician*
Taub, Aaron Myron *healthcare administrator, consultant*
Williams, Henry Ward, Jr. *lawyer*

### Plainview
Feller, Benjamin E. *actuary*
Fulton, Richard *lecture bureau executive*
Kelemen, John *neurologist, educator*
Krauss, Leo *urologist, educator*
Lieberman, Elliott *urologist*
Newman, Edwin Harold *news commentator*

### Plattsburgh
Cooper, Richard Francis *computer company executive*
Dossin, Ernest Joseph, III *credit consulting company executive*
Edwards, Peter *educator, writer*
Hanton, E(mile) Michael *public and personnel relations consultant*
Heintz, Roger Lewis *biochemist, educator, researcher*
Herod, Charles Carteret *Afro-American studies educator*
Lewis, Clyde A. *lawyer*
Myers, John Lytle *historian*
Ransom, Christina Roxane *librarian*
Rech, Susan Anita *obstetrician, gynecologist*
Smith, Noel Wilson *psychology educator*
Treacy, William Joseph *electrical and environmental engineer*

### Pleasantville
Ahrensfeld, Thomas Frederick *lawyer*
Annese, Domenico *landscape architect*
Antonecchia, Donald A. *principal*
Black, Percy *psychology educator*
Cober, Alan Edwin *artist, illustrator, printmaker, educator*
Coleman, Gregory G. *magazine publisher*
Eschweiler, Peter Quintus *planning consultant*
Howard, Carole Margaret Munroe *public relations executive*
Joseph, Harriet *English literature educator*
Keller, Mary Beth *advertising executive, researcher*
Kenney, Thomas Michael *publisher*
Needleman, Harry *lawyer*
Pike, John Nazarian *optical engineering consultant*
Reps, David Nathan *finance educator*
Schadt, James Phillip *consumer products executive*
Waletsky, Lucy Rockefeller *psychiatrist*
Willcox, Christopher Patrick *magazine editor*
Willis, William Henry *marketing executive*

### Poestenkill
Radley, Virginia Louise *humanities educator*

### Point Lookout
Stack, Maurice Daniel *retired insurance company executive*

### Pomona
Glassman, Lawrence S. *plastic surgeon*
Gordon, Edmund Wyatt *psychologist, educator*
Landau, Lauri Beth *accountant, tax consultant*
Zerin, Jay M. *lawyer*

### Port Chester
Ailloni-Charas, Dan *marketing executive*
†McKenna, John *computer company executive*
Oppenheimer, Suzi *state senator*
Penney, Linda Helen *music educator*
Rubin, Jacob Carl *mechanical research engineer*
Whaley, Christopher David *manufacturing engineer*

### Port Jefferson
Boucher, Louis Jack *retired dentist, educator*
Dranitzke, Richard J. *thoracic surgeon*

### Port Jefferson Station
Kaplan, Martin Paul *pediatrician, educator*

### Port Kent
Mc Kee, James, Jr. *retired bank executive*

### Port Washington
Anable, Anne Currier Steinert *journalist*
Blakeslee, Alton Lauren *scientific writer*
Brownstein, Martin Herbert *dermatopathologist*
Ciccariello, Priscilla Chloe *librarian*
Feldman, Jay Newman *lawyer, telecommunications executive*
Hackett, John Byron *advertising agency executive, lawyer*
Jay, Frank Peter *writer, educator*
Johnson, Tod Stuart *market research company executive*
Jones, Farrell *judge*
Kellner, Irwin L. *economist*
Oromaner, Daniel Stuart *marketing consultant*
Phelan, Arthur Joseph *financial executive*
Read, Frederick Wilson, Jr. *lawyer, educator*
Saltzman, Ellen S. *mediator*
Simmons, Lee Howard *book publishing company executive*
Sonnenfeldt, Richard Wolfgang *management consultant*
Tarleton, Robert Stephen *producer and distributor fine arts videos*
Taylor, Cecil Percival *pianist, composer, educator*
Williams, George Leo *retired secondary education educator*

### Portlandville
Munro, Janet Andrea *artist*

### Potsdam
Carroll, James Joseph *electrical and computer engineering educator*
Chin, Der-Tau *chemical engineer, educator*
Cotellessa, Robert Francis *retired electrical engineering educator, academic administrator*
Cross, John William *foreign language educator*
Ha, Andrew Kwangho *education educator*
Hanson, David Justin *sociology educator, researcher*
Harder, Kelsie Brown *retired language professional, educator*
Mackay, Raymond Arthur *chemist*
Matijevic, Egon *chemistry educator*
Mochel, Myron George *mechanical engineer, educator*
Ratliff, Gerald Lee *dean, speech and theater educator*
Rudiger, Lance Wade *secondary school educator*
Sathyamoorthy, Muthukrishnan *engineering researcher, educator*
Shen, Hung Tao *hydraulic engineering educator*
Stevens, Sheila Maureen *teachers union administrator*
†Stoltie, James Merle *academic administrator*
Washburn, Robert Brooks *university dean, composer*
Wells, David John *program director, academic administrator, mechanical engineer*

### Poughkeepsie
Agerwala, Tilak Krishna Mahesh *computer company executive*
Barker, Richard Alexander *organizational psychologist*
Bartlett, Lynn Conant *English literature educator*
Beck, Curt Werner *chemist, educator*
Berlin, Doris Ada *psychiatrist*
Brakas, Nora Jachym *education educator*
Carino, Aurora Lao *psychiatrist, hospital administrator*
Chu, Richard Chao-Fan *mechanical engineer*
Conklin, D(onald) David *academic administrator*
Daniels, Elizabeth Adams *English language educator*
Deiters, Sister Joan Adele *chemistry educator, nun*
Dolan, Thomas Joseph *judge*
Fergusson, Frances Daly *college president, educator*
Gardenier, Edna Frances *nursing educator*
Glasse, John Howell *retired philosophy and theology educator*
Griffen, Clyde Chesterman *retired history educator*
Handel, Bernard *accountant, actuarial and insurance consultant, lawyer*
Hansen, Karen Thornley *accountant*
Harris, Michael James *broadcasting executive*
Heller, Mary Bernita *psychotherapist*
Henley, Richard James *healthcare institution administrator and financial officer*
Hytier, Adrienne Doris *French language educator*
Johnson, M(aurice) Glen *political science educator*
Kanwit, Bert Alfred *retired surgeon*
Kelley, David Christopher *philosopher*
Kim, David Sang Chul *publisher, evangelist, retired seminary president*
Kohl, Benjamin Gibbs *historian, educator*
Lang, William Warner *physicist*
Lipschutz, Ilse Hempel *language educator*
Logue, Joseph Carl *electronics engineer, consultant*
Mack, John Edward, III *utility company executive*
Maling, George Croswell, Jr. *physicist*
Marshall, Natalie Junemann *economics educator*
McFadden, John Thomas *financial planner, insurance agent, investor*
Millman, Jode Susan *lawyer*
Opdycke, Leonard Emerson *retired secondary education educator, publisher*
O'Shea, John P. *insurance executive*
Ostertag, Robert Louis *lawyer*
Pliskin, William Aaron *physicist*
Rhodes, Geraldine Bryan *secondary school administrator*
Rosenblatt, Albert Martin *judge*
Slade, Bernard Newton *electronics company executive*
Stridsberg, Albert Borden *advertising consultant, educator, editor*
Tavel, Morton Allen *physics educator, researcher*
VanBuren, Denise Doring *media relations executive*
Van Zanten, Frank Veldhuyzen *retired library system director*
Willard, Nancy Margaret *writer, educator*
†Wilson, Richard Edward *composer, pianist, music educator*

### Pound Ridge
Ferro, Walter *artist*
Rubino, John Anthony *management and human resources consultant*
Schwebel, Renata Manasse *sculptor*
Throckmorton, Joan Helen *direct marketing consultant*
Webb, Richard Gilbert *financial executive*

### Purchase
Berman, Richard Angel *health and educational administrator*
Carleton, Robert L. *consumer products company executive*
Clark, Mary Twibill *philosopher, educator*
Daniel, Charles Timothy *transportation engineer, consultant*
Deering, Allan Brooks *beverage company executive*
Dillon, John T. *paper company executive*
Ehrman, Lee *geneticist*
Enrico, Roger A. *soft drink company executive*
Finnerty, Louise Hoppe *beverage and food company executive*
Gedeon, Lucinda Heyel *museum director*
Gioffre, Bruno Joseph *lawyer*
Guedry, James Walter *lawyer, paper corporation executive*
Hunziker, Robert McKee *paper company executive*
Kelly, Edmund Joseph *lawyer, investment banker*
Lacy, Bill *academic administrator*
Melican, James Patrick, Jr. *lawyer*
Noonan, Frank R. *business executive*
Panaro, Joseph *financial services company executive*
Ryan, Edward W. *economics educator*
Sandler, Irving Harry *art critic, art historian*
Schwerin, Warren Lyons *real estate developer*
Siegel, Nathaniel Harold *sociology educator*
†Staley, Harry L. *fund raising executive*
Turk, Milan Joseph *chemical company executive*
von der Heyden, Karl Ingolf Mueller *manufacturing company executive*
Wallach, Ira David *lawyer, business executive*
Wallin, James Peter *lawyer*
Wright, David L. *food and beverage company executive*

### Putnam Valley
Amram, David Werner *composer, conductor, musician*

### Queens Village
Le, Dan Hoang *data administrator, consultant*

### Queensbury
Bitner, William Lawrence, III *retired banker, educator*
Borgos, Stephen John *business educator, consultant, municipal administrator, real estate broker*
Lake, William Thomas *financial consultant*
Mead, John Milton *banker*

### Quogue
Cooke, Robert John *history and law educator*
Malabre, Alfred Leopold, Jr. *journalist, author*

### Randolph
Margesson, Maxine Edge *professor*

### Ransomville
Mayer, George Merton *elementary education educator*

### Ravena
Bower, Shelley Ann *business management consultant*

### Red Hook
Schulberg, Budd *author*

### Rego Park
Ben-Harari, Ruben Robert *research scientist, medical writer, medical communications consultant*
Cronyn, Hume *actor, writer, director*
Gudeon, Arthur *podiatrist*
LeFrak, Samuel J. *housing and building corporation executive*
Uter, Carmenlita *secondary education language educator, translator*

### Remsenburg
Billman, Irwin Edward *publishing company executive*
Edwards, Arthur Anderson *retired mechanical engineer*

### Rensselaer
Nack, Claire Durani *artist, author*
Semowich, Charles John *art historian, art dealer and appraiser, curator, artist*

### Rensselaerville
Dudley, George Austin *architect, planning consultant, educator*

### Rexford
Schmitt, Roland Walter *retired academic administrator*

### Rhinebeck
Barker, Barbara Yvonne *respiratory care administrator*
Clutz, William (Hartman Clutz) *artist, educator*
†Flexner, Kurt Fisher *economics educator*
Rabinovich, Raquel *artist, sculptor*
Smith, Lewis Motter, Jr. *advertising and direct marketing executive*

### Rhinecliff
Dierdorff, John Ainsworth *retired editor*
Meehan, John *artistic director*

### Ridgewood
Giambalvo, Vincent Salvatore *secondary education educator*
Jones, Harold Antony *banker*
Meehan, Richard Andrew *investment banker*

### Riverdale
Cammarata, Joan Frances *Spanish language and literature educator*
De La Cancela, Victor *psychologist*
Hollein, Helen Conway *chemical engineer, educator*
Hubley, Faith Elliott *filmmaker, painter, animator*
Itzkoff, Norman Jay *lawyer*

### Riverhead
Stark, Thomas Michael *state supreme court justice*

### Rochester
Abood, Leo George *biochemistry educator*
Adams, G. Rollie *museum executive*
†Afifi, Alaa Youssef *cardiothoracic surgeon*
Allen, Henry Lee *education educator, consultant*
Alling, Norman Larrabee *mathematics educator*
Alpert-Gillis, Linda Jayne *clinical psychologist*
Andolina, Lawrence J. *lawyer*
Annunziata, Frank *history educator*
Argenta, Joseph John *architect*
Balch, Glenn McClain, Jr. *academic administrator, minister, author*
Balderston, William, III *retired banker*
Bannon, Anthony Leo *museum director*
Barton, Russell William *psychiatrist, author*
Baum, John *physician*
Belgiorno, John *career consultant, educator*
Bennett, John Morrison *medical oncologist*
Berg, Robert Lewis *physician, educator*
Berman, Milton *history educator*
Bernhardt, Robert *music director, conductor*
Bernstein, Paul *retired academic dean*
Bessey, Palmer Quintard *surgeon*
Bigelow, Nicholas Pierre *physicist, educator*
Billings, Ronald J. *dental research administrator*
Bluhm, William Theodore *political scientist, educator*
Blyth, John E. *lawyer, educator*
Boeckman, Robert Kenneth, Jr. *chemistry educator, organic chemistry researcher*
Bonfiglio, Thomas Albert *pathologist, educator*
Borch, Richard Frederic *pharmacology and chemistry educator*
Bouyoucos, John Vinton *research and development company executive*
Bowen, William Henry *dental researcher, dental educator*
Braunsdorf, Paul Raymond *lawyer*
Brideau, Leo Paul *healthcare executive*
Brody, Bernard B. *physician, educator*
Brooks, Walter S. *dermatologist*
Brzustowicz, Richard John *neurosurgeon, educator*
Buckingham, Barbara Rae *educator*
Buckley, Michael Francis *lawyer*
Burgener, Francis André *radiology educator*
Burns, Stephen James *engineering educator, materials science researcher*
Burrill, William George *bishop*
Burton, Richard Irving *orthopedist, educator*
Bushinsky, David Allen *nephrologist, educator, researcher*
Cain, B(urton) Edward *chemistry educator*
Cain, Russell M. *psychiatrist*
Campbell, Alma Jacqueline Porter *elementary education educator*
Campbell, Vincent Bernard *municipal judge, lawyer*
Carlton, Charles Merritt *linguistics educator*
Carstensen, Edwin Lorenz *biomedical engineer, biophysicist*
Chang, Jack Che-man *photoscience research laboratory director*
Charles, Michael Harrison *architectural interior designer*
Chiarenza, Carl *art historian, critic, artist, educator*
Chu, Ellin Resnick *librarian, consultant*
Ciccone, J. Richard *psychiatrist*
Clark, Matthew Harvey *bishop*
Clarkson, Thomas William *toxicologist, educator*
Clement, Thomas Earl *lawyer*
Cline, Douglas *physicist, educator*
Cohen, Jules *academic dean, physician, educator*
Cohen, Nicholas *immunologist, educator*
Cokelet, Giles Roy *biomedical engineering educator*
Colby, William Michael *lawyer*
Coleman, Paul David *neurobiology researcher, educator*
Corio, Mark Andrew *electronics executive*
Crane, Irving Donald *pocket billiards player*
Crino, Marjanne Helen *anesthesiologist*
D'Agostino, Anthony Carmen *anthropologist, educator*
Deci, Edward Lewis *psychologist, educator*
DeMarco, Roland R. *foundation executive*
de Papp, Elise Wachenfeld *pathologist*
DeToro, Irving John *management consultant*
Diamond, David Leo *composer*
Dohanian, Diran Kavork *art historian, educator*
Donovan, Kreag *lawyer*
Doty, Robert William *neurophysiologist, educator*
Doyle, Justin P *lawyer*
Dreyfuss, Eric Martin *allergist*
Duarte, Francisco Javier *physicist, researcher*
DuBrin, Andrew John *behavioral sciences, management educator, author*
Eaves, Morris Emery *English language educator*
Eisenberg, Richard S. *chemistry educator*
Elder, Fred Kingsley, Jr. *physicist, educator*
Engelmann, Lothar Klaus *photographic science educator*
Engerman, Stanley Lewis *economist, educator, historian*
Everett, Claudia Kellam *special education educator*
Fagan, Garth *choreographer, artistic director, educator*
Fenno, Richard Francis, Jr. *political science educator*
Ferbel, Thomas *physics educator, physicist*
Fisher, George Myles Cordell *electronics equipment company executive, mathematician, engineer*
Forbes, Gilbert Burnett *physician, educator*
Frank, Irwin Norman *urologist, educator*
Frazer, John Paul *surgeon*
Freckleton, Jon Edward *engineering educator, consultant, retired military officer*
Friauf, Katherine Elizabeth *metal company executive*
Frisina, Robert Dana *sensory neuroscientist, educator*

Gans, Roger Frederick mechanical engineering educator
Garcia-Prichard, Diana research scientist, chemical physicist
Garg, Devendra financial executive
Gartner, Joseph Charles business systems administrator
Gates, Marshall DeMotte, Jr. chemistry educator
Gaudion, Donald Alfred former diversified manufacturing executive
Geertsma, Robert Henry psychologist, educator
George, Nicholas optics educator, researcher
George, Richard Neill lawyer
Goldman, Joel J. lawyer
Goldstein, David Arthur biophysicist, educator
Goldstein, Marvin Norman physician
Golisano, B. Thomas finance company director, human resources director
Gootnick, Margery Fischbein lawyer
Gordon, Dane Rex philosophy educator, minister
Griggs, Robert Charles physician
Gumaer, Elliott Wilder, Jr. lawyer
Gustina, Donna Elizabeth sign language educator, consultant
Hall, Dennis Gene optics educator
Hall, Donald S. retired planetarium administrator, pottery expert
Halpern, Werner Israel psychiatrist, educator
Hampson, Thomas Meredith lawyer
Hanushek, Eric Alan economics educator
Hargrave, Alexander Davidson banker, lawyer
Harris, Alfred social anthropologist, educator
Harris, Diane Carol merger and acquisition consulting firm executive
Harris, Wayne Manley lawyer
Hart-Piper, Lauren computer products professional
Harvey, Douglass Coate retired photographic company executive
Hauser, William Barry history educator, historian
Hayes, Charles Franklin, III museum research consultant
Haywood, Anne Mowbray pediatrics, virology, and biochemistry educator
Heinle, Robert Alan physician
Herminghouse, Patricia Anne foreign language educator
Herz, Marvin Ira psychiatrist
Hilf, Russell biochemist
Hoch, Edward Dentinger author
Hodkinson, Sydney Phillip composer, educator
Hoffberg, David Lawrence lawyer
Holcomb, Grant, III museum director
Holmes, Jay Thorpe lawyer
Hood, John B. lawyer
Hood, William Boyd, Jr. cardiologist, educator
Hopkins, Thomas Duvall economics educator
Hoskin, William Dickel physician
Howard, Hubert Wendell English language educator, academic administrator, choral conductor
Hoy, Cyrus Henry language professional, educator
Hunt, Roger Schermerhorn hospital administrator
Hutchins, Frank McAllister advertising executive
Hyman, Ralph Alan journalist, consultant
Jackson, Thomas Humphrey university president
Jacobs, Bruce political science educator
Jacobs, Laurence Stanton physician, educator
Jesserer, Henry L., III lawyer
Johns, J.C. health facility administrator, internist
Johnson, Bruce Marvin English language educator
Johnson, James William English educator, author
Johnson, Jean Elaine nursing educator
Johnson, William A., Jr. mayor
Johnston, Frank C. psychologist
Jones, Ronald Winthrop economics educator
Joyce, John Joseph English language educator
Joynt, Robert James academic administrator
Kampmeier, Jack August Carlos chemist, educator
Kehoe, L. Paul judge
Kende, Andrew Steven chemistry educator
Kingslake, Rudolf retired optical designer
Kinnen, Edwin electrical engineer, educator
Knauer, James Philip physicist
Knox, Robert Seiple physicist, educator
Kohrt, Carl Fredrick manufacturing executive, scientist
Kowalke, Kim H. music educator, musicologist, conductor, foundation executive
Kraus, Sherry Stokes lawyer
Kreilick, Robert W. chemist, educator
Kurland, Harold Arthur lawyer
Laires, Fernando concert piano educator
†Lank, Edith Handleman columnist, educator
Laties, Victor Gregory psychology educator
Law, Michael R. lawyer
Lawrence, Ruth Anderson pediatrician, clinical toxicologist
Lessen, Martin engineering educator, consulting engineer
Lewis, A. Duff, Jr. investment executive
Li, James Chen Min materials science educator
Lichtman, Marshall Albert medical educator
Loewen, Erwin G. precision engineer, educator, consultant
Long, John Broaddus, Jr. economist, educator
Loui, Alexander Chan Pong electrical engineer, researcher
Lundback, Staffan Bengt Gunnar lawyer
Makous, Walter Leon visual scientist, educator
Mandel, Leonard physics and optics educator
Maniloff, Jack biophysicist, educator
Mann, Alfred musicology educator, choral conductor
Marcellus, John Robert, III trombonist, educator
Margolis, Richard Martin photographer, educator
Marinetti, Guido V. biochemistry educator
Marriott, Marcia Ann human resources administrator, educator, consultant
Matzek, Richard Allan library director
McCall, Thomas Donald marketing communications company executive
McClure, Lucretia Walker medical librarian
McCrory, John Brooks retired lawyer
McCrory, Robert Lee physicist, mechanical engineering educator
McCurdy, Gilbert Geier retired retailer
Mc Donald, Joseph Valentine neurosurgeon
Mc Isaac, George Scott business policy educator, government official, former management consultant
Mc Kelvey, Jean Trepp industrial relations educator
Mc Kenzie, Lionel Wilfred economist, educator
McKie, W. Gilmore human resources executive
McMeekin, Thomas Owen dermatologist
McNamara, Timothy James secondary education educator
Mc Quillen, Michael Paul physician
Meloni, Andrew P. protective services official
Menguy, Rene surgeon, educator
Merritt, Howard Sutermeister retired art educator
Moore, Duncan Thomas optics educator
Moore, Matthew Scott publisher, deaf advocate, author
Morgan, William Lionel, Jr. physician, educator
Morrison, Patrice B. lawyer
Morrow, Paul Edward toxicology educator
Morton, John H. surgeon, educator
Moss, Arthur Jay physician
Muchmore, William Breuleux zoologist, educator
Mueller, John Ernest political science educator, dance critic and historian
Munson, Harold Lewis education educator
Nazarian, Lawrence Fred pediatrician
Newell, William James sign language educator
Niemi, Richard Gene political science educator
Nutter, David George urban planner
Oberdorster, Gunter toxicologist
Oberlies, John William physician organization executive
Olson, Russell L. pension fund administrator
O'Mara, Robert Edmund George radiologist, educator
Pacala, Leon retired association executive
Palermo, Anthony Robert lawyer
Paley, Gerald Larry lawyer
Palmer, Harvey John chemical engineering educator, consultant
Palmeri, Marlaina principal
Palvino, Jack Anthony broadcasting executive
Palvino, Nancy Mangin librarian
Panner, Bernard J. pathologist, educator
Parker, Kevin James electrical engineer educator
Parsons, George Raymond, Jr. lawyer
Paterson, Eileen radiation oncologist, educator
Pearce, William Joseph retired public broadcasting executive, consultant
Pearson, Thomas Arthur epidemiologist, educator
Pettee, Daniel Starr neurologist
Phelps, Charles Elliott economics educator
Plosser, Charles Irving university dean, economics educator
Pollicove, Harvey Myles manufacturing executive
Powers, James Matthew neuropathologist
Prosser, Michael Hubert communications educator
Przybylowicz, Edwin Paul chemical company executive, research director
Ramsey, Jarold William English language educator, author
Reed, James Alexander, Jr. lawyer
Regenstreif, S(amuel) Peter political scientist, educator
Reifler, Clifford Bruce psychiatrist, educator
Resnick, Alan Howard eye care executive
Richards, Thomas Savidge utility company executive
Risher, William Henry cardiothoracic surgeon
Robfogel, Susan Salitan lawyer
Rosenbaum, Richard Merrill lawyer
Rosett, Richard Nathaniel economist, educator
Rosner, Leonard Allen lawyer
Rothberg, Abraham author, educator, editor
Rothman-Marshall, Gail Ann counseling services administrator
Rouse, Christopher Chapman, III composer
Rowley, Peter Templeton physician, educator
Rulison, Joseph Richard investment advisor
Saisselin, Remy Gilbert fine arts educator
Sangree, Walter Hinchman social anthropologist, educator
Saunders, William Hundley, Jr. retired chemist, educator
Scalise, Francis Allen administrator, consultant
Schaffner, Robert Jay, Jr. nurse practitioner
Schmidhammer, Robert Howard environmental executive, engineering consultant
Schumacher, Jon Lee lawyer
Schwantner, Joseph composer, educator
Schwartz, Seymour Ira surgeon, educator
Scott, Joanna Jeanne writer, English language educator
Scutt, Robert Carl lawyer
Seager, Steven Albert small business owner, accountant
Segal, Sanford Leonard mathematics educator
Sherman, Charles Daniel, Jr. surgeon
Sherman, Fred biochemist, educator
Sieg, Albert Louis photographic company executive
Simon, Albert physicist, engineer, educator
Simon, Leonard Samuel banker
Simon, William biomathematician, educator
Simone, Albert Joseph academic administrator
Skupsky, Stanley laser fusion scientist
Smith, John Stuart lawyer
Smith, Julia Ladd medical oncologist, hospice physician
†Speranza, Paul Samuel, Jr. lawyer
Spurrier, Mary Eileen investment advisor, financial planner
Steamer, Robert Julius political science educator
Stewart, Sue S. lawyer
Stonehill, Eric lawyer
Strand, Marion Delores social service administrator
Swanton, Susan Irene library director
Telesca, Michael Anthony federal judge
Thomas, Garth Johnson psychology educator emeritus
Thomas, John Howard astrophysicist, engineer, educator
Thompson, Brian John university administrator, optics educator
Thorndike, Edward Harmon physicist
Toribara, Taft Yutaka radiation biologist, biophysicist, chemist, toxicologist
Trueheart, Harry Parker, III lawyer
Turner, Scott MacNeely lawyer
Turri, Joseph A. lawyer
Tyler, John Randolph lawyer
Underberg, Alan Jack lawyer
Utell, Mark Jeffrey medical educator
Van Graafeiland, Ellsworth Alfred federal judge
Von Holden, Martin Harvey psychologist
Waite, Stephen Holden lawyer
Walker, Michael Charles, Sr. retirement services executive
Watts, Ross Leslie accounting educator, consultant
Wayland-Smith, Robert Dean banker
Wegman, Robert B. food service executive
Weiss, Howard A. violinist, concertmaster, conductor, music educator
Wey, Jong-Shinn research laboratory manager
Whitten, David George chemistry educator
Wiedrick-Kozlowski, Jan Barbara communications executive
Wild, Robert Warren lawyer
Wiley, Jason LaRue, Jr. neurosurgeon
Willett, Thomas Edward lawyer
Williams, Thomas Franklin physician, educator
Witmer, George Robert, Jr. lawyer
Wolf, Emil physics educator
Wynne, Lyman Carroll psychiatrist
Yin, Fang-Fang medical physicist, educator
Young, Mary Elizabeth history educator
Zagorin, Perez historian, educator
Zamboni, Helen Attena lawyer, international telecommunications executive
Zax, Melvin psychologist, educator

### Rock Hill
Lombardi, Kent Bailey insurance company administrator
Williams, Annemarie Hauber secondary education educator

### Rockville Centre
Fitzgerald, Sister Janet Anne college president emeritus
Lerner, Steven Paul lawyer
McGann, John Raymond bishop

### Rome
Allen, Paul Christopher computer specialist
Campbell, Joann Cavo social worker
Coppola, Anthony electrical engineer
Gabelman, Irving Jacob consulting engineering executive, retired government official
Griffith, Emlyn Irving lawyer
Griffith, Mary L. Kilpatrick (Mrs. Emlyn I. Griffith) civic leader
Pflug, Donald Ralph electrical engineer
Simons, Richard Duncan lawyer
Waters, George Bausch newspaper publisher

### Ronkonkoma
Nussdorf, Bernard wholesale distribution executive
Townsend, Paul Brorstrom editor
Townsend, Terry publishing executive

### Roosevelt
Wisner, Roscoe William, Jr. retired human resources executive

### Roslyn
Barnathan, Julius broadcasting company executive
Cohen, Edward civil engineer
Damus, Paul Shibli cardiac surgeon
Epstein, Arthur Barry optometrist
Finke, Leonda Froehlich sculptor
Freedman, Joseph Mark optometrist
Levitan, David M(aurice) lawyer, educator
Risom, Ole Christian publishing company executive
Scollard, Patrick John hospital executive
Ulanoff, Stanley M. communications executive

### Roslyn Heights
Faber, Adele author, educator
Glickman, Franklin Sheldon dermatologist, educator
Jaffe, Melvin securities company executive
Rogatz, Peter physician
Tully, Michael J., Jr. state senator

### Rouses Point
Weierstall, Richard Paul pharmaceutical chemist

### Rye
Anderson, Allan architectural firm executive
Barker, Harold Grant surgeon, educator
Beldock, Donald Travis financial executive
Dixon, Paul Edward lawyer, metal products and manufacturing company executive
Erlick, Everett Howard broadcasting company executive
Finnerty, John Dudley investment banker, financial educator
Flanagan, Eugene John Thomas retired lawyer
Hopf, Frank Rudolph dentist
Kaulakis, Arnold Francis management consultant
Lehman, Lawrence Herbert consulting engineering executive
Marcus, Joel David pediatrician
Metzger, Frank management consultant
Mintz, Stephen Allan real estate company executive, lawyer
Mittelstadt, Charles Anthony advertising executive
Newburger, Howard Martin psychoanalyst
Pearson, Nathan Williams broadcast executive
Reader, George Gordon physician, educator
Sonneborn, Henry, III former chemical company executive, business consultant
Stoller, Ezra photojournalist
Troller, Fred graphic designer, painter, visual consultant, educator
Wagner, Edward Frederick, Jr. investment management company executive
Wessler, Stanford physician, educator
Wilmot, Irvin Gorsage former hospital administrator, educator, consultant

### Rye Brook
Cameron, Dort electronics executive
Cooper, Isabel Selma sculptor, writer, art historian
FitzSimons, Sharon Russell international financial and treasury executive
Garcia C., Elisa Dolores lawyer
Landegger, George F. engineering executive
Masson, Robert Henry paper company executive

### Sag Harbor
Baer, Jon Alan political scientist
Barry, Nada Davies retail business owner
Diamond, Mary E(lizabeth) B(aldwin) artist
Pierce, Lawrence Warren retired federal judge
Reeves, Richard writer, historian

### Sagaponack
Appleman, Marjorie (M. H. Appleman) playwright, educator, poet
Appleman, Philip poet, writer, educator
Butchkes, Sydney artist
Isham, Sheila Eaton artist

### Saint Bonaventure
Doyle, Mathias Francis university president, political scientist, educator
Khairullah, Zahid Yahya management sciences and marketing educator, consultant

### Saint James
Bigeleisen, Jacob chemist, educator
Irvine, Thomas Francis, Jr. mechanical engineering educator
Van Dover, Karen middle and elementary school educator, curriculum consultant, language arts specialist

### Saint Regis Falls
Lange, Robert John (Mutt Lange) producer

### Sanborn
Michalak, Janet Carol reading education educator
Schmidt-Bova, Carolyn Marie vocational school administrator, consultant

### Sands Point
Cohen, Ida Bogin (Mrs. Savin Cohen) import and export executive
Goodman, Edmund Nathan surgeon
Hoynes, Louis LeNoir, Jr. lawyer
Lear, Erwin anesthesiologist, educator
Olian, JoAnne Constance curator, art historian
Wurzel, Leonard retired candy manufacturing company executive

### Saranac Lake
North, Robert John biologist
Szwed, Beryl J. school system administrator, mathematics educator

### Saratoga Springs
Abrams, Kenneth Theodore academic administrator
Colangelo, Jayne Anne Parker accountant, auditor
Davis, John Eugene restaurant owner
Hall, James William college president
Higgins, Marika O'Baire nurse, educator, designer, writer, entrepreneur
Parthasarathy, Rajagopal writer, literature educator
Porter, David Hugh pianist, classicist, academic administrator, liberal arts educator
Ratzer, Mary Boyd secondary education educator, librarian
Stanley, Karen Francine Mary Lesniewski human resources professional
Upton, Richard Thomas artist
Wait, Charles Valentine banker

### Sayville
Blume, Sheila Bierman psychiatrist
Lippman, Sharon Rochelle art historian, curator, art therapist, writer

### Scarborough
Beglarian, Grant foundation executive, composer, consultant
Wittcoff, Harold Aaron chemist

### Scarsdale
Abbe, Colman investment banker
Bernstein, Irving international organization executive
Blinder, Abe Lionel management consultant
Blitman, Howard Norton construction company executive
Breinin, Raymond painter, sculptor
Buttinger-Fedeli, Catharine Sarina Caroline psychiatrist
Celliers, Peter Joubert public relations specialist
Clark, Merrell Mays management consultant
Cohen, Irwin economist
Eforo, John Francis financial officer
Fendelman, Helaine art appraiser
Florman, Samuel Charles civil engineer
Frackman, Noel art critic
Frankel, Stanley Arthur columnist, educator, business executive
Gerber, Roger Alan lawyer, business consultant
Glickenhaus, Sarah Brody speech therapist
Goldberg, Harriet David urban planner
Gollin, Stuart Allen accountant
Graff, Henry Franklin historian, educator
Griffiths, Daniel Edward dean emeritus
Hayman, Seymour former food company executive
Heese, William John music publishing company executive
Hines, William Eugene banker
Hoffman, Richard M. lawyer
Jensen, Grady Edmonds retired association executive
Johnson, Boine Theodore instruments company executive, mayor
Josevie, Arnold Jean Phillipe physicist, scientific consultant
Kaufman, Robert Jules communications consultant, lawyer
King, Robert Lucien lawyer
†Lehodey, John Francois hotel company executive
Liston, Mary Frances retired nursing educator
Marks, Barbara Hanzel publishing executive
Moser, Marvin physician, educator, author
Netter, Kurt Fred retired building products company executive
Newman, Fredric Alan plastic surgeon, educator
O'Brien, Edward Ignatius lawyer, private investor
O'Neill, Michael James editor, author
Oswald, George Charles advertising executive, management and marketing consultant
Paige, Susanne Lynn financial consultant
Paulin, Amy Ruth civic activist, consultant
Rapaport, Rita artist, sculpture, painter
Ries, Martin artist, educator
Rivlin, Richard Saul physician, educator
Rogalski, Lois Ann speech and language pathologist
Rosow, Jerome Morris institute executive
Rubin, A. Louis advertising executive
Sandell, Richard Arnold international trade executive, economist
Scheinberg, Labe Charles physician, educator
Schwartz, Harry journalist
Sheehan, Larry John lawyer
Topping, Seymour publishing executive, educator
Wile, Julius former corporate executive, educator

### Schenectady
Adler, Michael S. control systems and electronic technologies executive
Alpher, Ralph Asher physicist
Barthold, Lionel Olav engineering executive
Bedard, Donna Lee environmental microbiologist
Billmeyer, Fred Wallace, Jr. chemist, educator
Board, Joseph Breckinridge, Jr. political scientist, educator
Bucinell, Ronald Blaise mechanical engineer
Bulloff, Jack John physical chemist, consultant
Chestnut, Harold foundation administrator, engineering executive
Duncan, Stanley Forbes health care executive
Engeler, William Ernest physicist
Golub, Lewis supermarket company executive
Grant, Ian Stanley engineering company executive

Hebb, Malcolm Hayden *physicist*
Hedman, Dale Eugene *consulting electrical engineer*
Helmar-Salasoo, Ester Anette *literacy educator, researcher*
Hull, Roger Harold *college president*
Jarrett, Steven Ronald *physician, physical medicine and rehabilitation*
Jonas, Manfred *historian, educator*
Kambour, Roger Peabody *polymer physical chemist, researcher*
Kliman, Gerald Burt *electrical engineer*
Lambert, Stephen R. *electrical engineer, consultant*
Lawrence, Albert Weaver *insurance company executive*
Levine, Howard Arnold *state supreme court justice*
Levine, Sanford Harold *lawyer*
Luborsky, Fred Everett *research physicist*
Matta, Ram Kumar *aeronautical engineer*
Morris, John Selwyn *philosophy educator, college president emeritus*
Murphy, William Michael *literature educator, biographer*
Murray, Edward Rock *insurance broker*
Oliker, David William *healthcare management administrator*
Petersen, Kenneth Clarence *chemical company executive*
Philip, A. G. Davis *astronomer, editor, educator*
Ringlee, Robert James *consulting engineering executive*
Robb, Walter Lee *retired electric company executive, management company executive*
Rougeot, Henri Max *medical imaging engineer, physicist*
Schenck, John Frederic *physician*
Taub, Eli Irwin *lawyer, arbitrator*
Terry, Richard Allan *consulting psychologist, former college president*
Walsh, George William *engineering executive*
Wickerham, Richard Dennis *lawyer*
Wilson, Delano Dee *consultant*
Zheng, Maggie (Xiaoci) *materials scientist, vacuum coating specialist*

### Schoharie
Duncombe, Raynor Bailey *lawyer*
Stiver, Patricia Abare *elementary education educator*

### Scotia
Morris, Jason *Olympic athlete*
Pontius, James Wilson *foundation administrator*

### Scottsville
Dwyer, Ann Elizabeth *equine veterinarian*

### Sea Cliff
Popova, Nina *dancer, choreographer, director*

### Seaford
Schlossberg, Fred Paul *elementary education educator*
Setzler, William Edward *chemical company executive*

### Searingtown
Entmacher, Paul Sidney *insurance company executive, physician, educator*

### Selden
Paul, Carol Ann *academic administrator, biology educator*

### Seneca Falls
Norman, Mary Marshall *counselor, therapist, educator*

### Setauket
Irving, A. Marshall *marine engineer*
Levine, Sumner Norton *industrial engineer, educator, editor, author, financial consultant*
MacKay, Robert Battin *museum director*
Robinson, Richard M. *technical communication specialist*
Simpson, Louis Aston Marantz *English educator, author*

### Shady
Ruellan, Andree *artist*

### Shelter Island
Culbertson, Janet Lynn *artist*
Dowd, David Joseph *banker, builder*

### Sherburne
Birmingham, Kathleen Christina *secondary school educator*

### Sherrill
Rosendale, Suzanne Moore *library media specialist*

### Shokan
Schwartzberg, Paul David *lawyer*

### Shoreham
Reynolds, Carolyn Mary *elementary education educator*
Spier, Peter Edward *artist, author*

### Shrub Oak
Roston, Arnold *information specialist, educator, advertising executive, artist, editor*

### Sidney
Haller, Irma Tognola *secondary education educator*

### Silver Bay
Parlin, Charles C., Jr. *retired lawyer*

### Silver Creek
Schenk, Worthington George, Jr. *surgeon, educator*

### Slate Hill
Reber, Raymond Andrew *chemical engineer*

### Sleepy Hollow
Hyman, Leonard Stephen *finanical consultant, economist, author*
Maun, Mary Ellen *computer consultant*
Safian, Keith Franklin *hospital administrator*
Schmidt, Klaus Franz *advertising executive*

### Slingerlands
Fenton, William Nelson *anthropologist, anthropology educator emeritus*
Wilcock, Donald Frederick *mechanical engineer*

### Smithtown
Aleschus, Justine Lawrence *real estate broker*
Dvorkin, Ronald Alan *emergency physician*
Friedlander, Gerhart *nuclear chemist*
Goodman, Richard Shalem *lawyer, orthopedic surgeon*
Kreimer, Michael Walter *financial planner*
Leavy, Herbert Theodore *publisher*
Pruzansky, Joshua Murdock *lawyer*
Spellman, Thomas Joseph, Jr. *lawyer*
Sporn, Stanley Robert *retired electronic company executive*

### Snyder
Breverman, Harvey *artist*

### Somers
Banik, Douglas Heil *marketing executive*
Boudreaux, John *public relations specialist*
Carrick, Bruce Robert *publishing company executive*
Casey, Gerard William *food products company executive, lawyer*
Cloudman, Francis Harold, III *computer company executive*
Cohn, Howard *retired magazine editor*
Estefan, Nabil *business and finance executive*
Jacob, Alethea Marie *enterprise engineering consultant*
Joerger, Jay Herman *psychologist, entrepreneur*
Lane, David Oliver *retired librarian*
Miller, Alan *software executive, management specialist*
Rubin, Samuel Harold *physician, consultant*
Sayers, Ken W(illiam) *writer and public relations executive*
Sora, Sebastian Antony *business machines manufacturing executive, educator*
Wahl, William Joseph, Jr. *information systems specialist*

### South Salem
Cronin, Raymond Valentine *financial executive*
Howard, Joan Alice *artist*
Saurwein, Virginia Fay *international affairs specialist*

### Southampton
Atkins, Victor Kennicott, Jr. *investment banker*
Brokaw, Clifford Vail, III *investment banker, business executive*
Brophy, James David, Jr. *humanities educator*
Fuller, Sue *artist*
Graham, Howard Barrett *publishing company executive*
Joel, Billy (William Martin Joel) *musician*
Lerner, Abram *retired museum director, artist*
Lieberman, Carol *healthcare marketing communications consultant*
Robinson, Chester Hersey *retired dean*
Sims, Everett Martin *publishing company executive*
Smith, Dennis (Edward) *publisher, author*

### Southold
Bachrach, Howard L. *biochemist*
Callis, Jerry Jackson *veterinarian*
Curcuru, Edmond Harvey *management educator*

### Sparkill
Dahl, Arlene *actress, author, designer, cosmetic executive*

### Spencerport
Clarke, Stephan Paul *English language educator, writer*
Webster, Gordon Visscher, Jr. *minister*

### Spencertown
Dunne, John Richard *lawyer*
Lieber, Charles Donald *publisher*

### Springville
Balling, Louise Mary *social worker*

### Stafford
Moran, John Henry, Jr. *electrical engineer, consultant*

### Stamford
Bergleitner, George Charles, Jr. *investment banker*
Portland, Charles Denis *publishing executive*

### Stanfordville
Seborovski, Carole *artist*

### Stanley
Jones, Gordon Edwin *horticulturist*

### Staten Island
Auh, Yang John *librarian, academic administrator*
Banner, Burton *pediatrician*
Barton, Jerry O'Donnell *telecommunications executive*
Bocaya, Renato Biso *pharmaceutical sales and marketing executive*
Bruckstein, Alex Harry *internist, gastroenterologist, geriatrician*
Campbell, Craig John *podiatrist*
Chapin, Elliott Lowell *retired bank executive*
Connelly, Elizabeth Ann *state legislator*
Diamond, Richard Edward *publisher*
Fafian, Joseph, Jr. *management consultant*
Fernandes, Richard Louis *retired advertising agency executive*
Fung, Amy Shu-Fong *accountant*
Gokarn, Vijay Murlidhar *pharmacist, consultant*
Greco, Donna *educational administrator*
Harris, Allen *lawyer, educator, consultant*
Hartman, Joan Edna *English educator*
Henry, Paul James *lawyer, health care administrator*
Johansen, Robert John *electrical engineer*
Johnson, Frank Corliss *criminal psychologist*
Mayer, Andrew Mark *librarian, journalist*
Meltzer, Yale Leon *economist, educator*
Mirsepassi-Toloui, Shirley Shirin *pathologist, educator*
Nelson, Carey Boone *sculptor*
O'Connor, Robert James *gynecologist, consultant*
Paunov, Catherine Pennington *legal technology consultant*
Popler, Kenneth *behavioral healthcare executive, psychologist*
Porter, Darwin Fred *writer*
Rajakaruna, Lalith Asoka *civil engineer*
Robison, Paula Judith *flutist*
Shullich, Robert Harlan *systems analyst*
Smith, Norman Raymond *college president*
Springer, Marlene *university administrator, educator*
Toliver, Maxwell Doel *hypnotherapist*
Vu, Ha Manh *city official*
Wisniewski, Henryk Miroslaw *pathology and neuropathology educator, research facility administrator, research scientist*
Worth, Melvin H. *surgeon, educator*
Zayek, Francis Mansour *bishop*

### Sterling
Seawell, Thomas Robert *artist, retired educator*

### Stony Brook
Alexander, John Macmillan, Jr. *chemistry educator*
Anderson, Michael Thomas *mathematics researcher, educator*
Aronoff, Mark H. *linguistics educator, author, consultant*
Badalamenti, Fred Leopoldo *artist, educator*
Baron, Samuel *flutist*
Bilfinger, Thomas Victor *surgeon, educator*
Bonner, Francis Truesdale *chemist, educator, university dean*
Booth, George *cartoonist*
Brandwein, Ruth Ann *social welfare educator*
Brown, Gerald Edward *physicist, educator*
Cesa, Michael Peter *cardiologist, consultant*
Chen Ning Yang *physicist, educator*
Cleveland, Ceil Margaret *writer, journalist, education administrator, English language educator*
Cochran, James Kirk *dean, oceanographer, geochemist, educator*
Cope, Randolph Howard, Jr. *electronic research and development executive, educator*
Cottrell, Thomas Sylvester *pathology educator, university dean*
Davis, James Norman *neurologist, neurobiology researcher*
Dervan, John Patrick *cardiologist*
Edelman, Norman Herman *medical educator, university dean and official*
Erk, Frank Chris *biologist, educator*
Feinberg, Eugene Alexander *mathematics educator*
Fisher, David Woodrow *editor, publisher*
Fleagle, John Gwynn *anthropology and paleontology educator*
Fritts, Harry Washington, Jr. *physician, educator*
Glimm, James Gilbert *mathematician*
Goldberg, Homer Beryl *English language educator*
Goodman, Norman *sociologist, researcher*
Hanson, Gilbert Nikolai *geochemistry educator*
Harvey, Christine Lynn *publishing executive*
Herman, Herbert *materials science educator*
Ihde, Don *philosophy educator, university administrator*
Jonas, Steven *public health physician, medical educator, writer*
Kahn, Peter B. *physics educator*
Katkin, Edward Samuel *psychology educator*
Katz, Victoria Manuela *public relations executive, educator, consultant*
Kenny, Shirley Strum *university administrator*
Kim, Charles Wesley *microbiology educator*
Koppelman, Lee Edward *regional planner, educator*
Kuchner, Eugene Frederick *neurosurgeon, educator*
Kuspit, Donald Burton *art historian, art critic, educator*
Lane, Dorothy Spiegel *physician*
Laspina, Peter Joseph *computer resource educator*
Lawson, H(erbert) Blaine, Jr. *mathematician, educator*
Lennarz, William Joseph *research biologist, educator*
Levin, Richard Louis *English language educator*
Levinton, Jeffrey S. *biology educator, oceanographer*
Liang, Jerome Zhengrong *radiology educator*
Meyers, Morton Allen *physician, radiology educator*
Mignone, Mario B. *Italian studies educator*
Miller, Frederick *pathologist*
Neuberger, Egon *economics educator*
Ojima, Iwao *chemistry educator*
Pekarsky, Melvin Hirsch *artist*
Pindell, Howardena Doreen *artist*
Poppers, Paul Jules *anesthesiologist, educator*
Priebe, Cedric Joseph, Jr. *pediatric surgeon*
Rapaport, Felix Theodosius *surgeon, researcher, educator*
Rohlf, F. James *biometrician, educator*
Schneider, Mark *political science educator*
Semmel, Bernard *historian, educator*
Shamash, Yacov *dean, electrical engineering educator*
Silverman, Hugh J. *philosophy educator*
Sokoloff, Leon *pathology educator*
Solomon, Philip Myron *astronomer, atmospheric scientist*
Spector, Marshall *philosophy educator*
Sreebny, Leo M. *oral biology and pathology educator*
Steigbigel, Roy Theodore *infectious disease physician and scientist, educator*
Steinberg, Amy Wishner *dermatologist*
Stone, Elizabeth Caecilia *anthropology educator*
Swanson, Robert Lawrence *oceanographer, academic program administrator*
Tanur, Judith Mark *sociologist, educator*
Travis, Martin Bice *political scientist, educator*
Truxal, John Groff *electrical engineering educator*
Tucker, Alan Curtiss *mathematics educator*
Weidner, Donald J. *geophysicist educator*
Williams, George Christopher *biologist, ecology and evolution educator*
Wurster, Charles Frederick *environmental scientist, educator*
Yang, Chen Ning *physicist, educator*
Zemanian, Armen Humpartsoum *electrical engineer, mathematician*

### Stony Point
Ricci, Daniel Michael *protective services official*

### Stuyvesant
Tripp, Susan Gerwe *museum director*

### Suffern
Codispoti, Andre John *allergist, immunologist*
Commanday, Sue Nancy Shair *English language educator*
Jaffe, Elliot S. *women's clothing retail chain executive*
Longberg, Debra Lynn *dietitian, nutrition consultant*
Marcus, Janet Carol *cytotechnologist*
Monahan, Frances Donovan *nursing educator*
Schachter, Michael Ben *psychiatrist, complementary physician*
Sutherland, George Leslie *retired chemical company executive*
Unger, Barbara *poet, writer, educator*
Walsh, James Jerome *philosophy educator*
Zecca, John Andrew *retired association executive*

### Sunnyside
Giaimo, Kathryn Ann *performing arts company executive*
Privo, Alexander *finance educator, department chairman*
Wallmann, Jeffrey Miner *author*

### Swain
Robinson, Bina Aitchison *publisher, newsletter editor*

### Syosset
Bainton, Donald J. *diversified manufacturing company executive*
Barry, Richard Francis *retired life insurance company executive*
Guthart, Leo A. *electronics executive*
Hull, Gretchen Gaebelein *lay worker, writer, lecturer*
Kantor, Edwin *investment company executive*
Kendric, Deborah Ann *controller*
Kruse, Nancy Clarson *elementary education educator*
Lazor, Theodosius (His Beatitude Metropolitan Theodosius) *archbishop*
Nydick, David *school superintendent*
Roche, John Edward *human resources management consultant, educator*
†Rudman, Michael P. *publishing executive*
Streitman, Jeffrey Bruce *educational administrator*
Swenson, Eric David *town official, lawyer*
Vermylen, Paul Anthony, Jr. *oil company executive*

### Syracuse
Abbott, George Lindell *librarian*
Akiyama, Kazuyoshi *conductor*
Alston, William Payne *philosophy educator*
Baker, Bruce Edward *orthopedic surgeon, consultant*
Baldwin, John Edwin *chemistry educator*
Balk, Alfred William *journalist*
Barclay, H(ugh) Douglas *lawyer, former state senator*
Beeching, Charles Train, Jr. *lawyer*
Bellanger, Barbara Doris Hoysak *biomedical research technologist*
Berra, P. Bruce *computer educator*
Birge, Robert Richards *chemistry educator*
Birkhead, Guthrie Sweeney, Jr. *political scientist, university dean*
Black, Lois Mae *clinical psychologist, educator*
Blount-Cucchiaro, Lori *arts adminstrator, fundraiser*
†Boeheim, Jim *college basketball coach*
Bogart, William Harry *lawyer*
Bottar, Anthony Samuel *lawyer*
Braungart, Richard Gottfried *sociology and international relations educator*
Brennan, Paul Joseph *civil engineer, educator*
Bunn, Timothy David *newspaper editor*
Burgess, Robert Lewis *ecologist, educator*
Burstyn, Joan Netta *education educator*
†Carlson, William Clifford *defense company executive*
Charters, Alexander Nathaniel *retired adult education educator*
Cheng, David Keun *engineering educator*
Church, Philip Throop *mathematician, educator*
Cirando, John Anthony *lawyer*
Clausen, Jerry Lee *psychiatrist*
Cohen, William Nathan *radiologist*
Cole, Ned *bishop*
Coliz, James Russell *university administrator, telecommunications consultant*
Collette, Alfred Thomas *biology and science education educator*
Collins, William John *educational administrator*
Conan, Robert James, Jr. *chemistry educator, consultant*
Cooper, John Ambrose *management coordinator, international marketer*
Costello, Thomas Joseph *bishop*
Covillion, Jane Tanner *mathematics educator*
Crowley, John W(illiam) *English language educator*
Daly, Robert W. *psychiatrist, medical educator*
Daniels, Bruce Eric *library director*
Davis, William E. *utility executive*
De Dell, Gary Jerome *printing company executive, consultant*
Delmar, Mario *cardiac physiology educator*
Denise, Theodore Cullom *philosophy educator*
Diamond, Robert Mach *higher education administrator*
DiLorenzo, Louis Patrick *lawyer*
Dixon, John T. *food products company executive*
Drucker, Alan Steven *mechanical engineer*
Dudewicz, Edward John *statistician*
Dunham, Philip Bigelow *biology educator, physiologist*
Eisenberg, Michael Bruce *information studies educator*
Everett, Charles R., Jr. *airport executive*
Fendler, Janos Hugo *chemistry educator*
Ferguson, Tracy Heiman *lawyer, educational administrator*
Fitzgerald, Harold Kenneth *social work educator, consultant*
Fitzpatrick, James David *lawyer*
Fox, Geoffrey Charles *computer science and physics educator*
Fraser, Henry S. *lawyer*
Frazier, J(ohn) Phillip *manufacturing company executive*
Frohock, Fred Manuel *political science educator*
Gaal, John *lawyer*
Gilman, Karen Frenzel *legal assistant*
Gitsov, Ivan *chemist*
Gold, Joseph *medical researcher*
Graver, Jack Edward *mathematics educator*
Gray, Charles Augustus *banker*
Hamlett, James Gordon *electronics engineer, management consultant, educator*
Hancock, Stewart F., Jr. *state judge*
Hansen, Per Brinch *computer scientist*
Hayes, David Michael *lawyer*
Herzog, Peter Emilius *legal educator*

Higbee, Ann G. *public relations executive, consultant*
Hoffman, Arthur Wolf *English language educator*
Hole, Richard Douglas *lawyer*
Hollis, Susan Tower *college dean*
Honig, Arnold *physics educator, researcher*
Horst, Pamela Sue *medical educator, family physician*
Irwin, Martin *psychiatrist*
†Jabbour, John Jay *document product and services executive*
Jefferies, Michael John *retired electrical engineer*
Jensen, Robert Granville *geography educator, university dean*
Jump, Bernard, Jr. *economics educator*
Ketcham, Ralph *history and political science educator*
Kieffer, Stephen Aaron *radiologist, educator*
King, Bernard T. *lawyer*
Konski, James Louis *civil engineer*
Kopp, Robert Walter *lawyer*
Krathwohl, David Reading *education educator emeritus*
Kriebel, Mahlon Edward *physiology educator, inventor*
Kriesberg, Louis *sociologist, educator*
Landaw, Stephen Arthur *physician, educator*
Lawton, Joseph J., Jr. *lawyer*
Lemanski, Larry Fredrick *medical educator*
Levy, H. Richard *biochemistry educator*
Lichtblau, Myron Ivor *language educator*
Manning, J. Francis *school administrator*
Marcoccia, Louis Gary *accountant, university administrator*
Martonosi, Anthony Nicholas *biochemistry educator, researcher*
Mathewson, George Atterbury *lawyer*
Mazur, Allan Carl *sociologist, engineer, educator*
McCoubrey, Sarah *artist and art educator*
McCurn, Neal Peters *federal judge*
McGraw, James L. *retired ophthalmologist, educator*
Meiklejohn, Donald *philosophy educator*
Meinig, Donald William *geography educator*
Mesrobian, Arpena Sachaklian *publisher, editor, consultant*
Meyers, Peter L. *banker*
Mitchell, Robert Arthur *college president*
Monmonier, Mark *geographer, graphics educator, essayist*
Moses, Robert Edward *lawyer*
Mower, Eric Andrew *communications and marketing executive*
Muller, Ernest H. *geology educator*
Munson, Howard G. *federal judge*
Murray, David George *orthopedic surgeon, educator*
Nafie, Laurence Allen *chemistry educator*
Nast, Edward Paul *cardiac surgeon*
Naum, Christopher John *fire protection management and training consultant, educator*
Nelli, D. James *business school executive, accountant*
O'Day, Royal Lewis *former banker*
Ortiz, Fernando, Jr. *small business consultant*
Palmer, John L. *social sciences researcher, educator*
Pardee, Otway O'Meara *computer science educator*
Pearl, Harvey *psychologist*
Pennock, Donald William *retired mechanical engineer*
Perl, Andras *immunologist, educator, scientist*
Peters, Christopher Allen *computer consultant*
Phillips, Arthur William, Jr. *biology educator*
Phillips, Richard Hart *psychiatrist*
Pooler, Rosemary S. *federal judge*
Powell, James Matthew *history educator*
Prucha, John James *geologist, educator*
Rabuzzi, Daniel D. *medical educator*
Ramsey, Dan Steven *foundation and organization administrator*
Regan, Paul Michael *lawyer*
Robinson, Joseph Edward *geology educator, consulting petroleum geologist*
Rogers, Sherry Anne *physician*
Rogers, Stephen *newspaper publisher*
Rosenbaum, Arthur Elihu *neuroradiologist, educator*
Rountree, Patricia Ann *youth organization administrator*
Rubardt, Peter Craig *conductor, educator*
Russell-Hunter, Gus W(illiam) D(evigne) *zoology educator, research biologist, writer*
Sargent, Robert George *engineering educator*
Scheinman, Steven Jay *medical educator*
Schiess, Betty Bone *priest*
Schmidt, Patricia Ruggiano *education educator*
Schwartz, Richard Derecktor *sociologist, educator*
Scullin, Frederick James, Jr. *federal judge*
Serafin, John Alfred *art educator*
Shattuck, George Clement *lawyer*
Shaw, Kenneth Alan *university president*
Shedlock, Kathleen Joan Petrouskie *community health/research nurse*
Simmons, Roy, Jr. *university athletic coach*
Skoler, Louis *architect, educator*
Smardon, Richard Clay *landscape architecture and environmental studies educator*
Smith, Kenneth Judson, Jr. *chemist, theoretician, educator*
Smith, Robert L. *medical research administrator*
Stam, David Harry *librarian*
Sternlicht, Sanford *English and theater arts educator, writer*
Strutin, Kennard Regan *lawyer, educator, law librarian*
Sullivan, Michael Joachim *financial executive*
Sutton, Walter *English educator*
Szasz, Thomas Stephen *psychiatrist, educator, writer*
Tatham, David Frederic *art historian, educator*
Thomas, Sidney *fine arts educator, researcher*
Traylor, Robert Arthur *lawyer*
Turner, Christopher Edward *cell biology educator*
Verrillo, Ronald Thomas *neuroscientist*
Vook, Richard Werner *physics educator*
Wadley, Susan Snow *anthropologist*
Waite, Peter Arthur *literacy educator, educational consultant*
Waterman, Daniel *mathematician, educator*
Weiss, Volker *university administrator, educator*
Wellner, Marcel Nahum *physics educator, researcher*
Whaley, Ross Samuel *academic administrator*
Wiecek, William Michael *law educator*
Wiggins, James Bryan *religion educator*
Williams, William Joseph *physician, educator*
Zimmerman, Aaron Mark *lawyer*

**Tappan**
Dell, Robert Christopher *geothermal sculptor, scenic artist*
Fox, Muriel *public relations executive*
Nickford, Juan *sculptor, educator*

**Tarrytown**
Anderson, John Erling *chemical engineer*
Ashburn, Anderson *magazine editor*
Benjamin, Jeff *lawyer, pharmaceutical executive*
Bowen, Christopher Edward *library director*
Chu, Foo *physician*
Corbett, Gerard Francis *electronics executive*
Dobkin, John Howard *art administrator*
Dorland, Byrl Brown *civic worker*
Ferrari, Robert Joseph *business educator, former banker*
Field, Barry Elliot *internist, gastroenterologist*
Goldin, Milton *fund raising counsel, writer*
Gross, Stanislaw *environmental sciences educator, activist*
†Grufferman, Barbara Hannah *publishing executive*
Jarrett, Eugene Lawrence *chemical company executive*
Kane, Stanley Bruce *food products executive*
Kenney, John Michel *architect*
Kinigakis, Panagiotis *research principal scientist, engineer, author*
Kroll, Nathan *film producer, director*
LeGrice, Stephen *magazine editor*
Marcus, Sheldon *social sciences educator*
Neill, Richard Robert *retired publishing company executive*
Oelbaum, Harold *lawyer, corporate executive*
Raymond, George Marc *city planner, educator*
Scott, Richard Thurston *publishing executive*
Vagelos, Pindaros Roy *pharmaceutical company executive*
Whipple, Judith Roy *book editor*
†Wood, Roger *publishing executive*
Zegarelli, Edward Victor *retired dental educator, researcher*

**Thornwood**
Bassett, Lawrence C *management consultant*

**Ticonderoga**
Westbrook, Nicholas Kilmer *museum administrator, historian*

**Tonawanda**
Browning, James Franklin *professional society executive*
Dillman, Joseph John Thomas *electric utility executive*
Haller, Calvin John *banker*
Peterson, Dorothy Lulu *artist, writer*
Rovison, John Michael, Jr. *chemical engineer*
Vienne, Dorothy Titus *school principal*

**Troy**
Abetti, Pier Antonio *consulting electrical engineer, technology management and entrepreneurship educator*
Ahlers, Rolf Willi *philosopher, theologian*
Baron, Robert Alan *psychology and business educator, author*
Belfort, Georges *chemical engineering educator, consultant*
Berg, Daniel *science and technology educator*
Bergles, Arthur Edward *mechanical engineering educator*
Block, Robert Charles *nuclear engineering and engineering physics educator*
Bonney, William Lawless *data processing and telecommunications educator*
Brazil, Harold Edmund *political science educator*
Breed, Helen Illick *ichthyologist, educator*
Bunce, Stanley Chalmers *chemist, educator*
Caruso, Aileen Smith *managed care consultant*
Corelli, John Charles *physicist, educator*
Daves, Glenn Doyle, Jr. *science educator, chemist, researcher*
Desrochers, Alan Alfred *electrical engineer*
Diwan, Romesh Kumar *economics educator*
Doremus, Robert Heward *glass and ceramics processing educator*
Drew, Donald Allen *mathematical sciences educator*
Duquette, David Joseph *materials science and engineering educator*
Dvorak, George J. *mechanics and materials engineering educator*
Ehrlich, Henry Lutz *biology educator*
Ferris, James Peter *chemist, educator*
Fleischer, Robert Louis *physics educator*
Friedman, Sue Tyler *technical publications executive*
Gerhardt, Lester A. *engineering educator, dean*
Giaever, Ivar *physicist*
Gill, William Nelson *chemical engineering educator*
Glicksman, Martin Eden *materials engineering educator*
Graves, Robert John *industrial engineering educator*
Gutmann, Ronald J. *electrical engineering educator*
Haviland, David Sands *architectural educator, researcher, administrator*
Isaacs, Andrea *dancer, choreographer, former educator*
Jones, E. Stewart, Jr. *lawyer*
Jones, Owen Craven, Jr. *nuclear and mechanical engineer, educator*
Jordan, Mark Henry *consulting civil engineer*
Judd, Gary *university administrator*
Kahl, William Frederick *retired college president*
Krause, Sonja *chemistry educator*
Krempl, Erhard *mechanics educator, consultant*
Lahey, Richard Thomas, Jr. *nuclear engineer, fluid mechanics engineer*
Lemnios, Andrew Zachery *aerospace engineer, educator, researcher*
Levinger, Joseph Solomon *physicist, educator*
Littman, Howard *chemical engineer, educator*
McAllister, Edward William Charles *educator*
McDonald, John Francis Patrick *electrical engineering educator*
McNaughton, Robert Forbes, Jr. *computer science educator*
Medicus, Heinrich Adolf *physicist, educator*
Modestino, James William *electrical engineering educator*
Nelson, John Keith *electrical engineer*
Phelan, Thomas *clergyman, academic administrator, educator*
Potts, Kevin T. *emeritus chemistry educator*
Romond, James *principal*
Rubens, Philip *communications educator, technical writer*
Sanderson, Arthur Clark *engineering educator*
Saridis, George Nicholas *electrical engineer*
Schechter, Stephen L. *political scientist*
Schwartz, Robert William *management consultant*
Shephard, Mark Scott *civil and mechanical engineering educator*

Snyder, Patricia Di Benedetto *theater director and administrator*
Sperber, Daniel *physicist*
Stoloff, Norman Stanley *materials engineering educator, researcher*
Wait, Samuel Charles, Jr. *academic administrator, educator*
Whitburn, Merrill Duane *English literature educator*
White, Frederick Andrew *physics educator, physicist*
Wiberley, Stephen Edward *chemistry educator, consultant*
Wilson, Jack Martin *dean, scientific association executive, physics educator*
Woods, John William *electrical, computer and systems engineering educator, consultant*
Zimmie, Thomas Frank *civil engineer, educator*

**Trumansburg**
Billings, Peggy Marie *religious organization administrator, educator*
Wolf, Edward Dean *electrical engineering educator*

**Tuckahoe**
Brecher, Bernd *management consultant*
Doyle, Joellen Mary *special education educator*
Elliott, Dennis Dawson *communications executive*
Silk, Eleana S. *librarian*

**Tupper Lake**
Johnson, David Wesley *lawyer*
Welsh, Peter Corbett *museum consultant, historian*

**Tuxedo Park**
Brown, Walston Shepard *lawyer*
Domjan, Joseph (Spiri Domjan) *artist*
Friedman, Rodger *antiquarian bookseller, consultant*
Groskin, Sheila Marie Lessen *primary school educator*
Hall, Frederick Keith *chemist*
Heusser, Calvin John *biology educator, researcher*
Regan, Ellen Frances (Mrs. Walston Shepard Brown) *ophthalmologist*
Rossman, Toby Gale *genetic toxicology educator, researcher*

**Unadilla**
Compton, John Robinson *printing company executive*

**Uniondale**
Altimari, Frank X. *federal judge*
Arbour, Alger *professional hockey coach*
Brown, Kenneth Lloyd *lawyer*
Brustein, Martin *investment executive*
Cassidy, David Michael *lawyer*
†Milbury, Mike *professional hockey coach*
Mishler, Jacob *federal judge*
Platt, Thomas Collier, Jr. *federal judge*
Seybert, Joanna *federal judge*
Shapiro, Barry Robert *lawyer*
Spatt, Arthur Donald *federal judge*

**Upton**
Axe, John Donald, Jr. *physicist, researcher*
Blume, Martin *physicist*
Bond, Peter Danford *physicist*
Cronkite, Eugene Pitcher *physician*
Fthenakis, Vasilis *chemical engineer, consultant, educator*
Goldhaber, Maurice *physicist*
Hamilton, Leonard Derwent *physician, molecular biologist*
Hankes, Lawrence Valentine *biochemist*
Harbottle, Garman *chemist*
Hendrie, Joseph Mallam *physicist, nuclear engineer, government official*
Holroyd, Richard Allen *research scientist*
Kato, Walter Yoneo *physicist*
Lindenbaum, S(eymour) J(oseph) *physicist*
Lowenstein, Derek Irving *physicist*
Marr, Robert Bruce *physicist, educator*
McWhan, Denis Bayman *physicist*
Meinhold, Charles Boyd *health physicist*
Morris, Samuel Cary *environmental scientist, consultant, educator*
Ozaki, Satoshi *physicist*
Petrakis, Leonidas *research scientist, educator, administrator*
Radeka, Veljko *electronics engineer*
Rau, Ralph Ronald *retired physicist*
Ruckman, Mark Warren *physicist*
Samios, Nicholas Peter *physicist*
Setlow, Jane Kellock *biophysicist*
Setlow, Richard Burton *biophysicist*
Shutt, Ralph P. *research physicist*
Souw, Bernard Eng-Kie *physicist, consultant*
Steinberg, Meyer *chemical engineer*
Susskind, Herbert *biomedical engineer, educator*
Sutin, Norman *chemistry educator, scientist*
Van Tuyle, Gregory Jay *nuclear engineer*
Wolf, Alfred Peter *research chemist, educator*
Zarcone, Michael Joseph *experimental physicist, consultant*

**Utica**
Antzelevitch, Charles *research center executive*
Bowers, Roger Paul *radiologist*
Boyle, William Leo, Jr. *educational consultant, retired college president*
Brown, Thomas Glenn *college administrator*
Cardamone, Richard J. *federal judge*
Donovan, Donna Mae *newspaper publisher*
Ehre, Victor Tyndall *insurance company executive*
Gape, Serafina Vetrano *decorative artist and designer*
Iodice, Arthur Alfonso *biochemist*
Mortenson, Thomas Theodore *medical products executive, management consultant*
Pribble, Easton *artist*
Schrauth, William Lawrence *banker, lawyer*
Schweizer, Paul Douglas *museum director*
Simpson, Michael Kevin *academic administrator, political science educator*

**Vails Gate**
Fife, Betty H. *librarian*

**Valhalla**
Carter, Anne Cohen *physician*
Cimino, Joseph Anthony *physician, educator*
Couldwell, William Tupper *neurosurgeon, educator*
Del Guercio, Louis Richard Maurice *surgeon, educator, company executive*
Fink, Raymond *medical educator*
Frost, Elizabeth Ann McArthur *physician*

Hodgson, W(alter) John B(arry) *surgeon*
Hommes, Frits Aukustinus *biology educator*
Kilbourne, Edwin Dennis *virologist, educator*
Kline, Susan Anderson *medical school administrator, internist*
Levin, Aaron Reuben *pediatrician, educator*
Madden, Robert Edward *surgeon, educator*
McGiff, John C(harles) *pharmacologist*
Niguidula, Faustino Nazario *pediatric cardiothoracic surgeon*
Paik, John Kee *structural engineer*
Radeboldt-Daly, Karen Elaine *medical nurse*
Reed, George Elliott *surgery educator*
Weisburger, John Hans *medical researcher*
Williams, Gary Murray *medical researcher, pathology educator*
Wolin, Michael Stuart *physiology educator*

**Valley Cottage**
Atha, Stuart Kimball, Jr. *retired banker*
Shaderowfsky, Eva Maria *photographer, writer*
Stolldorf, Genevieve Schwager *media specialist*

**Valley Stream**
Blakeman, Royal Edwin *lawyer*
Grassi, Louis C. *accountant*
Greene, Howard Paul *communications executive*
Lehrer, Stanley *magazine publisher, editorial director, corporate executive*
Rachlin, Harvey Brant *author*
Robbins, Harvey Arnold *textile company executive*

**Valois**
Hurst, Kenneth Thurston *publisher*

**Vestal**
†Kuehl, Alexander *emergency physician, health facility administrator, medical educator, writer*
Piaker, Philip Martin *accountant, educator*
Wagner, Peter Ewing *physics and electrical engineering educator*

**Victor**
Abbott, Susan Alicia *elementary education educator*
Drummond, Malcolm McAllister *electronics engineer*

**Voorheesville**
Haydock, Michael Damean *building and code consultant, writer*

**Waccabuc**
Cross, William Redmond, Jr. *corporate director, foundation executive*
Hall, Elizabeth *writer*
Kislik, Richard William *publishing executive*
Thompson, Edward Thorwald *magazine editor*

**Wading River**
Hall, Kimball Parker *research scientist*
Marlow, Audrey Swanson *artist, designer*

**Wainscott**
Dubow, Arthur Myron *investor, lawyer*
Henderson, William Charles *editor*
Herzog, Arthur, III *author*
Russo, Alexander Peter *artist, educator*

**Walden**
Hanau, Kenneth John, Jr. *packaging company executive*
Hraniotis, Judith Beringer *artist*
Konior, Jeannette Mary *elementary school educator*

**Wallkill**
Bittner, Ronald Joseph *computer systems analyst, magician*
Chumas, Linda Grace *elementary school educator*
Koch, Edwin Ernest *artist, interior decorator*

**Walworth**
Reynolds, Lewis Dayton *administrator, pastor*

**Wantagh**
Dawson, George Glenn *economics educator emeritus*
DeNapoli, Anthony *middle school principal*
Glaser, David *painter, sculptor*
Kushner, Aileen *medical/surgical nurse*
Ross, Sheldon Jules *dentist*
Smits, Edward John *museum consultant*
Zinder, Newton Donald *stock market analyst, consultant*

**Wappingers Falls**
Engelman, Melvin Alkon *retired dentist, business executive, scientist*
Hogan, Edward Robert *financial services executive*
Johnson, Jeh Vincent *architect*
Maissel, Leon Israel *physicist, engineer*
Nolan, John Thomas, Jr. *retired oil industry administrator*

**Warsaw**
Dy-Ang, Anita C. *pediatrician*

**Warwick**
Altman, Eileen Shea *psychotherapist*
Franck, Frederick Sigfred *artist, author, dental surgeon*
Mack, Daniel Richard *furniture designer*
Simon, Dolores Daly *copy editor*

**Washingtonville**
Guarino, Iris Cooper *realtor, appraiser*
Guarino, Louis Joseph *mechanical engineer, consultant*

**Water Mill**
D'Urso, Joseph Paul *designer*

**Waterford**
Gold, James Paul *museum director*

**Watertown**
Coe, Benjamin Plaisted *retired state official*
Johnson, John Brayton *editor, publisher*
Militello, Samuel Philip *lawyer*
Waterston, William King *minister, educator, academic administrator*

**Webster**
Conwell, Esther Marly *physicist*
Duke, Charles Bryan *research and development manufacturing executive, physics educator*
Liebert, Arthur Edgar *retired hospital administrator*
McCormack, Stanley Eugene *financial consultant*
McWilliams, C. Paul, Jr. *engineering executive*
Nicholson, Douglas Robert *accountant*
Witmer, G. Robert *retired state supreme court justice*
Zirilli, Francesco *mechanical engineer, engineering educator*

**Weedsport**
Cichello, Samuel Joseph *architect*

**Wellsville**
Taylor, Theodore Brewster *physicist, business executive*
Van Tyne, Arthur Morris *geologist*

**West Bloomfield**
Charron, Helene Kay Shetler *nursing educator*

**West Chazy**
Cumiskey, Gerald John *radio communications technician*

**West Falls**
Lindemann, Edna Meibohm *museum director, art consultant*

**West Harrison**
Paul, Nancy Haworth *educator*

**West Haverstraw**
Cochran, George Van Brunt *physician, surgery educator, researcher*

**West Hempstead**
Guggenheimer, Heinrich Walter *mathematician, educator*

**West Henrietta**
Doty, Dale Vance *psychotherapist, hypnotherapist*

**West Hurley**
Martucci, Vincent James *composer, pianist*

**West Islip**
Carpenter, Angie M. *small business owner, editor*
Cokinos, Stephan George *cardiologist*
Coppola, Phyllis Gloria Cecire *special education educator*
Keller, Joyce *television and radio host, counselor*
Softness, Donald Gabriel *marketing and manufacturing executive*
Young, Morris *electrical engineering consultant*

**West Nyack**
Hornik, Joseph William *civil engineer*
Irwin, Ronald Gilbert *minister*
Kanyuk, Joyce Stern *secondary art educator*
Pringle, Laurence Patrick *writer*

**West Point**
Barr, Donald Roy *statistics and operations research educator, statistician*
Barrett, Lida Kittrell *mathematics educator*
Christman, Daniel William *military officer*
†Emmer, Jack *head coach men's lacrosse*
Leupold, Herbert August *physicist*
Meschutt, David Randolph *historian, curator*
Oldaker, Bruce Gordon *physicist, military officer*
Watson, Georgianna *librarian*

**West Valley**
Itzo, Ralph Francis *chemical engineer*

**Westbury**
Barboza, Anthony *photographer, artist*
Cullen, John B. *food products company executive*
De Pauw, Gommar Albert *priest, educator*
DiFiglia, Constance Joan *professional ethics executive, consultant, physician, researcher, writer, poet*
Eisenberg, Dorothy *federal judge*
Ente, Gerald *pediatrician*
Fogg, Joseph Graham, III *investment banking executive*
Fowler, Charles William *school administrator*
Martin, Daniel Richard *pharmaceutical company executive*
O'Sullivan, Kevin Patrick *foundation administrator*
Sandler, Gerald Howard *computer science educator, company executive*
Sherbell, Rhoda *artist, sculptor*
Tulchin, Stanley *banker, lecturer, author, business reorganization consultant*
Waterman, Diane Corrine *artist, educator, writer*

**Westfield**
Brown, Kent Louis, Sr. *surgeon*

**Westhampton Beach**
Maas, Jane Brown *advertising executive*

**White Plains**
Alin, Robert David *lawyer*
Allen, Ralph Dean *diversified company corporate executive*
Bader, Izaak Walton *lawyer*
Baum, Carol Grossman *physician*
Becker, Boris *professional tennis player*
Berlin, Alan Daniel *lawyer, international energy and legal consultant*
Biers, Martin Henry *physician*
Bijur, Peter I. *petroleum company executive*
Blank, H. Robert *psychiatrist*
Blass, John Paul *medical educator, physician*
Blumstein, William A. *insurance company executive*
Bober, Lawrence Harold *retired banker*
Bostin, Marvin Jay *hospital and health services consultant*
Brazell, James Ervin *oil company executive, lawyer*
Brieant, Charles La Monte *federal judge*
Cahill, William Joseph, Jr. *utility company executive*
Carey, John *lawyer, judge*
Castrataro, Barbara Ann *lawyer*
Cheng, Alexander Lihdar *computer scientist, researcher*
Colwell, Howard Otis *advertising executive*
Conner, William Curtis *judge*
Cooke, Lloyd Miller *former organization executive*
Davenport, Lindsay *professional tennis player*
Davidson, Carl B. *oil company executive*
Dent, Robert Alan *electrical engineer*
Ellenbogen, Milton Joseph *publishing executive, editor, writer*
Engen, D(onald) Travis *diversified telecommunications company executive*
Erla, Karen *artist, painter, collagist, printmaker*
Feder, Robert *lawyer*
Fernandez, Gigi *professional tennis player*
Flanigen, Edith Marie *materials scientist, consultant*
Flesher, Margaret Covington *corporate communications executive*
Fortini, V(ictor) Scott *sales and marketing executive*
Foster, John Horace *consulting environmental engineer*
Fowlkes, Nancy Lanetta Pinkard *social worker*
†Frazier, Amy *professional tennis player*
Fudge, Ann Marie *marketing executive*
Garrison-Jackson, Zina *retired tennis player*
Gilbert, Bradley *professional tennis player, Olympic athlete, professional tennis coach*
Gill, Patricia Jane *human resources executive*
Gjertsen, O. Gerard *lawyer*
Goodman, Walter *author, editor*
Graham, Lawrence Otis *lawyer, writer, television personality*
Greene, Leonard Michael *aerospace manufacturing executive, institute executive*
Greenspan, Leon Joseph *lawyer*
Greenspan, Michael Evan *lawyer*
Grossman, Ann *pressional tennis player*
Gurahian, Vincent *church official, former judge*
Halpern, Philip Morgan *lawyer*
Hardin, Adlai Stevenson, Jr. *judge*
Hoffman, Milton Sills *editor*
Jensen, Eric Finn *lawyer*
Johnston, Richard Boles, Jr. *pediatrician, educator, biomedical researcher*
Katz, Michael *pediatrician, educator*
Klein, Paul E. *lawyer*
Kourkoumelis, Nick *oil company analyst, consultant, finance educator*
Krasne, Charles A. *food products executive*
Krickstein, Aaron *professional tennis player*
Krowe, Allen Julian *oil company executive*
Ladjevardi, Hamid *fund manager*
Lapidus, Herbert *medical products executive*
Lauman, Richard H., Jr. *nuclear energy executive*
Machover, Carl *computer graphics consultant*
Maffeo, Vincent Anthony *lawyer, executive*
Magaziner, Elliot Albert *musician, conductor, educator*
Manville, Stewart Roebling *archivist*
Marano, Anthony Joseph *cardiologist*
Mareth, Paul *communications consultant*
Martin, Todd *professional tennis player*
McDowell, Fletcher Hughes *physician, educator*
McEnroe, Patrick *professional tennis player*
†McNeil, Lori Michelle *professional tennis player*
McQuaid, John Gaffney *lawyer*
Merritt, Susan Mary *computer science educator, university dean*
Mitchell, Robert Dale *consulting engineer*
Monteferrante, Judith Catherine *cardiologist*
Morris, Robert Warren *physician assistant*
Munneke, Gary Arthur *law educator, consultant*
Mutz, Steven Herbert *lawyer*
Nauert, Roger Charles *health care executive*
O'Rourke, Richard Lynn *lawyer*
Papp, Laszlo George *architect*
Patman, Jean Elizabeth *journalist*
Payson, Martin Fred *lawyer*
Peyton, Donald Leon *retired standards association executive*
Reap, James B. *judge*
Reneberg, Richard (Richey Reneberg) *professional tennis player*
Riha, William Edwin *beverage company executive*
Roll, Irwin Clifford (Win Roll) *advertising, marketing and publishing executive*
Rose, William Allen, Jr. *architect*
Rosenberg, Michael *lawyer*
Rostagno, Derrick *professional tennis player*
Rubin, Chanda *professional tennis player*
Sacco, John Michael *accountant*
Samii, Abdol Hossein *physician, educator*
Serchuk, Ivan *lawyer*
Silsverberg, Steven Mark *lawyer*
Sinsheimer, Warren Jack *lawyer*
Sive, David *lawyer*
†Slaughter, James C. *trading company executive*
Smith, Elizabeth Patience *oil industry executive, lawyer*
Smith, Gerard Peter *neuroscientist*
Soley, Robert Lawrence *plastic surgeon*
Stalerman, Ruth *civic volunteer, poet*
Tell, William Kirn, Jr. *oil company executive, lawyer*
Triffin, Nicholas *law librarian, law educator*
Vogel, Howard Stanley *lawyer*
Wahaab, Jay *entrepreneur*
Washington, MaliVai *professional tennis player*
Westerhoff, Garret Peter *environmental engineer, executive*
Wheaton, David *professional tennis player*
Worboys, Roger Dick *communications executive*

**Whitesboro**
Raymonda, James Earl *retired banker*

**Whitestone**
Brill, Steven Charles *financial advisor, lawyer*
Rahr, Stewart *health medical products executive*
Rosmarin, Leonard Alan *dermatologist*

**Williamson**
Ross, Kathleen Marie Amato *secondary school educator*

**Williamsville**
Alexander, Theodore William, III *venture capitalist*
Cloudsley, Donald Hugh *library administrator*
Danni, F. Robert *municipal official*
Greizerstein, Hebe Beatriz *research scientist, educator*
Jasiewicz, Ronald Clarence *physician*
Jensen, David Lynn *mathematician, infosystems specialist*
Jones, Robert Alfred *clergyman*
Paladino, Joseph Anthony *clinical pharmacist*
Reisman, Robert E. *physician, educator*
Whitcomb, James Stuart *videographer, photographer, production company executive*

**Willow**
Bley, Carla Borg *jazz composer*
Cox, James David *art gallery executive*

**Wolcott**
Bartlett, Cody Blake *lawyer, educator*

**Woodbury**
Agresti, Miriam Monell *psychologist*
Bell, William Joseph *cable television company executive*
Bleicher, Sheldon Joseph *endocrinologist, medical educator*
Doering, Charles Henry *research scientist, educator, editor, publisher*
Dolan, Charles Francis *cable systems company executive*
†Dolan, James *communications executive*
Guttenplan, Harold Esau *retired food company executive*
Lemle, Robert Spencer *lawyer*
McGovern, Thomas John *environmental engineer*
Stefancich, Donna Lee *information security specialist*
Sweeney, Daniel Thomas *cable television company executive*
Zirkel, Don *public information official*

**Woodhaven**
Bolster, Jacqueline Neben (Mrs. John A. Bolster) *communications consultant*
Krohley, Patricia Anne *realtor, artist, writer*

**Woodmere**
Abramson, Martin *author, journalist*
Bobroff, Harold *lawyer*
Natow, Annette Baum *nutritionist, author, consultant*
Raab, Ira Jerry *lawyer, judge*

**Woodsburgh**
Cohen, Lawrence Alan *real estate executive*

**Woodside**
Burchell, Jeanne Kathleen *primary school educator*
Vasilachi, Gheorghe Vasile *priest, vicar*

**Woodstock**
Banks, Rela *sculptor*
Berger, Karl Hans *composer, pianist, vibrafonist*
Currie, Bruce *artist*
Dolamore, Michael John *physician*
Doyle, Will Lee *writer, editor*
Godwin, Gail Kathleen *author*
Helioff, Anne Graile *painter*
Hoyt, Earl Edward, Jr. *industrial designer*
Kugler, E(rnest) Richard *management consultant*
Ober, Stuart Alan *investment consultant, book publisher*
Smith, Albert Aloysius, Jr. *electrical engineer, consultant*

**Wyandanch**
Barnett, Peter John *property development executive, educator*
Hodges-Robinson, Chettina M. *nursing administrator*

**Yaphank**
Ahern, John James *software company executive*

**Yonkers**
Agli, Stephen Michael *English language educator, literature educator*
Atkins, Leola Mae *special education educator*
Baumel, Herbert *violinist, conductor*
DeAngelis, Roger Thomas *surgeon*
Denver, Eileen Ann *magazine editor*
Drisko, Elliot Hillman *marriage and family therapist*
Eimicke, Victor W(illiam) *publishing company executive*
Goon, Gilbert *software consultant*
Gunner, Murray *Jewish organization administrator*
Hoar, Mary Margrette *gifted education educator*
Karpatkin, Rhoda Hendrick *consumer information organization executive, lawyer*
Liggio, Jean Vincenza *adult education educator, artist*
Lupiani, Donald Anthony *psychologist*
Miller, Karl A. *management counselor*
Pickover, Betty Abravanel *retired executive legal secretary, civic volunteer*
†Schnee, Alix Sandra *historic site administrator*
Singer, Cecile Doris *state legislator*
Smith, Aldo Ralston, Jr. *brokerage house executive*
Tuly, Charles A. *mathematics and computer science educator*
Varma, Baidya Nath *sociologist, broadcaster, poet*
Vergano, Lynn (Marilynn Bette Vergano) *artist*
Weston, Francine Evans *secondary education educator*
Williams, Ted Vaughnell *physical education educator*
Wolfson, Irwin M. *insurance company executive*

**York**
Coleman, David Cecil *financial executive*

**Yorkshire**
Smith, Barbara Jane *assistant school superintendent*

**Yorktown Heights**
Allen, Frances Elizabeth *computer scientist*
Bogdanoff, Stewart Ronald *physical education educator, coach*
Braddock, Nonnie Clarke *religious organization administrator*
Dennard, Robert Heath *engineering executive, scientist*
d'Heurle, François Max *research scientist, engineering educator*
Donovan, Andrew Joseph *financial analyst*
Fowler, Alan Bicksler *retired physicist*
Henle, Robert Athanasius *engineer*
Hoffman, Alan Jerome *mathematician, educator*
Hong, Se June *computer engineer*
Hsieh, Hazel Tseng *elementary and secondary education educator*
Jones, Lauretta Marie *artist, graphic designer, computer interface designer*
Keyes, Robert William *physicist*
Kirkpatrick, Edward Scott *physicist*
Klein, Richard Stephen *internist*
Landauer, Rolf William *physicist*
Lang, Norton David *physicist*
LaRussa, Joseph Anthony *optical company executive*
Lavenberg, Stephen S. *electrical engineer, researcher*
Laventhol, Henry L(ee) (Hank Laventhol) *artist, etcher*
Mandelbrot, Benoit B. *mathematician, scientist, educator*
Ning, Tak Hung *physicist, microelectronic technologist*
Rigoutsos, Isidore *computer scientist*
Romankiw, Lubomyr Taras *materials engineer*
Rosenblatt, Stephen Paul *marketing and sales promotion company executive*
Samalin, Edwin *lawyer, educator*
Sorokin, Peter Pitirimovich *physicist*
Spiller, Eberhard Adolf *physicist*
Terman, Lewis Madison *electrical engineer, researcher*
Troutman, Ronald R. *electrical engineer*
Wade, James O'Shea *publisher*
Winograd, Shmuel *mathematician*

**Youngstown**
Alpert, Norman *chemical company executive*
Polka, Walters S. *school superintendent*

## NORTH CAROLINA

**Advance**
Cochrane, Betsy Lane *state senator*
Herpel, George Lloyd *marketing educator*
Huber, Thomas Martin *container company executive*
Legere, Laurence Joseph *government official*
Meschan, Isadore *radiologist, educator*
Meschan, Rachel Farrer (Mrs. Isadore Meschan) *obstetrics and gynecology educator*

**Albemarle**
Bramlett, Christopher Lewis *academic administrator*
Ingram-Tinsley, Dorothy Catherine *library automation specialist, horse stables owner*

**Almond**
Strausbaugh, Scott David *Olympic athlete, canoeist*

**Angier**
Raynor, Wandra Adams *middle school educator*

**Apex**
Ellington, John David *retired state official*
Knapp, Richard Bruce *anesthesiologist*
Liu, Andrew Tze Chiu *chemical researcher and developer*
Rawlings, John Oren *statistician, researcher*

**Arden**
Adams, Pamela Jeanne *nurse, flight nurse*
Dowdell, Michael Francis *critical care and anesthesia nurse practitioner*

**Asheboro**
Davis, J. B. *furniture manufacturing executive*
Helsabeck, Eric H. *emergency physician*
Jones, David M. *zoological park director*

**Asheville**
Armstrong, Robert Baker *textile company executive*
Astler, Vernon Benson *surgeon*
Baldwin, Garza, Jr. *lawyer, manufacturing company executive*
Banks, James Barber *financial consultant*
Bissette, Winston Louis, Jr. *lawyer, mayor*
Bryson, Paula Kay *secondary school educator*
Coli, Guido John *chemical company executive*
Damtoft, Walter Atkinson *editor, publisher*
Davis, Roy Walton, Jr. *lawyer*
Deitch, D. Gregory *meteorologist*
Dillard, John Robert *lawyer*
Enriquez, Manuel Hipolito *physician*
Etter, Robert Miller *retired consumer products executive, chemist*
Everett, Durward R., Jr. *retired banker*
Fobes, John Edwin *international organization official*
Haggard, William Henry *meteorologist*
Hubbell, Elizabeth Wolfe *English language educator*
Hyde, Herbert Lee *lawyer*
Johnston, John Devereaux, Jr. *law educator, retired*
Jones, J. Kenneth *art dealer, former museum administrator*
King, Joseph Bertram *architect*
Korb, Elizabeth Grace *nurse midwife*
Lavelle, Brian Francis David *lawyer*
Morosani, George Warrington *real estate developer, realtor*
Pickard, Carolyn Rogers *secondary school educator*
Pinkerton, Linda F. *lawyer*
Powell, Norborne Berkeley *urologist*
Reed, Patsy Bostick *university administrator*
Roberts, Bill Glen *retired fire chief, investor, consultant*
Rufa, Robert Henry *writer, editor, photographer, artist*
Sharpe, Keith Yount *retired lawyer*
Smith, Norman Cutler *geologist, business executive, educator*
Vander Voort, Dale Gilbert *textile company executive*
Weed, Maurice James *composer, retired music educator*
Weil, Thomas P. *health services consultant*
White, Terry Edward *physician*
Wilkins, Rita Denise *researcher, multimedia design consultant*
Wilson, Herschel Manuel (Pete Wilson) *retired journalism educator*

**Atlantic Beach**
Barnes, James Thomas, Jr. *aquarium director*

**Ayden**
McElhinney, James Lancel *artist, educator*

**Bahama**
Epstein, David Lee *ophthalmologist, surgeon, educator*

**Banner Elk**
Thomas, John Edwin *retired academic administrator*

**Beaufort**
Cullman, Hugh *retired tobacco company executive*
Ellis, Michael *theatrical producer*

Hardee, Luellen Carroll Hooks school psychologist
Hayman, Carol Bessent poet, author
Ramus, Joseph S. marine biologist

### Belhaven
Boyette, Charles Otis family physician

### Belmont
Stowe, Robert Lee, III textile company executive

### Benson
Doyle, Sally A. controller

### Black Mountain
Cody, Hiram Sedgwick, Jr. retired telephone company executive
Kennedy, William Bean theology educator
Lathrop, Gertrude Adams chemist, consultant
Parker, Mary Althea painter, art educator

### Blowing Rock
Barnebey, Kenneth Alan food company executive

### Boiling Springs
Bennett, Elizabeth Susan music educator
Hearne, Stephen Zachary minister, educator
White, Martin Christopher academic administrator

### Bolivia
Horne, Lithia Brooks finance executive

### Boone
Borkowski, Francis Thomas university administrator
Bowden, Elbert Victor banking, finance and economics educator, author
Brown, Wade Edward lawyer, retired
Duke, Charles Richard academic dean
Jones, Dan Lewis psychologist
Singleton, Stella Wood educator and habilitation assistant

### Boonville
Reece, Joe Wilson engineering company executive

### Brevard
Flory, Margaret Martha retired religious organization administrator
Phillips, Euan Hywel publishing executive
Strongin, Theodore journalist
Wall, Robert Wilson, Jr. former utility executive

### Buies Creek
Davis, Ferd Leary, Jr. law educator, lawyer, consultant
Wiggins, Norman Adrian university administrator, legal educator

### Burlington
Buckley, J. Stephen newspaper publisher
Eddins, James William, Jr. marketing executive
Flagg, Raymond Osbourn biology executive
Holt, Bertha Merrill state legislator
Kee, Walter Andrew former government official
Mason, James Michael biomedical laboratories executive
Powell, James Bobbitt biomedical laboratories executive, pathologist
Tolley, Jerry Russell clinical laboratory executive
Turanchik, Michael research and development director
Wilson, William Preston psychiatrist, emeritus educator

### Burnsville
Bernstein, William Joseph glass artist, educator
Doyle, John Lawrence artist
Peterson, Allen Jay lawyer, educator
Snelling, George Arthur banker

### Calabash
Strunk, Orlo Christopher, Jr. psychology educator

### Camden
Hammond, Roy Joseph reinsurance company executive

### Camp Lejeune
†Howard, Patrick Gene marine corps officer

### Candler
Boggs, William Brady quality engineering and applied statistics consultant

### Canton
Furci, Joan Gelormino early childhood education educator

### Cape Carteret
Mullikin, Thomas Wilson mathematics educator

### Carolina Beach
Brown, Barry Stephen research psychologist

### Carrboro
Boggs, Robert Newell editor
Greenslade, Forrest Charles international health care executive

### Carthage
Thomas, Carol Taylor general services coordinator

### Cary
Ahmadieh, Aziz metallurgy materials science educator
Andrews, John Woodhouse newspaper publisher
Bat-haee, Mohammad Ali educational administrator, consultant
Conrad, Hans materials engineering educator
†Goodnight, James software company executive
Goodwin, Barry Kent economics educator
Hagan, John Aubrey financial executive
Jones, James Arthur retired utilities executive
Khan, Masrur Ali nuclear and chemical engineer, physicist
Martin, William Royall, Jr. association executive
McCarty, Thomas Joseph publishing company executive
Miranda, Constancio Fernandes civil engineering educator
Mochrie, Richard D. physiology educator
Montgomery, Charles Harvey lawyer
Nyce, David Scott electronics company executive
Reynolds, Edward book publisher
Smith, Roy Jordan religious organization administrator
Smith, Walter Sage environmental engineer, consultant
Sussenguth, Edward Henry computer company executive, computer network designer
Vick, Columbus Edwin, Jr. civil engineering design firm executive

### Cashiers
DeHority, Edward Havens, Jr. retired accountant, lawyer
O'Connell, Edward James, Jr. psychology educator, computer applications and data analysis consultant

### Chapel Hill
Andersen, Melvin Ernest toxicologist, consultant
Andrews, Richard Nigel Lyon environmental policy educator, environmental studies administrator
Andrews, William Leake English educator
Arnold, Roland R. dental educator and researcher
Azar, Henry Amin medical historian, educator
Baker, Charles Ray engineering and mathematics educator, researcher
Baker, Ronald Dale dental educator, surgeon, university administrator
Barker, Ben D. dentist, educator
Barnett, Thomas Buchanan physician, medical educator
Barnhill, Cynthia Diane accountant
Baroff, George Stanley psychologist, educator
Baron, Samuel Haskell historian
Bauer, Frederick Christian motor carrier executive
Bawden, James Wyatt dental educator, dental scientist
Betts, Doris June Waugh author, English language educator
Black, Stanley Warren, III economics educator
Blasius, Donald Charles retired appliance company executive
Blau, Peter Michael sociologist, educator
Bolas, Gerald Douglas art museum administrator, art history educator
Bolick, Ernest Bernard, Jr. housing administrator
Bondurant, Stuart physician, educational administrator
Boone, Franklin Delanor Roosevelt, Sr. cardiovascular perfusionist, realtor
Bowers, Thomas Arnold journalism educator
Briggaman, Robert Alan dermatologist, medical educator
Brinkhous, Kenneth Merle pathologist, educator
Brockington, Donald Leslie anthropologist, archaeologist, educator
Bromberg, Philip Allan internist, educator
Brookhart, Maurice S. chemist
Broun, Kenneth Stanley lawyer, educator
Brown, Frank social science educator
Brownlee, Robert Calvin pediatrician, educator
Bruck, Stephen Desiderius biochemist
Brummet, Richard Lee accounting educator
Buck, Richard Pierson chemistry educator, researcher
Bursey, Maurice M. chemistry educator
Calhoun, Richard James English language educator
Camp, Joseph Shelton, Jr. film producer, director, writer
Campbell, B(obby) Jack university official
Cance, William George surgeon
Carpenter, Raymond Leonard information science educator
Carroll, John Bissell psychologist, educator
Carroll, Roy academic administrator
Carson, Culley Clyde, III urologist
Cartwright, William Holman education educator emeritus
Cefalo, Robert Charles obstetrician, gynecologist
Churchill, Larry Raymond ethics educator
Clark, David Louis education educator, author
Clark, Richard Lee radiologist
Clemmons, David Robert internist, educator
Clyde, Wallace Alexander, Jr. pediatrics and microbiology educator
Cobb, Henry Van Zandt psychologist
Cole, Richard Ray university dean
Collier, Albert M. pediatric educator, child development center director
Coulter, Elizabeth Jackson biostatistician, educator
Coulter, Norman Arthur, Jr. biomedical engineering educator emeritus
Crane, Julia Gorham anthropology educator
Crassweller, Robert Doell retired lawyer, writer
Crohn, Max Henry, Jr. lawyer
Cromartie, William James medical educator, researcher
Cross, Dennis Wayne academic administrator
Cummings, Anthony William lawyer, educator
Cunningham, James William literacy education educator, researcher
Dahlstrom, William Grant psychologist, educator
Davis, Morris Schuyler astronomer
Daye, Charles Edward law educator
Debreczeny, Paul Slavic language educator, author
De Friese, Gordon H. health services researcher
Dennison, John Manley geologist, educator
Denny, Floyd Wolfe, Jr. pediatrician
De Rosa, Guy Paul orthopedic surgery educator
Dickman, Catherine Crowe retired human services administrator
Dixon, Frederick Dail architect
Dixon, John Wesley, Jr. retired religion and art educator
Dolan, Louise Ann physicist
Earley, Laurence Elliott medical educator
Easterling, William Ewart, Jr. obstetrician, gynecologist
Eaton, Charles Edward English language educator, author
Edwards, Richard LeRoy academic dean, social work educator, non-profit management consultant
Eifrig, David Eric ophthalmologist, educator
Eisenbud, Merril engineer, scientist
Eliel, Ernest Ludwig chemist, educator
Ellis, Fred Wilson retired pharmacology educator
Falk, Eugene Hannes foreign language educator emeritus
Farber, Rosann Alexander geneticist, educator
Farmer, Thomas Wohlsen neurologist, educator
Fine, J(ames) Allen insurance company executive
Flora, Joseph M(artin) English language educator
Fordham, Christopher Columbus, III university dean and chancellor, medical educator
Forman, Donald T. biochemist
Fowler, Wesley C., Jr. obstetrician, gynecologist
Fox, Ronald Ernest psychologist
Frampton, Paul Howard physics researcher, educator
Frelinger, Jeffrey Allen immunologist, educator
Freund, Cynthia M. dean, nursing educator
Friday, William Clyde university president emeritus
Friedman, James Winstein economist, educator
Fullagar, Paul David geology educator, geochemical consultant
Furst, Lilian Renee language professional, educator
Gallman, Robert Emil economics and history educator
Ganley, Oswald Harold university official
Gasaway, Laura Nell law librarian, educator
Gil, Federico Guillermo political science educator
Gilbert, Lawrence Irwin biologist, educator
Godschalk, David Robinson architect, urban development planner, educator
Goldman, Leonard Manuel physicist, engineering educator
Gottlieb, Gilbert psychobiologist, educator
Gottschalk, Carl William physician, educator
Goyer, Robert Andrew pathology educator
Graham, George Adams political scientist, emeritus educator
Graham, John Borden pathologist, writer, educator
Gray-Little, Bernadette psychologist
Greganti, Mac Andrew physician, medical educator
Gressman, Eugene lawyer
Grisham, Joe Wheeler pathologist, educator
Gulick, John anthropology educator
Hackenbrock, Charles R. cell biologist, educator
Hairston, Nelson George retired animal ecologist
Hammond, David Alan stage director, educator
Haskell, Paul Gershon law educator
Hawkins, David Rollo, Sr. psychiatrist
Hendrick, Randall linguist
Hendricks, Charles Henning retired obstetrics and gynecology educator
Heninger, Simeon Kahn, Jr. English language educator
Henson, Anna Miriam otolaryngology researcher, medical educator
Henson, O'Dell Williams, Jr. anatomy educator
Herman-Giddens, Gregory lawyer
Hershey, H(oward) Garland, Jr. university administrator, orthodontist
Hirsch, Philip Francis pharmacologist, educator
Hochbaum, Godfrey Martin retired behavioral scientist
Holley, Edward Gailon library science educator, former university dean
Hollister, William Gray psychiatrist
Hooker, Michael Kenneth university chancellor
Howell, James Theodore medical consultant, internist
Hubbard, Paul Stancyl, Jr. physics educator
Huber, Evelyne political science educator
Hulka, Barbara Sorenson epidemiology educator
Hulka, Jaroslav Fabian obstetrician, gynecologist
Ingram, James Carlton economist, educator
Irene, Eugene Arthur physical chemistry and materials science educator, researcher
Jackson, Blyden English language educator
Jerdee, Thomas Harlan business administration educator, organization psychology researcher and consultant
Johnson, George, Jr. physician, educator
Jones, Houston Gwynne history educator
Jones, Lyle Vincent psychology educator
Joyner, Leon Felix university administrator, retired
Judd, Burke Haycock geneticist
Juliano, Rudolph L. medical educator
Keagy, Blair Allen surgery educator
Kenan, Thomas Stephen, III philanthropist
Kilgour, Frederick Gridley librarian, educator
Kittredge, John Kendall retired insurance company executive
Klarmann, Dave university athletic coach
Kohn, Richard H. historian, educator
Kuenzler, Edward Julian ecologist and environmental biologist
Kuhn, Matthew engineering company executive
Kula, Katherine Sue dentist
Kusy, Robert Peter biomedical engineering and orthodontics educator
Langdell, Robert Dana medical educator
Langenderfer, Harold Quentin accountant, educator
Lauder, Valarie Anne editor, educator
Lauterborn, Robert F. advertising educator, consultant
Lawrence, David Michael lawyer, educator
Lawson, Edward Earle neonatologist
Lee, Kuo-Hsiung medicinal chemistry educator
Lee, Sherman Emery art historian, curator
Levine, Madeline Geltman Slavic literatures educator, translator
Ligett, Waldo Buford chemist
Lilley, Albert Frederick retired lawyer
Little, Loyd Harry, Jr. author
Loeb, Ben Fohl, Jr. lawyer, educator
Long, Douglas Clark philosophy educator
Lowman, Robert Paul psychology educator, academic administrator
Lucas, Carol Lee biomedical engineer
Ludington, Charles Townsend, Jr. English and American studies educator
Macdonald, James Ross physicist, educator
MacGillivray, Lois Ann organization executive
MacRae, Duncan, Jr. social scientist, educator
Manire, George Philip bacteriologist, educator
Markham, Jordan J. physicist, retired educator
Martin, Harry Corpening lawyer, retired state supreme court justice
McBay, Arthur John toxicologist, consultant
Mc Curdy, Harold Grier psychologist
McKay, Kenneth Gardiner physicist, electronics company executive
McMillan, Campbell White pediatric hematologist
Memory, Jasper Durham academic administrator, physics educator
Merzbacher, Eugen physicist, educator
Meyer, Thomas J. chemistry educator
Miller, C. Arden physician, educator
Miller, Daniel Newton, Jr. geologist, consultant
Mitchell, Earl Nelson physicist, educator
Moran, Barbara Burns librarian, educator
Mueller, Nancy Schneider retired biology educator
Munsat, Stanley Morris philosopher, educator
Murphy, James Lee college dean, economics educator
Murray, Royce Wilton chemistry educator
Nelson, Philip Francis musicology educator, consultant, choral conductor
Ness, Albert Kenneth artist, educator
Neumann, Andrew Conrad geological oceanography educator
Newman, William Stein music educator, author, pianist, composer
Okun, Daniel Alexander environmental engineering educator
Ontjes, David Ainsworth medicine and pharmacology educator
Pagano, Joseph Stephen physician, researcher, educator
Palmer, Gary Stephen health services administrator
Palmer, Jeffress Gary hematologist, educator
Parker, Scott Jackson theatre manager
Parr, Robert Ghormley chemistry educator
Perreault, William Daniel, Jr. business administration educator
Pfouts, Ralph William economist, consultant
Pillsbury, Harold Crockett otolaryngologist
Pollitzer, William Sprott anatomy educator
Powell, Carolyn Wilkerson music educator
Prange, Arthur Jergen, Jr. psychiatrist, neurobiologist, educator
Prather, Donna Lynn psychiatrist
†Price, David Eugene congressman, educator
Proffit, William Robert orthodontics educator
Pruett, James Worrell librarian, musicologist
Richardson, Richard Judson political science educator
Riggs, Timothy Allan museum curator
Rindfuss, Ronald Richard sociology educator
Roberts, Louis Douglas physics educator, researcher
Rogers, John James William geology educator
Rohe, William Michael urban planning educator
Rondinelli, Dennis A(ugust) business administration educator, research center director
Rosen, Benson business administration educator
Roth, Aleda Vender business educator
Rubin, Louis Decimus, Jr. English language and literature educator, writer, publisher
St. Jean, Joseph, Jr. micropaleontologist, educator
Sancar, Aziz research biochemist
Sanders, Charles Addison physician
Sanders, John Lassiter retired academic administrator
Scepanski, Jordan Michael librarian, administrator
Schier, Donald Stephen language educator
Schopler, John Henry psychologist, educator
Schoultz, Lars political scientist, educator
Scott, Tom Keck biologist, educator
Sharpless, Richard Kennedy lawyer
Sheldon, George F. medical educator
Simmons, Michael Anthony dean
Simpson, Richard Lee sociologist, educator
Singer, Philip C. environmental engineer, educator
Slack, Lewis organization administrator
Slifkin, Lawrence Myer physics educator
Smith, Dean Edwards university basketball coach
Smith, Sidney Rufus, Jr. linguist, educator
Smithies, Oliver geneticist, educator
Sorenson, James Roger public health educator
Spangler, Clemmie Dixon, Jr. business executive
Spencer, Elizabeth author
Spencer, Roger Felix psychiatrist, psychoanalyst, medical educator
Stadter, Philip Austin classicist, educator
Stamm, John William Rudolph dentist, educator, academic dean
Stanberry, Dosi Elaine English literature educator, writer
Stasheff, James Dillon mathematics educator
Stephens, Laurence David, Jr. linguist, investor, oil industry executive
Steponaitis, Vincas Petras archaeologist, anthropologist, educator
Stewart, Richard Edwin insurance consulting company executive
Stidham, Shaler, Jr. operations research educator
Stipe, Robert Edwin design educator
Stiven, Alan Ernest population biologist, ecologist
Stockman, James Anthony, III pediatrician
Strauss, Albrecht Benno English educator, editor
Stumpf, Walter Erich cell biology educator, researcher
Sugioka, Kenneth anesthesiologist educator
Suzuki, Kunihiko biomedical educator, researcher
Swanson, Michael Alan sales and marketing executive
Thakor, Haren Bhaskerrao manufacturing company executive
Thomas, Colin Gordon, Jr. surgeon, medical educator
Tillman, Rollie, Jr. university official
Tindall, George Brown historian, educator
Tolley, Aubrey Granville hospital administrator
Treml, Vladimir Guy economist, educator
Tunnessen, Walter William, Jr. pediatrician
Udry, J. Richard sociology educator
Upshaw, Harry Stephan psychology educator
Van Seters, John biblical literature educator
Van Wyk, Judson John endocrinologist, pediatric educator
Vogler, Frederick Wright French language educator
Wahl, Jonathan Michael mathematics educator
Ware, William Brettel education educator
Warren, Donald William physiology educator, dentistry educator
Waud, Roger Neil economics educator
Wegner, Judith Welch law educator, dean
Weinberg, Gerhard Ludwig history educator
Weiss, Charles Manuel environmental biologist
Weiss, Shirley F. urban and regional planner, economist, educator
Wheeler, Clayton Eugene, Jr. dermatologist, educator
White, Raymond Petrie, Jr. dentist, educator
Whybark, David Clay educational educator, researcher
Wicker, Marie Peachee civic worker
Wilcox, Benson Reid cardiothoracic surgeon, educator
Williams, Roberta Gay pediatric cardiologist, educator
Williamson, Joel Rudolph humanities educator
Wilson, Glenn economist, educator
Wilson, John Eric biochemistry educator
Wilson, Robert Neal sociologist, educator
Winfield, John Buckner rheumatologist, educator
Wogen, Warren Ronald mathematics educator
Wolfenden, Richard Vance biochemistry educator
Wood, Robert Emerson pediatrics educator
Wright, Deil Spencer political science educator
Wyrick, Priscilla Blakeney microbiologist
Yarnell, Richard Asa anthropologist
York, James Wesley, Jr. theoretical physicist, educator
Zeisel, Steven H. nutritionist, educator
Ziff, Paul philosophy educator

### Charlotte
Abelman, Henry Moss lawyer

Anderson, Gerald Leslie *financial executive*
Anoff, Jean Schoenstadt *advertising specialty company executive*
Ayscue, Edwin Osborne, Jr. *lawyer*
Barrows, Frank Clemence *newspaper editor*
Belk, John M. *retail company executive*
Belk, Thomas Milburn *apparel executive*
Belthoff, Richard Charles, Jr. *lawyer*
Bogues, Tyrone Curtis (Muggsy Bogues) *professional basketball player*
†Bosse, Michael Joseph *orthopedic trauma surgeon, retired medical officer*
Bowden, James Alvin *construction company financial executive*
Brackett, Martin Luther, Jr. *lawyer*
Bradshaw, Howard Holt *management consulting company executive*
Brazeal, Donna Smith *psychologist*
Brown, Tony *theater and dance critic*
Browning, Roy Wilson, III *mortgage banking executive*
Buchan, Jonathan Edward, Jr. *lawyer*
Burke, Mary Thomas *university administrator, educator*
Cannon, Robert Eugene *librarian, public administrator, fund raiser*
Capers, Dominic *professional football coach*
Carper, Barbara Anne *nursing educator*
Citron, David Sanford *physician*
Clark, Ann Blakeney *educational administrator*
Cogdell, Joe Bennett, Jr. *lawyer*
Colvard, Dean Wallace *emeritus university chancellor*
Cornick, Michael F(rederick) *accounting educator*
Crutchfield, Edward Elliott, Jr. *banking executive*
Curlin, William G. *bishop*
Dagenhart, Larry Jones *lawyer*
Daniels, William Carlton, Jr. *construction executive*
Davenport, Dona Lee *telecommunications consultant*
Davis, Eric Wayne *professional football player*
Davis, William Maxie, Jr. *lawyer*
Diamond, Harvey Jerome *machinery manufacturing company executive*
Doyle, Esther Piazza *critical care nurse, educator*
Edwards, Harold Mills *government official, lawyer*
Edwards, Irene Elizabeth (Libby Edwards) *dermatologist, educator, researcher*
†Eppes, Thomas Evans *advertising executive, public relations executive*
Ethridge, Mark Foster, III *writer, publisher, newspaper consultant*
Evans, Bruce Haselton *art museum director*
Ferebee, Stephen Scott, Jr. *architect*
Ferguson, James Elliot, II *lawyer*
Finley, Glenna *author*
Foss, Ralph Scot *mechanical engineer*
Freeman, Sidney Lee *minister, educator*
Freeman, Tyler Ira *physician*
Fretwell, Elbert Kirtley, Jr. *university chancellor emeritus, consultant*
Gage, Gaston Hemphill *lawyer*
†Gallo, Richard Anthony *electrical supply company executive*
Gambrell, Sarah Belk *retail executive*
Georgius, John R. *bank executive*
Glosson, Buster C. *venture capital, business development executive*
Goolkasian, Paula A. *psychologist, educator*
Goryn, Sara *textiles executive, real estate developer, psychologist*
Graham, Sylvia Angelenia *wholesale distributor, retail buyer*
Greene, William Henry L'Vel *academic administrator*
Grier, Joseph Williamson, Jr. *lawyer*
Griffith, Steve Campbell, Jr. *lawyer*
Grigg, William Humphrey *utility executive*
Hackler, John Byron, III *architect*
Haines, Kenneth H. *television broadcasting executive*
Halas, Paul Anthony, Jr. *business appraisal and valuation specialist, consultant*
Hall, Peter Michael *physics educator, electronics researcher*
Hanna, George Verner, III *lawyer*
Hannah, Thomas E. *textiles executive*
Hayes, Peter Charles *research chemist*
Hendrick, J. R., III *automotive executive*
Hill, Ruth Foell *language consultant*
Hinson, Jane Pardee Henderson *lactation consultant*
Huberman, Jeffrey Allen *architect*
Hudgins, Catherine Harding *business executive*
Hutcheson, J. Sterling *allergist, immunologist, physician*
Ismail, Raghib (Rocket Ismail) *professional football player*
Iverson, Francis Kenneth *metals company executive*
Johnson, Larry Demetric *professional basketball player*
Johnson, Phillip Eugene *mathematics educator*
Johnstone, Chauncey Olcott *pharmaceutical company executive*
Keanini, Russell Guy *mechanical engineering educator, researcher*
Kidda, Michael Lamont, Jr. *psychologist, educator*
Kim, Rhyn Hyun *engineering educator*
King, L. Ellis *civil engineer, educator, consultant*
Lapp, Charles Warren *internal medicine physician, pediatrician*
Latimer, Ben William *healthcare executive*
Lea, Scott Carter *retired packaging company executive*
Locke, Elizabeth Hughes *foundation administrator*
Loeffler, William George, Jr. *advertising executive*
Love, Franklin Sadler *retired trade association executive*
Lyerly, Elaine Myrick *advertising executive*
Maday, Clifford Ronald *insurance professional*
Martin, James Grubbs *medical research executive, former governor*
Mason, Anthony George Douglas *professional basketball player*
Mazze, Edward Mark *marketing educator, consultant*
McBryde, Neill Gregory *lawyer*
McCall, Billy Gene *charitable trust executive*
McColl, Hugh Leon, Jr. *bank executive*
McConnell, David Moffatt *lawyer*
McCrory, Patrick *mayor*
McLanahan, Charles Scott *neurosurgeon*
McVerry, Thomas Leo *manufacturing company executive*
Mendelsohn, Robert Victor *insurance company executive*
Mills, Samuel Davis, Jr. *professional football player*
Moland, Kathryn Johnetta *computer scientist, software engineer*
Monroe, Frederick Leroy *chemist*
Montague, Edgar Burwell, III (Monty Montague) *industrial designer*
Mueller, Werner Heinrich *organic chemist, chemical engineering technology administrator*
Mullen, Graham C. *federal judge*
Murray, Peter William *airline executive, educator, college administrator*
Nassar-McMillan, Sylvia C. *educator*
Neel, Richard Eugene *economics educator*
Neill, Rolfe *newspaper executive*
Nelson, Barbara Secrest *educational developer*
Nicholson, Henry Hale, Jr. *surgeon*
Orr, T(homas) J(erome) (Jerry Orr) *airport terminal executive*
Orsbon, Richard Anthony *lawyer*
Osborne, Richard Jay *electric utility company executive*
Pehl, Glen Eugene *risk and insurance consultant*
Phibbs, Garnett Ersiel *engineer, educator, minister, religious organization administrator*
Phillips, Sandra Allen *primary school educator*
Potter, Robert Daniel *federal judge*
Preston, James Young *lawyer*
Prosser, Bruce Reginal, Jr. (Bo Prosser) *minister, consultant*
Pyle, Gerald Fredric *medical geographer, educator*
Rajani, Prem Rajaram *transportation company financial executive*
Raper, William Cranford *lawyer*
Rathke, Dieter B. *construction company executive*
Regelbrugge, Roger Rafael *steel company executive*
Richards, Craig M. *wholesale distribution executive*
Risko, James Richard *business executive*
Rodite, Robert R.R. *engineering scientist*
Roels, Oswald Albert *oceanographer, educator, business executive*
Ross, David Edmond *church official*
Saikevych, Irene A. *pathologist*
Sanford, James Kenneth *public relations executive*
Schaffer, Eugene Carl *education educator*
Shah, Nandlal Chimanlal *physiatrist*
Shaul, Roger Louis, Jr. *health care consultant, executive, researcher*
Shinn, George *professional sports team executive*
Shive, Philip Augustus *architect*
Shoemaker, Raleigh A. *lawyer*
Short, Earl de Grey, Jr. *psychiatrist, consultant*
Siegel, Samuel *metals company executive*
Sintz, Edward Francis *librarian*
Smith, Arthur *radio and television producer, composer*
Smith, Elizabeth Hegeman *mental health therapist, hypnotherapist*
Stair, Frederick Rogers *retired foundation executive, former seminary president*
Sustar, T. David *college president*
Taylor, David Brooke *lawyer, banker*
Thies, Austin Cole *retired utility company executive*
Thigpen, Richard Elton, Jr. *lawyer*
Thompson, John Albert, Jr. *dermatologist*
Tillett, Grace Montana *ophthalmologist, real estate developer*
Turner, Thomas Patrick *architect*
Twisdale, Harold Winfred *dentist*
Van Allen, William Kent *lawyer*
Van Alstyne, Vance Brownell *arbitration management consultant*
Visser, Valya Elizabeth *physician*
Voorhees, Richard Lesley *chief federal judge*
Waggoner, William Johnson *lawyer*
Walker, Clarence Wesley *lawyer*
Walker, Kenneth Dale *automotive service company executive*
†Walls, Charles Wesley *football player*
Watkins, Carlton Gunter *retired pediatrician*
Webster, Murray Alexander, Jr. *sociologist*
Wenner, Gene Charles *arts management executive*
Wentz, Billy Melvin, Jr. *finance executive*
White, David Lee *journalist*
Wiggins, Nancy Bowen *real estate broker, market research consultant*
Williams, Edwin Neel *newspaper editor*
Williford, Donald Bratton *accounting company executive*
Wilson, Edward Cox *minister*
Wireman, Billy Overton *college president*
Wolf, Sara Hevia *art librarian*
Wood, William McBrayer *lawyer*
Woodward, James Hoyt *academic administrator, engineer*
Woolard, William Leon *lawyer, electrical distributing company executive*
Zeller, Michael Eugene *lawyer*

### Cherryville
Huffstetler, Palmer Eugene *retired transportation executive, lawyer*
Mayhew, Kenneth Edwin, Jr. *transportation company executive*

### China Grove
Baker, Ira Lee *journalist, former educator*
Hall, Telka Mowery Elium *educational administrator*

### Chocowinity
Castle, William Eugene *retired academic adminstrator*

### Clarkton
Wuebbels, Theresa Elizabeth *visual art educator*

### Clayton
Amy, James Borden *mechanical engineer*

### Clemmons
Cawood, Merton Campbell *investment management executive*

### Clyde
Parris, Donna Sands *secondary school educator*
Rogers, Frances Nichols *assistant principal*

### Columbus
Lee, Wallace Williams, Jr. *retired hotel executive*
Smith, Virginia Warren *artist, writer, educator*

### Concord
Campbell, Paul Thomas *cardiologist*
O'Toole, Michael Doran *psychologist*
†Wallace, Kenny *professional race car driver*

### Cornelius
†Mayfield, Jeremy *professional race car driver*

### Corolla
Schrote, John Ellis *retired government executive*

### Cove City
Hawkins, Elinor Dixon (Mrs. Carroll Woodard Hawkins) *retired librarian*

### Creedmoor
Cross, June Crews *music educator*

### Cullowhee
Bardo, John William *university administrator*
Blethen, Harold Tyler, III *history educator*
Coulter, Myron Lee *retired academic administrator*
Farwell, Harold Frederick, Jr. *English language educator*
Reed, Alfred Douglas *university director*
Willis, Ralph Houston *mathematics educator*

### Dallas
Blanton, Robert D'Alden *anthropology and history educator*
Green, Gayla Maxine *elementary school educator*

### Dana
Morgan, Lou Ann *physical education educator*

### Davidson
Burnett, John Nicholas *chemistry educator*
Cole, Richard Cargill *English language educator*
Jackson, Herb *artist, educator*
Jackson, Robert Bruce, Jr. *retired education educator*
Jones, Arthur Edwin, Jr. *library administrator, English and American literature educator*
Klein, Benjamin Garrett *mathematics educator*
Kuykendall, John Wells *academic administrator, educator*
Lester, Malcolm *historian, educator*
McKelway, Alexander Jeffrey *religion studies educator*
Mele, Alfred R. *philosophy educator*
Palmer, Edward L. *social psychology educator, television researcher, writer*
Park, Leland Madison *librarian*
Plyler, John Laney, Jr. *healthcare management professional*
Ramirez, Julio Jesus *neuroscientist*
Ratliff, Charles Edward, Jr. *economics educator*
Spencer, Samuel Reid, Jr. *educational consultant, former university president*
Tong, Rosemarie *medical humanities and philosophy educator, consultant and researcher*
Williams, Robert Chadwell *history educator*
Zimmermann, T. C. Price *historian, educator*

### Deep Gap
Tompkins, James Richard *special education educator*

### Dillsboro
Lefler, Lisa Jane *anthropologist and social sciences educator*

### Dobson
Smith, Richard Jackson *elementary education educator*

### Dunn
Blackman, Danny *religious organization administrator*
Davis, Dolly *religious organization administrator*
Heath, Preston *clergy member, religious organization administrator*
Taylor, David *clergy member, religious administrator*

### Durham
Abernathy, Margaret Denny *elementary school educator*
Aldrich, John Herbert *political science educator*
Alexander, C. Alex *physician*
Allard, William Kenneth *mathematician*
Amos, Dennis B. *immunologist*
Anderson, William Banks, Jr. *ophthalmology educator*
Anlyan, William George *surgeon, university administrator*
Baerg, Richard Henry *podiatric physician, surgeon*
Barber, James David *political scientist, retired educator*
Barry, David Walter *infectious diseases physician, researcher*
Bartlett, Katharine Tiffany *law educator*
Beckum, Leonard Charles *academic administrator*
Behn, Robert Dietrich *public policy educator, writer*
Bejan, Adrian *mechanical engineering educator*
Bell, Judith Carolyn Ott *interdisciplinary educator*
Bennett, Peter Brian *researcher, anesthesiology educator*
Bettman, James Ross *management educator*
Bevan, William *retired foundation executive*
Blazer, Dan German *psychiatrist, epidemiologist*
Blazing, Michael August *internist*
Blum, Jacob Joseph *physiologist, educator*
†Bolognesi, Dani Paul *virologist, educator*
Bradford, William Dalton *pathologist, educator*
Brahen, Leonard S. *psychiatrist*
Braibanti, Ralph John *political scientist, educator*
Britton, Charles Valentine *secondary education educator*
Brodie, Harlow Keith Hammond *psychiatrist, educator, past university president*
Bryan, Paul Robey, Jr. *musician, educator*
Buckley, Charles Edward, III *physician, educator*
Buckley, Rebecca Hatcher *physician, educator*
Budd, Isabelle Amelia *research economist*
Budd, Louis John *English language educator*
Burger, Robert Mercer *semiconductor device research executive*
Burmeister, Edwin *economics educator*
Busse, Ewald William *psychiatrist, educator*
Butters, Ronald Richard *English language educator*
Cady, Edwin Harrison *English language educator, author*
Caesar, Shirley *gospel singer, evangelist*
Campbell, Dennis Marion *theology dean, educator, university administrator*
Canada, Mary Whitfield *librarian*
Carlson, Alan Neil *ophthalmologist*
Carrington, Paul DeWitt *lawyer, educator*
Carter, James Harvey *psychiatrist, educator*
Cartmill, Matt *anthropologist, anatomy educator*
Casey, H(orace) Craig, Jr. *electrical engineering educator*
Chaddock, Jack Bartley *mechanical engineering educator*
Chafe, William Henry *history educator*
Chambers, Julius LeVonne *academic administrator, lawyer*
Chesnut, Donald Blair *chemistry educator*
Christie, George Custis *lawyer, educator, author*
Christmas, William Anthony *internist, educator*
Civello, Anthony Ned *retail drug company executive, pharmacist*
Clark, Arthur Watts *insurance company executive*
Clotfelter, Charles T. *economics educator*
Cocks, Franklin Hadley *materials scientist*
Cohen, Harvey Jay *physician, educator*
Coleman, Ralph Edward *nuclear medicine physician*
Collins, Bert *insurance executive*
Colton, Joel *historian, educator*
Colvin, O. Michael *medical director, medical educator*
Cook, Clarence Edgar *research facility scientist*
Cooper, Charles Howard *photojournalist, newspaper publishing company executive*
Copeland, Betty Marable *psychotherapist*
Cox, James D. *law educator*
Cruze, Alvin M. *research institute executive*
Culberson, William Louis *botany educator*
Danner, Richard Allen *law educator, dean*
Davis, Calvin De Armond *historian, educator*
Davis, James Evans *general and thoracic surgeon, parliamentarian, author*
Dawson, Robert Edward, Sr. *ophthalmologist*
Demott, Deborah Ann *lawyer, educator*
Dowell, Earl Hugh *university dean, aerospace and mechanical engineering educator*
Dunbar, Leslie Wallace *writer, consultant*
Dunteman, George Henry *psychologist*
Durden, Robert Franklin *history educator*
Elion, Gertrude Belle *research scientist, pharmacology educator*
Elliot, Jeffrey M. *political science educator, author*
Estes, Edward Harvey, Jr. *medical educator*
Evans, Ralph Aiken *physicist, consultant*
Fair, Richard Barton *electronics executive, educator*
Falletta, John Matthew *pediatrician, educator*
Feldman, Jerome Myron *physician*
Fish, Stanley Eugene *English language and literature educator*
Fisher, Charles Page, Jr. *consulting geotechnical engineer*
Fogle, G. Lee *credit union executive, consultant*
Foreman, John William *pediatrician, educator*
Franklin, John Hope *historian, educator, author*
Freemark, Michael Scott *pediatric endocrinologist and educator*
Fridovich, Irwin *biochemistry educator*
Frothingham, Thomas Eliot *pediatrician*
Gaede, Jane Taylor *pathologist*
Gann, Pamela Brooks *law educator*
Garg, Devendra Prakash *mechanical engineer, educator*
Georgiade, Nicholas George *physician*
Gillham, Nicholas Wright *geneticist, educator*
Gittler, Joseph Bertram *sociology educator*
Gleckner, Robert Francis *English language professional, educator*
Golding, Martin Philip *law and philosophy educator*
Goodwin, Frank Erik *materials engineer*
Graham, William Thomas *lawyer*
Gratz, Pauline *former nursing science educator*
Greenfield, Joseph Cholmondeley, Jr. *physician, educator*
Hamilton, Michael A. *medical educator*
Hammes, Gordon G. *chemistry educator*
Hammond, Charles Bessellieu *obstetrician, gynecologist, educator*
Han, Moo-Young *physicist*
Handy, Rollo Leroy *economics educator, research executive*
Harman, Charles Morgan *mechanical engineer*
Harmel, Merel Hilber *anesthesiologist, educator*
Harrell, Benjamin Carlton *columnist, retired editor*
Harris, Jerome Sylvan *pediatrician, pediatrics and biochemistry educator*
Havighurst, Clark Canfield *law educator*
Hawkins, William E. N. *newspaper editor*
Hayes, Brian Paul *editor, writer*
Hobbs, Marcus Edwin *chemistry educator*
Hochmuth, Robert Milo *mechanical and biomedical engineer, educator*
Holley, Irving Brinton, Jr. *historian, educator*
Holsti, Ole Rudolf *political scientist, educator*
Hopkins, Everett Harold *education educator*
Horowitz, Donald Leonard *lawyer, educator, researcher, political scientist, arbitrator*
†Hough, Jerry Fincher *political science educator*
Huestis, Charles Benjamin *former academic administrator*
†Israel, Michael David *healthcare executive*
Jacob, Jerry Rowland *airline executive*
Jaszczak, Ronald Jack *physicist, researcher, consultant*
Jennings, Robert Burgess *experimental pathologist, medical educator*
Johnson, Victoria Susan Kaprielian *medical educator*
Johnston, William Webb *pathologist, educator*
Joklik, Wolfgang Karl *biochemist, virologist, educator*
Katz, Samuel Lawrence *pediatrician, scientist*
Kaufman, Russell Eugene *hematologist, oncologist*
Kay, Richard Frederick *paleontology and biological anthropology educator*
Keene, Jack Donald *molecular genetics and microbiology educator*
Keepler, Manuel *mathematics educator, researcher*
Keller, Thomas Franklin *dean, management science educator*
Kelley, Allen Charles *economist, educator*
Keohane, Nannerl Overholser *university president, political scientist*
Keohane, Robert Owen *political scientist, educator*
King, Lowell Restell *pediatric urologist*
Kirshner, Norman *pharmacologist, researcher, educator*
Klitzman, Bruce *physiologist, plastic surgery educator, researcher*
Koepke, John Arthur *hematologist, clinical pathologist*
Krakauer, Thomas Henry *museum director*
†Kramer, Randall A. *economist, educator*
Kreps, Juanita Morris *economics educator, former government official*
Krishnan, Krishnaswamy Ranga Rama *psychiatrist*
Krzyzewski, Mike *university athletic coach*
Kuniholm, Bruce Robellet *university administrator*
Kylstra, Johannes Arnold *physician*
Lack, Leon *pharmacology and biochemistry educator*
Ladd, Marcia Lee *medical equipment and supplies company executive*

Land, Kenneth Carl sociology educator, demographer, statistician, consultant
Lange, David L. law educator
Langford, Thomas Anderson retired theology educator, academic administrator
Layish, Daniel T. internist
Leach, Richard Heald political scientist, educator
Lefkowitz, Robert Joseph physician, educator
Lerner, Warren historian
Lifton, Walter M. psychology and education consultant
Little, Larry Chatmon head football coach
Llewellyn, Charles Elroy, Jr. psychiatrist
Lockhead, Gregory Roger psychology educator
London, William Lord pediatrician
Loveland, Donald William computer science educator
Lozoff, Bo nonprofit organization administrator
Luney, Percy Robert, Jr. law educator, dean, lawyer, consultant
Lyerly, Herbert Kim surgical oncology educator, researcher
Malindzak, George Steve, Jr. cardiovascular physiology, biomedical engineer
Malpass, Leslie Frederick retired university president
Marchuk, Douglas Alan medical educator
Markham, Charles Buchanan lawyer
Mauskopf, Seymour Harold history educator
Maxwell, Richard Callender lawyer, educator
Mc Kinney, Ross Erwin civil engineering educator
McMahon, John Alexander law educator
Meyer, Horst physics educator
Meyers, Eric Mark religion educator
Michener, James Lloyd medical educator
Mickiewicz, Ellen Propper political science educator
Miller, David Edmond physician
Moon, Samuel David medical educator
Moore, John Wilson neurophysiologist, educator
Mosteller, Robert P. law educator
Murphy, Barbara Anne emergency physician, surgery educator
Murphy, Thomas Miles pediatrician
Murray, William James anesthesiology educator, clinical pharmacologist
Myers, George Carleton sociology and demographics educator
Nakarai, Charles Frederick Toyozo music educator, adjudicator
Naylor, Aubrey Willard botany educator
Nevins, Joseph Roy medical educator
Nicklas, Robert Bruce cell biologist
Nygard, Holger Olof English and folklore educator
Oates, John Francis classics educator
Odom, Guy Leary retired physician
Opara, Emmanuel Chukwuemeka biochemistry educator
Osterhout, Suydam physician, educator
Otterbourg, Robert Kenneth public relations consultant, writer
Page, Ellis Batten behavioral scientist, educator, corporate officer
Parker, Joseph B., Jr. psychiatrist, educator
Pearsall, George Wilbur materials scientist, mechanical engineer, educator, consultant
Pearsall, Samuel Haff, III landscape ecologist, geographer, foundation administrator
Perkins, Ronald Dee geologist, educator
Pinnell, Sheldon Richard physician, medical educator
Pirrung, Michael Craig chemistry educator, consultant
Pizzo, Salvatore Vincent pathologist
Plonsey, Robert electrical and biomedical engineer
Pratt, Philip Chase pathologist, educator
Preston, Richard Arthur historian
Raetz, Christian R. H. biochemistry educator
Redbone, Leon singer, musician
Reves, Joseph Gerald anesthesiology educator
Ricci, Robert Ronald manufacturing company executive
Richardson, Curtis John ecology educator
Richardson, Lawrence, Jr. Latin language educator, archeologist
Richardson, Stephen Giles biotechnology company executive
Ritter, Frederick Edmond plastic surgeon, educator
Roberson, Nathan Russell physicist, educator
Robertson, Horace Bascomb, Jr. law educator
Rollins, Edward Tyler, Jr. newspaper executive
Rose, Donald James computer science educator
Rosenthal, Julian Bernard association executive, lawyer
Roses, Allen David neurologist, educator
Rossiter, Alexander, Jr. news service executive, editor
Rouse, Doris Jane physiologist, research administrator
Rowe, Thomas Dudley, Jr. law educator
Ryals, Clyde de Loache humanities educator
Ryan, Gerard Spencer inn executive
Sabiston, David Coston, Jr. surgeon, educator
Sanford, David Hawley philosophy educator
Schanberg, Saul Murray pharmacology educator
Schiffman, Susan Stolte medical psychologist, educator
Schmalbeck, Richard Louis university dean, lawyer
Schmidt-Nielsen, Knut physiologist, educator
Schwarcz, Steven Lance lawyer
Scott, Anne Byrd Firor history educator
Searles, Richard Brownlee botany educator, marine biology researcher
Semans, Mary Duke Biddle Trent foundation administrator
Serafin, Donald plastic surgeon
Sessoms, Stuart McGuire physician, educator, retired insurance company executive
Severance, Harry Wells emergency medicine educator
Sheetz, Michael Patrick cell biology educator
Shelburne, John Daniel pathologist
Shimm, Melvin Gerald law educator
Sloan, Frank Allen economics educator
Smith, Grover Cleveland English language educator
Smith, Harmon Lee, Jr. clergyman, moral theology educator
Smith, Peter chemist, educator, consultant
Snyderman, Ralph medical educator, physician
Somjen, George Gustav physiologist
Spach, Madison Stockton cardiologist
Spock, Alexander pediatrician, professor
Squire, Alexander management consultant
Staddon, John Eric Rayner psychology, zoology, neurobiology educator
Staelin, Richard business administration educator
Stead, Eugene Anson, Jr. physician
Steinmetz, David Curtis religion educator, publisher, minister
Stiles, Gary Lester cardiologist, molecular pharmacologist, educator
Strohbehn, John Walter engineering science educator
Stroscio, Michael Anthony physicist, educator
Surwit, Richard Samuel psychology educator
Swaim, Mark Wendell molecular biologist, gastroenterologist
Sykes, Richard Brook microbiologist
Tebbel, John writer, educator
Tedder, Thomas Fletcher immunology educator, researcher
Thompson, John Herd history educator
Tiryakian, Edward Ashod sociology educator
Utku, Senol civil engineer, computer science educator
Vitter, Jeffrey Scott computer science educator, consultant
Walter, Richard Lawrence physicist, educator
Ward, Robert composer, conductor, educator
Wardropper, Bruce Wear language educator
Warner, Seth L. mathematician, educator
Warren, David Grant lawyer, educator
Watts, Charles DeWitt retired surgeon, corporate medical director
Weiner, Richard David psychiatrist, researcher
Welborn, Reich Lee lawyer
Werman, David Sanford psychiatrist, psychoanalyst, educator
Westbrook, Don Arlen minister
Wilder, Pelham, Jr. chemist, pharmacologist, educator, academic administrator
Wilkins, Robert Henry neurosurgeon, editor
Williams, George Walton English educator
Williams, Jocelyn Jones reading educator
Williams, Redford Brown medical educator
Wilson, Ruby Leila nurse, educator
Woodbury, Max Atkin polymath, educator
Yancy, William Samuel pediatrician

## Eden
Bishopric, Welsford Farrell textile executive
Staab, Thomas Robert textile company financial executive
Williams, Sue Darden library director

## Edenton
Rossman, Robert Harris management consultant
Walklet, John James, Jr. publishing executive

## Efland
Efland, Simpson Lindsay entrepreneur

## Elizabeth City
Baker, Jean M. cable television executive
Boyle, Terrence W. federal judge
Griffin, Gladys Bogues critical care nurse, educator

## Elizabethtown
Taylor, David Wyatt Aiken retired clergyman

## Elm City
Smith, Sue Parker media administrator

## Elon College
Knesel, Ernest Arthur, Jr. diagnostic company executive
Young, James Fred college president

## Fairmont
Byrne, James Frederick banker

## Fairview
Eck, David Wilson minister
Gaffney, Thomas Edward retired physician
Rhynedance, Harold Dexter, Jr. lawyer, consultant

## Fayetteville
Bowman, Charles Harwood, Jr. historian, educator
Chipman, Martin neurologist, retired army officer
Kendrick, Mark C. real estate executive
Kilgore, Joe Everett, Jr. army officer
Mayrose, Mona Pearl critical care nurse, flight nurse, educator
Mitchell, Ronnie Monroe lawyer
Resnick, Paul R. research chemist
Richardson, Emilie White manufacturing company executive, investment company executive, lecturer
Schaefer, Lewis George physicians assistant
Tyson-Autry, Carrie Eula legislative consultant, researcher, small business owner

## Flat Rock
Davidson, Clayton Leslie chemical engineer
Demartini, Robert John textile company executive

## Franklin
Earhart, Eileen Magie retired child and family life educator

## Franklinton
Lange, Niels Erik Krebs biotechnology company executive

## Fremont
Ackerman, Lennis Campbell management consultant retired
Smith, Mark Eugene architectural engineering service company executive

## Fuquay Varina
Hairston, William Michael manufacturing engineer

## Gastonia
Alala, Joseph Basil, Jr. lawyer, accountant
Carson, John Little historical theology educator, clergyman
Cox, Herbert Bartle natural gas company executive
Garland, James Boyce lawyer
Kimbrell, Willard Duke textile company executive
Kiser, Clyde Vernon retired demographer
Lawson, William David, III retired cotton company executive
McGlohon, Reeves education administrator
Prince, George Edward pediatrician
Stott, Grady Bernell lawyer
Teem, Paul Lloyd, Jr. savings and loan executive

## Gibsonville
Foster, C(harles) Allen lawyer

## Gloucester
Price, Marion Woodrow journalist

## Goldsboro
Barkley, Monika Johanna general contracting professional
Sauls, Don clergyman
Yelverton, Deborah Sue middle school art educator

## Graham
Lancaster, Carolyn Hohn secondary school educator

## Granite Falls
Humphreys, Kenneth King engineer, educator, association executive

## Greensboro
Ahmed, Fahim Uddin research fellow, scientist
Allen, Jesse Owen, III management development and organizational behavior
Almeida, José Agustín romance languages educator
Alston, Charlotte LeNora college administrator
Bailey, William Nathan systems engineer
Baird, Haynes Wallace pathologist
Banegas, Estevan Brown environmental biotechnology executive
Bardolph, Richard historian, educator
Barker, Walter William, Jr. artist, educator
Bell, Haney Hardy, III lawyer
Blackwell, William Ernest broadcast industry executive
Bullock, Frank William, Jr. federal judge
Carr, Howard Ernest retired insurance agency executive
Casterlow, Gilbert, Jr. mathematics educator
Cazel, Hugh Allen industrial engineer, educator
Chappell, Fred Davis English language educator, poet
Clark, Clifton Bob physicist
Clark, David M. lawyer
Coltrane, Tamara Carleane intravenous therapy nurse
Compton, John Carroll accountant
Conrad, David Paul business broker/retired restaurant chain executive
Crawford, Kathrine Nelson special education educator
Daughtry, Sylvester protective services official
Davidson, Gerard H., Jr. lawyer
Davis, Herbert Owen lawyer
Eason, Robert Gaston psychology educator
Edinger, Lois Virginia education educator emeritus
Englar, John David textile company executive, lawyer
Erwin, Martin Nesbitt lawyer
Floyd, Jack William lawyer
Formo, Brenda Terrell travel company executive
Gabriel, Richard Weisner lawyer
Gaines, Sarah Fore retired foreign language educator
Gill, Diane Louise psychology educator, university official
Gill, Evalyn Pierpoint writer, editor, publisher
Goldman, Bert Arthur psychologist, educator
Gordon, Eugene Andrew judge
Griffin, Haynes Glenn telecommunications industry executive
Gumbiner, Kenneth Jay lawyer
Hall, William Edward, Jr. insurance agency executive
Harllee, JoAnn Towery lawyer, educator
Harris-Offutt, Rosalyn Marie counselor, therapist, nurse, anesthetist, educator, writer
Helms-VanStone, Mary Wallace anthropology educator
Herman, Roger Eliot professional speaker, consultant, futurist, writer
Hidore, John Junior geographer, educator
Holton, Walter Clinton, Jr. U.S. attorney
Hopkins, John David lawyer
Houston, Frank Matt dermatologist
Howard, Paul Noble, Jr. retired construction company executive
Howard, Richard Turner construction company executive
Hunter, Bynum Merritt lawyer
Jellicorse, John Lee communications and theatre educator
Johnson, Andrew Myron pediatric immunologist, educator
Johnson, Marshall Hardy investment company executive
Johnson, Willie Spoon hospital administrator
Jones, Fred T., Jr. museum administrator
Kennedy, Charles G. wholesale distribution executive
Koonce, Neil Wright lawyer
Korb, William Brown, Jr. manufacturing company executive
Kornegay, Horace Robinson trade association executive, former congressman, lawyer
Kovacs, Beatrice library studies educator
Lolley, William Randall minister
Macon, Seth Craven retired insurance company executive
Mann, Lowell Kimsey retired manufacturing executive
McGinn, Max Daniel lawyer
McKissick-Melton, S. Charmaine mass communications educator
McNemar, Donald William academic administrator
Mecimore, Charles Douglas accounting educator
Melvin, Charles Edward, Jr. lawyer
Middleton, Herman David, Sr. theater educator
Miller, Robert Louis university dean, chemistry educator
Moore, Beverly Cooper lawyer
Morgenstern, Sheldon Jon symphony orchestra conductor
Morris, Edwin Alexander retired apparel manufacturing company executive
Nussbaum, V. M., Jr. former mayor
Osteen, William L., Sr. federal judge
Penninger, Frieda Elaine retired English language educator
Posey, Eldon Eugene mathematician, educator
Poteet, Daniel P(owell), II college provost
Prodan, James Christian university administrator
Reed, William Edward government official, educator
Reid, Charles Murry insurance company executive
Rights, Graham Henry minister
Ritter, Sandra Helen psychotherapist, counselor
Roberts, Rosemary journalist, columnist
Rogers, William Raymond college president emeritus, psychology educator
Rosser, Rhonda LaNae psychotherapist
Rowlenson, Richard Charles lawyer
Russell, Peggy Taylor soprano, educator
St. George, Nicholas James lawyer, manufactured housing company executive
Sanders, William Eugene marketing executive
Schell, Braxton lawyer
Schwenn, Lee William retired medical center executive
Sewell, Elizabeth author, English educator
Shelton, David Howard economics educator
Smith, John McNeill, Jr. lawyer
Smith, Lanty L(loyd) lawyer, business executive
Smith, Rebecca McCulloch human relations educator
Soles, William Roger insurance company executive
Spears, Alexander White, III tobacco company executive
Speight, Velma Ruth alumni affairs director
Stevens, Elliott Walker, Jr. allergist, pulmonologist
Stoodt, Barbara Dern education educator, magazine editor
Styles, Teresa Jo producer, educator
Sullivan, Patricia A. academic administrator
Thompson, James Howard historian, library administrator
Tilley, Norwood Carlton, Jr. federal judge
Watson, Robert Winthrop poet, English language educator
Williams, Irving Laurence physics educator
Willis, C. Paul minister
Wright, John Spencer school system administrator
Wright, Kieth Carter librarian, educator
Zopf, Paul Edward, Jr. sociologist

## Greenville
Bearden, James Hudson university official
Bolande, Robert Paul pathologist, scientist, educator
Chauncey, Beatrice Arlene music educator
Clemens, Donald Faull chemistry educator
Cramer, Robert Eli geography educator
†Donovan, Anne coach
Eakin, Richard Ronald academic administrator, mathematics educator
Flanagan, Michael Perkins lawyer
Frisell, Wilhelm Richard biochemist, educator
Furth, Eugene David physician, educator
Griffin, Linner Ward social work educator
Hallock, James Anthony pediatrician, school dean
Hines, Danny Ray accountant, educator
Howard, Malcolm Jones federal judge
Howell, John McDade retired university chancellor, political science educator
Hudgins, Herbert Cornelius, Jr. education educator
Jackson, Bobby Rand minister
Laing, Penelope Gamble art educator
Laupus, William Edward physician, educator
Lee, Kenneth Stuart neurosurgeon, educator
Leggett, Donald Yates academic administrator
Leggett, Nancy Porter university administrator
Lennon, Donald Ray archivist, historian
Maier, Robert Hawthorne biology educator
Mattsson, Ake psychiatrist, physician
Meggs, William Joel internist, emergency physician, educator
Metzger, W. James, Jr. physician, researcher, educator
Moseley, Sheryl Buck nursing administrator
Norris, H. Thomas pathologist, academic administrator
Pories, Walter Julius surgeon, educator
Sanchez, Rafael Camilo physician
Sayetta, Thomas Charles physics educator
Schellenberger, Robert Earl management educator and department chairman
Snyder, Scott William geology educator
Thurber, Robert Eugene physiologist, researcher
Tingelstad, Jon Bunde physician
Wallin, Leland Dean artist, educator
Waugh, William Howard biomedical educator
Williams, Melvin John sociologist, educator
Wood, Gerald David religious organization administrator
Wortmann, Dorothy Woodward physician
Zauner, Christian Walter university dean, exercise physiologist, consultant

## Hamlet
Walker, Wanda Gail special education educator

## Hampstead
Solomon, Robert Douglas pathology educator

## Harrisburg
Economaki, Chris Constantine (Christopher Economaki) publisher, editor

## Haw River
Poindexter, Richard Grover minister

## Henderson
Church, John Trammell retail stores company executive

## Hendersonville
Bastedo, Ralph W(alter) social science educator
Brittain, James Edward science and technology educator, researcher
Haynes, John Mabin retired utilities executive
Heltman, Robert Fairchild distribution executive
Jones, J(ohn) Charles education educator
Kehr, August Ernest geneticist, researcher
Payne, Gerald Oliver retired elementary education educator
Reinhart, John Belvin child and adolescent psychiatrist, educator
Saby, John Sanford physicist
Schooley, Charles Earl electrical engineer, consultant
Schwarz, Richard William historian, educator
Sims, Bennett Jones minister, educator

## Hickory
Crouch, Fred Michael physician, surgeon
George, Boyd Lee consumer products company executive
Gingrich-Petersen, Carolyn Ashcraft psychologist
Lefler, Wade Hampton, Jr. ophthalmologist
Loehr, Arthur William, Jr. healthcare executive, nurse
Lynn, Tony Lee import company executive
McDaniel, Michael Conway Dixon bishop, theology educator
Shuford, Harley Ferguson, Jr. furniture manufacturing executive
Sims, Janette Elizabeth Lowman educational director

## High Point
Bardelas, Jose Antonio allergist
Clark, Carol Ruth Jones secondary education educator
Draelos, Zoe D. dermatologist, consultant
Farlow, Joel Wray school system administrator

Fenn, Ormon William, Jr. *furniture company executive*
Foscue, James E. *commercial finance company executive*
Gay, David Braxton *stockbroker*
Howard, Lou Dean Graham *elementary education educator*
Huston, Fred John *retired automotive engineer*
Kleeman, Walter Benton, Jr. *interior and furniture designer, consultant, author*
Marsden, Lawrence Albert *retired textile company executive*
Martinson, Jacob Christian, Jr. *academic administrator*
McCaslin, Richard Bryan *history educator*
Phillips, Earl Norfleet, Jr. *financial services executive*
Sheahan, Robert Emmett *lawyer, consultant*
Wood, Stephen Wray *educator, legislator, minister, singer, songwriter*

**Highlands**
Sandor, George Nason *mechanical engineer, educator*
Sheehan, Charles Vincent *investment banker*
Watt, John Reid *retired mechanical engineering educator*

**Hillsborough**
Bolduc, Jean Plumley *journalist, education activist*
Goodwin, Craufurd David *economics educator*
Marzluff, William F. *medical educator*
†Moore, Edward Towson *electronics company executive, electrical engineer*
Pagano, Filippo Frank *financial broker, commercial loan consultant*
Stockstill, James William *secondary school educator*
†Taylor, Martha Croll *nursing adminstrator*

**Hope Mills**
Windham, Cuyler LaRue *police official*

**Horse Shoe**
Howell, George Washington *lawyer, consultant*

**Huntersville**
Evans, Trellany Victoria Thomas *entrepreneur*
Wilson, Milner Bradley, III *retired banker*

**Indian Beach**
Wiley, Albert Lee, Jr. *physician, engineer, educator*

**Jackson Springs**
Krebs, Max Vance *retired foreign service officer, educator*

**Jacksonville**
Daugherty, Robert Michael *music educator, composer*
Hutto, James Calhoun *retired financial executive*
†Kimball, Lynn Jerome *historian*

**Jefferson**
Franklin, Robert McFarland *book publisher*

**Kannapolis**
Ridenhour, Joseph Conrad *textile company executive*
Thigpen, Alton Hill *motor transportation company executive*

**Kernersville**
Litton, Daphne Napier Rudhman *special education educator*

**Kill Devil Hills**
Perry, Gaylord Jackson *former professional baseball player*

**Kinston**
Matthis, Eva Mildred Boney *college official*
Petteway, Samuel Bruce *college president*
Sanders, Brice Sidney *bishop*
†Woodall, Jim S. *hospital administrator*

**Kitty Hawk**
Sjoerdsma, Albert *research institute executive*

**Kure Beach**
Funk, Frank E. *retired university dean*
Lanier, James Alfred, III *aquarium administrator*

**Lake Junaluska**
Bryan, Monk *retired bishop*
Goodgame, Gordon Clifton *minister*
Hale, Joseph Rice *church organization executive*
Robinson, Mary Katherine *school system administrator*
Tullis, Edward Lewis *retired bishop*

**Lake Toxaway**
Gasperoni, Ellen Jean Lias *interior designer*
Morgan, Marianne *corporate professional*

**Laurel Springs**
Gilbert-Strawbridge, Anne Wieland *journalist*

**Laurinburg**
Bayes, Ronald Homer *English language educator, author*
Nance, Tony Max-Perry *designer, illustrator*
Snead, Eleanor Leroy Marks *secondary school educator*

**Lenoir**
Carswell, Jane Triplett *family physician*
Flaherty, David Thomas, Jr. *lawyer*
Mullis, Madeline Gail Herman *music educator, choir director*

**Liberty**
Feaster, Charlotte Josephine S. *school administrator*
Garner, Mildred Maxine *retired religious studies educator*

**Lincolnton**
Saine, Betty Boston *elementary school educator*

**Linwood**
Barnes, Melver Raymond *retired chemist*

**Little Switzerland**
Gross, Samson Richard *geneticist, biochemist, educator*

**Louisburg**
Boblett, Mark Anthony *civil engineering technician*

**Maiden**
Pruitt, Thomas P., Jr. *textiles executive*

**Manteo**
Berry, Russell W. *historic site administrator*
Miller, Judith Ann *retired financial executive*
Miller, William Lee, Jr. *minister*

**Marion**
Bergemann, Verna Elmyra *education educator*
Burgin, Charles E. *lawyer*

**Mars Hill**
Lennon, A. Max *food products company executive*

**Matthews**
Rivenbark, Jan Meredith *food service products corporate executive*

**Mebane**
Davidson, Lacinda Susan *materials engineer, chemist*
Langley, Ricky Lee *occupational medicine physician*

**Micro**
Loose, Vicky Dianne *special education educator*

**Monroe**
Rorie, Nancy Katheryn *elementary and secondary school educator*

**Montreat**
Robinson, Spencer, Jr. *retired service club executive, accountant*

**Mooresville**
Dausman, George Erwin *retired federal official, aeronautical engineer, consultant*
Davis, Courtland Harwell, Jr. *neurosurgeon*
Neill, Rita J. *elementary school educator*
†Spencer, Jimmy *professional race car driver*

**Morehead City**
Williams, Winton Hugh *civil engineer*

**Morganton**
Baden, Thomas James *dermatologist*
Ervin, Samuel James, III *federal judge*
Jokinen, John Victor *furniture company executive*
Sessa, Todd Raymond *marketing executive*
Simpson, Daniel Reid *lawyer*

**Morrisville**
Bursey, Joan Tesarek *chemist*
Richardson, Arline Annette *accountant, comptroller*

**Morven**
Jones, Sheila McLendon *construction company executive*

**Mount Airy**
Ratliff, Robert Barns, Jr. *mechanical engineer*
Thoppil, Cecil Koshey *pediatrician, educator*
Woltz, Howard Osler, Jr. *steel and wire products company executive*

**Mount Olive**
Boyd, Julia Margaret (Mrs. Shelton B. Boyd) *lay church worker*
Raper, William Burkette *retired college president*

**Mount Ulla**
Kluttz, Henry G. *principal*

**Murfreesboro**
Burke, Marguerite Jodi Larcombe *writer, computer consultant*
Whitaker, Bruce Ezell *college president*

**Murphy**
Bata, Rudolph Andrew, Jr. *lawyer*

**Nags Head**
Crow, Harold Eugene *physician, family medicine educator*

**New Bern**
Ash, William James *geneticist*
Baughman, Fred Hubbard *aeronautical engineer, former naval officer*
Davis, James Lee *lawyer*
Finnerty, Frances Martin *medical administrator*
Hemphill, Jean Hargett *college dean*
Hunt, William B. *cardiopulmonary physician*
Kellum, Norman Bryant, Jr. *lawyer*
Mack, Clifford Glenn *investment banker, management consultant*
Moeller, Dade William *environmental engineer, educator*
Overholt, Hugh Robert *lawyer, retired army officer*
Perdue, Beverly Moore *state legislator, geriatric consultant*
Sinning, Mark Alan *thoracic and vascular surgeon*
Skipper, Nathan Richard, Jr. *lawyer*
Stoller, David Allen *lawyer*
Ward, Thomas Monroe *lawyer, law educator*

**North Wilkesboro**
Herring, Leonard Gray *marketing company executive*
Pardue, Dwight Edward *venture capitalist*
Parsons, Irene *management consultant*

**Oak Ridge**
O'Bryant, Cecyle Arnold *secondary English educator*

**Oriental**
Sutter, John Richard *manufacturer, investor*

**Oxford**
Burnette, James Thomas *lawyer*

Spurr, Harvey W., Jr. *plant pathology research administrator*

**Pembroke**
Sexton, Jean Elizabeth *librarian*

**Pilot Mountain**
Ross, Norman Alexander *retired banker*

**Pine Knoll Shores**
Benson, Kenneth Victor *manufacturing company executive, lawyer*
Lynn, Otis Clyde *former army officer*

**Pinehurst**
Amspoker, James Mack *retired gas company executive*
Burris, Kenneth Wayne *biologist, educator*
Carroll, Kent Jean *retired naval officer*
Ellis, William Harold *former naval officer*
Gilmore, Voit *travel executive*
Henderson, Paul Audine *banker, consultant*
Huizenga, John Robert *nuclear chemist, educator*
Jacobson, Peter Lars *neurologist, educator*
Lebeck, Warren Wells *commodities consultant*
Nuzzo, Salvatore Joseph *defense, electronics company executive*
O'Neill, John Joseph, Jr. *business consultant, former chemical company executive*
Owings, Malcolm William *retired management consultant*
Paquette, Dean Richard *retired computer company executive, consultant*
Roberts, Francis Joseph *retired army officer, retired educational administrator, global economic advisor*
Stingel, Donald Eugene *management consultant*
Stroud, Richard Hamilton *aquatic biologist, scientist, consultant*

**Pinetops**
Robertson, Richard Blake *management consultant*

**Pisgah Forest**
Albyn, Richard Keith *retired architect*
Rierson, Robert Leak *retired broadcasting executive, television writer*

**Pittsboro**
Bailey, Herbert Smith, Jr. *retired publisher*
Doenges, Byron Frederick *economist, educator, former government official*
Hauser, Charles Newland McCorkle *newspaper consultant*
Lewis, Henry Wilkins *university administrator, lawyer, educator*
Magill, Samuel Hays *retired academic administrator, higher education consultant*
Quinn, Jarus William *physicist, former association executive*
Shurick, Edward Palmes *television executive, rancher*

**Pope AFB**
Conley, Raymond Leslie *English language educator*
Vaughan, Clyde Vernelson *program director*

**Raleigh**
Agrawal, Dharma Prakash *engineering educator*
Anderson, Amy Lee *realtor*
Anderson, Glenn Elwood *investment banker*
Aronson, Arthur Lawrence *veterinary pharmacology and toxicology educator*
Aspnes, David Erik *physicist, educator*
Atchley, William Reid *geneticist, evolutionary biologist, educator*
Baliga, Bantval Jayant *electrical engineering educator, research administrator*
Barish, Charles Franklin *internist, gastroenterologist, educator*
Beatty, Kenneth Orion, Jr. *chemical engineer*
Benson, D(avid) Michael *plant pathologist*
Berry, Joni Ingram *hospice pharmacist, educator*
Bishop, Paul Edward *microbiologist*
Bitzer, Donald Lester *electrical engineering educator, retired research laboratory administrator*
Boone, Stephen Christopher *neurosurgeon*
Bourham, Mohamed Abdelhay *electrical and nuclear engineering educator*
Boyles, Harlan Edward *state official*
Britt, W. Earl *federal judge*
Brooker, Lena Epps *human relations program administrator*
Buchanan, David Royal *associate dean*
Burns, Norma DeCamp *architect*
Burns, Robert Paschal *architect, educator*
Burris, Craven Allen *education administrator, educator*
Cameron, John Lansing *retired government official*
Carlton, Alfred Pershing, Jr. *lawyer*
Carter, Jean Gordon *lawyer*
Case, Charles Dixon *lawyer*
Cauthen, Carmen Wimberley *legislative staff member, jewelry designer*
Chou, Wushow *computer scientist, educator*
Chukwu, Ethelbert Nwakuche *mathematics educator*
Clark, Roger Harrison *architect, architecture educator*
Clarke, Lewis James *landscape architect*
Clauberg, Martin *research scientist*
Coggin, Michael Wright *insurance marketing and training executive*
Collins, G. Bryan, Jr. *lawyer*
Collins, Thomas Asa *minister*
Cook, Maurice Gayle *soil science educator, consultant*
Cooper, Arthur Wells *ecologist, educator*
Cresimore, James Leonard *food broker*
Cummings, Ralph Waldo *soil scientist, educator, researcher*
Cuomo, Jerome John *materials scientist*
Daniels, Frank Arthur, Jr. *newspaper publisher*
Daniels, Frank Arthur, III *publishing executive*
Dannelly, William David *lawyer*
Davey, Charles Bingham *soil science educator*
Davis, Egbert Lawrence, III *lawyer*
Davis, Thomas Hill, Jr. *lawyer*
Davis, William Robert *physicist*
De Hertogh, August Albert *horticulture educator, researcher*
DeJarnette, Fred Roark *aerospace engineer*
Denson, Alexander Bunn *federal magistrate judge*
Dixon, Daniel Roberts, Jr. *tax lawyer*
Dixon, Wright Tracy, Jr. *lawyer*
Doherty, Robert Cunningham *advertising executive*
Dolce, Carl John *education administration educator*

Drew, Nancy McLaurin Shannon *counselor, consultant*
Droessler, Earl George *geophysicist educator*
Dudziak, Donald John *nuclear engineer, educator*
Dunphy, Edward James *crop science extension specialist*
Eagles, Sidney Smith, Jr. *judge*
Easley, Michael F. *state attorney general*
Eason, Joseph W. *lawyer*
Eberly, Harry Landis *retired communications company executive*
Ebisuzaki, Yukiko *chemistry educator*
Edwards, Charles Archibald *lawyer*
Effron, Seth Alan *journalist*
Ellis, Lester Neal, Jr. *lawyer*
Ellis, Richard W. *lawyer*
Entman, Robert Mathew *communications educator, consultant*
Fang, Shu-Cherng *industrial engineering and operations research educator*
Fletcher, Oscar Jasper, Jr. *college dean*
Flournoy, William Louis, Jr. *landscape architect*
Foley, Gary J. *research chemical engineer, computer scientist, federal agency administrator*
Foley, Peter Michael *lawyer*
Freeman, Franklin Edward, Jr. *state agency administrator*
Frye, Henry E. *state supreme court justice*
Gardner, Robin Pierce *engineering educator*
Garrett, Leland Earl *nephrologist, educator*
Geller, Janice Grace *nurse*
Godwin, James Beckham *retired landscape architect*
Goldstein, Irving Solomon *chemistry educator, consultant*
Goodman, Major Merlin *botanical sciences educator*
Gordon, Morris Aaron *medical mycologist, microbiologist*
Gossman, Francis Joseph *bishop*
Graham, William Edgar, Jr. *lawyer, retired utility company executive*
Grubb, Donald Hartman *paper industry company executive*
Gwyn, William Blair, Jr. *lawyer*
Hanson, John M. *civil engineering and construction educator*
Hardin, Eugene Brooks, Jr. *retired banker*
Hardin, James W. *botanist, herbarium curator, educator*
Hauser, John Reid *electrical engineering educator*
Havner, Kerry Shuford *civil engineering and solid mechanics educator*
Henson, Glenda Maria *newspaper writer*
Hodgson, Ernest *toxicology educator*
Holding, Lewis R. *banker*
Holt, J. Darrin *corporate executive*
Holton, William Coffeen *electrical engineering executive*
Homick, Daniel John *financial executive, lawyer*
Horton, Horace Robert *biochemistry educator*
Howell, Bruce Inman *academic administrator*
Howell-Drake, Mindy Anne *administrative assistant*
Hughes, Barbara Ann *dietitian, public health administrator*
†Hughes, Francis P. *medical researcher*
Hugus, Z Zimmerman, Jr. *chemistry educator*
Hunt, James Baxter, Jr. *governor, lawyer*
Hunter, Margaret King *architect*
Jarrett, Polly Hawkins *secondary education educator, retired*
Jenkins, Clauston Levi, Jr. *college president*
Jessen, David Wayne *accountant*
Jividen, Loretta Ann Harper *secondary school educator*
Johnson, Charles Lavon, Jr. *clinical neuropsychologist, consultant*
Johnson, Janet Gray Andrews *clinical social worker*
Johnson, Marvin Richard Alois *architect*
Jolly, John Russell, Jr. *lawyer*
Joyner, Walton Kitchin *lawyer*
Kapp, Michael Keith *lawyer*
Kelman, Arthur *plant pathologist, educator*
Kimbrell, Odell Culp, Jr. *physician*
Kiser, Anita Hope *project team leader, technical writer*
Klein, Verle Wesley *corporate executive, retired naval officer*
†Knutson, Gary Herbert *advertising company executive*
Kriz, George James *agricultural research administrator, educator*
Kuhler, Renaldo Gillet *museum official, scientific illustrator*
Kurz, Mary Elizabeth *lawyer*
Leak, Robert E. *economic development consultant*
Leddicotte, George Comer *business executive, consultant*
Levine, Ronald H. *physician, state official*
Littleton, Isaac Thomas, III *retired university library administrator, consultant*
Maidon, Carolyn Howser *education director*
Malecha, Marvin John *architect, academic administrator*
Malone, Thomas Francis *academic administrator, meteorologist*
Markoff, Brad Steven *lawyer*
†Marshall, Elaine F. *state official*
Martin, Donnis Lynn *adult education educator*
Maupin, Armistead Jones *lawyer*
McGregor, Ralph *chemistry educator*
McKinney, Charles Cecil *investment company executive*
McPherson, Samuel Dace, III *computer scientist, instructor, consultant*
Meier, Wilbur Leroy, Jr. *industrial engineer, educator, former university chancellor*
Millberg, John C. *lawyer*
Miller, John Henry *clergyman*
Miller, Ralph Bradley *lawyer, state legislator*
Miller, Robert James *lawyer*
Mitchell, Burley Bayard, Jr. *state supreme court chief justice*
Mitchell, Gary Earl *physicist, educator*
Monteith, Larry King *university chancellor*
Moore, Jeannette Aileen *animal nutrition educator*
Moore, Thomas Lloyd *librarian*
Moreland, Donald Edwin *plant physiologist*
Murray, Elizabeth Davis Reid *writer, lecturer*
Murray, Raymond Le Roy *nuclear engineering educator*
Neely, Charles B., Jr. *lawyer*
Nelson, Larry A. *statistics educator, consultant*
Newman, Slater Edmund *psychologist, educator*
Ofner, J(ames) Alan *management consultant*
Orr, Robert F. *justice*
Page, Anne Ruth *gifted education educator, education specialist*
Parker, Joseph Mayon *printing and publishing executive*

Rauschenberg, Bradford Lee *museum research director*
Ray, Michael Edwin *lawyer*
Rodgman, Alan *chemist, consultant*
Rogers, Lee Frank *radiologist*
Roth, Marjory Joan Jarboe *special education educator*
Runnion, Howard J., Jr. *banker*
Sandridge, William Pendleton, Jr. *lawyer*
Scales, James Ralph *history educator, former university president*
Schollander, Wendell Leslie, Jr. *lawyer*
Shapere, Dudley *philosophy educator*
Simon, Jimmy Louis *pediatrician, educator*
Smith, Zachary Taylor, II *retired tobacco company executive*
Spach, Jule Christian *church executive*
Stein, Barry Edward *medical educator*
Sticht, J. Paul *retired food products and tobacco company executive*
Strayhorn, Ralph Nichols, Jr. *lawyer*
Strickland, Robert Louis *business executive*
Stroupe, Henry Smith *university dean*
Sullivan, Richard Leo *brokerage house executive*
Thompson, Cleon F., Jr. *university administrator*
Thrift, Julianne Still *academic administrator*
Toole, James Francis *medical educator*
Trautwein, George William *conductor*
Tursi, Frank Vincent *journalist*
Vance, Charles Fogle, Jr. *lawyer*
Veille, Jean-Claude *maternal-fetal medicine physician, educator*
Walker, George Kontz *law educator*
Walters, Doris Lavonne *pastoral counselor, counseling services facility administrator*
Wanders, Hans Walter *banker*
Ward, Hiram Hamilton *federal judge*
Ward, Marvin Martin *retired state senator*
Watlington, John Francis, Jr. *banker*
Wells, Dewey Wallace *lawyer*
Winn, Albert Curry *clergyman*
Womble, William Fletcher *lawyer*
Woods, James Watson, Jr. *cardiologist*
Worley, Bland Wallace *banker*
Zagoria, Sam D(avid) *arbitrator, author, educator*

### Winterville
Myers, Robert Durant *biologist, research director, medical educator*

### Wrightsville Beach
Block, Franklin Lee *lawyer*
Mc Ilwain, William Franklin *newspaper editor, writer*
Phull, B. S. *scientist*

### Yanceyville
Bowen, Audrey Lynn Harris *elementary education educator*

## NORTH DAKOTA

### Ashley
Kretschmar, William Edward *state legislator, lawyer*

### Bismarck
Carlisle, Ronald Dwight *nursery owner*
Carmichael, Virgil Wesly *mining, civil and geological engineer, former coal company executive*
Clark, Tony *state legislator*
Conmy, Patrick A. *federal judge*
Cornatzer, William Eugene *retired biochemistry educator*
Erickstad, Ralph John *judge, retired state supreme court chief justice*
Evanson, Barbara Jean *middle school education educator*
Gilbertson, Joel Warren *lawyer*
Gilmore, Kathi *state treasurer*
Heitkamp, Heidi *state attorney general*
Hook, William Franklin *radiologist*
Isaak, Larry A. *state agency administrator*
Jaeger, Alvin A. (Al Jaeger) *secretary of state*
Meschke, Herbert Leonard *state supreme court justice*
Montz, Florence Stolte *church official*
Murry, Charles Emerson *lawyer, official*
Myrdal, Rosemarie Caryle *state official, former state legislator*
Nelson, Keithe Eugene *lawyer, state court administrator*
Neumann, William Allen *judge*
Newborg, Gerald Gordon *historical agency administrator*
Olson, John Michael *lawyer*
Palmer, Richard Joseph *communications director*
†Renfrew, Joseph *communications technologist*
Rice, Jon Richard *state health officer, physician*
Sandstrom, Dale Vernon *state supreme court judge*
Sanstead, Wayne Godfrey *state superintendent, former lieutenant governor*
Schafer, Edward T. *governor*
Schobinger, Randy Arthur *state legislator*
Schuchart, John Albert, Jr. *utility company executive*
Solberg, Nellie Florence Coad *artist*
Strutz, William A. *lawyer*
Tabor, Sandra LaVonne *legal association administrator*
VandeWalle, Gerald Wayne *state supreme court chief justice*
Van Sickle, Bruce Marion *federal judge*

### Bottineau
Gorder, Steven F. *business executive*

### Crosby
Andrist, John M. *state senator*

### Dickinson
Conn, Philip Wesley *university president*
Kessel, Lloyd R. *acute care nursing director, educator*
Miller, Jean Patricia Salmon *art educator*

### Edgeley
Schimke, Dennis J. *state legislator*

### Edinburg
Melsted, Marcella H. *retired administrative assistant, civic worker*

### Fargo
Berg, Rick Alan *state legislator, real estate investor*
Bright, Myron H. *federal judge, educator*
Dill, William Joseph *newspaper editor*
Fairfield, Andrew H. *bishop*
Foss, Richard John *bishop*
Hill, William A(lexander) *judge*
Joppa, Leonard Robert *research geneticist, agronomist, educator*
Koppelman, Kim Arden *advertising executive, public relations consultant*
Lardy, Sister Susan Marie *academic administrator*
Littlefield, Robert Stephen *communication educator, training consultant*
Lohman, John Frederick *editor*
Magill, Frank John *federal judge*
Mathern, Tim *state senator, social worker*
Nickel, Janet Marlene Milton *geriatrics nurse*
Ommodt, Donald Henry *dairy company executive*
Orr, Steven R. *health facility administrator*
Paulson, John Doran *newspaper editor, retired*
Peet, Howard David *English language and literature educator, writer*
Query, Joy Marves Neale *medical sociology educator*
Revell, Dorothy Evangeline Tompkins *dietitian*
Riley, Thomas Joseph *anthropologist*
Risher, Stephan Olaf *investment officer*
Schmidt, Claude Henri *retired research administrator*
Spaeth, Nicholas John *lawyer, former state attorney general*
Sullivan, James Stephen *bishop*
Tallman, Robert Hall *investment company executive*
Wallwork, William Wilson, III *automobile executive*
Webb, Rodney Scott *judge*
Williams, Norman Dale *geneticist, researcher*
Zimmerman, Don Charles *plant physiologist, biochemist*

### Fessenden
Streibel, Bryce *state senator*

### Grand Forks
Anderson, Damon Ernest *lawyer*
Baker, Kendall L. *academic administrator*
Caldwell, Mary Ellen *English language educator*
Carlson, Edward C. *anatomy educator*
Cilz, Douglas Arthur *lawyer*
Clifford, Thomas John *university president*
Davis, W. Jeremy *dean, law educator, lawyer*
DeMers, Judy Lee *state legislator, university dean*
Fox, Carl Alan *research institute executive*
Gjovig, Bruce Quentin *manufacturing consultant*
Glassheim, Eliot Alan *grants officer*
Jacobs, Francis Albin *biochemist, educator*
Lindseth, Paul Douglas *aerospace educator, flight instructor, farmer*
Nielsen, Forrest Harold *research nutritionist*
Nordlie, Robert Conrad *biochemistry educator*
Penland, James Granville *psychologist*
Plaud, Joseph Julian *psychology educator*
Poolman, Jim *state legislator*
Rolshoven, Ross William *legal investigator, art photographer*
Senechal, Alice R. *judge, lawyer*
Sobus, Kerstin MaryLouise *physician, physical therapist*
Stenehjem, Wayne Kevin *state senator, lawyer*
Vogel, Robert *retired lawyer, educator*
Widdel, John Earl, Jr. *lawyer*
Wilson, H. David *dean*
Zahrly, Janice Honea *management educator*

### Jamestown
Kirby, Ronald Eugene *fish and wildlife research administrator*
Walker, James Silas *academic administrator*

### Mandan
Bair, Bruce B. *lawyer*
Halvorson, Ardell David *research leader, soil scientist*
Halvorson, Gary Alfred *soil scientist*
Hodge, Ann Linton *artist*

### Mayville
Karaim, Betty June *librarian*

### Minot
Armstrong, Phillip Dale *lawyer*
Danielson, David Gordon *health science facility administrator, general legal counsel*
Jermiason, John Lynn *elementary school educator, farmer, rancher*
Kerian, Jon Robert *judge*
Mickelson, Stacey *state legislator*
Mohler, Marie Elaine *nurse educator*
Shaar, H. Erik *academic administrator*
Turner, Jane Ann *federal agent*
Watne, Darlene Claire *state legislator*

### Regent
Krauter, Aaron Joseph *farmer, state senator*

### Rolla
Jacobsen-Theel, Hazel M. *historian*

### Rugby
Axtman, Benjamin J. *farmer*

### Saint Anthony
Tomac, Steven Wayne *state senator, farmer*

### Stanley
Piepkorn, Evonne Arlys *farmer, scriptwriter, producer, director*

### Tioga
Nelson, Marlow Gene *agricultural studies educator*

### Turtle Lake
Lindteigen, Susanna *rancher, state official*

### Valley City
Fischer, Mary Elizabeth *library director*
Sabby, Leland *state legislator*

### Wahpeton
Jensen, Delores (Dee Jensen) *physical education educator*

### Williston
Adducci, Joseph Edward *obstetrician, gynecologist*
Burdick, Eugene Allan *retired judge, lawyer, surrogate judge*
Rennerfeldt, Earl Ronald *state legislator, farmer, rancher*
Wenstrom, Frank Augustus *state senator*
Yockim, James Craig *state senator, oil and gas executive*

## OHIO

### Ada
Cooper, Ken Errol *management educator*
Freed, DeBow *college president*
Hanson, Eugene Nelson *judge*

### Akron
Arnett, James Edward *retired isurance company executive, retired secondary school educator*
Auburn, Norman Paul *university president*
Barker, Harold Kenneth *former university dean*
Bartlo, Sam D. *lawyer*
Bell, Samuel H. *federal judge*
Bohm, Georg G. A. *physicist*
Brock, James Robert *manufacturing company executive*
Brown, David Rupert *engineering executive*
Bryant, Keith Lynn, Jr. *history educator*
Byrne, Dennis Michael *economist, educator*
Cai, X. Sean *physical education educator*
Castronovo, Thomas Paul *architect, consultant*
Cheng, Stephen Zheng Di *chemistry educator, polymeric material researcher*
Childs, James William *lawyer, legal educator*
Coleman, Malina *law educator*
Collier, Alice Elizabeth *retired community organization executive*
Considine, William Howard *health care administrator*
Contie, Leroy John, Jr. *federal judge*
Coyne, Thomas Joseph *economist, finance educator*
Coz, Mary Kathleen *respiratory therapist*
Crawford, Robert John *credit company executive*
Dorsett, Roswell Branson, III *neurologist*
Dotson, John Louis, Jr. *newspaper executive*
Elliott, Peggy Gordon *university president*
Evans, Douglas McCullough *surgeon, educator*
Fisher, James Lee *lawyer*
Frank, John V. *foundation executive*
Friedman, Richard Everett *librarian*
Gent, Alan Neville *physicist, educator*
Gibara, Samir S. G. *manufacturing executive*
Gippin, Robert Malcolm *lawyer*
Glinsek, Gerald John *lawyer*
Hackbirth, David William *aluminum company executive*
Hale, Beverlee Ann *home care nurse*
Holland, Willard Raymond, Jr. *electric utility executive*
Hollis, William Frederick *information scientist*
Holloway, Donald Phillip *lawyer*
Isayev, Avraam Isayevich *polymer engineer, educator*
Jones, Robert Huhn *history educator*
Kahan, Mitchell Douglas *art museum director*
Kaufman, Donald Leroy *building products executive*
Keener, Polly Leonard *illustrator*
Kelley, Frank Nicholas *dean*
Kennedy, Joseph Paul *polymer scientist, researcher*
Knepper, George W. *history educator*
Lawrence, Alice Lauffer *artist, educator*
Lee, Brant Thomas *lawyer, federal official, educator*
Levy, Richard Philip *physician, educator*
Lombardi, Frederick McKean *lawyer*
Lynch, John Edward, Jr. *lawyer*
Martino, Frank Dominic *union executive*
Maximovich, Michael Joseph *chemist, consultant*
McCormick, William Edward *environmental consultant*
Mettler, Gerald Phillip *reliability engineer*
Miller, Irving Franklin *chemical engineering educator, biomedical engineering educator, academic administrator*
Milsted, Amy *medical educator*
Monacelli, Amieto *professional bowler*
Moss, Robert Drexler *lawyer*
Murphy, Bob *professional golfer*
Ozio, David *professional bowler*
Peavy, Homer Louis, Jr. *real estate executive, accountant*
Phillips, Dorothy Ormes *elementary education educator*
Piirma, Irja *chemist, educator*
Poll, Heinz *choreographer, artistic director*
Powell, Robert Eugene *computer operator*
Rebenack, John Henry *retired librarian*
Richert, Paul *law educator*
Rooney, George Willard *lawyer*
Rothmann, Bruce Franklin *pediatric surgeon*
Sam, David Fiifi *political economist, educator*
Sancaktar, Erol *engineering educator*
Schlichting, Nancy Margaret *hospital administrator*
Schrader, Helen Maye *retired municipal worker*
Schubert, Barbara Schuele *performing company executive*
Seiberling, John Frederick *former congressman, law educator, lawyer*
Shaffer, Oren George *manufacturing company executive*
Shea-Stonum, Marilyn *judge*
Showalter, Robert Earl *banker*
Smithkey, John, III *public health nurse, consultant*
Sonnecken, Edwin Herbert *management consultant*
Spetrino, Russell John *retired utility company executive, lawyer*
Staines, Michael Laurence *oil and gas production executive*
Stroll, Beverly Marie *elementary school principal*
†Tan, James *physician*
Timmons, Gerald Dean *pediatric neurologist*
Trotter, Thomas Robert *lawyer*
West, Michael Alan *hospital administrator*
White, Harold F. *bankruptcy judge, retired federal judge*

### Alliance
Clem, Harriet Frances *library director*
Dunagan, Gwendolyn Ann *special education educator*
Kitto, John Buck, Jr. *mechanical engineer*
Rockhill, Jack Kerrigan *collections company executive*
Rodman, James Purcell *astrophysicist, educator*
Woods, Rose Mary *former presidential assistant, consultant*

### Alpha
James, Francis Edward, Jr. *investment counselor*

### Amelia
Hayden, Joseph Page, Jr. *company executive*
Thoman, Henry Nixon *lawyer*

### Andover
Mathay, John Preston *elementary education educator*
Mole, Richard Jay *accounting company executive*

### Anna
Thompson, Virigina A. *elementary education educator*

### Archbold
Sauder, Erie Joseph *manufacturing executive*

### Ashland
Ford, Lucille Garber *economist, educator*
Waters, Ronald W. *educator, church executive, pastor*
Watson, JoAnn Ford *theology educator*

### Ashtabula
Hornbeck, Harold Douglas *psychotherapist*
Koski, Elizabeth Mitchell *arts center administrator*
Taylor, Norman Floyd *computer educator, administrator, band director*

### Ashville
Beckman, Judith *art educator*
Schilling, Eydie Anne *science educator, consultant*

### Athens
Ahrens, Kent *museum director, art historian*
Alsbrook, James Eldridge *journalist, educator*
Beale, William Taylor *engineering company executive*
Booth, Alan Rundlett *history educator*
Borchert, Donald Marvin *philosopher, educator*
Brehm, Sharon Stephens *psychology educator, university administrator*
Bruning, James Leon *university official, educator*
Chila, Anthony George *osteopathic educator*
Cohn, Norman Stanley *botany educator, university dean*
Crowl, Samuel Renninger *English language educator, author*
Dinos, Nicholas *engineering educator, administrator*
Eckelmann, Frank Donald *retired geology educator, dean emeritus*
Eckes, Alfred Edward, Jr. *historian, international trade analyst*
Gallaway, Lowell Eugene *economist, educator*
Glidden, Robert Burr *university president, musician, educator*
Hedges, Richard H. *epidemiologist, lawyer*
Klare, George Roger *psychology educator*
Lee, Hwa-Wei *librarian, educator*
Matthews, Jack (John Harold Matthews) *English educator, writer*
Metters, Thomas Waddell *sports writer*
Miller, Peggy McLaren *management educator*
Miller, Richard Irwin *education educator, university administrator*
Palmer, Brent David *environmental physiology educator, biologist*
Parmer, Jess Norman *university official, educator*
Patterson, Harlan Ray *finance educator*
Perdreau, Cornelia Ruth Whitener (Connie Perdreau) *English as a second language educator, international exchange specialist*
Ping, Charles Jackson *philosophy educator, retired university president*
Rakes, Ganas Kaye *finance and banking educator*
Robe, Thurlow Richard *engineering educator, university dean*
Scott, Charles Lewis *photojournalist*
Smith, Robert John, Jr. *real estate executive*
Stempel, Guido Hermann, III *journalism educator*
Torres-Labawld, Jose Dimas *institutional research director, service company executive, educator*
Ungar, Irwin Allan *botany educator*
Wagner, Eric Armin *sociology educator*
Wen, Shih-Liang *mathematics educator*
Werner, R(ichard) Budd *retired business executive*
Whealey, Lois Deimel *humanities scholar*

### Aurora
Hermann, Philip J. *lawyer*
Lawton, Florian Kenneth *artist, educator*
Lefebvre, Gabriel Felicien *retired chemical company executive*
Marshall, Lee Douglas *entertainment company executive*

### Avon Lake
Condon, George Edward *journalist*
Gwiazda, Caroline Louise *school system administrator*
Morton, David Ray *sales and marketing executive*

### Bannock
Gentile, Anthony *coal company executive*

### Barberton
Zbacnik, Raymond Eric *process engineer*

### Batavia
Bower, Kenneth Francis *electrical engineer*
McDonough, James Francis *civil engineer, educator*
Nichols, Marci Lynne *gifted education coordinator, educator, consultant*
Rosenhoffer, Chris *lawyer*

### Bath
Bowman-Dalton, Burdene Kathryn *education testing coordinator, computer consultant*

### Bay Village
Berger, James (Hank) *business broker*
Daly-Mattio, Barbara Ann *counselor, nurse*
Hiller, Deborah Lewis *long term care and retirement facility executive*
Woods, Dennis Craig *school superintendent*

### Beachwood
Charnas, Michael (Mannie Charnas) *packaging company executive*
Donnem, Roland William *lawyer, real estate owner and manager*
Fufuka, Natika Njeri Yaa *retail executive*

Leyda, James Perkins pharmaceutical company executive
Lichtin, (Judah) Leon pharmacist
Lienhart, David Arthur geologist, consultant, laboratory director
Lindberg, Charles David lawyer
Lindner, Robert David finance company executive
Linsey, Nathaniel L. bishop
Lintz, Robert Carroll financial holding company executive
Lippincott, Jonathan Ramsay healthcare executive
Liss, Herbert Myron newspaper publisher, communications company executive
Lockhart, John Mallery management consultant
Loggie, Jennifer Mary Hildreth medical educator, physician
Long, Phillip Clifford museum director
Longenecker, Mark Hershey, Jr. lawyer
Lopez-Cobos, Jesus conductor
Lucas, Stanley Jerome radiologist, physician
Luchette, Frederick A. surgeon
Lucke, Robert Vito merger and acquisition executive
Luckner, Herman Richard, III interior designer
Lutz, James Gurney lawyer
Macpherson, Colin R(obertson) pathologist, educator
Maier, Craig Frisch restaurant executive
Manley, Robert Edward lawyer, economist
Mann, David Scott lawyer
Mantel, Samuel Joseph, Jr. management educator, consultant
Martin, Daniel William acoustical physicist
Martin, John Bruce chemical engineer
Maruska, Edward Joseph zoo administrator
Maxwell, Robert Wallace, II lawyer
McClain, William Andrew lawyer
McCoy, John Joseph lawyer
McDowell, John Eugene lawyer
McGavran, Frederick Jaeger lawyer
Mc Henry, Powell lawyer
McKenny, Collin Grad banker
McNulty, John William retired public relations executive, automobile company executive
Meal, Larie chemistry educator, researcher, consultant
Mechem, Charles Stanley, Jr. former broadcasting executive, former golf association executive
Meisner, Gary Wayne landscape architect
Menyhert, Stephan retired chemist
Meranus, Leonard Stanley lawyer
Merchant, Mylon Eugene physicist, engineer
Meyer, Daniel Joseph machinery company executive
Meyer, Walter H. retired food safety executive, consultant
Meyers, Karen Diane lawyer, educator, corporate officer
Milligan, Lawrence Drake, Jr. consumer products executive
Million, Kenneth Rhea management consultant
Moler, James Clark marketing research executive
Molitor, Sister Margaret Anne nun, former college president
Monaco, John J. molecular genetics research educator
Moore, Alfred Anson corporate executive
Morgan, John Bruce hospital care consultant
Morgan, William Richard mechanical engineer
Muntz, Ernest Gordon historian, educator
Murphy, Eugene F. aerospace, communications and electronics executive
Naylor, Paul Donald lawyer
Neale, Henry Whitehead plastic surgery educator
Nebert, Daniel Walter molecular geneticist, research administrator
Nechemias, Stephen Murray lawyer
Nelson, David Aldrich federal judge
Nelson, Frederick Dickson lawyer
Neltner, Michael Martin lawyer
Nester, William Raymond, Jr. retired academic administrator and educator
Neumark, Michael Harry lawyer
Niehoff, Karl Richard Besuden financial executive
Nielsen, George Lee architect
Niesz, George Melvin tool and die company executive
Norman, Peter Minert fundraising consulting company executive
Olson, Robert Wyrick lawyer
O'Reilly, James Thomas lawyer, educator, author
Pancheri, Eugene Joseph chemical engineer
Parker, R. Joseph lawyer
Patterson, Claire Ann vocational educator
Peck, Abraham Joseph historian
Pelton, John Tom biochemist
Pendleton, Terry Lee baseball player
Pepper, John Ennis, Jr. consumer products company executive
Perlman, Burton judge
Perry, Norman Robert priest, magazine editor
Peters, Ann Louise accounting manager
Peterson, Gale Eugene historian
Petrie, Bruce Inglis lawyer
Phillips, T. Stephen lawyer
Pichler, Joseph Anton food products executive
Pilarczyk, Daniel Edward archbishop
Preiser, Wolfgang Friedrich Ernst architect, educator, consultant, researcher
Price, Thomas Emile investment company executive
Proffitt, Kevin archivist
Puthoff, Francis Urban insurance salesman
Qualls, Roxanne mayor
Rabe, Laura Mae mathematician, educator
Randman, Barry I. real estate developer
Randolph, Jackson Harold utility company executive
Rapoport, Robert Morton medical educator
†Rashkin, Mitchell Carl internist, pulmonary medicine specialist
Raskin, Fred Charles transportation and utility holding company executive
Reeb, Patricia A. nursing educator, administrator
Reed, D. Gary lawyer
Reichert, David lawyer
Reitter, Charles Andrew management consultant
Rexroth, Nancy Louise photographer
Rich, Robert Edward lawyer
Rockwell, R(onald) James, Jr. laser and electro-optics consultant
Roe, Clifford Ashley, Jr. lawyer
Rogers, James Eugene electric and gas utility executive
Rogers, Lawrence H., II retired television executive, investor, writer
Rogers, Millard Foster, Jr. retired art museum director
Roomann, Hugo architect
Rosato, Laura Marie toxicologist, educator
Rose, Donald McGregor lawyer
Rose, Peter Edward former professional baseball player and manager
Rubin, Robert Samuel lawyer
Rubin, Stanley Gerald aerospace engineering educator
Rudney, Harry biochemist, educator
Ryan, James Joseph lawyer
Saal, Howard Max clinical geneticist, pediatrician, educator
Saenger, Eugene Lange radiology educator, laboratory director
Safferman, Robert Samuel microbiologist
Sambi, Margaret Ann curator
Samuel, Gerhard orchestra conductor, composer
Sanders, Deion Luwynn baseball and football player
Sanders, Reginald Laverne (Reggie Sanders) professional baseball player
Sanford, Wilbur Lee elementary education educator
Sansbury, Blake Edward product development engineer
Sawyer, John professional football team executive
Schaefer, Frank William, III microbiologist, researcher
Schaefer, George A., Jr. bank executive
Schiff, John Jefferson insurance company executive
Schmidt, Thomas Joseph, Jr. lawyer
Schmit, David E. lawyer
Schneider, Harold Joel radiologist
Schott, Marge professional baseball team executive
Schreiner, Albert William physician, educator
Schrier, Arnold historian, educator
Schuck, Thomas Robert lawyer, farmer
Schuler, Robert Leo appraiser, consultant
Sedgwick-Hirsch, Carol Elizabeth financial executive
Semon, Warren Lloyd retired computer sciences educator
Senhauser, John Crater architect
Shenk, Richard Lawrence real estate developer, photographer, artist
Shore, Thomas Spencer, Jr. lawyer
Siekmann, Donald Charles accountant
Silbersack, Mark Louis lawyer
Silvers, Gerald Thomas publishing executive
Skilbeck, Carol Lynn Marie elementary educator and small business owner
Smale, John Gray diversified industry executive
Smith, C. LeMoyne publishing company executive
Smith, Gregory Allgire academic director
Smith, Leroy Harrington, Jr. mechanical engineer, aerodynamics consultant
Smith, Roger Dean pathologist
Smith, Stephen Dale safety engineer
Smittle, Nelson Dean electronics executive
Sodd, Vincent Joseph nuclear medicine researcher, educator
Sowder, Fred Allen foundation administrator, alphabet specialist
Sperelakis, Nicholas, Sr. physiology and biophysics educator, researcher
Sperzel, George E., Jr. personal care industry executive
Spiegel, S. Arthur federal judge
Spraley, Judith Ann nursing educator, administrator
Startup, William Harry chemist
Steger, Joseph A. university president
Steinberg, Janet Eckstein journalist
Stern, Joseph Smith, Jr. former footwear manufacturing company executive
Sterne, Bobbie Lynn city council member
Stoms, Donna Sue librarian
Strauss, William Victor lawyer
†Streck, Richard James medical administrator
Streckfuss, James Arthur lawyer, historian
Street, David Hargett investment company executive
Sullivan, Connie Castleberry artist, photographer
Sullivan, Dennis James, Jr. public relations executive
Sullivan, James F. physicist, educator
Suskind, Raymond Robert physician, educator
Sweeten, Gary Ray religious counseling educator
Swigert, James Mack lawyer
Terp, Thomas Thomsen lawyer
Thiemann, Charles Lee banker
Thompson, Herbert, Jr. bishop
Thompson, Morley Punshon textile company executive
Timpano, Anne museum director, art historian
Tobias, Charles Harrison, Jr. lawyer
Tobias, Paul Henry lawyer
Tocco, James pianist
Toftner, Richard Orville engineering executive
Toltzis, Robert Joshua cardiologist
Tomain, Joseph Patrick dean, law educator
Townsend, Robert J. lawyer
Trauth, Joseph Louis, Jr. lawyer
Tuttle, Martha Benedict artist
Vander Laan, Mark Alan lawyer
Vasholz, Lothar Alfred retired insurance company executive
Victor, William Weir retired telephone company executive, consultant
Vilter, Richard William physician, educator
Voet, Paul C. specialty chemical company executive
Vogel, Cedric Wakelee lawyer
Wales, Ross Elliot lawyer
Walker, Michael Claude finance educator
Walker, Ronald F. corporate executive
Ward, Sherman Carl, III (Buzz Ward) theater manager
Warm, Joel Seymour psychology educator
Watts, Barbara Gayle law academic administrator
Weber, Fredrick Louis, Jr. hepatologist, medical researcher
Weber, Herman Jacob federal judge
Weed, Ithamar Dryden life insurance company executive
Weeks, Steven Wiley lawyer
†Wehling, Robert Louis household products company executive
Weinrich, Alan Jeffrey occupational hygienist
Weiskittel, Ralph Joseph real estate executive
Weisman, Joel nuclear engineering educator, engineering consultant
Wellington, Jean Susorney librarian
Wentsler, Gertrude Josephine secondary school educator
Werner, Robert Joseph college dean, music educator
Weseli, Roger William lawyer
West, Clark Darwin pediatric nephrologist, educator
Whipple, Harry M. newspaper publishing executive
Whitaker, Glenn Virgil lawyer
White, Robert John journalist
Williams, James Case metallurgist
Wilsey, Philip Arthur computer science educator
Wilson, Frederic Sandford pharmaceutical company executive
Wilson, James Miller, IV cardiovascular surgeon, educator
Wilson, Lucy Jean librarian
Winchell, Margaret Webster St. Clair realtor
Winkler, Henry Ralph retired academic administrator, historian
Winternitz, Felix Thomas editor, educator
Wiot, Jerome Francis radiologist
Witten, Louis physics educator
Woodside, Frank C., III lawyer
Woodward, James Kenneth pharmacologist
Worachek, Susan music educator
Wygant, Foster Laurance art educator
Yund, George Edward lawyer
Yurchuck, Roger Alexander lawyer
Zafren, Herbert Cecil librarian, educator
Zanotti, John Peter broadcasting company executive
Zavatsky, Michael Joseph lawyer
Zierolf, Mary Louise nurse anesthetist
Zimmer, William Homer, Jr. retired insurance company executive
Zola, Gary Phillip religious educational administrator, rabbi,

## Circleville

Long, Jan Michael judge
Norman, Jack Lee church administrator, consultant
Scherer, Robert Davisson retired business and association executive
Tipton, Daniel L. religious organization executive

## Cleveland

Abid, Ann B. art librarian
Abram, Marian Christine lawyer
Adamo, Kenneth R. lawyer
Ainsworth, Joan Horsburgh university development director
Aldrich, Ann federal judge
Alfidi, Ralph Joseph radiologist, educator
Alfred, Stephen Jay lawyer
Alomar, Sandy, Jr. (Santos Velazquez Alomar) professional baseball player
Alspaugh, Robert Odo industrial management consultant
†Altose, Murray David physician
Anderson, David Gaskill, Jr. Spanish language educator
Anderson, Harold Albert engineering and building executive
Andorka, Frank Henry lawyer
Andrews, Oakley V. lawyer
Angus, John Cotton chemical engineering educator
Arlen, Mark Dale financial planner
Ashmus, Keith Allen lawyer
Atherton, James Dale publishing executive
Austin, Arthur Donald, II lawyer, educator
Awais, George Musa obstetrician, gynecologist
Bacon, Brett Kermit lawyer
Badal, Daniel Walter psychiatrist, educator
Baer, Eric engineering and science educator
Bahniuk, Eugene mechanical engineering educator
Bailey, John Turner public relations executive
Baker, Saul Phillip geriatrician, cardiologist, internist
Bambakidis, Peter neurologist, educator
Bamberger, David opera company executive
Bamberger, Richard H. lawyer
Banerjee, Amiya Kumar biochemist
Bass, Jonathan dermatologist
Bassett, John E. dean, English educator
Bates, Walter Alan former lawyer
Batt, John Paul lawyer
Baughman, R(obert) Patrick lawyer
Baxter, Howard H. lawyer
Baxter, Randolph judge
Beall, Cynthia anthropologist, educator
Beamer, Yvonne Marie psychotherapist, counselor
Behnke, William Alfred landscape architect, planner
Beling, Helen sculptor
Bennett, Michael newspaper editor
Benseler, David Price foreign language educator
Berger, Melvin allergist, immunologist
Berger, Sanford Jason lawyer, securities dealer, real estate broker
Bergholz, David foundation administrator
Bergman, Robert Paul museum administrator, art historian, educator, lecturer
Berick, James Herschel lawyer
Berry, Dean Lester lawyer
Bersticker, Albert Charles chemical company executive
Besse, Ralph Moore lawyer
Bidelman, William Pendry astronomer, educator
Bilchik, Gary B. lawyer
Binford, Gregory Glenn lawyer
Bingham, Richard Donnelly journal editor, director, educator
Binstock, Robert Henry public policy educator, writer, lecturer
Bixenstine, Kim Fenton lawyer
Blackstone, Patricia Clark bank officer, psychotherapist
Blackwell, John polymers scientist, educator
Blattner, Robert A. lawyer
Blodgett, Omer William electric company design consultant
Bluhm, Gene Elwood trade journal editor and publisher
Blum, Arthur social work educator
Bockhoff, Frank James chemistry educator
Bowen, Richard Lee architect
Bowerfind, Edgar Sihler, Jr. physician, medical administrator
Boyd, Richard Alfred school system administrator
Boyle, Kammer management psychologist
Brandon, Edward Bermetz retired banking executive
Brandt, John Reynold editor, journalist
Braverman, Herbert Leslie lawyer
Bravo, Kenneth Allan lawyer
Breen, John Gerald manufacturing company executive
Brennan, Maureen lawyer
Brentlinger, Paul Smith venture capital executive
†Bronson, David Leigh physician, educator
Brosilow, Coleman Bernard chemical engineering educator
Brown, Seymour R. lawyer
Brucken, Robert Matthew lawyer
Buchanan, D(aniel) Harvey art history educator
Budd, John Henry physician
Buhrow, William Carl religious organization administrator
Burghart, James Henry electrical engineer, educator
Burke, John Francis, Jr. economist
Burke, Kathleen B. lawyer
Burke, Lillian Walker retired judge
Butler, William E. retired manufacturing company executive
Cairns, James Donald lawyer
Calabrese, Leonard M. social services administrator
Calfee, John Beverly retired lawyer
Calfee, William Lewis lawyer
Calkins, Hugh foundation executive
Callsen, Christian Edward medical device company executive
Campbell, Paul Barton retired lawyer
Canary, Nancy Halliday lawyer
Caplan, Arnold I. biology educator
Carey, Paul Richard biophysicist
Carlsson, Bo Axel Vilhelm economics educator
Carrick, Kathleen Michele law librarian
Carter, James Rose, Jr. medical educator
Carter, John Dale organizational development executive
Carter, John Robert physician
Cartier, Charles Ernest alcohol and drug abuse services professional
Cascorbi, Helmut Freimund anesthesiologist, educator
Cassill, Herbert Carroll artist
Castele, Theodore John radiologist
Celebrezze, Anthony federal judge
Chandler, Everett Alfred lawyer
Chapman, Robert L. bishop
Chatterjee, Pranab social sciences educator
Chema, Thomas V. government official, lawyer
Clark, Gary R. newspaper editor
Clark, Robert Arthur mathematician, educator
Clarke, Charles Fenton lawyer
†Cleary, Martin Joseph real estate company executive
Climaco, Michael Louis lawyer
Clutter, Bertley Allen, III management company executive
Cole, Monroe neurologist, educator
Collin, Robert Emanuel electrical engineering educator
Collin, Thomas James lawyer
Collins, Duane E. manufacturing executive
Connors, Joanna film critic
Cooper, James Clinton social services administrator, consultant
Coquillette, William Hollis lawyer
Cornell, John Robert lawyer
Coulman, George Albert chemical engineer, educator
Courier, Jim (James Spencer Courier, Jr.) tennis player
Coyle, Martin Adolphus, Jr. lawyer
Crist, Paul Grant lawyer
Crosby, Fred McClellan retail home and office furnishings executive
Cudak, Gail Linda lawyer
Cullis, Christopher Ashley dean, biology educator
Cunningham, Pierce Edward lawyer, city planner
Currivan, John Daniel lawyer
Cutler, Alexander MacDonald manufacturing company executive
Dadley, Arlene Jeanne sleep technologist
Dampeer, John Lyell retired lawyer
Danco, Léon Antoine management consultant, educator
Dancyger, Ruth art historian
Daroff, Robert Barry neurologist
Davidson, James Wilson clinical psychologist
Davis, David Aaron journalist
Davis, Pamela Bowes pediatric pulmonologist
de Acosta, Alejandro Daniel mathematician, educator
Deissler, Robert George fluid dynamicist, researcher
Dell'Osso, Louis Frank neuroscience educator
De Marco, Thomas Joseph periodontist, educator
Denko, Joanne D. psychiatrist, writer
DesRosiers, Anne Booke performing arts administrator
Dipko, Thomas Earl minister, national church executive
Diskin, Michael Edward construction products company executive
Doershuk, Carl Frederick physician, professor of pediatrics
Dohnányi, Christoph von musician, conductor
Doris, Alan S(anford) lawyer
Dossey, Richard L. accountant
Dowell, Michael Brendan chemist
Drinko, John Deaver lawyer
Dunbar, Mary Asmundson communications executive, investor and public relations consultant
Duncan, Ed Eugene lawyer
Duvin, Robert Phillip lawyer
Dye, Sherman retired lawyer
Dylag, Helen Marie healthcare administrator
Dy Liacco, Tomas Enciso engineering consulting executive
Eastwood, Douglas William anesthesiologist
Eaton, Henry Felix public relations executive
Eberhard, William Thomas architect
Eiben, Robert Michael pediatric neurologist, educator
Ekelman, Daniel Louis lawyer
Elewski, Boni Elizabeth dermatologist, educator
Ellis, Lloyd H., Jr. emergency physician
Epp, Eldon Jay religion educator
Erb, Donald composer
Eski, John Robert residential appraiser, real estate consultant
Fabens, Andrew Lawrie, III lawyer
Fabris, James A. journalist
Faldo, Nick professional golfer
Faller, Dorothy Anderson international agency administrator
Falsgraf, William Wendell lawyer
Fay, Regan Joseph lawyer
Fay, Robert Jesse lawyer
Fazio, Victor Warren physician, colon and rectal surgeon
Feinberg, Paul H. lawyer
Fenton, Alan artist
Ferguson, Suzanne Carol English educator
Fernandez, René aerospace engineer
Fernandez, Tony (Octavio Antonio Castro Fernandez) baseball player
Finn, Robert writer, lecturer, broadcaster
Fisher, Thomas Edward lawyer
Fitzpatrick, Joyce J. dean, nursing educator
Fletcher, Robert lawyer, horologist
Fordyce, James Stuart non-profit organization executive
Fountain, Ronald Glenn management consultant
Fratello, Michael Robert professional basketball coach
Friedman, Barton Robert English educator
Friedman, Harold Edward lawyer
Friedman, James Moss lawyer
†Fusco, Diane Roman public relations executive
†Gallagher, Patrick Francis Xavier public relations executive
Gardner, Richard Kent retired librarian, educator, consultant
Garrison, William Lloyd cemetery executive
Gauff, Lisa broadcast journalist

White, Michael Reed *mayor*
Whiteman, Joseph David *lawyer, manufacturing company executive*
Whitney, Richard Buckner *lawyer*
†Whittlesey, Diana *surgeon*
Wiedemann, Herbert Pfeil *physician*
Williams, Arthur Benjamin, Jr. *bishop*
Williams, Clyde E., Jr. *lawyer*
Williams, Matt (Matthew Derrick Williams) *professional baseball player*
Wish, Jay Barry *nephrologist, specialist*
Wolfman, Alan *medical educator, researcher*
Wolinsky, Emanuel *physician, educator*
Woyczynski, Wojbor Andrzej *mathematician, educator*
Wright, Marshall *retired manufacturing executive, former diplomat*
Yeager, Ernest Bill *physical chemist, electrochemist, educator*
Young, James Edward *lawyer*
Young, Jess R. *physician*
Yurko, Joseph Andrew *chemical engineer*
Zambie, Allan John *lawyer*
Zangerle, John A. *lawyer*
Zdanis, Richard Albert *academic administrator*
Zimmerman, Michael Glenn *marketing and communications executive*
Zubal, John Thomas *book exchange executive, publisher, bibliographer*
Zung, Thomas Tse-Kwai *architect*

### Cleveland Heights

Banks, Melanie Anne *nutritionist, biochemist, educator*
Daroff, William C. *political consultant, public policy analyst*
Drane, Walter Harding *publishing executive, business consultant*
Gutfeld, Norman E. *lawyer*
Travis, Frederick Francis *academic administrator, historian*

### Coldwater

Kunz, Charles Alphonse *farm machinery manufacturing executive*

### Columbia Station

Pingatore, Sam Robert *systems analyst, consultant, business executive*

### Columbus

Ackerman, John Henry *health services consultant, physician*
Ackerman, Kenneth Benjamin *management consultant, writer*
Adams, John Marshall *lawyer*
Alban, Roger Charles *construction equipment distribution executive*
Aldridge, Mark Donald *financial advisor, investment counselor*
Alexander, Carl Albert *ceramic engineer*
Alger, Chadwick Fairfax *political scientist, educator*
Alutto, Joseph Anthony *university dean, management educator*
Anderson, Carole Ann *nursing educator*
Anderson, John Robert *state agency administrator*
Anderson, Jon Mac *lawyer*
Antler, Morton *consulting engineering executive, author, educator*
Armes, Walter Scott *vocational school administrator*
Arnold, Kevin David *psychologist, educational researcher*
Arps, David Foster *electronics engineer*
Ayers, James Cordon *lawyer*
Babcock, Charles Luther *classics educator*
Bachman, Sister Janice *health care executive*
Bahls, Steven Carl *law educator, university dean*
Bailey, Cecil Dewitt *aerospace engineer, educator*
Bailey, Daniel Allen *lawyer*
Banwart, George Junior *food microbiology educator*
Barker, Llyle James, Jr. *journalism educator, public relations executive, former military officer*
Barnes, Wallace Ray *retired lawyer*
Barry, James P(otvin) *writer, editor*
Barth, Rolf Frederick *pathologist, educator*
Barthelmas, Ned Kelton *investment and commercial real estate banker*
Battersby, James Lyons, Jr. *English language educator*
Baughman, George Washington, III *retired university official, financial consultant*
Beavers, John Parrish *lawyer*
Bechtel, Stephen E. *mechanical engineer, educator*
Beck, Paul Allen *political science educator*
Becker, Ralph Leonard *psychologist*
Beckholt, Alice *public health nurse*
Bedford, Keith Wilson *civil engineer, atmospheric science educator*
Behrman, Edward Joseph *biochemistry educator*
Beja, Morris *English literature educator*
Bell, George Edwin *retired physician, insurance company executive*
Beller, Stephen Mark *university administrator*
Bennett, Sharon Kay *music educator*
Bennett, Steven Alan *lawyer*
Benton-Borghi, Beatrice Hope *educational consultant, author, publisher*
Berggren, Ronald Bernard *surgeon, emeritus educator*
Bergstrom, Stig Magnus *geology educator*
Berntson, Gary Glen *psychiatry, psychology and pediatrics educator*
Berry, William Lee *business administration educator*
Beverley, Jane Taylor *artist*
Bhushan, Bharat *mechanical engineer*
Bibart, Richard L. *lawyer*
Billings, Charles Edgar *physician*
Binning, J. Boyd *lawyer*
Black, Larry David *library director*
Blackmore, Josiah H. *university president, lawyer, educator*
Blair, William Travis (Bud Blair) *retired organization executive*
Blickenstaff, Kathleen Mary *mental health nurse, nursing educator*
Boardman, William Penniman *lawyer, banker*
Boerner, Ralph E. J. *forest soil ecologist, plant biology educator*
Boh, Ivan *philosophy educator*
Böhm, Friedrich (Friedl) K.M. *architectural firm executive*
Boudoulas, Harisios *physician*
Boulger, Francis William *metallurgical engineer*
Bourguignon, Erika Eichhorn *anthropologist, educator*
Bowman, Louis L. *emergency physician*
Boyd, Barbara H. *state legislator*
Branscomb, Lewis Capers, Jr. *librarian, educator*
Bridgman, G(eorge) Ross *lawyer*
Brierley, Gerald P. *physiological chemistry educator*
Brinkman, Dale Thomas *lawyer*
Brittin, Marie Eleanor *communications, psychology, speech and hearing science educator*
Brodkey, Robert Stanley *chemical engineering educator*
Brooks, Keith *retired speech communication educator*
Brooks, Richard Dickinson *lawyer*
Brown, Firman Hewitt, Jr. *drama educator, theatrical director*
Brown, Herbert Russell *lawyer, writer*
Brown, Philip Albert *lawyer*
Brown, Rowland Chauncey Widrig *information systems, strategic planning and ethics consultant*
Brubaker, Robert Loring *lawyer*
Buchenroth, Stephen Richard *lawyer*
Buchsieb, Walter Charles *orthodontist*
Bullock, Joseph Daniel *pediatrician, educator*
Burke, Kenneth Andrew *advertising executive*
Burnham, John Chynoweth *historian, educator*
Cacioppo, John Terrance *psychology educator*
Calhoun, Donald Eugene, Jr. *federal judge*
Callander, Kay Eileen Paisley *business owner, retired gifted talented education educator, writer*
Campbell, Richard Rice *retired newspaper editor*
Capen, Charles Chabert *veterinary pathology educator, researcher*
Carnahan, John Anderson *lawyer*
Carpenter, Jot David *landscape architect, educator*
Carpenter, Michael H. *lawyer*
Carter, Cheryl A. *medical/surgical nurse*
Casey, John Frederick *lawyer*
Casey, Raymond Richard *agricultural business executive*
Chandrasekaran, Balakrishnan *computer and information science educator*
Charles, Bertram *radio broadcasting executive*
Chester, John Jonas *lawyer*
Chovan, John David *biomedical engineer*
Christensen, John William *lawyer*
Christoforidis, A. John *radiologist, educator*
Clovis, Albert Lee *lawyer, educator*
Colburn, Julia Katherine Lee *volunteer, educator*
Cole, Charles Chester, Jr. *educational administrator*
Cole, Clarence Russell *college dean*
†Cole, Ransey Guy, Jr. *judge*
Collier, David Alan *management educator*
Conrad, David Keith *lawyer*
Coopersmith, Jeffrey Alan *distribution corporation executive*
Copeland, William Edgar, Sr. *physician*
Corbato, Charles Edward *geology educator*
Cormanick, Rosa-Maria Moreno *academic program coordinator*
Cornwell, David George *biochemist, educator*
Cottrell, David Alton *school system administrator*
Cox, Mitchel Neal *editor*
Cramblett, Henry Gaylord *pediatrician, virologist, educator*
Crane, Jameson *plastics manufacturing company executive*
Cruz, Jose Bejar, Jr. *engineering educator*
Culbertson, Jack Arthur *education educator*
Cunnyngham, Jon *economist, information systems educator*
Cvetanovich, Danny L. *lawyer*
Daab-Krzykowski, Andre *pharmaceutical and nutritional manufacturing company administrator*
Daehn, Glenn Steven *materials scientist*
Dawson, Virginia Sue *newspaper editor*
Deep, Ira Washington *plant pathology educator*
De Lucia, Frank Charles *physicist, educator*
DeRousie, Charles Stuart *lawyer*
Dervin, Brenda Louise *communications educator*
DeSando, John Anthony *humanities educator*
Dieker, Lawrence L. *chemicals executive*
Dillon, Merton Lynn *historian, educator*
Di Lorenzo, John Florio, Jr. *lawyer*
Disinger, John Franklin *natural resources educator*
Douglas, Andrew *state supreme court justice*
Dowling, Thomas Allan *mathematics educator*
Drake, Grace L. *state senator*
Draper, E(rnest) Linn, Jr. *electric utility executive*
Dreher, Darrell L. *lawyer*
Druen, William Sidney *lawyer*
Drvota, Mojmir *cinema educator, author*
Duckworth, Winston Howard *retired ceramic engineer*
Dugan, Charles Francis, II *lawyer*
Dunham, Frank L. *accounting and consulting company executive*
Dunlay, Catherine Telles *lawyer*
Duryee, Harold Taylor *insurance executive*
Dwon, Larry *retired electrical engineer, educator, consultant*
Eaton, Michael Christopher *accounting technician*
Edwards, John White *lawyer*
Eickelberg, John Edwin *process control company executive*
Elam, John Carlton *lawyer*
Elliot, David Hawksley *geologist*
Elliot, Ernest Alexander *naval rear admiral*
Ellison, Edwin Christopher *physician, surgeon*
Emanuelson, James Robert *retired insurance company executive*
Ensminger, Dale *mechanical engineer, electrical engineer*
Epstein, Arthur Joseph *physics and chemistry educator*
Epstein, Erwin Howard *sociology and education educator*
Fahey, Richard Paul *lawyer*
Falcone, Robert Edward *surgeon*
Faure, Gunter *geology educator*
Fausey, Norman Ray *soil scientist*
Fawcett, Sherwood Luther *research laboratory executive*
Fay, Terrence Michael *lawyer*
Feck, Luke Matthew *utility executive*
Fenton, Robert Earl *electrical engineering educator*
Ferguson, Ronald Morris *surgeon, educator*
Firestone, Richard Francis *chemistry educator*
Fisher, Lawrence L. *lawyer*
Fisher, Lloyd Edison, Jr. *lawyer*
Floyd, Gary Leon *plant cell biologist*
Foland, Kenneth A. *geological sciences educator*
Fornshell, Dave Lee *educational broadcasting executive*
Frasier, Ralph Kennedy *lawyer, banker*
Frenzer, Peter Frederick *retired insurance company executive*
Fry, Donald Lewis *physiologist, educator*
Fu, Paul Shan *law librarian, consultant*
Fullerton, Charles William *retired insurance company executive*
Furney, Linda Jeanne *state legislator*
Furste, Wesley Leonard, II *surgeon, educator*
Galloway, Harvey Scott, Jr. *insurance company executive*
Gatewood, Buford Echols *retired educator, aeronautical and astronautical engineer*
Gee, Elwood Gordon *university administrator*
Gibson, Rankin MacDougal *lawyer*
Gilliom, Bonnie Lee *arts educator, consultant*
Gilliom, Morris Eugene *social studies and global educator*
Gillmor, Karen Lako *state legislator, strategic planner*
Glaser, Ronald *microbiology educator, scientist*
Goff, John *state agency administrator*
Goodman, Hubert Thorman *psychiatrist, consultant*
Goodridge, Alan Gardner *research biochemist, educator*
Goorey, Nancy Jane *dentist*
Gozon, Jozsef Stephan *engineering educator*
Graham, James Lowell *federal judge*
Grant, Michael Peter *electrical engineer*
Grapski, Ladd Raymond *accountant*
Greek, Darold I. *lawyer*
Gribble, Charles Edward *Slavic languages educator, editor*
Gross, James Howard *lawyer*
Grossberg, Michael Lee *theater critic, writer*
Gunnels, Lee O. *retired finance and management educator, manufacturing company executive*
Haddad, George Richard *musician, educator*
Hahm, David Edgar *classics educator*
Hamilton, Harold Philip *fund raising executive*
Hansen, Thomas Nanastad *pediatrician, health facility administrator*
Haque, Malika Hakim *pediatrician*
Hardymon, David Wayne *lawyer*
Hare, Robert Yates *music history educator*
Harris, Donald *composer*
Hayes, Edward F. *academic administrator*
Healy, Bernadine P. *physician, educator, federal agency administrator, scientist*
Hedrick, Larry Willis *airport executive*
Heffner, Grover Chester *retired corporate executive, retired naval officer*
Heinlen, Daniel Lee *alumni organization administrator*
Herbst, Eric *physicist, astronomer*
Hoberg, John William *lawyer*
Hobson, Harry E., Jr. *health care administrator*
Hoffmann, Charles Wesley *retired foreign language educator*
Hollenbaugh, H(enry) Ritchey *lawyer*
Hollister, Nancy *state official*
Holschuh, John David *federal judge*
Hooper, Kelley Rae *delivery service executive*
Horton, John Edward *periodontist, educator*
Hottinger, Jay *state legislator*
Houser, Donald Russell *mechanical engineering educator, consultant*
Hsu, Hsiung *engineering educator*
Huber, Joan Althaus *sociology educator*
Huff, C(larence) Ronald *criminology educator and public administration*
Hughes, Donald Allen, Jr. *law librarian and educator*
Hughes, James Sinclair *electronic engineer, writer*
Huheey, Marilyn Jane *ophthalmologist*
Ichiishi, Tatsuro *economics and mathematics educator*
Jackson, David Gordon *religious organization administrator*
Jackson, G. James *protective services official*
Jackson, Sally A(nn) *state official*
Jarvis, Gilbert Andrew *humanities educator*
Jenkins, George L. *lawyer, business executive*
Jenkins, John Anthony *lawyer*
Johnson, Mark Alan *lawyer*
Johnston, Jeffery W. *publishing executive*
Jolly, Daniel Ehs *dental educator*
Jones, Danny Clyde *healthcare products executive*
Jossem, Edmund Leonard *physics educator*
†Kakos, Gerard Stephen *thoracic and cardiovascular surgeon*
Kapral, Frank Albert *medical microbiology and immunology educator*
Kasper, Larry John *accountant, litigation support consultant*
Kasulis, Thomas Patrick *humanities educator*
Keaney, William Regis *engineering and construction services executive, consultant*
Kearns, Merle Grace *state senator*
Kefauver, Weldon Addison *publisher*
Keller, John Kistler *lawyer*
Kessel, John Howard *political scientist, educator*
Ketcham, Richard Scott *lawyer*
Kidder, C. Robert *food products executive*
Kiefer, Gary *newspaper editor*
Kim, Moon Hyun *physician, educator*
Kindig, Fred Eugene *statistics educator, arbitrator*
King, G. Roger *lawyer*
King, Norah McCann *federal judge*
Kinneary, Joseph Peter *federal judge*
Kirk, Ballard Harry Thurston *architect*
Knepper, William Edward *lawyer*
Knilans, Michael Jerome *supermarkets executive*
Knisely, Douglas Charles *accountant*
Koenigsknecht, Roy A. *education administrator*
Kolattukudy, Pappachan Ettoop *biochemist, educator*
Kolcio, Nestor *electrical engineer*
Kouyoumjian, Robert G. *electrical engineering educator*
Ksienski, Aharon Arthur *electrical engineer*
Kuehn, Edmund Karl *artist*
Kuehnle, Kenton Lee *lawyer*
Kuhn, Albert Joseph *English educator*
Kurtz, Charles Jewett, III *lawyer*
Ladman, Jerry R. *economist, educator*
LaLonde, Bernard Joseph *educator*
Lander, Ruth A. *medical group and association administrator*
Lashutka, Gregory S. *mayor, lawyer*
Laufman, Leslie Rodgers *hematologist, oncologist*
Lazar, Theodore Aaron *retired manufacturing company executive, lawyer*
Leach, Russell *judge*
Lehiste, Ilse *language educator*
Lehman, Harry Jac *lawyer*
Leier, Carl Victor *internist, cardiologist*
Leissa, Arthur William *mechanical engineering educator*
Leiter, William C. *banking executive*
Leland, Henry *psychology educator*
Leong, G. Keong *operations management educator*
Lewis, Richard Phelps *physician, educator*
Lim, Shun Ping *cardiologist*
Lince, John Alan *pharmacist*
Lindsay, Dianna Marie *educational administrator*
Ling, Ta-Yung *physics educator*
Liu, Ming-Tsan *computer engineering educator*
Long, Sarah Elizabeth Brackney *physician*
Long, Thomas Leslie *lawyer*
Lopez, A. Ruben *lawyer*
Lowe, Clayton Kent *visual imagery, cinema, and video educator*
Lowry, Bruce Roy *lawyer*
Lowther, Frank Eugene *research physicist*
Luck, James I. *foundation executive*
Lundstedt, Sven Bertil *behavioral and social scientist, educator*
Lynn, Arthur Dellert, Jr. *economist, educator*
Maddala, Gangadharrao Soundaryarao *economics educator*
Magliocca, Larry Anthony *education educator*
Maloney, Gerald P. *utility executive*
Maloon, Jerry L. *trial lawyer, physician, medicolegal consultant*
Marble, Duane Francis *geography educator, researcher*
Markham, Richard Lawrence *chemist*
Martin, William Giese *lawyer*
Marushige-Knopp, Yuka *food scientist*
Marzluf, George Austin *biochemistry educator*
Maser, Douglas James *lawyer*
Massie, Robert Joseph *publishing company executive*
Mayer, Victor James *earth system science educator*
Maynard, Robert Howell *lawyer*
Mayo, Elizabeth Broom *lawyer*
Mazzaferri, Ernest Louis *physician, educator*
McAlister, Robert Beaton *lawyer*
McClain, Thomas E. *communications executive*
McConnaughey, George Carlton, Jr. *lawyer*
Mc Cormac, John Waverly *judge*
Mc Coy, John Bonnet *banker*
McCoy, William Earl, Jr. *economic development training consultant*
McCutchan, Gordon Eugene *lawyer, insurance company executive*
McDermott, Kevin R. *lawyer*
McFerson, Diamond Richard *insurance company executive*
McKenna, Alvin James *lawyer*
McLin, Rhine Lana *state senator, funeral service executive, educator*
McMahon, John Patrick *lawyer*
McMaster, Robert Raymond *accountant*
McNealey, J. Jeffrey *lawyer, corporate executive*
Mead, Priscilla *state legislator*
Meites, Samuel *clinical chemist, educator*
Meredith, Meri Hill *retired librarian, educator*
Merwin, Harmon Turner *retired regional planner*
Meuser, Fredrick William *retired seminary president, church historian*
Meyer, Donald Ray *psychologist, brain researcher*
Meyer, Patricia Morgan *neuropsychologist, educator*
Milford, Frederick John *retired research company executive*
Miller, Don Wilson *nuclear engineering educator*
Miller, Malcolm Lee *retired lawyer*
Miller, Paul Dean *breeding company consultant, geneticist*
Miller, Terry Alan *chemistry educator*
Miller, Terry Morrow *lawyer*
Mills, Robert Laurence *physicist, educator*
Minor, Charles Daniel *lawyer*
Minor, Robert Allen *lawyer*
Mirman, Joel Harvey *lawyer*
Mitchell, Carol Elaine *publishing executive, writer, educator*
Moloney, Thomas E. *lawyer*
Mone, Robert Paul *lawyer*
Montgomery, Betty Dee *state official, former state legislator*
Moore, Jay Winston *director cytogenetics laboratory*
Morgan, Dennis Richard *lawyer*
Moritz, Michael Everett *lawyer*
Morrow, Grant, III *medical research director, physician*
Moser, Debra Kay *medical educator*
Moul, William Charles *lawyer*
Moulton, Edward Quentin *civil engineer, educator*
Moyer, Thomas J. *state supreme court chief justice*
Mueller, Charles Frederick *radiologist, educator*
Muller, Mervin Edgar *information systems educator, consultant*
Murphy, Andrew J. *managing news editor*
Myerowitz, P. David *cardiologist, cardiac surgeon*
Namboodiri, Krishnan *sociology educator*
Nasrallah, Henry Ata *psychiatry researcher, educator*
Nathan, Jerry E. *lawyer*
Naylor, James Charles *psychologist, educator*
Neckermann, Peter Josef *insurance company executive*
Needham, Glen Ray *entology and acarology educator*
Newman, Barbara Miller *psychologist, educator*
Newman, Diana S. *community foundation executive, consultant*
Newsom, Gerald Higley *astronomy educator*
Newton, William Allen, Jr. *pediatric pathologist*
Noe, Fred J. *sports association administrator*
Norris, Alan Eugene *federal judge*
Ockerman, Herbert W. *agricultural studies educator*
O'Donnell, F. Scott *banker*
Olesen, Douglas Eugene *research institute executive*
Oliphant, James S. *lawyer*
Oman, Richard Heer *lawyer*
O'Reilly, Michael Joseph *lawyer, real estate investor*
Osipow, Samuel Herman *psychology educator*
Otte, Paul John *academic administrator, consultant, trainer*
Ouzts, Dale Keith *broadcast executive*
Owsiany, David James *lawyer, lobbyist*
Oxley, Margaret Carolyn Stewart *elementary education educator*
Ozkan, Umit Sivrioglu *chemical engineering educator*
Pacht, Eric Reed *pulmonary and critical care physician*
Page, Linda Kay *banking executive*
Pappas, Peter William *zoology educator*
Patrick, Jane Austin *association executive*
Patterson, Samuel Charles *political science educator*
Peterle, Tony John *zoologist, educator*
Peters, Leon, Jr. *electrical engineering educator, research administrator*
Petricoff, M. Howard *lawyer, educator*
Petro, James Michael *lawyer, politician*
Petty, Richard Edward *psychologist, educator, researcher*
Pfeifer, Paul E. *state supreme court justice*
Pfening, Frederic Denver, III *manufacturing company executive*
Phillips, James Edgar *lawyer*

Pieper, Heinz Paul physiology educator
Pitzer, Russell Mosher chemistry educator
Plagenz, George Richard minister, journalist, columnist
Pohlman, James Erwin lawyer
Pointer, Peter Leon investment executive
Poirier, Frank Eugene physical anthropology educator
Pressley, Fred G., Jr. lawyer
Pyatt, Leo Anthony real estate broker
Quigley, John Bernard law educator
Radnor, Alan T. lawyer
Ramey, Denny L. bar association executive director
Rapp, Robert Anthony metallurgical engineering educator, consultant
Ray, Edward John economics educator, administrator
Ray, Frank Allen lawyer
Ray, Frank David government agency official
Reasoner, Willis Irl, III lawyer
Redmond, Robert Francis nuclear engineering educator
Reese, Douglas Wayne geologist
Reeve, John Newton molecular biology and microbiology educator
Reibel, Kurt physicist, educator
Relle, Ferenc Matyas chemist
Resnick, Alice Robie state supreme court justice
Richardson, Laurel Walum sociology educator
Ridgley, Thomas Brennan lawyer
Ripley, Randall Butler political scientist, educator
Robbins, Darryl Andrew pediatrician
Robinson, Barry R. lawyer
Robol, Richard Thomas lawyer
Rose, Michael Dean lawyer, educator
Rosenstock, Susan Lynn orchestra manager
Roth, Robert Earl environmental educator
Roth, Susan King design educator
Rowland, Robert Charles writer, clinical psychotherapist, researcher
Ruberg, Robert Lionel surgery educator
Rubin, Alan J. environmental engineer, chemist
Rudmann, Sally Vander Linden medical technology educator
Rule, John Corwin history educator
Rund, Douglas Andrew emergency physician, educator
Russell, William Fletcher, III opera company director
Ryan, Joseph W., Jr. lawyer
Ryan, Robert consulting company executive
Sahai, Yogeshwar engineering educator
St. Pierre, George Roland, Jr. materials science and engineering administrator, educator
St. Pierre, Ronald Leslie anatomy educator, university administrator
Santner, Thomas statistician, educator
Sawyers, Elizabeth Joan librarian, administrator
Sayers, Martin Peter pediatric neurosurgeon
Scanlan, James Patrick philosophy and Slavic studies educator
Schafer, William Harry electric power industry administrator
Schiavo, Mary Fackler news consultant, lawyer, educator
Schilling, David August management educator
Schottenstein, Jay L. retail executive
Schrag, Edward A., Jr. lawyer
Schuller, David Edward cancer center administrator, otolaryngology
Scott, Thomas Clevenger lawyer
Selby, Diane Ray Miller fraternal organization administrator
Sellers, Barbara Jackson federal judge
Senhauser, Donald A(lbert) pathologist, educator
Shamansky, Robert Norton lawyer
Sharp, Paul David institute administrator
Sherrill, Thomas Boykin, III retired newspaper publishing executive
Shook, Robert Louis business writer
Sidman, Robert John lawyer
Silbajoris, Frank Rimvydas Slavic languages educator
Silverman, Perry Raynard lawyer, consultant
Simms, Lowelle synod executive
Sims, Richard Lee hospital administrator
Simson, Bevlyn artist
Singh, Rajendra mechanical engineering educator
Skillman, Thomas Grant endocrinology consultant, former educator
Slettebak, Arne astronomer, educator
Sliger, Herbert Jacquemin, Jr. lawyer
Smith, George Curtis judge
Smith, George Leonard industrial engineering educator
Smith, Norman T. lawyer
Smith, Philip John industrial and systems engineering educator
Snyder, Robert Lyman materials scientist, educator
Sokol, Saul insurance agency executive
Soloway, Albert Herman medicinal chemist
Somani, Peter human service administrator
Speicher, Carl Eugene pathologist
Stedman, Richard Ralph lawyer
Stein, Jay Wobith legal research and education consultant, mediator arbitrator
Stephens, Thomas M(aron) education educator
Stern, Geoffrey lawyer, disciplinary counsel
Stevenson, Robert Benjamin, III prosthodontist, writer
Stinehart, Roger Ray lawyer
Stoner, Gary David pathology educator
Strode, George K. sports editor
Studer, William Joseph library director
Sugarbaker, Evan R. nuclear science research administrator
Sunami, John Soichi designer
Swanson, Gillian Lee law librarian
Sweeney, Asher William state supreme court justice
Sweeney, Francis E. state supreme court justice
Swetnam, Daniel Richard lawyer
Taaffe, Edward James geography educator
Tabor, Mary Leeba literary magazine editor, author
Taft, Bob state official
Taft, Sheldon Ashley lawyer
Taggart, Thomas Michael lawyer
Taiganides, E. Paul agricultural and environmental engineer, consultant
Tait, Robert E. lawyer
Tarpy, Thomas Michael lawyer
Taylor, Calvin Lee public administrator
Taylor, Celianna Isley information systems specialist
Taylor, Joel Sanford lawyer
Teater, Dorothy Seath county official
Thomas, Duke Winston lawyer
Thompson, Harold Lee lawyer
Tiefel, Virginia May librarian
Tipton, Clyde Raymond, Jr. communications and resources development consultant
Todd, William Michael lawyer
Triplehorn, Charles A. entomology educator, insects curator
Turano, David A. lawyer
Turchi, Peter John aerospace and electrical engineer, educator, scientist
Tzagournis, Manuel physician, educator, university administrator
Ultes, Elizabeth Cummings Bruce artist, retired art historian and librarian
Uotila, Urho Antti Kalevi geodesist, educator
Vassell, Gregory S. electric utility consultant
Vogel, Thomas Timothy surgeon, health care consultant, lay church worker
Voinovich, George V. governor
von Recum, Andreas F. bioengineer
Vorys, Arthur Isaiah lawyer
Voss, Anne Coble nutritional biochemist
Voss, Jerrold Richard city planner, educator, university official
Wagner, Robert Walter photography, cinema and communications educator, media producer, consultant
Wagoner, Robert Hall engineering educator, researcher
Waldron, Kenneth John mechanical engineering educator, researcher
Wali, Mohan Kishen environmental science and natural resources educator
Ware, Brendan John retired electrical engineer and utility executive
Warmbrod, James Robert agriculture educator, university administrator
Warner, Charles Collins lawyer
Weaver, Leah Ann journalist, speech writer
Webb, Thomas Evan biochemistry educator
Weinhold, Virginia Beamer interior designer
Weisberg, Herbert Frank political science educator
Weisgerber, David Wendelin editor, chemist
Wells, Richard Lewis insurance company executive
Wentworth, Andrew Stowell lawyer
Wexner, Leslie Herbert retail executive
Whipps, Edward Franklin lawyer
Whitacre, Caroline Clement immunologist, researcher
Wightman, Alec lawyer
Wigington, Ronald Lee retired chemical information services executive
Wilhelmy, Odin, Jr. insurance agent
Wilkins, John Warren physics educator
Williams, Gregory Howard lawyer, educator
Williams, Robert Roy trade association administrator
Wiseman, Randolph Carson lawyer
Wojcicki, Andrew Adalbert chemist, educator
Wolf, John Steven construction executive, land developer
Wood, Jackie Dale physiologist, educator, researcher
Wright, Harry, III retired lawyer
Yashon, David neurosurgeon, educator
Yeazel, Keith Arthur lawyer
Yenkin, Bernard Kalman coatings and resins company executive
Yohn, David Stewart virologist, science administrator
Yurcisin, John church official
Zakin, Jacques Louis chemical engineering educator
Zande, Richard Dominic civil engineering firm executive
Zapp, Robert Louis electronic test engineer
Zartman, David Lester animal sciences educator, researcher
Zuspan, Frederick Paul obstetrician, gynecologist, educator
Zweben, Stuart Harvey information scientist, educator

### Concord
Hanzak, Janice Chrisman accountant
Nielson, William Brooks clergyman
Whedon, Ralph Gibbs manufacturing executive

### Copley
Smith, Joan H. women's health nurse, educator

### Cortland
Lane, Sarah Marie Clark elementary education educator

### Coshocton
Parkhill, Harold Loyal artist

### Crestline
Maddy, Janet Marie retired educator, dean of students

### Cumberland
Reece, Robert William zoological park administrator

### Curtice
Hartman, Elizabeth Diane elementary education educator

### Cuyahoga Falls
Barsan, Robert Blake dentist
Haag, Everett Keith architect
Hahn, David Bennett hospital administrator, marketing professional
Moses, Abe Joseph international financial consultant
Shane, Sandra Kuli postal service administrator

### Dayton
Alexander, Roberta Sue history educator
Allen, Rose Letitia special education educator
†Ardis, David G. career officer
Arn, Kenneth Dale physician, city official
Ballal, Dilip Ramchandra mechanical engineering educator
Battino, Rubin chemistry educator, retired
Bedell, Kenneth Berkley computer specialist, educator
Berrey, Robert Forrest lawyer
Betz, Eugene William architect
Bohanon, Kathleen Sue neonatologist, educator
Bowman, Ed school administrator
Brown, William Milton electrical engineering educator
Burick, Lawrence T. lawyer
Byczkowski, Janusz Zbigniew toxicologist
Cawood, Albert McLaurin (Hap Cawood) newspaper editor
Chabali, Raul pediatrician
Chait, William librarian, consultant
Chelle, Robert Frederick electric power industry executive
Chernesky, Richard John lawyer
Christensen, Julien Martin psychologist, educator
Clark, William Alfred federal judge
†Cohen, Steven Michael internist, health facility administrator
Conway, Mark Allyn lawyer
Coulton, Martha Jean Glasscoe library consultant
Cowden, Roger Hugh, II systems engineer
Crowe, Shelby educational specialist, consultant
†Cruikshank, Stephen Herrick physician, consultant
Daley, Robert Emmett foundation executive, retired
†Dalrymple, Cheryl online information company executive
†Davies, Tim online information company executive
DeWall, Richard Allison retired surgeon
†Dunn, Margaret Mary general surgeon
Duval, Daniel Webster manufacturing company executive
Elliott, Daniel Whitacre surgeon, retired educator
Emrick, Donald Day chemist, consultant
Enouen, William Albert paper corporation executive
Fang, Zhaoqiang research physicist
Finn, Chester Evans lawyer
Fitz, Brother Raymond L. university president
Flack, Mignon Scott-Palmer elementary educator
Fridrick, M. Rogene gerontology educator, retired social worker
Fulton, Darrell Nelson information systems specialist
Garcia, Oscar Nicolas computer science educator
Gardner, Charles Clifford, Jr. colorectal surgeon
Gies, Frederick John education educator
Glasgow, D. Gerald polymer engineering researcher
Goldenberg, Kim university dean, internist
Gottschlich, Gary William lawyer
Gray, Edman Lowell metal distribution company executive
Gregor, Clunie Bryan geology educator
Gutmann, Max department store executive
Hadley, Robert James lawyer
Halki, John Joseph retired military officer, physician
Hanna, Marsha L. artistic director
Harden, Oleta Elizabeth English educator, university administrator
Harlan, Norman Ralph construction executive
Heath, Mariwyn Dwyer writer, legislative issues consultant
Heft, James Lewis academic administrator, theology educator
Heller, Abraham psychiatrist, educator
Heyman, Ralph Edmond lawyer
Hoge, Franz Joseph accounting firm executive
Houpis, Constantine Harry electrical engineering educator
Huffman, Dale journalist
Isaacson, Milton Stanley research and development company executive, engineer
Jacobs, Richard E. lawyer
Janning, John Louis research scientist, consultant
Jenefsky, Jack wholesale company executive
Jenks, Thomas Edward lawyer
Johnson, C. Terry lawyer
Kazimierczuk, Marian Kazimierz electrical engineer, educator
Kegerreis, Robert James management consultant, marketing educator
Khalimsky, Efim mathematics and computer science educator
Kinlin, Donald James lawyer
Klinck, Cynthia Anne library director
Knapp, James Ian Keith judge
Kogut, Maurice David pediatric endocrinologist
Ladehoff, Leo William metal products manufacturing executive
Langford, Roland Everett military officer, environmental scientist, author
Lashley, William Bartholomew county official
Lockhart, Gregory Gordon lawyer
Loughead, Jeffrey Lee physician
Macklin, Crofford Johnson, Jr. lawyer
Mandal, Anil Kumar nephrologist, medical educator
Martin, James Gilbert university provost emeritus
Mason, Steven Charles forest products company executive
Matheny, Ruth Ann editor
Mathews, David foundation executive
Mathile, Clayton Lee corporate executive
McCrabb, Donald Raymond religious ministry director
McCutcheon, Holly Marie accountant
McDonald, Bronce William community activist, advocate
McSwiney, Charles Ronald lawyer
Mc Swiney, James Wilmer retired pulp and paper manufacturing company executive
Merz, Michael federal judge
Miller, Kenneth Gregory retired air force officer
Miller, Tamara Dedra psychologist
Mitchell, Philip Michael aerospace engineer, consultant
Mohler, Stanley Ross physician, educator
Monk, Susan Marie physician, pediatrician
Nanagas, Maria Teresita Cruz pediatrician, educator
Nevin, Robert Charles information systems executive
Nixon, Charles William bioacoustician
Nyerges, Alexander Lee museum director
O'Malley, Patricia critical care nurse
Peterson, Skip (Orley R. Peterson, III) newspaper photographer
Pflum, Barbara Ann pediatric allergist
Ponitz, David H. academic administrator
Porter, Walter Arthur retired judge
Price, Harry Steele, Jr. construction materials company executive
Randall, Vernellia lawyer, nurse, educator
Rapp, Gerald Duane lawyer, manufacturing company executive
†Reading, Anthony John business executive, accountant
Reid, Marilyn Joanne state legislator, lawyer
Rogers, Richard Hunter lawyer, business executive
Rowe, Joseph Everett electrical engineering educator, administrator
Ruffer, David Gray museum director, former college president
Savage, Joseph Scott physician, career officer
Schmitt, George Frederick, Jr. materials engineer
Schnier, David Christian marketing executive, author
Schwartzhoff, James Paul foundation executive
Shaw, George Bernard consulting engineer, educator
Shuey, John Henry diversified products company executive
Siegel, Ira T. publishing executive
Singhvi, Surendra Singh finance and strategy consultant
Spicer, John Austin physicist
Stander, Joseph William mathematics educator, former university official
Taylor, Elisabeth Coler secondary school educator
Tillson, John Bradford, Jr. newspaper publisher
Uphoff, James Kent education educator
Versic, Linda Joan nurse educator, research company executive
Von Gierke, Henning Edgar biomedical science educator, former government official, researcher
Walden, James William accountant, educator
Walters, Jefferson Brooks musician, retired real estate broker
Weinberg, Sylvan Lee cardiologist, educator, author, editor
Wertz, Kenneth Dean real estate executive
Whitlock, David C. retired military officer
Williams, Michael Alan psychologist
Wilson, Robert M. financial executive
†Wilson, William C.M. gastroenterologist
Zahner, Mary Anne art educator

### Defiance
Harris, James Thomas, III college administrator, educator
Kane, Jack Allison physician, county administrator
Mirchandaney, Arjan Sobhraj mathematics educator
Thiede, Richard Wesley communications educator

### Delaware
Courtice, Thomas Barr academic administrator
Eells, William Hastings retired automobile company executive
Fry, Anne Evans zoology educator
Mendenhall, Robert Vernon mathematics educator
Schlichting, Catherine Fletcher Nicholson librarian, educator

### Delphos
Clark, Edward Ferdnand lawyer
Staup, John Gary safety engineer

### Delta
Miller, Beverly White past college president, education consultation

### Dresden
Reidy, Thomas Anthony lawyer

### Dublin
Baker, Mary Evelyn church librarian, retired academic librarian
Clement, Henry Joseph, Jr. diversified building products executive
Conrad, Marian Sue (Susan Conrad) special education educator
Cornwell, Paul M., Jr. architect
Freytag, Donald Ashe management consultant
Gores, Gary Gene credit union executive
Graham, Bruce Douglas pediatrician
Heffron, Robert F. manufacturing company executive
Heneman, Robert Lloyd management educator
Jolly, Barbara Lee home healthcare professional
Lamp, Benson J. tractor company executive
Madigan, Joseph Edward financial executive, consultant, director
Major, Coleman Joseph chemical engineer
Powell, Ernestine Breisch retired lawyer
Roeder, Rebecca Emily software engineer
Smith, K(ermit) Wayne computer company executive
Walter, Robert D. wholesale pharmaceutical distribution executive

### Duncan Falls
Cooper, April Helen nurse

### East Cleveland
Soule, Lucile Snyder pianist, music educator

### East Sparta
Cook, Martha Jane educator, counselor

### Eaton
Kendall, Susan Haines library director
Rinehart, Kathryn Ann principal
Thomas, James William lawyer

### Elyria
Eady, Carol Murphy (Mrs. Karl Ernest Eady) medical association administrator
Kennard, Emily Marie secondary school art educator, watercolor artist
Kreighbaum, John Scott banker
Kuchynski, Marie physician
Patton, Thomas James sales and marketing executive
Pucko, Diane Bowles public relations executive
Skillicorn, Judy Pettibone gifted and talented education coordinator
Wood, Jacalyn Kay education educator, educational consultant

### Englewood
Shearer, Velma Miller clergywoman

### Euclid
Clements, Mary Margaret retired educator
Keay, Charles Lloyd elementary school educator
Parks, John Morris metallurgist

### Fairborn
Leffler, Carole Elizabeth mental health nurse, women's health nurse
Nowak, John Michael retired air force officer, company executive
Seymour, Joyce Ann elementary school educator

### Fairfield
Goodman, Myrna Marcia school nurse
Lapp, Susan Bolster learning disability educator
Nichols, David L. retail executive
Robertson, Oscar Palmer (Big O Robertson) former professional basketball player, chemical company executive
Seed, Allen H. elementary and secondary education educator, science educator

### Fairlawn
Bonsky, Jack Alan chemical company executive, lawyer
Gibson, Charles Colmery former rubber manufacturing executive

**Fairport Harbor**
Kirchner, James William *retired electrical engineer*

**Findlay**
Gorr, Ivan William *retired rubber company executive*
Jetton, Girard Reuel, Jr. *lawyer, retired oil company executive*
Kremer, Fred, Jr. *manufacturing company executive*
Martin, Jim G. *church renewal consultant*
Rave, James A. *bishop*
Reynolds, Robert Gregory *toxicologist, management consultant*
Stephani, Nancy Jean *social worker, journalist*
Wilkin, Richard Edwin *clergyman, religious organization executive*
Yammine, Riad Nassif *oil company executive*

**Forest Park**
Ashley, Lynn *educator, consultant, administrator*

**Franklin**
Murray, Thomas Dwight *advertising agency executive*

**Fremont**
Bridges, Roger Dean *historical agency administrator*
Wethington, Norbert Anthony *medieval scholar*

**Gahanna**
Penn, Gerald Melville *pathologist*
Sherman, Ruth Todd *government advisor, counselor, consultant*
Smith, Brenda Joyce *author, editor, social studies educator*

**Galion**
Cobey, Ralph *industrialist*
Ross, Shirley S. *retired English educator*

**Gallipolis**
Clarke, Oscar Withers *physician*
Niehm, Bernard Frank *mental health center administrator*

**Gambier**
Sharp, Ronald Alan *English literature educator, author*

**Gates Mills**
Abbott, James Samuel, III *marketing executive*
Enyedy, Gustav, Jr. *chemical engineer*
Pace, Stanley Carter *retired aeronautical engineer*
Schanfarber, Richard Carl *real estate broker*
Veale, Tinkham, II *former chemical company executive, engineer*

**Geneva**
Gambill, Terry A. *manufacturing executive*

**Georgetown**
Rose, Beverly Anne *pharmacist*

**Germantown**
Lansaw, Charles Ray *sales industry executive*

**Girard**
Gaylord, Sanford Fred *physician*

**Granville**
Haubrich, Robert Rice *biology educator*
Myers, Michele Tolela *university president*
Santoni, Ronald Ernest *philosophy educator*

**Grove City**
Black, Frances Patterson *library administrator*
Funk, John William *emergency vehicle manufacturing executive, packaging company executive, lawyer*
Kilman, James William *surgeon, educator*
Purdy, Dennis Gene *insurance company executive, education consultant*

**Groveport**
Keck, Vicki Lynn *special education educator*
Ricart, Fred *automotive company executive*

**Hamilton**
Belew, David Lee *retired paper manufacturing company executive*
Conditt, Margaret Karen *scientist, policy analyst*
Erbe, Janet Sue *medical surgical, orthopedics and pediatrics nurse*
Johnson, Pauline Benge *nurse, anesthetist*
Marcum, Joseph LaRue *insurance company executive*
New, Rosetta Holbrock *home economics educator, nutrition consultant*
Patch, Lauren Nelson *insurance company, chief executive officer*
Pontius, Stanley N. *bank holding company executive*
Robertson, Jerald Lee *physicist*
Sebastian, Sandra Mary Thompson *mental health counselor, social worker*

**Harrison**
Everett, Karen J. *librarian*
Kocher, Juanita Fay *retired auditor*
Stoll, Robert W. *principal*

**Highland**
Taylor, Theresa Evereth *registered nurse, artist*

**Hilliard**
Cash, Francis Winford *hotel industry executive*
Cupp, David Foster *photographer, journalist*
†Longerbone, Doug *hotel executive*
Rahal, Robert W. *automotive company executive*

**Hillsboro**
Snyder, Harry Cooper *retired state senator*

**Hinckley**
Sprungl, Katherine Louise *nurse*

**Hiram**
Jagow, Elmer *retired college president*
Oliver, G(eorge) Benjamin *academic administrator, philosophy educator*

**Holland**
Kennedy, James L. *accountant*

**Holmesville**
Bolender, James Henry *tire and rubber manufacturing executive*

**Howard**
Lee, William Johnson *lawyer*

**Hubbard**
Rose, Ernst *dentist*

**Huber Heights**
Lee, Daniel Andrew *osteopathic physician, ophthalmologist*

**Hudson**
Galloway, Ethan Charles *technology development executive, former chemicals executive*
Giffen, Daniel Harris *lawyer, educator*
Goheen, Janet Moore *counselor, sales professional*
Kempe, Robert Aron *venture management executive*
Ong, John Doyle *lawyer*
Shaw, Doris Beaumar *film and video producer, executive recruiter*
Stec, John Zygmunt *real estate executive*
Wooldredge, William Dunbar *health facility administrator*

**Huron**
Clark, Thomas Garis *rubber products manufacturer*
Ruble, Ronald Merlin *humanities and theater communications educator*

**Independence**
Farling, Robert J. *utility company executive*
Hawkinson, Gary Michael *utility holding company executive*
Luciano, Gwendolyn Kaye *planning specialist, utility rates administrator*
Riedthaler, William Allen *risk management professional*

**Indian Springs**
Earley, Kathleen Sanders *municipal official*

**Jackson**
Lewis, Richard M. *lawyer*

**Jackson Center**
Thompson, Wade Francis Bruce *manufacturing company executive*

**Jamestown**
Liem, Darlene Marie *secondary education educator*

**Kent**
Anderson, William John, II *engineering and business management consultant*
†Andrews, Charles Forrest *radio station official*
Beer, Barrett Lynn *historian, educator*
Bissler, Richard Thomas *mortician*
Buttlar, Rudolph Otto *retired college dean*
Byrne, Frank Loyola *history educator*
Cartwright, Carol Ann *university president*
Centuori, Jeanine Gail *architecture educator*
Cooperrider, Tom Smith *botanist*
Cummins, Kenneth Burdette *retired science and mathematics educator*
Dante, Harris Loy *history educator*
Doane, J. William *physics educator and researcher, science administrator*
Fultz, John Howard *elementary school educator*
Gould, Edwin Sheldon *chemist, educator*
Harkness, Bruce *English language educator*
Hassler, Donald Mackey, II *English language educator, writer*
Heimlich, Richard Allen *geologist, educator*
James, Patricia Ann *philosophy educator*
Kwong, Eva *artist, educator*
Nome, William Andreas *lawyer*
Reid, Sidney Webb *English educator*
Rubin, Patricia *internist*
Schwartz, Michael *university president, sociology educator*
Smith, William Robert *utility company executive*
Stackelberg, Olaf Patrick Von *mathematician*
Stevenson, Thomas Herbert *management consultant, writer*
Tuan, Debbie Fu-Tai *chemistry educator*
Varga, Richard Steven *mathematics educator*
Williams, Harold Roger *economist, educator*
Zornow, William Frank *historian, educator*

**Kettering**
Caldabaugh, Karl *paper company executive*
Horn, Charles F. *state senator, lawyer, electrical engineer*
Mantil, Joseph Chacko *nuclear medicine physician, researcher*
Taylor, Billie Wesley *retired secondary education educator*

**Kingston**
Mathew, Martha Sue Cryder *retired education educator*

**Kirtland**
Munson, Richard Howard *horticulturist*
Skerry, Philip John *English educator*

**Lakewood**
Berman, Phillip Lee *religious institute administrator, author*
Bradley, J. F., Jr. *retired manufacturing company executive*
Cochran, Earl Vernon *retired manufacturing company executive*
O'Hara, Tamara Lynn *public health nurse, consultant*

**Lancaster**
Burns, Glenn Richard *dentist*
Fox, Robert Kriegbaum *manufacturing company executive*
Gault, Teressa Elaine *special education educator*
Gogate, Shashi Anand *pathologist*
Hurley, Samuel Clay, III *investment management company executive*
Huston, John Timothy *electrical engineer*
Katlic, John Edward *management consultant*

**Libert**, Donald Joseph *lawyer*
Phillips, Edward John *consulting firm executive*
Snider, Gordon B. *retired medical educator*
Varney, Richard Alan *medical office manager*
Voss, Jack Donald *international business consultant, lawyer*
Wagonseller, James Myrl *real estate executive*

**Lebanon**
Deyo, Wendel *sports association administrator*
Holtkamp, Dorsey Emil *medical research scientist*

**Lewis Center**
Strip, Carol Ann *gifted education specialist, educator*

**Lima**
Becker, Dwight Lowell *physician*
Collins, William Thomas *retired pathologist*
Cupp, Robert Richard *state senator, attorney*
Dicke, Candice Edwards *library educator*
Meek, Violet Imhof *dean*
Pranses, Anthony Louis *retired electric company executive, organization executive*
Robenalt, John Alton *lawyer*
Wangler, Mark Adrian *anesthesiologist*

**Lodi**
Cox, Hillery Lee *primary school educator*

**Logan**
Carmean, Jerry Richard *broadcast engineer*
Dillon, Neal Winfield *lawyer*

**London**
Hughes, Clyde Matthew *religious denomination executive*

**Lorain**
†Buzas, John William *hospital administrator, surgical nurse*

**Louisville**
Shadle, Donna A. Francis *principal*

**Loveland**
Anderson, Roy Alan *chemical engineer*

**Lucasville**
Reno, Ottie Wayne *former judge*

**Lyndhurst**
Dellas, Marie C. *retired psychology educator and consultant*

**Lyons**
Myers, John William *minister, poet, editor, publisher*

**Magnolia**
Zimmerman, Judith Rose *elementary art educator*

**Maineville**
Collins, Larry Wayne *small business owner, information systems specialist*

**Manchester**
McCluskey, Matthew Clair *physical chemist*

**Mansfield**
Beiter, Thomas Albert *crystallographer, research scientist, consultant*
Benham, Lelia *small business owner, social/political activist*
Ellison, Lorin Bruce *management consultant*
Gorman, James Carvill *pump manufacturing company executive*
Gregory, Thomas Bradford *mathematics educator*
Haldar, Frances Louise *business educator, accountant, treasurer*
Houston, William Robert Montgomery *ophthalmic surgeon*
Pesec, David John *data systems executive*
Reese, Wina Harner *speech pathologist, consultant*
Riedl, John Orth *university dean*
Shah, James M. *actuarial consultant*
Sheridan, Mark William *mechanical engineer, strategic planner*

**Mantua**
Ray, James Allen *research consultant*

**Maple Heights**
Sargent, Liz Elaine (Elizabeth Sargent) *safety consulting executive*

**Marblehead**
Haering, Edwin Raymond *chemical engineering educator, consultant*

**Marietta**
Fields, William Albert *lawyer*
Hausser, Robert Louis *lawyer*
Montgomery, Jerry Lynn *education educator*
Tipton, Jon Paul *allergist*
Wilbanks, Jan Joseph *philosopher*
Wilson, Lauren Ross *academic administrator*

**Martins Ferry**
Gracey, Robert William *account executive, minister*

**Marysville**
Baik-Kromalic, Sue S. *metallurgical engineer*
Covault, LLoyd R., Jr. *hospital administrator, psychiatrist*
Hines, Anthony Loring *automotive executive*
Jones-Morton, Pamela *human resources specialist*
Rogula, James Leroy *consumer products company executive*

**Mason**
Cettel, Judith Hapner *artist, secondary school educator*
Clements, Michael Craig *health services consulting executive, retired renal dialysis technician*

**Massillon**
Barr, Dixie Lou *geriatrics nurse*
Dawson, Robert Earle *utilities executive*
Fogle, Marilyn Louise Kiplinger *hospital administrator*

**Lin**, Edward Daniel *anesthesiologist, inventor*

**Materials Park**
Putnam, Allan Ray *association executive*

**Maumee**
Anderson, Richard Paul *agricultural company executive*
Kline, James Edward *lawyer*
Marsh, Benjamin Franklin *lawyer*
Tigges, Kenneth Edwin *retired financial executive*
Walrod, David James *retail grocery chain executive*
Zaliouk, Yuval Nathan *conductor*

**Mayfield Heights**
O'Brien, Frank B. *manufacturing executive*
Rankin, Alfred Marshall, Jr. *business executive*

**Mayfield Village**
Pavlovich, Donald *educator, support person*

**Mc Arthur**
Shuter, David Henry *foreign language educator*

**Mechanicsburg**
Maynard, Joan *education educator*

**Medina**
Ballard, John Stuart *retired law educator, former mayor*
Batchelder, Alice M. *federal judge*
Brown, Kathryn Lisbeth *secondary education educator*
Hunter, Brinca Jo *education specialist*
Noreika, Joseph Casimir *ophthalmologist*
Smith, Richey *chemical company executive*
Sullivan, Thomas Christopher *coatings company executive*
Walcott, Robert *healthcare executive, priest*

**Mentor**
Andrassy, Timothy Francis *trade association executive*
Barna, Kenneth James *design engineer*
Core, Harry Michael *psychiatric social worker, mental health therapist/administrator*
Davis, Barbara Snell *principal*
Driggs, Charles Mulford *lawyer*
Miller, Frances Suzanne *historic site curator*

**Miamisburg**
Northrop, Stuart Johnston *manufacturing company executive*

**Middleburg Heights**
Hartman, Lenore Anne *physical therapist*
Maciuszko, Kathleen Lynn *librarian, educator*

**Middletown**
Clinton, Mariann Hancock *educational association administrator*
Gilby, Steve *metallurgical engineering researcher*
Gilmore, June Ellen *psychologist*
Kemerling, James Lee *paper company executive*
Newby, John Robert *metallurgical engineer*
Rathman, William Ernest *lawyer, minister*
Redding, Barbara J. *nursing administrator, occupational health nurse*

**Milan**
Henry, Joseph Patrick *chemical company executive*

**Milford**
Donahue, John Lawrence, Jr. *paper company executive*
Kenton, James Alan *healthcare products executive*
Klosterman, Albert Leonard *technical development business executive, mechanical engineer*
Mechlem, Daphne Jo *vocational school educator*
Shipley, Tony L(ee) *software company executive*
Vorholt, Jeffrey Joseph *lawyer, software company executive*
Zimov, Bruce Steven *software engineer*

**Millersburg**
Childers, Lawrence Jeffrey *superintendent of schools*

**Minerva**
Koniecko, Mary Ann *elementary education educator*

**Mogadore**
Kelly, Janice Helen *elementary school educator*
Sonnhalter, Carolyn Therese *physical therapist, consultant*

**Mount Saint Joseph**
Roach, Sister Jeanne *nun, hospital administrator*

**Mount Vernon**
Nease, Stephen Wesley *college president*
Turner, Harry Edward *lawyer*

**Nelsonville**
Caplinger, James Clair *theatrical producer*

**New Albany**
Kessler, John Whitaker *real estate developer*

**New Carlisle**
Peters, Elizabeth Ann Hampton *nursing educator*

**New Concord**
Brown, Karen Rima *orchestra manager, Spanish language educator*
Speck, Samuel Wallace, Jr. *academic administrator*

**New Middletown**
Ade, Barbara Jean *secondary education educator*

**New Philadelphia**
Doughten, Mary Katherine (Molly Doughten) *retired secondary education educator*
Goforth, Mary Elaine Davey *secondary education educator*

**New Richmond**
Reynolds, Ronald Davison *family physician*
Scott, Michael Lester *artist, educator*

**Newark**
Fortaleza, Judith Ann *school system administrator*
Greenstein, Julius Sidney *zoology educator*
Hopson, James Warren *publishing executive*
Mantonya, John Butcher *lawyer*
McConnell, William Thompson *commercial banker*
Perera, Vicumpriya Sriyantha *mathematics educator*

**Newcomerstown**
Foley, Tracy Yevonne Lichtenfels *special education educator*

**Niles**
Cornell, William Harvey *clergyman*
Darlington, Oscar Gilpin *historian, educator*
Travaglini, Raymond Dominic *corporate executive*
Yancura, Ann Joyce *library director*

**North Canton**
Dettinger, Warren Walter *lawyer*
Foster, James Caldwell *academic dean, historian*
Lynham, C(harles) Richard *foundry company executive*

**North Olmsted**
Brady, Michael Cameron *investment consultant*
Galysh, Robert Alan *information systems analyst*
Hughes, Kenneth G. *elementary school educator*
Lundin, Bruce Theodore *engineering and management consultant*

**North Ridgeville**
Haddox, Arden Ruth Stewart *automotive aftermarket manufacturing executive*
Nagy, Robert David *tenor*

**North Royalton**
Michak, Helen Barbara *nurse, educator*

**Northfield**
Gupta, Kishan Chand *psychologist*

**Norwalk**
Burrell, Joel Brion *neuroimmunologist, researcher, clinician*
Carpenter, Paul Leonard *retired lawyer*
Germann, Richard Paul *pharmaceutical company chemist, executive*
Gutowicz, Matthew Francis, Jr. *radiologist*

**Norwood**
Wilson, William Alexander *manufacturing engineer*

**Novelty**
Miller, Dwight Richard *cosmetologist, corporate executive, hair designer*

**Oak Harbor**
Robertson, Jerry D. *lawyer*

**Oberlin**
Blodgett, Geoffrey Thomas *history educator*
Boe, David Stephen *musician, educator, college dean*
Care, Norman Sydney *philosophy educator*
Carlton, Terry Scott *chemist, educator*
Colish, Marcia Lillian *history educator*
Distelhorst, Garis Fred *trade association executive*
Dye, Nancy Schrom *academic administrator, history educator*
English, Ray *library administrator*
Friedman, William John *psychology educator*
Gladieux, Bernard Louis *management consultant*
Greenberg, Eva Mueller *librarian*
Jonesco, Jane Riggs *lawyer, development officer*
Layman, Emma McCloy (Mrs. James W. Layman) *psychologist, educator*
MacKay, Alfred F. *dean, philosophy educator*
Reinoehl, Richard Louis *artist, scholar, martial artist*
Simonson, Bruce Miller *geologist, educator*
Spear, Richard Edmund *art history educator*
Startup, Charles Harry *airline executive*
Stinebring, Warren Richard *microbiologist, educator*
Swank, Emory Coblentz *world affairs consultant, lecturer*
Tacha, Athena *sculptor, educator*
Taylor, Richard Wirth *political science educator*
Williams, Eleanor Joyce *government air traffic control specialist*
Young, David Pollock *humanities educator, author*
Zinn, Grover Alfonso, Jr. *religion educator*

**Oregon**
Crain, John Kip *school system administrator*
Culver, Robert Elroy *osteopathic physician*

**Oxford**
Baldwin, Arthur Dwight, Jr. *geology educator*
Brown, Edward Maurice *retired lawyer, business executive*
Cox, James Allan *chemistry educator*
Davis, Sherie Kay *special education educator*
Dizney, Robert Edward *retired secondary education educator*
Eshbaugh, W(illiam) Hardy *botanist, educator*
Gordon, Gilbert *chemist, educator*
Haley-Oliphant, Ann Elizabeth *science educator*
Heimsch, Charles *retired botany educator*
Macklin, Philip Alan *physics educator*
Miller, Harvey Alfred *botanist, educator*
Paulin, Henry Sylvester *antiques dealer, emeritus educator*
Pearson, Paul Guy *academic administrator emeritus*
Pont, John *football coach, educator*
Pratt, William Crouch, Jr. *English language educator, writer*
Pringle, Lewis Gordon *marketing professional, educator*
Rejai, Mostafa *political science educator*
Sanders, Gerald Hollie *communications educator*
Sessions, Judith Ann *librarian, university library dean*
Shriver, Phillip Raymond *academic administrator*
Siatra, Eleni *English educator*
Thompson, Bertha Boya *retired education educator, antique dealer and appraiser*
Ward, Roscoe Fredrick *engineering educator*
Williamson, Clarence Kelly *microbiologist, educator*
Wilson, James Ray *international business educator*
Winkler, Allan Michael *history educator*

**Painesville**
Clement, Daniel Roy, III *accountant, assistant nurse, small business owner*
Humphrey, George Magoffin, II *plastic molding company executive*
Jayne, Theodore Douglas *technical research and development company executive*
Lemr, James Charles *geriatrics nurse*
Lucier, P. Jeffrey *publishing and computer company executive*
Scozzie, James Anthony *chemist*

**Parma**
Bate, Brian R. *psychologist*
Cook, Jeanne Garn *historian, genealogist*
McFadden, Nadine Lynn *secondary education Spanish educator*
Moskal, Robert M. *bishop*
Mottl, Ronald M. *state legislator, lawyer*
Nemeth, Dian Jean *secondary school educator*
Tener, Carol Joan *retired secondary education educator*

**Peninsula**
Brobeck, David George *middle school administrator*
Ludwig, Richard Joseph *ski resort executive*

**Pepper Pike**
Bray, Pierce *business consultant*
Froelich, Wolfgang Andreas *neurologist*
Mc Call, Julien Lachicotte *banker*
Mc Innes, Robert Malcolm *lawyer, business consultant*
Vail, Thomas Van Husen *retired newspaper publisher and editor*

**Perrysburg**
Autry, Carolyn *artist, art history educator*
Barbe, Betty Catherine *financial analyst*
Eastman, John Richard *retired manufacturing company executive*
Khan, Amir U. *agricultural engineering consultant*
Schwier, Priscilla Lamb Guyton *television broadcasting company executive*
Weaver, Richard L., II *writer, speaker, educator*
Williamson, John Pritchard *utility executive*
Yager, John Warren *retired banker, lawyer*

**Pickerington**
Zacks, Gordon Benjamin *manufacturing company executive*

**Piketon**
Manuta, David Mark *research chemist*

**Port Clinton**
Subler, Edward Pierre *advertising executive*

**Portsmouth**
Christensen, Margaret Anna *nursing educator, consultant*
Davis, Donald W. *government official*
Horr, William Henry *lawyer*
Mirabello, Mark Linden *history educator*
Stead, Francesca Manuela Lewenstein *natural health care consultant, massage therapist*

**Powell**
Miller, Charles *business management research and measurements consultant*
Reed, Constance Louise *materials management and purchasing consultant*
Schwab, Glenn Orville *retired agricultural engineering educator, consultant*

**Randolph**
Pecano, Donald Carl *truck trailer manufacturing executive*

**Reynoldsburg**
Goostree, Robert Edward *political science and law educator*
Powell, Edward Lee *broadcasting company executive*
Serraglio, Mario *architect*
Woodward, Greta Charmaine *construction company executive*

**Richfield**
Calise, Nicholas James *lawyer*
Heider, Jon Vinton *lawyer, corporate executive*
Schulz, Mary Elizabeth *lawyer*
Tobler, D. Lee *chemical and aerospace company executive*

**Richmond**
Martin, Clara Rita *elementary education educator*

**Rocky River**
De Long, Erika Venta *psychiatrist*
Slaby, Lillian Frances *home finance counselor, real estate professional*

**Rootstown**
Blacklow, Robert Stanley *physician, medical college administrator*
Campbell, Colin *obstetrician, gynecologist, school dean*

**Saint Clairsville**
Bearce, Peter James *accountant*
Dankworth, Margaret Anne *management consultant*
Sidon, Claudia Marie *psychiatric and mental health nursing educator*

**Salem**
Barcey, Harold Edward Dean (Hal Barcey) *real estate counselor*
Fehr, Kenneth Manbeck *computer systems company executive*
Moss, Susan *nurse, retail store owner*

**Sandusky**
Duttera, Brian Cleve *financial consultant and sales manager*
Riedy, Virginia Kathleen *nursing educator*
Round, Alice Faye Bruce *school psychologist*

**Seven Hills**
Stanczak, Julian *artist, educator*

**Shaker Heights**
Boyd, Arthur Bernette, Jr. *surgeon, clergyman, beverage company executive*
Donnem, Sarah Lund *financial analyst, non-profit and political organization consultant*
†Eakin, Thomas Capper *sports promotion executive*
Ellett, Alan Sidney *real estate development company executive*
Feuer, Michael *office supply store executive*
Held, Lila M. *art appraiser*
McKenna, Kathleen Kwasnik *artist*

**Shelby**
Moore Moif, Florian Howard *electronics engineer*
Schaefer, Jon Patrick *judge, lawyer*

**Sidney**
Laurence, Michael Marshall *magazine publisher, writer*
Lawrence, Wayne Allen *publisher*
Stevens, Robert Jay *magazine editor*

**Solon**
Rosica, Gabriel Adam *corporate executive, engineer*
Stauffer, Thomas George *hotel executive*

**South Euclid**
Adler, Naomi Samuel *real estate counselor*
Conrad, Sister Linda *elementary school educator*

**Springboro**
Ramey, Rebecca Ann *elementary education educator*
Saxer, Richard Karl *metallurgical engineer, retired air force officer*

**Springfield**
Browne, William Bitner *lawyer*
Dominick, Charles Alva *college official*
Harkins, Daniel Conger *lawyer*
Kinnison, William Andrew *retired university president*
Kurian, Pius *physician*
Lagos, James Harry *lawyer*
Maddex, Myron Brown (Mike Maddex) *broadcasting executive*
Maki, Jerrold Alan *health system executive*
Patterson, Martha Ellen *artist, art educator*
Ryu, Kyoo-Hai Lee *physiologist*
Wood, Dirk Gregory *surgeon, physician, forensic consultant*

**Steubenville**
Hall, Alan Craig *library director*
Scanlan, Michael *priest, academic administrator*
Sheldon, Gilbert Ignatius *clergyman*

**Stow**
Hooper, Blake Howard *manufacturing executive*

**Streetsboro**
Kearns, Warren Kenneth *business executive*
Weiss, Joseph Joel *consulting company executive*

**Strongsville**
Mills, S. Loren *product safety manager, engineer*
Oltman, C. Dwight *conductor, educator*

**Sugar Grove**
Bonner, Herbert Dwight *construction management educator*
Young, Nancy Henrietta Moe *elementary education educator*

**Sunbury**
Jinks-Weidner, Janie *editor*

**Sylvania**
Bergsmark, Edwin Martin *mortgage bank executive*
Colasurd, Richard Michael *lawyer*
Heuschele, Sharon Jo *university program director*
Kneller, William Arthur *geologist, educator*
Lock, Richard William *packaging company executive*
Rabideau, Margaret Catherine *media center director*
Ring, Herbert Everett *management executive*
Sampson, Earldine Robison *education educator*
Sampson, Wesley Claude *auditor*
Verhesen, Anna Maria Hubertina *counselor*

**Terrace Park**
Madewell, Mary Ann *nursing educator*

**Tiffin**
Davison, Kenneth Edwin *American studies educator*
Einsel, David William, Jr. *retired army officer and consultant*
Kramer, Frank Raymond *classicist, educator*
Talbot-Koehl, Linda Ann *dancer, ballet studio owner*

**Tipp City**
Dallura, Sal Anthony *physician*
Panayirci, Sharon Lorraine *textiles executive, design engineer*
Taylor, Robert Homer *quality assurance professional, pilot*
Tighe-Moore, Barbara Jeanne *electronics executive*

**Toledo**
Anspach, Robert Michael *lawyer*
Attoh, Samuel Aryeetey *geographer, educator, planner*
Baker, Richard Southworth *lawyer*
Barrett, Michael John *anesthesiologist*
Batt, Nick *property and investment executive*
Bedell, Archie William *family physician, educator*
Billups, Norman Fredrick *college dean, pharmacist*
Binkley, Jonathan Andrew *secondary education educator, government educator*
Block, Allan James *communications executive*
Block, John Robinson *newspaper publisher*
Block, William K., Jr. *newspaper executive*
Boesel, Milton Charles, Jr. *lawyer, business executive*
Boggs, Ralph Stuart *lawyer*
Boller, Ronald Cecil *glass company executive*
Brockmeyer, Ann Hartmann *financial planner*
Brown, Charles Earl *lawyer*
Carpenter, John Edward *marketing professional*
Carr, James Gray *judge*
Carson, Samuel Goodman *retired banker, company director*
Chakraborty, Joana *physiology educator, research center administrator*

Cole, Jeffrey Clark *corporate public relations executive*
Craig, Harald Franklin *lawyer*
Dalrymple, Thomas Lawrence *retired lawyer*
Depew, Charles Gardner *research company executive*
Farison, James Blair *electrical biomedical engineer, educator*
Finkbeiner, Carlton S. (Carty Finkbeiner) *mayor*
Fisher, Donald Wiener *lawyer*
Fuhrman, Charles Andrew *country club proprietor, real estate management executive, lawyer*
Hauenstein, Henry William *civil engineer*
Hawkins, Donald Merton *lawyer*
Heinrichs, Mary Ann *former dean*
Heywood, William H. *lawyer*
Hiett, Edward Emerson *retired lawyer, glass company executive*
Hills, Arthur W. *architectural firm executive*
Hiner, Glen Harold, Jr. *materials company executive*
Hirsch, Carl Herbert *manufacturing company executive*
Hoffman, James R. *bishop*
Horton, Frank Elba *university official, geography educator*
Hutton, William *art historian*
James, William *bishop*
Katz, David Allan *judge, former lawyer, business consultant*
Klein, James Martin *law educator, labor arbitrator*
Kneen, James Russell *health care administrator*
Kozbial, Richard James *elementary education educator*
Kunze, Ralph Carl *savings and loan executive*
La Rue, Carl Forman *lawyer*
Lawrence, Edmund P., Jr. *neurosurgeon*
Leech, Charles Russell, Jr. *lawyer*
Leighton, Richard F. *retired dean*
Lemieux, Joseph Henry *manufacturing company executive*
Loeffler, William Robert *quality productivity specialist, engineering educator*
Machin, Barbara E. *lawyer*
Markwood, Sandra Reinsel *human services administrator*
Martin, John Thomas *physician, author, educator*
Martin, Robert Edward *architect*
Massey, Andrew John *conductor, composer*
Mayhew, Harry Eugene *physician, educator*
McCormick, Edward James, Jr. *lawyer*
McGlauchlin, Tom *artist*
Miller, Barbara Kaye *lawyer*
Moon, Henry *dean*
Morcott, Southwood J. *automotive parts manufacturing company executive*
Mulrow, Patrick Joseph *medical educator*
Northup, John David *management consultant, inventor*
O'Connell, Maurice Daniel *lawyer*
Oh, Keytack Henry *industrial engineering educator*
Paquette, Jack Kenneth *management consultant, antiques dealer*
Pletz, Thomas Gregory *lawyer*
Potter, John William *federal judge*
Quick, Albert Thomas *law educator, university dean*
Reins, Ralph Erich *automotive components supply company executive*
Rejent, Marian Magdalen *pediatrician*
Riseley, Martha Suzannah Heater (Mrs. Charles Riseley) *psychologist, educator*
Romanoff, Milford Martin *building contractor*
Rosenbaum, Kenneth E. *journalist, editor*
Royhab, Ronald *journalist, newspaper editor*
Rubin, Allan Maier *physician, surgeon*
Saffran, Murray *biochemist*
St. Clair, Donald David *lawyer*
Sanderson, David Alan *training and development administrator*
Schultz, Warren Robert *manufacturing administrator*
Shelley, Walter Brown *physician, educator*
Smith, Robert Freeman *history educator*
Smith, Robert Nelson *former government official, anesthesiologist*
Spitzer, John Brumback *lawyer*
Stankey, Suzanne M. *editor*
Steadman, David Wilton *museum official*
Strobel, Martin Jack *motor vehicle and industrial component manufacturing and distribution company executive*
†Talmage, Lance Allen *obstetrician/gynecologist, career military officer*
Thompson, Gerald E. *historian, educator*
Tuschman, James Marshall *lawyer*
Webb, Thomas Irwin, Jr. *lawyer*
Weikel, Malcolm Keith *health care company executive*
West, Ann Lee *clinical nurse specialist, educator, trauma nurse coordinator*
Wicklund, David Wayne *lawyer*
Willey, John Douglas *retired newspaper executive*
Wolff, Edwin Ray *construction engineer*
Zrull, Joel Peter *psychiatry educator*

**Toronto**
Hoffman, Janet N. *psychic counselor*

**Trotwood**
Kiefer, Jacqueline Lorraine *special education educator, consultant*

**Troy**
Davies, Alfred Robert *physician, educator*
Deering, Joseph William *manufacturing executive*

**Twinsburg**
Hill, Thomas Allen *lawyer*
Mohr, Eileen Theresa *environmental geologist*
Novak, Harry R. *manufacturing company executive*
Solganik, Marvin *real estate executive*

**Uniontown**
Naugle, Robert Paul *dentist*

**University Heights**
Bloch, Andrea Lynn *physical therapist*
Epstein, Marvin Morris *retired construction executive*
Rothschild, Beryl Elaine *mayor*

**Upper Arlington**
Snyder, Susan Leach *science educator*

**Upper Sandusky**
Baker, Harrison Scott *computer consultant*
Schmidt, Janis Ilene *elementary education educator*

**Urbana**
Bronkar, Eunice Dunalee *artist, art educator*

**Valley View**
Miller, Susan Ann *school system administrator*
Van Kirk, Robert John *nursing case manager, educator*

**Van Wert**
Duprey, Wilson Gilliland *retired librarian*
Liljegren, Frank Sigfrid *artist, art association official*

**Vandalia**
Davis, Pamela J. *nursing educator*
Smith, Marjorie Aileen Matthews *museum director*

**Warren**
Alli, Richard James, Sr. *manufacturing executive*
Auchterlonie, David Thomas *quality assurance professional*
Brodell, Robert Thomas *internal medicine educator*
Dennison, David Short, Jr. *lawyer*
Kandrac, Jo Ann Marie *school administrator*
McFarland, Leslie King *special education educator*
Nader, Robert Alexander *judge, lawyer*
Rizer, Franklin Morris *physician, otolarynogologist*
Rossi, Anthony Gerald *lawyer*
Thompson, Eric Thomas *manufacturing company executive*
VanAuker, Lana Lee *recreational therapist, educator*
White, Martin Fred *lawyer*

**Washington Court House**
Fichthorn, Fonda Gay *principal*
Fultz, Clair Ervin *former banker*

**Waterford**
Maltby, Sue Ellen *special education educator*
Montgomery, Gretchen Golzé *secondary education educator*
Riley, Nancy Mae *retired vocational home economics educator*

**Waterville**
Brumbaugh, Kathleen Semo *journalist, historian, lay minister*

**Wauseon**
McNulty, Roberta Jo *educational administrator*

**Waverly**
Squire, Russel Nelson *musician, retired educator*
Turner, Elvin L. *retired educational administrator*

**West Alexandria**
Scoville, George Richard *marketing professional*

**West Chester**
Bahrani, Neda Jean *programmer/analyst, consultant*
Capps, Dennis William *secondary school educator*
Rishel, James Burton *manufacturing executive*

**West Union**
Carr, George Francis, Jr. *lawyer*

**Westerville**
Barr, John Michael *investment adviser, training and management consultant*
Dadmehr, Nahid *neurologist*
DeVore, Carl Brent *college president, educator*
Diersing, Carolyn Virginia *educational administrator*
Goh, Anthony Li-Shing *business owner, consultant*
Golladay, Loy Edgar *emeritus special educator*
Kerr, Thomas Jefferson, IV *academic official*
Kollat, David Truman *management consultant*
Lancione, Bernard Gabe *lawyer*
Lattimore, Joy Powell *preschool administrator*
Lawrence, Ralph Waldo *manufacturing company executive*
Schultz, Arthur LeRoy *clergyman, educator*
Smith, C. Kenneth *business executive*
Thompson, Claire Louisa *nurse, educator, administrator*
VanSant, Joanne Frances *academic administrator*
Williams, John Michael *physical therapist, sports medicine educator*
Willke, Thomas Aloys *university official, statistics educator*

**Westfield Center**
Blair, Cary *insurance company executive*
Nance, James Clifton *business consulting company executive*
Spinelli, Anne Catherine *elementary education educator*

**Westlake**
Barker, Keith Rene *investment banker*
Bisson, Edmond Emile *mechanical engineer*
Connelly, John James *retired oil company technical specialist*
Huff, Ronald Garland *mechanical engineer*
Whitehouse, John Harlan, Jr. *systems software consultant, diagnostician*
†Wozniak, Donald Richard *information systems executive*

**Whitehouse**
Howard, John Malone *surgeon, educator*

**Wickliffe**
Anthony, Donald Barrett *engineering executive*
Bardasz, Ewa Alice *chemical engineer*
Crehore, Charles Aaron *lawyer*
Dunn, Horton, Jr. *organic chemist*
Kidder, Fred Dockstater *lawyer*
Pevec, Anthony Edward *bishop*

**Wilberforce**
Gupta, Vijay Kumar *chemistry educator*
Svager, Thyrsa Anne Frazier *university administrator, retired educator*

**Willoughby**
Abelt, Ralph William *bank executive*
Baker, Charles Stephen *music educator*
Campbell, Talmage Alexander *newspaper editor*
Combs, Steven Paul *orthopedic surgeon*
Grossman, Mary Margaret *elementary education educator*
Manning, William Dudley, Jr. *retired specialty chemical company executive*
Pazirandeh, Mahmood *rheumatologist, consultant*
Stern, Michael David *dentist*

**Wilmington**
Hackney, Howard Smith *retired county official*
Schutt, Walter Eugene *lawyer*

**Wintersville**
Becker, William A(lbert) *real estate developer*

**Wooster**
August, Robert Olin *journalist*
Childers, Susan Lynn Bohn *special education educator, administrator, human resources and transition specialist, consultant*
Colclaser, H. Alberta *lawyer, retired government official*
Degnan, Martin J. *rubber products corporation executive, lawyer*
Ferree, David Curtis *horticultural researcher*
Gates, Richard Daniel *manufacturing company executive*
Geho, Walter Blair *biomedical research executive*
Hickey, Damon Douglas *library director*
Kennedy, Charles Allen *lawyer*
Kuffner, George Henry *dermatologist*
Lafever, Howard Nelson *plant breeder, geneticist, educator*
Loess, Henry Bernard *psychology educator*
Madden, Laurence Vincent *plant pathology educator*
Payne, Thomas L. *university official*
Schmitt, Wolfgang Rudolf *consumer products executive*
Stuart, James Fortier *musician, artistic director*

**Worthington**
Bernhagen, Lillian Flickinger *school health consultant*
Bilderback, George Garrison, III *human services manager*
Castner, Linda Jane *instructional technologist, nurse educator*
Compton, Ralph Theodore, Jr. *electrical engineering educator*
Craig, Judith *bishop*
Giannamore, David Michael *electronics engineer*
Lentz, Edward Allen *consultant, retired health administrator*
Rowe, Lisa Dawn *computer programmer/analyst, computer consultant*
Stone, Linda Chapman *physician, consultant, medical educator*
Trevor, Alexander Bruen *computer company executive*
Winter, Chester Caldwell *physician, surgery educator*

**Wright Patterson AFB**
†Adams, Wade *materials engineer, researcher*
†Babbitt, George T. *career officer*
†Back, Donna J. *career officer*
†Batterman, Thomas W. *civilian military employee*
Boff, Kenneth Richard *engineering research psychologist*
D'Azzo, John Joachim *electrical engineer, educator*
Eastwood, DeLyle *chemist*
Haritos, George Konstantinos *engineering educator, military officer*
King, Paul Irvin *aerospace engineering educator*
Rinta, Christine Evelyn *nurse, air force officer*
Scriggins, Alan Lee *developmental pediatrician*
Szucs, Andrew Eric *training manager*
Turner, Wade Slover *biochemist, pilot*
†Worthington, Walter Thomas *career military officer*

**Wyoming**
Cooley, William Edward *regulatory affairs manager*

**Xenia**
Bigelow, Daniel James *aerospace executive*
Morrison, Robert Townsend *nephrologist*
Nutter, Zoe Dell Lantis *retired public relations executive*

**Yellow Springs**
Begin, Jacqueline Sue *college administrator*
Fogarty, Robert Stephen *historian, educator, editor*
Graham, Jewel Freeman *social worker, lawyer, educator*
Guskin, Alan E. *university president*
Hamilton, Virginia (Mrs. Arnold Adoff) *author*
Jensen, Roger Christian *industrial engineer*
Spokane, Robert Bruce *biophysical chemist*
Trolander, Hardy Wilcox *engineering executive, consultant*
Webb, Paul *physician, researcher, consultant, educator*

**Youngstown**
Ausnehmer, John Edward *lawyer*
Bartlett, Shirley Anne *accountant*
Becker, Karen Ann *university program administrator*
Bell, Carol Willsey *genealogist*
Biehl, Jane M. *rehabilitation services professional*
Bowers, Bege K. *English educator*
Brothers, Barbara *English language educator*
Carlomagno, Stephen Guido *insurance company executive*
Catoline, Pauline Dessie *small business owner*
Courtney, William Francis *food and vending service company executive*
DeBartolo, Edward John, Jr. *professional football team owner, real estate developer*
Fok, Thomas Dso Yun *civil engineer*
Kenner, Marilyn Sferra *civil engineer*
Lacivita, Michael John *safety engineer*
Marks, Esther L. *metals company executive*
Messenger, James Louis *lawyer*
Mumaw, James Webster *lawyer*
Nadler, Myron Jay *lawyer*
Powers, Paul J. *manufacturing company executive*
Przelomski, Anastasia Nemenyi *retired newspaper editor*
Roth, Daniel Benjamin *lawyer, business executive*
†Rubin, Jeffrey Reed *vascular surgeon*
Sokolov, Richard Saul *real estate company executive*
Stevens, Paul Edward *lawyer*
Trucksis, Theresa A. *retired library director*
Tucker, Don Eugene *retired lawyer*
Walton, Ralph Gerald *psychiatrist, educator*
Wellman, Thomas Peter *lawyer*

**Zanesville**
Micheli, Frank James *lawyer*
O'Sullivan, Christine *executive director social service agency*
Ray, John Walker *otolaryngologist, educator, broadcast commentator*
Truby, John Louis *computer, management and trucking consultant*

**Zoar**
Fernandez, Kathleen M. *cultural organization administrator*

## OKLAHOMA

**Ada**
Anoatubby, Bill *governor*
Davison, Victoria Dillon *real estate executive*
Gray, Edna Jane *elementary education educator*
Mildren, Jack *legal services company executive, former state official*
Stafford, Donald Gene *chemistry educator*
Van Burkleo, Bill Ben *osteopath, emergency physician*

**Afton**
Starbird, Lonnie Darryl *producer of custom car shows, designer and builder of custom automobiles*

**Altus**
Hensley, Stephen Ray *academic administrator*

**Anadarko**
Pain, Charles Leslie *lawyer*

**Antlers**
Stamper, Joe Allen *lawyer*

**Ardmore**
Brennen, Patrick Wayne *library director*
Mynatt, Cecil Ferrell *psychiatrist*
Thompson, John E. *principal*

**Bartlesville**
Allen, W. Wayne *oil industry executive*
Austerman, Donna Lynne *Spanish language educator*
Clay, Harris Aubrey *chemical engineer*
Cox, Glenn Andrew, Jr. *petroleum company executive*
Doty, Donald D. *retired banker*
Dunlap, James Robert *contractor, state legislator*
Dwiggins, Claudius William, Jr. *chemist*
Funk, Vicki Jane *librarian*
Gao, Hong Wen *chemical engineer*
Hedrick, Kirby L. *petroleum company executive*
Hogan, J(ohn) Paul *chemistry researcher, consultant*
Johnson, Marvin Merrill *chemical engineer, chemist*
Mihm, John Clifford *chemical engineer*
Roff, Alan Lee *lawyer, consultant*
Sauter, Marsha Jeanne *elementary school educator*
Silas, Cecil Jesse *retired petroleum company executive*
Woodruff, Wanda Lea *elementary education educator*
Woodruff, William Jennings *theology educator*

**Beaver**
Kachel, Harold Stanley *museum curator*

**Bethany**
Arnold, Donald Smith *chemical engineer, consultant*
Corvin, William Rayford *administrator, educator, minister*
Davis, Harrison Ransom Samuel, Jr. *English language educator*
Leggett, James Daniel *church administrator*
Shelton, Muriel Moore *religious education administrator*

**Broken Arrow**
Chambers, Richard Lee *geoscientist, researcher*
Everett, Carl Nicholas *management consulting executive*
Janning, Sister Mary Bernadette *nun, retired association executive*
Roberson, Deborah Kay *secondary school educator*
Striegel, Peggy Simsarian *advertising executive*
Westerman, Rosemary Matzzie *nurse, administrator*

**Buffalo**
Anthony, Jack Ramon *mechanical engineer, retired*

**Chandler**
Mather, Stephanie J. *lawyer*

**Cherokee**
Mitchell, Allan Edwin *lawyer*

**Chickasha**
Beets, Freeman Haley *retired government official*
Good, Leonard Phelps *artist*

**Claremore**
Cesario, Sandra Kay *women's health nurse, educator*
Davis, Carol Anderson *school counselor*
Marshall, Linda Lantow *pediatrics nurse*
McClain, Marilyn Russell *university student counselor*
Shrum, Alicia Ann *elementary school educator, librarian*

**Clinton**
Askew, Penny Sue *choreographer, artistic director, ballet instructor*

**Cushing**
Draughon, Scott Wilson *lawyer, social worker*
†Kyker, James Charles *engineering executive, computer programmer*

**Duncan**
Surjaatmadja, Jim Basuki *research engineer*

**Durant**
Kennedy, Elizabeth Carol *psychologist, educator*
Weiner, Kathy Carole *secondary educator*
Williams, Larry Bill *academic administrator*

**Edmond**
Aclin, Keith Andrew *radar meteorologist*
Binning, Gene Barton *educator, management consultant*
Brown, William Ernest *dentist*
Caire, William *biologist, educator*
Lester, Andrew William *lawyer*
Lewis, Gladys Sherman *nurse, educator*
Loman, Mary LaVerne *retired mathematics educator*
Loving, Susan B. *lawyer, former state official*
McLaughlin, Lisa Marie *educational administrator*
Necco, E(dna) Joanne *school psychologist*
Nelson, John Woolard *neurology educator, physician*
Pydynkowsky, Joan Anne *journalist*
Shadid, Randel Coy *lawyer*
Smock, Donald Joe *governmental liaison, political consultant*
Troutman, George William *geologist, geological consulting firm executive*
Zabel, Vivian Ellouise *secondary education educator*

**El Reno**
Buendia, Imelda Bernardo *clinical director, physician*
Grantham, Robert Edward *lawyer, educator*
Phillips, William A. *research animal scientist*

**Enid**
Dandridge, William Shelton *orthopedic surgeon*
Jones, Stephen *lawyer*
Lopez, Francisco, IV *health care administrator*
Musser, William Wesley, Jr. *lawyer*
Rider, John Allen, II *business educator, paralegal*
Tabbernee, William *academic administrator, theology educator*
Taylor, Donna Lynne *adult education coordinator*
Ward, Llewellyn O(rcutt), III *oil company executive*
Wyatt, Robert Lee, IV *lawyer*

**Eucha**
Cole, Harold Spencer *engineer*

**Fort Sill**
Livingston, Douglas Mark *lawyer*

**Fort Towson**
Pike, Thomas Harrison *plant chemist*

**Guthrie**
Davis, Frank Wayne *lawyer*
Jenkins, Ferguson Arthur, Jr. (Fergie Jenkins) *former baseball player*

**Guymon**
Wood, Donald Euriah *lawyer*

**Hodgen**
Brower, Janice Kathleen *library technician*

**Jenks**
Wootan, Gerald Don *osteopathic physician, educator*

**Jennings**
Nixon, Arlie James *oil and gas company executive*

**Keota**
Davis, Thomas Pinkney *secondary school educator*

**Kingfisher**
Buswell, Arthur Wilcox *physician, surgeon*

**Konawa**
Rains, Mary Jo *banker*

**Langston**
Mallik, Muhammad Abdul-Bari *soil microbiologist*
Simpson, Ocleris C. *agricultural research administrator*

**Lawton**
Brooks, (Leslie) Gene *cultural association administrator*
Cates, Dennis Lynn *education educator*
Cooke, Wanda (Cookie Cooke) *hearing aid specialist*
Davis, Don Clarence *university president*
Davis, Ellen Marie *business educator*
Hensley, Ross Charles *dermatologist*
Hooper, Roy B. *hospital administrator, insurance broker*
Klein, Scott Richard *acting and directing educator*
Mayes, Glenn *social worker*
McKeown, Rebecca J. *principal*
Moore, Roy Dean *judge*
Neptune, Richard Allan (Dick Neptune) *superintendent of schools*
Smiley, Frederick Melvin *education educator, consultant*
Webb, O(rville) Lynn *physician, pharmacologist, educator*
Young, J. A. *bishop*

**Mangum**
Ford, Linda Lou *dietitian*

**Maramec**
Blair, Marie Lenore *retired elementary school educator*

**Mc Loud**
Whinery, Michael Albert *physician*

**Mcalester**
Cornish, Richard Pool *lawyer*

**Miami**
Dicharry, James Paul *company official, retired air force officer*
Taylor, Vesta Fisk *real estate broker, educator*
Vanpool, Cynthia Paula *special education educator, special services consultant*

**Midwest City**
Bogardus, Carl Robert, Jr. *radiologist, educator*
Saulmon, Sharon Ann *college librarian*
Smith, Wayne Calvin *chemical engineer*

**Minco**
Strange, Frances Rathbun *financial aid administrator, therapist*

**Moore**
Harrington, Gary Burnes *retired controller*

**Muskogee**
Kendrick, Thomas Rudolph *chemist*
Kent, Bartis Milton *physician*
Meyer, Billie Jean *special education educator*
Robinson, Adelbert Carl *lawyer, judge*
Ruby, Russell (Glenn) *lawyer*
Seay, Frank Howell *federal judge*

**Mustang**
Laurent, J(erry) Suzanna *technical communications specialist*

**Norman**
Affleck, Marilyn *sociology educator*
Albert, Lois Eldora Wilson *archaeologist*
Altan, M(ustafa) Cengiz *mechanical engineering educator*
Atkinson, Gordon *chemistry educator*
Bell, Robert Eugene *anthropologist educator*
Bert, Charles Wesley *mechanical and aerospace engineer, educator*
Bluestein, Howard Bruce *meteorology educator*
Boren, David Lyle *academic administrator*
Brown, Sidney DeVere *history educator*
Campbell, John Morgan *retired chemical engineer*
Carey, Thomas Devore *baritone, educator*
Carpenter, Charles Congden *zoologist, educator*
Carver, Charles Ray *retired information systems company executive*
Cella, Francis Raymond *economist, research consultant*
Christian, Sherril D. *chemistry educator, administrator*
Ciereszko, Leon Stanley *chemistry educator*
Cochran, Gloria Grimes *pediatrician, retired*
Corr, Edwin Gharst *ambassador*
Cosier, Richard A. *business educator, consultant*
Crane, Robert Kendall *engineering educator, researcher, consultant*
Cross, George Lynn *foundation administrator, former university president*
Dalton, Deborah Whitmore *dean*
Dary, David Archie *journalism educator, author*
Dille, John Robert *physician*
Donahue, Hayden Hackney *mental health institute administrator, medical educator, psychiatric consultant*
Dryhurst, Glenn *chemistry educator*
Eek, Nathaniel Sisson *retired fine arts educator*
Egle, Davis Max *mechanical engineering educator*
Elkouri, Frank *law educator*
Evans, Rodney Earl *business educator*
Fairbanks, Robert Alvin *lawyer*
Fears, Jesse Rufus *historian, educator, academic dean*
Fuerbringer, Alfred Ottomar *clergyman*
Glad, Paul Wilbur *history educator*
Hagan, William Thomas *history educator*
Hemingway, Richard William *law educator*
Henderson, Arnold Glenn *architect, educator*
Henderson, George *educational sociologist, educator*
Hill, Loren G. *biology researcher*
Hiner, Gladys Webber *psychologist*
Hodgell, Murlin Ray *university dean*
Hodges, Thompson Gene *librarian, retired university dean*
Huntington, Penelope Ann *middle school educator*
Hutchison, Victor Hobbs *biologist, educator*
Kemp, Betty Ruth *librarian*
Kessler, Edwin *meteorology educator, consultant*
Kondonassis, Alexander John *economist, educator*
Lakshmivarahan, Sivaramakrishnan *computer science educator*
Lamb, Peter James *meteorology educator, researcher, consultant*
Lee, Sul Hi *library administrator*
Leonhardt, Thomas Wilburn *librarian, technical services director*
Lester, June *library and information management educator*
Lis, Anthony Stanley *business administration educator*
Lowitt, Richard *history educator*
MacFarland, Miriam Katherine (Mimi) *computer science consultant, writer*
Mankin, Charles John *geology educator*
Mares, Michael Allen *ecologist, educator*
McGuckin, Wendy Michelle Blassingame *accounting specialist*
Menzie, Donald E. *petroleum engineer, educator*
†O'Rear, Edgar Allen, III *chemical engineering educator*
Owens, Rochelle *poet, playwright*
Pain, Betsy M. *lawyer*
Pappas, James Pete *university administrator*
Perkins, Edward J. *diplomat*
Petersen, Catherine Holland *lawyer*
Pigott, John Dowling *geologist, geophysicist, geochemist, educator, consultant*
Ross, Allan Anderson *music educator, university official*
Scamehorn, John Frederick *chemical engineer*
Schindler, Barbara Francois *school administrator*
Schindler, Charles Alvin *microbiologist, educator*
Sharp, Paul Frederick *former university president, educational consultant*
Sherman, Mary Angus *public library administrator*
Sipes, James Lamoyne *landscape architect, educator*
Tackwell, Elizabeth Miller *social worker*
Toperzer, Thomas Raymond *art museum director*
Trimble, Preston Albert *retired judge*
Tussing, Marilee Appleby *music educator*
Tuttle, Arthur Norman, Jr. *architect, university administrator*
Van Auken, Robert Danforth *business administration educator, management consultant*
Van Horn, Richard Linley *academic administrator*
Velie, Lester *journalist*
Weber, Jerome Charles *education and human relations educator, former academic dean and provost*
Williams, David Samuel *insurance company executive*
Zaman, Musharraf *civil engineering educator*
Zapffe, Nina Byrom *retired elementary education educator*
Zelby, Leon Wolf *electrical engineering educator, consulting engineer*
Zelby, Rachel *realtor*

**Nowata**
Osborn, Ann George *retired chemist*

**Ochelata**
Hitzman, Donald Oliver *microbiologist*

**Oklahoma City**
Ackerman, Raymond Basil *advertising agency executive*
Alaupovic, Alexandra Vrbanic *artist, educator*
Alaupovic, Petar *biochemist, educator*
Alexander, Patrick Byron *zoological society executive*
Allbright, Karan Elizabeth *psychologist, consultant*
Allen, James Harmon, Jr. *civil engineer*
Allen, Robert Dee *lawyer*
Alley, Wayne Edward *federal judge, retired army officer*
Almond, David Randolph *lawyer, company executive*
Anderson, Kenneth Edwin *writer, educator*
Andrews, Robert Frederick *religious organization administrator, retired bishop*
Angel, Arthur Ronald *lawyer, consultant*
Anthony, Robert Holland *state official*
Bahr, Carman Bloedow *internist*
Bailey, Clark Trammell, II *public relations/public affairs professional*
Beltran, Eusebius Joseph *archbishop*
Beutler, Randy Leon *rancher, state legislator*
Blackwell, John Adrian, Jr. *computer company executive*
Bohanon, Luther L. *federal judge*
Boston, Billie *costume designer, costume history educator*
Boston, William Clayton *lawyer*
Boyd, Laura Wooldridge *state legislator*
Bozalis, John Russell *physician*
Branch, John Curtis *biology educator, lawyer*
Brandt, Edward Newman, Jr. *physician, educator*
Brawner, Lee Basil *librarian*
Brooks, Norma Newton *legal assistant, secondary school educator*
Brown, Kenneth Ray *banker*
Browne, John Robinson *banker*
Burns, Marion G. *management consultant, retired council executive*
Cameron, Charles Metz, Jr. *physician, medical educator*
Campbell, David Gwynne *petroleum executive, geologist*
Cantrell, Charles Leonard *lawyer, educator*
Cauthron, Robin J. *federal judge*
Champlin, Richard H. *lawyer, insurance company executive*
Chan, Peter P. *osteopathic physician*
Christiansen, Mark D. *lawyer*
Claflin, James Robert *pediatrician, allergist*
Clark, Robert Lloyd, Jr. *librarian*
Coats, Andrew Montgomery *lawyer, former mayor, dean*
Cole, Tom *state official*
Collins, William Edward *aeromedical administrator, researcher*
Comp, Philip Cinnamon *medical researcher*
Couch, James Russell, Jr. *neurology educator*
Court, Leonard *lawyer*
Cunningham, Stanley Lloyd *lawyer*
Danforth, Louis Fremont *banker, educator*
Davis, Emery Stephen *wholesale food company executive*
Denton, Michael David, Jr. *lawyer*
Dunlap, E.T. *retired educational administrator, consultant*
Dunn, Parker Southerland *retired chemical company consultant*
Durland, Jack Raymond *lawyer*
Edmondson, Drew *attorney general*
Edmondson, W. A. Drew *state attorney general*
Elder, James Carl *lawyer*
Ellis, Robert Smith *allergist, immunologist*
Emerson, Marvin Chester *legal association administrator*
England, Gary Alan *television meteorologist*
Epperson, Kraettli Quynton *lawyer, educator*
Everett, Mark Allen *dermatologist, educator*
Fair, Michael Edward *state senator*
Fallin, Mary Copeland *state official*
Felton, Warren Locker, II *surgeon*
Filley, Warren Vernon *allergist, immunologist*
Fishburne, John Ingram, Jr. *obstetrician-gynecologist, educator*
Fitch, Mark Keith *lawyer*
Ford, Charles Reed *state senator*
Ford, Michael Raye *lawyer*
Forni, Patricia Rose *nursing educator, university dean*
Frager, Norman *stockbroker*
Garrett, Kathryn Ann (Kitty Garrett) *legislative clerk*
Garrett, Sandy Langley *school system administrator*
Gavaler, Judith Ann Stohr Van Thiel *bio-epidemiologist*
Gaylord, Edward Lewis *publishing company executive*
George, James Noel *hematologist-oncologist, educator*
Gourley, James Leland *editor, publishing executive*
Griggy, Kenneth Joseph *food company executive*
Gumerson, Jean Gilderhus *health foundation executive*
Gumm, Jay Paul *media specialist*
Halverstadt, Donald Bruce *urologist, educator*
Hambrick, Marvin K. *energy company executive*
Hammons, Royce Mitchell *bank executive*
Harbour, Robert Randall *state agency administrator*
Hargrave, Rudolph *justice*
Harlin-Fischer, Gayle C. *elementary education educator*
Harper, Sandra Stecher *university administrator*
Hartsuck, Jean Ann *chemist*
Haywood, B(etty) J(ean) *anesthesiologist*
Hefner, William Johnson, Jr. (W. John Hefner, Jr.) *oil and gas industry executive*
Hemry, Jerome Eldon *lawyer*
Hendrick, Howard H. *lawyer, state senator*
Hennigan, George R. *chemicals executive*
Henry, Robert H. *federal judge, former attorney general*
Hodges, Ralph B. *state supreme court justice*
Hofener, Steven David *civil engineer*
Holder, Lee *educator and university dean emeritus*
Holloway, William Judson, Jr. *federal judge*
Holt, Karen Anita Young *English educator*
Horner, Russell Grant, Jr. *diversified company executive*
Horton, Donald *neurosurgeon*
Hough, Jack Van Doren *otologist*
Howeth, Lynda Carol *small business owner*
Hulseberg, Paul David *financial executive, educator*
Ille, Bernard Glenn *insurance company executive*
Irwin, Pat *federal magistrate judge*
Jackson, Gaines Bradford *environmental science educator*
Johnson, B(ruce) Connor *biochemist, educator, consultant*
Johnson, James Terence *college chancellor*
Johnson, Robert Max *lawyer*
†Johnson-Bailey, Marquita P. *nursing administrator, consultant*
Jones, Brenda Kaye *public relations executive*
Jones, Robert Lee *religion educator*
Kaufman, James Mark *lawyer*
Keating, Francis Anthony, II *governor, lawyer*
Keeth, Betty Louise *geriatrics nursing director*
Kelley, Carl Ed(win) *editor*
Kennedy, John H., Jr. *former state official*
Khaleeluddin, Mansoor *marketing professional*
Kimerer, Neil Banard, Sr. *psychiatrist, educator*
Kinasewitz, Gary Theodore *medical educator*
Kirkpatrick, John Elson *oil company executive, retired naval reserve officer*
Kline, David Adam *lawyer, educator, writer*
Kraker, Deborah Schovanec *special education educator*
†Kuner, Charles Michael *minister*
Lambird, Mona Salyer *lawyer*
Lambird, Perry Albert *pathologist*
LaMotte, Janet Allison *management specialist*
Larason, Timothy Manuel *lawyer*
Lavender, Robert Eugene *state supreme court justice*
Legg, William Jefferson *lawyer*
Leonard, Timothy Dwight *judge*
Lestina, Roger Henry *English language educator*
Lewis, Wilbur Curtis *surgeon*
Lynn, Thomas Neil, Jr. *retired medical center administrator, physician*
Macer, Dan Johnstone *retired hospital administrator*
Magarian, Robert Armen *medicinal chemist, researcher, educator*
Massion, Walter Herbert *anesthesiologist, educator*
Mather, Ruth Elsie *writer*
Maton, Anthea *education consultant*
McBride, Kenneth Eugene *lawyer, title company executive*
McClellan, Mary Ann *pediatrics nurse, educator*
McCoy, Wesley Lawrence *musician, conductor, educator*
McFadden, Robert Stetson *hepatologist*
McKenzie, Clif Allen *Indian tribe official, accountant*
Mc Pherson, Frank Alfred *manufacturing corporate executive*
Meeks, Patricia Lowe *secondary school educator*
Merritt, Kenni Barrett *lawyer*
Mikkelson, Dean Harold *geological engineer*
Miller, Herbert Dell *petroleum engineer*
Milsten, Robert B. *lawyer*
Minocha, Anil *physician, educator, researcher*
Moler, Edward Harold *lawyer*
Moody, Robert M. *bishop*
Moore, Joanne Iweita *pharmacologist, educator*
Necco, Alexander David *lawyer, educator*
Nesbitt, Charles Rudolph *lawyer, energy consultant*
Neuenschwander, Pierre Fernand *medical educator*
Nichols, J. Larry *energy company executive, lawyer*
Noakes, Betty L. *retired elementary school educator*
Nokes, Mary Triplett *former university president, counselor, artist*
Norick, Ronald J. *mayor*
Oehlert, William Herbert, Jr. *cardiologist, administrator, educator*
Opala, Marian P(eter) *state supreme court justice*
Owens, Barbara Ann *English educator*
Painton, Ira Wayne *retired securities executive*
Parke, David Wilkin, II *ophthalmologist, educator, healthcare executive*
Paul, William George *lawyer*
Payne, Gareld Gene *vocal music educator, medical transcriptionist*
Peace, H. W., II *oil company executive*
Perez-Cruet, Jorge *psychiatrist, psychopharmacologist, psychophysiologist, educator*
Petito, Victor Thomas, Jr. *credit bureau executive*
Pishkin, Vladimir *psychologist, educator*
Ponder, Alonza *church administrator*
Pope, Tim Lane *state legislator, consultant*
Rahhal, Donald K. *obstetrician, gynecologist*
Rayburn, William Frazier *obstetrician, gynecologist, educator*
Reynolds, Norman Eben *lawyer*
†Richardson, Dot *softball player*
Ridley, Betty Ann *educator, church worker*
Robinson, Malcolm *gastroenterologist*
Robison, Clarence, Jr. *surgeon*
Rockett, D. Joe *lawyer*
Ross, William Jarboe *lawyer*
Rossavik, Ivar Kristian *obstetrician, gynecologist*
Ruhrup, Clifton Brown *sales executive*
Rundell, Orvis Herman, Jr. *psychologist*
Rush, Richard P. *chamber of commerce executive*
Russell, David L. *federal judge*
Ryan, Patrick M. *prosecutor*
Sanders, Gilbert Otis *health and addictions psychologist, consultant*
Scott, Lawrence Vernon *microbiology educator*
Shirey, Margaret (Peggy Shirey) *elementary school educator*
Smith, Clodus Ray *academic administrator*
Smith, Robert Walter *food company executive*
Snider, John Joseph *lawyer*
Sookne, Herman Solomon (Hank Sookne) *human services executive*
Sowers, Wesley Hoyt *lawyer, management consultant*
Spencer, Melvin Joe *hospital administrator, lawyer*
Stauth, Robert Edward *food service executive*
Steinhorn, Irwin Harry *lawyer, educator, corporate executive*
Stephen, Michael *psychologist*
Sterban, Richard Anthony *singer*
Stringer, L.E. (Dean Stringer) *lawyer*
Sulc, Dwight George *investment advisor*
Summers, Hardy *state supreme court vice chiefjustice*
Taft, Richard George *lawyer*
Tang, Irving Che-hong *mathematician, educator*
Thadani, Udho *physician, cardiologist*
Thompson, Ralph Gordon *federal judge*
Thurman, William Gentry *medical research foundation executive, pediatric hematology and oncology physician, educator*
Todd, Joe Lee *historian*
Tolbert, James R., III *financial executive*
Tompkins, Raymond Edgar *lawyer*
Towery, Curtis Kent *lawyer*
Triplett, E. Eugene *editor*
Tuck-Richmond, Doletta Sue *prosecutor*
Turner, Eugene Andrew *manufacturing executive*
Turpen, Michael Craig *lawyer*
Underwood, Bernard Edward *religious organization administrator*
Valentine, Alan Darrell *symphony orchestra executive*
Van Rysselberge, Charles H. *organization administrator*
Walker, Clarence Eugene *psychology educator*
Walker, Jerald Carter *university administrator, minister*
Walsh, Lawrence Edward *lawyer*
Weigel, Paul Henry *biochemistry educator, researcher, consultant*
Weir, Richard Dale *elementary education educator*
Werries, E. Dean *food distribution company executive*
West, Lee Roy *federal judge*
Wheat, Willis James *retired university dean, management educator*
Wickens, Donald Lee *engineer executive, consultant, rancher*
Wilkerson, Matha Ann *oil company executive*
Williams, George Rainey *retired surgeon, educator*
Williams, Richard Donald *retired wholesale food company executive*
Williams, William Ralston *retired bank and trust company executive*
Wilson, Alma *state supreme court justice*
Woods, Pendleton *educational administrator*
Worsham, Bertrand Ray *psychiatrist*
Worthington, J.B. *business executive*
Zevnik-Sawatzky, Donna Dee *litigation coordinator*
Zuhdi, Nazih *surgeon, administrator*

**Oktaha**
Taylor, Clayton Charles *management and political legislative consultant*

**Oologah**
Knight, Gary Charles *mechanical engineer*

**Paden**
Adams, Darlene Agnes *secondary education educator*

**Park Hill**
Mankiller, Wilma Pearl *tribal leader*

**Pauls Valley**
Hope, Garland Howard *lawyer, retired judge*
Pesterfield, Linda Carol *school administrator, educator*

**Pawhuska**
Holloway, Sharon Kay Sossamon *vocational/secondary school educator*
Strahm, Samuel Edward *veterinarian*

**Perry**
Beers, Frederick Gordon *writer, retired corporate communications official*
Doughty, Michael Dean *insurance agent*

**Piedmont**
Clayton, Lawrence Otto *minister, writer*
Roberts, Kathleen Mary *school system administrator*

**Ponca City**
Bolene, Margaret Rosalie Steele *bacteriologist, civic worker*
Leonard, Samuel Wallace *oil company and bank executive*
Newport, L. Joan *clinical social worker, psychotherapist*
Northcutt, Clarence Dewey *lawyer*
Poole, Richard William, Jr. *secondary school educator*

**Poteau**
†Edwards, William Harold *manufacturing executive*

**Pryor**
Burdick, Larry G. *school system administrator*

**Purcell**
Lucas, Roy Edward, Jr. *minister*

**Quapaw**
Dawes, Charles Edward *retired manufacturing company executive*

**Sand Springs**
Ackerman, Robert Wallace *steel company executive*

**Sapulpa**
Barnes, Paulette Whetstone *school system administrator*
Geeslin, Robert Hawk *educational programming company executive*

**Shawnee**
Agee, Bob R. *university president, educator, minister*
Hill, Bryce Dale *school administrator*
Wilson, Robert Godfrey *radiologist*

**Stillwater**
Agnew, Theodore Lee, Jr. *historian, educator*
Ausburn, Lynna Joyce *vocational and technical curriculum developer, consultant*
Barfield, Billy Joe *agricultural engineer, educator*
Bell, Kenneth John *chemical engineer*
Berlin, Kenneth Darrell *chemistry educator, consultant, researcher*
Boger, Lawrence Leroy *university president emeritus*
Browning, Charles Benton *retired university dean, agricultural educator*
Brusewitz, Gerald Henry *agricultural engineering educator, researcher*
Bynum, Jack Edward, Jr. *sociology educator*
Campbell, John Roy *animal scientist educator, academic administrator*
Case, Kenneth Eugene *industrial engineering educator*
Confer, Anthony Wayne *veterinary pathologist, educator*
Cooper, Donald Lee *physician*
Curl, Samuel Everett *university dean, agricultural scientist*
Durham, Norman Nevill *microbiologist, scientist, educator*

Ewing, Sidney Alton *veterinary medical educator, parasitologist*
Fischer, LeRoy Henry *historian, educator*
Fischer, Richard Samuel *lawyer*
Gorin, George *retired chemistry educator*
Grischkowsky, Daniel Richard *research scientist, educator*
Halligan, James Edmund *university administrator, chemical engineer*
Hayes, Kevin Gregory *university administrator*
Hemberger, Glen James *university band director, music educator*
Hooper, Billy Ernest *medical association administrator*
Hughes, Michael *civil engineer*
Jaco, William H. *mathematics educator*
Johnson, Edward Roy *library director*
Kamm, Robert B. *former academic administrator, educator, author, diplomat*
Langwig, John Edward *retired wood science educator*
Lawson, F. D. *bishop*
Leach, Franklin Rollin *biochemistry educator*
Lu, Huizhu *computer scientist, educator*
Luebke, Neil Robert *philosophy educator*
Maddox, Robert Nott *chemical engineer, educator*
Matoy, Elizabeth Anne *personnel executive*
Maule, Charles Gough *retired industrial engineer, educator*
Mc Collom, Kenneth Allen *retired university dean*
Mc Farland, Frank Eugene *university official*
Mize, Joe Henry *industrial engineer, educator*
Monlux, Andrew W. *educator, veterinarian*
Moomaw, Ronald Lee *economics educator*
Noyes, Ronald Tacie *agricultural engineering educator*
Ownby, Charlotte Ledbetter *anatomy educator*
Poole, Richard William *economics educator*
Provine, Lorraine *mathematics educator*
Qualls, Charles Wayne, Jr. *veterinary pathology educator*
Quinn, Art Jay *veterinarian, retired educator*
Sandmeyer, Robert Lee *university dean, economist*
Shirley, Glenn Dean *writer*
Thompson, David Russell *engineering educator, academic dean*
Trennepohl, Gary Lee *finance educator*
Whitcomb, Carl Ervin *horticulturist, researcher*

**Taft**
Varner, Joyce Ehrhardt *librarian*

**Tahlequah**
Edmondson, Linda Louise *optometrist*
Ross, John *cultural organization administrator*
Wickham, M(arvin) Gary *optometry educator*

**Tinker AFB**
Goodman, Ernest Monroe *air force officer*

**Tulsa**
Abbott, William Thomas *claim specialist*
Alexander, John Robert *hospital administrator, internist*
Allen, Thomas Wesley *medical educator, dean*
Anderson, David Walter *physics educator, consultant*
Arrington, John Leslie, Jr. *lawyer*
Ashby, John Forsythe *retired bishop*
Atkinson, Michael Pearce *lawyer*
Bailey, Keith E. *petroleum pipeline company executive*
Ball, Rex Martin *urban designer, architect*
Barnes, Cynthia Lou *gifted education educator*
Barnes, James E. *energy company executive*
Beasley, William Rex *judge*
Belsky, Martin Henry *law educator, lawyer*
Bender, John Henry, Jr. (Jack Bender) *editor, cartoonist*
Berlin, Steven Ritt *oil company financial official*
Biolchini, Robert Fredrick *lawyer*
Blackstock, LeRoy *lawyer*
Blais, Roger Nathaniel *physics educator*
Blanton, Roger Edmund *mechanical engineer*
Bonsall, Joseph Sloan, Jr. *singer*
Bowen, William Augustus *financial consultant*
Braumiller, Allen Spooner *oil and gas exploration company executive, geologist*
Brett, Thomas Rutherford *federal judge*
Brightmire, Paul William *retired judge*
Brolick, Henry John *energy company executive*
Brown, Connie Yates *business owner*
Brunk, Samuel Frederick *oncologist*
Bryant, Dennis Michael *insurance executive*
Bryant, Hubert Hale *lawyer*
Buckley, Thomas Hugh *historian, educator*
Bynum, George T., III (Ted Bynum) *biomedical company executive*
Calvert, Delbert William *chemical company executive*
Calvert, Jon Channing *family practice physician*
Cardwell, Sandra Gayle Bavido *real estate broker*
Caroon, Lynne Stanley *secondary and elementary educator, coach*
Chaback, Joseph John *oil industry researcher*
Clark, Gary Carl *lawyer*
Clark, Roy *singer, musician, recording industry executive*
Collins, John Roger *transportation company executive*
Cook, Harold Dale *federal judge*
Cooke, Marvin Lee *sociologist, consultant, urban planner*
Cooper, Richard Casey *lawyer*
Cox, William Jackson *bishop*
Crawford, B(urnett) Hayden *lawyer*
Cremin, John Patrick *lawyer*
Daniel, Samuel Phillips *lawyer*
Davenport, Gerald Bruce *lawyer*
Davis, Annalee C. *clinical social worker*
Deihl, Michael Allen *federal agency administrator*
Dotson, George Stephen *drilling company executive*
Doverspike, Terry Richard *lawyer*
Earlougher, Robert Charles, Sr. *petroleum engineer*
Eaton, Leonard James, Jr. *banker*
Elkins, Lloyd Edwin, Sr. *petroleum engineer, energy consultant*
Ellison, James Oliver *federal judge*
Estill, John Staples, Jr. *lawyer*
Farrell, John L., Jr. *lawyer, business executive*
Frey, Martin Alan *lawyer, educator*
Frizzell, Gregory Kent *judge*
Gaberino, John Anthony, Jr. *lawyer*
Gable, G. Ellis *retired lawyer*
Gaddis, Richard William *management educator*
Gentry, Bern Leon, Sr. *minority consulting company executive*

Ginn, Connie Mardean *nurse*
Goodman, Jerry L(ynn) *judge*
Gottschalk, Sister Mary Therese *nun, hospital administrator*
Graham, Tony M. *lawyer*
Gregg, Lawrence J. *physician*
Hale, Richard Lee *magazine editor*
Hamilton, Carl Hulet *academic administrator*
Hannah, Barbara Ann *nurse, educator*
Haring, Robert Westing *newspaper editor*
Hawkins, Francis Glenn *banker, lawyer*
Hayes, Sharon LaRue (Shari Hayes) *clinical medical assistant, travel agent*
Helmerich, Hans Christian *oil company executive*
Henderson, James Ronald *industrial real estate developer*
Hill, Josephine Carmela *realtor*
Holmes, Sven Erik *federal judge*
Horkey, William Richard *retired diversified oil company executive*
Horn, Myron Kay *consulting petroleum geologist, author, educator*
Horvath, Carol Mitchell *home health administrator*
Howard, Gene Claude *lawyer, former state senator*
Huber, Fritz Godfrey *physical education educator, excercise physiologist*
Hulings, Norman McDermott, Jr. *energy consultant, former company executive*
Huttner, Sidney Frederick *librarian*
Imel, John Michael *lawyer*
Ingram, Charles Clark, Jr. *energy company executive*
Johnson, Gerald, III *cardiovascular physiologist, researcher*
Jones, Jenk, Jr. *editor, educator*
Jones, Jenkin Lloyd *retired newspaper publisher*
Jones, Robert Lawton *architect, planner, educator*
Kalbfleisch, John McDowell *cardiologist, educator*
Kelly, Vincent Michael, Jr. *orthodontist*
Kennedy, Nancy Louise *retired draftsman*
Kern, Terry C. *judge*
Kihle, Donald Arthur *lawyer*
Killin, Charles Clark *lawyer*
King, Peter Cotterill *former utilities executive*
Knaust, Clara Doss *retired elementary school educator*
Kothe, Charles Aloysius *lawyer*
Kruse, David Louis, II *transportation company executive*
Langholz, Robert Wayne *lawyer, investor*
Larkin, Moscelyne *retired artistic director, dancer*
Lawless, Robert William *academic administrator*
Lewis, Ceylon Smith, Jr. *physician, educator*
Lhevine, Dave Bernard *radiologist, educator*
Lindsay, Patricia Mae *physician, medical administrator*
Lowd, Judson Dean *oil and gas processing equipment manufacturing executive*
Lunev, Aleksandr (Sasha) *dancer*
Luthey, Graydon Dean, Jr. *lawyer*
Major, John Keene *radio broadcasting executive*
Manhart, Marcia Y(ockey) *art museum director*
Martin, Robert Finlay, Jr. *retired judge*
Matthews, Dane Dikeman *urban planner*
Mattocks-Whisman, Frances *nursing administrator, educator*
McGonigle, Richard Thomas *lawyer*
Miller, Gerald Cecil *immunologist, laboratory administrator, educator*
Moffett, J. Denny *lawyer*
Mojtabai, Ann Grace *author, educator*
Mourton, J. Gary *communications executive*
Narwold, Lewis Lammers *paper products manufacturer*
Naumann, William Carl *consumer products company executive*
Neas, John Theodore *petroleum company executive*
Nebergall, Robert William *orthopedic surgeon, educator*
Nero, Peter *pianist, conductor, composer, arranger*
Nettles, John Barnwell *obstetrics and gynecology educator*
Nixon, James Gregory *economic development consultant*
O'Brien, Darcy *English educator, writer*
O'Toole, Allan Thomas *electric utility executive*
Owens, Jana Jae *entertainer*
Palmer, Ron *police chief*
Parker, Robert Lee, Sr. *petroleum engineer, drilling company executive*
Parker, Robert Lee, Jr. *drilling company executive*
Payne, William Haydon *broadcasting executive*
Pippin, John Joseph *cardiologist*
Plunket, Daniel Clark *pediatrician*
Prayson, Alex Stephen *drafting and mechanical design educator*
Primeaux, Henry, III *automotive executive, author, speaker*
Quinn, Francis Xavier *arbitrator and mediator, author, lecturer*
Rex, Lonnie Royce *religious organization administrator*
Rippley, Robert *wholesale distribution executive*
Roberts, (Granville) Oral *clergyman*
Robertson, Vicki Dawn *adminstrative secretary, writer*
Roger, Jerry Lee *school system administrator*
Rubottom, Donald Julian *management consultant*
Rummerfield, Benjamin Franklin *geophysicist*
Saferite, Linda Lee *library director*
Sanditen, Edgar Richard *investment company executive*
Savage, M. Susan *mayor*
Say, Burhan *physician*
Schwartz, Bernard *law educator*
Seymour, Stephanie Kulp *federal judge*
Shane, John Marder *endocrinologist*
Slattery, Edward J. *bishop*
Smothers, William Edgar, Jr. *geophysical exploration company executive*
Spencer, Winifred May *art educator*
Stone, William Charles *surgeon*
Taylor, Joe Clinton *judge*
Thomas, Robert Eggleston *former corporate executive*
Thompson, Harold Jerome *counselor, mental retardation professional*
Tompkins, Robert George *physician*
Tubbs, David Eugene *mechanical engineer, marketing professional*
Upton, Howard B., Jr. *management writer, lawyer*
Wagner, John Leo *federal judge, lawyer*
Walker, Floyd Lee *lawyer*
†Warren, W. K., Jr. *oil industry executive*
Wesenberg, John Herman *professional society administrator*
Williams, David Rogerson, Jr. *engineer, business executive*

Williams, John Horter *civil engineer, oil, gas, telecommunications and allied products distribution company executive*
Williams, Joseph Hill *retired diversified industry executive*
Wood, Emily Churchill *gifted and talented education educator*
Woodrum, Patricia Ann *librarian*

**Vinita**
Curnutte, Mark William *lawyer*
Johnston, Oscar Black, III *lawyer*
Neer, Charles Sumner, II *orthopedic surgeon, educator*

**Wagoner**
Semore, Mary Margie *abstractor*

**Walters**
Flanagan, Michael Charles *lawyer*

**Wanette**
Thompson, Joyce Elizabeth *retired state education official*

**Washington**
Sliepcevich, Cedomir M. *engineering educator*

**Watonga**
Hoberecht, Earnest *abstract company executive, former newspaper executive*

**Wheatland**
Nance, Retha Hardison *reading specialist*

**Woodward**
Billings, Letha Marguerite *nurse*
Keith, Howard Barton *surgeon*
Selman, Minnie Corene Phelps *elementary school educator*

**Yale**
Berger, Billie David *corrosion engineer*

**Yukon**
Ford, Yvonne Ardella *barber stylist, entrepreneur*
Morgan, Robert Steve *mechanical engineer*

# OREGON

**Albany**
Bianchi, Charles Paul *technical and business executive, money manager, financial consultant*
Chowning, Orr-Lyda Brown *dietitian*
Dooley, George Joseph, III *metallurgist*
Wood, Kenneth Arthur *retired newspaper editor, writer*
Yau, Te-Lin *corrosion engineer*
Yu, Kitson Szewai *computer science educator*

**Aloha**
Rojhantalab, Hossein Mohammad *chemical engineer, researcher*

**Applegate**
Boyle, (Charles) Keith *artist, educator*

**Ashland**
Abrahams, Sidney Cyril *physicist, crystallographer*
Addicott, Warren Oliver *retired geologist, educator*
Bornet, Vaughn Davis *former history and social science educator, research historian*
Christianson, Roger Gordon *biology educator*
Farrimond, George Francis, Jr. *management educator*
Grover, James Robb *chemist, editor*
Hay, Richard Laurence *theater scenic designer*
Hirschfeld, Gerald Joseph *cinematographer*
Houston, John Albert *political science educator*
Kreisman, Arthur *higher education consultant, humanities educator emeritus*
Levy, Leonard Williams *history educator, author*
MacMillen, Richard Edward *biological sciences educator, researcher*
Mularz, Theodore Leonard *architect*
Smith, G(odfrey) T(aylor) *academic administrator*
Walt, Harold Richard *rancher*

**Astoria**
Bainer, Philip La Vern *retired college president*
Foster, Michael William *librarian*
Haskell, Donald McMillan *lawyer*

**Baker City**
Graham, Beardsley *management consultant*

**Beaverton**
Barnes, Keith Lee *electronics executive*
Bosch, Samuel Henry *computer company executive*
Chang, David Ping-Chung *business consultant, architect*
Chartier, Vernon Lee *electrical engineer*
Conn, P. Michael *pharmacologist, educator*
Donahue, Richard King *athletic apparel executive, lawyer*
Henderson, George Miller *foundation executive, former banker*
Hill, Wilmer Bailey *administrative law judge*
Knight, Philip H(ampson) *shoe manufacturing company executive*
Mersereau, Susan S. *clinical psychologist*
Mitchell, Bettie Phaenon *religious organization administrator*
Pond, Patricia Brown *library science educator, university administrator*
Robertson, Douglas Stuart *lawyer*
Swank, Roy Laver *physician, educator, inventor*

**Bend**
Connolly, Thomas Joseph *bishop*
Cooley, Wes *former congressman*
Kozak, Michael *real estate counselor, seminar instructor*
Mayer, Richard Dean *mathematics educator*
Nosler, Robert Amos *sports company executive*
Wonser, Michael Dean *retired public affairs director,*

**Boring**
Yatvin, Joanne Ina *school superintendent*

**Brookings**
Cross, Lynda Lee *health facility administrator, nurse*

**Canby**
Thalhofer, Paul Terrance *lawyer*

**Cannon Beach**
Greaver, Harry *artist*
Wismer, Patricia Ann *secondary education educator*

**Chiloquin**
Mead, Terry Eileen *clinic administrator, consultant*
Reed, David George *entrepreneur*
Siemens, Richard Ernest *retired metallurgy administrator, researcher*

**Clackamas**
Luchterhand, Ralph Edward *financial advisor*
Merrill, William Dean *retired architect, medical facility planning consultant*

**Cloverdale**
Jortner, Julius *materials engineer, consultant*

**Coos Bay**
Van Allen, Katrina Frances *painter*

**Coquille**
Taylor, George Frederick *newspaper publisher, editor*

**Corvallis**
Arp, Daniel James *biochemistry educator*
Becker, Robert Richard *biochemist, educator*
Blus, Lawrence John *biologist*
Brown, George *research forester and educator*
Bruce, Robert Kirk *college administrator*
Byrne, John Vincent *higher education consultant*
Castle, Emery Neal *agricultural and resource economist, educator*
Cerklewski, Florian Lee *human nutrition educator, nutritional biochemistry researcher*
Chambers, Kenton Lee *botany educator*
Dalrymple, Gary Brent *research geologist*
Davis, John Rowland *university administrator*
Drake, Charles Whitney *physicist*
Engelbrecht, Rudolf *electrical engineering educator*
Evans, Harold J. *plant physiologist, biochemist, educator*
Farkas, Daniel Frederick *food science and technology educator*
Forbes, Leonard *engineering educator*
Frakes, Rod Vance *plant geneticist, educator*
Gillis, John Simon *psychologist, educator*
Godfrey, Samuel Addison *retired telephone company executive*
Hafner-Eaton, Chris *health services researcher, educator*
Hall, Don Alan *editor, writer*
Hansen, Hugh Justin *agricultural engineer*
Harter, Lafayette George, Jr. *economics educator emeritus*
Healey, Deborah Lynn *education administrator*
Ho, Iwan *research plant pathologist*
Hunt, Donald R. *retired librarian*
Huyer, Adriana *oceanographer, educator*
Keller, George Henrik *marine geologist*
Knudsen, James George *chemical engineer, educator*
Leong, Jo-Ann Ching *microbiologist, educator*
Lubchenco, Jane *marine biologist, educator*
Mac Vicar, Robert William *retired university administrator*
Miner, John Ronald *bioresource engineer*
Mohler, Ronald Rutt *electrical engineering educator*
Moore, Thomas Carrol *botanist, educator*
Morita, Richard Yukio *microbiology and oceanography educator*
Nielson, Norma Lee *business educator*
Oldfield, James Edmund *nutrition educator*
Olleman, Roger Dean *industry consultant, former metallurgical engineering educator*
Parker, Donald Fred *college dean, human resources management educator*
Parks, Harold Raymond *mathematician, educator*
Pearson, Albert Marchant *food science and nutrition educator*
Petersen, Bent Edvard *mathematician, educator*
Rapier, Pascal Moran *chemical engineer, physicist*
Rounds, Donald Edwin *retired cell biologist*
Rygiewicz, Paul Thaddeus *plant ecologist*
Schmidt, Bruce Randolph *science administrator, researcher*
Sleight, Arthur William *chemist, educator*
Steele, Robert Edwin *orthopedic surgeon*
Steiner, Kenneth Donald *bishop*
Storvick, Clara Amanda *nutrition educator emerita*
Tarrant, Robert Frank *soil science educator, researcher*
Temes, Gabor Charles *electrical engineering educator*
Thomas, Thomas Darrah *chemistry educator*
Towey, Richard Edward *economics educator*
Trappe, James Martin *mycologist*
Van Holde, Kensal Edward *biochemistry educator*
Verts, Lita Jeanne *university administrator*
Wechsler, Susan Linda *software design engineer*
Westwood, Melvin Neil *horticulturist, pomologist*
Wilkins, Caroline Hanke *consumer agency administrator, political worker*
Willis, David Lee *radiation biology educator*
Yeats, Robert Sheppard *geologist, educator*
Yim, Solomon Chik-Sing *civil engineering educator, consultant*
Young, J. Lowell *soil chemist, biologist*
Young, Roy Alton *university administrator, educator*
Zobel, Donald Bruce *botany educator*
Zwahlen, Fred Casper, Jr. *journalism educator*

**Cottage Grove**
Miller, Joanne Louise *middle school educator*

**Cove**
Kerper, Meike *family violence, sex abuse and addictions abuse rehabilitation educator, consultant*

**Culver**
Siebert, Diane Dolores *author, poet*

**Dallas**
Calkins, Loren Gene *church executive, clergyman*

**Dayton**
Williams, Kenneth James *retired county official*

### Depoe Bay
Fish, Barbara Joan *investor, small business owner*

### Dexter
Myhre, Kathleen Randi *nurse*

### Eugene
Acker, Martin Herbert *psychotherapist, educator*
Aikens, C(lyde) Melvin *anthropology educator, archaeologist*
Andrews, Fred Charles *mathematics educator*
Bailey, Exine Margaret Anderson *soprano, educator*
Baker, Alton Fletcher, Jr. *retired newspaper publisher and editor*
Baker, Alton Fletcher, III *newspaper editor, publishing executive*
Baker, Bridget Downey *newspaper executive*
Baker, Edwin Moody *retired newspaper publisher*
Bascom, Ruth F. *former mayor*
Bennett, Robert Royce *engineering and management consultant*
Biglan, Anthony *medical educator*
Birn, Raymond Francis *historian, educator*
Boekelheide, Virgil Carl *chemistry educator*
Chambers, Carolyn Silva *communications company executive*
Chaney, James Alan *construction company executive*
Chezem, Curtis Gordon *physicist, former retail executive*
Clark, Chapin DeWitt *law educator*
Cox, Joseph William *academic administrator*
Crasemann, Bernd *physicist, educator*
Dasso, Jerome Joseph *real estate educator, consultant*
Davis, Richard Malone *economics educator*
Deshpande, Nilendra Ganesh *physics educator*
Donnelly, Marian Card *art historian, educator*
Donnelly, Russell James *physicist, educator*
Edwards, Ralph M. *librarian*
Flanagan, Latham, Jr. *surgeon*
Franklin, Jon Daniel *writer, journalist, educator*
Freyd, Jennifer Joy *psychology educator*
Frohnmayer, David Braden *university president*
Gall, Meredith Damien (Meredith Mark Damien Gall) *education educator, author*
Gillespie, Penny Hannig *business owner*
Girardeau, Marvin Denham *physics educator*
Griffith, Osbie Hayes *chemistry educator*
He, Xianguo *chemist, consultant*
Hess, Suzanne Harriet *newspaper administrator, photographer*
Hildebrand, Carol Ilene *librarian*
Hogan, Michael R(obert) *judge*
Holzapfel, Christina Marie *biologist*
Ismach, Arnold Harvey *journalism educator*
Khang, Chulsoon *economics educator*
Lansdowne, Karen Myrtle *retired English language and literature educator*
Lindholm, Richard Theodore *economics and finance educator*
Littman, Richard Anton *psychologist, educator*
Loescher, Richard Alvin *gastroenterologist*
Matthews, Brian W. *molecular biology educator*
Matthews, Esther Elizabeth *education educator, consultant*
Mazo, Robert Marc *chemistry educator, retired*
McConnaughey, Bayard Harlow *biology educator*
McGuire, Timothy William *economics and management educator, dean*
Mikesell, Raymond Frech *economics educator*
Miner, John Burnham *industrial relations educator, writer*
Morrison, Perry David *librarian, educator*
Moseley, John Travis *university administrator, research physicist*
Mowday, Richard Thomas *management educator*
Mumford, William Porter, II *lawyer*
Nissel, Martin *radiologist, consultant*
Osborn, Ronald Edwin *minister, church history educator*
Pascal, C(ecil) Bennett *classics educator*
Peticolas, Warner Leland *physical chemistry educator*
Phelps, Kathryn Annette *mental health counseling executive, consultant*
Piele, Philip Kern *education infosystems educator*
Rendall, Steven Finlay *language educator, editor, translator, critic*
Retallack, Gregory John *geologist educator*
Roe, Thomas Leroy Willis *pediatrician*
Sahlstrom, E(lmer) B(ernard) *retired lawyer*
Sanders, Jack Thomas *religious studies educator*
Schellman, John A. *chemistry educator*
Schroeder, Donald J. *orthopedic surgeon*
Scoles, Eugene Francis *law educator, lawyer*
Sherriffs, Ronald Everett *communication and film educator*
Sisley, Becky Lynn *physical education educator*
Sprague, George Frederick *geneticist*
Tykeson, Donald Erwin *broadcasting executive*
von Hippel, Peter Hans *chemistry educator*
Watson, Mary Ellen *ophthalmic technologist*
Wessells, Norman Keith *biologist, educator, university administrator*
White, David Olds *researcher, former educator*
Wickes, George *English language educator, writer*
Wilhelm, Kate (Katy Gertrude) *author*
Wood, Daniel Brian *educational consultant*
Woolley, Donna Pearl *timber and lumber company executive*
Youngquist, Walter Lewellyn *consulting geologist*

### Florence
Corless, Dorothy Alice *nurse educator*
Day, John Francis *city official, former savings and loan executive, former mayor*
Ericksen, Jerald Laverne *educator, engineering scientist*
Gray, Augustine Heard, Jr. *computer consultant*

### Forest Grove
Carson, William Morris *manpower planning and development advisor*
Gibby-Smith, Barbara *psychologist, nurse*
Singleton, Francis Seth *dean*

### Gladstone
Bradbury, William Chapman, III *former state senator*
Lavigne, Peter Marshall *environmentalist, lawyer, consultant*
Thomason, Scott *automobile executive*

### Gleneden Beach
Marks, Arnold *journalist*

### Gold Beach
Dillon, Robert Morton *retired association executive, architectural consultant*

### Grants Pass
Marchini, Claudia Cilloniz *artist*
Naylor, John Thomas *telephone company executive*
Petersen, Michael Kevin *internist, osteopathic physician*
Smith, Barnard Elliot *management educator*

### Gresham
Arney, James Douglas *forestry biometrics consultant*
Caldwell, Robert John *newspaper editor*
Kuney, Gary Wallace *elementary school educator, real estate agent*
Light, Betty Jensen Pritchett *former college dean*
Nicholson, R. Stephen *organization administrator*
Poulton, Charles Edgar *natural resources consultant*

### Hillsboro
Carruthers, John Robert *scientist*
Hurley, Bruce Palmer *artist*
Masi, Edward A. *computer company executive*
Yates, Keith Lamar *retired insurance company executive*

### Junction City
Humphry, Derek *association executive*

### Klamath Falls
Bohnen, Robert Frank *hematologist, oncologist, educator*
Buchanan, Walter Woolwine *electrical engineer, educator and administrator*
Crawford, Marcella *migrant bilingual resource educator*
Ehlers, Eleanor May Collier (Mrs. Frederick Burton Ehlers) *civic worker*
Klepper, Carol Herdman *mental health therapist*
Wendt, Richard L. *manufacturing executive*

### La Grande
Fanning, Edward John *soil scientist*
Gilbert, David Erwin *university president, physicist*
Joseph, Steven Jay *lawyer*

### Lake Oswego
Gawf, John Lee *foreign service officer*
Ladehoff, Robert Louis *bishop*
Le Shana, David Charles *retired academic administrator*
Loveless, Peggy Ann *social work administrator*
McPeak, Merrill Anthony *business executive, consultant, retired officer*
Meltebeke, Renette *career counselor*
Morse, Lowell Wesley *real estate executive, banking executive*
Mylnechuk, Larry Herbert *financial executive*
Salibello, Cosmo *optometrist, medical products executive*
Thong, Tran *biomedical company executive*

### Lebanon
Girod, Frank Paul *retired surgeon*
Kuntz, Joel Dubois *lawyer*
Pearson, Dennis Lee *optometrist*

### Lincoln City
Elliott, Scott *lawyer*
Gehrig, Edward Harry *electrical engineer, consultant*

### Lowell
Weathers, Warren Russell *forester, appraiser, consultant*

### Mcminnville
Blodgett, Forrest Clinton *economics educator*
McGillivray, Karen *elementary school educator*
Mc Kaughan, Howard Paul *linguistics educator*
Naylor-Jackson, Jerry *public relations consultant, retired, entertainer, broadcaster*
Roberts, Michael Foster *biology educator*
Walker, Charles Urmston *retired university president*

### Medford
Barnum, William Laird *pedodontist*
Bouquet, Francis Lester *physicist*
Cutler, Kenneth Ross *investment company and mutual fund executive*
Davenport, Wilbur Bayley, Jr. *electrical engineering educator*
Hennion, Reeve Lawrence *communications executive*
Keener, John Wesley *management consultant*
O'Connor, Karl William *lawyer*
Puckett, Richard Edward *artist, consultant, retired recreation executive*
Roy, Catherine Elizabeth *physical therapist*
Skelton, Douglas H. *architect*
†Smith, Robert F. (Bob Smith) *rancher, congressman*
Sours, James Kingsley *association executive, former college president*
Straus, David A. *architectural firm executive*
Thierolf, Richard Burton, Jr. *lawyer*

### Milwaukie
Anderson, Mark Alexander *lawyer*
McKay, Laura L. *banker, consultant*

### Monmouth
Forcier, Richard Charles *information technology educator, computer applications consultant*
Shay, Roshani Cari *political science educator*
White, Donald Harvey *physics educator emeritus*

### Myrtle Point
Walsh, Don *marine consultant, executive*

### Neotsu
Archer, Stephen Hunt *economist, educator*

### Netarts
Hartman-Irwin, Mary Frances *retired language professional*

### Newberg
Johnson, Thomas Floyd *college president, educator*
Keith, Pauline Mary *artist, illustrator, writer*
Stevens, Edward Franklin *college president*

### Newport
Gordon, Walter *architect*
Kennedy, Richard Jerome *writer*
Langrock, Karl Frederick *former academic administrator*
Richardson, Bruce LeVoyle *dentist*
Weber, Lavern John *marine science administrator, educator*

### North Bend
de Sá e Silva, Elizabeth Anne *secondary school educator*

### Oakland
Smelt, Ronald *retired aircraft company executive*

### Ontario
Tyler, Donald Earl *urologist*

### Otter Rock
Eaton, Leonard Kimball *retired architecture educator*
Kassner, Michael Ernest *materials science educator, researcher*

### Pendleton
Harper, Gloria Janet *artist, educator*
Klepper, Elizabeth Lee *physiologist*
Kottkamp, John Harlan *lawyer*
Smiley, Richard Wayne *research center administrator, researcher*

### Pleasant Hill
Kesey, Ken *writer*

### Port Orford
Drinnon, Richard *history educator*

### Portland
Abbott, Carl John *urban studies and planning educator*
Abbott, Robert Carl *management company executive*
Abel, William Edward *applied physicist, consultant*
Abravanel, Allan Ray *lawyer*
Ace, Katherine *artist*
Achterman, Gail Louise *lawyer*
Adams, Hilda Chaski *public health administrator, epidemiologist*
Ahuja, Jagdish Chand *mathematics educator*
Amon, Robert Bickford *physician, consultant*
Anderegg, Karen Klok *marketing executive*
Anderson, Herbert H. *lawyer, farmer*
Arthur, Michael Elbert *lawyer*
†Bagby, Grover Carlton *medical educator*
Bailey, Robert C. *opera company executive*
Baker, Allison Paige *photographer, musician, educator*
Baker, Diane R.H. *dermatologist*
Bakkensen, John Reser *lawyer*
Baldwin-Halvorsen, Lisa Rogene *community health and critical care nurse*
Balmer, Thomas Ancil *lawyer*
Barmack, Neal Herbert *neuroscientist*
Bates, Richard Mather *dentist*
Beatty, John Cabeen, Jr. *judge*
Becker, Bruce Douglas *mechanical engineer*
Bennett, William Michael *physician*
Benson, John Alexander, Jr. *physician, educator*
Berthelsdorf, Siegfried *psychiatrist*
Bhatia, Peter K. *editor, journalist*
Blackwell, Garland Wayne *retired military officer*
†Bley, Paul *jazz pianist, composer, producer*
Blumel, Joseph Carlton *university president*
Booth, Brian Geddes *lawyer*
Bragdon, Paul Errol *educator*
Brenneman, Delbert Jay *lawyer*
Brockley, John P. *state agency executive, airport executive*
Broughton, Ray Monroe *economic consultant*
Browne, Joseph Peter *retired librarian*
Bruce, John Allen *foundation executive, educator*
Brummett, Robert Eddie *pharmacology educator*
Burton, Mike *zoological park administrator*
Butler, Leslie Ann *advertising executive, portrait artist, writer*
Cable, John Franklin *lawyer*
Cameron, Gerry B. *banking executive*
Campbell, James, VII *patent lawyer*
Campbell, John Richard *pediatric surgeon*
Campbell, William Joseph *academic director*
Canaday, Richard A. *lawyer*
Carlsen, Clifford Norman, Jr. *lawyer*
Chrzanowska-Jeske, Malgorzata Ewa *electrical engineering educator, consultant*
Clarke, J(oseph) Henry *dental educator, dentist*
Claycomb, Cecil Keith *biochemist, educator*
Cohen, Joyce E. *former state senator, investment executive*
Cohen, Norm *chemist*
Cole-McCullough, Daniel *music educator, conductor, clinician*
Collins, Maribeth Wilson *foundation president*
Commerford, Kathleen Anne *psychologist*
Conkling, Roger Linton *consultant, business administration educator, retired utility executive*
Connor, William Elliott *physician, educator*
Cooper, Ginnie *library director*
Crabbs, Roger Alan *publisher, consultant, small business owner, educator*
Crawshaw, Ralph *psychiatrist*
Cronyn, Marshall William *chemistry educator*
Crowell, John B., Jr. *lawyer, former government official*
Dahl, Joyle Cochran *lawyer*
Dailey, Dianne K. *lawyer*
Daly, Donald F. *engineering company executive*
Darling, Lynda Karen *secondary education educator*
Davis, James Allan *gerontologist, educator*
Dean, E. Joseph *lawyer*
DeChaine, Dean Dennis *lawyer*
Deering, Thomas Phillips *lawyer*
†DeMots, Henry *cardiologist*
DePreist, James Anderson *conductor*
Dotten, Michael Chester *lawyer*
Drummond, Gerard Kasper *lawyer, retired minerals company executive*
Dryden, Robert D. *engineering educator*
DuBoff, Leonard David *lawyer*
Dunne, Thomas Gregory *chemistry educator, researcher*
Eakin, Margaretta Morgan *lawyer*
Edwards, Richard Alan *lawyer*
Eichinger, Marilynne H. *museum administrator*
Englert, Walter George *classics and humanities educator*
English, Stephen F. *lawyer*
Epstein, Edward Louis *lawyer*
Eshelman, William Robert *librarian, editor*
Fan, Lee Siu *business executive and vocational training program administrator*
Fell, James F. *lawyer*
Feuerstein, Howard M. *lawyer*
Foehl, Edward Albert *chemical company executive*
Foley, Ridgway Knight, Jr. *lawyer, writer*
Franklin, Dolores Roberts *elementary education educator*
Franzke, Richard Albert *lawyer*
Frasca, Robert John *architect*
Fraunfelder, Frederick Theodore *ophthalmologist, educator*
Frisbee, Don Calvin *retired utilities executive*
Froebe, Gerald Allen *lawyer*
Frolick, Patricia Mary *retired elementary education educator*
Fronk, William Joseph *retired machinery company executive*
Frye, Helen Jackson *judge*
Galbraith, John Robert *insurance company executive*
Georges, Maurice Ostrow *lawyer*
†Giffin, Sandra Lee *nursing administrator*
Gilkey, Gordon Waverly *curator, artist*
Glasgow, William Jacob *lawyer, venture capitalist*
Glass, Laurel Ellen *gerontologist, developmental biologist, physician, retired educator*
Glickman, Harry *professional basketball team executive*
Goldfarb, Timothy Moore *hospital administrator*
Grappe, Harold Hugo *civil engineer*
Grappelli, Stephane *jazz violinist*
Graves, Earl William, Jr. *journalist*
Gray, John Delton *retired manufacturing company executive*
Greene, Herbert Bruce *lawyer, merchant banker*
Greenlick, Merwyn Ronald *health services researcher*
Greenstein, Merle Edward *import and export company executive*
Greer, Monte Arnold *physician, educator*
Gren, Conrad Roger *accountant*
Gunsul, Brooks R. W. *architect*
Hacker, Thomas Owen *architect*
Hagenstein, William David *forester, consultant*
Hager, Orval O. *retired lawyer, consultant*
Hammer, Susan M. *lawyer*
Hanna, Harry Mitchell *lawyer*
Hardy, Randall Webster *utility executive*
Harris, Frederick Philip *retired philosophy educator*
Harrison, Howard F. *psychiatrist*
Hart, John Edward *lawyer*
Haselton, Rick Thomas *lawyer*
Hatfield, Mark O. *former senator*
Hay, Andrew Mackenzie *merchant banking and commodities company executive*
Held, Jay Allen *pastor*
Helmer, M. Christie *lawyer*
Hergenhan, Kenneth William *lawyer*
Hess, Henry Leroy, Jr. *bankruptcy judge*
Higdon, Polly Susanne *federal judge*
Hill, Andrew William *jazz musician, composer*
Hill, Ray Thomas, Jr. *import and export company executive*
Hinkle, Charles Frederick *lawyer, clergyman, educator*
Hoffman, Jack Leroy *lawyer*
Holman, Donald Reid *lawyer*
Howorth, David Bishop *lawyer*
Hudson, Jerry E. *university president*
Huenemann, Ruben Henry *clergyman*
Hutchens, Tyra Thornton *physician, educator*
Hyatt, Dan Richard *lawyer*
Jacob, Stanley Wallace *surgeon, educator*
Jenkins, Donald John *art museum administrator*
Jensen, Edmund Paul *bank holding company executive*
Johnson, Alexander Charles *lawyer, electrical engineer*
Johnston, Virginia Evelyn *editor*
Jones, Alan C. *grocery company executive*
Jones, Richard Theodore *biochemistry educator*
Jones, Robert Edward *federal judge*
Josephson, Richard Carl *lawyer*
Josselson, Frank *lawyer*
Juba, George E. *federal judge*
Julien, Robert Michael *anesthesiologist, author*
Jungers, Francis *oil consultant*
Katz, Vera *mayor, former college administrator, state legislator*
Kendall, John Walker, Jr. *medical educator, researcher, university dean*
Kennedy, Jack Leland *lawyer*
Kester, Randall Blair *lawyer*
Khalil, Mohammad Aslam Khan *environmental science and engineering educator*
Kilbourn, Lee Ferris *architect, specifications writer*
Kinzer, Donald Louis *retired historian, educator*
Knoll, James Lewis *lawyer*
Koblik, Stevens S. *academic administrator*
Kocaoglu, Dundar F. *engineering management educator, industrial and civil engineer*
Kolde, Bert *professional basketball team executive*
Kreinberg, Penelope Pettit *counselor*
Kristof, Ladis Kris Donabed *political scientist, author*
Kupel, Frederick John *counselor*
Lall, B. Kent *civil engineering educator*
Lang, Philip David *former state legislator, insurance company executive*
Larpenteur, James Albert, Jr. *lawyer*
Lawrence, Sally Clark *academic administrator*
Leavy, Edward *federal judge*
Leedy, Robert Allan, Sr. *retired lawyer*
Lees, Martin Henry *pediatrician, educator*
Lenderman, Joanie *elementary education educator*
Leupp, Edythe Peterson *retired education educator, administrator*
Leyden, Norman *conductor*
Li, Fu *electrical engineering educator, editor*
Lilly, Elizabeth Giles *mobile park executive*
Lincoln, Sandra Eleanor *chemistry educator*
Lindley, Thomas Ernest *environmental lawyer, law educator*
Linstone, Harold Adrian *management and systems science educator*
Livingston, Louis Bayer *lawyer*
Lobitz, Walter Charles, Jr. *physician, educator*
Loeb, Joyce Lichtgarn *interior designer, civic worker*
Loewenthal, Nessa Parker *communications educator*
Love, William Edward *lawyer*
Lynch, Nita Marie Smith *vocational curriculum developer*
Maclean, Charles (Bernard Maclean) *public affairs and marketing consultant*
Maloney, Robert E., Jr. *lawyer*
Mapes, Jeffrey Robert *journalist*

Marsh, John Harrison *environmental planner, lawyer*
Marsh, Malcolm F. *federal judge*
Martin, Ernest Lee *academic administrator, historian, theologian, writer*
Martin, Lucy Z. *public relations executive*
Marvin, Roy Mack *metal products executive*
Matarazzo, Joseph Dominic *psychologist, educator*
McCall, William Calder *oil and chemical company executive*
McClave, Donald Silsbee *professional society administrator*
McDaniel, Rickey David *senior living executive*
McKennon, Keith Robert *chemical company executive*
McKinley, Loren Dhue *museum director*
Meighan, Stuart Spence *hospital consultant, internist, writer*
Michael, Gary Linn *architect, artist*
Miller, Robert G. *retail company executive*
Miller, William Richey, Jr. *lawyer*
Mooney, Michael Joseph *college president*
Moore, Thomas Scott *lawyer*
Morgan, James Earl *librarian, administrator*
†Morris, Paul Francis *landscape architect*
Mowe, Gregory Robert *lawyer*
Murphy, Francis Seward *journalist*
Myers, Clay *retired investment management company executive*
Nash, Frank Erwin *lawyer*
Newman, Sharon Ann *principal*
Noonan, William Donald *lawyer*
Norby, Mark Alan *lawyer*
Nunn, Robert Warne *lawyer*
O'Hollaren, Paul Joseph *former international fraternity administrator*
Olejko, Mitchell J. *lawyer*
Olsen, Kurt *investment company executive, adviser*
Olson, Roger Norman *health service administrator*
Orloff, Chet *cultural organization administrator*
O'Scannlain, Diarmuid Fionntain *federal judge*
†Palmer, Earl A. *ophthalmologist, educator*
Pamplin, Robert Boisseau, Sr. *textile manufacturing executive, retired*
Pamplin, Robert Boisseau, Jr. *agricultural company executive, minister, writer*
Panner, Owen M. *federal judge*
Patterson, James Randolph *physician*
Pearson, David Petri *chemist*
Perkowski, Marek Andrzej *electrical engineering educator*
Pfeifer, Larry Alan *public health service coordinator*
†Pierson, Wayne George *trust company executive*
Porter, Elsa Allgood *writer, lecturer*
Press, Edward *consulting physician*
Purcell, John F. *lawyer*
Ramaley, Judith Aitken *academic administrator, endocrinologist*
Ramsby, Mark Delivan *lighting designer and consultant*
Rasmussen, Richard Robert *lawyer*
Rawlinson, Dennis Patrick *lawyer*
Redden, James Anthony *federal judge*
Reiten, Richard G. *natural gas industry executive*
Richards, Herbert East *minister emeritus, commentator*
Richardson, Campbell *lawyer*
Richter, Peter Christian *lawyer*
Ricks, Mary F(rances) *academic administrator, anthropologist*
Riker, William Kay *pharmacologist, educator*
Ritz, Richard Ellison *architect, architectural historian, writer*
Robbins, Donald Kenneth *real estate investment advisor, consultant*
†Rooks, Charles S. *foundation administrator*
Rooks, Judith Pence *family planning, maternal health care, midwifery consultant*
Rosenbaum, Lois Omenn *lawyer*
Roth, Phillip Joseph *retired judge*
Rowe, Sandra Mims *newspaper editor*
Rubin, Bruce Alan *lawyer*
Russell, Marjorie Rose *manufacturing company executive*
Rutherford, William Drake *investment executive, lawyer*
Rutsala, Vern A. *poet, English language educator, writer*
Rutzick, Mark Charles *lawyer*
Ryan, John Duncan *lawyer*
Sand, Thomas Charles *lawyer*
Saslow, George *psychiatrist, educator*
Schmidt, Stanley Eugene *retired speech educator*
Schmidt, Waldemar Adrian *pathologist, educator*
Schnitzer, Arlene Director *art dealer*
Schuster, Philip Frederick, II *lawyer, writer*
Seil, Fredrick John *neuroscientist, neurologist*
Sevetson, Donald James *retired minister, church administrator*
Sherrer, Charles David *college dean, clergyman*
Shireman, Joan Foster *social work educator*
Short, Robert Henry *retired utility executive*
Silver, Stephen Hal *stockbroker, financial planner*
Simpson, Robert Glenn *lawyer*
Skiens, William Eugene *electrical interconnect systems scientist, polymer engineer*
Sklovsky, Robert Joel *naturopathic physician, pharmacist, educator*
Skopil, Otto Richard, Jr. *federal judge*
Stalnaker, John Hulbert *physician*
Standring, James Douglas *real estate developer*
Staver, Leroy Baldwin *banker*
Steinfeld, Ray, Jr. *food products executive*
Steinman, Lisa Malinowski *English literature educator, writer*
Sterling, Donald Justus, Jr. *retired newspaper editor*
Stevens, Wendell Claire *anesthesiology educator*
Stewart, Janice Mae *judge*
Stewart, Milton Roy *lawyer*
Stickel, Frederick A. *publisher*
Stickel, Patrick Francis *publishing executive, newspaper*
Strader, Timothy Richards *lawyer*
Sugg, John Logan (Jack Sugg) *advertising executive*
Sullivan, Edward Joseph *lawyer, educator*
Sutherland, Donald Wood *cardiologist*
Suwyn, Mark A. *building products executive*
Swan, Kenneth Carl *surgeon*
Swindells, William, Jr. *lumber and paper company executive*
Taylor, Carson William *electrical engineer*
Taylor, J(ocelyn) Mary *museum administrator, zoologist, educator*
Taylor, Robert Brown *medical educator*
Terkla, Louis Gabriel *retired university dean*
Terry, Clark *musician*
Tomjack, T.J. *wholesale distribution executive*
Troutwine, Gayle Leone *lawyer*
Tufts, Robert B. *academic administrator*
Unis, Richard L. *state supreme court justice*
Van Hassel, Henry John *dentist, educator, university dean*
†Van Sickle, Sharon *public relations executive*
Van Valkenburg, Edgar Walter *lawyer*
Van Valkenburg, Mac Elwyn *retired electrical engineering educator*
Vaughan, Thomas James Gregory *historian*
Waddingham, John Alfred *artist, journalist*
†Walker, James Bradley *academic institution administrator*
Watkins, Charles Reynolds *medical equipment company executive*
Weaver, Delbert Allen *lawyer*
Webb, Jere Michael *lawyer*
Weber, George Richard *financial consultant, writer*
Weeks, Wilford Frank *retired geophysics educator, glaciologist*
†Weinberg, Lawrence *professional basketball team owner*
Westwood, James Nicholson *lawyer*
Wetzel, Karl Joseph *physics educator, university official and dean*
Whinston, Arthur Lewis *lawyer*
White, Douglas James, Jr. *lawyer*
Whiteley, Benjamin Robert *insurance company executive*
†Whitsitt, Robert James *professional basketball team executive*
†Wieden, Dan G. *advertising executive*
Wiener, Norman Joseph *lawyer*
Wiens, Arthur Nicholai *psychology educator*
Wiest, William Marvin *education educator, psychologist*
Wilson, Owen Meredith, Jr. *lawyer*
Wilson, Thomas Woodrow, III *research scientist, consultant*
Wineberg, Howard *research director*
Wood, Marcus Andrew *lawyer*
Woodward, Stephen Richard *newspaper reporter*
Workman, Norman Allan *accountant, graphic arts consultant*
Wright, Charles Edward *lawyer*
Wyse, William Walker *lawyer, real estate executive*
Yamayee, Zia Ahmad *engineering educator, dean*
Zalutsky, Morton Herman *lawyer*
Zerzan, Charles Joseph, Jr. *gastroenterologist*
Zimmerman, Earl Abram *physician, scientist, educator, neuroendocrinology researcher*
Zimmerman, Gail Marie *medical foundation executive*

### Prineville
Wick, Philip *wholesale distribution executive*

### Redmond
Rychetsky, Steve *civil and environmental engineer, consultant*

### Roseburg
Amnéus, John Sigfrid *retired research mechanical engineer*
Ferguson, John Franklin *music educator*
†Ford, Kenneth *lumber, wood products company executive*
Johnson, Doris Ann *educational administrator*
Jones, Henry Earl *dermatologist, direct patient care educator*

### Saint Helens
Van Horn, O. Frank *retired counselor, consultant*

### Salem
Bailey, Henry John, III *retired lawyer, educator*
Billman, Jennifer *elementsry school principal*
Breen, Richard F., Jr. *law librarian, lawyer, educator*
Brown, Kate *state legislator*
Butts, Edward Perry *civil engineer, environmental consultant*
Carson, Wallace Preston, Jr. *state supreme court chief justice*
Durham, Robert Donald, Jr. *judge*
Edge, James Edward *health care administrator*
Fadeley, Edward Norman *state supreme court justice*
Ferris, Evelyn Scott *lawyer*
Gold, Shirley Jeanne *state legislator, labor relations specialist*
Graber, Susan P. *judge*
Keisling, Phillip Andrew *state official*
Kenyon, Carleton Weller *librarian*
Kitzhaber, John Albert *governor, physician, former state senator*
Kulingoski, Theodore Ralph *lawyer*
Kulongoski, Theodore R. *state supreme court justice*
Mainwaring, William Lewis *publishing company executive, author*
Mannix, Kevin Leese *lawyer*
†Myers, William Hardy *attorney general*
Oberg, Larry Reynold *librarian*
O'Connell, Kenneth John *state justice*
Peterson, Edwin J. *retired supreme court justice, law educator*
Pierre, Joseph Horace, Jr. *commercial artist*
Rasmussen, Neil Woodland *insurance agent*
Taylor, Jacqueline Self *state legislator*
Tetzlaff, Karen Marie *state official*
Thornton, Dorothy Haberlach *artist, photographer*
Toran, Kay Dean *social services director*
Trueblood, Paul Graham *retired English educator, author, editor*
Turnbaugh, Roy Carroll *archivist*
Tweedt, Anne Elizabeth *lawyer, legislative policy analyst*
Van Hoomissen, George Albert *state supreme court justice*
VanLeeuwen, Liz Susan (Elizabeth VanLeeuwen) *state legislator, farmer*
Wallace, Julia Diane *newspaper editor*
Walsh, Richard Michael *lawyer*
Warnath, Maxine Ammer *organizational psychologist, mediator*
Weight, George Dale *banker, educator*

### Sandy
Thies, Lynn Wapinski *elementary education educator*

### Seaside
Andrews, Clarence Adelbert *historian, educator, writer, publisher*

### Siletz
Casey, Darla Diann *elementary school educator*
Jennings, Jesse David *anthropology educator*

### Sisters
Baxter, John Lincoln, Jr. *manufacturing company executive*
Keppler, Donald John *secondary education educator*

### Springfield
Detlefsen, William David, Jr. *chemicals executive*
Kimball, Reid Roberts *psychiatrist*
Lutes, Donald Henry *architect*

### Summerville
Hopkins, Gerald Frank *trade association administrator*

### Sunriver
Clough, Ray William, Jr. *civil engineering educator*
Fosmire, Fred Randall *retired forest products company executive*
Jamison, Harrison Clyde *former oil company executive, petroleum exploration consultant*

### Talent
McGill, Esby Clifton *former college official*

### Tigard
Berglund, Carl Neil *electronics company executive*
Heatherington, J. Scott *retired osteopathic physician and surgeon*
Longaker, Nancy *elementary school principal*
Nokes, John Richard *retired newspaper editor, author*

### Tualatin
Barnett, Baron Gale *prosthodontist*
Broome, John William *retired architect*
Brown, Robert Wallace *mathematics educator*
Harrington-Lloyd, Jeanne Leigh *interior designer*
Webster, Merlyn Hugh, Jr. *manufacturing engineer, information systems consultant*

### Waldport
Lemert, James Bolton *journalist, educator*

### Wallowa
Ray, Jenny *artist*
Wizard, Brian *publisher, author*

### West Linn
Bohrer, Richard William *religious writer, editor, educator*
Treffinger, Karl Edward *architectural firm executive*
Vinyard, Roy George, II *hospital administrator*

### White City
Moore, Charles August, Jr. *psychologist*

### Wilsonville
Bernard, Richard Montgomery *physician*
Gross, Hal Raymond *bishop*
Kimberley, A. G. *industrial products factory representative, management executive*
McMahon, Paul Francis *international management consultant*
Meyer, Jerome J. *diversified technology company executive*
Yacob, Yosef *lawyer, economist*

### Woodburn
Bradley, Lester Eugene *retired steel and rubber products manufacturing executive*

### Yachats
Gerdemann, James Wessel *plant pathologist, educator*
Robeck, Mildred Coen *educator, writer*

## PENNSYLVANIA

### Abington
Ayoub, Ayoub Barsoum *mathematician, educator*
Bell, H. Craig *psychiatrist*
Bildersee, Robert Alan *lawyer*
Pilla, Felix Mario *hospital administrator*
†Redmond, John *oncologist*
†Roediger, Paul M. *hospital administrator*
Schuster, Ingeborg Ida *chemistry educator*
Schwartz, Lita Linzer *psychologist, educator*

### Acme
Babcock, Marguerite Lockwood *addictions treatment therapist, writer*

### Akron
Lapp, John Allen *retired religious organization administrator*

### Albrightsville
Wilson, George Wharton *newspaper editor*

### Alcoa Center
Dobbs, Charles Luther *analytical chemist*
Kubisen, Steven Joseph, Jr. *marketing professional*
Lederman, Frank L. *scientist, research center administrator*
Stol, Israel *welding engineer*

### Aliquippa
Drobac, Nikola (Nick Drobac) *educator*

### Allensville
Yoder, Sara Ann *emergency nurse*

### Allentown
Agger, James H. *lawyer*
Armor, John N. *chemical company scientist and research manager*
Armstrong, W(illiam) Warren *advertising agency executive*
Baker, Dexter Farrington *manufacturing company executive*
Balog, Ibolya *accountant*
Bannon, George *retired economics educator, department chairman*
Baraket, Edmund S., Jr. *general contractor, contracting consultant*
Bednar, Charles Sokol *political scientist, educator*
Beltzner, Gail Ann *music educator*
Berman, Muriel Mallin *optometrist, humanities lecturer*
Berman, Philip I. *foundation administrator*
Blaney, Dorothy Gulbenkian *academic administrator*
Blume, Peter Frederick *museum director*
Brown, Robert Wayne *lawyer*
Cahn, Edward N. *federal judge*
Cavett, Van Andrew *journalist*
Chang, Chris C.N. *physician, pediatric surgeon*
Craig, Douglas Warren *food service industry executive*
DeFiore, Anthony Edward *administrative aide*
Donley, Edward *manufacturing company executive*
Farr, Lona Mae *non-profit executive, business owner*
Fitzgibbons, John P. *nephrologist*
Foster, Edward Paul (Ted Foster) *process industries executive*
Frank, Bernard *lawyer*
Gabel, Ronald Glen *telecommunications executive*
Gadomski, Robert Eugene *chemical and industrial gas company executive*
Gaylor, Donald Hughes *surgeon, educator*
Gewartowski, James Walter *electrical engineer*
Goldey, James Mearns *physicist*
Graham, Kenneth Robert *psychologist, educator*
Hansel, James Gordon *engineer, educator*
Heitmann, George Joseph *business educator, consultant*
Holt, Leon Conrad, Jr. *lawyer, business executive*
Huber, Carolyn Michelle *librarian*
Jodock, Darrell Harland *minister, religion educator*
Lesak, David Michael *safety engineer, educator, consultant*
LoCicero, Donald *language educator, writer*
McElroy, Janice Helen *government agency executive*
Moller, Hans *artist*
Nagel, Edward McCaul *lawyer, former utilities executive*
Pez, Guido Peter *research chemist*
Platt, William Henry *judge*
Russell, Alan Harold *computer specialist, educator*
Samuels, Abram *stage equipment manufacturing company executive*
Shire, Donald Thomas *retired air products and chemicals executive, lawyer*
Shorts, Gary K. *newspaper publisher*
Singhal, Kishore *engineering administrator*
Smith, Robert G., Jr. *public official, retired hotel executive*
Spering, Mark Andrew *optometrist*
Taylor, Arthur Robert *college president, business executive*
Tepper, Lloyd Barton *physician*
Tredinnick, Arthur Fred *private detective*
Wagner, Harold A. *industrial gas and chemical company executive*
†Wastak, John Rudolph *health care executive, educator*
Welsh, Thomas J. *bishop*
Wu, Pan *electrical engineer*
Yoder, Myron Eugene *secondary school educator*
Zeitlin, Bruce Allen *cryogenics technology executive*

### Allison Park
Backus, John King *former chemical company research administrator*
Craig, David W. *judge, author*
Guffey, Barbara Braden *elementary education educator*
Hadidian, Dikran Yenovk *librarian, clergyman*
Herrington, John David, III *lawyer*
LaDow, C. Stuart *consultant financial services*
Mc Dowell, John B. *bishop*
Ries, William Campbell *lawyer*
Soxman, Jane Ann *pediatric dentist*

### Altoona
Arbitell, Michelle Reneé *clinical psychologist, clinical neuropsychologist*
Clark, Threese Anne *occupational therapist, disability analyst*
Kinney, Janis Marie *librarian, consultant, storyteller*
Meadors, Allen Coats *health administrator, educator*
Sheetz, Stanton R. *retail executive*
Wright, Jerry Jaye *physical education educator*

### Ambler
Brandow, Theo *architect*
Crowell, Richard Lane *microbiologist*
Learnard, William Ewing *marketing executive*
Swansen, Donna Maloney *landscape designer, consultant*

### Ambridge
Frey, William Carl *retired bishop, academic administrator*

### Annville
McGill, William James, Jr. *academic administrator*
Synodinos, John Anthony *academic administrator*
Verhoek, Susan Elizabeth *botany educator*

### Ardmore
Bozzelli, Andrew Joseph, Jr. *retired valve company executive*
Giese, William Herbert *tax accountant*
Gutwirth, Marcel Marc *French literature educator*
Kline, George Louis *author, translator, retired philosophy and literature educator*
Lockett-Egan, Marian Workman *advertising executive*
Mirick, Henry Dustin *architect*
Ryan, Barbara Diane *management information systems director*
Scott, Bill *advertising agency executive*
Shaull, Richard *theologian, educator*
Stanley, Edward Alexander *geologist, forensic scientist, technical and academic administrator*
Zeit, Ruth Mae *foundation administrator*

### Aspers
Saltzman, Charles McKinley *educational consultant*

### Aston
Horvath, David B. *computer consultant, writer, educator*

### Athens
Luther-Lemmon, Carol Len *middle school educator*

### Avondale
Foster, Paul *playwright*
Friel, Daniel Denwood, Sr. *manufacturing executive*

**Bala Cynwyd**
Ackoff, Russell Lincoln *systems sciences educator*
Alter, Milton *neurologist, educator*
Bausher, Verne C(harles) *banker*
Bentivegna, Peter Ignatius *architectural company executive*
Blumberg, June Beth *artist*
Burland, J(ohn) Alexis *psychoanalyst*
Cades, Stewart Russell *lawyer, communications company executive*
Cander, Leon *physician, educator*
Chiusano, Michael Augustus *urologic surgeon, mechanical engineer*
Corliss, John Ozro *zoology educator*
Driscoll, Edward Carroll *construction management firm executive*
Ezold, Nancy O'Mara *lawyer*
Field, Joseph Myron *broadcast executive*
Furlong, Edward V., Jr. *paper company executive*
Garrity, Vincent Francis, Jr. *lawyer*
Gerber, Albert B. *lawyer, former legal association executive*
Kane-Vanni, Patricia Ruth *lawyer, consultant*
Kates, Gerald Saul *printing executive*
Lefton, Harvey Bennett *gastroenterologist, educator, author*
Lotman, Herbert *food processing executive*
Manko, Joseph Martin, Sr. *lawyer*
Marden, Philip Ayer *physician, educator*
McGill, Dan Mays *insurance business educator*
Michael, Gayle Granatir *English language educator, educational consultant*
Miller, L. Martin *accountant, financial planning specialist*
Newman, Andrew *physician*
Odell, Herbert *lawyer*
Potamkin, Meyer P. *mortgage banker*
Schwartz, Charles D. *broadcast executive*
Shepard, Geoffrey Carroll *insurance executive*
Strazzella, James Anthony *law educator*
Wiener, Thomas Eli *lawyer*

**Bangor**
Ceraul, David James *lawyer*
Wolf, Stewart George, Jr. *physician, medical educator*

**Barto**
Isett, Deborah Michele Gunther *elementary education educator*

**Beaver**
Helmick, Gayle Johnston *elementary education educator*
Ledebur, Linas Vockroth, Jr. *retired lawyer*

**Beaver Falls**
Copeland, Robert Marshall *music educator*

**Belle Vernon**
Kline, Bonita Ann *middle school guidance counselor, educator*
Wapiennik, Carl Francis *manufacturing firm executive, planetarium and science institute executive*

**Bensalem**
Bishop, Howard Stuart *management consultant*
Graf, William J. *entrepreneur*
Kang, Benjamin Toyeong *writer, clergyman*
Klingerman, Karen Nina *elementary school educator, teacher consultant, course coordinator*

**Berwick**
Crake, Roger F. *general surgeon*
Smith, Clara Jean *retired nursing home administrator*

**Berwyn**
Burch, John Walter *mining equipment company executive*
Ewing, Joseph Neff, Jr. *lawyer*
Fry, Clarence Herbert *retail executive*
Guenther, George Carpenter *travel company executive, retired*
Huffaker, John Boston *lawyer*
Lund, George Edward *retired electrical engineer*
Markle, John, Jr. *lawyer*
McIntyre, James Owen *insurance executive*
Reed, Clarence Raymond *retired association executive*
Silverman, Stanley Wayne *chemical company executive*
Swank, Annette Marie *software designer*
Watters, Edward McLain, III *lawyer*
Wood, Thomas E. *lawyer*

**Bethel Park**
Bohn, James Francis *physical education educator*
DeMay, Helen Louise *nursing services administrator*
Korchynsky, Michael *metallurgical engineer*
Marrs, Sharon Carter *librarian*
O'Donnell, William James *engineering executive*

**Bethlehem**
Alhadeff, Jack Abraham *biochemist, educator*
Allen, Eugene Murray *chemist*
Anderson, David Martin *environmental engineer*
Aronson, Jay Richard *economics educator, researcher, academic administrator*
Barnette, Curtis Handley *steel company executive, lawyer*
Barsness, Richard Webster *management educator, administrator*
Beedle, Lynn Simpson *civil engineering educator*
Beidler, Peter Grant *English educator*
Benz, Edward John *retired clinical pathologist*
Bergethon, Kaare Roald *retired college president*
Chen, John C. *chemical engineering educator*
Church, Thomas Trowbridge *former steel company executive*
Cole, Jack Eli *physician*
Dowling, Joseph Albert *historian, educator*
Durkee, Jackson Leland *civil engineer*
Evenson, Edward Bernard *geologist*
Fisher, John William *civil engineering educator*
Frankel, Barbara Brown *cultural anthropologist*
Gardiner, Keith Mattinson *engineering educator*
Geffe, Philip Reinhold *electrical engineer, consultant*
Georgakis, Christos *chemical engineer educator, consultant, researcher*
Ghosh, Bhaskar Kumar *statistics educator, researcher*
Gunton, James Douglas *physics educator*
Hartmann, Robert Elliott *manufacturing company executive, retired*
Haynes, Thomas Morris *philosophy educator*
Heindel, Ned Duane *chemistry educator*
Hertzberg, Richard Warren *materials science and engineering educator, researcher*
Hobbs, James Beverly *business administration educator, writer*
Jordan, John Allen, Jr. *steel company executive*
Kanofsky, Alvin Sheldon *physicist*
Karakash, John J. *engineering educator*
Kerchner, Charles Frederick, Jr. *electronics executive, engineer*
Levy, Edward Kenneth *mechanical engineering educator*
Lewis, Andrew Lindsay, Jr. (Drew Lewis) *transportation and natural resources executive*
Likins, Peter William *academic administrator*
Lindgren, John Ralph *philosophy educator*
McAulay, Alastair D. *electrical and computer engineer, educator*
Neti, Sudhakar *mechanical engineering educator*
Penny, Roger Pratt *management executive*
Pense, Alan Wiggins *metallurgical engineer, academic administrator*
Rivlin, Ronald Samuel *mathematics educator emeritus*
Roberts, Richard *mechanical engineering educator*
Rushton, Brian Mandel *chemical company executive*
Sacks, Patricia Ann *librarian, consultant*
Scanlon, Edward Charles *clinical psychologist*
Schwartz, Eli *economics educator, writer*
Sclar, Charles Bertram *geology educator, researcher*
Smolansky, Oles M. *humanities educator*
Smyth, Donald Morgan *chemical educator, researcher*
Sommers, Gordon L. *religious organization administrator*
Spillman, Robert Arnold *architect*
Steffen, Lloyd Howard *minister, religion educator*
Stuart, Gary Miller *railroad executive*
Tuzla, Kemal *mechanical engineer, scientist*
von Bernuth, Carl W. *diversified corporation executive, lawyer*
Watkins, George Daniels *physics educator*
Weidner, Richard Tilghman *physicist, educator*
Wenzel, Leonard Andrew *engineering educator*
Wolfgang, Lenora D. *foreign language educator*

**Birdsboro**
Hill, Lenora Mae *astrologer*
Mengle, Tobi Dara *mechanical engineer, consultant*

**Blakeslee**
Hayes, Alberta Phyllis Wildrick *retired health service executive*

**Bloomsburg**
Loncosky, Walter Beugger *real estate manager*
Lowthert, William Hughes, III *utility company executive*
Stropnicky, Gerard Patrick *theater director, consultant*
Traugh, Donald George, III *secondary education educator*
Vann, John Daniel, III *university dean, historian*

**Blue Bell**
Baine, Richard Joseph *vocational rehabilitation counselor*
Barron, Harold Sheldon *lawyer*
Bell, Michael G. *trade association administrator*
Brendlinger, LeRoy R. *college president*
Cherry, John Paul *science research association director, researcher*
Elliott, John Michael *lawyer*
Faden, Lee Jeffrey *technical advisory service executive*
Flaherty, Lois Talbot *psychiatrist, educator*
Gleklen, Donald Morse *investment company executive*
Lawrence, Gerald, Jr. *lawyer*
Minter, Philip Clayton *retired communications company executive*
Simon, David Frederick *lawyer*
Swansen, Samuel Theodore *lawyer*
Theis, Steven Thomas *executive safety director*
Unruh, James Arlen *business machines company executive*
Vollmar, John Raymond *electrical engineer*
Young, Charles Randall *software professional*

**Boiling Springs**
Clarke, Walter Sheldon *retired federal government official, educator*

**Boothwyn**
McLaughlin, Edward David *surgeon, medical educator*

**Boyertown**
Kuser, Edwin Charles *educational administrator, retired*
Novak, Darwin Albert, Jr. *engineering company executive, chemical engineer*
Slider, Dorla Dean (Freeman) *artist*

**Braddock**
Slack, Edward Dorsey, III *financial systems professional, consultant*

**Bradford**
Conley, Thomas Anthony *minister, counselor*
Hauser, Christopher George *lawyer*
Laroche, Roger Renan *psychiatrist*
Rice, Lester *electronics company executive*
Ross, Jean Louise *physical education educator*

**Bradfordwoods**
Davis, Nathan Tate *musician, educator*

**Brentwood**
Swanson, Fred A. *communications designer, borough councilman*

**Bridgeville**
Pappas, John George *secondary school educator*
Pearlman, Seth Leonard *civil engineer*

**Bristol**
Atkinson, Susan D. *producing artistic director, theatrical consultant*
Bush, Harold Ehrig *computer consultant*
Hutton, Ann Hawkes *state official*

**Brodbecks**
McMenamin, Helen Marie Foran *home health care, pediatric, maternal nurse*

**Broomall**
Dibianca, Joseph Philip *finance and tax executive*
Lerner, Julius *mechanical engineer*
Saunders, Sally Love *poet, educator*

**Bryn Mawr**
Ballam, Samuel Humes, Jr. *retired corporate director*
Berliner, Ernst *chemistry educator*
Braha, Thomas I. *business executive*
Brand, Charles Macy *history educator*
Broido, Arnold Peace *music publishing company executive*
Brunt, Manly Yates, Jr. *psychiatrist*
Carroll, Mary Colvert *corporate executive*
Clark, George Roberts *retired trust company executive*
Cooney, Patricia Ruth *civic worker*
Crawford, Maria Luisa Buse *geology educator*
Crawford, William Arthur *geologist*
Dorian, Nancy Currier *linguistics educator*
Driskill, John Ray *professional society administrator*
Dudden, Arthur Power *historian, educator*
Friedman, Arnold Carl *diagnostic radiologist*
Gaisser, Julia Haig *classics educator*
Goutman, Lois Clair *retired drama educator*
Grossman, William *medical researcher, educator*
Harkins, Herbert Perrin *otolaryngologist, educator*
Hoffman, Howard Stanley *experimental psychologist, educator*
Hoopes, Janet Louise *educator, psychologist*
Hung, Paul Porwen *biotechnologist, educator, consultant*
Huth, Edward Janavel *physician, editor*
King, Willard Fahrenkamp (Mrs. Edmund Ludwig King) *Spanish language educator*
Kraftson, Raymond Harry *business executive*
Krausz, Michael *philosopher, educator*
Lane, Barbara Miller (Barbara Miller-Lane) *humanities educator*
Lang, Mabel Louise *classics educator*
Ledwith, Sister Margaret Christine *nun, counselor*
Levitt, Robert E. *gastroenterologist*
Lewis, James Earl *investment banker*
Mallory, Frank Bryant *chemistry educator*
McPherson, Mary Patterson *academic administrator*
Moyer, F. Stanton *financial executive, advisor*
Noone, Robert Barrett *plastic surgeon*
Porter, Judith Deborah Revitch *sociologist, educator*
Salmon, John Hearsey McMillan *historian, educator*
Smith, Nona Coates *academic administrator*
Snider, Harlan Tanner *former manufacturing company executive*
Stapleton, Katharine Laurence *English literature educator, writer*
Stucky, Steven (Edward) *composer*
Tanis, James Robert *library director, history educator, clergyman*
Widzer, Steven J. *pediatric gastroenterologist*

**Buckingham**
Altier, William John *management consultant*

**Buffalo Mills**
Braendel, Douglas Arthur *healthcare executive*

**Bushkill**
Garretto, Leonard Anthony, Jr. *insurance company executive*
Muesing Ellwood, Edith Elizabeth *writer, researcher, publisher, editor*

**Butler**
Dodge, Ellen Elizabeth *community college official*
Kane, Marilyn Elizabeth *small business owner*
Kay, George Paul *environmental engineer*
Kendall, George Jason *accountant, financial planner, computer consultant*
Kosar, John E. *architectural firm executive*

**California**
Langham, Norma *playwright, educator, poet, composer, inventor*
Schwerdt, Lisa Mary *English language educator*

**Cambridge Springs**
Learn, Richard Leland *corrections school principal*

**Camp Hill**
Crider, Rudyard Lee *psychotherapist*
Crist, Christine Myers *consulting executive*
Crowe, John Carl *aviation consultant, retired airline executive*
Grass, Alexander *retail company executive*
Hughes, William Francis, Jr. *educational consultant*
Johnston, Thomas McElree, Jr. *church administrator*
Mead, James Matthew *insurance company executive*
Nowak, Jacquelyn Louise *administrative officer, realtor, consultant*
Peters, Ralph Edgar *architectural and engineering executive*
Robertson, James Colvert *insurance company executive*
Robinson, Ronald Michael *health care financial executive, financial consultant*
Scheiner, James Ira *engineering company executive*
Spiers, Tomas Hoskins, Jr. *architect*
Williams, Marie Cloney *rehabilitation nurse administrator, business owner*
Winberry, Joseph Paul, Jr. *optometrist*

**Canonsburg**
Harker, Joseph Edward *construction, industrial and steel company executive*
Mascetta, Joseph Anthony *principal*
Prado, Gerald M. *investment banker*

**Carlisle**
Davenny, Ward Leslie *artist, educator*
Fish, Chester Boardman, Jr. *retired publishing consultant, writer*
Fox, Arturo Angel *Spanish language educator*
Fritschler, A. Lee *college president, public policy educator*
Gorby, William Guy *anesthesiologist*
Graham, William Patton, III *plastic surgeon, educator*
Jacobs, Norman G(abriel) *sociologist, educator*
Jones, Oliver Hastings *consulting economist*
Laws, Kenneth L. *physics educator, author*
Laws, Priscilla Watson *physics educator*
Long, Howard Charles *physics educator emeritus*
Rossbacher, Lisa Ann *dean, geology educator, writer*
Russell, Theodore Emery *diplomat*
Schiffman, Joseph Harris *literary historian, educator*
Shrader, Charles Reginald *historian*
Talley, Carol Lee *newspaper editor*
Turo, Ron *lawyer*
Winkler, Ira Samuel *information security consultant, educator, author*

**Castle Shannon**
Selkowitz, Lucy Ann *security officer*

**Catasauqua**
Fogelson, Brian David *education educator*

**Center Valley**
Gambet, Daniel G(eorge) *college president, clergyman*
Smillie, Douglas James *lawyer*

**Central City**
Brown, Robert Alan *retired construction materials company executive*

**Centre Hall**
Rudy, Ruth Corman *former state legislator*

**Chadds Ford**
Cantwell, John Walsh *advertising executive*
Duff, James Henry *museum director, environmental administrator*
Isakoff, Sheldon Erwin *chemical engineer*
King, M. Jean *association executive*
Stewart, Allen Warren *lawyer*

**Chalfont**
Breslin, Elvira Madden *lawyer, educator*
Clifford, Maurice Cecil *physician, former college president, foundation executive*

**Chambersburg**
Boretz, Naomi Messinger *artist, educator*
Furr, Quint Eugene *marketing executive*
Gelbach, Martha Harvey *genealogist, writer, poet*
Holzman, Howard Eugene *health services executive*
Rumler, Robert Hoke *agricultural consultant, retired association executive*

**Cheltenham**
Weinstock, Walter Wolfe *systems engineer*

**Chester**
Bruce, Robert James *university president*
Buck, Lawrence Paul *academic administrator*
Frank, Amalie Julianna *computer science, electrical engineering and mathematics educator, consultant*
Kornfield, Nathaniel Richard *computer engineer educator*
Moll, Clarence Russel *retired university president, consultant*
O'Malley, John Patrick *dean*
Seidman, Marian Taylor *adult education educator*

**Chester Springs**
Quay, Thomas Emery *lawyer*
Scheer, R. Scott *physician*

**Chesterbrook**
Drake, William Frank, Jr. *lawyer*

**Clairton**
Dick, Douglas Patrick *construction company executive*

**Claridge**
Perich, Terry Miller *secondary school educator*

**Clarion**
Foreman, Thomas Alexander *dentist*
Siddiqui, Dilnawaz Ahmed *communications educator, international communication planning advisor, consultant*

**Clarks Summit**
Alperin, Irwin Ephraim *clothing company executive*
Beemer, John Barry *lawyer*
Firmin, Michael Wayne *counselor, educator*
Ross, Adrian E. *retired drilling manufacturing company executive*

**Clearfield**
Krebs, Margaret Eloise *publishing executive*
Pride, Douglas Spencer *minister*
Ulerich, William Keener *publishing company executive*

**Coatesville**
Ainslie, George William *psychiatrist, behavioral economist*
Burton, Mary Louise Himes *computer specialist*
DiBona, Margaret Rose *state official*
Fitzgerald, Susan Helena *elementary educator*
Giancola, Mary Ann *school nurse*
Smith, Patricia Anne *special education educator*
Sprague, William Douglas *lawyer, company executive*
Walker, Marie Fuller *elementary education educator*

**Cochranton**
Baldwin, Anthony Blair *systems theoretician, agricultural executive*

**Cochranville**
Sazegar, Morteza *artist*

**Collegeville**
Cawthorn, Robert Elston *health care executive*
De Rosen, Michel *pharmaceutical company executive*
Galie, Frank D. *sales executive*
Holder, Neville Lewis *chemist*
Kelly, Jeffrey Charles *materials engineer*
Kun, Kenneth A. *business executive*
Richter, Richard Paul *academic administrator*
Rothwell, Timothy Gordon *pharmaceutical company executive*
Strassburger, John Robert *academic administrator*

**Colmar**
Weber-Roochvarg, Lynn *English second language adult educator, communications consultant*

**Columbia**
McTaggart, Timothy Thomas *secondary education educator*
Steiner-Houck, Sandra Lynn *interior designer*

**Confluence**
Bower, Roy Donald *minister, counselor*

**Conshohocken**
Boenning, Henry Dorr, Jr. *investment banker*
Bramson, Robert Sherman *lawyer*
Cheung, Peter Pak Lun *investment company executive, chemistry educator*
Cunningham, James Gerald, Jr. *transportation company executive*
Gambescia, Stephen Francis *research administrator*
Gibson, Thomas Richard *automobile import company executive*
Naples, Ronald James *manufacturing company executive*
Rippel, Harry Conrad *mechanical engineer, consultant*
Schein, Philip Samuel *physician, educator, pharmaceutical executive*
Schumacher, Elizabeth Swisher *garden ornaments shop owner*
Spaeth, Karl Henry *retired chemical company executive, lawyer*
Tily, Stephen Bromley, III *bank executive*

**Coopersburg**
Eckardt, Arthur Roy *religion studies educator emeritus*
Peserik, James E. *electrical, controls and computer engineer, consultant, forensics and safety engineer, fire cause and origin investigator*
Siess, Alfred Albert, Jr. *engineering executive, management consultant*
Spira, Joel Solon *electronics company executive*

**Cooperstown**
Hogg, James Henry, Jr. *retired education educator*

**Coraopolis**
Giliberti, Michael Richard *financial planner*
Koepfinger, Joseph Leo *utilities executive*
Tannehill, Darcy Anita Bartins *academic administrator*

**Cornwall**
Ehrhart, Carl Yarkers *retired minister, retired college administrator*

**Corry**
Rathinavelu, Madi *manufacturing executive*

**Coudersport**
Kysor, Daniel Francis *psychologist*
†Rigas, John *broadcast executive*

**Cranberry Township**
Bashore, George Willis *bishop*
Birch, Jack Willard *psychologist, educator*
Hogberg, Carl Gustav *retired steel company executive*
St. John, Maria Ann *nurse anesthetist*
Tiller, Olive Marie *retired church worker*

**Dallas**
Baltimore, Ruth Betty *social worker*
Day, Maurice Jerome *automobile parts distributing company executive*
Hunter, Todd Lee *secondary school music educator*
Moran, Michael Lee *physical therapist, computer consultant*
Rockensies, Kenneth Jules *physicist, educator*
Sutton, Royal Keith *marketing professional*

**Danville**
Cochran, William John *physician, pediatrician, gastroenterologist, nutritionist, consultant*
Kazem, Ismail *radiation oncologist, educator, health science facility administrator*
Kleponis, Jerome Albert *dentist*
Lessin, Michael Edward *oral-maxillofacial surgeon*
Morgan, Howard Edwin *physiologist*
Pierce, James Clarence *surgeon*
Randall, Neil Warren *gastroenterologist*
Wert, Barbara J. Yingling *special education educator*

**Dayton**
Patterson, Madge Lenore *elementary education educator*

**Delaware Water Gap**
Woods, Philip Wells (Phil Woods) *jazz musician composer*

**Devon**
Burget, Dean Edwin, Jr. *plastic surgeon*
Carroll, Albert *retired corporate executive*

**Dickson City**
Carluccio, Sheila Cook *psychologist*

**Dillsburg**
Bowers, Glenn Lee *retired professional society administrator*
Jackson, George Lyman *nuclear medicine physician*

**Donora**
Todd, Norma Jean Ross *retired government official*

**Douglassville**
Haratunian, Michael *engineering company executive*

**Dover**
Hayek, William Edward *investment advisor, counsel*

**Doylestown**
Blewitt, George Augustine *physician, consultant*
Brink, Frank, Jr. *biophysicst, former educator*
Carson, John Thompson, Jr. *environmental consultant*
Cathcart, Harold Robert *hospital administrator*
Davis, Carole Joan *psychologist*
Elliott, Richard Howard *lawyer*
Haines, Bonnie Nadine *psychiatric nurse, visiting nurse*
Holstrom, Carleton Arthur *brokerage house executive*
Hoopes, Robert Patrick *lawyer*
King, Robert Edward *retired pharmacy educator*
Long, Ronald Alex *real estate and financial consultant, educator*
Maser, Frederick Ernest *clergyman*
McNulty, Carrell Stewart, Jr. *manufacturing company executive, architect*
McNutt, Richard Hunt *manufacturing company executive*
Miller, Lynne Marie *critical care nurse, administrator*
Mishler, John Milton (Yochanan Menashsheh ben Shaul) *natural sciences educator, academic administrator*
Morgnanesi, Lanny M. *journalist*
Purpura, Peter Joseph *museum curator, exhibition designer*
Smith, Charles Paul *newspaper publisher*
Thorne, John Watson, III *advertising and marketing executive*

**Drexel Hill**
Alexander, Lloyd Chudley *author*
Baessler, Christina A. *medical/surgical nurse*
Bomberger, John Henry Augustus *pediatrician*
Heilig, David *osteopathic physician*
Martino, Michael Charles *entertainer, musician*
Schiazza, Guido Domenic (Guy Schiazza) *educational association administrator*
Thompson, William David *minister, homiletics educator*
West, Kenneth Edward *lawyer*

**Duncannon**
Roach, Ralph Lee *human services and rehabilitation consultant*

**Dunmore**
Pencek, Carolyn Carlson *treasurer, educator*

**Eagles Mere**
Sample, Frederick Palmer *former college president*

**East Springfield**
Vadzemnieks, Michael Lester *plastics company executive*

**East Stroudsburg**
Brackbill, Nancy Lafferty *elementary education educator*
Briggs, Philip James *political science educator, author, lecturer*
Crackel, Theodore Joseph *historian*
Dillman, Robert John *academic administrator*
Truschel, Jack Henry, II *university official, consultant*

**Easton**
Ashby, Richard James, Jr. *bank executive, lawyer*
Belyea, Robert Combs *electrical engineer*
Brown, Robert Carroll *lawyer*
Coleman, John Macdonald *historian*
Cooke, Jacob Ernest *history educator, author*
Danjczek, Michael Harvey *social service adminstrator*
DiMatteo, Rhonda Lynn *speech-language pathologist, audiologist*
Grunberg, Robert Leon Willy *nephrologist*
Holmes, Larry, Jr. *professional boxer*
Kincaid, John *political science educator, editor*
Mamana, Joseph *editor*
Noel, Nicholas, III *lawyer*
Reibman, Jeanette Fichman *retired state senator*
Rohatgi, Rajeev *cardiologist*
Rothkopf, Arthur J. *college president*
Stitt, Dorothy Jewett *journalist*
Van Antwerpen, Franklin Stuart *federal judge*
Wimmer, Maureen Kathryn *chemical engineer*

**Ebensburg**
Ramsdell, Richard Adoniram *marine engineer*

**Edgemont**
Armani, Aida Mary *small business executive*

**Edinboro**
Cox, Clifford Laird *university administrator, musician*
Curry-Carlburg, Joanne Jeanne *elementary education educator*
Kemenyffy, Steven *artist, art educator*
Kinch, Janet Carolyn Brozic *English and German language/literature educator*
Miller, G(erson) H(arry) *research institute director, mathematician, computer scientist, chemist*
Paul, Charlotte P. *nursing educator*

**Eighty Four**
Capone, Alphonse William *retired industrial executive*

**Elizabethtown**
Brown, Dale Weaver *clergyman, theologian, educator*
Krut, Stephen Frank *trade association administrator*
Madeira, Robert Lehman *professional society administrator*
Ritsch, Frederick Field *academic administrator, historian*

**Elizabethville**
Romberger, John Albert *scientist, historian*

**Elkins Park**
Check, Jerome Harvey *reproductive endocrinologist*
Davidson, Abraham Aba *art historian, photographer*
Erlebacher, Martha Mayer *artist, educator*
Fussell, Catharine Pugh *biological researcher*
Glijansky, Alex *psychiatrist, psychoanalyst*
Kolansky, Harold *physician, psychiatrist, psychoanalyst*
Prince, Morton Bronenberg *physicist*
Rosen, Rhoda *obstetrician and gynecologist*
Simon, Marilyn Weintraub *art educator, sculptor*
Yun, Daniel Duwhan *physician, foundation administrator*

**Ellwood City**
Rorquist, Ivor Carl *mechanical engineer*

**Emmaus**
Beldon, Sanford T. *publisher*
Bowers, Klaus D(ieter) *retired electronics research development company executive*
Bricklin, Mark Harris *magazine editor, publisher*
Lafavore, Michael J. *magazine editor*
Rodale, Ardath *publishing executive*
†Vaughn, Lewis A. *magazine editor, writer*

**Enola**
Baumann, Matthew Louis *business education educator, elementary school educator*
Myers, Alfred Frantz *state education official*

**Erie**
Adovasio, J. M. *anthropologist, archeologist, educator*
Allshouse, Robert Harold *history educator*
Barber, Michele A. *special education educator*
Bentz, Warren Worthington *federal bankruptcy judge*
Boyes, Karl W. *state legislator*
Bracken, Charles Herbert *banker*
Duval, Albert Frank *paper company executive*
Egan, Corrine Halperin *trade association administrator*
Eiben, Gary *lawyer*
Gilloteaux, Jacques Jean-Marie Anthime *cell biologist, researcher*
Gray, Robert Beckwith *electrical engineer, consultant*
Hagen, Thomas Bailey *business owner, former state official, former insurance company executive*
Hey, John Charles *electronics company executive*
Hsu, Bertrand Dahung *mechanical engineer*
Kalkhof, Thomas Corrigan *physician*
Karlson, Eskil Leannart *biophysicist*
Kish, George Franklin *thoracic and cardiovascular surgeon*
Lilley, John Mark *academic administrator, dean*
Mason, Gregg C. *orthopedic surgeon, researcher*
Mencer, Glenn Everell *federal judge*
Moore, Christine Helen *critical care nurse*
Nash, Mary Alice *nursing educator*
Nygaard, Richard Lowell *federal judge*
Rowley, Robert Deane, Jr. *bishop*
Ryan, Gerald Anthony *financial advisor, venture capitalist*
Savocchio, Joyce A. *mayor*
Trautman, Donald W. *bishop*
Upton, Thomas Vernon *medical educator*
Vanco, John L. *art museum director*
Zamboldi, Richard Henry *lawyer*

**Erwinna**
Geldmacher, Robert Carl *engineering educator*
Richman, Joan F. *television consultant*

**Evans City**
Salisbury, Judith Muriel *marketing consultant*

**Everett**
Vollbrecht, Edward Alan *school superintendent*

**Exeter**
Stocker, Joyce Arlene *retired secondary school educator*

**Export**
Colborn, Harry Walter *electrical engineering consultant*
Wagner, Charles Leonard *electrical engineer, consultant*

**Exton**
Ashton, Mark Randolph *lawyer*
Burns, Richard James *marketing professional*
Falcone, Anthony *mechanical engineer*
Lewis, Thomas B. *specialty chemical company executive*
Penrose, Charles, Jr. *professional society administrator*
Pollock, Roy Van Horn *pharmaceutical company animal health researcher*
Sanford, Richard D. *computer company executive*
Walls, Thomas Francis *management consultant*

**Fairless Hills**
Decator, Carl James *transportation executive*
Marable, Simeon-David *artist*
Rosella, John Daniel *psychologist*

**Fairview**
Gorski, Brian C. *engineer, consultant*

**Fairview Village**
Filippini, Christine Marie *counselor*

**Fayetteville**
Kocek-McMurtray, Stephanie Susan *theater executive*

**Feasterville Trevose**
Faulkner, Henry, III *automotive executive*
McEvilly, James Patrick, Jr. *lawyer*
Sergey, John Michael, Jr. *manufacturing company executive*

**Felton**
Shoemaker, Eleanor Boggs *television production company executive*

**Ferndale**
Folk, James *sales executive*

**Fleetwood**
Buckalew, Robert Joseph *psychologist, consultant*
Lewis, Dana Kenneth *trading company executive, consultant, author*

**Flourtown**
Christy, John Gilray *financial company executive*
Lambert, Joan Dorety *elementary education educator*
Lee, Adrian Iselin, Jr. *journalist*
Moore, Sandra Kay *counselor, administrator*

**Fogelsville**
Ault, James Mase *bishop*

**Fort Washington**
Blumberg, Donald Freed *management consultant*
Blumberg, Judith Toplin *international consulting firm executive*
Deric, Arthur Joseph *management consultant, lawyer*
Hague, Stephen George *museum director*
Hess, Lawrence Eugene, Jr. *lawyer*
Keating, Frank J. *paper company executive*
Meyer, Andrew R. *manufacturing executive*
Pappas, Charles Engelos *plastic surgeon*
Pillai, Raviraj Sukumar *chemical engineer, researcher*
Shah, Bipin Chandra *banker*
Urbach, Frederick *physician, educator*

**Forty Fort**
Meeker, Robert Gardner *English language educator*

**Franklin Center**
Resnick, Stewart Allen *diversified company executive*

**Fredericktown**
Hess, Dolores J. *elementary education educator*

**Freeland**
Rudawski, Joseph George *educational administrator*

**Furlong**
Ide, John Edwin *physical education educator*

**Gaines**
Beller, Martin Leonard *retired orthopaedic surgeon*

**Gettysburg**
Coughenour, Kavin Luther *career officer, military historian*
Hallberg, Budd Jaye *management consulting firm executive*
Hendrix, Sherman Samuel *biology educator, researcher*
Hill, Hugh Kenneth *retired diplomat, former ambassador*
Holland, Koren Alayne *chemistry educator*
Latschar, John A. *historic site administrator*
Plischke, Elmer *political science educator*
Roach, James Clark *government official*
Schein, Virginia Ellen *psychologist, educator*
Schildknecht, Calvin E(verett) *chemist, consultant, educator*

**Gibsonia**
Cauna, Nikolajs *physician, medical educator*
Heilman, Carl Edwin *lawyer*
Shoub, Earle Phelps *chemical engineer, educator*

**Gladwyne**
Acton, David *lawyer*
Allen, Theresa Ohotnicky *neurobiologist, consultant*
Booth, Harold Waverly *finance and investment company executive, lawyer*
Geisel, Cameron Meade, Jr. *investment professional*
Gonick, Paul *urologist*
Mc Donald, Robert Emmett *company executive*
Patten, Lanny Ray *industrial gas industry executive*
Stick, Alyce Cushing *information systems consultant*

**Glen Mills**
Churchill, Stuart Winston *chemical engineering educator*
Turner, Janet Sullivan *painter*

**Glen Riddle**
Dunion, Celeste Mogab *township official, consultant*

**Glenmoore**
DeGuatemala, Joyce *sculptor*

**Glenside**
Bardliving, Clifford Lee, Jr. *graphic designer*
Carter, Ruth B. (Mrs. Joseph C. Carter) *foundation administrator*
Forman, Edgar Ross *mechanical engineer*
Frudakis, Zenos Antonios *sculptor, artist*
Hargens, Charles William, III *electrical engineer, consultant*
Hemenway, Aice Pearson *retired museum director*
Johnson, Waine Cecil *dermatologist*
Pelham, Fran O'Byrne *writer, teacher*
Reiss, George Russell, Jr. *physician*

**Gouldsboro**
Duricko, Erma O. *stage director, educator*
West, Daniel Jones, Jr. *hospital administrator, rehabilitaton counselor, health care consultant, educator*

**Grantham**
Falk, Noel Wesley *biology educator, radio and television program host, horticultural consultant*
Sider, Harvey Ray *minister, church administrator*

**Grantville**
Sudor, Cynthia Ann *marketing and corporate sponsorship consultant*

**Gratz**
Herb, Jane Elizabeth *banker*

**Greencastle**
Dietrich, Joyce Diane *librarian*

**Greensburg**
Boyd, Robert Wright, III *lamp company executive*
Duck, Patricia Mary *librarian*
Guyker, William Charles, Jr. *electrical engineer, researcher*
Harrell, Edward Harding *newspaper executive*
Lisowitz, Gerald Myron *neuropsychiatrist*
McDowell, Michael David *lawyer, utility executive*
Speedy, Eric Dawson *laboratory technician*

**Greentown**
Forcheskie, Carl S. *former apparel company executive*
Hall, Cathy E. *sales professional*

**Greenville**
Lillie, Marshall Sherwood *college safety and security director, educator*
Sakkal, Saad *endocrinologist, geriatrician*

Stuver, Francis Edward *former railway car company executive*

**Gwynedd**
Chasins, Edward A. *communications company executive*
Zumeta, Bertram William *retired economist*

**Gwynedd Valley**
Feenane, Sister Mary Alice *principal*
Giordano, Patricia J. *radiation therapist*

**Hamburg**
Schappell, Abigail Susan *speech, language and hearing therapist*

**Hanover**
Kline, Donald *food company executive*
Toft, Thelma Marilyn *secondary school educator*

**Harleysville**
Daller, Walter E., Jr. *banking executive*
Ruth, Alpheus Landis *dairy farmer*

**Harrisburg**
Allen, Heath Ledward *lawyer*
Armstrong, Gibson E. *state senator*
Armstrong, Thomas Errol *state legislator*
Baird, Irene Cebula *educational administrator*
Barto, Charles O., Jr. *lawyer*
Breslin, Michael Joseph, III *social services administrator, educator*
Brown, John Walter *vocational education supervisor*
Burcat, Joel Robin *lawyer*
Cadieux, Roger Joseph *physician, mental health care executive*
Campbell, Carl Lester *banker*
Carnahan, Frances Morris *magazine editor*
Cate, Donald James *mechanical engineer, consultant*
Cauley, Alvin Paul *state government administrator*
Chambers, Clarice Lorraine *clergy, educational consultant*
Chernicoff, David Paul *osteopath, educator*
Cline, Andrew Haley *lawyer*
Comoss, Patricia B. *cardiac rehabilitation nurse, consultant*
Cooper, Jane Todd (J. C. Todd) *poet, writer, educator*
Crall, Dale Eugene *accountant*
Cramer, John McNaight *lawyer*
Dattilo, Nicholas C. *bishop*
DeKok, David *writer, reporter*
Diehm, James Warren *lawyer, educator*
Dietz, John Raphael *consulting engineer executive*
Downey, Brian Patrick *lawyer*
Edmiston, Guy S., Jr. *bishop*
Edwards, JoAnn Louise *human resources executive*
Gallaher, William Marshall *dental laboratory technician*
Giusti, Joseph Paul *global human resource development director, retired university chancellor*
Glass, Brent D. *state commission administrator*
Goell, James Emanuel *electronics company executive*
Gover, Raymond Lewis *newspaper publisher*
Gruitza, Michael *state legislator, lawyer*
Hanson, Robert DeLolle *lawyer*
Hart, Melissa A. *state senator*
Hudson, William Jeffrey, Jr. *manufacturing company executive*
Huntington, Thomas Mansfield *editor*
Hyle, Jack Otto *orthomolecular psychologist*
Itkin, Ivan *state legislator*
Jeffries, Richard Haley *physician, broadcasting company executive*
Josephs, Babette *legislator*
Kaiser, Linda Susan *state commissioner, lawyer*
Kane, Yvette *state official, lawyer*
Kelly, Robert Edward, Jr. *lawyer*
Klein, Michael D. *lawyer*
Krobath, Krista Ann *pharmacist*
Kury, Franklin Leo *lawyer*
Lappas, Spero Thomas *lawyer*
Loedding, Peter Alfred *trade association executive*
Loeper, F. Joseph *state senator*
Logue, James Nicholas *epidemiologist*
Lourie, Norman Victor *government official, social worker*
Margo, Katherine Lane *physician*
McCormick, James Harold *academic administrator*
Megargee, Kathleen Anne *state public information officer, producer*
Moritz, Milton Edward *security consultant*
Neilson, Winthrop Cunningham, III *communications executive, financial communications consultant*
Newsome, William Roy, Jr. *state official*
Nyce, Robert Eugene *state legislator, tax accountant*
O'Donnell, John Joseph, Jr. *optometrist*
Ozereko-deCoen, Mary Therese *therapeutic recreation specialist and therapist*
Peechatka, Walter Norman *government official*
Rambo, Sylvia H. *federal judge*
Ridge, Thomas Joseph *governor, former congressman*
†Rudy, Frank R. *pathologist*
Sadlock, Richard Alan *lawyer*
Schore, Niles *lawyer*
Schweiker, Mark S. *lieutenant governor*
Settle, Eric Lawrence *lawyer*
Stabler, Donald Billman *business executive*
Stuckey, Susan Jane *perioperative nurse, consultant*
Trexler, Suzanne Frances *geriatrics nurse*
Tyson, Gail L. *health federation administrator*
Vaughn, Stephen Anthony *biochemist, physician, educator*
Warshaw, Allen Charles *lawyer*
Wei, I-Yuan *research and development consultant and director*
†Weiss, Stephen Max *health care administrator, surgeon, educator*
West, James Joseph *lawyer*
Woods, Willie G. *dean, English language and education educator*
Zook, Merlin Wayne *meteorologist*

**Harveys Lake**
Wolensky, Joan *occupational therapist, interfaith minister*

**Hatboro**
Hull, Lewis Woodruff *manufacturing company executive*
Marshall, Trevor John *engineering professional*
Quigley, Robert Charles *insurance industry consultant*

**Haverford**
Bogash, Richard *retired pharmaceutical company executive*
Boyer, Vincent Saull *energy consultant*
Brownlow, Donald Grey *private school educator*
Davison, John Herbert *music educator, academic administrator*
de Laguna, Frederica *anthropology educator emeritus, author, consultant*
Frick, Benjamin Charles *lawyer*
Gross, Stanley Carl *marketing consultant*
Jorden, Eleanor Harz *linguist, educator*
Jurney, Dorothy Misener *journalist, editor*
Kee, Howard Clark *religion educator*
McGlinn, Frank Cresson Potts *lawyer*
Mellink, Machteld Johanna *archaeologist, educator*
Merrill, Arthur Alexander *financial analyst*
Northrup, Herbert Roof *economist, business executive*
Perloe, Sidney Irwin *psychologist, primatologist, educator*
Rosefsky, Jonathan Benensohn *pediatrician*
Spielman, John Philip, Jr. *historian, educator*
Stroud, James Stanley *lawyer*
Szabad, George Michael *lawyer, former mayor*
Talucci, Samuel James *retired chemical company executive*
Young-Bruehl, Elisabeth *philosophy educator, psychoanalyst*
Zalinski, Edmund Louis Gray *insurance executive, mutual funds and real estate executive, investor*

**Havertown**
Beck, Elaine Kushner *elementary and secondary school educator*
Brinker, Thomas Michael *finance executive*
Godwin, Pamela June *financial services executive*
Prevoznik, Stephen Joseph *anesthesiologist, retired*
Sheppard, Walter Lee, Jr. *chemical engineer, consultant*

**Hawley**
Conley, Clare Dean *retired magazine editor*

**Hazleton**
Miller, David Emanuel *physics educator, researcher*
Stevens, Linda Tollestrup *academic director*

**Hellertown**
Claps, Judith Barnes *educational consultant*
McCullagh, James Charles *publishing company executive*
Viest, Ivan M(iroslav) *consulting structural engineer*

**Hermitage**
Havrilla, John William *middle school educator*

**Hershey**
Anderson, Allan Crosby *hospital executive*
Berlin, Cheston Milton, Jr. *pediatrician, educator*
Biebuyck, Julien Francois *anesthesiologist, educator*
Bomgardner, William Earl *retired association executive, photographer*
Brechbill, Joseph Albert *private school administrator*
†Caputo, Gregory Michael *physician, educator*
Cary, Gene Leonard *psychiatrist*
Chen, Qian *cell biologist, developmental biologist*
Davis, Dwight *cardiologist, educator*
Duncan, Charles Lee *food products company executive*
Eyster, Mary Elaine *hematologist, educator*
†Hamory, Bruce Hill *health facility administrator*
Jordan, Lois Wenger *university official*
Kauffman, Gordon Lee, Jr. *surgeon, educator*
King, Carolyn Marie *mathematics educator*
Lang, Carol Max *veterinarian, educator*
Leaman, David Martin *cardiologist*
Leventhal, Ruth *academic administrator, dean emeritus, educator*
Lindenberg, Steven Phillip *counselor, consultant*
Little, Rhoda Smeltzer *nursing administrator*
Madewell, John Edward *radiologist*
Marks, James Garfield, Jr. *dermatologist*
McInerney, Joseph John *biomedical engineer, educator*
Naeye, Richard L. *pathologist, educator*
Pierce, William Schuler *cardiac surgeon, educator*
Pincock, Garry LaMar *association administrator*
Reynolds, Herbert Young *physician, internist*
Rohner, Thomas John, Jr. *urologist*
Ruth, Edward B. *principal*
Schuller, Diane Ethel *allergist, immunologist, educator*
Severs, Walter Bruce *pharmacology educator, researcher*
Tan, Tjiauw-Ling *psychiatrist, educator*
Vary, Thomas Crispin *physiologist*
Vesell, Elliot Saul *pharmacologist, educator*
Waldhausen, John Anton *surgeon, editor*
Wassner, Steven Joel *pediatric nephrologist, educator*
Wolfe, Kenneth L. *food products manufacturing company executive*
Zelis, Robert Felix *cardiologist, educator*
Zimmerman, Richard Anson *food company executive*

**Holland**
Umbreit, Wayne William *bacteriologist, educator*

**Hollidaysburg**
Bloom, Lawrence Stephen *retired clothing company executive*
Robinson, Gary David *principal*

**Homestead**
King, Richard Wayne *principal*

**Honesdale**
Barbe, Walter Burke *education educator*
Brown, Kent Louis, Jr. *magazine editor*
Campbell, Linda Sue *guidance counselor*
Clark, Christine May *editor, author*
Stanton, Sara Baumgardner *retired secondary school educator*

**Horsham**
Beyland, Mark *publishing company executive*
Dariano, Joseph *publishing company executive*
Goff, Kenneth Wade *electrical engineer*
Hook, Jerry B. *pharmaceutical company executive*
Landberg, George Gustaf *mechanical engineer*
Logue, John J(oseph) *psychologist*
Neff, P. Sherrill *health care executive*
Rosoff, William A. *lawyer, executive*

Strock, Gerald E. *school system administrator*
Wesselink, David Duwayne *finance company executive*

**Hummelstown**
Bruhn, John Glyndon *university provost and dean*
Custer, John Charles *investment broker*
Moffitt, Charles William *insurance sales executive*
Smedley, Elizabeth *researcher, codifier, consultant, historian, writer*

**Hunlock Creek**
Zimmerman, Anita Eloise *elementary education educator*

**Huntingdon**
Buzminsky, David Andrew *school psychologist*
Durnbaugh, Donald Floyd *church history educator, researcher*
Neff, Robert Wilbur *academic administrator, educator*
Schock, William Wallace *pediatrician*

**Huntingdon Valley**
Altman, Brian David *pediatric ophthalmologist*
Antonell, Walter John *publishing executive*
Danielewski, Donna Krystyna *secondary school educator*
Edelman, Janice *artist, educator*
Forman, Howard Irving *lawyer, former government official*
Leibholz, Stephen Wolfgang *physicist, engineering company executive, entrepreneur*
Vollum, Robert Boone *management consultant*
West, A(rnold) Sumner *chemical engineer*

**Immaculata**
Manning, Kevin James *academic administrator*

**Indiana**
Jones, Shelley Pryce *chemical company executive, writer*
Kegel, William George *mining company executive*
Mc Cauley, R. Paul *criminologist, educator*
Miller, Vincent Paul, Jr. *geography and regional planning educator*
Nelson, Linda Shearer *child development and family relations educator*
Perlongo, Daniel James *composer*
Pettit, Lawrence Kay *university president*
Purdy, David Lawrence *biotechnical company executive*
Rocco, Domenic Patrick, Jr. *trust company executive, retired army officer*
Soule, Robert D. *safety and health educator, administrator*
Stevenson, Charles Beman *business educator*
Thibadeau, Eugene Francis *education educator, consultant*
Walker, Donald Anthony *economist, educator*

**Irwin**
Runser, Dianne Strong *music educator, music director*

**Jenkintown**
Baldwin, David Rawson *retired university administrator*
Beavers, Ellington McHenry *chemical company executive*
Coccagna, Fred Joseph, Jr. *flooring manufacturing executive*
Cohen, Alan *civil engineer*
Driehuys, Leonardus Bastiaan *conductor*
Friedman, Ralph David *lawyer*
Greenspan-Margolis, June E. *psychiatrist*
Hankin, Elaine Krieger *psychologist, researcher*
Haythornthwaite, Robert Morphet *civil engineer, educator*
Klock, Fred William *materials engineer*
Nerenberg, Aaron *lawyer*
Newburger, Frank L., Jr. *retired investment broker*
Potash, Jane *artist*
Reese, Francis Edward *retired chemical company executive, consultant*
Sadoff, Robert Leslie *psychiatrist*
Silver, Leonard J. *insurance and risk management company executive*
Smith, Francis Xavier *accountant*
Wilkinson, Harry J. *retired technical company executive*

**Jersey Shore**
Flayhart, Martin Albert *lawyer*
Nassberg, Richard T. *lawyer*

**Jim Thorpe**
Umbehocker, Kenneth Sheldon *priest*

**Johnstown**
Alcamo, Frank Paul *retired principal*
Glock, Earl Ferdinand *lawyer*
Glosser, William Louis *lawyer*
Grove, Nancy Carol *academic administrator*
Hull, Patricia Ann *nursing administrator*
Jones, Thomas William *secondary education educator, consultant*
Kaharick, Jerome John *lawyer*
Kuhn, Howard Arthur *engineering executive, educator*
Manty, Brian Alan *high technology company executive*
McKnight, Joyce Sheldon *adult educator, community organizer*
McNiesh, Lawrence Melvin *radiologist*
Miloro, Protopresbter Frank *church official, religious studies educator*
Nicholas, (Richard G. Smisko) *bishop*
Simmons, Elroy, Jr. *retired utility executive*
Smiach, Deborah *accountant, educator, consultant*
Smisko, Nicholas Richard *bishop, educator*
Smith, David Brooks *federal judge*
Smith, William Raymond *history educator, philosophy educator*
Straw, Gary Lee *construction company executive*
Untracht, Steven Harris *surgeon*
Wise, Robert Lester *utilities executive*

**Jones Mills**
Fish, Paul Waring *lawyer*

**Kempton**
Lenhart, Cynthia Rae *conservation organization executive*

**Kennett Square**
Allam, Mark Whittier *veterinarian, former university administrator*
Beck, Dorothy Fahs *social researcher*
Beddall, Barbara Gould *science historian, writer*
Bronner, Edwin Blaine *history educator*
Hennes, Robert Taft *former management consultant, investment executive*
Judson, Franklyn Sylvanus *lawyer, consultant*
Larmore, Catherine Christine *university official*
Leymaster, Glen R. *former medical association executive*
Lippincott, Sarah Lee *astronomer, graphologist*
Martin, George (Whitney) *writer*
May, Harold Edward *chemical company executive*
Naeve, Milo Merle *museum curator and trustee*
Nason, John William *retired college president, educational consultant*
Partnoy, Ronald Allen *lawyer*
Perera, George A. *physician*
Taylor, Bernard J., II *banker*
Vainstein, Rose *librarian, educator*

**Kimberton**
Douglas, Bryce *former pharmaceutical company executive*

**King Of Prussia**
Beausang, Michael Francis, Jr. *lawyer*
Brown, Emma Jean (EJ Brown) *medical editor, journalist*
Dee, Robert Forrest *retired pharmaceutical company executive*
Doniger, Irene G. *psychologist, business owner*
Draayer, Shari Lynn *sociologist*
Enge, Vernon Reier *editor health care publications*
Fitzgerald, Walter George *marketing executive*
Ghorpade, Ajit Kisanrao *chemical and environmental engineer*
Greenberg, Lon Richard *energy company executive, lawyer*
McLane, James Woods *healthcare executive*
†Middleton, Herbert Hunter, Jr. *tobacco manufacturing company executive*
Miller, Alan B. *hospital management executive*
Noonan, Gregory Robert *lawyer*
Ohnishi, Stanley Tsuyoshi *biomedical director, biophysicist*
Olexy, Jean Shofranko *English language educator*
Olson, Bob Moody *marketing executive*
Pope, Dale Allen *investment company executive*
Poste, George Henry *pharmaceutical company executive*
Quillen, Mary Ann *university administrator, consultant*
Stoughton, W. Vickery *healthcare executive*
Traynor, Sean Gabrial *manufacturing executive*
Volpe, Ralph Pasquale *insurance company executive*
Wachs, David V. *retired apparel executive*
Webb, Richard Stephen *manufacturing executive*

**Kingston**
Marko, Andrew Paul *school system administrator*
Weisberger, Barbara *choreographer, artistic director, educator*

**Knox**
Rupert, Elizabeth Anastasia *retired university dean*

**Kutztown**
Dougherty, Percy H. *geographer, educator, politician, planner*
Kuehne, Helenirene Anne *art educator*
McFarland, David E. *academic administrator*
Meyer, Susan Moon *speech language pathologist, educator*
Ogden, James Russell *marketing educator, consultant, lecturer, trainer*
Watrous, Robert Thomas *academic director*

**La Plume**
Boehm, Edward Gordon *university administrator, educator*

**Lafayette Hill**
Dixon, Fitz Eugene, Jr. *professional baseball team executive*
Green, Rose Basile (Mrs. Raymond S. Green) *poet, author, educator*
King, Leon *financial services executive*
Sehn, Susan Cleary *psychiatrist*

**Lake Ariel**
Caldwell, Nancy Ann *social worker, nurse*
Casper, Marie Lenore *middle school educator*
Tague, Charles Francis *retired engineering, construction and real estate development company executive*

**Lake Harmony**
Polansky, Larry Paul *court administrator, consultant*

**Lancaster**
Augsburger, Aaron Donald *clergyman*
Bernstein, Alan *retired virologist*
Brod, Roy David *ophthalmologist, educator*
Brunner, Lillian Sholtis *nurse, author*
Carlisle, James Patton *clergyman*
Cody, William Henry *retired newspaper editor*
Collins, Kathleen Anne *artistic director*
Daugherty, Ruth Alice *religious association consultant*
Dodge, Arthur Byron, Jr. *business executive*
Drum, Alice *college administrator*
Dunlap, Hallowell *data processing executive*
Duroni, Charles Eugene *retired lawyer, food products executive*
Ebersole, Mark Chester *emeritus college president*
Eshleman, Silas Kendrick, III *psychiatrist*
Freeman, Clarence Calvin *financial executive*
Gingerich, Naomi R. *emergency room nurse*
Glick, Garland Wayne *retired theological seminary president*
Hendrix, Stephen C. *financial executive*
Hess, Eugene Lyle *biologist, retired association executive*
High, S. Dale *diversified company executive*
Kelly, Robert Lynn *advertising agency executive*
Kneedler, Alvin Richard *academic administrator*

Liddell, W. Kirk *specialty contracting and distribution company executive, lawyer*
Lorch, George A. *manufacturing company executive*
McCollom, Herbert Forrest, Jr. *audiologist*
Nast, Dianne Martha *lawyer*
Pyfer, John Frederick, Jr. *lawyer*
Shaw, Charles Raymond *journalist*
Shenk, Willis Weidman *newspaper executive*
Simmons, Deidre Warner *performing company executive*
Steiner, Robert Lisle *language consultant, retired*
Stephenson, Donald Grier, Jr. *government studies educator*
Stewart, Arlene Jean Golden *designer, stylist*
Veitch, Boyer Lewis *printing company executive*
Whare, Wanda Snyder *lawyer*
Zimmerman, D(onald) Patrick *lawyer*

**Langhorne**
Babb, Wylie Sherrill *college president*
Brafford, William Charles *lawyer*
Brennan, John James *marketing executive*
Byrne, Jeffrey Edward *pharmacology researcher, educator, consultant*
Hillje, Barbara Brown *lawyer*
Lamonsoff, Norman Charles *psychiatrist*
Venable, Robert Ellis *crop scientist*

**Lansdale**
Cartlidge, Edward Sutterley *mechanical engineer*
Cusimano, Adeline Mary Miletti *educational administrator*
Esterhai, John Louis *lawyer*
Fawley, John Jones *retired banker*
Lovelace, Robert Frank *health facility administrator, researcher*
Madden, Theresa Marie *elementary education educator*
Reast, Deborah Stanek *ophthalmology center administrator*
Schnable, George Luther *chemist*
Schwartz, Louis Winn *ophthalmologist*
Strohecker, Leon Harry, Jr. *orthodontist*
Wittreich, Warren James *psychologist, consultant*

**Lansdowne**
Popovics, Sandor *civil engineer, educator, researcher*

**Latrobe**
Berardi, Ronald Stephen *pathologist, educator*
Conley, Edward Vincent, Jr. *metallurgical engineering researcher*
Zanotti, Marie Louise *hospital admininstrator*

**Laverock**
Block, Isaac Edward *professional society administrator*

**Lebanon**
Deysher, Paul Evans *training consultant*
Marshall, Marilyn Jean *social services director, consultant*
McMindes, Roy James *aggregate company executive*
Parrott, Charles Norman *bank executive*
Paul, Herman Louis, Jr. *valve manufacturing company executive*

**Lederach**
Hallman, H(enry) Theodore, Jr. *artist, textile designer*

**Leesport**
Jackson, Eric Allen *philatelist*
Otterman, Kenneth James *real estate investor, author, consultant*

**Lehigh Valley**
Kocsis, James Paul *artist, publisher*

**Lemoyne**
Deeg, Emil Wolfgang *manufacturing company executive, physicist*
Kirkwood, James Mace *pharmaceutical benefit management company executive*

**Leola**
McElhinny, Wilson Dunbar *banker*
Wedel, Paul George *retired hospital administrator*

**Levittown**
Halberstein, Joseph Leonard *retired associate editor*
Phillips, Edward John *computer scientist, writer*
Upton, Lorraine Frances *elementary education educator*

**Lewisburg**
Adams, William D. *university president*
Candland, Douglas Keith *educator*
Edgerton, Mills Fox, Jr. *foreign language educator*
†Jamieson, Sid *head coach men's lacrosse*
Jump, Chester Jackson, Jr. *clergyman, church official*
Little, Daniel Eastman *philosophy educator, university program director*
Main, A. Donald *bishop*
Neuman, Nancy Adams Mosshammer *civic leader*
Ondrusek, David Francis *discount store chain executive*
Payne, Michael David *English language educator*
Rich, Thomas Paul *engineering educator, administrator*
Rote, Nelle Fairchild Hefty *business consultant*
Sojka, Gary Allan *biologist, educator, university official*

**Ligonier**
Mellon, Seward Prosser *investment executive*
Pilz, Alfred Norman *manufacturing company executive*
Schmidt, Adolph William *retired ambassador*
Walters, Gomer Winston *lawyer*

**Lincoln University**
Dadson, William Kwame *economics and business administration educator*
Roberts, Lynn Ernest *theoretical physicist, educator*
Williams, Willie, Jr. *physicist, educator*

**Lititz**
Bolinger, Robert Stevens *banker*
Gasparich, Margaret Jo *interior designer*
Koch, Bruce R. *diplomat*
Lord, Kathleen Virginia *fundraising executive*
Smith, Thomas Clair *manufacturing company executive*

**Littlestown**
Plunkert, Donna Mae *business owner*

**Lock Haven**
Almes, June *retired education educator, librarian*
Congdon, Howard Krebs *philosopher, clergyman, educator*
Snowiss, Alvin L. *lawyer*
Willis, Craig Dean *academic administrator*

**Loretto**
Benham, Philip Owen, Jr. *business marketing educator, consultant*
Sackin, Claire *social work educator*

**Lower Burrell**
Kinosz, Donald Lee *quality consultant*
Rose, Robert Henry *arts education administrator*

**Lower Gwynedd**
Pendleton, Robert Grubb *pharmacologist*

**Lumberville**
Katsiff, Bruce *artist*

**Lyon Station**
Breidegam, DeLight Edgar, Jr. *battery company executive*

**Macungie**
Billingsley, Charles Edward *retired transportation company executive*
Gavin, Austin *retired lawyer*
Kocian, Nancy Jane *elementary education educator*

**Malvern**
Bogle, John Clifton *investment company executive*
Calabrese, Marylyn E. Jones *writing consultant*
Cameron, John Clifford *lawyer, health science facility administrator*
Churchill, Winston John *lawyer, investment firm executive*
Darby, Samuel Edward *guidance counselor*
Eagleson, William Boal, Jr. *banker*
Fisher, Sallie Ann *chemist*
Fredrick, Susan Walker *tax company manager*
Popp, James Alan *toxicologist, toxicology executive*
Smalley, Christopher Joseph *pharmaceutical company professional*
Swymer, Stephen *principal*
Weisman, Harlan Frederick *pharmaceutical company executive*
Wolfe, Jean Elizabeth *medical illustrator, artist*

**Manchester**
Owens, Marilyn Mae *elementary school educator, secondary school educator*

**Manheim**
Critz, Richard Laurens *magazine editor, architectural consultant*
Frederick, Susan Louise *preschool educator*

**Mc Donald**
Tannehill, Norman Bruce, Jr. *consultant, educator*

**Mc Murray**
Brzustowicz, John Cinq-Mars *lawyer*

**Meadowbrook**
Kiesel, Harry Alexander *physician*

**Meadville**
Adams, Earl William, Jr. *economics educator*
Cable, Charles Allen *mathematician*
Foster, Catherine Rierson *manufacturing company executive*
Hogan, James Charles *classicist, educator*
Katope, Christopher George *English language educator*
Kilgallon, Robert Donald *company executive, author, screenwriter*
Lotze, Barbara *physicist*
Thorson, Connie Capers *library educator*
Wharton, William Polk *psychologist, consultant*

**Mechanicsburg**
Bitner, Jerri Lynne *information systems professional*
Chamberlin, Edward Robert *career officer, educator*
Kinney, Linford Nelson *retired army officer*
Pearsall, Gregory Howard *naval officer*
Rudolph, Robert Norman *secondary school educator, adult education educator*

**Mechanicsville**
Bye, Ranulph DeBayeux *artist, author*

**Media**
Ackerman, Alvin S. *lawyer*
Barnett, Samuel Treutlen *international company executive*
Behbehanian, Mahin Fazeli *surgeon*
Bosacco, David N. *orthopedic surgeon*
Comeforo, Jean Elizabeth *hearing-impaired educator*
Cooke, M(erritt) Todd *banker*
D'Amico, Andrew J. *lawyer*
Dunlap, Richard Frank *school system administrator*
Elman, Gerry Jay *lawyer*
Ewing, Robert Clark *lawyer*
Fehnel, Edward Adam *chemist, educator*
Garrison, Susan Kay *lawyer*
Hart, William C. *insurance underwriter, educator, writer*
Heilig, Margaret Cramer *nurse, educator*
Hemphill, James S. *investment management executive, financial advisor*
Kahrmann, Robert George *educational administrator*
King, Kathleen Palombo *computer technology and adult education educator, consultant*
Klinefelter, Hylda Catharine *obstetrician and gynecologist*
Lerner, Daniel Merril *broadcasting company executive*
Lewandowski, Theodore Charles *psychology educator*
Peabody, William Tyler, Jr. *retired paper manufacturing company executive*
Reuschlein, Harold Gill *university dean*
Salo, Harry A. *health care executive*
Schuller, Edwin Arthur *osteopathic physician*
Smith, David Gilbert *political science educator*
Strunk, Betsy Ann Whitenight *education educator*
Wood, Richard D., Jr. *retail executive*

**Mendenhall**
Reinert, Norbert Frederick *patent lawyer, retired chemical company executive*

**Mercer**
Brady, Wray Grayson *mathematician, educator*
Inman, Thomas Leroy *county auditor*

**Mercersburg**
Coffman, Patricia JoAnne *school nurse, counselor*

**Merion Station**
Amado, Ralph David *physics educator*
de Pasquale, Joseph *musician, educator*
Lewis, Paul Le Roy *pathology educator*
Littell, Franklin Hamlin *theologian, educator*
Littell, Marcia Sachs *educator, educational administrator*

**Middletown**
Kaynak, Erdener *marketing educator, consultant editor*
Pannebaker, James Boyd *lawyer*
Ross, Cheri Louise *English language educator*

**Milford**
Eckert, Allan Wesley *writer*
Le Guin, Ursula Kroeber *author*
Reynolds, Edwin Wilfred, Jr. *retired secondary education educator*

**Millersburg**
Kirkwood, Nancy Lynne *elementary education educator*

**Millersville**
Caputo, Joseph Anthony *university president*
Mallery, Anne Louise *elementary education educator, consultant*
Miller, Steven Max *humanities educator*

**Milton**
Ellis, Jane Marie *real estate manager*

**Mohnton**
Bowers, Richard Philip *manufacturing executive*

**Monaca**
Jaskiewicz, David Walter *optometrist*

**Monongahela**
Brandon, John Mitchell *physician*

**Monroeville**
Carney, Ann Vincent *secondary education educator*
Jacobi, William Mallett *nuclear engineer, consultant*
Lin, Ming Shek *allergist, immunologist*
Maclay, William Nevin *retired manufacturing and construction company executive*
Mandel, Herbert Maurice *civil engineer*
Marasco, Joseph A., Jr. *radiologist*
Parker, James Roger *chemist*
Penman, Paul Duane *nuclear power laboratory executive*

**Mont Alto**
Russo, Peggy Anne *English language educator*
Sourbier, James Henry, IV *police chief*
Wagaman, James Brian *environmentalist*

**Montoursville**
Woolever, Naomi Louise *retired editor*

**Moon Township**
Alstadt, Lynn Jeffery *lawyer*
Rabosky, Joseph George *engineering consulting company executive*

**Morrisville**
Clark, William Roger *artist, educator*
Denslow, Deborah Pierson *primary education educator*
Heefner, William Frederick *lawyer*
Lineberry, Paul F., Jr. *secondary education music educator*
Marsh, Frederick William *accountant*

**Mount Gretna**
Newman, Richard August *psychiatrist, educator*

**Mount Joy**
Steinhart, Dean Raymond *educational administrator*

**Mount Pleasant**
Dangelo, Eugene Michael *elementary school educator*

**Mountainhome**
Buttz, Charles William *outdoor advertising executive*

**Murrysville**
McWhirter, James Herman *consulting engineering business executive, financial planner*

**Narberth**
Fenichel, Richard Lee *retired biochemist*
Grenald, Raymond *architectural lighting designer*
Knapp, Nancy Hay *mental health administrator*
Madow, Leo *psychiatrist, educator*
Mezvinsky, Edward M. *lawyer*
Nathanson, Neal *virologist, epidemiologist, educator*
Newhall, John Harrison *management consultant*
Pedersen, Darlene Delcourt *health science publishing consultant*
Strom, Brian Leslie *internist, educator*
Wagner, Frederick Balthas, Jr. *historian, retired surgery educator*

**Natrona Heights**
Stanger, Robert Henry *psychiatrist, educator*

**Nazareth**
Herrick, Robert Ford *personnel consultant*
Rayner, Robert Martin *financial executive*

**New Bethlehem**
Fedak, John G. *biology education educator*

**New Castle**
Denniston, Marjorie McGeorge *retired elementary education educator*
Flannery, Harry Audley *lawyer*
Flannery, Wilbur Eugene *health science association administrator, internist*
Grzebieniak, John Francis *psychologist*
Mangino, Matthew Thomas *lawyer*
Roux, Mildred Anna *retired secondary school educator*

**New Florence**
Olson, Clinton Louis *foreign service officer, former ambassador*

**New Galilee**
Randza, Jason Michael *engineer*

**New Holland**
Amor, James Michael *dentist*
Papadakis, Emmanuel Philippos *physicist, consultant*
West, Daniel Charles *lay worker, dentist*

**New Hope**
Knight, Douglas Maitland *educational administrator, optical executive*
Lee, Robert Earl *retired physician*
Stahl, Stephen Lee *theater director, writer, producer*
Williamson, Frederick Beasley, III *rubber company executive*

**New Kensington**
Blair, Karen Elaine *respiratory care practitioner, health educator*
Hahn, William Orr *psychologist, consultant*
Jarrett, Noel *chemical engineer*
Joseph, Daniel *lawyer*
Li, Nai-Yi *mechanical engineer, researcher*
Miller, Albert Jay *retired librarian, educator*
Pien, Shyh-Jye John *mechanical engineer*

**New Stanton**
Black, Cora Jean *evangelist, wedding consultant*

**New Wilmington**
Deegan, John, Jr. *academic administrator, educator*
Pitman, Grover Allen *music educator*
Remick, Oscar Eugene *academic administrator*

**Newfoundland**
Sked, Marie Josephine *financial service owner, nurse*

**Newtown**
Bohning, Elizabeth Edrop *foreign language educator*
Carlson, David Emil *physicist*
Carpenter, Esther *biological science educator*
Coale, Ansley Johnson *economics educator*
Cohen, Myer *former international organization official*
Denoon, Clarence England, Jr. *business executive*
Duncan, Stephen Robert *elementary education educator*
Henshaw, Jonathan Cook *manufacturing company executive*
Keenan, Terrance *foundation executive*
Keyes, Fenton *educational consultant, writer*
Messerschmidt, Gerald Leigh *pharmaceutical industry executive, physician*
Muth, Robert James *metal company executive, lawyer*
Palmer, Robert Roswell *historian, educator*
Pfeiffer, John Edward *author*
Ross, Edwin William *rubber company executive*
Selden, William Kirkpatrick *retired educational administrator*
Smith, Karen Ann *artist, graphic designer, educator*
Somers, Anne Ramsay *medical educator*

**Newtown Square**
Benenson, James, Jr. *manufacturer*
Bower, Ward Alan *management consultant, lawyer*
Graf, Arnold Harold *employee benefits executive, financial planner*
Perrone, Nicholas *mechanical engineer, business executive*
Staats, Dean Roy *retired reinsurance executive*
Steinman, Robert Cleeton *accountant*
Strausz-Hupé, Robert *ambassador, author*
Tipka, Karen *obstetric and women's health nurse*
Turner, George Pearce *consulting company executive*
Yeh, George Chiayou *engineering company executive*

**Newville**
Rand, Sharon Kay *elementary education educator*

**Nineveh**
Quackenbush, Robert Dean *management consultant*

**Norristown**
Aman, George Matthias, III *lawyer*
Bergmann, Donald Gerald *pharmaceutical company executive*
Burtt, Anne Dampman *special education educator*
Clemens, Alvin Honey *insurance company executive*
Folmar, Larry John *lawyer*
Genuardi, Charles A. *retail executive*
Gregg, John Pennypacker *lawyer*
Hunter, Patricia Phelps *physician assistant*
Lafredo, Stephen Christopher *consultant*
Mirabile, Carolyn Rose *lawyer*
Nelson, Dawn Marie *middle school science and math educator*
Oliver, James John *lawyer*
Quinn-Kerins, Catherine *psychologist*
Rounick, Jack A. *lawyer*
Seiderman, Arthur Stanley *optometrist, consultant, author*
Steinberg, Arthur Irwin *periodontist, educator*
Tsou, Walter Hai-tze *physician*
Wetherill, Eikins *lawyer, stock exchange executive*
Williamson, Ronald Thomas *lawyer*

**North East**
Ayrault, Evelyn West *psychologist, writer*

**North Huntingdon**
Kukovich, Allen Gale *legislator, lawyer*

Glazer, Ronald Barry lawyer
Glick, Jane Mills biochemistry educator
Glick, John H. oncologist, medical educator
Glusker, Jenny Pickworth chemist
Goldberg, Jay Lenard lawyer
Goldberg, Martin physician, educator
Goldberg, Marvin Allen lawyer, business consultant
Goldberg, Richard Robert lawyer
Golden, Gerald Samuel national medical board executive
Goldfarb, Stanley internist, educator
Goldin, Judah Hebrew literature educator
Goldman, Jerry Stephen lawyer
Goldsmith, Howard Michael lawyer
Goldsmith, Nancy Carrol business and health services management educator
Goldsmith, Sidney physician, scientist, inventor
Goldstein, William Marks lawyer
Goldstine, Herman Heine mathematician, association executive
Goodchild, John Charles, Jr. advertising and public relations executive
Goodenough, Ward Hunt anthropologist, educator
Goodman, Charles Schaffner marketing educator
Goodman, David Barry Poliakoff physician, educator
Goodman, Stephen Murry lawyer
Goodrich, Herbert Funk, Jr. lawyer
Gordesky, Morton lawyer
Graessle, William Rudolf physician, educator
Graffman, Gary pianist, music educator
Graham, Alexander John classics educator
Granoff, Gail Patricia lawyer
Grant, M. Duncan lawyer
Grant, Richard W. lawyer
Gray, Edward Anthony lawyer
Graziani, Leonard Joseph pediatric neurologist, researcher
Green, Clifford Scott federal judge
Greenberg, Marshall Gary marketing research consultant
Greene, Ronald Barry orthopedic surgeon
Greenfield, Bruce Harold lawyer, banker
Greenfield, Val Shea ophthalmologist
Greenstein, Jeffrey Ian neurologist
Griswold, Idawease Johnson librarian
Gross, Larry Paul communications educator
Grossman, Sanford Jay economics educator
Grove, David Lavan lawyer
Gueson, Emerita Torres obstetrician, gynecologist
Gusoff, Patricia Kearney elementary education educator
Gustafson, Sandra Lynne secondary education educator
Haas, Charles Nathan environmental engineering educator
Hackney, Francis Sheldon university president
Hagan, Mary Ann lawyer
Hailey, Jacob Joseph bank executive
Hairston, Harold B. protective services official
Haley, Vincent Peter lawyer
Hall, Robert J. newspaper executive
Hameka, Hendrik Frederik chemist, educator
Hamilton, Stephen David Derwent lawyer
Hamlin, Arthur Tenney librarian
Hamme, David Codrington architect
Hammond, Benjamin Franklin microbiologist, educator
Hammond, Charles Ainley clergyman
Hand, Christopher Michael cancer research scientist, medical consultant, educator
Hand, Peter James neurobiologist, educator
Hangley, William Thomas lawyer
Hanle, Paul Arthur museum administrator
Hansen-Flaschen, John Hyman medical educator, researcher
Hanuschak, Lee Nicholas physician
Harbater, David mathematician
Harkins, John Graham, Jr. lawyer
Harris, Raymond Jesse retired government official
Harvey, Colin Edwin veterinary medicine educator
Harvey, John Adriance psychology and pharmacology educator, researcher, consultant
Harvey, William J. religious service organization, religious publication editor
Haskin, Donald Lee bank executive
Hatoff, Howard Ira retired labor lawyer
Haugaard, Niels pharmacologist
Hauptfuhrer, George Jost, Jr. lawyer
Havard, Bernard theatrical producer
Havas, Peter physicist, educator
Haviland, Bancroft Dawley lawyer
Haydanek, Ronald Edward lawyer and consultant
Hayes, John Freeman architect
Haynes, Gary Allen photographer, journalist, newspaper editor
Hazard, Geoffrey Cornell, Jr. law educator
Heilig, William Wright coal and manufacturing company executive
Helfand, Arthur E. podiatrist
Henderson, J(oseph) Welles lawyer
Henrich, William Joseph, Jr. lawyer
Henry, Rene Arthur, Jr. environmental agency administrator
Hernandez, Marissa physicist
Hess, Hans Ober lawyer
Hickey, Gregory Joseph priest, educational administrator
Hildebrand, David Kent statistics educator
Hillgren, Sonja Dorothy journalist
Hirschmann, Ralph Franz chemist
Hoelscher, Robert James lawyer
Hoenigswald, Henry Max linguist, educator
Hoffman, Alan Jay lawyer
Hoffman, Daniel (Gerard) literature educator, poet
Holloway, Hiliary Hamilton lawyer, banker
Holzbaur, Erika L. medical educator
Hoskins, Alexander L. (Pete Hoskins) zoological park administrator
Howard, Gerald Kenneth minister
Humenuk, William Anzelm lawyer
Humes, James Calhoun lawyer, communications consultant, author
Hunter, James Austen, Jr. lawyer
Hurvich, Leo Maurice experimental psychologist, educator, vision researcher
Hussain, M. Mahmood medical educator
Hussar, Daniel Alexander pharmacy educator
Hutton, Herbert J. federal judge
Iams, David Aveling journalist, columnist
Iannotti, Joseph Patrick orthopedic surgeon
Iglewicz, Boris statistician, educator
Intemann, Robert Louis physics educator, researcher
Iskrant, John Dermot lawyer
Izenour, Steven architect
Jackson, Laird Gray physician, educator
Jacobson, Sheldon emergency medicine physician, medical administrator
Jaffe, Paul Lawrence judge, lawyer
Jameson, Dorothea sensory neuroscientist
Jamieson, Kathleen Hall dean, communications educator
Jaron, Dov biomedical engineer, educator
Jefferies, Gregory Scott professional baseball player
Jellinek, Miles Andrew lawyer
Jensh, Ronald Paul anatomist, educator
Jimenez, Sergio A. physician
Johnson, Craig Norman investment banker
Johnson, E(lmer) Marshall biology educator, reproductive toxicologist
Johnson, Joseph Eggleston, III physician, educator
Joner, Bruno aeronautical engineer
Jones, Loren Farquhar electronics executive
Jones, O. T. bishop
Jones, Robert Jeffries lawyer
Jones, Robert Mead, Jr. lawyer
Jordan, Clifford Henry management consultant
Jordan, Joe J. architect
Joseph, Rosaline Resnick hematologist and oncologist
Joshi, Aravind Krishna computer educator, information scientist
Joyner, J(ames) Curtis federal judge
Justice, Jack Burton retired lawyer
Kadison, Richard Vincent mathematician, educator
Kahn, James Robert lawyer
†Kaiser, Roy artistic director
Kaji, Akira microbiology scientist, educator
Kaji, Hideko Katayama pharmacology educator
Kane, Jonathan lawyer
Kantner, Theodore Robert family physician
Kardon, Robert mortgage company executive
Katherine, Robert Andrew chemical company executive
Katz, Julian gastroenterologist, educator
Katz, Marvin federal judge
Kauffman, Bruce William lawyer, former state supreme court justice
Kauffman, Leon A. internist, educator
Kaufman, David Joseph lawyer
Kaufman, Denise Norma psychologist, addictions counselor, educator
Kaye, Donald physician, educator
Kaye, Janet Miriam psychologist
Kaye, Robert pediatrics educator
Kazazian, Haig Hagop, Jr. medical scientist, physician, educator
Keenan, Mary Ann orthopedic surgeon, researcher
Keene, John Clark lawyer, educator
Kefalides, Nicholas Alexander physician, educator
Kelley, Mark Albert internal medicine educator, university official
Kelley, William Nimmons physician, educator
Kelley, William Thomas marketing educator
Kelly, James McGirr federal judge
Kelly, Robert F. federal judge
Kempin, Frederick Gustav, Jr. lawyer, educator
Kendall, Robert Louis, Jr. lawyer
Kennedy, David William otolaryngologist, educator
Kessler, Alan Craig lawyer
Kim, Sangduk biochemistry educator, researcher
Kimball, Harry Raymond medical association executive, educator
Kimberly, John Robert management educator, consultant
King, David Roy lawyer
King, Gwendolyn S. utility company executive, former federal official
King, Maxwell E. P. newspaper editor
Kise, James Nelson architect, urban planner
Klasko, Herbert Ronald lawyer, law educator, writer
Klaus, William Robert lawyer
Klausner, Samuel Zundel sociologist, educator
Klayman, Barry Martin lawyer
Klein, Abraham physics educator, researcher
Klein, Arthur foundation executive
Klein, Howard Bruce lawyer, law educator
†Klein, Jonathan broadcast engineer
Klein, Julia Meredith newspaper reporter
Klein, Lawrence Robert economist, educator
Klein, Michael Lawrence research chemist, educator
Klein, Samuel Edwin lawyer
Kleinzeller, Arnost physiologist, physician, emeritus educator
Kligerman, Morton M. radiologist
Klinghoffer, June Florence physician, educator
Knapton, David Robert city planner
Knauer, Georg Nicolaus classical philologist
Knopp, Marvin Isadore mathematics educator
Knudson, Alfred George, Jr. medical geneticist
Koelle, George Brampton university pharmacologist, educator
Kogan, Deen artistic director
Kohn, Harold Elias lawyer
Kopecky, Kenneth John economics educator
Koprowski, Hilary microbiologist, educator
Kormes, John Winston lawyer
Korsyn, Irene Hahne marketing executive
Kotler, Ronald Lee physician, educator
Kozlowski, Bette Marie accountant
Kraemer, Michael Frederick lawyer
Kraft, Robert Alan history of religion educator
Kramer, Meyer lawyer, editor, clergyman
Krampf, John Edward lawyer
Krebs, Hope Paula tax consultant, lawyer
Kritchevsky, David biochemist, educator
Kritikos, Haralambos N. electrical engineering educator
Krutsick, Robert Stanley science center executive
Krzyzanowski, Richard Lucien lawyer, corporate executive
Ksansnak, James E. service management company executive
Kupperman, Louis Brandeis lawyer
Kurtz, Alfred Bernard radiologist
La Blanc, Charles Wesley, Jr. financial consultant
Laddon, Warren Milton lawyer
Ladman, A(aron) J(ulius) anatomist, educator
Lambertsen, Christian James environmental physiologist, physician, educator
Lande, Kenneth physicist, astronomer, educator
Landis, Edgar David services business company executive
Lang, Norma M. dean, nursing educator
Lang, Richard Warren economist
Langacker, Paul George physics educator
Lanza, Donald Charles otolaryngologist, rhinologist
Larsen, Terrance A. bank holding company executive
Larson, Donald Clayton physics educator, consultant
Laverty, Bruce curator
Lawley, Alan materials engineering educator
Lawson, John Quinn architect
Lawton, Lois health facility administrator
Leary, Michael Warren journalist
Leatherbarrow, David architecture department chair
Le Clair, Charles George artist, retired university dean
Ledwith, James Robb lawyer
Ledwith, John Francis lawyer
Lee, Charles retired English language and literature educator, arts critic
Lee, Chong-Sik political scientist, educator
Leech, Noyes Elwood lawyer, educator
Lefer, Allan Mark physiologist
Legido, Agustin pediatric neurologist
Leiter, Robert Allen journalist, magazine editor
Lent, John Anthony journalist, educator
Leonard, Thomas Aloysius lawyer
Leventhal, Lawrence Jay rheumatologist, educator
Levin, A. Leo law educator, retired government official
Levin, Murray Simon lawyer
Levine, Rhea Joy Cottler anatomy educator
Levinson, Arnold Irving allergist, immunologist
Levit, Edithe Judith physician, medical association administrator
Levitt, Israel Monroe astronomer
Levitt, Jerry David medical educator
Levy, Dale Penneys lawyer
Levy, Robert Isaac physician, educator, research director
Levy, Rochelle Feldman artist
Lewin, Moshe historian, educator
Lewin, Peter Andrew electrical engineer, educator
Lewis, Claude Aubrey columnist
Lewis, George Withrow business executive
Lewis, John Hardy, Jr. lawyer
Libby, Ronald Theodore political science educator, consultant, researcher
Liberati, Maria Theresa fashion production company executive
Libonati, Michael Ernest lawyer, educator, writer
Lichtenstein, Robert Jay lawyer
Lien, Eric L. pharmaceutical executive
Lillie, Charisse Ranielle lawyer, educator
Lindros, Eric Bryan professional hockey player
Lindsey, Jack Lee, III curator
Lipman, Frederick D. lawyer, writer, educator
Listgarten, Max Albert periodontics educator
Litt, Mitchell chemical engineer, educator, bioengineer
Little, Brian W. pathology educator, administrator
Litwack, Gerald biochemistry researcher, educator, administrator
Lloyd, Albert Lawrence, Jr. German language educator
Lodish, Leonard Melvin marketing educator, entrepreneur
Loewenstein, Benjamin Steinberg lawyer
Logan, Marie-Rose van Stynvoort literature educator, editor
Lombard, John James, Jr. lawyer
Long, Mary Louise retired government official
Long, Sarah S. pediatrician, educator
Longnecker, David Eugene anesthesiologist, educator
Lotsch, Richard Charles osteopath
Loveless, George Group lawyer
Lowery, William Herbert lawyer
Lu, Ponzy molecular biology educator
Lucey, John David, Jr. lawyer
Lucid, Robert Francis English educator
Ludwig, Edmund Vincent federal judge
Lundy, Joseph E. lawyer
Lurie, Jeffrey professional sports team executive
Luscombe, Herbert Alfred physician, educator
Lynch, William Francis, Jr. secondary mathematics educator
Lyon, William Carl sports columnist
Macdonald, John Stephen oncologist, educator
Mac Ewen, George Dean physician, medical institute executive
Mack, Wayne A. lawyer
Maclay, Donald Merle lawyer
Madaio, Michael P. medical educator, investigator, physician
Madeira, Edward W(alter), Jr. lawyer
Madva, Stephen Alan lawyer
Magarge, W(illiam) Scott, III lawyer
Magaziner, Fred Thomas lawyer
Magaziner, Henry Jonas architect
Magee, Wayne Edward biochemistry educator, researcher
Mai, Elizabeth Hardy lawyer
Maitin, Sam(uel Calman) (Sam Maitin) artist
Malamud, Daniel biochemistry educator
Malhotra, Davinder Kumar finance educator, consultant, researcher
Mancall, Elliott Lee neurologist, educator
Manganiello, Janice Marie peri-operative nurse
Mangione, Jerre Gerlando author, educator
Mann, Theodore R. lawyer
Mannino, Edward Francis lawyer
Mansfield, Edwin economist, educator
Maratea, James Michael healthcare administrator, editor, consultant
Marino, Paul Lawrence physician, researcher
Marple, Dorothy Jane retired church executive
Marshall, Bryan Edward anesthesiologist, educator
Maschak-Carey, Barbara Jean clinical nurse specialist
Mason, Theodore W. lawyer
Mastroianni, Luigi, Jr. physician, educator
Mathes, Stephen Jon lawyer
Matsumoto, Teruo surgeon, educator
Mattoon, Peter Mills lawyer
Matz, Kenneth H., Jr. newscaster
Maurer, Paul Herbert biochemist, educator
Maxman, Susan Abel architect
Mayock, Robert Lee internist
Mazzarella, James Kevin business administration educator
Mazzatenta, Rosemary Dorothy school administrator
McCormick, Rod sculptor, art educator
McCrae, Keith R. medical educator, researcher
McEachron, Donald Lynn biology educator, researcher
McGinley, Joseph Patrick brokerage house executive
McGlynn, Joseph Leo, Jr. federal judge
McHarg, Ian Lennox landscape architect, regional planner, educator
McIntosh, L(orne) William marketing executive
McKee, Theodore A. federal judge
McKeever, John Eugene lawyer
McKenna, Michael Joseph manufacturing company executive
McKenna, Thomas Morrison, Jr. social services organization executive
Mc Mahon, Charles Joseph, Jr. materials science educator
McMichael, Lawrence Grover lawyer
McNeill, Corbin Asahel, Jr. utility executive
McQuiston, Robert Earl lawyer
McRae, Hal (Harold Abraham McRae) former major league baseball team manager
Means, John Barkley foreign language educator, association executive
Meigs, John Forsyth lawyer
Mella, Arthur John insurance company executive
Mellman, Leonard real estate investor and advisor
Mellon, Thomas S. lawyer
Menken, Jane Ava demographer, educator
Mesirov, Leon Isaac lawyer
Messa, Joseph Louis, Jr. lawyer
Metcalf, Bruce Barber visual artist, craft critic
Metzker, Ray K. photographer
Meyer, Leonard B. musician, educator
Meyer, Paul William arboretum director, horticulturist
Meyers, Howard L. lawyer
Meyerson, Martin university executive, professor, urban and regional planner
Michael, Henry N. geographer, anthropologist
Micko, Alexander S. financial executive
Micozzi, Marc Stephen health executive, physician, educator
Milbourne, Walter Robertson lawyer
Miller, Henry Franklin lawyer
Miller, Leonard David surgeon
Miller, Leslie Anne lawyer
Miller, Ronald Eugene regional science educator
Ming, Si-Chun pathologist, educator
Minisi, Anthony S. lawyer
Mirabello, Francis Joseph lawyer
Mitchell, Ehrman Burkman, Jr. architect
Mitchell, Howard Estill human resources educator, consultant
Miyamoto, Curtis Trent medical educator
Mode, Charles J. mathematician, educator
Monos, Dimitrios medical educator, researcher
Montgomery, David Paul professional baseball team executive
Moore, Acel journalist
Morahan, Page S. microbiologist, educator
Morardini, Michael Robert professional baseball player
Morello, Celeste Anne historian, educator, criminologist
Morgan, Arlene Notoro newspaper editor, reporter, recruiter
Morlok, Edward Karl engineering educator, consultant
Morrison, Donald Franklin statistician, educator
Mortimer, Richard Walter mechanical engineering educator
Moss, Arthur Henshey lawyer
Moss, Roger William, Jr. historian, writer, administrator
Mostovoy, Marc Sanders conductor
Mulholland, S. Grant urologist
Mullinix, Edward Wingate lawyer
Murdoch, Lawrence Corlies, Jr. retired banker, economist
Murphey, Murray Griffin history educator
Murphey, Sheila Ann infectious diseases physician, educator, researcher
Murphy, Mary Marguerite artist
Murray, Terry (Terence Rodney Murray) professional hockey team coach
Muzykantov, Vladimir Rurick immunochemist, researcher
Myers, Allen Richard rheumatologist
Nadley, Harris Jerome accountant, educator, writer
Nalle, Peter Devereux publishing company executive
Narin, Stephen B. lawyer
Neilson, Eric Grant physician, educator, health facility administrator
Neubauer, Joseph food services company executive
Newman, Cory Frank clinical psychologist
Niewiarowski, Stefan physiology educator, biomedical research scientist
Nimoityn, Philip cardiologist
Nix, Robert N(elson) C(ornelius), Jr. state supreme court chief justice
Nixon, Eugene Ray chemist, educator
Nofer, George Hancock lawyer
Noordergraaf, Abraham biophysics educator
Nowell, Peter Carey pathologist, educator
Nussbaum, Paul Eugene journalist
O'Brien, Charles P. psychiatrist, educator
O'Brien, William Jerome, II lawyer
O'Connor, John Joseph insurance company executive
O'Connor, Joseph A., Jr. lawyer
O'Donnell, G. Daniel lawyer
O'Leary, Dennis Joseph lawyer
Olenginski, Jan Anthony surgeon
Oliva, Terence Anthony marketing educator
Olshin, Samuel E. architect
Ominsky, Alan Jay lawyer, medical educator
Ominsky, Harris lawyer
O'Neill, Thomas Newman, Jr. federal judge
O'Reilly, Timothy Patrick lawyer
Orne, Emily Carota psychologist
Osborne, Frederick Spring, Jr. academic administrator, artist
Oswald, Stanton S. lawyer
Othmer, David Artman television and radio station executive
Otvos, Laszlo Istvan, Jr. organic chemist
Padova, John R. federal judge
Padulo, Louis university administrator
Paglia, Camille writer, humanities educator
Pagliaro, James Domenic lawyer
Pak, Hyung Woong foundation executive
Palmer, Richard Ware lawyer
Palmer, Russell Eugene investment executive
Panzer, Mitchell Emanuel lawyer
Paone, Peter artist
Papadakis, Constantine N. university executive
Parish, Lawrence Charles physician, editor
Parker, Grace Patrice insurance specialist
Parry, Lance Aaron newspaper executive
Parry, William DeWitt lawyer
Patel, Ronald Anthony newspaper editor
Patterson, Donald Floyd human, medical and veterinary genetics educator
Peachey, Lee DeBorde biology educator
Peck, Robert McCracken naturalist, science historian, writer
Peirce, Donald Oluf elementary education educator
Pepe, Frank A. cell and developmental biology educator
Perkins, George Holmes architectural educator, architect
Perry, Robert Palese molecular biologist, educator
Peters, Edward Murray history educator
Pew, Robert Anderson retired real estate corporation officer
Phillips, Dorothy Kay lawyer
Phillips, Stephen S. lawyer
Piccolo, Joseph Anthony hospital administrator
Pietra, Giuseppe Giovanni pathology educator
Pilborough, Barbara Jean healthcare consultant

Brunson, Kenneth Wayne *cancer biologist*
Bryant, Randal Everitt *computer science educator, consultant*
Buchanan, James Junkin *classics educator*
Burger, Herbert Francis *advertising agency executive*
Burke, Leah Weyerts *physician*
Burke, Linda Beerbower *lawyer, aluminum manufacturing company executive, mining executive*
Burke, Timothy Francis, Jr. *lawyer*
Burnham, Donald Clemens *manufacturing company executive*
Buyny, Marianne Jo *eating disorders therapist, addictions counselor*
Cagney, William Robert *psychologist*
Cahouet, Frank Vondell *banking executive*
Candris, Laura A. *lawyer*
Capobianco, Tito *opera director*
Carbo, Toni (Toni Carbo Bearman) *information scientist, university dean*
Cardenes, Andres Jorge *violinist, music educator*
Caretto, Albert Alexander *chemist, educator*
Carr, Walter James, Jr. *research physicist, consultant*
Carroll, Holbert Nicholson *political science educator*
Carter, Donald K. *architectural firm executive*
Carter-Jones, Sheila Lorraine *secondary school educator*
Casasent, David Paul *electrical engineering educator, data processing executive*
Cassidy, William Arthur *geology and planetary science educator*
Casturo, Don James *venture capitalist*
Charap, Stanley Harvey *electrical engineering educator*
Cheever, George Martin *lawyer*
Chiang, Shiao-Hung *chemical engineering educator*
Chigier, Norman *mechanical engineering educator*
Choyke, Wolfgang Justus *physicist*
Christiano, Paul P. *academic administrator, civil engineering educator*
Cindrich, Robert James *judge*
Clack, Jerry *classics educator*
Clyde, Larry Forbes *banker*
Cohen, Bernard Leonard *physicist, educator*
Cohen, Henry C. *lawyer*
Cohill, Maurice Blanchard, Jr. *federal judge*
Colen, Frederick Haas *lawyer*
Collins, Rose Ann *minister*
Coltman, John Wesley *physicist*
Colville, Robert E. *lawyer*
Coney, Aims C., Jr. *lawyer, labor-management negotiator*
Conley, Martha Richards *lawyer*
Connolly, Ruth Carol *critical care nurse*
Connors, Eugene Kenneth *lawyer*
Conti, Joy Flowers *lawyer*
Conti, Ronald Samuel *electronics engineer, fire prevention engineer*
Cooper, Thomas Louis *lawyer*
Cooper, William Marion *physician*
Cosetti, Joseph Louis *federal judge*
Courtsal, Donald Preston *manufacturing company executive, financial consultant*
Cowan, Barton Zalman *lawyer*
Cowher, Bill *professional football coach*
Craig, John Gilbert, Jr. *newspaper editor*
Cressman, Michael David *internist, researcher*
Croan, Robert James *music critic, singer*
Culhane, M. Bridget *nursing society executive, oncology clinical nurse specialist*
Culyba, Michael John *physician, medical administrator*
Curry, Nancy Ellen *educator, psychoanalyst, psychologist*
Curtis, Gregory Dyer *investment company executive, foundation administrator, lawyer, author, poet*
Cutler, John Charles *physician, educator*
Cyert, Richard Michael *former academic administrator, economist*
Dameshek, H(arold) Lee *physician*
Damianos, Sylvester *architect, sculptor*
Daniel, Robert Michael *lawyer*
Davidson, George A., Jr. *utility company executive*
Davis, John Phillips, Jr. *lawyer*
Davis, Otto Anderson *economics educator*
Dawes, Robyn Mason *psychology educator*
Dawson, Dermontti Farra *professional football player*
Dawson, Mary Ruth *curator*
DeForest, Walter Pattison, III *lawyer*
deGroat, William Chesney *pharmacology educator*
DeKosky, Steven Trent *neurologist*
Delaney, John Francis *neurologist, psychiatrist*
Demmler, John Henry *lawyer*
Dempsey, Jacqueline Lee *special education director*
Dempsey, Jerry Edward *service company executive*
Deskins, Wilbur Eugene *mathematician, educator*
Detre, Thomas *psychiatrist, educator*
Diamond, Gustave *federal judge*
Dick, David E. *construction company executive*
Dillon, W. Daniel *radio broadcast producer*
Dinman, Bertram David *consultant, retired aluminum company executive*
Dixit, Balwant Narayan *pharmacology and toxicology educator*
Dobos, Sister Marion *parochial school educator*
Doerfler, Leo G. *audiology educator*
Donahoe, David Lawrence *state and city official*
Donahue, John Francis *investment company executive*
Donaldson, William Fielding, Jr. *orthopedic surgeon*
Donnelly, Thomas Joseph *lawyer*
Doty, Robert Walter *lawyer*
Drescher, Seymour *history educator, writer*
Dugan, John F. *lawyer*
Duval, Robert *leasing company executive*
Dybeck, Alfred Charles *labor arbitrator*
Eaton, Joseph W. *sociology educator*
Edelman, Harry Rollings, III *engineering and construction company executive*
Egler, Frederick Norton *lawyer*
Ehrenwerth, David Harry *lawyer*
Emmerich, Werner Sigmund *physicist*
Epperson, David Ernest *dean, educator*
Eskenazi, Maxine Solomon *speech researcher*
Evans, Bruce Dwight *lawyer*
Evey, Lois Reed *psychiatric nurse*
Ewalt, Henry Ward *lawyer*
Fairbanks, Frank Bates *manufacturing company executive*
Fararo, Thomas John *sociologist, educator*
Farley, Andrew Newell *lawyer*
Farrow, Robert Scott *economist, educator*
Feingold, David Sidney *microbiology educator*
Feller, Robert Livingston *chemist, art conservation scientist*
Fenves, Steven Joseph *civil engineer*
Ferguson, Donald Guffey *radiologist*
Ferguson, Mary Anne Heyward *language professional, educator*
Ferguson, Sanford Barnett *lawyer*
Fernsler, John Paul *lawyer*
Fienberg, Stephen Elliott *statistician*
Fine, Milton *hotel company executive, lawyer*
Finn, Frances Mary *biochemistry researcher*
Fireman, Philip *pediatrician, allergist, immunologist, medical association executive*
Fischer, Richard Lawrence *metal products executive*
Fischhoff, Baruch *psychologist, educator*
Fisher, Bernard *surgeon, educator*
Fisher, D. Michael *state senator, lawyer*
Fisher, Henry *investment banker*
Fisher, James Aiken *industrial marketing executive*
Fitzgerald, Judith Klaswick *federal judge*
Flaherty, John P., Jr. *chief justice*
Flatley, Lawrence Edward *lawyer*
Fletcher, Ronald Darling *microbiologist educator*
Flinn, Michael James *lawyer*
Foreman, John Daniel *financial executive*
Fort, James Tomlinson *lawyer*
Foxen, Richard William *manufacturing company executive*
Francis, Ron *professional hockey player*
Frank, Alan I. W. *manufacturing company executive*
Frank, Ronald W. *lawyer, financier*
Franklin, Kenneth Ronald *franchise company executive, consultant*
Freudenrich, David Robert *civil engineer, traffic engineer*
Friday, Gilbert Anthony, Jr. *pediatrician*
Friday, Paul J(ohn) *psychologist*
Friedberg, Simeon Adlow *physicist, educator*
Froehlich, Fritz Edgar *telecommunications educator and scientist*
Frolik, Lawrence Anton *law educator, lawyer, consultant*
Gaffney, Paul Cotter *retired physician*
Gale, Robert Lee *retired American literature educator and critic*
Geeseman, Robert George *lawyer*
Geibel, Sister Grace Ann *college president*
Geiger, Gene Edward *engineer, educator*
Genge, William Harrison *advertising executive, writer*
Geraghty, Andrea *lawyer*
Gerhard, Harry E., Jr. *counter trader, management and trade consultant*
Gerjuoy, Edward *physicist, lawyer*
Gerlach, G. Donald *lawyer*
Gernert, Eric Vincent *telecommunications analyst*
Giel, James Arthur, Jr. *steel company executive*
Gill, Thomas James, III *physician, educator*
Gindroz, Raymond L. *architect*
Ginsburg, Mark Barry *sociology of education educator*
Gold, Harold Arthur *lawyer*
Goldberg, Mark Joel *lawyer*
Goldstein, Donald Maurice *historian, educator*
Goldstein, Gerald *research psychologist*
Gollin, Susanne Merle *cytogeneticist, cell biologist*
Gottfried, Byron Stuart *engineering educator*
Grady, James Stran *financial planner*
Graf, Edward Louis, Jr. *lawyer, finance executive*
Graham, Laurie *editor*
Gray, Charles Buffum *theatrical director, producer*
Greene, Kevin Darwin *professional football player*
Grefenstette, Carl G. *medical products and real estate executive*
Griffin, Donald Spray *mechanical engineer, consultant*
Griffiths, Robert Budington *physics educator*
Grossman, Ignacio E. *chemical engineering educator*
Grossmann, Ignacio Emilio *chemical engineering educator*
Grunbaum, Adolf *philosophy educator, author*
Gurtin, Morton Edward *mathematics educator*
Hackney, William Pendleton *lawyer*
Haggerty, Gretchen R. *petroleum and steel industry executive*
Haley, Roy W. *financial services executive*
Hall, Charles Allan *numerical analyst, educator*
Hallen, Philip Burgh *foundation administrator*
Halpern, Richard I. *lawyer*
Hamilton, Howard Britton *electrical engineer, educator*
Hammer, Harold Harlan *oil company financial executive*
Hammond, Paul Young *political scientist, educator*
Hannan, Robert William *retail pharmaceutical company executive*
Hardesty, Robert Lynch *surgeon, educator*
Hardie, James Hiller *lawyer*
Harff, Charles Henry *lawyer, retired diversified industrial company executive*
Harper, Gladys Coffey *health services adviser*
Harris, Ann Birgitta Sutherland *art historian*
Harrold, Ronald Thomas *research scientist*
Harvey, Calvin Rea *lawyer*
Heath, David Clay *mathematics educator, consultant*
Heckler, Frederick Roger *plastic surgeon*
Heindl, Mary Lynn *magazine editor*
Heller, Lawrence Aaron *business owner, association executive*
Hellman, Arthur David *law educator, consultant*
Hendrickson, Chris Thompson *civil and environmental engineering educator, researcher*
Henry, Susan Armstrong *biology educator, university dean*
Herndon, James Henry *orthopedic surgeon, educator*
Herrington, Donald Francis *financial services executive*
Hershey, Colin Harry *management consultant*
Hershey, Dale *lawyer*
Hershey, Nathan *lawyer, educator*
Hickman, Leon Edward *lawyer, business executive*
Hicks, Wendell Leon *history educator, publisher, political scientist*
Higgins, James Henry *retired banker*
Hill, John Howard *lawyer*
Hillman, Henry L. *investment company executive*
Hingson, Robert Andrew *physician, educator, inventor, farmer, poet*
Hitt, Leo N. *lawyer, educator*
Hlawati, Joyce F. *elementary education educator*
Ho, Chien *biological sciences educator*
Hoburg, James Frederick *electrical engineering educator*
Hodges, Margaret Moore *author, educator*
Hoffman, Ronald Robert *aluminum company executive*
Hoffstot, Henry Phipps, Jr. *lawyer*
Holcomb, Philo *steel company executive*
Hollingsworth, Samuel Hawkins, Jr. *bassist*
Hollinshead, Earl Darnell, Jr. *lawyer*
Holzner, Burkart *sociologist, educator*
Horan, Justin Thomas *retired association executive*
Horowitz, Carole Spiegel *interior designer*
Horowitz, Don Roy *landscape company executive*
Howard, Lawrence Cabot *international affairs educator*
Howse, W. Frances *academic administrator*
Hsu, Cho-yun *history educator*
Humphrey, Watts Sherman *technical executive, author*
Hung, Tin-Kan *engineering educator, researcher*
Hunter, David Wittmer *security brokerage executive*
Huntington, James Cantine, Jr. *equipment manufacturing company executive*
Hyman, Lewis Neil *investment company executive, investment advisor*
Ijiri, Yuji *accounting and economics educator*
Ismail, Yahia Hassan *dentist, educator*
Jagr, Jaromir *professional hockey player*
Janis, Allen Ira *retired physicist, educator*
Jannetta, Peter Joseph *neurosurgeon*
Johnson, Micah William *television newscaster, director*
Johnson, Robert Alan *lawyer*
Johnston, Edward Joseph *professional hockey team coach, former team executive, former player*
Jones, Craig Ward *lawyer*
Jones, Elizabeth Winifred *biology educator*
Jordan, Angel Goni *electrical and computer engineering educator*
Jordan, Michael Hugh *electrical and electronics company executive*
Josephs, Eileen Sherle *mediator, financial consultant*
Josey, E(lonnie) J(unius) *librarian, educator, former state administrator*
Joyner, Claude Reuben, Jr. *physician, medical educator*
Junker, Edward P., III *diversified financial services company executive*
Kadane, Joseph B. *statistics educator*
Kalnicki, Shalom *radiologist, educator*
Kang, Yoogoo *anesthesiologist*
Kaplan, John *photojournalist, consultant, educator*
Karis, William George *coal company executive*
Karol, Meryl Helene *immunologist, educator*
Katz, Arnold *economics educator*
Kaufman, William Morris *research institute administrator, engineer*
Kearns, John J., III *lawyer*
Keefe, William Joseph *political science educator*
Keleti, Georg *retired microbiologist, researcher*
†Kendall, Jason Daniel *professional baseball player*
Kenkel, James Lawrence *economics educator*
Kenrick, Charles William *lawyer*
Keshavan, Matcheri *psychiatrist*
Ketchum, David Storey *retired fundraising executive*
Ketter, David Lee *lawyer*
Kiger, Robert William *botanist, science historian, educator*
Kilmann, Ralph Herman *business educator*
King, Elaine A. *curator, art historian, critic*
King, William Richard *business educator, consultant*
†Kirkland, Lorenzo Levon *football player*
Kisslinger, Leonard Sol *physicist, educator*
Klett, Edwin Lee *lawyer*
Knapp, George Robert *investment executive, business advisor, lawyer*
Knox, Charles Graham *lawyer*
Kochanek, Patrick Michael *pediatrician, educator*
Koedel, Robert Craig *minister, historian, educator*
Kraus, John Delbert *investment advisor*
Krause, Helen Fox *physician, otolaryngologist*
Kriebel, Charles Hosey *management sciences educator*
Krutz, Ronald L. *computer engineer*
Kupfer, David J. *psychiatry educator*
Kuster, Janice Elizabeth *biology educator, researcher*
Lake, Carnell Augustino *professional football player*
Langenberg, Frederick Charles *business executive*
La Rue, Henry Aldred *consultant, former oil company executive*
Laughlin, David Eugene *materials science educator, metallurgical consultant*
Lauterbach, Robert Emil *steel company executive*
Lave, Judith Rice *economics educator*
Lave, Lester Bernard *economist, educator, researcher*
LeBoeuf, Raymond Walter *manufacturing company executive*
Lee, Donald John *federal judge*
Lego, Paul Edward *retired corporation executive*
Lehoczky, John Paul *statistics educator*
Leibowitz, Marvin *lawyer*
Lemieux, Mario *former professional hockey player*
Leo, Peter Andrew *newspaper columnist, writing educator*
Levine, Macy Irving *physician*
Lewis, Jessica Helen (Mrs. Jack D. Myers) *physician, educator*
Lewis, Richard Allan *financial planner, business consultant*
Lewis, Timothy K. *federal judge*
Li, Ching-Chung *electrical engineering, computer science educator*
Libman, Steven Bradley *performing arts administrator*
Limbach, Walter F. *construction company executive*
†Linaberger, Anne *television producer*
Lippard, Thomas Eugene *lawyer*
Litman, Roslyn Margolis *lawyer, educator*
Lloyd, Gregory Lenard *professional football player*
Loftness, Vivian Ellen *architecture educator*
Longest, Beaufort Brown *health services administration educator, research director*
Lotze, Michael Thomas *surgeon*
Lowery, Willa Dean *obstetrician-gynecologist*
Ludwig, Karl David *psychiatrist*
Lundquist, Dana R. *health insurance executive*
Luthy, Richard Godfrey *environmental engineering educator*
Lyjak Chorazy, Anna Julia *pediatrician, medical administrator, educator*
Machatzke, Heinz Wilhelm *dean, science administrator*
MacLeod, Gordon Kenneth *physician, educator*
Majors, Johnny (John Terrill Majors) *university athletic coach*
Mansmann, Carol Los *federal judge, law educator*
Mansmann, J. Jerome *lawyer*
Marino, Ignazio Roberto *transplant surgeon, researcher*
Marts, Terri Louise *management executive*
Mason, Craig Watson *corporate planning executive*
Massalski, Thaddeus Bronislaw *material scientist, educator*
Matchett, Janet Reedy *psychologist*
Mathieson, Andrew Wray *investment management executive*
Mattison, Donald Roger *dean, physician, military officer*
Matyjaszewski, Krzysztof *chemist, educator*
Matzke, Gary Roger *pharmacist*
Maurer, Richard Michael *investment company executive*
Maximos, (Maximos Demetrios Aghiorgoussis) *bishop*
McAvoy, Bruce Ronald *engineer, consultant*
McCall, Dorothy Kay *social worker, psychotherapist*
McCallum, Bennett Tarlton *economics educator*
McCartney, Robert Charles *lawyer*
McClelland, James Lloyd *psychology educator, cognitive scientist*
McCoid, Donald James *bishop*
McConomy, James Herbert *lawyer*
McCullough, Lauren Fink *aluminum company manager*
McCullough, M. Bruce *judge*
McDuffie, Keith A. *literature educator, magazine director*
Mc Featters, Dale Stitt *retired electric company executive*
McGough, Walter Thomas, Jr. *lawyer*
McGovern, John Joseph *retired air pollution control executive*
McGuinn, Martin Gregory *banker, lawyer*
McHoes, Ann McIver *technical writer, computer systems consultant*
McIntosh, DeCourcy Eyre *museum director*
McKenna, J. Frank, III *lawyer*
Mc Kenzie, Ray *anesthesiologist, educator*
McKenzie, Thomas James *lawyer, insurance consultant*
McLaughlin, John Sherman *lawyer*
McMichael, Francis Clay *civil engineering educator, environmental engineering consultant*
†Mc Vicker, Charles Taggart *artist*
McWilliams, Betty Jane *science administrator, communication disorders educator, researcher*
Mehrabian, Robert *academic administrator*
Meiksin, Zvi H. *electrical engineering educator*
Meisel, Alan *law educator*
Mellon, Richard Prosser *charitable foundation executive*
Meltzer, Allan H. *economist, educator*
Mendelson, Leonard M. *lawyer*
Mesa-Lago, Carmelo *economist, educator*
Messner, Robert Thomas *lawyer, banking executive*
Miles, Leon F. (Lee Miles) *vocational education educator*
Miller, David William *historian, educator*
Miller, Donald *art critic*
Miller, Harbaugh *lawyer*
Miller, James Robert *lawyer*
Miller, Mildred *opera singer, recitalist*
Milnes, Arthur George *electrical engineer, educator*
Milsom, Robert Cortlandt *banker*
Minnigh, Joel Douglas *library director*
Missiriotis, Irene *recreational activities director, artist*
Modell, John *historian, educator*
Moeller, Audrey Carolyn *energy company executive, corporate secretary*
Moore, Daniel Edmund *psychologist, educator, retired educational administrator*
Moore, Pearl B. *nurse*
Moore, Richard Allan *mathematics educator*
Moore, Robert Yates *neuroscience educator*
Moriarty, Richard William *pediatrician*
Morice, Joseph Richard *history educator*
Mortimer, James Winslow *analytical chemist*
Morton, James Davis *lawyer*
Moura, José Manuel Fonseca *electrical engineer*
Mueller, Gerd Dieter *financial and administrative executive*
Mulloney, Peter Black *steel, oil and gas executive*
Mulvihill, David Brian *lawyer*
Mulvihill, John Joseph *medical geneticist*
Murdoch, David Armor *lawyer*
Murphy, John Nolan *mining executive, researcher, electrical engineer*
Murphy, Thomas J., Jr. *mayor*
Murray, Davina Ann *financial analyst, accounting officer*
Murray, John Edward, Jr. *lawyer, educator, university president*
Murray, Philip Joseph, III *lawyer*
Murray, Sandra Ann *biology research scientist, educator*
Murrin, Regis Doubet *lawyer*
Muto, Susan Annette *religion educator, academic administrator*
Myers, Eugene Nicholas *otolaryngologist, otolaryngology educator*
Myers, Jack Duane *physician*
Nathanson, Harvey Charles *electrical engineer*
Needleman, Herbert Leroy *psychiatrist, pediatrician*
Neel, John Dodd *memorial park executive*
Neuman, Charles P. *electrical and computer engineering educator*
Noll, Charles Henry *former professional football coach*
Nordenberg, Mark Alan *law educator, university official*
Norris, James Harold *lawyer*
Norton, Eunice *pianist*
Ober, Russell John, Jr. *lawyer*
O'Brien, Thomas Henry *bank holding company executive*
O'Connor, Donald Thomas *lawyer*
O'Connor, Edward Gearing *lawyer*
Ogul, Morris Samuel *political science educator, consultant*
O'Hare, Virginia Lewis *legal administrator*
Olson, Stephen M(ichael) *lawyer*
Omiros, George James *medical foundation executive*
O'Neill, Paul Henry *aluminum company executive*
O'Reilly, Anthony John Francis *food company executive*
Ostern, Wilhelm Curt *retired holding company executive*
Pacifico, Diane Alane *ophthalmic nurse*
Packard, Rochelle Sybil *elementary school educator*
Page, Lorne Albert *physicist, educator*
Parkes, Kenneth Carroll *ornithologist*
Partanen, Carl Richard *biology educator*
Pasnick, Raymond Wallace *labor union official, editor*
Patrick, Craig *professional hockey team executive*
Patten, Charles Anthony *management consultant, retired manufacturing company executive, author*
Patton, Nancy Matthews *elementary education educator*
Patton, Robert Frederick *lawyer, banker*
Paul, Robert Arthur *steel company executive*
Paulston, Christina Bratt *linguistics educator*
Pearson, Nathan Williams *investment management executive*
†Pepe, Paul Ernest *emergency physician, educator*
Perlman, Mark *economist, educator*

Perloff, Robert psychologist, educator
Petersen, Jean Snyder association executive
Pettit, Frederick Sidney metallurgical engineering educator, researcher
Pezacka, Ewa Hanna biochemist, educator
Pham, Si Mai cadiothoracic surgeon, medical educator
Phillips, James Macilduff material handling company executive, engineering and manufacturing executive
Phillips, Larry Edward lawyer
Plazek, Donald John materials science educator
Plowman, Jack Wesley lawyer
Pohl, Paul Michael lawyer
Pohland, Frederick George environmental engineering educator, researcher
Pois, Joseph lawyer, educator
Pollock, Bruce Godfrey psychiatrist, educator
†Pompeani, Bruce Patrick television reporter
†Posvar, Wesley Wentz university president, educator, consultant
Powderly, William H., III lawyer
Pratt, Richard Houghton physics educator
Price, Fredric Victor physician, educator, researcher
Price, Trevor Robert Pryce psychiatrist, educator
Procyk, Judson M. metropolitan archbishop
Prosperi, Louis Anthony lawyer
Pugliese, Robert Francis lawyer, business executive
Puhala, James Joseph lawyer
Purcupile, John Stephen lawyer
Pushinsky, Jon lawyer
Puskar, Milan pharmaceuticals executive
Pyeritz, Reed Edwin medical geneticist, educator, research director
Rabin, Bruce Stuart immunologist, physician, educator
Rago, Ann D'Amico public relations professional, educator
Raimondi, Albert Anthony mechanical engineer
Ramm, Douglas Robert psychologist
Ramsey, David Allen psychologist
Randolph, Robert DeWitt lawyer
Rao, Abdul Sohail transplant immunologist, researcher
Rawski, Evelyn Sakakida history educator
Raynovich, George, Jr. lawyer
Reed, W. Franklin lawyer
Reichblum, Audrey Rosenthal public relations executive
Renk, Carol Ann secondary education educator
Rescher, Nicholas philosophy educator
Restivo, James John, Jr. lawyer
Reznik, Alan A. petroleum engineering educator
Rheinboldt, Werner Carl mathematics educator, researcher
Rimer, John Thomas foreign language educator, academic administrator, writer, translator
Ritchey, Patrick William lawyer
Rogers, Bryan Leigh artist, art educator
Rogers, Fred McFeely television producer and host
Rogers, Robert Mark physician
Roman, Andrew Michael lawyer, educator
Romoff, Jeffrey Alan university officer, health care executive
Roof, Robert L. broadcast executive, sales executive
Rooney, Daniel M. professional football team executive
Rosenberg, Jerome Laib chemist, educator
Rosenberger, Bryan David lawyer
Rosenkranz, Herbert S. environmental toxicology educator
Ross, Eunice Latshaw judge
Ross, Madelyn Ann newspaper editor
Roth, Alvin Eliot economics educator
Roth, Loren H. psychiatrist
Roth, William George manufacturing company executive
Rubin, Robert Terry physician, researcher
Rust, William James retired steel company executive
Ruttenberg, Harold Joseph manufacturing executive
Ryan, Stephen Michael, Jr. professional hockey team executive
Sante, William Arthur, II electronics manufacturing executive
Sanzo, Anthony Michael health care executive
Sashin, Donald physicist, radiological physicist, educator
Sauer, Georgia Booras newspaper writer
†Scaife, Richard Mellon philanthropist
Schaub, Marilyn McNamara religion educator
Scheinholtz, Leonard Louis lawyer
Schliebs, Charles Allan lawyer
Schmeler, Mark Raymond occupational therapist
Schmidt, Edward Craig lawyer
Schorr-Ribera, Hilda Keren psychologist
Schultz, Jerome Samson biochemical engineer, educator
Schwab, Arthur James lawyer
Schwendeman, Paul William lawyer
Sekerka, Robert Floyd physics educator, scientist
Seligson, Mitchell A. Latin American studies educator
Sell, William Edward legal educator
Sensenich, Ila Jeanne magistrate judge
Shane, Peter Milo law educator
Shapira, David S. food chain executive
Shapiro, Alvin Philip physician, educator
Shaw, Mary M. computer science educator
Sheon, Aaron art historian, educator
Siker, Ephraim S. anesthesiologist
Silverman, Arnold Barry lawyer
Simaan, Marwan A. electrical engineering educator
Simmermon, James Everett credit bureau executive
Simmons, Richard L. surgeon
Simon, Herbert A(lexander) social scientist
Simonds, John Ormsbee landscape architect
Sinclair, Glenn Bruce mechanical engineering educator, researcher
Slifkin, Malcolm microbiologist
Smartschan, Glenn Fred school system administrator
Smith, Phillip Hartley steel company executive
Sokol, Stephen M. lawyer
Sorensen, Raymond Andrew physics educator
Southworth, Horton Coe educational educator, education scholar
Spanovich, Milan civil engineer
Spina, Horacio Anselmo physician
Spohn, Janice elementary education educator, consultant
Stahl, Laddie L. electrical engineer, manufacturing company executive
Standish, William Lloyd judge
Stargell, Willie (Wilver Dornel Stargell) professional sports team coach, former baseball player
Stark, Rohn Taylor professional football player
Stearns, Peter Nathaniel history educator
Stella, Janet Louise special education educator
Stephenson, Robert Clay real estate company executive
Stiff, Robert Henry dentist, educator
Strader, James David lawyer
Strauss, Robert Philip economics educator
Stroyd, Arthur Heister lawyer
Stuckeman, Herman Campbell architectural engineer
Sussna, Edward economist, educator
Suzuki, Jon Byron dean, periodontist, educator
Swaim, Joseph Carter, Jr. lawyer
Swain, William Grant landscape architect
Swann, Lynn Curtis sportscaster, former professional football player
Sweeney, Clayton Anthony lawyer, business executive
Symons, Edward Leonard, Jr. lawyer, educator, investment advisor
Tarasi, Louis Michael, Jr. lawyer
Tarr, Joel Arthur history and public policy educator
Taylor, D. Lansing cell biology educator
†Taylor, Mark Chandlee choreographer
Thomas, Richard Irwin lawyer
Thomas, W(illiam) Bruce retired steel, oil, gas company executive
Thompson, Gerald Luther operations research and applied mathematics educator
Thompson, Kay Francis dentist
Thompson, Thomas Martin lawyer
Thorne, John Reinecke business educator, venture capitalist
†Thorner, John professional society administrator
Thorpe, Leon Ferber real estate investment company executive
Thurman, Andrew Edward lawyer
Tierney, John William chemical engineering educator
Toeplitz, Gideon symphony society executive
Toker, Franklin K. art history educator, archaeologist, foundation executive
Touhill, C. Joseph environmental engineer
Trapp, Frank Anderson art educator
Troen, Philip physician, educator
Trottier, Bryan John professional sports team coach, former professional hockey player
Tucker, Richard Blackburn, III lawyer
Tung, Frank Yao-Tsung microbiologist educator
Turbeville, Robert Morris engineering executive
Turner, Harry Woodruff lawyer
Ubinger, John W., Jr. lawyer
Udler, Rubin Yakovlevitch linguist
Ummer, James Walter lawyer
Usher, Thomas James steel executive, energy executive
Van Dusen, Albert Clarence university official
Van Kirk, Thomas L. lawyer
Vater, Charles J. lawyer
Veeder, Peter Greig lawyer
Verlich, Jean Elaine writer, public relations consultant
Vidovich, Danko Victor neurosurgeon, researcher
Vogel, Victor Gerald medical educator, researcher
Vogeley, Clyde Eicher, Jr. engineering educator, artist, consultant
von Waldow, Arnd N. lawyer
Voss, James Frederick psychologist, educator
Wagner, Florence Zeleznik telecommunications executive
Wald, Niel medical educator
Wallace, Richard Christopher, Jr. school system administrator, educator
Wallace, William Edward engineering educator, scientist
Wallman, George hospital and food services administrator
Walsh, Arthur Campbell psychiatrist
Walsh, Michael Francis advertising executive
Walton, James M. investment company executive
Walton, Jon David lawyer
Ward, Thomas Jerome lawyer
Warner, Judith (Anne) Huss educator
Weaver, Charles Henry business consulting executive
Wehmeier, Helge H. chemical, health care and imaging technologies company executive
Weidman, John Carl, II education educator, consultant
Weingartner, Rudolph Herbert philosophy educator
Weis, Joseph Francis, Jr. federal judge
Welfer, Thomas, Jr. utility company executive
Westerberg, Arthur William chemical engineering educator
White, Robert Marshall physicist, educator
Wilde, Patricia artistic director
Wilkins, David George fine arts educator
Will, James Fredrick steel company executive
Williams, Charles David oil and steel company executive
Williams, John Wesley fine arts educator
Williams, Lisle Edward civil and structural engineer
Williams, Louis Stanton glass and chemical manufacturing executive
Williams, Nathaniel, Jr. elementary education educator
Williams, Robert Brickley lawyer
Wilson, Charles Reginald real estate executive
Winnie, Glenna Barbara pediatric pulmonologist
Winter, Peter Michael physician, anesthesiologist, educator
Wishart, Alfred Wilbur, Jr. foundation administrator
Wohleber, Lynne Farr archivist, librarian
Wolken, Jerome Jay biophysicist, educator
Woo, Savio Lau-Yuen bioengineering educator
Woodson, Roderick Kevin professional football player
Woodward, Thomas Aiken lawyer
Wuerl, Donald W. bishop
Wycoff, William Mortimer lawyer
Wylie, Mary Evelyn psychiatrist, retired anesthesiologist, educator
Wynstra, Nancy Ann lawyer
Yang, Wen-Ching chemical engineer
Yates, John Thomas, Jr. chemistry educator, research director
Yorsz, Stanley lawyer
Young, Hugh David physics educator, writer, organist
Youngner, Julius Stuart microbiologist, educator
Yu, Victor Lin-Kai physician, educator
Zanardelli, John Joseph healthcare services executive
Zappala, Stephen A. state supreme court justice
Ziegler, Donald Emil chief federal judge
Zoffer, H. Jerome business educator, university dean
Zoghby, Guy Anthony lawyer

**Plains**
Elias, Joseph secondary school educator

**Plymouth Meeting**
Brownstone, Hugh Michael technology executive
Clemmer, Leon architect, planner
Gilstein, Jacob Burrill physicist
Guckes, William Ruhland, Jr. insurance executive
Kostinsky, Harvey clinical and electrical engineer
Litman, Raymond Stephen financial services consultant
Nobel, Joel J. biomedical researcher
Schott, Jeffrey Brian software engineer
Siegal, Jacob J. management and financial consultant
Suydam, Peter R. clinical engineer, consultant
Thomsen, Thomas Richard retired communications company executive
Yarnall, D. Robert, Jr. entrepreneur, investor

**Pocopson**
Mulligan, James Francis retired business executive, lawyer

**Polk**
Hall, Richard Clayton retired psychologist

**Port Royal**
Wert, Jonathan Maxwell, II management consultant

**Pottstown**
Hylton, Thomas James author
Kelly, Thomas Joseph, III photojournalist
Ruth, Thomas Griswold history educator
White, Thomas David, II academic administrator

**Pottsville**
Ackalusky, Hazel Ethel artist
Boran, Robert Paul, Jr. orthopedic surgeon
Garloff, Samuel John psychiatrist
Jones, Joseph Hayward lawyer
Walsh, James William mental health professional

**Preston Park**
†Janowich, Ron artist

**Punxsutawney**
Dinsmore, Roberta Joan Maier library director
Graffius, Richard Stewart, II elementary educator
Lorenzo, Nicholas Francis, Jr. lawyer

**Quakertown**
Ambrus, Lorna medical, surgical and geriatrics nurse
de Limantour, Clarice Barr food scientist
McDaniel, Robert Stephen technical professional
Wartella, Rosanne Karen occupational therapy assistant

**Quarryville**
Bird, L. Raymond investor

**Radnor**
Baxter, John Michael editor
†Buck, James Mahlon, Jr. venture capital executive
Burtis, Theodore Alfred oil company executive
Castle, Joseph Lanktree, II energy company executive, consultant
Draeger, Kenneth W. high technology company executive
Frankson-Kendrick, Sarah Jane publisher
Harrison, Robert Drew management consultant
Humes, Graham investment banker
Marland, Alkis Joseph leasing company executive, computer science educator, financial planner
Mestre, Oscar Luis financial consultant
Paier, Adolf Arthur computer software and services company executive
Rothrock, Robert William physician assistant
Stearns, Milton Sprague, Jr. financial executive
Templeton, John Marks, Jr. pediatric surgeon, foundation executive
Vanarsdall, Robert Lee, Jr. orthodontist, educator

**Reading**
Alexander, Robert William radiologist
Beaver, Howard Oscar, Jr. wrought specialty alloys manufacturing company executive
Bell, Frances Louise medical technologist
Blue, John James psychotherapist, consultant
Boscov, Albert retail executive
Breidegam, Mary Ellen energy company professional
Canning, Traci A. designer
Cottrell, G. Walton manufacturing executive
Dersh, Rhoda E. management consultant, business executive
Dietrich, Bruce Leinbach planetarium and museum administrator, astronomer, educator
Ehlerman, Paul Michael industrial battery manufacturing company executive
Erdman, Carl L. N. retired banker
Fiore, Nicholas Francis special alloys and materials company executive
Gebbia, Robert James tax executive
Hedegard, Victor Christian, III clinical psychologist
Hildreth, Eugene A. physician, educator
Hollander, Herbert I. consulting engineer
Huyett, Daniel Henry, III federal judge
Linton, Jack Arthur lawyer
Lusch, Charles Jack physician
Mattern, Donald Eugene retired association executive
Mengel, Philip R(ichard) investment banker
Rochowicz, John Anthony, Jr. mathematician, mathematics and physics educator
Roedel, Paul Robert steel company executive
Roesch, Clarence Henry banker
Rothermel, Daniel Krott lawyer, holding company executive
Sauer, Elissa Swisher nursing educator
Smith, John Wilson, III newspaper editor, columnist, statistician
Snyder, Clair Allison banker
Troutman, E. Mac federal judge
Welty, John Rider lawyer
White, Timothy Paul brokerage house executive
Williams, Sandra Keller postal service executive

**Reedsville**
Miller, Mary Lois retired nurse midwife

**Reynoldsville**
Wheeler, Mark Andrew, Sr. lawyer

**Ridley Park**
Brittell-Whitehead, Diane Peeples secondary education educator, addiction counselor
Clark, John H., Jr. lawyer
Walls, William Walton, Jr. management consultant

**Riegelsville**
Banko, Ruth Caroline library director

**Roaring Spring**
Smith, Larry Dennis paper mill stores executive

**Robesonia**
Houck, Charleen McClain education educator

**Rochester**
Goulait, John Joseph aircraft maintenance specialist

**Rockledge**
Bacon, George Hughes consultant

**Rosemont**
Bolger, Stephen Garrett English and American studies educator
Kline, Harriet Dennis psychologist, school psychologist
Nixon, Agnes Eckhardt television writer, producer

**Roseto**
Coppolella, Anthony S. songwriter, poet, singer, model

**Russellton**
Curtis, Paula Annette elementary and secondary education educator

**Rydal**
Black, Thomas Donald retired religious organization administrator
Kirkland, Bryant Mays clergyman
Roediger, Janice Anne artist, educator

**Saint Davids**
Baird, John Absalom, Jr. college official
Bertsch, Frederick Charles, III business executive
Heebner, Albert Gilbert economist, banker, educator
Maahs, Kenneth Henry, Sr. religion educator
Rogers, James Gardiner accountant, educator
Sheftel, Roger Terry merchant bank executive
Shurkin, Lorna Greene writer, publicist

**Saint Marys**
Johnson, J. M. Hamlin manufacturing company executive
Shobert, Erle Irwin, II management consultant

**Saltsburg**
Buseck, Larry Allen music educator
Pidgeon, John Anderson headmaster

**Sayre**
Moody, Robert Adams neurosurgeon

**Schuylkill Haven**
Sarno, Patricia Ann biology educator

**Scottdale**
Miller, Levi publishing administrator

**Scranton**
Bianca, Joanne Marie elementary and early childhood educator
Cimini, Joseph Fedele law educator, lawyer, former magistrate
Clymer, Jay Phaon, III science educator
Culliney, John James radiologist, educator
De Celles, Charles Edouard theologian, educator
Haggerty, James Joseph lawyer
Hoffman, Barbara Ann English language educator
Howley, James McAndrew lawyer
Janoski, Henry Valentine banker, former investment counselor, realtor
Lepore, Marie Ann home care nurse
Lynett, George Vincent newspaper publisher
Lynett, William Ruddy publishing, broadcasting company executive
Maislin, Isidore hospital administrator
Myers, Morey Mayer lawyer
Narsavage, Georgia Roberts nursing educator, researcher
Nealon, William Joseph, Jr. federal judge
Nee, Sister Mary Coleman college president emeritus
Newman, Samuel trust company executive
O'Malley, Carlon Martin judge
Panuska, Joseph Allan academic administrator
Parente, William Joseph political science educator
Passon, Richard Henry academic administrator
Powell, Robert Ellis mathematics educator, college dean
Reap, Sister Mary Margaret college administrator
Rhiew, Francis Changnam radiologist
Rogers, Edwin Earl newspaper editor
Sebastianelli, Carl Thomas clinical psychologist
Shipula, Anthony James, II church diocese administrator
Shovlin, Joseph Patrick optometrist
Sposito, James A. lawyer, consultant
Timins, Bonita Lea interior decorator
Timlin, James Clifford bishop
Vanaskie, Thomas Ignatius judge
Volk, Thomas accountant
Wood, Kathleen Marie physical therapist

**Selinsgrove**
Cunningham, Joel Luther university president
Diers, Hank H. drama educator, playwright, director
Kolbert, Jack foreign language educator, French literature educator, humanities educator

**Sellersville**
Loux, Norman Landis psychiatrist
Rilling, David Carl surgeon

**Seneca**
Spring, Paull E. bishop

**Sewickley**
Chaplin, James Crossan, IV securities firm executive
Jehle, Michael Edward financial executive
Newell, Byron Bruce, Jr. retired theological seminary dean, clergyman
Snyder, William Penn, III manufacturing company executive
Wilkinson, James Allan lawyer, healthcare executive

**Sharon**
Epstein, Louis Ralph retired wholesale grocery executive
Rosenblum, Harold Arthur grocery distribution executive

Ullrich, Linda J. *medical technologist*

**Sharpsville**
Durek, Dorothy Mary *retired English language educator*

**Shickshinny**
Luksha, Rosemary Dorothy *art educator*

**Shippensburg**
Ceddia, Anthony Francis *university administrator*
Collier, Duaine Alden *manufacturing, distribution company executive*
Fogelsonger, Ned Raymond *insurance agency executive*
Luhrs, H. Ric *toy manufacturing company executive*
Thompson, Elizabeth Jane *small business owner*

**Shrewsbury**
Martin, Debra Michele *nurse*

**Sinking Spring**
Wilson, Terrence Raymond *manufacturing executive*

**Slippery Rock**
Aebersold, Robert Neil *university president*
Smith, Grant Warren, II *academic administrator, physical sciences educator*

**Solebury**
Anthonisen, George Rioch *sculptor, artist*
Gilleo, Sandra V. *elementary education educator*
Valentine, H. Jeffrey *legal association executive*

**Somerset**
Nair, Velupillai Krishnan *cardiologist*

**Souderton**
Delp, R. Lee *meat packing company executive*
Hoeflich, Charles Hitschler *banker*
Lapp, James Merrill *clergyman, marriage and family therapist*

**South Williamsport**
Bryant, Martha J. *reading specialist*

**Southampton**
Appell, Kathleen Marie *management consultant, legal administrator*
Bendiner, Robert *writer, editor*
DaCosta, Edward Hoban *plastics and electronics manufacturing company executive*
Zocholl, Stanley Ernest *electronics executive*

**Southeastern**
Hawley, Linda Donovan *advertising executive*

**Spring City**
Blanchard, Norman Harris *retired pharmaceutical company executive*
Mayerson, Hy *lawyer*
Middleton, Dawn E. *education educator*

**Spring Grove**
Helberg, Shirley Adelaide Holden *artist, educator*

**Spring House**
Frederick, Clay Bruce *toxicologist, researcher*
Hart, Alex Way *banker*
Klotz, Wendy Lynnett *analytical chemist*
Payn, Clyde Francis *technology company executive, consultant*
Reitz, Allen Bernard *organic chemist*
van Steenwyk, John Joseph *health care plan consultant, educator*

**Springfield**
Carter, Frances Moore *educator, writer*
Gordon, Robert Bruce *mechanical engineer*
Parmiter, James Darlin *safety engineer*
Wilkinson, William Durfee *museum director*

**Springtown**
Hunt, John Wesley *English language educator*

**Star Junction**
Baldwin, Clarence Jones, Jr. *electrical engineer, manufacturing company executive*

**State College**
Arnold, Douglas Norman *mathematics educator*
Asbell, Bernard *author, English language educator*
Barnoff, Robert Mark *civil engineering educator*
Bergman, Ernest L. *retired horticulture educator*
Bittner, Carl S. *retired university educator*
Chiswick, Nancy Rose *psychologist*
Coppersmith Fredman, Marian Ungar *magazine publisher*
Deering, Anne-Lise *artist, real estate salesperson*
DeVoss, James Thomas *community foundation administrator, retired*
Farr, Jo-Ann Hunter *psychologist*
Foderaro, Anthony Harolde *nuclear engineering educator*
Forth, Stuart *librarian*
Garrett, Steven Lurie *physicist*
German, Randall Michael *materials science educator, consultant*
Gould, Peter Robin *geographer, educator*
Haas, John C. *architect*
Heldman, Louis Marc *newspaper publisher and executive*
Hettche, L. Raymond *research director*
Hoffa, Harlan Edward *retired university dean, art educator*
Johnstone, Henry Webb, Jr. *philosophy educator*
Kenealy, Matthew H., III *hydrogeologist*
Kockelmans, Joseph J. *philosopher, educator*
Kulakowski, Bohdan Tadeusz *mechanical engineering educator*
Lamb, Robert Edward *diplomat*
Lawrence, Ken *columnist*
Luther, William Lee *construction company executive*
Maneval, David Richard *mineral engineering consultant*
Miller, E. Willard *geography educator*
Morrow, David Austin, III *veterinary medical educator*
Nollau, Lee Gordon *lawyer*
Olson, Donald Richard *mechanical engineering educator*

Phillips, Janet Colleen *educational association executive, editor*
Remick, Forrest Jerome, Jr. *former university official*
Robinett, Betty Wallace *linguist*
Santavicca, Pamela Ferguson *social welfare administrator*
Thompson, Fred Clayton *engineering executive, consultant*
Wysk, Richard A. *engineering educator, researcher*
Yoder, Stanley Jonas *orthopedic surgeon*

**Stevens**
Shenk, Lois Landis *writer, caregiver*

**Stewartstown**
Kandra, Joseph *retired federal agency administrator*

**Strasburg**
Lewis, Marilyn Ware *water company executive*
Lindsay, George Carroll *former museum director*

**Stroudsburg**
Batistoni, Ronald *educational association administrator*
Gasink, Warren Alfred *speech communication educator*
Macmillan, Robert Francis *director university service*
Sherman, Ruth Tenzer *artist, fixtures company executive*

**Sunbury**
†Weis, Robert Freeman *supermarket company executive*

**Swarthmore**
Bannister, Robert Corwin, Jr. *history educator*
Beeman, Richard Roy *historian, educator*
Berger, Dianne Gwynne *educator*
Bilaniuk, Oleksa Myron *physicist, educator*
Blackburn, Thomas Harold *English language professional, educator*
Bloom, Alfred Howard *college president*
Carey, William Bacon *pediatrician, educator*
Cornelsen, Rufus *clergyman*
Devin, (Philip) Lee *dramaturg, theater educator*
Frost, Jerry William *religion and history educator, library administrator*
Gilbert, Scott Frederick *biologist, educator, author*
Hammons, James Hutchinson *chemistry educator, researcher*
Heaps, Marvin Dale *food services company executive*
Hopkins, Raymond Frederick *political science educator*
Kaufman, Antoinette D. *business services company executive*
Keith, Jennie *anthropology educator and administrator, writer*
Kelemen, Charles F. *computer science educator*
Krendel, Ezra Simon *systems and human factors engineering consultant*
Lacey, Hugh Matthew *philosophy educator*
North, Helen Florence *classicist, educator*
Oneal, Glen, Jr. *retired physicist*
Ostwald, Martin *classics educator emeritus*
Pagliaro, Harold Emil *English language educator*
Pasternack, Robert Francis *chemistry educator*
Saffran, Bernard *economist, educator*
Sawyers, Claire Elyce *arboretum administrator*
Sing, Robert Fong *physician*
Swearer, Donald Keeney *Asian religions educator, writer*

**Sweet Valley**
Aldrow-Liput, Priscilla R. *elementary education educator*

**Swiftwater**
Melling, Jack *biotechnologist*
Woods, Walter Earl *biomedical manufacturing executive*

**Swissvale**
Martoni, Charles J. *dean*

**Tannersville**
Moore, James Alfred *ski company executive, lawyer*

**Telford**
Hagey, Walter Rex *retired banker*
†Kamnitsis, Gus *electronic industry executive*

**Thorndale**
Hodess, Arthur Bart *cardiologist*

**Throop**
Karluk, Lori Jean *craft designer, copy editor*

**Titusville**
Peaslee, Margaret Mae Hermanek *zoology educator*

**Topton**
Haskell, Ellery Bickford *retired philosophy educator*

**Transfer**
Miller, Gayle D. *health facility administrator, nurse, health educator*

**Troy**
Hulslander, Marjorie Diane *auditor*

**Turtle Creek**
Collins, Carrie Linda Clark *administrative assistant*

**Tyrone**
Lewis, Kathryn Huxtable *pediatrician*
Shaw, Marilyn Margaret *artist, photographer*
Spewock, Theodosia George *reading specialist, educator*
Stoner, Philip James *hospital administrator*

**Uniontown**
Eberly, Robert Edward *oil and gas production company executive*
Prescott, Janelle *medical and surgical nurse*

**Unionville**
De Marino, Donald Nicholson *international business executive, former federal agency administrator*
Forney, Robert Clyde *retired chemical industry executive*

**University Park**
Albinski, Henry Stephen *academic research center director, writer*
Allcock, Harry R. *chemistry educator*
Ameringer, Charles D. *history educator*
Anderson, John Mueller *retired philosophy educator*
Andrews, George Eyre *mathematics educator*
Antle, Charles Edward *statistics educator*
Aplan, Frank Fulton *metallurgical engineering educator*
Askov, Eunice May *adult education educator*
Badding, John Victor *chemistry educator*
Baisley, Robert William *music educator*
Barnes, Hubert Lloyd *geochemistry educator*
Barron, Eric *earth scientist*
Benkovic, Stephen James *chemist*
Bennett, Peter Dunne *marketing educator*
Bernheim, Robert Allan *chemistry educator*
Blackadar, Alfred Kimball *meteorologist, educator*
Bollag, Jean-Marc *soil biochemistry educator, consultant*
Bose, Nirmal Kumar *electrical engineering, mathematics educator*
Brault, Gerard Joseph *French language educator*
Brenchley, Jean Elnora *microbiologist, researcher*
Brown, John Lawrence, Jr. *electrical engineering educator*
Buskirk, Elsworth Robert *physiologist, educator*
Cahir, John Joseph *meteorologist, educational administrator*
Castleman, Albert Welford, Jr. *physical chemist, educator*
Cavanagh, Peter Robert *science educator, researcher*
Chang, Parris Hsu-cheng *government official, political science educator, writer*
Coleman, Michael Murray *polymer science educator*
Cowen, Barrett Stickney *microbiology educator*
Davids, Norman *engineering science and mechanics educator, researcher*
De Armas, Frederick Alfred *foreign language educator*
Duda, John Larry *chemical engineering educator*
Dunson, William Albert *biology educator*
Dupuis, Victor Lionel *retired curriculum and instruction educator*
Durrenberger, Edward Paul *anthropologist educator*
Dutton, John Altnow *meteorologist, educator*
Eaton, Nancy Ruth Linton *librarian, dean*
†Elliott, Herschel *agricultural engineer, educator*
Epp, Donald James *economist, educator*
Erickson, Rodney Allen *dean, educator*
Fedoroff, Nina Vsevolod *research scientist, consultant*
Feller, Irwin *think-tank executive, economics educator*
Feng, Tse-yun *computer engineer, educator*
Ford, Donald Herbert *psychologist, educator*
Fowler, H(oratio) Seymour *retired science educator*
Frank, Robert Worth, Jr. *English language educator*
Frankl, Daniel Richard *physicist, educator*
Friedman, Robert Sidney *political science educator*
Golany, Gideon Salomon *urban designer*
Goldschmidt, Arthur Eduard, Jr. *historian, educator*
Gouran, Dennis Stephen *communications educator*
Guthrie, Helen A. *nutrition educator, registered dietitian*
Hagen, Daniel Russell *physiologist, educator*
Hager, Hellmut Wilhelm *art history educator*
Ham, Inyong *industrial engineering educator*
Hammond, J. D. *university executive, educator*
Helfferich, Friedrich G. *chemical engineer, educator*
Herrmann, Carol *university administrator*
Hogg, Richard *mineral/particle process engineering educator*
Holl, John William *engineering educator*
Hood, Lamartine Frain *agriculture educator, former dean*
Hosler, Charles Luther, Jr. *meteorologist, educator*
Howell, Benjamin Franklin, Jr. *geophysicist, educator*
Jackman, Lloyd Miles *chemistry educator*
Jaffe, Austin Jay *business administration educator*
Jeffery, William Richard *developmental biology educator, researcher*
Jordan, Bryce *corporate director, retired university president*
Kabel, Robert Lynn *chemical engineering educator*
Kasting, James Fraser *research meteorologist, physicist*
Kim, Ke Chung *entomology, systematics, and biodiversity educator, researcher*
Klein, Philip Alexander *economist*
Knott, Kenneth *engineering educator, consultant*
Koopmann, Gary Hugo *educational center administrator, mechanical engineering educator*
Kuhns, Larry J. *horticulturist, educator*
Lakshminarayana, Budugur *aerospace engineering educator*
Lampe, Frederick Walter *chemistry educator, consultant*
Larson, Russell Edward *university provost emeritus, consultant agriculture research and development*
Lee, Robert Dorwin *public affairs educator*
Leslie, Donald Wilmot *landscape architecture educator*
Lewis, Peirce Fee *geographer, educator*
Lima, Robert *Hispanic studies and comparative literature educator*
Lindsay, Bruce George *statistics educator*
Lusht, Kenneth Michael *business administration educator*
Macdonald, Digby Donald *scientist, science administrator*
Manbeck, Harvey B. *agricultural and biological engineer, wood engineer, educator*
Martorana, Sebastian Vincent *educator, educational consultant*
Mathews, John David *electrical engineering educator, research director, consultant*
Mayers, Stanley Penrose, Jr. *public health educator*
McCormick, Barnes Warnock *aerospace engineering educator*
McDonnell, Archie Joseph *environmental engineer*
McKeown, James Charles *accounting educator, consultant*
McWhirter, John Ruben *chemical engineering educator*
Mentzer, John Raymond *electrical engineer, educator*
Mészáros, Peter Istvan *astrophysicist, researcher, astronomy educator*
Morris, Philip John *aerospace engineering educator*
Nelsen, Hart Michael *sociologist, educator*
Nicely, Robert Francis, Jr. *education educator, administrator*
Nisbet, John Stirling *electrical engineering educator*
Pashek, Robert Donald *economics educator emeritus*
Paterno, Joseph Vincent *college football coach*
Pazur, John Howard *biochemist, educator*

Porterfield, Neil Harry *landscape architect, educator*
Ramani, Raja Venkat *mining engineering educator*
Rao, Calyampudi Radhakrishna *statistician, educator*
Rashid, Kamal A. *program director, researcher*
Ray, William Jackson *psychologist*
Reed, Joseph Raymond *civil engineering educator, academic administrator*
Rigby, Paul Herbert *management educator, college dean*
Rose, Adam Zachary *economist, educator*
Rosenberger, James Landis *statistician, educator, consultant*
Roy, Rustum *interdisciplinary materials researcher, educator*
Rusinko, Frank, Jr. *fuels and materials scientist*
Ruud, Clayton Olaf *engineering educator*
Scanlon, Andrew *structural engineering educator*
Schaie, K(laus) Warner *human development and psychology educator*
Schmalstieg, William Riegel *Slavic languages educator*
Schrader, William Joseph *accountant, educator*
Snow, Dean Richard *anthropology educator, archaeologist*
Spanier, Graham Basil *academic administrator, family sociologist, demographer, marriage and family therapist*
Starling, James Lyne *university administrator, retired*
Stern, Robert Morris *gastrointestinal psychophysiology researcher, psychology educator*
Stinson, Richard Floyd *retired horticulturalist, educator*
Tammen, James F. *plant pathologist, educator*
Taylor, William Daniel *biophysics educator, university dean*
Thatcher, Sanford Gray *publishing executive*
Thompson, William, Jr. *engineering educator*
Thuering, George Lewis *industrial engineering educator*
Tittmann, Bernhard Rainer *engineering science and mechanics educator*
Traverse, Alfred *palynology educator, clergyman*
Tukey, Loren Davenport *pomology educator, researcher*
Van Dommelen, David B. *artist, educator*
Vannice, M. Albert *chemical engineering educator, researcher*
Walden, Daniel *humanities and social sciences educator*
Webb, Ralph Lee *mechanical engineering educator*
Weintraub, Stanley *arts and humanities educator, author*
Wheeler, C. Herbert *architect, consultant, educator*
White, William Blaine *geochemist, educator*
Whitko, Jean Phillips *academic administrator*
Williams, Edward Vinson *music history educator*
Willumson, Glenn Gardner *curator, art historian*
Winograd, Nicholas *chemist*
Witzig, Warren Frank *nuclear engineer, educator*
Yoder, Edgar Paul *education educator*

**Upland**
Ridout, Daniel Lyman, III *physician, educator*

**Upper Darby**
Clemens, David Allen *minister*
Gasparro, Frank *sculptor*
Hudiak, David Michael *educational administrator, lawyer*
Hurley, Harry James, Jr. *dermatologist*
Leiby, Bruce Richard *secondary education educator, writer*
Livingston, Margery Elsie *missionary, clinical psychologist*

**Upper Saint Clair**
Dunkis, Patricia B. *principal*

**Valley Forge**
Atilgan, Timur Faik *structural engineer*
Bovaird, Brendan Peter *lawyer*
Carlson, Beverly Clark *historical society administrator*
Corchin, Mark Alan *lawyer*
Cuzzolina, Michael Joseph *financial executive*
Dachowski, Peter Richard *manufacturing executive*
Erb, Doretta Louise Barker *polymer applications scientist*
Erb, Robert Allan *physical scientist*
Hergert, Herbert Lawrence *chemist*
Hilyard, James Emerson *manufacturing company executive*
LaBoon, Lawrence Joseph *personnel consultant*
Mauch, Robert Carl *gas industry executive*
Miller, Betty Brown *freelance writer*
Penfield, Carole H. (Kate Penfield) *minister, church official*
Rassbach, Herbert David *marketing executive*
Schaefer, Adolph Oscar, Jr. *advertising agency executive*
Simmons, James Charles *lawyer*
Smith, G. Elaine *religious organization executive*
Smith, Gordon E. *religious organization executive*
Sundquist, John A. *religious organization executive*
Walters, Bette Jean *lawyer*
Weiss, Daniel Edwin *clergyman, educator*
Wright-Riggins, Aidsand F., III *religious organization executive*

**Valley View**
Holmes, David James *elementary education educator*

**Vandergrift**
Bullard, Ray Elva, Jr. *retired psychiatrist, hospital administrator*
Kulick, Richard John *computer scientist, researcher*
Quader, Patricia Ann *elementary education educator*

**Verona**
Bruno, Louis Vincent *special education educator*
Matthews, Jack *psychologist, speech pathologist, educator*

**Villanova**
Beck, Robert Edward *computer scientist, educator*
Beletz, Elaine Ethel *nurse, educator*
Bergquist, James Manning *history educator*
Bersoff, Donald Neil *lawyer, psychologist*
Caputo, John David *philosophy educator*
Dobbin, Edmund J. *university administrator*
Dorian, Harry Aram *financial consultant, former bank executive*
Edwards, John Ralph *chemist, educator*
Fitzpatrick, M. Louise *nursing educator*

Friend, Theodore Wood, III foundation executive, historian
Hadley, Judith Marie archaeologist, educator
Heitzmann, Wm. Ray education educator
Helmetag, Charles Hugh foreign language educator
Hunt, John Mortimer, Jr. classical studies educator
Johannes, John Roland political science educator, college dean
Lambert, William G. journalist, consultant
Langran, Robert Williams political scientist
Lesch, Ann Mosely political scientist, educator
Malik, Hafeez political scientist, educator
Maule, James Edward law educator, lawyer
McDiarmid, Lucy English educator, author
McLaughlin, Philip VanDoren, Jr. mechanical engineering educator, researcher, consultant
Mullins, James Lee library director
Mulroney, Michael lawyer, law educator, graduate program director
Nolan, Patrick Joseph screenwriter, playwright, educator
Palmer, Donald Curtis interdenominational missionary society executive
Perritt, Henry Hardy, Jr. law educator
Phares, Alain Joseph physicist, educator
Scott, Robert Montgomery museum executive, lawyer
Steg, Leo research and development executive
Termini, Roseann Bridget lawyer
Thomas, Deborah Allen English educator
Tomlinson, J. Richard engineering services company executive
Vander Veer, Suzanne aupair business executive
Whitman, Alan Morris mechanical engineering educator

### Wallingford
Clauss, Alfred architect
Parker, Jennifer Ware chemical engineer, researcher
Severdia, Anthony George chemistry research investigator

### Warminster
Carroll, Lucy Ellen choral director, music coordinator, educator
Koch, Nancy Joy music educator, choral director, vocal coach
Tatnall, George Jacob aeronautical engineer

### Warrendale
Buckley, Deborah Jeanne Morey technical marketing specialist
Friede, Samuel A(rnold) health care executive
Hartwig, Thomas Leo civil engineer
Rumbaugh, Max Elden, Jr. professional society administrator
Scott, Alexander Robinson engineering association executive
Snyder, Linda Ann marketing specialist

### Warrington
Shaw, Milton Herbert conglomerate executive

### Washington
Allison, Jonathan retired lawyer
Burnett, Howard Jerome college president
Erdner, Jon W. small business owner, securities trader
Hays, Lewis W. amateur baseball executive, writer
Kastelic, Robert Frank aerospace company executive
Mc Cune, Barron Patterson federal judge
Piatt, Jack Boyd manufacturing executive
Richman, Stephen I. lawyer

### Waverly
Tosti, Sally T. artist, educator

### Waymart
Giambrone, Angela C. psychologist

### Wayne
Agersborg, Helmer Pareli K. pharmaceutical company executive, researcher
Andes, Charles Lovett direct marketing executive
†Annenberg, Leonore A. foundation administrator
Baldwin, Frank Bruce, III lawyer
Bartholdson, John Robert industrial company executive
Brodsky, Julian A. broadcasting services, telecommunications company executive
Carroll, Robert W. retired business executive
Carter, Edward Carlos, II librarian, historian
Clelland, Richard Cook statistics educator, university administrator
Coane, James Edwin, III information technology executive
Crofford, Bonnie Ann rehabilitation clinical specialist
Curry, Thomas James manufacturers representative
de Rivas, Carmela Foderaro psychiatrist, hospital administrator
Emory, Hugh Mercer lawyer
Etris, Samuel Franklin trade association administrator
Garrison, Guy Grady librarian, educator
Green, Norman Marston, Jr. minister
Griffith, Edward, II lawyer
Grigg, William Clyde electrical engineer
Guernsey, Louis Harold retired oral and maxillofacial surgeon, educator
Hill, Virgil Lusk, Jr. academic administrator, naval officer
Horwitz, Orville cardiologist, educator
Lefevre, Thomas Vernon retired utility company executive, lawyer
Lief, Harold Isaiah psychiatrist
MacNeal, Edward Arthur economic consultant
Martino, Peter Dominic software company executive, military officer
Mudry, Michael pension and benefit consultant
Rubley, Carole A. state legislator
Simms, Amy Lang writer, educator
Thelen, Edmund research executive
Townsend, Philip W., Jr. library director
Warshell, Jay systems engineer
Wolcott, Robert Wilson, Jr. consulting company executive
Woodbury, Alan Tenney lawyer
Yoskin, Jon William, II insurance company executive
Youman, Roger Jacob editor, writer

### Waynesboro
Benchoff, James Martin manufacturing company executive
Kirk, Daniel Lee physician, consultant
Stefenelli, George Edward physician

Swartz, William Rick school psychologist

### Wellsboro
Baker, Matthew Edward state legislator

### Wernersville
Himmelberger, Richard Charles vocational school educator
Mackey, Sheldon Elias minister
Worley, Jane Ludwig lawyer

### Wescosville
Rienzo, Robert James radiologist

### West Chester
Adler, Madeleine Wing academic administrator
Aiken, Robert McCutchen retired chemical company executive, management consultant
Bartlett, Desmond William engineering company executive
Bogle, Hugh Andrew chemical company executive
Burton, John Bryan music educator
Dinniman, Andrew Eric county commissioner, history educator, academic program director, international studies educator
Dorchester, Jane Elizabeth historic researcher
Dunlop, Edward Arthur computer company executive
Dwyer, Francis Gerard chemical engineer, researcher
Flood, Dorothy Garnett neuroscientist
Gaadt, Suzanne DeMott graphic designer
Gibson, JoAnn Marie psychotherapist, consultant, personal mentor
Gougher, Ronald Lee foreign language educator and administrator
Green, Andrew Wilson economist, lawyer, educator
Hajcak, Frank psychologist, cartoonist, writer, photographer, consultant
Hammonds, Jay A. retired secondary education educator, administrator
Handzel, Steven Jeffrey accountant
Harrington, Anne Wilson medical librarian
Hickman, Janet Susan college administrator, educator
Hipple, Walter John English language educator
Hurd-Graham, Robin J. sales and marketing executive, consultant
Jamison, Philip artist
Mahoney, William Francis editor
McMeen, Albert Ralph, Jr. investment advisor
Murphy, Stephan David electrical engineer
Osborn, John Edward lawyer, former government official, writer
Pettigrew, Claire Rudolph music educator
Segel, Joseph M. broadcasting executive
Sommer, Jeffrey Robert lawyer
Swope, Charles Evans banker, lawyer
Tomlinson, Charles Wesley, Jr. advertising executive
Weston, Roy Francis environmental consultant
Young, Franklin biochemistry educator

### West Conshohocken
Brenner, Ronald John pharmaceutical industry executive
Miller, Paul Fetterolf, Jr. retired investment company executive
Mullen, Eileen Anne human resources executive
Richard, Scott F. portfolio manager
Teillon, L. Pierre, Jr. lawyer

### West Mifflin
Ardash, Garin mechanical engineer
Clayton, John Charles scientist, researcher
DiCioccio, Gary F. secondary education educator
Gerity, Patrick Emmett college director
Smith, Stewart Edward physical chemist

### West Point
Abrams, William Bernard pharmaceutical company executive, physician
Caskey, Charles Thomas biology and genetics educator
Chen, I-Wu pharmaceutical researcher
Hilleman, Maurice Ralph virus research scientist
Sherwood, Louis Maier physician, scientist, pharmaceutical company executive
Teltser, Michael chemical engineer
Vickers, Stanley biochemical pharmacologist

### Wexford
DoVale, Fern Louise civil engineer
Hutchinson, Barbara Winter middle school educator
Osby, Larissa Geiss artist

### Wilkes Barre
Bart, Georgiana Cray artist, educator
Bevevino, Frank finance company executive
Denaro, Anthony Thomas psychiatrist
Harter, Robert Jackson, Jr. lawyer
Hayes, Wilbur Frank biology educator
Hobbs, William Barton Rogers company executive
Lackenmier, James Richard college president, priest
Mech, Terrence Francis library director
Musto, Joseph John lawyer
Ogren, Robert Edward biologist, educator
Reilly, Michael James law librarian
Rosenn, Max federal judge
Roth, Eugene lawyer
Ru Dusky, Basil Michael cardiologist, consultant
Van Scoy, Gary social services administrator

### Williamsport
Bellmore, Lawrence Robert, Jr. financial planner
Douthat, James Evans college administrator
Ertel, Allen Edward lawyer, former congressman
Facey, Karlyle Frank financial executive, consultant
Foucart Vincenti, Valerie art educator
Kane, Joseph Patrick lawyer, financial planner
Largen, Joseph retailer, furniture manufacturer, book wholesaler
Lattimer, Gary Lee physician
McClure, James Focht, Jr. federal judge
Meyers, Judith Ann education educator
Muir, Malcolm federal judge
Schultz, Carole Lamb community volunteer
Van Voorst, Robert E. theology educator, minister

### Willow Grove
Asplundh, Christopher B. tree service company executive
Duff, Donald James religious organization administrator
Emory, Thomas Mercer, Jr. data communications equipment manufacturing executive

Kulicke, C(harles) Scott business executive
†Schiffman, Louis F. management consultant
Suer, Marvin David architecture, consultant

### Willow Street
Stright, I. Leonard educational consultant

### Windber
Furigay, Rodolfo Lazo surgeon

### Worcester
McAdam, Will electronics consultant

### Wrightsville
Johnson, Clarence Ray minister

### Wyncote
Baldridge, Robert Crary retired biochemistry educator
Bersh, Philip Joseph psychologist, educator
Burton, DeWitt A. bishop

### Wyndmoor
Pfeffer, Philip Elliot biophysicist
Uemura, Teruki child brain developmentalist
Wint, Dennis Michael museum director

### Wynnewood
Belinger, Harry Robert business executive, retired
Connor, James Edward, Jr. retired chemical company executive
Doherty, Henry Joseph anesthesiologist, medical hypnotist
Flanagan, Joseph Charles ophthalmologist
Frankl, Razelle management educator
Freeman, Morton S. former bar association executive, retired lawyer
Hodges, John Hendricks physician, educator
Khouri, Fred John political science educator
Koprowska, Irena cytopathologist, cancer researcher
Meyers, Mary Ann writer, consultant
Phillips, Almarin economics educator, consultant
Russell, Horace Orlando dean of chapel, theology educator
Sider, Ronald J. theology educator, author
Singer, Samuel L(oewenberg) journalist
Weinhouse, Sidney biochemist, educator

### Wyoming
Singer, Sandra Maria forensic scientist

### Wyomissing
Boyer, Robert Allen physics educator
Cellucci, Peter T. principal
Garr, Carl Robert manufacturing company executive
Moll, Lloyd Henry banker
Moran, William Edward academic administrator
Pellecchia, Eve Wassall management consultant
Pugh, Lawrence R. apparel executive
Smith, Raymond Leigh plastic surgeon
Stephen, Dennis John financial planner

### Yardley
Crane, Barbara Joyce author, editor, publishing consulting executive
Desai, Cawas Jal distribution company executive
Elliott, Frank Nelson retired college president
Kaska, Charles Powers psychologist
Newsom, Carolyn Cardall management consultant
Patel, Mukund Ranchhodlal electrical engineer, researcher
Somma, Beverly Kathleen medical and marriage educator
Terry, John Joseph transportation investor
Watson, Joyce Leslie elementary educator
Zulker, Charles Bates broadcasting company executive

### York
Bartels, Bruce Michael health care executive
Chronister, Virginia Ann school nurse, educator
Garner, Edward Markley, II manufacturing and engineering executive
†Greisler, David Scott healthcare executive
Grossman, Robert Allen transportation executive
Hamilton, Shirley Ann nursing administrator
Horn, Russell Eugene engineering executive, consultant
Horn, Russell Eugene, Jr. business executive
Keiser, Paul Harold hospital administrator
Macdonald, Andrew manufacturing company executive
McMillan, Wendell Marlin agricultural economist
Nau, Douglas Scott psychotherapist
Page, Sean Edward emergency medical care provider, educator
Pokelwaldt, Robert N. manufacturing company executive
Rosen, Raymond health facility executive
Snyder, Jan Louise administrative aide, retired
Thornton, George Whiteley investment company executive

### Youngstown
Palmer, Arnold Daniel professional golfer

### Zionsville
Fleming, Richard chemical company executive

## RHODE ISLAND

### Barrington
Carpenter, Charles Colcock Jones physician, educator
Deakin, James writer, former newspaperman
Graser, Bernice Erckert elementary school principal
Mihaly, Eugene Bramer corporate executive, consultant, writer, educator
O'Toole, John Dudley retired utility executive, consultant
Paolino, Ronald Mario clinical psychologist, consultant, psychopharmacologist, pharmacist

### Block Island
Coxe, Weld management consultant
Gasner, Walter Gilbert retired dermatologist
Kingsbury, Read Austin retired journalist
Stone, Robert Anthony author

### Bristol
Chaim, Robert Alex dean, educator
Esty, David Cameron marketing and communications executive
Quinn, Anthony Rudolph Oaxaca actor, writer, artist
Schipper, Michael academic administrator
Wilcox, Harry Wilbur, Jr. retired corporate executive

### Charlestown
Ungaro, Joseph Michael newspaper publishing executive, consultant

### Coventry
Traficante, Daniel Dominick chemist

### Cranston
Cardi, Vincenzo marketing professional, financial and investment consultant, pharmacist
Coletti, John Anthony lawyer, furniture and realty company executive
Crooks, W. Spencer artist, educator
Feinstein, Alan Shawn writer, financial adviser
Ferguson, Christine C. lawyer, state agency administrator
Gardner, Ann Jeannette family and child therapist
Mruk, Charles Karzimer agronomist
Parravano, Amelia Elizabeth (Amy Beth) recording industry executive
Simonian, John S. lawyer
Stark, Dennis Edwin banker
Terry, Brian R. counselor, academic administrator
Thielsch, Helmut John engineering company executive
Vavala, Domenic Anthony medical scientist, educator, retired air force officer

### Cumberland
LaFlamme-Zurowski, Virginia M. secondary school special education educator
Wyman, James Vernon newspaper executive

### East Greenwich
Dence, Edward William, Jr. lawyer, banker
Deutsch, Stephen R. real estate development executive, retired state senator
Flynn, Richard James lawyer
Hunter, Garrett Bell investment banker
†Juechter, John William retired mechanical engineer, consultant

### East Providence
McGee, Mary Alice health science research administrator
Tripp, Michael Windsor accountant

### Greenville
Calo, Joseph Manuel chemical engineering educator

### Harrisville
Jubinska-Christiansen, Patricia Ann ballet instructor, choreographer

### Jamestown
Logan, Nancy Allen library media specialist
Potter, Clarkson Nott publishing consultant
Todd, Thomas Abbott architect, urban designer
Worden, Katharine Cole sculptor

### Johnston
D'Ambra, Diane M. nursing educator

### Kingston
Alexander, Lewis McElwain geographer, educator
Berman, Allan psychologist, educator
Biller, Henry Burt psychologist, educator
Carothers, Robert Lee academic administrator
Driver, Rodney David mathematics educator, former state legislator
Gaulin, Lynn experiential education educator
Gelles, Richard James sociology and psychology educator
Goos, Roger Delmon mycologist
Harlin, Marilyn Miler marine botany educator, researcher, consultant
Harrick, Jim university athletic coach
Harrison, Robert William zoologist, educator
Hufnagel, Linda Ann biology educator, researcher
Kim, Yong Choon philosopher, theologian, educator
Lee, Kang-Won Wayne engineer, educator
Leete, William White artist
MacLaine, Allan Hugh English language educator
Nixon, Scott West oceanography science educator
Polk, Charles electrical engineer, educator, biophysicist
Rohm, Robert Hermann sculptor, educator
Roxin, Emilio Oscar mathematics educator
Schmidt, Charles T., Jr. labor and industrial relations educator
Seifer, Marc Jeffrey psychology educator
Tufts, Donald Winston electrical engineering educator
Youngken, Heber Wilkinson, Jr. former university administrator, pharmacy educator
Zucker, Norman Livingston political scientist, educator, author

### Lincoln
Barlow, August Ralph, Jr. minister
Burgdoerfer, Jerry J. marketing and distribution executive
Carter, Wilfred Wilson financial executive, controller
Lyle, John William, Jr. former state senator, lawyer, social studies educator
Marsden, Herci Ivana classical ballet artistic director

### Little Compton
Bullerjahn, Eduard Henri architect
MacKowski, John Joseph retired insurance company executive

### Middletown
Mellberg, Leonard Evert physicist
Ning, John Tse-Tso urologic surgeon
Whitman, Ruth poet, educator, translator

### Narragansett
Apperson, Jack Alfonso retired army officer, business executive
McGreevy, Robert Michael oil company executive, owner

Pilson, Michael Edward Quinton *oceanography educator*

### Newport
Bergstrom, Albion Andrew *army officer, federal official*
Brennan, Joseph Gerard *philosophy educator*
Burgin, William Lyle *architect*
Cohen, Arthur Abram *lawyer*
Graziano, Catherine Elizabeth *nursing educator*
Haas, William Paul *humanities educator, former college president*
Hamblet, Charles Albert *educational administrator, educator*
Holloway, Jerome Knight *publisher, former military strategy educator, retired foreign service officer*
Jackson, John Edward *naval officer, educator, logistician*
Koch, Robert Michael *research scientist, consultant, educator*
Levie, Howard S(idney) *lawyer, educator, author*
Malkovich, Mark Paul, III *musician, artistic director, scientist, sports agent*
Nelligan, Kenneth Egan *lawyer*
Peters, Lauralee Milberg *diplomat*
Schnare, Robert Edey, Jr. *library director*
Sundlun, Bruce *former governor*
Wurman, Richard Saul *architect*
Yates, Elsie Victoria *retired secondary English educator*

### North Kingstown
Apostal, Michael Christopher *structural engineer*
Sharpe, Henry Dexter, Jr. *retired manufacturing company executive*

### North Scituate
Stubbs, Donald Clark *secondary education educator*

### Pawtucket
Carleton, Richard Allyn *cardiologist*
Davison, C. Hamilton *greeting card executive*
Davison, Charles Hamilton *financial executive*
Hassenfeld, Alan Geoffrey *toy company executive*
Herman, Steven David *cardiologist, educator, researcher*
Holden, Raymond Henry *clinical psychologist*
Kranseler, Lawrence Michael *lawyer*
Metivier, Robert Emmett *mayor*
Neff, Edward August *manufacturing company executive*
O'Neill, John T. *toy company executive*
Plotz, Richard Douglas *pathologist*
Tarpy, Eleanor Kathleen *social worker*
Tracy, Allen Wayne *manufacturing company executive*

### Portsmouth
Baker, Walter Louis *engineering company executive*
Becken, Bradford Albert *engineering executive*
Pearson, Oscar Harris *plant breeder, geneticist*

### Providence
Ackerman, Felicia *philosophy educator, writer*
Adams, Thomas Randolph *bibliographer, librarian, historian*
Adler, Jane Eve *columnist, cartoonist and illustrator*
Algiere, Dennis L. *state senator*
Almeida, Victoria Martin *lawyer*
Almond, Lincoln *governor*
Amaral, Joseph Ferreira *surgeon*
Ames, Robert San *retired manufacturing company executive*
Anderson, James Alfred *psychology educator*
Anderson, James Arthur *humanities educator, academic director*
Anton, Thomas Julius *political science and public policy educator, consultant*
Arant, Patricia *Slavic languages and literature educator*
Aronson, Stanley Maynard *physician, educator*
Avery, Donald Hills *metallurgist, educator, ethnographer*
Banchoff, Thomas Francis *mathematics educator*
Barnhill, James Orris *theater educator*
Bensmaia, Reda *French studies educator, researcher*
Berghahn, Volker Rolf *history educator*
Biron, Christine Anne *medical science educator, researcher*
Blasing, Mutlu Konuk *English language educator*
Block, Stanley Hoyt *pediatrician, allergist*
Blough, Donald S. *psychology educator*
Boegehold, Alan Lindley *classics educator*
Boekelheide, Kim *pathologist*
Borod, Richard Melvin *lawyer*
Borts, George Herbert *economist, educator*
Boyle, Francis Joseph *federal judge*
Bray, Philip James *physicist*
Breda, John Alexander *physician, musician*
Briant, Clyde Leonard *metallurgist, researcher*
Burns, Robert E. *bank executive*
Burrows, Richard Henry *lawyer*
Calabresi, Paul *pharmacologist, oncologist, educator*
Caldwell, Ann Wickins *academic administrator*
Caldwell-Wood, Naomi Rachel *library media specialist*
Carlotti, Stephen Jon *lawyer*
Carpenter, Gene Blakely *crystallography and chemistry educator*
Charniak, Eugene *computer scientist, educator*
Choquette, Paul Joseph, Jr. *construction company executive*
Church, Russell Miller *psychology educator*
Coffey, Sean Owen *former state senator, lawyer*
Cook, Albert Spaulding *comparative literature and classics educator, writer*
Cooper, Gordon Mayo *retired manufacturing company executive*
Cooper, Leon N. *physicist, educator*
Coover, Robert *writer, scriptwriter, educator*
Courage, Thomas Roberts *lawyer*
Crowley, James Patrick *hematologist*
Curran, Joseph Patrick *lawyer*
Dafermos, Constantine Michael *applied mathematics educator*
Dahlberg, Albert Edward *biochemistry educator*
Damon, William Van Buren *developmental psychologist, educator, writer*
Davis, Philip J. *mathematician*
Davis, Robert Paul *physician, educator*
†Dempsey, Raymond Leo, Jr. *radio and television producer, moderator, writer*
Donnelly, Kevin William *lawyer*
Donovan, Bruce Elliot *classics educator, university dean*
Dowben, Robert Morris *physician, scientist*
Dujardin, Richard Charles *journalist*
Easton, J(ohn) Donald *neurologist, educator*
Eddy, Edward Danforth *academic administrator, educator*
Edens, Myra Jim *health facility nursing administrator*
Elbaum, Charles *physicist, educator, researcher*
Enteman, Willard Finley *philosophy educator*
Erikson, G(eorge) E(mil) (Erik Erikson) *anatomist, archivist, historian, educator, information specialist*
Estrup, Peder Jan *physics and chemistry educator*
Eustis, Oskar (Paul Jefferson Eustis) *performing company executive*
Farmer, Susan Lawson *broadcasting executive, former secretary of state*
Farrell, Margaret Dawson *lawyer*
Feldman, Walter Sidney *artist, educator*
Field, Noel Macdonald, Jr. *lawyer*
Fleming, Wendell Helms *mathematician, educator*
Fogarty, Charles Joseph *state senator*
Fornara, Charles William *historian, classicist, educator*
Freiberger, Walter Frederick *mathematics educator, actuarial science consultant, educator*
Frerichs, Ernest Sunley *religious studies educator*
Freund, Lambert Ben *engineering educator, researcher, consultant*
Gale, Edwin John *prosecutor*
Galletti, Pierre Marie *medical science educator, artificial organ scientist*
Gardner, Thomas Earle *investment banker, managment/financial consultant*
Gasbarro, Pasco, Jr. *lawyer*
Geckle, Robert Alan *manufacturing company executive*
Geisser, Peter James *artist, educator for hearing impaired*
Gelineau, Louis Edward *bishop*
Gerbi, Susan Alexandra *biology educator*
Germani, Elia *lawyer*
Gerritsen, Hendrik Jurjen *physics educator, researcher*
Gibbs, June Nesbitt *state senator*
Gilbane, Jean Ann (Mrs. Thomas F. Gilbane) *construction company executive*
Gilmore, Judith Marie *physician*
Gleason, Abbott *history educator*
Glicksman, Arvin S(igmund) *radiologist, physician*
Glicksman, Maurice *engineering educator, former dean and provost*
Goldstein, Sidney *sociology educator, demographer*
Goodman, Elliot Raymond *political scientist, educator*
Gorham, Bradford *lawyer*
Gorton, Arlene Elizabeth *physical education educator*
Gottschalk, Walter Helbig *mathematician, educator*
Greene, Edward Forbes *chemistry educator*
Greer, David S. *university dean, physician, educator*
Gregorian, Vartan *academic administrator*
Grenander, Ulf *mathematics educator*
Grossman, Herschel I. *economics educator*
Gurland, Joseph *engineering educator*
Hagopian, Jacob *federal judge*
Hamblett, Stephen *newspaper publishing executive*
Hamolsky, Milton William *physician*
Hardymon, James Franklin *diversified products company executive*
Harleman, Ann *English educator, writer*
Harris, Richard John *diversified holding company executive*
Hawkins, Brian L. *academic administrator, educator*
Hay, Susan Stahr Heller *museum curator*
Hazeltine, Barrett *electrical engineer, educator*
Heath, Dwight Braley *anthropologist, educator*
Heyman, Lawrence Murray *printmaker, painter*
Hitt, Mary Frances Lyster *environmentalist, deacon*
Hogan, Dennis Patrick *sociology educator*
Honig, Edwin *comparative literature educator, poet*
Hopmann, Philip Terrence *political science educator*
Houghton, Anthony *physics educator, research scientist*
Howes, Lorraine de Wet *fashion designer, educator*
Jackson, Benjamin Taylor *surgeon, educator, medical facility administrator*
Jackvony, Bernard A. *lawyer*
Johnson, Maxine Frahm *bank executive*
Johnson, Vahe Duncan *lawyer*
Jones, Ferdinand Taylor, Jr. *psychologist, educator*
Jordy, William Henry *art history educator*
Joukowsky, Artemis A. W. *private investor*
Juchatz, Wayne Warren *lawyer*
Kacir, Barbara Brattin *lawyer*
Kane, Agnes Brezak *pathologist, educator*
Kean, John Vaughan *lawyer*
Kersh, DeWitte Talmadge, Jr. *lawyer*
Kim, Jaegwon *philosophy educator*
Klyberg, Albert Thomas *historical society administrator*
Konstan, David *classics and comparative literature educator, researcher*
Kushner, Harold Joseph *mathematics educator*
†LaButti, Gerald Michael *company executive*
Lagueux, Ronald Rene *federal judge*
Langevin, James R. *state official*
Lanou, Robert Eugene, Jr. *physicist, educator*
Lederberg, Victoria *judge, former state legislator, lawyer, psychology educator*
Lekas, Mary Despina *retired otolaryngologist*
Lesko, Leonard Henry *Egyptologist, educator*
Levin, Frank S. *physicist, educator*
Lewis, David Carleton *medical educator, university center director*
Licht, Richard A. *lawyer*
Lipsey, Howard Irwin *law educator, justice, lawyer*
Lisi, Mary M. *federal judge*
Long, Beverly Glenn *lawyer*
Lynden, Frederick Charles *librarian*
Manchester, Robert D. *venture capitalist*
Mandle, Earl Roger *academic administrator, former museum administrator*
Marsh, Donald Jay *college dean, medical educator*
Marsh, Robert Mortimer *sociologist, educator*
Marshall, Jean McElroy *physiologist*
Mates, Susan Onthank *physician, medical educator, writer, violinist*
Mayer, Nancy J. *state official*
McCann, Gail Elizabeth *lawyer*
McCard, Harold Kenneth *aerospace company executive*
McCartney, James Robert *psychiatrist*
Mc Donald, Charles J. *physician, educator*
McIntyre, Jerry L. *lawyer*
McMahon, Eleanor Marie *education educator*
McWalters, Peter *state agency administrator*
Mehlman, Edwin Stephen *endodontist*
Merlino, Anthony Frank *orthopedic surgeon*
Metrey, George David *social work educator, academic administrator*
Milhaven, John Giles *religious studies educator*
Miller, Kenneth Raymond *biologist, educator*
Monteiro, George *English educator, writer*
Monteiro, Lois Ann *medical science educator*
Mulvee, Robert Edward *bishop*
Mumford, David Bryant *mathematics educator*
Nazarian, John *academic administrator, mathematics educator*
Needleman, Alan *mechanical engineering educator*
Nelson, Ron *composer, conductor, educator*
Neu, Charles Eric *historian, educator*
Newman, Janet Elaine *elementary education educator*
Ockerse, Thomas *graphic design educator*
Oh, William *physician*
Olmsted, Audrey June *communications educator*
Olsen, Hans Peter *lawyer*
Parks, Robert Emmett, Jr. *medical science educator*
Parmentier, E. M. (Marc) *geophysics educator*
Parris, Thomas Godfrey, Jr. *medical facility administrator*
Paster, Benjamin G. *lawyer*
Patinkin, Terry Allan *physician*
Pearce, George Hamilton *archbishop*
Pendergast, John Joseph, III *lawyer*
Perkins, Whitney Trow *political science educator emeritus*
Perroni, Carol *artist, painter*
Pierce, Richard Hilton *lawyer*
Pieters, C.M. *geology educator, planetary scientist, researcher*
Pine, Jeffrey Barry *state attorney general*
Pomerantz, James Robert *psychology educator, academic admininstrator*
Poole, William *economics educator, consultant*
Preparata, Franco Paolo *computer science and engineering educator*
Pueschel, Siegfried M. *pediatrician, educator*
Putnam, Michael Courtney Jenkins *classics educator*
Putterman, Louis G. *economics educator*
Resmini, Ronald Joseph *lawyer*
Ribbans, Geoffrey Wilfrid *Spanish educator*
Richardson, Peter Damian *mechanical engineering educator*
Richman, Marc Herbert *forensic engineer, educator*
Rieger, Philip Henri *chemistry educator*
Risen, William Maurice, Jr. *chemistry educator*
Robinson, William Philip, III *lawyer*
Rohr, Donald Gerard *history educator*
Rosenberg, Alan Gene *newspaper editor*
Rosenberg, Bruce Alan *English language educator, author*
Rothman, Frank George *biology educator, biochemical genetics researcher*
Rueschemeyer, Dietrich *sociology educator*
Russell, Bill *former professional basketball team executive, former professional basketball player*
Saint-Amand, Pierre Nemours *humanities educator*
Salesses, John Joseph *university executive*
Salter, Lester Herbert *lawyer*
Sanderson, Edward French *state official*
Sapinsley, Lila Manfield *state official*
Satterthwaite, Franklin Bache, Jr. *management educator, consultant*
Savage, John Edmund *computer science educator, researcher*
Scharf, Peter Mark *Sanskrit and Indian studies educator*
Schevill, James Erwin *poet, playwright*
Schmitt, Johanna Marie *plant population biologist, educator*
Schottland, Edward Morrow *hospital adminstrator*
Schulz, Juergen *art history educator*
Selya, Bruce Marshall *federal judge*
Shepp, Bryan Eugene *psychologist, educator*
Sherman, Deming Eliot *lawyer*
Shu, Chi-Wang *mathematics educator, researcher*
Silverman, Joseph Hillel *mathematics educator*
Silverstein, Michael Alan *judge*
Sinclair, Joseph Samuels *broadcasting company executive, retail merchant*
Siqueland, Einar *psychology educator*
Sizer, Theodore R. *educational director*
Sosa, Ernest *philosopher, educator*
Souney, Paul Frederick *pharmacist*
Soutter, Thomas Douglas *retired lawyer*
Spilka, Mark *retired English language educator*
Staples, Richard Farnsworth *lawyer*
Stein, Jerome Leon *economist, educator*
Stratt, Richard Mark *chemistry researcher, educator*
Stultz, Newell Maynard *political science educator*
Suuberg, Eric Michael *chemical engineering educator*
Svengalis, Kendall Frayne *law librarian*
Symonds, Paul Southworth *mechanical engineering educator, researcher*
Tauc, Jan *physics educator*
Terras, Victor *Slavic languages and comparative literature educator*
Tillinghast, Charles Carpenter, Jr. *aviation and financial consultant*
Torres, Ernest C. *federal judge*
Trueblood, Alan Stubbs *former modern language educator*
Vezeridis, Michael Panagiotis *surgeon, educator*
Waldrop, Bernard Keith *English educator*
Walker, Howard Ernest *lawyer*
Watkins, John Chester Anderson *newspaper publisher*
Watkins, William, Jr. *electric power industry executive*
Weaver, Barbara Frances *librarian*
Webb, Thompson *geological sciences educator, researcher*
Weiner, Jerome Harris *mechanical engineering educator*
Weisberger, Joseph Robert *state supreme court chief justice*
Westervelt, Peter Jocelyn *physics educator*
Weygand, Robert A. *congressman*
Whitcomb, Robert Bassett *journalist, editor*
White, Benjamin Vroom, III *lawyer*
Widgoff, Mildred *physicist, educator*
Williams, Lea Everard *history educator*
Wilmeth, Don Burton *theatre arts educator, theatre historian, administrator, editor*
Wood, Craig Breckenridge *paleobiologist, natural science educator*
Wood, Gordon Stewart *historian, educator*
Wrenn, James Joseph *East Asian studies educator*
Wunderlich, Alfred Leon *artist, art educator*
Zarrella, Arthur M. *superintendent*

### Rumford
Findley, William Nichols *mechanical engineering educator*

### Saunderstown
Donovan, Gerald Alton *retired academic administrator, former university dean*
Leavitt, Thomas Whittlesey *museum director, educator*

### Tiverton
Constance, Barbara Ann *financial planner, small business owner, consultant*
Davis, Stephen Edward *lawyer, educator*

### Wakefield
Boothroyd, Geoffrey *industrial and manufacturing engineering educator*
Mason, Scott MacGregor *entrepreneur, inventor, consultant*
Moore, George Emerson, Jr. *geologist, educator*
Morrison, Fred Beverly *real estate consultant*
Pouliot, Assunta Gallucci *retired business school owner and director*
Rothschild, Donald Phillip *lawyer, arbitrator*

### Warwick
Baffoni, Frank Anthony *biomedical engineer, consultant*
Blount, William Allan *broadcasting executive*
Carlin, David R., Jr. *state senator*
Charette, Sharon Juliette *library administrator*
Halperson, Michael Allen *publishing company executive*
Knowles, Charles Timothy *lawyer, state legislator*
Lachapelle, Cleo Edward *real estate broker*
Polselli, Linda Marie *elementary education educator*
Reilly, John B. *lawyer*
Revens, John Cosgrove, Jr. *state senator, lawyer*
Sholes, David Henry *lawyer, former state senator*
Stockar, Helena Marie Magdalena *artist*

### West Greenwich
Anderson, Theodore Robert *physicist*
Markowicz, Victor *video company executive*

### West Kingston
Haring, Howard Jack *newsletter editor*

### West Warwick
Galkin, Robert Theodore *company executive*
Pollock, Bruce Gerald *lawyer*

### Westerly
Bachmann, William Thompson *dermatologist*
Christy, Nicholas Pierson *physician*
Day, Chon *cartoonist*
Hennessy, Dean McDonald *lawyer, multinational corporation executive*
Hirsch, Larry Joseph *retail executive, lawyer*
Looper, George Kirk *religious society executive*
Newman, Edward Henry *judge, lawyer*
Reiland, Lowell Keith *sculptor*

### Woonsocket
Eno, Paul Frederick *editor*
Goldstein, Stanley P. *retail company executive*

## SOUTH CAROLINA

### Aiken
Alexander, Robert Earl *university chancellor, educator*
Dickson, Paul Wesley, Jr. *physicist*
Hanna, Carey McConnell *securities and investments executive*
Hofstetter, Kenneth John *research chemist*
Hootman, Harry Edward *retired nuclear engineer, consultant*
Kanne, Elizabeth Ann Arnold *secondary school educator*
Miller, Phillip Edward *environmental scientist*
Naifeh, Steven Woodward *writer*
Neiswander, Linda Carol *realtor, interior decorator*
Rudnick, Irene Krugman *lawyer, former state legislator, educator*
Salter, David Wyatt *secondary school educator*
Simons, Charles Earl, Jr. *federal judge*
Smith, Gregory White *writer*
von Buedingen, Richard Paul *urologist*
Williamson, Thomas Garnett *nuclear engineering and engineering physics educator*
Zubillaga, Jose Gustavo *education specialist*

### Anderson
Anderson, George Ross, Jr. *federal judge*
Apinis, John *chemist*
Bergmann, Warren Clarence *mechanical engineer*
Campbell, Susan Rebecca *psychotherapist, educator*
Carroll, Edward Perry *instrumental music educator, conductor*
†Elzerman, Alan William *environmental chemistry educator*
Goodner, Homer Wade *process systems failure risk consultant*
Harllee, Mary Beth *social worker, educator*
Vaughan, Dennis J. *business executive*
Watkins, William Law *retired lawyer*
Wisler, Darla Lee *pastor*

### Arcadia
Dent, Frederick Baily *mill executive, former ambassador, former secretary of commerce*

### Barnwell
Loadholt, Miles *lawyer*

### Batesburg
Drafts, James Pickens, III *financial and actuarial examiner*

### Beaufort
Day, John Sidney *management sciences educator*
Harvey, William Brantley, Jr. *lawyer, former lieutenant governor*
Ogburn, Charlton *writer*
Pinkerton, Robert Bruce *mechanical engineer*
Plyler, Chris Parnell *dean*
Richards, Charlene Anna *computer manufacturing company executive*
†Rowland, Lawrence Sanders *history educator*
Sheldon, Jeffrey Andrew *college official*

### Bennettsville
Kinney, William Light, Jr. newspaper editor, publisher

### Bluffton
Brown, Dallas Coverdale, Jr. retired army officer, retired history educator

### Camden
Barker, Martha Smith retired mental health nurse
Craig, Joanna Burbank historic site director
Daniels, John Hancock agricultural products company executive
Jacobs, Rolly Warren lawyer
Reich, Merrill Drury intelligence consultant, writer

### Cayce
Byars, Merlene Hutto accountant, visual artist, writer, publisher
McElveen, William Lindsay broadcasting executive, lecturer
McGill, Cathy Broome gifted and talented education educator
Paynter, Vesta Lucas pharmacist

### Central
Reid, William James retired physicist, educator
Smith, Elizabeth Shelton art educator

### Chapin
Branham, Mack Carison, Jr. retired theological seminary educator, minister

### Charleston
Addlestone, Nathan Sidney metals company executive
Adelman, Saul Joseph astronomy educator, researcher
Adelson, Gloria Ann financial executive
Anderson, Ivan Verner, Jr. newspaper publisher
Anderson, Marion Cornelius surgeon, medical educator
Ashley, Franklin Bascom theater educator, writer
Austin, Charles John health services educator
Barclay, James Ralph psychologist, educator
Baron, Seymour engineering and research executive
Basler, Thomas G. librarian, administrator, educator
Bell, Norman Howard physician, endocrinologist, educator
Bissada, Nabil Kaddis urologist, educator, researcher, author
Blatt, Solomon, Jr. federal judge
Bolin, Edmund Mike electrical engineer, franchise engineering consultant
Bowman, Daniel Oliver psychologist
Brewerton, Timothy David psychiatrist
Brumgardt, John Raymond museum administrator
Brusca, Richard Charles zoologist, researcher, educator
Burrell, Victor Gregory, Jr. marine scientist
Buvinger, Jan library director
Cannon, Hugh lawyer
Carabello, Blase Anthony cardiology educator
Carek, Donald J(ohn) child psychiatry educator
Chapin, Fred airport executive
Cheng, Kenneth Tat-Chiu pharmacy educator
Cheng, Thomas Clement parasitologist, immunologist, educator, author
Crawford, Fred Allen, Jr. cardiothoracic surgeon, educator
Crout, Robert Rhodes historian, educator
Cuddy, Brian Gerard neurosurgeon
Curtis, Marcia university dean
Daniell, Herman Burch pharmacologist
Delli Colli, Humbert Thomas chemist, product development specialist
De Wolff, Louis management consultant
Dobson, Richard Lawrence dermatologist, educator
Dominick, Paul Allen lawyer
Donehue, John Douglas interdenominational ministries executive
Edwards, James Burrows university president, oral surgeon
Evans, Allen Donald investment real estate company executive
Favaro, Mary Kaye Asperheim (Mrs. Biagino Philip Favaro) pediatrician
Fenn, Jimmy O'Neil physicist
Finn, Albert Frank, Jr. physician
Franklin, Paul Deane financial consultant, financial planner
French, Kenneth Wayne radio station executive, consultant
Gadsden, Richard Hamilton clinical biochemistry educator
Gaillard, John Palmer, Jr. former government official, former mayor
Geentiens, Gaston Petrus, Jr. former construction management consultant company executive
Gettys, Thomas Wigington medical researcher
Gilbreth, Frank Bunker, Jr. retired communications executive, writer
Goff, R. Garey architect
Good, Joseph Cole, Jr. lawyer
Greenberg, Raymond Seth academic administrator, educator
Grimball, William Heyward retired lawyer
Grimsley, James Alexander, Jr. university administrator, retired army officer
Groves, Stephen Peterson, Sr. lawyer
Haines, Stephen John neurological surgeon
Harding, Enoch, Jr. clothing executive
Hastie, J. Drayton plantation and garden owner, director
Hawkins, Falcon Black, Jr. federal judge
Hogan, Arthur James portfolio manager
Hogan, Edward Leo neurologist
Hollis, Bruce Warren experimental nutritionist, industrial consultant
Hughes, Blake retired architectural institute administrator, publisher
Hunter, Jairy C., Jr. academic administrator
Ivey, Robert Carl artistic director, educator, choreographer
Jaffa, Ayad A. medical educator, medical researcher
Jaffe, Murray Sherwood surgeon, retired
Jenrette, Joseph Malphus, III radiation oncologist
Kahn, Ellis Irvin lawyer
Kaplan, Allen P. physician, educator, researcher
Kent, Harry Ross construction executive, lay worker
Key, Janice Dixon physician, medical educator
Kirschner-Bromley, Victoria Ann clinical counselor
Langdale, Emory Lawrence physician
Langley, Lynne Spencer newspaper editor, columnist
La Via, Mariano Francis physician, pathology and laboratory medicine educator
LeRoy, Edward Carwile rheumatologist
Lucas, Frank Edward architect
Lutz, Myron Howard obstetrician, gynecologist, surgeon, educator
†Mahoney, John Joseph business executive, educator
Manigault, Peter media executive
Margolius, Harry Stephen pharmacologist, physician
Martin, Roblee Boettcher retired cement manufacturing executive
McCurdy, Layton medical educator
McGee, Hall Thomas, Jr. newspaper, radio and television executive
Meggett, Linda Linette reporter
Mohr, Lawrence Charles physician
Moore, William Vincent political science educator
Norton, David C. federal judge
O'Brien, Paul Herbert surgeon
Ogawa, Makio physician
Othersen, Henry Biemann, Jr. pediatric surgeon, physician, educator
Patrick, Charles William, Jr. lawyer
Perry, Evelyn Reis communications company executive
Ray, Paul DuBose lawyer
Redden, Nigel A. performing company executive
Reed, Stanley Foster editor, writer, publisher, lecturer
Reilly, David Henry university dean
Richburg, W. Edward nurse educator
Robinson, Jakie Lee human services administrator
Robinson, Neil Cibley, Jr. lawyer
Roof, Betty Sams internist
Rupp, Frank A., III association executive
Rustin, Dowse Bradwell, III credit union executive
Rustin, Rudolph Byrd, III physician
Salinas, Carlos Francisco dentist, educator
Salmon, Edward Lloyd, Jr. bishop
Sanders, Alexander Mullings, Jr. judge
Schreadley, Richard Lee writer, retired newspaper editor
Schuman, Stanley H. epidemiologist, educator
†Shealy, Ralph McKeetha emergency physician, educator
Simms, Lois Averetta retired secondary education educator, musician
Simons, Albert, Jr. retired lawyer
Simson, Jo Anne anatomy and cell biology educator
Smith, J. Roy education educator
Smith, W. Stuart strategic planning director
Spence, Edward Lee publisher, historian, archaeologist
Suggars, Candice Louise special education educator
Swift, Steven Edward gynecologist, educator
Tarleton, Larry Wilson newspaper editor
Thompson, David B. bishop
Thompson, W(ilmer) Leigh pharmaceutical company executive, physician, pharmacologist
Warrick, Kenneth Ray dermatologist, cosmetic surgeon
Watts, Claudius Elmer, III retired air force officer
Whelan, Wayne Louis higher education administrator
Wilcox, Arthur Manigault newspaper editor
Wilson, Frederick Allen medical educator, medical center administrator, gastroenterologist
Winthrop, John investment company executive
Wyrick, Charles Lloyd, Jr. publisher, writer, editor

### Clemson
Adams, John Quincy, III nuclear engineer
Boykin, Joseph Floyd, Jr. librarian
Bunn, Joe Millard agricultural engineering educator
Burch, Elmer Earl management educator
Chisman, James Allan industrial engineering educator, consultant
Clayton, Donald Delbert astrophysicist, nuclear physicist, educator
Couch, James Houston industrial engineer, educator
Cox, Headley Morris, Jr. lawyer, educator
Curris, Constantine William university president
Gangemi, J(oseph) David microbiology educator, biomedical researcher, research administrator, hospital administrator
Griffin, Villard Stuart, Jr. geology educator
Halfacre, Robert Gordon landscape architect, horticulturist, educator
Han, Young Jo agricultural engineer, educator
Hays, Sidney Brooks retired entomology educator
Hicks, Edwin Hugh accountant
Kelly, John William, Jr. university adminstrator
Kenelly, John Willis, Jr. mathematician, educator
Krause, Lois Ruth Breur chemistry educator
Leonard, Michael Steven industrial engineering educator
Paul, Frank Waters mechanical engineer, educator, consultant
Petzel, Florence Eloise textiles educator
Pursley, Michael Bader electrical engineering educator, communications systems research and consulting
Riley, Helene Maria Kastinger Germanist
Sheriff, Jimmy Don accounting educator, academic dean
Trevillian, Wallace Dabney economics educator, retired dean
Vogel, Henry Elliott retired university dean and physics educator
†Wehrenberg, William Busse agricultural studies educator
Williamson, Robert Elmore agricultural engineering educator
Young, Joseph Laurie architecture educator
Zumbrunnen, David Arnold mechanical engineering educator, consultant

### Clinton
Cornelson, George Henry, IV retired textile company executive
Skinner, James Lister, III English language educator
Vance, Robert Mercer textile manufacturing company executive, banker

### Columbia
Abel, Anne Elizabeth Sutherland pediatrician
Abel, Francis Lee physiology educator
Adams, John Hurst bishop
Adams, Weston diplomat, lawyer
Adcock, David Filmore radiologist, educator
Aelion, C. Marjorie educator
Almond, Carl Herman surgeon, physician, educator
Amidon, Roger Lyman health administration educator
Anderson, Joseph Fletcher, Jr. federal judge
Ashley, Perry Jonathan journalism educator
Aull, James Stroud retired bishop
Averyt, Gayle Owen insurance executive
Bailey, George Screven lawyer
Baker, Carleton Harold physiology educator
Baum, Marsha Lynn law educator
Beasley, David Muldrow governor
Belasco, Simon French language and linguistics educator
Best, Robert Glen geneticist
Bjontegard, Arthur Martin, Jr. foundation executive
Bland, Annie Ruth (Ann Bland) nursing educator
Blanton, Hoover Clarence lawyer
Blount, Evelyn religious organization administrator
Boggs, Jack Aaron banker, municipal government official
Bristow, Walter James, Jr. retired judge
Brooker, Jeff Zeigler cardiologist
Broome, Michael Cortes college administrator
Brubaker, Lauren Edgar minister, educator
Bruccoli, Matthew Joseph English educator, publisher
Bryant, Douglas E. public health service official
Burnettt, E. C., III state supreme court justice
Callaham, Betty Elgin librarian
Case, George Tilden, Jr. marketing professional
Chapman, Robert Foster federal judge
Chappell, Barbara Kelly child welfare consultant
Cilella, Salvatore George, Jr. museum director
Clark, David Randolph wholesale grocer
Clower, Robert Wayne economics educator, consultant
Cohn, Elchanan economics educator
Cole, Benjamin Theodore biologist
Condon, Charles Molony state attorney general
Conrad, Paul Ernest transportation consultant
Cooper, William Allen, Jr. audiologist
Corey, David Thomas invertebrate zoology specialist
Cork, Holly A. state legislator
Coursey, Joy Hammond critical care nurse
Courson, John Edward state senator, insurance company executive
da Silva, Ercio Mario physician
Davis, Barbara Langford financial advisor
Davis, Keith Eugene psychologist, educator, consultant
Dawson, Wallace Douglas, Jr. geneticist
Donald, Alexander Grant psychiatrist, educator
Drafts, Norma Shealy medical foundation executive
Duffie, Virgil Whatley, Jr. state agency administrator
Duffy, John Joseph academic administrator, history educator
Duggan, Carol Cook library director
Eastman, Caroline Merriam computer science educator
Edgar, Walter Bellingrath historian
Edge, Ronald Dovaston physics educator
Edwards, James Benjamin accountant, educator
Ernst, Edward Willis electrical engineering educator
Feinn, Barbara Ann economist
Ferillo, Charles Traynor, Jr. public relations executive
Fields, Harriet Gardin counselor, educator, consultant
Finkel, Gerald Michael lawyer
Flanagan, Clyde Harvey, Jr. psychiatist, psychoanalyst, educator
Floyd, Frank Albert, Jr. management executive
Foster, Robert Watson, Sr. law educator
Friedman, Myles Ivan education educator
Fry, Catherine Howard publishing executive
Gandy, James Thomas meteorologist
Gasque, Diane Phillips funding specialist
Geckle, George Leo, III English language educator
Giese, Warren Kenneth health and physical education educator, state senator
Ginsberg, Leon Herman social work educator
Gray, Katherine Wilson newspaper editor
Gressette, Lawrence M., Jr. utilities executive
Griffin, Mary Frances retired library media consultant
Haimbaugh, George Dow, Jr. lawyer, educator
Hamilton, Clyde Henry federal judge
Hand, Herbert Hensley management educator, executive, consultant, inventor
Hardin, James Neal German and comparative literature educator, publisher
Harvin, Charles Alexander, III state legislator
Hatch, David Lincoln sociology educator
Hatch, Mary Gies German language educator
Helsley, Alexia Jones archivist
Henderson, Robert Edward research institute director
Horger, Edgar Olin, III obstetrics and gynecology educator
Howard-Hill, Trevor Howard English language educator
Hultstrand, Charles John architect
Humphries, John O'Neal physician, educator, university dean
Inkley, Scott Russell, Jr. state agency administrator
Jaco, Thomas Wright hazardous materials administrator
Jedziniak, Lee Peter lawyer, educator, state insurance administrator
Jervey, Harold Edward, Jr. medical education consultant, retired
Johnson, Herbert Alan history and law educator, lawyer, chaplain
Johnson, James Bek, Jr. library director
Kay, Carol McGinnis literature educator
Kiker, Billy Frazier economics educator
King, John Ethelbert, Jr. education educator, former academic administrator
Lander, James Albert retired military officer, state senator
Leatherman, Hugh Kenneth, Sr. state senator, business executive
LeFever, Michael Grant state agency administrator
List, Noel David medical educator
Long, Eugene Thomas, III philosophy educator, administrator
Lumpkin, John Henderson retired banker
MacIlwinen, William Lee, Jr. executive search consultant
Madden, Arthur Allen nuclear pharmacist, educator
Manwill, Diane Rachel counselor
Marchant, Trelawney Eston retired national guard officer, lawyer
Martell, Denise Mills lay worker
Martin, Charles Wallace travel executive, retired university administrator
Matthews, Steve Allen lawyer
Mc Cullough, Ralph Clayton, II lawyer, educator
McGill, Jennifer Houser non-profit association administrator
McNeely, Patricia Gantt journalism educator
Melton, Gary Bentley psychology and law educator
Meriwether, James Babcock retired English language educator
Miles, Jim state official
Morris, Earle Elias, Jr. state official, business executive
Morris, James Aloysius economist, educator
Morrison, Stephen George lawyer
Myerson, Joel Arthur English language educator, researcher
Newton, Rhonwen Leonard writer, microcomputer consultant
Nexsen, Julian Jacobs lawyer
Nolte, William Henry English language educator
Norton, Hugh Stanton economist, educator
O'Connor, James Arthur theatre educator
Osman, Mary Ella Williams journal editor
Palms, John Michael academic administrator, physicist
Patterson, Grady Leslie, Jr. financial advisor
Peeler, Bob state official
Pritchett, Samuel Travis finance and insurance educator, researcher
Rawlinson, Helen Ann librarian
Reeves, George McMillan, Jr. comparative literature educator, educational administrator
Reisz, Howard Frederick, Jr. seminary president, theology educator
Resch, Mary Louise social services administrator
Robinson, Christopher Thomas artist
Rone, William Eugene, Jr. newspaper editor, retired
Schuette, Oswald Francis physics educator
Scott, Ronald Charles lawyer
Secor, Donald Terry, Jr. geologist, educator
Shabazz, Aiysha Muslimah social work administrator
Shannon, David Thomas, Sr. academic administrator
Shedd, Dennis W. federal judge
Sheftman, Howard Stephen lawyer
Sheheen, Fred Roukos education agency administrator
Sheppe, Joseph Andrew surgeon
Shmunes, Edward dermatologist
Sigmon, Daniel Ray foundation administrator
Sloan, Frank Keenan lawyer, writer
Smith, Franklin Sumner, Jr. retired insurance executive
Smith, James Roland state legislator
Spector, Joseph Robert retired diversified manufacturing executive
Sproat, John Gerald historian
Starr, Harvey political scientist
†Stewart, Nathaniel Johnson emergency medicine physician
Still, Charles Neal neurologist, consultant
Strom, J. Preston, Jr. lawyer
Synnott, Marcia Graham history educator
Tate, Harold Simmons, Jr. lawyer
Teague, Peyton Clark chemist, educator
Thee, Christian artist, designer
Thelen, Gil newspaper editor
Toal, Jean Hoefer state supreme court justice, lawyer
Toombs, Kenneth Eldridge librarian
Vernberg, Frank John marine and biological sciences educator
Waites, Candy Yaghjian former state official
Waldron, Robert Leroy, II radiologist, educator
Walker, Richard Louis former ambassador, educator, author
Warren, Charles David library administrator
Watabe, Norimitsu biology and marine science educator
Watt, (Arthur) Dwight, Jr. computer programming and microcomputer specialist
Weatherbee, Donald Emery political scientist, educator
Wells, Robert Steven law association executive
Wilder, Ronald Parker economics educator
Willoughby, William, II retired nuclear engineer
Wilson, Karen Wilkerson paralegal

### Conway
Moore, Richard Harlan biology educator, university official
Nale, Julia Ann nursing educator
Sharples, D. Kent college administrator
Skinner, Samuel Ballou, III physics educator, researcher
Suggs, Michael Edward lawyer
Talbert, Roy, Jr. history educator
Wiseman, Dennis Gene university dean

### Darlington
Holt, Robert LeRoi philosophy educator

### Dillon
Labbe, Patrick Charles legal nursing consultant

### Due West
Koonts, Jones Calvin retired education educator
Ruble, Randall Tucker theologian, educator, academic administrator

### Easley
Cole, Lois Lorraine retired elementary school educator
Failing, George Edgar editor, clergyman, educator
Goldman, Joseph Elias advertising executive
Spearman, David Hagood veterinarian
Sundstrom, Harold Walter public relations executive
Urakami, Akio manufacturing company executive

### Eastover
Sullivan, Neil Maxwell oil and gas company executive

### Edgefield
†Allen, Jerry Wayne organization executive

### Edisto Island
Van Metre, Margaret Cheryl retired artistic director

### Elgin
Peake, Frank middle school educator

### Fairfax
McCarthy, Timothy Michael career non-commissioned officer

### Florence
Brewer, Mary Dean medical foundation executive
Burns, William A. museum administrator, author
Currie, Cameron McGowan judge
Dixon, Gale Harllee drug company executive
Houck, Charles Weston federal judge
Imbeau, Stephen Alan allergist
Kittrell, Benjamin Upchurch agronomist
Rutherford, Vicky Lynn special education educator
Sanderson, Dennis Carl theater director, educator

Smith, Walter Douglas *retired college president*
Strong, Roger Lee *mathematics educator*
Wagner, John Garnet *pharmacologist, educator*

### Folly Beach
Overton, Marcus Lee *performing arts administrator, actor, writer*
Shutrump, Mary Jill *writer, editor, photographer, educator*

### Fort Mill
Brooks, Jerry Claude *safety engineer, educator*
Hodge, Bobby Lynn *mechanical engineer, bearing company executive*
Horten, Carl Frank *textile manufacturing company executive*

### Gaffney
Davis, Lynn Hambright *culinary arts educator*
Harrison, Richard Dean *minister, counselor*
Jones, Nancy Gale *retired biology educator*
Wheeler, William Earl *general surgeon*

### Georgetown
Allison, Christopher FitzSimons *bishop*
Isbell, Robert *writer*
McGrath, James Charles, III *financial services company executive, lawyer, consultant*
Moore, Albert Cunningham *lawyer, insurance company executive*
Rogers, Rynn Mobley *community health nurse*

### Goose Creek
Floss, Mark Thaddeus *civil engineer, computer scientist*
Johnson, Johnnie *bishop*
Kershner, Jerry Wayne *human resources director*
†Lindquist, Michael Adrian *career military officer*
Sullivan, James *consultant*

### Green Pond
Ittleson, H(enry) Anthony *bicycle vacation company executive*

### Greenville
†Anderson, Greg Richard *broadcasting executive*
Armstrong, Joanne Marie *clinical and consulting psychologist, business advisor, mediator*
Barash, Anthony Harlan *lawyer*
Bauknight, Clarence Brock *wholesale and retail company executive*
Bonner, Jack Wilbur, III *psychiatrist, educator, administrator*
Carlay, Ronald Leon *mechanical engineer*
Cloer, Carl Thomas, Jr. *education educator*
Crabtree, John Henry, Jr. *retired English educator*
Cureton, Claudette Hazel Chapman *biology educator*
Davis, Joan Carroll *museum director*
DeLoache, William Redding *pediatrician*
Dozier, Herbert Randall *school system administrator*
Edwards, Harry LaFoy *lawyer*
Eskew, Rhea Taliaferro *newspaper publisher*
Fayonsky, James Leon *financial planner*
Fitzgerald, Eugene Francis *management consultant*
Foulke, Edwin Gerhart, Jr. *lawyer*
Frampton, Lisa *elementary education educator*
Friedman, Steven M. *textile company executive*
Frist, Thomas Ferran *philanthropic organization executive*
Gerretsen, Gilbert Wynand (Gil Gerretsen) *marketing and management consultant*
Gilkerson, Yancey Sherard *retired writer, former editor*
Hagood, William Milliken, III *lawyer*
Herlong, Henry Michael, Jr. *federal judge*
Hill, Grace Lucile Garrison *education educator, consultant*
Hipp, William Hayne *insurance and broadcasting executive*
Horton, James Wright *retired lawyer*
Jones, Bob, Jr. *academic administrator, educator, lecturer, minister*
Jones, Robert Thaddues *principal*
Kilgore, Donald Gibson, Jr. *pathologist*
Kondra, Emil Paul *transportation components manufacturing executive*
Kowalski, Paul Randolph *minister*
LeBlanc, L(ouis) Christian *architect*
Lloyd, Wanda Smalls *newspaper editor*
Maguire, D.E. *electronics executive*
Manly, Sarah Letitia *state legislator, ophthalmic photographer, angiographer*
Mann, James Robert *congressman*
McKnight, Edgar Vernon *religion educator*
Miller, Cecelia Smith *chemist*
Morton, James Carnes, Jr. *public relations executive*
Neal, James Austin *architect*
Nemirow, Arnold Myles *manufacturing executive*
Pate, Frances Valerie *psychotherapist, clinical social worker*
Plumstead, William Charles *quality engineer, consultant*
Roe, Thomas Anderson *building supply company executive*
Selvy, Barbara *dance instructor*
Smith, Morton Howison *religious organization administrator, educator*
Smith, Philip Daniel *academic administrator, education educator*
Smith, Willie Tesreau, Jr. *retired judge, lawyer*
Steed, Connie Mantle *nurse*
Taylor, John L. *communications executive*
Todd, John Dickerson, Jr. *lawyer*
Townes, Bobby Joe *travel agency executive*
Traxler, William Byrd *retired lawyer*
Traxler, William Byrd, Jr. *federal judge*
Varin, Roger Robert *textile executive*
Walker, Wesley M. *lawyer*
Walters, Johnnie McKeiver *lawyer*
Wilkins, William Walter, Jr. *federal judge*
Workman, William Douglas, III *former mayor*
Wyche, Bradford Wheeler *lawyer*
Wyche, Cyril Thomas *lawyer*
Wyche, Madison Baker, III *lawyer*
Wyche, Marguerite Ramage *realtor*

### Greenwood
Abercrombie, Stoney Alton *family physician*
Jackson, Larry Artope *retired college president*
Marino, Sheila Burris *education educator*
Moore, James E. *state supreme court justice*
Self, W. M. *textile company executive*
Williams, Sylvester Emanual, III *elementary school educator, consultant*

### Greer
Gallman, Clarence Hunter *textile executive*
Gregg, Marie Byrd *retired farmer*
Howell, Maxine Dill *women's health nurse*
Lane, James Garland, Jr. *diversified industry executive*
Scruggs, Jack Gilbert *retired chemical executive*

### Hampton
Platts, Francis Holbrook *plastics engineer*

### Hartsville
Browning, Peter Crane *packaging company executive*
Coker, Charles Westfield *diversified manufacturing company executive*
Daniels, James Douglas *academic administrator*
DeLoach, Harris E(ugene), Jr. *lawyer, manufacturing company executive*
Edson, Herbert Robbins *foundation and hospital executive*
Menius, Espie Flynn, Jr. *electrical engineer*
Terry, Stuart L(ee) *research manager*

### Hilton Head Island
Adams, William Hensley *ecologist, educator*
Ambler, Ernest *government official*
Batten, William Milfred *retired stock exchange executive*
Baumgardner, Barbara Borke *publishing consultant*
Becker, Karl Martin *lawyer, investment company executive*
Birk, Robert Eugene *retired physician, educator*
Brock, Karena Diane *ballerina, educator, choreographer*
Brown, Arthur Edmon, Jr. *retired army officer*
Cunningham, William Henry *retired food products executive*
Davis, Milton Wickers, Jr. *chemical engineer, educator*
Engelman, Karl *physician*
Exley, Winston Wallace *middle school educator*
Flemister, Launcelot Johnson *physiologist, educator*
Gruchacz, Robert S. *real estate executive*
Gui, James Edmund *architect*
Hagoort, Thomas Henry *lawyer*
Harty, James D. *former manufacturing company executive*
Huckins, Harold Aaron *chemical engineer*
Humphrey, Edward William *surgeon, medical educator*
Kaley, Arthur Warren *financial consulting company executive*
Klein, James Ronald *international consulting company executive*
Lachenauer, Robert Alvin *retired school superintendent*
Lindner, Joseph, Jr. *physician, medical administrator*
Little, Thomas Mayer *public relations executive*
Love, Richard Emerson *equipment manufacturing company executive*
Male, Roy Raymond *English language educator*
Margileth, Andrew Menges *physician, former naval officer*
McKay, John Judson, Jr. *lawyer*
McKeldin, William Evans *management consultant*
McKinney, Donald Lee *magazine editor*
Mersereau, Hiram Stipe *wood products company consultant*
Mirse, Ralph Thomas *former college president*
Mulhollan, Paige Elliott *academic administrator emeritus*
Ouellette, Bernard Charles *pharmaceutical company executive*
Patton, Joseph Donald, Jr. *management consultant*
Patton, Susan Oertel *clinical social worker, educator*
Perdunn, Richard Francis *management consultant*
Pritchard, Dalton Harold *retired electronics research engineer*
Pustilnik, Jean Todd *elementary education educator*
Radest, Howard Bernard *clergyman, educator*
Ranney, Maurice William *chemical company executive*
Rapp, Fred *virologist*
Rose, William Shepard, Jr. *lawyer*
Rulis, Raymond Joseph *manufacturing company executive, consultant*
Russell, Allen Stevenson *retired aluminum company executive*
Santos, George Wesley *physician, educator*
Scarminach, Charles Anthony *lawyer*
Simpson, John Wistar *energy consultant, former manufacturing company executive*
Stockard, Joe Lee *public health service officer, consultant*
Stoll, Richard Edmund *retired manufacturing executive*
Tucker, Frances Laughridge *civic worker*
Urato, Barbra Casale *entrepreneur*
Wesselmann, Glenn Allen *retired hospital executive*
West, John Carl *lawyer, former ambassador, former governor*
Windman, Arnold Lewis *retired mechanical engineer*
Wood, Donald Craig *retired marketing professional*

### Hopkins
Clarkson, Jocelyn Adrene *medical technologist*

### Inman
Kunze, Dolores Johanna *veterinarian*

### Isle Of Palms
Wohltmann, Hulda Justine *pediatric endocrinologist*

### Johns Island
Behnke, Wallace Blanchard, Jr. *consultant, engineer, retired utility executive*
Cameron, Thomas William Lane *investment company executive*
Failla, Patricia McClement *biomedical and environmental research adminstrator*
Mackaness, George Bellamy *retired pharmaceutical company executive*

### Kershaw
Lucas, Dean Hadden *retired educator*

### Kiawah Island
Reed, Rex Raymond *retired telephone company executive*

### Ladson
Cannon, Major Tom *special education educator*

### Lake City
TruLuck, James Paul, Jr. *dentist, vintner*

### Lancaster
Bundy, Charles Alan *foundation executive*

### Landrum
Hilton, Ordway *retired document examiner*
Pauley, Robert Reinhold *broadcasting executive, financial executive*
Wyche, Samuel David *sportscaster*

### Langley
Bell, Robert Morrall *lawyer*

### Leesville
Crumley, James Robert, Jr. *retired clergyman*

### Lexington
DuVall, Richard *elementary school educator*
Gatch, Charles Edward, Jr. *academic administrator*
Kelehear, Carole Marchbanks Spann *legal administrator*
Love, Kenneth Edward *real estate, investment and business consultant*
Wilkins, Robert Pearce *lawyer*

### Little River
Ehrlich, John Gunther *writer*

### Marion
Kirkpatrick, Donald Robert *middle school educator*
Waller, John Henry, Jr. *judge*

### Mauldin
Harris, Daniel Frederick *biomechanical analyst, educator*
Phillips, James Oscar *minister*

### Moncks Corner
Deavers, James Frederick *optometrist*
Morris, Henry Allen, Jr. *publisher*

### Moore
Simmons, Sharon Dianne *elementary education educator*

### Mount Pleasant
Gilbert, James Eastham *academic administrator*
Hill, Larkin Payne *real estate company data processing executive*
McConnell, John William, Jr. *lawyer*

### Mullins
Stonesifer, Richard James *retired humanities and social science educator*

### Murrells Inlet
Noble, Joseph Veach *fine arts administrator*

### Myrtle Beach
Dail, Hilda Lee *psychotherapist*
Harwell, David Walker *retired state supreme court chief justice*
Madory, James Richard *hospital administrator, former air force officer*
Naumoff, Philip *physician*
Uzenda, Jara Carlow *technical writer*

### Newberry
Pope, Thomas Harrington, Jr. *lawyer*

### North
Moran, John Bernard *government official*

### North Augusta
Pritchard, Constance Jenkins *human resources/ organizion development trainer*

### North Charleston
Fei, James Robert *engineer*
Mc Aleece, Donald John *mechanical engineering educator*
Zucker, Jerry *polymer systems manufacturing executive*

### North Myrtle Beach
Atkinson, Harold Witherspoon *utilities consultant, real estate broker*

### Orangeburg
Babb, Julius Wistar, III *cardiovascular surgeon*
Benson, Sarah D. *rehabilitation services professional*
Clark, Paul Buddy *management information systems educator, consultant*
Creekmore, Verity Veirs *media specialist*
Graule, Raymond (Siegfried) *metallurgical engineer*
Grimes, Tresmaine Judith Rubain *psychology educator*
Johnson, Alex Claudius *English language educator*
Sims, Edward Howell *editor, publisher*
Staley, Frank Marcellus, Jr. *mathematics educator*
Williams, Karen Johnson *federal judge*

### Pawleys Island
Alexander, William D., III *civil engineer, consultant, former army air force officer*
Kay, Thomas Oliver *agricultural consultant*
Proefrock, Carl Kenneth *academic medical administrator*
Tarbox, Gurdon Lucius, Jr. *retired museum executive*

### Pendleton
Shanahan, Elizabeth Anne *art educator*
Spain, James Dorris, Jr. *biochemist, educator*

### Ridgeland
Gardner, James *recreational management executive, personal care industry executive*
Kadar, Karin Patricia *librarian*
Smart, Jacob Edward *management consultant*

### River Hills
Peacock, A(lvin) Ward *textile company executive*

### Rock Hill
Bristow, Robert O'Neil *writer, educator*
Click, John William *communication educator*
Di Giorgio, Anthony J. *college president*
Du Bois, Paul Zinkhan *library director*
Hardin, James Carlisle, III *lawyer, educator*
Hardin, William Beamon, Jr. *electrical engineer*
Stewart, Lyn Varn *critical care nurse*
Viault, Birdsall Scrymser *history educator*

### Saint Helena Island
Austin-Long, Jean Audrey *psychiatric department administrator*
Herzbrun, David Joseph *retired advertising executive, consultant*

### Salem
Gentry, Robert Cecil *meteorological consultant, research scientist*
Jones, Charles Edward *mechanical engineer*
Van Buren, William Benjamin, III *retired pharmaceutical company executive*

### Seneca
Clausen, Hugh Joseph *retired army officer*
Fleming, Mack Gerald *lawyer*
Uden, David Elliott *cardiologist, educator*

### Shaw AFB
Mingo, Joe Louis *elementary school educator*

### Sheldon
Goss, Richard Henry *lawyer*

### Simpsonville
Dean, Virginia Agee *principal*
Drummond, Julia Elaine Butler *middle school educator*
Gilstrap, Leah Ann *media specialist*

### Society Hill
King, Amanda Arnette *elementary school educator*

### Spartanburg
Adamson, James *restaurant holding company executive*
Adamson, James B. *business executive*
Bullard, John Moore *religion educator, church musician*
Deku, Afrikadzata *Afrikan-centric scholar, international speaker*
Ely, Duncan Cairnes *non profit human services executive, civic leader*
Fowler, Paul Raymond *physician, lawyer*
Gray, Gwen Cash *real estate broker*
Hatley, Amy Bell *elementary education educator, broadcast journalist*
Hilton, Theodore Craig *computer scientist, computer executive*
Leonard, Walter Raymond *retired biology educator*
Lesesne, Joab Mauldin, Jr. *college president*
Mahaffey, James Perry *education educator, consultant*
Mc Gehee, Larry Thomas *university administrator*
Milliken, Roger *textile company executive*
Patterson, Elizabeth Johnston *former congresswoman*
Russell, Donald Stuart *federal judge*
Sovenyhazy, Gabor Ferenc *surgeon*
Stephens, Bobby Gene *college administrator, consultant*
Wilde, Edwin Frederick *mathematics educator*
Williams, John Cornelius *lawyer*

### Sullivans Island
Humphreys, Josephine *novelist*
Romaine, Henry Simmons *investment consultant*

### Summerville
Diamond, Michael Shawn *science and math educator, computer consultant*
Duffy, Margaret McLaughlin *nephrology nurse, educator*
Mortimer, Rory Dixon *lawyer*
Reisman, Rosemary Moody Canfield *writer, humanities educator*
Stasiukaitis, Brenda Hodge *physical therapist*
Vorwerk, E. Charlsie *artist*
Young, Margaret Aletha McMullen (Mrs. Herbert Wilson Young) *social worker*

### Sumter
Blakely, Delores Phinella *financial consultant, business advisor*
Finney, Ernest Adolphus, Jr. *state supreme court chief justice*
Kieslich, Anita Frances *school system administrator*
Olsen, Thomas Richard, Sr. *air force officer*

### Surfside Beach
McCrensky, Edward *international consultant, former organization executive*
Turner, Gloria Townsend Burke *social services association executive*

### Taylors
Vaughn, John Carroll *minister, educator*

### Townville
Wright, George Cullen *electronics company executive*

### Union
Lorenz, Latisha Jay *elementary education educator*

### Ware Shoals
Webb, Patricia Dyan W. *speech and language pathologist, sign language educator*

### Wedgefield
McLaurin, Hugh McFaddin, III *military officer, historian consultant*

### West Columbia
Brown, Opal Diann *medical technologist, nurse*
Carter, Saralee Lessman *immunologist, microbiologist*
Coker, Gurnelle Sheely *retired secondary education educator*
Ochs, Robert David *history educator*
Parker, Harold Talbot *history educator*
Wilson, Addison Graves (Joe Wilson) *state senator, lawyer*

**Westminster**
Duncan, Gwendolyn McCurry elementary education educator

**Winnsboro**
King, Robert Thomas editor, free-lance writer

**Woodruff**
Childers, Bob Eugene educational association executive

**York**
Blackwell, Paul Eugene army officer
Clinch, Nicholas assistant principal
Lee, Joseph Edward history educator

## SOUTH DAKOTA

**Aberdeen**
Hahnemann, Barbara K. family nurse practitioner

**Bison**
Wishard, Della Mae state legislator

**Black Hawk**
Maicki, G. Carol former state senator, consultant

**Box Elder**
Schmidt, Laura Lee elementary and middle school gifted and talented educator, special education educator

**Britton**
Farrar, Frank Leroy lawyer, former governor

**Brookings**
Bailey, Harold Stevens, Jr. retired educational administrator
Duffey, George Henry physics educator
Gilbert, Howard Alden economics educator
Hugghins, Ernest Jay biology educator
Janssen, Larry Leonard economics educator, researcher
MacFarland, Craig George natural resource management professional
Marquardt, Steve Robert library director
McClure-Bibby, Mary Anne former state legislator
Moore, Raymond A. consultant, retired agriculture educator
Morgan, Walter retired poultry science educator
Spease, Loren William chiropractor
Storry, Junis Oliver retired engineering educator
Swiden, Ladell Ray travel company executive
Sword, Christopher Patrick microbiologist, university dean
Wagner, Mary Kathryn sociology educator, former state legislator
Wagner, Robert Todd university president, sociology educator
Williams, Elizabeth Evenson writer

**Burbank**
Simmons, Joseph Thomas accountant, educator

**Centerville**
Thomson, John Wanamaker bank executive

**Chamberlain**
Gregg, Robert Lee pharmacist

**Dakota Dunes**
Putney, Mark William lawyer, utility executive

**Eagle Butte**
Tays, Glenny Mae secondary education educator

**Elk Point**
Chicoine, Roland Alvin farmer, state official

**Freeman**
Waltner, John Randolph banker

**Hartford**
Murray, Barbara Ann bank officer

**Hot Springs**
Hiller, William Clark retired physics educator, engineering educator

**Huron**
Kuhler, Deborah Gail grief counselor, former state legislator
Wilkens, Robert Allen utilities executive, electrical engineer

**Lake Andes**
Dolliver, Mary Gwen medical, surgical nurse

**Lemmon**
Grey Eagle, Sandra Lee special education educator

**Madison**
Tunheim, Jerald Arden academic administrator, physics educator

**Miller**
Morford-Burg, JoAnn state senator, investment company executive

**Minot**
Larson, Michael Len newspaper editor

**Mitchell**
Gaede, James Ernest physician, medical educator
Randall, Ronald Fisher grocery store chain executive
Widman, Paul Joseph insurance agent

**North Sioux City**
Grant, Judith Iversen family health nurse, nursing administrator
Waitt, Ted W. computer company executive

**Parker**
Zimmer, John Herman lawyer

**Pierre**
Barnett, Mark William state attorney general
Dunn, James Bernard mining company executive, state legislator
Hazeltine, Joyce state official
Hillard, Carole state official
Janklow, William John governor
Johnson, Julie Marie lawyer/lobbyist
Kolbe, Jane Boegler state librarian
Miller, Robert Arthur state supreme court chief justice
Moser, Jeffery Richard state official
Pederson, Gordon Roy state legislator, retired military officer
Sabers, Richard Wayne state supreme court justice
Thompson, Charles Murray lawyer

**Platte**
Pennington, Beverly Melcher financial services company executive

**Rapid City**
Battey, Richard Howard judge
Bogue, Andrew Wendell federal judge
Corwin, Bert Clark optometrist
Erickson, John Duff educational association administrator
Foye, Thomas Harold lawyer
Gowen, Richard Joseph electrical engineering educator, academic administrator
Gries, John Paul geologist
Hughes, William Lewis former university official, electrical engineer
Lien, Bruce Hawkins minerals and oil company executive
†Murphy, Joseph Timothy army officer
Quinn, Robert Henry surgeon, medical school administrator
Ramakrishnan, Venkataswamy civil engineer, educator
Riemenschneider, Albert Louis engineering educator
Schleusener, Richard August college president
Scofield, Gordon Lloyd mechanical engineer, educator
Smith, Paul Letton, Jr. geophysicist
Strand, Neal Arnold retired county government official
Sykora, Harold James military officer
Undlin, Charles Thomas banker
Viken, Linda Lea Margaret lawyer

**Selby**
Akre, Donald J. school system administrator

**Sioux Falls**
Balcer, Charles Louis college president emeritus, educator
Brendtro, Larry Kay psychologist, educator
Carlson, Robert James bishop
Carlson Aronson, Marilyn A. English language educator
Christensen, David Allen manufacturing company executive
Cowles, Ronald Eugene church administrator
Crawford, Thomas Williams, Jr. information scientist, soil scientist
DeGeus, Wendell Ray photographer
Dertien, James LeRoy librarian
Ecker, Peder Kaloides former judge
Fenton, Lawrence Jules pediatric educator
Flora, George Claude retired neurology educator, neurologist
Garson, Arnold Hugh newspaper publisher
Gibbs, Frank P. retired federal judge
Grupp, Carl Alf art educator, artist
Hiatt, Charles Milton seminary president
Hoskins, John H. urologist, educator
Huseboe, Arthur Robert American literature educator
Jaqua, Richard Allen pathologist
Johnson, Warren R. marketing executive, consultant
Jones, John Bailey federal judge
Kilian, Thomas Randolph rural economic developer, consultant
Koch, Ralph Richard architect
LaFave, LeAnn Larson lawyer
Marsh, John S., Jr. newspaper editor
Morse, Peter Hodges ophthalmologist, educator
Paisley, Keith Watkins state senator, small business owner
Piersol, Lawrence L. federal judge
Richards, LaClaire Lissetta Jones (Mrs. George A. Richards) social worker
Smith, Murray Thomas transportation company executive
Staggers, Kermit LeMoyne, II history and political science educator, state senator
Taplett, Lloyd Melvin human resources management consultant
Thompson, Ronelle Kay Hildebrandt library director
Trujillo, Angelina endocrinologist
Tucker, William Vincent vocational evaluator, former college president
Wagoner, Ralph Howard academic administrator, educator
Wegner, Karl Heinrich physician, educator
Williams, W. Vail psychologist
Witzke, David John plastic surgeon, educator
Wollman, Roger Leland federal judge
Zawada, Edward Thaddeus, Jr. physician, educator

**Spearfish**
Anderson, Thomas Caryl financial and administrative systems professional
Erickson, Richard Ames physicist, emeritus educator

**Sturgis**
Daane, Kathryn D. retired nursing administrator
Ingalls, Marie Cecelie former state legislator, retail executive

**Vermillion**
Carlson, Loren Merle political science educator
Clem, Alan Leland political scientist
Clifford, Sylvester retired communication educator
Dahlin, Donald C(lifford) political science educator
Freeman, Jeffrey Vaughn (Jeff Freeman) art educator, artist
Hagen, Arthur Ainsworth pharmacologist
Langworthy, Thomas Allan microbiologist, educator
Milton, Leonharda Lynn elementary and secondary school educator
Neuhaus, Otto Wilhelm biochemistry educator
Rotert, Denise Anne occupational therapist, army officer, educator

**Volga**
Moldenhauer, William Calvin soil scientist

**Watertown**
Meyer, Todd Kent secondary school educator
Witcher, Gary Royal minister, educator

**Wessington**
Lockner, Vera Joanne farmer, rancher, legislator

**Yankton**
Hirsch, Robert William lawyer

## TENNESSEE

**Alamo**
Finch, Evelyn Vorise financial planner

**Anderson**
Olson, Carol Lea lithographer, educator, photographer

**Antioch**
Vallance, James church administrator, religious publication editor
Waddell, R. Eugene minister
Wisehart, Mary Ruth academic administrator
Worthington, Melvin Leroy minister, writer

**Arnold AFB**
Chapman, Randall Allen research engineer
Davis, John William government science and engineering executive

**Athens**
Wilson, Ben elementary school principal

**Bartlett**
Huffman, Delton Cleon, Jr. pharmaceuticals executive

**Big Sandy**
Chastain, Kenneth Duane retired foreign language educator

**Bolivar**
Buchanan, Bennie Lee Gregory special education educator
Morson, Philip Hull, III psychiatrist, osteopath
Wingate, Robert Lee, Jr. internist

**Brentwood**
Abernathy, Sue Eury physical education educator
Bates, George William obstetrician, gynecologist, educator
Bennett, Harold Clark clergyman, religious organization administrator
Dalton, James Edgar, Jr. health facility administrator
Flanagan, Van Kent journalist
Hearn, Billy Ray recording industry executive
Provine, John C. lawyer
Ragsdale, Richard Elliot healthcare management executive
Raskin, Edwin Berner real estate executive
Schreiber, Kurt Gilbert lawyer
†Stow, Gerald Lynn human services executive, speaker
Tucker, Tanya Denise singer
†White, Steve Allen health facility administrator
Zimmerman, Raymond retail chain executive

**Brighton**
King, James Andrew protective services educator and administrator

**Bristol**
Anderson, Jack Oland retired college official
Cauthen, Charles Edward, Jr. retail executive, business consultant
Harkrader, Charles Johnston, Jr. surgeon
McIlwain, William Anthony orthopedic surgeon
Sessoms, Stephanie Thompson accountant
Weeden, Debbie Sue early childhood education educator

**Brownsville**
Kalin, Robert retired mathematics educator

**Chapel Hill**
Christman, Luther Parmalee retired university dean, consultant

**Chattanooga**
Anderson, Lee Stratton newspaper publisher, editor
Arndt, Steven Andrew nuclear engineer
Baker, Merl engineering educator
Bechtel, Sherrell Jean psychotherapist
Bush, Patricia Ann occupational health nurse
Callahan, North author, educator
Chandler, J. Harold insurance company executive
Charlton, Shirley Marie instructional supervisor
Collier, Curtis Lynn lawyer
Copeland, Floyd Dean lawyer
Corey, Charles William investment banker
Cox, Ronald Baker engineering and management consultant, university dean
Cress, George Ayers artist, educator
Derthick, Alan Wendell architect
Duckworth, Jerrell James electrical engineer
Durham, J(oseph) Porter, Jr. lawyer, educator
Edgar, R(obert) Allan federal judge
Feinberg, Edward Burton ophthalmologist, educator
Fody, Edward Paul pathologist
Fortenberry, Elizabeth Waller private school educator
Goodman, Michael Frederick advertising executive
Gore, Barry Maurice electrical engineer
Holmberg, Albert William, Jr. publishing company executive
Holmberg, Ruth Sulzberger publishing company executive
Howe, Lyman Harold, III chemist
Hughes, Michael Randolph evangelist
James, Stuart Fawcett lawyer
Johnson, Joseph Erle mathematician
Kaplan, Hyman M. internist
Kelley, Ralph Houston judge
Kiser, Thelma Kay analytical chemist
Kittlitz, Rudolf Gottlieb, Jr. chemical engineer
Knight, Ralph H. consumer products company executive
MacManus, Yvonne Cristina editor, videoscripter, writer, consultant
Martin, Chester Y. sculptor, painter
McFarland, Jane Elizabeth librarian
Milburn, Herbert Theodore federal judge
Mills, Olan, II photography company executive
Mohney, Ralph Wilson minister
Neely, Paul newspaper editor
Obear, Frederick Woods academic administrator
Pinkerton, Helen Jeanette health care executive
Porter, Dudley, Jr. environmentalist, foundation executive, lawyer
Powers, John Y. federal judge
Proctor, John Franklin lawyer
Quinn, Patrick tranportation executive
Rabin, Alan Abraham economics educator
Ragon, Robert Ronald clergyman
St. Goar, Herbert food corporation executive
Scarbrough, Cleve Knox, Jr. museum director
Scott, Mark Alden hospital network executive
Shuck, Edwin Haywood, III surgeon
Smith, David Yarnell financial consultant
Summitt, Robert Murray circuit judge
Thow, George Bruce surgeon
Tracy, Carol Cousins association executive, former educator
Tucker, Stanley R. headmaster
Waring, Mary Louise social work administrator
Weinmann, Judy Munger nurse
Witherspoon, John Knox, Jr. investment banking executive
Witt, Raymond Buckner, Jr. lawyer
Young, Sonia Winer public relations director
Zodhiates, Spiros George association executive

**Clarksville**
Birdsong, William Herbert, Jr. retired brigadier general
Carlin, James Boyce elementary education educator, consultant
Tsambassis, Nicholas Alexander pediatrician

**Cleveland**
Albert, Leonard religious organization executive
Alford, Delton L. religious organization executive
Baker, Michael Lyndon minister
Breuer, William Bentley writer
Chambers, O. Wayne religious organization executive
Clowers, Evelyn civic worker
Fisher, Richard Ashley lawyer
Fisher, Robert Elwood minister, church official
Gillum, Perry Eugene college president, minister
Jackson, Joseph Essard religious organization administrator
Murray, Billy Dwayne, Sr. church administrator
Rayburn, Billy J. Church administrator
Reyes, Jose Antonio, Sr. minister
Robinson, Julian B. church administrator
Taylor, William Al church administrator
Vaughan, Roland church administrator
Vest, R. Lamar church administrator

**Clinton**
Birdwell, James Edwin, Jr. retired banker
Tyndall, Richard Lawrence microbiologist, researcher

**Collegedale**
Bennett, Peggy Elizabeth librarian, library director, educator
McKee, Ellsworth food products executive

**Collierville**
Hendren, Gary E. retail executive
†Ludwig, Charles T. technical company executive
Springfield, James Francis retired lawyer, banker

**Columbia**
Chafin, William Vernon, Jr. retired public housing manager
Curry, Beatrice Chesrown English educator
Loper, Linda Sue learning resources center director

**Cookeville**
Campana, Phillip Joseph German language educator
Chowdhuri, Pritindra electrical engineer, educator
Elkins, Donald Marcum dean, agronomy educator
Forest, Herman Silva biology educator
Hearn, Edell Midgett university dean, teacher educator
Nash, Sheena Ann Hargis flight nurse
Peters, Ralph Martin education educator
Porter, Wilma Jean educational consultant
Sissom, Leighton Esten engineering educator, dean, consultant
Smaili, Ahmad mechanical engineering educator
Swartling, Daniel Joseph chemistry educator, researcher
Volpe, Angelo Anthony university administrator, chemistry educator

**Cordova**
Bellantoni, Maureen Blanchfield manufacturing executive
Colbert, Robert B., Jr. apparel company executive
Cooke, Edward William corporate executive, former naval officer
Dean, Jimmy meat processing company executive, entertainer
Echols, James agricultural products supplier
Hunt, Gregory Lynn writer, author

**Corryton**
Hooper, William Edward broadcast journalist

**Crossville**
Marlow, James Allen lawyer
Moore, Harold Blaine middle school educator
Rollason, Mary Katherine artist, art educator

**Dandridge**
Comer, Evan Philip manufacturing company executive
Trent, Wendell Campbell business owner

**Dickson**
Peterson, Bonnie Lu mathematics educator
Thomas, Janey Sue elementary school principal

**Ducktown**
Hopkins, David Lee medical manufacturing executive

### Dyersburg
Baker, Kerry Allen *management consultant*
Wiggins, Jerome Meyer *apparel textile industry financial executive*

### East Ridge
Hodge, Raymond Douglas *minister*

### Elizabethton
Claussen, Lisa Renee *engineering executive*
Taylor, Wesley Alan *accountant, consultant*

### Elkton
Newman, Sharon Lynn *elementary education educator*

### Englewood
Jones, Vivian M. *secondary and elementary education educator*

### Erwin
Shults-Davis, Lois Bunton *lawyer*

### Fairfield Glade
Gillis, Bernard Thomas *retired chemistry educator*

### Fayetteville
Dickey, John Harwell *lawyer, public defender*

### Franklin
Guthrie, Glenda Evans *educational company executive*
Huey, George Irving, Jr. *computer senior systems consultant*
Moessner, Harold Frederic *allergist*
Waltrip, Darrell Lee *professional stock car driver*
Woodside, Donna J. *nursing educator*

### Gallatin
Bradley, Nolen Eugene, Jr. *personnel executive, educator*
Ellis, Joseph Newlin *retired distribution company executive*
Evans, Robert Byron *software engineer, educator*
Glover, Nancy Elliott *elementary school administrator*
Ramer, Hal Reed *academic administrator*

### Gatlinburg
Cave, Kent R. *national park ranger*
Pope, Randall Ray *retired national park superintendent*
†Wade, Karen *national parks administrator*

### Georgetown
Geren, Brenda L. *business educator*

### Germantown
Allison, Beverly Gray *seminary president, evangelism educator*
Hamilton, David Eugene *minister, educator*
Tutko, Robert Joseph *radiology administrator, educator*

### Greenbrier
Newell, Paul Haynes, Jr. *engineering educator, former college president*

### Greeneville
Hull, Thomas Gray *federal judge*
Parsons, Marcia Phillips *judge*
Smith, Myron John, Jr. *librarian, author*

### Hampton
McClendon, Fred Vernon *real estate professional, business consultant, equine and realty appraiser, financial consultant*

### Harrogate
Robertson, Edwin Oscar *banker*

### Hartsville
Todd, Mary Patricia *nursing administrator*

### Hendersonville
Allen, Duane David *singer*
Bare, Robert Joseph (Bobby Bare) *country music singer, songwriter*
Cash, June Carter *singer*
Davis, Robert Norman *hospital administrator*
Gregory, Sandra K. *accountant, consultant*
Hill, William Thomas *geological consultant*
Leslie, Lynn Marie *secondary education educator*
McCaleb, Joe Wallace *lawyer*
Poynor, Robert Allen, Jr. *guidance counselor*
Sanders, Steve *singer*
Thomas, Roberta Will *home care agency administrator*

### Hermitage
Chambers, Curtis Allen *clergyman, church communications executive*
Lockmiller, David Alexander *lawyer, educator*

### Huntsville
Boardman, Maureen Bell *community health nurse*

### Jackson
Bailey, James Andrew *middle school educator*
Barefoot, Hyran Euvene *academic administrator, educator, minister*
Drew, Gayden, IV *lawyer*
Hazlehurst, George Edward *physician*
Katz, Norman *manufacturing company executive*
Maynard, Terrell Dennis *minister*
Mitchell, Elizabeth Marelle *nursing educator, medical, surgical nurse*
Smith, Geri Garrett *nurse educator*
Taylor, Ronald Fulford *physician*
Todd, James Dale *federal judge*
Troupe, Marilyn Kay *education educator*
Woodall, Gilbert Earl, Jr. *medical administrator*

### Jefferson City
Bahner, Carl Tabb *retired chemistry educator, researcher*
Ball, Louis Oliver, Jr. *music educator*
Baumgardner, James Lewis *history educator*
Maddox, Jesse Cordell *academic administrator*
Muncy, Estle Pershing *physician*

### Jellico
Chitwood, Helen Irene *elementary education educator*
Hausman, Keith Lynn *hospital administrator, physical therapist*

### Johnson City
Adebonojo, Festus O. *medical educator*
Alfonso, Robert John *university administrator*
Coogan, Philip Shields *pathologist*
Dyer, Allen Ralph *psychiatrist*
Fukuda, Aisaku (Isaac Fukuda) *reproductive endocrinologist*
Greninger, Edwin Thomas *former history educator*
Hamdy, Ronald Charles *geriatrician*
Isaac, Walter Lon *psychology educator*
Jenkins, Ronald Wayne *lawyer*
Kostrzewa, Richard Michael *pharmacology educator*
Larkin, Donald Wayne *clinical psychologist*
McIntosh, Cecilia Ann *biochemist, educator*
Miller, Barney E. *biochemist*
Paxton, J. Willene *retired university counseling director*
Rasch, Ellen Myrberg *cell biology educator*
Roark, Edith Humphreys *private school language arts educator, reading specialist*
Schneider, Valerie Lois *speech educator*
Schueller, William Alan *dermatologist*
Shaw, Angus Robertson, III *minister*
Shurbaji, M. Salah *pathologist*
Skalko, Richard Gallant *anatomist, educator*
Wiebe, Richard Herbert *reproductive endocrinologist, educator*
Wyatt, Doris Fay Chapman *English language educator*
Zayas-Bazan, Eduardo *foreign language educator*

### Jonesborough
Broyles, Ruth Rutledge *principal*
Weaver, Kenneth *gynecologist, researcher*

### Kingsport
Adams, W. G. *chemicals executive*
Bremer, Louis Henry, Jr. *health care administrator*
Coover, Harry Wesley *manufacturing company executive*
Davis, Tammie Lynette *music educator, director*
Deavenport, Earnest W., Jr. *chemical executive*
Egan, Martha Avaleen *history educator, archivist*
Findley, Don Aaron *manufacturing company executive*
Germinario, Louis Thomas *materials scientist*
Gose, William Christopher *chemist*
Head, William Iverson, Sr. *retired chemical company executive*
Hull, E. Patrick *lawyer*
Kiss, Mary Catherine Clement *writer*
Lunsford, Marvin Carl *chemical company executive*
Meyerrose, Sarah Louise *bank holding company executive*
Moore, Marilyn Patricia *community counselor*
Reasor, Roderick Jackson *industrial engineer*
Rex, David Lawrence *project manager*
Scott, H(erbert) Andrew *retired chemical engineer*
Siirola, Jeffrey John *chemical engineer*
Wolfe, Margaret Ripley *historian, educator, consultant*
Young, Howard Seth *chemist, researcher*

### Kingston
Manly, William Donald *metallurgist*
Oran, Geraldine Ann *assistant principal*

### Knoxville
Acker, Joseph Edington *retired cardiology educator*
Adams, Linas Jonas *gastroenterologist*
Ailor, Earl Starnes *lawyer*
Alexeff, Igor *physicist, electrical engineer, educator emeritus*
Ambrester, Marcus LaRoy *communication educator, program administrator*
Anderson, Ilse Janell *clinical geneticist*
Armistead, Willis William *university administrator, veterinarian*
Arnett, Foster Deaver *lawyer*
Bailey, Bridget *lawyer*
Bailey, John Milton *electrical engineering educator*
Bateman, Veda Mae *industrial psychologist, management consultant*
Bell (Jarratt), Corinne *psychologist*
Blake, Gerald Rutherford *banker*
Blass, William Errol *physics and astronomy educator*
Bly, Robert Maurice *lawyer*
Boling, Edward Joseph *university president emeritus, educator*
Borden, Eugene Owen *software engineer*
Borie, Bernard Simon, Jr. *physicist, educator*
Bose, Bimal Kumar *electrical engineering educator*
Brady, Patrick *French literature educator, novelist*
Bressler, Marcus N. *consulting engineer*
Brockett, Ralph Grover *adult education educator*
Brott, Walter Howard *cardiac surgeon, educator, retired army officer*
Brown, Kevin James *real estate broker*
Burkhart, John Henry *physician*
Caponetti, James Dante *botany educator*
Chen, James Pai-fun *biology educator, researcher*
Christenbury, Edward Samuel *lawyer*
Cole, William Edward *economics educator, consultant*
Conger, Bob Vernon *plant and soil science educator*
Cottrell, Jeannette Elizabeth *retired librarian*
Coulson, Patricia Bunker *endocrinologist*
Crowell, Craven H., Jr. *federal agency administrator*
Cutler, Everette Wayne *history educator*
Dean, John Aurie *chemist, author, chemistry educator emeritus*
DePersio, Richard John *otolaryngologist, plastic surgeon*
Diamond, Daniel Lloyd *surgeon*
Dickey, Joseph William *utility executive, engineer*
Dillard, W. Thomas *lawyer*
Draughon, Frances Ann *microbiology educator*
Drinnon, Janis Bolton *volunteer*
Faires, Ross N. *manufacturing company executive*
Filston, Howard Church *pediatric surgeon, educator*
Fisher, John Hurt *English language educator*
Froula, James DeWayne *national honor society director, engineer*
Garrison, Arlene Allen *engineering executive, engineering educator*
Gonzalez, Rafael Ceferino *electrical engineering educator*
Gotcher, Jack Everett, Jr. *oral and maxillofacial surgeon*
Hagood, Lewis Russell *lawyer*
Hammond, Edwin Hughes *geography educator*
Harris, Charles Edgar *retired wholesale distribution company executive*
Harris, Diana Koffman *sociologist, educator*
Harris, William Franklin, III *biologist, environmental science director and educator*
Harrison, Faye Venetia *anthropologist, educator*
Herndon, Anne Harkness *sales executive*
Hohenberg, John *journalist, educator*
Holton, Raymond William *botanist, educator*
Howard, Lewis Spilman *lawyer*
Hung, James Chen *engineer, educator, consultant*
Igoe, Terence B. *airport terminal executive*
Jacobs, Kenneth A. *composer, educator*
Jarvis, James Howard, II *judge*
Jenkins, Roger Lane *retail executive, consultant*
Jordan, Robert Leon *federal judge*
Klein, Milton Martin *history educator*
Kliefoth, A(rthur) Bernhard, III *neurosurgeon*
Lange, Robert Dale *internist, educator, medical researcher*
Laroussi, Mounir *electrical engineer*
LeVert, Francis Edward *nuclear engineer*
Lietzke, Milton Henry *chemistry educator*
Mahan, Gerald Dennis *physics educator, researcher*
Mankel, Francis Xavier *former principal, priest*
Martin, James Robert *identification company executive*
Maxson, Linda Ellen *biologist, educator*
Mayfield, T. Brient, IV *media and computer executive*
Mc Carty, Bruce *architect*
Mc Dow, John Jett *agricultural engineering educator*
Mc Hargue, Carl Jack *research laboratory administrator*
Mikels, J(ames) Ronald *bank executive*
Moor, Anne Dell *education director*
Moser, Harold Dean *historian*
Murray, Rebecca Brake *lawyer*
Murrian, Robert Phillip *magistrate, judge, educator*
Natelson, Stephen Ellis *neurosurgeon*
Oberman, Steven *lawyer*
O'Connell, Anthony J. *bishop*
Olmstead, Francis Henry, Jr. *plastics industry executive*
Owenby, Phillip H. *learning and communications consultant*
Ownby, Jere Franklin, III *lawyer*
Painter, Linda Robinson *physics educator, dean*
Penn, Dawn Tamara *entrepreneur*
Phillips, Jerry Juan *law educator*
Phillips, Thomas Wade *judge, lawyer*
Pollard, Dennis Bernard *lawyer, educator*
Rayson, Edwin Hope *lawyer*
Renshaw, Amanda Frances *retired physicist, nuclear engineer*
Reynolds, Glenn Harlan *law educator*
Reynolds, Marjorie Lavers *nutrition educator*
Richards, Stephen Harold *engineering educator*
Richardson, Don Orland *agricultural educator*
Rosinski, Jan *mathematics educator*
Roth, J(ohn) Reece *electrical engineer, educator, researcher-inventor*
Rukeyser, William Simon *journalist*
Sanger, Herbert Shelton, Jr. *lawyer, former government official*
Schuler, Theodore Anthony *retired civil engineer, retired city official*
Schweitzer, George Keene *chemistry educator*
Sharp, Aaron John *botanist, educator*
Sherman, Gordon Rae *computer science educator*
Siler, Susan Reeder *communications educator*
Smith, Leonard Ware *lawyer*
Sorrells, Frank Douglas *mechanical engineer, consultant*
South, Stephen A. *academic administrator*
Springer, John K. *securities representative*
Stegmayer, Joseph Henry *housing industry executive*
Stooksbury, William Claude *minister*
Stringfield, Hezz, Jr. *contractor, financial consultant*
Sublett, Carl Cecil *artist*
Sullenberger, Donald Shields *air force officer, business executive*
†Summitt, Patricia Head *college basketball coach*
Swanson, Lorna Ellen *physical therapist, athletic trainer, researcher*
Swingle, Homer Dale *horticulturist, educator*
Teeter, Dwight Leland, Jr. *journalism educator*
Trevor, Kirk David Niell *orchestra conductor, cellist*
Tschantz, Bruce Allen *civil engineer, educator*
Uhrig, Robert Eugene *nuclear engineer, educator*
Vance, Stanley Charles *management educator*
Walsh, Joanne Elizabeth *art educator, librarian*
Ward, Robert Cleveland *research mathematician, science administrator*
Wasserman, Jack F. *exercise science educator*
Watson, Patricia L. *library director*
Wehlitz, Ralf *physicist*
Wheeler, John Watson *lawyer*
White, David Cleaveland *microbial ecologist, environmental toxicologist*
Williams, Thomas Ffrancon *chemist, educator*
Wunderlich, Bernhard *physical chemistry educator*

### La Follette
Eads, Ora Wilbert *clergyman, church official*
McDonald, Miller Baird *management consultant, columnist, historian*
Williams, Jane Crouch *mental health counselor, social worker*

### La Vergne
†Ingram, David *entertainment company executive*
†Ingram, John *publishing company executive*
†Ingram, Orrin H., III *entertainment company executive*
Walker, Phillip R. *agricultural products supplier*

### Lawrenceburg
Calvert, Lois Prince *nursing home administrator, registered nurse*

### Lebanon
Daniels, Charlie *musician, songwriter*
Toombs, Cathy West *assistant principal*

### Lenoir City
Brown, Donald Vaughn *technical educator, engineering consultant*

### Linden
Yarbro, Billy Ray *elementary school educator, basketball coach*

### Livingston
Harrison, Jim Rush, Jr. *minister of music*

### Lookout Mountain
Hardy, Thomas Cresson *insurance company executive*
Leitner, Paul R. *lawyer*
Rymer, S. Bradford, Jr. *retired appliance manufacturing company executive*
Wyeth, Andrew *artist*

### Loudon
Jones, Robert Gean *religion educator*
Morton, Jerome Holdren *school psychologist*

### Louisville
Wheeler, George William *university provost, physicist, educator*

### Luttrell
Milligan, Mancil Wood *mechanical and aerospace engineering educator*

### Madison
Kennedy, Matthew Washington *pianist, educator*
Wells, Kitty (Muriel Deason Wright) *country western singer*

### Martin
Smith, Robert Mason *university dean*

### Maryville
Bradford, Tutt Sloan *retired publisher*
Brigance, Albert Henry *educational writer*
Davis, William Walter *recruiter, trainer*
Hall, Marion Trufant *botany educator, arboretum director*
Howard, Cecil Byron *pediatrician*
Inscho, Barbara Pickel *mathematics educator*
Koella, Carl Ohm, Jr. *retired state senator, lawyer*
Lawson, Fred Raulston *banker*
Lucas, Melinda Ann *pediatrician, educator*
Mosher, Donald Raymond *chemical engineer, consultant*
Oakes, Lester Cornelius *retired electrical engineer, consultant*
Stone, Hubert Dean *editor, journalist*

### Maynardville
Smith, Fred Doyle *nurse*

### Mc Minnville
Martin, Ron *editor, superintendent of schools, consultant, minister*
Potter, Clement Dale *public defender*

### Memphis
Abston, Dunbar, Jr. *management executive*
Allen, James Henry *magistrate*
Allen, Newton Perkins *lawyer*
Andrews, William Eugene *construction products manufacturing executive*
Babin, Richard Weyro *surgeon, educator*
Battle, Allen Overton, Jr. *psychologist, educator*
Bernstein, Janna S. Bernheim *art educator*
Bland, James Theodore, Jr. *lawyer*
Booker, Bruce Robert *theology educator, author, educational consultant*
Booth, Robert Lee, Jr. *banker*
Broadhurst, Jerome Anthony *lawyer*
Brooks, Kathleen *journalist*
Brooks, P. A., II *bishop*
Brown, Bailey *federal judge*
Buchignani, Leo Joseph *lawyer*
Buckman, Robert Henry *chemical company executive*
Butts, Herbert Clell *dentist, educator*
Byrd, Paula Strickland *mental health nurse clinician, educator*
Carmean, E. A., Jr. *art museum director, art historian*
Carroll, Billy Price *artist*
Carter, Michael Allen *college dean, nursing educator*
Chesney, Russell Wallace *pediatrician*
Christopher, Robert Paul *physician*
Chung, King-Thom *microbiologist, educator*
Cicala, Roger Stephen *physician, educator*
Clark, Ross Bert, II *lawyer*
Clarkson, Andrew MacBeth *retail executive*
Cody, Walter James Michael *lawyer, former state official*
Coleman, Veronica Freeman *prosecutor*
Connolly, Matthew B., Jr. *conservationist*
Cooper, Irby *real estate development company executive*
Copper, John Franklin *Asian studies educator, consultant*
Cowan, George Sheppard Marshall, Jr. *surgeon, educator, research administrator*
Cox, Clair Edward, II *urologist, medical educator*
†Cox, Larry D. *airport terminal executive*
Crane, Laura Jane *research chemist*
Creel, Wesley S. *museum director*
Cunningham, David Coleman *career officer*
Curran, Thomas *molecular biologist, educator*
Czestochowski, Joseph Stephen *museum administrator*
Daniel, Coldwell, III *economist, educator*
Daughdrill, James Harold, Jr. *academic administrator*
Davis, Frederick Benjamin *law educator*
Depperschmidt, Thomas Orlando *economist, educator*
Desiderio, Dominic Morse, Jr. *chemistry and neurochemistry educator*
Diggs, Walter Whitley *health science facilty administrator*
Dobbs, James K., III *automotive executive*
Doherty, Peter Charles *immunologist*
Drescher, Judith Altman *library director*
Dunathan, Harmon Craig *college dean*
Dunavant, William Buchanan, Jr. *textiles executive*
Dunnigan, T. Kevin *electrical and electronics manufacturing company executive*
Elfervig, Lucie Theresa Savoie *ophthalmic nursing consultant*
Emery, Sue McHam *bulletin editor, owner bridge studio*
Evans, James Mignon *architect*
Fain, John Nicholas *biochemistry educator*
Fields, W(ade) Thomas *dental educator*
Finch, Larry *university athletic coach*
Foote, Shelby *author*
Forell, David Charles *financial executive*
Franklin, Stanley Phillip *computer scientist, cognitive scientist, mathematician, educator*
Freeman, Bob A. *retired microbiology educator, retired dean*

French, Louis Bertrand *engineering educator*
Gagne, Ann Marie *special education educator*
Gentry, Gavin Miller *lawyer*
Gerald, Barry *radiology educator, neuroradiologist*
Gibbons, Julia Smith *federal judge*
Gilman, Ronald Lee *lawyer*
Godsey, William Cole *physician*
Goldstein, Jerome Arthur *mathematics educator*
Gourley, Dick R. *college dean*
Granger, David Mason *broadcasting and communications executive*
Griffin, Tom *former editor, writer*
Haight, Scott Kerr *lawyer*
Haizlip, Henry Hardin, Jr. *real estate consultant, former banker*
Hall, Johnnie Cameron *pathologist*
Hamilton, W. W. *church administrator*
Harpster, James Erving *lawyer*
Harris, Edward Frederick *orthodontics educator, physical anthropologist*
Harvey, Albert C. *lawyer*
Hathcock, John Edward *vocalist*
Hedgeman, Lulah M. *secondary education educator*
Heimberg, Murray *pharmacologist, biochemist, physician, educator*
Herenton, Willie W. *mayor*
Herrod, Henry Grady, III *allergist, immunologist*
Hester, James David *academic administrator*
Hofmann, Polly A. *physiology educator*
Horn, Ralph *bank executive*
Horton, Odell *federal judge*
Howe, Martha Morgan *microbiologist, educator*
Huget, Eugene Floyd *dental educator, researcher*
Hughes, Walter Thompson *physician, pediatrics educator*
Hunt, James Calvin *academic administrator, physician*
Hyde, Joseph R., III *retail auto parts executive*
Ingram, Alvin John *surgeon*
Jarvis, Daphne Eloise *laboratory administrator*
Jenkins, Ruben Lee *chemical company executive*
Jerry, Robert Howard, II *law educator*
Johnson, Johnny *research psychologist, consultant*
Jolly, William Thomas *foreign language educator*
Jones, Marguerite Jackson *English language educator*
Jones, Walk Claridge, III *architect*
Jurand, Jerry George *periodontology educator, researcher*
Kahane, Joel Carl *speech pathologist*
Kellogg, Frederic Hartwell *civil engineer, educator*
Knight, H. Stuart *law enforcement official, consultant*
†Korones, Sheldon Bernarr *physician, educator*
Krieger, Robert Lee, Jr. *management consultant, educator, writer, political analyst*
Lasslo, Andrew *medicinal chemist, educator*
Latta, George Haworth, III *neonatologist*
Lawson, Katherine Elaine *minister, counselor, psychologist*
Lazar, Rande Harris *otolaryngologist*
Ledsinger, Charles Albert, Jr. *hotel, gaming executive*
Lewin, Ann White *museum director, educator*
Macklin, F. Douglas *bishop*
Magrill, Joe Richard, Jr. *religious organization administrator, minister*
Manire, James McDonnell *lawyer*
Martin, Daniel C. *surgeon, educator*
Mauer, Alvin Marx *physician, medical educator*
McCalla, Jon P. *federal judge*
McEachran, Angus *newspaper editor*
McGlown, Brenda Pryor *special education educator*
McMahan, Gary Lynn *medical foundation executive*
McNabb, Darcy LaFountain *medical management company executive*
McPherson, Larry E(ugene) *photographer, educator*
McRae, Robert Malcolm, Jr. *federal judge*
Mealor, William Theodore, Jr. *geography educator, university administrator, consultant*
Mendel, Maurice *audiologist, educator*
Meredith, Donald Lloyd *librarian*
Miller, Neil Austin *biology educator*
Mirvis, David Marc *health administrator, cardiologist, educator*
Monypeny, David Murray *lawyer*
Mulholland, Kenneth Leo, Jr. *health care facility administrator*
Neely, Charles Lea, Jr. *retired physician*
Nesin, Jeffrey D. *academic administrator*
Nienhuis, Arthur Wesley *physician, researcher*
Noble, Douglas Ross *museum administrator*
Noel, Randall Deane *lawyer*
Nolly, Robert J. *hospital administrator, pharmaceutical science educator*
O'Donnell, William Hugh *English educator*
Piazza, Marguerite *opera singer, actress, entertainer*
Porter, W. L. *bishop*
Pourciau, Lester John *librarian*
Pugh, Dorothy Gunther *ballet company executive*
Pulido, Miguel Lazaro *marketing professional*
Ramirez, Michael P. *editorial cartoonist*
Ramsey, Marjorie Elizabeth *early childhood education educator*
Ranta, Richard Robert *university dean*
Rice, George Lawrence, III (Larry Rice) *lawyer*
Riely, Caroline Armistead *physician, medical educator*
Riss, Murray *photographer, educator*
Runyan, John William, Jr. *medical educator*
Russell, James Franklin *lawyer*
Ryan, Kevin William *research virologist, educator*
Shanklin, Douglas Radford *physician*
Sharpe, Robert F., Sr. *writer, lecturer, educator, consultant, publisher*
Shochat, Stephen Jay *pediatric surgeon*
Sigler, Lois Oliver *retired educator*
Smith, Charles E. *protective services official*
Smith, Frederick Wallace *transportation company executive*
Smith, Joseph Philip *lawyer*
Smith, Whitney Bousman *music and drama critic*
Solomon, Solomon Sidney *endocrinologist, pharmacologist, scientist*
Spitznagel, John Keith *periodontist, researcher*
Spore, Richard Roland, III *lawyer, educator*
Stagg, Louis Charles *English language and literature educator*
Steib, James Terry *bishop*
Stokes, Henry Arthur *journalist*
Streibich, Harold Cecil *lawyer*
Sullivan, Eugene Joseph *food service company executive*
Sullivan, Jay Michael *medical educator*
Summitt, Robert Layman *pediatrician, educator*
Tate, Stonewall Shepherd *lawyer*
Terry, Ronald Anderson *bank holding company executive*
Thomas, Nathaniel Charles *clergyman*
Todd, Virgil Holcomb *clergyman, religion educator*
†Tuckman, Howard Paul *economics educator, consultant*
Turner, Jerome *federal judge*
Vest, James Murray *foreign language and literature educator*
Wagner, Samuel, V *secondary school English language educator*
Wallis, Carlton Lamar *librarian*
Walsh, Thomas James, Jr. *lawyer*
Ward, Jeannette Poole *psychologist, educator*
Wellford, Harry Walker *federal judge*
Wheeler, Orville Eugene *university dean, civil and mechanical engineering educator*
Whitesell, Dale Edward *retired association executive, natural resources consultant*
Wilcox, Harry Hammond *retired medical educator*
Wildman, Gary Cecil *chemist*
Williams, David Russell *music educator*
Wilson, Charles Glen *zoo administrator*
Woodson, Gayle Ellen *otolaryngologist*
Yawn, David McDonald *journalist*
Yeates, Zeno Lanier *retired architect*

**Millington**
Lecuyer, Robert Raymond *aviation maintenance administrator*
Melcher, Jerry William Cooper *clinical psychologist, army officer*

**Morristown**
Harmon, David Eugene *optometrist, geneticist*
Johnson, Evelyn Bryan *flying service executive*

**Moscow**
Crawford, Sheila Jane *education educator, consultant*

**Mount Juliet**
Holloway, Susan Master *elementary education educator*
Masters, John Christopher *psychologist, educator, writer*

**Mountain Home**
McCoy, Sue *surgeon*

**Murfreesboro**
Berry, Mary Tom *education educator*
Childress, Elizabeth Lush *community volunteer, investor*
Doyle, Delores Marie *elementary education educator*
Eckles, George Love, Jr. *surgeon*
Ford, William F. *banker*
Hayes, Janice Cecile *education educator*
Huhta, James Kenneth *historian, university administrator, educator, consultant*
Lee, John Thomas *finance educator, financial planner*
Rupprecht, Nancy Ellen *historian, educator*
Walker, David Ellis, Jr. *educator, minister, consultant*
Westwick, Carmen Rose *retired nursing educator, consultant*
Wyatt, Robert Odell *journalism educator*

**Nashville**
Abstein, William Robert, II *minister*
Allbritton, Cliff *national consultant*
Allen, George Sewell *neurosurgery educator*
Allison, Fred, Jr. *physician, educator*
Altman, David Wayne *geneticist*
Anderson, Edward Riley *state supreme court justice*
Anderson, Lynn (Rene Anderson) *singer*
Arnold, Eddy *singer*
Atchison, David Warren *church officer*
Atkins, Chester Burton *record company executive, guitarist, publisher*
Aubrey, Roger Frederick *psychology and education educator*
Barnett, Joey Victor *pharmacologist, educator, researcher*
Bass, James Orin *lawyer*
Battle, William Robert (Bob Battle) *newspaper executive*
Bayuzick, Robert J. *materials scientist*
Beck, Robert Beryl *real estate executive*
Belton, Robert *law educator*
Bender, Harvey W., Jr. *cardiac and thoracic surgeon*
Benson, Edwin Welburn, Jr. *trade association executive*
Bernard, Louis Joseph *surgeon, educator*
Berry, William Wells *lawyer*
†Betts, Virginia Trotter *nursing educator, policy researcher*
Birch, Adolpho A., Jr. *judge*
Black, Clint *country singer, musician*
Blair, Joyce Allsmiller *computer science educator*
Bloch, Frank Samuel *law educator*
Blumstein, James Franklin *legal educator, lawyer, consultant*
Bogguss, Suzy *country music singer, songwriter*
Bolian, George Clement *health care executive, physician*
Bolinger, John C., Jr. *management consultant*
Bond, Sherry Louise *trade association administrator*
Boorman, Howard Lyon *history educator*
Bostick, Charles Dent *lawyer, educator*
Bottorff, Dennis C. *banker*
Boyd, Theophilus Bartholomew, III *publishing company executive*
Bradford, James C., Jr. *brokerage house executive*
Bragg, John Thomas *state legislator, retired businessman*
Bramlett, Paul Kent *lawyer*
Bredesen, Philip Norman *mayor*
Brigham, Kenneth Larry *medical educator*
Brodersen, Arthur James *electrical engineer*
Brooks, Garth (Troyal Garth Brooks) *country music singer*
Brophy, Jeremiah Joseph *financial company official, former army officer*
Brown, J. Aaron *producer, publisher*
Brown, Joe Blackburn *lawyer*
Brown, Tony Ersic *record company executive*
Buckles, Stephen Gary *economist, educator*
Burk, Raymond Franklin, Jr. *physician, educator, researcher*
Burnett, Lonnie Sheldon *obstetrics and gynecology educator*
Burson, Charles W. *state attorney general*
Burt, Alvin Miller, III *anatomist, cell biologist, educator, writer*
Butler, Javed *internist*
Butler, Merlin Gene *physician, medical geneticist, educator*
Buttrick, David Gardner *religion educator*
Byrd, Benjamin Franklin, Jr. *surgeon, educator*
Cadzow, James Archie *engineering educator, researcher*
Carr, Davis Haden *lawyer*
Carter, James McCord *television producer, personality*
Cawthon, William Connell *operations management consultant*
Chambers, Carol Tobey *elementary school educator*
Chapman, John Edmon *university dean, pharmacologist, physician*
Chapman, Morris Hines *denominational executive*
Charney, Jonathan Isa *law educator, lawyer*
Cheek, James Howe, III *lawyer, educator*
Chytil, Frank *biochemist*
Cleveland, Ashley *musician*
Clinton, Barbara Marie *university health services director, social worker*
Clinton, Mary Ellen *neurologist*
Clouse, Robert Wilburn *communication executive, educator*
Cobb, Stephen A. *lawyer*
Cohen, Stanley *biochemistry educator*
Collier, Simon *history educator*
Compton, John Joseph *philosophy educator*
Conkin, Paul Keith *history educator*
Cook, Ann Jennalie *English language educator*
Cook, Charles Wilkerson, Jr. *banker, former county official*
Cook, George Edward *electrical engineering educator, consultant*
Cooney, Charles Hayes *lawyer*
Cordaro, Matthew Charles *utility executive, energy developer, engineer*
Covington, Robert Newman *law educator*
Crabtree, Bruce Isbester, Jr. *architect*
Crooke, Philip Schuyler *mathematics educator*
Cross, Christopher *recording artist, songwriter, singer*
Crowell, Rodney J. *country music recording artist, songwriter*
Culbertson, Katheryn Campbell *lawyer*
Cunningham, Leon William *biochemist, educator*
Cyrus, Billy Ray *country music performer*
Daane, James Dewey *banker*
Dale, Kathy Gail *rehabilitation rheumatology nurse*
Darnell, Riley Carlisle *state government executive, lawyer*
Daughtrey, Martha Craig *federal judge*
Davis, James Verlin *insurance brokerage executive*
Dedman, Bertram Cottingham *retired insurance company executive*
Dettbarn, Wolf-Dietrich *neurochemist, pharmacologist, educator*
Diffie, Joe *country singer, songwriter*
Dobbs, George Albert *funeral director, embalmer*
Dohrmann, Richard Martin *high technology manufacturing and publishing executive*
Doody, Margaret Anne *English language educator*
Doran, James Marion, Jr. *lawyer*
Doyle, Don Harrison *history educator*
Draper, James Thomas, Jr. (Jimmy Draper) *clergyman*
Driscoll, Joseph Francis *real estate executive*
Du Bois, Tim *recording industry executive*
Dupont, William Dudley *biostatistician, educator*
Dykes, Archie Reece *financial services executive*
Earle, Steve *country rockabilly musician, songwriter*
Echols, Robert L. *federal judge*
Elam, Lloyd Charles *psychiatrist*
Elberry, Zainab Abdelhaliem *insurance company executive*
Ely, James Wallace, Jr. *law educator*
Emans, Robert LeRoy *academic administrator, education educator*
Faust, A. Donovan *communications executive*
Fazio, Sergio *medical educator, researcher*
Fenichel, Gerald Mervin *neurologist, educator*
Fenner, Catherine Munro *association administrator*
Fields, James Perry *dermatologist, dermatopathologist, allergist*
Finegan, Thomas Aldrich *economist*
Fischer, Patrick Carl *computer scientist, educator*
Fitzgerald, Edmund Bacon *electronics industry executive*
Fleck, Bela *country musician*
Fleming, Samuel M. *banker*
Fondaw, Elizabeth Louise *vocational school educator*
Forlines, Franklin Leroy *minister, educator*
Forstman, Henry Jackson *theology educator, university dean*
Fort, Tomlinson *chemist, chemical engineering educator*
Foster, Henry Wendell *medical educator*
Fowinkle, Eugene W. *physician, medical center administrator*
Franks, John Julian *anesthesiology educator, medical investigator*
Frey, Herman S. *publishing company executive*
Galloway, Kenneth Franklin *electrical engineering educator*
Gaultney, John Orton *life insurance agent, consultant*
Geisel, Martin Simon *college dean, educator*
Gentry, Teddy *country musician*
George, Alfred L., Jr. *medical educator, researcher*
Gibbs, Jack Porter *sociologist, educator*
Gill, Vince *country musician, singer*
Gillmor, John Edward *lawyer*
Girgus, Sam B. *English literature educator*
Gleaves, Edwin Sheffield *librarian*
Gobbell, Ronald Vance *architect*
Gove, Walter R. *sociology educator*
Graham, George J., Jr. *political scientist, educator*
Graham, Hugh Davis *history educator*
Graham, Thomas Pegram, Jr. *pediatric cardiologist*
Grant, Amy *singer, songwriter*
Grantham, Dewey Wesley *historian, educator*
Graves, Rebecca O. *public health nurse, consultant*
Green, Lisa Cannon *business editor*
Greenwood, Lee Melvin *singer*
Griffith, James Leigh *lawyer*
Griffith, Jerry Lynn *physical education educator*
Griffith, Nanci *singer, songwriter*
Guinsburg, Philip Fried *psychologist*
Gulmi, James Singleton *apparel manufacturing company executive*
Guthrie, James Williams *education educator*
Guy, Sharon Kaye *state agency executive*
Hahn, George Thomas *materials engineering educator, researcher*
†Hall, Douglas Scott *astronomy educator*
Halperin, John William *English literature educator*
Hamilton, Joseph Hants, Jr. *physicist, educator*
Hamilton, Russell George, Jr. *academic dean, Spanish and Portuguese language educator*
Hancock, M(arion) Donald *political science educator*
Hanselman, Richard Wilson *entrepreneur*
Hardin, Hal D. *lawyer, former United States attorney, former judge*
Hardman, Joel Griffeth *pharmacologist*
Hargrove, Erwin Charles, Jr. *political science educator*
Harrawood, Paul *civil engineering educator*
Harris, Alice Carmichael *linguist, educator*
Harris, Emmylou *singer*
Harris, J(acob) George *health care company executive*
Harris, Thomas Munson *chemistry educator, researcher*
Harris, Thomas Raymond *biomedical engineer, educator*
Harrison, Clifford Joy, Jr. *banker*
Harrod, Howard Lee *religion educator*
Hart, Richard Banner *lawyer*
Hartford, John Cowan *singer, songwriter*
Harwell, Aubrey Biggs *lawyer*
Hass, Joseph Monroe *automotive executive*
Hassel, Rudolph Christopher *English language educator*
Hazelip, Herbert Harold *academic administrator*
Hazlehurst, Franklin Hamilton *fine arts educator*
Heard, (George) Alexander *retired educator and chancellor*
Hefner, James A. *academic administrator*
Heiser, Arnold Melvin *astronomer*
Henderson, Milton Arnold *professional society administrator*
Hercules, David Michael *chemistry educator, consultant*
Hester, Bruce Edward *library media specialist, lay worker*
Hieronymus, Clara Booth Wiggins *journalist*
Higgins, Thomas A. *federal judge*
Hildebrand, Donald Dean *lawyer*
Holladay, Wendell Gene *physics educator*
Holmquest, Donald Lee *physician, astronaut, lawyer*
Holsen, Robert Charles *accountant*
Hood, Howard Allison *law librarian*
†Houk, Benjamin Noah *ballet dancer*
House, Robert William *technology management educator*
Huffman, William Raymond *emergency physician*
Hughes, Gayle Womack *civil engineer, educator*
Hummell, Burton Howard *food distribution company executive*
Hutchison, Barbara Bailey *children's entertainer*
Inagami, Tadashi *biochemist, educator*
†Ingram, Martha R. *company executive*
Jackson, Alan *country songwriter, singer*
Jackson, Kenneth Monroe *lawyer, actor*
James, Kay Louise *management consultant, healthcare executive*
Jamison, Connie Joyce *sociology educator*
Jarman, Mark Foster *English language educator*
Jennings, Henry Smith, III *cardiologist*
Johnson, Albert William *mortgage banker, real estate broker*
Johnson, David *medical administrator*
Johnson, Hollis Eugene, III *foundation executive*
Jones, Kathryn Cherie *pastor*
Jonsson, Bjarni *mathematician, educator*
Judd, Naomi *country music entertainer, singer, songwriter, author*
Kaas, Jon H. *psychology educator*
Kaludis, George *management consultant, book company executive, educator*
†Kaplan, Peter Robert *cardiologist*
Kenner, William Davis, III *psychiatrist*
Kephart, Floyd W. *corporate strategist*
Kisber, Matthew Harris *state legislator*
Klein, Christopher Carnahan *economist*
Kmiec, Edward Urban *bishop*
Kono, Tetsuro *biochemist, physiologist, educator*
Krantz, Sanford Burton *physician*
Kreyling, Christine Moorman *museum curator, writer*
Kuhn, Paul Hubert, Jr. *investment counsel*
Kurek, Michael Henry *music educator*
Lachs, John *philosopher, educator*
Laczko, Brian John *theater director*
Land, Rebekah Ruth *marriage and family therapist*
Langstaff, George Quigley, Jr. *retired footwear company executive*
Lawrence, Thomas Patterson *public relations executive*
Lawton, Alexander Robert, III *immunologist, educator*
Lazenby, Fred Wiehl *insurance company executive*
Ledyard, Robins Heard *lawyer*
Lee, Brenda (Brenda Mae Tarpley) *singer, entertainer*
Lee, Douglas A. *music educator*
Leftwich, Russell Bryant *allergist, immunologist, consultant*
Lehman, David R. *children's entertainer*
Levinson, L(eslie) Harold *lawyer, educator*
Lukehart, Charles Martin *chemistry educator*
Lynch, John Brown *plastic surgeon, educator*
Lyon, Philip K(irkland) *lawyer*
Madu, Leonard Ekwugha *lawyer, human rights officer, newspaper columnist*
Mahanes, David James, Jr. *retired distillery executive*
Maier, Harold Geistweit *law educator, lawyer*
Maihafer, Harry James *retired banker, former army officer, writer*
Mandrell, Barbara Ann *singer, entertainer*
Manning, David Lee *health care executive*
Marney, Samuel Rowe *physician, educator*
Martin, Henry Alan *lawyer*
Martin, Peter Robert *psychiatrist, pharmacologist*
Mathews, Robert C.H. *state agency executive*
Mattea, Kathy *vocalist, songwriter*
May, James M. *medical educator, medical researcher*
May, Joseph Leserman (Jack) *lawyer*
Mayden, Barbara Mendel *lawyer*
Mayhew, Aubrey *music industry executive*
McClanahan, Larry Duncan *civil engineer, consultant*
Mc Creary, James Franklin *lawyer, mediator*
McKinney, Jane-Allen *artist and educator*
McMurry, Idanelle Sam *educational consultant*
Meltzer, Herbert Yale *psychiatry educator*
Meredith, Owen Nichols *public relations executive, genealogist*
Merritt, Gilbert Stroud *federal judge*
Miller, Calvin Francis *geology educator*
Miller, Richard L. *architectural executive*
Mills, Liston Oury *theology educator*
Mizell, Andrew Hooper, III *concrete company executive*
Moore, William Grover, Jr. *management consultant, former air freight executive, former air force officer*
Morgan, Lorrie (Loretta Lynn Morgan) *country singer*

Morrow, Jason Drew *medical and pharmacology educator*
Needham, Maureen *dance educator, writer*
Neel, Jasper Phillip *English educator*
Nelson, Edward Gage *merchant banking investment company executive*
Nixon, John Trice *judge*
Oates, John Alexander, III *medical educator*
Oates, Sherry Charlene *portraitist*
O'Day, Denis Michael *ophthalmologist, educator*
Oldfield, Russell Miller *lawyer*
O'Neill, James Anthony, Jr. *pediatric surgeon, educator*
Orgebin-Crist, Marie-Claire *biology educator*
Osborne, Charles William (Bill Osborne) *transportation executive*
Oslin, K. T. (Kay Toinette Oslin) *country singer*
Ossoff, Robert Henry *otolaryngological surgeon*
Overton, Stanley Dixon *banking executive*
Palmer-Hass, Lisa Michelle *state official*
Panvini, Robert S. *physics researcher/educator*
Parker, Frank Leon *environmental engineering educator, consultant*
Partain, Clarence Leon *radiologist, nuclear medicine physician, educator, administrator*
Partlett, David F. *law educator*
Pellegrino, James William *college dean, psychology educator*
Pendergrass, Henry Pancoast *physician, radiology educator*
Perry, Lewis Curtis *historian, educator*
Person, Curtis S., Jr. *state senator, lawyer*
Phillips, John A(tlas), III *geneticist, educator*
Pichois, Claude P. *classical studies educator*
Picirilli, Robert Eugene *clergyman, college dean, writer*
Pinson, Charles Wright *transplant surgeon, educator*
Potter, John Leith *mechanical and aerospace engineer, educator, consultant*
Prine, John *singer, songwriter*
Purcell, William Paxson, III *association administrator*
Rabbitt, Edward Thomas *singer, songwriter*
Ramsaur, Allan Fields *lawyer, lobbyist*
Ransom, Nancy Alderman *sociology and women's studies educator, university administrator*
Ray, Wayne Allen *epidemiologist*
Rayburn, Ted Rye *newspaper editor*
Reed, Millard C. *academic administator*
Reid, Donna Joyce *small business owner*
Reid, Lyle *judge*
Richmond, Samuel Bernard *management educator*
Ridley, Carolyn Fludd *social studies educator*
Riley, Harris DeWitt, Jr. *pediatrician, educator*
Roberts, Kenneth Lewis *investor, lawyer, foundation administrator*
Roberts, Sandra *editor*
Robertson, David *pharmacologist, physician, educator*
Robinson, Roscoe Ross *nephrologist, educator*
Roden, Dan Mark *cardiologist, medical educator*
Rogers, Roy (Leonard Franklin Slye) *country musician, actor*
Ross, Joseph Comer *physician, educator, academic administrator*
Russell, Clifford Springer *economics and public policy educator*
Russell, Fred McFerrin *journalist, author, lawyer*
Sanders, Jay William *audiology educator*
Sanders, Paul Hampton *lawyer, retired educator, arbitrator/mediator*
Sawyers, John Lazelle *surgeon*
Scheffman, David Theodore *economist, management educator, consultant*
Schnelle, Karl Benjamin, Jr. *chemical engineering educator, consultant, researcher*
Schoggen, Phil H(oward) *psychologist, educator*
Schumaker, Larry Lee *mathematics educator*
Scott, Richard L. *health and medical products company executive*
†Shack, R. Bruce *plastic surgeon*
Sharp, Bert Lavon *retired education educator, retired university dean*
Sharp, Vernon Hibbett *psychiatrist*
Shelton, Ricky Van *country music singer, songwriter*
Sherborne, Robert *editor*
Silberman, Enrique *physics researcher and administrator*
Sims, Wilson *lawyer*
Skaggs, Ricky *country musician*
Sloan, Reba Faye *dietitian, consultant*
Smith, Charles Edward *state agency administrator*
Smith, Dani Allred *sociologist, educator*
†Smith, Joseph A. *urologic surgeon*
Smith, Michael W. *popular musician*
Smith, Samuel Boyd *history educator*
Smith, William Barney *allergist*
Snoddy, Chris Raymond *athletic trainer*
Snyders, Dirk Johan *electrophysiologist, biophysicist, educator*
Soderquist, Larry Dean *lawyer, educator*
South, Mary Ann *pediatrics educator*
Speece, Richard Eugene *civil engineer, educator*
Spengler, Dan Michael *orthopedic surgery educator, researcher, surgeon*
Spinella, Judy Lynn *healthcare administrator*
Spores, Ronald Marvin *anthropology educator, ethnohistorian*
Stahlman, Mildred Thornton *pediatrics and pathology educator, researcher*
Stepnoski, Mark Matthew *professional football player*
Stewart, David Marshall *librarian*
Stone, Lawrence Mynatt *publishing executive*
Stone, Robert Edward, Jr. *speech pathologist*
Stringfield, Charles David *hospital administrator*
Strupp, Hans Hermann *psychologist, educator*
†Strupp, John Allen *oncologist*
Stuart, Marty *country music singer, musician, songwriter*
Stubbs, Gerald *biochemist, educator*
Stumpf, Samuel Enoch *philosophy educator*
Sullivan, Allen Trousdale *securities company executive*
Sullivan, Walter Laurence *writer, educator*
Sundquist, Donald *governor, former congressman, sales corporation executive*
Sutherland, Frank *publishing executive, editor*
Sutton, Barrett Boulware *former insurance company executive*
Swensson, Earl Simcox *architect*
Szarwark, Ernest John *lawyer*
Tarbell, Dean Stanley *chemistry educator*
Thackston, Edward Lee *engineer, educator*
Thornton, Spencer P. *ophthalmologist, educator*
Tippin, Aaron *country music singer, songwriter*
Tolk, Norman Henry *physics educator*
Torrey, Claudia Olivia *lawyer*
Trauger, Aleta Arthur *judge*
Trautman, Herman Louis *lawyer, educator*
Travis, Randy Bruce *musician*
Tuke, Robert Dudley *lawyer, educator*
Twain, Shania *country musician*
Ullestad, Merwin Allan *tax services executive*
Unger, Gary A. *recording industry executive, singer, lyricist*
Van, George Paul *international money management consultant*
van Eys, Jan *retired pediatrician, educator, administrator*
Van Mol, Louis John, Jr. *public relations executive*
Voegeli, Victor Jacque *history educator, dean*
von Raffler-Engel, Walburga (Walburga Engel) *linguist, lecturer, writer*
Wadley, Fredia Stovall *state commissioner*
Wagoner, Porter *country music singer, composer*
†Walkup, John Knox *state official*
Walters, Jane *state agency administrator*
Wang, Taylor Gunjin *science administrator, astronaut, educator*
Wasserman, David H. *medical educator, researcher*
Weeks, Robet Andrew *materials science researcher, educator*
Weingartner, H(ans) Martin *finance educator*
Weiss, Judith Miriam *psychologist*
Wendell, Earl W. *entertainment company executive*
Wert, James Junior *materials scientist, educator*
Westfield, Fred M. *economics educator*
Whitefield, Anne C. *secondary school principal*
†Whitworth, Thomas C. *neonatologist*
Wilder, John Shelton *state official, state legislator*
Wilkinson, Grant Robert *pharmacology educator*
Williams, Lester Frederick, Jr. *general surgeon*
Wilson, David James *chemistry researcher, educator*
Wilson, Sheryl A. *pharmacist*
Winstead, George Alvis *law librarian, biochemist, educator, consultant*
Wire, William Shidaker, II *retired apparel and footwear manufacturing company executive*
Wiseman, Thomas Anderton, Jr. *federal judge*
Wolraich, Mark Lee *pediatrician*
Wyatt, Joe Billy *academic administrator*
Young, Tommie Morton *social psychology educator, writer*
Youngblood, Elaine Michele *lawyer*
Zibart, Michael Alan *wholesale book company executive*
Zierdt, John Graham, Jr. *transportation company executive*

### Newport
Ball, Travis, Jr. *educational systems administrator, consultant, editor*
Bunnell, John Blake *lawyer*
Dykeman, Wilma *writer, lecturer*
Kridler, Jamie Branam *children's advocate, social psychologist*

### Oak Ridge
Auerbach, Stanley Irving *ecologist, environmental scientist, educator*
Beasley, Cloyd Orris, Jr. *physicist, researcher*
Boyle, William R. *science administrator*
Cain, Victor Ralph *nuclear engineer*
Cawley, Charles Nash *enviromental scientist*
Clapp, Neal Keith *experimental pathologist*
Dickens, Justin Kirk *nuclear physicist*
Felton, Lewis A. *career officer*
Gardiner, Donald Andrew *statistician, consultant*
Garrett, Jerry Dale *nuclear physicist*
Gifford, Franklin Andrew, Jr. *meteorologist*
Grimes, James Gordon *geologist*
Hosker, Rayford Peter, Jr. *air pollution research scientist*
Huff, Dale Duane *hydrologist, educator*
Jasny, George Roman *retired energy company executive*
Jones, Virginia McClurkin *social worker*
Kasten, Paul Rudolph *nuclear engineer, educator*
Kliewer, Kenneth Lee *computational scientist, research administrator*
Krause, Manfred Otto *physicist*
Larson, Bennett Charles *solid state physicist, researcher*
Luxmoore, Robert John *soil and plant scientist*
Maienschein, Fred C. *physicist*
Mazur, Peter *cell physiologist, cryobiologist*
Mulkey, Charles Eric *environmental engineer*
O'Neil, Charlotte Cooper *environmental education administrator*
Penniman, W. David *information scientist, educator, consultant*
Plasil, Franz *physicist*
Postma, Herman *physicist, consultant*
Poutsma, Marvin L. *chemical research administrator*
Raridon, Richard Jay *computer specialist*
Rivera, Angel Luis *chemical engineer*
Rosenthal, Murray Wilford *chemical engineer, science administrator*
Satchler, George Raymond *physicist*
Slusher, Kimberly Goode *researcher*
Spray, Paul Elsworth *surgeon*
Stevens, George M., III *surgeon*
Totter, John Randolph *biochemist*
Trauger, Donald Byron *nuclear engineering laboratory administrator*
Trivelpiece, Alvin William *physicist, corporate executive*
Turov, Daniel *financial writer, investment executive*
Weinberg, Alvin Martin *physicist*
Whittle, Charles Edward, Jr. *consultant, lecturer*
Wilkinson, Michael Kennerly *physicist*
Wise, Edmund Joseph *physician assistant, industrial hygienist*
Yalcintas, M. Güven *medical physicist*
Zucker, Alexander *physicist, administrator*

### Oliver Springs
Davis, Sara Lea *pharmacist*
Hecker, Thelma Weaks *retired elementary school educator*

### Ooltewah
Harris, Pamela Maize *journalism educator*

### Parsons
Franks, Hollis Berry *retired investment executive*

### Portland
Miller, Sandra Perry *middle school educator*

### Powell
Gentry, Robert Vance *physicist, researcher, writer*
Hyman, Roger David *lawyer*

### Pulaski
Dowdy, Ronald Raymond *academic administrator*

### Sevierville
Waters, John B. *lawyer*
Witucki, Janet Marie *nursing educator, geriatric researcher*

### Sewanee
Croom, Frederick Hailey *college administrator, mathematics educator*
Croom, Henrietta Brown *biology educator*
Dunkly, James Warren *theological librarian*
Hughes, Robert Davis, III *theological educator*
Kepple, Thomas Ray, Jr. *college administrator*
Lorenz, Anne Partee *special education educator, consultant*
Lytle, Guy Fitch, III *priest, educator, dean*
Mohiuddin, Yasmeen Niaz *economics educator*
Patterson, William Brown *university dean, history educator*
Pierce, Donna L. *lawyer*
Puckette, Stephen Elliott *mathematics educator, mathematician*
Spears, Monroe Kirk *English educator, author*
Williamson, Samuel Ruthven, Jr. *historian, university administrator*
Yeatman, Harry Clay *biologist, educator*

### Seymour
Steele, Ernest Clyde *retired insurance company executive*

### Shelbyville
Austin, Margaret Cully *school administrator*
Cooper, James Hayes Shofner (Jim Cooper) *investment company executive, former congressman, lawyer*
White, James Claiborne *manufacturing engineer executive*
Yates, Patricia England *employment company executive*

### Shiloh
Hawke, Paul Henry *historian*

### Signal Mountain
Cooper, Robert Elbert *state supreme court justice*
Hall, Thor *religion educator*
Reading, Sadie Ethel *retired public health nurse*

### Smithville
DeMay, Susan Ann *ceramic artist*
Enoch, Leslie Blythe, II *gas industry executive, lawyer*

### Soddy Daisy
Hamrick, Rita Gale *elementary school educator*
Watson, James Stanley *secondary education educator*

### Sparta
Langford, Jack Daniel *elementary school educator*
Pearson, Margaret Donovan *former mayor*

### Springfield
Fagan, A. Rudolph *minister*
Nutting, Paul John *city official*
Wilks, Larry Dean *lawyer*

### Summertown
Emanuel, William Gilbert *electrical engineer*

### Trenton
McCullough, Kathryn T. Baker *social worker, utility commissioner*

### Tullahoma
Antar, Basil Niman *engineering educator*
Butler, R. W. *engineering company executive*
Collins, S(arah) Ruth *education educator*
Dahotre, Narendra Bapurao *materials scientist, researcher, educator*
Gossick, Lee Van *consultant, executive, retired air force officer*
McCay, Thurman Dwayne *university administrator*
Moulton, Dawn G. *English language educator*
Wu, Ying Chu Lin Susan *engineering company executive, engineer*

### Vonore
Lownsdale, Gary Richard *mechanical engineer*

### Wartburg
Freytag, Addie Lou *nurse*

### Waverly
Williams, John Lee *lawyer*

### Waynesboro
Davis, Sharon Denise (Sherry Davis) *editor*

### White House
Ruth, Bryce Clinton, Jr. *lawyer*

### Williamsport
Dysinger, Paul William *physician, educator, health consultant*

## TEXAS

### Abilene
Boone, Billy Warren *lawyer, judge*
Boone, Celia Trimble *lawyer*
Booth, Linda Leigh *vocational educator*
Boyll, David Lloyd *broadcasting company executive*
Calvert, Linda Darnell *women's health nurse, educator*
Clayton, Lawrence Ray *university dean, literary critic, biographer*
Crowell, Sherry Diegel *clinical psychologist*
Crymes, Mary Cooper *secondary school educator*
Davis, Burl Edward *social sciences research consulting company executive, communications educator*
Fryer, William Neal *retired psychologist*
Hennig, Charles William *psychology educator*
Hunter, Robert Dean (Bob Hunter) *state legislator, retired university official*
Kyker, Christine White (Chris Kyker) *human services administrator*
McCaleb, Gary Day *university official*
McClain, Sylvia Nancy *voice educator, classical vocalist*
McWhiney, Grady *history educator*
Morgan, Clyde Nathaniel *dermatologist*
Morrison, Shirley Marie *nursing educator*
Richert, Harvey Miller, II *ophthalmologist*
Russell, Byron Edward *physical therapy educator*
Shimp, Robert Everett, Jr. *academic administrator, historian*
Specht, Alice Wilson *library director*
Warren, Russell Glen *academic administrator*
Wilson, Stanley P. *retired lawyer*

### Addison
McElvain, David Plowman *retired manufacturing company financial executive*

### Alamo
Forina, Maria Elena *gifted education educator*

### Aledo
Barton, Charles David *religious studies educator, author, researcher, historian*
Lindsay, John, IV *principal*
Rowe, Sheryl Ann *librarian*

### Alice
Tetlie, Harold *priest*

### Allen
Dawes, Robert Leo *research company executive*
Garner, Julie Lowrey *occupational therapist*
Gilliland, Mary Margarett *healthcare consultant*
Wilhelm, Walter Tinkham *information systems consultant*
Wynn, Robert E. *retired career officer, electronics executive*

### Alpine
Morgan, Raymond Victor, Jr. *academic administrator, mathematics educator*

### Amarillo
Ayad, Joseph Magdy *psychologist*
Ball, Charles Elihue *association consultant*
Berry, Rita Kay *medical technologist*
Borchardt, Paul Douglas *recreational executive*
Bowling, Joyce Blankenchip *retired critical care nurse*
Brainard, Jayne Dawson (Mrs. Ernest Scott Brainard) *civic worker*
Bull, Walter Stephen *police officer*
Crain, Mary Tom *volunteer*
Jones, Michael Wayne *health services administrator*
Keaton, Lawrence Cluer *safety engineer, consultant*
Klein, Jerry Lee, Sr. *religion educator, minister*
Laur, William Edward *retired dermatologist*
Madden, Wales Hendrix, Jr. *lawyer*
Marupudi, Sambasiva Rao *surgeon, educator*
Matthiesen, Leroy Theodore *bishop*
McDougall, Gerald Duane *lawyer*
Myers, Terry Lewis *clinical geneticist, educator*
Neal, A. Curtis *retired lawyer*
Norrid, Henry Gail *osteopath, surgeon, researcher*
Parker, Lynda Michele *psychiatrist*
Pratt, Donald George *physician*
Robinson, Mary Lou *federal judge*
Saadeh, Constantine Khalil *internist, health facility administrator, educator*
Smithee, John True *lawyer, state legislator*
Spies, Dennis J. *editor*
Sprowls, Robert Wayne *veterinarian, laboratory administrator*
Streu, Raymond Oliver *financial planner, securities executive*
Strickland, Anita Maurine *retired business educator, librarian*
Sutterfield, Deborah Kay *special education educator*
Taylor, Wesley Bayard, Jr. *retired army officer*
White, Sharon Elizabeth *lawyer*
Woods, John William *retired lawyer*

### Angleton
Panitz, Lawrence Herbert *lawyer*

### Anson
Kilpatrick, Martha Sue *speech-language pathologist*

### Aransas Pass
Stehn, Lorraine Strelnick *physician*

### Argyle
Merritt, Joe Frank *industrial supply executive*

### Arlington
Anderson, Dale Arden *aerospace engineer, educator*
Boyer, Vincent Lee *engineering executive*
Bunten, Brenda Arlene *geriatrics nurse*
Burkart, Burke *geology educator, researcher*
Burkett, John David *professional baseball player*
Burson, Betsy Lee *librarian*
Carey, Milburn Ernest *musician, educator*
Chen, Mo-Shing *electrical engineering educator*
Chong, Vernon *surgeon, physician, Air Force officer*
Clark, Dayle Meritt *civil engineer*
Clark, Will (William Nuschler Clark, Jr.) *professional baseball player*
Cole, Richard Louis *political scientist, educator*
Deaver, Pete Eugene *civil and aeronautical engineer*
Dickinson, Roger Allyn *business administration educator*
Dingwerth, Joan H. *religious organization administrator*
Ferrier, Richard Brooks *architecture educator, architect*
Fung, Adrian Kin-Chiu *electrical engineering educator, researcher*
Gelinas, Marc Adrien *healthcare administrator*
Glisson, Melissa Ann *dietitian*
Goelden-Bowen, Michelle Marie *occupational therapist*
Gonzalez, Juan (Alberto Vazquez) *professional baseball player*
Greenspan, Donald *mathematician, educator*
Grzesiak, Robert Charles *therapist*
Han, Chien-Pai *statistics educator*
†Harris, Ronald Leon *minister, communications executive*
Hawkins, Robert A. *college administrator*
Henderson, Arvis Burl *data processing executive, biochemist*

Kemp, Thomas Joseph *electronics company executive*
Kendall, Jillian D. *information systems specialist, program developer, educator, consultant*
Kubecka, Ronna Denise *English language and art educator, psychotherapist*
Lingerfelt, B. Eugene, Jr. *minister*
†Machle, Edward Johnstone *emeritus educator*
Malone, Edwin Scott, III *radio and television producer, public relations consultant*
McCall, Tina *critical care nurse*
McCuistion, Peg Orem *hospice administrator*
McCuistion, Robert Wiley *lawyer, hospital administrator, management consultant*
Mc Elroy, John Harley *electrical engineering educator*
McNairn, Peggi Jean *speech pathologist, educator*
†Melvin, Robert Douglas *professional sports team executive*
Moore, Tresi Lea *lawyer*
Mullendore, Walter Edward *economist*
Nelson, Wallace Boyd *economics and business administration educator*
Oates, Johnny Lane *professional baseball team manager*
†Pavlik, Roger Allen *professional baseball player*
Payne, Fred R(ay) *aerospace engineering educator, researcher*
Pickard, Myrna Rae *dean*
Pomerantz, Martin *chemistry educator, researcher*
Ptaszkowski, Stanley Edward, Jr. *civil engineer, structural engineer*
Qasim, Syed Reazul *civil engineering educator, researcher*
Quant, Harold Edward *financial services company executive, rancher*
Rajeshwar, Krishnan *chemist, educator*
Ramsey, Charles Eugene *sociologist, educator*
Rodriguez, Ivan *professional baseball player*
Rose, Edward W. (Rusty Rose) *professional sports team executive*
Rosenberry, William Kenneth *lawyer, educator*
Russell, Andrew Milo *music educator*
Ryan, Nolan *former professional baseball player*
Savage, Ruth Hudson *poet, writer, speaker*
†Sawyer, Dolores *motel facility executive*
Schieffer, J. Thomas *professional baseball team executive*
Smith, Charles Isaac *geology educator*
Sobol, Harold *retired dean, manufacturing executive, consultant*
Spears, Georgann Wimbish *marketing executive*
Stevens, Gladstone Taylor, Jr. *industrial engineer*
Swanson, Peggy Eubanks *finance educator*
Watkins, Ted Ross *social work educator*
Wetteland, John Karl *professional baseball player*
Wiig, Elisabeth Hemmersam *audiologist, educator*
Wright, James Edward *judge*

**Austin**
Adcock, Willis Alfred *electrical engineer, educator*
Aggarwal, Jagdishkumar Keshoram *electrical and computer engineering educator, research administrator*
Ahlschwede, Arthur Martin *church educational official*
Albin, Leslie Owens *biology educator*
Alexander, Drury Blakeley *architectural educator*
Alich, John Arthur, Jr. *manufacturing company executive*
Allday, Martin Lewis *lawyer*
Alpert, Mark Ira *marketing educator*
Anderson, David Arnold *law educator*
Anderson, Urton Liggett *accounting educator*
Antokoletz, Elliott Maxim *music educator*
Argo, William Frank *automotive executive*
Armbrust, David B. *lawyer*
Armstrong, Neal Earl *civil engineering educator*
Ashworth, Kenneth Hayden *state educational commissioner*
Austin, David Mayo *social work educator*
Austin, John Riley *surgeon, educator*
Auvenshine, Anna Lee Banks *school system administrator*
Ayres, Robert Moss, Jr. *retired university president*
Baade, Hans Wolfgang *legal educator, law expert*
Baird, Charles F. *judge*
Baker, Lee Edward *biomedical engineering educator*
Banks, Virginia Anne (Ginger Banks) *association administrator*
Bard, Allen Joseph *chemist, educator*
Barker, Daniel Stephen *geology educator*
Barnes, Jay William, Jr. *architect, rancher*
Barnes, Thomas Joseph *migration program administrator*
Barr, Howard Raymond *architect*
Barrera, Elvira Puig *counselor, therapist, educator*
Bash, Frank Ness *astronomer, educator*
Beard, Leo Roy *civil engineer*
Benavides, Fortunato Pedro (Pete Benavides) *federal judge*
Bengtson, Roger Dean *physicist*
Berdahl, Robert Max *academic administrator, historian, educator*
Bernstein, Robert *retired physician, state official, former army officer*
Biesele, John Julius *biologist, educator*
Billings, Harold Wayne *librarian, editor*
Blair, Calvin Patton *retired business administration educator*
Blake, Robert Rogers *psychologist, behavioral science company executive*
Blodgett, Warren Terrell *public affairs educator*
Bobbitt, Philip Chase *lawyer, educator, writer*
Boeker, Herbert Ralph, Jr. *urban planner*
Boggs, James Ernest *chemistry educator*
Bona, Jerry Lloyd *mathematician, educator*
Bonevac, Daniel Albert *philosopher, author*
Bonjean, Charles Michael *foundation executive, sociologist, educator*
Bordie, John George *linguistics educator*
Boswell, Gary Taggart *investor, former electronics company executive*
Box, John Harold *architect, educator, academic dean*
Boyd, Carolyn Patricia *history educator*
Boyer, Mildred Vinson *retired foreign language educator*
Brager, Walter S. *retired food products corporation executive*
Branch, Brenda Sue *library director*
Braybrooke, David *philosopher, educator*
Bredemeyer, Loretta Jeane *public relations, vocational and academic consultant*
Breen, John Edward *civil engineer, educator*
Brender, Jean Diane *epidemiologist, nurse*
Brewer, Thomas Bowman *retired university president*
Brock, James Rush *chemical engineering educator*
Brockett, Oscar Gross *theatre educator*
Bronaugh, Edwin Lee *electromagnetic compatibility engineer, consultant*
Bronson, Franklin H. *zoology educator*
Brown, Frank Beverly, IV *lawyer, accountant*
Brown, J. E. (Buster Brown) *state senator, lawyer*
Brown, Norman Donald *history educator*
Brown, Stephen Neal *computer engineer*
Buchanan, Bruce, II *political science educator*
Buerschinger, Charles Albert *state commissioner*
Bullock, Robert D. (Bob Bullock) *state legislator, lieutenant governor, lawyer*
Bunten, William Daniel *retired banker*
Burnham, Walter Dean *political science educator*
Burns, Ned Hamilton *civil engineering educator*
Bush, George W. *governor*
Byrd, Linward Tonnett *lawyer, rancher*
Caldwell, William McNeilly *insurance agent*
Calhoun, Frank Wayne *lawyer, former state legislator*
Campion, Alan *chemistry educator*
Cannon, William Bernard *retired university educator*
Cantilo, Patrick Herrera *lawyer*
Cardozier, Virgus Ray *higher education educator*
Carey, Graham Francis *engineering educator*
Carleton, Don Edward *history center administrator, educator, writer*
Carlton, Donald Morrill *research, development and engineering executive*
Carpenter, Elizabeth Sutherland *journalist, author, equal rights leader, lecturer*
Casey, James Francis *management consultant*
Castaldi, Frank James *environmental engineer, consultant*
Causey, Robert Louis *philosopher, educator, consultant*
Chavarria, Ernest Montes, Jr. *international trade, business and finance consultant, lecturer*
Churgin, Michael Jay *law educator*
Clark, Charles T(aliferro) *retired business statistics educator*
Cleaves, Peter Shurtleff *academic administrator*
Cleland, Charles Carr *psychologist, educator*
Cline, Clarence Lee *language professional*
Clinton, Sam Houston *retired judge*
Conine, Ernest *newspaper commentator, writer*
Cook, Chauncey William Wallace *retired food products company executive*
Cook, J. Rowland *lawyer*
Cooke, Carlton Lee, Jr. *mayor*
Crain, William Henry *retired curator*
Crenshaw, Ben *professional golfer*
Crosby, Alfred Worcester *history educator*
Crum, Lawrence Lee *banking educator*
Culp, George Hart *computer executive, consultant*
Culp, Joe C(arl) *electronics executive*
Cundiff, Edward William *marketing educator*
Cunningham, William Hughes *academic administrator, marketing educator*
Dalton, Caryl *school psychologist*
Dalton, Don *principal*
Dalziel, Ian William Drummond *geologist, educator, researcher*
Danielson, Wayne Allen *journalism and computer science educator*
Davis, Creswell Dean *lawyer, consultant*
Davis, David Murrel *lawyer*
Davis, Donald Gordon, Jr. *librarian, educator*
Davis, Donald Robert *nutritionist, researcher, consultant*
Davis, Edward Mott *anthropology educator and researcher*
Davis, Tony Robert *investment company executive*
Deal, Ernest Linwood, Jr. *banker*
Debold, Cynthia Ann *sculptor*
Deisler, Paul Frederick, Jr. *retired oil company executive*
Delevoryas, Theodore *botanist, educator*
Deming, David Lawson *art educator*
Denham, William Ernest, Jr. *minister*
Denius, Franklin Wofford *lawyer*
Denny, Mary Craver *state legislator, rancher*
Derounian, Steven Boghos *retired judge, lawyer*
de Wette, Frederik Willem *physics educator*
DeWitt-Morette, Cécile *physicist*
Dicus, Duane A. *physicist, educator*
Dijkstra, Edsger Wybe *computer science educator, mathematician*
Divine, Robert Alexander *history educator*
Doenges, Rudolph Conrad *finance educator*
Doluisio, James Thomas *pharmacy educator*
Doolittle, William Emery, III *geography educator*
Dorsen, Michael *physician*
Dougal, Arwin Adelbert *electrical engineer, educator*
Dougherty, John Chrysostom, III *lawyer*
Drake, Stephen Douglas *clinical psychologist, health facility administrator*
Drummond Borg, Lesley Margaret *clinical geneticist*
Dulles, John Watson Foster *history educator*
Duncombe, Raynor Lockwood *astronomer*
Durbin, Richard Louis, Sr. *healthcare admnistration consultant*
Dusansky, Richard *economist, educator*
†Eaton, David *natural resource policy studies educator*
Edwards, Wayne Forrest *paper company executive*
Elder, Patricia Anne *nursing educator, nurse midwife*
Eldredge, Linda Gaile *psychologist*
Elequin, Cleto, Jr. *retired physician*
Ellison, Samuel Porter, Jr. *geologist, educator*
Enoch, Craig Trively *state supreme court justice*
Epstein, Jeremiah Fain *anthropologist, educator*
Ersek, Robert Allen *plastic surgeon, inventor*
Erskine, James Lorenzo *physics educator*
Evans, Walter Reed *engineering executive, consultant*
Fair, Harry David *academic administrator, physicist*
Fair, James Rutherford, Jr. *chemical engineering educator, consultant*
Farrell, Edmund James *English language educator, author*
Fearing, William Kelly *art educator, artist*
Fischer, Norman, Jr. *media broker, appraiser, broadcast consultant*
Fisher, William Lawrence *geologist, educator*
Fleeger, David Clark *colon and rectal surgeon*
Folk, Robert Louis *geologist, educator*
Fonken, Gerhard Joseph *retired chemistry educator, academic administrator*
Fowler, David Wayne *architectural engineering educator*
Fox, Marye Anne *chemistry educator*
Franke, Wayne Thomas *government affairs director, lobbyist*
Franklin, Billy Joe *international higher education specialist*
Franklin, G(eorge) Charles *academic administrator*
Friedman, Alan Warren *humanities educator*
Fryxell, Greta Albrecht *marine botany educator, oceanographer*
Fults, Kenneth Wyatt *civil engineer, surveyor*
Galinsky, Gotthard Karl *classicist, educator*
Gambrell, James Bruton, III *lawyer, educator*
Gammage, Robert Alton (Bob Gammage) *lawyer*
Gangstad, John Erik *lawyer*
Gans, Carl *zoologist, educator*
Gardiner, William Cecil, Jr. *chemist, educator*
Gardner, Joan *medical, surgical nurse*
Garner, Harvey Louis *computer scientist, consultant, electrical engineering educator*
Garrido, Augie *university athletic coach*
Garwood, William Lockhart *federal judge*
Garza, Antonio O. *state official*
Gates, Charles W., Sr. *city official*
Gavenda, J(ohn) David *physicist*
Gentle, Kenneth William *physicist*
George, Walter Eugene, Jr. *architect*
Getman, Julius Gerson *law educator, lawyer*
Gibbins, Bob *lawyer*
Gibson, William Willard, Jr. *law educator*
Gilbert, Lucia Albino *psychology educator*
Gill, Clark Cyrus *retired education educator*
Gillman, Leonard *mathematician, educator*
Girling, Bettie Joyce Moore *home health executive*
Girling, Robert George William, III *business owner*
Glade, William Patton, Jr. *economics educator*
Glenn, Norval Dwight *sociologist, educator*
Gloyna, Earnest Frederick *environmental engineer, educator*
Golden, Edwin Harold *insurance company executive*
Golden, Kimberly Kay *critical care, flight nurse*
Goldstein, E. Ernest *lawyer*
Goldstein, Peggy R. *sculptor*
Golemon, Ronald Kinnan *lawyer*
Gonzalez, Raul A. *state supreme court justice*
Goodenough, John Bannister *engineering educator, research physicist*
Gould, Lewis Ludlow *historian*
Grace, James Martin *insurance company executive*
Gracy, David Bergen, II *archivist, information science educator, writer*
Graglia, Lino Anthony *lawyer, educator*
Grangaard, Daniel Robert *psychologist*
Granof, Michael H. *accounting educator*
Grant, Verne Edwin *biology educator*
Graydon, Frank Drake *retired accounting educator, university administrator*
Green, Peter Morris *classics educator, writer, translator*
Greene, John Joseph *lawyer*
Greenhill, Joe Robert *former chief justice state supreme, lawyer*
Greig, Brian Strother *lawyer*
Griffy, Thomas Alan *physics educator*
Grimm, Clayford Thomas *architectural engineer, consultant*
Guerin, John William *artist*
†Gurasich, Stephen William, Jr. *advertising executive*
Gustafsson, Lars Erik Einar *writer, educator*
Haas, Joseph Marshall *petroleum consultant*
Hale, Arnold Wayne *religious studies educator, army officer, clergyman, psychotherapist*
Hall, Beverly Adele *nursing educator*
Hamermesh, Daniel Selim *economics educator*
Hamilton, Dagmar Strandberg *lawyer, educator*
Hamilton, Robert Woodruff *law educator*
Hammer, Katherine Gonet *software company executive*
Hancock, Ian Francis (O Yanko le Redžosko) *linguistics educator*
Hardin, Dale Wayne *retired law educator*
Hardin, Sheryl Dawn *elementary education educator*
Harms, Robert Thomas *linguist, educator*
Harris, Ben M. *education educator*
Harris, Richard Lee *engineering executive, retired army officer*
Harrison, Richard Wayne *lawyer*
Hart, Roderick P. *communications educator, researcher, author*
Hatgil, Paul Peter *artist, sculptor, educator*
Hayes, Patricia Ann *university president*
Hazel, Joseph Patrick *law educator*
Hazeltine, Richard Deimel *physics educator, university institute director*
Hecht, Nathan Lincoln *state supreme court justice*
Heffley, James Dickey *nutrition counselor*
Hefner, Robert Eugene *technology management consultant*
Helburn, Isadore B. *arbitrator, mediator, educator*
Heller, Adam *chemist, researcher*
Helman, Stephen Jody *lawyer*
Henderson, George Ervin *lawyer*
Herman, Robert *physics educator*
Hester, Thomas Roy *anthropologist*
High, Timothy Griffin *artist, educator, writer*
Hill, David Wayne *geologist*
Himmelblau, David Mautner *chemical engineer*
Hinojosa-Smith, Roland *English language educator, writer*
Hixson, Elmer L. *engineering educator*
Ho, Paul Siu-Chung *physics educator*
Hodge, Ann F. *environmental company executive*
Holtzman, Wayne Harold *psychologist, educator*
Holz, Robert Kenneth *geography educator*
Hopper, Robert William *speech communication educator*
Horton, Claude Wendell *physicist, educator*
Houston, Samuel Lee *computer software company executive*
Howell, John Reid *mechanical engineering educator*
Huang, Yee-Wei *strategic analyst, chemical engineering educator*
Hubbs, Clark *zoologist, researcher*
Hudspeth, Emmett LeRoy *physicist, educator*
Huff, David L. *geography educator*
Hull, David George *aerospace engineering educator, researcher*
Hurley, Laurence Harold *medicinal chemistry educator*
Huston, Ted Laird *psychology educator*
Hutchins, Karen Leslie *psychotherapist*
Ikard, Frank Neville, Jr. *lawyer*
Ingram, Denny Ouzts, Jr. *lawyer, educator*
Inman, Bobby Ray *investor, former electronics executive*
Iscoe, Ira *psychology educator*
Ivins, Molly *columnist, writer*
Jackson, Eugene Bernard *librarian*
Jackson, William Vernon *library science and Latin American studies educator*
Jacobson, Antone Gardner *zoology educator*
Jannuzi, F. Tomasson *economics educator*
Jazayery, Mohammad Ali *foreign languages and literature educator emeritus*
Jefferys, William Hamilton, III *astronomer*
Jeffords, Edward Alan *former state attorney general*
Jeffrey, Robert Campbell *university dean*
Jennings, Coleman Alonzo *dramatics educator*
Jentz, Gaylord Adair *law educator*
Johnson, Corwin Waggoner *law educator*
Johnson, Lady Bird (Mrs. Lyndon Baines Johnson) *widow of former President of United States*
Johnson, Mildred Snowden *retired nursing educator*
Johnson, Patrick D. *human resources executive*
Johnson, Sam D. *federal judge*
Jones, William Richard *open systems product support representative*
Jordan, Terry Gilbert *geography educator*
Juricic, Davor *mechanical engineering educator*
Justiz, Manuel Jon *educator, researcher*
Katz, Michael Ray *Slavic languages educator*
Kendrick, David Andrew *economist, educator*
Kennamer, Lorrin Garfield, Jr. *retired university dean*
Kennan, Kent Wheeler *composer, educator*
Kilgore, Joe Madison *former congressman, lawyer*
Kimberlin, Sam Owen, Jr. *financial institutions consultant*
King, Robert D. *linguistics educator*
Kirk, Lynda Pounds *biofeedback therapist, neurotherapist*
Knapp, Mark Lane *communications educator, consultant*
Knight, Gary *lawyer, educator, publisher, trader*
Koen, Billy Vaughn *mechanical engineering educator*
Koepsel, Wellington Wesley *electrical engineering educator*
Kopp, Debra Lynn *manufacturing engineer, consultant*
Koros, William John *chemical engineering educator*
Kozmetsky, George *computer science educator*
Krishna, Hari J. *engineer*
Lagowski, J(oseph) J(ohn) *chemist*
LaGrone, Alfred Hall *electrical engineering educator*
Lam, Simon Shin-Sing *computer science educator*
Lamb, Jamie Parker, Jr. *mechanical engineer, educator*
Lariviere, Richard Wilfred *Asian studies educator, consultant*
Larkam, Peter Howard *electric utility executive, entrepreneur*
Larson, Kermit Dean *accounting educator*
Lary, Banning Kent *video producer, publisher*
Laycock, Harold Douglas *law educator, writer*
Lehmann, Ruth Preston Miller *literature educator*
Lehmann, Winfred Philipp *linguistics educator*
Leiden, Carl *political scientist, educator*
Le Maistre, Charles Aubrey *internist, epidemiologist, educator*
Levy, Michael Richard *publishing executive*
Lewis, Nancy Louine Lambert *school counselor*
Little, Emily Browning *architect*
Livingston, William Samuel *university administrator, political scientist*
Lochridge, Lloyd Pampell, Jr. *lawyer*
Loehlin, John Clinton *psychologist, educator*
Lopreato, Joseph *sociology educator, author*
Louis, William Roger *historian, educator, editor*
Luedecke, William Henry *mechanical engineer, company executive*
Lundelius, Ernest Luther, Jr. *vertebrate paleontologist, educator*
Mackey, Louis Henry *philosophy educator*
Mackovic, John *college football coach, athletic director*
Maloney, Frank *judge, lawyer*
Manosevitz, Martin *psychologist*
Mansfield, Stephen W. *judge*
Manson, Lewis Auman *energy research executive*
Mark, Hans Michael *aerospace engineering educator, physicist*
Martin, David Hugh *private investigator, business executive, writer*
Martin, Frederick Noel *audiology educator*
Mathias, Reuben Victor (Vic Mathias) *real estate executive, investor*
Matthews, Jay Arlon, Jr. *publisher, editor*
Mautz, Karl Emerson *engineering executive*
Mauzy, Oscar Holcombe *lawyer, retired state supreme court justice*
Maxwell, Arthur Eugene *oceanographer, marine geophysicist, educator*
Mayer, Susan Martin *art educator*
Mayes, Wendell Wise, Jr. *broadcasting company executive*
Mc Carthy, John Edward *bishop*
McCormick, Michael Jerry *judge*
McDaniel, Myra Atwell *lawyer, former state official*
Mc Donald, Stephen Lee *economics educator*
McFadden, Dennis *experimental psychology educator*
McGinnis, Charles Irving *civil engineer*
Mc Ketta, John J., Jr. *chemical engineering educator*
Mc Kinney, Michael Whitney *trade association executive*
Meacham, Standish *historian, educator*
Megaw, Robert Neill Ellison *English educator*
Mersky, Roy Martin *law educator, librarian*
Metcalfe, Tom Brooks *chemical engineering educator*
Meyers, Lawrence Edward *judge*
Michener, James Albert *author*
Middleton, Christopher *Germanic languages and literature educator*
Middleton, Harry Joseph *library administrator*
Miller, John Eddie *lawyer*
Misra, Jayadev *computer science educator*
Moag, Rodney Frank *language educator, country music singer*
Mohrmann, Leonard Edward, Jr. *chemist, chemical engineer*
Montgomery, William J. *finance company executive*
Moore, Rebecca Ann Rucker *marketing executive*
Morales, Dan *state attorney general*
Morgante, John-Paul *state government training administrator*
Moses, Mike *commissioner*
Moss, Bill Ralph *lawyer, publisher*
Mullen, Ron *insurance company executive*
Mullenix, Linda Susan *lawyer, educator*
Mullins, Charles Brown *physician, academic administrator*
Nation, Floyd Reuben *lawyer*
Nelson, Steven Douglas *construction company executive*
Nevola, Roger Paul *lawyer*
Newton, Charles Chartier *architect*
Nguyen, Truc Chinh *analytical chemist*
Nichols, Steven Parks *mechanical engineer, university official*
Northington, David Knight, III *research center director, botanist, educator*
Nowlin, James Robertson *federal judge*
Oram, Robert W. *library administrator*
Owen, Priscilla Richman *judge*
Painter, Theophilus Shickel, Jr. *physician*
Painton, Russell Elliott *lawyer, mechanical engineer*

Papadakis, Myron Philip lawyer, educator, pilot
Paredes, Americo English language educator
Pate, Jacqueline Hail retired data processing company executive
Paul, Donald Ross chemical engineer, educator
Payne, Eugene Edgar insurance company executive
Payne, John Ross rare books and archives appraisal consulting company executive, library science educator
Payne, Tyson Elliott, Jr. retired insurance executive
Perkins, Richard Burle, II chemical engineer, international consultant
Peterson, Robert Allen marketing educator
Phelps, Gerry Charlotte economist, minister
Phillips, Frances Marie history educator
Phillips, Thomas Royal judge
Pickens, Franklin Ace lawyer
†Pingree, Dianne sociologist, educator, mediator
Polomé, Edgar Charles foreign language and linguistics educator
Pope, Andrew Jackson, Jr. (Jack Pope) retired judge
Pope, Ingrid Bloomquist sculptor, lecturer, poet
Pope, Marvin Hoyle language educator, writer
Poulsen, Lawrence LeRoy research scientist
Preeg, William Edward oil company executive
Prentice, Norman Macdonald clinical psychologist
Probus, Michael Maurice, Jr. lawyer
Rabago, Karl Roger lawyer
Ragsdale, Keith Ellen nurse, educator, administrator
Raina, Rajesh computer engineer
Rascoe, Paul Stephen librarian, researcher
Ray, Cread L., Jr. retired state supreme court justice
Reavley, Thomas Morrow federal judge
Reed, Lester James biochemist, educator
Reeves, Dianne L. artist
Reid, Jackson Brock psychologist, educator
Rentz, Tamara Holmes software consultant
Rhyne, Vernon Thomas, III electrical engineer, consultant
Rich, John Martin humanities educator, researcher
Richards, Ann Willis former governor
Richards-Kortum, Rebecca Rae biomedical engineering educator
Rider, Brian Clayton lawyer
Roach, James Robert retired political science educator
Robertson, Jack Clark accounting educator
Rogers, Lorene Lane university president emeritus
Rostow, Walt Whitman economist, educator
Roueche, John Edward, II education educator, leadership program director
Royal, Darrell K. university official, former football coach
Ruud, Millard Harrington former legal association administrator, retired educator
Rylander, Henry Grady, Jr. mechanical engineering educator
Sager, Thomas William statistics research administrator
Sanchez, Isaac Cornelius chemical engineer, educator
Sandberg, Irwin Walter electrical and computer engineering educator
Sansom, Andrew federal agency administrator
Sawyer, Margo Lucy artist, educator
Schapery, Richard Allan engineering educator
Schechter, Robert Samuel chemical engineer, educator
Schmandt-Besserat, Denise archaeologist, educator
Schmidt, Philip S. mechanical engineering educator
Schmitt, Karl Michael retired political scientist
Schulz, Russell Eugene musician, educator, composer
Schulze, Eric William lawyer, legal publications editor, publisher
Science, Carroll Thomas chemical engineer
Seung, Thomas Kaehao philosophy educator
Shapiro, David L. lawyer
Shapiro, Sander Wolf lawyer
Sharir, Yacov artistic director, choreographer
Shaw, James computer systems analyst
Shipley, George Corless political consultant
Simpson, Beryl Brintnall botany educator
Sims, Robert Barry lawyer
Smith, Alfred Goud anthropologist, educator
Smith, Todd Malcolm political consultant
Snell, Esmond Emerson biochemist
Sparks, Sam federal judge
Speck, Lawrence W. architect
†Spence, Roy advertising executive
Spertus, Philip investment company executive
Spielman, Barbara Helen New editor, consultant
Staley, Thomas Fabian language professional, academic administrator
Starr, Richard Cawthon botany educator
Steinfink, Hugo chemical engineering educator
Stephen, John Erle lawyer, consultant
Stewart, Kent Kallam analytical biochemistry educator
Stice, James Edward chemical engineer, educator
Stone, Leon banker
Stoner, James Lloyd retired foundation executive, clergyman
Straiton, Archie Waugh electrical engineering educator
Strauser, Robert Wayne lawyer
Streetman, Ben Garland electrical engineering educator
Sturdevant, Wayne Alan computer-based training development administrator
Sturley, Michael F. law educator
Sullivan, Teresa Ann law and sociology educator, academic administrator
Sutherland, William Owen Sheppard English language educator
Sutton, Harry Eldon geneticist, educator
Sutton, John F., Jr. law educator, university dean, lawyer
Swartzlander, Earl Eugene, Jr. engineering educator, former electronics company executive
Swinney, Harry Leonard physics educator
Szebehely, Victor G. aeronautical engineer
Taber, Patrick E. computer programmer
Tapley, Byron Dean aerospace engineer, educator
Teague, Hyman Faris former publishing company executive
Temple, Larry Eugene lawyer
Tesar, Delbert machine systems and robotics educator, researcher, manufacturing consultant
Thiessen, Delbert Duane psychologist
Thomajan, Robert lawyer, management and financial consultant
Thornton, Joseph Scott research institute executive, materials scientist
Thurston, George Butte mechanical and biomedical engineering educator
Todd, Bruce M. mayor
Todd, William Burton English language and literature educator
Trafton, Laurence Munro astronomer
Trevino, Jerry Rosalez secondary school principal
Tucker, Richard Lee civil engineer, educator
Turner, Billie Lee botanist, educator
Turner, Sylvester state legislator, lawyer
Turney, James Edward computer scientist
Tyler, Noel geological researcher and educator
Tyler, Ronnie Curtis historian
Uhlenbeck, Karen Keskulla mathematician, educator
Vande Hey, James Michael corporate executive, former air force officer
Velz, John William literature educator
Vishniac, Ethan Tecumseh astronomy educator
Vliet, Gary Clark mechanical engineering educator
Vykukal, Eugene Lawrence wholesale drug company executive
Wadlington, Warwick Paul English language educator
Wahlberg, Philip Lawrence former bishop
Walker, James Roy microbiologist
Walls, Carl Edward, Jr. communications company official
Walton, Charles Michael civil engineering educator
Warlick, Charles Henry mathematician/computer science educator
Watson, Elizabeth Marion protective services official
Weddington, Sarah Ragle lawyer, educator
Wehring, Bernard William nuclear engineering educator
Weinberg, Louise law educator, author
Weintraub, Russell Jay lawyer, educator
Weintraub, Sidney economist, educator
Weismann, Donald Leroy art educator, artist, filmmaker, writer
Welch, Ashley James engineering educator
Wellborn, Olin Guy, III law educator
Welsch, Glenn Albert accounting educator
Werbow, Stanley Newman language educator
Werner, Gerhard pharmacologist, psychoanalyst, educator
West, Glenn Edward business organization executive
Westbrook, Jay Lawrence law educator
Wheeler, John Craig astrophysicist, writer
Wheeler, Marshall Ralph zoologist, educator
Whitbread, Thomas Bacon English educator, author
White, John Michael chemistry educator
White, Michael Lee lawyer
Williams, Mary Pearl judge, lawyer
Willson, C. Grant chemistry educator, engineering educator
Wilson, James William lawyer
Winegar, Albert Lee computer systems company executive
Winters, J. Sam lawyer, federal government official
Wolf, Harold Arthur finance educator
Woodson, Herbert Horace retired electrical engineering educator
Worthing, Carol Marie minister
Wright, Charles Alan law educator, author
Wright, Stephen Gailord civil engineering educator, consultant
Young, Harrison, II software development and marketing executive
Young, Phyllis Casselman music educator
Young, William David computer scientist
Yudof, Mark G. law educator, academic administrator
Ziegler, Daniel Martin chemistry educator
Zimmerman, Louis Seymour lawyer

### Baird
Rodenberger, Charles Alvard aerospace engineer, consultant

### Barker
Atchley, Daniel Gene business executive

### Bartonville
Spies, Jacob John health care executive

### Bastrop
Shurley, Jay Talmadge psychiatrist, medical educator, administrator, behavioral sciences researcher, polar explorer, author, genealogist

### Bay City
Aylin, Elizabeth Twist Pabst real estate broker, developer

### Baytown
Gardner, Kerry Ann librarian
Leiper, Robert Duncan protective services official
Mendelson, Robert Allen polymer scientist, rheologist
Percoco, Thelma Ann nurse, educator
Williams, Drew Davis surgeon

### Beaumont
Allums, James A. retired cardiovascular surgeon
†Brejot, John radio station executive
Brentlinger, William Brock college dean
Brooks, Jack Bascom congressman
Cobb, Howell federal judge
Coe, (Matchett) Herring sculptor
Fisher, Joseph Jefferson federal judge
Gagne, Mary secondary school principal
Galante, Joseph A. bishop
Gray, Enid Maurine city official, director of libraries
Lee, Shung-Man nephrologist
Long, Alfred B. retired oil company executive, consultant
Lord, Evelyn Marlin former mayor
Lozano, Jose nephrologist
Marshall, Nina Colleen Clubb elementary school educator
McGary, Betty Winstead minister, counselor, individual, marriage, and family therapist
Phan, Tâm Thanh medical educator, psychotherapist, consultant, researcher
Scofield, Louis M., Jr. lawyer
Smith, David Ryan museum director
Smith, Floyd Rodenbeck retired utilities executive
Stansel, James W. agricultural research administrator
Tucker, Gary Wilson nurse educator

### Bedford
Harrison, Jerry Ann nursing administration
Lewis, Frank Leroy electrical engineer, educator, researcher
Lieber, David Leslie journalist

### Bedias
Williamson, Norma Beth adult education educator

### Bellaire
Haywood, Theodore Joseph physician, educator
Lancaster, Carroll Townes, Jr. business executive
Mayo, Clyde Calvin organizational psychologist, educator
Moore, Pat Howard engineering and construction company executive
Mote, Marie Therese reference librarian
Skaggs, Arline Dotson elementary school educator
Smeal, Janis Lea operating room nurse, health facility administrator
Soffar, William Douglas lawyer
Thorne, Lawrence George allergist, immunologist, pediatrician
Weyandt, Linda Jane anesthetist
Wisch, David John structural engineer

### Bellville
Dittert, J. Lee, Jr. lawyer

### Belton
Bumpus, Floyd David, Jr. microcomputer analyst
Christoff, Beth Graves artist
Ham, Clarence Edward university administrator
Harrison, Benjamin Leslie retired army officer
Parker, Bobby Eugene, Sr. college president
Shoemaker, Robert Morin retired army officer, county government official
Wallace, Aliceanne civic worker

### Bertram
Albert, Susan Wittig writer, English educator

### Big Spring
Fryrear, Donald William agricultural engineer
Morrison, Walton Stephen lawyer
Simmons, Lorna Womack elementary school educator

### Blanco
Finley, James Edward independent oil operator

### Boerne
Goode, Bobby Claude retired secondary education educator, writer
Mitchelhill, James Moffat civil engineer
Morton, Michael Ray retail company consultant
Price, John Randolph writer
Wittmer, James Frederick preventive medicine physician, educator

### Borger
Schneck, Gary Alan securities broker

### Brenham
Moorman, Robert Lawson real estate appraiser and broker
Pipes, Paul Ray county commissioner

### Brooks AFB
Convertino, Victor Anthony physiologist, educator, research scientist, civil servant
Cox, Ann Bruger biological scientist, editor, researcher
Monk, Richard Francis air force officer, health care administrator
Olsen, Richard Galen biomedical engineer, researcher
Patterson, John C. clinical psychology researcher
Wilde, James Dale archaeologist, educator

### Brownfield
†Jany, Richard Wayne railroad executive
Moore, Bradford L. lawyer

### Brownsville
Boze, Betsy Vogel university dean, marketing educator
Cohen, Barry Mendel financial executive, educator
Farst, Don David zoo director, veterinarian
Fitzpatrick, John J. bishop
French, Bertha Doris medical, surgical and geriatrics nurse
Garza, Reynaldo G. federal judge
Pena, Raymundo Joseph bishop
Santa-Coloma, Bernardo secondary school educator, counselor
Tijerina, Raul Martin physics and mathematics educator
Vela, Filemon B. federal judge

### Brownwood
Chapman, Dan G. minister
DeHay, Jerry Marvin business educator

### Bryan
Bear, Robert Emerson elementary education educator
Branson, Robert Earl marketing economist
Dirks, Kenneth Ray pathologist, medical educator, army officer
Hoskins, Earl R., Jr. geophysics department dean
Hubert, Frank William Rene retired university system chancellor
Kellett, William Hiram, Jr. retired architect, engineer, educator
Lusas, Edmund William food processing research executive
Lynch, Thomas Francis archeologist, educator
Owens, Harold B. former state agency consultant
Röller, Herbert Alfred biology and medical scientist, educator
Samson, Charles Harold, Jr. (Car Samson) retired engineering educator, consultant
Steelman, Frank (Sitley) lawyer
Sulik, Edwin (Pete Sulik) health care administrator

### Bullard
Buckner, John Hugh retired real estate broker, retired construction company executive, retired air force officer

### Burleson
Johnstone, Deborah Blackmon lawyer
Prior, Boyd Thelman management consultant
Robin, Clara Nell (Claire Robin) English language educator

### Burnet
Gomes, Norman Vincent retired industrial engineer

### Bushland
Howell, Terry Allen agricultural engineer
Unger, Paul Walter soil scientist

### Candelaria
Chambers, Johnnie Lois (Tucker) elementary school educator, rancher

### Canton
White, Jeffery Howell lawyer

### Canyon
Long, Russell Charles academic administrator
Roper, Beryl Cain writer, publisher, retired library director

### Canyon Lake
Phelan, Charlotte Robertson journalist, book critic

### Carrollton
Ali, Odeh Said petroleum geologist
Bentley, Clarence Edward savings and loan executive
Foster, William Edwin (Bill Foster) nonprofessional basketball coach
Grimes, Mary Woodworth special educational consultant
Heath, Jinger L. cosmetics executive
Hulbert, Paul William, Jr. paper, lumber company executive
Kelly, Ralph Whitley emergency physician, health facility administrator
Last, Susan Walker training developer
Maher, Sheila secondary school principal
Miller, Marvin Edward building materials company executive
Nichols, Gerry Lynn occupational therapist
Schulz, Richard Burkart electrical engineer, consultant
Varner, Bruce H., Jr. fire department official, educator
Withrow, Lucille Monnot nursing home administrator

### Castroville
Strickland, Sandra Jean Heinrich nursing educator

### Cedar Hill
Hickman, Traphene Parramore library director, storyteller, library and library building consultant
Kilgore, Janice Kay musician, educator

### Cedar Park
Guzma'n, Ana Margarita university administrator
Koop, Tobey Kent research consultant, educational psychologist
Lam, Pauline Poha library director

### Chandler
Sanders, Sharon Raye (Sharri Sanders) telecommunications executive, educator

### Channelview
Courville, Susan Kay secondary education educator

### Childress
Mayes, Ila Laverne minister

### Chillicothe
Brock, Helen Rachel McCoy retired mental health and community health nurse

### Cibolo
Newsom, Melvin Max retired research company executive

### Cleburne
MacLean, John Ronald lawyer
Urban, Carlyle Woodrow retired lawyer

### Coleman
Needham, Judy Len artist, art educator

### College Station
Adkisson, Perry Lee university system chancellor
Anderson, Aubrey Lee oceanographer, educator
Anderson, Duwayne Marlo earth and polar scientist, university administrator
Armstrong, Robert Beall physiologist
Arnowitt, Richard Lewis physics educator, researcher
Baskharone, Erian Aziz mechanical and aerospace engineering educator
Bass, George Fletcher archaeology educator
Beaver, Bonnie Veryle veterinarian, educator
Berg, Robert Raymond geologist, educator
Berner, Leo De Witte, Jr. retired oceanographer
Berthold, Dennis Alfred English language educator
Bhattacharyya, Shankar Prashad electrical engineer, educator
Black, Samuel Harold microbiology and immunology educator
Blakley, George Robert, Jr. mathematician, computer scientist
Bond, Jon Roy political science educator
Borlaug, Norman Ernest agricultural scientist
Bowen, Ray Morris academic administrator, engineering educator
Bryant, Vaughn Motley, Jr. botany and anthropology educator
Buth, Carl Eugene civil engineer
Calhoun, John C., Jr. academic administrator
Cannon, Garland English language educator
Carpenter, Delbert Stanley educational administration educator
Chiou, George Chung-Yih pharmacologist, educator
Christiansen, James Edward agricultural educator
Chui, Charles K. mathematics educator
Cocanougher, Arthur Benton university dean, former business administration educator
Cochran, Robert Glenn nuclear engineering educator
Conway, Dwight Colbur chemistry educator
Copp, James Harris sociologist, educator
Cotton, Frank Albert chemist, educator
Davenport, Manuel Manson philosophy educator
Dethloff, Henry Clay history educator
Douglas, Ronald George mathematician
Duce, Robert Arthur atmospheric chemist, university administrator
Duff, Michael James physicist
Ehsani, Mehrdad (Mark Ehsani) electrical engineering educator, consultant

Erlandson, David Alan education administration educator
Ewing, Richard Edward mathematics, chemical and petroleum engineering educator
Fackler, John Paul, Jr. chemistry educator
Feagin, Clarence Elmer, Jr. microbiologist
Fedorchik, Bette Joy Winter foreign language professional
Fisher, Richard Forrest soils educator
Fletcher, Leroy Stevenson mechanical engineer, educator
Furubotn, Eirik Grundtvig economics educator
Godbey, Luther David architectural and engineering executive
Goodman, David Wayne research chemist
Greenhut, Melvin Leonard economist, educator
Gunn, Clare Alward travel consultant, writer, retired educator
Haden, Clovis Roland university administrator, engineering educator
Hall, Kenneth Richard chemical engineering educator, consultant
Hall, Timothy C. biology educator, consultant
Hardy, John Christopher physicist
Harvey, Roger Bruce veterinary toxicologist, researcher
Heidelbaugh, Norman Dale veterinary medicine educator, consultant, author, inventor
Herbich, John Bronislaw engineering educator
Hiler, Edward Allan agricultural and engineering educator
Holland, Charles Donald chemical engineer, educator
Isdale, Charles Edwin chemical engineer
Kennedy, Robert Alan educational administrator
Kern-Foxworth, Marilyn Louise journalism educator
Knight, James Allen psychiatrist, educator
Knutson, Ronald Dale economist, educator, academic adminstrator
Kohel, Russell James geneticist
Kubacak, Lawrence Don energy efficient design and construction company executive
Kunze, Otto Robert retired agricultural engineering educator
Kuo, Lih medical educator
Kuo, Way industrial engineer, researcher
Laane, Jaan chemistry educator
Lee, William John petroleum engineering educator, consultant
Lowery, Lee Leon, Jr. civil engineer
Luepnitz, Roy Robert psychologist, consultant, small business owner, entrepreneur
Lytton, Robert Leonard civil engineer, educator
Manning, Walter Scott accountant, former educator, consultant
Martell, Arthur Earl chemistry educator
Mathewson, Christopher Colville engineering geologist, educator
McCrady, James David veterinarian, educator
McIntyre, John Armin physics educator
McIntyre, Peter Mastin physicist, educator
Milford, Murray Hudson soil science educator
Monroe, Haskell M., Jr. university educator
Nachman, Ronald James research chemist
Nance, Joseph Milton history educator
Natowitz, Joseph B. chemistry educator, research administrator
Neff, Ray Quinn electric power educator, consultant
Neill, William Harold, Jr. biological science educator and researcher
O'Connor, Rod chemist, inventor
Ogburn, Wayne Lee health science facility administrator
Page, Robert Henry engineer, educator, researcher
Painter, John Hoyt electrical engineer
Parzen, Emanuel statistical scientist
Patton, Alton DeWitt electrical engineering educator, consultant, research administrator
Perrone, Ruth Ellyn university administrator
Pierce, Kenneth Ray veterinary medicine educator
Pitt, Woodrow Wilson, Jr. engineering educator
Plum, Charles Walden retired business executive and educator
Prescott, John Mack biochemist, retired university administrator
Rabins, Michael Jerome mechanical engineer, educator
Reddell, Donald Lee agricultural engineer
Reed, Raymond Deryl architect
Rezak, Richard geology and oceanography educator
Richardson, Herbert Heath mechanical engineer, educator, institute director
Roeseler, Wolfgang Guenther Joachim city planner
Rosberg, David William plant sciences educator
Rotell, Thomas M. publishing executive
Sadoski, Mark Christian education educator
Sanchez, David Alan mathematics educator
Scott, Alastair Ian chemistry educator
Sis, Raymond Francis veterinarian, educator
Slocum, R.C. university athletic coach
Smith, Roberta Hawking plant physiologist
Solecki, R. Stefan anthropologist, educator
Stanton, Robert James, Jr. geologist, educator
Steffy, John Richard nautical archaeologist, educator
Stewart, Robert Henry oceanographer, educator
Stipanovic, Robert Douglas chemist, researcher
Summers, Max (Duanne) entomologist, scientist, educator
Toler, Ray Edward conductor, band director
Unterberger, Betty Miller history educator, writer
Urbanik, Thomas, II research civil engineer
Vandiver, Frank Everson institute administrator, former university president, author, educator
Van Riper, Paul Pritchard political science educator
Way, James Leong pharmacology and toxicology educator
Weese, John Augustus mechanical engineer, educator
Wendler, Walter V. dean
Wichern, Dean William business educator
Wild, James Robert biochemistry and genetics educator
Wilding, Lawrence Paul pedology educator, soil science consultant
Wilson, Don Whitman archivist, historian
Woodcock, David Geoffrey architect, educator
Wu, Guoyao animal science, nutrition and physiology educator
Yao, James Tsu-Ping civil engineer
Yeung, Albert Tak-Chung civil engineering educator

## Colleyville
Driscoll, Diana Sanderson optometrist, consultant
Johnson, Zoe Ann accounting executive
Love, Ben Howard retired organization executive
Pavony, William H. retail executive
Thompson, James Richard human resources management consultant

## Comanche
Droke, Edna Faye elementary school educator

## Commerce
Grimshaw, James Albert, Jr. English language educator
Linck, Charles Edward, Jr. English language educator
Lutz, Frank Wenzel education administration educator
Morris, Jerry Dean academic administrator
Perry, Thomas Amherst English literature and language educator
Schmidt, L. Lee, Jr. university official

## Conroe
Bruce, Rachel Mary Condon nurse practitioner
Cabaret, Joseph Ronald defense company executive
Corley, Donna Jean education educator, language arts educator
Little, Don Barron clergyman
Westmoreland, Thomas Delbert, Jr. chemist

## Converse
Droneburg, Nancy Marie geriatrics nurse
Vontur, Ruth Poth elementary school educator

## Coppell
Auerbach, Ernest Sigmund lawyer, company executive, writer
Miiller, Susan Diane artist
Minyard, Liz food products executive
Smothermon, Peggi Sterling middle school educator

## Copperas Cove
Barnes, Sara Lynn school system administrator
Townsend, Linda Ladd mental health nurse
Wagner, Susan Elizabeth secondary school educator
Wright, David Ray secondary school educator

## Corpus Christi
Allison, Joan Kelly music educator, pianist
Appel, Truman Frank surgeon
Bateman, John Roger investment holding company executive
Berkebile, Charles Alan geology educator, hydrogeology researcher
Berryhill, Henry Lee, Jr. geologist
Bonilla, Tony lawyer
Branscomb, Harvie, Jr. lawyer
Bucklin, Leonard Herbert lawyer
Clark, Joyce Naomi Johnson nurse
Cole, June Robertson psychotherapist
Cox, William Andrew cardiovascular thoracic surgeon
Cutlip, Randall Brower retired psychologist, college president emeritus
de Wys, Egbert Christiaan geochemist
Doty, James Edward pastor, psychologist
Early, William James education educator
Eddleman, Bobby Ross agriculturist, economist
Fancher, Rick lawyer
Fender, Freddy (Baldemar Huerta) singer
French, Dorris Towers Bryan volunteer
Furgason, Robert Roy university president, engineering educator
Gracida, Rene Henry bishop
Haas, Paul Raymond petroleum company executive
Hall, Ralph Carr lawyer, real estate consultant
Hamilton, Paul Martin psychologist
Harte, Edward Holmead retired newspaper publisher
Head, Hayden Wilson, Jr. district judge
Heinz, Walter Ernst Edward retired chemical executive
House, David Augusta newspaper editor
Jack, Janis Graham judge
Kane, Sam meat company executive
Kenna, John Thomas priest
Lim, Alexander Rufasta neurologist, clinical investigator, educator, writer
Long, Ralph Stewart clinical psychologist
Miller, Carroll Gerard, Jr. (Gerry Miller) lawyer
Morales, John Mark cardiac surgeon
Parker, Roy Denver, Jr. entomologist
Paulson, Bernard Arthur oil company executive, consultant
Pérez-Gonzalez, Esmeralda principal, educator
Pinkel, Donald Paul pediatrician
Pivonka, Leonard Daniel priest
Rhodes, Mary mayor
Schake, Lowell Martin animal science educator
Sharp, John Lewis oil industry executive, geologist
†Shook, Donald Ray health care administrator
Sisley, Nina Mae physician, public health officer
Snouffer, Nancy Kendall English and reading educator
Sommers, Maxine Marie Bridget writer, educator, publisher
Trybul, Theodore Nicholan education educator
Turner, Elizabeth Adams Noble (Betty Turner) healthcare executive, former mayor
Ullberg, Kent Jean sculptor
Umfleet, Lloyd Truman electrical engineering technology educator
Walraven, Joseph William (Bill Walraven) writer, publisher
Ward, Harold William Cowper oncologist, educator
Wood, James Allen lawyer
Wooster, Robert history educator
Worden, Elizabeth Ann artist, comedy writer, singer

## Corsicana
Dyer, James Mason, Jr. investment company executive
Roberts, Nancy Mize retired librarian, composer, pianist

## Crane
Dohlman, Dennis Raye oil company executive

## Crockett
LaClair, Patricia Marie physical education director, medical technician

## Crosby
Cole, Edith Fae dietitian, consultant
Ohsol, Ernest Osborne consulting chemical engineer

## Crowell
Binnion, John Edward education educator

## Crystal Beach
Dunn, Glennis Mae writer, lyricist

## Cypress
Day, Robert Michael oil company executive
Hamilton, Phyllis principal

## Daisetta
Ursprung, Deborah Lynn special education educator

## Dallas
Abney, Frederick Sherwood lawyer
Acker, Rodney lawyer
Agnich, Richard John lawyer, electronics company executive
Allen, Terry Devereux urologist, educator
Allison, Stephen Galender broadcast executive
Anders, John newspaper columnist
Anderson, Barbara McComas lawyer
Anderson, E. Karl lawyer
Anderson, Robert Theodore music educator, organist
Anderson, Ron Joe hospital administrator, physician, educator
Anderson-Mann, Shelley N. institutional review specialist
Anglin, Michael Williams lawyer
Aranas, Noel Bautista systems analyst, consultant
Ardoin, John Louis music editor
Armour, James Lott lawyer
Arnold, George Lawrence advertising company executive
Ash, Mary Kay cosmetics company executive
Atkinson, Bill artistic director
Augur, Marilyn Hussman distribution executive
Austin, Ann Sheree lawyer
Babcock, Charles Lynde, IV lawyer
Baggett, W. Mike lawyer
Bailon, Gilbert newspaper editor
Baker, Robert Woodward airline executive
Barbee, Linton E. lawyer
Barnes, Robert Vertreese, Jr. masonry contractor executive
Barnett, Barry Craig lawyer
Barnett, Patricia Ann public relations professional
Barnett, Peter Ralph health science facility administrator, dentist
Barnhouse, Ruth Tiffany priest, psychiatrist
Bartlett, Richard Chalkley cosmetics executive, writer
Bashour, Fouad Anis cardiology educator
Bass, John Fred lawyer
†Beard, Alfred (Butch) former basketball player, former commentator
Beck, Abe Jack retired business executive, retired air force officer
Beck, Luke Ferrell Wilson insurance specialist
Behrens, Richard John real estate executive
Bell, John Lewis McCulloch manufacturing executive
Bell-Tolliver, LaVerne social worker
Benge, Raymond Doyle, Jr. astronomy educator
Benn, Douglas Frank information technology and computer science executive
Berkeley, Marvin H. management educator, former university dean
Bersano, Bob newspaper editor
Betts, Dianne Connally economist, educator
Beuttenmuller, Rudolf William lawyer
Bickel, John W., II lawyer
Birkeland, Bryan Collier lawyer
Bishop, Bryan Edwards lawyer
Bishop, Gene Herbert corporate executive
Blachly, Jack Lee lawyer
Blackistone, Kevin sports columnist
Blakeley, Kellie Elder accountant, small business owner
Blattner, Wolfram Georg Michael meteorologist
Blau, Charles William lawyer, former government official
Blessen, Karen Alyce free-lance illustrator, designer
Blessing, Edward Warfield petroleum company executive
Bliss, Robert Harms lawyer
Blomquist, Carl Gunnar cardiologist
Blount, Charles William, III lawyer
Blow, Steve newspaper columnist
Blue, J(ohn) Ronald evangelical mission executive
Blumenthal, Karen newspaper executive
Bockstruck, Lloyd DeWitt librarian
†Bonelli, Anthony Eugene former university dean
Bonesio, Woodrow Michael lawyer
Bonney, Samuel Robert lawyer
Bonte, Frederick James radiology educator, physician
Boone, Oliver Kiel lawyer
Boren, Bryant C., Jr. lawyer
Brachman, Malcolm K. oil company executive
†Bradford, William Edward oil field equipment manufacturing company executive
Bradley, John Andrew hospital management company executive
Bradshaw, Lillian Moore retired library director
Brand, Julia Marie occupational health nurse
Brin, Royal Henry, Jr. lawyer
Britton, Wesley Alan English language educator
Bromberg, Henri Louie, Jr. lawyer
Bromberg, John E. lawyer
Brooks, E. R. (Dick Brooks) utility company executive
Brooks, James Elwood geologist, educator
Brown, A.C., Jr. electrical engineer
Brown, Benjamin A. gas, oil industry executive
Brown, Gloria Vasquez banker
Brown, Michael Stuart geneticist, educator, administrator
Brown, Ronald Lee lawyer
Brown, Stephen Bryan real estate editor
Browne, Richard Harold statistician, consultant
Bruene, Warren Benz electronic engineer
Bryant, L. Gerald health care administrator
Buchmeyer, Jerry federal judge
Bucy, J. Fred, Jr. retired electronics company executive
Bumpas, Stuart Maryman lawyer
Bunker, Anthony Louis health science executive
Burke, William Temple, Jr. lawyer
Burlingame, David Hartley software development manager
Burns, Scott columnist
Burnside, John Wayne medical educator, university official
Busbee, Kline Daniel, Jr. law educator, lawyer
Buzzell, Barbara Feder public relations executive
Cain, David state senator, lawyer
Campfield, Regis William law educator
Campillo, Fred Grover naval officer
Cansler, Denise Ann real estate executive
Carlton, Dean lawyer
Carman, George Henry retired physician
Carson, Virginia Hill oil and gas executive
Carter, Donald J. wholesale distribution, manufacturing executive
†Carty, Donald J. airline company executive
Cavanagh, Harrison Dwight ophthalmic surgeon
Cave, Skip company executive
Chae, Don B. judge, educator, lawyer
Champion, Michael Ray health facility administrator
Cheney, Dick (Richard Bruce Cheney) former secretary of defense, former congressman
Cherryholmes, James Gilbert construction consultant, real estate agent
Cirilo, Amelia Medina educational consultant, supervisor
Cissik, John Henry medical research director, consultant
Clark, Robert Murel, Jr. lawyer
Cleveland, Linda Joyce delivery service executive
Click, Bennie R. protective services official
Cline, Bobby James insurance company executive
Closser, Patrick Denton radio evangelist, artist
Cloud, Robert Royce surgeon
Cochran, George Calloway, III retired banker
Cochran, Kendall Pinney economics educator
Coggins, Paul Edward, Jr. prosecutor
Cohn, Linkie Seltzer professional speaker, author
Coldwell, Philip Edward financial consultant
Coleman, Robert Winston lawyer
Collins, Michael James investment company executive
Comini, Alessandra art historian, educator
Compton, Robert D. newspaper editor
Conant, Allah B., Jr. lawyer
Contreras, Israel manufacturing executive
Cook, Gary Raymond university president, clergyman
Copley, Edward Alvin lawyer
Cottingham, Jennifer Jane city official
Countryman, Edward Francis historian, educator
Courtney, Constance E. lawyer
Cowart, T(homas) David lawyer
Cox, James William newspaper executive
Cox, Richard D. lawyer
Cox, Rody P(owell) medical educator, internist
Crain, Christina Melton lawyer
Crain, Gayla Campbell lawyer
Crain, John Walter historian
Creany, Cathleen Annette television station executive
Creel, Luther Edward, III lawyer
Cromartie, Eric Ross lawyer
Crotty, Robert Bell lawyer
Crowley, James Worthington retired lawyer, business consultant, investor
Cruikshank, Thomas Henry energy services and engineering executive
Cullum, Colin Munro psychiatry and neurology educator
Cummings, Brian Thomas public relations company executive
Cummins, James Duane correspondant, media executive
Curran, Geoffrey Michael lawyer
Dalton, Harry Jirou, Jr. (Jerry Dalton) public relations executive
Davis, Clarice McDonald lawyer
†Davis, Gregory T. radio station executive
Davis, Patricia Ann school system administrator
Davis, Patricia M. literacy educator
Dawson, Edward Joseph merger and acquisition executive
Decherd, Robert William newspaper and broadcasting executive
Dedman, Robert Henry sales executive
Demarest, Sylvia M. lawyer
Denur, Jack Boaz scientific researcher, scientific consultant
DeOre, Bill editorial cartoonist
DePaola, Dominick Philip academic administrator
Dillard, Robert Lionel, Jr. lawyer, former life insurance executive
Dillon, David Anthony journalist, lecturer
Dillon, Donald Ward management consultant
†Dobbs, James Frederick marketing professional
Doke, Marshall J., Jr. lawyer
Doran, Mark Richard real estate financial executive
Dorris, Carlos Eugene chemicals executive
Dozier, David Charles, Jr. marketing public relations and advertising executive
Drach, George Wisse urology educator
Drumm, David Gary lawyer
Dudley, George William behavioral scientist, writer
Dufner, Edward Joseph business newswriter
Durham, Michael Jonathan information technology company executive
Dutta, Paritosh Chandra immunologist
Dutton, Diana Cheryl lawyer
Dyess, Bobby Dale lawyer
Dykeman, Alice Marie public relations executive
Dykes, Virginia Chandler occupational therapist
Eads, John A. accountant
Eagar, Stephen Wade television news anchor, reporter
Eaton, Michael William lawyer, educator
Eddleman, William Roseman lawyer
Edwards, George Alva physician, educator
Eggers, Paul Walter lawyer
Eichenwald, Heinz Felix physician
Einspruch, Burton Cyril psychiatrist
Eisenberg, David H. automotive executive
Elam, Andrew Gregory, II convention and visitors bureau executive
Ellis, Alfred Wright (Al Ellis) lawyer
Ellis, James Alvis, Jr. lawyer
Ellis, June B. human resource consultant
Ellison, Luther Frederick oil company executive
Emerson, Walter Caruth artist, educator
Emery, Herschell Gene lawyer
Emmett, Michael physician
Engels, Lawrence Arthur metals company executive
Engleman, Donald James lawyer, corporate executive
Enix, Agnes Lucille editorial consultant
Ericson, Ruth Ann psychiatrist
Esquivel, Agerico Liwag research physicist
Estabrook, Ronald Winfield chemistry educator
Etgen, Ann ballet educator
†Evans, Linda Perryman foundation adminstrator
Evans, Roger lawyer
Evans, William Wilson journalism educator, retired newspaper editor
Everbach, Otto George lawyer
Eyerman, David John software engineer
Fanning, Barry Hedges lawyer
Farquhar, Robert Michael lawyer
Farrington, Jerry S. utility holding company executive
Farris, Edward Thompson dentist, medical researcher, real estate developer and broker
Fegan, Jeffrey P. airport executive
Feiner, Joel S. psychiatrist

Feld, Alan David *lawyer*
Feldman, H. Larry *lawyer*
Feldman, Robert C. *lawyer*
Fenner, Suzan Ellen *lawyer*
Ferguson, Hugh W., III *lawyer*
Fiddick, Paul William *broadcasting company executive*
Fielder, Charles Robert *oil industry executive*
Fifield, William O. *lawyer*
Finn, Peter Michael *television production executive*
Fish, A. Joe *federal judge*
Fishman, Edward Marc *lawyer*
Fitzwater, Sidney Allen *federal judge*
Fix, Douglas Martin *electrical engineer*
Flanagan, Christie Stephen *lawyer*
Flanary, Donald Herbert, Jr. *lawyer*
Flatt, Adrian Ede *surgeon*
Flegle, Jim L. *lawyer*
Fleming, Jon Hugh *psychology educator, business executive, educational consultant*
Flood, Joan Moore *paralegal*
Flores, Marion Thomas *advertising executive*
Flournoy, John Craig *newspaper reporter*
Fogelman, Morris Joseph *physician*
Fontana, Robert Edward *electrical engineering educator, retired air force officer*
Fortado, Michael George *lawyer*
France, Newell Edwin *former hospital administrator, consultant*
Free, Mary Moore *anthropologist*
French, Joseph Jordan, Jr. *lawyer*
Frenkel, Eugene Phillip *physician*
Friedberg, Errol Clive *pathology educator, researcher*
Friedheim, Jan V. *education administrator*
Friedheim, Stephen Bailey *public relations executive*
Fritze, Julius Arnold *marriage counselor*
Fry, Edward Irad *anthropology educator*
Gage, Tommy Wilton *pharmacologist, dentist, pharmacist, educator*
Galloway, Randy *newspaper sports columnist*
Galt, John William *actor, writer*
Galvin, Charles O'Neill *law educator*
Gant, Norman Ferrell, Jr. *obstetrician, gynecologist*
Gantt, James Raiford *thoracic surgeon*
Gibbs, James Alanson *geologist*
Gibby, Mabel Enid Kunce *psychologist*
Gidel, Robert Hugh *real estate investor*
Gifford, Porter William *retired construction materials manufacturing company executive*
Gilchrist, Henry *lawyer*
Gilman, Alfred Goodman *pharmacologist, educator*
Gilmore, Jerry Carl *lawyer*
Ginsburg, Lawrence David *lawyer*
Girards, James Edward *lawyer*
†Glade, Thomas *radio station executive*
Glancy, Walter John *lawyer*
Glatt, Linnea Elizabeth *artist*
Glendenning, Don Mark *lawyer*
Glines, Carroll Vane, Jr. *magazine editor*
Godfrey, Cullen Michael *lawyer*
Goldstein, Joseph Leonard *physician, medical educator, molecular genetics scientist*
Gonwa, Thomas Arthur *nephrologist, transplant physician*
Goodell, Sol *retired lawyer*
Goodson, Shannon Lorayn *behavioral scientist, author*
Goodstein, Barnett Maurice *lawyer*
Goodwin, Joel Franklin, Sr. *dentist*
Gores, Christopher Merrel *lawyer*
Goss, James Walter *oil company executive*
Gossen, Emmett Joseph, Jr. *motel chain executive, lawyer*
Gouge, Betty Merle *family therapist*
Govett, Brett Christopher *lawyer*
†Grant, Lester Howard *retired physician*
Grayson, Walton George, III *retired lawyer*
Green, Cecil Howard *geophysicist, consultant, educator*
Greenstone, James Lynn *psychotherapist, police psychologist, mediator, consultant, author, educator*
Griffith, Dotty (Dorothy Griffith Stephenson) *journalist, speaker*
†Griffith, Rachel *neonatologist*
Grimes, David Lynn *communications company executive*
Grissom, Gerald Homer *lawyer, mediator, arbitrator*
Gross, Gary Neil *allergist, physician*
Gruebel, Barbara Jane *internist, pulmonologist*
Guerin, Dean Patrick *food products executive*
Guthrie, M. Philip *insurance company executive*
Haayen, Richard Jan *university official, insurance company executive*
Haddock, Ronald Wayne *oil company executive*
Hafner, Dudley H. *health agency executive*
Halbreich, Jeremy L. *newspaper publishing executive*
Hall, Cheryl *newspaper editor*
Hallam, Robert G. *wholesale distribution executive*
Halpin, James *retail computer stores executive*
Halpin, James F. *business executive*
Halter, Kevin B. *communications executive*
Hamilton, David Lee *retired environmental company executive*
Hamon, Richard Grady *lawyer*
Harasta, Cathy Ann *journalist*
Harbaugh, Lois Jensen *secondary education educator*
Harbin, John Pickens *oil well company executive*
Hardy, Tom Charles, Jr. *medical equipment company*
Harper, Harlan, Jr. *lawyer*
Harrell, Roy Harrison, Jr. *minister*
Harrington, Marion Ray *ophthalmologist*
Harris, Leon A., Jr. *writer*
Harrison, Frank *former university president*
Hart, John Clifton *lawyer*
Hartnett, Thomas Robert, III *lawyer*
Hartnett, Will Ford *lawyer*
Hartt, Grover, III *lawyer*
Haworth, Charles Ray *lawyer*
Hay, Jess Thomas *retired finance company executive*
Haynes, J. Neauell *clergyman, bishop*
Head, Mark D. *insurance and employee benefit broker*
Healy, Margaret Mary *retail marketing executive*
Heileman, Sandra Marie *health facility administrator, educator*
Helm, Phala Aniece *physiatrist*
Henderson, David Allen *lawyer*
Henkel, Kathryn G. *lawyer*
Hennessy, Daniel Kraft *lawyer*
Herbener, Mark Basil *bishop*
Hester, Linda Hunt *university dean, counselor*
Hewett, Arthur Edward *real estate developer, lawyer*
Hewlett, Gloria Louise *rancher, retired educator, civic volunteer*
Heydrick, Linda Carol *consulting company executive, editor*
Hicks, Marion Lawrence, Jr. (Larry Hicks) *lawyer*
Higginbotham, Patrick Errol *federal judge*
Hilgemann, Donald William *medical educator*
Hillis, Robert Gregory *investment executive*
Hinshaw, Chester John *lawyer*
Hirsch, Laurence Eliot *construction executive, mortgage banker*
Hirsh, Bernard *supply company executive, consultant*
Hitt, David Hamilton *hospital executive*
Hoffman, Harold Wayne *advertising agency executive*
Holl, Dee Lynn *career counselor, psychotherapist, management consultant*
Holman, James *allergist, immunologist*
Holmes, Bert Otis E., Jr. *retired newspaperman*
Honkanen, Jari Olavi *electrical engineer*
Hopkins, Zora Clemons *training and development specialist*
Horchow, S(amuel) Roger *marketing consultant*
Horton, Paul Bradfield *lawyer*
Howe, Beverly Jeanne *nurse*
Howell, Bradley Sue *librarian*
Howie, John Robert *lawyer*
Howland, Grafton Dulany *financial counselor*
Huang, Yen Ti *civil engineer*
Hudgins, Louise Nan *art educator*
Hudspeth, Albert James *biomedical researcher, educator*
Huey, Ward L(igon), Jr. *media executive*
Huffman, Gregory Scott Combest *lawyer*
Hughes, Joe Kenneth *retired beverage company executive*
Hughes, Vester Thomas, Jr. *lawyer*
Humann, Walter Johann *corporation executive*
Humble, Monty Garfield *lawyer*
Hunt, Ray L. *petroleum company executive*
Hunter, Kermit *writer, former university dean*
Hunter, Robert Grams *retired English language educator*
Hurd, Eric Ray *rheumatologist, internist, educator*
Ibach, Robert Daniel, Jr. *library director*
Jayson, Melinda Gayle *lawyer*
Jeffett, Frank Asbury *former oil company and insurance company executive, business consultant*
Jenkins, Chester Phillip *religious organization, church administration*
Jennings, Susan Jane *lawyer*
Jialal, Ishwarlal *medical educator*
Jobe, Larry Alton *financial company executive*
Johnson, Hubert Dee *retired lawyer*
Johnson, James Harold *lawyer*
Johnson, James Joseph Scofield *lawyer, judge, educator*
Johnson, Judith Kay *lawyer*
Johnson, Murray H. *optometrist, researcher, consultant, lecturer*
Johnson, Richard Clayton *engineer, physicist*
Johnson, Robert Lee, Jr. *physician, educator, researcher*
Jones, Everett Riley, Jr. *oil company executive*
Joplin, Julian Mike *lawyer*
Jordan, Karen Leigh *newspaper travel editor*
Jordan, William Davis *lawyer*
†Jorns, Steven D. *hotel executive*
Juergens, Bonnie Kay *not-for-profit company executive*
Keiser, Robert Lee *gas and oil industry executive*
Keith, Camille Tigert *airline marketing executive*
Keithley, Bradford Gene *lawyer*
Kelleher, Herbert David *airline executive, lawyer*
†Keller, William L. *lawyer*
Kemper, Robert Van *anthropologist, educator*
Kendall, Joe *federal judge*
Kennedy, Marc J. *lawyer*
Kent, David Charles *lawyer*
Kessler, Tom *newspaper editor*
Kilby, Jack St. Clair *electrical engineer*
Killam, Jill Minervini *oil and gas company executive*
Kimbrough, Allen Wayne *lawyer*
Kindberg, Shirley Jane *pediatrician*
†King, C(larence) Carleton, II *health care executive*
Kinnebrew, Jackson Metcalfe *lawyer*
Kirby, James Edmund, Jr. *theology educator*
Kirk, Ron *mayor, lawyer*
Kitner, David N. *lawyer*
Klehfoth, Jay Gordon *publisher, writer, consultant*
Kneipper, Richard Keith *lawyer*
Kobdish, George Charles *lawyer*
Kohl, Kathleen Allison Barnhart *lawyer*
Kolb, Nathaniel Key, Jr. *architect*
Kollmeyer, Kenneth Robert *surgeon*
Konrad, Dusan *chemist*
Korba, Robert W. *communications executive*
Kostas, Evans *manufacturing executive*
Kramer, Robert Ivan *pediatrician*
Kruse, Ann Gray *computer programer*
Kuhn, Willis Evan, II *lawyer, mediator*
Kutner, Janet *art critic, book reviewer*
Lacy, John Ford *lawyer*
Lafving, Brian Douglas *lawyer*
Lambert, Joseph Parker *dentist*
Lan, Donald Paul, Jr. *lawyer*
Lancaster, John Lynch, III *lawyer*
Lancaster, Sally Rhodus *non-profit consultant*
Land, Geoffrey Allison *science administrator*
Landry, Jane Lorenz *architect*
Landry, Tom (Thomas Wade Landry) *former professional football coach*
Lane, Alvin Huey, Jr. *management consultant*
Lane, Marvin Maskall, Jr. *electronics company executive*
Lang, Douglas Steward *lawyer*
Langer, Ralph Ernest *journalist, newspaper executive and editor*
Lang-Miers, Elizabeth Ann *lawyer*
Langston, Roy A. *insurance company consultant*
Le, Can *mechanical engineer, inventor, author*
Leedom, John Nesbett *state senator, distribution company executive*
Leeper, Harold Harris *arbitrator*
Leigh-Manuell, Robert Allen *training executive, educator*
Lenox, Roger Shawn *lawyer*
Lersch, DeLynden Rife *computer engineering executive*
Levenson, Stanley Richard *public relations and advertising executive*
Le Vieux, Jane Stuart *pediatrics nurse*
Levin, Richard C. *lawyer*
Levine, Harold *lawyer*
Lewis, Jerry M. *psychiatrist, educator*
Lichliter, Warren Eugene *surgeon, educator*
Lindsey, Tanya Jamil *secondary education administrator*
Livingston, Grover D. *newspaper publishing executive*
Lomax, John H. *financial service company executive*
Lombard, Richard Spencer *lawyer*
Lopez, Francisca Uy *elementary education educator*
Loveless, Kathy Lynne *client services executive*
Lowe, John Stanley *lawyer, educator*
Lucier, James Alfred *advertising executive*
Lumry, William Raymond *physician, allergist*
Lundy, Victor Alfred *architect, educator*
Lutz, Gretchen Kay *English language educator*
Lynch, William Wright, Jr. *investment executive, engineer*
MacMahon, Paul *advertising executive*
Madden, Teresa Darleen *insurance agency owner*
Maddrey, Willis Crocker *medical educator, internist, academic administrator, consultant, researcher*
Mahr, George Joseph *financial service executive, real estate developer*
Maloney, Robert B. *federal judge*
Malorzo, Thomas Vincent *lawyer*
Mankoff, Ronald Morton *lawyer*
Margerison, Richard Wayne *diversified industrial company executive*
Margolin, Solomon Begelfor *pharmacologist*
Maris, Stephen S. *lawyer, educator*
Marks, James Frederic *pediatric endocrinologist, educator*
Marshall, John Harris, Jr. *geologist, oil company executive*
Martin, Boe Willis *lawyer*
Martin, Carol Jacquelyn *educator, artist*
Martin, Jack *physician*
Martin, Richard Kelley *lawyer*
Mason, Barry Jean *retired banker*
Massman, Richard Allan *lawyer*
Matelan, Mathew Nicholas *software engineer*
Matthews, Clark J(io), II *retail executive, lawyer*
Maycock, Ian David *oil executive*
Maza, Michael William *newspaper editor, columnist*
McCall, Clyde Samuel, Jr. *petroleum engineer*
McCally, Charles Richard *construction company executive*
McCarthy, Michael Joseph *communications company executive*
Mc Clelland, Robert Nelson *surgeon, educator*
McClure, Frederick Donald *public affairs consultant, lawyer*
McCord, Don Lewis *surgeon*
McCord, William Charles *retired diversified energy company executive*
McCormick, James Edward *oil company executive*
McCormick, James Hillman *retired broadcast executive*
McCracken, Alexander Walker *pathologist*
McDonald, Michael Scott *lawyer*
McDougall, Ronald Alexander *restaurant executive*
Mc Elhaney, John Hess *lawyer*
McElyea, Jacquelyn Suzanne *accountant, real estate consultant*
McGowan, Patrick Francis *lawyer*
McKennon, Richard Otey *lawyer*
McKnight, Joseph Webb *law educator, historian*
McKnight, Steven Lanier *molecular biologist*
McLane, David Glenn *lawyer*
McLean, Susan Ralston *lawyer, federal government*
McNamara, Anne H. *lawyer, corporate executive*
McNamara, Lawrence John *lawyer*
McNamara, Martin Burr *lawyer, oil and gas company executive*
McNeely, Patricia Morse *middle school educator, poet, writer*
McTeer, Robert D., Jr. *banker*
McWhorter, Kathleen *orthodontist*
McWilliams, Mike C. *lawyer*
Meadows, Patricia Blachly *art curator, civic worker*
Mears, Rona Robbins *lawyer*
Mebus, Robert Gwynne *lawyer*
Meek, Paul Derald *oil and chemical company executive*
Mickey, Bruce Edward *neurosurgeon*
Middleton, Linda Jean Greathouse *lawyer*
Mighell, Kenneth John *lawyer*
Miller, Brian Keith *airline executive*
Miller, Clint *technology company executive*
Mills, Jerry Woodrow *lawyer*
Mitchell, Teddy Lee *physician*
Moneypenny, Edward William *oil and gas mining executive*
†Monserrate, Jennifer Kratzer *healthcare administrator*
Moore, Stanley Ray *lawyer*
Moore, Thomas Joseph *financial company executive*
Morgan, Larry Ronald *minister*
Morgan, Timi Sue *lawyer*
Morris, Rebecca Robinson *lawyer*
Mow, Robert Henry, Jr. *lawyer*
Mueller, James Bernhard *anesthesiologist, pain managememt consultant*
Mueller, Mark Christopher *lawyer*
Mullinax, Otto B. *retired lawyer*
Murad, John Louis *clinical microbiology educator*
Murphy, John Carter *economics educator*
Murphy, John Joseph *manufacturing company executive*
Murphy, Randall Kent *training consultant*
Murray, John William, Jr. *writer, legal investigator*
Murray, Suzanne Marie *accountant*
New, William Neil *physician, retired naval officer*
Nichols, Henry Louis *lawyer*
Nolan, John Michael *lawyer*
Nordlund, William Chalmers *lawyer*
Norris, John Windsor, Jr. *manufacturing company executive*
Nye, Erle Allen *utilities executive, lawyer*
Oden, William Bryant *bishop, educator*
Odom, Floyd Clark *surgeon*
Olinger, Sheff Daniel *neurologist, educator*
Osborne, Burl *newspaper publisher, editor*
Owen, Robert Randolph *accountant*
Owens, Robin Maria *management consultant*
Owens, Rodney Joe *lawyer*
Page, Richard Leighton *cardiologist, medical educator, researcher*
Palmer, Christine (Clelia Rose Venditti) *operatic singer, performer, pianist, vocal instructor, lecturer, entertainer*
Parent, David Hill *investment company executive*
Parker, Angelo Pan *lawyer*
Parker, James Francis *lawyer, airline executive*
Parkey, Robert Wayne *radiology and nuclear medicine educator, research radiologist*
Pastine, Maureen Diane *librarian*
Patterson, Joseph Redwine *lawyer*
Patterson, Ronald Paul *publishing company executive, clergyman*
Patton, Bob J. *oil industry executive*
Pearce, Ronald *retired cosmetic company executive*
Pederson, Rena *newspaper editor*
Peiser, John George *accountant, consultant*
Pell, Jonathan Laurence *artistic administrator*
Perry, George Wilson *oil and gas company executive*
Perry, Malcolm Oliver *vascular surgeon*
Peterson, Edward Adrian *lawyer*
Pettey, Walter Graves, III *lawyer*
Petty, Charles Sutherland *pathologist*
Pew, John Glenn, Jr. *lawyer*
Phelan, Robin Eric *lawyer*
Philipson, Herman Louis, Jr. *investment banker*
Phillips, Bettie Mae *elementary school educator*
Phillips, Betty Lou (Elizabeth Louise Phillips) *author, interior designer*
Phillips, Margaret A. *pharmacology educator*
Pike, Kenneth Lee *linguist, educator*
Pingree, Bruce Douglas *lawyer*
Pinson, William Meredith, Jr. *pastor, writer*
Pistor, Charles Herman, Jr. *former banker, academic administrator*
Pleasant, James Scott *lawyer*
Portman, Glenn Arthur *lawyer*
Powell, Boone, Jr. *hospital administrator*
Powell, Larry Randall *columnist*
Powell, Michael Vance *lawyer*
Price, John Aley *lawyer*
Price, Robert Eben *judge*
Pride, Charley *singer*
Prince, Frank Michael *lawyer*
Pryor, Richard Walter *telecommunications executive, retired air force officer*
Purnell, Charles Giles *lawyer*
Purnell, Maurice Eugene, Jr. *lawyer*
Qualls, June Carol *elementary education educator*
Race, George Justice *pathology educator*
Raggio, Kenneth Gaylord *lawyer, mediator*
Raggio, Louise Ballerstedt *lawyer*
Rainey, William E., II *medical educator*
Ram, Chitta Venkata *physician*
Ray, George Einar *lawyer*
Reagan, Barbara Benton *economics educator*
Reed, Jesse Francis *entrepreneur, artist, inventor, theologian, business consultant*
Rees, Frank William, Jr. *architect*
Reeser, Rachel Anne Everson *graphic designer, artist*
Reid, Langhorne, III *merchant banker*
Reinert, James A. *entomologist, educator*
Rice, Darrel Alan *lawyer*
Richards, Jeanne Herron *artist*
Riehm, Sarah Lawrence *writer, arts administrator*
Ries, Edward Richard *petroleum geologist, consultant*
Riggs, Arthur Jordy *retired lawyer*
Ringle, Brett Adelbert *lawyer, petroleum company executive*
Rinne, Austin Dean *insurance company executive*
Roach, John D. C. *manufacturing company executive*
Robbins, Ray Charles *manufacturing company executive*
Roberts, Harry Morris, Jr. *lawyer*
Roberts, Lynne Jeanine *physician*
Robertson, Beverly Carruth *steel company executive*
Robertson, Ted Zanderson *judge*
Robinson, Hugh Granville *consulting management company executive*
Rochon, John Philip *cosmetics company executive*
Rogers, Ralph B. *industrial business executive*
Rose, Charles David *consulting company executive*
Rosenberg, Roger Newman *neurologist, educator*
Rosson, Glenn Richard *building products and furniture company executive*
Routman, Daniel Glenn *marketing and business development professional, lawyer*
Roy, Clarence Leslie *landscape architect*
Rubottom, Roy Richard, Jr. *retired diplomat and educator, consultant*
Ryan, Timothy Christopher *anchor, reporter*
St. Claire, Frank Arthur *lawyer*
St. John, Bill Dean *diversified equipment and services company executive*
St. John, Bob *journalist, columnist, author*
Salazar, Ramiro S. *library administrator*
Salyer, Kenneth E. *surgeon*
Sammons, Elaine D. *corporate executive*
Sanders, Harold Barefoot, Jr. *federal judge*
Savage, Wallace Hamilton *lawyer*
Schenkel, Peter *food company executive*
Schreiber, Sally Ann *lawyer*
Schulze, Richard Hans *engineering executive, environmental engineer*
Schwartz, Irving Donn *architect*
Schwartz, Marilyn *columnist*
Scott, John Roland *lawyer, oil company executive*
Scott, Terry Lee *communications company executive*
See, Robert Fleming, Jr. *lawyer*
Selinger, Jerry Robin *lawyer*
Semmler, Caryl J. *occupational therapist*
Shapiro, Robert Alan *retail executive*
Sharp, William Wheeler *geologist*
Sheinberg, Israel *computer company executive*
Shimer, Daniel Lewis *corporate executive*
Shoup, Andrew James, Jr. *oil company executive*
Shower, Robert Wesley *financial executive*
Sibley, William Ruck, III (Trey Sibley) *lawyer, oil and gas executive*
Sides, Jack Davis, Jr. *lawyer*
Siegel, Thomas Louis *lawyer*
Siegfried, Tom *newspaper editor*
Silcox, Frances Eleanor *museum and exhibits planning consultant*
Simon, Theodore Ronald *physician, medical educator*
Sims, Konstanze Olevia *social worker, case manager*
Sizer, Phillip Spelman *consultant, retired oil field services executive*
Skaggs, Merton Melvin, Jr. *environmental engineer*
Smiles, Ronald *management educator*
Smith, Barry Samuel *physiatrist*
Smith, Cece *venture capitalist*
Smith, David Lee *newspaper editor*
Smith, Edwin Ide *medical educator*
Smith, Nancy Lynne *journalist, real estate agent*
Smith, Sue Frances *newspaper editor*
Smith, Valerie Gay *school counselor*
Smith, William Randolph (Randy Smith) *health care management association executive*
Snead, Richard Thomas *restaurant company executive*
†Snyder, William D. *photojournalist*
Solender, Robert Lawrence *financial, newsprint manufacturing executive*
Solis, Jorge Antonio *federal judge*
Solomon, Risa Greenberg *video software industry executive*
Solomon, William Tarver *general construction company executive*
Sparkman, Robert Satterfield *retired surgeon, educator*
Spiegel, Lawrence Howard *advertising executive*

Sprague, Charles Cameron medical foundation president
Stacy, Dennis William architect
Stalcup, Joe Alan lawyer, clergyman
Steinberg, Lawrence Edward lawyer
Stembridge, Vernie A(lbert) pathologist, educator
Stephens, Marjorie Johnsen lawyer
Stilwell, John Quincy lawyer
Stinnett, Mark Allan lawyer
Stockard, James Alfred lawyer
Stone, Donald James retired retail executive
Stone, Marvin Jules physician, educator
Storey, Charles Porter lawyer
Stratton, Robert financial company executive
Swanson, Wallace Martin lawyer
Sweeney, Mark Owen publisher
Talley, Linda Jean food scientist, dietitian
Taylor, Barbara Alden public relations executive
Taylor, William Berley history educator
Termini, Deanne Lanoix research company executive
Terry, Marshall Northway, Jr. English language educator, author
Thau, William Albert, Jr. lawyer
Thomas, Robert Ray management consultant
Thomas, Sarah Elaine elementary music educator
Thompson, Charles Kerry company executive
Thompson, Jesse Eldon vascular surgeon
Tong, Alex Waiming immunologist
Trevino, Lee Buck professional golfer
True, Roy Joe lawyer
Tubb, James Clarence lawyer
Tucker, L. Dan lawyer
Turley, Linda lawyer
Turner, Robert Gerald university president
Tygrett, Howard Volney, Jr. lawyer
Udashen, Robert N. lawyer
Unger, Roger Harold physician, scientist
Valentine, Foy Dan clergyman
Vanatta, John Crothers, III physiologist, physician, educator
Vanderveld, John, Jr. waste disposal company executive
Vestal, Tommy Ray lawyer
Vetter, James George, Jr. lawyer
Villareal, Patricia lawyer
Vogel, Donald Stanley gallery executive, artist
Walden, Linda Lee lawyer
Walkowiak, Vincent Steven lawyer
Wallace, William C. airline executive
Wallenstein, James Harry lawyer
Walvoord, John Flipse academic administrator, theologian
Walwer, Frank Kurt dean, legal educator
Warren, Thomas Paul consulting executive
Wassenich, Linda Pilcher health policy analyst, fund raiser
Wasserman, Richard Lawrence pediatrician, educator
Weekley, Frederick Clay, Jr. lawyer
Weeks, Jerome Christopher writer, drama critic
Weiner, Myron Frederick psychiatrist, educator, clinical investigator
Weinkauf, William Carl communications company executive
Wells, Leonard Nathaniel David, Jr. lawyer
Wenrich, John William college president
Werner, Seth Mitchell advertising executive
West, William Beverley, III lawyer
Wheeler, Clarence Joseph, Jr. physician
White, James Richard lawyer
Whitson, James Norfleet, Jr. diversified company executive
Whitt, Robert Ampudia, III advertising executive, marketing professional
Wilber, Robert Edwin corporate executive
Wildenthal, C(laud) Kern physician, educator
Wileman, George Robert lawyer
Wiles, Charles Preston minister
Wiles, William Dixon, III lawyer
Williams, Bryan university dean, medical educator
Williams, James Alexander lawyer
Williams, Martha Spring psychologist
Willingham, Clark Suttles lawyer
Wilson, Claude Raymond, Jr. lawyer
Wilson, Jean Donald endocrinologist, educator
Winters, J. Otis oil industry consultant
Wise, Marvin Jay lawyer
Witmer, John Albert librarian
Woodward, David Luther lawyer, consultant
Wuntch, Philip Samuels journalist, film critic
Wyly, Charles Joseph, Jr. corporate executive
Yanagisawa, Samuel Tsuguo electronics executive
Yeslow, Rosemarie real estate professional
Young, Barney Thornton lawyer
Zammit, John P. financial planner
Ziff, Morris internist, rheumatologist, educator
Zisman, Barry Stuart lawyer
Zumwalt, Richard Dowling flour mill executive

## De Soto
Ball, Millicent Joan (Penny Ball) multimedia developer
Cupp, Marilyn Marie sales executive
Jackson, Johnny W. minister
Judah, Frank Marvin retired school system administrator

## Decatur
Jordan, Linda Susan Darnell elementary school educator

## Deer Park
Mujica, Mary Bernadette mechanical engineer

## Del Rio
Prather, Gerald Luther management consultant, retired air force officer, judge
Thurmond, George Murat judge

## Denison
Farr, Reeta Rae special education administrator

## Denton
Baier, John Leonard university educator
Berry, Linda Segraves paralegal educator
Brock, Horace Rhea accounting educator
Brostow, Witold Konrad materials scientist, educator
Brownell, Blaine Allison university administrator, history educator
Carlson, William Dwight college president emeritus
Cissell, William Bernard health studies educator
Crocker, Betty Charlotte education educator
Davidson, Norma Lewis concert violinist, composer, music educator, psychologist
Elder, Mark Lee university research administrator, writer
Garcia-Heras, Jaime clinical cytogeneticist, researcher
Greenlaw, Marilyn Jean education educator, consultant, writer
Hurley, Alfred Francis retired military officer, university administrator
Jackson, Stephen Eric police official
Kamman, William historian, educator
Kesterson, David Bert English language educator
Latham, William Peters composer, former educator
Lawhon, John E., III lawyer, former county official
Lawhon, Tommie Collins Montgomery child development and family living educator
McDonald-West, Sandi M. headmaster, consultant
Miller, Tom Polk retired architect
Newell, Charldean public administration educator
Owen, William Michael real estate developer
Palmer, Leslie Howard literature educator
Pickett, Stephen Wesley university official, lecturer and consultant
Poole, Eva Duraine librarian
Preston, Thomas Ronald English language educator, researcher
Rektorik-Sprinkle, Patricia Jean Latin language educator
Saleh, Farida Yousry chemistry educator
Schumacker, Randall Ernest educational psychology educator
Schwalm, Fritz Ekkehardt biology educator
Smith, Howard Wellington education educator, dean
Snapp, Elizabeth librarian, educator
Snapp, Harry Franklin historian
Swigger, Keith dean
Taylor, Sherrill Ruth management educator
Thompson, Leslie Melvin college dean, educator
Toulouse, Robert Bartell retired college administrator
Turner, Philip Michael university official and dean, author
Vaughn, William Preston historian, educator
Vick, Frances Brannen publishing executive
Waage, Mervin Bernard lawyer

## Denver City
Taylor, Sharon Kay elementary school counselor

## Diboll
Ericson, Roger Delwin lawyer, forest resource company executive
Grum, Clifford J. manufacturing company executive
Harbordt, Charles Michael forest products executive

## Dickinson
Bush, Robert Thomas shipping company executive

## Dilley
McMillian, Marilyn Lindsey elementary educator, health, home economics

## Dripping Springs
Ballard, Mary Melinda financial communications and investment banking firm executive
Delph, Shirley Cox artist, designer, illustrator, consultant
Gallerano, Andrew John lawyer
Rios, Evelyn Deerwester columnist, musician, artist, writer

## Duncanville
Bilhartz, James Rohn, Jr. independent oil producer

## Dyess AFB
Lawson, Melanie Kay management administrator, early childhood consultant

## Eastland
Quinn, Janita Sue city secretary

## Eden
Boyd, John Hamilton osteopath

## Edinburg
Barrera, Eduardo Spanish language and literature educator
Diong, Billy Ming control engineering researcher
Esparza, Thomas, Sr. academic athletics administrator
Hinojosa, Federico Gustavo, Jr. judge
Libbey, Darlene Hensley artist, educator
Nieto, Beatriz Chavez nursing educator
Wilson, Bruce Keith men's health nurse

## Egypt
Krenek, Mary Louise political science researcher, educator

## El Paso
Adams, Nancy R. nurse, military officer
Ainsa, Francis Swinburne lawyer
Bailey, Kenneth Kyle history educator
Bartlett, Janet Sanford (Walz) school nurse
Blevins, Leon Wilford political science educator, minister
Carroll, Edwin Winford architect
Cassidy, Richard Thomas hotel executive, defense industry consultant, retired army officer
Coleman, Edmund Benedict university dean
Cook, Clarence Sharp physics educator
Crossen, John Jacob radiologist, educator
Cuevas, David psychologist
Day, James Milton foundation executive, English educator
Dinsmoor, Robert Davidson judge
Drake, James sculptor
Dyer, Travis Neal defense consultant, retired army officer
Feuille, Richard Harlan lawyer
Foley, John Donald physician
Francis, Larry mayor
Friedkin, Joseph Frank consulting engineering executive
Gainer, Barbara Jeanne radiology educator
Gianelli, Victor F. mathematics and physics educator
Grieves, Robert Belanger engineering educator
Grimes, William Gaylord adult education educator
Groat, Charles George geologist, science administrator
Hardaway, Robert Morris, III physician, educator, retired army officer
Harris, Arthur Horne biology educator
Hedrick, Wyatt Smith pharmacist
Heger, Herbert Krueger education educator
Heide, John Wesley engineering executive
Hoagland, Jennifer Hope accountant
Huchton, Paul Joseph, Jr. pediatrician
Hudspeth, Harry Lee federal judge
Ingle, Henry Thomas communications educator, university administrator
Jaraba, Martha E. (Betty Jaraba) secondary school educator
Johnson, Jerry Douglas biology educator
Juarez, Antonio psychotherapist, consultant, counselor, educator
Kelley, Sylvia Johnson financial services firm executive
Kimmel, Herbert David psychology educator
Korth, Fred lawyer
Lujan, Rosa Emma bilingual specialist, trainer, consultant
Lyle, James Arthur real estate broker
Marshall, Richard Treeger lawyer
Mason, Richard Clyde landscape architect
McCarthy, Cormac writer
McCotter, James Rawson lawyer
Melton, Melinda Wallace archaeologist, laboratory director
Miller, Deane Guynes salon and cosmetic studio owner
Mitchell, Paula Rae nursing educator
Mrochek, Michael J. physician
Natalicio, Diana Siedhoff academic administrator
Pazmiño, Patricio Augusto physician, scientist, consultant
Prendergast, Thomas A. investments and management consultant
Quevedo, Hector Adolf operations research analyst, environmental scientist
Rankin, William Brown, II airport administrator
Riter, Stephen university administrator, electrical engineer
Roark, Charles Elvis healthcare executive
Roberts, Ernst Edward marketing consultant
Salewski, Ruby Marie Graf nursing educator
Shapiro, Stephen Richard retired air force officer, physician
Showery, Charles George, Jr. financial services company executive, consultant
Simon, Doris Marie Tyler nurse
Simpson, Michael Homer dermatologist
Sipiora, Leonard Paul retired museum director
Smith, Tad Randolph lawyer
Stoddard, Ellwyn R. sociology and anthropology educator
Tackett, Stephen Douglas education services specialist
Treadwell, Hugh Wilson publishing executive
Verghese, Abraham Cheeran internist, writer, educator
†Vines, Georgiana Fry editor
von Tungeln, George Robert retired university administrator, economics consultant
Vowell, Jack C. former state legislator, investor
Wang, Paul Weily materials science and physics educator
Ward DiDio, Patty special education educator, educational diagnostician
Weitz, Jeanne Stewart artist, educator
Williams, Darryl Marlowe medical educator
Wise, William Allan oil company executive, lawyer

## Elgin
Osborne, Michael James real estate executive, energy executive, author

## Euless
Leding, Anne Dixon artist, educator
Paran, Mark Lloyd lawyer
Warwick, Sharon Brenda elementary art educator

## Fair Oaks Ranch
Dixon, Robert James aerospace consultant, former air force officer, former aerospace company executive

## Farwell
Franse, Jean Lucille secondary school educator

## Floresville
Alvarez, Olga Mendoza elementary school educator

## Flower Mound
Hunt, David Ford lawyer
Kolodny, Stanley Charles oral surgeon, air force officer
Morrish, Thomas Jay golf course architect

## Floydada
Hinton, Sharon Tonya Curtis nursing educator

## Fort Hood
Hughes, William Foster career officer, surgeon, obstetrician, gynecologist
Sprabary, Larry Drew military analyst

## Fort Sam Houston
Cohen, David John cardiothoracic surgeon

## Fort Worth
Ahmed, M. Basheer psychiatrist, educator
Allmand, Linda F(aith) library director
Al-Shakhshir, Ragheb Hilmi pharmaceutical engineer
Appel, Bernard Sidney marketing consultant
Ard, Harold Jacob library administrator
Arena, M. Scott pharmaceutical company executive
Asher, Garland Parker investment holding company executive
Auping, Michael G. curator
Barr, Kenneth L. mayor
Bass, Perry Richardson oil company executive
Bean, Jack Vaughan author, publisher
Berenson, William Keith lawyer
Bickerstaff, Mina March Clark university administrator
Brannon, Treva Lee (Wood) insurance company executive
Braudaway, Gary Wayne secondary school educator
Brockman, Leslie Richard social worker
Brooks, Lloyd William, Jr. osteopath, interventional cardiologist, educator
Brown, C. Harold lawyer
Brown, Richard Lee lawyer
Buckley, Betty Bob journalist, consultant
Bush, Alan Clifford computer company executive
Byas, Teresa Ann Uranga healthcare professional
Caldwell, Billy Ray geologist
Chalk, John Allen, Sr. lawyer
Clark, Emory Eugene financial planning executive
Cliburn, Van (Harvey Lavan Cliburn, Jr.) concert pianist
Collins, Whitfield James lawyer
Cox, James Sidney physician
Crandall, Robert Lloyd airline executive
Crumley, John Walter lawyer
Cunningham, Atlee Marion, Jr. aeronautical engineer
Curry, Donald Robert lawyer, oil company executive
Danilow, Deborah Marie rancher, singer, songwriter, musician
Dean, Beale lawyer
Dees, Sandra Kay Martin psychologist, research consultant
Delaney, Joseph P. bishop
Dent, Edward Dwain lawyer
Desha, Doris Hollingsworth retired elementary education educator
de Tonnancour, Paul Roger Godefroy library administrator
†Dewar, Thomas Norman gastroenterologist
Dominiak, Geraldine Florence accounting educator
Doran, Robert Stuart mathematician, educator
Durham, Carolyn Richardson foreign language and literature educator
Edwards, Samuel Lee religious organization executive
Eliasoph, Jeffrey Paul television news anchor
Elliott, John Franklin clergyman
Erisman, Fred Raymond English literature educator
Faherty, John Kevin insurance broker, consultant
Fleshman, Linda Eilene Scalf private investigator, writer, columnist, consultant, communications and marketing executive
Ford, Kathleen Marie home health nurse, trainer
Geren, Pete (Preston Geren) former congressman
Geren, Preston Murdoch, Jr. architect, engineer
Gideon, Randall Clifton architectural firm executive
Gilbert, James Cayce minister
Gillette, Paul Crawford pediatric cardiologist
Giordano, John Read conductor
Griffith, Richard Lattimore lawyer
Gross, John Birney retired minister
Gutsche, Carl David chemistry educator
Harcrow, E. Earl lawyer
Hayes, Larry B. lawyer
Hendricks, William Lawrence theology educator
Herlihy, James Edward retail executive
Hill, Mark C. lawyer
Hurley, Linda Kay psychologist
Hyde, Clarence Brodie, II oil company executive
Jensen, Harlan Ellsworth veterinarian, educator
Joe, George Washington clinical researcher, quantitative methodologist
Jones, Evelene Manns principal, minister
Jones, Kathryn Ann writer, artist
Jurgensen, Warren Peter retired psychiatrist, educator
Kelly, Dee J. lawyer
Kenderdine, John Marshall petroleum engineer, retired army officer
Killingsworth, Maxine Armatha special education educator
Koger, David Gordon oil and gas exploration, analyst, consultant
Krebs, Robert Duncan transportation company executive
Lale, Cissy Stewart (Lloyd Lale) freelance writer
Landolt, Robert George chemistry educator
Law, Thomas Hart lawyer
Leone, George Frank pharmaceutical executive
Lipkin, Seymour pianist, conductor, educator
Livengood, Charlotte Louise employee development specialist
Lorenzetti, Ole John pharmaceutical research executive, ophthalmic research and development executive
Mack, Theodore lawyer
Mahon, Eldon Brooks federal judge
Malone, Dan F. journalist
Martin, Harold Eugene publishing executive, consultant
Mays, Glenda Sue retired education educator
McBryde, John Henry federal judge
McConnell, Michael Arthur lawyer
McInnes, Donald Gordon railroad executive
McKimmey, Martha Anne elementary education educator
McKinney, James Carroll baritone, educator
McLane, William Delano mechanical engineer
Means, Terry Robert federal judge
Messman, Jack L. oil executive
Michero, William Henderson retired retail trade executive
Miller, Travis Milton association executive, accountant
Mills, John James research director
Minton, Jerry Davis lawyer, former banker
Moncrief, William Alvin, Jr. oil and gas producer
Mowery, Anna Renshaw state legislator
Mullanax, Milton Greg lawyer
Munn, Cecil Edwin lawyer
Newport, John Paul philosophy of religion educator, former academic administrator
Nichols, James Richard civil engineer, consultant
Otto, Donald R. museum director
Owens, Merle Wayne executive search consultant
Peipert, James Raymond journalist
Phillips, Robert James, Jr. corporate executive
Pillsbury, Edmund Pennington museum director
Pray, Donald George aerospace engineer
Price, Debbie Mitchell journalist, newspaper editor
Price, Michael Howard journalist, critic, composer, cartoonist
Quarles, Carroll Adair, Jr. physicist, educator
†Rainwater, Richard financial consultant, investor
Randle, Rolinda Carol elementary education educator
Ray, Paul Richard, Jr. executive search consultant
Reade, Kathleen Margaret paralegal
Record, Phillip Julius newspaper executive
Reinecke, Manfred G. chemistry educator
Reuter, Frank Theodore history educator
Rhodes, Ann L. theatrical producer, investor
Roach, John Vinson, II retail company executive
Roberts, Leonard H. retail executive
Robinson, Nell Bryant nutrition educator
Rogers, Charles Ray minister, religious organization administrator
Roland, Billy Ray electronics company executive
Romine, Thomas Beeson, Jr. consulting engineering executive
Saenz, Michael college president
Sartain, James Edward lawyer
Sasser, William Jack retired federal agency administrator, consultant
Schrum, Jake Bennett university administrator
Scott-Wabbington, Vera V. elementary school educator

Shannon, Larry Redding administrative assistant
Sharpe, James Shelby lawyer
Sheets, John Wesley, Jr. research scientist
Shoemaker, Sandra Kaye aerospace executive
Shosid, Joseph Lewis government official
Simpson, Dennis Dwayne psychologist, educator
Smith, Thomas Hunter ophthalmologist, ophthalmic plastic and orbital surgeon
Smith, William Burton chemist, educator
Stormdancer, Rowan Ehlenfeldt traditional herbalist, management consultant
Strength, Danna Elliott nursing educator
Suggs, Marion Jack minister, college dean
Sullenberger, Ara Broocks mathematics educator
Tade, George Thomas university dean
Talley, Jane artist, educator
Teegarden, Kenneth Leroy clergyman
Thompson, Carson R. retail, manufacturing company executive
Thornton, Charles Victor metals executive
Tilley, Rice M(atthews), Jr. lawyer
Tinsley, Jackson Bennett newspaper editor
Tobey, Martin Alan cardiologist
Tracy, Barbara Marie lawyer
Treviño, Fernando Manuel medical educator
Tucker, William Edward academic administrator, minister
Turner, Loyd Leonard advertising executive, public relations executive
Von Rosenberg, Gary Marcus, Jr. parochial school educator
Webb, Theodore Stratton, Jr. aerospace scientist, consultant
Wertz, Spencer K. philosophy educator
Wilkie, Valleau, Jr. foundation executive
Williamson, Philip apparel executive
Willis, Doyle Henry state legislator, lawyer
Wilson, Ronald James geologist
Wilson-Webb, Nancy Lou adult educational administrator
Worcester, Donald Emmet history educator, author
Wynn, Susan Rudd physician
Yanni, John Michael pharmacologist
Yarbro, James Wesley financial executive
Zeigler, Vicki Lynn pediatrics nurse

### Fredericksburg
Malec, William Frank utilities company executive

### Freeport
Baskin, William Gresham counselor, music educator, vocalist
Duncan, Dan L. gas company executive
Tsai, Tom Chunghu chemical engineer

### Friendswood
Arnaud, Sandra financial advisor
Lampton, Robert Donald, Jr. chemical engineer, consultant

### Galveston
Arens, James F. anesthesiologist, educator
Bailey, Byron James otolaryngologist, medical association executive
Baker, Robert Ernest, Jr. foundation executive
Banet, Charles Henry academic administrator, clergyman
Barratt, Ernest Stoelting psychologist, educator
Baskaran, Mahalingam marine science educator
Bernier, George Matthew, Jr. physician, medical educator, medical school dean
Bonchev, Danail Georgiev chemist, educator
Brasier, Allan R. medical educator
Budelmann, Bernd Ulrich zoologist, educator
Bungo, Michael William physician, educator, science administrator
Burns, Chester Ray medical history educator
Caldwell, Garnett Ernest lawyer
Calverley, John Robert physician, educator
Carrier, Warren Pendleton retired university chancellor, writer
Chonmaitree, Tasnee pediatrician, educator, infectious disease specialist
Clayton, William Howard retired university president
Dawson, Earl Bliss obstetrician/gynecologist, educator
Ewing, George H. pipeline company executive
Felthous, Alan Robert psychiatrist
Fisher, Seymour psychologist, educator
Giam, Choo-Seng marine science educator
Gibson, Hugh federal judge
Gold, Daniel Howard ophthalmologist, educator
Goodwin, Jean McClung psychiatrist
Goodwin, Sharon Ann academic administrator
Gorenstein, David G. chemistry and biochemistry educator
Grant, J(ohn) Andrew, Jr. medical educator, allergist
Herndon, David N. surgeon
Hillman, Gilbert Rothschild medical educator
Hilton, James Gorton pharmacologist
Jahadi, Mohammad Reza surgeon
James, Thomas Naum cardiologist, educator
Johnson, Howard Eugene (Stretch Johnson) educator, consultant
Kent, Samuel B. federal judge
Kurosky, Alexander biochemist, educator
Levin, William Cohn hematologist, former university president
Mader, Jon Terry physician
McLeod, E. Douglas real estate developer, lawyer
Merrell, William John, Jr. oceanography educator
Millikan, Charles Reagan pastor
Neves, Kerry Lane lawyer
†Newman, Frances Moody foundation executive
Ogra, Pearay L. physician, educator
Otis, John James civil engineer
Pearl, William Richard Emden pediatric cardiologist
Phillips, Linda Goluch plastic surgeon, educator, researcher
Powell, Don Watson medical educator, physician, physiology researcher
Powell, Leslie Charles, Jr. obstetrics and gynecology educator
Prakash, Satya biology educator
Ryan, James Gilbert historian, educator, writer
Sandstead, Harold Hilton medical educator
Santschi, Peter Hans marine sciences educator
Schoenbucher, Bruce health physicist
Schreiber, Melvyn Hirsh radiologist
Schwartz, Aaron Robert lawyer, former state legislator
Shannon, Mary Lou adult health nursing educator
Sheppard, Louis Clarke biomedical engineer, educator
Shope, Robert Ellis epidemiology educator
Smith, David English physician, educator
Smith, Edgar Benton physician
Smith, Eric Morgan virology educator
Smith, Jerome Hazen pathologist
Thomas, Leelamma Koshy women's health care nurse
Thompson, Edward Ivins Brad biological chemistry and genetics educator, molecular endocrinologist, department chairman
Tyson, Kenneth Robert Thomas surgeon, educator
Welch, Ronald J. actuary
White, Robert Brown medical educator
Willis, William Darrell, Jr. neurophysiologist, educator
Würsig, Bernd Gerhard marine biology educator
Zimmerman, Roger Joseph fishery biologist

### Garland
Christensen, Allan Robert electrical engineer, enrolled agent
Driver, Joe L. state legislator, insurance agent
Duren, Michael cardiologist
Evans, Patricia M. performing arts association administrator
Foster, Rebecca Anne Hodges secondary school educator
Hockett, Sheri Lynn radiologist
McGill, Maurice Leon financial executive
McGrath, James Thomas real estate investment company executive
Michaels, Cindy Whitfill (Cynthia G. Michaels) educational consultant, telecommunications representative
Shugart, Jill school system administrator
Stimpson, Ritchie Ples retired military officer

### Garrison
Herrington, Dale Elizabeth lay worker

### Gary
Speer, James religious organization administrator

### Georgetown
Browning, Grayson Douglas philosophy educator
Busfield, Roger Melvil, Jr. retired trade association executive, educator
Comola, James Paul legislative and environmental consultant
Davis, O. L., Jr. education educator, researcher
Gerding, Thomas Graham medical products company executive
Girvin, Eb Carl biology educator
Lord, William Grogan financial holding company executive
Neville, Gwen Kennedy anthropology educator
Shilling, Roy Bryant, Jr. academic administrator
Welch, William Henry oil service company executive, consultant
Weyrauch, Paul Turney retired army officer

### Gilmer
Green, Douglas Alvin retired library director

### Gladewater
Cox-Beaird, Dian Sanders middle school educator

### Graham
Ritchlin, Martha Ann occupational therapist

### Granbury
Adams, Christopher Steve, Jr. retired defense electronics corporation executive, former air force officer
Fletcher, Riley Eugene lawyer
Garrison, Truitt B. architect
Ketron, Carrie Sue secondary school educator
†Mainord, William Ronald pilot
McWilliams, Chris Pater Elissa elementary school educator
Scogin, Martha Aduddell public information officer
Wisler, Charles Clifton, Jr. retired cotton oil company executive

### Grand Prairie
Childs, Hymen broadcasting corporation executive
Frost, James Hamner health facility administrator
Loo, Maritta Louise military officer, nurse
Ritterhouse, Kathy Lee librarian
Wietholter, William James automotive parts manufacturing company executive

### Grapevine
Arnott, Ellen Marie medical case management and occupational health executive
Franks, Jon Michael lawyer, mediator
Gibbons, Michael Lawrence software engineer
Hirsh, Cristy J. school counselor
Holley, Cyrus Helmer management consulting service executive
Killebrew, James Robert architectural engineering firm executive
Kraft, Karen Ann secondary school educator
Smith, Lee Herman business executive
Stack, George Joseph philosophy educator

### Greenville
Brown, Harley Mitchell retired computer company executive, writer
Peters, Ted Hopkins insurance company executive
White, William Dudley safety engineer

### Gun Barrel City
Smith, Thelma Tina Harriette gallery owner, artist

### Hale Center
Courtney, Carolyn Ann school librarian

### Hallettsville
Baber, Wilbur H., Jr. lawyer

### Hallsville
Hutcherson, Donna Dean music educator

### Haltom City
Deering, Brenda Florine secondary education educator

### Harlingen
Ephraim, Charles lawyer
Farris, Robert Gene transportation company executive
Godfrey, Aline Lucille music specialist, church organist
Johnson, Orrin Wendell lawyer
†Klein, Garner Franklin cardiologist, internist
Martin, Leland Morris (Pappy Martin) history educator
Pope, William L. lawyer, judge
Zaslavsky, Robert secondary school educator

### Hawkins
Lewis, Annice Moore middle school language arts educator

### Hearne
Moore, Loretta Westbrook banker
Williams, Mary Lee elementary school educator

### Heath
Kolodey, Fred James lawyer

### Henderson
McDonald, Benna J. nursing educator, critical care nurse

### Hereford
Langford, Karen Soltis counselor, family therapist

### Hermleigh
Barnes, Maggie Lue Shifflett (Mrs. Lawrence Barnes) nurse

### Hico
Blankenship, Jenny Mary public relations executive, publisher, editor-in-chief

### Highland Village
Coogan, Melinda Ann Strank chemistry educator
Wiedemann, Ramona Diane occupational therapist

### Hillsboro
Auvenshine, William Robert academic administrator

### Hondo
Swort, Arlowayne retired nursing educator and administrator

### Horseshoe Bay
Lesikar, Raymond Vincent business administration educator
Moore, Lawrence Jack lawyer
Ramey, James Melton chemist

### Houston
Aarons-Holder, Charmaine Michele lawyer
Abbott, Lawrence E. lawyer
†Abbruzzese, James Lewis medical oncologist
Able, Luke William retired pediatric surgeon, consultant
†Acree, G. Handy airport executive
†Adams, Kenneth Stanley, Jr. (Bud Adams) energy company executive, football executive
Agraz, Francisco Javier lawyer, public affairs representative
Aguilar, Melissa Ward newspaper editor
Ahart, Jan Fredrick electrical manufacturing company executive
Akers, William Walter chemical engineering educator
Alderman, Richard Mark legal educator, lawyer, television and radio commentator
†Alexander, Leslie Lee professional sports team executive
Alexander, Michael Lee music educator, cellist
Alexanian, Raymond hematologist
Alford, Bobby Ray physician, educator, university official
Allen, Don Lee dentistry educator
Allen, John Timothy mechanical engineer
Allender, John Roland lawyer
Allman, Mark C. engineer, physicist
Amundson, Neal Russell chemical engineer, mathematician, educator
Anderson, Eric Severin lawyer
Anderson, Richard Carl geophysical exploration company executive
Anderson, Thomas Dunaway retired lawyer
Anderson, William (Albion), Jr. investment banker
Andrews, Lavone Dickensheets architect
Antalffy, Leslie Peter mechanical engineer
Appel, Stanley Hersh neurologist
Arnold, Daniel Calmes finance company executive
Arnold, James Phillip religious studies educator, history educator
Askew, William Earl chemist, educator
Atlas, Nancy Friedman judge
Atlas, Scott Jerome lawyer
Auchmuty, Giles applied mathematics educator
Austin, Harry Guiden engineering and construction company executive
Auston, David Henry university administrator, educator
Bagwell, Jeff (Jeffrey Robert Bagwell) professional baseball player
Bahl, Saroj Mehta nutritionist, educator
Bailar, Benjamin Franklin academic administrator, administration educator
Bailey, Charles Lyle insurance company executive
†Bailey, Harold Randolph surgeon
Bair, Royden Stanley architect
Baird, David Leach, Jr. lawyer, petroleum and chemical company executive
Baker, Stephen Denio physics educator
Ballantyne, Christie Mitchell medical educator
Bambace, Robert Shelly lawyer
Banks, Evelyn Yvonne middle school educator
Banks, John Robert, Jr. lawyer
Baranowski, Tom public health educator, researcher
Barcenas, Camilo Gustavo internist, educator
Bargfrede, James Allen lawyer
Barkley, Charles Wade professional basketball player
Barlow, Jim B. newspaper columnist
Barnett, Edward William lawyer
Barracano, Henry Ralph retired oil company executive, consultant
Barrett, Michael Joseph priest
Barrow, Thomas Davies oil and mining company executive
Barry, Allan Ronald ship pilot, corporate executive
Bartling, Phyllis McGinness oil company executive
Baskin, David Stuart neurosurgeon
Bast, Robert Clinton, Jr. medical researcher, medical educator
Baugh, John Frank wholesale company executive
Baughn, Robert Elroy microbiology educator
Bayko, Emil Thomas lawyer
Bean, Alan LaVern retired astronaut, artist
Beasley, Robert Palmer epidemiologist, dean, educator
Bech, Douglas York lawyer
Becher, Andrew Clifford lawyer
Beck, John Robert pathologist, information scientist
Beck, Robert James editor, energy economist, author, consultant
Becker, Frederick Fenimore cancer center administrator, pathologist
Beckingham, Kathleen Mary education educator, researcher
Beirne, Martin Douglas lawyer
Bellatti, Lawrence Lee lawyer
Bennett, George Nelson biochemistry educator
Bentsen, Kenneth Edward architect
Berg, David Howard lawyer
Berra, Yogi (Lawrence Peter Berra) professional baseball coach
Berry, Michael A. physician, consultant
Bethea, Louise Huffman allergist
Bethune, Gordon airline executive
Bickel, Stephen Douglas insurance company executive
Biggio, Craig professional baseball player
Bilger, Bruce R. lawyer
Billingsley, David Stuart chemical engineer, researcher
Bircher, Edgar Allen lawyer
Bischoff, Susan Ann newspaper editor
†Bishop, Blaine Elwood football player
Bishop, David Nolan electrical engineer
Bishop, Thomas Ray retired mechanical engineer
Bistline, F. Walter, Jr. lawyer
Bjornson, Carroll Norman business owner
Black, Kent March aerospace and electronics company executive
Black, Norman William federal judge
Blacklock, Jerry Bob neurosurgeon
Blackshear, A. T., Jr. lawyer
Blanco, Jorge Desiderio physician, medical educator, researcher
Bland, John L. lawyer
Bliss, Ronald Glenn lawyer
Bluestein, Edwin A., Jr. lawyer
Boardman, Robert B. author
Bodey, Gerald Paul medical educator, physician
Bonderman, David airline company executive
Bonilla-Felix, Melvin A. pediatrician, educator
Bonner, Billy Edward physics educator
Bonner, David Calhoun chemical company executive
Bonneville, Richard Briggs retired petroleum exploration and production executive
†Booker, Ronald Joseph physician practice management
Boone, James A. lawyer
Boren, William Meredith manufacturing executive
Borget, Lloyd George architect
Bostic, Jacqueline Whiting management consultant, retired postmaster, association executive
Boudreaux, Bob broadcast journalist
Bousquet, Thomas Gourrier lawyer
Bovay, Harry Elmo, Jr. retired engineering company executive
Bowen, W. J. retired gas company executive
Bowersox, Thomas H. lawyer
Bowman, Jeffrey Neil podiatrist
Bowron, Edgar Peters art museum curator, administrator
Bozeman, Ross Elliot engineering executive
Brandl, Ernest David civil engineer
Brandt, I. Marvin chemist, engineer
Brann, Richard Roland lawyer
Brantley, John Randolph lawyer
Brents, Daniel Rugel architectural firm executive
Bridges, David Manning lawyer
Brinsmade, Lyon Louis lawyer
Brinson, Gay Creswell, Jr. lawyer
Brito, Dagobert Llanos economics educator
Brooks, Philip Russell chemistry educator, researcher
Brotzen, Franz Richard materials science educator
Brouse, Michael petroleum engineer, management consultant
†Brown, Dale, Jr. obstetrician, educator, health facility adminstrator
Brown, Glenda Ann Walters ballet director
Brown, Jack Harold Upton physiology educator, university official, biomedical engineer
Brown, Lee Patrick federal official, law enforcement educator
Bryan, James Lee oil field service company executive
Bryant, John Bradbury economics educator, consultant
Buchanan, Dennis Michael manufacturing and holding company executive
Buckingham, Edwin John, III lawyer
Bue, Carl Olaf, Jr. retired federal judge
Bui, Khoi Tien college counselor
Bui, Long Van church custodian, translator
Bunch, Fred newspaper picture editor
Burch, Voris Reagan retired lawyer
Burdette, Walter James surgeon, educator
Burdine, John A. hospital administrator, nuclear medicine educator
Burguieres, Philip energy service and manufacturing company executive
Burke, Kevin Charles Antony geologist
Burzynski, Stanislaw Rajmund internist
Busch, Harris medical educator
Bush, George Herbert Walker former President of the United States
Buster, John Edmond gynecologist, medical researcher
Butel, Janet Susan virology educator
Butler, Ian John neurologist
Butler, William Thomas college chancellor, physician, educator
Bux, William John lawyer
Buyse, Leone Karena orchestral musician, educator
Caddy, Michael Douglas lawyer
Cadwalder, Hugh Maurice psychology educator
Caldwell, Rodney K. lawyer
Calhoun, Harold architect
Callender, Norma Anne psychology educator, counselor
Cameron, William Duncan plastics company executive
Camfield, William Arnett art educator
Campbell, Andrew William immunotoxicology physician
Campbell, Bert Louis lawyer
Campbell, Carl David oil industry executive, landman
Cantrell, William Allen psychiatrist, educator
Capps, Ethan LeRoy oil company executive
Carameros, George Demitrius, Jr. natural gas company executive
Cardus, David physician
Carlquist, Robert E. newspaper publishing executive
Carlson, Warren Ore civil engineer
Carmody, James Albert lawyer

Carr, Edward A. lawyer
Carroll, Philip Joseph oil company executive
Carter, James Sumter oil company executive, tree farmer
Carter, John Boyd, Jr. oil operator, bank executive
Carter, John Francis, II lawyer
Carter, John Loyd lawyer
Casscells, Samuel Ward, III cardiologist, educator
Castañeda, James Agustín Spanish language educator, university golf coach
Catlin, Francis Irving physician
Chaku, Pran Nath international consulting metallurgist
Chalmers, David B. petroleum executive
Chamberlain, Joseph Wyan astronomer, educator
Chance, Jane English literature educator
Chang, Robert Huei library director
Chapman, Alan Jesse mechanical engineering educator
Chavez, J. Anthony lawyer
Chavez, Victor Manuel process engineer
Cheatham, John Bane, Jr. retired mechanical engineering educator
Chu, Paul Ching-Wu physicist
Chu, Wei-Kan physicist, educator
Cizek, John Gary safety and fire engineer
Cizik, Robert manufacturing company executive
Claiborn, Stephen Allan investment banker
Clark, John William, Jr. electrical engineer, educator
Clark, Pat English lawyer
Clark, Ron D(ean) cosmetologist
Clark, Scott newspaper editor
†Clarke, Jeff television station executive
Clarke, Robert Logan lawyer
Clemenceau, Paul B. lawyer
Cline, Vivian Melinda lawyer
Clore, Lawrence H. lawyer
Cofran, George Lee management consultant
Coghlan, Kelly Jack lawyer
Cole, Aubrey Louis management consultant, forest products company executive
Coleman, Bryan Douglas lawyer, educator, arbitrator, mediator
Collins, Vincent Patrick radiologist, physician, educator
Collipp, Bruce Garfield ocean engineer, consultant
Condit, Linda Faulkner economist
Conway, Sharon Elizabeth lawyer
Cook, B. Thomas lawyer
Cook, Eugene Augustus lawyer
Cooley, Denton Arthur surgeon, educator
Cope-Gibbs, Amy Michelle paralegal
Corral, Edward Anthony fire marshal
Corriere, Joseph N., Jr. urologist, educator
Couch, J. O. Terrell lawyer, former oil company executive
Couch, Jesse Wadsworth retired insurance company executive
Couch, Robert Barnard physician, educator
Cox, Frank D. (Buddy Cox) oil company executive, exploration consultant
Cox, James Talley lawyer
Craig, Robert Mark, III lawyer, educator
Crain, Richard Charles school district music director
Crawford, David Coleman retired diversified manufacturing company executive
Crenshaw, Corinne Burrowes kindergarten educator
Crisp, Jennifer Ann Clair neurosurgical nurse
Crispin, Andre Arthur international trading company executive
Criswell, Ann newspaper editor
Crites, Omar Don, Jr. lawyer
Crone, Marcia Ann judge
Crooker, John H., Jr. lawyer
Cui, Michael Minqin mechanical engineer
Cunningham, R. Walter venture capitalist
Cunningham, Tom Alan lawyer
Curl, Robert Floyd, Jr. chemistry educator
Currie, John Thornton (Jack Currie) retired investment banker
Curry, Alton Frank lawyer
Cuthbertson, Gilbert Morris political science educator
Cutler, John Earl landscape architect
D'Agostino, James Samuel, Jr. financial executive
Daily, James L., Jr. retired financial executive
Daily, Louis ophthalmologist
Dampier, Harold Dean, Jr. lawyer
Danburg, Jerome Samuel oil company executive
Danos, Robert McClure retired oil company executive
Dantone, W. Bryan real estate investor, principal
Darby, Anita Loyce secondary school educator
Davenport, Joseph Dale insurance executive
David, Yadin B. biomedical engineer, health care technology consultant
Davidson, Chandler sociologist, educator
Davis, Bruce Gordon retired principal
Davis, Leon oil company executive
Davis, Martha Algenita Scott lawyer
Davis, Michael Jordan civil engineer, natural gas company executive
Davis, Rex Lloyd insurance company executive
Dawn, Frederic Samuel chemical and textile engineer
Dean, Robert Franklin insurance company executive
Dean, Warren Michael construction company executive
DeBakey, Lois science communications educator, writer, editor
DeBakey, Michael Ellis cardiovascular surgeon, educator, scientist
DeBakey, Selma science communications educator, writer, editor, lecturer
De Bremaecker, Jean-Claude geophysics educator
†de Castro, Jimmy radio station executive
Decker, Hannah Shulman history educator
de Hostos, Eugenio Luis cell biologist
DeMent, James Alderson, Jr. lawyer
DeMoss, Harold R., Jr. federal judge
DeVault, John Lee oil company executive, geophysicist
DeVilla, Lucena M. home healthcare nurse, administrator, business owner
Devlin, Robert Manning financial services company executive
de Vries, Douwe oil company executive
de Vries, Robbie Ray Parsons author, illustrator, international consultant
De Wree, Eugene Ernest manufacturing company executive
Diaz-Arrastia, George Ravelo lawyer
Dice, Bruce Burton retired exploration company executive
DiCorcia, Edward Thomas oil industry executive
Dillon, Clifford Brien retired lawyer
Dimitry, Theodore George lawyer
Dinkins, Carol Eggert lawyer
DiRosa, Linda Mary education specialist, diagnostic company executive
Dishman, Cris Edward professional football player
Dodson, D. Keith engineering and construction company executive
Donie, Scott Olympic athlete, platform diver
Donnelly, Edward James, Jr. medical services company executive
Dosher, John Rodney consulting management consultant
Doubleday, Charles William dermatologist, educator
Douglas, Frank Fair architect, graphic designer
Douglas, James Matthew law educator
Douglass, James academic administrator
Douglass, John Jay lawyer, educator
Doyle, Joseph Francis, III art educator
Drew, Katherine Fischer history educator
Drexler, Clyde professional basketball player
Drury, Leonard Leroy retired oil company executive
Drutz, Jan Edwin pediatrics educator
Duerr, David civil engineer
Duke, Michael B. aerospace scientist
Duncan, Charles William, Jr. investor, former government official
Dunlop, Fred Hurston lawyer
Dunn, James Randolph chief financial officer
DuPont, Herbert Lancashire medical educator, researcher
Dwight, Kenneth Harlan metallurgical engineer
Dworsky, Clara Weiner merchandise brokerage executive, lawyer
Dykes, Osborne Jefferson, III lawyer
Ebaugh, Helen Rose sociology educator, researcher
Edens, Donald Keith oil company executive
Edwards, Blaine Douglass lawyer
Edwards, Victor Henry chemical engineer
Eichberger, LeRoy Carl mechanical engineer, consultant, stress analyst
Eiland, Gary Wayne lawyer
Eisner, Diana pediatrician
Elkins, James Anderson, Jr. banker
Elkins, James Anderson, III banker
Ellis, Rodney Glenn investment banking firm director
Elwood, William Norelli medical researcher
Engelhardt, Hugo Tristram, Jr. physician, educator
England, Rudy Alan lawyer
Englesmith, Tejas actor, producer, curator
Epstein, Jon David lawyer, educator
Estle, Thomas Leo physicist, educator
Eubank, J. Thomas lawyer
Eusibio, Raul Antonio professional baseball player
Evans, Harry Launius pathology educator
Ewoh, Andrew Ikeh Emmanuel political science educator
Fabricant, Jill Diane technology company executive
Faison, Holly state agency administrator
Farenthold, Frances Tarlton lawyer
Farr, Walter Emil, Jr. insurance agent
Feigin, Ralph David medical school president, pediatrician, educator
Feigon, Judith Tova ophthalmologist, surgeon, educator
Feldcamp, Larry Bernard lawyer
Fenn, Sandra Ann programmer, analyst
Ferrand, Jean C. oil company executive
Ferrendelli, James Anthony neurologist, educator
Finch, Michael Paul lawyer
Finney, Clifton Donald publishing executive
Fiorenza, Joseph A. bishop
†Fisher, Jeff professional football coach
Fishman, Marvin Allen pediatrician, neurologist, educator
Fitzgerald, William Terry lawyer
Flack, Joe Fenley county and municipal official, former insurance executive
Flato, William Roeder, Jr. software development company executive
Florio, Ermanno conductor, music administrator
Focht, John Arnold, Jr. geotechnical engineer
Foreman, George boxer, nondenominational christian minister, boxing broadcaster
Fort, John Franklin, III manufacturing company executive
Fortenbach, Ray Thomas retired lawyer
Foster, Charles Crawford lawyer, educator
Foster, Dale Warren political scientist, educator, management consultant, real estate
Foster, Joe B. oil company executive
Fowler, Robert Asa diplomat, consultant, business executive
Foyt, A(nthony) J(oseph), Jr. auto racing crew chief, former professional auto racer
Frank, Hilda Rhea Kaplan dancer
Frankhouser, Homer Sheldon, Jr. engineering and construction company executive
Freeman, Marjorie Schaefer mathematics educator
Freireich, Emil J hematologist, educator
French, Layne Bryan lawyer, investor, community volunteer
Frenger, Paul Fred medical computer consultant, physician
Frieden, Kit newspaper editor
Friedkin, Thomas H. automotive executive
Friedrich, Katherine Rose educational researcher
Fritsch, Derek Adrian nurse anesthetist
Frost, John Elliott minerals company executive
Fullenweider, Donn Charles lawyer
Fuller, Theodore, Jr. elementary education educator
Fulwiler, Robert Neal oil company executive
†Ganter, Garland radio station executive
Garcia, Hector David toxicologist
Gardner, Dale Ray lawyer
Gardner, Everette Shaw, Jr. information sciences educator
Garten, David Burton lawyer
Gattis, James Ralph engineering company executive
Gayle, Gibson, Jr. lawyer
Geer, Ronald Lamar mechanical engineering consultant, retired oil company executive
Geis, Duane Virgil retired investment banker
George, Deveral D. editor, journalist, advertising consultant
Georgiades, William Den Hartog educational administrator
Gerraughty, David R. newspaper editor
Giacalone, Frank Thomas energy and environmental company executive
Gibson, Everett Kay, Jr. space scientist, geochemist
Gibson, Jerry Leigh oil company executive
Gibson, Kathleen Rita anatomy and anthropology educator
Gibson, Michael Addison chemical engineering company executive
Gibson, Quentin Howieson biochemist
Gidley, John Lynn engineering executive
Gigli, Irma physician, educator, academic administrator
Gilbert, Harold Stanley warehousing company executive
Gildenberg, Philip Leon neurosurgeon
Gillis, (Stephen) Malcolm academic administrator, economics educator
Gilmore, Vanessa D. federal judge
Gipson, Robert Malone oil industry executive
Girouard, Peggy Jo Fulcher ballet educator
Gissel, L. Henry, Jr. lawyer
Glass, Douglas B. lawyer
Glassell, Alfred Curry, Jr. investor
Glassman, Armand Barry physician, pathologist, scientist, educator, administrator
Glowinski, Roland mathematics educator
†Goerke, Glenn Allen university administrator
Goff, Robert Burnside retired food company executive
Goldberg, William Jeffrey accountant
Goldman, Nathan Carliner lawyer, educator
Goldman, Stanford Milton medical educator
Goldman, William Alexander computer engineer
Goldsmith, Billy Joe real estate broker
Goldstein, Jack Charles lawyer
Goldstein, Margaret Ann biologist
Gomez, Lucas assistant treasurer, credit manager
Gonynor, Francis James lawyer
†Gonzalez, Georgina S. insurance executive, actuary
Goodman, Herbert Irwin petroleum company executive
Gordon, Wendell Chaffee economics educator
Gordon, William Edwin physicist, engineer, educator, university official
Gore, Thomas Jackson construction executive
Gormley, W. Clarke lawyer
Gorry, G. Anthony medical educator
Gorski, Daniel Alexander art educator
Gould, Kenneth Lance physician, educator
Gover, Alan Shore lawyer
Grace, James Martin, Jr. lawyer
Graham, David Yates gastroenterologist
Graham, Michael Paul lawyer
Graving, Richard John law educator
Gray, Mel professional football player
Gray, Robert Steele publishing executive, editor
Green, Gene congressman
Griffin, Oscar O'Neal, Jr. writer, former oil company executive
Grossett, Deborah Lou psychologist, behavior analyst, consultant
Grossman, Herbert Barton urologist, researcher
Grossman, Robert George physician, educator
Gruber, Ira Dempsey historian, educator
Gubbin, Barbara Ashley Brendon librarian
Guinn, David Crittenden petroleum engineer, drilling and exploration company executive
Gunn, Albert Edward, Jr. internist, educator, lawyer, hospital and university administrator
Gunn, Joan Marie health care administrator
Gupta, Kaushal Kumar internist
Guynn, Robert William psychiatrist, educator
Haas, Merrill Wilber geologist, oil company executive
Hackerman, Norman chemist, consultant, academic administrator
Hafner, Joseph A., Jr. food company executive
Halbouty, Michel Thomas geologist, petroleum engineer, petroleum operator
Hale, Leon newspaper columnist
Hall, Charles Washington lawyer
Hall, Robert Joseph physician, medical educator
Halloran, Bernard Thorpe lawyer
Hamblet, Carole Orr artist
Hamel, Lee lawyer
Hamilton, Lorraine Rebekah adult education consultant
Hammack, Gladys Lorene Mann reading specialist, educator
Hammond, Ken newspaper magazine editor
Hammond, Michael Peter music educator, dean
Hanania, Nicola Alexander physician
Hansen, Paula Renee healthcare administrator
Hardin, George Cecil, Jr. petroleum consultant
Hargrove, James Ward financial consultant
Harle, Thomas Stanley radiologist
Harmon, Melinda Furche federal judge
Harper, Alfred John, II lawyer
Harrell, James Earl, Sr. radiologist, educator
Harrell, Robert S. lawyer
Harrington, Bruce Michael lawyer, investor
Harris, Richard Foster, Jr. insurance company executive
Hart, James Whitfield, Jr. corporate public affairs executive, lawyer
Hartrick, Janice Kay lawyer
Hartsfield, Henry Warren, Jr. astronaut
Harvey, F. Reese mathematics educator
Harvin, David Tarleton lawyer
Harvin, William Charles lawyer
Haskell, Thomas Langdon history educator
†Haslam, Charles Linn aerospace executive, lawyer, educator
Hasling, Jill Freeman meteorologist
Haymes, Robert C. physicist, educator
Haymond, Paula J. psychologist, diagnostician, hypnotherapist
Haynie, Thomas Powell, III physician
Heiker, Vincent Edward information systems executive
Heinrich, Randall Wayne lawyer, investment banker
Heinsen, Lindsay newspaper editor
Heit, Raymond Anthony civil engineer
Helland, George Archibald, Jr. management consultant, manufacturing executive, former government official
Hellums, Jesse David chemical engineering educator and researcher
Hempel, John P. mathematics educator
Henderson, Nathan H. bishop
Hendrix, Dennis Ralph energy company executive
Henington, David Mead library director
Henkel, Jenny Saucier neurovirologist
Henning, Susan June biomedical researcher
Henry, John Cooper journalist
Hermann, Robert John lawyer, corporate executive
Hesse, Martha O. natural gas company executive
Hewitt, Lester L. lawyer
Hightower, Joe Walter chemical engineering educator, consultant
Hinton, Paula Weems lawyer
Hirsch, Edward Mark poet, English language educator
Hitchman, Cal McDonald, Sr. secondary education educator
Hittner, David federal judge
Ho, Yhi-Min university dean, economics educator
Hoang, Hung Manh information systems analyst, consultant
Hobby, William Pettus broadcast executive, retired
†Hodge, Etta Lee director of surgical services, nurse
Hodges, Ann television editor, newspaper columnist
Hodo, Edward Douglas university president
Hoffman, Philip Guthrie former university president
Hoglund, Forrest Eugene petroleum company executive
Holcomb, William A. retired oil and gas exploration, pipeline executive, retired real estate broker, consultant
Holderness, Algernon Sidney, Jr. lawyer
Hollister, Leo Edward physician, educator
Holloway, Gordon Arthur lawyer
Holloway, Tommy W. government agency administrator
Hollyfield, John Scoggins lawyer
Holmes, Ann Hitchcock journalist
Holmes, Cecile Searson religion editor
Holmes, Darrell tourism consultant
Holmes, Harry Dadisman health facility administrator
Holovak, Mike sports association exec
Holstead, John Burnham lawyer
Honea, T. Milton gas industry executive
Honeycutt, George Leonard photographer, retired
Hong, Waun Ki medical oncologist, clinical investigator
Hook, Harold Swanson insurance company executive
Hornak, Anna Frances library administrator
Horvitz, Paul Michael finance educator
†Howard, Allan E. television station executive
Howell, Paul Neilson oil company executive
Hoyt, Kenneth M. federal judge
Hoyt, Mont Powell lawyer
Hsu, Katharine Han Kuang pediatrics educator
Hsu, Thomas Tseng-Chuang civil engineer, educator
Huang, Huey Wen physicist, educator
Huck, Lewis Francis lawyer, real estate consultant and developer
Hudspeth, Chalmers Mac lawyer, educator
Huelbig, Larry Leggett lawyer
Huff, John Rossman oil service company executive
Hughes, Lynn Nettleton federal judge
Hult, Susan Freda history educator
Hung, Mien-Chie cancer biologist
Hungerford, Ed Vernon, III physics educator
†Hunsicker, Gerry professional sports executive
Huston, John Dennis English educator
Hutcheson, Joseph Chappell, III lawyer
Hutcheson, Thad Thomson, Jr. international executive
Hyman, Harold M. history educator, consultant
Ibrahim, Nuhad Khalil oncologist
†Ilft, Lewis George, III company administrator
Ignatiev, Alex physics researcher
Irelan, Robert Withers metal products executive
Irwin, John Robert oil and gas drilling executive
Ivins, Marsha S. aerospace engineer, astronaut
†Jackson, Ernest, Jr. broadcasting executive
Jackson, Gilchrist L. surgeon
Jackson, R. Graham architect
Jacobus, Charles Joseph lawyer, title company executive, author
Jamail, Joseph Dahr, Jr. lawyer
Jamieson, John Kenneth oil company executive
Jankovic, Joseph neurologist, educator, scientist
Jansen, Donald Orville lawyer
Janssens, Joe Lee controller
Jeanneret, Paul Richard management consultant
Jenkins, Daniel Edwards, Jr. physician, educator
Jenkins, Judith Alexander bank consultant
Jennings, Gray lawyer
Jetton, Steve newspaper editor
Jewell, George Hiram lawyer
Jhin, Michael Kontien health care executive
Johnson, Frederick Dean former food company executive
Johnson, Judy Dianne elementary education educator
Johnson, Kenneth Oscar oil company executive
Johnson, Richard James Vaughan newspaper executive
Johnson, Thomas David pharmacologist
Johnson, Wayne D. gas industry executive
Johnston, Ben Earl veterinarian
Johnston, Marguerite journalist, author
Jones, Dan B. ophthalmologist, educator
Jones, Edith Hollan federal judge
Jones, Edith Irby physician
Jones, Florence M. music educator
Jones, Frank Griffith lawyer
Jones, James Wilson physician, cell biologist
Jones, Larry Leroy oil company executive
Jones, Lincoln, III army officer
Jones, Samuel conductor
Jordan, Charles Milton lawyer
Jordan, Don D. electric company executive
Jordan, W. Carl lawyer
Jorden, James Roy retired oil company engineering executive
Jordon, Robert Earl physician
Joyce, James Daniel clergyman
Jurtshuk, Peter, Jr. microbiologist
Justice, (David) Blair psychology educator, author
Kahan, Barry Donald surgeon, educator
Kalmaz, Errol Ekrem environmental scientist
Kaplan, Lee Landa lawyer
Kaptopodis, Louis supermarket chain executive
Karff, Samuel Egal rabbi
Katrana, David John plastic and reconstructive surgeon
Kaufman, Raymond Henry physician
Kay, Joel Phillip lawyer
Kaye, Howard business executive
Kean, James Campbell lawyer
Kellaway, Peter neurophysiologist, researcher
Kellison, Stephen George insurance executive
Kelly, Hugh Rice lawyer
Kelly, William Franklin, Jr. lawyer
Kenley, Elizabeth Sue commerce and transportation executive
Kennedy, Ken computer science educator
†Kenney, Belinda Jill Forseman electronics executive
Kerr, Baine Perkins oil company executive
Kershaw, Carol Jean psychologist
Ketchand, Robert Lee lawyer
Kevan, Larry chemistry educator
Key, James Everett ophthalmologist
Kientz, Renee newspaper editor
King, Carolyn Dineen federal judge
King, Jonathan architectural researcher, educator
King, Kay Wander design educator, fashion designer, consultant
King, Robert Augustin engineering executive
Kinnaird, Susan Marie special education educator
Kinsey, James Lloyd chemist, educator
Kirby, Sarah Ann Van Deventer aerospace engineer
Kirkland, John David oil and gas company executive, lawyer
Kit, Saul biochemist, educator

Kitowski, Vincent Joseph medical consultant, former physical medicine and rehabilitation physician
Klausmeyer, David Michael scientific instruments manufacturing company executive
Kline, Allen Haber, Jr. lawyer
Kline, John William retired air force officer, management consultant
Knapp, David Hebard banker
Knauss, Robert Lynn international business educator, corporate executive
Knight, J. Vernon medicine and microbiology educator
Kobayashi, Riki chemical engineer, educator
Kobs, Alfred W. engineer
Kochi, Jay Kazuo chemist, educator
Koenig, Rodney Curtis lawyer, rancher
Kollaer, Jim C. real estate executive, architect
Konisky, Jordan microbiology educator
Kors, R. Paul search company executive
Kouri, Donald Jack chemist, educator
Kraft, Irvin Alan psychiatrist
Krakower, Terri Jan biochemist, researcher
Kratochvil, L(ouis) Glen lawyer
Krause, William Austin engineering executive
Kraus-Friedmann, Naomi biochemistry educator
Krebs, Arno William, Jr. lawyer
Krieger, Paul Edward lawyer
Krishen, Kumar aerospace research technologist
Kulkarni, Venkatesh author
Kuntz, Edward Lawrence health care executive
Kuntz, Hal Goggan petroleum exploration company executive
Kutka, Nicholas nuclear medicine physician
LaBoon, Robert Bruce lawyer
Lake, Kathleen C. lawyer
Lake, Simeon Timothy, III federal judge
Lamb, Sydney MacDonald linguistics and cognitive science educator
Lane, Montague physician, educator
†Lanier, Bob mayor
Lanier, Robert C. (Bob Lanier) mayor
Lankford, Olga Juanita gifted and talented and elementary educator
Larkin, Lee Roy lawyer
Larkin, William Vincent, Jr. service company executive
Larks, Jack forensic engineer, consultant
Larrey, Inge Harriette jazz and blues freelance photographer
Larson, Peter L. legal assistant, investigator
Latimer, Roy Truett museum executive
Lawhon, Susan Harvin lawyer
Lawson, Ben F. lawyer, international legal consultant
Lay, Kenneth Lee diversified energy company executive
Lee, Janie C. curator
Lee, William Gentry lawyer
Lehrer, Kenneth Eugene real estate advisor, economic consultant
Lenox, Angela Cousineau healthcare consultant
Leonard, Gilbert Stanley oil company executive
Lerup, Lars G. architecture educator, college dean
Letsou, George Vasilios cardiothoracic surgeon
Levin, Bernard physician
Levit, Max food service executive
Levit, Milton grocery supply company executive
Lewis, Carl (Frederick Carlton Lewis) Olympic track and field athlete
Lewis, Edward Sheldon chemistry educator
Liang, Edison Parktak astrophysicist, educator, researcher
Lichtman, David Michael military officer, health care administrator, orthopedist, educator
Liddell, Leon Morris librarian, educator
Lienhard, John Henry, IV mechanical engineering educator
Lindig, Bill M. food distribution company executive
Lindner, Kenneth Edward academic administrator and chemistry educator emeritus
Lindsey, John Horace insurance executive, museum official
Loeffler, James Joseph lawyer
Loftis, Jack D. newspaper editor, newspaper executive
Long, William Everett retired utility executive
Lopez, David Tiburcio lawyer, educator, arbitrator, mediator
Lopez-Nakazono, Benito chemical and industrial engineer
Loria, Christopher Joseph marine officer
Louck, Lisa Ann lawyer
Love, Jeffrey Benton lawyer
Lovelace, Byron Keith lawyer, management consultant
Loveland, Eugene Franklin petroleum executive
Low, Morton David physician, educator
Lowry, William Randall executive recruiter
Lucid, Shannon W. biochemist, astronaut
Luigs, Charles Russell gas and oil drilling industry executive
Luss, Dan chemical engineering educator
Mackey, William Sturges, Jr. investor, consultant
Maligas, Manuel Nick metallurgical engineer
Maloney, James Edward lawyer
Mampre, Virginia Elizabeth communications executive
Mansell, Joyce Marilyn special education educator
†Marcus, Jerry broadcasting executive
Margrave, John Lee chemist, educator, university administrator
Marley, Everett Armistead, Jr. lawyer
Marshall, Gailen Daugherty, Jr. physician, scientist, educator
Marshall, Jane Pretzer newspaper editor
Marshall, Margo artistic director
Marshall, Thom columnist
Marston, Edgar Jean, III lawyer
Martin, J. Landis manufacturing company executive, lawyer
Martin, James Kirby historian, educator
Martin, Jerry C. oil company executive
Martin, Randi Christine psychology educator
Martin, William C. sociology educator, writer
Marzio, Peter Cort museum director
Mason, Franklin Rogers automotive executive
Massad, Stephen Albert lawyer
Masters, Ronald G. dentist, educator
Mateker, Emil Joseph, Jr. geophysicist
Matney, William Brooks, VII electrical engineer, marine engineer
Matthews, Bruce Rankin professional football player
Matthews, Charles Sedwick petroleum engineering consultant, research advisor
Matthews, Kathleen Shive biochemistry educator
Matthews, Thomas Michael energy company executive
Mattox, Kenneth Leon surgeon, educator, medical scientist
Mauck, William M., Jr. executive recruiter, small business owner
Max, Ernest surgeon
May, Beverly elementary school educator
May, Henry Stratford, Jr. lawyer
May, John Andrew petrophysicist, geologist
Mayor, Richard Blair lawyer
McCleary, Henry Glen geophysicist
McClung, J(ames) David corporate executive, lawyer
McClure, Daniel M. lawyer
McCollum, Gary Wayne government official
McDaniel, Jarrel Dave lawyer
Mc David, George Eugene (Gene Mc David) newspaper executive
McEvilly, Michael James civil engineer
Mc Fadden, Joseph Michael academic administrator
Mc Ginty, John Milton architect
McGregor, Martin Luther, Jr. lawyer
McGuire, Dianne Marie psychotherapist
McIntire, Larry Vern chemical engineering educator
McIntosh, Susan Keech anthropology educator
McKim, Paul Arthur management consultant, retired petroleum executive
†McLane, Drayton, Jr. professional baseball team executive
McMahon, Catherine Driscoll lawyer
†McNair, Robert C. communications executive
McPhail, JoAnn Winstead writer, publisher, art dealer
Mc Pherson, Alice Ruth ophthalmologist
Meddleton, Francis Charles elementary and secondary school educator
Meeks, Herbert Lessig, III pastor, former school system administrator
Mehra, Jagdish physicist
Meindl, Max J., III environmental consultant, professional inspector
Meinke, Roy Walter electrical engineer, consultant
Mendelsohn, John oncologist, hematologist, educator
Menscher, Barnet Gary steel company executive
Menzies, John Alexander mechanical and chemical engineer
Mermelstein, Isabel Mae Rosenberg financial consultant
Meyer, Dianne Scott Wilson secondary school educator, librarian
Meyer, John Stirling neurologist, educator
Mian, Farouk Aslam chemical engineer, educator
Michaels, Kevin Richard lawyer
Miele, Angelo engineering educator, researcher, consultant, author
Milam, John Daniel pathologist, educator
Millar, Jeffery Lynn columnist
Miller, Charles Rickie thermal and fluid systems analyst, engineering manager
Miller, Gary Evan psychiatrist, mental health services administrator
Miller, Janel Howell psychologist
Miller, Kenneth William holding company executive, financier
Miner, Michael E. neurosurgery educator
Minter, David Lee English literature educator
Mithoff, Richard Warren lawyer
Moehlman, Michael Scott lawyer
Moncure, John Lewis lawyer
Monroe, L. A. J. oil well drilling company executive
Montle, Paul Joseph entrepreneur
Moore, Lois Jean health science facility administrator
Moore, Walter Parker, Jr. civil engineering company executive
Moorhead, Gerald Lee architect
Morehead, James Caddall, Jr. architect, educator
Morgenstern, Lewis B. medical educator
Morris, (William) Carloss lawyer, insurance company executive
Morris, Malcolm Stewart title company executive, lawyer
Morris, Owen Glenn engineering corporation executive
Morris, Seth Irwin architect
Morrison, Scott David computer company executive
Moya, Olga Lydia law educator
Mueller, Carl Gustav, Jr. lawyer
Müller-Eberhard, Hans Joachim medical research scientist, administrator
Munisteri, Joseph George construction executive
Munk, Zev Moshe allergist, researcher
†Murphy, Calvin Jerome professional sports team executive
Murphy, Ewell Edward, Jr. lawyer
Murphy, William Alexander, Jr. diagnostic radiologist, educator
Musgrave, Story astronaut, surgeon, pilot, physiologist, educator
Musher, Daniel Michael physician
Myers, Franklin lawyer, oil service company executive
Myers, James Clark advertising and public relations executive
Myers, Norman Allan marketing professional
Nacol, Mae lawyer
Nanz, Robert Hamilton petroleum consultant
Nations, Howard Lynn lawyer
Neeld, Elizabeth Harper author
Nelson, David Loren geneticist, educator
Nelson, John Robert theology educator, clergyman
Nesbitt, Vance Gordon computer software company executive
Nestvold, Elwood Olaf oil and gas industry executive
Neuhaus, Philip Ross investment banker
Neuhaus, William Oscar, III architect
Newberry, Robert Curtis, Sr. communications executive, newspaper editor
Newbold, Benjamin Millard, Jr. library manager, education consultant
Newman, Mary Thomas communications educator, management consultant
Nicandros, Constantine Stavros business consultant, retired oil company executive
Nichols, Buford Lee, Jr. physiologist
Nielsen, Niels Christian, Jr. theology educator
Nolen, Roy Lemuel lawyer
Nordgren, Ronald Paul engineering educator, researcher
Norton, Norman James exploration geologist
Nuss, Eldon Paul casket manufacturer
Nyberg, Donald Arvid oil company executive
Obiora, Chris Sunny architect
O'Connor, Ralph Sturges investment company executive
O'Donnell, Lawrence, III lawyer
O'Kehie, Collins Emeka lawyer, consultant
Olajuwon, Hakeem Abdul professional basketball player
Oldham, Darius Dudley lawyer
O'Malley, Bert William cell biologist, educator, physician
O'Neil, John artist
O'Neil, Sharon Lund educator
Onstead, Randall consumer goods company executive
Onstead, Robert R. consumer goods company executive
Ordonez, Nelson Gonzalo pathologist
Oren, Bruce Clifford newspaper editor, artist
Orr, Joseph Newton recreational guide, outdoor educator
Orton, John Stewart lawyer
Orton, Stewart retail company executive, merchant
Ostrofsky, Benjamin business and engineering management educator, industrial engineer
Ostrow, Stuart theatrical producer, educator
O'Toole, Austin Martin lawyer
Overfield, Robert Edward physicist
Owsley, William Clinton, Jr. radiologist
Oxer, John Paul Daniell civil engineer
Palmer, James Edward public relations executive
Parker, Norman Neil, Jr. software systems analyst, mathematics educator
Parsons, Edmund Morris investment company executive
Pasternak, Joanna Murray special education and gifted and talented educator
Pate, James Leonard oil company executive
Pate, Stephen Patrick lawyer
Patin, Michael James oil company executive
Patten, Robert Lowry English language educator
Patterson, Donald Eugene research scientist
Patterson, Ronald R(oy) health care systems executive
Patterson, Steve professional hockey team executive
Paul, Gordon Lee behavioral scientist, psychologist
Paul, Thomas Daniel lawyer
Pearson, James Boyd, Jr. electrical engineering educator
Pearson, Michael P. lawyer
Peck, Edwin Russell real estate management executive
Pederson, Tony Weldon newspaper editor
Pelaez, Rolando Federico economics educator, consultant
Pennell, Linda Bennett secondary school educator
Pester, Jack Cloyd oil company executive
Peterkin, George Alexander, Jr. marine transportation company executive
Pfeiffer, Eckhard computer company executive
Phillippi, Elmer Joseph, Jr. data communications analyst
Phillips, Linda Lou pharmacist
Phung, Nguyen Dinh medical educator
Pickering, James Henry, III academic administrator
Pierce, George Foster, Jr. architect
Pinson, Artie Frances elementary school educator
Pittman, Katherine Anne Atherton elementary education educator
Pitts, Gary Benjamin lawyer
Pluff, Stearns Charles, III investment banker
Plunkett, Jack William writer, publisher
Poston, Walker Seward, II medical educator, researcher
Poulos, Michael James insurance company executive
Powell, Alan mechanical engineer, scientist
Powell, Michael Robert biophysicist, physicist, chemist
Powers, Hugh William newspaper executive
Prats, Michael petroleum engineer, educator
Pravel, Bernarr Roe lawyer
Prentice, James Stuart energy company executive, chemical engineer
Prescott, William Bruce minister
Pryor, William Daniel Lee humanities educator
Pugsley, Frank Burruss lawyer
Pyle, Jerry automotive executive
Quick, Lisa R. accountant, scheduler
†Raber, Martin health facility administrator, medical educator
Radke, Jan Rodger pulmonologist, hospital program administrator
Radnofsky, Barbara A. lawyer, mediator/arbitrator
Radoff, Leonard Irving librarian, consultant
Raijman, Isaac gastroenterologist, endoscopist, educator
Rainey, John David federal judge
Rakel, Robert Edwin physician, educator
Ransom, Clifton Louis, Jr. lawyer, real estate investor
Ray, Hugh Massey, Jr. lawyer
Raymer, Warren Joseph retired allergist
Read, Michael Oscar editor, consultant
Reasoner, Barrett Hodges lawyer
Reasoner, Harry Max lawyer
Redmon, Agile Hugh, Jr. allergist
Reed, Kathlyn Louise occupational therapist, educator
†Reese, Floyd professional sports team executive
Reif, Louis Raymond lawyer, utilities executive
Reiff, Patricia Hofer space physicist, educator
Reso, Anthony geologist, earth resources economist
Reynolds, John Terrence oil industry executive
Ribble, Anne Hoerner communications executive
Ribble, John Charles medical educator
Rice, Emily Joy retired secondary school and adult educator
Rich, Robert Regier immunology educator, physician
Richardson, Frank H. retired oil industry executive
Riedel, Alan Ellis manufacturing company executive, lawyer
Riesser, Gregor Hans arbitrage investment advisor
Rigsby, Carolyn Erwin music educator
Riley, William John neurologist
Ro, Jae Yun pathologist
Roach, Robert Michael, Jr. lawyer
Robbins, Earl L. oil operator
Roberts, Cecil Kenneth lawyer
Robertson, James Woolsey lawyer
Robins, W. Ronald lawyer
Robinson, Esther Martin secondary school educator
Roby, Reginald Henry professional football player
Rock, Douglas Lawrence manufacturing executive
Rockwell, Elizabeth Dennis retirement specialist, financial planner
Roff, J(ohn) Hugh, Jr. energy company executive
Rogers, Arthur Hamilton, III lawyer
Romsdahl, Marvin Magnus surgeon, educator
Roorda, John Francis, Jr. business consultant
Rose, Beatrice Schroeder (Mrs. William H. Rose) harpist, educator
Rosenthal, Lee H. federal judge
Ross, Patti Jayne obstetrics and gynecology educator
Rossler, Willis Kenneth, Jr. petroleum company executive
Roth, Jack Alan thoracic surgeon
Rozzell, Scott Ellis lawyer
Rudolph, Andrew Henry dermatologist, educator
Rudolph, Frederick Byron biochemistry educator
Runge, Barbara Kay lawyer, arbitrator, mediator
Russell, John Francis retired librarian
Russman, Thomas Anthony philosophy educator
Ryan, Cornelius O'Brien lawyer
Rypien, David Vincent welding engineer
Saizan, Paula Theresa oil company executive
Salch, Steven Charles lawyer
Sales, James Bohus lawyer
Sampson, Franklin Delano minister
Sapp, Walter William lawyer, energy company executive
Sass, Ronald Lewis biology and chemistry educator
Saunders, Charles Albert lawyer
Scharold, Mary Louise psychoanalyst, educator
Schechter, Arthur Louis lawyer
Scheuerle, Angela Elizabeth geneticist
Schier, Mary Jane science writer
Schiflett, Mary Fletcher Cavender health facility executive, researcher, educator
Schneider, David J. psychology educator, academic administrator
Schneider, Karen Lee psychotherapist
Schoolar, Joseph Clayton psychiatrist, pharmacologist, educator
Schroepfer, George John, Jr. biochemistry educator
Schultz, Stanley George physiologist, educator
Schulze, Arthur Edward biomedical engineer, researcher
Schwartz, Charles Walter lawyer
Schwartzel, Charles Boone lawyer
Schwarz, Paul Winston judge, lawyer, business company executive
Scott, David Warren statistics educator
Scott, Ronald lawyer
Scuseria, Gustavo Enrique theoretical chemist
Seale, Robert Arthur, Jr. lawyer
Seaman, Roual Duane data processing company executive
Seaton, Alberta Jones biologist, consultant
Sebastian, Michael James retired manufacturing company executive
Segner, Edmund Peter, III natural gas company executive
Selke, Oscar O., Jr. physiatrist, educator
Shaddock, Carroll Sidney lawyer
Shankel, Gerald Marvin professional society administrator
Sharp, Douglas Andrew secondary school educator
Shearer, William Thomas pediatrician, educator
Sheehan, Linda Suzanne educational administrator
Sheinfeld, Myron M. lawyer, educator
Shen, Liang Chi electrical engineer, educator, researcher
Sher, George Allen philosophy educator
Shirley, Dennis Lynn education educator
Shulman, Robert Jay physician
Silva, Eugene Joseph lawyer
Simmons, Lawrence William health care company executive
Simon, Barry Philip lawyer, airline executive
Simpson, Joe Leigh obstetrics and gynecology educator
Sims, Rebecca Gibbs accountant, certified fraud examiner
Sing, William Bender lawyer
Singleton, John Virgil, Jr. retired federal judge, lawyer
Sisson, Virginia Baker geology educator
Skalla, John Lionell insurance agent
Skolnick, Malcolm Harris biophysics researcher, educator, patent lawyer, mediator
Skov, Arlie Mason petroleum engineer, consultant
Slaugh, Lynn H. chemist
Sloan, Harold David chemical engineering consultant
Smalley, Arthur Louis, Jr. engineering and construction company executive
Smalley, Richard Errett chemistry and physics educator, researcher
Smith, Arthur Kittredge, Jr. academic administrator, political science educator
Smith, David Kingman retired oil company executive, consultant
Smith, Frank Forsythe, Jr. lawyer
Smith, Jerry Edwin federal judge
Smith, Ken A. physicist
Smith, Michael Alexis petroleum geologist
Smith, Richard Joseph history educator
†Smith, Tal sports association administrator
Smith, William Randolph lawyer
Smythe, Cheves McCord dean, medical educator
Solymosy, Edmond Sigmond Albert international marketing executive, retired army officer
Sondock, Ruby Kless retired judge
Sonfield, Robert Leon, Jr. lawyer
SoRelle, Ruth Doyle medical writer, journalist
Sorrels, Randall Owen lawyer
Spalding, Andrew Freeman lawyer
Spanos, Pol Dimitrios engineering educator
Spencer, Albert Franklin physical education and education educator
Spencer, William A. physician, educational administrator
Spincic, Wesley James oil company executive, consultant
Spira, Melvin plastic surgeon
Staine, Ross lawyer
Steele, James Harlan former public health veterinarian, educator
Steen, Wesley Wilson former judge, lawyer
Stehlin, John Sebastian, Jr. surgeon
Stephens, Carson Wade minister
Stevenson, Ben artistic director
Stewart, Pamela L. lawyer
Stinemetz, Steven Douglas lawyer
Stralem, Pierre retired stockbroker
Streng, William Paul lawyer, educator
Strudler, Robert Jacob real estate development executive
Stryker, Steven Charles lawyer
Stuart, Walter Bynum, IV lawyer
Sudbury, John Dean religious foundation executive, petroleum chemist
Susman, Morton Lee lawyer
Susman, Stephen Daily lawyer
Sutej, Vjekoslav conductor
Suter, Jon Michael academic library director, educator
Sweeney, John W., III newspaper executive
Sweet, James Brooks oral and maxillofacial surgeon
Symons, James Martin environmental engineer, educator
Szalkowski, Charles Conrad lawyer
Talwani, Manik geophysicist, educator
Taylor, James B. securities trader, financial planner

Temkin, Larry Scott philosopher, educator
Templeton, Robert Earl engineering and construction company executive
Terrell, G. Irvin lawyer
Tesarek, William Paul business consultant, writer, financial executive
Thagard, Norman E. astronaut, physician, engineer
Thomas, Marilyn Jane insurance company executive
Thomas, Orville C. physician
Thompson, Ewa M. foreign language educator
Thorn, Terence Hastings gas industry executive
Thorne, Joye Holley special education administrator
Toedt, D(ell) C(harles), III lawyer
Tomjanovich, Rudolph professional athletic coach
Tooker, Carl E. department store executive
Touchy, Deborah K. P. lawyer, accountant
Travis, Andrew David lawyer
†Trimble, Eddie Don television executive
Tripp, Karen Bryant lawyer
Tucker, Randolph Wadsworth engineering executive
Tulloch, Brian Robert endocrinologist
Tullos, Hugh Simpson orthopedic surgeon, educator
Tung, Shih-Ming Samuel medical physicist
Turner, William Wilson hospital administrator
Urbina, Manuel, II legal research historian, history educator
Vaden, Frank Samuel, III lawyer, engineer
Vallbona, Carlos physician
Vallbona, Rima-Gretel Rothe Spanish language educator, writer
Van Caspel, Venita Walker retired financial planner
Vance, Carol Stoner lawyer
Vanderploeg, James M. preventive medicine physician
Van Fleet, George Allan lawyer
Vassilopoulou-Sellin, Rena medical educator
Vest, G. Waverly, Jr. lawyer
Vogel, Susan Michelle physician
Waggoner, James Virgil chemicals company executive
Wagner, Donald Bert health care consultant
Wagner, Paul Anthony, Jr. education educator
Wainerdi, Richard Elliott medical center executive
Wakefield, Stephen Alan lawyer
Wakil, Salih Jawad biochemistry educator
Walbridge, Willard Eugene broadcasting executive
Walker, Esper Lafayette, Jr. civil engineer
Walker, Sammie Lee retired elementary education educator
Walker, William Easton surgeon, educator, lawyer
†Wall, Matthew J., Jr. surgeon, scientist
Walls, Carmage newspaper publishing executive
Walls, Martha Ann Williams (Mrs. B. Carmage Walls) newspaper executive
Wang, Chao-Cheng mathematician, engineer
Ward, David Henry (Dave Ward) television news reporter
Ward, Jo Alice computer consultant, educator
†Wasserman, Steve broadcast executive
†Watson, Bob professional baseball executive
Watson, John Allen lawyer
Watson, Max P., Jr. computer software company executive
Waycaster, Bill chemicals executive
Webb, Jack M. lawyer
Webb, Marty Fox principal
Weber, Fredric Alan lawyer
Weber, Owen broadcast executive
Weberpal, Michael Andrew lawyer
Weekley, David real estate developer
Weinstein, Roy physics educator, researcher
Welch, Byron Eugene communications educator
Welch, Harry Scoville lawyer, retired gas pipeline company executive
Welch, Robert Morrow, Jr. lawyer
Wells, Benjamin Gladney lawyer
Wells, Damon, Jr. investment company executive
Wells, Raymond O., Jr. mathematics educator, researcher
Werlein, Ewing, Jr. federal judge, lawyer
West, Thomas Lowell, Jr. insurance company executive
Westby, Timothy Scott lawyer
Wheelan, R(ichelieu) E(dward) lawyer
Wheless, James Warren neurologist
Whitaker, Gilbert Riley, Jr. academic administrator, business economist
Wickliffe, Jerry L. lawyer
Wiemer, David Robert plastic surgeon
Wiener, Martin Joel historian
Wilde, Carlton D. lawyer
Wilde, William Key lawyer
Wilhelm, Marilyn private school administrator
Wilkinson, Harry Edward management educator and consultant
Wilks, William Lee retired educator, dean
Willcott, Mark Robert, III chemist, educator, researcher
Williams, Edward Earl, Jr. entrepreneur, educator
Williams, James Lee financial industries executive
Williams, Robert Henry oil company executive
Williams, Robert Lyle corporate executive, consultant
Williams, Temple Weatherly, Jr. internist, educator
Williamson, Peter David lawyer
Willis, Kevin Alvin professional basketball player
Wilson, Edward Converse, Jr. oil and natural gas production company executive
Wilson, Patricia Potter library science and reading educator, educational and library consultant
Wilson, Rick Keith political science educator
Wilson, Thomas Leon physicist
Wold, Finn biochemist, educator
Wolff, Dee Ivona artist
Wolinsky, Ira nutritionist
Wong, Daniel On-Cheong geotechnical and environmental engineer
Wong-Liang, Eirene Ming psychologist
Woodhouse, John Frederick food distribution company executive
Woods, Donna Sue education educator, reading consultant, state agency administrator
Woodson, Benjamin Nelson, III insurance executive
Woodward, Katherine Anne secondary education educator
Wray, Thomas Jefferson lawyer
Wren, Robert James aerospace engineering manager
Wright, Robert Payton lawyer
Wu, Gary G. petroleum engineer, consultant
Wyatt, Oscar Sherman, Jr. energy company executive
Wyschogrod, Edith philosophy educator
Yang, Chao Yuh chemistry educator
Yokubaitis, Roger T. lawyer
York, James Martin judge
Young, Frank Mitchell musical theater producer
Young, Jeanette Cochran corporate planner, reporter, analyst
Young, John Watts astronaut
Yu, Aiting Tobey engineering executive
Yuen, Benson Bolden airline management consultant, software executive
Zeff, Stephen Addam accounting educator
Zhang, Jingwu immunologist
Zlatkis, Albert chemistry educator

## Hughes Springs
Koelker, Gail family nurse practitioner

## Humble
Brinkley, Charles Alexander geologist
Brown, Samuel Joseph, Jr. scientist, engineer
Fields, Jack Milton, Jr. former congressman
Fortney, Thomas Kent cost and petroleum engineer, management consultant
Hawk, Phillip Michael service corporation executive
Trowbridge, John Parks physician

## Hunt
Price, Donald Albert veterinarian, consultant

## Huntsville
Bowers, Elliott Toulmin university president
Flanagan, Timothy James criminal justice educator, university official
Gutermuth, Mary Elizabeth foreign language educator
†Karolyi, Bela gymnastics coach
Lea, Stanley E. artist, educator
Raymond, Kay E(ngelmann) Spanish language educator, consultant
Smyth, Joseph Philip travel industry executive
Warner, Laverne education educator

## Hurst
Bishara, Amin Tawadros mechanical engineer, technical services executive
Dodd, Sylvia Bliss special education educator
Marling, Lynwood Bradley lawyer
Mc Keen, Chester M., Jr. business executive
Owen, Cynthia Carol sales executive

## Industry
Huitt, Jimmie L. rancher, oil, gas, real estate investor

## Ingram
Hughes, David Michael oil service company executive, rancher

## Irving
Aikman, Troy professional football player
†Allen, Larry Christopher football player
Anastasi, Richard Joseph computer software consultant
Anderson, Michael Curtis computer industry analyst
Andrews, Judy Coker electronics company executive
Armey, Richard Keith (Dick Armey) congressman
Baum, Herbert Merrill motor oil company executive
Bayne, James Elwood oil company executive
Cannon, Francis V., Jr. academic administrator, electrical engineer, economist
Card, Hugh Cleveland, III city official
Chris, Harry Joseph architect, architectural company executive
Clark, Priscilla Alden elementary school educator
Collins, Stephen Barksdale health care executive
Cooper, Kathleen Bell economist
Dinicola, Robert consumer products company executive
Donnelly, Barbara Schettler medical technologist
Elliott, Frank Wallace lawyer, educator
†Evans, Michael David clergyman, author
Glober, George Edward, Jr. lawyer
Gretzinger, Ralph Edwin, III management consultant
Haley, Charles Lewis professional football player
Halter, Jon Charles magazine editor, writer
Helm, Terry Allen telecommunications consultant
Hendrickson, Constance Marie McRight chemist, consultant
Hess, Edwin John oil company executive
Holdar, Robert Martin chemist
Hughes, Keith William banking and finance company executive
Irvin, Michael Jerome professional football player
Jones, Jerry (Jerral Wayne Jones) professional football team executive
Lett, Leon professional football player
Le Vine, Duane Gilbert petroleum company executive
Lieberman, Mark Joel lawyer
Lifson, Kalman Alan management consultant, retail executive
Lites, James professional hockey team executive
Longwell, H.J. petroleum engineer
Lutz, Matthew Charles oil company executive, geologist
Martin, Thomas Lyle, Jr. university president
†McClain, Dennis Douglas advertising executive
Mobley, William Hodges management educator, researcher
†Moog, Donald Andrew professional hockey player
Newton, Nate professional football player
Novacek, Jay McKinley professional football player
Nurenberg, David oil company executive
Olson, Herbert Theodore trade association executive
†Owen, Joe David editor
Pickett, Edwin Gerald financial executive
Plaskett, Thomas G. transportation company executive
Potter, Robert Joseph technical and business executive
Rainwater, R. Steven systems engineer
Robinson, Charles Emanuel systems engineer, consultant
Robinson, Edgar Allen oil company executive
Sasseen, Robert Francis university educator
Serverian, Heidi Sue Whitaker accountant, systems developer
Smith, Emmitt J., III professional football player
Sommerfeldt, John Robert historian
Swinburn, John S. professional association executive
Switzer, Barry professional football coach, former university athletic coach
†Tolbert, Tony Lewis football player
Tucker, Phyllis Anita sales representative, guidance counselor
Tuinei, Mark Pulemau professional football player
Walker, Herschel professional football player
Wicks, William Withington retired public relations executive
Williams, Erik George professional football player
Wood, Joseph George neurobiologist, educator
Woodson, Darren Ray professional football player
Zahn, Donald Jack lawyer

## Jacksonville
Blaylock, James Carl clergyman, librarian
Pruitt, William Charles, Jr. minister, educator

## Johnson City
Pollock, Margaret Landau Peggy elementary school educator

## Katy
Fudge, Edward William lawyer
Harbour, Patricia Ann Monroe poet
Mitchell, Leona Pearl soprano
†Thorne, Melvin Quentin managed healthcare executive

## Kaufman
Legg, Reagan Houston lawyer

## Kelly AFB
†Kelly, Gary Michael career military officer
Stringer, Jerry Ray magazine editor

## Kemp
Wurlitzer, Fred Pabst physician, surgeon

## Kerrville
Cremer, Richard Eldon marketing professional
Dozier, William Everett, Jr. newspaper editor and publisher
Frudakis, Evangelos William sculptor
Harkey, Ira Brown, Jr. newspaperman, educator, author
Holloway, Leonard Leveine former university president
Kunz, Sidney entomologist
Lich, Glen Ernst writer, consultant, business executive
Matlock, (Lee) Hudson civil engineer, educator
Rhodes, James Devers psychotherapist
Shaw, Alan Bosworth geologist, paleontologist, retired
Sinninger, Dwight Virgil engineer
Tomlin, Linton court reporter
Williams, William Henry, II publisher

## Kilgore
Rorschach, Richard Gordon lawyer
Wilcox, Nancy Diane nurse, administrator

## Killeen
Harvey, Hilda Ruth special education educator
Reid, Sharon Lea educational facilitator
Vancura, Stephen Joseph radiologist

## Kingsville
Cecil, David Rolf mathematician, educator
Ibanez, Manuel Luis university official, biological sciences educator
Morey, Philip Stockton, Jr. mathematics educator
Perez, John Carlos biology educator
Robins, Gerald Burns education educator
Stanford, Jane Herring business administration educator

## Kingwood
Ramsey, William Dale, Jr. technology and regulatory consultant

## Klein
Slater, Joan Elizabeth secondary education educator

## La Feria
Philip, Sunny Koipurathu municipal official

## Lackland AFB
Carlton, Paul Kendall, Jr. air force officer, physician

## Lago Vista
Kinsey, Julia Catherine medical records coding specialist

## Lake Dallas
Coleman, Brenda Forbis gifted and talented educator

## Lake Jackson
Elbert, James Peak independent insurance agent, minister
McCutchen, Charles William chemical engineer
Tasa, Kendall Sherwood chemistry educator

## Lampasas
Harvey, Leigh Kathryn lawyer

## Lancaster
Fewel, Harriett lawyer
Wendorf, Denver Fred, Jr. anthropology educator

## Laredo
Black, Clifford Merwyn academic administrator, sociologist, educator
Cavazos, Hilda Valdez nursing administrator, educator
Colón, Phyllis Janet city official
Condon, Maria del Carmen retired elementary school educator
Heimes, Charmaine Marie elementary school educator
Jones, James Robert ambassador, former congressman, lawyer
Kazen, George Philip federal judge
Knapp, Thomas Edwin sculptor, painter
Wood, Jack Calvin health care consultant, lawyer
Zaffirini, Judith state senator

## League City
Faget, Maxime A(llan) aeronautical engineer
Lawson, Randall Clayton, II financial executive

## Leander
Erickson, Ralph D. retired physical education educator, small business owner, consultant

## Levelland
Sears, Edward L. English language educator
Walker, James Kenneth judge

## Lewisville
Bickel, Herbert Jacob, Jr. corporation executive
Ferguson, R Neil computer systems consultant
Vacca, John Joseph, Jr. television executive
Whiteley, Harold Lee director

## Liberty Hill
Vance, Zinna Barth artist, writer
West, Felton retired newspaper writer

## Lindale
Bockhop, Clarence William retired agricultural engineer
Carter, Thomas Smith, Jr. retired railroad executive
Wilson, Leland Earl petroleum engineering consultant

## Littlefield
Driskell, Charles Mark principal

## Livingston
Oliver, Debbie Edge elementary education educator
Perkins, Sue Dene editor

## Llano
Anderson, Janet Ann women's health care nurse practitioner
Walter, Virginia Lee psychologist, educator

## Lockhart
Williams, Margaret Lu Wertha Hiett nurse

## Longview
Anderson, Linda Kay elementary education educator
Brannon, Clifton Woodrow, Sr. evangelist, lawyer
Hearne, Carolyn Fox art and history educator, artist
Mann, Jack Matthewson bottling company executive
Martin, Ulrike Balk laboratory analyst

## Lubbock
Allison, Cecil Wayne insurance company executive
Archer, James Elson engineering educator
Askins, Billy Earl education educator, consultant
Beck, George Preston anesthesiologist, educator
Bobylev, Alexandre Vasiliy mathematician, researcher
Bricker, Donald Lee surgeon
Bronwell, Nancy Brooker writer
Broselow, Linda Latt medical office technician, aviculturist
Buesseler, John Aure ophthalmologist, management consultant
Cochran, Joseph Wesley law librarian, educator
Collins, Harker economist, manufacturing executive, publisher, marketing, financial, business and legal consultant
Connor, Seymour Vaughan historian, educator, writer
Conover, William Jay statistics educator
Cooke, Alex "Ty", Jr. mayor
Crowson, James Lawrence lawyer, financial company executive
Cummings, Sam R. federal judge
Dudek, Richard Albert engineering educator
Duncan, Robert Lloyd lawyer
Eddleman, Floyd Eugene retired English language educator
Frazier, Eugene Richard designer
Gilliam, John Charles economist, educator
Glass, Carson McElyea lawyer
Haragan, Donald Robert university administrator, geosciences educator
Havens, Murray Clark political scientist, educator
Heath, Brent Alan electrical engineer
Hennessey, Audrey Kathleen computer researcher, educator
Hentges, David John microbiology educator
Hulsey, Sam Byron bishop
Illner-Canizaro, Hana physician, oral surgeon, researcher
Ishihara, Osamu electrical engineer, physicist, educator
Jackson, Francis Charles physician, surgeon
Jackson, Raymond Carl cytogeneticist
Johnson, Ronda Janice fundraising consultant
Jonish, James Edward economist, educator
Kelsey, Clyde Eastman, Jr. philosophy and psychology educator
Ketner, Kenneth Laine philosopher, educator
Kimbrough, Robert Cooke, III infectious diseases physician
Kristiansen, Magne electrical engineer, educator
Kurtzman, Neil A. medical educator
Li, Hua Harry computer scientist
Marx, John Norbert chemistry educator
May, Donald Robert Lee ophthalmologist, retina and vitreous surgeon, educator, academic administrator
McManigal, Shirley Ann university dean
Mittemeyer, Bernhard Theodore urology and surgery educator
Montford, John Thomas state legislator, academic administrator, lawyer
Murray, Grover Elmer geologist, educator
Nagy, Joe Howard lawyer
Pasewark, William Robert author, management consultant
Pearce, William Martin history educator
Pike, Douglas Eugene educator
Portnoy, William Manos electrical engineering educator
Purdom, Thomas James lawyer
Reeves, A. Sue Windsor healthcare administrator
Robinson, G. Wilse molecular physicist, educator
Rodriguez, Placido bishop
Rose, Sharon Marie critical care nurse
Rushing, Jane Gilmore writer
Schmidly, David J. university official and dean, biology educator
Sears, Robert Stephen finance educator
†Sharp, Marsha basketball coach
Skillern, Frank Fletcher law educator
Skoog, Gerald Duane science educator
Smith, Doris Corinne Kemp retired nurse
Snell, Robert retail executive
Stein, William Warner anthropology educator
Stem, Carl Herbert business educator
Stuart, Frank Adell county official
Walker, Warren Stanley English educator
Way, Barbara Haight dermatologist
Wendt, Charles William soil physicist, educator
Willingham, Mary Maxine retail store executive

Wilson, Margaret Eileen *retired physical education educator*
Wolfe, Verda Nell *pension consultant, financial planner*
Wood, Richard Courtney *library director, educator*
Woolam, Gerald Lynn *surgeon*

**Lufkin**
Perry, Lewis Charles *emergency medicine physician, osteopath*

**Mabank**
Beets, Hughla Fae *retired secondary school educator*

**Magnolia**
Ramsey, Kathleen Sommer *toxicologist*

**Mansfield**
Rivera, Angel (Andy) Manuel *retired career officer, city official*

**Marble Falls**
Simpson, H. Richard (Dick Simpson) *retailer*

**Marshall**
Gilstrap, James Rodney *lawyer, judge*
Hawkins, Audrey Denise *academic administrator, educator*
Magrill, Rose Mary *library director*
Sudhivoraseth, Niphon *pediatrician, allergist, immunologist*
Thames, Earl Glenn *accounting educator*
Weathers, Melba Rose *hospital utilization review coordinator*

**Mc Kinney**
Berry, Brian Joe Lobley *geographer, political economist, urban planner*
Brewer, Ricky Lee *investment broker, estate planner*
Dickinson, Richard Raymond *retired oil company executive*
Gill, David Brian *electrical engineer, educator*
White, Nathan Emmett, Jr. *judge, lawyer*

**Mcallen**
Carrera, Victor Manuel *lawyer*
Connors, Joseph Aloysius, III *lawyer*
Figgs, Linda Sue *principal*
Gonzalez, Rolando Noel *secondary school educator, religion educator, photographer*
†Guilliouma, Larry Jay, Jr. *performing arts administrator, music educator*
Hinojosa, Ricardo H. *federal judge*
McGee, William Howard John *library system coordinator*
Ramirez, Mario Efrain *physician*
Sutton, William Blaylock *pastor*

**McQueeney**
Gunter, Edwin Dale, Jr. *pilot*

**Mercedes**
Alaniz, Theodora Villarreal *elementary education educator*

**Mesquite**
Mc Gregor, Donald Thornton *newspaper editor, journalist*
Montgomery, Marvin *musical producer*
Pratt, Sharon L. *secondary and elementary education educator*
Tabor, Beverly Ann *elementary school educator*
Vaughan, Joseph Lee, Jr. *education educator, consultant*
Zook, Bill *lawyer*

**Mico**
Shockey, Thomas Edward *real estate executive, engineer*

**Midland**
Best, Alynda Kay *conflict resolution mediator*
Bullock, Maurice Randolph *lawyer*
Craddick, Thomas Russell *state representative, investor*
Crawford, Roger Brentley *industrial executive, inventor, author*
Estes, Andrew Harper *lawyer*
Frost, Wayne N. *lawyer*
Furgeson, William Royal *federal judge*
Groce, James Freelan *financial consultant*
Grover, Rosalind Redfern *oil and gas company executive*
Hackler, Teri Cecilia *elementary education educator*
King, Mary Lou *artist, medical technologist*
Lohmann, George Young, Jr. *neurosurgeon, hospital executive*
Morrow, William Clarence lawyer, *mediator*
Rebik, James Michael *otolaryngologist*
Smith, Robin Doyle *judge*
Sullivan, Patricia G. *maternal, child and women's health nursing educator*
Wegner, Sandra Sue *library director*

**Missouri City**
Hodges, Jot Holiver, Jr. *lawyer, business executive*
Mathur, Rupa Ajwani *former state official, risk management consultant*
Strier, Murray Paul *chemist, consultant*
Trichel, Mary Lydia *middle school educator*

**Montgomery**
Brown, Lewis Arnold *realtor*
Gooch, Carol Ann *psychotherapist consultant*
Holman, Charles Richardson *chemical company executive*
Snider, Robert Larry *management consultant*
Tharp, Benjamin Carroll, Jr. *architect*

**Mount Pleasant**
Palmer, Robert Blunden *newspaper, printing executive*

**Munday**
Bennett, Rodney Dee *music educator*

**Nacogdoches**
Cart-Rogers, Katherine Cooper *emergency nurse*
Clagett, Arthur F(rank) *psychologist, sociologist, qualitative research writer, retired sociology educator*

Fish, Stewart Allison *retired obstetrician and gynecologist*
Kallsen, Theodore John *retired English language educator*
Mallot, Michael E. *gastroenterologist*
Migl, Donald Raymond *therapeutic optometrist, pharmacist*
Schwei, Michael Allen *doctoral student*
Worrell, Albert Cadwallader *forest economics educator*

**New Braunfels**
Krueger, Robert Charles *ambassador, former senator, former congressman*
Oestreich, Charles Henry *president emeritus*
Pharis, Ruth McCalister *retired banker*
Wilson, James Lee *retired geology educator, consultant*

**Newton**
Hopkins, Sallye F. *women's health nurse*

**North Richland Hills**
Cunningham, Larry J. *city official*
Hinkley Thompson, Carol Joyce *philanthropy consultant, motivational speaker*

**Odessa**
Bailey, Keith Stewart *insurance company executive*
Boyd, Claude Collins *educational specialist, consultant*
Folsom, Hyta Prine *educational grant writer, consultant*
Gilliland, William Elton *retired lawyer*
Jackson, Dorothy Faye Greene *nursing educator*
Lane, Daniel McNeel *pediatric hematologist, lipidologist*
Lee, Nelda S. *art appraiser and dealer, film producer*
Miller, Margaret Joanne *pediatrics nurse*
Sorber, Charles Arthur *academic administrator*

**Omaha**
Moos, Verna Vivian *special education educator*

**Orange**
Adkins, John E(arl), Jr. *chemist*

**Overton**
Randel, Ronald Dean *physiologist, educator*

**Palestine**
Williams, Franklin Cadmus, Jr. *bibliographer*

**Pampa**
Cain, Donald Ezell *judge*
Lane, Jerry Ross *alcohol and drug abuse service counselor*
Willingham, Jeanne Maggart *dance educator, ballet company executive*

**Panhandle**
Sherrod, Lloyd B. *nutritionist*

**Pantego**
Schimelpfenig, C(larence) W(illiam), Jr. *retired chemistry educator*

**Paris**
Proctor, Richard Owen *public health administrator, army officer*
Sawyer, Mary Catherine *hospital administrator*

**Pasadena**
D'Andrea, Mark *radiation oncologist*
Gilley, Mickey Leroy *musician*
Moon, John Henry, Sr. *banker*
Root, M. Belinda *chemist*
Shapiro, Edward Muray *dermatologist*

**Pearland**
Jones, Lionel Troy, Jr. *electronic engineer*
Smith, Annie Lee Northern *retired school system administrator*

**Pecan Gap**
Williams, Jessie Willmon *lay religious worker, retired librarian*

**Pecos**
Weinacht, John William *lawyer*

**Plainview**
Galle, Richard Lynn *association executive, former municipal official*
Porter, Joan Margaret *elementary education educator*

**Plano**
Ahmad, Syeda Sultana *physician*
Alberthal, Lester M., Jr. *information processing services executive*
Bain, Travis Whitsett, II *manufacturing and retail executive*
Bode, Richard Albert *retired financial executive*
Bonet, Frank Joseph *lawyer*
Brock, Dee Sala *television executive, educator, writer, consultant*
Broyles, Michael Lee *geophysics and physics educator*
Carmicle, Linda Harper *psychotherapist*
Clement, Clarence Clark, Jr. *petroleum engineer*
Collumb, Peter John *communications company executive*
Conrad, Philip Jefferson *software development engineer*
Crowley, Daniel Francis, Jr. *food products manufacturing executive*
Cumming, Marilee *apparel company executive*
Dahiya, Jai Bhagwan *chemist*
Fleming, Christina Samusson *special education educator*
Gallardo, Henrietta Castellanos *writer*
Grant, Joseph Moorman *finance executive*
Grogan, Timothy James *information technology executive*
Hinton, Norman Wayne *information services executive*
Kranzow, Ronald Roy *lawyer*
Lee, Allan Wren *clergyman*
Mackenzie, John *retired oil industry executive*
Moore, Christopher Robertson Kinley *petroleum geologist*
Neppl, Walter Joseph *retired retail store executive*

Oesterreicher, James E. *department stores executive*
Pointon, Mary Lou *special education educator*
Schuh, Frank Joseph *drilling engineering company executive, consultant*
Senderling, Jon Townsend *journalist, public affairs specialist*
Statman, Jackie C. *career consultant*
Taylor, Paul Peak *pediatric dentist, educator*
Vengrow, Michael Ian *neurologist*
Wilke, Chet *real estate executive*

**Port Aransas**
Cook, Marilyn Jane *elementary school educator*
Goodwin, Mary McGinnis *secondary education educator*
Lehmann, William Leonardo *electrical engineer, educator*
Noble, James Kendrick, Jr. *media industry consultant*
Wohlschlag, Donald Eugene *zoologist, marine ecologist, educator emeritus*

**Post**
Earl, Lewis Harold *economics and management consultant, lawyer*

**Pottsboro**
Hanning, Gary William *utility executive, water company executive, consultant*
Thomas, Ann Van Wynen *law educator*

**Prairie View**
Boyd-Brown, Lena Ernestine *history educator, education consultant*
Jones, Barbara Ann Posey *college dean*
Prestage, Jewel Limar *political science educator*
Server, Ronald Douglas *criminologist, political scientist, lawyer, educator*

**Premont**
Cisneros, Marc Anthony *military officer*

**Quinlan**
Black, Sheryl Elaine Hale *author*
Gross, Paul Allan *health service executive*

**Randolph AFB**
†Anderson, Kurt B. *career officer*
Blankenbeker, Joan Winifred *communications computer/information management executive*
Carroll, Robert Eugene *senior flight surgeon*

**Ranger**
Jones, Roger Walton *English language educator, writer*

**Ravenna**
Greene, Jennifer *elementary school counselor*

**Redwater**
Hammer, Richard Lee *music educator*

**Rhome**
Brammer, Barbara Rhudene *retired secondary education educator*

**Richardson**
Adamson, Dan Klinglesmith *science association executive*
Akmakjian, Alan Paul *English language, literature and creative writing educator*
Andrews, Melinda Wilson *human development researcher*
Bellamy, Jennifer Rachelle *artist*
Biard, James Robert *electrical engineer*
Bick, David Greer *healthcare marketing executive*
Brady, Vicki Lee *dental assistant*
Brown, Ollie Dawkins *marriage, family and child therapist, scientific researcher*
Burke, Thomas William *executive benefits consulting company official*
Conrad, Flavius Leslie, Jr. *minister*
Cordell, Robert James *retired geologist*
DeBusk, Manuel Conrad *lawyer*
Douglas, John Paul *lawyer, commercial and family law mediator*
Dunn, David E. *university dean*
Edwards, Carl Elmo, Jr. *lawyer*
Ellwanger, J. David *lawyer*
Fahrlander, Henry William, Jr. *management consultant*
Garreans, Leonard Lansford *protective services official, criminal justice professional*
Gary, John *singer*
Gray, Donald Melvin *molecular and cell biology educator*
Hagan, Joseph Lawrence *communications executive*
Harp, Rose Marie *secondary education educator*
Hiegel, James Edward *apparel executive*
Johnson, Francis Severin *physicist*
Kelly, Rita Mae *academic administrator, researcher*
Li, Shu *business executive*
Lovelace, Julianne *library director*
Lutz, Raymond Price *industrial engineer, educator*
McDaniel, Dolan Kenneth *oil exploration service company executive*
Neely, Vicki Adele *legal assistant, poet*
Nevill, William Albert *chemistry educator*
Nugent, John Hilliard *communications executive*
Olson, Dennis Oliver *lawyer*
Pervin, William Joseph *computer science educator*
Redman, Timothy Paul *English language educator, author, chess federation administrator*
Rutford, Robert Hoxie *geoscience educator*
Schrimsher, Jerry James *diversified financial services company executive*
Standel, Richard Reynold, Jr. *lawyer, communications executive*
Thomas, Robert Lee *financial services company executive, consultant*
Urquhart, Sally Ann *environmental scientist, chemist*
Weaver, Jo Nell *elementary school educator*
Wildenthal, Bryan Hobson *university administrator*
Williams, James Francis, Jr. *religious organization administrator*
Witherspoon, W(illiam) Tom *engineering consultant*
Wyman, Richard Thomas *information services consultant*
†Yang, Yueh Sam *electronics company executive*
Young, Malcolm Eugene, Jr. *social studies secondary educator*

**Richmond**
Barratt, Cynthia Louise *pharmaceutical company executive*
Hay, Richard Carman *retired anesthesiologist*
Willis, David Edwin *retired geophysicist*

**Roanoke**
Kleinkort, Joseph Alexius *physical therapist, consultant*
Steward, Jerry Wayne *air transportation executive, consultant*

**Rockport**
Jones, Lawrence Ryman *retired research chemist*
Minor, Joseph Edward *civil engineer, educator*
Mulle, George Ernest *petroleum geologist*

**Rockwall**
Fisher, Gene Jordan *retired chemical company executive*
Griffith, James William *engineer, consultant*
House, Robert William *music educator*
Wallace, Mary Elaine *opera director, author*

**Rosenberg**
Jaunal, Bridget Kennedy *energy and environmental company executive, consultant*

**Round Rock**
Aadnesen, Christopher *railroad company executive, consultant*
Bruce-Juhlke, Debbie *nursing consultant, social worker*
Chavez, Dorothy Vaughan *elementary school educator, environmental educator*
Dell, Michael S. *manufacturing executive*
LaShelle, Charles Stanton *lawyer, insurance company executive*
Schneider, Dennis Ray *microbiology educator*

**Round Top**
Dick, James Cordell *concert pianist*
Lentz, Edwin Lamar *art historian*

**Rowlett**
Ogden, LouAnn Marie *dietitian, consultant*

**Rusk**
Jones, Janet Valeria *psychiatric nurse*

**Salado**
Greene, A(lvin) C(arl) *author*
Mackie, Donald John, Jr. *real estate developer*
Parks, Lloyd Lee *oil company executive*

**San Angelo**
Coe, Robert Stanford *retired management educator*
Davison, Elizabeth Jane Linton *education educator*
Henry, William Charles *manufacturing company supervisor*
Person, Ruth Janssen *academic administrator*
Pfeifer, Michael David *bishop*
Sutton, John Ewing *judge*
Tillery-Tate, Johnnie Lea *mental health and geriatrics nurse*

**San Antonio**
Abramson, Hyman Norman *engineering and science research executive*
Ahart-Walls, Pamela *elementary school principal*
Ahmad, Shair *mathematics educator*
Akujuobi, Cajetan Maduabuchukwu *research engineer, electrical engineering educator*
Aldave, Barbara Bader *law educator, lawyer*
Allison, Stephen Philip *lawyer*
Anderson, Bruce Edwin. *lawyer*
Armstrong, William Tucker, III *lawyer*
Arnold, Marie Collette *elementary school educator*
Arnold, Stephen Paul *investment professional*
Aust, Joe Bradley *surgeon, educator*
Baker, Floyd Wilmer *surgeon, retired army officer*
Ball, M(ary) Isabel *chemistry educator, dean*
Barrow, Charles Wallace *university dean*
Barton, James Cary *lawyer*
Beckmann, Charles Henry *cardiologist, educator*
Belgin, Harvey Harry *photojournalist*
Bellows, Thomas John *political scientist, educator*
Belzung, Paul Edward *engineering executive*
Benninger, Edward C., Jr. *petroleum and natural gas company executive*
Benz, George Albert *economic consultant, retired educator*
Berg, Thomas *manufacturing executive*
Betts, Austin Wortham *retired research company executive*
Bhandari, Basant *biochemist, molecular biologist, chemical engineer, food technologist, chemist*
Biery, Evelyn Hudson *lawyer*
Biery, Fred *judge*
Blaylock, Neil Wingfield, Jr. *applied statistics educator*
Blystone, Robert Vernon *developmental cell biologist, educator, textbook consultant*
Boyers, John Martin *principal*
Bramble, Ronald Lee *business and legal consultant*
Branton, James LaVoy *lawyer*
Brown, Robert *manufacturing executive*
Bryan, Richard Ray *real estate development executive, construction executive*
Budalur, Thyagarajan Subbanarayan *chemistry educator*
Burch, James Leo *science research institute executive*
Burke, Michael Donald *oil and gas company executive*
Burns, Leslie Kaye *documentary video producer and director*
Burton, Russell Rohan *aerospace scientist, researcher*
Buster, Alan Adair *control engineer*
Butt, Charles Clarence *food service executive*
Calgaard, Ronald Keith *university president*
Carroll, William Marion *financial services executive*
Castleberry, James Newton, Jr. *legal educator*
Catto, Henry Edward *former government official, former ambassador*
Caudill, Howard Edwin *bishop, educator*
Celmer, Virginia *psychologist*
Chan, Kwai Shing *materials engineer, researcher*
Clark, Leif Michael *federal judge*
Cloud, Bruce Benjamin, Sr. *construction company executive*
Colyer, Kirk Klein *insurance executive, real estate investment executive*
†Conly, Michael J. *communications company executive, television executive*

Hardin, James *retail food company executive*
Hatfield, James Allen *theater arts educator*
Juneau, Stafford Gerard, III *bank officer*
Justice, William Wayne *federal judge*
Kronenberg, Richard Samuel *physician, educator*
Lassiter, Charles Whitfield *construction executive*
Marsh, Owen Robert *education educator*
Ott, Wendell Lorenz *art museum director, artist*
Parker, Robert M. *federal judge*
Resnik, Linda Ilene *marketing and information executive, consultant*
Sharpe, Aubrey Dean *college administrator*
Smith, Howard Thompson *business executive*
Steger, William Merritt *federal judge*
Trent, Warren C. *mechanical engineer*
Walsh, Kenneth Albert *chemist*
Warner, John Andrew *foundry executive*

### Universal City
Atchley, Curtis Leon *mechanical engineer*
Lamoureux, Gloria Kathleen *nurse, air force officer*
Smith, James Earlie, Jr. *accountant*

### Uvalde
Ramsey, Frank Allen *veterinarian, retired army officer*
Wilson, Benjamin Franklin, Jr. *education educator*
Wood, James Albert *foreign language educator*

### Van Alstyne
Daves, Don Michael *minister*

### Vernon
Cook, Marcella Kay *drama educator*
Roberson, Mark Allen *physicist, educator*
Slosser, Jeffery Eric *research entomologist*

### Victoria
Chapman, J. Milton *lawyer*
Fellhauer, David E. *bishop*
Haynes, Karen Sue *university president, social work educator*
Stubblefield, Page Kindred *banker*
Weber, Michael James *conductor*

### Waco
Achor, Louis Joseph Merlin *psychology and neuroscience educator*
Baird, Robert Malcolm *philosophy educator, researcher*
Belew, John Seymour *academic administrator, chemist*
Bonnell, Pamela Gay *library administrator*
Brooks, Roger Leon *university president*
Chewning, Richard Carter *religious business ethics educator*
Collmer, Robert George *English language educator*
Colvin, (Otis) Herbert, Jr. *musician, educator*
Cutter, Charles Richard, III *retired classics educator*
Denton, Betty *lawyer, state representative*
Dow, David Sontag *retired ophthalmologist*
Flanders, Henry Jackson, Jr. *religious studies educator*
Garland, Meg *advertising executive*
Goode, Clement Tyson *English language educator*
Henke, Emerson Overbeck *accountant, educator*
Herring, Jack William *English language educator*
Hillis, William Daniel *university administrator*
Hynan, Linda Susan *psychology educator*
Jackson, Janis Lynn *biology educator*
Kagle, Joseph Louis, Jr. *artist, arts administrator*
Lamkin, Bill Dan *psychologist, educator, consultant*
Lindsey, Jonathan Asmel *development executive, educator*
Miller, Carl Chet *business educator*
Mitchell, William Allen *air force officer, political geography educator*
Moseley, Mary Prudence *educator*
Odell, Patrick Lowry *mathematics educator*
Osborne, Harold Wayne *sociology educator, consultant*
Pedrotti, Leno Stephano *physics educator*
Preddy, Raymond Randall *retired newspaper publisher, educator*
Progar, Dorothy *retired library director*
Rapoport, Bernard *life insurance company executive*
Reynolds, Herbert Hal *academic administrator*
Richie, Rodney Charles *critical care and pulmonary medicine physician*
Rolf, Howard Leroy *mathematician, educator*
Rose, John Thomas *finance educator*
Sharp, Ronald Arvell *sociology educator*
Smith, Cornelia Marschall *retired biology educator*
Smith, Cullen *lawyer*
Smith, Walter S., Jr. *federal judge*
Stauber, Donna Beth *education educator*
Sternberg, Daniel Arie *musician, conductor, educator*
Thomson, Basil Henry, Jr. *lawyer, university general counsel*
Weems, John Edward *writer*
Wendorf, Hulen Dee *law educator, author, lecturer*
Whaley, Carolyn Louise *primary school educator*
Wilson, John Ross *retired law educator*
Wood, James E., Jr. *religion educator, author*

### Warda
Kunze, George William *retired soil scientist*

### Waxahachie
Cockerham, Sidney Joe *professional society administrator*
Tschoepe, Thomas *bishop*

### Weatherford
Buckner-Reitman, Joyce *psychologist, educator*
McMahon, Robert Lee, Jr. (Bob McMahon) *information systems executive*

### Webster
Farnam, Jafar *allergist, immunologist, pediatrician*
Rappaport, Martin Paul *internist, nephrologist, educator*
Stephens, Douglas Kimble *chemical engineer*
Terry, Reese *engineering executive*

### Weslaco
Legaspi, Jesusa Crisostomo *agricultural scientist, entomologist*
Lingle, Sarah Elizabeth *research scientist*

### West
Eisma, Jose Albarracin *pulmonary physician*

### Westlake
Pitts, Joe W., III (Chip Pitts) *lawyer, law educator*

### Wharton
Gonzalez, Antonio *academic administrator, mortgage company executive*

### Whiteface
Lamb, Stacie Thompson *elementary school educator*

### Whitehouse
Baker, Rebecca Louise *musician, music educator, consultant*

### Wichita Falls
Bourland, D(elphus) David, Jr. *linguist*
Cagle, Paulette Bernice *mental health administrator and psychologist*
Harvill, Melba Sherwood *university librarian*
Jones, William Houston *stock brokerage executive, financial consultant*
Rodriguez, Louis Joseph *university president, educator*
Silverman, Gary William *financial planner*
Todd, Richard D. R. *lawyer*
Walker, Randall Wayne *lawyer*

### Wimberley
Ellis, John *small business owner*
Skaggs, Wayne Gerard *financial services company executive, retired*
Upchurch, Garland Rudolph, Jr. *paleontologist, researcher*

### Winnsboro
Boyd, Joe Dan *journal editor*
Fairchild, Raymond Eugene *oil company executive*

### Woodsboro
Rooke, Allen Driscoll, Jr. *civil engineer*

### Yoakum
Williams, Walter Waylon *lawyer, pecan grower*

## UTAH

### Bingham Canyon
Callender, Jonathan Ferris *environmental engineer, consultant*

### Bountiful
Burningham, Kim Richard *former state legislator*
Carter, Richard Bert *retired church official, retired government official*
Clement, Walter Hough *retired railroad executive*
Oveson, W(ilford) Val *state official, accountant*

### Brigham City
Fife, Dennis Jensen *military officer, chemistry educator*
McCullough, Edward Eugene *patent agent, inventor*

### Cedar City
Hamlin, Alan Russell *financial educator*
Hunter, R. Haze *former state legislator*
Sherratt, Gerald Robert *university president*
Veigel, Jon Michael *science administrator*

### Corinne
Ferry, Miles Yeoman *state official*

### Draper
Averett, Robert Lee *educator, information system professional*
Partridge, William Schaubel *retired physicist, research company executive*

### Fort Duchesne
Cameron, Charles Henry *petroleum engineer*

### Garrison
Beeston, Joseph Mack *metallurgist*

### Heber City
Day, Gerald W. *wholesale grocery company executive*

### Layton
†Yates, Jay Reese *physician*

### Logan
Anderson, Jay LaMar *horticulture educator, researcher, consultant*
Aust, Steven Douglas *biochemistry, biotechnology and toxicology educator*
Bennett, James Austin *retired animal science educator*
Bowles, David Stanley *engineering educator, consultant*
Cheng, Heng-Da *computer scientist*
Ellsworth, Samuel George *historian, educator*
Gay, Charles W., Jr. *academic administrator*
Hargreaves, George Henry *civil and agricultural engineer, researcher*
Hillyard, Lyle William *lawyer*
Honaker, Jimmie Joe *lawyer, ecologist*
Hunsaker, Scott Leslie *gifted and talented education educator*
Keller, Jack *agricultural engineering educator, consultant*
Lye, William Frank *history educator*
McKell, Cyrus M. *college dean, plant physiologist, consultant*
Milner, Clyde A., II *historian*
Price, Susan Kay Lind *employment training organization administrator*
Rasmussen, Harry Paul *horticulture and landscape educator*
Salisbury, Frank Boyer *plant physiologist, educator*
Schunk, Robert Walter *space physics research administrator*
Scouten, William Henry *chemistry educator, academic administrator*
†Sharik, Terry L. *forest resources educator*
Shaver, James Porter *education educator, university dean*
Van Dusen, Lani Marie *psychologist*
Vest, Hyrum Grant, Jr. *horticultural sciences educator*

Watterson, Scott *home fitness equipment manufacturer*

### Manti
Petersen, Benton Lauritz *paralegal*

### Midway
Zenger, John Hancock *retired publishing company executive*

### Mount Pleasant
Schade, Wilbert Curtis *educational administrator*

### Murray
Cannell, Cyndy Michelle *elementary school principal*
Volberg, Herman William *electronics engineer, consultant*

### Ogden
Browning, Roderick Hanson *banker*
Buckner, Elmer La Mar *insurance executive*
Buss, Walter Richard *geology educator*
Davidson, Thomas Ferguson *chemical engineer*
Dilley, William Gregory *aviation company executive*
Evans, Keith Edward *government official, researcher*
Evans, Robert John *retired biochemistry educator, researcher*
Garrison, U. Edwin *military, space and defense products manufacturing company executive*
Harrington, Mary Evelina Paulson (Polly Harrington) *religious journalist, writer, educator*
Howard, Sherwin Ward *theatre educator*
Kaufman, Steven Michael *lawyer*
Larson, Brent T. *broadcasting executive*
Maughan, Willard Zinn *dermatologist*
Mecham, Glenn Jefferson *lawyer, mayor*
Mecham, Steven Ray *school system administrator*
Montgomery, Robert F. *state legislator, retired surgeon, cattle rancher*
Nickerson, Guy Robert *lumber company executive*
Paralez, Linda Lee *technology management consultant*
Ritchey, Harold W. *retired chemical engineer*
Schow, Terry D. *state official*
Smith, Robert Bruce *college administrator*
Spencer, LaVal Wing *physician*
Thompson, Paul Harold *university president*
Trundle, W(infield) Scott *publishing executive newspaper*
Welch, Garth Larry *chemistry educator, retired*

### Orderville
Zornes, Milford *artist*

### Orem
Abbott, Charles Favour, Jr. *lawyer*
Brower, Gerald Grant *architect, software developer*
Green, John Alden *university director study abroad program*
Hall, Blaine Hill *retired librarian*
Harris, Michael James *software engineer*
Jacobson, Alfred Thurl *petroleum executive*
Moore, Hal G. *mathematician, educator*
Morey, Robert Hardy *communications executive*
Sawyer, Thomas Edgar *management consultant*
Snow, Marlon O. *trucking executive, state agency administrator*

### Park City
Ebbs, George Heberling, Jr. *management consulting company executive*
Edwards, Howard Lee *retired petroleum company executive, lawyer*
Kennicott, James W. *lawyer*
Moe, Tommy (Thomas Sven Moe) *skier, former Olympic athlete*
Roffe-Steinrotter, Diann *Olympic athlete*
Wardell, Joe Russell, Jr. *pharmacologist*

### Provo
Alexander, Thomas Glen *history educator*
Allred, Ruel Acord *education educator*
Arrington, Leonard James *history educator*
Bahr, Howard Miner *sociologist, educator*
Barker, Dee H. *chemical engineering educator*
Bartlett, Leonard Lee *communications educator, retired advertising agency executive, advertising historian*
†Bateman, Merrill Joseph *university president*
Beckham, Janette Hales *religious organization administrator*
Bennett, Bill *publishing company executive*
Bergin, Allen Eric *clinical psychologist, educator*
Blake, George Rowland *soil science educator, water resources research administrator*
Buck, William Fraser, II *marketing executive*
Christensen, Bruce LeRoy *academic administrator, former public broadcasting executive*
Christiansen, John Rees *sociologist, educator*
Clark, Bruce Budge *humanities educator*
Clark, Loyal Frances *public affairs specialist*
Conlee, Robert Keith *physical education educator*
Fleming, Joseph Clifton, Jr. *university dean, law educator*
Forster, Merlin Henry *foreign languages educator, author, researcher*
Fry, Earl Howard *political scientist, educator*
Hall, Howard Tracy *chemist*
Hansen, H. Reese *law school dean, educator*
Hansen, James Vernon *computer science, information systems educator*
Hart, Edward LeRoy *poet, educator*
Hill, Richard Lee *lawyer*
Hunt, H(arold) Keith *business management educator, marketing consultant*
Jensen, Clayne R. *university administrator*
Jensen, Richard Dennis *librarian*
Jonsson, Jens Johannes *electrical engineering educator*
Kimball, Edward Lawrence *law educator, lawyer*
Kunz, Phillip Ray *sociologist, educator*
Lang, William Edward *mathematics educator*
Lee, Blaine Nelson *executive consultant, educator, author*
Lyon, James Karl *German language educator*
Marchant, Maurice Peterson *librarian, educator*
McArthur, Eldon Durant *geneticist, researcher*
Merritt, LaVere Barrus *engineering educator, civil engineer*
Peer, Larry Howard *literature educator*
Pope, Bill Jordan *chemical engineering educator, business executive*
Porter, Blaine Robert Milton *sociology and psychology educator*
Porter, Bruce Douglas *federal agency administrator, educator, writer*
Pratt, Rosalie Rebollo *harpist, educator*
Schofield, Anthony Wayne *judge*
Skinner, Andrew Charles *history educator, religious writer*
Smith, H(oward) Duane *zoology educator*
Smith, Maurice Edward *lawyer, business consultant*
Smith, Nathan McKay *library and information sciences educator*
Smoot, Leon Douglas *chemical engineering educator, research director, former university dean*
Snow, Karl Nelson, Jr. *public management educator, university administrator, former state senator*
Stahmann, Robert F. *education educator*
Stanford, Melvin Joseph *retired dean, educator*
Tata, Giovanni *publishing executive*
Thomas, David Albert *law educator*
Tolman, Richard Robins *zoology educator*
Valentine, John Lester *state legislator, lawyer*
Whatcott, Marsha Rasmussen *elementary education educator*
Whitman, Dale Alan *lawyer, educator*
Wilde, James L. *lawyer*
Wilson, Ramon B. *educator, administrator*
Woodbury, Lael Jay *theater educator*

### Richfield
Murphy, Millene Freeman *psychiatric rehabilitation nurse, business executive*

### Riverdale
Anderson, Byron Floyd *business and political consultant*

### Riverside
Reveal, Arlene Hadfield *retired librarian, consultant*

### Saint George
Beesley, H(orace) Brent *savings and loan executive*
Chilow, Barbara Gail *social worker*
Collett, Farrell Reuben *art educator*
Day, John Denton *retired company executive, cattle and horse rancher, trainer, wrangler, actor, educator*
†Day, Steven M. *accounting educator, accountant*
Gallian, Russell Joseph *lawyer*
Martin, George Wilbur *trade association administrator*
Potwin, Juanita R. *marketing professional, dental hygienist*

### Salt Lake City
Abildskov, J. A. *cardiologist, educator*
Adams, Joseph Keith *lawyer*
Alter, Edward T. *state treasurer*
Anderson, Charles Ross *civil engineer*
Anderson, Joseph Andrew, Jr. *retired apparel company executive, retail consultant*
Anderson, Kent Taylor *lawyer*
Anderson, Stephen Hale *federal judge*
Anspaugh, Lynn Richard *research biophysicist*
†Ballard, Melvin Russell, Jr. *investment executive, church official*
Balthaser, Anita Young *legal assistant*
Barker, Ronald C. *lawyer*
Baucom, Sidney George *lawyer*
Bauer, A(ugust) Robert, Jr. *surgeon, educator*
Beall, Burtch W., Jr. *architect*
Benjamin, Lorna Smith *psychologist*
Bennett, Janet Huff *legislative staff member*
Benson, Dee Vance *federal judge*
Benson, Joan Ellen *dietetics educator, researcher*
Berman, Daniel Lewis *lawyer*
Bhayani, Kiran Lilachand *environmental engineer, programs manager*
Black, Rosa Vida *writer, educator*
Black, Wilford Rex, Jr. *state senator*
Blackner, Boyd Atkins *architect*
Bozich, Anthony Thomas *transportation industry consultant, retired motor freight company executive*
Brady, Rodney Howard *broadcast company executive, holding company executive, former college president, former government official*
Bragg, David Gordon *physician, radiology educator*
Brandon, Kathryn Elizabeth Beck *pediatrician*
Bremer, Ronald Allan *geneologist, historian*
Brems, David Paul *architect*
Brewer, Stanley R. *wholesale grocery executive*
Brown, Carolyn Smith *communications educator, consultant*
Buchi, Mark Keith *lawyer*
Burdette, Robert Soelberg *accountant*
Buttars, Gerald Anderson *librarian*
Caldwell, Karin D. *biochemist educator*
Callister, Louis Henry, Jr. *lawyer*
Carey, John Clayton *pediatrician*
Carlson, Ralph Jennings *communications executive*
Carnahan, Orville Darrell *state legislator, retired college president*
Cash, R(oy) Don *gas and petroleum company executive*
Chivers, Laurie Alice *state educational administrator*
Chong, Richard David *architect*
Christensen, Ray Richards *lawyer*
Christiansen, Joyce L. Soelberg *newspaper editor*
Christopher, James Walker *architect, educator*
Clark, Deanna Dee *civic leader and volunteer*
Clark, Jeffrey Raphiel *research and development company executive*
Clark, Scott H. *lawyer*
Colessides, Nick John *lawyer*
Cook, M(elvin) Garfield *chemical company executive*
Cornaby, Kay Sterling *lawyer, former state senator*
Corradini, Deedee *mayor*
Creer, James Read *financial officer*
Curtis, LeGrand R., Jr. *lawyer*
Dahlstrom, Donald Albert *chemical and metallurgical engineering educator, former equipment manufacturing company executive*
Davis, Brian Adam *physician*
Davis, Gene *public relations professional, state legislator*
Davis, Loyd Evan *defense industry marketing professional*
Davis, Roy Kim *otolaryngologist, health facility administrator*
De Vries, Kenneth Lawrence *mechanical engineer, educator*
Dibb, Roger Alan *accountant*
Dick, Bertram Gale, Jr. *physics educator*
Drew, Clifford James *university administrator, special education and educational psychology educator*

Freeman, Stephen Albert *retired foreign language educator*
Gibson, Eleanor Jack (Mrs. James J. Gibson) *retired psychology educator*
Jacobs, Travis Beal *historian, educator*
Lamberti, Marjorie *history educator*
Landgren, Craig Randall *academic administrator*
Langrock, Peter Forbes *lawyer*
Lynch, Peter *biology educator*
O'Brien, George Dennis *retired university president*
Patterson, William Bradford *surgical oncologist*
Saul, George Brandon, II *biology educator*
Vail, Van Horn *German language educator*
Wilson, George Wilton *economics educator*
Winkler, Paul Frank, Jr. *astrophysicist, educator*
Wonnacott, (Gordon) Paul *economics educator*

### Montpelier
Barbieri, Christopher George *professional society administrator*
Bertrand, Frederic Howard *insurance company executive*
Brock, James Sidney *lawyer*
Dean, Howard *governor*
Diamond, M. Jerome *lawyer, former state official*
Good, Jeffrey *journalist*
Guild, Alden *lawyer*
Klinck, Patricia Ewasco *state official*
Leland, Lawrence *insurance executive*
Morse, James L. *state supreme court justice*
Paquin, Edward H., Jr. *state legislator*
Serrani, Thom *contracting trade association executive*
†Sorrell, William H. *state official*
Steele, Karen Kiarsis *state legislator*
Wood, Barbara Louise Champion *state legislator, retired*

### Morrisville
Lechevalier, Hubert Arthur *microbiology educator*
Lechevalier, Mary Pfeil *retired microbiologist, educator*
Simonds, Marshall *lawyer*

### Moscow
Kende, Stephen James *insurance sales executive*

### Newbury
McGarrell, James *artist, educator*

### Newport
Guerrette, Richard Hector *priest, psychotherapist, management consultant, writer*

### North Bennington
Belitt, Ben *poet, educator*
Noland, Kenneth Clifton *artist*

### North Clarendon
Freed, Walter Everett *petroleum company executive, state representative*

### Northfield
Wick, William Shinn *clergyman, chaplain*

### Norwich
Fitzhugh, William Wyvill, Jr. *printing company executive*
Naumann, Robert Bruno Alexander *chemistry and physics educator*
Post, Avery Denison *retired church official*
Smith, Markwick Kern, Jr. *management consultant*
Snapper, Ernst *mathematics educator*
Stetson, Eugene William, III *film producer*
White, Cleveland Stuart, Jr. *architect*

### Pawlet
Buechner, Carl Frederick *minister, author*

### Peacham
Engle, James Bruce *ambassador*

### Perkinsville
Freeburg, Richard Gorman *financial derivatives company executive*
Harris, Christopher *publisher, designer, editor*

### Plainfield
Harding, John Hibbard *retired insurance company executive*

### Pownal
Gibson, Sarah Ann Scott *art librarian*

### Putney
Loring, Honey *small business owner*

### Quechee
Baney, John Edward *insurance company executive*

### Randolph
Angell, Philip Alvin, Jr. *lawyer*

### Randolph Center
Ryerson, W. Newton *association executive*

### Rutland
Chalidze, Lisa Leah *lawyer*
Ferraro, Betty Ann *corporate administrator, state senator*
Griffin, James Edwin *utilities executive*
Keyser, Frank Ray, Jr. *lawyer, former governor*
Stafford, Robert Theodore *lawyer, former senator*
Wright, William Bigelow *financial executive*

### Saint Albans
Johnson, Paula Bouchard *preschool administrator, educator, consultant*

### Saint Johnsbury
Crosby, George Miner *state legislator*
Mandelstein, Paul Stanley *book publishing executive*
Mayo, Bernier L. *secondary school principal*
Toll, David *pediatrician*

### Shaftsbury
Williams, Robert Joseph *museum director, educator*

### Shelburne
Carpenter, Donald Blodgett *real estate appraiser*
Ross, Charles Robert *lawyer, consultant*
Sawabini, Wadi Issa *retired dentist*

### South Burlington
Hackett, Luther Frederick *insurance company executive*
Hamilton, John J., Jr. *airport executive*
Johnson, Robert Eugene *physiologist*
Kebabian, Paul Blakeslee *librarian*
Pizzagalli, James *construction executive*
Terris, Milton *physician, educator*

### South Hero
Bisson, Roger *middle school educator*

### South Londonderry
Spiers, Ronald Ian *diplomat*

### South Pomfret
Arkin, William Morris *military and political analyst, writer*

### South Royalton
Kempner, Maximilian Walter *law school dean, lawyer*
Powers, Thomas Moore *author*
Wroth, L(awrence) Kinvin *lawyer, educator*

### South Strafford
Novick, Sheldon M. *author, lawyer*

### South Woodstock
Crowl, John Allen *retired publishing company executive*
Kennan, Elizabeth Topham *university executive*

### Springfield
Charest, Gabrielle Marya *educational administrator*
Guité, J. C. Michel *telephone company executive*
Putnam, Paul Adin *retired government agency official*

### Stowe
Fiddler, Barbara Dillow *sales and marketing professional*
Taplin, Winn Lowell *historian, retired senior intelligence operations officer*

### Swanton
Chaim, Linda Susan *school system administrator*
Wooding, William Minor *medical statistics consultant*

### Thetford
Brown, Susan Elizabeth S. *secondary education educator*
Cummings Rockwell, Patricia Guilbault *psychiatric nurse*
Hoagland, Mahlon Bush *biochemist, educator*
Paley, Grace *author, educator*

### Underhill
Danforth, Elliot, Jr. *medical educator*
Panner, Jeannie Harrigan *electrical engineer*

### Vergennes
Grant, Edwin Randolph *retail and manufacturing executive*

### Waitsfield
Clark, Samuel Smith *urologist*
Raphael, Albert Ash, Jr. *lawyer*

### Wallingford
Bluhm, Norman *artist*

### Waterbury
Adams, Charles Jairus *lawyer*
Bunting, Charles I. *academic administrator*
Pelton, Joan Elisabeth Mason *music company owner*

### Waterbury Center
Amestoy, Jeffrey Lee *judge*

### West Burke
Van Vliet, Claire *artist*

### West Danville
Somers, Melvin Claude *retired mathematics educator and dean*

### West Dover
Humphreys, George H., II *surgery educator*

### Weston
Kasnowski, Chester Nelson *artist, educator*
Neff, Walter Perry *financial consultant*
Stettler, Stephen F. *performing company executive*

### White River Junction
Halperin, George Bennett *education educator, retired naval officer*
Linnell, Robert Hartley *environment, safety consultant*
Myers, Warren Powers Laird *physician, educator*
Rutter, Frances Tompson *publisher*

### Williamstown
Dickinson, Charles Arthur *manufacturing company executive*

### Williston
†Cote, David Orman *career officer, health facility administrator*

### Windsor
Forbes, Georgina *artist, psychotherapist*
Furnas, Howard Earl *business executive, educator, retired government official*

### Winooski
Wilson, Mary Louise *publishing executive*

### Woodstock
Billings, Franklin Swift, Jr. *federal judge*
Blackwell, David Jefferson *insurance company executive*
Hoyt, Coleman Williams *postal consultant*
Lash, James William (Jay Lash) *embryology educator*
Wollman, Harry *health care and executive search consultant*

## VIRGINIA

### Abingdon
Graham, Howard Lee, Sr. *corporate executive*
Johnson, Janet Droke *legal secretary*
Ramos-Cano, Hazel Balatero *caterer owner, innkeeper, entrepreneur*
Taylor, Alfred Raleigh *geologist*
Widener, Hiram Emory, Jr. *federal judge*
Williams, Glen Morgan *federal judge*

### Accomac
Reid-Roberts, Dayl Helen *mental health counselor*

### Afton
Anderson, Donald Norton, Jr. *retired electrical engineer*

### Alexandria
Abbott, Preston Sargent *psychologist*
Abell, Richard Bender *lawyer, federal official*
Abernathy, Mary Gates *elementary school educator*
Ackerman, Roy Alan *research and development executive*
Adams, Ranald Trevor, Jr. *retired air force officer*
†Agronsky, Martin Zama *radio and TV news analyst*
Alderson, Margaret Northrop *arts administrator, educator, artist*
Alexander, Fred Calvin, Jr. *lawyer*
Allen, Fred Cary *retired army officer*
Alloway, Robert Malcombe *computer consulting executive*
Anderson, Ann Davis *curriculum and staff development specialist*
Babcock, Jack Emerson *retired army officer, educator, corporate executive*
Bachus, Walter Otis *retired army general, former association executive*
Bailey, Steven Scott *operations research analyst*
Ball, Robert M. *social security, welfare and health policy specialist, writer, lecturer*
Ballard, Edward Brooks *landscape architect*
Baroody, Michael Elias *trade association executive*
Battle, Timothy Joseph *lawyer*
Berger, Patricia Wilson *retired librarian*
Bergheim, Laura Ann *writer*
Berman, Alan *physicist*
Bezold, Clement *think tank executive*
Biberman, Lucien Morton *physicist*
Birely, William Cramer *investment banker*
Black, Beverly Holstun *psychiatric social worker*
Boge, Walter Edward *retired army civilian official, private consultant*
Bolger, Robert Joseph *retired trade association executive*
Bostetter, Martin V. B., Jr. *bankruptcy court judge*
Bowman, Richard Carl *defense consultant, retired air force officer*
Brackett, James Vincent *electrical engineer*
Brandell, Sol Richard *electrical power and control system engineer, research mathematician*
Brenner, Alfred Ephraim *physicist*
Brickhill, William Lee *international finance consultant*
Brinkema, Leonie Milhomme *federal judge*
Brittigan, Robert Lee *lawyer*
Brockert, Joseph Paul *government administrator, writer, editor, design consultant*
Broide, Mace Irwin *public affairs consultant*
Brown, Ann Herrell *secondary school educator*
Brown, Frederic Joseph *army officer*
Brown, Quincalee *professional society administrator*
Brownfeld, Allan Charles *columnist*
Bryan, Albert V., Jr. *federal judge*
Budde, Mitzi Marie Jarrett *librarian*
Buhain, Wilfrido Javier *medical educator*
Burch, Michael Ira *public relations executive, former government official*
Burke, Kelly Howard *former air force officer, business executive*
Byrd, Barbara A. *professional society administrator*
Byrne, John Edward *writer, retired government official*
Byrnside, Oscar Jehu, Jr. *professional society administrator*
Cacheris, James C. *federal judge*
Campbell, Francis James *retired chemist*
Carlson, J(ohn) Philip *lawyer*
Carter, Gene R. *professional society administrator*
Carter, Richard Dennis *lawyer, educator*
Casey, Michael Kirkland *business executive, lawyer*
Chamberlain, Adrian Ramond *trade association executive*
Chapman, Anthony Bradley *psychiatrist*
Chatelier, Paul Richard *aviation psychologist, training company officer*
Christie, Thomas Philip *federal agency administrator, research manager*
Clinger, William Floyd, Jr. *former congressman*
Clinkscales, William Abner, Jr. *government administrator*
Clower, William Dewey *trade association administrator*
Clubb, Bruce Edwin *retired lawyer*
Cohen, Bernard S. *lawyer*
Collins, Cardiss *former congresswoman*
Comeau, Kathy Darr *publishing executive*
Condrill, Jo Ellaresa *professional speaker*
Connally, Ernest Allen *retired federal agency administrator*
Connell, John Gibbs, Jr. *former government official*
Cook, Charles William *aerospace consultant, educator*
Cooney, David Martin *organization administrator, retired naval officer*
Cooper, B. Jay *public relations executive*
Cooper, Charles Donald *association executive, editor, retired career officer*
Cooper, Kenneth Banks *business executive, former army officer*
Cooper, Roger Merlin *information technology executive, federal government official, educator*
Corson, Walter Harris *sociologist*
Costagliola, Francesco *former government official, macro operations analyst*
Covone, James Michael *automotive parts manufacturer and distribution company executive*
Coyne, James Kitchenman, III *engineering executive*
Crane, Stephen Charles *professional society administrator*
Cross, Eason, Jr. *architect*
Culkin, Charles Walker, Jr. *trade association administrator*
Curtin, Gary Lee *air force officer*
Darling, Thomas, Jr. *retired rural electrification specialist*
David, Joseph Raymond, Jr. *writer, periodical editor*
Dawson, Samuel Cooper, Jr. *retired motel company executive*
De Barbieri, Mary Ann *nonprofit management consultant*
Devine, Donald J. *management and political consultant*
DeZarn, Guy David *English language educator*
Dietrich, Laura Jordan *international policy advisor*
Dietrich, Paul George *lawyer*
Dobson, Donald Alfred *electrical engineer*
Doeppner, Thomas Walter *electrical engineer, consultant*
Donohue, Thomas Joseph *transportation association executive*
Dorsey, James Francis, Jr. *naval officer*
Downs, Michael Patrick *retired marine corps officer*
Dunn, Bernard Daniel *former naval officer, consultant*
Dyer, Joseph Wendell *career officer*
Eckhart, Myron, Jr. (Max Myron) *marine engineer*
Edgell, Karin Jane *reading specialist, special education educator*
Ellis, Thomas Selby, III *federal judge*
Emely, Charles Harry *trade association executive*
Ensslin, Robert Frank, Jr. *retired association executive and military officer*
Entzminger, John Nelson, Jr. *federal agency administrator, electronic engineer, researcher*
Evans, Grose *former curator, retired educator*
Evans, H(arold) Bradley, Jr. *lawyer*
Fichenberg, Robert Gordon *newspaper editor, consultant*
Finnell, Dallas Grant *fundraising executive*
Fisher, Donald Wayne *medical association executive*
Fitton, Harvey Nelson, Jr. *former government official, publishing consultant*
Fleming, Douglas Riley *journalist, publisher, public affairs consultant*
Foster, Robert Francis *communications executive*
Francis, Samuel Todd *columnist*
Gaynor, Margaret Cryor *program director*
Girouard, Shirley Ann *nurse, policy analyst*
Goldstein, Jerome Charles *professional association executive, surgeon, otolaryngologist*
Good, Phillip *think-tank executive*
Gray, Dorothy Louise Allman Pollet *librarian*
Gray, John Edmund *chemical engineer*
Greenstein, Ruth Louise *research institute executive, lawyer*
Gurke, Sharon McCue *naval officer*
Haas, Ward John *research and development executive*
Hagan, Robert Leslie *retired consulting company executive*
†Hammad, Alam E. *international business consultant, educator*
Hampton, E. Lynn *municipal finance administrator*
Hanft, Ruth S. Samuels (Mrs. Herbert Hanft) *health care consultant, educator, economist*
Hansan, Mary Anne *marketing professional*
Harris, David Ford *management consultant, retired government official*
Hartsock, Linda Sue *educational and management development executive*
Hathaway, Fred William *lawyer*
Havens, Harry Stewart *former federal assistant comptroller general, government consultant*
Heacock, Phillip Kaga *aerospace executive*
Helman, Gerald Bernard *government official*
Hewitt, Charles C. *broadcast executive*
Hilton, Claude Meredith *federal judge*
Hilton, Robert Parker, Sr. *national security affairs consultant, retired naval officer*
Hixson, Stanley G. *speech, language and computer technology educator*
Hobbs, Michael Edwin *broadcasting company executive*
Holland, Dianna Gwin *real estate broker*
Hoyt, F(rank) Russell *professional society administrator*
Hughes, Grace-Flores *former federal agency administrator, management consulting executive*
Hume, Ellen Hunsberger *broadcast executive, media analyst, journalist*
Hurtado, Rodrigo Claudio *allergist, immunologist*
Hussey, Ward MacLean *lawyer, former government official*
Hutzelman, Martha Louise *lawyer*
Jagoda, Barry Lionel *media adviser, communications consultant*
Jameson, Paula Ann *lawyer*
Jarrard, James Paul *school program administrator*
Johnson, Edgar McCarthy *psychologist*
Johnson, Robert Gerald *federal agency consultant*
Johnson, William David *retired university administrator*
Jokl, Alois Louis *electrical engineer*
Jones, Russel Cameron *civil engineer*
Justesen, Benjamin Ray, II *foreign service officer*
Keith, Donald Raymond *business executive, retired army officer*
Kelso, John Hodgson *former government official*
Kemble, James Richard *engineering services executive, retired*
Kennedy, Mary Virginia *diplomat*
Kennedy, Roger George *museum director, park service executive*
Kingston, Robert Charles *retired army officer*
Kolar, Mary Jane *professional society administrator*
Kollander, Mel *social scientist, statistician*
Kopp, Eugene Paul *lawyer*
Krosin, Kenneth E. *lawyer*
Krueger, Gerald Peter *psychologist*
Kyprios, Tina Slocum *auditor*
Lajoie, Roland *army officer*
Lantz, Phillip Edward *corporate executive, consultant*
Lasser, Howard Gilbert *chemical engineer, consultant*
Laurent, Lawrence Bell *communications executive, former journalist*
Le, Thuy Xuan *financial control systems developer, consultant, metaphysics scientist*
†Lennon, Thomas John *retired air force officer, company executive*
Lenz, Edward Arnold *trade association executive, lawyer*
Locigno, Paul Robert *public affairs executive*

Losey, Michael Robert *professional society administrator*
Loving, William Rush, Jr. *public relations company executive, consultant*
Lund, Rita Pollard *aerospace consultant*
Lundeberg, Philip Karl Boraas *curator*
Mandil, I. Harry *nuclear engineer*
Mann, Seymour Zalmon *political science and public administration educator emeritus, union official*
†Mar, Eugene *lawyer*
Marino, Ann Dozier *real estate broker*
Martinez, Ricardo *federal agency administrator*
Masterson, Kleber Sanlin, Jr. *physicist*
Mathews, Mary Kathryn *retired government official*
Mathis, William Lowrey *lawyer*
Matthews, Sir Stuart *aviation industry executive*
Maves, Michael Donald *medical association executive*
Mayo, Louis Allen *corporation executive*
McClure, Roger John *lawyer*
McCulloch, William Leonard *trade association administrator*
McDowell, Charles Eager *lawyer, retired military officer*
McFarland, Janet Chapin *consulting company executive*
McKinney, James Clayton *electronics executive, electrical engineer*
Mc Lucas, John Luther *aerospace company executive*
McMillan, Charles William *consulting company executive*
Mc Mullen, Thomas Henry *retired air force officer*
McNair, Carl Herbert, Jr. *army officer, aeronautical engineer*
Megivern, Kathleen *association director, lawyer*
Merrick, Roswell Davenport *educational association administrator*
Milling, Marcus Eugene, Sr. *geologist*
Minor, Mary Ellen *civilian military employee*
Montgomery, Gillespie V. (Sonny Montgomery) *former congressman*
Mosely, Linda Hays *surgeon*
Muir, Warren Roger *chemist, toxic substances specialist*
Mulvihill, John Gary *information services administrator*
Murray, Robert John *think-tank executive*
Murray, Russell, II *aeronautical engineer, defense analyst, consultant*
Myers, Denys Peter, Jr. *architectural historian*
Naylor, Kenneth Glen *federal agency administrator*
Needels, Christopher James *sports association administrator*
Nekritz, Leah Kalish *dean, college administrator*
Noland, Royce Paul *association executive, physical therapist*
O'Brien, Patrick Michael *library administrator*
O'Hara, John Patrick *lawyer, accountant*
Olson, Warren Kinley *operations research analyst, engineer, physicist*
Pabarcius, Algis *investment executive*
Palma, Dolores Patricia *urban planner*
Parsons, Henry McIlvaine *psychologist*
Pastin, Mark Joseph *executive consultant, association executive*
Paul, Andrew Robert *trade association executive*
Pavlick, Charles Raleigh *architect, engineer, retired air force officer*
Payne, Nancy Sloan *visual arts educator*
Powell, Colin Luther *retired military officer, author*
Pulling, Ronald Wilson, Sr. *aviation systems planner, civil engineer, consultant*
Puscheck, Herbert Charles *social sciences educator*
Radewagen, Fred *publisher, organization executive*
Rall, Lloyd Louis *civil engineer*
Rector, John Michael *association executive, lawyer*
Reid, Ralph Waldo Emerson *management consultant*
Revere, Virginia Lehr *clinical psychologist*
Richards, Darrie Hewitt *investment company executive*
Richardson, Robert Charlwood, III *management consultant, retired air force officer*
Ritter, James William *architect, educator*
Rose, Susan Porter *federal commissioner*
Rowden, William Henry *naval officer*
Saint, Crosbie Edgerton *retired army officer*
Sayre, Edward Vale *chemist*
Scheupelein, Robert John *government official*
Schultz, Franklin M. *retired lawyer*
Scurlock, Arch Chilton *chemical engineer*
Senese, Donald Joseph *former government official*
Shapiro, Maurice Mandel *astrophysicist*
Sheetz, Richard LaTrelle *retired association executive*
Shrier, Stefan *mathematician, educator*
Simmons, Richard De Lacey *mass media executive*
Smith, Carl Richard *association executive, former air force officer*
Smith, Jeffrey Greenwood *industry executive, retired army officer*
Spar, Edward Joel *demographer*
Stafford, Thomas Patten *retired military officer, former astronaut*
Stanley, Robert Warren *association executive*
Stempler, Jack Leon *government and aerospace company executive*
Straub, Peter Thornton *lawyer*
Straus, Leon Stephan *physicist*
Strickland, Nellie B. *library program director*
Strunz, Kim Carol *military officer*
Studebaker, John Milton *utilities engineer, consultant, educator*
Sturtevant, Brereton *retired lawyer, former government official*
Swinburn, Charles *lawyer*
Tatham, Julie Campbell *writer*
Thomas, William Griffith *lawyer*
Thompson, LeRoy, Jr. *radio engineer, military reserve officer*
Ticer, Patricia *state senator*
Toulmin, Priestley *geologist*
Trent, Darrell M. *academic and corporate executive*
Tucker, John Robert *financial executive*
Turner, Mary Jane *educational administrator*
Vance, Bernard Wayne *lawyer, government official*
Van Cleve, Ruth Gill *retired lawyer, government official*
Vander Myde, Paul Arthur *technology and engineering services executive*
Vander Myde, Philip Louis *architectural design firm executive*
Von Drehle, Ramon Arnold *lawyer*
Wagner, Louis Carson, Jr. *retired army officer*
Wallace, Barbara Brooks *writer*
Wasko-Flood, Sandra Jean *artist, educator*
Wegner, Helmuth Adalbert *lawyer, retired chemical company executive*
Weiner, Robert Michael *engineering design company executive, consulting engineer*
Wendel, Charles Allen *lawyer*
White, Gordon Eliot *historian*
Widner, Ralph Randolph *civic executive*
Wilding, James Anthony *airport administrator*
Williams, Emma Crawford *business owner*
Williams, Justin W. *government official*
Wilner, Morton Harrison *retired lawyer*
Wilson, Kathy *principal*
Woelflein, Kevin Gerard *banker*
Wolfe, Thad Allison *air force officer*
Wolicki, Eligius Anthony *nuclear physicist, consultant*
Womack, Joseph Donald, Sr. *manufacturing and telecommunications executive, consultant*
Woolley, Mary Elizabeth *research administrator*
Wright, Mary James *multimedia instructional designer*
Wurzel, Mary V. *past association executive*
Yaworsky, George Myroslaw *physicist, technical and management consultant*
Yoder, Edwin Milton, Jr. *columnist, educator, editor, writer*
Zarro, Janice Anne *lawyer*
Ziegler, Ronald Louis *association executive, former government official*
Zook, Theresa Fuetterer *gemologist, consultant*

## Altavista
Jones, Susan Renee *counselor, mental health services professional*

## Amelia Court House
Wallace, John Robert *county administrator*

## Amherst
Herbert, Amanda Kathryn *special education educator*

## Annandale
Abdellah, Faye Glenn *retired public health service executive*
Binder, Richard Allen *hematologist, oncologist*
Christianson, Geryld B. *government relations consultant*
Connair, Stephen Michael *financial analyst*
Faraday, Bruce John *scientific research company executive, physicist*
Freitag, Robert Frederick *retired government official*
Geiger, Richard Bernard *engineer, retired federal agency administrator*
Gingrich, Lisa Cox *advertising and marketing executive, consultant*
Greinke, Everett Donald *corporate executive, international programs consultant*
Guthrie, John Reiley *retired army officer, business executive*
Hedrick, Floyd Dudley *government official, author*
Herbst, Robert LeRoy *organization executive*
Heyer, Laura Miriam *special education educator*
Jarvis, Elbert, II (Jay Jarvis) *employee benefits specialist*
Kaufmanas, Petras G. *biomedical researcher, psychologist*
Khim, Jay Wook *high technology systems integration executive*
†Lefrak, Edward Arthur *cardiovascular surgeon*
Mandeville, Robert Clark, Jr. *former naval officer, business executive*
Matuszko, Anthony Joseph *research chemist, administrator*
McCaffree, Burnham Clough, Jr. *retired naval officer*
McGuire, Edward David, Jr. *lawyer*
McKee, Fran *retired naval officer*
Nowak, Jan Zdzislaw *writer, consultant*
Osborn, Len *business executive*
Raab, Harry Frederick, Jr. *physicist*
Richstein, Abraham Richard *lawyer*
Rogers, Stephen Hitchcock *former ambassador*
Santi, Ellyn E. (Ellyn E. Wagner) *mathematics educator*
Scott, Hugh Patrick *physician, naval officer*
Shamburek, Roland Howard *physician*
Simonian, Simon John *surgeon, scientist, educator*
Speakes, Larry Melvin *public relations executive*
Tontz, Robert L. *government official*
Watts, Helena Roselle *military analyst*
Wilhelmi, Mary Charlotte *education educator, college official*
Williams, James Arthur *retired army officer, information systems company executive*
Yaffe, David Philip *lawyer*

## Arlington
Adams, John Hanly *retired magazine editor, writer, consultant*
Adreon, Beatrice Marie Rice *pharmacist*
Adreon, Harry Barnes *architect*
Aggrey, Orison Rudolph *former ambassador, university administrator*
Alford, Paula N. *federal agency administrator*
Allard, Dean Conrad *historian, retired naval history center director*
Allen, David *government official*
Allen, Harry Roulon, Jr. *data processing and storage company executive*
Anderson, David Lawrence *lawyer*
Anthony, Robert Armstrong *law educator*
Arndt, Roger Edward Anthony *hydraulic engineer, educator*
Ascunce, Gil *physician*
Aukland, Elva Dayton *retired biologist, educator*
Bader, Michael Haley *lawyer, telecommunications, broadcasting executive*
Bailey, Amos Purnell *clergyman, syndicated columnist*
Banister, G. Huntington *federal official*
Bardon, Marcel *government official*
Barnhart, Beverly Jean *physicist*
Bartlett, Elizabeth Susan *audio-visual specialist*
Bast, James Louis *trade association executive*
Basu, Sunanda *scientific administrator, researcher in space physics*
Bautz, Laura Patricia *astronomer*
Beggs, James Montgomery *former government official*
Behney, Clyde Joseph *health services researcher*
Belen, Frederick Christopher *lawyer*
Bennett, John Joseph *professional services company executive*
Benzinger, Raymond Burdette *lawyer, educator*
Berg, John Richard *chemist, former federal government executive*
Berg, Sister Marie Majella *university chancellor*
Berry, Fred Clifton, Jr. *author, magazine editor, book packager*
Bevill, Tom *retired congressman, lawyer*
Beyer, Barbara Lynn *aviation consultant*
Bird, Caroline *author*
Bloomer, William Arthur *security industry executive*
Bodley, Harley Ryan, Jr. *editor, writer, broadcaster*
Bold, Frances Ann *librarian*
Bolster, Archie Milburn *retired foreign service officer*
Borchers, Robert Reece *physicist and administrator*
Bordogna, Joseph *engineer, educator*
Boyle, Robert Patrick *retired government agency consultant, lawyer*
Bradunas, John Joseph *marine corps officer*
Brandt, Werner William *federal agency official*
Brehm, William Keith *information systems company executive*
Brenner, Edgar H. *legal administrator*
Bridgewater, Albert Louis *science foundation administrator*
Brown, Elliott Rowe *physicist*
Brown, James Harvey *neuroscientist, government research administrator*
Brown, Robert Lyle *foreign affairs consultant*
Brown-Black, Lillian (Rusty) *volunteer*
Brunson, Burlie Allen *aerospace executive*
Bullard, Marcia Lynn *publishing executive*
Busby, Morris D. *ambassador*
Bussmann, Charles Haines *publisher*
Cameron, Maryellen *science association administrator, geologist, educator*
Cargo, William Ira *ambassador, retired*
Carr, Kenneth Monroe *naval officer*
Cavanaugh, Margaret Anne *chemist*
Chapman, Donald D. *retired naval officer, lawyer*
Chapple, Thomas Leslie *lawyer*
Chipman, Susan Elizabeth *psychologist*
Ciment, Melvyn *mathematician*
Clarke, Frederic B., III *risk analysis consultant*
Clayton, James Edwin *journalist*
Coady, Philip James, Jr. *naval officer*
Cocolis, Peter Konstantine *business development executive*
Cohen, Eliot Dorsey *electrical engineer*
Cole, Benjamin Richason *newspaper executive*
Collins, Eileen Louise *economist*
Collins, Philip Reilly *lawyer, educator*
Conger, Clement Ellis *foreign service officer, curator*
Conklin, Kenneth Edward *lawyer, industry executive*
Contis, George *medical services company executive*
Coronado, Gil *federal official*
Covington, James Edwin *government agency administrator, psychologist*
Cox, Geraldine Vang *engineering executive*
Cox, Henry *research company executive, research engineer*
Crittenden, Danielle Ann *editor, journalist*
Crystal, Lester Martin *television producer*
Curley, John J. *diversified media company executive*
Curley, Thomas *newspaper executive*
Curtis, Richard A. *newspaper editor*
Damich, Edward John *law educator*
Davis, Michael *engineering company executive*
DeFrancesco, Gerry *broadcasting company executive*
DeHarde, William M. *business consultant, pension plan administrator*
†Denman, Gary L. *mechanical engineer*
Dennis, Everette Eugene, Jr. *foundation executive, journalism educator*
Dickman, Robert Laurence *physicist, researcher*
Dillaway, Robert Beacham *engineering and management consultant*
Dillon, Francis Richard *air force officer, retired*
Dolan, William David, Jr. *physician*
Drake, Diana Ashley *financial planner*
Drayton, William *lawyer, management consultant*
Dunham, Frank Willard *lawyer*
Dunn, Loretta Lynn *lawyer*
Duryee, William Rankin *retired cell physiology educator, consultant*
Eastin, Keith E. *lawyer*
Edmonds, Albert J. *career officer*
Edmondson, William Brockway *retired foreign service officer*
Ehrman, Madeline Elizabeth *federal agency administrator*
Elam, Fred Eldon *career army officer, retired*
Endahl, Lowell Jerome *retired electrical cooperative executive*
England, Robert Stowe *writer*
Ensminger, Luther Glenn *chemist*
Erb, Karl Albert *physicist, government official*
Erwin, Frank William *personnel research and publishing executive*
Everett, Warren Sylvester *consultant, former government official*
Fabian, John McCreary *non-profit company executive, former astronaut, former air force officer*
Faris, Frank Edgar *marketing executive*
†Feld, Donald H. *management consultant*
Feller, Mimi *newspaper publishing executive*
Fernandez, Henry A. *professional association administrator, lawyer*
Fisher, Farley *federal agency administrator, chemist*
Flowers, Harold Lee *aerospace engineer, consultant*
Forrester, Eugene Priest *former army officer, management marketing consultant*
Freeman, Neal Blackwell *communications corporation executive*
Friedheim, Jerry Warden *museum executive*
Fuchs, Roland John *geography educator, university science official*
Fulton, Diann Marie *financial consultant*
Funseth, Robert Lloyd Eric Martin *international consultant, lecturer, retired senior foreign service officer*
†Gabrielson, Charles *publishing executive*
†Gauvin, Charles F. *professional society administrator*
Gergely, Tomas *astronomer*
Gergen, David Richmond *federal official, magazine editor*
Gianturco, Delio E. *management consultant*
†Gibbons, Miles J., Jr. *foundation administrator*
Gilbert, Arthur Charles *aerospace engineer, consulting engineer*
Giles, Scott Andrew *federal agency staff member*
Gilmore, Marjorie Havens *civic worker, lawyer*
Gniewek, Raymond Louis *newspaper editor*
Golladay, Mary Jean *statistician*
Gonzalez, Eduardo *federal agency administrator*
Gormley, Dennis Michael *consulting company executive*
Gottschalk, John Simison *biologist*
Gracey, James Steele *corporate director, retired coast guard officer, consultant*
Graham, William Pierson *investment banker, entrepreneur*
Green, Judy *mathematics educator*
Gregg, David, III *investment banker*
Hagn, George Hubert *electrical engineer, researcher*
Hall, Carl William *agricultural and mechanical engineer*
Hall, Douglas K. *conservation official*
Hamor, Kathy Virginia *consultant*
Hansen, Kenneth D. *lawyer, ophthalmologist*
Haq, Bilal Ul *national science foundation program director, researcher*
Harper, Michael John Kennedy *obstetrics and gynecology educator*
Harrison, Jerry Calvin *retired army officer*
Hartley, Craig Sheridan *dean, mechanical engineering educator*
Hartley, David Minor *physicist*
Hartmanis, Juris *computer scientist, educator*
Heineken, Frederick George *biochemical engineer*
Held, Joe Roger *veterinarian, epidemiologist*
Henderson, John Brown *economist*
Henderson, Robert Earl *mechanical engineer, educator, consultant*
Hendrickson, Jerome Orland *trade association executive, lawyer*
Henle, Peter *retired economic consultant, arbitrator*
Hickman, Elizabeth Podesta *retired counselor, educator*
Hill, Donald Wain *education accreditation commission executive*
Hittle, James Donald *writer, business consultant*
Hugler, Edward C. *lawyer, federal and state government*
Infosino, Iara Ciurria *management consultant*
Ingrassia, Anthony Frank *human resource specialist*
Jackson, William Paul, Jr. *lawyer*
Jankowski, John Edward, Jr. *government administrator*
Johnson, Charles Nelson, Jr. *physicist*
Johnson, John A. *communications company executive*
Junker, Bobby Ray *research and development executive, physicist*
Jurgensen, Karen *newspaper editor*
Kaiser, Philip Mayer *diplomat*
Kane, Cheryl Chase *education program developer*
Katona, Peter Geza *biomedical engineer, educator*
Kauffman, Thomas Richard *lawyer, consultant*
Kaufman, Paul *physician, former naval officer, association executive*
Keating, John Richard *bishop*
Keel, Alton Gold, Jr. *ambassador*
Kelley, Paul Xavier *retired marine corps officer*
Kelly, John James *lawyer*
Kem, Richard Samuel *retired army officer*
Kern, Paul John *army officer*
Kerns, Wilmer Lee *social science researcher*
Khosla, Rajinder Paul *physicist*
Kilduff, Bonnie Elizabeth *director of expositions*
Kiraly, Karch (Charles Kiraly) *professional volleyball player*
Kirk, Robert L. *aerospace and transportation company executive*
Kirtley, Jane Elizabeth *professional society administrator, lawyer*
Knipling, Edward Fred *retired research entomologist, agricultural administrator*
Knowlton, William Allen *business executive, consultant*
Korman, James William *lawyer*
Kosarin, Jonathan Henry *lawyer*
Koury, Agnes Lillian *real estate property manager*
Kovacic, William Evan *law educator*
Krys, Sheldon Jack *retired foreign service officer, career minister*
Kuelbs, John Thomas *lawyer*
Kull, Joseph *government administrator*
Kuwamoto, Roderick Dean, Jr. *physician assistant, perfusionist, educator*
Lambert, Richard Bowles, Jr. *national science foundation program director, oceanographer*
Lane, Neal Francis *university provost, physics researcher, federal administrator*
Langworthy, Everett Walter *association executive, natural gas exploration company executive*
Larsen-Basse, Jorn *mechanical and materials engineering educator, researcher, consultant*
Lau, Clifford *electrical engineer, researcher*
Lawrence, Ray Vance *chemist*
Leland, Marc Ernest *trust advisor, lawyer*
Lester, Barnett Benjamin *editor, foreign affairs officer*
Levinson, Lawrence Edward *lawyer, corporation executive*
Lewis, Hunter *financial advisor, publisher*
Lisanby, James Walker *retired naval officer*
Lockard, John Allen *naval officer*
Long, Madeleine J. *mathematics and science educator*
Lorell, Monte *newspaper editor*
†Luftig, Stephen D. *federal agency administrator*
Lynch, John Thomas *science foundation administrator, physicist*
Lynn, Larry (Verne Lauriston Lynn) *engineering executive*
MacDougall, William Lowell *magazine editor*
MacNeil, Robert Breckenridge Ware *retired broadcast journalist*
Malone, William Grady *lawyer*
†Maness, Stephen Ray *manufacturing engineer, retired army officer*
Marcuccio, Phyllis Rose *association executive, editor*
Marini, Elizabeth Ann *civilian military executive*
Marks, Robert Hutchinson *publishing executive*
Marshall, Charles Burton *political science consultant*
Marshall, James John *publishing executive*
Marzetti, Loretta A. *government agency executive, policy analyst*
Mason, Phillip Howard *aircraft company executive, retired army officer*
Mater, Gene P. *communications consultant*
Mathis, Mark Jay *lawyer*
Mazzarella, David *newspaper editor*
McDermott, Francis Owen *lawyer*
McDonald, Bernard Robert *federal agency administrator*
McMasters, Paul Kenneth *foundation executive*
McNamara, Tom *newspaper editor*
McWethy, John Fleetwood *journalist*
McWethy, Patricia Joan *educational association administrator*
Melickian, Gary Edward *trade association executive*
Merrifield, Dudley Bruce *business educator, former government official*
Merritt, Jack Neil *retired army officer*
Meyer, Richard Townsend *service company executive*
Meyers, Sheldon *engineering company executive*
Milburn, Richard Allan *aerospace company executive*

Miller, Thomas Hulbert, Jr. *former marine corps officer*
Mills, Elizabeth Shown *genealogist editor, writer*
Mirrielees, James Fay, III *publishing executive*
Mooney, John Bradford, Jr. *oceanographer, engineer, consultant*
Moore, Julia Alice *federal government executive*
Moraff, Howard *science foundation program director*
Morgan, Bruce Ray *international consultant*
Morris, John Woodland, II *businessman, former army officer*
Moshier, David Irwin *church administrator*
Muris, Timothy Joseph *law educator*
Murphy, Donn Brian *theater educator*
Murray, Arthur Joseph *engineering executive, lecturer*
Murray, Jeanne Morris *computer scientist, educator, consultant*
Nalen, Craig Anthony *government official*
Neikirk, William Robert *journalist*
Nejelski, Paul Arthur *judge*
Neuharth, Allen Harold *newspaper publisher*
Newburger, Beth Weinstein *medical telecommunications company executive*
Nickle, Dennis Edwin *electronics engineer, church deacon*
Nida, Jane Bolster (Mrs. Dow Hughes Nida) *retired librarian*
Nielsen, Aldon Dale *retired government agency official, economist*
Nodeen, Janey Price *government official*
Obermayer, Herman Joseph *newspaper publisher*
†O'Connell, Patrick Michael *naval officer*
Oleson, Ray Jerome *computer service company executive*
O'Neill, Brian *research organization administrator*
Ordway, Frederick Ira, III *educator, consultant, researcher, author*
Otstott, Charles Paddock *company executive, retired army officer*
Palor, John *media group executive*
Parker, Jeffrey Scott *law educator, university official*
Paynter, Harry Alvin *retired trade association executive*
Perry, Bill *photojournalist*
Peterson, Paul Quayle *retired university dean, physician*
†Pippen, Harvey G. *government official*
Poehlein, Gary Wayne *chemical engineering educator*
Porter, Barbara *anchorwoman, writer, educator*
Putnam, George W., Jr. *army officer*
Pyatt, Everett Arno *government official*
Quinn, John Collins *publishing executive, newspaper editor*
Quinn, William Wilson *army officer, manufacturing executive*
Rabun, John Brewton, Jr. *social services agency administrator*
Rahman, Muhammad Abdur *mechanical engineer*
Reed, Paul Allen *artist*
Reeder, Franklin S. *retired federal agency administrator*
Rees, Clifford Harcourt, Jr. (Ted Rees) *association executive, retired air force officer*
Reiss, Susan Marie *editor, writer*
Reynik, Robert J. *materials scientist, research and education administrator*
Reynolds, Peter James *physicist*
Richtol, Herbert Harold *science foundation program director*
Rieken, Danny Michael *naval officer, aerospace and systems engineer*
Rimpel, Auguste Eugene, Jr. *management and technical consulting executive*
Ritter, Hal *newspaper editor*
Roberts, James Milnor, Jr. *professional society administrator*
Rockefeller, Sharon Percy *broadcast executive*
Roco, Mihail Constantin *mechanical engineer, educator*
Rogers, James Frederick *banker, management consultant*
Romney, Carl F. *seismologist*
Rose, Charles Grandison, III (Charlie Rose) *former congressman*
Rosenker, Mark Victor *trade association executive*
Saalfeld, Fred Erich *naval researcher*
Samburg, A. Gene *security company executive*
Sancetta, Constance Antonina *oceanographer*
Sands, Frank Melville *investment manager*
Sawhill, John Crittenden *conservationist, economist, university president, government official*
Scarborough, Robert Henry, Jr. *coast guard officer*
Schafer, Alice Turner *retired mathematics educator*
†Schaffer, Teresita Currie *federal official*
Scott, Suzanne *writer, artist*
Seamans, Andrew Charles *editorial and public relations consultant, columnist, author*
Secular, Sidney *federal agency administrator, procurement analyst*
Seely, James Michael *defense consultant, retired naval officer, small business owner*
Shannon, Thomas Alfred *retired educational association administrator emeritus*
Sibley, William Arthur *academic administrator, physics educator, consultant*
Simms, Frances Bell *elementary education educator*
Simonson, David C. *retired newspaper association executive*
Simpson, John Mathes *newspaper editor*
Sinclair, Rolf Malcolm *physicist*
Singstock, David John *military officer*
Smalley, Robert Manning *government official*
Smith, Elise Fiber *international non-profit development agency administrator*
Smith, John Michael *lawyer*
Soderquist, Ronald Bruce *minister, ministry director*
Sowle, Donald Edgar *management consultant*
†Spooner, Richard Edward *aerospace company executive*
Stahl, O(scar) Glenn *writer, lecturer, former government official*
Stanley, Scott, Jr. *editor*
Stevens, Donald King *aeronautical engineer*
Stokes, B. R. *retired transportation consultant*
Stolgitis, William Charles *professional society executive*
Stover, David Frank *lawyer*
Strandquist, John Herbert *association executive*
Strean, Bernard M. *retired naval officer*
Stuart, Charles Edward *electrical engineer, oceanographer*
Sullivan, Cornelius Wayne *marine biology educator, research foundation administrator, government agency administrator*
Sullivan, Terry T. *newspaper publishing executive*
Sutton, George Walter *research laboratory executive, mechanical engineer*
Taggart, G. Bruce *government program executive*
Talmadge, John Barnes *science foundation administrator*
Tanzer, Lester *editor*
Tarbell, David S. *federal agency administrator*
Teem, John McCorkle *retired association executive*
Terzian, Grace Paine *publisher*
Thomas, Jimmy Lynn *financial executive*
Thompson, Jonathan Sims *army officer*
Tice, Raphael Dean *army officer*
Tyrrell, Robert Emmett, Jr. *editor-in-chief, writer*
Umminger, Bruce Lynn *government official, scientist, educator*
Van Doren, Emerson Barclay *administrative judge*
Van Horn, Hugh *physicist, astronomer*
Van Landingham, Leander Shelton, Jr. *lawyer*
Van Lare, Wendell John *lawyer*
Vaught, Wilma L. *foundation executive, retired air force officer*
Verburg, Edwin Arnold *federal agency administrator*
Vesper, Carolyn F. *newspaper publishing executive*
Violand-Sanchez, Emma Natividad *school administrator, educator*
Voigt, Robert Gary *numerical analyst*
Volkmer, Harold L. *former congressman*
Wakefield, Richard Alan *energy consulting firm executive*
Walker, John Denley *foundation director, former government official*
Walker, Walter Gray, Jr. *small business owner, program statistician*
Wall, Barbara Wartelle *lawyer*
Watson, Alexander Fletcher *organization executive, former ambassador*
Wayland, Russell Gibson, Jr. *retired geology consultant, government official*
Webb, Clifton Alan *media consultant*
Weidemann, Celia Jean *social scientist, international business and financial development consultant*
Weiss, Susan *newspaper editor*
Wells, Christine *foundation executive*
Werbos, Paul John *neural net research director*
Whitcomb, James Hall *geophysicist, foundation administrator*
Widener, Peri Ann *business development executive*
Willenson, Kim Jeremy *publisher, journalist, author*
Williams, Luther Steward *science foundation administrator*
Wilson, Minter Lowther, Jr. *retired officers association executive*
Wodarczyk, Francis John *chemist*
Yankwich, Peter Ewald *chemistry educator*
Zakheim, Dov Solomon *economist, government official*
Zirkind, Ralph *physicist, educator*
Zorthian, Barry *communications executive*
Zumwalt, Elmo Russell, Jr. *retired naval officer*

**Ashburn**
Bennett, Lawrence Herman *physicist*
Boyne, Walter James *writer, former museum director*
Cooke, John Kent *professional sports management executive*
Gold, George Myron *lawyer, editor, writer, consultant*
Walsh, Geraldine Frances *nursing administrator*

**Ashland**
Henshaw, William Raleigh *middle school educator*
Inge, Milton Thomas *American literature and culture educator, author*
Martin, Roger Harry *college president*
Payne, Ladell *college president*
Stevenson, Carol Wells *secondary education educator*

**Beaumont**
Jackson, Hermoine Prestine *psychologist*

**Bedford**
Haymes, Harmon Hayden *economist, educator*

**Belle Haven**
Ross, Charles Worthington, IV *metals company executive*

**Berryville**
Croswell, Clyde Vernard, Jr. *human resources educator, researcher*
White, Eugene Vaden *pharmacist*

**Blacksburg**
Ash, Philip *psychologist*
Barden, John Allan *horticulturist*
Batra, Romesh Chander *engineering mechanics educator, researcher*
Bauer, Henry Hermann *chemistry and science educator*
Baumgartner, Frederic Joseph *history educator*
Blackwell, William Allen *electrical engineering educator*
Bliznakov, Milka Tcherneva *architect*
Boardman, Gregory Dale *environmental engineer, educator*
Brown, Gary Sandy *electrical engineering educator*
Brown, Gregory Neil *university administrator, forest physiology educator*
Brozovsky, John A. *accounting educator*
Bryant, Clifton Dow *sociologist, educator*
Cairns, John, Jr. *environmental science educator, researcher*
Campbell, Joan Virginia Loweke *secondary school educator, language educator*
Cannell, Robert Quirk *agricultural sciences , educator*
Carlisle, Ervin Frederick *university provost, educator*
Colmano, Germille *physiology educator, biophysics researcher*
Cowles, Joe Richard *biology educator*
Crawford, Peggy Smith *design educator*
De Datta, Surajit Kumar *soil scientist, agronomist, educator*
de Wolf, David Alter *electrical engineer, educator*
Doswald, Herman Kenneth *German language educator, academic administrator*
Edwards, Patricia K. *dean*
Fabrycky, Wolter Joseph *engineering educator, author, industrial and systems engineer*
Foster, Bill Carey *collegiate basketball team coach*
Fox, Edward Alan *computer science educator*
Glasser, Wolfgang Gerhard *wood science and chemical engineering researcher, educator*
Good, Irving John *statistics educator, mathematician, philosopher of science*
Graybeal, Jack Daniel *chemist, educator*
Grover, Norman LaMotte *theologian, philosopher*
Haugh, Clarence Gene *agricultural engineering educator*
Herndon, James Francis *retired political science educator*
Hibbard, Walter Rollo, Jr. *retired engineering educator*
Inman, Daniel John *mechanical engineer, educator*
Jensen, Walter Edward *lawyer, educator*
Jones, James Beverly *retired mechanical engineering educator, consultant*
Killough, Larry Neil *accounting educator*
Kincade, Doris Helsing *apparel marketing educator*
Krutchkoff, Richard Gerald *statistics educator, researcher*
Landen, Robert Geran *historian, university administrator*
Lee, Fred C. *electrical engineering educator*
Lucas, J. Richard *retired mining engineering educator*
McGrath, James Edward *chemistry educator*
Meirovitch, Leonard *engineering educator*
Minckler, Leon Sherwood *forestry and conservation educator, author*
Mitchell, James Kenneth *civil engineer, educator*
Mo, Luke Wei *physicist, educator*
Moore, James Mendon *industrial engineering educator, consultant*
Moore, Laurence John *business educator*
Murray, Thomas Michael *civil engineering educator, consultant*
Ogliaruso, Michael Anthony *chemist, educator*
Olin, Robert Floyd *mathematics educator and reseacher*
Peacock, Markham Lovick, Jr. *English educator*
Pitt, Joseph Charles *philosophy educator*
Price, Dennis Lee *industrial engineer, educator*
Purswell, Beverly Jean *veterinary medicine educator, theriogenologist*
Randall, Clifford Wendell *civil engineer*
Robertson, James Irvin, Jr. *historian, educator*
Rodriguez-Camilloni, Humberto Leonardo *architect, historian, educator*
Ross, James Barrett *finance and insurance educator*
Sgro, Joseph Anthony *psychologist, educator*
Shepard, Jon Max *sociologist*
Smeal, Paul Lester *retired horticulture educator*
Smith, Charles William *engineering educator*
Smith, Robert McNeil *university dean*
Squires, Arthur Morton *chemical engineer, educator*
Steger, Charles William *university administrator*
Stutzman, Warren Lee *electrical engineer, educator*
Swiger, L. A. *agricultural studies educator*
Terhune, Robert William *optics scientist*
Torgersen, Paul Ernest *academic administrator, educator*
Ulloa, Justo Celso *Spanish educator*
Wall, Robert Thompson *secondary school educator*
Weaver, Pamela Ann *hospitality research professional*
Wilkins, Tracy Dale *microbiologist, educator*

**Blackstone**
Walton, G. Clifford *family practice physician*

**Bluemont**
Weisman, John *author*

**Boston**
Knoche, Douglas Andrew *marketing executive, consultant*

**Bridgewater**
Geisert, Wayne Frederick *educational consultant, retired administrator*
Richardson, John MacLaren, Jr. *school superintendent*

**Brightwood**
Skelton, Dorothy Geneva Simmons (Mrs. John William Skelton) *art educator*

**Bristol**
Creger, David L. *financial planner, insurance executive*
McGlothlin, James W. *wholesale distribution executive*
Muller, William Albert, III *library director*

**Broad Run**
Hinkle, Barton Leslie *retired electronics company executive*
Kube, Harold Deming *retired financial executive*

**Broadway**
Keeler, James Leonard *food products company executive*

**Brookneal**
Elson, James Martin *historic foundation director, college music educator, fine arts administrator*

**Buena Vista**
Ripley, John Walter *academic administrator*

**Burgess**
Towle, Leland Hill *retired government official*

**Burke**
Bayer, Ada-Helen *industrial and organizational psychologist, educator*
Daski, Robert Steven *federal agency executive*
Dean, John Wilson, Jr. *business consultant, retired army officer*
Forster, William Hull *aerospace executive*
Lynch, Charles Theodore, Sr. *materials science engineering researcher, consultant, educator*
O'Connor, Edward Cornelius *army officer*
Pfister, Cloyd Harry *consultant, former career officer*
Smeeton, Thomas Rooney *governmental affairs consultant*

**Cape Charles**
†Brookshire, James Knox, Jr. *transportation facility administrator*

**Castleton**
Hahn, James Maglorie *former librarian, farmer*

**Catlett**
Broderick, Anthony James *air transportation executive*
Scheer, Julian Weisel *business executive, author*

**Centreville**
Amerault, James F. *military officer*
Bucciero, Joseph Mario, Jr. *executive engineering firm*
Kelly, John Joseph, Jr. *career officer*
Nong *artist, sculptor*

**Chantilly**
Dowdy, Dorothy Williams *political science educator*
Evans, Richard Taylor *aerospace engineer, consultant*
Harris, Paul Lynwood *aerospace transportation executive*
Miller, Donald Eugene *aerospace electronics executive*
O'Brien, Robert John, Jr. *public relations executive, former government official, air force officer*
Priem, Richard Gregory *writer, information systems executive, entertainment company executive*
Rowe, Audrey *postal service administrator*
Saunders, Norman Thomas *military officer*
Slayton, Gus *foundation administrator*
Sroka, John Walter *trade association executive*
Stone, Thomas Edward *defense consultant, retired rear admiral*

**Charles City**
Tyler, Payne Bouknight *museum executive*

**Charlotte Court House**
Hoffman, William *author*
Prophett, Andrew Lee *political science educator*

**Charlottesville**
Abbot, William Wright *history educator*
Abraham, Henry Julian *political science educator*
Abraham, Kenneth Samuel *law educator*
Alden, Douglas William *French language educator*
Anderson, Robert Barber *architect*
Arnold, A. James *foreign language educator*
Aylor, James Hiram *electrical engineering educator, department chair*
Barnett, Benjamin Lewis, Jr. *physician*
Barolsky, Paul *art history educator*
Battestin, Martin Carey *English language educator*
Bednar, Michael John *architecture educator*
Beller, George Allan *medical educator*
Berkeley, Edmund, Jr. *archivist, educator*
Berkeley, Francis Lewis, Jr. *retired archivist*
Berne, Robert Matthew *physiologist, educator*
Bierstedt, Robert *sociologist, author*
Biltonen, Rodney Lincoln *biochemistry and pharmacology educator*
Bloomfield, Louis Aub *physicist, educator*
Blotner, Joseph Leo *English language educator*
Bly, Charles Albert *nuclear engineer, research scientist*
Bonnie, Richard Jeffrey *legal educator, lawyer*
Boring, John Wayne *physicist, educator*
Bosserman, Joseph Norwood *architecture educator*
†Bouchard, Ronald A. *health care administrator*
Bovet, Eric David *economist, consultant*
Bradbeer, Clive *biochemistry and microbiology educator, research scientist*
Brame, Joseph Robert, III *lawyer*
Brandt, Richard Martin *education educator*
Breneman, David Worthy *dean, educator*
Brill, Arthur Sylvan *biophysics educator*
Broome, Oscar Whitfield, Jr. *accounting educator, administrator*
Brown, Rita Mae *author*
Bull, George Albert *retired banker*
Bunch, John Blake *photographer, writer, educator*
Bunker, Linda Kay *dean, physical education educator*
Campbell, Stephen Donald Peter *retired university administrator*
Cano-Ballesta, Juan *Spanish language educator*
Cantrell, Robert Wendell *otolaryngologist, head and neck surgeon, educator*
Carey, Robert Munson *university dean, physician*
Carpenter, Richard Amon *chemist*
Casey, John Dudley *writer, English language educator*
Casteen, John Thomas, III *university president*
Catlin, Avery *engineering and computer science educator, writer*
Chalam, Ann *healthcare administrator*
Chandler, Lawrence Bradford, Jr. *lawyer*
Chapel, Robert Clyde *stage director, theater educator*
Cherno, Melvin *humanities educator*
Chevalier, Robert Louis *pediatric nephrologist, educator, researcher*
Chevalier, Roger Alan *astronomy educator, consultant*
Childress, James Franklin *theology and medical educator*
Claude, Inis Lothair, Jr. *political scientist, educator*
Clay, Jenny Strauss *classics educator*
Cohen, Edwin Samuel *lawyer, educator*
Cohen, Helen Herz *camp owner, director*
Colker, Marvin Leonard *classics educator*
Colley, John Leonard, Jr. *educator, author, management consultant*
Conrad, Paul Edward *lawyer, army officer*
Conway, Brian Peter *ophthalmologist, educator*
Cooper, James Michael *education educator*
Corse, John Doggett *university official, lawyer*
Courtney, Edward *classics educator*
Cowles, Roger William *federal agency administrator*
Craig, James William *physician, educator, university dean*
Crigler, B. Waugh *federal judge*
Dalton, Claudette Ellis Harloe *anesthesiologist, educator, university official*
Davis, Edward Wilson *business administration educator*
Deese, James Earle *psychologist, educator*
DeMong, Richard Francis *finance and investments educator*
Denommé, Robert Thomas *foreign language educator*
DeSilvey, Dennis Lee *cardiologist, educator, university administrator*
Detmer, Don Eugene *medical educator, health policy researcher, surgeon*
Dickman, James Earl *financial services executive*
Dodson, Claudia Lane *athletic administrator*
Dooley, Michael P. *law educator*
Dorning, John Joseph *nuclear engineering, engineering physics and applied mathematics educator*
Dove, Rita Frances *poet, English language educator*
Dreifuss, Fritz Emanuel *neurologist, educator*
Du Bar, Jules Ramon *geologist, retired educator*

†Lavine, Thelma Zeno *philosophy educator*
Levis, Alexander Henry *systems engineer educator, consultant*
Levitt, Serena Farr *nursing administrator*
Lipset, Seymour Martin *sociologist, political scientist, educator*
Lipton, Eric *reporter*
Lott, Wayne Thomas *systems engineer*
Madry-Taylor, Jacquelyn Yvonne *educational administrator*
Marohn, Ann Elizabeth *health information professional*
McCormick, Robert Junior *company executive, former government official*
Merten, Alan Gilbert *academic administrator*
Miller, Emilie F. *former state senator, consultant*
Morowitz, Harold Joseph *biophysicist, educator*
Mund, Richard Gordon *foundation executive*
Newsome, George Marvin *lawyer*
Noto, Lucio R. *gas and oil industry executive*
Palmer, James Daniel *information technology educator*
Pedersen, George J. *engineering company executive, computer support company executive*
Peters, Esther Caroline *aquatic toxicologist, pathobiologist, consultant*
Pitchell, Robert J. *business executive*
Priesman, Elinor Lee Soll *family dynamics administrator, mediator, educator*
Rosenkranz, Robert Bernard *military officer*
Rossotti, Charles Ossola *computer consulting company executive*
Rubin, Robert Joseph *physician, health care consultant*
Sage, Andrew Patrick, Jr. *systems information and software engineering educator*
Sanderson, Douglas Jay *lawyer*
Santore, Carrie-Beth *computer management professional*
Saverot, Pierre-Michel *nuclear waste management company executive*
Scanlon, Charles Francis *army officer, retired, defense consultant*
Schilling, William Richard *aerospace engineer, research and development company executive*
Schneck, Paul Bennett *computer scientist*
Schrock, Simon *retail executive*
Sheehan, Edward James *technical consultant, former government official*
Sheehy, Vincent *automotive executive*
Singer, S(iegfried) Fred *geophysicist, educator*
Sisodia, Rajendra Singh *business educator, researcher, consultant*
Smith, Robert Keith *exchange program associate*
Snyder, Thomas Daniel *retired electronics engineer, consultant*
Sowder, Donald Dillard *chemicals executive*
Spitzberg, Irving Joseph, Jr. *lawyer, corporate executive*
Stage, Thomas Benton *psychiatrist*
Stitt, David Tillman *judge*
Strauch, Barry Stuart *physician, educator*
Swenson, Harold Francis *crisis management consultant*
Tucker, Dewey Duane *systems analyst*
Vaughn, Karen Iversen *economics educator*
Verheyen, Egon *art historian, educator*
Walker, Betsy Ellen *consulting and systems integration company executive*
Ward, Charles Raymond *systems engineer*
Ward, George Truman *architect*
Warfield, John Nelson *engineering educator, consultant*
West, Bob *pharmaceutical company executive*
†Whitcomb, Darrel Dean *pilot*
Williams, Thomas Rhys *anthropologist, educator*
Wolff, Edward A. *electronics engineer*
Wood, C(harles) Norman *air force officer*
†Woodle, Roy V. *services company executive*
Woodruff, C(harles) Roy *professional association executive*

**Fairfax Station**
Jackson, Vaughn Lyle *artist, consultant*
Johansen, Eivind Herbert *special education services executive, former army officer*
Ross, Jimmy Douglas *army officer*
Sielicki-Korczak, Boris Zdzislaw *political educator, investigative consultant*
Starry, Donn Albert *former aerospace company executive, former army officer*
Taylor, Eldon Donivan *government official*

**Falls Church**
Bankson, Marjory *religious association administrator*
Barkley, Paul Haley, Jr. *architect*
Beach, Robert Oliver, II *computer company executive*
Becker, James Richard *lawyer*
Benson, William Edward (Barnes) *geologist*
Benton, Nicholas Frederick *publisher*
Blanck, Ronald Ray *hospital administrator, internist, career officer*
Block, John Rusling *former secretary of agriculture*
Brady, Rupert Joseph *lawyer*
Bucur, John Charles *neurological surgeon*
Cain, David Lee *corporate executive*
Calkins, Gary Nathan *lawyer, retired*
Calkins, Susannah Eby *retired economist*
Carney, Daniel L. *program and financial management consultant*
Cetron, Marvin Jerome *management executive*
Christman, Bruce Lee *lawyer*
Cleland, Sherrill *college president*
Connery, Robert Howe *author, educator*
Cooper, Arthur Irving *former association executive*
Cromley, Allan Wray *journalist*
†Cuddy, John James *deputy surgeon general*
Diamond, Robert Michael *lawyer*
Dodd, Steven Louis *systems engineer*
Dole, Elizabeth Hanford *charitable organization administrator, former secretary of labor, former secretary of transportation*
Duesenberg, Robert H. *lawyer*
Dunton, James Gerald *association executive*
Ehrlich, Bernard Herbert *lawyer, association executive*
Ehrlich, Geraldine Elizabeth *service management consultant*
Ehrlich, S(aul) Paul, Jr. *physician, consultant, former government official*
Elderkin, Helaine Grace *lawyer*
Evans, Peter Yoshio *ophthalmologist, educator*
Feldmann, Edward George *pharmaceutical chemist*
Fink, Charles Augustin *behavioral systems scientist*
Frazier, Walter Ronald *real estate investment company executive*

Geithner, Paul Herman, Jr. *banker*
Glass, Lawrence *business executive*
Gorges, Heinz August *research engineer*
Graves, Howard Dwayne *army officer, academic administrator, educator*
Gray, D'Wayne *retired marine corps officer*
Green, Gerald *editor, consultant*
Green, James Wyche *sociologist, anthropologist, psychotherapist*
†Gruggel, John Stuart, Jr. *judge*
Hahn, Thomas Joonghi *accountant*
Harley, William Gardner *retired communications consultant*
Harrison, Virginia Florence *retired anatomist and educator, investment advisor, publisher, philanthropist*
Hart, C(harles) W(illard), Jr. *zoologist, curator*
Haynes, William J(ames), II *lawyer*
Honigberg, Carol Crossman *lawyer*
Ibañez, Alvaro *patent design company executive, artist*
Imburg, Irving Jerome *dentist*
Inglefield, Joseph T., Jr. *allergist, immunologist, pediatrician*
Isaac, William Michael *investment firm executive, former government official*
Jennings, Thomas Parks *lawyer*
Kalleres, Michael Peter *career officer*
Kaplow, Herbert Elias *journalist*
Kroesen, Frederick James *retired army officer, consultant*
Laqueur, Maria *educational association administrator*
Layman, Lawrence *naval officer*
LeBlanc, Hugh Linus *political science educator, consultant*
Leighton, Frances Spatz *writer, journalist*
Livingstone, Susan Morrisey *nonprofit administrator*
Lorenzo, Michael *engineer, government official, real estate broker*
Lyman, Robert Howard *veterans association executive*
Masterson, Kleber Sandlin *former organization executive, retired naval officer*
McVay, Mary Frances *portfolio manager*
Mellor, James Robb *electronics executive*
Morrison, H. Robert *writer, editor, politician*
Morse, Marvin Henry *judge*
Mortensen, Robert Henry *landscape architect*
Moscato, Anthony Charles *federal official*
Nach, James Peter *foreign service officer*
Nashman, Alvin Eli *computer company executive*
Nelson, Thomas William *former management consultant, government official*
Okay, John Louis *telecommunications executive*
Orben, Robert *editor, writer*
Orkand, Donald Saul *management consultant*
O'Sullivan, Judith Roberta *lawyer, author*
Pendleton, Elmer Dean, Jr. *retired military officer, international consultant*
Perkins, Jack Edwin *lawyer*
Persinger, Judith Eileen *management plan clerk*
Post, Howard Allen *forest industry specialist*
Rosenberg, Theodore Roy *financial executive*
Salvatori, Vincent Louis *corporate executive*
Schaer, Werner *computer services executive*
Schmidt, Paul Wickham *lawyer*
Simokaitis, Frank Joseph *air force officer, lawyer*
Simpson, John Arol *retired government executive, physicist*
Spector, Louis *retired federal judge, lawyer, arbitrator, consultant*
Spindel, William *chemist, consultant*
Stone, Marvin Lawrence *journalist, government official*
Theismann, Joseph Robert *former professional football player, announcer*
Todd, Shirley Ann *school system administrator*
Van Nelson, Nicholas Lloyd *business council executive*
Villarreal, Carlos Castaneda *engineering executive*
Waldo, (Clifford) Dwight *political science educator*
Webb, William John *public relations counsel*
Weiss, Armand Berl *economist, association management executive*
Werner, Stuart Lloyd *computer services company executive*
Whitehead, Kenneth Dean *author, translator, retired federal government official*
Winzer, P.J. *lawyer*
Young, John Hardin *lawyer*
Zirkle, William Vernon *philanthropist*

**Farmville**
Boyer, Calvin James *librarian*
Dorrill, William Franklin *political scientist, educator*

**Farnham**
Durham, James Michael, Sr. *marketing consultant*

**Fishersville**
Geiman, Stephen Royer *secondary school educator, coach*

**Flint Hill**
Dietel, William Moore *former foundation executive*

**Floyd**
McBroom, Diane Craun *accountant, horse trainer*

**Fort Belvoir**
Barnholdt, Terry Joseph *chemical, industrial, and general engineer*
Diercks, Frederick Otto *government official*
Gould, Jay William, III *management development educator, lecturer, author, international consultant*
Molholm, Kurt Nelson *federal agency administrator*
Reed, William H. *federal agency administrator*
†Richbourg, Donna S. *federal agency adminstrator*
Smith, Margherita *writer, editor*
Suycott, Mark Leland *naval flight officer*

**Fort Defiance**
Livick, Malcolm Harris *school administrator*

**Fort Lee**
Johnson, Harry Watkins *defense analyst*
Sterling, Keir Brooks *historian, educator*

**Fort Monroe**
Miller, John Edward *army officer, educational administrator*

**Fort Myer**
Hart, Herbert Michael *military officer*
Shalikashvili, John Malchase *military career officer*

**Franconia**
Keating, Gladys Brown *state legislator*

**Franklin**
Cobb, G. Elliott, Jr. *lawyer*
Sprouse, Earlene Pentecost *educational diagnostician*

**Fredericksburg**
Anderson, Roberta June *computer engineer*
Dennis, Donald Daly *retired librarian*
Dorman, John Frederick *genealogist*
Farmer, James *civil rights leader, former trade union official*
Funk, Ella Frances *genealogist, author*
Geary, Patrick Joseph *naval security administrator*
Hajek, Otomar *mathematics educator*
Herndon, Cathy Campbell *artist, art educator*
Hickman, Margaret Capellini *advertising executive*
Hickman, Richard Lonnie *advertising executive*
Ivey, David Lamar *trade association executive*
Jamison, John Ambler *retired circuit judge*
Jenks-Davies, Kathryn Ryburn *retired daycare provider and owner, civic worker*
Jones, Julia Pearl *elementary school educator*
Jones, Owaiian Maurice *lawyer*
Medding, Walter Sherman *environmental engineer*
Rowe, Charles Spurgeon *newspaper publishing and broadcasting executive*
Schmutzhart, Berthold Josef *sculptor, educator, art and education consultant*
Snapp, Roy Baker *lawyer*

**Free Union**
Hart, Jean Hardy *international business operations systems specialist, consultant*

**Front Royal**
Andes, Larry Dale *minister*
Douglas, J(ocelyn) Fielding *toxicologist, consultant*
Greco, Barbara Ruth Gomez *literacy organization administrator*
Marx, Paul Benno *author, social service administrator, missionary*

**Gainesville**
Steger, Edward Herman *chemist*

**Galax**
Kapp, John Paul *lawyer, physician, educator*
Sense, Karl August *physicist, educator*

**Glasgow**
Riegel, Kurt Wetherhold *environmental protection executive*

**Glen Allen**
Batzli, Terrence Raymond *lawyer*
Fairbank, Richard *diversified financial services company executive*
Farrell, Joseph Christopher *mining executive, services executive*
Fife, William Franklin *retired drug company executive*
Minor, George Gilmer, III *drug and hospital supply company executive*
Murphey, Robert Stafford *pharmaceutical company executive*
Weaver, Mollie Little *lawyer*

**Gloucester**
Fang, Joong *philosopher, mathematician, educator*
Powell, Bolling Raines, Jr. *lawyer, educator*

**Goldvein**
Peterson, Barbara Mae Bittner Owecke *artist, nurse, realtor*

**Goode**
Brown, John Robert, Jr. *international marketing executive, consultant*

**Great Falls**
Foryst, Carole *mortgage broker*
Garrett, Wilbur (Bill) *magazine editor*
Jacobson, Richard Lee *lawyer, educator*
Litton, Robert Clifton *marine engineer, consultant*
MacGowan, Charles Frederic *retired chemical company executive*
Neidich, George Arthur *lawyer*
Railton, William Scott *lawyer*
Savage, Michael Thomas *federal executive*
Schreiner, George E. *nephrologist, educator, writer*
Schwartz, Robert Terry *professional association executive*
Somers, James Wilford *information management company executive*
Zimmermann, Warren *former foreign service officer*

**Grundy**
Smith, Jack *food service executive*

**Halifax**
Anderson, Howard Palmer *former state senator*
Greenbacker, John Everett *retired lawyer*

**Hampden Sydney**
Bagby, George Franklin, Jr. *English language educator*
Jagasich, Paul Anthony *language educator, translator*
Joyner, Weyland Thomas *physicist, educator, business consultant*
Kniffen, Donald Avery *astrophysicist, educator, researcher*
Porterfield, William Wendell *chemist, educator*
Wilson, Samuel V. *academic adminstrator*

**Hampton**
Barnes, Myrtle Sue Snyder *editor*
Bartels, Robert Edwin *aerospace engineer*
Brown, Loretta Ann Port *physician, geneticist*
Coombs, Vanessa Moody *journalism educator, lawyer*
Cravens, James J., Jr. *military officer*
Deepak, Adarsh *meteorologist, aerospace engineer, atmospheric scientist*
Drummond, James Everman *technology transfer company executive, former army officer*

Duberg, John Edward *retired aeronautical engineer, educator*
Dula, Brett M. *military officer*
Dwoyer, Douglas Leon *engineering executive*
Goers, Melvin Armand *retired army officer*
Harvey, William Robert *university president*
Henderson, Salathiel James *minister, clergy*
†Heuser, George Kelly *physician*
Hightower, John Brantley *arts administrator*
Houbolt, John Cornelius *physicist*
Joshi, Suresh Meghashyam *research engineering executive*
Kelly, Jeffrey Jennings *mechanical engineer*
Keyes, David Elliot *scientific computing educator, researcher*
Knewstep, Nancy Gay *language educator*
Looges, Peter John *systems engineer, architect*
Maher, Kim Leverton *museum administrator*
Mehrotra, Sudhir C. *engineering company executive*
Noblitt, Nancy Anne *aerospace engineer*
Pandey, Dhirendra Kumar *mechanical engineer, scientist*
Pulaski, Lori Jaye *career officer*
Schauer, Catharine Guberman *public affairs specialist*
Schon, Alan Wallace *lawyer, actor*
Sobieski, Jaroslaw *aerospace engineer*
Whitesides, John Lindsey, Jr. *aerospace engineering educator, researcher*
Wiedman, Timothy Gerard *management educator*

**Harrisonburg**
Arthur, Thomas Hahn *theater educator, director*
†Burkholder, Owen Eugene *religious organization administrator*
Carrier, Ronald Edwin *university administrator*
Cline, Paul Charles *political science educator, state legislator*
Gill, Gerald Lawson *librarian*
Hodges, Ronald Dexter *lawyer*
Ivory, Ming Marie *political scientist*
Palmer, Forrest Charles *librarian, educator*
Ramsey, Jackson Eugene *management educator*
Rollman, Steven Allan *communication educator*
Slye, Carroll James *instructional supervisor*

**Hartfield**
Lovell, Robert R(oland) *engineering executive*

**Hayes**
Dixon, Thomas Francis *aviation company executive*

**Haymarket**
Crafton-Masterson, Adrienne *real estate executive, writer, poet*
Doolittle, Warren T. *retired federal official*
Douglas, Clarence James, Jr. *corporation executive, management consultant*

**Haysi**
Deel, George Moses *elementary school educator*

**Heathsville**
McKerns, Charles Joseph *lawyer*
Sisson, Jean Cralle *middle school educator*
Stubbs, Susan Conklin *statistician*
Winkel, Raymond Norman *avionics manufacturing executive, retired naval officer*

**Herndon**
Altalib, Omar Hisham *sociologist*
Arena, Bruce *university coach*
Crossfield, Albert Scott *aeronautical science consultant, pilot*
Gorog, William Francis *corporate executive*
Guerreri, Carl Natale *electronic company executive*
Gullace, Marlene Frances *information engineer, systems analyst, consultant*
Hermansen, John Christian *computational linguist*
Houston, Brian Christopher Michael *small business owner*
Kunkel, David Nelson *lawyer*
Larese, Edward John *company executive*
Larson, Arvid Gunnar *electrical engineer*
Lynch, George Michael *family practice physician*
Payne, Fred J. *physician, educator*
Scripps, Edward Wyllis *newspaper publisher*
Sherwin, Michael Dennis *government official*
Spragens, William Clark *public policy educator, consultant*
Vogel, Frederick John *diplomat*

**Hillsboro**
Farwell, Byron Edgar *writer*

**Hopewell**
Leake, Preston Hildebrand *tobacco research executive*

**Huddleston**
Kopp, Richard Edgar *electrical engineer*
Saunders, Dorothy Ann *insurance company executive, sales management*

**Ivy**
Wilcox, Harvey John *lawyer*

**Keswick**
Baratz, Morton Sachs *economic consultant, writer*
Markman, Sherman *investment banker, venture capitalist, corporate financier*
Massey, Donald Wayne *Episcopal minister, small business owner*
Norgren, C. Neil *retired manufacturing company executive*
Owen, Jack Walden *retired hospital association administrator*

**Kilmarnock**
Maxwell, W(ilbur) Richard *management consultant, retired*

**King George**
Hoglund, Richard Frank *research and technical executive*
Newhall, David, III *former federal government official*
Storke, Dwight Clifton, Jr. *government official*

**Ladysmith**
Provencher, Roger Arthur *international consultant*

Bateman, Fred Willom retired judge
Camp, Hazel Lee Burt artist
Cardman, Lawrence S. physics educator
Coleman, James Eugene national laboratory administrator
Corlett, William Albert retired aerospace engineer
Cox, Alvin Earl shipbuilding executive
Cuthrell, Carl Edward lawyer, educator, clergyman
Davis, Jack Wayne, Jr. newspaper publisher
Donaldson, Coleman duPont aerodynamics and aerospace consulting engineer
Feldt, Glenda Diane educational administrator
Fisher, Denise Butterfield marketing executive
Fricks, William Peavy shipbuilding company executive
Guastaferro, Angelo company executive
Hawkins, J. Michael housing development administrator
Hubbard, Harvey Hart aeroacoustician, noise control engineer, consultant
Isgur, Nathan Gerald physicist, educator
Kale, Wallace Wilford, Jr. journalist, communicator, administrator
Le Mons, Kathleen Ann portfolio manager, investment broker
Levy, Robin Carole elementary guidance counselor
Luke, James Phillip manufacturing executive
Mazur, Rhoda Himmel community volunteer
Meade, Angela Kaye special education educator
Miller, W. Marshall, II insurance consultant
Morris, James Matthew history educator
Otis, Glenn Kay retired army officer
Patty, Anna Christine middle school educator
Perry, Donald A. cable television consultant
Phillips, Denise critical care nurse
Santoro, Anthony Richard academic administrator
Saunders, Bryan Leslie lawyer
Summerville, Richard M. mathematician, retired academic administrator
Trible, Paul Seward, Jr. former United States senator
Young, Maurice Isaac mechanical and aerospace engineering educator

## Norfolk
Adams, David Huntington judge
Agnew, Christopher Mack minister
Ahrari, M. Ehsan political science educator, researcher, consultant
Andrews, Mason Cooke mayor, obstetrician, gynecologist, educator
Andrews, William Cooke physician
Baird, Edward Rouzie, Jr. lawyer
Barry, Richard Francis, III media executive
Batten, Frank newspaper publisher, cable broadcaster
Bernsen, Harold John marketing executive, political affairs consultant, retired naval officer
Bishop, Bruce Taylor lawyer
Blount, Robert Haddock corporate executive, retired naval officer
Bonko, Larry Walter columnist, writer, radio personality
Bonney, Hal James, Jr. federal judge
Brignoni, Gladys foreign language educator
Bullington, James R. ambassador
Cason, James Caldwell diplomat
Clark, Morton Hutchinson lawyer
Clarke, J. Calvitt, Jr. federal judge
Cooper, Charles Neilson lawyer
Cranford, Page Deronde lawyer, educator, executive
Crenshaw, Francis Nelson lawyer
Cutchins, Clifford Armstrong, III banker
Dandoy, Suzanne Eggleston physician, academic administrator, educator
Devine, Charles Joseph, Jr. urologist, educator
Doumar, Robert George judge
El-Mahdi, Anas Morsi radiation oncologist
Ershler, William Baldwin biogerontologist, educator
Faulconer, Robert Jamieson pathologist, educator
Fitzpatrick, William Henry retired journalist
Fox, Thomas George academic adminstrator, health science educator
Frieden, Jane Heller art educator
Garlette, William Henry Lee army officer
Glickman, Albert Seymour psychologist, educator
Goode, David Ronald transportation company executive
Goode, Stacy J. real estate broker
Green, Janice Strickland emergency services nurse
Hailstork, Adolphus Cunningham composer
Harrell, Charles Lydon, Jr. lawyer
Haug, James Charles business and management educator
Hennessey, William John art museum director
Hund, Barbara Maurer speech broadcasting and English educator
Jackson, Raymond A. federal judge
Jones, Franklin Ross education educator
Jones, Howard Wilbur, Jr. gynecologist
Jones, Leon Herbert, Jr. (Herb Jones) artist
Katz, Douglas Jeffrey naval officer
Knox, Richard Douglas, Jr. healthcare executive
Koch, James Verch academic administrator, economist
Krantz, Kenneth Allan military officer, judge
†Larry, Wendy head coach women's basketball
Lester, Richard Garrison radiologist, educator
Lind, James Forest surgeon, educator
Maly, Kurt John computer science educator
Marchello, Joseph Maurice mathematics and physical science educator
Mark, Peter director, conductor
Martin, Mary Coates genealogist, writer, volunteer
Martin, Roy Butler, Jr. museum director, retired broker
Mc Gaughy, John Bell civil engineer
McKee, Timothy Carlton taxation educator
McKinnon, Arnold Borden transportation company executive
Melvin C., High protective services official
Miller, Yvonne Bond state senator, educator
Morgan, Henry Coke, Jr. judge
Morrison, Ashton Byrom pathologist, medical school official
Musgrave, Thea composer, conductor
Myers, Donald Allen university dean
Myers, Sue Bartley artist
Nicholson, Myreen Moore artist, researcher
Oberne, Sharon Brown elementary education educator
Oelberg, David George neonatologist, biomedical researcher
Pearson, John Y., Jr. lawyer
Power, Edward Francis broadcast executive
Prince, William Taliaferro federal judge
Proctor, Ronald Eugene academic administrator, educator, consultant
Rephan, Jack lawyer
Reynolds, Pamela Preston historian, physician
Ritter, Alfred Francis, Jr. communications executive
Rohn, Reuben David pediatric educator and administrator
Rump, Kendall E. air transportation executive
Russell, C. Edward, Jr. lawyer
Russell, Susan Webb elementary and middle school education educator
Ryan, John M. lawyer
Ryan, Louis Farthing lawyer
Schellenberg, Karl Abraham biochemist
Schneider, Daniel Scott pediatric cardiologist
Scott, Kenneth R. transportation executive
Shannon, John Sanford retired railway executive, lawyer
Sizemore, William Howard, Jr. newspaper editor
Smith, Rebecca Beach federal judge
Smith, Richard Muldrow lawyer
Tolmie, Donald McEachern lawyer
Train, Harry Depue, II retired naval officer
Valentine, Herman Edward computer company executive
Vest, Frank Harris, Jr. bishop
Wei, Benjamin Min engineering educator
Wheeler, Jock R. dean
Wilson, Lloyd Lee organization administrator
Wiltse, James Clark civil engineer
Wolcott, Hugh Dixon obstetrics and gynecology educator
Wooldridge, William Charles lawyer
Wynne, John Oliver newspaper, broadcast and cable executive

## North Garden
Moses, Hamilton, III neurology educator, hospital executive, management consultant

## Norton
Bowen, Bill Monroe educational administrator
Jessee, Roy Mark lawyer
Kendrick, Richard Lofton university administrator, consultant
Shortridge, Judy Beth lawyer
Vest, Gayle Southworth obstetrician and gynecologist
Vest, Steven Lee gastroenterologist, hepatologist, internist

## Oakton
Anderson, William Robert career naval officer
Brauer, Gwendolyn Gail real estate broker
Curry, Thomas Fortson electronics engineer, defense industry executive
Mosemann, Lloyd Kenneth, II government official
Trifoli-Cunniff, Laura Catherine psychologist, consultant

## Orange
Cortada, James N. mayor, former diplomat
Duncan, Douglas Allen educator
Dunnington, Walter Grey, Jr. lawyer, retired food and tobacco executive
Mallison, N Daniele elementary school educator
Soderbergh, Steven Andrew filmmaker

## Orlean
Kulski, Julian Eugeniusz architect, planner, educator

## Palmyra
Brown, Nan Marie clergywoman
Cawley, William Arthur research educator
Chapin, Suzanne Phillips retired psychologist
Leslie, William Cairns metallurgical engineering educator
Mulckhuyse, Jacob John energy conservation and environmental consultant
Ramsey, Forrest Gladstone, Jr. engineering company executive
Sahr, Morris Gallup financial planner
Southworth, R. Morrison development counsel
White, Luther Wesley lawyer

## Pearisburg
Adams, Jimmy Wayne osteopath

## Penn Laird
Wise, Charles Conrad, Jr. educator, past government official, author

## Petersburg
Burns, Cassandra Stroud prosecutor
Dance, Gloria Fenderson dance studio executive, ballet administrator
Edmunds, Cecelia Powers health facility administrator
Franklin, Virgil L. school administrator, education educator
Miles, Ruby Williams secondary education educator
Northrop, Mary Ruth mental retardation nurse
Ryan, James Herbert security and retail services company executive
Smith, Paul Edmund, Jr. philosophy and religion educator
Spangler, Vera Mae mental health nurse
Stronach, Carey Elliott physicist, educator
Young, Estelle Irene dermatologist

## Philomont
Conte, Joseph John, II meteorologist, management consultant

## Poquoson
Holloway, Paul Fayette retired aerospace executive
Moore, Sandra Bucher mathematics educator
Parry, Thomas Herbert, Jr. school system administrator, educational consultant
Yard, Rix Nelson former athletic director

## Portsmouth
Brown, James Andrew naval architect
Geib, Philip Oldham physician, retired naval officer
Mapp, Alf Johnson, Jr. writer, historian
†Mason, Jon Donavon military career officer, physician
Mintz, Susan Ashinoff menswear manufacturing comapany executive
Moody, Willard James, Sr. lawyer
Rowley, William Robert surgeon
Spong, William Belser, Jr. lawyer, educator
Thomas, Ted, Sr. minister
Williams, Lena Harding English language educator
Wolf, Jeffrey Stephen physician

## Powhatan
Huff, Cynthia Fae medical and orthopedic nurse

## Purcellville
Mainwaring, Thomas Lloyd motor freight company executive
Sharples, Winston Singleton automobile importer and distributor

## Quantico
Van Riper, Paul Kent marine corps officer

## Radford
Davis, Richard Waters lawyer
Hanna, Mary Ann education educator
Henderson, Nancy Carr dietitian, medical transcriber, writer
James, Clarity (Carolyne Faye James) mezzo-soprano
Kessler, Kendall Seay Feriozi artist
Owens, Charles Wesley university executive
Pribram, Karl Harry psychology educator, brain researcher
Reed, Helen I. medical, surgical nurse
Shell, Robert Edward Lee photographer, writer
Thomas, Robert Wilburn broadcasting and advertising executive
Wille, Lois Jean retired newspaper editor

## Rapidan
Grimm, Ben Emmet former library director and consultant

## Reedville
Westbrook, Walter Winfield minister

## Reston
Ackerson, Jeffrey Townsend computer systems executive
Arnberg, Robert Lewis mathematician
Bannister, Dan R. professional and technical services company executive
Basinger, William Daniel computer programmer
Blanchard, Townsend Eugene service companies executive
Bredehoft, Elaine Charlson lawyer
Bredehoft, John Michael lawyer
Brennan, Norma Jean professional society publications director
Brett, Robin geologist
Brosseau, Irma Finn management consultant
Brown, James Robert retired air force officer
Burton, James Samuel physical chemist
Calio, Anthony John scientist, business executive
Cerf, Vinton Gray telecommunications company executive
Chattman, Raymond Christopher foundation administrator
Christ, Thomas Warren electronics research and development company executive, sociologist
Clark, Sandra Helen Becker geologist
Cohen, Philip retired hydrogeologist
Cramer, James Perry management consultant, publisher
Crawford, Lawrence Robert aviation and aerospace consultant
Curry, John Joseph professional organization executive
Dantone, Joseph John, Jr. naval officer
†Davis, James E. professional association executive
Dyer, Timothy J. educational association administrator
Easton, Glenn Hanson, Jr. management and insurance consultant, federal official, naval officer
Eaton, Gordon Pryor geologist, research director
Foster, William Anthony management consultant, educator
Fredette, Richard Chester computer specialist
Fullagar, Paul Richard medical association administrator
Gates, James David retired association executive, consultant
Goodwin, Robert Delmege retired association executive
Hamilton, Robert Morrison geophysicist
Harvey, Aubrey Eaton, III industrial engineer
Heginbotham, Jan Sturza sculptor
Hope, Samuel Howard accreditation organization executive
Huebner, John Stephen geologist
Humphreys, David John lawyer, trade association executive
Hutchin, Nancy Lee reengineering process business consultant
Jaffe, Russell Merritt pathologist, research director
Jaynes, Robert Henry, Jr. retired military officer
Johnson, Thea Jean internet and intranet security service provider
Kader, Nancy Stowe nurse, consultant
Keefe, James Washburn educational researcher, consultant
Kelly, Robert William economist
Kramish, Arnold technical consultant, historian, author
Lewis, Gene Evans retired medical equipment company executive
Mahlmann, John James music education association administrator
Mallette, Malcolm Francis newspaper editor, educator
Miller, Donald Lane publishing executive
Miller, Edward David non-profit association administrator
Minton, Joseph Paul retired safety organization executive
Naeser, Nancy Dearien geologist, researcher
Payne, Roger Lee geographer
Peck, Dallas Lynn retired geologist
Polemitou, Olga Andrea accountant
Pyle, Thomas Alton instructional television and motion picture executive
Richard, Oliver, III (Rick Richard) gas company executive
Ross, Malcolm mineralogist, crystallographer
Ryan, Mary Catherine pediatrician
Sarreals, Sonia data processing consultant
Sato, Motoaki geologist, researcher
Scharff, Joseph Laurent lawyer
Scheeler, James Arthur architect
Schleede, Glenn Roy energy market and policy consultant
Schwolsky, Peter M. gas industry executive, lawyer, partner
Seiberlich, Carl Joseph retired naval officer
Sherman, William Courtney foreign service officer
Showalter-Keefe, Jean data processing executive
Uffelman, Malcolm Rucj electronics company executive, electrical engineer
Wessner, Deborah Marie telecommunications executive, computer consultant
White, Rosanne Teresa educational association executive
Wiegley, Roger Douglas lawyer
Wilkinson, Edward Anderson, Jr. retired naval officer, business executive
Zollar, Carolyn Catherine lawyer

## Richlands
Peralta, Antonio Martinez family physician
Witten, Thomas Jefferson, Jr. mathematics educator

## Richmond
Ackell, Edmund Ferris university president
Ackerly, Benjamin Clarkson lawyer
Adams, John Buchanan, Jr. advertising agency executive
Addison, David Dunham lawyer
Aigner, Emily Burke lay worker
Albanese, Jay Samuel criminologist, educator
Allen, George Felix governor
Altschul, B. J. public relations counselor
Anderson, James Frederick clergyman
Anderson, Leonard Gustave retired lawyer, retired business executive
Aron, Mark G. transportation executive, lawyer
Ashworth, Lawrence Nelson bank executive
Ayres, Stephen McClintock physician, educator
Bagby, Daniel Gordon religious studies educator, clergyman
Baker, Donald Parks journalist, educator
Baliles, Gerald L. lawyer, former governor
Balster, Robert Louis pharmacologist
Baretski, Charles Allan political scientist, librarian, educator, historian, municipal official
Barker, Thomas Carl retired health care administration educator, executive
Barocci, Robert Louis advertising agency executive
Barton, Jonathan Miller clergyman
Bates, Hampton Robert, Jr. pathologist
Bates, John Wythe, III lawyer
Beamer, Betsy Davis state official
Belcher, Dennis Irl lawyer
Berry, William Willis retired utility executive
Beyer, Donald Sternoff, Jr. state official
Bing, Richard McPhail lawyer
Black, Robert Perry retired banker, executive
Blanchard, Lawrence Eley, Jr. lawyer, corporation executive
Blank, Florence Weiss literacy educator, editor
Blumberg, Michael Zangwill allergist
Bohannon, Sarah Virginia personnel assistant
Booker, Lewis Thomas lawyer
Bourke, William Oliver retired metal company executive
Brasfield, Evans Booker lawyer
Brissette, Martha Blevins lawyer
Broaddus, John Alfred, Jr. bank executive, economist
Brockenbrough, Henry Watkins lawyer
Brooks, Robert Franklin, Sr. lawyer
Brown, Aubrey Neblett, Jr. minister, editor
Brush, Carey Wentworth retired college administrator, history educator
Bryan, David Tennant media company executive
Bryan, John Stewart, III newspaper publisher
Buford, Robert Pegram lawyer
Bunzl, Rudolph Hans retired diversified manufacturing company executive
Burke, John K(irkland), Jr. lawyer
Burrus, Robert Lewis, Jr. lawyer
Bush, Thomas Norman lawyer
Bustard, Clarke music critic, newswriter, radio producer
Campbell, Thomas Corwith, Jr. economics educator
Capps, Thomas Edward utilities company executive, lawyer
Capps, Thos E. diversified financial services company executive
Carr, David Turner physician
Carrell, Daniel Allan lawyer
Carrico, Harry Lee state supreme court chief justice
Carter, Joseph Carlyle, Jr. lawyer
Catlett, Richard H., Jr. retired lawyer
Charlesworth, Arthur Thomas mathematics and computer science educator
Chavis, Larry Eugene mayor
Christie, Laurence Glenn, Jr. surgeon
Clement, Alvis Macon former utilities executive
Clinard, Robert Noel lawyer
Coffman, Edward Nathaniel accounting educator
Cohn, David Stephen lawyer
Coleman, Ronald Lee insurance claims executive
Compton, Asbury Christian state supreme court justice
Compton, Olin Randall consulting electrical engineer, researcher
Cox, Edwin, III chemical engineer
Cramer, Morgan Joseph, Jr. international management executive
Dabney, H. Slayton, Jr. lawyer
Dahlenburg, Lyle Marion investment company executive
Daniel, Beth professional golfer
David, Ronald Brian child neurologist
Dell, Willie Jones social services executive, educator
Denny, Collins, III lawyer
Dessypris, Emmanuel Nicholas hematologist-oncologist
Dickinson, Alfred James realtor
Dilworth, Robert Lexow career military officer, adult education educator
Dray, Mark S. lawyer
Edmonds, Thomas Andrew state bar executive director
Ellis, Andrew Jackson, Jr. lawyer
Elmore, Edward Whitehead lawyer
Epps, Augustus Charles lawyer
Estes, Gerald Walter newspaper executive
Fields, William Jay investment banker
Fischer, Carl Robert health care facility administrator
Flannagan, Benjamin Collins, IV lawyer
Ford, Barbara Jean library studies educator
Framme, Lawrence Henry, III lawyer
Franko, Bernard Vincent pharmacologist
Freed, David Clark artist
Freund, Emma Frances medical technologist
Fuller, Reginald Horace clergyman, biblical studies educator
Gandy, Gerald Larmon rehabilitation counseling educator, psychologist, writer
Gary, Richard David lawyer

Geary, David Patrick *criminal justice educator, consultant, author*
Geraghty, Patrick James *organ recovery coordinator*
Gerrish, Brian Albert *theologian, educator*
Gewanter, Harry Lewis *pediatric rheumatologist*
Gilmore, James Stuart, III *state attorney general*
Goff, Stephen Charles *retail and franchise executive*
Goodpasture, Philip Henry *lawyer*
Goodykoontz, Charles Alfred *newspaper editor, retired*
Gordon, John L., Jr. *historian, educator*
Gordon, Thomas Christian, Jr. *former justice*
Gorr, Louis Frederick *investment consultant*
Gottwald, Bruce Cobb *chemical company executive*
†Gottwald, Bruce Cobb, Jr. *treasurer analyst*
Gottwald, Floyd Dewey, Jr. *chemical company executive*
Graves, H. Brice *lawyer*
Gray, Clarence Jones *foreign language educator, dean emeritus*
Gresham, Ann Elizabeth *retailer, horticulturist executive, consultant*
†Grover, Peter Dun *cultural organization administrator*
Hackney, Virginia Howitz *lawyer*
Hagan, Randall Lee *manufacturing executive*
Hall, James Curtis *economics and business educator*
Hall, Stephen Charles *lawyer*
Ham, William Taylor, Jr. *biophysics educator, researcher*
Hamel, Dana Bertrand *academic administrator*
Hanneman, Rodney Elton *metallurgical engineer*
Hardage, Page Taylor *health care administrator*
Hardy, Richard Earl *rehabilitation counseling educator, clinical psychologist*
Harris, Henry Hiter, Jr. *banker*
Hassell, Leroy Rountree, Sr. *state supreme court justice*
Hatch, Robert Norris *banker*
Heilman, E. Bruce *academic administrator*
Helwig, Arthur Woods *chemical company executive*
Hemingway, Beth Rowlett *author, columnist, lecturer*
Henderson, Bernard Levie, Jr. *former state official, funeral service executive*
Henley, Vernard William *banker*
Hettrick, George Harrison *lawyer*
Hicks, C. Flippo *lawyer*
Hintz, Robert Louis *transportation company executive*
Holcomb, Richard D. *state commissioner*
Hong, James Ming *industrialist, venture capitalist*
Horsley, Waller Holladay *lawyer*
Howell, George Cook, III *lawyer*
Hull, Rita Prizler *accounting educator*
Jacobs, Harry Milburn, Jr. *advertising executive*
Jacobs, James Paul *retired insurance executive*
James, Allix Bledsoe *retired university president*
Jandl, Henry Anthony *architect, educator*
Joel, William Lee, II *interior and lighting designer*
Johnston, Francis Claiborne, Jr. *lawyer*
Jones, Catesby Brooke *retired banker*
Jones, Jeanne Pitts *director early childhood school*
Kallar, Surinder Kaur *anesthesiologist*
Kaplowitz, Lisa Glauser *physician, educator*
Kay, Saul *pathologist*
Kearfott, Joseph Conrad *lawyer*
Kendig, Edwin Lawrence, Jr. *physician, educator*
Kevorkian, Richard *artist*
King, Robert Leroy *business administration educator*
Kline, Robert H. *foundation administrator*
Kontos, Hermes *dean*
Kyle, Penelope Ward *state administrator, lawyer*
Lacy, Elizabeth Bermingham *state supreme court justice*
Lanahan, John Stevenson *management consultant*
Lanam, Linda Lee *lawyer*
Laskin, Daniel M. *oral and maxillofacial surgeon, educator*
Laverge, Jan *tobacco company executive*
Lawrence, Walter, Jr. *surgeon*
Leary, David Edward *university dean*
Ledbetter, David Oscar *lawyer*
Lee, Peter James *bishop*
Leggett, Gloria Jean *minister*
Leith, John Haddon *clergyman, theology educator*
Levit, Heloise B. (Ginger Levit) *art dealer, fine arts and media consultant*
Levit, Jay J(oseph) *lawyer*
Lindholm, John Victor *business executive*
Linkonis, Suzanne Newbold *pretrial case manager, counselor*
Mackenzie, Ross *newspaper editor*
Maneker, Deanna Marie *advertising executive*
†Marsh, Miles L. *textile company executive*
Marshall, Wayne Keith *anesthesiology educator*
Martin, Bernard Murray *painter, educator*
Mathews, Roderick Bell *lawyer*
Mattauch, Robert Joseph *electrical engineering educator*
Mauck, Henry Page, Jr. *medical and pediatrics educator*
McClard, Jack Edward *lawyer*
McClenahan, Mary Tyler Freeman *civic and community volunteer*
Mc Cue, Carolyn Moore *retired pediatric cardiologist*
McDermott, William Thomas *accountant, lawyer*
McDonough, Reginald Milton *religious organization executive*
McElligott, James Patrick, Jr. *lawyer*
McFarlane, Walter Alexander *lawyer, educator*
McGee, Henry Alexander, Jr. *university official*
Mc Grath, Lee Parr *public relations executive, author*
McMurray, Carol Dolber *human services administrator*
McVey, Henry Hanna, III *lawyer*
Mellette, M. Susan Jackson *physician, educator, researcher*
Merhige, Robert Reynold, Jr. *federal judge*
Mezzullo, Louis Albert *lawyer*
Miller, Lewis Nelson, Jr. *banker*
Miller, Nan Louise *museum director*
Millner, Wallace B., III *banker*
Milmoe, Patrick Joseph *lawyer*
Minardi, Richard A., Jr. *lawyer*
Minisi, Anthony Joseph *cardiologist, educator*
Modlin, George Matthews *university chancellor emeritus*
Mollen, Edward Leigh *pediatrician, allergist and clinical immunologist*
Moore, Andrew Taylor, Jr. *banker*
Moore, John Sterling, Jr. *minister*
Moore, Thurston Roach *lawyer*
Morrill, Richard Leslie *university administrator*
Morris, James Carl *architect*
Moyne, Yves M. *water treatment executive*
Mullinax, Perry Franklin *rheumatologist, allergist, immunologist*
Musick, Robert Lawrence, Jr. *lawyer*
Neal, Marcus Pinson, Jr. *radiologist, medical educator*
Negus, Lucy Newton Boswell *foundation executive*
Neman, Daniel Louis *movie critic*
Newbrand, Charles Michael *advertising firm executive*
Nielsen, Steven B. *medical products executive*
Nunn, Charles Burgess *religious organization executive*
Oakey, John Martin, Jr. *lawyer*
Owen, Duncan Shaw, Jr. *physician, medical educator*
Owen, Howard Wayne *journalist, writer*
Palik, Robert Richard *mechanical engineer*
Palmore, Fred Wharton, III *lawyer*
Pasco, Hansell Merrill *retired lawyer*
Pauley, Stanley Frank *manufacturing company executive*
Payne, Robert E. *federal judge*
Pendleton, Eugene Barbour, Jr. *business executive*
Peters, David Frankman *lawyer*
Phillips, Thomas Edworth, Jr. *investment executive, senior consultant*
Pinckney, C. Cotesworth *lawyer*
Plaisted, Harris Merrill, III *real estate executive*
Poff, Richard Harding *state supreme court justice*
Pollard, Overton Price *state agency executive, lawyer*
Pope, Robert Dean *lawyer*
Powell, Kenneth Edward *investment banker*
Powell, Lewis Franklin, III *lawyer*
Rainey, Gordon Fryer, Jr. *lawyer*
Reveley, Walter Taylor, III *lawyer*
Reynolds, David Parham *metals company executive*
Richardson, David Walthall *cardiologist, educator, consultant*
Richerson, Stephen Wayne *minister*
Rigsby, Linda Flory *lawyer*
Rilling, John Robert *history educator*
Roach, Edgar Mayo, Jr. *lawyer*
Robert, Joseph Clarke *historian, consultant*
Robertson, William Franklin *publishing executive*
Rogers, Isabel Wood *religious studies educator*
Rogers, James Edward *paper company executive*
Rolfe, Robert Martin *lawyer*
Roop, Ralph Goodwin *retired oil marketing company executive*
Rosenblum, John William *dean*
Rowley, Frank Selby, Jr. *artist*
Rubinstein, Phyllis M. *lawyer*
Rudlin, David Alan *lawyer*
Sasser, Ellis A. *gifted and talented education educator*
Savage, William Woodrow *education educator*
Schaar, Susan Clarke *state legislative staff member*
Seals, Margaret Louise *newspaper editor*
Self, Phyllis C. *library director*
Sgro, Beverly Huston *state official, educator*
Shands, William Ridley, Jr. *lawyer*
Shapiro, Gary Michael *philosophy educator*
Sharer, John Daniel *lawyer*
Sharp, Richard L. *retail company executive*
Simmons, S. Dallas *university president*
Simpson, John Noel *healthcare administrator*
Sirica, Alphonse Eugene *pathology educator*
Slater, Thomas Glascock, Jr. *lawyer*
Slaughter, Alexander Hoke *lawyer*
Smith, R. Gordon *lawyer*
Smith, Ted Jay, III *mass communications educator*
Sniffin, John Harrison *retail executive*
Spahn, Gary Joseph *lawyer*
Spain, Jack Holland, Jr. *lawyer*
Spencer, James R. *federal judge*
Sprinkle, William Melvin *engineering administrator, audio-acoustical engineer*
Starke, Harold E., Jr. *lawyer*
Stephenson, Roscoe Bolar, Jr. *state supreme court justice*
Stoyko, William Nelson *lawyer*
Strickland, William Jesse *lawyer*
Suleymanian, Mirik *biophysicist*
Sullivan, Walter Francis *bishop*
Sweeney, Arthur Hamilton, Jr. *metal manufacturing executive, retired army officer*
Swezey, Charles Mason *Christian ethics educator, administrator*
Taliaferro, Nancy Ellen Taylor *artist*
Talley, Charles Richmond *commercial banking executive*
Taylor, Welford Dunaway *English language educator*
Thomas, John Charles *lawyer, former state supreme court justice*
Thompson, Francis Neal *financial services consultant*
Thompson, Paul Michael *lawyer*
Thornhill, Barbara Cole *marketing executive*
Thorp, Benjamin A., III *paper manufacturing company executive*
Tice, Douglas Oscar, Jr. *federal judge*
Tiedemann, Albert William, Jr. *chemist*
Tilghman, Richard Granville *banker*
Toler, Ann Patrick *public relations executive*
Towne, Alan Raymond *neurologist, educator*
Trani, Eugene Paul *academic administrator, educator*
Treadway, John David *history educator*
Trott, Sabert Scott, II *marketing professional*
Troy, Anthony Francis *lawyer*
Trumble, Robert Roy *business educator*
Tuck, Grayson Edwin *real estate agent, former natural gas transmission executive*
Tunner, William Sams *urological surgeon*
Turner, Elaine S. *allergist, immunologist*
Turner, James Wesley *minister, former church administrator*
Ukrop, James E. *retail executive*
Urofsky, Melvin Irving *historian, educator, director*
Wakeham, Helmut Richard Rae *chemist, consulting company executive*
Walsh, William Arthur, Jr. *lawyer*
Ward, John Wesley *retired pharmacologist*
Warthen, Harry Justice, III *lawyer*
Watkins, Hays Thomas *retired railroad executive*
Watts, Robert Glenn *retired pharmaceutical company executive*
Watts, Stephen Hurt, II *lawyer*
Wechsler, Andrew Stephen *surgery educator*
White, Ann Stewart *language educator, consultant*
White, Hugh Vernon, Jr. *lawyer*
†White, John Douglas *emergency physician*
White, Kenneth Ray *health administration educator, consultant*
Whiting, Henry H. *state supreme court justice*
Williams, Richard Leroy *federal judge*
Williams, Robert C. *company executive*
†Winslett, Stoner *artistic director*
Wist, Abund Ottokar *biomedical engineer, radiation physicist, educator*
Witschey, Walter Robert Thurmond *science museum administrator, archaeologist, computer systems consultant*
Witt, Walter Francis, Jr. *lawyer*
Wolf, Barry *genetics, pediatric educator*
Wood, Jeanne Clarke *charitable organization executive*
Wood, Maurice *medical educator*
Yu, Robert Kuan-jen *biochemistry educator*

## Roanoke

Al-Zubaidi, Amer Aziz *physicist, educator*
Bates, Harold Martin *lawyer*
Beagle, Benjamin Stuart, Jr. *columnist*
Berry, John Coltrin *insurance executive*
Butler, Manley Caldwell *lawyer*
Coleman, Sallye Terrell *retired social studies educator*
Densmore, Baron Douglas Warren *lawyer*
Denton, Judy Holley *elementary education educator*
Deppen, Douglas *bank executive*
Dillard, Richard Henry Wilde *English language professional, educator, author*
Duff, Doris Eileen (Shull) *critical care nurse*
Fishwick, John Palmer *lawyer, retired railroad executive*
Fulton, George Henry, Jr. *automobile and truck retail company executive*
Guerrant, Helen Orzel *artist*
Hammond, Glenn Barry, Sr. *lawyer*
Hamrick, Joseph Thomas *mechanical engineer, aerospace company executive*
Henn, Shirley Emily *retired librarian*
Hooper, M. David *protective services official*
Husted, John Edwin *geologist, educator*
†Hutcheson, Jack Robert *hematologist, medical oncologist*
Jackson, Daniel Wyer *electrical engineer*
†Kennedy, Stephen Smith *hematologist, oncologist, educator*
King, Stephen Emmett *educational administrator*
Landon, Forrest Malcolm *retired newspaper executive*
Marmion, William Henry *retired bishop*
McKenna, John Dennis *environmental testing engineer*
Nickens, Harry Carl *academic administrator*
Noblett, Russell Don *medical and computer consultant*
Pearson, Henry Clyde *judge*
Rugaber, Walter Feucht, Jr. *newspaper executive*
Shaffner, Patrick Noel *architectural engineering executive*
Shaftman, Fredrick Krisch *telephone communications executive*
Sowers, William Armand *civil engineer*
Stanley, Ralph *bluegrass musician*
Turk, James Clinton *federal judge*
Warren, William Kermit *electronic publishing consultant*
Wilson, Samuel Grayson *federal judge*
Woodrum, Clifton A., III *lawyer, state legislator*
Woods, Walter Ralph *retired agricultural scientist, administrator*
Word, Eliza Switzer *critical care nurse, administrator*

## Rockbridge Baths

Patteson, Roy Kinneer, Jr. *clergyman, administrator*

## Roseland

Arey, William Griffin, Jr. *former government official*
Stemmler, Edward Joseph *physician, retired association executive, retired academic dean*

## Round Hill

Bergeman, Clarissa Hellman *special education educator*
Pugh, Marion Stirling *archaeologist, author*

## Salem

Bansemer, Richard Frederick *bishop*
Brand, Edward Cabell *retail executive*
Chakravorty, Ranes Chandra *surgeon, educator*
Dagenhart, Betty Jane Mahaffey *nursing educator, administrator*
Fisher, Charles Harold *chemistry educator, researcher*
Gring, David M. *academic administrator*
Koontz, Lawrence L., Jr. *judge*
Perkins, Marvin Earl *psychiatrist, educator*
Russell, Douglas Campbell *cardiologist*

## Seaford

Jenkins, Margaret Bunting *human resources executive*

## South Hill

Taylor, Jean Mull *home economics educator, secondary educator*

## Sperryville

Armor, David J. *sociologist*

## Spotsylvania

Arnhoff, Franklyn Nathaniel *psychologist, sociologist, educator*
Hardy, Dorcas Ruth *government relations and public policy consultant*

## Spottswood

Fredricksen, Cleve Laurance *thoroughbred horse farm owner, real estate investor*

## Spring Grove

Daniel, Robert Williams, Jr. *business executive, former congressman*

## Springfield

Baker, George Harold, III *physicist*
Bond, William Jennings, Jr. *air force officer*
Broome, Paul Wallace *engineering research and development executive*
Bruen, John Dermot *business management consultant*
Casazza, John Andrew *electrical engineer, business executive*
Chappell, Milton Leroy *lawyer*
De Nigris, Anna Maria Theresa *middle school educator*
Doe, Bruce Roger *geologist*
Doyle, James Stephen *publishing company executive, journalist*
Duff, William Grierson *electrical engineer*
Eastman, Donna Kelly *composer, music educator*
Fedewa, Lawrence John *information technology company executive*
Finkel, Karen Evans *school transportation association executive, lawyer*
Fowler, Ray Harland *engineering consultant*
Gawalt, Gerard W(ilfred) *historian, writer*
Hastings, Melanie (Melanie Jean Wotring) *television news anchor*
Hillis, John David *television news executive, producer, writer*
Hughes, James Charles *lawyer*
Johnson, Donald Rex *research institute administrator*
Larson, Reed Eugene *foundation administrator*
Leavitt, Mary Janice Deimel *special education educator, civic worker*
Meikle, Philip G. *retired government agency executive*
†Norman, Jean Reid *journalist*
Patterson, Veda Malia *equal opportunity specialist*
Rankin, Jacqueline Annette *communications expert, educator*
Sebastian, Richard Lee *physicist, executive*
Shuster, Robert G. *electronics company executive, consultant*
Sproul, Joan Heeney *elementary school educator*
Steele, Lendell Eugene *research scientist*
Stottlemyer, David Lee *government official*
Tomlinson, Ian *software engineer*
Whitener, Lawrence Bruce *political consultant, consumer advocate, educator*

## Stafford

Brown, Harold Eugene *district chief magistrate*
Lambert, Linda Margaret *reading specialist*
Tallent, Robert Glenn *chemical and environmental engineer, entrepreneur*
Woldt, Gerald D. (Jay Woldt) *nurse anesthetist*

## Stanardsville

Anns, Philip Harold *international trading executive, former pharmaceutical company executive*

## Stanleytown

Stanley, Thomas Bahnson, Jr. *investor*

## Staunton

Balsley, Philip Elwood *entertainer*
Cochran, George Moffett *retired judge*
Farrell, Larry Charles *management consultant, author, speaker*
Hammaker, Paul M. *retail executive, business educator, author*
Sweetman, Beverly Yarroll *physical therapist*
Tyson, Cynthia Haldenby *academic administrator*

## Sterling

Block, Robert Michael *endodontist, educator, researcher*
Blum, John Curtis *agricultural economist*
Brewster-Walker, Sandra JoAnn *public relations executive, publishing executive, genealogist, historian, consultant*
Finn, Gloria Inez *geriatrics nurse*
Gunberg, Edwin Woodrow, Jr. *counseling psychologist, consultant, researcher*
McPherson, John Barkley *aerospace consultant, retired military officer*
Munger, Paul David *educational administrator*
Murchie, Edward Michael *accountant*
Oller, William Maxwell *retired energy company executive, retired naval officer*
Padgett, Gail Blanchard *lawyer*
Port, Arthur Tyler *retired government administrator, lawyer*
Sabosik, Patricia Elizabeth *publisher, editor*
Sanfelici, Arthur H(ugo) *editor, writer*
Witek, James Eugene *public relations executive*

## Suffolk

Birdsong, George Yancy *manufacturing company executive*
Carroll, George Joseph *pathologist, educator*
Gray, Marcia Lanette *health, physical education and recreation educator*
Hines, Angus Irving, Jr. *petroleum marketing executive*
Hope, James Franklin *mayor, civil engineer, consultant*
Matson, Virginia Mae Freeberg (Mrs. Edward J. Matson) *retired special education educator, author*
Parker, James Fletcher *middle school educator*
Tritten, James John *national security educator*

## Surry

Wachsmann, Elizabeth Rideout *reading specialist*

## Susan

Ambach, Dwight Russell *retired foreign service officer*

## Sweet Briar

Armstrong, Gregory Timon *religious studies educator, minister*
Baldwin, Nancy Godwin *program director*
McClenon, John Raymond *chemistry educator*
Miller, Reuben George *economics educator*
Shea, Brent Mack *social science educator*

## Tazewell

Garner, June Brown *journalist*
Weeks, Ross Leonard, Jr. *museum executive, consultant*

## Timberville

Barnard, Robert Edward *potter, writer*

## University Of Richmond

Hall, James H(errick), Jr. *philosophy educator, author*
Terry, Robert Meredith *foreign language educator*

## Upperville

di Zerega, Thomas William *former energy company executive, lawyer*
Smart, Stephen Bruce, Jr. *business and government executive*

## Urbanna

Hudson, Jesse Tucker, Jr. *financial executive*
Salley, John Jones *university administrator, oral pathologist*

### Vienna
Argow, Keith Angevin *association executive,forester*
Bajpai, Sanjay Kumar *pharmaceutical executive, consultant*
Bartlett, John Wesley *consulting firm executive*
Bauer, Karen Mary *accountant, consultant*
Blevins, Charles Russell *publishing executive*
Brandel, Ralph Edward *management consultant*
Cantus, H. Hollister *government relations consultant*
Cartier, Brian Evans *association executive*
†Case, Steve *business executive*
Chamberlain, Diane *psychotherapist, author, clinical social worker*
Chandler, Hubert Thomas *former army officer*
Clark, Katherine Karen *software company executive*
Davis, Cabell Seal, Jr. *naval officer*
Dewar, James McEwen *film director, writer, former marketing, aerospace and defense executive, consultant*
DeWitt, Charles Barbour *federal government official*
Dodson, Louis Raymond *computer systems engineer*
Fasser, Paul James, Jr. *labor arbitrator*
†Feld, Kenneth *performing company executive*
Gardenier, John Stark, II *statistician, management scientist*
Gardner, Joel Sylvanus *tempest products company executive*
Giovacchini, Robert Peter *toxicologist, manufacturing executive, retired*
Hale, Thomas Morgan *professional services executive*
Hatch, Harold Arthur *retired military officer*
Heller, John Roderick, III *lawyer, business executive*
Higginbotham, Wendy Jacobson *political adviser, writer*
Hood, William Clarence *international banking official*
Howard, Daggett Horton *lawyer*
Hubbell, Katherine Jean *marketing consultant*
Jackson, Dempster McKee *retired naval officer*
Jahn, Laurence Roy *retired biologist, institute executive*
†Jayne, Edward Randolph, II *executive search consultant*
Kautt, Glenn Gregory *financial planner*
Keiser, Bernhard Edward *engineering company executive, consulting telecommunications engineer*
Kohler, Karl Eugene *architect*
Kumar, Verinder *accountant, financial executive*
Leonsis, Ted *communications company executive, publishing company executive*
Lewis, Boyd De Wolf *publisher,editor, writer*
Lillard, Mark Hill, III *computer consulting executive, former air force officer*
Lyons, Paul Michael *producer, film*
Mc Arthur, George *journalist*
McCabe, Thomas Edward *lawyer*
McKinley, Sarah Elizabeth *journalist*
Meisinger, Henry Peter *electronics engineer*
Miller, Claire Ellen *periodical editor*
Molineaux, Charles Borromeo *lawyer, arbitrator, columnist, poet*
Palmer, Stephen Eugene, Jr. *government official*
Peltz, Paulette Beatrice *corporate lawyer*
Phillips, Richard L(overidge) *marine corps officer*
Price, Ilene Rosenberg *lawyer*
Razzano, Frank Charles *lawyer*
Rothery, Chet *business executive*
Rovis, Christopher Patrick *clinical social worker, psychotherapist*
Salah, Sagid *retired nuclear engineer*
Sanbrailo, John A. *mission director*
Savoca, Antonio Litterio *technology company executive*
Schneider, Peter Raymond *political scientist*
Schwartz, Richard Harvey *pediatrician*
Sheinbaum, Gilbert Harold *international management consultant*
Sirpis, Andrew Paul *insurance company executive*
Smith, Esther Thomas *management consultant*
Spiro, Robert Harry, Jr. *foundation and business executive, educator*
Strohm, Robert Dean *publications executive*
†Van Patten, Mark *environmentalist*
Van Stavoren, William David *management consultant, retired government official*
Veasey, Byron Keith *information systems consultant*
Vreeland, Russell Glenn *accountant, consultant*
Walker, Edward Keith, Jr. *business executive, retired naval officer*
Webb, William Loyd, Jr. *army officer*
West, Richard Luther *military association executive, defense consultant, retired army officer*
Whitaker, Thomas Patrick *lawyer*
Woodward, Kenneth Emerson *retired mechanical engineer*
Yarborough, William Glenn, Jr. *military officer, forest farmer, defense and international business executive*
Zehl, Otis George *optical physicist*
Zoeller, Jack Carl *financial executive*

### Virginia Beach
Abbott, Regina A. *neurodiagnostic technologist, consultant, business owner*
Alexander, William Powell *business advisor*
Barriskill, Maudanne Kidd *primary school educator*
Brennan, Patrick Jeremiah *computer system architect*
Burgess, Marvin Franklin *human resources specialist, consultant*
Carlston, John A. *allergist*
Cheng, Richard Tien-ren *computer scientist, educator*
Christy, Larry Todd *publisher*
Corbat, Patricia Leslie *special education educator*
DeVenny, Lillian Nickell *trophy company executive*
Dumville, S(amuel) Lawrence *lawyer*
Farrell, Paul Edward *dentist, retired naval officer, educator*
Fischer, Daniel Edward *psychiatrist*
Freyss, David *producer, director*
Goodwin, Robert *human resources specialist*
Green, Barbara-Marie *publisher, journalist, poet*
Halpin, Timothy Patrick *former air force officer*
Happy, J. Nelson *legal educator, law school dean*
Harrison, William Wright *retired banker*
Ives, Ronn Brian *artist, educator*
Jones, Robert Clair *middle school educator*
Kodis, Mary Caroline *marketing consultant*
Kornylak, Harold John *osteopathic physician*
Kreyling, Edward George, Jr. *railroad executive*
Lawson, Beth Ann Reid *strategic planner*
Mallenbaum, Sidney *neurologist*
Markson, Daniel Ben *real estate developer, consultant, syndicator*
McDaniel, David Henry *physician*
Merchant, Donald Joseph *microbiologist*
Oberndorf, Meyera E. *mayor*
O'Brien, Robert James *financial consultant, business owner*
Oldfield, Edward Charles, Jr. *retired naval officer, communications company executive*
Onsanit, Tawachai *physician*
Ratajski, Magda Anne *public relations executive*
Richardson, Daniel Putnam *headmaster, history, economics and criminal law educator*
Robertson, Pat (Marion Gordon Robertson) *religious broadcasting executive*
Robertson, Timothy B. *cable television executive*
Sanderson, James Richard *naval officer, planning and investment company consultant*
Sekulow, Jay Alan *lawyer*
Selig, William George *university official*
Seward, William W(ard), Jr. *author, educator*
Smith, A. Robert *editor, author*
Stephan, Charles Robert *retired ocean engineering educator, consultant*
Stevens, Suzanne Duckworth *artist, educator*
Stevenson, Amanda (Sandy Stevens) *librettist, composer*
Tarbutton, Lloyd Tilghman *motel executive, franchise consultant*
Wick, Robert Thomas *retired supermarket executive*
Wiggins, Samuel Paul *education educator*
Wootten, Thomas Franklin *criminal justice administrator*
Yurso, Joseph Francis *engineering manager*

### Warm Springs
Orem, Henry Philip *retired chemist, chemical engineer, consultant*

### Warrenton
Andresen, Mark Nils *electrical engineer*
Brenken, Hanne Marie *artist*
†Estaver, Paul Edward *writer, poet*
Fox, Raymond Graham *educational administrator*
Haley, Jeanne Ackerman *preschool director*
Sass, Arthur Harold *educational executive*
vom Baur, Francis Trowbridge *retired lawyer*
Watkins, Birge Swift *real estate investment executive*

### Washington
Weinberg, Robert Lester *lawyer, law educator*

### Waterford
Harper, James Weldon, III *finance executive, consultant*
Pollack, Reginald Murray *painter, sculptor*

### Waynesboro
Aronson, Mark Theodore *chemical engineer*
Lane, Lawrence Jubin *retired electrical engineer, consultant*
McNair, John William, Jr. *civil engineer*
Prye, Ellen Ross *graphic designer*
Rippe, Peter Marquart *museum administrator*
Tynes, Theodore Archibald *educational administrator*

### Weems
LaPrade, Carter *lawyer*

### White Stone
Wroth, James Melvin *former army officer, computer company executive*

### Williamsburg
Aaron, Bertram Donald *corporation executive*
Austin, Sigrid Linnevold *counselor*
Axtell, James Lewis *history educator*
Ball, Donald Lewis *retired English language educator*
Baranowski, Frank Paul *energy consultant, former government official*
Becker, Lawrence Carlyle *philosopher, educator, author*
Bernhardt, John Bowman *banker*
Birney, Robert Charles *retired academic administrator, psychologist*
Blouet, Brian Walter *geography educator*
Brackenridge, N. Lynn *public relations and development specialist*
Brinkley, Joseph Willard *social services administrator*
Cantlay, George Gordon *retired army officer*
Cell, Gillian Townsend *historian, educator*
Chappell, Miles Linwood, Jr. *art history educator*
Coleman, Henry Edwin *art educator, artist*
Connell, Alastair McCrae *physician*
Crapol, Edward P. *history educator*
Davis, Emma-Jo Levey *retired government executive, publishing executive*
Davis, Richard Bradley *internal medicine, pathology educator, physician*
†Dhillon, Avtar Singh *psychiatrist*
Dittman, Duane Arthur *educational consultant*
Emerson, Philip G. *museum director*
Esler, Anthony James *historian, novelist, educator*
Finn, A. Michael *public relations executive*
Fisher, Chester Lewis, Jr. *retired lawyer*
Fraser, Howard Michael *foreign language educator, editor*
Fulmer, Robert M. *business educator, management consultant*
Garrison, George Hartranft Haley *curator*
Geddy, Vernon Meredith, Jr. *lawyer*
Goodwin, Bruce Kesseli *geology educator, researcher*
Gordon, Baron Jack *stockbroker*
Griffith, Melvin Eugene *entomologist, public health official*
Gross, Robert Alan *history educator*
Herbert, Albert Edward, Jr. *interior and industrial designer*
Herrmann, Benjamin Edward *former insurance executive*
Hess, Donald K. *academic administrator*
Hoegerman, Stanton Fred *cytogeneticist*
Holmes, David L. *religious educator*
Hornsby, Bruce Randall *composer, musician*
Hughes, George Farant, Jr. *retired safety engineer*
Jacoby, William Jerome, Jr. *internist, retired military officer*
Johnston, Robert Atkinson *psychologist, educator*
Kelly, William E. *psychoanalyst*
Kelm, Bonnie G. *art museum director, educator*
Kevelson, Roberta *philosopher, educator*
Kottas, John Frederick *business administration educator*
Lange, Carl James *psychology educator*
Longsworth, Charles R. *foundation administrator*
Lutzer, David John *mathematics professor*
Maccubbin, Robert Purks *literature and culture educator*
Maloney, Milford Charles *retired internal medicine educator*
Marcus, Paul *lawyer, educator*
Marshall, Nancy Haig *library administrator*
McGiffert, Michael *history educator, editor*
Mc Kean, John Rosseel Overton *university dean*
Mc Knight, John Lacy *physics educator*
McLane, Henry Earl, Jr. *philosophy educator*
Messmer, Donald Joseph *business management educator, marketing consultant*
Mouser, Grant Earl, III *retired foreign service officer*
Nettels, Elsa *English language educator*
Noël Hume, Ivor *retired archaeologist, consultant*
O'Connell, William Edward, Jr. *finance educator*
Orwoll, Robert Arvid *chemistry educator*
Papenthien, Ruth Mary *fiber artist, retired educator*
Parkany, John *business educator, international financial consultant*
Parker, Donald Howard *landscape architect*
Petersen, Richard Herman *government executive, aeronautical engineer*
Polk-Matthews, Josephine Elsey *school psychologist*
Price, Richard *anthropologist, author*
Refinetti, Roberto *physiological psychologist*
Regan, Donald Thomas *financier, writer, lecturer*
Roberson, Robert S. *investment company executive*
Robinson, Jay (Thurston) *artist*
Rodman, Leiba *mathematics educator*
Roseberg, Carl Andersson *sculptor, educator*
Rosen, Ellen Freda *psychologist, educator*
Ruppel, George Robert *accountant*
Scholnick, Robert J. *college dean, English language educator*
Shaver, Kelly G. *psychology educator*
Sherman, Richard Beatty *history educator*
Siegel, Robert Ted *physicist*
Smith, James Brown, Jr. *secondary school educator*
Smith, Roger Winston *political theorist, educator*
Smolla, Rodney Alan *lawyer, educator*
Spitzer, Cary Redford *avionics consultant, electrical engineer*
Starnes, William Herbert, Jr. *chemist, educator*
Strong, John Scott *finance educator*
Sullivan, Timothy Jackson *law educator, academic administrator*
Tate, Thaddeus W(ilbur), Jr. (Thad Tate) *history educator, historical institute executive, historian*
Van Tassel-Baska, Joyce Lenore *education educator*
Wallach, Alan *art historian, educator*
Warren, William Herbert *business administration educator*
Webster, Robert Louis *insurance company executive*
Wegner, Samuel Joseph *museum executive*
Whyte, James Primrose, Jr. *former law educator*
Wilburn, Robert Charles *institute executive*
Williams, Ruth Elizabeth (Betty Williams) *retired secondary school educator*
Winstead, Joy *journalist, consultant*
Zhang, Xiaodong *computer science educator and researcher*

### Winchester
Bechamps, Gerald J. *surgeon*
Billeter, Marianne *pharmacy educator*
Byrd, Harry Flood, Jr. *newspaper executive, former senator*
Engelage, James Roland *management and educational consultant*
Holland, James Tulley *plastic products company executive*
Hughes, Donna Jean *librarian*
Jamison, Richard Bryan *airport consultant*
Jolly, Bruce Dwight *manufacturing company executive*
Ludwig, George Harry *physicist*
Murtagh, John Edward *alcohol production consultant*
Pavsek, Daniel Allan *banker, educator*
Pleacher, David Henry *secondary school educator*
Proe, John David *business educator, consultant, administrator*
Smith, Virginia A. *marketing communications professional*
Tisinger, Catherine Anne *college dean*

### Wise
Gibson, David Allen *civil engineer*
Lemons, L. Jay *academic administrator*
Smiddy, Joseph Charles *retired college chancellor*

### Woodbridge
Carvalho, Julie Ann *psychologist*
Cosner, David Dale *plastics industry executive, marketing executive*
Dillaber, Philip Arthur *budget and resource analyst, economist, consultant*
Englert, Helen Wiggs *writer*
Flori, Anna Marie DiBlasi *nurse anesthetist, educational administrator*
Garon, Richard Joseph, Jr. *chief of staff, political worker*
†Hood, Ronald Chalmers, III *historian, writer*
Packard, Mildred Ruth *middle school educator*
Peck, Dianne Kawecki *architect*
Richardson, Sharon Young *marketing professional*
Rose, Marianne Hunt *business educator*
†Scofield, Thomas Carey *retired army officer*
Townsend, Kenneth Ross *retired priest*
Vachher, Prehlad Singh *psychiatrist*

### Woodstock
Walker, Charles Norman *retired insurance company executive*

### Woodville
Mc Carthy, Eugene Joseph *writer, former senator*

### Wytheville
Baird, Thomas Bryan, Jr. *lawyer*
Hansen, B(obby) J. *management consultant, real estate investor and developer*

### Yorktown
Behlmar, Cindy Lee *business manager, consultant*
Edwards, Richard Charles *oral and maxillofacial surgeon*

## WASHINGTON

### Anacortes
Higgins, Robert (Walter) *military officer, physician*
Kuure, Bojan Marlena *operating room nurse*
Mc Cracken, Philip Trafton *sculptor*
Randolph, Carl Lowell *chemical company executive*
Spaulding, John Pierson *public relations executive, marine consultant*

### Ashford
Briggle, William James *federal agency administrator*
Ingle, John Ide *dental educator*

### Auburn
Overholt, Miles Harvard *cable television consultant*
Sata, Lindbergh Saburo *psychiatrist, physician, educator*
Sims, Marcie Lynne *English language educator, writer*
Westbo, Leonard Archibald, Jr. *electronics engineer, educator*
Whitmore, Donald Clark *retired engineer*

### Bainbridge Island
Bowden, William Darsie *retired interior designer*
Fox, Kenneth *naval engineer, shipbuilder, water transit consultant*
Grisham, Jeannie *artist*
Huntley, James Robert *government official, international affairs scholar and consultant*
Milander, Henry Martin *educational consultant*
Nagle, James Francis *lawyer*
Otorowski, Christopher Lee *lawyer*
Randlett, Mary Willis *photographer*
Schmidt, Karen Anne *travel company executive, state legislator*

### Battle Ground
Hansen, James Lee *sculptor*
Morris, William Joseph *paleontologist, educator*

### Belfair
Walker, E. Jerry *retired clergyman*

### Bellevue
Akutagawa, Donald *psychologist, educator*
Allen, Paul *computer executive, professional sports team owner*
Andersen, James A. *retired state supreme court justice*
Arnold, Robert Lloyd *investment broker*
Bates, Charles Walter *human resources executive, lawyer, internal auditor*
Benveniste, Jacob *retired physicist*
Bergstrom, Marianne Elisabeth *program coordinator, special education educator*
Berkley, James Donald *clergyman*
Boespflug, John Francis, Jr. *lawyer*
Carlson, Curtis Eugene *orthodontist, periodontist*
Chen, Ching-Hong *medical biochemist, biotechnology company executive*
Clark, Richard Walter *education consultant*
Clay, Orson C. *insurance company executive*
Davidson, Robert William *merchant banker*
Douglas, Diane Miriam *museum director*
Dow, Daniel Gould *electrical engineering educator*
Dunn, Jeffrey Edward *neurologist*
Dykstra, David Charles *management executive, consultant, accountant, author, educator*
Edde, Howard Jasper *retired engineering executive*
Eigsti, Roger Harry *insurance company executive*
Faris, Charles Oren *civil engineer*
Fremouw, Edward Joseph *physicist*
Gosslee, Mary June *chiropractor*
Graham, John Robert, Jr. *financial executive*
Groten, Barnet *energy company executive*
Hackett, Carol Ann Hedden *physician*
Hall, Eleanor Williams *public relations executive*
Hannah, Lawrence Burlison *lawyer*
Hoag, Paul Sterling *architect*
Hovind, David J. *manufacturing company executive*
Knoepfler, Peter Tamas *psychiatrist, organizational consultant*
Ladd, James Roger *international management consultant, accountant*
Liang, Jeffrey Der-Shing *retired electrical engineer, civil worker, diplomat*
Lipkin, Mary Castleman Davis (Mrs. Arthur Bennett Lipkin) *retired psychiatric social worker*
McAleer, William Harrison *software venture capitalist*
Melby, Orville Erling *retired banker*
Metz, Marilyn Joyce *bank executive*
Mitchell, Gloria Jean *elementary school principal, educator*
Mutschler, Herbert Frederick *retired librarian*
O'Keefe, Kathleen Mary *state government official*
Olson, Hilding Harold *surgeon, educator*
Otterholt, Barry L. *technology management consultant*
Parks, Donald Lee *mechanical engineer, human factors engineer*
Phillips, Zaiga Alksnis *pediatrician*
Pigott, Charles McGee *transportation equipment manufacturing executive*
Puckett, Allen Weare *health care information systems executive*
Rice, Kay Diane *elementary education educator, consultant*
Roddis, Richard Stiles Law *insurance company executive, consultant, legal educator*
Ryles, Gerald Fay *private investor, business executive*
Schairer, George Swift *aeronautical engineer*
Sebris, Robert, Jr. *lawyer*
Smith, George Lester *lawyer*
Smith, Lester Martin *broadcasting executive*
Szablya, Helen Mary *author, language professional, lecturer*
Szablya, John Francis *electrical engineer, consultant*
Traister, Robert Edwin *naval officer, engineer*
Treacy, Gerald Bernard *lawyer*
Wallentine, Mary Kathryn *secondary school educator*
Warren, James Ronald *retired museum director, author, columnist*
Watson, Mathew D. *optical scientist*
Weaver, William Schildecker *electric power industry executive*
Wright, Theodore Otis *forensic engineer*

### Bellingham
Albrecht, Albert Pearson *electronics engineer, consultant*
Bestwick, Warren William *retired construction company executive*
Burdge, Rabel James *sociology educator*
De Lorme, Roland L. *university provost and vice president*
Diers, Carol Jean *psychology educator*

GEOGRAPHIC INDEX 5027 WASHINGTON


Doerper, John Erwin *publisher, editor*
Fullmer, Donald Kitchen *insurance executive*
Gabay, Elizabeth Lee *infectious diseases physician*
Haensly, Patricia A. *psychology educator*
Haggen, Donald E. *food products executive*
Howe, Warren Billings *physician*
Jansen, Robert Bruce *consulting civil engineer*
Johnson, Jennifer Lucky *psychotherapist*
Krmpotich, Frank Zvonko *fiberglass company executive, consultant*
Landis, Wayne G. *environmental toxicologist*
Masland, Lynne S. *university official*
Morse, Joseph Grant *chemistry educator*
Morse, Karen Williams *academic administrator*
Olsen, Mark Norman *small business owner*
Packer, Mark Barry *lawyer, financial consultant, foundation official*
Pierce, George Adams *university administrator, educator*
Ross, June Rosa Pitt *biologist*
Self, Charles Edwin *financial consultant, retail company executive*
Skinner, Knute Rumsey *poet, English educator*
Wayne, Marvin Alan *emergency medicine physician*
Whisenhunt, Donald Wayne *history educator*

**Bothell**
Banks, Cherry Ann McGee *education educator*
Cothern, Barbara Shick *real estate investor*
Fortier, Sharon Murphy *special education educator*
Garr, Cheryl Denise *research chemist*
Icenhower, Rosalie B. *retired elementary school principal*
Jaundalderis, Julia Lee *software engineer*
McDonald, Michael Lee *clinic administrator, retired naval officer*
Sengupta, Mritunjoy *mining engineer, educator*

**Bremerton**
Joseph, James Edward *engineering technician*
Pliskow, Vita Sari *anesthesiologist*
Rickerson, Jean Marie *video producer, journalist, photographer*

**Burlington**
Herbaugh, Roger Duane *computer and software company executive*
Zeretzke, Frederick Frank H. *artist, educator*

**Camas**
Howe, Robert Wilson *education educator*

**Carnation**
Beshur, Jacqueline E. *pet training consultant, writer*

**Cathlamet**
Torget, Arne Odmund *retired electrical engineer*

**Centralia**
Kirk, Henry Port *academic administrator*
Miller, James McCalmont *pediatrician*

**Chehalis**
Burrows, Robert Paul *optometrist*
Neal-Parker, Shirley Anita *obstetrician and gynecologist*

**Cheney**
Drummond, Marshall Edward *business educator, university administrator*
Gerber, Sanford Edwin *audiologist*
Hegi, Ursula *writer*

**Clarkston**
Chinchinian, Harry *pathologist, educator*
Ramsden, Norma La Vonne Huber *nurse*

**Clinton**
Forward, Robert L(ull) *physicist, writer, consultant*

**Colfax**
Webster, Ronald B. *lawyer*
Young, Joann Elizabeth *veterinarian*

**Coupeville**
Canfield, Stella Stojanka *artist*
Lotzenhiser, George William *music educator, university administrator, composer*

**Dayton**
McFarland, Jon Weldon *retired county commissioner*

**Des Moines**
Harper, Vera Jean *retirement home activity director, music therapist*
Wilson, Donna Mae *foreign language educator, administrator*

**Dupont**
Pettit, Ghery St. John *electronics engineer*

**Eastsound**
Anders, William Alison *aerospace and defense manufacturing executive*
Fowles, George Richard *physicist, educator*

**Edmonds**
Eisenzimmer, Betty Wenner *insurance agency executive*
Galster, Richard W. *engineering geologist*
Holcomb, M. Staser *insurance executive*
Landau, Henry Groh *geoenvironmental consulting engineer*
Owen, John *retired newspaper editor*
Paul, Ronald Stanley *research institute executive*
Peckol, James Kenneth *consulting engineer*
Sankovich, Joseph Bernard *cemetery management consultant*
Schmit, Lucien André, Jr. *structural engineer*
Terrel, Ronald Lee *civil engineer, business executive, educator*
Thyden, James Eskel *diplomat, educator*
Walker, Doris Ann *education educator*
Wood, David Bruce *naturopathic physician*

**Ellensburg**
Comstock, Dale Robert *mathematics educator*
Housner, Jeanette Ann *artist, jeweler*
Jones, Gail Kathleen *educational administrator*
Legere, Diane J. *art association administrator, alpaca breeder*
Nelson, Ivory Vance *academic administrator*
Rosell, Sharon Lynn *physics and chemistry educator, researcher*
Yu, Roger Hong *physics educator*

**Enumclaw**
Goff, Thomas M. *secondary education educator*
Vernier, Richard *educator, author*

**Everett**
Bowden, George Newton *lawyer*
Callaghan, Mary Anne *secondary school educator*
King, Indle Gifford *industrial designer, educator*
Labayen, Louie Anthony Lopez *information analyst, consultant*
Nelson, Gary *county councilman, engineer*
Oliver, William Donald *orthodontist*
Sandahl, Bonnie Beardsley *pediatric nurse practitioner, clinical nurse specialist, nurse manager*
Toyer, Richard Henry *accountant*
Valentine, Mark Conrad *dermatologist*
Van Ry, Ginger Lee *school psychologist*

**Federal Way**
Boling, Joseph Edward *numismatist, retired military officer*
Creighton, John W., Jr. *forest products company executive*
Cunningham, John Randolph *systems analyst*
Curtis, Arnold Bennett *lumber company executive*
Jemelian, John Nazar *retail and financial executive*
Muzyka-McGuire, Amy *marketing professional, nutrition consultant*
Scott, Otto *writer*
Seiple, Robert Allen *Christian relief organization executive*
Studebaker, Irving Glen *mining engineering consultant*

**Fort Lewis**
Davis, Harley Cleo *retired military officer*
Tille, James Eugene *army chaplain*

**Freeland**
Freehill, Maurice F. *retired educational psychology educator*

**Friday Harbor**
Blinks, John Rogers *physiology and biophysics educator*
Buck, Robert Follette *retired banker, lawyer*
Daum, David Ernest *machinery manufacturing company executive*
de Vries, Rimmer *economist*
Geyman, John Payne *physician, educator*
MacGinitie, Walter Harold *psychologist*
Waite, Ric *cinematographer*

**Gig Harbor**
Canter, Ralph Raymond *psychology educator, research director*
Huyler, Jean Wiley *media and interpersonal communications consultant, hypnotherapist*
McGill, Charles Morris *physician, consultant*
Minnerly, Robert Ward *retired headmaster*
Ramsey, Jerry Virgil *educator, financial planner, radio broadcaster*
Robinson, James William *retired management consultant*

**Goldendale**
Maxwell, William Stirling *retired lawyer*

**Grayland**
Ransom, Bill *author*

**Greenbank**
Grant, Robert Yearington *former government official*
Tuell, Jack Marvin *retired bishop*

**Hansville**
Blalock, Ann Bonar *policy analyst, evaluation researcher*
Griffin, DeWitt James *architect, real estate developer*
Strahilevitz, Meir *inventor, researcher, psychiatry educator*

**Hoquiam**
Kessler, Keith Leon *lawyer*

**Indianola**
Nelson, John Howard *food company research executive*

**Issaquah**
Barchet, Stephen *physician, former naval officer*
Benoliel, Joel *lawyer*
Brotman, Jeffrey H. *variety stores executive*
Newbill, Karen Margaret *elementary school educator, education educator*
Reid, John Mitchell *biomedical engineer, researcher*
Sinegal, James D. *variety store wholesale business executive*
Tenenbaum, Michael *steel company executive*
Wainwright, Paul Edward Blech *construction company executive*

**Kalama**
Liang, Jason Chia *research chemist*

**Kennewick**
Cobb, William Thompson *environmental consultant*
Fontana, Sharon Marie *early childhood education educator*
Gates, Thomas Edward *civil engineer, waste management administrator*
Stevens, Henry August *insurance agent, educator*
Wistisen, Martin J. *agricultural business executive*

**Kent**
Goo, Abraham Meu Sen *retired aircraft company executive*
Hebeler, Henry Koester *retired aerospace and electronics executive*
Irwin, Deborah Jo *secondary education educator, flutist*
Johnson, Dennis D. *elementary school principal*
O'Bara, Kenneth J. *physician*
Pierce, Danny Parcel *artist, educator*
Williams, Max Lea, Jr. *engineer, educator*

**Kingston**
Pichal, Henri Thomas *electronics engineer, physicist, consultant*

**Kirkland**
Ayars, Albert Lee *retired school superintendent*
Barto, Deborah Ann *physician*
Blades, Horatio Benedict (Bennie Blades) *professional football player*
Brandenstein, Daniel Charles *astronaut, retired naval officer*
Davis, Dennis Albert *college president*
Dorkin, Frederic Eugene *lawyer*
Erickson, Dennis *professional football coach, former university football coach*
Forsen, Harold Kay *retired engineering executive*
Goldman, Ralph Morris *political science educator*
Look, Janet K. *psychologist*
McDonald, Joseph Lee *insurance broker*
Mitchell, Joseph Patrick *architect*
Rosett, Ann Doyle *librarian*
†Sinclair, Michael Glenn *football player*
Strode, Gerald Marvin *physician assistant*
Tuten, Richard Lamar *professional football player*
Warren, Christopher Collins *professional football player*
Wenk, Edward, Jr. *civil engineer, policy analyst, educator, writer*

**La Center**
Holley, Lawrence Alvin *retired labor union official*

**La Conner**
Knopf, Kenyon Alfred *economist, educator*
Robbins, Thomas Eugene *author*

**Lacey**
Breytspraak, John, Jr. *management consultant*
Cosand, Joseph Parker, Jr. *education educator emeritus*
Felger, Ralph William *educator, retired military officer*
Kuniyasu, Keith Kazumi *secondary education educator*
Smith, Donald Evans *library consultant*
Spangler, David Robert *college administrator, engineer*
Wells, Roger Stanley *software engineer*

**Lake Forest Park**
Favorite, Felix *oceanographer*
Keith, Donald Malcolm *physician*
Polonis, Douglas Hugh *engineering educator*

**Langley**
Bitts, Todd Michael *sales and marketing consultant*

**Longview**
Algra, Ronald James *dermatologist*
Kenagy, John Warner *surgeon*
Wollenberg, Richard Peter *paper manufacturing company executive*

**Lummi Island**
Ewing, Benjamin Baugh *environmental engineering educator, consultant*

**Lynnwood**
Araki, Takaharu *editor, mineralogist, crystallographer, consultant*
Bear, Gregory Dale *writer, illustrator*
Benzel, Brian L. *superintendent*
Edwards, Kirk Lewis *real estate company executive*
Jenes, Theodore George, Jr. *retired military officer*
Krause, Thomas Evans *record promotion and radio consultant*
Olsen, Kenneth Harold *geophysicist, astrophysicist*
Vierheller, Todd *software engineering consultant*

**Malaga**
Nanto, Roxanna Lynn *marketing professional, management consulstant*

**Manchester**
Fearon, Lee Charles *chemist*

**Maple Valley**
Brown, Thomas Andrew *retired aircraft/weaponry manufacturing executive*

**Marysville**
Philpott, Larry La Fayette *horn player*

**Mazama**
Hogness, John Rusten *physician, academic administrator*

**Medical Lake**
Grub, Phillip Donald *business educator*
Taylor, Eldon *psychologist researcher*

**Medina**
Schlotterbeck, Walter Albert *manufacturing company executive, lawyer*

**Mercer Island**
Bridgforth, Robert Moore, Jr. *aerospace engineer*
Coe, Robert Campbell *surgeon*
Elgee, Neil Johnson *retired internist and endocrinologist, educator*
Gould, Alvin R. *international business executive*
Haviland, James West *physician*
Herres, Phillip Benjamin *computer software executive*
Langhout-Nix, Nelleke *artist*
Noe, James Alva *retired judge*
Spitzer, Jack J. *banker*
Steinhardt, Henry *photographer*

**Mill Creek**
Corbally, John Edward *foundation director*
Larson, Mary Bea *elementary education educator*

**Moses Lake**
Leadbetter, Mark Renton, Jr. *orthopedic surgeon*

**Mount Vernon**
Cammock, Earl E. *surgeon*
Garcia, John *psychologist, educator*
Hall, David Ramsay *architect*
Klein, Henry *architect*
Moser, C. Thomas *lawyer*
Poppe, Patricia Lee *clinical social worker, consultant*

**Mountlake Terrace**
Imamura, Eugene Hachiro *osteopathic physician, surgeon*

**Napavine**
Morgan-Fadness, Corrina May *staff charge nurse*

**Nine Mile Falls**
Payne, Arlie Jean *parent education administrator*

**Nordland**
Kepner, Rita Marie *sculptor, writer, editor, educator, public affairs officer, marketing and communications professional, education manager, agency spokesperson*

**North Seattle**
Spafford, Michael Charles *artist*

**Oak Harbor**
Crampton, George Harris *science educator, retired army officer*
Miller, Robert Scott *mental health administrator, social worker*
Piercy, Gordon Clayton *bank executive*

**Ocean Shores**
Morgan, Audrey *architect*

**Olympia**
Alfers, Gerald Junior *bank executive, retired*
Allen, Robert Mark *lawyer*
Beck, Gordon Eugene *art history educator, consultant*
Blake, Ann Beth *psychologist*
Bloomquist, Rodney Gordon *geologist*
Boruchowitz, Stephen Alan *health policy analyst*
Dolliver, James Morgan *state supreme court justice*
Durham, Barbara *state supreme court justice*
Flemming, Stanley Lalit Kumar *family practice physician, mayor, state legislator*
Foley, Thomas Michael *financial executive*
Guy, Richard P. *state supreme court justice*
Haseltine, James Lewis *artist, consultant*
Humphrey, Camilla Marie *retired special education educator*
Inverso, Marlene Joy *optometrist*
Jervis, Jane Lise *college official, science historian*
Johnson, Charles William *justice*
Kessler, Lynn Elizabeth *state legislator*
Kohl, Jeanne Elizabeth *state senator, sociologist, educator*
Lind, Carl Bradley *retired museum director*
†Locke, Gary *governor*
Loftness, Marvin O. *electrical engineer*
Long, Jeanine Hundley *state legislator*
Manning, Farley *retired public relations executive*
Munro, Ralph Davies *state government official*
Myers, Sharon Diane *auditor*
Mylroie, Willa Wilcox *transportation engineer, regional planner*
Nesbit, Robert Carrington *historian*
Nichols, James Raymond, Jr. *civil engineer*
Norwood, Deborah Anne *law librarian*
O'Brien, Robert S. *state official*
Ogden, Valeria Juan *management consultant, state representative*
†Owen, Bradley Scott *lieutenant governor*
Ponder, William Stanley *university administrator*
Reilly, Robert Joseph *counselor*
Smith, Charles Z. *state supreme court justice*
Spanel, Harriet Rosa Albertsen *state senator*
Steiger, Gretchen Helene *marine mammalogist, research biologist*
Stewart, Jeffree Robert *environmental planner, artist*
Walker, Francis Joseph *lawyer*

**Orcas**
Greever, John *retired mathematics educator*

**Pasco**
Yoshino, George *food products executive*

**Port Angeles**
Chase, John David *university dean, physician*
Muller, Willard C(hester) *writer*
Osborne, Richard Hazelet *anthropology and medical genetics educator*
Youmans, William Barton *physiologist*

**Port Ludlow**
Gullander, Werner Paul *retired consultant, retired corporate executive*
Ward, Louis Emmerson *retired physician*

**Port Orchard**
Crawford, William Matterson *lawyer*

**Port Townsend**
Buhler, Jill Lorie *editor, writer*
Harrington, LaMar *curator, museum director*
Woolf, William Blauvelt *retired association executive*

**Poulsbo**
Meyer, Roger Jess Christian *pediatrics educator*
Tozer, William Evans *entomologist, educator*

**Prosser**
Boyle, Steven Leonard *secondary school educator*
Deffenbaugh, Kay Anne *secondary education art educator*
Proebsting, Edward Louis, Jr. *retired research horticulturist*

**Pullman**
Baugh, Bradford Hamilton *occupational and environmental health advisor*
Bennett, Edward Moore *historian, educator*
Bertramson, B. Rodney *agronomist*
Bustad, Leo Kenneth *veterinary educator, college administrator*
Carlson, James Roy *animal science educator*
Catton, William Robert, Jr. *sociology educator*
Crosby, Glenn Arthur *chemistry educator*
Crowe, Clayton T. *engineering educator*
Davis, Fred *journalist, educator*

Dillman, Donald Andrew *sociologist, educator*
Dodgen, Harold Warren *chemistry and physics educator*
Funk, William Henry *environmental engineering educator*
Gustafsson, Borje Karl *veterinarian, educator*
Halvorson, Alfred Rubin *retired mayor, consultant, education educator*
Henson, James Bond *veterinary pathologist*
Hildebrandt, Darlene Myers *information scientist*
Hirth, John Price *metallurgical engineering educator*
Hosick, Howard Lawrence *cell biology educator, academic administrator*
Kallaher, Michael Joseph *mathematics educator*
Lewis, Norman G. *academic administrator, researcher, consultant*
Lutz, Julie Haynes *astronomy and mathematics educator*
McSweeney, Frances Kaye *psychology educator*
Michaelis, Karen Lauree *law educator*
Mitchell, Madeleine Enid *nutritionist, educator*
Randall, Linda Lea *biochemist, educator*
Ryan, Clarence Augustine, Jr. *biochemistry educator*
Sheldon, Charles Harvey *political science educator*
Smith, Robert Victor *university administrator*
Smith, Samuel Howard *academic administrator, plant pathologist*
Stock, David Earl *mechanical engineering educator*
Warner, Dennis Allan *psychology educator*
Watkinson, Patricia Grieve *museum director*
Wilson, Robert Burton *veterinary and medical educator*
Young, Francis Allan *psychologist*

**Puyallup**
Brandner, (Mary Ann) Joyce *retired nurse educator*
Chalk, Earl Milton *retired art director*
DeBock, Ronald Gene *real estate company executive*
Kutscher, Kathleen Ann *social welfare administrator, social worker*
Lurie, Hugh James *psychiatrist, educator*
Ruff, Lorraine Marie *public relations executive*
Tate, Randall J. (Randy Tate) *former congressman*
Veatch, John William *Reiki educator, educational administrator*
Walize, Reuben Thompson, III *health research administrator*

**Redmond**
Beeson, Paul Bruce *physician*
Butler-Thomas, Jannette Sue *human resources professional*
Erxleben, William Charles *lawyer, data processing executive*
Gates, William Henry, III *software company executive*
Gilmore, A. Douglas *retail sales executive*
Kimmich, Jon Bradford *computer science program executive*
MacKenzie, Peter Sean *instructional designer*
Malik, Sohail *chemistry educator, researcher, consultant*
Nagel, Daryl David *retail executive*
Oaks, Lucy Moberley *retired social worker*
Pacholski, Richard Francis *retired securities company executive, financial advisor, consultant*
Ransdell, Tod Elliot *pharmaceutical, parenteral and in vitro diagnostics validation specialist*
Rossano, August Thomas *environmental engineering educator*
Rushmer, Estella Virginia Dix (Dixie Rushmer) *artist*
Sasenick, Joseph Anthony *health care company executive*
Sowder, Robert Robertson *architect*
Teeter, Rob R. *regulatory affairs specialist*
Welke, Elton Grinnell, Jr. *publisher, writer*

**Renton**
Barber, Mark Edward *lawyer*
Tajon, Encarnacion Fontecha (Connie Tajon) *retired educator, association executive*

**Richland**
Albaugh, Fred William *nuclear engineer, retired research and development executive*
Bair, William J. *radiation biologist*
Barr, Carlos Harvey *lawyer*
Bevelacqua, Joseph John *physicist, researcher*
Bush, Spencer Harrison *metallurgist*
Campbell, Milton Hugh *chemist*
Chikalla, Thomas David *retired science facility administrator*
Cochran, James Alan *mathematics educator*
Colson, Steven Douglas *research director, chemistry educator*
Elderkin, Charles Edwin *retired meteorologist*
Evans, Ersel Arthur *consulting engineer executive*
Fraser, Frederick Ewart *art educator*
Jacobsen, Gerald Bernhardt *biochemist*
Liu, Yosen *nuclear engineer*
McGinley, Edward Stillman, II *former naval officer, engineering executive*
Moore, Emmett Burris, Jr. *physical chemist*
Nolan, John Edward *retired electrical corporation executive*
Piippo, Steve *educator*
Ramesh, Kalahasti Subrahmanyam *materials scientist*
Schwinkendorf, Kevin Neil *nuclear engineer*
Trent, Donald Stephen *thermo fluids engineer*
Zirkle, Lewis Greer *physician, executive*

**Ritzville**
Schoesler, Mark Gerald *state legislator, farmer*

**Rollingbay**
Young, Jeffry *psychologist, gerontologist, educator, statistician*

**Seattle**
Aagaard, George Nelson *medical educator*
Abbott, Robert Dean *education scientist*
Ackerley, Barry *professional basketball team executive, communications company executive*
Adams, Hazard Simeon *English educator, author*
Adams, Julie Karen *clinical psychologist*
Alberg, Tom Austin *communications executive, lawyer*
Albrecht, Richard Raymond *airplane manufacturing company executive, lawyer*
Albright, Douglas Eaton *lawyer*
Aldrich, Robert Anderson *physician*
Alexander, Edward Russell *disease research administrator*
Alkire, John D. *lawyer*
Allen, Joanna Cowan *lawyer*
Allen, Thomas Joseph *treasurer*
Anang, Amma Cecilia *dance company administrator*
Andersen, Niels Hjorth *chemistry educator, biophysics researcher, consultant*
Anderson, Arthur G., Jr. *chemistry educator*
Anderson, Peter MacArthur *lawyer*
Anderson, Ross *columnist*
Andreasen, Steven W. *lawyer*
Andrew, Lucius Archibald David, III *bank executive*
Andrews, J. David *lawyer*
Andrews, Richard Otis *museum director*
Andrews, Robert Goff *pediatrician, medical educator*
Ansell, Julian S. *physician, retired urology educator*
Armstrong, Charles G. *professional baseball executive, lawyer*
Arnold, Robert Morris *banker*
Arons, Arnold Boris *physicist, educator*
Arthur, William Lynn *environmental foundation administrator*
Averill, Lloyd James, Jr. *religion educator*
Babb, Albert Leslie *biomedical engineer, educator*
†Bagley, George D. *aerospace transportation executive*
Bagshaw, Bradley Holmes *lawyer*
Bain, William James, Jr. *architect*
Ballweg, Ruth Milligan *physician assistant, educator*
Banks, James Albert *educational research director, educator*
Banse, Karl *retired oceanography educator*
Bargreen, Melinda Lueth *music critic*
Barnes, Susan Lewis *lawyer*
†Bartels, Juergen E. *hotel company executive*
Bassett, Edward Powers *university official*
Bassetti, Fred Forde *architect*
Bassingthwaighte, James Bucklin *physiologist, educator, medical researcher*
Baum, William Alvin *astronomer, educator*
Bayley, Christopher T. *public affairs consultant*
Beetham, Stanley Williams *international management consultant*
Beezer, Robert Renaut *federal judge*
Behnke, Carl Gilbert *beverage franchise executive*
Beighle, Douglas Paul *business executive*
Benirschke, Stephen Kurt *orthopedic surgeon*
Bensussen, Estelle Esther *writer, illustrator, artist*
Berg, Margarete Claire *banker*
Berger, Paul Eric *artist, photographer*
Bernard, Eddie Nolan *oceanographer*
Bevan, Donald Edward *retired marine science educator, university dean*
Beyers, William Bjorn *geography educator*
Bichsel, Hans *physicist, consultant, researcher*
Bierman, Charles Warren *physician, educator*
Bigos, Stanley James *orthopedic surgery spine specialist, educator*
Bird, Thomas D. *neurologist*
Birmingham, Richard Joseph *lawyer*
Black, W. L. Rivers, III *lawyer*
Blagg, Christopher Robin *nephrologist*
Blais, Robert Howard *lawyer*
Blake, Robert Wallace *aeronautical engineer, consultant*
Blandau, Richard Julius *physician, educator*
Blase, Nancy Gross *librarian*
Blethen, Frank A. *newspaper publisher*
Blethen, William Kingsley, Jr. *newspaper publishing executive*
Bliss, Lawrence Carroll *botany educator*
Blom, Daniel Charles *lawyer, investor*
Blomdahl, Sonja *artist*
Blumenfeld, Charles Raban *lawyer*
Boardman, David *newspaper editor*
Boaz, Doniella Chaves *psychotherapist, consultant*
Bodansky, David *physicist, educator*
Boeder, Thomas L. *lawyer*
Boersma, P. Dee *zoology educator*
Borden, Weston Thatcher *chemistry educator*
Borgatta, Edgar F. *social psychologist, educator*
Bornstein, Paul *physician, biochemist*
Bosworth, Thomas Lawrence *architect, educator*
Bourque, Philip John *business economist, educator*
Bowden, Douglas McHose *neuropsychiatric scientist, educator, research center administrator*
Bowen, Jewell Ray *chemical engineering educator*
Bowman, Patricia Lynn *lawyer*
Boyko, Edward John *internist, medical researcher*
Boylan, Merle Nelson *librarian*
Brammer, Lawrence Martin *psychology educator*
Brandauer, Frederick Paul *Asian language educator*
Breslow, Norman Edward *biostatistics educator, researcher*
Bridge, Herbert Marvin *jewelry executive*
Bringman, Joseph Edward *lawyer*
Brockenbrough, Edwin Chamberlayne *surgeon*
Brooke, Francis John, III *foundation administrator*
Brown, Craig William *physical chemist*
Brown, Frederick Calvin *physicist, educator*
Brown, Janiece Alfreida *pilot*
Brown, Kristi *principal*
Brown, Lillie McFall *elementary school principal*
Brown, Lowell Severt *physicist, educator*
Brown, Robert Alan *atmospheric science educator, research scientist*
Brownlee, Donald Eugene, II *astronomer, educator*
Brownstein, Barbara Lavin *geneticist, educator, university official*
Buckner, Philip Franklin *newspaper publisher*
Buffington, John Douglas *ecologist, researcher*
Bunting, Robert Louis *accounting firm executive, management consultant*
Burgess, Charles Orville *history educator*
Burke, William Thomas *law educator, lawyer*
Burkhart, William Henry *lawyer*
Burns, Robert Carter *psychologist, author*
Burrows, Elizabeth MacDonald *religious organization executive, educator*
Bursten, Stuart Lowell *physician, biochemist*
Butow, Robert Joseph Charles *history educator*
Byers, Peter H. *geneticist*
Cameron, Mindy *newspaper editor*
Campbell, Robert Hedgcock *investment banker*
Carlson, Dale Arvid *university dean*
Carlyon, Diane Claire *nurse*
Caro, Ivor *dermatologist*
Castanes, James Christopher *architect*
Catterall, William A. *pharmacology, neurobiology educator*
Cavanaugh, Michael Everett *lawyer, arbitrator*
Celentano, Francis Michael *artist, art educator*
Cella, John J. *freight company executive*
Chang, Taiping *marketing executive, magazine publisher*
Char, Patricia Helen *lawyer*
Charlson, Robert Jay *atmospheric sciences educator, scientist*
Chirot, Daniel *sociology and international studies educator*
Chisholm, Margaret Elizabeth *retired library education administrator*
Christian, Gary Dale *chemistry educator*
Christiansen, Walter Henry *aeronautics educator*
Cichanski, Gerald *golf course architect*
Claflin, Arthur Cary *lawyer*
Clark, Kenneth Courtright *retired physics and geophysics educator*
Clark, Robert Newhall *electrical and aeronautical engineering educator*
Clarkson, Lawrence William *airplane company executive*
Cleland, Robert Erksine *plant physiologist, educator*
Cline, Robert Stanley *air freight company executive*
Clinton, Gordon Stanley *lawyer*
Clinton, Richard M. *lawyer*
Clowes, Alexander Whitehill *surgeon, educator*
Coburn, Robert Craig *philosopher*
Cochran, Wendell *science editor*
Cockburn, John F. *retired banker*
Coffman, Sandra Jeanne *psychologist*
Coldewey, John Christopher *English literature educator*
Collett, Robert Lee *financial company executive*
Condit, Philip Murray *aerospace executive, engineer*
Cook, Victor *physics educator, researcher*
Corker, Charles Edward *retired lawyer, educator*
Coughenour, John Clare *federal judge*
Couser, William Griffith *medical educator, academic administrator, nephrologist*
Cox, Frederick Moreland *retired university dean, social worker*
Coyle, Marie Bridget *microbiology educator, laboratory director*
Cramer, John Gleason, Jr. *physics educator, experimental physicist*
Creager, Joe Scott *geology and oceanography educator*
Criminale, William Oliver, Jr. *applied mathematics educator*
Cross, Harry Maybury *retired law educator, consultant*
Crumb, Robert *cartoonist*
Cullen, Bruce F. *anesthesiologist*
Cullen, James Douglas *banker, finance company executive*
Culp, Gordon Louis *consulting engineer*
Culp, Mildred Louise *corporate executive*
Cunningham, Joel Dean *lawyer*
Curley, Jonathan Edward *small business owner*
Dagnon, James Bernard *human resources executive*
Dahl, Lance Christopher *lawyer*
Dale, David C. *physician, medical educator*
Dalton, Thomas George *paralegal, social worker, legal consultant*
Dash, J. Gregory *physicist, educator*
Davis, Earl James *chemical engineering educator*
Davis, John MacDougall *lawyer*
Davis, Patricia *state agency executive*
Dawson, Patricia Lucille *surgeon*
Day, Robert Winsor *cancer research administrator*
De Alessi, Ross Alan *lighting designer*
Dear, Ronald Bruce *social work educator*
Debro, Julius *university dean, sociology educator*
Dederer, Michael Eugene *public relations company executive*
Dehmelt, Hans Georg *physicist*
del Moral, Roger *botany educator, ecologist, wetland consultant*
Denny, Brewster Castberg *retired university dean*
Derham, Richard Andrew *lawyer*
de Tornyay, Rheba *nurse, former university dean, educator*
DeVore, Paul Cameron *lawyer*
Dickinson, Calhoun *lawyer*
Dietrich, William Alan *reporter*
Diggs, Bradley C. *lawyer*
Dillard, Marilyn Dianne *property manager*
Dimmick, Carolyn Reaber *federal judge*
Dolan, Andrew Kevin *lawyer*
Donaldson, James Adrian *otolaryngology educator*
Donaldson, Lauren R. *fisheries biology and radiobiology educator emeritus*
Donohue, James Patrick *lawyer*
Dorpat, Theodore Lorenz *psychoanalyst*
Drew, Jody Lynne *secondary education educator*
Dubes, Michael John *insurance company executive*
Duckworth, Tara Ann *insurance company executive*
Duncan, Elizabeth Charlotte *marriage and family therapist, educator*
Dunnell, Robert Chester *archaeologist, educator*
Dunner, David Louis *medicine educator*
Du Pen, Everett George *sculptor, educator*
Duryee, David Anthony *management consultant*
Dworkin, Samuel Franklin *dentist, psychologist*
Dwyer, William L. *federal judge*
Dyer, Philip E. *insurance company executive*
Edmondson, W(allace) Thomas *retired limnologist, educator*
Ellegood, Donald Russell *publishing executive*
Ellings, Richard James *political and economic research institution executive*
Elliott, Jeanne Marie Koreltz *transportation executive*
Ellis, James Reed *lawyer*
Ellis, John W. *professional baseball team executive, utility company executive*
Ellis, Stephen D. *physics educator*
Ellison, Herbert Jay *history educator*
Emory, Meade *lawyer*
Engel, Thomas *chemistry educator*
Ernst, Chadwick Ellsworth *fastener company executive*
†Espinoza, Lynn R. *journalist*
Etcheson, Warren Wade *business administration educator*
Evans, Bernard William *geologist, educator*
Evans, Charles Albert *microbiology educator*
Evans, Daniel Jackson *former senator*
Evans, Ellis Dale *psychologist, educator*
Evans, Trevor Heiser *advertising executive*
Fancher, Michael Reilly *newspaper editor, newspaper publishing executive*
Farrell, Anne Van Ness *foundation executive*
Farris, Jerome *federal judge*
Faulstich, James R. *bank executive*
Feiss, George James, III *financial services company executive*
Fiedler, Fred Edward *organizational psychology educator, consultant*
Figley, Melvin Morgan *radiologist, physician, educator*
Fine, James Stephen *physician*
Finlayson, Bruce Alan *chemical engineering educator*
Fischer, Edmond Henri *biochemistry educator*
Fischer, Fred Walter *physicist, engineer, educator*
Fischer, Mary E. *special education educator*
Fitzpatrick, Thomas Mark *lawyer*
Fix, Wilbur James *department store executive*
Fleagle, Robert Guthrie *meteorologist, educator*
Fletcher, Betty B. *federal judge*
Floss, Heinz G. *chemistry educator, scientist*
Forbes, David Craig *musician*
Fortson, Edward Norval *physics educator*
Freedman, Bart Joseph *lawyer*
Freeman, Antoinette Rosefeldt *lawyer*
Freeny, Patrick Clinton *radiology educator, consultant*
Gabbe, Steven Glenn *physician, educator*
Galvan, Elias Gabriel *bishop*
Galvin, Elias *bishop*
Gandara, Daniel *lawyer*
Gardiner, T(homas) Michael *artist*
Gardner, Jill Christopher *neuroscientist, bioengineer*
Gartz, Paul Ebner *systems engineer*
Geballe, Ronald *physicist, university dean*
Gerberding, William Passavant *retired university president*
Gerhart, James Basil *physics educator*
Gerrodette, Charles Everett *real estate company executive, consultant*
Gerstenberger, Donna Lorine *humanities educator*
Gibaldi, Milo *university dean*
Giblett, Eloise Rosalie *hematology educator*
Giedt, Walvin Roland *epidemiologist, educator*
Gilbert, Paul H. *engineering executive, consultant*
Gilchrist, James Beardslee *banker*
Giles, Robert Edward, Jr. *lawyer*
Gist, Marilyn Elaine *organizational behavior and human resource management educator*
Gittinger, D. Wayne *lawyer*
Givan, Boyd Eugene *aircraft company executive*
Glover, Karen E. *lawyer*
Godden, Jean W. *columnist*
Goeltz, Thomas A. *lawyer*
Goodlad, John Inkster *education educator, author*
Gorans, Gerald Elmer *accountant*
Gordon, Milton Paul *biochemist, educator*
Gore, William Jay *political science educator*
Gores, Thomas C. *lawyer*
Gouldthorpe, Kenneth Alfred Percival *publisher, state official*
Gouterman, Martin Paul *chemistry educator*
Govedare, Philip Bainbridge *artist, educator*
Graham, Clyde Benjamin, Jr. *physician*
Graham, Stephen Michael *lawyer*
Gray, Marvin Lee, Jr. *lawyer*
Grayston, J. Thomas *medical and public health educator*
Green, G. Dorsey *psychologist, author*
Green, Joshua, III *banker*
Greenan, Thomas J. *lawyer*
Greene, John Burkland *lawyer*
Greenwood, Wilbur R., III *investment banker*
Greggs, Elizabeth May Bushnell (Mrs. Raymond John Greggs) *retired librarian*
Gregory, Norman Wayne *chemistry educator, researcher*
Griffey, Ken, Jr. (George Kenneth Griffey, Jr.) *professional baseball player*
Griffin, Thomas W. *physician*
Grimley, Janet Elizabeth *newspaper editor*
Grinstein, Gerald *transportation executive*
Groman, Neal Benjamin *microbiology educator*
Gross, Edward *retired sociologist, educator, lawyer*
Grossman, Robert James *architect*
Gunter, Laurie M. *retired nurse educator*
Guntheroth, Warren Gaden *physician*
Gustafson, Alice Fairleigh *lawyer*
Guy, Andrew A. *lawyer*
Guy, Arthur William *electrical engineering educator, researcher*
Gwinn, Mary Ann *newspaper reporter*
Hackman, Robert Cordell *pathology educator, researcher*
Haggard, Joel Edward *lawyer*
Halferty, Frank Joseph *middle school music educator*
Halver, John Emil *nutritional biochemist*
Haman, Raymond William *lawyer*
Hampton, Philip McCune *banker*
Hampton, Shelley Lynn *hearing impaired educator*
Han, Mao-Tang *surgeon, researcher*
Hansen, Wayne W. *lawyer*
Hanson, Kermit Osmond *business administration educator, university dean emeritus*
Haralick, Robert Martin *electrical engineering educator*
Harder, Virgil Eugene *business administration educator*
Hargiss, James Leonard *ophthalmologist*
Harmon, Daniel Patrick *classics educator*
Harrison, Don Edmunds *oceanographer, educator*
Hart, Paul *retired dean and educator, poet*
Hartl, John George *film critic*
†Hartley, Robert *public relations executive*
Hartmann, Dennis Lee *atmospheric science educator*
Harwick, Dennis Patrick *lawyer*
Hastings, L(ois) Jane *architect, educator*
Hazelton, Penny Ann *law librarian, educator*
Heer, Nicholas Lawson *Arabist and Islamist educator*
Hegyvary, Sue Thomas *dean nursing school*
Henderson, Dan Fenno *lawyer, law educator*
Henderson, Maureen McGrath *medical educator*
Hendrickson, Anita Elizabeth *biology educator*
Henkel, Cathy *newspaper sports editor*
Henley, Ernest Mark *physics educator, university dean emeritus*
Herman, Lloyd Eldred *curator, consultant, writer*
Herring, Susan Weller *dental educator, oral anatomist*
Hertzberg, Abraham *aeronautical engineering educator, university research scientist*
Hewitt, Edwin *mathematician, educator*
Hiatt, Peter *librarian studies educator*
Hill, G. Richard *lawyer*
Hill, Gary *video artist*
Hille, Bertil *physiology educator*
Hills, Regina J. *journalist*
Hilpert, Edward Theodore, Jr. *lawyer*
Hinshaw, Mark Larson *architect, urban planner*
Hirschman, Charles, Jr. *sociologist, educator*
Hodge, Paul William *astronomer, educator*
Hoffman, Allan Sachs *chemical engineer, educator*
Hofmann, Douglas Allan *lawyer*
Holm, Vanja Adele *developmental pediatrician, educator*
Holmes, King Kennard *medical educator*
Holtby, Kenneth Fraser *manufacturing executive*
Hornbein, Thomas Frederic *anesthesiologist*
Horton, Elliott Argue, Jr. *lawyer, business consultant*
†Hough, John *public relations executive*
Howard, Heather *corporate secretary*
Hudson, Leonard Dean *physician*

Huey, Constance Anne Berner *mental health counselor*
Huff, Gary D. *lawyer*
Hunkins, Francis Peter *education educator*
Hunter, Theodore Paul *lawyer, energy consultant*
Huston, John Charles *law educator*
Hutcheson, Mark Andrew *lawyer*
Ingalls, Robert Lynn *physicist, educator*
Inlow, Edgar Burke *political science educator*
Isaki, Lucy Power Slyngstad *lawyer*
Ishimaru, Akira *electrical engineering educator*
Israel, Allen D. *lawyer*
Jackson, Dillon Edward *lawyer*
Jacobson, Phillip Lee *architect, educator*
Jaeger, David Arnold *aerospace company executive*
Jameson, Henry C. *lawyer*
Jenkins, Speight *opera company executive, writer*
Jennerich, Edward John *university official and dean*
Jensen, Helen *musical artists management company executive*
Johnson, Bruce Edward Humble *lawyer*
Johnson, Janice Susan Gallik *finance executive*
Johnson, Mildred Grace Mash *investment company executive*
Johnson, Randall David (Randy Johnson) *professional baseball player*
Johnson, Wayne Eaton *writer, editor, former drama critic*
Johnston, Norman John *architecture educator*
Johnston, William Frederick *emergency services administrator*
Jonassen, James O. *architect*
Jones, Edward Louis *historian, educator*
Jones, Grant Richard *landscape architect, planner*
Jonsen, Albert R. *medical ethics educator*
Joppa, Robert Glenn *aeronautics educator*
Judson, C(harles) James (Jim Judson) *lawyer*
Kahn, Steven Emanuel *medical educator*
Kalina, Robert Edward *physician, educator*
Kane, Alan Henry *lawyer*
Kane, Christopher *nonprofit organization executive, lawyer, legal consultant*
Kane, Karen Marie *public affairs consultant*
Kaplan, Barry Martin *lawyer*
Kapur, Kailash Chander *industrial engineering educator*
Karl, George *professional basketball coach*
Karr, James Richard *ecologist, educator, research director*
Kasama, Hideto Peter *accountant, advisor, real estate consultant*
Katz, Charles J., Jr. *lawyer*
Keegan, John E. *lawyer*
Kelley, John F. *airline executive*
Kellogg, Kenyon P. *lawyer*
Kelly, Carolyn Sue *newspaper executive*
Kemp, Shawn T. *professional basketball player*
Kenney, Richard Laurence *poet, English language educator*
Kevorkian, Jirair *applied mathematics, aeronautics and astronautics educator*
Keyt, David *philosophy and classics educator*
Killinger, Kerry Kent *bank executive*
Kim, Yongmin *electrical engineering educator*
King, Mary-Claire *geneticist, educator*
Kippenhan, Charles Jacob *mechanical engineer, retired educator*
Kirby, William Murray Maurice *medical educator*
Kirkendall, Richard Stewart *historian, educator*
Klebanoff, Seymour Joseph *medical educator*
Klee, Victor La Rue *mathematician, educator*
Klein, Otto G., III *lawyer*
†Kleisner, Fred *hotel executive*
Kobayashi, Albert Satoshi *mechanical engineering educator*
Koehler, Reginald Stafford, III *lawyer*
Kohn, Alan J. *zoology educator*
Kolb, Keith Robert *architect, educator*
Kolbeson, Marilyn Hopf *holistic practioner, educator, artist, retired organization and management consultant*
Korg, Jacob *English literature educator*
†Kraft, Donald B. *advertising executive*
Kraft, George Howard *physician, educator*
Krebs, Edwin Gerhard *biochemistry educator*
Krohn, Kenneth Albert *radiology educator*
Kruckeberg, Arthur Rice *botanist, educator*
Kruse, Paul Robert *retired librarian, educator*
Kuhl, Patricia K. *science educator*
Kuhrau, Edward W. *lawyer*
Kuvshinoff, Bertha Horne *painter, sculptor*
Kwiram, Alvin L. *physical chemistry educator, university official*
Lacitis, Erik *journalist*
Laird, Charles David *zoology and genetics educator, researcher*
Lang, Kurt *sociologist, educator, writer*
LaPoe, Wayne Gilpin *retired business executive*
Lauritzen, Peter Owen *electrical engineering educator*
LaVeck, Gerald DeLoss *physician, educator*
Lawrence, Jacob *artist, educator*
Leale, Olivia Mason *import marketing company executive*
Lee, John Marshall *mathematics educator*
Lee, Qwihee Park *plant physiologist*
Lee, Ronald Eugene *international air transportation supply executive*
Leitzell, Terry Lee *lawyer*
Lemly, Thomas Adger *lawyer*
Liljebeck, Roy C. *transportation company executive*
Lingafelter, Edward Clay, Jr. *chemistry educator*
Loeser, John David *neurosurgeon, educator*
Loftus, Thomas Daniel *lawyer*
Lombard, David Norman *lawyer*
Loper, Robert Bruce *theater director, educator*
Lord, Jere Johns *retired physics educator*
Lovett, Wendell Harper *architect*
Lowry, Mike *former governor, former congressman*
Lubatti, Henry Joseph *physicist, educator*
MacDonald, Andrew Stephen *management consulting firm executive*
MacLachlan, Douglas Lee *marketing educator*
Mah, Feng-hwa *economics educator*
Malcolm, Garold Dean *architect*
Mallory, V(irgil) Standish *geologist, educator*
Mankoff, David A. *nuclear medicine physician*
Margon, Bruce Henry *astrophysicist, educator*
Marks, William H. *organ transplant program director, pharmacologist, pharmacognosist, director for laboratory transplantation biology*
Marriott, David M. *public relations executive*
Martin, George Coleman *aeronautical engineer*
Martin, George M. *pathologist, gerontologist, educator*
Martinez, Edgar *professional baseball player*
Mason, James Tate *surgeon*
Matchett, William H(enry) *English literature educator*
Matsen, Frederick Albert, III *orthopedic educator*
Matthews, Donald Rowe *political scientist, educator*
McCann, Richard Eugene *lawyer*
McConnell, J. Daniel *sports marketing professional*
Mc Donald, James Michael, Jr. *research institute consultant*
Mc Feron, Dean Earl *mechanical engineer*
Mc Govern, Walter T. *federal judge*
McHugh, Heather *poet*
McKay, Michael Dennis *lawyer*
McKey, Thomas J. *lawyer*
McKinnon, James Buckner *real estate sales executive, writer, researcher*
McMillan, John A. *retail executive*
McMillan, Nathaniel *professional basketball player*
McReynolds, Neil Lawrence *public affairs consultant*
Meditch, James Stephen *electrical engineering educator*
Medved, Michael *film critic, author*
Meeuse, Bastiaan Jacob Dirk *biologist, educator, researcher*
Merendino, K. Alvin *surgical educator*
Michael, Ernest Arthur *mathematics educator*
Miller, Robert Carmi, Jr. *microbiology educator, university administrator*
Mizrahi, Yves *retail executive*
Moberly, David Lindsey *retired foundation executive*
Moch, Robert Gaston *lawyer*
†Mogelgaard, Michael *creative director*
Monsen, Elaine Ranker *nutritionist, educator, editor*
Moore, Benjamin *theatrical producer*
Moore, Daniel Charles *physician*
Moore, James R. *lawyer*
Morrill, Richard Leland *geographer, educator*
Morse, John Moore *architect, planner*
Mottet, Norman Karle *pathologist, educator*
Motulsky, Arno Gunther *geneticist, physician, educator*
Muilenburg, Robert Henry *hospital administrator*
Murphy, Thomas Joseph *archbishop*
Murray, James Dickson *mathematical biology educator*
Mussehl, Robert Clarence *lawyer*
Nalder, Eric Christopher *investigative reporter*
Narver, John Colin *business administration educator*
Nash, Cynthia Jeanne *journalist*
Nellermoe, Leslie Carol *lawyer*
Nelson, James Alonzo *radiologist, educator*
Nelson, Walter William *computer programmer, consultant*
Newmeyer, Frederick Jaret *linguist, educator*
Niemi, Janice *lawyer, former state legislator*
Nijenhuis, Albert *mathematician, educator*
Ning, Xue-Han (Hsueh-Han Ning) *physiologist, researcher*
Nishitani, Martha *dancer*
Noble, Phillip D. *lawyer*
Noe, Jerre Donald *computer science educator*
Nordstrom, Bruce A. *department store executive*
Nordstrom, John N. *department store executive*
Nostrand, Howard Lee *language and literature educator*
Oehler, Richard William *lawyer*
O'Leary, Thomas Howard *resources executive*
Oles, Stuart Gregory *lawyer*
Olmstead, Marjorie Ann *physics educator*
Olsen, Harold Fremont *lawyer*
Olson, David John *political science educator*
Olson, James William Park *architect*
Olstad, Roger Gale *science educator*
Olver, Michael Lynn *lawyer*
O'Malley, Robert Edmund, Jr. *mathematics educator*
Oman, Henry *retired electrical engineer, engineering executive*
Omenn, Gilbert Stanley *university dean, physician*
Orcutt, James Craig *ophthalmologist*
Orians, Gordon Howell *biology educator*
Overstreet, Hon. Karen A. *federal bankruptcy judge*
Page, Roy Christopher *periodontist, educator*
Painter, Diana Jean *urban designer, consultant*
Palm, Gerald Albert *lawyer*
Palmer, Douglas S., Jr. *lawyer*
Parker, Omar Sigmund, Jr. *lawyer*
Parks, Patricia Jean *lawyer*
Parrish, John Brett *manufacturing executive*
Parsons, A. Peter *lawyer*
Paul, Thomas Frank *lawyer*
Payne, Ancil Horace *retired broadcasting executive*
Payton, Gary Dwayne *professional basketball player*
Perkin, Gordon Wesley *international health agency executive*
Perrin, Edward Burton *health services researcher, biostatistician, public health educator*
Petersdorf, Robert George *physician, medical educator*
Peterson, Jane White *nursing educator, anthropologist*
Petrie, Gregory Steven *lawyer*
Pettigrew, Edward W. *lawyer*
Phillips, Josef Clayton *insurance and investment company executive*
Phillips, William Robert *physician*
Pigott, George Morris *food engineering educator, consulting engineer*
Piniella, Louis Victor *professional baseball team manager*
Pitts, Barbara Towle *accountant, painter*
Piven, Peter Anthony *architect, management consultant*
Plotnick, Robert David *educator, economic consultant*
Pocker, Yeshayau *chemistry, biochemistry educator*
Pollack, Gerald Harvey *bioengineering educator*
Pollack, Sylvia Byrne *educator, researcher, counselor*
Porad, Laurie Jo *jewelry company official*
Porter, Stephen Cummings *geologist, educator*
Porter, Walter Thomas, Jr. *bank executive*
Potter, Karl Harrington *philosophy educator*
Prentke, Richard Ottesen *lawyer*
Pressly, Thomas James *history educator*
Price, John Richard *lawyer, law educator*
Prins, David *speech pathologist, educator*
Pritchard, Llewelyn G. *lawyer*
Pusch, William Gerard *lawyer*
Pyke, Ronald *mathematics educator*
Pyle, Kenneth Birger *historian, educator*
Pym, Bruce Michael *lawyer*
Rabinovitch, Benton Seymour *chemist, educator emeritus*
Raible, Peter Spilman *minister*
Raisbeck, James David *engineering company executive*
Ramanathan, Kavasseri Vaidianatha *accounting educator, researcher, consultant*
Ramsey, Paul Glenn *internist*
Ratner, Buddy Dennis *bioengineer, educator*
Ravenholt, Reimert Thorolf *epidemiologist*
Ray, Charles Kendall *retired university dean*
Redman, Eric *lawyer*
Reed, Richard John *retired meteorology educator*
Reinhardt, William Parker *chemical physicist, educator*
Reis, Jean Stevenson *administrative secretary*
Rhines, Peter Broomell *oceanographer, atmospheric scientist*
Rice, Norman B. *mayor*
Riddiford, Lynn Moorhead *zoologist, educator*
Rieke, Paul Victor *lawyer*
Rinearson, Peter Mark *journalist, author, software developer*
Ritter, Daniel Benjamin *lawyer*
Robb, Bruce *former insurance company executive*
Robb, John Wesley *religion educator*
Robertson, Robert Graham Hamish *physicist*
Rodin, Michael F. *lawyer, corporate*
Rosen, Jon Howard *lawyer*
Ross, Russell *pathologist, educator*
Rothstein, Barbara Jacobs *federal judge*
Rubbert, Paul Edward *engineering executive*
Ruckelshaus, William Doyle *investment group executive*
Rummage, Stephen Michael *lawyer*
Russell, Francia *ballet director, educator*
Sale, George Edgar *physician*
Sandman, Irvin W(illis) *lawyer*
Sarason, Irwin G. *psychology educator*
Sateren, Terry *theater technical production*
Saunders, William Lockwood *financial consultant*
Saxberg, Borje Osvald *management educator*
Scafe, Lincoln Robert, Jr. *retired sales executive*
Schall, Lawrence Delano *economics educator, consultant*
Schaller, Joanne F. *nursing consultant*
Schilling, John Albert *surgeon*
Schmidt, Peter Gustav *shipbuilding industry executive*
Schoenfeld, Walter Edwin *manufacturing company executive*
Schulte, Henry Gustave *college administrator*
Scott, John Carlyle *gynecologist, oncologist*
Scribner, Belding Hibbard *medical educator, nephrologist*
Segal, Jack *mathematics educator*
Shepard, Thomas Hill *physician, educator*
Shrontz, Frank Anderson *airplane manufacturing executive*
Shulkin, Jerome *lawyer*
Silbergeld, Jerome Leslie *art historian, educator*
Silver, Michael *school superintendent*
Simcox, Craig Dennis *aeronautical engineer*
Simkin, Peter Anthony *physician, educator*
Singer, Sarah Beth *poet*
Sizemore, Herman Mason, Jr. *newspaper executive*
Skidmore, Donald Earl, Jr. *government official*
Skilling, John Bower *structural and civil engineer*
Sleicher, Charles Albert *chemical engineer*
Smith, Andrew Vaughn *telephone company executive*
Smith, Jeffrey L. (The Frugal Gourmet) *cook, writer*
Smith, Orville Auverne *physiology educator*
Soltys, John Joseph *lawyer*
Spindel, Robert Charles *electrical engineering educator*
Spinrad, Bernard Israel *physicist, educator*
Spitzer, Hugh D. *lawyer*
Springer, Floyd Ladean *architect*
Squires, William Randolph, III *lawyer*
Staheli, Lynn Taylor *pediatric orthopedist, educator*
Stanton, Michael John *newspaper editor*
Staryk, Steven S. *violinist, concertmaster, educator*
Stear, Edwin Byron *corporate executive*
Stearns, Susan Tracey *lighting design company executive, lawyer*
Steers, George W. *lawyer*
Steinberg, Jack *lawyer*
Stenchever, Morton Albert *physician, educator*
Stern, Edward Abraham *physics educator*
Stevens, Clyde Benjamin, Jr. *property manager, retired naval officer*
†Stewart, Thomas J. *wholesale distribution executive*
Stoebuck, William Brees *law educator*
Stolov, Walter Charles *physician, rehabilitation educator, physiatrist*
Stowell, Kent *ballet director*
Strandjord, Paul Edphil *physician, educator*
Strandness, Donald Eugene, Jr. *surgeon*
Stringer, William Jeremy *academic administrator*
Stroup, Elizabeth Faye *librarian*
Stuiver, Minze *geological sciences educator*
Su, Judy Ya Hwa Lin *pharmacologist*
Sugar, Peter Frigyes *historian*
Sullivan, Daniel J. *artistic director*
Sutter, Joseph F. *aeronautical engineer, consultant, retired aircraft company executive*
Swanson, August George *physician, retired association executive*
Swanson, Phillip Dean *neurologist*
Sweeney, David Brian *lawyer*
Szkody, Paula *astronomy educator, researcher*
Taketomi, Susamu *physicist, researcher*
Tallman, Richard C. *lawyer*
Talvi, Ilkka Ilari *violinist*
Tapper, David *pediatric surgeon*
Terrell, W(illiam) Glenn *university president emeritus*
Thiel, Arthur Warren *journalist*
Thomas, David Phillip *forestry educator, college administrator*
Thomas, Edward Donnall *physician, researcher*
Thomas, Karen P. *composer, conductor*
Thompson, Arlene Rita *nursing educator*
Thorne, David W. *lawyer*
Thorne, Frank Leadley *plastic surgeon*
Thornton, Dean Dickson *retired airplane company executive*
Thorson, Lee A. *lawyer*
Thouless, David James *physicist, educator*
Todaro, George Joseph *pathologist*
Tollett, Glenna Belle *accountant, mobile home park operator*
Treiger, Irwin Louis *lawyer*
†Trimpin *artist*
Tucker, Gary Jay *physician, educator*
Tukey, Harold Bradford, Jr. *horticulture educator*
Turner, Wallace L. *reporter*
Turnovsky, Stephen John *economics educator*
Van Citters, Robert Lee *medical educator, physician*
van den Berghe, Pierre Louis *sociologist, anthropologist*
Varanasi, Usha *environmental scientist*
Veblen, John Elvidge *lawyer*
Vesper, Karl Hampton *business and mechanical engineering educator*
Vestal, Josephine Burnet *lawyer*
Voget, Jane J. *city official, lawyer*
Voorhees, John Lloyd *columnist*
Voorhees, Lee R., Jr. *lawyer*
Wagner, Patricia Hamm *lawyer*
Wagoner, David Russell *author, educator*
Waldman, Bart *lawyer*
Walker, Walter Frederick *professional basketball team executive*
Wallerstein, George *astronomy educator*
Wallis, Richard James *lawyer*
Walsh, Kenneth Andrew *biochemist*
Walters, Dennis H. *lawyer*
Warner, Vincent W. *bishop*
Warren, Patricia J. *arts association executive*
Washington, James Winston, Jr. *artist, sculptor*
Webb, Eugene *English language educator*
Wechsler, Mary Heyrman *lawyer*
Weinberg, John Lee *federal judge*
Weissman, Eugene Yehuda *chemical engineer*
Weitkamp, William George *retired nuclear physicist*
Wells, Christopher Brian *lawyer*
Wells, Judee Ann *lawyer*
West, Richard Vincent *art museum official*
Whalen, Jerome Demaris *lawyer*
Whitacre, John *apparel executive*
Whitehead, James Fred, III *lawyer*
Whitford, Joseph P. *lawyer*
Wilets, Lawrence *physics educator*
Williams, J. Vernon *lawyer*
Williams, Robert Walter *physics educator*
Williams, Walter Baker *mortgage banker*
Wilske, Kenneth Ray *internist, rheumatologist, researcher*
Wilson, David Eugene *magistrate judge*
Winn, H. Richard *surgeon*
Winnowski, Thaddeus Richard (Ted Winnowski) *bank executive*
Wolfle, Dael Lee *public affairs educator*
Wood, Stuart Kee *retired engineering manager*
Woodruff, Gene Lowry *nuclear engineer, university dean*
Woods, James Sterrett *toxicologist*
Woods, Nancy Fugate *women's health nurse, educator*
Wooster, Warren S(criver) *marine science educator*
Wott, John Arthur *arboretum and botanical garden executive, horticulture educator*
Wright, Eugene Allen *federal judge*
Wright, Willard Jurey *lawyer*
Yarington, Charles Thomas, Jr. *surgeon, administrator*
Yue, Agnes Kau-Wah *otolaryngologist*
Zehr, Clyde James *church administrator*
Ziadeh, Farhat J. *Middle Eastern studies educator*
Zilly, Thomas Samuel *federal judge*
Zunker, Richard E. *insurance company executive*

### Sequim
Barton, Jay *university administrator, biologist*
Beaton, Roy Howard *retired nuclear industry executive*
Laube, Roger Gustav *retired trust officer, financial consultant*
McMahon, Terrence John *retired foriegn service officer*
Meacham, Charles Harding *government official*
Woodruff, Truman O(wen) *physicist, emeritus educator*

### Shelton
Barnard, Michael Dana *orthopedic surgeon*
Wolbrink, Donald Henry *landscape architect, city planner*

### Shoreline
Freed, Aaron David *architect*
Privat, Jeannette Mary *bank librarian*
Treseler, Kathleen Morrison *retired nursing educator*

### Silverdale
Horn, Thomas Carl *retired banker*
Walske, M(ax) Carl, Jr. *physicist*

### Snohomish
Frohnen, Richard Gene *journalism educator*

### South Bend
Heinz, Roney Allen *civil engineering consultant*

### Spanaway
Campbell, Thomas J. *chiropractor, former legislator*
Loete, Steven Donald *pilot*
Westbrook, T. L. *bishop*

### Spokane
Bakker, Cornelis B. *psychiatrist, educator*
Bender, Betty Wion *librarian*
Benson, Allen B. *chemist, educator, consultant*
Bray, R(obert) Bruce *music educator*
Burr, Robert Lyndon *information services specialist*
Burton, Robert Lyle *accounting firm executive*
Carriker, Robert Charles *history educator*
Cohen, Arnold Norman *gastroenterologist*
Coker, Charlotte Noel *political activist*
Connolly, K. Thomas *lawyer*
Coughlin, Bernard John *university chancellor*
Cowles, William Stacey *publisher*
Dellwo, Dennis A. *state legislator*
Eliassen, Jon Eric *utility company executive*
Evoy, John Joseph *psychology educator*
Fosseen, Neal Randolph *business executive, former banker, former mayor*
Foster, Ruth Mary *dental association administrator*
Fowler, Betty Janmae *dance company director, editor*
Gibson, Melvin Roy *pharmacognosy educator*
Glynn, Edward *college administrator*
Gray, Alfred Orren *journalism educator, communications specialist*
Green, Dale Monte *retired judge*
Harbaugh, Daniel Paul *lawyer*
Hendershot, Carol Miller *physical therapist*
Higgins, Shaun O'Leary *media executive*
Imbrogno, Cynthia *judge*
Johnson, Theodore *physician*
Kafentzis, John Charles *journalist, educator*
Keller, Robert M. *bishop*
Kirschbaum, James Louis *real estate company administrator*
Koegen, Roy Jerome *lawyer*
Kossel, Clifford George *retired philosophy educator, clergyman*
Kunkel, Richard Lester *public radio executive*
Lamp, John Ernest *lawyer*
Lee, Hi Young *physician, acupuncturist*
Lindsay, Donald Parker *former savings bank executive*
Linn, Diana Patricia *elementary education educator*

Matters, Clyde Burns *former college president*
Maus, John Andrew *computer systems engineer*
Mayer, Herbert Carleton, Jr. *computer consultant*
McManus, Patrick Francis *educator, writer*
McWilliams, Edwin Joseph *banker*
Mielke, Clarence Harold, Jr. *hematologist*
Moe, Orville Leroy *racetrack executive*
Murphy, William Schaefer *cardiologist*
Murray, James Michael *librarian, law librarian, legal educator, lawyer*
Nicolai, Eugene Ralph *public relations consultant, editor, writer*
Nielsen, William Fremming *federal judge*
Novak, Terry Lee *public adminstration educator*
Nyman, Carl John, Jr. *university dean and official*
Polley, Harvey Lee *retired missionary and educator*
Quackenbush, Justin Lowe *federal judge*
Richard, Gerald Lawrence *soil scientist*
Robinson, Herbert Henry, III *educator, psychotherapist*
Robinson, William P. *academic administrator, consultant, speaker*
Rowe, Marjorie Douglas *retired social services administrator*
Sayre, Richard Layton *lawyer*
Schlicke, Carl Paul *retired surgeon*
Skylstad, William S. *bishop*
Stackelberg, John Roderick *history educator*
Steele, Karen Dorn *journalist*
Symmes, William Daniel *lawyer*
Terry, Frank Jeffrey *bishop*
Van Sickle, Frederick L. *federal judge*
Vaux, Dora Louise *sperm bank official, consultant*
Wagner, Teresa Ann *business owner*
Weatherhead, Leslie R. *lawyer*
Wirt, Michael James *library director*
Woodard, Alva Abe *business consultant*

### Stevenson
Clausel, Nancy Karen *minister*

### Sumas
Hemry, Larry Harold *former federal agency official, writer*

### Sunnyside
Capener, Regner Alvin *minister, electronics engineer, author, inventor*

### Tacoma
Ames, Kenneth Carl *hydrologist, geology educator*
Arreola, Philip *police officer*
Barcus, Benjamin Franklin *lawyer*
Brevik, J. Albert *communications consultant*
Browning, Christopher R. *historian, educator*
Bryan, Robert J. *federal judge*
Carlson, Frederick Paul *electronics executive*
Champ, Stanley Gordon *scientific company executive*
Cheah, Keong-Chye *psychiatrist*
Chen, Stephen Shau-tsi *psychiatrist, physiologist*
Collier, Richard Bangs *philosopher, foundation executive*
Crisman, Mary Frances Borden *librarian*
Ernst, John Allan *clinical neuropsychologist*
Fetters, Norman Craig, II *banker*
Flick, Gervase Mead *surgeon*
Franklin, William Emery *forest products company executive*
Garner, Carlene Ann *fundraising consultant*
Gordon, Joseph Harold *lawyer*
Graves, Ray *lawyer*
Graybill, David Wesley *chamber of commerce executive*
Gregory, Arthur Stanley *retired chemist*
Guilmet, Glenda Jean *artist*
Habedank, Gary L. *brokerage house executive*
Hansen, Edward Allen *music educator, organist*
Harris, James Martin *architect*
Holman, Kermit Layton *chemical engineer*
Holt, William E. *lawyer*
Hutchings, George Henry *food company executive*
Ingram, Artonyon S. *mental health professional, therapist*
Jungkuntz, Richard Paul *university provost emeritus*
Kaltinick, Paul R. *trust company executive*
King, Gundar Julian *retired university dean*
Lane, Robert Casey *lawyer*
Le Roy, Bruce Murdock *historian*
Licens, Lila Louise *administrative assistant*
Liddle, Alan Curtis *architect*
Maloney, Patsy Loretta *university official, nursing educator*
Maynard, Steven Harry *writer*
Meyer, Richard Schlomer *food company executive*
Miller, Judson Frederick *lawyer, former military officer*
Mohler, Georgia Ann *geriatrics nurse practitioner*
Nance, John Joseph *lawyer, writer, air safety analyst, broadcaster, consultant*
Nazaire, Michel Harry *physician*
Noll, Anna Cecilia *curator*
Odlin, Richard Bingham *retired banker*
Owen, Thomas Walker *banker, broker*
Pierce, Susan Resneck *academic administrator, English educator*
Ragan, Betty Sapp *artist, educator*
Reisberg, Leon Elton *education educator*
Rieke, William Oliver *foundation director, medical educator, former university president*
Rudnick, Rebecca Sophie *lawyer, educator*
Shipman, Keith Bryan *sportscaster*
Smith, Leo Gilbert *hospital administrator*
Steele, Anita Martin (Margaret Anne Martin) *law librarian, legal educator*
Strege, Timothy Melvin *economic consultant*
Tanner, Jack Edward *federal judge*
Taylor, Mary D. *counselor*
Taylor, Peter van Voorhees *advertising and public relations consultant*
Thompson, Ronald Edward *lawyer*
Tonn, Sheri Jeanne *chemistry educator, dean*
Verhey, Joseph William *psychiatrist, educator*
Waldo, James Chandler *lawyer*
Wang, Arthur Ching-li *law educator, lawyer*
Weyerhaeuser, George Hunt *forest products company executive*
Wiegman, Eugene William *minister, former college administrator*
Wold, David C. *bishop*

### Tenino
Orsini, Myrna J. *sculptor, educator*

### Toppenish
Ross, Kathleen Anne *academic administrator*

### University Place
Bourgaize, Robert G. *economist*

### Vancouver
Campbell, Scott *newspaper publishing company executive*
Craven, James Michael *economist, educator*
Dodds, Michael Bruce *lawyer*
Firstenburg, Edward William *banker*
†Fishman, Neill Timothy *medical services administrator*
Graffis, Julie Anne *interior designer, entrepreneur*
Howsley, Richard Thornton *regional government administrator, lawyer*
Hulburt, Lucille Hall *artist, educator*
Kleweno, Gilbert H. *lawyer*
Lollar, Katherine Louise *social worker, therapist*
Mangino, Kristin Mikalson *secondary education educator*
Matlock, John Hudson *science administrator, materials engineer*
Ogden, Daniel Miller, Jr. *government official, educator*
Perlstein, Abraham Phillip *psychiatrist*
Simontacchi, Carol Nadine *nutritionist, retail store executive*
Smith, Milton Ray *computer company executive, lawyer*
Smith, Sam Corry *retired foundation executive, consultant*
Vogel, Ronald Bruce *food products executive*

### Vashon
Biggs, Barry Hugh *lawyer*

### Walla Walla
Carlsen, James Caldwell *musicologist, educator*
Corfield, Timothy Lynn *college rodeo executive, educator*
Cronin, Thomas Edward *academic administrator*
Edwards, Glenn Thomas *history educator*
Hayner, Herman Henry *lawyer*
Jonish, Arley Duane *retired bibliographer*
Perry, Louis Barnes *retired insurance company executive*
Potts, Charles Aaron *management executive, writer*
Stevens, David *economics educator*
Yaple, Henry Mack *library director*

### Washougal
†Davis, Paul Rick *military career officer*

### Wenatchee
Bennett, Grover Bryce *engineering consultant*
Elfving, Don C. *horticulturist, administrator*
Miller, David Eugene *soil scientist, researcher*
Schrader, Lawrence Edwin *plant physiologist, educator*

### Winlock
Brown, Stephan Mark *international fundraising and resource development executive, consultant*

### Woodinville
Pihl, James Melvin *electrical engineer*
Sanders, Richard Kinard *actor*

### Woodland
Brown, Alan Johnson *chemicals executive*

### Yakima
Aldridge, Geanie Black *bank executive*
Bruenn, Ronald Sherman *financial company executive*
Cleary, Sean Fulton *radiation oncologist*
Grandy, Jay Franklin *fruit processing executive*
Hovis, James Brunton *federal judge*
Jongeward, George Ronald *retired systems analyst*
McDonald, Alan Angus *federal judge*
Meshke, George Lewis *drama and humanities educator*
Newland, Ruth Laura *small business owner*
Newstead, Robert Richard *urologist*
Shuman, Mark Samuel *environmental and electroanalytical chemistry educator*
Simonson, Susan Kay *hospital administrator*
Suko, Lonny Ray *judge*
Sveinsson, Johannes *former city and county government official*
Tanner, Patricia Ruth *gerontology nurse*
Vujovic, Mary Jane *education and employment training planner*
Wright, J(ames) Lawrence *lawyer*

## WEST VIRGINIA

### Athens
†Beasley, Jerry L. *academic administrator*
Marsh, Joseph Franklin, Jr. *emeritus college president, educational consultant*

### Beaver
Baligar, Virupax C. *research soil scientist*
Voigt, Paul Warren *research geneticist*

### Beckley
Dinh, Anthony Tung *internist*
Hallanan, Elizabeth V. *senior federal judge*
Thompson, Novella Woodrum *college administrator, psychotherapist*

### Berkeley Springs
Weinberger, Leon Walter *sanitary engineer*

### Bethany
Cummins, Delmer Duane *academic administrator, historian*
Krug, John Carleton (Tony Krug) *college administrator, library consultant*
Sandercox, Robert Allen *college official, clergyman*

### Bluefield
Barsi, Louis Michael *college dean*
Davenport, Dorothy Dean *nurse*
Evans, Wayne Lewis *lawyer*
Faber, David Alan *federal judge*
Feinberg, Mary Stanley *judge*
Kantor, Isaac Norris *lawyer*
Scott, Nina Ogle *nurse*

### Charles Town
McDonald, Angus Wheeler *farmer*

### Charleston
Arrington, Carolyn Ruth *school system administrator*
Bennett, Robert Menzies *retired gas pipeline company executive*
Betts, Rebecca A. *lawyer*
Bhasin, Madan Mohan *chemical research scientist*
Boland, James Pius *surgeon, educator*
Brown, James Knight *lawyer*
Chapman, John Andrew *association executive*
Chilton, Elizabeth Easley Early *newspaper executive*
Clark, Hanley C. *state insurance commissioner*
Cleckley, Franklin D. *judge*
Coe, Pam *educational researcher*
Conlin, Thomas (Byrd) *conductor*
Copenhaver, John Thomas, Jr. *federal judge*
Davis, James Hornor, III *lawyer*
Deitzler, Harry G. *lawyer*
Douglass, Gus Ruben *state agency administrator*
Gage, Charles Quincey *lawyer*
Goodwin, Claude Elbert *lawyer, former gas utility executive*
Goodwin, Phillip Hugh *hospital administrator*
Grimes, Richard Stuart *editor, writer*
Gunnoe, Nancy Lavenia *food executive, artist*
Haden, Charles H., II *federal judge*
Hall, Kenneth Keller *federal judge*
Hambrick, Arlene *school system administrator, minister*
Haught, James Albert, Jr. *journalist, newspaper editor, author*
Hechler, Ken *state official, former congressman, political science educator, author*
Heck, Albert Frank *neurologist*
Ives, Samuel Clifton *minister*
Keith, Steven Jeffrey *newspaper editor*
Kizer, John Oscar *lawyer*
Knapp, Dennis Raymond *federal judge*
Koleske, Joseph Victor *chemical engineer, consultant*
Krotseng, Marsha Van Dyke *higher education administrator*
Lamb, Patrick John *research associate, accountant*
Lipton, Allen David *retail executive*
Maddox, Timothy Dwain *natural gas company manager*
Manning, Charles W. *academic administrator*
Marockie, Henry R. *state school system administrator*
McClaugherty, John Lewis *lawyer*
Mc Gee, John Frampton *communications company executive*
Mc Graw, Darrell Vivian, Jr. *state attorney general*
Melton, G. Kemp *mayor*
Michael, M. Blane *federal judge*
Michelson, Gail Ida *lawyer*
Moore, Jeanne *arts educator and administrator*
Neely, Richard *lawyer*
Recht, Arthur *judge*
Scott, Olof Henderson, Jr. *priest*
Seiber, William Joseph *financial and insurance consultant*
Stacy, Charles Brecknock *lawyer*
Stephenson, Ann Watz *artist*
Sterling, Donald Eugene *retired civil engineer*
Tomblin, Earl Ray *state official*
Trupo, Frank J. *plastic surgeon*
Underwood, Cecil H. *governor, company executive*
Victorson, Michael Bruce *lawyer*
Welch, Edwin Hugh *academic administrator*
Whittington, Bernard Wiley *electrical engineer, consultant*
Workman, Margaret Lee *state supreme court justice, chief justice*
Zak, Robert Joseph *lawyer*

### Clarksburg
Highland, Cecil Blaine, Jr. *newspaper publisher, lawyer, banker*
Keeley, Irene Patricia Murphy *federal judge*
Murphy, Jeanne Ann *parochial school educator*
Ona-Sarino, Milagros Felix *physician, pathologist*
Sarino, Edgardo Formantes *physician*

### Clay
Gillespie, Larry *secondary school principal*

### Dellslow
Allamong, Betty D. *academic administrator*

### Dunbar
Russell, James Alvin, Jr. *college administrator*

### Elkins
Khatter, Prithipal Singh *radiologist*
MacConkey, Dorothy I. *academic administrator*
Maxwell, Robert Earl *federal judge*
Payne, Gloria Marquette *business educator*
Spears, Jae *state legislator*

### Elkview
Banonis, Edward Joseph *gas industry executive*

### Fairmont
Brizendine, Anthony Lewis *civil engineering educator*
Hardway, Wendell Gary *former college president*
Stalder, Florence Lucille *secondary education educator*
Swiger, Elizabeth Davis *chemistry educator*

### Falling Waters
Schellhaas, Linda Jean *toxicologist, consultant*
Schellhaas, Robert Wesley *counselor, songwriter, musician*

### Glen Jean
Beverly, Laura Elizabeth *special education educator*

### Glenville
Tubesing, Richard Lee *library director*

### Greenville
Warner, Kenneth Wilson, Jr. *editor, association publications executive*

### Hamlin
Barrett, Brian Lee *minister, evangelist*

### Harpers Ferry
Blue, Kathy Jo *elementary school educator*
Startzell, David N. *sports association executive*

### Hillsboro
Pierce, William Luther *association executive, writer*

### Huntington
Bagley, Charles Frank, III *lawyer*
Barenklau, Keith Edward *safety services company executive*
Bowdler, Anthony John *physician, educator*
Cocke, William Marvin, Jr. *plastic surgeon, educator*
deBarbadillo, John Joseph *metallurgist, management executive*
Evers, Martin Louis *internist*
Gould, Alan Brant *academic administrator*
Hayes, Robert Bruce *former college president, educator*
Hooper, James William *educator*
Hubbard, John Lewis *chemist, educator, researcher*
Justice, Franklin Pierce, Jr. *oil company executive*
Kent, Calvin Albert *university administrator*
Mason, Bert E. *podiatrist*
McKown, Charles H. *dean*
Morabito, Rocco Anthony *urologist*
Mufson, Maurice Albert *physician, educator*
Reynolds, Marshall Truman *printing company executive*
St. Clair, James William *lawyer*

### Hurricane
Nance, Martha McGhee *rehabilitation nurse*

### Institute
DasSarma, Basudeb *chemistry educator*
Scott, John Edward *librarian*
Wohl, David *humanities educator, college dean-theatre director*

### Inwood
Cloyd, Helen Mary *accountant, educator*

### Kearneysville
Biggs, Alan Richard *plant pathologist, educator*
Le Roy, L. David *journalist*

### Kingwood
Rock, Gail Ann *obstetrical/gynecological nurse*

### Lahmansville
Snyder, Robert Martin *agriculture consultant, retired government official*

### Lewisburg
Byrd, Julie Anderson *nurse*
Ford, Richard Edmond *lawyer*
Hooper, Anne Dodge *pathologist, educator*
Seifer, Judith Huffman *sex therapist, educator*
Willard, Ralph Lawrence *surgery educator, physician, former college president*

### Mannington
Schumacher, Theresa Rose *singer, musician*

### Martinsburg
†Aitken, Percy W. *cardiologist*
Ayers, Anne Louise *small business owner, retired education specialist, consultant*
Bovey, Lisa Dawn *special education educator*
†Farrar, John Thruston *health facility adminstrator*
Malin, Howard Gerald *podiatrist*
Rice, Lacy I., Jr. *lawyer*
Yoe, Harry Warner *retired agricultural economist*

### Milton
Roebuck, Judith Lynn *secondary school educator*

### Montgomery
Keenan, Mary Elizabeth *vocational education educator*

### Morgantown
Adler, Lawrence *mining engineering consultant*
Albrink, Margaret Joralemon *medical educator*
Bajura, Richard Albert *university administrator, engineering educator*
Barba, Roberta Ashburn *retired social worker*
Beattie, Diana Scott *biochemistry educator*
Biddington, William Robert *university administrator, dental educator*
Blaydes, Sophia Boyatzies *English language educator*
Brooks, Dana D. *dean*
Bucklew, Neil S. *educator, past university president*
Butcher, Donald Franklin *statistics educator, computer scientist*
Butcher, Fred R. *biochemistry educator, university administrator*
Cochrane, Robert Lowe *biologist*
Cogley, Allen C. *mechanical engineering educator, administrator*
Dadyburjor, Dady B. *chemical engineering educator, researcher*
D'Alessandri, Robert M. *dean*
Davis, Leonard McCutchan *speech educator*
De Vore, Paul Warren *technology educator*
Drvar, Margaret Adams *vocational education educator*
Ducatman, Alan Marc *physician*
Eck, Ronald Warren *civil engineer, educator*
Fisher, John Welton, II *law educator, magistrate judge, university official*
Fleming, William Wright, Jr. *pharmacology educator*
Fodor, Gábor Béla *chemistry educator, researcher*
Friedland, Billie Louise *former human services administrator*
Friedline, John Allen *pathologist*
Fusco, Andrew G. *lawyer*
Gagliano, Frank Joseph *playwright*
Gelhausen, Marvin Duane *editor*
Gladfelter, Wilbert Eugene *physiology educator*
Guthrie, Hugh Delmar *chemical engineer*
†Haggett, Rosemary R. *dean*
Hill, Ronald Charles *surgeon, educator*
Holtan, Boyd DeVere *mathematics educator*
Iammarino, Richard Michael *pathologist, student support services director*
Jackson, Ruth Moore *academic administrator*
Keller, Edward Clarence, Jr. *foundation executive, ecologist, statistician, geneticist, educator*
Kent, James A. *consulting chemical engineer, author, consultant*
Klein, Ronald Lloyd *electrical engineer, educator*
Mansmann, Paris Taylor *medical educator*
Martin, James Douglas *neurologist*
Maxwell, Robert Haworth *agriculture educator, university administrator*

McAvoy, Rogers *educational psychology educator, consultant*
Meitzen, Manfred Otto *religious studies educator*
Morris, William Otis, Jr. *lawyer, educator, author*
Nath, Joginder *genetics and biology educator, researcher*
Overman, Dennis Orton *anatomist, educator*
Peterson, Sophia *international studies educator*
Pyles, Rodney Allen *archivist, county official*
Reese, Hayne Waring *psychologist*
Schroder, John L., Jr. *retired mining engineer*
Seehra, Mohindar Singh *physics educator, researcher*
Singer, Armand Edwards *foreign language educator*
Stewart, Guy Harry *university dean emeritus, journalism educator*
Vest, Marvin Lewis *mathematical educator*
Warden, Herbert Edgar *surgeon, educator*
Witt, Tom *economics researcher, educator*

### Mount Gay
Earnest, Carmella Lynn *art educator, artist*

### Mullens
Lee, Debora Ann *elementary school educator, reading specialist*

### Nitro
Lucas, Panola *elementary education educator*
Magaw, Roger Wayne *construction company executive*

### Parkersburg
Brum, Brenda *state legislator, librarian*
Crooks, Dorena May (Dee Crooks) *administrative assistant, social worker*
Fahlgren, H(erbert) Smoot *advertising agency executive*
Meadows, Lois Annette *elementary education educator*
Miller, Steven Douglas *federal agency executive*
Poling, Kermit William *minister*
Powell, Eric Karlton *lawyer, researcher*
Wakley, James Turner *manufacturing company executive*

### Paw Paw
Palmer, Robert Jeffrey *special education educator*

### Philippi
Shearer, Richard Eugene *educational consultant*

### Pineville
Maxey, Nigel Aaron *publisher*

### Point Pleasant
Vance, Thomas Ray *engineer*

### Pratt
Terrell-McDaniel, Robin F. *cardiac rehabilitation and critical care nurse*

### Princeton
de la Piedra, Jorge *orthopedic surgeon*
†Spracher, John C. *banking executive*

### Rainelle
Scott, Pamela Moyers *physician assistant*

### Ridgeley
Hammond, Anna Josephine *nurse practitioner*
Unger, Roberta Marie *special education educator*

### Saint Albans
Alderson, Gloria Frances Dale *rehabilitation specialist*
McKittrick, William David Parrish *lawyer*
Richards, John Dale *sociology and philosophy educator, counselor*

### Salem
Frasure, Carl Maynard *political science educator*
Ohl, Ronald Edward *academic administrator*
Raad, Virginia *pianist, lecturer*

### Shady Spring
Reed, Cathy Lorraine *elementary education educator*

### Shepherdstown
Elliott, Jean Ann *library administrator*
Hendricks, Ida Elizabeth *mathematics educator*
Snyder, Joseph John *editor, historian, author, lecturer, consultant*
Strasser, William Carl, Jr. *retired college president, educator*
Wilson, Miriam Janet Williams *publishing executive*

### South Charleston
Nielsen, Kenneth Andrew *chemical engineer*

### Spencer
Parker, Theresa Ann *special education educator*

### Sprague
Rhoades, Marye Frances *paralegal*

### Summersville
Yeager, Charles William *lawyer, newspaper publisher*

### Summit Point
Taylor, Harold Allen, Jr. *industrial mineral marketing consultant*

### Union
Sprouse, James Marshall *retired federal judge*

### Washington
Pace, John Edward, III *chemical engineer*

### Weirton
Adamczyk, Edmond David *metallurgical engineer*
Robinson, Charles Warren *controller*

### Wellsburg
Wellman, Gerald Edwin, Jr. *safety and fire inspector*

### West Liberty
Hunter, John Alfred *English educator*

### Weston
Sumpter, Sonja Kay *elementary school educator*

### Westover
Trythall, Harry Gilbert *music educator, composer*

### Wheeling
Bontos, George Emmanuel *physician*
Campbell, Clyde Del *academic administrator*
Exley, Ben, III *pharmaceutical company executive*
Good, Laurance Frederic *company executive*
Heceta, Estherbelle Aguilar *anesthesiologist*
Hughes, Mary Elizabeth *interior designer*
Kirkpatrick, Forrest Hunter *management consultant*
Marquart, Christopher Louis *neurosurgeon*
Nutting, George Ogden *newspaper publisher*
Phillips, John Davisson *retired lawyer*
Phillis, Marilyn Hughey *artist*
Ritz, Lorraine Isaacs *nursing administrator*
Schmitt, Bernard W. *bishop*
Stidd, Linda Marie *rehabilitation nurse*
Urval, Krishna Raj *health facility administrator, educator*
Welker, William Andrew *reading specialist*
Wilmoth, William David *prosecutor*

### White Sulphur Springs
Kappa, Margaret McCaffrey *resort hotel consultant*

### Williamson
Shaw, Laurie Jo *grant project director*

## WISCONSIN

### Algoma
Golomski, William Arthur *consulting company executive*

### Altoona
James, Henry Thomas *former foundation executive, educator*
Powell, Christopher Robert *systems engineer/ manager, computer scientist*

### Amery
Mickelson, Arnold Rust *consultant, religious denominational official*

### Appleton
Amm, Sophia J. *artist, educator*
Barlow, F(rank) John *mechanical contracting company executive*
Boldt, Oscar Charles *construction company executive*
†Boren, Clark Henry, Jr. *general and vascular surgeon*
Chaney, William Albert *historian, educator*
†Crowley, Geoffrey T. *airline executive*
Froehlich, Harold Vernon *judge, former congressman*
Goldgar, Bertrand Alvin *literary historian, educator*
Gunderson, Richard L. *insurance company executive*
Herscher, Susan Kay *English language educator*
Kolbe-Mims, Margie Loretta *safety and health engineer*
Luther, Thomas William *physician*
McManus, John Francis *association executive, writer*
Murray, John Daniel *lawyer*
Petinga, Charles Michael *business executive*
Rankin, Arthur David *paper company executive*
Spiegelberg, Harry Lester *retired paper products company executive*
Suarez, Louis A. *cardiothoracic surgeon*
Van den Akker, Johannes Archibald *physicist*
Warch, Richard *academic administrator*

### Argyle
Daley, Ron (Ronald) Eugene (Ron ) *playwright, poet, director, producer*

### Athelstane
Outcalt, David Lewis *academic administrator, mathematician, educator*

### Baraboo
Aderhold, Louise Kathryn *art educator*

### Bayfield
Gallinat, Michael Paul *fisheries biologist*
Wilhelm, Sister Phyllis *principal*

### Beaver Dam
Butterbrodt, John Ervin *real estate executive*

### Belgium
Murphy, Greta Werwath *retired academic administrator*
Slater, John Greenleaf *financial consultant*

### Beloit
Davis, Harry Rex *political science educator*
Ferrall, Victor Eugene, Jr. *college administrator, lawyer*
Gates, Crawford Marion *conductor, composer*
Hendricks, Kenneth *wholesale distribution executive*
Melvin, Charles Alfred, III *superintendent of schools*
Simon, Michael Alexander *photographer, educator*

### Brodhead
O'Neil, J(ames) Peter *elementary education educator, computer software designer*

### Brookfield
Corby, Francis Michael, Jr. *manufacturing company executive*
Curfman, Floyd Edwin *engineering educator, retired*
DeLuca, Donald Paul *manufacturing company executive*
Gradeless, Donald Eugene *secondary education educator*
Grove, Richard Charles *power tool company executive*
Hardman, Harold Francis *pharmacology educator*
Jenkins, William Atwell *university chancellor*
Kraut, Joanne Lenora *computer programmer, analyst*
Lessiter, Frank Donald *magazine editor*
†Nickerson, Greg *public relations executive*
Payne, Howard James *insurance company executive*
Roder, Ronald Ernest *accountant*
Trytek, David Douglas *insurance company executive*

Welnetz, David Charles *human resources executive*
Zander, Gaillienne Glashow *psychologist*

### Burlington
Oestmann, Mary Jane *retired senior radiation specialist*

### Cable
MacCarty, Collin Stewart *neurosurgeon*

### Cedarburg
Clark, Harry Wilber *church administrator*
Hazelwood, John A. *lawyer*
Mielke, Jon Alan *elementary school administrator*
Schaefer, Gordon Emory *food company executive*
Steffens, Donna Irene *gifted and talented education coordinator*

### Chippewa Falls
Copeland, Christine Susan *therapist*

### Darien
Miller, Malcolm Henry *manufacturing sales executive, real estate developer*

### De Pere
Manion, Thomas A. *college president*
Ngo, Paul Y.L. *psychology educator*
Schaupp, Joan Pomprowitz *trucking company executive, writer*

### Delavan
Armstrong, Kevin William *marketing executive, researcher*
Nichols, Greg Mark *systems analyst*

### Dodgeville
Fry, David Francis *computing educator*

### Eagle River
Nieuwendorp, Judy Lynell *special education educator*

### Eau Claire
Davidson, John Kenneth, Sr. *sociologist, educator, researcher, author, consultant*
Dick, Raymond Dale *psychology educator*
Dunlap, William Phillip *education educator*
Larson, Brian Foix *architect*
Menard, John R. *lumber company executive*
Patterson, Donald Lee *music educator*
Richards, Jerry Lee *academic administrator, religious educator*
Schenk, Quentin Frederick *retired social work educator, mayor*
Schnack, Larry Gene *university chancellor*
Thompson, Glenn Judean *library science educator*
Thompson, Lynn Renee *chiropractor*
Wantland, William Charles *bishop, lawyer*
Weil, D(onald) Wallace *business administration educator*

### Edgerton
Peck, David Blackman *electrical engineer*

### Elkhorn
Dunn, Walter Scott, Jr. *writer, former museum director, consultant*
Head, Henry Buchen *physician*
Reinke, Doris Marie *retired elementary education educator*
Sweet, Lowell Elwin *lawyer*

### Ellison Bay
MacKinney, Arthur Clinton, Jr. *retired university official, psychologist*

### Elm Grove
Barth, Karl Luther *retired seminary president*
Gorske, Robert Herman *retired lawyer*
Halvorsen, Morrie Edward *trade association administrator*
Headlee, Raymond *psychoanalyst, educator*

### Elroy
Gavin, Joan Elaine *special education educator*

### Exeland
Engelhardt-Alvarez, Madeline *retired preschool administrator*

### Ferryville
Tedeschi, John Alfred *historian, librarian*

### Fish Creek
Abegg, Martin Gerald *retired university president*
Henke, Robert John *lawyer, mediator, consultant, engineer*

### Fond Du Lac
Bespalec, Dale Anthony *clinical psychologist*
Chamberlain, Robert Glenn *retired tool manfacturing executive*
Hayes, Elizabeth Lamb *biology educaotr*
Henken, Willard John *retired university dean*
Ingle, Sud Ranganath *management consultant*
Kaufman, Harvey Isidore *neuropsychology consultant*
Lambert, Eugene Kent *oncologist, hematologist*
Treffert, Darold Allen *psychiatrist, author, hospital director*

### Fontana
Kummer, Daniel William *insurance executive*

### Fort Atkinson
Albaugh, John Charles *hospital executive*
Knox, William David *publishing company executive*
Meyer, Eugene Carlton *retired editor*
Nesbitt, Arthur Wallace *mail order and manufacturing executive*
Sager, Donald Jack *publisher, former librarian*

### Frederic
Rudell, Milton Wesley *aerospace engineer*

### Fredonia
Diesem, John Lawrence *business executive*

### Germantown
Statkus, Jerome Francis *lawyer*

### Gleason
Raash, Kathleen Forecki *artist*

### Glendale
Moeser, Elliott *principal*

### Glidden
Palecek, Sandra Marie *reading education specialist*

### Green Bay
Banks, Robert J. *bishop*
†Bollom, Daniel A. *energy executive*
Bush, Robert G. *food service executive*
Butler, Robert Andrews *clinical psychologist*
Daley, Arthur James *retired magazine publisher*
Favre, Brett Lorenzo *professional football player*
Finesilver, Alan George *rheumatologist*
Geisendorfer, James Vernon *author*
Green, Mark Andrew *state legislator, lawyer*
Harlan, Robert Ernest *professional football team executive*
Heaster, Arlene L. *chemical engineer*
Hempel, Kathleen Jane *paper company executive*
Holmgren, Mike *professional football coach*
Kress, George F. *packaging company executive*
Kress, William F. *manufacturing company executive*
Kuehne, Carl W. *food products executive*
Martens, Lyle Charles *state education administrator*
McIntosh, Elaine Virginia *nutrition educator*
Meng, Jack *food products executive*
Olson, James Richard *transportation company executive*
Parkinson, Ethelyn Minerva *author*
Poppenhagen, Ronald William *newspaper editor, publishing executive*
Schneider, Donald J. *trucking company executive*
Shebesta, Lynn Marie *school administrator*
Swetlik, William Philip *orthodontist*
Vesta, Richard V. *meat packing company executive*
†Weyers, Larry L. *energy executive*
White, Reggie (Reginald Howard White) *professional football player*
Zemke, William A. *farm management educator*

### Greendale
†Kuhn, Roseann *sports association administrator*
Tucker, William Thomas, III *computer software company executive*

### Greenfield
Neal, Jon C(harles) *accountant, consultant*

### Greenwood
Kern-Ystad, Carol Rae *special education educator*

### Hales Corners
Kuwayama, S. Paul *physician, allergist, immunologist*
Michalski, (Żurowski) Wacław *adult education educator*

### Hartford
Babbitt, Donald Patrick *radiologist*

### Hartland
Stamsta, Jean F. *artist*
Wilson, Peter Michael *insurance company executive*

### Hollandale
Myers, Frances *artist*

### Hurley
Nicholls, Thomas Maurice *business owner*

### Iola
Krause, Chester Lee *publishing company executive*
Mishler, Clifford Leslie *publisher*
Rulau, Russell *numismatist, consultant*

### Janesville
Detert-Moriarty, Judith Anne *graphic artist, civic activist*
Fitzgerald, James Francis *cable television executive*
Steil, George Kenneth, Sr. *lawyer*
Wood, Wayne W. *state legislator*

### Jefferson
Morgan, Gaylin F. *public realtions executive*

### Juneau
Carpenter, David Erwin *county planner*
Fitzgerald, Scott *state legislator*

### Kaukauna
Janssen, Gail Edwin *banking executive*

### Kenosha
Adler, Seymour Jack *social services administrator*
Baker, Douglas Finley *library director*
Campbell, F(enton) Gregory *college administrator, historian*
Grover, Robert Lawrence *tool company executive*
Huml, Donald Scott *manufacturing company executive*
Infusino, Achille Francis *construction company executive*
Kolb, Vera M. *chemistry educator*
Levis, Richard George *middle school educator*
Morrone, Frank *electronic manufacturing executive*
Potente, Eugene, Jr. *interior designer*
Schultz, Clarence John *minister*
Smith, Eleanor Jane *university chancellor*
Steigerwaldt, Donna Wolf *clothing manufacturing company executive*
Tielke, James Clemens *retail and manufacturing management consultant*
Zuhlke, Marybeth *elementary school curriculum consultant, educator*

### Kohler
Brands, Robert Franciscus *marketing executive*
Kohler, Herbert Vollrath, Jr. *diversified manufacturing company executive*

### La Crosse
Anderson, Mary Ann *hospital nursing administrator*
Bubar, Joseph Bedell, Jr. *church official*
Corser, David Hewson *pediatrician*

Gelatt, Charles Daniel *manufacturing company executive*
Klos, Jerome John *lawyer*
Larson, April Ulring *bishop*
Lindesmith, Larry Alan *physician, administrator*
Medland, William James *college president*
Morehouse, Richard Edward *psychology educator*
Nix, Edmund Alfred *lawyer*
Novotney, Donald Francis *superintendent of schools*
Paul, John Joseph *bishop*
Rausch, Joan Mary *art historian*
Rozelle, Lee Theodore *physical chemist*
Sleik, Thomas Scott *lawyer*
Webster, Stephen Burtis *physician, educator*

**Lake Geneva**
Braden, Berwyn Bartow *lawyer*
O'Hare, Linda Parsons *management consultant*
Weed, Edward Reilly *marketing executive*

**Lake Nebagamon**
Meyer, Karl William *retired university president*

**Lancaster**
Johnson, Hal Harold Gustav *marketing educator emeritus*

**Little Chute**
Rice, Ferill Jeane *writer, civic worker*

**Lodi**
Schereck, William John *retired historian, consultant*

**Madison**
Abrahamson, Shirley Schlanger *state supreme court justice*
Adler, Julius *biochemist, biologist, educator*
Albert, Daniel Myron *ophthalmologist, educator*
Aldag, Ramon John *management and organization educator*
Ammerman, Robert Ray *philosopher, educator*
Anderson, Louis Wilmer, Jr. *physicist, educator*
Anderson, Michael Steven *lawyer*
Anderson, Odin Waldemar *sociologist, educator*
Andreano, Ralph Louis *economist, educator*
Armstrong, Gregory Davenport *arboretum administrator*
Askey, Richard Allen *mathematician*
Atkinson, Richard Lee, Jr. *internal medicine educator*
Bablitch, William A. *state supreme court justice*
Baldwin, Gordon Brewster *lawyer, educator*
Baldwin, Robert Edward *economics educator*
Barger, Vernon Duane *physicist, educator*
Barish, Lawrence Stephen *nonpartisan legislative staff administrator*
Barnes, Robert F. *agronomist*
Barnhill, Charles Joseph, Jr. *lawyer*
Barnick, Helen *retired judicial clerk*
Baron, Alma Fay S. *management educator*
Barr, Jim, III *telecommunications company executive*
Barrows, Richard Lee *economics educator, academic administrator*
Bartell, Jeffrey Bruce *lawyer*
Bass, Paul *pharmacology educator*
Beachley, Norman Henry *mechanical engineer, educator*
Beck, Anatole *mathematician, educator*
Beck, Stanley Dwight *retired entomology educator, researcher*
Becker, David *artist, educator*
Bell/Jackson, Marianne Jeanne *elementary education educator*
Bennett, Kenneth Alan *biological anthropologist*
Benson, John T. *state agency administrator*
Bentley, Charles Raymond *geophysics educator*
Berg, William James *French language educator, writer, translator*
Bernstine, Daniel O'Neal *law educator, university dean*
Berthouex, Paul Mac *civil and environmental engineer, educator*
Beyer-Mears, Annette *physiologist*
Bird, Robert Byron *chemical engineering educator, author*
Bisgard, Gerald Edwin *biosciences educator, researcher*
Bloodworth, J(ames) M(organ) Bartow, Jr. *physician, educator*
Bochert, Linda H. *lawyer*
Bogue, Allan G. *history educator*
Bohnhoff, David Roy *agricultural engineer, educator*
Botez, Dan *physicist*
Boutwell, Roswell Knight *oncology educator*
Boyle, William Charles *civil engineering educator*
Brembeck, Winston Lamont *retired speech communication educator*
Bremer, Howard Walter *consulting patenting and licensing lawyer*
Bretherton, Francis P. *atmospheric and oceanic sciences educator*
Brock, Thomas Dale *microbiology educator*
Brock, William Allen, III *economics educator, consultant*
Bromley, Daniel Wood *economics educator, consultant*
Brown, Arnold Lanehart, Jr. *pathologist, educator, university dean*
Bruhn, Hjalmar Diehl *retired agricultural engineer, educator*
Bryson, Reid Allen *earth sciences educator*
Bubenzer, Gary Dean *agricultural engineering educator, researcher*
Bugge, Lawrence John *lawyer*
Bula, Raymond J. *agronomist*
Bullock, William Henry *bishop*
Bunge, Charles Albert *library science educator*
Burgess, James Edward *newspaper publisher, executive*
Burgess, Richard Ray *oncology educator, molecular biology researcher, biotechnology consultant*
Burke, Brian B. *state senator, lawyer*
Burkholder, Wendell Eugene *retired entomology educator, researcher*
Burns, Elizabeth Murphy *media executive*
Burris, Robert Harza *biochemist, educator*
Busby, Edward Oliver *retired dean*
Caldwell, Barrett Scott *industrial engineering educator*
Carbon, Max William *nuclear engineering educator*
Carbone, Paul Peter *oncologist, educator, administrator*
Cassens, Robert Gene *food scientist*
Cassidy, Frederic Gomes *humanities educator*
Cassinelli, Joseph Patrick *astronomy educator*
Chang, Y. Austin *materials engineer, educator*

Chapman, Loren J. *psychology educator*
Chow, Tse-Tsung *foreign language and literature educator, author, poet*
Christensen, Nikolas Ivan *geophysicist, educator*
Churchwell, Edward Bruce *astronomer, educator*
Ciplijauskaite, Birute *humanities educator*
Clark, David Leigh *marine geologist, educator*
Clay, Clarence Samuel *acoustical oceanographer*
Cleland, W(illiam) Wallace *biochemistry educator*
Coberly, Camden Arthur *chemical engineering educator*
Coe, Christopher Lane *psychology researcher*
Cohen, Bernard Cecil *political scientist, educator*
Cohen, Marcus *allergist*
Colás, Antonio Espada *medical educator*
Colescott, Warrington Wickham *artist, printmaker, educator*
Connors, Kenneth Antonio *retired chemistry educator*
Converse, James Clarence *agricultural engineering educator*
Cornwell, Charles Daniel *physical chemist, educator*
Crabb, Barbara Brandriff *federal judge*
Craddock, (John) Campbell *geologist, educator*
Crandall, Lee Walter *civil and structural engineer*
Cronin, Patti Adrienne Wright *state agency administrator*
Cronon, E(dmund) David, Jr. *history educator, historian*
Cronon, William *history educator*
Culbertson, John Mathew *economist, educator*
Curry, Robert Lee *lawyer*
Curtiss, Charles Francis *chemist, educator*
Daie, Jaleh *scientist, educator*
Darling, Alberta Statkus *state legislator, marketing executive, former art museum executive*
Davis, Erroll Brown, Jr. *utility executive*
Davis, Richard *musician, music educator*
Day, Roland Bernard *retired chief justice state supreme court*
de Boor, Carl *mathematician*
Deininger, David George *judge*
De Main, John *conductor, music director*
Dembo, Lawrence Sanford *English educator*
Dembski, Stephen Michael *composer, university music composition professor*
DeMets, David L. *medical educator, biomedical researcher*
DeNovo, John August *history educator*
Denton, Frank M. *newspaper editor*
Derzon, Gordon M. *hospital administrator*
Deutsch, Harold Francis *biochemist, researcher, educator*
DeVries, Marvin Frank *mechanical engineering educator*
DeWerd, Larry Albert *medical physicist, educator*
Dick, Elliot Colter *virologist, epidemiologist, educator*
Dietmeyer, Donald Leo *electrical engineer*
Dodson, Vernon Nathan *physician, educator*
Dott, Robert Henry, Jr. *geologist, educator*
Downs, Donald Alexander, Jr. *political scientist, educator*
Doyle, James E(dward) *state attorney general*
Draper, Norman Richard *statistician, educator*
Duffie, John Atwater *chemical engineer, educator*
Dunham, Michael Herman *managed care executive*
Dunwoody, Sharon Lee *journalism and communications educator*
DuRose, Stanley Charles, Jr. *insurance executive*
Earl, Anthony Scully *former governor of Wisconsin, lawyer*
Easterday, Bernard Carlyle *veterinary medicine educator*
Ebben, James Adrian *college president*
Ediger, Mark D. *chemistry educator*
Eisinger, Peter K(endall) *political science educator*
Ellis, Arthur Baron *chemist, educator*
Emmert, Gilbert Arthur *engineer, educator*
Enslin, Jon S. *bishop*
Epstein, William *experimental psychologist*
Eriksson, Larry John *electrical engineer*
Evanson, Elizabeth Moss *editor*
Evenson, Merle Armin *chemist, educator*
Evert, Ray Franklin *botany educator*
Fahien, Leonard August *physician, educator*
Farrar, Thomas C. *chemist, educator*
Farrell, Philip M. *physician, educator, researcher*
Farrow, Margaret Ann *state legislator*
Felstehausen, Herman Henry *natural resources-land planning educator*
Felten, Edward Joseph *business executive accountant*
Fennema, Owen Richard *food chemistry educator*
Ferry, John Douglass *retired chemist, educator*
Fiedler, Patrick James *circuit court judge*
Field, Henry Augustus, Jr. *lawyer*
Finman, Ted *lawyer, educator*
Fitchen, Allen Nelson *publisher*
Fleischman, Stephen *art center director*
Foell, Wesley Kay *engineer, energy and environmental scientist, educator, consultant*
Ford, Charles Nathaniel *otolaryngologist, educator*
Forster, Francis Michael *physician, educator*
Foster, George William, Jr. *lawyer, educator*
Fowler, Barbara Hughes *classics educator*
Fox, Michael Vass *Hebrew educator, rabbi*
Frautschi, Walter Albert *contract and publications printing company executive*
Freudenburg, William R. *sociology educator*
Fritz, Bruce Morrell *photographer*
Fry, William Frederick *physics educator*
Frykenberg, Robert Eric *historian*
Garner, Jac Buford *management executive*
Garver, Thomas Haskell *curator, art consultant, writer*
Gavin, Mary Jane *medical, surgical nurse*
Gehl, Eugene O. *power company executive, lawyer*
Gilboe, David Dougherty *physiology educator*
Glesner, Richard Charles *lawyer*
Goldberger, Arthur Stanley *economics educator*
Goodman, Robert Merwin *microbiologist, plant biologist, educator*
Goodman, Stuart Lauren *lawyer*
Googins, Louise Paulson *financial planner*
Gorski, Jack *biochemistry educator*
Graf, Truman Frederick *agricultural economist, educator*
Graham, James Miller *physiology researcher*
Graziano, Frank Michael *medical educator, researcher*
Greaser, Marion Lewis *science educator*
Greenfield, Norman Samuel *psychologist, educator*
Greenwald, Caroline Meyer *artist*
Guillery, Rainer Walter *anatomy educator*
Gustafson, David Harold *industrial engineering and preventive medicine educator*
Hachten, William Andrews *journalism educator, author*

Hagedorn, Donald James *phytopathologist, educator, agricultural consultant*
Hall, David Charles *zoo director, veterinarian*
Haller, Archibald Orben *sociologist, educator*
Hamalainen, Pekka Kalevi *historian, educator*
Hamerow, Theodore Stephen *history educator*
Hamers, Robert J. *chemistry educator, researcher*
Hansen, W. Lee *economics educator, author*
Hanson, David James *lawyer*
Harkness, Donald Richard *hematologist, educator*
Harr, Lucy Loraine *professional society administrator*
Harvey, John Grover *mathematics educator*
Haslanger, Philip Charles *journalist*
Haveman, Robert Henry *economics educator*
†Hayner, Stephen A. *religious organization administrator*
Hearn, John Patrick *biologist, educator*
Hedden, Gregory Dexter *environmental science educator, consultant*
Heffernan, Nathan Stewart *retired state supreme court chief justice*
Helgeson, John Paul *plant physiologist, researcher*
Helstad, Orrin L. *lawyer, legal educator*
Herndon, Terry Eugene *insurance executive*
Hester, Donald Denison *economics educator*
Hetsko, Cyril Michael *physician*
Heymann, S. Richard *lawyer*
Hickman, James Charles *business and statistics educator, business school dean*
Higby, Gregory James *historical association administrator, historian*
Hildebrand, Daniel Walter *lawyer*
Hill, Charles Graham, Jr. *chemical engineering educator*
Hofeldt, John W. *lawyer*
Hokin, Lowell Edward *biochemist, educator*
Holbrook, John Scott, Jr. *lawyer*
Hopen, Herbert John *horticulture educator*
Houghton, David Drew *meteorologist, educator*
Howe, Herbert Marshall *classics educator*
Hoyt, James Lawrence *journalism educator, athletic administrator*
Hurst, James Willard *law educator*
Ihde, Aaron John *history of science educator emeritus*
Iltis, Hugh Hellmut *plant taxonomist-evolutionist, educator*
Ishikawa, Jesse Steven *lawyer*
Javid, Manucher J. *neurosurgery educator*
Jeanne, Robert Lawrence *entomology educator*
Johnson, Alton Cornelius *management educator*
Johnson, Millard Wallace, Jr. *mathematics and engineering educator*
Johnson, Richard Arnold *statistics educator, consultant*
Johnson, Roland A. *conductor, music director*
Jones, James Edward, Jr. *retired law educator*
Kaesberg, Paul Joseph *virology researcher*
Keenan, John Paul *management educator, consultant, psychologist*
Kelly, Douglas *medieval and foreign literature educator*
Kepecs, Joseph Goodman *physician, educator*
Kingdon, Robert McCune *historian, educator*
Klein, Sheldon *computational linguist, educator*
Kleinhenz, Christopher *foreign language educator, researcher*
Klug, Scott Leo *congressman*
Knowles, Richard Alan John *English language educator*
Koval, Charles Francis *entomologist, agricultural administrator, educator*
Kraushaar, William Lester *physicist, educator*
Kreuter, Gretchen V. *academic administrator*
Krusick, Margaret Ann *state legislator*
Kulcinski, Gerald LaVerne *nuclear engineer, educator*
Kutler, Stanley Ira *history and law educator, author*
Laessig, Ronald Harold *pathology educator, state official*
La Follette, Douglas J. *secretary of state*
Lagally, Max Gunter *physics educator*
Langer, Richard J. *lawyer*
Lardy, Henry A(rnold) *biochemistry educator*
Larsen, Edwin Merritt *retired chemist, educator*
Larson, John David *life insurance company executive, lawyer*
Lasseter, Robert Haygood *electrical engineering educator, consultant*
Launder, Yolanda Marie *graphic design director*
Lautenschlager, Peggy Ann *prosecutor*
Lawler, James Edward *physics educator*
Lawson, David E. *architect*
Leavitt, Lewis A. *pediatrician, educator*
Lee, Leslie Warren *marketing executive*
Lemanske, Robert F., Jr. *allergist, immunologist*
Lemberger, August Paul *university dean, pharmacy educator*
Levin, Jacob Joseph *mathematician, educator*
Levine, Solomon Bernard *business and economics educator*
Lewis, Herbert Samuel *anthropologist, educator*
†Lillesand, Thomas Martin *remote sensing educator*
Link, O(gle) Winston *photographer*
Linstroth, Tod B. *lawyer*
Lipo, Thomas A. *electrical engineer, educator*
Littlefield, Vivian Moore *nursing educator, administrator*
Lobeck, Charles Champlin, Jr. *pediatrics educator*
Long, Willis Franklin *electrical engineering educator, researcher*
Lonnebotn, Trygve *battery company executive*
Loper, Carl Richard, Jr. *metallurgical engineer, educator*
Lovell, Edward George *mechanical engineering educator*
Luening, Robert Adami *agricultural economics educator emeritus*
Lyall, Katharine C(ulbert) *academic administrator, economics educator*
MacDougall, Priscilla Ruth *lawyer*
MacKendrick, Paul Lachlan *classics educator*
Mackie, Frederick David *retired utility executive*
Mac Kinney, Archie Allen, Jr. *physician*
Magnuson, John Joseph *zoology educator*
Maher, Louis James, Jr. *geologist, educator*
Maki, Dennis G. *medical educator, researcher, clinician*
Malkus, David Starr *mechanics educator, applied mathematician*
Maloney, Michael James *research scientist*
Malter, James Samuel *pathologist, educator*
Marks, Elaine *French language educator*
Marlett, Judith Ann *nutritional sciences educator, researcher*
Marrett, Cora B. *university educator, science educator*

Marth, Elmer Herman *bacteriologist, educator*
Martin, Robert David *judge, educator*
Marton, Laurence Jay *clinical pathologist, educator, researcher*
Mathwich, Dale F. *insurance company executive*
McBeath, Andrew Alan *orthopedic surgery educator*
McCallum, James Scott *lieutenant governor, former state senator*
McCallum, Laurie Riach *lawyer, state government*
McCallum, Scott *state official*
McCarty, Donald James *retired education educator*
McKinnon, Robert Harold *retired insurance company executive*
McNelly, John Taylor *journalist, educator*
Melli, Marygold Shire *law educator*
Merrick, William Andrew *neuropsychologist*
Metz, Mary Haywood *sociologist*
Miller, Frederick William *publisher, lawyer*
Miller, James Alexander *oncologist, educator*
Mitby, Norman Peter *college president*
Moen, Rodney Charles *state senator, retired naval officer*
Moore, Edward Forrest *computer scientist, mathematician, former educator*
Moore, John Ward *chemistry educator*
Moore, Judy Kay *media relations specialist*
Morton, Stephen Dana *chemist*
Moss, Richard L. *physiology educator*
Mosse, George Lachmann *history educator, author*
Mueller, Willard Fritz *economics educator*
Mukerjee, Pasupati *chemistry educator*
Murphy, Robert Brady Lawrence *lawyer*
Nagy, Joanne Elizabeth Berg *associate dean university*
Nelson, Oliver Evans, Jr. *geneticist, educator*
Netzer, Lanore A(gnes) *retired educational administration educator*
Nevin, John Robert *business educator, consultant*
Newcomb, Eldon Henry *retired botany educator*
Nicholas, Robert Leon *foreign language educator*
Nichols, Donald Arthur *economist, educator*
Niemann, Bernard John, Jr. *land and geographical system educator, researcher, consultant*
Nordby, Eugene Jorgen *orthopedic surgeon*
Novotny, Donald Wayne *electrical engineering educator*
O'Brien, James Aloysius *foreign language educator*
Odden, Allan Robert *education educator*
Olson, Norman Fredrick *food science educator*
Panzer, Mary E. *state legislator*
Pariza, Michael Willard *research institute executive, microbiology and toxicology educator*
Parrino, Cheryl Lynn *state agency administrator*
Pella, Milton Orville *retired science educator*
Penniman, Clara *political scientist, educator*
Perkins, Merle Lester *French language educator*
Perlman, D(avid) *biochemist, educator*
Peters, Henry Augustus *neuropsychiatrist*
Peterson, David Maurice *plant physiologist, research leader*
Piliavin, Jane Allyn *social psychologist*
Pitot, Henry Clement, III *physician, educator*
Policano, Andrew J. *university dean*
Pondrom, Lee Girard *physicist, educator*
Porter, Andrew Calvin *educational administrator, psychology educator*
Porter, Cloyd Allen *state representative*
Potter, Kevin *former United States attorney*
Powell, Barry Bruce *classicist*
Prange, Roy Leonard, Jr. *lawyer*
Pray, Lloyd Charles *geologist, educator*
Prieve, E. Arthur *arts administration educator*
Ragatz, Thomas George *lawyer*
Raushenbush, Walter Brandeis *law educator*
Ray, Dennis Jay *utilities and business educator, researcher*
Reuschlein, Robert William *accountant, researcher*
Reynolds, Ernest West *physician, educator*
Rice, Joy Katharine *psychologist, educational policy studies and women's studies educator*
Rich, Daniel Hulbert *chemistry educator*
Richards, Hugh Taylor *physics educator*
Rideout, Walter Bates *English educator*
Ring, Gerald J. *real estate developer, insurance executive*
Ris, Hans *zoologist, educator*
Roberson, Linda *lawyer*
Roberts, Leigh Milton *psychiatrist*
Robertson, James Magruder *geological research administrator*
Robins, H(enry) Ian *medical oncologist*
Robinson, Arthur Howard *geography educator*
Robinson, Stephen Michael *applied mathematician, educator*
Roessler, Carol Ann *state senator*
Rosenshield, Gary *Russian literature educator*
Rosser, Annetta Hamilton *composer*
Rowe, George Giles *cardiologist, educator*
Rowe, John Westel *retired organic chemist*
Rowlands, Robert Edward *engineering educator*
Rude, Brian David *state legislator*
Rueckert, Roland Rudyard *virologist, educator*
Rutkowski, James Anthony *state legislator*
Sackett, Joseph Frederic *radiologist, educator, administrator*
Sample, Nathaniel Welshire *architect*
Sanders, Keith R. *university chancellor*
Satter, Larry Dean *biochemist, scientific research administrator*
Savage, Blair deWillis *astronomer, educator*
Schatten, Gerald Phillip *cell biologist, reproductive biologist, educator*
Scheidler, James Edward *business executive*
Schmidt, John Richard *agricultural economics educator*
Schoeller, Dale Alan *nutrition research educator*
Schultz, Dale Walter *state senator*
Schutta, Henry Szczesny *neurologist, educator*
Schutze, Charles R. *lawyer*
Seireg, Ali A(bdel Hay) *mechanical engineer*
Sequeira, Luis *plant pathology educator*
Sewell, Richard Herbert *historian, educator*
Sewell, William Hamilton *sociologist*
Shain, Irving *retired chemical company executive and university chancellor*
Sharkey, Thomas David *educator, botanist*
Shaw, Joseph Thomas *Slavic languages educator*
Sih, Charles John *pharmaceutical chemistry educator*
Singer, Marcus George *philosopher, educator*
Skiles, James Jean *electrical and computer engineering educator*
Skinner, James Lauriston *chemist, educator*
Skoog, Folke Karl *botany educator*
Smalley, Eugene Byron *plant pathology educator, forest pathologist, mycologist*
Smith, Michael James *industrial engineering educator*
Smith, Morton Edward *ophthalmology educator, dean*

Sobkowicz, Hanna Maria *neurology researcher*
Sondel, Paul Mark *pediatric oncologist, educator*
Sonnedecker, Glenn Allen *historian of pharmacy*
Spear, Thomas Turner *history educator*
Stewart, Warren Earl *chemical engineer, educator*
Still, Thomas Wayne *newspaper editor, columnist*
Stites, Susan Kay *human resources consultant*
Stone, John Timothy, Jr. *writer*
Strasma, John Drinan *economist, educator*
Strier, Karen Barbara *anthropology educator*
Sunde, Milton Lester *retired poultry science educator*
Susman, Millard *geneticist, educator*
Swoboda, Lary Joseph *state legislator*
Szybalski, Waclaw *molecular geneticist, educator*
Szymanski, Edna Mora *rehabilitation psychology and special education educator*
Taylor, Carolyn L. *principal*
Temkin, Harvey L. *lawyer*
Thesen, Arne *industrial engineering educator*
Thiesenhusen, William Charles *agricultural economist*
Thompson, Howard Elliott *business educator*
Thompson, Tommy George *governor*
Tibbitts, Theodore William *horticulturist, researcher*
Tishler, William Henry *landscape architect, educator*
Tomar, Russell Herman *pathologist, educator, researcher*
Tracy, Alan Thomas *government official*
Turner, Robert Lloyd *state legislator*
Uselmann, Catherine Rose (Kit Uselmann) *small business owner, network marketer, behavioral researcher, financial independence consultant*
Valdivia, Hector Horacio *medical educator*
Vandell, Deborah Lowe *educational psychology educator*
Vandell, Kerry Dean *real estate and urban economics educator*
Vaughan, Michael Richard *lawyer*
Vaughan, Worth Edward *chemistry educator*
Voight, Jack C. *state official*
Voos, Paula Beth *economics educator*
Vowles, Richard Beckman *literature educator*
Wade, Royce Allen *financial services representative*
Wagner, Burton Allan *lawyer*
Wahba, Grace *statistician, educator*
Waldo, Robert Leland *retired insurance company executive*
Waldron, Ellis Leigh *retired political science educator*
Walker, Duard Lee *medical educator*
Walsh, David Graves *lawyer*
Wang, Herbert Fan *geophysics educator*
Ward, David *academic administrator, educator*
Webster, John Goodwin *biomedical engineering educator, researcher*
Weinbrot, Howard David *English educator*
Weiss, Mareda Ruth *dean*
Welker, Wallace Irving *neurophysiologist, educator*
West, Robert Culbertson *chemistry educator*
Westman, Jack Conrad *child psychiatrist, educator*
Westphal, Klaus Wilhelm *university museum administrator*
Whiffen, James Douglass *surgeon, educator*
White, William Fredrick *lawyer*
Whitney, Robert Michael *lawyer*
Wilcox, Jon P. *justice*
Wilcox, Michael Wing *lawyer*
Wilson, Franklin D. *sociology educator*
Wilson, Pamela Aird *physician*
Wineke, William Robert *reporter, clergyman*
Wirz, George O. *bishop*
Witiak, Donald Theodore *medicinal chemistry educator*
Wolman, J. Martin *retired newspaper publisher*
Wynn, Robert Louis, II *state government official, business owner*
Wyse, Roger Earl *physiologist*
Young, Merwin Crawford *political science educator*
†Young, Raymond Allen *chemist, educator*
Young, Rebecca Mary Conrad *state legislator*
Yuill, Thomas MacKay *university administrator, microbiology educator*
Zimmerman, Howard Elliot *chemist, educator*
Zobel, Robert Leonard *state government official*
Zweifel, David Alan *newspaper editor*

### Manitowish Waters
Laidig, William Rupert *retired paper company executive*

### Manitowoc
Plank, William Brandt *minister*
Sfat, Michael Rudolph *retired biochemical engineer*
Trader, Joseph Edgar *orthopedic surgeon*

### Marinette
Staudenmaier, Mary Louise *banker, lawyer*

### Marion
Simpson, Vinson Raleigh *manufacturing company executive*

### Markesan
Jahns, Arthur William *retired educational administrator*

### Marshfield
Fye, W. Bruce, III *cardiologist*
Jaye, David Robert, Jr. *retired hospital administrator*
Stueland, Dean Theodore *emergency physician*

### Mayville
Bell, Scott William *private school educator, principal*

### Medford
Sebold, Duane David *food manufacturing executive*

### Menasha
Baird, Roger Allen *retired corporation executive*

### Menomonee Falls
Kellogg, William S. *retail executive*
Walters, Ronald Ogden *finance company executive*

### Menomonie
Shaw, Dennis Lee *academic administrator*
Steans, Phillip Michael *lawyer*

### Mequon
Berry, William Martin *financial consultant*
Bloom, James Edward *commodity trading and financial executive*
Burroughs, Charles Edward *lawyer*
Dohmen, Frederick Hoeger *retired wholesale drug company executive*
Dohmen, Mary Holgate *retired primary school educator*
Elias, Paul S. *marketing executive*
Ellis, William Grenville *academic administrator, management consultant*
Locklair, Gary Hampton *computer science educator*
Miller, Scott Joseph *software executive*
Ryan, Mary Nell H. *training consultant*
Watson-Boone, Rebecca A. *library & information studies educator, researcher*
Wray, Gail Miller *government agency administrator, environmentalist*

### Merrill
Whitburn, Gerald *insurance company executive*
Wulf, William Arthur *lawyer*

### Middleton
Berman, Ronald Charles *lawyer, accountant*
Conaway, Jane Ellen *elementary education educator*
Conklin, Charles D. *marketing executive*
Ferry, James Allen *physicist, electrostatics company executive*
Foss, Karl Robert *auditor*
Hinsdill, Ronald Dwight *bacteriology educator, immunotoxicologist*
Jefferson, James Walter *psychiatry educator*
McDermott, Molly *lay minister*
Ostrom, Meredith Eggers *retired geologist*
Senn, Richard Allan *environmental safety professional*
Wills, Robert Hamilton *retired newspaper executive*

### Milton
Hosler, Russell John *retired education educator*

### Milwaukee
Abraham, William John, Jr. *lawyer*
Aita, Carolyn Rubin *materials scientist*
Alexander, Janice Hoehner *physician, educator*
Alverson, William H. *lawyer*
Aman, Mohammed Mohammed *university dean, library and information science educator*
Arbit, Bruce *direct marketing executive, consultant*
Armstrong, Douglas Dean *journalist*
Armstrong, Leona May Bottrell *counselor, teacher*
Auer, James Matthew *art critic, journalist*
Babler, Wayne E., Jr. *lawyer*
Bacon, John Stuart *biochemical engineer*
Bader, Alfred Robert *chemist*
Baker, John Edward *cardiac biochemist, educator*
Balbach, George Charles *technology company executive*
Ballweg, Mary Lou *nonprofit association administrator and founder, writer, consultant*
Bannen, John T. *lawyer*
Barbee, Lloyd Augustus *lawyer*
Barnes, Paul McClung *lawyer*
Bartel, Fred Frank *consulting engineer executive*
Bartels, Jean Ellen *nursing educator*
Basquin, Mary Smyth (Kit Basquin) *museum curator*
†Bateman, C. Barry *airport terminal executive*
Battocletti, Joseph Henry *electrical engineer, biomedical engineer, educator*
Bauer, Chris Michael *banker*
Baumann, Carol Edler *political science educator*
Beals, Vaughn Le Roy, Jr. *motorcycle and recreational vehicle manufacturing executive*
Beckwith, David E. *lawyer*
Behrendt, David Frogner *journalist*
Bergmann, Linda J. *marketing professional*
Berkoff, Marshall Richard *lawyer*
Bhore, Jay Narayan *psychiatrist*
Bicha, Karel Denis *historian, educator*
Biehl, Michael Melvin *lawyer*
Biller, Joel Wilson *lawyer, former foreign service officer*
Bishop, Charles Joseph *manufacturing company executive*
Blum, Lawrence Philip *educational psychology educator*
Boese, Gilbert Karyle *cultural organization executive*
Boettcher, Harold Paul *engineer, educator*
Bowen, Michael Anthony *lawyer, writer*
Bremer, John M. *lawyer*
Brown, Edith *social worker*
Browning, Carol Anne *pediatrician, educator*
Bruce, Jackson Martin, Jr. *lawyer*
Buck, David Douglas *historian*
Burkert, Robert Randall *retired artist*
Burstein, Sol *consultant, retired utility company executive, engineer*
Busch, John Arthur *lawyer*
Cannon, David Joseph *lawyer*
Carozza, Davy Angelo *Italian language educator*
Carr, Charles Lee Glenn, Jr. (Chuck Carr) *professional baseball player*
Carter, Martha Eloise *retired curriculum specialist, reading consultant*
Case, Karen Ann *lawyer*
Casey, John Alexander *lawyer*
Casper, Richard Henry *lawyer*
Chait, Jon Frederick *corporate executive, lawyer*
Chan, Shih Hung *mechanical engineering educator, consultant*
Chapman, William Paul *retired automatic control manufacturing company executive*
Christiansen, Keith Allan *lawyer*
Clark, James Richard *lawyer*
Cleary, John Washington *lawyer*
Coffman, Terrence J. *academic administrator*
Cohn, Lucile *psychotherapist, nurse*
Colbert, Virgis William *brewery company executive*
Condon, Robert Edward *surgeon, educator*
Connolly, Gerald Edward *lawyer*
Coogan, Frank Neil *health and social services administrator*
Cooper, Richard Alan *hematologist, college dean, health policy analyst*
†Counsell, Paul S. *advertising executive*
Croak, Francis R. *lawyer*
Crowe-Hagans, Natonia *manufacturing executive, engineer*
Curran, Thomas J. *federal judge*
Cutler, Richard Woolsey *lawyer*
Daily, Frank J(erome) *lawyer*
Dallman, Robert E. *lawyer*
Davis, Thomas William *steel industry executive*
Davis, Walter Stewart *lawyer*
Demerdash, Nabeel Aly Omar *electrical engineer*
Dionisopoulos, George Allan *lawyer*
Doehr-Blanck, Denise Louise *special education educator*
Downey, John Wilham *composer, pianist, conductor, educator*
Drummond, Robert Kendig *lawyer*
Duback, Steven Rahr *lawyer*
Dunleavy, Michael Joseph *professional basketball coach*
Dunn, Michael T. *dean*
Dziewanowski, Marian Kamil *history educator*
Ehlinger, Ralph Jerome *lawyer*
Eisenberg, Howard Bruce *law educator*
Ericson, James Donald *lawyer, insurance executive*
Esterly, Nancy Burton *physician*
Evans, Terence Thomas *federal judge*
Falconer, Judith Ann *public health and occupational therapist, educator*
Farris, Trueman Earl, Jr. *retired newspaper editor*
Feinsilver, Donald Lee *psychiatry educator*
Feitler, Robert *shoe company executive*
Felde, Martin Lee *advertising agency executive, accountant*
Fibich, Howard Raymond *retired newspaper editor*
Ficken, Millicent Sigler *zoology educator*
Fitzsimonds, Roger Leon *bank holding company executive*
Florsheim, Richard Steven *lawyer*
Foster, Richard *journalist*
Fournelle, Raymond Albert *engineering educator*
Frank, Kristy Louise *English educator*
Frautschi, Timothy Clark *lawyer*
†Frey, James Severin *educational association executive*
Friedman, James Dennis *lawyer*
Fromstein, Mitchell S. *temporary office services company executive*
Fuller, Howard *education educator, academic administrator*
Gaggioli, Richard Arnold *mechanical engineering educator*
Gallagher, Richard S. *lawyer*
Gallop, Jane (Anne) *women's studies educator, writer*
Garbaciak-Bobber, Joyce Katherine *news anchor*
Garner, Phil *professional baseball manager*
Garnier, Robert Charles *management consultant*
Gefke, Henry Jerome *lawyer*
Gemignani, Joseph Adolph *lawyer*
Gengler, Sister M. Jeanne *hospital administrator*
Ghiardi, James Domenic *lawyer, educator*
Goblirsch, Dean Edmund *otolaryngologist*
Goetsch, John Hubert *consultant and retired utility company executive*
Goldin, Martin Bruce *financial executive, consultant*
Gonnering, Russell Stephen *ophthalmic plastic surgeon*
Goodkind, Conrad George *lawyer*
Goodstein, Aaron E. *federal magistrate judge*
Gordon, Myron L. *federal judge*
Graef, Luther William *civil engineer*
Green, Edward Anthony *museum director*
Greenler, Robert George *physics educator, researcher*
Greenstreet, Robert Charles *architect, educator*
Griffith, Owen Wendell *biochemistry educator*
Grim, Clarence Ezra *medical educator, internist, researcher*
Grochowski, Mary Ann *psychotherapist*
Groethe, Reed *lawyer*
Groiss, Fred George *lawyer*
Haas, George Edward *lawyer*
Haberman, F. William *lawyer*
Habush, Robert Lee *lawyer*
Hachey, Thomas Eugene *British and Irish history educator, consultant*
Haggerty, Nancy Leary *lawyer*
Halloran, William Frank *English educator*
Handelman, Howard *political scientist, educator*
Hansen-Rachor, Sharon Ann *conductor, choral music educator*
Hanthorn, Dennis Wayne *performing arts association administrator*
Harrington, John Timothy *lawyer*
Harvieux, Anne Marie *psychotherapist*
Harvitt, Adrianne Stanley *lawyer*
Hase, David John *lawyer*
Hawkins, Brett William *political science educator*
Haworth, Daniel Thomas *chemistry educator*
Heiloms, May (Mrs. Samuel Heiloms) *artist*
Heinen, James Albin *electrical engineering educator*
Helbert, Clifford L. *graphic designer, journalism educator*
Hendee, William Richard *medical physics educator, university official*
Hill, Dennis P. *information technology executive*
Hinshaw, Edward Banks *broadcasting company executive*
Hoffman, Nathaniel A. *lawyer*
Hoffmann, Gregg J. *journalist, author*
Horsman, Reginald *history educator*
†Hosenpud, Jeffrey *cardiovascular physician*
Hudson, Katherine Mary *manufacturing company executive*
Huff, Marsha E. *lawyer*
Humber, Wilbur James *psychologist*
Hunter, Victor Lee *marketing executive, consultant*
Huntington, David Mack Goode *foundation administrator*
Huston, Kathleen Marie *library administrator*
Huston, Margo *journalist*
Jache, Albert William *retired chemistry educator, scientist*
†Jake, Richard *editor periodicals*
James, Charles Franklin, Jr. *engineering educator*
Jansen, Daniel Ervin *professional speedskater, marketing professional, former Olympic athlete*
Jaques, Damien Paul *theater critic*
Johannes, Robert J. *lawyer*
Joseph, Jules K. *retired public relations executive*
Joslyn, Jay Thomas *retired arts critic*
Jost, Lawrence John *lawyer*
Kahlor, Robert A. *communications company executive*
Kaiser, George Chapin *investment company executive*
Kampine, John P. *anesthesiologist*
Kamps, Charles Q. *lawyer*
Kao, Sue Fei *ophthalmologist*
Karkheck, John Peter *physics educator, researcher*
Kelly, Francis Daniel *lawyer*
Kendall, Leon Thomas *finance and real estate educator, retired insurance company executive*
Kerr, Dorothy Marie Burmeister *marketing executive, consultant*
Kessler, Joan F. *lawyer*
Keuler, Roland Leo *retired shoe company executive*
Keulks, George William *university dean, chemistry educator*
Keyes, James Henry *manufacturing company executive*
Killian, William Paul *industrial corporate executive*
King, Guadalupe Vasquez *psychology and social work educator*
Kinnamon, David Lucas *lawyer*
Kochar, Mahendr Singh *physician, educator, administrator, scientist, writer, consultant*
Krausen, Anthony Sharnik *surgeon*
Krieger, Robert Alan *software engineer*
Kringel, Jerome Howard *lawyer*
Kritzer, Paul Eric *media executive, communications lawyer*
Krueger, Raymond Robert *lawyer*
Kubale, Bernard Stephen *lawyer*
Kupst, Mary Jo *psychologist, researcher*
Kurtz, Harvey A. *lawyer*
LaBudde, Roy Christian *lawyer*
Landis, Fred *mechanical engineering educator*
Lange, Marilyn *social worker*
Lanier, Bob *former professional sports team executive, former basketball player*
†Larson, David Lee *surgeon*
Lawrence, Willard Earl *mathematics, statistics and computer science educator emeritus*
Leonard, Richard Hart *journalist*
Levit, William Harold, Jr. *lawyer*
Lietz, Jeremy Jon *educational administrator, writer*
Listach, Patrick Alan *professional baseball player*
Long, Robert Eugene *banker*
Lueders, Wayne Richard *lawyer*
Lydolph, Paul Edward *geography educator*
MacGregor, David Lee *lawyer*
Machulak, Edward Leon *real estate, mining and advertising company executive*
MacIver, John Kenneth *lawyer*
Manko, Wesley Daniel *financial advisor*
Manning, Kenneth Paul *food company executive*
Marcus, Richard Steven *lawyer*
Marringa, Jacques Louis *manufacturing company executive*
Martin, Quinn William *lawyer*
Martin, Vincent Lionel *manufacturing company executive*
Mayer, Henry Michael *mass transit consultant*
Maynard, John Ralph *lawyer*
McCanles, Michael Frederick *English language educator*
McCann, Dennis John *columnist*
McCormick, Kenneth L. *pediatrics educator, researcher*
McGaffey, Jere D. *lawyer*
McKinney, Venora Ware *librarian*
McSweeney, Maurice J. (Marc) *lawyer*
Medved, Paul Stanley *lawyer*
Meier, Kenneth J. *political science journal editor*
Meldman, Clifford Kay *lawyer*
Meldman, Robert Edward *lawyer*
Melin, Robert Arthur *lawyer*
Meyer, Jon Keith *psychiatrist, psychoanalyst, educator*
Miller, David Hewitt *environmental scientist, writer*
Moberg, David Oscar *sociology educator*
Montgomery, Robert Renwick *medical association administrator, educator*
Morris, G. Ronald *industrial executive*
Mosher, George Allan *manufacturing company executive*
Moynihan, William J. *museum executive*
Mulcahy, Charles Chambers *lawyer, educator*
Mulcahy, Robert William *lawyer*
Murphy, Judith Chisholm *trust company executive*
Namdari, Bahram *surgeon*
Noelke, Paul *lawyer*
Norquist, John Olof *mayor*
Novak, Victor Anthony *semi-retired manufacturing company executive*
Obenberger, Thomas E. *lawyer*
Olson, Frederick Irving *retired history educator*
Ovitsky, Steven Alan *musician, symphony orchestra executive*
Paige, Norma *lawyer, corporate executive*
Panenka, James Brian Joseph *financial company executive*
Parker, Charles Walter, Jr. *consultant, retired equipment company executive*
Paull, Richard Allen *geologist, educator*
Paulson, Belden Henry *political scientist*
Pelisek, Frank John *lawyer*
Perlman, Richard Wilfred *economist, educator*
Phillips, Thomas John *lawyer*
Pindyck, Bruce Eben *lawyer, corporate executive*
Pisciotta, Anthony Vito *physician, educator*
Poehlmann, JoAnna *artist, illustrator, book designer, educator*
Powell, Edmund William *lawyer*
Quade, Quentin Lon *political science educator*
Rabbat, Guy *electronics company executive, inventor*
†Rader, I. A. *electronic components manufacturing company executive*
Randa, Rudolph Thomas *judge*
Randall, William Seymour *leasing company executive*
Raynor, John Patrick *university administrator*
Read, Sister Joel *academic administrator*
Reedy, George Edward *educator, author, lecturer*
Reid, Robert Lelon *college dean, mechanical engineer*
Remsen, Charles Cornell, III *microbiologist, educator, research administrator*
Renner, Richard Henry *industrial engineer*
Reynolds, John W. *federal judge*
Rheams, Annie Elizabeth *education educator*
Rich, Robert C. *manufacturing executive*
Richman, Stephen Erik *lawyer*
Ritz, Esther Leah *civic worker, volunteer, investor*
Roeming, Robert Frederick *foreign language educator*
Rosenberg, Susan *lawyer*
Ryan, Patrick Michael *lawyer*
Samson, Allen Lawrence *bank executive*
Samson, Richard Max *investments and real estate executive*
Sanfilippo, Jon Walter *lawyer*
Sankovitz, James Leo *development director, lobbyist*
Schaleben, Arville *newspaper editor, writer, educator*
Schaub, Theresa Marie *early childhood educator*
Scheinfeld, James David *travel agency executive*
Schenker, Eric *university dean, economist*
Schmitz, Francis David *lawyer*
Schneider, Thomas Paul *prosecutor*
Schnoll, Howard Manuel *investment banking and managed asset consultant*
Schnur, Robert Arnold *lawyer*
Schrader, Thomas F. *utilities executive*
Schroeder, John H. *university chancellor*
Schultz, Richard Otto *ophthalmologist, educator*
Schur, Leon Milton *economist, educator*
Schwartz, Joseph *English language educator*
Scrabeck, Jon Gilmen *dental eductor*
Scrivner, Thomas William *lawyer*

Selig, Allan H. (Bud Selig) *professional baseball team executive*
Shapiro, James Edward *judge*
Shapiro, Robyn Sue *lawyer, educator*
Shea, Donald Richard *political science educator*
Shields, James Richard *alcohol and drug counselor, consultant*
Shiely, John Stephen *company executive, lawyer*
Shindell, Sidney *medical educator, physician*
Shriner, Thomas L., Jr. *lawyer*
Siegesmund, Kenneth August *forensic anatomist, consultant, educator*
Silverman, Franklin Harold *speech pathologist, educator*
Simms, John Carson *logic, mathematics and computer science educator*
Smith, David Bruce *lawyer*
Smith, James John *physiologist*
Smith, Jane Farwell *civic worker*
Smith, Lois Ann *real estate executive*
Soergel, Konrad Hermann *physician*
Solomon, Donald William *mathematician, educator, consultant*
†Squires, Joan H. *orchestra executive*
Stadtmueller, Joseph Peter *federal judge*
Steinmiller, John F. *professional basketball team executive*
Stephenson, Robert Baird *energy company executive*
Sterner, Frank Maurice *industrial executive*
Stokes, Kathleen Sarah *dermatologist*
Stomma, Peter Christopher *lawyer*
Stromberg, Roland Nelson *historian*
†Sullivan, Edward *periodical editor*
Swanson, Roy Arthur *classicist, educator*
Szmanda, Lucille Marie *retired vocational school educator*
†Taylor, Allen M. *community foundation executive*
Taylor, Donald *retired manufacturing company executive*
Taylor, Robin Lynn *anchorperson, reporter*
Terry, Leon Cass *neurologist, educator*
Teuschler, Michael Alexander *computer company executive, consultant*
Theis, William Harold *lawyer, educator*
Thrall, Arthur Alvin *artist*
Titley, Robert L. *lawyer*
Tolan, David J. *insurance corporation executive*
†Towne, Jonathan Baker *vascular surgeon*
Van Antwerpen, Regina Lane *underwriter, insurance company executive*
Van Vugt, Eric J. *lawyer*
Vice, Jon Earl *hospital executive*
Viets, Hermann *college president, consultant*
Wagner, Diane M(argaret) *theology educator*
Wake, Madeline Musante *nursing educator*
Waldbaum, Jane Cohn *art history educator*
Walmer, Edwin Fitch *lawyer*
Walters, William LeRoy *physics educator*
Warren, Richard M. *experimental psychologist, educator*
Warren, Robert Willis *federal judge*
Weakland, Rembert G. *archbishop*
†Weifbecker, Robert T. *healthcare administrator*
Weise, Charles Martin *zoology educator*
Wells, Carolyn Cressy *social work educator*
Whyte, George Kenneth, Jr. *lawyer*
Widera, Georg Ernst Otto *materials engineering educator, consultant*
Wiley, Edwin Packard *lawyer*
Will, Trevor Jonathan *lawyer*
Wilsdon, Thomas Arthur *product development engineer, administrator*
Winsten, Saul Nathan *lawyer*
†Wisniewski, Robert Jude *publishing company sales and marketing executive*
Yontz, Kenneth Fredric *medical and chemical company executive*
Zeidler, Frank P. *former association administrator, mayor, arbitrator, mediator, fact-finder*
Zelazo, Nathaniel K. *engineering executive*
Ziperski, James Richard *trucking company executive, lawyer*
Zore, Edward John *insurance company investment executive*

### Minocqua
Utt, Glenn S., Jr. *motel investments and biotech industry company executive*

### Monroe
Bishop, Carolyn Benkert *public relations counselor*
Brown, Sandra Lee *educational consultant, watercolorist*
Kittelsen, Rodney Olin *lawyer*

### Montello
Burns, Robert Edward *editor, publisher*

### Muskego
Stefaniak, Norbert John *business administration educator*

### Nashotah
Kriss, Gary W(ayne) *Episcopal priest*
Vincent, Norman L. *retired insurance company executive*

### Neenah
Bergstrom, Dedric Waldemar *retired paper company executive*
Bero, R.D. *manufacturing executive*
Fetzer, Edward Frank *transportation company executive*
Hansen, Nick Dane *lawyer*
Hanson, Charles R(ichard) *manufacturing company executive*
Stanton, Thomas Mitchell *lawyer, educator*
Talbot, John Dudley *college administrator*
Underhill, Robert Alan *consumer products company executive*
Workman, Jerome James, Jr. *chemist*

### Nekoosa
Sigler, LeRoy Walter *banker, lawyer, entrepreneur*

### New Berlin
Nelson, Kay Ellen *speech and language pathologist*
Winkler, Dolores Eugenia *retired hospital administrator*

### New Franken
Weidner, Edward William *university chancellor, political scientist*

### New Glarus
Marsh, Robert Charles *writer, music critic*

### New Holstein
Tyunaitis, Patricia Ann *elementary school educator*

### New London
Fitzgerald, Laurine Elisabeth *university dean, educator*

### New Richmond
Schwan, LeRoy Bernard *artist, retired educator*

### Oak Creek
Giblin, Louis *stockbroker*
Robertson, Michael Swing *religious association administrator*

### Oconomowoc
Kneiser, Richard John *accountant*
Morgan, Donna Jean *psychotherapist*
Reich, Rose Marie *retired art educator*
Vespa, Ned Angelo *photographer*

### Oconto Falls
Schlieve, Hy C. J. *principal*

### Omro
Turner, Mildred Edith *day care owner*

### Onalaska
Waite, Lawrence Wesley *osteopathic physician*

### Oregon
Dorner, Peter Paul *retired economist, educator*

### Oshkosh
Barwig, Regis Norbert James *priest*
Burr, John Roy *philosophy educator*
Drebus, Richard William *pharmaceutical company executive*
Goodson, Raymond Eugene *automotive executive*
Gruberg, Martin *political science educator*
Herzog, Barbara Jean *secondary school educator, administrator*
Hulsebosch, Charles Joseph *truck manufacturing company executive*
Jones, Norma Louise *librarian, educator*
Kerrigan, John E. *academic administrator*
Urch, Diane Sherman *librarian*
Wilde, William Richard *lawyer*

### Osseo
Wright, Rodney H. *architect*

### Park Falls
Westphal, William Henry *staff nurse*

### Pewaukee
Andacht, Herman William *retired educator and counselor*
Dupies, Donald Albert *retired civil engineer*
Lee, Jack (Jim Sanders Beasley) *broadcast executive*
Lestina, Gerald F. *wholesale grocery executive*
Loteyro, Corazon Bigata *physician*
Quadracci, Harry V. *printing company executive, lawyer*
Tessmann, Cary Annette *controller*

### Platteville
Lindahl, Thomas Jefferson *university dean*

### Plymouth
Gentine, Lee Michael *marketing professional*
Woythal, Constance Lee *psychologist*

### Princeton
Sylke, Loretta Clara *artist*

### Racine
Bray, Charles William, III *foundation executive*
Campbell, Edward Joseph *retired machinery company executive*
Coates, Glenn Richard *lawyer*
Coyle-Rees, Margaret Mary *chemist*
Gunnerson, Robert Mark *manufacturing company executive, accountant, lawyer*
Henley, Joseph Oliver *manufacturing company executive*
Johnson, Samuel Curtis *wax company executive*
Klein, Gabriella Sonja *communications executive*
Konz, Gerald Keith *manufacturing company executive*
Langenegger, Armin *radiation physicist*
Moles, Randall Carl *orthodontist*
Stephens, James Linton *mechanical engineer*
Stewart, Richard Donald *internist, educator*
Swanson, Robert Lee *lawyer*
Wright, Betty Ren *children's book writer*

### Rhinelander
Saari, John William, Jr. *lawyer*

### Ripon
Ashley, Robert Paul, Jr. *English literature educator*
Miller, George H. *historian, educator*
Prissel, Barbara Ann *paralegal, law educator*

### River Falls
DeLorenzo, David Joseph *retired public relations executive*
Johnston, Randy James *artist*
LeCapitaine, John Edward *counseling psychology educator, researcher*
Smith, Clyde Curry *historian, educator*
Thibodeau, Gary A. *academic administrator*

### River Hills
Silverman, Albert A. *retired lawyer, manufacturing company executive*

### Saint Croix Falls
Rimmereide, Arne Magnar *engineering executive*

### Shawano
Lyon, Thomas L. *agricultural organization administrator*

### Sheboygan
Buchen, John Gustave *retired judge*
Kohler, Ruth DeYoung *arts center executive*
Ladiges, Lori Jean *learning disabilities specialist*

### Shorewood
Surridge, Stephen Zehring *lawyer, writer*

### Solon Springs
Kleven, Bruce Alan *academic administrator*
Robek, Mary Frances *business education educator*

### South Milwaukee
Kitzke, Eugene David *research management executive*

### Spooner
Frey, Paul Howard *chemical engineer, engineering consultants company executive*
Schaeffer, Brenda Mae *psychologist, author*

### Stevens Point
Copps, Michael William *retail and wholesale company executive*
Dougherty, Daniel Allan *insurance claims manager*
Garber, David J. *sports association executive, marketing consultant*
George, Thomas Frederick *chemistry educator*
Makholm, Mark Henry *lawyer, former insurance company executive*
Paul, Justus Fredrick *historian, educator*
Stevens, Dwight Marlyn *educational administrator*

### Stoddard
Hollenbeck, Sue J. *elementary education educator*

### Stone Lake
Kissinger, Harold Arthur *retired army officer*

### Stoughton
Brenz, Gary Jay *publishing executive*
Huber, David Lawrence *physicist, educator*
Kuhn, Peter Mouat *atmospheric physicist*

### Sturgeon Bay
Becker, Bettie Geraldine *artist*
Wallestad, Philip Weston *retired business owner*

### Sun Prairie
Berkenstadt, James Allan *lawyer*
Eustice, Francis Joseph *lawyer*

### Superior
Feldman, Egal *historian, educator*

### Sussex
Dantzman, Gregory Peter *design engineer*
Stromberg, Gregory *printing company executive*

### Thiensville
Kostecke, B. William *utilities executive*
Roselle, William Charles *librarian*

### Three Lakes
Bauknecht, Barbara Belle *educator*

### Tomah
†Due, James M. *pharmacist*

### Twin Lakes
Fleischer, John Richard *retired secondary education educator*

### Valders
Fabian, Thomas Robert *superintentent of schools*

### Verona
Hoffmeister, Ann Elizabeth *elementary education educator*
Kieser, Randall John *family practice, addiction medicine and emergency medicine physician*
Schroeder, Henry William *publisher*

### Walworth
Sissons, John Roger *educational administrator*

### Washington Island
Raup, David Malcolm *paleontology educator*

### Waterford
Gunderson, Scott L. *state legislator*

### Waterloo
Burke, Richard A. *manufacturing executive*
Kay, Dennis Matthew *publishing company official*

### Watertown
Henry, Carl Ferdinand Howard *theologian*
Henry, Helga Irmgard *liberal arts educator*
Leitzke, Jacque Herbert *psychologist, corporate executive*
Thompson, Richard Lloyd *pastor*
Wallman, Charles James *historian*

### Waukesha
Burgess, William R. *food service executive*
Falcone, Frank S. *academic administrator*
Gruber, John Edward *editor, railroad historian, photographer*
Larson, Russell George *magazine and book publisher*
Macy, John Patrick *lawyer*
Mielke, William John *civil engineer*

### Waunakee
Berthelsen, John Robert *printing company executive*

### Wausau
Builer, Dorothy Marion *business owner*
Derwinski, Dennis Anthony *dentist*
Fleming, Thomas Michael *artist, educator*
Huebner, Suzanne M. *insurance company executive*
Orr, San Watterson, Jr. *lawyer*
Plein, Kathryn Anne *secondary educator*
Rogers, James Thomas *lawyer*
Slayton, John Arthur *electric motor manufacturing executive*

### Wauwatosa
Alexander, Robert Gardner *lawyer*
Hollister, Winston Ned *pathologist*
Janzen, Norine Madelyn Quinlan *medical technologist*
Jasiorkowski, Robert Lee *real estate broker, computer consultant*
Ladd, Louise Elizabeth *investments company executive*
White, Herbert Charles *psychiatrist*

### West Bend
Fraedrich, Royal Louis *magazine editor, publisher*
Gardner, Robert Joseph *general and thoracic surgeon*
Huff, Gayle Compton *advertising agency executive*
Rodney, Joel Morris *dean*
Styve, Orloff Wendell, Jr. *electrical engineer*

### Whitewater
Bhargava, Ashok *economics educator*
Busse, Eileen E. *special education educator*
Culbertson, Frances Mitchell *psychology educator*
Greenhill, H. Gaylon *academic administrator*
Gulgowski, Paul William *German language, social science, and history educator*
Refior, Everett Lee *labor economist, educator*

### Williams Bay
Hobbs, Lewis Mankin *astronomer*

### Windsor
Baumer, Martha Ann *minister*

### Winneconne
Gust, Joyce Jane *artist*

### Wisconsin Rapids
Brennan, Patrick Francis *retired printing paper manufacturing executive*
Engelhardt, LeRoy A. *retired paper company executive*
Kenney, Richard John *paper company finance executive*
McGrath, Cheryl Julia *elementary education educator*
Mead, George Wilson, II *paper company executive*
Olson-Hellerud, Linda Kathryn *elementary education educator*

### Woodruff
Agre, James Courtland *physical medicine and rehabilitation educator*
Polasek, Edward John *electrical engineer, consultant*
Rosenberg, Douglas Owen *healthcare management executive*

## WYOMING

### Afton
Hunsaker, Floyd B. *accountant*

### Basin
Kennette, Jennie Laura Fakes *medical and surgical nurse*

### Casper
Bostwick, Richard Raymond *retired lawyer*
Donley, Russell Lee, III *former state representative*
Hinchey, Bruce Alan *environmental engineering company executive*
Hjelmstad, William David *lawyer*
Jozwik, Francis Xavier *agricultural business executive*
Keim, Michael Ray *dentist*
Lowe, Robert Stanley *lawyer*
Meenan, Patrick Henry *state legislator*
Mobley, Karen Ruth *art gallery director*
Reed, James Earl *fire department commander*
Seeger, Sondra Joan *artist*
Seese, William Shober *chemistry educator*
Smith, Dick Martin *oil field service company executive, owner*
Stroock, Thomas Frank *manufacturing company executive*
True, Jean Durland *entrepreneur, oil company executive*
Wilkes, Shar (Joan Charlene Wilkes) *elementary education educator*
Wold, John Schiller *geologist, former congressman*

### Centennial
Russin, Robert Isaiah *sculptor, educator*

### Cheyenne
Barrett, James Emmett *federal judge*
Brimmer, Clarence Addison *federal judge*
Brorby, Wade *federal judge*
Brown, Charles Stuart *retired state supreme court justice*
Cardine, Godfrey Joseph *state supreme court justice*
Carlson, Kathleen Bussart *law librarian*
Catchpole, Judy *state agency administrator*
Freudenthal, Steven Franklin *lawyer*
Geringer, James E. *governor*
Golden, Michael *state supreme court justice*
Hanes, John Grier *lawyer, state legislator*
Hardway, James Edward *vocational and rehabilitative specialist*
Hart, Joseph H. *bishop*
Hill, William U. *lawyer, prosecutor*
Hirst, Wilma Elizabeth *psychologist*
Hunton, Donald Bothen *retired internist*
Johnson, Alan Bond *federal judge*
Johnson, Wayne Harold *librarian, county official*
Knight, Robert Edward *banker*
Macy, Richard J. *state judge*
Mc Clintock, Archie Glenn *lawyer*
McDowell, Sherrie Lorraine *secondary education educator*
Moore, Mary French (Muffy Moore) *potter, community activist*
Noe, Guy *social services administrator*
Ohman, Diana J. *state official, former school system administrator*
Robertson, Susan Joyce Coe *special education educator*
Rose, Robert R., Jr. *lawyer*
Schuman, Gerald Eugene *soil scientist*
Smith, Stanford Sidney *state treasurer*
Southworth, Rod Brand *computer science educator*
Taylor, William Al *judge*

GEOGRAPHIC INDEX 5035 MILITARY ADDRESSES OF THE UNITED STATES


Thomson, Thyra Godfrey *former state official*
Wagner, Samuel Albin Mar *records management executive, educator*
Wittler, Shirley Joyce *former state official, state commissioner*

**Cody**
Coe, Margaret Louise Shaw *community service volunteer*
Fritjofson, Sarah Marie *reporter, columnist*
Grimes, Daphne Buchanan *priest, artist*
Housel, Jerry Winters *lawyer*
Jackson, Harry Andrew *artist*
Patrick, H. Hunter *lawyer, judge*
Price, B. Byron *museum director*
Riley, Victor J., Jr. *financial services company executive*
Shreve, Peg *state legislator, retired elementary educator*

**Douglas**
Harrop, Diane Glaser *shop owner, mayor*
Sanford, Leroy Leonard *rancher*

**Gillette**
Garry, James B. *historian, storyteller, researcher, writer*
Gilbertz, Larry E. *state legislator, entrepreneur*
Naramore, James Joseph *family practice physician, educator*

**Green River**
Marty, Lawrence A. *magistrate*
Thoman, Mary E. *business and marketing educator, rancher*
Thompson, Josie *nurse*

**Jackson**
Davis, Randy L. *soil scientist*
Downer, Eugene Debs, Jr. *editor, publisher*
Furrer, John Rudolf *retired manufacturing business executive*
Gordon, Stephen Maurice *manufacturing company executive, rancher*
Herrick, Gregory Evans *technology corporation executive*
Hirschfield, Alan J. *entrepreneur*
LaLonde, Robert Frederick *state senator, retired*
Law, Clarene Alta *innkeeper, state legislator*
Schuster, Robert Parks *lawyer*
Spence, Gerald Leonard *lawyer, writer*
Thulin, Walter Willis *real estate company executive*

**Jackson Hole**
Paulson, Glenn *environmental scientist*

**Kemmerer**
Clark, Michael *artist, educator*

**Lander**
Raynolds, David Robert *buffalo breeder, author*
Tipton, Harry Basil, Jr. *state legislator, physician*

**Laramie**
Bellamy, John Cary *civil engineer, meteorologist*
Boresi, Arthur Peter *author, educator*
Caldwell, Daniel Ralston *microbiology educator*
Chai, Winberg *political science educator, foundation chair*
Chisum, Emmett Dewain *historian, archeologist, researcher*
Christensen, Martha *mycologist, educator*
Cottam, Keith M. *librarian, educator, administrator*
Crocker, Thomas Dunstan *economics educator*
Dickman, Francois Moussiegt *former foreign service officer, educator*
Flach, Victor Hugo *designer, writer*
Forster, Bruce Alexander *dean*
Gill, George Wilhelm *anthropologist*
Grandy, Walter Thomas, Jr. *physicist, educator*
Gressley, Gene Maurice *history educator*
Hardy, Deborah Welles *history educator*
Kinney, Lisa Frances *lawyer*
Laman, Jerry Thomas *mining company executive*
Lewis, Randolph Vance *molecular biologist, researcher*
Maxfield, Peter C. *state legislator, law educator, lawyer*
Meyer, Edmond Gerald *energy and natural resources educator, resources scientist, entrepreneur, former chemistry educator, university administrator*
Meyer, Joseph B. *academic administrator, former state attorney general*
Mingle, John Orville *engineer, educator, lawyer, consultant*
Nelson, Elmer Kingsholm, Jr. *educator, writer, mediator, consultant*
Nord, Thomas Allison *hospital administrator*
Nye, Eric William *English language and literature educator*
Rechard, Paul Albert *civil engineering consulting company executive*
Reif, (Frank) David *artist, educator*
Roark, Terry Paul *academic administrator, physicist*
Roberts, Philip John *history educator, editor*
Shaffer, Sherrill Lynn *economist*
Smith, Thomas Shore *lawyer*
Speight, James Glassford *research company executive*
Spiegelberg, Emma Jo *business education educator*
Sutherland, Robert L. *engineering company executive, educator*
Williams, Roger Lawrence *historian, educator*

**Mills**
Kennerknecht, Richard Eugene *marketing executive*

**Moose**
Craighead, Frank Cooper, Jr. *ecologist*

**Newcastle**
Sample, Bette Jeane *elementary educator*

**Powell**
Brophy, Dennis Richard *psychology and philosophy educator*

**Riverton**
Bebout, Eli Daniel *oil executive*
Clark, Stanford E. *accountant*
Girard, Nettabell *lawyer*
Mulholland, Barbara Ann *school director*
Peck, Robert A. *newspaper publisher*

**Rock Springs**
Blackwell, Samuel Eugene *state legislator*
Chadey, Henry F. *museum director*
Kathka, David Arlin *director educational services*

**Saratoga**
Collamer, Sonja Mae Soreide *veterinary facility administrator*

**Sheridan**
Goodwin, Doris Helen Kearns *history educator, writer*
Taylor, Judith Ann *marketing and sales executive*

**Story**
Mc Ewan, Leonard *former judge*

**Teton Village**
Ellwood, Paul Murdock, Jr. *health policy analyst, consultant*

**Wheatland**
Bunker, John Birkbeck *cattle rancher, retired sugar company executive*
Hunkins, Raymond Breedlove *lawyer, rancher*
Morrison, Samuel Ferris *secondary school educator*
Whitney, Ralph Royal, Jr. *financial executive*

**Wilson**
Breitenbach, Mary Louise McGraw *psychologist, chemical dependency counselor*
Chrystie, Thomas Ludlow *investor*
Fritz, Jack Wayne *communications and marketing company executive*
Lawroski, Harry *nuclear engineer*
Sage, Andrew Gregg Curtin, II *corporate investor, manager*

**Worland**
Woods, Lawrence Milton *airline company executive*

## TERRITORIES OF THE UNITED STATES

### AMERICAN SAMOA

**Pago Pago**
Ili, Esther Kaili *principal*
Lutali, A. P. *governor of American Samoa*
Lutu, Afoa Moega *legislator, lawyer*
Sunia, Tausese *governor*
Tulafono, Togiola T.A. *senator*
Varghese, Mary *secondary education educator*
Weitzel, John Quinn *bishop*

### FEDERATED STATES OF MICRONESIA

**Chuuk**
Marcus, Mariano Nakamura *secondary school principal*
Neylon, Martin Joseph *retired bishop*
Samo, Amando *bishop*

**Pohnpei**
Eu, March Fong *ambassador, former California state official*

### GUAM

**Agana**
Apuron, Anthony Sablan *archbishop*
Black, Frederick A. *prosecutor*
Bordallo, Madeleine Mary (Mrs. Ricardo Jerome Bordallo) *lieutenant governor of Guam, wife of former governor of Guam*
Gutierrez, Carl T. C. *Guamanian government official*
Hardin, Ann *marriage and family therapist*
Maraman, Katherine Ann *judge*
Tock, Joseph *lawyer*
Unpingco, John Walter Sablan *federal judge*

**Dededo**
Diaz, Ramon Valero *retired judge*

**Mangilao**
Colfax, Richard Schuyler *business management and marketing educator*
Hamerly, Michael T. *librarian*
Lee, Chin-Tian *academic administrator, agricultural studies educator*

**Perez Acres**
Duenas, Laurent Flores *health and nursing consultant*

**Sinajana**
Toves, Jo Ann Villamor *nursing supervisor*

**Talofofo**
Taylor, James John *academic adminstrator*

**Tamuning**
Camacho, Eduardo Garcia *finance company executive, insurance agent*

### NORTHERN MARIANA ISLANDS

**Saipan**
Aldan, Tomas Benavente *pension fund administrator*
Camacho, Tomas Aguon *bishop*
Dela Cruz, Jose Santos *retired state supreme court chief justice*
Munson, Alex Robert *judge*
Siemer, Deanne Clemence *lawyer*

### PUERTO RICO

**Aguadilla**
Gómez-Jiménez, Carlos *science educator, microbiologist, geneticist*
Jaramillo, Juana Segarra *dean*

**Bayamon**
Berio, Blanca *editor*
Herrans-Perez, Laura Leticia *psychologist, educator, research consultant*

**Cabo Rojo**
Rivera-Martinez, Socorro *retired educator, assistant principal*

**Caparra Terrace**
León, Felix Ivan *pulmonologist*

**Carolina**
Velázquez de Cancel, Lourdes *religious organization executive, educator, interpreter, translator, poet*

**Dorado**
Spector, Michael Joseph *agribusiness executive*

**Guayama**
Febres-Santiago, Samuel F. *university chancellor*
Flores-Nazario, Margarita *human resources director*

**Guaynabo**
Flores-Lopez, Auremir *microbiologist*

**Gurabo**
Morales-Borges, Raul Hector *physician*

**Hato Rey**
Acosta, Raymond Luis *federal judge*
Ferrer, Miguel Antonio *brokerage firm and investment bank executive*

**Humacao**
Castrodad, Felix A. *university administrator*
Delgado-Rodriguez, Manuel *secondary school educator*

**Manati**
Silva-Ruíz, Sergio Andrés *biochemist*

**Mayaguez**
Casiano Vargas, Ulises *bishop*
Collins, Dennis Glenn *mathematics educator*
Deliz-Alvarez, Jose Rinaldo *industrial engineering educator, consultant*
Del Valle, Harry Fred Imzarry *minister, economist*
Rodríguez-Arias, Jorge Herminio *retired agricultural engineering educator*
Romaguera, Mariano Antonio *consulting engineer*
Sahai, Hardeo *medical statistics educator*

**Ponce**
Cummings, Luis Emilio *anesthesiologist, consultant*
Figueroa-Roman, Betsy *medical records administrator*
Sala, Luis Francisco *surgeon, educator*
Torres-Aybar, Francisco Gualberto *medical educator*
Torres Oliver, Juan Fremiot *bishop*

**Rio Piedras**
Davila, Norma *developmental psychologist and program evaluator*
López de Mendez, Annette Giselda *education educator*
Medina-Diaz, Maria del Rosario *education educator*

**San German**
Mojica, Agnes *academic administrator*

**San Juan**
Acevedo-Vilá, Aníbal *state legislator, lawyer*
Andreu-Garcia, Jose Antonio *judge*
Antonetti-Zequeira, Salvador *lawyer*
Bangdiwala, Ishver Surchand *statistician, educator*
Basols, Jose Andres *school director, priest*
†Callen, Tarquin M. *hotel executive*
Carreras, Francisco José *retired university president, foundation executive*
Cerezo, Carmen Consuelo *federal judge*
Corrada del Río, Baltasar *state official, lawyer, former mayor, former congressman*
Diaz-Cruz, Jorge Hatuey *lawyer, former state supreme court justice*
Fajardo, Victor *state commissioner*
Fernández-Coll, Fred *microbiologist, food technology laboratory director*
Fernández-V., Juan Ramon *university chancellor*
Fusté, José Antonio *federal judge*
Ghaly, Evone Shehata *pharmaceutics and industrial pharmacy educator*
Gierbolini-Ortiz, Gilberto *federal judge*
†Gonzales, Edgardo A. *lawyer*
†Gonzalez, Edgardo Antonio *lawyer*
Gonzalez, Jose Ramón *academic administrator*
Hernandez-Denton, Federico *commonwealth supreme court justice*
Irizarry-Yunque, Carlos Juan *lawyer, educator*
Laffitte, Hector Manuel *federal judge*
Marvel, Thomas Stahl *architect*
Matheu, Federico Manuel *university chancellor*
Muñoz Dones Carrascal, Eloisa *hospital administrator, pediatrician, consultant, educator*
Muñoz-Solá, Haydeé Socorro *library administrator*
†Ocasio Belén, Félix E. *real estate development company executive*
Ocasio-Melendez, Marcial Enrique *history educator*
Orkand, Richard Kenneth *neurobiologist, researcher, educator*
Perez-Gimenez, Juan Manuel *federal judge*
Pierluisi, Pedro R. *lawyer*
Piovanetti, Simon *pediatrician*
Prevor, Ruth Claire *psychologist*
Ramirez-Rivera, Jose *physician*
Ramos, Carlos E. *law educator*
Rodriguez, Agustin Antonio *surgeon*
Soltero-Harrington, Luis Rubén *surgeon, educator*
Thompson, Annie Figueroa *academic director, educator*
Torruella, Juan R. *federal judge*
Weinstein-Bacal, Stuart Allen *lawyer, educator*

**Santurce**
Aponte Martinez, Luis Cardinal *archbishop*
Fleisher, T. Lawrence *dermatologist*

**Trujillo Alto**
Antoun, Mikhail *medicinal chemistry and pharmacognosy educator*

**Vega Alta**
Matos, Cruz Alfonso *environmental consultant*

### REPUBLIC OF MARSHALL ISLAND

**Majuro**
Plaisted, Joan M. *diplomat*
Zackhras, Ruben *Marshallese government official*

### VIRGIN ISLANDS

**Charlotte Amalie**
Aubain, Joseph F. *municipal official*
Bolt, Thomas Alvin Waldrep *lawyer*
Mapp, Kenneth E. *lieutenant governor of Virgin Islands*
Moore, Thomas Kail *chief judge*

**Christiansted**
Baar, James A. *public relations and corporate communications executive, author, consultant, internet publisher, software developer*
Finch, Raymond Lawrence *judge*
Resnick, Jeffrey Lance *federal magistrate judge*

**Frederiksted**
Petrait, Brother James Anthony *secondary education educator, clergy member*

**Kingshill**
Crossman, Stafford Mac Arthur *agronomist, researcher*

**Saint John**
Walker, Ronald R. *writer, newspaper editor, educator*

**Saint Thomas**
Creque, Linda Ann *non-profit educational and research executive, former education commissioner*
Ferguson, Glenn Walker *educational consultant, lecturer*
Feuerzeig, Henry Louis *lawyer*
Henneman, Carol O'Bryan *secondary school educator*
Hodge, Verne Antonio *judge*
Mabe, Hugh Prescott, III *prosecutor*
Miner, Robert Gordon *creative promotional consultant, auctioneer, writer, publisher, actor, educator*
Mitton, Michael Anthony *environmental technology company executive*
Schneider, Roy *United States Virgin Islands government official*
Shuck, Annette Ulsh *education educator*

## MILITARY ADDRESSES OF THE UNITED STATES

### ATLANTIC

**APO**
Alexander, Leslie M. *ambassador*
Baltimore, Richard Lewis, III *foreign service officer*
Bracete, Juan Manuel *diplomat, lawyer*
Bruno, George C. *ambassador*
Carner, George *foreign service executive, economic strategist*
Creagan, James Francis *diplomat*
Darnell, Susan Laura Browne *career officer*
de Vos, Peter Jon *ambassador*
Dyal, William M., Jr. *federal agency administrator*
Frechette, Myles Robert Rene *ambassador*
Gutierrez, Lino *diplomat*
Hughes, William John *former congressman, diplomat*
Jett, Dennis Coleman *foreign service officer*
Kadunc, Edward Louis, Jr. *federal government official*
Kamman, Curtis Warren *ambassador*
Knowlton, Nancy *biologist*
Magruder, Lawson William, III *military officer*
Maisto, John F. *ambassador*
Rubinoff, Ira *biologist, research administrator, conservationist*
Service, Robert E. *ambassador*

**FPO**
Hyde, Jeanette W. *ambassador*

### EUROPE

**APO**
Aaron, David L. *diplomat*
Archard, Douglas Bruce *foreign service officer*
Astriab, Steven Michael *army officer*
Bikales, Norbert M. *chemist, science administrator*
Bindenagel, James Dale *diplomat*
Blinken, Alan John *ambassador*
Carney, Timothy Michael *diplomat*
Charlip, Ralph Blair *career officer*
Connell, Mary Ellen *diplomat*
Cook, Frances D. *diplomat*
Crocker, Ryan C. *ambassador*
Cunningham, James Blair *foreign service officer*
Dickey, James Stuart *retired military officer*
Dornbush, K. Terry *ambassador*
Doyle, Justin Emmett *lawyer, government official*
Eastham, Alan Walter, Jr. *foreign service officer, lawyer*
Elson, Edward Elliott *diplomat*
Evans, John Marshall *diplomat*
Flynn, Raymond Leo *ambassador to the Holy See, former mayor*
†Fowler, Wyche, Jr. *ambassador*
Frawley-Bagley, Elizabeth *ambassador*
Ginsberg, Marc C. *ambassador*

Gresham, Dorothy Ann *operating room nurse, educator*
Harriman, Pamela Digby Churchill *diplomat, philanthropist*
Indyk, Martin S. *ambassador*
Kinnan, Timothy Alan *air force officer*
Kunin, Madeleine May *ambassador to Switzerland, former governor*
Loftus, Thomas Adolph *ambassador*
Meigs, Montgomery Cunningham, Jr. *military officer*
Moloff, Alan Lawrence *army officer, physician*
Niles, Thomas Michael Tolliver *ambassador*
Ray, Norman Wilson *career officer*
Scholes, Edison Earl *army officer*
Simpson, Daniel H. *ambassador*
Terry, Wayne Gilbert *healthcare executive, hospital administrator*
Tompkins, Tain Pendleton *foreign service official*
Walker, Edward S., Jr. *diplomat*
Westley, John Richard *foreign service officer*
Wilson, Joseph Charles, IV *ambassador*
Wood, Roberta Susan *foreign service officer*

### FPO

Chaiklin, Amy Lynn *childhood education program developer*
Griffin, Paul, Jr. *navy officer, engineer, educator*
Madison, Kenneth Edward *career officer*
Ransom, David Michael *diplomat*

## PACIFIC

### APO

Harvey, Barbara Sillars *foreign service officer*
Hicks, Robert Ruiz, Jr. *army officer*
†Holmes, Genta Hawkins *diplomat*
Itoh, William H. *ambassador*
McCarthy, Sean Michael *air force officer, pilot*
McGuire, Roger Alan *foreign service officer*
Mirick, Robert Allen *military officer*
Mondale, Joan Adams *wife of former vice president of United States*
Moser, Gregg Anthony *career officer*

### FPO

Beeman, Josiah Horton *diplomat*
Burghardt, Raymond Francis, Jr. *foreign service officer*
Chorba, Timothy A. *ambassador to Singapore*
Haskins, Michael Donald *naval officer*
Murray, Julia Kaoru (Mrs. Joseph E. Murray) *occupational therapist*
Sasser, James Ralph (Jim Sasser) *ambassador, former senator*
†Zacharias, David Alexander *career military officer*

## CANADA

## ALBERTA

### Athabasca
Rodnunsky, Sidney *lawyer, educator*

### Banff
Fruchtman, Milton Allen *film and television producer, director*

### Brooks
Krahn, Thomas Richard *horticultural research administrator*

### Calgary
Armstrong, David Anthony *physical chemist, educator*
Ballem, John Bishop *lawyer, novelist*
†Bartlett, Grant A. *professional sports team executive*
Calkin, Joy Durfée *healthcare consultant, educator*
Campbell, Finley Alexander *geologist*
†Clark, Charles Joseph (Joe Clark) *Canadian government official, former prime minister*
Cumming, Thomas Alexander *stock exchange executive*
Curtis, John Barry *archbishop*
†Duerr, Alfred *mayor*
†Edwards, N. Murray *professional sports team owner*
Forbis, Richard George *archaeologist*
Furnival, George Mitchell *petroleum and mining consultant*
Gish, Norman Richard *oil industry executive*
Glockner, Peter G. *civil and mechanical engineering educator*
Graf, Hans *conductor*
Hagerman, Allen Reid *mining executive*
Haskayne, Richard Francis *petroleum company executive*
Heidemann, Robert Albert *chemical engineering educator, researcher*
Holman, J(ohn) Leonard *retired manufacturing corporation executive*
Hotchkiss, Harley N. *professional hockey team owner*
Hriskevich, Michael Edward *oil and gas consultant*
Hughes, Margaret Eileen *law educator, former dean*
Hume, James Borden *corporate professional, foundation executive*
Hyne, James Bissett *chemistry educator, industrial scientist, consultant*
Izzo, Herbert John *language and linguistics educator, researcher*
Janes, Robert Roy *museum executive, archaeologist*
Jones, Geoffrey Melvill *physiology research educator*
†Joyce, Ronald V. *professional sports team executive*
Kelley, Jane Holden *archaeology educator*
Kentfield, John Alan *mechanical engineering educator*
King, Frank *investment company executive*
LaHay, David George Michael *ballet company director*
Lederis, Karolis Paul (Karl Lederis) *pharmacologist, educator, researcher*
†Libin, Alvin G. *business executive*
Little, Brian F. *oil company executive*
Lougheed, Peter *lawyer, former Canadian official*
MacDonald, Alan Hugh *librarian, university administrator*
Maclagan, John Lyall *retired petroleum company executive*
Maher, Peter Michael *university dean*

Maier, Gerald James *natural gas transmission and marketing company executive*
Malik, Om Parkash *electrical engineering educator, researcher*
†Markin, Allan P. *professional sports team executive*
Matthews, Francis Richard *lawyer*
McCaig, Jeffrey James *transportation company executive*
McCaig, John Robert *transportation executive*
McDaniel, Roderick Rogers *petroleum engineer*
McEwen, Alexander Campbell *cadastral studies educator, former Canadian government official, surveying consultant*
McIntyre, Norman F. *petroleum industry executive*
Mc Kinnon, F(rancis) A(rthur) Richard *utility executive*
Melvill-Jones, Geoffrey *physician, educator*
Meyers, Marlene O. *hospital administrator*
Milavsky, Harold Phillip *real estate executive*
Monk, Allan James *baritone*
Mossop, Grant Dilworth *geological institute director*
Neale, E(rnest) R(ichard) Ward *retired university official, consultant*
Nigg, Benno Maurus *biomechanics educator*
O'Brien, David Peter *oil company executive*
O'Byrne, Paul J. *bishop*
Paquette, Richard *airport executive*
†Peltier, John Wayne (Jack ) *oil and gas industry executive*
Pick, Michael Claude *international exploration consultant*
Pierce, Robert Lorne *petrochemical, oil and gas company executive*
Poole, Robert Anthony *journalist*
Raeburn, Andrew Harvey *performing arts association executive, record producer*
Rasporich, Anthony Walter *university dean*
Rattner, Jerome Bernard *biologist, anatomist, educator*
Reid, David Evans *pipeline company executive*
Rewcastle, Neill Barry *neuropathology educator*
Risebrough, Doug *professional hockey team executive*
Roberts, John Peter Lee *cultural advisor, administrator, educator, writer*
Seaman, Daryl Kenneth *oil company executive*
Seaman, Donald Roy *investment company executive*
†Shaw, James Robert *broadcast executive*
†Shaw, Jim, Jr. *broadcast executive*
Smith, Eldon *dean*
Southern, Ronald D. *diversified corporation executive*
Stebbins, Robert Alan *sociology educator*
Stell, William Kenyon *neuroscientist, educator*
Thorsteinsson, Raymond *geology research scientist*
Travis, Vance Kenneth *petroleum business executive*
Wagner, Norman Ernest *corporate education executive*
Watanabe, Mamoru *former university dean, physician, researcher*
White, Terrence Harold *academic administrator, sociologist*
Yoon, Ji-Won *virology, immunology and diabetes educator, research administrator*

### Camrose
Campbell, John Douglas *minister*

### Canmore
Wood, Sharon *mountaineer*

### Cochrane
Schmidt, Allen Edward *religious denomination administrator*

### De Winton
Shutiak, James *management consultant*

### Drumheller
Currie, Philip John *research paleontologist, museum program director*
Naylor, Bruce Gordon *museum director*

### Edmonton
Adams, Peter Frederick *university president, civil engineer*
Bateman, William Maxwell *retired construction company executive*
†Cardinal, Melvin Percy Joseph *government official*
†Christian, Ralph Gordon *agricultural research administrator*
Cook, David Alastair *pharmacology educator*
Cossins, Edwin Albert *biology educator, academic administrator*
Davis, Wayne Alton *computer science educator*
Day, Stockwell Burt *government official*
Dewhurst, William George *psychiatrist, educator, research director*
†Ekelund, Michael William *government official*
Fields, Anthony Lindsay Austin *health facility administrator, oncologist, educator*
Folinsbee, Robert Edward *retired geology educator*
Forsyth, Joseph *Canadian government official*
Fraser, Catherine Anne *Canadian chief justice*
Freeman, Milton Malcolm Roland *anthropology educator*
Gough, Denis Ian *geophysics educator*
Harris, Walter Edgar *chemistry educator*
Hiruki, Chuji *plant virologist, science educator*
Hislop, Mervyn Warren *health advocate administrator, psychologist*
Horton, William Russell *retired utility company executive*
Hughes, Linda J. *newspaper publisher*
Hughes, Monica *author*
Jones, Richard Norman *physical chemist, researcher*
†Joseph, Curtis Shayne *professional hockey player*
Jungkind, Walter *design educator, writer, consultant*
Kay, Cyril Max *biochemist*
Khanna, Faqir Chand *physics educator*
Klein, Ralph *premier of Alberta*
Koval, Don O. *electrical engineering educator*
Kratochvil, Byron George *chemistry educator, researcher*
Krotki, Karol Jozef *sociology educator, demographer*
Lechelt, Eugene Carl *psychology educator*
Lemieux, Raymond Urgel *chemistry educator*
Lock, Gerald Seymour Hunter *retired mechanical engineering educator*
Low, Ron Albert *professional hockey coach*
Mac Neil, Joseph Neil *archbishop*
†Marcotte, Brian *transportation executive*
†McCrank, Michael Neil *government official*
McDougall, Donald Blake *retired librarian, government official*
McDougall, John Roland *civil engineer*

McMaster, Juliet Sylvia *English language educator*
Miller, Jack David R. *radiologist, physician, educator*
Offenberger, Allan Anthony *electrical engineering educator*
Otto, Fred Douglas *chemical engineering educator*
Patrick, Lynn Allen *lawyer, construction company executive*
†Pocklington, Peter H. *business executive*
Rajotte, Ray V. *biomedical engineer, researcher*
Reimer, Jan Rhea *former mayor*
Rostoker, Gordon *physicist, educator*
Rutter, Nathaniel Westlund *geologist, educator*
Sather, Glen Cameron *professional hockey team executive, coach*
Shoctor, Joseph Harvey *barrister, producer, civic worker*
Smith, Peter John *geographer, educator*
Stelck, Charles Richard *geology educator*
Stevenson, William Alexander *retired justice of Supreme Court of Canada*
Stollery, Robert *construction company executive*
Sykes, Brian Douglas *biochemistry educator, researcher*
Thompson, Gordon William *dentist, educator, administrator*
Tyrell, Lorne S. *dean*
Vance, Dennis Edward *biochemistry educator*
†Ward Neville, Johanna (Anne) *government official*
†Weight, Doug *professional hockey player*

### Lethbridge
Cho, Hyun Ju *veterinary research scientist*
Rand, Duncan D. *librarian*

### McLennan
Légaré, Henri Francis *archbishop*

### Red Deer
Donald, Jack C. *oil company executive*

### Saint Paul
Roy, Raymond *bishop*

### Waterton Lakes Park
Russell, Andrew George Alexander *author, naturalist*

## BRITISH COLUMBIA

### Abbotsford
Fredeman, Betty Coley (Betty Coley) *retired librarian*
Holdcroft, Leslie Thomas *clergyman, educator*

### Bamfield
Druehl, Louis Dix *biology educator*

### Bowen Island
Lambert, Michael Malet *investment and hospitality consultant*

### Brentwood Bay
Carrothers, Alfred William Rooke *retired law educator*

### Burnaby
Bender, Graham I. *forest products executive*
Borden, John Harvey *entomologist, educator*
Borwein, Peter Benjamin *mathematician*
Brantingham, Patricia Louise *criminology educator*
Brantingham, Paul Jeffrey *criminology educator*
Buitenhuis, Peter Martinus *language professional, educator*
Copes, Parzival *economist, researcher*
Kitchen, John Martin *historian, educator*
Tung, Rosalie Lam *business educator, consultant*

### Cobble Hill
Cox, Albert Reginald *academic administrator, physician, retired*

### Duncan
Hughes, Edward John *artist*

### Kaleden
Siddon, Thomas Edward *Canadian government official, environmental consultant*

### Kamloops
Cruickshank, James David *bishop*
Sabatini, Lawrence *bishop*

### Kelowna
Muggeridge, Derek Brian *dean, engineering consultant*

### Maple Ridge
Wainwright, David Stanley *intellectual property professional*

### Nanaimo
Meadows, Donald Frederick *librarian*
Ricker, William Edwin *biologist*

### New Westminster
Fair, James Stanley *hospital administrator*

### North Saanich
Weichert, Dieter Horst *seismologist, researcher*

### North Vancouver
†Anderson, Gillian *actress*
Gibbs, David George *retired food processing company executive*
Grunder, Arthur Neil *forest products industry executive, retired*
Wedepohl, Leonhard Martin *electrical engineering educator*

### Powell River
Carsten, Arlene Desmet *financial executive*

### Prince Rupert
Hannen, John Edward *bishop*

### Qualicum Beach
Little, Carl Maurice *performing arts administrator*

### Richmond
Colton, Sterling Don *lawyer, business executive, missionary*
Halsey-Brandt, Greg *mayor*
†Pfeifer, Joann *hotel executive*
Plomp, Teunis (Tony Plomp) *minister*
Zeigler, Earle Frederick *physical education-kinesiology educator*

### Saanichton
Crozier, Lorna *poet, educator*

### Salt Spring Island
Raginsky, Nina *artist*
Shepherd, R. F. *retired bishop*

### Sidney
Bigelow, Margaret Elizabeth Barr *mycologist educator*
Davis, John Christopher *zoologist, aquatic toxicologist*
Kendrick, William Bryce *biology educator, author, publisher*
Mann, Cedric Robert *retired institute administrator, oceanographer*
Petrie, William *physicist*
Saddlemyer, Ann (Eleanor Saddlemyer) *educator, critic, theater historian*
van den Bergh, Sidney *astronomer*

### Sooke
Booth, Andrew Donald *retired university administrator, scientist*
Howard, John Lindsay *lawyer, forest industry company executive*

### Summerland
Looney, Norman Earl *pomologist, plant physiologist*

### Surrey
Farley, Lawrence *clergyman*
Kinsella, William Patrick *author, educator*

### Vancouver
Aalto, Madeleine *library director*
Aberle, David Friend *anthropologist, educator*
Alleyne, John *dancer, choreographer*
Andrews, John Hobart McLean *education educator*
Aubke, Friedhelm *chemistry educator*
Baird, Patricia Ann *physician, educator*
Bates, David Vincent *physician, medical educator*
Batts, Michael Stanley *German language educator*
Beagrie, George Simpson *dentist, educator, dean emeritus*
Belzberg, Samuel *real estate investment professional*
Bennett, Winslow Wood *mechanical engineer*
Bentley, Peter John Gerald *forest industry company executive*
Bentley, Thomas Roy *English educator, writer, consultant*
Birch, Murray Patrick *oil industry executive*
Blair, Robert *animal science administrator, educator, researcher*
Bloom, Myer *physicist, educator*
Bonner, Robert William *lawyer*
Bowering, George Harry *writer, English literature educator*
Boyd, David William *mathematician, educator*
Budzinsky, Armin Alexander *investment banker*
Bure, Pavel *professional hockey player*
Campbell, Bruce Alan *market research consultant*
Campbell, Jack James Ramsay *microbiology educator*
Chapple, John H. *professional sports team executive*
Chitty, Dennis Hubert *zoology educator*
Chow, Anthony Wei-Chik *physician*
Clark, Colin Whitcomb *mathematics educator*
Clarke, Garry Kenneth Connal *geophysics educator*
Collins, Mary *health association executive, former Canadian legislator*
Conway, John S. *history educator*
Copp, Douglas Harold *physiologist, educator*
Cormier, Jean G. *communications company executive*
Craig, Kenneth Denton *psychologist, educator, researcher*
Crawford, Carl Benson *retired civil engineer, government research administrator*
Cynader, Max Sigmund *psychology, physiology, brain research educator, researcher*
de Weerdt, Mark Murray *retired judge*
Doyle, Patrick John *otolaryngologist*
†Duncan, Mark *government official*
Durrant, Geoffrey Hugh *retired English language educator*
Eaves, Allen Charles Edward *hematologist, medical agency administrator*
Elkins, David J. *political science educator*
Erickson, Arthur Charles *architect*
Ericson, Richard Victor *social science-law educator, university official*
Exner, Adam *archbishop*
Feaver, George A. *political science educator*
Feldman, Joel Shalom *mathematician*
Finnegan, Cyril Vincent *retired university dean, zoology educator*
Freeman, Hugh James *gastroenterology educator*
Friedman, Sydney M. *anatomy educator, medical researcher*
Gardiner, William Douglas Haig *bank executive*
Gilbert, John Humphrey Victor *audiologist, speech scientist, educator*
Goldberg, Michael Arthur *land policy and planning educator*
Grace, John Ross *chemical engineering educator*
Granirer, Edmond Ernest *mathematician, educator*
Griffiths, Arthur R. *professional hockey team executive*
Hallam, Robert J. *performing company executive, consultant*
Hardwick, David Francis *pathologist*
Hardy, Walter Newbold *physics educator, researcher*
Harwood, Brian Dennis *securities industry executive*
Haycock, Kenneth Roy *education administrator*
Head, Ivan Leigh *law educator*
Hoar, William Stewart *zoologist, educator*
Holsti, Kalevi Jacque *political scientist, educator*
Jackson, Stu *professional sports team executive, former university basketball coach*
James, Brian Robert *chemistry educator*
Johnson, Michael E. *stock exchange executive*
Jones, David Robert *zoology educator*
Jull, Edward V. *electrical engineer, radio scientist, educator*
Keevil, Norman Bell *mining executive*

Kesselman, Jonathan Rhys *economics educator, public policy researcher*
Klohn, Earle Jardine *engineering company executive, consultant*
Klonoff, Harry *psychologist*
Knobloch, Ferdinand J. *psychiatrist, educator*
Ladner, Thomas E. *lawyer*
Langdon, Frank Corriston *political science educator, researcher*
Laponce, Jean Antoine *political scientist*
Lindsey, Casimir Charles *zoologist*
Lipsey, Richard George *economist, educator*
Lusztig, Peter Alfred *university dean, educator*
Lysyk, Kenneth Martin *judge*
Mahler, Richard T. *finance executive*
March, Beryl Elizabeth *animal scientist, educator*
Marchak, Maureen Patricia *anthropology and sociology educator*
Mattessich, Richard Victor (Alvarus) *business administration educator*
McBride, Barry Clarke *microbiology and oral biology educator, research microbiologist*
McCaw, John E., Jr. *professional sports team executive*
McEachern, Allan *Canadian justice*
McGeer, Edith Graef *neurological science educator emerita*
Mc Lean, Donald Millis *microbiology, pathology educator, physician*
McLean, Kirk *professional hockey player*
McNeill, John Hugh *pharmaceutical sciences educator*
McWhinney, Edward Watson *Canadian government legislator*
Meisen, Axel *chemical engineering educator, university dean*
Miura, Robert Mitsuru *mathematician, researcher, educator*
Mizgala, Henry F. *physician*
†Mogilny, Alexander *professional hockey player*
Murray, Anne *singer*
Newman, Murray Arthur *aquarium administrator*
Oberlander, Cornelia Hahn *landscape architect*
Overmyer, Daniel Lee *Asian studies educator*
Ozier, Irving *physicist, educator*
Pacheco-Ransanz, Arsenio *Hispanic and Italian studies educator*
Patkau, John *architect*
Patkau, Patricia *architect, architecture educator*
Paty, Donald Winston *neurologist*
Pearson, Richard Joseph *archaeologist, educator*
Peters, Ernest *metallurgy educator, consultant*
Peterson, Leslie Raymond *barrister*
Petrina, Anthony J. *retired mining executive*
Phillips, Anthony George *neurobiology educator*
Phillips, Edwin Charles *gas transmission company executive*
Phillips, John Edward *zoologist, educator*
Pickard, George Lawson *physics educator*
Pincock, Richard Earl *chemistry educator*
Piternick, Anne Brearley *librarian, educator*
Pulleyblank, Edwin George *history educator emeritus, linguist*
Radler, Franklin David *publishing holding company executive*
Raffi, (Raffi Cavoukian) *folksinger, children's entertainer*
Randall, David John *physiologist, zoologist, educator*
Rennie, Paul Steven *research scientist*
Riedel, Bernard Edward *retired pharmaceutical sciences educator*
Robinson, John Lewis *geography educator*
Rootman, Jack *ophthalmologist, surgeon, pathologist, oncologist, artist*
Rothstein, Samuel *librarian, educator*
Roy, Chunilal *psychiatrist*
Russell, Richard Doncaster *geophysicist, educator, geoscientist*
Saint-Jacques, Bernard *linguistics educator*
Salcudean, Martha Eva *mechanical engineer, educator*
Saunders, Peter Paul *investor*
Saywell, William George Gabriel *foundation administrator*
Seymour, Brian Richard *mathematician*
Shaw, Michael *biologist, educator*
Shearer, Ronald Alexander *economics educator*
Sinclair, Alastair James *geology educator*
Sion, Maurice *mathematics educator*
Slaymaker, H. Olav *geography educator*
Slonecker, Charles Edward *anatomist, medical educator, author*
Smethurst, Robert Guy *retired lawyer*
Smith, Michael *biochemistry educator*
Snider, Robert F. *chemistry educator, researcher*
Solloway, C. Robert *forest products company executive*
Splane, Richard Beverley *social work educator*
Stankiewicz, Wladyslaw Jozef *political philosopher, educator*
Stewart, Ross *chemistry educator*
Stone, Robert Ryrie *financial executive*
Suedfeld, Peter *psychologist, educator*
Sutter, Morley Carman *medical scientist*
Swanson, Charles Andrew *mathematics educator*
Tees, Richard Chisholm *psychology educator, researcher*
Thurlbeck, William Michael *retired pathologist, retired medical educator*
Tingle, Aubrey James *pediatric immunologist, research administrator*
Tyers, Geddes Frank Owen *surgeon*
Underhill, Anne Barbara *astrophysicist*
Unger, Richard Watson *history educator*
Vogt, Erich Wolfgang *physicist, academic administrator*
Wakefield, Wesley Halpenny *church official*
Warren, Harry Verney *geological sciences educator, consulting geological engineer*
Webber, William Alexander *university administrator, physician*
Wellington, William George *plant science and ecology educator*
Wheeler, John Oliver *geologist*
Willson, John Michael *mining company executive*
Wilson, Graham McGregor *energy company executive*
†Winters, Brian Joseph *professional sports team executive*
Yaffe, Barbara Marlene *journalist*
Young, Lawrence *electrical engineering educator*

**Victoria**
Antoniou, Andreas *electrical engineering educator*
Barber, Clarence Lyle *economics educator*
Barkley, William Donald *museum executive director*
Barnes, Christopher Richard *geologist*

Batten, Alan Henry *astronomer*
Best, Melvyn Edward *geophysicist*
Boone, Lois Ruth *legislator*
Chard, Chester Stevens *archaeologist, educator*
De Roo, Remi Joseph *bishop*
Finlay, James Campbell *retired museum director*
Gardom, Garde Basil *lieutenant governor of British Columbia*
Harris, Christie Lucy *author*
Harvey, Donald *artist, educator*
Horn, Paul Joseph *musician*
Hutchings, John Barrie *astronomer, researcher*
Israel, Werner *physics educator*
Kroetsch, Robert Paul *English language educator, author*
Leffek, Kenneth Thomas *chemist, educator*
Lind, Niels Christian *civil engineering educator*
Mac Diarmid, William Donald *physician*
MacLeod, John Munroe *radio astronomer*
†MacPhail, Joy K. *provincial agency administrator*
†Maloney, Maureen *government official*
Manning, Eric *computer science and engineering educator, university dean, researcher*
Mc Carter, John Alexander *biochemistry educator*
McCoppin, Peter *symphony orchestra conductor*
†McIntosh, Gordon Andrew *local government official*
Morton, Donald Charles *astronomer*
Oke, John Beverley *astronomy educator*
Partridge, Bruce James *lawyer, educator*
Payne, Robert Walter *psychologist, educator*
Richards, Vincent Philip Haslewood *librarian*
Segger, Martin Joseph *museum director, art history educator*
Stetson, Peter Brailey *astronomer*
Strong, David F. *university administrator*
Tighe, James C. *publisher*
Weisgerber, John Sylvester *provincial legislator*
Welch, S(tephen) Anthony *university dean, Islamic studies and arts educator*
Wiles, David McKeen *chemist*
Wright, Kenneth Osborne *retired astronomer*

**West Vancouver**
Donaldson, Edward Mossop *research scientist, aquaculture consultant*
Kloepfer, Clarence Victor *oil company executive*
Rae, Barbara Joyce *former employee placement company executive*
Wynne-Edwards, Hugh Robert *entrepreneur, scientist*

**White Rock**
Cooke, Herbert Basil Sutton *geologist, educator*
Huntington, A. Ronald *retired coal terminal executive*

## MANITOBA

**Churchill**
Rouleau, Reynald *bishop*

**Headingley**
Gerrard, Jon *Canadian government official*

**Otterburne**
McKinney, Larry *religious organization administrator*

**Pinawa**
Allan, Colin James *research and development company manager*

**Saint Boniface**
Hacault, Antoine Joseph Leon *archbishop*

**The Pas**
Sutton, Peter Alfred *archbishop*

**Winnipeg**
Alexander, Norman James *investment consultant*
Anderson, David Trevor *law educator*
Angel, Aubie *physician, academic administrator*
Barber, Robert Charles *physics educator*
Bigelow, Charles Cross *biochemist, university administrator*
Brennan, Robert Bryan *utility company executive*
†Buchko, Garth *broadcasting executive*
Burt, Christopher Murray *former newspaper editor, communications consultant*
†Chalmers, Jane *broadcast executive*
Cheff, Michel Vincent *art museum executive*
Cherniack, Saul Mark *retired barrister, solicitor*
Cohen, Albert Diamond *retail executive*
Cohen, Harley *civil engineer, science educator*
Converse, William Rawson Mackenzie *librarian*
Curtis, Charles Edward *Canadian government official*
Downey, James Erwin *government official*
Dumont, W. Yvon *provincial official*
Eales, John Geoffrey *zoology educator*
†Edwards, Clifford Henry Coad *law educator*
†Ernst, James Arthur *cabinet minister*
Eyre, Ivan *artist*
Ferguson, Robert Bury *mineralogy educator*
Filmon, Gary Albert *Canadian provincial premier, civil engineer*
Findlay, Glen Marshall *agrologist*
†Forand, Liseanne *government official*
Fraser, John Foster *management company executive*
Frey, Marvin *religious organization administrator*
Gilbertson, Leon Charles *church administrator*
Harder, Helmut George *religious organization administrator*
Haworth, James Chilton *pediatrics educator*
Hogan, Terrence Patrick *psychologist, university administrator*
Israels, Lyonel Garry *hematologist, medical educator*
Kanfer, Julian Norman *biochemist, educator*
Kuffel, Edmund *electrical engineering educator*
Lang, Otto E. *industry executive, former Canadian cabinet minister*
Lewis, Andre Leon *artistic director*
Liba, Peter Michael *communications executive*
Lyon, Sterling Rufus Webster *justice*
MacKenzie, George Allan *diversified company executive*
Mantsch, Henry Horst *chemistry educator*
McAlpine, Phyllis Jean *genetics educator, researcher*
†McBride, Matthew Gordon *broadcasting executive*
McKie, Francis Paul *journalist*
Morris, Jorden Walter *dancer, educator*
Morrish, Allan Henry *electrical engineering educator*

Naimark, Arnold *medical educator, physiologist, educator*
Oberman, Sheldon Arnold *writer, educator*
Olds, Elizabeth *dancer*
Persaud, Trivedi Vidhya Nandan *anatomy educator, researcher, consultant*
Poettcker, Henry *retired seminary president*
†Praznik, Darren Thomas *provincial legislator*
Roblin, Duff *former Canadian senator, health facility administrator*
Ronald, Allan Ross *internal medicine and medical microbiology educator, researcher*
Ross, Robert Thomas *neurologist, educator*
Rubio, Suzanne Sarah *ballet dancer*
Salgado, Lissette *dancer*
Savchenko, Alla *ballet mistress*
Schacter, Brent Allan *oncologist, health facility administrator*
Schaefer, Theodore Peter *chemistry educator*
†Schnoor, Jeffrey Arnold *lawyer*
Seifert, Blair Wayne *clinical pharmacist*
Smith, Ian Cormack Palmer *biophysicist*
Spohr, Arnold Theodore *artistic director, choreographer*
Stalker, Jacqueline D'Aoust *academic administrator, educator*
Suzuki, Isamu *microbiology educator, researcher*
Thompson, Susan A. *mayor*
Thorfinnson, A. Rodney *hospital administrator*
Tipples, Keith Howard *research director*
Turner, Robert Comrie *composer*
Wall, Leonard J. *bishop*
Watchorn, William Ernest *diversified manufacturing executive*
Weismiller, David R. *library administrator*
Wolfart, H.C. *linguistics scholar, author, editor*
Wreford, David Mathews *magazine editor*
Zhang Wei-Qiang *dancer*

## NEW BRUNSWICK

**Charters Settlement**
Easterbrook, James Arthur *psychology educator*

**Douglas**
Cogswell, Frederick William *English language educator, poet, editor, publisher*

**Fredericton**
Blanchard, Edmond P. *Canadian government official*
†Bourgeois, Maryanne *public administration executive*
Faig, Wolfgang *survey engineer, engineering educator*
Grotterod, Knut *retired paper company executive*
Kennedy, Richard Frederick *English language educator*
Kenyon, Gary Michael *gerontology educator, researcher*
†LeBreton, Paul M. *government official*
Lemmon, George Colborne *bishop*
Lewell, Peter A. *international technology executive, researcher*
†Loughrey, Carol Elaine Ashfield *government official*
Lumsden, Ian Gordon *art gallery director*
McCain, Margaret *province official*
†McGreal, Rory Patrick *educational administrator*
McKenna, Frank Joseph *Canadian government official, lawyer*
Parr-Johnston, Elizabeth *academic administrator*
Valenta, Zdenek *chemistry educator*
Vaníček, Petr *geodesist*

**Moncton**
McGeorge, Ronald Kenneth *hospital executive*

**Mouth of Keswick**
†Hoyt-Hallett, Bonny *health facility administrator*

**Oromocto**
Strange, Henry Hazen *judge*

**Rothesay**
Fairweather, Robert Gordon Lee *lawyer*

**Saint Andrews**
Anderson, John Murray *operations executive, former university president*
†Taylor, R. William *foundation administrator*

**Saint John**
Condon, Thomas Joseph *university historian*

**Sussex**
Secord, Lloyd Douglas *healthcare administrator*

**Westfield**
Logan, Rodman Emmason *retired jurist*

## NEWFOUNDLAND

**Corner Brook**
Payne, Sidney Stewart *archbishop*

**Saint John's**
†Aylward, Kevin *economist*
Clark, Jack I. *civil engineer, researcher*
Davis, Charles Carroll *aquatic biologist, educator*
†Gibbons, Rex Vincent *government official*
Grattan, Patricia Elizabeth *art gallery director*
Harvey, Donald Frederick *bishop*
†Matthews, Lloyd *government official*
May, Arthur W. *university president*
Murphy, John Joseph *city official, retail executive*
Rochester, Michael Grant *geophysics educator*
Russell, Frederick William *Canadian provincial official*
Troy, J. Edward *bishop*
†Vivian, Gladys Lily *administrator social services*
†Wells, Clyde Kirby *Canadian provincial government official*
Williams, Harold *geology educator*

## NORTHWEST TERRITORIES

**Yellowknife**
Croteau, Denis *bishop*
†LeBlanc, Pierre Gabriel *military officer*

## NOVA SCOTIA

**Antigonish**
Campbell, Colin *bishop*

**Bedford**
Hennigar, David J. *investment broker*

**Dartmouth**
Bhartia, Prakash *defense research management executive, researcher, educator*
Callaghan, J. Clair *corporate executive*
Elliott, James A. *oceanographer, researcher*
Horrocks, Norman *library science educator, editor*
Keen, Charlotte Elizabeth *marine geophysicist, researcher*
Mann, Kenneth Henry *marine ecologist*
†Norrie, Eleanor E. *government official*
Platt, Trevor Charles *oceanographer, scientist*

**Halifax**
Birdsall, William Forest *librarian*
Borgese, Elisabeth Mann *political science educator, author*
Burke, Austin E. *archbishop*
Carrigan, David Owen *history educator*
Cosman, Francene Jen *government official*
Dahn, Jeff R. *physics educator*
Dexter, Robert Paul *lawyer*
Dykstra Lynch, Mary Elizabeth *library and information science educator*
Fillmore, Peter Arthur *mathematician, educator*
Fowler, Charles Allison Eugene *architect, engineer*
Geldart, Donald James Wallace *physics educator*
†Gillis, John William *geologist, provincial government legislator*
Glube, Constance Rachelle *Canadian chief justice*
Gold, Edgar *marine affairs educator, mariner, lawyer*
Gold, Judith Hammerling *psychiatrist*
Goldbloom, Richard Ballon *pediatrics educator*
Gratwick, John *management consulting executive, writer, consultant*
Gray, James *English literature educator*
Hall, Brian Keith *biology educator, author*
Jackson, Sarah Jeanette *sculptor, graphic artist, copier artist, bookmaker*
Kinley, John James *government official*
Langley, George Ross *medical educator*
†MacGillivray, Frederick Richard *executive*
MacIntosh, Charles William *property development company executive*
Mingo, James William Edgar *lawyer*
Murray, Thomas John (Jock Murray) *medical humanities educator, medical researcher, neurologist*
O'Dor, Ron *physiologist, marine biology educator*
Ozmon, Kenneth Lawrence *university president, educator*
Pincock, Douglas George *electronics company executive*
Renouf, Harold Augustus *business consultant*
Savage, John Patrick *provincial official*
Shaw, Timothy Milton *political science educator*
Smith, Ronald Emory *telecommunications executive*
Sparling, Mary Christine *foundation executive*
Stairs, Denis Winfield *political science educator*
Stevenson, Candace J. *museum director*
Stewart, Ronald Daniel *medical educator, government official*
Tonks, Robert Stanley *pharmacology and therapeutics educator, former university dean*
Winham, Gilbert Rathbone *political science educator*

**Kentville**
Baker, George Chisholm *engineering executive, consultant*

**Lawrencetown**
Pottie, Roswell Francis *Canadian federal science and technology consultant*

**Liscomb**
Hemlow, Joyce *language and literature educator, author*

**Lower Sackville**
Ortlepp, Bruno *marine navigation educator, master mariner*

**Lunenburg**
Morrow, James Benjamin *retired sea products company executive*

**Mahone Bay**
Tolmie, Kenneth Donald *artist, author*

**North Sydney**
Nickerson, Jerry Edgar Alan *manufacturing executive*

**Parrsboro**
Hatfield, Leonard Fraser *retired bishop*

**Stellarton**
Gogan, James Wilson *corporate executive*
Rowe, Allan Duncan *food products executive*
Sobey, David Frank *food company executive*
Sobey, Donald Creighton Rae *real estate developer*

**Timberlea**
Verma, Surjit K. *school system administrator*

**Truro**
Mac Rae, Herbert Farquhar *retired college president*

**Wallace**
Boyle, Willard Sterling *physicist*

**Waverley**
†Grady, Wayne J. *government official*

**Wolfville**
Bishop, Roy Lovitt *physics and astronomy educator*
Colville, David Alexander *artist*
Elliott, Robbins Leonard *consultant*
Ogilvie, Kelvin Kenneth *university president, chemistry educator*
Toews, Daniel Peter *zoologist*
Zeman, Jarold Knox *history educator*

### Yarmouth
Wingle, James Mathew *bishop*

## ONTARIO

### Agincourt
Lutgens, Harry Gerardus *food company executive*

### Almonte
Hugessen, James K. *judge*
Morrison, Angus Curran *aviation executive*

### Ancaster
Brockhouse, Bertram Neville *physicist, retired educator*

### Aurora
Lanthier, Ronald Ross *retired manufacturing company executive*

### Barrie
Clune, Robert Bell *bishop*

### Blenheim
Thompson, Wesley Duncan *grain merchant*

### Bracebridge
MacKenzie, Lewis Wharton *military officer*

### Brampton
Allen, Clive Victor *lawyer, communications company executive*
Bastian, Donald Noel *bishop, retired*
Greenhough, John Hardman *business forms company executive*
Prevost, Edward James *paint manufacturing executive*
Robertson, Peter Barrie *mayor*
Toole, David George *pulp and paper products executive*

### Brantford
Inns, Harry Douglas Ellis *optometrist*
Woodcock, Richard Beverley *health facility administrator*

### Burlington
Cragg, Laurence Harold *chemist, former university president*
Elgersma, Ray *relief and development organization executive*
Hamilton, Donald Gordon *religious association administrator*
Harris, Philip John *engineering educator*
Karsten, Albert *religious organization administrator*
McMulkin, Francis John *steel company executive*

### Caledon
Fallis, Albert Murray *microbiology educator*

### Cambridge
Hooper, Wayne Nelson *clergy member*
MacBain, William Halley *minister, theology educator, seminary chancellor*
Turnbull, Robert Scott *manufacturing company executive*
White, Joseph Charles *manufacturing and retailing company executive*

### Campbellville
Georgije, Djokic *bishop*

### Cavan
Young, Scott Alexander *television journalist, author*

### Chalk River
Milton, John Charles Douglas *nuclear physicist*
Torgerson, David Franklyn *chemist, research facility administrator*

### Chatham
McKeough, William Darcy *investment company executive*

### Cornwall
La Rocque, Eugene Philippe *bishop*

### Deep River
Hanna, Geoffrey Chalmers *nuclear scientist*
Newcombe, Howard Borden *biologist, consultant*

### Don Mills
Applebaum, Louis *composer, conductor*
Atwood, Margaret Eleanor *author*
Budrevics, Alexander *landscape architect*
French, William Harold *retired newspaper editor*
Hickey, Brian Edward *publishing executive*

### Downsview
Bakht, Baidar *civil engineer, researcher, educator*
Burton, Ian *environmentalist, consultant, educator, writer*
Endler, Norman Solomon *psychology educator*
Forer, Arthur H. *biology educator, researcher, editor*
Moens, Peter B. *biology researcher and educator*
Pritchard, Huw Owen *chemist, educator*
Ribner, Herbert Spencer *physicist, educator*
Tennyson, Roderick C. *aerospace scientist*
Thomas, Clara McCandless *retired English language educator, biographer*

### Dundas
Jones, Frank Edward *sociology educator*
Shaw, John Firth *orchestra administrator*

### Dunrobin
Dickson, Brian *retired chief justice of Canada*

### Elgin
Lafave, Hugh Gordon John *medical association executive, psychiatrist, educator, consultant*

### Etobicoke
Bahadur, Birendra *display specialist, liquid crystal researcher*
Coleman, K. Virginia *diaconal minister*
Ecroyd, Lawrence Gerald *trade association administrator*
Gulden, Simon *lawyer, foods and beverages company executive*
Holyday, Douglas Charles *mayor*
Howe, James Tarsicius *retired insurance company executive*
Hyland, Geoffrey Fyfe *energy company executive*
Stojanowski, Wiktor J. *mechanical engineer*
Wykes, Edmund Harold *retired insurance company executive*

### Fort Erie
Watson, Stewart Charles *construction company executive*

### Galt
Dobbie, George Herbert *retired textile manufacturing executive*

### Gloucester
†Bailey, Donovan *Olympic athlete*
Boisvert, Laurier J. *communications executive*
Browning, Kurt *figure skating champion*
Marsters, Gerald Frederick *retired aerospace science and technology executive*

### Grimsby
Morgan, Wayne Philip *art and popular culture exhibition producer*

### Guelph
Benn, Denna M. *veterinarian*
Beveridge, Terrance James *microbiology educator, researcher*
Bewley, John Derek *botany researcher, educator*
Dickinson, William Trevor *hydrologist, educator*
Jorgensen, Erik *forest pathologist, educator, consultant*
Karl, Gabriel *physics educator*
Kasha, Kenneth John *crop science educator*
Land, Reginald Brian *library administrator*
Oaks, B. Ann *plant physiologist, educator*
Osen, Gregory Alan *water conditioning company executive*
Sells, Bruce Howard *biomedical sciences educator*
Simpson, John Joseph *physics educator, researcher*

### Hamilton
Asbil, Walter *bishop*
Banaschewski, Bernhard *mathematics educator*
Bandler, John William *electrical engineering educator, consultant*
Basinski, Zbigniew Stanislaw *metal physicist, educator*
Basmajian, John Varoujan *medical scientist, educator, physician*
Bienenstock, John *physician, educator*
Blewett, David Lambert *English literature educator*
Campbell, Colin Kydd *electrical and computer engineering educator, researcher*
Childs, Ronald Frank *chemistry educator, science administrator*
Collins, John Alfred *obstetrician-gynecologist, educator*
Crowe, Cameron Macmillan *chemical engineering educator*
Datars, William Ross *physicist, educator*
Davies, John Arthur *physics and engineering educator, scientist*
Garland, William James *engineering physics educator*
George, Peter James *economist, educator*
Gillespie, Ronald James *chemistry educator, researcher, writer*
Hill, Graham Roderick *librarian*
King, Leslie John *geography educator*
Lee, Alvin A. *literary educator, scholar, author*
Lipton, Daniel Bernard *conductor*
MacLean, David Bailey *chemistry educator, researcher*
Mc Kay, Alexander Gordon *classics educator*
Mueller, Charles Barber *surgeon, educator*
Parnas, David Lorge *computer scientist, engineer, educator*
Pietrzak, Ted S. *art gallery director*
Roland, Charles Gordon *physician, medical historian, educator*
Ryan, Ellen Bouchard *psychology educator, gerontologist*
Schwarcz, Henry Philip *geologist, educator*
Shaw, Denis Martin *university dean, former geology educator*
Smith, Stuart Lyon *psychiatrist, corporate executive*
Spenser, Ian Daniel *chemist educator*
Sprung, Donald Whitfield Loyal *physics educator*
Stanbury, Robert Douglas George *lawyer, executive*
Telmer, Frederick Harold *steel products manufacturing executive*
Tonnos, Anthony *bishop*
Uchida, Irene Ayako *cytogenetics educator, researcher*
Walker, Roger Geoffrey *geology educator, consultant*
Welch, Douglas Lindsay *physics educator*

### Hanover
Adams, John David Vessot *manufacturing company executive*

### Hillier
Lunn, Janet Louise Swoboda *writer*

### Islington
Foster, John Stanton *nuclear engineer*
White, Adrian Michael Stephen *financial executive*

### Keswick
Macdonald, John Barfoot *research foundation executive*

### Kingston
Akenson, Donald Harman *historian, educator*
Bacon, David Walter *chemical engineering educator*
Batchelor, Barrington de Vere *civil engineer, educator*
Berry, John Widdup *psychologist*
Bisby, Mark Ainley *physiology educator*
Boag, Thomas Johnson *physician*
Campbell, L(ouis) Lorne *mathematics educator*
Coleman, Albert John *mathematics educator*
Dick, Susan Marie *English language educator*
Ewan, George Thomson *physicist, educator*
Furter, William Frederick *chemical engineer, educator, university dean*
Glynn, Peter Alexander Richard *hospital administrator*
Hamilton, Albert Charles *English language educator*
Kaliski, Stephan Felix *economics educator*
Kaufman, Nathan *pathology educator, physician*
Leggett, William C. *biology educator, academic administrator*
Low, James A. *physician*
Mac Kenzie, Norman Hugh *retired English educator, writer*
Manning, Charles Terrill *retired lawyer*
McDonald, Arthur Bruce *physics educator*
McGeer, James Peter *research executive, consultant*
Meisel, John *political scientist*
Read, Allan Alexander *minister*
Riley, Anthony William *German language and literature educator*
Sayer, Michael *physics educator*
Sen, Paresh Chandra *electrical engineering educator*
Spence, Francis John *archbishop*
Spencer, John Hedley *biochemistry educator*
Stanley, James Paul *printing company executive*
Stewart, Alec Thompson *physicist*
Szarek, Walter Anthony *chemist, educator*
Turpin, David Howard *biologist, educator*
Wyatt, Gerard Robert *biology educator, researcher*

### Kitchener
Coles, Graham *conductor, composer*
Huras, William David *bishop*
MacDonald, Wayne Douglas *publisher*
Pollock, John Albon *broadcasting and manufacturing company executive*
Rittinger, Carolyne June *newspaper editor*
Winger, Roger Elson *church administrator*

### Kleinburg
Tyler, Barbara A. *museum director*

### Leamington
Epp, Menno Henry *clergyman*

### Lindsay
Evans, John David Daniel *judge*

### Lions Bay
Bartholomew, Gilbert Alfred *retired physicist*

### London
Allan, Ralph Thomas Mackinnon *insurance company executive*
Bancroft, George Michael *chemical physicist, educator*
Banks, Margaret Amelia *author, consultant, retired law educator-librarian*
Bauer, Michael Anthony *computer scientist, educator*
Borwein, David *mathematics educator*
Brooks, Vernon Bernard *neuroscientist, educator, author*
Buck, Carol Kathleen *medical educator*
Carroll, Kenneth Kitchener *biochemist, nutritionist, educator*
Carruthers, S. George *medical educator, physician*
Collins, Thomas Joseph *English language educator*
Cornies, Larry Alan *journalist, educator*
Creighton, Dale Edward *retired insurance company executive*
Creighton, Douglas George *French language educator*
Crncich, Tony Joseph *retired pharmacy chain executive*
Davenport, Alan Garnett *civil engineer, educator*
Davenport, Paul *university administrator, economics educator*
Desbarats, Peter Hullett *journalist, academic administrator*
Dreimanis, Aleksis *emeritus geology educator*
Dunn, Wesley John *dental educator*
Ehrman, Joachim Benedict *mathematics educator*
Fyfe, William Sefton *geochemist, educator*
Gerber, Douglas Earl *classics educator*
Haskett, Dianne Louise *mayor, lawyer*
Inculet, Ion I. *electrical engineering educator, research director, consultant*
Kimura, Doreen *psychology educator, researcher*
Laidler, David Ernest William *economics educator*
Lala, Peeyush Kanti *medical scientist, educator*
Livick, Stephen *fine art photographer*
Locke, Michael *zoology educator*
Marotta, Joseph Thomas *medical educator*
McLeod, Philip Robert *publishing executive*
McMurty, Robert Y. *academic dean*
McWhinney, Ian Renwick *physician, medical educator*
Orser, Earl Herbert *insurance company executive*
Osbaldeston, Gordon Francis *business educator, former government official*
Pearson, Norman *urban and regional planner, administrator, academic and planning consultant, writer*
Peterson, Leslie Ernest *bishop*
Poole, Nancy Geddes *art gallery curator*
Reaney, James Crerar *dramatist, poet, educator*
Roach, Margot Ruth *biophysicist, educator*
Scott, W. Peter *bishop*
Sherlock, John Michael *bishop*
Stafford, Earl *conductor*
Stewart, Harold Brown *biochemist*
Stillman, M. J. *physical science rsch. administrator, bioinorganic chemist*
Stothers, John B. *chemistry educator*
Valberg, Leslie Stephen *medical educator, physician, researcher*
Weedon, Alan Charles *chemist, educator, university dean*
Widdrington, Peter Nigel Tinling *environmental and energy company executive*
William, David *director, actor*
Wilson, Gerald Einar *mechanical and industrial engineer, business executive*
Wonnacott, Ronald Johnston *economics educator*

### Maberly
Kennett, William Alexander *retired Canadian government official, consultant*

### Manotick
Hobson, George Donald *retired geophysicist*
Prince, Alan Theodore *former government official, engineering consultant*

### Markham
Burns, H. Michael *health care company executive*
Marshall, Donald Stewart *computer systems company executive*
Nelson, William George, IV *software company executive*
Stronach, Frank *automobile parts manufacturing executive*
Wardell, David Joseph *travel industry specialist*

### Mississauga
Astington, John Harold *English educator*
Barkin, Martin *pharmaceutical company executive, physician*
Beckley, Michael John *hotel executive*
Burrell, Carol Ann *trade association executive*
Davies, Michael Norman Arden *lawyer, business executive*
†Farrell, Craig *hotel executive*
Griffin, William Arthur *clergyman, religious organization executive*
Hornby-Anderson, Sara Ann *metallurgical engineer, marketing professional*
Lewis, William Leonard *food products executive*
†McCallion, Hazel *mayor*
Mills, Donald McKenzie *librarian*
Morden, John Reid *Canadian government corporation administrator*
†Ortt, Terry *hotel executive*
Pelley, Marvin Hugh *mining executive*
Peterson, Oscar Emmanuel *pianist*
Ross, Thomas McCallum *professional society administrator*
Ryan, Noel *librarian, consultant*
Sonnenberg, Hardy *data processing company research and development executive, engineer*
Strachan, Graham *pharmaceutical company executive*
Thibault, J(oseph) Laurent *service company executive*
Tobias, Kal *transportation executive*
Turnbull, Adam Michael Gordon *financial executive, accountant*

### Nepean
†Adams, Gabrielle *biologist*
†Alfredsson, Daniel *professional hockey player*
Beare-Rogers, Joyce Louise *former research executive*
Bishop, Claude Titus *retired biological sciences research administrator, editor*
Cornell, Peter McCaul *economic consultant, former government official*
Kallmann, Helmut Max *music historian, retired music librarian*
†Pokotylo, August Elmer *government official*
Stanford, Joseph Stephen *diplomat, lawyer, educator*

### Newmarket
Wood, Neil Roderick *real estate development company executive*

### Niagara-on-the-Lake
Newton, Christopher *artistic director*
Olley, Robert Edward *economist, educator*
Scott, Campbell *artist*

### Nobleton
Embleton, Tony Frederick Wallace *retired Canadian government official*

### North Town
†Morgan, Beverly *publishing company executive*

### North York
Adelman, Howard *philosophy educator*
Arthurs, Harry William *legal educator, former university president*
Bohme, Diethard Kurt *chemistry educator*
Bryant, Josephine Harriet *library executive*
Buzacott, John Alan *engineering educator*
Carrothers, Gerald Arthur Patrick *environmental and city planning educator*
Carswell, Allan Ian *physics educator*
Castel, Jean Gabriel *lawyer*
Coles, Don Langdon *English literature educator*
Cumming, Glen Edward *art gallery director*
Davey, Kenneth George *biologist, university official*
Denham, Frederick Ronald *management consultant*
Hanna, William Brooks *book publisher*
Harris, Sydney Malcolm *retired judge*
Lastman, Melvin D. *mayor*
Macdonald, Hugh Ian *university president emeritus, economist, educator*
MacKenzie, Donald Murray *hospital administrator*
Mann, Susan *history educator*
Regan, David *brain researcher, educator*
Richmond, Anthony Henry *sociologist, emeritus educator*
Tulving, Endel *psychologist, educator*
Turnbull, John Cameron *pharmacist, consultant*
Wleugel, John Peter *manufacturing company executive*
Yarlow, Loretta *art museum director*

### Oakville
Barlow, Kenneth James *management consultant*
Holmes, James *investment company executive*

### Ontario
†DeQuetteville, Allan M. *career officer*

### Orillia
O'Grady, Thomas B. *Canadian provincial official*

### Oshawa
Drynan, Margaret Isobel *music teacher, retired consultant*

### Ottawa
†Adams, John L. *retired career officer, federal agency administrator*
Alper, Howard *chemistry educator*
Anderson, David *Canadian government official*
Andrew, Bryan Haydn *astronomer*
†Archambault, Pierre Guy *judge*
Armstrong, Henry Conner *former Canadian government official, consultant*
Austin, Jacob (Jack Austin) *Canadian senator*
Axworthy, Chris *Canadian government official*
Axworthy, Lloyd *Canadian government official*
Batra, Tilak Raj *research scientist*
Beatty, Perrin *broadcasting company executive*
Beaudoin, Gérald-A(rmand) *lawyer, educator, senator*
Beehan, Cathy *government official, lawyer*
Bélisle, Paul *Canadian government official*

Goring, David Arthur Ingham *chemical engineering educator, scientist*
Goring, Peter Allan Elliott *real estate executive*
Gotlieb, Allan E. *former ambassador*
Gotlieb, Calvin Carl *computer scientist, educator*
Gotlieb, Phyllis Fay Bloom *author*
Graham, James Edmund *service management executive*
Graham, John Webb *lawyer*
Graham, Victor Ernest *French language educator*
Granatstein, Jack Lawrence *history educator*
Grayson, Albert Kirk *Near Eastern studies educator*
Greben, Stanley Edward *psychiatrist, educator, author, editor*
Greenwood, Lawrence George *banker*
Gregor, Tibor Philip *management consultant*
Greig, Thomas Currie *retired financial executive*
Greiner, Peter Charles *mathematics educator, researcher*
Grendler, Paul Frederick *history educator*
Grier, Ruth *environmentalist*
Grinspun, Ricardo *economist, educator*
Grosland, Emery Layton *banker*
†Hall, Barbara *mayor*
Halperin, John Stephen *mathematics educator*
Ham, James Milton *engineering educator*
Hanson, Erik Brian *professional baseball player*
Harris, Nicholas George *publisher*
Harvey, George Edwin *communications company executive*
Hayes, Derek Cumberland *banking executive, lawyer*
Hayhurst, James Frederick Palmer *career and business consultant, inspirational speaker, writer*
Haynes, Robert Hall *biophysicist, educator*
Heath, Michele Christine *botany educator*
Helleiner, Gerald Karl *economics educator*
Hentgen, Patrick George *professional baseball player*
Herbert, Stephen W. *hospital executive*
Hirst, Peter Christopher *consulting actuary*
Hodgson, Chris *Canadian provincial official*
Hofmann, Theo *biochemist, educator*
Hollander, Samuel *economist, educator*
Honderich, John Allen *newspaper publisher*
Hore, John Edward *commodity futures educator*
Hudson, Alan Roy *neurosurgeon, medical educator, hospital administrator*
Innanen, Larry John *lawyer, food products executive*
Irwin, Samuel Macdonald *toy company executive*
Israelievitch, Jacques H. *violinist, conductor*
Ivey, Donald Glenn *physics educator*
Jackman, Henry Newton Rowell *former Canadian provincial official*
Jacob, Ellis *entertainment company executive*
Jagt, Jack *trading company executive*
Janischewskyj, Wasyl *electrical engineering educator*
Jay, Charles Douglas *religion educator, college administrator, clergyman*
Jervis, Robert E. *chemistry educator*
Johnson, Robert Eugene *historian, academic administrator*
Johnston, Malcolm Carlyle *bank executive*
Johnston, Robert Donaghy *cultural organization administrator*
Kain, Karen Alexandria *ballet dancer*
Kalant, Harold *pharmacology educator, physician*
Kalow, Werner *pharmacologist, toxicologist*
Keenan, Anthony Harold Brian *catalog company executive*
Kerr, David Wylie *natural resource company executive*
King, John Charles Peter *newspaper editor*
Kirby, Charles William, Jr. *dancer, choreographer*
Kluge, Holger *bank executive*
Korey-Krzeczowski, George J. M. Kniaz *university administrator, management consultant*
Kosich, George John *retail executive*
Kossuth, Selwyn Barnett *trade association consultant*
Kramer, Burton *graphic designer, educator*
Kresge, Alexander Jerry *chemistry educator*
Kudelka, James *choreographer, artistic director*
Kuerti, Anton Emil *pianist, composer*
Kunov, Hans *biomedical and electrical engineering educator*
Kushner, Donn Jean *microbiologist, children's author*
Kushner, Eva *academic administrator, educator, author*
Lamy, Martine *dancer*
Landsberg, Michele *journalist*
Lasker, David Raymond *newspaper editor, musician*
Lavoie, Serge *principal dancer*
Leech, James William *technology company executive*
Lewis, Robert *periodical editor, journalist*
Lindsay, Roger Alexander *investment executive*
Lindsay, William Kerr *surgeon*
List, Roland *physicist, educator, former UN official*
Litherland, Albert Edward *physics educator*
Liversage, Richard Albert *cell biologist*
Lombardi, John Barba-Linardo *broadcasting executive*
Lowe, Donald Cameron *corporate executive*
Lowe, Robert Edward *financial company executive*
Lucas, Cynthia *ballet mistress, dancer*
Macdonald, Donald Stovel *lawyer*
MacDougall, Hartland Molson *corporate director, retired bank executive*
Mackiw, Vladimir Nicholaus *metallurgical consultant*
MacLennan, David Herman *research scientist, educator*
MacMillin, James *religious organization administrator*
Mann, George Stanley *real estate and financial services corporation executive*
Martin, Robert William *corporate director*
McAuliffe, Jane Dammen *Middle Eastern and Islamic studies educator*
McCoomb, Lloyd Alexander *transportation executive*
McCoubrey, R. James *advertising executive*
Mc Culloch, Ernest Armstrong *physician, educator*
McKenna, Marianne *architect*
McLean, (Andrew) Stuart *educator, journalist*
McMurtry, R. Roy *chief justice*
McNeill, John *botanist*
McNeill, K(enneth) G(ordon) *medical physicist*
Meadows, George Lee *communications company executive*
Meagher, George Vincent *mechanical engineer*
Mercier, Eileen Ann *management consultant*
Miller, Anthony Bernard *physician, medical researcher*
Miller, Kenneth Merrill *computing services company executive*
Millgate, Jane *language professional*
Millgate, Michael (Henry) *retired English educator*
Mills, Robert Harry *church administrator*
Moffat, John William *physics educator*

Montgomery, Donald Russell *labor consulting firm executive*
Moore, Carole Irene *librarian*
Moore, Christopher Hugh *writer*
Morey, Carl Reginald *musicologist, academic administrator*
Mowatt, E. Ann *women's voluntary leader, lawyer*
Munk, Peter *mining executive*
Munro, John Henry Alexander *economics educator, writer*
Murasugi, Kunio *mathematician, educator*
Mustard, James Fraser *research institute executive*
Naldrett, Anthony James *geology educator*
Nesbitt, Lloyd Ivan *podiatrist*
Nesbitt, Mark *management consultant*
Norris, Geoffrey *geology educator, consultant*
Novak, David *Judaic studies educator, rabbi*
Ogilvie, Richard Ian *clinical pharmacologist*
Oliphant, Betty *ballet school director*
Olive, David Michael *magazine writer, magazine editor*
Olsen, Richard W. *advertising executive*
Osler, Gordon Peter *retired utility company executive*
Ostry, Sylvia *academic administrator, economist*
Ottaway, Terri Louise *geologist, gemologist*
Ottmann, Peter *choreologist, ballet master*
Owens, Joseph *clergyman*
Packer, Katherine Helen *retired library educator*
Packham, Marian Aitchison *biochemistry educator*
Parr, James Gordon *writer*
Pawson, Anthony J. *molecular biologist*
Payton, Thomas William *corporate finance consultant executive*
Pedersen, Paul Richard *composer, educator*
Peterson, David Robert *lawyer, former Canadian government official*
Peterson, Robert B. *petroleum company executive*
Petrillo, Leonard Philip *corporate securities executive, lawyer*
Pilliar, Robert Mathews *metallurgy educator, materials scientist*
Plaut, Wolf Gunther *minister, author*
Polanyi, John Charles *chemist, educator*
†Poprawa, Andrew *financial services executive, accountant*
Potvin, Felix *professional hockey player*
Pratt, Robert Cranford *political scientist, educator*
Prichard, John Robert Stobo *academic administrator, law educator*
Prugovecki, Eduard *mathematical physicist, educator, author*
Rakoff, Vivian Morris *psychiatrist, writer*
Ransom, Jeremy *ballet dancer*
Rapoport, Anatol *peace studies educator, mathematical biologist*
Rasky, Harry *producer, director, writer*
Rauhala, Ann Elaine *reporter*
Redford, Donald Bruce *historian, archaeologist*
Redway, Alan Arthur Sydney *Canadian legislator, lawyer*
Reid, Terence C. W. *corporation executive*
Rickerd, Donald Sheridan *foundation executive*
Rimrott, Friedrich Paul Johannes *engineer, educator*
†Roberts, William D. *broadcasting executive*
Rogers, Edward Samuel *communications company executive*
Ronald, Thomas Iain *financial services executive*
Ronald, William *artist*
Rooney, Paul George *mathematics educator*
Rose, Jeffrey Raymond *economist, educator, negotiator*
Ross, Henry Raymond *advertising executive and legal counsel*
Ross, Murray George *social science educator, university president emeritus*
Rothstein, Aser *radiation biology educator*
Rowe, David John *physics educator*
Runnalls, (Oliver) John (Clyve) *nuclear engineering educator*
Runte, Roseann *academic administrator*
Ryan, James Franklin *retail executive*
Salama, C. Andre Tewfik *electrical engineering educator*
Santiago, Benito Rivera *professional baseball player*
Saunderson, William *Canadian provincial official*
†Schneider, Mathieu *hockey player*
Schogt, Henry Gilius *foreign language educator*
Scholefield, Peter Gordon *health agency executive*
Schramek, Tomas *ballet dancer*
Schwenger, Frances *library director*
Seagram, Norman Meredith *corporate executive*
Seaquist, Ernest Raymond *astronomy educator*
Sedra, Adel Shafeek *electrical engineering educator, university administrator*
Semak, Michael William *photographer, educator*
Semlyen, Adam *electrical engineering educator*
Sessle, Barry John *university administrator, researcher*
Shaw, Ian Alexander *mining company executive, accountant*
Shearing, Clifford Denning *criminology and sociology educator*
Shearing, George Albert *pianist, composer*
Shields, Carol Ann *writer, educator*
Sierra, Ruben Angel Garcia *professional baseball player*
Sigal, Israel Michael *scientist*
Silk, Frederick C.Z. *financial consultant*
Silver, Malcolm David *pathologist, educator*
Silverman, Melvin *medical research administrator*
†Siminovitch, Louis *biophysics educator, scientist*
Singleton-Wood, Allan James *communications executive*
Skinner, Alastair *accountant*
Skvorecky, Josef Vaclav *English literature educator, novelist*
†Slaight, Gary *broadcasting executive*
Slemon, Gordon Richard *electrical engineering educator*
Sloan, David Edward *retired corporate executive*
Smith, David Todd *publishing company executive*
Smith, Peter William Ebblewhite *electrical engineering educator, scientist*
Smith, Stephen Alexander *retail and wholesale food distribution company executive*
Sole, Michael Joseph *cardiologist*
Sopko, Michael D. *mining company executive*
Spooner, Ed Thornton Casswell *geology educator and researcher*
Stadelman, William Ralph *chemical institution executive*
Staines, Mavis Avril *artistic director, ballet principal*
Stavro, Steve A. *professional hockey team executive*
Stefanschi, Sergiu *dancer*
Stoicheff, Boris Peter *physicist, educator*
Styles, Richard Geoffrey Pentland *retired banker*
†Sundin, Mats Johan *professional hockey player*

Synan, Edward Aloysius, Jr. *clergyman, former institute president*
Tall, Franklin David *mathematics educator*
Taman, Larry *Canadian provincial official*
†Tanaka, Ron S. *hotel executive*
Taylor, Allan Richard *retired banker*
Taylor, Paul Albert *banker*
Ten Cate, Arnold Richard *dentistry educator*
Thall, Burnett Murray *newspaper executive*
Thomas, Alan Richard *natural resources products executive*
Thomas, Isiah Lord, III *former professional basketball player, basketball team executive*
Thomas, Kenneth Glyndwr *mining executive*
Thomson, Kenneth R. (Lord Thomson of Fleet) *publishing executive*
Thomson, Richard Murray *banker*
Thornley, Shirley Blumberg *architect*
Tidwell, Thomas Tinsley *chemistry educator*
Till, James Edgar *medical educator, researcher*
Tindal, Douglas *religious organization administrator*
Tobe, Stephen Solomon *zoology educator*
Todres, Elaine Meller *foundation administrator*
Tremaine, Scott Duncan *astrophysicist*
Troubetzkoy, Alexis Serge *foundation administrator, educator*
Tsubouchi, David H. *Canadian provincial official*
Tsui, Lap-Chee *molecular genetics educator*
Turner, Gerald Phillip *hospital administrator*
Turner, John Napier *former prime minister of Canada, legislator*
Turner, Peter Merrick *retired manufacturing company executive*
Turner, Robert Edward *psychiatrist, educator*
Turpen, Louis A. *airport terminal executive*
van Ginkel, Blanche Lemco *architect, educator*
Van Houten, Stephen H. *manufacturing company executive*
Venetsanopoulos, Anastasios Nicolaos *electrical engineer, educator*
Volpé, Robert *endocrinologist, researcher, educator*
Watson, Paul *photojournalist, correspondent*
Webb, Anthony Allan *banker*
Webster, Jill Rosemary *historian, educator*
Weldon, David Black *financial executive*
Weston, W. Galen *diversified holdings executive*
Wetzel, Heinz *foreign language educator*
Wevers, John William *retired Semitic languages educator*
Whittington, Stuart Gordon *chemistry educator*
Wicks, Frederick John *research mineralogist, museum curator*
Wilder, Valerie *ballet company administrator*
†Wildman, C.J. (Bud) *political organization official*
Wilkins, Ormsby *music director, conductor, pianist*
Wilson, Ian Edwin *cultural organization administrator, archivist*
Wilson, Jim *Canadian provincial official*
Wilson, Lois M. *minister*
Wilson, Thomas Arthur *economics educator*
Winter, Frederick Elliot *fine arts educator*
Witkowsky, Gizella *dancer*
Wolfe, Harold Joel *lawyer, business executive*
Wolfe, Jonathan A. *food wholesaler, retailer*
Wonham, Walter Murray *electrical engineer, educator*
Yip, Cecil Cheung-Ching *biochemist, educator*
Zemans, Joyce Pearl *art historian, arts administrator*

### Unionville
Nichols, Harold Neil *corporate executive, former pipeline company executive*
Rusnak, Michael *bishop*

### Waterloo
Aczel, Janos Dezso *mathematics educator*
Berczi, Andrew Stephen *academic administrator*
Cornell, Paul Grant *history educator*
Cowan, Donald Douglas *mathematician, educator, computer scientist*
Downey, James *university president*
Fallding, Harold Joseph *sociology educator*
Gladwell, Graham Maurice Leslie *mathematician, civil engineering educator*
Haworth, Lawrence Lindley *philosophy educator*
Hynes, Hugh Bernard Noel *biology educator*
Kay, Jeanne *dean, educator*
Masterman, Jack Verner *insurance company executive*
Mills (Kutz-Harder), Helga *religious organization executive*
Morgan, Alan Vivian *geologist, educator*
Nash, Peter Hugh John *geographer, educator, planner*
Nelson, J. Gordon *geography educator*
Paldus, Josef *mathematics educator*
Penlidis, Alexander *chemical engineering educator*
Pindera, Jerzy Tadeusz *mechanical and aeronautical engineer*
Rempel, Garry Llewellyn *chemical engineering educator, consultant*
Sherbourne, Archibald Norbert *civil engineering educator*
Smith, Rowland James *educational administrator*
Sprott, David Arthur *statistics and psychology educator*
Stewart, Cameron Leigh *mathematics educator*
Suits, Bernard Herbert *philosophy educator*
Urquhart, Tony *artist, educator*
Vlach, Jiri *electrical engineering educator, researcher*
Warner, Barry Gregory *geographer, educator*
Wright, Douglas Tyndall *former university administrator, civil engineer*

### Welland
Wintermans, Joseph Jack Gerard Francis *financial services executive*

### Weston
McIntyre, John George Wallace *real estate development and management consultant*

### Willowdale
Binder, Herbert R. *drug store chain executive*
Bloom, David Ronald *retail drug company executive*
Bulloch, John Frederick Devon *foundation administrator*
Dean, Geoffrey *book publisher*
Irwin, John Wesley *publisher*
Kerner, Fred *book publisher, writer*
MacDonald, Brian Scott *management consultant*
McDonald, William Henry *financial executive*

### Windsor
Auld, Frank *psychologist, educator*
Drake, Gordon William Frederic *physics educator*

Hackam, Reuben *electrical engineering educator*
Ianni, Ronald William *university president and vice chancellor, lawyer*
Jones, William Ernest *chemistry educator*
Landry, G. Yves *automotive company executive*
Thibert, Roger Joseph *clinical chemist, educator*
Whitney, Barry Lyn *religious studies educator*

### Yarker
Smallman, Beverley N. *biology educator*

## PRINCE EDWARD ISLAND

### Charlottetown
†Beck, Rory *government agency administrator*
Carruthers, Norman Harry *Canadian province supreme court justice*
†Hicken, Barry W. *environmental legislator*
MacAulay, Lawrence A. *Canadian government official*
Severance, Christopher Churchill *museum director*

## QUEBEC

### Amos
Drainville, Gerard *bishop*

### Athelstan
Ness, Owen McGregor *retired aluminum company executive*

### Ayers Cliff
Beament, Thomas Harold (Tib Beament) *artist, printmaker, educator*

### Beaconsfield
Harder, Rolf Peter *graphic designer, painter*

### Beauport
Parent, André *neurobiology educator, researcher*

### Boucherville
Martel, Jacques G. *engineer, adminstrator*

### Brockville
Spalding, James Stuart *retired telecommunications company executive*

### Brossard
Allen, Harold Don *education educator, science writer, monetary historian*

### Charlesbourg
†Gignac, Jean-Pierre *lawyer, judge*
Paradis, Andre *librarian*

### Chelsea
Warren, Jack Hamilton *former diplomat and trade policy advisor*

### Chicoutimi
Couture, Jean Guy *bishop*

### Dollard
Des Roches, Antoine *retired newspaper executive*

### Dorval
Brown, Robert Ellis *transportation company executive, former Canadian government official*

### Haute-Ville
Fortier, Jean-Marie *retired archbishop*

### Hull
Blondin-Andrew, Ethel *Canadian government official*
Boyer, Denis *library director*
†Cappe, Melvin Samuel *economist*
†Chartier, Jean *federal public service administrator*
Ebacher, Roger *archbishop*
Gagliano, Alfonso *Canadian government official*
Gruchy, Charles George *Canadian government official*
Irwin, Ronald A. *Canadian government official*
†Isenberg, Seymour *government agency administrator*
MacDonald, George Frederick *anthropologist, Canadian museum director*
Marchi, Sergio Sisto *Canadian government official*
Marleau, Diane *Canadian government official*
†Ostry, Adam Knelman *public information office*

### Ile des Soeurs
Dagenais, Marcel Gilles *economist, educator*

### Ile Perrot
Tomlinson, George Herbert *retired industrial company research executive*

### Joliette
Audet, Rene *bishop*

### Laval
David, Michel Louis *geostatistician, consultant*
Kluepfel, Dieter *microbiologist*
Pavilanis, Vytautas *microbiology educator, physician*
Pichette, Claude *former banking executive, university rector, research executive*

### Leclercville
Morin, Pierre Jean *retired management consultant*

### Longueuil
Caplan, L(azarus) David *manufacturing company executive*
Smith, Elvie Lawrence *corporate director*

### Mont Laurier
Gratton, Jean *clergyman*

### Montpellier
Poirier, Louis Joseph *neurology educator*

### Montreal
Aguayo, Albert Juan *neuroscientist*
Alain, Robert *foundation administrator*

Gauthier, Serge Gaston *neurologist*
Lessard, Michel M. *finance company executive*

### Wakefield
Roots, Ernest Frederick *scientific advisor emeritus*

### Westmount
Fortier, L. Yves *barrister*
Gordonsmith, John Arthur Harold *collection agency executive*
Jasper, Herbert Henri *neuroscience researcher, consultant, writer*
Kessler, Jacques Isaac *gastroenterologist, educator*
Lussier, Jean-Paul *dentistry educator*

## SASKATCHEWAN

### Moose Jaw
Moore, Yvette M. *artist, illustrator*

### Muenster
Novecosky, Peter Wilfred *abbot*

### Prince Albert
Burton, Anthony John *bishop*
Morand, Blaise E. *bishop*

### Regina
†Atkinson, Patricia *minister of education*
Balfour, Reginald James *lawyer*
Barber, Lloyd Ingram *retired university president*
Bayda, Edward Dmytro *judge*
Bays, Eric *retired bishop*
†Clayton, Raymond Edward *government official*
Dalla-Vicenza, Mario Joseph *steel company financial executive*
Davis, Gordon Richard Fuerst *retired biologist, translator*
Holm, Roy K. *church administrator*
Hughes, Robert Lachlan *newspaper executive*
†Kuziak, Myron A. *government official, lawyer*
Laschuk, Roy Bogdan *lawyer*
MacKay, Harold Hugh *lawyer*
Mallon, Peter *archbishop*
Mollard, John Douglas *engineering and geology executive*
Nuttall, Richard Norris *state agency administrator*
Penikett, Antony David John *Canadian government official*
Phillips, Roger *steel company executive*
Powell, Trevor John David *archivist*
Romanow, Roy John *provincial government official, barrister, solicitor*
Shillington, Edward Blain *government official*
Sonntag, Bernard H. *agrologist, research executive*
†Stengler, Ron Joseph *gaming corporation executive*
Teichrob, Carol *Canadian provincial official*
†Warriner, William Ernest *government official*
Wiebe, J. E. N. *province official*
†Zukowsky, Ronald James *environmental regulator*

### Saltcoats
Farquharson, Walter Henry *minister, church official*

### Saskatoon
Babiuk, Lorne Alan *virologist, immunologist, research administrator*
Bell, John Milton *agricultural science educator*
Belovanoff, Olga *retired health care facility administrator*
Billinton, Roy *engineering educator*
Blakeney, Allan Emrys *Canadian government official, lawyer*
Bornstein, Eli *artist, sculptor*
Brewster, Elizabeth Winifred *English language educator, poet, novelist*
Carr, Roy Arthur *agricultural products applied research, development and commercialization processing organization executive*
Childers, Charles Eugene *mining company executive*
Filevich, Basil *bishop*
Gupta, Madan Mohan *engineering educator, researcher*
Harvey, Bryan Laurence *crop science educator*
Hirose, Akira *physics educator, researcher*
Houston, C(larence) Stuart *radiologist, educator*
Huang, Pan Ming *soil science educator*
Irvine, Vernon Bruce *accounting educator, administrator*
Ish, Daniel Russell *law educator, academic adminstrator*
Jacobson, Sverre Theodore *retired minister*
Jaques, Louis Barker *pharmacologist*
Kennedy, Marjorie Ellen *librarian*
Kent, Christopher Andrew *history educator*
Knight, Arthur Robert *technical institute administrator*
Knott, Douglas Ronald *college dean, agricultural sciences educator, researcher*
Kumar, Surinder *electrical engineering educator, consultant*
Kupsch, Walter Oscar *geologist*
Morgan, Thomas Oliver *bishop*
Nikiforuk, Peter N. *university dean*
Popkin, David Richard *academic dean, obstetrician, gynocologist*
Randhawa, Bikkar Singh *psychologist, educator*
Sachdev, Mohindar Singh *engineering educator*
Shokeir, Mohamed Hassan Kamel *medical geneticist, educator*
Steck, Warren Franklin *chemical company executive, former biochemistry researcher*
Stewart, John Wray Black *college dean*

## YUKON TERRITORY

### Whitehorse
Lobsinger, Thomas *bishop*

## MEXICO

### Chetumal
Rosado-May, Francisco Javier *agricultural studies educator, researcher*

### Chihuahua
Almeida Merino, Adalberto *archbishop*

### Coahuila
Whelan, James Robert *communications executive, international trade and investment consultant, author, educator, mining executive, writer*

### Coyoacan
Paz, Octavio *poet, Mexican diplomat*

### Cuernavaca
Illich, Ivan *educator, researcher*
Mora, Francisco *artist, printmaker*

### Guadalajara
Godinez Flores, Ramon *auxiliary bishop*
Levine, Guillermo *computer scientist, educator*
Sandoval Iñiguez, Juan Cardinal *archbishop*

### Jalisco
Wolf, Charlotte Elizabeth *sociologist*

### Matamoros
Chavolla Ramos, Francisco Javier *bishop*

### Mexico City
Aramburo-de-la-Hoz, Carlos *biochemist, researcher*
Arellano, Hector *telecommunications consulting company executive*
Aspe, Pedro *former Mexican government official*
Baer, George Martin *veterinarian, researcher*
Blanco, Herminio *Mexican government official*
Bruton, John Macaulay *trade association executive*
†Camacho, Hector *boxer*
Castillo Garcia, Luis Fernando *science and technology educator*
Cervantes Aguirre, Enrique *Mexican government official*
†Chavez, Julio Cesar *professional boxer*
de Brun, Shauna Doyle *investment banker, industrialist*
de la Fuente Ramirez, Juan Ramon *Mexican government official*
del Conde, Teresa *museum director, art historian, researcher*
Dudley, Craig James *executive recruiter*
†Duran, Roberto *boxer*
Hernandez, Silvia *mexican government official*
†Hill, Virgil *professional boxer*
†Holmes, Keith *professional boxer*
†Joppy, William *professional boxer*
†Liles, Frank *professional boxer*
Limón Rojas, Miguel *Mexican government official*
†Lopez, Ricardo *professional boxer*
†Martens, Ernesto *air, aerospace transportation executive*
†Martin, Christy *professional boxer*
Martinez de la Escalera, Gonzalo *neuroendocrinologist*
Mendelejis, Leonardo Nierman *artist*
†Miller, Nate *professional boxer*
Peimbert, Manuel *astronomer*
†Randall, Frankie *professional boxer*
Rodriguez, Adolfo *library director, historian*
Rojas Gutierrez, Carlos *Mexican government official*
Ruiz Sacristán, Carlos *Mexican government official*
Schinkel, Claus *chemical company executive*
†Taylor, Quincy *professional boxer*
Warman, Arturo Gryj *Mexican government official*
Weber, Ernesto Juan *counselor, educator, industrialist*
Whitaker, Pernell (Sweet Pea Whitaker) *professional boxer*
†Zarazoga, Daniel *professional boxer*
Zedillo Ponce de León, Ernesto *president of Mexico*

### Morelia
Warren, J. Benedict *retired history educator*

### Morelos
Cauduro, Rafael *painter, muralist*

### Nuevo Leon
Garza Garza, Rómulo *livestock breeder and writer, agriculturist*

### Puebla
Zehe, Alfred Fritz Karl *physics educator*

### Saltillo
Villalobos Padilla, Francisco *bishop*

### San Nicolas de Garza
Suarez Rivera, Adolfo Antonio *archbishop*

### Veracruz
Ranzahuer, Guillermo Gonzalez *bishop*

### Zapopan
Garibay-Gutierrez, Luis *physician, educator*

## ARGENTINA

### Buenos Aires
Balve, Beba Carmen *research center administrator*
Bergel, Meny *physician, researcher*
Cascales, José María *bank executive*
Sacerdote, Manuel Ricardo *banker*

## ARMENIA

### Yerevan
Gilmore, Harry J. *ambassador*

## AUSTRALIA

### Avalon
West, Morris Langlo *novelist*

### Belair
Briggs, Geoffrey Hugh *retired librarian*

### Bundoora
James, Bruce David *chemistry educator*

### Canberra
Gani, Joseph Mark *statistics educator, administrator, researcher*
†Keith, Leroy Allen *aviation safety executive*
Taylor, Stuart Ross *geochemist, author*

### Kensington
Rayward, Warden Boyd *librarian, educator*

### Melbourne
Lawson, Francis Colin *chemical company executive*
Mc Gimpsey, Ronald Alan *oil company executive*

### Nedlands
Oxnard, Charles Ernest *anatomist, anthropologist, human biologist, educator*

### Randwick
Hall, Peter Francis *physiologist*

### Ringwood
Base, Graeme Rowland *illustrator, author*

### Strawberry Hills
Bonynge, Richard *opera conductor*

### Sydney
Barusch, Ronald Charles *lawyer*
Guerin, Didier *magazine executive*
Melkonian, Harry G. *insurance executive, rancher*
Miller, George *film director*
Murdoch, (Keith) Rupert *publisher*
Salsbury, Stephen Matthew *historian, educator*

## AUSTRIA

### Graz
Weisstein, Ulrich Werner *English literature educator*

### Laxenburg
MacDonald, Gordon James Fraser *geophysicist*

### Maria Enzersdorf
Vetter, Herbert *physician, educator*

### Salzburg
Mueller, Ulrich *literature educator*

### Vienna
Coufal, Franz Anton *sculptor*
†de Maria y Campos, Mauricio *United Nations official*
Frankl, Viktor E. *psychiatrist, author*
Hunt, Swanee G. *ambassador*
Lo Bello, Nino *author, journalist*
Niederreiter, Harald Guenther *mathematician, researcher*
Oberhuber, Konrad Johannes *art museum curator, educator*
Pohl, Adolf Leopold *clinical chemist, quality assurance consultant*
Steinbruckner, Bruno Friedrich *foreign language educator*

## BAHAMAS

### Grand Cayman
McIntire, Jerald Gene *investment executive, former municipal official*

### Nassau
Cates, Nelia Barletta de *diplomat*
Dingman, Michael David *industrial company executive, international investor*
Ford, John Seabury *diplomat*
Templeton, John Marks *investment counsel, financial analyst*

## BARBADOS

### Christ Church
Goodine, Isaac Thomas *development executive, educator*

## BELGIUM

### Brussels
Arion, Georges Julien *retired commercial organization executive*
Barnum, John Wallace *lawyer*
Branegan, James Augustus, III *journalist*
Bustin, George Leo *lawyer*
Glazer, Barry David *lawyer*
Hanotiau, Bernard Raoul *lawyer*
Hunter, Robert Edwards *ambassador, scholar*
Jadot, Jean Lambert Octave *clergyman*
Kempe, Frederick Schumann *newspaper editor, author*
Liebman, Howard Mark *lawyer*
Murdock, Robert McClellan *military officer*
Oberreit, Walter William *lawyer*
Pendleton, Mary Catherine *foreign service officer*
Prigogine, Vicomte Ilya *physics educator*
Rose, Merrill *public relations counselor*
†Solana Madariaga, Javier *Spanish government official*

### Lens
Peat, Randall Dean *defense analysis company executive, retired air force officer*

### Liege
Mosora, Florentina Ioana *physics educator*

### Strombeek Bever
Mancel, Claude Paul *household product company executive*

## BELIZE

### San Ignacio
Ripinsky-Naxon, Michael *archaeologist, art historian, ethnologist*

## BERMUDA

### Flatts
Smith, Wendell Murray *graphic arts control and equipment manufacturing executive*

### Hamilton
Kramer, Donald *insurance executive*
Stempel, Ernest Edward *insurance executive*

### Pembroke
Wiedemann, Joseph Robert *insurance company executive*

### Tuckers Town
Heizer, Edgar Francis, Jr. *venture capitalist*

## BRAZIL

### Brasilia
Ventura, Manuel Mateus *biochemist, educator*

### Rio Claro
Christofoletti, Antonio *geography educator*
Potter, Paul Edwin *geologist, educator, consultant*

### Rio de Janeiro
Sales, Eugenio de Araujo Cardinal *archbishop*

### São Paulo
Fernicola, Nilda Alicia Gallego Gándara de *pharmacist, biochemist*
Marino, Raul, Jr. *neurosurgeon*
Martins, Nelson *physics educator*

### Salvador
Davidson, Ralph Kirby *economist, retired foundation executive, consultant*

### Santa Maria
Radharamanan, Ramachandran *mechanical and industrial engineering educator*

### Sao Jose dos Campos
Berman, Marcelo Samuel *mathematics and physics educator, cosmology researcher*

## CAPE VERDE

### Praia
McNamara, Francis T. *ambassador*

## CAYMAN ISLANDS

### Grand Cayman
Crockett, James Grover, III *musician, former music publisher*

## CHILE

### Concepcion
Trzebiatowski, Gregory L. *education educator*

### Santiago
Beshears, Charles Daniel *consultant, former insurance executive*
Wilkey, Malcolm Richard *retired ambassador, former federal judge*

### Zapallar
Silbaugh, Preston Norwood *lawyer, consultant*

## CHINA

### Beijing
†Li, Gong-song *cardiac surgeon, educator*
Melville, Richard Allen *investment company executive*
Shu, Wenlong *environmental engineer, educator*

### Chengdu
Zeng, Xuegang *telecommunications enginer, engineering educator*
Zhou, Kang-Wei *physics educator*

### Guangzhou
Mundorf, Nancy Knox *early childhood educator*

### Hong Kong
Laurie, James Andrew *journalist, broadcaster*
Lehner, Urban Charles *journalist*
Ligare, Kathleen Meredith *strategy and marketing executive*
Magarity, Russell Lynn *banker*

### Nanjing
Wang, Xinwei *aeronautics educator*

### Shanghai
Li, Guosong *mechanical engineering educator*

### Taiwan
Meyer, Richard Jonah *broadcast executive, consultant*

## COSTA RICA

### Nicoya
Brunson, Joel Garrett *retired pathologist, educator*

**San Jose**
Hoffman, Irwin *orchestra conductor*

## CROATIA

**Zagreb**
Galbraith, Peter W. *ambassador*

## CUBA

**Havana**
Kouri, Gustavo Pedro *virologist*

## CZECH REPUBLIC

**Prague**
Kalkus, Stanley *librarian, administrator, consultant*

## DENMARK

**Birketinget**
†Larsen, Poul Steen *library educator*

**Copenhagen**
Alsted, Peter *lawyer*
Benjamin, David Nicholas *architect, researcher*
Bundesen, Claus Mogens *psychologist, educator*
Hansen, Elisa Marie *art historian*
Hansen, Ole *physicist*
Massolo, Arthur James *banker*
Pethick, Christopher John *physicist*
Skylv, Grethe Krogh *rheumatologist, anthropologist*

**Grasted**
Wiin-Nielsen, Aksel Christopher *meteorologist educator*

**Hoersholm**
Sørensen, Erik *international company executive*

**Vedbaek**
Nordqvist, Erik Askbo *shipping company executive*
Rasmussen, Gunnar *engineer*

## DOMINICAN REPUBLIC

**Santo Domingo**
†Marichal, Juan Antonio Sanchez *retired baseball player, agency administrator*
Piantini, Carlos *conductor*

## EGYPT

**Cairo**
Boutros-Ghali, Boutros *former United Nations official*
Callison, Charles Stuart *retired foreign service officer, development economist*
Miller, Harry George *education educator*

## ENGLAND

**Ascot Berkshire**
Grubman, Wallace Karl *chemical company executive*

**Balcombe**
Scofield, Paul *actor*

**Bedford**
Glassburn, Tracy Ann *geochemist, researcher*

**Berryhill**
Barlow, Matthew Blaise Joseph *merchant banker*

**Birmingham**
Casson, Alan Graham *thoracic surgeon, researcher*
Fry, Maxwell John *economist, educator*
Hick, John Harwood *theologian, philosopher, educator*

**Brighton**
Oldham, Charles Herbert Geoffrey *physicist, science consultant*
Watkin, David *film director, cinematographer*

**Buckinghamshire**
Elegant, Robert Sampson *journalist, author*
Pierce-Roberts, Tony *cinematographer*

**Burford**
Blackney, Arthur Bruce *Middle East defense and aviation consultant*

**Cambridge**
Acheson, Roy Malcolm *epidemiologist, educator*
Bream, Julian *classical guitarist and lutanist*
Hogwood, Christopher Jarvis Haley *music director, educator*
Kermode, (John) Frank *literary critic, educator*
Steiner, George (Francis Steiner) *author, educator*

**Carshalton**
Das, Sankar Kumar *cardiopulmonologist*

**Claverton Down**
Buchanan, Robert Angus *archaeology educator*

**Cornwall**
Dark, Philip John Crosskey *anthropologist, educator*

**Coventry**
Monberg, Jay Peter *management consultant*
Trigg, Roger Hugh *philosophy educator*

**Cranbrook**
Hattersley-Smith, Geoffrey Francis *retired government research scientist*

**Devon**
Rossmiller, George Eddie *agricultural economist*

**Eastbourne**
Baylen, Joseph O. *retired history educator*

**Hartlepool**
Smyth, Reginald (Reggie Smythe) *cartoonist*

**Heathfield**
Wilson, Leroy *retired glass manufacturing company executive*

**Hingham**
Pollini, Francis *author*

**Hove**
Kitchin, Laurence Tyson *liberal arts and drama educator, author*

**Isle of Wight**
Stigwood, Robert Colin *theater, movie, television and record producer*

**Iver Heath**
Kubrick, Stanley *producer, director, writer*

**Kettering**
Dellis, Frédy Michel *travel exchange company executive*

**Leeds**
Phillips, Oliver *tropical biodiversity scientist*

**Leicester**
Harijan, Ram *computer scientist, technology transfer researcher*

**Liverpool**
Reilly, Thomas *humanities educator*

**London**
Ackland-Snow, Terry *art director*
Adams, Douglas Noel *writer*
Albert, Robert Alan *lawyer*
Aliki, (Aliki Liacouras Brandenberg) *author, illustrator children's books*
Ambler, Eric *writer*
Ashkenazy, Vladimir Davidovich *concert pianist, conductor*
Barren, Bruce Willard *merchant banker*
Barshai, Rudolf Borisovich *conductor*
Bart, Lionel *composer, lyricist*
Bates, Malcolm Rowland *corporate director*
Batla, Raymond John, Jr. *lawyer*
Batty, J. Michael *geographer, educator*
Bawden, Nina (Mary) *author*
Baxendell, Sir Peter (Brian) *petroleum engineer*
Beck, Jeff *musician, composer, vocalist*
Beharrell, Steven Roderic *lawyer*
Berger, Andrew L. *investment banker, lawyer*
Berger, Thomas Jan *financial company executive*
Bertolucci, Bernardo *film director*
Bigbie, John Taylor *lawyer, banker*
Billings, Donald Franklin *international banking consultant*
Binney, Robert Harry *bank executive*
Bischoff, Winfried Franz Wilhelm *merchant banker*
Brownwood, David Owen *lawyer*
Bruce, Robert Rockwell *lawyer*
Catto of Cairncatto, Baron Stephen Gordon *banker*
Cellan-Jones, James Gwynne *television producer, director*
Chappell, Anthony Gordon *banker*
Clarke, Arthur Charles *author*
Cleese, John Marwood *writer, businessman, comedian*
Codron, Michael Victor *theatrical producer*
Cole, Richard A. *lawyer*
Collins, Paul John *banker*
Comfort, Alexander *physician, author*
Conti, Tom *actor, writer, director*
Cook, Jan *recording industry executive, film executive*
Cope, Wendy *poet, journalist*
Cowles, Fleur (Mrs. Tom M. Meyer) *author, artist*
Crowe, William James, Jr. *diplomat, think tank executive*
Dearden, James *director, screenwriter*
Deighton, Len *author*
Dickinson, Peter *composer*
Diem, William Roy, III *editor, playwright*
Dorman, Craig Emery *oceanographer, academic administrator*
Douglas, Mary Tew *anthropology and humanities educator*
Dowell, Anthony James, Sr. *ballet dancer*
Downing, Danielle Santander *brokerage house executive*
Doyle, Patrick *composer*
Drabble, Margaret *writer*
Dudley, Anne *composer*
†Dupee, Paul Rich, Jr. *business executive*
Elizabeth, Her Majesty II (Elizabeth Alexandra Mary) *Queen of United Kingdom of Great Britain and Northern Ireland, and her other Realms and Territories, head of the Commonwealth, defender of the faith*
Ellis, Peter Hudson *management consultant*
Elson, Sarah Lee *art historian*
Estes, Simon Lamont *opera singer, bass-baritone*
Fabricant, Arthur E. *lawyer, corporate executive*
Fine, Anne *author*
Follett, Kenneth Martin *author*
Foster, Sir Norman Robert *architect*
Fowles, John *author*
Fox, Hazel Mary *barrister, editor*
Francis, Freddie *film producer and director*
Freni, Mirella *soprano*
Gaines, Peter Mathew *lawyer*
Galloway, Janice *writer, editor*
Gielgud, Sir (Arthur) John *actor, director*
Gilbert, Patrick Nigel Geoffrey *organization executive*
Gillam, Patrick John *oil company executive*
Gleichauf, John George *ophthalmologist*
Godden, Rumer *author*
Grade, Lord Lew *entertainment corporation executive*
Green, Richard *psychiatrist, lawyer, educator*
Green, Richard Lancelyn (Gordon) *editor, writer*
Greener, Anthony *beverage company executive*
Gummer, Baron Peter Selwyn *public relations executive*
Gyllenhammar, Pehr Gustaf *finance company executive, retired automobile company executive, writer*
Habgood, Anthony John *corporate executive*
Hale, Charles Martin *stockbroker*
Hall, Peter Geoffrey *urban and regional planning educator*
Hallissey, Michael *accounting company executive*
Hare, David *playwright*
Haubold, Samuel Allen *lawyer*
Hawthorne, Nigel Barnard *actor*
Hayden, Richard Michael *investment banker*
Hendricks, Barbara *opera singer, recitalist*
Hinton, Leslie Frank *media executive*
Hoban, Russell Conwell *author*
Hoge, Warren M. *newspaper and magazine correspondent, editor*
Holm, Ian *actor*
Hornyak, Eugene Augustine *bishop*
Hoskins, Bob (Robert William Hoskins) *actor*
Hudson, Manley O., Jr. *lawyer*
Hughes, Ted *poet, author*
Hughes, Winifred Shirley *writer, illustrator*
Hunter Blair, Pauline Clarke *author*
Hurt, John Vincent *actor*
Irons, Jeremy John *actor*
Irvine, Ian Alexander Noble *publishing company executive, director*
Jackson, Felicity Anne *performing arts organization administrator*
Jalili, Mahir *lawyer*
James, P(hyllis) D(orothy) (Baroness James of Holland Park of Southwold in County of Suffolk ) *author*
John, Elton Hercules (Reginald Kenneth Dwight) *musician*
Johnson, Thomas Edward *lawyer*
Jourdren, Marc Henri *investment banking company executive*
Junz, Helen B. *economist*
Kingham, Richard Frank *lawyer*
Kitaj, R. B. *artist*
Kuper, Adam Jonathan *anthropologist, educator*
Lahr, John *author*
Leaf, Robert Stephen *public relations executive*
le Carré, John (David John Moore Cornwell) *author*
Lennox, Annie *rock musician*
Lessing, Doris (May) *writer*
Levi, Yoel *orchestra conductor*
Le Vien, John Douglas (Jack Le Vien) *motion picture and television producer, director*
Lloyd-Webber, Baron Andrew *composer*
Lynne, Gillian Barbara *choreographer, dancer, actress, director*
MacHale, Joseph P. *financial executive*
Mackerras, Sir (Alan) Charles (Maclaurin) *conductor*
Mackintosh, Cameron *musical theater producer*
MacLaren, Roy *Canadian government official, publisher*
Mallinckrodt, George W. *bank executive*
Markoski, Joseph Peter *lawyer*
Marriner, Sir Neville *orchestra conductor*
Marsden, William *government official*
Martines, Lauro *historian, writer*
Mathias, Christopher Joseph *physician, educator, researcher, consultant*
Mathias, Sean Gerard *author, director*
McIntyre, Donald Conroy *opera singer, baritone*
McKellen, Ian *actor*
McNulty, Dermot *public relations executive*
Mellon, John *publishing executive*
Menges, Chris *cinematographer, film director*
Miller, Jonathan Wolfe *theater and film director, physician*
Minton, Yvonne Fay *mezzo-soprano*
Mirageas, Evans John *record company executive*
Mirren, Helen *actress*
Montero, Fernan Gonzalo *advertising executive*
Montgomery, John Warwick *law educator, theologian*
Moreno, Glen Richard *banker*
Morris, Desmond *author*
Morrison, William David *lawyer*
Mulford, David Campbell *finance company executive*
Naipaul, Vidiadhar Surajprasad *author*
Nelson, Bernard Edward *lawyer*
Nelson, John Wilton *symphonic conductor*
Nucci, Leo *baritone*
Nunn, Trevor Robert *director*
Oliver, Diane Frances *publisher, writer*
Orr, Bobette Kay *diplomat*
Oxenbury, Helen *children's writer, illustrator*
Pacter, Paul Allan *accounting standards researcher*
Palin, Michael Edward *actor, screenwriter, author*
Paton Walsh, Jill *author*
Pecorino, Lauren Teresa *biologist*
Pennant-Rea, Rupert Lascelles *banker*
Perkin, Harold James *retired social historian, educator*
Phocas, George John *international lawyer, business executive*
Pickle, James C. *hospital administrator*
Pinter, Harold *playwright*
Pleasants, Henry *music critic*
Pletcher, John Harold, Jr. *career officer*
Plowright, Joan Anne *actress*
Pryce, Jonathan *actor*
Puttnam, Sir David Terence *film producer*
Ralston, Anthony *computer scientist, mathematician, educator*
Rattle, Simon *conductor*
Rea, Stephen *actor*
Read, Piers Paul *author*
Ricci, Ruggiero *violinist, educator*
Ricciarelli, Katia *soprano*
Russell, Thomas *British government official*
Rutter, Michael Llewellyn *child psychiatry educator*
Sainsbury of Preston Candover, Lord (John Davan Sainsbury) *food retailer executive, art patron*
Scardino, Albert James *journalist*
Scardino, Marjorie Morris *publishing company executive*
Schaufuss, Peter *dancer, producer, choreographer, ballet director*
Shaw, Sir Neil McGowan *sugar, cereal and starch refining company executive*
Slocombe, Douglas *cinematographer*
Smalley, David Vincent *lawyer*
Smernoff, Richard Louis *oil company executive*
Smith, Dame Maggie *actress*
Solomon, Andrew Wallace *author*
Sorrell, Martin Stuart *advertising and marketing executive*
Spark, Dame D. B. E. Muriel Sarah *writer*
Stapleton, Nigel John *multinational information publishing executive*
Starr, Ringo (Richard Starkey) *musician, actor*
Stevens, Robert Bocking *lawyer, educator*
Sting, (Gordon Matthew Sumner) *musician, songwriter, actor*
Stoppard, Tom (Tomas Straussler) *playwright*
Streator, Edward *diplomat*
Sutherland, Dame Joan *retired soprano*
Taylor, Jonathan Francis *agribusiness executive*
Tennstedt, Klaus *conductor*
Thomas, Allen Lloyd *lawyer, private investor*
Treasure, John Albert Penberthy *advertising executive*
Van Culin, Samuel *religious organization administrator*
Vaness, Carol *soprano*
Van Meter, John David *lawyer*
Wallis, Diana Lynn *artistic director*
Warr, Robert *producer*
†Webber, Andrew Lloyd *composer*
Weller, Michael *playwright, screenwriter*
Winner, Michael Robert *film director, writer, producer*
Wyman, William George *musician*

**London Bridge**
Nauheim, Stephen Alan *lawyer*

**Malmesbury**
Shober, Edward Wharton *bioscience company executive*

**Manchester**
Wilson, Keith Dudley *media and music educator*

**Milford on Sea**
Styan, John Louis *English literature and theater educator*

**Milton Keynes**
Daniel, Sir John Sagar *academic administrator, metallurgist*

**Newcastle upon Tyne**
Cookson, Dame Catherine Ann *author*

**Oxford**
Aldiss, Brian (Wilson) *writer*
Cairncross, Sir Alexander Kirkland *economist*
Carey, John *English language educator, literary critic*
Gulbrandsen, Natalie Webber *religious association administrator*
Heilbron, John L. *historian*
Hirsch, Peter Bernhard *metallurgist*
Howe, Daniel Walker *historian, educator*
†Pullman, Philip Nicholas *author, educator*
Tureck, Rosalyn *concert performer, author, editor, educator*
Williams, William Stanley Cossom *physics educator and researcher*

**Poole**
Stokes, Donald Gresham *vehicle company executive*

**Richmond**
Attenborough, Baron Richard Samuel *actor, producer, director, goodwill ambassador*

**Rottingdean**
Matthews, John Floyd *writer, educator*

**Stroud**
Robinson, John Beckwith *development management consultant*

**Suffolk**
Clement, John *food products company executive*

**Surrey**
Godwin, Naomi Nadine *editor*
Petrek, William Joseph *college president emeritus*

**Tunbridge Wells**
Howden, Frank Newton *Episcopal priest, humanities educator*

**Warwick**
Hands, Terence David (Terry Hands) *theater director*

**West Sussex**
Aiken, Joan (Delano) *author*

**Whitchurch**
Adams, Richard George *writer*

**Wiltshire**
Symon, Lindsay *retired neurological educator*

**Windsor**
Hall, Sir Arnold Alexander *aeronautical, mechanical and electrical executive*
Zabriskie, John L. *healthcare and agricultural products manufacturing company executive*

**York**
Grant, Patrick Oliver *priest*

## ETHIOPIA

**Addis Ababa**
Hicks, Irvin *ambassador*

## FIJI

**Suva**
Usher, Sir Leonard Gray *retired news association executive*

## FINLAND

**Helsinki**
Saraste, Jukka-Pekka *conductor*
Siimestö, Orvo Kalervo *financial executive*

**Kuopio**
Hakola, Hannu Panu Aukusti *psychiatry educator*
Sen, Chandan Kumar *physiologist, scientist, educator*

**Tampere**
Pöntinen, Pekka Juhani *anesthesiologist, consultant*

## FRANCE

**Alpes Maritimes**
Morley, Roger Hubert *company executive, consultant*

**Angers**
Chauvet, Gilbert André *mathematics educator*

**Arles**
Clergue, Lucien Georges *photographer*

**Aveyron**
Roudybush, Franklin *diplomat, educator*

**Avignon**
De Mori, Renato *computer science educator, researcher*

**Beduer**
Ezelle, Robert Eugene *diplomat*

**Belves**
Raphael, Frederic Michael *author*

**Créteil**
Renoux, André *physician educator*

**Dijon**
Poli, Rinaldo *chemist, researcher and educator*

**Ferney-Voltaire**
Greer, Joseph Epps *architect*

**Fontainebleu**
Ayres, Robert Underwood *environmental economics and technology educator*

**Genlis**
van Raalte, John A. *research and engineering management executive*

**La Couture Boussey**
Karnath, Lorie Mary Lorraine *bank officer, consultant*

**Lauris**
Spivak, Jonathan M. *journalist*

**Levallois-Perret**
de Pouzilhac, Alain Duplessis *advertising executive*

**Lyon**
Rice, Jerry Mercer *biochemist*

**Marseilles**
Azzopardi, Marc Antoine *astrophysicist, scientist*
Vague, Jean Marie *endocrinologist*

**Nanterre**
Nguyen-Trong, Hoang *physician, consultant*

**Neuilly sur Seine**
Hewes, Thomas Francis *physician*
Ophuls, Marcel *film director and producer*

**Orsay**
Deutsch, Claude David *physicist, educator*
Fiszer-Szafarz, Berta (Berta Safars) *research scientist*

**Palaiseau**
†Basdevant, Jean-Louis Henri *physicist, educator*

**Paris**
Abboud, Ann Creelman *lawyer*
Baum, Axel Helmuth *lawyer*
Biala, Janice *artist*
Blondeau, Jacques Patrick Adrien *reinsurance company executive*
Boulez, Pierre *composer, conductor*
Bourdais de Charbonn, Eric *financial executive*
Chachques, Juan Carlos *cardiac surgeon, researcher*
Cochran, John M., III *lawyer*
Collomb, Bertrand Pierre *cement company executive*
Craig, William Laurence *lawyer*
Dahlburg, John-Thor Theodore *newspaper correspondent*
Davidson, Alfred Edward *lawyer*
Dean, John Gunther *diplomat*
Degos, Laurent *hematologist, educator*
de Havilland, Olivia Mary *actress*
De Lyrot, Alain Herve *editor*
Dubs, Patrick Christian *publisher*
Ferriter, John Pierce *diplomat*
Gallant, Mavis *author*
Gontier, Jean Roger *medicine and physiology educator*
Goupy, Jacques Louis *chemiometrics engineer*
Herzog, Brigitte *lawyer*
Jaclot, Francois Charles *utility company executive*
Jolas, Betsy *composer*
Kurtz, Eugene Allen *composer, educator, consultant*
Lacroix, Christian Marie Marc *fashion designer*
Landers, Steven E. *lawyer*
Lecerf, Olivier Maurice Marie *construction company executive*
LeGoffic, Francois *biotechnology educator*
Levee, John Harrison *artist, designer*
Levy, David Alfred *immunology educator, physician, scientist*
Lewis, Flora *journalist*
Lubell, Harold *economic consultant*
Lucas, Georges *physicist, researcher*

MacCrindle, Robert Alexander *lawyer*
Marceau, Marcel *pantomimist, actor, director, painter, poet*
Marcus, Claude *advertising executive*
Marton, Eva *opera singer*
Marx, Kathryn *photographer, author*
Masurel, Jean-Louis Antoine Nicolas *investment company executive*
McGurn, William Barrett, III *lawyer*
Mestrallet, Gérard *professional society administrator*
Michel, James H. *ambassador, lawyer*
Myerson, Jacob Myer *former foreign service officer*
Peugeot, Patrick *insurance executive*
Raimondi, Ruggero *opera singer*
Reeves, Van Kirk *lawyer*
Renouf, Edda *artist*
Robert, Leslie (Ladislas) *research center administrator, consultant*
Rosenberg, Pierre Max *museum director*
Roussel, Lee Dennison *economist*
Salans, Carl Fredric *lawyer*
Shapiro, Isaac *lawyer*
Ungaro, Emanuel Matteotti *fashion designer*
Williams, C(harles) K(enneth) *poet, literature and writing educator*
Yuechiming, Roger Yue Yuen Shing *mathematics educator*

**Ramatuelle**
Collins, Larry *author, journalist*

**Rognac**
Castel, Gérard Joseph *physician*

**Sannois**
Cornell, Robert Arthur *retired international government official, consultant*

**Sevres**
Asscher, Jean Claude *electronic executive*

**Strasbourg**
Shea, William Rene *historian, science philosopher, educator*

**Toulouse**
Courtés, Joseph Jean-Marie *humanities educator, writer, semiotician*

**Vence**
Polk, William Roe *historian*

**Villeneuve d'Ascq**
Allain, Louis *literature educator, scientific advisor*

## GERMANY

**Berlin**
Abbado, Claudio *conductor*
Anderson, David *former ambassador*
Fischer-Dieskau, Dietrich *baritone*
Goodman, Alfred *composer, musicologist*
Iannone, Dorothy *visual artist, writer*
Wenders, Wim *film director*

**Bielefeld**
Lauven, Peter Michael *anesthesiologist*

**Bonn**
Fleming, Joseph Benedict *newspaperman*
Hutton, Winfield Travis *management consultant, educator*
Walker, Ruth Ann *journalist*
Wohlleben, Rudolf *microwave and antenna researcher*

**Cologne**
Ungers, Oswald M. *architect, educator*

**Darmstadt**
Hofmann, Karl Heinrich *mathematics educator*

**Dortmund**
Freund, Eckhard *electrical engineering educator*

**Dresden**
Schreier, Peter *tenor*

**Duedenbuettel**
Pfennigstorf, Werner *lawyer*

**Dusseldorf**
Stuhl, Oskar Paul *scientific and regulatory consultant*

**Erlangen**
Lips, H. Peter *systems engineer director*

**Finning**
English, Charles Brand *retired lawyer*

**Frankfurt**
Ammann, Jean-Christophe *art director*
Fozzati, Aldo *automobile manufacturing company executive*
Simitis, Spiros *legal educator*

**Freiburg**
Schaefer, Hans-Eckart *pathologist*

**Gethles**
Frank, Dieter *technical consultant, retired chemical company executive*

**Gottingen**
Sheldrick, George Michael *chemistry educator, crystallographer*
Tietze, Lutz Friedjan *chemist, educator*

**Groebenzell**
Chandrasekhar, B(ellur) S(ivaramiah) *physics educator*

**Grunwald**
Semm, Kurt Karl *obstetrics & gynecology researcher/department head*

**Gutersloh**
Wössner, Mark Matthias *business executive*

**Halle-Saale**
Schmoll, Hans Joachim *internal medicine, hematology, oncology educator*

**Hamburg**
Jensen, Elwood Vernon *biochemist*
Lehne, Pascal Horst *chemistry educator, consultant*
Neumeier, John *choreographer, ballet company director*
Ramsey, Bill (William McCreery) *singer, actor, composer-lyricist, television executive*
Vogel, Carl-Wilhelm Ernst *immunologist, biochemistry educator*

**Hannover**
Döhler, Klaus Dieter *pharmaceutical and development company executive*
Monroy, Victor M. *polymer scientist*

**Hemsbach**
Froessl, Horst Waldemar *business executive, data processing developer*

**Ingersheim**
Philippi, Dieter Rudolph *academic administrator*

**Kaiserslautern**
Immesberger, Helmut *lawyer*

**Katlenburg**
Hagfors, Tor *institute director*

**Leipzig**
Hielscher, Udo Artur *business administration and finance educator*

**Luneburg**
Linde, Robert Hermann *economics educator*

**Mannheim**
Henn, Fritz Albert *psychiatrist*

**Moglingen**
Meyberg, Bernhard Ulrich *entrepreneur*

**Münster**
Spevack, Marvin *English educator*

**Munich**
Berg, Jan Mikael *science educator*
Born, Gunthard Karl *aerospace executive*
Fassbaender, Brigitte *opera singer*
Fischer, Ernst Otto *chemist, educator*
Giacconi, Riccardo *astrophysicist, educator*
Horak, Jan-Christopher *film studies educator, curator*
Saur, Klaus G. *publisher*
von Minckwitz, Bernhard *publishing company executive*
Whetten, Lawrence Lester *international relations educator*

**Nuremberg**
Doerries, Reinhard René *modern history educator*

**Paderborn**
Belli, Fevzi *computing science educator, consultant*

**Stuttgart**
Anderson, Reid Bryce *ballet company artistic director*
Bettisch, Johann *linguist, researcher*
Nagel, Joachim Hans *biomedical engineer, educator*

**Tübingen**
Fahle, Manfred *ophthalmology researcher*

**Wachtberg**
Pitrella, Francis Donald *human factors professional*

**Wiesbaden**
Handy, Robert Maxwell *patent lawyer*

**Witten**
Gaengler, Peter Wolfgang *dentist, researcher*

**Wuppertal**
Schubert, Guenther Erich *pathologist*

**Wurzburg**
Hölldobler, Berthold Karl *zoologist, educator*

## GHANA

**Accra**
Brocke, Eunice Miranda *foundation executive*

## GREECE

**Athens**
Adamenko, Victor Gregory *biophysics researcher and educator*
Arnis, Efstathios Constatine *space naval designer*
Greene-Mercier, Marie Zoe *sculptor*
Halkias, Christos Constantine *electronics educator*
Hatzakis, Michael *retired electrical engineer, research executive*
Iakovidis, Spyros Eustace *archaeologist*
Kalamotousakis, George John *economist*
Larounis, George Philip *manufacturing company executive*
Ligomenides, Panos Aristides *electrical and computer engineering educator, consultant*
Panaretos, John *mathematics and statistics educator*

**Patras**
Makios, Vasilios *electronics educator*

## GRENADA

**Saint George's**
Barrett, James Thomas *immunologist, educator*
Helgerson, John Walter *lawyer*

## GUATEMALA

**Guatemala City**
Mayora-Alvarado, Eduardo Rene *lawyer, law educator*

## HONG KONG

**Causeway Bay**
Ignatius, Alan (Adi) *magazine editor*

**Clear Water Bay**
Tang, Wilson Hon-chung *engineering educator*

**Hong Kong**
Allen, Richard Marlow *lawyer*
Blevans, John *lawyer*
Chen, Concordia Chao *mathematician*
Chiang, Samuel Edward *theological educator, humanities educator*
Chu, Franklin Dean *lawyer*
Chun, Wendy Sau Wan *investment company executive*
Gargan, Edward A. *journalist*
Kwong, Peter Kong Kit *bishop*
Mueller, Richard Walter *foreign service officer*
Pisanko, Henry Jonathan *command and control communications company executive*
Rowe, Kevin S. *banker*
Solberg, Ronald Louis *investment banker, fixed-income strategist*
Tanner, Douglas Alan *lawyer*
Torres, Cynthia Ann *banker*
Tse, Edmund Sze-Wing *insurance company executive*
van Hoften, James Dougal Adrianus *business executive, former astronaut*
Wang, Jun *engineering educator*
Wong, Wing Keung *trading, electronics company executive, physician*

**Kowloon**
Hsieh, Din-Yu *applied mathematics educator*
Kung, Shain-dow *molecular biologist, academic administrator*
Liou, Ming-Lei *electrical engineer*
McNaughton, William Frank *translator, educator*

**Sha Tin**
Chang, Shu Ting *fungal geneticist, mushroom biologist*
Kao, Charles Kuen *electrical engineer, educator*
Larr, Peter *banker*
†Xu, Lei *computer scientist, educator*

## HUNGARY

**Budapest**
Mazzucelli, Colette Grace Celia *author, university adminstrator, educator*
Peterson, Trudy Huskamp *archivist*
Rice, Kenneth Lloyd *environmental services executive, educator*

## INDIA

**Yavatmal**
Ward, Daniel Thomas *bishop*

## INDONESIA

**Irian Jaya**
Sowada, Alphonse Augustus *bishop*

**Jakarta**
Hamidjaja, Wiriadi (Willy Hamidjaja) *finance executive*
Roy, J(ames) Stapleton *ambassador*

**Palembang**
Saputra, Daniel *agricultural engineering educator*

## IRAN

**Tehran**
Dinkha, Mar, IV *church administrator*

## IRELAND

**Arklow**
Barber, Jerry Randel *medical device company executive*

**Ballyvaughan**
Wicks, Eugene Claude *college president, art educator*

**Donegal**
Friel, Brian (Bernard Patrick Friel) *author*

**Dublin**
Sheridan, Jim *director, screenwriter*
Smith, Jean Kennedy *ambassador*
Toibin, Colm *journalist, writer*
Voss, Katherine Evelyn *international management consultant*

**Mullingar**
Donleavy, James Patrick *writer, artist*

**Wicklow**
McCaffrey, Anne Inez *author*

## NEW CALEDONIA

**Noumea**
Curlook, Walter *mining company executive*

## NEW ZEALAND

**Bay of Islands**
Veysey, Arthur Ernest *reporter, administrator, biographer*

## NORWAY

**Asker**
Fitzpatrick, Whitfield Westfeldt *lawyer*

**Lillestrøm**
Borgen, Ole Edvard *bishop, educator*

**Oslo**
Christensen, Hans Christian *retired chemist*
Fleischer, Carl August *law educator, consultant*

**Trondheim**
Lindmo, Tore *biophysicist*

## PAKISTAN

**Karachi**
Ahmed, Akhtar *neurologist, educator*
Shroff, Firoz Sardar *merger and acquisition professional*

**Lahore**
Geoffrey, Iqbal (Mohammed Jawaid Iqbal Jafree) *artist, lawyer*

## PANAMA

**Panama City**
Fletcher Arancibia, Pablo Enrique *internal medicine endocrinology physician, educator*

## PERU

**Lima**
French, Edward Ronald *plant pathologist*

## THE PHILIPPINES

**Calookan City**
Dado, Jose Butial *railway company executive*

**Manila**
Llamanzares, Magda Carolina Go Vera *nurse, clinical child psychologist*
Metzger, Barry *lawyer*
Siguion-Reyna, Leonardo *lawyer, business executive*
Stepanich, Fred Charles *civil and water resources engineer*

**Pasay**
Lim, Sonia Yii *minister*

## POLAND

**Warsaw**
Koscielak, Jerzy *scientist, science administrator*
Romney, Richard Bruce *lawyer*

## PORTUGAL

**Coimbra**
dos Reis, Luciano Sérgio Lemos *surgeon*

**Funchal**
Mayda, Jaro *lawyer, educator, author, consultant*

**Lisbon**
Berger, Jason *artist, printmaker*
De Jesus, Fernando *science administrator*
Thore, Sten Anders *economics and aerospace engineering educator*

**Vila Nova de Gaia**
Moura-Relvas, Joaquim M.M.A. *electrical engineer, educator*

## REPUBLIC OF KOREA

**Pohang**
Choi, Sang-il *physics educator, researcher*

**Pusan**
Ha, Chang Sik *polymer science educator*

**Seoul**
Kang, Woo Sik *medical association administrator*
Kim, Kwang-Iel *psychiatrist, educator*
Rhi, Sang-Kyu *lawyer, educator*
Steinberg, David Isaac *economic development consultant, educator*
Surh, Young-Joon *medical educator*

**Suwon**
Lee, Tong Hun *economics educator*

**Taegu**
Park, Soong-Kook *internist, researcher*

**Taejon**
Kim, Sung Chul *polymer engineering educator*
Lee, Choochon *physics educator, researcher*

## ROMANIA

**Bucharest**
Moses, Alfred Henry *lawyer*

## RUSSIA

**Moscow**
Knaus, Jonathan Charles *manufacturing executive*

**Novosibirsk**
Aleksandrov, Leonid Naumovitsh *physicist, educator, researcher*

## SAINT LUCIA

**Castries**
Felix, Kelvin Edward *archbishop*

## SAUDI ARABIA

**Dhahran**
Warne, Ronson Joseph *mathematics educator*

**Jeddah**
Hussain, Kazi Fareeduddin *engineering executive*

**Riyadh**
Chaudhary, Shaukat Ali *ecologist, plant taxonomist*
Olayan, Suliman Saleh *finance company executive*
Taylor, Frederick William, Jr. (Fritz Taylor) *lawyer*
Uygur, Mustafa Eti *materials and mechanical engineering educator*

## SCOTLAND

**Aberdeen**
Rice, Charles Duncan *university official*
Rousseau, George Sebastian *eighteenth century studies educator, chamber musician*

**Argyll**
Reeves, Daniel McDonough *video artist*

**Cellardyke**
Roff, William Robert *history educator, writer*

**Edinburgh**
Macneil, Ian Roderick *lawyer, educator*
McMaster, Brian John *artistic director*
Miller, James *construction company executive*
Singer, Norman A. *government official, former diplomat*

**Gullane**
Collins, Jeffrey Hamilton *research facility administrator, electrical engineering educator*

**Kinross**
Finlay, Robert Derek *food company executive*

**Peebles**
Hooper, John Edward *retired physicist, researcher*

**Saint Andrews**
Lenman, Bruce Philip *historian, educator*

## SINGAPORE

**Henderson Industrial Park**
Shima, Larry Mitsuru *health facility administrator*

**Singapore**
Brown, Kenneth Charles *manufacturing company executive*
Edwards, Stephen Allen *lawyer*
Enlow, Fred Clark *banker*
Ho, Yik Hong *colon and rectal surgeon*
Skodon, Emil Mark *diplomat*

## SOUTH AFRICA

**Arcadia**
Berry, Ann Roper *diplomat*

**Auckland Park**
Koekemoer, Carl Lodewicus *university official, business consultant*

**Capetown**
Benatar, Solomon Robert *internist*

**Johannesburg**
†Berk, Philip Woolf *journalist*
Crockett, Phyllis Darlene *communications executive*
Hunter-Gault, Charlayne *journalist*

**Klippoortjie**
Els, Theodore Ernest *professional golfer*

**Mamelodi West**
Ntlola, Peter Makhwenkwe *retired translator*

**Marshalltown**
Chen, Philip Minkang *investment banker, corporate executive, lawyer, engineer*

**Medunsa**
Walubo, Andrew *clinical pharmacologist, researcher*

## SPAIN

**Barcelona**
de Larrocha, Alicia *concert pianist*
Jackson, Gabriel *historian*

**Caceres**
Long, Bert Louis, Jr. *artist*

**Madrid**
Berganza Vargas, Teresa *mezzo-soprano*
De Reyna, Luis *oil drilling company executive*
Feltenstein, Harry David, Jr. *chemical executive*
Frühbeck de Burgos, Rafael *conductor*
Trueba, Fernando *film director and producer, screenwriter*

**Santander**
Ballesteros, Severiano *professional golfer*

**Santiago De Compostela**
Balseiro Gonzalez, Manuel *management executive, consultant*

**Segovia**
Harter, Hugh Anthony *foreign language educator*

**Seville**
Sanchez, Leonedes Monarrize Worthington (Duke de Leonedes) *fashion designer*

**Tacoronte**
Kardas, Sigmund Joseph, Jr. *secondary education educator*

## SRI LANKA

**Colombo**
Smyth, Richard Henry *foreign service officer*
Spain, James William *political scientist, writer, investor*

## SWEDEN

**Bralanda**
Emilson, Henry Bertil *artist*

**Goteborg**
Bona, Christian M. *dentist, psychotherapist*
Norrby, Klas Carl Vilhelm *pathology educator*

**Hasselby**
Wasell, Gösta *retired auditor*

**Lerum**
Borei, Sven Hans Emil *translator*

**Lund**
Grimmeiss, Hermann Georg *physics educator, researcher*
Welin, Walter *financial advisor*

**Malmo**
Cronberg, Stig *infectious diseases educator*

**Stockholm**
Bergström, K. Sune D. *biochemist*
Johnson, Antonia Axson *corporate executive*
Schröder, Harald Bertel *aerospace industry executive*
Siebert, Thomas L. *ambassador*
Soederstrom, Elisabeth Anna *opera singer*

## SWITZERLAND

**Basel**
Gerber, Fritz *insurance company executive, diversified financial services company executive*
Ghiglia, Oscar Alberto *classical guitarist*
Marti, Erwin Ernst *physicochemist, researcher*
Moret, Marc *chemicals executive*
†Rosenthal, David *media executive, publicist*

**Berne**
Krauss, Joachim Kurt *neurosurgeon, researcher*
†Leavey, Thomas E. *international organization administrator*

**Burgdorf**
Haeberlin, Heinrich Rudolf *electrical engineering educator*

**Busingen**
Friede, Reinhard L. *neuropathologist, educator*

**Chambesy**
Spiegel, Daniel Leonard *lawyer*

**Cologny**
Maglacas, A. Mangay *nursing researcher, educator*

**Fribourg**
Gurley, Franklin Louis *lawyer, military historian*

**Geneva**
Abram, Morris Berthold *lawyer, educator, diplomat*
Agostinelli, Robert Francesco *investment banker*
Barenboim, Daniel *conductor, pianist*
Bogsch, Arpad *diplomat*
Brown, Kent Newville *ambassador*
†Casey, John W. *association executive*
De Pfyffer, Andre *lawyer*
Farman-Farmaian, Ghaffar *investment company executive*
Halle, Louis Joseph *author, educator*
Harigel, Gert Günter *physicist*
Hedstrom, Mitchell Warren *banker*
Henderson, Ralph Hale *physician*
Kessinger, Tom G. *academic administrator*
Ledogar, Stephen J. *diplomat*
O'Regan, Richard Arthur *editor, retired foreign correspondent*
Overseth, Oliver Enoch *physicist, educator*
†Piot, Peter *medical microbiologist, public health officer*
Polunin, Nicholas *environmentalist, author, editor*
Purcell, James Nelson, Jr. *international organization administrator*
Rohrer, Maurice Pierre *journalist*
Schweitzer, Theodore Gottlieb, III *United Nations administrator*

Twarog, Sophia Nora *international association administrator*
†Weber, George *international social welfare administrator*

**Lausanne**
Bloemsma, Marco Paul *investor*
Borel, Georges Antoine *gastroenterologist, consultant*
Stingelin, Valentin *research center director, mechanical engineer*

**Lucerne**
Sherwin, James Terry *lawyer, window covering company executive*

**Lugano**
Ricci, Giovanni Mario *finance company executive*

**Lyss**
Scheftner, Gerold *marketing executive*

**Montreux**
Cronin, Robert Francis Patrick *physician, educator*

**Signy**
Murphy, Edmund Michael *federal agency administrator, demographer*

**Versoix**
Mahler, Halfdan Theodor *physician, health organization executive*

**Zurich**
Bailey, James Edwin *chemical engineer*
Barnevik, Percy Nils *electrical company executive*
Diederich, Francois Nico *chemistry educator*
Gut, Rainer Emil *banker*
Kalman, Rudolf Emil *research mathematician, system scientist*
Lanford, Oscar Erasmus, III *mathematics educator*
Nievergelt, Jurg *computer science educator*

## TAIWAN

**Chung Li**
Hong, Zuu-Chang *engineering educator*

**Hsinchu**
Chang, Chin-An *research chemist*

**Taichung**
Lu, Shih-Peng *history educator*

**Tainan**
Huang, Ting-Chia *chemical engineering educator, researcher*
Shih, Tso Min *mining engineering educator*

**Taipei**
Ho, Low-Tone *physician, researcher, educator*
Hsu, Kuo-Pang *physician, educator*
O'Hearn, James Francis *chemical company executive*
Tung, Phoebus Che-Se *biomedical educator*
Yang, Shang Fa *biochemistry educator, plant physiologist*
Yeh, K. H. *bank executive*
Yin, Shih-Jiun *biochemist*
Young, Der-Liang Frank *civil engineering educator, researcher*

**Yung-Ho**
Liu, Shi-Kau *microbiologist, research scientist*

## THAILAND

**Bangkok**
Cheosakul, Pradisth *chemist*
Kruck, Donna Jean *special education educator, consultant*
Lyman, David *lawyer*
Pahnichaputt, Momluang Ananchanok *English and American literature educator*

**Pathum Thani**
Stueart, Robert D. *university information services director, educator*

## TONGA

**Nuku'alofa**
Cook, Beth Marie *writer, poet, volunteer*

## TRINIDAD AND TOBAGO

**Diego Martin**
Walcott, Derek Alton *poet, playwright*

## TURKEY

**Ankara**
Inalcik, Halil *historian, educator*

**Istanbul**
Rountree, George Denton *health services managemtent consultant*

## TURKS AND CAICOS ISLANDS

**Provinciales**
Johnston, Samuel Thomas *entertainment company executive*

## UKRAINE

**Kiev**
Miller, William Green *ambassador*

**Lviv**
†Lubachivsky, Myroslav Ivan Cardinal *archbishop*

## UNITED ARAB EMIRATES

**Al Ain**
Voth, Douglas W. *academic dean*

**Dubai**
Bieber-Roberts, Peggy Eilene *communications editor, journalist, researcher*

## VATICAN CITY

**Vatican City**
John Paul, His Holiness Pope, II (Karol Jozef Wojtyla) *bishop of Rome*
Szoka, Edmund Casimir Cardinal *archbishop*

## VENEZUELA

**Caracas**
Chang-Mota, Roberto *electrical engineer*
Mendelovici, Efraim Eliahu *materials chemistry and earth sciences researcher*
Nakano, Tatsuhiko *chemist, educator*

## VIETNAM

**Hanoi**
Peterson, Douglas Pete (Pete Peterson) *ambassador, former congressman*
†Peterson, Pete *ambassador, former congressman*

## WALES

**Gwynedd**
Owen, Walter Shepherd *materials science and engineering educator*

## WEST INDIES

**Plymouth Montserrat**
Diggs, J(esse) Frank *retired magazine editor*

**Roseau**
Jeffries, Charles Dean *microbiology educator, scientist*

## WESTERN SAMOA

**Apia**
†Alesana, Tofilau Eti *Samoan prime minister*

## ZAIRE

**Kinshasa**
†Seko, Mobutu Sese *President Zaire*

## ZAMBIA

**Mumbwa**
Hansen, Florence Marie Congiolosi (Mrs. James S. Hansen) *social worker*

## ADDRESS UNPUBLISHED

Aaron, Lynn *dancer*
Aaron, Roy Henry *lawyer, arbitrator, business consultant*
Aaslestad, Halvor Gunerius *university official*
Abadi, Fritzie *artist, educator*
Abajian, John Christian *anesthesiologist*
Abbe, Elfriede Martha *sculptor, graphic artist*
Abdoo, Raymond Thomas *preventive health consultant*
Abel, Harold *psychologist, educator, academic administrator*
Abell, Murray Richardson *retired medical association administrator*
Abercrombie, Stanley *magazine editor*
Abere, Andrew Evan *economist*
Abernathy, Vicki Marie *nurse*
Ablin, Richard Joel *immunologist, educator*
Abramowicz, Janet *painter, print-maker*
Abzug, Bella Savitzky *lawyer, former congresswoman*
Achorn, Robert Comey *retired newspaper publisher*
Acker, Raymond Abijah *retired minister and army officer*
Ackerman, Jack Rossin *investment banker*
Ackerman, Melvin *investment company executive*
Adam, John, Jr. *insurance company executive emeritus*
Adam, Orval Michael *retired financial executive, lawyer*
Adamovich, Shirley Gray *retired librarian, state official*
Adams, Arlin Marvin *retired judge, counsel to law firm*
Adams, Bryan *vocalist, composer*
Adams, Edwin Melville *former foreign service officer, actor, author, lecturer*
Adams, Gregory James *insurance company executive*
Adams, James Blackburn *former state government official, former federal government official, lawyer*
Adams, James Thomas *surgeon*
Adams, John Andrew *physicist, engineering company executive*
Adams, Michael John *air force non-commissioned officer*
Adams, Robert McCormick *anthropologist, educator*
Adams, Thomas Lynch, Jr. *lawyer*
Adams, Warren Sanford, II *retired food company executive, lawyer*
Adams, William White *retired manufacturing company executive*
Adaskin, Murray *composer*
Adato, Perry Miller *documentary producer, director, writer*
Adcock, Richard Paul *lawyer*
Addiss, Susan Silliman *public health consultant*
Addy, Frederick Seale *retired oil company executive*
Adelman, Richard Charles *gerontologist, educator*
Adelman, Robert Paul *retired construction company executive, lawyer*
Adelson, Merv Lee *entertainment and communication industry executive*
Aden, Arthur Laverne *retired office systems company executive*
Adisman, I. Kenneth *prosthodontist*
Adkins, Terry R. *artist*
†Adkisson, Gregory Hugh *anesthesiologist*
Adler, Richard Melvin *architect, planner*
Adler, Samuel Hans *retired conductor, composer*
Adsit, Russell Allan *landscape architect*
Aehlert, Barbara June *health services executive*
Affatato, Joseph Frank *marketing professional*
Agarwal, Suman Kumar *editor*
Ahearne, John Francis *scientific research administrator, researcher*
Ahl, Janyce Barnwell *historian, writer, speaker, retired educator*
Ahlquist, Paul Gerald *molecular biology researcher, educator*
Ajemian, Robert Myron *journalist*
Akasofu, Syun-Ichi *geophysicist*
Akbarian, Shah-Rokh *management consultant*
Akel, Ollie James *oil company executive*
Aladjem, Daniel *policy analyst*
Albert, Margaret Cook *communications executive*
Alberts, David *artistic director, mime*
Albino, George Robert *business executive*
Aldredge, Theoni Vachliotis *costume designer*
Aldrich, Franklin Dalton *research physician*
Aldrich, Patricia Anne Richardson *retired magazine editor*
Alexander, Jonathan *cardiologist, consultant*
Alig, Frank Douglas Stalnaker *construction company executive*
Aljian, James Donovan *investment company executive*
Alker, Hayward R. *political science educator*
Allan, Hugh James Pearson *retired bishop*
Allegra, Francis *federal government official*
Allen, Charles Eugene *college administrator, agriculturist*
Allen, Eric Andre *professional football player*
Allen, Henry L. *pathologist*
Allen, John Lyndon *social studies educator*
Allen, Kenneth Dale *insurance executive, corporate counsel*
Allen, Lew, Jr. *laboratory executive, former air force officer*
Allen, Marilyn Myers Pool *theater director, video producer*
Allen, Theodore Earl *marketing consultant*
Allerton, John Stephen *association executive*
Alligood, Elizabeth H. *retired special education educator*
Allison, Andrew Marvin *church executive*
Allison, John McComb *retired aeronautical engineer*
Almeida, Evelyn *retired elementary education educator*
Almen, Louis Theodore *retired college president*
Almgren, Herbert Philip *bank executive*
Aloff, Mindy *writer*
Alpern, Andrew *lawyer, architect, architectural historian*
Alpert, Ann Sharon *insurance claims examiner*
Al-Qadi, Imad Lutfi *civil engineering educator, researcher*
Alsop, Marin *conductor*
Alston, Eugene Benson *communications company executive*
Altamura, Carmela Elizabeth *concert artist, philanthropist*
Altan, Taylan *engineering educator, mechanical engineer, consultant*
Altekruse, Joan Morrissey *retired preventive medicine educator*
Altman, Irwin *psychology educator*
Altshuler, Alan Anthony *dean, political scientist*
Altshuler, Kenneth Z. *psychiatrist*
Alvernaz, Rodrigo *insurance company executive*
Alvord, Joel Barnes *bank executive*
Amann, Charles Albert *mechanical engineer*
Ambrose, James Richard *consultant, retired government official*
Ambrozic, Aloysius Matthew *archbishop*
Amdahl, Byrdelle John *business consulting executive*
Ames, Donald Paul *retired aerospace company executive, researcher*
Ames, Oakes *physicist, educator*
Amstutz, Daniel Gordon *trade association administrator, former grain dealer, government official*
Amundson, Robert A. *state supreme court justice*
Anaple, Elsie Mae *medical, surgical and geriatrics nurse*
Anastasi, William Joseph *artist*
Anastos, Anna Vedouras *federal lawyer*
Ancheta, Caesar Paul *software developer*
Ancona, George E. *photographer, film producer, author*
Anderer, Joseph Henry *textile company executive*
Andersen, Morten *football player*
Anderson, Bernard E. *economist*
Anderson, Charles D. *former bishop*
Anderson, Dianne Jean *nursing administrator*
Anderson, Donald Lloyd *weapon systems consultant*
Anderson, Dorothy Fisher *social worker, psychotherapist*
Anderson, Fletcher Neal *chemical executive*
Anderson, Geoffrey Allen *retired lawyer*
Anderson, Glen Robert *federal official*
Anderson, Iris Anita *retired secondary education educator*
Anderson, John Firth *church administrator, librarian*
Anderson, John Gaston *electrical engineer*
Anderson, John Rogers *Canadian diplomat*
Anderson, Joseph Norman *executive consultant, former food company executive, former college president*
Anderson, Keith *retired lawyer, retired banker*
Anderson, Kenneth Ward *investor, consultant*
Anderson, Laurie *performance artist*
Anderson, Mark Robert *data processing executive, biochemist*
Anderson, Mary Theresa *investment manager*
Anderson, Michael L. *financial planning manager*
Anderson, Ned, Sr. *Apache tribal chairman*
Anderson, Nils, Jr. *former government official, retired business executive, industrial historian*
Anderson, Ollie Palmer, Jr. *former diplomat*
Anderson, Robert Orville *oil and gas company executive*
Anderson, Thomas Patrick *mechanical engineer, educator*
Anderson, Vernon Russell *technology company executive, entrepreneur*
Anderson, Violet Henson *artist, educator*
Anderson, Wayne Carl *public information officer*
Anderson-Spivy, Alexandra *writer, editor*
Andersson, Craig Remington *retired chemical company executive*
Andrade, Edna *artist, art educator*
Andre, (Kenneth) Michael *editor, publisher, writer*
Andreas, Dwayne Orville *business executive*
Andreoli, Thomas Eugene *physician*
Andretti, John *professional race car driver*
Andretti, Mario (Gabriele) *race car driver*
Andretti, Michael Mario *professional race car driver*
Andrews, Julie *actress, singer*
Andrews, William Frederick *manufacturing executive*
Andriole, Stephen John *information systems executive*
Andrisani, John Anthony *editor, author, golf consultant*
Angell, Richard Bradshaw *philosophy educator*
Anguiano, Lupe *business executive*
Angulo, Gerard Antonio *publisher, investor*
Angus, Robert Carlyle, Jr. *health facility administrator*
Anker, Peter Louis *retired securities executive*
Anker, Robert Alvin *insurance company executive*
Annenberg, Walter H. *philanthropist, diplomat, editor, publisher, broadcaster*
Annus, John Augustus *artist*
Ansbro, John Joseph *philosophy educator*
Anshaw, Carol *writer*
Anspach, Herbert Kephart *retired appliance company executive, patent attorney*
Anthony, Earl Roderick *professional bowler*
Apel-Brueggeman, Myrna L. *entrepreneur*
Appelbaum, Jacob Gregory *physicist*
Appell, Louise Sophia *consulting company executive*
Appenzeller, Otto *neurologist, researcher*
Apted, Michael David *film director*
Aptekar, Sheldon I. *speech and theatre educator*
Aptheker, Herbert *historian, lecturer*
Aquino-Kaufman, Florence (Florence Anglin) *actress, playwright*
Arbelbide, C(indy) L(ea) *historian, author*
Archer, Anne *actress*
Archer, Jeffrey Howard *author, politician*
Archibald, Nolan D. *household and industrial products company executive*
Arden, Bruce Wesley *computer science and electrical engineering educator*
Arden, Sherry W. *publishing company executive*
Areen, Judith Carol *law educator*
Arenal, Julie (Mrs. Barry Primus) *choreographer*
Arenberg, Julius Theodore, Jr. *retired accounting company executive*
Arenella, Peter Lee *law educator*
Arenstein, Walter Alan *environmental scientist*
Argun, Fatima Hatice *international business and marketing consultant*
Arkin, Mara J. *social studies educator*
Arlen, Michael J. *writer*
Arlidge, John Walter *utility company executive*
Armacost, Mary-Linda Sorber Merriam *former college president*
Armas, Jennifer Villareal *nurse*
Armistead, Katherine Kelly (Mrs. Thomas B. Armistead, III) *interior designer, travel consultant, civic worker*
Armistead, Thomas Boyd, III *television and film producer*
Armour, David Edward Ponton *trade association administrator*
Armstrong, Anne Legendre (Mrs. Tobin Armstrong) *former ambassador, corporate director*
Armstrong, F(redric) Michael *insurance company executive, consultant*
Armstrong, John Allan *business machine company research executive*
Armstrong, Karen Lee *special education educator*
Armstrong, Lloyd, Jr. *university official, physics educator*
Armstrong, Thomas Newton, III *American art and garden specialist, consultant*
Armstrong, Warren Bruce *university president, historian, educator*
Armstrong, William Henry *lawyer*
Arnaud, Claude Donald, Jr. *physician, educator*
Arndt, Dianne Joy *artist, photographer*
Arnold, Deborrah Ann *human services director*
Arnold, Henri *cartoonist*
Arnold, Jerome Gilbert *lawyer*
Arnold, P. A. *special education educator*
Arnold, Sheila *former state legislator*
Arnold, William Howard *retired nuclear fuel executive*
Arnott, Howard Joseph *biology educator, university dean*
Aronson, Luann Marie *actress*
Arquette, Rosanna *actress*
Arthur, Beatrice *actress*
Arthur, John Morrison *retired utility executive*
Arthur, Rochelle Linda *association executive*
Arutyunyan, Emma *radio-broadcaster*
Aschauer, Charles Joseph, Jr. *corporate director, former company executive*
Ashby, Clifford Charles *theatre arts educator, historian*
Ashby, Norma Rae Beatty *journalist, beauty consultant*
Ashe, Bernard Flemming *lawyer, educator*
†Ashford, Nickolas *singer, songwriter*
Ashley, Jim R(ay) *newspaper editor*
Ashton, Harris John *business executive*
Askey, William Hartman *federal judge, lawyer*
Askins, Wallace Boyd *manufacturing company executive*
Aspen, Alfred William *agricultural import/export products, company executive*
Assante, Armand *actor*
Astaire, Carol Anne Taylor *artist, educator*
Atchison, Richard Calvin *trade association director*
Atherton, William *actor*
Atkins, John *concert pianist, voice teacher*
Atwood, Genevieve *geologist*
Au, Tung *civil engineer, educator, consultant*
Auberjonois, René Murat *actor*
Audet, Paul Andre *retired newspaper executive*
Aulbach, George Louis *property investment company executive*
Auriemma, Louis Francis *printing company executive*
Aurin, Robert James *entrepreneur*
Austin, Robert Clarke *naval officer*
Autin, Ernest Anthony, II *chemist, educator, consultant*
Autorino, Anne Turnbull *retired social worker*
Avalon, Frankie *singer, actor*
Aved, Barry *retail executive, consultant*
Avian, Bob *choreographer, producer*
Avnet, Jonathan Michael *motion picture company executive, film director*
Axelrad, Irving Irmas *lawyer, motion picture producer*
Axilrod, Stephen Harvey *financial markets consultant, economist*
Ayres, Jayne Lynn Ankrum *community health nurse*
Azarnoff, Daniel Lester *pharmaceutical company consultant*
Babao, Donna Marie *community health, psychiatric nurse, educator*
Babb, Frank Edward *lawyer, executive*
Babbitt, Samuel Fisher *retired university administrator*
Babitzke, Theresa Angeline *health facility administrator*
Bach, Mária-Cathérine *writer, researcher, translator*
Bacharach, Burt *composer, conductor*
Bacharach, Melvin Lewis *retired venture capitalist*
Bacon, Caroline Sharfman *investor relations consultant*
Bader, Lorraine Greenberg *textile designer, consultant*
Badham, John MacDonald *motion picture director*
Baer, Robert J. *transportation company executive*
Baeumer, Maximilian Lorenz *literature historian*
Baggett, Donnis Gene *journalist, editor*
Baghaei-Rad, Nancy Jane Bebb *elementary educator*
Bagley, William Thompson *lawyer*
Bagwill, John Williams, Jr. *retired pension fund company executive*
Bahre, Jeannette *education educator, librarian*
Baier, Edward John *former public health official, industrial hygiene engineer, consultant*
Bailey, Francis Lee *lawyer*
Bailey, Joselyn Elizabeth *physician*
Bailey, Rita Maria *investment advisor, psychologist*
Bailey-Jones, Carla Lynn *nursing administrator*
Bailin, David William *educational administrator*
Bain, William Donald, Jr. *lawyer, chemical company executive*
Bainbridge, Dona Bardelli *international marketing executive*
Baird, William David *retired anesthesiologist*
†Baiul, Oksana *figure skater*
Baker, Charles DeWitt *research and development company executive*
Baker, Donald *lawyer*
Baker, Edward Kevin *retail executive*
Baker, Ginger Lee *oncological and cardiac nurse*
Baker, Henry S., Jr. *retired banker*
Baker, Howard Henry, Jr. *former senator, lawyer*
Baker, Joe Don *actor*
Baker, Laurence Howard *oncology educator*
Baker, Mark Allen *author, historian*
Baker, Patricia (Jean) *lawyer, mediator*
Baker, Richard Hugh *congressman*
Baker, Ronald James *English language educator, university administrator*
Baker, William Thompson, Jr. *lawyer*
Baker, Zachary Moshe *librarian*
Bakshi, Ralph *film and television producer, director*
Balaban, Bob *actor, director*
Balaban-Perry, Eleanor *retired advertising executive*
Baldrige, Letitia *writer, management training consultant*
Baldwin, Alec (Alexander Rae Baldwin, III) *actor*
Baldwin, C. Andrew, Jr. *retired science educator*
Baldwin, Deanna Louise *dietitian*
Baldwin, DeWitt Clair, Jr. *physician, educator*
Baldwin, George Curriden *physicist, educator*
Baldwin, William Russell *optometrist, foundation executive*
Balet, Jan *artist*
Balke, Robert Roy *architect*
Ball, Howard Guy *education specialist educator*
Ball, Lawrence *retired physical scientist*
Ballard, Marion Scattergood *software development professional*
Ballhaus, William Francis *retired scientific instruments company executive*
Balsamello, Joseph Vincent *information services manager*
Baltazzi, Evan Serge *engineering research consulting company executive*
Balter, Alan *conductor, music director*
Bamberger, Gerald Francis *plastics marketing consultant*
Bambrick, James Joseph *labor economist, labor relations executive*
Bandeen, William Reid *retired meteorologist*
Bangs, John Kendrick *lawyer, foundation executive, former chemical company executive*
Banks, Ernest (Ernie Banks) *retired professional baseball player*
Banks, Robert Sherwood *lawyer*
Bansak, Stephen A., Jr. *investment banker, financial consultant*
Bantry, Bryan *entrepreneur*
Barabino, William Albert *science and technology researcher, inventor*
Baranski, Christine *actress*
Barbee, George E. L. *financial services and business executive*
Barca, George Gino *winery executive, finanial investor*
Barcenas, Jude R. L. *financial services company executive*
Bar-Cohen, Avram *mechanical engineering educator*
Bardin, Clyde Wayne *biomedical researcher, developer of contraceptives*
Bare, Bruce *retired life insurance company executive*
Barger, William James *management consultant*
Barham, Charles Dewey, Jr. *electric utility executive, lawyer*
Barham, Patte (Mrs. Harris Peter Boyne) *publisher, author, columnist*
Barhydt, Sally J. *publishing company executive*
Barker, Clive *artist, screenwriter, director, producer, writer*
Barker, Virginia Lee *nursing educator*
Barkin, Ellen *actress*
Barkley, Richard Clark *ambassador*
Barlascini, Cornelius Ottavio, Jr. *physician*
Barlow, John Sutton *neurophysiologist, electroencephalographer, lexicographer*
Barnard, Donald Roy *entomologist*
Barnes, Joanna *author, actress*

Barnett, Linda Kay Smith vocational guidance counselor
Barnett, Vincent MacDowell, Jr. political science educator
Barney, Austin Cornelius Dunham, II estate planner
Barnhart, Jo Anne B. government official
Barnhill, Howard Eugene insurance company executive
Barnhouse, Lillian May Palmer retired medical surgical nurse, researcher, civic worker
Barnum, William Milo architect
Barone, John Anthony university provost emeritus
Barr, Burt artist
Barrack, William Sample, Jr. petroleum company executive
Barreda, William Eloy retired government official
Barrett, Barbara McConnell ranch owner, community leader, lawyer
Barrett, Izadore retired fisheries research administrator
Barrett, Jane Hayes lawyer
Barrett, Janet Tidd academic administrator
Barro, Mary Helen marketing professional, consultant
Barron, Charles Elliott retired electronics executive
Barrow, Frank Pearson, Jr. retired energy company executive
Barrs, James Thomas speech, language educator
Barry, Janet Cecilia retired elementary school educator
Barry, Rick (Richard Francis Dennis Barry, III) sportscaster, retired professional basketball player, marketing professional
Barselou, Paul Edgar actor, writer
Bartenieff, George producer, actor
Barth, Frances Dorothy artist
Bartholomew, Donald Dekle engineering executive, inventor
Bartlett, David Conant journalist
Bartlett, James Williams psychiatrist, educator
Bartling, Theodore Charles oil company executive
Barton, Ann Elizabeth retired financial executive
Barton, Joe Linus congressman
Barton, Peter Richard, III communications executive
†Bartrem, Duane Harvey retired military officer, designer, building consultant
Bartunek, Joseph Wenceslaus magistrate, judge
Barzun, Jacques author, literary consultant
Basch, Reva information services company executive
Bascom, Willard Newell engineer, scientist, underwater archaeologist
Basford, Robert Eugene retired biochemistry educator, researcher
Basham-Tooker, Janet Brooks retired geropsychologist, educator
Bashore, Irene Saras research institute administrator
Basia, (Basia Trzetrzelewska) musician, vocalist
Baskin, Stuart Jay lawyer
Bass, Lynda D. medical/surgical nurse, educator
Bass, Robert Olin manufacturing executive
Bassett, Carol Ann journalism educator, freelance and writer, producer
Bassett, Elizabeth Ewing (Libby Bassett) writer, editor
Batalden, Paul Bennett pediatrician, health care educator
Bateman, Mildred Mitchell psychiatrist
Bateman, Robert McLellan artist
Bates, Charles Turner lawyer, educator
Bateson, Mary Catherine anthropology educator
Batignani, Laurie A. communications professional
Batson, David Warren lawyer
Battat, Felix A. retired orthopedic surgeon
Battistelli, Joseph John electronics executive
Battle, Frank Vincent, Jr. lawyer
Bauer, Barbara Ann marketing consultant
Bauer, Caroline Feller author
Bauer, Richard Carlton nuclear engineer
Baughman, J. Ross photographer, writer, educator
Bauman, Richard Arnold coast guard officer
Bauman, Robert Patten diversified company executive
Baumann-Sinacore, Patricia Lynn nursing administrator
Baumgartner, John H. refining and petroleum products company executive
Baur, Isolde Nacke translator, freelance writer, public speaker
Baxter, Cecil William, Jr. retired college president
Baxter, Stephen Bartow retired history educator
†Baxter, Thomas Gregory cable television executive
Bayer, Robert Edward retired defense department official
Baym, Gordon Alan physicist, educator
Beach, Edward Latimer writer, retired military officer
Beadle, John Grant retired manufacturing company executive
Beal, Merrill David conservationist, museum director
†Beale, Richard Ewing, Jr. career military officer
Beals, Nancy Farwell state legislator
Beasley, Barbara Starin sales executive, marketing professional
Beasley, James W., Jr. lawyer
Beattie, Charles Robert, III lawyer
Beattie, Edward James surgeon, educator
Beattie, Nora Maureen insurance company executive, actuary
Beatts, Anne Patricia writer, producer
Becerra-Fernandez, Irma electrical engineer, researcher, educator
Becich, Raymond Brice healthcare consultant, mediator, trainer, educator
Beck, Isha Manna researcher, performing company executive, actress
Beck, Jeffrey Dengler banking executive
Beck, John Roland environmental consultant
Beck, John Ryder ambassador
Beck, Mary Virginia lawyer, public official
Becker, JoAnn Elizabeth insurance company executive
Becker, Richard Charles retired college president
Becker, Walter Heinrich vocational educator, planner
Beckjord, Eric Stephen nuclear engineering educator, energy researcher
Beckman, James Wallace Bim economist, marketing executive
Beebe, John Eldridge financial service executive
Begley, Ed, Jr. actor
Behlmer, Rudy H., Jr. director, writer, film educator
Beighey, Lawrence Jerome packaging company executive
Beiser, Helen Ruth psychiatrist
Belafonte, Harry singer, concert artist, actor
Belanger, Luc oncologist
Beldock, Myron lawyer
Bell, Clarence Deshong state senator, lawyer
Bell, Clarence Elmo former state senator

Bell, David Eugene investment company executive
Bell, H. Jenkins clergyman, bishop
Bell, John William lawyer
Bell, P. Jackson computer executive
Bell, Susan Jane nurse
Bellamy, Everett law school administrator
Bellamy, James Carl insurance company executive
Belle Isle, Albert Pierre electronics company executive
Beller, Luanne Evelyn accountant
Belles, Donald Arnold pastoral therapist, mental health counselor
Bellow, Donald Grant mechanical engineering educator
Bellow, Saul C. writer
Belluomini, Frank Stephen accountant
Belmont, Larry Miller health association executive
Belnap, Nuel Dinsmore, Jr. philosophy educator
Beltz, Herbert Allison retired financial consultant
Bender, James Frederick psychologist, educator, university dean
Bender, Ross Thomas minister
Bendix, Helen Irene lawyer
Benediktson, Stephan Vilberg oil company executive
Benenson, Esther Siev (Mrs. William Benenson) nursing home administrator, gerontologist
Benfey, Otto Theodor chemist, educator, editor, historian of science
Benfield, Ann Kolb lawyer
Benjamin, Edward A. lawyer
Benjamin, James Cover controller, manufacturing company executive
Benjamin, Richard actor, director
Benjaminson, James Albert protective services official
†Benn, Caroline M. public relations executive, advertising executive
Bennett, Elsie Margaret music school administrator
Bennett, Geraldine Mae Paulette publisher, author
Bennett, John Roscoe computer company executive
Bennett, Richard Thomas retired manufacturing executive
Bennett, Saul public relations agency executive
Benney, Douglas Mabley direct marketing executive, consultant
Benson, James Carl retired accountant
Benton, Robert Dean educational organization executive
Bentsen, Lloyd former government official, former senator
Benzle, Curtis Munhall artist, art educator
Berdanier, Carolyn Dawson nutrition educator, researcher
Berezin, Tanya acting coach, actress
Bergan, William Luke lawyer
Bergau, Frank Conrad real estate, commercial and investment properties executive
Bergen, Candice actress, writer, photojournalist
Berger, Anita Hazel psychotherapist, adult educator, organizational consultant
Berger, Frank Stanley management executive
Berger, Lawrence Douglas lawyer
Berger, William Ernest newspaper publisher
Berger-Kraemer, Nancy speech and language pathologist, artist
Bergfield, Gene Raymond engineering educator
Bergin, Colleen Joan medical educator
Bergman, Claire Alice violist
Bergman, Hermas John (Jack Bergman) retired college administrator
Bergman, Klaus retired utility executive, lawyer
Bergson, Maria designer
Bergstein, Stanley Francis horse racing executive
Bergstrom, Robert William lawyer
Beringer, William Ernst mediator, arbitrator, lawyer
Berke, Judie publisher, editor
Berkholtz, Nicholas Evald engineering manager, consultant
Berkley, Mary Corner neurologist
Berkovich, Gary A. architect
Berle, Peter Adolf Augustus lawyer, media director
Berlin, Beatrice Winn visual artist, printmaker
Berlincourt, Marjorie Alkins government official, retired
Berlinger, Warren actor
Berlowitz Tarrant, Laurence biotechnologist, university administrator
Berman, Aaron art appraiser, director, consultant
Berman, Eleanore artist
Berman, Lori Beth legislative staff member
Berman, Sanford Solomon motion picture sound designer, composer, arranger, artist
Berman, Siegrid Visconti interior designer
Berman, William H. publishing company executive
Bern, Lynda Kaplan women's health and pediatric nurse
Bernard, Jami film critic, author
Bernard, Richard Lawson geneticist, retired
Bernfield, Lynne psychotherapist
Bernhardt, Arthur Dieter building industry executive and consultant
Bernhardt, Melvin theater director
Bernstein, George L. lawyer, accountant
Bernstein, I(rving) Melvin university official and dean, materials scientist
Bernstein, Richard Allen publishing company executive
Berra, Robert Louis human resources consultant
Berry, Laurie Ann critical care nurse
Berry, Richard Lewis author, magazine editor, lecturer, programmer
Berry, Richard Stephen chemist
Berry, Robert Vaughan retired electrical manufacturing company executive
Berry, Robert Worth lawyer, educator, retired army officer
Bers, Abraham electrical engineering and physics educator
Bers, Donald Martin physiology educator
Bersin, Richard Lewis physicist, plasma process technologist
Bertelsman, William Odis federal judge
Berthaud, Vladimir physician
Bertin, John Joseph aeronautical engineer, educator, researcher
Bertles, John Francis physician, educator
Bertolett, Craig Randolph mechanical engineer consultant
Berzin, Russell Frank land and housing developer
Berzon, Betty psychotherapist
Beston, Rose Marie college president
Betlach, Mary Carolyn biochemist, molecular biologist
Betsinger, Peggy Ann oncological nurse
Betti, John Anso federal official, former automobile manufacturing company executive
Betts, Elaine Wiswall retired headmistress
Beukema, John Frederick lawyer

Beyer, Gordon Robert foreign service officer
Biagi, Richard Charles retail executive, real estate consultant
Bick, Katherine Livingstone scientist, international liaison, consultant
Bidwell, Roger Grafton Shelford biologist, educator
Biegel, David Eli social worker, educator
Bierce, James Malcolm retired judge
Bierley, Paul Edmund musician, author, publisher
Bierwirth, John Cocks retired aerospace manufacturing executive
Bigelow, Robert P. lawyer, arbitrator, mediator, journalist
Bigelow-Lourie, Anne Edwige graphic designer
Biggs, Arthur Edward retired chemical manufacturing company executive
Bigham, Cecilia Beth retired communications and marketing professional
Bilbray, James Hubert former congressman, lawyer, consultant
Biljetina, Richard chemical engineering researcher
Binch, Caroline Lesley illustrator, photographer
Bingham, Jinsie Scott broadcast company executive
Bini, Dante Natale architect, industrial designer
Birchem, Regina cell biologist, environment consultant, educator, writer
Bird, Harrie Waldo, Jr. psychiatrist, educator
Birk, John R. marketing/financial services consultant
Birkenstock, James Warren business machine manufacturing company executive
Birkett, Cynthia Anne theater company executive
Birman, Linda Lee elementary education educator
Bishop, Cecil bishop
Bishop, Charles Edwin university president emeritus, economist
Bishop, Gordon Bruce journalist
Bishop, Raymond Holmes, Jr. physician, retired army officer
Bishop, (Ina) Sue Marquis psychiatric and mental health nurse educator, researcher, administrator
Bissell, Allen Morris engineer, consultant
Bissell, James Dougal, III motion picture production designer
Bistline, Stephen retired state supreme court justice
Bixler, Margaret Triplett former manufacturing executive
Biziou, Peter cinematographer
Bjerknes, Michael Leif dancer
Bjorndahl, David Lee electrical engineer
Bjornson, Maria theatrical designer
Blacher, Joan Helen psychotherapist, educator
Blachman, Nelson M(erle) physicist
Black, David R. superintendent
Black, Rhonda Stout special education educator
Black, Richard Bruce business executive, consultant
Blackbourn, David Gordon history educator
Blacker, Harriet public relations executive
Blackmun, Harry Andrew retired United States supreme court justice
Blaine, Davis Robert valuation consultant executive
Blair, Charles Melvin manufacturing company executive, scientist
Blair, Fred Edward social services administrator
Blair, Frederick David interior designer
Blake, John Edward retired car rental company executive
Blake, Ran jazz pianist, composer
Blanchard, David Lawrence aerospace executive, real estate developer
Blanchard, Richard Frederick construction executive
Blank, Richard Glenn religious organization administrator, counselor
†Blankenship, Jayne author
Blasco, Alfred Joseph business and financial consultant
Blatt, Harold Geller lawyer
Blausey, Jeanne Martha accountant, financial systems analyst, fraud examiner
Blazina, Janice Fay transfusion medicine physician
Blazzard, Norse Novar lawyer
Blevins, Gary Lynn architect, real estate broker, real estate appraiser
Bliley, Thomas Jerome, Jr. congressman
Blinder, Janet art dealer
Bliss, William Stanley, Jr. corporate financial and marketing consultant
Bloch, Erich retired electrical engineer, former science foundation administrator
Block, Emil Nathaniel, Jr. military officer
Block, William newspaper publisher
Blood, Archer Kent retired foreign service officer
Bloodworth, Gladys Leon educator
Bloom, Frank corporation executive, consultant
Bloomquist, Kenneth Gene music educator, university bands director
Blossom, Beverly choreographer, dance educator
Blount, David Laurence lawyer
Blow, George lawyer
Bluechel, Alan state senator, wood structural components manufacturing company executive
Blum, Barbara Davis banker
Blumberg, Mark Stuart health care researcher
Blumengold, Jeffrey Gene health care financial reimbursement expert
Blumenthal, William lawyer
Boal, Dean retired arts center administrator, educator
Boam, Jeffrey David screenwriter
Boan, Bobby Jack chemist
Bochner, Hart actor
Bock, Jerry (Jerrold Lewis) composer
Bodanszky, Miklos chemist, educator
Bodea, Andy S(orin) financial services and manufacturing executive
Bodner, Bruce Ira ophthalmologist
Boehle, William Randall music educator emeritus
Boeker, Paul Harold academic official, diplomat
Bogart, Carol Lynn small business owner, writer, talk show host, poet
Bogart, Judith Saunders public relations executive
Bogdan, Victor Michael mathematics educator, scientist
Bogosian, Eric actor, writer
Bogosian, Mark Jerome investment company executive
Bogue, Philip Roberts consultant
Bohannan, Paul James anthropologist, writer, former university administrator
†Bohle, Robert Henry journalism educator
Boho, Dan L. lawyer
Bok, Sissela philosopher, writer
Boling, Robert Bruce physical education educator
Bolla, Karen Irene neuropsychologist, educator
Bollback, Anthony George minister
Bolliger, Eugene Frederick retired surgeon
Bolsterli, Margaret Jones English educator, farmer
Bond, Victoria Ellen conductor, composer
Bondi, Harry Gene lawyer

Bonerz, Peter actor, director
Boni, Miki artist
†Bonifay, Cam professional sports team executive
Bonn, Ethel May psychiatrist, educator
Bonnard, Raymond theater director
Bonnell, Victoria Eileen sociologist
Bonner, Jack public relations company executive
Bonner, John Tyler biology educator
Bonner, Patricia J. academic dean, educator
Bonnet, John David physician, medical facility administrator
Bono, Sonny Salvatore congressman, singer, composer, former mayor
Booher, Alice Ann lawyer
Booker, Nana Laurel public relations executive
Bootle, William Augustus retired federal judge
Boozer, Howard Rai retired state education official
Borchers, Mary Amelia middle school educator
Borda, Richard Joseph management consultant
Borecky, Isidore bishop
Borg, Ruth I. home nursing care provider
Borges, William, III environmental scientist
Borgstahl, Kaylene Denise health facility administrator
Bork, Robert Heron lawyer, author, educator, former federal judge
Borne, Bonita H. ballet dancer, assistant artistic director
Bornhorst, Kenneth Frank electrical and systems engineer
Borow, Richard Henry lawyer
Borowitz, Albert Ira lawyer, author
Borst, Philip West academic administrator
Borten, William H. research company executive
Bortz, Paul Isaac media, sport and entertainment consultant
Borum, Rodney Lee financial business executive
Borwein, Jonathan Michael mathematics educator
Borysewicz, Mary Louise editor
Bosco, Anthony Gerard bishop
Bose, Anjan electrical engineering educator, academic administrator
Boslaugh, Leslie retired judge
Bosmajian, Haig Aram speech communication educator
Bosse, Malcolm Joseph, Jr. professional language educator, author
Bost, Raymond Morris retired college president
Bost, Thomas Glen lawyer
Boston, Gretha mezzo-soprano, actress
Boswell, Thomas Murray sports columnist, writer
Boswell, Winthrop Palmer writer
Bothwell, John Charles archbishop
Bottone, JoAnn health services executive
Boucher, Laurence James university dean, chemist
Bouchey, L. Francis publicist, diplomat
Bova, Benjamin William author, editor, educator
Bowden, Ann bibliographer, educator
Bowen, Douglas Glenn electrical engineer, consultant
Bowen, James Ronald banker
Bower, Jean Ramsay lawyer
Bower, Sandra Irwin communications executive
Bowie, E(dward) J(ohn) Walter hematologist, researcher
Bowles, Paul Frederick composer, author
Bowman, Charles Hay petroleum company executive
Bowne, Shirlee Pearson credit union executive, real estate executive
Box, Dwain D. former judge
Box, George Edward Pelham statistics educator
Boxer, Stanley Robert artist, sculptor
Boyatt, Thomas David former ambassador
Boyd, Edward Lee financial executive
Boyd, Francis Virgil retired accounting educator
Boyd, Julianne Mamana theater director
Boyd, Liona Maria musician
Boyes, Stephen Richard hydrogeologic consultant
Boykin, Robert Heath banker
Boyle, Betsy H. educational administrator
Boyle, Bryan Douglas computer and network systems architect
Boyle, R. Emmett metal products executive
Boyles, James Kenneth retired banker
Boylston, Benjamin Calvin retired steel company executive
Boysen, Thomas Cyril state school system administrator
Bracken, Peg author
Brackenhoff, Lonnie Sue principal
Braden, Charles Hosea physicist, university administrator
Braden, George Walter, II (Lord of Carrigaline) company executive
Braden, Joan Kay mental health counselor
Braden, Thomas Wardell news commentator
Bradford, Barbara Reed lawyer
Bradford, Robert Edward supermarket executive, retired
Bradley, Carol Ann nursing administrator
Bradley, Jean Eleanor newspaper executive, public relations consultant
Bradley, Patricia Ellen professional golfer
Bradunas, Edward Terence data processing management and technology management consultant
Brady, George Moore real estate executive, mortgage banker
Brady, Jean Stein retired librarian
Braen, Bernard Benjamin psychology educator
Brain, George Bernard university dean
Braithwaite, Ralph Rhey organizational consultant
Bramson, Phyllis Halperin artist, educator
Branagan, James Joseph lawyer
Brancato, Leo John manufacturing company executive
Brand, John Charles chemistry educator
Brandl, John Edward public affairs educator
Brando, Marlon, Jr. actor
Brandt, Grace Borgenicht art dealer
Brandt, James Bradford producer
Brandt, Ronald Stirling education association executive
Branson, Harley Kenneth finance executive, motion picture producer
Brantley, Benjamin David drama critic
Brantz, George Murray retired lawyer
Branyan, Robert Lester retired university administrator
Braswell, Arnold Webb retired military officer
Braswell, Jackie Terry medical, surgical nurse
Bratsch, Steven Gary chemistry educator
Bratt, Nicholas investment management and research company executive
Bratzler, Mary Kathryn desktop publisher
Brauer, Rhonda Lyn lawyer
Braugher, Andre actor
Braun, Jerome Irwin lawyer

Braun, Mary Lucile Dekle (Lucy Braun) therapist, consultant, counselor
Braun, Robert Alexander retired psychiatrist
Brawn, Linda Curtis political consultant, former state legislator
Brawner, Gerald Theodore lawyer
Bray, Sharon Ann management company executive
Brazier, Don Roland retired railroad executive
Breathed, Berkeley cartoonist
Bredfeldt, John Creighton economist, financial analyst, retired air force officer
Breen, Janice DeYoung health services executive, community health nurse
Brekke, Gail Louise broadcasting administrator
Bremner, John McColl agronomy and biochemistry educator
Brennan, Ciaran Brendan accountant, independent oil producer, real estate developer
Brennan, Donna Lesley public relations company executive
Brennan, Maryann business consulting executive
Brennan, T. Casey writer
Brennen, Stephen Alfred international business consultant
Brenner, Albert production designer, sculptor
Brent, Robert Leonard radiology and pediatrics educator
Breslin, Evalynne L. W. retired psychiatric nurse
Brett, Barbara Jeanne publisher
Brettell, Richard Robson art historian, museum consultant
Bretthauer, Erich Walter chemist, educator
Brewer, Carey retired academic administrator
Brewer, Timothy Francis, III retired cardiologist
Brickell, Charles Hennessey, Jr. marine engineer, retired military officer
Bricker, William Rudolph organization executive
Brickman, Ravelle public relations writer and consultant
Bridger, Baldwin, Jr. electrical engineer
Bridges, Roy Dubard, Jr. career officer
Bright, Harold Frederick university provost emeritus, consultant
Briles, Judith writer, speaker, consultant
Brill, Winston Jonas microbiologist, educator, research director, publisher and management consultant
Brimacombe, James Keith metallurgical engineering educator, researcher, consultant
Brin, Pamela Yale art dealer, mirror and glass designer
Brinberg, Herbert Raphael information management, publishing company executive
Brinckerhoff, Richard Charles retired manufacturing company executive
Brink, John William financial corporation executive
Brink, Richard Edward lawyer
Brinkley, Fred Sinclair, Jr. state agency administrator, pharmacist
Britt, John Roy banker
Broadwater, James E. publisher
Brock, Mary Anne research biologist, consultant
Brodhead, David Crawmer lawyer
Brodian, Laura broadcasting and illustration studio executive, professional illustrator
Brodie, Howard artist
Brodie, Theodore Hamilton construction company executive
Brodkin, Alan Keith investment company executive
Brodsky, David M. lawyer
Brodsky, Richard Louis state legislator
Brody, Edward Norman molecular biologist, educator
Brody, Martin food service company executive
Broedling, Laurie Adele human resources executive, psychologist, educator
Brogan, Frank T. state agency administrator
Brohammer, Richard Frederic psychiatrist
Brooke, Ralph Ian dental educator, vice provost, university dean
Brooker, Robert Elton, Jr. manufacturing company executive
Brookner, Anita writer, educator
Brooks, Albert (Albert Einstein) actor, writer, director
Brooks, James Sprague retired national guard officer
†Brooks, Kenneth N. forestry educator
Brooks, Mark Hunter systems engineering manager, consultant
Brooks, Michael Paul urban planning educator
Brooks, Thomas Aloysius, III retired naval officer, telecommunications company executive
Brophy, Theodore Frederick telephone company executive
Brosz, Margaret Headley pediatrics nurse
Broude, Ronald music publisher
Browder, Felix Earl mathematician, educator
Brower, Charles Nelson lawyer, judge
Brower, Forrest Allen retired health facility administrator
Brown, Anne Rhoda Wiesen civic worker
Brown, Barbara June hospital and nursing administrator
Brown, Beulah Louise retired elementary educator
Brown, Brice Norman surgeon, educator
Brown, Britt retired publishing company executive
Brown, Bruce Maitland philanthropy consultant
Brown, Carol Rentiers health facility administrator
Brown, Carol Rose artist
Brown, Donald Douglas transportation company executive, retired air force officer, consultant
Brown, Elizabeth Ruth neonatologist
Brown, Geraldine nurse, freelance writer
Brown, Henry Bedinger Rust financial management company executive
Brown, Herbert Graham entrepreneur
Brown, Jim (James Nathaniel Brown) film actor, former professional football player
Brown, Kay (Mary Kathryn Brown) former state official, talk radio host
Brown, Marcia Joan author, artist, photographer
Brown, Robert Laidlaw state supreme court justice
Brown, Sandra Jean banker
Brown, William Ferdinand artist, writer
Browne, Diana Gayle artist, social services
Browne, Edmund John Phillip oil company executive
Browne, Patti Ann journalist
Browning, Colin Arrott retired banker
Browning, Jesse Harrison entrepreneur
Brown-Whittington, Vanessa Elizabeth educator
Brubaker, Crawford Francis, Jr. government official, aerospace consultant
Bruce, James Edmund retired utility company executive
Bruggeman, Lewis LeRoy radiologist
Bruinsma, Theodore August retired business executive
Brumberg, G. David historical center administrator, history bibliographer
Brune, David Hamilton financial corporation executive, lawyer
Brune, Eva fundraiser
Bruno, Barbara Altman social worker
Brunt, Harry Herman, Jr. psychiatrist
Bruzda, Francis Joseph investment executive, former banker
Bryan, Lawrence Dow college administrator
Bryant, Bertha Estelle retired nurse
Bryant, Cecil Farris lawyer, retired insurance company executive
Bryant, Gail Annette Grippen nurse, educator
Bryant, Roy, Sr. bishop
Bubrick, Melvin Phillip surgeon
Buchanan, John Clark bishop
Buchanan, John MacLennan Canadian provincial official
Buchanan, Patrick Joseph journalist
Buchbinder, Sharon Bell health science educator
Buchin, Jean psychologist
Buckels, Marvin Wayne savings and loan executive
Buckler, Marilyn Lebow school psychologist, educational consultant
Buckley, Linda Anne critical care and psychiatric-mental health, chemical dependency nurse
Buckley, William Elmhirst publishing consultant
Buechel, William Benjamin retired lawyer
Buell, James Richard, Jr. investment management company executive
Buenaventura, Milagros Paez psychiatrist
Bueno, Ana (Marie) marketing executive, writer
Buffkins, Archie Lee public television executive
Bugbee, Joan Barthelme retired corporate communications executive
Bugella, Barbara Ann psychiatric nurse therapist
Bujold, Tyrone Patrick lawyer
Bukar, Margaret Witty physician assistant, healthcare administrator, civic leader
Buker, Robert Hutchinson, Sr. army officer, thoracic surgeon
Bull, Bergen Ira retired equipment manufacturing company executive
Bulla, Clyde Robert writer
Bullins, Ed author
Bullock, Theodore Holmes biologist, educator
Bullough, Vern LeRoy nursing educator, historian, sexologist, researcher
Bumbery, Joseph Lawrence diversified telecommunications company executive
Bumpus, Frederick Joseph retired insurance company executive
Bunch, Franklin Swope architect
Bunch, Jennings Bryan, Jr. electrical engineer
Bundalo, Milan Richard manufacturing executive
Bundi, Renee art director, graphic designer
Bundschuh, George August William retired insurance company executive
Bundy, Mary Lothrop retired social worker
Bunim, Mary-Ellis television producer
Bunning, Jim congressman, former professional baseball player
Bunton, Lucius Desha, III federal judge
Bunyan, Ellen Lackey Spotz chemist, educator
Burbridge, Ann Arnold elementary school educator
Burcher, Hilda Beasley librarian
Burchman, Leonard government official
Burden, Ordway Partridge investment banker
Burdett, Barbra Elaine biology educator
Burge, John Wesley, Jr. management consultant
Burger, Robert Eugene author, chess expert
Burgess, Marjorie Laura protective services official
Burk, Sylvia Joan petroleum landman, freelance writer
Burke, Edmond Wayne retired judge, lawyer
Burke, Joseph C. university administrator
Burke, Mona sales engineer
Burke, Thomas Edmund retired lawyer
Burkett, Thomas O. manufacturing executive
Burki, Fred Albert labor union official
Burlant, William Jack retired chemical company executive
Burlingame, James Montgomery, III lawyer
Burlingame, John Hunter lawyer
Burnett, Iris Jacobson corporate communications specialist
Burney, Mary Ann mental health nurse
Burnham, J. V. sales executive
Burnham, Sophy writer
Burns, Bebe Lyn journalist
Burns, James F. social work therapist
Burns, James Milton retired educator
Burns, Marie T. retired secondary education educator
Burns, Mary Ferris finance executive
Burns, Richard Francis mechanical engineer
Burroughs, John Townsend lawyer
Burton, Al producer, director, writer
Burton, Joseph Alfred state legislator
Büsch, Annemarie mental health nurse
Bush, Charles Vernon telecommunications executive
Bush, Grace Villanueva dancer, dance instructor, choreographer
Bush, Guy Louis biology educator
Bush, Kate (Catherine Bush) singer, songwriter
Busho, Elizabeth Mary nurse, consultant, educator
Busse, Leonard Wayne banker, financial consultant
Bussgang, Julian Jakob electronics engineer
Butler, Eugene L. oil field equipment company executive
Butler, George Frank editor, literary historian
Butler, Jack Fairchild semiconductors company executive
Butler, Robert Leonard sales executive
Butler, Robert Thomas retired advertising executive
Butson, Alton Thomas mathematics educator
Butterfield, Alexander Porter former business executive, government official
Butts, Virginia corporate public relations executive
Buxton, Winslow Hurlbert diversified manufacturing company executive
Buzard, James Albert healthcare management consultant
Bynes, Frank Howard, Jr. physician
Bynum, Richard Cary publishing consultant, author
Byrd, Lloyd Garland civil engineer
Byrne, David musician, composer, artist, director
Cachia, Pierre Jacques Middle East languages and culture educator, researcher
Caddeo, Maria Elizabeth critical care nurse
Cahn, Robert Nathan physicist
Caine, Raymond William, Jr. retired public relations executive
Calamita, Kathryn Elizabeth nursing administrator
Calcaterra, Edward Lee construction company executive
Caldwell, Louise Phinney historical researcher, community volunteer
Caldwell, Warren Frederick investment company executive
Calegari, Maria ballerina
Califano, Joseph Anthony, Jr. lawyer, public health policy educator, writer
Callan, Richard John elementary school educator
Callander, Bruce Douglas journalist, free-lance writer
Callard, Carole Crawford librarian, educator
Callard, David Jacobus investment banker
Calleo, David Patrick political science educator
Callow, Keith McLean judge
Callow, William Grant retired state supreme court justice
Calvert, James Francis manufacturing company executive, retired admiral
Calvert, Marilyn Rose Stewart nursing consultant
Camayd-Freixas, Yoel management, strategy & planning consultant
Cambrice, Robert Louis lawyer
Camdessus, Michel (Jean) federal agency administrator, international organization executive
Cameron, David Brian health service administrator
Cameron, J. Elliot retired parochial educational system administrator
†Cameron, Kay director music
Cameron, Lucille Wilson retired dean of libraries
Cameron, Roy Eugene scientist
Caminiti, Kenneth Gene professional baseball player
Camisa, George Lincoln beverage company executive
Camm, Gertrude Elizabeth physician, writer
Camp, Clifton Durrett, Jr. newspaper consultant, rancher
Campanelli, Pauline Eble artist
Campbell, Addison James, Jr. writer
Campbell, Alan Keith business educator
Campbell, Alice Shaw retired accountant, poet
Campbell, Arthur Andrews retired government official
Campbell, Byron Chesser publishing company executive
Campbell, Craig Stewart landscape architect, town planner
Campbell, Demarest Lindsay artist, designer, writer
Campbell, Donald Alfred retired government official
Campbell, Edward Clinton small business owner, violin maker
Campbell, Edwin Denton consultant
Campbell, Henry Cummings librarian
Campbell, Margaret M. retired social work educator
Campbell, Mary Ann social psychologist
Campbell, Naomi model
Campbell, Patton stage designer, educator
Campbell, Richard Alden electronics company executive
Campbell, Sarah elementary education educator, special education specialist
Canan, Michael James lawyer, author
Cane, David E. chemistry educator
Cannon, Isabella Walton mayor
Cantliffe, Jeri Miller artist, art educator
Cantone, Vic political cartoonist
Cantus, Jane Scott management consultant
Capice, Philip Charles television production executive
Capps, James Leigh, II lawyer, military career officer
Caputo, Salvatore critic
Caras, Roger Andrew author, motion picture company executive, television correspondent, radio commentator
Carder, Paul Charles advertising executive
Cardwell, Nancy Lee editor, writer
Cardy, Andrew Gordon hotel executive
Carey, Dennis Clarke executive search consultant
Carey, Martin Conrad gastroenterologist, molecular biophysicist, educator
†Carillo, Mary broadcaster, tennis analyst
Carlin, Betty educator
Carlquist, Sherwin biology and botany educator
Carlsen, Mary Baird clinical psychologist
Carlson, Charlotte Booth book illustrator
Carlson, Janet Frances psychologist, educator
Carlson, Marguerite T. science educator
Carlson, Natalie Traylor publisher
Carlyss, Earl Winston musician
Carmack, Mildred Jean retired lawyer
Carmody, Thomas Roswell business products company executive
Carney, Arthur William Matthew actor
Carney, Kate actress, director, educator, playwright
†Carollo, Joe mayor
Carpenter, Derr Alvin landscape architect
Carpenter, Kenneth John nutrition educator
Carpenter, Myron Arthur manufacturing company executive
Carr, Albert Anthony retired organic chemist
Carr, David Robert oil trading company executive
Carr, Harold Noflet investment corporation executive
Carr, Jesse Metteau, III lawyer, engineering executive
Carradine, Keith Ian actor, singer, composer
Carraher, Mary Lou Carter art educator
Carreker, John Russell retired agricultural engineer
Carrell, Heather Demaris foundation executive
Carrell, Terry Eugene manufacturing company executive
Carrier, W(illiam) David, III geotechnical engineer
†Carrison, Dale Mitchell emergency medicine physician
Carroll, Karen Jeorgianna fund administrator
Carroll, Margaret Ann retired chemist
Carroll, Marie-Jean Greve educator, artist
Carroll, Marshall Elliott architect
Carruthers, Claudelle Ann occupational and physical therapist
Carson, Johnny television personality
Carson, Regina Edwards healthcare administrator, pharmacist, educator
Carter, David LaVere soil scientist, researcher, consultant
Carter, Elliott Cook, Jr. composer
Carter, Herbert Edmund former university official
Carter, (William) Hodding, III television and newspaper journalist, educator
Carter, Hugh Clendenin mechanical consulting engineer
Carter, Jaine M(arie) human resources development company executive
Carter, Nanette Carolyn artist
Carter, Orwin L. chemical executive
Carter, Richard Duane business educator
Carter, Ronald musician
Carter, Ronald Gary academic administrator
Carter, Rosalynn Smith wife of former President of United States
Carter, William George, III army officer
Carter, Yvonne Pickering art educator
Cartier, Celine Paule librarian, administrator, consultant
Cartwright, Talula Elizabeth writing and career development educator, communication and leadership consultant
Carver, Calvin Reeve public utility company director
Carver, Kendall Lynn insurance company executive
Cary, Anne O. diplomat
Casadesus, Penelope Ann advertising executive, film producer
Case, Gerard Ramon drafting technologist, paleontologist
Casei, Nedda mezzo-soprano
Casey, Robert J. international trade association executive
Casey, Robert Reisch lawyer
Casey, Shannon Gloria visual effects producer
Cashel, Thomas William retired lawyer, educator
Cashen, J. Frank professional baseball team executive
Cashman, William James, Jr. information processing marketing executive
Casler, Frederick Clair academic administrator, law enforcement educator
Cason, Nica Virginia nursing educator
Casper, Gerhard academic administrator, law educator
Cassell, William Comyn college president
Casselman, William E., II lawyer
Cassidy, Carl Eugene physician
Cassidy, James Mark construction company executive
Cassidy, John Harold lawyer
Cassill, (Karilyn) Kay artist, writer
Castagna, William John federal judge
Castiglione, Kathie Anne accountant
Castile, Jesse Randolph (Rand) retired museum director
Castle, James Cameron information systems executive
Caston, J(esse) Douglas medical educator
†Castor, Betty academic administrator
Castro, Alejandro F. retired surgeon
Castro, Amuerfina Tantiongco geriatrics nurse
Castruita, Rudy school system administrator
Catacosinos, William James utility company executive
Catalano, Louis William, Jr. neurologist
Cates, Dalton Reede electronics company official, consultant
Catlin, B. Wesley microbiologist
Cattani, Maryellen B. lawyer
Caudill, Maureen author and computer consultant
Cauthorne-Burnette, Tamera Dianne family nurse practitioner, healthcare consultant
Cavallaro, Mary Caroline retired physics educator
Cavnar, Margaret Mary (Peggy Cavnar) business executive, former state legislator, nurse, consultant
Cecchi, David Robert farmer, graphic designer
Ceci, Louis J. former state supreme court justice
Cecil, Maxine critical care nurse
Cerny, Louis Thomas civil engineer, association executive
Cesnik, James Michael union official, newspaperman, printer
Chafkin, Rita M. physician, dermatologist
Chaikin, A. Scott public relations executive
Chaikof, Elliot Lorne vascular surgeon
Chajet, Lori Menschel secondary education educator
Chalfant, Richard Dewey hypnotherapist, composer, insurance consultant
Chamberlain, George Arthur, III manufacturing company executive, venture capitalist
Chamberlain, William Edwin, Jr. management consultant
Chamberlin, Michael Meade lawyer
Chambers, Judith Tarnpoll speech pathologist, audiologist
Chamblee, Mary Jane management specialist
Chambliss, Lavonda Jo Eastup writer, poet, songwriter
Chance, Kenneth Donald engineer
Chandler, Alfred Dupont, Jr. historian, educator
Chandler, Alice university president, educator
Chandler, Harry Edgar author
Chandler, John Herrick college president
Chandra, Abhijit engineering educator
Chandra, Pramod art history educator
Chao, James Min-Tzu architect
Chapanis, Alphonse human factors engineer, ergonomist
Chapman, Hope Horan psychologist
Chapman, Kristin Heilig public relations consultant
Chapman, William baritone
Charleston, Steve bishop
Charlton, Betty Jo retired state legislator
Charlton, Gordon Taliaferro, Jr. retired bishop
Charlton, Jesse Melvin, Jr. management educator, lawyer
Charry, Michael R(onald) musician, conductor
Chase, Clinton Irvin psychologist, educator, business executive
Chase, James Richard retired college president
Chase, Seymour M. lawyer
Chastain, Denise Jean process improvement engineer
Chater, Shirley Sears former vice chancellor, federal commissioner
Chawla, Krishan Kumar materials engineer, educator, consultant
Chaykin, Robert Leroy manufacturing and marketing executive
Cheesman, John Michael aeronautics company administrator, civic leader
Chegini, Nasser cell biology educator, reproductive endocrinologist
Chelberg, Bruce Stanley holding company executive
Chelberg, Robert Douglas army officer
Chellas, Brian Farrell philosophy educator
Chen, Di electro-optic company executive, consultant
Chen, Kuen Hai physician
Chenhall, Robert Gene former museum director, consultant, author
Chercover, Murray television executive
Cherenzia, Bradley James radiologist
Chernichaw, Mark television, film and interactive multimedia executive producer, director, international media consultant
Chernoff, Amoz Immanuel hematologist, consultant
Cherryh, C. J. writer
Cheston, Theodore C. electrical engineer
Chevalier, Paul Edward retired retail executive, lawyer, art gallery executive
Chia, Felipe Humberto management marketing educator, author, consultant
Child, Carroll Cadell research nursing administrator
Chinitz, Benjamin economics educator
Chinn, Thomas Wayne typographic company executive

Chinni, Peter Anthony *artist*
Chinoy, Helen Krich *theater historian*
Chinula, Donald McLean *religious studies educator*
Chmielinski, Edward Alexander *electronics company executive*
Choi, Man-Duen *mathematics educator*
Chojnowski, Donna A. *cardiac transplant nurse, administrator*
Chorpenning, Frank Winslow *immunology educator, researcher*
Choukas-Bradley, Melanie *writer, photographer*
Chow, Rita Kathleen *nurse consultant*
†Chris, McKendry *sports anchor*
†Christen, Paul Richert *financial company executive*
Christenson, Gregg Andrew *bank executive*
Christenson, William Newcome *retired physician*
Christian, James Wayne *economist*
Christoffersen, Ralph Earl *chemist*
Christopher, Russell Lewis *baritone*
Christopher, Sharon A. Brown *bishop*
Christy, Thomas Patrick *human resources executive, educator*
Chrysostomos, (González-Alexopoulos) *archbishop, clergyman, psychologist, educator*
Chryssis, George Christopher *engineering executive*
Chu, Benjamin Thomas Peng-Nien *chemistry educator*
Chu, Steven *physics educator*
Church, Eugene Lent *physicist, consulting scientist*
Churchill, Robert Wilson *state legislator, lawyer*
Cibbarelli, Pamela Ruth *information executive*
Cima, Brooks Dement *art educator*
Cioczek, Henryk Antoni *internist*
Cittone, Henry Aron *hotel and restaurant management educator*
Claes, Gayla Christine *writer, editorial consultant*
Claiborne, Craig *author, editor cookbooks*
Clanon, Thomas Lawrence *retired hospital administrator*
Clapper, Lyle Nielsen *magazine publisher*
Clark, Alicia Garcia *political party official*
Clark, Caleb Morgan *political scientist, educator*
Clark, Candy *actress*
Clark, Carolyn Archer *aerosopace technologist, life scientist*
Clark, Claudia J. *educational administration, speech, language and learning disabilities professional*
Clark, James Milford *college president, retired*
†Clark, Jeffrey Ray *surgeon*
Clark, Larry *photographer*
Clark, Mary Higgins *author, business executive*
Clark, Maxine *retail executive*
Clark, Peter Bruce *newspaper executive*
Clark, Philip Raymond *nuclear utility executive, engineer*
†Clark, Richard Harry Jr. *clinic administrator*
Clark, Rick Gene *radiologist, osteopath*
Clark, Robert Phillips *newspaper editor, consultant*
Clark, Thomas Lloyd *English linguistics educator*
Clarke, Edward Owen, Jr. *lawyer*
Clarke, Hope *choreographer, director, actress*
Clarke, John Patrick *retired newspaper publisher*
Clarke, Lambuth McGeehee *academic administrator*
Clarke, W. Hall *engineer*
Clauser, Angela Frances *medical surgical, pediatrics and geriatrics nurse*
Clauser, Kenneth Alton *professional photographer, banjo player*
Claver, Robert Earl *television director, producer*
Claxton, Bradford Wayne *professional society administrator*
Claytor, Richard Anderson *retired federal agency executive, consultant*
Cleaveland, John Riddle *architect*
Cleaver, James Edward *radiologist, educator*
Clemendor, Anthony Arnold *obstetrician, gynecologist, educator*
Clemens, Charles Joseph *insurance agent*
Clement, Alain Gérard *photographer*
Clement, Hope Elizabeth Anna *librarian*
Clemetson, Charles Alan Blake *physician*
Cleveland, Charlene S. *community health nurse*
Cliff, Judith Anita *author, biblical studies lecturer*
Cliff, Ronald Laird *energy company executive*
Clifford, Brother Peter *academic administrator, religious educator*
Clifton, Russell B. *banking and mortgage lending consultant, retired mortgage company executive*
Cline, Linda Jean *reading educator*
Closset, Gerard Paul *forest products company executive*
Cloud, Stanley Wills *journalist, editor, writer*
Clouston, Ross Neal *retired food and related products company executive*
Clover-Lee, Shevonne Jones *geriatrics nurse*
Cluff, E. Dale *librarian, educator, administrator*
Clymer, Wayne Kenton *bishop*
Cobb, John Boswell, Jr. *clergyman, educator*
Cobb, Miles Alan *retired lawyer*
Cobb, Millicent Amelia *special education educator*
Cobb, Ruth *artist*
Cobb, Virginia Horton *artist, educator*
Coble, Howard *congressman, lawyer*
Coburn, D(onald) L(ee) *playwright*
Cochran, Thad *senator*
Cochrane, Walter E. *education administrator, writer*
Cockrum, William Monroe, III *investment banker, consultant, educator*
Coffee, Joseph Denis, Jr. *college chancellor emeritus*
Coffey, John Louis *federal judge*
Coffman, Stanley Knight, Jr. *English educator, former college president*
Cograve, John Edwin *retired judge*
Cohen, Alexander H. *theatrical and television producer*
Cohen, Allan Richard *broadcasting executive*
Cohen, B. Stanley *physician*
†Cohen, Ellis Avrum *producer, writer*
Cohen, Mark Herbert *broadcasting company executive*
Cohen, Melvin Joseph *neuroscientist, educator*
†Cohen, Roberta Jane *government executive*
Cohen, Sharleen Cooper *interior designer, writer*
Cohn, Avern Levin *federal judge*
Cohn, Leonard Allan *retired chemical company executive*
Cohn, Marianne Winter Miller *civic activist*
Cohn, Martin *advertising executive, consultant*
Coke, Frank Van Deren *museum director, photographer*
Colaianni, Joseph Vincent *judge*
Colangelo, James Joseph *psychotherapist*
Colburn, Harold Lewis *dermatologist, state legislator*
Cole, Brady Marshall *retired naval officer*
Cole, Clifford Adair *clergyman*
Cole, Jerome Foster *research company executive*
Coleman, Arlene Florence *nurse practitioner*
Coleman, Barbara Helene *secondary education educator*
Coleman, Claire Kohn *public relations executive*
Coleman, Lewis Waldo *bank executive*
Coleman, Malcolm James, Jr. *band director, music educator, flute educator*
Coleman, Nancy Catherine *actress*
Coleman, Robert Elliott *retired secondary education educator*
Coleman, Robert Lee *retired lawyer*
Coleman, Ronald D. (Ron Coleman) *former congressman*
Colgate, Stephen *small business owner*
Colgate-Lindberg, Catharine Pamella *educator*
Collier, Herman Edward, Jr. *retired college president*
Collier, Oscar *literary agency consultant, writer*
Collins, Allen Howard *psychiatrist*
Collins, Eileen Marie *astronaut*
Collins, Joan Henrietta *actress*
Collins, John Francis *landscape architect, educator*
Collins, William Michael *public relations executive*
Colodny, Edwin Irving *lawyer, retired airline executive*
Colonnier, Marc Leopold *neuroanatomist, educator*
Colosimo, Mary Lynn Sukurs *psychology educator*
Colton, Victor Robert *real estate developer, investor,*
Coluccio, Josephine Catherine *primary and elementary school educator*
Colvin, Burton Houston *mathematician, government official*
Comden, Betty *writer, dramatist, lyricist, performer*
Comissiona, Sergiu *conductor*
Como, Perry *singer*
Compton, Norma Haynes *retired university dean*
Compton, W. Dale *physicist*
Condayan, John *retired foreign service officer, consultant*
Condie, Vicki Cook *nurse, educator*
Condit, Doris Elizabeth *historian*
Condry, Robert Stewart *retired hospital administrator*
Cone, Edward Toner *composer, emeritus music educator*
Connell, George Edward *former university president, scientist*
Connell, Shirley Hudgins *public relations professional*
Connell, William D. *lawyer*
Connelly, Margery Annette *research pathologist, educator*
Connelly, Sharon Rudolph *lawyer, federal official*
†Connolly, Gerald E. *company executive*
Conole, Clement Vincent *business administrator*
Conomikes, Melanie Remington *marketing consultant*
Conover, Nancy Anderson *secondary school counselor*
Conrad-England, Roberta Lee *pathologist*
Conran, James Michael *consumer advocate, public policy consultant*
Consoli, Marc-Antonio *composer*
Conte, Andrea *retail executive, health care consultant*
Contillo, Lawrence Joseph *financial and computer company executive*
Conway, James Valentine Patrick *forensic document examiner, former postal service executive*
Conway, Richard Ashley *environmental engineer*
Cook, Alexander Burns *museum curator, artist, educator*
Cook, Charles Emerson *electrical engineer*
Cook, Fielder *producer, director*
Cook, Fred James *journalist, author*
Cook, Julian Abele, Jr. *federal judge*
Cook, Quentin LaMar *healthcare executive, lawyer*
Cooke, Eileen Delores *retired librarian*
Cooke, Susan Marie *lawyer*
Cookson, Albert Ernest *telephone and telegraph company executive*
Cooley, James William *retired executive researcher*
Cooney, John Thomas *retired banker*
Coons, Marion McDowell *retail food stores executive*
Coonts, Stephen Paul *novelist*
Coop, Frederick Robert *retired city manager*
Cooper, Allen David *research scientist, educator*
Cooper, Austin Morris *chemist, chemical engineer, consultant, researcher*
Cooper, Carol Diane *publishing company executive*
Cooper, Charles Gordon *insurance consultant, former executive*
Cooper, David Wayne *aerospace engineer*
Cooper, Francis Loren *advertising executive*
Cooper, Hal *television director*
Cooper, Hal Dean *lawyer*
Cooper, John Miller *retired biomechanics lab director*
Cooper, John Milton, Jr. *history educator, author*
Cooper, Norton J. *liquor, wine and food company executive*
Cooper, Rebecca *art dealer*
Cooper, Sarah Jean *nursing educator*
Cooper, Signe Skott *retired nurse educator*
Cooper-Lewter, Nicholas Charles *psychotherapist, educator, minister, author*
Cope, Alfred Haines *political scientist, educator*
Copeland, Henry Jefferson, Jr. *former college president*
Copeland, Terrilyn Denise *speech pathologist*
Coplans, John Rivers *artist*
Coplin, Mark David *lawyer*
Copperfield, David (David Kotkin) *illusionist, director, producer, writer*
Coppie, Comer Swift *state official*
Coppolecchia, Rosa *internist*
Corcoran, Barbara Asenath *author*
Corey, Jeff *actor, director, educator*
Corey, Kenneth Edward *geography and urban planning educator, researcher*
Coriell, Lewis Lemon *physician, research institute administrator*
Cork, Edwin Kendall *business and financial consultant*
Corkery, James Caldwell *retired Canadian government executive, mechanical engineer*
Cormican, M. Alma *elementary education educator*
Cornell, David Roger *health care executive*
Cortese, Richard Anthony *computer company executive*
Corwell, Ann Elizabeth *public relations executive*
Cosby, Bill *actor, entertainer*
Cossa, Dominic Frank *baritone*
Costa-Gavras, (Konstaninos Gavras) *director, writer*
Costantino, Lorine Protzman *woodworking company executive*
Costas, Robert Quinlan (Bob Costas) *sportscaster*
Costello, Daniel Walter *retired bank executive*
Costello, James Joseph *retired electrical manufacturing company executive*
Costello, Thomas Patrick *manufacturing executive*
Coté, Kathryn Marie *psychotherapist, stress management educator*
Cotrubas, Ileana *opera singer, lyric soprano, retired*
Cotsonas, Nicholas John, Jr. *physician, medical educator*
Cotter, Richard Vern *management consultant, author, educator*
Cotting, James Charles *manufacturing company executive*
Cottrell, Mary-Patricia Tross *banker*
Couchman, Robert George James *human services consultant*
Coughlan, William David *professional society administrator*
Cougill, Roscoe McDaniel *mayor, retired air force officer*
Counsil, William Glenn *electric utility executive*
Courtheoux, Richard James *management consultant*
Courtnay, Wiliam Gerard *osteopathic physician*
Coval-Apel, Naomi Miller *dentist*
Coven, Berdeen *psychotherapist*
Cover, Franklin Edward *actor*
Covington, Gary Wayne *accountant*
Cowan, Andrew Glenn *television writer, producer, performer*
Cox, David Brummal *accounting firm executive*
Cox, J. William *retired physician, health services administrator*
Cox, John Curtis *healthcare and educational administrator*
Cox, John Francis *retired cosmetic company executive*
Cox, John Michael *cardiologist*
Cox, Wilford Donald *retired food company executive*
Coyle, John J. *publishing executive*
Cozan, Lee *clinical research psychologist*
Cozen, Lewis *orthopedic surgeon*
Crable, John V. *chemist*
Crabtree, Davida Foy *minister*
Craft, Edmund Coleman *automotive parts manufacturing company executive*
Craig, Carol Mills *marriage, family and child counselor*
Cramer, Robert Vern *retired college administrator, consultant*
Crampton, Esther Larson *sociology and political science educator*
Crandall, Albert Earl *retail executive, accountant, entrepreneur*
Cranin, Marilyn Sunners *landscape designer*
Craw, Freeman (Jerry Craw) *graphic artist*
Crawford, Carol Tallman *government executive*
Crawford, Kenneth Charles *educational institute executive, retired government official*
Crawford, Muriel Laura *lawyer, author, educator*
Crawford, Pamela J. *critical care nurse*
Crawford, William Walsh *retired consumer products company executive*
Cray, Robert *popular blues guitarist, singer, songwriter*
Creech, John Lewis *retired scientist, consultant*
Creigh, Thomas, Jr. *utility executive*
Crews, Esca Holmes, Jr. *utility company executive*
Criscuolo, Wendy Laura *lawyer, interior design consultant*
Critoph, Eugene *retired physicist, nuclear research company executive*
Cromwell, Florence Stevens *occupational therapist*
Cronkhite, Leonard Wolsey, Jr. *physician, consultant, research foundation executive*
Cronson, Robert Granville *lawyer*
Crooker, Diane Kay *accountant*
Crooks, Bruce Philip *retired bank executive*
Crosby, John Griffith *investment banker*
Crosby, Norman Lawrence *comedian*
Cross, Alexander Dennis *business consultant, former chemical and pharmaceutical executive*
Cross, Harold Dick *physician*
Crossley, Francis Rendel Erskine *engineering educator*
Crouse, Carol K. Mavromatis *elementary education educator*
Crowder, Eleanor Louise McElheny *nursing educator*
Crowe, James Joseph *lawyer*
Crowley, Joseph Michael *electrical engineer, educator*
Crowther, James Earl *radio and television executive, lawyer*
Crowther, Richard Layton *architect, consultant, researcher, author, lecturer*
Croxton, Fred(erick) E(mory), Jr. *retired information specialist, consultant*
Crudup, W. *bishop*
Cruise, Tom (Tom Cruise Mapother, IV) *actor*
Cruz Aponte, Ramón Aristides *foundation administrator, educator*
Cruz-Romo, Gilda *soprano*
Culbertson, Phillip Edgar *aerospace company executive, consultant*
Cull, Robert Robinette *electric products manufacturing company executive*
Cullen, James Thaddeus, Jr. *broadcast executive*
Cullen, Robert John *publishing executive, financial consultant*
Culp, William Newton *retired insurance executive*
Culverwell, Albert Henry *historian*
Culwell, Charles Louis *retired manufacturing company executive*
Cummer, William Jackson *former oil company executive, investor*
Cumming, Robert Hugh *artist, photographer*
Cummings, Constance *actress*
Cummings, David William *artist, educator*
Cummiskey, J. Kenneth *former college president*
Cunningham, William Francis, Jr. *English language educator, university administrator*
Curley, Elmer Frank *librarian*
Curran-Smith, Anita Stiles *public health medicine educator, dean*
Currier, Ruth *dancer, choreographer and educator*
Curry, Richard Orr *history educator and freelance writer*
Curson, Theodore *musician*
Curtin, David Stephen *newswriter*
Curtis, James L. *psychiatrist*
Curtis, James Richard *flight engineer*
Curtis, Mary Ellen (Mary Curtis Horowitz) *publishing company executive*
†Curtis, Peter J. *government official*
Cushing, Frederic Sanford *publishing company executive*
Cushman, Paul *physician, educator*
Cushwa, William Wallace *retired machinery parts company executive*
Cyr, Conrad Keefe *federal judge*
Czarnecki, Gerald Milton *investment banking and venture capital*
Dabbs, Henry Erven *television and film producer, educator*
Dackow, Orest Taras *insurance company executive*
D'Agostino, Stephen I. *bottling company executive*
Dahl, Bren Bennington *photo retoucher*
Dahlgren, Carl Herman Per *educator, arts administrator*
Dailey, Irene *actress, educator*
Dailey, Janet *novelist*
Dake, Marcia Allene *retired nursing educator, university dean*
Dale, Wesley John *chemistry educator*
Dale Riikonen, Charlene Boothe *international health administrator*
D'Alesandro, Philip Anthony *parasitologist, immunologist, retired educator*
Dally, James William *mechanical engineering educator, consultant*
Dalton, Robert Edgar *mathematician, computer scientist*
Daly, William James *retired health industry distributing company executive*
Dalziel, Robert David *telecommunications consultant*
Damaschino, Ann Toothman *development consultant*
D'Amato, Anthony Roger *recording company executive*
Dangerfield, Rodney (Jack Roy Dangerfield) *comedian, actor, author*
Dangoor, David Ezra Ramsi *consumer goods company executive*
Daniel, Elbert Clifton *journalist*
Daniels, Arlene Kaplan *sociology educator*
Daniels, James Maurice *physicist*
Daniels, Kurt R. *speech and language pathologist*
Daniels, Ronald George *theater director*
Danielson, Patricia Rochelle Frank *urban planner*
Danilowicz, Delores Ann *pediatric cardiologist, pediatrics educator*
Dannenberg, Martin Ernest *retired insurance company executive*
Danner, Blythe Katharine *actress*
Danza, Tony *actor*
Danzig, Joan *newspaper editor*
Darany, Michael Anthony *financial executive*
D'Arcangelo, Allan Matthew *artist*
Darien, Steven Martin *technology company executive*
Darke, Charles Bruce *academic administrator, dentist*
Darkey, Kermit Louis *association executive, lawyer*
Dasburg, John Harold *airline executive*
Dash, Robert (Warren) *artist, writer*
Datcu, Ioana *artist*
Daugherty, Frederick Alvin *federal judge*
Davenport, Ernest Harold *university official, accountant*
Davenport, L. B. *bishop*
Davenport, Lawrence Franklin *school system administrator*
Davenport, William Harold *mathematics educator*
David, Larry *television scriptwriter*
David, Marilyn Hattie *lawyer, retired military officer*
Davidovsky, Mario *composer*
Davidow, Jenny Jean *counselor, writer*
Davidson, Jeannie *costume designer*
Davidson, John *financial advisory executive*
Davidson, Mayer B. *medical educator, researcher*
Davis, Alphonse *health facility administrator, special education counselor*
Davis, Andrew Frank *conductor*
Davis, Carolyne Kahle *health care consultant*
Davis, Danny (George Joseph Nowlan) *musician*
Davis, Darrell L. *automotive executive*
Davis, Gay Ruth *psychotherapist, social welfare educator, author, researcher, consultant*
Davis, George Linn *banker*
Davis, George Lynn *retired aerospace company executive*
Davis, Henry Jefferson, Jr. *former naval officer*
Davis, James Richard *retired military officer*
Davis, Joseph Lloyd *educational administrator, consultant*
Davis, Luther *writer, producer*
Davis, Mac *singer, songwriter*
Davis, Marguerite Herr *judge*
Davis, Mary Helen *psychiatrist, psychoanalyst, educator*
Davis, Robert Aldine *academic administrator*
Davis, Roger Edwin *lawyer, retired discount chain executive*
Davis, Russell Haden *association executive, pastoral psychotherapist*
Davis, Sandra Bernice *nurse anesthetist*
Davis, Theodore Roosevelt *bishop, contractor*
Davis, Wanda Rose *lawyer*
Davison, Beaumont *retired university administrator*
Dawes, Carol J. *retired psychologist*
Dawkins, Marva Phyllis *psychologist*
Dawson, Horace Greeley, Jr. *former diplomat, government official*
Deacon, David Emmerson *advertising executive*
Deal, Lynn Hoffmann *interior designer*
DeAlessandro, Joseph Paul *insurance company executive*
Dean, Dearest (Lorene Glosup) *songwriter*
Dean, Francis Hill *landscape architect, educator*
Dean, Leesa Jane *musician*
De Antoni, Edward Paul *cancer control research scientist*
De Blasi, Tony (Anthony Armando De Blasi) *artist*
de Blasis, James Michael *artistic director, producer, stage director*
de Blij, Harm Jan *geography educator, editor*
Debs, Barbara Knowles *former college president, consultant*
deButts, Robert Edward Lee *corporate development and real estate executive*
DeCamp, Graydon *journalist*
deCastro, Fernando Jose *pediatrics educator*
Dechar, Peter Henry *artist*
Decker, Gilbert Felton *manufacturing company executive*
Decker, Oscar Conrad, Jr. *retired army officer*
Decker, Walter Johns *toxicologist*
De Concini, Dennis *lawyer, former U.S. senator, consultant*
Dedman, Bill *journalist*
Deely, Maureen Cecelia *community health nurse*
Deering, Fred Arthur *retired insurance company executive*
Dees, Lynne *artist*
Dees, Susan Coons *physician, educator*
DeFelice, Jonathan Peter *college president, priest*
De Felitta, Frank Paul *producer, writer, director*

Fanos, Kathleen Hilaire *osteopathic physician, podiatrist*
Fanwick, Ernest *lawyer*
Farah, Joseph Francis *newspaper editor, writer*
Farah, Tawfic Elias *political scientist, educator*
Farber, Neal Mark *biotechnologist, molecular biologist*
Farinella, Paul James *retired arts institution executive*
Faris, James Vannoy *cardiology educator, hospital executive*
Fariss, Bruce Lindsay *endocrinologist, educator*
Farley, Barbara Suzanne *lawyer*
Farley, John Michael *steel industry executive, consultant*
Farmakides, John Basil *lawyer*
Farmer, Deborah Kiriluk *marketing professional*
Farmer, Elaine Frazier *state legislator*
Farnsworth, Elizabeth *broadcast journalist*
Farnsworth, Michael Edward *mechanical engineer*
Farquhar, Robin Hugh *former university president*
Farrall, Harold John *retired accountant*
Farrar, Elaine Willardson *artist*
Farren, Patricia *lawyer, producer*
Farrington, Bertha Louise *nursing administrator*
Farris, Robert Earl *transportation consultant*
Farrow, Mia Villiers *actress*
Farrug, Jay (Eugene Joseph Farrug, Jr.) *technology executive, consultant*
Faruqui, G. Ahmad *engineering consultant*
Fasick, Adele Mongan *information services consultant*
Fassio, Virgil *newspaper publishing company executive*
Fasullo, Eugene Jack *state official*
Faub, Kenneth James *school nurse practitioner*
Faulkenberry, Virgil Thomas *retired naval officer, educator*
Faulkner, Julia Ellen *opera singer*
Faust, John Joseph, Jr. *theatre educator, director*
Faverty, Patrick William *principal*
Fawcett, Farrah Leni *actress, model*
Fawcett, John Thomas *archivist*
Fay, Conner Martindale *management consultant*
Fazio, Evelyn M. *publisher*
Fearrington, Ann Peyton *writer, illustrator, newspaper reporter*
Federici, William Vito *newspaper reporter*
Fehr, Donald M. *baseball union executive*
Fehr, Lola Mae *nursing association director*
Feiffer, Jules *cartoonist, writer, playwright*
Feiler, Jo Alison *artist*
Fein, Adrienne Myra *nursing educator*
Fein, Seymour Howard *pharmaceutical executive*
Feinberg, Herbert *apparel and beverage executive*
Feld, Carole Leslie *marketing executive*
Feld, Kenneth J. *entertainment executive*
Feldstein, Joshua *academic administrator*
Felix, Richard James *engineering executive, consultant*
Fell, Jennifer Anne *technical writer*
Feller, Robert William Andrew *baseball team public relations executive, retired baseball player*
Fellingham, David Andrew *retired mortgage banker*
Fellman, Barry L. *real estate developer*
Felts, Margaret Davis *librarian, bibliographer*
Fenger, Manfred *retired manufacturing executive*
Fenwick, William Augustus *lawyer*
Ference-Valenta, Mary Jean *osteopath*
Ferguson, Earl Wilson *cardiologist, physiologist, medical executive*
Ferguson, Emmet Fewell, Jr. *surgeon*
Ferguson, Maynard *trumpeter, band leader*
Ferguson, Robert *financial services executive, educator, writer*
Ferman, Irving *lawyer, educator*
Fernald, Harold Allen *publishing executive*
Fernandez, Dennis Sunga *lawyer, electrical engineer, entrepreneur*
†Fernandez, Mary Joe *professional tennis player*
Ferraro, Geraldine Anne *lawyer, former congresswoman*
Ferre, Antonio Luis *newspaper publisher*
Ferreira, Armando Thomas *sculptor, educator*
Ferrera, Robert James *superintendent of schools*
Fetler, Andrew *author, educator*
Fetrow, George Lawrence *retired plans engineer*
Fetterly, Lynn Lawrence *real estate broker, developer*
Fiala, David Marcus *lawyer*
Fiala, Dennison Fairchild *technical consultant*
Fibiger, John Andrew *life insurance company executive*
Field, Arthur Norman *lawyer*
Field, Charles William *metallurgical engineer, small business owner, consultant*
Field, Julia Allen *futurist, conceptual planner*
Field, Sally *actress*
Fielding, Harold Preston *bank executive*
Fields, Douglas Philip *building supply and home furnishings wholesale company executive*
Fields, Freddie *producer, agent*
Fields, Keith Allen *secondary education educator*
Fields, Leo *former jewelry company executive, investor*
Fife, Jonathan Donald *higher education educator*
Filchock, Ethel *education educator, poet*
Filerman, Michael Herman *television producer*
Findley, Troy Ray *state legislator*
Fine, Vivian *composer, retired educator*
Finger, Harold B. *energy, space, nuclear energy and urban affairs consultant*
Fink, John Francis *retired newspaper editor*
Finkelstein, Seymour *business consultant*
Finn, Mary Ralphe *artist*
Finnegan, Sara Anne *publisher*
Finney, Essex Eugene, Jr. *agricultural research administrator*
Finocchiaro, Alfonso G. *bank executive*
Fiorito, Edward Gerald *lawyer*
Fires, Earlie Stancel *jockey*
Firestone, Evan Richard *art educator, historian*
Fischer, A(lbert) Alan *family physician*
Fischer, Eugene H. *air force officer*
Fischer, Linda Marie *nursing educator*
Fischl, Eric *artist*
Fischmar, Richard Mayer *resort executive, financial consultant*
Fish, Janet Isobel *artist*
Fisher, Ann L. *pro tem judge*
Fisher, Linda Alice *physician*
Fisher, Robert Charles *publishing company executive, editor*
Fisher, Vernon *artist, educator*
Fisherman, Nina Yarlovsky *nursing administrator*
Fishman, Bernard *mechanical engineer*
Fitch, Robert McLellan *business and technology consultant*
Fitting-Gifford, Marjorie Ann *mathematician, educator, consultant*
Fitzgeorge, Harold James *former oil and gas company executive*
Fitzgerald, Edward Earl *publishing executive, author*
Fitzgerald, James Richard *naval officer*
Fitzpatrick, Nancy Hecht *magazine editor*
Fitzpatrick, William Allen *pharmacist*
Fitzwater, Ivan W. *retired superintendant*
Fix, John Neilson *banker*
Flanagan, Mary Haley *nursing administrator, mental health nurse*
Flanagan, William Stanley, Jr. *banker, lawyer*
Flaschen, Steward Samuel *high technology company executive*
Flaxman, Howard Richard *lawyer*
Fleischer, Gerald Albert *industrial engineer, educator*
Fleischman, Herman Israel *lawyer*
Fleming, Charles Clifford, Jr. *retired airline and jet aircraft sales company executive*
Fleming, Ronald Lee *urban designer, administrator, preservation planner, environmental educator*
Flemming, David Paul *biologist*
Fletcher, J. Sue *health educator*
Fletcher, Louise *actress*
Fletcher, Mary Ann *immunologist, educator*
Flick, Carl *electrical engineer, consultant*
Flick, John Edmond *lawyer*
Flinner, Beatrice Eileen *retired library and media sciences educator*
Flint, John E. *historian, educator*
Flint, Kenneth Brian *singer, songwriter*
Flipse, John Edward *naval architect, mechanical engineer*
Flitcraft, Richard Kirby, II *former chemical company executive*
†Flohr, Bruce M. *freight company executive*
Florence, Paul Smith *agronomist, business owner*
Florian, Marianna Bolognesi *civic leader*
Flowers, Anna *writer*
Flynn, Paul Bartholomew *foundation executive*
Fogelberg, Daniel Grayling *songwriter, singer*
Fogg, Richard Lloyd *food products company executive*
Foldi, Andrew Harry *retired singer, educator*
Folkman, David H. *retail, wholesale and consumer products consultant*
Foltiny, Stephen Vincent *special education educator*
Fomon, Samuel Joseph *physician, educator*
Fondo, Edwin Young *surgical oncologist*
Fong, Wen Chih *art historian, educator, author, museum curator*
Foote, Evelyn Patricia *retired army officer, consultant*
Foote, William Chapin *executive officer*
Ford, Ashley Lloyd *lawyer, retired consumer products company executive*
Ford, E(mma) Jane *public relations executive*
Ford, Ford Barney *retired government official*
Ford, Harrison *actor*
Ford, Jerry Lee *service company executive*
Ford, Judith Ann Tudor *retired natural gas distribution company executive*
Ford, Kenneth William *physicist*
Ford, Nancy Louise *composer, scriptwriter*
Ford, Wendell Hampton *senator*
†Ford, William Clay, Jr. *professional sports team executive*
Ford, William Francis *retired bank holding company executive*
Forest, Eva Brown *nurse, supervisor and paralegal*
Forest, Harvey *electronics executive*
Forester, Jean Martha Brouillette *innkeeper, retired librarian and educator*
Forester, Russell *artist*
Forman-Mason, Monica N. *speech and language pathologist*
Fornaess, John Erik *mathematics educator*
Forney, Ronald Dean *elementary school educator, consultant*
Forster, Ann Dorothy *publicist*
Forsythe, Henderson *actor*
Foss, Lukas *composer, conductor, pianist*
Fossier, Mike Walter *consultant, retired electronics company executive*
Foster, Charles Henry Wheelwright *former foundation officer, consultant,author*
Foster, Edson L. *retired mining and manufacturing company executive*
Foster, Frances *actress*
Foster, Martha Tyahla *educational administrator*
Foster, Robert Lawson *retired judge, deacon*
Foster, Stephen Kent *banker*
Foulk, David Wingerd *retired military civilian executive*
Foulkes, William David *psychologist, educator*
Fowler, Donald Raymond *retired lawyer, educator*
Fowler, Raymond David *financial executive*
Fowler, Robert Joseph *financial company executive, consultant*
Fox, Edward A. *retired college dean*
Fox, John David *educator, physicist*
Fox, Michael Wilson *veterinarian, animal behaviorist*
Fox, William Richard *retired physician*
Foy, Charles Daley *retired soil scientist*
Fradkin, David Milton *physicist, educator*
Frailey, Stephen A. *photographer*
Frame, Russell William *retired electronics executive*
Franciosa, Anthony (Anthony Papaleo) *actor*
Franciosa, Joseph Anthony *health care consultant*
Francke, Linda Bird *journalist*
Franco, Alexander *construction company executive*
Frank, Edgar Gerald *retired financial executive*
Frank, James Stuart *lawyer*
Frank, Jerome David *psychiatrist, educator*
Frank, Sanders Thalheimer *physician, educator*
Frankel, Glenn *journalist*
Frankenberger, Bertram, Jr. *investor, consultant*
Frankenheimer, John Michael *film and stage director*
Frank-Fitzner, Fontaine Lynne *geriatrics nurse, health insurance utilization reviewer*
Franklin, Barbara Kipp *financial advisor*
Franklin, Inga Sivills Knupp *special education educator*
Franklin, Margaret Lavona Barnum (Mrs. C. Benjamin Franklin) *civic leader*
Franklin, Michael Harold *arbitrator, lawyer, consultant*
Franklin-Griffin, Cathy Lou Hinson *nursing educator*
Franks, David Bryan *internist, emergency physician*
Franks, Gary Alvin *former congressman, real estate professional*
Franz, John E. *bio-organic chemist, researcher*
Franzetti, Lillian Angelina *former automobile dealership owner*
Fraser, Campbell *business consultant*
Fraser, Donald MacKay *former mayor, former congressman, educator*
Fraser, Kathleen Joy *poet, creative writing educator*
Frauenfelder, Hans *physicist, educator*
Frawley, Patrick Joseph, Jr. *health care executive*
Frazier, Henry Bowen, III *retired government official, lawyer*
Freberg, Stan(ley) (Victor Freberg) *satirist*
Fredricks, Richard *baritone*
Fredrickson, Donald Sharp *physician, scientist*
Freedman, Russell Bruce *author*
Freeman, Arthur *veterinarian, retired association administrator*
Freeman, Meredith Norwin *former college president, education educator*
Freeman, Ralph Carter *management consultant*
Freeman, Russell Adams *lawyer*
Freilicher, Jane *artist*
Freitag, Harlow *retired computer scientist and corporate executive*
Freitag, Peter Roy *transportation specialist*
Freitas, Beatrice B(otty) *musician, educator*
Fremont-Smith, Thayer *judge*
French, Clarence Levi, Jr. *retired shipbuilding company executive*
French, Earl Allan *principal*
French, Marilyn *author, critic*
Freston, Thomas E. *cable television programming executive*
Freter, Mark Allen *marketing and public relations executive*
Frey, Katie Manciet *educational administrator*
Frey, Margo Walther *career counselor, columnist*
Frick, Ivan Eugene *college president emeritus, education consultant*
Fricke, Janie (Jane Marie Fricke) *singer*
Fricklas, Anita Alper *religious organization administrator*
Friday, Katherine Orwoll *artist*
Frieder, Gideon *computer science and engineering educator*
Friedlander, Charles Douglas *investment company executive, space consultant*
†Friedman, Eugene Warren *surgeon*
Friedman, Howard W. *retired real estate company executive*
Friedman, Martin *museum director, arts adviser*
Friedman, Mildred *designer, educator, curator*
Friedman, Paul Richard *lawyer*
Friedman, Richard Lee *lumberyard owner*
Frieling, Gerald Harvey, Jr. *specialty steel company executive*
Frierson, Jimmie Lou *retired vocational education educator*
Fries, Raymond Sebastian *manufacturing company executive*
Fritz, Mark *reporter, journalist*
Fritz, Rene Eugene, Jr. *manufacturing executive*
Frizzell, Linda Diane Bane *exercise physiologist*
Froberg, Brent Malcolm *classics educator*
Froehlke, Robert Frederick *financial services executive*
Frost, Anne *real estate broker, author, publisher*
Frost, Carolyn Dean *critical care nurse, nursing administrator*
Frost, Sir David (Paradine) *author, producer, columnist*
Frost, Everett Lloyd *academic administrator*
Frost, J. Ormond *otolaryngologist, educator*
Frost, Sterling Newell *arbitrator, mediator, management consultant*
Fry, Malcolm Craig *retired clergyman*
Fryburger, Lawrence Bruce *lawyer, mediator, writer*
Fryer, Thomas Waitt, Jr. *writer and editor*
Fuchs, Joseph Louis *retired magazine publisher*
Fuchs, Michael Joseph *television executive*
Fuentes, Carlos *writer, former ambassador*
Fuerstner, Fiona Margaret Anne *ballet company executive, ballet educator*
Fuld, Richard Severin, Jr. *investment banker*
Fuller, Gayle Barnes *psychotherapist*
Fuller, James Chester Eedy *retired chemical company executive*
Fuller, Margaret Jane *medical technologist*
Fuller, Robert Ferrey *lawyer, investor*
Fuller, Stephen Herbert *business administration educator*
Fullwood, Altburg Marie *women's health nurse*
Fulton, James Franklin *industrial designer*
Funnell, Kevin Joseph *lawyer*
Fusciardi, Katherine *nursing administrator*
Futter, Victor *lawyer*
Gabel, Creighton *retired anthropologist, educator*
Gable, Karen Elaine *health occupations educator*
Gaffney, Thomas *banker*
Gage, John *opera company executive*
Gagnon, Edith Morrison *ballerina, singer, actress*
Gainey, Robert Michael *professional hockey coach, former player*
Gainor, Thomas Edward *banker*
Galan, Vincent *anethesiologist*
Galas, David John *molecular biology educator, researcher, administrator*
Galbraith, John Semple *history educator*
Galdi-Weissman, Natalie Ann *secondary education educator*
Gallegly, Elton William *congressman*
Galliher, Clarice A. Andrews *secondary education educator*
Gallo, Robert Charles *research scientist*
Gallucci, Robert Louis *diplomat, federal government official*
Galvao, Louis Alberto *import and export corporation executive, consultant*
Gamble, E. James *lawyer, accountant*
Gambrell, Luck Flanders *corporate executive*
Gammon, Samuel Rhea, III *association executive, former ambassador*
Gangarosa, Raymond Eugene *epidemiologist, engineer*
Gangriwala, Huned Ahmedi *engineering executive*
Gannon, James Patrick *newspaper editor*
Gantz, Carroll Melvin *industrial design consultant, consumer product designer*
Ganz, Lowell *screenwriter, television producer*
Garahan, Peter Thomas *software company executive*
Garber, Sharon N. *medical/surgical nurse*
Garcia, Alexander *orthopedic surgeon*
Garcia-Granados, Sergio Eduardo *brokerage house executive*
Gard, Judy Richardson *artist, educator*
Gardner, Anne Lancaster *lawyer*
Gardner, Clyde Edward *health care executive, consultant, educator*
Gardner, John Howland, III *neurologist*
Gardner, Kathryn Johanna *nursing educator, community health nurse*
Gardner, Lee Robbins *psychiatrist*
†Gardner, Meredith Lee *communication consultant*
Gardner, Richard Hartwell *oil company executive*
Gardner, Warner Winslow *lawyer*
Gardner, Wilford Robert *physicist, educator*
Garfield, Brian Wynne *author*
Garfield, Robert Edward *newspaper columnist*
Garfinkel, Fran Sylvia *professional business coach, financial planner*
Garfunkel, Art *singer, actor*
Garnett, Linda Kopec *nurse, researcher*
Garrett, Shirley Gene *nuclear medicine technologist*
Garrison, Richard Christopher *advertising agency executive*
Garrity, Wendell Arthur, Jr. *federal judge*
Garten, Wayne Philip *financial executive*
Gartenberg, Seymour Lee *retired recording company executive*
Gartner, William Joseph *company executive, business owner*
Garvey, Evelyn Jewel *retired mental health nurse*
Garza, Deborah Jane *bilingual education educator*
Gasper, Jo Ann *consulting firm executive*
Gates, Donna Marie *special education educator*
Gatlin, Larry Wayne *singer, songwriter*
†Gaugler, Robert Walter *retired career military officer*
Gauthier, Mary Elizabeth *librarian, researcher, secondary education educator*
Gavin, Herbert James *consultant, retired air force officer*
Gay, Carlo Teofilo Eberhard *art historian*
Gay, William Ingalls *veterinarian, health science administrator*
Geddes, Jane *professional golfer*
Geddes, Robert *architect, educator*
Geer, Stephen DuBois *retired journalist*
Gehm, Denise Charlene *ballerina, arts administrator*
Geis, Bernard *book publisher*
Geiselhart, Lorene Annetta *English language educator*
Geissinger, Frederick Wallace *investment banker*
Geitgey, Doris Arlene *retired nursing educator, dean*
Geller, Seymour *retired educator, researcher*
Gelles, Harry P. *investment banker, land investor*
Gellman, Isaiah *environmental consultant*
Gelman, Larry *actor, director*
Gelman, Norman Ira *public policy consultant*
Gemignani, Michael Caesar *clergyman, retired educator*
Gendell, Gerald Stanleigh *retired public affairs executive*
Gennaro, Antonio L. *biology educator*
Genovese, Lawrence Matthew *secondary education educator*
Gens, Ralph Samuel *electrical engineering consultant*
Gentilcore, Eileen Marie Belsito *elementary school principal*
Gentilcore, John C. *school principal*
Gentry, Francis G. *German language educator*
Geoffroy, Charles Henry *retired business executive*
George, Joyce Jackson *lawyer, former judge*
George, William Douglas, Jr. *retired consumer products company executive*
Gerald, Michael Charles *pharmacy educator, college dean*
Gerard, Roy Dupuy *oil company executive*
Gerber, Seymour *retired publishing company executive*
Gereau, Mary Condon *corporate executive*
Gerhardt, Heinz Adolf August *aircraft design engineer*
Gerhardt, Jon Stuart *mechanical engineer, engineering educator*
Gerlach, Luther Paul *anthropologist*
Germany, Daniel Monroe *aerospace engineer*
Gerou, Phillip Howard *architect*
Gerry, Debra Prue *psychotherapist*
Gers, Seymour *psychiatrist*
Gerson, Carol Roberts *pediatric otolaryngologist*
Gerstein, Esther *sculptor*
Gerstner, Mary Jane *nurse*
Gertenbach, Robert Frederick *medical research organization executive, accountant, lawyer*
Gervais, Marcel Andre *bishop*
Gerwin, Leslie Ellen *public affairs and community relations executive, lawyer*
Getchius, June Katherine *customer service administrator*
Getting, Ivan Alexander *physicist, former aerospace company executive*
Giacomini, Giuseppe *tenor*
Giancaterino, Linda DeMarsico *social worker*
Giardina, Paul Anthony *environmental nuclear engineer, thoroughbred horse investment specialist*
Gibb, Roberta Louise *lawyer, artist*
Gibbons, Michael Eugene *investment banker*
Gibson, Denice Yvonne *telecommunications, networking and computer executive*
Gidwitz, Gerald *retired hair care company executive*
Giebel, Miriam Catherine *librarian, genealogist*
Gier, Patricia Chapman *elementary education educator*
Gierlasinski, Kathy Lynn *accountant*
Gilb, Corinne Lathrop *history educator*
Gilb, Dagoberto *writer, carpenter*
Gilbert, Frederick E. *international development planner, consultant*
Gilbert, Kenneth Albert *harpsichordist*
Gilbert, Nancy Louise *librarian*
Gilbert, Ronald Rhea *lawyer*
Gilchrest, Thornton Charles *retired association executive*
Gilchrist, Ellen Louise *writer*
Giles, Susan Michele *medical/surgical nurse*
Giles, Walter Edmund *alcohol and drug treatment executive*
Gilford, Leon *business executive and consultant*
Gilinsky, Victor *physicist*
Gill, Henry Herr *photojournalist*
Gill, William Robert *soil scientist*
Gillespie, Gerald Ernest Paul *comparative literature educator, writer*
Gillespie, Nellie Redd *academic administrator, state official*
Gillespie, Robert James *manufacturing company executive*
Gillett, Mary Caperton *military historian*
Gillette, Stanley C. *apparel manufacturing company executive*
Gilliam, Terry Vance *film director, actor, illustrator, writer*
Gillice, Sondra Jupin (Mrs. Gardner Russell Brown) *sales and marketing executive*
†Gilman, Steven A. *management consultant*
Gilreath, Warren Dean *retired packaging company executive*
Gilroy, Frank Daniel *playwright*
Gilson, Barbara Frances *editor*

Hartman, John Wheeler publisher
Hartman, Margaret J. biologist, educator, university official
Hartman, Phil Edward actor
Hartmann, George Herman retired manufacturing company executive
Harton, John James utility executive, consultant
Hartsell, Samuel David insurance agent
Harville Smith, Martha Louise special education educator
Harwood, Vanessa Clare ballet dancer
Haskin, Larry Allen earth and planetary scientist, educator
Haskins, James English language educator, writer
Hasselmeyer, Eileen Grace medical research administrator
Hasselmo, Nils university official, linguistics educator
Hast, Adele editor, historian
Hatch, Orrin Grant senator
Haug, Marilyn Ann reading and mathematics educator
Hausdorfer, Gary Lee management consultant
Hausman, Arthur Herbert electronics company executive
Hausman, Bruce lawyer
Hauver, Constance Longshore lawyer
Havener, Robert Dale agricultural institute administrator
Havens, Keith Cornell artist
Havlicek, John J. (Hondo Havlicek) former professional basketball player
Havoc, June actress
Hawk, Carole Lynn insurance company executive, research/analyst
Hawk, Robert Dooley wholesale grocery company executive
Hawkes, John humanities educator, author
Hawkes, Kevin Cliff illustrator, author
Hawkins, Lawrence Charles management consultant, educator
Hawkins, Mary Ellen Higgins (Mary Ellen Higgins) former state legislator, public relations consultant
Hawkins, Michael Daly federal judge
Hawkins, Osie Penman, Jr. former baritone, former performing company executive
Hawkins, Willis Moore aerospace and astronautical consultant
Haworth, Dale Keith art history educator, gallery director
Hawryluk, Christine Joanne school nurse
Hayek, Carolyn Jean retired judge
Hayes, David Vincent sculptor
Hayes, George J. retired neurosurgeon
Hayes, Janet Gray retired business manager, former mayor
Hayes, John Patrick retired manufacturing company executive
Hayes, Judith psychotherapist, educator
Hayes, Peter Lind actor, writer
Haynes, Michael Scott, Sr. resource specialist
Haynes, Thomas Joseph marketing executive
Hays, Thomas Chandler holding company executive
Hazard, Thomas Pierrepont conflict resolution consultant
Hazuda, Ronald A. church administrator
Headley, Anne Renouf technology commercialization financier
Healton, Donald Carney retired government official
Healy, Sonya Ainslie health facility administrator
Heard, Ronald Roy motion picture producer
Hearn, Joyce Camp retired state legislator, educator
Heath, Richard Eddy lawyer
Heath, Richard Murray retired hospital administrator
Heaton-Marticorena, Jean early childhood educator
Hecht, Chic ambassador, former senator
Hecht, Sylvia Lillian pianist, educator
Heck, James Baker university official
Heckart, Eileen actress
Heckel, John Louis (Jack Heckel) aerospace company executive
Heckler, John Maguire stockbroker, investment company executive
Hedahl, Gorden Orlin theatre educator, university dean
Hedrick, Basil Calvin state agency administrator, ethnohistorian, educator, museum and multicultural institutions consultant
Heeschen, David Sutphin astronomer, educator
Heestand, Diane Elissa educational technology educator, medical educator
Hefferan, Colien Joan economist
Heffron, Howard A. lawyer
Hegarty, George John university president, English educator
Heidt-Dunwell, Debra Sue vocational education educator
Heilmann, Christian Flemming corporate executive
Heiman, Grover George, Jr. magazine editor, author
Heimbold, Margaret Byrne publisher, marketing professional, business executive
Heine, Ursula Ingrid biologist, researcher, artist
Heiney, John Weitzel former utility executive
Heinicke, Peter Hart computer consultant
Heinsman, Raymond Edward land surveyor
Heit, Ivan packaging equipment company executive
Heitz, Edward Fred freight traffic consultant
Helander, Bruce Paul artist, private art dealer
Held, Nancy B. perinatal nurse, lactation consultant
Helfgott, Roy B. economist, educator
Helford, Paul Quinn communications educator, academic administrator
Helfrich, Wauneta Meyne retired school social worker
Heller, Dorothy artist
†Heller, Richard H. writer, editor, book critic, publisher
Heller, Ronald Gary manufacturing company executive, lawyer
Hellmers, Norman Donald historic site director
Helm, DeWitt Frederick, Jr. consultant, professional society administrator
Helm, Lewis Marshall public affairs executive
Helman, Alfred Blair retired college president, education consultant
Helms, J. Lynn former government agency administrator
Helms, W. Richard lawyer
Helprin, Mark author
Hemmer, James Paul lawyer
Hemond, Roland A. professional baseball team executive
Henderson, Charles Brooke research company executive
Henderson, Melford J. epidemiologist, molecular biologist, chemist
Hendl, Walter conductor, pianist, composer
Hendricks, Leonard D. emergency medicine physician, consultant
Hendrickson, Louise retired association executive, retired social worker
Henes, Donna celebration artist, ritualist, writer
Henig, Robin Marantz journalist
Henkel, Arthur John, Jr. investment banker
Henkel, Cynthia Leigh preschool educator
Henry, Charles Jay library director
Hentic, Yves Frank Mao investment banker, industrial engineer
Heppe, Karol Virginia lawyer, educator
Hepper, Carol artist, educator
Heptinstall, Robert Hodgson physician
Herbert, Carol Sellers farming executive, lawyer
Herbig, Günther conductor
Herbst, Jurgen history and education educator
Heredia, Wilson Jermaine actor
Hering, Doris Minnie dance critic
Heris, Toni psychologist, psychotherapist
Herkner, Bernadette Kay occupational health nurse
Herman, Chester Joseph physician
Herman, David Jay orthodontist
Herman, Hank writer
Herman, Kenneth Neil journalist
Herman, William Arthur physics and engineering laboratory administrator
Hermance, Betty Jean special education educator
Herranen, Kathy artist, graphic designer
Herrera, Guillermo Antonio pathologist
Herring, Andrew Michael research chemist
Herriott, David Neil aerospace engineer
Herrmann, Thomas Francis database administrator
Herrmann, Walter retired laboratory administrator
Hersey, David Kenneth theatrical lighting designer
Hershberger, Steven Kaye controller
Hersher, Richard Donald management consultant
Herson, Arlene Rita producer, journalist, television program host
Hertel, Howard Jay photographer
Hertz, Kenneth Theodore health care executive
Herz, George Peter chemical engineer, industrial consultant
Herz, Michael Joseph marine environmental scientist
Herzberg, Thomas artist, illustrator
Herzfeld, Charles Maria physicist
Hess, David Willard journalist
Hess, Sidney Wayne management consultant
Hess, Ulrich Edward electrical engineer
Hesse, Christian August mining and underground construction consultant
Hester, Nancy Elizabeth county government official
Hetfeld, Elizabeth Ann industrial engineer
Hetzron, Robert linguist, educator
Hewes, Laurence Ilsley, III lawyer, management, development, legal consultant
Heyman, Ira Michael federal agency administrator, museum executive, law educator
Heymann, C(lemens) David author
Heymann, Philip Benjamin law educator, academic director
Heywood, Elizabeth Z. nurse educator, nurse manager
Hiatt, Arnold shoe manufacturer, importer, retailer
Hiatt, Robert Nelson consumer products executive
Hibbs, Robert Andrews analytical chemistry educator
Hichens, Walter Wilson former state senator
Hickcox, Leslie Kay health educator, consultant, counselor
Hickey, Joseph Michael investment banker
Hickey, Winifred E(spy) former state senator, social worker
Hickson, Ernest Charles financial executive
Higby, Edward Julian safety engineer
Higginbotham, John Taylor lawyer
Higginson, Jerry Alden, Jr. bank executive
Hightower, Jack English former state supreme court justice and congressman
Hiler, Monica Jean sociology and reading educator
Hill, Anita Carraway retired state legislator
Hill, George James physician, educator
Hill, Harold Nelson, Jr. lawyer
Hill, John Edward, Jr. investment banker, small business owner
Hill, Shirley Ann mathematics educator
Hille, Robert Arthur healthcare executive
Hillerman, Tony writer, former journalism educator
Hilliard, Sam Bowers geography educator
Hilsman, Roger government educator
Hilton, Clifford Thomas clergyman
Himes, John Harter medical researcher, educator
Himmelfarb, Milton editor, educator
Hinderliter, Richard Glenn electrical engineer
Hinds, Edward Dee insurance and investment professional, financial planner
Hiner, Elizabeth Ellen pharmacist
Hines, JoAnn R. professional association executive and consultant
Hingle, Pat actor
Hinkley, Everett David, Jr. physicist, business executive
Hinman, Charles Baldwin artist
†Hinojosa, Rubén congressman
Hinson, Howard Houston petroleum company executive
Hinson, Sue Ann legal assistant, orthopedic nurse
Hirayama, Chisato retired physician, educator, healthcare facility administrator
Hires, William Leland psychologist, consultant
Hirondelle, Anne Elizabeth ceramic artist
Hirose, Teruo Terry surgeon, educator
Hirsch, Horst Eberhard business consultant
Hirschberg, Vera Hilda writer
Hirsh, Norman Barry management consultant
Hirst, Heston Stillings former insurance company executive
Hitchborn, James Brian telecommunications executive
Hitchcock, Walter Anson educational consultant, retired educational administrator
Hite, Elinor Kirkland oil company human resources manager
Hixon, Allen Wentworth landscape architect, land planner
Hlywa, Jennifer Lyn secondary educator
Ho, Chih-Ming physicist, educator
†Ho, Geoffrey Bo Ning lawyer
Ho, John Wing-Shing biochemistry educator, researcher
Ho, Louis Ting retired mechanical engineer
Hoag, Kevin Lane engineering education administrator
Hoban, Lillian author, illustrator
Hobbs, Avaneda Dorenza publishing company executive, minister, singer
Hoch, Frederic Louis medical educator
Hock, Morton entertainment advertising executive
Hockeimer, Henry Eric business executive
Hodson, Nancy Perry real estate agent
Hoeg, Donald Francis chemist, consultant, former research and development executive
Hoeppner, David William mechanical engineering educator
Hoeprich, Paul Daniel physician educator
Hoewing, Mark Wesley real estate association executive
Hoffer, Alma Jeanne nursing educator
Hoffer, Roy Daniel electrical engineer
Hoffman, Alan Craig lawyer, consultant
Hoffman, Jerry Irwin dental educator
Hoffman, S. David lawyer, engineer, educator
Hoffman, Stanley Marc composer, music engraver
Hoffmann, Malcolm Arthur lawyer
Hofmann, Paul Bernard health care consultant
Hofmeyr, Harold David yacht construction company executive
Hogan, Charles Marshall lawyer
Hogan, Mark investment company executive
Hogan, Neville John mechanical engineering educator, consultant
Hogan, Richard Phillips lawyer
Hogan, Robert Henry trust company executive, investment strategist
Hogan, Thomas Francis federal judge
Hogg, Judith E. neurologist, educator
Hogg, Karen Sue telecommunications and information systems executive
Hoggard, Lara Guldmar conductor, educator
Hogue, Carol Jane Rowland epidemiologist
Hoke, Sheila Wilder retired librarian
Holch, Eric Sanford artist
Holden, Rebecca Lynn artist
Holder, Richard Gibson metal products executive
Holiday, Edith Elizabeth former presidential adviser, cabinet secretary
Holland, David Thurston former editor
Holland, Henry Norman marketing consultant
Holland, James Paul lawyer
Holland, Randy James state supreme court justice
Holland, Robert Campbell anatomist, educator
Hollander, Anne writer
†Hollandsworth, Todd Mathew professional baseball player
Holle, Reginald Henry retired bishop
Holleb, Doris B. urban planner, economist
Holliday, Robert Kelvin retired state senator, former newspaper executive
Hollis, Mary Fern Caudill community health nurse
Holloran, Thomas Edward business educator
Holloway, James Curtis military officer
Holloway, Julia Bolton professor emerita, theologian
Holloway, Richard Lawrence marriage-family therapist, college official
Holloway, Robert Ross archaeologist, educator
Holm, Celeste actress
Holmes, Jerry Dell retired organic chemist
Holmes, Michael Gene lawyer
Holmes, Paul Luther political scientist, educational consultant
Holmes, Robert Wayne service executive, consultant, biological historian
Holmes, Wilhelmina Kent community health nurse
Holt, Marjorie Sewell lawyer, retired congresswoman
Holtkamp, Susan Charlotte elementary education educator
Holton, Grace Holland accountant
Holton, Robert Page publishing executive
Holtsberg, Philip gerontologist, lawyer, psychologist
Holtzschue, Karl Bressem lawyer, author, educator
Homestead, Susan E. (Susan Freedlender) psychotherapist
Honeystein, Karl lawyer, entertainment company executive
Honnold, John Otis law educator
Honour, Lynda Charmaine research scientist, educator, psychotherapist
Hood, Luann Sandra special education educator
Hooper, Gerry Don information systems specialist, consultant
Hooper, Roger Fellowes architect, retired
Hoopes, Townsend Walter business consultant, former government official
Hoops, William James clergyman
Hoover, Francis Louis retired educator, gemologist, jewelry designer, fine arts appraiser , writer
Hoover, John Elwood former military officer, consultant, writer
Hopkins, Jacques Vaughn lawyer, retired
Hopkins, Maureen Muriel labor union official
Horn, Andrew Warren lawyer
Horner, Matina Souretis retired college president, corporate executive
Hornick, Katherine Joyce Kay artist, small business owner
Horovitz, Zola Philip pharmaceutical company executive
Horsch, Kathleen Joanne social services administrator, educator, consultant
Horton, James David critical care and emergency nurse
Horton, Patricia Mathews artist, violist and violinist
Horton, Sir Robert Baynes (Sir ) railroad company executive
Horton, Wilfred Henry mathematics educator
Horwitz, Donald Paul lawyer
Hosea, Julia Hiller communications executive, paralegal
Hostettler, Stephen John naval officer
Houghtaling, Pamela Ann public relations executive
Houghton, Katharine actress
Houlihan, Patrick Thomas museum director
House, Stephen Eugene information systems consultant
Houser, William Douglas telecommunications company executive, former naval officer
Houstoun, Lawrence Orson, Jr. development consultant
Howard, Charles L. chemist, educator
Howard, Dean Denton electrical engineer, researcher, consultant
Howard, Donald Searcy banker
Howard, George, Jr. federal judge
Howard, James Joseph, III utility company executive
Howard, James Webb investment banker, lawyer, engineer
Howard, John Wayne lawyer
Howard, Joseph Harvey retired librarian
Howard, Michael Eliot historian, educator
Howard, Robert Elliott former federal official, consultant, educator
Howe, John Perry materials science educator, research consultant
Howe, John Prentice, III health science center executive, physician
Howe, Virginia Hoffman nurse administrator
Howell, Barbara Fennema retired research chemist
Howell, Donald Lee lawyer
Howell, Embry Martin researcher
Howell, Joel DuBose physician, educator
Howell, Saralee Fisher pilot
Howell, William Robert retail company executive
Howes, Sophia DuBose writer, editorial associate
Hoy, Harold Joseph marketing educator, retail executive, management consultant, author, military officer
Hoyt, Mary Finch author, editor, media consultant, former government official
Hoyt, William Lloyd chief justice
Hsiao, Kwang-Jen genetics and biochemistry educator
Hsin, Victor Jun-Kuan information systems and telecommunications consultant
Hubbard, Elizabeth actress
Hubbard, Stevan Ralph biophysicist, educator
Hubbe, Henry Ernest financial forecaster, funds manager
Huber, Douglas Crawford pathologist
Huber, Vida S. nursing educator
Hubley, Reginald Allen publisher
Hudak, Thomas F(rancis) finance company executive
Huddleston, Marilyn Anne international financier, merchant banker, educator, author
Hudson, Donald J. retired stock exchange executive
Hudson, Franklin Donald diversified company executive, consultant
Hudson, Jerry Charles communications educator
Hudson, Sharon Marie credit and collections specialist
Huff, Janet House special education educator
Hufferd, Linda M. nurse
Huffman, Carol Koster retired middle school educator
Huffman, James Thomas William oil exploration company executive
Hufschmidt, Maynard Michael resources planning educator
Hughes, Eugene Morgan university president
Hughes, Michaela Kelly actress, dancer
Hughes, Richard Gene computer executive, consultant
Hughes, Sue Margaret retired librarian
Hughes, Thomas Parke history educator
Hughey, Richard Kohlman lawyer, author
Hukins-Rodrigue, Dana Ann community health nurse
Humke, Ramon L. utility executive
Hummel, Gene Maywood retired bishop
Humphrey, Arthur Earl university administrator, retired
Humphrey, Shirley Joy state education administrator
Humphreys, Robert Russell lawyer, consultant, arbitrator
Huning, Devon Gray actress, dancer, audiologist, photographer, video producer and editor
Hunt, Donald Edward planning and engineering executive
Hunt, Donnell Ray retired agricultural engineering educator
Hunt, George Nelson bishop
Hunt, Martha sales executive, researcher
Hunt, Oliver Raymond, Jr. thoracic and cardiovascular surgeon
Hunt, Ronald Duncan veterinarian, educator, pathologist
Hunt, Ronald Forrest lawyer
Hunt, William Edward neurosurgeon, educator
Hunte, Beryl Eleanor mathematics educator, consultant
Hunter, Duncan Lee congressman
Hunter, Holly actress
Hunter, Kim (Janet Cole) actress
Hunter, Rachel model
Huntley, Robert Edward Royall lawyer, business executive, former university president
Huntley, Robert Ross physician, educator
Hurd, Byron Thomas newspaper executive, retired
Hurd, Richard Nelson pharmaceutical company executive
Hurn, Raymond Walter minister, religious order administrator
Hurst, John Emory, Jr. retired airline executive
Hurst, Leland Lyle natural gas company executive
Husain, Taqdir mathematics educator
Huston, Nancy Louise writer, educator
Hutcheon, Linda Ann English language educator
Hutchins, Robert Ayer architectural consultant
Hutchinson, John Woodside applied mechanics educator, consultant
Hutchison, Kay Bailey senator
Hutner, Herbert L. financial consultant, lawyer
Huttenback, Robert Arthur academic administrator, educator
Huttner, Richard M. publishing executive
Hutzler, Lisa Ann mental health nurse, adult clinical psychologist
Hybl, William Joseph lawyer, foundation executive
Hyde, Robert Burke, Jr. retired oil industry executive
Hyman, Richard Roven composer, jazz musician
Hyman, Seymour C(harles) arbitrator
Iasiello, Dorothy Barbara brokerage company executive
Ichaporia, Pallan R. pharmaceutical marketing executive
Ichino, Yoko ballet dancer
Idaszak, Jerome Joseph economic journalist
Iklé, Richard Adolph lawyer
Iles, Eileen Marie bank executive, controller
Iman, (Iman Abudulmajid) model
Indenbaum, Dorothy musician, researcher
Ingersoll, Paul Mills banker
Ingle, James Chesney, Jr. geology educator
Inglis, James telecommunications company executive
Inman, Cullen Langdon telecommunications scientist
Inouye, David William zoology educator
Intilli, Sharon Marie television director, small business owner
Inui, Thomas Spencer physician, educator
Ipsen, Grant Ruel insurance and investments professional
Iqbal, Zafar biochemist, neurochemist
Irani, Raymond Reza electro-mechanical company executive
Irey, Charlotte York dance educator
Irvine, John Alexander lawyer
Irving, Amy actress
Irving, George Steven actor
Irving, John Winslow writer
Irving, Terry (Edward B. Irving, III) television producer
Irwin, Linda Belmore marketing consultant
Isaac, Steven Richard communications executive
Isaacs, Kenneth S(idney) psychoanalyst, educator

Isaacs, Susan *novelist, screenwriter*
Isaacson, Edith Lipsig *civic leader*
Isacson, Ole *neuroscientist, educator*
Isom, Dotcy Ivertus, Jr. *bishop*
Isom, Harriet Winsar *ambassador*
Israel, Robert Allan *statistician*
Issari, M(ohammad) Ali *film producer, educator, consultant*
Ivry, Alfred Lyon *foreign language and literature educator*
Izlar, Robert Lee *forester*
Jackman, Jay M. *psychiatrist*
Jackson, Carmault Benjamin, Jr. *physician*
Jackson, Elmer Joseph *lawyer, oil and gas company executive*
Jackson, Nagle *stage director, playwright*
Jackson, Robert William *utility company executive, retired*
Jackson, Rudolph Ellsworth *pediatrician, educator*
Jackson, Victor Louis *retired naturalist*
Jacobowitz, Ellen Sue *museum and temple administrator*
Jacobs, Abigail Conway *toxicologist*
Jacobs, Herbert Howard *investor*
Jacobs, Hyde Spencer *soil chemistry educator*
Jacobs, Linda Rotroff *elementary school educator*
Jacobs, Marion Kramer *psychologist*
Jacobs, Wilbur Ripley *writer, history educator*
Jacobs, William Jay *historian, writer*
Jacobson, Herbert Laurence *diplomat*
Jacobson, James Bassett *insurance executive*
Jacoby, Stanley Arthur *retired manufacturing executive*
Jacques, Andre Charles *financial consultant*
Jaicks, Frederick Gillies *retired steel company executive*
Jakubauskas, Edward Benedict *college president*
Jaller, Michael M. *retired orthopedic surgeon*
Jamieson, Michael Lawrence *lawyer*
Jamison, John Callison *business educator, investment banker*
Janis, Conrad *actor, jazz musician, art dealer, film producer, director*
Janklow, Linda LeRoy *civic worker, volunteer*
Janko, May *graphic artist*
Janos, James Donald *broadcast engineer*
Jansen, Angela Bing *artist, educator*
Jaquette, Peter Barnes *economist*
Jarrett, Keith *pianist, composer*
Jarvis, Barbara Ann *conference planner, conference manager*
Jarvis, William Esmond *retired Canadian government official*
Jaw, Andrew Chung-Shiang *software analyst*
Jeansonne, Angela Lynne *senior analyst*
Jebsen, Joan Helene *medical senior secretary*
Jedenoff, George Alexander *steel consultant*
Jedju, Linda Jo-Anne *writer, poet, nurse*
Jefferies, William McKendree *internist, educator*
Jenkins, Anthony Curtis *sales executive*
Jenkins, Darrell Lee *librarian*
Jenkins, James William *osteopath*
Jenney, Neil Franklin, Jr. *artist, philosopher*
Jennings, Elizabeth Moomaw *social worker*
Jennings, Joseph Ashby *banker*
Jennings, Max *newspaper editor*
Jennings, Waylon *country musician*
Jensen, Barbara Wood *interior design business owner*
Jensen, Erik Hugo *pharmaceutical quality control consultant*
Jensen, Jack Michael *publishing executive*
Jensen, Marvin Eli *retired agricultural engineer*
Jensen, Mogens Reimer *psychologist*
Jensen, Robert Trygve *lawyer*
Jepson, Robert Scott, Jr. *international investment banking specialist*
Jernstedt, Richard Don *public relations executive*
Jerrytone, Samuel Joseph *trade school executive*
Jessup, Harley William *production designer*
Jewell, Florence Eva *telecommunications administrator*
Jiler, William Laurence *publisher*
Jinks, Robert Larry *retired newspaper publisher*
Joanou, Phillip *advertising executive*
Jobe, Muriel Ida *medical technologist, educator*
Jochner, Michele Melina *lawyer*
John, K. K. (John Kuruvilla Kaiyalethe) *minister*
John, Ralph Candler *retired college president, educator*
Johnson, Albert Wesley *consultant on governance*
Johnson, Arnold Ivan *civil engineer*
Johnson, Bruce *state legislator*
Johnson, Charlene Elizabeth *adult education educator*
Johnson, Clifton Herman *historian, archivist, former research center director*
Johnson, Cyrus Edwin *grain farmer, former food products executive*
Johnson, Daniel, Jr. *lawyer*
Johnson, Delores *special education educator*
Johnson, Dewey E(dward), Jr. *dentist*
Johnson, Diane Lain *novelist, critic*
Johnson, Frank Edward *former newspaper editor*
Johnson, Geneva Bolton *retired human service organization executive*
Johnson, Irving Stanley *pharmaceutical company executive, scientist*
Johnson, Joe William *engineering educator, consultant*
Johnson, John Prescott *philosophy educator*
Johnson, Kay Durbahn *real estate manager, consultant*
Johnson, Keith Gilbert *retired heavy equipment company executive*
†Johnson, Kenneth Lance *professional baseball player*
Johnson, Kirsten Denise *elementary education educator*
Johnson, Linda Kaye *art educator*
Johnson, Malcolm Clinton, Jr. *publishing consultant*
Johnson, Marlene M. *furniture company executive*
Johnson, Mary Elizabeth Susan *consulting engineer*
Johnson, Mary Murphy *social services administrator, writer*
Johnson, Maryl Rae *cardiologist*
Johnson, Michael Warren *international relations specialist*
Johnson, Philip *investment banking executive*
Johnson, Ralph Raymond *ambassador, federal agency administrator*
Johnson, Robert Walter *marine engineer, priest*
Johnson, Rogers Bruce *retired chemical company executive*
Johnson, Silas R., Jr. *air force officer*
Johnson, Stewart Willard *civil engineer*
Johnson, Sylvia Sue *university administrator, educator*
Johnson, Warren Donald *retired pharmaceutical executive, former air force officer*
Johnston, James Monroe, III *air force officer*
Johnston, Julia Ann *writer*
Johnston, Ralph Kennedy, Sr. *aerospace engineer*
Jones, Anita Katherine *computer scientist, educator*
Jones, Billy Ernest *dermatology educator*
Jones, Claire Burtchaell *artist*
Jones, David Charles *retired air force officer, former chairman Joint Chiefs of Staff*
Jones, Donna Marie *public administrator, lawyer, consultant*
Jones, Gerre Lyle *marketing and public relations consultant*
Jones, Jack Dellis *oil company executive*
Jones, Joan Megan *anthropologist*
Jones, Keith Alden *lawyer*
Jones, Lawrence Neale *university dean, minister*
Jones, Leonade Diane *media publishing company executive*
Jones, Margaret Louise *supervisory production analyst*
Jones, Peter d'Alroy *history educator, author*
Jones, Phyllis Gene *judge*
Jones, Regina Nickerson *public relations executive*
Jones, Richard Melvin *bank executive, former retail executive*
Jones, Robert Henry *automotive distribution executive*
Jones, Shirley *actress, singer*
Jones, Shirley Ann *psychiatric nurse*
Jones, Suejette Albritton *basic skills educator*
Jones, Thornton Keith *research chemist*
Jones, Walton Linton *internist, former government official*
Jones, William Augustus, Jr. *retired bishop*
Jontz, Polly *retired college official, museum director*
Jordan, Fred *publishing company executive*
Jordan, Howard Emerson *retired engineering executive, consultant*
Jordan, Sharie Cecilia *small business owner*
Jordan, Thomas Fredrick *physics educator*
Jordan, William Bryan, Jr. *art historian*
Jorden, William John *writer, retired diplomat*
Joseph, Jean *artist*
Joseph, Michael Thomas *broadcast consultant*
Joseph, Shirley Troyan *retired executive*
Josephs, Melvin Jay *retired professional society administrator*
Joslin, David Bruce *bishop*
†Joulwan, George A. *career military officer*
Jourdain, Alice Marie *philosopher, retired educator*
Judelson, David N. *company executive*
Judge, Jean Frances *management consultant*
Judge, Rosemary Ann *oil company executive*
Juenemann, Sister Jean *hospital executive*
Juister, Barbara Joyce *retired mathematics educator*
Jukes, Betty C. *performing arts consultant, fundraiser*
Just, Ward Swift *author*
Juviler, Peter Henry *political scientist, educator*
Kadota, Takashi Theodore *mathematician, electrical engineer*
Kahan, Rochelle Liebling *lawyer, concert pianist*
Kahana, Eva Frost *sociology educator*
Kahn, Albert Michael *artist, designer*
Kahn, Charles Howard *architect, educator*
Kahn, David *dermatologist, educator*
Kahn, Irwin William *industrial engineer*
Kaiser, Jean Morgan *real estate broker*
Kaiser, Nina Irene *health facility administrator*
Kalin, D(orothy) Jean *artist, educator*
Kalina, Richard *artist*
Kalish, Donald *philosophy educator*
Kalkwarf, Leonard V. *minister*
Kampmeier, Curt *management consultant*
Kandel, Joan Ellen *osteopath*
Kane, Loana *foreign language educator*
Kane, Patricia Lanegran *language professional, educator*
Kane, Ryan Thomas *association executive, law enforcement officer*
Kaneko, Mitsuru *production company executive, animation producer*
Kanin, Fay *screenwriter*
Kanin, Garson *writer, theatrical director*
Kannenstine, Margaret Lampe *artist*
Kantrowitz, Susan Lee *lawyer*
Kapcsandy, Louis Endre *building construction and manufacturing executive, chemical engineering consultant*
Kapitan, Mary L. *retired nursing administrator, educator*
Kaplan, Leonard Eugene *accountant*
Kaplan, Robert B. *linguistics educator, consultant, researcher*
Kapnick, Richard Bradshaw *lawyer*
Kaprielian, Walter *advertising executive*
Karalekas, Anne *media executive*
Karalis, John Peter *computer company executive, lawyer*
Karawina, Erica *artist, stained glass designer*
Karber, Johnnie Faye *elementary education educator*
Karlin, Myron D. *motion picture executive*
Karlson, Dixie D. *gifted and talented education educator*
Karp, David *communications executive, writer*
Karp, Sherman *aerospace consultant*
Karson, Samuel *psychologist, educator*
†Karsten, Adrian *reporter*
Kasberger-Mahoney, Elvera A. *educational administrator*
Kaser, David *retired librarian, educator, consultant*
Kash, Wyatt Keith *publishing executive*
Kaskowitz, Edwin *social services executive*
Kasperbauer, Isabel Giles *art educator*
Kass, Jerome Allan *writer*
Kaster, Laura A. *lawyer*
Kastner, Marc Aaron *physics educator*
Kastor, Frank Sullivan *English language educator*
Kasulka, Larry Herman *management consultant*
Katayama, Toshihiro *artist, educator*
Katz, Anne Harris *biologist, educator, writer, aviator*
Katz, Leon *packaging company executive*
Katz, Martin Howard *lawyer*
Katz, Phyllis Alberts *developmental research psychologist*
Katz, Robert David *architecture educator*
Katz, Roberta R. *lawyer*
Katz, Sanford Noah *lawyer, educator*
Katzenbach, John Strong Miner *author*
Kauffman, Dagmar Elisabeth *writer, researcher*
Kaufman, Paula T. *librarian*
Kaufman, Raymond L. *energy company executive*
Kauger, Yvonne *state supreme court justice*
Kavalek, Lubomir *chess expert*
Kaye, Jennifer Lynn *healthcare executive*
Kaylan, Howard Lawrence *musical entertainer, composer*
Kazan, Elia *theatrical, motion picture director and producer, author*
Kazmarek, Linda Adams *secondary education educator*
Keach, Stacy, Sr. *producer, director*
Keala, Francis Ahloy *security executive*
Kearney, Patricia Michal *retired natural sciences educator, poet, consultant*
Kearns, James Joseph *artist*
Kebblish, John Basil *retired coal company executive, consultant*
Kebe, Sara *psychiatrist*
Keebler, Lois Marie *elementary school educator*
Keegan, Kenneth Donald *financial consultant, retired oil company executive*
Keehner, Michael Arthur Miller *banker*
Keeler, William Henry *cardinal*
Keenan, Mike *professional hockey team coach*
Keigler, John E. *aerospace engineer*
Keil, M. David *retired international association executive*
Keiper, Marilyn Morrison *elementary education educator*
Keister, Stephen Lee *artist*
Keith, Brian Thomas *automobile executive*
Keith, Leroy, Jr. *former college president*
Kellam, Norma Dawn *medical, surgical nurse*
Kelleher, Richard Cornelius *marketing and communications executive*
Keller, Paul *advertising agency executive*
Kellerman, Faye Marder *novelist, dentist*
Kelley, Albert Benjamin *author, consultant*
Kelley, Jackson DeForest *actor*
Kelley, Larry Dale *retired army officer*
Kelley, Mary Elizabeth (LaGrone) *computer specialist*
Kellogg, Carol Kay *neuroscientist, researcher*
Kelly, Anthony Odrian *flooring manufacturing company executive*
Kelly, Aurel Maxey *retired judge*
Kelly, Ellsworth *painter, sculptor*
Kelly, Nancy Folden *arts administrator*
Kelly, Robert Thomas *publisher*
Kelso, Frank Benton, II *naval officer*
Kemper, John Dustin *mechanical engineering educator*
Kempf, Cecil Joseph *naval officer*
Kempner, Walter *retired physician*
Kendall, Christopher (Christopher Wolff) *conductor, lutenist, educator, university official*
Kendig, William L. *retired government official, accountant*
Kendrick, Budd Leroy *psychologist*
Kendrick, Daniel Frederick, III *real estate executive*
Kendrick, Joseph Trotwood *former foreign service officer, writer, consultant*
Kennedy, Adrienne Lita *playwright*
Kennedy, Harvey Edward *science information publishing executive*
Kennedy, Jerrie Ann Preston *public relations executive*
Kennedy, Keith Clyde *mechanical engineer, entrepreneur, administrator*
Kennedy, Leo Raymond *engineering executive*
Kennedy, Thomas J. *lawyer*
Kennedy, Thomas Patrick *financial executive*
Kenney, George *writer*
Kenny, Patrick Edward *publishing executive*
Kent, Donald Charles *physician*
Kent, E(verett) Allen *performing arts administrator*
Kent, Gary Warner *film director, writer*
Kent, Howard Lees *obstetrician, gynecologist*
Kent, Jack Thurston *retired mathematics educator*
Kenyhercz, Thomas Michael *pharmaceutical company executive*
Kenyon, Daphne Anne *economics educator*
Kepes, Gyorgy *author, painter, photographer, educator*
Kerber, Ronald Lee *industrial corporation executive*
Kerins, Francis Joseph *college president*
Kern, Irving John *retired food company executive*
Kernan, Barbara Desind *senior government executive*
†Kernan, Joseph E. *state official*
Kerns, Stephen Rimmer *insurance executive*
Kerr, Deborah Jane *actress*
Kerr, James Winslow *pipe line company executive*
Kerstetter, Michael James *retired manufacturing company executive*
Kersting, Edwin Joseph *retired university dean*
Kertz, Hubert Leonard *telephone company executive*
Kerwin, Larkin *retired physics educator*
Ketchum, Milo Smith *civil engineer*
Kettelkamp, Donald Benjamin *retired surgeon and educator*
Key, Ted *cartoonist*
Keyes, Margaret Naumann *home economics educator*
Keyes, Saundra Elise *newspaper editor*
Keys, Jerry Malcom *lawyer*
Keyser, Charles Lovett, Jr. *bishop*
Kezer, Pauline Ryder *ballet company executive*
Kezlarian, Nancy Kay *social services administrator, family counselor*
Khachadurian, Avedis *physician*
Khalidi, Rashid Ismail *history educator*
Khan, Arfa *radiologist, educator*
Kidd, A. Paul *hospital administrator, government official*
Kidd, Robert Hugh *financial executive, accountant*
Kidder, Margot *actress*
Kidder, (John) Tracy *writer*
Kiefer, Helen Chilton *neurologist, psychiatrist*
Kieffer, Joyce Loretta *health science facility administrator, educator*
Kiley, Richard Paul *actor*
Killeen, Michael John *lawyer*
Killhour, William Gherky *paper company executive*
Kilmer, Joseph Charles *secondary school educator*
Kilpatrick, James Jackson, Jr. *columnist, author*
Kimes, Beverly Rae *editor, writer*
Kindness, Thomas Norman *former congressman, lawyer, consultant*
King, Algin Braddy *marketing educator*
King, Annie Roberts *elementary and secondary education educator*
King, Edward William *retired transportation executive*
King, Frances *education educator*
King, Imogene M. *nurse, educator*
King, James B. *federal official*
King, John Quill Taylor *science center administrator, college administrator emeritus*
King, Larry L. *playwright, actor*
King, Morgana *jazz vocalist*
King, Philip Gordon *public relations consultant*
King, S(anford) MacCallum *business owner, consultant*
King, Stephen Edwin *novelist, screenwriter, director*
King, Susan Bennett *retired glass company executive*
King, William Collins *oil company executive*
King, William Douglas *retired executive*
Kingsbery, Walton Waits, Jr. *retired accountant*
Kinney, Marjorie Sharon *marketing executive, artist*
Kinslow, Margie Ann *volunteer worker*
Kinsman, Frank Ellwood *engineering executive*
Kinzer, James Raymond *retired pipeline company executive*
Kipniss, Robert *artist*
Kippur, Merrie Margolin *lawyer*
Kirk, Judd *real estate development executive*
Kirkby, Maurice Anthony *oil company executive*
Kirkland, Geoffrey Alan *motion picture production designer*
Kirkpatrick, Dorothy Louise *retired education educator, program coordinator*
Kirschenmann, Henry George, Jr. *management consultant, former government official, accountant*
Kirsteuer, Ernst Karl Eberhart *biologist, curator*
Kirven, Gerald *lawyer*
Kisak, Paul Francis *engineering company executive*
Kiselik, Paul Howard *manufacturing company executive*
Kish, Michael Louis *transportation executive*
Kissinger, Henry Alfred *former secretary of state, international consulting company executive*
Klafter, Cary Ira *lawyer*
Klagholz, Leo F. *state agency administrator*
Klapper, Carol Lorraine *magazine publisher*
Klass, Morton *anthropology educator, consultant*
Klatt, Melvin John *library consultant*
Klauberg, William Joseph *technical services company executive*
Klaus, Charles *retired lawyer*
Kleckner, Willard Richards *electrical engineer, consultant, educator*
Kleiman, Alan Boyd *artist*
Kleiman, Bernard *lawyer*
Klein, Charlotte Conrad *public relations executive*
Klein, Edward Joel *editor, author, lecturer*
Klein, Fay Magid *health administrator*
Klein, Martin *ocean engineering consultant*
Klein, Stephen Thomas *performing arts executive*
Kleinberg, Howard J. *newspaper columnist*
Kleinberg, Judith G. *lawyer, children's advocate*
Kleinberg, Lawrence H. *food industry executive*
Klement, Vera *artist*
Klett, Gordon A. *retired savings and loan association executive*
Kleven, Marguerite *state senator*
Kliebhan, Sister M(ary) Camille *academic administrator*
Klinetob, Carson Wayne *physical therapist*
Klink, Robert Michael *consulting engineer, management consultant, financial consultant, property developer*
Klippstatter, Kurt L. *conductor, music director*
Klivington, Kenneth Albert *research administrator*
Klombers, Norman *retired podiatrist, association executive*
Klotzkin, Charles Edward *secondary school educator*
Kloze, Ida Iris *lawyer*
Kluge, Cheryle Darlene Jobe *secondary education educator*
Klute, Allan Aloys *physicist, economist, consultant*
Knabenshue, Catherine Sue *special education educator*
Knapp, Lonnie Troy *elementary education educator*
Knauer, Virginia Harrington (Mrs. Wilhelm F. Knauer) *consumer consultant, former government official*
Knell, Gary Evan *media executive, lawyer*
Knight, Alice Dorothy Tirrell *state legislator*
Knight, Thomas Jefferson, Jr. *computer consultant, trainer*
Knipp, Helmut *hospitality industry executive*
Knittel, Diane Lynne *insurance marketing executive*
Knoll, Florence Schust *architect, designer*
Knowles, Elizabeth Pringle *art museum director*
Knox, Ernest Rudder *retired college president*
Knudsen, William Claire *geophysicist*
Knuth, Eric Joseph *lawyer*
Kocher, Margaret *technical writer*
Kochta, Ruth Martha *art gallery owner*
Kodali, Hari Prasad *electrical engineer*
Koehler, George Applegate *broadcasting company executive*
Koelmel, Lorna Lee *data processing executive*
Koenig, Allen Edward *higher education consultant*
Kogut, John Anthony *retail/wholesale executive*
Kohlmeyer, Ida Rittenberg *artist*
Kolasa, Kathryn Marianne *food and nutrition educator, consultant*
Kolb, Dorothy Gong *elementary education educator*
Kolda, Thomas Joseph *non-profit organization executive*
Koller, Loren D. *veterinary medicine educator*
Kolm, Henry Herbert *physicist, electric research company executive*
Koltai, Stephen Miklos *mechanical engineer, consultant, economist, writer, educator*
Kolton, Paul *business executive*
†Komar Storey, Charlene Mary *editor*
Komidar, Joseph Stanley *librarian*
Komisar, David Daniel *retired university provost*
Kondo, Masatoshi S. *pharmaceutical executive, educator*
Koner, Pauline *dancer, choreographer, author*
Kongabel, H. Fred *industrial construction company executive*
Konigsburg, Elaine Lobl *author*
Koning, Hans (Hans Koningsberger) *author*
Konnyu, Ernest Leslie *former congressman*
†Konstantinov, Vladimir *professional hockey player*
Kontny, Vincent L. *rancher, engineering executive*
Kooken, John Frederick *retired bank holding company executive*
Kooloian, Elizabeth *construction company executive*
Koppett, Leonard *columnist, journalist, author*
Korab, Arnold Alva *engineering executive*
Korgaonkar, Pradeep Kashinath *marketing educator*
Kormondy, Edward John *university official, biology educator*
Korn, Peter A. *city manager, public administration educator*
Korpal, Eugene Stanley *banker, former army officer*
Korsgaard, Christine Marion *philosophy educator*
Korwek, Alexander Donald *management consultant*
Kost, Gerald Joseph *physician, scientist*
Kostka, Janice Ellen *automotive wholesale company administrator*
Kotler, Steven *investment banker*
Kottler, Raymond George Michael *economist, researcher*

Kousparis, Dimitrios oil consulting company executive
Kozlowski, Theodore Thomas botany educator, research director, author, editor
Kraemer, Linda Gayle associate dean
Kraft, Arthur academic dean
Kraichnan, Robert Harry theoretical physicist, consultant
Kramer, Constance Ann songwriter
Kramer, Dale Vernon retired English language educator
Kramer, Peter Robin computer company executive
Krantz, Judith Tarcher novelist
Krantz, Steven George mathematics educator
Kraslow, David retired newspaper publishing executive, reporter, author, consultant
Kratt, Peter George lawyer
Krause, Werner William plastics company executive
Krauthammer, Charles columnist, editor
Kravitz, Rubin chemist
Krawitz, Herman Everett television producer
Kreitzer, Lois Helen personal investor
Kremer, Honor Frances (Noreen Kremer) real estate broker, small business owner
Kretschmer, Frank Frederick, Jr. electrical engineer, researcher, consultant
Kreutzer, S. Stanley lawyer
Krey, Robert Dean education educator emeritus
Kriegsman, Sali Ann arts administrator, artistic director, writer, consultant
Krisher, Patterson Howard management consultant
Kristensen, Marlene early childhood education educator
Kristofferson, Karl Eric writer
Krogius, Tristan Ernst Gunnar international marketing consultant, lawyer
Krongard, Howard J. lawyer
Kropp, David Arthur retired landscape architect
Krueger, Eugene Rex academic program consultant
Kruizenga, Richard John retired energy company executive
Krupansky, Blanche retired judge
Kryder, Mark Howard computer and electrical engineering educator, consultant
Kryza, E(lmer) Gregory financial planner, international affairs advisor, former ambassador
Kubiak, John Michael academic administrator
Kubo, Edward Hachiro, Jr. lawyer
Kucera, Daniel William retired bishop
Kuehn, James Marshall newspaper editor
Kuesel, Thomas Robert civil engineer
Kuhl, Walter James, Jr. physician
Kulik, Rosalyn Franta food company executive, consultant
Kultermann, Udo architectural and art historian
Kumar, Kaplesh materials scientist
†Kump, Warren Lee diagnostic radiologist
Kundel, Harold Louis radiologist, educator
Kundera, Milan writer, educator
Kunin, Jacqueline Barlow art educator
Kunstadter, Geraldine Sapolsky foundation executive
Kupcinet, Essee Solomon performing arts producer
Kuper, George Henry research and development institute executive
Kupferman, Meyer composer
Kurfess, Thomas Roland mechanical engineering educator
Kuriansky, Judy television and radio talk show host, reporter, psychologist, writer, lecturer
Kurtz, Gary Douglas film producer
Kushner, Harvey David management consultant
Kusserow, Richard Phillip government official, business consultant
Kussrow, Nancy Esther educational association administrator
Kutrzeba, Joseph S. theatrical and film producer, director
Kutyna, Donald Joseph air force officer
Kwak, Sung conductor, music director
Kwiat, Joseph J. English literature and American studies educator
Kyle, John Hamilton publishing executive
LaBarre, Carl Anthony retired government official
Labins, Deborah Lynne maternal women's health nurse
La Blanc, Robert Edmund consulting company executive
Laboda, Amy Sue writer
Labrecque, Richard Joseph industrial executive
Lacey, Cloyd Eugene retired insurance company executive
Lacey, John William Charles management consultant
Lackland, John lawyer
Lacy, Joseph Newton architect
Lacy, Steve jazz musician
Laczko, Robert Matthias cook
Ladd, Cheryl (Cheryl Stopplemoor) actress
Ladd, Joseph Carroll retired insurance company executive
Lader, Philip government official, business executive
Ladly, Frederick Bernard health services and financial services company executive
Laemmle, Cheryl Marie Vicario artist
Lafley, Alan Frederick retired banker
Lafontant-Mankarious, Jewel (Mrs. Naguib S. Mankarious) diplomat, lawyer
Lahourcade, John Brosius retired service company executive
Laible, Jon Morse retired mathematics educator, dean
Laidlaw, Robert Richard publishing company executive
Laird, Bradley Duane social services administrator, psychotherapist
Laitin, Joseph journalist, former government spokesman and public relations consultant
Lakritz, Isaac management consultant
Lalli, Mary Schweitzer writer, artist
Lally, Michael David writer, actor
Lamalie, Robert Eugene retired executive search company executive
Lamb, Gordon Howard music educator
Lamb, Joann Isabel adult nurse practitioner
Lamb, Katie A. nursing educator
Lamberg, Stanley Lawrence medical technologist, educator
Lambert, Samuel Waldron, III lawyer
Lamel, Linda Helen insurance company executive, former college president, lawyer, consultant
Lamm, Harriet A. mathematics educator
Lampert, Eleanor Verna retired human resources specialist
Lampson, Butler Wright computer scientist
Lancaster, John Howard civil engineer
Lancaster, Robert Samuel lawyer, educator
Landel, Robert Franklin physical chemist, rheologist
Lander, Howard entertainment newspaper publisher
Landes, George Miller biblical studies educator
Landesman, Fredric Rocco theatre executive
Landgren, George Lawrence electrical engineer, consultant
Landis, James David publishing company executive, retired, author
Landon, Robert Gray retired manufacturing company executive
Landy, Lisa Anne lawyer
Lane, Bernard Bell furniture company executive
Lane, Burton (Burton Levy) composer
Lane, Debra Ann critical care nurse
Lane, Lilly Katherine museum staff member
Lane, William W. electronics executive
Langdale, John Wesley timber executive
Langerak, Esley Oren retired research chemist
Langford, Walter Martin retired greeting card and gift wrap manufacturing executive
Langley, Joellen S. music educator
Langworthy, William Clayton college official
Laning, J. Halcombe retired computer scientist
Lankford, Duane Gail investment banker, mountaineer
Lantz, Joanne Baldwin academic administrator emeritus
Lantz, Kenneth Eugene consulting firm executive
Lanzillotti, Robert Franklin economist, educator
Lardner, Ring Wilmer, Jr. author
Larizadeh, M(ohammed) R(eza) business educator
Larkin, Joan poet, English educator
La Rocca, Isabella artist, educator
LaRock, Terrance Edmond health facility administrator
Larson, David Bruce research epidemiologist
Larson, Janice Talley computer science educator
Larson, Richard Smith pathologist, researcher
Lasry, Jean-Michel mathematics educator
Lassiter, Kenneth T. photography educator, consultant
Latham, James Richard research scientist
Lathlaen, Robert Frank retired construction company executive
Latimer, Helen information resource manager, writer, researcher
Lauber, John K. research psychologist
Laughlin, Louis Gene economic analyst, consultant
Laurenzo, Vincent Dennis industrial management company executive
Lautenbacher, Conrad Charles, Jr. naval officer
Lauterbach, Christine radio producer
Lauterbach, Edward Charles psychiatric educator
Lavidge, Robert James marketing research executive
Lavin, Roxanna Marie finance executive
Lavington, Michael Richard venture capital company executive
Lawrence, Glenn Robert arbitrator, mediator
Lawrence, Jerome playwright, director, educator
Lawrence, Linda Hiett retired school system administrator, writer
Lawrence, Margery H(ulings) marketing consultant
Lawrence, Vicki Schultz singer, dancer, comedienne
Lawson Donadio, Carolina Anna foreign language educator, translator
Lawton, Kim Audrey freelance journalist
Lay, Elizabeth Marian health association administrator
Laycraft, James Herbert judge
Layton, Robert lawyer
Lazarus, Margaret Louise film producer and director
Lazay, Paul Duane telecommunications manufacturing company executive
Lazechko, D. M. (Molly Lazechko) former state legislator
Lea, Lorenzo Bates lawyer
Leach, Kay T. critical care nurse, administrator
Leak, Nancy Marie artist
Leal, Herbert Allan Borden former university chancellor, former government official
Leaman, Jack Ervin landscape architect, community and regional planner
Lear, Evelyn soprano
Leason, Jody Jacobs newspaper columnist
Leath, Kenneth Thomas research plant pathologist, educator, agricultural consultant
Leather, Victoria Potts college librarian
Leb, Arthur Stern lawyer
LeBaron, Edward Wayne, Jr. lawyer
LeBlond, Paul Henri oceanographer, educator
Lebor, John F(rancis) retired department store executive
†LeClair, John Clark professional hockey player
Lecocke, Suzanne Elizabeth lawyer
Le Dain, Gerald Eric retired Canadian Supreme Court justice
Leddy, Susan nursing educator
Leder, Mimi television director
Leder, Philip geneticist, educator
Lederman, Marie Jean English language educator
Ledford, Jack Clarence retired aircraft company executive, former air force officer
Ledford, Janet Marie Smalley real estate appraiser, consultant
Lee, Barbara A. retired federal magistrate judge
Lee, Benny Y. C. import and export company executive
Lee, Chester Maurice government official
Lee, Dan M. state supreme court justice
Lee, David Stoddart investment counselor
Lee, J. Daniel, Jr. retired insurance company executive
Lee, James Matthew Canadian politician
Lee, Jen-shih biomedical engineering educator
Lee, Joseph William sales executive
Lee, Michele actress
Lee, Mordecai political scientist, educator
Lee, Thomas Henry electrical engineer, educator
Lee, William Saul (Bill Lee) artist, writer
Leean, Joseph social services administrator
Leff, Joseph Norman yarn manufacturing company executive
Leff, Sandra H. gallery director, consultant
Lefferts, George producer, writer, director
Lefranc, Margaret (Margaret Schoonover) artist, illustrator, editor, writer
Leggett, Roberta Jean (Bobbi Leggett) social services administrator
Legington, Gloria R. middle school educator
Lehman, Christopher M. international business consultant
Lehman, John F., Jr. industrialist
Lehtinen, Merja Helen Kokkonen journalist, researcher, publisher
Leibowitz, Ann Galperin lawyer
Leigh, Margie mortgage company originator
Leis, Henry Patrick, Jr. surgeon, educator
Leith, James Clark economics educator
Leizear, Charles William retired information services executive
Lejins, Peter Pierre criminologist, sociologist, educator
Le Mehaute, Bernard Jean marine physics educator
Lemke, James Underwood physicist
Lenahan, Walter Clair retired foreign service officer
Lennon, Joseph Luke college official, priest
Lennox, Donald D(uane) automotive and housing components company executive
León, Tania Justina composer, music director, pianist
Leonard, Guy Meyers, Jr. international holding company executive
Lepage, Robert actor, director, playwright
L'Eplattenier, Nora Sweeny Hickey nursing educator
Leppig, Mary Louise artist
Lerner-Lam, Eva I-Hwa transportation executive
leRoux, Betty Von Moore elementary education educator
LeRoy, G. Palmer art dealer
Lesher, John Lee, Jr. consulting services company executive
Lesko, Harry Joseph transportation company executive
Leslie, Gerrie Allen immunologist
Lester, Virginia Laudano advocate civil rights consumer protection
Letcher, Naomi Jewell quality engineer, educator, counselor
Le Van, Daniel Hayden retired gas industry executive
Leveille, Gilbert Antonio food products executive
Levenson, Marc David optics and lasers specialist, scientist
Leventhal, Ellen Iris portfolio manager, financial services executive
Leventhal, Nathan performing arts executive, lawyer
Levering, Emma Gertrude special education educator
Levetown, Robert Alexander lawyer
Levi, Barbara Goss physicist, editor
Levi, Josef Alan artist
Levi, Maurice David economics educator
Levien, David Harold surgeon
Levin, Jack physician, educator, biomedical investigator
Levin, Morton D(avid) artist, printmaker, educator
Levine, Beryl Joyce state supreme court justice
Levine, Carl Morton motion picture exhibition, real estate executive
Levine, David M. newspaper editor
Levine, Jack artist
Levine, Meldon Edises lawyer, former congressman
Levine, Philip poet, educator
Levinson, Herbert Sherman civil and transportation engineer
Levinson, Stephen Eliot electrical engineer
Levitsky, Melvyn ambassador
Levitt, B. Blake medical and science writer
Levy, Arthur James public relations executive, writer
Levy, David lawyer, insurance company executive
Levy, Ezra Cesar aerospace scientist, real estate broker
Levy, Leah Garrigan federal official
Levy, Louis Edward retired accounting firm executive
Levy, Robert Edward engineering consultant
Lewcock, Ronald Bentley architect, educator
Lewin, K(atherine) Tamar reporter
Lewis, Alexander, Jr. oil company executive
Lewis, Arthur Dee corporation executive
Lewis, Brock investment company executive
Lewis, C. A. church administrator
Lewis, Charles Arlen financial services company executive
Lewis, Charles Leonard psychologist
Lewis, Dale Kenton retired lawyer, mediator
Lewis, Dennis Carroll public relations executive
Lewis, Emanuel Raymond historian, psychologist, retired librarian
Lewis, Floyd Wallace former electric utility executive
Lewis, Gordon Carter auditor
Lewis, James Lee, Jr. actuary
Lewis, John Furman retired lawyer, oil company executive
Lewis, Lois A. health services administrator
Lewis, Lucinda musician
Lewis, Martin Edward shipping company executive, foreign government concessionary
Lewis, Martin R. paper company executive, consultant
Lewis, Norman English language educator, writer
Lewis, Rita Hoffman plastic products manufacturing company executive
Lewis, Russell Carl, Jr. family nurse practitioner
Lewis, Samuel Winfield retired government official, former ambassador
Liacos, Paul Julian retired state supreme judicial court chief justice
Liard, Jean-Francois cardiovascular physiologist, researcher, educator
Liberman, Gail Jeanne editor
Libertiny, Thomas Gabor mechanical engineer, administrator
Lichtenberg, Byron K. futurist, manufacturing executive, space flight consultant, pilot
Lichtenstein, Sarah Carol lawyer
Liddell, Jane Hawley Hawkes civic worker
Liebeler, Susan Wittenberg lawyer
Lieberman, Louis (Karl Lieberman) artist
†Liebler, Arthur C. automotive executive
Liebman, Nina R. economic developer
Liffers, William Albert retired chemical company executive
Liftin, John Matthew lawyer
Light, Arthur Heath bishop
Lightburn, Faye Marie genealogist
Lightfoot, James Ross former congressman
Lightstone, Ronald lawyer
Lillibridge, John Lee retired airline executive
Lilly, Edward Guerrant, Jr. retired utility company executive
Lilly-Hersley, Jane Anne Feeley nursing researcher
Liman, Ellen painter, writer, arts advocate
Linda, Gerald advertising and marketing executive
Lindars, Laurence Edward retired health care products executive
Lindburg, Daytha Eileen physician assistant
Linde, Hans Arthur state supreme court justice
Linde, Maxine Helen lawyer, business executive, private investor
Lindegren, Jack Kenneth elementary and secondary education educator
Lindgren, Kermit Lyle nurse
Lindgren, William Dale librarian
Lindsay, Carol Frances Stockton art specialist
Lindsay, Dale Richard research administrator
Lindsay, Franklin Anthony business executive, author
Lindsay, John Vliet former mayor, former congressman, author, lawyer
Lindsey, D. Ruth physical education educator
Lindsey, Dottye Jean marketing executive
Lindsey, Roberta Lewise music researcher, historian
Lindsley, John Martin chemical engineer
Lindstedt-Siva, (Karen) June marine biologist, environmental consultant
Linhares, Judith Yvonne artist, educator
Link, Arthur Stanley history educator, editor
Link, William Theodore television writer, producer
Linz, Anthony James osteopathic physician, consultant, educator
Lipman, Ira Ackerman security service company executive
Lipowski, Zbigniew Jerzy retired psychiatrist, educator
Lippert, Christopher Nelson dentist, consultant
Lippert, John Richard magazine editor
Lippincott, Philip Edward retired paper products company executive
Lipscomb, Rosalind Tarver artist
Lipscomb-Brown, Edra Evadean retired childhood educ.
Lipsey, Joseph, Jr. water bottling company executive, retail and wholesale corporation executive
Lipsitt, Lewis Paeff psychology educator
Lipsky, Stephen Edward engineering executive, electronic warfare engineer
Lipton, Susan Lytle investment banker, lawyer
Lish, Gordon author, educator, editor
Liskamm, William Hugo architect, urban planner, educator
Lisnek, Margaret Debbeler artist, educator
Lister, Keith Fenimore publishing executive
Litow, Joel David strategic planning and financial analyst
Little, Loren Everton musician, ophthalmologist
Littler, Gene Alec professional golfer
Littleton, Harvey Kline artist
Littman, Earl advertising and public relations executive
Liu, Ernest K. H. international banking executive, international financial consultant
Liu, Katherine Chang artist, art educator
Liu, Young King biomedical engineering educator
Lively, Edwin Lester retired oil company executive
Livezey, Mark Douglas physician
Livingston, Alan Wendell communications executive
Livingstone, Trudy Dorothy Zweig dancer, educator
Lloyd, Joseph Wesley physicist, researcher
Lloyd, Michael Jeffrey recording producer
Lloyd, Walt cinematographer
Lloyd-Jones, Donald J. transportation executive
Lo, Shui-yin physicist
Loach, Paul Allen biochemist, biophysicist, educator
Lobanov-Rostovsky, Oleg arts association executive
Localio, Marcia Judith medical/surgical nurse
Locke, Norton hotel management and construction company executive
Lockhart, Aileene Simpson retired dance, kinesiology and physical education educator
Lockhart, James Bicknell, III company executive
Locklear, Brenda Louise mathematics educator
Lockwood, Robert W. management consultant
Lockwood, Theodore Davidge former academic administrator
Loder, Victoria Kosiorek information broker
Lodge, Arthur Scott mechanical engineering educator
Logan, James Kenneth federal judge
Logan, John Francis electronics company executive, management consultant
Lohmuller, Martin Nicholas bishop
Lohrer, Richard Baker investment consultant
Loiello, John Peter public affairs executive, consultant
LoIudice, Thomas Anthony gastroenterologist, researcher
Lokmer, Stephanie Ann public relations counselor
Lomas, Bernard Tagg college president emeritus
Long, Alvin William title insurance company executive
Long, Charles William child and adolescent psychiatrist
Long, Robert Livingston retired photographic equipment executive
Longo, Kathryn Milani pension consultant
Longobardo, Anna Kazanjian engineering executive
Longstreet, Harry Stephen television producer, director, scriptwriter
Longstreet, Stephen (Chauncey Longstreet) author, painter
Longsworth, Robert Morrow English educator
Lonneke, Michael Dean radio and television marketing executive
†Looney, John G. mental health services administrator
Lopez, Barry Holstun writer
Lopina, Lawrence Thomas retired manufacturing executive
Loppnow, Milo Alvin clergyman, former church official
Lord, Roy Alvin retired publisher
Lord, Walter author
Lordo, Phillip James telecommunications professional
Loren, Mary Rooney controller
Lorenzo Franco, José Ramón Mexican government official
Loring, Gloria Jean singer, actress
Los, Marinus retired agrochemical researcher
Loser, Joseph Carlton, Jr. dean, retired judge
Loss, John C. architect, retired educator
Losten, Basil Harry bishop
Loube, Samuel Dennis physician
Loughlin, Mary Anne Elizabeth television news anchor
Loughran, James Newman philosophy educator, college president
Louison, Deborah Finley public affairs consultant
Love, Miron Anderson retired judge
Lovelace, Alan Mathieson aerospace company executive
Lovell, Walter Carl engineer, inventor
Lovett, John Robert retired chemical company executive
Lovinger, Warren Conrad emeritus university president
Low, Emmet Francis, Jr. mathematics educator
Low, Harry William judge
Lowden, John L. retired corporate executive
Lowe, John, III consulting civil engineer
†Lowell, Juliet author
Lowery, Dominic Gerald (Nick ) professional football player
Lowrie, Walter Olin management consultant
Loy, Richard Franklin civil engineer
Lubic, Ruth Watson association executive, nurse midwife

Lubin, Steven concert pianist, musicologist
Lubinsky, Menachem Yechiel communications executive
Lucas, Beth Anne television producer
Lucas, Rhett Roy artist, lawyer, chemical engineer
Lucas, William Ray aerospace consultant
Luche, Thomas Clifford foreign service officer
Luciano, Roselle Patricia advertising executive, editor
Luckey, Doris Waring civic volunteer
Ludden, John Franklin retired financial economist
Ludlam, James Edward, III insurance company executive
Ludwig, Allan Ira photographer, artist, author
Ludwig, Christa mezzo-soprano
Ludwikowski, Rett Ryszard law educator, researcher
Lueke, Donna Mae national retail company manager
Luetkehoelter, Gottlieb Werner (Lee) retired bishop, clergyman
Luger, Donald R. engineering company executive
Lugt, Hans Josef physicist
Luhn, Robert Kent writer, magazine editor
Luke, David Lincoln, III retired paper company executive
Luke, Douglas Sigler business executive
Lumet, Sidney film director
Lund, David Nathan artist
Lunde, Katherine LaMontagne educational consultant
Lundgren, Leonard, III retired secondary education educator
Lundin, Richard Allen career military officer, federal government administrator, educator
Lupberger, Edwin Adolph utility executive
Lupu, Radu pianist
Lurix, Paul Leslie, Jr. chemist
Luttner, Edward F. consulting company executive
Lutts, Ralph Herbert museum administrator, scholar, educator
Lutz, Carl Freiheit academic administrator
Lutz, Lawrence Joseph family practice physician
Lyman, Ruth Ann psychologist
Lynch, Charles Andrew chemical industry consultant
Lynch, Charlotte Andrews communications executive
Lynch, John Daniel secondary education educator, state legislator
Lynch, Michael Edward medical facility administrator
Lynch, Patricia Gates broadcasting organization executive consultant, former ambassador
Lynch, Peter George artist
Lynch, Phyllis Anne stockbroker
Lynch, Thomas Peter securities executive
Lynch, Thomas Wimp lawyer
Lynch, Virginia Anne (Virginia A. Red Hawk) forensic nurse, educator, consultant
Lynds, Beverly Turner retired astronomer
Lyne, Dorothy-Arden educator
Lyng, Richard Edmund former secretary of agriculture
Lyngbye, Jørgen hospital administrator, researcher
Lynn, Mark Wayne secondary school educator, assistant principal
Lynn, Sheilah Ann service executive, consultant
Lynne, Jeff rock musician, composer
Lyons, Natalie Beller family counselor
Lyshak-Stelzer, Francie artist
Maas, Anthony Ernst pathologist
Maatman, Gerald Leonard insurance company executive
Maazel, Lorin conductor, composer, violinist
Macaulay, David (Alexander) author, illustrator
MacCarthy, Talbot Leland civic volunteer
MacDonald, Robert Alan language educator
Macdonald, Sheila de Marillac transaction management company executive
Macek, Anna Michaella cosmetics executive
MacFarlane, Andrew Walker media specialist, educator
Machida, Curtis A. research molecular neurobiologist
Mack, Charles Daniel, III labor union executive
Mack, Sandra Lee secondary school educator
Mackenzie, Malcolm Lewis marketing executive
MacLachlan, Patricia author
MacLaine, Shirley actress
Maclaren, Noel Keith pathologist, pediatrician, educator
MacLean, John Angus former premier of Prince Edward Island
MacLennan, Beryce Winifred psychologist
MacMillan, Kip Van Metre foundation executive
Macmillan, William Hooper university dean, educator
MacMinn, Aleene Merle B(arnes) newspaper editor, columnist, educator
MacNaughton, John David Francis aerospace company executive
Macon, Carol Ann Gloeckler micro-computer data base management company executive
MacPhee, Donald Albert academic administrator
MacQueen, Robert Moffat solar physicist
Madden, Richard Blaine forest products executive
Maddin, Robert metallurgist educator
Madeira, Francis King Carey conductor, educator
Madera, Joseph J. bishop
Madison, T. Jerome business executive
Maehl, William Harvey historian, educator
Maehr, Martin Louis psychology educator
Maestrone, Frank Eusebio diplomat
Magafas, Diania Lee geriatrics nurse consultant, administrator
Maglich, Bogdan Castle physicist
Magnabosco, Louis Mario chemical engineer, researcher, consultant
Magnano, Salvatore Paul retired financial executive, treasurer
Magnuson, Robert Martin retired hospital administrator
Magor, Louis Roland conductor
Maguire, Robert Francis, III real estate investor
Magurno, Richard Peter lawyer
Mahey, John Andrew museum director
Mahle, Christoph Erhard electrical engineer
Mahoney, Donald Scott financial industry marketing executive
Mahoney, Linda Kay mathematics educator
Mai, Chao Chen engineer
Mai, Harold Leverne retired judge
Maier, Alfred neuroscientist
Maillet, Antonine author, educator
Main, Myrna Joan mathematics educator
Maio, F. Anthony lawyer
Mair, Douglas Dean medical educator, consultant
Maitra, Subir Ranjan medical educator
Major, André radio producer, writer, educator
Major, Patrick Webb, III principal
Majors, Nelda Faye physical therapist
†Mak, Ben Bohdan engineer
Makepeace, Darryl Lee consulting company executive
Makowski, Edgar Leonard obstetrician and gynecologist
Maksymowicz, John electrical engineer
Malakhov, Vladimir dancer
Malakoff, James Leonard management information executive
Malkinson, Frederick David dermatologist
Mallenbaum, Allan Eliyahu marketing executive
Mallo-Garrido, Josephine Ann advertising agency owner
Mallory, Arthur Lee university dean, retired state official
Mallory, William Barton, III lawyer
Malloy, Craig Riggs physician, educator
Malloy, John Richard lawyer, chemical company executive
Malloy, Michael Terrence journalist, newspaper editor
Malluche, Hartmut Horst nephrologist, medical educator
Malone, Edward H. financial executive
Malone, James William retired bishop
Maloney, Diane Marie legal nurse consultant
Maloney, John William lawyer, retired
Maloney, Therese Adele insurance company executive
Malott, Adele Renee editor
Malphurs, Roger Edward biomedical marketing executive
Malson, Rex Richard drug and health care corporation executive
Mamet, David Alan playwright, director, essayist
Mañas, Rita educational administrator
Mancher, Rhoda Ross federal agency administrator, strategic planner
Manchester, Kenneth Edward electronics executive, consultant
Mand, Martin G. financial executive
Mandell, Arlene Linda writing and communications educator
Manganaro, Francis Ferdinand naval officer
Mangione, Chuck (Charles Frank Mangione) jazz musician, composer
Mangler, Robert James lawyer
Mangold, Sylvia Plimack artist
Manley, Joan A(dele) Daniels retired publisher
Manley, John Hugo computing technology executive, educator
Mann, Clarence Charles real estate company official
Mann, Emily Betsy writer, artistic director, theater and film director
Mann, Herbie flutist
Mann, Jim (James William Manousos) editor, publisher
Mann, Jonathan Max international agency administrator
Mann, Lowell D. religious organization executive
Manne, Henry Girard lawyer, educator
Mannering, Jerry Vincent agronomist, educator
Mannes, Elena Sabin film and television producer, director
Manning, Deborah A. physician
Manning, Richard Dale writer
Mansouri, Lotfollah (Lotfi Mansouri) opera stage director, administrator
Maradona, Remigio Martin international diplomat
Maranda, Pierre Jean anthropologist, writer
Marble, Melinda Smith writer, editor
March, Jacqueline Front retired chemist
Marchand, Nancy actress
Marchione, Sharyn Lee computer scientist
Marcinek, Margaret Ann nursing educator
Marcoux, Julia A. midwife
Marcus, Greil Gerstley critic
Marcus, Ruth Barcan philosopher, educator, writer, lecturer
Marcuse, Dietrich retired physicist
Marden, Anne Elliott Roberts paralegal, estates and trusts specialist
Maree, Wendy painter, sculptor
Marinaccio, Paul John, Jr. marketing professional
Marini, Frank Nicholas political science and public administration educator
Marinis, Thomas Paul, Jr. lawyer
Marino, Joseph Anthony retired publishing executive
Marion, Marjorie Anne English educator
Marion, Mildred Ruth honor society executive
Mark, Alan Samuel lawyer
Marken, William Riley magazine editor
Markinson, Martin theatre owner, producer
Markle, Roger A(llan) retired oil company executive
Markovich, Patricia economist, art consultant
Markovitz, Alvin molecular biologist, geneticist
Marks, Leonard, Jr. retired corporate executive
Marks, Stanley Jacob lawyer, historian, lecturer, author
Marler, Larry John private investor
Maroni, Donna Farolino biologist, researcher
Marple, Gary Andre management consultant
Marr, Carmel Carrington retired lawyer, retired state official
Marr, Jack Wayne lawyer
Marrington, Bernard Harvey retired automotive company executive
Marsee, Susanne Irene lyric mezzo-soprano
Marshak, Robert Reuben former university dean, medical educator, veterinarian
Marshall, Charles Noble railroad consultant
Marshall, Donald Thomas medical technologist
Marshall, George Dwire retired supermarket chain executive
Marshall, Gerald Francis optical engineer, consultant, physicist
Marshall, John Crook internal medicine educator
Marshall, Julie W. Gregovich engineering executive
Marshall, Kathryn Sue lawyer
Marshall, L. B. clinical lab scientist
Marshall, (C.) Penny actress, director
Marshall, Richard art historian, curator
Marshall, Robert Charles computer company executive
Martin, Alan Edward gasket company executive
Martin, Albert Charles manufacturing executive, lawyer
Martin, Catherine Elizabeth anthropology educator
Martin, George Conner pomology educator
Martin, Judy Brackin Hereford higher education administrator
Martin, Lee mechanical engineer
Martin, LeRoy E. finance company executive
Martin, Murray Simpson librarian, writer, consultant
Martin, Noel graphic design consultant, educator
Martin, Patricia Ann music educator
Martin, Preston financial services executive
†Martin, Tony football player
†Martinez, Buck baseball analyst
Martini, Robert Edward wholesale pharmaceutical and medical supplies company executive
Martino, Joseph Paul research scientist
Martino, Rocco Leonard computer systems executive
Marty, John state senator, writer
Martyl, (Mrs. Alexander Langsdorf, Jr.) artist
†Martz, Judy state official
Marvel, Wanda Faye home health clinical consultant
Marvin, William Glenn, Jr. former foreign service officer
Marx, Anne (Mrs. Frederick E. Marx) poet
Mascheroni, Eleanor Earle investment company executive
Masiello, Rocco Joseph airlines and aerospace manufacturing executive
Maskell, Donald Andrew contracts administrator
Maslansky, Carol Jeanne toxicologist
Masnari, Nino Antonio electrical engineer, educator
Mason, Frank Henry, III automobile company executive, leasing company executive
Mason, James Albert museum director, former university dean
Mason, John Latimer engineering executive
Massa, Salvatore Peter psychologist
Massachi, Albert (David Massachi) financial strategist
Massey, William Walter, Jr. sales executive
Masson, Gayl Angela airline pilot
Mast, Stewart Dale retired airport manager
Masterson, Peter actor, director
Matasovic, Marilyn Estelle business executive
Matera, Frances Lorine elementary educator
Materson, Richard Stephen physician, educator
Mathay, Mary Frances marketing executive
Matheny, Adam Pence, Jr. child psychologist, educator, consultant, researcher
Matherlee, Thomas Ray health care consultant
Matheson, Scott Milne, Jr. lawyer
Mathew, Porunelloor Abraham molecular biologist, educator
Mathews, Harry Burchell poet, novelist, educator
Mathis, Sharon Bell author, elementary educator, librarian
Matsuda, Fujio technology research center administrator
Matthau, Charles Marcus film director
Matthews, L. White, III railroad executive
Matthews, Wendy Schempp psychologist, researcher
Matthiessen, Peter author
Mattingly, Mack F. former ambassador, former senator, entrepreneur
Mattson, Richard Henry neurologist, educator
Maulding, Barry Clifford lawyer
Maunder, Addison Bruce agronomic research company executive
Maurer, Beverly Bennett school administrator
Mauzy, Michael Philip environmental consultant, chemical engineer
Maxwell, Barbara Sue systems analyst consultant, educator
May, Kenneth Nathaniel food industry consultant
May, Phyllis Jean financial executive
Mayer, Allan magazine editor, writer
Mayer, Patricia Lynn Sorci mental health nurse, educator
Mayfield, Robert Charles university official, geography educator
Mayhew, Lawrence Lee electronics company executive
Maynard, E. Rose retired school health services coordinator
Mayo, Robert Porter banker
Mayoras, Donald Eugene corporate executive, speaker, consultant, educator
Mayron, Melanie actress, writer
Mazankowski, Donald Frank Canadian government official
Mazzarella, Rosemary Louise business administration executive
McBean, Sharon Elizabeth church administrator
McBee, Robert Levi retired federal government official, writer, consultant
McBurney, Margot B. librarian
McCabe, Charles Law retired manufacturing company executive, management consultant
McCandless, J(ane) Bardarah retired religion educator
McCann, Elizabeth Ireland theater, television and motion picture producer, lawyer
McCann, Jack Arland former construction and mining equipment company executive, consultant
McCann, Michael F. industrial hygienist
McCargar, Eleanor Barker portrait painter
†McCarthy, Carolyn congresswoman
McCarthy, Daniel William management consultant
McCarthy, J. Thomas lawyer, educator
Mc Carthy, Jean Jerome retired physical education educator
McCarthy, Joanne Mary reading specialist
McCarthy, Vincent Paul lawyer
Mc Carthy, Walter John, Jr. retired utility executive
McCartney, (James) Paul musician
McCartt, Susan Stockton medical, surgical nurse
McCarty, Dennis L. insurance executive
McCauley, Floyce Reid psychiatrist
McCauley, Jane Reynolds journalist
McClaron, Louisianna Clardy retired secondary school educator
Mc Clellan, Catharine anthropologist, educator
McClendon, Sarah Newcomb news service executive, writer
McClinton, James Leroy city administrator
McClinton, Wendell C. religious organization administrator
Mc Closkey, Robert artist
McClure, Ann Crawford lawyer, judge
McCobb, John Bradford, Jr. lawyer
McConnell, Calvin Dale clergyman
McConnell, Edward Bosworth legal organization administrator, lawyer
McConnell, Elliott Bonnell, Jr. oil company executive
McCormick, David Arthur lawyer
McCormick, John Owen retired comparative literature educator
McCormick, Robert William court reporting educator
McCormick, Susan Konn retired publishing executive
McCown, Hale retired judge
McCoy, Georgia Sideris magazine editor, writing consultant
†McCoy, Helen Thomas civilian military employee
McCoy, Mary Ann state official
McCoy, Patricia A. psychology educator, writer, art critic
Mc Coy, Tidal Windham former government official
McCracken, John Harvey painter, sculptor
McCready, Kenneth Frank past electric utility executive
McCue, Howard McDowell, III lawyer, educat
McCullough, Colleen author
McCullough, David L. urologist
McCullough, R. Michael management consulta
†McCully, Emily Arnold illustrator, writer
McCurdy, Michael Charles illustrator, author
Mc Curley, Robert Lee, Jr. lawyer
McDaniel, Geraldine Howell nursing administra
McDarrah, Gloria Schoffel editor, author
McDermott, Agnes Charlene Senape philosophy educator
McDermott, Kevin J. engineering educator, consultant
McDermott, Lucinda Mary ecumenical minister teacher, philosopher, poet, author
McDonagh, Thomas Joseph physician
Mc Donough, John Richard lawyer
McDowell, Malcolm actor
McEntire, Reba N. country singer
Mc Fadden, George Linus retired army officer
McFadden, Nancy Elizabeth lawyer
McFall, Catherine Gardner poet, critic, educato
McFarland, Robert Edwin lawyer
McFarlin, Diane H. newspaper editor
McFate, Patricia Ann foundation executive, scie educator
Mc Fee, Thomas Stuart retired government ager administrator
McGann, Lisa B. Napoli language educator
McGaw, Kenneth Roy wholesale distribution executive
McGervey, Teresa Ann technology information specialist
Mc Gill, Archie Joseph venture capitalist
McGillis, Kelly actress
McGillivray, Donald Dean agricultural products executive
McGonigle, John Leo, Jr. civil engineer
McGough, Duane Theodore economist, retired government official
McGovern, Frances retired lawyer
Mc Govern, George Stanley former senator
Mc Gowan, James Atkinson business executive, financial consultant
McGrady, Stephanie Jill speech communications educator
McGraw, Deloss Holland illustrator, painter
McGregor, F. Daniel education educator
†McGuire, Hunter Holmes, Jr. surgeon, educator
McGuire, John Murray chemist, researcher
McGuirk, Terrence former broadcasting company executive
McHale, Paul congressman, lawyer
McHenry, Robert (Dale) editor
McHugh, Betsy Baldwin sociologist, educator, journalist, business owner
McHugh, Earl Stephen dentist
McHugh, Edward Francis, Jr. lawyer
McIlvaine, Joseph Peter professional baseball tea executive
McIntosh, Carolyn Meade retired educational administrator
Mc Intosh, James Eugene, Jr. interior designer
McIntosh, Joyce Eubanks special education educa
McIntyre, Douglas Alexander magazine publisher
McIntyre, Guy Maurice professional football play
†McIntyre, Mike congressman
Mc Kay, Dean Raymond computer company executive
McKayle, Donald Cohen choreographer, director, writer, dance educator
McKean, Robert Jackson, Jr. retired lawyer
Mc Kelvey, John Jay, Jr. retired foundation executive
McKenna, David Loren academic administrator, clergyman, consultant, author
McKenna, Richard Henry healthcare managemen consultant
McKenna, Terence Patrick insurance company executive
McKennee, Arden Norma art educator, retired, consultant
McKenzie, Herbert A(lonza) pharmaceutical company executive
McKinley, Ellen Bacon priest
McKinney, Donald art gallery director, art dealer
McKinney, Elizabeth Anne government purchasing professional
McKinnon, Daniel Wayne, Jr. naval officer
McKinnon, Kathleen Ann software engineer
McKnight, Thomas Frederick artist
McLaren, Susan Smith therapist, healing touch practitioner, instructor
McLarnon, Mary Frances neurologist
McLaughlin, Ann public policy, communications executive
McLaughlin, Robert Bruce software designer
McLean, Walter Franklin international consultant, pastor, former Canadian government official
McLendon, Dorothy school psychologist
McLendon, George Leland chemistry educator, researcher
McLeskey, Charles Hamilton anesthesiology educator
McLoone, Eugene P. education educator
Mc Mahon, George Joseph academic administrator
McManus, Jason Donald editor, retired
†McMaster, Sam professional sports team official
McMenamy, Kristen model
McMillan, Terry L. writer, educator
McMillen, Elizabeth Cashin artist
McNeely, Donald Robert steel company executive
McNeil, Heidi Loretta lawyer
McNeil, Steven Arthur food company executive
McNeill, Robert Patrick investment counselor
McNully, Lynnette Larkin elementary education educator
Mc Phee, John Angus writer
Mc Pheeters, Edwin Keith architect, educator
McPherson, James Alan writer, educator
Mc Pherson, Peter academic administrator
Mc Pherson, Robert Donald retired lawyer
Mc Quade, Lawrence Carroll lawyer, corporate executive
McQuilkin, John Robertson religion educator, academic administrator, writer
McRae, Thomas Kenneth retired investment company executive
McShefferty, John retired research company executive, consultant
McSorley, Cisco lawyer
McSweeny, William Francis petroleum company executive, author
McVay, John Edward professional football club executive

McVeigh-Pettigrew, Sharon Christine *communications consultant*
McVey, Diane Elaine *accountant*
McVicker, Jesse Jay *artist, educator*
McWilliams, Bruce Wayne *marketing professional*
Mead, Beverley Tupper *physician, educator*
Mead, Loren Benjamin *writer, consultant*
Meade, Everard Kidder, Jr. *retired broadcasting and publishing executive*
Meads, Donald Edward *management services company executive*
Meagher, Mark Joseph *publishing company executive*
Meahl, Barbara *occupational health nurse*
Meaker, Marijane Agnes *author*
Meara, Anne *actress, playwright, writer*
Medalie, Marjorie Lynn *educational administrator, consultant*
Medavoy, Mike *motion picture company executive*
Medina, Kathryn Bach *book editor*
Medley, Donald Matthias *retired education educator, consultant*
Mednick, Murray *playwright*
Mednick, Robert *accountant*
Meehan, John Joseph, Jr. *hospital administrator*
Meek, Forrest Burns *oil industry executive, trading company executive*
Meeker, Guy Bentley *banker*
Mehne, Paul Randolph *associate dean, medical educator*
Mehta, Peshotan Rustom *magnetobiologist*
Meier, Gustav *symphony conductor*
Meier, Henry George *architect*
Meiling, Gerald Stewart *materials scientist*
Meilman, Edward *physician*
Meister, Steven Gerard *cardiologist, educator*
Mekenney, C. Robert *management analyst, tax accountant*
Melady, Thomas Patrick *academic administrator, ambassador, author, public policy expert, educator*
Melamid, Alexander *artist*
Melczek, Dale J. *bishop*
Melillo, Joseph Vincent *producer, performing arts*
†Mellanby, Scott Edgar *professional hockey player*
Mellema, Donald Eugene *retired radio news reporter and anchor*
Melnick, Joseph L. *virologist, educator*
Melody, Michael Edward *publishing company executive*
Melsheimer, Mel P(owell) *consumer products business executive*
Melton, Marie Frances *retired university dean*
Melvin, Ben Watson, Jr. *petroleum and chemical manufacturing executive*
Melvin, Billy Alfred *clergyman*
Mench, John William *retail store executive, electrical engineer*
Mende, Robert Graham *retired engineering association executive*
Mendelson, Sol *physical science educator, consultant*
Mendez, Albert Orlando *industrialist, financier*
Mendonsa, Arthur Adonel *retired city official*
Mendoza, George *poet, author*
Meneeley, Edward Sterling *artist*
Menhall, Dalton Winn *lawyer, insurance executive, professional association administrator*
Menn, Julius Joel *research scientist*
Meo, Roxanne Marie *critical care nurse*
Mercer, Edwin Wayne *lawyer*
Mercoun, Dawn Denise *human resources executive*
Mercurio, Renard Michael *real estate corporation executive*
Meredith, Alice Foley *publisher, consultant*
Meredith, Ellis Edson *association and business executive*
Merenbloom, Robert Barry *hospital and medical school administrator*
Merilan, Jean Elizabeth *statistics educator*
Merk, Elizabeth Thole *sales representative*
†Merriam, Robert W. *engineering executive, educator*
Merrick, Dorothy Susan *interior designer*
Merrill, Jean Fairbanks *writer*
Merritt, Joshua Levering, Jr. *retired engineering executive, consultant*
Meserve, Walter Joseph *drama studies educator, publisher*
Meshel, Harry *state senator, political party official*
Messenkopf, Eugene John *real estate and business consultant*
Messmore, David William *construction executive, former psychologist*
Metcalfe, Robert Davis, III *lawyer*
Metz, Frank Andrew, Jr. *data processing executive*
Metz, Steven William *small business owner*
Metzner, Charles Miller *federal judge*
Metzner, Richard Joel *psychiatrist, psychopharmacologist, educator*
Meyer, Daniel Kramer *real estate executive*
Meyer, Frances Margaret Anthony *elementary and secondary school educator, health education specialist*
Meyer, Greg Charles *psychiatrist*
Meyer, Harry Martin, Jr. *retired health science facility administrator*
Meyer, Henry Lewis, III *banker*
Meyer, Kathleen Marie *English educator*
Meyer, L. Donald *retired agricultural engineer, researcher, educator*
Meyer, Lasker Marcel *retail executive*
Meyer, Louis B. *superior court judge, retired state supreme court justice*
Meyer, Mary-Louise *art gallery executive*
Meyer, Max Earl *lawyer*
Meyer, Robert Lee *secondary education educator*
Meyer, Ursula *retired library director*
Meyers, Richard James *landscape architect*
Miah, Abdul Malek *electrical engineer, educator*
Mian, Ahmad Zia *economist*
Miaskiewicz, Theresa Elizabeth *secondary education educator*
Mich, Connie Rita *mental health nurse, educator*
Michael, Donald Nelson *social scientist, educator*
Michael, Harold Kaye (Bud Michael) *sales and marketing executive*
Michalski, Carol Ann *medical, surgical and psychiatric nurse, writer, poet*
Michelson, Harold *production designer*
Micks, Don Wilfred *biologist, educator*
Middaugh, Robert Burton *artist*
Miele, Anthony William *retired librarian*
Migden, Chester L. *professional society administrator*
Mike, Deborah Denise *systems engineering consultant*
Mikel, Thomas Kelly, Jr. *laboratory administrator*
Mikitka, Gerald Peter *investment banker, financial consultant*
Mikulski, Barbara Ann *senator*
Milanovich, Norma JoAnne *training company executive, occupational educator*
Miles, Cynthia Lynn *theatrical costume designer, consultant*
Miles, Elsie E. *counselor, educator*
Miles, Jeanne Patterson *artist*
Miles, John Frederick *retired manufacturing company executive*
Miles, Laveda Ann *advertising executive*
Miles, Leland Weber *university president*
Miles-LaGrange, Vicki Lynn *federal judge*
Milewski, Barbara Anne *pediatrics nurse, neonatal intensive care nurse*
Milhouse, Paul William *bishop*
Millane, Lynn *town official*
Millard, Charles Warren, III *museum director, writer*
Miller, Alan Jay *financial consultant, author*
Miller, Arjay *retired university dean*
Miller, Charles Edmond *library administrator*
Miller, Donald Muxlow *accountant, administrator*
Miller, Ellen S. *marketing communications executive*
Miller, Frank William *legal educator*
†Miller, Gary *sports network host, sports anchor*
Miller, Hainon Alfred *lawyer, investor*
Miller, Harold Edward *retired manufacturing conglomerate executive, consultant*
Miller, Herman Lunden *retired physicist*
Miller, Jack Conway *landscape artist, art gallery director, owner*
Miller, Jacqueline Winslow *library director*
Miller, James Vince *university president*
Miller, Jeffrey Veach *biochemist, researcher*
Miller, Jerry Huber *retired university chancellor*
Miller, Judith *federal official*
Miller, Kenneth William, II *business consultant, educator*
Miller, Leland Bishop, Jr. *food processing and financial consultant*
Miller, Lillie M. *nursing educator*
Miller, Lowell Donald *pharmaceutical company research executive*
Miller, Marilyn Lea *library science educator*
Miller, Pamela Lynn *sales director*
Miller, Patricia Anne *speech and language pathologist*
Miller, Reed *lawyer*
Miller, Reginald Wayne *professional basketball player*
Miller, Richard Alan *lawyer, former merger and acquisition and forest products company executive*
Miller, Robert Branson, Jr. *retired newspaper publisher*
Miller, Robert Stevens, Jr. *finance professional*
Miller, Ross Hays *retired neurosurgeon*
Miller, Thormund Aubrey *lawyer*
Miller, Vel *artist*
Millett, Ralph Linwood, Jr. *retired newspaper editor*
†Millhauser, Steven *writer*
Milligan, Arthur Achille *banker*
Millikan, Clark Harold *physician*
Millimet, Erwin *lawyer*
Mills, Celeste Louise *hypnotherapist, professional magician*
Mills, Eugene Sumner *college president*
Mills, Inga-Britta *artist*
Mills, Kevin Lee *government executive*
Mills, Mike *popular musician*
Mills, Robert Lee *president emeritus*
Millsaps, Fred Ray *investor*
Milner, Irvin Myron *lawyer*
Mims, Edward Trow *electronics industry executive*
Minami, Robert Yoshio *artist, graphic designer*
Mindlin, Paula Rosalie *retired reading educator*
Miner, A. Bradford *journalist*
Miner, Mary Elizabeth Hubert *retired secondary school educator*
Mingle, James John *lawyer*
Minners, Howard Alyn *physician, research administrator*
Minnix, Bruce Milton *television and theatre director*
Mints, Grigori Efroim *specialist in mathematical logic*
Mintz, M. J. *lawyer*
Mintz, Morton Abner *author, former newspaper reporter*
Miracle, Robert Warren *retired banker*
Mirisch, Walter Mortimer *motion picture producer*
Mischke, Carl Herbert *religious association executive, retired*
Miskowski, Lee R. *retired automobile executive*
Mislow, Kurt Martin *chemist, educator*
Misrach, Richard Laurence *photographer*
Missan, Richard Sherman *lawyer*
Mitchel, F(rederick) Kent *retired food company executive*
Mitchell, Ada Mae Boyd *legal assistant*
Mitchell, Briane Nelson *lawyer*
Mitchell, Carol Ann *nursing educator*
Mitchell, Claybourne, Jr. *retired utilities executive*
Mitchell, Rick *journalist, writer*
Mitchell, Robert Edward *urban planner, international development specialist, educator*
Mitchell, Tonja Keashavel *physical education educator, nutritional consultant*
Mitchem, Mary Teresa *publishing executive*
Mitzner, Kenneth Martin *electrical engineering consultant*
Mixon, Alan *actor*
Mlyniec, Wallace John *law educator, lawyer, consultant*
Modano, Michael *professional hockey player*
Modigliani, Franco *economics and finance educator*
Moeckel, Bill Reid *retired university dean*
Moeller, Robert John *management consultant*
Moffatt, Hugh McCulloch, Jr. *hospital administrator, physical therapist*
Moffatt, Katy (Katherine Louella Moffatt) *musician, vocalist, songwriter*
Moffet, Hugh Lamson *pediatrician*
Mogel, Leonard Henry *author*
Mogelever, Bernard *public relations executive*
Mogielski, Phyllis Ann *health association administrator, psychotherapist*
Mogil, H(arvey) Michael *meteorologist, educator*
Mohamed, Joseph *real estate broker*
Mohler, Brian Jeffery *diplomat*
Molden, Herbert George *publisher*
Mollo, John *film costume designer, military historian*
Molloy, Sylvia *Latin American literature educator, writer*
Monacelli, Gianfranco *publishing executive*
Monahan, Edward Charles *academic administrator, marine science educator*
Mondale, Walter Frederick *former vice president of United States, diplomat, lawyer*
Monfils-Clark, Maud Ellen *analyst*
Monk, Nancy Dina *artist, educator*
Monninger, Robert Harold George *ophthalmologist, educator*
Monroe, Murray Shipley *lawyer*
Monsen, Raymond Joseph, Jr. *economist, educator, art patron*
Monsma, Robbie Elizabeth *lawyer, mediator, arbitrator, real estate executive*
Monson, David Carl *school superintendent, farmer, state legislator*
Montgomery, James Morton *public relations, marketing executive, association executive*
Montgomery, John Richard *pediatrician, educator*
Montgomery, Roy Delbert *retired gas utility company executive*
Montgomery, Seth David *retired state supreme court chief justice*
Monty, Charles Embert *utility company executive*
Monty, Gloria *television producer*
Moody, Evelyn Wilie *consulting geologist, educator, artist*
Moody, Graham Blair *lawyer*
Moody, Roland Herbert *retired librarian*
Moore, E. Harris *bishop*
Moore, Emily Allyn *pharmacologist*
Moore, George Elliott *management consultant*
Moore, John Cordell *retired lawyer*
Moore, John Plunkett Dennis *publisher*
Moore, John Runyan *agricultural and resource economics educator*
Moore, Matthew Emerson *environmental program planning management specialist*
Moore, Powell Allen *former government official, consultant*
Moore, Richard Alan *landscape architect*
Moore, Richard Earl *communications creative director*
Moore, Robert Henry *insurance company executive*
Moore, Robert William *professional organization executive*
Moore, Thomas David *academic administrator*
Moore, Tom *film and theater director*
Moore, Vernon Lee *agricultural consultant, retired food products company executive*
Moore, William Jason *museum director*
Moore, William Leroy, Jr. *career officer, physician*
Moossy, John *neuropathologist, neurologist, consultant*
Moradi, Ahmad F. *software company executive, consultant*
Moran, Charles A. *securities executive*
Moran, John Arthur *oil company executive*
Morandi, John Arthur, Jr. *nursing administrator, educator, nurse*
Morang, Diane Judy *writer, television producer, business entrepreneur*
Mordecai, Benjamin *theatrical producer, drama educator*
Morelan, Paula Kay *choreographer*
Moreland, Alvin Franklin *veterinarian*
Morello, Joseph Albert *musician, educator*
Moreton, Thomas Hugh *minister*
Morgan, Edmund Sears *history educator*
Morgan, Elizabeth *plastic and reconstructive surgeon*
Morgan, Jane Hale *retired library director*
Morgan, Mary Lou *retired education educator, civic worker*
Morgan, Robert Arthur *accountant*
Morgan, Ruth Prouse *academic administrator, educator*
Morgan, Thomas Rowland *retired marine corps officer*
Morgenroth, Earl Eugene *entrepreneur*
Morgenstein, William *shoe company executive*
Moriarty, Donald William, Jr. *banker*
Morin, William James *management consultant*
Morin-Miller, Carmen Aline *writer*
Morita, Toshiyasu *technical manager*
Morning, John *graphic designer*
Morrell, Gene Paul *liquid terminal company executive*
Morrill, Thomas Clyde *insurance company executive*
Morris, Albert Jerome *pest control company executive*
Morris, Frank Eugene *banker*
Morris, Jane Elizabeth *home economics educator*
Morris, Richard Ward *author*
Morris, Robert G(emmill) *retired foreign service officer*
Morris, Willie *author, editor*
Morrison, Ian A(lastair) *foundation executive*
Morrison, James R. *retired banker*
Morrison, Margaret Louise *artist*
Morrison, Shelley *actress*
Morrison, Van *musician, songwriter*
Morrissey, Charles Thomas *historian, educator*
Morrow, Barry Nelson *screenwriter, producer*
Morrow, George Lester *retired oil and gas executive*
Morrow, Ralph Ernest *historian, educator*
Morrow, Rob *actor*
Morse, Leon William *traffic, physical distribution and transportation management executive, consultant*
†Morse, Robert Harry *lawyer*
Morse, Susan Edwina *film editor*
Mortensen, Peter *banker*
Mortimer, David William *communications engineer*
Mortola, Edward Joseph *academic administrator emeritus*
Mosca, Christopher Patrick *principal*
Moscona, Aron Arthur *biology educator, scientist*
Moser, Robert Lawrence *pathologist, health facility administrator*
Moses, Edward Crosby *artist*
Moses, Jeffrey Michael *customer services executive*
Mosler, John *retired financial planner*
Mossawir, Harve H., Jr. *retired lawyer*
Moszkowicz, Virginia Marie *quality administrator*
Mott, Stewart Rawlings *business executive, political activist*
Motto, Jerome Arthur *psychiatry educator*
Mount, Thomas H(enderson) *motion picture and stage producer*
Mountain, Clifton Fletcher *surgeon, educator*
Mow, Douglas Farris *former naval officer, consultant*
Moynahan, John Daniel, Jr. *retired insurance executive*
Mrkonic, George Ralph, Jr. *retail executive*
Muckerman, Norman James *priest, writer*
Mudd, Roger Harrison *news broadcaster, educator*
Mudd, Sidney Peter *former beverage company executive*
Mueller, Barbara Stewart (Bobbie Mueller) *youth drug use prevention specialist, volunteer*
†Mueller, Lisel *writer, poet*
Mueller, Robert Louis *business executive*
Mugridge, David Raymond *lawyer*
Mujica, Mauro E. *architect*
Mulcahy, Robert Edward *management consultant*
Muldoon, Thomas Lyman *writer*
Mullan, Donald William *bishop*
Mullen, William Joseph, III *military analyst, retired army officer*
Muller, Frederica Daniela *psychology educator*
Muller, Margie Hellman *financial services consultant*
Muller, Peter *lawyer, entertainment company executive, retail company executive, consultant*
Mulvihill, Peter James *fire protection engineer*
Mumma, Albert Girard, Jr. *architect*
Munera, Gerard Emmanuel *manufacturing company executive*
Munger, Bryce L. *physician, educator*
Munic, Rachelle Ethel *health services administrator*
Munier, William Boss *medical service executive*
Muñoz, Carlos Ramón *bank executive*
Munsey, Virdell Everard, Jr. *retired utility executive*
Murdock, Mary-Elizabeth *history educator*
Muren, Dennis E. *visual effects director*
Murphy, Benjamin Edward *actor*
Murphy, Charles Haywood, Jr. *retired petroleum company executive*
Murphy, Francis *English language educator*
Murphy, Lewis Curtis *lawyer, former mayor*
Murphy, Mary Kathleen *nursing educator*
Murphy, Sandra Robison *lawyer*
Murr, James Coleman *federal government official*
Murray, Albert L. *writer, educator*
Murray, David George *architect*
Murray, Florence Kerins *retired state supreme court justice*
Murray, Fred F. *lawyer*
Murray, Herbert Frazier *retired federal judge*
Murray, Leonard Hugh *railroad executive*
Murray, Robert Gray *sculptor*
Murrill, Paul Whitfield *former utility executive, former university administrator*
Musante, Tony (Anthony Peter Musante, Jr.) *actor*
Muson, Howard Henry *writer, editor*
Mutafova-Yambolieva, Violeta Nikolova *pharmacologist*
Mutombo, DiKembe (Dikembe Mutombo Mpolondo Mukamba Jean Jacque Wamutombo) *professional basketball player*
Myatt, Clifford E. *federal official*
Mydland, Gordon James *judge*
Myers, Albert G., Jr. *textile manufacturer*
Myers, Ann Margaret *state agency supervisor*
Myers, Harold Mathews *academic administrator*
Myers, Jack Edgar *biologist, educator*
Myers, Jesse Jerome *lawyer*
Myers, John Herman *investment management executive*
Myers, John Thomas *retired congressman*
Myers, Phillip Fenton *financial services and technology company executive*
Myers, Phillip Samuel *mechanical engineering educator*
Myers, Shirley Diana *art book editor*
Myers, Walter Dean *young adult book author*
Myerson, Alan *director, film and television writer*
Myhand, Wanda Reshel *paralegal, legal assistant*
Myhren, Trygve Edward *communications company executive*
Nabholz, Mary Vaughan *rehabilitation nurse*
Nabrit, Samuel Milton *retired embryologist*
Nagel, Thomas *philosopher, educator*
Nahman, Norris Stanley *electrical engineer*
Nair, Raghavan D. *accountant, educator*
Nakagawa, Allen Donald *radiologic technologist*
Nakamura, Kazuo *artist*
Nalls, Gayil Lynn *artist*
Nance, Mary Joe *secondary education educator*
Nangle, Carole Folz *counselor*
Nank, Lois Rae *financial executive*
Napodano, Rudolph Joseph *internist, medical educator*
Naquin, Patricia Elizabeth *employee assistance consultant*
Nara, Bonnie A. *psychologist*
Nardi Riddle, Clarine *association administrator, judge*
Narita, Hiro *cinematographer*
Nasgaard, Roald *museum curator*
Natale, Laurel A. *nursing case manager*
Natcher, Stephen Darlington *lawyer, business executive*
Nattras, Ruth A(nn) *school nurse*
Naughton, James *actor*
Naughton, Patricia J. *gerontological nurse, administrator, consultant*
Naylor, Thomas Herbert *economist, educator, consultant*
Neal, Margaret Sherrill *writer, editor*
Neame, Ronald *director, producer*
Nearine, Robert James *educational psychologist*
Neary, Patricia Elinor *ballet director*
Nebel, Henry Martin, Jr. *literature historian, educator*
Nedelman, Dorothy O'Flaherty *primary care nurse*
Nederlander, James Laurence *theater owner, producer*
Needham, Lucien Arthur *musician, educator*
Needleman, Philip *cardiologist, pharmacologist*
Needles, Belverd Earl, Jr. *accountant, educator*
Neel, James Van Gundia *geneticist, educator*
Neelankavil, James Paul *international business educator, researcher and consultant*
Neely, Mark Edward, Jr. *writer*
Neff, Diane Irene *naval officer*
Neff, Donald Lloyd *news correspondent, writer*
Neff, Francine Irving (Mrs. Edward John Neff) *former federal government official*
Neff, Jack Kenneth *apparel manufacturing company executive*
Negron, Carlos Daniel *lawyer*
Nehrt, Lee Charles *management educator*
Neilson, Benjamin Reath *lawyer*
Neimark, Philip John *financial consultant, editor*
Nelson, Ben, Jr. *retired air force officer*
Nelson, Carl Roger *retired lawyer*
Nelson, Dennis George Anthony *dental researcher, life scientist*
Nelson, Edwin Clarence *academic administrator, emeritus*
Nelson, Harvey Frans, Jr. *retired foreign service officer*
Nelson, Helen Martha *retired library director*
Nelson, Kaye Lynn *healthcare consultant*
Nelson, Martha Jane *magazine editor*
Nelson, Norman Daniel *government official*
Nelson, Ralph Stanley *lawyer*
Nelson, Robert Charles *newspaper executive*
†Nelson, Theresa *writer*
Nelson, Wallace Warren *retired superintendent experimental station, agronomy educator*

Pinkney, D. Timothy *investment company executive*
Pinter, Gabriel George *physiologist*
Pionke, Harry Bernhard *research leader and soil scientist*
Piore, Nora Kahn *economist, health policy analyst*
Piper, Margarita Sherertz *retired school administrator*
Pippin, James Adrian, Jr. *middle school educator*
Pirkle, Earl Charnell *geologist, educator*
Pisney, Raymond Frank *international consulting services executive*
Pitcher, Griffith Fontaine *lawyer*
Pitrelli, Ellen Jane *secondary school educator*
Pitts, Terence Randolph *curator and museum director*
Pizzuro, Salvatore Nicholas *special education educator*
Plane, Robert Allen *academic administrator, chemistry educator, author*
Plangere, Jules Leon, Jr. *media company executive*
Plaskonos, Anne *school nurse*
Platou, Joanne (Dode) *retired museum director*
Platti, Rita Jane *educator, draftsman, author, inventor*
Pleming-Yocum, Laura Chalker *religion educator*
Pleshette, Suzanne *actress, writer*
Pletcher, Eldon *editorial cartoonist*
Plummer, Daniel Clarence, III *insurance consultant*
Pniakowski, Andrew Frank *structural engineer*
Pockell, Leslie M. *publishing company executive*
Pocock, Frederick James *environmental scientist, engineer, consultant*
Podhoretz, Norman *magazine editor, writer*
Pogue, Richard Welch *lawyer*
Pohlman, Janet Elizabeth *healthcare executive, consultant*
Poledouris, Basil K. *composer*
Poliakoff, Gary A. *lawyer, educator*
Policinski, Eugene Francis *author, newspaper editor*
Polikoff, Benet, Jr. *lawyer*
Polk, James Ray *journalist*
Poll, Martin Harvey *film producer*
Pollack, Gerald Alexander *economist, government official*
Pollack, Ronald F(rank) *foundation executive, lawyer*
Pollard, Henry *lawyer*
Pollock, Karen Anne *computer analyst*
Polston, Barbara *principal, educational psychologist*
Pomeroy, Kent Lytle *physical medicine and rehabilitation physician*
Pomraning, Gerald Carlton *engineering educator*
Pond, Phyllis Joan Ruble *state legislator*
Pool, Philip Bemis, Jr. *investment banker*
Pooley, Beverley John *law educator, librarian*
Poor, Anne *artist*
Poor, Janet Meakin *landscape designer*
Pop, Iggy (James Newell Osterberg) *composer, singer, musician*
Porges, Walter Rudolf *television news executive*
Porretta, Emanuele Peter *retired bank executive*
Portal, Gilbert Marcel Adrien *oil company executive*
Porter, Charles Henry *photographer*
Porter, Daniel Reed, III *museum director*
Porter, Marie Ann *neonatal nurse, labor and delivery nurse*
Porter, Marsha Kay *Language professional and educator, English*
Porter, Michael Pell *lawyer*
Porter, Philip Thomas *retired electrical engineer*
Portis, Alan Mark *physicist, educator*
Portnoy, Sara S. *lawyer*
Poser, Ernest George *psychologist, educator*
Posin, Daniel Q. *physics educator, television lecturer*
Post, Boyd Wallace *forester*
Post, Richard Bennett *retired human resources executive*
Poster, Steven Barry *cinematographer, photgrapher, publisher, digital imaging consultant*
Poston, Tom *actor*
Poteat, James Donald *diaconal minister, retired military officer*
Potok, Chaim *author, artist, editor*
Potter, James Earl *retired international hotel management company executive*
Potter, William Blake *language professional, educator*
Potts, Annie *actress*
Potts, Douglas Gordon *neuroradiologist*
Potts, Gerald Neal *manufacturing company executive*
Potts, Sandra Dell *elementary education educator*
Potvin, Alfred Raoul *engineering executive*
Pouncey, Peter Richard *academic administrator, classics educator*
Pound, Robert Vivian *physics educator*
Povish, Kenneth Joseph *retired bishop*
Powell, Clinton Cobb *radiologist, physician, former university administrator*
Powell, Earl Alexander, III *art museum director*
Powell, Sara Jordan *musician, religious worker*
Powell, Thomas Edward, III *biological supply company executive*
Powers, Thomas Edward *managed care executive*
Powledge, Fred Arlius *freelance writer*
Pozzatti, Rudy Otto *artist*
Pracht, Drenda Kay *psychologist*
Prady, Norman *journalist, advertising executive, writer, marketing consultant*
Prager, David *retired state supreme court chief justice*
Prakapas, Eugene Joseph *art gallery director*
Prange, Hilmar Walter *neurology educator*
Pratt, Alice Reynolds *retired educational administrator*
Pratt, David Terry *mechanical engineering educator, combustion researcher*
Pratte, Lise *lawyer, corporate secretary*
Precopio, Frank Mario *chemical company executive*
Preece, Warren Eversleigh *editor*
Press, Aida Kabatznick *former editor, writer*
Preston, Alda S. *academic administrator, nursing educator*
Preston, Seymour Stotler, III *manufacturing company executive*
Preszler, Sharon Marie *psychiatric home health nurse*
Preusser, Joseph William *academic administrator*
Prezzano, Wilbur John *retired photographic products company executive*
Price, Alfred Lee *lawyer, mining company executive*
Price, Annie Laurie *senior health program manager*
Price, Clifford Warren *retired metallurgist, researcher*
Price, Griffith Baley *mathematician, educator*
Price, Jeannine Alleenica *clinical psychologist, retired computer consultant*
Price, Paul Buford *physicist, educator*
Price, Robert *electronics consultant*
Price, Robert Ira *coast guard officer*
Price, Thomas Frederick *theatre educator*
Price, Tom *journalist*
Pridmore, Roy Davis *government official*
Primosch, James Thomas *music educator, composer, musician*
Prince, Andrew Steven *lawyer, former government official*
Prince, Milton S. *investment company executive*
Principal, Victoria *actress*
Principe, Helen Mary *medical case manager*
Prins, Robert Jack *academic administrator*
Prisco, Frank J. *psychotherapist*
Pritchard, Claudius Hornby, Jr. *retired university president*
Pritchard, Kathleen Jo *not-for-profit association administrator*
Pritikin, David T. *lawyer*
Pritts, Kim Derek *state conservation officer, writer*
Pritz, Michael Burton *neurological surgeon*
Pritzker, Leon *statistician, consultant*
Procter, John Ernest *former publishing company executive*
Proctor, Richard J. *geologist, consultant*
Proft, Pat *screenwriter, film producer*
Prokasy, William Frederick *academic administrator*
Prokopis, Emmanuel Charles *computer company executive*
Propst, Harold Dean *retired academic administrator*
Prosky, Robert Joseph *actor*
Protigal, Stanley Nathan *lawyer*
Provensen, Alice Rose Twitchell *artist, author*
Proxmire, William *former senator*
Prugh, George Shipley *lawyer*
Pruis, John J. *business executive*
Prusiner, Stanley Ben *neurology and biochemistry educator, researcher*
Pryce, Deborah D. *congresswoman*
†Pryor, Bill *attorney general*
Pryor, Harold S. *retired college president*
Przybylski, Sandra Marie *speech pathologist*
Psillos, Susan Rose *artist, educator*
Pugliese, Karen Olsen *freelance public relations counsel*
Pullen, Penny Lynne *non-profit administrator, former state legislator*
Pullen, Richard Owen *lawyer, communications company executive*
Purcell, George Richard *artist, postal inspector*
Purdy, Teddy George, Jr. *programmer, analyst, researcher, consultant*
Pursey, Derek Lindsay *physics educator*
Purtle, John Ingram *lawyer, former state supreme court justice*
Puryear, Alvin Nelson *management educator*
Pusateri, Lawrence Xavier *lawyer*
Pustilnik, David Daniel *lawyer*
Putnam, Linda Lee *communication educator, researcher*
Pyle, Donald Alan *music educator, tenor*
Quaid, Dennis *actor*
Quaife, Marjorie Clift *nursing educator*
Quarles, Peggy Delores *secondary school educator*
Quattrone-Carroll, Diane Rose *clinical social worker*
Queenan, Joseph Martin, Jr. *writer, magazine editor*
Quehl, Gary Howard *association executive, consultant*
Quesnel, Gregory L. *transportation company executive*
Quetglas, Moll Juan *plastic and maxillofacial surgeon*
Quick, Norman *bishop*
Quigley, Leonard Vincent *lawyer*
Quillen, Cecil Dyer, Jr. *lawyer, consultant*
Quillen, William Tatem *judge, lawyer, educator*
Quinlan, J(oseph) Michael *lawyer*
Quinlan, Kathleen *actress*
Quinn, Charles Nicholas *journalist*
Quirico, Francis Joseph *retired state supreme court justice*
Quirk, Kenneth Paul *accountant*
Qutub, Musa Yacub *hydrogeologist, educator, consultant*
Raab, Herbert Norman *retail executive*
Rabó, Jule Anthony *chemical researcher, consultant*
Rabson, Robert *plant physiologist, retired science administrator*
Rader, Dotson Carlyle *author, journalist*
Radice, Anne-Imelda *museum director*
Radkowsky, Karen *advertising/marketing research executive*
Rae, John Joseph *lawyer*
Rafael, Ruth Kelson *archivist, librarian, consultant*
Rafelson, Bob *film director*
Ragland, Terry Eugene *emergency physician*
Ragsdale, Carl Vandyke *motion picture producer*
Ragucci, John Albert *family practice physician*
Ragusea, Stephen Anthony *psychologist, educator*
Raichle, Marcus Edward *radiology, neurology educator*
Rainey, Claude Gladwin *retired health care executive*
Rairdin, Craig Allen *software company executive, software developer*
Rajski, Peggy *film director, film producer*
Ramanarayanan, Madhava Prabhu *science administrator, researcher, educator*
Ramis, Harold Allen *film director, screenwriter, actor*
Ramo, Virginia M. Smith *civic worker*
Ramos, Eleanor Lacson *transplant nephrologist*
Ramos, Gerardo Ernesto *Spanish teacher*
Ramsay, Karin Kinsey *publisher, educator*
Ramsey, Henry, Jr. *university official, lawyer, retired judge*
Ramsey, Lynn Allison *public relations executive*
Ramsey, Sandra Lynn *psychotherapist*
Ramsey, Stephen Douglas *lawyer, environmental manager*
Randall, Richard Harding, Jr. *art gallery director*
Randall, Richard Rainier *geographer*
Randinelli, Tracey Anne *magazine editor*
Randolph, Judson Graves *pediatric surgeon*
Randolph, Nancy Adele *nutritionist, consultant*
Rank, Larry Gene *management consultant*
Rankin, Elizabeth Anne DeSalvo *nurse, psychotherapist, educator, consultant*
Rankin, Scott David *artist, educator*
Ransome, Ernest Leslie, III *retail company executive*
Rappach, Norma Jeanne *health occupations educator*
Rappaport, Theodore Scott *electrical engineering educator*
Raskin, Michael A. *retail company executive*
Rasmussen, Dennis Loy *sales and marketing executive*
Rasmussen, Gail Maureen *critical care nurse*
Rasmussen, Wayne Roger *law educator, consultant*
Rasmusson, Gary Henry *medicinal chemist*
Rasor, Dina Lynn *investigator, journalist*
Rassman, Joel H. *real estate company executive, accountant*
Rast, Walter, Jr. *hydrologist, water quality management*
Rataj, Elizabeth Ann *artist*
Ratcliff, James Lewis *administrator*
Rathmell, Sandra Lee *women's health nurse*
Ratliff, Lois L. *secondary school educator*
Ratny, Ruth Lucille *publishing company executive, writer*
Rattley, Jessie Menifield *former mayor, educator*
Raubicheck, Charles Joseph *lawyer, educator*
Raucher, Herman *novelist, screenwriter*
Raval, Dilip N. *retired pharmaceutical executive*
Ravetch, Irving *screenwriter*
Rawdon, Cheryl Ann *elementary school educator*
Ray, Gayle Elrod *sheriff*
Ray, Jeanne Cullinan *lawyer, insurance company executive*
Rayfiel, David *screenwriter*
Raymond, Lee R. *oil company executive*
Rayner, William Alexander *retired newspaper editor*
Raynolds, Harold, Jr. *retired state education commissioner*
Reath, George, Jr. *lawyer*
Reaves, Ray Donald *civil engineer*
Rechy, John Francisco *author*
Recine, Judy Ann *surgical nurse*
Redda, Kinfe Ken *chemist, educator*
Redgrave, Vanessa *actress*
Redmond, Douglas Michael *diversified company executive*
Redmont, Bernard Sidney *university dean, journalism educator*
Reece, Geraldine Maxine *elementary education educator*
Reed, Adam Victor *psychologist, engineer*
Reed, Cynthia Kay *minister*
Reed, David Fredrick *artist*
Reed, David Patrick *infosystems specialist*
Reed, Diane Marie *psychologist*
Reed, Leon Samuel *policy analyst*
Reed, Nancy Binns *composer, poet, artist*
Reed, Thomas Lee, II *minister, elementary education educator*
Reeder, James Arthur *lawyer*
Reeder, Robert Harry *retired lawyer*
Rees, Morgan Rowlands *engineer, educator*
Reetz, Harold Frank, Jr. *industrial agronomist*
Reeves, Lucy Mary *retired secondary school educator*
Reeves, Nancy Alice *critical care nurse*
Reeves, Peggy Lois Zeigler *accountant*
Regalado, Raul L. *airport parking executive*
Regan, Paul Jerome, Jr. *manufacturing company executive, consultant*
Regenstreif, Herbert *lawyer*
Regn Fraher, Bonnie *special education educator*
Rehm, Leo Frank *civil engineer*
Rehmus, Charles Martin *law educator, arbitrator*
Reich, Robert Bernard *federal official, political economics educator*
Reiche, Frank Perley *lawyer, former federal commissioner*
Reichman, Fredrick Thomas *artist*
Reichmanis, Elsa *chemist*
Reid, Harry *senator*
Reid, Lorene Frances *middle school educator*
Reid-Bills, Mae *editor, historian*
Reidenbaugh, Lowell Henry *retired sports editor*
Reifsnider, Kenneth Leonard *metallurgist, educator*
Reilly, Edward Francis, Jr. *former state senator, federal agency administrator*
Reinhardt, John Edward *former international affairs specialist*
Reinhardt, Stephen Roy *federal judge*
Reinke, Ralph Louis *retired academic administrator*
Reisch, Michael Stewart *social work educator*
Reiser, Paul *actor, comedian*
Reister, Ruth Alkema *lawyer, business executive*
Reitan, Daniel Kinseth *electrical and computer engineering educator*
Reiter, Glenn Mitchell *lawyer*
Religa, James Paul *software engineer*
Remer, Donald Sherwood *engineering economist, cost estimator, educator*
Reminger, Richard Thomas *lawyer*
Remley, Audrey Wright *retired educational administrator, psychologist*
Renaud, Bernadette Marie Elise *author*
Renda, Dominic Phillip *airline executive*
Renda, Rosa A. *special education educator*
Renson, Jean Felix *psychiatry educator*
Reppen, Norbjorn Dag *electrical engineer, consultant*
Resnick, Myron J. *retired insurance company executive, lawyer*
Resnik, Regina *operatic singer*
Retz, William Andrew *retired naval officer*
Reuber, Grant Louis *banking insurance company executive*
Reuman, Robert Everett *philosophy educator*
Revor, Barbara Kay *secondary school educator*
Rey, Nicholas Andrew *ambassador*
†Reyes, Silvestre *congressman*
Reynolds, Billie Iles *financial representative and counselor, former association executive*
Reynolds, Carl Christiansen *government official*
Reynolds, Geneva B. *special education educator*
Reynolds, Jack W. *retired utility company executive*
Reynolds, John Francis *insurance company executive*
Reynolds, Louise Maxine Kruse *retired school nurse*
Reynolds, R. John *university administrator*
Reynolds, William Bradford *lawyer*
Rhame, Thomas Gene *army officer*
Rhein, Murray Harold *management consultant*
Rhett, John Taylor, Jr. *government official, civil engineer*
Rhoads, James Berton *archivist, former government official, consultant, educator*
Rhodes, John Jacob *lawyer, former congressman*
Rhodes, Peter Edward *label company executive*
Riasanovsky, Nicholas Valentine *historian, educator*
Ricards, June Elaine *nursing consultant, administrator*
Rice, Gary Russell *special education educator*
Rice, Joseph Albert *banker*
Rice, Patricia Oppenheim Levin *special education educator, consultant*
Rice, Richard Campbell *retired state official, retired army officer*
Rice, Richard Lee *retired architect*
Rice, Roger Douglas *television executive, artist*
Rice, Stanley Travis, Jr. *poet, painter, English language educator*
Rice, Stuart Alan *chemist, educator*
Rice, Walter Herbert *federal judge*
Rich, David Barry *city official, auditor, accountant, entertainer*
Rich, John *film and television producer, director*
Richard, Edward H. *manufacturing company executive, former municipal government official*
Richard, Susan Mathis *communications executive*
Richards, Kenneth Edwin *management consultant*
Richards, Paul Linford *physics educator, researcher*
Richardson, Charles Clifton *biochemist, educator*
Richardson, Elsie Helen *retired elementary education educator*
Richardson, John Carroll *lawyer, tax legislative consultant*
Richardson, Kenneth T., Jr. *psychotherapist, consultant, educator, author*
Richardson, Natasha Jane *actress*
Richardson, Richard Thomas *retired banker*
Richardson, Robert Dale, Jr. *English language educator*
Richardson, Roy *management consultant*
Richardson, Wanda Louise Gibson *family practice nurse*
†Richey, Thomas Adam *advertising executive*
Richman, Alan *magazine editor*
Richman, Gertrude Gross (Mrs. Bernard Richman) *civic worker*
Richman, Marvin Jordan *real estate developer, investor, educator*
Richman, Paul *semiconductor industry executive, educator*
Richman, Peter *electronics executive*
Richmond, Julius Benjamin *retired physician, health policy educator emeritus*
Richstone, Beverly June *psychologist*
Richter, Susan Mary *medical and surgical nurse*
Rickard, Norman Edward *office equipment company executive*
Rickard, Ruth David *retired history and political science educator*
Rickel, Annette Urso *psychology educator*
Rickert, Jonathan Bradley *foreign service officer*
Rickey, George Warren *artist, sculptor, educator*
Ridder, Paul Anthony *newspaper executive*
Riddle, Donald Husted *former university chancellor*
Riddle, James Douglass *retired academic administrator*
Rideout, Patricia Irene *operatic, oratorio and concert singer*
Ridloff, Richard *real estate executive, lawyer, consultant*
Riecken, Henry William *psychologist, research director*
Riehecky, Janet Ellen *writer*
Ries, Barbara Ellen *alcohol and drug abuse services professional*
Rifkin, Ned *museum director*
Riggs, Jacki Pieracci *educational consultant*
Riggs, Sonya Woicinski *elementary school educator*
Righter, Walter Cameron *bishop*
Riker, Walter F., Jr. *pharmacologist, physician*
Rimel, Rebecca Webster *foundation executive*
Rimpila, Charles Robert *physician*
Ring, Victoria A. *small business owner*
Rinzel, Daniel Francis *lawyer*
Risk, John Fred *banker, investment banker*
Riss, Robert Bailey *real estate investor*
Ritcheson, Charles Ray *university administrator, history educator*
Ritchie, Anne *educational administrator*
Ritter-Clough, Elise Dawn *consultant, private investor*
Rivas, Ernesto *newspaper columnist*
Rivers, Kenneth Jay *judicial administrator, consultant*
Rivkind, Perry Abbot *federal railroad agency administrator*
Roaden, Arliss Lloyd *retired higher education executive director, former university president*
Robb, Lynda Johnson *writer*
Robbins, Frances Elaine *educational administrator*
Roberson, James O. *foundation executive*
Roberts, Alfred Wheeler, III *law firm executive*
Roberts, Delmar Lee *editor*
Roberts, Doris *actress*
Roberts, Francis Joy *educational consultant*
Roberts, James G. *foundation executive*
Roberts, Joan I. *social psychologist, educator*
Roberts, John Benjamin, II *public policy consultant, television producer, writer*
Roberts, John Glover, Jr. *lawyer*
Roberts, Marie Dyer *computer systems specialist*
Roberts, Maura M. *secondary school educator*
Roberts, Paul Craig, III *economics educator, author, columnist*
Roberts, Thomas Morgan *former government official*
Roberts, Wess *author*
Robertson, A. Haeworth *actuary, benefit consultant, foundation executive*
Robertson, Cliff *actor, writer, director*
Robertson, John Archibald Law *nuclear scientist*
Robertson, Mark Wayne *investment specialist*
Robertson, Mary Virginia *retired elementary education educator*
Robertson, R(ita) Kae *nurse, administrator*
Robertson, Wyndham Gay *university official*
Robins, Norman Alan *strategic planning consultant, former steel company executive*
Robinson, Angela Tomei *clinical laboratory scientist*
Robinson, Bob Leo *international investment services executive*
Robinson, Bruce Butler *physicist*
Robinson, Charlotte Hill *artist*
Robinson, David Adair *neurophysiologist*
Robinson, Gail Patricia *mental health counselor*
Robinson, James Arthur *university president emeritus, political scientist*
Robinson, Linda Gosden *communications executive*
Robinson, Marshall Alan *economics educator, foundation executive*
Robinson, Phil Alden *director*
Robison, James Everett *management consulting company executive*
Robson, Marian Lorraine *Canadian federal official*
Rochberg, George *composer, educator*
Rock, Richard Rand *lawyer, former state senator*
Rockburne, Dorothea Grace *artist*
†Rockefeller, Winthrop P. *state official*
Rockstein, Morris *science writer, editor, consultant*
Rodbell, Clyde Armand *distribution executive*
Rodenberg-Roberts, Mary Patricia *advocacy services administrator, lawyer*
Rodgers, Lawrence Rodney *physician, educator*
Rodgers, Nancy Lucille *corporate executive*
Rodrigues, Alfred Benjamin Kameeiamoku *marketing consultant*
†Rodriguez, Alexander Emmanuel *professional baseball player*
Rodriguez, Elena Garcia *retired pension fund administrator*
Rodriguez, Elias C. *judge*
Rodriguez, Nora *social worker*

Shanahan, Eileen Frances *secondary education educator*
Shanahan, Michael George *police officer*
Shank, Maurice Edwin *aerospace engineering executive, consultant*
Shanks, Ann Zane *filmmaker, producer/director, photographer, writer*
Shanks, Kathryn Mary *health care administrator*
Shannon, Margaret T. *nursing administrator, educator*
Shapiro, Ivan *lawyer*
Shapiro, Karl Jay *poet, former educator*
Shapiro, Leo J. *social researcher*
Shapiro, Marcia Haskel *speech and language pathologist*
Shapiro, Michael Edward *museum administrator, curator, art historian*
Shapiro, Richard Charles *sales and marketing executive*
Shapiro, Sumner *retired naval officer, business executive*
Sharick, Merle Dayton, Jr. *mortgage insurance company executive*
Sharkey, Leonard Arthur *automobile company executive*
Sharpe, Sterling *former professional football player, sports commentator*
Sharpe, William Forsyth *economics educator*
Sharwell, William Gay *retired university president and company executive*
Shasteen, Donald Eugene *government official*
Shatin, Judith *music composing educator*
Shattuck, Cathie Ann *lawyer, former government official*
Shattuck, Roger Whitney *author, educator*
Shaw, Artie *musician, writer, lecturer*
Shaw, David Elliot *financial executive*
Shaw, Dean Alvin *architect*
Shaw, Helen Lester Anderson *university dean*
Shaw, John Frederick *retired naval officer*
Shaw, Melvin Phillip *physicist, engineering educator, psychologist*
Shaw, Ronald Ahrend *physician, educator*
Shea, Bernard Charles *retired pharmaceutical company executive*
Sheaff, Richard Dana *graphic designer*
Shearer, Charles Livingston *academic administrator*
Shearing, Miriam *justice*
Sheedy, Patrick Thomas *judge*
Sheehy, Gail Henion *author*
Sheeline, Paul Cushing *hotel executive*
Sheh, Robert Bardhyl *environmental management company executive*
Shelan, Debbie Levin *travel agency administrator, school system administrator*
Sheldon, Terry Edwin *lawyer, business consultant, advisor*
Shelet, Dawn Ardelle *financial analyst*
Shellman-Lucas, Elizabeth C. *special education educator, researcher*
Shelton, Karl Mason *management consultant*
Shelton, Philip Anderson *criminal investigator, writer*
Shelton, Sloane *actress*
Shelton, Stephani *broadcast journalist, consultant*
Shemansky, Cindy Ann *nursing educator*
Shepard, Alan Bartlett, Jr. *former astronaut, real estate developer*
Shepherd, Mark, Jr. *retired electronics company executive*
Shepherd, Robert James *plant pathology researcher, retired educator*
Shepherd, Steven Stewart *auditor, consultant*
Sheppard, Harold Lloyd *gerontologist, educator*
Sher, Paul Phillip *physician, pathologist*
Sherf, Sandee Croft *real estate corporation executive*
Sheridan, Diane Frances *public policy facilitator*
Sheridan, Patrick Michael *finance company executive*
Sheridan, Sonia Landy *artist, retired art educator*
Sherin, Edwin *theatrical and film director, actor*
Sherman, John Foord *biomedical consultant*
Sherman, Joseph Howard *clergyman*
Sherman, Joseph Owen *pediatric surgeon*
Sherman, Kathryn Ann *communication professional*
Sherman, Richard H. *education educator*
Shernoff, Elise Rubin *special education educator*
†Sherrer, Gary *state official*
Sherwood, (Peter) Louis *retail executive*
Shields, H. Richard *tax consultant,business executive*
Shields, Rana Colleen *special education educator*
Shikuma, Eugene Yujin *travel agency executive*
Shillingsburg, Miriam Jones *English educator, academic administrator*
Shils, Maurice Edward *physician, educator*
Shimoda, Jerry Yasutaka *retired national historic park superintendent*
Shin, Edward Sung-Shik *bilingual education educator*
Shindler, Merrill Karsh *writer, radio personality*
Shipley, Lucia Helene *retired chemical company executive*
Shirley, David Arthur *chemistry educator, science administrator*
Shirley-Quirk, John *concert and opera singer*
Shockley, Edward Julian *aerospace company executive*
Shook, Ann Jones *lawyer*
Shoop, Glenn Powell *investment consultant*
Shore, Harvey Harris *business educator*
Shore, Stephen *photographer*
Shotwell, Malcolm Green *retired minister*
Shreiner, Curt *educational technologist, consultant*
Shreve, Susan Richards *author, English literature educator*
Shughart, Donald Louis *lawyer*
Shull, Claire *documentary film producer, casting director*
Shultis, Robert Lynn *finance educator, cost systems consultant, retired professional association executive*
Shultz, Linda Joyce *retired library director*
Shumacker, Harris B., Jr. *surgeon, educator, author*
Shuman, Samuel Irving *lawyer, law educator*
Shur, Michael *electrical engineer, educator, consultant*
Shure, Myrna Beth *psychologist, educator*
Shuster, John A. *civil engineer*
Shute, Richard Emil *government official, engineer*
Shyer, Charles Richard *screenwriter, film director*
Sices, David *language educator, translator*
Sicuro, Natale Anthony *academic and financial administrator, consultant*
Siddayao, Corazón Morales *economist, educator, energy and environment consultant*
Siefer, Stuart B. *architect*
Siegel, Jack Morton *retired biotechnology company executive*
Siegel, Laurence Gordon *conductor*
Sifontes, Jose E. *pediatrics educator*
Sigmond, Carol Ann *lawyer*
Sikes, Cynthia Lee *actress, singer*
Silberberg, Inga *dermatologist*
Silberman, Curt C. *lawyer*
Silberman, Laurence Hirsch *federal judge*
Siljak, Dragoslav D. *engineering educator*
Silkett, Robert Tillson *food business consultant*
Sills, Richard Reynolds *scientist, educator*
Silva, Omega Logan *physician*
Silverberg, Stuart Owen *obstetrician, gynecologist*
Silverman, Michael *manufacturing company executive*
Silverstein, Barbara Ann *conductor*
Silverstein, Martin Elliot *surgeon, author, consultant*
Silvestri, Alan Anthony *film composer*
Silvius, Donald Joe *educational consultant*
Simecka, Betty Jean *marketing executive*
Simeral, William Goodrich *retired chemical company executive*
Simmons, Raymond Hedelius *lawyer*
Simmons, Ted Conrad *writer*
Simms, Maria Ester *health services administrator*
Simon, Melvin *real estate developer, professional basketball executive*
Simone, Regina *family practice physician*
Simonet, John Thomas *banker*
Simons, Lewis Martin *journalist*
Simons, Thomas W., Jr. *ambassador*
Simpson, Alan Kooi *former senator*
Simpson, Bob G. *retired quality assurance professional*
Simpson, Frederick James *retired research administrator*
Simpson, Madeline Louisa *psychologist*
Simpson, Murray *engineer, consultant*
Simpson, O. J. (Orenthal James Simpson) *former professional football player, actor, sports commentator*
Sims, Albert Maurice *marketing professional*
Sims, Keith *professional football player*
Sims, Kent Otway *economist*
Sinclair, Carole *publisher, editor, author*
Sinclair, Virgil Lee, Jr. *judge, writer*
Sincoff, Michael Z. *human resources and marketing professional*
Singer, David Michael *marketing and public relations company executive*
Singer, Markus Morton *retired trade association executive*
Singleton, Philip Arthur *corporate executive*
Sinicropi, Anthony Vincent *industrial relations and human resources educator*
Sinining, Vicente C. *education educator*
Siper, Cynthia Dawn *special education educator*
Siskel, Gene (Eugene Kal Siskel) *film critic*
Sisto, Elena *artist, educator*
Sjostrand, Fritiof Stig *biologist, educator*
Skaff, Joseph John *state agency administrator, retired army officer*
Skaggs, Bebe Rebecca Patten *college dean, clergywoman*
Skala, Gary Dennis *electric and gas utilities executive management consultant*
Skinner, James Stanford *physiologist, educator*
Skinner, Patricia Morag *state legislator*
†Skolnick, Lawrence *neonatologist, medical administrator*
Skolovsky, Zadel *concert pianist, educator*
Skowronski, Vincent Paul *concert violinist, recording artist, executive producer, producer classical recordings*
Skratek, Sylvia Paulette *mediator, arbitrator, dispute systems designer*
Skromme, Lawrence H. *consulting agricultural engineer*
Slagle, Jacob Winebrenner, Jr. *food products executive*
Slavitt, David Walton *retired lawyer*
Slayton, William Larew *planning consultant, former government official*
Slewitzke, Connie Lee *retired army officer*
Sloyan, Gerard Stephen *religious studies educator, priest*
Smally, Donald Jay *consulting engineering executive*
Smietana, Walter *educational research director*
Smith, Ann C. *nursing educator*
Smith, Barbara Anne *healthcare management company consultant*
Smith, Carter Blakemore *broadcaster*
Smith, Charles Conard *refractory company executive*
Smith, Charles Haddon *geoscientist, consultant*
Smith, Charlotte Reed *retired music educator*
Smith, Chester *broadcasting executive*
Smith, Christine *author, lecturer, former pharmaceutical executive*
Smith, Dentye M. *library media specialist*
Smith, Doris Victoria *educational agency administrator*
Smith, Edward K. *economist, consultant*
Smith, Edward Reaugh *retired lawyer, cemetery and funeral home consultant*
Smith, Elmer W. *retired federal government administrator*
Smith, Fern M. *federal judge*
Smith, Floyd Leslie *insurance company executive*
Smith, Frederick Coe *manufacturing executive*
Smith, George Drury *publisher, editor, collagist, writer*
Smith, George Patrick, II *lawyer, educator*
Smith, Goff *industrial equipment manufacturing executive*
Smith, Gregory Scott *medical researcher, educator*
Smith, Hedrick Laurence *journalist, television commentator, author, lecturer*
Smith, Howard McQueen *librarian*
Smith, Ileene A. *book editor*
Smith, James A. *lawyer*
Smith, Jane Wardell *historian, philanthropist, entrepreneur*
Smith, Jonathan David *medical educator*
Smith, Kathleen Ann *mathematics educator*
Smith, Kathryn Ann *advertising executive*
Smith, Kenneth Blose *former financial executive*
Smith, Lauren Ashley *lawyer, journalist, clergyman, physicist*
Smith, Lawrence Leighton *conductor*
Smith, Leighton Warren, Jr. *naval officer*
Smith, Leonard, Jr. *medical/surgical and oncology nurse*
Smith, Leonore Rae *artist*
Smith, Lois Arlene *actress, writer*
Smith, Loren Allan *federal judge*
Smith, Loretta Mae *contracting officer*
Smith, Margaret Taylor *volunteer*
Smith, Martin Bernhard *journalist*
Smith, Martin Cruz *author*
Smith, Martin Henry *pediatrician*
Smith, Martin Lane *biomedical researcher*
Smith, Marya Jean *writer*
Smith, Paul Vergon, Jr. *corporate executive, retired oil company executive*
Smith, Paula Marion *urology and medical/surgical nurse*
Smith, Philip Luther *patent information scientist*
Smith, Richard Anthony *investment banker*
Smith, Richard Grant *retired telecommunications executive, electrical engineer*
Smith, Robert Hugh *engineering construction company executive*
Smith, Robert Powell *former ambassador, former foundation executive*
Smith, Ronald Ehlbert *lawyer, referral-based distributor, public speaker, writer and motivator*
Smith, Ronald Lynn *health system executive*
Smith, Russell Francis *transportation executive*
Smith, Sallye Wrye *librarian*
Smith, Seymour Maslin *financial advisor, investment banker*
Smith, Thomas Winston *cotton marketing executive*
Smith, V. Kerry *economics educator*
Smith, Verna Mae Edom *sociology educator, freelance writer, photographer*
Smith, Wilburn Jackson, Jr. *retired bank executive*
Smither, Howard Elbert *musicologist*
Smock, Raymond William *historian*
Smoot, Hazel Lampkin *retired piano teacher, poet*
Smoot, Wendell McMeans, Jr. *investment counselor*
Snelling, Robert Orren, Sr. *franchising executive*
Snelson, Kenneth Duane *sculptor*
Snetsinger, David Clarence *retired animal feed company executive*
Snider, L. Britt *government executive*
†Snoddon, Larry Erle *public relations executive*
Snortland, Howard Jerome *educational financial consultant*
Snow, John William *railroad executive*
Snow, Marina Sexton *author*
Snow, W. Sterling *secondary education educator, retired sports coach*
Snowden, Lawrence Fontaine *retired aircraft company executive, retired marine corps general officer*
Snyder, Alan Carhart *insurance company executive*
Snyder, Gary Sherman *poet*
Snyder, Stephen Edward *lawyer, mediator*
Snyder, Susan Brooke *retired English literature educator*
Snyder, William Burton *insurance executive*
Sobczak, Darlene Marie *police officer*
Soderberg, Nancy *federal agency administrator*
Sodolski, John *retired association administrator*
Soeth, Sarah Laverne Reedy McMillan *psychiatric nurse*
Sokal, Robert Reuven *biology educator, author*
Soles, Ada Leigh *former state legislator, government advisor*
Sollender, Joel David *management consultant, financial executive*
Sollid, Faye Eising *volunteer*
Sollon, Phillip Benedict *pharmacist, computer specialist*
Solo, Joyce R. *volunteer*
Solomon, Amelia Kroll *artist*
Solomon, Julius Oscar Lee *pharmacist, hypnotherapist*
Solomon, Robert Charles *philosopher, educator*
Solow, Herbert Franklin *film producer, writer*
Solzhenitsyn, Aleksandr Isayevich *author*
Somasundaran, Ponisseril *surface and colloid engineer, applied science educator*
Somers, Louis Robert *retired food company executive*
Somes, Grant William *statistician, biomedical researcher*
Sommer, Barbara *school administrator*
Sommer, Howard Ellsworth *textile executive*
Sommers, Louise *lawyer*
Sonderegger, Theo Brown *psychology educator*
Sondheim, Stephen Joshua *composer, lyricist*
Sonnenschein, Hugo Freund *academic administrator, economics educator*
Sontag, Susan *writer*
Soper, Anne Marie *psychologist*
Soper, James Herbert *botanist, curator*
Sorel, Edward *artist*
Sorensen, Sheila *state senator*
Sorgi, Deborah Bernadette *educational software company executive*
Soro, Mar Bawai *bishop*
Sorter, Bruce Wilbur *federal program administrator, educator, consultant*
Sotirhos, Michael *ambassador*
Souders, Jean Swedell *artist, educator*
Soule, Sallie Thompson *retired state official*
Souter, David Hackett *United States supreme court justice*
South, Frank Edwin *physiologist, educator*
Southerland, S. Duane *manufacturing company executive*
Southwick, Charles Henry *zoologist, educator*
Southworth, Jamie MacIntyre *education educator*
Souveroff, Vernon William, Jr. *business executive, author*
Soyke, Jennifer Mae *emergency and family physician*
Spada, James *author, publisher*
Spaeth, C. Edmond *library media specialist*
Spagnuolo, Pasqualina Marie *rehabilitation nurse*
Spain, Jayne Baker *corporate executive*
Spain, Steve Randall *secondary school educator*
Spanninger, Beth Anne *lawyer*
Spatta, Carolyn Davis *mediator, consultant*
Spaulding, Frank Henry *librarian*
Speaker, Susan Jane *lawyer*
Speer, Max Michael *special education educator*
Speers, Roland Root, II *lawyer*
Speier, John Leo, Jr. *retired chemist*
Spejewski, Eugene Henry *physicist, educator*
Spence, Andrew *artist, painter*
Spence, Dianna Jeannene *software engineer, educator*
Spence, Glen Oscar *clergyman*
Spence, William Allen *lawyer*
Spencer, David Mills *library administrator*
Spencer, Milton Harry *economics and finance educator*
†Spencer, Peter LeValley, Sr. *editor*
Spencer-Dahlem, Anita Joyce *medical, surgical and critical care nurse*
Spero, Nancy *artist*
Spiekerman, James Frederick *lawyer*
Spiesicke, Margrit Herma *counselor*
Spinelli, Jerry *writer*
Spingola, Jeannie Saundra *college, special education and adult educator, counselor*
Spinner, Robert Jay *orthopedic surgeon*
Spirn, Michele Sobel *communications professional, writer*
Spitaleri, Vernon Rosario *newspaper publisher*
Spitzer, Lyman, Jr. *astronomer*
Spliethoff, William Ludwig *chemical company executive*
Splitstone, George Dale *retired hospital administrator*
Sprenger, Curtis Donald *choir conductor, educator*
Springer, Paul David *lawyer, motion picture company executive*
Springer, Robert Dale *retired air force officer, consultant, lecturer*
Sprinthall, Norman Arthur *psychology educator*
Sprouse, Robert Allen, II *retail chain executive*
Squibb, Samuel Dexter *chemistry educator*
Sreenivasan, Katepalli Raju *mechanical engineering educator*
Srinivasan, Venkataraman *marketing and management educator*
Sroge, Maxwell Harold *marketing consultant, publishing executive*
Stabile, Benedict Louis *retired academic administrator, retired coast guard officer*
Stackhouse, Robert *sculptor*
Stacy, Bill Wayne *academic administrator*
Stadler, Craig Robert *professional golfer*
Staker, Robert Jackson *senior federal judge*
Stallings, Henry E., II *state legislator*
Stallone, Thomas Michael *clinical psychologist*
Stallworth-Barron, Doris A. Carter *librarian, educator*
Stalon, Charles Gary *retired economics educator, institute administrator*
Stamos, John James *judge*
Stamp, Frederick Pfarr, Jr. *federal judge*
Stamper, Malcolm Theodore *aerospace company executive*
Stancil, Irene Mack *family counselor*
Stanfill, Dennis Carothers *business executive*
Stanfill, Shelton G. *performing arts administrator*
Stanley, Margaret King *performing arts administrator*
Stans, Maurice Hubert *retired business consultant, former government official*
Stansell, Ronald Bruce *investment banker*
Stanton, John Jeffrey *editor, broadcast journalist, government programs director, analyst, professional society administrator*
Stanton, Robert John *corporate bank executive, lawyer*
Stapleton, Maureen *actress*
Starer, Robert *composer*
Stark, Diana *public relations and promotion executive*
Stark, Helen Morton *secondary education educator*
Stark, Nellie May *forest ecology educator*
Starkweather, Teresa Madery *artist, educator*
Starnes, Susan Smith *elementary education educator*
Starr, David *newspaper editor, publisher*
Starr, Leon *retired chemical research company executive*
Stavely, Keith Williams Fitzgerald *librarian*
Stearns, Robert Leland *curator*
Steel, Kuniko June *retired artist*
Steen, Carlton Duane *private investor, former food company executive*
Stefano, George B. *neurobiologist, researcher*
Steffens, Dorothy Ruth *political economist*
Steiger, Dale Arlen *publishing executive*
Stein, Dale Franklin *retired university president*
Steinberg, Joan Emily *retired middle school educator*
Steinberg, Melvin Allen *lieutenant governor, lawyer*
Steiner, Michael Louis *pediatrician*
Steinmetz, John Charles *geologist, paleontologist*
Stemberg, Thomas George *retail executive*
Sten, Johannes Walter *control systems engineer, consultant*
Stendahl, Krister *retired bishop*
Stengel, Ronald Francis *management consultant*
Stennett, William Clinton (Clint Stennett) *radio/TV station executive, state senator*
Stephens, C. Michael *service executive*
Stephens, Donald R(ichards) *banker*
Stephens, Edward Carl *communications educator, writer*
Stephens, Elton Bryson *bank executive, service and manufacturing company executive*
Stephenson, Bette Mildred *physician, former Canadian legislator*
Stephenson, Toni Edwards *publisher, investment management executive*
Steptoe, Mary Lou *lawyer*
Stern, Arthur Paul *electronics company executive, electrical engineer*
Stern, Charles *retired foreign trade company executive*
Stern, Daniel *author, executive, educator*
Stern, Marilyn *picture editor, photographer, writer*
Stern, Milton *chemical company executive*
Stern, Nancy Fortgang *mathematics and computer science, educator*
Sternhagen, Frances *actress*
Stevens, Berton Louis, Jr. *data processing manager*
Stevens, John Flournoy *priest*
Stevens, Lisa Gay *minister, choral director*
Stevens, May *artist*
Stevens, Shane *novelist*
Stevens, Warren *actor*
Stevenson, Bryan Allen *lawyer*
Stevenson, Elizabeth *author, educator*
Stevenson, Paul Michael *physics educator, researcher*
Stewart, Arthur Irving, III (Art Stewart) *communications executive*
Stewart, Barbara Ellen *media specialist*
Stewart, Barbara Lynne *geriatrics nursing educator*
Stewart, Carleton M. *banker, corporate director*
Stewart, Cindy Kathleen *school social worker, educator*
Stewart, Clinton Eugene *adult education educator*
Stewart, Daniel Robert *retired glass company executive*
Stewart, Dorothy K. *educator, librarian*
Stewart, Gordon Curran *insurance information association executive*
†Stewart, James Percy *safety and risk management consultant*
Stewart, Joe J. *manufacturing executive*
Stewart, John Ezell *educational and business consultant*
Stewart, Peter Beaufort *retired beverage company executive*
Stewart, Richard Alfred *business executive*
Stewart, Robert Gordon *former museum curator*
Stewart, Thomas James, Jr. *baritone*
Stewart-Pérez, Renice Ann *writer*
Stickle, David Walter *microbiologist*
Stickler, Fred Charles *manufacturing company executive*
Stickler, Gunnar Brynolf *pediatrician*

Vecchione, Jane Frances school nurse
Vega, J. William aerospace engineering executive, consultant
Velzy, Charles O. mechanical engineer
Vermeule, Emily Townsend (Mrs. Cornelius C. Vermeule, III) classicist, educator
Verney, Judith La Baie health program administrator
Vernon, Carl Atlee, Jr. retired wholesale food distributor executive
Veronis, George geophysicist, educator
Verplanck, William Samuel psychologist, educator
Vessey, John William, Jr. army officer
Vestal, Thelma Shaw history educator
Vidal, Gore writer
Vila, Adis Maria corporate executive, former government official, lawyer
Villella, Edward Joseph ballet dancer, educator, choreographer, artistic director
Villoch, Kelly Carney art director
Vincent, Hal Wellman marine corps officer, investor
Vinroot, Richard Allen lawyer, mayor
Viorst, Milton writer
Virkhaus, Taavo symphony orchestra conductor
Vitaliano, Charles J(oseph) geologist, educator
Vitt, David Aaron medical manufacturing company executive
Vittetoe, Marie Clare retired clinical laboratory science educator
Viverito, Louis S. state legislator
Voelker, Margaret Irene (Meg Voelker) gerontology, medical, surgical nurse
Vogel, H. Victoria psychotherapist, educator
Vohs, James Arthur health care program executive
Voight, Elizabeth Anne lawyer
Voigt, Cynthia author
Voketaitis, Arnold Mathew bass-baritone, educator
Volcker, Paul A. economist
Volkhardt, John Malcolm food company executive
Vollmer, Richard Wade federal judge
Volpe, Edmond L(oris) college president
Voltz, Jeanne Appleton author
von Hoffman, Nicholas writer, former journalist
von Schwarz, Carolyn M. Geiger psychotherapist, educator
Vook, Frederick Ludwig physicist, consultant
Voorhees, James Dayton, Jr. lawyer
Vorous, Margaret Estelle primary and secondary school educator
Vosburgh, Margaret Murphy hospital administrator
Voss, Omer Gerald truck company executive
Vradenburg, George, III lawyer
Waddell, Harry Lee editor, publisher
Waddle, John Frederick former retail chain executive
Wademan, Patsy Ann psychiatric, geriatrics nurse
Wadley, M. Richard consumer products executive
Wadsworth, Jacqueline Dorèt private investor
Wagman, Robert John journalist, author
Wagner, Julia A(nne) retired editor
Wagner, Marilyn Faith elementary school educator
Wagner, Richard business executive, former baseball team executive
Wagner, Sigurd electrical engineering educator, researcher
Wagoner, Geraldine Vander Pol music educator
Wahl, Floyd Michael geologist
Wain, Christopher Henry Fairfax Moresby actuary, insurance and investment consultant
Wakeman, Olivia Van Horn marketing professional
Walash, Eileen Robin (Lee Walash) promotions and public relations specialist
Wald, Francine Joy Weintraub (Mrs. Bernard J. Wald) physicist, academic administrator
Waldman, Paul artist
Waldo, Burton Corlett lawyer
Waldon, Alton Ronald, Jr. state senator
Waldrop, Gideon William composer, conductor, former president music school
Waldrop, Linda McGill medical administrator
Walenga, Jeanine Marie medical educator, researcher
Walker, Bradford C. architect
Walker, Craig Michael lawyer
Walker, John Neal agricultural engineering educator
Walker, John Sumpter, Jr. lawyer
Walker, Lannon foreign service officer
Walker, Lawrence D. lawyer
Walker, Leroy Tashreau university chancellor, coach
Walker, Loren Haines electrical engineer
Walker, Mark A. lawyer
Walker, Mary L. lawyer
Wall, M. Danny finance company executive
Wallace, F. Blake aerospace executive, mechanical engineer
Wallace, William Augustine philosophy and history educator
Wallach, Amei Marione journalist, art critic
Wallach, Eli actor
Wallack, Rina Evelyn lawyer
Wallen, Lina Hambali educator, consultant
Waller, Ephraim Everett retired professional association executive
Waller, Gary Fredric English language educator, administrator, poet
Walls, Carmage Lee, Jr. newspaper executive, consultant
Walner, Robert Joel lawyer
Walsh, Diane pianist
Walsh, Edward Patrick federal agency administrator
Walsh, Thomas A. production designer
Walsh, William Albert management consultant, former naval officer
Walston, Ray actor
Walter, J. Jackson foundation executive, consultant
Walter, John Robert printing company executive
Walthall, Lee Wade artistic director, dancer
Walton, Harold Vincent former agricultural engineering educator, academic administrator
Wambaugh, Joseph author
Ward, Edward Wells telecommunications executive
Ward, Elaine artist
Ward, Fred actor
Ward, Lynda Sue Scoville special education educator, writer
Ward, Susan Marie cultural organization administrator
Warder, Richard Currey, Jr. dean, mechanical aerospace engineering educator
Warfel, John Hiatt medical educator, retired
Warlick, Roger Kinney history educator, assistant dean
Warner, Heidi C. clinical research nurse
Warner, Walter Duke corporate executive
Warshawsky, Isidore physicist, consultant
Wartella, Ellen Ann communications educator, consultant
Washington, Grover, Jr. musician, producer, composer, arranger
Washington, Valora foundation administrator
Washington, Walter retired academic administrator
Wasseen, Marjorie rehabilitation nurse, administrator
†Wasserman, Anthony Ira software company executive, educator
Wasserman, Helene Waltman art dealer, artist
Wasserstein, Wendy playwright
Wasson, James Walter aircraft manufacturing company executive
Waters, Betty Lou newspaper reporter, writer
Waters, Cheryl Diane accountant
Waters, Donald Eugene academic administrator
Waters, John film director, writer, actor
Wathen, Daniel Everett state supreme court chief justice
Watkins, Cheryl Denise special education educator
Watkins, James David food products executive
Watkins, James David government official, naval officer
Watring, Watson Glenn gynecologic oncologist, educator
Watson, Keith Stuart lawyer
Watson, W. H. bishop
Watson, W(allace) Robert financial executive
Watt, John H. financial executive
Wattenberg, Albert physicist, educator
Watts, Dave Henry retired corporate executive
Watts, Glenn Ellis union official
Watts, Ronald Lester retired military officer
Waymouth, John Francis physicist, consultant
Weadon, Donald Alford, Jr. lawyer
Wearn, Wilson Cannon retired media executive
Weatherstone, Sir Dennis bank executive
Weaver, Charles Horace educator
Weaver, Edward T. foundation executive, educator
Weaver, Esther Ruth medical and surgical, geriatrics and oncology nurse
Weaver, Howard C. newspaper executive
Weaver, Peggy (Marguerite McKinnie Weaver) plantation owner
Weaver, William Charles retired industrial executive
Webb, John Gibbon, III lawyer
Weber, Arthur magazine executive
Weber, Eugen historian, educator, author
Weber, Fred J. retired state supreme court justice
Weber, John Walter insurance company executive
Weber, Julian L. lawyer, former publishing and entertainment company executive
Weber, Mary Ellen Healy economist
Webster, John Kingsley Ohl, II health administrator, rehabilitation manager
Wechsler, Arnold osteopathic obstetrician, gynecologist
Wechter, Vivienne Thaul artist, poet, educator
Weckesser, Ernest Prosper, Jr. publisher, educator
Wedeen, Marvin Meyer hospital executive
Weichler, Nancy Karen pediatric nurse
Weidner, Roswell Theodore artist
Weightman, Esther Lynn emergency trauma nurse
Weigle, Robert Edward civil engineer, research director
Weikart, David Powell educational research foundation administrator
Weil, Peter Henry lawyer
Weil, Rolf Alfred economist, university president emeritus
Weiland, Charles Hankes lawyer
Weimer, Gary W. academic administrator, consultant
Weinberg, Steven physics educator
Weinberger, Arnold retired electrical engineer
Weinberger, Siegbert Jacob food company executive
Weiner, Louis Max retired mathematics educator
Weiner-Heuschkel, Sydell theater educator
Weingarten, Joseph Leonard aerospace engineer
Weinhauer, William Gillette retired bishop
Weinkauf, Mary Louise Stanley clergywoman
Weinschel, Bruno Oscar engineering executive, physicist
Weinsier, Philip David electronics educator
Weinstock, Ronald Jay research and development company executive
Weir, Kenneth Wynn marine corps officer, experimental test pilot
Weir, Thomas Charles banker
Weisburger, Elizabeth Kreiser chemist, editor
Weisinger, Ronald Jay economic development consultant, real estate developer
Weisman, Lorenzo David investment banker
Weismantel, Gregory Nelson management consultant and software executive
Weiss, Alan musician, educator
Weiss, Bruce Jordan academic administrator
Weiss, Kenneth Jay education educator, reading specialist, administrator
Weiss, Max Tibor retired aerospace company executive
Weiss, Michael James chemistry educator
Weiss, Robert M. urologist, educator
Weissman, Jack (George Anderson) editor
Welch, Oliver Wendell retired pharmaceutical executive
Weldon, Jeffrey Alan lawyer
Weldon, William Forrest electrical and mechanical engineer, educator
Welles, John Galt retired museum director
Wells, Robert Hartley chemistry professional
Wells, Toni Lynn accountant
Welsome, Eileen journalist
Welton, Alice Gordon (Guilfoy) artist
Welton, Theodore Allen retired theoretical physics educator, consultant
Wendt, Marilynn Suzann elementary school educator, principal
Wenger, Vicki interior designer
Wengert, Norman Irving political science educator
Wentworth, Malinda Ann Nachman former small business owner, real estate broker
Wenzel, Richard Putnam internist
Wenzel, Sandra Lee Ann pediatrics nurse
Werkman, Rosemarie Anne past public relations professional, civic worker
Werman, Thomas Ehrlich record producer
Werner-Jacobsen, Emmy Elisabeth developmental psychologist
Werth, Andrew M. telecommunications executive
Wesely, Marissa Celeste lawyer
Wessel, Morris Arthur pediatrics educator
Wessel, Peter lawyer
Wessler, Richard Lee psychology educator, psychotherapist
West, Gregory Alan physician
West, Kathleen Shea special education educator, reading specialist
West, Rexford Leon banker
Westmoreland, Barbara Fenn neurologist, electroencephalographer, educator
Wettig, Patricia actress
Wetzel, Donald Truman engineering company executive
Wexler, Jacqueline Grennan (Mrs. Paul J. Wexler) former association executive and college president
Whalen, Charles William, Jr. author, business executive, educator
Whalen, Loretta Theresa religious educational administrator
Whalen-Blaauwgeers, Herma-Jozé financial analyst
Whaley-Buckel, Marnie social service administrator
Wharton, Margaret Agnes artist
Wharton, Thomas William mining executive
Wheatley, George Milholland medical administrator
Wheeler, Albin Gray U.S. Army career officer, educator, retail executive, law firm executive
Wheeler, Burton M. literature educator, higher education consultant, college dean
Wheeler, David Laurie university dean
Wheeler, George Charles materials and processes engineer
Wheeler, Jack Cox army officer
Wheeler, R(ichard) Kenneth lawyer
Whistler, Roy Lester chemist, educator, industrialist
White, Augustus Aaron, III orthopedic surgeon
White, Charles Olds aeronautical engineer
White, Devon Markes professional baseball player
White, Erskine Norman, Jr. management company executive
White, Gerald Andrew retired chemical company executive
White, Jane See journalist
†White, John Kiernan lighting company executive
†White, Julie Ann foundation executive
White, Kerr Lachlan retired physician, foundation director
White, Leslie Miles parochial school educator
White, Loray Betty public relations executive, writer, actress, producer
White, Renee Allyn judge
White, Richard Clarence lawyer
White, Thomas Edward retired government park official
White, Willis Sheridan, Jr. retired utilities company executive
Whitehouse, Alton Winslow, Jr. retired oil company executive
Whitesell, John Edwin motion picture company executive
Whitley, Nancy O'Neil retired radiology educator
Whitlock, Bennett Clarke, Jr. retired association executive
Whitlock, William Abel retired lawyer
Whitman, Marland Hamilton, Jr. lawyer
Whitmer, Joseph Morton benefits consulting firm executive, retired
Whitmore, James Allen actor
Whitney, Jane foreign service officer
Whitten, Dolphus, Jr. former university administrator, educational consortium executive
Wiatr, Christopher L. microbiologist
Wiatt, James Anthony theatrical agency executive
Wicker, Thomas Grey retired journalist
Wickman, Herbert Hollis physical chemist, condensed matter physicist
Widmark, Richard actor
Wiebe, Leonard Irving radiopharmacist, educator
Wiebenson, Dora Louise architectural historian, educator, author
Wien, Stuart Lewis retired supermarket chain executive
Wies, Barbara editor, publisher
Wiese, Neva critical care nurse
Wiesen, Donald Guy retired diversified manufacturing company executive
Wieser, Siegfried planetarium executive director
Wiesner, John Joseph retail executive
Wiessler, David Albert correspondent
Wigdor, Lawrence Allen chemical company executive
Wiggins, Charles Edward federal judge
Wigler, Andrew Jeffrey lawyer
Wikarski, Nancy Susan information technology consultant
Wilburn, Mary Nelson retired lawyer, writer
Wilde, John artist, educator
Wildhack, John Robert producer, broadcast executive
Wildhack, William August, Jr. lawyer
Wiley, Carl Ross timber company executive
Wiley, Myra mental health nurse, educator
Wiley, Richard Arthur lawyer
Wilhelmsen, Harold John accountant, operations controller
Wilkens, Leonard Randolph, Jr. (Lenny Wilkens) professional basketball coach
Wilkerson, Charles Edward architect
Wilkins, Roger Carson retired insurance company executive
Wilkinson, Doris medical sociology educator
Wilkinson, Rebecca Elaine human resources application specialist
Wilkinson, Stanley Ralph agronomist
Wilks, Duffy Jean counselor, educator
Will, Joanne Marie food and consumer services executive, communications consultant, writer
Wille, Wayne Martin retired editor
Willenbecher, John artist
Willey, Gordon Randolph retired anthropologist, archaeologist, educator
Williams, Carolyn Elizabeth manufacturing executive
Williams, Charles Wesley technical executive, researcher
Williams, David Keith technical trainer
Williams, Earle Carter retired professional services company executive
Williams, Ervin Eugene religious organization administrator
Williams, Henry Stratton radiologist, educator
Williams, James Orrin university administrator, educator
Williams, John Christopher Richard bishop
Williams, Joseph Theodore oil and gas company executive
Williams, Louis Clair, Jr. public relations executive
Williams, Patrick Moody composer
Williams, Richard Clarence retired librarian
Williams, Robert Leon psychiatrist, neurologist, educator
Williams, Roger Stewart physician
Williams, Ronald Lee pharmacologist
Williams, Ronald Oscar systems engineer
Williams, Thomas Lloyd psychiatrist
Williams, William John, Jr. lawyer
Williams Jones, Elizabeth financial planner, business consultant
Williams-Monegain, Louise Joel science educator, administrator, retired
Williamson, Edwin Dargan lawyer, former federal official
Williamson, Fletcher Phillips real estate executive
Williamson, Laird stage director, actor
Williamson, Myrna Hennrich retired army officer, lecturer, consultant
Willig, Karl Victor computer firm executive
Willis, Bruce Walter actor, singer
Willis, Selene Lowe electrical engineer, software consultant
Wills, Charles Francis former church executive, retired career officer
Wills, William Ridley, II former insurance company executive, historian
Wilmore, Douglas Wayne physician, surgeon
Wilner, Judith journalist
Wilner, Thomas Bernard lawyer
Wilson, Almon Chapman surgeon, physician, retired naval officer
Wilson, Brandon Laine writer, advertising and public relations consultant, explorer
Wilson, Colin Henry writer
Wilson, Dwight Liston former military officer, investment advisor
Wilson, Gary Lee airline company executive
Wilson, Geneva June gerontology nurse, consultant
Wilson, Hugh Steven lawyer
Wilson, Jane artist
Wilson, Kenneth Geddes physics research administrator, educator
Wilson, Lanford playwright
Wilson, Melvin Edmond civil engineer
Wilson, Nancy singer
Wilson, Paul W., Jr. lawyer, entrepreneur
Wilson, Richard Alexander career officer
Wilson, Robert James Montgomery investment company executive
Wilson, Robin Scott university president, writer
Wilson, Sloan author, lecturer
Wilson, William Glenn, Jr. graphic designer
Wimmer, Nancy T. lawyer
Winder, Robert Owen retired mathematician, computer engineer executive
Wing, James David lawyer
Wing, Lilly Kelly Raynor health services administrator
Wingate, Bettye Faye librarian, educator
Wink, Doreen Musto interior designer
Winslow, John Franklin lawyer
Winter, Alan retired publishing company executive
Winter, Harland Steven pediatric gastroenterologist
Winters, Jonathan actor
Winters, Nola Frances food company executive
Wintle, Rosemarie bio-medical electronic engineer
Winton, Howard Phillip optometrist
Winwood, Stephen Lawrence musician, composer
Winzenried, Jesse David retired petroleum executive
Wise, Patricia lyric coloratura
Wiseman, Jay Donald photographer, mechanical contractor, designer
Witcher, Daniel Dougherty retired pharmaceutical company executive
Witmer, Diane F. communication educator
Witt, Hugh Ernest technology consultant
Witte, Merlin Michael oil company executive
Witte, Raymond Henry psychologist, educator
Wittebort, Robert John, Jr. lawyer, writer, business executive
Wittich, John Jacob retired college president, corporation consultant
Wittner, Loren Antonow lawyer, former public relations executive
Woerner, Robert Lester landscape architect
Wolf, Dale Edward state official
Wolf, Hans Abraham retired pharmaceutical company executive
Wolf, Rosalie Joyce financial executive
Wolf, William Martin computer company executive, consultant
Wolfberg, Melvin Donald optometrist, educational administrator, consultant
Wolfe, Gregory Baker international relations educator
Wolff, Brian Richard metal manufacturing company executive
Wolff, Manfred Ernst medicinal chemist, pharmaceutical company executive
Wolff, Peter Adalbert physicist, educator
†Wolfgang, Gary L. orthopaedic surgeon
Wolfman, Ira Joel editor, writer
Wollert, Gerald Dale retired food company executive, investor
Wolner, Rena Meryl publisher
Wolotkiewicz, Marian M. program director
Wolters, Oliver William history educator
Womach, Emily Hitch retired banker and marketing and public relations executive
Wommack, W(illiam) W(alton) retired manufacturing company executive
Wonders, William Clare geography educator
Wong, David Yue academic administrator, physics educator
Wood, Allen John electrical engineer, consultant
Wood, Andrée Robitaille archaeologist, researcher
Wood, Diane Pamela federal judge
Wood, Elwood Steven, III chemical company executive
Wood, Margaret Gray dermatologist, educator
Wood, Marian Starr publishing company executive
Wood, Robert Coldwell political scientist
Woodall, Jack David manufacturing company executive
Woodard, Nina Elizabeth banker
Wooden, John Robert former basketball coach
Woodhouse, Derrick Fergus ophthalmologist
Woodland, Irwin Francis lawyer
Woodruff, Martha Joyce home health agency executive
Woodruff, Virginia broadcast journalist, writer
Woods, Geraldine Pittman health education consultant, educational consultant
Woods, Harriett Ruth retired political organization president
Woods, Phyllis Michalik elementary school educator
Woods, Reginald Foster management consulting executive
Woodward, Clinton Benjamin, Jr. civil engineering educator
Woodward, Thomas Morgan actor
Woosnam, Ian Harold professional golfer
Work, William retired association executive
Workman, Kayleen Marie special education educator
Worley, Gordon Roger retail chain financial executive
Wormwood, Richard Naughton retired naturalist
Worrell, Audrey Martiny geriatric psychiatrist
Worth, Gary James communications executive
Worthen, John Edward academic administrator
Worthey, Carol composer
Wright, Beth Segal art historian, educator
Wright, Charles Spaulding, II writer, communications consultant

Wright, Connie Sue *special education educator*
Wright, Earl Jerome *pastor, bishop*
Wright, Gladys Stone *music educator, composer, writer*
Wright, James David *sociology educator, writer*
Wright, Jeffrey *actor*
Wright, Linda Jean *manufacturing company executive*
Wright, Sir (John) Oliver *retired diplomat*
Wright, Philip Lincoln *zoologist, educator*
Wright, Randolph Earle *retired petroleum company executive*
Wriston, Kathryn Dineen *lawyer, business executive*
Wroble, Lisa Ann *writer, educator*
Wroblowa, Halina Stefania *electrochemist*
Wruck, Erich-Oskar *retired German language educator*
Wrucke-Nelson, Ann C. *elementary school educator*
Wulf, Janie Scott McIlwaine *gifted and talented education educator*
Wussler, Robert Joseph *broadcasting executive, media consultant*
Wustenberg, Wendy Wiberg *public affairs specialist, consultant*
Wyer, Peter Charles *emergency physician*
Wylan, Barbara *artist*
Wyman, Louis Crosby *judge, former senator, former congressman*
Wynette, Tammy *singer*
Wyngaarden, James Barnes *physician*
Wynn, Karla Wray *artist, agricultural products company executive*
Wynne, Linda Marie *administrative assistant, artist*
Yamane, George Mitsuyoshi *oral diagnosis and radiology educator*
Yancey, Jimmie Isaac *marketing professional*
Yanchyshyn, Madelyn *poet, writer*
Yang, Xiangzhong *research scientist, administrator, educator*
Yarbro, Alan David *lawyer*
Yarrow, Peter *folksinger*
Yates, Charles Richardson *former arts center executive*
Yates, David John C. *chemist, researcher*
Yates, Elton G. *retired petroleum industry executive*
Yeager, Mark L. *lawyer*
Yellen, Linda *film director, writer, producer*
Yeo, Ronald Frederick *librarian*
Yielding, K. Lemone *physician*
Ying, John L. *manufacturing executive*
Yntema, Mary Katherine *retired mathematics educator*
Yoakam, Dwight *country western musician*
Yocam, Delbert Wayne *software products company executive*
Yochelson, Bonnie Ellen *museum curator, art historian*
Yodaiken, Ralph E. *pathologist, occupational medicine physician*
Yollick, Bernard Lawrence *otolaryngologic surgeon*
Yolton, John William *philosopher, educator*
York, Shirley Marie *artist*
Yoshiuchi, Ellen Haven *childbirth educator*
Yost, William Albert *psychology educator, hearing researcher*
Yother, Anthony Wayne *critical care nurse, nurse manager*
Young, Edwin S. W. *federal agency official*
Young, Elizabeth Bell *consultant*
Young, John Alan *electronics company executive*
Young, Leo *electrical engineer*
Young, Margaret Chong *elementary education educator*
Young, Michael Kent *lawyer, educator*
Young, Patrick *writer, editor*
Young, Richard Alan *publishing company executive*
Young, Virgil M. *education educator*
Younger, Betty Nichols *social worker*
Youngs, Diane Campfield *learning disabilities specialist, educator*
Yovicich, George Steven Jones *civil engineer*
Yue, Alfred Shui-choh *metallurgical engineer, educator*
Yun, Hsing *head religious order*
Yun, James Kyoon *electrical engineer*
Zacks, Sumner Irwin *pathologist*
Zaffaroni, Alejandro C. *biochemist, medical research company executive*
Zagorin, Janet Susan *professional development director*
Zaillian, Steven *screenwriter, director*
Zajac, Jack *sculptor, painter*
Zajas, J. Jonathan R. *management consulting company executive, principal*
Zaleski, Jean *artist*
Zanetti, Joseph Maurice, Jr. *corporate executive*
Zapf, Hermann *book and type designer*
Zarb, Frank Gustave *insurance brokerage executive*
Zarzour, Robin Ann *special education educator*
Zehring, Karen *information executive*
Zeiger, Scott Leslie *commercial theater executive*
Zeigler, L(uther) Harmon *political science educator*
Zeilinger, Elna Rae *elementary educator, gifted-talented education educator*
Zekman, Terri Margaret *graphic designer*
Zelinsky, Paul O. *illustrator, painter, author*
Zeller, Joseph Paul *advertising executive*
Zenner, Nico *air transportation executive*
Zentz, Patrick James *artist, rancher*
Zhao, Li *fine arts company executive, teacher, consultant*
Zheng, Lisa Liqing *computer consultant*
Zhou, Ming De *aeronautical scientist, educator*
Zhu, Yong *research scientist*
Zick, John Walter *retired accounting company executive*
Ziegenhorn, Eric Howard *lawyer, legal writer*
Ziegler, Jack (Denmore) *cartoonist*
Ziegler, Richard Ferdinand *lawyer*
†Zilbert, Allen Bruce *education educator, computer consultant*
Zimet, Lloyd *psychologist, health planner, educator*
Zimm, Bruno Hasbrouck *physical chemistry educator*
Zimmerman, Harold Samuel *retired state senator, state administrator, newspaper executive*
Zimmerman, Lydia *community health nurse, retired*
Zimny, Max *labor union administrator, lawyer*
Zinnen, Robert Oliver *general management executive*
Ziock, Klaus Otto Heinrich *retired physics educator*
Zischke, Douglas Arthur *foreign service officer*
Zizza, Salvatore J. *diversified company executive*
Zoellick, Robert Bruce *corporate executive, lawyer*
Zohn, Martin Steven *lawyer*
Zoritch, George *dance educator*
Zox, Larry *artist*
Zuck, Alfred Miller *association executive*
Zucker, Jean Maxson *nurse*

Zuckerman, Martin Harvey *personnel director*
Zufryden, Fred S. *academic administrator, marketing educator, researcher*
Zuiches, James Joseph *academic administrator*
Zukin, Paul *retired health research educator*
Zupsic, Matthew Michael *insurance company executive*
Zusy, Catherine *curator*
Zweck, Ruth Edna Feeney *human services administrator, psychiatric nurse*
Zwerver, Peter John *linguistics educator*
Zwislocki, Jozef John *neuroscience educator, researcher*

# Professional Index

†New name in *Who's Who in America*, 52nd Edition

---

## AGRICULTURE

### UNITED STATES

#### ALABAMA

**Tuskegee Institute**
Hill, Walter A. *agricultural sciences educator, researcher*

#### ARKANSAS

**Hot Springs National Park**
Baer, Kenneth Peter *farmer cooperative executive*

**Humphrey**
Wilson, Victoria Jane Simpson *farmer, former nurse*

#### CALIFORNIA

**Arvin**
Pankey, Edgar Edward *rancher*

**Davis**
Carter, Harold O. *agricultural economics educator*
Schneeman, Barbara Olds *agricultural studies educator*

**Hanford**
Hall, Richard Dennis *agribusiness and international trade writer*

**Modesto**
Crawford, Charles McNeil *winery science executive*
Gallo, Ernest *vintner*

**Napa**
Chiarella, Peter Ralph *vintner*

**Sacramento**
Wightman, Thomas Valentine *rancher, researcher*

**San Francisco**
Hills, Austin Edward *vineyard executive*

**San Jose**
D'Arrigo, Stephen, Jr. *agricultural company executive*

**San Luis Obispo**
McCorkle, Robert Ellsworth *agribusiness educator*

**Sierra Madre**
Whittingham, Charles Edward *thoroughbred race horse owner and trainer*

**Trinity Center**
Hartman, Ruth Gayle *rancher*

#### COLORADO

**Fort Collins**
Heird, James C. *agricultural studies educator*

**Kersey**
Guttersen, Michael *ranching and investments professional*

**Ridgway**
Decker, Peter Randolph *rancher, former state official*

**Springfield**
Wessler, Melvin Dean *farmer, rancher*

#### DELAWARE

**Dover**
Carey, V. George *farmer, state legislator*

#### DISTRICT OF COLUMBIA

**Washington**
†Boyd, F. Allen, Jr. *farmer, congressman*
Schmidt, Berlie Louis *agricultural research administrator*

#### FLORIDA

**Cape Canaveral**
Bell, James Bacon *business executive*

**Mount Dora**
Chandler, Robert Flint, Jr. *international agriculture consultant*

**Punta Gorda**
Parvin, Philip E. *retired agricultural researcher and educator*

#### GEORGIA

**Atlanta**
Brooks, David William *farmer cooperative executive*
Stimpert, Michael Alan *agricultural products company executive*
Wright, Daniel *wine specialist, consultant*

#### HAWAII

**Honolulu**
Ching, Chauncey Tai Kin *agricultural economics educator*

**Waialua**
Singlehurst, Dona Geisenheyner *horse farm owner*

#### IDAHO

**Buhl**
Ray, Leo Eldon *fish breeding and marketing company executive*

**Twin Falls**
Jones, Douglas Raymond *farming executive, state legislator*

#### ILLINOIS

**Bloomington**
Jones, Norman Thomas *agricultural products company executive*
Stonier, Daryle L. *agricultural supplies company executive*
Webb, O. Glenn *farm supplies company executive*

**Champaign**
Bentley, Orville George *retired agricultural educator, dean emeritus*

**Homewood**
Reed, Michael A. *agricultural products supplier*

**Jacksonville**
Randall, Robert Quentin *nursery executive*

**Northfield**
Bruns, Nicolaus, Jr. *retired agricultural chemicals company executive, lawyer*

**Pekin**
Frison, Rick *agricultural company executive*

**Urbana**
Cheryan, Munir *agricultural studies educator, biochemical engineering educator*
Hill, Lowell Dean *agricultural marketing educator*

#### INDIANA

**Indianapolis**
Hegel, Carolyn Marie *farmer, farm bureau executive*

**West Lafayette**
Lechtenberg, Victor L. *agricultural studies educator*

#### IOWA

**Ames**
Jacobson, Norman L. *retired agricultural educator, researcher*
Topel, David Glen *agricultural studies educator*

**Charles City**
McCartney, Rhoda Huxsol *farm manager*

**Mason City**
Kuhlman, James Weldon *county extension education director*

**Muscatine**
Kautz, Richard Carl *chemical and feed company executive*

**Vinton**
Jorgensen, Ann *farmer*

#### KANSAS

**Atchison**
Cray, Cloud Lanor, Jr. *grain products company executive*

**Claflin**
Burmeister, Paul Frederick *farmer*

**Haven**
Schlickau, George Hans *cattle breeder, professional association executive*

**Manhattan**
McKee, Richard Miles *animal studies educator*

#### KENTUCKY

**Port Royal**
Berry, Wendell *farmer, author*

#### MARYLAND

**College Park**
Fretz, Thomas A. *agricultural studies educator*

#### MINNESOTA

**Minneapolis**
Joseph, Burton M. *retired grain merchant*

**Saint Paul**
Zylstra, Stanley James *farmer, food company executive*

#### MISSISSIPPI

**Clarksdale**
Williams, Kenneth Ogden *farmer*

**Starkville**
Gregg, Billy Ray *seed industry executive, consultant*

#### MISSOURI

**Springfield**
Strickler, Ivan K. *dairy farmer*

#### MONTANA

**Polson**
Marchi, Jon *cattle rancher, former investment brokerage executive*

**Pony**
Anderson, Richard Ernest *agribusiness development executive, rancher*

#### NEBRASKA

**Lincoln**
Sheffield, Leslie Floyd *retired agricultural educator*

**Scottsbluff**
Weichenthal, Burton A. *beef cattle specialist*

#### NEVADA

**Yerington**
Scatena, Lorraine Borba *rancher, women's rights advocate*

#### NEW YORK

**Canandaigua**
Sands, Marvin *wine company executive*

**Elmont**
Stephens, Woodford Cefis (Woody Stephens) *horse trainer, breeder*

**Ithaca**
Bail, Joe Paul *agricultural educator emeritus*

#### NORTH DAKOTA

**Bismarck**
Carlisle, Ronald Dwight *nursery owner*

**Regent**
Krauter, Aaron Joseph *farmer, state senator*

**Rugby**
Axtman, Benjamin J. *farmer*

**Stanley**
Piepkorn, Evonne Arlys *farmer, scriptwriter, producer, director*

**Tioga**
Nelson, Marlow Gene *agricultural studies educator*

**Turtle Lake**
Lindteigen, Susanna *rancher, state official*

#### OHIO

**Columbus**
Casey, Raymond Richard *agricultural business executive*
Ockerman, Herbert W. *agricultural studies educator*

#### OKLAHOMA

**Oklahoma City**
Beutler, Randy Leon *rancher, state legislator*

#### OREGON

**Ashland**
Walt, Harold Richard *rancher*

**Lowell**
Weathers, Warren Russell *forester, appraiser, consultant*

**Medford**
†Smith, Robert F. (Bob Smith) *rancher, congressman*

#### PENNSYLVANIA

**Harleysville**
Ruth, Alpheus Landis *dairy farmer*

**University Park**
Hood, Lamartine Frain *agriculture educator, former dean*

#### SOUTH CAROLINA

**Charleston**
Hastie, J. Drayton *plantation and garden owner, director*

**Clemson**
†Wehrenberg, William Busse *agricultural studies educator*

**Greer**
Gregg, Marie Byrd *retired farmer*

**Pawleys Island**
Kay, Thomas Oliver *agricultural consultant*

#### SOUTH DAKOTA

**Brookings**
Moore, Raymond A. *consultant, retired agriculture educator*

**Elk Point**
Chicoine, Roland Alvin *farmer, state official*

**Wessington**
Lockner, Vera Joanne *farmer, rancher, legislator*

#### TENNESSEE

**Cordova**
Echols, James *agricultural products supplier*

**La Vergne**
Walker, Phillip R. *agricultural products supplier*

#### TEXAS

**Beaumont**
Stansel, James W. *agricultural research administrator*

**College Station**
Christiansen, James Edward *agricultural educator*
Hiler, Edward Allan *agricultural and engineering educator*

**Dallas**
Hewlett, Gloria Louise *rancher, retired educator, civic volunteer*

**Fort Worth**
Danilow, Deborah Marie *rancher, singer, songwriter, musician*

**Industry**
Huitt, Jimmie L. *rancher, oil, gas, real estate investor*

**San Antonio**
†Petty, Scott, Jr. *rancher*

#### VIRGINIA

**Blacksburg**
Cannell, Robert Quirk *agricultural sciences, educator*
Swiger, L. A. *agricultural studies educator*

**Burke**
Dean, John Wilson, Jr. *business consultant, retired army officer*

**Chesapeake**
Shirley, Charles William *farm owner*

**Montross**
Fountain, Robert Roy, Jr. *farmer, industrial executive, naval officer*

**Spottswood**
Fredricksen, Cleve Laurance *thoroughbred horse farm owner, real estate investor*

## WASHINGTON

**Walla Walla**
Corfield, Timothy Lynn *college rodeo executive, educator*

**Yakima**
Grandy, Jay Franklin *fruit processing executive*

## WEST VIRGINIA

**Charles Town**
McDonald, Angus Wheeler *farmer*

**Lahmansville**
Snyder, Robert Martin *agriculture consultant, retired government official*

**Morgantown**
Maxwell, Robert Haworth *agriculture educator, university administrator*

## WISCONSIN

**Green Bay**
Zemke, William A. *farm management educator*

**Madison**
Felstehausen, Herman Henry *natural resources-land planning educator*

## WYOMING

**Douglas**
Sanford, Leroy Leonard *rancher*

**Lander**
Raynolds, David Robert *buffalo breeder, author*

**Wheatland**
Bunker, John Birkbeck *cattle rancher, retired sugar company executive*

## CANADA

## ONTARIO

**Blenheim**
Thompson, Wesley Duncan *grain merchant*

## MEXICO

**Chetumal**
Rosado-May, Francisco Javier *agricultural studies educator, researcher*

**Nuevo Leon**
Garza Garza, Rómulo *livestock breeder and writer, agriculturist*

## ADDRESS UNPUBLISHED

Barrett, Barbara McConnell *ranch owner, community leader, lawyer*
†Brooks, Kenneth N. *forestry educator*
Erwin, Elmer Louis *vintager, cement consultant*
Johnson, Cyrus Edwin *grain farmer, former food products executive*
Kontny, Vincent L. *rancher, engineering executive*
Sello, Allen Ralph *forest products executive*
Weaver, Peggy (Marguerite McKinnie Weaver) *plantation owner*

---

## ARCHITECTURE AND DESIGN

## UNITED STATES

## ALABAMA

**Auburn**
Millman, Richard George *architect, educator*

**Birmingham**
Barrow, Richard Edward *architect*

**Huntsville**
Jones, Harvie Paul *architect*

**Mobile**
Winter, Arch Reese *architect*

**Tuskegee**
Pryce, Edward Lyons *landscape architect*

## ARIZONA

**Carefree**
Beadle, Alfred Newman *architect*
Johnson, Charles Foreman *architect, architectural photographer, planning architecture and system engineering consultant*
Robbins, Conrad W. *naval architect*

**New River**
Bruder, William Paul *architect*

**Phoenix**
DeBartolo, Jack, Jr. *architect*
Elmore, James Walter *architect, retired university dean*
Gwozdz, Kim Elizabeth *interior designer*
Ham, Stephanie Ann *interior architect*
Hawkins, Jasper Stillwell, Jr. *architect*
Schiffner, Charles Robert *architect*
Winslow, Paul David *architect*

**Scottsdale**
Blumer, Harry Maynard *architect*
Douglas, John Clifton *architect*
Hooker, Jo *interior designer*
Rutes, Walter Alan *architect*

**Sedona**
Iverson, Wayne Dahl *landscape architect, consultant*

**Sonoita**
Cook, William Howard *architect*

**Sun City West**
Madson, John Andrew *architect*
Mc Cune, John Francis, III *retired architect*

**Tempe**
Abell, James Logan *architect*
Mc Sheffrey, Gerald Rainey *architect, educator, city planner*

**Tucson**
Breckenridge, Klindt Duncan *architect*
Dinsmore, Philip Wade *architect*
Gourley, Ronald Robert *architect, educator*
Hershberger, Robert Glen *architect, educator*
McConnell, Robert Eastwood *architect, educator*
Nelson, Edward Humphrey *architect*
Wallach, Leslie Rothaus *architect*
Zube, Ervin Herbert *landscape architect, geographer, educator*

## ARKANSAS

**Fayetteville**
Burggraf, Frank Bernard, Jr. *landscape architect, retired educator*
Jones, Euine Fay *architect, educator*

**Little Rock**
Blass, Noland, Jr. *retired architect*
Chilcote, Lugean Lester *architect*
Cromwell, Edwin Boykin *architect*
Levy, Eugene Pfeifer *architect*
Truemper, John James, Jr. *retired architect*

## CALIFORNIA

**Altadena**
Ziegler, Raymond Stewart *retired architect*

**Bakersfield**
McAlister, Michael Hillis *architect*

**Belvedere**
Gale, Daniel Bailey *architect*

**Berkeley**
Brocchini, Ronald Gene *architect*
Burger, Edmund Ganes *architect*
Burk, Gary Maurice *health care facility planner*
Cardwell, Kenneth Harvey *architect, educator*
Hester, Randolph Thompson, Jr. *landscape architect, educator*
Stoller, Claude *architect*

**Beverly Hills**
Eisenshtat, Sidney Herbert *architect*
Myers, Barton *architect*

**Bodega Bay**
King, Leland W. *architect*

**Burbank**
Naidorf, Louis Murray *architect*

**Burlingame**
Tanzi, Carol Anne *interior designer*

**Calabasas**
Broderick, Marsha *interior designer, general contractor*

**Carmel**
Merrill, William Dickey *architect*

**Corona**
Ohmert, Richard Allan *architect*

**Corona Del Mar**
Yeo, Ron *architect*

**Coronado**
Wagener, Hobart D. *retired architect*
Weiss-Cornwell, Amy *interior designer*

**Costa Mesa**
Dougherty, Betsey Olenick *architect*
Olson, Cal Oliver *golf architect*

**Culver City**
Moss, Eric Owen *architect*

**Dillon Beach**
Caddy, Edmund H.H., Jr. *architect*

**El Cerrito**
Komatsu, S. Richard *architect*

**Encinitas**
Geier, Susan Asid *interior designer*

**Encino**
Rance, Quentin E. *interior designer*

**Eureka**
Van Fleet, William Mabry *retired architect*

**Fresno**
Darden, Edwin Speight, Sr. *architect*
Patnaude, William E. *architect*
Pings, Anthony Claude *architect*
Putman, Robert Dean *golf course architect*

**Glen Ellen**
Rockrise, George Thomas *architect*

**Glendale**
Colby, Barbara Diane *interior designer, consultant*

**Irvine**
Jacobs, Donald Paul *architect*
Kraemer, Kenneth Leo *architect, urban planner, educator*

**La Jolla**
Baesel, Stuart Oliver *architect*

**Los Angeles**
Adams, William Wesley, III *architect*
Aroni, Samuel *architecture and urban planning educator*
Axon, Donald Carlton *architect*
Berry, Richard Douglas *architectural educator, urban planner and designer*
Blankenship, Edward G. *architect*
Bobrow, Michael Lawrence *architect*
Brotman, David Joel *architectural firm executive*
Dillard, Suzanne *interior designer*
Dworsky, Daniel Leonard *architect*
†Holdsworth, Ray W. *architectural firm executive*
Kline, Lee B. *architect*
Li, Gerald *architect, film producer and director*
Maltzan, Michael Thomas *architect*
Martin, Albert Carey *architect*
Miller, Victoria Loren *marketing and communications design executive*
Moe, Stanley Allen *architect, consultant*
Nelson, Mark Bruce *interior designer*
Neutra, Dion *architect*
Phelps, Barton Chase *architect, educator*
Tanzmann, Virginia Ward *architect*
Thoman, John Everett *architect, mediator*
Verger, Morris David *architect, planner*

**Los Gatos**
Zacher, Valerie Irene *interior designer*

**Manhattan Beach**
Blanton, John Arthur *architect*

**Marshall**
Evans, Robert James *architect*

**Mill Valley**
D'Amico, Michael *architect, urban planner*

**Mountain View**
Kobza, Dennis Jerome *architect*

**Newport Beach**
Bissell, George Arthur *architect*
Richardson, Walter John *architect*
Strock, Arthur Van Zandt *architect*

**Oakland**
Eckbo, Garrett *landscape architect, urban designer*
Matsumoto, George *architect*
Nicol, Robert Duncan *architect*

**Oxnard**
O'Connell, Hugh Mellen, Jr. *retired architect*

**Palm Desert**
Chambers, Milton Warren *architect*

**Palm Springs**
Frey, Albert *architect*

**Palo Alto**
Ivester, (Richard) Gavin *industrial designer*
Linn, Gary Dean *golf course architect*

**Pasadena**
Goei, Bernard Thwan-Poo (Bert Goei) *architectural and engineering firm executive*
Thomas, Joseph Fleshman *architect*

**Pleasant Hill**
Hassid, Sami *architect, educator*

**Pleasanton**
Fehlberg, Robert Erick *architect*

**Pomona**
Lyle, John Tillman *landscape architecture educator*

**Redondo Beach**
Shellhorn, Ruth Patricia *landscape architect*

**Sacramento**
Cox, Whitson William *architect*
Dahlin, Dennis John *landscape architect*
Hallenbeck, Harry C. *architect*
Lionakis, George *architect*
Muller, David Webster *architectural designer*
Nacht, Daniel Joseph *architect*
Wasserman, Barry L(ee) *architect*

**San Diego**
Blumenfeld, Alfred Morton *industrial design consultant, educator*
Delawie, Homer Torrence *architect*
Harmon, Harry William *architect, former university administrator*
Henderson, John Drews *architect*
Holl, Walter John *architect, interior designer*
Livingston, Stanley C. *architect*
Paderewski, Clarence Joseph *architect*
Wilson, Richard Allan *landscape architect*

**San Francisco**
Bull, Henrik Helkand *architect*
Del Campo, Martin Bernardelli *architect*
Emmons, Donn *architect*
Field, John Louis *architect*
Hardison, Donald Leigh *architect*
Horan, Joseph Patrick *interior designer*
Kriken, John Lund *architect*
MacDonald, Donald William *architect*
Moris, Lamberto Giuliano *architect*
Raeber, John Arthur *architect, construction specifier consultant*
Ream, James Terrill *architect, sculptor*
Rockwell, Burton Lowe *architect*
Simon, Cathy Jensen *architect*
Thistlethwaite, David Richard *architect*
Turnbull, William, Jr. *architect*
Valentine, William Edson *architect*
Werner, William Arno *architect*

**San Jose**
Richards, Lisle Frederick *architect*
Tanaka, Richard Koichi, Jr. *architect, planner*

**San Juan Capistrano**
Paul, Courtland Price *landscape architect, planner*

**San Luis Obispo**
Deasy, Cornelius Michael *architect*

**San Marino**
Man, Lawrence Kong *architect*

**San Rafael**
Badgley, John Roy *architect*
Elliott, Edward Procter *architect*
Thompson, Peter L. H. *golf course architect*

**Santa Barbara**
Frizzell, William Kenneth *architect*
Kruger, Kenneth Charles *architect*

**Santa Clara**
Kwock, Royal *architect*

**Santa Monica**
Eizenberg, Julie *architect*
†Friedrichs, Edward C. *architect*
Gehry, Frank Owen *architect*
Koning, Hendrik *architect*
Miller, Leroy Benjamin *architect*

**Sausalito**
Leefe, James Morrison *architect*

**Seal Beach**
Rossi, Mario Alexander *architect*

**Somerset**
Setzekorn, William David *retired architect, consultant, author*

**Sonoma**
Allen, Rex Whitaker *architect*
Woodbridge, John Marshall *architect, urban planner*

**South Pasadena**
Girvigian, Raymond *architect*

**Stanton**
Polk, Benjamin Kauffman *retired architect, composer, educator*

**Tarzana**
Smith, Mark Lee *architect*

**Venice**
Naga, Tarek A. *architect, educator*

**Ventura**
Okuma, Albert Akira, Jr. *architect*

**West Hollywood**
Luckman, Charles *architect*

## COLORADO

**Aspen**
Caudill, Samuel Jefferson *architect*

**Aurora**
Hynek, Frederick James *architect*

**Boulder**
Carlson, Devon McElvin *architect, educator*

**Colorado Springs**
Kelsey, Floyd Lamar, Jr. *architect*
Phibbs, Harry Albert *interior designer, professional speaker, lecturer*

**Crestone**
Temple, Lee Brett *architect*

**Denver**
Abo, Ronald Kent *architect*
Anderson, John David *architect*
Brownson, Jacques Calmon *architect*
Cowley, Gerald Dean *architect*
Decker, David B. *architect, educator*
Dominick, Peter Hoyt, Jr. *architect*
Fuller, Kenneth Roller *architect*
Hatami, Marvin *architect, educator, urban designer*
Havekost, Daniel John *architect*
Hoover, George Schweke *architect*

## INDIANA

**Carmel**
Eden, Barbara Janiece *commercial and residential interior designer*
Mc Laughlin, Harry Roll *architect*

**Chesterton**
Wilkes, Delano Angus *architect*

**Fort Wayne**
Cole, Kenneth Duane *architect*

**Indianapolis**
Conly, Michael Frederick *architect*
Woollen, Evans *architectural firm executive*

**Michigan City**
Brockway, Lee J. *architect*

**Mishawaka**
Ponko, William Reuben *architect*
Troyer, LeRoy Seth *architect*

**Muncie**
Sappenfield, Charles Madison *architect, educator*

**Notre Dame**
Stroik, Duncan Gregory *architect, architectural design educator*

**South Bend**
Horsbrugh, Patrick *architect, educator*

**West Lafayette**
Molnar, Donald Joseph *landscape architecture educator*

## IOWA

**Ames**
Kainlauri, Eino Olavi *architect*
Palermo, Gregory Sebastian *architect*

**Cedar Rapids**
Healey, Edward Hopkins *architect*
Stone, Herbert Marshall *architect*

**Clear Lake**
Broshar, Robert Clare *architect*

**Des Moines**
Lewis, Calvin Fred *architect, educator*
Vande Krol, Jerry Lee *architect*

**Fairfield**
Lipman, Jonathan *architect, historic preservationist*

**Iowa City**
Neumann, Roy Covert *architect*

**Mount Vernon**
Elliott, Candice K. *interior designer*

## KANSAS

**Lawrence**
Grabow, Stephen Harris *architecture educator*

**Manhattan**
Foerster, Bernd *architecture educator*
Kremer, Eugene R. *architecture educator*

**Pittsburg**
Fish, David Carlton *architect*

**Topeka**
Karst, Gary Gene *architect*
Schneider, Raymond Clinton *architect, educator*

**Wichita**
Ellington, Howard Wesley *architect*

## KENTUCKY

**Covington**
Thrun, Robert Read *architect*

**Lexington**
Girone, Vito Anthony *architect, city planner, educator emeritus, artist*
Loghry, Richard M. *architecture and engineering services executive*
Romanowitz, Byron Foster *architect, engineer*

**Salvisa**
Lancaster, Clay *architecture/design educator, writer*

## LOUISIANA

**Baton Rouge**
Desmond, John Jacob *architect*
Reich, Robert Sigmund *landscape architect*

**Lafayette**
Perkins, David Layne, Sr. *architect*

**Metairie**
Colbert, Charles Ralph *architect*

**New Orleans**
Blitch, Ronald Buchanan *architect*
Filson, Ronald Coulter *architect, educator, college dean*
Frantz, Phares Albert *architect*
Klingman, John Philip *architect, educator*
Latorre, Robert George *naval architecture and engineering educator*
Steinmetz, Robert Charles *architect*

**Shreveport**
Haas, Lester Carl *architect*

## MAINE

**Canaan**
Zikorus, Albert Michael *golf course architect*

**Edgecomb**
Carlson, Suzanne Olive *architect*

**New Harbor**
Fradley, Frederick Macdonell *architect*

## MARYLAND

**Annapolis**
Jansson, John Phillip *architect, consultant*
Lee, T. Girard *church growth consultant*
Miller, Richards Thorn *naval architect, engineer*
Nicholson, William Mac *naval architect, marine engineer, consultant*
Wilkes, Joseph Allen *architect*

**Baltimore**
Adams, Harold Lynn *architect*
Anderson, Gary Dean *architect, planner, educator*
Brodie, M. J. (Jay Brodie) *architect, city planner, government executive*
Donkervoet, Richard Cornelius *architect*
Ford, John Gilmore *interior designer*
Snead, James Arrington *architect*
Trostel, Michael Frederick *architect*

**Bethesda**
Auerbach, Seymour *architect*
Dawson, John Frederick *retired architect*
Hoenack, August Frederick *architect*
Morgan, William Bruce *naval architect*

**Bowie**
Stone, Edward Harris, II *landscape architect*

**Chevy Chase**
Freeman, Raymond Lee *landscape architect, planning consultant*
Oudens, Gerald Francis *architect, architectural firm executive*

**College Park**
Lewis, Roger Kutnow *architect, educator, author*

**Columbia**
Askew, Laurin Barker, Jr. *architect*
Slater, John Blackwell *landscape architect*

**Fort Washington**
Miller, John Richard *interior designer*

**Olney**
Delmar, Eugene Anthony *architect*

**Port Republic**
Miller, Ewing Harry *architect*

**Rockville**
Elliott, Benjamin Paul *architect*
Horowitz, Harold *architect*

**Silver Spring**
Senseman, Ronald Sylvester *architect*
Ware, Thomas Earle *building consultant*

**West Bethesda**
Spurling, Everett Gordon, Jr. *architect, construction specifications consultant*

## MASSACHUSETTS

**Amherst**
Cornish, Geoffrey St. John *golf course architect*
Rupp, William John *architect*

**Boston**
Alexander, James Garth *architect*
Anthony, Ethan *architect*
Bargmann, Joel David *architect*
Elkus, Howard Felix *architect*
Finegold, Maurice Nathan *architect*
Flansburgh, Earl Robert *architect*
Fletcher, Norman Collings *architect*
Forbes, Peter *architect*
Glassman, Herbert Haskel *architect*
Goody, Joan E. *architect*
Harkness, John Cheesman *architect*
Joseph, J. Jonathan *interior designer*
Manfredi, David Peter *architect*
Rawn, William Leete, III *architect*
Shepley, Hugh *architect*
Stull, Donald LeRoy *architect*
Tappé, Albert Anthony *architect*
Wallace, David Dunsmore *architect*
Wolf, Gary Herbert *architect*
Wood, Henry Austin *architect*

**Cambridge**
Anderson, Stanford Owen *architect, architectural historian, educator*
Bluestone, Hugh Lawrence *architect*
Bruck, Ferdinand Frederick *architect*
Bruck, Phoebe Ann Mason *landscape architect*
Burns, Carol J. *architect, educator*
Campbell, Robert *architect, writer*
Dewart, Christopher *architectural educator, furniture maker*
Green, Richard John *architect*
Hamner, W. Easley *architect*
Hass, Michael Shepherdson *architect*
Kobus, Richard Lawrence *architect, designer, executive*
Krieger, Alex *architecture and design educator*
Kruger, Kenneth *architect*
McCue, Gerald Mallon *architect*
Moneo, José Rafael *architecture educator*
Newman, John Nicholas *naval architect educator*

Pollock, Wilson F. *architectural firm executive*
Porter, William Lyman *architect, educator*
Rosenfeld, Walter David, Jr. *architect, writer*
Rowe, Peter Grimmond *architecture educator, researcher*
Sekler, Eduard Franz *architect, educator*
Szabo, Albert *architect, educator*
Tsoi, Edward Tze Ming *architect, interior designer, urban planner*
Ward, Robertson, Jr. *architect*

**Concord**
Cutting, Heyward *designer, planner*
Daley, Royston Tuttle *architect*

**Duxbury**
Phipps, Lynne Bryan *interior architect, clergywoman, parent educator*

**Essex**
McMillen, Louis Albert *architect*

**Lexington**
Frey, John Ward *landscape architect*

**Lincoln**
Merrill, Vincent Nichols *landscape architect*
Payne, Harry Morse, Jr. *architect*

**Nantucket**
Lethbridge, Francis Donald *architect*

**Newton**
Oles, Paul Stevenson (Steve Oles) *architect, perspectivist, educator*

**North Andover**
Goldstein, Charles Henry *architect, consultant*

**Shirley**
Field, Hermann Haviland *architect, educator, author*

**Somerville**
Korobkin, Barry Jay *architect*
Safdie, Moshe *architect*

**Stoughton**
Ross, Edward Joseph *architect*

**Topsfield**
Peirce, John Wentworth *architect*

**Waltham**
Notkin, Leonard Sheldon *architect*

**Watertown**
Dawson, Stuart Owen *landscape architect, urban designer*

**Wayland**
Huygens, Remmert William *architect*

**West Springfield**
Engebretson, Douglas Kenneth *architect*

**Weston**
Sturgis, Robert Shaw *architect*

**Winchester**
Jabre, Eddy-Marco *architect*

**Winthrop**
Costantino, Frank Mathew *architectural illustrator*

**Worcester**
Herman, Barbara Rose *interior decorator*

## MICHIGAN

**Ann Arbor**
Beckley, Robert Mark *architect, educator*
Benford, Harry Bell *naval architect*
Flowers, Damon Bryant *architect, facility planner*
Fry, Richard E. *architectural firm executive*
Malkawi, Ali Mahmoud *architecture educator, researcher*
Marans, Robert Warren *architect, planner*
Metcalf, Robert Clarence *architect, educator*
Paulsen, Serenus Glen *architect, educator*
Vakalo, Emmanuel-George *architecture and planning educator, researcher*

**Birmingham**
Bublys, Algimantas Vladas *architect*
Van Dine, Harold Forster, Jr. *architect*

**Bloomfield Hills**
Allen, Maurice Bartelle, Jr. *architect*
Birkerts, Gunnar *architect*
Brown, Jack Wyman *architect*

**Detroit**
Cox, John William *architect, educator*
Francis, Edward D. *architect*
Kessler, William Henry *architect*
Roehling, Carl David *architect*

**Fair Haven**
Wittbrodt, Frederick Joseph, Jr. *automotive designer*

**Flint**
Tomblinson, James Edmond *architect*

**Grand Rapids**
Dickerson, Allen Bruce *interior designer, consultant*
Vrancken, Robert Danloy *facilities planner, designer and educator*
Wold, Robert Lee *architect, engineer*

**Gregory**
Frank, Richard Calhoun *architect*

**Jackson**
Kendall, Kay Lynn *interior designer*

**Kalamazoo**
Carver, Norman Francis, Jr. *architect, photographer*
O'Boyle, Robert L. *landscape architect*

**Saint Joseph**
Keech, Elowyn Ann *interior designer*

**Southfield**
Redstone, Daniel Aaron *architect*
Redstone, Louis Gordon *architect*

**Traverse City**
Brown, Paul Bradley *architect*

## MINNESOTA

**Duluth**
Salmela, David Daniel *architect*
Whiteman, Richard Frank *architect*

**Minneapolis**
Chilton, William David *architect*
Clemence, Roger Davidson *landscape architect, educator*
Degenhardt, Robert Allan *architectural and engineering firm executive*
Eyberg, Donald Theodore, Jr. *architect*
Jacob, Bernard Michel *architect*
Martin, Roger Bond *landscape architect, educator*
Parker, Leonard S. *architect, educator*
Rand, Peter Anders *architect*
†Sjoblad, Steven A. *architectural firm executive*
Susanka, Sarah Hills *architect*
Van Housen, Thomas Corwin, III *architect, designer, builder*

**Northfield**
Sovik, Edward Anders *architect, consultant*

**Saint Paul**
Close, Elizabeth Scheu *architect*
Close, Winston Arthur *retired architect*
Faricy, Richard Thomas *architect*
Lein, Malcolm Emil *architect*

## MISSISSIPPI

**Columbus**
Kaye, Samuel Harvey *architect, educator*

**Hattiesburg**
Traylor, Joan Sadler *interior design educator*

**Jackson**
Biggs, Thomas Jones *architect*
Burns, Robert, Jr. *architect, freelance writer, artist*
Timmer, Wayne Francis *architectural firm executive*

**Mississippi State**
Bishop, Calvin Thomas *landscape architect, educator*
Martin, Edward Curtis, Jr. *landscape architect, educator*

**Starkville**
Ford, Robert MacDonald, III *architect, educator*

## MISSOURI

**Ballwin**
Kern, Gary L. *golf course architect*

**Clayton**
Christner, Theodore Carroll *architect*
Turner, Terry Madison *architect*

**Kansas City**
Baker, Robert Thomas *interior designer*
Conrad, William Merrill *architect*
Patty, R. Bruce *architect*
Seligson, Theodore H. *architect, interior designer, art consultant*

**Saint Louis**
Becker, Rex Louis *architect*
Burks, Verner Irwin *architect*
Cameron, Paul Scott *architect*
Chivetta, Anthony Joseph *architect*
Cotton, W(illiam) Philip, Jr. *architect*
Hellmuth, George Francis *architect*
Ittner, H. Curtis *architect*
Lickhalter, Merlin Eugene *architect*
Lovelace, Eldridge Hirst *retired landscape architect, city planner*
Mertz, Stuart Moulton *landscape architect*
Michaelides, Constantine Evangelos *architect, educator*
Self, Larry Douglas *architectural firm executive*
†Sincoff, Jerome J. *architect*
Thalden, Barry E. *architect*
Weese, Cynthia Rogers *architect, educator*

**Springfield**
Liu, Yuan Hsiung *drafting and design educator*
Ownby, Jerry Steve *landscape architect, educator*

**Webster Groves**
Kramer, Gerhardt Theodore *architect*

## MONTANA

**Bozeman**
DeHaas, John Neff, Jr. *retired architecture educator*

**Great Falls**
Davidson, David Scott *architect*
Hoiland, Andrew Calvin *architect*

PROFESSIONAL INDEX 5071 ARCHITECTURE AND DESIGN


## NEBRASKA

**Lincoln**
Morrow, Andrew Nesbit *interior designer, business owner*
Stange, James Henry *architect*
Steward, Weldon Cecil *architecture educator, architect, consultant*

**Omaha**
Bowen, Gary Roger *architect*
Polsky, Donald Perry *architect*
Ryan, Mark Anthony *architect*

## NEVADA

**Las Vegas**
Serfas, Richard Thomas *architecture educator, urban planner, county official*

## NEW HAMPSHIRE

**Fremont**
Richardson, Artemas P(artridge) *landscape architect*

**Goffstown**
Gillmore, Robert *landscape designer, author, editor, publisher*

**Hanover**
Brooks, H. Allen *architectural educator, author, lecturer*

**Holderness**
Cutler, Laurence Stephan *architect, urban designer, advertising executive, educator*

**Jaffrey**
Alderman, Bissell *architect*

**New London**
Sheerr, Deirdre McCrystal *architectural firm executive*

**Portsmouth**
Lyman, William Welles, Jr. *retired architect*

## NEW JERSEY

**Bernardsville**
Lazor, Patricia Ann *interior designer*

**Clifton**
Held, George Anthony *architect*
Rigolo, Arthur Emil *architect*

**East Orange**
Fielo, Muriel Bryant *interior designer, space engineer*

**Englewood**
Schmidt, Ronald Hans *architect*

**Jamesburg**
Zeigen, Spencer Steven *architect*

**Medford**
Dunn, Roy J. *landscape architect*

**Montclair**
Jones, Rees Lee *golf course architect*

**Morristown**
Nadaskay, Raymond *architect*

**Newark**
Goldman, Glenn *architecture educator, architect*
Greenfield, Sanford Raymond *architect*

**Paramus**
DiGeronimo, Suzanne Kay *architect*

**Princeton**
Ford, Jeremiah, III *architect*
Hillier, J(ames) Robert *architect*
Holt, Philetus Havens, III *architect*
Kehrt, Allan W. *architectural firm executive*
Lerner, Ralph *architect, university dean*
Mills, Michael James *architect*

**Ridgefield**
Wolchko, Matthew John *architect*

**Roseland**
Mahler, Harry Bez *architect, planner*

**Somerville**
Shive, Richard Byron *architect*

**South Orange**
DeVaris, Panayotis Eric *architect*

**Summit**
Bottelli, Richard *retired architect*

## NEW MEXICO

**Albuquerque**
Campbell, C(harles) Robert *architect*
Hakim, Besim Selim *architecture and urban design educator, researcher*
Hooker, Van Dorn *architect, artist*
Sabatini, William Quinn *architect*

**Placitas**
Pirkl, James Joseph *industrial designer, educator, writer*

**Santa Fe**
Conron, John Phelan *architect*
Leon, Bruno *architect, educator*

## NEW YORK

**Armonk**
Behr, Richard Henry *architect, educator*

**Bedford**
Benedek, Armand *landscape architect*
Damora, Robert Matthew *architect*

**Berlin**
Stephens, Donald Joseph *retired architect*

**Binghamton**
Bearsch, Lee Palmer *architect, city planner*

**Brooklyn**
Delson, Sidney Leon *architect*
Weston, I. Donald *architect*
Woolley, Margaret Anne (Margot Woolley) *architect*
Zivari, Bashir *architect, industrial designer*

**Buffalo**
Coles, Robert Traynham *architect*
Freschi, Bruno Basilio *architect, educator*

**Carmel**
Carruth, David Barrow *landscape architect*

**Cold Spring**
Brill, Ralph David *architect, real estate developer, venture capitalist*

**Corning**
Nary, John Henry *interior designer*

**Cranberry Lake**
Glavin, James Edward *landscape architect*

**East Hampton**
Damaz, Paul F. *architect*

**Fayetteville**
Sears, Bradford George *landscape architect*

**Flushing**
Shirvani, Hamid *architect, educator, author, administrator*

**Garden City**
Accordino, Frank Joseph *architect, car rental company executive*

**Great Neck**
Turofsky, Charles Sheldon *landscape architect*

**Greenlawn**
Stevens, John Richard *architectural historian*

**Hastings On Hudson**
Weinstein, Edward Michael *architect, consultant*

**Ithaca**
Becherer, Richard John *architecture educator*
Sims, William Riley *design and facility management educator, consultant*

**Katonah**
Baker, John Milnes *architect*

**Locust Valley**
Bentel, Frederick Richard *architect, educator*
Bentel, Maria-Luise Ramona Azzarone (Mrs. Frederick R. Bentel) *architect, educator*
Webel, Richard Karl *landscape architect*

**Long Island City**
Sadao, Shoji *architect*

**Manhasset**
Corva, Angelo Francis *architect*
Grossi, Olindo *architect, educator*
Schiller, Arthur A. *architect, educator*

**Marcellus**
Lafferty, Richard Thomas *architect*

**Millerton**
Burgee, John Henry *architect*

**New Rochelle**
Menzies, Henry Hardinge *architect*

**New York**
Abramovitz, Max *architect*
Aldea, Patricia *architect*
Baker, James Barnes *architect*
Barnes, Edward Larrabee *architect*
Barnett, Jonathan *architect, city planner*
Barratt, Michael Scott *architect*
Barrett, Celia Elizabeth *interior designer*
Beckhard, Herbert *architect*
Beckmann, John *architect, industrial designer*
Beer, David Wells *architect*
Berg, Wayne *architect, educator*
Bland, Frederick Aves *architect*
Blinder, Richard Lewis *architect*
Bond, J. Max, Jr. *architect, educational administrator*
Bookhardt, Fred Barringer, Jr. *architect*
Borrelli, John Francis *architect*
Breines, Simon *architect*
Brennan, Henry Higginson *architect*
Broches, Paul Elias *architect*
Buatta, Mario *interior designer*
Butler, Jonathan Putnam *architect*
Buttrick, Harold *architect*
Cavaglieri, Giorgio *architect*
Chan, Lo-Yi Cheung Yuen *architect*
Cobb, Henry Nichols *architect*
Dattner, Richard *architect, educator*
David, Theoharis Lambros *architect, educator*
Decker, Dennis Dale *industrial designer*
De Vido, Alfredo Eduardo *architect*
Edelman, Harold *architect*
Edelman, Judith H. *architect*
Eisenman, Peter David *architect, educator*
Fitch, James Marston *architectural preservationist, architectural historian, critic*
†Fitzsimmons, Sophie Sonia *interior designer*
Fleischer, Joseph Linden *architect*
Franzen, Ulrich J. *architect*
Freed, James Ingo *architect*
Friedberg, Marvin Paul *landscape architect*
Gatje, Robert Frederick *architect*
Genaro, Donald Michael *industrial designer*
Georgopoulos, Maria *architect*
Gibbs, Jamie *landscape architect, interior designer*
Ginsberg, David Lawrence *architect*
Glaser, Milton *graphic designer and illustrator*
Guise, David Earl *architect, educator*
Gwathmey, Charles *architect*
Halpin, Anna Marie *architect*
Halsband, Frances *architect*
Hardy, Hugh *architect*
Hariri, Gisue *architect, educator*
Heisel, Ralph Arthur *architect*
Hinz, Theodore Vincent *architect*
Holub, Martin *architect*
Holzman, Malcolm *architect*
Hoog, Marjorie *architect*
Ivanov, Lyuben Dimitrov *naval architecture researcher, educator*
Ivy, Robert Adams, Jr. *architect, editor-in-chief*
Johansen, John MacLane *architect*
Kinnear, John Kenyon, Jr. *architect*
Kissiloff, William *industrial designer*
Kliment, Robert Michael *architect*
Kliment, Stephen Alexander *architect, editor*
Knowles, Edward F(rank) *architect*
Kohn, A. Eugene *architect*
Kondylis, Costas Andrew *architect*
Ladau, Robert Francis *architect, planner*
Lee, Sarah Tomerlin *design executive*
Lefferts, Gillet, Jr. *architect*
Leigh, Stephen *industrial designer*
Liebman, Theodore *architect*
Masey, Jack *exhibition designer*
Meier, Richard Alan *architect*
Palermo, Robert James *architect, consultant, inventor*
Pasanella, Giovanni *architect, architectural educator*
Pei, Ieoh Ming *architect*
Peretz, Eileen *interior designer*
Perkins, Lawrence Bradford, Jr. *architect*
Pesce, Gaetano *architectural, interior, industrial and graphic designer*
Platt, Charles Adams *architect, planner*
Pomeroy, Lee Harris *architect*
Pool, Mary Jane *design consultant, writer*
Quennell, Nicholas *landscape architect, educator*
Rice, Richard Lee, Jr. *architect*
Rosenblatt, Arthur Isaac *architect, former museum director*
Rosenblatt, Lester *naval architect*
Rossant, James Stephane *architect, artist*
Rutkin, Seymour *architect*
Slomanson, Lloyd Howard *architect, musician*
Smith, G. E. Kidder *architect, author*
Smith, Ken *landscape architect*
Smotrich, David Isadore *architect*
Snibbe, Richard W. *architect*
Stephens, Olin James, II *naval architect, yacht designer*
Stern, Robert Arthur Morton *architect, educator, writer*
†Stoddard, Alexandra *designer, writer, lecturer*
Tabler, William Benjamin *architect*
Tafel, Edgar *architect*
Tayar, Memduh Ali *architect*
Todd, David Fenton Michie *architect*
Varney, Carleton Bates, Jr. *interior designer, columnist, educator*
Viemeister, Tucker L. *industrial designer*
Vignelli, Massimo *architecture and design executive*
Voorsanger, Bartholomew *architect*
Walker, Kenneth Henry *architect*
Willis, Beverly Ann *architect*

**Nyack**
Degenshein, Jan *architect, planner*

**Pleasantville**
Annese, Domenico *landscape architect*

**Rensselaerville**
Dudley, George Austin *architect, planning consultant, educator*

**Rochester**
Argenta, Joseph John *architect*
Charles, Michael Harrison *architectural interior designer*

**Rye**
Anderson, Allan *architectural firm executive*

**Syracuse**
Skoler, Louis *architect, educator*
Smardon, Richard Clay *landscape architecture and environmental studies educator*

**Tarrytown**
Kenney, John Michel *architect*

**Troy**
Haviland, David Sands *architectural educator, researcher, administrator*

**Wappingers Falls**
Johnson, Jeh Vincent *architect*

**Warwick**
Mack, Daniel Richard *furniture designer*

**Water Mill**
D'Urso, Joseph Paul *designer*

**Weedsport**
Cichello, Samuel Joseph *architect*

**White Plains**
Papp, Laszlo George *architect*
Rose, William Allen, Jr. *architect*

**Woodstock**
Hoyt, Earl Edward, Jr. *industrial designer*

## NORTH CAROLINA

**Asheville**
King, Joseph Bertram *architect*

**Chapel Hill**
Dixon, Frederick Dail *architect*
Godschalk, David Robinson *architect, urban development planner, educator*

**Charlotte**
Ferebee, Stephen Scott, Jr. *architect*
Hackler, John Byron, III *architect*
Huberman, Jeffrey Allen *architect*
Montague, Edgar Burwell, III (Monty Montague) *industrial designer*
Shive, Philip Augustus *architect*
Turner, Thomas Patrick *architect*

**High Point**
Kleeman, Walter Benton, Jr. *interior and furniture designer, consultant, author*

**Lake Toxaway**
Gasperoni, Ellen Jean Lias *interior designer*

**Pisgah Forest**
Albyn, Richard Keith *retired architect*

**Raleigh**
Burns, Norma DeCamp *architect*
Burns, Robert Paschal *architect, educator*
Clark, Roger Harrison *architect, architecture educator*
Clarke, Lewis James *landscape architect*
Flournoy, William Louis, Jr. *landscape architect*
Godwin, James Beckham *retired landscape architect*
Hunter, Margaret King *architect*
Johnson, Marvin Richard Alois *architect*
Malecha, Marvin John *architect, academic administrator*

**Robbinsville**
Ginn, Ronn *architect, urban planner, general contractor*

**Winston Salem**
Butner, Fred Washington, Jr. *architect*
Oppermann, Joseph Kay *architect*

## OHIO

**Akron**
Castronovo, Thomas Paul *architect, consultant*

**Berea**
Pattison, Robert Maynicke *architect*

**Celina**
Fanning, Ronald Heath *architect, engineer*

**Chagrin Falls**
Cordes, Loverne Christian *interior designer*
Dunning, Ann Marie *architect*

**Cincinnati**
Alexander, James Marshall, Jr. *architect, retired educator*
Cole, Thomas Ferguson *architect*
Glendening, Everett Austin *architect*
Goetzman, Bruce Edgar *architecture educator*
Gosling, David *architect, urban design educator*
Luckner, Herman Richard, III *interior designer*
Meisner, Gary Wayne *landscape architect*
Nielsen, George Lee *architect*
Preiser, Wolfgang Friedrich Ernst *architect, educator, consultant, researcher*
Roomann, Hugo *architect*
Senhauser, John Crater *architect*

**Cleveland**
Behnke, William Alfred *landscape architect, planner*
Bowen, Richard Lee *architect*
Eberhard, William Thomas *architect*
Gibans, James David *architect*
Kelly, John Terence *architect*
Little, Robert Andrews *architect, designer, painter*
Madison, Robert Prince *architect*
Melsop, James William *architect*
Sande, Theodore Anton *architect, educator, foundation executive*
Zung, Thomas Tse-Kwai *architect*

**Columbus**
Böhm, Friedrich (Friedl) K.M. *architectural firm executive*
Carpenter, Jot David *landscape architect, educator*
Kirk, Ballard Harry Thurston *architect*
Weinhold, Virginia Beamer *interior designer*

**Cuyahoga Falls**
Haag, Everett Keith *architect*

**Dayton**
Betz, Eugene William *architect*

**Dublin**
Cornwell, Paul M., Jr. *architect*

**Kent**
Centuori, Jeanine Gail *architecture educator*

**Reynoldsburg**
Serraglio, Mario *architect*

**Toledo**
Hills, Arthur W. *architectural firm executive*
Martin, Robert Edward *architect*

## OKLAHOMA

**Norman**
Henderson, Arnold Glenn *architect, educator*
Sipes, James Lamoyne *landscape architect, educator*
Tuttle, Arthur Norman, Jr. *architect, university administrator*

**Tulsa**
Ball, Rex Martin *urban designer, architect*
Jones, Robert Lawton *architect, planner, educator*
Kennedy, Nancy Louise *retired draftsman*

## OREGON

**Ashland**
Mularz, Theodore Leonard *architect*

**Clackamas**
Merrill, William Dean *retired architect, medical facility planning consultant*

**Medford**
Skelton, Douglas H. *architect*
Straus, David A. *architectural firm executive*

**Newport**
Gordon, Walter *architect*

**Otter Rock**
Eaton, Leonard Kimball *retired architecture educator*

**Portland**
Frasca, Robert John *architect*
Gunsul, Brooks R. W. *architect*
Hacker, Thomas Owen *architect*
Kilbourn, Lee Ferris *architect, specifications writer*
Loeb, Joyce Lichtgarn *interior designer, civic worker*
Michael, Gary Linn *architect, artist*
†Morris, Paul Francis *landscape architect*
Ritz, Richard Ellison *architect, architectural historian, writer*

**Springfield**
Lutes, Donald Henry *architect*

**Tualatin**
Broome, John William *retired architect*
Harrington-Lloyd, Jeanne Leigh *interior designer*

**West Linn**
Treffinger, Karl Edward *architectural firm executive*

## PENNSYLVANIA

**Ambler**
Brandow, Theo *architect*
Swansen, Donna Maloney *landscape designer, consultant*

**Ardmore**
Mirick, Henry Dustin *architect*

**Bala Cynwyd**
Bentivegna, Peter Ignatius *architectural company executive*

**Bethlehem**
Spillman, Robert Arnold *architect*

**Butler**
Kosar, John E. *architectural firm executive*

**Camp Hill**
Peters, Ralph Edgar *architectural and engineering executive*
Spiers, Tomas Hoskins, Jr. *architect*

**Columbia**
Steiner-Houck, Sandra Lynn *interior designer*

**Lancaster**
Stewart, Arlene Jean Golden *designer, stylist*

**Lititz**
Gasparich, Margaret Jo *interior designer*

**Philadelphia**
Aquaro, Angelo Ralph *architect, consultant*
Brown, Denise Scott *architect, urban planner*
Cooke, R(ichard) Caswell, Jr. *architect*
Dagit, Charles Edward, Jr. *architect, educator*
Eiswerth, Barry Neil *architect, educator*
Hamme, David Codrington *architect*
Hayes, John Freeman *architect*
Izenour, Steven *architect*
Jordan, Joe J. *architect*
Kise, James Nelson *architect, urban planner*
Lawson, John Quinn *architect*
Leatherbarrow, David *architecture department chair*
Magaziner, Henry Jonas *architect*
Maxman, Susan Abel *architect*
McHarg, Ian Lennox *landscape architect, regional planner, educator*
Mitchell, Ehrman Burkman, Jr. *architect*
Olshin, Samuel E. *architect*
Perkins, George Holmes *architectural educator, architect*
Rauch, John Keiser, Jr. *architect*
Rybczynski, Witold Marian *architect, educator, writer*
Rykwert, Joseph *architecture and art history educator*
Santos, Adele Naude *architect, educator*
Saylor, Peter M. *architect*
Tyng, Anne Griswold *architect*
Venturi, Robert *architect*
Vernon, Shirley Jane *architect, educator*
Vinh, Binh *architect*
Wheatley, William Arthur *architect, musician*

**Pittsburgh**
Carter, Donald K. *architectural firm executive*
Damianos, Sylvester *architect, sculptor*
Gindroz, Raymond L. *architect*
Horowitz, Carole Spiegel *interior designer*
Horowitz, Don Roy *landscape company executive*
Loftness, Vivian Ellen *architecture educator*
Simonds, John Ormsbee *landscape architect*
Swain, William Grant *landscape architect*

**Plymouth Meeting**
Clemmer, Leon *architect, planner*

---

**Scranton**
Timins, Bonita Lea *interior decorator*

**State College**
Haas, John C. *architect*

**University Park**
Leslie, Donald Wilmot *landscape architecture educator*
Porterfield, Neil Harry *landscape architect, educator*
Wheeler, C. Herbert *architect, consultant, educator*

**Wallingford**
Clauss, Alfred *architect*

**Willow Grove**
Suer, Marvin David *architecture, consultant*

## RHODE ISLAND

**Jamestown**
Todd, Thomas Abbott *architect, urban designer*

**Little Compton**
Bullerjahn, Eduard Henri *architect*

**Newport**
Burgin, William Lyle *architect*
Wurman, Richard Saul *architect*

## SOUTH CAROLINA

**Charleston**
Goff, R. Garey *architect*
Lucas, Frank Edward *architect*

**Clemson**
Halfacre, Robert Gordon *landscape architect, horticulturist, educator*
Young, Joseph Laurie *architecture educator*

**Columbia**
Hultstrand, Charles John *architect*

**Greenville**
LeBlanc, L(ouis) Christian *architect*
Neal, James Austin *architect*

**Hilton Head Island**
Gui, James Edmund *architect*

## SOUTH DAKOTA

**Sioux Falls**
Koch, Ralph Richard *architect*

## TENNESSEE

**Chattanooga**
Derthick, Alan Wendell *architect*

**Knoxville**
Mc Carty, Bruce *architect*

**Memphis**
Evans, James Mignon *architect*
Jones, Walk Claridge, III *architect*
Yeates, Zeno Lanier *retired architect*

**Nashville**
Crabtree, Bruce Isbester, Jr. *architect*
Gobbell, Ronald Vance *architect*
Miller, Richard L. *architectural executive*
Swensson, Earl Simcox *architect*

## TEXAS

**Arlington**
Ferrier, Richard Brooks *architecture educator, architect*

**Austin**
Alexander, Drury Blakeley *architectural educator*
Barnes, Jay William, Jr. *architect, rancher*
Barr, Howard Raymond *architect*
Box, John Harold *architect, educator, academic dean*
George, Walter Eugene, Jr. *architect*
Little, Emily Browning *architect*
Newton, James Chartier *architect*
Speck, Lawrence W. *architect*

**Bryan**
Kellett, William Hiram, Jr. *retired architect, engineer, educator*

**College Station**
Reed, Raymond Deryl *architect*
Woodcock, David Geoffrey *architect, educator*

**Dallas**
Kolb, Nathaniel Key, Jr. *architect*
Landry, Jane Lorenz *architect*
Lundy, Victor Alfred *architect, educator*
Rees, Frank William, Jr. *architect*
Roy, Clarence Leslie *landscape architect*
Schwartz, Irving Donn *architect*
Stacy, Dennis William *architect*

**Denton**
Miller, Tom Polk *retired architect*

**El Paso**
Carroll, Edwin Winford *architect*
Mason, Richard Clyde *landscape architect*

**Flower Mound**
Morrish, Thomas Jay *golf course architect*

---

**Fort Worth**
Geren, Preston Murdoch, Jr. *architect, engineer*
Gideon, Randall Clifton *architectural firm executive*

**Granbury**
Garrison, Truitt B. *architect*

**Houston**
Andrews, Lavone Dickensheets *architect*
Bair, Royden Stanley *architect*
Bentsen, Kenneth Edward *architect*
Borget, Lloyd George *architect*
Brents, Daniel Rugel *architectural firm executive*
Calhoun, Harold *architect*
Cutler, John Earl *landscape architect*
Douglas, Frank Fair *architect, graphic designer*
Jackson, R. Graham *architect*
King, Jonathan *architectural researcher, educator*
Lerup, Lars G. *architecture educator, college dean*
Mc Ginty, John Milton *architect*
Moorhead, Gerald Lee *architect*
Morehead, James Caddall, Jr. *architect, educator*
Morris, Seth Irwin *architect*
Neuhaus, William Oscar, III *architect*
Obiora, Chris Sunny *architect*
Pierce, George Foster, Jr. *architect*

**Irving**
Chris, Harry Joseph *architect, architectural company executive*

**Lubbock**
Frazier, Eugene Richard *designer*

**Montgomery**
Tharp, Benjamin Carroll, Jr. *architect*

**San Antonio**
Frazer, Robert Lee *landscape architect*
Haywood, Norcell Dan *architect*
Perez, Andrew, III *architect*
Pfanstiel Parr, Dorothea Ann *interior designer*

**Southlake**
George, David Webster *architect*

**Spring**
Green, Sharon Jordan *interior decorator*

## UTAH

**Orem**
Brower, Gerald Grant *architect, software developer*

**Salt Lake City**
Beall, Burtch W., Jr. *architect*
Blackner, Boyd Atkins *architect*
Brems, David Paul *architect*
Chong, Richard David *architect*
Christopher, James Walker *architect, educator*

## VERMONT

**Charlotte**
Kiley, Daniel Urban *landscape architect, planner*

**Chester**
Farrar, Aili R. *cartographic draftsperson*

**Norwich**
White, Cleveland Stuart, Jr. *architect*

## VIRGINIA

**Alexandria**
Ballard, Edward Brooks *landscape architect*
Cross, Eason, Jr. *architect*
Pavlick, Charles Raleigh *architect, engineer, retired air force officer*
Ritter, James William *architect, educator*
Vander Myde, Philip Louis *architectural design firm executive*

**Arlington**
Adreon, Harry Barnes *architect*

**Blacksburg**
Bliznakov, Milka Tcherneva *architect*
Rodriguez-Camilloni, Humberto Leonardo *architect, historian, educator*

**Charlottesville**
Anderson, Robert Barber *architect*
Bednar, Michael John *architecture educator*
Bosserman, Joseph Norwood *architecture educator*
Root, James Benjamin *landscape architect*
Swofford, Donald Anthony *architect*

**Fairfax**
Ward, George Truman *architect*

**Falls Church**
Barkley, Paul Haley, Jr. *architect*
Mortensen, Robert Henry *landscape architect*

**Mc Lean**
Bass, Roger William *architect*
Freyer, Victoria C. *fashion and interior design executive*

**Orlean**
Kulski, Julian Eugeniusz *architect, planner, educator*

**Portsmouth**
Brown, James Andrew *naval architect*

**Reston**
Scheeler, James Arthur *architect*

**Richmond**
Jandl, Henry Anthony *architect, educator*
Joel, William Lee, II *interior and lighting designer*
Morris, James Carl *architect*

---

**Vienna**
Kohler, Karl Eugene *architect*

**Williamsburg**
Herbert, Albert Edward, Jr. *interior and industrial designer*
Parker, Donald Howard *landscape architect*

**Woodbridge**
Peck, Dianne Kawecki *architect*

## WASHINGTON

**Bainbridge Island**
Bowden, William Darsie *retired interior designer*

**Bellevue**
Hoag, Paul Sterling *architect*

**Everett**
King, Indle Gifford *industrial designer, educator*

**Hansville**
Griffin, DeWitt James *architect, real estate developer*

**Kirkland**
Mitchell, Joseph Patrick *architect*

**Mount Vernon**
Hall, David Ramsay *architect*
Klein, Henry *architect*

**Ocean Shores**
Morgan, Audrey *architect*

**Redmond**
Sowder, Robert Robertson *architect*

**Seattle**
Bain, William James, Jr. *architect*
Bassetti, Fred Forde *architect*
Bosworth, Thomas Lawrence *architect, educator*
Castanes, James Christopher *architect*
Cichanski, Gerald *golf course architect*
Grossman, Robert James *architect*
Hastings, L(ois) Jane *architect, educator*
Hinshaw, Mark Larson *architect, urban planner*
Jacobson, Phillip Lee *architect, educator*
Johnston, Norman John *architecture educator*
Jonassen, James O. *architect*
Jones, Grant Richard *landscape architect, planner*
Kolb, Keith Robert *architect, educator*
Lovett, Wendell Harper *architect*
Malcolm, Garold Dean *architect*
Morse, John Moore *architect, planner*
Olson, James William Park *architect*
Piven, Peter Anthony *architect, management consultant*
Springer, Floyd Ladean *architect*

**Shelton**
Wolbrink, Donald Henry *landscape architect, city planner*

**Shoreline**
Freed, Aaron David *architect*

**Tacoma**
Harris, James Martin *architect*
Liddle, Alan Curtis *architect*

**Vancouver**
Graffis, Julie Anne *interior designer, entrepreneur*

## WEST VIRGINIA

**Wheeling**
Hughes, Mary Elizabeth *interior designer*

## WISCONSIN

**Eau Claire**
Larson, Brian Foix *architect*

**Kenosha**
Potente, Eugene, Jr. *interior designer*

**Madison**
Lawson, David E. *architect*
Niemann, Bernard John, Jr. *land and geographical system educator, researcher, consultant*
Sample, Nathaniel Welshire *architect*
Tishler, William Henry *landscape architect, educator*

**Milwaukee**
Greenstreet, Robert Charles *architect, educator*

**Osseo**
Wright, Rodney H. *architect*

## TERRITORIES OF THE UNITED STATES

## PUERTO RICO

**San Juan**
Marvel, Thomas Stahl *architect*

## CANADA

## BRITISH COLUMBIA

**Vancouver**
Erickson, Arthur Charles *architect*
Oberlander, Cornelia Hahn *landscape architect*
Patkau, John *architect*

Patkau, Patricia *architect, architecture educator*

## NOVA SCOTIA

### Halifax
Fowler, Charles Allison Eugene *architect, engineer*

## ONTARIO

### Don Mills
Budrevics, Alexander *landscape architect*

### Toronto
Akazawa-Eguchi, Miyuki Rei Real *landscape architect, environmental artist*
Diamond, Abel Joseph *architect*
Fife, Edward H. *landscape architecture educator*
Flanagan-Eguchi, Barbara L. *landscape architect, theme park designer*
McKenna, Marianne *architect*
Thornley, Shirley Blumberg *architect*
van Ginkel, Blanche Lemco *architect, educator*

## QUEBEC

### Montreal
Jacobs, Peter Daniel Alexander *architecture and landscape architecture educator*
Marsan, Jean-Claude *architect, urban planner, educator*

### Senneville
Prus, Victor Marius *architect, urbanist*

## DENMARK

### Copenhagen
Benjamin, David Nicholas *architect, researcher*

## ENGLAND

### London
Foster, Sir Norman Robert *architect*

## FRANCE

### Ferney-Voltaire
Greer, Joseph Epps *architect*

## GERMANY

### Cologne
Ungers, Oswald M. *architect, educator*

## JAPAN

### Tokyo
Azuma, Takamitsu *architect, educator*
Taguchi, Yoshitaka *architect*

## KUWAIT

### Safat
Boyer, Lester Leroy, Jr. *architecture educator, consultant*

## ADDRESS UNPUBLISHED

Adler, Richard Melvin *architect, planner*
Adsit, Russell Allan *landscape architect*
Armistead, Katherine Kelly (Mrs. Thomas B. Armistead, III) *interior designer, travel consultant, civic worker*
Balke, Robert Roy *architect*
Barnum, William Milo *architect*
Berkovich, Gary A. *architect*
Berman, Siegrid Visconti *interior designer*
Bini, Dante Natale *architect, industrial designer*
Blair, Frederick David *interior designer*
Blevins, Gary Lynn *architect, real estate broker, real estate appraiser*
Bunch, Franklin Swope *architect*
Campbell, Craig Stewart *landscape architect, town planner*
Carpenter, Derr Alvin *landscape architect*
Carroll, Marshall Elliott *architect*
Case, Gerard Ramon *drafting technologist, paleontologist*
Chao, James Min-Tzu *architect*
Cleaveland, John Riddle *architect*
Cohen, Sharleen Cooper *interior designer, writer*
Collins, John Francis *landscape architect, educator*
Cranin, Marilyn Sunners *landscape designer*
Crowther, Richard Layton *architect, consultant, researcher, author, lecturer*
Deal, Lynn Hoffmann *interior designer*
Dean, Francis Hill *landscape architect, educator*
De Reineck, Marie *interior designer*
Dermanis, Paul Raymond *architect*
Dibner, David Robert *architect*
Diffrient, Niels *industrial designer*
Dobbel, Rodger Francis *interior designer*
Ely, Marica McCann *interior designer*
End, Henry *interior and industrial designer*
Flipse, John Edward *naval architect, mechanical engineer*
Friedman, Mildred *designer, educator, curator*
Fulton, James Franklin *industrial designer*
Gantz, Carroll Melvin *industrial design consultant, consumer product designer*
Geddes, Robert *architect, educator*
Gerou, Phillip Howard *architect*
Gordon, Ezra *architect, educator*
Hampton, Mark *interior designer*
Hixon, Allen Wentworth *landscape architect, land planner*
Hooper, Roger Fellowes *architect, retired*
Hutchins, Robert Ayer *architectural consultant*
Kahn, Charles Howard *architect, educator*
Katz, Robert David *architecture educator*
Knoll, Florence Schust *architect, designer*
Kropp, David Arthur *retired landscape architect*
Kultermann, Udo *architectural and art historian*
Lacy, Joseph Newton *architect*
Leaman, Jack Ervin *landscape architect, community and regional planner*
Lewcock, Ronald Bentley *architect, educator*
Liskamm, William Hugo *architect, urban planner, educator*
Loss, John C. *architect, retired educator*
Mc Intosh, James Eugene, Jr. *interior designer*
Mc Pheeters, Edwin Keith *architect, educator*
Meier, Henry George *architect*
Merrick, Dorothy Susan *interior designer*
Meyers, Richard James *landscape architect*
Miller, Jack Conway *landscape artist, art gallery director, owner*
Moore, Richard Alan *landscape architect*
Mujica, Mauro E. *architect*
Mumma, Albert Girard, Jr. *architect*
Murray, David George *architect*
Odermatt, Robert Allen *architect*
Peters, Robert Woolsey *architect*
Pettitt, Jay S. *architect, consultant*
Poor, Janet Meakin *landscape designer*
Rice, Richard Lee *retired architect*
Roegner, George Peter *industrial designer*
Rogers, Kate Ellen *interior design educator*
Ryan, John Michael *landscape architect*
Shadbolt, Douglas *architecture educator, administrator*
Shaw, Dean Alvin *architect*
Siefer, Stuart B. *architect*
Sullivan, Robert Scott *architect, graphic designer*
Tomasi, Donald Charles *architect*
Walker, Bradford C. *architect*
Wenger, Vicki *interior designer*
Wiebenson, Dora Louise *architectural historian, educator, author*
Wilkerson, Charles Edward *architect*
Wilson, William Glenn, Jr. *graphic designer*
Wink, Doreen Musto *interior designer*
Woerner, Robert Lester *landscape architect*

# ARTS: LITERARY. *See also* COMMUNICATIONS MEDIA.

## UNITED STATES

## ALABAMA

### Birmingham
Stallworth, Anne Nall *writer, writing educator*

### Huntsville
Smith, Philip Wayne *writer, communications company executive*

## ALASKA

### Anchorage
Haines, John Meade *poet, translator, writer*
Strohmeyer, John *writer, former editor*
Thomas, Lowell, Jr. *author, lecturer, former lieutenant governor, former state senator*

### Fairbanks
Helmericks, Harmon R. *author, explorer*

## ARIZONA

### Cave Creek
Gose, Celeste Marlene *writer*

### Flagstaff
Cline, Platt Herrick *author*

### Paradise Valley
Cussler, Clive Eric *author*

### Phoenix
Ellison, Cyril Lee *literary agent, publisher*
Estes, Mark Wayne *corporate communications writer, editor*

### Snowflake
Freyermuth, Gundolf S. *writer*

### Tempe
Raby, William Louis *author*

### Tucson
Butcher, Russell Devereux *author, photographer*
Ingalls, Jeremy *poet, educator*
†Kingsolver, Barbara Ellen *writer*
Leydet, François Guillaume *writer*
Russ, Joanna *author*
Vicker, Ray *writer*

## ARKANSAS

### Eureka Springs
Dragonwagon, Crescent (Ellen Zolotow) *writer*

### Fayetteville
Jones, Douglas Clyde *author*
Williams, Miller *poet, translator*

### Flippin
Modeland, Phyllis Jo *author*

### Hot Springs National Park
Stuber, Irene Zelinsky *writer, researcher*

### Little Rock
Brown, Dee Alexander *author*
Serbus, Pearl Sarah Dieck *former freelance writer, former editor*

## CALIFORNIA

### Altadena
Burden, Jean (Prussing) *poet, writer, editor*

### Antioch
Chu, Valentin Yuan-ling *author*

### Arcadia
Sloane, Beverly LeBov *writer, consultant*

### Belmont
Morris, Bruce Dorian *technical writer, literary historian, educator*

### Berkeley
Callenbach, Ernest *writer, editor*
Clark, Thomas Willard *poet*
Dundes, Alan *writer, folklorist, educator*
Guest, Barbara *author, poet*
†Katzen, Mollie *writer, artist*
Kingston, Maxine Hong *author*
Meltzer, David *author, musician*
Milosz, Czeslaw *poet, author, educator*
Peoples, David Webb *screenwriter*
Temko, Allan Bernard *writer*

### Beverly Hills
Bass, Ronald *screenwriter*
Benedek, Barbara *screenwriter*
Bochco, Steven *screenwriter, television producer*
Carpenter, John Howard *screenwriter, director*
Crichton, (John) Michael *author, film director*
Darabont, Frank *screenwriter, director*
Epstein, Julius J. *screenwriter, playwright, producer*
Essex, Harry J. *screenwriter, novelist*
Fisher, Terry Louise *television writer*
Frank, Harriet, Jr. *screenwriter*
Gelbart, Larry *writer, producer*
Getchell, Robert *screenwriter*
Goldman, Bo *screenwriter, director*
Goldman, William *writer*
Graff, Todd *screenwriter*
Green, Walon *screenwriter*
Leonard, Elmore John *novelist, screenwriter*
Lloyd, Christopher *television writer and producer*
Mandel, Babaloo *scriptwriter*
Mann, Ted *screenwriter*
Mazursky, Paul *screenwriter, theatrical director and producer*
Meyer, Nicholas *screenwriter, director*
Oldfield, A(rthur) Barney *writer, radio commentator*
Rabe, David William *playwright*
Roth, Eric *screenwriter*
Schulian, John (Nielsen Schulian) *screenwriter, author*
Shepard, Sam (Samuel Shepard Rogers) *playwright, actor*
Silverman, David Alan *screenwriter, television story consultant*
Stern, Gardner *television writer and producer*
Tally, Ted *screenwriter*
Towne, Robert *screenwriter*
Ward, David Schad *screenwriter, film director*

### Burbank
Schumacher, Joel *film writer, director*

### Carson
Davidson, Mark *writer, educator*

### Chico
Keithley, George *writer*

### Claremont
Mezey, Robert *poet, educator*

### Coronado
Stockdale, James Bond *writer, research scholar, retired naval officer*

### Covina
Phillips, Jill Meta *novelist, critic, astrologer*

### Cromberg
Kolb, Ken Lloyd *writer*

### Culver City
Crowe, Cameron *screenwriter, film director*
McNeill, Daniel Richard *writer*

### Cupertino
Zobel, Louise Purwin *author, educator, lecturer, writing consultant*

### Cypress
Edmonds, Ivy Gordon *writer*

### Davis
Beagle, Peter Soyer *writer*
Major, Clarence Lee *novelist, poet, educator*
McPherson, Sandra Jean *poet, educator*

### Encino
Kanter, Hal *television and film writer, producer, director*

### Fair Oaks
Inglis, Andrew Franklin *author, consultant*

### Fairfax
Gores, Joseph Nicholas *novelist, scriptwriter*
Novello, Don *writer, comedian, actor*

### Georgetown
Lengyel, Cornel Adam (Cornel Adam) *author*

### Healdsburg
Erdman, Paul Emil *author*

### Irvine
Shusterman, Neal Douglas *author, screenwriter*
Wolff, Geoffrey Ansell *novelist, critic, educator*

### Kensington
Nathan, Leonard Edward *writer, educator*

### La Jolla
Antin, David *poet, critic*
Havis, Allan Stuart *playwright, theatre educator*
Movius, Alison Whitney Burton (Alison Whitney) *writer, educator, publisher, speaker, poet, songwriter*

### Laguna Beach
Taylor, Theodore Langhans *author*

### Landers
Landers, Vernette Trosper *writer, educator, association executive*

### Los Angeles
Anderson, Jane A. *scriptwriter*
Avallone, Michael Angelo *author*
Basil, Douglas Constantine *author, educator*
Bayless, Raymond *writer, artist, parapsychologist*
Cecchetti, Giovanni *poet, Italian language educator, literary critic*
Chetwynd, Lionel *screenwriter, producer, director*
Cohen, Leonard (Norman Cohen) *poet, novelist, musician, songwriter*
Corwin, Norman *writer, director, producer*
Crow, John Armstrong *writer, educator*
†France, Richard Xavier *playwright, educator, narrator*
Fraser, Brad *playwright, theatrical director, screenwriter*
Fuller, Samuel (Michael) *scriptwriter, film director*
Highwater, Jamake *author, lecturer*
Hotz, Robert Lee *science writer, editor*
Lachman, Morton *writer, theatrical director and producer*
Lee, David C. *screenwriter*
Mooser, Stephen *author*
Myers, Katherine Donna *writer, publisher*
Nelson, Anna Masterton *writer*
Noguchi, Thomas Tsunetomi *author, forensic pathologist*
Pollock, David *television writer and producer*
Puzo, Mario *author*
Richter, W. D. *screenwriter, director, producer*
Robert, Patrick *playwright*
Ross, Stanley Ralph *writer, publisher, producer, software manufacturing executive*
Rubin, Bruce Joel *screenwriter, director, producer*
Russell, Pamela Redford *writer, film documentarian*
Schulman, Tom *screenwriter*
Shapiro, Mel *playwright, director, drama educator*
Shore, Herbert *writer, poet, educator*
Steel, Ronald Lewis *author, historian, educator*
Thomas, Shirley *author, educator, business executive*
Westheimer, David Kaplan *novelist*
Yoshiki-Kovinick, Marian Tsugie *author*

### Mariposa
Shields, Allan Edwin *writer, photographer, retired educator*

### Newport Beach
Dovring, Karin Elsa Ingeborg *author, poet, playwright, communication analyst*
Wentworth, Diana von Welanetz *author*

### North Hollywood
Kuter, Kay E. *writer, actor*

### Novato
†Goldstein, Kenneth F. *entertainment executive, software executive*

### Oakland
Foley, Jack (John Wayne Harold Foley) *poet, writer, editor*
Grzanka, Leonard Gerald *writer, consultant*
Schacht, Henry Mevis *writer, consultant*
Silverberg, Robert *author*

### Oceanside
Humphrey, Phyllis A. *writer*

### Pacific Grove
Fleischman, Paul *children's author*
O'Shaughnessy, Ellen Cassels *writer*

### Palm Springs
Minahan, John English *author*

### Palomar Mountain
Day, Richard Somers *author, editorial consultant, video producer*

### Pasadena
Butler, Octavia Estelle *free-lance writer*

### Petaluma
Hill, Debora Elizabeth *author, journalist, screenwriter*
Pronzini, Bill John (William Pronzini) *author*

### Ramona
Cesinger, Joan *author*

### Rancho Santa Fe
Simon, William Leonard *film and television writer and producer, author*

### Redondo Beach
Battles, Roxy Edith *novelist, consultant, educator*

### Reedley
Carey, Ernestine Gilbreth (Mrs. Charles E. Carey) *writer, lecturer*

### San Carlos
Morrison, Ellen M. *writer, researcher*

### San Diego
Broening, Elise Hedwig *writer*
Crumpler, Hugh Allan *author*
Krull, Kathleen *juvenile fiction and nonfiction writer*
Lederer, Richard Henry *writer, educator, columnist*
Linn, Edward Allen *writer*
March, Marion D. *writer, astrologer, consultant*

## San Francisco
Bowers, Edgar *poet, educator*
Ferlinghetti, Lawrence *poet*
Ferris, Russell James, II *freelance writer*
Field, Carol Hart *writer, journalist, foreign correspondent*
Gunn, Thom(son) (William) *poet*
Lippitt, Elizabeth Charlotte *writer*
O'Connor, Sheila Anne *freelance writer*
Olsen, Tillie *author*
Patterson, Richard North *writer, lawyer*
Quick, William Thomas *author, consultant*
Sachs, Marilyn Stickle *author, lecturer, editor*
Whalen, Philip Glenn *poet, novelist*

## San Jose
Loventhal, Milton *writer, playwright, lyricist*
Steele, Shelby *writer, educator*

## San Juan Capistrano
Kleiner, Richard Arthur *writer, editor*

## San Luis Obispo
Bunge, Russell Kenneth *writer, poet, editor*

## San Luis Rey
Williams, Elizabeth Yahn *author, lecturer, lawyer*

## San Marcos
Sauer, David Andrew *writer, computer consultant*

## San Mateo
Korn, Walter *writer*

## San Rafael
Turner, William Weyand *author*

## Santa Ana
Kinosian, Janet Marie *journalist*

## Santa Barbara
Bock, Russell Samuel *author*
Branch, Taylor *writer*
Davidson, Eugene Arthur *author*
Easton, Robert (Olney) *author, environmentalist*
Jackson, Beverley Joy Jacobson *columnist, lecturer*
Smith, Michael Townsend *author, editor, stage director*

## Santa Cruz
Sherman, Frieda Frances *writer*

## Santa Monica
Barry, Julian *playwright, screenwriter*
Launer, Dale Mark *screenwriter*
O'Donnell, Lawrence Francis, Jr. *author*
Stone, Oliver William *screenwriter, director*

## Santa Rosa
Gioia, (Michael) Dana *poet, literary critic*

## Sebastopol
Kherdian, David *author*

## Sherman Oaks
Ellison, Harlan Jay *author, screenwriter*
MacMullen, Douglas Burgoyne *writer, editor, retired army officer, publisher*

## Sonoma
Jayme, William North *writer*
Kizer, Carolyn Ashley *poet, educator*

## Stanford
Conquest, (George) Robert (Acworth) *writer, historian, poet, critic, journalist*
Gardner, John William *writer, educator*
Girard, René Noel *author, educator*
Lindenberger, Herbert Samuel *writer, literature educator*
Wolff, Tobias (Jonathan Ansell Wolff) *author*

## Studio City
Parish, James Robert *author, cinema historian*
Ribman, Ronald Burt *playwright*
Shavelson, Melville *writer, theatrical producer and director*

## Tiburon
Drury, Allen Stuart *author*

## Trinidad
Schaaf, Miv *writer, graphic designer, composer*

## Venice
Eliot, Alexander *author, mythologist*
Seger, Linda Sue *script consultant, writer*

## West Hollywood
Black, David *writer, educator, producer*
Black, Shane *screenwriter*
Dorsey, Helen Danner (Johna Blinn) *writer, author, educator*
Grasshoff, Alex *writer, producer, director*
Ranberg, Chuck Alan *television writer, producer*

## COLORADO

## Aurora
Bower, Donald Edward *author*

## Boulder
Kaye, Evelyn Patricia (Evelyn Patricia Sarson) *author, publisher, travel expert*
Metzger, H(owell) Peter *writer*
Waldman, Anne Lesley *poet, performer, editor, publisher, educational administrator*

## Canon City
Bendell, Donald Ray *writer, director, poet*

## Colorado Springs
Dassanowsky, Robert von *writer, editor, educator, producer*
Yaffe, James *author*

## Denver
Ducker, Bruce *novelist, lawyer*
MacGregor, George Lescher, Jr. *freelance writer*
Nemiro, Beverly Mirium Anderson *author, educator*
Stephens, Phillip *screenwriter, producer*

## Estes Park
Hillway, Tyrus *author, educator*

## Greeley
Willis, Connie (Constance E. Willis) *author*

## Vail
Knight, Constance Bracken *writer, realtor, corporate executive*

## CONNECTICUT

## Danbury
Weiner, Jonathan David *writer*

## East Haven
Scarf, Margaret (Maggie Scarf) *author*

## Easton
Maloney, John Joseph *writer*

## Essex
Keppel, John *writer, former diplomat*
Soule, Gardner Bosworth *writer*

## Fairfield
Barone, Rose Marie Pace *writer, retired educator, entertainer*

## Greens Farms
St. Marie, Satenig *writer*

## Greenwich
Ewald, William Bragg, Jr. *author, consultant*
Hoberman, Mary Ann *author*

## Guilford
Peters, William *author, producer, director*

## Hanover
†Cheney, Glenn Alan *writer, educator*

## Hartford
Hedrick, Joan Doran *writer*

## Madison
Carlson, Dale Bick *writer*

## Middletown
Manchester, William *writer*

## New Canaan
Prescott, Peter Sherwin *writer*

## New Haven
Gallup, Donald Clifford *bibliographer, educator*

## Old Lyme
St. George, Judith Alexander *author*

## Old Saybrook
Hamilton, Donald Bengtsson *author*

## Preston
Gibson, Margaret Ferguson *poet, educator*

## Roxbury
Anderson, Robert Woodruff *playwright, novelist, screenwriter*
Gurney, Albert Ramsdell *playwright, novelist, educator*
Miller, Arthur *playwright, author*

## Storrs Mansfield
Rimland, Lisa Phillip *writer, composer, lyricist, artist*

## Suffield
Tobin, Joan Adele *writer*

## Waterford
Commire, Anne *playwright*

## West Cornwall
Klaw, Spencer *writer, editor, educator*

## Westbrook
Hall, Jane Anna *writer, model, artist*

## Weston
Diforio, Robert G. *literary agent*
Kilty, Jerome Timothy *playwright, stage director, actor*

## Westport
Hotchner, Aaron Edward *author*
Martin, Ralph Guy *writer*
Safran, Claire *writer, editor*

## DISTRICT OF COLUMBIA

## Washington
Alperovitz, Gar *author*
Arndt, Richard T. *writer, consultant*
Barnet, Richard Jackson *author, educator*
Birnbaum, Norman *author, humanities educator*
Black, Charlie J. *technical writer, author, educator, business consultant*
Blair, Patricia Wohlgemuth *economics writer*
Burnham, David Bright *writer*
Burns, David Mitchell *writer, musician, former diplomat*
Cashmore, Patsy Joy *speechwriter, editor, author, consultant, educator*
Cavnar, Samuel Melmon *author, publisher, activist*
Childs, Timothy Winston *writer*
Friedan, Betty Naomi *author, feminist leader*
George, Gerald William *author, administrator*

Goldberg, Kirsten Boyd *science journalist*
Haggerty, James Joseph *writer*
Hecht, Anthony Evan *poet*
Innis, Pauline *writer, publishing company executive*
Lilienthal, Alfred M(orton) *author, historian, editor*
May, Stephen *writer, former government official*
McCarthy, Abigail Quigley *writer, columnist, educator*
Merrell, Jesse Howard *writer*
Miller, Hope Ridings *author*
Ramsay, William Charles *writer*
Richardson, David Bacon *writer, journalist*
Rosenbaum, Alvin Robert *writer*
Sattler, Stephen Charles *writer, editor, communications consultant*
Shaw, Russell Burnham *author, journalist*
Small, Jennifer Jean *writer, journalist*
Smith, Stuart Seaborne *writer, government official, union official*
Tannen, Deborah Frances *writer, linguist*
Taquey, Charles Henri *writer, consultant*
Van Dyk, Frederick Theodore *writer, consultant*
Viorst, Judith Stahl *author*
Wouk, Herman *writer*
Yarrow, Andrew Louis *writer, journalist, educator, international relations consultant*

## FLORIDA

## Babson Park
Morrison, Kenneth Douglas *author, columnist*

## Belleair Beach
Fuentes, Martha Ayers *playwright*

## Boca Raton
Keyes, Daniel *author*

## Boynton Beach
Heckelmann, Charles Newman (Charles Lawton) *author, publishing consultant*

## Captiva
Fadiman, Clifton *writer, editor, radio and television entertainer*

## Coconut Grove
Alschuler, Al *freelance writer, public relations counselor*

## Daytona Beach
Chesnut, Nondis Lorine *writer, consultant, reading educator*
Mc Collister, John Charles *writer, clergyman, educator, executive producer*

## Delray Beach
Burbank, Kershaw *writer*
Coyle, William *educator*
Robinson, Richard Francis *writer, author*

## Eustis
Chorosinski, Eugene Conrad *writer, poet, author*

## Fort Lauderdale
Martínez-Solanas, Gerardo Enrique *reporting service reviser, writer*
Maurer, Yolanda Tahar *publisher*

## Fort Myers
Powell, Richard Pitts *writer*

## Gainesville
Haldeman, Joe William *novelist*
Holland, Norman Norwood *literary critic*
Smith, Jo Anne *writer, retired educator*

## Hallandale
Geller, Bunny Zelda *poet, writer, publisher, sculptor, artist*

## Hollywood
Blate, Michael *author, lecturer*

## Indialantic
Lewis, Richard Stanley *author, former editor*

## Jacksonville
Slaughter, Frank Gill *author, physician*

## Largo
Craft Davis, Audrey Ellen *writer, educator*

## Lynn Haven
Leonard, Venelda Hall *writer*

## Melbourne
Lederer, William Julius *author*
Stone, Elaine Murray *author, composer, television producer*

## Miami
Morgan, Marabel *author*
Robinson, David Bradford *poet, scientific writer*

## Miami Beach
Angel-Junguito, Antonio *writer*

## Milton
Tarvin, Albert Leon *writer*

## Mount Dora
Hart, Valerie Gail *writer*

## Naples
Alpert, Hollis *writer*
Card, Orson Scott (Byron Walley) *writer*
Montgomery, Ruth Shick *author*
Thompson, Didi Castle (Mary Bennett) *writer, editor*

## Nokomis
Wendt, Lloyd *writer*

## Orlando
Raffa, Jean Benedict *author, educator*

## Palm Beach
Hall, Kathryn Evangeline *writer, lecturer*

## Pensacola
Klepper, Robert Kenneth *writer, silent film historian, journalist*
Sargent, James O'Connor *freelance writer*

## Saint Augustine
Edwards, Page Lawrence, Jr. *author, archivist, historical society administrat*
Oliver, Elizabeth Kimball *writer, historian*

## Saint Petersburg
Bryant, John *author, publisher*
Carlson, Jeannie Ann *writer*
Meinke, Peter *writer, retired educator*

## Sarasota
Hayes, Joseph *author*
Weeks, Albert Loren *author, educator, journalist*

## Tallahassee
Bagley, James Robert *freelance writer*

## Tampa
Battle, Jean Allen *writer, educator*
Dunn, Henry Hampton *writer, former television commentator, former editor*
Hanford, Grail Stevenson *writer*

## Tequesta
Ragno, Nancy Nickell *educational writer*

## Venice
Shaw, Bryce Robert *author*

## Winter Park
Hill, Elizabeth Starr *writer*

## GEORGIA

## Atlanta
Chapman, Paul H. *author*
Dunn, John Clinton *writer, editor*
Geigerman, Clarice Furchgott *writer, actress, consultant*
Horsman, David A. Elliott *writer, financial services executive, educator*

## Augusta
Taylor, Janelle Diane Williams *writer*

## Savannah
Thomas, Dwight Rembert *writer*

## Statesboro
Ragans, Rosalind Dorothy *textbook author, retired art educator*

## HAWAII

## Honolulu
Edel, (Joseph) Leon *biographer, educator*
Halloran, Richard Colby *writer, former research executive, former news correspondent*
Statler, Oliver Hadley *writer*

## IDAHO

## Sun Valley
Briley, John Richard *writer*

## ILLINOIS

## Abbott Park
Devine, Barbara Armstrong *medical writing administrator*

## Chicago
Brooks, Gwendolyn *writer, poet*
Buehler, Evelyn Judy *poet*
Carpenter, Allan *author, editor, publisher*
Hoover, Paul *poet*
Kolkey, Eric Samuel *screenwriter*
Lach, Alma Elizabeth *food and cooking writer, consultant*
Litweiler, John Berkey *writer, editor*
Manelli, Donald Dean *screenwriter, film producer*
Nims, John Frederick *writer, educator*
Paretsky, Sara N. *writer*
Phillips, Ethel C. (Mrs. Lloyd J. Phillips) *writer*
Stern, Richard Gustave *author, educator*
Terkel, Studs (Louis Terkel) *author, interviewer*
Wade, Edwin Lee *writer, lawyer*

## Evanston
Gibbons, William Reginald, Jr. *poet, novelist, editor*

## Lake Forest
Swanton, Virginia Lee *author, publisher, bookseller*

## Lanark
Etter, David Pearson *poet, editor*

## Marengo
Mrkvicka, Edward Francis, Jr. *financial writer, publisher, consultant*

## Morton Grove
Vega, Steve *poet*

## North Riverside
Sedlak, S(hirley) A(gnes) *freelance writer*

## Oak Park
Bowman, James Henry *writer*
Kotlowitz, Alex *writer, journalist*

## Palatine
Pohl, Frederik *writer*

**Park Forest**
Putnam, Robert E. *writer, editor*

**Peru**
Kurtz, James Eugene *freelance writer, minister*

**South Barrington**
Kissane, Sharon Florence *writer, consultant*

**Springfield**
Hines, Daisy Marie *writer*

**Urbana**
Lieberman, Laurence *poet, educator*

**Waukegan**
Marks, Martha Alford *author*

**INDIANA**

**Bloomington**
Kibbey, Hal Stephen *science writer*
Komunyakaa, Yusef (James Willie Brown, Jr.) *poet*
Mitchell, Bert Breon *literary translator*

**Chesterton**
Petrakis, Harry Mark *author*

**Crown Point**
Palmeri, Sharon Elizabeth *freelance writer, community educator*

**Frankfort**
Borland, Kathryn Kilby *author*

**Howe**
Bowerman, Ann Louise *author, genealogist, educator*

**Indianapolis**
Altman, Joseph *author, neuroscientist*
Budniakiewicz, Therese *author*
Wise, Rita J. *writer, poet*

**La Porte**
Madsen, Dorothy Louise (Meg Madsen) *writer*

**Muncie**
Eddy, Darlene Mathis *poet, educator*

**South Bend**
Black, Virginia Morrow *writer*

**IOWA**

**Ames**
Smiley, Jane Graves *author, educator*

**Iowa City**
Bell, Marvin Hartley *poet, English language educator*
Graham, Jorie *author*
Johnson, Nicholas *writer, lawyer, lecturer*
Justice, Donald Rodney *poet, educator*
†Stein, Robert A. *writer*
Stern, Gerald Daniel *poet*

**KANSAS**

**Manhattan**
Davis, Kenneth Sidney *writer*

**Wichita**
Page, Thomas Leslie *poet, writer*

**KENTUCKY**

**Lexington**
Davenport, Guy Mattison, Jr. *author, retired educator*

**Louisville**
Davenport, Gwen (Mrs. John Davenport) *author*

**Utica**
Henry, Loretta M. *writer*

**West Paducah**
Simmons, Gary M. *writer, small business owner*

**LOUISIANA**

**Baton Rouge**
Madden, David *author*

**Lafayette**
Webb, Bernice Larson *writer, consultant, press owner, publisher*

**Lake Charles**
Butler, Robert Olen *writer, educator*

**Mandeville**
Harton, Merle Carter, Jr. *writer*

**New Orleans**
Grau, Shirley Ann (Mrs. James Kern Feibleman) *writer*
Pizer, Donald *author, educator*

**Quitman**
Maxwell, Patricia Anne *writer*

**Zachary**
Blevins, Donna Caton *writer*

**MAINE**

**Blue Hill**
Minarik, Else Holmelund (Bigart Minarik) *author*

**Brooklin**
Yglesias, Helen Bassine *author, educator*

**East Blue Hill**
Taylor, Samuel A. *playwright*

**Milbridge**
Enslin, Theodore Vernon *poet*

**Orono**
Wilson, Dorothy Clarke *author*

**Phippsburg**
Mc Lanathan, Richard (Barton Kennedy) *author, consultant*

**South Berwick**
Carroll, Gladys Hasty *author*

**Union**
Taylor, Roger Conant *writer*

**MARYLAND**

**Aberdeen**
Schueler, Betty Jane *writer, counselor*

**Baltimore**
Barth, John Simmons *writer, educator*
Eisenberg, Gerson G. *author, historian*
Epstein, Daniel Mark *poet, dramatist*
Livingstone, Harrison Edward *writer*
Tyler, Anne (Mrs. Taghi M. Modarressi) *author*

**Bethesda**
Dyer, Frederick Charles *writer, consultant*
Free, Ann Cottrell *writer*
Hartmann, Robert Trowbridge *author, consultant*
Henze, Paul Bernard *author, former government official*
Naylor, Phyllis Reynolds *author*
Simonds, Peggy Muñoz *writer, lecturer, retired literature educator*
Vosburgh, Frederick George *writer, editor*

**Burtonsville**
Peck, Carol Faulkner *poet, writer, publisher, educator*

**Chevy Chase**
Bacon, Donald Conrad *author, editor*
Cron, Theodore Oscar *writer, editor, educator*
McNamara, Francis John *writer*

**College Park**
Whittemore, Edward Reed, II *poet, retired educator*

**Fort Washington**
Cameron, Rita Giovannetti *writer, publisher*

**Garrett Park**
Kornberg, Warren Stanley *science journalist*

**Huntingtown**
Clancy, Thomas L., Jr. *novelist*

**Potomac**
Kessler, Ronald Borek *author*
Pastan, Linda Olenik *poet*
Sowalsky, Patti Lurie *author*

**Rockville**
Nilsson, Nancy Mitchell *playwright*

**Severna Park**
Davis, Clayton *writer, pilot*

**Silver Spring**
Whitten, Leslie Hunter, Jr. *author, newspaper reporter, poet*

**Upper Marlboro**
Smith, Ralph Lee *author, musician*

**MASSACHUSETTS**

**Amherst**
Bagg, Robert Ely *poet*
Commager, Henry Steele *retired writer, history educator*
Jenkins, Paul Randall *poet, editor*
Langland, Joseph Thomas *author, emeritus educator*
Lester, Julius B. *author*
Tate, James Vincent *poet, English educator*

**Bedford**
Kennedy, X. J. (Joseph Kennedy) *writer*

**Belmont**
Cavarnos, Constantine Peter *writer, philosopher*

**Boston**
Andre, Rae *writer, organizational behavior educator*
Angelou, Maya *author*
Ballas, Nadia S. *writer, poet*
Carroll, James *author*
Davis, William Arthur *writer, editor*
Greenwald, Sheila Ellen *writer, illustrator*
Hailey, Arthur *author*
Headding, Lillian Susan (Sally Headding) *writer, forensic clairvoyant*
Kindl, Patrice *writer*
Lowry, Lois (Hammersberg) *author*
Pinsky, Robert Neal *poet, educator*
Pynchon, Thomas Ruggles, Jr. *author*
Say, Allen *children's writer, illustrator*
Sklar, Holly L(yn) *nonfiction writer*
Terrill, Ross Gladwin *author, educator*
Van Allsburg, Chris *author, artist*
Warren, Rosanna *poet*

Wiesel, Elie *writer, educator*
Wind, Herbert Warren *writer*

**Byfield**
Kozol, Jonathan *writer*

**Cambridge**
Alfred, William *author, educator*
Bernays, Anne Fleischman *writer, educator*
Desai, Anita *writer*
Gaulin, Kenneth *writer, designer*
Heaney, Seamus Justin *poet, educator*
Kaplan, Justin *author*
Lamport, Felicia (Mrs. Benjamin Kaplan) *writer*
Yergin, Daniel Howard *writer, consultant*

**Concord**
Edmonds, Walter Dumaux *author*
Moore, Robert Lowell, Jr. (Robin Moore) *author*

**Cummington**
Smith, William Jay *author*
Wilbur, Richard Purdy *writer, educator*

**Dover**
Smith, William Henry Preston *writer, editor, former corporate executive*

**Edgartown**
Treat, Lawrence *author*

**Everett**
Wright, Franz *poet, writer, translator*

**Gardner**
Wagenknecht, Edward *author*

**Gloucester**
Erkkila, Barbara Howell Louise *writer, photographer*

**Hatfield**
Yolen, Jane *author*

**Leominster**
Cormier, Robert Edmund *writer*

**Lincoln**
Donald, David Herbert *author, history educator*

**Montague**
Andersen, Richard Arnold *writer, consultant*

**Natick**
Sutcliffe, Marion Shea *writer*

**Needham**
Walworth, Arthur *author*

**Newton**
Zohn, Harry *author, educator*

**Newton Highlands**
Porter, Jack Nusan *writer, sociologist, educator*

**North Egremont**
Le Comte, Edward Semple *author, educator*

**Norton**
Norris, Curtis Bird *writer, journalist*

**Orleans**
Hughes, Libby *author*

**Osterville**
El-Fayoumy, J.P.G. *writer, poet*

**Provincetown**
Doty, Mark *poet*
Oliver, Mary *poet*

**Revere**
Herron, Carolivia *novelist, English educator*

**Rockport**
Deedy, John Gerard, Jr. *writer*

**Somerville**
Wheeler, Katherine Frazier (Kate Wheeler) *writer*

**South Hadley**
Viereck, Peter *poet, historian, educator*

**Springfield**
Miller, J(ohn) Wesley, III *lawyer, author*

**Truro**
Cassill, Ronald Verlin *author*
Woolley, Catherine (Jane Thayer) *writer*

**Waltham**
Ellenbogen, George *poet, educator*
Hindus, Milton *writer, literature educator*

**Wellesley**
Jacobs, Ruth Harriet *poet, playwright, sociologist, gerontologist*

**Wellfleet**
Piercy, Marge *poet, novelist, essayist*

**West Newbury**
Dooley, Ann Elizabeth *freelance writers cooperative executive, editor*

**Westport**
Howard, James Merriam, Jr. *education writer*

**Worcester**
Vick, Susan *playwright, educator*

**Yarmouth Port**
Gorey, Edward St. John *author, artist*

**MICHIGAN**

**Ann Arbor**
Fraser, Russell Alfred *author, educator*

**Battle Creek**
Cline, Charles William *poet, pianist, rhetoric and literature educator*

**Detroit**
Madgett, Naomi Long *poet, editor, educator*
McWilliams, Michael G. *writer, television critic*

**East Lansing**
Wakoski, Diane *poet, educator*

**Kalamazoo**
Arnold Hubert, Nancy Kay *writer*
Light, Christopher Upjohn *freelance writer, computer musician*

**Mackinac Island**
Mc Cabe, John Charles, III *writer*

**Okemos**
Janicki, Gregory John *writer, consultant*

**Traverse City**
Abeel, Samantha Lynn *juvenile fiction author*

**Union Pier**
Howland, Bette *writer*

**MINNESOTA**

**Collegeville**
Powers, James Farl *author*

**Edina**
Schwarzrock, Shirley Pratt *author, lecturer, educator*

**Minneapolis**
Baker, John Stevenson (Michael Dyregrov) *writer*
Bly, Robert *poet*
Boylan, Brian Richard *author, producer, photographer, director, literary agent*
Hull, William Henry *author, retired publishing executive*
Korotkin, Fred *writer, philatelist*

**Richfield**
Thompson, Steve Allan *writer*

**Spring Grove**
Hellyer, Clement David *writer*

**MISSISSIPPI**

**Jackson**
Welty, Eudora *author*

**MISSOURI**

**Bloomfield**
Ferrell, Paul Cleveland *author*

**Columbia**
Windsor, Margaret Eden *writer*

**Florissant**
Basler, Theodore Eugene *poet*

**Kansas City**
Callo, Joseph Francis *writer*
Martin-Bowen, (Carole) Lindsey *freelance writer*

**Saint Charles**
Castro, Jan Garden *author, arts consultant, educator*

**Saint Louis**
Broeg, Bob (Robert William Broeg) *writer*
Early, Gerald *writer*
Finkel, Donald *poet*
Gass, William H. *author, educator*
†McKissack, Patricia Carwell *children's book author*
Schlafly, Phyllis Stewart *author*

**Sweet Springs**
Long, Helen Halter *author, educator*

**Viburnum**
West, Roberta Bertha *writer*

**MONTANA**

**Livingston**
Clarke, Urana *writer, musician, educator*

**Mc Leod**
Hjortsberg, William Reinhold *author*
McGuane, Thomas Francis, III *author, screenwriter*

**NEVADA**

**Las Vegas**
Eikenberry, Arthur Raymond *writer, service executive, researcher*
King, Gary Curtis *author, lecturer*

**NEW HAMPSHIRE**

**Bradford**
Hersh, Burton David *author*

**Concord**
Yates, Elizabeth (Mrs. William McGreal) *author, editor*

**Cornish**
Atkinson, James Blakely *writer, editor*

**Durham**
Ford, Daniel (Francis) *writer*

**Lyme**
Demarest, Chris Lynn *writer, illustrator*

**Merrimack**
Vogt, Sharon Madonna *author, educator*

**Suncook**
Weiss, Joanne Marion *writer*

**Walpole**
Gooding, Judson *writer*

## NEW JERSEY

**Andover**
Gioseffi, (Dorothy) Daniela *poet, performer, author, educator*

**Basking Ridge**
Allen, Katherine Spicer *writer, former chemist*

**Bergenfield**
Knowles, John *author*

**Cape May Court House**
Cohen, Daniel Edward *writer*
Cohen, Susan Lois *author*

**Cherry Hill**
Gardner, Joel Robert *writer, historian*

**Elizabeth**
Willis, Ben *writer, artist*

**Englewood**
Downes, John *writer, editor*

**Fort Lee**
Locke, Virginia Otis *freelance writer, editor*

**Hopewell**
Halpern, Daniel *poet, editor, educator*

**Lawrenceville**
Wiater, Teresa Veronica *writer*

**Long Valley**
Collins, Kathleen *writer*

**Madison**
Gibson, William Ford *author*

**Montclair**
Alexander, Fernande Gardner *writer, photographer*

**New Brunswick**
Ostriker, Alicia Suskin *poet*

**Newark**
Dickson, Jim *playwright, stage director, arts consultant*
Hadas, Rachel *poet, educator*
Moskowitz, Sam (Sam Martin) *author, editor, publisher*

**Oradell**
Dinsmore, Gordon Griffith *writer*

**Paramus**
Fader, Shirley Sloan *writer*

**Parsippany**
Harris, Margaret Elizabeth *writer*

**Plainsboro**
Norback, Craig Thomas *writer*

**Princeton**
Morrison, Toni (Chloe Anthony Morrison) *novelist*
Muldoon, Paul *creative writing educator, poet*
Putnam, Peter Brock *author, lecturer*
Twichell, Chase *poet*
Weiss, Theodore Russell *poet, editor*

**Princeton Junction**
Pollard-Gott, Lucy *writer*

**Ringwood**
Murphy, Gloria Walter *novelist, screenwriter*

**Rockaway**
Ruch, William Vaughn *writer, educator, consultant*

**Secaucus**
Gomes, Celeste Regina *writer, editor*

**Ship Bottom**
Turkot, Dorothy Regester Felton *writer, illustrator*

**Short Hills**
Middleton, Timothy George *writer*

**Skillman**
†Kluger, Richard *author, editor*

**Somerset**
Plenty, Royal Homer *writer*

**Stockton**
Tunley, Roul *author*

**Teaneck**
Rizio, Ronald R. *writer, information specialist*

**West Orange**
Rayfield, Gordon Elliott *playwright, political risk consultant*

**Westfield**
Devlin, Wende Dorothy *writer, artist*
Smith, Joan Lowell *writer, public relations consultant*

## NEW MEXICO

**Albuquerque**
Evans, Max Allen *writer, artist*
Whiddon, Carol Price *writer, editor, consultant*

**Corrales**
Page, Jake (James K. Page, Jr.) *writer, editor*

**Galisteo**
Lippard, Lucy Rowland *writer, lecturer*

**Las Cruces**
Medoff, Mark Howard *playwright, screenwriter, novelist*

**Placitas**
Dunmire, William Werden *author, photographer*

**Portales**
Williamson, Jack (John Stewart ) *writer*

**Ranchos De Taos**
Dickey, Robert Preston *author, educator, poet*

**Santa Fe**
Bergé, Carol *author*
Connell, Evan Shelby, Jr. *author*
Tarn, Nathaniel *poet, translator, educator*

## NEW YORK

**Albany**
Kennedy, William Joseph *novelist, educator*

**Amherst**
Kurtz, Paul *publisher, philosopher, educator*

**Annandale On Hudson**
Achebe, Chinua *writer, humanities educator*
Kelly, Robert *poet, novelist, educator*
Manea, Norman *writer, educator*

**Ballston Spa**
Barba, Harry *author, educator, publisher*

**Barrytown**
Higgins, Dick (Richard Carter Higgins) *writer, publisher, composer, artist*

**Bedford Hills**
Ludlum, Robert *author*

**Brewster**
Barnhart, Robert Knox *writer, editor*

**Briarcliff**
Hopkins, Lee Bennett *writer, educator*

**Bronx**
Greenberg, Blu *author*

**Brooklyn**
Chernow, Ron *writer, columnist*
Cunningham, Julia Woolfolk *author*
Lewin, Ted Bert *writer, illustrator*
Mulvihill, Maureen Esther *writer, educator, scholar*
Purdy, James *writer*
Sainer, Arthur *writer, theater educator*

**Buffalo**
Creeley, Robert White *author, English educator*
Federman, Raymond *novelist, English and comparative literature educator*
Feldman, Irving *poet*
Schatz, Lillian Lee *playwright, molecular biologist, educator*

**Cedarhurst**
Solymosy, Hattie May *writer, publisher, storyteller, educator*

**Chappaqua**
George, Jean Craighead *author, illustrator*
Kingsley, Emily Perl *writer*

**Circleville**
Hazan, Marcella Maddalena *author, educator, consultant*

**Cold Spring Harbor**
Freeman, Ira Henry *author, journalist*

**Croton on Hudson**
Henderson, Harry Brinton, Jr. *author, editor*

**East Hampton**
Gaddis, William *writer*
Ignatow, David *poet*

**Erieville**
Snodgrass, W. D. *writer, educator*

**Esopus**
Tetlow, Edwin *author*

**Flushing**
Allen, Ralph Gilmore *dramatist, producer, drama educator*
Goldsmith, Howard *writer, consultant*

**Fort Covington**
Dunwich, Gerina *author, magazine editor, astrologer*

**Fulton**
Long, Robert Emmet *author*

**Garden City**
DeMille, Nelson Richard *writer*

**Great Neck**
Hurwitz, Johanna (Frank) *author, librarian*

**Greenfield Center**
Fonseca, John dos Reis *writer, former law educator*

**Guilderland**
Persico, Joseph Edward *author*

**Hamilton**
Berlind, Bruce Peter *poet, educator*
Busch, Frederick Matthew *writer, literature educator*

**Hastings on Hudson**
Cooney, Patrick Louis *writer*

**Hicksville**
Kneitel, Thomas Stephen *writer, consultant, editor*

**Hudson Falls**
Bronk, William *writer, retail businessman*

**Interlaken**
Bleiler, Everett Franklin *writer, publishing company executive*

**Irvington**
Massie, Robert Kinloch *author*

**Ithaca**
Ammons, Archie Randolph *poet, English educator*
Lurie, Alison *author*

**Jamaica**
Paolucci, Anne Attura *playwright, poet, English and comparative literature educator*

**Jamesville**
Mazer, Norma Fox *writer*

**Keene Valley**
Neville, Emily Cheney *author*

**Kings Point**
Bloom, Murray Teigh *author*

**Lockport**
Cull, John Joseph *novelist, playwright*

**Locust Valley**
McGee, Dorothy Horton *writer, historian*

**Montauk**
Lavenas, Suzanne *writer, editor, consultant*

**Munnsville**
Carruth, Hayden *poet*

**New Rochelle**
Branch, William Blackwell *playwright, producer*
Saperstein, David *novelist, screenwriter, film director*

**New York**
Adams, Alice *writer*
Albee, Edward Franklin *author, playwright*
Allen, Jay Presson *writer, producer*
Allen, Roberta L. *fiction and nonfiction writer, conceptual artist*
Amory, Cleveland *writer*
Andersen, Kurt Byars *writer*
Anderson, Poul William *author*
Angell, Roger *writer, magazine editor*
Ashdown, Marie Matranga (Mrs. Cecil Spanton Ashdown, Jr.) *writer, lecturer*
Ashton, Dore *author, educator*
Auchincloss, Louis Stanton *writer*
Auel, Jean Marie *author*
Auster, Paul *writer*
Balliett, Whitney *writer, critic*
Bauer, Marion Dane *writer*
Beattie, Ann *author*
Beim, Norman *playwright, actor, director*
Bel Geddes, Joan *writer*
Benchley, Peter Bradford *author*
Benedikt, Michael *poet, educator, author, editor, free-lance consultant*
Benn, T(heodore) Alexander (Alec Benn) *writer*
Berendt, John Lawrence *writer, editor*
Berg, David *author, artist*
Berkow, Ira Harvey *author, journalist*
Bernard, Kenneth (Otis Bernard) *poet, author, playwright*
Birstein, Ann *writer, educator*
Bliven, Bruce, Jr. *writer*
Block, Francesca Lia *writer*
Block, Lawrence *author*
Blume, Judy Sussman *author*
Bolt, Thomas *writer, artist*
Bourjaily, Vance *novelist*
†Bradbury, Ray Douglas *author*
Bradford, Barbara Taylor *writer, journalist, novelist*
Bradford, Richard Roark *writer*
Braudy, Susan Orr *writer*
Brenner, Erma *author*
Breuer, Lee *playwright, theatrical director, producer, actor*
Brickman, Marshall *screenwriter, director*
Brown, Kevin *writer*
Bujold, Lois McMaster *science fiction writer*
Burland, Brian Berkeley *novelist, poet, painter, scenarist*
Burnshaw, Stanley *writer*
Calisher, Hortense (Mrs. Curtis Harnack) *writer*
Caputo, Philip Joseph *author, journalist, screenwriter*
Carlson, P(atricia) M(cElroy) *writer*
Caro, Robert Allan *author*
Cartland, Barbara *author*
Christopher, Nicholas *poet, novelist*
Cisneros, Sandra *poet, short story writer, essayist*
Clark, Matt *science writer*
Cleary, Beverly Atlee (Mrs. Clarence T. Cleary) *author*
Cohen, Mark Daniel *poet, communications company executive*
Conroy, Pat (Donald Patrick Conroy) *writer*
†Cook, Robin *author*
Cooper, Paulette Marcia *writer*
Corn, Alfred DeWitt *poet, educator*
†Cornwell, Patricia Daniels *author*
Creech, Sharon *children's author*
†Crews, Harry Eugene *author*
Cryer, Gretchen *playwright, lyricist, actress*
Cummings, Josephine Anna *writer*
Curie, Eve *writer, lecturer*
Curry, Jane Louise *writer*
Cushman, Karen Lipski *writer*
Danto, Arthur Coleman *author, philosopher, art critic*
Danziger, Paula *author*
Davis, Lorraine Jensen *writer, editor*
Decter, Midge *writer*
de Hartog, Jan *writer*
Denker, Henry *playwright, author, director*
Diamonstein-Spielvogel, Barbaralee *writer, television interviewer/ producer*
Didion, Joan *author*
Dillard, Annie *author*
Doctorow, Edgar Lawrence *novelist, English educator*
Doerr, Harriet *writer*
Donaldson, Stephen Reeder *author*
Duffy, James Henry *writer, former lawyer*
Dunne, John Gregory *author*
Ephron, Nora *writer, director*
Espy, Willard Richardson *author*
Fallaci, Oriana *writer, journalist*
Fast, Howard Melvin *author*
Fast, Julius *author, editor*
Fierstein, Harvey Forbes *playwright, actor*
Flanagan, William Francis *writer and editor*
Fleischman, Albert Sidney (Sid Fleischman) *writer*
Fleming, Alice Carew Mulcahey (Mrs. Thomas J. Fleming) *author*
Fleming, Thomas James *writer*
Flexner, James Thomas *author*
Foote, Horton *playwright, scriptwriter*
Fornes, Maria Irene *playwright, director*
Fox, Paula (Mrs. Martin Greenberg) *author*
Francis, Dick (Richard Stanley Francis) *novelist*
†Frazier, Ian *writer*
Friedman, B(ernard) H(arper) *writer*
Fulghum, Robert L. *author, lecturer*
Fuller, Charles *playwright*
Gelber, Jack *playwright, director*
Giblin, James Cross *author, editor*
Gill, Brendan *writer*
Goldman, James *playwright, screenwriter, novelist*
Goldstein, Lisa Joy *writer*
Goodman, George Jerome Waldo (Adam Smith) *author, television journalist, editor*
Gordimer, Nadine *author*
Gordon, David *playwright, director, choreographer*
Gordon, Mary Catherine *author*
Goulden, Joseph Chesley *author*
Grant, Cynthia D. *writer*
Green, Adolph *playwright, lyricist*
Grisham, John *writer*
Grumbach, Doris *novelist, editor, critic, educator, bookseller*
Guare, John *playwright*
Hadley, Leila Eliott-Burton (Mrs. Henry Luce, III) *author*
†Hague, William Edward *editor, author*
Hall, Susan *author, film producer*
Hamburger, Philip (Paul) *writer*
Hannibal, Edward Leo *copywriter*
Hardwick, Elizabeth *author*
†Harris, E. Lynn *writer*
Haskell, Molly *author*
Hauptman, William *playwright*
Haynes, Todd *film writer, producer, director*
Hazzard, Shirley *author*
Heller, Joseph *writer*
Henley, Arthur *author, editor, television consultant*
Henley, Beth *playwright, actress*
Hentoff, Nathan Irving *writer*
Hernández, Roger Emilio *newspaper columnist*
Hesse, Karen (Sue) *writer, educator*
Hijuelos, Oscar *novelist*
†Hillman, Howard Budrow *author, editor, publisher, consultant*
Hines, Anna Grossnickle *author, illustrator*
Hinton, S(usan) E(loise) *author*
Hinz, Dorothy Elizabeth *writer, editor, international corporate communications and public affairs specialist*
Hoffman, William M(oses) *playwright, editor*
Holland, Isabelle Christian *writer*
Holmes, Doloris Grant *writer, social worker, theater director*
Holroyd, Michael *author*
Holzer, Hans *author*
Horovitz, Israel Arthur *playwright*
Hudlin, Warrington *writer, producer, director*
Hwang, David Henry *playwright, screenwriter*
Inez, Colette *poet*
Iselin, Sally Cary *writer*
Jacker, Corinne Litvin *playwright*
Jakes, John *author*
Janeway, Elizabeth Hall *author*
Jhabvala, Ruth Prawer *author*
Jones, Diana Wynne *writer*
Jones, Sally Daviess Pickrell *writer*
Jong, Erica Mann *writer, poet*
Katz, William Loren *author*
Kauffmann, Stanley Jules *author*
Kaufman, Bel *author, educator*
Kazin, Alfred *writer*
Keene, Donald *writer, translator, language educator*
Kehret, Peg *writer*
Kinnell, Galway *poet, translator*
Kisner, Jacob *poet, editor*
Klein, T(heodore) E(ibon) D(onald) *writer*
Kobler, John *writer*
Koch, Kenneth *poet, playwright*
Koke, Richard Joseph *author, exhibit designer, museum curator*
Koontz, Dean Ray *writer*
Kopit, Arthur *playwright*
Kostelanetz, Richard *writer, artist*
Kotlowitz, Robert *writer, editor*
Kumin, Maxine Winokur *poet, author*
Kunitz, Stanley Jasspon *poet, editor, educator*
Kushner, Tony *playwright*
Lader, Lawrence *writer*
Lapierre, Dominique *writer, historian, philanthropist*
Lapine, James Elliot *playwright, director*
Lauber, Patricia Grace *writer*
Laurents, Arthur *playwright*
Lelchuk, Alan *author, educator*
L'Engle, Madeleine (Mrs. Hugh Franklin) *author*
Levin, Ira *author, playwright*
Levine, Israel E. *writer*
Levoy, Myron *author*
Linney, Romulus *author, educator*
Lord, M. G. *writer*

Maas, Peter *writer*
Macer-Story, Eugenia Ann *writer, artist*
Mailer, Norman *author*
Mason, Bobbie Ann *novelist, short story writer*
Matzner, Chester Michael *writer*
Maupin, Armistead Jones, Jr. *writer*
McCullough, David *author*
Mcdonald, Gregory Christopher *author*
McMeen, Albert Ralph, III *writer, lecturer*
McMurtry, Larry Jeff *author*
McNally, Terrence *playwright*
McQuown, Judith Hershkowitz *author, financial advisor*
Mee, Charles L. *playwright, historian, editor*
Mehta, Ved (Parkash) *writer, literature and history educator*
Meltzer, Milton *author*
Meyers, Nancy Jane *screenwriter, producer*
Mitgang, Herbert *author, journalist*
Mooney, Richard Emerson *writer*
Moore, Brian *writer*
Morgan, (George) Frederick *poet, editor*
Morgan, Robin Evonne *poet, author, journalist, activist, editor*
Morris, Wright *novelist, critic*
Morrison, Patricia Kennealy *author*
Morton, Frederic *author*
Munro, Alice *author*
†Neier, Aryeh *author, human rights organization administrator*
Nelson, Richard John *playwright*
Norman, Marsha *playwright*
Oates, Joyce Carol *author*
O'Doherty, Brian *playwright, filmmaker*
Offit, Sidney *writer, educator*
Oppenheimer, Paul Eugene *English comparative literature educator, poet, author*
O'Rourke, P. J. (Patrick Jake O'Rourke) *writer, humorist*
Osborne, Mary Pope *writer*
Ozick, Cynthia *author*
Paterson, Katherine Womeldorf *writer*
Patterson, Jerry Eugene *author*
Peacock, Molly *poet*
Peck, Richard Wayne *novelist*
Pérez-Rivera, Francisco *writer*
Phillips, Thomas H. *writer, journalism educator, editor*
Pirsig, Robert Maynard *author*
Plain, Belva *writer*
Plimpton, George Ames *writer, editor, television host*
Pogrebin, Letty Cottin *writer, lecturer*
Polacco, Patricia *children's author, illustrator*
Pollitt, Katha *writer, poet, educator*
Pomerantz, Charlotte *writer*
Price, Reynolds *novelist, poet, playwright, essayist, educator*
Proulx, Edna Annie *writer*
Ratcliff, Carter Goodrich *writer, art critic, poet*
†Rathmann, Peggy *author, illustrator*
Reed, Ishmael Scott (Emmett Coleman) *writer*
Regan, Sylvia *playwright*
Reig, June Wilson *writer, director, producer*
Reiss, Alvin *writer*
Rhodes, Richard Lee *writer*
Rice, Anne *author*
Rich, Adrienne *writer*
Ripley, Alexandra Braid *author*
Robbins, Harold *author*
Rollin, Betty *author, television journalist*
Rooney, Andrew Aitken *writer, columnist*
Root, William Pitt *poet, educator*
Rothenberg, Jerome *author, visual arts and literary educator*
Rudman, Mark *poet, educator*
Rylant, Cynthia *author*
Salant, Ari *medical advertising writer*
Sale, (John) Kirkpatrick *writer*
Salinger, Jerome David *author*
Salter, Mary Jo *poet*
Sanders, Lawrence *author*
Sargent, Pamela *writer*
Saul, John Woodruff, III *writer*
Saylor, Steven Warren *writer prose, fiction*
Schaffner, Cynthia Van Allen *writer, researcher*
Schisgal, Murray Joseph *playwright*
Schlein, Miriam *author*
Schlesinger, Arthur (Meier), Jr. *writer, educator*
Schrader, Paul Joseph *film writer, director*
Schulman, Grace *poet, English language educator*
Schwartz, Arthur Robert *food writer, critic, consultant*
Schwed, Peter *author, retired editor and publisher*
Seaman, Barbara (Ann Rosner) *author*
Segal, Lore *writer*
Sendak, Maurice Bernard *writer, illustrator*
Shaffer, Peter Levin *playwright*
Shange, Ntozake (Paulette Williams) *playwright, poet*
Shapiro, Harvey *poet*
Shawn, Wallace *playwright, actor*
Sheehan, Susan *writer*
Sheldon, Sidney *author, producer*
Shepard, Elaine Elizabeth *writer, lecturer*
Shulevitz, Uri *author, illustrator*
Silverstein, Shelby (Shel Silverstein) *author, cartoonist, composer, folksinger*
Simmons, Charles *author*
Simon, Neil *playwright, television writer*
Slade, Bernard *playwright*
Smith, Betty *writer, nonprofit foundation executive*
Smith, Robert Kimmel *author*
Sonnenberg, Ben *playwright, poet, editor, producer*
Sourian, Peter *writer, educator*
Southall, Ivan Francis *author*
Spiegelman, Art *author, cartoonist*
Spillane, Mickey (Frank Morrison Spillane) *author*
Spoto, Donald *writer, educator*
Steel, Danielle Fernande *author*
Stein, Joseph *playwright*
Steinem, Gloria *writer, editor, lecturer*
Stevenson, William Henri *author*
Stewart, Mary Florence Elinor *author*
Stone, Peter *playwright, scenarist*
Stowers, Carlton Eugene *writer*
Swann, Brian *writer, humanities educator*
Swenson, Karen *poet, journalist*
Talese, Gay *writer*
Taylor, Clyde Calvin, Jr. *literary agent*
†Taylor, Mildred D. *author*
Terry, Megan *playwright, performer, photographer*
†Thomas, Elizabeth Marshall *writer*
Thompson, Hunter Stockton *author, political analyst, journalist*
Tomkins, Calvin *writer*
Trillin, Calvin Marshall *writer, columnist*
Uhry, Alfred Fox *playwright*
Uris, Leon Marcus *author*
Vonnegut, Kurt, Jr. *writer*
Wager, Walter Herman *author, communications director*
Wakefield, Dan *author, screenwriter*
Walker, Alice Malsenior *author*
Waller, Robert James *writer*
Ward, Geoffrey Champion *author, editor*
Wasserman, Albert *writer, director*
Wasserman, Dale *playwright*
Watt, Douglas (Benjamin Watt) *writer, critic*
Weidman, Jerome *author*
Wender, Phyllis Bellows *literary agent*
Weschler, Lawrence Michael *writer, journalist*
†West, Dorothy *writer*
West, Paul Noden *author*
Whitney, Phyllis Ayame *author*
Wiener, Solomon *writer, consultant, former city official*
Wilds, Bonnie *author, community volunteer*
Wilson, August *playwright*
Wilson, F(rancis) Paul *novelist, screenwriter*
Windsor, Patricia (Katonah Summertree) *author, educator, lecturer*
Winsor, Kathleen *writer*
Wise, David *author, journalist*
Woiwode, Larry (Alfred Woiwode) *writer, poet*
Wolfe, Thomas Kennerly, Jr. *writer, journalist*
Wolff, Virginia Euwer *writer, secondary education educator*
Wright, Laurali R. (Bunny Wright) *writer*
Yorinks, Arthur *children's author, writer, director*
Zahn, Timothy *writer*
Zara, Louis *author, editor*
Zolotow, Charlotte Shapiro *author, editor*

**Newburgh**
Severo, Richard *writer*

**Niagara Falls**
Gromosiak, Paul *author, historian, science & mathematics educator*
Powers, Bruce Raymond *author, English language educator, consultant*

**North Boston**
Herbert, James Alan *writer*

**Nyack**
Hendin, David Bruce *literary agent, author, consultant, numismatist*

**Oceanside**
Mills, James Spencer *author*

**Palisades**
Berger, Thomas Louis *author*
Davis, Dorothy Salisbury *author*

**Port Washington**
Blakeslee, Alton Lauren *scientific writer*

**Poughkeepsie**
Willard, Nancy Margaret *writer, educator*

**Red Hook**
Schulberg, Budd *author*

**Rochester**
Hoch, Edward Dentinger *author*
Rothberg, Abraham *author, educator, editor*
Scott, Joanna Jeanne *writer, English language educator*

**Roslyn Heights**
Faber, Adele *author, educator*

**Sag Harbor**
Reeves, Richard *writer, historian*

**Sagaponack**
Appleman, Marjorie (M. H. Appleman) *playwright, educator, poet*
Appleman, Philip *poet, writer, educator*

**Saratoga Springs**
Parthasarathy, Rajagopal *writer, literature educator*

**Staten Island**
Porter, Darwin Fred *writer*

**Suffern**
Unger, Barbara *poet, writer, educator*

**Sunnyside**
Wallmann, Jeffrey Miner *author*

**Valley Stream**
Rachlin, Harvey Brant *author*

**Waccabuc**
Hall, Elizabeth *writer*

**Wainscott**
Herzog, Arthur, III *author*

**West Nyack**
Pringle, Laurence Patrick *writer*

**Woodmere**
Abramson, Martin *author, journalist*

**Woodstock**
Doyle, Will Lee *writer, editor*
Godwin, Gail Kathleen *author*

## NORTH CAROLINA

**Beaufort**
Hayman, Carol Bessent *poet, author*

**Chapel Hill**
Betts, Doris June Waugh *author, English language educator*
Little, Loyd Harry, Jr. *author*
Spencer, Elizabeth *author*

**Charlotte**
Finley, Glenna *author*

**Durham**
Dunbar, Leslie Wallace *writer, consultant*
Tebbel, John *writer, educator*

**Greensboro**
Sewell, Elizabeth *author, English educator*
Watson, Robert Winthrop *poet, English language educator*

**Murfreesboro**
Burke, Marguerite Jodi Larcombe *writer, computer consultant*

**Raleigh**
Murray, Elizabeth Davis Reid *writer, lecturer*

**Southern Pines**
Yarborough, William Pelham *writer, lecturer, retired army officer, consultant*

**Winston Salem**
Ehle, John Marsden, Jr. *writer*
Hanes, Frank Borden *author, farmer, former business executive*

## OHIO

**Canton**
Sowd, David Howard *writer*

**Cincinnati**
Birmingham, Stephen *writer*
Hornbaker, Alice Joy *author*
Steinberg, Janet Eckstein *journalist*

**Cleveland**
Finn, Robert *writer, lecturer, broadcaster*
Gleisser, Marcus David *author, lawyer, journalist*
Kovel, Ralph M. *author, antiques expert*
Kovel, Terry Horvitz (Mrs. Ralph Kovel) *author, antiques authority*
Moore, Dan Tyler *writer*
Sandburg, Helga *author*
Stadtler, Beatrice Horwitz *author*
†Stannfe, Helen *writer*

**Dayton**
Heath, Mariwyn Dwyer *writer, legislative issues consultant*

**Gahanna**
Smith, Brenda Joyce *author, editor, social studies educator*

**Mayfield Village**
Pavlovich, Donald *educator, support person*

**Perrysburg**
Weaver, Richard L., II *writer, speaker, educator*

**Yellow Springs**
Hamilton, Virginia (Mrs. Arnold Adoff) *author*

## OKLAHOMA

**Norman**
Owens, Rochelle *poet, playwright*

**Oklahoma City**
Anderson, Kenneth Edwin *writer, educator*
Mather, Ruth Elsie *writer*

**Perry**
Beers, Frederick Gordon *writer, retired corporate communications official*

**Stillwater**
Shirley, Glenn Dean *writer*

**Tulsa**
Mojtabai, Ann Grace *author, educator*

## OREGON

**Culver**
Siebert, Diane Dolores *author, poet*

**Eugene**
Wilhelm, Kate (Katy Gertrude) *author*

**Newport**
Kennedy, Richard Jerome *writer*

**Pleasant Hill**
Kesey, Ken *writer*

**Portland**
Porter, Elsa Allgood *writer, lecturer*
Rutsala, Vern A. *poet, English language educator, writer*

## PENNSYLVANIA

**Ardmore**
Kline, George Louis *author, translator, retired philosophy and literature educator*

**Avondale**
Foster, Paul *playwright*

**Broomall**
Saunders, Sally Love *poet, educator*

**Bushkill**
Muesing Ellwood, Edith Elizabeth *writer, researcher, publisher, editor*

**California**
Langham, Norma *playwright, educator, poet, composer, inventor*

**Drexel Hill**
Alexander, Lloyd Chudley *author*

**Glenside**
Pelham, Fran O'Byrne *writer, teacher*

**Harrisburg**
Cooper, Jane Todd (J. C. Todd) *poet, writer, educator*

**Kennett Square**
Martin, George (Whitney) *writer*

**Lafayette Hill**
Green, Rose Basile (Mrs. Raymond S. Green) *poet, author, educator*

**Malvern**
Calabrese, Marylyn E. Jones *writing consultant*

**Milford**
Eckert, Allan Wesley *writer*
Le Guin, Ursula Kroeber *author*

**Newtown**
Pfeiffer, John Edward *author*

**Philadelphia**
Fussell, Paul *author, English literature educator*
Mangione, Jerre Gerlando *author, educator*
Paglia, Camille *writer, humanities educator*
Pipes, Daniel *writer, editor*
Willis, Arthur Clifton *writer, educator*

**Pittsburgh**
Hodges, Margaret Moore *author, educator*
McHoes, Ann McIver *technical writer, computer systems consultant*
Verlich, Jean Elaine *writer, public relations consultant*

**Pottstown**
Hylton, Thomas James *author*

**Rosemont**
Nixon, Agnes Eckhardt *television writer, producer*

**Saint Davids**
Shurkin, Lorna Greene *writer, publicist*

**Southampton**
Bendiner, Robert *writer, editor*

**State College**
Asbell, Bernard *author, English language educator*

**Stevens**
Shenk, Lois Landis *writer, caregiver*

**Valley Forge**
Miller, Betty Brown *freelance writer*

**Villanova**
Nolan, Patrick Joseph *screenwriter, playwright, educator*

**Wayne**
Simms, Amy Lang *writer, educator*

**Wynnewood**
Meyers, Mary Ann *writer, consultant*

**Yardley**
Crane, Barbara Joyce *author, editor, publishing consulting executive*

## RHODE ISLAND

**Barrington**
Deakin, James *writer, former newspaperman*

**Block Island**
Stone, Robert Anthony *author*

**Cranston**
Feinstein, Alan Shawn *writer, financial adviser*

**Middletown**
Whitman, Ruth *poet, educator, translator*

**Providence**
Coover, Robert *writer, scriptwriter, educator*
Schevill, James Erwin *poet, playwright*

## SOUTH CAROLINA

**Aiken**
Naifeh, Steven Woodward *writer*
Smith, Gregory White *writer*

**Beaufort**
Ogburn, Charlton *writer*

**Columbia**
Newton, Rhonwen Leonard *writer, microcomputer consultant*

**Folly Beach**
Shutrump, Mary Jill *writer, editor, photographer, educator*

**Georgetown**
Isbell, Robert *writer*

**Greenville**
Gilkerson, Yancey Sherard *retired writer, former editor*

**Little River**
Ehrlich, John Gunther *writer*

**Myrtle Beach**
Uzenda, Jara Carlow *technical writer*

**Rock Hill**
Bristow, Robert O'Neil *writer, educator*

**Sullivans Island**
Humphreys, Josephine *novelist*

**Summerville**
Reisman, Rosemary Moody Canfield *writer, humanities educator*

## SOUTH DAKOTA

**Brookings**
Williams, Elizabeth Evenson *writer*

## TENNESSEE

**Chattanooga**
Callahan, North *author, educator*

**Cleveland**
Breuer, William Bentley *writer*

**Cordova**
Hunt, Gregory Lynn *writer, author*

**Kingsport**
Kiss, Mary Catherine Clement *writer*

**Maryville**
Brigance, Albert Henry *educational writer*

**Memphis**
Foote, Shelby *author*
Sharpe, Robert F., Sr. *writer, lecturer, educator, consultant, publisher*

**Nashville**
Sullivan, Walter Laurence *writer, educator*

**Newport**
Dykeman, Wilma *writer, lecturer*

**Oak Ridge**
Turov, Daniel *financial writer, investment executive*

## TEXAS

**Arlington**
Savage, Ruth Hudson *poet, writer, speaker*

**Austin**
Gustafsson, Lars Erik Einar *writer, educator*
Michener, James Albert *author*

**Bertram**
Albert, Susan Wittig *writer, English educator*

**Boerne**
Price, John Randolph *writer*

**Canyon**
Roper, Beryl Cain *writer, publisher, retired library director*

**Corpus Christi**
Sommers, Maxine Marie Bridget *writer, educator, publisher*
Walraven, Joseph William (Bill Walraven) *writer, publisher*

**Crystal Beach**
Dunn, Glennis Mae *writer, lyricist*

**Dallas**
Cohn, Linkie Seltzer *professional speaker, author*
Harris, Leon A., Jr. *writer*
Hunter, Kermit *writer, former university dean*
Murray, John William, Jr. *writer, legal investigator*
Phillips, Betty Lou (Elizabeth Louise Phillips) *author, interior designer*
Riehm, Sarah Lawrence *writer, arts administrator*
Weeks, Jerome Christopher *writer, drama critic*

**El Paso**
McCarthy, Cormac *writer*

**Fort Worth**
Bean, Jack Vaughan *author, publisher*
Jones, Kathryn Ann *writer, artist*
Lale, Cissy Stewart (Lloyd Lale) *freelance writer*

**Houston**
Boardman, Robert B. *author*
de Vries, Robbie Ray Parsons *author, illustrator, international consultant*
Hirsch, Edward Mark *poet, English language educator*
Kulkarni, Venkatesh *author*
McPhail, JoAnn Winstead *writer, publisher, art dealer*
Neeld, Elizabeth Harper *author*
Plunkett, Jack William *writer, publisher*
Schier, Mary Jane *science writer*
SoRelle, Ruth Doyle *medical writer, journalist*

**Katy**
Harbour, Patricia Ann Monroe *poet*

**Kerrville**
Lich, Glen Ernst *writer, consultant, business executive*

**Liberty Hill**
West, Felton *retired newspaper writer*

**Lubbock**
Bronwell, Nancy Brooker *writer*
Pasewark, William Robert *author, management consultant*
Rushing, Jane Gilmore *writer*

**Plano**
Gallardo, Henrietta Castellanos *writer*

**Quinlan**
Black, Sheryl Elaine Hale *author*

**Salado**
Greene, A(lvin) C(arl) *author*

**San Antonio**
Laurence, Dan H. *author, literary and dramatic specialist*
Stuart, Lillian Mary *writer*
Swiggett, Harold E. (Hal Swiggett) *writer, photographer*

**Spring**
†Berriault, Gina *writer*

**Waco**
Weems, John Edward *writer*

## UTAH

**Provo**
Hart, Edward LeRoy *poet, educator*

**Salt Lake City**
Black, Rosa Vida *writer, educator*
Ghiselin, Brewster *author, English language educator emeritus*
Lueders, Edward George *author, poet, educator, editor*

**Springville**
Hickman, Craig Ronald *author*

## VERMONT

**Bennington**
Glazier, Lyle *writer, educator*
Sandy, Stephen *writer, educator*

**Burlington**
Carlisle, Lilian Matarose Baker (Mrs. E. Grafton Carlisle, Jr.) *author, lecturer*
Hearon, Shelby *writer, lecturer, educator*

**North Bennington**
Belitt, Ben *poet, educator*

**Norwich**
Stetson, Eugene William, III *film producer*

**South Royalton**
Powers, Thomas Moore *author*

**South Strafford**
Novick, Sheldon M. *author, lawyer*

**Thetford**
Paley, Grace *author, educator*

## VIRGINIA

**Alexandria**
Bergheim, Laura Ann *writer*
David, Joseph Raymond, Jr. *writer, periodical editor*
Tatham, Julie Campbell *writer*
Wallace, Barbara Brooks *writer*

**Annandale**
Nowak, Jan Zdzislaw *writer, consultant*

**Arlington**
Bird, Caroline *author*
England, Robert Stowe *writer*
Hittle, James Donald *writer, business consultant*
Scott, Suzanne *writer, artist*
Stahl, O(scar) Glenn *writer, lecturer, former government official*

**Ashburn**
Boyne, Walter James *writer, former museum director*

**Bluemont**
Weisman, John *author*

**Chantilly**
Priem, Richard Gregory *writer, information systems executive, entertainment company executive*

**Charlotte Court House**
Hoffman, William *author*

**Charlottesville**
Brown, Rita Mae *author*
Casey, John Dudley *writer, English language educator*
Dove, Rita Frances *poet, English language educator*
Simpson, R(obert) Smith *author, retired diplomat*

**Christiansburg**
Roberts, Ruby Altizer *poet, author*

**Fairfax**
Bausch, Richard Carl *writer, educator*

**Falls Church**
Connery, Robert Howe *author, educator*
Leighton, Frances Spatz *writer, journalist*
Morrison, H. Robert *writer, editor, politician*
Orben, Robert *editor, writer*
Whitehead, Kenneth Dean *author, translator, retired federal government official*

**Fort Belvoir**
Smith, Margherita *writer, editor*

**Hillsboro**
Farwell, Byron Edgar *writer*

**Lexington**
Stuart, Walker Dabney, III *poet, author, English language educator*

**Manassas**
Holmes, Marjorie Rose *author*

**Midlothian**
Rodgers, Eugene *writer*

**Portsmouth**
Mapp, Alf Johnson, Jr. *writer, historian*

**Richmond**
Hemingway, Beth Rowlett *author, columnist, lecturer*

**Virginia Beach**
Seward, William W(ard), Jr. *author, educator*

**Warrenton**
†Estaver, Paul Edward *writer, poet*

**Woodbridge**
Englert, Helen Wiggs *writer*

**Woodville**
Mc Carthy, Eugene Joseph *writer, former senator*

## WASHINGTON

**Bellevue**
Szablya, Helen Mary *author, language professional, lecturer*

**Bellingham**
Skinner, Knute Rumsey *poet, English educator*

**Cheney**
Hegi, Ursula *writer*

**Federal Way**
Scott, Otto *writer*

**Grayland**
Ransom, Bill *author*

**La Conner**
Robbins, Thomas Eugene *author*

**Lynnwood**
Bear, Gregory Dale *writer, illustrator*

**Port Angeles**
Muller, Willard C(hester) *writer*

**Seattle**
Bensussen, Estelle Esther *writer, illustrator, artist*
Kenney, Richard Laurence *poet, English language educator*
McHugh, Heather *poet*
Singer, Sarah Beth *poet*
Wagoner, David Russell *author, educator*

**Tacoma**
Maynard, Steven Harry *writer*

## WEST VIRGINIA

**Morgantown**
Gagliano, Frank Joseph *playwright*

## WISCONSIN

**Argyle**
Daley, Ron (Ronald) Eugene (Ron ) *playwright, poet, director, producer*

**Elkhorn**
Dunn, Walter Scott, Jr. *writer, former museum director, consultant*

**Green Bay**
Parkinson, Ethelyn Minerva *author*

**Little Chute**
Rice, Ferill Jeane *writer, civic worker*

**Madison**
Stone, John Timothy, Jr. *writer*

**Racine**
Wright, Betty Ren *children's book writer*

## WYOMING

**Laramie**
Boresi, Arthur Peter *author, educator*

## CANADA

## ALBERTA

**Edmonton**
Hughes, Monica *author*

**Waterton Lakes Park**
Russell, Andrew George Alexander *author, naturalist*

## BRITISH COLUMBIA

**Saanichton**
Crozier, Lorna *poet, educator*

**Surrey**
Kinsella, William Patrick *author, educator*

**Vancouver**
Bowering, George Harry *writer, English literature educator*

**Victoria**
Harris, Christie Lucy *author*

## MANITOBA

**Winnipeg**
Oberman, Sheldon Arnold *writer, educator*

## ONTARIO

**Don Mills**
Atwood, Margaret Eleanor *author*

**Hillier**
Lunn, Janet Louise Swoboda *writer*

**London**
Reaney, James Crerar *dramatist, poet, educator*

**Ottawa**
Jackson, Charles Ian *writer, consultant*
†Khalid, Samy *writer*
Major, Jean-Louis *author, French literature educator*

**Owen Sound**
Bradford, Karleen *writer*

**Port Hope**
Mowat, Farley McGill *writer*

**Richmond Hill**
Gilman, Phoebe *author, illustrator*

**Scarborough**
Hunter, Bernice Thurman *writer*

**Sudbury**
Havel, Jean Eugène Martial *author, educator*

**Toronto**
Bodsworth, Fred *author, naturalist*
Colombo, John Robert *poet, editor, writer*
Gotlieb, Phyllis Fay Bloom *author*
Moore, Christopher Hugh *writer*
Parr, James Gordon *writer*
Shields, Carol Ann *writer, educator*

## QUEBEC

**Montreal**
Bruemmer, Fred *writer, photographer*
Richler, Mordecai *writer*

## MEXICO

**Coyoacan**
Paz, Octavio *poet, Mexican diplomat*

## AUSTRALIA

**Avalon**
West, Morris Langlo *novelist*

## AUSTRIA

**Vienna**
Lo Bello, Nino *author, journalist*

## ENGLAND

**Cambridge**
Steiner, George (Francis Steiner) *author, educator*

**Hingham**
Pollini, Francis *author*

**London**
Adams, Douglas Noel *writer*
Aliki, (Aliki Liacouras Brandenberg) *author, illustrator children's books*
Ambler, Eric *writer*
Bawden, Nina (Mary) *author*
Clarke, Arthur Charles *author*
Cleese, John Marwood *writer, businessman, comedian*
Cope, Wendy *poet, journalist*
Cowles, Fleur (Mrs. Tom M. Meyer) *author, artist*
Deighton, Len *author*
Drabble, Margaret *writer*
Fine, Anne *author*
Follett, Kenneth Martin *author*
Fowles, John *author*
Galloway, Janice *writer, editor*
Godden, Rumer *author*
Hare, David *playwright*
Hoban, Russell Conwell *author*
Hughes, Ted *poet, author*
Hughes, Winifred Shirley *writer, illustrator*
Hunter Blair, Pauline Clarke *author*
James, P(hyllis) D(orothy) (Baroness James of Holland Park of Southwold in County of Suffolk ) *author*
Lahr, John *author*
le Carré, John (David John Moore Cornwell) *author*
Lessing, Doris (May) *writer*

## ARTS: PERFORMING


### UNITED STATES


### ALABAMA

### ALASKA

### ARIZONA

### ARKANSAS

### CALIFORNIA

**Antioch**
Adams, Liliana Osses music performer, harpist

**Anza**
Skelton, Red (Richard Skelton) comedian, artist

**Apple Valley**
Beller, Gerald Stephen professional magician, former insurance company executive

**Bakersfield**
Owens, Buck (Alvis Edgar, Jr.) singer, musician, songwriter

**Belvedere Tiburon**
Power, Jules television producer

**Berkeley**
Dresher, Paul Joseph composer, music educator, performer
Dugger, Edwin Ellsworth composer, educator
Hutcherson, Bobby jazz vibraphonist
Imbrie, Andrew Welsh composer, educator
Ridgway, David Wenzel educational film producer, director
Smith, James Oscar (Jimmy Smith) jazz organist
Thow, John H. music educator, composer
Wood, David Kennedy Cornell choreographer, educator
Zaentz, Saul motion picture producer

**Beverly Hills**
Ahmad, Maher film production designer
Alexander, Jason (Jay Scott Greenspan) actor
Allen, Dede (Dorothea Carothers Allen) film editor
Allen, Joan actress
Amis, Suzy actress
Anders, Allison film director, screenwriter
Anderson, Richard Dean actor
Angell, David L. television producer, screenwriter
Aniston, Jennifer actress
Ann-Margret, (Ann-Margret Olsson) actress, performer
Arau, Alfonso film producer and director, writer
Arnold, Tom actor, comedian, producer
Arquette, Patricia actress
Asner, Edward actor
Avary, Roger Roberts film director, writer
Avildsen, John Guilbert film director
Aykroyd, Daniel Edward actor, writer
Bacon, Kevin actor
Bailey, John cinematographer
Baker, Kathy Whitton actress
Bakula, Scott actor
Baldwin, Daniel actor
Baldwin, William actor
Banderas, Antonio actor
Barrie, Barbara Ann actress
Barrymore, Drew actress
Bates, Kathy actress
Bauer, Marty agent
Baxter, Meredith actress
†Bay, Michael film director
Beals, Jennifer actress
Beatty, (Henry) Warren actor, producer, director
Becks, Ronald Arthur film producer
Bedelia, Bonnie actress
Bellisario, Donald P. television director
Belushi, James A. actor
Bening, Annette actress
Bergman, Andrew motion picture director
†Berkeley, Elizabeth actress
Berry, Halle actress
†Binoche, Juliette actress
Bishop, Joey (Joseph Abraham Gottlieb) comedian
Blades, Ruben singer, songwriter, composer
Branagh, Kenneth actor, director
Braun, Zev motion picture and television producer
Brillstein, Bernie J. producer, talent manager
Broderick, Matthew actor
Brokaw, Norman Robert talent agency executive
Bullock, Sandra actress
Burnett, Carol actress, comedienne, singer
Burrell, Orville Richard popular musician
Burstyn, Ellen (Edna Rae Gillooly) actress
Burwell, Carter composer
Byrne, Gabriel actor
Cage, Nicolas (Nicolas Coppola) actor
Caine, Michael actor
Campion, Jane director, screenwriter
Carreras, José tenor
Carrey, Jim actor
†Carter, Chris producer, director
Cates, Phoebe actress
Channing, Carol actress
Chapman, Michael cinematographer, director
Cher, (Cherilyn Sarkisian) singer, actress
Chong, Thomas comedian, writer, director, musician
Chritton, George A. film producer
Clooney, George actor
Close, Glenn actress
Coen, Ethan film producer, writer
Coen, Joel film director, writer
Coleman, Dabney W. actor
Columbus, Chris Joseph film director, screenwriter
Connery, Sean (Thomas Connery) actor
Coolidge, Martha film director
Corman, Eugene Harold motion picture producer
Cox, Courteney actress
Crawford, Cindy model
Crowe, Christopher director, screenwriter
†Crowe, Russell actor
Cundey, Dean cinematographer
Curtis, Jamie Lee actress
Cusack, John actor
†D'Abo, Olivia actress
Daly, Timothy actor
D'Angelo, Beverly actress
Danson, Ted actor
Dante, Joe film director
Davis, Andrew film director, screenwriter
Davis, Judy actress
Dawber, Pam actress
DeBont, Jan cinematographer, director
Delany, Dana actress
Demme, Jonathan director, producer, writer
De Niro, Robert actor
Depardieu, Gérard actor
Depp, Johnny actor
Dern, Bruce MacLeish actor
Deschanel, Caleb cinematographer, director
DeVito, Danny Michael actor
†D'Onofrio, Vincent Philip actor
†Donovan, Tate actor
†Douglas, Ileana actress
Douglas, Kirk (Issur Danielovitch Demsky) actor, motion picture producer
Douglas, Michael Kirk actor, film producer, director
†Dutton, Charles S. actor
Duvall, Shelley actress
Eastwood, Clint actor, director, former mayor
Eikenberry, Jill actress
Elliott, Chris actor
Elliott, Paul cinematographer
Elliott, Sam actor
Elwes, Cary actor
†Epps, Omar actor
Estevez, Emilio actor, writer, director
†Everett, Rupert actor
Evigan, Greg actor, musician
Fahey, Jeff actor
Feldshuh, Tovah S. actress
Fiennes, Ralph Nathaniel actor
†Fincher, David film director
Finfer, David film editor
Flanagan, Fionnula Manon actress, writer, producer
Flaum, Marshall Allen television producer, writer, director
Fleischer, Richard O. film director
Foch, Nina actress, creative consultant, educator, director
†Foley, James film director
Fonda, Bridget actress
†Forsythe, William actor
Foster, Lawrence concert and opera conductor
Foxworth, Robert Heath actor, director
Friedkin, William film director
Friendly, Ed television producer
Gassner, Dennis production designer
Gillard, Stuart Thomas film and television director, writer
Glover, John actor
Grant, Hugh actor
Graves, Peter actor
Graysmark, John production designer
Green, Guy Mervin Charles film director
Green, Jack N. cinematographer
Greenberg, Gerald B. film editor
†Grey, Brad producer, agent
Griffin, Merv Edward former entertainer, television producer, entrepreneur
Guttenberg, Steve actor
Hagar, Sammy musician, vocalist, composer
Hagman, Larry actor
Hall, Arsenio television talk show host, comedian
Hall, Roger production designer
Hallowell, Todd art director, production designer
Hamel, Veronica actress
Hamlin, Harry Robinson actor
Hanks, Tom actor
Hanley, Daniel film editor
Harlin, Renny (Renny Lauri Mauritz Harjola) film director
Harrelson, Woody actor
Harris, Ed(ward Allen) actor
Harris, Julie (Ann) actress
Harris, Mel (Mary Ellen Harris) actress
Harrison, Gregory actor
Haskell, Peter Abraham actor
Hawn, Goldie actress
Headly, Glenne Aimée actress
Helmond, Katherine actress
Henderson, Florence (Florence Henderson Bernstein) actress, singer
Hepburn, Katharine Houghton actress
Hershey, Barbara (Barbara Herzstein) actress
Hill, Michael J. film editor
Hoenig, Dov film editor
Hopkins, Sir Anthony (Philip) actor
Howard, Ron director, actor
Hudlin, Reginald Alan director, writer, producer
Hughes, John W. film producer, screenwriter, film director
Hunt, Helen actress
Hurd, Gale Anne film producer
Hutshing, Joe film editor
Isham, Mark composer, jazz musician
Jackson, Samuel L. actor
Jarre, Maurice Alexis composer
Jones, David Hugh theater, film and television director
Jones, Robert C. film editor
Jones, Terry film director, author
Jordan, Glenn director
Kahn, Michael film editor
Kasdan, Lawrence Edward film director, screenwriter
Kaufman, Philip film director
Keaton, Diane actress
Keaton, Michael actor, comedian
Kemper, Victor J. cinematographer
Kilmer, Val actor
Kravitz, Lenny singer, guitarist
Kudrow, Lisa actress
Lahti, Christine actress
Landis, John David film director, writer
Lane, Nathan (Joseph Lane) actor
Langella, Frank actor
Lee, Peggy (Norma Delores Egstrom) singer, actress
Lehmann, Michael Stephen film director
Leigh, Jennifer Jason (Jennifer Leigh Morrow) actress
Lester, Richard film director
Levine, Alan J. entertainment company executive
Levy, Eugene actor, director, screenwriter
Levy, Peter cinematographer
Lewis, Juliette actress
Limato, Edward Frank talent agent
†Lindo, Delroy actor
Linkletter, Arthur Gordon radio and television broadcaster
Liotta, Ray actor
Littleton, Carol film editor
Lloyd, Emily (Emily Lloyd Pack) actress
Locklear, Heather actress
Loggia, Robert actor
Loggins, Kenny (Kenneth Clarke Loggins) singer, songwriter
Lombardo, Tony film editor
Long, Shelley actress
†Lopez, Jennifer actress, dancer
Lottman, Evan film editor
Loughnane, Lee David trumpeter
Louis-Dreyfus, Julia actress
Lovejoy, Ray film editor
Lyne, Adrian director
MacMillan, Kenneth cinematographer
Madsen, Michael actor
†Maffia, Roma actress
Mann, Michael K. producer, director, writer
Manoff, Dinah Beth actress
Manulis, Martin film producer
Marsh, Terence production designer
Martin, Steve comedian, actor
Mason, Marsha actress, director, writer
Masterson, Mary Stuart actress
Mastrantonio, Mary Elizabeth actress
†Masur, Richard actor
Matlin, Marlee actress
McAlpine, Andrew production designer
†McDermott, Dylan actor
Mc Mahon, Ed television personality
Mc Tiernan, John film director
Miller, Dennis comedian
Mirkin, David television producer
Mischer, Donald Leo television director and producer
Moore, Demi (Demi Guynes) actress
Moore, Dudley Stuart John actor, musician
Moore, Michael film director
Murphy, Eddie comedian, actor
Musky, Jane Michelle film production designer
†Nava, Gregory film director
Neeson, Liam actor
Neill, Sam actor
Nelligan, Kate (Patricia Colleen Nelligan) actress
Nesmith, Michael film producer, video specialist
Neuwirth, Bebe dancer, actress
Nichols, Mike stage and film director
Nicita, Rick agent
Nitzsche, Jack composer
Noble, (Terry) Thom film editor
Norris, Chuck (Carlos Ray) actor
Novak, Kim (Marilyn Novak) actress
Noyce, Phillip film director
Nykvist, Sven Vilhem cinematographer
Oakley, Bill television producer
O'Donnell, Rosie comedienne, actress
Ondricek, Miroslav cinematographer
Pacino, Al (Alfredo James Pacino) actor
Palance, Jack actor
Palminteri, Chazz actor
Paquin, Anna actress
Parker, Alan William film director, writer
Parker, Sarah Jessica actress
†Patric, Jason actor
Paull, Lawrence G. production designer
†Paymer, David actor
Peck, Eldred Gregory actor
Penderecki, Krzysztof composer, conductor
Perez, Rosie actress
Perkins, Elizabeth Ann actress
Perry, Matthew actor
Pfeiffer, Michelle actress
†Pinkett, Jada actress
Pitt, Brad actor
Platt, Oliver actor
Plummer, (Arthur) Christopher (Orme) actor
Polanski, Roman film director, writer, actor
†Pollak, Kevin actor
Portman, Rachel Mary Berkeley composer
Presley, Priscilla actress
Pressman, Michael film director
Priestley, Jason actor
Ptak, John Anthony talent agent
Pullman, Bill actor
Rafkin, Alan television and film director
Raimi, Samuel M. film director
Rapke, Jack agent
Reiner, Rob actor, writer, director
Reitman, Ivan film director, producer
Reynolds, William Henry film editor
†Rhames, Ving actor
†Ricci, Christina actress
Rickman, Tom screenwriter, director
Rivers, Joan entertainer
Robbins, Richard composer
Roberts, Eric actor
†Roberts, Julia Fiona actress
†Rodriguez, Robert filmmaker
Roeg, Nicolas Jack film director
Rolf, Tom film editor
Romero, George A. film director
Ross, Herbert David film director
Rossellini, Isabella actress, model
Rotunno, Giuseppe cinematographer
Rubeo, Bruno production designer
Ryan, Meg actress
Ryder, Winona (Winona Laura Horowitz) actress
Sakamoto, Ryuichi composer
Schepisi, Fred producer, director, screenwriter
Schlatter, George H. producer, director, writer
Schlesinger, John Richard film, opera and theater director
†Schneider, Rob actor
Schwarzenegger, Arnold Alois actor, author
Schwimmer, David actor
Scott, Ridley film director
Seagal, Steven actor
Seinfeld, Jerry comedian
†Shaham, Gil violinist
Shandling, Garry comedian, scriptwriter, actor
Shue, Elisabeth actress
Singleton, John director, screenwriter
Sinise, Gary actor, director
†Sizemore, Tom actor
Skerritt, Tom actor
†Smith, John N. film director
†Smith, Kevin film director, writer
Smith, Roy Forge art director, production designer
Smith, Will actor, rapper
Snyder, David L. film production designer
Sonnenfeld, Barry cinematographer, film director
Sorvino, Mira actress
Spacek, Sissy (Mary Elizabeth Spacek) actress
Spader, James actor
Spheeris, Penelope film director
Spielberg, Steven motion picture director, producer
Stack, Robert Langford actor
Stallone, Sylvester Enzio actor, writer, director
Steenburgen, Mary actress
Stefano, Joseph William film and television producer, author
Steinkamp, Fredric film editor
Stewart, Patrick actor
Stoltz, Eric actor
Stowe, Madeleine actress
Strauss, Peter actor
Streep, Meryl (Mary Louise Streep) actress
Streisand, Barbra Joan singer, actress, director
Stringfield, Sherry actress
Suschitzky, Peter cinematographer
Sutherland, Kiefer actor
†Sweeney, A.B. actor
Thompson, Caroline Warner film director, screenwriter
Thompson, Larry Angelo producer, lawyer, personal manager
Thorin, Donald E. cinematographer
†Thornton, Billy Bob actor, director
Thurman, Uma Karuna actress
Tilly, Jennifer actress
Tomei, Marisa actress
Travis, Nancy actress
Trumbull, Douglas film director, writer, creator special effects
†Tucci, Stanley actor
Turner, Tina (Anna Mae Bullock) singer
†Turteltaub, Jon film director
Turturro, John actor
Tyson, Cicely actress
Van Ark, Joan actress
Van Sant, Gus, Jr. director, screenwriter
Virkler, Dennis M. film editor
Von Wright, Victor, Sr. actor, film producer
Wagner, Lindsay J. actress
Walker, Lesley film editor
Washington, Denzel actor
Weaver, Sigourney (Susan Alexandra Weaver) actress
†Weber, Steven actor
Weir, Peter Lindsay film director
Whaley, Frank actor
White, Betty actress, comedienne
Wilder, Billy motion picture director, writer, producer
Wilder, Gene actor, director, writer
Wilson, Brian Douglas recording artist, composer, record producer
Wincer, Simon film director
Winger, Debra actress
Winkler, Henry Franklin actor
Winkler, Irwin motion picture producer
Winningham, Mare actress
Winslet, Kate actress
Wise, Robert film producer, director
Woods, James Howard actor
Wright, John film editor
Yorkin, Bud (Alan Yorkin) producer, director
†Zane, Billy actor
Zimmerman, Don film editor
Zwick, Edward M. director, producer, scriptwriter

**Bolinas**
Murch, Walter Scott director, writer, film editor, sound designer

**Burbank**
Allen, Tim actor, comedian
Becker, Walter guitarist, record producer
Berman, Bruce entertainment company executive
Berry, Bill popular musician
Buck, Peter musician, guitarist
Chierighino, Brianne Siddall voice-over, actress, assistant location manager
Clark, Dick performer, producer
Clark, Susan (Nora Goulding) actress
Clements, Ronald Francis animation director
Costello, Elvis (Declan Patrick McManus) musician, songwriter
Costner, Kevin actor
de Cordova, Frederick Timmins television producer, director
Dodd, Richard sound recording engineer
Donner, Richard film director, producer
Feldman, Edward S. producer
Ferry, Bryan singer, songwriter
Flanagan, Tommy (Lee) jazz pianist
Gibson, Mel actor, director
Gold, Jeffrey Alan record company executive
Goldthwait, Bob comedian, actor
Greene, Shecky entertainer
Guy, Buddy blues guitarist
Hope, Bob actor, comedian
Isaak, Chris popular musician, singer, songwriter, actor
Karras, Alex actor, former professional football player
Kellman, Barnet Kramer film, stage and television director
Ketchum, Hal Michael country music singer, songwriter
Kleiser, (John) Randal motion picture director
Lamas, Lorenzo actor, race car driver
Lanois, Daniel record producer, musician, popular
Leno, Jay (James Douglas Muir Leno) television personality, comedian, writer
Levin, Mark Jay director of photography, lighting designer, cinematographer, writer
Levinson, Barry L. film director
Lurie, Rod film critic, writer, film director
Mark, Laurence Maurice film producer
Mathis, Johnny singer
Mc Vie, Christine Perfect musician
Michael, George (Gergios Kyriakou Panayiotou) musician, singer, songwriter
Milchan, Arnon film producer
Newman, Randy singer, songwriter, musician
Nicks, Stevie (Stephanie Nicks) singer, songwriter
Ohlmeyer, Donald Winfred, Jr. film and television producer
Petty, Tom rock guitarist, band leader, composer
†Rauch, Paul David television producer
Sanborn, David alto saxophonist
Sandell, William production designer
Scott, Jim sound recording engineer
Seals, Dan Wayland country music singer
Shuler Donner, Lauren film producer
Silver, Joel producer
Stipe, Michael musician
Tritt, Travis country music singer, songwriter
Weintraub, Jerry motion picture producer, executive
Wonder, Stevie (Stevland Morris) singer, musician, composer
York, Michael (Michael York-Johnson) actor

**Burlingame**
Ward, William Reed composer, educator

**Calabasas**
Landau, Martin actor
Revell, Graeme composer

**Calistoga**
Sassoon, Janet ballerina, educator

**Carmel Valley**
Meckel, Peter Timothy arts administrator, educator

**Century City**
O'Neal, Tatum actress

**Chatsworth**
Woodruff, Tom, Jr. special effects designer

**Claremont**
Herschensohn, Bruce film director, writer

**Concord**
Bellson, Louis Paul *drummer*
Burrell, Kenneth Earl *guitarist, composer*
Clooney, Rosemary *singer*
Jackson, Milton (Bags Jackson) *jazz musician*
McConnell, Rob *jazz musician, composer*

**Coronado**
Neblett, Carol *soprano*

**Culver City**
Bancroft, Anne (Mrs. Mel Brooks) *actress*
†Besson, Luc *film director*
Brooks, James L. *writer, director, producer*
Brooks, Mel *producer, director, writer, actor*
†Calley, John *film producer*
Copeland, Stewart *composer, musician*
Gregg, David Paul *information storage media specialist*
Guber, Peter *producer*
Jaffe, Stanley Richard *film producer, director*
Marshall, Garry *film producer, director, writer*
Melnick, Daniel *film producer*
Rich, Lee *entertainment industry executive*
Stark, Ray *motion picture producer*
Tarantino, Quentin *film director, screenwriter*
Tisch, Steven E. *movie producer*
Trebek, Alex *television game show host*
Zucker, David *director*
Zucker, Jerry *producer, director*

**Davis**
Swift, Richard G(ene) *composer, educator*

**El Cerrito**
Jiménez, Leonardo *popular accordionist*

**Encino**
Broughton, Bruce Harold *composer*
Colombier, Michel *composer*
Conway, Tim *comedian*
Eves, Jeffrey Parvin *entertainment industry executive*
Franklin, Bonnie Gail *actress*
Hubbard, Frederick Dewayne *trumpeter*
Kazan, Lainie (Lainie Levine) *singer, actress*
Nicholson, Jack *actor, director, producer*
Pryor, Richard *actor, writer*
Westmore, Michael George *make-up artist*
Zsigmond, Vilmos *cinematographer, director*

**Escondido**
Rockwell, Elizabeth Goode *dance company director, consultant, educator*

**Fish Camp**
Schneider, Arthur Paul *retired videotape and film editor, author*

**Fresno**
Gerster, Robert Gibson *composer*

**Fullerton**
Karson, Burton Lewis *musician*
Linahon, James Joseph *music educator, musician*

**Glendale**
Rabe, Elizabeth Rozina *hair stylist, horse breeder*

**Hemet**
Bible, Frances Lillian *mezzo-soprano, educator*

**Hollywood**
Cannell, Stephen Joseph *television writer, producer, director*
Crow, Sheryl *singer/songwriter, musician*
Gibbons, Leeza *television talk show host, entertainment reporter*
Hall, Allen *special effects expert*
Harris, Susan *television producer*
Jordan, Stanley *musician*
Lewis, Huey (Hugh Anthony Cregg, III) *singer, composer, bandleader*
Little Richard, (Richard Wayne Penniman) *recording artist, pianist, songwriter, minister*
†Miles, Joanna *actress, playwright*
Robertson, Robbie *musician, popular*
Safan, Craig Alan *film composer*
Salomon, Mikael *cinematographer, director*
Secada, Jon *musician*

**Irvine**
Cohen, Robert Stephen *drama educator*
Penrod, James Wilford *choreographer, dancer*
Ruyter, Nancy Lee Chalfa *dance educator*

**Joshua Tree**
Styles, Beverly *entertainer*

**Kentfield**
Halprin, Anna Schuman (Mrs. Lawrence Halprin) *dancer*

**La Crescenta**
Purcell, Lee *actress, producer*

**La Jolla**
Harkins, Edwin L. *music educator, performer*
Moore, F. Richard *music educator*
Ogdon, Wilbur *composer, music educator*
Reynolds, Roger Lee *composer*

**La Quinta**
Harbert, Edward Wesley, II *television producer, writer, director*

**Lafayette**
Oliveira, Elmar *violinist*

**Laguna Hills**
Herold, Ralph Elliott *motion picture arts educator*

**Lake Hughes**
La Mont-Wells, Tawana Faye *camera operator, video director*

**Lake Isabella**
Mansbridge, Mark *art director, production designer*

**Los Angeles**
Allen, Karen Jane *actress*
Alley, Kirstie *actress*
Amos, John *actor, producer, director*
Anderson, Daryl *actor*
Anderson, Richard Norman *actor, film producer*
Anka, Paul *singer, composer*
Bain, Conrad Stafford *actor*
Ballard, Glen *composer*
Banner, Bob *television producer, director*
Barbera, Joseph *motion picture and television producer, cartoonist*
Barker, Robert William *television personality*
†Barnes, Priscilla *actress*
Barry, Gene *actor*
Barry, Philip Semple *television and film producer*
Bartel, Paul *film director*
Bass, Barbara DeJong *film assistant director, free-lance writer*
Bassett, Angela *actress*
Beatty, Ned *actor*
Bell, Lee Phillip *television personality, television producer*
Belzer, Richard *comedian, TV show host, actor*
Black, Lisa Hartman (Lisa Hartman Black) *actress, singer*
Bogart, Paul *film director*
Bogdanovich, Peter *film director, writer, producer, actor*
Bosley, Tom *actor*
Brest, Martin *film director*
Brosnan, Peter Lawrence *documentary filmmaker*
Buckley, Betty Lynn *actress*
Burrows, James *television and motion picture director, producer*
Burton, Tim *film director*
Bymel, Suzan Yvette *talent manager, film producer*
Caan, James *actor, director*
Campbell, Glen *singer, entertainer*
Campbell, Malcolm *film editor*
Carlin, George Denis *comedian*
†Carmen, Julie *actress*
Carr, Allan *film and stage producer, celebrity representative*
Carter, Richard *production designer*
Casey, Peter William *television producer, screenwriter*
Cates, Gilbert *film, theater, television producer and director*
Chaffin, Cean *producer*
Champlin, Charles Davenport *television host, book critic, writer*
Charles, Glen *television producer*
Charles, Les *television producer*
Chase, Chevy (Cornelius Crane Chase) *comedian, actor, author*
Cocker, Joe *popular musician*
Cole, Natalie Maria *singer*
Conniff, Ray *popular musician, conductor, composer, arranger*
Cooder, Ry *recording artist, guitarist*
Corea, Chick (Armando Corea) *pianist, composer*
Corman, Roger William *motion picture producer, director*
Crockett, Donald Harold *composer, university educator*
Cromwell, James *actor*
Curry, Daniel Francis Myles *filmmaker*
D'Accone, Frank Anthony *music educator*
Daniels, Jeff *actor*
†D'Arbanville, Patti *actress*
†Dash, Stacey *actress*
Davidson, Gordon *theatrical producer, director*
Davis, Don *composer*
Davis, Ossie *actor, author*
Dee, Ruby (Ruby Dee Davis) *actress, writer, director*
†Del Toro, Benicio *actor*
De Luise, Dom *actor*
DiCaprio, Leonardo *actor*
Dickerson, Ernest *cinematographer, director*
Dolenz, Mickey (George Michael Dolenz) *singer, actor, television producer*
Domino, Fats (Antoine Domino) *pianist, singer, songwriter*
Dr. Dre, (Andre Young) *rapper, record producer*
Edelman, Randy *composer*
Edwards, Blake *film director*
Everhart, Angie *model*
Faltermeyer, Harold *composer*
Farrell, Mike *actor*
Ferrell, Conchata Galen *actress, acting teacher and coach*
Finerman, Wendy *film producer*
Fleischmann, Ernest Martin *music administrator*
Fodor, Eugene Nicholas *concert violinist*
Folk, Robert *composer*
Foster, David *composer, record producer*
Foster, Jodie (Alicia Christian Foster) *actress*
Franke, Christopher *composer*
Franz, Dennis *actor*
Fuller, Larry *choreographer, director*
Furth, George *actor, playwright*
Garcia, Andy *actor*
Getty, Estelle *actress*
Gibbs, Marla (Margaret Gibbs) *actress*
Gibbs, Richard *composer*
Gimbel, Norman *lyricist, music publisher, television producer*
Gimble, Johnny *country musician*
Goldenthal, Elliot *composer*
Goldsmith, Jerry *composer*
Goldwyn, Samuel John, Jr. *motion picture producer*
Gooding, Cuba, Jr. *actor*
Goodman, David Bryan *musician, educator*
Gore, Michael *composer*
Gorman, Cliff *actor*
Gould, Harold *actor*
Grammer, Kelsey *actor*
Grant, Lee (Lyova Haskell Rosenthal) *actress, director*
Gruska, Jay *composer*
Hackman, Gene *actor*
Haden, Charles *jazz bassist, composer*
Halsey, Richard *film editor*
Hammer, (Stanley Kirk Burrell) *musician*
Hancock, Herbert Jeffrey (Herbie Hancock) *composer, pianist, publisher*
Hart, Mary *television talk show host*
Hartke, Stephen Paul *composer, educator*
Hemion, Dwight Arlington *television producer, director*
Hemmings, Peter William *orchestra and opera administrator*
†Henriksen, Lance *actor*
Hiatt, John *musician, country, popular*
Hicklin, Ronald Lee *music production company executive*
Hiller, Arthur *motion picture director*
Holman, Bill *composer*
Horner, James *composer*
Howard, James Newton *composer*
Howard, Sandy *motion picture producer*
Howe, John Thomas *film director, educator*
Hoy, William *film editor*
Hunt, Peter Roger *film director, writer, editor*
Ice Cube, (O'Shea Jackson) *rap singer, actor*
Iglesias, Julio (Julio Jose Iglesias De La Cueva) *singer, songwriter*
Ingels, Marty *theatrical agent, television and motion picture production executive*
Ireland, Kathy *actress*
Jackson, Isaiah *conductor*
Jackson, Janet Damita *singer, dancer*
Jackson, Mary *actress*
Jackson, Michael (Joseph) *singer*
Jarrott, Charles *film and television director*
Johansen, David (Buster Poindexter) *popular musician, actor*
Jones, Henry *actor*
Jones, James Earl *actor*
Jones, Tom *singer*
Kamen, Michael *composer, musician, conductor*
Kaplan, Jonathan Stewart *film director, writer*
Kidman, Nicole *actress*
Kirkwood, Gene *motion picture producer*
Koch, Howard W., Jr. *film producer*
Koch, Howard Winchel *film and television producer*
Kopelson, Arnold *film producer*
Korman, Harvey Herschel *actor*
Kramer, Stanley E. *motion picture producer, director*
Krieg, Dorothy Linden *soprano, performing artist, educator*
Kurtz, Swoosie *actress*
Lambro, Phillip *composer, conductor, pianist*
Lamont, Peter *production designer, art director*
Lansing, Sherry Lee *motion picture production executive*
Lawrence, Martin *actor, comedian*
Lear, Norman Milton *producer, writer, director*
Leigh, Janet (Jeanette Helen Morrison) *actress*
Leighton, Robert *film editor*
Lepine, Jean *cinematographer*
Levy, Norman *motion picture company executive*
Lew, Joycelyne Mae *actress*
Lewis, Richard *actor, comedian*
Lewis, Shari *puppeteer, entertainer*
Lewitzky, Bella *choreographer*
Linder, Stu *film editor*
London, Andrew Barry *film editor*
†Love, Courtney *singer, actress*
Lowry-Johnson, Junie *casting director*
Madonna, (Madonna Louise Veronica Ciccone) *singer, actress*
Maher, Bill *talk show host, comedian, producer*
Malden, Karl (Malden Sekulovich) *actor*
Mann, Delbert *film, theater, television director and producer*
Marsalis, Branford *musician*
Matthau, Walter *actor*
Mc Coy, Frank Milton *concert pianist, educator, lecturer*
Mc Guire, Dorothy Hackett *actress*
McQueen, Justice Ellis (L. Q. Jones) *actor, director*
Medak, Peter *film director*
Merlis, George *television producer*
Metheny, Patrick Bruce *musician*
Mirisch, Lawrence Alan *motion picture agent*
Moreno, Rita *actress*
Morissette, Alanis *musician*
Morriss, Frank *film editor*
Mossman, Thomas Mellish, Jr. *television manager*
Mueller, Carl Richard *theater arts educator, author*
Muldaur, Diana Charlton *actress*
Mulligan, Richard M. *actor, writer*
Mulligan, Robert Patrick *film director, producer*
Neville, Aaron *musician*
Neville, Art *musician*
Neville, Charles *musician*
Neville, Cyril *musician*
Newhart, Bob *entertainer*
Newman, Thomas *composer*
Niehaus, Lennie *composer, jazz saxophonist*
Noble, James Wilkes *actor*
Nyman, Michael Lawrence *composer*
O'Connor, Carroll *actor, writer, producer*
O'Day, Anita Belle Colton *entertainer, singer*
O'Steen, Sam *film editor, director*
Pappe, Stuart H. *film editor*
Paxton, Bill *actor, writer, director*
Perry, Joe *guitarist*
Perry, Luke (Coy Luther Perry, III) *actor*
Phillips, Julia Miller *film producer*
Pollack, Daniel *concert pianist*
Pollack, Sydney *film director*
Ponty, Jean-Luc *violinist, composer, producer*
Post, Mike *composer*
Raitt, Bonnie Lynn *blues singer, guitarist*
†Rapaport, Michael *actor*
Reaney, Gilbert *musician, educator*
Reeves, Keanu *actor*
Reynolds, Burt *actor, director*
Richards, Michael *actor, comedian*
Richie, Lionel B., Jr. *singer, songwriter, producer*
Richman, Peter Mark *actor, painter, writer*
Rickles, Donald Jay *comedian, actor*
Riley, Jack *actor, writer*
Riva, J. Michael *art director, production designer*
Robinson, Smokey *singer, composer*
Rogers, Kenneth Ray *entertainer, recording artist*
Rollins, Henry *musician, author, publisher*
Rosen, Charles *production designer*
Rosenthal, Laurence *composer*
Ross, Diana *singer, actress, entertainer, fashion designer*
Rosten, Irwin *writer, producer, director*
Rubin, Stanley Creamer *producer*
Rudin, Scott *film and theatre producer*
Rundgren, Todd *musician, record producer*
Ruskin, Joseph Richard *actor, director*
Saltzman, Barry *actor*
Salzman, David Elliot *entertainment industry executive*
†San Giacomo, Laura *actress*
Schmidt, Arthur *film editor*
Seidelman, Arthur Allan *director*
Seymour, Michael *production designer*
Shaiman, Marc *composer, arranger, orchestrator*
Shatner, William *actor*
Shire, David Lee *composer*
Shore, Howard Leslie *composer*
Silverman, Fred *television producer*
†Silverstone, Alicia *actress*
Skotak, Robert F. *film production company executive*
Slash, (Saul Hudson) *guitarist*
Smith, Howard *film editor*
Smits, Jimmy *actor*
Spelling, Aaron *film and television producer, writer, actor*
Stapleton, Jean (Jeanne Murray) *actress*
Steel, Dawn *motion picture producer*
Steinberg, David *comedian, author, actor*
Steinkamp, William *film editor*
Stevens, Connie *actress, singer*
Stevenson, Robert Murrell *music educator*
Stone, Sharon *actress*
Strock, Herbert Leonard *motion picture producer, director, editor, writer*
Suhrstedt, Tim *cinematographer*
Summers, Andy (Andrew James Somers) *popular musician*
Sutherland, Donald *actor*
Swit, Loretta *actress*
Tewkesbury, Joan F. *film director, writer*
Torme, Mel(vin) (Howard Torme) *musician, jazz vocalist*
Townsend, Robert *film director*
Trembly, Dennis Michael *musician*
Tyler, Steven *singer*
Urioste, Frank J. *film editor*
Waits, Thomas Alan *composer, actor, singer*
Waterston, Samuel Atkinson *actor*
Weinstein, Josh *television producer*
Welch, Robert W. *production designer, art director*
Wellburn, Timothy *film editor*
Williams, John Towner *composer, conductor*
Williams, Robin *actor, comedian*
Winfield, Paul Edward *actor*
Winters, Barbara Jo *musician*
Winters, Ralph E. *film editor*
Woessner, Frederick T. *composer, pianist*
†Yared, Gabriel *composer*
Yates, Peter *director, producer*
Zemeckis, Robert L. *film director*
Zentner, Anne Diener *flutist*
Ziskin, Laura *film producer*

**Los Osos**
Mehring, Margaret *filmmaker, retired educator*

**Malibu**
Almond, Paul *film director, producer, writer*
Downey, Robert, Jr. *actor*
Nolte, Nick *actor*
Vereen, Ben *actor, singer, dancer*

**Menlo Park**
Baez, Joan Chandos *folk singer*

**Mill Valley**
Padula, Fred David *filmmaker*

**Montecito**
McShirley, Marjorie Stone *art director*

**North Hollywood**
Badalamenti, Angelo *composer, conductor*
Baker, Rick *make-up artist*
Clarke, Stanley Marvin *musician, composer*
Diller, Phyllis *actress, author*
Duffield, Thomas Andrew *art director, production designer*
Kahn, Sheldon F. *film editor, producer*
LaBelle, Patti *singer*
Lantieri, Michael *special effects expert*
Levin, Alvin Irving *composer*
Lynn, Loretta Webb (Mrs. Oliver Lynn, Jr.) *singer*
McMartin, John *actor*
Meat Loaf, (Marvin Lee Aday) *popular musician, actor*
Meyer, Ron *agent*
Mirisch, Marvin Elliot *motion picture producer*
Neill, Ve *make-up artist*
Newton-John, Olivia *singer, actress*
Omens, Sherwood *cinematographer*
Pike, (John) Kevin *special effects expert*
Reynolds, Debbie (Mary Frances Reynolds) *actress*
Robinson, John Peter *film composer, keyboardist*
Smothers, Dick *actor, singer*
Smothers, Tom *actor, singer*
Spencer, James H. *art director, production designer*
Walker, Mallory Elton *tenor*
Yearwood, Trisha *country music singer, songwriter*
Zappa, Gail *record producer*

**Northridge**
Berger, Peter E. *film editor*
Mouzon, Alphonse *actor, composer, record producer, instrumentalist*

**Oakland**
DeFazio, Lynette Stevens *dancer, choreographer, educator, chiropractor, author, actress, musician*
Zschau, Marilyn *singer*

**Oxnard**
Frodsham, Olaf Milton *music educator*

**Pacific Palisades**
Albert, Eddie (Edward Albert Heimberger) *actor*
Brown, Robert N. *film editor*
Burum, Stephen H. *cinematographer*
Francis-Bruce, Richard *film editor*
Gosnell, Raja *film editor*
Hirsch, Paul Frederick *film editor*
Kovacs, Laszlo *cinematographer*
Malley, William *production designer*
Milsome, Douglas *cinematographer*
Primes, Robert *cinematographer*
Spinotti, Dante *cinematographer*
Washington, Dennis *production designer*

**Palm Springs**
Lees, Benjamin *composer*

**Palo Cedro**
Haggard, Merle Ronald *songwriter, recording artist*

**Palos Verdes Peninsula**
Giles, Allen *pianist, composer, music educator*
Lima, Luis Eduardo *tenor*

**Pasadena**
McClellan, Bennett Earl *producer*

**Pebble Beach**
Cameron, JoAnna *actress, director*

**Quartz Hill**
McKain, Mary Margaret *musician*

**Sacramento**
Nice, Carter *conductor, music director*

**San Bernardino**
Little, Thomas Warren *broadcast executive*
Robertson, Stewart *conductor*

**San Diego**
Burge, David Russell *concert pianist, composer, piano educator*
Campbell, Ian David *opera company director*
Flettner, Marianne *opera administrator*
Noehren, Robert *organist, organ builder*
Price, Betty Jeanne *choirchime soloist, writer*
Sasaki, Tatsuo *musician*
Sutowski, Thor Brian *choreographer*
Ward-Steinman, David *composer, music educator, pianist*

**San Francisco**
Allemann, Sabina *ballet dancer*
Allman, Gregg *musician*
Balin, Marty (Martyn Jerel Buchwald) *musician*
Bennett, William *oboist*
Berman, Joanna *dancer*
Breeden, David *clarinetist*
Brubeck, David Warren *musician*
Caniparoli, Val William *choreographer, dancer*
Castilla, Antonio *ballet dancer*
Cisneros, Evelyn *dancer*
Coppola, Francis Ford *film director, producer, writer*
De Coteau, Denis *music director, conductor*
Eilenberg, Lawrence Ira *theater educator, artistic director*
Festinger, Richard *music educator, composer*
George, Vance *conductor*
Getty, Gordon Peter *composer, philanthropist*
Haire, James *theatrical producer*
Hastings, Edward Walton *theater director*
Hooker, John Lee *blues singer, guitarist*
Jacobus, Arthur *dance company administrator*
Jenkins, Margaret Ludmilla *choreographer, dancer*
Kantner, Paul *musician*
Kobler, Raymond *concertmaster*
LeBlanc, Tina *dancer*
Legate, Stephen *ballet dancer*
Loscavio, Elizabeth *dancer*
Maffre, Muriel *ballet dancer*
Mahal, Taj (Henry St. Clair Fredericks) *composer, musician*
Palmer, David *dancer*
Pastreich, Peter *orchestra executive director*
Peterson, Wayne Turner *composer, pianist*
Posokhov, Iouri *ballet dancer, educator*
Runnicles, Donald *conductor*
Sheinfeld, David *composer*
Smuin, Michael *choreographer, director, dancer*
Stowell, Christopher R. *dancer*
Tiano, Anthony Steven *television producer, book publishing executive*
Tomasson, Helgi *dancer, choreographer, dance company executive*
Van Dyck, Wendy *dancer*
Wheater, Ashley *dancer*
†Yu, Jessica *director, producer, writer, editor*
Zhukov, Yuri *ballet dancer*

**San Jose**
Dalis, Irene *mezzo-soprano, opera company administrator, music educator*
†DeGrande, Kenneth P. *production company executive*

**San Rafael**
Brevig, Eric *special effects expert, executive*
Carson, Dave *special effects expert, executive*
Farrar, Scott *special effects expert, executive*
Goldman, Clint Paul *producer*
Gorman, Ned *film producer*
Kennedy, Thomas *executive producer*
Lesh, Philip Chapman *musician, composer*
Lucas, George W., Jr. *film director, producer, screenwriter*
Murphy, George *special effects expert*
Nicholson, Bruce *graphics expert, executive*
Santana, Carlos *guitarist*
Sheldon, Gary *conductor, music director*
Squires, Scott William *special effects expert, executive*

**Santa Ana**
St. Clair, Carl *conductor, music director*

**Santa Barbara**
Brant, Henry *composer*
Snyder, Allegra Fuller *dance educator*
Wayland, Newton Hart *conductor*

**Santa Clarita**
Powell, Mel *composer*
Senter, Jack *art director, production designer*

**Santa Cruz**
Mumma, Gordon *composer, educator, author*
Winston, George *pianist, guitarist, harmonica player*

**Santa Monica**
Abdul, Paula (Julie) *singer, dancer, choreographer*
Anderson, Loni Kaye *actress*
Bergman, Alan *lyricist, writer*
Bergman, Marilyn Keith *lyricist, writer*
Black, Noel Anthony *television and film director*
Bruckheimer, Jerry *producer*
Cameron, James *film director, screenwriter, producer*
Chartoff, Robert Irwin *film producer*
Cooper, Jackie *actor, director, producer*
Diamond, Neil Leslie *singer, composer*
†Dobson, Kevin James *film director*
Edwards, Sarah Anne *radio and cable television personality, clinical social worker*
Goldberg, Leonard *television and movie producer*
Ho, Alexander Kitman *producer*
Kalb, Benjamin Stuart *television producer, director*
Kempster, Victor *art director, production designer*
Kennedy, Kathleen *film producer*
Leaf, Paul *producer, director, writer*
Lebenzon, Chris *film editor*
Marshall, Frank W. *film producer, director*
Nathanson, Michael *film company executive*

Norris, David Randolph *recording artist, philanthropist*
Pisano, A. Robert *entertainment company executive, lawyer*
Random, Ida *production designer*
Redford, Robert (Charles Robert Redford) *actor, director*
Reynolds, Norman *production designer, art director*
Rydell, Mark *film director, producer, actor*
Schultz, Michael *stage and film director, film producer*
Smith, Anna Deavere *actress, playwright*
Vacano, Jost *cinematographer*
Watrous, William Russell *trombonist, composer, conductor*
Watson, Doc (Arthel Lane Watson) *vocalist, guitarist, banjoist, recording artist*
Weber, Samuel Lloyd *tap dancer, choreographer*
Wexler, Haskell *film producer, cameraman*

**Sherman Oaks**
Atwood, Colleen *costume designer*
Buckingham, Lindsey *musician*
Conrad, Robert (Conrad Robert Falk) *actor, singer, producer, director*
Easton, Sheena *rock vocalist*
Farnsworth, Richard *actor, former stuntman*
Gibbs, Antony (Tony) *film editor*
Gilmore, Art *television performer*
Hall, Deidre *actress*
Harper, Valerie *actress*
Kennedy, Burt Raphael *film director*
Tesh, John *television talk show host*

**Simi Valley**
Brock, James Wilson *drama educator, playwright, researcher*
Hoover, Richard *special effects expert, film director*
Shartle, Keith Robert *producer*
Yeatman, Hoyt *special effects expert, executive*

**Somis**
Woodruff, Donald B. *motion picture art director, production designer*

**Sonoma**
Pollack, Phyllis Addison *ballerina*

**Stanford**
Cohen, Albert *musician, educator*
Cole, Wendell Gordon *speech and drama educator*
Lyons, Charles R. *drama educator and critic*

**Stockton**
Tregle, Linda Marie *dance educator*

**Studio City**
Autry, Gene (Orvon Gene Autry) *actor, entertainer, broadcasting executive, baseball team executive*
Barrett, Dorothy *performing arts administrator*
Basinger, Kim *actress*
Bergen, Polly *actress*
Bloodworth-Thomason, Linda *television producer, writer*
Bumstead, Henry *art director, production designer*
Carradine, David *actor, director*
Carsey, Marcia Lee Peterson *television producer*
Cockrell, Frank Boyd, II *film production company executive*
Coolidge, Rita *singer*
English, Diane *television producer, writer, communications executive*
Gautier, Dick *actor, writer*
Haber, David M. *art director, production designer*
Hasselhoff, David *actor*
Hole, Fred *art director*
Hutman, Jon *art director, production designer*
Jacobs, Ronald Nicholas *television and motion picture producer/director*
Kenney, H(arry) Wesley, Jr. *producer, director*
Kilvert, Lilly *film production designer*
Malone, Nancy *actor, director, producer*
Mansbridge, John B. *art director, production designer*
Needham, Hal *director, writer*
Peerce, Larry *film director*
Roseanne *actress, comedienne, producer, writer*
Rosenberg, Philip *production designer*
Scarfiotti, Ferdinando *production designer*
Sertner, Robert Mark *producer*
Shepherd, Cybill *actress, singer*
†Sinbad *actor, comedian*
Smith, Peter Lansdown *art director*
Sylbert, Paul *production designer, art director*
Sylbert, Richard *production designer, art director*
Taylor, Jack G., Jr. *art director*
Thomas, Wynn P. *art director, production designer*
Tomkins, Alan *art director, production designer*
von Zerneck, Frank Ernest *television producer*
Wedgeworth, Ann *actress*
Werner, Tom *television producer, professional baseball team executive*

**Sylmar**
Foster, Dudley Edwards, Jr. *musician, educator*

**Tarzana**
Abbott, Philip *actor*

**Thousand Oaks**
Miller, Jim *film editor*
Rooney, Mickey (Joe Yule, Jr.) *actor*

**Topanga**
Redgrave, Lynn *actress*
Warner, Mark Roy *film editor*

**Torrance**
Harness, William Edward *tenor*

**Turlock**
Goedecke, David Stewart *music educator, band educator, trumpet player*
Klein, James Mikel *music educator*

**Universal City**
Bishop, Stephen *singer, songwriter*
Buffett, Jimmy *singer, songwriter, author*
Ely, Joe *singer and songwriter*
Frey, Glenn *songwriter, vocalist, guitarist*
Judd, Wynonna *vocalist, musician*
Lansbury, Angela Brigid *actress*
Metheny, Pat *jazz musician*

Michelson, Lillian *motion picture researcher*

**Van Nuys**
Allen, Stephen Valentine Patrick William *television comedian, author, pianist, songwriter*
Ferguson, Jay A. *composer*
Ivey, Judith *actress*
Newborn, Ira *composer*

**Venice**
Bill, Tony *producer, director*
Chomsky, Marvin J. *director*
Ferry, April *costume designer*
Young, Christopher *composer*

**West Hollywood**
Bloom, Claire *actress*
Blumofe, Robert Fulton *motion picture producer, association executive*
De Palma, Brian Russell *film director, writer*
Elfman, Danny *composer*
Henley, Don *singer, drummer, songwriter*
Males, William James *film producer, make-up artist*
Marsalis, Wynton *musician*
McKagan, Duff (Michael McKagan) *bassist*
McLaughlin, Stephen *sound recording engineer*
Ronstadt, Linda Marie *singer*
Rose, W. Axl (William Bruce Bailey) *singer*
Shaye, Robert Kenneth *cinema company executive*
Sherman, Robert B(ernard) *composer, lyricist, screenwriter*
Taylor, James Vernon *musician*
Verhoeven, Paul *film director*

**Winnetka**
Peirson, George Ewell *film producer, art director, educator*

**Woodland Hills**
Felton, Norman Francis *motion picture producer*
Pendergrass, Teddy (Theodore D. Pendergrass) *musician*
Ross, Marion *actress*
Scheimer, Louis *film and television producer*
Small, Michael *composer*
Wester, Keith Albert *film and television recording engineer, television executive*

**Yreka**
Beary, Shirley Lorraine *retired music educator*

## COLORADO

**Arvada**
Ozaki, Nancy Junko *performance artist, former educator*

**Aspen**
Harth, Robert James *music festival executive*

**Basalt**
Sinatra, Frank (Francis Albert Sinatra) *singer, actor*

**Boulder**
Brakhage, James Stanley *filmmaker, educator*
Duckworth, Guy *musician, educator*
Fink, Robert Russell *music theorist, former university dean*
Sable, Barbara Kinsey *former music educator*
Sarson, John Christopher *television producer, director, writer*
Schwarz, Josephine Lindeman *retired ballet company director, choreographer*
Symons, James Martin *theater and dance educator*

**Cherry Hills Village**
Stapleton, Katharine Hall (Katie Stapleton) *food broadcaster, author*

**Denver**
Bearden, Thomas Howard *news program producer, correspondent*
Burshtan, John Willis *television producer*
Ceci, Jesse Arthur *violinist*
Fredmann, Martin *ballet artistic director, educator, choreographer*
Keats, Donald Howard *composer, educator*
Rawls, Eugenia *actress*

**Evergreen**
White, John David *composer, theorist, cellist*

**Loveland**
Balsiger, David Wayne *television-video director, researcher, producer, writer*

**Ridgway**
Weaver, Dennis *actor*

## CONNECTICUT

**Bristol**
†Campbell, Dave *baseball analyst*
†Clement, Bill *hocket analyst*
†Conley, Larry *basketball analyst*
†Davis, Rece *anchor, reporter*
†Edwards, Jack *anchor, reporter*
†Fowler, Chris *anchor, reporter*
†Franklin, Ron *anchor, reporter*
†Goldberg, Hank *sports analyst*
†Gottfried, Mike *sports analyst*
†Griffin, Mimi *basketball analyst*
†Herbstreit, Kirk *sports analyst*
†Jackson, Jason *anchor, reporter*
†Jackson, Tom *anchor, reporter*
†Jarrett, Ned *auto racing analyst*
†Jaworski, Ron *sports analyst*
†Jones, Mark *sports network host*
†Kellogg, Clark *basketball analyst*
†Levy, Steve *sports anchor, studio host*
†Ley, Bob *sports network anchor, reporter*
†Mayne, Kenny *sports anchor*
†Miller, Jon *sports commentator*
†Mortensen, Chris *sports analyst, reporter*
†Myers, Chris *network host*
†Nessler, Brad Ray *sports commentator*
†Pang, Darren *hockey analyst*
†Paolantonio, Sal *sports correspondent*

**Chester**
Hays, David Arthur *theater producer, stage designer*

**Danbury**
Jennings, Alfred Higson, Jr. *music educator, actor, singer*
Nelson, Willie *musician, songwriter*

**East Haddam**
Borton, John Carter, Jr. (Terry Borton) *producer, theater*

**Fairfield**
Wolff, Steven Alexander *arts and entertainment consultant*

**Greenwich**
Fates, Joseph Gilbert *television producer*
Rutgers, Katharine Phillips (Mrs. Frederik Lodewijk Rutgers) *dancer*
Tiegs, Cheryl *model, designer*

**Hartford**
Lamos, Mark *artistic director, administrator, actor*
Lyman, Peggy *dancer, choreographer, educator*
Mc Lean, Jackie *jazz saxophonist, educator, composer, community activist*
Osborne, George Delano *performing arts company director*

**Litchfield**
Winter, Paul Theodore *musician*

**New Canaan**
Richardson, Dana Roland *video producer*

**New Haven**
Baker, Robert Stevens *organist, educator*
Brainard, Paul Henry *musicologist, music educator*
Brown, Arvin Bragin *theater director*
French, Richard Frederic *retired music educator*
Gilman, Richard *drama educator, author*
Laderman, Ezra *composer, educator, college dean*
Morgan, Robert P. *music theorist, educator*
Nolan, Victoria *theater director*
Tirro, Frank Pascale *music educator, author, composer*
Wojewodski, Stan, Jr. *artistic director, dean*

**Norwalk**
Albanese, Licia *retired operatic soprano*
Eagan, Sherman G. *producer, communications executive*

**Ridgefield**
Wyton, Alec *composer, organist*

**Southport**
Walker, Charles Dodsley *conductor, organist*

**Stamford**
Karp, Steve *artistic director*
†Mitzner, Donald H. *cable television executive*
Nierenberg, Roger *symphony conductor*
Preiss-Harris, Patricia *music educator, composer, pianist*

**Storrs Mansfield**
Birdman, Jerome Moseley *drama educator, consultant*
Wood, Wendy Deborah *filmmaker*

**Thomaston**
Kirshner, Hal *cinematographer*

**Washington**
Pendleton, Moses Robert Andrew *dancer, choreographer*

**Washington Depot**
Chase, Alison Becker *modern dancer, choreographer, teacher*
Mandler, Susan Ruth *dance company administrator*
Tracy, Michael Cameron *choreographer, performer*

**Waterford**
White, George Cooke *theater director, foundation executive*

**West Redding**
Kipnis, Igor *harpsichordist, fortepianist, pianist, critic*

**Weston**
Fredrik, Burry *theatrical producer, director*
Schnitzer, Robert C. *theater administrator*

**Westport**
Hersey, Marilyn Elaine *performing company executive*
Rose, Reginald *television writer, producer*

## DELAWARE

**Wilmington**
Gunzenhauser, Stephen Charles *conductor*
Wesler, Ken *theater company manager*

## DISTRICT OF COLUMBIA

**Washington**
Ames, Frank Anthony *percussionist, film producer*
Carpenter, Mary Chapin *singer, songwriter*
Crowther, G(eorge) Rodney, III *television production company executive, writer, photographer*
Day, Doris (Doris von Kappelhoff) *singer, actress*
Day, Mary *artistic director, ballet company executive*
Doty, Shayne Taylor *organist*
Dukert, Betty Cole *television producer*
Farrell, Suzanne *ballerina*
Forrest, Sidney *clarinetist, music educator*
Fricke, Heinz *conductor*
Gruber, Brian Keith *disk jockey, entertainment agent*

PROFESSIONAL INDEX 5083 ARTS: PERFORMING

Guggenheim, Charles E. *film, television producer*
Hancock, Richard B. *symphony orchestra executive*
Harpham, Virginia Ruth *violinist*
Hay, George Austin *actor, producer, director, musician, artist*
Hewitt, Frankie Lea *theater producer*
Kahn, Michael *stage director*
Kendall, Peter Landis *television news executive*
Makris, Andreas *composer*
Mosettig, Michael David *television producer, writer*
Mossel, Patricia L. *opera executive*
Myers, Margaret Jane (Dee Dee Myers) *television personality, editor*
Parris, Robert *composer*
Pasmanick, Kenneth *bassoonist*
Ratner, Ellen Faith *radio talk show host, writer*
Royle, David Brian Layton *television producer, journalist*
Russell, Mark *comedian*
†Schaefer, James Lee *television news producer*
Slatkin, Leonard Edward *conductor, music director, pianist*
Stevens, George, Jr. *film and television producer, writer, director*
Stevens, Milton Lewis, Jr. *trombonist*
Stevens, Roger Lacey *theatrical producer*
Thayer, Edwin Cabot *musician*
Thulean, Donald Myron *symphony conductor*
Wager, Douglas Charles *artistic director*
Weidenfeld, Sheila Rabb *television producer, author*
Wilker, Lawrence J. *performing arts association administrator*

## FLORIDA

### Boca Raton
Blanton, Jeremy *dance company director*
Fengler, John Peter *television producer, director, advertising executive*
Gold, Catherine Anne Dower *music history educator*
Wallis, John James (Jimmy Wallis) *comedian, impressionist, ventriloquist, comedy writer, video production executive*

### Bradenton
Powers, Dudley *musician*

### Brooksville
Manieri-Harvey, Michele Dawn *musician, educator*

### Clearwater
Dukore, Bernard Frank *theatre arts and humanities educator, writer*

### Deerfield Beach
Waldman, Alan I. (Alawana) *songwriter, composer, lyricist, computer programmer*

### Deland
Sorensen, Jacki Faye *choreographer, aerobic dance company executive*

### Fort Lauderdale
Davis-Wexler, Ginia *singer, association executive*
Gill, Richard Thomas *opera singer, economic analyst*
Holland, Beth *actress*
LeRoy, Miss Joy *model, designer*
Levy, Marvin David *composer*
Randi, James (Randall James Hamilton Zwinge) *magician, writer, educator*

### Fort Pierce
Herd, Charmian June *singer, actress*
Norton, Robert Howard *entertainer, musical arranger, author*

### Gainesville
Bodine, Willis Ramsey, Jr. *music educator, organist*

### Hollywood
Polivnick, Paul *conductor, music director*

### Jacksonville
Swenson, Courtland Sevander *musician*

### Key West
Mitchell, John Dietrich *theatre arts institute executive*

### Lake Worth
Newton, Wayne *entertainer, actor, recording artist*

### Miami
Allen, Charles Norman *television, film and video producer*
Brady, Alexander Childs *dancer*
Catanzaroedu, Tony *dancer*
Gibb, Robin *vocalist, songwriter*
Heuer, Robert Maynard, II *opera company executive*
Lawson, Eve Kennedy *ballet mistress*
Reed, Alfred *composer, conductor*

### Naples
White, Roy Bernard *theater executive*

### North Palm Beach
Hayman, Richard Warren Joseph *conductor*

### Odessa
Lister, Thomas Mosie *composer, lyricist, publishing company executive, minister*

### Orlando
Grant, Raymond Thomas *arts administrator*
Swedberg, Robert Mitchell *opera company director*
Walsh, James Anthony (Tony Walsh) *theater and film educator*

### Port Charlotte
Clark, Keith Collar *musician, educator*
Spatz, Hugo David *film producer*

### Punta Gorda
Kavanaugh, Frank James *film producer, educator*

### Saint Petersburg
Carroll, Charles Michael *music educator*

### Sarasota
McCollum, John Morris *tenor*

### Shalimar
Sublette, Julia Wright *music educator, performer, adjudicator*

### Spring Hill
Burnim, Kalman Aaron *theatre educator emeritus*
Youngman, Henny *comedian*

### Surfside
Berman, Mona S. *actress, playwright, theatrical director and producer*

### Tallahassee
Harsanyi, Janice *soprano, educator*
Housewright, Wiley Lee *music educator*
Kirk, Colleen Jean *conductor, educator*
McConnell, Michael *opera company director*

### Tampa
Hankenson, E(dward) Craig, Jr. *performing arts executive*
Kase-Polisini, Judith Baker *theater educator, playwright*

### Umatilla
Lange, Billie Carola *aquatic exercise video creator and specialist*

### West Palm Beach
Robinson, Raymond Edwin *musician, music educator, writer*

## GEORGIA

### Americus
Nichols, Harold James *theatre educator*

### Athens
Staub, August William *drama educator, theatrical producer, director*

### Atlanta
Bell, Jack Atkins *percussionist, educator*
Bridgewater, Herbert Jeremiah, Jr. *radio host*
Holder, Beth D. *ballet company administrator*
Holliday, Jennifer Yvette *singer, actress*
Johnson, J. J. *trombonist*
Kamm, Laurence Richard *television producer, director*
Lane, Louis *musician, conductor*
Rex, Christopher Davis *classical musician*
Shaw, Robert Lawson *symphony orchestra conductor*
Swartz, Christopher John *musician, instrument designer/builder*
Turner, Ed Sims *broadcast executive, writer*

### Clarkston
Downs, Jon Franklin *theater educator, director*

### Columbus
Patrick, Carl Lloyd *theatre executive*
Patrick, Michael Wynn *theatre executive*

### Conyers
Smith, Michael Joseph *composer, pianist, lecturer*

### Cumming
Pirkle, George Emory *television and film actor, director*

### Decatur
Hamilton, Frank S. *jazz musician, folksinger, composer and arranger, educator*

### Dunwoody
Clark, Faye Louise *drama and speech educator*

### Mableton
Rowe, Bonnie Gordon *music company executive*

### Macon
Marshall, Howard Lowen *music educator, musicologist*
Rich, Arthur Lowndes *music educator*

### Marietta
East, Nancy McKinley *private primary music educator*
Wells, Palmer Donald *performing arts executive*

### Millen
Cremer, Thomas Gerhard *music educator*

### Roswell
Siepi, Cesare *opera singer*

## HAWAII

### Honolulu
Baker, Kent Alfred *broadcasting company executive*
Greenberg, Marvin *retired music educator*
Ho, Donald Tai Loy *entertainer, singer*
Langhans, Edward Allen *drama and theater educator*
Smith, Barbara Barnard *music educator*

## IDAHO

### Pocatello
Stanek, Alan Edward *music educator, performer, music administrator*

## ILLINOIS

### Alton
Schnabel, John Henry *retired music educator*

### Bloomington
Brown, Jared *theater director, educator, writer*
Vayo, David Joseph *composer, music educator*

### Bourbonnais
York, Joseph Russell *media production technician, & film*

### Buffalo Grove
Denov, Sam *musician*
Siegel, Sid *composer, lyricist*

### Champaign
Fredrickson, L(awrence) Thomas *composer*
Garvey, John Charles *violist, conductor, retired music educator*

### Chicago
Aitay, Victor *concert violinist, music educator*
Akos, Francis *violinist*
Arpino, Gerald Peter *performing company executive*
†Barr, David *actor, playwright*
Bartoletti, Bruno *conductor*
Baudendistel, Daniel *dancer*
Bratton, Christopher Alan *video and art educator*
Duell, Daniel Paul *artistic director, choreographer, lecturer*
Eaton, John C. *composer, educator*
Falls, Robert Arthur *artistic director*
†Farina, Dennis *actor*
Favors, Malachi *jazz musician, bassist*
Fogel, Henry *orchestra administrator*
Guastafeste, Roberta Harrison *cellist*
Hillis, Margaret *conductor, musician*
Johns, Catherine *radio personality*
Knapp, Donald Roy *musician, educator*
LaPointe-Peterson, Kittie Vadis *choreographer, ballet school director, educator*
Lazar, Ludmila *concert pianist, pedagogue*
Lewis, Ramsey Emanuel, Jr. *pianist, composer*
Maggio, Michael John *artistic director*
Moffatt, Joyce Anne *performing arts executive*
Peck, Donald Vincent *musician*
Peters, Gordon Benes *musician*
Pikler, Charles *musician*
†Price, Henry Escoe *broadcast executive*
Ran, Shulamit *composer*
Schnell, Joseph *dancer*
Schweikert, Norman Carl *musician*
Scott, Stephen Brinsley *theater producer*
Sedelmaier, John Josef *film director, cinematographer*
Shapey, Ralph *composer, conductor, educator*
Solti, Sir Georg *conductor*
Tallchief, Maria *ballerina*
Turner, Lynne Alison (Mrs. Paul H. Singer) *harpist*
Walker, John Patrick *theater producer, actor*
Wang, Albert James *violinist, educator*
Warfield, William Caesar *singer, actor, educator*
Winfrey, Oprah *television talk show host, actress, producer*
Winter, John Dawson, III *blues guitarist, singer*
Zajicek, Jeronym *music educator*
Zlatoff-Mirsky, Everett Igor *violinist*

### Coal City
Major, Mary Jo *dance school artistic director*

### De Kalb
Bach, Jan Morris *composer, educator*

### Downers Grove
†Shen, Sin-Yan *conductor, acoustics specialist, music director*

### Elgin
Dodohara, Jean Noton *music educator*

### Evanston
Citron, Michelle *filmmaker, educator*
Eberley, Helen-Kay *opera singer, classical record company executive, poet*
Galati, Frank Joseph *stage and opera director, educator, screen writer, actor*
Giordano, August Thomas (Gus Giordano) *choreographer, dancer*
Hemke, Frederick L. *music educator, university administrator*
Karlins, M(artin) William *composer, educator*
Kujala, Walfrid Eugene *musician, educator*
Reimer, Bennett *music educator, writer*
Yoder, John Clifford *producer, consultant*

### Highland Park
Grimmer, Margot *dancer, choreographer, director*
Mehta, Zarin *music festival administrator*

### Mount Prospect
DeVol, Skip *entertainer*

### Northbrook
Magad, Samuel *orchestra concertmaster, conductor*
Slattery, James Joseph (Joe Slattery) *actor*

### Oak Park
Mason, Barbara E. Suggs *educator*

### Park Forest
Billig, Etel Jewel *theater director, actress*

### River Forest
Rimbach, Evangeline Lois *retired music educator*

### Rock Island
Thompson, Joyce Elizabeth *arts management educator*

### Rockford
Larsen, Steven *orchestra conductor*
Robinson, Donald Peter *musician, retired electrical engineer*

### Saint Charles
Zinn, Marcie Lynn *music educator, pianist*

### Skokie
Vandenbroucke, Russell James *theatre director*

### Springfield
Ellis, Michael Eugene *documentary film producer, writer, director*
Nanavati, Grace Luttrell *dancer, choreographer, instructor*

### Urbana
Boardman, Eunice *music educator*
Brün, Herbert *composer*
Elyn, Mark *opera singer, educator*
Hedlund, Ronald *baritone*
Hobgood, Burnet McLean *theater educator*
Melby, John B. *composer, educator*
Wisniewski, Thomas Joseph *music educator*

### Wilmette
Merrier, Helen *actress, writer*
Miller, Frederick Staten *music educator, academic administrator*

## INDIANA

### Bloomington
Brown, Keith *musician, educator*
Klotman, Robert Howard *music educator*
Mac Watters, Virginia Elizabeth *singer, music educator, actress*
Orrego-Salas, Juan Antonio *composer, retired music educator*
Pagels, Jürgen Heinrich *balletmaster, dance educator, dancer, choreographer, author*
Phillips, Harvey *musician, soloist, music educator, arts consultant*
Rousseau, Eugene Ellsworth *musician, music educator, consultant*
Samuelsen, Roy *bass-baritone*
Sebok, Gyorgy *pianist, educator*
Sharrow, Leonard *musician, educator*
Svetlova, Marina *ballerina, choreographer, educator*
Williams, Camilla *soprano, voice educator*
Wittlich, Gary Eugene *music theory educator*

### Crawfordsville
Fisher, A. James *theater educator, director, actor*

### Fort Wayne
Franklin, Al *artistic director*
Sack, James McDonald, Jr. *radio and television producer, marketing executive*

### Indianapolis
Aliev, Eldar *artistic director, choreographer, educator*
Alvarez, Thomas *film and video producer, director*
Bolin, Daniel Paul *music educator*
Hammack, Julia Dixon *music educator*
Johnson, David Allen *singer, songwriter, investor, minister*
Schellen, Nando *opera director*
Suzuki, Hidetaro *violinist*
Thomas, John David *musician, composer, arranger, photographer, recording engineer, producer*

### Knox
Weiss, Randall A. *television producer, supermarket executive*

### Kokomo
Highlen, Larry Wade *music educator, piano rebuilder, tuner*

### Notre Dame
Haimo, Ethan T. *music educator*

### Rolling Prairie
Eggleston, Alan Edward *musician, opera singer, Boy Scout executive*

### South Bend
Yeh, Tsung *orchestral conductor*

### West Lafayette
Wright, Alfred George James *band symphony orchestra conductor, educator*

## IOWA

### Anita
Everhart, Robert Phillip (Bobby Williams) *entertainer, songwriter, recording artist*

### Cedar Falls
Gordon, Debra Gwen *music educator*

### Davenport
DCamp, Charles Barton *musician, educator*

### Des Moines
Giunta, Joseph *conductor, music director*

### Dubuque
Hemmer, Paul Edward *musician, composer, broadcasting executive*

### Indianola
Larsen, Robert LeRoy *artistic director*

### Iowa City
Kottick, Edward Leon *music educator, harpsichord maker*
Mather, Betty Bang *musician, educator*
Mather, Roger Frederick *music educator, writer*

### Marion
McDonald, Carolyn Ann *dance educator, choreographer*

### Muscatine
Strand, Dean Paul *disc jockey, audio engineer*

## KANSAS

### Hutchinson
Wendelburg, Norma Ruth *composer*

## KENTUCKY

**Lawrence**
Duerksen, George Louis *music educator, music therapist*
Heller, George Norman *music educator*
Hilding, Jerel Lee *music and dance educator, former dancer*
Pozdro, John Walter *music educator, composer*
Tsubaki, Andrew Takahisa *theater director, educator*

**Shawnee Mission**
Julien, Gail Leslie *model, public relations professional*

**Wichita**
Chen, Zuohuang *conductor*

## KENTUCKY

**Louisville**
Luvisi, Lee *concert pianist*
Slater, Marilee Hebert *theatre administrator, producer, director, consultant*
Smillie, Thomson John *opera producer*

## LOUISIANA

**Baton Rouge**
Constantinides, Dinos Demetrios (Constantine Constantinides) *music educator, composer, conductor*
Mathews, Sharon Walker *artistic director, secondary school educator*
Norem, Richard Frederick, Sr. *musician, music educator*
Willett, Anna Hart *composer*
Yarbrough, Martha Cornelia *music educator*

**New Orleans**
Baron, John Herschel *music educator, musicologist*
Cosenza, Arthur George *opera director*
Fountain, Peter Dewey, Jr. (Pete Fountain) *clarinetist*
Gonzales, Brother Alexis (Joseph M. Gonzales) *theater and communications educator*

**Pineville**
Sennett, Henry Herbert, Jr. *theatre arts educator and consultant*

**Thibodaux**
Klaus, Kenneth Sheldon *choral conductor, vocalist, music educator*

## MAINE

**Bangor**
Libbey, Robert David *television producer*

**Blue Hill Falls**
Stookey, Noel Paul *folksinger, composer*

**Boothbay Harbor**
Lenthall, Franklyn *theatre historian*

**Brunswick**
Schwartz, Elliott Shelling *composer, author, music educator*

**Castine**
Davis, Peter Frank *filmmaker, author*

**Portland**
Goodman, Craig Stephen *musician*
Shimada, Toshiyuki *orchestra conductor, music director*

**Surry**
Sopkin, George *cellist, music educator*

**West Baldwin**
Simmonds, Rae Nichols *musician, composer, educator*

## MARYLAND

**Annapolis**
Holmberg, Lawrence Oscar, Jr. *documentary film producer, photographer, writer*
Marton, Michael *cinematographer*

**Baltimore**
Beer, Alice Stewart (Mrs. Jack Engeman) *retired musician, educator*
Harrison, Michael *opera company executive*
Hopps, Raymond, Jr. *film producer*
Southern, Hugh *performing arts consultant*
Yannuzzi, William A(nthony) *conductor*
Zinman, David Joel *conductor*

**Bethesda**
†Keefe, Gary P.J. *televison producer, director, scriptwriter*
Mastny-Fox, Catherine Louise *administrator, consultant*

**Chestertown**
Clarke, Garry Evans *composer, educator, musician, administrator*

**College Park**
Feinstein, Martin *performing arts educator*
Moss, Lawrence Kenneth *composer, educator*

**Davidsonville**
Mahaffey, Redge Allan *movie producer, director, writer, actor, scientist*

**Gaithersburg**
Whallon, Evan Arthur, Jr. *orchestra conductor*

**Hagerstown**
Tuckwell, Barry Emmanuel *musician, music educator*

**Lutherville Timonium**
Hambleton, Thomas Edward *theatrical producer*

**Olney**
Graham, William Howard *theatre producer, consultant*

**Rockville**
Cain, Karen Mirinda *musician, educator*

**Silver Spring**
Crawford-Mason, Clare Wootten *television producer, journalist*

**Towson**
Mark, Michael Laurence *music educator*

## MASSACHUSETTS

**Amherst**
Bestor, Charles Lemon *composer, educator*
Brandon, Liane *filmmaker, educator*

**Boston**
Armand, Patrick *dancer*
Bauer, Elaine Louise *ballet dancer*
Cassilly, Richard *tenor, voice educator*
Cogan, Robert David *composer, school official*
Curtin, Phyllis *music educator, former dean, operatic singer*
Dederer, William Bowne *music educator, administrator*
Di Domenica, Robert Anthony *musician, composer*
Hampton, Henry Eugene *film and television producer*
Harvey, Les *composer, producer*
Hoyt, Herbert Austin Aikins *television producer*
Jochum, Veronica *pianist*
Lesser, Laurence *musician, educator*
Lockhart, Keith Alan *conductor*
MacCombie, Bruce Franklin *composer, college administrator*
Marks, Bruce *artistic director, choreographer*
Maso, Michael Harvey *managing director*
McKinley, William Thomas *composer, performer, educator*
McPhee, Jonathan *music director, conductor, composer, arranger*
Miller, J. Philip *television producer, director, educator*
Moriarty, John *opera administrator, artistic director*
Rotenberg, Sheldon *violinist*
Row, Peter Lyman *musician, educator*
Scofield, John *jazz guitarist*
Sharp, William Leslie *performing arts educator*
Totenberg, Roman *violinist, music educator*
†Wahlberg, Mark *actor*
Wheeler, W(illiam) Scott *composer, conductor, music educator*
Young, Laura *dance educator, choreographer*

**Brookline**
Epstein, Alvin *actor, director, singer, mime*

**Cambridge**
Cleary, David Michael *composer, library assistant*
de Varon, Lorna Cooke *choral conductor*
Epstein, David Mayer *composer, conductor, educator*
Erdely, Stephen Lajos *music educator*
Harbison, John *composer*
Langstaff, John Meredith *musician*
Layton, Billy Jim *composer*
Martino, Donald James *composer, educator*
Orchard, Robert John *theater producer, educator*
Pinkham, Daniel *composer*
Rands, Bernard *composer, educator*
Russell, George Allen *composer, theoritician, author, conductor*
Sims, Ezra *composer*
Wiseman, Frederick *filmmaker*
Wunderlich, Renner *film producer, cinematographer*

**Charlestown**
Armstrong, Nancy L. *soprano, voice coach*

**Dedham**
Firth, Everett Joseph *timpanist*

**Framingham**
Bogard, Carole Christine *lyric soprano*

**Gloucester**
Zawinul, Josef *bandleader, composer, keyboardist, synthesist*

**Lenox**
Curtis, William Edgar *conductor, composer*

**Marstons Mills**
Vila, Robert Joseph *television host, designer, real estate developer*

**Medford**
Anderson, Thomas Jefferson, Jr. *composer, educator*

**Nantucket**
Rorem, Ned *composer, author*

**Natick**
Gomberg, Sydelle *dancer educator*

**Newton**
Brilliant, Barbara *television host, producer, columnist, consultant, journalist*

**Newton Center**
Schuller, Gunther Alexander *composer*

**North Dartmouth**
Dace, Tish *drama educator*

**Northampton**
Naegele, Philipp Otto *violinist, violist, music educator*

**Pittsfield**
Liveright, Betty Fouch *actress, director, writer*

**Plymouth**
Gregory, Dick *comedian, civil rights activist*

**Stockbridge**
Storch, Arthur *theater director*

**Truro**
Falk, Lee Harrison *performing arts executive, cartoonist*

**Waltham**
Boykan, Martin *composer, music educator*
Titcomb, Caldwell *music and theatre historian*
Wyner, Yehudi *composer, pianist, conductor, educator*

**Williamstown**
Shainman, Irwin *music educator, musician*

**Worcester**
Curran, Louis Jerome, Jr. *choral master*

## MICHIGAN

**Ann Arbor**
Bassett, Leslie Raymond *composer, educator*
Bolcom, William Elden *musician, composer, educator, pianist*
Boylan, Paul Charles *music educator, academic administrator*
Nugent, Theodore Anthony *musician*
Rosseels, Gustave Alois *music educator*
Scharp-Radovic, Carol Ann *choreographer, classical ballet educator, artistic director*
Sparling, Peter David *dancer, dance educator*

**Battle Creek**
Matthews, Wyhomme S. *music educator, college administrator*

**Bloomfield Hills**
Haidostian, Alice Berberian *concert pianist, civic volunteer and fundraiser*

**Cedar**
Kunkel, Dorothy Ann *music educator*

**Charlotte**
LeDoux, Chris Lee *country musician*

**Detroit**
Alpert, Daniel *television executive*
Di Chiera, David *performing arts impresario*
Jarvi, Neeme *conductor*
†Lamka, Philip Charles *broadcasting company executive*
Young, Gordon Ellsworth *composer, organist*

**East Lansing**
Johnson, Theodore Oliver, Jr. *musician, educator*
Kirk, Edgar Lee *musician, educator*

**Grand Rapids**
Arthur Estner, Charthel *artistic director*
Comet, Catherine *conductor*
Hardy, Michael C. *performing arts administrator*
Smith, Peter Wilson *symphony orchestra administrator*

**Kalamazoo**
Zupko, Ramon *composer, music professor*

**Lansing**
Kluge, Len H. *director, actor, theater educator*

**Livonia**
Swift, Jonathan *television personality, education educator, tenor*

**Redford**
Goslin, Gerald Hugh *concert pianist, teacher*

**Rochester**
Bajor, James Henry *musician, jazz pianist*

**Rochester Hills**
Daniels, David Wilder *conductor, music educator*

**Saginaw**
Najar, Leo Michael *conductor, arranger, educator*

**Westland**
Harris, Frances Alvord (Mrs. Hugh W. Harris) *retired radio and television broadcaster, consultant*

## MINNESOTA

**Bloomington**
Smith, Henry Charles, III *symphony orchestra conductor*

**Duluth**
Coffman, Phillip Hudson *music educator, arts administrator*

**Litchfield**
Snelling, Norma June *retired music educator, English educator*

**Mankato**
Hustoles, Paul John *theater educator*

**Minneapolis**
Argento, Dominick *composer*
Bouassida, Hafed *director, producer*
Fetler, Paul *composer*
Fleezanis, Jorja Kay *violinist, educator*
Larsen, Elizabeth B. (Libby Larsen) *composer*
Miller, John William, Jr. *bassoonist*
Porter, Jennifer Madeleine *producer, director*
Skrowaczewski, Stanislaw *conductor, composer*
Ware, D. Clifton *singer, educator*

**Moorhead**
Revzen, Joel *conductor*
Rothlisberger, Rodney John *music educator*

**Plymouth**
Checker, Chubby (Ernest Evans) *musician*

**Saint Paul**
Anderson, Clyde Bailey *musician, educator*
Best, Eugene Crawford, Jr. *musician*
Elliott, Jack *folk musician*
Paulus, Stephen Harrison *composer*
Tecco, Romuald Gilbert Louis Joseph *violinist, concertmaster*

**Sunfish Lake**
Corn, Joseph Edward, Jr. *arts management consultant*

**White Bear Lake**
Gutchë, Gene *composer*

## MISSISSIPPI

**Hattiesburg**
Wood, Vivian Poates *mezzo soprano, voice educator*

**Jackson**
Pearce, Colman Cormac *conductor, pianist, composer*

**Purvis**
Young, Raymond Guinn *music educator*

## MISSOURI

**Arrow Rock**
Bollinger, Michael *artistic director*

**Branson**
Tillis, Mel(vin) *musician, songwriter*
Williams, Andy *entertainer*

**Columbia**
Archer, Stephen Murphy *theater educator*

**Kansas City**
Bolender, Todd *choreographer*
Costin, James D. *performing arts company executive*
Londré, Felicia Mae Hardison *theater educator*
Patterson, Russell *conductor, opera executive*
Whitener, William Garnett *dancer, choreographer*
Williams, Wade Hampton, III *motion picture producer, director, distributor*

**Liberty**
Harriman, Richard Lee *performing arts administrator, educator*

**Maryland Heights**
Dokoudovsky, Nina Ludmila *dance educator*

**Saint Louis**
Briccetti, Joan Therese *theater manager, arts management consultant*
DuMaine, Daniel Jerome *musician, composer, musical director*
Ehrlich, Ava *television executive producer*
Graham, Colin *stage director*
Haley, Johnetta Randolph *musician, educator, university administrator*
Stewart, John Harger *music educator*
Vonk, Hans *conductor*
Waddington, Bette Hope (Elizabeth Crowder) *violinist, educator*

**Springfield**
Moulder, T. Earline *musician*
Spicer, Holt Vandercook *speech and theater educator*

**Warrensburg**
Smith, Dolores Maxine Plunk *retired dancer, educator*

## MONTANA

**Billings**
Barnea, Uri N. *music director, conductor, composer, violinist*
Pihlaja, Maxine Muriel Mead *orchestra executive*

**Missoula**
Knowles, William Leroy (Bill Knowles) *television news producer, journalism educator*
Listerud, (Lowell) Brian *choir director, music educator*

## NEBRASKA

**Beatrice**
Alesio, Vena Beth *music educator*

**Lincoln**
Dixon, Wheeler Winston *film and video studies educator, writer*
Miller, Tice Lewis *theatre educator*

**Omaha**
Johnson, James David *concert pianist, organist, educator*
Schmidman, Jo Ann *artistic director*

## NEVADA

**Carson City**
Zetter, Lois C. *personal manager*

**Henderson**
Knight, Gladys (Maria) *singer*

Riske, William Kenneth *producer, cultural services consultant*

**Las Vegas**
Baker, Anita *singer*
Castro, Joseph Armand *music director, pianist, composer, orchestrator*
Goulet, Robert Gerard *singer, actor*
Healy, Mary (Mrs. Peter Lind Hayes) *singer, actress*
Lewis, Jerry (Joseph Levitch) *comedian*
Shields, Brooke Christa Camille *actress, model*
Wiemer, Robert Ernest *film and television producer, writer, director*

## NEW HAMPSHIRE

**Hanover**
Dodge, Charles Malcolm *composer, music educator*
Ehrlich, David Gordon *film director, educator*
Sabinson, Mara Beth *theatre educator, director, actress*

**Lyme**
Darion, Joe *librettist, lyricist*

**Plymouth**
Swift, Robert Frederic *music educator*

**Walpole**
Burns, Kenneth Lauren *filmmaker, historian*

## NEW JERSEY

**Allendale**
Hampton, Lionel Leo *composer, conductor, entertainer*

**Atlantic City**
McKee, Mary Elizabeth *producer*

**Belle Mead**
Carroll, David Joseph *actor*

**Brigantine**
Carlson, Marsha George *performing company executive*

**Cliffside Park**
Perhacs, Marylouise Helen *musician, educator*

**Denville**
Fisher, Sharon Mary *musician*

**East Brunswick**
Mooney, William Piatt *actor*
Yttrehus, Rolv Berger *composer, educator*

**Englewood**
Zwilich, Ellen Taaffe *composer*

**Florham Park**
Atkins, Richard Bart *film, television producer*

**Fort Lee**
Houston, Whitney *vocalist, recording artist*

**Freehold**
Topham, Sally Jane *ballet educator*

**Glen Ridge**
Bracken, Eddie (Edward Vincent) *actor, director, writer, singer, artist*

**Leonia**
Deutsch, Nina *pianist*

**Little Silver**
Sizer, Rebecca Rudd *performing arts educator, arts coordinator*

**Livingston**
Bertenshaw, Bobbi Cherrelle *producer*

**Madison**
Monte, Bonnie J. *performing company executive, director, educator*

**Maplewood**
Weston, Randy (Randolph Edward Weston) *pianist, composer*

**Montclair**
Sierra, Roberto *composer, music educator*
Walker, George Theophilus, Jr. *composer, pianist, music educator*

**Mount Laurel**
Torres, Robert Alvin *dancer, singer, actor, sign language interpreter*

**New Brunswick**
Hurst, Gregory Squire *artistic director, director, producer*
Lettvin, Theodore *concert pianist*
Webre, Septime *ballet company artistic director, choreographer*

**Newark**
Jones, Etta *singer*
Morgenstern, Dan Michael *jazz historian, educator, editor*
Silipigni, Alfredo *opera conductor*
Storrer, William Allin *consultant*

**Princeton**
Estey, Audree Phipps *artistic director*
Levy, Kenneth *music educator*
Orphanides, Nora Charlotte *ballet educator*
Spies, Claudio *composer, educator*
Westergaard, Peter Talbot *composer, music educator*

**Red Bank**
Hughes, Barnard *actor*

**Ridgewood**
Fokine, Irine *ballet educator*

**River Vale**
Moderacki, Edmund Anthony *music educator, conductor*

**Rockaway**
Laine, Cleo (Clementina Dinah Dankworth) *singer*

**Shamong**
Knight, Margaret Elizabeth *music educator*

**Somerville**
Dixon, Joanne Elaine *music educator*

**Teaneck**
Bullough, John Frank *organist, music educator*
Koszarski, Richard *film historian, writer*
†Reid, Rufus Lamar *jazz bassist, educator*

**Warren**
Maull, George Marriner *music director, conductor*

**Wayne**
Law, Janet Mary *music educator*

**Woodcliff Lake**
Morath, Max Edward *entertainer, composer, writer*

## NEW MEXICO

**Albuquerque**
Evans, Bill (James William Evans) *dancer, choreographer, educator, arts administrator*

**Edgewood**
Hamilton, Jerald *musician*

**Portales**
Paschke, Donald Vernon *music educator*

**Santa Fe**
Ballard, Louis Wayne *composer*
Baustian, Robert Frederick *conductor*
Brockway, Merrill LaMonte *television producer and director*
Crosby, John O'Hea *conductor, opera manager*
Gaddes, Richard *performing arts administrator*
Reggio, Godfrey *film director*
Rubenstein, Bernard *orchestra conductor*

**Taos**
Murphey, Michael Martin *country western singer, songwriter*

## NEW YORK

**Albany**
Kristofferson, Kris *singer, songwriter, actor*

**Amherst**
Beahan, Susan Nancy *video producer*
Coover, James Burrell *music educator*

**Astoria**
Morrow, Scott Douglas *choreographer, educator*

**Auburn**
Sayles, Edward Thomas *theatrical producer*

**Bayside**
Zinn, William *violinist, composer, business executive*

**Beacon**
Flagello, Ezio Domenico *basso*

**Bronx**
Mittler, Diana (Diana Mittler-Battipaglia) *music educator and administrator, pianist*
Sherman, Judith Dorothy *producer, recording company owner, recording engineer*
Sprecher, Baron William Gunther *pianist, composer, conductor, diplomat*

**Bronxville**
Biscardi, Chester *composer, educator*
Farber, Viola Anna *dancer, choreographer, educator*

**Brooklyn**
Borel, Ludmila Ivanovna *ballerina, educator*
Gordon, Edward Harrison *choral conductor, educator*
Hopkins, Karen Brooks *performing arts executive*
Jarman, Joseph *jazz musician*
Jenkins, Leroy *violinist, composer*
Kazan, Basil Gibran *religious music composer*
Koppel, Audrey Feiler *electrologist, educator*
Lichtenstein, Harvey *performing arts executive*
Poster, June *performing company executive*
Salzman, Eric *composer, writer*

**Buffalo**
Manes, Stephen Gabriel *concert pianist, educator*
Valdes, Maximiano *conductor*

**Clifton Park**
Orsini, Paul Vincent *music educator*

**Cornwall**
Gentile, Melanie Marie *record producer, marketing and public relations consultant, writer*

**Crugers**
Norman, Jessye *soprano*

**Deer Park**
Gorme, Eydie *singer*
Lawrence, Steve *entertainer*

**Dobbs Ferry**
Kapp, Richard P. *conductor, arts administrator*

**East Hampton**
Dello Joio, Norman *composer*

**East Syracuse**
Duffy, Nancy Keogh *television broadcast professional*

**Elmira**
Wavle, Elizabeth Margaret *music educator, college official*

**Flushing**
Grossman, Julius *conductor*
Smaldone, Edward Michael *composer*

**Forest Hills**
Janson, Patrick *singer, actor, conductor, educator*
Polakoff, Abe *baritone*
Prager, Alice Heinecke *music company executive*
Silver, Sheila Jane *composer, music educator*

**Fredonia**
Jordan, Robert *concert pianist, educator*

**Geneva**
Berta, Joseph Michel *music educator, musician*

**Germantown**
Rollins, (Theodore) Sonny *composer, musician*

**Gilbertsville**
Roos, Casper *actor*

**Glen Head**
Sutherland, Denise Jackson (Denise Suzanne Jackson) *ballerina*

**Great Neck**
Brand, Oscar *folksinger, author, educator*
Kraft, Leo Abraham *composer*
Weisgall, Hugo David *composer, conductor*

**Greenfield Center**
Conant, Robert Scott *harpsichordist, music educator*

**Hastings On Hudson**
Wolfe, Stanley *composer, educator*

**Hempstead**
Chapman, Ronald Thomas *musician, educator*
Graffeo, Mary Thérèse *music educator, performer*

**Hewlett**
Wolff, Eleanor Blunk *actress*

**Hopewell Junction**
Walden, Stanley Eugene *composer, clarinetist*

**Hurley**
Bedford, Brian *actor*

**Irvington**
Angelakis, Manos G(eorge) *filmmaker, communications executive*

**Ithaca**
Hsu, John Tseng Hsin *music educator, cellist, gambist, barytonist, conductor*
Husa, Karel Jaroslav *composer, conductor, educator*

**Jamaica**
Desser, Maxwell Milton *artist, art director, filmstrip producer*

**Jamaica Estates**
Rose, Jodi *opera company founder and artistic director*

**Larchmont**
Swire, Edith Wypler *music educator, musician, violist, violinist*

**Long Eddy**
Hoiby, Lee *composer, concert pianist*

**Margaretville**
Brockway-Henson, Amie *producing artistic director*
Matalon, Vivian *theatrical director*

**Massapequa Park**
Zizzo, Alicia *concert pianist*

**Massena**
Schroll, Edwin John *theater educator, stage director*

**Millerton**
Hastings, Donald Francis *actor, writer*

**New Rochelle**
Cleary, James Charles, Jr. *audio-visual producer*
Klein, Arthur Luce *theatrical company executive*
Merrill, Robert *baritone*

**New York**
Abrams, Muhal Richard *pianist, composer*
Adams, Joey *comedian, author*
Adler, Richard *composer, lyricist*
Alcantara, Theo *conductor*
Alexopoulos, Helene *ballet dancer*
Allen, Betty (Mrs. Ritten Edward Lee, III) *mezzo-soprano*
Allen, Nancy *musician, educator*
Allen, Woody (Allen Stewart Konigsberg) *actor, filmmaker, author*
Alvary, Lorenzo *bass*
Amara, Lucine *opera and concert singer*
Amos, Tori *singer, musician*
Anderson, Cherine Esperanza *television and film production manager, special events planner*
Araiza, Francisco (José Francisco Araiza Andrade) *opera singer*
Arkin, Alan Wolf *actor*
Asakawa, Takako *dancer, dance teacher, director*
Ashley, Elizabeth *actress*
Ashley, Merrill *ballerina*
Aucoin, Kevyn J. *make-up artist*
Ax, Emanuel *pianist*
†Azzoli, Val *music company executive*
Babyface, (Kenny Edmonds) *popular musician*
Bacall, Lauren *actress*
Baker-Riker, Margery *television executive*
Baldwin, Stephen *actor*
Banks, Helen Augusta *singer, actress*
Barbee, Victor *ballet dancer*
Barber, Russell Brooks Butler *television producer*
Barker, Charles *conductor*
Barker, Edwin Bogue *musician*
Barsalona, Frank Samuel *theatrical agent*
Baryshnikov, Mikhail *ballet dancer*
Basden, Cameron *ballet mistress, dancer*
Becofsky, Arthur Luke *arts administrator, writer*
Beeson, Jack Hamilton *composer, educator, writer*
Behrens, Hildegard *soprano*
Belkin, Boris David *violinist*
Bennett, Tony (Anthony Dominick Benedetto) *entertainer*
Benton, Nicholas *theater producer*
Berger, Miriam Roskin *creative arts therapy director, educator, therapist*
Bergeret, Albert Hamilton *artistic director, conductor, singer*
Bergonzi, Carlo *tenor, voice educator*
Berlind, Roger Stuart *stage and film producer*
Berman, Lazar *pianist*
Bernardi, Mario *conductor*
Bernstein, Elliot Louis *television executive*
Berry, Walter *baritone*
Betts, Dicky (Richard Forrest Betts) *guitarist, songwriter, vocalist*
Bikel, Theodore *actor, singer*
Birkenhead, Thomas Bruce *theatrical producer and manager, educator*
Bishop, André *artistic director, producer*
Black, Shawn Morgado *dancer*
Boal, Peter Cadbury *dancer*
Boelzner, Gordon *orchestral conductor*
Boggs, Gil *principal ballet dancer*
Bohrman, David Ellis *television news producer*
Bolton, Michael *singer, songwriter*
Bonazzi, Elaine Claire *mezzo-soprano*
Bon Jovi, Jon *rock singer, composer*
Borge, Victor *entertainer, comedian, pianist*
Bosco, Philip Michael *actor*
Bowden, Sally Ann *choreographer, teacher, dancer*
Bradford, Robert Ernest *motion picture producer*
Braun, Craig Allen *producer*
Braxton, Toni *popular musician*
Brechner, Stanley *artistic director*
Brecker, Michael *saxophonist*
Bregman, Martin *film producer*
Brendel, Alfred *concert pianist*
Brewster, Robert Gene *concert singer, educator*
Brightman, Sarah *singer, actress*
Brinkley, Christie *model*
Brooks, Tyrone *dancer*
Brothers, Joyce Diane *television personality, psychologist*
Brown, David *motion picture producer, writer*
Brown, Trisha *dancer*
Browning, John *pianist*
Bumbry, Grace *soprano*
Button, Richard Totten *television and stage producer, former figure skating champion*
Byer, Diana *performing arts company executive*
Calabrese, Rosalie Sue *arts management consultant, writer*
†Cannon, John *actor, performing arts association executive*
Cantrell, Lana *actress, singer, lawyer*
Capalbo, Carmen Charles *director, producer*
Caples, Richard James *dance company executive, lawyer*
Carelli, Gabor Paul *opera singer*
Carey, Mariah *vocalist, songwriter*
Carlson, Marvin Albert *theater educator*
Carney, Michael *orchestra leader*
Carpenter, Patricia *music educator*
Carter, Bennett Lester (Benny Carter) *musician, composer, conductor*
Carter, Betty (Lillie Mae Jones) *jazz singer, songwriter*
†Carter, James *musician, jazz*
Cash, Rosanne *country singer, songwriter*
Castel, Nico *tenor, educator*
Cazeaux, Isabelle Anne Marie *retired musicology educator*
Chapman, Wes *dancer*
Charnin, Martin *theatrical director, lyricist, producer*
Chaya, Masazumi *dancer*
Christensen, Dieter *ethnomusicologist*
Clapton, Eric *musician*
Cobham, William Emanuel, Jr. *musician*
Cohen, Selma Jeanne *dance historian*
Cohn, Sam *motion picture and theatrical agent*
Coigney, Martha Wadsworth *theater executive*
Colbath, Brian (Brian Colbath Watson) *actor, script and live performance writer*
Cole, Vinson *tenor*
Coleman, Cy *pianist, composer, producer*
Coleman, George Edward *tenor, alto and soprano saxophonist*
Coleman, Ornette *jazz musician*
Collins, Judy Marjorie *singer, songwriter*
Comfort, Jane *choreographer, director*
Conlon, James Joseph *conductor*
Connick, Harry, Jr. *jazz musician, actor, singer*
Conway, Kevin *actor, director*
Coolio *popular musician*
Cooper, Alice (Vincent Furnier) *popular musician*
Corigliano, John Paul *composer*
Corsaro, Frank Andrew *theater, musical and opera director*
Cory, Jeffrey *television, film, stage, event and creative director*
Cruz, Celia *vocalist*
Cunningham, Merce *dancer*
Curtin, Jane Therese *actress, writer*
Curtis, Paul James *mime*
Dakin, Christine Whitney *dancer, educator*
Dale, Jim *actor*
Dalrymple, Jean Van Kirk *theatrical producer, publicist, author*
Daltrey, Roger *musician*
Daly, Tyne *actress*
d'Amboise, Jacques Joseph *dancer, choreographer*
Danitz, Marilynn Patricia *choreographer, videographer*
Darling, Robert Edward *designer, stage director*
Darvarova, Elmira *violinist, concertmaster*
David, Hal *lyricist*
Davidovich, Bella *pianist*
Davidson, Joy Elaine *mezzo-soprano*
Davies, Dennis Russell *conductor, music director, pianist*
Davis, Anthony *composer, pianist, educator*
Davis, Leonard *violist*

De Johnette, Jack *musician*
de la Falaise, Lucie *model*
DeLay, Dorothy (Mrs. Edward Newhouse) *violinist, educator*
Denver, John (Henry John Deutschendorf, Jr.) *singer, songwriter*
Diaz, Justino *bass-baritone*
Dichter, Misha *concert pianist*
Dicterow, Glenn Eugene *violinist*
Di Franco, Loretta Elizabeth *lyric coloratura soprano*
Diggins, Peter Sheehan *arts administrator*
Dillon, Matt *actor*
Dispeker, Thea *artists' representative*
Dissette, Alyce Marie *television and multimedia producer, non-profit foundation executive*
Dlugoszewski, Lucia *artistic director*
Dodson, Daryl Theodore *ballet administrator, arts consultant*
Domingo, Placido *tenor*
Donahue, Phil *television personality*
Downes, Edward Olin Davenport *musicologist, critic, radio broadcaster*
Downs, Hugh Malcolm *radio and television broadcaster*
Druck, Mark *director, producer, writer*
Duchin, Peter Oelrichs *musician*
Duddy, Joan Frances *performing arts administrator, dancer*
Dufour, Val (Albert Valery Dufour) *actor*
Dukakis, Olympia *actress*
Dulaine, Pierre *ballroom dancer*
Duncan, Sandy *actress*
Dunham, Christine *dancer*
Dunleavy, Rosemary *ballet dancer*
Dunn, Mignon *mezzo-soprano*
Dunn, Susan *singer*
Duquesnay, Ann *actress, singer*
Dylan, Bob (Robert Allen Zimmerman) *singer, composer*
Eger, Joseph *conductor, music director*
Elias, Rosalind *mezzo-soprano*
Englander, Roger Leslie *television producer, director*
Entremont, Philippe *conductor, pianist*
Epstein, Matthew *performing company director*
Eschenbach, Christoph *conductor, pianist*
Estefan, Gloria Maria *singer, songwriter*
Etheridge, Melissa Lou *singer, songwriter*
Evangelista, Linda *model*
Evans, Jerry Norman *television director*
Everly, Jack *conductor*
Ewing, Maria Louise *soprano*
Fairbanks, Douglas Elton, Jr. *actor, producer, writer, corporation director*
Falletta, Jo Ann *musician*
Farberman, Harold *conductor, composer*
Farley, Carole *soprano*
Feist, Gene *theater director*
Feld, Eliot *dancer, choreographer*
Ferber, Laurence Robert *television producer*
Ferri, Alessandra Maria *ballet dancer*
Feuer, Cy *motion picture and theatrical producer, director*
Fiorato, Hugo *conductor*
Fisher, Jules Edward *producer, lighting designer, theatre consultant*
Flack, Roberta *singer*
Fleming, Renée L. *opera singer*
Fontana, Thomas Michael *producer, scriptwriter*
Ford, Eileen Otte (Mrs. Gerard W. Ford) *modeling agency executive*
Foreman, Laura *dancer, choreographer, conceptual artist, writer, educator*
Foreman, Richard *theater director, playwright*
Forst, Judith Doris *mezzo-soprano*
Frankel, Gene *theater director, author, producer, educator*
Frassetto, Floriana Domina *performer, choreographer, costume designer*
Freizer, Louis A. *radio news producer*
Frisell-Schröder, Sonja Bettie *opera producer, stage director*
Fryer, Robert Sherwood *theatrical producer*
Fugate, Judith *ballet dancer*
Galway, James *flutist*
Gamson, Annabelle *dancer*
Garcia, Josefina Margarita *dancer, nurse, educator*
Gayle, Crystal *singer*
Gazzara, Ben *actor*
Gersten, Bernard *theatrical producer*
Ghiaurov, Nicolai *opera singer*
Gifford, Kathie Lee *television personality, singer*
Glass, Philip *composer, musician*
Glazer, Esther *violinist*
Glover, Savion *actor, dancer*
Goldberg, Gary David *producer, writer*
Goldsmith, Merwin *actor, theater director*
†Gong, Li *actress*
Goodacre, Jill *model*
Goode, Richard Stephen *pianist, educator*
Goodman, Roger Mark *television director*
Gordon, David Jamieson *tenor*
Gottlieb, Morton Edgar *theatrical and film producer*
Graff, Randy *actress*
Graffeo, John Jude *musician, actor*
Graffin, Guillaume *ballet dancer*
Grant, Merrill Theodore *producer*
Gray, Diane *dancer, choreographer*
Greco, Jose *choreographer*
Green, Al *soul and gospel singer*
Grillo, Joann Danielle *mezzo-soprano*
Grizzard, George *actor*
Grove, Barry *theater executive*
Guettel, Henry Arthur *retired arts executive*
Hackett, Buddy *actor*
Hadley, Jerry *opera singer*
Hagen, Uta Thyra *actress*
Hall, Daryl *musician*
Hancock, Gerre Edward *musician*
Hardy, Gordon Alfred *music educator, music school president*
Harkarvy, Benjamin *artistic director*
Harnick, Sheldon Mayer *lyricist*
Harrell, Lynn Morris *cellist*
Harris, Rosemary Ann *actress*
Harrow, Nancy (Mrs. Jan Krukowski) *jazz singer, songwriter, editor*
Harry, Deborah Ann *singer*
Harth, Sidney *musician, educator*
Hartley, Hal *film director*
Hasso, Signe Eleonora Cecilia *actress*
Hastings, Baird *conductor, music educator, writer*
Hastings, Deborah *bass guitarist*
Haubert, Alaine *ballet dancer, educator*
Hayes, Isaac *rhythm and blues singer, composer*
Hearn, George *actor*
Hebert, Bliss Edmund *opera director*
Henderson, Joe *jazz tenor saxophonist*
Henderson, Skitch (Lyle Russell Cedric) *pianist, conductor*
Herman, Jerry *composer, lyricist*
Herrera, Paloma *dancer*
Herstand, Theodore *theatre artist, educator*
Hetfield, James *singer*
Hewitt, Don S. *television news producer*
Heyward, Andrew John *television producer*
Hill, George Roy *film director*
Hill, Robert Arthur *ballet dancer*
Hirsch, Judd *actor*
Holbrook, Anna *actress*
Holder, Geoffrey Lamont *dancer, actor, choreographer, director*
Hollander, Lorin *pianist*
Holliday, Polly Dean *actress*
Holloway, David *baritone*
Horn, Shirley *vocalist, pianist*
Horne, Marilyn *mezzo-soprano*
Houghton, Charles Norris *stage director, author, educator*
Howard, David *ballet school administrator*
Hubbe, Nikolaj *dancer*
Huffstodt, Karen *opera singer, recitalist*
Humperdinck, Engelbert (Arnold George Dorsey) *singer*
Hupp, Robert Martin *artistic director, educator*
†Ienner, Don *music company executive*
†Imus, Don *radio host*
Istomin, Marta Casals *performing arts administrator, former educator*
Ivory, James Francis *film director*
Jackson, Anne (Anne Jackson Wallach) *actress*
Jackson, Joe *musician, singer, composer, songwriter*
Jacobs, Jim *playwright, composer, lyricist, actor*
Jaffe, Susan *ballerina*
Jagger, Mick (Michael Philip Jagger) *singer, musician*
Jamison, Judith *dancer*
Jarmusch, Jim *director*
Jefferson, Denise *dance school director*
Johanos, Donald *orchestra conductor*
Johnson, James M. *orchestra executive*
Johnson, Virginia Alma Fairfax *ballerina*
Jones, Bill T. *dancer, choreographer*
Jones, Cherry *actress*
Jones, George *country music singer, songwriter*
Jones, Gwyneth *soprano*
Jones, Rickie Lee *singer, songwriter*
Jung, Doris *dramatic soprano*
Kalmanoff, Martin *composer*
Kamlot, Robert *performing arts executive*
Kander, John Harold *composer*
Kaplan, Richard James *producer, director, writer, educator, consultant*
Karchin, Louis Samuel *composer*
Kassel, Virginia Weltmer *television producer, writer*
Keating, Charles *actor*
Keeshan, Bob *television producer, actor*
Kellogg, Cal Stewart, II *conductor, composer*
Kelm, Linda *opera singer*
Kent, Julie *ballet dancer, actress, model*
Kent, Linda Gail *dancer*
Kernis, Aaron Jay *composer*
Khan, Chaka (Yvette Marie Stevens) *singer*
Khanzadian, Vahan *tenor*
Kidd, Michael (Milton Greenwald) *choreographer, director*
Kinberg, Judy *television producer, director*
King, B. B. (Riley B. King) *singer, guitarist*
King, Carole *songwriter, singer*
King, Woodie, Jr. *producer, actor, director*
Kistler, Darci Anna *ballet dancer*
Klein, Joseph Michelman *musical director*
Klein, Robert *comedian, actor*
Kness, Richard Maynard *tenor*
Kolpakova, Irina *dancer, educator, coach*
Kono, Toshihiko *cellist*
Krauss, Alison *country musician*
Krosnick, Joel *cellist*
Krupska, Danya (Mrs. Ted Thurston) *theater director, choreographer*
Krzyzanowski, Eve *video production company executive*
Kulin, Keith David *cinematographer*
Kusmin, Ellyn Sue *music administrator*
La Fosse, Robert *ballet dancer, choreographer*
†Lake, Ricki *talk show host, actress*
lang, k. d. (Katherine Dawn Lang) *country music singer, composer*
Lang, Pearl *dancer, choreographer*
Langham, Michael *theatrical director*
Langsam, Ida S. *press agent, consultant*
Lansbury, Edgar George *theatrical producer*
Larmore, Jennifer *mezzo-soprano*
Laufer, Beatrice *composer*
Lauper, Cyndi *musician*
Leach, Robin *producer, writer, television host*
Leavitt, Michael P(aul) *arts manager, concert producer, records marketer*
Leber, Steven Edward *film producer, corporate executive*
LeCompte, Elizabeth *theater director*
†Lee, Ang *filmmaker*
Lee, Dai-Keong *composer*
Legrand, Michel Jean *composer*
Leiber, Jerry *songwriter*
Leland, Sara *ballet dancer*
Lemesh, Nicholas Thomas *designer, filmmaker*
†Lemon, Ralph *choreographer*
Leppard, Raymond John *conductor, harpsichordist*
Leritz, Lawrence R. *choreographer, dancer, actor*
Letterman, David *television personality, comedian, writer*
Levine, James *conductor, pianist, artistic director*
Lewis, Jerry Lee *country-rock singer, musician*
Libin, Paul *theatre executive, producer*
Liebermann, Lowell *composer, pianist, conductor*
Limbaugh, Rush Hudson *radio and talk show host*
Livengood, Victoria Ann *opera singer*
Livingston, Jay Harold *composer, lyricist*
LL Cool J, (James Todd Smith) *rap singer, actor*
Loney, Glenn Meredith *drama educator*
Lopez, Lourdes *ballerina*
Lortel, Lucille *theatrical producer*
Loudon, Dorothy *actress*
Louis, Murray *dancer, choreographer, dance teacher*
Loveless, Patty (Patty Ramey) *country music singer*
Lubovitch, Lar *dancer, choreographer*
Lucas, James E(vans) *operatic director*
Luders, Adam *ballet dancer*
Ludgin, Chester Hall *baritone, actor*
Lunden, Joan *television personality*
LuPone, Patti *actress*
Ma, Yo-Yo *cellist*
Macero, Teo *composer, conductor*
Macpherson, Elle *model*
Macurdy, John Edward *basso*
Malkin, Barry *film editor, consultant*
Maltby, Richard Eldridge, Jr. *theater director, lyricist*
Mamlok, Ursula *composer, educator*
Manilow, Barry *singer, composer, arranger*
Mann, Theodore *theatrical producer and artistic director*
Maraynes, Allan Lawrence *filmmaker, television producer*
Marceau, Yvonne *ballroom dancer*
Mardin, Arif *musician*
Marsh, Jean Lyndsey Torren *actress, writer*
Marshall, Susan *choreographer*
Martin, Elliot Edwards *theatrical producer*
Martini, Richard K. *theatrical producer*
Martins, Nilas *dancer*
Martins, Peter *ballet master, choreographer, dancer*
Mason, Jackie *comedian, actor*
Masur, Kurt *conductor*
Maxwell, Carla Lena *dancer, choreographer, educator*
May, Elaine *actress, theatre and film director*
Maynard, Parrish *ballet dancer*
Mazzo, Kay *ballet dancer, educator*
Mazzola, John William *former performing arts center executive, consultant*
McDormand, Frances *actress*
McFerrin, Bobby *singer, musician, composer and conductor*
McKay, Craig *film editor*
McKenzie, Kevin Patrick *artistic director*
McKerrow, Amanda *ballet dancer*
Mc Lean, Don *singer, instrumentalist, composer*
Meadow, Lynne (Carolyn Meadow) *theatrical producer and director*
Mellencamp, John (John Cougar) *singer, songwriter*
Menken, Alan *composer*
Menotti, Gian Carlo *composer*
Menuhin, Yehudi *violinist*
Merchant, Ismail Noormohamed *film producer and director*
Michaels, Lorne *television writer, producer*
Midler, Bette *singer, entertainer, actress*
Midori, (Midori Goto) *classical violinist*
Milnes, Sherrill E. *baritone*
Mintz, Shlomo *conductor, violist, violinist*
Mitchell, Arthur *dancer, choreographer, educator*
Monk, Debra *actress*
Monk, Meredith Jane *artistic director, composer, choreographer, film maker, director*
Moore, Kathleen *dancer*
Moore, Michael Watson *musician, string bass, educator*
Morris, James Peppler *bass*
Morris, John *composer, conductor, arranger*
Morris, Mark William *choreographer*
Moseley, Carlos DuPre *former music executive, musician*
Moss, Kate *model*
Muller, Jennifer *choreographer, dancer*
Munzer, Cynthia Brown *mezzo-soprano*
Murphy, Donna Jeanne *actress*
Murphy, Rosemary *actress*
Murphy, Russell Stephen *theater company executive*
Nagano, Kent George *conductor*
Nash, Graham William *singer, composer*
†Ndour, Youssou *musician*
Neal, Philip *dancer*
Nederlander, James Morton *theater executive*
Nichols, Kyra *ballerina*
Nicola, James B. *stage director, composer, playwright, lyricist*
Niesen, James Louis *theater director*
Nugent, Nelle *theater, film and television producer*
Nussbaum, Jeffrey Joseph *musician*
O'Brien, Conan *writer, performer, talk show host*
O'Connor, Sinead *singer, songwriter*
Ohira, Kazuto *theatre company executive, writer*
O'Horgan, Thomas Foster *composer, director*
O'Neal, Hank *entertainment producer, business owner*
Orr, Terrence S. *dancer*
Osbourne, Ozzy (John Osbourne) *vocalist*
Ostrum, Dean Gardner *actor, writer, calligrapher*
Owen, Michael *ballet dancer*
Oz, Frank (Frank Richard Oznowicz) *puppeteer, film director*
Ozawa, Seiji *conductor, music director*
Pakula, Alan J. *producer, director*
Papadakos, Dorothy Jean *composer, organist*
Pardee, Margaret Ross *violinist, violist, educator*
Parker, Alice *composer, conductor*
Parker, Maceo *jazz musician, alto saxophone*
Parkinson, Georgina *ballet mistress*
Parks, Gordon Roger Alexander Buchanan *film director, author, photographer, composer*
Parseghian, Gene *talent agent*
Parsons, David *artistic director, choreographer*
Parsons, Estelle *actress*
Parton, Dolly Rebecca *singer, composer, actress*
Paul, Les *entertainer, inventor*
Pavarotti, Luciano *lyric tenor*
Pellegrini, Anna Maria *soprano*
Penn, Arthur Hiller *film and theatre producer*
Perahia, Murray *pianist*
Peress, Maurice *symphony conductor, musicologist*
Perkins, Leeman Lloyd *music educator, musicologist*
Perlman, Itzhak *violinist*
Perlmutter, Alvin Howard *television and film producer*
Perry, Douglas *opera singer*
Peters, Roberta *soprano*
Philbin, Regis *television personality*
Poor, Peter Varnum *producer, director*
Popchristov, Damyan Christov *theater director and educator*
Porizkova, Paulina *model, actress*
Porter, Karl Hampton *orchestra musical director, conductor*
Porter, Stephen Winthrop *stage director*
Posin, Kathryn Olive *choreographer*
Previn, Andre *composer, conductor*
Price, Leontyne *concert and opera singer, soprano*
Prince, (Prince Rogers Nelson) *musician, actor*
Prince, Harold *theatrical producer*
Protas, Ron *dance company executive*
Queler, Eve *conductor*
Questel, Mae *actress*
Quilico, Louis *baritone*
Quintero, Jose *theatrical director*
Rachleff, Owen Spencer (Owen Spencer Rackleff) *actor, author*
Ramey, Samuel Edward *bass soloist*
Ramirez, Tina *artistic director*
Ramsay, Gustavus Remak *actor*
Ramsier, Paul *composer, psychotherapist*
Rand, Calvin Gordon *arts and education producer and consultant*
Randall, Tony (Leonard Rosenberg) *actor*
Randazzo, Anthony *dancer*
Randolph, David *conductor*
Raphael, Sally Jessy *talk-show host*
†Reed, Lou *musician*
Reich, Steve *composer*
Reid, Antonio (L. A. Reid) *musician, songwriter*
†Reinking, Ann H. *actress, dancer*
Renick, Kyle *artistic director*
†Reznor, Trent *musician*
Rhodes, Samuel *violist, educator*
Richard, Ellen *theater executive*
Richards, Keith *musician*
Richards, Lloyd George *theatrical director, university administrator*
Rivera, Chita (Conchita del Rivero) *actress, singer, dancer*
Rivera, Geraldo *television personality, journalist*
Rizzo, Francis *arts administrator, writer, stage director*
Roach, Maxwell Lemuel *musician*
Robards, Jason Nelson, Jr. *actor*
Robbins, Jerome *choreographer, director*
Rodriguez, Beatriz *ballerina*
Roney, Wallace *musician*
Rosen, Nathaniel Kent *cellist*
Rosenberger, Carol *concert pianist*
Rosenblum, M. Edgar *theater director*
Rostropovich, Mstislav Leopoldovich *musician*
Rothschild, Amalie Randolph *filmmaker, producer, director, digital artist, photographer*
Rotter, Stephen A. *film editor*
Roy, Melinda *dancer*
Rudel, Julius *conductor*
RuPaul, (Andre Charles) *model, singer*
Rysanek, Leonie *soprano*
Saddler, Donald Edward *choreographer, dancer*
Sade, (Helen Folasade Adu) *singer, songwriter*
Sagami, Kim *dancer*
Salerno-Sonnenberg, Nadja *violinist*
Salonga, Lea *actress, singer*
Sandler, Jenny *dancer*
Santiago-Hudson, Ruben *actor*
Saunders, Arlene *opera singer*
Savich, René *broadway theater executive, producer*
Schechner, Richard *theater director, author, educator*
Scheeder, Louis *theater producer, director, educator*
Schickele, Peter *composer*
Schiffer, Claudia *model*
Schoonmaker Powell, Thelma *film editor*
Schorer, Suki *ballet teacher*
Schrade, Rolande Maxwell Young *composer, pianist, educator*
Schroeder, Aaron Harold *songwriter*
Schwartz, Stephen Lawrence *composer, lyricist*
Scorsese, Martin *film director, writer*
Scott, Tom *musician*
Scott, Willard Herman *radio and television performer*
Scotto, Renata *soprano*
Seal *popular musician*
Sedaka, Neil *singer, songwriter*
Sedares, James L. *conductor*
Seeger, Pete *folk singer, songwriter*
Seidelman, Susan *film director*
Seldes, Marian *actress*
Seltzer, Leo *documentary filmmaker, educator, lecturer*
Serebrier, José *musician, conductor, composer*
Serkin, Peter *pianist*
Severs, William *actor*
Shaffer, Paul *musician, bandleader*
Shane, Rita *opera singer, educator*
Shaw, (Francis) Harold *performing arts administrator*
Shelley, Carole *actress*
Shellman, Eddie J. *ballet dancer, teacher, choreographer*
Sherman, Arthur *theater educator, writer, actor, composer*
Short, Robert Waltrip (Bobby Short) *entertainer, author*
Shostakovich, Maxim Dmitriyevich *symphonic conductor*
Shull, Richard Bruce *actor*
Sidney, Sylvia (Sophia Kossow) *actress*
Siegel, Marc Monroe *television and film producer, writer, director*
Silverman, Ira Norton *news producer*
Silvers, Sally *choreographer, performing company executive*
Simmons, Gene *musician*
Simon, Carly *singer, composer, author*
Sitomer, Sheila Marie *television producer, director*
Smith, Anna Nicole *model*
Smith, Malcolm Sommerville *bass*
Snipes, Wesley *actor*
Solomon, Maynard Elliott *music historian, former recording company executive*
Solomons, Gus, Jr. (Gustave Martinez) *choreographer, dancer, writer*
Solov, Zachary *choreographer, ballet artist*
Sorel, Claudette Marguerite *pianist*
Soto, Jock *dancer*
Soviero, Diana Barbara *soprano*
Soyer, David *cellist, music educator*
Spacey, Kevin *actor*
Springsteen, Bruce *singer, songwriter, guitarist*
Stapp, Olivia Brewer *opera singer*
Stern, Howard Allan *radio disc jockey, television show host*
Stern, Isaac *violinist*
Stewart, Roderick David *singer*
Stiefel, Ethan *dancer*
Stilwell, Richard Dale *baritone*
Stoltzman, Richard Leslie *clarinetist*
Strasfogel, Ian *stage director*
Stratas, Teresa (Anastasia Strataki) *opera singer, soprano*
Stutzmann, Nathalie *classical vocalist*
Swados, Elizabeth A. *composer, director, writer*
Swan, William *actor*
Talmi, Yoav *conductor, composer*
Taylor, Elizabeth Rosemond *actress*
Taylor, Nicole Renée *model*
Taylor, Paul *choreographer*
Te Kanawa, Kiri *opera and concert singer*
Tetley, Glen *choreographer*
Thomas, Richard *actor*
Thorne, Francis *composer*
Tillis, Pam *country singer, songwriter*
Tilson Thomas, Michael *symphony conductor*
Townshend, Peter *musician, composer, singer*
Tracey, Margaret *dancer*
Tree, Michael *violinist, violist, educator*
Tregellas, Patricia *musical director, composer*
Tune, Tommy (Thomas James Tune) *musical theater director, dancer, choreographer, actor*

Turk, Patricia Avedon *dance company executive*
Turrentine, Stanley William *musician*
Tyner, McCoy *jazz pianist, composer*
Ulrich, Lars *drummer*
Upbin, Shari *theatrical producer, director, agent, educator*
Uppman, Theodor *concert and opera singer, voice educator*
Upshaw, Dawn *soprano*
Vai, Steve *guitarist*
Vandross, Luther *singer*
Van Halen, Eddie *guitarist, rock musician*
Vedder, Eddie *singer*
Verdon, Gwen (Gwyneth Evelyn) *actress, dancer, choreographer*
VerDorn, Jerry *actor*
Viertel, Jack *theatrical producer, writer*
Volpe, Joseph *opera company administrator*
Von Brandenstein, Patrizia *production designer*
von Furstenberg, Betsy *actress, writer*
Von Stade, Frederica *mezzo-soprano*
Wadsworth, Charles William *pianist*
Wagner, Alan Cyril *television and film producer*
Wakeman, Rick *musician, composer*
Walker, Sandra *mezzo-soprano*
Warfield, Gerald Alexander *composer, writer*
Warwick, Dionne *singer*
Washington, Shelley Lynne *dancer*
Waters, Roger *rock musician*
Waters, Sylvia *dance company artistic director*
Waters, Willie Anthony *opera and orchestra conductor*
Watts, André *concert pianist*
Webb, Veronica *fashion model, journalist*
Wexler, Peter John *producer, director, set designer*
Whelan, Wendy *ballet dancer*
Whitehead, Robert *theatrical producer*
Wilkin, Miles Clifford *theatrical group executive*
Williams, Donald Maxey *dancer, singer, actor*
Williams, Stanley *ballet dancer and teacher*
Williams, Vanessa *recording artist, actress*
Wilson, Robert M. *theatre artist*
Wincenc, Carol *concertizing flutist, educator*
Wittstein, Edwin Frank *stage and film production designer*
Woetzel, Damian Abdo *ballet dancer, educator*
Wolfe, George C. *theater director, producer, playwright*
Wood, Ronald *musician*
Worth, Irene *actress*
Wuorinen, Charles Peter *composer*
Wurtzel, Alan Henry *television executive*
Yellin, Victor Fell *composer, music educator*
Yeston, Maury *composer, lyricist, educator*
Young, Neil *musician, songwriter*
†Yuriko, (Yuriko Kikuchi) *dancer, choreographer*
Zevon, Warren *singer, songwriter*
Zhu, Ai-Lan *opera singer*
Zosike, Joanie Fritz *theater director, actor*
Zucker, Stefan *tenor, writer, radio broadcaster*
Zukerman, Pinchas *concert violinist, violist, conductor*

### Niagara Falls
Kuciewski, Patrick Michael *music educator*

### Oswego
Nesbitt, Rosemary Sinnett *theatre educator*

### Palisades
Cavett, Dick *entertainer*
Krainin, Julian Arthur *film director, producer, writer, cinematographer*

### Pittsford
Benson, Warren Frank *composer, educator*

### Port Washington
Tarleton, Robert Stephen *producer and distributor fine arts videos*
Taylor, Cecil Percival *pianist, composer, educator*

### Poughkeepsie
†Wilson, Richard Edward *composer, pianist, music educator*

### Putnam Valley
Amram, David Werner *composer, conductor, musician*

### Rego Park
Cronyn, Hume *actor, writer, director*

### Rhinecliff
Meehan, John *artistic director*

### Riverdale
Hubley, Faith Elliott *filmmaker, painter, animator*

### Rochester
Bernhardt, Robert *music director, conductor*
Diamond, David Leo *composer*
Fagan, Garth *choreographer, artistic director, educator*
Hodkinson, Sydney Phillip *composer, educator*
Kowalke, Kim H. *music educator, musicologist, conductor, foundation executive*
Laires, Fernando *concert piano educator*
Marcellus, John Robert, III *trombonist, educator*
Rouse, Christopher Chapman, III *composer*
Schwantner, Joseph *composer, educator*
Weiss, Howard A. *violinist, concertmaster, conductor, music educator*

### Saint Regis Falls
Lange, Robert John (Mutt Lange) *producer*

### Saratoga Springs
Porter, David Hugh *pianist, classicist, academic administrator, liberal arts educator*

### Sea Cliff
Popova, Nina *dancer, choreographer, director*

### Southampton
Joel, Billy (William Martin Joel) *musician*

### Sparkill
Dahl, Arlene *actress, author, designer, cosmetic executive*

### Staten Island
Robison, Paula Judith *flutist*

### Stony Brook
Baron, Samuel *flutist*

### Sunnyside
Giaimo, Kathryn Ann *performing arts company executive*

### Syracuse
Akiyama, Kazuyoshi *conductor*
Rubardt, Peter Craig *conductor, educator*

### Tarrytown
Kroll, Nathan *film producer, director*

### Troy
Isaacs, Andrea *dancer, choreographer, former educator*
Snyder, Patricia Di Benedetto *theater director and administrator*

### West Hurley
Martucci, Vincent James *composer, pianist*

### White Plains
Magaziner, Elliot Albert *musician, conductor, educator*

### Willow
Bley, Carla Borg *jazz composer*

### Woodstock
Berger, Karl Hans *composer, pianist, vibrafonist*

### Yonkers
Baumel, Herbert *violinist, conductor*

## NORTH CAROLINA

### Asheville
Weed, Maurice James *composer, retired music educator*

### Beaufort
Ellis, Michael *theatrical producer*

### Boiling Springs
Bennett, Elizabeth Susan *music educator*

### Chapel Hill
Camp, Joseph Shelton, Jr. *film producer, director, writer*
Hammond, David Alan *stage director, educator*
Newman, William Stein *music educator, author, pianist, composer*
Parker, Scott Jackson *theatre manager*
Powell, Carolyn Wilkerson *music educator*

### Charlotte
Smith, Arthur *radio and television producer, composer*

### Creedmoor
Cross, June Crews *music educator*

### Durham
Bryan, Paul Robey, Jr. *musician, educator*
Caesar, Shirley *gospel singer, evangelist*
Nakarai, Charles Frederick Toyozo *music educator, adjudicator*
Redbone, Leon *singer, musician*
Ward, Robert *composer, conductor, educator*

### Greensboro
Middleton, Herman David, Sr. *theater educator*
Morgenstern, Sheldon Jon *symphony orchestra conductor*
Russell, Peggy Taylor *soprano, educator*
Styles, Teresa Jo *producer, educator*

### Greenville
Chauncey, Beatrice Arlene *music educator*

### Jacksonville
Daugherty, Robert Michael *music educator, composer*

### Lenoir
Mullis, Madeline Gail Herman *music educator, choir director*

### Raleigh
Zimmermann, Gerhardt *conductor*

### Warrenton
Weddington, Elizabeth Gardner (Liz Gardner) *actress, editor*

### Winston Salem
Perret, Peter James *symphony conductor*
Trautwein, George William *conductor*

## OHIO

### Akron
Poll, Heinz *choreographer, artistic director*
Schubert, Barbara Schuele *performing company executive*

### Aurora
Marshall, Lee Douglas *entertainment company executive*

### Berea
Strew, Suzanne Claflin *choreographer, dance educator*

### Cincinnati
Belew, Adrian *guitarist, singer, songwriter, producer*
†DeLaura, Kathleen J. *performing company executive*
DeLeone, Carmon *conductor, musician, composer, educator*
Hoffman, Joel Harvey *composer*
James, Jefferson Ann *performing company executive, choreographer*
Kunzel, Erich, Jr. *conductor, arranger, educator*
Lopez-Cobos, Jesus *conductor*
Samuel, Gerhard *orchestra conductor, composer*
Tocco, James *pianist*
Ward, Sherman Carl, III (Buzz Ward) *theater manager*
Worachek, Susan *music educator*

### Cleveland
Bamberger, David *opera company executive*
DesRosiers, Anne Booke *performing arts administrator*
Dohnányi, Christoph von *musician, conductor*
Erb, Donald *composer*
Giannetti, Louis Daniel *film educator, film critic*
Gladden, Dean Robert *arts administrator, educator, consultant*
Hruby, Frank Michael *musician, critic, educator*
Mc Farlane, Karen Elizabeth *concert artists manager*
Morris, Thomas William *symphony orchestra administrator*
Nahat, Dennis F. *artistic director, choreographer*

### Columbus
Bennett, Sharon Kay *music educator*
Brown, Firman Hewitt, Jr. *drama educator, theatrical director*
Drvota, Mojmir *cinema educator, author*
Haddad, George Richard *musician, educator*
Harris, Donald *composer*
Lowe, Clayton Kent *visual imagery, cinema, and video educator*
Rosenstock, Susan Lynn *orchestra manager*
Russell, William Fletcher, III *opera company director*
Wagner, Robert Walter *photography, cinema and communications educator, media producer, consultant*

### Dayton
Hanna, Marsha L. *artistic director*
Walters, Jefferson Brooks *musician, retired real estate broker*

### East Cleveland
Soule, Lucile Snyder *pianist, music educator*

### Hudson
Shaw, Doris Beaumar *film and video producer, executive recruiter*

### Maumee
Zaliouk, Yuval Nathan *conductor*

### Nelsonville
Caplinger, James Clair *theatrical producer*

### New Concord
Brown, Karen Rima *orchestra manager, Spanish language educator*

### North Ridgeville
Nagy, Robert David *tenor*

### Novelty
Miller, Dwight Richard *cosmetologist, corporate executive, hair designer*

### Oberlin
Boe, David Stephen *musician, educator, college dean*

### Strongsville
Oltman, C. Dwight *conductor, educator*

### Tiffin
Talbot-Koehl, Linda Ann *dancer, ballet studio owner*

### Toledo
Massey, Andrew John *conductor, composer*

### Waverly
Squire, Russel Nelson *musician, retired educator*

### Willoughby
Baker, Charles Stephen *music educator*

### Wooster
Stuart, James Fortier *musician, artistic director*

## OKLAHOMA

### Clinton
Askew, Penny Sue *choreographer, artistic director, ballet instructor*

### Lawton
Klein, Scott Richard *acting and directing educator*

### Norman
Carey, Thomas Devore *baritone, educator*
Eek, Nathaniel Sisson *retired fine arts educator*
Ross, Allan Anderson *music educator, university official*
Tussing, Marilee Appleby *music educator*

### Oklahoma City
McCoy, Wesley Lawrence *musician, conductor, educator*
Payne, Gareld Gene *vocal music educator, medical transcriptionist*
Sterban, Richard Anthony *singer*
Valentine, Alan Darrell *symphony orchestra executive*

### Stillwater
Hemberger, Glen James *university band director, music educator*

### Tulsa
Bonsall, Joseph Sloan, Jr. *singer*
Clark, Roy *singer, musician, recording industry executive*
Larkin, Moscelyne *retired artistic director, dancer*
Lunev, Aleksandr (Sasha) *dancer*
Nero, Peter *pianist, conductor, composer, arranger*
Owens, Jana Jae *entertainer*

## OREGON

### Ashland
Hirschfeld, Gerald Joseph *cinematographer*

### Eugene
Bailey, Exine Margaret Anderson *soprano, educator*

### Portland
Bailey, Robert C. *opera company executive*
†Bley, Paul *jazz pianist, composer, producer*
Cole-McCullough, Daniel *music educator, conductor, clinician*
DePreist, James Anderson *conductor*
Grappelli, Stephane *jazz violinist*
Hill, Andrew William *jazz musician, composer*
Leyden, Norman *conductor*
Terry, Clark *musician*

### Roseburg
Ferguson, John Franklin *music educator*

## PENNSYLVANIA

### Allentown
Beltzner, Gail Ann *music educator*

### Beaver Falls
Copeland, Robert Marshall *music educator*

### Bloomsburg
Stropnicky, Gerard Patrick *theater director, consultant*

### Bradfordwoods
Davis, Nathan Tate *musician, educator*

### Bristol
Atkinson, Susan D. *producing artistic director, theatrical consultant*

### Bryn Mawr
Goutman, Lois Clair *retired drama educator*
Stucky, Steven (Edward) *composer*

### Delaware Water Gap
Woods, Philip Wells (Phil Woods) *jazz musician composer*

### Drexel Hill
Martino, Michael Charles *entertainer, musician*

### Fayetteville
Kocek-McMurtray, Stephanie Susan *theater executive*

### Gouldsboro
Duricko, Erma O. *stage director, educator*

### Haverford
Davison, John Herbert *music educator, academic administrator*

### Indiana
Perlongo, Daniel James *composer*

### Irwin
Runser, Dianne Strong *music educator, music director*

### Jenkintown
Driehuys, Leonardus Bastiaan *conductor*

### Kingston
Weisberger, Barbara *choreographer, artistic director, educator*

### Lancaster
Collins, Kathleen Anne *artistic director*
Simmons, Deidre Warner *performing company executive*

### Merion Station
de Pasquale, Joseph *musician, educator*

### New Hope
Stahl, Stephen Lee *theater director, writer, producer*

### New Wilmington
Pitman, Grover Allen *music educator*

### Philadelphia
Allman, William Berthold *musician, engineer, consultant*
Barfield, Dede *ballerina*
Blavat, Jerry (Gerald Joseph Blavat) *radio and television personality, actor*
Bookspan, Michael Lloyd *musician*
Borovik, Alexei Peter *ballet dancer, educator*
Clauser, Donald Roberdeau *musician*
Coppock, Ada Gregory *theatre executive*
Crumb, George Henry *composer, educator*
Garfield, Bernard Howard *musician, composer*
Garonzik, Sara Ellen *stage director*
Gates, Jodie *dancer*
Graffman, Gary *pianist, music educator*
Havard, Bernard *theatrical producer*
†Kaiser, Roy *artistic director*
Kogan, Deen *artistic director*
Meyer, Leonard B. *musician, educator*
Mostovoy, Marc Sanders *conductor*
Sawallisch, Wolfgang *conductor*
Smith, Lloyd *musician*
Wernick, Richard Frank *composer, conductor*

### Phoenixville
Landis, Linda Kay *music educator*

### Pittsburgh
Balada, Leonardo *composer, educator*

Bardyguine, Patricia Wilde *ballerina, ballet theatre executive*
Capobianco, Tito *opera director*
Cardenes, Andres Jorge *violinist, music educator*
Croan, Robert James *music critic, singer*
Gray, Charles Buffum *theatrical director, producer*
Hollingsworth, Samuel Hawkins, Jr. *bassist*
Libman, Steven Bradley *performing arts administrator*
†Linaberger, Anne *television producer*
Miller, Mildred *opera singer, recitalist*
Norton, Eunice *pianist*
Rogers, Fred McFeely *television producer and host*
†Taylor, Mark Chandlee *choreographer*
Toeplitz, Gideon *symphony society executive*
Wilde, Patricia *artistic director*

### Roseto
Coppolella, Anthony S. *songwriter, poet, singer, model*

### Saltsburg
Buseck, Larry Allen *music educator*

### Selinsgrove
Diers, Hank H. *drama educator, playwright, director*

### Swarthmore
Devin, (Philip) Lee *dramaturg, theater educator*

### University Park
Baisley, Robert William *music educator*

### Warminster
Carroll, Lucy Ellen *choral director, music coordinator, educator*
Koch, Nancy Joy *music educator, choral director, vocal coach*

### West Chester
Burton, John Bryan *music educator*
Pettigrew, Claire Rudolph *music educator*

## RHODE ISLAND

### Bristol
Quinn, Anthony Rudolph Oaxaca *actor, writer, artist*

### Harrisville
Jubinska-Christiansen, Patricia Ann *ballet instructor, choreographer*

### Lincoln
Marsden, Herci Ivana *classical ballet artistic director*

### Newport
Malkovich, Mark Paul, III *musician, artistic director, scientist, sports agent*

### Providence
Barnhill, James Orris *theater educator*
†Dempsey, Raymond Leo, Jr. *radio and television producer, moderator, writer*
Eustis, Oskar (Paul Jefferson Eustis) *performing company executive*
Nelson, Ron *composer, conductor, educator*
Wilmeth, Don Burton *theatre arts educator, theatre historian, administrator, editor*

## SOUTH CAROLINA

### Anderson
Carroll, Edward Perry *instrumental music educator, conductor*

### Charleston
Ashley, Franklin Bascom *theater educator, writer*
Ivey, Robert Carl *artistic director, educator, choreographer*
Redden, Nigel A. *performing company executive*

### Columbia
O'Connor, James Arthur *theatre educator*

### Edisto Island
Van Metre, Margaret Cheryl *retired artistic director*

### Florence
Sanderson, Dennis Carl *theater director, educator*

### Folly Beach
Overton, Marcus Lee *performing arts administrator, actor, writer*

### Greenville
Selvy, Barbara *dance instructor*

### Hilton Head Island
Brock, Karena Diane *ballerina, educator, choreographer*

## TENNESSEE

### Brentwood
Tucker, Tanya Denise *singer*

### Hendersonville
Allen, Duane David *singer*
Bare, Robert Joseph (Bobby Bare) *country music singer, songwriter*
Cash, June Carter *singer*
Sanders, Steve *singer*

### Jefferson City
Ball, Louis Oliver, Jr. *music educator*

### Kingsport
Davis, Tammie Lynette *music educator, director*

### Knoxville
Jacobs, Kenneth A. *composer, educator*
Trevor, Kirk David Niell *orchestra conductor, cellist*

### La Vergne
†Ingram, David *entertainment company executive*
†Ingram, Orrin H., III *entertainment company executive*

### Lebanon
Daniels, Charlie *musician, songwriter*

### Madison
Kennedy, Matthew Washington *pianist, educator*
Wells, Kitty (Muriel Deason Wright) *country western singer*

### Memphis
Hathcock, John Edward *vocalist*
Piazza, Marguerite *opera singer, actress, entertainer*
Pugh, Dorothy Gunther *ballet company executive*
Williams, David Russell *music educator*

### Nashville
Anderson, Lynn (Rene Anderson) *singer*
Arnold, Eddy *singer*
Black, Clint *country singer, musician*
Bogguss, Suzy *country music singer, songwriter*
Brooks, Garth (Troyal Garth Brooks) *country music singer*
Brown, J. Aaron *producer, publisher*
Carter, James McCord *television producer, personality*
Cleveland, Ashley *musician*
Cross, Christopher *recording artist, songwriter, singer*
Crowell, Rodney J. *country music recording artist, songwriter*
Cyrus, Billy Ray *country music performer*
Diffie, Joe *country singer, songwriter*
Earle, Steve *country rockabilly musician, songwriter*
Fleck, Bela *country musician*
Gentry, Teddy *country musician*
Gill, Vince *country musician, singer*
Grant, Amy *singer, songwriter*
Greenwood, Lee Melvin *singer*
Griffith, Nanci *singer, songwriter*
Harris, Emmylou *singer*
Hartford, John Cowan *singer, songwriter*
†Houk, Benjamin Noah *ballet dancer*
Hutchison, Barbara Bailey *children's entertainer*
Jackson, Alan *country songwriter, singer*
Judd, Naomi *country music entertainer, singer, songwriter, author*
Kurek, Michael Henry *music educator*
Laczko, Brian John *theater director*
Lee, Brenda (Brenda Mae Tarpley) *singer, entertainer*
Lee, Douglas A. *music educator*
Lehman, David R. *children's entertainer*
Mandrell, Barbara Ann *singer, entertainer*
Mattea, Kathy *vocalist, songwriter*
Morgan, Lorrie (Loretta Lynn Morgan) *country singer*
Needham, Maureen *dance educator, writer*
Oslin, K. T. (Kay Toinette Oslin) *country singer*
Prine, John *singer, songwriter*
Rabbitt, Edward Thomas *singer, songwriter*
Rogers, Roy (Leonard Franklin Slye) *country musician, actor*
Shelton, Ricky Van *country music singer, songwriter*
Skaggs, Ricky *country musician*
Smith, Michael W. *popular musician*
Stuart, Marty *country music singer, musician, songwriter*
Tippin, Aaron *country music singer, songwriter*
Travis, Randy Bruce *musician*
Twain, Shania *country musician*
Unger, Gary A. *recording industry executive, singer, lyricist*
Wagoner, Porter *country music singer, composer*

## TEXAS

### Abilene
McClain, Sylvia Nancy *voice educator, classical vocalist*

### Arlington
Carey, Milburn Ernest *musician, educator*
Malone, Edwin Scott, III *radio and television producer, public relations consultant*
Russell, Andrew Milo *music educator*

### Austin
Antokoletz, Elliott Maxim *music educator*
Brockett, Oscar Gross *theatre educator*
Jennings, Coleman Alonzo *dramatics educator*
Kennan, Kent Wheeler *composer, educator*
Lary, Banning Kent *video producer, publisher*
Schulz, Russell Eugene *musician, educator, composer*
Sharir, Yacov *artistic director, choreographer*
Young, Phyllis Casselman *music educator*

### Cedar Hill
Kilgore, Janice Kay *musician, educator*

### College Station
Toler, Ray Edward *conductor, band director*

### Corpus Christi
Allison, Joan Kelly *music educator, pianist*
Fender, Freddy (Baldemar Huerta) *singer*

### Dallas
Anderson, Robert Theodore *music educator, organist*
Atkinson, Bill *artistic director*
Eagar, Stephen Wade *television news anchor, reporter*
Etgen, Ann *ballet educator*
Galt, John William *actor, writer*
Palmer, Christine (Clelia Rose Venditti) *operatic singer, performer, pianist, vocal instructor, lecturer, entertainer*
Pell, Jonathan Laurence *artistic administrator*
Pride, Charley *singer*

### Denton
Davidson, Norma Lewis *concert violinist, composer, music educator, psychologist*
Latham, William Peters *composer, former educator*

### Fort Worth
Cliburn, Van (Harvey Lavan Cliburn, Jr.) *concert pianist*
Giordano, John Read *conductor*
Lipkin, Seymour *pianist, conductor, educator*
McKinney, James Carroll *baritone, educator*
Rhodes, Ann L. *theatrical producer, investor*

### Garland
Evans, Patricia M. *performing arts association administrator*

### Hallsville
Hutcherson, Donna Dean *music educator*

### Harlingen
Godfrey, Aline Lucille *music specialist, church organist*

### Houston
Alexander, Michael Lee *music educator, cellist*
Brown, Glenda Ann Walters *ballet director*
Buyse, Leone Karena *orchestral musician, educator*
Clark, Ron D(ean) *cosmetologist*
Crain, Richard Charles *school district music director*
Englesmith, Tejas *actor, producer, curator*
Florio, Ermanno *conductor, music administrator*
Frank, Hilda Rhea Kaplan *dancer*
Girouard, Peggy Jo Fulcher *ballet educator*
Hammond, Michael Peter *music educator, dean*
Jones, Florence M. *music educator*
Jones, Samuel *conductor*
Marshall, Margo *artistic director*
Ostrow, Stuart *theatrical producer, educator*
Rigsby, Carolyn Erwin *music educator*
Rose, Beatrice Schroeder (Mrs. William H. Rose) *harpist, educator*
Stevenson, Ben *artistic director*
Šutej, Vjekoslav *conductor*
Young, Frank Mitchell *musical theater producer*

### Katy
Mitchell, Leona Pearl *soprano*

### Mcallen
†Guilliouma, Larry Jay, Jr. *performing arts administrator, music educator*

### Mesquite
Montgomery, Marvin *musical producer*

### Munday
Bennett, Rodney Dee *music educator*

### Pampa
Willingham, Jeanne Maggart *dance educator, ballet company executive*

### Pasadena
Gilley, Mickey Leroy *musician*

### Redwater
Hammer, Richard Lee *music educator*

### Richardson
Gary, John *singer*

### Rockwall
House, Robert William *music educator*
Wallace, Mary Elaine *opera director, author*

### Round Top
Dick, James Cordell *concert pianist*

### San Antonio
Burns, Leslie Kaye *documentary video producer and director*
Greenberg, Nat *orchestra administrator*
Mairs, David *symphony conductor*
Marek, Vladimir *ballet director, educator*
Powell Hill, Dr. Queen Elizabath T. *singer, small business owner*

### Tyler
Hatfield, James Allen *theater arts educator*

### Vernon
Cook, Marcella Kay *drama educator*

### Victoria
Weber, Michael James *conductor*

### Waco
Colvin, (Otis) Herbert, Jr. *musician, educator*
Sternberg, Daniel Arie *musician, conductor, educator*

### Whitehouse
Baker, Rebecca Louise *musician, music educator, consultant*

## UTAH

### Ogden
Howard, Sherwin Ward *theatre educator*

### Provo
Pratt, Rosalie Rebollo *harpist, educator*
Woodbury, Lael Jay *theater educator*

### Salt Lake City
Ewers, Anne *opera company director*
Hart, John *artistic director*
Jiang, Qi *ballet dancer, educator*
Leedom, Erin *dancer*
Maidon, Gilles *dancer*
Morey, Charles Leonard, III *theatrical director*
Ottley, Jerold Don *choral conductor, educator*
Robinson, Pamela *dancer*
Rogers, Jeffrey *dancer*
St. John, Katherine Iva *artistic director, dance educator*
Silverstein, Joseph Harry *conductor, musician*
Van Mason, Raymond *dancer, choreographer*
Wood, Jane *dancer*

## VERMONT

### Burlington
Whitehill, Angela Elizabeth *artistic director*

### Weston
Stettler, Stephen F. *performing company executive*

## VIRGINIA

### Arlington
Crystal, Lester Martin *television producer*
Murphy, Donn Brian *theater educator*

### Charlottesville
Chapel, Robert Clyde *stage director, theater educator*
Ross, Walter Beghtol *music educator, composer*

### Chester
Gray, Frederick Thomas, Jr. ('Rick Gray) *actor, educator*

### Harrisonburg
Arthur, Thomas Hahn *theater educator, director*

### Lexington
Seeger, Michael *musician, singer, folklorist*

### Manassas
Bahner, Sue (Florence Suzanna Bahner) *radio broadcasting executive*

### Mc Lean
Drummond, Carol Cramer *voice educator, singer, artist, writer*
Rugala, Karen Francis (Karen Francis) *television producer, painter*
Youngs, William Ellis *motion picture engineer, projectionist*

### Moneta
Pfeuffer, Robert John *musician*

### Norfolk
Hailstork, Adolphus Cunningham *composer*
Mark, Peter *director, conductor*
Musgrave, Thea *composer, conductor*

### Orange
Soderbergh, Steven Andrew *filmmaker*

### Petersburg
Dance, Gloria Fenderson *dance studio executive, ballet administrator*

### Radford
James, Clarity (Carolyne Faye James) *mezzo-soprano*

### Richmond
Levit, Heloise B. (Ginger Levit) *art dealer, fine arts and media consultant*
†Winslett, Stoner *artistic director*

### Roanoke
Stanley, Ralph *bluegrass musician*

### Springfield
Eastman, Donna Kelly *composer, music educator*

### Staunton
Balsley, Philip Elwood *entertainer*

### Vienna
Dewar, James McEwen *film director, writer, former marketing, aerospace and defense executive, consultant*
†Feld, Kenneth *performing company executive*
Lyons, Paul Michael *producer, film*

### Virginia Beach
Freyss, David *producer, director*
Stevenson, Amanda (Sandy Stevens) *librettist, composer*

### Williamsburg
Hornsby, Bruce Randall *composer, musician*

## WASHINGTON

### Auburn
Overholt, Miles Harvard *cable television consultant*

### Bremerton
Rickerson, Jean Marie *video producer, journalist, photographer*

### Coupeville
Lotzenhiser, George William *music educator, university administrator, composer*

### Friday Harbor
Waite, Ric *cinematographer*

### Gig Harbor
Ramsey, Jerry Virgil *educator, financial planner, radio broadcaster*

### Lynnwood
Krause, Thomas Evans *record promotion and radio consultant*

### Marysville
Philpott, Larry La Fayette *horn player*

### Seattle
Anang, Amma Cecilia *dance company administrator*
Forbes, David Craig *musician*
Jenkins, Speight *opera company executive, writer*
Jensen, Helen *musical artists management company executive*
Loper, Robert Bruce *theater director, educator*
Moore, Benjamin *theatrical producer*
Nishitani, Martha *dancer*
Russell, Francia *ballet director, educator*
Sateren, Terry *theater technical production*
Staryk, Steven S. *violinist, concertmaster, educator*
Stowell, Kent *ballet director*
Sullivan, Daniel J. *artistic director*

Talvi, Ilkka Ilari *violinist*
Thomas, Karen P. *composer, conductor*

**Spokane**
Bray, R(obert) Bruce *music educator*
Fowler, Betty Janmae *dance company director, editor*

**Tacoma**
Hansen, Edward Allen *music educator, organist*

**Woodinville**
Sanders, Richard Kinard *actor*

## WEST VIRGINIA

**Charleston**
Conlin, Thomas (Byrd) *conductor*

**Falling Waters**
Schellhaas, Robert Wesley *counselor, songwriter, musician*

**Mannington**
Schumacher, Theresa Rose *singer, musician*

**Salem**
Raad, Virginia *pianist, lecturer*

**Westover**
Trythall, Harry Gilbert *music educator, composer*

## WISCONSIN

**Beloit**
Gates, Crawford Marion *conductor, composer*

**Eau Claire**
Patterson, Donald Lee *music educator*

**Madison**
Burns, Elizabeth Murphy *media executive*
Davis, Richard *musician, music educator*
De Main, John *conductor, music director*
Dembski, Stephen Michael *composer, university music composition professor*
Johnson, Roland A. *conductor, music director*
Rosser, Annetta Hamilton *composer*

**Milwaukee**
Downey, John Wilham *composer, pianist, conductor, educator*
Hansen-Rachor, Sharon Ann *conductor, choral music educator*
Hanthorn, Dennis Wayne *performing arts association administrator*
Ovitsky, Steven Alan *musician, symphony orchestra executive*
†Squires, Joan H. *orchestra executive*

### CANADA

## ALBERTA

**Banff**
Fruchtman, Milton Allen *film and television producer, director*

**Calgary**
Graf, Hans *conductor*
LaHay, David George Michael *ballet company director*
Monk, Allan James *baritone*

## BRITISH COLUMBIA

**North Vancouver**
†Anderson, Gillian *actress*

**Qualicum Beach**
Little, Carl Maurice *performing arts administrator*

**Vancouver**
Alleyne, John *dancer, choreographer*
Hallam, Robert J. *performing company executive, consultant*
Murray, Anne *singer*
Raffi, (Raffi Cavoukian) *folksinger, children's entertainer*

**Victoria**
Horn, Paul Joseph *musician*
McCoppin, Peter *symphony orchestra conductor*

## MANITOBA

**Winnipeg**
Lewis, Andre Leon *artistic director*
Morris, Jorden Walter *dancer, educator*
Olds, Elizabeth *dancer*
Rubio, Suzanne Sarah *ballet dancer*
Salgado, Lissette *dancer*
Savchenko, Alla *ballet mistress*
Spohr, Arnold Theodore *artistic director, choreographer*
Turner, Robert Comrie *composer*
Zhang Wei-Qiang *dancer*

## ONTARIO

**Don Mills**
Applebaum, Louis *composer, conductor*

**Dundas**
Shaw, John Firth *orchestra administrator*

**Hamilton**
Lipton, Daniel Bernard *conductor*

**Kitchener**
Coles, Graham *conductor, composer*

**London**
Stafford, Earl *conductor*
William, David *director, actor*

**Mississauga**
Peterson, Oscar Emmanuel *pianist*

**Niagara-on-the-Lake**
Newton, Christopher *artistic director*

**Oshawa**
Drynan, Margaret Isobel *music teacher, retired consultant*

**Ottawa**
Franca, Celia *ballet director, choreographer, dancer, narrator*
Gillingham, Bryan Reginald *music educator*

**Thornhill**
Nimmons, Phillip Rista *composer, conductor, clarinetist, educator*

**Toronto**
Augustyn, Frank Joseph *dancer, artistic director*
Beckwith, John *musician, composer, educator*
Boswell, Philip John *opera administrator*
Bradshaw, Richard James *conductor*
Chan Hon Goh *ballerina*
Colgrass, Michael Charles *composer*
Crawley, Alexander Radford *actor*
Doherty, Tom (Thomas Storen, Jr.) *art director, set designer*
Domb, Daniel *cellist, educator*
Drabinsky, Garth Howard *entertainment company executive*
Eklof, Svea Christine *ballet dancer*
Eldred, Gerald Marcus *performing arts association executive*
Freedman, Harry *composer*
Geddes, Lorna *ballet mistress*
Girard, Francois *film director*
Glasco, Kimberly *ballet dancer*
Israelievitch, Jacques H. *violinist, conductor*
Kain, Karen Alexandria *ballet dancer*
Kirby, Charles William, Jr. *dancer, choreographer*
Kudelka, James *choreographer, artistic director*
Kuerti, Anton Emil *pianist, composer*
Lamy, Martine *dancer*
Lavoie, Serge *principal dancer*
Lucas, Cynthia *ballet mistress, dancer*
Oliphant, Betty *ballet school director*
Ottmann, Peter *choreologist, ballet master*
Pedersen, Paul Richard *composer, educator*
Ransom, Jeremy *ballet dancer*
Rasky, Harry *producer, director, writer*
Schramek, Tomas *ballet dancer*
Shearing, George Albert *pianist, composer*
Staines, Mavis Avril *artistic director, ballet principal*
Stefanschi, Sergiu *dancer*
Wilder, Valerie *ballet company administrator*
Wilkins, Ormsby *music director, conductor, pianist*
Witkowsky, Gizella *dancer*

## QUEBEC

**Montreal**
Dutoit, Charles *conductor*
Gulkin, Harry *arts administrator, film producer*
Nault, Fernand *choreographer*
Obomsawin, Alanis *director, producer*
Rhodes, Lawrence *artistic director*
Trogani, Monica *ballet mistress*
Uzan, Bernard *general and artistic director*
Woszczyk, Wieslaw Richard *audio engineering educator, researcher*

**Sainte Foy**
Pasquier, Joël *music educator*

### AUSTRALIA

**Strawberry Hills**
Bonynge, Richard *opera conductor*

**Sydney**
Miller, George *film director*

### CAYMAN ISLANDS

**Grand Cayman**
Crockett, James Grover, III *musician, former music publisher*

### COSTA RICA

**San Jose**
Hoffman, Irwin *orchestra conductor*

### DOMINICAN REPUBLIC

**Santo Domingo**
Piantini, Carlos *conductor*

### ENGLAND

**Balcombe**
Scofield, Paul *actor*

**Brighton**
Watkin, David *film director, cinematographer*

**Buckinghamshire**
Pierce-Roberts, Tony *cinematographer*

**Cambridge**
Bream, Julian *classical guitarist and lutanist*
Hogwood, Christopher Jarvis Haley *music director, educator*

**Isle of Wight**
Stigwood, Robert Colin *theater, movie, television and record producer*

**Iver Heath**
Kubrick, Stanley *producer, director, writer*

**London**
Ackland-Snow, Terry *art director*
Ashkenazy, Vladimir Davidovich *concert pianist, conductor*
Barshai, Rudolf Borisovich *conductor*
Bart, Lionel *composer, lyricist*
Beck, Jeff *musician, composer, vocalist*
Bertolucci, Bernardo *film director*
Cellan-Jones, James Gwynne *television producer, director*
Codron, Michael Victor *theatrical producer*
Conti, Tom *actor, writer, director*
Dearden, James *director, screenwriter*
Dickinson, Peter *composer*
Dowell, Anthony James, Sr. *ballet dancer*
Doyle, Patrick *composer*
Dudley, Anne *composer*
Estes, Simon Lamont *opera singer, bass-baritone*
Francis, Freddie *film producer and director*
Freni, Mirella *soprano*
Gielgud, Sir (Arthur) John *actor, director*
Hawthorne, Nigel Barnard *actor*
Hendricks, Barbara *opera singer, recitalist*
Holm, Ian *actor*
Hoskins, Bob (Robert William Hoskins) *actor*
Hurt, John Vincent *actor*
Irons, Jeremy John *actor*
Jackson, Felicity Anne *performing arts organization administrator*
John, Elton Hercules (Reginald Kenneth Dwight) *musician*
Lennox, Annie *rock musician*
Levi, Yoel *orchestra conductor*
Le Vien, John Douglas (Jack Le Vien) *motion picture and television producer, director*
Lloyd-Webber, Baron Andrew *composer*
Lynne, Gillian Barbara *choreographer, dancer, actress, director*
Mackerras, Sir (Alan) Charles (Maclaurin) *conductor*
Mackintosh, Cameron *musical theater producer*
Marriner, Sir Neville *orchestra conductor*
McIntyre, Donald Conroy *opera singer, baritone*
McKellen, Ian *actor*
Menges, Chris *cinematographer, film director*
Miller, Jonathan Wolfe *theater and film director, physician*
Minton, Yvonne Fay *mezzo-soprano*
Mirren, Helen *actress*
Nelson, John Wilton *symphonic conductor*
Nucci, Leo *baritone*
Nunn, Trevor Robert *director*
Palin, Michael Edward *actor, screenwriter, author*
Plowright, Joan Anne *actress*
Pryce, Jonathan *actor*
Puttnam, Sir David Terence *film producer*
Rattle, Simon *conductor*
Rea, Stephen *actor*
Ricci, Ruggiero *violinist, educator*
Ricciarelli, Katia *soprano*
Schaufuss, Peter *dancer, producer, choreographer, ballet director*
Slocombe, Douglas *cinematographer*
Smith, Dame Maggie *actress*
Starr, Ringo (Richard Starkey) *musician, actor*
Sting, (Gordon Matthew Sumner) *musician, songwriter, actor*
Sutherland, Dame Joan *retired soprano*
Tennstedt, Klaus *conductor*
Vaness, Carol *soprano*
Wallis, Diana Lynn *artistic director*
Warr, Robert *producer*
†Webber, Andrew Lloyd *composer*
Winner, Michael Robert *film director, writer, producer*
Wyman, William George *musician*

**Manchester**
Wilson, Keith Dudley *media and music educator*

**Oxford**
Tureck, Rosalyn *concert performer, author, editor, educator*

**Richmond**
Attenborough, Baron Richard Samuel *actor, producer, director, goodwill ambassador*

**Warwick**
Hands, Terence David (Terry Hands) *theater director*

### FINLAND

**Helsinki**
Saraste, Jukka-Pekka *conductor*

### FRANCE

**Neuilly sur Seine**
Ophuls, Marcel *film director and producer*

**Paris**
Boulez, Pierre *composer, conductor*
de Havilland, Olivia Mary *actress*
Jolas, Betsy *composer*
Kurtz, Eugene Allen *composer, educator, consultant*
Marceau, Marcel *pantomimist, actor, director, painter, poet*
Marton, Eva *opera singer*
Raimondi, Ruggero *opera singer*

### GERMANY

**Berlin**
Abbado, Claudio *conductor*
Fischer-Dieskau, Dietrich *baritone*

Goodman, Alfred *composer, musicologist*
Wenders, Wim *film director*

**Dresden**
Schreier, Peter *tenor*

**Hamburg**
Neumeier, John *choreographer, ballet company director*
Ramsey, Bill (William McCreery) *singer, actor, composer-lyricist, television executive*

**Munich**
Fassbaender, Brigitte *opera singer*
Horak, Jan-Christopher *film studies educator, curator*

**Stuttgart**
Anderson, Reid Bryce *ballet company artistic director*

### IRELAND

**Dublin**
Sheridan, Jim *director, screenwriter*

### ISRAEL

**Tel Aviv**
Mehta, Zubin *conductor, musician*

### ITALY

**Pontedera**
Grotowski, Jerzy *theater director, acting educator*

**Rome**
Antonioni, Michelangelo *film director*
Loren, Sophia *actress*
Storaro, Vittorio *cinematographer*
Zeffirelli, Franco *theater and film director*

### JAPAN

**Yokohama**
Kurosawa, Akira *film director*

### MONACO

**Monaco**
Zylis-Gara, Teresa Gerarda *soprano*

### THE NETHERLANDS

**Hilversum**
De Waart, Edo *conductor*

**The Hague**
Kylián, Jiri *choreographer*

### SCOTLAND

**Edinburgh**
McMaster, Brian John *artistic director*

### SPAIN

**Barcelona**
de Larrocha, Alicia *concert pianist*

**Madrid**
Berganza Vargas, Teresa *mezzo-soprano*
Frühbeck de Burgos, Rafael *conductor*
Trueba, Fernando *film director and producer, screenwriter*

### SWEDEN

**Stockholm**
Soederstrom, Elisabeth Anna *opera singer*

### SWITZERLAND

**Basel**
Ghiglia, Oscar Alberto *classical guitarist*

**Geneva**
Barenboim, Daniel *conductor, pianist*

### ADDRESS UNPUBLISHED

Aaron, Lynn *dancer*
Adams, Bryan *vocalist, composer*
Adaskin, Murray *composer*
Adato, Perry Miller *documentary producer, director, writer*
Adelson, Merv Lee *entertainment and communication industry executive*
Adler, Samuel Hans *retired conductor, composer*
Alberts, David *artistic director, mime*
Allen, Marilyn Myers Pool *theater director, video producer*
Alsop, Marin *conductor*
Altamura, Carmela Elizabeth *concert artist, philanthropist*
Anderson, Laurie *performance artist*
Andrews, Julie *actress, singer*
Apted, Michael David *film director*
Aquino-Kaufman, Florence (Florence Anglin) *actress, playwright*
Archer, Anne *actress*

Schwary, Ronald Louis *motion picture producer*
Schwarz, Gerard *conductor, musician*
Scruggs, Earl Eugene *entertainer*
Seale, John Clement *director, cinematographer*
Shanks, Ann Zane *filmmaker, producer/director, photographer, writer*
Shatin, Judith *music composing educator*
Shaw, Artie *musician, writer, lecturer*
Shelton, Sloane *actress*
Sherin, Edwin *theatrical and film director, actor*
Shirley-Quirk, John *concert and opera singer*
Shull, Claire *documentary film producer, casting director*
Siegel, Laurence Gordon *conductor*
Sikes, Cynthia Lee *actress, singer*
Silverstein, Barbara Ann *conductor*
Silvestri, Alan Anthony *film composer*
Skolovsky, Zadel *concert pianist, educator*
Skowronski, Vincent Paul *concert violinist, recording artist, executive producer, producer classical recordings*
Smith, Carter Blakemore *broadcaster*
Smith, Lawrence Leighton *conductor*
Smith, Lois Arlene *actress, writer*
Smoot, Hazel Lampkin *retired piano teacher, poet*
Solow, Herbert Franklin *film producer, writer*
Sondheim, Stephen Joshua *composer, lyricist*
Sprenger, Curtis Donald *choir conductor, educator*
Stanfill, Shelton G. *performing arts administrator*
Stanley, Margaret King *performing arts administrator*
Stapleton, Maureen *actress*
Starer, Robert *composer*
Sternhagen, Frances *actress*
Stevens, Warren *actor*
Stewart, Thomas James, Jr. *baritone*
Stiller, Jerry *actor*
Strait, George *country music vocalist*
Stuart, Mary *actress*
Sutherland, Bruce *composer, pianist, music educator*
Sutton, Dolores *actress, writer*
Sylvester, Michael Lane *vocalist*
Taylor, Guy Watson *symphonic conductor*
Terrell, Dominique Lara *dramatic soprano, actress, real estate and marketing executive*
Tharp, Twyla *dancer, choreographer*
Thomas, Marlo (Margaret Julia Thomas) *actress*
Thomson, Alex *cinematographer*
Thorstenberg, (John) Laurence *oboe and English horn player*
Tilly, Meg *actress*
Timmons, William Milton *producer, freelance writer, retired cinema arts educator, publisher, film maker*
Tinker, Mark Christian *producer, director*
Tokofsky, Jerry Herbert *film producer*
Topaz, Muriel *dance educator, author*
Topilow, Carl S. *conductor*
Travanti, Daniel John *actor*
Travis, Neil *film editor*
Travolta, John *actor*
Turkin, Marshall William *symphony orchestra, festival and opera administrator, arranger, composer*
Turok, Paul Harris *composer, music reviewer*
Ullman, Tracey *actress, singer*
Ustinov, Sir Peter Alexander *actor, director, writer*
Vallone, John Charles *motion picture production designer*
Vandusen, Blanche Baker *actress, sculptor*
Van Ness, Patricia Catheline *composer, violinist*
Van Patten, Joyce Benignia *actress*
Villella, Edward Joseph *ballet dancer, educator, choreographer, artistic director*
Virkhaus, Taavo *symphony orchestra conductor*
Voketaitis, Arnold Mathew *bass-baritone, educator*
Waldrop, Gideon William *composer, conductor, former president music school*
Wallach, Eli *actor*
Walsh, Diane *pianist*
Walsh, Thomas A. *production designer*
Walston, Ray *actor*
Walthall, Lee Wade *artistic director, dancer*
Ward, Fred *actor*
Washington, Grover, Jr. *musician, producer, composer, arranger*
Waters, John *film director, writer, actor*
Weiner-Heuschkel, Sydell *theater educator*
Weiss, Alan *musician, educator*
Wettig, Patricia *actress*
Whitmore, James Allen *actor*
Wiatt, James Anthony *theatrical agency executive*
Widmark, Richard *actor*
Wildhack, John Robert *producer, broadcast executive*
Williams, Patrick Moody *composer*
Williamson, Laird *stage director, actor*
Willis, Bruce Walter *actor, singer*
Wilson, Nancy *singer*
Winters, Jonathan *actor*
Winwood, Stephen Lawrence *musician, composer*
Wise, Patricia *lyric coloratura*
Woodward, Thomas Morgan *actor*
Worthey, Carol *composer*
Wright, Gladys Stone *music educator, composer, writer*
Wright, Jeffrey *actor*
Wynette, Tammy *singer*
Yarrow, Peter *folksinger*
Yellen, Linda *film director, writer, producer*
Yoakam, Dwight *country western musician*
Zeiger, Scott Leslie *commercial theater executive*
Zhao, Li *fine arts company executive, teacher, consultant*
Zoritch, George *dance educator*


## ARTS: VISUAL

### UNITED STATES

#### ALABAMA


**Birmingham**
Fleming, Frank *sculptor*
Price, Rosalie Pettus *artist*

**Decatur**
Bennett, Rebecca Eaton *artist*
Braswell, Paula Ann *artist*

**Huntsville**
Wilson, Allan Byron *graphics company executive*

**Montgomery**
Schwarz, Joseph Edmund *artist*

**Trussville**
Best, Frederick Napier *artist, designer, educator*

**Tuscaloosa**
Gourley, Paula Marie *art educator, artist, designer bookbinder*

**Tuskegee**
Thomas, Elaine Freeman *artist, educator*


#### ALASKA


**Anchorage**
Shadrach, (Martha) Jean Hawkins *artist*

**Cordova**
Bugbee-Jackson, Joan *sculptor*


#### ARIZONA


**Fountain Hills**
†York, Tina *painter*

**Green Valley**
Page, John Henry, Jr. *artist, educator*

**Lake Montezuma**
Burkee, Irvin *artist*

**Oracle**
Rush, Andrew Wilson *artist*

**Oro Valley**
Loeh, Corinne Genevieve *artist*

**Paradise Valley**
Heller, Jules *artist, writer, educator*

**Phoenix**
Dignac, Geny (Eugenia M. Bermudez) *sculptor*
Lawes, Patricia Jean *art educator*
Schmieder, Carl *jeweler*
Swensen, Mary Jean Hamilton *graphic artist*
Whitman, Kathy Velma Rose (Elk Woman Whitman) *artist, sculptor, jeweler, painter, educator*

**Prescott**
Stasack, Edward Armen *artist*

**Scottsdale**
Blanchet, Jeanne Ellene Maxant *artist, educator, performer*
Brock, Lonnie Rex *landscape and nature photographer*
Chase, James Keller *retired artist, museum director, educator*
Curtis, Philip C. *artist*
Fratt, Dorothy *artist*
Golden, Libby *artist*
Lang, Margo Terzian *artist*
Scholder, Fritz *artist*

**Sedona**
Ware, Peggy Jenkins *photographer, writer, artist, dancer*

**Tempe**
Grigsby, Jefferson Eugene, Jr. *artist, educator*
Klett, Mark C. *photographer, educator*
Turk, Rudy Henry *artist, retired museum director*

**Tucson**
Conant, Howard Somers *artist, educator*
Doren, Henry Julius Thaddeus *artist, painter*
Flint, Willis Wolfschmidt (Willi Wolfschmidt) *artist*
Golden, Judith Greene *artist, educator*
Kingery, William David *ceramics and anthropology educator*
Root, Nile *photographer, educator*


#### ARKANSAS


**Fayetteville**
Wilson, Charles Banks *artist*

**State University**
Lindquist, Evan *artist, educator*


#### CALIFORNIA


**Acampo**
Eger, Marilyn Rae *artist*

**Albion**
Martin, Bill *artist, art educator*

**Aptos**
Woods, Gurdon Grant *sculptor*

**Arcadia**
Danziger, Louis *graphic designer, educator*

**Aromas**
Nutzle, Futzie (Bruce John Kleinsmith) *artist, author, cartoonist*

**Avalon**
Burns, Denise Ruth *artist*

**Bakersfield**
Reep, Edward Arnold *artist*

**Belmont**
Pava, Esther Shub *artist, educator*

**Berkeley**
Genn, Nancy *artist*
Hartman, Robert Leroy *artist, educator*
Kasten, Karl Albert *painter, printmaker*
†Klein, Lynn Ellen *artist*
McNamara, John Stephen *artist, educator*
Miyasaki, George Joji *artist*
Rapoport, Sonya *artist*
Shoichi, Ida *artist*
Simpson, David William *artist, educator*
Washburn, Stan *artist*

**Beverly Hills**
De Anda, Alicia *artist*
Ringwald, Lydia Elaine *artist, poet*

**Big Bear Lake**
Essman, Robert Norvel *artist, graphic designer*

**Bodega**
Hedrick, Wally Bill *artist*

**Bolinas**
Harris, Paul *sculptor*

**Boonville**
Hanes, John Ward *sculptor, civil engineer consultant*

**Brisbane**
Anargyros, Spero *sculptor*

**Burbank**
Merrill, Thomas St. John *medical photographer*

**Cambria**
Harden, Marvin *artist, educator*

**Canoga Park**
Rosenfeld, Sarena Margaret *artist*

**Carmel**
Andreason, Sharon Lee *sculptor*
Bullock, Edna Jeanette *photographer*
Kenna, Michael *photographer*
Kennedy, John Edward *art dealer, appraiser, curator*

**Carmel Valley**
Sands, Sharon Louise *graphic design executive, art publisher, artist*

**Carmichael**
Sahs, Majorie Jane *art educator*

**Carpinteria**
Hansen, Robert William *artist, educator*
Rosas, Susan Jane *designer, graphic artist, illustrator, art director*

**Carson**
Hirsch, Gilah Yelin *artist, writer*

**Claremont**
Benjamin, Karl Stanley *art educator*
Blizzard, Alan *artist*
Casanova, Aldo John *sculptor*
Watson, Helen Richter *educator, ceramic artist*

**Corona Del Mar**
Brandt, Rexford Elson *artist*
Delap, Tony *artist*

**Coronado**
Hubbard, Donald *marine artist, writer*

**Costa Mesa**
Muller, Jerome Kenneth *photographer, art director, editor*

**Crescent City**
Swart, Bonnie Blount *artist*

**Culver City**
Pittard, William Blackburn (Billy Pittard) *television graphic designer*

**Daggett**
Bailey, Katherine Christine *artist, writer*

**Daly City**
Leong, Lam-Po (Lanbo Liang) *artist, educator*

**Dana Point**
Hodara, Eden *artist*

**Davis**
DePaoli, Geri M. *artist, art historian*
Petersen, Roland *artist, printmaker*

**Escondido**
Sternberg, Harry *artist*

**Fairfax**
Toney, Anthony *artist*

**Fallbrook**
Ragland, Jack Whitney *artist*

**Folsom**
Campbell, Ann Marie *artist*

**Fullerton**
Curran, Darryl Joseph *photographer, educator*
Woodhull, Patricia Ann *artist*

**Glen Ellen**
Anderson, Catherine *artist*

**Greenbrae**
Blatt, Morton Bernard *medical illustrator*

**Hayward**
Jordahl, Geir Arild *photographer, educator*
Jordahl, Kathleen Patricia (Kate Jordahl) *photographer, educator*
Ramos, Melvin John *artist, educator*

**Inverness**
Welpott, Jack Warren *photographer, educator*

**Irvine**
†Giannulli, Mossimo *designer, apparel business executive*

**Kelseyville**
Fletcher, Leland Vernon *artist*

**Kensington**
Loran, Erle *artist*

**Kingsburg**
Olson, Maxine Louise *artist, lecturer*

**La Canada Flintridge**
Drees, Elaine Hnath *artist and educator*

**La Jolla**
Antin, Eleanor *artist*
Cohen, Barbara Ann *artist*
Imana, Jorge Garron *artist*
Inverarity, Robert Bruce *artist*
Low, Mary Louise (Molly Low) *documentary photographer*
Merrim, Louise Meyerowitz *artist, actress*
Monaghan, Eileen *artist*
Silva, Ernest R. *visual arts educator, artist*
Whitaker, Eileen Monaghan *artist*

**La Quinta**
Barr, Roger Terry *sculptor*

**Lafayette**
Beaumont, Mona *artist*
Kapp, Eleanor Jeanne *impressionistic artist, writer, researcher*

**Laguna Beach**
Powers, Runa Skötte *artist*

**Laguna Niguel**
Apt, Charles *artist*
Pierce, Hilda (Hilda Herta Harmel) *painter*

**Lagunitas**
Holman, Arthur Stearns *artist*

**Larkspur**
Napoles, Veronica Kleeman *graphic designer, consultant*

**Long Beach**
Viola, Bill *artist, writer*

**Los Angeles**
Abeles, Kim Victoria *artist*
Anderson, Isabel *artist, educator*
Bangs, Cate (Cathryn Margaret Bangs) *film production designer, interior designer*
Bothwell, Dorr *artist*
Boyett, Joan Reynolds *arts administrator*
Caroompas, Carole Jean *artist, educator*
Chappel, Timothy Paul *costume designer*
Chen, Edna Lau *art educator, artist*
Ewing, Edgar Louis *artist, educator*
Frame, John Fayette *sculptor*
Galanos, James *fashion designer*
Hayes, Vertis Clemon *painter, sculptor, educator*
Hockney, David *artist*
Ida, Shoichi *painter, printmaker*
Johnston, Ynez *artist*
Ketchum, Robert Glenn *photographer, print maker*
Kienholz, Lyn Shearer *international arts projects coordinator*
Klausen, Raymond *sculptor, television and theatre production designer*
Lark, Raymond *artist, art scholar*
Layton, Harry Christopher *artist, lecturer, consultant, hypnotherapist, poet*
Lem, Richard Douglas *painter*
Manolakas, Stanton Peter *watercolor artist*
McAuley, Skeet *artist*
Miller, Harriet Sanders *art center director*
Natzler, Otto *ceramic artist*
Pederson, Con *animator*
Rankaitis, Susan *artist*
Saar, Alison *sculptor*
Smith, Alexis *artist, educator*
Tyler, Richard *fashion designer*
Welles, Melinda Fassett *artist, educator*
With, Gerda Becker *artist*
Woelffer, Emerson Seville *artist*
†Wyland, (Robert ) *artist*
Young, Joseph Louis *artist*

**Lucerne Valley**
Johnson, Jane Oliver *artist*

**Mariposa**
Bruce, John Anthony *artist*
Rogers, Earl Leslie *artist, educator*

**Mendocino**
Alexander, Joyce Mary *illustrator*

**Merced**
LeCocq, Karen Elizabeth *artist*

**Mill Valley**
Hahner, Linda R. R. *artist, creative director*

**Mission Hills**
Jones, John Harding *photographer*

**Mission Viejo**
Samuelson, Norma Graciela *architectural illustrator, artist*

**Modesto**
Bucknam, Mary Olivia Caswell *artist*

**Monterey**
Bowman, Dorothy Louise *artist*
Bradford, Howard *graphic artist, painter*

**Moraga**
Schmaltz, Roy Edgar, Jr. *artist, art educator*

**Morgan Hill**
Freimark, Robert (Bob Freimark) *artist*

**Napa**
Garnett, William *photographer*
Norman, Sheri Hanna *artist, educator, cartographer*

**Newport Beach**
Spitz, Barbara Salomon *artist*

**Norco**
Kromka, James Thomas Michael *designer, illustrator*

**North Hollywood**
Prince, Donna Jean *artist*

**Northridge**
Bassler, Robert Covey *artist, educator*

**Oakland**
Alba, Benny *artist*
Beasley, Bruce Miller *sculptor*
Bowen-Forbes, Jorge Courtney *artist, author, poet*
Brewster, Andrea B. *artist*
Dickinson, Eleanor Creekmore *artist, educator*
Frey, Viola *sculptor, educator*
Melchert, James Frederick *artist*
O'Hare, Marilynn Ryan *artist*
Okamura, Arthur *artist, educator, writer*
Rath, Alan T. *sculptor*

**Orinda**
Epperson, Stella Marie *artist*

**Pacific Palisades**
Chesney, Lee Roy, Jr. *artist*
Zamparelli, Elsa Maria Johanna Elisabeth *costume designer, art director*
Zivelonghi, Kurt Daniel *artist, painter*

**Palm Desert**
Moroles, Jesus Bautista *sculptor*

**Palo Alto**
Weakland, Anna Wu *artist, art educator*

**Pasadena**
Howe, Graham Lloyd *photographer, curator*
Newman, Joyce Kligerman *sculptor*
Pashgian, Margaret Helen *artist*
Zammitt, Norman *artist*

**Pebble Beach**
Mortensen, Gordon Louis *artist, printmaker*

**Petaluma**
McChesney, Robert Pearson *artist*
Reichek, Jesse *artist*

**Pinole**
Gerbracht, Robert Thomas (Bob Gerbracht) *painter, educator*

**Placentia**
Galvez, William *artist*

**Ramona**
Decker, George John *litigation photographer, videographer, journalist*

**Richmond**
Wessel, Henry *photographer*

**Riverside**
Smith, Dorothy Ottinger *jewelry designer, civic worker*

**Sacramento**
Couzens, Julia *artist*
Dalkey, Fredric Dynan *artist*

**San Diego**
Barone, Angela Maria *artist, researcher*
†Diaz, David *illustrator*
Lebadang *artist*
Linton, Roy Nathan *graphic arts company executive*
Sorrentino, Renate Maria *illustrator*

**San Francisco**
Allan, William George *painter, educator*
Autio, Rudy *artist educator*
Beall, Dennis Ray *artist, educator*
Bowers, Jack (John Burton Bowers, Jr.) *artist, graphics and digital color executive*
Buck, John *sculptor*
Buck, John E. *sculptor, print maker, educator*
Chin, Sue Soone Marian (Suchin Chin) *conceptual artist, portraitist, photographer, community affairs activist*
Gerzso, Gunther *painter, graphic artist*
Hershman, Lynn Lester *artist*
Hobbs, C. Fredric *artist, filmmaker, author*
Howard, David E. *artist*
Jones, Pirkle *photographer, educator*
Kehlmann, Robert *artist, critic*
Lobdell, Frank *artist*
Marioni, Tom *artist*
Martin, Fred *artist, college administrator*
Mayeri, Beverly *artist, ceramic sculptor, educator*
Muranaka, Hideo *artist, educator*
Piccolo, Richard Andrew *artist, educator*
Raciti, Cherie *artist*
Rascón, Armando *artist*
Salzman, Richard William *artists representative*
Stermer, Dugald Robert *designer, illustrator, writer, consultant*
Van Hoesen, Beth Marie *artist, printmaker*
Wall, Brian Arthur *sculptor*

**San Jose**
Ellner, Michael William *art educator*
Estabrook, Reed *artist, educator*
Gunther, Barbara *artist, educator*

**San Leandro**
Chilcoat, Dale Allen *artist, visual and performing arts educator*

**San Luis Obispo**
Dickerson, Colleen Bernice Patton *artist, educator*

**San Marino**
Medearis, Roger Norman *artist*

**San Mateo**
Xiong, Jean Z. *artist, consultant*

**San Pedro**
Crutchfield, William Richard *artist, educator*

**San Rafael**
Tift, Mary Louise *artist*

**Santa Barbara**
Eguchi, Yasu *artist*

**Santa Clara**
Lane, Holly Diana *artist*

**Santa Cruz**
Rydell, Amnell Roy *artist, landscape architect*
Summers, Carol *artist*

**Santa Monica**
Fukuhara, Henry *artist, educator*
Gilbert-Rolfe, Jeremy Denton *artist, art critic, educator*
Jenkins, George *stage designer, film art director*
Kaminski, Janusz Zygmuni *photographer*

**Santa Rosa**
Monk, Diana Charla *artist, stable owner*
Rider, Jane Louise *artist, educator*
†Wells, Annie *photographer*

**Saratoga**
Sherwood, Patricia Waring *artist, educator*

**Sausalito**
Kuhlman, Walter Egel *artist, educator*

**Sherman Oaks**
Weiss, Julie *costume designer*

**Sierra Madre**
Converse, Elizabeth Sheets *artist, writer*

**Solana Beach**
Dieffenbach, AliceJean *artist*

**Somis**
Kehoe, Vincent Jeffré-Roux *photographer, author, cosmetic company executive*

**Sonora**
Price, Joe (Allen) *artist, former educator*

**South Pasadena**
Askin, Walter Miller *artist, educator*
Zagon, Laurie *artist, writer, color consultant*

**Stockton**
Oak, Claire Morisset *artist, educator*

**Studio City**
Manders, Susan Kay *artist*
Wissner, Gary Charles *motion picture art director, production designer*

**Summerland**
Calamar, Gloria *artist*

**Sylmar**
Scheib, Gerald Paul *fine art educator, jeweler, metalsmith*

**Torrance**
Everts, Connor *artist*

**Tustin Ranch**
Ortlieb, Robert Eugene *sculptor*

**Upper Lake**
Twitchell, Kent *mural artist*

**Valencia**
Fiskin, Judith Anne *artist, educator*

**Van Nuys**
Corinblit, Nita Green *artist, educator*

**Venice**
Bengston, Billy Al *artist*
Chipman, Jack *artist*
Eversley, Frederick John *sculptor, engineer*
Hartley, Corinne *painter, sculptor, educator*

**Victorville**
Grogan, Suzann Jeanette-Wyman *artist*

**Walnut Creek**
Neacsu, Maria *artist*

**West Hills**
Freas, Frank Kelly *illustrator*

**Westlake Village**
Newman, Ruth Tantlinger *artist*

**Woodland**
Nye, Gene Warren *art educator*

**Woodland Hills**
Bonassi, Jodi *artist, marketing consultant*

**Woodside**
Gallaway, Marthine S. *artist*

**Yreka**
McFadden, Leon Lambert *artist, inventor*

## COLORADO

**Aspen**
Berkó, Ferenc *photographer*
Soldner, Paul Edmund *artist, ceramist, educator*

**Boulder**
Bolomey, Roger Henry *sculptor*
Chong, Albert Valentine *artist, educator*
Matthews, Eugene Edward *artist*
Matthews, Wanda Miller *artist*

**Colorado Springs**
Budd, Barbara Tews *sculptor*
Goehring, Kenneth *artist*

**Cortez**
Winterer-Schulz, Barbara Jean *art designer, author*

**Denver**
Enright, Cynthia Lee *illustrator*
Nesheim, Dennis Warren *art educator, artist, writer, instructional materials producer*
Norman, John Barstow, Jr. *designer, educator*

**Englewood**
Lamb, Darlis Carol *sculptor*

**Granby**
Rienhoff, Joanne Winkenwerder *artist*

**Larkspur**
Bierbaum, Janith Marie *artist*

**LaVeta**
Zehring, Peggy Johnson *artist*

**Littleton**
Barnes, Cloyd Ray *sculptor, retired engineer*

**Longmont**
Adams, Robert Hickman *photographer*
King, Jane Louise *artist*

**Louisville**
Day, Robert Edgar *retired artist, educator*
Qualley, Charles Albert *fine arts educator*

**Morrison**
Graham, Pamela Smith *artist, distributing company executive*

**Telluride**
Smith, Samuel David *artist, educator*

**Woodland Park**
Cockrille, Stephen *art director, business owner*

## CONNECTICUT

**Bethel**
Ajay, Abe *artist*

**Bloomfield**
Hammer, Alfred Emil *artist, educator*

**Brookfield**
Rowe, Edward Lawrence, Jr. *graphic designer*

**Colebrook**
Ash, Hiram Newton *graphic designer*

**Cornwall Bridge**
Pfeiffer, Werner Bernhard *artist, educator*

**Cos Cob**
Kane, Margaret Brassler *sculptor*
Neal, Irene Collins *artist, educator*

**Danbury**
Saghir, Adel Jamil *artist, painter, sculptor*

**East Hartford**
Soppelsa, George Nicholas Angelo *artist*

**Essex**
Curtis, Alva Marsh *artist*
Rooney, Maria Dewing *photographer*

**Fairfield**
Trager, Philip *photographer, lawyer*

**Falls Village**
Cronin, Robert Lawrence *sculptor, painter*

**Farmington**
Smith, Cary Christopher *artist*

**Georgetown**
Roberts, Priscilla Warren *artist*

**Greenwich**
Perless, Robert L. *sculptor*

**Hartford**
Glasson, Lloyd *sculptor, educator*
Menses, Jan *artist, draftsman, etcher, lithographer, muralist*
Uccello, Vincenza Agatha *artist, director, educator emerita*

**Madison**
Cappetta, Anna Maria *art educator*

**Meriden**
Bertolli, Eugene Emil *sculptor, goldsmith, designer, consultant*

**Middletown**
Baker, Lucy *artist*

**Monroe**
Wheatley, Sharman B. *art educator, artist*

**New Britain**
Kot, Marta Violette *artist, art educator*

**New Canaan**
Caesar, Henry A., II *sculptor*
Kovatch, Jak Gene *artist*
Rendl-Marcus, Mildred *artist, economist*
Richards, Walter DuBois *artist, illustrator*

**New Haven**
Bailey, William Harrison *artist, educator*
Johnson, Lester Fredrick *artist*
Lindroth, Linda (Linda Hammer) *artist, curator, writer*
Papageorge, Tod *photographer, educator*
Pease, David Gordon *artist, educator*

**Noank**
Bates, Gladys Edgerly *sculptor*

**Norwalk**
Babcock, Catherine Evans *artist, educator*
Glidden, Germain G. *artist*
Perry, Charles Owen *sculptor*

**Old Greenwich**
Kelley, Wendy Thue *fine art advisor, consultant*

**Old Lyme**
Chandler, Elisabeth Gordon (Mrs. Laci De Gerenday) *sculptor, harpist*
de Gerenday, Laci Anthony *sculptor*

**Redding**
Isley, Alexander Max *graphic designer, lecturer*

**Sherman**
Goodspeed, Barbara *artist*

**South Norwalk**
Rodriguez, Carmen Vila *artist, art educator, art historian*

**Stamford**
Koch, Robert *art educator*
Maruyama, Karl Satoru *graphic designer*
Rudman, Joan Eleanor *artist, educator*
Strosahl, William Austin *artist, art director*

**Storrs Mansfield**
Zelanski, Paul John *art educator, author*

**Voluntown**
Caddell, Foster *artist*

**Warren**
Abrams, Herbert E. *artist*
Gray, Cleve *artist*

**West Cornwall**
Prentice, Tim *sculptor, architect*
Simont, Marc *artist*

**Weston**
Bleifeld, Stanley *sculptor*
Cadmus, Paul *artist, etcher*
Reinker, Nancy Clayton Cooke *artist*

**Westport**
Chernow, Ann Levy *artist, art educator*
Chernow, Burt *artist, educator, writer*
Fisher, Leonard Everett *artist, writer, educator*
Kraus, Hilda *designer, artist*
Reilly, Anne Caulfield (Nancy Reilly) *painter*
Silk, George *photographer*

## DELAWARE

**Greenville**
Reynolds, Nancy Bradford duPont (Mrs. William Glasgow Reynolds) *sculptor*

**Hockessin**
Sawin, Nancy Churchman *art educator, artist, historian*

**New Castle**
Almquist, Don *illustrator, artist*

**Newark**
†Brown, Hilton *visual arts educator, artist*
Moss, Joe Francis *sculptor, painter*
Rowe, Charles Alfred *artist, designer, educator*

**Wilmington**
Bounds-Seemans, Pamella J. *artist*

## DISTRICT OF COLUMBIA

**Washington**
Blair, James Pease *photographer*
Brown, John Carter *art and education consultant, federal agency administrator*
Cleary, Manon Catherine *artist, educator*
Costigan, Constance Frances *artist, educator*
Danziger, Joan *sculptor*
DiPerna, Frank Paul *photographer, educator*
Donaldson, Jeff Richardson *visual artist, educator*
Forrester, Patricia Tobacco *artist*
Gossage, John Ralph *photographer*
Gumpert, Gunther *artist*
Krebs, Rockne *artist*
Millon, Henry Armand *fine arts educator, architectural historian*
Perlmutter, Jack *artist, lithographer*
Polan, Annette Lewis *artist*
Power, Mark *journalist, photographer, educator*
Shinolt, Eileen Thelma *artist*
Stamm, Geoffrey Eaton *arts administrator*
Stevenson, A. Brockie *artist*
Summerford, Ben Long *retired artist, educator*
Truitt, Anne Dean *artist*
Ulvestad, Anne Elizabeth *art director*

## FLORIDA

**Aventura**
Cerri, Robert Noel *photographer*

**Bal Harbour**
Bernay, Betti *artist*

**Boca Raton**
Amen, Irving *artist*
Langfield, Helen Elion *artist, radio commentator*
Ortlip, Mary Krueger *artist*
Ortlip, Paul Daniel *artist*
Russo, Kathleen Marie *art educator*

**Boynton Beach**
Birkenstock, Joyce Ann *artist*

**Bradenton**
Doenecke, Carol Anne *artist*
Hodgell, Robert Overman *artist, art educator*

**Coral Gables**
Bannard, Walter Darby *artist, art critic*

**Dania**
Abbott, Linda Joy *stained glass artisan, educator*

**Delray Beach**
Mills, Agnes Eunice Karlin *artist, printmaker, sculptor*
Ross, Beatrice Brook *artist*

**Englewood**
Morphew, Dorothy Richards-Bassett *artist, real estate broker*
Sisson, Robert F. *photographer, writer, lecturer, educator*

**Fernandina Beach**
D'Agnese, Helen Jean *artist*

**Fort Lauderdale**
Gillam, Paula Sample *artist, educator*

**Fort Myers**
Dean, Jean Beverly *artist*
Frank, Elizabeth Ahls *art educator, artist*
Schwartz, Carl Edward *artist, printmaker*

**Fort Pierce**
Cassens, Susan Forget *artist*

**Gainesville**
Kerslake, Kenneth Alvin *artist, printmaker, art educator*
Murray, Ernest Don *artist, educator*
Williams, Hiram Draper *artist, educator*

**Gulfport**
Marshall, Nathalie *artist, writer, educator*

**Hollywood**
Sadowski, Carol Johnson *artist*

**Holmes Beach**
Neustadt, Barbara Mae *artist, illustrator, etcher*

**Indian Harbor Beach**
Traylor, Angelika *stained glass artist*

**Islamorada**
Poons, Larry *artist*

**Jacksonville**
Eden, F(lorence) Brown *artist*
Mikulas, Joseph Frank *graphic designer, educator, painter*

**Key Largo**
Fundora, Thomas *artist, journalist, composer*

**Key West**
Barnard, Scott *artist consultant*

**Lake Park**
Heaton, Janet Nichols *artist, art gallery director*

**Lakeland**
Stark, Bruce Gunsten *artist*

**Margate**
Albert, Calvin *sculptor*

**Melrose**
Harley, Ruth *artist, educator*

**Miami**
Alexenberg, Mel *artist, art educator*
Hanna, Ronald Everette *art educator, consultant*
Morgan, Andrew Wesley *artist, educator*
Ralis, Paraskevy *art educator, artist*
Strickland, Thomas Joseph *artist*

**Naples**
Eldridge, David Carlton *art appraiser*

**New Smyrna**
Leeper, Doris Marie *sculptor, painter*

**North Miami**
Henry, John Raymond *sculptor*

**Odessa**
Broderick, Patrick Rodney *artist*

**Orlando**
Haxton, David *computer graphics educator, computer animator, photographer*
Renee, Lisabeth Mary *art educator, artist, galley director*
Terwilliger, Julia Anne *art educator, artist*
Warren, Dean Stuart *artist*

**Osprey**
Robinson, Sally Winston *artist*

**Palm Beach**
Kaplan, Muriel Sheerr *sculptor*
Krois, Audrey *artist*
Myers, Eugene Ekander *art consultant*
Wenzel, Joan Ellen *artist*

**Palm City**
Sloan, Richard *artist*

**Pensacola**
Albrecht, Carol Heath *artist, educator*

**Plant City**
Holland, Gene Grigsby (Scottie Holland) *artist*

**Plantation**
Ballantyne, Maree Anne Canine *artist*
Oxell, Loie Gwendolyn *fashion and beauty educator, consultant, columnist*

**Safety Harbor**
Banks, Allan Richard *artist, art historian, researcher*

**Saint Augustine**
Gilliland, Thomas *art gallery director*
Portman, Nancy Ann *artist, art educator*
Quirke, Lillian Mary *retired art educator*

**Saint Petersburg**
Ransom, Brian Charles *artist, educator, musician, composer*

**Sanibel**
Keogh, Mary Cudahy *artist*

**Sarasota**
Altabe, Joan Augusta Berg *artist, writer, art and architecture critic*
Burkett, Helen *artist*
Harmon, (Loren) Foster *art consultant*
Held, Philip *artist*
Krate, Nat *artist*
Putterman, Florence Grace *artist, printmaker*
Savenor, Betty Carmell *painter, printmaker*
Winterhalter, Dolores August (Dee Winterhalter) *art educator*

**Sebastian**
Pieper, Patricia Rita *artist, photographer*

**Tampa**
Cardoso, Anthony Antonio *artist, educator*
Wilson, Wallace *art educator, artist*

**Tarpon Springs**
Giavis, Theodore Demetrios *commercial illustrator, artist*

**Vero Beach**
Polan, Nancy Moore *artist*

**Winter Springs**
San Miguel, Manuel *painter, historian, composer, poet*

## GEORGIA

**Alpharetta**
Wu, Wayne Wen-Yau *artist*

**Athens**
Edison, Diane *artist, educator*
Herbert, James Arthur *artist, filmmaker*
Paul, William Dewitt, Jr. *artist, educator, photographer, museum director*

**Atlanta**
Alexander, Constance Joy (Connie Alexander) *stone sculptor*
Artemis, Maria *sculptor, educator*
Beattie, George *artist*
Callahan, Harry Morey *photographer*
Grumet, Priscilla Hecht *fashion specialist, consultant, writer*
Guberman, Sidney Thomas *painter, writer*
James, Rose Victoria *sculptor, poet*
Lucero, Michael *sculptor*
McLean, James Albert *artist, educator*

**Augusta**
Rosen, James Mahlon *artist, art historian, educator*

**Carrollton**
Barr, Mary Jeanette *art educator*
Romain, Bella Mary *graphic designer*

**Decatur**
Loehle, Betty Barnes *artist, painter*

**Macon**
Weaver, Jacquelyn Kunkel Ivey *artist, educator*

**Marietta**
Daresta, Pamela Beagle *artist*

**Mount Berry**
Mew, Thomas Joseph, III (Tommy Mew) *artist, educator*

**Peachtree City**
Robben, Mary Margaret *portrait artist*

**Powder Springs**
Collins, Lisa Diane *art educator*

**Roswell**
Dalia, Vesta Mayo *artist*
Huckeba, Karen Kaye *crafts designer, consultant*
Sherman, Ron *photographer*

**Savannah**
Alley, James Pinckney, Jr. *computer art and graphic design educator*
Aquadro, Jeana Lauren *graphic designer, educator*
Gabeler-Brooks, Jo *artist*

**Stone Mountain**
Brown, Jane Bowden *artist, educator*
Honea, Nance *artist, educator*

**Waycross**
Stock, Maxine *sculptor, librarian, art therapist*

## HAWAII

**Honolulu**
Amor, Simeon, Jr. *photographer*
Belknap, Jodi Parry *graphic designer, business owner, writer*
Betts, Barbara Stoke *artist, educator*
Chang, Rodney Eiu Joon *artist, dentist*
Guthrie, Edgar King *artist*
Pedesky, Geraldine Golick *design project professional*

**Kapaau**
Jankowski, Theodore Andrew *artist*

**Lahaina**
Killingsworth, Kathleen Nola *artist, photographer, company executive*
Sato, Tadashi *artist*

**Lihue**
Lai, Waihang *art educator*

## IDAHO

**Harrison**
Carlson, George Arthur *artist*

## ILLINOIS

**Carbondale**
Feldman, Joel Benet *artist, educator*

**Champaign**
Jackson, Billy Morrow *artist, retired art educator*
Kotoske, Roger Allen *artist, educator*

**Chicago**
Bender, Janet Pines *artist*
Boggess, Thomas Phillip, III *graphic arts company executive*
Bowman, Leah *fashion designer, consultant, photographer, educator*
Castillo, Mario Enrique *artist, educator*
Coffey, Susanna Jean *artist, educator*
Feeley, Henry Joseph, Jr. (Hank Feeley) *artist, former advertising agency executive*
Gehr, Mary *illustrator, painter, printmaker*
Gray, Richard *art dealer, consultant, holding company executive*
Heinecken, Robert Friedli *art educator, artist*
Himmelfarb, John David *artist*
Hoffman, William August *art educator*
Jachna, Joseph David *photographer, educator*
Josephson, Kenneth Bradley *artist, educator*
Kearney, John Walter *sculptor, painter*
King, Andre Richardson *architectural graphic designer*
Koga, Mary *artist, photographer, social worker*
Kolkey, Gilda P. *artist*
Lerner, Nathan Bernard *artist*
Look, Dona Jean *artist*
Marshall, Kerry James *artist*
Novak, Marlena *artist, educator, writer, curator*
Olson, Patricia Joanne *artist, educator*
Pallasch, Magdalena Helena (Mrs. Bernhard Michael Pallasch) *artist*
Paul, Arthur *artist, graphic designer, illustrator, art and design consultant*
Regensteiner, Else Friedsam (Mrs. Bertold Regensteiner) *textile designer, educator*
Sigler, Hollis *artist, educator*
Skrebneski, Victor *photographer*
Stanley, Robert Anthony *artist, educator*
Tessing, Louise Scire *graphic designer*
Wilson, Anne Gawthrop *artist, educator*
Workman, Robert Peter *artist, cartoonist*

**De Kalb**
Even, Robert Lawrence *art educator*
Rollman, Charlotte *artist, educator*

**Des Plaines**
Banach, Art John *graphic artist*

**Dixon**
Huber, Marianne Jeanne *art dealer*

**Edwardsville**
Malone, Robert Roy *artist, art educator*

**Evanston**
Conger, William Frame *artist, educator*
Nakoneczny, Michael Martin *artist*
Vanderstappen, Harrie Albert *Far Eastern art educator*

**Highland Park**
Slavick, Ann Lillian *art educator, arts*

**Hudson**
Mills, Frederick VanFleet *art educator, watercolorist*

**Lombard**
Ahlstrom, Ronald Gustin *artist*
Hudson, Samuel Campbell, Jr. *art educator, artist, sculptor*

**Park Forest**
Cribbs, Maureen Ann *artist, educator*

**River Forest**
Sloan, Jeanette Pasin *artist*
White, Philip Butler *artist*

**Riverside**
Howlett, Carolyn Svrluga *art educator*

**Scales Mound**
Lieberman, Archie *photographer, writer*

**Winnetka**
Lang, Lenore Schulman *visual artist*
Plowden, David *photographer*
Sharboneau, Lorna Rosina *artist, educator, author, poet, illustrator*

**Woodhull**
Lotspeich, Ellin Sue *art specialist, educator*

## INDIANA

**Bloomington**
Lowe, Marvin *artist*
Markman, Ronald *artist, educator*
O'Hearn, Robert Raymond *stage designer*
Stirratt, Betsy Alison *gallery director*
Wolin, Jeffrey Alan *artist*

**Evansville**
Roth, Carolyn Louise *art educator*

**Gary**
Rosen, Kay *painter*

**Indianapolis**
Block, Amanda Roth *artist*

**Madison**
Gunter, Frank Elliott *artist*

**Morgantown**
Boyce, Gerald G. *artist, educator*

**Muncie**
Connally, Sandra Jane Oppy *art educator*

**Notre Dame**
Lauck, Anthony Joseph *artist, retired art educator, priest*

**Purdue University**
Bannatyne, Mark William McKenzie *technical graphics educator*

**Richmond**
Ronald, Pauline Carol *art educator*

**Terre Haute**
Lamis, Leroy *artist, retired educator*

**Valparaiso**
Olson, Lynn *sculptor, painter, writer*

**West Lafayette**
Ichiyama, Dennis Yoshihide *design educator, consultant*

## IOWA

**Bettendorf**
Herdman, Susan *art educator, artist*

**Davenport**
Jecklin, Lois Underwood *art corporation executive, consultant*

**Des Moines**
Reece, Maynard Fred *artist, author*

**Grinnell**
Cervene, Richard T. *art educator*

**Iowa City**
Schmidt, Julius *sculptor*
Stratton, Margaret Mary *art educator*

## KANSAS

**Lawrence**
Papanek, Victor *designer, educator, writer*

**Liberal**
Rosel, Carol Ann *artist*

**Ottawa**
Howe, William Hugh *artist*

**Topeka**
Menninger, Rosemary Jeanetta *art educator, writer*

## KENTUCKY

**Lexington**
Boyer, Lillian Buckley *artist, educator*
Henderson, Hubert Platt *fine arts association executive*
Sandoval, Arturo Alonzo *art educator, artist*
Snowden, Ruth O'Dell Gillespie *artist*

## LOUISIANA

**Covington**
Rohrbough, Elsa Claire Hartman *artist*

**Houma**
Babin, Regina-Champagne *artist, educator, consultant*

**Lake Charles**
Dentler, Anne Lillian *artist*

**Metairie**
Burshell, Sandra *artist*

**New Orleans**
Bailey, Barry Stone sculptor, educator
Lovejoy, Barbara Campbell sculptor, architectural designer
O'Meallie, Kitty artist
Simons, Dona artist
Thornell, Jack Randolph photographer
Weiss, Susette Marie technical consultant, specialist in imaging

**Shreveport**
Hughes, Mary Sorrows artist
Wray, Geraldine Smitherman (Jerry Wray) artist

**Slidell**
Bishop, Mary Lou artist

## MAINE

**Alfred**
Benson, S. Patricia artist, educator

**Bath**
Webb, Todd (Charles Clayton Webb) photographer, writer

**Boothbay Harbor**
Cavanaugh, Tom Richard artist, antiques dealer, retired art educator
Eames, John Heagan etcher
Grossman, Morton S. artist

**Cushing**
Magee, A. Alan artist

**Damariscotta**
Robinson, Walter George arts management and funding consultant

**East Boothbay**
Peters, Andrea Jean artist

**Georgetown**
Ipcar, Dahlov illustrator, painter, author

**Gorham**
Bearce, Jeana Dale artist, educator

**Jefferson**
Fiore, Joseph Albert artist

**Kennebunk**
Betts, Edward artist

**Lincolnville**
Pattison, Abbott Lawrence sculptor

**Monhegan Island**
Hudson, Jacqueline artist

**New Harbor**
Lyford, Cabot sculptor

**Port Clyde**
Thon, William artist

**Rangeley**
Conwill, Joseph Dillard photographer

**Scarborough**
Warg, Pauline artist, educator

**South Portland**
Huntoon, Abby Elizabeth artist, teacher

**Wells**
Hero, Barbara Ferrell visual and sound artist, writer

**Wiscasset**
Leslie, Seaver artist

**York**
Hallam, Beverly (Beverly Linney) artist

**York Beach**
Davison, Nancy Reynolds artist

## MARYLAND

**Annapolis**
Alderdice, Cynthia Lou artist
Fowler, Terri (Marie Therese Fowler) artist
Koscianski, Leonard Joseph artist

**Arnold**
Kellogg-Smith, Peter educator, sculptor, inventor

**Baltimore**
Bryan, Sukey artist
Carper, Gertrude Esther artist, marina owner
Hartigan, Grace artist
Mericle, Sally Diane graphic artist
Rothschild, Amalie Rosenfeld artist

**Bethesda**
Day, Marylouise Muldoon (Mrs. Richard Dayton Day) appraiser
Kranking, Margaret Graham artist
Safer, John artist, lecturer
Sarnoff, Lili-Charlotte Dreyfus (Lolo Sarnoff) artist, business executive

**Centreville**
Amos, James Lysle photographer

**Chevy Chase**
Asher, Lila Oliver artist
Duvall, Bernice Bettum artist, exhibit coordinator, jewelry designer
Kainen, Jacob artist, former museum curator

**College Park**
DeMonte, Claudia Ann artist, educator

**Lapinski, Tadeusz Andrew** artist, educator

**Columbia**
Blackwell, Camellia Ann art educator

**Gaithersburg**
Bochicchio, Jill Arden photographer

**Hagerstown**
Paxton, Alice Adams artist, architect, interior designer

**Hyattsville**
Raines, Charlotte Austine Butler artist, poet

**North East**
Marie, Linda artist, photographer

**Owings**
Oring, Stuart August visual information specialist, writer, photographer

**Owings Mills**
Kissel, William Thorn, Jr. sculptor

**Potomac**
Keil, Marilyn Martin artist

**Silver Spring**
Barkin, Robert Allan graphic designer, newspaper executive, consultant
Peiperl, Adam kinetic sculptor, photographer

**Upper Fairmount**
Dougherty, Barbara Lee artist, writer

## MASSACHUSETTS

**Amherst**
Hendricks, James Powell artist
Lasch, Pat artist, educator
Liebling, Jerome photographer, educator
Yarde, Richard Foster art educator

**Andover**
Lloyd, Robert Andrew art educator

**Ashland**
Gohlke, Frank William photographer

**Beverly**
Ghen, Edythe Solberg artist

**Boston**
Ablow, Joseph artist, educator
Avison, David photographer
Fink, Aaron artist
Gibran, Kahlil sculptor
Grassl, Anton Maria artist
Handford, Martin John illustrator, author
Parker, Olivia photographer
Preston, Malcolm artist, art critic
Stone, James J. photographer
†Wiesner, David illustrator, children's writer
Yanoff, Arthur Samuel artist, art therapist

**Braintree**
Conlon, Eugene artist, administrator

**Brookfield**
Couture, Ronald David art administrator, design consultant

**Brookline**
Barron, Ros artist
Schiller, Sophie artist, graphic designer
Swan, Barbara artist
Wilson, John artist

**Burlington**
DeCrosta, Susan Elyse graphic designer

**Cambridge**
Ackerman, James Sloss fine arts educator
Alcalay, Albert S. artist, design educator
Bakanowsky, Louis Joseph visual arts educator, architect, artist
Bapst, Sarah artist, educator
Feininger, Theodore Lux artist
Hadzi, Dimitri sculptor, educator
Mazur, Michael artist
Mc Kie, Todd Stoddard artist
Piene, Otto artist, educator
Reimann, William Page artist, educator

**Chilmark**
Geyer, Harold Carl artist, writer
Low, Joseph artist

**Concord**
Ihara, Michio sculptor

**East Falmouth**
Selman, Jan Collins artist

**Gloucester**
Curtis, Roger William artist, educator
Duca, Alfred Milton artist
Hancock, Walker Kirtland sculptor

**Hull**
Burgess, David Lowry artist

**Leeds**
Baskin, Leonard sculptor, graphic artist

**Lenox**
LiMarzi, Joseph artist

**Lowell**
Sullivan, Anne Dorothy Hevner artist

**Lynn**
Denzler, Nancy J. artist

**Manchester**
Lothrop, Kristin Curtis sculptor

**Marblehead**
Heins, Esther botanical artist, painter

**Montague**
Coughlin, Jack printmaker, sculptor, art educator

**Natick**
Geller, Esther (Bailey Geller) artist
Morgan, Betty Mitchell artist, educator

**Needham**
Carr, Iris Constantine artist, writer

**Newtonville**
Polonsky, Arthur artist, educator

**North Attleboro**
Cote, Louise Roseann creative director, designer

**North Brookfield**
Neal, Avon artist, author
Parker, Ann (Ann Parker Neal) photographer, graphic artist

**North Eastham**
DeMuth, Vivienne Blake McCandless artist, illustrator
Simmel, Marianne Lenore graphic designer

**Northampton**
Rupp, Sheron Adeline photographer, educator

**Norwell**
Brett, Jan Churchill illustrator, author
Wentworth, Murray Jackson artist, educator

**Orange**
Bate, Judith Ellen artist

**Orleans**
Lawton, Nancy artist

**Peabody**
Dee, Pauline Marie artist

**Plymouth**
Joseph, Rodney Randy artist, arts society executive

**Provincetown**
Harmon, Lily artist, author

**Rockport**
Nicholas, Thomas Andrew artist
Strisik, Paul artist

**Sharon**
Kahn, Marilyn Zeldin artist, art educator

**Sherborn**
Pickhardt, Carl Emile, Jr. artist

**Somerville**
Halevi, Marcus photographer

**South Dartmouth**
Backes, Joan artist

**Springfield**
Frey, Mary Elizabeth artist

**Sudbury**
Aronson, David artist, retired art educator
Nyman, Georgianna Beatrice painter

**Topsfield**
Webster, Larry Russell artist

**Vineyard Haven**
McIntosh, Jon Charles illustrator

**Walpole**
Hunter, Elizabeth Ives-Valsam fashion consultant

**Waltham**
Bohlen, Nina artist

**Wayland**
Dergalis, George artist, educator

**Wellesley**
O'Gorman, James Francis art educator, writer

**West Brookfield**
Higgins, Brian Alton art gallery executive

**Westport**
Somerson, Rosanne artist

**Westwood**
Philbrick, Margaret Elder artist

**Winchester**
Neuman, Robert Sterling art educator, artist

## MICHIGAN

**Ann Arbor**
Cassara, Frank artist, printmaker
Kamrowski, Gerome artist
Weddige, Emil Albert lithographer, art educator

**Birmingham**
Ashleigh, Caroline art and antiques appraiser
Ortman, George Earl artist

**Brethren**
Crandell, Deborah Lynne Kaskinen art educator

**Capac**
Wagner, Dorothy Marie retired senior creative designer, artist

**Commerce Township**
Wager, Paula Jean artist

**Dearborn**
Cape, James Odies E. fashion designer

**Detroit**
Kachadoorian, Zubel artist, educator
McWhorter, Sharon Louise business executive, inventor, consultant
Moldenhauer, Judith A. graphic design educator

**East Lansing**
Berding, Thomas George art educator
Leepa, Allen artist, educator

**Farmington Hills**
Donald, Edward Milton, Jr. graphic designer

**Glenn**
Rizzolo, Louis B. M. artist, educator

**Grand Rapids**
Blovits, Larry John retired art educator
Bolt, Eunice Mildred DeVries artist

**Harsens Island**
Slade, Roy artist, college president, museum director

**Howell**
Watkins, Curtis Winthrop artist

**Lake Ann**
Monteith, Clifton James artist

**Plainwell**
Flower, Jean Frances art educator

**Port Huron**
Rowark, Maureen fine arts photographer

**Riverdale**
Kirby, Kent Bruce artist, educator

**Roseville**
Geck, Francis Joseph furniture designer, educator, author

**Royal Oak**
Eisner, Gail Ann artist, educator
Fredericks, Marshall Maynard sculptor

**Wyandotte**
Dunn, Gloria Jean artist

## MINNESOTA

**Duluth**
Chee, Cheng-Khee artist

**Edina**
Saltzman, William painter, sculptor, designer

**Mankato**
Frink, Brian Lee artist, educator

**Minneapolis**
Hallman, Gary L. photographer, educator
Larkin, Eugene David artist, educator
Myers, Malcolm Haynie artist, art educator
Preuss, Roger E(mil) artist
Rose, Thomas Albert artist, art educator
Weinberger, Adrienne artist

**Northfield**
Lloyd, Timothy L. art educator

**Saint Paul**
Bloch, Ricardo Adrian visual artist
Matteson, Clarice Chris artist, educator

## MISSISSIPPI

**Belzoni**
Halbrook, Rita Robertshaw artist, sculptor

**Meridian**
Marshall, John Steven artist, educator, museum administrator

## MISSOURI

**Columbia**
Larson, Sidney art educator, artist, writer, painting conservator

**Des Peres**
Smith, Barbara Martin art educator

**Hermann**
Mahoney, Catherine Ann artist, educator

**Kansas City**
Bransby, Eric James muralist, educator
Lee, Margaret Norma artist
Mast, Kande White artist

**Rogersville**
Davis, Evelyn Marguerite Bailey artist, organist, pianist

**Saint Louis**
Burkett, Randy James lighting designer
Duhme, H(erman) Richard, Jr. sculptor, educator
Dunivent, John Thomas artist, educator
Pulitzer, Emily S. Rauh (Mrs. Joseph Pulitzer, Jr.) art consultant

**Springfield**
Delaney, Jean Marie art educator
King, (Jack) Weldon photographer

**Webster Groves**
Osver, Arthur artist

## MONTANA

**Billings**
Butterfield, Deborah Kay sculptor
Deschner, Jane Waggoner collage artist, public relations consultant

**Bozeman**
Hoffman, Franklin Thomas artist, printmaker, retired army officer

**Helena**
Clarkson, Robert Noel commercial photographer, magician

**Hot Springs**
Erickson, James Gardner retired artist, cartoonist

**Missoula**
Rippon, Thomas Michael art educator, artist

## NEBRASKA

**Auburn**
Biggerstaff, Myra artist, designer, educator

**Kearney**
Hoffman, M. Kathy graphic designer, packaging designer

**Omaha**
Spencer, Jeffrey Paul art educator

## NEVADA

**Carson City**
Alcorn, Karen Zefting Hogan artist, art educator, analyst

**Henderson**
Turner, Florence Frances ceramist

**Reno**
Harder, Kelsie T. artist, educator
Newberg, Dorothy Beck (Mrs. William C. Newberg) portrait artist
Waddell, Theodore painter

## NEW HAMPSHIRE

**Exeter**
Dailey, Daniel Owen artist, educator, designer

**Hancock**
Pollaro, Paul Philip artist

**Hanover**
Boghosian, Varujan Yegan sculptor
Moss, Ben Frank, III art educator, painter

**Salem**
Flanagan, Anne Patricia art educator, artist

## NEW JERSEY

**Asbury**
Konrad, Adolf Ferdinand artist

**Basking Ridge**
Frediani, Diane Marie graphic designer, interior designer

**Bayonne**
Gorman, William David artist, graphic artist
Searle, Ronald artist

**Bernardsville**
Coheleach, Guy Joseph artist
Spofford, Sally Hyslop artist

**Blairstown**
Bean, Bennett artist

**Bridgewater**
Glesmann, Sylvia-Maria artist
Patton, Diana Lee Wilkoc artist

**Califon**
Rosen, Carol Mendes artist

**Chatham**
Glover, Janet Briggs artist

**Closter**
Soroka, Cynthia Anne photographer, writer

**Cresskill**
Smyth, Craig Hugh fine arts educator

**Denville**
Coes, Kent Day artist

**Edison**
Behr, Marion Ray artist, author

**Englewood**
Anuszkiewicz, Richard Joseph artist
Casarella, Edmond sculptor, printmaker
Grom, Bogdan sculptor, painter, illustrator

**Fair Lawn**
Parker, Adrienne Natalie art educator, art historian

**Freehold**
Flynn, Pamela artist, educator

**Hightstown**
Howard, Barbara Sue Mesner artist
Raichle, Elaine Lucas retired art educator

**Hoboken**
Rose, Roslyn artist

**Holmdel**
Slovik, Sandra Lee art educator

**Iselin**
Tice, George A(ndrew) photographer

**Jersey City**
Gurevich, Grigory visual artist, educator
Hakeem, Muhammad Abdul artist, educator

**Keasbey**
Hari, Kenneth Stephen painter, sculptor, writer

**Keyport**
Graupe-Pillard, Grace artist, educator

**Long Branch**
Stamaty, Clara Gee Kastner artist

**Manalapan**
Hurley, Anne Irène medical illustrator

**Marlton**
Cullen, Mary Lynne artist

**Mercerville**
Pitynski, Andrzej Piotr sculptor

**Milford**
Carter, Clarence Holbrook artist

**Montclair**
Beerman, Miriam artist, educator

**Morristown**
Prince, Leah Fanchon art educator and research institute administrator

**New Brunswick**
Goffen, Rona art educator
Goodyear, John Lake artist, educator
Ortiz, Raphael Montañez performance artist, educator

**Park Ridge**
De Pol, John artist

**Pemberton**
Witkin, Isaac sculptor

**Penns Grove**
Reilley, James Clark artist, cartoonist, small business owner

**Phillipsburg**
Richards, Jay Claude commercial photographer, news service executive, historian

**Piscataway**
Young, James Earl ceramics educator, educational administrator

**Princeton**
Bunnell, Peter Curtis photography and art educator, museum curator
George, Thomas artist
Grabar, Oleg art educator
Seawright, James L., Jr. sculptor, educator
Wilmerding, John art history educator, museum curator

**Ringwood**
Day, Ann Elizabeth artist, educator

**Roosevelt**
Landau, Jacob artist

**Rumson**
Cocker, Barbara Joan marine artist, interior designer

**Rutherford**
Petrie, Ferdinand Ralph illustrator, artist

**Short Hills**
Good, Joan Duffey artist

**Shrewsbury**
Abel, Mary Elizabeth art educator, artist

**Sparta**
Seaman, Emma Lucy artist, poet

**Springfield**
DeVone, Denise artist, educator

**Stillwater**
Finkelstein, Louis retired art educator

**Stockton**
Mahon, Robert photographer
Schoenherr, John (Carl) artist, illustrator
Taylor, Rosemary artist

**Summit**
Rousseau, Irene Victoria artist, sculptor

**Tenafly**
Heghinian, Elizabeth Alban Trumbower artist, educator
Koons, Irvin Louis design and marketing executive, graphic artist, consultant

**Trenton**
Brearley, Candice fashion designer
Chavooshian, Marge artist, educator

**Ventnor City**
Robbins, Hulda Dornblatt artist, printmaker

**Verona**
Ayaso, Manuel artist

**Waldwick**
Samuelson, Billie Margaret artist

**Wayne**
Katz, Leandro artist, filmmaker

**West Orange**
Schreiber, Eileen Sher artist

**West Paterson**
Seiffer, Neil Mark photographer

**Whippany**
Petitto, Barbara Buschell artist

**Whiting**
Case, Elizabeth artist, writer

## NEW MEXICO

**Albuquerque**
Adams, Clinton artist, historian
Antreasian, Garo Zareh artist, lithographer, art educator
Aubin, Barbara Jean artist
Barrow, Thomas Francis artist, educator
Coleman, Barbara McReynolds artist
Culpepper, Mabel Claire artist
Hahn, Betty artist, photographer, educator
Hovel, Esther Harrison art educator
Lee-Smith, Hughie artist, educator
Multhaup, Merrel Keyes artist
Nagatani, Patrick Allan Ryoichi artist, art educator
Witkin, Joel-Peter photographer

**Arroyo Hondo**
Davis, Ronald artist, printmaker

**Corona**
Steen, Nancy artist

**Corrales**
Eaton, Pauline artist

**Galisteo**
Holt, Nancy Louise artist

**Las Cruces**
Ritter, Sallie painter, sculptor

**Ranchos De Taos**
Marx, Nicki Diane sculptor, painter

**Roswell**
Avery, Keith Willette artist, educator
Wiggins, Kim Douglas artist, art dealer

**Santa Fe**
Allen, Terry artist
Barrett, Bill sculptor
Burk, Yvonne Turner artist, educator
Clift, William Brooks, III photographer
Dechert, Peter photographer, writer, foundation administrator
Erdman, Barbara visual artist
Longley, Bernique artist, painter, sculptor
Loriaux, Maurice Lucien artist, ecclesiologist
Scheinbaum, David photography educator
Shubart, Dorothy Louise Tepfer artist, educator
Steinke, Bettina artist
Sturgen, Winston photographer, printmaker, artist

**Taos**
Bell, Larry Stuart artist
Martin, Agnes artist

## NEW YORK

**Afton**
Schwartz, Aubrey Earl artist

**Alfred**
Billeci, Andre George art educator, sculptor
Higby, (Donald) Wayne artist, educator

**Amityville**
Banks, Marilyn Kellogg sculptor

**Ancramdale**
Weinstein, Joyce artist

**Annandale On Hudson**
Sullivan, Jim artist

**Ardsley**
Sokolow, Isobel Folb sculptor

**Armonk**
Elson, Charles stage designer, educator

**Babylon**
Haley, Priscilla Jane artist, printmaker

**Bedford**
Weinman, Robert Alexander sculptor

**Bedford Hills**
Jensen-Carter, Philip Scott advertising and architectural photographer, medical photographer

**Bloomington**
Ruffing, Anne Elizabeth artist

**Bridgehampton**
Jackson, Lee artist

**Bronx**
Adams, Alice sculptor
Kassoy, Hortense (Honey Kassoy) artist
Kitt, Olga artist
Pearlman, Barbara artist, educator
Schwam, Marvin Albert graphic design company executive

**Brooklyn**
Allman, Avis Louise artist, Turkish and Islamic culture educator
Amendola, Sal John artist, educator, writer
Battle, Turner Charles, III art educator, educational association administrator
Bosman, Richard painter, printmaker
Carlile, Janet Louise artist, educator
Colker, Edward artist, educator
Cornell, Thomas Browne artist, educator
Daley, Sandra Dakota retired artist, filmmaker, photographer
Delson, Elizabeth artist
Dinnerstein, Harvey artist
Dinnerstein, Simon Abraham artist, educator
Grado, Angelo John artist
Jones, Susan Emily fashion educator, administrator, educator
Lederman, Stephanie Brody artist
Pearlstein, Seymour artist
Peker, Elya Abel artist
Rocco, Ron artist
Schaefer, Marilyn Louise artist, writer, educator
Scherer, Suzanne Marie artist, educator
Shechter, Ben-Zion artist, illustrator
Shechter, Laura Judith artist
Silverstein, Louis art director, designer, editor
Sonenberg, Jack artist
von Rydingsvard, Ursula Karoliszyn sculptor
Zakanitch, Robert Rahway artist

**Buffalo**
Krims, Leslie Robert photographer, art educator
Piccillo, Joseph artist
Rogovin, Milton photographer, retired optometrist
St. Pierre, Cheryl Ann art educator

**Buskirk**
Johanson, Patricia Maureen artist, architect, park designer

**Campbell Hall**
Greenly, Colin artist

**Canaan**
Walker, William Bond painter, retired librarian

**Clarence**
Hubler, Julius artist

**Climax**
Adler, Lee artist, educator, marketing executive

**Corning**
Buechner, Thomas Scharman artist, retired glass manufacturing company executive, museum director

**Cornwall On Hudson**
Abrams-Collens, Vivien artist
Grant, Joanne Catherine auctioneer, fine art appraiser

**Croton On Hudson**
Rubinfien, Leo H. photographer, filmmaker

**Cutchogue**
Dank, Leonard Dewey medical illustrator, audio-visual consultant

**Deer Park**
Martone, Jeanette Rachele artist

**Douglaston**
Costa, Ernest Fiorenzo graphic designer

**East Hampton**
Jaudon, Valerie artist
Praetorius, William Albert, Sr. artist, former advertising and real estate executive
Richenburg, Robert Bartlett artist, retired art educator
Scott, Rosa Mae artist, educator
Stein, Ronald Jay artist, airline transport pilot

**East Islip**
Rogers, Jeanne Valerie art educator, artist

**Elmhurst**
Wachsteter, George illustrator

**Flushing**
Bruder, Harold Jacob artist, educator
Carlson, Cynthia Joanne artist, educator
Goldstein, Milton art educator, printmaker, painter
Laderman, Gabriel artist
Nicotra, Joseph Charles artist

**Fly Creek**
Dusenbery, Walter Condit sculptor

**Forest Hills**
Baral, Lillian artist, retired educator
Crystal, Boris artist
Immerman, Mia Fendler artist
Tewi, Thea sculptor

**Franklin Square**
Indiviglia, Salvatore Joseph artist, retired naval officer

**Freeport**
Terris, Albert metal sculptor

**Great Neck**
Seidler, Doris artist

**Greenvale**
Leipzig, Arthur photographer, educator emeritus

**Hartsdale**
Brozak-McMann, Edith May performing and visual artist

**Hawthorne**
Sandbank, Henry photographer, film director

**Hillsdale**
Richards, Joseph Edward artist

**Holland**
Blair, Robert Noel artist

**Hoosick Falls**
Hatfield, David Underhill artist

**Hudson**
Avedisian, Edward artist

**Hudson Falls**
Leary, Daniel artist

**Huntington**
Maglione, Lili fine artist, art consultant
Twardowicz, Stanley Jan artist, photographer

**Irvington**
Holden, Donald artist, author

**Ithaca**
Grippi, Salvatore William artist
Mikus, Eleanore Ann artist
Poleskie, Stephen Francis artist, educator, writer
Squier, Jack Leslie sculptor, educator

**Jackson Heights**
Schiavina, Laura Margaret artist
Schuyler, Jane fine arts educator

**Jamaica**
Jones, Cynthia Teresa Clarke artist
Zenbopwe, (Walter Cade), III artist, musician, singer, actor

**Jamestown**
David, Christine A. artist, marketing consultant

**Jeffersonville**
Craft, Douglas Durwood artist
Finn, David Thurman artist, sculptor
Harms, Elizabeth Louise artist
Wooddell, Philo Glenn fine arts educator, radio broadcaster and producer

**Katonah**
Giobbi, Edward Giacchino artist

**Larchmont**
Tobey, Alton Stanley artist

**Lawrence**
Sklarin, Ann H. artist

**Lockwood**
McMahon, Maria Driscoll artist

**Locust Valley**
DeRegibus, William artist
Lippold, Richard sculptor

**Long Island City**
Donneson, Seena Sand artist
Gussow, Roy sculptor, educator
Villinski, Paul Stephen artist

**Lynbrook**
Amorosi, Teresa artist

**Mamaroneck**
Pugh, Grace Huntley artist

**Marcellus**
Baker, Bruce Roy retired art educator, artist

**Merrick**
Cariola, Robert Joseph artist

**Middle Village**
Meyers, Edward photographer, writer, publisher

**Middletown**
Blumenthal, Fritz printmaker, painter

**Monroe**
Karen, Linda Tricarico fashion designer

**Montour Falls**
Stillman, Joyce L. artist, educator, writer, illustrator, consultant

**New Paltz**
Schneemann, Carolee painter, performing artist, filmmaker, writer

**New Rochelle**
Mallary, Robert sculptor
Nienburg, George Frank photographer
Slotnick, Mortimer H. artist

**New York**
Abboud, Joseph M. fashion designer
Abeles, Sigmund M. artist, printmaker
Abish, Cecile artist
Abularach, Rodolfo Marco Antonio artist
Adam, Ken production designer
Adams, Dennis Paul artist
Adams, Edward Thomas (Eddie Adams) photographer
Adri, (Adrienne Steckling) fashion designer
Adrian, Barbara (Mrs. Franklin C. Tramutola) artist
Allard, Linda Marie fashion designer
Allner, Walter Heinz designer, painter, art director
Alpert, William Harold artist
Alten, Jerry art director
Altman, Harold artist educator
Andre, Carl sculptor
Anthony, William Graham artist
Antonakos, Stephen sculptor
Antupit, Samuel Nathaniel art director
Applebroog, Ida artist
Aptekar, Ken painter
Arcilesi, Vincent Jasper artist
Armstrong, Jane Botsford sculptor
Avedon, Richard photographer
Baechler, Donald painter
Baranik, Rudolf artist
Barnes, Jhane Elizabeth fashion design company executive, designer
Barnet, Will artist, educator
Barrasi, Susan artist
Bartle, Annette Gruber (Mrs. Thomas R. Bartle) artist, writer, photographer
Bartlett, Jennifer Losch artist
Barton, John Murray artist, appraiser, consultant, lecturer
Baumgardner, Matthew Clay artist
Beal, Jack artist
Beck, Rosemarie artist, educator
Bellin, Milton Rockwell artist
Benglis, Lynda artist, sculptor
Ben-Haim, Zigi artist
Berlind, Robert Elliot artist
Berman, Ariane R. artist
Bernard, Walter art director
Bernstein, Theresa artist
Berthot, Jake artist
Bhavsar, Natvar Prahladji artist
†Billington, Ken lighting designer
Blanc, Peter (William Peters Blanc) sculptor, painter
Blechman, R. O. artist, filmmaker
Block, John Douglas auction house executive
Boardman, Seymour artist
Bohnen, Blythe artist
Bonino, Fernanda art dealer
Boutis, Tom artist, painter, print maker
Brach, Paul Henry artist
Bradley, Lisa M. artist
Brandt, Warren artist
Brett, Nancy Heléne artist
Brown, Christopher artist
Bunts, Frank Emory artist
Burke, Mary Griggs (Mrs. Jackson Burke) art collector
Burlingame, Lloyd Lamson design instructor
Cajori, Charles Florian artist, educator
Campbell, Ronald Neil magazine designer
Carnase, Thomas Paul graphic designer, typographic consultant
Casebere, James Edward artist
Casella, Margaret Mary artist, photographer
Castoro, Rosemarie sculptor
Cesarani, Sal fashion designer
†Chase, Doris Totten sculptor, video artist, filmmaker
Chen, Chi (Chen Chi) artist
Chermayeff, Ivan graphic designer
Chia, Sandro painter
Christo, (Christo Vladimirov Javacheff) artist
Chwast, Seymour graphic artist
Clarke, John Clem artist
Clemente, Francesco artist
Cohen, Arthur Morris artist
Cohen, Cora artist
Cole, Max artist
Cole, Sylvan, Jr. art dealer
Colp, Norman Barry photographic artist, curator
Conover, Robert Fremont artist, educator
Cooper, Paula art dealer
Cortor, Eldzier artist, printmaker
Costa, Victor Charles fashion designer
Cowles, Charles art dealer
Cutler, Ronnie artist
Dallmann, Daniel F. artist, educator
Dana, F(rank) Mitchell theatrical lighting designer
Daphnis, Nassos artist
Davidovich, Jaime video artist, researcher
Davidson, Nancy Brachman artist, educator
Davis, Stephen Arnold artist, educator
de Champlain, Vera Chopak artist, painter
Deem, George artist
De Forest, Roy Dean artist, sculptor
de la Renta, Oscar fashion designer
†Demaria, Walter sculptor
Denhof, Miki graphic designer
Dennis, Donna Frances sculptor, art educator
des Rioux, Deena Victoria Coty artist, graphics designer
Dill, Lesley sculptor
Di Meo, Dominick artist, sculptor, painter
Dintenfass, Terry art dealer
Dobbs, John Barnes artist, educator
Dodd, Lois artist, art professor
Donati, Enrico artist
Drasler, Gregory John artist
Drexler, Joanne Lee art appraiser
Drucker, Mort commercial artist
Duff, John Ewing sculptor
Dunkelman, Loretta artist
Dyyon, Frazier (LeRoy Frazier) artist
Edelson, Mary Beth artist, educator
Egielski, Richard illustrator
Eins, Stefan painter, conceptual artist, arts curator, sculptor
Eisenberg, Sonja Miriam artist
Elder, Eldon stage designer, theatre consultant
Eliot, Lucy artist
Elliott, Inger McCabe designer, textile company executive, consultant
Elman, Naomi Geist artist, producer
Enders, Elizabeth McGuire artist
Escobar, Marisol sculptor
Estes, Richard artist
Faurer, Louis photographer
Feigen, Richard L. art dealer
Feininger, Andreas Bernhard Lyonel photographer
Findlay, Michael Alistair auction house executive, poet
Fischer, Carl graphic designer, photographer
Fleischman, Lawrence Arthur art dealer, publisher, consultant
Forbes, Colin Ames graphic design consultant
Foster, Kim art dealer, gallery owner
Fredericks, Wendy Ann graphic designer
Freeman, Elaine Lavalle sculptor
Freeman, Mark artist
French, Stephanie Taylor arts administrator
Frumkin, Allan art dealer
Fugate-Wilcox, Tery artist
Gechtoff, Sonia artist
Geismar, Thomas H. graphic designer
Geissbuhler, Stephan graphic designer
Georges, Paul Gordon artist
Gibson, Ralph H(olmes) photographer
Gisondi, John Theodore theater and television design
Gittler, Wendy artist, art historian, writer
Goertz, Augustus Frederick, III artist
Gold, Albert artist
Goldin, Leon artist, educator
Goldsmith, Caroline L. arts executive
Golub, Leon Albert artist
Gottschall, Edward Maurice graphic arts company executive
Graham, Robert sculptor
Gramatte, Joan Helen graphic designer, art director, photographer
Graves, Morris Cole artist
Gray, George mural painter
Grefé, Richard graphic design executive
Griefen, John Adams artist, educator
†Grooms, Red artist
Grossman, Nancy artist
Gutman, Robert William retired educator
Haacke, Hans Christoph Carl artist, educator
Haas, Richard John artist
Haber, Ira Joel artist, art educator
Hacklin, Allan artist, art educator
Haerer, Carol artist
Haessle, Jean-Marie Georges artist
Halley, Peter painter, educator
Hamoy, Carol artist
Hardy, Thomas Austin sculptor
Hasen, Burton Stanley artist
Held, Al artist, educator
Henselmann, Caspar Gustav Fidelis sculptor
Henson Scales, Meg Diane artist, writer, publisher
Highstein, Jene Abel sculptor
Hightower, Caroline Warner arts management consultant
Hill, Clinton artist
Hios, Theodore painter, graphic artist
Hirschfeld, Albert artist
Holland, Bradford Wayne artist, writer
Holzer, Jenny artist
Hull, Cathy artist, illustrator
Hultberg, John artist
Hutsaliuk, Liuboslav artist
Incandela, Gerald Jean-Marie artist
Ireland, Patrick artist
Jackson, Ward artist
Jacquette, Yvonne Helene artist
Jenkins, Paul artist
Johns, Jasper artist
Johnson, Betsey Lee fashion designer
Jones, Edward Powis artist
†Judge, Mike animator
Judson, Jeannette Alexander artist
Juszczyk, James Joseph artist
Kahn, Susan Beth artist
Kahn, Wolf artist
Kaish, Luise Clayborn sculptor, former educator
Kaish, Morton artist, educator
Kamali, Norma fashion designer
Kan, Diana Artemis Mann Shu artist
Kanovitz, Howard artist
Kaplan, Phyllis computer artist, painter
Karan, Donna (Donna Faske) fashion designer
Karp, Marshall Warren creative director, writer
Katz, Alex artist
Katz, Hilda (Hulda Weber) artist, poet
Katz, Morris artist, entertainer
Katzman, Herbert Henry artist
Keller, Martha Ann artist, painter
Kelly, James artist
Kendall, Dolores Diane Pisapia artist, author, marketing executive
Kepets, Hugh Michael artist
Kingman, Dong artist, educator
Kinstler, Everett Raymond artist
Kirk, Alexis Vemian designer
Klein, Calvin Richard fashion designer
Klotz, Florence costume designer
Kner, Andrew Peter art director
Komar, Vitaly artist
†Koons, Jeff artist
Koppelman, Chaim artist
Koppelman, Dorothy Myers artist, consultant
Koutroulis, Aris George artist, educator
Krementz, Jill photographer, author
Kruger, Barbara artist, art critic
Krulik, Barbara S. director, curator
Kunc, Karen artist, educator
Kushner, Robert Ellis artist
Lang, Daniel S. artist
La Noue, Terence David artist, educator
Lanyon, Ellen (Mrs. Roland Ginzel) artist, educator
Lash, Stephen Sycle auction company executive
Lasker, Jonathan Lewis artist
Lassen, Robert Maurie graphic artist, photographer, editor
Lauren, Ralph fashion designer
Lechay, James artist, emeritus art educator
Lee, Catherine sculptor, painter
Lehr, Janet art dealer, publisher, author
Lehrer, Leonard artist, educator
Leiber, Gerson August artist
Leiber, Judith Maria designer, manufacturer
Leve, Samuel scenic designer
LeWitt, Sol artist
Lichtenstein, Roy artist
Linn, Judy NMN photographer
Loengard, John Borg photographer, editor
Loring, John Robbins artist
Lucas, Christopher artist
MacIver, Loren artist
Mackie, Robert Gordon costume and fashion designer
Mackler, Tina artist
Madsen, Loren Wakefield sculptor
Mann, Sally photographer
Manning, Jack photographer, columnist, author
Marion, John Louis fine arts auctioneer and appraiser
Marisol, (Marisol Escobar) sculptor
Massey, Stephen Charles auctioneer
McCarthy, Denis artist, educator
McCollum, Allan Lloyd artist
McCredie, James Robert fine arts educator
McDarrah, Fred William photographer, editor, writer, photography reviewer
Mc Gowin, William Edward artist
McHugh, Caril Dreyfuss art dealer, gallery director, consultant
McKenzie, Mary Beth artist
Meisel, Louis Koenig art dealer, art historian, writer
Meisel, Steven advertising photographer
Meiselas, Susan Clay photographer
Mendelson, Haim artist, educator, art gallery director
Mesches, Arnold artist
Miller, Harry Brill scenic designer, director, acting instructor, lyricist, interior designer
Miller, Richard Kidwell artist, actor, educator
Miller, Richard McDermott sculptor
Milonas, Minos artist, designer, poet
Moeller, Achim Ferdinand Gerd art dealer, curator, consultant, publisher
Morales, Armando artist
Morath, Inge photographer
Morgan, Jacqui illustrator, painter, educator
Murphy, John Cullen illustrator
Musser, Tharon theatrical lighting designer, theatre consultant
Neiman, LeRoy artist
Newman, Bruce Murray antiques dealer
Newman, Elias artist
Norvell, Patsy artist
Notarbartolo, Albert artist
Ohlson, Douglas Dean artist
Oldenburg, Claes Thure artist
Oldham, Todd fashion designer
Olitski, Jules artist
Owsley, David Thomas art consultant, appraiser, lecturer, author
Pace, Stephen Shell artist, educator
Papi, Liza artist, writer, educator
Parker, Nancy Winslow artist, writer
Pascal, David artist
Pearson, Henry Charles artist
Peckolick, Alan graphic designer
Pepper, Beverly artist, sculptor
Perlis, Donald M. artist
Plavinskaya, Anna Dmitrievna artist
Porter, Liliana Alicia artist, printmaker, photographer
†Pran, Dith photographer, social activist
Quackenbush, Robert Mead artist, author, psychoanalyst
Quaytman, Harvey painter
Rabinowitch, David George sculptor
Rankin-Smith, Pamela photographer
Rauschenberg, Robert artist
Reddy, Krishna Narayana artist, educator
Reininghaus, Ruth artist
Remington, Deborah Williams artist
Resika, Paul artist
Ringgold, Faith artist, writer
Rivelli, William Raymond Allan photographer
Rivera, Sophie photographer
Rivers, Larry artist
Rodriguez, Geno (Eugene Rodriguez) artist, arts administrator
Rose, Leatrice artist, educator
Rosenhouse, Irwin J. artist, designer
Rosenthal, Tony (Bernard) sculptor
Ross, Charles artist
Ross, Rhoda artist
Ruscha, Edward artist
Ryman, Robert Tracy artist
St. Clair, Michael art dealer
Santlofer, Jonathan artist, educator
Schapiro, Miriam artist
Schneider, Jane Harris sculptor
Schneider, JoAnne artist
Schwartz, Daniel Bennett artist
Segal, George sculptor
Seliger, Mark Alan photographer
Semmel, Joan artist, educator
Shapiro, Ellen Marie graphic designer, writer
Shapiro, Joel Elias artist
Sharp, Anne Catherine artist, educator
Shaw, (George) Kendall artist, educator
Sherman, Cindy artist
Silverman, Burton Philip artist
Simonds, Charles Frederick artist
Singer, Barbara Helen photographer
Sis, Peter illustrator, children's book author, artist, filmmaker
Skupinski, Bogdan Kazimierz artist
Slavin, Arlene artist
Sleigh, Sylvia artist, educator
Slone, Sandi artist
Smith, Shirley artist
Smith, Vincent DaCosta artist
Snider, Stephen William art director, graphic designer
Sobell, Nina R. artist
Solé, Maria Jesus (Xusca Solé) visual artist
Solman, Joseph artist
Sonneman, Eve artist
Soreff, Stephen Mayer artist
Southworth, Linda Jean artist, critic, educator
Sperakis, Nicholas George artist
Stanley, Bob artist
Starr, Steven Dawson photographer
Steir, Pat Iris artist
Sterling, David Mark graphic designer
Stiebel, Gerald Gustave art dealer
Stine, Catherine Morris artist
Stolzenberg, Pearl fashion designer
Surls, James sculptor
Surrey, Milt artist
Sutton, Pat Lipsky artist, educator
Swain, Robert artist
Tàpies, Antoni painter, sculptor
Tate, Barbara Marie art director
Thrall, Donald Stuart artist
Tilton, James Floyd theatrical designer, art director
Tipton, Jennifer lighting designer
Tisma, Marija Stevan artist
Tobias, Julius sculptor
Toledo, Francisco painter, printmaker
Tooker, George artist
Torffield, Marvin artist
†Trakas, George sculptor
Trigere, Pauline fashion designer
Tscherny, George graphic designer
Upright, Diane Warner art dealer
Vaadia, Boaz sculptor
Vass, Joan fashion designer
Vicente, Esteban artist
Viviano, Sam Joseph illustrator
Von Furstenberg, Diane Simone Michelle fashion designer, writer, entrepreneur
Von Ringelheim, Paul Helmut sculptor
Wagner, Robin Samuel Anton stage and set designer
Wald, Sylvia artist
Walton, Anthony John (Tony Walton) theater and film designer, book illustrator
Webb, Patrick McIvor artist, educator
Wechsler, Gil lighting designer
Wegman, William George artist
Weiner, Lawrence Charles sculptor
Weitz, John fashion designer, writer
Welch, (William) Roger artist
Wenegrat, Saul S. arts administrator, art educator, consultant
Weschler, Anita sculptor, painter

Wesley, John Mercer *artist*
White, Faith *sculptor*
Williams, William Thomas *artist, educator*
Willis, Thornton Wilson *painter*
Wolins, Joseph *artist*
Wright, Faith-dorian *artist*
Wunderman, Jan Darcourt *artist*
Wurmfeld, Sanford *artist, educator*
Wyeth, James Browning *artist*
York, Richard Travis *art dealer*
Youngerman, Jack *artist, sculptor*
Zimmerman, Kathleen Marie *artist*
Zipprodt, Patricia *costume designer*
Zlowe, Florence Markowitz *artist*
Zuniga, Francisco *sculptor, graphic artist*

**Newark**
Hughes, Owen Willard *artist*

**Northport**
Hohenberger, Patricia Julie *fine arts and antique appraiser, consultant*

**Norwich**
Berman, Ethel Wargotz *artist, educator*

**Old Chatham**
Teng, Juliet *artist*

**Old Westbury**
Kurlander, Honey Wachtel *artist, educator*

**Oneonta**
Freckelton, Sondra *artist*

**Oswego**
Fox, Michael David *art educator, visual imagist artist*

**Owego**
McCann, Jean Friedrichs *artist, educator*

**Oyster Bay**
Prey, Barbara Ernst *artist*

**Palisades**
Knowlton, Grace Farrar *sculptor, photographer*

**Peekskill**
Rosenberg, Marilyn Rosenthal *artist, visual poet*

**Pelham**
Conroy, Tamara Boks *artist, special education educator, former nurse*
Ralston, Lucy Virginia Gordon *artist*

**Piermont**
Berkon, Martin *artist*
Gussow, Alan *artist, sculptor*

**Pittsford**
Lyttle, Douglas Alfred *photographer, educator*

**Pleasantville**
Cober, Alan Edwin *artist, illustrator, printmaker, educator*

**Portlandville**
Munro, Janet Andrea *artist*

**Pound Ridge**
Ferro, Walter *artist*
Schwebel, Renata Manasse *sculptor*

**Rensselaer**
Nack, Claire Durani *artist, author*

**Rhinebeck**
Clutz, William (Hartman Clutz) *artist, educator*
Rabinovich, Raquel *artist, sculptor*

**Rochester**
Engelmann, Lothar Klaus *photographic science educator*
Margolis, Richard Martin *photographer, educator*
Merritt, Howard Sutermeister *retired art educator*
Saisselin, Remy Gilbert *fine arts educator*

**Roslyn**
Finke, Leonda Froehlich *sculptor*

**Rye**
Troller, Fred *graphic designer, painter, visual consultant, educator*

**Rye Brook**
Cooper, Isabel Selma *sculptor, writer, art historian*

**Sag Harbor**
Diamond, Mary E(lizabeth) B(aldwin) *artist*

**Sagaponack**
Butchkes, Sydney *artist*
Isham, Sheila Eaton *artist*

**Saratoga Springs**
Upton, Richard Thomas *artist*

**Scarsdale**
Breinin, Raymond *painter, sculptor*
Fendelman, Helaine *art appraiser*
Rapaport, Rita *artist, sculpture, painter*
Ries, Martin *artist, educator*

**Shady**
Ruellan, Andree *artist*

**Shelter Island**
Culbertson, Janet Lynn *artist*

**Shoreham**
Spier, Peter Edward *artist, author*

**Snyder**
Breverman, Harvey *artist*

**South Salem**
Howard, Joan Alice *artist*

**Southampton**
Fuller, Sue *artist*

**Stanfordville**
Seborovski, Carole *artist*

**Staten Island**
Nelson, Carey Boone *sculptor*

**Sterling**
Seawell, Thomas Robert *artist, retired educator*

**Stony Brook**
Badalamenti, Fred Leopoldo *artist, educator*
Pekarsky, Melvin Hirsch *artist*
Pindell, Howardena Doreen *artist*

**Syracuse**
McCoubrey, Sarah *artist and art educator*
Thomas, Sidney *fine arts educator, researcher*

**Tappan**
Dell, Robert Christopher *geothermal sculptor, scenic artist*
Nickford, Juan *sculptor, educator*

**Tonawanda**
Peterson, Dorothy Lulu *artist, writer*

**Tuxedo Park**
Domjan, Joseph (Spiri Domjan) *artist*

**Utica**
Gape, Serafina Vetrano *decorative artist and designer*
Pribble, Easton *artist*

**Valley Cottage**
Shaderowfsky, Eva Maria *photographer, writer*

**Wading River**
Marlow, Audrey Swanson *artist, designer*

**Wainscott**
Russo, Alexander Peter *artist, educator*

**Walden**
Hraniotis, Judith Beringer *artist*

**Wallkill**
Koch, Edwin Ernest *artist, interior decorator*

**Wantagh**
Glaser, David *painter, sculptor*

**Warwick**
Franck, Frederick Sigfred *artist, author, dental surgeon*

**Westbury**
Barboza, Anthony *photographer, artist*
Sherbell, Rhoda *artist, sculptor*
Waterman, Diane Corrine *artist, educator, writer*

**White Plains**
Erla, Karen *artist, painter, collagist, printmaker*

**Williamsville**
Whitcomb, James Stuart *videographer, photographer, production company executive*

**Woodstock**
Banks, Rela *sculptor*
Currie, Bruce *artist*
Helioff, Anne Graile *painter*

**Yonkers**
Vergano, Lynn (Marilynn Bette Vergano) *artist*

**Yorktown Heights**
Jones, Lauretta Marie *artist, graphic designer, computer interface designer*
Laventhol, Henry L(ee) (Hank Laventhol) *artist, etcher*

## NORTH CAROLINA

**Asheville**
Jones, J. Kenneth *art dealer, former museum administrator*
Rufa, Robert Henry *writer, editor, photographer, artist*

**Ayden**
McElhinney, James Lancel *artist, educator*

**Black Mountain**
Parker, Mary Althea *painter, art educator*

**Burnsville**
Bernstein, William Joseph *glass artist, educator*
Doyle, John Lawrence *artist*

**Chapel Hill**
Ness, Albert Kenneth *artist, educator*
Stipe, Robert Edwin *design educator*

**Clarkton**
Wuebbels, Theresa Elizabeth *visual art educator*

**Columbus**
Smith, Virginia Warren *artist, writer, educator*

**Davidson**
Jackson, Herb *artist, educator*

**Greensboro**
Barker, Walter William, Jr. *artist, educator*

**Greenville**
Laing, Penelope Gamble *art educator*
Wallin, Leland Dean *artist, educator*

**Laurinburg**
Nance, Tony Max-Perry *designer, illustrator*

**Sanford**
Higgins, George Edward *sculptor*

**Williamston**
Wobbleton, Judy Karen *artist, educator*

**Wilmington**
Jones, Sarah Downing *visual arts educator*

**Winston Salem**
Faccinto, Victor Paul *artist, gallery administrator*

## NORTH DAKOTA

**Bismarck**
Solberg, Nellie Florence Coad *artist*

**Dickinson**
Miller, Jean Patricia Salmon *art educator*

**Mandan**
Hodge, Ann Linton *artist*

## OHIO

**Akron**
Keener, Polly Leonard *illustrator*
Lawrence, Alice Lauffer *artist, educator*

**Ashville**
Beckman, Judith *art educator*

**Aurora**
Lawton, Florian Kenneth *artist, educator*

**Bowling Green**
Ocvirk, Otto George *artist*

**Chagrin Falls**
Ross, Sally Price *artist, mural painter*

**Chesterland**
Wood, Ruth Diehm *artist, design consultant*

**Cincinnati**
Attee, Joyce Valerie Jungclas *artist*
Brod, Stanford *graphic designer, educator*
Daniels, Astar *artist*
Knipschild, Robert *artist, educator*
Rexroth, Nancy Louise *photographer*
Sullivan, Connie Castleberry *artist, photographer*
Tuttle, Martha Benedict *artist*
Wygant, Foster Laurance *art educator*

**Cleveland**
Beling, Helen *sculptor*
Cassill, Herbert Carroll *artist*
Fenton, Alan *artist*
Schorgl, Thomas Barry *arts administrator*
Seltzer, Phyllis Estelle *painter, printmaker*

**Columbus**
Beverley, Jane Taylor *artist*
Gilliom, Bonnie Lee *arts educator, consultant*
Kuehn, Edmund Karl *artist*
Roth, Susan King *design educator*
Simson, Bevlyn *artist*
Sunami, John Soichi *designer*
Ultes, Elizabeth Cummings Bruce *artist, retired art historian and librarian*

**Coshocton**
Parkhill, Harold Loyal *artist*

**Dayton**
Zahner, Mary Anne *art educator*

**Hilliard**
Cupp, David Foster *photographer, journalist*

**Kent**
Kwong, Eva *artist, educator*

**Mason**
Cettel, Judith Hapner *artist, secondary school educator*

**New Richmond**
Scott, Michael Lester *artist, educator*

**Oberlin**
Reinoehl, Richard Louis *artist, scholar, martial artist*
Tacha, Athena *sculptor, educator*

**Perrysburg**
Autry, Carolyn *artist, art history educator*

**Seven Hills**
Stanczak, Julian *artist, educator*

**Shaker Heights**
Held, Lila M. *art appraiser*
McKenna, Kathleen Kwasnik *artist*

**Springfield**
Patterson, Martha Ellen *artist, art educator*

**Toledo**
McGlauchlin, Tom *artist*

**Urbana**
Bronkar, Eunice Dunalee *artist, art educator*

**Van Wert**
Liljegren, Frank Sigfrid *artist, art association official*

## OKLAHOMA

**Chickasha**
Good, Leonard Phelps *artist*

**Oklahoma City**
Alaupovic, Alexandra Vrbanic *artist, educator*
Boston, Billie *costume designer, costume history educator*

**Tulsa**
Spencer, Winifred May *art educator*

## OREGON

**Applegate**
Boyle, (Charles) Keith *artist, educator*

**Ashland**
Hay, Richard Laurence *theater scenic designer*

**Cannon Beach**
Greaver, Harry *artist*

**Coos Bay**
Van Allen, Katrina Frances *painter*

**Grants Pass**
Marchini, Claudia Cilloniz *artist*

**Hillsboro**
Hurley, Bruce Palmer *artist*

**Medford**
Puckett, Richard Edward *artist, consultant, retired recreation executive*

**Newberg**
Keith, Pauline Mary *artist, illustrator, writer*

**Pendleton**
Harper, Gloria Janet *artist, educator*

**Portland**
Ace, Katherine *artist*
Baker, Allison Paige *photographer, musician, educator*
Ramsby, Mark Delivan *lighting designer and consultant*
Waddingham, John Alfred *artist, journalist*

**Salem**
Pierre, Joseph Horace, Jr. *commercial artist*
Thornton, Dorothy Haberlach *artist, photographer*

**Wallowa**
Ray, Jenny *artist*

## PENNSYLVANIA

**Allentown**
Moller, Hans *artist*

**Bala Cynwyd**
Blumberg, June Beth *artist*

**Boyertown**
Slider, Dorla Dean (Freeman) *artist*

**Carlisle**
Davenny, Ward Leslie *artist, educator*

**Chambersburg**
Boretz, Naomi Messinger *artist, educator*

**Cochranville**
Sazegar, Morteza *artist*

**Edinboro**
Kemenyffy, Steven *artist, art educator*

**Elkins Park**
Erlebacher, Martha Mayer *artist, educator*
Simon, Marilyn Weintraub *art educator, sculptor*

**Fairless Hills**
Marable, Simeon-David *artist*

**Glen Mills**
Turner, Janet Sullivan *painter*

**Glenmoore**
DeGuatemala, Joyce *sculptor*

**Glenside**
Bardliving, Clifford Lee, Jr. *graphic designer*
Frudakis, Zenos Antonios *sculptor, artist*

**Huntingdon Valley**
Edelman, Janice *artist, educator*

**Jenkintown**
Potash, Jane *artist*

**Kutztown**
Kuehne, Helenirene Anne *art educator*

**Lederach**
Hallman, H(enry) Theodore, Jr. *artist, textile designer*

**Lehigh Valley**
Kocsis, James Paul *artist, publisher*

**Lumberville**
Katsiff, Bruce *artist*

**Malvern**
Wolfe, Jean Elizabeth *medical illustrator, artist*

**Mechanicsville**
Bye, Ranulph DeBayeux *artist, author*

**Morrisville**
Clark, William Roger *artist, educator*

**Narberth**
Grenald, Raymond *architectural lighting designer*

**Newtown**
Smith, Karen Ann *artist, graphic designer, educator*

**Philadelphia**
Cramer, Richard Charles *artist, educator*
Fine, Miriam Brown *artist, educator, poet, writer*
Le Clair, Charles George *artist, retired university dean*
Levy, Rochelle Feldman *artist*
Maitin, Sam(uel Calman) (Sam Maitin) *artist*
McCormick, Rod *sculptor, art educator*
Metcalf, Bruce Barber *visual artist, craft critic*
Metzker, Ray K. *photographer*
Murphy, Mary Marguerite *artist*
Paone, Peter *artist*
Remenick, Seymour *artist, educator*
†Saul, April *photographer*
Schaff, Barbara Walley *artist*
Schwarz, Robert Devlin *art dealer*
Solomon, Vita Petrosky *artist*
Spandorfer, Merle Sue *artist, educator, author*

**Phoenixville**
Allen, Carol Linnea Ostrom *art educator*

**Pittsburgh**
Arkus, Leon Anthony *art consultant, former museum director*
†Mc Vicker, Charles Taggart *artist*
Rogers, Bryan Leigh *artist, art educator*
Trapp, Frank Anderson *art educator*
Wilkins, David George *fine arts educator*
Williams, John Wesley *fine arts educator*

**Pottsville**
Ackalusky, Hazel Ethel *artist*

**Preston Park**
†Janowich, Ron *artist*

**Reading**
Canning, Traci A. *designer*

**Rydal**
Roediger, Janice Anne *artist, educator*

**Shickshinny**
Luksha, Rosemary Dorothy *art educator*

**Solebury**
Anthonisen, George Rioch *sculptor, artist*

**Spring Grove**
Helberg, Shirley Adelaide Holden *artist, educator*

**State College**
Deering, Anne-Lise *artist, real estate salesperson*

**Stroudsburg**
Sherman, Ruth Tenzer *artist, fixtures company executive*

**Throop**
Karluk, Lori Jean *craft designer, copy editor*

**Tyrone**
Shaw, Marilyn Margaret *artist, photographer*

**University Park**
Van Dommelen, David B. *artist, educator*

**Upper Darby**
Gasparro, Frank *sculptor*

**Waverly**
Tosti, Sally T. *artist, educator*

**West Chester**
Gaadt, Suzanne DeMott *graphic designer*
Jamison, Philip *artist*

**Wexford**
Osby, Larissa Geiss *artist*

**Wilkes Barre**
Bart, Georgiana Cray *artist, educator*

**Williamsport**
Foucart Vincenti, Valerie *art educator*

**RHODE ISLAND**

**Cranston**
Crooks, W. Spencer *artist, educator*

**Jamestown**
Worden, Katharine Cole *sculptor*

**Kingston**
Leete, William White *artist*
Rohm, Robert Hermann *sculptor, educator*

**Providence**
Feldman, Walter Sidney *artist, educator*
Geisser, Peter James *artist, educator for hearing impaired*
Heyman, Lawrence Murray *printmaker, painter*
Howes, Lorraine de Wet *fashion designer, educator*
Ockerse, Thomas *graphic design educator*
Perroni, Carol *artist, painter*
Wunderlich, Alfred Leon *artist, art educator*

**Warwick**
Stockar, Helena Marie Magdalena *artist*

**Westerly**
Reiland, Lowell Keith *sculptor*

**SOUTH CAROLINA**

**Central**
Smith, Elizabeth Shelton *art educator*

**Clemson**
Petzel, Florence Eloise *textiles educator*

**Columbia**
Robinson, Christopher Thomas *artist*
Thee, Christian *artist, designer*

**Pendleton**
Shanahan, Elizabeth Anne *art educator*

**Summerville**
Vorwerk, E. Charlsie *artist*

**SOUTH DAKOTA**

**Sioux Falls**
DeGeus, Wendell Ray *photographer*
Grupp, Carl Alf *art educator, artist*

**Vermillion**
Freeman, Jeffrey Vaughn (Jeff Freeman) *art educator, artist*

**TENNESSEE**

**Anderson**
Olson, Carol Lea *lithographer, educator, photographer*

**Chattanooga**
Cress, George Ayers *artist, educator*
Martin, Chester Y. *sculptor, painter*
Mills, Olan, II *photography company executive*

**Crossville**
Rollason, Mary Katherine *artist, art educator*

**Knoxville**
Sublett, Carl Cecil *artist*
Walsh, Joanne Elizabeth *art educator, librarian*

**Lookout Mountain**
Wyeth, Andrew *artist*

**Memphis**
Bernstein, Janna S. Bernheim *art educator*
Carroll, Billy Price *artist*
McPherson, Larry E(ugene) *photographer, educator*
Riss, Murray *photographer, educator*

**Nashville**
Hazlehurst, Franklin Hamilton *fine arts educator*
McKinney, Jane-Allen *artist and educator*
Oates, Sherry Charlene *portraitist*

**Smithville**
DeMay, Susan Ann *ceramic artist*

**TEXAS**

**Austin**
Debold, Cynthia Ann *sculptor*
Deming, David Lawson *art educator*
Fearing, William Kelly *art educator, artist*
Goldstein, Peggy R. *sculptor*
Guerin, John William *artist*
Hatgil, Paul Peter *artist, sculptor, educator*
High, Timothy Griffin *artist, educator, writer*
Mayer, Susan Martin *art educator*
Pope, Ingrid Bloomquist *sculptor, lecturer, poet*
Reeves, Dianne L. *artist*
Sawyer, Margo Lucy *artist, educator*
Weismann, Donald Leroy *art educator, artist, filmmaker, writer*

**Beaumont**
Coe, (Matchett) Herring *sculptor*

**Belton**
Christoff, Beth Graves *artist*

**Coleman**
Needham, Judy Len *artist, art educator*

**Coppell**
Miiller, Susan Diane *artist*

**Corpus Christi**
Ullberg, Kent Jean *sculptor*
Worden, Elizabeth Ann *artist, comedy writer, singer*

**Dallas**
Blessen, Karen Alyce *free-lance illustrator, designer*
Emerson, Walter Caruth *artist, educator*
Glatt, Linnea Elizabeth *artist*
Hudgins, Louise Nan *art educator*
Reeser, Rachel Anne Everson *graphic designer, artist*
Richards, Jeanne Herron *artist*

**Dripping Springs**
Delph, Shirley Cox *artist, designer, illustrator, consultant*

**Edinburg**
Libbey, Darlene Hensley *artist, educator*

**El Paso**
Drake, James *sculptor*
Weitz, Jeanne Stewart *artist, educator*

**Euless**
Leding, Anne Dixon *artist, educator*

**Fort Worth**
Talley, Jane *artist, educator*

**Houston**
Camfield, William Arnett *art educator*
Gorski, Daniel Alexander *art educator*
Hamblet, Carole Orr *artist*
Honeycutt, George Leonard *photographer, retired*
King, Kay Wander *design educator, fashion designer, consultant*
Larrey, Inge Harriette *jazz and blues freelance photographer*
O'Neil, John *artist*
Wolff, Dee Ivona *artist*

**Huntsville**
Lea, Stanley E. *artist, educator*

**Kerrville**
Frudakis, Evangelos William *sculptor*

**Laredo**
Knapp, Thomas Edwin *sculptor, painter*

**Liberty Hill**
Vance, Zinna Barth *artist, writer*

**Longview**
Hearne, Carolyn Fox *art and history educator, artist*

**Midland**
King, Mary Lou *artist, medical technologist*

**Odessa**
Lee, Nelda S. *art appraiser and dealer, film producer*

**Richardson**
Bellamy, Jennifer Rachelle *artist*

**San Antonio**
Groover, Deborah Kate *artist, educator*
Stephens, Martha Lockhart *writer, researcher*
Thompson, Mary Koleta *sculptor, non-profit organization director*
Willson, Robert (William) *glass sculpture and watercolor artist*

**Sonora**
Earwood, Barbara Tirrell *artist*

**Waco**
Kagle, Joseph Louis, Jr. *artist, arts administrator*

**UTAH**

**Orderville**
Zornes, Milford *artist*

**Saint George**
Collett, Farrell Reuben *art educator*

**Salt Lake City**
Goldstein, Barbara Joan *sculptor*

**Smithfield**
Rasmuson, Brent (Jacobsen) *photographer, graphic artist*

**VERMONT**

**Bennington**
Adams, Pat *artist, educator*

**Cavendish**
Shapiro, David *artist, art historian*

**East Calais**
Gahagan, James Edward, Jr. *artist*

**Lyndonville**
Robbins, Elizabeth *stained glass artist, designer*

**Newbury**
McGarrell, James *artist, educator*

**North Bennington**
Noland, Kenneth Clifton *artist*

**Wallingford**
Bluhm, Norman *artist*

**West Burke**
Van Vliet, Claire *artist*

**Weston**
Kasnowski, Chester Nelson *artist, educator*

**Windsor**
Forbes, Georgina *artist, psychotherapist*

**VIRGINIA**

**Alexandria**
Alderson, Margaret Northrop *arts administrator, educator, artist*
Payne, Nancy Sloan *visual arts educator*
Wasko-Flood, Sandra Jean *artist, educator*

**Arlington**
Reed, Paul Allen *artist*

**Blacksburg**
Crawford, Peggy Smith *design educator*

**Brightwood**
Skelton, Dorothy Geneva Simmons (Mrs. John William Skelton) *art educator*

**Centreville**
Nong *artist, sculptor*

**Charlottesville**
Bunch, John Blake *photographer, writer, educator*
Priest, Hartwell Wyse *artist*
Ruben, Leonard *retired art educator*

**Clifton**
Hennesy, Gerald Craft *artist*

**Draper**
Whitehurst, Mary Tarr *artist, poet, writer*

**East Stone Gap**
Combs, Jo Karen Kobeck *artist, writer*

**Fairfax**
Hammond, Mary Sayer *art educator*

**Fairfax Station**
Jackson, Vaughn Lyle *artist, consultant*

**Fredericksburg**
Herndon, Cathy Campbell *artist, art educator*
Schmutzhart, Berthold Josef *sculptor, educator, art and education consultant*

**Goldvein**
Peterson, Barbara Mae Bittner Owecke *artist, nurse, realtor*

**Lynchburg**
Hudson, Walter Tiree *artist*
Massie, Anne Adams Robertson *artist*

**Mc Lean**
Harrison, Carol Love *fine art photographer*
Johnson, Mary Zelinda *artist*

**Middleburg**
Robinson, Michael Francis *private art dealer and appraiser*

**Newport News**
Camp, Hazel Lee Burt *artist*

**Norfolk**
Frieden, Jane Heller *art educator*
Jones, Leon Herbert, Jr. (Herb Jones) *artist*
Myers, Sue Bartley *artist*
Nicholson, Myreen Moore *artist, researcher*

**Radford**
Kessler, Kendall Seay Feriozi *artist*
Shell, Robert Edward Lee *photographer, writer*

**Reston**
Heginbotham, Jan Sturza *sculptor*

**Richmond**
Freed, David Clark *artist*
Kevorkian, Richard *artist*
Martin, Bernard Murray *painter, educator*
Rowley, Frank Selby, Jr. *artist*
Taliaferro, Nancy Ellen Taylor *artist*

**Roanoke**
Guerrant, Helen Orzel *artist*

**Timberville**
Barnard, Robert Edward *potter, writer*

**Virginia Beach**
Ives, Ronn Brian *artist, educator*
Stevens, Suzanne Duckworth *artist, educator*

**Warrenton**
Brenken, Hanne Marie *artist*

**Waterford**
Pollack, Reginald Murray *painter, sculptor*

**Waynesboro**
Prye, Ellen Ross *graphic designer*

**Williamsburg**
Coleman, Henry Edwin *art educator, artist*
Papenthien, Ruth Mary *fiber artist, retired educator*
Robinson, Jay (Thurston) *artist*
Roseberg, Carl Andersson *sculptor, educator*

**WASHINGTON**

**Anacortes**
Mc Cracken, Philip Trafton *sculptor*

**Bainbridge Island**
Grisham, Jeannie *artist*
Randlett, Mary Willis *photographer*

**Battle Ground**
Hansen, James Lee *sculptor*

**Burlington**
Zeretzke, Frederick Frank H. *artist, educator*

**Coupeville**
Canfield, Stella Stojanka *artist*

**Ellensburg**
Housner, Jeanette Ann *artist, jeweler*

**Kent**
Pierce, Danny Parcel *artist, educator*

**Mercer Island**
Langhout-Nix, Nelleke *artist*
Steinhardt, Henry *photographer*

**Nordland**
Kepner, Rita Marie *sculptor, writer, editor, educator, public affairs officer, marketing and communications professional, education manager, agency spokesperson*

**North Seattle**
Spafford, Michael Charles *artist*

**Olympia**
Haseltine, James Lewis *artist, consultant*

**Puyallup**
Chalk, Earl Milton *retired art director*

**Redmond**
Rushmer, Estella Virginia Dix (Dixie Rushmer) *artist*

**Richland**
Fraser, Frederick Ewart *art educator*

**Seattle**
Berger, Paul Eric *artist, photographer*
Blomdahl, Sonja *artist*
Celentano, Francis Michael *artist, art educator*
De Alessi, Ross Alan *lighting designer*
Du Pen, Everett George *sculptor, educator*
Gardiner, T(homas) Michael *artist*
Govedare, Philip Bainbridge *artist, educator*
Hill, Gary *video artist*
Kuvshinoff, Bertha Horne *painter, sculptor*
Lawrence, Jacob *artist, educator*
†Mogelgaard, Michael *creative director*
†Trimpin *artist*
Washington, James Winston, Jr. *artist, sculptor*

**Tacoma**
Guilmet, Glenda Jean *artist*
Ragan, Betty Sapp *artist, educator*

**Tenino**
Orsini, Myrna J. *sculptor, educator*

**Vancouver**
Hulburt, Lucille Hall *artist, educator*

**WEST VIRGINIA**

**Charleston**
Stephenson, Ann Watz *artist*

**Mount Gay**
Earnest, Carmella Lynn *art educator, artist*

**Wheeling**
Phillis, Marilyn Hughey *artist*

**WISCONSIN**

**Appleton**
Amm, Sophia J. *artist, educator*

**Baraboo**
Aderhold, Louise Kathryn *art educator*

**Beloit**
Simon, Michael Alexander *photographer, educator*

**Gleason**
Raash, Kathleen Forecki *artist*

**Hartland**
Stamsta, Jean F. *artist*

**Hollandale**
Myers, Frances *artist*

**Janesville**
Detert-Moriarty, Judith Anne *graphic artist, civic activist*

**Madison**
Becker, David *artist, educator*
Colescott, Warrington Wickham *artist, printmaker, educator*
Fritz, Bruce Morrell *photographer*
Greenwald, Caroline Meyer *artist*
Launder, Yolanda Marie *graphic design director*
Link, O(gle) Winston *photographer*

**Milwaukee**
Burkert, Robert Randall *retired artist*
Heiloms, May (Mrs. Samuel Heiloms) *artist*
Helbert, Clifford L. *graphic designer, journalism educator*
Poehlmann, JoAnna *artist, illustrator, book designer, educator*
Thrall, Arthur Alvin *artist*

**New Richmond**
Schwan, LeRoy Bernard *artist, retired educator*

**Oconomowoc**
Vespa, Ned Angelo *photographer*

**Princeton**
Sylke, Loretta Clara *artist*

**River Falls**
Johnston, Randy James *artist*

**Sturgeon Bay**
Becker, Bettie Geraldine *artist*

**Wausau**
Fleming, Thomas Michael *artist, educator*

**Winneconne**
Gust, Joyce Jane *artist*

**WYOMING**

**Casper**
Seeger, Sondra Joan *artist*

**Centennial**
Russin, Robert Isaiah *sculptor, educator*

**Cheyenne**
Moore, Mary French (Muffy Moore) *potter, community activist*

**Cody**
Jackson, Harry Andrew *artist*

**Kemmerer**
Clark, Michael *artist, educator*

**Laramie**
Flach, Victor Hugo *designer, writer*
Reif, (Frank) David *artist, educator*

**CANADA**

**ALBERTA**

**Edmonton**
Jungkind, Walter *design educator, writer, consultant*

**BRITISH COLUMBIA**

**Duncan**
Hughes, Edward John *artist*

**Salt Spring Island**
Raginsky, Nina *artist*

**Victoria**
Harvey, Donald *artist, educator*

**MANITOBA**

**Winnipeg**
Eyre, Ivan *artist*

**NOVA SCOTIA**

**Halifax**
Jackson, Sarah Jeanette *sculptor, graphic artist, copier artist, bookmaker*

**Mahone Bay**
Tolmie, Kenneth Donald *artist, author*

**Wolfville**
Colville, David Alexander *artist*

**ONTARIO**

**Grimsby**
Morgan, Wayne Philip *art and popular culture exhibition producer*

**Hamilton**
Pietrzak, Ted S. *art gallery director*

**London**
Livick, Stephen *fine art photographer*

**Niagara-on-the-Lake**
Scott, Campbell *artist*

**Ottawa**
Karsh, Yousuf *photographer*

**Toronto**
Astman, Barbara Ann *artist, educator*
Kramer, Burton *graphic designer, educator*
Ronald, William *artist*
Semak, Michael William *photographer, educator*
Winter, Frederick Elliot *fine arts educator*

**Waterloo**
Urquhart, Tony *artist, educator*

**QUEBEC**

**Ayers Cliff**
Beament, Thomas Harold (Tib Beament) *artist, printmaker, educator*

**Beaconsfield**
Harder, Rolf Peter *graphic designer, painter*

**Montreal**
Charney, Melvin *artist, architect, educator*
McEwen, Jean *painter*

**Pontiac**
Hlavina, Rasto R(astislav) *sculptor, writer*

**Saint Lambert**
Archambault, Louis *sculptor*

**SASKATCHEWAN**

**Moose Jaw**
Moore, Yvette M. *artist, illustrator*

**Saskatoon**
Bornstein, Eli *artist, sculptor*

**MEXICO**

**Cuernavaca**
Mora, Francisco *artist, printmaker*

**Mexico City**
Mendelejis, Leonardo Nierman *artist*

**Morelos**
Cauduro, Rafael *painter, muralist*

**AUSTRALIA**

**Ringwood**
Base, Graeme Rowland *illustrator, author*

**AUSTRIA**

**Vienna**
Coufal, Franz Anton *sculptor*

**ENGLAND**

**London**
Kitaj, R. B. *artist*

**FRANCE**

**Arles**
Clergue, Lucien Georges *photographer*

**Paris**
Biala, Janice *artist*
Lacroix, Christian Marie Marc *fashion designer*
Levee, John Harrison *artist, designer*
Marx, Kathryn *photographer, author*
Renouf, Edda *artist*
Ungaro, Emanuel Matteotti *fashion designer*

**GERMANY**

**Berlin**
Iannone, Dorothy *visual artist, writer*

**Frankfurt**
Ammann, Jean-Christophe *art director*

**GREECE**

**Athens**
Greene-Mercier, Marie Zoe *sculptor*

**ITALY**

**Florence**
Cecil, Charles Harkless *artist, educator*

**Milan**
Ferré, Gianfranco *fashion designer, artistic director*

**JAPAN**

**Kanagawa**
Swarz, Sahl *sculptor*

**Tokyo**
Kusama, Yayoi *sculptor, painter*

**THE NETHERLANDS**

**Amsterdam**
Baer, Jo *painter*

**PAKISTAN**

**Lahore**
Geoffrey, Iqbal (Mohammed Jawaid Iqbal Jafree) *artist, lawyer*

**PORTUGAL**

**Lisbon**
Berger, Jason *artist, printmaker*

**SCOTLAND**

**Argyll**
Reeves, Daniel McDonough *video artist*

**SPAIN**

**Caceres**
Long, Bert Louis, Jr. *artist*

**Seville**
Sanchez, Leonedes Monarrize Worthington (Duke de Leonedes) *fashion designer*

**SWEDEN**

**Bralanda**
Emilson, Henry Bertil *artist*

**ADDRESS UNPUBLISHED**

Abadi, Fritzie *artist, educator*
Abbe, Elfriede Martha *sculptor, graphic artist*
Abramowicz, Janet *painter, print-maker*
Adkins, Terry R. *artist*
Aldredge, Theoni Vachliotis *costume designer*
Anastasi, William Joseph *artist*

Ancona, George E. *photographer, film producer, author*
Anderson, Violet Henson *artist, educator*
Andrade, Edna *artist, art educator*
Annus, John Augustus *artist*
Arndt, Dianne Joy *artist, photographer*
Astaire, Carol Anne Taylor *artist, educator*
Bader, Lorraine Greenberg *textile designer, consultant*
Balet, Jan *artist*
Barr, Burt *artist*
Barth, Frances Dorothy *artist*
Bateman, Robert McLellan *artist*
Baughman, J. Ross *photographer, writer, educator*
Benzle, Curtis Munhall *artist, art educator*
Bergson, Maria *designer*
Berlin, Beatrice Winn *visual artist, printmaker*
Berman, Aaron *art appraiser, director, consultant*
Berman, Eleanore *artist*
Bigelow-Lourie, Anne Edwige *graphic designer*
Binch, Caroline Lesley *illustrator, photographer*
Bissell, James Dougal, III *motion picture production designer*
Bjornson, Maria *theatrical designer*
Blinder, Janet *art dealer*
Boni, Miki *artist*
Boxer, Stanley Robert *artist, sculptor*
Bramson, Phyllis Halperin *artist, educator*
Brandt, Grace Borgenicht *art dealer*
Brenner, Albert *production designer, sculptor*
Brin, Pamela Yale *art dealer, mirror and glass designer*
Brodie, Howard *artist*
Brown, Carol Rose *artist*
Brown, William Ferdinand *artist, writer*
Browne, Diana Gayle *artist, social services*
Bundi, Renee *art director, graphic designer*
Campanelli, Pauline Eble *artist*
Campbell, Demarest Lindsay *artist, designer, writer*
Campbell, Patton *stage designer, educator*
Cantliffe, Jeri Miller *artist, art educator*
Carlson, Charlotte Booth *book illustrator*
Carraher, Mary Lou Carter *art educator*
Carroll, Marie-Jean Greve *educator, artist*
Carter, Nanette Carolyn *artist*
Carter, Yvonne Pickering *art educator*
Cassill, (Karilyn) Kay *artist, writer*
Cecchi, David Robert *farmer, graphic designer*
Chinni, Peter Anthony *artist*
Cima, Brooks Dement *art educator*
Clark, Larry *photographer*
Clauser, Kenneth Alton *professional photographer, banjo player*
Clement, Alain Gérard *photographer*
Cobb, Ruth *artist*
Cobb, Virginia Horton *artist, educator*
Coplans, John Rivers *artist*
Craw, Freeman (Jerry Craw) *graphic artist*
Cumming, Robert Hugh *artist, photographer*
Cummings, David William *artist, educator*
Dahl, Bren Bennington *photo retoucher*
D'Arcangelo, Allan Matthew *artist*
Dash, Robert (Warren) *artist, writer*
Datcu, Ioana *artist*
Davidson, Jeannie *costume designer*
De Blasi, Tony (Anthony Armando De Blasi) *artist*
Dechar, Peter Henry *artist*
Dees, Lynne *artist*
de Kooning, Willem *artist*
De Looper, Willem Johan *artist, museum curator*
Dembeck, Mary Grace *artist, writer*
Der Manuelian, Lucy *art and architecture educator*
Deutsch, David Allan *artist*
Dickau, Keith Michael (Mike Dickau) *artist, secondary school educator*
Dill, Laddie John *artist*
Dogançay, Burhan C. *artist, photographer, sculptor*
Donath, Therese *artist, author*
Downes, Rackstraw *artist*
Doyle, Tom *sculptor, retired educator*
Drysdale, Nancy Allensworth *art dealer*
Dyer, Geraldine A. (Geri A. Dyer) *artist, poet*
Eddy, Don *artist*
Emmons, Beverly *lighting designer*
Engle, Steve E. *artist*
Enriquez, Nora Olague *artist, educator*
Erden, Sybil Isolde *artist*
Farrar, Elaine Willardson *artist*
Feiler, Jo Alison *artist*
Ferreira, Armando Thomas *sculptor, educator*
Finn, Mary Ralphe *artist*
Firestone, Evan Richard *art educator, historian*
Fischl, Eric *artist*
Fish, Janet Isobel *artist*
Fisher, Vernon *artist, educator*
Forester, Russell *artist*
Frailey, Stephen A. *photographer*
Freilicher, Jane *artist*
Friday, Katherine Orwoll *artist*
Gard, Judy Richardson *artist, educator*
Gerstein, Esther *sculptor*
Giusti, Robert George *artist, educator*
Gleason, John James *theatrical lighting designer*
Goldberger, Blanche Rubin *sculptor, jeweler*
Goodstadt, Suzanne Louise *artist*
Goodwill, Margaret Jane *artist*
Goulet, Lorrie *sculptor*
Graham, Kathleen Margaret (K. M. Graham) *artist*
Greenberg, Albert *art director*
Greene, Lynne Jeannette *fashion designer*
Gregory, Eleanor Anne *artist, educator*
Grim, Ellen Townsend *artist, retired art educator*
Gumen, Murad *artist, writer, film director and producer*
Gurney, James Marshall *artist, writer*
Gurwitz-Hall, Barbara Ann *artist*
Halaby, Samia Asaad *artist, educator, computer artist*
Hall, Susan Laurel *artist, educator*
Halsey, William *artist, educator*
Hanson, Jo *artist*
Harari, Hananiah *artist*
Harbutt, Charles *photographer*
Harrington, Michaele Mary *art educator, graphic designer, consultant*
Havens, Keith Cornell *artist*
Hawkes, Kevin Cliff *illustrator, author*
Hayes, David Vincent *sculptor*
Helander, Bruce Paul *artist, private art dealer*
Heller, Dorothy *artist*
Hepper, Carol *artist, educator*
Herranen, Kathy *artist, graphic designer*
Hersey, David Kenneth *theatrical lighting designer*
Hertel, Howard Jay *photographer*
Herzberg, Thomas *artist, illustrator*
Hinman, Charles Baldwin *artist*
Hirondelle, Anne Elizabeth *ceramic artist*
Holch, Eric Sanford *artist*

Holden, Rebecca Lynn *artist*
Hoover, Francis Louis *retired educator, gemologist, jewelry designer, fine arts appraiser, writer*
Hornick, Katherine Joyce Kay *artist, small business owner*
Horton, Patricia Mathews *artist, violist and violinist*
Janko, May *graphic artist*
Jansen, Angela Bing *artist, educator*
Jenney, Neil Franklin, Jr. *artist, philosopher*
Johnson, Linda Kaye *art educator*
Jones, Claire Burtchaell *artist*
Joseph, Jean *artist*
Kahn, Albert Michael *artist, designer*
Kalin, D(orothy) Jean *artist, educator*
Kalina, Richard *artist*
Kannenstine, Margaret Lampe *artist*
Karawina, Erica *artist, stained glass designer*
Kasperbauer, Isabel Giles *art educator*
Katayama, Toshihiro *artist, educator*
Kearns, James Joseph *artist*
Keister, Stephen Lee *artist*
Kelly, Ellsworth *painter, sculptor*
Kipniss, Robert *artist*
Kleiman, Alan Boyd *artist*
Klement, Vera *artist*
Kohlmeyer, Ida Rittenberg *artist*
Kunin, Jacqueline Barlow *art educator*
Laemmle, Cheryl Marie Vicario *artist*
La Rocca, Isabella *artist, educator*
Lassiter, Kenneth T. *photography educator, consultant*
Leak, Nancy Marie *artist*
Lee, William Saul (Bill Lee) *artist, writer*
Lefranc, Margaret (Margaret Schoonover) *artist, illustrator, editor, writer*
Leppig, Mary Louise *artist*
LeRoy, G. Palmer *art dealer*
Levi, Josef Alan *artist*
Levin, Morton D(avid) *artist, printmaker, educator*
Levine, Jack *artist*
Lieberman, Louis (Karl Lieberman) *artist*
Liman, Ellen *painter, writer, arts advocate*
Lindsay, Carol Frances Stockton *art specialist*
Linhares, Judith Yvonne *artist, educator*
Lipscomb, Rosalind Tarver *artist*
Lisnek, Margaret Debbeler *artist, educator*
Littleton, Harvey Kline *artist*
Liu, Katherine Chang *artist, art educator*
Lucas, Rhett Roy *artist, lawyer, chemical engineer*
Ludwig, Allan Ira *photographer, artist, author*
Lund, David Nathan *artist*
Lynch, Peter George *artist*
Lyshak-Stelzer, Francie *artist*
Mangold, Sylvia Plimack *artist*
Maree, Wendy *painter, sculptor*
Martin, Noel *graphic design consultant, educator*
Martyl, (Mrs. Alexander Langsdorf, Jr.) *artist*
McCargar, Eleanor Barker *portrait painter*
Mc Closkey, Robert *artist*
McCracken, John Harvey *painter, sculptor*
†McCully, Emily Arnold *illustrator, writer*
McCurdy, Michael Charles *illustrator, author*
McGraw, Deloss Holland *illustrator, painter*
McKennee, Arden Norma *art educator, retired, consultant*
McKnight, Thomas Frederick *artist*
McMillen, Elizabeth Cashin *artist*
McVicker, Jesse Jay *artist, educator*
Melamid, Alexander *artist*
Meneeley, Edward Sterling *artist*
Middaugh, Robert Burton *artist*
Miles, Cynthia Lynn *theatrical costume designer, consultant*
Miles, Jeanne Patterson *artist*
Miller, Vel *artist*
Mills, Inga-Britta *artist*
Minami, Robert Yoshio *artist, graphic designer*
Misrach, Richard Laurence *photographer*
Mollo, John *film costume designer, military historian*
Monk, Nancy Dina *artist, educator*
Morning, John *graphic designer*
Morrison, Margaret Louise *artist*
Moses, Edward Crosby *artist*
Murray, Robert Gray *sculptor*
Nakamura, Kazuo *artist*
Nalls, Gayil Lynn *artist*
Neuwirth, Allan Charles *designer, director, screenwriter*
Newman, Muriel Kallis Steinberg *art collector*
Nichols, Iris Jean *illustrator*
O'Brien, John Thomas *illustrator, cartoonist*
Olkinetzky, Sam *artist, retired museum director and educator*
Onslow Ford, Gordon Max *painter*
Ord, Linda Banks *artist*
Oritsky, Mimi *artist, educator*
Pack, Susan Joan *art consultant*
Palausi Galinat, Nicole *artist*
Patterson, Marion Louise *photographer, educator*
Pearlstein, Philip *artist*
Péladeau, Marius Beaudoin *art consultant, retired museum director*
Perman, Norman Wilford *graphic designer*
Phelan, Ellen *artist*
Phillips, Billy Saxton *artist, designer, painter*
Poor, Anne *artist*
Porter, Charles Henry *photographer*
Pozzatti, Rudy Otto *artist*
Provensen, Alice Rose Twitchell *artist, author*
Psillos, Susan Rose *artist, educator*
Purcell, George Richard *artist, postal inspector*
Rankin, Scott David *artist, educator*
Rataj, Elizabeth Ann *artist*
Reed, David Fredrick *artist*
Reichman, Fredrick Thomas *artist*
Rickey, George Warren *artist, sculptor, educator*
Robinson, Charlotte Hill *artist*
Rockburne, Dorothea Grace *artist*
Roe, Wanda Jeraldean *artist, retired educator, lecturer*
Root, Doris Smiley *portrait artist*
Ross, Gloria Frankenthaler *tapestry artist, consultant*
Ross, Molly Owings *gold and silversmith, jewelry designer, small business owner*
Rossman, Ruth Scharff *artist, educator*
Rowe, Michael Duane *artist*
Rubello, David Jerome *artist*
Rubin, Sandra Mendelsohn *artist*
Rubinstein, Eva (Anna) *photographer*
Saar, Betye (Irene Saar) *artist*
Sand Lee, Inger *artist*
Scharf, William *artist*
Schley, Reeve, III *artist*
Schmalz, Carl Nelson, Jr. *artist, educator, printmaker*
Schnackenberg, Roy Lee *artist*
Schultz, Eileen Hedy *graphic designer*
Schwartz, Lillian Feldman *artist, filmaker, art analyst, author, nurse*
Schwegman, Monica Joan *artist*
Sheaff, Richard Dana *graphic designer*
Sheridan, Sonia Landy *artist, retired art educator*
Shore, Stephen *photographer*
Sisto, Elena *artist, educator*
Smith, Leonore Rae *artist*
Snelson, Kenneth Duane *sculptor*
Solomon, Amelia Kroll *artist*
Sorel, Edward *artist*
Souders, Jean Swedell *artist, educator*
Spence, Andrew *artist, painter*
Spero, Nancy *artist*
Stackhouse, Robert *sculptor*
Starkweather, Teresa Madery *artist, educator*
Steel, Kuniko June *retired artist*
Stevens, May *artist*
Streeter, Tal *sculptor*
Strider, Marjorie Virginia *artist, educator*
Sugar, Sandra Lee *art consultant*
Sumichrast, Jozef *illustrator, designer*
Swig, Roselyne Chroman *art advisor*
Tamburro, Giovanna M. *artist*
Tardos, Anne *artist, composer, writer*
Taylor, Elouise Christine *artist*
Terpening, Virginia Ann *artist*
Thiel, Philip *design educator*
Tomkow, Gwen Adelle *artist*
Tovish, Harold *sculptor*
Tsai, Wen-Ying *sculptor, painter, engineer*
Turner, Bonese Collins *artist, educator*
Underwood, Martha Jane Menke *artist, educator*
†Unithan, Dolly *visual artist*
Vassil, Pamela *graphic designer*
Villoch, Kelly Carney *art director*
Waldman, Paul *artist*
Ward, Elaine *artist*
Wasserman, Helene Waltman *art dealer, artist*
Wechter, Vivienne Thaul *artist, poet, educator*
Weidner, Roswell Theodore *artist*
Welton, Alice Gordon (Guilfoy) *artist*
Wharton, Margaret Agnes *artist*
Wilde, John *artist, educator*
Willenbecher, John *artist*
Wilson, Jane *artist*
Wiseman, Jay Donald *photographer, mechanical contractor, designer*
Wylan, Barbara *artist*
Wynn, Karla Wray *artist, agricultural products company executive*
York, Shirley Marie *artist*
Zajac, Jack *sculptor, painter*
Zaleski, Jean *artist*
Zapf, Hermann *book and type designer*
Zekman, Terri Margaret *graphic designer*
Zelinsky, Paul O. *illustrator, painter, author*
Zentz, Patrick James *artist, rancher*
Zox, Larry *artist*

## ASSOCIATIONS AND ORGANIZATIONS. *See also* specific fields.

### UNITED STATES

### ALABAMA

**Auburn**
Teague, Sam Fuller *association executive, educator,*

**Birmingham**
Bonfield, Barbara Goldstein *non-profit organization administrator*
Carter, Frances Tunnell (Fran Carter) *fraternal organization administrator*
Moran, William Madison *fundraising executive*
Newton, Don Allen *chamber of commerce executive*
Parker, Israel Frank *national association consultant*
Rynearson, W. John *foundation administrator*

**Huntsville**
Fries, Helen Sergeant Haynes *civic leader*

**Mobile**
McCann, Clarence David, Jr. *special events coordinator, museum curator and director, artist*

**Montgomery**
Jones, Charles William *association executive*

**Tuscaloosa**
Summersell, Frances Sharpley *organization worker*

### ALASKA

**Anchorage**
Devens, John Searle *natural resources administrator*
Jones, Mark Logan *educational association executive, educator*
Moore, Faye Annette *social services professional*
O'Regan, Deborah *association executive, lawyer*

**Fairbanks**
Wilkniss, Peter E. *foundation administrator, researcher*

### ARIZONA

**Dewey**
Burch, Mary Lou *organization consultant, housing advocate*

**Phoenix**
DeMenna, Kevin Bolton *lobbyist*

**Scottsdale**
Carney, Richard Edgar *foundation executive*
Jacobson, Frank Joel *cultural organization administrator*
Muller, H(enry) Nicholas, III *foundation executive*

**Sedona**
Keane, Mark Edward *public executive and educator*
Stoufer, Ruth Hendrix *community volunteer*

**Sun City**
Jones, Alexander Elvin *retired foundation executive*

**Tempe**
Baker, Roland Jerald *trade association administrator*

**Tucson**
Dresher, William Henry *research association executive*
Grand, Marcia *civic worker*
Lauver, Edith Barbour *nonprofit organization administrator*
Riggs, Frank Lewis *foundation executive*
Ross, Robert *health agency administrator*
Tirrell, John Albert *organization executive, consultant*

### ARKANSAS

**Fayetteville**
Stephens, Wanda Brewer *social services administrator, investor*

**Mountain Home**
Seevers, Charles Junior *foundation executive, psychologist*

### CALIFORNIA

**Aliso Viejo**
Sanford, Sarah J. *healthcare executive*

**Atherton**
King, Jane Cudlip Coblentz *volunteer educator*

**Bakersfield**
Drake, Stanley Joseph *association executive*

**Beverly Hills**
Brenner, Esther Lerner *fundraiser*

**Brea**
Tamura, Cary Kaoru *fundraiser*

**Canoga Park**
Lederer, Marion Irvine *cultural administrator*

**Carlsbad**
Liddicoat, Richard Thomas, Jr. *professional society administrator*
Swoap, David Bruce *children's relief official, art gallery director*

**Carmel**
Chester, Lynne *foundation executive, artist*
Pinkham, Frederick Oliver *foundation executive, consultant*

**Claremont**
Rankin, Robert *retired educational foundation executive*
Warder, Michael Young *think tank executive*

**Culver City**
Netzel, Paul Arthur *fundraising management executive, consultant*

**Dana Point**
Reed, David Andrew *foundation executive*

**Davis**
Redenbach, Sandra Irene *educational consultant*

**Hawthorne**
Gruenwald, James Howard *association executive, consultant*

**Irvine**
Fouste, Donna H. *association executive*
Young, Robert Anthony *association director*

**Keene**
Rodriguez, Arturo Salvador *labor union official*

**Kentfield**
Blum, Joan Kurley *fundraising executive*

**La Jolla**
Knox, Elizabeth Louise *community volunteer, travel consultant*

**Lancaster**
Roths, Beverly Owen *organization executive*

**Long Beach**
Brown, Lester B. *social work educator*
Lee, Isaiah Chong-Pie *social worker, educator*
Muchmore, Don Moncrief *museum, foundation, educational, financial fund raising and public opinion consulting firm administrator, banker*
Patino, Douglas Xavier *foundation and university administrator*

**Los Alamitos**
Jones, Dorothy Joanne *social services professional*

**Los Altos**
Orr, Susan Packard *foundation administrator*
Wickham, Kenneth Gregory *retired institute official, army officer*
Wilbur, Colburn Sloan *foundation administrator, chief executive officer*

**Los Angeles**
Berenbaum, Michael G. *foundation adminstrator, theology educator*
Chassman, Leonard Fredric *labor union administrator*
Christopher, James Roy *executive director*
Gottlieb, Leonard *foundation administrator*
Harris, Barbara Hull (Mrs. F. Chandler Harris) *social agency administrator*
Headlee, Rolland Dockeray *professional society administrator*
Hubbs, Donald Harvey *foundation executive*
Lindley, F(rancis) Haynes, Jr. *foundation president, lawyer*
Mack, J. Curtis, II *civic organization administrator*
Marshall, Mary Jones *civic worker*
Orsatti, Alfred Kendall *organization executive*
Reagan, Nancy Davis (Anne Francis Robbins) *volunteer, wife of former President of United States*
Reed, Donald Anthony *executive*
Rice, Susan F. *fundraising counsel executive*
†Shestock, Linda *community foundation executive*
Smith, Jean Webb (Mrs. William French Smith) *civic worker*
Walton, Brian *labor union executive*
Watkins, Sydney Lynn *sports administrator*
Williams, Harold Marvin *foundation official*

**Menlo Park**
Altman, Drew E. *foundation executive*
Nichols, William Ford, Jr. *foundation executive, business executive*
Pallotti, Marianne Marguerite *foundation administrator*

**Modesto**
Richardson, Ernest Ray (Rocky Richardson) *housing program supervisor*

**Moffett Field**
Scott, Donald Michael *educational association administrator, educator*

**Mountain View**
Michalko, James Paul *library association administrator*

**Newport Beach**
Kallman, Burton Jay *foods association director*

**North Hollywood**
Grasso, Mary Ann *theater association executive*

**Oakland**
Dozier, Flora Grace *civil and human rights activist, entrepreneur*
Macmeeken, John Peebles *foundation executive, educator*
Misner, Charlotte Blanche Ruckman *community organization administrator*
Rosen, Corey M. *professional association executive*

**Oceanside**
Roberts, James McGregor *retired professional association executive*

**Orange**
Zweifel, Donald Edwin *civic affairs volunteer, consultant*

**Orinda**
Fisher, Robert M. *foundation administrator, university administrator*

**Palm Springs**
Hearst, Rosalie *philanthropist, foundation executive*

**Pasadena**
Staehle, Robert L. *foundation executive*

**Pauma Valley**
Magee, Dennis *cultural organization administrator*

**Pebble Beach**
Gianelli, William Reynolds *foundation administrator, civil engineering consultant, former federal agency commissioner*

**Pleasanton**
Brooks, Stephen Volume *foundation executive*
Whisnand, Rex James *housing association executive*

**Pomona**
Thompson, Earlene *civic volunteer*

**Riverside**
Hodgen, Maurice Denzil *foundation executive*
Pick, Arthur Joseph, Jr. *chamber of commerce executive*

**Sacramento**
Black, Barbara Crowder *educational consultant*
Meyer, Rachel Abijah *foundation director, artist, theorist, poet*
Naglestad, Frederic Allen *legislative advocate*

**San Andreas**
Breed, Allen Forbes *correctional administrator*

**San Diego**
Ballinger, Charles Edwin *educational association administrator*
Carleson, Robert Bazil *public policy consultant, corporation executive*
Dolan, James Michael, Jr. *zoological society executive*
Grosser, T.J. *administrator, developer, fundraiser*
Hinsvark, Don George *social services agency professional*
Lane, Gloria Julian *foundation administrator*

**San Francisco**
Collins, Dennis Arthur *foundation executive*
Du Bain, Myron *foundation administrator*
Eastham, Thomas *foundation administrator*
Evankovich, George Joseph *labor union administrator*
Giovinco, Joseph *nonprofit administrator, writer*
Hayes, Randall L. *environmental organizer, lecturer*
Hickman, Maxine Viola *social services administrator*
Jacobs, John Howard *professional society administrator*
Marquardt, Sandra Mary *activist, lobbyist, researcher*
McCuaig, Ian Carruthers *fundraising consultant*
†Pope, Carl *professional society administrator*

Tobin, Gary Allan *cultural organization educator*

**San Jose**
Bennett, Charles Turner *social welfare administrator*

**San Juan Capistrano**
Horn, Deborah Sue *organization administrator, writer, editor*

**San Luis Obispo**
Jamieson, James Bradshaw *foundation administrator*

**San Marino**
Hull, Suzanne White *retired administrator, author*

**San Rafael**
Bobb, Richard Allen *non-profit executive*
Lee, Robert *association executive, former theological educator, consultant, author*

**Santa Barbara**
Krieger, David Malcolm *peace foundation executive, lawyer*
Mc Coy, Lois Clark *emergency services executive, retired county official, magazine editor*
Shobe, Nancy *fundraising consultant, small business owner*

**Santa Monica**
Abarbanel, Gail *social service administratior, educator*
Greene, Michael C. *art association administrator*
Rich, Michael David *research corporation executive, lawyer*
Thomson, James Alan *research company executive*

**Santa Rosa**
Harris, David Joel *foundation executive*

**Sherman Oaks**
Barron, Tiana Luisa *foundation developer, fundraiser, educator*

**Simi Valley**
Bumgardner, Larry G. *foundation administrator, law and political science educator*

**Sonoma**
Stadtman, Verne August *former foundation executive, editor*

**Sonora**
Coffill, Marjorie Louise *civic leader*

**South Lake Tahoe**
Nason, Rochelle *conservation organization administrator*
Prescott, Barbara Lodwich *educational administrator*

**Stanford**
Lyman, Richard Wall *foundation and university executive, historian*
Stone, William Edward *association executive*

**Studio City**
Frumkin, Simon *political activist and columnist*

**Sunnyvale**
Bills, Robert Howard *political party executive*
Karp, Nathan *political activist*

**Tiburon**
Cook, Lyle Edwards *retired fund raising executive, consultant*

**Trinidad**
Marshall, William Edward *historical association executive*

**Truckee**
Johnston, Bernard Fox *foundation executive*

**Tustin**
Parker, Kimberly Jane *nonprofit association executive, paralegal*

**Watsonville**
Cane, William Earl *nonprofit organization executive*

**COLORADO**

**Aurora**
Fish, Ruby Mae Bertram (Mrs. Frederick Goodrich Fish) *civic worker*
Motz, Kenneth Lee *former farm organization official*

**Boulder**
Jonsen, Richard Wiliam *educational administrator*
Neinas, Charles Merrill *athletic association executive*

**Castle Rock**
Graf, Joseph Charles *retired foundation executive*

**Colorado Springs**
Killian, George Ernest *educational association administrator*
Libby, Lauren Dean *foundation executive*
Loux, Gordon Dale *organization executive*
MacLeod, Richard Patrick *foundation administrator*
Miller, Zoya Dickins (Mrs. Hilliard Eve Miller, Jr.) *civic worker*
†Payne, Kevin Joseph *association executive*
Rochette, Edward Charles *retired association executive*

**Denver**
Bryan, A(lonzo) J(ay) *service club official*
Groff, JoAnn *organization administrator*
Hirschfeld, Arlene F. *civic worker, homemaker*
Hixon, Janet Kay Erickson *education specialist*
Hogan, Curtis Jule *union executive, industrial relations consultant*
Jones, Jean Correy *organization administrator*
Loeup, Kong *cultural organization administrator*
Nelson, Bernard William *foundation executive, educator, physician*

Reynolds, Collins James, III *foundation administrator*
Smith, Rita Sue *administrator*
Ward, Lester Lowe, Jr. *arts executive, lawyer*

**Englewood**
Chesser, Al H. *union official*
Reese, Monte Nelson *agricultural association executive*

**Fort Collins**
Cummings, Sharon Sue *state extension service youth specialist*

**Golden**
Shimanski, Charles Stuart *organization executive*

**Grand Junction**
McCarthy, Mary Frances *hospital foundation administrator*

**Greenwood Village**
Walker, Eljana M. du Vall *civic worker*

**Guffey**
Ward, Larry Thomas *social program administrator*

**Highlands Ranch**
Massey, Leon R. *professional society administrator*

**Lakewood**
Isely, Henry Philip *association executive, integrative engineer, writer, educator, businessman*

**Snowmass**
Lovins, L. Hunter *public policy institute executive*

**CONNECTICUT**

**Branford**
Hegyi, Albert Paul *association executive, lawyer*
Resnick, Idrian Navarre *foundation administrator*

**Bridgeport**
Hendricks, Edward David *speaker, consultant*

**Fairfield**
Rilla, Donald Robert *social services administrator*

**Falls Village**
Toomey, Jeanne Elizabeth *animal activist*

**Farmington**
Thibodeau, Robin Ann *union official, mail carrier*

**Groton**
Kennedy, Evelyn Siefert *foundation executive, textile restoration specialist*

**Guilford**
Schaffer, James Mason *foundation administrator*

**Hartford**
Decko, Kenneth Owen *trade association administrator*
Flynn, Barbara Lois *developer*
Francis, Paul Wilbur, Jr. *former professional society administrator*

**Lyme**
Greene, Joseph Nathaniel, Jr. *former foundation executive, former diplomat*

**Madison**
Houghton, Alan Nourse *association executive, educator, consultant*

**Milford**
Frazier, Howard Thomas *professional society administrator*
Wall, Robert Emmet *educational administrator, novelist*

**Mystic**
Connell, Hugh P. *foundation executive*
Smith, Norman Clark *fund raising consultant*

**New Canaan**
Davis, Emma Laura *social services specialist*
Mountcastle, Katharine Babcock *foundation executive*
Thomsen, Donald Laurence, Jr. *institute executive, mathematician*

**New Fairfield**
Meyers, Abbey S. *foundation administrator*

**New Haven**
Brewster, Carroll Worcester *fund administrator*
Dechant, Virgil C. *fraternal organization administrator*
Theodore, Eustace D. *alumni association executive, management consultant*

**Newington**
†Sumner, David George *association executive*

**North Branford**
Logan, John Arthur, Jr. *retired foundation executive*

**Norwalk**
Fulweiler, Patricia Platt *civic worker*

**Old Greenwich**
Bonner, Charles William, III *community services executive, newspaper writer*
Scullion, Tsugiko Yamagami *non-profit organization executive*

**Old Lyme**
Bond, Niles Woodbridge *cultural institute executive, former foreign service officer*

**Old Saybrook**
Spencer, William Courtney *foundation executive, international business executive*

**Ridgefield**
Weese, Bruce Eric *pharmaceutical industry lobbyist, human services manager*

**Riverside**
Coulson, Robert *retired association executive, arbitrator, author*

**Southbury**
Sallani, Marion Davis (Mrs. Werner Sallani) *social work administrator, therapist*

**Stamford**
Brakeley, George Archibald, Jr. *fundraising consultant*
Chisolm, Barbara Wille *world affairs organization executive*
†Gorman, Maureen *foundation administrator*
Hathaway, Lynn McDonald *education advocate, administrator*
Kaufman, John E. *retired association executive*
McNamara, Francis Joseph, Jr. *foundation executive, lawyer*
Wunsch, Bonnie Rubenstein *fraternal organization executive*

**Suffield**
Connelly, William Howard *retired foundation executive*

**Westport**
Milton, Catherine Higgs *public service entrepreneur*

**Willimantic**
Loin, E. Linnea *social work administrator*

**Wilton**
Forger, Robert Durkin *retired professional association administrator*
Sullivan, Adèle Woodhouse *organization official*

**DELAWARE**

**Dover**
Ornauer, Richard Lewis *retired educational association administrator*

**Newark**
Curtis, James C. *cultural organization administrator/history educator*
Mitchell, Peter Kenneth, Jr. *educational consultant, association administrator*

**Rehoboth Beach**
Warden, Richard Dana *government labor union official*

**Wilmington**
Peterson, Russell Wilbur *former association executive, former state governor*
Wheeler, M. Catherine *organization executive*

**DISTRICT OF COLUMBIA**

**Washington**
Able, Edward H. *association executive*
Abrams, Elliott *think-tank executive, writer, foreign affairs analyst*
Ahmann, Mathew Hall *social action organization administrator, consultant*
Ambach, Gordon Mac Kay *educational association executive*
Anderson, Dean William *educational administrator*
Andrews, Laureen E. *foundation administrator*
Appleberry, James Bruce *higher education association executive*
Arlook, Ira Arthur *public interest association executive*
†Armacost, Michael Hayden *research institution executive, ambassador*
Arnold, William Edwin *foundation administrator, consultant*
Atherton, Alfred Leroy, Jr. *foundation executive, former foreign service officer*
Babby, Ellen Reisman *education administrator*
Bagge, Carl Elmer *association executive, lawyer, consultant*
Banzhaf, John F., III *organization executive, lawyer*
Barbour, Haley *political organization administrator, lawyer*
Barrow, Robert Earl *retired agricultural organization administrator*
Barry, John J. *labor union leader*
Bartlett, Charles L. *think-tank executive*
Bartlett, Charles Leffingwell *foundation executive, former newspaperman*
Barto, Cheryl *educational association administrator, researcher*
Beazley, Hamilton Scott *volunteer health organization executive*
Bender, David Ray *library association executive*
†Berman, Ellen *foundation administrator*
†Berry, Morrell John *cultural organization administrator*
Biller, Morris (Moe Biller) *union executive*
Blitzer, Charles *educational administrator*
Boaz, David Douglas *foundation executive*
Bode, Barbara *foundation executive, consultant*
Bond, Julian *civil rights leader*
Bonosaro, Carol Alessandra *professional association executive, former government official*
Book, Edward R. *consultant, retired association executive*
Bookbinder, Hyman H(arry) *public affairs counselor*
Borut, Donald J. *professional society administrator*
Bourne, Francis Stanley *foundation administrator*
Boyle, John Edward Whiteford *cultural organization administrator*
Boyle, Renée Kent *cultural organization executive, translator, editor*
Bradley, Mitchell Hugh *retired professional society administrator, retired career officer*
Brightup, Craig Steven *lobbyist*
Brobeck, Stephen James *consumer advocate*

Brosnan, Carol Raphael Sarah *arts administrator, musician*
Brown, David R. *think-tank executive*
Brown, Lawrence Clifton, Jr. *foundation administrator*
Brown, William Robert *association executive, consultant*
Brownlee, Paula Pimlott *professional society administrator*
Bush, Barbara Pierce *volunteer, wife of former President of the United States*
†Bush, James T. *professional organization executive*
Cain, Becky C. *association executive*
Calhoun, John Alfred *social services administrator*
Calingaert, Michael *international consultant*
Cameron, Don R. *educational association administrator*
Canes, Michael Edwin *trade association administrator, economist*
Carey, Ronald *labor union leader*
Chan, Wing-Chi *cultural organization administrator, musicologist*
Chavez-Thompson, Linda *labor union administrator*
Clark, Margaret Pruitt *education and advocacy executive administrator*
Cochran, John Thomas *professional association executive*
Coia, Arthur A. *labor union executive*
Colbert, Robert Ivan *education association administrator*
Collins, Winifred Quick (Mrs. Howard Lyman Collins) *organizational executive, retired navy officer*
Cooper, Josephine Smith *trade association and public relations executive*
Cope, James Dudley *trade association administrator*
Crane, Edward Harrison, III *institute executive*
Croser, Mary Doreen *educational association executive*
Crutchfield, Sam Shaw, Jr. *association executive, lawyer*
Dambach, Charles Frederick *foundation administrator, management consultant*
Damgard, John Michael *trade association executive*
Dando, George William *professional association executive*
Danzansky, Joan Cox *child and family advocate and consultant, riding therapist*
Deets, Horace *association executive*
Denney, George Covert, Jr. *organization administrator*
DiBona, Charles Joseph *professional society administrator*
Dillon, Robert Sherwood *non-profit educational organization executive*
Ditlow, Clarence M. *think-tank executive*
Dolibois, Robert Joseph *trade association administrator*
Donahue, Thomas Reilly *trade union official*
†Dooley, Betty Parsons *educational association administrator*
Dorn, Jennifer Lynn *charitable organization administrator*
Dudley, Barbara *environmental association administrator*
Eisenberg, Pablo Samuel *non-profit organization executive*
Elliott, Thomas Michael *executive, educator, consultant*
Elsey, George McKee *foundation administrator*
Engel, Ralph *manufacturers association executive*
Farrell, William Christopher *lobbyist*
Fink, Matthew Pollack *trade association executive, lawyer*
Finkle, Jeffrey Alan *professional association executive*
Foard, Douglas W. *educational association administrator*
Forkan, Patricia Ann *professional society administrator*
Fowler, Donald L. *political committee chairman*
†Fowler, Raymond Dalton *professional association executive, psychologist*
Francois, Francis Bernard *association executive, lawyer*
Friedman, Miles *trade association executive, financial services company executive, university lecturer*
Fritz, Thomas Vincent *association and business executive, accountant*
Frye, LaRue *trade association executive*
Fujito, Wayne Takeshi *international business company executive*
Fuller, Kathryn Scott *environmental association executive, lawyer*
Gans, Curtis B. *think tank administrator*
†Gaviria, Cesar *political organization administrator*
Georgine, Robert Anthony *union executive*
Gershman, Carl Samuel *foundation administrator*
Gilliam, Arleen Fain *labor union administrator, finance executive*
Goldman, Aaron *foundation executive, writer*
Goldstein, Sheldon Robert *retired professional association administrator*
Golodner, Jack *labor association official*
Gore, Tipper (Mary Elizabeth Gore) *wife of vice president of the United States*
Gorham, William *organization executive*
Green, Shirley Moore *public affairs and communications executive*
Greenstein, Robert M. *non-profit organization director*
Griffenhagen, George Bernard *trade association executive*
Guenther, Kenneth Allen *business association executive, economist*
Harrison, Monika Edwards *business development executive*
Hartman, Arthur A. *international business consultant*
Healey, John G. *human services organization executive*
†Heinz, Teresa F. *foundation administrator*
Hill, Jim Tom *association executive*
Hills, John Merrill *public policy research center executive, former educational administrator*
Holbrook, Douglas Cowen *labor union administrator*
Holloway, James Lemuel, III *foundation executive, retired naval officer*
Holmer, Alan Freeman *trade association executive, lawyer*
Hosie, Stanley William *foundation executive, writer*
Howard, Barbara Viventi *research foundation executive*
Howard, Glen Scott *foundation executive, lawyer*
Howard, Jack *consultant*
Hoyt, John Arthur *humane society executive*
Huband, Frank Louis *educational association executive*

Hudnut, William Herbert, III *senior resident fellow, political scientist*
Hughes, Thomas Lowe *foundation executive*
Imig, David Gregg *educational association executive*
Ireland, Patricia *association executive*
Isaacs, Amy Fay *political organization executive*
Jacobson, Michael Faraday *consumer advocate, writer*
Johnston, Laurance Scott *foundation director*
Jones, George Fleming *foundation executive*
Kamber, Victor Samuel *political consultant*
Kamikawa, Alden Tanemitsu *trade association executive*
Kane, Michael Barry *social science research executive*
Karpinski, Gene Brien *non-profit group administrator, think tank executive*
Kavanaugh, Everett Edward, Jr. *trade association executive*
Keeny, Spurgeon Milton, Jr. *association executive*
Kemp, John D. *professional society administrator*
Kempner, Jonathan L. *professional society administrator*
Kleinknecht, Christian Frederick *Masonic official*
Knapp, Richard Maitland *association executive*
Knippers, Diane LeMasters *organization administrator*
Kolb, Charles Chester *humanities administrator*
Kossak, Shelley *think-tank executive*
Kratovil, Jane Lindley *think tank associate, developer/fundraiser*
Kreig, Andrew Thomas *trade association executive*
Krepinevich, Andrew F. *organization administrator*
†Kressley, Larry *foundation administrator*
†Ku, Charlotte *professional association administrator*
Kullberg, John Francis *foundation administrator*
Lampl, Peggy Ann *social services administrator*
LaPidus, Jules Benjamin *educational association administrator*
Larson, Charles Fred *trade association executive*
Lawson, Richard Laverne *trade association executive, retired military officer*
LeBlanc, James Leo *business executive, consultant*
Ledwig, Donald Eugene *professional society administrator*
Lesher, Richard Lee *association executive*
Leven, Ann Ruth *arts administrator*
Liederman, David Samuel *child welfare administrator*
Limon, Lavinia *social services administrator*
Lively, Carol A. *professional society administrator*
Longin, Thomas Charles *education association administrator*
Low, Stephen *foundation executive, educator, former diplomat*
Loy, Frank Ernest *conservation organization executive*
Lucas, C. Payne *development organization executive*
Luciano, Peter Joseph *professional society administrator*
†Lynch, Robert L. *art association administrator*
Magazine, Alan Harrison *association executive, consultant*
Magrath, C. Peter *educational association executive*
Marshall, Brian Laurence *trade association executive*
Marshall, William, III *think tank executive*
Martin, Jerry Lee *organization executive, philosophy educator*
Masters, Edward E. *association executive, former foreign service officer*
†Maury, Samuel L. *association executive*
Maynes, Charles William *foundation administrator*
McCarroll, Jeanne Louise *association executive*
McClintic, Howard Gresson *foundation executive*
McCloskey, J(ohn) Michael *association administrator*
McElroy, Edward J. *union officer*
McEntee, Gerald W. *labor union official*
Mc Kay, Emily Gantz *civil and human rights professional*
McNulty, Robert Holmes *non-profit executive*
McSteen, Martha Abernathy *organization executive*
Melendez, Sara E. *non-profit organization executive*
Messner, Howard Myron *professional association executive*
Miller, John Francis *association executive, social scientist*
Miller, Margaret Alison *education association administrator*
Moore, Jacquelyn Cornelia *labor union official, editor*
Morrison, James William, Jr. *lobbyist, government relations consultant*
Mtewa, Mekki *foundation administrator*
Muir, Patricia Allen *educational association administrator*
Munson, Richard Jay *congressional policy analyst*
Murphy, Kenneth Ray *non-governmental organization executive*
Murray, James Joseph, III *association executive*
Myers, William Gerry, III *advocate, lawyer*
Nader, Ralph *consumer advocate, lawyer, author*
Nicholson, Richard Selindh *educational association administrator*
Nikkel, Ronald Wilbert *social services administrator*
Norton, James J. *union official*
O'Brien, Margaret Hoffman *educational administrator*
O'Day, Paul Thomas *trade association executive*
Ogilvie, Donald Gordon *bankers association executive*
Ottley, William Henry *professional association director, consultant*
†Paal, Douglas H. *educational association administrator*
Paulson, Stanley Fay *educational association administrator*
Pearson, Roger *organization executive*
Pelavin, Sol Herbert *research company executive*
Peterson, Esther *consumer advocate*
Pings, Cornelius John *educational association administrator*
Pinstrup-Andersen, Per *educational administrator*
Platts, Howard Gregory *scientific, educational organization executive*
†Portney, Paul R. *research and educational organization executive*
†Posner, Roni D. *professional organization executive*
Radin, Alex *former association executive, consultant*
Reger, Lawrence Lee *trade association administrator*
Reich, Alan Anderson *foundation administrator*
Rich, Dorothy Kovitz *educational administrator, author*
Richardson, Ann Bishop *foundation executive, lawyer*
Riehle, B. Hudson *trade association administrator*
Robey, Kathleen Moran (Mrs. Ralph West Robey) *civic worker*
Robinson, Kenneth Leonard, Jr. *trade association executive*
Robinson, Leonard Harrison, Jr. *international government consultant, business executive*
Rodgers, Kirk Procter *international organization executive, environmentalist*
Rodman, Peter Warren *foreign policy specialist*
Rosenberg, Sarah Zacher *institute arts administration executive, humanities administration consultant*
Rudder, Catherine Estelle *political science association administrator*
Russell, William Joseph *educational association administrator*
†Salisbury, Dallas L. *research institute administrator*
Samuel, Howard David *union official*
Sandler, Bernice Resnick *women's rights specialist*
Scanlon, Terrence Maurice *public policy foundation administrator*
Scheibel, James Allen *volunteer service executive*
Schlickeisen, Rodger Oscar *non-profit environmental organization executive*
Schubert, Richard Francis *consultant*
Scott, Helen Kinard *corporate executive*
Seldman, Neil Norman *cultural organization administrator*
Semler Strong, Margot *association administrator*
Sever, Tom *labor union administrator*
†Shuman, Michael *think tank executive, attorney*
Siciliano, Rocco Carmine *institute executive*
Sieverts, Frank Arne *association executive*
Simmons, Caroline Thompson *civic worker*
Sims, Robert Bell *professional society administrator, public affairs official, newspaper publisher*
Smedley, Lawrence Thomas *retired organization executive*
†Soller, R. William *association executive, pharmacologist*
Sombrotto, Vincent R. *postal union executive*
Spence, Sandra *professional administrator*
Spink, Frank Henry, Jr. *association manager, publisher, urban planner,*
Splete, Allen Peterjohn *association executive, educator*
Staats, Elmer Boyd *foundation executive, former government official*
Stephens, John Frank *association executive, researcher*
Stern, Paula *international trade advisor*
Stone, Jeremy Judah *professional society administrator*
Strachan, David E. *trade association executive*
Strong, Henry *foundation executive*
Sugarman, Jule M. *children's services consultant, former public administrator*
Sulc, Jean Luena (Jean L. Mestres) *lobbyist, consultant*
Sutherland, Alan Roy *foundation administrator*
†Sweeney, John Joseph *labor union administrator*
Szaz, Zoltan Michael *association executive*
Tarr-Whelan, Linda *policy center executive*
Taylor, Helen Lavon Hollingshed *association executive, early childhood consultant*
Taylor, Robert William *professional society administrator*
Thompson, Otis Nathaniel, Jr. *professional society executive*
Thomsen, Samuel Borron *non-profit executive, consultant*
Tipton, E. Linwood *trade association executive*
Tobias, Robert Max *labor leader, lawyer*
Tonkin, Leo Sampson *educational foundation administrator*
Topping, John Carruthers, Jr. *environmental organization administrator, lawyer*
Townsend, Ann Van Devanter *foundation administrator, art historian*
Trumka, Richard Louis *labor leader, lawyer*
Ture, Norman Bernard *public policy research organization executive*
Uehling, Barbara Staner *educational administrator*
Unsell, Lloyd Neal *energy organization executive, former journalist*
Vander Horst, Kathleen Purcell *nonprofit association administrator*
Vanderryn, Jack *philanthropic foundation administrator*
Veliotes, Nicholas Alexander *professional association executive, former ambassador and assistant secretary of state*
Vladeck, Bruce Charney *charitable organization executive*
von Kann, Clifton Ferdinand *aviation and space executive, software executive*
Ward, Michael Delavan *social services administrator, former Congressman*
Warren, David Liles *educational association executive*
Weinstein, Allen *educator, historian, non-profit administrator*
Wertheimer, Fredric Michael *public policy advocate*
Weyrich, Paul Michael *political organizations executive*
White, Margita Eklund *television association executive*
Willging, Paul Raymond *trade association executive*
Williams, Eddie Nathan *research institution executive*
Williams, Lawrence Floyd *conservation organization official*
Williams, Maurice Jacoutot *development organization executive*
Williams, Neville *international development organization executive*
Williams, Ronald L. *pharmaceutical association executive*
Wilson, Glen Parten *professional society administrator*
Wiseman, Laurence Donald *foundation executive*
Wolfe, Leslie R. *think-tank executive*
Woodall, Samuel Roy, Jr. *trade association executive*
Work, Jane Magruder *professional society administrator*
Yost, Paul Alexander, Jr. *foundation executive, retired coast guard officer*
Yzaguirre, Raul Humberto *civil rights leader*
Zielinski, Paul Bernard *grant program administrator, civil engineer*

## FLORIDA

### Arcadia
Turnbull, David John (Chief Piercing Eyes-Penn) *cultural association executive*

### Bal Harbour
Ash, Dorothy Matthews *civic worker*

### Boca Raton
Fey, Dorothy (Mrs. George Jay Fey) *former association executive*
Jessup, Jan Amis *arts volunteer, writer*
Williams, Charlotte Evelyn Forrester *civic worker*

### Boynton Beach
Rogers, John S. *retired union official*

### Coral Springs
Burg, Ralph *art association executive*

### Daytona Beach
Collyer, Robert B. *trade association administrator*

### Delray Beach
Stewart, Patricia Carry *foundation administrator*

### Destin
De Revere, David Wilsen *professional society administrator*

### Englewood
Schultz, Arthur Joseph, Jr. *retired trade association executive*

### Fort Lauderdale
McAusland, Randolph M. N. *arts administrator*
White, Mary Lou *fundraiser, writer, educator*
Wynne, Brian James *former association executive, consultant*

### Gainesville
Baughman, George Fechtig *foundation executive*

### Hallandale
Contney, John Joseph *trade association administrator*

### Heathrow
†Darbelnet, Robert Louis *automobile association executive*

### Hollywood
Graves, Walter Albert *retired association executive, editor*

### Jacksonville
Glover, Richard Bernard *foundation administrator*
Johnson, Leland "Lee" Harry *social services administrator*
Morris, Max King *foundation executive, former naval officer*

### Lake Park
McBride, Nancy Allyson *child resource center administrator*

### Lake Worth
Moore, Alderine Bernice Jennings (Mrs. James F. Moore) *association and organization administrator*

### Lakeland
Spencer, Mary Miller *civic worker*

### Longwood
Dunne, Nancy Anne *retired social services administrator*

### Melbourne
Dale, Cynthia Lynn Arpke *educational administrator*

### Miami
Beckley, Donald K. *fundraiser*
Berger, Arthur Seymour *cultural organization executive, vice-mayor, lawyer, author*
Berger, Joyce Muriel *foundation executive, author, editor*
Brinkman, Paul Del(bert) *foundation executive*
Courshon, Carol Biel *civic worker*
Cullom, William Otis *trade association executive*
Dickason, John Hamilton *foundation executive*
Hills, Lee *foundation administrator, newspaper executive, consultant*
Lynch, Catherine Gores *social work administrator*
Rosenberg, Mark B. *think-tank executive*
VanBrode, Derrick Brent, IV *trade association administrator*
Weber, Nancy Walker *charitable trust administrator*

### Naples
Bageant, Martha Dyer *retired volunteer*
Rowe, Herbert Joseph *retired trade association executive*

### North Palm Beach
Crawford, Roberta *association administrator*

### Orlando
Grant, Joanne Cummings *social service agency administrator*

### Oviedo
Ferguson, Carmela *social services administrator*

### Palm Beach
Chittick, Elizabeth Lancaster *association executive, women's rights activist*
Mallardi, Vincent *organization executive*
Mandel, Carola Panerai (Mrs. Leon Mandel) *foundation trustee*
Rinker, Ruby Stewart *foundation administrator*

### Palm Beach Gardens
Falk, Bernard Henry *trade association executive*

### Panama City Beach
Schafer, John Stephen *foundation administrator*

### Pensacola
Furlong, George Morgan, Jr. *museum foundation executive, retired naval officer*

### Pinellas Park
West, Wallace Marion *cultural organization administrator*

### Ponte Vedra
Watson, John Lawrence, III *former trade association executive*

### Saint Augustine
Baker, Norman Henderson *professional association administrator*
Marsolais, Harold Raymond *trade association administrator*
Rountree, John Griffin Richardson *association and retail executive*

### Saint Petersburg
Dickson, Suzanne Elizabeth (Sue Dickson) *educational administrator*
Giffin, Barbara Haines *education coordinator*

### Sanibel
Ball, Armand Baer *former association executive, consultant*

### Sarasota
Balter, Frances Sunstein *civic worker*
Spencer, Lonabelle (Kappie Spencer) *political agency administrator, lobbyist*

### Stuart
Hutchinson, Janet Lois *historical society administrator*

### Tallahassee
Bishop, Barney Tipton, III *political consultant, lobbyist*
Campbell, Frances Harvell *foundation administrator*
Ryll, Frank Maynard, Jr. *professional society administrator*

### Tampa
Lowe, Peter Stephen *non-profit company executive*
Tapp, Mamie Pearl *educational association administration*

### Tequesta
Luster, George Orchard *professional society administrator*

### Wesley Chapel
Holloway, Marvin Lawrence *retired automobile club executive, rancher, vintager*

### West Palm Beach
Borchers, Karen Lily *child welfare administrator*
Engh, Fredric Charles *educational association administrator*
Moody, Cheryl Anne *social services administrator, social worker, educator*

### Winter Haven
Gobie, Henry Macaulay *philatelic researcher, retired postal executive*

### Winter Park
Olsson, Nils William *former association executive*

## GEORGIA

### Americus
Fuller, Millard Dean *charitable organization executive, lawyer*

### Atlanta
†Avery, Byllye Yvonne *health association administrator*
Axon, Michael *education association field representative*
Barnes, Harry G., Jr. *human rights activist, conflict resolution specialist, retired ambassador*
Beard, Rick *cultural organization administrator*
Bell, Ronald Mack *university foundation administrator*
Birdsong, Alta Marie *volunteer*
DeConcini, Barbara *association executive, religious studies educator*
Elson, Suzanne Goodman *community activist*
Foster, Andrew Nichols, Jr. *professional society administrator*
Glassick, Charles Etzweiler *academic foundation administrator*
Harrison, John Raymond *foundation executive, retired newspaper executive*
Johnston, John Philip *social services executive*
Kelly, William Watkins *educational association executive*
King, Coretta Scott (Mrs. Martin Luther King, Jr.) *educational association administrator, lecturer, writer, concert singer*
King, Jennie Louise *research director*
McTier, Charles Harvey *foundation administrator*
Neiss, Edgar *civic organization administrator*
†Philipp, Alicia *community foundation executive*
Rucker, Kenneth Lamar *public administrator, educator*
Scott, William Fred *cultural organization administrator*
Sears, Curtis Thornton, Jr. *educational administrator*
Thumann, Albert *association executive, engineer*
Tipping, William Malcolm *social services administrator*
White, Ann Wells *community activist*
Wylly, Barbara Bentley *performing arts association administrator*

### Augusta
Davison, Frederick Corbet *foundation executive*
Grier, Leamon Forest *social services administrator*

### Cordele
Wade, Benny Bernar *educational administrator*

### Duluth
Gullickson, Nancy Ann *art association administrator*

### La Grange
Gresham, James Thomas *foundation executive*

PROFESSIONAL INDEX 5103 ASSOCIATIONS AND ORGANIZATIONS

**Macon**
Mills, Cynthia Spraker *association executive*

**Norcross**
LaFramboise, Patrick Joseph *trade association administrator*

**Sautee Nacoochee**
Hill, Ronald Guy *non-profit organization consultant*

**Savannah**
Beals, L(oren) Alan *association executive*

**Stone Mountain**
Wingate, Henry Taylor, Jr. *foundation administrator, fundraiser*

**Valdosta**
McRae, John Henry *educational administrator*

**Winterville**
Shockley, W. Ray *travel trade association executive*

**HAWAII**

**Honolulu**
Jordan, Amos Azariah, Jr. *foreign affairs educator, retired army officer*
Lee, Beverly Ing *educational administrator*
Mirikitani, John Masa *foundation administrator*
Olmsted, Ronald David *foundation executive, consultant*
Robinson, Robert Blacque *foundation administrator*

**Kapaa**
Atkins, William Theodore *community volunteer, retired insurance executive*

**Lihue**
Pironti, Lavonne De Laere *developer, fundraiser*

**IDAHO**

**Boise**
Hennessey, Alice Elizabeth *community foundation executive*

**Coeur D Alene**
Sanderson, Holladay Worth *domestic violence advocate*

**Meridian**
Patterson, Beverly Ann Gross *fund raising consultant, grant writer, federal grants administrator, social services administrator, poet*

**Moscow**
Samaniego, Pamela Susan *organization administrator*

**ILLINOIS**

**Arlington Heights**
Nerlinger, John William *trade association administrator*

**Barrington**
Howlett, Phyllis Lou *athletics conference administrator*

**Carlinville**
Bellm, Joan *civic worker*

**Champaign**
Clark, Roger Gordon *educational administrator*

**Chicago**
Barker, Emmett Wilson, Jr. *trade association executive*
Bloch, Ralph Jay *professional association executive*
Bourdon, Cathleen Jane *executive director*
Bushman, Mary Laura Jones *developer, fundraiser*
Chacko, Samuel *association official*
Creighton, Neal *foundation administrator, retired army officer*
Cyr, Arthur I. *institute executive*
Detmer, Lawrence McCormick *professional society administrator*
Dolan, Thomas Christopher *professional society administrator*
Donnell, Harold Eugene, Jr. *professional society administrator*
Donovan, Margaret *educational association administrator*
Dykla, K.H.S. Edward George *social services administrator*
Feldstein, Charles Robert *fund raising consultant*
Fetridge, Bonnie-Jean Clark (Mrs. William Harrison Fetridge) *civic volunteer*
Harvey, Katherine Abler *civic worker*
Hayes, Richard Johnson *association executive, lawyer*
Heineman, Natalie (Mrs. Ben W. Heineman) *civic worker*
Herbert, Victor James *foundation administrator*
Jackson, Jesse Louis *civic and political leader, clergyman*
Jonas, Harry S. *professional society administrator*
Koenig, Bonnie *non-profit organization consultant*
Krug, Judith Fingeret *association administrator*
Kudo, Irma Setsuko *not-for-profit executive director*
†Leff, Deborah *foundation executive*
Lerner, Alexander Robert *association executive*
MacDougal, Gary Edward *corporate director, foundation trustee*
†Martinez, Elizabeth *professional association administrator*
Mercer, David Robinson *cultural organization administrator*
Miller, Jay Alan *civil rights association executive*
Minow, Josephine Baskin *civic worker*
Murphy, Ellis *association management executive*
Newman, Wade Davis *trade association executive*
Olsen, Rex Norman *trade association executive*
Peterson, Mildred Othmer (Mrs. Howard R. Peterson) *civic leader, lecturer, writer, librarian*
Richman, Harold Alan *social welfare policy educator*
Rielly, John Edward *educational association administrator*
Rodgers, James Foster *association executive, economist*
Scalish, Frank Anthony *labor union administrator*
Schimberg, Barbara Hodes *organizational development consultant*
Sigmon, Joyce Elizabeth *professional society administrator*
†Smith, Almon R. *labor union administrator*
Vogelzang, Jeanne Marie *professional association executive, attorney*
Wilhelm, David C. *political organization administrator*
Wright, Helen Kennedy *professional association administrator, publisher, editor, librarian*

**Crystal Lake**
Chamberlain, Charles James *railroad labor union executive*
Linklater, Isabelle Stanislawa Yarosh-Galazka (Lee Linklater) *foundation administrator*

**Des Plaines**
Neel, Judy Murphy *association executive*

**Du Quoin**
Smith, Lucius Skinner, III *educational foundation administrator*

**Elgin**
Kelly, Matthew Edward *association executive, retired*

**Elmhurst**
Hildreth, R(oland) James *foundation executive, economist*
John, Richard C. *enterprise development organization executive*

**Evanston**
Abnee, A. Victor *trade association executive*
Gordon, Julie Peyton *foundation administrator*
Kreml, Franklin Martin *educational administrator, association executive*
Thrash, Patricia Ann *educational association administrator*
Yoder, Frederick Floyd *fraternity executive*

**Galena**
Hermann, Paul David *retired association executive*

**Glencoe**
Carr, Barbara Whitney *foundation administrator*

**Harvey**
Dunn, Eraina Burke *non-profit organization administrator, city official*

**Hoffman Estates**
Biggins, James J. *fundraiser*
Roach, William Russell *training and education executive*

**La Grange Park**
Brown, Helen Sauer *fund raising executive*

**Lake Bluff**
Schreiber, George Richard *association executive, writer*

**Lake Forest**
Smith, Wendy L. *foundation executive*
Taylor, Barbara Ann *educational consultant*

**Long Grove**
Connor, James Richard *foundation administrator*

**Mooseheart**
Ross, Donald Hugh *fraternal organization executive*

**Naperville**
L'Allier, James Joseph *educational multimedia company executive, instructional designer*

**Northbrook**
Degen, Bernard John, II *association executive*

**Northfield**
Cartwright, Howard E(ugene) *retired association executive*

**Palatine**
Brod, Catherine Marie *foundation administrator*

**Park Forest**
McDonnell, Rosemary Cynthia *social services administrator*

**Park Ridge**
Bailey, Marianne Therese *social service administrator*
Kleckner, Dean Ralph *trade association executive*
Kukla, Robert John *professional society administrator educator*

**Peoria**
Bussone, Frank Joseph *foundation executive, television broadcaster*

**Riverside**
Dengler, Robert Anthony *professional association executive*

**Rockford**
Lukac, George Joseph *fundraising executive*

**Rosemont**
Good, William Allen *professional society executive*

**Schaumburg**
Boston, Leona *organization executive*
Pandak, Carol Ann *fraternal organization administrator*
Tompson, Marian Leonard *professional society administrator*

**Skokie**
Gleason, John Patrick, Jr. *trade association executive*

**Springfield**
Blackman, Jeanne A. *policy advisor*
Puckett, Carlissa Roseann *non-profit association executive*

**Urbana**
Myers, Miles A. *educational association administrator*
Sturtevant, William T. *fundraising executive, consultant*

**Vernon Hills**
Michalik, John James *legal educational association executive*

**Waukegan**
Drapalik, Betty Ruth *civic worker, artist*

**Wheaton**
Votaw, John Frederick *educational foundation executive, educator*

**Wilmette**
Brink, Marion Francis *trade association administrator*
Hansen, Andrew Marius *retired library association executive*

**Winfield**
McNutt, Kristen Wallwork *consumer affairs executive*

**Winnetka**
Andersen, Kenneth Benjamin *retired association executive*

**INDIANA**

**Bloomington**
Wilson, Kathy Kay *foundation executive*

**Evansville**
Early, Judith K. *social services director*
Halterman, Martha Lee *social services administrator, counselor*

**Fishers**
Gatto, Louis Constantine *educational authority executive*

**Greenwood**
Means, George Robert *organization executive*

**Hanna**
Stephenson, Dorothy Maxine *volunteer*

**Indianapolis**
Barcus, Robert Gene *educational association administrator*
Braun, Robert Clare *retired association and advertising executive*
Burnett, Judith Jane *foundation administrator, consultant*
Clark, Charles M., Jr. *research institution adminstrator*
Dortch, Carl Raymond *former association executive*
Dunn, Sidney N. *fraternity administrator*
Honor, Noël Evans *social services supervisor*
McDonell, Katherine Mandusic *professional society administrator*
Poray, John Lawrence *professional association executive*
Recker, Thomas Edward *fraternal organization executive*
†Robbins, N. Clay *foundation administrator*
Shaffer, Alfred Garfield (Terry) *service organization executive*
Sweezy, John William *political party official*
Throgmartin, Dianne *educational foundation executive*
Vereen, Robert Charles *retired trade association executive*

**Martinsville**
†Miller, John *foundation administrator*

**Michigan City**
Blake, George Alan, Jr. *non-profit association executive*

**Moores Hill**
Ramsey, William Ray *professional society administrator*

**Santa Claus**
Platthy, Jeno *cultural association executive*

**Shelby**
Kurzeja, Richard Eugene *professional society administrator*

**Terre Haute**
Aldridge, Sandra *civic volunteer*

**IOWA**

**Cedar Rapids**
Huber, Rita Norma *civic worker*

**Center Point**
Neenan, Thomas Francis *association executive, consultant*

**Davenport**
Campagna, Timothy Nicholas *institute executive*

**Decorah**
Price, Lucile Brickner Brown *retired civic worker*

**Des Moines**
Nelson, Charlotte Bowers *public administrator*
Powell, Sharon Lee *social welfare organization administrator*
Smith, Mary Louise *politics and public affairs consultant*

**Iowa City**
Ferguson, Richard L. *educational administrator*

**West Branch**
Forsythe, Patricia Hays *development professional*

**KANSAS**

**Fort Riley**
Spurrier, Patricia Ann *executive director*

**Kansas City**
Campbell, Joseph Leonard *trade association executive*

**Larned**
Hewson, Mary McDonald *civic volunteer*

**Lawrence**
Bowman, Laird Price *retired foundation administrator*
†Mona, Stephen Francis *golf association executive*

**Prairie Village**
Pew, Kevin Dale *association executive*

**Shawnee Mission**
Green, John Lafayette, Jr. *education executive*
Stock, Gregg Francis *retired association executive*

**Topeka**
Menninger, Roy Wright *medical foundation executive, psychiatrist*
Powers, Ramon Sidney *historical society administrator, historian*

**Wichita**
Lowrey, Annie Tsunee *retired cultural organization administrator*

**Winfield**
Gray, Ina Turner *fraternal organization administrator*

**KENTUCKY**

**Corbin**
Barton-Collings, Nelda Ann *political activist, newspaper, bank and nursing home executive*

**Frankfort**
Cody, Wilmer St. Clair *educational administrator*
Klotter, James C. *state historical organization administrator, consultant*

**Lexington**
Lewis, Robert Kay, Jr. *fundraising executive*
Sexton, Robert Fenimore *educational organization executive*

**Louisville**
Watts, Beverly L. *civil rights executive*

**LOUISIANA**

**Baton Rouge**
Robertson, George Leven *retired association executive*
Warren, John William *professional society administrator*

**Lake Charles**
Fourcard, Inez Garey *foundation executive, artist*

**New Orleans**
Monroe, James Walter *organization executive*
Rathke, Dale Lawrence *community organizer and financial analyst*

**MAINE**

**Augusta**
Billings, Richard Whitten *professional society administrator*
Gervais, Paul Nelson *foundation administrator, psychotherapist, public relations executive*
Trites, Donald George *human service consultant*

**Friendship**
Merrill, Mary Lee *professional society administrator*

**Georgetown**
Chapin, Maryan Fox *civic worker*

**Kittery Point**
Howells, Muriel Gurdon Seabury (Mrs. William White Howells) *volunteer*

**Orrs Island**
Porter, Maxiene Helen Greve *civic worker*

**Portland**
Nosanow, Barbara Shissler *art association administrator*

**Rangeley**
Hunter, J(ohn) Robert *insurance consumer advocate*

**Windham**
Mulvey, Mary C. *retired adult education director, gerontologist, senior citizen association administrator*

**York**
Smart, Mary-Leigh Call (Mrs. J. Scott Smart) *civic worker*

## MARYLAND

### Aberdeen Proving Ground
Tobin, Aileen Webb *educational administrator*

### Accokeek
Dorsch, Roberta Funk *association executive, volunteer coordinator*

### Annapolis
Brady, Frank Benton *retired technical society executive*
Forkin, Sister Jean Louise *organization administrator*
Stahl, David Edward *trade association administrator, retired*

### Baltimore
Backas, James Jacob *foundation administrator*
Evers-Williams, Myrlie *cultural organization administrator*
Freeze, James Donald *administrator, clergyman*
Fuentealba, Victor William *professional society administrator*
Hartman, Charles Henry *association executive, educator*
Jernigan, Kenneth *social services administrator*
Maurer, Marc Morgan *federation administrator, lawyer*
Safran, Linda Jacqueline *fundraising consultant*
Viall, J(ohn) Thomas *non-profit organization executive, fundraiser*

### Beltsville
Kasprick, Lyle Clinton *volunteer, financial executive*

### Bethesda
Beall, Robert Joseph *foundation executive*
Briggs, Shirley Ann *retired organization executive, writer*
Brouha, Paul *association executive, fishery-wildlife biologist*
Buhler, Leslie Lynn *institute administrator*
Cleary, Timothy Finbar *professional society administrator*
Day, Robert Dwain, Jr. *foundation executive, lawyer*
Grandy, Fred *foundation administrator, former congressman, former actor*
Grau, John Michael *trade association executive*
Hershaft, Alex *organization executive*
Hodes, Richard J. *think tank executive, immunologist, researcher*
Kalish, Susan Jean *professional society administrator*
King, Charles McDonald, Jr. *association foundation executive*
Larson, Clarence Edward *foundation administrator*
Nelligan, William David *professional association executive*
Oddis, Joseph Anthony *social services administrator*
Oliver, Daniel *foundation fellow, lawyer*
Pogue, Mary Ellen E. (Mrs. L. Welch Pogue) *youth and community worker*
Rogul, June Audrey *fundraising executive, government relations specialist*
Salisbury, Tamara Paula *foundation executive*
Saunders, Charles Baskerville, Jr. *retired association executive*
Tape, Gerald Frederick *former association executive*
Thursz, Daniel *retired service organization executive, consultant*
Wolf, R. Peter *fundraising executive, harpsichordist*
Wright, Helen Patton *professional society administrator*

### Chevy Chase
Carey, Stephen Clayton *foundation administrator*
Cross, Christopher T. *professional society administrator*
Dulin, Maurine Stuart *volunteer*
Sauer, Richard John *developer fundraiser*

### College Park
Stover, Carl Frederick *foundation executive*

### Columbia
Bailey, John Martin *retired transportation planner, educator*
Gray, Kirk Lamond *social investment firm executive, anthropologist*

### Crofton
Ross, E(dwin) Clarke *association executive, educator*

### Elkton
Scherf, Christopher N. *foundation administrator*

### Fort Washington
Coffey, Matthew B. *professional society administrator*

### Frederick
Keefe, Arthur Thomas, III *non-profit fund raising executive*

### Germantown
Price, William James *organization executive*

### Lanham
Littlefield, Roy Everett, III *association executive, legal educator*

### Lexington Park
Sprague, Edward Auchincloss *retired association executive, economist*

### Linthicum Heights
Lavin, Charles Blaise, Jr. *association executive*

### Mitchellville
Kendall, Katherine Anne *social worker*

### Owings Mills
Siegel, Bernard *foundation administrator*

### Parkville
Payne, Winfield Scott *national security policy research executive*

### Potomac
Noonan, Patrick Francis *conservation executive*

### Rockville
Anderson, Walter Dixon *trade association management consultant*
Cypess, Raymond Hardd *think tank executive*
Hawkins, James Alexander, II *mental health fund executive*
Huber, John Michael *director non-profit organization*
Kline, Raymond Adam *professional organization executive*
Leshner, Alan Irvin *science foundation administrator*
Murphy, Gerard Norris *trade association executive*
†Spahr, Frederick Thomas *association executive*
Standing, Kimberly Anna *educational researcher*
Sumberg, Alfred Donald *professional association executive*

### Silver Spring
Camphor, James Winky, Jr. *educational administrator*
Fanelli, Joseph James *retired public affairs executive, consultant*
Fockler, Herbert Hill *foundation executive*
Goldstein, Laurence Alan *trade association executive*
Hayman, Harry *association executive, electrical engineer*
Hermanson Ogilvie, Judith *foundation executive*
Hunt, Mary Elizabeth *association executive*
Kirkland, (Joseph) Lane *labor union official*
Rasi, Humberto Mario *educational administrator, editor, minister*
Winston, Michael Russell *foundation executive, historian*

### Takoma Park
Lancaster, Alden *educational consultant*

### Towson
Barton, Meta Packard *business executive, financial planner*

### Upper Marlboro
Beasley, Diana Lee *educational administrator*

## MASSACHUSETTS

### Amherst
Hewlett, Horace Wilson *former educational administrator, association executive*
Holmes, Helen Bequaert *association administrator*

### Boston
Cabot, Louis Wellington *foundation trustee*
Deissler, Mary A. *foundation executive*
Diener, Betty Jane *trade association administrator*
Franks, Peter John *educational administrator*
†Garcia, Frieda *community foundation executive*
Glass, Renée *educational health foundation executive*
Guild, Richard Samuel *trade association management company executive*
Meacham, Brian Jay *professional society administrator*
Sullivan, James Leo *organization executive*
Tarlov, Alvin Richard *former philanthropic foundation administrator, physician, educator, researcher*
Tucker, Louis Leonard *historical society administrator*

### Brookline
Alvino, Gloria *charitable organization administrator, speaker*
Wax, Bernard *research and development consultant, lecturer*

### Brookline Village
Zoll, Miriam Hannah *activist, writer, communication specialist*

### Cambridge
†Chen, Martha Alter *international development, gender and poverty specialist*
de Marneffe, Barbara Rowe *volunteer*
Harris, William Wolpert *treasurer political action committee*
Kovach, Bill *educational foundation administrator*
Orlen, Joel *professional society administrator*
Wenger, Luke Huber *educational association executive, editor*

### Chestnut Hill
Daniel-Dreyfus, Susan B. Russe *civic worker*

### Dorchester
Daly, Charles Ulick *foundation executive*

### Essex
Broome, Roger Greville Brooke, IV *fundraiser*

### Fitchburg
Niemi, Beatrice Neal *social services professional*

### Great Barrington
Gilmour, Robert Arthur *foundation executive, educator*

### Holyoke
Hedrick, Janet Lee *fundraising executive*

### Ipswich
Bryant, Edward Curtis *education consultant*

### Lenox
Slavin, Simon *social administration educator*

### Lincoln
Payne, Roger S. *conservation organization executive*

### Marlborough
Ryan, John William *association executive*

### Mattapan
Deen, Alusaine *foundation administrator*

### Medford
O'Connell, Brian *community organizer, public administrator, writer, educator*

### Shrewsbury
Forde, Mary Margaret *foundation executive*

### Wellesley
Hornig, Lilli Schwenk *educational administrator, researcher*
Tagge, Anne Katherine *not-for-profit organization administrator*

## MICHIGAN

### Adrian
Henricks, Roger Lee *social services administrator*

### Ann Arbor
Diana, Joseph A. *retired foundation executive*
Dirks, Nicholas B. *cultural research organization administrator/history educator*
Kennedy, David Boyd *foundation executive, lawyer*
Radock, Michael *foundation executive*
Ware, Richard Anderson *foundation executive*

### Battle Creek
Davis, Laura Arlene *foundation administrator*
DeVries, Robert Allen *foundation administrator*
Grace, Helen Kennedy *foundation administrator*
Hollenbeck, Karen Fern *foundation executive*
Mawby, Russell George *retired foundation executive*
Richardson, William Chase *foundation executive*
Wendt, Linda M. *educational association administrator*

### Bloomfield Hills
Bianco, Joseph Paul, Jr. *foundation and art museum executive*

### Brighton
Darlington, Judith Mabel *clinical social worker, Christian counselor*

### Dearborn
Brennan, Leo Joseph, Jr. *foundation executive*

### Detroit
Noland, Mariam Charl *foundation executive*
Scherer, Karla *foundation executive, venture capitalist*
Schuster, Elaine *civil rights professional, state official*
Vaitkevicius, Vainutis Kazys *foundation administrator, medical educator*
Wyse, Roy *labor union administrator*

### East Lansing
Mitstifer, Dorothy Irwin *honor society administrator*
Munger, Benson Scott *professional society administrator*

### Farmington Hills
Leyh, George Francis *association executive*

### Flint
Belcher, Max *social services administrator*
White, William Samuel *foundation executive*

### Fremont
Melonakos, Christine Marie *educational administrator*

### Grosse Pointe Shores
Smith, Frank Earl *retired association executive*

### Hickory Corners
Brown, Norman A. *consultant, educator*

### Lansing
Croxford, Lynne Louise *social services administrator*
Lobenherz, William Ernest *association executive, legislative counsel, lawyer*

### Madison Heights
O'Hara, Thomas Edwin *professional administrator executive*

### Manistee
Behring, Daniel William *educational and business professional*

### Okemos
Luecke, Eleanor Virginia Rohrbacher *civic volunteer*

### Saint Joseph
Butt, Jimmy Lee *retired association executive*
Phenix, Gloria Gayle *educational association administrator*

### Southfield
Fleming, Mac Arthur *labor union administrator*

### Troy
Hunia, Edward Mark *foundation executive*
Marshall, John Elbert, III *foundation executive*

### University Center
Miller, Roberta Balstad *science administrator*

### Ypsilanti
Porter, John Wilson *education executive*

## MINNESOTA

### Minneapolis
Johnson, John Warren *retired association executive*
†King, Reatha Clark *community foundation executive*
King, Robert Cotton *professional society consultant*
Kolehmainen, Jan Waldroy *professional association administrator*
O'Keefe, Thomas Michael *foundation executive*
Schanfield, Fannie Schwartz *community volunteer*
Skillingstad, Constance Yvonne *social services administrator, educator*
Speer, Nancy Girouard *educational administrator*

### Minnetonka
Fogelberg, Paul Alan *continuing education company executive*

### Rochester
Shulman, Carole Karen *professional society administrator*
Wojcik, Martin Henry *foundation development official*

### Roseville
Hughes, Jerome Michael *education foundation executive*

### Saint Cloud
Henry, Edward LeRoy *former foundation executive, consultant, college president, public official*

### Saint Paul
Anderson, Gordon Louis *foundation administrator*
Archabal, Nina M(archetti) *historical society director*
Aune, Benjamin *health association administrator*
Doermann, Humphrey *foundation administrator*
Fesler, David Richard *foundation director*
Goff, Lila Johnson *historical society administrator*
McNamee, Sister Catherine *educational association executive*
Parsons, Mark Frederick *college development officer*

### Saint Peter
Nelsen, William Cameron *foundation president, former college president*

### Wayzata
Shannon, James Patrick *foundation consultant, retired food company executive*

## MISSISSIPPI

### Fayette
La Salle, Arthur Edward *historic foundation executive*

### Jackson
Bates, Lura Wheeler *trade association executive*
Penick, George Dial, Jr. *foundation executive*
Risley, Rod Alan *education association executive*
Sullivan, John Magruder, II *government affairs administrator*
Thrash, Edsel E. *educational administrator*

### Long Beach
Kanagy, Steven Albert *foundation administrator*

### Pontotoc
Roberts, Rose Harrison *social services administrator, consultant*

## MISSOURI

### Bucklin
Payne, Flora Fern *retired social service administrator*

### Columbia
Francis, Lee, III *trade association administrator*
McFate, Kenneth Leverne *trade association administrator*
Palo, Nicholas Edwin *professional society administrator*

### Earth City
Anderhalter, Oliver Frank *educational organization executive*

### Independence
Potts, Barbara Joyce *historical society executive*

### Ironton
Douma, Harry Hein *social service agency administrator*

### Jefferson City
McDaniel, Sue Powell *cultural organization administrator*

### Kansas City
Bugher, Robert Dean *professional society administrator*
Colaizzi, Joseph John *homeless services professional, clergyman*
Davis, Florea Jean *social worker*
Dickenson, H. H. *professional society administrator*
Fries, James Lawrence *trade association executive*
Levi, Peter Steven *chamber of commerce executive, lawyer*
Slater, William Adcock *retired social services organization executive*
Sparks, Donald Eugene *interscholastic activities association executive*
Switzer, Samuel Thomas *non-profit administrator*
Wilson, Eugene Rolland *foundation executive*

### Kirksville
French, Michael Francis *non-profit education agency administrator*

### O'Fallon
Lottes, Patricia Joette Hicks *foundation administrator, retired nurse*

### Richmond Heights
Chandler, James Barton *international education consultant*

### Saint Louis
Bascom, C. Perry *foundation administrator*
Duhme, Carol McCarthy *civic worker*
Hall, Mary Taussig *volunteer*
Hunter, Earle Leslie, III *professional association executive*
†MacArthur, Robert S. *foundation administrator, Episcopalian priest*
Pope, Robert E(ugene) *fraternal organization administrator*

**Springfield**
Himstedt, Ronald Eugene *union official*
Morris, Ann Haseltine Jones *social welfare administrator*

## MONTANA

**Billings**
Abrams, Ossie Ekman *fundraiser*
Sample, Joseph Scanlon *foundation executive*

**Bozeman**
Sanddal, Nels Dodge *foundation executive, consultant*

**Great Falls**
Ebbinga, Crystalle Yvonne *social services administrator*

**Harrison**
Jackson, Peter Vorious, III *retired association executive*

**Helena**
Marquardt, Kathleen Patricia *professional society administrator*

**Missoula**
Kemmis, Daniel Orra *cultural organization administrator, author*

## NEBRASKA

**Bancroft**
Neihardt, Hilda *foundation administrator, writer, educator*

**Boys Town**
Peter, Val Joseph *social services administrator, author*

**Lincoln**
Rosenow, John Edward *foundation executive*
Swartz, Jack *chamber of commerce executive*

**Omaha**
Ansorge, Luella M. *retired association administrator*
Bell, C(lyde) R(oberts) (Bob Bell) *foundation administrator*
Flickinger, Thomas Leslie *hospital alliance executive*
Monasee, Charles Arthur *retired healthcare foundation executive*
Prince, Frances Anne Kiely *civic worker*

**Seward**
Vrana, Verlon Kenneth *retired professional society administrator, conservationist*

## NEVADA

**Carson City**
Ayres, Janice Ruth *social service executive*

**Henderson**
Freyd, William Pattinson *fund raising executive, consultant*

**Incline Village**
DuBois, L(uther) Carl *development company executive*

**Las Vegas**
Horner, Lee *foundation executive, speaker, consultant, computer specialist*

**Minden**
Jackson, John Jay *denomination administrator, clergyman*

**Pahrump**
Hersman, Marion Frank *professional administrator, lawyer*

**Reno**
†Getty, J. Paul *foundation executive*

## NEW HAMPSHIRE

**Concord**
Crosier, John David *trade association administrator*

**Francestown**
Hamel, Elizabeth Cecil *volunteer, educator*

**Hancock**
Carney, David Mitchel *political party official*

**Londonderry**
Michaud, Norman Paul *association administrator, logistics consultant*

**Marlborough**
Walton, Russell Sparey *foundation administrator*

**Randolph**
Bradley, William Lee *retired foundation executive, educator*

**Washington**
Halverson, Wendell Quelprud *former educational association executive, clergyman, educator*

## NEW JERSEY

**Avalon**
Emmert, Richard Eugene *professional association executive, retired*

**Bernardsville**
Cooperman, Saul *foundation administrator*

**Camden**
Wellington, Judith Lynn *cultural organization administrator*

**Cape May Court House**
Gronka, M(artin) Steven *educational association executive, film and television producer*

**Cedar Grove**
Brownstein, Alan P. *health foundation executive, consultant*

**Cliffside Park**
Pushkarev, Boris S. *research foundation director, writer*

**Cranbury**
Copleman, Rosalyn Rosenberg *volunteer*
Rector, Milton Gage *social work educator, former association executive*

**East Rutherford**
Kempner, Michael W. *public relations executive*

**Englewood**
Orlando, George (Joseph) *union executive*

**Glen Ridge**
Pendley, Donald Lee *association executive*

**Glen Rock**
Riggs, Gina Ginsberg *educational association administrator*

**Hoboken**
Buckman, Thomas Richard *foundation executive, educator*

**Jersey City**
Degatano, Anthony Thomas *educational association administrator*
Niemiec, Edward Walter *professional association executive*

**Kendall Park**
Goldberg, Bertram J. *social agency administrator*

**Lebanon**
O'Neill, Elizabeth Sterling *trade association administrator*

**Locust**
Freeman, David Forgan *retired foundation executive*

**Lyndhurst**
Ridenour, James Franklin *fund raising consultant*

**Millburn**
Tinning, Herbert Peter *association executive*

**Montclair**
Campbell, Stewart Fred *foundation executive*
Mason, Lucile Gertrude *fundraiser, consultant*

**Montvale**
Scopes, Gary Martin *professional association executive*

**New Vernon**
Dugan, John Leslie, Jr. *foundation executive*

**Pennington**
Calvo, Roque John *professional society administrator*

**Plainfield**
Limpert, John H., Jr. *fundraising executive*

**Princeton**
Balch, Stephen Howard *professional society administrator*
Brief, Henry *trade association consultant*
Hearn, Ruby Puryear *foundation executive*
Jellinek, Paul S. *foundation executive, health economist*
Kenyon, Regan Clair *research foundation executive*
Stern, Gail Frieda *historical association director*

**Ramsey**
Eklund, Donald Arthur *trade association executive*

**Red Bank**
Meredith, George (Marlor) *association executive, writer*

**River Edge**
Jacobson, Gilbert H. *association executive, lawyer*

**Roseland**
Hochberg, Mark S. *foundation president, cardiac surgeon*

**Rumson**
Brenner, Theodore Engelbert *retired trade association executive*

**Scotch Plains**
Ungar, Manya Shayon *volunteer, education consultant*

**Short Hills**
Rinsky, Judith Lynn *foundation administrator, educator consultant*

**Springfield**
Stoller, Mitchell Robert *non-profit organization administrator*

**Trenton**
Binder, Elaine Kotell *consultant to associations*

## NEW MEXICO

**Albuquerque**
Cole, Terri Lynn *organization administrator*
Roberts, Dennis William *trade association administrator*

**Las Cruces**
Eriksson, Anne-Marie *social services executive, educator*

## NEW YORK

**Albany**
Bellizzi, John J. *law enforcement association administrator, educator, pharmacist*
Carovano, John Martin *not-for-profit adminstrator, conservationist*

**Amagansett**
†Frankl, Jeanne Silver *educational association administrator*

**Amherst**
Clark, Donald Malin *professional society administrator*

**Armonk**
Bergson, Henry Paul *professional association administrator*
Cannella, Nancy Anne *educational administrator*

**Astoria**
Davidson, Rex L. *association executive*

**Bedford Hills**
Waller, Wilhelmine Kirby (Mrs. Thomas Mercer Waller) *civic worker, organization official*

**Briarcliff Manor**
Luck, Edward Carmichael *professional society administrator*

**Bronx**
Holland, Darryl Boyd *foundation executive*
Vassel, Lee Hylton *urbanist, social services administrator, writer*

**Brooklyn**
Crawford, Patricia Alexis *healthcare and social justice advocate, writer*
Prince, Leslie Francis *lobbyist, activist*

**Buffalo**
Clarkson, Elisabeth Ann Hudnut *civic worker*
Glickman, Marlene *non-profit organization administrator*

**Chappaqua**
de Janosi, Peter Engel *research manager*

**Clinton**
Couper, Richard Watrous *foundation executive, educator*

**Cortlandt Manor**
Rath, Bernard Emil *trade association executive*

**Dobbs Ferry**
Miss, Robert Edward *fundraiser*

**East Hampton**
Fulbright, Harriet Mayor *foundation administrator*

**East Islip**
Chassman, Karen Moss *educational administrator*

**East Quogue**
Weiss, Elaine Landsberg *community development management official*

**Elizabethtown**
Lawrence, Richard Wesley, Jr. *foundation executive*

**Elmhurst**
Matsa, Loula Zacharoula *social services administrator*

**Flushing**
Fichtel, Rudolph Robert *retired association executive*
Madden, Joseph Daniel *trade association executive*
Rathbone, Susan Wu *social services administrator*

**Garrison**
Pierpont, Robert *fund raising executive, consultant*

**Harrison**
Herrick, Doris Eileen Schlesinger *sports association administrator*
Wadsworth, Frank Whittemore *foundation executive, literature educator*

**Hudson**
Miner, Jacqueline *political consultant*

**Huntington**
Schulz, William Frederick *human rights association executive*

**Lagrangeville**
Sedlak, James William *organization administrator*

**Larchmont**
Hinerfeld, Ruth J. *civic organization executive*

**Merrick**
Doyle, James Aloysius *retired association executive*

**Montauk**
Butler, Thomas William *retired health and social services administrator*

**Mount Kisco**
Keesee, Patricia Hartford *volunteer*

**New Rochelle**
Black, Page Morton *civic worker*

**New York**
Allmendinger, Paul Florin *retired engineering association executive*
Angle, Richard Warner, Jr. *not-for-profit administrator, publishing executive*
Appel, Marsha Ceil *association executive*
Aronson, Esther Leah *association administrator, psychotherapist*
Barnes, Jack Whittier *political party official*
Bausch, James John *foundation executive*
Beckham, Edgar Frederick *foundation administrator*
Belden, David Leigh *professional association executive, engineering educator*
Bell, Thomas Devereaux, Jr. *public relations company executive*
Bellamy, Carol *international organization executive*
Benner, Mary Wright *lobbyist*
Berkman, Lillian *foundation executive, corporation executive, art collector*
Berresford, Susan Vail *philanthropic foundation executive*
Berry, Nancy Michaels *philanthropy consultant*
Bird, Mary Lynne Miller *professional society administrator*
Bjornson, Edith Cameron *foundation executive, communications consultant*
Bloch, Julia Chang *foundation administrator, former government official*
Braverman, Robert Jay *international consultant, public policy educator*
Brown, Terrence Charles *art association executive, researcher, lecturer*
Campbell, Colin Goetze *foundation president*
Canada, Geoffrey *social welfare administrator*
Cashin, Richard Marshall *international aid official*
Cassella, William Nathan, Jr. *organization executive*
Catley-Carlson, Margaret *professional organization administrator*
Chapin, Schuyler Garrison *cultural affairs executive, university dean*
Chatfield-Taylor, Adele *arts administrator, historic preservationist*
Christopher, Maurine Brooks *foundation administrator, writer, editor*
Cicerchi, Eleanor Ann Tomb *fundraising executive*
Clarke, Garvey Elliott *educational association administrator, lawyer*
Cole, Elma Phillipson (Mrs. John Strickler Cole) *social welfare executive*
Collett, Stephen Wallace *social services organization executive*
†Cook, John Wesley *foundation administrator*
Cornell, Thomas Charles *peace activist, writer*
Couture, Josie Balaban *foundation director, insurance executive*
David, Miles *association and marketing executive*
Davis, Karen Padgett *fund executive*
Davis, Kathryn Wasserman *foundation executive, writer, lecturer*
Dean, Diane D. *youth service agency executive, fund development consultant*
Deffenbaugh, Ralston H., Jr. *immigration agency executive, lawyer*
DeVita, M. Christine *foundation administrator*
Diamond, Irene *foundation administrator*
†Drake, Owen Burtch Winters *association administrator*
Dressner, Howard Roy *foundation executive, lawyer*
Easum, Donald Boyd *consultant, educator, former institute executive, diplomat*
Eisenberg, Alan *professional society administrator*
Ekman, Richard *foundation executive, educator*
Elliott, Eleanor Thomas *foundation executive, civic leader*
Engelhardt, Sara Lawrence *organization executive*
Eppes, William David *civic worker, writer*
Feeney, Maryann McHugh *fundraiser*
Feurey, Claudia Packer *not-for-profit executive*
Finberg, Barbara Denning *foundation executive*
Fisher, Florence Anna *association executive, author, lecturer*
†Flicker, John *foundation executive*
Foerst, John George, Jr. *fundraising executive*
Fox, Daniel Michael *foundation administrator, author*
Foxman, Abraham H. *advocacy organization administrator*
Franklin, Phyllis *professional association administrator*
Freid, Jacob *association executive, educator*
Freund, Gerald *foundation administrator*
Gallagher, Edward Peter *foundation administrator*
Garrison, John Raymond *organization executive*
Gaudieri, Millicent Hall *association executive*
Gilmore, Louise Jacobson *labor union director*
Glasser, Ira Saul *civil liberties organization executive*
Goldblatt, Eileen Witzman *arts administrator, executive director*
Goldmark, Peter Carl, Jr. *foundation executive*
Granik, Russell T. *sports association executive*
Gray, Robert Loren *professional society administrator*
Grimaldi, Nicholas Lawrence *social services administrator*
Guenther, Paul Bernard *volunteer*
Guttentag, Lucas *advocate, lawyer*
Handberg, Irene Deak *educational executive*
Harris, David Alan *not-for-profit organization executive*
Hart, Kitty Carlisle *arts administrator*
Heatley, Connie La Motta *association executive*
Helton, Arthur Cleveland *advocate*
Hesselbein, Frances Richards *foundation executive, consultant, editor*
Hester, James McNaughton *foundation administrator*
†Hoffman, Linda R. *social services administrator*
Holman, Margaret Mezoff *fundraising consultant*
Holtzman, Ellen A. *foundation executive*
Innis, Roy Emile Alfredo *organization executive*
Jacobsen, Theodore H. (Ted H. Jacobsen) *labor union official, educator*
Jacobson, Gaynor I. *retired association executive*
Jerome, Fred Louis *science organization executive*
Johns, William Potter *non-profit organization administrator*
Kaggen, Lois Sheila *non-profit organization executive*
Kahan, Marlene *professional association executive*
Kahn, Alfred Joseph *social worker and policy scholar, educator*
Kane, Herman William *research company executive, political scientist*
Kaplan, Robert Arthur *trade association executive*

Kardon, Peter Franklin *foundation administrator*
Karr, Norman *trade association executive*
Kaskell, Peter Howard *association executive, lawyer*
Kennedy, John Joseph *trade association executive*
Kennedy, Moorhead *foundation administrator*
Krasno, Richard Michael *educational organization executive, educator*
Kuh, Joyce Dattel *education administrator*
Kuyper, Joan Carolyn *foundation administrator*
Labunski, Stephen Bronislaw *professional society administrator*
Lamb, George Richard *foundation executive*
Landy, Joanne Veit *foreign policy analyst*
Lawson-Johnston, Peter Orman *foundation executive*
Lee, Clement William Khan *trade association administrator*
Letzig, Betty Jean *association executive*
Lewis, Sylvia Davidson *association executive*
Linder, Bertram Norman *foundation administrator, horse-breeder, actor*
Luce, Henry, III *foundation executive*
Luks, Allan Barry *executive director*
Mahoney, Margaret Ellerbe *foundation executive*
Mangan, Mona *association executive, lawyer*
Marchi, Lorraine June *social services executive*
Marks, Edward B. *international social service administrator*
Marlin, Alice Tepper *research organization administrator*
Maynard, Virginia Madden *charitable organization executive*
Mazur, Jay J. *trade union official*
McCormack, Elizabeth J. *foundation administrator*
McCrary, Eugenia Lester (Mrs. Dennis Daughtry McCrary) *civic worker, writer*
McNamara, Mary E. *nonprofit executive, asset manager, minister*
Metcalf, Karen *foundation executive*
Milbank, Jeremiah *foundation executive*
Miller, Harvey S. Shipley *foundation trustee*
Miller, Lenore *labor union official*
Millett, Kate (Katherine Murray Millett) *political activist, sculptor, artist, writer*
Mintz, Dale Leibson *health education executive*
Moran, Martin Joseph *fundraising company executive*
Morrisett, Lloyd N. *foundation executive*
Nadler, Allan Lawrence *institute director*
Neal, Leora Louise Haskett *social services administrator*
Odenweller, Robert Paul *philatelist, association executive, airline pilot*
Olyphant, David *cultural, educational association executive*
O'Neil Bidwell, Katharine Thomas *fine arts association executive, performing arts executive*
Oppenheimer-Nicolau, Siobhan *think tank executive*
Ovadiah, Janice *cultural institute administrator*
Owens, Alexandra Cantor *professional society administrator*
Peters, Robert Wayne *organization executive, lawyer*
Phillips, Russell Alexander, Jr. *foundation executive*
Preston, Frances Williams *performing rights organization executive*
†Price, Hugh B. *foundation executive, lawyer*
Rattazzi, Serena *art museum and association administrator*
†Riordan, John Thomas *trade association executive*
Robinson, David Zav *non-profit agency consultant*
Robinson, Nan Senior *not-for-profit organization consultant*
Rose, Joanna Semel *civic activities worker*
Rosoff, Jeannie I. *foundation administrator*
Roy, Robin Jennifer *educational fund raiser, marketing professional*
Scaffidi, Judith Ann *school volunteer program administrator*
Schlittler, Gilberto Bueno *former United Nations official, lecturer*
Schubart, Mark Allen *arts and education executive*
Schwalbe, Mary Anne *nonprofit committee executive*
Seessel, Thomas Vining *nonprofit organization executive*
Sharp, Daniel Asher *foundation executive*
Sheinkman, Jack *union official, lawyer*
Sherrod, Lonnie Ray *foundation administrator, researcher, psychologist*
Siegman, Henry *association executive, foreign policy analyst*
Singer, Arthur Louis, Jr. *foundation executive*
Singh, Jyoti Shankar *political organization director*
Slater, Joseph Elliott *educational institute administrator*
Slutsky, Lorie Ann *foundation executive*
Smith, Datus Clifford, Jr. *former foundation executive, publisher*
Smith, J. Kellum, Jr. *foundation executive, lawyer*
Sokol, Marc Jeffrey *arts administrator*
Solender, Stephen David *philanthropic organization executive*
Spero, Joan Edelman *foundation president*
Spira, Patricia Goodsitt *performing arts association executive*
Steedman, Doria Lynne Silberberg *organization executive*
Straus, Oscar S., II *foundation executive*
Sultanik, Kalman *professional society administrator*
Sussman, Leonard Richard *foundation executive*
Swing, John Temple *association executive, lawyer*
Touborg, Margaret Earley Bowers *non-profit executive*
Tudryn, Joyce Marie *professional society administrator*
Wanner, Eric *foundation executive*
Weeks, David Frank *foundation administrator*
Weintraub, Daniel Ralph *social welfare administrator*
Weisl, Edwin Louis, Jr. *foundation executive, lawyer*
Wellington, Sheila Wacks *foundation administrator, psychiatry educator*
Wiener, Malcolm Hewitt *foundation executive*
Wohlgelernter, Beth *organization executive*
Wray, Gilda Gates *foundation administrator*
Wright, Hugh Elliott, Jr. *association executive, writer*
Zollar, Jawole Willa Jo *art association administrator*

**Oneonta**
Zachmeyer, Richard Frederick *administrator*

**Ossining**
Chervokas, John Vincent *chamber of commerce executive*
Weintz, Caroline Giles *non-profit association consultant, travel writer*

**Oyster Bay**
Russell, Mary Wendell Vander Poel *non-profit organization executive, interior*

**Pittsford**
Dorsey, Eugene Carroll *former foundation and communications executive*

**Potsdam**
Stevens, Sheila Maureen *teachers union administrator*

**Purchase**
†Staley, Harry L. *fund raising executive*

**Rochester**
DeMarco, Roland R. *foundation executive*
Pacala, Leon *retired association executive*
Strand, Marion Delores *social service administrator*

**Rome**
Griffith, Mary L. Kilpatrick (Mrs. Emlyn I. Griffith) *civic leader*

**Scarborough**
Beglarian, Grant *foundation executive, composer, consultant*

**Scarsdale**
Bernstein, Irving *international organization executive*
Jensen, Grady Edmonds *retired association executive*
Paulin, Amy Ruth *civic activist, consultant*
Rosow, Jerome Morris *institute executive*
Wile, Julius *former corporate executive, educator*

**Schenectady**
Chestnut, Harold *foundation administrator, engineering executive*

**Scotia**
Pontius, James Wilson *foundation administrator*

**Stony Brook**
Brandwein, Ruth Ann *social welfare educator*

**Suffern**
Zecca, John Andrew *retired association executive*

**Syracuse**
Blount-Cucchiaro, Lori *arts adminstrator, fundraiser*
Ramsey, Dan Steven *foundation and organization administrator*
Rountree, Patricia Ann *youth organization administrator*

**Tarrytown**
Dobkin, John Howard *art administrator*
Dorland, Byrl Brown *civic worker*
Goldin, Milton *fund raising counsel, writer*

**Tonawanda**
Browning, James Franklin *professional society executive*

**Waccabuc**
Cross, William Redmond, Jr. *corporate director, foundation executive*

**Westbury**
O'Sullivan, Kevin Patrick *foundation administrator*

**White Plains**
Cooke, Lloyd Miller *former organization executive*
Stalerman, Ruth *civic volunteer, poet*

**Yonkers**
Karpatkin, Rhoda Hendrick *consumer information organization executive, lawyer*

## NORTH CAROLINA

**Asheville**
Fobes, John Edwin *international organization official*

**Carrboro**
Greenslade, Forrest Charles *international health care executive*

**Cary**
Martin, William Royall, Jr. *association executive*

**Chapel Hill**
Dickman, Catherine Crowe *retired human services administrator*
Kenan, Thomas Stephen, III *philanthropist*
MacGillivray, Lois Ann *organization executive*
Slack, Lewis *organization administrator*
Wicker, Marie Peachee *civic worker*

**Charlotte**
Locke, Elizabeth Hughes *foundation administrator*
Love, Franklin Sadler *retired trade association executive*
McCall, Billy Gene *charitable trust executive*
Stair, Frederick Rogers *retired foundation executive, former seminary president*

**Durham**
Bevan, William *retired foundation executive*
Lozoff, Bo *nonprofit organization administrator*
Rosenthal, Julian Bernard *association executive, lawyer*
Semans, Mary Duke Biddle Trent *foundation administrator*

**Greensboro**
Kornegay, Horace Robinson *trade association executive, former congressman, lawyer*

**Montreat**
Robinson, Spencer, Jr. *retired service club executive, accountant*

**Raleigh**
Brooker, Lena Epps *human relations program administrator*

**Research Triangle Park**
†Harvey, Glenn F. *association executive*
Miller, Robert Reese *trade association executive*

**Sanford**
Skadden, Donald Harvey *professional society executive, accounting educator*

**Smithfield**
Taylor, Ellen Borden Broadhurst *civic worker*

**Weaverville**
Mankoff, Albert William *cultural organization administrator, consultant*

**Wilson**
McCain, Betty Landon Ray (Mrs. John Lewis McCain) *political party official*

**Winston Salem**
Carter, Henry Moore, Jr. *foundation executive*
Jones, F(rancis) Whitney *fund raising executive, consultant*
Lambeth, Thomas Willis *foundation executive*

## OHIO

**Akron**
Collier, Alice Elizabeth *retired community organization executive*
Frank, John V. *foundation executive*
Martino, Frank Dominic *union executive*

**Bryan**
Nelson, Sandra Kay *foundation administrator*

**Canton**
Lyon, James Hugh *educational rights specialist, legislative consultant, political strategist*

**Chagrin Falls**
Vail, Iris Jennings *civic worker*

**Chardon**
Langer, Edward L. *trade association administrator*
Reinhard, Sister Mary Marthe *educational organization administrator*

**Cincinnati**
Hiatt, Marjorie McCullough *service organization executive*
Norman, Peter Minert *fundraising consulting company executive*
Sowder, Fred Allen *foundation administrator, alphabet specialist*
Zola, Gary Phillip *religious educational administrator, rabbi,*

**Circleville**
Scherer, Robert Davisson *retired business and association executive*

**Cleveland**
Bergholz, David *foundation administrator*
Calabrese, Leonard M. *social services administrator*
Calkins, Hugh *foundation executive*
Cooper, James Clinton *social services administrator, consultant*
Faller, Dorothy Anderson *international agency administrator*
Fordyce, James Stuart *non-profit organization executive*
Garrison, William Lloyd *cemetery executive*
Hartley, Duncan *fundraising executive*
Jenson, Jon Eberdt *association executive*
Minter, Steven Alan *foundation executive, social worker*

**Columbus**
Benton-Borghi, Beatrice Hope *educational consultant, author, publisher*
Blair, William Travis (Bud Blair) *retired organization executive*
Colburn, Julia Katherine Lee *volunteer, educator*
Cole, Charles Chester, Jr. *educational administrator*
Hamilton, Harold Philip *fund raising executive*
Luck, James I. *foundation executive*
Newman, Diana S. *community foundation executive, consultant*
Patrick, Jane Austin *association executive*
Selby, Diane Ray Miller *fraternal organization administrator*
Sharp, Paul David *institute administrator*
Williams, Robert Roy *trade association administrator*

**Dayton**
Daley, Robert Emmett *foundation executive, retired*
Mathews, David *foundation executive*
McDonald, Bronce William *community activist, advocate*
Schwartzhoff, James Paul *foundation executive*

**Materials Park**
Putnam, Allan Ray *association executive*

**Mentor**
Andrassy, Timothy Francis *trade association executive*

**Middletown**
Clinton, Mariann Hancock *educational association administrator*

**Oberlin**
Distelhorst, Garis Fred *trade association executive*
Swank, Emory Coblentz *world affairs consultant, lecturer*

**Portsmouth**
Stead, Francesca Manuela Lewenstein *natural health care consultant, massage therapist*

**Toledo**
Markwood, Sandra Reinsel *human services administrator*

**Yellow Springs**
Graham, Jewel Freeman *social worker, lawyer, educator*

**Zoar**
Fernandez, Kathleen M. *cultural organization administrator*

## OKLAHOMA

**Edmond**
McLaughlin, Lisa Marie *educational administrator*

**Lawton**
Brooks, (Leslie) Gene *cultural association administrator*

**Oklahoma City**
Gumerson, Jean Gilderhus *health foundation executive*
Maton, Anthea *education consultant*
Van Rysselberge, Charles H. *organization administrator*
Woods, Pendleton *educational administrator*

**Tahlequah**
Ross, John *cultural organization administrator*

**Tulsa**
Wesenberg, John Herman *professional society administrator*

## OREGON

**Beaverton**
Henderson, George Miller *foundation executive, former banker*

**Corvallis**
Wilkins, Caroline Hanke *consumer agency administrator, political worker*

**Gold Beach**
Dillon, Robert Morton *retired association executive, architectural consultant*

**Gresham**
Nicholson, R. Stephen *organization administrator*

**Junction City**
Humphry, Derek *association executive*

**Klamath Falls**
Ehlers, Eleanor May Collier (Mrs. Frederick Burton Ehlers) *civic worker*

**Medford**
Sours, James Kingsley *association executive, former college president*

**Portland**
Bruce, John Allen *foundation executive, educator*
Collins, Maribeth Wilson *foundation president*
McClave, Donald Silsbee *professional society administrator*
O'Hollaren, Paul Joseph *former international fraternity administrator*
Orloff, Chet *cultural organization administrator*
†Rooks, Charles S. *foundation administrator*

**Salem**
Toran, Kay Dean *social services director*

**Summerville**
Hopkins, Gerald Frank *trade association administrator*

## PENNSYLVANIA

**Allentown**
Berman, Philip I. *foundation administrator*
Farr, Lona Mae *non-profit executive, business owner*

**Ardmore**
Zeit, Ruth Mae *foundation administrator*

**Aspers**
Saltzman, Charles McKinley *educational consultant*

**Berwyn**
Reed, Clarence Raymond *retired association executive*

**Blue Bell**
Bell, Michael G. *trade association administrator*

**Bryn Mawr**
Carroll, Mary Colvert *corporate executive*
Cooney, Patricia Ruth *civic worker*
Driskill, John Ray *professional society administrator*

**Camp Hill**
Hughes, William Francis, Jr. *educational consultant*

**Chadds Ford**
King, M. Jean *association executive*

**Conshohocken**
Gambescia, Stephen Francis *research administrator*

**Dillsburg**
Bowers, Glenn Lee *retired professional society administrator*

**Drexel Hill**
Schiazza, Guido Domenic (Guy Schiazza) *educational association administrator*

**Easton**
Danjczek, Michael Harvey *social service adminstrator*

**Elizabethtown**
Krut, Stephen Frank *trade association administrator*
Madeira, Robert Lehman *professional society administrator*

**Erie**
Egan, Corrine Halperin *trade association administrator*

**Exton**
Penrose, Charles, Jr. *professional society administrator*

**Glenside**
Carter, Ruth B. (Mrs. Joseph C. Carter) *foundation administrator*

**Harrisburg**
Breslin, Michael Joseph, III *social services administrator, educator*
Loedding, Peter Alfred *trade association executive*

**Hershey**
Bomgardner, William Earl *retired association executive, photographer*
Pincock, Garry LaMar *association administrator*

**Kempton**
Lenhart, Cynthia Rae *conservation organization executive*

**Laverock**
Block, Isaac Edward *professional society administrator*

**Lewisburg**
Neuman, Nancy Adams Mosshammer *civic leader*

**Lititz**
Lord, Kathleen Virginia *fundraising executive*

**Media**
Kahrmann, Robert George *educational administrator*

**Newtown**
Keenan, Terrance *foundation executive*

**Philadelphia**
Bodine, James Forney *retired civic leader*
Ciociola, Cecilia Mary *science education specialist*
Dolnick, Sandy Friedman *cultural organization administrator*
Foti, Margaret Ann *association executive, publisher, editor*
Friedman, Murray *civil rights official, historian*
Klein, Arthur *foundation executive*
McKenna, Thomas Morrison, Jr. *social services organization executive*
Pak, Hyung Woong *foundation executive*
Pizzi, Charles Peter *association president*
Polland, Rebecca Robbins *foundation executive*
Scheffer, Ludo Carel Peter *educational researcher, consultant*
†Shmavonian, Nadya Kay *administrative services administrator*
Tise, Larry Edward *historical organization administrator, historian*
Tucker, Cynthia Delores Nottage (Mrs. William M. Tucker) *political party official, former state official*
†Watson, Bernard Charles *foundation administrator*

**Pittsburgh**
Dybeck, Alfred Charles *labor arbitrator*
Hallen, Philip Burgh *foundation administrator*
Horan, Justin Thomas *retired association executive*
Ketchum, David Storey *retired fundraising executive*
Mellon, Richard Prosser *charitable foundation executive*
Pasnick, Raymond Wallace *labor union official, editor*
Petersen, Jean Snyder *association executive*
†Scaife, Richard Mellon *philanthropist*
†Thorner, John *professional society administrator*
Wishart, Alfred Wilbur, Jr. *foundation administrator*

**Reading**
Mattern, Donald Eugene *retired association executive*

**Rockledge**
Bacon, George Hughes *consultant*

**State College**
DeVoss, James Thomas *community foundation administrator, retired*
Phillips, Janet Colleen *educational association executive, editor*
Santavicca, Pamela Ferguson *social welfare administrator*

**Stroudsburg**
Batistoni, Ronald *educational association administrator*

**University Park**
Feller, Irwin *think-tank executive, economics educator*

**Valley Forge**
Carlson, Beverly Clark *historical society administrator*

**Villanova**
Friend, Theodore Wood, III *foundation executive, historian*

**Warrendale**
Rumbaugh, Max Elden, Jr. *professional society administrator*
Scott, Alexander Robinson *engineering association executive*

**Wayne**
†Annenberg, Leonore A. *foundation administrator*
Etris, Samuel Franklin *trade association administrator*

**Williamsport**
Schultz, Carole Lamb *community volunteer*

**Wynnewood**
Freeman, Morton S. *former bar association executive, retired lawyer*

## RHODE ISLAND

**Kingston**
Schmidt, Charles T., Jr. *labor and industrial relations educator*

**Providence**
Klyberg, Albert Thomas *historical society administrator*

## SOUTH CAROLINA

**Charleston**
Hughes, Blake *retired architectural institute administrator, publisher*
Rupp, Frank A., III *association executive*

**Columbia**
Bjontegard, Arthur Martin, Jr. *foundation executive*
Chappell, Barbara Kelly *child welfare consultant*
Drafts, Norma Shealy *medical foundation executive*
McGill, Jennifer Houser *non-profit association administrator*
Resch, Mary Louise *social services administrator*
Shabazz, Aiysha Muslimah *social work administrator*
Sheheen, Fred Roukos *education agency administrator*
Sigmon, Daniel Ray *foundation administrator*

**Edgefield**
†Allen, Jerry Wayne *organization executive*

**Florence**
Brewer, Mary Dean *medical foundation executive*

**Greenville**
Frist, Thomas Ferran *philanthropic organization executive*

**Hilton Head Island**
Tucker, Frances Laughridge *civic worker*

**Lancaster**
Bundy, Charles Alan *foundation executive*

**Spartanburg**
Ely, Duncan Cairnes *non profit human services executive, civic leader*

**Surfside Beach**
McCrensky, Edward *international consultant, former organization executive*
Turner, Gloria Townsend Burke *social services association executive*

**Woodruff**
Childers, Bob Eugene *educational association executive*

## SOUTH DAKOTA

**Rapid City**
Erickson, John Duff *educational association adimnistrator*

## TENNESSEE

**Chattanooga**
Tracy, Carol Cousins *association executive, former educator*
Zodhiates, Spiros George *association executive*

**Cleveland**
Clowers, Evealyn *civic worker*

**Knoxville**
Drinnon, Janis Bolton *volunteer*
Froula, James DeWayne *national honor society director, engineer*

**Memphis**
Whitesell, Dale Edward *retired association executive, natural resources consultant*

**Murfreesboro**
Childress, Elizabeth Lush *community volunteer, investor*

**Nashville**
Benson, Edwin Welburn, Jr. *trade association executive*
Bond, Sherry Louise *trade association administrator*
Henderson, Milton Arnold *professional society administrator*
Johnson, Hollis Eugene, III *foundation executive*
Purcell, William Paxson, III *association administrator*

**Newport**
Kridler, Jamie Branam *children's advocate, social psychologist*

## TEXAS

**Abilene**
Kyker, Christine White (Chris Kyker) *human services administrator*

**Amarillo**
Ball, Charles Elihue *association consultant*
Brainard, Jayne Dawson (Mrs. Ernest Scott Brainard) *civic worker*
Crain, Mary Tom *volunteer*

**Austin**
Banks, Virginia Anne (Ginger Banks) *association administrator*
Barnes, Thomas Joseph *migration program administrator*
Bonjean, Charles Michael *foundation executive, sociologist, educator*
Mc Kinney, Michael Whitney *trade association executive*
Stoner, James Lloyd *retired foundation executive, clergyman*
West, Glenn Edward *business organization executive*

**Belton**
Wallace, Aliceanne *civic worker*

**College Station**
Vandiver, Frank Everson *institute administrator, former university president, author, educator*

**Colleyville**
Love, Ben Howard *retired organization executive*

**Corpus Christi**
French, Dorris Towers Bryan *volunteer*

**Dallas**
Anderson-Mann, Shelley N. *institutional review specialist*
†Evans, Linda Perryman *foundation adminstrator*
Juergens, Bonnie Kay *not-for-profit company executive*
Lancaster, Sally Rhodus *non-profit consultant*
Wassenich, Linda Pilcher *health policy analyst, fund raiser*

**El Paso**
Day, James Milton *foundation executive, English educator*

**Fort Worth**
Miller, Travis Milton *association executive, accountant*
Wilkie, Valleau, Jr. *foundation executive*

**Galveston**
Baker, Robert Ernest, Jr. *foundation executive*
†Newman, Frances Moody *foundation executive*

**Georgetown**
Busfield, Roger Melvil, Jr. *retired trade association executive, educator*

**Houston**
Crispin, Andre Arthur *international trading company executive*
Shankel, Gerald Marvin *professional society administrator*

**Irving**
Olson, Herbert Theodore *trade association executive*
Swinburn, John S. *professional association executive*

**Lubbock**
Johnson, Ronda Janice *fundraising consultant*

**North Richland Hills**
Hinkley Thompson, Carol Joyce *philanthropy consultant, motivational speaker*

**Odessa**
Boyd, Claude Collins *educational specialist, consultant*

**Plainview**
Galle, Richard Lynn *association executive, former municipal official*

**Richardson**
Adamson, Dan Klinglesmith *science association executive*

**San Antonio**
Krier, Joseph Roland *chamber of commerce executive, lawyer*
Leal, Barbara Jean Peters *fundraising executive*
Mc Giffert, John Rutherford *retired cultural institute director, retired army officer*
Montecel, Maria Robledo (Cuca Robledo Montecel) *educational association administrator*
White, Mary Ruth Wathen *social services administrator*

**South Houston**
Miller, Robert James *educational association administrator*

**Sugar Land**
Hosley, Marguerite Cyril *volunteer*

**Texarkana**
Hines, Betty Taylor *women's center administrator*

**Waxahachie**
Cockerham, Sidney Joe *professional society administrator*

## UTAH

**Provo**
Lee, Blaine Nelson *executive consultant, educator, author*

**Saint George**
Martin, George Wilbur *trade association administrator*

**Salt Lake City**
Clark, Deanna Dee *civic leader and volunteer*
Evans, Max Jay *historical society administrator*
Ingles, Joseph Legrand *social services administrator, political science educator*

## VERMONT

**Bennington**
Perin, Donald Wise, Jr. *former association executive*

**Bradford**
Mallary, Gertrude Robinson *civic worker*

**Brattleboro**
Akins, Zane Vernon *association executive*

**Montpelier**
Barbieri, Christopher George *professional society administrator*

**Randolph Center**
Ryerson, W. Newton *association executive*

## VIRGINIA

**Alexandria**
Bachus, Walter Otis *retired army general, former association executive*
Ball, Robert M. *social security, welfare and health policy specialist, writer, lecturer*
Baroody, Michael Elias *trade association executive*
Bezold, Clement *think tank executive*
Bolger, Robert Joseph *retired trade association executive*
Brown, Quincalee *professional society administrator*
Byrd, Barbara A. *professional society administrator*
Byrnside, Oscar Jehu, Jr. *professional society administrator*
Carter, Gene R. *professional society administrator*
Clower, William Dewey *trade association administrator*
Cooney, David Martin *organization administrator, retired naval officer*
Cooper, Charles Donald *association executive, editor, retired career officer*
Crane, Stephen Charles *professional society administrator*
Culkin, Charles Walker, Jr. *trade association administrator*
De Barbieri, Mary Ann *nonprofit management consultant*
Dietrich, Laura Jordan *international policy advisor*
Emely, Charles Harry *trade association executive*
Finnell, Dallas Grant *fundraising executive*
Goldstein, Jerome Charles *professional association executive, surgeon, otolaryngologist*
Gould, Phillip *think-tank executive*
Greenstein, Ruth Louise *research institute executive, lawyer*
Hoyt, F(rank) Russell *professional society administrator*
Kolar, Mary Jane *professional society administrator*
Lenz, Edward Arnold *trade association executive, lawyer*
Losey, Michael Robert *professional society administrator*
McCulloch, William Leonard *trade association administrator*
Megivern, Kathleen *association director, lawyer*
Merrick, Roswell Davenport *educational association administrator*
Murray, Robert John *think-tank executive*
Noland, Royce Paul *association executive, physical therapist*
Pastin, Mark Joseph *executive consultant, association executive*
Paul, Andrew Robert *trade association executive*
Rector, John Michael *association executive, lawyer*
Sheetz, Richard LaTrelle *retired association executive*
Smith, Carl Richard *association executive, former air force officer*
Stanley, Robert Warren *association executive*
Turner, Mary Jane *educational administrator*
Wurzel, Mary V. *past association executive*
Ziegler, Ronald Louis *association executive, former government official*

**Annandale**
Herbst, Robert LeRoy *organization executive*

**Arlington**
Bast, James Louis *trade association executive*
Brown-Black, Lillian (Rusty) *volunteer*
Dennis, Everette Eugene, Jr. *foundation executive, journalism educator*
Fabian, John McCreary *non-profit company executive, former astronaut, former air force officer*
Fernandez, Henry A. *professional association administrator, lawyer*
†Gauvin, Charles F. *professional society administrator*
†Gibbons, Miles J., Jr. *foundation administrator*
Gilmore, Marjorie Havens *civic worker, lawyer*
Hendrickson, Jerome Orland *trade association executive, lawyer*
Hickman, Elizabeth Podesta *retired counselor, educator*
Jankowski, John Edward, Jr. *government administrator*
Kane, Cheryl Chase *education program developer*
Kirtley, Jane Elizabeth *professional society administrator, lawyer*
Langworthy, Everett Walter *association executive, natural gas exploration company executive*
Marcuccio, Phyllis Rose *association executive, editor*
McMasters, Paul Kenneth *foundation executive*
McWethy, Patricia Joan *educational association administrator*
Melickian, Gary Edward *trade association executive*
Paynter, Harry Alvin *retired trade association executive*
Rees, Clifford Harcourt, Jr. (Ted Rees) *association executive, retired air force officer*
Richtol, Herbert Harold *science foundation program director*
Roberts, James Milnor, Jr. *professional society administrator*
Rosenker, Mark Victor *trade association executive*
Shannon, Thomas Alfred *retired educational association administrator emeritus*
Smith, Elise Fiber *international non-profit development agency administrator*
Stolgitis, William Charles *professional society executive*
Strandquist, John Herbert *association executive*
Teem, John McCorkle *retired association executive*

Vaught, Wilma L. *foundation executive, retired air force officer*
Walker, John Denley *foundation director, former government official*
Watson, Alexander Fletcher *organization executive, former ambassador*
Wells, Christine *foundation executive*
Wilson, Minter Lowther, Jr. *retired officers association executive*

**Brookneal**
Elson, James Martin *historic foundation director, college music educator, fine arts administrator*

**Chantilly**
Slayton, Gus *foundation administrator*
Sroka, John Walter *trade association executive*

**Charlottesville**
Jones, Constance Ann *educational association administrator*
Jordan, Daniel Porter, Jr. *foundation administrator, history educator*
Wilson, Mitchell B. *fraternal organization administrator*

**Chesapeake**
†Reed, Ralph Eugene, Jr. *association executive, writer*

**Culpeper**
Landa, William Robert *foundation executive*

**Fairfax**
Bartlow, Gene Steven *association executive, retired air force officer*
Blanken, Sarah Stuber *retired foundation administrator*
Cullison, Alexander C. (Doc Cullison) *society administrator*
Gray, William H., III *association executive, former congressman*
Grunder, Fred Irwin *program administrator, industrial hygienist*
†Hammer, Marion Price *association administrator*
Hollans, Irby Noah, Jr. *retired association executive*
Madry-Taylor, Jacquelyn Yvonne *educational administrator*
Mund, Richard Gordon *foundation executive*
Woodruff, C(harles) Roy *professional association executive*

**Falls Church**
Cooper, Arthur Irving *former association executive*
Dole, Elizabeth Hanford *charitable organization administrator, former secretary of labor, former secretary of transportation*
Laqueur, Maria *educational association administrator*
Livingstone, Susan Morrisey *nonprofit administrator*
Lyman, Robert Howard *veterans association executive*
Masterson, Kleber Sandlin *former organization executive, retired naval officer*
Van Nelson, Nicholas Lloyd *business council executive*

**Flint Hill**
Dietel, William Moore *former foundation executive*

**Fredericksburg**
Farmer, James *civil rights leader, former trade union official*
Ivey, David Lamar *trade association executive*

**Front Royal**
Greco, Barbara Ruth Gomez *literacy organization administrator*
Marx, Paul Benno *author, social service administrator, missionary*

**Great Falls**
Schwartz, Robert Terry *professional association executive*

**Keswick**
Owen, Jack Walden *retired hospital association administrator*

**Louisa**
Small, William Edwin, Jr. *association and recreation executive*

**Lynchburg**
Johnson, Robert Bruce *historic preservationist*

**Manassas Park**
Emely, Mary Ann *association executive*

**Mc Lean**
Finberg, Donald Richard *international consultant*
Friel, Thomas Patrick *trade association administrator*
Gary, Charles Lester *professional association consultant, educator*
Kurth, Walter Richard *trade association administrator*
Landry, James Edward *trade association administrator*
McInerney, James Eugene, Jr. *trade association administrator*
Rogers, Thomas Francis *foundation administrator*
Schweiker, Richard Schultz *trade association executive, former senator, former cabinet secretary*
Sudarkasa, Michael Eric Mabogunje *lawyer, consultant*
Weinert, Donald G(regory) *association executive, engineer*
Whipple, David Doty *professional society administrator*

**Mount Jackson**
Wait, Carol Grace Cox *organization administrator*

**Newport News**
Feldt, Glenda Diane *educational administrator*
Hawkins, J. Michael *housing development administrator*
Mazur, Rhoda Himmel *community volunteer*

**Norfolk**
Wilson, Lloyd Lee *organization administrator*

**Palmyra**
Southworth, R. Morrison *development counsel*

**Reston**
Brennan, Norma Jean *professional society publications director*
Chattman, Raymond Christopher *foundation administrator*
Curry, John Joseph *professional organization executive*
†Davis, James E. *professional association executive*
Dyer, Timothy J. *educational association administrator*
Gates, James David *retired association executive, consultant*
Goodwin, Robert Delmege *retired association executive*
Hope, Samuel Howard *accreditation organization executive*
Mahlmann, John James *music education association administrator*
Miller, Edward David *non-profit association administrator*
Minton, Joseph Paul *retired safety organization executive*
White, Rosanne Teresa *educational association executive*

**Richmond**
Dell, Willie Jones *social services executive, educator*
†Grover, Peter Dun *cultural organization administrator*
Kline, Robert H. *foundation administrator*
Linkonis, Suzanne Newbold *pretrial case manager, counselor*
McClenahan, Mary Tyler Freeman *civic and community volunteer*
Negus, Lucy Newton Boswell *foundation executive*
Wood, Jeanne Clarke *charitable organization executive*

**Spotsylvania**
Hardy, Dorcas Ruth *government relations and public policy consultant*

**Springfield**
Larson, Reed Eugene *foundation administrator*

**Sterling**
Munger, Paul David *educational administrator*

**Vienna**
Argow, Keith Angevin *association executive, forester*
Cartier, Brian Evans *association executive*
Spiro, Robert Harry, Jr. *foundation and business executive, educator*
West, Richard Luther *military association executive, defense consultant, retired army officer*

**Warrenton**
Fox, Raymond Graham *educational administrator*
Sass, Arthur Harold *educational executive*

**Williamsburg**
Brinkley, Joseph Willard *social services administrator*
Longsworth, Charles R. *foundation administrator*
Wilburn, Robert Charles *institute executive*

## WASHINGTON

**Ellensburg**
Legere, Diane J. *art association administrator, alpaca breeder*

**Federal Way**
Seiple, Robert Allen *Christian relief organization executive*

**La Center**
Holley, Lawrence Alvin *retired labor union official*

**Mill Creek**
Corbally, John Edward *foundation director*

**Port Townsend**
Woolf, William Blauvelt *retired association executive*

**Puyallup**
Kutscher, Kathleen Ann *social welfare administrator, social worker*

**Seattle**
Arthur, William Lynn *environmental foundation administrator*
Brooke, Francis John, III *foundation administrator*
Moberly, David Lindsey *retired foundation executive*

**Spokane**
Coker, Charlotte Noel *political activist*
Rowe, Marjorie Douglas *retired social services administrator*

**Tacoma**
Garner, Carlene Ann *fundraising consultant*
Graybill, David Wesley *chamber of commerce executive*
Rieke, William Oliver *foundation director, medical educator, former university president*

**Vancouver**
Smith, Sam Corry *retired foundation executive, consultant*

**WEST VIRGINIA**

**Charleston**
Chapman, John Andrew *association executive*

**Hillsboro**
Pierce, William Luther *association executive, writer*

**Morgantown**
Friedland, Billie Louise *former human services administrator*

## WISCONSIN

**Altoona**
James, Henry Thomas *former foundation executive, educator*

**Elm Grove**
Halvorsen, Morrie Edward *trade association administrator*

**Kenosha**
Adler, Seymour Jack *social services administrator*

**Madison**
Harr, Lucy Loraine *professional society administrator*
Higby, Gregory James *historical association administrator, historian*
Porter, Andrew Calvin *educational administrator, psychology educator*

**Milwaukee**
Ballweg, Mary Lou *nonprofit association administrator and founder, writer, consultant*
†Frey, James Severin *educational association executive*
Huntington, David Mack Goode *foundation administrator*
Ritz, Esther Leah *civic worker, volunteer, investor*
Smith, Jane Farwell *civic worker*
†Taylor, Allen M. *community foundation executive*
Zeidler, Frank P. *former association administrator, mayor, arbitrator, mediator, fact-finder*

**Monroe**
Brown, Sandra Lee *educational consultant, watercolorist*

**Racine**
Bray, Charles William, III *foundation executive*

**Shawano**
Lyon, Thomas L. *agricultural organization administrator*

## WYOMING

**Cheyenne**
Noe, Guy *social services administrator*

**Cody**
Coe, Margaret Louise Shaw *community service volunteer*

## TERRITORIES OF THE UNITED STATES

### VIRGIN ISLANDS

**Saint Thomas**
Creque, Linda Ann *non-profit educational and research executive, former education commissioner*

## CANADA

### ALBERTA

**Calgary**
Raeburn, Andrew Harvey *performing arts association executive, record producer*
Roberts, John Peter Lee *cultural advisor, administrator, educator, writer*

**Edmonton**
†Christian, Ralph Gordon *agricultural research administrator*

### BRITISH COLUMBIA

**Vancouver**
Saywell, William George Gabriel *foundation administrator*

### NEW BRUNSWICK

**Fredericton**
Lewell, Peter A. *international technology executive, researcher*

**Saint Andrews**
†Taylor, R. William *foundation administrator*

### NEWFOUNDLAND

**Saint John's**
†Vivian, Gladys Lily *administrator social services*

### NOVA SCOTIA

**Halifax**
Sparling, Mary Christine *foundation executive*

**Wolfville**
Elliott, Robbins Leonard *consultant*

### ONTARIO

**Etobicoke**
Ecroyd, Lawrence Gerald *trade association administrator*

**Mississauga**
Burrell, Carol Ann *trade association executive*
Ross, Thomas McCallum *professional society administrator*

**Ottawa**
Bezanson, Keith Arthur *administrative educational executive*
Davies, Gareth John *trade executive, lawyer*

**Pontypool**
Kniewasser, Andrew Graham *company director*

**Toronto**
Goodenow, Robert W. *labor union administrator*
Johnston, Robert Donaghy *cultural organization administrator*
Kossuth, Selwyn Barnett *trade association consultant*
Montgomery, Donald Russell *labor consulting firm executive*
Rickerd, Donald Sheridan *foundation executive*
Troubetzkoy, Alexis Serge *foundation administrator, educator*
†Wildman, C.J. (Bud) *political organization official*
Wilson, Ian Edwin *cultural organization administrator, archivist*

**Willowdale**
Bulloch, John Frederick Devon *foundation administrator*

### QUEBEC

**Hull**
†Chartier, Jean *federal public service administrator*

**Montreal**
Alain, Robert *foundation administrator*
Hobday, John Charles *foundation administrator*

**Outremont**
Letourneau, Jean-Paul *business association executive and consultant*

**Quebec**
†Simard, Cyril *cultural organization administrator, architect*

**Rosemere**
Hopper, Carol *trade show administrator*

**Thetford Mines**
†Cartier, Benoît *professional society administrator*

### MEXICO

**Mexico City**
Bruton, John Macaulay *trade association executive*

### FRANCE

**Paris**
Mestrallet, Gérard *professional society administrator*

### GHANA

**Accra**
Brocke, Eunice Miranda *foundation executive*

### ITALY

**Rome**
Hjort, Howard Warren *international organization official, economist*
Wilson, George Peter *international organization executive*

### SWITZERLAND

**Berne**
†Leavey, Thomas E. *international organization administrator*

**Geneva**
†Casey, John W. *association executive*
Purcell, James Nelson, Jr. *international organization administrator*
Schweitzer, Theodore Gottlieb, III *United Nations administrator*
†Weber, George *international social welfare administrator*

### ADDRESS UNPUBLISHED

Allerton, John Stephen *association executive*
Allison, Andrew Marvin *church executive*
Amstutz, Daniel Gordon *trade association administrator, former grain dealer, government official*
Anguiano, Lupe *business executive*
Annenberg, Walter H. *philanthropist, diplomat, editor, publisher, broadcaster*
Armour, David Edward Ponton *trade association administrator*
Arthur, Rochelle Linda *association executive*
Atchison, Richard Calvin *trade association director*
Bailin, David William *educational administrator*
Bashore, Irene Saras *research institute administrator*
Benton, Robert Dean *educational organization executive*
Blair, Fred Edward *social services administrator*

## ATHLETICS

## UNITED STATES

### ALABAMA

**Auburn**
Reeve, Thomas Gilmour *physical education educator*

**Bessemer**
Allison, Robert Arthur *retired professional stock car driver*

**Birmingham**
Huff, Sherri Lynn *physical education educator*
Salant, Nathan Nathaniel *athletic conference commissioner*

**Jacksonville**
Wilson, Barbara T. *physical education educator*

**Mobile**
Jackson, Bo (Vincent Edward Jackson) *professional baseball, former football player*

**Tuscaloosa**
†Moody, Rick *collegiate basketball coach*

### ARIZONA

**Phoenix**
Bidwill, William V. *professional football executive*
†Colangelo, Bryan *professional sports team executive*
Colangelo, Jerry John *professional basketball team executive*
†Dozer, Richard H. *professional sports team executive*
Fitzsimmons, (Lowell) Cotton *professional basketball executive, broadcaster, former coach*
Gartner, Michael Alfred *professional hockey player*
Johnson, Kevin Maurice *professional basketball player*
Jones, Lucia Jean *physical education educator*
Joyner, Seth *professional football player*
Kidd, Jason *professional basketball player*
†King, Kris *professional hockey player*
Love, Duval Lee *professional football player*
Manning, Daniel Ricardo *professional basketball player*
†Mitchell, Don *professional sports team executive*
Paddock, John *professional hockey team head coach*
Schoenfeld, Jim *professional hockey coach*
†Selanne, Teemu *hockey player*
Showalter, Buck (William Nathaniel Showalter, III) *major league baseball team manager*
Simmons, Clyde *professional football player*
Starks, Rosalyn June *physical education and health educator*
Swann, Eric Jerrod *professional football player*
†Tkachuk, Keith *professional hockey player*
†Tobin, Vincent Michael *professional sports team executive*
†Ueberroth, Peter Victor *former baseball commissioner*
Van Arsdale, Dick *professional basketball team executive*
Williams, Aeneas Demetrius *professional football player*
Wilson, Lawrence Frank (Larry Wilson) *professional football team executive*

**Tempe**
Hoke, Judy Ann *physical education educator*
Moore, Rob *professional football player*
†Snyder, Lester M. *sports association executive*

**Tucson**
Kearney, Joseph Laurence *retired athletic conference administrator*
Olson, Lute *university athletic coach*

### ARKANSAS

**Conway**
Titlow, Larry Wayne *physical education and kinesiology educator*

**Fayetteville**
Richardson, Nolan *university athletic coach*

**Strong**
Nunnally, Dolores Burns *retired physical education educator*

### CALIFORNIA

**Alameda**
Gossett, Jeffrey Alan *professional football player*
Herrera, John *professional football team executive*
Jaeger, Jeff Todd *professional football player*
Swilling, Pat *professional football player*
Wisniewski, Stephen Adam *professional football player*

**Alta Loma**
Tolan, Vicki Irvena *physical education educator*

**Anaheim**
Alicea, Luis Rene *professional baseball player*
†Bavasi, William Joseph *professional sports team executive*
DiSarcina, Gary Thomas *professional baseball player*
Edmonds, James Patrick (Jim Edmonds) *professional baseball player*
Finley, Chuck (Charles Edward Finley) *professional baseball player*
Hollins, David Michael *professional baseball player*
†Kariya, Paul *professional hockey player*
Lachemann, Marcel *professional baseball manager*
Langston, Mark Edward *professional baseball player*
Murray, Eddie Clarence *professional baseball player*
Salmon, Timothy James *professional baseball player*
Tavares, Tony *professional hockey team executive*
Wilson, Ronald Lawrence *professional hockey coach*

**Beverly Hills**
Lott, Ronnie (Ronald Mandel Lott) *professional football player*
Shoemaker, Bill (William Lee Shoemaker) *retired jockey, horse trainer*
Stevens, Gary *professional jockey*
Winfield, David Mark *former professional baseball player, commentator*

**Camarillo**
Griffith Joyner, Florence DeLorez *track and field athlete*

**Coronado**
Axelson, Joseph Allen *professional athletics executive, publisher*

**Danville**
Behring, Kenneth E. *professional sports team owner*

**El Segundo**
Brown, Timothy Donell *professional football player*
Davis, Allen *professional football team executive*
Rock, Angela *volleyball player*

**Englewood**
†Kupchak, Mitchell *professional sports team executive*

**Inglewood**
†Ferraro, Ray *hockey player*

†Harris, Del William *professional basketball coach*
O'Neal, Shaquille Rashaun *professional basketball player*
Robinson, Larry Clark *professional hockey coach*
†Roski, Edward P. *professional sports team executive*
Sharman, William *professional basketball team executive*
†Tocchet, Rick *professional hockey player*
Van Exel, Nickey Maxwell *professional basketball player*
West, Jerry Alan *professional basketball team executive*

**La Jolla**
Bavasi, Peter Joseph *professional baseball team executive*

**Long Beach**
Brisco, Valerie *track and field athlete*
Fornia, Dorothy Louise *physical education educator*

**Los Angeles**
†Bardt, Harry M. *sports association administrator*
Barretta-Keyser, Jolie *professional athletics coach, author*
Baylor, Elgin Gay *professional basketball team executive*
Chamberlain, Wilton Norman *retired professional basketball player*
Fitch, William C. *professional basketball coach*
Hamill, Dorothy Stuart *professional ice skater*
†Hurtado, Eduardo *soccer player*
Karros, Eric Peter *professional baseball player*
Lasorda, Thomas Charles (Tommy Lasorda) *professional baseball team manager*
Martinez, Ramon Jaime *professional baseball player*
Mondesi, Raul *professional baseball player*
Nomo, Hideo *professional baseball player*
O'Malley, Peter *professional baseball club executive*
†Osiander, Lothar *soccer coach*
Piazza, Michael Joseph *professional baseball player*
Sterling, Donald T. *professional basketball team executive*
Watts, Quincy Dushawn *track and field athlete*

**Malibu**
Louganis, Greg E. *former Olympic athlete, actor*
Wilkins, (Jacques) Dominique *professional basketball player*

**Marina Del Rey**
Hovland, Tim (The Hov) (The Hov) *volleyball player*
Steffes, Kent *volleyball player*
Stoklos, Randy (Stokey Stoklos) *volleyball player*
Timmons, Steve (Red) *volleyball player*

**Menlo Park**
Walsh, William *former football coach*

**Mentone**
Stockton, David Knapp *professional golfer*

**Napa**
Miller, John Laurence *professional golfer*

**Oakland**
Alderson, Richard Lynn (Sandy Alderson) *professional baseball team executive*
Bordick, Michael Todd *professional baseball player*
Canseco, Jose *professional baseball player*
Carlesimo, P. J. (Peter J. Carlesimo) *former college basketball coach, professional basketball coach*
Cohan, Christopher *professional sports team executive*
Gates, Brent Robert *professional baseball player*
†Howard, Desmond Kevin *professional football player*
†Howe, Art (Arthur Henry Howe, Jr.) *professional baseball manager*
McGwire, Mark David *professional baseball player*
Mullin, Chris(topher) Paul *professional basketball player*
Price, (William) Mark *professional basketball player*
†White, Mike *professional sports team executive*

**Pacific Palisades**
Smith, Sinjin *beach volleyball player*

**Palm Springs**
Jumonville, Felix Joseph, Jr. *physical education educator, realtor*

**Sacramento**
Benner, Rick *professional basketball team executive*
†Fox, Ned *professional sports team owner*
Grant, Brian Wade (General Grant) *professional basketball player*
Petrie, Geoff *professional basketball team executive*
Richmond, Mitchell James *professional basketball player*
Thomas, Jim *professional basketball team executive*

**San Diego**
†Beathard, Bobby *professional football team executive*
†Bochy, Bruce *professional sports team executive*
Carney, John Michael *professional football player*
Fuller, William Henry, Jr. *professional football player*
Gwynn, Anthony Keith (Tony Gwynn) *professional baseball player*
Henderson, Rickey Henley *professional baseball player*
†Moores, John *professional sports team executive*
O'Neal, Leslie Cornelius *professional football player*
Reed, Jody Eric *professional baseball player*
Seau, Junior (Tiana Seau, Jr.) *professional football player*
Spanos, Alexander Gus *professional football team executive*
Vaughn, Gregory Lamont *professional baseball player*

**San Francisco**
Baker, Dusty (Johnnie B. Baker, Jr.) *professional baseball team manager*
Beck, Rodney Roy *professional baseball player*
Bonds, Barry Lamar *professional baseball player*
Kent, Jeffrey Franklin *baseball player*
Magowan, Peter Alden *professional baseball team executive, grocery chain executive*

Mays, Willie Howard, Jr. (Say Hey Kid) *former professional baseball player*
Mc Covey, Willie Lee *former professional baseball player*
†Quinn, Bob *professional baseball team executive*
Vizcaino, Jose Luis Pimental *professional baseball player*

### San Jose
McEnery, Tom *professional sports team executive*
†Nicholls, Bernard Irvine *hockey player*
†Nolan, Owen *professional hockey player*

### Santa Clara
Anderson, Gary Allan *professional football player*
Cooper, Adrian *football player*
Gogan, Kevin *professional football player*
Hanks, Merton Edward *professional football player*
Jones, Brent Michael *professional football player*
McDonald, Tim *professional football player*
Norton, Kenneth Howard *professional football player*
†Policy, Carmen A. *professional sports team executive*
Rice, Jerry Lee *professional football player*
Sapolu, Manase Jesse *professional football player*
Stubblefield, Dana William *professional football player*
Woodall, Lee *professional football player*
†Young, Bryant Colby *football player*
Young, Steven *professional football player*

### Sausalito
Casals, Rosemary *professional tennis player*

### Sherman Oaks
Hamilton, Scott Scovell *professional figure skater, former Olympic athlete*

### Stanford
Van Derveer, Tara *university athletic coach*

### Sunnyvale
Cognata, Joseph Anthony *football commissioner*

### Walnut Creek
Hallock, C. Wiles, Jr. *athletic official*

### Westminster
Treadway-Dillmon, Linda Lee *athletic trainer, actress*

## COLORADO

### Aspen
Sullivan, Danny *professional race car driver*

### Colorado Springs
Armstrong, Lance *professional cyclist*
Barrowman, Mike *Olympic athlete, swimmer*
Barton, Gregory Mark *Olympic athlete, kayak racer*
Bates, Michael *Olympic athlete, track and field*
†Beard, Amanda *swimmer, Olympic athlete*
Berkoff, David *Olympic athlete, swimmer*
Biondi, Matt *Olympic athlete, swimmer*
†Botsford, Beth *swimmer, Olympic athlete*
†Bridgewater, Brad *Olympic athlete*
Burgess, Greg *Olympic athlete, swimming*
Byrd, Chris *Olympic athlete, boxer*
Byrne, Catherine *swimmer*
Conley, Mike *track and field athlete*
Dees, Tony *Olympic athlete, track and field*
Dello Joio, Norman *olympic athlete, equestrian*
Diebel, Nelson *Olympic athlete, swimmer*
Dimas, Trent *Olympic athlete, gymnast*
Doehrin, James *Olympic athlete, track and field*
Eldredge, Todd *figure skater*
Evans, Janet *Olympic swimmer*
Foth, Bob *Olympic athlete, riflery*
Gray, Johnny *Olympic athlete, track and field*
Groebli, Werner Fritz (Mr. Frick) *professional ice skater, realtor*
Jacobi, Joe *Olympic athlete, canoeist*
Jager, Tom *Olympic athlete, swimmer*
Johnson, Dave *Olympic athlete, track and field*
†Kwan, Michelle *professional skater*
Lenzi, Mark *Olympic athlete, springboard diver*
Lewis, Steve *Olympic athlete, track and field*
†Lucia, Don *head coach men's ice hockey*
Marsh, Michael *track and field athlete*
McIntyre, Elizabeth Geary *Olympic athlete*
Mitchell, Dennis A. *Olympic athlete, track and field*
Morales, Pablo *Olympic athlete, swimmer*
Murray, Ty (The Kid Murray) *professional rodeo cowboy*
Peterson, Amy *Olympic athlete*
Pierce, Jack *Olympic athlete, track and field*
†Reid, David *Olympic athlete*
Rouse, Jeff *Olympic athlete, swimmer*
Sanders, Summer *Olympic athlete*
†Scherr, James E. *sports association executive*
Schultz, Richard Dale *national athletic organizations executive*
Stewart, Melvin *Olympic athlete, swimmer*
Street, Picabo *Olympic athlete*
Stulce, Mike *Olympic athlete, track and field*
Turner, Cathy *Olympic athlete*
†Van Dyken, Amy *swimmer, Olympic athlete*
Young, Kevin *track and field athlete*

### Denver
Baylor, Don Edward *professional baseball manager*
Bichette, Alphonse Dante *professional baseball player*
Castilla, Vinivio Soria *professional baseball player*
Crawford, Marc *professional hockey coach*
Forsberg, Peter *professional hockey player*
Galarraga, Andres Jose *professional baseball player*
Gebhard, Bob *professional baseball team executive*
†Issel, Daniel Paul *former professional basketball coach*
Johnson, Mary Bettina Black *physical education educator, athletic trainer*
†Lacroix, Pierre *professional sports team professional*
Lemieux, Claude *professional hockey player*
Lyons, Charles *professional hockey team executive*
Roy, Patrick *professional hockey player*
†Sakic, Joseph Steve *professional hockey player*
Swift, William Charles *professional baseball player, Olympic athlete*
Walker, Larry Kenneth Robert *professional baseball player*

### Englewood
Atwater, Stephen Dennis *professional football player*
Beake, John *professional football team executive*
Craw, Nicholas Wesson *motor sports association executive*
Elway, John Albert *professional football player*
Gordon, Darrien X. Jamal *professional football player*
Perry, Michael Dean *professional football player*
Shanahan, Mike *professional football coach*
Sharpe, Shannon *professional football player*
Smith, Neil *professional football player*

### Fort Collins
Lubick, Sonny *college football coach*

## CONNECTICUT

### Branford
Agassi, Andre Kirk *tennis player*

### Bristol
Abdul-Jabbar, Kareem (Lewis Ferdinand Alcindor) *retired professional basketball player, sports commentator*
†Carter, Frederick James *professional basketball coach*
†Corso, Lee *former football coach, football analyst*
†Phelps, Richard Frederick *basketball coach*
†Reynolds, Harold Craig *professional baseball player*

### Hartford
†Karmanos, Peter, Jr. *professional sports team executive*
Rutherford, Jim *professional sports team executive*
†Shanahan, Brendan Frederick *professional hockey player*

### New London
Pinhey, Frances Louise *physical education educator*

### Norwich
Heinrich, Carl Chester *physical education educator*

### Stamford
Taylor, Stephen Hosmer *sports entertainment executive, photographer*
Worcester, Anne Person *sports association executive*

### Storrs Mansfield
Auriemma, Geno *university athletic coach*
†Calhoun, Jim *college basketball coach*

## DELAWARE

### Wilmington
Miller, Christine Talley *physical education educator*

## DISTRICT OF COLUMBIA

### Washington
†Allen, Terry Thomas, Jr. *football player*
Casserly, Charley *professional football team executive*
Chin, Allen E., Sr. *athletic administrator, educator*
Green, Darrell *professional football player*
Harvey, Kenneth Ray *professional football player*
Hathaway, Carmrid Glaston *sports association executive, real estate investor*
Johnson, Tim *professional football player*
Lachey, James Michael *professional football player*
Thompson, John *college basketball coach*
†Turk, Matt *football player*
Turner, Norv *professional football coach*
Upshaw, Gene *sports association executive*

## FLORIDA

### Boca Raton
Evert, Christine Marie (Chris Evert) *retired professional tennis player*

### Boynton Beach
Spannuth, John Roy *aquatics association executive*

### Davie
Emtman, Steven Charles *professional football player*
Johnson, Jimmy *professional football coach*
†Jones, Eddie J. *professional football team executive*
Shula, Don Francis *former professional football coach, team executive*

### Daytona Beach
Alcott, Amy Strum *professional golfer*
†Benson, Johnny *professional race car driver*
†Bodine, Brett *professional race car driver*
†Bodine, Geoff *professional race car driver*
†Burton, Brandie *professional golfer*
†Craven, Ricky *professional race car driver*
Earnhardt, (Ralph) Dale *professional race car driver*
Gordon, Jeff *race car driver*
Inkster, Juli *professional golfer*
†Irvan, Ernie (Swervin' Irvan) *professional race car driver*
†Jarrett, Dale *professional race car driver*
King, Betsy *professional golfer*
†Klein, Emilee *professional golfer*
†Labonte, Bobby *professional race car driver*
†Labonte, Terry *professional race car driver*
Mallon, Meg *professional golfer*
Marlin, Sterling *professional race car driver*
†Martin, Mark *professional race car driver*
†McGann, Michelle *professional golfer*
Mochrie, Dottie *professional golfer*
†Neumann, Liselotte *professional golfer*
Petty, Kyle *professional stock car driver*
Reeves, Donna Andrews *golfer*
†Ritts, Jim *professional sports team executive*
†Rudd, Ricky *professional race car driver*
†Schrader, Ken *professional race car driver*
Sheehan, Patty *professional golfer*
†Shepherd, Morgan *professional race car driver*
†Sorenstam, Annika *professional golfer*
†Speed, Lake *professional race car driver*
Stephenson, Jan Lynn *professional golfer*
Wallace, Rusty *race car driver*
†Webb, Karrie *professional golfer*
Whitworth, Kathrynne Ann *professional golfer*
Yarborough, William Caleb *former professional stock car race driver*

### Fort Lauderdale
†Clark, Mary Ellen *Olympic athlete*
Fitzpatrick, Mark *professional hockey player*
MacLean, Doug *hockey coach*
Murray, Bryan Clarence *professional sports team executive*
†Torrey, William Arthur *professional hockey team executive*
Tyson, Mike G. *professional boxer*
Vanbiesbrouck, John *professional hockey player*

### Gainesville
Lopez, Andy *university athletic coach*
Singer, Robert Norman *motor behavior educator*
Spurrier, Steve *university athletic coach, former professional football player*

### Hobe Sound
Norman, Gregory John *professional golfer*

### Hollywood
Di Maggio, Joseph Paul *former professional baseball player*
King, Alma Jean *former health and physical education educator*

### Jacksonville
Coughlin, Tom *professional football coach*
†Weaver, Wayne *professional sports team executive*

### Lady Lake
Hartzler, Genevieve Lucille *physical education educator*

### Miami
Bonilla, Bobby (Roberto Martin Antonio Bonilla) *professional baseball player*
Brown, James Kevin *professional baseball player*
Conine, Jeffrey Guy *professional baseball player*
Hardaway, Timothy Duane *basketball player*
Leyland, James Richard *professional baseball team manager*
Mourning, Alonzo *professional basketball player*
Nen, Robert Allen (Robb Nen) *professional baseball player*
Riley, Patrick James *professional basketball coach*
Sheffield, Gary Antonian *professional baseball player*
Webb, Richmond Jewel *professional football player*

### North Palm Beach
Nicklaus, Jack William *professional golfer*

### Opa Locka
†Dombrowski, David *baseball team executive*
Marino, Daniel Constantine, Jr. *professional football player*

### Orlando
Hardaway, Anfernee Deon (Penny Hardaway) *professional basketball player*
Sharkey, Colleen Mary *sports association administrator*
†Vander Weide, Bob *professional sports team executive*
†Williams, Pat *professional basketball team executive*

### Ormond Beach
Wendelstedt, Harry Hunter, Jr. *umpire*

### Palm Beach Gardens
Awtrey, Jim L. *sports association executive*
†Beck, Chip *professional golfer*
†Brooks, Mark David *professional golfer*
Calcavecchia, Mark *professional golfer*
Couples, Fred *professional golfer*
Daly, John *professional golfer*
†Haas, Jay *professional golfer*
†Henninger, Brian *professional golfer*
†Hoch, Scott *professional golfer*
†Huston, John *professional golfer*
†Jacobsen, Peter Erling *professional golfer*
Janzen, Lee *professional golfer*
†Langer, Bernhard *professional golfer*
†Lehman, Tom *professional golfer*
†Leonard, Justin *professional golfer*
†Mickelson, Phil *professional golfer*
Mize, Larry *professional golfer*
†Montgomerie, Colin *professional golfer*
†Olazabal, Jose Maria *professional golfer*
†O'Meara, Mark *professional golfer*
†Perry, Kenny *professional golfer*
Price, Nick *professional golfer*
Rodriguez, Chi Chi (Juan Rodriguez) *professional golfer*
†Simpson, Scott *professional golfer*
Snead, Samuel Jackson *former professional golfer*
†Woods, Tiger (Eldrick Woods) *professional golfer*

### Palm City
†Mc Hale, John Joseph *baseball club executive*

### Pompano Beach
Elder, Robert Lee *professional golfer*

### Ponte Vedra
Love, Davis, III *professional golfer*
Sampras, Pete *tennis player*

### Ponte Vedra Beach
Azinger, Paul *professional golfer*
Cook, John *professional golfer*
Edberg, Stefan *former professional tennis player*
†Elkington, Steve *professional golfer*
Faxon, Brad *professional golfer*
Floyd, Raymond *professional golfer*
Forsman, Dan *professional golfer*
†Frost, David *professional golfer*
Kite, Thomas O., Jr. *professional golfer*
Pavin, Corey *professional golfer*
†Singh, Vijay *professional golfer*
Stewart, (William) Payne *professional golfer*
†Tway, Bob *professional golfer*
Wadkins, Lanny *professional golfer*
Zoeller, Fuzzy *professional golfer*

### Saint Petersburg
†Moore, Mike *baseball league executive*
†Pierce, Mary *professional tennis player*
Sabatini, Gabriela *retired tennis player*

### Sarasota
Graham, Otto Everett, Jr. *retired athletic director*

### Starke
Loper, George Wilson, Jr. *physical education educator*

### Tallahassee
Bowden, Bobby *university athletic coach*

### Tampa
†Bergeron, Jean-Claude *professional hockey player*
Crisp, Terry Arthur *professional hockey coach*
†Dungy, Tony *professional sports team executive*
†Glazer, Malcolm *professional sports team executive*
†Hamrlik, Roman *professional hockey player*
†Kowalski, John *soccer coach*
†Lassiter, Roy *soccer player*
†Nickerson, Hardy Otto *football player*
†Sakiewicz, Nick *professional sports team executive*

### West Palm Beach
Player, Gary Jim *professional golfer, businessman, golf course designer*

## GEORGIA

### Athens
Dooley, Vincent Joseph *college athletics administrator*
†Landers, Andy *head coach women's basketball*
†Smith, (Tubby) Orlando Henry *college basketball coach*

### Atlanta
Aaron, Henry L. (Hank Aaron) *professional baseball team executive*
Arani, Ardy A. *professional sports marketing executive, lawyer*
Babcock, Peter Heartz *professional sports executive*
Blauser, Jeffrey Michael *professional baseball player*
Cox, Bobby (Robert Joe Cox) *professional baseball manager*
†Cremins, Bobby *college basketball coach*
Cunningham, Randall *professional football player*
Gearon, John Michael *professional basketball team executive*
Glavine, Tom (Thomas Michael Glavine) *professional baseball player*
Grissom, Marquis Dean *professional baseball player*
Harvey, Bryan Stanley *professional baseball player*
Kasten, Stanley Harvey *sports association executive*
Laettner, Christian Donald *professional basketball player*
Maddux, Greg(ory Alan) *professional baseball player*
McGriff, Fred (Frederick Stanley McGriff) *baseball player*
Moses, Edwin *former track and field athlete*
Neagle, Dennis Edward (Denny Neagle) *professional baseball player*
†Schuerholz, John Boland, Jr. *professional baseball executive*
Smith, Janet Marie *professional sports team executive*
Smith, Steven Delano *professional basketball player*
Smoltz, John Andrew *professional baseball player*

### Fort Valley
Porter, Douglas Taylor *athletic administrator*

### Marietta
Wrege, Julia Bouchelle *tennis professional, physics educator*

### Suwanee
Doleman, Christopher John *professional football player*
Hebert, Bobby Joseph, Jr. *professional football player*
Jones, June *professional football coach*
Mathis, Terance *professional football player*
Reeves, Daniel Edward *professional football coach*
Shell, Art *professional football team coach*
Shelley, Elbert Vernell *professional football player*
†Smith, Rankin M., Jr. *professional football team executive*
Smith, Taylor *professional football team executive*
Tuggle, Jessie Lloyd *professional football player*

## ILLINOIS

### Belleville
Connors, Jimmy (James Scott Connors) *former professional tennis player*

### Carbondale
Hart, James Warren *university athletic director, restaurant owner, former professional football player*

### Chicago
†Akers, Michelle Anne *soccer player*
Amonte, Anthony Lewis *professional hockey player*
Baines, Harold Douglass *professional baseball player*
Belfour, Ed *professional hockey player*
Belle, Albert Jojuan *professional baseball player*
Bevington, Terry Paul *professional baseball manager*
Chelios, Christos K *professional hockey player*
†Daze, Eric *professional hockey player*
†DiCicco, Tony *soccer coach*
Drabek, Doug (Douglas Dean Drabek) *baseball player*
Dunston, Shawon Donnell *professional baseball player*
Einhorn, Edward Martin (Eddie Einhorn) *professional baseball team executive*
Fisk, Carlton Ernest *retired professional baseball player*
Fournier, Maureen Mary *physical education educator*
Grace, Mark Eugene *professional baseball player*
Guillen, Oswaldo Jose Barrios (Ozzie Guillen) *baseball player*
†Hamm, Mariel Margaret *soccer player*

Hartsburg, Craig William *professional hockey coach*
Henning, Lorne Edward *professional hockey coach*
Himes, Laurence Austin *professional baseball executive*
Ivan, Thomas Nathaniel *professional hockey team executive*
Jackson, Philip Douglas *professional basketball coach*
Jordan, Michael Jeffery *professional basketball player, retired baseball player*
King, Billie Jean Moffitt *former professional tennis player*
Krause, Jerry (Jerome Richard Krause) *professional basketball team executive*
Lilly, Kristine Marie *soccer player*
†Lynch, Edward Francis *professional sports team executive*
Meyer, Raymond Joseph *former college basketball coach*
Mulholland, Terence John (Terry Mulholland) *professional baseball player*
Parish, Robert Lee (Chief Parish) *professional basketball player*
Pippen, Scottie *professional basketball player*
Pizer, Howard Charles *sports and entertainment executive*
Reinsdorf, Jerry Michael *professional sports teams executive, real estate executive, lawyer, accountant*
†Reyna, Claudio *soccer player*
Riggleman, James David *professional baseball team manager*
Rodman, Dennis Keith *basketball player*
Roenick, Jeremy *professional hockey player*
Sampson, Steve *professional soccer coach*
Sandberg, Ryne *professional baseball player*
Savard, Denis Joseph *professional hockey player*
Schwartz, Alan Gifford *sport company executive*
†Scurry, Briana Collette *amateur soccer player*
†Smith, James Stephen *hockey player*
Sosa, Samuel (Sammy Sosa) *professional baseball player*
†Sutter, Brent Colin *hockey player*
Thomas, Frank Edward *professional baseball player*
Ventura, Robin Mark *professional baseball player*
Wirtz, Arthur Michael, Jr. *professional hockey team executive*

### Evanston
Barnett, Gary *football coach*

### Glendale Heights
Spearing, Karen Marie *physical education educator, coach*

### Highland Park
Mordini, Marilyn Heuer *physical education educator*

### Lake Forest
Carrier, Mark Anthony *professional football player*
Cox, Bryan Keith *professional football player*
McCaskey, Edward W. *professional football team executive*
McCaskey, Michael B. *professional football team executive*
Salaam, Rashaan *professional football player*
Wannstedt, David Raymond *professional football team coach*
Woolford, Donnell *professional football player*

### Lincolnshire
Schauble, John Eugene *physical education educator*

### Moline
Carls, Judith Marie *physical education educator, golf coach*

### Mundelein
Carr, Bonnie Jean *professional ice skater*

### Saint Charles
Felt, Jennifer Ruth *elementary physical education educator*

### Sterling
Moran, Joan Jensen *physical education and health educator*

### Urbana
Thompson, Margaret M. *physical education educator*

## INDIANA

### Bloomington
Counsilman, James Edward *physical education educator*
Knight, Bob *college basketball coach*

### Indianapolis
†Adkins, Derrick Ralph *Olympic athlete*
Ashford, Evelyn *former track and field athlete*
†Austin, Charles *Olympic athlete*
†Barnes, Eric Randolph *Olympic athlete*
Bird, Larry Joe *retired professional basketball player, coach*
†Blanchard, Cary *football player*
Burrell, Leroy Russel *track and field athlete*
Cason, Andre Royal *track and field athlete*
Conway, Hollis *track and field athlete, Olympic athlete*
†Dawes, Dominique *gymnast, Olympic athlete*
Decker Slaney, Mary Teresa *Olympic athlete*
Dent, Richard Lamar *professional football player*
†Donaldson, Raymond Canute *professional football player*
Faulk, Marshall William *professional football player*
Favor-Hamilton, Suzanne Marie *track and field athlete, Olympian*
†Gardocki, Christopher *football player*
Greene, Joe *Olympic athlete, track and field*
Harbaugh, James Joseph *professional football player*
†Infante, Lindy *professional football coach*
Irsay, James Steven *professional football team executive*
†Johnson, Allen *Olympic athlete*
†Johnson, Michael *Olympic athlete*
†Lynch, Jair *Olympic athlete*
O'Brien, Daniel Dion *track and field athlete, Olympic athlete*
Pierce, Ricky Charles *professional basketball player*
Rose, Jalen *professional basketball player*
†Scanlan, Kathy *sports association administrator*
Simon, Herbert *professional basketball team executive*
Torrence, Gwen *Olympic athlete*
Walsh, Donnie *sports club executive*

### Notre Dame
†Poulin, David James *hockey coach*

### Ogden Dunes
Mulvaney, Mary Jean *physical education educator*

### South Bend
MacLeod, John *college basketball coach*
Thomas, Debi (Debra J. Thomas) *ice skater*

### Speedway
Unser, Alfred, Jr. *professional race car driver*

### Terre Haute
Campbell, Judith May *physical education educator*

## IOWA

### Des Moines
Foster, James Franklin *professional sports management executive*

### Iowa City
Balukas, Jean *professional pocket billiard player*
Davis, Tom *university athletic coach*
Fry, Hayden *university athletic coach*
†Lee, Angie *basketball coach*

## KANSAS

### Lawrence
Williams, Roy *university athletic coach*

### Overland Park
Dempsey, Cedric W. *sports association administrator*

### Shawnee Mission
Byers, Walter *athletic association executive*
Watson, Thomas Sturges *professional golfer*

## KENTUCKY

### Lexington
Boucher, Larry Gene *sports association commissioner*
Krone, Julie *jockey*

### Louisville
Crum, Denny (Denzel Edwin Crum) *collegiate basketball coach*

### Richmond
Morgan, Tim Dale *physical education educator*

## LOUISIANA

### Baton Rouge
Brown, Dale Duward *basketball coach*

### Grambling
Robinson, Eddie Gay *college football coach*

### Metairie
Benson, Tom *professional football executive*
Del Rio, Jack *professional football player*
Martin, Gerald Wayne *professional football player*
Roaf, William Layton *professional football player*
Turnbull, Renaldo *professional football player*

## MAINE

### Orono
†Cronin, Greg *ice hockey coach*

## MARYLAND

### Baltimore
Alomar, Roberto Velazquez *professional baseball player*
Davis, Eric Keith *former professional baseball player*
†Foss, Joseph E. *professional sports team executive*
Gillick, Patrick *professional baseball team executive*
Hoiles, Christopher Allen *professional baseball player*
Johnson, Davey (David Allen Johnson) *baseball team manager*
Key, Jimmy (James Edward Key) *professional baseball player*
Mussina, Michael Cole *professional baseball player*
Myers, Randall Kirk (Randy Myers) *professional baseball player*
Palmeiro, Rafael Corrales *professional baseball player*
Ripken, Calvin Edwin, Jr. (Cal Ripken) *professional baseball player*
†Runk, Carl *head coach men's lacrosse*
Seaman, Tony *university athletic coach*
Shriver, Pamela Howard *professional tennis player*

### Bethesda
Leonard, Sugar Ray (Ray Charles Leonard) *retired professional boxer*
Palmer, James Alvin *baseball commentator*

### Bridgeton
Devers, Gail *track and field athlete*

### College Park
Williams, Gary *collegiate basketball team coach*

### Columbia
Maier, William Otto *martial arts school administrator, educator, consultant*

### Landover
Bickerstaff, Bernard Tyrone, Sr. *professional basketball team coach*
†Carey, Jim *professional hockey player*
Howard, Juwan *professional basketball player*
O'Malley, Susan *professional basketball team executive*
Pollin, Abe *professional basketball team executive, builder*
Unseld, Westley Sissel *professional sports team executive, former professional basketball coach, former professional basketball player*
Webber, Chris, III (Mayce Edward Christopher Webber) *professional basketball player*

### Owings Mills
Burnett, Robert Barry *professional football player*
Green, Bernard Eric *professional football player*
Marchibroda, Ted (Theodore Joseph Marchibroda) *professional football coach*
Modell, Arthur B. *professional football team executive*
Thompson, Bennie *professional football player*
Turner, Eric Ray *professional football player*

## MASSACHUSETTS

### Amherst
†Flint, James *university head basketball coach*

### Arlington
†Samuelson, Joan *professional runner*

### Boston
Auerbach, Arnold (Red Auerbach) *professional basketball team executive*
Avery, Steven Thomas *professional baseball player*
Bourque, Ray *professional hockey player*
Carr, Michael Leon *professional sports team executive, former professional basketball player*
Cordero, Wilfredo Nieva *professional baseball player*
†Crowder, Bruce *collegiate ice hockey coach*
†Duquette, Daniel F. *professional baseball team executive*
Gaston, Paul E. *professional basketball team executive*
Harrington, John Leo *baseball company executive*
Kasper, Stephen Neil *professional hockey coach*
Neely, Cameron Michael *professional hockey player*
Oates, Adam R. *professional hockey player*
Orr, Bobby (Robert Gordon Orr) *former hockey player*
O'Sullivan, Chris *collegiate hockey player*
Parker, Jack *collegiate athletic coach*
Pitino, Richard *college basketball coach*
Saberhagen, Bret William *professional baseball player*
Schram, Stephen C. *professional basketball team executive*
Sinden, Harry *professional hockey team executive*
Slocumb, Heathcliff *professional baseball player*
Stanley, Robert Michael *professional baseball player*
Valentin, John William *professional baseball player*
Vaughn, Maurice Samuel (Mo Vaughn) *professional baseball player*
Volk, Jan *professional sports team executive*
Yastrzemski, Carl Michael *former baseball player, public relations executive*

### Cambridge
Parker, Harry Lambert *university rowing coach*
†Tomassoni, Ronn *men's ice hockey coach*

### Foxboro
Coates, Ben Terrence *professional football player*
†Kraft, Robert K. *professional sports team executive*
Lalas, Alexi *professional soccer player*
Martin, Curtis *professional football player*

### Springfield
†Archibald, Nathaniel *retired basketball player*
†Bellamy, Walter Jones *retired basketball player*
†Blazejowski, Carol *retired basketball player*
†Gallatin, Harry Junior *retired basketball player*
†Gates, William *retired baseball player*
†Gola, Tom *retired basketball player*
†Goodrich, Gail Charles, Jr. *retired basketball player*
†Greer, Harold Everett *retired basketball player*
†Hagan, Clifford *retired basketball player*
†Harris-Stewart, Lusia *retired basketball player*
†Hawkins, Cornelius L. (Connie) *retired basketball player*
†Hayes, Elvin Ernest *retired basketball player*
†Holzman, William *retired basketball player*
†Houbregs, Bob *retired basketball player*
†Jones, Samuel *retired basketball player*
†Kundla, John *coach, retired*
†Lieberman-Cline, Nancy *retired basketball player*
†Lovellette, Clyde *retired basketball player*
†Lucas, Jerry *retired basketball player*
†Martin, Slater Nelson, Jr. *retired basketball player*
†McGuire, Richard Joseph *retired basketball player*
†Mikan, George *retired basketball player*
†Mikkelsen, Arlid Verner Agerskov *retired basketball player*
†Miller, Ralph *coach, retired*
†Newell, Peter *retired basketball coach*
†Pettit, Robert *retired basketball player*
†Ramsey, Frank *retired basketball player*
†Schayes, Adolf *retired basketball player*
†Taylor, Fred *retired basketball coach*
†Thompson, David O'Neal *retired basketball player*
†Wanzer, Robert *retired basketball player*
†White, Nera *retired basketball player*

### Taunton
White, Christine *physical education educator*

### Wakefield
Kerrigan, Nancy *professional figure skater, former Olympic athlete*

### Wilmington
Hayes, Carol Jeanne *physical education educator*

## MICHIGAN

### Ada
†De Vos, Daniel G. *sports team executive, marketing professional*
†Vander Weide, Cheri DeVos *sports team executive, marketing professional*

### Ann Arbor
†Berenson, Gordon *head coach men's ice hockey*
Fisher, Stephen Louis *collegiate basketball team coach*

### Auburn Hills
Dumars, Joe, III *professional basketball player*
Hill, Grant *professional basketball player*
Thorpe, Otis Henry *professional basketball player*

### Berrien Springs
Ali, Muhammad (Cassius Marcellus Clay) *retired professional boxer*

### Detroit
Anderson, Sparky (George Lee Anderson) *former professional baseball team manager*
†Bell, David Gus (Buddy Bell) *professional baseball manager*
†Bing, David *retired basketball player, metal products executive*
Bowman, Scotty *professional hockey coach*
†Ciccarelli, Dino *professional hockey player*
Coffey, Paul *professional hockey player*
Devellano, James Charles *professional hockey manager*
†Fedotov, Sergei *professional hockey player*
†Fetisov, Slava *professional hockey player*
Fryman, David Travis *professional baseball player*
Hearns, Thomas *professional boxer*
Ilitch, Marian *professional hockey team executive*
Ilitch, Michael *professional hockey team executive*
†Osgood, Chris *professional hockey player*
†Vernon, Mike *professional hockey player*
Yzerman, Steve *professional hockey player*

### East Lansing
van der Smissen, M. E. Betty *physical education educator*

### Pontiac
Carter, Anthony *football player*
†Glover, Kevin *football player*
Sanders, Barry *football player*
Schmidt, Chuck *professional football team executive*
Thomas, Henry Lee, Jr. *professional football player*

### Traverse City
Howe, Gordon *former professional hockey player, sports association executive*

## MINNESOTA

### Bloomington
Allen, Mary Louise Hook *physical education educator*

### Eden Prairie
Carter, Cris *professional football player*
Grant, Bud (Harry Peter Grant) *retired professional football coach*
Green, Dennis *professional football coach*
Headrick, Roger Lewis *professional sports executive*
Randle, John *professional football player*
Reveiz, Fuad *professional football player*
Skoglund, John C. *former professional football team executive*
Talley, Darryl Victor *professional football player*

### Mankato
Taylor, Glen *professional sports team executive, printing and graphics company executive*

### Minneapolis
Aguilera, Richard Warren (Rick Aguilera) *professional baseball player*
Bell, Jerry *professional sports team executive*
Carlton, Steven Norman *retired professional baseball player*
Cordova, Martin Keevin (Marty Cordova) *professional baseball player*
Fox, Howard Tall, Jr. *professional baseball team executive*
Kelly, Roberto Conrado (Bobby Kelly) *professional baseball player*
Kelly, Tom (Jay Thomas Kelly) *major league baseball club manager*
Knoblauch, Edward Charles *professional baseball player*
McHale, Kevin Edward *former professional basketball player*
Molitor, Paul Leo *professional baseball player*
Moor, Rob *professional basketball team executive*
Nanne, Louis Vincent *professional hockey team executive*
Pohlad, Carl R. *professional baseball team executive, bottling company executive*
Porter, Terry *professional basketball player*
Puckett, Kirby *professional baseball team executive, former player*
†Ryan, Terry *professional sports team executive*
Saunders, Philip D. *professional basketball team executive*
Steinbach, Terry Lee *professional baseball player*
†Woog, Doug *collegiate ice hockey coach*

### Saint Paul
Swanson-Schones, Kris Margit *developmental adapted physical education educator*

## MISSISSIPPI

### Itta Bena
Ware, William Levi *physical education educator, researcher*

## MISSOURI

### Bridgeton
Joyner Kersee, Jacqueline *track and field athlete*
Lohmiller, John M. (Chip Lohmiller) *professional football player*

**Earth City**
Frontiere, Georgia *professional football team executive*
Landeta, Sean *professional football player*

**Florissant**
Hicks, Ritchie B. *physical education educator*

**Kansas City**
Allen, Marcus *professional football player*
Alt, John *football player*
Appier, (Robert) Kevin *professional baseball player*
Bell, Jay Stuart *professional baseball player*
Boone, Robert Raymond *professional baseball coach*
Brett, George Howard *baseball executive, former professional baseball player*
Carter, Dale Lavelle *professional football player*
Collins, Mark *professional football player*
Cooper, Scott Kendrick *professional baseball player*
Davis, Charles Theodore *professional baseball player*
Hunt, Lamar *professional football team executive*
Kanaby, Robert F. *sports association administrator*
†Kauffman, Larry *professional sports team executive*
†Kreamer, Janice C. *sports association executive*
†McGuff, Joseph Thomas *professional sports team executive*
Montgomery, Jeffrey Thomas *professional baseball player*
Offerman, Jose Antonio Dono *professional baseball player*
Peterson, Carl *professional football team executive*
Robinson, Spencer T. (Herk Robinson) *professional baseball team executive*
Schottenheimer, Martin Edward *professional football coach*
†Shields, Will Herthie *football player*
†Smith, Louis *sports association administrator*
Steadman, Jack W. *professional football team executive*
Thomas, Derrick Vincent *professional football player*

**Lees Summit**
Ferguson, Julie Ann *physical education educator*

**Saint Louis**
Benes, Andrew Charles *professional baseball player*
Caron, Ronald Jacques *professional sports team executive*
†Corson, Shayne *professional hockey player*
Eckersley, Dennis Lee *professional baseball player*
Fuhr, Grant *professional hockey player*
Gant, Ron (Ronald Edwin Gant) *professional baseball player*
Hull, Brett A. *professional hockey player*
Irwin, Hale S. *professional golfer*
†Jocketty, Walt *professional sports team executive*
†Kroenke, Stan *sports association administrator*
†Lamping, Mark *professional sports team executive*
†Lankford, Raymond Lewis *professional baseball player*
La Russa, Tony, Jr. (Anthony La Russa, Jr.) *professional baseball manager*
†MacInnis, Al *professional hockey player*
†MacTavish, Craig *hockey player*
Quinn, Jack J. *professional hockey team executive*
Schoendienst, Albert Fred (Red Schoendienst) *professional baseball coach, former baseball player*
†Shaw, John *sports association administrator*
Smith, Ozzie (Osborne Earl Smith) *professional baseball player*

## NEBRASKA

**Lincoln**
Osborne, Tom *college football coach*

## NEVADA

**Las Vegas**
Allen, Vicki Lynette *physical education educator*
De La Hoya, Oscar *Olympic athlete, professional boxer*
Holmes, David Leo *recreation and leisure educator*
Schneiter, George Malan *golf professional, development company executive*

## NEW JERSEY

**Cherry Hill**
Erving, Julius Winfield, II (Dr. J. Erving) *business executive, retired professional basketball player*

**East Orange**
†Carbajal, Michael *boxer*
†Gatti, Arturo *professional boxer*
Gibson, Althea *retired professional tennis player, golfer, state official*
†Hopkins, Bernard *professional boxer*
†Johnson, Tom *boxer*
†Norris, Terry *professional boxer*
†Pazienza, Vinny *professional boxer*
†Romero, Danny, Jr. *boxer*
†Trinidad, Felix *professional boxer*

**East Rutherford**
Aufzien, Alan L. *professional sports team executive*
†Brodeur, Martin *professional hockey player*
Calipari, John *collegiate basketball team coach*
†Cohen, Jerry L. *professional sports team executive*
Gilmour, Doug *professional hockey player*
Hampton, Rodney *professional football player*
Lamoriello, Louis Anthony *professional hockey team executive*
Lemaire, Jacques *professional hockey coach*
†MacLean, John *professional hockey player*
Mann, Bernard (Bernie Mann) *professional basketball team executive*
Mara, Wellington T. *professional football team executive*
McMullen, John J. *professional hockey team executive*
Montross, Eric Scott *professional basketball player*
Nash, John N. *professional basketball team executive*
O'Bannon, Ed *professional basketball player*
Reed, Willis *professional basketball team executive, former head coach*
†Stevens, Scott *professional hockey player*
Young, George Bernard, Jr. *professional football team executive*

**Edison**
Ensor, Richard Joseph *athletic conference commissioner, lawyer*
Torchia, Karin G. *sports association administrator*

**Far Hills**
Fay, David B. *sports association executive*
Laing, Beverly Ann *sports administrator*

**Gladstone**
†Standish, Robert C. *professional sports team executive*

**Milltown**
Bradley, Edward William *sports foundation executive*

**Montclair**
Lucenko, Leonard Konstantyn *sport, recreation management, and safety educator, coach, consultant*

**New Brunswick**
Dougherty, Neil Joseph *physical education educator, safety consultant*

**North Bergen**
Marth, Fritz Ludwig *sports association executive*

**Philadelphia**
Hextall, Ron *professional hockey player*

**Princeton**
Tierney, Bill *university athletic coach*

**Secaucus**
†Donaldoni, Roberto *soccer player*
Meola, Tony *professional soccer player, actor*
†Parreira, Carlos Alberto *soccer coach*

**Totowa**
Holyfield, Evander *boxer*
Moorer, Michael *professional boxer*

**Trenton**
†Case, Richard W. *professional sports team executive*

**Union**
Pasvolsky, Richard Lloyd *parks, recreation, and environment educator*

**West Orange**
Nessel, Edward Harry *swimming coach*

## NEW MEXICO

**Albuquerque**
Unser, Al *professional auto racer*

**Las Cruces**
Dudenhoeffer, Frances Tomlin *physical education educator*

## NEW YORK

**Astoria**
Frazier, Walter, Jr. (Clyde Frazier) *radio announcer, television analyst, retired professional basketball player*

**Bronx**
Boggs, Wade Anthony *professional baseball player*
Constantine, Gus *physical education educator, coach*
Duncan, Mariano *professional baseball player*
Fielder, Cecil Grant *professional baseball player*
†Girardi, Joseph Elliott *professional baseball player*
Hayes, Charles Dewayne *professional baseball player*
Hurwitz, Ted H. *sports conference administrator*
†Jeter, Derek *professional baseball player*
Kelly, Patrick Franklin *professional baseball player*
†Martinez, Constantino *professional baseball player*
†Molloy, Joseph A. *professional sports team executive*
O'Neill, Paul Andrew *professional baseball player*
Raines, Timothy *professional baseball player*
Richman, Arthur Sherman *sports association executive*
†Rivera, Mariano *professional baseball player*
Steinbrenner, George Michael, III *professional baseball team executive, shipbuilding company executive*
†Watson, Robert *professional sports team executive*
Wells, David Lee *professional baseball player*
Williams, Bernabe Figueroa *professional baseball player*
Zimmer, Donald William *coach professional athletics, former professional baseball manager*

**Buffalo**
Hasek, Dominik *professional hockey player*
Holzinger, Brian *professional hockey player*
Lafontaine, Pat *professional hockey player*
Moss, Douglas G. *professional hockey team executive*
Muckler, John *professional hockey coach, professional team executive*
Nolan, Theodore John *professional hockey coach*

**Cooperstown**
†Aparicio, Luis Ernesto *retired baseball player*
†Ashburn, Don Richard *retired baseball player, broadcaster*
†Barlick, Al *retired baseball umpire*
Carew, Rodney Cline *batting coach, former professional baseball player*
†Doerr, Robert Pershing *retired baseball player*
†Early, Wynn *retired baseball player*
†Ferrell, Rick *retired baseball player*
†Fingers, Roland Glen *retired baseball player*
†Ford, Edward Charles (Whitey Ford) *retired baseball player*
†Hunter, James Augustus *retired baseball player*
†Irvin, Monte *retired baseball player*
†Kaline, Albert William *retired baseball player*
†Koufax, Sandy *retired baseball player*
†Lemon, Robert Granville *retired baseball player*
†Leonard, Buck *retired baseball player*
†Lopez, Alfonso Ramon *retired baseball player*
†Mathews, Edwin Lee *retired baseball player*
†Newhouser, Hal *retired baseball player*
†Reese, Harold Henry *retired baseball player*
Schmidt, Michael Jack *former professional baseball player*
†Slaughter, Enos *retired baseball player*
†Snider, Edwin D. *retired baseball player*
†Spahn, Warren *retired baseball player*
†Wilhelm, James Hoyt *retired baseball player*
Williams, Ted (Theodore Samuel Williams) *former baseball player, former manager, consultant*

**Corona**
Saunders, Adah Wilson *physical education educator*

**Delmar**
Collins, Sandra Dee *physical education educator*

**Fallsburg**
Carey, Janet L. *physical education educator*

**Flushing**
Doubleday, Nelson *professional baseball team executive*
†Hundley, Todd Randolph *professional baseball player*
†Katz, Saul B. *professional sports team executive*
Olerud, John Garrett *professional baseball player*
†Tepper, Marvin B. *professional sports team executive*

**Garden City**
Feingold, Ronald Sherwin *physical education educator*

**Hempstead**
Gutman, Steve *professional football team executive*
Lewis, Mo *professional football player*
Parcells, Bill (Duane Charles Parcells) *professional football coach*

**Lake Placid**
†Rossi, Ronald Aldo *sports association administrator, Olympic athlete*

**New Hartford**
Kelley, Sharon Lee *physical education educator*

**New York**
Austrian, Neil R. *football league executive*
†Beeston, Paul *professional baseball executive*
Campbell, Colin (Soupy Campbell) *professional hockey coach*
Capriati, Jennifer Maria *professional tennis player*
Checketts, David Wayne *professional basketball team executive*
Coleman, Leonard S., Jr. *sports association executive*
Cone, David Brian *professional baseball player*
†Driver, Bruce *professional hockey player*
Evans, James Bremond (Jim Evans) *major league baseball umpire*
Ewing, Patrick Aloysius *professional basketball player*
Gamble, Harry T. *professional football team executive*
Gibbs, Joe Jackson *former professional football coach, broadcaster, professional sports team executive*
Gourdine, Simon Peter *professional basketball executive*
Graves, Adam *professional hockey player*
Gretzky, Wayne Douglas *professional hockey player*
†Grunfeld, Ernie *professional sports team executive*
Holtz, Louis Leo *former college football coach, sports commentator*
Jackson, Reginald Martinez *former professional baseball player*
†Jones, K. C. *professional basketball coach*
Jones, Roy *professional boxer*
Leetch, Brian Joseph *hockey player*
†Lobo, Rebecca *basketball player*
†Lowe, Kevin Hugh *professional hockey player*
Martin, Michael Townsend *racing horse stable executive, sports marketing executive*
McClelland, Timothy Reid *baseball umpire*
McEnroe, John Patrick, Jr. *retired professional tennis player, commentator*
Messier, Mark Douglas *professional hockey player*
Pelé, (Edson Arantes do Nascimento) *professional soccer player*
Powell, Mike *olympic athlete, track and field*
Richter, Michael Thomas *professional hockey player*
Robinson, Frank *professional baseball team executive, former coach, former player*
Robitaille, Luc *professional hockey player*
Scott, Dale Allan *major league umpire*
Seaver, Tom (George Thomas Seaver) *former professional baseball player*
†Smith, Neil *professional sports team executive*
Spinks, Michael *retired professional boxer*
†Steinfeld, Allan *sports association administrator*
Stern, David Joel *basketball association executive*
Stram, Hank Louis *former professional football coach, television and radio commentator*
†Straus, Eric L. *sports association administrator*
Tagliabue, Paul John *national football league commissioner*
Van Gundy, Jeff *coach*
Weiss, Donald L(ogan) *retired sports association executive*
Welts, Rick *sports association executive*
Williams, Charles Linwood (Buck Williams) *professional basketball player*
Yamaguchi, Kristi Tsuya *ice skater*
Zahnd, Richard Hugo *professional sports executive, lawyer*

**Newburgh**
Orbacz, Linda Ann *physical education educator*

**Orchard Park**
†Brown, Ruben Pernell *football player*
†Butler, John *professional sports team executive*
Hull, Kent *professional football player*
Levy, Marvin Daniel *professional football coach, sports team executive*
Paup, Bryce Eric *professional football player*
Reed, Andre Darnell *professional football player*
Smith, Bruce *professional football player*
Spielman, Chris *professional football player*
Tasker, Steven Jay *professional football player*
Thomas, Thurman *professional football player*

**Rochester**
Crane, Irving Donald *pocket billiards player*

**Scotia**
Morris, Jason *Olympic athlete*

**Syracuse**
†Boeheim, Jim *college basketball coach*
Simmons, Roy, Jr. *university athletic coach*

**Uniondale**
Arbour, Alger *professional hockey coach*
†Milbury, Mike *professional hockey coach*

**West Point**
†Emmer, Jack *head coach men's lacrosse*

**White Plains**
Becker, Boris *professional tennis player*
Davenport, Lindsay *professional tennis player*
Fernandez, Gigi *professional tennis player*
†Frazier, Amy *professional tennis player*
Garrison-Jackson, Zina *retired tennis player*
Gilbert, Bradley *professional tennis player, Olympic athlete, professional tennis coach*
Grossman, Ann *pressional tennis player*
Krickstein, Aaron *professional tennis player*
Martin, Todd *professional tennis player*
McEnroe, Patrick *professional tennis player*
†McNeil, Lori Michelle *professional tennis player*
Reneberg, Richard (Richey Reneberg) *professional tennis player*
Rostagno, Derrick *professional tennis player*
Rubin, Chanda *professional tennis player*
Washington, MaliVai *professional tennis player*
Wheaton, David *professional tennis player*

**Yonkers**
Williams, Ted Vaughnell *physical education educator*

**Yorktown Heights**
Bogdanoff, Stewart Ronald *physical education educator, coach*

## NORTH CAROLINA

**Almond**
Strausbaugh, Scott David *Olympic athlete, canoeist*

**Chapel Hill**
Klarmann, Dave *university athletic coach*
Smith, Dean Edwards *university basketball coach*

**Charlotte**
Bogues, Tyrone Curtis (Muggsy Bogues) *professional basketball player*
Capers, Dominic *professional football coach*
Davis, Eric Wayne *professional football player*
Ismail, Raghib (Rocket Ismail) *professional football player*
Johnson, Larry Demetric *professional basketball player*
Mason, Anthony George Douglas *professional basketball player*
Mills, Samuel Davis, Jr. *professional football player*
Shinn, George *professional sports team executive*
†Walls, Charles Wesley *football player*

**Concord**
†Wallace, Kenny *professional race car driver*

**Cornelius**
†Mayfield, Jeremy *professional race car driver*

**Dana**
Morgan, Lou Ann *physical education educator*

**Durham**
Krzyzewski, Mike *university athletic coach*
Little, Larry Chatmon *head football coach*

**Greenville**
†Donovan, Anne *coach*

**Kill Devil Hills**
Perry, Gaylord Jackson *former professional baseball player*

**Mooresville**
†Spencer, Jimmy *professional race car driver*

**Raleigh**
Yow, Kay *university athletic coach*

**Randleman**
Petty, Richard *retired professional race car driver*

**Trinity**
Weeks, Marie Cook *health and physical education educator*

**Winston Salem**
†Gaines, Clarence E., Sr. *coach, retired, school system administrator*
Odoms, Dave *collegiate athletic coach*

## NORTH DAKOTA

**Wahpeton**
Jensen, Delores (Dee Jensen) *physical education educator*

## OHIO

**Akron**
Cai, X. Sean *physical education educator*
Monacelli, Amieto *professional bowler*
Murphy, Bob *professional golfer*
Ozio, David *professional bowler*

**Canton**
Dorsett, Anthony Drew (Tony Dorsett) *former professional football player*

Elliott, Peter R. *athletic organization executive, retired*
Greene, Joe (Charles Edward Greene) *former professional football player, professional football coach*
†Haynes, Michael James Heflin *professional football player*
Johnson, Jimmy *former professional football player*
†Joiner, Charlie *retired football player*
Kelly, Leroy *former professional football player*
†Renfro, Mel *retired football player*
†Selmon, Lee Roy *retired football player*
Smith, Jackie *former professional football player*

**Cincinnati**
†Ambrose, Ashley Avery *football player*
Bench, Johnny Lee *retired professional baseball player*
Blake, Jeff *professional football player*
Boone, Bret Robert *professional baseball player*
†Bowden, Jim *professional sports team executive*
Brantley, Jeffrey Hoke *professional baseball player*
Brown, Mike *professional sports team executive*
Coslet, Bruce N. *professional football coach*
†Huggins, Bob *college basketball coach*
†Knight, (Charles) Ray *professional sports team executive*
Knowlton, Austin E. (Dutch Knowlton) *professional football team executive*
Larkin, Barry Louis *professional baseball player*
Pendleton, Terry Lee *baseball player*
Rose, Peter Edward *former professional baseball player and manager*
Sanders, Deion Luwynn *baseball and football player*
Sanders, Reginald Laverne (Reggie Sanders) *professional baseball player*
Sawyer, John *professional football team executive*
Schott, Marge *professional baseball team executive*

**Cleveland**
Alomar, Sandy, Jr. (Santos Velazquez Alomar) *professional baseball player*
Courier, Jim (James Spencer Courier, Jr.) *tennis player*
Faldo, Nick *professional golfer*
Fernandez, Tony (Octavio Antonio Castro Fernandez) *baseball player*
Fratello, Michael Robert *professional basketball coach*
Hargrove, Mike (Dudley Michael Hargrove) *professional baseball team manager*
Hart, John *professional sports team executive*
Hershiser, Orel Leonard, IV *professional baseball player*
Hill, Tyrone *professional basketball player*
Jackson, Michael Ray *professional baseball player*
Justice, David Christopher *baseball player*
Lofton, Kenneth *professional baseball player*
Lopez, Nancy *professional golfer*
McDowell, Jack Burns *professional baseball player*
Mesa, Jose Ramon *professional baseball player*
Montana, Joseph C., Jr. *former professional football player*
Navratilova, Martina *former professional tennis player*
Ramirez, Manuel Aristides (Manny Ramirez) *professional baseball player*
Rothstein, Ronald *professional basketball coach*
Rubins, Alex *physical education educator*
Seitzer, Kevin Lee *professional baseball player*
Seles, Monica *tennis player*
Strange, Curtis Northrop *professional golfer*
Thompson, Robert Randall (Robby Thompson) *professional baseball player*
Vizquel, Omar Enrique *professional baseball player*
Williams, Matt (Matthew Derrick Williams) *professional baseball player*

**Columbus**
Noe, Fred J. *sports association administrator*

**Fairfield**
Robertson, Oscar Palmer (Big O Robertson) *former professional basketball player, chemical company executive*

**Lebanon**
Deyo, Wendel *sports association administrator*

**Oxford**
Pont, John *football coach, educator*

**Shaker Heights**
†Eakin, Thomas Capper *sports promotion executive*

**Youngstown**
DeBartolo, Edward John, Jr. *professional football team owner, real estate developer*

### OKLAHOMA

**Guthrie**
Jenkins, Ferguson Arthur, Jr. (Fergie Jenkins) *former baseball player*

**Oklahoma City**
†Richardson, Dot *softball player*

**Tulsa**
Huber, Fritz Godfrey *physical education educator, excercise physiologist*

### OREGON

**Eugene**
Sisley, Becky Lynn *physical education educator*

**Portland**
Glickman, Harry *professional basketball team executive*
Kolde, Bert *professional basketball team executive*
†Weinberg, Lawrence *professional basketball team owner*
†Whitsitt, Robert James *professional basketball team executive*

### PENNSYLVANIA

**Altoona**
Wright, Jerry Jaye *physical education educator*

**Bethel Park**
Bohn, James Francis *physical education educator*

**Bradford**
Ross, Jean Louise *physical education educator*

**Easton**
Holmes, Larry, Jr. *professional boxer*

**Furlong**
Ide, John Edwin *physical education educator*

**Lafayette Hill**
Dixon, Fitz Eugene, Jr. *professional baseball team executive*

**Lewisburg**
†Jamieson, Sid *head coach men's lacrosse*

**Philadelphia**
†Betz, Claire S. *professional sports team executive*
Brind'Amour, Rod Jean *professional hockey player*
Brown, Lawrence Harvey (Larry Brown) *basketball coach*
†Buck, Alexander K. *professional sports team executive*
†Buck, William C. *professional sports team executive*
Cheveldae, Tim *professional hockey player*
Clarke, Robert Earle (Bobby Clarke) *hockey executive*
Coleman, Derrick D. *professional basketball player*
Daulton, Darren Arthur *professional baseball player*
Dykstra, Lenny (Leonard Kyle Dykstra) *professional baseball player*
Fryar, Irving Dale *professional football player*
Garcia, Richard Raul *major league umpire*
Giles, William Yale *professional baseball team executive*
Jefferies, Gregory Scott *professional baseball player*
Lindros, Eric Bryan *professional hockey player*
Lurie, Jeffrey *professional sports team executive*
McRae, Hal (Harold Abraham McRae) *former major league baseball team manager*
Montgomery, David Paul *professional baseball team executive*
Morardini, Michael Robert *professional baseball player*
Murray, Terry (Terence Rodney Murray) *professional hockey team coach*
†Rhodes, Raymond Earl *professional sports team executive*
Runge, Paul Edward *baseball umpire, realtor*
Rypien, Mark Robert *professional football player*
Scott, Joseph C. *professional hockey team executive*
Snider, Edward Malcolm *professional hockey club executive*
†Thomas, Lee *professional sports team executive*
Thomas, William Harrison *professional football player*
Watters, Richard James *professional football player*

**Pittsburgh**
Bettis, Jerome Abram *professional football player*
†Brown, Chadwick Everett *football player*
Cowher, Bill *professional football coach*
Dawson, Dermontti Farra *professional football player*
Francis, Ron *professional hockey player*
Greene, Kevin Darwin *professional football player*
Jagr, Jaromir *professional hockey player*
Johnston, Edward Joseph *professional hockey team coach, former team executive, former player*
†Kendall, Jason Daniel *professional baseball player*
†Kirkland, Lorenzo Levon *football player*
Lake, Carnell Augustino *professional football player*
Lemieux, Mario *former professional hockey player*
Lloyd, Gregory Lenard *professional football player*
Majors, Johnny (John Terrill Majors) *university athletic coach*
Noll, Charles Henry *former professional football coach*
Patrick, Craig *professional hockey team executive*
Rooney, Daniel M. *professional football team executive*
Ryan, Stephen Michael, Jr. *professional hockey team executive*
Stargell, Willie (Wilver Dornel Stargell) *professional sports team coach, former baseball player*
Stark, Rohn Taylor *professional football player*
Trottier, Bryan John *professional sports team coach, former professional hockey player*
Woodson, Roderick Kevin *professional football player*

**University Park**
Paterno, Joseph Vincent *college football coach*

**Washington**
Hays, Lewis W. *amateur baseball executive, writer*

**Youngstown**
Palmer, Arnold Daniel *professional golfer*

### RHODE ISLAND

**Kingston**
Harrick, Jim *university athletic coach*

**Providence**
Gorton, Arlene Elizabeth *physical education educator*
Russell, Bill *former professional basketball team executive, former professional basketball player*

### SOUTH CAROLINA

**Columbia**
Giese, Warren Kenneth *health and physical education educator, state senator*

### TENNESSEE

**Brentwood**
Abernathy, Sue Eury *physical education educator*

**Franklin**
Waltrip, Darrell Lee *professional stock car driver*

**Knoxville**
†Summitt, Patricia Head *college basketball coach*
Wasserman, Jack F. *exercise science educator*

**Memphis**
Finch, Larry *university athletic coach*

**Nashville**
Griffith, Jerry Lynn *physical education educator*
Snoddy, Chris Raymond *athletic trainer*
Stepnoski, Mark Matthew *professional football player*

### TEXAS

**Arlington**
Burkett, John David *professional baseball player*
Clark, Will (William Nuschler Clark, Jr.) *professional baseball player*
Gonzalez, Juan (Alberto Vazquez) *professional baseball player*
†Melvin, Robert Douglas *professional sports team executive*
Oates, Johnny Lane *professional baseball team manager*
†Pavlik, Roger Allen *professional baseball player*
Rodriguez, Ivan *professional baseball player*
Rose, Edward W. (Rusty Rose) *professional sports team executive*
Ryan, Nolan *former professional baseball player*
Schieffer, J. Thomas *professional baseball team executive*
Wetteland, John Karl *professional baseball player*

**Austin**
Crenshaw, Ben *professional golfer*
Garrido, Augie *university athletic coach*
Mackovic, John *college football coach, athletic director*

**Carrollton**
Foster, William Edwin (Bill Foster) *nonprofessional basketball coach*

**College Station**
Slocum, R.C. *university athletic coach*

**Dallas**
†Beard, Alfred (Butch ) *former basketball player, former commentator*
Landry, Tom (Thomas Wade Landry) *former professional football coach*
Trevino, Lee Buck *professional golfer*

**Houston**
†Alexander, Leslie Lee *professional sports team executive*
Bagwell, Jeff (Jeffrey Robert Bagwell) *professional baseball player*
Barkley, Charles Wade *professional basketball player*
Berra, Yogi (Lawrence Peter Berra) *professional baseball coach*
Biggio, Craig *professional baseball player*
†Bishop, Blaine Elwood *football player*
Dishman, Cris Edward *professional football player*
Donie, Scott *Olympic athlete, platform diver*
Drexler, Clyde *professional basketball player*
Eusibio, Raul Antonio *professional baseball player*
†Fisher, Jeff *professional football coach*
Foreman, George *boxer, nondenominational christian minister, boxing broadcaster*
Foyt, A(nthony) J(oseph), Jr. *auto racing crew chief, former professional auto racer*
Gray, Mel *professional football player*
Holovak, Mike *sports association exec*
†Hunsicker, Gerry *professional sports executive*
Lewis, Carl (Frederick Carlton Lewis) *Olympic track and field athlete*
Matthews, Bruce Rankin *professional football player*
†McLane, Drayton, Jr. *professional baseball team executive*
†Murphy, Calvin Jerome *professional sports team executive*
Olajuwon, Hakeem Abdul *professional basketball player*
Patterson, Steve *professional hockey team executive*
†Reese, Floyd *professional sports team executive*
Roby, Reginald Henry *professional football player*
†Smith, Tal *sports association administrator*
Spencer, Albert Franklin *physical education and education educator*
Tomjanovich, Rudolph *professional athletic coach*
†Watson, Bob *professional baseball executive*
Willis, Kevin Alvin *professional basketball player*

**Huntsville**
†Karolyi, Bela *gymnastics coach*

**Irving**
Aikman, Troy *professional football player*
†Allen, Larry Christopher *football player*
Haley, Charles Lewis *professional football player*
Irvin, Michael Jerome *professional football player*
Jones, Jerry (Jerral Wayne Jones) *professional football team executive*
Lett, Leon *professional football player*
Lites, James *professional hockey team executive*
†Moog, Donald Andrew *professional hockey player*
Newton, Nate *professional football player*
Novacek, Jay McKinley *professional football player*
Smith, Emmitt J., III *professional football player*
Switzer, Barry *professional football coach, former university athletic coach*
†Tolbert, Tony Lewis *football player*
Tuinei, Mark Pulemau *professional football player*
Walker, Herschel *professional football player*
Williams, Erik George *professional football player*
Woodson, Darren Ray *professional football player*

**Leander**
Erickson, Ralph D. *retired physical education educator, small business owner, consultant*

**Lubbock**
†Sharp, Marsha *basketball coach*
Wilson, Margaret Eileen *retired physical education educator*

**San Antonio**
†Diller, John C. *professional athletics executive*
Elliot, Sean Michael *professional basketball player*
Robinson, David Maurice *professional basketball player*

### UTAH

**Park City**
Moe, Tommy (Thomas Sven Moe) *skier, former Olympic athlete*
Roffe-Steinrotter, Diann *Olympic athlete*

**Provo**
Conlee, Robert Keith *physical education educator*

**Salt Lake City**
Hornacek, Jeffrey John *professional basketball player*
†Howells, R. Tim *professional sports team executive*
Layden, Francis Patrick (Frank Layden) *professional basketball team executive, former coach*
Majerus, Rick *collegiate basketball team coach*
Malone, Karl *professional basketball player*
Miller, Larry H. *professional sports team executive, automobile dealer*
Sloan, Jerry (Gerald Eugene Sloan) *professional basketball coach*
Stockton, John Houston *professional basketball player*

### VIRGINIA

**Alexandria**
Needels, Christopher James *sports association administrator*

**Arlington**
Kiraly, Karch (Charles Kiraly) *professional volleyball player*

**Ashburn**
Cooke, John Kent *professional sports management executive*

**Blacksburg**
Foster, Bill Carey *collegiate basketball team coach*

**Charlottesville**
Dodson, Claudia Lane *athletic administrator*
Ryan, Debbie *university athletic coach*

**Falls Church**
Theismann, Joseph Robert *former professional football player, announcer*

**Herndon**
Arena, Bruce *university coach*

**Mc Lean**
Chang, Michael *tennis player*

**Norfolk**
†Larry, Wendy *head coach women's basketball*

**Richmond**
Daniel, Beth *professional golfer*

**Suffolk**
Gray, Marcia Lanette *health, physical education and recreation educator*

### WASHINGTON

**Kirkland**
Blades, Horatio Benedict (Bennie Blades) *professional football player*
Erickson, Dennis *professional football coach, former university football coach*
†Sinclair, Michael Glenn *football player*
Tuten, Richard Lamar *professional football player*
Warren, Christopher Collins *professional football player*

**Seattle**
Ackerley, Barry *professional basketball team executive, communications company executive*
Armstrong, Charles G. *professional baseball executive, lawyer*
Ellis, John W. *professional baseball team executive, utility company executive*
Griffey, Ken, Jr. (George Kenneth Griffey, Jr.) *professional baseball player*
Johnson, Randall David (Randy Johnson) *professional baseball player*
Karl, George *professional basketball coach*
Kemp, Shawn T. *professional basketball player*
Martinez, Edgar *professional baseball player*
McMillan, Nathaniel *professional basketball player*
Payton, Gary Dwayne *professional basketball player*
Piniella, Louis Victor *professional baseball team manager*
Walker, Walter Frederick *professional basketball team executive*

**Spokane**
Moe, Orville Leroy *racetrack executive*

### WEST VIRGINIA

**Harpers Ferry**
Startzell, David N. *sports association executive*

### WISCONSIN

**Green Bay**
Favre, Brett Lorenzo *professional football player*

Harlan, Robert Ernest *professional football team executive*
Holmgren, Mike *professional football coach*
White, Reggie (Reginald Howard White) *professional football player*

**Greendale**
†Kuhn, Roseann *sports association administrator*

**Milwaukee**
Carr, Charles Lee Glenn, Jr. (Chuck Carr) *professional baseball player*
Dunleavy, Michael Joseph *professional basketball coach*
Garner, Phil *professional baseball manager*
Jansen, Daniel Ervin *professional speedskater, marketing professional, former Olympic athlete*
Lanier, Bob *former professional sports team executive, former basketball player*
Listach, Patrick Alan *professional baseball player*
Selig, Allan H. (Bud Selig) *professional baseball team executive*
Steinmiller, John F. *professional basketball team executive*

**Stevens Point**
Garber, David J. *sports association executive, marketing consultant*

## CANADA

### ALBERTA

**Calgary**
†Bartlett, Grant A. *professional sports team executive*
†Edwards, N. Murray *professional sports team owner*
Hotchkiss, Harley N. *professional hockey team owner*
†Joyce, Ronald V. *professional sports team executive*
†Libin, Alvin G. *business executive*
†Markin, Allan P. *professional sports team executive*
Risebrough, Doug *professional hockey team executive*

**Canmore**
Wood, Sharon *mountaineer*

**Edmonton**
†Joseph, Curtis Shayne *professional hockey player*
Low, Ron Albert *professional hockey coach*
Sather, Glen Cameron *professional hockey team executive, coach*
†Weight, Doug *professional hockey player*

### BRITISH COLUMBIA

**Richmond**
Zeigler, Earle Frederick *physical education-kinesiology educator*

**Vancouver**
Bure, Pavel *professional hockey player*
Chapple, John H. *professional sports team executive*
Griffiths, Arthur R. *professional hockey team executive*
Jackson, Stu *professional sports team executive, former university basketball coach*
McCaw, John E., Jr. *professional sports team executive*
McLean, Kirk *professional hockey player*
†Mogilny, Alexander *professional hockey player*
†Winters, Brian Joseph *professional sports team executive*

### ONTARIO

**Gloucester**
†Bailey, Donovan *Olympic athlete*
Browning, Kurt *figure skating champion*

**Nepean**
†Alfredsson, Daniel *professional hockey player*

**Toronto**
†Ash, Gordon *professional sports team executive*
Carter, Joe (Joseph Chris Carter) *professional baseball player*
†Clark, Wendel *hockey player*
Clemens, William Roger *professional baseball player*
Fletcher, Cliff *professional hockey team executive*
Gaston, Cito *professional baseball manager*
Hanson, Erik Brian *professional baseball player*
Hentgen, Patrick George *professional baseball player*
Potvin, Felix *professional hockey player*
Santiago, Benito Rivera *professional baseball player*
†Schneider, Mathieu *hockey player*
Sierra, Ruben Angel Garcia *professional baseball player*
Stavro, Steve A. *professional hockey team executive*
†Sundin, Mats Johan *professional hockey player*
Thomas, Isiah Lord, III *former professional basketball player, basketball team executive*

### QUEBEC

**Montreal**
Alou, Felipe Rojas *professional baseball manager*
†Beattie, James Louis *professional sports team executive*
†Blanchet, Claude *professional sports team executive*
Brochu, Claude Renaud *professional baseball team executive*
Corey, Ronald *professional hockey team executive*
Damphousse, Vincent *professional hockey player*
Fletcher, Darrin Glen *professional baseball player*
†Grudzielanek, Mark James *professional baseball player*
King, W. David *professional hockey coach*
Martinez, Pedro Jaime *professional baseball player*
†Menard, Louis Jacques *professional sports team executive*
Perez, Carlos Gross *professional baseball player*
†Proteau, Jocelyn *professional sports team executive*
Smith, Lee Arthur *professional baseball player*
Stoneman, William Hambly, III *professional baseball team executive*
†Turgeon, Pierre *professional hockey player*

**Saint Lazare**
Fanning, William James *professional baseball team executive, radio and television broadcaster*

**Sainte Foy**
Lagassé, Pierre Philippe *exercise science educator*

## MEXICO

**Mexico City**
†Camacho, Hector *boxer*
†Chavez, Julio Cesar *professional boxer*
†Duran, Roberto *boxer*
†Hill, Virgil *professional boxer*
†Holmes, Keith *professional boxer*
†Joppy, William *professional boxer*
†Liles, Frank *professional boxer*
†Lopez, Ricardo *professional boxer*
†Martin, Christy *professional boxer*
†Miller, Nate *professional boxer*
†Randall, Frankie *professional boxer*
†Taylor, Quincy *professional boxer*
Whitaker, Pernell (Sweet Pea Whitaker) *professional boxer*
†Zarazoga, Daniel *professional boxer*

## DOMINICAN REPUBLIC

**Santo Domingo**
†Marichal, Juan Antonio Sanchez *retired baseball player, agency administrator*

## SOUTH AFRICA

**Klippoortjie**
Els, Theodore Ernest *professional golfer*

## SPAIN

**Santander**
Ballesteros, Severiano *professional golfer*

## ADDRESS UNPUBLISHED

Allen, Eric Andre *professional football player*
Andersen, Morten *football player*
Andretti, John *professional race car driver*
Andretti, Mario (Gabriele) *race car driver*
Andretti, Michael Mario *professional race car driver*
Anthony, Earl Roderick *professional bowler*
†Baiul, Oksana *figure skater*
Banks, Ernest (Ernie Banks) *retired professional baseball player*
Boling, Robert Bruce *physical education educator*
†Bonifay, Cam *professional sports team executive*
Bradley, Patricia Ellen *professional golfer*
Caminiti, Kenneth Gene *professional baseball player*
Cashen, J. Frank *professional baseball team executive*
Cooper, John Miller *retired biomechanics lab director*
†Desjardins, Eric *professional hockey player*
Embry, Wayne Richard *basketball executive*
Esposito, Philip Anthony (Phil Esposito) *professional sports team executive, former hockey broadcaster, former professional hockey player*
†Fernandez, Mary Joe *professional tennis player*
Fires, Earlie Stancel *jockey*
†Ford, William Clay, Jr. *professional sports team executive*
Gainey, Robert Michael *professional hockey coach, former player*
Geddes, Jane *professional golfer*
Graf, Steffi *professional tennis player*
Guthrie, Janet *professional race car driver*
Harding, F(red) Victor *fitness consultant*
Havlicek, John J. (Hondo Havlicek) *former professional basketball player*
Hemond, Roland A. *professional baseball team executive*
†Hollandsworth, Todd Mathew *professional baseball player*
†Johnson, Kenneth Lance *professional baseball player*
Kavalek, Lubomir *chess expert*
Keenan, Mike *professional hockey team coach*
†Konstantinov, Vladimir *professional hockey player*
†LeClair, John Clark *professional hockey player*
Lindsey, D. Ruth *physical education educator*
Littler, Gene Alec *professional golfer*
Lowery, Dominic Gerald (Nick ) *professional football player*
†Martin, Tony *football player*
Mc Carthy, Jean Jerome *retired physical education educator*
McIlvaine, Joseph Peter *professional baseball team executive*
McIntyre, Guy Maurice *professional football player*
†McMaster, Sam *professional sports team official*
McVay, John Edward *professional football club executive*
†Mellanby, Scott Edgar *professional hockey player*
Miller, Reginald Wayne *professional basketball player*
Mitchell, Tonja Keashavel *physical education educator, nutritional consultant*
Modano, Michael *professional hockey player*
Mutombo, DiKembe (Dikembe Mutombo Mpolondo Mukamba Jean Jacque Wamutombo) *professional basketball player*
Parins, Robert James *professional football team executive, judge*
Payton, Walter (Sweetness Payton) *professional race car driver, former professional football player*
†Rodriguez, Alexander Emmanuel *professional baseball player*
Rogers, Kenneth Scott *professional baseball player*
Ross, Robert Joseph *head professional football coach*
Rutherford, John Sherman, III (Johnny Rutherford) *professional race car driver*
Schrempf, Detlef *professional basketball player*
†Seldin, David *professional sports team executive*
Sharpe, Sterling *former professional football player, sports commentator*
Sims, Keith *professional football player*
Stadler, Craig Robert *professional golfer*
Tewksbury, Robert Alan *professional baseball player*
Thompson, Craig Dean *sports association executive*
Vanatta, Bob *athletic administrator*
White, Devon Markes *professional baseball player*
Wilkens, Leonard Randolph, Jr. (Lenny Wilkens) *professional basketball coach*
Wooden, John Robert *former basketball coach*
Woosnam, Ian Harold *professional golfer*

---

## BUSINESS. *See* FINANCE; INDUSTRY.

---

## COMMUNICATIONS. *See* COMMUNICATIONS MEDIA; INDUSTRY: SERVICE.

---

## COMMUNICATIONS MEDIA. *See also* ARTS: LITERARY.

---

## UNITED STATES

### ALABAMA

**Anniston**
Ayers, Harry Brandt *editor, publisher, columnist*

**Birmingham**
Carlton, Michael *magazine editor*
Casey, Ronald Bruce *journalist*
Crichton, Douglas Bentley *editor, writer*
Griffin, Eleanor *magazine editor*
Hanson, Victor Henry, II *newspaper publisher*
Jacobson, James Edmund *newspaper editor*
Kennedy, Joe David, Jr. (Joey Kennedy) *editor*
†Lynch, Kevin *publishing executive*
Nunnelley, Carol Fishburne *editor newspaper*
Scarritt, Thomas Varnon *newspaper editor*
Seitz, Karl Raymond *editor*
Sheppard, Scott *magazine publisher*
Stephens, James T. *publishing executive*
Walker, Evelyn *retired television executive*

**Huntsville**
Barros-Smith, Deborah Lynne *publishing executive, editor, journalist*

**Jacksonville**
Merrill, Martha *instructional media educator*

**Mobile**
Hearin, William Jefferson *newspaper publishing company executive*

**Monroeville**
Kniskern, Maynard *editor, writer*

**Montgomery**
Brown, William Blake *newspaper editor*
Hayes, John Edward *broadcasting executive*
Teague, Larry Gene *editor*

**Tuscaloosa**
Mac Donald, Malcolm Murdoch *editor, publisher*
Reinhart, Kellee Connely *journalist*
Thomson, H. Bailey *editor*

### ALASKA

**Anchorage**
Atwood, Robert Bruce *publisher*
Lindauer, John Howard, II *newspaper publisher*
Pearson, Larry Lester *journalism educator, internet presence provider*

**Fairbanks**
Hatch, Kelley Marie *journalist, television news anchor, writer*

### ARIZONA

**Bisbee**
Eppele, David Louis *columnist, author*

**Casa Grande**
Kramer, Donovan Mershon, Sr. *newspaper publisher*

**Flagstaff**
Hammond, Howard David *retired botanist and editor*

**Gilbert**
Kenney, Thomas Frederick *broadcasting executive*

**Glendale**
Joseph, Gregory Nelson *media critic*

**Green Valley**
Lasch, Robert *former journalist*
Perry, Roger Lawrence *printing executive*

**Phoenix**
Benson, Stephen R. *editorial cartoonist*
†Berkery, Dan *television station executive*
Cook, Neil D. *publishing executive*
Edens, Gary Denton *broadcasting executive*
Genrich, Mark L. *newspaper editorial writer, columnist*
Godwin, Mary Jo *editor, librarian consultant*
Gunty, Christopher James *newspaper editor*
Harelson, Hugh *publishing and tourism consultant*
Kolbe, John William *newspaper columnist*
Leach, John F. *newspaper editor, journalism educator*
Might, Thomas Owen *newspaper company executive*
Moyer, Alan Dean *retired newspaper editor*
Murian, Richard Miller *book company executive*
Oppedahl, John Fredrick *publisher*
Schatt, Paul *newspaper editor*
Stahl, Richard G. C. *journalist, editor*
Steckler, Phyllis Betty *publishing company executive*
Weil, Louis Arthur, III *newspaper publishing executive*

**Prescott**
Casserly, John Joseph *author, journalist*

**Scottsdale**
Frischknecht, Lee Conrad *retired broadcasting executive*
Reidy, Richard Robert *publishing company executive*
Searight, Patricia Adelaide *retired radio and television executive*
Walsh, Mason *retired newspaperman*

**Sedona**
Chicorel, Marietta Eva *publisher*
Edwards, F(loyd) Kenneth *journalist, educator, management consultant, marketing executive*
Sasmor, James Cecil *publishing representative, educator*

**Tempe**
†Allen, Charles R. *television station executive*
Rankin, William Parkman *communications educator, former publishing company executive*
Sabine, Gordon Arthur *educator, writer*

**Tucson**
Coffman, Roy Walter, III *publishing company executive*
Hutchinson, Charles Smith, Jr. *book publisher*
Martin, June Johnson Caldwell *journalist*
Neal, James Madison, Jr. *retired editor and educator*
Roos, Nestor Robert *consultant*
Silva, John Philip Costa *newspaper editor*
Weber, Samuel *editor, retired*

### ARKANSAS

**Eureka Springs**
Sackett, Ross DeForest *publisher*

**Fayetteville**
Masterson, Michael Rue *journalist, educator, editor*

**Fort Smith**
Flippin, Perry Welch *publishing executive*

**Harrisburg**
Sanders, Barbara Heeb *writer, consultant*

**Little Rock**
Greenberg, Paul *newspaperman*
Hobbs, Ray David *editor*
Lutgen, Robert Raymond *newspaper editor*
Portis, Charles McColl *reporter, writer*
Simmons, Bill *political editor*
Smith, Griffin, Jr. *editor*
Starr, John Robert *retired newspaper editor, political columnist*

**Mountain Home**
Anderson, Kenneth Norman *retired magazine editor, author*

**Springdale**
Martin, Becca Bacon *editor, journalist*

### CALIFORNIA

**Agoura Hills**
Chagall, David *journalist, author*
Teresi, Joseph *publishing executive*

**Alameda**
Mewhinney, Bruce Harrison Nicholas *publisher*

**Albany**
Sikora, Stephen Theodore *publisher*

**Alhambra**
Duke, Donald Norman *publisher*

**Alpine**
Greenberg, Byron Stanley *newspaper and business executive, consultant*
Sharits, Dean Paul *motion picture company executive*

**Avila Beach**
Kamm, Herbert *journalist*

**Belmont**
Carlson, Gary R. *publishing executive*

**Belvedere**
Lake, David S. *publisher, lawyer*

**Belvedere Tiburon**
Kramer, Lawrence Stephen *journalist*

**Berkeley**
Bagdikian, Ben Haig *journalist, emeritus university educator*
Browne, G.M. Walter Shawn Browne *journalist, chess player*
Clark, James Henry *publishing company executive*
Fulton, Katherine Nelson *journalist, consultant*
Helson, Henry Berge *publisher, retired mathematics educator*
Lesser, Wendy *literary magazine editor, writer, consultant*

Light, Ken *photojournalist, educator*
Littlejohn, David *journalism educator, writer*
Matthews, Mildred Shapley *scientific editor, freelance writer*

### Beverly Hills
Beck, Marilyn Mohr *columnist*
Bradshaw, Terry *sports announcer, former professional football player*
Chernin, Peter *motion picture company executive*
Corwin, Stanley Joel *book publisher*
Filosa, Gary Fairmont Randolph V., II *multimedia executive, financier, columnist*
Harris, Jordan *record company executive*
Hefner, Hugh Marston *editor-in-chief*
Heller, Paul Michael *film company executive, producer*
Hill, David *broadcast executive*
Israel, David *journalist, screenwriter, producer*
Jenner, Bruce *sportscaster, former Olympic athlete*
Kuhn, Michael *motion picture company executive*
Levy, David *broadcasting executive*
Lond, Harley Weldon *editor, publisher*
Madden, John *television sports commentator, former professional football coach*
Mark, John *film company executive*
Mechanic, William M. *television and motion picture industry executive*
Pedersen, Ken *recording industry executive*
Quartararo, Phil *recording industry executive*
Rifkin, Arnold *film company executive*
Rosenzweig, Richard Stuart *publishing company executive*
Rush, Herman E. *television executive*
Schneider, Charles I. *newspaper executive*
Sheinberg, Sidney Jay *producer, entertainment company executive*
Spikings, Barry Peter *film company executive, producer*
Zanuck, Richard Darryl *motion picture company executive*

### Brisbane
England, Cheryl *editor-in-chief*

### Burbank
†Black, Carole *broadcast executive*
Brogliatti, Barbara Spencer *television and motion picture executive*
Chiolis, Mark Joseph *television executive*
†DiBonaventure, Lorenzo *film company executive*
Disney, Roy Edward *broadcasting company executive*
Eisner, Michael Dammann *entertainment company executive*
†Gerber, William Norman *motion picture executive*
Hashe, Janis Helene *editor*
Kellner, Jamie *broadcasting executive*
Littlefield, Warren *television executive*
Mestres, Ricardo A., III *motion picture company executive*
Robinson, James G. *film production executive*
Roth, Joe *motion picture company executive*
†Schneider, Peter *film company executive*
†Schumacher, Thomas *film company executive*
†Thyret, Russ *recording industry executive*
Wolper, David Lloyd *motion picture and television executive*

### Burlingame
Mendelson, Lee M. *film company executive, writer, producer, director*

### Camarillo
DePatie, David Hudson *motion picture company executive*
Doebler, Paul Dickerson *publishing management executive*

### Cambria
Blundell, William Edward *journalist, consultant*

### Camino
Miller, Carole Ann Lyons *editor, publisher, marketing specialist*

### Carlsbad
Brown, Jack *magazine editor*

### Carmel
Bohannon-Kaplan, Margaret Anne *publisher, lawyer*
Koeppel, Gary Merle *publisher, art dealer, writer, marketing consultant*
Mollman, John Peter *book publisher, consultant electronic publishing*

### Century City
Harbert, Ted *broadcast executive*

### Chico
Greb, Gordon Barry *writer, educator*

### Chino
Hemenway, Stephen James *record producer, author*

### Chula Vista
Pasqua, Thomas Mario, Jr. *journalism educator*

### Claremont
Miles, Jack (John Russiano) *journalist, educator*

### Cool
Toren, Robert *photojournalist*

### Corona Del Mar
Crump, Spencer *publisher, business executive*
Michaels, Patrick Francis *broadcasting company executive*

### Costa Mesa
Billiter, William Overton, Jr. *journalist*

### Cotati
Carroll, Bonnie *publisher, editor*

### Culver City
Buyse, Emile Jules *film company executive*
Fisher, Lucy J. *motion picture company executive*
Martin, Gary O. *film company executive*
†Pascal, Amy *film company executive*
Sagansky, Jeff *broadcast executive*

### Danville
Reed, John Theodore *publisher, writer*

### Del Mar
Faludi, Susan C. *journalist, scholarly writer*
Kaye, Peter Frederic *television editor*

### El Centro
Lokey, Frank Marion, Jr. *broadcast executive, consultant*

### El Segundo
Conrad, Paul Francis *editorial cartoonist*

### Encino
Holman, Harland Eugene *retired motion picture company executive*
Rawitch, Robert Joe *journalist, educator*

### Flintridge
Fry, Donald Owen *broadcasting company executive*

### Forestville
Benyo, Richard Stephen *magazine editor, writer*

### Foster City
Alvarez, Robert Smyth *editor, publisher*
Ball, John Paul *publishing company executive*
Goldstein, Morris *publishing company executive*

### Frazier Park
Nelson, Harry *journalist, medical writer*

### Fresno
Hart, Russ Allen *telecommunications educator*
Orr, Jim (James D. Orr) *columnist, writer, publicist*
Rehart, Burton Schyler *journalism educator, freelance writer*

### Hayward
Hammerback, John Clark *communications educator*

### Hollywood
†Greene, Stanley H. *broadcasting executive*
†Heftel, Richard *radio station executive*
Sarley, John G. *broadcast executive, writer*
Schaefer, Carl George Lewis *writer, public relations and advertising executive*

### Huntington Beach
Frye, Judith Eleen Minor *editor*

### Inglewood
Rogers, James Curtis *publisher, psychologist, screenwriter*

### Inyokern
Stallknecht-Roberts, Clois Freda *publisher, publicist*

### Irvine
Bartkus, Richard Anthony *magazine publisher*
Hardie, Robert C. *newspaper publishing executive*
†Jones, Chuck *cartoonist, writer, director*
Lesonsky, Rieva *editor-in-chief*
Power, Francis William *newspaper publisher*
Rosse, James N. *newspaper publishing executive*

### La Canada
Paniccia, Patricia Lynn *television news reporter, lawyer*

### La Habra
Maxwell, Donald Stanley *publishing executive*

### La Jolla
Copley, David C. *newspaper publishing company executive*
Copley, Helen Kinney *newspaper publisher*
Harris, T. George *magazine editor*

### La Puente
Thornburg, Lee Ellis *film executive, director*

### Lafayette
Alexander, Kenneth Lewis *editorial cartoonist*

### Laguna Hills
James, Sidney Lorraine *television executive*

### Lake Elsinore
Corral, Jeanie Beleyn *journalist, school board administrator*

### Lodi
Wyrick, Daniel John *science/health textbook editor, science specialist*

### Loma Linda
Bell, Denise Louise *newspaper reporter, photographer, librarian*

### Long Beach
Adler, Jeffrey D. *political consultant, public affairs consultant, crisis management expert*
Crutchfield, James N. *publishing executive*
Lobdell, Robert Charles *retired newspaper executive*
Ruszkiewicz, Carolyn Mae *newspaper editor*
Zappe, John Paul *city editor, educator*

### Los Alamitos
Ayling, Henry Faithful *writer, editor, consultant*

### Los Altos
Burkhart, Dorothy P. *art critic, catalog essayist*
Miller, Ronald Grant *journalist*

### Los Angeles
†Angotti, Mark Everett *broadcast executive*
Archerd, Army (Armand Archerd) *columnist, television commentator*
Bart, Peter Benton *newspaper editor, film producer, novelist*
†Bean, Donna *television station executive*
†Beard, John Jackson, III *journalist*
Belnap, David Foster *journalist*
Bernstein, William *film company executive*
Berry, Stephen Joseph *reporter*
Boyarsky, Benjamin William *journalist*
Boyle, Barbara Dorman *motion picture company executive*
Cafaro, Albert *recording industry executive*
Cardone, Bonnie Jean *photojournalist*
Charen, Mona *syndicated columnist*
Clarke, Peter *communications and health educator*
Coffey, C. Shelby, III *newspaper editor*
Cole, Jay N. *magazine publisher*
Cort, Robert W. *film company executive*
Crippens, David Lee *broadcast executive*
Darling, Juanita Marie *correspondent*
Day, Anthony *newspaper writer*
Del Olmo, Frank *newspaper editor*
Delugach, Albert Lawrence *journalist*
de Passe, Suzanne *record company executive*
Dolgen, Jonathan L. *motion picture company executive*
Dreyfuss, John Alan *journalist*
Dunnahoo, Terry (Mrs. Thomas William Dunnahoo) *editor, author*
Dwyre, William Patrick *journalist, public speaker*
Fein, Irving Ashley *television and motion picture executive*
Field, Ted (Frederick Field) *film and record industry executive*
Fifield, James G. *recording industry executive*
Firstenberg, Jean Picker *film institute executive*
Flanigan, James J(oseph) *journalist*
Foster, Mary Christine *motion picture and television executive*
Friedman, Arthur Meeker *magazine editor, professional motorcycle racer*
Friedman, Robert Lee *film company executive*
Garry, William James *magazine editor*
Garza, Oscar *newspaper editor*
Gates, Susan Inez *magazine publisher*
Gilmore, Mikal George *critic, journalist, author*
Glass, Herbert *music critic, lecturer, editor*
Gordon, Rob *recording industry executive*
Gray, Thomas Stephen *newspaper editor*
Grazer, Brian *film company executive*
Groves, Martha *newspaper writer*
Gudea, Darlene *publishing company executive*
Hall, Jeffrey Stuart *newspaper executive*
Hart, John Lewis (Johnny Hart) *cartoonist*
Hester, John W. *motion picture company executive*
Horowitz, David Charles *consumer commentator, newspaper columnist*
Hudson, Christopher John *publisher*
Iovine, Jimmy *recording industry executive*
Isinger, William R. *newspaper publishing executive*
Jarmon, Lawrence *developmental communications educator*
Jones, Quincy *producer, composer, arranger, conductor, trumpeter*
Katleman, Harris L. *television executive*
Kaye, Jhani *radio station manager, director*
Knight, Christopher Allen *art critic*
Knittle, William Joseph, Jr. *media executive, psychologist, religious leader, management and marketing consultant*
Kraft, Scott Corey *correspondent*
Kristof, Kathy M. *journalist*
Ladd, Alan Walbridge, Jr. *motion picture company executive*
Laird, Jere Don *news reporter*
Laventhol, David Abram *newspaper editor*
Lazarus, Mell *cartoonist*
Lee, Stan (Stanley Martin Lieber) *cartoon publisher, writer*
Leider, Gerald J. *motion picture and television company executive*
Lipstone, Howard Harold *television executive*
Loehwing, Rudi Charles, Jr. *publicist, marketing, advertising, internet, commerce, radio broadcasting executive, journalist, broadcast journalist*
Maltin, Leonard *television commentator, writer*
Mann, Wesley F. *newspaper editor*
Margulies, Lee *newspaper editor*
Marsh, Dave *writer, publisher, editor*
Martinez, Al *journalist, screenwriter*
Masket, Edward Seymour *television executive*
Masters, Lee *broadcast executive*
Matoian, John *broadcasting company executive*
Michel, Donald Charles *editor*
Miller, Norman Charles, Jr. *newspaper editor*
Moonves, Leslie *television company executive*
†Mottek, Frank *broadcaster, journalist*
Murphy, Philip Edward *broadcast executive*
Neufeld, Mace *film company executive*
Nogales, Luis Guerrero *communications company executive*
Obst, Lynda Rosen *film company executive, producer, screenwriter*
O'Reilly, Richard Brooks *journalist*
Parks, Michael Christopher *journalist*
Perenchio, Andrew Jerrold *film and television executive*
Perlmutter, Donna *music and dance critic*
Petersen, Robert E. *publisher*
Phillips, Geneva Ficker *editor*
Plate, Thomas Gordon *newspaper columnist, educator*
Purcell, Patrick B. *motion picture company executive*
Radloff, William Hamilton *editor, writer*
Rehme, Robert G. *film company executive*
Reich, Kenneth Irvin *journalist*
Rense, Paige *editor, publishing company executive*
Rich, Alan *music critic, editor, author*
Rosenberg, Howard Anthony *journalist*
Russell, James Brian *broadcast executive*
Salhany, Lucille S. *broadcast executive*
Saltzman, Joseph *journalist, producer, educator*
Sarnoff, Thomas Warren *television executive*
Saylor, Mark Julian *editor*
Schifsky, Charles Mark *magazine editor*
†Schlosberg, Richard T., III *newspaper publishing executive*
Scott, Kelly *newspaper editor*
Scully, Vincent Edward *sports broadcaster*
Shapazian, Robert Michael *publishing executive*
Shaw, David Lyle *journalist, author*
Shuster, Alvin *journalist, newspaper editor*
Sigband, Norman Bruce *management communication educator*
Sinay, Hershel David *publisher*
Smith, Lane Jeffrey *automotive journalist, technical consultant*
Sperling-Orseck, Irene *publishing company executive*
Stern, Leonard Bernard *television and motion picture production company executive*
†Stern, Mitchell *broadcast executive*
Tartikoff, Brandon *broadcast executive*
Thomas, Robert Joseph *columnist, author*
Trembly, Cristy *television executive*
Unterman, Thomas E. *newspaper publishing company executie, lawyer*
Van Buren, Abigail (Pauline Friedman Phillips) *columnist, author, writer, lecturer*
Verdery, David Norwood *broadcast programming executive*
Ward, Leslie Allyson *journalist, editor*
Wasserman, Steve *editor*
White, Leonard *motion picture company executive*
Willes, Mark Hinckley *media industry executive*
Wilson, Charles Zachary, Jr. *newspaper publisher*
Wolinsky, Leo C. *newspaper editor*
Wright, Donald Franklin *newspaper executive*
†Youpa, Donald G. *broadcast executive*
Zwick, Barry Stanley *newspaper editor, speechwriter*

### Los Gatos
Monday, Jon Ellis *music publishing company executive*

### Malibu
MacLeod, Robert Fredric *editor, publisher*
Price, Frank *motion picture and television company executive*

### Manhattan Beach
Dworetzky, Thomas Alan *publishing executive*

### Marina
Grenfell, Gloria Ross *freelance journalist*

### Menlo Park
Wright, Rosalie Muller *magazine and newspaper editor*

### Mill Valley
Leslie, Jacques Robert, Jr. *journalist*
McNamara, Stephen *newspaper executive*

### Modesto
LaMont, Sanders Hickey *journalist*

### Monterey
Britton, Eve Marchant *newspaper reporter*
Dedini, Eldon Lawrence *cartoonist*
Ketcham, Henry King *cartoonist*
Miller, Susan Heilmann *publishing executive*

### Monterey Park
Stapleton, Jean *journalism educator*

### Mountain View
Dorsch, Jeffrey Peter *journalist*

### Napa
Muedeking, George Herbert *editor*

### Newport Beach
Bryant, Thomas Lee *magazine editor*
Dean, Paul John *magazine editor*
Snow, Alan Albert *publisher*
Van Mols, Brian *publishing executive*

### North Hollywood
Cramer, Douglas Schoolfield *broadcasting executive*
Horowitz, Zachary I. *entertainment company executive*
Hulse, Jerry *journalist*
Katzenberg, Jeffrey *motion picture studio executive*
Koran, Dennis Howard *publisher*
Lindheim, Richard David *television company executive*
Loper, James Leaders *broadcasting executive*
Paul, Charles S. *motion picture and television company executive*
Wasserman, Lew R. *film, recording and publishing company executive*
Yablans, Frank *film company executive, motion picture producer*

### Northridge
Devol, Kenneth Stowe *journalism educator*

### Novato
Pfeiffer, Phyllis Kramer *newspaper company executive*

### Oakland
Burt, Christopher Clinton *publisher*
Conway, Nancy Ann *editor*
Dailey, Garrett Clark *publisher, lawyer*
Haiman, Franklyn Saul *author, communications educator*
McKinney, Judson Thad *broadcast executive*
Torrez, Naomi Elizabeth *editor, librarian*
Wood, Larry (Mary Laird) *journalist, author, university educator, public relations executive, environmental consultant*

### Oceanside
Howard, Robert Staples *newspaper publisher*

### Orinda
Lesher, Margaret *newspaper publisher, songwriter*

### Pacific Grove
Davis, Robert Edward *retired communication educator*

### Pacific Palisades
Bernheimer, Martin *music critic*

### Palm Desert
Hartman, Ashley Powell *publishing executive, journalist, educator*

### Palm Springs
Browning, Norma Lee (Mrs. Russell Joyner Ogg) *journalist*
Jones, Milton Wakefield *publisher*

### Palos Verdes Peninsula
King, Nancy *communications educator*

### Paradise
Fulton, Len *publisher*

### Pasadena
Bergholz, Richard Cady *political writer*
Diehl, Digby Robert *journalist*
Spector, Phil *record company executive*

Wood, Nathaniel Fay *editor, writer, public relations consultant*

**Paso Robles**
Brown, Benjamin Andrew *journalist*

**Richmond**
Doyle, William Thomas *retired newspaper editor*

**Riverside**
Foreman, Thomas Elton *drama critic*
Hays, Howard H. (Tim Hays) *editor, publisher*
Locke, Francis Philbrick *retired editorial writer*
MacQueen, Cher *newscaster, sportscaster*
Mc Laughlin, Leighton Bates, II *journalism educator, former newspaperman*
McQuern, Marcia Alice *newspaper publishing executive*
Opotowsky, Maurice Leon *newspaper editor*
Sokolsky, Robert Lawrence *journalist, entertainment writer*

**Ross**
Godwin, Sara *writer, author*

**Sacramento**
Baltake, Joe *film critic*
Blum, Deborah *reporter*
Bottel, Helen Alfea *columnist, writer*
Endicott, William F. *journalist*
Glackin, William Charles *arts critic, editor*
Knudson, Thomas Jeffery *journalist*
Lundstrom, Marjie *newspaper editor*
McClatchy, James B. *editor, newspaper publisher*
Potts, Erwin Rea *newspaper executive*
Schrag, Peter *editor, writer*
Shaw, Eleanor Jane *newspaper editor*
Swatt, Stephen Benton *communications executive, consultant*
Walsh, Denny Jay *reporter*
Walters, Daniel Raymond *political columnist*
Williams, Arthur Cozad *broadcasting executive*

**Salinas**
Duncan, James Richard *systems administrator*

**San Bernardino**
Burgess, Mary Alice (Mary Alice Wickizer) *publisher*
Fairley Raney, Rebecca *journalist*

**San Carlos**
Barnard, William Calvert *retired news service executive*

**San Clemente**
Dinkel, John George *magazine editor*
Lewis, Jack (Cecil Paul Lewis) *publishing executive, editor*
Singer, Kurt Deutsch *news commentator, author, publisher*

**San Diego**
Bell, Gene *newspaper publishing executive*
Bennett, Ronald Thomas *photojournalist*
Da Rosa, Alison *travel editor*
Fike, Edward Lake *newspaper editor*
Freedman, Jonathan Borwick *journalist, author, lecturer*
†Glickenhaus, Mike *radio station executive*
Hope, Douglas Olerich *newspaper editor*
Jones, Welton H., Jr. *critic*
Kaufman, Julian Mortimer *broadcasting company executive, consultant*
Klein, Herbert George *newspaper editor*
Kopp, Harriet Green *communication specialist*
Krulak, Victor Harold *newspaper executive*
Lee, Marianna *editor*
Mickelson, Sig *broadcasting executive, educator*
Morgan, Neil *author, newspaper editor, lecturer, columnist*
†Myrland, Doug *broadcast executive*
Pfeffer, Rubin Harry *publishing executive*
Pincus, Robert Lawrence *art critic, cultural historian*
†Quinn, Edward J. *broadcasting company executive*
Ristine, Jeffrey Alan *reporter*
Rowe, Peter A. *newspaper columnist*
Scher, Valerie Jean *music critic*
Simms, Maria Kay *publishing and computer services executive*
Steen, Paul Joseph *retired broadcasting executive*
Winner, Karin *newspaper editor*

**San Francisco**
Baker, Kenneth *art critic, writer*
Batlin, Robert Alfred *editor*
Bauer, Michael *newspaper editor*
Bitterman, Mary Gayle Foley *broadcasting executive*
Blakey, Scott Chaloner *journalist, writer*
Bonetti, David *art critic*
Brown, Kathan *publisher of artists' etchings and woodcuts*
Carroll, Jon *newspaper columnist*
Chapin, Dwight Allan *columnist, writer*
Chimsky, Mark Evan *editorial executive*
Close, Sandy *journalist*
†Cohen, Jeffrey Mark *media company executive*
Curley, John Peter *sports editor*
Dickey, Glenn Ernest, Jr. *sports columnist*
Donnally, Patricia Broderick *newspaper editor*
Duscha, Julius Carl *journalist*
Eastwood, Susan *medical scientific editor*
Freeman, Marshall *publishing executive*
Garchik, Leah Lieberman *journalist*
George, Donald Warner *online columnist and editor, freelance writer*
German, William *newspaper editor*
Graham, Robert Arlington *newspaper entertainment editor*
Graysmith, Robert *political cartoonist, author*
Guittar, Lee John *newspaper executive*
Hill, Greg *newspaper bureau chief*
Hochschild, Adam *writer, commentator, journalist*
Hoppe, Arthur Watterson *columnist*
Horne, Grant Nelson *corporate communications specialist*
Hoyem, Andrew Lewison *publisher*
Jenkins, Bruce *sportswriter*
Kees, Beverly *newspaper editor*
Kelly, Kevin *editor*
†Klein, Jeffrey *editor-in-chief*
Klein, Jeremy Stephen *editor*
Klein, Marc S. *newspaper editor and publisher*
Kobayashi, Tom Toru *motion picture company executive*
Lara, Adair *columnist, writer*
Lefevre, Greg *bureau chief*
Marino, Richard J. *publishing executive*
Meyer, Thomas James *editorial cartoonist*
Minton, Torri *journalist*
Nachman, Gerald Weil *columnist, critic, author, lecturer*
Nichols, Alan *newspaper publishing executive*
O'Flaherty, Terrence *journalist*
Osterhaus, William Eric *television executive*
Perlman, David *science editor, journalist*
Reed, Robert Daniel *publisher*
Rice, Jonathan C. *retired educational television executive*
Rosenheim, Daniel Edward *journalist, television news director*
Rubenstein, Steven Paul *newspaper columnist*
Rusher, William Allen *writer, commentator*
Saunders, Debra J. *columnist*
Schwarz, Glenn Vernon *editor*
Shulgasser, Barbara *writer*
Sias, John B. *multi-media company executive, newspaper publisher, publishing executive*
Spander, Art *sportswriter*
Steinberg, Michael *music critic, educator*
Susskind, Teresa Gabriel *publisher*
†Swanson, Jack *broadcast executive*
Tulsky, Fredric Neal *journalist*
Watkins, Rufus Nathaniel *newspaper professional*
Wilner, Paul Andrew *journalist*
Wilson, Matthew Frederick *newspaper editor*
Winchester, Kenneth James *publisher*
Winn, Steven Jay *critic*
Wolaner, Robin Peggy *internet and magazine publisher*
Yamamoto, Michael Toru *journalist*

**San Jose**
Baseman, Sandra Libbie *editor*
Bentel, Dwight *journalism educator emeritus*
Carey, Peter Kevin *reporter*
Ceppos, Jerome Merle *newspaper editor*
Doctor, Kenneth Jay *editor*
Edmonds, Charles Henry *publisher*
Elder, Robert Laurie *newspaper editor*
Frymer, Murry *columnist, theater critic, critic-at-large*
Ingle, Robert D. *newspaper editor, newspaper executive*
Lovell, Glenn Michael *film critic*
Migielicz, Geralyn *photojournalist*
Pulcrano, Dan Michael *newspaper and online services executive*
Ritzheimer, Robert Alan *educational publishing executive*
Sumrall, Harry *journalist*
Trounstine, Philip J. *editor, journalist*

**San Marcos**
Barnes, Howard G. *film company executive, film and video producer*

**San Mateo**
Berkowitz, Steve *publishing company executive*
Golding, George Earl *journalist*
†Martin, Jim *publishing executive*

**San Rafael**
Roffman, Howard *motion picture company executive*
Sansweet, Stephen Jay *journalist, author, marketing executive*

**Santa Ana**
Cheverton, Richard E. *newspaper editor*
Katz, Tonnie *newspaper editor*
†Schueler, John R. *newspaper executive*
†Treshie, R. David *newspaper publishing executive*

**Santa Barbara**
Ackerman, Marshall *publishing company executive*
Brantingham, Barney *journalist, writer*
Cameron, Heather Anne *publishing executive*
Campbell, William Steen *writer, magazine publisher*
Gallagher, James Wes *journalist*
Gibney, Frank Bray *publisher, editor, writer, foundation executive*
Segal, Helene R. *editor*
Tapper, Joan Judith *magazine editor*
Wiemann, John Moritz *communications educator, executive, consultant*

**Santa Clara**
Charles, Mary Louise *newspaper columnist, photographer, editor*

**Santa Monica**
Alpert, Herb *musician, painter, recording artist, theatrical producer, philanthropist*
Ansen, David B. *critic, writer*
Baer, Walter S. *research executive*
Holzman, D. Keith *record company executive, producer, arts consultant*
Jacobson, Sidney *editor*
Kerkorian, Kirk *motion picture company executive, consultant*
Mancuso, Frank G. *entertainment company executive*
Pleskow, Eric Roy *motion picture company executive*
Snedaker, Catherine Raupagh (Kit Snedaker) *editor*

**Santa Rosa**
Locher, Richard Earl *editorial cartoonist*
Person, Evert Bertil *newspaper and radio executive*
Schulz, Charles Monroe *cartoonist*
Swofford, Robert Lee *newspaper editor, journalist*

**Sausalito**
Brand, Stewart *editor, writer*

**Seal Beach**
Caesar, Vance Roy *newspaper executive*

**Sherman Oaks**
Yasnyi, Allan David *media communications executive*

**Sierra Madre**
Dewey, Donald William *magazine publisher, editor, writer*

**Simi Valley**
Killion, Jack Charles *newspaper columnist*

**Sonoma**
Beckmann, Jon Michael *publisher*

**South Pasadena**
Mantell, Suzanne Ruth *editor*

**South San Francisco**
†Tawg, Manyin *editor, periodical*

**Stanford**
Andreopoulos, Spyros George *writer*
Barnes, Grant Alan *book publisher*
Breitrose, Henry S. *communications educator*
Chaffee, Steven Henry *communication educator*
Maharidge, Dale Dimitro *journalist, educator*
Nelson, Lyle Morgan *communications educator*
Risser, James Vaulx, Jr. *journalist, educator*
Roberts, Donald Frank, Jr. *communications educator*

**Stockton**
Whittington, Robert Bruce *retired publishing company executive*

**Studio City**
Tortorici, Peter Frank *television executive*
†Wardlow, Bill *record industry consultant, entertainer*

**Summerland**
Cannon, Louis Simeon *journalist, author*
Hall, Lee Boaz *publishing company consultant, author*

**Tarzana**
Shaw, Carole *editor, publisher*
Shaw-Cohen, Lori Eve *magazine editor*

**Temecula**
Yankee, Marie *educator, publishing executive*

**Thousand Oaks**
Falk, EuGene L. *publishing executive*
Hale, William Bryan, Jr. *newspaper editor*
McCune, David Franklin *publisher*

**Toluca Lake**
†Firestone, Roy *sportscaster*

**Torrance**
Adelsman, (Harriette) Jean *newspaper editor*
Trousdale, Stephen Richard *newspaper editor*

**Union City**
Funston, Gary Stephen *publishing and advertising executive*

**Universal City**
Geffen, David *recording company executive, producer*
†Silver, Casey *broadcast executive*

**Van Nuys**
Sludikoff, Stanley Robert *publisher, writer*

**Ventura**
Greig, William Taber, Jr. *publishing company executive*
Kirman, Charles Gary *photojournalist*

**Walnut Creek**
Satz, Louis K. *publishing executive*

**West Hollywood**
Lowy, Jay Stanton *music industry executive*

**Whittier**
Loughrin, Jay Richardson *mass communications educator, consultant*

**Winnetka**
Robbins, Karen Diane *editor*

**Woodland Hills**
DeWitt, Barbara Jane *journalist*

## COLORADO

**Boulder**
Birkenkamp, Dean Frederick *editor, publishing executive*
Bowers, John Waite *communication educator*
Gaines, James Russell *magazine editor, author*
Quint, Bert *journalist*
Rienner, Lynne Carol *publisher*

**Castle Rock**
Henry, Frances Ann *journalist, educator*

**Colorado Springs**
Dahlman, Simon Jacques *magazine editor, minister*
Nolan, Barry Hance *publishing company executive*
Ogrean, David William *sports executive*
Zapel, Arthur L. *book publishing executive*

**Crawford**
Mosher, Lawrence Forsyth *journalist*

**Denver**
Ballentine, Lee Kenney *writer, publishing company executive*
Barnewall, Gordon Gouverneur *news analyst, marketing educator*
Bates, James Robert *newspaper editor*
Bradley, Jeff(rey) Mark *arts critic*
Brom, Libor *journalist, educator*
Cubbison, Christopher Allen *editor*
Dallas, Sandra *correspondent, writer*
Dance, Francis Esburn Xavier *communication educator*
Dobbs, Gregory Allan *journalist*
Drake, Sylvie (Jurras Drake) *theater critic*
Dubroff, Henry Allen *newspaper editor*
Engdahl, Todd Philip *newspaper editor*
Giffin, Glenn Orlando, II *music critic, writer, newspaper editor*
Hamblin, Kenneth Lorenzo *radio talk show host, columnist*
May, Clifford Daniel *newspaper editor, journalist*
McGowan, Joseph Anthony, Jr. *news executive*
McKibben, Ryan Timothy *newspaper executive*
Movshovitz, Howard Paul *film critic, educator*
Otto, Jean Hammond *journalist*
Price, Kathleen McCormick *book editor, writer*
†Romero, Lynette Denise *news reporter, anchor*
Saltz, Howard Joel *newspaper editor*
Sardella, Edward Joseph *television news anchor*
Scudder, Richard B. *newspaper executive*
Strutton, Larry D. *newspaper executive*
Ulevich, Neal Hirsh *photojournalist*
Zeilig, Nancy Meeks *magazine editor*
†Zimmer, Lawrence William, Jr. *sports announcer*

**Dillon**
Follett, Robert John Richard *publisher*

**Durango**
Ballantine, Morley Cowles (Mrs. Arthur Atwood Ballantine) *newspaper editor*
Hansen, Leonard Joseph *author, journalist, marketing consultant*

**Englewood**
Hall, Kurt *movie theatre executive*
†O'Brian, James *broadcast executive*

**Fort Collins**
Christiansen, Norman Juhl *retired newspaper publisher*
MacLauchlin, Robert Kerwin *communications artist, educator*
Sons, Raymond William *journalist*

**Georgetown**
Stern, Mort(imer) P(hillip) *journalism and communications educator, academic administrator, consultant*

**Glenwood Springs**
Musselman, Norman Burkey *retired editor*

**Golden**
Baron, Robert Charles *publishing executive*

**Granby**
Johnson, William Potter *newspaper publisher*

**Greeley**
Roberts, David Lowell *journalist*

**Lakewood**
Hosokawa, William K. *newspaper columnist, author*

**Littleton**
Udevitz, Norman *publishing executive*

**Longmont**
Davis, Donald Alan *author, news correspondent, lecturer*
Hibler, Jude Ann *photojournalist*
Stewart, William Gene *broadcast executive*

**Mc Coy**
Hastings, Merrill George, Jr. *publisher, marketing consultant*

**Morrison**
Myers, Harry J., Jr. *retired publisher*

**Pueblo**
Rawlings, Robert Hoag *newspaper publisher*

## CONNECTICUT

**Bridgeport**
Henderson, Albert Kossack *publishing company executive, dairy executive, consultant*

**Bristol**
†Adamle, Mike *sports commentator*
†Aldridge, David *sports announcer*
†Beil, Larry *sports announcer*
†Berman, Chris *sports anchor*
†Bernstein, Al *sports commentator*
†Bernstein, Bonnie *reporter*
Bornstein, Steven M. *broadcast executive*
†Cyphers, Steve *reporter*
†Eisen, Rich *reporter*
†Gammons, Peter *columnist*
†Kernan, John *auto racing reporter*
†Kiper, Mel *sports commentator*
†Kremer, Andrea *sports correspondent*
†Malone, Mark *sports reporter*
Melrose, Barry James *sportscaster, former professional hockey team coach*
†Morganti, Al *reporter*
Olbermann, Keith *sportcaster*
†Parsons, Benny *auto racing commentator*
†Patrick, Bill *sports network host*
Patrick, Dan *sportscaster*
†Patrick, Mike *sports commentator*
†Pidto, Bill *sports network anchorman*
†Punch, Jerry *sports reporter*
†Raftery, Bill *basketball analyst*
†Ramsay, John T. *professional basketball team coach*
†Ravech, Karl *sports anchor, reporter*
†Roberts, Jimmy *sports correspondent*
Roberts, Robin *sportcaster*
†Saunders, John *broadcast network host*
†Schwarz, Mark *sports correspondent*
†Scott, Stuart *sports anchor*
Steiner, Charles Harris *sports broadcaster, journalist*
†Thorne, Gary *sports commentator*
Tirico, Mike *sportscaster*
†Varsha, Bob *sports commentator*
†Visser, Lesley *sports correspondent*

**Brookfield**
Reynolds, Jean Edwards *publishing executive*

**Chester**
Cobb, Hubbard Hanford *magazine editor, writer*
Plotnik, Arthur *author, editorial consultant*

PROFESSIONAL INDEX 5117 COMMUNICATIONS MEDIA


**Cos Cob**
Hauptman, Michael *broadcasting company executive*
Senter, William Joseph *publishing company executive*

**Danbury**
Leish, Kenneth William *publishing company executive*
Primm, Earl Russell, III *publishing executive*

**Darien**
Allen, Joseph Henry *retired publishing company executive*
Becker, Ralph Edward *broadcast executive, consultant*
Brooke, Avery Rogers *publisher, writer*

**Essex**
Kenyon, Charles Moir *publishing company executive*

**Fairfield**
Cox, Richard Joseph *former broadcasting executive*
Kaff, Albert Ernest *journalist, author*
Limpitlaw, John Donald *retired publishing executive, clergyman*
Spence, Barbara E. *publishing company executive*

**Greens Farms**
Deford, Frank *sportswriter, television and radio commentator, author*

**Greenwich**
†Buckley, Rick *broadcast executive*
Collins, Richard Lawrence *magazine editor, publisher, author*
Goldmann, Peter D. *editor*
Keogh, James *journalist*
Lurie, Ranan Raymond *political cartoonist, political analyst, artist, lecturer*
†Moffly, John Wesley, IV *magazine publishing executive*
Pfeiffer, Jane Cahill *former broadcasting company executive, consultant*
Rukeyser, Louis Richard *economic commentator*
Schutz, Herbert Dietrich *publishing executive*
Shepard, Thomas Rockwell, Jr. *publishing consultant*
Sweeney, Michael Andrew *newspaper editor*

**Hartford**
Endrst, James Bryan *television critic, columnist*
Englehart, Robert Wayne, Jr. *cartoonist*
Golden, Louis Joseph *former business news editor, newspaper executive*
Grant, Stephen Scott *journalist*
Harden, Jon Bixby *publishing executive*
Hershfield, Lotte Cassel *writer, editor*
Horgan, Denis Edward *journalist*
King, Richard Hood *newspaper executive*
Koupal, Raymond *newspaper publishing executive*
Lumsden, Lynne Ann *publishing company executive*
Noel, Don Obert, Jr. *newspaper columnist*
Pach, Peter Barnard *newspaper columnist and editor*
Renner, Gerald Anthony *journalist*
Roessner, Barbara *journalist*
Zakarian, John J. *journalist*

**Ivoryton**
Bendig, William Charles *editor, artist, publisher*

**Lakeville**
Estabrook, Robert Harley *journalist*

**Litchfield**
Phillips, Kevin Price *columnist, author*

**Lyme**
Bessie, Simon Michael *publisher*

**Madison**
Azarian, Martin Vartan *publishing company executive*
Egbert, Emerson Charles *retired publisher*
Platt, Sherman Phelps, Jr. *publishing consultant*
Purcell, Bradford Moore *publishing company executive*

**Middletown**
Balay, Robert Elmore *editor, reference librarian*
Cumming, Robert Emil *editor*
D'Oench, Russell Grace, Jr. *publishing consultant*

**New Canaan**
Keating, Cornelius Francis *record company executive*

**New Haven**
Leeney, Robert Joseph *newspaper editor*
McClatchy, J. D. *editor, writer, educator*
Rush, William John *newspaper executive*
Ryden, John Graham *publishing executive*

**New London**
MacCluggage, Reid *newspaper editor, publisher*
McGinley, Morgan *newspaper editor*

**Newtown**
Cayne, Bernard Stanley *editor*

**North Haven**
Walker, Fred Elmer *broadcasting executive*

**Norwalk**
Britt, David Van Buren *educational communications executive*
DeCesare, Donald E. *broadcasting executive*
Dolson, Patricia *publishing company executive*
Howatson, Marianne *publisher*
Partch, Kenneth Paul *editor, consultant*

**Old Greenwich**
Dixon, John Morris *magazine editor*
Islan, Gregory deFontaine *cable television executive*

**Old Saybrook**
Jensen, Oliver Ormerod *editor, writer*

**Ridgefield**
Forbes, James Wendell *publishing consultant*
Kelley, Edward Allen *publisher*
Lewis, Gerri *newspaper columnist*

**Riverside**
Isaacson, Gerald Sidney *publishing company executive*

**Salem**
Diamond, Sigmund *editor, educator*

**Sharon**
Gordon, Nicholas *broadcasting executive*

**Shelton**
Forbes, Richard E. *retired publishing company executive*
Wham, William Neil *publisher*

**Sherman**
Valeriani, Richard Gerard *news broadcaster*

**Stamford**
Britt, Glenn Alan *media company executive*
Chiddix, James Alan *cable television engineering executive*
†Collins, Joseph J. *television services company executive*
Conover, Harvey *retired publisher*
†Doolittle, James H. *cable television systems company executive*
Kisseberth, Paul Barto *retired publishing executive*
Paul, Thomas A. *book publisher*
Rowe, William John *newspaper publishing executive*
Sayers, Richard James *newspaper editor*
Veronis, Peter *publisher*
Wilensky, Julius M. *publishing company executive*

**Storrs Mansfield**
Breen, John Joseph *journalism educator*

**Trumbull**
†Brown, Tom *publishing executive*
FitzGerald, James W. (Jay) *magazine publisher*
Seitz, Nicholas Joseph *magazine editor*
Tarde, Gerard *magazine editor*

**Waterbury**
Pape, William James, II *newspaper publisher*

**West Cornwall**
Klaw, Barbara Van Doren *author, editor*

**West Granby**
Conland, Stephen *publishing company executive*

**West Haven**
Ellis, Lynn Webster *management educator, telecommunications consultant*

**Westport**
Bronson, Carole *publishing executive*
Brooks, Andrée Aelion *journalist, educator, author*
Brooks, Babert Vincent *publisher*
Davis, Joel *publisher*
Enos, Randall *cartoonist, illustrator*
Hagelstein, Robert Philip *publisher*
Joseloff, Gordon Frederic *journalist, editor*
Knopf, Alfred, Jr. *retired publisher*
Kramer, Sidney B. *publisher, lawyer, literary agent*
McCormack, Donald Paul *newspaper consultant*
McCormack, Patricia Seger *independent press service editor, journalist*
Meckler, Alan Marshall *publisher, author*
Murphy, Thomas John *publishing executive*
Ross, John Michael *editor, magazine publisher*
Stewart, Martha Kostyra *editor-in-chief, lecturer, author*

**Wilton**
Cutler, Theodore John *cable company executive*

## DELAWARE

**Dover**
Smyth, Joel Douglas *newspaper executive*

**New Castle**
Cansler, Leslie Ervin *retired newspaper editor*

## DISTRICT OF COLUMBIA

**Washington**
Abel, Elie *reporter, broadcaster, educator*
Adams, Lorraine *reporter*
†Adams, Noah *broadcaster*
Adams, Robert Edward *journalist*
Agres, Theodore Joel *editor*
Allen, William L. *editor*
Amolsch, Arthur Lewis *publishing executive*
Andrews, John Frank *editor, author, educator*
Angier, Natalie Marie *science journalist*
Apple, Raymond Walter, Jr. *journalist*
Aquino, John Thomas *publishing executive, lawyer*
Arana-Ward, Marie *editor, writer*
†Archeson, Richard *editor*
Arena, Kelli *news correspondent*
Arnett, Peter *journalist*
Arnold, Gary Howard *film critic*
Arnovitz, Benton Mayer *editor*
Attkisson, Sharyl T. *newscaster, correspondent, writer*
Auerbach, Stuart Charles *journalist*
Aukofer, Frank Alexander *journalist*
Bailey, Charles Waldo, II *journalist, author*
Bancroft, Elizabeth Abercrombie *publisher, analytical chemist*
Bandow, Douglas Leighton *editor, columnist, policy consultant*
Barbash, Fred *journalist, author*
Barber, Ben Bernard Andrew *journalist*
Barnes, Frederic Wood, Jr. *journalist*
Barone, Michael D. *journalist*
Barrett, Laurence Irwin *journalist*
Beach, Walter Eggert *publishing organization executive*
Beale, Betty (Mrs. George K. Graeber) *columnist, writer*
Begleiter, Ralph J. *correspondent*
Beltz, William Albert *publisher*
Bennett, Carolyn L. *journalist, writer*
Bentley, James Luther *journalist*
Bern, Paula Ruth *syndicated columnist*
Bierbauer, Charles *correspondent, news analyst*
Block, Herbert Lawrence (Herblock) *editorial cartoonist*
Blodgett, Todd Alan *publisher, marketing consultant*
Bradlee, Benjamin Crowninshield *executive editor*
Braestrup, Peter *editor*
Branigin, William Joseph *journalist*
Brant, Donna Marie *journalist*
Braverman, Jordan *columnist*
Brazaitis, Thomas Joseph *journalist*
Bredemeier, Kenneth Herbert *journalist*
Brinkley, David McClure *news commentator*
Brock, Gerald Wayne *telecommunications educator*
Broder, David Salzer *reporter*
Brown, John Patrick *newspaper executive, financial consultant*
Brown, Richard Laurence *broadcast executive*
†Browning, Charles *publishing executive*
†Browning, Charles M. *publisher*
Bruno, Harold Robinson, Jr. *journalist*
Buchwald, Art *columnist, writer*
Butterworth, Ritajean Hartung *broadcast executive*
Carlson, Richard Warner *journalist, diplomat, federal agency administrator, broadcast executive*
Carmody, John *newspaper columnist*
†Carr, David Michael *editor, writer*
Chronister, Gregory Michael *newspaper editor*
Clift, Eleanor *magazine correspondent*
Clurman, Michael *newspaper publishing executive*
Cocco, Marie Elizabeth *journalist*
Cohen, Richard Martin *journalist*
Cohn, Victor Edward *journalist*
Coll, Stephen Wilson *journalist*
Compton, Ann Woodruff *news correspondent*
Conroy, Sarah Booth *columnist, novelist, speaker*
Cosgrove, John Patrick *editor*
Cowan, Edward *journalist*
Cowen, Eugene Sherman *broadcasting executive*
Crenshaw, Albert Burford *journalist*
Crewdson, John Mark *journalist, author*
Cromley, Raymond Avolon *syndicated columnist*
Curry, George Edward *journalist*
†Curtiss, Richard Holden *magazine editor*
Cutler, Bernard Joseph *editor-in-chief, writer*
Daniel, Leon *journalist, newspaper columnist, editor*
Dasch, Pat (Anne) *magazine editor*
Dash, Leon DeCosta, Jr. *journalist*
Davis, Evelyn Y. *editor, writer, publisher, investor*
Davis, Garry (S. Gareth Davis) *publishing executive*
Davis, Sid *journalist*
Deane, James Garner *magazine editor, conservationist*
de Borchgrave, Arnaud *editor, writer, lecturer*
Deeb, Mary-Jane *editor, educator*
Denlinger, John Kenneth *journalist*
Devens, Richard Mather *publishing executive, economist*
Dillman, Grant *journalist*
Dirda, Michael *book critic*
Doan, Michael Frederick *editor*
Donaldson, Samuel Andrew *journalist*
Donovan, Robert John *retired journalist*
Dorn, James Andrew *editor*
†Dowd, Maureen *columnist*
Downie, Leonard, Jr. *newspaper editor, author*
Drew, Elizabeth *television commentator, journalist, author*
Dujack, Stephen Raymond *editor*
Dunton, James Raynor *publisher*
Eaton, Sabrina C. E. *journalist*
Edsall, Thomas Byrne *reporter*
Edwards, Bob (Robert Alan Edwards) *radio news anchor*
Elfin, Mel *magazine editor*
Engberg, Eric Jon *news correspondent*
Epstein, Joseph *editor, writer, educator*
Epstein, Kalman Noel *newspaper publishing company executive*
Epstein, Sidney *editor*
Erlanger, Steven Jay *journalist*
Evans, Rowland, Jr. *columnist, commentator*
Faherty, Robert Louis *publishing executive*
Fahey, John M., Jr. *book publishing executive*
Faucheux, Ronald Anthony *publisher, editor*
Feld, Karen Irma *columnist, journalist, broadcaster, public speaker*
Fenwick, James H(enry) *editor*
Ferguson Kennedy, Barbara Brownell *journalist*
Fernandez, Lillian *broadcast executive, lawyer*
†Finley, Skip *broadcast executive*
Foote, Timothy Gilson *editor*
Forgey, Benjamin Franklin *architecture and art critic*
Frank, Richard Sanford *retired magazine editor*
Franzen, Byron T. (John Franzen) *media specialist*
Fritts, Edward O. *broadcast executive*
Furgurson, Ernest Baker, Jr. (Pat Furgurson) *journalist*
Gart, Murray Joseph *journalist*
Geyer, Georgie Anne *syndicated columnist, educator, author, biographer, TV commentator*
Gilliam, Dorothy Butler *columnist*
Gilmour, Craddock Matthew, Jr. (Sandy Gilmour) *television news correspondent*
Glaser, Vera Romans *journalist*
Glass, Andrew James *newspaper editor*
Glassman, James Kenneth *editor, writer, publishing executive*
Gonzales, Richard Steven *broadcast executive*
Gorman, Patricia Jane *editor*
Graham, Donald Edward *publisher*
Graham, Fred Patterson *journalist, lawyer*
Graham, Katharine *newspaper executive*
Gray, Ralph *editor, writer*
Grecich, Daryl George *publishing executive, editor-in-chief*
Greenfield, Meg *journalist*
Greenhouse, Linda Joyce *journalist*
Greenwood, William Warren *journalist*
Gregory, Bettina Louise *journalist*
Griffith, Patricia King *journalist*
Grosvenor, Gilbert Melville *journalist, educator, business executive*
Gutman, Roy William *reporter*
Guzy, Carol *photojournalist*
Gwaltney, Corbin *editor, publishing executive*
Hager, Robert *journalist*
Hales, Linda *newspaper editor*
Hallinan, Joseph Thomas *journalist, correspondent*
Halsey, Ashley, III *newspaper editor*
Halsey, Linda *newspaper editor*
Harden, Blaine Charles *journalist*
Hartman, (Howard) Carl *newspaperman*
Harwood, Richard Lee *journalist, newspaper editor*
Hassan, Aftab Syed *education specialist, author, editor*
Hecht, Marjorie Mazel *editor*
Herbers, Tod Arthur *publisher*
Herman, Andrea Maxine *newspaper editor*
Herman, George Edward *radio and television correspondent*
Hey, Robert Pierpont *editor association bulletin*
Hinden, Stanley Jay *newspaper editor*
Hoagland, Jimmie Lee *newspaper editor*
Hodgson, Frederick Kimmel *radio station executive*
Hume, Brit (Alexander Britton Hume) *journalist*
Hunt, Albert R. *newspaper executive*
Innerst, Preston Eugene *newspaper editor, journalist*
Irvine, Reed John *media critic, corporation executive*
Johnson, Haynes Bonner *author, journalist, television commentator*
Johnson, Robert Louis *media company executive*
Jones, Philip Howard *broadcast journalist*
†Jordan, Anne E. Dollerschell *journalist*
Joyce, Anne Raine *editor, director of publications*
Judd, Jacqueline Dee (Jackie Judd) *journalist, reporter*
Kaiser, Robert Greeley *newspaper editor*
Karmin, Monroe William *editor*
Kaulkin, Donna Brookman *editor, writer*
†Keena, J. Bradley *political commentator*
Kempley, Rita A. *film critic, editor*
Kempster, Norman Roy *journalist*
Kennedy, Davis Lee *newspaper editor, publisher*
Kilborn, Peter Thurston *journalist*
Kilian, Michael David *journalist, columnist, writer*
King, Larry (Larry Zeiger) *broadcaster, radio personality*
King, Llewellyn Willings *publisher, lecturer, journalist*
King, Nina Davis *journalist*
Kiplinger, Knight A. *journalist, publisher*
Kirk, Donald *journalist*
Klass, Philip Julian *technical journalist, electrical engineer*
Knight, Athelia Wilhelmenia *journalist*
Koppel, Ted *broadcast journalist*
Kornheiser, Anthony I. *journalist*
Kotz, Nathan Kallison (Nick Kotz) *news correspondent*
Krebsbach, Karen Anton *editor*
Kristol, William *editor, publisher*
Laden, Susan *publisher, consultant*
Laessig, Walter Bruce *publishing executive*
Lambro, Donald Joseph *columnist*
Landers, James Michael (Jim Landers) *news editor, bureau chief*
Lanouette, William John *writer, public policy analyst*
Lardner, George, Jr. *journalist, author*
Larson, George Charles *magazine editor, writer*
Lawson, Jennifer *broadcast executive*
LeBrecht, Thelma Jane Mossman *reporter*
Leeds, Charles Alan *publishing executive*
Lehrer, James Charles *television journalist*
Lehrman, Margaret McBride *television news executive, producer*
Lepkowski, Wil (Wilbert Charles Lepkowski) *journalist*
Leubsdorf, Carl Philipp *newspaper executive*
Levey, Robert Frank *newspaper columnist*
Lewis, Charles Joseph *journalist*
Lewis, Delano Eugene *broadcast executive*
Lewis, Robert David Gilmore *editor*
Liebert, Larry Steven *journalist*
Lillie, Helen *journalist, novelist*
Lindberg, Tod Marshall *editor, writer*
Loker, Elizabeth St. John *newspaper executive*
Lorsung, Thomas Nicholas *news service editor*
Lubar, Jeffrey Stuart *journalist, trade association executive*
Luxenberg, Steven Marc *newspaper editor*
†Lynker, John Paul *newscaster*
Mack, Raymond Francis *newspaper executive*
Malarkey, Martin Francis, Jr. *cable television executive*
Malone, Julia Louise *news reporter, White House correspondent*
Maraniss, David *reporter*
Martin, John Joseph *journalist*
Maxa, Rudolph Joseph, Jr. *journalist*
McAllister, William Howard, III *newspaper reporter, columnist*
McBee, Susanna Barnes *journalist*
McCartney, James Harold *retired newspaper columnist, educator, journalist*
McCormally, Kevin Jay *editor*
Mc Curdy, Patrick Pierre *editor, consultant*
McDowell, Charles R. *columnist, news analyst, lecturer*
McElveen, Joseph James, Jr. *author, journalist, public broadcasting executive*
Mc Grory, Mary *columnist*
McLellan, Joseph Duncan *critic, journalist*
McLoughlin, Merrill *publishing executive*
Means, Marianne *political columnist*
Mears, Walter Robert *journalist*
Melendy, David Russell *broadcast journalist*
†Melton, Carol A. *publishing executive*
Merry, Robert William *publishing executive*
Meszar, Frank *publishing executive, former army officer*
Meyer, Cord *columnist*
Meyer, Lawrence Robert *journalist*
Meyerson, Adam *magazine editor, foundation executive*
Miklaszewski, James Alan *television news correspondent*
Miller, Loye Wheat, Jr. *journalist, corporate communications specialist*
Miller, Mark Karl *journalist*
Millie, Harold Raymond *editor*
Mitchell, Andrea *journalist*
Morris, Daniel Kearns *journalist*
Moser, Donald Bruce *magazine editor*
Moss, Madison Scott *editor*
Murphy, Frances Louise, II *newspaper publisher*
Murphy, Reg *publishing executive*
Murray, Alan Stewart *publishing executive*
Myers, Elissa Matulis *publisher, association executive*
Naylor, Brian *news correspondent*
†Neale, Tracey D. *news anchor*
Nelson, John Howard (Jack Howard Nelson) *journalist*
Nelson, Lars-Erik *newspaperman*
Newman, Barbara Pollock *journalist, television writer, producer*
†North, David Morgan *editor*
Novak, Robert David Sanders *newspaper columnist, television commentator*
O'Brien, Timothy Andrew *writer, journalist, lawyer*
Orr, J. Scott *newspaper correspondent*
Packard, George Randolph *journalist, educator*
Page, Clarence E. *newspaper columnist*
†Page, Tim *music critic*
Palmer, Stacy Ella *periodical editor*

Pancake, John *newspaper editor*
Parshall, Gerald *journalist*
Paxson, Richard *newspaper editor*
Perkins, Lucian *photographer*
Peter, Frances Marchbank *editor, research agency administrator, writer, strategic planner*
Peters, Charles Given, Jr. *editor*
Phlegar, Benjamin Focht *retired magazine editor*
Pincus, Walter Haskell *editor*
Plante, William Madden *news correspondent*
Podhoretz, John *writer, editor*
Potter, Blair Burns *editor*
Povich, Shirley Lewis *columnist, former sports editor*
Powell, Anne Elizabeth *editor*
Prah, Pamela Marie *journalist*
Prina, L(ouis) Edgar *journalist*
Pruden, James Wesley *newspaper editor, columnist*
Putzel, Michael *journalist, consultant*
Rabel, Ed *news correspondent*
Randall, Gene *news correspondent, anchor*
Rankin, Robert Arthur *journalist*
Richard, Paul *art critic*
Richburg, Keith Bernard *journalist, foreign correspondent*
Richman, Phyllis Chasanow *newspaper critic*
Ridgeway, James Fowler *journalist*
Roberts, Corinne Boggs (Cokie Roberts) *correspondent, news analyst*
Rogers, Warren Joseph, Jr. *journalist*
Rooney, William Richard *magazine editor*
Roos, Joseph Charles, III *publisher, pastor*
Roosevelt, Edith Kermit *journalist*
Rose, Lloyd *theatre critic*
Rosen, Gerald Robert *editor*
Rosenbloom, Morris Victor *author, publisher, public relations executive, government official*
Rosenfeld, Stephen Samuel *newspaper editor*
Rosenthal, Andrew *newspaper editor*
Ross, Robinette Davis *publisher*
Ross, Wendy Clucas *newspaper editor, journalist*
Rowan, Carl Thomas *columnist*
Rowson, Richard Cavanagh *publisher*
Rushnell, Squire Derrick *television executive*
Russert, Timothy John *broadcast journalist, executive*
Safire, William *journalist, author*
Salhani, Claude *photojournalist*
Scheibel, Kenneth Maynard *journalist*
Schiff, Margaret Scott *newspaper publishing executive*
Schram, Martin Jay *journalist*
Schwartz, Amy Elizabeth *editorial writer, columnist*
Scully, Malcolm Griffin *editor, writer*
Seidman, L(ewis) William *television commentator*
Serafin, Barry D. *television news correspondent*
Shales, Thomas William *writer, journalist, television and film critic*
Shanks, Hershel *editor, writer*
Shanks, Judith Weil *editor*
Shannon, Donald Hawkins *retired newspaperman*
Shapiro, Walter Elliot *political columnist*
Sharpe, Rochelle Phyllis *journalist*
Shaw, Bernard *television journalist*
Shaw, Gaylord *newspaper executive*
Sheehan, Neil *reporter, scholarly writer*
Sherman, Charles Edwin *broadcasting executive, educator*
Shogan, Robert *news correspondent*
Shosky, John Edwin *communications consultant, speechwriter*
Shribman, David Marks *editor*
Sidey, Hugh Swanson *correspondent*
Siegel, Robert Charles *broadcast journalist*
Silano, Robert Anthony *editor, defense analyst, educator*
Simpson, Carole Estelle *broadcast journalist*
Singer, Suzanne Fried *editor*
Skene, Neil *publishing executive*
Slenker, Richard Dreyer, Jr. *broadcast executive*
Sloyan, Patrick Joseph *journalist*
Smith, Dean *communications advisor, arbitrator*
Smith, Jack Prescott *journalist*
Smith, Stephen Grant *journalist*
Snow, Robert Anthony *journalist*
Solomon, George M. *newspaper editor*
Sperling, Godfrey, Jr. *journalist*
Spoon, Alan Gary *communications and publishing executive*
Stamberg, Susan Levitt *radio broadcaster*
Staples, Edward Taylor *reporter*
Steele, John Lawrence *journalist*
Stepp, Laura Sessions *journalist*
Stern, Carl Leonard *former news correspondent, federal official*
Stolberg, Sheryl Gay *journalist*
Sullivan, John Fox *publisher*
Sullivan, Steve Joseph *editor, journalist*
Suskind, Ronald Steven *journalist*
Sweet, Lynn D. *journalist*
Szulc, Tad *journalist, commentator*
Talbott, Strobe *journalist*
Terzian, Philip Henry *journalist*
Thomas, Helen A. (Mrs. Douglas B. Cornell) *newspaper bureau executive*
Thomas, Jacqueline Marie *journalist, editor*
Tiede, Tom Robert *journalist*
Tillery, Richard Lee *television executive*
Toedtman, James Smith *newspaper editor, journalist*
Tolchin, Martin *newspaper reporter, author*
Toledano, Ralph de *columnist, author, poet*
Tolson, John J. *editor*
Totenberg, Nina *journalist*
Toth, Robert Charles *polling consultant, journalist*
Trafford, Abigail *editor, writer, columnist*
Tufty, Harold Guilford *editor, publisher*
Turner, Douglas Laird *writer, editor, columnist*
Valenti, Jack Joseph *motion picture executive*
Von Drehle, David James *journalist*
Walker, Ronald C. *magazine publisher*
Wallace, Christopher *broadcast television correspondent*
†Walsh, Kenneth T. *journalist*
Warren, Albert *publishing executive*
†Warren, Clay *communication educator*
Watson, George Henry, Jr. *broadcast executive, journalist*
Weinberger, Caspar Willard *publishing executive, former secretary of defense*
Weiner, Timothy Emlyn *newspaper journalist*
West, Marvin Leon *managing editor*
†Whitcomb, Vanessa Lide *editor*
White, Robert M., II *newspaper executive, editor, columnist*
Will, George Frederick *editor, political columnist, news commentator*
Willis, Clayton *broadcaster, author, corporation executive, former government official, educator, arts consultant, photojournalist, lecturer, author*
†Winch, Terence Patrick *publications director, writer*
Winneker, Craig Anthony *journalist*
Winter, Thomas Swanson *editor, newspaper executive*
Witcover, Jules Joseph *newspaper columnist, author*
Woodruff, Judy Carline *broadcast journalist*
Woodward, Robert Upshur *newspaper reporter, writer*
Yardley, Jonathan *journalist, columnist*
Young, Thomas Wade *journalist*
Zelnick, Carl Robert *Congressional correspondent*
Zimmerman, Richard Gayford *journalist*

## FLORIDA

### Apopka
Brandner, John William *publishing company executive, insurance company executive*

### Aventura
Babson, Irving K. *publishing company executive*

### Boca Grande
Geoghegan, John Joseph *retired publisher*

### Boca Raton
Frank, Stanley Donald *publishing company executive*
Johnson, Martin Allen *publisher*
Levine, Irving Raskin *news commentator, university dean, author, lecturer*
McQueen, Scott Robert *broadcasting company executive*
Rukeyser, M. S., Jr. *television consultant, writer*

### Boynton Beach
Beisel, Daniel Cunningham *former newspaper publisher*
Klein, Bernard *publishing company executive*

### Bradenton
Blancett, Suzanne Smith *editor-in-chief*
Crouthamel, Thomas Grover, Sr. *editor*
Godfrey, Paul *publisher*
McFarland, Richard Macklin *retired journalist*
White, Dale Andrew *journalist*

### Clearwater
Darack, Arthur J. *editor*
VanMeer, Mary Ann *publisher, writer, researcher*

### Coral Gables
Eisner, Peter Norman *journalist, author, news agency executive*

### Daytona Beach
Davidson, Herbert M. (Tippen), Jr. *newspaper publisher*
Gardner, Joseph Lawrence *editor, writer*
†O'Reilly, Don *reporter, writer, photographer*

### Deerfield Beach
Hochberger, Simon *communications educator*

### Delray Beach
Cary, James Donald *journalist*
Peoples, Thomas Edward *publisher, executive, writer*
Salsberg, Arthur Philip *publishing company executive*

### Dover
Pearson, Walter Donald *editor, columnist*

### Dunedin
Geer, James Hamilton *retired broadcasting company executive*

### Fort Lauderdale
Aleff, Andrea Lee (Andy Aleff) *newspaper editor*
Eisner, Will *publishing company executive*
Greenberger, Sheldon Lee *newspaper advertising executive*
Hartz, Deborah Sophia *editor, critic*
Maucker, Earl Robert *newspaper editor, newspaper executive*
Perkel, Robert Simon *photojournalist, educator*
Pettijohn, Fred Phillips *retired newspaper executive, consultant*
Schulte, Frederick James *newpaper editor*
Smith, James Edward *newspaper company executive*
Soeteber, Ellen *journalist, newspaper editor*

### Fort Myers
Barbour, Hugh Revell *book publisher*
Barbour, William Rinehart, Jr. *retired book publisher*
Jacobi, Fredrick Thomas *newspaper publisher*
Rogliano, Aldo Thomas *publishing executive*

### Gainesville
Barber, Charles Edward *newspaper executive, journalist*
Bedell, George Chester *retired publisher, educator, priest*
Davis, Horance Gibbs, Jr. *retired educator, journalist*
Henson, (Betty) Ann *media specialist, educator*
Hollien, Harry Francis *speech and communications scientist, educator*

### Goldenrod
Carmichael, William Jerome *publishing company executive*

### Hialeah
Hernandez, Roland *broadcast executive*

### Hollywood
Anger, Paul *newspaper editor*
Fell, Frederick Victor *publisher*
Korngold, Alvin Leonard *broadcasting company executive*

### Homestead
Crouse, John Oliver, II *journalist, publisher*

### Jacksonville
Brown, Lloyd Harcourt, Jr. *newspaper editor*
Fredrickson, Arthur Allan *retired publishing company executive*
Hartmann, Frederick William *newspaper editor*
Kress, Mary Elizabeth *newspaper editor*
Loomis, Henry *former broadcasting company executive, former government official*
Vincent, Norman Fuller *broadcasting executive*
Walters, John Sherwood *retired newspaperman*

### Juno Beach
Robe, Lucy Barry *editor, educator*

### Jupiter
Anderson, Thomas Jefferson *publisher, rancher, public speaker, syndicated columnist*
Barhyte, Donald James *retired newspaper executive*

### Key West
Heuer, Kenneth John *publishing company executive*

### Lake Mary
Strang, Stephen Edward *magazine editor, publisher*

### Lake Worth
Calder, Iain Wilson *publishing company executive*
†Coz, Steve *editor*
Policy, Joseph J. *publisher, television producer*

### Lakeland
Perez, Louis Michael *newspaper editor*

### Longwood
Argirion, Michael *editor*

### Marco Island
Figge, Frederick Henry, Jr. *retired publishing executive*
Lavin, John Halley *editor, author*
Wheeler, Warren G(age), Jr. *retired publishing executive*

### Melbourne
Jarrell, Patricia Lynn *photojournalist*
Krieger, Robert Edward *publisher*
Spezzano, Vincent Edward *newspaper publisher*

### Melrose
Burt, Alvin Victor, Jr. *journalist*

### Miami
Balmaseda, Liz *columnist*
Barry, Dave *columnist, author*
Black, Creed Carter *newspaper executive*
Chapman, Alvah Herman, Jr. *newspaper executive*
Clifton, Douglas C. *newspaper editor*
Cohen, Alex *retired publisher*
Dickey, Arden *newspaper publishing executive*
Dolen, Christine Arnold *theater critic*
Fichtner, Margaria *journalist*
Fontaine, John C. *newspaper company executive, corporate lawyer*
Foster, Kathryn Warner *newspaper editor*
Goldberg, Bernard R. *news correspondent*
Hampton, John Lewis *newspaper editor*
Harris, Douglas Clay *newspaper executive*
Hoyt, Clark Freeland *journalist, newspaper editor*
Ibarguen, Alberto *newspaper executive*
Lawrence, David, Jr. *newspaper editor, publisher*
Lew, Salvador *radio station executive*
Lewis, John Milton *cable television company executive*
Meyer, Sylvan Hugh *editor, magazine executive, author*
Miller, Gene Edward *newspaper reporter and editor*
Morin, James Corcoran *editorial cartoonist*
Muir, Helen *journalist, author*
Natoli, Joe *newspaper publishing executive*
O'Bryon, Linda Elizabeth *television station executive*
Pope, John Edwin, III *newspaper sports editor*
Randolph, Jennings, Jr. (Jay Randolph) *sportscaster*
Reisinger, Sandra Sue *journalist, lawyer*
†Rodriguez, Ray *broadcast executive*
Russell, James Webster, Jr. *newspaper editor, columnist*
†Sanchez, Rick *newscaster*
Sanchez, Robert Francis *journalist*
Savage, James Francis *editor*
Shroder, Tom *newspaper editor*
Smiley, Logan Henry *journalist, public concern consultant*
Steinback, Robert Lamont *newspaper columnist*
Terilli, Samuel A., Jr. *newspaper publishing executive*
Wax, William Edward *photojournalist*
Wickstrom, Karl Youngert *publishing company executive*
Williamson, William Paul, Jr. *journalist*

### Mount Dora
Goodwin, Harry Eugene *journalist, educator*
Trussell, Charles Tait *columnist*

### Naples
Arthur, William Bolling *retired editor*
Clapp, Roger Howland *retired newspaper executive*
Hedberg, Paul Clifford *broadcasting executive*
Norins, Leslie Carl *publisher*
Taishoff, Lawrence Bruce *publishing company executive*
Wodlinger, Mark Louis *broadcast executive*
Wyant, Corbin A. *newspaper publisher*

### New Smyrna Beach
Makela, Benjamin R. *editor, research director*

### North Palm Beach
Edwards, William James *broadcasting executive*

### Ocala
Stock, Stephen Michael *broadcast journalist*

### Orlando
Clark, James Covington *journalist, historian*
Dunn, William Bruna, III *journalist*
Guest, Larry Samuel *newspaper columnist*
Haile, L. John, Jr. *journalist, newspaper executive*
Healy, Jane Elizabeth *newspaper editor*
Ivey, James Burnett *political cartoonist*
Maupin, Elizabeth Thatcher *theater critic*
Puerner, John *newspaper publishing executive*
Quinn, Jane *journalist*
Reese, Charles Edgar *columnist*

### Osprey
Allen, George Howard *publishing management consultant*

### Oviedo
Linhart, Letty Lemon *editor*

### Palm Beach
Gowdy, Curtis *sportscaster*
†Pryor, Hubert *editor, writer*
Roberts, Margaret Harold *editor, publisher*

### Palm City
Wirsig, Woodrow *magazine editor, trade organization executive, business executive*

### Palmetto
Castleman, Tonya Kay *journalist*

### Penney Farms
Meyer, Marion M. *editorial consultant*

### Pensacola
Bowden, Jesse Earle *newspaper editor, author, cartoonist, journalism educator*

### Pompano Beach
Legler, Bob *publishing company executive*
Roen, Sheldon R. *publisher, psychologist*

### Port Saint Lucie
Sommers, Robert Thomas *editor, publisher, author*

### Saint Augustine
Nolan, Joseph Thomas *journalism educator, communications consultant*

### Saint Petersburg
Barnes, Andrew Earl *newspaper editor*
Belich, John Patrick, Sr. *journalist*
Benbow, Charles Clarence *retired writer, critic*
Corty, Andrew P. *publishing executive*
Foley, Michael Francis *newspaper executive*
Haiman, Robert James *newspaper editor, journalism educator, media consultant*
Hooker, Robert Wright *journalist*
Hull, Anne Victoria *journalist*
Jenkins, Robert Norman *newswriter, editor*
Johnson, Edna Ruth *editor*
Martin, Susan Taylor *newspaper editor*
Naughton, James Martin *journalist*
Patterson, Eugene Corbett *retired editor, publisher*
Pittman, Robert Turner *retired newspaper editor*
Potter, Deborah Ann *news correspondent, educator*
Tash, Paul C. *editor-in-chief*

### Sarasota
Burket, Harriet (Mrs. Francis B. Taussig) *editor*
Estrin, Richard William *newspaper editor*
Grubbs, Elven Judson *retired newspaper publisher*
Hackl, Alphons J. *publisher*
Loomis, Wesley Horace, III *former publishing company executive*
MacDonald, Robert Taylor *newspaper executive*
Marino, Eugene Louis *publishing company executive*
North, Marjorie Mary *columnist*
Proffitt, Waldo, Jr. *newspaper editor*
Silberman, Charles Eliot *magazine editor, author*
Wilson, Kenneth Jay *writer*

### Stuart
Murchake, John *publishing executive*
Slade, Gerald Jack *publishing company executive*

### Summerland Key
Thomas, Vincent Cox *editor*

### Sun City Center
Fleischman, Sol Joseph, Sr. *retired television broadcasting executive*

### Tallahassee
†Brunais, Andrea *newspaper editor*
Dadisman, Joseph Carrol *newspaper executive*
McBride, Donna Jannean *publisher*
Morgan, Lucy W. *journalist*
Semion, A. Kay *editor*

### Tampa
Benjamin, Robert Spiers *foreign correspondent, writer, publicist*
Friedlander, Edward Jay *journalism educator*
Locker, Raymond Duncan *editor*
Nevins, Albert J. *publisher, editor, author*
Roberts, Edwin Albert, Jr. *newspaper editor, journalist*
Ruth, Daniel John *journalist*
Shevy, Allen Earl, Jr. *publishing executive*
Tully, Darrow *newspaper publisher*
White, Nancy G. *journalism educator*

### Venice
Corrigan, William Thomas *retired broadcast news executive*
Jackel, Lawrence *publishing company executive*

### Vero Beach
Michelson, Edward J. *journalist*
Parkyn, John William *editor, writer*
Shadek, Arthur Joseph *radio station executive*

### West Palm Beach
Fairbanks, Richard Monroe *broadcasting company executive*
Lavine, Alan *columnist, writer*
O'Hara, Thomas Patrick *managing editor*
Passy, Charles *arts critic*
Rivers, Marie Bie *broadcasting executive*
Sears, Edward Milner, Jr. *newspaper editor*
Wright, Donald Conway *editorial cartoonist*

### Winter Springs
Diamond, James Thomas, Jr. *publishing executive*

## GEORGIA

### Albany
Stultz, Thomas Joseph *newspaper executive*

**Athens**
Agee, Warren Kendall *journalism educator*
Feldman, Edmund Burke *art critic*
Fink, Conrad Charles *journalism educator, communications consultant*
Holder, Howard Randolph, Sr. *broadcasting company executive*
Koppes, Steven Nelson *public information officer, science writer*

**Atlanta**
Bisher, James Furman *journalist, author*
Brady, Kimberly Ann *editorial director*
Burgess, Chester Francis, III *journalist, television producer*
Campbell, Colin McLeod *journalist*
Chambers, Anne Cox *newspaper executive, former diplomat*
Chong, Bruce Simon *broadcast executive*
Cross, Joyce Annette Oscar *newscaster*
Daly, Chuck (Charles Jerome Daly) *sports commentator, former professional basketball coach*
Dobson, Bridget McColl Hursley *television executive and writer*
Dollar, Steve *music critic*
Dotson, Robert Charles *news correspondent*
Dowden, Thomas Clark *telecommunication executive*
Drennen, Eileen Moira *editor*
Easterly, David Eugene *communications executive*
Eckert, Michael Joseph *cable and broadcast television executive*
Ellis, Elmo Israel *broadcast executive, consultant, columnist*
Evans, Gail Hirschorn *television news executive*
Gilmer, Harry Wesley *publishing executive, educator*
Grogan, Paula Cataldi *newspaper editor*
Hall, Sarah E. *magazine editor, educator*
†Harmon, Mark Thomas *sports anchor*
Harris, Henry Wood *cable television executive*
Henderson, Charles William *health and medical publishing executive*
Holliman, John *news broadcaster*
Holzel, David Benjamin *newspaper editor*
Hulbert, Daniel J. *theater critic, entertainment writer*
†Johnson, Ben *editor, periodical*
Johnson, Wyatt Thomas, Jr. (Tom Johnson) *cable news executive*
Jones, J. Kenley *journalist*
Kennedy, James C. *publishing and media executive*
Kloer, Philip Baldwin *television critic*
Lamkin, William Pierce *editor*
Landess, Mike (Malcolm Lee Landess, III) *television news anchorman*
Merdek, Andrew Austin *publishing/media executive, lawyer*
†Murray, Sonia Yvette *newswriter*
Nelson, Brian James *broadcast journalist*
Phillips, John D. *media company executive*
Pucket, Susan *newspaper editor*
Ringel, Eleanor *film critic*
Rosenfeld, Arnold Solomon *newspaper editor*
Schwartz, William A(llen) *broadcasting and cable executive*
Sibley, Celestine (Mrs. John C. Strong) *columnist, reporter*
Sink, John Davis *leadership consultant, scientist, minister*
Skube, Michael *journalist, critic*
Tarver, Jackson Williams *newspaper executive*
Teepen, Thomas Henry *newspaper editor, journalist*
Tharpe, Frazier Eugene *journalist*
Thomas, Barbara Ann *record company executive*
Tierney, Michael Stewart *newspaper editor, journalist*
Toner, Michael F. *journalist*
Tucker, Cynthia Anne *journalist*
Turner, Ted (Robert Edward Turner) *television executive*
†Waffenschmidt, Lori Ann *television executive producer*
Walden, Philip Michael *recording company executive, publishing company executive*
Walter, John *newspaper editor*
Ward, Janet Lynn *magazine editor, sports wire reporter*
Waters, Lou *anchorman, correspondent*
Whitt, Richard Ernest *reporter*
Yother, Michele *publisher*

**Augusta**
Hill, Michael John *newspaper editor*
Morris, William Shivers, III *newspaper executive*

**Carrollton**
Williams, Mary Eleanor Nicole *writer*

**Decatur**
Knight, Walker Leigh *editor, publisher, clergyman*
Shaw, Jeanne Osborne *editor, poet*

**Douglasville**
Turnipseed, Barnwell Rhett, III *journalist, public relations consultant*

**Macon**
Savage, Randall Ernest *journalist*

**Marietta**
Bemis, Royce Edwin *publishing executive*
Dunwoody, Kenneth Reed *magazine editor*

**Norcross**
Garwood, Robert Ashley, Jr. *network communications analyst*

**Oxford**
Sitton, Claude Fox *newspaper editor*

**Roswell**
Peterson, Donald Robert *magazine editor, vintage automobile consultant*

**Savannah**
Coffey, Thomas Francis, Jr. *editor*
Tobey, Carl Wadsworth *retired publisher*

**Sea Island**
Carter, Don Earl *newspaper editor, publisher*

**Smyrna**
Waters, Cynthia Winfrey *media advertising specialist*

**Stone Mountain**
Speed, Billie Cheney (Mrs. Thomas S. Speed) *retired editor, journalist*

**Sylvania**
Johnson, Daniel McDonald (Dan Johnson) *newspaper editor*

## HAWAII

**Aiea**
Walker, Welmon, Jr. (Rusty Walker) *publisher, consultant*

**Honolulu**
Chaplin, George *newspaper editor*
Flanagan, John Michael *editor, publisher*
Fuller, Lawrence Robert *newspaper publisher*
Jellinek, Roger *editor*
Kamemoto, Garett Hiroshi *reporter*
Kim, Joung-Im *communication educator, consultant*
Krauss, Bob *newspaper columnist, author*
Lewis, Mary Jane *communication educator, writer*
Simonds, John Edward *newspaper editor*
Smyser, Adam Albert *newspaper editor*
Sparks, Robert William *retired publishing executive*
Tehranian, Majid *political economy and communications educator*
Twigg-Smith, Thurston *newspaper publisher*
Wiley, Bonnie Jean *journalism educator*

**Kailua**
Bone, Robert William *writer, photojournalist*

**Kailua Kona**
Wageman, Virginia Farley *editor, writer*

**Kaneohe**
McGlaughlin, Thomas Howard *publisher, retired naval officer*

**Lahaina**
Arnold, Joan Dean *publisher*

## IDAHO

**Boise**
Lemmon, Philip Douglas *publishing company executive*

**Caldwell**
Gipson, Gordon *publishing company executive*

**Idaho Falls**
Harris, Darryl Wayne *publishing executive*

**Moscow**
Anderson, Clifton Einar *writer, communications consultant*

**Sandpoint**
Bowne, Martha Hoke *publishing consultant*

## ILLINOIS

**Arlington Heights**
Baumann, Daniel E. *newspaper executive*
Lampinen, John A. *newspaper editor*
Ray, Douglas *newspaper executive*
Shuman, Nicholas Roman *journalist, educator*

**Barrington**
Bash, Philip Edwin *publishing executive*

**Belleville**
Berkley, Gary Lee *newspaper publisher*

**Bloomington**
Merwin, Davis Underwood *newspaper executive*

**Brookfield**
Hansen, Donald Marty *journalist, accountant*

**Burr Ridge**
Sund, Jeffrey Owen *publishing company executive*

**Carol Stream**
Myra, Harold Lawrence *publisher*
Taylor, Kenneth Nathaniel *publishing executive, author*

**Champaign**
Christians, Clifford Glenn *communications educator*
McCulloh, Judith Marie *editor*
Meyer, August Christopher, Jr. *broadcasting company executive, lawyer*
Vedder, Byron Charles *newspaper executive*
†Wentworth, Richard Leigh *editor*

**Chicago**
Agema, Gerald Walton *broadcasting company executive*
†Ahern, Joseph A. *television station executive*
Allen, Richard Blose *legal editor, lawyer*
Anderson, Jon Stephen *newswriter*
Anderson, Karl Stephen *newspaper executive*
Artner, Alan Gustav *art critic, journalist*
Balz, Douglas Charles *journalist*
†Banks, Lyle *television station executive*
Beck, Joan Wagner *journalist*
Bell, Clark Wayne *business editor, educator*
Bennett, Lerone, Jr. *magazine editor, author*
Boers, Terry John *sportswriter, radio and television personality*
Brickhouse, John B. (Jack Brickhouse) *sports broadcaster*
Brotman, Barbara Louise *columnist, writer*
Brumback, Charles Tiedtke *retired newpaper executive*
Brummel, Mark Joseph *magazine editor*
Callaway, Karen A(lice) *journalist*
Camper, John Jacob *writer, university administrator*
Cappo, Joseph C. *publisher*
Caray, Harry Christopher *sports announcer*
Chapman, Stephen James *columnist*
Christiansen, Richard Dean *newspaper editor*
Ciccone, Richard *newspaper editor*
Coffey, Raymond Richard *newspaper editor, journalist*
Cohodes, Eli Aaron *publisher*
Conklin, Michael L. *newspaper columnist*
Connors, Dorsey *television and radio commentator, newspaper columnist*
Constant, Anita Aurelia *publisher*
Cooper, Ilene Linda *magazine editor, author*
Cross, Robert Clark *journalist*
Curwen, Randall William *journalist, editor*
Darby, Edwin Wheeler *retired newspaper financial columnist*
DeBat, Donald Joseph *media consultant*
Dimond, Robert Edward *publisher*
Dodds, Claudette La Vonn *radio executive and consultant*
Dold, Robert Bruce *journalist*
Donovan, Dianne Francys *journalist*
Ebert, Roger Joseph *film critic*
Essex, Joseph Michael *visual communication planner*
†Evans, Mariwyn *periodical editor*
†Everhart, Bruce *radio station executive*
Feder, Robert *television and radio columnist*
Fetridge, Clark Worthington *publisher*
Field, Marshall *business executive*
Flock, Jeffrey Charles *news bureau chief*
Fuller, Jack William *writer, publishing executive*
Gaines, William Chester *journalist*
Goldberg, Stephanie Benson *editor, magazine writer, lawyer*
Goldsborough, Robert Gerald *publishing executive, author*
Gradowski, Stanley Joseph *retired newspaper publishing company executive*
Graham, Jarlath John *publishing executive*
Grant, Dennis *newspaper publishing executive*
Greene, Robert Bernard, Jr. (Bob Greene) *broadcast television correspondent, columnist, author*
Grenesko, Donald C. *publishing company executive*
Griffin, Jean Latz *newspaper reporter*
Gruber, William Paul *journalist*
Haddix, Carol Ann Mighton *journalist*
Harvey, Paul *news commentator, author, columnist*
Hefner, Christie Ann *publishing and marketing executive*
Hengstler, Gary Ardell *publisher, editor, lawyer*
Herguth, Robert John *columnist*
Hewitt, Brian *journalist*
Higgins, Jack *editorial cartoonist*
Huntley, Robert Stephen *newspaper editor*
Husar, John Paul *newspaper columnist, television panelist*
Iglauer, Bruce *record company executive*
†Jones, Zemira *radio station executive*
Judge, Bernard Martin *law bulletin editor, publisher*
Kaiserlian, Penelope Jane *publishing company executive*
Kazik, John Stanley *newspaper executive*
Kelley, Michael John *newspaper editor*
†Kelly, James *radio station executive*
Kennett, Robert L. *publisher*
Kirshner, Julius *journal editor*
Kisor, Henry Du Bois *newspaper editor, critic, columnist*
Klaviter, Helen Lothrop *magazine editor*
Koester, Robert Gregg *record company executive*
Kotulak, Ronald *newspaper science writer*
†Kramer, Weezie Crawford *broadcast executive*
Krueger, Bonnie Lee *editor, writer*
Kupcinet, Irv *columnist*
Kyle, Robert Campbell, II *publishing executive*
Landers, Ann (Mrs. Esther P. Lederer) *columnist*
Lazarus, George Milton *newspaper columnist*
Lehrman, Nat *magazine editor*
†Lemon, Jim *radio station executive*
Lewis, Sylvia Gail *journalist*
Lincicome, Bernard Wesley *journalist*
Lipinski, Ann Marie *newspaper editor*
Loesch, Katharine Taylor (Mrs. John George Loesch) *communication and theatre educator*
Longworth, Richard Cole *journalist*
Lundberg, George David, II *medical editor, pathologist*
Lyon, Jeffrey *journalist, author*
Lythcott, Marcia A. *newspaper editor*
Mac Nelly, Jeffrey Kenneth *cartoonist*
Madigan, John William *publishing executive*
Mariotti, Jay Anthony *journalist*
Markus, Robert Michael *journalist, retired*
McCarron, John Francis *columnist*
†McCarter, William J., Jr. *broadcasting executive*
McDaniel, Charles-Gene *journalism educator, writer*
McDougal, Alfred Leroy *publishing executive*
†Meade, Robin Michele *news anchor, reporter*
Migala, Lucyna Jozefa *broadcast journalist, arts administrator, radio station executive*
Nault, William Henry *publishing executive*
Neal, Steven George *journalist*
Nebenzahl, Paul *broadcast executive*
Neubauer, Charles Frederick *investigative reporter*
O'Dell, James E. *newspaper publishing executive*
†O'Laughlin, Donna *editor periodical*
Orr, Richard Tuttle *journalist*
Parisi, Joseph (Anthony) *magazine editor, writer-consultant, educator*
Peerman, Dean Gordon *magazine editor*
Peres, Judith May *journalist*
†Philipson, Morris *university press director*
Pierson, Don *sports columnist*
Pilchen, Ira A. *journal editor*
Pitt, Judson Hamilton *publisher, author*
Plotnick, Harvey Barry *publishing executive*
Pope, Kerig Rodgers *magazine executive*
Quaal, Ward Louis *broadcast executive*
Quade, Victoria Catherine *editor, writer*
Rapoport, Ronald Jon *journalist*
Reedy, Jerry Edward *editor, writer*
Rice, Linda Johnson *publishing executive*
Rice, William Edward *newspaper columnist*
Robinson, Martin (Marty) *television and radio broadcaster, media consultant*
Rodenkirk, Robert Francis, Jr. *journalist*
Roeper, Richard *columnist*
Rosenbloom, Steve *sportswriter*
Rynkiewicz, Stephen Michael *journalist*
Sachs, Lloyd Robert *entertainment critic, writer*
Scanlan, Thomas Cleary *publishing executive, editor*
Schultz, Paul Neal *electronic publishing executive*
Shere, Dennis *publishing executive*
Smith, Sam Pritzker *columnist, author*
Sneed, Michael (Michele) *columnist*
Stone, Steven Michael *sports announcer, former baseball player*
Tyner, Howard A. *publishing executive, newspaper editor, journalist*
†Uukas, Ronald *publishing executive*

Varro, Barbara Joan *editor*
Verdi, Robert William *sports columnist*
Voedisch, Lynn Andrea *reporter*
von Rhein, John Richard *music critic, editor*
Wasik, John Francis *editor, writer, publisher*
Wasiolek, Edward *literary critic, language and literature educator*
Weinberg, Lila Shaffer *writer, editor*
Weintraub, Joseph Barton *publishing executive*
Weiss, Hedy *theater critic*
Wells, Joel Freeman *editor, author*
Wier, Patricia Ann *publishing executive, consultant*
Wolfe, Sheila A. *journalist*
Wycliff, Noel Don *journalist, newspaper editor*
Youngman, Owen Ralph *newspaper executive*
Zaslow, Jeffrey Lloyd *syndicated columnist*
Zekman, Pamela Lois (Mrs. Fredric Soll) *reporter*
Zorn, Eric John *newspaper columnist*
Zwecker, William Rene, Jr. (Bill Zwecker) *newspaper columnist, television reporter*

**Crystal Lake**
Keller, William Francis *publishing consultant*

**De Kalb**
Vance Siebrasse, Kathy Ann *newspaper publishing executive*

**Deerfield**
Smith, Carole Dianne *legal editor, writer, product developer*

**Des Plaines**
Carper, James David *magazine editor*
Clapper, Marie Anne *magazine publisher*
Grahn, Barbara Ascher *publisher*
Harrington, Richard J. *newspaper publishing executive*
Henrikson, Lois Elizabeth *photojournalist*
Hlavacek, Roy George *publishing executive, magazine editor*
Kelly, Timothy Michael *magazine publisher*
Tory, John A. *newspaper publishing executive*

**Dixon**
Shaw, Thomas Douglas *newspaper executive*

**Elmhurst**
Ephland, John Russell *magazine editor*
Pruter, Margaret Franson *editor*

**Evanston**
Borcover, Alfred Seymour *journalist*
Downing, Joan Forman *editor*
Galvin, Kathleen Malone *communications educator*
Jacobs, Norman Joseph *publishing company executive*
Jones, Robert Russell *magazine editor*
Kuenster, John Joseph *magazine editor*
Larson, Roy *journalist, publisher*
Lavine, John M. *journalism educator, management educator*
McCleary, Elliott Harold *magazine editor*
Otwell, Ralph Maurice *retired newspaper editor*
Peck, Abraham *editor, writer, educator, magazine consultant*
Schwarzlose, Richard Allen *journalism educator*
Wagner, Durrett *former publisher, picture service executive*
Whitaker, Charles F. *journalism educator*
White, Willmon Lee *magazine editor*
Wills, Garry *journalist, educator*
Ziomek, Jonathan S. *journalist, educator*

**Glen Ellyn**
Beers, V(ictor) Gilbert *publishing executive*
Kirkpatrick, Clayton *former newspaper executive*

**Glenview**
Biedron, Theodore John *newspaper executive*
Mabley, Jack *newspaper columnist, communications consultant*
†Witting, Christian James, Jr. (Chris Witting) *broadcast executive*

**Highland Park**
Johnson, Curtis Lee *publisher, editor, writer*
Pattis, S. William *publisher*
Rutenberg-Rosenberg, Sharon Leslie *retired journalist*

**Kenilworth**
Cook, Stanton R. *media company executive*

**Lake Bluff**
Felknor, Bruce Lester *editorial consultant, writer*

**Lake Forest**
Krouse, Ann Wolk *publishing executive*
Mc Cutcheon, John Tinney, Jr. *journalist*
Rentschler, William Henry *publisher, editor, columnist, writer, corporate executive*
Schulze, Franz, Jr. *art critic, educator*

**Lincolnwood**
Astrin, Marvin H. *retired broadcasting company executive*

**Litchfield**
Jackson, David Alonzo *retired newspaper editor*
Talley, Brian Chandler *broadcasting executive*

**Mount Vernon**
Withers, W. Russell, Jr. *broadcast executive*

**Mundelein**
Terris, William *publishing executive*

**Naperville**
†Raccah, Dominique Marcelle *publisher*
Spiotta, Raymond Herman *editor*

**Normal**
Mc Knight, William Warren, Jr. *publisher*

**Northbrook**
Elleman, Barbara *editor*
Klemens, Thomas Lloyd *editor*
Pesmen, Sandra (Mrs. Harold William Pesmen) *editor*
Snader, Jack Ross *publishing company executive*

Wasserman, Stephen Miles *communications manager*

**Northfield**
Hotze, Charles Wayne *publisher, printer*
Tenuta, Jean Louise *sports reporter, medical technologist*

**Oak Lawn**
Laird, Jean Elouise Rydeski (Mrs. Jack E. Laird) *columnist, adult education educator*

**Oak Park**
Forst, Edmund Charles, Jr. *communications educator, consultant*

**Palatine**
Lindberg, Richard Carl *editor, author, historian*

**Park Ridge**
Johnson, Kenneth Stuart *publisher, printer*
Peterson, Richard Elton *publisher*

**Peoria**
Dancey, Charles Lohman *newspaper executive*
Duncan, Royal Robert *publisher*
McConnell, John Thomas *newspaper executive, publisher*
Slane, Henry Pindell *retired broadcasting executive*

**River Grove**
Litzsinger, Paul Richard *publishing company executive*

**Riverside**
Gwinn, Robert P. *publishing executive*

**Rolling Meadows**
Miles, Frank Charles *retired newspaper executive*

**Schaumburg**
Edmunds, Jane Clara *communications consultant*

**Skokie**
Manos, John *editor-in-chief*
McNally, Andrew, IV *publishing executive*
Steele, Kurt D. *publishing company executive*

**Sutton**
Babb, Michael Paul *engineering magazine editor*

**Urbana**
Andersen, Kenneth Eldon *speech communication educator, consultant*
Helle, Steven James *journalism educator, lawyer*
Littlewood, Thomas Benjamin *retired journalism educator*
Peterson, Theodore Bernard *retired journalism educator*

**Vernon Hills**
Strother, Jay D. *legal editor*

**West Chicago**
Franzen, Janice Marguerite Gosnell *magazine editor*

**Wheaton**
†Hollingsworth, Pierce *publishing executive*
Taylor, Mark Douglas *publishing executive*

**Wheeling**
Kuennen, Thomas Gerard *journalist*

## INDIANA

**Anderson**
Nuwer, Henry Joseph (Hank Nuwer) *journalist, educator*

**Bloomington**
Gough, Pauline Bjerke *magazine editor*
Jacobi, Peter Paul *journalism educator, author*
Lee, Don Yoon *publisher, academic researcher and writer*
Schurz, Scott Clark *journalist, publisher*
Weaver, David Hugh *journalism educator, communications researcher*

**Cicero**
Poindexter, Beverly Kay *media and communications professional*

**Crawfordsville**
Karg, Thelma Aileen *writer, retired educator*

**Evansville**
Jackson, Bill D. *newspaper editor*
Mathews, Walter Garret *columnist*
Ryder, Thomas Michael *newspaper editor*

**Fort Wayne**
Klugman, Stephan Craig *newspaper editor*
Lockwood, Robert Philip *publishing executive*
Pellegrene, Thomas James, Jr. *editor, researcher*
Sandeson, William Seymour *cartoonist*

**Franklin**
Jacobs, Harvey Collins *newspaper editor, writer*

**Gary**
Bosley, John Scott *editor*

**Greensburg**
Small, Ralph Milton *publisher, clergyman*

**Huntingburg**
Matthews, William Edmund *newspaper and travel magazine publisher*

**Indianapolis**
Allan, Marc David *music critic*
Applegate, Malcolm W. *newspaper executive*
Birky, Nathan Dale *publishing company executive*
Caperton, Albert Franklin *newspaper editor*
Cohen, Gabriel Murrel *editor, publisher*
Fleming, Marcella *journalist*
Fortune, William Lemcke *journalist*
Garmel, Marion Bess Simon *journalist*
Griggs, Ruth Marie *retired journalism educator, writer, publications consultant*
McKeand, Patrick Joseph *newspaper publisher, educator*
Phillippi, Wendell Crane *editor*
Pratt, Arthur D. *printing company executive*
Price, (John) Nelson *journalist*
Pulliam, Eugene Smith *newspaper publisher*
Russell, Frank Eli *newspaper publishing executive*
Schilling, Emily Born *editor, association executive*
SerVaas, Beurt Richard *corporate executive*
Staff, Charles Bancroft, Jr. *music and theater critic*
Wheeler, Daniel Scott *management executive, editor*
Wright, David Burton *retired newspaper publishing company executive*

**Lafayette**
Finch, Robert Jonathan *communications engineering consultant*

**Martinsville**
Kendall, Robert Stanton *newspaper editor, journalist*

**Muncie**
Bell, Stephen Scott (Steve Bell) *journalist, educator*
Kumbula, Tendayi Sengerwe *journalism educator*

**Munster**
Moore, Carolyn Lannin *video specialist*

**New Haven**
Chapman, Reid Gillis *former broadcasting company executive*

**Notre Dame**
Langford, James Rouleau *university press administrator*
Rice, (Ethel) Ann *publishing executive, editor*

**Peru**
Stackhouse, John Wesley *publishing executive*

**Richmond**
Talbot, Ardith Ann *editor*

**South Bend**
Schurz, Franklin Dunn, Jr. *media executive*
Wensits, James Emrich *newspaper editor*

## IOWA

**Ames**
Gartner, Michael Gay *editor, television executive*

**Cedar Falls**
Carlson, Jerry Alan *editor*

**Cedar Rapids**
Quarton, William Barlow *broadcasting company executive*

**Davenport**
Brocka, Bruce *editor, educator, software engineer*
Gottlieb, Richard Douglas *media executive*

**Des Moines**
Boyle, Bruce James *publisher*
Burnett, Robert A. *publisher*
†Byal, Nancy Louise *food editor*
DeAngelo, Anthony James *media specialist, architect*
Graham, Diane E. *newspaper editor*
Kaplan, Jerry *magazine publisher*
Kerr, William T. *publishing and broadcasting executive*
Kruidenier, David *newspaper executive*
Lawless, James L. *editor, columnist*
Leach, Dave Francis *editor, musician*
Lemmon, Jean Marie *editor-in-chief*
MacDonald, Kenneth *journalist, former editor*
McLane, Peter *broadcast executive*
Myers, Mary Kathleen *publishing executive*
†Pannier, Cheryl Jane *radio broadcast executive*
Peterson, David Charles *photojournalist*
Van Zante, Shirley M(ae) *magazine editor*
Witke, David Rodney *newspaper editor*

**Dubuque**
Kolz, Beverly Anne *publishing executive*

**Iowa City**
Duck, Steve Weatherill *communications educator*
Hardt, Hanno Richard Eduard *communications educator*
Keller, Eliot Aaron *broadcasting executive*
Zimmer, Paul Jerome *publisher, editor, poet*

**Mason City**
Collison, Jim *business executive*

**Urbandale**
Alumbaugh, JoAnn McCalla *magazine editor*

**West Des Moines**
Dooley, Donald John *publishing executive*
Soth, Lauren Kephart *journalist, economist*

**Zearing**
Britten, William Harry *editor, publisher*

## KANSAS

**Coffeyville**
Seaton, Richard Melvin *newspaper and broadcasting executive*

**Hutchinson**
Baumer, Beverly Belle *journalist*
Buzbee, Richard Edgar *newspaper editor*

**Lawrence**
Dickinson, William Boyd, Jr. *editorial consultant*
Ginn, John Charles *journalism educator, former newspaper publisher*
Levine, Stuart George *editor, English literature educator, author*
Morgan, Scott Ellingwood *publisher, lawyer*
Orel, Harold *literary critic, educator*
Pickett, Calder Marcus *retired journalism educator*
Simons, Dolph Collins, Jr. *newspaper publisher*
Woodward, Frederick Miller *publisher*

**Manhattan**
Seaton, Edward Lee *newspaper editor and publisher*
Watt, Willis Martin (Bill Watt) *academic administrator, communications educator*

**Marion**
Meyer, Bill *newspaper publisher, editor*

**Prairie Village**
Franking, Holly Mae *software publisher*
Jacobs, Vernon Kenneth *publisher*

**Topeka**
Peavler, Nancy Jean *editor*
Powers, Harris Pat *broadcasting executive*
Sipes, Karen Kay *newspaper editor*
Stauffer, Stanley Howard *retired newspaper and broadcasting executive*

**Wichita**
Claassen, Sherida Dill *newspaper executive*
Curtright, Robert Eugene *newspaper critic and columnist*
Getz, Robert Lee *newspaper columnist*
Hatteberg, Larry Merle *photojournalist*

## KENTUCKY

**Carlisle**
Wolf, John Howell *retired publisher*

**Covington**
Trimble, Vance Henry *retired newspaper editor*

**Fort Knox**
Barnes, Larry Glen *journalist, editor, educator*

**Fort Mitchell**
Oppmann, Andrew James *newspaper editor*

**Frankfort**
Cross, Alvin Miller (Al Cross) *political columnist, writer*

**Goshen**
Strode, William Hall, III *photojournalist, publisher*

**Lexington**
Allison, James Claybrooke, II *broadcasting executive*
Glixon, David M(orris) *editor, writer*
Keeling, Larry Dale *journalist*
Kelly, Timothy Michael *newspaper publisher*
Kissling, Fred Ralph, Jr. *publishing executive, insurance agency executive*

**Louisville**
Bullard, Claude Earl *newspaper, commercial printing and radio and television executive*
Ellison, Rebecca Linda Raymond *newspaper editor*
Hawpe, David Vaughn *newspaper editor, journalist*
Haynie, Hugh *editorial cartoonist*
Lewis, Ronald Chapman *record company executive*
Melnykovych, Andrew O. *journalist*
†Nash, Alanna Kay *critic, writer*
Scheu, Lynn McLaughlin *scientific publication editor*
Tinsley, Tuck, III *book publishing executive*
Towles, Donald Blackburn *retired newspaper publishing executive*
Woolsey, Frederick William *retired journalist, music critic*

**Owensboro**
Mong, Robert William, Jr. *publisher*

**Pewee Valley**
Gill, George Norman *newspaper publishing company executive*

**Trappist**
Hart, Patrick Joseph *editor*

## LOUISIANA

**Alexandria**
Smilie, James William, Jr. *editor*
Smith, Joe Dorsey, Jr. *retired newspaper executive*

**Baker**
Roberson, Patt Foster *mass communications educator*

**Baton Rouge**
Giles, William Elmer *journalism educator, former newspaper editor*
Gilmore, Clarence Percy *writer, magazine editor*
Jenkins, Louis (Woody Jenkins) *television executive, state legislator*
Manship, Douglas *broadcast and newspaper executive*
Phillabaum, Leslie Ervin *publisher*
Windhauser, John William *journalism educator*

**Covington**
Stroup, Sheila Tierney *columnist*

**Gonzales**
Young, David Nelson *media and business consultant*

**Gretna**
Calhoun, Milburn *publishing executive, rare book dealer, physician*

**Hammond**
Kemp, John Randolph *journalist, author, academic administrator*

**Lake Charles**
Beam, James C. (Jim Beam) *editor, newspaper*

**Mandeville**
†Bellas, Stephen C. *broadcast meteorologist, reporter*

**Metairie**
Costello, Joseph Mark, III *broadcasting and motion picture executive*
Sandmel, Ben *journalist, musician*

**New Orleans**
Amoss, Walter James, III *editor*
Ball, Millie (Mildred Porteous Ball) *editor, journalist*
Barker, Larry Lee *communications educator*
Curry, Dale Blair *journalist*
Dodds, Richard Crofton *theater critic*
Ferguson, Charles Austin *retired newspaper editor*
†Handelsman, Walt *cartoonist*
Phelps, Ashton, Jr. *newspaper publisher*
Pope, John M. *journalist*
Toussaint, Allen Richard *recording studio executive, composer, pianist*
Turner, Kathleen J. *communication educator, consultant*

**Shreveport**
Beaird, Charles T. *publishing executive*
Lazarus, Allan Matthew *retired newspaper editor*

## MAINE

**Bangor**
Warren, Richard Jordan *newspaper publisher*
Warren, Richard Kearney *newspaper publisher*

**Brunswick**
Lowndes, Janine Marie Herbert *journalist*

**Camden**
Anderson, George Harding *broadcasting company executive*
Thomas, (Charles) Davis *editor*

**Cape Elizabeth**
Emerson, Paul Carlton *retired publishing executive*

**Castine**
Hall, David *sound archivist, writer*

**Chebeague Island**
Traina, Albert Salvatore *publishing executive*

**Damariscotta**
Blake, Bud (Julian Watson) *cartoonist*

**Ellsworth**
Dudman, Richard Beebe *communications company executive, journalist*
Wiggins, James Russell *newspaper editor*

**Lincoln**
Kneeland, Douglas Eugene *retired newspaper editor*

**Portland**
Neavoll, George Franklin *newspaper editor*

**Rockport**
Jackson, David Pingree *publishing executive*

**Sebago Lake**
Murray, Wallace Shordon *publisher, educator*

**Sedgwick**
Schroth, Thomas Nolan *editor*

**Thorndike**
Treleaven, Phillips Albert *retired publishing company executive*

## MARYLAND

**Annapolis**
Casey, Edward Dennis *newspaper editor*
Chambers, Ronald D. *book publishing executive*
Holmes, David Charles *broadcasting company executive*
Miller, John Grider *magazine editor*
Wyman, L. Pilar *indexer*

**Baltimore**
Baker, Barry *broadcast executive*
Beckenstein, Myron *journalist*
Bor, Jonathan Steven *journalist*
Bready, James Hall *reporter*
Brunson, Dorothy Edwards *broadcasting executive*
Carroll, John Sawyer *newspaper editor*
Digges, Dudley Perkins *retired editor*
Dorsey, John Russell *journalist*
Glasgow, Jesse Edward *newspaper editor*
Heldrich, Eleanor Maar *publisher*
Hirsh, Allan Thurman, Jr. *publishing executive*
Jackson, Harold *journalist*
Junck, Mary *newspaper publishing executive*
Marimow, William Kalmon *journalist*
Miller, Donald LeSessne *publishing executive*
†Miller, Jayne Ellen *journalist, educator*
Montgomery, Paula Kay *publisher*
Passano, E. Magruder, Jr. *publishing executive*
Passano, Edward Magruder *printing company executive*
†Pollak, Lisa *columnist*
Rodricks, Daniel John *columnist, television commentator*
Rousuck, J. Wynn *theater critic*
Scott, Frederick Isadore, Jr. *editor, business executive*
Steinbach, Alice *journalist*
Sterne, Joseph Robert Livingston *newspaper editor, educator*
Stevens, Elisabeth Goss (Mrs. Robert Schleussner, Jr.) *writer, journalist*
Tepper, Michael Howard *publishing company executive*
Williams, Harold Anthony *retired newspaper editor*

**Bel Air**
Klett, Shirley Louise *columnist, writer, critic, researcher*

Ginsburg, Scott *radio station executive*
Hill, Draper *editorial cartoonist*
Kelleher, Timothy John *publishing company executive*
Kiska, Timothy Olin *newspaper columnist*
Kramer, Mary Louise *journalist*
Kushma, David William *journalist*
Laughlin, Nancy *newspaper editor*
McGruder, Robert *newspaper publishing executive*
Meriwether, Heath J. *newspaper publisher*
Newman, Jay *broadcast executive*
Parry, Dale D. *newspaper editor*
Pepper, Jonathon L. *newspaper columnist*
Ruffner, Frederick G., Jr. *book publisher*
Smyntek, John Eugene, Jr. *newspaper editor*
Stark, Susan R. *film critic*
Stroud, Joe Hinton *newspaper editor*
Talbert, Bob *newspaper columnist*
Teagan, John Gerard *newspaper executive*
Turnley, David Carl *photojournalist*
Vega, Frank J. *newspaper publishing executive*
Vincent, Charles Eagar, Jr. *sports columnist*
Visci, Joseph Michael *newspaper editor*
Waldmeir, Peter Nielsen *journalist*
White, Joseph B. *reporter*

**East Lansing**
Freedman, Eric *journalist*
Greenberg, Bradley Sander *communications educator*
Johnson, J. David *communication educator*
Ralph, David Clinton *communications educator*

**Farmington Hills**
Ethridge, James Merritt *editor, former publishing company executive, writer*
Harwell, William Earnest (Ernie Harwell) *broadcaster*

**Grand Rapids**
Baker, Richard Lee *book publishing company executive*
Kaczmarczyk, Jeffrey Allen *journalist, classical music critic*
Lloyd, Michael Stuart *newspaper editor*
Ryskamp, Bruce E. *publishing executive*

**Grosse Pointe**
Christian, Edward Kieren *broadcasting station executive*
McWhirter, Glenna Suzanne (Nickie McWhirter) *retired newspaper columnist*
Whittaker, Jeanne Evans *former newspaper columnist*

**Jackson**
Weaver, Franklin Thomas *newspaper executive*

**Kalamazoo**
Cogswell, Kenneth Mark *newspaper executive*
Gilmore, James Stanley, Jr. *broadcast executive*
Jamison, Frank Raymond *communications educator*

**Lansing**
Brown, Nancy Field *editor*
McCoy, Bernard Rogers *television anchor*
Mitzelfeld, Jim *commentor, legal assistant*

**Livonia**
Campbell, Barbara Ann *editor*

**Marquette**
Manning, Robert Hendrick *media consultant*

**Mears**
Binder, Leonard James *magazine editor, retired*

**Mount Pleasant**
Orlik, Peter Blythe *media educator, author, musician*

**Plymouth**
Scott, George Ernest *publisher, writer*

**Pontiac**
†Wilson, Thomas S. *professional basketball team administrator*

**Royal Oak**
Opre, Thomas Edward *magazine editor, film company executive, corporate travel company executive*

**Saginaw**
Chaffee, Paul Charles *newspaper editor*
Puravs, John Andris *journalist*
Thatcher, Rex Howard *newspaper publisher*

**Saint Clair Shores**
Shine, Neal James *journalism educator, former newspaper editor, publisher*

**Southfield**
Makupson, Amyre Porter *television station executive*
†Spinola, John *broadcast executive*

**Sturgis**
Hair, Robert Eugene *editor, writer, historian*

**Suttons Bay**
Skinner, Thomas *broadcasting and film executive*

**Troy**
Donald, Larry Watson *sports journalist*
Moore, Oliver Semon, III *publishing executive, consultant*

**Williamston**
Landis, Elwood Winton *retired newspaper editor*

**Ypsilanti**
Evans, Gary Lee *communications educator and consultant*

## MINNESOTA

**Annandale**
Johnson, Jon E. *magazine editor and publisher*

**Bloomington**
Miller, Alan M. *editor*

**Duluth**
Billig, Thomas Clifford *publishing and marketing executive*
Latto, Lewis M., Jr. *broadcasting company executive*

**Edina**
Ryan, Allan James *publishing executive, editor*

**Excelsior**
Kaufman, Jeffrey Allen *publisher*

**Fergus Falls**
Rinden, David Lee *editor*

**Maple Lake**
Andrus, Theresa Kester *photojournalist, communications specialist*

**Minneapolis**
Anderson, Albert Esten *publisher*
Bisping, Bruce Henry *photojournalist*
Boyd, Belvel James *newspaper editor*
Buoen, Roger *newspaper editor*
Carter, Roy Ernest, Jr. *journalist, educator*
Cope, Lewis *journalist*
Cowles, John, Jr. *publisher, women's sports promoter*
Crosby, Jacqueline Garton *newspaper editor, journalist*
Degnan, Joseph *magazine editor*
Flanagan, Barbara *journalist*
Franklin, Robert Brewer *journalist*
Huntzicker, William Edward *journalism educator*
Ison, Christopher John *investigative reporter*
Johnson, Cheryl *newspaper columnist*
Jones, Will(iam) (Arnold) *writer, former newspaper columnist*
Kinderwater, Joseph C. (Jack Kinderwater) *publishing company executive*
Kramer, Joel Roy *journalist, newspaper executive*
Laing, Karel Ann *magazine publishing executive*
Lerner, Harry Jonas *publishing company executive*
Marshall, Sherrie *newspaper editor*
McEnroe, Paul *reporter*
Meador, Ron *newspaper editor, writer*
Mohr, L. Thomas *newspaper executive*
Moraczewski, Robert Leo *publisher*
Murphy, Joseph Edward, Jr. *broadcast executive*
Opperman, Dwight Darwin *publishing company executive*
Salyer, Stephen Lee *broadcast executive*
Scallen, Thomas Kaine *broadcasting executive*
Seaman, William Casper *retired news photographer*
Slovut, Gordon *reporter*
Strickler, Jeff *newspaper movie critic*
Swartz, Donald Everett *television executive*
Vaughan, Peter Hugh *theater critic*
Watson, Catherine Elaine *journalist*
White, Robert James *newspaper columnist*
Wright, Frank Gardner *newspaper editor*
Youngblood, Richard Neil *columnist*
Ziebarth, E. William *news analyst, educator*

**Minnetonka**
Ehlert, John Ambrose *publisher*

**Northfield**
Hvistendahl, Joyce Kilmer *journalism and communications educator*

**Saint Joseph**
Rowland, Howard Ray *mass communications educator*

**Saint Paul**
Clark, Ronald Dean *newspaper editor*
Fryxell, David Allen *publishing executive, newspaper editor*
Henry, John Thomas *retired newspaper executive*
Hubbard, Stanley Stub *broadcast executive*
Keillor, Garrison Edward *writer, radio host, storyteller*
Kling, William Hugh *broadcasting executive*
Lund, Bert Oscar, Jr. *publisher*
Lundy, Walker *newspaper editor*
Ridder, Bernard Herman, Jr. *newspaper publisher*
†Rockstroh, Robert John *broadcast television executive*
Wehrwein, Austin Carl *newspaper reporter, editor, writer*

**West Saint Paul**
Bremer, Victor John *broadcasting executive*
Cento, William Francis *retired newspaper editor*

## MISSISSIPPI

**Biloxi**
Weeks, Roland, Jr. *newspaper publisher*

**Brandon**
Buckley, Frank Wilson *newspaper executive*

**Gulfport**
Hash, John Frank *broadcasting executive*

**Jackson**
Downing, Margaret Mary *newspaper editor*

**Yazoo City**
Brown, Marion Lipscomb, Jr. *publisher, retired chemical company executive*

## MISSOURI

**Clayton**
Marcus, Larry David *broadcasting executive*
Richmond, Richard Thomas *journalist*

**Columbia**
Brooks, Brian Shedd *journalist, educator*
Loory, Stuart Hugh *journalist*
Sanders, Keith Page *journalism educator*
Taft, William Howard *journalism educator*

**Harrisonville**
James, William Edward *publishing executive*

**Kansas City**
Anderson, James Keith *retired magazine editor*
Andrews, Kathleen W. *book publishing executive*
Batiuk, Thomas Martin *cartoonist*
Brisbane, Arthur Seward *newspaper editor*
Busby, Marjorie Jean (Marjean Busby) *journalist*
Cantrell, (Thomas) Scott *newspaper music critic*
Davis, James Robert *cartoonist*
Diuguid, Lewis Walter *editor, columnist*
Fox, Thomas Charles *editor, publisher, writer*
Gusewelle, Charles Wesley *journalist*
Ingram, Robert Palmer *magazine publisher*
Kipp, Robert Almy *greeting card company executive*
Larson, Gary *cartoonist*
Martin, Donna Lee *publishing company executive*
Mc Meel, John Paul *newspaper syndicate and publishing executive*
McSweeney, William Lincoln, Jr. *retired publishing executive*
Oliphant, Patrick *cartoonist*
Palmer, Cruise *newspaper editor*
Petosa, Jason Joseph *publisher*
Stephens, Joe Alan *investigative reporter*
Stites, C. Thomas *journalist, publisher*
Tammeus, William David *journalist, columnist*
Thornton, Thomas Noel *publishing executive*
Townsend, Harold Guyon, Jr. *publishing company executive*
Wilson, Tom *cartoonist, greeting card company executive*

**Saint Louis**
Barnes, Harper Henderson *movie critic, editor*
Bauman, George Duncan *former newspaper publisher*
Bohle, Bruce William *editor*
Buck, Jack *sportscaster, broadcast executive*
Dames, Joan Foster (Mrs. Urban L. Dames) *magazine editor, columnist*
Dill, John Francis *retired publishing company executive*
Domjan, Laszlo Karoly *newspaper editor*
Elkins, Ken Joe *broadcasting executive*
Engelhardt, Thomas Alexander *editorial cartoonist*
Ferguson, Gary Warren *editorial consultant*
Gauen, Patrick Emil *newspaper correspondent*
Godsey, C. Wayne *broadcasting executive*
Goldberg, Norman Albert *music publisher, writer*
Graham, Lester Lynn *radio executive*
Higgins, Edward Aloysius *retired newspaper editor*
Kanne, Marvin George *newspaper publishing executive*
Killenberg, George Andrew *newspaper consultant, former newspaper editor*
Korando, Donna Kay *journalist*
Lipman, David *multimedia consultant for publishing company*
†Middleton, Leslie Lyles *journalist*
Norman, Charles Henry *broadcasting executive*
Olshwanger, Ron *photojournalist*
Olson, Clarence Elmer, Jr. *newspaper editor*
Penniman, Nicholas Griffith, IV *newspaper publisher*
Pollack, Joe *retired newspaper critic and columnist, writer*
Pulitzer, Michael Edgar *publishing executive*
Waters, Richard *retired publishing company executive*
Wiley, Gregory Robert *publisher*
Willnow, Ronald Dale *editor*

**Springfield**
Booze, Joyce Wells *retired publishing executive*
Champion, Norma Jean *communications educator, state legislator*
Dearmore, Thomas Lee *retired journalist*
Glazier, Robert Carl *publishing executive*
Sylvester, Ronald Charles *newspaper writer*

**University City**
Benson, Joseph Fred *journalist, legal historian*

## MONTANA

**Bigfork**
Blumberg, Nathan(iel) Bernard *journalist, educator, writer and publisher*

**Bozeman**
O'Donnell, Victoria J. *communication educator*

**Helena**
Malcolm, Andrew Hogarth *journalist, writer*

**Kalispell**
Ruder, Melvin Harvey *retired newspaper editor*

**Livingston**
Feldstein, Albert B. *retired editor, artist, writer*

**Whitefish**
James, Marion Ray *magazine founder, editor*

## NEBRASKA

**Kearney**
Wice, Paul Clinton *news director, educator*

**Lincoln**
Dyer, William Earl, Jr. *retired newspaper editor*
Ebel, A. James *broadcasting consultant*
†Hillegass, Clifton Keith *publisher*
Raz, Hilda *editor-in-chief periodical, educator*

**Omaha**
Andersen, Harold Wayne *contributing editor, newspaper executive*
Batchelder, Anne Stuart *former publisher, political party official*
Davis, Chip *record producer, arranger*
Donaldson, William L. *newspaper publishing company executive*
Howe, G(ary) Woodson (Woody Howe) *newspaper editor, newspaper executive*

**York**
Givens, Randal Jack *communications educator*

## NEVADA

**Boulder City**
Kidd, Hillery Gene *educational publisher*

**Henderson**
Martin, Donald Walter *author, publisher*

**Las Vegas**
Baker, Chuck *journalist, author*
Cling, Carol Susan *movie critic, writer*
Jaffe, Herb *retired newspaper editor, columnist*
Rossin, Herbert Yale *television producer*

**Reno**
Clark-Jackson, Susan *publishing executive*
Miller, Newton Edd, Jr. *communications educator*
Pagliarini, James *broadcast executive*

## NEW HAMPSHIRE

**Alstead**
Fiske, Edward B. *editor, journalist, educational consultant*

**Bristol**
Peirce, Neal R. *journalist*

**Concord**
Brown, Tom Christian *newspaper publisher*

**Dover**
Wentworth, William Edgar *journalist*

**Dublin**
Hale, Judson Drake, Sr. *editor*

**Freedom**
Bickford, Gail Holmgren *publishing executive*

**Hanover**
Mc Farland, Thomas L. *book publishing executive*
Olcott, William Alfred *magazine editor*

**Hollis**
Lerner, Arnold Stanley *radio station executive*

**Jackson**
Johnson, Ned (Edward Christopher Johnson) *publishing company executive*

**Jaffrey**
Schulte, Henry Frank *journalism educator*

**Lyme**
Dwight, Donald Rathbun *newspaper publisher, corporate communications executive*

**Manchester**
Loeb, Nackey Scripps *publisher*
McQuaid, Joseph Woodbury *newspaper executive*
Perkins, Charles, III *newspaper editor*

**Merrimack**
Kotelly, George Vincent *editor, writer*

**Portsmouth**
Hopkins, Jeannette Ethel *book publisher, editor*
Silverman, George Alan *broadcasting executive*
Thornhill, Arthur Horace, Jr. *retired book publisher*

## NEW JERSEY

**Barnegat Light**
Sparano, Vincent Thomas *editor*

**Bridgewater**
Freeman, Henry McCall *newspaper publisher*
Healey, Lynne Kover *editor, writer, broadcaster, educator*

**Califon**
Hannigan, Frank *sportswriter, television writer and commentator, golf course design consultant*

**Cherry Hill**
Callaway, Ben Anderson *journalist*
Rudman, Solomon Kal *magazine publisher*

**Cranbury**
Reichek, Morton Arthur *retired magazine editor, writer*
Yoseloff, Julien David *publishing company executive*
Yoseloff, Thomas *publisher*

**Cranford**
Bodian, Nat G. *publishing, marketing consultant, author, lecturer, lexicographer*

**Deal**
Becker, Richard Stanley *music publisher*

**Dover**
†Kassell, Paula Sally *editor, publisher*

**East Brunswick**
Kabela, Frank, Jr. *broadcast executive*

**Edgewater**
Lape, Robert Cable *broadcast journalist*

**Edison**
Comstock, Robert Ray *journalism educator, newspaper editor*
Hunter, Michael *publishing executive*

**Englewood**
Friedman, Emanuel *publishing company executive*

**Englewood Cliffs**
Guiher, James Morford, Jr. *publisher*
Haltiwanger, Robert Sidney, Jr. *book publishing executive*

Saible, Stephanie *magazine editor*
Vane, Dena *magazine editor-in-chief*

**Fair Lawn**
Mazel, Joseph Lucas *publications consultant*

**Fanwood**
Whitaker, Joel *publisher*

**Florham Park**
Mott, Vincent Valmon *publisher, author*

**Fords**
Blond, Stuart Richard *newsletter editor*

**Fort Lee**
Fischel, Daniel Norman *publishing consultant*
Gharib, Susie *television newscaster*
McCullough, Kevin *news anchor, correspondent*

**Guttenberg**
Pesin, Ella Michele *journalist, public relations professional*

**Hackensack**
Ahearn, James *newspaper columnist*
Blomquist, David Wels *journalist*
Margulies, James Howard *editorial cartoonist*
Pennington, William Mark *sportswriter*
Waixel, Vivian *journalist*

**Hackettstown**
DeAngelis, Margaret Scalza *publishing executive*

**Haddonfield**
Cheney, Daniel Lavern *retired magazine publisher*

**Hightstown**
Frank, Betty Pope *editor*

**Hoboken**
Regazzi, John James, III *publishing executive*

**Holmdel**
Wyndrum, Ralph W., Jr. *communications company executive*

**Iselin**
Krebs, Gary Michael *editor, author*

**Jackson**
Hunter, Lynn *publications company executive*

**Jersey City**
Callum, Myles *magazine editor, writer*
Ingrassia, Paul Joseph *publishing executive*
Katz, Colleen *editor in chief*
Levine, Richard James *publishing executive*
Wagner, Douglas Walker Ellyson *journal editor*
Williams, Alan Davison *publishing company executive*

**Lebanon**
Goulazian, Peter Robert *retired broadcasting executive*
Suchodolski, Ronald Eugene *publishing company executive*

**Linwood**
McCormick, Robert Matthew, III *newspaper executive*

**Little Falls**
Glasser, Lynn Schreiber *publisher*
Glasser, Stephen Andrew *publishing executive, lawyer*

**Long Branch**
Lagowski, Barbara Jean *writer, book editor*

**Mahwah**
Bram, Leon Leonard *publishing company executive*
Eiger, Richard William *publisher*

**Manahawkin**
Scully, Paula Constance *journalist*

**Maplewood**
Dennis, Anita Anna *journalist*

**Margate City**
Kennedy, Berenice Connor (Mrs. Jefferson Kennedy, Jr.) *magazine executive, writer, consultant*

**Marlton**
Forbes, Gordon Maxwell *sports journalist, commentator*

**Medford**
Hogan, Thomas Harlan *publisher*

**Metuchen**
Daub, Albert Walter *publishing executive*

**Midland Park**
Koster, John Peter, Jr. *journalist, author*

**Millville**
De Bevoise, Lee Raymond *editor, nurse, writer, photographer*

**Montclair**
Brownrigg, Walter Grant *cartoonist, corporate executive*
Gogick, Kathleen Christine *magazine editor, publisher*
Jacoby, Tamar *journalist, author*
Sabin, William Albert *editor*

**Montvale**
Friis, Erik Johan *editor, publisher*
Sifton, David Whittier *magazine editor*

**Montville**
Teubner, Ferdinand Cary, Jr. *retired publishing company executive*

**Morris Plains**
O'Neill, Robert Edward *business journal editor*

**Morristown**
Ahl, David Howard *writer, editor*

**Mount Holly**
Brown, Hershel M. *retired newspaper publisher*

**Mount Laurel**
†Sabol, Steve *film company executive*

**Mountain Lakes**
LaForce, William Leonard, Jr. *photojournalist*

**Mountainside**
Horner, Shirley Jaye *columnist, writing and publishing consultant*

**Neptune**
Clurfeld, Andrea *editor, food critic*
Ollwerther, William Raymond *newspaper editor*
Plangere, Jules L., III *newspaper company executive*

**New Brunswick**
Horowitz, Irving Louis *publisher, educator*
Reeling, Patricia Glueck *library educator, educational consultant*
Wilson, Donald Malcolm *publishing executive*

**New Providence**
Barnes, Sandra Henley *publishing company executive*
Fisher, Darryl *information services company executive*
†Goff, Neal *publishing company executive*
Hollister, Dean *publishing company executive*
Meyer, Andrew W. *publishing executive*
Mysel, Randy Howard *publishing company executive*
Roycroft, Edward J. *publishing company executive*
Sullivan, Barbara *publishing company executive*
Walker, Stanley P. *publishing executive*
Williams, Alun Gwyn *publishing company executive*

**Newark**
Aregood, Richard Lloyd *editor*
Bartner, Martin *newspaper executive*
Dauth, Frances Kutcher *journalist, newspaper editor*
Everett, Richard G. *newspaper editor*
Harrison, Charles R. *retired newspaper editor*
Hooper-Perkins, Marlene *technical editor, educator*
Kanzler, George *journalist, critic*
Lenehan, Art *newspaper editor*
Martinez, Arturo *newspaper editor*
Newhouse, Donald E. *newspaper publishing executive*
Newhouse, Mark William *publishing executive*
Shoup, Michael C. *newspaper reporter, editor*
Steinbaum, Robert S. *publisher, lawyer*
Willse, James Patrick *newspaper editor*

**Newton**
Carstens, Harold Henry *publisher*

**Northvale**
Aronson, Jason *publisher*
Kurzweil, Arthur *publisher, writer, educator*

**Oldwick**
Snyder, Arthur *publishing company executive*

**Paramus**
Brissie, Eugene Field, Jr. *publisher*

**Parsippany**
Geyer, Thomas Powick *newspaper publisher*

**Paterson**
Deffaa, Chip *jazz critic*

**Pennington**
Harris, Frederick George *publishing company executive*

**Piscataway**
Fogiel, Max *publishing executive*

**Pleasantville**
Bennett, Eileen Patricia *copy editor, reporter*
Briant, Maryjane *newspaper editor*
Pollock, Michael Jeffrey *periodical editor*

**Pompton Plains**
Costello, Gerald Michael *editor*

**Princeton**
Buttenheim, Edgar Marion *publishing executive*
†Cushmore, Carole Lee *publisher*
Doherty, Leonard Edward *financial publishing company executive*
Grossman, Allen Neil *publishing executive*
Lippincott, Walter Heulings, Jr. *publishing executive*
O'Donnell, Laurence Gerard *editorial consultant*
Weiss, Renée Karol *editor, writer, musician*

**Ramsey**
Underwood, Steven Clark *publishing executive*

**Ridgewood**
Anderson, Thomas Kemp, Jr. *editor*
Kiernan, Richard Francis *publisher*

**Rumson**
Macdonald, Donald Arthur *publishing executive*
Robinson, William Wheeler *editor*

**Saddle River**
Buckler, Beatrice *editor*
Dowden, Carroll Vincent *publishing company executive*
Gorham, David L. *newspaper executive*

**Secaucus**
Bailey, Steven Frederick *publishing executive*
Bender, Bruce F. *book publishing executive*
Black, Hillel Moses *publisher*
†Fredericks, Alan *editor-in-chief*
Highet, Mac *publishing company executive*
Nathan, Martin *publishing company executive*
Povich, Lynn *journalist, magazine editor*
Thomas, Ian Leslie Maurice *publisher*
Verdi, David Joseph *broadcast news executive*

**Short Hills**
Soderlind, Sterling Eugene *newspaper industry consultant*
Winter, Ruth Grosman (Mrs. Arthur Winter) *journalist*

**Somerville**
Yuster-Freeman, Leigh Carol *publishing company executive*

**Sparta**
Spence, Robert Leroy *publishing executive*

**Stockholm**
dePaolo, Ronald Francis *editor, publisher*

**Summit**
Scudder, Edward Wallace, Jr. *newspaper and broadcasting executive*

**Tenafly**
Vinocur, M. Richard *publisher*

**Tinton Falls**
Canfield, William Newton *retired editorial cartoonist*

**Toms River**
Wagner, Edward Kurt *publishing company executive*

**Trenton**
Christopherson, Elizabeth Good *broadcast executive*
Joseph, Edith Hoffman *retired editor*
†Manahan, Kent *newscaster*

**Tuckerton**
Egan, Roger Edward *publishing executive*

**Upper Saddle River**
Butterfield, Bruce Scott *publishing company executive*
Dojny, Richard Francis *publishing company executive*

**Verona**
Meyer, Helen (Mrs. Abraham J. Meyer) *retired editorial consultant*

**Vineland**
DeVivo, Sal J. *newspaper executive*

**Westwood**
Noyes, Robert Edwin *publisher, writer*

## NEW MEXICO

**Albuquerque**
Danziger, Jerry *broadcasting executive*
Davidson, Juli *creativity consultant*
Friedenberg, Walter Drew *journalist*
Goldston, Barbara M. Harral *editor*
Guthrie, Patricia Sue *newspaper reporter, free-lance writer*
Hadas, Elizabeth Chamberlayne *publisher*
Johnson, Robert Hersel *journalist*
Lang, Thompson Hughes *publishing company executive*
Mc Million, John Macon *retired newspaper publisher*
Wilde, David *publisher, writer, biographer*

**Glenwood**
Tackman, Arthur Lester *newspaper publisher, management consultant*

**Glorieta**
Mc Coy, Robert Baker *publisher*

**Las Cruces**
Merrick, Beverly Childers *journalism, communications educator*

**Los Alamos**
Mendius, Patricia Dodd Winter *editor, educator, writer*

**Santa Fe**
Anderson, Denice Anna *editor*
Atkinson, John Christopher *magazine editor, critic, writer*
Calloway, Larry *columnist*
Dirks, Lee Edward *newspaper executive*
Forsdale, (Chalmers) Louis *education and communication educator*
Lichtenberg, Margaret Klee *publishing company executive*
Mc Kinney, Robert Moody *newspaper editor and publisher*
Stieber, Tamar *journalist*

**Taos**
Bacon, Wallace Alger *speech communications educator, author*

## NEW YORK

**Albany**
Morga Bellizzi, Celeste *editor*
Ortloff, George Christian, Sr. (Chris Ortloff) *journalist, state legislator*
Rosenfeld, Harry Morris *editor*
Smith, Rex William *journalist*

**Albertson**
Ferber, Samuel *publishing executive*

**Annandale On Hudson**
Chace, James Clarke *editor*

**Armonk**
Sharpe, Myron Emanuel *publisher, editor, writer*

**Baldwin Place**
Kurian, George Thomas *publisher*

**Ballston Lake**
Silverman, Gerald Bernard *journalist*

**Bayport**
Poli, Kenneth Joseph *editor*

**Bedford**
Bowman, James Kinsey *publishing company executive, rare book specialist*

**Bellport**
Hughes, Elinor Lambert *drama and film critic*

**Brewster**
Shepard, Jean Heck *author, publishing company consultant, agent*

**Briarcliff Manor**
Zimmar, George Peter *publishing executive, psychology educator*

**Briarwood**
Danna, Jo J. *publisher, author, anthropologist*

**Bridgehampton**
Phillips, Warren Henry *publisher*

**Bronx**
Moritz, Charles Fredric *book editor*
Rizzuto, Philip Francis (Scooter ) *sports broadcaster, former professional baseball player*
Zalaznick, Sheldon *editor, journalist*

**Bronxville**
Greenwald, Martin *publishing company executive*
Keller, LeRoy *journalist, consultant*
Lombardo, Philip Joseph *broadcasting company executive*
Shuker, Gregory Brown *publishing and production company executive*

**Brooklyn**
Bianco, Anthony Joseph, III *newswriter*
Bode, Walter Albert *editor*
Newbauer, John Arthur *editor*
Reynolds, Nancy Remick *editor, writer*
Sanford, David Boyer *writer, editor*
Schmidt, Fred (Orval Frederick Schmidt) *editor*
Walsh, George William *publishing company executive, editor*

**Buffalo**
Brady-Borland, Karen *reporter*
Collins, J. Michael *public broadcasting executive*
Goldhaber, Gerald Martin *communication educator, author, consultant*
Halpert, Leonard Walter *retired editor*
Huntington, Richard (John) *art critic*
Ireland, Barbara Hennig *newspaper editor*
Light, Murray Benjamin *newspaper editor*
Robinson, David Clinton *reporter*
Spencer, Foster Lewis *newspaper editor*
Toles, Thomas Gregory *editorial cartoonist*
Trotter, Herman Eager, Jr. (Herman Trotter) *music critic*
Urban, Henry Zeller *newspaperman*
Vogel, Michael N. *journalist, writer, historian*
Woelfel, Joseph Donald *communications educator*

**Campbell Hall**
Ottaway, James Haller, Jr. *newspaper publisher*

**Centerport**
Stevens, Martin Brian *publisher*

**Chappaqua**
Brennan, Terrence Michael *publisher*
Gstalder, Herbert William *publisher*

**Cooperstown**
Gibson, Robert *broadcaster, former baseball player*

**Croton On Hudson**
Coleman, Earl Maxwell *publishing company executive*
Kahn, Roger *author*
Miranda, Robert Nicholas *publishing company executive*
Needham, Richard Lee *magazine editor*
Nelson, Charles Arthur *publisher, consultant*
Shatzkin, Leonard *publishing consultant*
Straka, Laszlo Richard *publishing consultant*
Turner, David Reuben *publisher, author*

**Dobbs Ferry**
Holtz, Sidney *publishing company executive*
Simon, Lothar *publishing company executive*

**East Hampton**
De Bruhl, Marshall *writer, editor, publishing consultant*
Harmon, Marian Sanders *writer, sculptor*

**East Northport**
Reed, Robert Monroe *publishing executive*

**Farmingdale**
Steckler, Larry *publisher, editor, author*

**Flushing**
Cathcart, Robert Stephen *mass media consultant*
Chook, Paul Howard *publishing executive*
Kiner, Ralph McPherran *sports commentator, former baseball player*

**Garden City**
Brooks, Helene Margaret *editor-in-chief*
Egan, Frank T. *writer, editor*

**Garrison**
Duncan, Thomas Webb *magazine publishing executive*

**Glen Head**
Huber, Don Lawrence *publisher*

**Glendale**
Pipia, Rosaria Anna *publishing executive, consultant*

**Golden's Bridge**
Ambrose, Daniel Michael *publishing executive*

**Goshen**
Goodreds, John Stanton *newspaper publisher*

**Grand Island**
White, Ralph David *retired editor and writer*

**Great Neck**
Fiel, Maxine Lucille *journalist, behavioral analyst, lecturer*
Panes, Jack Samuel *publishing company executive*
Roth, Harvey Paul *publisher*
Rubin, Irving *pharmaceutical editor*

**Hamilton**
Edmonston, William Edward, Jr. *publisher, educator*

**Hastings On Hudson**
Reich, Herb *editor*

**Hauppauge**
Reis, Don *publishing executive*

**Hempstead**
Masheck, Joseph Daniel *art critic, educator*

**Hicksville**
Horowitz, Barry Allan *music company executive*

**Huntington**
Connor, Joseph Robert *editor*
Holahan, Richard Vincent *former magazine and book publisher*

**Irvington**
Lugenbeel, Edward Elmer *publisher*

**Ithaca**
Bourne, Russell *publisher, author*
Kendler, Bernhard *editor*
Schwartz, Donald Franklin *communication educator*

**Jackson Heights**
Sklar, Morty E. *publisher, editor*

**Jamaica**
Wetherington, Roger Vincent *journalism educator, newspaper copy editor*

**Jamestown**
Goldman, Simon *broadcasting executive*

**Jericho**
†Faletra, Robert *editor*
†Mannion, Kevin *publishing executive*

**Katonah**
Fry, John *magazine editor*
Krefting, Robert J(ohn) *publishing company executive*
Raymond, Jack *journalist, public relations executive, foundation executive*

**Kinderhook**
Lankhof, Frederik Jan *publishing executive*

**Kings Park**
Greene, Robert William *journalism educator, media consultant*

**Larchmont**
Rainier, Robert Paul *publisher*
Vitt, Samuel Bradshaw *communications media services executive*

**Liverpool**
Mitchell, John David *journalism educator*

**Locust Valley**
Zulch, Joan Carolyn *retired medical publishing company executive, consultant*

**Long Beach**
Bernstein, Lester *editorial consultant*
Robbins, Jeffrey Howard *media consultant, research writer, educator*

**Malverne**
Pollio, Ralph Thomas *editor, writer, magazine consultant*

**Mamaroneck**
Flagg, Jeanne Bodin *editor*
Meadow, Susan Ellen *publisher*

**Manhasset**
Cavill, Karen A. *publishing executive*
McGreal, Joseph A., Jr. *publishing company executive*
Moran, Timothy *newspaper editor*
Rostky, George Harold *editor*
Wallace, Richard *editor, writer*

**Maryknoll**
Gormley, Robert John *book publisher*

**Mattituck**
Gazouleas, Panagiotis J. *journalist*

**Melville**
Bass, Elizabeth Ruth *editor*
Brandt, Robert Frederic, III *newspaper editor, journalist*
Carter, Sylvia *journalist*
†Cole, Kirstin Elizabeth *television news anchor*
Cooke, Robert William *science journalist*
Donovan, Brian *reporter, journalist*
Dooley, James C. *newspaper editor, director of photography*
Drewry, Elizabeth *newspaper publishing executive*
†Garrett, Laurie *science correspondent*
Grebow, Edward *television company executive*
Hall, Charlotte Hauch *newspaper editor*
Hildebrand, John Frederick *newspaper columnist*
Jansen, Raymond A., Jr. *newspaper publishing executive*
†Kahn, David *editor, author*
Klurfeld, James Michael *journalist*
Lynn, James Dougal *newspaper editor, journalist*
Marro, Anthony James *newspaper editor*
Moran, Paul James *journalist, columnist*
Payne, Leslie *newspaper editor, columnist, journalist, author*
Phelps, Timothy Miller *reporter*
Richards, Carol Ann Rubright *editor, columnist*
Robins, Marjorie Kaplan *newspaper editor*
Roel, Ron *newspaper editor*
Saul, Stephanie *journalist*

**Middle Village**
Kolatch, Alfred Jacob *publisher*

**Middletown**
Bedell, Barbara Lee *journalist*
Sprick, Dennis Michael *critic, copy editor*

**Mineola**
Cirker, Hayward *publisher*

**Montauk**
First, Wesley *publishing company executive*

**Monticello**
Lubrecht, Heinz D. *publishing company executive, antiquarian book expert, appraiser*

**Mount Kisco**
Pastorelle, Peter John *film company executive, radiological services and waste management company executive*

**Mount Vernon**
Mc Neill, Charles James *publishing executive*

**New City**
Elberg, Darryl Gerald *publisher, educator*

**New Rochelle**
Hoxter, Allegra Branson *radio news and freelance writer*
Iarocci, Kent Alexander *newswriter, home improvement contractor*
Saunders, Rubie Agnes *former magazine editor, author*

**New York**
Aaron, Betsy *journalist*
Abatemarco, Fred *editor in chief*
Abelson, Alan *columnist*
Abrahams, William Miller *editor, author*
Abrams, Pamela Nadine *magazine editor*
Adams, Edward A. *legal journalist*
†Adams, Scott *cartoonist*
Addison, Herbert John *publishing executive*
Adler, Margot Susanna *journalist, radio producer*
Alabiso, Vincent *photojournalist*
†Alarcon, Raul, Jr. *broadcast executive*
Albert, Marv *sportscaster, program director*
Alexander, Shana *journalist, author, lecturer*
Alpern, David Mark *magazine editor, broadcast journalist and producer*
Alter, Jonathan Hammerman *journalist*
Amdur, Neil Lester *sports editor, writer*
Amster, Linda Evelyn *newspaper executive, consultant*
Anderson, Bradley Jay *cartoonist*
Anderson, David Poole *sportswriter*
Anderson, Gloria Faye *editor*
Anderson, Walter Herman *magazine editor*
Andrews, Frederick Franck *newspaper editor*
Antilla, Susan *journalist*
Appleton, Myra *magazine editor, writer*
Arcara, James Amadeus *retired broadcasting company executive*
Arledge, Roone *television executive*
Arnold, Audrey Jayne *communications company editor, record and cassette producer*
Arnold, C. Stuart *publishing executive*
Arnold, Kenneth Lloyd *publisher, playwright*
Arnold, Martin *journalist*
Asahina, Robert James *editor, publishing company executive*
Asher, Aaron *editor, publisher*
Astor, David Warren *journalist*
Atlas, James Robert *magazine editor, writer*
Auchincloss, Kenneth *magazine editor*
Austin, Danforth Whitley *newspaper executive*
Austin, Gabriel Christopher *publisher*
Bache, Theodore Stephen *recording company executive*
Bahr, Lauren S. *publishing company executive*
Bailey, Janet Dee *publishing company executive*
Bakal, Carl *writer, public affairs consultant, photojournalist*
Baker, Elizabeth Calhoun *magazine editor*
Baker, Russell Wayne *columnist, author*
Baker, William Franklin *public broadcasting company executive*
Baldassano, Corinne Leslie *radio executive*
Baquet, Dean Paul *newspaper editor*
Baranski, Joan Sullivan *publisher*
Barnes, Clive Alexander *drama and dance critic*
Barnes, Duncan *magazine editor, writer*
Barolini, Teodolinda *literary critic*
Baron, Carolyn *editor, author, publishing executive*
Barrett, Loretta Anne *publishing executive*
Barron, James Turman *journalist*
Barry, Edward William *publisher*
Bartley, Robert LeRoy *newspaper editor*
Baruch, Ralph M. *communications executive*
†Bauman, Steve *television station executive*
Bazell, Robert Joseph *science correspondent*
Beardsley, Charles William *engineering publisher, editor, writer*
Becker, Don Crandall *newspaper executive*
Begell, William *publisher*
Bemis, Mary Ferguson *magazine editor*
Benderly, Beryl Lieff *journalist, author*
Bennack, Frank Anthony, Jr. *publishing company executive*
Berman, Philip Averill *journalist, consultant*
Berner, Mary *publisher*
Bernstein, Laurel *publishing executive*
Bernstein, Robert Louis *publishing company executive*
Berry, John Nichols, III *publishing executive, editor*
Berry, Joyce Charlotte *university press editor*
Bertelle, Jeanne T. *publishing company executive, human resources director*
Bewkes, Jeff *television broadcasting company executive*
Birsh, Arthur Thomas *publisher*
Black, Cathleen Prunty *publishing executive*
Black, Rosemary *newspaper editor*
†Blackford, John *magazine editor*
Blair, William Granger *retired newspaperman*
Bleiberg, Robert Marvin *retired financial editor*
Bliven, Naomi *book reviewer*
Bloch, Peter *editor*
†Bloomfield, Louise Anne *editor*
Blyth, Myrna Greenstein *publishing executive, editor, author*
Blythe, William LeGette, II *editor, writer*
Boccardi, Louis Donald *news agency executive*
Bocchino, Lisa *magazine editor*
†Bodow, Warren G. *radio station executive*
Boehm, David Alfred *publisher, producer*
Borders, William Alexander *journalist*
Boultinghouse, Marion Craig Bettinger *editor*
Bourdon, David *art critic, writer*
Boyce, Joseph Nelson *journalist*
Brack, Reginald Kufeld, Jr. *publisher*
Bradford, John Carroll *retired magazine executive*
Bradley, Edward R. *news correspondent*
Brant, Sandra J. *magazine publisher*
Brecher, John *newspaper editor*
Breindel, Eric Marc *communications executive, television moderator, columnist*
Brenner, Beth Fuchs *publishing executive*
Brewer, John Charles *journalist*
Bridges, Linda Kay *journalist*
Briggs, Jean Audrey *publishing company executive*
Brill, Steven *magazine editor*
Brimelow, Peter *journalist*
Brock, Kerry Lynn *broadcast executive*
Brody, Jacqueline *editor*
Brody, Jane Ellen *journalist*
Brown, Darrell James *publishing executive*
Brown, Helen Gurley *editor, writer*
Brown, Jeffrey Wisner *publishing company executive*
Brown, Les (Lester Louis) *journalist*
Brown, Tina *magazine editor*
†Brown, William Anthony (Tony) *broadcast executive*
Browne, Arthur *newspaper editor*
Browne, Malcolm Wilde *journalist*
Brydon, Donald James *media consultant, former news service executive*
Buckley, Christopher Taylor *editor, author*
Buckley, Kevin *magazine editor*
Buckley, Priscilla Langford *magazine editor*
Buckley, Virginia Laura *editor*
Buckley, William Frank, Jr. *magazine editor, writer*
Buford, Bill *editor, writer*
Buhagiar, Marion *editor, author*
Burenga, Kenneth L. *publishing executive*
Burgheim, Richard Allan *magazine editor*
Burns, John F. *reporter*
Buttner, Jean Bernhard *publishing company executive*
Bylinsky, Gene Michael *magazine editor*
Byrne, Gerard Anthony *publishing company executive, marketing consultant*
Calame, Byron Edward *journalist*
Callahan, Robert F., Jr. *radio network executive*
Campbell, Robert Chambers *critic, playwright*
Campi, John G. *newspaper publishing executive*
Campos, Fernando *editor-in-chief*
Canby, Vincent *film critic*
Cannistraro, Nicholas, Jr. *newspaper executive*
Cantwell, Mary *journalist*
Capano, Edward Andrew *publishing company executive*
†Carey, Bud *television station executive*
Carr, Gladys Justin *publishing company executive, editor, writer*
Carter, Betsy L. *magazine editor*
Carter, Edward Graydon *editor*
Carter, John Mack *publishing company executive*
Cassidy, John Joseph *journalist*
Cavender, Catherine C. *magazine editor*
Chandler, Kenneth A. *newspaper editor*
Chang, Jeannette *publishing executive*
Chardiet, Bernice Kroll *juvenile books publisher, editor, record and cassette producer*
Charnin, Jade Hobson *magazine executive*
Chase, Sylvia B. *journalist*
Cherry, Rona Beatrice *magazine editor, writer*
Chesnutt, Jane *publishing executive*
Chopey, Nicholas P. *editor*
Christian, Darrell L. *journalist*
Chung, Connie (Constance Yu-hwa Chung) *broadcast journalist*
Church, George John *journalist*
Churgin, Amy *publishing executive*
Clinton, Michael *magazine publisher*
Cohane, Heather Christina *magazine publisher*
Colton, James K. *photojournalist*
Conde, Yvonne Menéndez *freelance journalist*
†Conlon, Peggy Eileen *publisher*
Connolly, William Gerard *newspaper editor*
Cook, James *magazine editor*
Cooke, Alfred Alistair *correspondent, broadcaster*
Cooney, Joan Ganz *broadcasting executive*
Cooper, Arthur Martin *magazine editor*
Cooper, Gloria *editor, press critic*
Corcoran, David *newspaper editor*
Corliss, Richard Nelson *critic, magazine editor*
Corporon, John Robert *broadcasting executive*
†Coryat, Sonja Heinze *journalist, freelance writer*
Cose, Ellis *journalist, author*
Couric, Katherine *broadcast journalist*
Cowley, Robert William *editor, writer*
Crandell, Susan *magazine editor*
Crawford, Harold Bernard *publisher*
Crist, Judith *film and drama critic*
Croce, Arlene Louise *critic*
†Crocker, Frankie *radio broadcast executive*
Cronkite, Walter *radio and television news correspondent*
Cross, Theodore Lamont *publisher, author*
Crow, Elizabeth Smith *publishing company executive*
Crowdus, Gary Alan *film company executive*
Culhane, John William *journalist, author, film historian*
Cunningham, Jeffrey Milton *publishing executive*
Cuozzo, Steven David *newspaper editor*
Curry, Ann *correspondent, anchor*
Curry, Jack *magazine editor*
Daly, Charles Patrick *publishing company executive*
Daly, Cheryl *broadcast executive*
Daly, Joe Ann Godown *publishing company executive*
Daly, Robert Anthony *film executive*
D'Angelo, Joseph Francis *publishing company executive*
Danzig, Frederick Paul *newspaper editor*
Danziger, Jeff *political cartoonist, writer*
Darnton, John Townsend *journalist*
Dauten, Dale Alan *newspaper columnist*
Davila, Jaime *broadcast executive*
Davis, Clive Jay *record company executive*
De Angelis, Judy *anchorwoman*
DeFranco, Elizabeth Carol *editor*
Deitz, Paula *magazine editor*
Dekker, Marcel *publishing company executive*
Delbourgo, Joëlle Lily *publishing executive*
Derow, Peter Alfred *publishing company executive*
†Desiato, Michael *editor-in-chief, periodical*
Deutsch, Martin Bernard Joseph *editor, publisher*
Diamond, Edwin *journalism educator, editor, columnist*
Dierdorf, Daniel Lee (Dan Dierdorf) *football analyst, sports commentator, former professional football player*
DiGuido, Al *publishing executive*
Dillingham, Robert Bulger *publishing executive*
Dionne, Joseph Lewis *publishing company executive*
Disney, Anthea *publishing executive*
Dobelis, Inge Nachman *editor*
Dobell, Byron Maxwell *magazine consultant*
Dodge, Geoffrey A. *magazine publisher*
Doherty, Thomas *publisher*
Dolger, Jonathan *editor, literary agent*
Dolice, Joseph Leo *multimedia publisher, exhibition director*
Donald, Roger Thomas *publishing executive*
Dormann, Henry O. *magazine publisher*
Dornemann, Michael *book publishing executive*
Douglas, Andra Christine *entertainment company executive*
Drasner, Fred *newspaper publishing executive*
Drawbaugh, Kevin Alan *journalist*
Duggan, Dennis Michael *newspaper editor*
Dunn, James Joseph *magazine publisher*
Dwyer, Jim *reporter, columnist*
Dystel, Jane Dee *literary agent*
Eaker, Sherry Ellen *entertainment newspaper editor*
Ebersol, Dick *television broadcasting executive*
Eckman, Fern Marja *journalist*
†Edelstein, Robert Glenn *magazine editor*
Edmiston, Mark Morton *publishing company executive*
Ellerbee, Linda *broadcast journalist*
†Elliman, Donald M., Jr. *magazine publisher and executive*
Elliott, Osborn *journalist, educator, urban activist, former dean*
Ellis, Charles Richard *publishing executive*
Engstrom, Erik *publishing company executive*
Epstein, Barbara *editor*
Epstein, Jason *publishing company executive*
Erbsen, Claude Ernest *journalist*
Ertegun, Ahmet Munir *record company executive*
Esposito, Richard Joseph *journalist, executive*
Esterow, Milton *magazine editor, publisher*
Evans, Linda Kay *publishing company executive*
Evans, Thomas R. *magazine publisher*
Fairchild, John Burr *publisher*
Farber, Jackie *editor*
Fargis, Paul McKenna *publishing consultant, book developer, editor*
Farney, Dennis *journalist*
Feders, Sid *journalist, television producer*
Feingold, Michael E. *critic, translator, stage director*
Feniger, Jerome Roland, Jr. *broadcasting executive*
Fennell, John *magazine publisher*
Fenton, Thomas Trail *journalist*
Ferm, David G. *magazine publisher*
Fertig, Howard *publisher, editor*
†Findlen, Barbara J. *magazine editor*
Fine, Donald Irving *editor, publisher, writer*
Fine, Michael Joseph *publishing company executive*
Finn, Edwin, Jr. *publishing executive*
Fiori, Pamela *publishing executive, magazine editor*
Fischler, Stan *sportswriter, sportscaster*
Fisher, Arthur *magazine editor*
Fisher, Gary Alan *publishing executive*
Flanagan, Dennis *journalist*
Florio, Steven T. *magazine executive*
Florio, Thomas *magazine publisher*
†Flynn-Connors, Elizabeth Kathryn *editor*
Fondiller, David Stewart *journalist*
Forbes, Christopher (Kip Forbes) *publisher*
Forbes, Steve (Malcolm Stevenson Forbes, Jr.) *publishing executive*
Forbes, Timothy Carter *publisher*
Forden, Diane Claire *magazine editor*
Fox, Mitchell *magazine publisher*
Fox, Sylvan *journalist*
Frank, James Aaron *magazine editor, author*
Frankel, Max *journalist*
Franks, Lucinda Laura *journalist*
Frawley, Sean Paul *publishing executive*
Freedman, Albert Z. *publishing company executive*
Freudenheim, Milton B. *journalist*
Friedheim, Eric Arthur *publisher, editor*
Friedman, J. Roger *publisher*
Friend, David *publishing executive*
Fritz, Maura Kathleen *magazine editor*
Fuchs, Anne Sutherland *magazine publisher*
†Fuller, Bonnie *editor*
Gainsburg, Roy Ellis *publishing executive*
Galassi, Jonathan White *book publishing company executive*
Galazka, Jacek Michal *publishing company executive*
Gallick, Sarah Patricia *editor, writer*
Gallo, William Victor *cartoonist*
Galotti, Ronald A. *magazine publisher*
Gandolf, Raymond L. *media correspondent*
Garagiola, Joe *sports broadcaster*
Gardino, Vincent Anthony *broadcast executive*
†Gardner, Andre V. *broadcast executive*
Gardner, Janet Paxton *journalist, video producer*
Garratt, Graham *publishing executive*
Gehringer, Richard George *publishing executive*
Geiser, Elizabeth Able *publishing company executive*
Gelb, Arthur *newspaper editor*
Gelb, Leslie Howard *organization president, lecturer*
Germano, William Paul *publisher*
†Gershon, Bernard *broadcast executive*
Gerson, Robert Elisha *periodical editor-in-chief*
Gewirtz, Gerry *editor*
Gibson, Charles DeWolf *broadcast journalist*
Giddins, Gary Mitchell *music critic, columnist*
Gifford, Frank Newton *sportscaster, commentator, former professional football player*
Giles, Robert Hartmann *foundation executive*
Gilman, Richard H. *newspaper publishing executive*
Giniger, Kenneth Seeman *publisher*
Giraldi, Robert Nicholas *film director*
Giroux, Robert *editor, book publisher, author*

Shier, Shelley M. *production company executive*
Shnayerson, Robert Beahan *editor*
Shortz, Will *puzzle editor*
Siegal, Allan Marshall *newspaper editor*
Siegel, Joel Steven *television news correspondent*
Siegel, Marvin *newspaper editor*
Siek, Rainer *broadcast executive*
†Sikorsky, Robert Bellarmine *syndicated columnist*
Silberman, James Henry *editor, publisher*
Silberstein, Diane *publishing executive*
Silver, Shelly Andrea *media artist*
Silverman, Al *editor*
Silverman, Stephen Meredith *journalist, screenwriter, producer*
Silvers, Robert Benjamin *editor*
Simmons, Russell *recording industry executive*
Simon, John Ivan *film and drama critic*
Simonson, Lee Stuart *broadcast company executive*
Singer, Niki *publishing executive, public relations executive*
†Singerman, Martin *newspaper publishing executive*
Singleton, Donald Edward *journalist*
Sischy, Ingrid Barbara *magazine editor, art critic*
Skillin, Edward Simeon *magazine publisher*
Sleed, Joel *columnist*
Sloan, Allan Herbert *journalist*
Smith, Charles Carter, Jr. *publishing executive*
Smith, Corlies Morgan *publishing executive*
Smith, Joseph Phelan *film company executive*
Smith, Liz (Mary Elizabeth Smith) *newspaper columnist, broadcast journalist*
Smith, Patrick John *editor, writer*
Smith, Richard Mills *editor in chief, magazine executive*
Smith, Warren Allen *editor*
Snyder, Richard Elliot *publishing company executive*
†Sonenberg, David A. *personal manager*
Soren, Tabitha L. *television newscaster, writer*
Speller, Robert Ernest Blakefield *publishing executive*
Spence, James Robert, Jr. *television sports executive*
Spring, Michael *editor, writer*
Stahl, Lesley R. *journalist*
Stamaty, Mark Alan *cartoonist, author, artist*
Stanger, Ila *writer, editor*
†Steele, Bruce Carl *editor*
Steiger, Paul Ernest *newspaper editor, journalist*
Steinfeld, Thomas Albert *publisher*
Steinfels, Peter Francis *newspaper correspondent, writer*
Stephenson, Michele *photographer*
Stepler, Richard Lewis *magazine editor*
Stern, Robert D. *publishing executive*
Stern, Roslyne Paige *magazine publisher*
Steves, Gale C. *editor-in-chief*
Stossel, John *news analyst*
Straus, Roger W., Jr. *publishing company executive*
Stringer, Howard *television executive*
Stuart, Carole *publishing executive*
Stuart, Lyle *publishing company executive*
†Studin, Jan *publishing executive*
Sturtevant, Peter Mann, Jr. *television news executive*
Sugihara, Kenzi *publishing executive*
Sugiyama, Kazunori *music producer*
†Sullivan, Timothy J. *journalist*
Sulzberger, Arthur Ochs *newspaper executive*
Sulzberger, Arthur Ochs, Jr. *newspaper publisher*
Summerall, Pat (George Allan Summerall) *sportscaster*
Sussman, Gerald *publishing company executive*
Sustendal, Diane *editor, consultant*
Sutton-Straus, Joan M. *journalist*
Sweed, Phyllis *publishing executive*
Sweezy, Paul Marlor *editor, publisher*
Swenson, Eric Pierson *publishing company executive*
†Sykes, Jolene *publishing executive*
Talese, Nan Ahearn *publishing company executive*
Talley, Truman Macdonald *publisher*
Tash, Martin Elias *publishing company executive*
Tatum, Wilbert Arnold *editor, publisher*
Taylor, Sherril Wightman *broadcasting company executive*
†Taylor, Susan L. *editor, magazine*
Taylor, Terry R. *editor, educator*
Temple, Wick *journalist*
Thomas, Brooks *publishing company executive*
Thompson, Martin Christian *news service executive*
Tilberis, Elizabeth *editor-in-chief*
Tober, Barbara D. (Mrs. Donald Gibbs Tober) *editor*
Toepfer, Susan Jill *editor*
Toff, Nancy Ellen *book editor*
Tomlinson, James Francis *retired news agency executive*
Townsend, Charles H. *publishing executive*
Treaster, Joseph B. (Bland) *journalist*
Tuchman, Gary Robert *television news correspondent*
Tuchman, Phyllis *critic*
Tucker, Alan David *publisher*
Turner, Craig *journalist*
Ubell, Robert Neil *editor, publisher, consultant, literary agent*
Uchitelle, Louis *journalist*
†Udell Turshen, Rochelle Marcia *publishing executive*
Ungaro, Susan Kelliher *magazine editor*
Urdang, Alexandra *book publishing executive*
Valenti, Carl M. *newspaper publisher*
Vanden Heuvel, Katrina *magazine editor*
Van Sant, Peter Richard *news correspondent*
Vaughan, Samuel Snell *editor, author, publisher*
Vecsey, George Spencer *sports columnist*
Vega, Marylois Purdy *journalist*
Vitale, Alberto Aldo *publishing company executive*
Vitale, Dick *commentator, sports writer*
Vittorini, Carlo *publishing company executive*
Vizard, Frank Joseph *journalist*
von Mehren, Jane *editor, publisher*
Voorhees, David William *editor, historian*
Wald, Richard Charles *broadcasting executive*
Walker, Mort *cartoonist*
Wallace, G. David *magazine editor*
Wallace, Ken *magazine publisher*
Wallace, Mike *television interviewer and reporter*
Wallace, Thomas C(hristopher) *editor, literary agent*
Walters, Barbara *television journalist*
Walters, Raymond, Jr. *newspaper editor, author*
Walton, Bill (William Theodore Walton, III) *sportscaster, former professional basketball player*
Walzog, Nancy Lee *film and television executive*
Wang, Arthur Woods *publisher*
Warner, Peter David *publishing executive*
Waxenberg, Alan M. *publisher*
Weber, Robert Maxwell *cartoonist*
Weins, Leo Matthew *retired publishing executive*
Weinstein, Harvey *film company executive*
Weinstein, Robert *film company executive*
Weintz, Walter Louis *book publishing company executive*
Welling, Kathryn Marie *editor*
Wells, Linda Ann *editor-in-chief*
Welsh, Donald Emory *publisher*
Wenner, Jann Simon *editor, publisher*
Westin, David *broadcast executive*
†Wetschler, Ed *editor*
Wham, George Sims *publishing executive*
White, Kate *editor-in-chief*
White, Timothy Thomas Anthony *writer, editor, broadcaster*
Whiteman, Douglas E. *publisher*
Whitney, Ruth Reinke *magazine editor*
Whittell, Polly (Mary) Kaye *editor, writer*
Wiener, Hesh (Harold Frederic Wiener) *publisher, editor, consultant*
Wiggers, Charlotte Suzanne Ward *magazine editor*
Wilford, John Noble, Jr. *news correspondent*
Willis, John Alvin *editor*
Windsor, Laurence Charles, Jr. *publishing executive*
Winfrey, Carey Wells *journalist, magazine editor*
Winship, Frederick Moery *journalist*
Winstead, Clint *financial publisher*
Wintour, Anna *editor*
†Wittenberg, Kate *editor*
Wogan, Robert *broadcasting company executive*
Wolmer, Bruce Richard *magazine editor*
Wolper, Allan L. *journalist, educator*
Wordsman, Elizabeth Schmitt *senior manager print production*
Wright, Bob *broadcasting executive*
Wright, Robert *broadcast executive*
Yablon, Leonard Harold *publishing company executive*
Young, Genevieve Leman *publishing executive, editor*
Zackheim, Adrian Walter *editor*
Zanetti, Richard Joseph *editorial director*
Zeldin, Richard Packer *publisher*
Zevon, Susan Jane *editor*
Ziff, William Bernard, Jr. *retired publishing executive*
Zimbalist, Efrem, III *publishing company executive*
Zimmerman, William Edwin *newspaper editor, publisher, writer*
Zinsser, William Knowlton *editor, writer, educator*
Zuckerman, Mortimer Benjamin *publisher, editor, real estate developer*
†Zweigenthal, Gail *magazine editor*

### North Salem
Burlingame, Edward Livermore *book publisher*
Larsen, Jonathan Zerbe *journalist*

### Nyack
Flood, (Hulda) Gay *editor, consultant*
Leiser, Ernest Stern *journalist*

### Old Brookville
Fairman, Joel Martin *broadcasting executive*

### Oneonta
Knudson, Richard Lewis *editor*

### Ossining
Carter, Richard *publisher, writer*
Ravis, Howard Shepard *conference planner and publishing consultant*
Stein, Sol *publisher, writer, editor in chief*

### Pelham
Decker, Carol Arne *magazine publishing consultant*
Minick, Michael *publishing executive*

### Piermont
Fox, Matthew Ignatius *publishing company executive*

### Plainview
Newman, Edwin Harold *news commentator*

### Pleasantville
Coleman, Gregory G. *magazine publisher*
Kenney, Thomas Michael *publisher*
Willcox, Christopher Patrick *magazine editor*

### Port Washington
Anable, Anne Currier Steinert *journalist*
Jay, Frank Peter *writer, educator*
Simmons, Lee Howard *book publishing company executive*

### Poughkeepsie
Kim, David Sang Chul *publisher, evangelist, retired seminary president*
VanBuren, Denise Doring *media relations executive*

### Purchase
Sandler, Irving Harry *art critic, art historian*

### Quogue
Malabre, Alfred Leopold, Jr. *journalist, author*

### Remsenburg
Billman, Irwin Edward *publishing company executive*

### Rhinecliff
Dierdorff, John Ainsworth *retired editor*

### Rochester
Hyman, Ralph Alan *journalist, consultant*
†Lank, Edith Handleman *columnist, educator*
Moore, Matthew Scott *publisher, deaf advocate, author*
Palvino, Jack Anthony *broadcasting executive*
Pearce, William Joseph *retired public broadcasting executive, consultant*
Prosser, Michael Hubert *communications educator*

### Rome
Waters, George Bausch *newspaper publisher*

### Ronkonkoma
Townsend, Paul Brorstrom *editor*
Townsend, Terry *publishing executive*

### Roslyn
Barnathan, Julius *broadcasting company executive*
Risom, Ole Christian *publishing company executive*

### Rye
Erlick, Everett Howard *broadcasting company executive*
Pearson, Nathan Williams *broadcast executive*
Stoller, Ezra *photojournalist*

### Scarsdale
Frackman, Noel *art critic*
Frankel, Stanley Arthur *columnist, educator, business executive*
Heese, William John *music publishing company executive*
Marks, Barbara Hanzel *publishing executive*
O'Neill, Michael James *editor, author*
Schwartz, Harry *journalist*
Topping, Seymour *publishing executive, educator*

### Setauket
Robinson, Richard M. *technical communication specialist*

### Smithtown
Leavy, Herbert Theodore *publisher*

### Somers
Boudreaux, John *public relations specialist*
Carrick, Bruce Robert *publishing company executive*
Cohn, Howard *retired magazine editor*

### Southampton
Graham, Howard Barrett *publishing company executive*
Sims, Everett Martin *publishing company executive*
Smith, Dennis (Edward) *publisher, author*

### Spencertown
Lieber, Charles Donald *publisher*

### Staten Island
Diamond, Richard Edward *publisher*

### Stony Brook
Booth, George *cartoonist*
Cleveland, Ceil Margaret *writer, journalist, education administrator, English language educator*
Fisher, David Woodrow *editor, publisher*
Harvey, Christine Lynn *publishing executive*

### Swain
Robinson, Bina Aitchison *publisher, newsletter editor*

### Syosset
†Rudman, Michael P. *publishing executive*

### Syracuse
Balk, Alfred William *journalist*
Bunn, Timothy David *newspaper editor*
Mesrobian, Arpena Sachaklian *publisher, editor, consultant*
Rogers, Stephen *newspaper publisher*

### Tarrytown
Ashburn, Anderson *magazine editor*
†Grufferman, Barbara Hannah *publishing executive*
LeGrice, Stephen *magazine editor*
Neill, Richard Robert *retired publishing company executive*
Scott, Richard Thurston *publishing executive*
Whipple, Judith Roy *book editor*
†Wood, Roger *publishing executive*

### Troy
Friedman, Sue Tyler *technical publications executive*
Rubens, Philip *communications educator, technical writer*

### Utica
Donovan, Donna Mae *newspaper publisher*

### Valley Cottage
Stolldorf, Genevieve Schwager *media specialist*

### Valley Stream
Lehrer, Stanley *magazine publisher, editorial director, corporate executive*

### Valois
Hurst, Kenneth Thurston *publisher*

### Waccabuc
Kislik, Richard William *publishing executive*
Thompson, Edward Thorwald *magazine editor*

### Wainscott
Henderson, William Charles *editor*

### Warwick
Simon, Dolores Daly *copy editor*

### Watertown
Johnson, John Brayton *editor, publisher*

### West Islip
Keller, Joyce *television and radio host, counselor*

### White Plains
Ellenbogen, Milton Joseph *publishing executive, editor, writer*
Goodman, Walter *author, editor*
Hoffman, Milton Sills *editor*
Patman, Jean Elizabeth *journalist*

### Woodbury
Bell, William Joseph *cable television company executive*
Dolan, Charles Francis *cable systems company executive*
Sweeney, Daniel Thomas *cable television company executive*

### Yonkers
Denver, Eileen Ann *magazine editor*
Eimicke, Victor W(illiam) *publishing company executive*

### Yorktown Heights
Wade, James O'Shea *publisher*

## NORTH CAROLINA

### Asheville
Damtoft, Walter Atkinson *editor, publisher*
Wilkins, Rita Denise *researcher, multimedia design consultant*
Wilson, Herschel Manuel (Pete Wilson) *retired journalism educator*

### Brevard
Phillips, Euan Hywel *publishing executive*
Strongin, Theodore *journalist*

### Burlington
Buckley, J. Stephen *newspaper publisher*

### Carrboro
Boggs, Robert Newell *editor*

### Cary
Andrews, John Woodhouse *newspaper publisher*
McCarty, Thomas Joseph *publishing company executive*
Reynolds, Edward *book publisher*

### Chapel Hill
Bowers, Thomas Arnold *journalism educator*
Lauder, Valarie Anne *editor, educator*

### Charlotte
Barrows, Frank Clemence *newspaper editor*
Brown, Tony *theater and dance critic*
Ethridge, Mark Foster, III *writer, publisher, newspaper consultant*
Haines, Kenneth H. *television broadcasting executive*
Neill, Rolfe *newspaper executive*
White, David Lee *journalist*
Williams, Edwin Neel *newspaper editor*

### China Grove
Baker, Ira Lee *journalist, former educator*

### Durham
Cooper, Charles Howard *photojournalist, newspaper publishing company executive*
Harrell, Benjamin Carlton *columnist, retired editor*
Hawkins, William E. N. *newspaper editor*
Hayes, Brian Paul *editor, writer*
Rollins, Edward Tyler, Jr. *newspaper executive*
Rossiter, Alexander, Jr. *news service executive, editor*

### Edenton
Walklet, John James, Jr. *publishing executive*

### Elizabeth City
Baker, Jean M. *cable television executive*

### Gloucester
Price, Marion Woodrow *journalist*

### Greensboro
Blackwell, William Ernest *broadcast industry executive*
Gill, Evalyn Pierpoint *writer, editor, publisher*
Herman, Roger Eliot *professional speaker, consultant, futurist, writer*
Jellicorse, John Lee *communications and theatre educator*
McKissick-Melton, S. Charmaine *mass communications educator*
Roberts, Rosemary *journalist, columnist*

### Harrisburg
Economaki, Chris Constantine (Christopher Economaki) *publisher, editor*

### Hillsborough
Bolduc, Jean Plumley *journalist, education activist*

### Jefferson
Franklin, Robert McFarland *book publisher*

### Laurel Springs
Gilbert-Strawbridge, Anne Wieland *journalist*

### Pisgah Forest
Rierson, Robert Leak *retired broadcasting executive, television writer*

### Pittsboro
Bailey, Herbert Smith, Jr. *retired publisher*
Hauser, Charles Newland McCorkle *newspaper consultant*
Shurick, Edward Palmes *television executive, rancher*

### Raleigh
Daniels, Frank Arthur, Jr. *newspaper publisher*
Daniels, Frank Arthur, III *publishing executive*
Effron, Seth Alan *journalist*
Entman, Robert Mathew *communications educator, consultant*
Henson, Glenda Maria *newspaper writer*
Parker, Joseph Mayon *printing and publishing executive*
Powell, Drexel Dwane, Jr. *editorial cartoonist*
Reeves, Ralph B., III *publisher, editor*

### Research Triangle Park
May, Michael Lee *magazine editor*

### Sparta
Johnson, Jessie Jones *newspaper columnist, writer*

### Spindale
Trautmann, Patricia Ann *communications educator, storyteller*

### Tryon
Thayer, Lee *educator, author, consultant*

**Waxhaw**
Lamparter, William C. *printing and publishing consultant, digital printing and information systems specialist*

**Winston Salem**
Brill, Frank Patrick *journalist*
Tursi, Frank Vincent *journalist*

**Wrightsville Beach**
Mc Ilwain, William Franklin *newspaper editor, writer*

## NORTH DAKOTA

**Bismarck**
†Renfrew, Joseph *communications technologist*

**Fargo**
Dill, William Joseph *newspaper editor*
Littlefield, Robert Stephen *communication educator, training consultant*
Lohman, John Frederick *editor*
Paulson, John Doran *newspaper editor, retired*

## OHIO

**Akron**
Dotson, John Louis, Jr. *newspaper executive*

**Athens**
Alsbrook, James Eldridge *journalist, educator*
Metters, Thomas Waddell *sports writer*
Scott, Charles Lewis *photojournalist*
Stempel, Guido Hermann, III *journalism educator*

**Avon Lake**
Condon, George Edward *journalist*

**Bowling Green**
Clark, Robert King *communications educator emeritus, lecturer, consultant, actor, model*

**Bucyrus**
Moore, Thomas Paul *broadcast executive*

**Chagrin Falls**
Lange, David Charles *journalist*

**Cincinnati**
Beaupre, Lawrence Kenneth *newspaper editor*
Beckwith, Barbara Jean *journalist*
Blake, George Rowell *newspaper executive*
Burleigh, William Robert *newspaper executive*
Engebrecht, Julie *newspaper sports editor*
Harmon, Patrick *newspaperman*
Knue, Paul Frederick *newspaper editor*
Liss, Herbert Myron *newspaper publisher, communications company executive*
Mechem, Charles Stanley, Jr. *former broadcasting executive, former golf association executive*
Rogers, Lawrence H., II *retired television executive, investor, writer*
Silvers, Gerald Thomas *publishing executive*
Smith, C. LeMoyne *publishing company executive*
Whipple, Harry M. *newspaper publishing executive*
White, Robert John *journalist*
Winternitz, Felix Thomas *editor, educator*
Zanotti, John Peter *broadcasting company executive*

**Cleveland**
Atherton, James Dale *publishing executive*
Bennett, Michael *newspaper editor*
Bingham, Richard Donnelly *journal editor, director, educator*
Bluhm, Gene Elwood *trade journal editor and publisher*
Brandt, John Reynold *editor, journalist*
Clark, Gary R. *newspaper editor*
Connors, Joanna *film critic*
Davis, David Aaron *journalist*
Fabris, James A. *journalist*
Gauff, Lisa *broadcast journalist*
Gilbert, Harold Frederick *publishing executive, art lecturer*
Gordon, Anne Kathleen *editor*
Greer, Thomas H. *newspaper executive*
Hall, David *newspaper editor*
Harayda, Janice *newspaper book editor, author*
Jensen, Kathryn Patricia (Kit) *public radio station executive*
Jindra, Christine Ann *editor*
Kanzeg, David George *radio programming director*
Kovacs, Rosemary *newpaper editor*
Lebovitz, Harold Paul (Hal Lebovitz) *journalist*
Long, Robert M. *newspaper publishing executive*
Machaskee, Alex *newspaper publishing company executive*
Marr, David Francis *television announcer, former professional golfer, journalist*
Miyares, Benjamin David *editor, publisher, consultant*
Modic, Stanley John *business editor, publisher*
Molyneaux, David Glenn *newspaper travel editor*
Pascarella, Perry James *author, editor, speaker*
Shaw, Scott Alan *photojournalist*
Strang, James Dennis *editor*
Strassmeyer, Mary *newspaper columnist*
Wells, Charlena Renee *editor, writer*
Zubal, John Thomas *book exchange executive, publisher, bibliographer*

**Cleveland Heights**
Drane, Walter Harding *publishing executive, business consultant*

**Columbus**
Barker, Llyle James, Jr. *journalism educator, public relations executive, former military officer*
Barry, James P(otvin) *writer, editor*
Campbell, Richard Rice *retired newspaper editor*
Charles, Bertram *radio broadcasting executive*
Cox, Mitchel Neal *editor*
Dawson, Virginia Sue *newspaper editor*
Dervin, Brenda Louise *communications educator*
Fornshell, Dave Lee *educational broadcasting executive*
Grossberg, Michael Lee *theater critic, writer*
Johnston, Jeffery W. *publishing executive*
Kefauver, Weldon Addison *publisher*
Kiefer, Gary *newspaper editor*
Massie, Robert Joseph *publishing company executive*
Mitchell, Carol Elaine *publishing executive, writer, educator*
Murphy, Andrew J. *managing news editor*
Ouzts, Dale Keith *broadcast executive*
Schiavo, Mary Fackler *news consultant, lawyer, educator*
Sherrill, Thomas Boykin, III *retired newspaper publishing executive*
Strode, George K. *sports editor*
Tabor, Mary Leeba *literary magazine editor, author*
Weaver, Leah Ann *journalist, speech writer*
Weisgerber, David Wendelin *editor, chemist*

**Dayton**
Cawood, Albert McLaurin (Hap Cawood) *newspaper editor*
Huffman, Dale *journalist*
Matheny, Ruth Ann *editor*
Peterson, Skip (Orley R. Peterson, III) *newspaper photographer*
Siegel, Ira T. *publishing executive*
Tillson, John Bradford, Jr. *newspaper publisher*

**Defiance**
Thiede, Richard Wesley *communications educator*

**Kent**
†Andrews, Charles Forrest *radio station official*

**Newark**
Hopson, James Warren *publishing executive*

**Oxford**
Sanders, Gerald Hollie *communications educator*

**Pepper Pike**
Vail, Thomas Van Husen *retired newspaper publisher and editor*

**Perrysburg**
Schwier, Priscilla Lamb Guyton *television broadcasting company executive*

**Reynoldsburg**
Powell, Edward Lee *broadcasting company executive*

**Sidney**
Laurence, Michael Marshall *magazine publisher, writer*
Lawrence, Wayne Allen *publisher*
Stevens, Robert Jay *magazine editor*

**Springfield**
Maddex, Myron Brown (Mike Maddex) *broadcasting executive*

**Sunbury**
Jinks-Weidner, Janie *editor*

**Toledo**
Block, John Robinson *newspaper publisher*
Block, William K., Jr. *newspaper executive*
Rosenbaum, Kenneth E. *journalist, editor*
Royhab, Ronald *journalist, newspaper editor*
Stankey, Suzanne M. *editor*
Willey, John Douglas *retired newspaper executive*

**Waterville**
Brumbaugh, Kathleen Semo *journalist, historian, lay minister*

**Willoughby**
Campbell, Talmage Alexander *newspaper editor*

**Wooster**
August, Robert Olin *journalist*

**Youngstown**
Przelomski, Anastasia Nemenyi *retired newspaper editor*

## OKLAHOMA

**Afton**
Starbird, Lonnie Darryl *producer of custom car shows, designer and builder of custom automobiles*

**Edmond**
Pydynkowsky, Joan Anne *journalist*

**Norman**
Dary, David Archie *journalism educator, author*
Velie, Lester *journalist*

**Oklahoma City**
Gaylord, Edward Lewis *publishing company executive*
Gourley, James Leland *editor, publishing executive*
Gumm, Jay Paul *media specialist*
Kelley, Carl Ed(win) *editor*
Triplett, E. Eugene *editor*

**Sapulpa**
Geeslin, Robert Hawk *educational programming company executive*

**Tulsa**
Bender, John Henry, Jr. (Jack Bender) *editor, cartoonist*
Hale, Richard Lee *magazine editor*
Haring, Robert Westing *newspaper editor*
Jones, Jenk, Jr. *editor, educator*
Jones, Jenkin Lloyd *retired newspaper publisher*
Major, John Keene *radio broadcasting executive*
Payne, William Haydon *broadcasting executive*
Upton, Howard B., Jr. *management writer, lawyer*

## OREGON

**Albany**
Wood, Kenneth Arthur *retired newspaper editor, writer*

**Coquille**
Taylor, George Frederick *newspaper publisher, editor*

**Corvallis**
Hall, Don Alan *editor, writer*
Zwahlen, Fred Casper, Jr. *journalism educator*

**Eugene**
Baker, Alton Fletcher, Jr. *retired newspaper publisher and editor*
Baker, Alton Fletcher, III *newspaper editor, publishing executive*
Baker, Bridget Downey *newspaper executive*
Baker, Edwin Moody *retired newspaper publisher*
Franklin, Jon Daniel *writer, journalist, educator*
Hess, Suzanne Harriet *newspaper administrator, photographer*
Ismach, Arnold Harvey *journalism educator*
Sherriffs, Ronald Everett *communication and film educator*
Tykeson, Donald Erwin *broadcasting executive*

**Gleneden Beach**
Marks, Arnold *journalist*

**Gresham**
Caldwell, Robert John *newspaper editor*

**Portland**
Bhatia, Peter K. *editor, journalist*
Crabbs, Roger Alan *publisher, consultant, small business owner, educator*
Graves, Earl William, Jr. *journalist*
Johnston, Virginia Evelyn *editor*
Loewenthal, Nessa Parker *communications educator*
Mapes, Jeffrey Robert *journalist*
Murphy, Francis Seward *journalist*
Rowe, Sandra Mims *newspaper editor*
Sterling, Donald Justus, Jr. *retired newspaper editor*
Stickel, Frederick A. *publisher*
Stickel, Patrick Francis *publishing executive, newspaper*
Woodward, Stephen Richard *newspaper reporter*

**Salem**
Mainwaring, William Lewis *publishing company executive, author*
Wallace, Julia Diane *newspaper editor*

**Tigard**
Nokes, John Richard *retired newspaper editor, author*

**Waldport**
Lemert, James Bolton *journalist, educator*

**Wallowa**
Wizard, Brian *publisher, author*

## PENNSYLVANIA

**Albrightsville**
Wilson, George Wharton *newspaper editor*

**Allentown**
Cavett, Van Andrew *journalist*
Shorts, Gary K. *newspaper publisher*

**Bala Cynwyd**
Field, Joseph Myron *broadcast executive*
Kates, Gerald Saul *printing executive*
Schwartz, Charles D. *broadcast executive*

**Bensalem**
Kang, Benjamin Toyeong *writer, clergyman*

**Bryn Mawr**
Broido, Arnold Peace *music publishing company executive*

**Carlisle**
Fish, Chester Boardman, Jr. *retired publishing consultant, writer*
Talley, Carol Lee *newspaper editor*

**Clarion**
Siddiqui, Dilnawaz Ahmed *communications educator, international communication planning advisor, consultant*

**Clearfield**
Krebs, Margaret Eloise *publishing executive*
Ulerich, William Keener *publishing company executive*

**Coudersport**
†Rigas, John *broadcast executive*

**Doylestown**
Morgnanesi, Lanny M. *journalist*
Smith, Charles Paul *newspaper publisher*

**Easton**
Mamana, Joseph *editor*
Stitt, Dorothy Jewett *journalist*

**Emmaus**
Beldon, Sanford T. *publisher*
Bricklin, Mark Harris *magazine editor, publisher*
Lafavore, Michael J. *magazine editor*
Rodale, Ardath *publishing executive*
†Vaughn, Lewis A. *magazine editor, writer*

**Erwinna**
Richman, Joan F. *television consultant*

**Felton**
Shoemaker, Eleanor Boggs *television production company executive*

**Flourtown**
Lee, Adrian Iselin, Jr. *journalist*

**Greensburg**
Harrell, Edward Harding *newspaper executive*

**Harrisburg**
Carnahan, Frances Morris *magazine editor*
DeKok, David *writer, reporter*
Gover, Raymond Lewis *newspaper publisher*
Huntington, Thomas Mansfield *editor*

**Haverford**
Jurney, Dorothy Misener *journalist, editor*

**Hawley**
Conley, Clare Dean *retired magazine editor*

**Hellertown**
McCullagh, James Charles *publishing company executive*

**Honesdale**
Brown, Kent Louis, Jr. *magazine editor*
Clark, Christine May *editor, author*

**Horsham**
Beyland, Mark *publishing company executive*
Dariano, Joseph *publishing company executive*

**Huntingdon Valley**
Antonell, Walter John *publishing executive*

**King Of Prussia**
Brown, Emma Jean (EJ Brown) *medical editor, journalist*
Enge, Vernon Reier *editor health care publications*

**Lancaster**
Cody, William Henry *retired newspaper editor*
Shaw, Charles Raymond *journalist*
Shenk, Willis Weidman *newspaper executive*

**Levittown**
Halberstein, Joseph Leonard *retired associate editor*

**Manheim**
Critz, Richard Laurens *magazine editor, architectural consultant*

**Media**
Lerner, Daniel Merril *broadcasting company executive*

**Montoursville**
Woolever, Naomi Louise *retired editor*

**Oaks**
Lenfest, Harold Fitz Gerald *cable television executive, lawyer*

**Paoli**
Gallagher, Terrence Vincent *editor*

**Philadelphia**
Biddle, Daniel R. *editor, reporter*
Binzen, Peter Husted *columnist*
Boasberg, Leonard W. *reporter*
Boldt, David Rhys *journalist*
Breitenfeld, Frederick, Jr. *public broadcasting executive, educator*
Broom, William Wescott *retired newspaper executive*
Bykofsky, Stuart Debs *newspaper columnist*
Carey, Arthur Bernard, Jr. *editor, writer, columnist*
†Claus, Chris *radio station executive*
Cooper, Richard Lee *newspaper editor, journalist*
†Cortes, Ron *reporter*
Drake, Donald Charles *journalist*
Fancher, Charles B., Jr. *newspaper publishing executive*
Foreman, Gene Clemons *newspaper editor*
Gerbner, George *communications educator, university dean emeritus*
Gross, Larry Paul *communications educator*
Hall, Robert J. *newspaper executive*
Haynes, Gary Allen *photographer, journalist, newspaper editor*
Hillgren, Sonja Dorothy *journalist*
Iams, David Aveling *journalist, columnist*
King, Maxwell E. P. *newspaper editor*
†Klein, Jonathan *broadcast engineer*
Klein, Julia Meredith *newspaper reporter*
Leary, Michael Warren *journalist*
Leiter, Robert Allen *journalist, magazine editor*
Lent, John Anthony *journalist, educator*
Lewis, Claude Aubrey *columnist*
Lyon, William Carl *sports columnist*
Matz, Kenneth H., Jr. *newscaster*
Moore, Acel *journalist*
Morgan, Arlene Notoro *newspaper editor, reporter, recruiter*
Nalle, Peter Devereux *publishing company executive*
Nussbaum, Paul Eugene *journalist*
Othmer, David Artman *television and radio station executive*
Parry, Lance Aaron *newspaper executive*
Patel, Ronald Anthony *newspaper editor*
Porter, Jill *journalist*
Prendergast, John Thomas *editor, writer*
Randall, Roger David *publishing executive*
Rogers, Mary Martin *publishing company executive*
Rosenthal, Robert Jon *newspaper editor, journalist*
Rossi, Steven B. *newspaper publishing executive*
Ryan, Desmond *film critic*
Samsot, Robert Louis *newspaper editor, consultant*
Searcy, Jarrell D. (Jay) *sportswriter*
Shapiro, Howard *newspaper editor*
Spikol, Art *editor, writer, illustrator*
Stalberg, Zachary *newspaper editor*
Storm, Jonathan Morris *television critic*
Tait, Elaine *restaurant critic*
Toolan, Brian Paul *newspaper editor*
Turow, Joseph Gregory *communication educator*
†Vitez, Michael *reporter*
Ward, Hiley Henry *journalist, educator*
Wilkinson, Signe *cartoonist*
Winfrey, Marion Lee *television critic*
Woestendiek, (William) John, Jr. *columnist*

**Pittsburgh**
Alexander, James Eckert *editor*
Apone, Carl Anthony *journalist*
Craig, John Gilbert, Jr. *newspaper editor*
Dillon, W. Daniel *radio broadcast producer*
Graham, Laurie *editor*
Heindl, Mary Lynn *magazine editor*
Johnson, Micah William *television newscaster, director*

Kaplan, John *photojournalist, consultant, educator*
Leo, Peter Andrew *newspaper columnist, writing educator*
Miller, Donald *art critic*
†Pompeani, Bruce Patrick *television reporter*
Roof, Robert L. *broadcast executive, sales executive*
Ross, Madelyn Ann *newspaper editor*
Sauer, Georgia Booras *newspaper writer*
Swann, Lynn Curtis *sportscaster, former professional football player*

**Pottstown**
Kelly, Thomas Joseph, III *photojournalist*

**Radnor**
Baxter, John Michael *editor*
Frankson-Kendrick, Sarah Jane *publisher*

**Reading**
Smith, John Wilson, III *newspaper editor, columnist, statistician*

**Scottdale**
Miller, Levi *publishing administrator*

**Scranton**
Lynett, George Vincent *newspaper publisher*
Lynett, William Ruddy *publishing, broadcasting company executive*
Rogers, Edwin Earl *newspaper editor*

**State College**
Coppersmith Fredman, Marian Ungar *magazine publisher*
Heldman, Louis Marc *newspaper publisher and executive*
Lawrence, Ken *columnist*

**Stroudsburg**
Gasink, Warren Alfred *speech communication educator*

**University Park**
Thatcher, Sanford Gray *publishing executive*

**Villanova**
Lambert, William G. *journalist, consultant*

**Wayne**
Brodsky, Julian A. *broadcasting services, telecommunications company executive*
Youman, Roger Jacob *editor, writer*

**West Chester**
Mahoney, William Francis *editor*
Segel, Joseph M. *broadcasting executive*

**Wynnewood**
Singer, Samuel L(oewenberg) *journalist*

**Yardley**
Zulker, Charles Bates *broadcasting company executive*

## RHODE ISLAND

**Block Island**
Kingsbury, Read Austin *retired journalist*

**Charlestown**
Ungaro, Joseph Michael *newspaper publishing executive, consultant*

**Cranston**
Parravano, Amelia Elizabeth (Amy Beth) *recording industry executive*

**Cumberland**
Wyman, James Vernon *newspaper executive*

**Jamestown**
Potter, Clarkson Nott *publishing consultant*

**Newport**
Holloway, Jerome Knight *publisher, former military strategy educator, retired foreign service officer*

**Providence**
Adler, Jane Eve *columnist, cartoonist and illustrator*
Dujardin, Richard Charles *journalist*
Farmer, Susan Lawson *broadcasting executive, former secretary of state*
Hamblett, Stephen *newspaper publishing executive*
Olmsted, Audrey June *communications educator*
Rosenberg, Alan Gene *newspaper editor*
Sinclair, Joseph Samuels *broadcasting company executive, retail merchant*
Watkins, John Chester Anderson *newspaper publisher*
Whitcomb, Robert Bassett *journalist, editor*

**Warwick**
Blount, William Allan *broadcasting executive*
Halperson, Michael Allen *publishing company executive*

**West Greenwich**
Markowicz, Victor *video company executive*

**West Kingston**
Haring, Howard Jack *newsletter editor*

**Westerly**
Day, Chon *cartoonist*

**Woonsocket**
Eno, Paul Frederick *editor*

## SOUTH CAROLINA

**Bennettsville**
Kinney, William Light, Jr. *newspaper editor, publisher*

**Cayce**
McElveen, William Lindsay *broadcasting executive, lecturer*

**Charleston**
Anderson, Ivan Verner, Jr. *newspaper publisher*
French, Kenneth Wayne *radio station executive, consultant*
Gilbreth, Frank Bunker, Jr. *retired communications executive, writer*
Langley, Lynne Spencer *newspaper editor, columnist*
Manigault, Peter *media executive*
McGee, Hall Thomas, Jr. *newspaper, radio and television executive*
Meggett, Linda Linette *reporter*
Reed, Stanley Foster *editor, writer, publisher, lecturer*
Schreadley, Richard Lee *writer, retired newspaper editor*
Spence, Edward Lee *publisher, historian, archaeologist*
Tarleton, Larry Wilson *newspaper editor*
Wilcox, Arthur Manigault *newspaper editor*
Wyrick, Charles Lloyd, Jr. *publisher, writer, editor*

**Columbia**
Fry, Catherine Howard *publishing executive*
Gray, Katherine Wilson *newspaper editor*
McNeely, Patricia Gantt *journalism educator*
Osman, Mary Ella Williams *journal editor*
Rone, William Eugene, Jr. *newspaper editor, retired*
Thelen, Gil *newspaper editor*

**Easley**
Failing, George Edgar *editor, clergyman, educator*
Urakami, Akio *manufacturing company executive*

**Greenville**
Eskew, Rhea Taliaferro *newspaper publisher*
Lloyd, Wanda Smalls *newspaper editor*

**Hilton Head Island**
Baumgardner, Barbara Borke *publishing consultant*
McKinney, Donald Lee *magazine editor*

**Landrum**
Pauley, Robert Reinhold *broadcasting executive, financial executive*
Wyche, Samuel David *sportscaster*

**Moncks Corner**
Morris, Henry Allen, Jr. *publisher*

**Orangeburg**
Sims, Edward Howell *editor, publisher*

**Simpsonville**
Gilstrap, Leah Ann *media specialist*

**Winnsboro**
King, Robert Thomas *editor, free-lance writer*

## SOUTH DAKOTA

**Minot**
Larson, Michael Len *newspaper editor*

**Sioux Falls**
Garson, Arnold Hugh *newspaper publisher*
Marsh, John S., Jr. *newspaper editor*

## TENNESSEE

**Brentwood**
Flanagan, Van Kent *journalist*
Hearn, Billy Ray *recording industry executive*

**Chattanooga**
Anderson, Lee Stratton *newspaper publisher, editor*
Holmberg, Albert William, Jr. *publishing company executive*
Holmberg, Ruth Sulzberger *publishing company executive*
MacManus, Yvonne Cristina *editor, videoscripter, writer, consultant*
Neely, Paul *newspaper editor*

**Corryton**
Hooper, William Edward *broadcast journalist*

**Knoxville**
Ambrester, Marcus LaRoy *communication educator, program administrator*
Hohenberg, John *journalist, educator*
Rukeyser, William Simon *journalist*
Teeter, Dwight Leland, Jr. *journalism educator*

**La Vergne**
†Ingram, John *publishing company executive*

**Maryville**
Bradford, Tutt Sloan *retired publisher*
Stone, Hubert Dean *editor, journalist*

**Mc Minnville**
Martin, Ron *editor, superintendent of schools, consultant, minister*

**Memphis**
Brooks, Kathleen *journalist*
Emery, Sue McHam *bulletin editor, owner bridge studio*
Griffin, Tom *former editor, writer*
McEachran, Angus *newspaper editor*
Ramirez, Michael P. *editorial cartoonist*
Smith, Whitney Bousman *music and drama critic*
Stokes, Henry Arthur *journalist*
Yawn, David McDonald *journalist*

**Murfreesboro**
Wyatt, Robert Odell *journalism educator*

**Nashville**
Allbritton, Cliff *national consultant*
Atkins, Chester Burton *record company executive, guitarist, publisher*
Battle, William Robert (Bob Battle) *newspaper executive*
Boyd, Theophilus Bartholomew, III *publishing company executive*
Du Bois, Tim *recording industry executive*
Frey, Herman S. *publishing company executive*
Green, Lisa Cannon *business editor*
Hieronymus, Clara Booth Wiggins *journalist*
Mayhew, Aubrey *music industry executive*
Rayburn, Ted Rye *newspaper editor*
Roberts, Sandra *editor*
Russell, Fred McFerrin *journalist, author, lawyer*
Sherborne, Robert *editor*
Stone, Lawrence Mynatt *publishing executive*
Sutherland, Frank *publishing executive, editor*

**Ooltewah**
Harris, Pamela Maize *journalism educator*

**Waynesboro**
Davis, Sharon Denise (Sherry Davis) *editor*

## TEXAS

**Abilene**
Boyll, David Lloyd *broadcasting company executive*

**Amarillo**
Spies, Dennis J. *editor*

**Austin**
Carpenter, Elizabeth Sutherland *journalist, author, equal rights leader, lecturer*
Conine, Ernest *newspaper commentator, writer*
Danielson, Wayne Allen *journalism and computer science educator*
Fischer, Norman, Jr. *media broker, appraiser, broadcast consultant*
Ivins, Molly *columnist, writer*
Levy, Michael Richard *publishing executive*
Matthews, Jay Arlon, Jr. *publisher, editor*
Mayes, Wendell Wise, Jr. *broadcasting company executive*
Spielman, Barbara Helen New *editor, consultant*
Teague, Hyman Faris *former publishing company executive*

**Beaumont**
†Brejot, John *radio station executive*

**Bedford**
Lieber, David Leslie *journalist*

**Canyon Lake**
Phelan, Charlotte Robertson *journalist, book critic*

**College Station**
Kern-Foxworth, Marilyn Louise *journalism educator*
Rotell, Thomas M. *publishing executive*

**Corpus Christi**
Harte, Edward Holmead *retired newspaper publisher*
House, David Augusta *newspaper editor*

**Dallas**
Allison, Stephen Galender *broadcast executive*
Anders, John *newspaper columnist*
Ardoin, John Louis *music editor*
Bailon, Gilbert *newspaper editor*
Bersano, Bob *newspaper editor*
Blackistone, Kevin *sports columnist*
Blow, Steve *newspaper columnist*
Blumenthal, Karen *newspaper executive*
Brown, Stephen Bryan *real estate editor*
Burns, Scott *columnist*
Compton, Robert D. *newspaper editor*
Cox, James William *newspaper executive*
Creany, Cathleen Annette *television station executive*
Cummins, James Duane *correspondant, media executive*
†Davis, Gregory T. *radio station executive*
Decherd, Robert William *newspaper and broadcasting executive*
DeOre, Bill *editorial cartoonist*
Dillon, David Anthony *journalist, lecturer*
Dufner, Edward Joseph *business newswriter*
Enix, Agnes Lucille *editorial consultant*
Evans, William Wilson *journalism educator, retired newspaper editor*
Fiddick, Paul William *broadcasting company executive*
Finn, Peter Michael *television production executive*
Flournoy, John Craig *newspaper reporter*
Galloway, Randy *newspaper sports columnist*
†Glade, Thomas *radio station executive*
Glines, Carroll Vane, Jr. *magazine editor*
Griffith, Dotty (Dorothy Griffith Stephenson) *journalist, speaker*
Halbreich, Jeremy L. *newspaper publishing executive*
Hall, Cheryl *newspaper editor*
Harasta, Cathy Ann *journalist*
Holmes, Bert Otis E., Jr. *retired newspaperman*
Huey, Ward L(igon), Jr. *media executive*
Jordan, Karen Leigh *newspaper travel editor*
Kessler, Tom *newspaper editor*
Klehfoth, Jay Gordon *publisher, writer, consultant*
Kutner, Janet *art critic, book reviewer*
Langer, Ralph Ernest *journalist, newspaper executive and editor*
Livingston, Grover D. *newspaper publishing executive*
Maza, Michael William *newspaper editor, columnist*
McCormick, James Hillman *retired broadcast executive*
Osborne, Burl *newspaper publisher, editor*
Patterson, Ronald Paul *publishing company executive, clergyman*
Pederson, Rena *newspaper editor*
Powell, Larry Randall *columnist*
Ryan, Timothy Christopher *anchor, reporter*
St. John, Bob *journalist, columnist, author*
Schwartz, Marilyn *columnist*
Siegfried, Tom *newspaper editor*
Smith, David Lee *newspaper editor*
Smith, Nancy Lynne *journalist, real estate agent*
Smith, Sue Frances *newspaper editor*
†Snyder, William D. *photojournalist*
Sweeney, Mark Owen *publisher*
Weinkauf, William Carl *communications company executive*
Wuntch, Philip Samuels *journalist, film critic*

**Denton**
Vick, Frances Brannen *publishing executive*

**Dripping Springs**
Rios, Evelyn Deerwester *columnist, musician, artist, writer*

**El Paso**
Ingle, Henry Thomas *communications educator, university administrator*
Treadwell, Hugh Wilson *publishing executive*
†Vines, Georgiana Fry *editor*

**Fort Worth**
Buckley, Betty Bob *journalist, consultant*
Eliasoph, Jeffrey Paul *television news anchor*
Malone, Dan F. *journalist*
Martin, Harold Eugene *publishing executive, consultant*
Peipert, James Raymond *journalist*
Price, Debbie Mitchell *journalist, newspaper editor*
Price, Michael Howard *journalist, critic, composer, cartoonist*
Record, Phillip Julius *newspaper executive*
Tinsley, Jackson Bennett *newspaper editor*

**Grand Prairie**
Childs, Hymen *broadcasting corporation executive*

**Houston**
Aguilar, Melissa Ward *newspaper editor*
Barlow, Jim B. *newspaper columnist*
Beck, Robert James *editor, energy economist, author, consultant*
Bischoff, Susan Ann *newspaper editor*
Boudreaux, Bob *broadcast journalist*
Bunch, Fred *newspaper picture editor*
Carlquist, Robert E. *newspaper publishing executive*
Clark, Scott *newspaper editor*
†Clarke, Jeff *television station executive*
Criswell, Ann *newspaper editor*
†de Castro, Jimmy *radio station executive*
Frieden, Kit *newspaper editor*
†Ganter, Garland *radio station executive*
George, Deveral D. *editor, journalist, advertising consultant*
Gerraughty, David R. *newspaper editor*
Gray, Robert Steele *publishing executive, editor*
Griffin, Oscar O'Neal, Jr. *writer, former oil company executive*
Hale, Leon *newspaper columnist*
Hammond, Ken *newspaper magazine editor*
Heinsen, Lindsay *newspaper editor*
Henry, John Cooper *journalist*
Hobby, William Pettus *broadcast executive, retired*
Hodges, Ann *television editor, newspaper columnist*
Holmes, Ann Hitchcock *journalist*
Holmes, Cecile Searson *religion editor*
†Howard, Allan E. *television station executive*
†Jackson, Ernest, Jr. *broadcasting executive*
Jetton, Steve *newspaper editor*
Johnson, Richard James Vaughan *newspaper executive*
Johnston, Marguerite *journalist, author*
Kientz, Renee *newspaper editor*
Loftis, Jack D. *newspaper editor, newspaper executive*
Marshall, Jane Pretzer *newspaper editor*
Marshall, Thom *columnist*
Mc David, George Eugene (Gene Mc David) *newspaper executive*
†McNair, Robert C. *communications executive*
Millar, Jeffery Lynn *columnist*
Newman, Mary Thomas *communications educator, management consultant*
Oren, Bruce Clifford *newspaper editor, artist*
Pederson, Tony Weldon *newspaper editor*
Powers, Hugh William *newspaper executive*
Read, Michael Oscar *editor, consultant*
Sweeney, John W., III *newspaper executive*
Walbridge, Willard Eugene *broadcasting executive*
Walls, Carmage *newspaper publishing executive*
Walls, Martha Ann Williams (Mrs. B. Carmage Walls) *newspaper executive*
Ward, David Henry (Dave Ward) *television news reporter*
†Wasserman, Steve *broadcast executive*
Weber, Owen *broadcast executive*

**Irving**
Halter, Jon Charles *magazine editor, writer*
†Owen, Joe David *editor*

**Kelly A F B**
Stringer, Jerry Ray *magazine editor*

**Kerrville**
Dozier, William Everett, Jr. *newspaper editor and publisher*
Harkey, Ira Brown, Jr. *newspaperman, educator, author*
Williams, William Henry, II *publisher*

**Lewisville**
Vacca, John Joseph, Jr. *television executive*

**Livingston**
Perkins, Sue Dene *editor*

**Mesquite**
Mc Gregor, Donald Thornton *newspaper editor, journalist*

**Mount Pleasant**
Palmer, Robert Blunden *newspaper, printing executive*

**Plano**
Brock, Dee Sala *television executive, educator, writer, consultant*
Senderling, Jon Townsend *journalist, public affairs specialist*

**Port Aransas**
Noble, James Kendrick, Jr. *media industry consultant*

**San Antonio**
Belgin, Harvey Harry *photojournalist*
Davis, Jolene Bryant *magazine publishing executive*
†Emerson, Arthur *broadcast executive*
†Giust, Steve *television station executive*

PROFESSIONAL INDEX 5129 COMMUNICATIONS MEDIA

†Gwathmey, Joe Neil, Jr. *broadcasting executive*
Harte, Houston Harriman *newspaper, broadcasting executive*
†Jones, Jay, II *radio station executive*
†Joslyn, James *television station executive*
Kilpatrick, Charles Otis *newspaper editor, publisher*
†Kocurek, Betty *radio station executive*
Lenke, Joanne Marie *publishing executive*
Luter, John *news correspondent, educator*
Mammen, Sam *publishing executive, entrepreneur*
Manning, Noel Thomas *publishing company executive*
Marbut, Robert Gordon *communications and broadcast executive*
†Marrou, Chris René *television newscaster*
Mays, Lester Lowry *broadcast executive*
Michaels, Willard A. (Bill Michaels) *retired broadcasting executive*
Ostmo, David Charles *broadcasting executive*
Polunsky, Bob A. *movie critic, talk show host*
†Walker, W. Lawrence, Jr. *newspaper publishing executive*
Yerkes, Susan Gamble *newspaper columnist*

**Schulenburg**
Clark, I. E. *publisher*

**Spring**
Mohalley, Patricia JoAnn *library media specialist*

**Stephenville**
King, Clyde Richard *journalism educator, writer*

**The Woodlands**
Anderson, Dale *film production executive*
Logan, Mathew Kuykendall *journalist*

**Tyler**
Berry, David Val *newspaper editor*

**Waco**
Preddy, Raymond Randall *retired newspaper publisher, educator*

**Winnsboro**
Boyd, Joe Dan *journal editor*

## UTAH

**Midway**
Zenger, John Hancock *retired publishing company executive*

**Ogden**
Larson, Brent T. *broadcasting executive*
Trundle, W(infield) Scott *publishing executive newspaper*

**Provo**
Bennett, Bill *publishing company executive*
Tata, Giovanni *publishing executive*

**Salt Lake City**
Brady, Rodney Howard *broadcast company executive, holding company executive, former college president, former government official*
Brown, Carolyn Smith *communications educator, consultant*
Christiansen, Joyce L. Soelberg *newspaper editor*
Fehr, J. Will *newspaper editor*
Gale, G(len) Donald *broadcast company executive*
Gallivan, John William *publisher*
Hatch, George Clinton *television executive*
Hatch, Wilda Gene *broadcast company executive*
Mortimer, William James *newspaper publisher*
Robison, Barbara Ann *retired newspaper editor*
Shelledy, James Edwin, III *editor*
Smith, Donald E. *broadcast engineer, manager*

**Sandy**
Fullmer, Timothy Shawn *printing company executive*

## VERMONT

**Barre**
Falzarano, James Vincent *newspaper editor*

**Bennington**
Brownell, David Wheaton *editor*

**Burlington**
Guma, Greg William *editor, writer, administrator*

**Calais**
Elmslie, Kenward Gray *publishing company executive, writer*

**Charlotte**
†Monsarrat, Nicholas *newspaper editor, writer*

**Chester**
Coleman, John Royston *newspaper publisher*

**Colchester**
Green, Hope Stuart *public television executive*

**Dorset**
Ketchum, Richard Malcolm *editor, writer*

**Hartland Four Corners**
Brady, Upton Birnie *editor, literary agent*

**Lincoln**
Kompass, Edward John *consulting editor*

**Montpelier**
Good, Jeffrey *journalist*

**Perkinsville**
Harris, Christopher *publisher, designer, editor*

**Saint Johnsbury**
Mandelstein, Paul Stanley *book publishing executive*

**South Woodstock**
Crowl, John Allen *retired publishing company executive*

**White River Junction**
Rutter, Frances Tompson *publisher*

**Winooski**
Wilson, Mary Louise *publishing executive*

## VIRGINIA

**Alexandria**
†Agronsky, Martin Zama *radio and TV news analyst*
Brownfeld, Allan Charles *columnist*
Comeau, Kathy Darr *publishing executive*
Fichenberg, Robert Gordon *newspaper editor, consultant*
Fleming, Douglas Riley *journalist, publisher, public affairs consultant*
Foster, Robert Francis *communications executive*
Francis, Samuel Todd *columnist*
Hewitt, Charles C. *broadcast executive*
Hobbs, Michael Edwin *broadcasting company executive*
Hume, Ellen Hunsberger *broadcast executive, media analyst, journalist*
Radewagen, Fred *publisher, organization executive*
Wright, Mary James *multimedia instructional designer*
Yoder, Edwin Milton, Jr. *columnist, educator, editor, writer*

**Arlington**
Adams, John Hanly *retired magazine editor, writer, consultant*
Berry, Fred Clifton, Jr. *author, magazine editor, book packager*
Bodley, Harley Ryan, Jr. *editor, writer, broadcaster*
Bullard, Marcia Lynn *publishing executive*
Bussmann, Charles Haines *publisher*
Clayton, James Edwin *journalist*
Cole, Benjamin Richason *newspaper executive*
Crittenden, Danielle Ann *editor, journalist*
Curley, John J. *diversified media company executive*
Curley, Thomas *newspaper executive*
Curtis, Richard A. *newspaper editor*
DeFrancesco, Gerry *broadcasting company executive*
Feller, Mimi *newspaper publishing executive*
†Gabrielson, Charles *publishing executive*
Giles, Scott Andrew *federal agency staff member*
Gniewek, Raymond Louis *newspaper editor*
Jurgensen, Karen *newspaper editor*
Lester, Barnett Benjamin *editor, foreign affairs officer*
Lorell, Monte *newspaper editor*
MacDougall, William Lowell *magazine editor*
MacNeil, Robert Breckenridge Ware *retired broadcast journalist*
Marks, Robert Hutchinson *publishing executive*
Marshall, James John *publishing executive*
Mater, Gene P. *communications consultant*
Mazzarella, David *newspaper editor*
McNamara, Tom *newspaper editor*
McWethy, John Fleetwood *journalist*
Mirrielees, James Fay, III *publishing executive*
Neikirk, William Robert *journalist*
Neuharth, Allen Harold *newspaper publisher*
Obermayer, Herman Joseph *newspaper publisher*
Palor, John *media group executive*
Perry, Bill *photojournalist*
Porter, Barbara *anchorwoman, writer, educator*
Quinn, John Collins *publishing executive, newspaper editor*
Reiss, Susan Marie *editor, writer*
Ritter, Hal *newspaper editor*
Rockefeller, Sharon Percy *broadcast executive*
Seamans, Andrew Charles *editorial and public relations consultant, columnist, author*
Simonson, David C. *retired newspaper association executive*
Simpson, John Mathes *newspaper editor*
Stanley, Scott, Jr. *editor*
Sullivan, Terry T. *newspaper publishing executive*
Tanzer, Lester *editor*
Terzian, Grace Paine *publisher*
Tyrrell, Robert Emmett, Jr. *editor-in-chief, writer*
Vesper, Carolyn F. *newspaper publishing executive*
Webb, Clifton Alan *media consultant*
Weiss, Susan *newspaper editor*
Willenson, Kim Jeremy *publisher, journalist, author*

**Charlottesville**
Foard, Susan Lee *editor*
Loo, Beverly Jane *publishing company executive*
Mayes, Bernard Duncan *broadcast journalist, educator, dramatist*
McQueeney, Thomas A. *publisher*
Parrish, David Walker, Jr. *legal publishing company executive*
Worrell, Anne Everette Rowell *newspaper publisher*

**Chesapeake**
Collins, Carolyn Herman *school media specialist, legislative aide*

**Culpeper**
Utnik, David Alan *newspaper editor, journalist*

**Dulles**
Pittman, Robert Warren *entertainment executive*

**Faber**
Friede, Eleanor Kask *editor, publisher*

**Fairfax**
Lipton, Eric *reporter*

**Falls Church**
Benton, Nicholas Frederick *publisher*
Cromley, Allan Wray *journalist*
Green, Gerald *editor, consultant*
Kaplow, Herbert Elias *journalist*
Stone, Marvin Lawrence *journalist, government official*

**Fredericksburg**
Rowe, Charles Spurgeon *newspaper publishing and broadcasting executive*

**Great Falls**
Garrett, Wilbur (Bill) *magazine editor*

**Hampton**
Barnes, Myrtle Sue Snyder *editor*
Coombs, Vanessa Moody *journalism educator, lawyer*

**Harrisonburg**
Rollman, Steven Allan *communication educator*

**Herndon**
Scripps, Edward Wyllis *newspaper publisher*

**Lively**
Gallimore, Robert Stephenson *news service executive*

**Luray**
Burzynski, Norman Stephen *editor*

**Manassas**
Wilson, Robert Spencer *magazine editor*

**Mc Lean**
Fromm, Joseph *retired magazine editor, foreign affairs consultant*
Salzinger, Mark Alan *editor, violinist*
Wong, Andrew *telecommunications company executive*

**Middleburg**
Evans, John Derby *telecommunications company executive*

**Midlothian**
Chapman, Gilbert Whipple, Jr. *publishing company executive*

**Mineral**
Speer, Jack Atkeson *publisher*

**Moneta**
Armistead, Moss William, III *retired newspaper executive*

**Mount Vernon**
Brownson, Anna Louise Harshman *publishing executive, editor*

**Newport News**
Davis, Jack Wayne, Jr. *newspaper publisher*
Kale, Wallace Wilford, Jr. *journalist, communicator, administrator*
Perry, Donald A. *cable television consultant*

**Norfolk**
Barry, Richard Francis, III *media executive*
Batten, Frank *newspaper publisher, cable broadcaster*
Bonko, Larry Walter *columnist, writer, radio personality*
Fitzpatrick, William Henry *retired journalist*
Power, Edward Francis *broadcast executive*
Ritter, Alfred Francis, Jr. *communications executive*
Sizemore, William Howard, Jr. *newspaper editor*
Wynne, John Oliver *newspaper, broadcast and cable executive*

**Radford**
Thomas, Robert Wilburn *broadcasting and advertising executive*
Wille, Lois Jean *retired newspaper editor*

**Reston**
Mallette, Malcolm Francis *newspaper editor, educator*
Miller, Donald Lane *publishing executive*
Pyle, Thomas Alton *instructional television and motion picture executive*

**Richmond**
Baker, Donald Parks *journalist, educator*
Bryan, David Tennant *media company executive*
Bryan, John Stewart, III *newspaper publisher*
Bustard, Clarke *music critic, newswriter, radio producer*
Estes, Gerald Walter *newspaper executive*
Goodykoontz, Charles Alfred *newspaper editor, retired*
Mackenzie, Ross *newspaper editor*
Neman, Daniel Louis *movie critic*
Owen, Howard Wayne *journalist, writer*
Robertson, William Franklin *publishing executive*
Seals, Margaret Louise *newspaper editor*
Smith, Ted Jay, III *mass communications educator*

**Roanoke**
Beagle, Benjamin Stuart, Jr. *columnist*
Landon, Forrest Malcolm *retired newspaper executive*
Rugaber, Walter Feucht, Jr. *newspaper executive*
Warren, William Kermit *electronic publishing consultant*

**Springfield**
Doyle, James Stephen *publishing company executive, journalist*
Hastings, Melanie (Melanie Jean Wotring) *television news anchor*
Hillis, John David *television news executive, producer, writer*
†Norman, Jean Reid *journalist*
Rankin, Jacqueline Annette *communications expert, educator*

**Sterling**
Sabosik, Patricia Elizabeth *publisher, editor*
Sanfelici, Arthur H(ugo) *editor, writer*

**Tazewell**
Garner, June Brown *journalist*

**Vienna**
Blevins, Charles Russell *publishing executive*
Lewis, Boyd De Wolf *publisher,editor, writer*
Mc Arthur, George *journalist*
McKinley, Sarah Elizabeth *journalist*
Miller, Claire Ellen *periodical editor*
Strohm, Robert Dean *publications executive*

**Virginia Beach**
Christy, Larry Todd *publisher*
Green, Barbara-Marie *publisher, journalist, poet*
Robertson, Pat (Marion Gordon Robertson) *religious broadcasting executive*
Robertson, Timothy B. *cable television executive*
Smith, A. Robert *editor, author*

**Williamsburg**
Winstead, Joy *journalist, consultant*

**Winchester**
Byrd, Harry Flood, Jr. *newspaper executive, former senator*

## WASHINGTON

**Bellevue**
Berkley, James Donald *clergyman*
Smith, Lester Martin *broadcasting executive*

**Bellingham**
Doerper, John Erwin *publisher, editor*

**Edmonds**
Owen, John *retired newspaper editor*

**Lynnwood**
Araki, Takaharu *editor, mineralogist, crystallographer, consultant*

**Port Townsend**
Buhler, Jill Lorie *editor, writer*

**Pullman**
Davis, Fred *journalist, educator*

**Redmond**
Welke, Elton Grinnell, Jr. *publisher, writer*

**Seattle**
Anderson, Ross *columnist*
Bargreen, Melinda Lueth *music critic*
Blethen, Frank A. *newspaper publisher*
Blethen, William Kingsley, Jr. *newspaper publishing executive*
Boardman, David *newspaper editor*
Buckner, Philip Franklin *newspaper publisher*
Cameron, Mindy *newspaper editor*
Cochran, Wendell *science editor*
Crumb, Robert *cartoonist*
Culp, Mildred Louise *corporate executive*
Dietrich, William Alan *reporter*
Ellegood, Donald Russell *publishing executive*
†Espinoza, Lynn R. *journalist*
Fancher, Michael Reilly *newspaper editor, newspaper publishing executive*
Godden, Jean W. *columnist*
Gouldthorpe, Kenneth Alfred Percival *publisher, state official*
Grimley, Janet Elizabeth *newspaper editor*
Gwinn, Mary Ann *newspaper reporter*
Hartl, John George *film critic*
Henkel, Cathy *newspaper sports editor*
Hills, Regina J. *journalist*
Johnson, Wayne Eaton *writer, editor, former drama critic*
Kelly, Carolyn Sue *newspaper executive*
Lacitis, Erik *journalist*
Medved, Michael *film critic, author*
Nalder, Eric Christopher *investigative reporter*
Nash, Cynthia Jeanne *journalist*
Payne, Ancil Horace *retired broadcasting executive*
Rinearson, Peter Mark *journalist, author, software developer*
Sizemore, Herman Mason, Jr. *newspaper executive*
Stanton, Michael John *newspaper editor*
Thiel, Arthur Warren *journalist*
Turner, Wallace L. *reporter*
Voorhees, John Lloyd *columnist*

**Snohomish**
Frohnen, Richard Gene *journalism educator*

**Spokane**
Cowles, William Stacey *publisher*
Gray, Alfred Orren *journalism educator, communications specialist*
Kafentzis, John Charles *journalist, educator*
Kunkel, Richard Lester *public radio executive*
Steele, Karen Dorn *journalist*

**Tacoma**
Shipman, Keith Bryan *sportscaster*

**Vancouver**
Campbell, Scott *newspaper publishing company executive*

## WEST VIRGINIA

**Charleston**
Chilton, Elizabeth Easley Early *newspaper executive*
Grimes, Richard Stuart *editor, writer*
Haught, James Albert, Jr. *journalist, newspaper editor, author*
Keith, Steven Jeffrey *newspaper editor*

**Clarksburg**
Highland, Cecil Blaine, Jr. *newspaper publisher, lawyer, banker*

**Greenville**
Warner, Kenneth Wilson, Jr. *editor, association publications executive*

**Huntington**
Reynolds, Marshall Truman *printing company executive*

**Kearneysville**
Le Roy, L. David *journalist*

**Morgantown**
Gelhausen, Marvin Duane *editor*

**Pineville**
Maxey, Nigel Aaron *publisher*

**Shepherdstown**
Snyder, Joseph John *editor, historian, author, lecturer, consultant*
Wilson, Miriam Janet Williams *publishing executive*

**Wheeling**
Nutting, George Ogden *newspaper publisher*

## WISCONSIN

**Brookfield**
Lessiter, Frank Donald *magazine editor*

**Fort Atkinson**
Knox, William David *publishing company executive*
Meyer, Eugene Carlton *retired editor*
Sager, Donald Jack *publisher, former librarian*

**Green Bay**
Daley, Arthur James *retired magazine publisher*
Poppenhagen, Ronald William *newspaper editor, publishing executive*

**Iola**
Krause, Chester Lee *publishing company executive*
Mishler, Clifford Leslie *publisher*

**Janesville**
Fitzgerald, James Francis *cable television executive*

**Madison**
Burgess, James Edward *newspaper publisher, executive*
Denton, Frank M. *newspaper editor*
Dunwoody, Sharon Lee *journalism and communications educator*
Evanson, Elizabeth Moss *editor*
Fitchen, Allen Nelson *publisher*
Hachten, William Andrews *journalism educator, author*
Haslanger, Philip Charles *journalist*
Hoyt, James Lawrence *journalism educator, athletic administrator*
McNelly, John Taylor *journalist, educator*
Miller, Frederick William *publisher, lawyer*
Still, Thomas Wayne *newspaper editor, columnist*
Wineke, William Robert *reporter, clergyman*
Wolman, J. Martin *retired newspaper publisher*
Zweifel, David Alan *newspaper editor*

**Middleton**
Wills, Robert Hamilton *retired newspaper executive*

**Milwaukee**
Armstrong, Douglas Dean *journalist*
Auer, James Matthew *art critic, journalist*
Behrendt, David Frogner *journalist*
Farris, Trueman Earl, Jr. *retired newspaper editor*
Fibich, Howard Raymond *retired newspaper editor*
Foster, Richard *journalist*
Garbaciak-Bobber, Joyce Katherine *news anchor*
Hinshaw, Edward Banks *broadcasting company executive*
Hoffmann, Gregg J. *journalist, author*
Huston, Margo *journalist*
†Jake, Richard *editor periodicals*
Jaques, Damien Paul *theater critic*
Joslyn, Jay Thomas *retired arts critic*
Kritzer, Paul Eric *media executive, communications lawyer*
Leonard, Richard Hart *journalist*
McCann, Dennis John *columnist*
Meier, Kenneth J. *political science journal editor*
Reedy, George Edward *educator, author, lecturer*
Schaleben, Arville *newspaper editor, writer, educator*
†Sullivan, Edward *periodical editor*
Taylor, Robin Lynn *anchorperson, reporter*
†Wisniewski, Robert Jude *publishing company sales and marketing executive*

**Montello**
Burns, Robert Edward *editor, publisher*

**New Glarus**
Marsh, Robert Charles *writer, music critic*

**Pewaukee**
Lee, Jack (Jim Sanders Beasley) *broadcast executive*

**Stoughton**
Brenz, Gary Jay *publishing executive*

**Verona**
Schroeder, Henry William *publisher*

**Waterloo**
Kay, Dennis Matthew *publishing company official*

**Waukesha**
Gruber, John Edward *editor, railroad historian, photographer*
Larson, Russell George *magazine and book publisher*

**West Bend**
Fraedrich, Royal Louis *magazine editor, publisher*

## WYOMING

**Cody**
Fritjofson, Sarah Marie *reporter, columnist*

**Jackson**
Downer, Eugene Debs, Jr. *editor, publisher*

**Riverton**
Peck, Robert A. *newspaper publisher*

## TERRITORIES OF THE UNITED STATES

**PUERTO RICO**

**Bayamon**
Berio, Blanca *editor*

**VIRGIN ISLANDS**

**Saint John**
Walker, Ronald R. *writer, newspaper editor, educator*

## CANADA

**ALBERTA**

**Calgary**
Poole, Robert Anthony *journalist*
†Shaw, James Robert *broadcast executive*
†Shaw, Jim, Jr. *broadcast executive*

**Edmonton**
Hughes, Linda J. *newspaper publisher*

**BRITISH COLUMBIA**

**Vancouver**
Radler, Franklin David *publishing holding company executive*
Yaffe, Barbara Marlene *journalist*

**Victoria**
Tighe, James C. *publisher*

**MANITOBA**

**Winnipeg**
†Buchko, Garth *broadcasting executive*
Burt, Christopher Murray *former newspaper editor, communications consultant*
†Chalmers, Jane *broadcast executive*
†McBride, Matthew Gordon *broadcasting executive*
McKie, Francis Paul *journalist*
Wreford, David Mathews *magazine editor*

**ONTARIO**

**Cavan**
Young, Scott Alexander *television journalist, author*

**Don Mills**
French, William Harold *retired newspaper editor*
Hickey, Brian Edward *publishing executive*

**Kitchener**
MacDonald, Wayne Douglas *publisher*
Rittinger, Carolyne June *newspaper editor*

**London**
Cornies, Larry Alan *journalist, educator*
Desbarats, Peter Hullett *journalist, academic administrator*
McLeod, Philip Robert *publishing executive*

**North Town**
†Morgan, Beverly *publishing company executive*

**North York**
Hanna, William Brooks *book publisher*

**Ottawa**
Beatty, Perrin *broadcasting company executive*
Clever, W(arren) Glenn *editor, publishing executive, poet, writer, educator*
Davey, Clark William *newspaper publisher*
Macklem, Michael Kirkpatrick *publisher*
Mills, Russell Andrew *newspaper publisher*
†Saucier, Guylaine *broadcast executive*
Stone, Jeffrey Jay *film critic, journalist, writer*

**Scarborough**
Besse, Ronald Duncan *publishing company executive*
†Carson, Edward John *book publisher*
Knycha, Josef *journalist*
Mitchell, Arthur Harris *newspaper columnist*

**Toronto**
†Alvarez, Frank *radio station executive*
Berton, Pierre *journalist, author*
Black, Conrad Moffat *publishing corporate executive*
†Bosel, Val *radio station executive*
Boultbee, John Arthur *publishing executive*
Bregg, Peter *photojournalist*
†Cassaday, John Michael *television network executive*
Chodos, Robert Irwin *editor, writer*
Clancy, Louis John *newspaper editor, journalist*
Downing, John Henry *columnist, journalist*
Egan, Vincent Joseph *journalist, newspaper columnist*
Galloway, David Alexander *publishing company executive*
Harris, Nicholas George *publisher*
Honderich, John Allen *newspaper publisher*
King, John Charles Peter *newspaper editor*
Landsberg, Michele *journalist*
Lasker, David Raymond *newspaper editor, musician*
Lewis, Robert *periodical editor, journalist*
Lombardi, John Barba-Linardo *broadcasting executive*
McLean, (Andrew) Stuart *educator, journalist*
Olive, David Michael *magazine writer, magazine editor*
Rauhala, Ann Elaine *reporter*
†Roberts, William D. *broadcasting executive*
†Slaight, Gary *broadcasting executive*
Smith, David Todd *publishing company executive*
Thall, Burnett Murray *newspaper executive*
Thomson, Kenneth R. (Lord Thomson of Fleet) *publishing executive*
Watson, Paul *photojournalist, correspondent*

**Willowdale**
Dean, Geoffrey *book publisher*
Irwin, John Wesley *publisher*
Kerner, Fred *book publisher, writer*

**QUEBEC**

**Dollard**
Des Roches, Antoine *retired newspaper executive*

**Montreal**
†Beaubien, Philippe de Gaspe, II *communications executive*
†Beaudoin, Claude *radio station executive*
Braide, Robert David *broadcast executive*
Juneau, Pierre *broadcasting company executive*
†La Arcand, Pierre *radio station executive*
Landry, Roger D. *publishing company executive*
Peladeau, Pierre *publishing company executive*
Pépin, Marcel *broadcast executive*
Romanelli, G. Jack *journalist*
Webster, Norman Eric *journalist, charitable foundation administrator*

**SASKATCHEWAN**

**Regina**
Hughes, Robert Lachlan *newspaper executive*

## AUSTRALIA

**Sydney**
Guerin, Didier *magazine executive*
Murdoch, (Keith) Rupert *publisher*

## BELGIUM

**Brussels**
Branegan, James Augustus, III *journalist*
Kempe, Frederick Schumann *newspaper editor, author*

## CHINA

**Hong Kong**
Laurie, James Andrew *journalist, broadcaster*
Lehner, Urban Charles *journalist*

**Taiwan**
Meyer, Richard Jonah *broadcast executive, consultant*

## ENGLAND

**Buckinghamshire**
Elegant, Robert Sampson *journalist, author*

**Cambridge**
Kermode, (John) Frank *literary critic, educator*

**Hartlepool**
Smyth, Reginald (Reggie Smythe) *cartoonist*

**London**
Cook, Jan *recording industry executive, film executive*
Diem, William Roy, III *editor, playwright*
Grade, Lord Lew *entertainment corporation executive*
Green, Richard Lancelyn (Gordon) *editor, writer*
Hinton, Leslie Frank *media executive*
Hoge, Warren M. *newspaper and magazine correspondent, editor*
Irvine, Ian Alexander Noble *publishing company executive, director*
Mellon, John *publishing executive*
Mirageas, Evans John *record company executive*
Oliver, Diane Frances *publisher, writer*
Pleasants, Henry *music critic*
Scardino, Albert James *journalist*
Scardino, Marjorie Morris *publishing company executive*
Stapleton, Nigel John *multinational information publishing executive*

**Surrey**
Godwin, Naomi Nadine *editor*

## FIJI

**Suva**
Usher, Sir Leonard Gray *retired news association executive*

## FRANCE

**Lauris**
Spivak, Jonathan M. *journalist*

**Paris**
Dahlburg, John-Thor Theodore *newspaper correspondent*
De Lyrot, Alain Herve *editor*
Dubs, Patrick Christian *publisher*
Lewis, Flora *journalist*

## GERMANY

**Bonn**
Fleming, Joseph Benedict *newspaperman*
Walker, Ruth Ann *journalist*

**Munich**
Saur, Klaus G. *publisher*

von Minckwitz, Bernhard *publishing company executive*

## HONG KONG

**Causeway Bay**
Ignatius, Alan (Adi) *magazine editor*

**Hong Kong**
Gargan, Edward A. *journalist*

## IRELAND

**Dublin**
Toibin, Colm *journalist, writer*

## ISRAEL

**Haifa**
Farrell, Naomi *editor, journalist, medical writer, nurse researcher, poet*

**Savyon**
Bushinsky, Jay (Joseph Mason) *journalist, radio/TV correspondent, columnist*

## ITALY

**Rome**
Wynn, Coy Wilton *journalist*

## JAPAN

**Tokyo**
Akutsu, Yoshihiro *communications educator*
Krisher, Bernard *foreign correspondent*
Nagata, Akira *publishing executive*
WuDunn, Sheryl *journalist, correspondent*

## THE NETHERLANDS

**Aerdenhout**
Vinken, Pierre Jacques *publishing executive, neurosurgeon*

**Amsterdam**
Bruggink, Herman *publishing executive*

## NEW ZEALAND

**Bay of Islands**
Veysey, Arthur Ernest *reporter, administrator, biographer*

## SOUTH AFRICA

**Johannesburg**
†Berk, Philip Woolf *journalist*
Hunter-Gault, Charlayne *journalist*

## SWITZERLAND

**Geneva**
O'Regan, Richard Arthur *editor, retired foreign correspondent*
Rohrer, Maurice Pierre *journalist*

## TURKS AND CAICOS ISLANDS

**Provinciales**
Johnston, Samuel Thomas *entertainment company executive*

## UNITED ARAB EMIRATES

**Dubai**
Bieber-Roberts, Peggy Eilene *communications editor, journalist, researcher*

## WEST INDIES

**Plymouth Montserrat**
Diggs, J(esse) Frank *retired magazine editor*

## ADDRESS UNPUBLISHED

Abercrombie, Stanley *magazine editor*
Achorn, Robert Comey *retired newspaper publisher*
Agarwal, Suman Kumar *editor*
Ajemian, Robert Myron *journalist*
Aldrich, Patricia Anne Richardson *retired magazine editor*
Andre, (Kenneth) Michael *editor, publisher, writer*
Andrisani, John Anthony *author, golf consultant*
Angulo, Gerard Antonio *publisher, investor*
Arden, Sherry W. *publishing company executive*
Arnold, Henri *cartoonist*
Arutyunyan, Emma *radio-broadcaster*
Ashby, Norma Rae Beatty *journalist, beauty consultant*
Ashley, Jim R(ay) *newspaper editor*
Audet, Paul Andre *retired newspaper executive*
Avnet, Jonathan Michael *motion picture company executive, film director*
Baggett, Donnis Gene *journalist, editor*
Barham, Patte (Mrs. Harris Peter Boyne) *publisher, author, columnist*
Barhydt, Sally J. *publishing company executive*

Barry, Rick (Richard Francis Dennis Barry, III) sportscaster, retired professional basketball player, marketing professional
Bartlett, David Conant journalist
Batignani, Laurie A. communications professional
†Baxter, Thomas Gregory cable television executive
Bennett, Geraldine Mae Paulette publisher, author
Berger, William Ernest newspaper publisher
Berke, Judie publisher, editor
Berman, William H. publishing company executive
Bernard, Jami film critic, author
Bernstein, Richard Allen publishing company executive
Bingham, Jinsie Scott broadcast company executive
Bishop, Gordon Bruce journalist
Block, William newspaper publisher
†Bohle, Robert Henry journalism educator
Bortz, Paul Isaac media, sport and entertainment consultant
Borysewicz, Mary Louise editor
Boswell, Thomas Murray sports columnist, writer
Braden, Thomas Wardell news commentator
Bradley, Jean Eleanor newspaper executive, public relations consultant
Brantley, Benjamin David drama critic
Bratzler, Mary Kathryn desktop publisher
Breathed, Berkeley cartoonist
Brekke, Gail Louise broadcasting administrator
Brett, Barbara Jeanne publisher
Brinberg, Herbert Raphael information management, publishing company executive
Broadwater, James E. publisher
Brodian, Laura broadcasting and illustration studio executive, professional illustrator
Broude, Ronald music publisher
Brown, Britt retired publishing company executive
Browne, Patti Ann journalist
Buchanan, Patrick Joseph journalist
Buckley, William Elmhirst publishing consultant
Buffkins, Archie Lee public television executive
Burns, Bebe Lyn journalist
Butler, George Frank editor, literary historian
Bynum, Richard Cary publishing consultant, author
Callander, Bruce Douglas journalist, free-lance writer
Camp, Clifton Durrett, Jr. newspaper consultant, rancher
Campbell, Byron Chesser publishing company executive
Cantone, Vic political cartoonist
Caputo, Salvatore critic
Cardwell, Nancy Lee editor, writer
†Carillo, Mary broadcaster, tennis analyst
Carlson, Natalie Traylor publisher
Chercover, Murray television executive
Chernichaw, Mark television, film and interactive multimedia executive producer, director, international media consultant
Clapper, Lyle Nielsen magazine publisher
Clark, Peter Bruce newspaper executive
Clark, Robert Phillips newspaper editor, consultant
Clarke, John Patrick retired newspaper publisher
Cloud, Stanley Wills journalist, editor, writer
Cohen, Allan Richard broadcasting executive
Cohen, Mark Herbert broadcasting company executive
Cook, Fred James journalist, author
Cooper, Carol Diane publishing company executive
Costas, Robert Quinlan (Bob Costas) sportscaster
Coyle, John J. publishing executive
Crowther, James Earl radio and television executive, lawyer
Cullen, James Thaddeus, Jr. broadcast executive
Cullen, Robert John publishing executive, financial consultant
Curtin, David Stephen newswriter
Curtis, Mary Ellen (Mary Curtis Horowitz) publishing company executive
Cushing, Frederic Sanford publishing company executive
Dahlgren, Carl Herman Per educator, arts administrator
D'Amato, Anthony Roger recording company executive
Daniel, Elbert Clifton journalist
Danzig, Joan newspaper editor
DeCamp, Graydon journalist
Dedman, Bill journalist
de Leon, Lidia Maria magazine editor
Dickman, James Bruce photojournalist
Dills, James Arlof retired publishing company executive
Disbrow, Lynn Marie communication educator
Douglas, Eileen news broadcaster, writer, television producer
Downs, Steven Edward magazine editor
Draznin, Jules Nathan journalism and public relations educator, consultant
Drew, Elizabeth Heineman publishing executive
†Dreyfuss, Joel Philippe magazine editor
Duerr, Herman George retired publishing executive
Dunham, Benjamin Starr editor, arts administrator
Eaker, Ira publishing executive
Edelson, Zelda Sarah Toll retired editor
Edwards, Geoffrey Hartley newspaper publisher
Ehrlich, Amy editor, writer
Elliman, Donald magazine company executive
Elsner, Sidney Edgar journalist
Emery, Sherman Raymond editorial consultant
Erbacher, Kathryn Anne editor, art and design writer, marketing consultant
Erlicht, Lewis Howard broadcasting company executive
Erwin, John Seymour writer, editor, composer
Esposito, Joseph John publishing company executive
Everingham, Harry Towner editor, publisher
Ewell, Miranda Juan journalist
Farah, Joseph Francis newspaper editor, writer
Farnsworth, Elizabeth broadcast journalist
Fassio, Virgil newspaper publishing company executive
Fazio, Evelyn M. publisher
Federici, William Vito newspaper reporter
Feiffer, Jules cartoonist, writer, playwright
Fernald, Harold Allen publishing executive
Ferre, Antonio Luis newspaper publisher
Fink, John Francis retired newspaper editor
Finnegan, Sara Anne publisher
Fisher, Robert Charles publishing company executive, editor
Fitzgerald, Edward Earl publishing executive, author
Francke, Linda Bird journalist
Frankel, Glenn journalist
Fritz, Mark reporter, journalist
Fuchs, Joseph Louis retired magazine publisher
Fuchs, Michael Joseph television executive
Gannon, James Patrick newspaper editor
Garfield, Robert Edward newspaper columnist
Gartenberg, Seymour Lee retired recording company executive
Geer, Stephen DuBois retired journalist
Geis, Bernard book publisher
Gerber, Seymour retired publishing company executive
Gill, Henry Herr photojournalist
Gilson, Barbara Frances editor
Giuffrida, Tom A. publisher
Glover, William Harper theater critic
Goellner, Jack Gordon publishing executive
Gold, Sylviane entertainment editor, writer, critic
Goldsmith, Arthur Austin magazine editor
Goldwater, John Leonard publisher, writer
Goode, Stephen Hogue publishing company executive
Goodkin, Michael Jon publishing company executive
†Graff, Gail Svensson television producer
Gralla, Milton publisher
Gray, Gordon L. communications educator
Grayson, Richard Steven (Lord of Mursley) foreign correspondent, international legal and political management consultant, educator
Gretser, George Westfall publisher
Hagel, Raymond Charles publishing company executive, educator
Hahn, Helene B. motion picture company executive
Haimovitz, Jules broadcasting company executive
Halfen, David publishing executive
Hamill, (William) Pete newspaper columnist, author, editor
Harkness, Peter Anthony editor, publisher
Harris, Louis public opinion analyst, columnist
Harrison, Gerald publisher
Hartman, John Wheeler publisher
Hast, Adele editor, historian
Heiman, Grover George, Jr. magazine editor, author
Heimbold, Margaret Byrne publisher, marketing professional, business executive
Helford, Paul Quinn communications educator, academic administrator
†Heller, Richard H. writer, editor, book critic, publisher
Henig, Robin Marantz journalist
Hering, Doris Minnie dance critic
Herman, Kenneth Neil journalist
Hess, David Willard journalist
Himmelfarb, Milton editor, educator
Hobbs, Avaneda Dorenza publishing company executive, minister, singer
Holland, David Thurston former editor
Holton, Robert Page publishing executive
Hubley, Reginald Allen publisher
Hudson, Jerry Charles communications educator
Hurd, Byron Thomas newspaper executive, retired
Huttner, Richard M. publishing executive
Idaszak, Jerome Joseph economic journalist
Janos, James Donald broadcast engineer
Jennings, Max newspaper editor
Jensen, Jack Michael publishing executive
Jiler, William Laurence publisher
Jinks, Robert Larry retired newspaper publisher
Johnson, Frank Edward former newspaper editor
Johnson, Malcolm Clinton, Jr. publishing consultant
Jones, Leonade Diane media publishing company executive
Jordan, Fred publishing company executive
Joseph, Michael Thomas broadcast consultant
Karlin, Myron D. motion picture executive
†Karsten, Adrian reporter
Kash, Wyatt Keith publishing executive
Kelly, Robert Thomas publisher
Kennedy, Harvey Edward science information publishing executive
Kenny, Patrick Edward publishing executive
Key, Ted cartoonist
Keyes, Saundra Elise newspaper editor
Kilpatrick, James Jackson, Jr. columnist, author
Kimes, Beverly Rae editor, writer
Klapper, Carol Lorraine magazine publisher
Klein, Edward Joel editor, author, lecturer
Kleinberg, Howard J. newspaper columnist
Knell, Gary Evan media executive, lawyer
Koehler, George Applegate broadcasting company executive
†Komar Storey, Charlene Mary editor
Koppett, Leonard columnist, journalist, author
Kraslow, David retired newspaper publishing executive, reporter, author, consultant
Krauthammer, Charles columnist, editor
Kuehn, James Marshall newspaper editor
Kyle, John Hamilton publishing executive
Laidlaw, Robert Richard publishing company executive
Laitin, Joseph journalist, former government spokesman and public relations consultant
Lander, Howard entertainment newspaper publisher
Landis, James David publishing company executive, retired, author
Lauterbach, Christine radio producer
Lawton, Kim Audrey freelance journalist
Leason, Jody Jacobs newspaper columnist
Lehtinen, Merja Helen Kokkonen journalist, researcher, publisher
Levine, David M. newspaper editor
Lewin, K(atherine) Tamar reporter
Liberman, Gail Jeanne editor
Lippert, John Richard magazine editor
Lister, Keith Fenimore publishing executive
Lloyd, Michael Jeffrey recording producer
Lonneke, Michael Dean radio and television marketing executive
Lord, Roy Alvin retired publisher
Loughlin, Mary Anne Elizabeth television news anchor
Lynch, Patricia Gates broadcasting organization executive consultant, former ambassador
MacFarlane, Andrew Walker media specialist, educator
MacMinn, Aleene Merle B(arnes) newspaper editor, columnist, educator
Mallo-Garrido, Josephine Ann advertising agency owner
Malloy, Michael Terrence journalist, newspaper editor
Malott, Adele Renee editor
Manley, Joan A(dele) Daniels retired publisher
Mann, Jim (James William Manousos) editor, publisher
Manning, Richard Dale writer
Marcus, Greil Gerstley critic
Marino, Joseph Anthony retired publishing executive
Marken, William Riley magazine editor
Mayer, Allan magazine editor, writer
McCauley, Jane Reynolds journalist
McClendon, Sarah Newcomb news service executive, writer
McCormick, Susan Konn retired publishing executive
McCoy, Georgia Sideris magazine editor, writing consultant
McDarrah, Gloria Schoffel editor, author
McFarlin, Diane H. newspaper editor
McGuirk, Terrence former broadcasting company executive
McHenry, Robert (Dale) editor
McIntyre, Douglas Alexander magazine publisher
McManus, Jason Donald editor, retired
Meade, Everard Kidder, Jr. retired broadcasting and publishing executive
Meagher, Mark Joseph publishing company executive
Medavoy, Mike motion picture company executive
Medina, Kathryn Bach book editor
Mellema, Donald Eugene retired radio news reporter and anchor
Melody, Michael Edward publishing company executive
Meredith, Alice Foley publisher, consultant
Miller, Robert Branson, Jr. retired newspaper publisher
Millett, Ralph Linwood, Jr. retired newspaper editor
Miner, A. Bradford journalist
Mitchell, Rick journalist, writer
Mitchem, Mary Teresa publishing executive
Molden, Herbert George publisher
Monacelli, Gianfranco publishing executive
Moore, John Plunkett Dennis publisher
Mudd, Roger Harrison news broadcaster, educator
Myers, Shirley Diana art book editor
Neff, Donald Lloyd news correspondent, writer
Nelson, Martha Jane magazine editor
Nelson, Robert Charles newspaper executive
Nicholls, David G. editor, scholar, educator
Nichols, Carl Michael interactive media executive
Novick, Julius Lerner theater critic, educator
Nyquist, Kathleen A. publishing executive
Nytko, Edward C. printing company executive
Oakley, Andrew Arthur journalist, educator
O'Grady, Mary J. editor, foundation consultant
Orr, Carol Wallace book publishing executive
Ortner, Everett Howard magazine editor, writer
Osrin, Raymond Harold retired political cartoonist
Otis, Denise Marie editor, writer
Pack, Richard Morris broadcasting executive
Paglio, Lydia Elizabeth editor
Paulson, Kenneth Alan journalist, lawyer, business executive
Peacock, Mary Willa magazine editor
Peeples, Rufus Roderick, Jr. (Roddy Peeples) farm and ranch news radio broadcaster
Pepper, Jeffrey Mackenzie publishing executive
Perlis, Michael Steven magazine publisher
Perrin, Gail editor
Peterson, Kevin Bruce newspaper editor, publishing executive
Phillips, Glynda Ann editor
Pierce, James Robert magazine executive
Plangere, Jules Leon, Jr. media company executive
Pletcher, Eldon editorial cartoonist
Pockell, Leslie M. publishing company executive
Podhoretz, Norman magazine editor, writer
Policinski, Eugene Francis author, newspaper editor
Polk, James Ray journalist
Porges, Walter Rudolf television news executive
Powledge, Fred Arlius freelance writer
Prady, Norman journalist, advertising executive, writer, marketing consultant
Preece, Warren Eversleigh editor
Press, Aida Kabatznick former editor, writer
Price, Tom journalist
Putnam, Linda Lee communication educator, researcher
Quinn, Charles Nicholas journalist
Ramsay, Karin Kinsey publisher, educator
Randinelli, Tracey Anne magazine editor
Ratny, Ruth Lucille publishing company executive, writer
Rayner, William Alexander retired newspaper editor
Reid-Bills, Mae editor, historian
Reidenbaugh, Lowell Henry retired sports editor
Rice, Roger Douglas television executive, artist
Richman, Alan magazine editor
Ridder, Paul Anthony newspaper executive
Ritter-Clough, Elise Dawn consultant, private investor
Rivas, Ernesto newspaper columnist
Roberts, Delmar Lee editor
Rosenberg, Shirley Sirota publications and public relations executive
Rosenthal, Arthur Jesse publisher
Rosset, Lisa Krug editor
Rubin, Rick record producer
Ruby, Michael magazine executive
Ryan, Tom Kreusch cartoonist
Sackett, Susan Deanna film and television production associate, writer
Salinger, Pierre Emil George journalist
Samuelson, Robert Jacob journalist
Sanders, Marlene anchor, journalism educator
Sapsowitz, Sidney H. entertainment and media company executive
Sarris, Andrew George film critic
Savage, Scott David broadcast executive
Schacht, Linda Joan broadcast journalist
Schorr, Daniel Louis broadcast journalist, author, lecturer
Schrader, Martin Harry retired publisher
Schrand, Richard Henry broadcaster
Schwartz, Lloyd Marvin newspaper and magazine correspondent, broadcaster
Scruggs, Charles G. editor
Sendler, David Alan magazine editor
Serwatka, Walter Dennis publishing executive
Shelton, Stephani broadcast journalist, consultant
Shreiner, Curt educational technologist, consultant
Simons, Lewis Martin journalist
Simpson, O. J. (Orenthal James Simpson) former professional football player, actor, sports commentator
Sinclair, Carole publisher, editor, author
Siskel, Gene (Eugene Kal Siskel) film critic
Smith, Chester broadcasting executive
Smith, George Drury publisher, editor, collagist, writer
Smith, Hedrick Laurence journalist, television commentator, author, lecturer
Smith, Ileene A. book editor
Smith, Martin Bernhard journalist
†Spencer, Peter LeValley, Sr. editor
Spitaleri, Vernon Rosario newspaper publisher
Stanton, John Jeffrey editor, broadcast journalist, government programs director, analyst, professional society administrator
Starr, David newspaper editor, publisher
Steiger, Dale Arlen publishing executive
Stennett, William Clinton (Clint Stennett) radio/TV station executive, state senator
Stephens, Edward Carl communications educator, writer
Stephenson, Toni Edwards publisher, investment management executive
Stern, Marilyn picture editor, photographer, writer
Stewart, Barbara Ellen media specialist
Stiff, Robert Martin newspaper editor
Stines, Fred, Jr. publisher
Stolley, Richard Brockway journalist
Stricklin, Alix publishing executive, writer, actor
Strothman, James Edward editor
Sullivan, Daniel Joseph journalist
Switzer, Maurice Harold publisher
Tallichet, Leon Edgar retired publishing executive, financial administrator
Taylor, Kristin Clark media specialist
Taylor-Pickell, Lavonne Troy editor
Terry, Clifford Lewis journalist
Thomas, Katherine Jane newspaper business columnist
Threlkeld, Richard Davis broadcast journalist
Tiedge-Lafranier, Jeanne Marie editor
Tobias, Andrew Previn columnist, lecturer
Triece, Anne Gallagher magazine publisher
Trudeau, Garretson Beekman (Garry Trudeau) cartoonist
Trueman, William Peter Main broadcaster, newspaper columnist
Tuohy, William correspondent
Ubell, Earl magazine health editor
Uman, Sarah Dungey editor
Urdang, Laurence lexicographer, publisher
Vandenberg, Peter Ray magazine publisher
Van Horn, Lecia Joseph newswriter
Vargas, Pattie Lee author, editor
Vaughan, Linda publishing executive
Voltz, Jeanne Appleton author
Waddell, Harry Lee editor, publisher
Wagman, Robert John journalist, author
Wagner, Julia A(nne) retired editor
Wallach, Amei Marione journalist, art critic
Walls, Carmage Lee, Jr. newspaper executive, consultant
Wartella, Ellen Ann communications educator, consultant
Waters, Betty Lou newspaper reporter, writer
Wearn, Wilson Cannon retired media executive
Weaver, Howard C. newspaper executive
Weber, Arthur magazine executive
Weckesser, Ernest Prosper, Jr. publisher, educator
Weissman, Jack (George Anderson) editor
Welsome, Eileen journalist
Werman, Thomas Ehrlich record producer
White, Jane See journalist
Whitesell, John Edwin motion picture company executive
Wicker, Thomas Grey retired journalist
Wies, Barbara editor, publisher
Wiessler, David Albert correspondent
Wille, Wayne Martin retired editor
Wilner, Judith journalist
Winter, Alan retired publishing company executive
Witmer, Diane F. communication educator
Wolfman, Ira Joel editor, writer
Wolner, Rena Meryl publisher
Wood, Marian Starr publishing company executive
Woodruff, Virginia broadcast journalist, writer
Wussler, Robert Joseph broadcasting executive, media consultant
Young, Patrick writer, editor
Young, Richard Alan publishing company executive
Ziegler, Jack (Denmore) cartoonist

## EDUCATION. For postsecondary education, *See also* specific fields.

### UNITED STATES

### ALABAMA

**Athens**
Ruth, Betty Muse school system administrator

**Auburn**
Alderman, Charles Wayne university dean
Galbraith, Ruth Legg retired university dean, home economist
Miller, Wilbur Randolph university educator and administrator
Muse, William Van academic administrator
Owens, John Murry dean
Philpott, Harry Melvin former university president
Rouse, Roy Dennis retired university dean
Voitle, Robert Allen college dean, physiologist
Yang, Baiyin adult education educator

**Birmingham**
Barker, Samuel Booth former university dean, physiology and biology educator
Berte, Neal Richard college president
Carter, John Thomas retired educational administrator, writer
Clarke, Juanita M. Waiters education educator
Corts, Thomas Edward university president
Fincher, John Albert college official, consultant
Goldman, Jay industrial engineer, educator, dean
Gross, Michael S. secondary school principal
Hames, Carl Martin educational administrator, art dealer, consultant
Hendley, Dan Lunsford retired university official
Lee, James Michael religious education educator, publisher
Mc Callum, Charles Alexander university official

**Childersburg**
Sappington, Sharon Anne school librarian

**Decatur**
Davis, Marian Bloodworth secondary school educator

**Dothan**
Cross, Steven Jasper dean, educator
Garner, Alto Luther retired education educator

**Florence**
Gillaspie, Lynn Clara *education educator, director clinical experience*
Howard, G. Daniel *university administrator*
Potts, Robert Leslie *academic administrator*
Zarate, Ann Gairing *academic administrator, lawyer*

**Guntersville**
Patterson, Harold Dean *superintendent of schools*
Sparkman, Brandon Buster *educator, writer, consultant*

**Hanceville**
Bailey, James Curtis *college administrator*
Galin, Jerry Dean *college dean*

**Homewood**
Hart, Virginia Wade *elementary education educator*

**Hoover**
Parrish, Sherry Dye *elementary school educator*

**Hueytown**
Gilbert, Melba Caldwell *special education and early childhood educator*

**Huntsville**
Billings, Nancy Carter *secondary education educator*
Elliott, Sally Ann *special education educator*
Franz, Frank Andrew *university president, physics educator*
Helton, Norma Jean *special education educator*
Hollowell, Jan Bennett *adult education educator*
Leslie, Lottie Lyle *retired secondary education educator*
Lundquist, Charles Arthur *university official*
Morgan, Beverly Hammersley *middle school educator, artist*
Quick, Jerry Ray *academic administrator*

**Jacksonville**
Boswell, Rupert Dean, Jr. *retired academic administrator, math educator*
Dunaway, William Preston *retired academic administration educator*
Hale, Judy Ann *education educator*
McGee, Harold Johnston *academic administrator*

**Jasper**
Rowland, David Jack *academic administrator*

**Livingston**
Green, Asa Norman *university president*

**Madison**
Brannan, Eulie Ross *education consultant*

**Maxwell AFB**
Kline, John Alvin *academic administrator*

**Mobile**
Baker, Amanda Sirmon *university dean, nursing educator*
Byrd, Gwendolyn Pauline *school system superintendent*
Copeland, Lewis *principal*
Pruitt, Albert W. *dean*
Strodl, Peter *educational administrator, educator*
Vacik, James Paul *university administrator*
Whiddon, Frederick Palmer *university president*

**Montgomery**
Bigham, Wanda Ruth *college president*
Deaton, Cheryl Davis *school system administrator*
Harris, William Hamilton *academic administrator*
Johnson, Andrew Emerson, III *educational administrator*
Kurth, Ronald James *university president, retired naval officer*
Ritvo, Roger Alan *university dean, health management-policy educator*
Saigo, Roy Hirofumi *university chancellor*
Stanley, Janice Faye *special education educator*
Tracy, Patricia Ann Koop *secondary school educator*
Walker, Annette *counseling administrator*
Wright, Cathy Hess *secondary education educator*

**Muscle Shoals**
Smith, Harry Delano *educational administrator*

**Orange Beach**
Bennett, James Jefferson *higher education consultant*

**Rainsville**
Reece, Marilyn King *college dean*

**Scottsboro**
McGill, Judy Annell McGee *early childhood and elementary educator*

**Southside**
Hill, Anita Griffith *principal*

**Sylacauga**
Moore, Penelope *school librarian*

**Talladega**
Anderson, Sharon Rice *special education educator*
Johnson, Joseph Benjamin *university president*
Paris, Virginia Hall (Ginger Paris) *elementary school educator*

**Troy**
Adams, Ralph Wyatt, Sr. *university chancellor emeritus*
Hawkins, Jack, Jr. *academic administrator*
Long, John Maloy *university dean*
Marsicano, Hazel Elliott *education educator*

**Tuscaloosa**
Barrett, Nancy Smith *university administrator*
Dolly, John Patrick *university dean, educational psychologist*
Gunther, William David *university administrator, economics educator*
Jackson, Cynthia Williford *special education educator*
Meredith, Thomas C. *academic administrator*
Mitchell, Herbert Hall *former university dean, educational consultant*
Sorensen, Andrew Aaron *academic administrator*
Taaffe, James Griffith *university administrator, educator*
Thomas, Joab Langston *academic administrator, biology educator*

**Tuskegee**
Green, Elbert P. *university official*
Payton, Benjamin Franklin *college president*

**Vestavia Hills**
Jacobs, Delores Hamm *secondary education educator*

**Wetumpka**
Curlee, Robert Glen, Jr. *special education educator*

## ALASKA

**Anchorage**
Behrend, Donald Fraser *university administrator*
Brunstad, Michael Lewis *elementary education educator*
Byrd, Milton Bruce *college president, former business executive*
Collins, Michael Paul *secondary school educator, earth science educator, consultant*
Matsui, Dorothy Nobuko *elementary education educator*
Mitchell, Michael Kiehl *elementary and secondary education educator, minister*
Young, Bettye Jeanne *retired secondary education educator*

**Chiniak**
Griffin, Elaine B. *educator*

**Fairbanks**
Abels, Michael Alan *university administrator*
Alexander, Vera *dean, marine science educator*
Doran, Timothy Patrick *educational administrator*
Komisar, Jerome Bertram *university administrator*
Reichardt, Paul Bernard *dean, chemistry educator*
Wadlow, Joan Krueger *academic administrator*
Wood, William Ransom *retired university president, city official, corporate executive*

**Juneau**
Lind, Marshall L. *academic administrator*
May, Scott C. *special education educator*

**Old Harbor**
O'Brien, Annmarie *education educator*

**Tuntutuliak**
Daniel, Barbara Ann *elementary and secondary education educator*

## ARIZONA

**Arizona City**
Donovan, Willard Patrick *retired elementary education educator*

**Avondale**
Thompson, Bonnie Ransa *secondary educator, chemistry educator*

**Chandler**
Barnard, Annette Williamson *elementary school educator*
Rowe, Ernest Ras *education educator, academic administrator*

**Chinle**
Reed, Leonard Newton *secondary school educator*

**Flagstaff**
Hooper, Henry Olcott *academic administrator, physicist*
Lovett, Clara Maria *university administrator, historian*
Ratzlaff, Vernon Paul *elementary education educator, consultant*

**Fort Huachuca**
Adams, Frank *education specialist*

**Fountain Hills**
Humes, Charles Warren *counselor educator*

**Glendale**
Altersitz, Janet Kinahan *principal*
Bret, Donna Lee *elementary education educator*
Shuck, Lola Mae *retired elementary school educator*
Voris, William *academic administrator emeritus*

**Green Valley**
Barich, Dewey Frederick *emeritus educational administrator*
Carpenter, John Everett *retired principal, educational consultant*
Shafer, Susan Wright *retired elementary school educator*
Smith, Raymond Lloyd *former university president, consultant*

**Kayenta**
Parrott, Sharon Lee *elementary educator*

**Mesa**
Carter, Sally Packlett *elementary education educator*
Garwood, John Delvert *former college administrator*
Ramirez, Janice L. *assistant school superintendent*

**Naco**
Davies, Daniel R. *retired educator*

**Page**
Hart, Marian Griffith *retired reading educator*
Tsinigine, Allen *educator*

**Peoria**
Jesse, Sandra Elizabeth *special education educator*

**Phoenix**
Cain, Robert Joseph *elementary school educator*
Culnon, Sharon Darlene *reading specialist, special education educator*
Davis, Colleen Teresa *elementary education educator, reading educator*
Dewalt, Judith K. *elementary school principal*
Donnelly, Charles Robert *retired college president*
Ebert, Richard J. *principal*
Fitzgerald, Joan *principal*
Gibbs, William Harold *university administrator*
Hutchinson, Ann *development director*
Meddles, Sharon Diane Gunstream *school counselor*
Peabody, Debbie Kay *elementary school educator*
Williams, Bill *academic administrator*
Wood, Barbara Butler *secondary language arts and television production educator*
Woods, Cyndy Jones *junior high educator, researcher*

**Prescott**
Halvorson, Mary Ellen *education educator, writer*

**Roll**
Jorajuria, Elsie Jean *elementary education educator*

**Safford**
Riddlesworth, Judith Himes *elementary education educator*

**San Manuel**
Hawk, Dawn Davah *secondary education educator*

**Scottsdale**
Cherney, Elaine Ethel *education educator*
Cianfarano, Sam Anthony, Jr. *principal, educator*
Esquer, Deborah Anne *elementary education educator*
Hill, Louis Allen, Jr. *former university dean, consultant*
Wright, C. T. Enus *former university president*

**Sedona**
Hoffmann, Joan Carol *retired academic dean*
Richards, Wanda Jamie *education educator*

**Shonto**
Haviland, Marlita Christine *elementary school educator*

**Sun City**
Corcoran, Eileen Lynch *special education educator emerita*

**Sun City West**
Cohen, Abraham J. (Al Cohen) *educational administrator*

**Sun Lakes**
Cunningham, Arthur Francis *university dean, marketing educator*
Thompson, Loring Moore *retired college administrator, writer*

**Tempe**
Coor, Lattie Finch *university president*
Forsyth, Ben Ralph *academic administrator, medical educator*
Guzzetti, Barbara Jean *education educator*
Haggerson, Nelson Lionel, Jr. *education educator*
Marsh, Roberta Reynolds *elementary education educator, consultant*
Overman, Glenn Delbert *college dean emeritus*
Richardson, Richard Colby, Jr. *higher education educator, researcher*
Scott, Judith Myers *elementary education educator*
Simmons, Howard Lee *education educator*
Thompson, Anna Blanche *retired educator*
Thor, Linda Maria *college president*
Wills, J. Robert *academic administrator, drama educator, writer*

**Tucson**
Bowlan, Nancy Lynn *elementary and secondary school educator*
Brousseau, Georgia Cole *school principal*
Cate, Rodney Michael *academic administrator*
Chidester, Otis Holden *retired secondary education educator*
Clement, Nicholas I. *principal*
Dyer-Raffler, Joy Ann *special education diagnostician, educator*
Eribes, Richard *dean*
Fountain, Linda *secondary education educator*
Gallagher, Rosanna Bostick *elementary educator, administrator*
Harcleroad, Fred Farley *education educator*
Hawk, Floyd Russell *secondary school educator*
Heins, Marilyn *college dean, pediatrics educator, author*
Humphrey, John Julius *university program director, historian, writer*
Johnson, John Gray *retired university chancellor*
Kaltenbach, C(arl) Colin *dean, educator*
Leavitt, Jerome Edward *childhood educator*
Madden, James A. *gifted and talented educator*
Maker, Carol June *gifted and talented educator*
Pacheco, Manuel Trinidad *academic administrator*
Padilla, Elsa Norma *school system administrator*
Porreca, Betty Lou *education educator*
Reid, Charles Phillip Patrick *academic administrator, researcher, educator*
Smerdon, Ernest Thomas *academic administrator*
Starr, Melvin Lee *counselor*
Stoffle, Carla Joy *university library dean*
Tomoeda, Cheryl Kuniko *academic researcher*
Weaver, Albert Bruce *university administrator*
Wilson, John Lewis *university official*

**Vail**
Wallach-Levy, Wendee Esther *retired secondary school educator*

**Whiteriver**
Clark, John Munro *superintendent of schools*

## ARKANSAS

**Arkadelphia**
Dunn, Charles DeWitt *academic administrator*
Elrod, Ben Moody *academic administrator*
Grant, Daniel Ross *retired university president*
Hicks, Billy Ferrell *retired educator, minister*
Thomas, Herman L. *school system administrator*

**Batesville**
Griffith, John Vincent *academic official*

**Camden**
Bradshaw, Otabel *retired primary school educator*

**Conway**
Die, Ann Marie Hayes *college president, psychology educator*
Horton, Joseph Julian, Jr. *academic dean, educator*
Thompson, Winfred Lee *university president, lawyer*

**DeQueen**
Brinson, Harold Thomas *retired university president emeritus*

**Fayetteville**
Ferritor, Daniel E. *university official*
Henry, Ann Rainwater *education educator*
Jones, Susan Matthews *elementary educator educator*
Knowles, Malcolm Shepherd *education educator*
Madison, Bernard L. *academic dean, mathematics educator*
Oxford, Charles William *university dean, chemical engineer*
Schoppmeyer, Martin William *education educator*
Van Patten, James Jeffers *education educator*
Vorsanger, Fred S. *university administrator*
Williams, Doyle Z. *university dean, educator*

**Fort Smith**
Gooden, Benny L. *school system administrator*

**Glenwood**
Klopfenstein, Philip Arthur *high school educator*

**Hot Springs National Park**
Farris, Jefferson Davis *university administrator*

**Hot Springs Village**
Robinson, Donald Walter *university dean*

**Jonesboro**
Smith, Eugene Wilson *retired university president and educator*

**Little Rock**
Anderson, Joel E., Jr. *university administrator*
Fribourgh, James Henry *university administrator*
Gray, John Wylie *university dean, consultant*
Hathaway, Charles E. *academic administrator*
Sawyer, Anita Dawn *special education educator*
Smith, Charles Wilson, Jr. *university dean*
Truex, Dorothy Adine *retired university administrator*
Wilson, I. Dodd *dean*

**Magnolia**
Gamble, Steven G. *academic administrator*

**Pine Bluff**
Davis, Lawrence A. *academic administrator*
Scott, Vicki Sue *school system administrator*

**Rogers**
Searles, Anna Mae Howard *educator, civic worker*
Spainhower, James Ivan *retired college president*

**Russellville**
Morris, Lois Lawson *education educator*

**Searcy**
Burks, David Basil *academic administrator, educator*

**Sherwood**
Vogler, Diane Clark *elementary school principal*

**Springdale**
Cordell, Beulah Faye *special education educator*
Hill, Peggy Sue *principal*
Rollins, Jimmy Don *school system administrator*

**Stamps**
Moore-Berry, Norma Jean *secondary school educator*

**State University**
Fowler, Gilbert L. *dean, educator*
Wyatt, James Leslie, III *university president*
Wyatt, Leslie *academic administrator*

**Van Buren**
Breeden, Betty Loneta *secondary school educator*

## CALIFORNIA

**Albany**
Chook, Edward Kongyen *university official, disaster medicine educator*

**Alhambra**
Porché-Burke, Lisa Marie *chancellor*

**Anaheim**
Grose, Elinor Ruth *retired elementary education educator*
Jackson, David Robert *school system administrator*

**Angwin**
Maxwell, Donald Malcolm *college president, minister*

**Apple Valley**
Tishner, Keri Lynn *secondary education educator*

**Aptos**
Bohn, Ralph Carl *educational consultant, retired educator*
Hirsch, Bette G(ross) *college administrator, foreign language educator*

### Arcata
Bowker, Lee Harrington academic administrator
Geyer, Dennis Lynn university administrator and registrar
McCrone, Alistair William university president

### Atherton
Lane, Joan Fletcher educational administrator

### Azusa
Felix, Richard E. academic administrator
Gray, Paul Wesley university dean

### Bakersfield
Arciniega, Tomas Abel university president
Hefner, John principal
Thompson, Joyce Ann education consultant

### Bayside
Bank, Ron principal

### Bel Air
Wexler, Robert university administrator

### Bellflower
Cook, Karla Joan elementary education educator

### Ben Lomond
Sikora, James Robert educational business consultant

### Berkeley
Bender, Richard university dean, architect, educator
Bowker, Albert Hosmer retired university chancellor
Buffler, Patricia Ann dean
Cieslak, William academic administrator
Clifford, Geraldine Joncich (Mrs. William F. Clifford) education educator
Cross, Kathryn Patricia education educator
Freedman, Sarah Warshauer education educator
Glenny, Lyman Albert retired education educator
Kerr, Clark academic administrator emeritus
Linn, Marcia Cyrog education educator
Maslach, George James former university official
Merrill, Richard James educational director
Miles, Raymond Edward former university dean, organizational behavior and industrial relations educator
Montgomery, Roger dean
Ralston, Lenore Dale academic policy and program analyst
Rice, Robert Arnot school administrator
Rohwer, William D., Jr. university dean
Tien, Chang-Lin chancellor

### Beverly Hills
Grant, Michael Ernest educational administrator, institutional management educator

### Bloomington
Llanusa, Steven Michael elementary education educator

### Brea
Shell, Billy Joe retired university president

### Buena Park
Papin, Nancy Sue educational computer coordinator
Turkus-Workman, Carol Ann educator

### Burbank
Godwin, Annabelle Palkes retired early childhood education educator
Kelly, Michael Joseph academic administrator, consultant

### Burlingame
Raffo, Susan Henney elementary education educator

### Calabasas
Dworkoski, Robert John headmaster

### Calexico
Dixon, Michel L. educational administrator
Patterson, Melissa elementary education educator

### Camarillo
Derr, Jeannie Combs bilingual educator, anthropology educator
El Shami, Patricia Ann elementary school tutor
Knapp-Philo, Joanne school system administrator

### Campo
Charles, Blanche retired elementary education educator
Jermini, Ellen educational administrator, philosopher

### Canyon Lake
Knight, Vick, Jr. (Ralph Knight) dean, education educator, counselor

### Carmel
Faul, George Johnson former college president
Faul, June Patricia education specialist
Longman, Anne Strickland special education educator, consultant

### Carson
Brownell, John Arnold retired university president
Detweiler, Robert Chester university president, historian
Quijada, Angélica María elementary educator

### Castro Valley
Kinee-Krohn, Patricia special education educator

### Chatsworth
Miller, Robert Steven secondary school educator

### Chico
Esteban, Manuel Antonio university administrator, educator

### Chula Vista
Hanson, Eileen principal
Steele, Nancy Eden Rogers educator

### Claremont
Alexander, John David, Jr. college administrator
Bekavac, Nancy Yavor academic administrator, lawyer
Faranda, John Paul college administrator
Fucaloro, Anthony Frank academic dean
Liggett, Thomas Jackson retired seminary president
Maguire, John David academic administrator, educator, writer
Platt, Joseph Beaven former college president
Riggs, Henry Earle academic administrator, engineering management educator
Stanley, Peter William academic administrator
Stark, Jack Lee academic administrator
Strauss, Jon Calvert academic administrator
Wettack, F. Sheldon academic administrator

### Clayton
Bower, Fay Louise retired academic administrator, nursing educator

### Clovis
Driscoll, Glen Robert former university president

### Colton
Dybowski, Douglas Eugene education educator, economist
Slider, Margaret Elizabeth elementary education educator

### Concord
Thall, Richard Vincent school system administrator

### Corcoran
Roberts, Alice Noreen educational administrator

### Coronado
Heap, Suzanne Rundio elementary school educator

### Costa Mesa
Hansen, Sally Jo school system coordinator

### Coulterville
Henderson, Pamela Mason elementary education educator

### Culver City
Kamm, Jacqueline Ann elementary reading specialist

### Danville
Penner-Sekera, Cynthia Dawn secondary education educator

### Davis
Pritchard, William Roy former university system administrator
Smiley, Robert Herschel university dean
Vanderhoef, Larry Neil academic administrator

### Diamond Bar
Domeño, Eugene Timothy elementary education educator, principal

### Downey
De Lorca, Luis E. educational administrator, educator, speaker
Ruecker, Martha Engels retired special education educator

### Duarte
Tse, Man-Chun Marina special education educator

### El Cajon
Palafox, Mari Lee private school educator
Thomas, Esther Merlene elementary education educator

### El Centro
Kussman, Eleanor (Ellie Kussman) retired educational superintendent

### Encino
Bach, Cynthia educational program director, writer
O'Connor, Patricia Ranville secondary and special education educator

### Escondido
Gorsline, Samuel Gilbert, Jr. school administrator
Moore, Marc Anthony university administrator, writer, retired military officer

### Eureka
Harvey, Carol Sammons educator

### Fair Oaks
Branch, Robert Lee retired educational administrator

### Fontana
Donica, Cheryl Marie elementary education educator
Rynearson, Patricia Heaviside elementary school educator

### Fortuna
Fisher, Bruce David elementary school educator
Fullerton, Gail Jackson university president emeritus

### Foster City
Berman, Daniel K(atzel) educational consultant, university official

### Fremont
Brown, David Richard school system administrator, minister

### Fresno
Andresen, Claudia principal
Dandoy, Maxima Antonio education educator emeritus
Haak, Harold Howard university president
Howard, Katsuyo Kunugi counselor, educator, consultant
Klassen, Peter James academic administrator, history educator
Welty, John Donald academic administrator

### Fullerton
Barchi, Barbara Ann education educator
Beers, Susan Alice dean
Donoghue, Mildred Ransdorf education educator
Gordon, Milton Andrew academic administrator
Hopping, Richard Lee college president
Hugstad, Paul Steven college dean
Smith, Ephraim Philip university dean, educator

### Glendale
Odier, Pierre Andre educator, writer, photographer, artist
Whalen, Lucille academic administrator

### Glendora
Lindly, Douglas Dean elementary school educator, administrator
Schiele, Paul Ellsworth, Jr. educational business owner, writer

### Grass Valley
Stewart-Finocchiaro, Penny Morris secondary school educator

### Hayward
McCune, Ellis E. retired university system chief administrator, higher education consultant
Rees, Norma S. academic administrator

### Hemet
Masters, Judith Anne elementary school educator
Shea, Robert Stanton retired academic administrator

### Huntington Beach
Davidson-Shepard, Gay secondary education educator
Gruner, George Richard secondary education educator
Watts, Judith-Ann White academic administrator

### Indian Wells
Trotter, F(rederick) Thomas retired academic administrator

### Inglewood
Guzy, Marguerita Linnes secondary education educator
Logan, Lynda Dianne elementary education educator
Moghadam, Amir consultant, educational administrator

### Inyokern
Norris, Lois Ann elementary school educator

### Irvine
Fleischer, Everly Borah academic administrator
Garcia, Stephen Gregory vice chancellor, finance administrator
Peltason, Jack Walter former university president, educator
Wilkening, Laurel Lynn academic administrator, planetary scientist

### Kelseyville
Berry, John Joseph educational administrator

### La Canada Flintridge
Lamson, Robert Woodrow retired school system administrator

### La Crescenta
Winter-Neighbors, Gwen Carole special education educator, art educator

### La Jolla
Alksne, John F. dean
Dreilinger, Charles Lewis (Chips Dreilinger) dean
Frieman, Edward Allan university administrator, educator
Lee, Jerry Carlton university administrator
Masys, Daniel Richard medical school director
Stewart, John Lincoln university administrator
Talke, Frank Eberhard education educator

### La Mesa
Black, Eileen Mary elementary school educator
Tarson, Herbert Harvey university administrator emeritus

### La Mirada
Lingenfelter, Sherwood Galen university provost, anthropology educator

### La Palma
Akubuilo, Francis Ekenechukwu secondary school educator

### La Verne
Fleck, Raymond Anthony, Jr. retired university administrator
Morgan, Stephen Charles academic administrator

### Laguna Beach
Fry, Edward Bernard retired education educator

### Laguna Niguel
Teitelbaum, Marilyn Leah special education educator

### Lakewood
Bogdan, James Thomas secondary education educator, electronics researcher and developer

### Lebec
Shelby, Tim Otto secondary education educator

### Lemoore
Krend, William John secondary education educator

### Livermore
Lucas, Linda Lucille dean

### Loma Linda
Klooster, Judson academic administrator, dentistry educator

### Lompoc
Maxwell, Marilyn Julia elementary education educator

### Long Beach
Anatol, Karl W. E. provost
Armstrong, Joanna education educator
Beljan, John Richard university administrator, medical educator
Dean, Charles Thomas industrial arts educator, academic administrator
Feldman, Stephen university president
Hext, Kathleen Florence internal audit college administrator
Hobgood, E(arl) Wade college dean
Lathrop, Irvin Tunis retired academic dean, educator
Lauda, Donald Paul university dean
Martinez, Patricia Ann middle school educator, administrator
McDonough, Patrick Dennis academic administrator
Munitz, Barry university administrator, English literature educator, business consultant
Thompson, William Ancker intramural-recreational sports director, educator

### Los Altos
Puder, Janice special education educator

### Los Angeles
Anastos, Rosemary Park retired higher education educator
Ansley, Julia Ette elementary school educator, consultant, poet, writer
Bratt, Bengt Erik academic administrator, consulting engineer
Cobb, Jewel Plummer former college president, educator
Dewey, Donald Odell university dean
Ellsworth, Frank L. university administrator, non-profit executive
Gothold, Stuart E. school system administrator, educator
Harris, F. Chandler retired university administrator
Hayes, Robert Mayo university dean, library and information science educator
Hirson, Estelle retired school educator
Hoffman, Neil James academic administrator
Houser, Gerald Burnett university administrator
Hubbard, John Randolph university president emeritus, history educator, diplomat
Jackson, Kingsbury Temple educational contract consultant
Kennelly, Sister Karen Margaret college administrator
Kleingartner, Archie founding dean, educator
Lieber, David Leo university president
Lucente, Rosemary Dolores educational administrator
Lynch, Beverly Pfeifer education and information studies educator
Mandel, Joseph David university official, lawyer
†McCabe, Edward R. B. academic administrator, educator, physician
Merrifield, Donald Paul university chancellor
Mitchell, Theodore R. academic administrator
Money, Ruth Rowntree child development specialist, consultant
Moran, Thomas Harry academic administrator
Mori, Allen Anthony university dean, consultant, researcher
Pierskalla, William Peter university dean, management-engineering educator
Prager, Susan Westerberg dean, law educator
Rosser, James Milton academic administrator
Ryan, Stephen J. academic dean
Saito-Furukawa, Janet Chiyo primary school educator
Sample, Steven Browning university executive
Shearer, Derek N. international studies educator, diplomat, administrator
Shutler, Mary Elizabeth academic administrator
Silverman, Leonard M. university dean, electrical engineering educator
Slaughter, John Brooks university administrator
Spitzer, William George university dean, physicist, educator, researcher
Steinberg, Warren Linnington principal
Stevens, Gerald D. secondary education educator, consultant
Taylor, Leigh Herbert college dean
Tuckson, Reed V. university president
Ungar, Roselva May primary and elementary educator
Venis, Linda Diane academic administrator, educator
Wagner, William Gerard university dean, physicist, consultant, information scientist, investment manager
Wazzan, A(hmed) R(assem) Frank engineering educator, dean
Young, Charles Edward university chancellor
Zamir, Frances Roberta (Frances Roberta Weiss-Swede) principal

### Los Gatos
Hartinger, Patricia Bernardine elementary school educator
Simonson, Ted principal

### Malibu
Davenport, David university president, lawyer
Greer, Cynthia Faye university administrator, legal educator, mediator
Young, Matt Norvel, Jr. university chancellor emeritus

### Manhattan Beach
Brooks, Edward Howard college administrator

### Menlo Park
Cody, Frank Joseph secondary school administrator, teacher education educator

### Milpitas
Lobig, Janie Howell special education educator

### Mission Viejo
McGinnis, Joán Adell retired secondary school educator
Sabaroff, Rose Epstein retired education educator

### Modesto
Bairey, Marie principal
Reberg, Rosalie vice principal

### Montebello
Dible, Rose Harpe McFee special education educator

### Monterey
Kadushin, Karen D. dean

Oder, Broeck Newton *school emergency management consultant*

**Monterey Park**
Choyke, George Raymond *safety educator, consultant*
Meysenburg, Mary Ann *principal*

**Moraga**
Anderson, Brother Mel *academic administrator*

**Moreno Valley**
Moran, Patricia Eileen *special education educator*
Moulthrop, Rebecca Lee Stilphen *elementary education educator*

**Morgan Hill**
Desimone, Richard Louis *school assistant principal*

**Mountain View**
Craig, Joan Carmen *secondary school educator, drama teacher*

**Napa**
Rada, Alexander *university official*

**Newcastle**
Hill, Bonnie Guiton *dean*

**North Hollywood**
Chang, Wung *researcher, lecturer, business advisor*

**Northridge**
Curzon, Susan Carol *university administrator*
Ellner, Carolyn Lipton *university dean, consultant*
Tanis, Norman Earl *retired university dean, library expert*
Wilson, Blenda Jacqueline *academic administrator*

**Novato**
Patterson, W. Morgan *college president*

**Oakland**
Atkinson, Richard Chatham *university president*
Diaz, Sharon *education administrator*
Dibble, David Van Vlack *visually impaired educator, lawyer*
Farley, Thelma *principal*
Fries, Lita Linda *school system administrator*
Goldstine, Stephen Joseph *college administrator*
Gomes, Wayne Reginald *academic administrator*
Heydman, Abby Maria *dean*
Miller, Barry *research administrator, psychologist*
Saxton, Ruth Olsen *educator, dean*
Tomlinson-Keasey, Carol Ann *university administrator*

**Oceanside**
Pena, Maria Geges *academic services administrator*

**Ontario**
Kennedy, Mark Alan *middle and secondary school educator*
Morton, Laurel Anne *elementary education educator*

**Orange**
Doti, James L. *academic administrator*
Gerhard, Nancy Lucile Dege *school counselor, educator*
Hamilton, Harry Lemuel, Jr. *academic administrator*
Schrodi, Tom *instructional services director*

**Orinda**
Glasser, Charles Edward *university president*

**Oroville**
Tamori, David Isamu *secondary education educator*

**Oxnard**
Steele, Julius Raynard *special education educator*

**Palm Springs**
Aikens, Donald Thomas *educational administrator, consultant*
Gill, Jo Anne Martha *middle school educator*
Hartman, Rosemary Jane *special education educator*

**Palmdale**
Bowen, Jimmie Carl *vocational education educator*

**Palo Alto**
Antuna-Munoz, Mary Josephine *elementary education educator*
Attig, John Clare *secondary education educator, consultant*
Bohrnstedt, George William *educational researcher*
Case, Robbie *education educator, author*
Dance, Maurice Eugene *college administrator*
Gibbons, James Franklin *university dean, electrical engineering educator*
Loveless, Edward Eugene *education educator, musician*

**Palos Verdes Estates**
Lazzaro, Anthony Derek *university administrator*

**Palos Verdes Peninsula**
Copeland, Phillips Jerome *former university administrator, former air force officer*
Miller, Francie Loraditch *college counselor*

**Pasadena**
Almore-Randle, Allie Louise *special education educator*
Everhart, Thomas Eugene *academic administrator, engineering educator*
Freise, Earl Jerome *univeristy administrator, materials engineering educator*
Gabel, Katherine *academic administrator*
Gilman, Richard Carleton *retired college president*
Lawler, Alice Bonzi (Mrs. Oscar T. Lawler) *retired college administrator, civic worker*
Levy, David Steven *college administrator*
Meye, Robert Paul *retired seminary administrator, writer*
Stolper, Edward Manin *secondary education educator*

**Pebble Beach**
Sullivan, James Francis *university administrator*

**Petaluma**
O'Hare, Sandra Fernandez *elementary education educator, adult education educator*

**Pinole**
Grogan, Stanley Joseph *educational consultant*

**Playa Del Rey**
Hite, Janet Sue *elementary education educator*

**Pleasanton**
Aladeen, Lary Joe *secondary school educator*

**Pomona**
Amaya, Patricia Mojarro *elementary education educator*
Demery, Dorothy Jean *secondary school educator*
Eaves, Ronald Weldon *university administrator*
Lawrence, William, Jr. *elementary education educator*
Markham, Reed B. *education educator, consultant*
Suzuki, Bob H. *university president*

**Porterville**
Hayes, Shirley Ann *special education educator*

**Portola Valley**
Oscarson, Kathleen Dale *writing assessment coordinator, educator*

**Poway**
Brose, Cathy *principal*
Shippey, Lyn *reading center director*

**Rancho Palos Verdes**
Fischer, Robert Blanchard *university administrator, researcher*
McFadden, Thomas *academic administrator*

**Redlands**
Appleton, James Robert *university president, educator*
Proffitt, Lawrence Alan *secondary school educator*

**Redondo Beach**
Mahrenholtz, Dayla Dianne *elementary school principal*
Marsee, Stuart (Earl) *educational consultant, retired*

**Reseda**
Anstad, Neil *director*

**Rialto**
Johnson, Ruth Floyd *university educator, consultant*

**Ridgecrest**
Matulef, Gizelle Terese *secondary education educator*

**Riverside**
Balow, Irving Henry *retired education educator*
Diamond, Richard *secondary education educator*
Geraty, Lawrence Thomas *academic administrator, archaeologist*
Hendrick, Irving Guilford *dean, education educator*
Lacy, Carolyn Jean *elementary education educator, secondary education educator*
Morris, Stephen Allen *elementary school educator*
Prosser, Michael Joseph *community college staff member*
Reardon, James Louis *education educator, consultant*
Yacoub, Ignatius I. *university dean*

**Rohnert Park**
Arminana, Ruben *university president, educator*
Babula, William *university dean*
Gordon, Sharon J. *special education educator*

**Rowland Heights**
Perfetti, Robert Nickolas *educational services administrator*

**Sacramento**
Gerth, Donald Rogers *university president*
Grimes, Pamela Rae *elementary school educator*
McKinley, Donald Robert *former school system administrator, education advisor*
O'Leary, Marion Hugh *university dean, chemist*
Riles, Wilson Camanza *educational consultant*
Stegenga, Preston Jay *international education consultant*
West, Linda Lea *administrator*

**San Anselmo**
Enfield, Susan Ann *secondary education educator*

**San Bernardino**
Butler, Arthur Maurice *university administrator*
Evans, Anthony Howard *university president*
Kaisershot, Edward Joseph *elementary education educator, coach*
Norton, Ruth Ann *education educator*

**San Diego**
Ashton, Tamarah M. *learning disabilities specialist, consultant*
Charles, Carol Morgan *education educator*
Clement, Betty Waidlich *literacy educator, consultant*
Feinberg, Lawrence Bernard *university dean, psychologist*
Golding, Brage *former university president*
Hayes, Alice Bourke *university official, biology educator*
Hays, Garry D. *academic administrator*
King, Verna St. Clair *retired school counselor*
Kuc, Joseph A. *education educator, consultant*
Lauer, Jeanette Carol *college dean, history educator, author*
Maurer, Lawrence Michael *acting school administrator, educator*
Morris, Henry Madison, Jr. *education educator*
Schade, Charlene Joanne *adult and early childhood education educator*
Schwartz, Alfred *university dean*
Shearer, Rick Leland *academic administrator*
Till, Franklin L. *school system administrator*
Trybus, Raymond J. *academic administrator, psychology educator, rehabilitation services professional*
Walker, Donald Ezzell *retired academic administrator*
Weber, Stephen Lewis *university president*

**San Francisco**
Adcock, Muriel W. *special education educator*
Albino, Judith E.N. *university president*
Ammiano, Tom *school system administrator*
Buidang, George (Hada Buidang) *educator, administrator, consultant, writer*
Cain, Leo Francis *retired special education educator*
Corrigan, Robert Anthony *academic administrator*
Counelis, James Steve *education educator*
Dullea, Charles W. *university chancellor emeritus, priest*
Fleishhacker, David *school administrator*
Gray, Frances M. *retired college president, lecturer*
Kleinberg, David Lewis *education administrator*
Kozloff, Lloyd M. *university dean, educator, scientist*
Krevans, Julius Richard *university administrator, physician*
LaBelle, Thomas Jeffrey *academic administrator*
Lo Schiavo, John Joseph *university executive*
Manson, Malcolm Hood *educational administrator*
Naegele, Carl Joseph *university academic administrator, educator*
Pagano, Anthony J. *university dean*
Rippel, Clarence W. *academic administrator*
Schlegel, John Peter *academic administrator*
Stauffer, Thomas Michael *university president*
Stephens, Elisa *art college president, lawyer*
Wallace, Arthur, Jr. *college dean*

**San Jose**
Caret, Robert Laurent *university president*
Collett, Jennie *principal*
Cruz, B. Robert *academic administrator*
Elsorady, Alexa Marie *secondary education educator*
Martin, Bernard Lee *former college dean*
Meegan, Brother Gary Vincent *school administrator, music educator*
Merriam, Janet Pamela *special education educator*
Okerlund, Arlene Naylor *university official*
Sanders, Adrian Lionel *educational consultant*

**San Leandro**
Nehls, Robert Louis, Jr. *school system administrator*

**San Lorenzo**
Glenn, Jerome T. *secondary school principal*

**San Luis Obispo**
Baker, Warren J(oseph) *university president*
Ericson, Jon Meyer *academic administrator, rhetoric theory educator*
Haile, Allen Cleveland *educator and administrator*
Zingg, Paul Joseph *university provost*

**San Marcos**
Lilly, Martin Stephen *university dean*

**San Marino**
Footman, Gordon Elliott *educational administrator*
Mothershead, J. Leland, III *dean*

**San Pablo**
Colfack, Andrea Heckelman *elementary education educator*

**San Pedro**
Matich, Matthew P. *secondary school English educator*

**San Rafael**
Fink, Joseph Richard *college president*
Hill, Nathan Scott *educator, writer, cultural consultant*

**Santa Barbara**
Boyan, Norman J. *retired education educator*
Korenic, Lynette Marie *librarian*
Louis, Barbra Schantz *dean*
Mac Intyre, Donald John *college president*
O'Dowd, Donald Davy *retired university president*
Sinsheimer, Robert Louis *retired university chancellor and educator*
Sprecher, David A. *university administrator, mathematician*
Tettegah, Sharon Yvonne *education educator*
Yang, Henry T. *university chancellor, educator*

**Santa Clara**
Abdaljabbar, Abdalhameed A. *educational administrator*
DiUlio, Albert Joseph *university president, priest*
Facione, Peter Arthur *dean, philosophy and education educator*
Locatelli, Paul Leo *university administrator*

**Santa Clarita**
Lavine, Steven David *academic administrator*
Volpe, Eileen Rae *special education educator*

**Santa Cruz**
Keizer, Lewis Stewart *headmaster*

**Santa Maria**
Dunn, Judith Louise *secondary school educator*

**Santa Monica**
Dickerson, Joe Bernard *principal, educator*

**Santa Rosa**
Christiansen, Peggy *principal*
Webb, Charles Richard *retired university president*

**Saratoga**
Wood, Gladys Blanche *retired secondary education educator, journalist*

**Selma**
Jura, Debra Dowell *bilingual educator*

**Sherman Oaks**
O'Neill, Sallie Boyd *educator, business owner, sculptor*

**South Pasadena**
Patterson, Dawn Marie *dean, consultant, author, educator*

**South San Francisco**
Shelton, Leslie Habecker *adult literacy program director*

**Stanford**
Baron, James Neal *organizational behavior and human resources educator, researcher*
Bridges, Edwin Maxwell *education educator*
Gross, Richard Edmund *education educator*
Henriksen, Thomas Hollinger *university official*
Kays, William Morrow *university administrator, mechanical engineer*
Kirst, Michael Weile *education educator, researcher*
Massy, William Francis *education educator, academic administrator*
†Naimark, Norman M. *academic administrator*
Noddings, Nel *education educator, writer*
Palm, Charles Gilman *university official*
Perry, William James *educator, former federal official*
Raisian, John *university institute director, economist*
Spence, Andrew Michael *dean, finance educator*
Strena, Robert Victor *retired university research laboratory manager*
Strober, Myra Hoffenberg *education educator, consultant*
Whitney, Rodger Franklin *university housing director*

**Stinson Beach**
Metz, Mary Seawell *university dean, retired college president*

**Stockton**
DeRicco, Lawrence Albert *college president emeritus*
Jantzen, J(ohn) Marc *retired education educator*
Klinger, Wayne Julius *secondary education educator*
O'Brien, Sister Maureen *school system administrator*
Sorby, Donald Lloyd *university dean*
Thompson, Thomas Sanford *former college president*
Washburn, Harriet Caroline *secondary education educator*

**Sun Valley**
Mayhue, Richard Lee *dean, pastor, writer*

**Tarzana**
Yablun, Ronn *secondary education educator, small business owner*

**Temecula**
Randall, John Albert, III *elementary and secondary education educator*

**Torrance**
Culton, Paul Melvin *retired counselor, educator, interpreter*
McNamara, Brenda Norma *secondary education educator*

**Turlock**
Amrhein, John Kilian *dean*
Hughes, Marvalene *academic administrator*

**Tustin**
Gray, Sandra Rae *retired secondary school educator*

**Twentynine Palms**
Clemente, Patrocinio Ablola *psychology educator*

**Ukiah**
Elberg, Sanford Samuel *retired university dean and bacteriology educator*

**Union City**
Lockhart, Patsy Marie *secondary education educator*

**Vacaville**
Wisneski, Mary Jo Elizabeth *reading specialist, educator*

**Valencia**
Looney, Claudia Arlene *academic administrator*

**Vallejo**
Baker, Christine Marie *secondary education educator*
Marshall, Roberta Navarre *middle school educator*

**Van Nuys**
Altshiller, Arthur Leonard *secondary education educator*

**Venice**
Dixon, Neil Edward *elementary school educator, paleo-anthropologist*

**Ventura**
Evans, James Handel *university administrator, architect, educator*
Lawson, William Harold *college dean, labor economist*
Williamson, John Henry, III *school administrator*

**Visalia**
Dixon, Andrew Derart *retired academic administrator*
Sickels, William Loyd *secondary educator*

**Vista**
Tiedeman, David Valentine *education educator*

**Walnut**
Spencer, Constance Marilyn *secondary education educator*

**Walnut Creek**
Carver, Dorothy Lee Eskew (Mrs. John James Carver) *retired secondary education educator*
Mackay, Patricia McIntosh *counselor*

**Weimar**
Kerschner, Lee R(onald) *academic administrator, political science educator*

**West Covina**
Perez, Mary Angelica *bilingual specialist, educational administrator*

**Westlake Village**
Steadman, Lydia Duff *elementary school educator, symphony violinist*

**Westminster**
Ryan, James Edwin *industrial arts educator*

**Whittier**
Ash, James Lee, Jr. *academic administrator*
Drake, E. Maylon *academic administrator*
Tunison, Elizabeth Lamb *education educator*
Zanetta, Joseph Michael *university administrator, lawyer*

**Woodland Hills**
Swaim, Ruth Carolyn *secondary education educator*
Zeitlin, Eugenia Pawlik *educator, librarian, writer*
Zeitlin, Herbert Zakary *retired college president, private pilot*

**Yorba Linda**
Sternitzke-Holub, Ann *elementary school educator*

## COLORADO

**Arvada**
Rusch, Pamela Jean *middle school educator*

**Aurora**
Cowee, John Widmer *retired university chancellor*
Fedak, Barbara Kingry *technical center administrator*
Jarvis, Mary G. *principal*
Matson, Merwyn Dean *educational consultant*

**Bellvue**
Bennett, Jim *retired university official*

**Boulder**
Anderson, Ronald Delaine *education educator*
Buechner, John C. *academic administrator*
Dilley, Barbara Jean *college administrator, choreographer, educator*
Enarson, Harold L. *university presidentemeritus*
Fletcher, James Andrew *vice chancellor*
Park, Roderic Bruce *academic administrator*
Sirotkin, Phillip Leonard *educational administrator*
Williams, James Franklin, II *university dean, librarian*
Williams, Pamela R. *secondary school administrator*

**Broomfield**
Rodriguez, Linda Takahashi *secondary school educator, administrator*

**Colorado Springs**
Adams, Bernard Schroder *retired college president*
Grady, Dolores Anne *academic administrator, educator, consultant*
Mohrman, Kathryn *academic administrator*
Reddel, Carl Walter *education adminstration*
Ruch, Marcella Joyce *educator, biographer*
Wilcox, Rhoda Davis *elementary education educator*

**Creede**
Carter, Shirley Raedelle *retired elementary school educator*

**Deer Trail**
Malson, Verna Lee *special education educator*

**Denver**
Bautista, Michael Phillip *school system administrator*
Brainard, Edward Axdal *academic administrator*
Craine, Thomas Knowlton *academic administrator*
DePew, Marie Kathryn *retired secondary school educator*
Fielden, C. Franklin, III *early childhood education consultant*
Fulginiti, Vincent *university dean*
Fulkerson, William Measey, Jr. *college president*
Goss, Patricia Elizabeth *secondary education educator*
Greenspahn, Barbara *university administrator, law educator, librarian*
Grounds, Vernon Carl *seminary administrator*
Hafenstein, Norma Lu *education educator*
Halgren, Lee A. *academic administrator*
Hill, Kathleen Lois *performing art school executive*
Hinkle, Betty Ruth *educational administrator*
Jacobson, Eugene Donald *educator, administrator, researcher*
Koto, Paul *multicultural educator*
Mc Clenney, Byron Nelson *community college administrator*
Messer, Donald Edward *theological school president*
Mornes, Amber J. Bishop *consultant, computer software trainer, analyst*
Palmreuter, Kenneth Richard Louis *principal*
Ritchie, Daniel Lee *academic administrator*
Ryman, Ruth (Stacie) Marie *primary education educator*
Tucker, James Raymond *primary education educator*
Zaranka, William F. *academic administrator, author*

**Durango**
Candelaria, Angie Mary *special education educator*
Jones, Joel Mackey *college president*

**Englewood**
Dawson, Eugene Ellsworth *university president emeritus*
Zernial, Susan Carol *education educator*

**Fort Collins**
Anderson, B(enard) Harold *educational administrator*
Harper, Judson Morse *university administrator, consultant, educator*
Holcomb, Edie L. *educational administrator, consultant*
Jaros, Dean *university official*
Yates, Albert Carl *academic administrator, chemistry educator*

**Fort Morgan**
Perdue, James Everett *university vice chancellor emeritus*

**Golden**
Mueller, William Martin *former academic administrator, metallurgical engineering educator*

**Grand Junction**
Bergen, Virginia Louise *principal, language arts educator*
Kribel, Robert Edward *academic administrator, physicist*
Moberly, Linden Emery *educational administrator*

**Greeley**
Bond, Richard Randolph *foundation administrator, legislator*
Duff, William Leroy, Jr. *university dean emeritus, business educator*
Hause, Jesse Gilbert *retired college president*
Murry, Francie Roberta *special education educator*
Townsend, Susan Louise *elementary school administrator*

**Hotchkiss**
Perry, Jeanne Elyce *principal*

**Iliff**
Nichols, Lee Ann *library media specialist*

**Lakewood**
Beckman, L. David *university chancellor*
Mc Bride, Guy Thornton, Jr. *college president emeritus*
Milan, Marjorie Lucille *early childhood education educator*
Reed, Joan-Marie *special education educator*
West, Marjorie Edith *elementary education educator*

**Littleton**
Bush, Stanley Giltner *secondary school educator*
Greenberg, Elinor Miller *college offocial, consultant*
Lening, Janice Allen *physical education educator*
Lucero, Scott Alan *special education educator*
Pearlman, Mitzi Ann *elementary education educator*
Rockwell, Kay Anne *elementary education educator*
Schmidt, Ronald R. *academic administrator*

**Monte Vista**
Tillman, John Lee *principal*

**Northglenn**
Shaeffer, Thelma Jean *primary school educator*
Straub, Kenneth Richard *educator*

**Pueblo**
Lightell, Kenneth Ray *education educator*
Shirley, Robert Clark *retired university president, strategic planning consultant, educator*
Sisson, Ray L. *retired dean*
Vest, Rosemarie Lynn Torres *secondary school educator*

**Trinidad**
Amari, Kathryn Jane *elementary education educator*
Palovich, Marilyn Lee *elementary education educator*

**U S A F Academy**
Cubero, Ruben Anthony *dean, military officer*

**Westminster**
Eaves, Stephen Douglas *educator, vocational administrator*
Reed, John Howard *school administrator*

**Yuma**
Pfalmer, Charles Elden *secondary school educator*

## CONNECTICUT

**Bloomfield**
Hilsenrath, Baruch M. *principal*

**Branford**
Milgram, Richard Myron *music school administrator*

**Bridgeport**
Dworkin, Irma-Theresa *school system administrator, researcher*
Pitzschler, Kathryn Van Duren *secondary school educator*

**Bristol**
Roberts, Alida Jayne *elementary school educator*

**Cheshire**
Wallace, Ralph *superintendent*

**Cos Cob**
Fishman, Claire *media specialist*

**Danbury**
Arbitelle, Ronald Alan *elementary education educator*
Hawkes, Carol Ann *university dean*
Roach, James R. *university president*
Roach, James Richard *academic administrator*
Stewart, Albert Clifton *college dean, marketing educator*

**Fairfield**
Cernera, Anthony Joseph *academic administrator*
Kelley, Aloysius Paul *university administrator, priest*
Michael, Mary Amelia Furtado *retired educator, freelance writer*

**Falls Village**
Purcell, Dale *college president, consultant*

**Farmington**
Deckers, Peter John *dean*
Jestin, Heimwarth B. *retired university administrator*

**Glastonbury**
Hatch, D. Patricia P. *principal*
Juchnicki, Jane Ellen *secondary education educator*

Roy, Kenneth Russell *school system administrator, educator*

**Greens Farms**
Johnson, Jamieson Dregallo *women's athletics director*

**Groton**
English, James Fairfield, Jr. *former college president*

**Hamden**
Bennett, Harry Louis *college educator*
Loro, Lauren Marguerite *secondary education educator*

**Hartford**
Cross, Vivian Alicia *school system administrator, educator*
†Dobelle, Evan Samuel *college administrator*
Frost, James Arthur *former university president*
Perez-Silva, Glaisma *special education teacher*
Reynolds, Scott Walton *academic administrator*
Stoker, Warren Cady *university president*
Tonkin, Humphrey Richard *academic administrator*

**Madison**
Peterkin, Albert Gordon *retired education educator*

**Meriden**
Brandt, Irene Hildegard *secondary education educator*
Cassidy, LeAnn Murphy *elementary educator*

**Middletown**
Bennet, Douglas Joseph, Jr. *university president*
Kerr, Clarence William *retired university administrator*

**Milford**
Palochko, Eleanor LaRivere *retired secondary education educator*

**New Britain**
Rybczyk, Edward Joseph *university director, consultant*

**New Canaan**
Norman, Christina Reimarsdotter *secondary education language educator*

**New Haven**
Farquhar, Doris Irene Davis *academic administrator*
Hull, John McAllister *educator, painter*
Lamar, Howard Roberts *educational administrator, historian*
Levin, Richard Charles *academic administrator, economist*
Lorimer, Linda Koch *university educator*
Mullen, Frank Albert *university official, clergyman*
Simone, Angela Paolino *elementary education educator*
Walker-LaRose, Linda Waleska *elementary education educator*
Yandle, Stephen Thomas *law school dean*

**New London**
Gaudiani, Claire Lynn *academic administrator*

**Newington**
Vassar, William Gerald *gifted and talented education educator*

**Newtown**
Kotecki, Joanna Krystyna Emerle *primary school educator*

**Niantic**
Ashley, Eleanor Tidaback *retired elementary educator*

**North Haven**
Fuggi, Gretchen Miller *education educator*
McCauley, Lisa Francine *secondary education educator*
Montagna, Bernice Donna *education educator*

**North Stonington**
Keane, John Patrick *retired secondary education educator*

**Northford**
James, Virginia Stowell *retired elementary, secondary education educator*

**Norwalk**
Perschino, Arthur J. *elementary school principal*
Wiggins, Charles *secondary education educator*

**Preston**
Makara, Carol Pattie *education educator, consultant*

**Prospect**
Thornley, Wendy Ann *educator, sculptor*

**Ridgefield**
Leonard, Sister Anne C. *superintendent, education director*
Robertson, Suzanne Marie *primary education educator*

**Simsbury**
Barnicle, Stephan Patrick *secondary school educator*
DiCosimo, Patricia Shields *art educator*

**Stamford**
Bonina, Sally Anne *secondary school educator*
Castrignano, Robert Anthony *retired dean, retired broadcasting company executive*

**Storrs**
Nieforth, Karl Allen *university dean, educator*

**Storrs Mansfield**
Austin, Philip Edward *university president*
Gray, Robert Hugh *college dean*
Gutteridge, Thomas G. *academic administrator, consultant and labor arbitrator*

**Stratford**
Hageman, Richard Philip, Jr. *educational administrator*

**Suffield**
Savoie, Ronald E. *secondary educator*

**Trumbull**
Nevins, Lyn (Carolyn A. Nevins) *educational supervisor, trainer, consultant*
Norcel, Jacqueline Joyce Casale *educational administrator*

**Wallingford**
Hay, Leroy E. *school system administrator*

**Waterbury**
Cable, Richard Charles *education administrator, educator, consultant*
Farrell, Brian E. *school psychologist*
Higgins, Dorothy Marie *academic dean*

**West Haven**
DeNardis, Lawrence J. *academic administrator*
Farquharson, Patrice Ellen *primary school educator*

**Wethersfield**
Edwards, Kenneth S. *principal*
Gaudreau, Gayle Glanert *computer resource educator*

**Willimantic**
Carter, David George, Sr. *university administrator*
Enggas, Grace Falcetta *university administrator*
Peagler, Owen F. *college administrator*

**Wilton**
Grunewald, Donald *former college president, educator*
Jessep, Jane Nordli *elementary education educator*

**Windsor Locks**
Coelho, Sandra Signorelli *secondary school educator*

**Wolcott**
Gerace, Robert F. *secondary school principal*

## DELAWARE

**Delmar**
Czernik, Joanne *elementary and secondary education educator*

**Dover**
Braverman, Ray Howard *secondary school educator*
Delauder, William B. *academic administrator*
Sorenson, Liane Beth McDowell *women's affairs director, state legislator*

**Hockessin**
Moyer, Calvin Lyle *adult educator*

**Lewes**
Lane, William Harry, Jr. *principal*

**Millsboro**
Derrickson, Shirley Jean Baldwin *elementary school educator*

**New Castle**
Olden, Anna Beatrice *former educator*

**Newark**
Kessler, Betty Dean *elementary school educator, reading resource educator*
McLain, William Tome *principal*
Schiavelli, Melvyn David *academic administrator, chemistry educator, researcher*

**Ocean View**
Parler, Anne Hemenway *elementary education educator, horse trainer*

**Wilmington**
Desien, Mary Donna *principal*
Graves, Thomas Ashley, Jr. *educational administrator*
Heald, Debbie Ann *special education educator, counselor*
Houseman, Ann Elizabeth Lord *educational administrator, state official*
Olson, Leroy Calvin *retired educational administration educator*
Renshaw, John Hubert *retired secondary education educator*

## DISTRICT OF COLUMBIA

**Washington**
Adams, Linette M. *principal*
Alatis, James Efstathios *university dean emeritus*
Alton, Bruce Taylor *educational consultant*
Arnez, Nancy Levi *educational leadership educator*
August, Diane L. *educational program consultant, policy researcher*
Bader, Rochelle Linda (Shelley Bader) *educational administrator*
Barrett, Richard David *university director, consultant, bank executive*
Battle, Lucius Durham *retired educational institution administrator, former diplomat*
Baylor, Valoria E. *educational administrator, school counselor*
Bulger, Roger James *academic health center executive*
Burgin, Walter Hotchkiss, Jr. *educational administrator*
Burris, James Frederick *academic dean, educator*
Chambliss, William Joseph *educator, sociologist, author*
Chandler, John Wesley *educational consultant*
Collins, Herbert, Jr. *retired elementary education educator*
Collins, Naomi F. *higher education administrator*
Cornett, Richard Orin *research educator, consultant*
Covington, Eileen Queen *secondary education educator*

Dougherty, Jude Patrick dean
Elliot, Peggy Gordon academic administrator
Elliott, Emerson John education consultant, policy analyst
Ellis, Brother Patrick (H. J. Ellis) academic administrator
Fisher, Miles Mark, IV education and religion educator, minister
Fosler, R. Scott academic administrator
Futrell, Mary Alice Hatwood dean, education association administrator
Gaff, Jerry Gene academic administrator
Gentry, Barbara Beatrice educational consultant
Goldfarb, Mark Leonard education program specialist
Graves, Ruth Parker educational executive, educator
Halperin, Samuel education and training policy analyst
Harrison, Earl Grant, Jr. educational administrator
Herbert, James Charles education executive
Herbster, William Gibson university administrator, consultant
Hoi, Samuel Chuen-Tsung art school dean
Holden, John Bernard former college president, educator
Horan, Harold Eugene university administrator, former diplomat
Ikenberry, Stanley Oliver education educator, former university president
Ingold, Catherine White academic administrator
Jenkins, John Smith academic dean, lawyer
Jones-Wilson, Faustine Clarisse education educator emeritus
Keeley, Robert Vossler retired academic administrator, retired ambassador
Kelly, Eugene Walter, Jr. counseling educator
Kent, Jill Elspeth academic administrator, lawyer, art dealer, former government official
Kirkien-Rzeszotarski, Alicia Maria academic administrator, researcher, educator
Kramer, Robert dean
Leon, Donald Francis university dean, medical educator
Livingston, Robert Gerald university official, political scientist
MacDonald, John Thomas educational administrator
Malveaux, Floyd Joseph academic dean
Martin, David Standish education educator
Mattar, Philip institute director, editor
Maxted, William C. dean
Maxwell, David E. academic administrator, educator
Miller, Carroll Lee Liverpool educational researcher
Moore, Marsha Lynn elementary education educator
Myers, Marjorie Lora elementary school principal
Nelson, Charles J. university administrator, international consultant, diplomat, consultant
Newsome, Sandra Singleton secondary education educator, principal
O'Connor, John Dennis academic administrator
O'Donovan, Leo Jeremiah university president, theologian, priest
Ostar, Allan William academic administrator, higher education consultant
Preer, Jean Lyon associate dean, information science educator
Pruitt, Anne Loring academic administrator, education educator
Ross, Marlene educator
Salamon, Linda Bradley university administrator, English literature educator
Scott, Joyce Alaine university official
Sibolski, Elizabeth Hawley academic administrator
Smuckler, Ralph Herbert university dean, political science educator
Solomon, Henry university dean
Starr, Stephen Frederick academic administrator, historian
Steigman, Andrew L. academic dean
Stein, Paul E. superintendent
Stone, Elizabeth Wenger retired dean
Sullivan, Charles university dean, educator, author
Thompson, Bernida Lamerle principal, consultant, educator
Tlou, Josiah S. education educator
Trachtenberg, Stephen Joel university president
Turaj, Frank university dean, literature and film educator
Wilson, Carolyn Ross school administrator
Young, Kenneth Evans educational consultant

## FLORIDA

### Alachua
Marston, Robert Quarles university president
Thornton, J. Ronald technology center director

### Altamonte Springs
Harner, David Paul development administrator
Poland, Phyllis Elaine secondary school educator, consultant

### Atlantic Beach
Herge, Henry Curtis, Sr. education educator, dean emeritus

### Avon Park
Cornelius, Catherine Petrey college president

### Babson Park
Cloud, Linda Beal retired secondary school educator

### Bartow
Mercadante, Anthony Joseph special education educator
Wean, Karla Denise middle school educator, secondary education educator

### Boca Raton
Arden, Eugene retired university provost
Arnold, Walter Martin vocational education educator
Averett-Short, Geneva Evelyn college administrator
Burns, Gerald Phillip higher education educator
Caputi, Marie Antoinette university official
Catanese, Anthony James academic administrator
Guglielmino, Lucy Margaret Madsen education educator, researcher, consultant
Miller, Eugene university official, business executive
Murray, John Ralph former college president
Ross, Donald Edward university administrator
Tennies, Robert Hunter headmaster

### Bonita Springs
Johnson, Franklyn Arthur academic administrator

### Bradenton
Brown, David Edward elementary and environmental education educator
Pedersen, Norman Arno, Jr. retired headmaster, literary club director
Reagan, Larry Gay dean

### Brandon
Blomgren, David Kenneth dean, pastor

### Brooksville
Warsick-Rinzivillo, Mary Katrina counselor, educator

### Bryceville
Tippins, Susan Smith elementary school principal

### Cape Coral
Lane, William C., Jr. principal

### Clearwater
Jacobs, Marilyn Arlene Potoker gifted education educator, consultant, author
Mattice, Howard LeRoy education educator
Stilwell, Charlotte Finn vocational counselor
Youngberg, Robert Stanley principal, consultant

### Coconut Grove
Cotton, John Pierce principal

### Coral Gables
Moss, Ambler Holmes, Jr. academic administrator, educator, lawyer, former ambassador
Parry, Barbara Drepperd educational administrator
Yarger, Sam Jacob dean, educator

### Coral Springs
Caserta, Jean Kilsheimer elementary education educator, family counselor
Heydet, Nathalie Durbin gifted and talented education educator

### Daytona Beach
Cool, Mary L. elementary education educator

### Deland
Brakeman, Louis Freeman retired university administrator
Dascher, Paul Edward university dean, accounting educator
Duncan, Pope Alexander college administrator
Gill, Donald George education educator
Langston, Paul T. music educator, university dean, composer
Lee, Howard Douglas academic administrator
Morland, Richard Boyd retired educator

### Delray Beach
Knapp, Janis Ann elementary school educator

### Deltona
Neal, Dennis Melton middle school educator
Venuti, Ruth Louise secondary school educator, counselor

### Destin
Asher, Betty Turner academic administrator

### Estero
Brush, George W. college president

### Fernandina Beach
Fishbaugh, Carole Sue secondary school educator

### Fort Lauderdale
Adams, Alfred Hugh college president
Fershleiser, Steven Buckler secondary education educator
Fischler, Abraham Saul education educator, retired university president
Ginn, Vera Walker educational administrator
McCan, James Lawton education educator
Ornstein, Libbie Allene primary school educator
Young, William Benjamin special education educator

### Fort Myers
Cyphert, Frederick Ralph academic administrator
Hoffman, Nelson Miles, Jr. retired academic administrator, consultant
Tyrer, John Lloyd retired headmaster
Whittaker, Douglas Kirkland school system administrator

### Fort Myers Beach
Waetjen, Walter Bernhard academic administrator emeritus

### Fort Walton Beach
Sanders, Jimmy Devon public administration and health services educator

### Gainesville
App, James Leonard educator
Bryan, Robert Armistead university administrator, educator
Chait, Andrea Melinda special education educator
Challoner, David Reynolds university official, physician
Chapin, Kenneth Lee middle school educator
Cheek, Jimmy Geary university administrator, agricultural education and communications educator
Clark, Elmer J. education educator
Davidson, James Melvin academic administrator, researcher, educator
Hale, James Pierce education educator
†Humphrey, Stephen college dean
Ketts, Sharon Davis elementary education educator
Kirkland, Nancy Childs secondary education educator, consultant
Lombardi, John V. university administrator, historian
Lowenstein, Ralph Lynn university dean emeritus
Meyer, Harvey Kessler, II retired academic administrator
Neims, Allen Howard univeristy dean, medical scientist
Penland, Arnold Clifford, Jr. college dean, educator
Phillips, Winfred Marshall dean, mechanical engineer
Price, Donald Ray university official, agricultural engineer
Slattery, William Joseph school psychologist
Viessman, Warren, Jr. academic dean, civil engineering educator, researcher
York, E. Travis academic administrator, former university chancellor, consultant

### Graceville
Collier, Evelyn Myrtle elementary school educator
Kinchen, Thomas Alexander college president

### Green Cove Springs
Yelton, Eleanor O'Dell retired reading specialist

### Hilliard
Clough, Lauren C. special education educator

### Hollywood
Goldberg, Icchok Ignacy retired special education educator

### Homestead
Bachmeyer, Steven Allan secondary education educator
Brammer, Barbara Allison secondary school educator, consultant

### Indian Harbor Beach
Barr, Constance Ransick school system administrator

### Indian Rocks Beach
Rocheleau, James Romig academic administrator

### Jacksonville
Beytagh, Francis Xavier, Jr. college dean, lawyer
Boyles, Carol Ann Patterson career development educator
Brann, William Paul retired university official
Colby, Lestina Larsen secondary education educator
Cook, Mary Shepard education educator
Gunning, John Thaddeus retired superintendent
Herbert, Adam William, Jr. university president
Kinne, Frances Bartlett chancellor emeritus
MacDonald, Carolyn Helms gifted education educator
Osborn, Marvin Griffing, Jr. educational consultant

### Jupiter
Moseley, Karen Frances F. retired school system administrator, educator
Sproull, Robert Lamb retired university president, physicist
Strom, Carla Castaldo elementary education educator

### Kissimmee
Boswell, Tommie C. middle school educator
Evans-O'Connor, Norma Lee secondary school educator, consultant
Toothe, Karen Lee elementary and secondary school educator

### Lady Lake
Belok, Michael Victor education educator

### Lake Wales
Hodapp, Shirley Jeaniene curriculum administrator

### Lakeland
Hammond, Vernon Francis school administrator
Wade, Ben Frank college administrator

### Largo
Gall, Keith M. director
Hinesley, J. Howard superintendent
Weatherby, Susan Moormann elementary school educator

### Lecanto
Walker, Mary Diane secondary school educator

### Leesburg
Burns, Diane gifted education educator

### Longboat Key
Atwell, Robert Herron higher education executive

### Maitland
MacKenzie, Charles Sherrard academic administrator
Whitlock, Luder Gradick, Jr. seminary president

### Marianna
Flowers, Virginia Anne academic administrator emerita

### Melbourne
Delisio, Sharon Kay secondary school educator, school administrator
Edwards, David Northrop retired university administrator
Hollingsworth, Abner Thomas university dean
Noonan, Norine Elizabeth academic administrator, researcher
Weaver, Lynn Edward academic administrator, consultant, editor

### Merritt Island
Martin, Judson Phillips retired education educator
McClanahan, Leland academic administrator

### Miami
Bitter, John university dean emeritus, musician, businessman, diplomat
Breman, Joseph Eliot school administrator, lawyer
Brenner, Esther Hannah elementary school educator
Clarke, Donald Duhaney secondary education educator
Cohen, Eugene Erwin university health institute administrator, accounting educator emeritus
Cornelius, Vicki Lynn middle school educator
Dottin, Erskine S. education educator
Foote, Edward Thaddeus, II university president, lawyer
Halberg, F. David principal
Henderson, William Eugene education educator
Lee, J. Patrick academic administrator
Maidique, Modesto Alex academic administrator
McCabe, Robert Howard college president
Morales, Carlota Eloisa principal
O'Laughlin, Sister Jeanne university administrator
Pyles, Carol DeLong dean, consultant, educator
Quigley, John Joseph special education educator
Stern, Joanne Thrasher elementary school educator
†Stiehm, Judith Hicks university official, political science educator

### Miami Beach
Gitlow, Abraham Leo retired university dean

### Mount Dora
Santini, John Amedeo educational consultant

### Mulberry
Bowman, Hazel Lois retired English language educator

### Naples
Abbott, John Sheldon law school dean and chancellor emeritus
Cantelon, John Edward academic administrator
Loft, Bernard Irwin education educator, consultant

### Navarre
Korn, Irene Elizabeth retired elementary education educator, consultant

### Nokomis
Myers, Virginia Lou education educator

### Ocala
Hodges, Elizabeth Swanson educational consultant, tutor
Tait, Patricia Ann secondary education educator

### Ocoee
Mabie, Susan (Susse ) secondary education educator

### Okeechobee
Raulerson, Phoebe Hodges school superintendent

### Oldsmar
Fernandez, Joseph Anthony educational administrator

### Opa Locka
Hopton, Janice elementary school principal
Sample, Althea Merritt secondary education educator, conductor

### Orange Park
Oglesby, Beverly Clayton kindergarten educator
Ratzlaff, Judith L. secondary school educator

### Orlando
Ady, Laurence Irvin academic administrator
Clinton, Stephen Michael academic administrator
Colbourn, Trevor retired university president, historian
Hitt, John Charles university president
Wright, Martha Helen elementary education educator

### Osprey
Weathermon, Sidney Earl elementary school educator

### Palm Bay
Colman, Charles Kingsbury academic administrator, criminologist

### Palm Beach
Steere, Anne Bullivant retired student advisor

### Palm City
Ammarell, John Samuel retired college president, former security services executive

### Palm Coast
Dickson, David Watson Daly retired college president
Godfrey, Eutha Marek elementary school educator, consultant
Myckaniuk, Maria Anna elementary and special education educator

### Palm Harbor
Wolfe, Elizabeth Anne elementary education educator

### Pensacola
Abercrombie, Charlotte Manning reading specialist, supervisor
Marx, Morris Leon academic administrator
McLeod, Stephen Glenn education educator, language educator
Wyss, Norma Rose Topping counselor, supervisor, educator, writer

### Pinellas Park
Athanson, Mary Catheryne elementary school principal
Pellegrino, Nancy Davis middle school educator

### Pompano Beach
Hoffman, Lynn Renee elementary education educator

### Ponte Vedra Beach
Hartzell, Karl Drew retired university dean, historian

### Port Charlotte
Gravelin, Janesy Swartz elementary education educator
Hennessy, Brother Paul Kevin religion school president
Norris, Dolores June elementary school educator

### Port Saint Lucie
Centerbar, Alberta Elaine education educator, research specialist

### Punta Gorda
Goodman, Donald C. university administrator
Hill, Richard Earl academic administrator

**Saint Augustine**
Proctor, William Lee *college president*
Sullivan, Mary Jean *elementary school educator*

**Saint Petersburg**
Allshouse, Merle Frederick *higher education executive*
Armacost, Peter Hayden *college president*
Jacob, Bruce Robert *dean, academic administrator, law educator*
Kuttler, Carl Martin, Jr. *academic administrator*
Meisels, Gerhard George *academic administrator, chemist, educator*
Nussbaum, Leo Lester *retired college president, consultant*
Peterson, Arthur Laverne *former college president*
Southworth, William Dixon *retired education educator*
Westall, Sandra Thornton *special education educator*

**Sanford**
Luna, Charaline *superintendent of schools*

**Sarasota**
Adams, Richard Towsley *university president, educational consultant*
Christ-Janer, Arland Frederick *college president*
Downey, John Charles *university dean, zoology educator*
Gourley, Mary E. *education educator*
Highland, Marilyn M. *principal*
Pillot, Gene Merrill *retired school system administrator*
Russell, Margaret Jones (Peg Russell) *secondary school educator, retired writer*
Tatum, Joan Glennalyn John *secondary school educator*

**Sebastian**
Mauke, Otto Russell *retired college president*

**Spring Hill**
Rojas, Victor Hugo Macedo *retired vocational education educator*

**Stuart**
Bourque, Anita Mary *school principal, health facility administrator*

**Sun City Center**
Stanton, Vivian Brennan (Mrs. Ernest Stanton) *retired educator*

**Tallahassee**
Adams, Perry Ronald *former college administrator*
Baum, Werner A. *former academic administrator, meteorologist*
Bert, Clara Virginia *home economics educator, administrator*
Burkman, Ernest, Jr. *education educator*
Burnette, Ada M. Puryear *educational administrator*
Bye, Raymond Erwin, Jr. *academic administrator*
D'Alemberte, Talbot (Sandy D'Alemberte) *academic administrator, lawyer*
Foss, Donald John *university dean, research psychologist*
Gil, Lazier *university dean*
Hafner, Lawrence Erhardt *education educator*
Humphries, Frederick S. *university president*
Lick, Dale Wesley *educator*
Lynn, Gwendolyn Renaye *educator*
Mills, Belen Collantes *early childhood education educator*
Morgan, Robert Marion *educational research educator*
Reed, Charles Bass *academic administrator*
Voran, James F. *principal*

**Tampa**
Anderson, Robert Henry *education educator*
Baldwin, Maryann Powell *school counselor, educator*
Bondi, Joseph Charles, Jr. *education educator, consultant*
Brown, John Lott *educator*
Cannella, Deborah Fabbri *elementary school educator*
Daniel, Patricia Lynne *educator, consultant*
Givens, Paul Ronald *former university chancellor*
Hegarty, Thomas Joseph *academic administrator, history educator*
Luddington, Betty Walles *library media specialist*
Mc Alister, Linda Lopez *educator, philosopher*
McCook, Kathleen de la Peña *university educator*
Reese-Brown, Brenda *primary education educator, mathematics specialist*
Sanchez, Mary Anne *secondary school educator*
Streeter, Richard Barry *academic official*
Weiner, Irving Bernard *university administrator, psychologist, educator*

**Tarpon Springs**
Byrne, Richard Hill *counselor, educator*
Green, May Clayman *early childhood educator and administrator*

**Tierra Verde**
Schmitz, Dolores Jean *primary education educator*

**Titusville**
Linscott, Jacqueline C. *education consultant, retired educator*

**Valrico**
Benjamin, Sheila Pauletta *secondary education educator*

**Venice**
Jamrich, John Xavier *retired university administrator*
Thomas, David Ansell *retired university dean*

**West Palm Beach**
Corts, Paul Richard *college president*
Russell, Joyce Weber *principal*
Turner, Arthur Edward *college administrator*

**Winter Haven**
Peck, Maryly VanLeer *college president, chemical engineer*

**Winter Park**
Bornstein, Rita *academic administrator*
Mc Kean, Keith Ferguson *former education educator*

**Zephyrhills**
Jernstrom, Joan *secondary education educator*

## GEORGIA

**Albany**
Hart, Mary *educator*

**Americus**
Capitan, William Harry *university president emeritus*
McGrady, Clyde A. *secondary school principal*
Stanford, Henry King *college president*

**Athens**
Andrews, Grover Jene *adult education educator, administrator*
Cole, David Akinola *academic administrator*
Crowley, John Francis, III *university dean*
Douglas, Dwight Oliver *university administrator*
Kleiner, Heather Smith *academic administrator*
Meeks, Carol Jean *educator*
Mixon, Deborah Lynn Burton *elementary school educator*
Newsome, George Lane, Jr. *education educator*
Speering, Robin *educator, computer specialist*
West, Marsha *elementary school educator*
Younts, Sanford Eugene *university administrator*

**Atlanta**
Aaberg, Thomas M., Sr. *academic administrator, ophthalmology educator*
Alexander, Cecil Abraham *college official, retired architect, consultant*
Bickerton, Jane Elizabeth *university research coordinator*
Bright, David Forbes *academic administrator, classics and comparative literature educator*
Chace, William Murdough *university administrator*
Clough, Gerald Wayne *academic administrator*
Cole, Johnnetta Betsch *academic administrator*
Cole, Thomas Winston, Jr. *chancellor, college president, chemist*
Curry, Toni Griffin *counseling center executive, consultant*
Dees, Julian Worth *academic/research administrator*
Ferris, James Leonard *academic administrator*
Fowler, Andrea *teachers academy administrator*
Frye, Billy Eugene *university administrator, biologist*
Galloway, Thomas D. *dean*
Henry, Ronald James Whyte *university official*
Hershatter, Andrea Silver *university official*
Higgins, Richard J. *educational administrator*
Hogan, John Donald *college dean, finance educator*
Jolley, Samuel Delanor, Jr. *academic administrator*
Keiller, James Bruce *college dean, clergyman*
Lopez, Antonio Vincent *education educator*
Lucido, Chester Charles, Jr. *educational consultant*
Parko, Edith Margaret *special education educator*
Pattillo, Manning Mason, Jr. *academic administrator*
Patton, Carl Vernon *academic administrator, educator*
Pound, E. Jeanne *school psychologist, consultant*
Stanton, Donald Sheldon *academic administrator*
Suttles, William Maurrelle *university administrator, clergyman*
Truly, Richard H. *academic administrator, former federal agency administrator*
Walker, Carolyn Smith *college services administrator, counselor*
White, Annette Jones *early childhood education administrator*

**Auburn**
Clines, Cindy Collins *elementary school administrator, educator*

**Augusta**
Bloodworth, William Andrew, Jr. *academic administrator*
Kirch, Darrell G. *dean*
Lambert, Vickie Ann *dean*
Martin, Willie Pauline *elementary school educator, illustrator*
Puryear, James Burton *college administrator*
Tedesco, Francis Joseph *university administrator*

**Bremen**
McBrayer, Laura Jean H. *school media specialist*

**Brunswick**
Harper, Janet Sutherlin Lane *educational administrator, writer*
Holder, Kathleen *elementary education educator*

**Buford**
Carswell, Virginia Colby *primary school educator, special education educator*

**Carrollton**
Johnson, Harris Tucker *university administrator*
Morris, Robert Christian *education educator*
Sethna, Beheruz Nariman *university president, marketing, management educator*

**Cartersville**
Cleveland, Julia Lynn *elementary school educator*
Wheeler, Susie Weems *retired educator*

**Chatsworth**
Witherow, Jimmie David *secondary school educator*

**Clarkesville**
Melichar, Barbara Ehrlich *educational administrator*

**Clarkston**
Conway, Edward Gerald, Jr. *university educational technology administrator*

**Cochran**
Halaska, Thomas Edward *academic administrator, director, engineer*
Welch, Joe Ben *academic administrator*

**College Park**
Ferguson, Wendell *private school educator*

**Columbus**
Averill, Ellen Corbett *secondary education science educator, administrator*
Brown, Frank Douglas *academic administrator*
Cook, Mary Gooch *elementary school educator*
Edmondson, Michael Herman *secondary school educator*
Montgomery, Anna Frances *elementary school educator*
Riggsby, Dutchie Sellers *education educator*
Robbins, Brenda Sue *early childhood educator*

**Cornelia**
Reabold, Anthony Maurice *school system administrator*

**Covington**
Griffey, Karen Rose *special education educator*

**Crawford**
Bower, Douglas William *pastoral counselor, psychotherapist, clergyman*

**Cumming**
Benson, Betty Jones *school system administrator*

**Cuthbert**
Swinson, Sue Whitlow *secondary education educator*
Treible, Kirk *college president*

**Dacula**
Reid, Ginger Meredith *school counselor, educator*

**Dallas**
Calhoun, Patricia Hanson *secondary education educator*

**Danielsville**
Bond, Joan *elementary school educator*

**Decatur**
Baker, Stephen M. *school system administrator*
Carey, John Jesse *academic administrator, religion educator*
Fletcher, Regina Roberson *school system administrator*
Jones, Sherman J. *academic administrator, management educator, investment executive*
Keaton, Mollie M. *elementary school educator*
Myers, Orie Eugene, Jr. *university official*
Wilkinson, Ben *chancellor, evangelist, ministry organizer, writer*

**Douglas**
Pugh, Joye Jeffries *educational administrator*

**Dublin**
Fatum, Delores Ruth *school counselor*
Watson, Mary Alice *academic administrator*

**Duluth**
Neuman, Ted R. *principal*

**Ellijay**
Davis, Janet Holmes *special education educator*

**Evans**
Shrader, Lynne Ann *secondary school educator, coach*

**Gainesville**
Burd, John Stephen *academic administrator, music educator*
Embry, Karen Thompson *elementary education educator*
Hastings, Trish D. *clinical counselor, marriage counselor*

**Jasper**
Parrish, Carmelita *secondary school educator*

**Jonesboro**
Pulliam, Brenda Jane *secondary school educator*
Sprayberry, Roslyn Raye *secondary school educator*
Ziegler, Robert Oliver *special education educator*

**Kennesaw**
Siegel, Betty Lentz *college president*
Whitworth, Elaine Atkins *counselor*

**La Fayette**
Hendrix, Bonnie Elizabeth Luellen *elementary school educator*

**La Grange**
Ault, Ethyl Lorita *special education educator, consultant*

**Lilburn**
Magill, Dodie Burns *early childhood education educator*

**Lithonia**
Flanagan, James Lee *educational administrator*

**Locust Grove**
Short, Betsy Ann *elementary education educator*

**Lyons**
Cancer, Cathy Lynn *elementary education educator*

**Macon**
Ackerman, Robert Kilgo *college president, historian*
Bayliss, Sister Mary Rosina *principal*
Dantzler, Deryl Daugherty *dean, law educator*
Dessem, R. Lawrence *dean, law educator*
Godsey, R(aleigh) Kirby *university president*
Innes, David Lyn *university official, educator*
Mitchell, Carolyn Cochran *college official*
Popper, Virginia Sowell *education educator*
Smith, Constance Lewis *secondary school educator*
Steeples, Douglas Wayne *university dean, consultant, researcher*

**Manchester**
McIntyre, Richard Rawlings, II *elementary school educator*

**Marietta**
Brown, Billy Charlie *secondary school educator*
Cheshier, Stephen Robert *university president, electrical engineer*
Laframboise, Joan Carol *middle school educator*
Matias, Patricia Trejo *secondary education educator*
Veatch, Sheila Williamson *counselor*

**Millwood**
King, Mary Ann *secondary education educator*

**Morrow**
Becker, Robert Dean *academic administrator, educator, author, consultant*

**Mount Berry**
Mathis, Luster Doyle *college administrator, political scientist*
Shatto, Gloria McDermith *academic administrator*

**Newnan**
Johnson, Hardwick Smith, Jr. *school psychologist*

**Norcross**
Burnett, Cassie Wagnon *middle school educator*
Wingate, Thomas Marie Joseph *assistant headmaster*

**Ocilla**
Miller, Mavis Moss *school administrator, social worker*

**Perry**
Hinnant, Tony *superintendent*

**Riverdale**
Lambert, Ethel Gibson Clark *secondary school educator*

**Robins AFB**
Hunnicutt, Victoria Anne Wilson *school system administrator*

**Roswell**
Causey, Susan Marie *health educator*
Smith, Sheryl Velting *elementary school executive director*

**Saint Simons Island**
Tomberlin, William G. *principal*

**Savannah**
Burnett, Robert Adair *university administrator, history educator*
Coberly, Patricia Gail *elementary education educator, adult education educator*
Strauser, Beverly Ann *education educator*
Wolfe, John Thomas, Jr. *university president*

**Statesboro**
Black, Charlene Rushton *university official, sociology educator*
Henry, Nicholas Llewellyn *college president, political science educator*

**Thomson**
English, John Rife *educational administrator*
Smith, Robert L. *principal*

**Toccoa**
Gardner, William Wayne *academic administrator*

**Toccoa Falls**
Alford, Paul Legare *college and religious foundation administrator*

**Tunnel Hill**
Martin, Teresa Ann Hilbert *special education educator*

**Valdosta**
Bailey, Hugh Coleman *university president*
Cripe, Juliann Woods *education educator*

**Warner Robins**
Owens, Helen Dawn *elementary school educator, reading consultant*

**Washington**
Wills, Olive Boline *elementary education educator*

**Watkinsville**
Kennon, Pamela Canerday *secondary school educator*

**Waycross**
Losty, Barbara Paul *college official*

**Winder**
Allen, B. Janice *elementary educator*
Hutchins, Cynthia Barnes *special education educator*

**Winterville**
Anderson, David Prewitt *retired university dean*

**Young Harris**
Yow, Thomas Sidney, III *college administrator*

**Zebulon**
Bizzell Yarbrough, Cindy Lee *school counselor*

## HAWAII

**Eleele**
Takanishi, Lillian K. *elementary school educator*

**Hilo**
Best, Mary Lani *university program coordinator*

**Honolulu**
Alm, Richard Sanford *education educator*
Bess, Henry David *dean*
Gee, Chuck Yim *dean*
Gulbrandsen, Christian L. *academic dean*
Hee, Vivian Sanae Mitsuda *principal*
Inaba, Lawrence Akio *educational director*

Jackson, Miles Merrill *retired university dean*
Kaiser-Botsai, Sharon Kay *early chilhood educator*
Keith, Kent Marsteller *academic administrator, corporate executive, government official, lawyer*
King, Arthur R., Jr. *education educator, researcher*
Meyer, Robert Allen *human resource management educator*
Pickens, Alexander Legrand *education educator*
Ramler, Siegfried *educator*
Wright, Chatt Grandison *academic administrator*

**Kailua**
Tokumaru, Roberta *principal*

**Kailua Kona**
Clewett, Kenneth Vaughn *college official*
Diama, Benjamin *retired educator, artist, composer, writer*
Feaver, Douglas David *university dean, classics educator*

**Lihue**
Shigemoto, April Fumie *English educator secondary school*

**Makawao**
Mascho, George Leroy *education educator emeritus*

**Pearl City**
Rhinelander, Esther Richard *secondary school educator*

## IDAHO

**Boise**
Andrus, Cecil Dale *academic administrator*
Barr, Robert Dale *university dean, educator*
Cook, Sharon Evonne *university official*
Griffin, Gloria Jean *elementary school educator*
Griffin, Sylvia Gail *reading specialist*
Maloof, Giles Wilson *academic administrator, educator, author*
Ruch, Charles P. *academic administrator*
Steinfort, James Richard *university program director*
Woodard, Larry L. *college official*
Young, Katherine Ann *education educator*

**Caldwell**
Hendren, Robert Lee, Jr. *academic administrator*

**Coeur D Alene**
Medved, Sandra Louise *elementary education educator*

**Idaho Falls**
Woodruff, Shirley *middle school educator*

**Lewiston**
Duley, Charlotte Dudley *vocational counselor*

**Mc Call**
Evans, Darrell J. *secondary education educator*

**Middleton**
Brown, Ilene De Lois *special education educator*

**Moscow**
Bartlett, Robert Watkins *academic dean, metallurgist*
†Hatch, Charles R. *university dean*
Hendee, John Clare *university research educator*

**Pocatello**
Bowen, Richard Lee *academic administrator, political science educator*
Eichman, Charles Melvin *career assessment educator, school counselor*
Lawson, Jonathan Nevin *academic administrator*
Sagness, Richard Lee *education educator, former academic dean*

**Twin Falls**
Anderson, Marilyn Nelle *elementary education educator, librarian, counselor*

## ILLINOIS

**Anna**
McMahan, Gale Ann Scivally *school system administrator*
Wolfe, Martha *elementary education educator*

**Aurora**
Nespechal, Susan Mary *community college administrator*
Thomas, James Patrick *special education educator*
Zarle, Thomas Herbert *academic administrator*

**Bloomington**
Gregor, Marlene Pierce *primary education educator, elementary science consultant*
Myers, Minor, Jr. *academic administrator, political science educator*
Watkins, Lloyd Irion *university president*

**Calumet City**
Jandes, Kenneth Michael *superintendent of schools*
Palagi, Robert Gene *college administrator*

**Carbondale**
Casey, John P. *special education educator*
Covington, Patricia Ann *university administrator*
Dixon, Billy Gene *academic administrator*
Guyon, John Carl *university administrator*
Mead, John Stanley *university administrator*
Quisenberry, Nancy Lou *university administrator, educator*
Snyder, Carolyn Ann *university dean, librarian*

**Carlinville**
Pride, Miriam R. *academic administrator*

**Carol Stream**
Choice, Priscilla Kathryn Means (Penny Choice) *gifted education educator, international consultant*

**Cary**
Passaglia, Candace V. *special education educator*

**Catlin**
Asaad, Kolleen Joyce *special education educator*

**Champaign**
Cammack, Trank Emerson *retired university dean*
Dulany, Elizabeth Gjelsness *university press administrator*
Espeseth, Robert D. *park and recreation planning educator*
Feinberg, Walter *philosophy educator*
Loeb, Jane Rupley *university administrator, educator*
Schowalter, William Raymond *college dean, educator*
Spodek, Bernard *early childhood educator*
Ward, James Gordon *education administration educator*

**Charleston**
Buckellew, William Franklin *retired education educator*
Jorns, David Lee *university president*
Rives, Stanley Gene *university president emeritus*

**Chester**
Gross, Melissa Kay *elementary education educator*

**Chicago**
Ayman, Iraj *international education consultant*
Baker, Robert J. *medical academic dean, surgeon*
Beane, Marjorie Noterman *academic administrator*
Beck, Irene Clare *educational consultant, writer*
Beck, John Matthew *education educator*
Bloom, Benjamin S. *education educator*
Blumenthal, Carlene Margaret *vocational-technical school educator*
Bornholdt, Laura Anna *university administrator*
Bowman, Barbara Taylor *institute president*
Brown, Carlos *secondary education educator, psychology educator*
Caldwell, Ethel Louise Lynch *academic administrator*
Champagne, Ronald Oscar *academic administrator, mathematics educator*
Chapman, Delores *elementary education educator*
Coduti, Philip James *legal association administration*
Coe, Donald Kirk *university official*
Coleman, Roy Everett *secondary education educator, computer programmer*
Collens, Lewis Morton *university president, legal educator*
Cooper, Jo Marie *elementary school administrative assistant*
Coy, Patricia Ann *special education director, consultant*
Cross, Dolores Evelyn *university administrator, educator*
Culp, Kristine Ann *dean, theology educator*
Cummings, Maxine Gibson *elementary school educator*
Dempsey, James Randall *academic administrator*
Diaz-Gemmati, Griselle Maritza *secondary education educator*
Driskell, Claude Evans *college director, educator, dentist*
Dunlap, Patricia Pearl *elementary school educator*
Dye, Carl Melvyn *academic administrator, educational association executive, insurance consultant*
Felton, Cynthia *principal*
Finch, Herman Manuel *academic administrator*
Fruchter, Rosalie Klausner *elementary school educator*
Gamwell, Franklin I. *dean, educator*
Graham, Patricia Albjerg *education educator, foundation executive*
Gross, Theodore Lawrence *university administrator, author*
Hawkins, Loretta Ann *secondary school educator, playwright*
Henikoff, Leo M., Jr. *academic administrator, medical educator*
Heuer, Michael Alexander *dean, endodontist educator*
Iwanski, Mary *parochial school educator*
Jegen, Sister Carol Frances *religion educator*
Johnson, Barbara Elaine Spears *education educator*
Kloc, Emily Alvina *retired elementary school principal*
Kozanecki, Robert Francis *educator*
Kubistal, Patricia Bernice *educational consultant*
Lester, Robin Dale *educator, author, former headmaster*
Lewis, Philip *educational and technical consultant*
Long, Earline Davis *elementary education educator*
Lynn, Laurence Edwin, Jr. *university administrator, educator*
Maresh, Alice Marcella *retired educational administrator*
Mason, Gregory Wesley, Jr. *secondary education educator*
Matasar, Ann B. *former dean, business and political science educator*
Meyers, Dorothy *education consultant, writer*
Mindes, Gayle Dean *education educator*
Minogue, John P. *academic administrator, priest, educator*
Moss, Gerald S. *dean, medical educator*
Mulligan, Robert William *university official, clergyman*
O'Reilly, Charles Terrance *university dean*
Page, Dozzie Lyons *vocational secondary school educator*
Panko, Jessie Symington *education educator*
Perry, Edna Burrell *retired elementary school principal*
Piderit, John J. *university educator*
Pillarella, Deborah Ann *elementary education educator, consultant*
Reinke, John Henry *educational administrator, clergyman*
Reynolds, Ruth Carmen *school administrator, secondary school educator*
Richardson, John Thomas *academic administrator, clergyman*
Rosenbluth, Marion Helen *educator, consultant, psychotherapist*
Schieser, Hans Alois *education educator*
Schommer, Carol Marie *principal*
Schubert, William Henry *curriculum studies educator*
Schwarzkopf, Gloria A. *education educator, psychotherapist*
Scrimshaw, Susan *dean*
Sizemore, Barbara Ann *Black studies educator*
Smith, Kenneth Bryant *seminary administrator*
Spearman, David Leroy *elementary education educator, administrator*
Standberry, Herman Lee *school system administrator, consultant*
Steven, Donald Anstey *dean, educator*
Stowell, Joseph, III *academic administrator*
Stukel, James Joseph *academic administrator, mechanical engineering educator*
Sulkin, Howard Allen *college president*
Swanson, Don Richard *university dean*
Swanson, Patricia K. *university official*
Taylor, John Wilkinson *education educator*
Wallace, Helen Marie *secondary school educator, coach*
Wasan, Darsh Tilakchand *university official, chemical engineer educator*
Watts, John Ransford *university administrator*
Weiman, Heidi *early childhood education educator*
Wooten-Bryant, Helen Catherine *academic administrator*
Yamakawa, Allan Hitoshi *academic administrator*

**Darien**
Meyer, James Philip *secondary education social studies educator*

**De Kalb**
King, Kenneth Paul *secondary education educator*
La Tourette, John Ernest *academic administrator*
Monat, William Robert *university official*
Zar, Jerrold H(oward) *academic administrator, biology educator, statistician*

**Decatur**
McCray, Curtis Lee *university president*

**Deerfield**
Meyer, Mara Ellice *special education educator, consultant*

**Des Plaines**
Coburn, James LeRoy *educational administrator*
Lakier, Thelma *child development specialist, librarian*
Lee, Margaret Burke *college administrator, English educator*

**East Moline**
Adams, Stewart Lee *special education educator*

**East Peoria**
Dries, Colleen Patricia *adult education educator*

**East Saint Louis**
Wright, Katie Harper *school system administrator*

**Edwardsville**
Lazerson, Earl Edwin *academic administrator emeritus*
May, Mary Louise *elementary education educator*

**Elgin**
Didier, James William *academic administrator, consultant*
Patterson, Paul M. *school administrator*
Weber, Harm Allen *college chancellor, former college president*

**Elmhurst**
Begando, Joseph Sheridan *retired university chancellor, educator*
Cureton, Bryant Lewis *college president, educator*
Latzel, Lynn Marina *college administrator*

**Erie**
Latham, LaVonne Marlys *physical education educator*

**Eureka**
Hearne, George Archer *academic administrator*

**Evanston**
Boye, Roger Carl *academic administrator, journalism educator, writer*
Bufe, Noel Carl *program director*
Christian, Richard Carlton *university dean, former advertising agency executive*
Gellman, Aaron Jacob *management educator, transportation center administrator*
Herron, Orley R. *college president*
Ihlanfeldt, William *university administrator, consultant*
Kern, Charles William *university official, chemistry educator*
Lewis, Dan Albert *education educator*
McCoy, Marilyn *university official*
Miller, Thomas Williams *former university dean*
Slaughter-Defoe, Diana Tresa *education educator*
Weber, Arnold R. *academic administrator*
Worthy, James Carson *management educator*
Zarefsky, David Harris *academic administrator, communication studies educator*

**Evergreen Park**
Sochacki, Tina Marie *secondary education educator*

**Flossmoor**
Ferreira, Daniel Alves *secondary education Spanish language educator*
Schillings, Denny Lynn *history educator*

**Fox Lake**
Galitz, Laura Maria *secondary education educator*

**Frankfort**
Ruggles, Barbara Ann *elementary education educator*

**Galesburg**
Haywood, Bruce *retired college president*

**Geneseo**
Simonich, Sandra Sue *elementary education educator*

**Glen Ellyn**
Patten, Ronald James *university dean*

**Glenview**
Corley, Jenny Lynd Wertheim *elementary education educator*
Traudt, Mary B. *elementary education educator*

**Granite City**
Humphrey, Owen Everett *retired education administrator*

**Greenville**
Stephens, William Richard *college president emeritus*

**Hazel Crest**
Roberts, Jo Ann Wooden *school system administrator*

**Highland Park**
Hoffman, Sharon Lynn *adult education educator*

**Hinsdale**
Burrows, Donald Albert *college dean, artist, painter,*

**Hoffman Estates**
Starzynski, Christine Joy *secondary educator*

**Homer**
Gilhaus, Barbara Jean *secondary education home economics educator*

**Ingleside**
Krentz, Eugene Leo *university president, educator, minister*

**Jacksonville**
Pfau, Richard Anthony *college president*
Welch, Rhea Jo *special education educator*

**Joliet**
Caamano, Kathleen Ann Folz *gifted education professional*
Gamble, Thomas Ellsworth *academic administrator*
Johnson, Mary Ann *computer training vocational school owner*
Scott, Linda Ann *assistant principal, elementary education educator*

**Kankakee**
Bowling, John C. *academic administrator*

**Kildeer**
Muffoletto, Mary Lu *retired school program director, consultant, editor*

**La Grange Park**
Stone, Gail Susan *retired gifted, talented education educator*

**Lake Forest**
Adelman, Pamela Bernice Kozoll *education educator*
Bermingham, John Scott *associate dean*
Bransfield, Joan *principal*
DuBose, Cornelius Bates *educational director*
Hotchkiss, Eugene, III *college president emeritus*

**Lansing**
Guzak, Debra Ann *special education educator*

**Lemont**
Urban, Patricia A. *former elementary school educator*

**Libertyville**
Kremkau, Paul *principal*
Price, Sandra Hoffman *secondary school educator*

**Lincolnshire**
DuFour, Richard P. *school system administrator*

**Lombard**
Winterstein, James Fredrick *academic administrator*

**London Mills**
McKinley Balfour, Stephanie Ann *learning resources director, librarian*

**Lynwood**
Dyer-Dawson, Diane Faye *educational administrator*

**Macomb**
Goehner, Donna Marie *university dean*
Witthuhn, Burton Orrin *university official*

**Madison**
Pope, Sarah Ann *elementary education educator*
Purdes, Alice Marie *adult education educator, retired*

**Markham**
Ruffolo, Marilyn Claire *primary education educator*

**Mattoon**
Sherline, Harold Albert *adult education professional*

**Metamora**
Crow, Mary Jo Ann *elementary education educator*

**Midlothian**
Cagala, M. Therese *assistant principal*

**Milan**
Yeggy-Davis, Geraldine Marie *elementary reading and special education educator*

**Montgomery**
Butcher, Ann Patrice *elementary school educator*

**Morton**
Corey, Judith Ann *educator*

**Murphysboro**
Hall, James Robert *secondary education educator*

**Naperville**
Florence, Ernest Estell, Jr. *special education educator*
Wilde, Harold Richard *college president*

PROFESSIONAL INDEX 5139 EDUCATION

**Normal**
Bolen, Charles Warren *university dean*
Hickrod, George Alan Karnes Wallis *educational administration educator*
Matsler, Franklin Giles *higher education educator*

**Norridge**
Karlin, Bernard Richard *retired educational administrator*

**Northbrook**
Cerveny, Kathryn M. *educational administrator*

**Northfield**
Fodrea, Carolyn Wrobel *educational researcher, publisher, consultant*
Hestad, Marsha Anne *educational administrator*

**O'Fallon**
Bradley, Thomas Michael *school system administrator*

**Oak Brook**
Baar, John Greenfield, II *school educator*

**Oak Forest**
Hull, Charles William *special education educator*

**Oak Lawn**
Surma, Jane Ann *secondary education educator*

**Oak Park**
Adelman, William John *university labor and industrial relations educator*
Davis, Christine Eurich *elementary education educator*
Patricks, Edward J *elementary education educator*
Venerable, Shirley Marie *gifted education educator*

**Oakbrook Terrace**
Cason, Marilynn Jean *technological institute official, lawyer*

**Oglesby**
Zeller, Francis Joseph *dean*

**Palos Hills**
Crawley, Vernon Obadiah *academic adminstrator*

**Palos Park**
Lawler, Susan George *elementary education educator*
Nicholls, Richard Allen *middle school social studies educator*

**Paris**
Essinger, Susan Jane *special education educator*

**Patoka**
Borgmann, Norma Lee *school superintendent*

**Pekin**
Herbstreith, Yvonne Mae *primary education educator*
Novak, Martha Lois *elementary education educator*

**Peoria**
Brazil, John Russell *academic administrator*
Francis, John Elbert *university dean*
McMullen, David Wayne *education educator*
Murphy, Sharon Margaret *university official, educator*
Smith, Clyde R. *counselor educator*

**Peru**
Benning, Joseph Raymond *principal*

**Quincy**
Toal, James Francis *academic administrator*

**River Forest**
Lund, Sister Candida *college chancellor*

**River Grove**
Stein, Thomas Henry *social science educator*

**Robinson**
Wolfe, Ellen Darlene *school librarian, elementary school educator*

**Rock Island**
Brauch, Merry Ruth Moore *gifted education consultant*
Horstmann, James Douglas *college official*
Tredway, Thomas *college president*

**Rockford**
Howard, John Addison *former college president, institute executive*
Marelli, Sister M. Anthony *secondary school principal*
Rauch, Janet Melodie *elementary school educator*
Steele, Carl Lavern *academic administrator*
Whitsell, Doris Benner *retired educator*
Wilke, Duane Andrew *educator*

**Roselle**
Gomopoulos, Mary *elementary school educator*

**Saint Charles**
Alfini, James Joseph *dean, educator, lawyer*
Libka, Robert John *educational director, consultant*

**Saint Joseph**
McDade, Linna Springer *retired academic program administrator*

**Schaumburg**
Hlousek, Joyce B(ernadette) *school system administrator*
Roderick, William Rodney *academic administrator*

**Shelbyville**
Storm, Sandy Lamm *secondary education educator*

**Springfield**
Cowles, Ernest Lee *academic administrator, educator, consultant, researcher*
Craig, John Charles *educational researcher, consultant*
Lynn, Naomi B. *academic administrator*
Moy, Richard Henry *academic dean, educator*
Penning, Patricia Jean *elementary education educator*
Phillips, John Robert *college administrator, political scientist*
Poorman, Robert Lewis *education educator, consultant, academic administrator*

**Sterling**
Albrecht, Beverly Jean *special education educator*

**Sycamore**
Johnson, Yvonne Amalia *elementary education educator, science consultant*

**Urbana**
Aiken, Michael Thomas *academic administrator*
Bloomfield, Daniel Kermit *college dean, physician*
Holt, Donald A. *university administrator, agronomist, consultant, researcher*
Mc Conkie, George Wilson *education educator*
Rogers, Paula Ann *secondary school educator*
Shuman, R(obert) Baird *academic program director, writer, English language educator, educational consultant*
Wedgeworth, Robert *dean, university librarian, former association executive*
Weir, Morton Webster *retired academic administrator, educator*

**Villa Park**
Peterson, Elaine Grace *technology director*
Smith, Barbara Ann *gifted education coordinator*
Taylor, Ronald Lee *school administrator*

**Washington**
McKinney-Keller, Margaret Frances *retired special education educator*

**Wheaton**
Algeo, John Thomas *retired educator, association executive*

**Wilmette**
Kohl, Dolores *educator, administrator*
Smutny, Joan Franklin *academic director, educator*

**Winnetka**
Huggins, Charlotte Susan Harrison *secondary education educator, author, travel specialist*

**Woodridge**
Krugly, Andrew *elementary school principal*

## INDIANA

**Anderson**
Nicholson, Robert Arthur *college president*

**Angola**
Lin, Ping-Wha *engineering educator, consultant*

**Batesville**
Volk, Cecilia Ann *elementary education educator*

**Bloomington**
Arnove, Robert Frederick *education educator*
Bain, Wilfred Conwell *former university dean, music educator, opera theater director*
Barnes, A. James *academic dean*
Brand, Myles *academic administrator*
Crowe, James Wilson *university administrator, educator*
Gros Louis, Kenneth Richard Russell *university chancellor*
Hopkins, Jack Walker *former university administrator, environmental educator*
Johnson, Owen Verne *program director*
Mehlinger, Howard Dean *education educator*
Mobley, Tony Allen *university dean, recreation educator*
Otteson, Schuyler Franklin *former university dean, educator*
Ryan, John William *retired university president*
Smith, Carl Bernard *education educator*
Webb, Charles Haizlip, Jr. *university dean*
Wells, Herman B *university chancellor*
Williams, Edgar Gene *university administrator*

**Cambridge City**
Schwartz, Susan Lynn Hill *principal*

**Churubusco**
Deck, Judith Therese *elementary school educator*

**Crawfordsville**
Ford, Andrew Thomas *academic administrator*

**Crown Point**
Jones, Walter Dean *community program director*

**Culver**
Manuel, Ralph Nixon *private school executive*

**East Chicago**
Platis, James G. *secondary school educator*

**Elkhart**
Meyer, Albert James *educational researcher*

**Elwood**
Barnett, Marilyn Doan *secondary education business educator*

**Evansville**
Thompson, Robin Jill *special education educator*
Vinson, James Spangler *academic administrator*

**Fort Branch**
Bertram, Michael Wayne *secondary education educator*

**Fort Wayne**
Andorfer, Donald Joseph *university president*
Lewark, Carol Ann *special education educator*
Pease, Ella Louise *elementary education educator*
Stebbins, Vrina Grimes *elementary school educator, counselor*
Weicker, Jack Edward *educational administrator*

**Franklin**
Farrar, Susan Lee *special education educator, consultant*
Martin, William Bryan *chancellor, lawyer*

**Fremont**
Elliott, Carl Hartley *former university president*

**Gary**
Hall, James Rayford, III *adult education educator*
Richards, Hilda *academic administrator*
Smith, Vernon G. *education educator, state representative*
Thomas, Carolyn Harper *elementary educator*
Wells, Charles Robert *secondary education educator*
Williams, Mary Elizabeth *elementary school educator*

**Georgetown**
Dailey, Donald Harry *adult education educator, volunteer*

**Goshen**
Stoltzfus, Victor Ezra *retired university president, academic consultant*

**Greencastle**
Bottoms, Robert Garvin *academic administrator*
Houck, Carolyn Marie Kumpf *special education educator*

**Hammond**
Delph, Donna Jean (Maroc) *education educator, consultant, university administrator*
Yovich, Daniel John *educator*

**Indianapolis**
Bannister, Geoffrey *university president, geographer*
Barcus, Mary Evelyn *primary school educator*
Bepko, Gerald Lewis *university administrator, law educator, lecturer, consultant, lawyer*
Brash, Susan Kay *principal*
Brooks, Patricia Scott *principal*
Dickeson, Robert Celmer *retired university president, corporation president, political science educator*
Fadely, James Philip *admissions and financial aids director, educator, writer*
Felicetti, Daniel A. *academic administrator, educator*
Galbraith, Bruce W. *educational administrator*
Gilmore, H. William *college dean, dentistry educator*
Gooldy, Patricia Alice *elementary education educator*
Hefler, William Louis *elementary education educator*
Huffman-Hine, Ruth Carson *adult education administrator, educator*
Ilchman, Warren Frederick *university administrator, political science educator*
Johnstone, Joyce Visintine *education educator*
Rand, Leon *academic administrator*
Scannell, Dale Paul *education educator*
Silver, David Mayer *former university official*
Solomon, Marilyn Kay *educator, consultant*
Watkins, Sherry Lynne *elementary school educator*
Williams, Gloria Louise *gifted and talented education educator*
Woody, John Frederick *secondary education educator*
Wynn, Sherri Lorraine *educational administrator*

**Jamestown**
Waymire, John Thomas *principal*

**Kokomo**
Daniels, Doral Lee *education educator*
Hill, Emita Brady *academic administrator*

**La Porte**
Heiden, Susan Jane *elementary education educator*

**Lafayette**
Andrews, Frederick Newcomb *emeritus university administrator*
Vaughn, Vicki Lynn *education educator*

**Lagrange**
Young, Rebecca Lee *special education educator*

**Leesburg**
Pryor, Dixie Darlene *elementary education educator*

**Linden**
Lefebvre, Gren Gordon *school superintendent*

**Marion**
Barnes, James Byron *university president*
Philbert, Robert Earl *secondary school educator*

**Merrillville**
Magry, Martha J. *elementary education educator*
Roberts, Samuel Alden *secondary school educator*

**Monroeville**
Sorgen, Elizabeth Ann *retired educator*

**Monticello**
McTaggart, Patrick William *principal*

**Muncie**
Wagner, Joseph Crider *retired academic administrator*

**Munster**
Fies, James David *elementary education educator*
†Platis, Chris Steven *educator*
Sherman, Mona Diane *school system administrator*

**New Albany**
Crooks, Edwin William *former academic administrator*
Riehl, Jane Ellen *education educator*

**New Carlisle**
Serpe-Schroeder, Patricia L. *elementary education educator*

**Noblesville**
Thacker, Jerry Lynn *school administrator*

**Notre Dame**
Castellino, Francis Joseph *university dean*
Crosson, Frederick James *former university dean, humanities educator*
Hatch, Nathan Orr *university administrator*
O'Meara, Onorato Timothy *academic administrator, mathematician*
Truesdell, Timothy Lee *research director, consultant, real estate investor*

**Pendleton**
Phenis, Nancy Sue *educational administrator*

**Portage**
Zuick, Diane Martina *elementary education educator*

**Rensselaer**
Shannon, Albert Joseph *education educator*

**Richmond**
Bennett, Douglas Carleton *academic administrator*
Porter, Patrick Kevin *secondary education educator, administrator*
Robinson, Dixie Faye *school system administrator*

**Saint Mary Of The Woods**
Doherty, Sister Barbara, S.P. (Ann Doherty) *academic administrator*

**Schererville**
Griffin, Anita Jane *elementary education educator*

**South Bend**
Charles, Isabel *university administrator*
Mills, Nancy Anne *elementary education educator*
Perrin, Kenneth Lynn *university chancellor*

**Terre Haute**
Gilman, David Alan *education educator, editor*
Grimley, Liam Kelly *special education educator*
Hulbert, Samuel Foster *college president*
Hunt, Effie Neva *former college dean, former English educator*
Jerry, Robert Howard *education educator*
Kicklighter, Clois Earl *academic administrator*
Landini, Richard George *university president, emeritus English educator*
Leach, Ronald George *educational administration educator*
Moore, John W. *academic administrator*
Moore, John William *university president*
Van Til, William *education educator, writer*

**Upland**
Kesler, Jay Lewis *academic administrator*

**Valparaiso**
Foley, Jane Deborah *educational administrator*
Harre, Alan Frederick *university president*
Hillila, Bernhard Hugo Paul *education educator*
Maletta, Diane Stanley *gifted and talented educator, education educator*
Miller, John Albert *university administrator, consultant*
Mundinger, Donald Charles *college president retired*
Schnabel, Robert Victor *retired academic administrator*

**Vincennes**
Nead, Karen L. *university professor*

**West Lafayette**
Baumgardt, Billy Ray *university official, agriculturist*
Beering, Steven Claus *academic administrator, medical educator*
Ford, Frederick Ross *university official*
Frick, Gene Armin *university administrator*
Gappa, Judith M. *university administrator*
Gentry, Don Kenneth *academic dean*
Haring, Marilyn Joan *academic dean*
Moskowitz, Herbert *management educator*
Moyars-Johnson, Mary Annis *university official*
Newby, Timothy James *education educator, researcher*
Ringel, Robert Lewis *university administrator*
Shertzer, Bruce Eldon *education educator*
Stone, Beverley *former university dean, former dean of students*
Tacker, Willis Arnold, Jr. *academic administrator, medical educator, researcher*
Weidenaar, Dennis Jay *college dean*

**Westville**
Alspaugh, Dale William *university administrator, aeronautics and astronautics educator*

**Whiting**
Fies, Ruth Elaine *media specialist*

**Williamsport**
Baysinger, Jane Ann *elementary school music educator*

**Zionsville**
Hansen, Arthur Gene *former academic administrator, consultant*

## IOWA

**Ames**
Beisser, Sally Rapp *education educator*
Christensen, George Curtis *retired university official*
Crabtree, Beverly June *college dean*
Ebbers, Larry Harold *education educator*
Jischke, Martin C. *academic administrator*
Manatt, Richard *education educator*
Mattila, Mary Jo Kalsem *elementary and art educator*
Snow, Joel Alan *research director*

**Ankeny**
Nash, John Joseph *secondary education educator, real estate manager*

**Burlington**
Brocket, Judith Ann *elementary education mathematics educator*
Lundy, Sherman Perry *secondary school educator*

**Cedar Falls**
Schneider, Melvin Frederick *retired secondary music educator*

**Cedar Rapids**
Feld, Thomas Robert *academic administrator*
Plagman, Ralph *principal*
Rosberg, Merilee Ann *education educator*

**Charter Oak**
Kutschinski, Dorothy Irene *elementary education educator*

**Clinton**
Winkler, Joann Mary *secondary school educator*

**Corydon**
Olson, Diane Louise *secondary education educator*

**Council Bluffs**
Roberts, Antonette *special education educator*

**Davenport**
Currence, Glennda Kay *elementary education educator*
Rogalski, Edward J. *university administrator*

**Des Moines**
Davilla, Donna Elaine *school system administrator*
Ferrari, Michael Richard, Jr. *university administrator*
Marker, David George *university president*
Mattern, David Bruce *elementary education educator*
Webb-Groe, Mary Christine *special education educator*

**Dubuque**
Agria, John Joseph *retired college official*
Dunn, M. Catherine *college administrator, educator*
Peterson, Walter Fritiof *academic administrator*
Toale, Thomas Edward *school system administrator, priest*

**Dunkerton**
Wede, Richard J. *school superintendent*

**Elliott**
Hunt, Colleen A. *college administrator*

**Fort Dodge**
Pratt, Diane Adele *elementary education educator*

**Fort Madison**
Carroll, Melody Jane *educator, writer*

**Gilmore City**
Worthington, Patricia *elementary education educator*

**Greenfield**
Wilson, Wendy Melgard *primary and elementary school educator*

**Grimes**
Harper, Karen Beidelman *elementary school educator*

**Grinnell**
Fitzgerald, Michael J. *secondary school principal*
Walker, Waldo Sylvester *academic administrator*

**Harlan**
Ahrenholtz, Mary Mickelson *special education educator*

**Indianola**
Jennings, Stephen Grant *academic administrator*

**Iowa City**
Brennan, Robert Lawrence *educational director, psychometrician*
Bruch, Delores Ruth *education educator, musician*
Feldt, Leonard Samuel *university educator and administrator*
Paulina, Diana *alternative school educator*
Schulz, Rudolph Walter *university dean emeritus*
Skorton, David Jan *university official, physician, educator, researcher*
Vaughan, Emmett John *academic dean, insurance educator*
Whitmore, Jon Scott *university official, play director*

**Keokuk**
Mills, Sylvia Janet *secondary education educator*

**Lockridge**
Wolfe, Eva Agnes *retired educator*

**Muscatine**
Yoder, Anna Mary *reading educator*

**New Sharon**
Sullivan, Mary Jane *elementary school educator*

**Oakdale**
Spriestersbach, Duane Caryl *university administrator, speech pathology educator*

**Remsen**
Hamil, Lynn Ray *secondary education educator*

**Sioux Center**
Schut, Donna Sue *elementary education educator*

**Sioux City**
Nichols, Roger Sabin *school counselor*
Rants, Carolyn Jean *college official*
Rooney, Gail Schields *college administrator*
Tommeraasen, Miles *college president*
Wick, Sister Margaret *college administrator*

**Sloan**
Ullrich, Roxie Ann *special education educator*

**Storm Lake**
Hetzler, Susan Elizabeth Savage *educational administrator*

**Story City**
Kruger, Vicki Henry *elementary education educator*

**Walnut**
Myers, Gloria J. *elementary education educator*

**Waterloo**
Kober, Arletta Refshauge (Mrs. Kay L. Kober) *educational administrator*

**Waverly**
Vogel, Robert Lee *college administrator, clergyman*

## KANSAS

**Alta Vista**
Grimsley, Bessie Belle Gates *special education educator*

**Baldwin City**
Lambert, Daniel Michael *academic administrator*

**Bonner Springs**
Jarrett, Gracie Mae *junior high school guidance counselor*

**Coffeyville**
Brittain, Sister Janelle Ann *parochial school educator*

**Colby**
Squibb, Sandra Hildyard *special education educator*

**Derby**
Sandwell, Kristin Ann *special education educator*

**El Dorado**
Edwards, James Lynn *college dean*

**Emporia**
Glennen, Robert Eugene, Jr. *university president*
Schallenkamp, Kay *academic administrator*
Torrens, Peggy Jean *technical school coordinator*

**Goodland**
Sharp, Glenn (Skip Sharp) *technical education administrator*

**Great Bend**
Rittenhouse, Nancy Carol *elementary education educator*

**Hays**
Hammond, Edward H. *university president*
Harman, Nancy June *elementary education educator*

**Hiawatha**
Pennel, Marie Lucille Hunziger *elementary education educator*

**Horton**
Kirschner, Rod *secondary education educator*

**Hutchinson**
Green, Thereasa Ellen *elementary education educator*

**Kansas City**
Clifton, Thomas E. *seminary president, minister*
†Hagen, Donald Floyd *university administrator, former military officer*
Whelan, Richard J. *director special education and pediatrics programs, academic administrator*

**Lawrence**
Crowe, William Joseph *academic administrator, dean, educator*
Frederickson, Horace George *former college president, public administration educator*
Hemenway, Robert E. *university administrator, language educator*
Locke, Carl Edwin, Jr. *academic administrator, engineering educator*
Pinet, Frank Samuel *former university dean*
Turnbull, Ann Patterson *special education educator, consultant*
Wiechert, Allen LeRoy *educational planning consultant, architect*

**Leawood**
Briscoe, Keith G. *retired college president*

**Lenexa**
Starr, Darlene R. *special education educator, education educator*

**Liberal**
Wilkerson, Rita Lynn *special education educator, consultant*

**Manhattan**
Coffman, James Richard *academic administrator, veterinarian*
Flaherty, Roberta D. *university official*
Hahn, Richard Ray *academic administrator*
Kruh, Robert F. *university administrator*
Lee, William Franklin, III *association administrator*
Muir, William Lloyd, III *academic administrator*

**Mc Pherson**
Mason, Stephen Olin *academic administrator*

**Newton**
Hymer, Martha Nell *elementary education educator*

**Oakley**
Wolfe, Mindy René *early childhood education educator*

**Olathe**
Goodwin, Becky K. *secondary education educator*
Hackler, Ruth Ann *retired educator*
Shelton, Jody *educational executive director*

Stevens, Diana Lynn *elementary education educator*

**Pittsburg**
Darling, John Rothburn, Jr. *university administrator, educator*
Huddleston, Michael Ray *counseling administrator, consultant, educator*
Smoot, Joseph Grady *university administrator*
Sullivan, F(rank) Victor *university administrator, retired educator*

**Pomona**
Gentry, Alberta Elizabeth *elementary education educator*

**Salina**
Stanton, Marshall P. *academic administrator, minister*

**Shawnee Mission**
Coleman, Timothy Stewart *middle school principal*
Kaplan, Marjorie Ann Pashkow *school district administrator*

**Topeka**
Concannon, James M. *dean, law educator*
Thompson, Hugh Lee *academic administrator*
Young, Betty Mae *special education educator*

**Vassar**
Visser, John Evert *university president emeritus, historian*

**Wichita**
Groff, Susan Carole *elementary education educator*
Willon, Mychael Cole *school system administrator*

**Winfield**
Willoughby, John Wallace *former college dean, provost*

## KENTUCKY

**Bardstown**
Carter, Carmen M. *elementary education educator, consultant*

**Berea**
Hager, Paul Calvin *retired college administrator, educator*

**Bowling Green**
Carlock, Janet Lynne *middle school educator*
Murrell, Estelle C. *elementary school educator*

**Covington**
Bensman, Charles J. *academic administrator*

**Crestwood**
Upchurch, Paul *principal*

**Danville**
Adams, Michael F. *academic administrator, political communications specialist*
Breeze, William Hancock *college administrator*
Rowland, Robert E. *secondary school principal*

**Fairdale**
Steffen, Pamela Bray *secondary school educator*

**Falmouth**
Mudd, Sheryl Kay *secondary school educator, guidance counselor*

**Fordsville**
Upchurch, Sally Ann *school counselor*

**Fort Thomas**
Kukulinsky, Nancy Elaine *academic administrator*

**Frankfort**
Bennett, Ivan Stanley *school administrator*
McDaniel, Karen Jean *university library administrator*
Smith, Mary Levi *academic administrator*

**Georgetown**
Powell, Rebecca Gaeth *education educator*

**Harlan**
Greene, James S., III *school administrator*

**Harrodsburg**
Lunger, Irvin Eugene *university president emeritus, clergyman*

**Henderson**
Mattingly, L. Sharon *elementary principal*

**Highland Heights**
Boothe, Leon Estel *university president emeritus*

**Hindman**
Thompson, Marcia Slone *choral director, educator*

**Lexington**
Blackburn, Vickie Carlee *vocational rehabilitation counselor*
Blanton, Jack Christopher *academic administrator*
Bosomworth, Peter Palliser *university medical administrator*
Casey, Elberta *secondary education educator*
Cole, Henry Philip *educational psychology educator*
Fleming, Juanita W. *academic administrator*
Lawson, Frances Gordon *child guidance specialist*
Logan, Joyce Polley *education educator*
Matheny, Samuel Coleman *academic administrator*
Shipley, David Elliott *university dean, lawyer*
Singletary, Otis Arnold, Jr. *university president emeritus*
Thelin, John Robert *academic administrator, education educator, historian*
Walters-Parker, Kimberly Kay *secondary school educator*
Wethington, Charles T., Jr. *academic administrator*
Williams, Jackson Jay *education consultant*

Wilson, Emery Allen *university dean, obstetrician-gynecologist, educator*
Zinser, Elisabeth Ann *academic administrator*

**London**
Early, Jack Jones *college administrator*
Ridner, Kathleen Rader *elementary education educator*

**Louisville**
Carden, Joy Cabbage *educational consultant*
Copes, Marvin Lee *college president*
Ekstrom, William Ferdinand *college administrator*
Ferguson, Duncan Sheldon *education administrator*
Garfinkel, Herbert *university official*
Hazen, Elizabeth Frances *retired special education educator*
Kmetz, Donald R. *academic administrator*
McKinney, Owen Michael *special education educator, training and security consultant*
Mohler, Richard Albert, Jr. *academic administrator, theologian*
Nystrand, Raphael Owens *university dean, educator*
Oates, Thomas R. *university executive*
Schneider, Jayne B. *school librarian*
Shumaker, John William *academic administrator*
Swain, Donald Christie *retired university president, history educator*
Taylor, Robert Lewis *academic administrator*

**Mayfield**
Harris, Isaac Henson *university dean*

**Morehead**
Berry, Lemuel, Jr. *university dean*

**Murray**
Bumgardner, Cloyd Jeffrey *school principal*
Herndon, Donna Ruth Grogan *educational administrator*
Hunt, Charles Brownlow, Jr. *university dean, musician*

**Nicholasville**
Crouch, Dianne Kay *secondary school guidance counselor*

**Owensboro**
Hooks, Vandalyn Lawrence *former elementary school educator*
Martin, Barbara Ann *secondary education educator*
Poling, Wesley Henry *college president*

**Partridge**
Burton, Sharon Kay *primary education educator*

**Richmond**
Funderburk, H(enry) Hanly, Jr. *college president*

**Union**
Cook, Janice Eleanor Nolan *elementary school educator*

**Vanceburg**
Phillips, Susan Diane *secondary school educator*

**Winchester**
Dulin, Teresa Dianne *primary school educator*

## LOUISIANA

**Alexandria**
Goldich, Sandra McGinty *secondary school educator, consultant*

**Baton Rouge**
Boyce, Bert Roy *university dean, library and information science educator*
Brun, Judith *principal*
Caffey, H(orace) Rouse *university official, agricultural consultant*
Copping, Allen Anthony *university president*
Davis, William Eugene *university administrator*
Doty, Gresdna Ann *education educator*
Harrelson, Clyde Lee *secondary school educator*
Mc Cameron, Fritz Allen *retired university administrator*
Phills, Bobby Ray *dean, agricultural research director*
Prestage, James Jordan *university chancellor*
Rabideau, Peter Wayne *university dean, chemistry educator*
Wheeler, Otis Bullard *academic administrator, educator emeritus*
Williams, Hulen Brown *former university dean*
Wilson, Roosevelt Ledell *secondary education educator*
Woodin, Martin Dwight *retired university system president*

**Bossier City**
Darling, Shannon Ferguson *special education educator*

**Boutte**
Breaux, Marion Mary *secondary education educator*

**Destrehan**
Greene, Glen Lee, Jr. *secondary school educator*

**Franklin**
Fairchild, Phyllis Elaine *school counselor*

**Hammond**
Parker, Clea Edward *retired university president*

**Houma**
Lemoine, Pamela Allyson *assistant principal*

**Kenner**
Cook, Willie Chunn *elementary school educator*

**Lafayette**
Andrew, Catherine Vige *elementary school educator*
Cosper, Sammie Wayne *educational consultant*
Redding, Evelyn A. *dean, nursing educator*

**Lake Charles**
Fields, Anita *dean*
Hebert, Robert D. *academic administrator*
Leder, Sandra Juanita *elementary school educator*

**Marrero**
Love, Gayle Magalene *special education educator, adult education educator*

**Metairie**
Caruso, Kay Ann Pete *elementary education educator*
Flake, Leone Elizabeth *special education educator*
Gennaro, Glenn Joseph *principal*
Johnson, Beth Michael *principal*
Murphy, Alvin Leo *educational administrator*
Piper, Claudia Rosemary *academic administrator*

**Minden**
Doerge, Everett Gail *retired school system admistrator, state rep*

**Monroe**
Martin, Diane Caraway *school librarian*

**Natchitoches**
Alost, Robert Allen *university executive*
Wolfe, George Cropper *retired private school educator, artist, author*

**New Iberia**
Ledbetter, Deidre Leday *special education educator*

**New Llano**
Boren, Lynda Sue *gifted education educator*

**New Orleans**
Carter, James Clarence *university administrator*
Chambers, Thomas Edward *college president, psychologist*
Cook, Samuel DuBois *academic administrator, political scientist*
Danahar, David C. *academic administrator, history educator*
Davillier, Brenda Bozant *university administrator*
Gordon, Joseph Elwell *university official, educator*
Hamlin, James Turner, III *university dean, physician*
Hassenboehler, Donalyn *principal*
Jefferson, Patrick O'Neal *university program director, administrative assistant*
Johnson, Lee Harnie *dean, educator*
Jones, John Anderson, Jr. *school system administrator*
Kelly, Eamon Michael *university president*
†Kilroy, James Francis *dean provost*
Levitt, Gregory Alan *education educator*
Mackin, Cooper Richerson *university chancellor*
McCall, John Patrick *college president, educator*
McFarland, James W. *academic administrator*
McMahon, Maeve *middle school administrator*
Novakov, George John, Jr. *gifted and talented educator*
O'Brien, Gregory Michael St. Lawrence *university official*
Vanselow, Neal Arthur *university administrator, physician*
Walsh, John Joseph *medical school administrator, physician*
Washington, Robert Orlanda *educator, former university official*

**Pearl River**
Pendarvis, Donna Kaye *elementary secondary school educator, admnistrator*

**Pineville**
Matthews, Betty Parker *special education educator*

**Pride**
Jones, LaCinda *assistant principal*

**Quitman**
Davis, Ella Delores *special education educator, elementary school educator*

**Ruston**
Benedict, Barry Arden *dean*
Freasier, Aileen W. *special education educator*
Maxfield, John Edward *retired university dean*
Reneau, Daniel D. *university administrator*
Taylor, Foster Jay *retired university president*

**Shreveport**
Schwab, Kenneth Lynn *college president*
Thomas, Bessie *primary education educator*
Whitehead, Barbara Ann *secondary school educator*
Witt, Elizabeth Nowlin (Beth Witt) *special education educator, speech-language pathologist*

**Slidell**
Faust, Marilyn B. *elementary college school principal*

**Thibodaux**
Nunn, Thomas Calvin *school supervisor, retired army officer*
Worthington, Janet Evans *academic director, English language educator*

## MAINE

**Bar Harbor**
Swazey, Judith Pound *institute president, sociomedical science educator*

**Biddeford**
Featherman, Sandra *university president, political science educator*
Ford, Charles Willard *university administrator, educator*

**Brownfield**
Kloskowski, Vincent John, Jr. *educational consultant, writer, educator*

**Brunswick**
Edwards, Robert Hazard *college president*
Greason, Arthur LeRoy, Jr. *university administrator*

**Cumberland Foreside**
Dill, William Rankin *college president*

**Damariscotta**
Johnson, Arthur Menzies *retired college president, historian, educator*

**Fairfield**
Douglas, Jeanne Masson *academic administrator, education educator*

**Farmington**
Kalikow, Theodora June *university president*

**Hebron**
Farwell, Margaret Wheeler *elementary education educator*

**Kennebunk**
McConnell, David M. *secondary school principal*

**Lewiston**
Harward, Donald *academic official*

**Machias**
Rosen, David Matthew *education educator*

**Milbridge**
Heath, Douglas Hamilton *educational consultant*

**Millinocket**
Steeves, Eric William *school administrator*

**North Yarmouth**
Fecteau, Rosemary Louise *educational administrator, educator, consultant*

**Old Orchard Beach**
Bartner, Jay B. *school system administrator*

**Orono**
Bartel, Lavon Lee *university administrator, foods and nutrition scientist*
Butterfield, Stephen Alan *education educator*
Phippen, Sanford Edwin *secondary school educator, writer*
Wiersma, G. Bruce *dean, forest resources educator*

**Palermo**
Robbins, Marjorie Jean Gilmartin *elementary education educator*

**Portland**
Gilmore, Roger *college president*
Pattenaude, Richard Louis *academic administrator*

**Presque Isle**
Huffman, Durward Roy *college president, electrical engineer, educator*

**Spruce Head**
Bird, John Adams *educational consultant*

**Waterville**
Cotter, William Reckling *college president*

**Yarmouth**
Bischoff, David Canby *retired university dean*
Bissonnette, Jean Marie *elementary school educator, polarity therapist*
Hart, Loring Edward *academic administrator*

## MARYLAND

**Adelphi**
Langenberg, Donald Newton *academic administrator, physicist*

**Annapolis**
Brann, Eva Toni Helene *educator*
Ness, Frederic William *former academic administrator, educator, consultant*
Nuesse, Celestine Joseph *retired university official*
Parham, Carol Sheffey *school system administrator*
Rosenthal, Michael Ross *academic administrator, dean*

**Baltimore**
Behm, Mark Edward *university administrator, consultant*
Bianco, Frederick Anthony *dean*
Boughman, Joann Ashley *dean*
Bryan, Thelma Jane *dean, English educator*
Buser, Carolyn Elizabeth *correctional education administrator*
Donaldson, Sue Karen *dean, nursing educator*
Donovan, Sharon Ann *educator*
Ferrara, Steven *educational administrator, researcher, consultant*
Fishbein, Estelle Ackerman *lawyer*
Fitzgerald, Thomas Rollins *university administrator*
Fletcher, Sherryl Ann *higher education administrator*
Gifford, Donald George *academic dean*
Gleichmann, Frances Evangeline *retired elementary educator*
Grasmick, Nancy S. *superintendent of schools*
Hall, Merrill Souel, III *head master*
Jackson, Stanley Edward *retired special education educator*
Jancuk, Kathleen Frances *principal*
Keller, George Charles *higher education consultant, editor*
King, Ora Sterling *education educator*
Klitzke, Theodore Elmer *former college dean, arts consultant*
Lafferty, Joyce G. Zvonar *retired middle school educator*
Laric, Michael Victor *academic administrator*
Lazarus, Fred, IV *college president*
Leonard, John Wirth *English educator, retailer*
Levine, Robert Joseph *secondary school administrator*
McPartland, James Michael *university official*
Mohraz, Judy Jolley *college president*
Moszkowski, Lena Iggers *secondary school educator*
Nwofor, Ambrose Onyegbule *vocational assessment evaluator*
Ranney, Richard Raymond *dental educator, researcher*
Rose, Sara Margaret *English as a second language educator*
Ross, Richard Starr *medical school dean emeritus, cardiologist*
Schoenrich, Edyth Hull *academic administrator, physician*
Smith, Hoke LaFollette *university president*
Stenberg, Carl W(aldamer), III *academic program director, educator*
Sunshine, Eugene Samuel *university and public administrator*
Taylor, Janet Winona Mills *secondary school educator*
Wortham, Deborah Lynne *school system director, principal*

**Bel Air**
Hagenbuch, Stephen Lee *principal*
Miller, Dorothy Eloise *education educator*
Nye, Daniel William *elementary school educator*
Phillips, Bernice Cecile Golden *retired vocational education educator*
Riley, Catherine Irene *university official, cosultant, former state senator*

**Berlin**
Crawford, Norman Crane, Jr. *academic administrator, consultant*

**Bethesda**
Buccino, Alphonse *university dean emeritus, consultant*
Corn, Milton *academic dean, physician*
Dykstra, Vergil Homer *retired academic administrator*
Gleazer, Edmund John, Jr. *retired education educator*
Havlicek, Sarah Marie *educator, artist, small business owner*
Hemming, Val G. *university dean*
Jameson, Sanford Chandler *education educator*
Lystad, Robert Arthur Lunde *retired university dean, educator*
Reichard, John Francis *educational consultant*
Sober, Sidney *retired diplomat, education educator*

**Bowie**
Francis, Maxine Beth *special education educator*

**Boyds**
Carpenter, Dorothy Schenck *special education educator*

**Brookeville**
West, Gail Marcia Weiss *special education educator*

**Centreville**
Wharton, Kay Karole *special education educator*

**Chevy Chase**
Ferguson, James Joseph, Jr. *academic administrator, researcher*
Holloway, William Jimmerson *retired educator*
Meltzer, Jack *consultant, retired college dean*

**Clinton**
Jones, Sandra LaVern *day care administrator, small business owner*

**Cobb Island**
Rudy, Linda Mae *secondary school educator*

**College Park**
Berman, Louise Marguerite *education educator*
Collinson, Vivienne Ruth *education educator, researcher*
Dieter, George Elwood, Jr. *university official*
Dorsey, John Wesley, Jr. *university administrator, economist*
Finkelstein, Barbara *education educator*
Geoffroy, Gregory L. *academic administrator*
Hey, Nancy Henson *educational administrator*
Jackson, Vivian Michele *school administrator*
Massey, Thomas Benjamin *educator*
Polakoff, Murray Emanuel *university dean, economics and finance educator*
Prentice, Ann Ethelynd *academic adminstrator*
Schwab, Susan Carroll *university dean*
Seefeldt, Carol *education educator*
Stumpff, Robert Thomas *academic administrator*
Toll, John Sampson *university administrator, physics educator*

**Columbia**
Bruley, Duane Frederick *academic administrator, consultant, engineer*
Driggs, Margaret *educator*
Hartman, Lee Ann Walraff *educator*
Welty, Gail Ann Harper *physical education educator*
Whiting, Albert Nathaniel *former university chancellor*

**Crofton**
Eastman, John Robert *educator*

**Cumberland**
Shelton, Bessie Elizabeth *school system administrator*

**Eldersburg**
Bastress, Robert Lewis *principal*

**Emmitsburg**
Houston, George R. *college president*

**Forestville**
Stewart, Teresa Elizabeth *elementary school educator*

**Frederick**
Brown, Frederick James *education educator*

**Frostburg**
Gira, Catherine Russell *university president*
Root, Edward Lakin *education educator, university administrator*

**Gaithersburg**
Horman, Karen Loeb *elementary education educator*

**Glen Burnie**
Picken, Edith Daryl *school principal*

**Glenwood**
Rossetti, Linda Elaine *special education educator*

**Greenbelt**
Boarman, Gerald L. *principal*

**Helen**
Carter, Gale Denise *elementary education educator*

**Hyattsville**
Moylan, John L. *secondary school principal*
Rodgers, Mary Columbro *academic administrator, English educator, author*

**Kennedyville**
Schiff, Gary Stuart *academic administrator, educator*

**Kensington**
Hudson, Yvonne Morton *elementary education educator*
Jackson, Mary Jane McHale Flickinger *principal*

**Landover**
Fortson-Rivers, Tina E. (Thomasena Elizabeth Fortson-Rivers) *computer educator*

**Lanham**
Williams, Gladys Tucker *elementary school principal*

**Laurel**
Wales, Patrice *school system administrator*

**Lusby**
Ladd, Culver Sprogle *secondary education educator*

**Mardela Springs**
Harcum, Louise Mary Davis *retired elementary education educator*

**Marriottsville**
Pryseski, Gary Michael *secondary school educator*

**Mountain Lake Park**
Forrester, Donald Dean *university adminstrator, educator, consultant*

**Owings Mills**
Berg, Barbara Kirsner *health education specialist*

**Oxon Hill**
Christian, Mary Jo Dinan *educator, real estate professional*

**Potomac**
Ahmad, Sharmin *elementary education educator*
Jung, Richard Kieth *headmaster*
Karch, Karen Brooke *principal*

**Prince Frederick**
Karol, Victoria Diane *educational administrator*

**Queenstown**
Mc Laughlin, David Thomas *academic administrator, business executive*
Ryans, Reginald Vernon *music education educator*

**Randallstown**
Myers, Debra Taylor *elementary school educator, writer*

**Rockville**
Generlette, Bertram B. *elementary school educator*
Krear, Gail Richardson *elementary education educator, consultant*
Levine, Barbara Gershkoff *early childhood education educator, consultant*
Rohr, Karolyn Kanavas *school system administrator*
Rosenberg, Judith Lynne *middle school educator*
Sparks, David Stanley *university administrator*
Stansfield, Charles W. *educational administrator*
Stenger, Judith Antoinette *middle school educator*

**Sandy Spring**
Cope, Harold Cary *former university president, higher education association executive*

**Silver Spring**
Cheek, King Virgil, Jr. *educational administrator, lawyer*
Coles, Anna Louise Bailey *university official, nurse*
McGinn, Cherie M. *secondary education educator*
McLurkin-Harris, Kimberly Elana *secondary education educator*
Moseley, Theresa *guidance counselor, actress*
Poinsett-White, Sadie Ruth *elementary education educator*
Ryan, Patrick Andrew *educator*
Schick, Irvin Henry *academic administrator, educator*
Shih-Carducci, Joan Chia-mo *cooking educator, biochemist, medical technologist*
Shira, Robert Bruce *university administrator, oral surgery educator*
Whalen, John Philip *retired educational administrator*

**Suitland**
McKinney-Ludd, Sarah Lydelle *middle school education, librarian*

**Takoma Park**
Porter, Clarence A. *academic dean*

**Towson**
Chappell, Annette M. *university dean*
Hildebrand, Joan Martin *education educator*

**Upper Marlboro**
Clark, Jerome *educational administrator*
Dortch, Susan Madeline *elementary education educator*
Reed, Jacqueline K(emp) *educational researcher*
Street, Patricia Lynn *secondary education educator*

**Waldorf**
Robey, Sherie Gay Southall Gordon *secondary education educator, consultant*

**Westminster**
Chambers, Robert Hunter, III *college president, American studies educator*
LeGates, Gary A. *secondary education educator*

## MASSACHUSETTS

**Acton**
Tamaren, Michele Carol *special education educator*

**Agawam**
Schilling-Nordal, Geraldine Ann *secondary school educator*

**Amherst**
Adrion, William Richards *academic administrator, computer and information sciences educator, author*
Anderson, Ronald Trent *art educator*
Gerety, Tom *college administrator, educator*
Prince, Gregory Smith, Jr. *academic administrator*

**Andover**
Chase, Barbara Landis *school administrator*
Wise, Kelly *private school educator, photographer, critic*

**Arlington**
Freeland, Richard Middleton *academic affairs administrator, historian*
Fulmer, Vincent Anthony *retired college president*

**Babson Park**
Glavin, William Francis *academic administrator*

**Belmont**
Haselkorn, David *educator, recruiting executive*

**Beverly**
Marion, John Martin *academic administrator*
Murray, Mary *early childhood, elementary and secondary educator*

**Boston**
Argyris, Chris *organizational behavior educator*
Backus, Ann Swift Newell *education educator, consultant*
Banks, Henry H. *academic dean, physician*
Carfora, John Michael *university administrator, economics and political science educator*
Chobanian, Aram Van *medical school dean, cardiologist*
Curry, John Anthony, Jr. *university educator*
Davies, Don *education educator*
Dluhy, Deborah Haigh *college dean*
Eisner, Sister Janet Margaret *college president*
Greene, Robert Allan *former university administrator*
Hall, David *dean, law educator*
Henry, Joseph Louis *university dean*
Hyatt, Raymond Russell, Jr. *educator*
Kirkpatrick, Edward Thomson *college administrator, mechanical engineer*
Lerner, Richard Martin *academic administrator, educator*
O'Neil, William Francis *academic administrator*
Penney, Sherry Hood *university president, educator*
Pereira, Julio Cesar *middle school educator*
Rittner, Carl Frederick *educational administrator*
Rittner, Stephen Lee *academic administrator*
Ronayne, Michael Richard, Jr. *academic dean*
Sargent, David Jasper *university executive, lawyer*
Shattuck, Lawrence William *admissions director*
Silber, John Robert *academic administrator*
Simmons, Sylvia Jeanne Quarles (Mrs. Herbert G. Simmons, Jr.) *university administrator, educator, senior manager*
Van Domelen, John Francis *academic administrator*
Watts, Charles Henry, II *university administrator*
Westling, Jon *university administrator*

**Braintree**
Gittleman, Sol *university official, humanities educator*

**Bridgewater**
Barry, Marilyn White *dean, educator*
Cost, Richard Willard *university administrator, educator*
Fitzpatrick, Ruth Ann *education educator*
Tinsley, Adrian *college president*
Troupe, Bonnie Lee *college program coordinator, teacher*

**Brookline**
Weinstein, Rhonda Kruger *elementary mathematics educator, administrator*

**Burlington**
Dubois, Cindy A. *guidance counselor*

**Byfield**
Bragdon, Peter Wilkinson *headmaster*

**Cambridge**
Arnesen, Deborah Arnie *educator*
Bruce, James Donald *academic administrator*
Clendenning, Bonnie Ryon *college administrator*
†Cooney, James Allen *international educator*
Dickson, William Robert *academic administrator*
Emerson, Anne Devereux *university administrator*
Eurich, Nell P. *educator, author*
Fischer, Kurt Walter *education educator*
Fox, Ellen *academic administrator*
Fox, John Bayley, Jr. *university dean*
Gray, Paul Edward *academic official*
Hausman, Leonard J. *university official, educator*
†Howitt, Arnold Martin *university researcher, administrator, educator*
Johnson, Howard Wesley *former university president, business executive*
Landry, John Marsdale *university fundraiser, consultant*
McKenna, Margaret Anne *college president*
Mitchell, William J. *dean, architecture educator*
Ragone, David Vincent *former university president*
Rowe, Mary P. *academic administrator, management educator*
Rudenstine, Neil Leon *academic administrator, educator*
Seaman, Jeffrey Richard *academic administrator*
Sharp, Phillip Allen *academic administrator, biologist, educator*
Smith, David Julian *educational consultant*
Thiemann, Ronald Frank *dean, religion educator*
Vest, Charles Marstiller *academic administrator*
Whitlock, Charles Preston *former university dean*
Wilson, Linda Smith *academic administrator*

**Centerville**
Kiernan, Owen Burns *educational consultant*

**Chestnut Hill**
Altbach, Philip *higher education director, educator*
Hunt-Clerici, Carol Elizabeth *academic administrator*
†Leahy, William P. *academic administrator, educator*
Monan, James Donald *university administrator*

**Chicopee**
Czerwiec, Irene Theresa *gifted education educator*

**Concord**
Brown, Linda Weaver *academic administrator*
Lilien, Elliot Stephen *secondary education educator*

**Danvers**
Traicoff, George *college president*

**Duxbury**
Mc Carthy, D. Justin *emeritus college president*

**Easthampton**
Grubbs, Dennis H. *secondary school principal*

**Fall River**
Ingles, James H. *dean*

**Fitchburg**
Mara, Vincent Joseph *college president*
Riccards, Michael Patrick *academic administrator*

**Gardner**
Coulter, Sherry Parks *secondary education educator*

**Grafton**
Tite, John Gregory *secondary school educator*

**Great Barrington**
Rodgers, Bernard F., Jr. *academic administrator, dean*

**Haverhill**
Charlesworth, Marion Hoyen *secondary school educator*
Dimitry, John Randolph *academic administrator*

**Holliston**
O'Connor, Jude *special education educator, consultant*

**Hyde Park**
Harris, Emily Louise *special education educator*

**Jamaica Plain**
Tirella, Theresa Mary *special education educator*

**Kingston**
Hybertson, Beverly Blaisdell *elementary education educator*
Squarcia, Paul Andrew *school superintendent*

**Lakeville**
Chase, Karen Humphrey *middle school education educator*

**Lenox**
Smith, Elske Van Panhuys *retired university administrator*

**Leominster**
Libby, Sandra Chiavaras *special education educator*

**Lexington**
France-Litchfield, Ruth A. *reading and literacy specialist*
Hedlund, Ronald David *academic administrator, researcher, educator*

**Longmeadow**
Leary, Carol Ann *academic administrator*

**Lowell**
Hayes, Donald Paul, Jr. *elementary and secondary education educator*

**Lynn**
Astuccio, Sheila Margaret *educational administrator*

**Marshfield Hills**
Johnson, Margaret Hill *retired educational administrator, consultant*

**Mattapoisett**
Andersen, Laird Bryce *retired university administrator*

**Medford**
DiBiaggio, John A. *university administrator*
Mumford, George Saltonstall, Jr. *former university dean, astronomy educator*
Swap, Walter Charles *academic dean, psychology educator*

**Methuen**
Conran, Lisa Ann *educational administrator*

**Mill River**
Haworth, Donald Robert *educator, retired association executive*

**Milton**
Warren, John Coolidge *private school dean, history educator*

**Monson**
St. Louis, Paul Michael *foreign language educator*

**North Andover**
McGovern, Barbara Elizabeth Ann *elementary education educator*

**Northampton**
Heartt, Charlotte Beebe *university official*
Lightburn, Anita Louise *dean, social work educator*
†Simmons, Ruth J. *academic administrator*

**Norton**
Marshall, Dale Rogers *college president, political scientist, educator*

**Oakham**
Poirier, Helen Virginia Leonard *elementary education educator*

**Osterville**
Malayery, Nasrin *educator, consultant*

**Peabody**
Stahl, William Martin *professional training director*

**Petersham**
Kenney, Joseph Edmund *special education educator*

**Plymouth**
Freyermuth, Virginia Karen *secondary art educator*
Taylor, Maryann Courtney *elementary education educator*

**Provincetown**
Wolfman, Brunetta Reid *education educator*

**Quincy**
Hill, Kent Richmond *college president*

**Reading**
Terilli, Joseph Anthony *secondary education educator*

**Revere**
Pennacchio, Linda Marie *secondary school educator*

**Rockport**
Bakrow, William John *college president emeritus*

**Rowe**
Foshay, Arthur Wellesley *retired educator*

**Roxbury**
Gamer, Frances *elementary educator*
Short, Janet Marie *principal*

**Salem**
Harrington, Nancy D. *college president*

**Saugus**
Austill, Allen *dean emeritus*

**South Dartmouth**
Ward, Richard Joseph *university official, educator, author*

**South Hadley**
Creighton, Joanne Vanish *academic administrator*

**South Weymouth**
Milley, Jane Elizabeth *academic administrator*

**Southwick**
MacEwan, Barbara Ann *middle school educator*

**Springfield**
Caprio, Anthony S. *university president*
Cleland, Thomas Edward, Jr. *secondary school educator*
Miller, Leroy Paul, Jr. *secondary English educator*
Vella, Sandra Rachael *principal*

**Taunton**
Buote, Rosemarie Boschen *special education educator*
Donly, Michael J. *headmaster*

**Tewksbury**
DeAngelis, Michele F. *school system administrator*

**Walpole**
Marshall, Virginia Mary *technology educator*

**Waltham**
Adamian, Gregory Harry *academic administrator*
Reinharz, Jehuda *academic administrator, history educator*

**Wellesley**
Auerbach, Jerold S. *university educator*
Stannard, Jan Gregory *academic administrator*
Walsh, Diana Chapman *academic administrator, social and behavioral sciences educator*

**Westborough**
Atsumi, Ikuko *management school administrator, educator*
Jackson, Frederick Herbert *educational administrator*

**Whitman**
Delaney, Matthew Michael *school administrator, fine arts educator*

**Wilbraham**
Woloshchuk, Candace Dixon *secondary school educator, artist, consultant*

**Winchester**
Casey, Norine Therese *school principal*

**Worcester**
Berth, Donald Frank *university official, consultant*
Brooks, John Edward *college president emeritus*
Grogan, William Robert *university dean*
Hagan, Joseph Henry *college president*
Onorato, Nicholas Louis *program director, economist*
Plummer, Edward Bruce *college librarian*
Sinkis, Deborah Mary *principal*
Traina, Richard Paul *academic administrator*

**Yarmouth Port**
Hall, James Frederick *retired college president*

## MICHIGAN

**Adrian**
Caine, Stanley Paul *college administrator*

**Albion**
Vulgamore, Melvin L. *college president*

**Allendale**
Lubbers, Arend Donselaar *academic administrator*
Niemeyer, Glenn Alan *academic administrator, history educator*

**Alma**
Moerdyk, Charles Conrad *school system administrator*
Stone, Alan Jay *college administrator*
Swanson, Robert Draper *college president*

**Ann Arbor**
Anderson, Austin Gothard *university administrator, lawyer*
Beaulieu, Carol Marie *special education educator*
Behmer, Kevin Shea *mathematics educator*
Cole, David Edward *university administrator*
Copeland, Carolyn Abigail *retired university dean*
Davis, Wayne Kay *university dean, educator*
Duderstadt, James Johnson *academic administrator, engineering educator*
Dumas, Rhetaugh Etheldra Graves *university official*
Fleming, Suzanne Marie *university official, chemistry educator*
Iadipaolo, Donna Marie *secondary school educator, writer, director, artist*
Paul, Ara Garo *university dean*
Robbins, Jerry Hal *educational administration educator*
Stark, Joan Scism *education educator*
Tice, Carol Hoff *middle school educator, consultant*
Turner, Hazel M. *educator*
Van Houweling, Douglas Edward *university administrator, educator*
Warner, Robert Mark *university dean, archivist, historian*
Watkins, Paul B. *academic research center administrator, medical educator*

**Auburn Hills**
Etefia, Florence Victoria *academic and behavior specialist*

**Berrien Springs**
Lesher, William Richard *retired academic administrator*

**Birch Run**
Radwick, Melissa Jane *elementary counselor*

**Bloomfield Hills**
Doyle, Jill J. *elementary school principal*

**Brighton**
Jensen, Baiba *principal*

**Cadillac**
McKay, Laurie Marie *special education educator*

**Carsonville**
Kummerow, Arnold A. *superintendent of schools*

**Clinton Township**
Darby, Lewis Randal *special education educator*

**Coloma**
Tallman, Clifford Wayne *school system administrator, consultant*

**Dearborn**
Fair, Jean Everhard *education educator*
LeVasseur, Susan Lee Salisbury *secondary education educator*
Orlowska-Warren, Lenore Alexandria *art educator*
Presley, John Woodrow *academic administrator*

**Detroit**
Alford, Sandra Elaine *university official*
Boykin, Nancy Merritt *former academic administrator*
Brynski, Christina Halina *school system administrator, consultant, educator*
Cox, Clifford Ernest *deputy superintendent, chief information officer*
Edelstein, Tilden Gerald *academic administrator, history educator*
Fay, Sister Maureen A. *university president*
Hagman, Harlan Lawrence *education educator*
Hough, Leslie Seldon *educational administrator*
Lee, James Edward, Jr. *educational administrator*
Paul, Rhonda Elizabeth *university program director, career development counselor*
Rogers, Richard Lee *educator*
Semanik, Anthony James *university program administrator*
Shay, John E., Jr. *academic administrator*
Skoney, Sophie Essa *educational administrator*
Snead, David L. *superintendent*
Syropoulos, Mike *school system director*

**Dowagiac**
Mulder, Patricia Marie *education educator*

**East Lansing**
Abbett, William S. *dean*
Brophy, Jere Edward *education educator, researcher*
Byerrum, Richard Uglow *college dean*
Harrison, Jeremy Thomas *dean*
Honhart, Frederick Lewis, III *academic director*
Mackey, Maurice Cecil *university president, economist, lawyer*

McPherson, Melville Peter *academic administrator, former government official*
Moore, Kathryn McDaniel *education educator*
Pierre, Percy Anthony *university president*
Rudman, Herbert Charles *education educator*
Snoddy, James Ernest *education educator*
Wronski, Stanley Paul *education educator*

### Edwardsburg
Stuck, Wanda Marie *special education educator*

### Escanaba
Ling, Robert William, Jr. *academic director*

### Farmington Hills
Allen, Janet Louise *school system administrator*
Faxon, Jack *headmaster*
Hartman-Abramson, Ilene *adult education educator*

### Flint
Green, Allison Anne *retired secondary education educator*
Hayes, Joyce Merriweather *secondary education educator*
Lorenz, John Douglas *college official*
Nelms, Charlie *academic administrator*

### Flushing
Barnes, Robert Vincent *elementary and secondary school art educator*

### Fort Gratiot
Stevens, Brenda Joy *educator*

### Frankfort
Acker, Nathaniel Hull *retired educational administrator*

### Gaylord
Magsig, Judith Anne *early childhood education educator*

### Grand Rapids
Diekema, Anthony J. *college president, educational consultant*
Monsma, Marvin Eugene *library director*
VanHarn, Gordon Lee *college administrator and provost*

### Grosse Pointe
Robie, Joan *elementary school principal*

### Gwinn
Lasich, Vivian Esther Layne *secondary education educator*

### Hancock
Puotinen, Arthur Edwin *college president, clergyman*

### Harrison Township
Cobb, Cecelia Annette *counselor*
Kennard, Margaret Anne *middle school educator*
Suchecki, Lucy Anne *elementary education educator*

### Haslett
Hotaling, Robert Bachman *community planner, educator*

### Hillsdale
Kline, Faith Elizabeth *college administrator*
Roche, George Charles, III *college administrator*
Trowbridge, Ronald Lee *college admininstrator*

### Holland
Hill, JoAnne Francis *elementary education educator*
Jacobson, John Howard, Jr. *college president*
Nyenhuis, Jacob Eugene *college official*
Van Wylen, Gordon John *former college president*

### Houghton
Tompkins, Curtis Johnston *university president*

### Jackson
Haglund, Bernice Marion *elementary school educator*

### Jenison
Roberts Harvey, Bonita *secondary school educator*

### Kalamazoo
Burns, James W. *education educator*
Cline, Sandra Williamson *elementary education educator*
Inselberg, Rachel *retired educator, researcher*
Johnson, Tom Milroy *academic dean, medical educator, physician*
Jones, James Fleming, Jr. *college president, Roman language and literature educator*
Lennon, Elizabeth M. *retired educator*
McCarthy, Catherine Therese *elementary educator*
Stufflebeam, Daniel LeRoy *education educator*

### Kincheloe
Light, Kenneth Freeman *college administrator*

### Lambertville
Korthuis, Kathleen E. *dean*

### Lansing
Brennan, Thomas Emmett *law school president*
Carter, Pamela Lee *school system administrator*
Doty, Brant Lee *academic administrator*
Warrington, Willard Glade *former university official*

### Lewiston
Ruehle, Dianne Marie *retired elementary education educator*

### Livonia
Van de Vyver, Sister Mary Francilene *academic administrator*

### Ludington
Puffer, Richard Judson *retired college chancellor*

### Macomb
Farmakis, George Leonard *education educator*

### Madison Heights
Pricer, Wayne Francis *counseling administrator*

### Maple City
Morris, Donald Arthur Adams *college president*

### Marquette
Harrington, Lucia Marie *elementary education educator*
Jajich, James Gary *elementary and middle school educator*
Suomi, Paul Neil *alumni association director*
Vandament, William Eugene *academic administrator, educator*

### Midland
Barker, Nancy Lepard *university official*
Chen, Catherine Wang *provost*
Hyde, Geraldine Veola *retired secondary education educator*
McDaniels, Peggy Ellen *special education educator*
Powell, Rebecca Ann *secondary school educator*

### Monroe
Siciliano, Elizabeth Marie *secondary education educator*

### Mount Pleasant
Lippert, Robert J. *administrator and culinary arts educator, consultant*

### Muskegon
Hadiaris, Marie Ellen *special education educator*

### Okemos
Hickey, Howard Wesley *retired education educator*
Velicer, Janet Schafbuch *elementary school educator*

### Olivet
Bassis, Michael Steven *academic administrator*
Fuller, Judith Kay Altenhein *special education educator*
Mahmoudi, Hoda *academic administrator, sociology educator*

### Pinckney
Duquet, Suzanne Frances *special education educator*

### Plymouth
Belobraidich, Sharon Lynn Goul *elementary education educator*

### Pontiac
Decker, Peter William *academic administrator*
Love, Sharon Irene *elementary education educator*

### Portage
Rainey, John Mark *administrator*

### Portland
Adams, Bill *principal*

### Rochester
Loh, Robert N. K. *academic administrator, engineering educator*
Packard, Sandra Podolin *education educator, consultant*
Polis, Michael Philip *university dean*

### Saint Clair Shores
Black, Patricia Anne *special education educator*

### Saint Joseph
Skale, Linda Dianne *elementary education educator*

### Southfield
Chambers, Charles MacKay *university president*
Olsen, Douglas H. *superintendent*

### Stanton
Winchell, George William *curriculum and technology educator*

### Sterling Heights
Cutter, Jeffrey S. *secondary education educator, music educator*

### Taylor
Beebe, Grace Ann *special education educator*

### Temperance
Jan, Colleen Rose *secondary school educator*
Kinney, Mark B. *fellowship executive, educator*

### Traverse City
Halsted, Judith Ann Wynn *educational consultant*
Petersen, Evelyn Ann *education consultant*
Rosser, Richard Franklin *company executive*
Stepnitz, Susan Stephanie *special education educator*
Zimmerman, Paul Albert *retired college president, minister*

### University Center
Gilbertson, Eric Raymond *academic administrator, lawyer*
Lange, Crystal Marie *academic administrator, nursing educator*

### Warren
Lorenzo, Albert L. *academic administrator*

### Watervliet
Peal, Christopher John *educational administrator*

### Williamsburg
Goodell, Warren Franklin *retired university administrator*

### Wixom
Boynton, Irvin Parker *educational administrator*

### Ypsilanti
Boone, Morell Douglas *academic administrator, information and instructional technology educator*
Cantrell, Linda Maxine *counselor*
Corriveau, Arlene Josephine *educational specialist*
Gwaltney, Thomas Marion *education educator, researcher*
Lewis-White, Linda Beth *elementary school educator*
Olmsted, Patricia Palmer *education educator, researcher*
Shelton, William Everett *university president*
Sullivan, Thomas Patrick *academic administrator*
Tobias, Tom, Jr. *elementary school educator*
Walker, Michael Leon *education educator*
Washington, Adrienne Marie *elementary school educator*

## MINNESOTA

### Albert Lea
Rechtzigel, Sue Marie (Suzanne Rechtzigel) *child care center executive*

### Annandale
Schilplin, Yvonne Winter *educational administrator*

### Bemidji
Martel, Petra Jean Hegstad *elementary school educator*

### Bertha
Peterson, Myra M. *special education educator*

### Cloquet
Ellison, David Charles *special education educator*

### Cokato
Thomas, Paul S. *principal*

### Collegeville
Reinhart, Dietrich Thomas *university president, history educator*

### Dassel
Kay, Craig *principal*

### Duluth
Franks, Ronald Dwyer *university dean, psychiatrist, educator*

### Eden Prairie
McCoy, Gerald Leo *superintendent of schools*

### Eden Valley
Stringer, Patricia Anne *retired secondary educator*

### Elysian
Nickerson, James Findley *retired educator*

### Grand Marais
Kreitlow, Burton William *retired adult education educator*

### Grand Rapids
King, Sheryl Jayne *secondary education educator, counselor*

### Hermantown
Leland, Paula Susan *educational administrator, educator*

### Hopkins
Hedberg, Laurentius Arthur *educator*
Passi, Beth *school administrator*

### Lakeland
Helstedt, Gladys Mardell *vocational education educator*

### Mankato
Rush, Richard R. *academic administrator*

### Minneapolis
Anderson, Charles S. *college president, clergyman*
Bowie, Norman Ernest *university official, educator*
Cerra, Frank Bernard *dean*
Davis, Julia McBroom *college dean, speech pathology and audiology educator*
DiGangi, Frank Edward *academic administrator*
Kidwell, David Stephen *academic administrator*
Lindell, Edward Albert *former college president, religious organization administrator*
Matson, Wesley Jennings *educational administrator*
Morrow, Dennis Robert *school system administrator, consultant*
Nolting, Earl *academic administrator*
Rand, Sidney Anders *retired college administrator*
Schuh, G(eorge) Edward *university dean, agricultural economist*
Slorp, John S. *academic administrator*
Wehrwein-Hunt, Jeri Lynn *elementary education educator*

### Minnetonka
Vanstrom, Marilyn June *retired elementary education educator*

### Moorhead
Barden, Roland Eugene *university administrator*
Dille, Roland Paul *college president*
Treumann, William Borgen *university dean*

### Morris
Johnson, David Chester *university chancellor, sociology educator*

### Northfield
Berwald, Helen Dorothy *education educator*
Edwards, Mark U., Jr. *college president, history educator, author*
Jorgensen, Daniel Fred *academic director*
McKinsey, Elizabeth *college dean*

### Perham
Kingsbury, Rex Alan *elementary education educator, administrator*

### Preston
Hokenson, David Leonard *secondary school educator*

### Remer
McNulty-Majors, Susan Rose *special education administrator*

### Richfield
Devlin, Barbara Jo *school district administrator*

### Rochester
Sherman, Thomas Francis *education educator*

### Saginaw
Stauber, Marilyn Jean *secondary and elementary school*

### Saint Cloud
Bates, Margaret Helena *special education educator*
Berling, John George *academic dean*
Wertz, John Alan *secondary school educator*

### Saint Louis Park
Dooley, David J. *elementary school principal*
Porter, Jeannette Upton *elementary education educator*
Svendsbye, Lloyd August *college president, clergyman, educator*

### Saint Paul
Brushaber, George Karl *academic president, minister*
Dykstra, Robert *retired education educator*
Graham, Charles John *university educator, former university president*
Huber, Sister Alberta *college president*
Keffer, Charles Joseph *academic administrator*
Kerr, Sylvia Joann *educator*
Osnes, Larry G. *academic administrator*
Pampusch, Anita Marie *academic administrator*
Sullivan, Alfred Dewitt *academic administrator*
Willis, Wesley Robert *college administrator*

### Spring Park
Nelson, Craig Wayne *academy administrator*

### Waseca
Frederick, Edward Charles *university official*

### Wayzata
Fish, James Stuart *college dean, advertising consultant*

### White Bear Lake
Gabrick, Robert William *secondary education educator*

### Winona
Beyer, Mary Edel *primary education educator*
DeThomasis, Brother Louis *college president*
Krueger, Darrell William *university president*
Preska, Margaret Louise Robinson *education educator, district service professional*
Towers, James Mc *education educator*

## MISSISSIPPI

### Ackerman
Coleman, Frances McLean *secondary school educator*

### Batesville
Neal, Joseph Lee *vocational school educator*

### Biloxi
Brown, Sheba Ann *elementary education educator*
Manners, Pamela Jeanne *middle school educator*

### Cleveland
Baker-Branton, Camille B. *counselor, educator*
Wyatt, Forest Kent *university president*

### Columbus
Rent, Clyda Stokes *academic administrator*

### Hattiesburg
Fleming, Horace Weldon, Jr. *higher education administrator, educator*
Lucas, Aubrey Keith *university president*
Noonkester, James Ralph *retired college president*
Saucier Lundy, Karen *college dean, educator*

### Holly Springs
Beckley, David Lenard *academic administrator*

### Indianola
Crigler, Sammie Mae *secondary school English language educator*
Gary, Toni Berryhill *school counselor, psychotherapist*

### Jackson
Burnham, Tom *state school system administrator*
Chambers-Mangum, Fransenna Ethel *special education educator*
Conerly, Albert Wallace *academic administrator, dean*
Harmon, George Marion *college president*
LeTourneau, Richard Howard *retired college president*
McLin, Hattie Rogers *school system administrator*
Rogers, Oscar Allan, Jr. *academic administrator*
Summers, Tracy Yvonne *assistant principal*

### Kosciusko
May, Cecil Richard, Jr. *academic adminstrator*

### Lorman
Waters, Rudolph Earl *university administrator*

### Meridian
Phillips, Patricia Jeanne *retired school administrator, consultant*
Reed, Vanessa Regina *secondary education educator*

### Mississippi State
†Gunter, John E. *dean*
Hawkins, Merrill Morris, Sr. *college administrator*
Hughes, Patricia Newman *academic administrator*
Mabry, Donald Joseph *university administrator, history educator*
McGilberry, Joe Herman, Sr. *university administrator*
Watson, James Ray, Jr. *education educator*
Zacharias, Donald Wayne *academic administrator*

**Natchez**
Profice, Rosena Mayberry *elementary school educator*

**Oxford**
Knight, Aubrey Kevin *vocational education educator*
Moorhead, Sylvester Andrew *education educator retired*

**Pascagoula**
McKee, Ronald Gene *vocational education educator*

**Starkville**
Hunt, Pamela Stafford *secondary school educator*
Martin, Theodore Krinn *former university administrator (deceased)*

**Tupelo**
Rupert, Daniel Leo *elementary education consultant*

**University**
Ferris, William Reynolds *folklore educator*
Khayat, Robert C. *chancellor*
Leary, William James *educational administrator*
Meador, John Milward, Jr. *university dean*
Sam, Joseph *retired university dean*
Smith, Allie Maitland *university dean*

**Vicksburg**
Aarons, Cecilia *retired secondary school educator*

**Waveland**
Jackson, Judith Ann *elementary education educator*

**Yazoo City**
Cartlidge, Shriley Ann Bell *school administrator*

## MISSOURI

**Ballwin**
Waskow, Joyce Ann *school administrator*

**Blue Springs**
Hatley, Patricia Ruth *school system administrator*
Shover, Joan *secondary school educator*

**Boonville**
Cline, Dorothy May Stammerjohn (Mrs. Edward Wilburn Cline) *educator*

**Cape Girardeau**
Haugland, Susan Warrell *education educator*

**Chesterfield**
Goodwin, Leslie Diane *elementary education educator*

**Chula**
Murphy, Jenny Lewis *special education educator*

**Clayton**
Kohm, Barbara *principal*

**Columbia**
Adams, Algalee Pool *college dean, art educator*
Bay, Marjorie Seaman *secondary school educator*
Brouder, Gerald T. *academic administrator*
Dyrenfurth, Michael John *vocational technical and industrial arts educator, consultant*
Fluharty, Charles William *policy research institute director, consultant, researcher*
George, Melvin Douglas *retired university president*
Gysbers, Norman Charles *education educator*
Hatley, Richard V(on) *education educator*
Keith, Everett Earnest *educator, education administrator*
Kierscht, Marcia Selland *academic administrator, psychologist*
McCollum, Clifford Glenn *college dean emeritus*
Miller, Paul Ausborn *adult education educator*
Staley, Marsha Lynn *elementary school educator*
Wheeler, Otis V., Jr. *public school principal*

**Cottleville**
Shepperd, Susan Abbott *special education educator*

**Delta**
Burton, Drenna Lee O'Reilly *kindergarten educator*

**Fair Grove**
Pickering, Becky Ruth Thompson *special education educator*

**Fayette**
Inman, Marianne Elizabeth *college administrator*

**Florissant**
Barnes, Rebecca Marie *assistant principal*
Bartlett, Robert James *principal*
Johnson, Mary Elizabeth *retired elementary education educator*
Ordinachev, Joann Lee *special education counselor and administrator*
Payuk, Edward William *elementary education educator*

**Fulton**
Barnett, Jahnae Harper *academic administrator*
Davidson, Robert Laurenson Dashiell *college president emeritus, philatelist*

**Gallatin**
Wilsted, Joy *elementary education educator, reading specialist, parenting consultant*

**Hannibal**
Wilhoit, Carol Diane *special education educator*

**Hayti**
Skelton, Diann Clevenger *elementary education educator*

**Hazelwood**
Martin, Barbara Jean *elementary education educator*

**Hillsboro**
Adkins, Gregory D. *higher education administrator*

**Hollister**
Head, Mary Mae *elementary education educator*

**Houston**
Ruckert, Rita E. *elementary education educator*

**Independence**
Fraker, Barbara J. *elementary education educator, school system administrator, middle school education educator*
Henley, Robert Lee *school system administrator*
Muñoz, Margaret Ellen *reading specialist*

**Jefferson City**
Scott, Gary Kuper *retired academic administrator*

**Jennings**
Robards, Bourne Rogers *elementary education educator*

**Joplin**
Allman, Margaret Ann Lowrance *counselor*
Pulliam, Frederick Cameron *educational administrator*

**Kansas City**
Bodinson, Nancy Sue *art educator*
Doyle, Wendell E. *retired band director, educator*
Durig, James Robert *college dean*
Eubanks, Eugene Emerson *education educator, consultant*
Hall, Rochelle Denise *elementary school educator*
Kramer, Lawrence John *college president*
Martin, Deanna Coleman *university director*
Maxwell, Delores Young *elementary school principal*
Sherwood, Joan Karolyn Sargent *career counselor*
Stubbs, Marilyn Kay *education administrator*
Van Ackeren, Maurice Edward *college administrator*

**Kirksville**
Ediger, Marlow *education educator*
Smith, Dwyane *university administrator*

**Kirkwood**
Warner, Alvina (Vinnie Warner) *principal*

**Lees Summit**
Boehm, Toni Georgene *seminary dean, nurse*
Griffith-Thompson, Sara Lynn *resource reading educator*

**Lexington**
Terrill, Julia Ann *elementary education educator*

**Liberty**
Tanner, Jimmie Eugene *college dean*

**Linn**
Gove, Peter Charles *special education educator*

**Marionville**
Estep, Mark Randall *secondary education educator*

**Marshall**
Wymore, Luann Courtney *education educator*

**Maryland Heights**
Hampton, Margaret Josephine *secondary education educator, decorating consultant*

**Maryville**
Hubbard, Dean Leon *university president*

**Mountain Grove**
Smith, Martha Virginia Barnes *elementary school educator*

**New Florence**
Francis, Albert W. *elementary education educator*

**Pilot Grove**
Betteridge, Elizabeth Ann *elementary education educator*

**Plato**
Wood, Joetta Kay *special education educator*

**Rolla**
Warner, Don Lee *dean emeritus*

**Saint Charles**
Cassy, Catherine Mary *elementary school educator*
Huckshold, Wayne William *elementary education educator*

**Saint Joseph**
Murphy, Janet Gorman *college president*

**Saint Louis**
Allen, Renee *principal*
Biondi, Lawrence *university administrator, priest*
Bloomberg, Terry *early childhood education administrator*
Bohne, Jeanette Kathryn *mathematics and science educator*
Brennan, Donald George *university dean, research administrator*
Byrnes, Christopher Ian *academic dean, researcher*
Cain, James Nelson *arts school and concert administrator*
Conaway, Mary Ann *dean*
Danforth, William Henry *retired academic administrator, physician*
Deal, Joseph Maurice *university dean, art educator, photographer*
Dodge, Paul Cecil *academic administrator*
Earle, James A. *educational administrator*
Ellis, Dorsey Daniel, Jr. *dean, lawyer*
Fowler, Marti *secondary education educator*
Gerdine, Leigh *retired academic administrator*
Gilligan, Sandra Kaye *private school director*
Hunter, Thom Hugh *seminary administrator*
Kelly, Ann Terese *elementary education educator*
Koff, Robert Hess *program director*
Lovin, Keith Harold *university administrator, philosophy educator*
Mahan, David James *school superintendent*
Marsh, James C., Jr. *secondary school principal*
Maupin, Stephanie Zeller *French language educator*
McFarland, Mary A. *elementary and secondary school educator, administrator*
McGannon, John Barry *university chancellor*
Monteleone, Patricia *academic dean*
Morgan, Lawrence Allison *headmaster, educational administrator*
O'Neill, Sheila *principal*
Parks, Beatrice Griffin *elementary school educator*
Patton, Thomas F. *academic administrator, pharmaceutical chemist*
Pfefferkorn, Michael Gene, Sr. *secondary school educator, writer*
Pfefferkorn, Sandra Jo *secondary school educator*
Ramming, Michael Alexander *school system administrator*
Reinert, Paul Clare *university chancellor emeritus*
Stodghill, Ronald *school system administrator*
Thomas, Pamela Adrienne *special education educator*
Touhill, Blanche Marie *university chancellor, history-education educator*
Truitt, William Harvey *private school educator*
Turner, Harold Edward *education educator*
Watkins, Hortense Catherine *middle school educator*
Weiss, Robert Francis *former academic administrator, religious organization administrator, consultant*
Wood, Samuel Eugene *college administrator, psychology educator*

**Sainte Genevieve**
Cantu, Dino Antonio *secondary education history educator*

**Salem**
Dent, Catherine Gale *secondary education educator*

**Sedalia**
Noland, Gary Lloyd *vocation educational administrator*

**Seymour**
Wallace, Dorothy Alene *special education administrator*

**Springfield**
Ames, Jimmy Ray *education educator*
Good, Stephen Hanscom *academic administrator*
Groves, Sharon Sue *elementary education educator*
Moore, John Edwin, Jr. *college president*
Petersen, George James *educational administration educator*
Smith, Donald L. *social sciences educator*
Tarr, Delbert Howard, Jr. *seminary president, clergyman*

**Stella**
Davidson, Cynthia Ann *elementary school educator*

**Troy**
Dattilo, Linda Kathleen *elementary education educator*

**University City**
Flanagan, Joan Wheat (Maggie Flanagan) *educational therapist*

**Valley Park**
Benedict, Gary Clarence *school system administrator, psychotherapist*

**Warrensburg**
Alewel, Teresa Fine *university director*
Elliott, Eddie Mayes *academic administrator*
Limback, E(dna) Rebecca *vocational education educator*

**Washington**
Chambers, Jerry Ray *school system administrator*

**Waynesville**
Learmann, Judith Marilyn *secondary education educator*

**Webster Groves**
Schenkenberg, Mary Martin *principal*
Zimmerman, Harold Seymour *elementary school educator*

**West Plains**
Gunter, DeVona Elizabeth (Betty Gunter) *special education educator*

**Willow Springs**
Evins, Marylou *retired special education educator*

**Windyville**
Condron, Daniel Ralph *academic administrator, metaphysics educator*

## MONTANA

**Antelope**
Olson, Betty-Jean *elementary education educator*

**Bigfork**
Keller, Barbara Lynn *special education educator, reading teacher*

**Billings**
DeRosier, Arthur Henry, Jr. *college president*

**Bozeman**
Goering, Kenneth Justin *college administrator*
Malone, Michael Peter *academic administrator, historian*
Monaco, Paul *academic administrator, educator, artist, writer*

**Crow Agency**
Pease-Pretty On Top, Janine B. *community college administrator*

**Dayton**
Catalfomo, Philip *university dean*

**Hardin**
Alvarado, Rebecca Jane *secondary education educator*

**Havre**
Lanier, William Joseph *college program director*

**Helena**
Morton, Claudette *education administrator*

**Kalispell**
Ormiston, Patricia Jane *elementary education educator*

**Miles City**
Emilsson, Elizabeth Maykuth *special education educator*

**Missoula**
†Brown, Perry Joe *university dean*
Dennison, George Marshel *academic administrator*
Fisher, William Henry *education educator*
Kindrick, Robert LeRoy *university official and dean, English educator*
Mercer, Chet Atom *retired elementary educator*

**Victor**
Stewart, JoAnne *secondary school educator*

## NEBRASKA

**Auburn**
Winegardner, Rose Mary *special education educator*

**Bellevue**
Muller, John Bartlett *university president*

**Blair**
Christopherson, Myrvin Frederick *college president*

**Columbus**
Rieck, Janet Rae *special education educator*

**Concord**
Fritschen, Robert David *educational administrator, animal science educator, researcher*

**Grand Island**
Roehrkasse, Pauline Catherine Holtorf *retired secondary education educator*
Zichek, Shannon Elaine *secondary school educator*

**Gretna**
Riley, Kevin M. *principal*

**La Vista**
Phillips, Kimberly Kay *educator*

**Lincoln**
Bradley, Richard Edwin *retired college president*
Elwood, Brian Clay *educational purchasing agent, computer consultant*
Grew, Priscilla Croswell *university official, geology educator*
Hendrickson, Kent Herman *university administrator*
Hermance, Lyle Herbert *college official*
Janzow, Walter Theophilus *retired college administrator*
Laursen, Paul Herbert *retired university educator*
Liggett, Twila Marie Christensen *college official, public television executive*
Lingle, Muriel Ellen *elementary education educator*
Nelson, Darrell Wayne *university administrator, scientist*
Powers, David Richard *educational administrator*
Rogers, Vance Donald *former university president*
Smith, Lewis Dennis *academic administrator*
White, John Wesley, Jr. *university president*

**Mc Cook**
Creasman, Virena Welborn (Rene Creasman) *retired elementary and secondary school educator, genealogist, researcher*
Koetter, Leila Lynette *college administrator*

**Morrill**
Steele, Sarah Jane *elementary school educator*

**Newcastle**
Myers, Kenneth L(eRoy) *secondary education educator*

**Norfolk**
Mortensen-Say, Marlys (Mrs. John Theodore Say) *school system administrator*

**Omaha**
Bauer, Otto Frank *university official, communication educator*
Cinque, Thomas J. *dean*
Fjell, Mick *principal*
Haselwood, Eldon LaVerne *education educator*
Hill, John Wallace *special education educator*
Jacobs, Henrietta Marie *early childhood educator, consultant*
McEniry, Robert Francis *education educator*
Morrison, Michael Gordon *university president, clergyman, history educator*
Newton, John Milton *acadmeic administrator, psychology educator*
O'Brien, Richard L(ee) *academic administrator, physician, cell biologist*
Peck, Ernest James, Jr. *academic administrator*
Rosse, Therese Marie *reading and special education educator, curriculum and instruction specialist*
Schlessinger, Bernard S. *retired university dean*
Schuerman, Norbert Joel *school superintendent*
Tucker, Michael *elementary school principal*
Weber, Delbert Dean *academic administrator*

**Plainview**
Mauch, Jeannine Ann *elementary education educator*

**South Sioux City**
Wilson, Esther Elinore *technical college educator*

**Wayne**
Mash, Donald J. *college president*

## NEVADA

**Boulder City**
Holmes, BarbaraAnn Krajkoski *secondary education educator*

**Carson City**
Wadman, William Wood, III *educational director, technical research executive, consulting company executive*

**Elko**
Lovell, Walter Benjamin *secondary education educator*

**Fallon**
Plants, Walter Dale *elementary education educator, minister*

**Glenbrook**
Buscaglia, (Felice) Leo(nardo) *special education educator, author*

**Hawthorne**
Graham, Lois Charlotte *retired educator*

**Henderson**
Benson, James DeWayne *university administrator*

**Incline Village**
Hiatt, Robert Worth *former university president*

**Las Vegas**
Brown, Lori Lipman *secondary school educator*
Cram, Brian Manning *school system administrator*
Dax, Betty Joyce *primary education educator*
Gaspar, Anna Louise *retired elementary school teacher, consultant*
Harter, Carol Clancey *university president, English language educator*
Horner, Sandra Marie Groce (Sandy Heart) *educator, poet, songwriter, lyricist*
Iorio, John Emil *retired education educator*
Opfer, Neil David *construction educator, consultant*
Ozi, Elizabeth *private school administrator*
Rice, Stephen Landon *university official*

**Lovelock**
Kiley, James P. *retired school system administrator*

**North Las Vegas**
Williams, Mary Irene *dean*

**Reno**
Cain, Edmund Joseph *education educator, emeritus dean*
Cathey-Gibson, Sharon Sue Rinn *principal, educator*
Clarke, Janice Cessna *principal*
Crowley, Joseph Neil *university president, political science educator*
Daugherty, Robert Melvin, Jr. *university dean, medical educator*
Dupree, Marsha Anne *academic administrator*
Humphrey, Neil Darwin *university president, retired*
Perry, Jean Louise *dean*

## NEW HAMPSHIRE

**Amherst**
Collins, Paul D. *principal*

**Chester**
Preston, Faith *college president*

**Concord**
Lord, Marion Manns *retired academic director*

**Durham**
DeMitchell, Todd Allan *education educator*
Farrell, William Joseph *university chancellor*
Lawson, John H. *university official*
Leitzel, Joan Ruth *university president*
Perry, Bradford Kent *academic administrator*

**Exeter**
Erickson, Raymond Leroy *dean, psychologist*
McLaughlin, Anne Elizabeth *secondary education educator*

**Goffstown**
Glines, Jon Malcolm *secondary education educator*

**Hanover**
Byrne, Patrick Michael *writer, educator, entrepreneur*
Freedman, James Oliver *university president, lawyer*
Hennessey, John William, Jr. *academic administrator*
Howe, Harold, II *academic administrator, former foundation executive, educator*
Rieser, Leonard Moos *college administrator, physics educator*
Wright, James Edward *dean, history educator*

**Hooksett**
Gustafson, Richard Alrick *college president*

**Keene**
Hickey, Delina Rose *education educator*
Yarosewick, Stanley J. *academic administrator, physicist*

**Lebanon**
Jillette, Arthur George, Jr. *school system administrator*

**Littleton**
McGruder-Houlihan, Ruby Lee *special education educator*

**Londonderry**
Kennedy, Ellen Woodman *elementary and home economics educator*

**Lyman**
Kaplan, Frada M. *retired principal, special education educator*

**Manchester**
Gallagher, Nancy Anne *college official*
Stefanik, Jean Marianne *secondary school educator, naturalist*
Sullivan, Robert Martin *educational fundraiser*

**Nashua**
Mitsakos, Charles Leonidas *education educator, consultant*

**North Haverhill**
Charpentier, Keith Lionel *school system administrator*

**Pelham**
Holmes, Richard Dale *secondary education educator, historical consultant*

**Penacook**
Denham, Robin Richardson *secondary school educator*

**Plymouth**
Wiseman, Douglas Carl *education educator*

**Rindge**
Palmer, Bruce Harrison *college director*

**Walpole**
Harris, Grant Warren *principal*

**Wolfeboro**
Pierce, Edward Franklin *retired academic administrator*

## NEW JERSEY

**Alloway**
Tackett, William Edward *school system administrator*

**Atlantic Highlands**
Crowley, Cynthia Johnson *secondary school educator*

**Belleville**
Weyland, Deborah Ann *learning disabilities teacher consultant*

**Bellmawr**
Wilke, Constance Regina *elementary education educator*

**Bergenfield**
Alfieri, John Charles, Jr. *educational administrator*

**Berkeley Heights**
Older, Richard Samuel *elementary school music educator*
Shaffer, Gail Dorothy *secondary education educator*

**Bloomfield**
Chagnon, Joseph V. *school system administrator*

**Bloomsbury**
Clymer, Jerry Alan *educational administrator*

**Boonton**
DiGiovachino, John *special education educator*

**Bound Brook**
Kish, Elissa Anne *educational administrator*

**Brick**
Zalinsky, Sandra H. Orlofsky *school counselor*

**Bridgewater**
Baldwin, Dorothy Leila *secondary school educator*
Mack, Robert William *secondary school educator*

**Brigantine**
Kickish, Margaret Elizabeth *elementary education educator*

**Caldwell**
Simplicio, Joseph S.C. *education educator*
Werner, Patrice (Patricia Ann Werner) *college president*

**Camden**
Coney, Stephné Reniá *education educator*
Gordon, Walter Kelly *retired provost, English language educator*

**Cherry Hill**
Brenner, Lynnette Mary *reading specialist, educator*
Bryan, Richard Arthur *special education educator*
Carter, Catherine Louise *elementary school educator*
Teare, Bernice Adeline *elementary school educator, reading specialist*

**Clifton**
Charsky, Thomas Robert *elementary education educator*
McCoy, Linda Korteweg *media specialist*

**Delaware**
Hill-Rosato, Jane Elizabeth *elementary education educator*

**East Brunswick**
Fisher, Lucille *principal*
Haupin, Elizabeth Carol *retired secondary school educator*

**East Hanover**
Tamburro, Peter James, Jr. *social studies secondary school educator*

**East Orange**
Jones Gregory, Patricia *secondary art educator*

**Edison**
Maeroff, Gene I. *academic administrator, journalist*

**Elizabeth**
Rocha, Pedro, Jr. *academic administrator*

**Fair Lawn**
Aitchison, Suann *elementary school educator*
Wallace, Mary Monahan *elementary and secondary schools educator*

**Fort Lee**
Sugarman, Alan William *educational administrator*

**Franklinville**
DiGregory, Nicholas A. *secondary educator, coach*

**Glassboro**
Gephardt, Donald Louis *university official*
James, Herman Delano *college administrator*
Letki, Arleen *secondary school educator*
Marcus, Laurence Richard *education leadership and policy educator*

**Hackensack**
Cicchelli, Joseph Vincent *secondary education educator*
Daut, Eleanor Gilmore *vocational education educator*

**Haddon Heights**
Gwiazda, Stanley John *university dean*

**Haddonfield**
Cheney, Eleanora Louise *retired secondary education educator*

**Highland Park**
Broggi, Barbara Ann *elementary education educator, staff developer*
Collier, Albert, III *school system administrator*

**Hopatcong**
Cullen, Lawrence David *elementary education educator*

**Jersey City**
Foster, Delores Jackson *elementary school principal*
Stencer, Mark Joseph *academic administrator, consultant*

**Johnsonburg**
Cioffi, Eugene Edward, III *educational administrator*

**Kearny**
Meissner, Dorothy Theresa *reading specialist*

**Lakewood**
Rodgers, Dianna Sue *private school educator*
Williams, Barbara Anne *college president*

**Lawrenceville**
Leonard, Patricia Louise *education educator, consultant*
Megna, Jerome Francis *university dean*
Stehle, Edward Raymond *secondary education educator, school system administrator*

**Leonia**
Penin, Linda Margaret *elementary education educator*

**Lincroft**
Pollock, William John *secondary school administrator*
Sullivan, Brother Jeremiah Stephen *former college president*

**Linden**
Bedrick, Bernice *retired science educator, consultant*

**Little Falls**
Regan-Geraci, Theresa Elizabeth *learning disability educator, consultant*

**Livingston**
Batshaw, Marilyn Seidner *educational administrator*

**Lyndhurst**
DeBellis, Francine Darnel *elementary education educator*

**Mahwah**
Scott, Robert Allyn *academic administrator*

**Matawan**
Rodgers, John Joseph, III *school administrator*

**Mays Landing**
Pizzuto, Debra Kay *secondary school mathematics educator*

**Medford**
Cerulli, Patricia Ann *secondary school educator*
Galbraith, Frances Lynn *educational administrator*

**Mendham**
Posunko, Barbara *retired elementary education educator*
Posunko, Linda Mary *retired elementary education educator*

**Middletown**
Shields, Patricia Lynn *educational broker, consultant*

**Monmouth Junction**
Lawton, Deborah Simmons *educational media specialist*

**Montclair**
Egan, Patricia Jane *former university director of development, writer*

**Morganville**
Karp, Stefanie *special education educator*

**Morristown**
Burton, Valerie Diane *elementary education educator*

**New Brunswick**
Dill, Ellis Harold *university dean*
Durnin, Richard Gerry *education educator*
Garner, Charles William *educational administration educator, consultant*
Kansfield, Norman J. *seminary president*
Lee, Barbara Anne *academic administrator, lawyer*
Nelson, Jack Lee *education educator*
Tanner, Daniel *curriculum theory educator*

**New Providence**
Miskiewicz, Susanne Piatek *elementary education educator*

**Newark**
Abrams, Roger Ian *university dean, law educator, arbitrator*
Bergen, Stanley Silvers, Jr. *university president, physician*
Fenster, Saul K. *university president*
Healy, Phyllis M. Cordasco *school social worker*
Hollander, Toby Edward *education educator*
Mullin, Mary Ann *career counselor*
Pfeffer, Edward Israel *educational administrator*
Thomas, Gary L. *academic administrator*
Wolfe, Lilyan *special education clinical educator*

**Newton**
MacMurren, Margaret Patricia *secondary education educator, consultant*

**North Bergen**
Zondler, Joyce Evelyn *kindergarten educator*

**North Branch**
Gartlan, Philip M. *secondary school director*

**North Brunswick**
Kahrmann, Linda Irene *child care supervisor*

**Nutley**
Smith, Susan Elizabeth *guidance director*

**Ocean City**
Gross, Kathleen Frances *parochial school mathematics educator*

**Old Bridge**
Swett, Stephen Frederick, Jr. *principal*

**Old Tappan**
Gaffin, Joan Valerie *secondary school educator*

**Paramus**
Plucinsky, Constance Marie *school counselor, supervisor*

**Paterson**
Pulhamus, Marlene Louise *retired elementary school educator*

**Paulsboro**
Banks, Theresa Ann *elementary education educator*

**Perth Amboy**
Richardson-Melech, Joyce Suzanne *secondary school educator, singer*

**Phillipsburg**
Stull, Frank Walter *elementary school educator*

**Piscataway**
Colaizzi, John Louis *college dean*
Coppola, Sarah Jane *special education educator*
Rudczynski, Andrew B. *academic administrator, medical researcher*

**Plainfield**
Montford, Claudian Hammond *gifted and talented education educator*

**Pleasantville**
London, Charlotte Isabella *secondary education educator, reading specialist*

**Pomona**
Colijn, Geert Jan *academic administrator, political scientist*
Farris, Vera King *college president*

**Princeton**
Church, Martha Eleanor *retired academic administrator, scholar*
Cole, Nancy Stooksberry *educational research executive*
Gillespie, Thomas William *theological seminary administrator, religion educator*
Howarth, William (Louis) *education educator, writer*
Labalme, Patricia Hochschild *educational administrator*
Malkiel, Nancy Weiss *college dean, history educator*
Shapiro, Harold Tafler *academic administrator, economist*
Timpane, Philip Michael *education educator, foundation official*
†Trussell, James *dean*

**Ridgefield Park**
Ranone, John Louis *school board executive*

**Ridgewood**
Friedrich, Margret Cohen *guidance and student assistance counselor*
Riccio-Sauer, Joyce *art educator*

**River Edge**
Meldonian, Susan Lucy *elementary education educator*

**Rockaway**
Allen, Dorothea *secondary education educator*

**Roselle**
Bizub, Barbara L. *elementary school educator*
Di Marco, Barbaranne Yanus *multiple handicapped special education educator*

**Roselle Park**
Zahumeny, Janet Mae *secondary education educator*

**Saddle River**
Lehmann, Doris Elizabeth *elementary education educator*

**Scotch Plains**
Gross, Ruth Chaiken *educational administrator*

**Short Hills**
Danzis, Rose Marie *emeritus college president*
King, Charles Thomas *retired school superintendent, educator*
Robbins-Wilf, Marcia *educational consultant*

**Skillman**
Rhett, Haskell Emery Smith *educator*

**Somerville**
McCoy, Eileen Carey *academic dean*

**South Amboy**
Kosmoski, Mary Lou Teresa *special education educator*
Moskal, Anthony John *former dean, professor, management and education consultant*

**South Orange**
Gruenwald, Renee *special education educator*

**South Plainfield**
Munger, Janet Anne *education administrator*

**Sparta**
Harrison, Alice Kathleen *retired elementary educator*
Saxe, Thelma Richards *secondary school educator, consultant*

**Spring Lake**
Connor, Frances Partridge *education educator*

**Springfield**
Merachnik, Donald *superintendent of schools*

**Stanhope**
Scala, John Charles *secondary education educator, astronomer*

**Stone Harbor**
Koss, Rosabel Steinhauer *retired education educator*

**Stratford**
Rollins, Sandra L. *academic administrator*

**Summit**
Rossey, Paul William *school superintendent, university president*
Starks, Florence Elizabeth *retired special education educator*
Williams, Sandra Castaldo *elementary school educator*

**Surf City**
Sommer, Joseph William *retired middle school educator*

**Teaneck**
Bukovec, Joseph Aloysius *special education educator*
Mertz, Francis James *academic administrator*
Pischl, Adolph John *school administrator*

**Trenton**
Donahue, Donald Francis *secondary education educator*
Eickhoff, Harold Walter *college president, humanities educator*
Glass, Michael George *college administrator*
Pruitt, George Albert *academic administrator*
Ranck, Edna Runnels *academic administrator, researcher*
Stefane, Clara Joan *business education secondary educator*
Stein, Sandra Lou *educational psychologist, educator*

**Tuckerton**
DeCicco, James Joseph *media specialist*

**Union**
Applbaum, Ronald Lee *academic administrator*
French, Kathleen Patricia *educational evaluator, consultant*
Hennings, Dorothy Grant (Mrs. George Hennings) *education educator*
†Lederman, Susan Sturc *public administration educator*

**Union City**
Bull, Inez Stewart *special education and gifted music educator, coloratura soprano, pianist, editor, author*
Feingold, Janice Ann *elementary education educator*
Makar, Nadia Eissa *secondary education educator, educational administrator*
Ortizio, Debra Louise *elementary education educator*

**Washington**
De Sanctis, Vincent *college president*

**Wayne**
†Goldstein, Marjorie Tunick *special education educator*
Speert, Arnold *college president, chemistry educator*
†Wepner, Shelley Beth *education educator, software developer*
†Younie, William John *special education educator, researcher*

**West Long Branch**
Lutz, Francis Charles *university dean, civil engineering educator*
Rouse, Robert Sumner *former college official*
Stafford, Rebecca *academic administrator, sociologist*

**West Milford**
Kinney, Dorothy Jean *retired elementary educator*

**Westfield**
Besch, Lorraine W. *special education educator*
Fitts, Leonard Donald *educational administrator*

**Westwood**
Cullen, Ruth Enck *reading specialist, elementary education educator*

**Whippany**
Morris, Patricia Smith *media specialist, author, educator*

**Woodbridge**
Chesky, Pamela Bosze *school system administrator, curriculum specialist*

**Wyckoff**
Rice, Richard Charles *academic administrator, educator, consultant*

**Yardville**
Telencio, Gloria Jean *elementary education educator*

## NEW MEXICO

**Alamogordo**
Lee, Joli Fay Eaton *elementary education educator*
McFadin, Helen Lozetta *retired elementary education educator*

**Albuquerque**
Anaya, Rudolfo *educator, writer*
Benson, Sharon Stovall *primary school educator*
Caplan, Edwin Harvey *university dean, accounting educator*
Drummond, Harold Dean *education educator*
Fleury, Paul Aimé *university dean, physicist*
Garcia, F. Chris *academic administrator, political science educator, public opinion researcher*
Hadley, William Melvin *college dean*
Hull, McAllister Hobart, Jr. *retired university administrator*
Lattman, Laurence Harold *retired academic administrator*
May, Gerald William *university administrator, educator, civil engineering consultant*
Miller, Mickey Lester *retired school administrator*
Peck, Richard Earl *academic administrator, playwright, novelist*
Skipp, Tracy John *academic advisor, counselor*
Travelstead, Chester Coleman *former educational administrator*
Zink, Lee B. *academic administrator, economist, educator*

**Artesia**
Sarwar, Barbara Duce *school system administrator*

**Gallup**
Lindenmeyer, Mary Kathryn *secondary education educator*
Swain, Melinda Susan *elementary education educator*

**Grants**
Ward, Katherine Marie *school system administrator*

**Las Cruces**
Easterling, Kathy *school system administrator*
Gale, Thomas Martin *university dean*

**Loco Hills**
Sánchez, Frank Perez *elementary education educator*

**Los Alamos**
Engel, Emily Flachmeier *school administrator, educator*

**Mesilla Park**
Shutt, Frances Barton *special education educator*

**Montezuma**
Geier, Philip Otto, III *college president*

**Portales**
Byrnes, Lawrence William *dean*

**Raton**
Robinson, Janie Monette *education educator*

**Rio Rancho**
Meyerson, Barbara Tobias *elementary school educator*

**Ruidoso**
Coe, Elizabeth Ann *elementary education educator*
Stover, Carolyn Nadine *middle school educator*

**Santa Fe**
Agresto, John *college president*
Kasbeer, Stephen Frederick *retired university official*
Perkins, Van L. *university administrator, educator, conservationist*

**Silver City**
French, Laurence Armand *social science educator, psychology educator*
Moses-Foley, Judith Ann *special education educator*
Snedeker, John Haggner *university president*

**Tohatchi**
Hansen, Harold B., Jr. *elementary school educator*

## NEW YORK

**Albany**
Chonski, Denise Theresa *primary school educator, artist*
Edmonds, Richard *dean*
Kadamus, James Alexander *educational administrator*
Kinney, Thomas J. *adult education educator*
Lobosco, Anna Frances *state development disabilities program planner*
Quackenbush, Roger E. *retired secondary school educator*

**Robbins**, Cornelius (Van Vorse) *education administration educator*
Sbuttoni, Karen Ryan *reading specialist*
Thornton, Maurice *academic administrator*
Vaccaro, Louis Charles *college president*

**Alfred**
Coll, Edward Girard, Jr. *university president*
Ott, Walter Richard *academic administrator*

**Alfred Station**
Love, Robert Lyman *educational consulting company executive*

**Amherst**
Anisman, Martin Jay *academic administrator*
Vanderwerf, Mary Ann *elementary school educator, consultant*

**Amityville**
Gicola, Paul *middle school science educator, administrator*

**Annandale On Hudson**
Botstein, Leon *college president, historian, conductor, music critic*

**Auburn**
Eldred, Thomas Gilbert *secondary education educator, historian*

**Baldwinsville**
Kline, Carole June *special education educator*

**Barrytown**
Shimmyo, Theodore Tadaaki *seminary president*

**Batavia**
Steiner, Stuart *college president*

**Berne**
Lounsbury, Helen Marie *education educator, consultant*

**Binghamton**
Beach, Beth *elementary educator*
DeFleur, Lois B. *university president, sociology educator*
Feisel, Lyle Dean *university dean, electrical engineering educator*

**Bohemia**
Ortiz, Germaine Laura De Feo *secondary education educator, counselor*

**Bridgehampton**
McMenamin, Joan Stitt *headmistress*

**Bridgeport**
Sheldon, Thomas Donald *academic administrator*

**Brockport**
Stier, William Frederick, Jr. *academic administrator*
Van de Wetering, John E(dward) *academic administrator*

**Bronx**
Fernandez, Ricardo R. *university administrator*
Flam, Bernard Vincent *secondary education educator*
Hilliard, John Mauk *university official*
Ianniello, Peter Louis *school system administrator*
Murray, Phyllis Cynthia *educator*
Nathanson, Melvyn Bernard *university provost, mathematician*
Reichert, Marlene Joy *secondary school educator*
Riba, Netta Eileen *secondary school educator*
Scanlan, Thomas Joseph *college president, educator*
Smith, Sharon Patricia *university dean*
Wertheim, Mary Danielle *elementary education coordinator*
Williams, Lovie Jean *elementary education educator*

**Bronxville**
Ilchman, Alice Stone *college president, former government official*

**Brooklyn**
Alfano, Edward Charles, Jr. *elementary education educator*
Birenbaum, William M. *former university president*
Bugliarello, George *university chancellor*
Curry, David *guidance staff developer*
Gresser, Carol A. *school system administrator*
Kimmich, Christoph Martin *academic administrator, educator*
Moore, Martin *educator*
O'Connor, Sister George Aquin (Margaret M. O'Connor) *college president, sociology educator*
Williams, Vida Veronica *guidance counselor*
Williams, William Magavern *headmaster*
Wolfe, Ethyle Renee (Mrs. Coleman Hamilton Benedict) *college administrator*

**Buchanan**
Somerstein, Aurora Abrera *preschool administrator, educator*

**Buffalo**
Gemmett, Robert James *university dean, English language educator*
Gephart, Michele Marie *elementary education educator*
Greiner, William Robert *university administrator, educator, lawyer*
Gress, Edward J(ules) *academic program director, consultant*
Oak, H. Lorraine *academic administrator, geography educator*
Petrie, Hugh Gilbert *university dean, philosophy of education educator*
Reece-Porter, Sharon Ann *global education educator*
Seidl, Fredrick William *dean, social work educator*
Singletary, James, Jr. *principal*
Swanson, Austin Delain *educational administration educator*
Thurston, John Thomas *university advancement official*
Triggle, David John *university dean, consultant*
Vitagliano, Kathleen Alyce Fuller *secondary education educator*

**Wilbur**, Barbara Marie *elementary education educator*

**Canandaigua**
Malinowski, Patricia A. *community college educator*
Williams, Carolyn Woodworth *retired elementary education educator, consultant*

**Canton**
Fleming, Barbara Joan *university official*

**Carmel**
Caporino, Grace Connolly *secondary education educator, consultant*

**Castleton On Hudson**
Lanford, Oscar Erasmus, Jr. *retired university vice chancellor*

**Cazenovia**
Durgin, Patricia Harte *college administrator, chemistry educator, counselor*

**Centereach**
Cutrone, Dee T(heresa) *elementary education educator*

**Centerport**
Mallett, Helene Gettler *elementary education educator*

**Central Islip**
Griffith, Philip Arthur *elementary school educator*
Rodriguez, Teresa Ida *elementary education educator, educational consultant*

**Cicero**
Webster, Michael Lee *academic administrator*

**Clarence**
Trinkus, Laima Mary *special education educator*

**Clifton Park**
Murphy, Mary Patricia *elementary education educator*

**Clinton**
Fuller, Ruthann *principal*

**Cohoes**
Tabner, Mary Frances *secondary school educator*

**Commack**
Cohen, Judith W. *academic administrator*

**Congers**
Nelson, Marguerite Hansen *special education educator*

**Corona**
Cole, Donald H. *middle school educator*

**Coxsackie**
Amado, Lisa *elementary education educator*

**Crown Point**
Dajany, Innam *academic administrator*

**Dix Hills**
Schultheis, Edwin Milford *dean, business educator*

**Dobbs Ferry**
Pap, Beatriz Diaz *secondary education educator*

**East Aurora**
Spahn, Mary Attea *retired educator*
Weidemann, Julia Clark *principal, educator*
Woodard, Carol Jane *educational consultant*

**East Islip**
Somerville, Daphine Holmes *elementary education educator*

**East Meadow**
Beyer, Norma Warren *secondary education educator*

**East Setauket**
Barcel, Ellen Nora *secondary school educator, free-lance writer, indexer*

**East Williston**
Abernethy, Ann Lawson *retired elementary education educator*

**Elmhurst**
Lester, Lance Gary *education educator, researcher*

**Elmira**
Meier, Thomas Keith *college president, English educator*

**Endicott**
Goodwin, Charles Hugh *technology education educator*

**Fairport**
Gorzka, Margaret Rose *elementary education educator*
Halpern, David Rodion *special education administrator, principal*
Lavoie, Dennis James *secondary education educator*

**Farmingdale**
Cipriani, Frank Anthony *college president*

**Fayetteville**
Hiemstra, Roger *adult education educator, writer, networker*

**Floral Park**
Scricca, Diane Bernadette *principal*

**Flushing**
Erickson, Raymond *academic dean*

### Forest Hills
Kane, Sydell *elementary school principal*
Pinto, Rosalind *retired educator, civic volunteer*

### Fredonia
Mac Vittie, Robert William *retired college administrator*

### Freeport
Martorana, Barbara Joan *secondary education educator*

### Friendship
Kingdon, Mary Oneida Grace *elementary education educator*

### Gainesville
MacWilliams, Debra Lynne *secondary reading specialist, consultant*

### Garden City
Okulski, John Allen *principal*
Webb, Igor Michael *academic administrator*
Weinrich, Gloria Joan Castoria *retired elementary education educator*

### Garrison
Grossman, Allen, III *educational administrator*

### Geneseo
Moore, Gary Alan *academic administrator, educator*

### Geneva
Hersh, Richard H. *academic administrator*

### Glen Head
Boyrer, Elaine M. *principal*

### Glenmont
Block, Murray Harold *educational consultant*

### Great Neck
Feiler Goldstein, Paulette *secondary education educator, researcher*

### Greenvale
Cook, Edward Joseph *college president*
Shenker, Joseph *academic administrator*
Steinberg, David Joel *academic administrator, historian, educator*
Woodsworth, Anne *university dean, librarian*

### Greenwood
Rollins, June Elizabeth *elementary education educator*

### Hamilton
Cappeto, Michael Arnold *dean*
Grabois, Neil Robert *college president*
Jones, Howard Langworthy *educational administrator, consultant*

### Hammond
Deno, Lawrence M. *academic administrator*

### Hempstead
Berliner, Herman Albert *university provost and dean, economics educator*
Conway-Gervais, Kathleen Marie *reading specialist, educational consultant*
Haynes, Ulric St. Clair, Jr. *university dean*
Shuart, James Martin *academic administrator*

### Hicksville
Kremin, Daniel Paul *educational administrator*
Reedy, Catherine Irene *library and media specialist*

### Hilton
Ratigan, Hugh Lewis *middle school and elementary school educator*

### Holbrook
Senholzi, Gregory Bruce *secondary school educator*

### Hopewell Junction
Coppola, Patricia L. (Scheffel) *elementary school educator*

### Houghton
Chamberlain, Daniel Robert *college president*
Luckey, Robert Reuel Raphael *retired academic administrator*

### Howard Beach
Livingston, Barbara *special education educator*

### Huntington
D'Addario, Alice Marie *school administrator*

### Huntington Station
Boxwill, Helen Ann *primary and secondary education educator*
Braun, Ludwig *educational technology consultant*

### Irvington
Harris, Maria Loscutoff *special education educator, consultant*

### Island Park
Feir-Stillitano, Elisabeth *gifted/talented education educator*

### Ithaca
Ben Daniel, David Jacob *entrepreneurship educator, consultant*
Cooke, William Donald *university administrator, chemistry educator*
Corson, Dale Raymond *retired university president, physicist*
Cotton, Dorothy Foreman *former director student activities, consultant*
Craft, Harold Dumont, Jr. *university official, radio astronomer*
Firebaugh, Francille Maloch *university official*
Halpern, Bruce Peter *academic administrator*
Hopcroft, John Edward *dean, computer science educator*
Nesheim, Malden C. *academic administrator, nutrition educator*
Peterson, Patti McGill *academic administrator*
Rawlings, Hunter Ripley, III *university president*
Rhodes, Frank Harold Trevor *university president emeritus, geologist*
Rhodin, Thor Nathaniel *educational administrator*
Scott, Norman Roy *academic administrator, agricultural engineering educator*
Streett, William Bernard *university dean, engineering educator*
Weinstein, Leonard Harlan *institute program director*
Whalen, James Joseph *college president*

### Jamaica
Bartilucci, Andrew Joseph *university administrator*
Cline, Janice Claire *education educator*
Davis-Jerome, Eileen George *principal*
Faust, Naomi Flowe *education educator, poet*
Harrington, Donald James *university president*
Mangru, Basdeo *secondary school educator*
McKenzie, André *academic administrator, educator*
Sciame, Joseph *university administrator*

### Jamestown
Benke, Paul Arthur *college president*
Seguin, David Gerard *community college official*

### Jericho
Mandery, Mathew M. *principal*
Martin, David S. *educator, administrator*

### Kenmore
Bates Stoklosa, Evelynne (Eve Bates Stoklosa) *educational consultant, educator*

### Kings Park
Smith, Norma Jane *elementary education educator*

### Kings Point
Matteson, Thomas T. *academic administrator*
Mazek, Warren F(elix) *academic administrator, economics educator*

### Kingston
Bruck, Arlene Lorraine *secondary education educator*
Steller, Arthur Wayne *educational administrator*

### Lake Placid
Reiss, Paul Jacob *college president*

### Latham
Garner, Doris Traganza *educator*

### Levittown
Dwyer, Mary Elizabeth *nursery school director*
Rode, Helen Jane *special education educator*

### Liverpool
Mann, Linda Marie *elementary school educator*
Miller, Eileen Renee *counselor*
Williams, John Alan *secondary education educator, coach*

### Lockport
Godshall, Barbara Marie *special education educator*

### Long Beach
Thompson, Dorothy Barnard *elementary school educator*

### Long Eddy
Van Swol, Noel Warren *secondary education educator*

### Long Island City
Bowen, Raymond Cobb *academic administrator*
Rothman, Barbara Schaeffer *education director*

### Lynbrook
Pagillo, Carl Robert *elementary school educator*

### Mahopac
Silbert, Linda Bress *educational counselor, therapist*

### Manhasset
Scala, Marilyn Campbell *special education educator, writer, consultant*

### Massapequa
McCann, Susan Lynn *elementary education educator*

### Massena
Vazquez, Sue Ellen *elementary education educator*

### Mastic Beach
Casciano, Paul *school system administrator*
Pagano, Alicia I. *education educator*

### Middle Island
Ferrara, Frank Gregory *middle school educator*
Mastrion, Guy *secondary school principal*

### Middleport
Massaro, Joseph James *secondary school educator*

### Middletown
Isseks, Evelyn *retired educational administrator*
McCord, Jean Ellen *secondary art educator, coach*
Shaw, Roslyn Lee *elementary education educator*

### Montrose
Lee, Edna Pritchard *education educator*

### New City
Schaefer, Rhoda Pesner *elementary school educator*

### New Paltz
Emanuel-Smith, Robin Lesley *special education educator*
Whittington-Couse, Maryellen Frances *education administrator*

### New Rochelle
Capasso, Frank Louis *secondary school educator*
Donahue, Richard James *secondary school educator*
Gallagher, John Francis *education educator*
Kelly, Sister Dorothy Ann *college president*
Maher, Vincent F. *academic administrator, educator, lawyer*
Veith, Mary Roth *assistant dean*
Wolotsky, Hyman *retired college dean*

### New York
Alpern, Mildred *history educator, consultant*
Bouton, Marshall Melvin *academic administrator*
Boylan, Elizabeth Shippee *academic administrator, biology educator*
Brademas, John *retired university president, former congressman*
Brenner, Egon *university official, education consultant*
†Budig, Gene Arthur *former chancellor, professional sports executive*
Burton, John Campbell *university dean, educator, consultant*
Campbell, Mary Schmidt *dean art school*
Caputo, David Armand *university president, political scientist educator*
Carey, James William *university dean, educator, researcher*
Chelstrom, Marilyn Ann *political education consultant*
Claster, Jill Nadell *university administrator, history educator*
Cohen, Saul Bernard *former college president, geographer*
Consagra, Sophie Chandler *academy administrator*
Daly, George Garman *college dean, educator*
Durst, Carol Goldsmith *educator*
Einiger, Carol Blum *university administrator*
Elster, Samuel Kase *college dean, medical educator, physician*
Ewers, Patricia O'Donnell *university administrator*
Feldberg, Meyer *university dean*
Gartner, Alan P. *university official, author*
Gatto, John Taylor *educational consultant, writer*
Gillespie, John Thomas *university administrator*
Goren, Arnold Louis *educator, former university official*
Haffner, Alden Norman *university official*
Hejduk, John Quentin *dean, architect*
Heslin, James J. *counseling career planning administrator*
Hoffner, Marilyn *university administrator*
Hollister, Juliet Garretson *educator*
Hood, Donald Charles *university administrator, psychology educator*
Horowitz, Frances Degen *academic administrator, psychology educator*
Hoxie, Ralph Gordon *educational administrator, author*
Iselin, John Jay *university president*
Jelinek, Vera *university director*
Jeynes, Mary Kay *college dean*
Katsh, Abraham Isaac *university president emeritus, educator*
Klopf, Gordon John *educational consultant, former college dean*
Konner, Joan Weiner *university administrator, educator, broadcasting executive, television producer*
Kopp, Wendy *teaching program administrator*
†Lamm, Norman *academic administrator, rabbi*
Lange, Phil C. *retired education educator*
Levine, Arthur Elliott *academic administrator, educator*
Levine, Naomi Bronheim *university administrator*
Lewis, Enid Selena *educator*
Lynch, Gerald Weldon *academic administrator, psychologist*
Macchiarola, Frank Joseph *academic administrator*
Marcus, Steven *dean, English educator*
Marcuse, Adrian Gregory *academic administrator*
Marshall, Geoffrey *university official*
Martin, Joseph Paul *university department director*
Maubert, Jacques Claude *headmaster*
Molholt, Pat *academic administrator, associate dean*
Nelson, Iris Dorothy *retired guidance and rehabilitation counselor*
Nentwich, Michael Andreas Erhart *educator, consultant*
O'Hare, Joseph Aloysius *academic administrator, priest*
Oliva, Lawrence Jay *academic administrator, history educator*
Oreskes, Susan *private school educator*
Pawliczko, George Ihor *academic administrator*
Pedraza, Pedro *research director*
Pigott, Irina Vsevolodovna *educational administrator*
Polisi, Joseph W(illiam) *academic administrator*
Potter, Elizabeth Stone *academic administrator*
Pratt, Richardson, Jr. *retired college president*
Pulanco, Tonya Beth *special education educator*
Reissman, Rose Cherie *elementary education educator*
Reutter, Eberhard Edmund, Jr. *education and law educator*
Reynolds, W(ynetka) Ann *academic administrator, educator*
Rinsland, Roland DeLano *retired university dean and registrar*
Rosenthal, Albert Joseph *university dean, law educator, lawyer*
Rowe, John Wallis *medical school president, hospital administrator*
Rowland, Esther E(delman) *college dean, retired*
Rupp, George Erik *academic administrator*
Rust, Frances O'Connell *education educator*
Schor, Laura Strumingher *academic administrator, historian*
Seidenberg, Rita Nagler *education educator*
Seitz, Frederick *former university administrator*
Selby, Cecily Cannan *dean, educator, scientist*
Shea, Dion Warren Joseph *university official, fund raiser*
Shields, James Joseph *educational administrator, educator, author*
Silverman, Martin Morris Bernard *secondary education educator*
Smith, John Brewster *teaching program administrator*
Socol, Sheldon Eleazer *university official*
†Soros, Susan Weber *educational administrator*
Tapley, Donald Fraser *university official, physician, educator*
Tschumi, Bernard *dean*
Tsui, Soo Hing *educational research consultant*
Vernon, Arthur *educational administrator*
Violenus, Agnes A. *retired school system administrator*
Walzer, Judith Borodovko *academic administrator, educator*
Waren, Stanley A. *university administrator, theatre and arts center administrator, director*
Weiner, Annette Barbara *university dean, anthropology educator*
Weinstein, Sidney *university program director*
Williams, Harriet Clarke *retired academic administrator, artist*
Yetman, Leith Eleanor *academic administrator*

### Newburgh
Joyce, Mary Ann *principal*
Saturnelli, Annette Miele *school system administrator*
Weiss, Barry Ronald *education administrator*

### Niagara Falls
Bundy-Iannarelli, Barbara Ann *educational administrator*
Sheeran, Thomas Joseph *education educator, writer, consultant, judge*

### Niagara University
O'Leary, Daniel Francis *university dean*

### North Bellmore
Chun, Arlene Donnelly *special education educator*

### North Rose
Anderson, Nancy Marie Greenwood *special education educator*

### Oakdale
Meskill, Victor Peter *college president, educator*

### Old Westbury
Dibble, Richard Edward *academic administrator*
Pettigrew, L. Eudora *academic administrator*
Saueracker, Edward *academic administrator*
Schure, Matthew *college president*

### Oneonta
Detweller, Richard Allen *college president*
Donovan, Alan Barton *college president*

### Orangeburg
Hennessy, James Ernest *academic administrator, telecommunications executive, retired*

### Oswego
Gerber, Barbara Ann Witter *university dean, educator*
Moody, Florence Elizabeth *education educator, retired college dean*

### Patchogue
Fogarty, James Vincent, Jr. *special education administrator, educator*
Orlowski, Karel Ann *elementary education educator*

### Plattsburgh
Edwards, Peter *educator, writer*

### Pleasantville
Antonecchia, Donald A. *principal*

### Port Chester
Penney, Linda Helen *music educator*

### Port Washington
Williams, George Leo *retired secondary education educator*

### Potsdam
Ha, Andrew Kwangho *education educator*
Ratliff, Gerald Lee *dean, speech and theater educator*
Rudiger, Lance Wade *secondary school educator*
†Stoltie, James Merle *academic administrator*
Washburn, Robert Brooks *university dean, composer*
Wells, David John *program director, academic administrator, mechanical engineer*

### Poughkeepsie
Brakas, Nora Jachym *education educator*
Conklin, D(onald) David *academic administrator*
Fergusson, Frances Daly *college president, educator*
Opdycke, Leonard Emerson *retired secondary education educator, publisher*
Rhodes, Geraldine Bryan *secondary school administrator*

### Purchase
Lacy, Bill *academic administrator*

### Randolph
Margesson, Maxine Edge *professor*

### Ransomville
Mayer, George Merton *elementary education educator*

### Rego Park
Uter, Carmenlita *secondary education language educator, translator*

### Rexford
Schmitt, Roland Walter *retired academic administrator*

### Ridgewood
Giambalvo, Vincent Salvatore *secondary education educator*

### Rochester
Allen, Henry Lee *education educator, consultant*
Balch, Glenn McClain, Jr. *academic administrator, minister, author*
Bernstein, Paul *retired academic dean*
Buckingham, Barbara Rae *educator*
Campbell, Alma Jacqueline Porter *elementary education educator*
Cohen, Jules *academic dean, physician, educator*
Everett, Claudia Kellam *special education educator*
Jackson, Thomas Humphrey *university president*
Joynt, Robert James *academic administrator*
Mc Isaac, George Scott *business policy educator, government official, former management consultant*

McNamara, Timothy James *secondary education educator*
Munson, Harold Lewis *education educator*
Newell, William James *sign language educator*
Palmeri, Marlaina *principal*
Plosser, Charles Irving *university dean, economics educator*
Rothman-Marshall, Gail Ann *counseling services administrator*
Scalise, Francis Allen *adminstrator, consultant*
Simone, Albert Joseph *academic administrator*
Thompson, Brian John *university administrator, optics educator*

### Rock Hill
Williams, Annemarie Hauber *secondary education educator*

### Rockville Centre
Fitzgerald, Sister Janet Anne *college president emeritus*

### Saint Bonaventure
Doyle, Mathias Francis *university president, political scientist, educator*

### Saint James
Van Dover, Karen *middle and elementary school educator, curriculum consultant, language arts specialist*

### Sanborn
Schmidt-Bova, Carolyn Marie *vocational school administrator, consultant*

### Saranac Lake
Szwed, Beryl J. *school system administrator, mathematics educator*

### Saratoga Springs
Abrams, Kenneth Theodore *academic administrator*
Hall, James William *college president*
Ratzer, Mary Boyd *secondary education educator, librarian*

### Scarsdale
Griffiths, Daniel Edward *dean emeritus*

### Schenectady
Helmar-Salasoo, Ester Anette *literacy educator, researcher*
Hull, Roger Harold *college president*

### Schoharie
Stiver, Patricia Abare *elementary education educator*

### Seaford
Schlossberg, Fred Paul *elementary education educator*

### Selden
Paul, Carol Ann *academic administrator, biology educator*

### Sherburne
Birmingham, Kathleen Christina *secondary school educator*

### Shoreham
Reynolds, Carolyn Mary *elementary education educator*

### Sidney
Haller, Irma Tognola *secondary education educator*

### Southampton
Robinson, Chester Hersey *retired dean*

### Staten Island
Greco, Donna *educational administrator*
Smith, Norman Raymond *college president*
Springer, Marlene *university administrator, educator*

### Stony Brook
Cochran, James Kirk *dean, oceanographer, geochemist, educator*
Kenny, Shirley Strum *university administrator*
Shamash, Yacov *dean, electrical engineering educator*

### Syosset
Kruse, Nancy Clarson *elementary education educator*
Nydick, David *school superintendent*
Streitman, Jeffrey Bruce *educational administrator*

### Syracuse
Burstyn, Joan Netta *education educator*
Charters, Alexander Nathaniel *retired adult education educator*
Coliz, James Russell *university administrator, telecommunications consultant*
Collins, William John *educational administrator*
Diamond, Robert Mach *higher education administrator*
Hollis, Susan Tower *college dean*
Krathwohl, David Reading *education educator emeritus*
Manning, J. Francis *school administrator*
Mitchell, Robert Arthur *college president*
Nelli, D. James *business school executive, accountant*
Schmidt, Patricia Ruggiano *education educator*
Serafin, John Alfred *art educator*
Shaw, Kenneth Alan *university president*
Waite, Peter Arthur *literacy educator, educational consultant*
Weiss, Volker *university administrator, educator*
Whaley, Ross Samuel *academic administrator*

### Tonawanda
Vienne, Dorothy Titus *school principal*

### Troy
Judd, Gary *university administrator*
Kahl, William Frederick *retired college president*
McAllister, Edward William Charles *educator*
Romond, James *principal*
Wait, Samuel Charles, Jr. *academic administrator, educator*

Wilson, Jack Martin *dean, scientific association executive, physics educator*

### Tuckahoe
Doyle, Joellen Mary *special education educator*

### Tuxedo Park
Groskin, Sheila Marie Lessen *primary school educator*

### Utica
Boyle, William Leo, Jr. *educational consultant, retired college president*
Brown, Thomas Glenn *college administrator*
Simpson, Michael Kevin *academic administrator, political science educator*

### Victor
Abbott, Susan Alicia *elementary education educator*

### Walden
Konior, Jeannette Mary *elementary school educator*

### Wallkill
Chumas, Linda Grace *elementary school educator*

### Wantagh
DeNapoli, Anthony *middle school principal*

### West Harrison
Paul, Nancy Haworth *educator*

### West Islip
Coppola, Phyllis Gloria Cecire *special education educator*

### West Nyack
Kanyuk, Joyce Stern *secondary art educator*

### Westbury
Fowler, Charles William *school administrator*

### Williamson
Ross, Kathleen Marie Amato *secondary school educator*

### Woodside
Burchell, Jeanne Kathleen *primary school educator*

### Yonkers
Atkins, Leola Mae *special education educator*
Hoar, Mary Margrette *gifted education educator*
Liggio, Jean Vincenza *adult education educator, artist*
Tuly, Charles A. *mathematics and computer science educator*
Weston, Francine Evans *secondary education educator*

### Yorkshire
Smith, Barbara Jane *assistant school superintendent*

### Yorktown Heights
Hsieh, Hazel Tseng *elementary and secondary education educator*

### Youngstown
Polka, Walters S. *school superintendent*

## NORTH CAROLINA

### Albemarle
Bramlett, Christopher Lewis *academic administrator*

### Angier
Raynor, Wandra Adams *middle school educator*

### Asheville
Bryson, Paula Kay *secondary school educator*
Pickard, Carolyn Rogers *secondary school educator*
Reed, Patsy Bostick *university administrator*

### Banner Elk
Thomas, John Edwin *retired academic administrator*

### Boiling Springs
White, Martin Christopher *academic administrator*

### Boone
Borkowski, Francis Thomas *university administrator*
Duke, Charles Richard *academic dean*

### Buies Creek
Wiggins, Norman Adrian *university administrator, legal educator*

### Canton
Furci, Joan Gelormino *early childhood education educator*

### Cary
Bat-haee, Mohammad Ali *educational administrator, consultant*

### Chapel Hill
Campbell, B(obby) Jack *university official*
Carroll, Roy *academic administrator*
Cartwright, William Holman *education educator emeritus*
Clark, David Louis *education educator, author*
Cole, Richard Ray *university dean*
Cross, Dennis Wayne *academic administrator*
Cunningham, James William *literacy education educator, researcher*
Edwards, Richard LeRoy *academic dean, social work educator, non-profit management consultant*
Fordham, Christopher Columbus, III *university dean and chancellor, medical educator*
Freund, Cynthia M. *dean, nursing educator*
Friday, William Clyde *university president emeritus*
Ganley, Oswald Harold *university official*
Hooker, Michael Kenneth *university chancellor*
Joyner, Leon Felix *university administrator, retired*
Memory, Jasper Durham *academic administrator, physics educator*

Murphy, James Lee *college dean, economics educator*
Sanders, John Lassiter *retired academic administrator*
Simmons, Michael Anthony *dean*
Spangler, Clemmie Dixon, Jr. *business executive*
Tillman, Rollie, Jr. *university official*
Ware, William Brettel *education educator*
Whybark, David Clay *educational educator, researcher*

### Charlotte
Burke, Mary Thomas *university administrator, educator*
Clark, Ann Blakeney *educational administrator*
Colvard, Dean Wallace *emeritus university chancellor*
Fretwell, Elbert Kirtley, Jr. *university chancellor emeritus, consultant*
Greene, William Henry L'Vel *academic administrator*
Nassar-McMillan, Sylvia C. *educator*
Phillips, Sandra Allen *primary school educator*
Schaffer, Eugene Carl *education educator*
Wireman, Billy Overton *college president*
Woodward, James Hoyt *academic administrator, engineer*

### China Grove
Hall, Telka Mowery Elium *educational administrator*

### Chocowinity
Castle, William Eugene *retired academic adminstrator*

### Clyde
Parris, Donna Sands *secondary school educator*
Rogers, Frances Nichols *assistant principal*

### Cullowhee
Bardo, John William *university administrator*
Coulter, Myron Lee *retired academic administrator*
Reed, Alfred Douglas *university director*

### Dallas
Green, Gayla Maxine *elementary school educator*

### Davidson
Jackson, Robert Bruce, Jr. *retired education educator*
Kuykendall, John Wells *academic administrator, educator*
Spencer, Samuel Reid, Jr. *educational consultant, former university president*

### Deep Gap
Tompkins, James Richard *special education educator*

### Dobson
Smith, Richard Jackson *elementary education educator*

### Durham
Abernathy, Margaret Denny *elementary school educator*
Beckum, Leonard Charles *academic administrator*
Bell, Judith Carolyn Ott *interdisciplinary educator*
Britton, Charles Valentine *secondary education educator*
Chambers, Julius LeVonne *academic administrator, lawyer*
Dowell, Earl Hugh *university dean, aerospace and mechanical engineering educator*
Hopkins, Everett Harold *education educator*
Huestis, Charles Benjamin *former academic administrator*
Keller, Thomas Franklin *dean, management science educator*
Keohane, Nannerl Overholser *university president, political scientist*
Kuniholm, Bruce Robellet *university administrator*
Malpass, Leslie Frederick *retired university president*
Schmalbeck, Richard Louis *university dean, lawyer*

### Elon College
Young, James Fred *college president*

### Gastonia
McGlohon, Reeves *education administrator*

### Goldsboro
Yelverton, Deborah Sue *middle school art educator*

### Graham
Lancaster, Carolyn Hohn *secondary school educator*

### Greensboro
Alston, Charlotte LeNora *college administrator*
Crawford, Kathrine Nelson *special education educator*
Edinger, Lois Virginia *education educator emeritus*
McNemar, Donald William *academic administrator*
Miller, Robert Louis *university dean, chemistry educator*
Poteet, Daniel P(owell), II *college provost*
Prodan, James Christian *university administrator*
Rogers, William Raymond *college president emeritus, psychology educator*
Speight, Velma Ruth *alumni affairs director*
Stoodt, Barbara Dern *education educator, magazine editor*
Sullivan, Patricia A. *academic administrator*
Wright, John Spencer *school system administrator*

### Greenville
Bearden, James Hudson *university official*
Eakin, Richard Ronald *academic administrator, mathematics educator*
Howell, John McDade *retired university chancellor, political science educator*
Hudgins, Herbert Cornelius, Jr. *education educator*
Leggett, Donald Yates *academic administrator*
Leggett, Nancy Porter *university administrator*
Zauner, Christian Walter *university dean, exercise physiologist, consultant*

### Hamlet
Walker, Wanda Gail *special education educator*

### Hendersonville
Jones, J(ohn) Charles *education educator*

Payne, Gerald Oliver *retired elementary education educator*

### Hickory
Sims, Janette Elizabeth Lowman *educational director*

### High Point
Clark, Carol Ruth Jones *secondary education educator*
Farlow, Joel Wray *school system administrator*
Howard, Lou Dean Graham *elementary education educator*
Martinson, Jacob Christian, Jr. *academic administrator*

### Hillsborough
Stockstill, James William *secondary school educator*

### Kernersville
Litton, Daphne Napier Rudhman *special education educator*

### Kinston
Matthis, Eva Mildred Boney *college official*
Petteway, Samuel Bruce *college president*

### Kure Beach
Funk, Frank E. *retired university dean*

### Lake Junaluska
Robinson, Mary Katherine *school system administrator*

### Laurinburg
Snead, Eleanor Leroy Marks *secondary school educator*

### Liberty
Feaster, Charlotte Josephine S. *school administrator*

### Lincolnton
Saine, Betty Boston *elementary school educator*

### Marion
Bergemann, Verna Elmyra *education educator*

### Micro
Loose, Vicky Dianne *special education educator*

### Monroe
Rorie, Nancy Katheryn *elementary and secondary school educator*

### Mooresville
Neill, Rita J. *elementary school educator*

### Mount Olive
Raper, William Burkette *retired college president*

### Mount Ulla
Kluttz, Henry G. *principal*

### Murfreesboro
Whitaker, Bruce Ezell *college president*

### New Bern
Hemphill, Jean Hargett *college dean*

### Oak Ridge
O'Bryant, Cecyle Arnold *secondary English educator*

### Pittsboro
Lewis, Henry Wilkins *university administrator, lawyer, educator*
Magill, Samuel Hays *retired academic administrator, higher education consultant*

### Pope AFB
Vaughan, Clyde Vernelson *program director*

### Raleigh
Buchanan, David Royal *associate dean*
Burris, Craven Allen *education administrator, educator*
Dolce, Carl John *education administration educator*
Drew, Nancy McLaurin Shannon *counselor, consultant*
Fletcher, Oscar Jasper, Jr. *college dean*
Howell, Bruce Inman *academic administrator*
Jarrett, Polly Hawkins *secondary education educator, retired*
Jenkins, Clauston Levi, Jr. *college president*
Jividen, Loretta Ann Harper *secondary school educator*
Maidon, Carolyn Howser *education director*
Malone, Thomas Francis *academic administrator, meteorologist*
Martin, Donnis Lynn *adult education educator*
Monteith, Larry King *university chancellor*
Page, Anne Ruth *gifted education educator, education specialist*
Parramore, Barbara Mitchell *education educator*
Poulton, Bruce Robert *former university chancellor*
Robinson, Prezell Russell *academic administrator*
Shaw, Talbert O. *university president*
Stewart, Debra Wehrle *university dean and official, educator*
Toole, William Bell, III *college dean, retired, writer*
Winstead, Nash Nicks *university administrator, phytopathologist*
Wynne, Johnny Calvin *university dean, plant breeding researcher*

### Rockingham
Robertson, Ralph S. *secondary school principal*

### Rosman
Dutton, Sharon Gail *elementary school educator*

### Rural Hall
McDermon, Linda Garrett *elementary school educator*

### Shelby
Edgar, Ruth R. *retired educator*

### Spruce Pine
Rensink, Jacqueline B. *secondary school educator*

PROFESSIONAL INDEX 5149 EDUCATION

**Statesville**
Heymann, Hans Paulsen *community college administrator*

**Taylorsville**
Leonhardt, Debbie Ann *counselor, writer, minister*

**Troy**
Gasper, Theodore Howard, Jr. *college president*

**Wake Forest**
Buchanan, Edward A. *education educator*

**Waynesville**
Boyd, Charles Lee *horticulture educator*

**Weaverville**
Boyce, Emily Stewart *retired library and information science educator*

**Whiteville**
Scott, Stephen Carlos *academic administrator*

**Wilmington**
Cahill, Charles L. *university administrator, chemistry educator*
Dewey, Ralph Jay *headmaster*
Leutze, James Richard *academic administrator, television producer and host*
McManus, Hugh F. *principal*

**Wilson**
Bailey, Grace Daniel *retired secondary school educator*
Howell, Maria DeLane *elementary physical education educator*

**Wingate**
McGee, Jerry Edward *academic administrator*

**Winston Salem**
Ewing, Alexander Cochran *chancellor*
Janeway, Richard *university official*
Liner, Ronald Sims *middle school administrator*
Roth, Marjory Joan Jarboe *special education educator*
Stroupe, Henry Smith *university dean*
Thompson, Cleon F., Jr. *university administrator*
Thrift, Julianne Still *academic administrator*

**Yanceyville**
Bowen, Audrey Lynn Harris *elementary education educator*

NORTH DAKOTA

**Bismarck**
Evanson, Barbara Jean *middle school education educator*

**Dickinson**
Conn, Philip Wesley *university president*

**Fargo**
Lardy, Sister Susan Marie *academic administrator*

**Grand Forks**
Baker, Kendall L. *academic administrator*
Clifford, Thomas John *university president*
Davis, W. Jeremy *dean, law educator, lawyer*
Wilson, H. David *dean*

**Jamestown**
Walker, James Silas *academic administrator*

**Minot**
Jermiason, John Lynn *elementary school educator, farmer, rancher*
Shaar, H. Erik *academic administrator*

OHIO

**Ada**
Freed, DeBow *college president*

**Akron**
Auburn, Norman Paul *university president*
Barker, Harold Kenneth *former university dean*
Elliott, Peggy Gordon *university president*
Kelley, Frank Nicholas *dean*
Phillips, Dorothy Ormes *elementary education educator*
Stroll, Beverly Marie *elementary school principal*

**Alliance**
Dunagan, Gwendolyn Ann *special education educator*

**Andover**
Mathay, John Preston *elementary education educator*

**Anna**
Thompson, Virigina A. *elementary education educator*

**Ashville**
Schilling, Eydie Anne *science educator, consultant*

**Athens**
Bruning, James Leon *university official, educator*
Glidden, Robert Burr *university president, musician, educator*
Miller, Richard Irwin *education educator, university administrator*
Parmer, Jess Norman *university official, educator*
Torres-Labawld, Jose Dimas *institutional research director, service company executive, educator*

**Avon Lake**
Gwiazda, Caroline Louise *school system administrator*

**Batavia**
Nichols, Marci Lynne *gifted education coordinator, educator, consultant*

**Bath**
Bowman-Dalton, Burdene Kathryn *education testing coordinator, computer consultant*

**Bay Village**
Woods, Dennis Craig *school superintendent*

**Beavercreek**
Geier, Sharon Lee *special education educator*

**Berea**
Malicky, Neal *college president*

**Bloomingburg**
Lester, Richard Lee *elementary education educator, consultant*

**Brecksville**
Johnson, L. Neil *school system administrator*

**Brooklyn**
Clapp, Gayle Laurene *school administrator*

**Bucyrus**
Bowlby, Linda Arlene *secondary school educator*
Frey, Judith Lynn *elementary education educator*

**Canton**
Herritt, David R. *elementary education educator*

**Chagrin Falls**
Bernard, Lowell Francis *academic administrator, educator, consultant*
Brown, Jeanette Grasselli *university official*

**Chesapeake**
Harris, Bob L(ee) *educational administrator*

**Chillicothe**
Atwood, Joyce Charlene *curriculum and instruction administrator, consultant*

**Cincinnati**
Briggs, Henry Payson, Jr. *headmaster*
Clutter, Timothy John *secondary language arts educator*
De Courten-Myers, Gabrielle Marguerite *education educator, researcher*
Fischer, Patricia Ann *middle school educator*
Gottschalk, Alfred *college chancellor*
Greengus, Samuel *academic administrator, religion educator*
Hamler, Shelley Jefferson *administrator*
Harrison, Donald Carey *university official, cardiology educator*
Hoff, James Edwin *university president*
Hoke, Eugena Louise *special education educator*
Johnson, Betty Lou *secondary education educator*
Kohl, David *dean, librarian*
Nester, William Raymond, Jr. *retired academic administrator and educator*
Patterson, Claire Ann *vocational educator*
Sanford, Wilbur Lee *elementary education educator*
Skilbeck, Carol Lynn Marie *elementary educator and small business owner*
Smith, Gregory Allgire *academic director*
Steger, Joseph A. *university president*
Tomain, Joseph Patrick *dean, law educator*
Wentsler, Gertrude Josephine *secondary school educator*
Werner, Robert Joseph *college dean, music educator*
Winkler, Henry Ralph *retired academic administrator, historian*

**Cleveland**
Ainsworth, Joan Horsburgh *university development director*
Bassett, John E. *dean, English educator*
Boyd, Richard Alfred *school system administrator*
Cullis, Christopher Ashley *dean, biology educator*
Fitzpatrick, Joyce J. *dean, nursing educator*
Jirkans, Maribeth Joie *school counselor*
Jones, Byrd, Jr. *registrar*
Jones, Rosemary *education director*
Loehr, Marla *spiritual care coordinator*
Mayer, Robert Anthony *college president*
McArdle, Richard Joseph *academic administrator*
McCullough, Joseph *college president emeritus*
Nickerson, Gary Lee *secondary education educator*
Parker, Robert Frederic *university dean emeritus*
Prater-Fipps, Eunice Kay *educational administrator*
Pytte, Agnar *academic administrator*
Samson, Gordon Edgar *educator, consultant*
Van Ummersen, Claire A(nn) *academic administrator, biologist, educator*
Weidenthal, Maurice David (Bud Weidenthal) *educational administrator, journalist*
Zdanis, Richard Albert *academic administrator*

**Cleveland Heights**
Travis, Frederick Francis *academic administrator, historian*

**Columbus**
Alutto, Joseph Anthony *university dean, management educator*
Armes, Walter Scott *vocational school administrator*
Baughman, George Washington, III *retired university official, financial consultant*
Beller, Stephen Mark *university administrator*
Blackmore, Josiah H. *university president, lawyer, educator*
Cole, Clarence Russell *college dean*
Cormanick, Rosa-Maria Moreno *academic program coordinator*
Cottrell, David Alton *school system administrator*
Culbertson, Jack Arthur *education educator*
Gee, Elwood Gordon *university administrator*
Hayes, Edward F. *academic administrator*
Heinlen, Daniel Lee *alumni organization administrator*
Koenigsknecht, Roy A. *education administrator*
Lindsay, Dianna Marie *educational administrator*
Magliocca, Larry Anthony *education educator*
Meuser, Fredrick William *retired seminary president, church historian*
Otte, Paul John *academic administrator, consultant, trainer*
Oxley, Margaret Carolyn Stewart *elementary education educator*
Stephens, Thomas M(aron) *education educator*

**Cortland**
Lane, Sarah Marie Clark *elementary education educator*

**Crestline**
Maddy, Janet Marie *retired educator, dean of students*

**Curtice**
Hartman, Elizabeth Diane *elementary education educator*

**Dayton**
Allen, Rose Letitia *special education educator*
Bowman, Ed *school administrator*
Crowe, Shelby *educational specialist, consultant*
Fitz, Brother Raymond L. *university president*
Flack, Mignon Scott-Palmer *elementary educator*
Gies, Frederick John *education educator*
Goldenberg, Kim *university dean, internist*
Heft, James Lewis *academic administrator, theology educator*
Martin, James Gilbert *university provost emeritus*
Ponitz, David H. *academic administrator*
Taylor, Elisabeth Coler *secondary school educator*
Uphoff, James Kent *education educator*

**Defiance**
Harris, James Thomas, III *college administrator, educator*

**Delaware**
Courtice, Thomas Barr *academic administrator*

**Delta**
Miller, Beverly White *past college president, education consultation*

**Dublin**
Conrad, Marian Sue (Susan Conrad) *special education educator*

**East Sparta**
Cook, Martha Jane *educator, counselor*

**Eaton**
Rinehart, Kathryn Ann *principal*

**Elyria**
Kennard, Emily Marie *secondary school art educator, watercolor artist*
Skillicorn, Judy Pettibone *gifted and talented education coordinator*
Wood, Jacalyn Kay *education educator, educational consultant*

**Euclid**
Clements, Mary Margaret *retired educator*
Keay, Charles Lloyd *elementary school educator*

**Fairborn**
Seymour, Joyce Ann *elementary school educator*

**Fairfield**
Lapp, Susan Bolster *learning disability educator*
Seed, Allen H. *elementary and secondary education educator, science educator*

**Forest Park**
Ashley, Lynn *educator, consultant, administrator*

**Granville**
Myers, Michele Tolela *university president*

**Groveport**
Keck, Vicki Lynn *special education educator*

**Harrison**
Stoll, Robert W. *principal*

**Hiram**
Jagow, Elmer *retired college president*
Oliver, G(eorge) Benjamin *academic administrator, philosophy educator*

**Hudson**
Goheen, Janet Moore *counselor, sales professional*

**Jamestown**
Liem, Darlene Marie *secondary education educator*

**Kent**
Buttlar, Rudolph Otto *retired college dean*
Cartwright, Carol Ann *university president*
Fultz, John Howard *elementary school educator*
Schwartz, Michael *university president, sociology educator*

**Kettering**
Taylor, Billie Wesley *retired secondary education educator*

**Kingston**
Mathew, Martha Sue Cryder *retired education educator*

**Lakewood**
Berman, Phillip Lee *religious institute administrator, author*

**Lancaster**
Gault, Teressa Elaine *special education educator*

**Lewis Center**
Strip, Carol Ann *gifted education specialist, educator*

**Lima**
Meek, Violet Imhof *dean*

**Lodi**
Cox, Hillery Lee *primary school educator*

**Louisville**
Shadle, Donna A. Francis *principal*

**Magnolia**
Zimmerman, Judith Rose *elementary art educator*

**Mansfield**
Riedl, John Orth *university dean*

**Marietta**
Montgomery, Jerry Lynn *education educator*
Wilson, Lauren Ross *academic administrator*

**Mechanicsburg**
Maynard, Joan *education educator*

**Medina**
Hunter, Brinca Jo *education specialist*

**Mentor**
Davis, Barbara Snell *principal*

**Milford**
Mechlem, Daphne Jo *vocational school educator*

**Millersburg**
Childers, Lawrence Jeffrey *superintendent of schools*

**Minerva**
Koniecko, Mary Ann *elementary education educator*

**Mogadore**
Kelly, Janice Helen *elementary school educator*

**Mount Vernon**
Nease, Stephen Wesley *college president*

**New Concord**
Speck, Samuel Wallace, Jr. *academic administrator*

**New Middletown**
Ade, Barbara Jean *secondary education educator*

**New Philadelphia**
Doughten, Mary Katherine (Molly Doughten) *retired secondary education educator*
Goforth, Mary Elaine Davey *secondary education educator*

**Newark**
Fortaleza, Judith Ann *school system administrator*

**Newcomerstown**
Foley, Tracy Yevonne Lichtenfels *special education educator*

**North Canton**
Foster, James Caldwell *academic dean, historian*

**North Olmsted**
Hughes, Kenneth G. *elementary school educator*

**Oberlin**
Dye, Nancy Schrom *academic administrator, history educator*
MacKay, Alfred F. *dean, philosophy educator*

**Oregon**
Crain, John Kip *school system administrator*

**Oxford**
Davis, Sherie Kay *special education educator*
Dizney, Robert Edward *retired secondary education educator*
Pearson, Paul Guy *academic administrator emeritus*
Shriver, Phillip Raymond *academic administrator*
Thompson, Bertha Boya *retired education educator, antique dealer and appraiser*

**Parma**
McFadden, Nadine Lynn *secondary education Spanish educator*
Nemeth, Dian Jean *secondary school educator*
Tener, Carol Joan *retired secondary education educator*

**Peninsula**
Brobeck, David George *middle school administrator*

**Richmond**
Martin, Clara Rita *elementary education educator*

**South Euclid**
Conrad, Sister Linda *elementary school educator*

**Springboro**
Ramey, Rebecca Ann *elementary education educator*

**Springfield**
Dominick, Charles Alva *college official*
Kinnison, William Andrew *retired university president*

**Sugar Grove**
Young, Nancy Henrietta Moe *elementary education educator*

**Sylvania**
Heuschele, Sharon Jo *university program director*
Rabideau, Margaret Catherine *media center director*
Sampson, Earldine Robison *education educator*

**Toledo**
Billups, Norman Fredrick *college dean, pharmacist*
Binkley, Jonathan Andrew *secondary education educator, government educator*
Heinrichs, Mary Ann *former dean*
Horton, Frank Elba *university official, geography educator*
Kozbial, Richard James *elementary education educator*
Leighton, Richard F. *retired dean*
Moon, Henry *dean*

**Trotwood**
Kiefer, Jacqueline Lorraine *special education educator, consultant*

**Upper Sandusky**
Schmidt, Janis Ilene *elementary education educator*

**Valley View**
Miller, Susan Ann *school system administrator*

**Warren**
Kandrac, Jo Ann Marie *school administrator*
McFarland, Leslie King *special education educator*

**Washington Court House**
Fichthorn, Fonda Gay *principal*

**Waterford**
Maltby, Sue Ellen *special education educator*
Montgomery, Gretchen Golzé *secondary education educator*

**Wauseon**
McNulty, Roberta Jo *educational administrator*

**Waverly**
Turner, Elvin L. *retired educational administrator*

**West Chester**
Capps, Dennis William *secondary school educator*

**Westerville**
DeVore, Carl Brent *college president, educator*
Diersing, Carolyn Virginia *educational administrator*
Kerr, Thomas Jefferson, IV *academic official*
Lattimore, Joy Powell *preschool administrator*
VanSant, Joanne Frances *academic administrator*
Willke, Thomas Aloys *university official, statistics educator*

**Westfield Center**
Spinelli, Anne Catherine *elementary education educator*

**Wilberforce**
Svager, Thyrsa Anne Frazier *university administrator, retired educator*

**Willoughby**
Grossman, Mary Margaret *elementary education educator*

**Wooster**
Childers, Susan Lynn Bohn *special education educator, administrator, human resources and transition specialist, consultant*
Payne, Thomas L. *university official*

**Yellow Springs**
Begin, Jacqueline Sue *college administrator*
Guskin, Alan E. *university president*

**Youngstown**
Becker, Karen Ann *university program administrator*

## OKLAHOMA

**Ada**
Gray, Edna Jane *elementary education educator*

**Altus**
Hensley, Stephen Ray *academic administrator*

**Ardmore**
Thompson, John E. *principal*

**Bartlesville**
Sauter, Marsha Jeanne *elementary school educator*
Woodruff, Wanda Lea *elementary education educator*

**Bethany**
Corvin, William Rayford *administrator, educator, minister*

**Broken Arrow**
Roberson, Deborah Kay *secondary school educator*

**Claremore**
Davis, Carol Anderson *school counselor*
McClain, Marilyn Russell *university student counselor*
Shrum, Alicia Ann *elementary school educator, librarian*

**Durant**
Weiner, Kathy Carole *secondary educator*
Williams, Larry Bill *academic administrator*

**Edmond**
Zabel, Vivian Ellouise *secondary education educator*

**Enid**
Tabbernee, William *academic administrator, theology educator*
Taylor, Donna Lynne *adult education coordinator*

**Keota**
Davis, Thomas Pinkney *secondary school educator*

**Lawton**
Cates, Dennis Lynn *education educator*
Davis, Don Clarence *university president*
McKeown, Rebecca J. *principal*
Neptune, Richard Allan (Dick Neptune) *superintendent of schools*
Smiley, Frederick Melvin *education educator, consultant*

**Maramec**
Blair, Marie Lenore *retired elementary school educator*

**Miami**
Vanpool, Cynthia Paula *special education educator, special services consultant*

**Midwest City**
Saulmon, Sharon Ann *college librarian*

**Minco**
Strange, Frances Rathbun *financial aid administrator, therapist*

**Muskogee**
Meyer, Billie Jean *special education educator*

**Norman**
Boren, David Lyle *academic administrator*
Dalton, Deborah Whitmore *dean*
Hodgell, Murlin Ray *university dean*
Huntington, Penelope Ann *middle school educator*
Pappas, James Pete *university administrator*
Schindler, Barbara Francois *school administrator*
Sharp, Paul Frederick *former university president, educational consultant*
Van Horn, Richard Linley *academic administrator*
Zapffe, Nina Byrom *retired elementary education educator*

**Oklahoma City**
Dunlap, E.T. *retired educational administrator, consultant*
Garrett, Sandy Langley *school system administrator*
Harlin-Fischer, Gayle C. *elementary education educator*
Harper, Sandra Stecher *university administrator*
Holder, Lee *educator and university dean emeritus*
Johnson, James Terence *college chancellor*
Kraker, Deborah Schovanec *special education educator*
Meeks, Patricia Lowe *secondary school educator*
Noakes, Betty L. *retired elementary school educator*
Nokes, Mary Triplett *former university president, counselor, artist*
Shirey, Margaret (Peggy Shirey) *elementary school educator*
Smith, Clodus Ray *academic administrator*
Walker, Jerald Carter *university administrator, minister*
Weir, Richard Dale *elementary education educator*
Wheat, Willis James *retired university dean, management educator*

**Paden**
Adams, Darlene Agnes *secondary education educator*

**Pauls Valley**
Pesterfield, Linda Carol *school administrator, educator*

**Pawhuska**
Holloway, Sharon Kay Sossamon *vocational/secondary school educator*

**Piedmont**
Roberts, Kathleen Mary *school system administrator*

**Ponca City**
Poole, Richard William, Jr. *secondary school educator*

**Pryor**
Burdick, Larry G. *school system administrator*

**Sapulpa**
Barnes, Paulette Whetstone *school system administrator*

**Shawnee**
Agee, Bob R. *university president, educator, minister*
Hill, Bryce Dale *school administrator*

**Stillwater**
Ausburn, Lynna Joyce *vocational and technical curriculum developer, consultant*
Boger, Lawrence Leroy *university president emeritus*
Browning, Charles Benton *retired university dean, agricultural educator*
Curl, Samuel Everett *university dean, agricultural scientist*
Halligan, James Edmund *university administrator, chemical engineer*
Hayes, Kevin Gregory *university administrator*
Kamm, Robert B. *former academic administrator, educator, author, diplomat*
Mc Collom, Kenneth Allen *retired university dean*
Mc Farland, Frank Eugene *university official*
Sandmeyer, Robert Lee *university dean, economist*

**Tulsa**
Barnes, Cynthia Lou *gifted education educator*
Caroon, Lynne Stanley *secondary and elementary educator, coach*
Hamilton, Carl Hulet *academic administrator*
Knaust, Clara Doss *retired elementary school educator*
Lawless, Robert William *academic administrator*
Roger, Jerry Lee *school system administrator*
Wood, Emily Churchill *gifted and talented education educator*

**Wheatland**
Nance, Retha Hardison *reading specialist*

**Woodward**
Selman, Minnie Corene Phelps *elementary school educator*

## OREGON

**Ashland**
Kreisman, Arthur *higher education consultant, humanities educator emeritus*
Smith, G(odfrey) T(aylor) *academic administrator*

**Astoria**
Bainer, Philip La Vern *retired college president*

**Bend**
Wonser, Michael Dean *retired public affairs director,*

**Boring**
Yatvin, Joanne Ina *school superintendent*

**Cannon Beach**
Wismer, Patricia Ann *secondary education educator*

**Corvallis**
Bruce, Robert Kirk *college administrator*
Byrne, John Vincent *higher education consultant*
Davis, John Rowland *university administrator*
Healey, Deborah Lynn *education administrator*
Mac Vicar, Robert William *retired university administrator*
Parker, Donald Fred *college dean, human resources management educator*
Verts, Lita Jeanne *university administrator*
Young, Roy Alton *university administrator, educator*

**Cottage Grove**
Miller, Joanne Louise *middle school educator*

**Eugene**
Cox, Joseph William *academic administrator*
Frohnmayer, David Braden *university president*
Gall, Meredith Damien (Meredith Mark Damien Gall) *education educator, author*
Matthews, Esther Elizabeth *education educator, consultant*
Moseley, John Travis *university administrator, research physicist*
Piele, Philip Kern *education infosystems educator*
Wood, Daniel Brian *educational consultant*

**Forest Grove**
Singleton, Francis Seth *dean*

**Gresham**
Kuney, Gary Wallace *elementary school educator, real estate agent*
Light, Betty Jensen Pritchett *former college dean*

**Klamath Falls**
Crawford, Marcella *migrant bilingual resource educator*

**La Grande**
Gilbert, David Erwin *university president, physicist*

**Lake Oswego**
Le Shana, David Charles *retired academic administrator*
Meltebeke, Renette *career counselor*

**Mcminnville**
McGillivray, Karen *elementary school educator*
Walker, Charles Urmston *retired university president*

**Newberg**
Johnson, Thomas Floyd *college president, educator*
Stevens, Edward Franklin *college president*

**North Bend**
de Sá e Silva, Elizabeth Anne *secondary school educator*

**Portland**
Blumel, Joseph Carlton *university president*
Bragdon, Paul Errol *educator*
Campbell, William Joseph *academic director*
Darling, Lynda Karen *secondary education educator*
Fan, Lee Siu *business executive and vocational training program administrator*
Franklin, Dolores Roberts *elementary education educator*
Frolick, Patricia Mary *retired elementary education educator*
Hudson, Jerry E. *university president*
Koblik, Stevens S. *academic administrator*
Kreinberg, Penelope Pettit *counselor*
Lawrence, Sally Clark *academic administrator*
Lenderman, Joanie *elementary education educator*
Leupp, Edythe Peterson *retired education educator, administrator*
Lynch, Nita Marie Smith *vocational curriculum developer*
Martin, Ernest Lee *academic administrator, historian, theologian, writer*
Mooney, Michael Joseph *college president*
Newman, Sharon Ann *principal*
Ramaley, Judith Aitken *academic administrator, endocrinologist*
Ricks, Mary F(rances) *academic administrator, anthropologist*
Sherrer, Charles David *college dean, clergyman*
Terkla, Louis Gabriel *retired university dean*
Tufts, Robert B. *academic administrator*
†Walker, James Bradley *academic institution administrator*
Wiest, William Marvin *education educator, psychologist*
Wineberg, Howard *research director*

**Roseburg**
Johnson, Doris Ann *educational administrator*

**Salem**
Billman, Jennifer *elementsry school principal*

**Sandy**
Thies, Lynn Wapinski *elementary education educator*

**Siletz**
Casey, Darla Diann *elementary school educator*

**Sisters**
Keppler, Donald John *secondary education educator*

**Talent**
McGill, Esby Clifton *former college official*

**Tigard**
Longaker, Nancy *elementary school principal*

**Yachats**
Robeck, Mildred Coen *educator, writer*

## PENNSYLVANIA

**Aliquippa**
Drobac, Nikola (Nick Drobac) *educator*

**Allentown**
Blaney, Dorothy Gulbenkian *academic administrator*
Taylor, Arthur Robert *college president, business executive*
Yoder, Myron Eugene *secondary school educator*

**Allison Park**
Guffey, Barbara Braden *elementary education educator*

**Annville**
McGill, William James, Jr. *academic administrator*
Synodinos, John Anthony *academic administrator*

**Athens**
Luther-Lemmon, Carol Len *middle school educator*

**Barto**
Isett, Deborah Michele Gunther *elementary education educator*

**Beaver**
Helmick, Gayle Johnston *elementary education educator*

**Belle Vernon**
Kline, Bonita Ann *middle school guidance counselor, educator*

**Bensalem**
Klingerman, Karen Nina *elementary school educator, teacher consultant, course coordinator*

**Bethlehem**
Bergethon, Kaare Roald *retired college president*
Likins, Peter William *academic administrator*

**Bloomsburg**
Traugh, Donald George, III *secondary education educator*
Vann, John Daniel, III *university dean, historian*

**Blue Bell**
Brendlinger, LeRoy R. *college president*

**Boyertown**
Kuser, Edwin Charles *educational administrator, retired*

**Bridgeville**
Pappas, John George *secondary school educator*

**Bryn Mawr**
McPherson, Mary Patterson *academic administrator*
Smith, Nona Coates *academic administrator*

**Butler**
Dodge, Ellen Elizabeth *community college official*

**Cambridge Springs**
Learn, Richard Leland *corrections school principal*

**Canonsburg**
Mascetta, Joseph Anthony *principal*

**Carlisle**
Fritschler, A. Lee *college president, public policy educator*
Rossbacher, Lisa Ann *dean, geology educator, writer*

**Catasauqua**
Fogelson, Brian David *education educator*

**Center Valley**
Gambet, Daniel G(eorge) *college president, clergyman*

**Chester**
Bruce, Robert James *university president*
Buck, Lawrence Paul *academic administrator*
Moll, Clarence Russel *retired university president, consultant*
O'Malley, John Patrick *dean*
Seidman, Marian Taylor *adult education educator*

**Claridge**
Perich, Terry Miller *secondary school educator*

**Coatesville**
Fitzgerald, Susan Helena *elementary educator*
Smith, Patricia Anne *special education educator*
Walker, Marie Fuller *elementary education educator*

**Collegeville**
Richter, Richard Paul *academic administrator*
Strassburger, John Robert *academic administrator*

**Columbia**
McTaggart, Timothy Thomas *secondary education educator*

**Cooperstown**
Hogg, James Henry, Jr. *retired education educator*

**Coraopolis**
Tannehill, Darcy Anita Bartins *academic administrator*

**Dallas**
Hunter, Todd Lee *secondary school music educator*

**Danville**
Wert, Barbara J. Yingling *special education educator*

**Dayton**
Patterson, Madge Lenore *elementary education educator*

**Eagles Mere**
Sample, Frederick Palmer *former college president*

**East Stroudsburg**
Brackbill, Nancy Lafferty *elementary education educator*
Dillman, Robert John *academic administrator*
Truschel, Jack Henry, II *university official, consultant*

**Easton**
Rothkopf, Arthur J. *college president*

**Edinboro**
Cox, Clifford Laird university administrator, musician
Curry-Carlburg, Joanne Jeanne elementary education educator

**Elizabethtown**
Ritsch, Frederick Field academic administrator, historian

**Enola**
Myers, Alfred Frantz state education official

**Erie**
Barber, Michele A. special education educator
Lilley, John Mark academic administrator, dean

**Everett**
Vollbrecht, Edward Alan school superintendent

**Exeter**
Stocker, Joyce Arlene retired secondary school educator

**Fairview Village**
Filippini, Christine Marie counselor

**Flourtown**
Lambert, Joan Dorety elementary education educator
Moore, Sandra Kay counselor, administrator

**Fredericktown**
Hess, Dolores J. elementary education educator

**Freeland**
Rudawski, Joseph George educational administrator

**Greenville**
Lillie, Marshall Sherwood college safety and security director, educator

**Gwynedd Valley**
Feenane, Sister Mary Alice principal

**Hanover**
Toft, Thelma Marilyn secondary school educator

**Harrisburg**
Baird, Irene Cebula educational administrator
Brown, John Walter vocational education supervisor
Giusti, Joseph Paul global human resource development director, retired university chancellor
McCormick, James Harold academic administrator
Woods, Willie G. dean, English language and education educator

**Haverford**
Brownlow, Donald Grey private school educator

**Havertown**
Beck, Elaine Kushner elementary and secondary school educator

**Hazleton**
Stevens, Linda Tollestrup academic director

**Hellertown**
Claps, Judith Barnes educational consultant

**Hermitage**
Havrilla, John William middle school educator

**Hershey**
Brechbill, Joseph Albert private school administrator
Jordan, Lois Wenger university official
Leventhal, Ruth academic administrator, dean emeritus, educator
Ruth, Edward B. principal

**Hollidaysburg**
Robinson, Gary David principal

**Homestead**
King, Richard Wayne principal

**Honesdale**
Barbe, Walter Burke education educator
Stanton, Sara Baumgardner retired secondary school educator

**Horsham**
Strock, Gerald E. school system administrator

**Hummelstown**
Bruhn, John Glyndon university provost and dean

**Hunlock Creek**
Zimmerman, Anita Eloise elementary education educator

**Huntingdon**
Neff, Robert Wilbur academic administrator, educator

**Huntingdon Valley**
Danielewski, Donna Krystyna secondary school educator

**Immaculata**
Manning, Kevin James academic administrator

**Indiana**
Pettit, Lawrence Kay university president
Thibadeau, Eugene Francis education educator, consultant

**Jenkintown**
Baldwin, David Rawson retired university administrator

**Johnstown**
Alcamo, Frank Paul retired principal
Grove, Nancy Carol academic administrator
Jones, Thomas William secondary education educator, consultant

McKnight, Joyce Sheldon adult educator, community organizer

**Kennett Square**
Larmore, Catherine Christine university official
Nason, John William retired college president, educational consultant

**King Of Prussia**
Olexy, Jean Shofranko English language educator
Quillen, Mary Ann university administrator, consultant

**Kingston**
Marko, Andrew Paul school system administrator

**Knox**
Rupert, Elizabeth Anastasia retired university dean

**Kutztown**
McFarland, David E. academic administrator
Watrous, Robert Thomas academic director

**La Plume**
Boehm, Edward Gordon university administrator, educator

**Lake Ariel**
Casper, Marie Lenore middle school educator

**Lancaster**
Drum, Alice college administrator
Ebersole, Mark Chester emeritus college president
Kneedler, Alvin Richard academic administrator

**Langhorne**
Babb, Wylie Sherrill college president

**Lansdale**
Cusimano, Adeline Mary Miletti educational administrator
Madden, Theresa Marie elementary education educator

**Levittown**
Upton, Lorraine Frances elementary education educator

**Lewisburg**
Adams, William D. university president

**Lock Haven**
Almes, June retired education educator, librarian
Willis, Craig Dean academic administrator

**Lower Burrell**
Rose, Robert Henry arts education administrator

**Macungie**
Kocian, Nancy Jane elementary education educator

**Malvern**
Darby, Samuel Edward guidance counselor
Swymer, Stephen principal

**Manchester**
Owens, Marilyn Mae elementary school educator, secondary school educator

**Manheim**
Frederick, Susan Louise preschool educator

**Mechanicsburg**
Rudolph, Robert Norman secondary school educator, adult education educator

**Media**
Comeforo, Jean Elizabeth hearing-impaired educator
Dunlap, Richard Frank school system administrator
Reuschlein, Harold Gill university dean
Strunk, Betsy Ann Whitenight education educator

**Merion Station**
Littell, Marcia Sachs educator, educational administrator

**Milford**
Reynolds, Edwin Wilfred, Jr. retired secondary education educator

**Millersburg**
Kirkwood, Nancy Lynne elementary education educator

**Millersville**
Caputo, Joseph Anthony university president
Mallery, Anne Louise elementary education educator, consultant

**Monroeville**
Carney, Ann Vincent secondary education educator

**Morrisville**
Denslow, Deborah Pierson primary education educator
Lineberry, Paul F., Jr. secondary education music educator

**Mount Joy**
Steinhart, Dean Raymond educational administrator

**Mount Pleasant**
Dangelo, Eugene Michael elementary school educator

**New Castle**
Denniston, Marjorie McGeorge retired elementary education educator
Roux, Mildred Anna retired secondary school educator

**New Hope**
Knight, Douglas Maitland educational administrator, optical executive

**New Wilmington**
Deegan, John, Jr. academic administrator, educator

Remick, Oscar Eugene academic administrator

**Newtown**
Duncan, Stephen Robert elementary education educator
Keyes, Fenton educational consultant, writer
Selden, William Kirkpatrick retired educational administrator

**Newville**
Rand, Sharon Kay elementary education educator

**Norristown**
Burtt, Anne Dampman special education educator
Nelson, Dawn Marie middle school science and math educator

**Northampton**
Bartholomew, Gordon Wesley health and physical education educator
Greenleaf, Janet Elizabeth principal

**Oakdale**
Gilden, Robin Elissa elementary education educator

**Orefield**
Zellner, Kenneth Kermit elementary education educator

**Perkasie**
Ferry, Joan Evans school counselor

**Philadelphia**
Aversa, Dolores Sejda educational administrator
Ball, Earl John, III school administrator
Bates, James Earl academic administrator
Blumberg, Baruch Samuel academic research scientist
Brucker, Paul C. academic administrator, physician
Bryan, Henry Collier secondary school educator, clergyman
Burnley, June Williams secondary school educator
Cohen, David Walter academic administrator, periodontist, educator
Cooke, Sara Mullin Graff daycare provider, kindergarten teacher, doctor's assistant
Cooperman, Barry S. educational administrator, educator, scientist
Davidson, Rhonda Elizabeth preschool educator
Delacato, Carl Henry education educator
Diver, Colin S. dean, educator
Eddy, Julia Veronica educator
Gerrity, Thomas P. dean
†Giegengack, Robert university administrator
Gusoff, Patricia Kearney elementary education educator
Gustafson, Sandra Lynne secondary education educator
Hackney, Francis Sheldon university president
Jamieson, Kathleen Hall dean, communications educator
Kim, Sangduk biochemistry educator, researcher
Lang, Norma M. dean, nursing educator
Lynch, William Francis, Jr. secondary mathematics educator
Mazzatenta, Rosemary Dorothy school administrator
Meyerson, Martin university executive, professor, urban and regional planner
Osborne, Frederick Spring, Jr. academic administrator, artist
Padulo, Louis university administrator
Papadakis, Constantine N. university executive
Peirce, Donald Oluf elementary education educator
Reisman, Fredricka Kauffman education educator
Rodin, Judith Seitz academic administrator, psychology educator
Sheehan, Donald Thomas academic administrator
Smith, Robert Rutherford university dean, communication educator
Solmssen, Peter academic administrator
Spencer, Priscilla James physical education educator
Styer, Antoinette Cardwell middle school counselor
Sutman, Francis Xavier university dean
Sutnick, Alton Ivan dean, educator, researcher, physician
Toto, Mary elementary and secondary education educator
Vargus, Ione Dugger retired university administrator
Wachman, Marvin university chancellor
Wagner, Daniel A. human developement educator, academic administrator
Woodside, Lisa Nicole academic administrator
Zambone, Alana Maria special education educator

**Philipsburg**
Reiter, Daisy K. elementary education educator, retired

**Phoenixville**
Brethauer, Alma Winifred secondary school educator

**Pittsburgh**
Boyce, Doreen Elizabeth education, civic development foundation executive
Carter-Jones, Sheila Lorraine secondary school educator
Christiano, Paul P. academic administrator, civil engineering educator
Curry, Nancy Ellen educator, psychoanalyst, psychologist
Cyert, Richard Michael former academic administrator, economist
Dempsey, Jacqueline Lee special education director
Dobos, Sister Marion parochial school educator
Epperson, David Ernest dean, educator
Geibel, Sister Grace Ann college president
Hlawati, Joyce F. elementary education educator
Howse, W. Frances academic administrator
Machatzke, Heinz Wilhelm dean, science administrator
Mattison, Donald Roger dean, physician, military officer
McDuffie, Keith A. literature educator, magazine director
Mehrabian, Robert academic administrator
Miles, Leon F. (Lee Miles) vocational education educator
Packard, Rochelle Sybil elementary school educator
Patton, Nancy Matthews elementary education educator
†Posvar, Wesley Wentz university president, educator, consultant
Rago, Ann D'Amico public relations professional, educator
Renk, Carol Ann secondary education educator

Smartschan, Glenn Fred school system administrator
Southworth, Horton Coe educational educator, education scholar
Spohn, Janice elementary education educator, consultant
Stella, Janet Louise special education educator
Suzuki, Jon Byron dean, periodontist, educator
Van Dusen, Albert Clarence university official
Wallace, Richard Christopher, Jr. school system administrator, educator
Warner, Judith (Anne) Huss educator
Weidman, John Carl, II education educator, consultant
Williams, Nathaniel, Jr. elementary education educator

**Plains**
Elias, Joseph secondary school educator

**Pottstown**
White, Thomas David, II academic administrator

**Punxsutawney**
Graffius, Richard Stewart, II elementary educator

**Ridley Park**
Brittell-Whitehead, Diane Peeples secondary education educator, addiction counselor

**Robesonia**
Houck, Charleen McClain education educator

**Russellton**
Curtis, Paula Annette elementary and secondary education educator

**Saint Davids**
Baird, John Absalom, Jr. college official

**Saltsburg**
Pidgeon, John Anderson headmaster

**Scranton**
Bianca, Joanne Marie elementary and early childhood educator
Nee, Sister Mary Coleman college president emeritus
Panuska, Joseph Allan academic administrator
Passon, Richard Henry academic administrator
Reap, Sister Mary Margaret college administrator

**Selinsgrove**
Cunningham, Joel Luther university president

**Sewickley**
Newell, Byron Bruce, Jr. retired theological seminary dean, clergyman

**Shippensburg**
Ceddia, Anthony Francis university administrator

**Slippery Rock**
Aebersold, Robert Neil university president
Smith, Grant Warren, II academic administrator, physical sciences educator

**Solebury**
Gilleo, Sandra V. elementary education educator

**South Williamsport**
Bryant, Martha J. reading specialist

**Spring City**
Middleton, Dawn E. education educator

**Springfield**
Carter, Frances Moore educator, writer

**State College**
Hoffa, Harlan Edward retired university dean, art educator
Remick, Forrest Jerome, Jr. former university official

**Stroudsburg**
Macmillan, Robert Francis director university service

**Swarthmore**
Berger, Dianne Gwynne educator
Bloom, Alfred Howard college president

**Sweet Valley**
Aldrow-Liput, Priscilla R. elementary education educator

**Swissvale**
Martoni, Charles J. dean

**Tyrone**
Spewock, Theodosia George reading specialist, educator

**University Park**
Albinski, Henry Stephen academic research center director, writer
Askov, Eunice May adult education educator
Dupuis, Victor Lionel retired curriculum and instruction educator
Erickson, Rodney Allen dean, educator
Hammond, J. D. university executive, educator
Herrmann, Carol university administrator
Koopmann, Gary Hugo educational center administrator, mechanical engineering educator
Larson, Russell Edward university provost emeritus, consultant agriculture research and development
Martorana, Sebastian Vincent educator, educational consultant
Nicely, Robert Francis, Jr. education educator, administrator
Spanier, Graham Basil academic administrator, family sociologist, demographer, marriage and family therapist
Starling, James Lyne university administrator, retired
Whitko, Jean Phillips academic administrator
Yoder, Edgar Paul education educator

**Upper Darby**
Hudiak, David Michael educational administrator, lawyer
Leiby, Bruce Richard secondary education educator, writer

**Upper Saint Clair**
Dunkis, Patricia B. *principal*

**Valley View**
Holmes, David James *elementary education educator*

**Vandergrift**
Quader, Patricia Ann *elementary education educator*

**Verona**
Bruno, Louis Vincent *special education educator*

**Villanova**
Dobbin, Edmund J. *university administrator*
Heitzmann, Wm. Ray *education educator*

**Washington**
Burnett, Howard Jerome *college president*

**Wayne**
Hill, Virgil Lusk, Jr. *academic administrator, naval officer*

**Wernersville**
Himmelberger, Richard Charles *vocational school educator*

**West Chester**
Adler, Madeleine Wing *academic administrator*
Hammonds, Jay A. *retired secondary education educator, administrator*
Hickman, Janet Susan *college administrator, educator*

**West Mifflin**
DiCioccio, Gary F. *secondary education educator*
Gerity, Patrick Emmett *college director*

**Wexford**
Hutchinson, Barbara Winter *middle school educator*

**Wilkes Barre**
Lackenmier, James Richard *college president, priest*

**Williamsport**
Douthat, James Evans *college administrator*
Meyers, Judith Ann *education educator*

**Willow Street**
Stright, I. Leonard *educational consultant*

**Wyomissing**
Cellucci, Peter T. *principal*
Moran, William Edward *academic administrator*

**Yardley**
Elliott, Frank Nelson *retired college president*
Watson, Joyce Leslie *elementary educator*

## RHODE ISLAND

**Barrington**
Graser, Bernice Erckert *elementary school principal*

**Bristol**
Chaim, Robert Alex *dean, educator*
Schipper, Michael *academic administrator*

**Cumberland**
LaFlamme-Zurowski, Virginia M. *secondary school special education educator*

**Kingston**
Carothers, Robert Lee *academic administrator*
Gaulin, Lynn *experiential education educator*
Youngken, Heber Wilkinson, Jr. *former university administrator, pharmacy educator*

**Newport**
Hamblet, Charles Albert *educational administrator, educator*
Yates, Elsie Victoria *retired secondary English educator*

**North Scituate**
Stubbs, Donald Clark *secondary education educator*

**Providence**
Caldwell, Ann Wickins *academic administrator*
Greer, David S. *university dean, physician, educator*
Gregorian, Vartan *academic administrator*
Hawkins, Brian L. *academic administrator, educator*
Mandle, Earl Roger *academic administrator, former museum administrator*
Marsh, Donald Jay *college dean, medical educator*
McMahon, Eleanor Marie *education educator*
Nazarian, John *academic administrator, mathematics educator*
Newman, Janet Elaine *elementary education educator*
Salesses, John Joseph *university executive*
Sizer, Theodore R. *educational director*
Zarrella, Arthur M. *superintendent*

**Saunderstown**
Donovan, Gerald Alton *retired academic administrator, former university dean*

**Wakefield**
Pouliot, Assunta Gallucci *retired business school owner and director*

**Warwick**
Polselli, Linda Marie *elementary education educator*

## SOUTH CAROLINA

**Aiken**
Alexander, Robert Earl *university chancellor, educator*
Kanne, Elizabeth Ann Arnold *secondary school educator*
Salter, David Wyatt *secondary school educator*
Zubillaga, Jose Gustavo *education specialist*

**Beaufort**
Plyler, Chris Parnell *dean*
Sheldon, Jeffrey Andrew *college official*

**Cayce**
McGill, Cathy Broome *gifted and talented education educator*

**Charleston**
Curtis, Marcia *university dean*
Edwards, James Burrows *university president, oral surgeon*
Greenberg, Raymond Seth *academic administrator, educator*
Grimsley, James Alexander, Jr. *university administrator, retired army officer*
Hunter, Jairy C., Jr. *academic administrator*
Reilly, David Henry *university dean*
Simms, Lois Averetta *retired secondary education educator, musician*
Smith, J. Roy *education educator*
Suggars, Candice Louise *special education educator*
Whelan, Wayne Louis *higher education administrator*

**Clemson**
Curris, Constantine William *university president*
Kelly, John William, Jr. *university admnistrator*
Vogel, Henry Elliott *retired university dean and physics educator*

**Columbia**
Aelion, C. Marjorie *educator*
Broome, Michael Cortes *college administrator*
Duffy, John Joseph *academic administrator, history educator*
Fields, Harriet Gardin *counselor, educator, consultant*
Friedman, Myles Ivan *education educator*
King, John Ethelbert, Jr. *education educator, former academic administrator*
Palms, John Michael *academic administrator, physicist*
Reisz, Howard Frederick, Jr. *seminary president, theology educator*
Shannon, David Thomas, Sr. *academic administrator*

**Conway**
Sharples, D. Kent *college administrator*
Wiseman, Dennis Gene *university dean*

**Due West**
Koonts, Jones Calvin *retired education educator*

**Easley**
Cole, Lois Lorraine *retired elementary school educator*

**Elgin**
Peake, Frank *middle school educator*

**Florence**
Rutherford, Vicky Lynn *special education educator*
Smith, Walter Douglas *retired college president*

**Gaffney**
Davis, Lynn Hambright *culinary arts educator*

**Greenville**
Cloer, Carl Thomas, Jr. *education educator*
Dozier, Herbert Randall *school system administrator*
Frampton, Lisa *elementary education educator*
Hill, Grace Lucile Garrison *education educator, consultant*
Jones, Bob, Jr. *academic administrator, educator, lecturer, minister*
Jones, Robert Thaddues *principal*
Smith, Philip Daniel *academic administrator, education educator*

**Greenwood**
Jackson, Larry Artope *retired college president*
Marino, Sheila Burris *education educator*
Williams, Sylvester Emanual, III *elementary school educator, consultant*

**Hartsville**
Daniels, James Douglas *academic administrator*

**Hilton Head Island**
Exley, Winston Wallace *middle school educator*
Lachenauer, Robert Alvin *retired school superintendent*
Mirse, Ralph Thomas *former college president*
Mulhollan, Paige Elliott *academic administrator emeritus*
Pustilnik, Jean Todd *elementary education educator*

**Kershaw**
Lucas, Dean Hadden *retired educator*

**Ladson**
Cannon, Major Tom *special education educator*

**Lexington**
DuVall, Richard *elementary school educator*
Gatch, Charles Edward, Jr. *academic administrator*

**Marion**
Kirkpatrick, Donald Robert *middle school educator*

**Moore**
Simmons, Sharon Dianne *elementary education educator*

**Mount Pleasant**
Gilbert, James Eastham *academic administrator*

**Orangeburg**
Creekmore, Verity Veirs *media specialist*

**Pawleys Island**
Proefrock, Carl Kenneth *academic medical administrator*

**Rock Hill**
Di Giorgio, Anthony J. *college president*

**Shaw AFB**
Mingo, Joe Louis *elementary school educator*

**Simpsonville**
Dean, Virginia Agee *principal*
Drummond, Julia Elaine Butler *middle school educator*

**Society Hill**
King, Amanda Arnette *elementary school educator*

**Spartanburg**
Hatley, Amy Bell *elementary education educator, broadcast journalist*
Lesesne, Joab Mauldin, Jr. *college president*
Mahaffey, James Perry *education educator, consultant*
Mc Gehee, Larry Thomas *university administrator*
Stephens, Bobby Gene *college administrator, consultant*

**Summerville**
Diamond, Michael Shawn *science and math educator, computer consultant*

**Sumter**
Kieslich, Anita Frances *school system administrator*

**Union**
Lorenz, Latisha Jay *elementary education educator*

**West Columbia**
Coker, Gurnelle Sheely *retired secondary education educator*

**Westminster**
Duncan, Gwendolyn McCurry *elementary education educator*

**York**
Clinch, Nicholas *assistant principal*

## SOUTH DAKOTA

**Box Elder**
Schmidt, Laura Lee *elementary and middle school gifted and talented educator, special education educator*

**Brookings**
Bailey, Harold Stevens, Jr. *retired educational administrator*
Wagner, Robert Todd *university president, sociology educator*

**Eagle Butte**
Tays, Glenny Mae *secondary education educator*

**Lemmon**
Grey Eagle, Sandra Lee *special education educator*

**Madison**
Tunheim, Jerald Arden *academic administrator, physics educator*

**Rapid City**
Hughes, William Lewis *former university official, electrical engineer*
Schleusener, Richard August *college president*

**Selby**
Akre, Donald J. *school system administrator*

**Sioux Falls**
Balcer, Charles Louis *college president emeritus, educator*
Hiatt, Charles Milton *seminary president*
Tucker, William Vincent *vocational evaluator, former college president*
Wagoner, Ralph Howard *academic administrator, educator*

**Vermillion**
Milton, Leonharda Lynn *elementary and secondary school educator*

**Watertown**
Meyer, Todd Kent *secondary school educator*

## TENNESSEE

**Antioch**
Wisehart, Mary Ruth *academic administrator*

**Athens**
Wilson, Ben *elementary school principal*

**Bolivar**
Buchanan, Bennie Lee Gregory *special education educator*

**Bristol**
Anderson, Jack Oland *retired college official*
Weeden, Debbie Sue *early childhood education educator*

**Chapel Hill**
Christman, Luther Parmalee *retired university dean, consultant*

**Chattanooga**
Charlton, Shirley Marie *instructional supervisor*
Fortenberry, Elizabeth Waller *private school educator*
Obear, Frederick Woods *academic administrator*
Tucker, Stanley R. *headmaster*

**Clarksville**
Carlin, James Boyce *elementary education educator, consultant*

**Cleveland**
Gillum, Perry Eugene *college president, minister*

**Columbia**
Loper, Linda Sue *learning resources center director*

**Cookeville**
Elkins, Donald Marcum *dean, agronomy educator*
Hearn, Edell Midgett *university dean, teacher educator*
Peters, Ralph Martin *education educator*
Porter, Wilma Jean *educational consultant*
Volpe, Angelo Anthony *university administrator, chemistry educator*

**Crossville**
Moore, Harold Blaine *middle school educator*

**Dickson**
Thomas, Janey Sue *elementary school principal*

**Elkton**
Newman, Sharon Lynn *elementary education educator*

**Englewood**
Jones, Vivian M. *secondary and elementary education educator*

**Franklin**
Guthrie, Glenda Evans *educational company executive*

**Gallatin**
Glover, Nancy Elliott *elementary school administrator*
Ramer, Hal Reed *academic administrator*

**Germantown**
Allison, Beverly Gray *seminary president, evangelism educator*

**Hendersonville**
Leslie, Lynn Marie *secondary education educator*
Poynor, Robert Allen, Jr. *guidance counselor*

**Jackson**
Bailey, James Andrew *middle school educator*
Barefoot, Hyran Euvene *academic administrator, educator, minister*
Troupe, Marilyn Kay *education educator*

**Jefferson City**
Maddox, Jesse Cordell *academic administrator*

**Jellico**
Chitwood, Helen Irene *elementary education educator*

**Johnson City**
Alfonso, Robert John *university administrator*
Paxton, J. Willene *retired university counseling director*
Roark, Edith Humphreys *private school language arts educator, reading specialist*

**Jonesborough**
Broyles, Ruth Rutledge *principal*

**Kingston**
Oran, Geraldine Ann *assistant principal*

**Knoxville**
Armistead, Willis William *university administrator, veterinarian*
Boling, Edward Joseph *university president emeritus, educator*
Brockett, Ralph Grover *adult education educator*
Mankel, Francis Xavier *former principal, priest*
Moor, Anne Dell *education director*
Owenby, Phillip H. *learning and communications consultant*
Reynolds, Marjorie Lavers *nutrition educator*
South, Stephen A. *academic administrator*

**Lebanon**
Toombs, Cathy West *assistant principal*

**Linden**
Yarbro, Billy Ray *elementary school educator, basketball coach*

**Louisville**
Wheeler, George William *university provost, physicist, educator*

**Martin**
Smith, Robert Mason *university dean*

**Memphis**
Carter, Michael Allen *college dean, nursing educator*
Daughdrill, James Harold, Jr. *academic administrator*
Dunathan, Harmon Craig *college dean*
Gagne, Ann Marie *special education educator*
Gourley, Dick R. *college dean*
Hedgeman, Lulah M. *secondary education educator*
Hester, James David *academic administrator*
Hunt, James Calvin *academic administrator, physician*
McGlown, Brenda Pryor *special education educator*
Nesin, Jeffrey D. *academic administrator*
Ramsey, Marjorie Elizabeth *early childhood education educator*
Ranta, Richard Robert *university dean*
Sigler, Lois Oliver *retired educator*
Wagner, Samuel, V *secondary school English language educator*
Wheeler, Orville Eugene *university dean, civil and mechanical engineering educator*

**Moscow**
Crawford, Sheila Jane *education educator, consultant*

**Mount Juliet**
Holloway, Susan Master *elementary education educator*

**Murfreesboro**
Berry, Mary Tom *education educator*
Doyle, Delores Marie *elementary education educator*
Hayes, Janice Cecile *education educator*

### Nashville
Chambers, Carol Tobey elementary school educator
Chapman, John Edmon university dean, pharmacologist, physician
Clinton, Barbara Marie university health services director, social worker
Emans, Robert LeRoy academic administrator, education educator
Fondaw, Elizabeth Louise vocational school educator
Geisel, Martin Simon college dean, educator
Guthrie, James Williams education educator
Hamilton, Russell George, Jr. academic dean, Spanish and Portuguese language educator
Hazelip, Herbert Harold academic administrator
Heard, (George) Alexander retired educator and chancellor
Hefner, James A. academic administrator
McMurry, Idanelle Sam educational consultant
Pellegrino, James William college dean, psychology educator
Reed, Millard C. academic administrator
Ridley, Carolyn Fludd social studies educator
Sharp, Bert Lavon retired education educator, retired university dean
Whitefield, Anne C. secondary school principal
Wyatt, Joe Billy academic administrator

### Newport
Ball, Travis, Jr. educational systems administrator, consultant, editor

### Oak Ridge
O'Neil, Charlotte Cooper environmental education administrator

### Oliver Springs
Heacker, Thelma Weaks retired elementary school educator

### Portland
Miller, Sandra Perry middle school educator

### Pulaski
Dowdy, Ronald Raymond academic administrator

### Sewanee
Croom, Frederick Hailey college administrator, mathematics educator
Kepple, Thomas Ray, Jr. college administrator
Lorenz, Anne Partee special education educator, consultant
Patterson, William Brown university dean, history educator

### Shelbyville
Austin, Margaret Cully school administrator

### Soddy Daisy
Hamrick, Rita Gale elementary school educator
Watson, James Stanley secondary education educator

### Sparta
Langford, Jack Daniel elementary school educator

### Tullahoma
Collins, S(arah) Ruth education educator
McCay, Thurman Dwayne university administrator

## TEXAS

### Abilene
Booth, Linda Leigh vocational educator
Clayton, Lawrence Ray university dean, literary critic, biographer
Crymes, Mary Cooper secondary school educator
McCaleb, Gary Day university official
Shimp, Robert Everett, Jr. academic administrator, historian
Warren, Russell Glen academic administrator

### Alamo
Forina, Maria Elena gifted education educator

### Aledo
Lindsay, John, IV principal

### Alpine
Morgan, Raymond Victor, Jr. academic administrator, mathematics educator

### Amarillo
Sutterfield, Deborah Kay special education educator

### Arlington
Hawkins, Robert A. college administrator
Pickard, Myrna Rae dean
Sobol, Harold retired dean, manufacturing executive, consultant

### Austin
Auvenshine, Anna Lee Banks school system administrator
Ayres, Robert Moss, Jr. retired university president
Barrera, Elvira Puig counselor, therapist, educator
Berdahl, Robert Max academic administrator, historian, educator
Brewer, Thomas Bowman retired university president
Cannon, William Bernard retired university educator
Cardozier, Virgus Ray higher education educator
Cleaves, Peter Shurtleff academic administrator
Cunningham, William Hughes academic administrator, marketing educator
Dalton, Don principal
Fair, Harry David academic administrator, physicist
Franklin, Billy Joe international higher education specialist
Franklin, G(eorge) Charles academic administrator
Gill, Clark Cyrus retired education educator
Hardin, Sheryl Dawn elementary education educator
Harris, Ben M. education educator
Hayes, Patricia Ann university president
Jeffrey, Robert Campbell university dean
Justiz, Manuel Jon educator, researcher
Kennamer, Lorrin Garfield, Jr. retired university dean
Lewis, Nancy Louine Lambert school counselor
Livingston, William Samuel university administrator, political scientist
Rogers, Lorene Lane university president emeritus
Roueche, John Edward, II education educator, leadership program director
Royal, Darrell K. university official, former football coach
Trevino, Jerry Rosalez secondary school principal

### Beaumont
Brentlinger, William Brock college dean
Gagne, Mary secondary school principal
Marshall, Nina Colleen Clubb elementary school educator

### Bedias
Williamson, Norma Beth adult education educator

### Bellaire
Skaggs, Arline Dotson elementary school educator

### Belton
Ham, Clarence Edward university administrator
Parker, Bobby Eugene, Sr. college president

### Big Spring
Simmons, Lorna Womack elementary school educator

### Boerne
Goode, Bobby Claude retired secondary education educator, writer

### Brownsville
Boze, Betsy Vogel university dean, marketing educator
Santa-Coloma, Bernardo secondary school educator, counselor

### Bryan
Bear, Robert Emerson elementary education educator
Hubert, Frank William Rene retired university system chancellor

### Candelaria
Chambers, Johnnie Lois (Tucker) elementary school educator, rancher

### Canyon
Long, Russell Charles academic administrator

### Carrollton
Grimes, Mary Woodworth special educational consultant
Last, Susan Walker training developer
Maher, Sheila secondary school principal

### Cedar Park
Guzma'n, Ana Margarita university administrator

### Channelview
Courville, Susan Kay secondary education educator

### College Station
Adkisson, Perry Lee university system chancellor
Bowen, Ray Morris academic administrator, engineering educator
Calhoun, John C., Jr. academic administrator
Carpenter, Delbert Stanley educational administration educator
Cocanougher, Arthur Benton university dean, former business administration educator
Erlandson, David Alan education administration educator
Haden, Clovis Roland university administrator, engineering educator
Kennedy, Robert Alan educational administrator
Monroe, Haskell M., Jr. university educator
Perrone, Ruth Ellyn university administrator
Sadoski, Mark Christian education educator
Wendler, Walter V. dean

### Comanche
Droke, Edna Faye elementary school educator

### Commerce
Lutz, Frank Wenzel education administration educator
Morris, Jerry Dean academic administrator
Schmidt, L. Lee, Jr. university official

### Conroe
Corley, Donna Jean education educator, language arts educator

### Converse
Vontur, Ruth Poth elementary school educator

### Coppell
Smothermon, Peggi Sterling middle school educator

### Copperas Cove
Barnes, Sara Lynn school system administrator
Wagner, Susan Elizabeth secondary school educator
Wright, David Ray secondary school educator

### Corpus Christi
Early, William James education educator
Furgason, Robert Roy university president, engineering educator
Pérez-Gonzalez, Esmeralda principal, educator
Trybul, Theodore Nicholan education educator

### Crockett
LaClair, Patricia Marie physical education director, medical technician

### Crowell
Binnion, John Edward education educator

### Cypress
Hamilton, Phyllis principal

### Daisetta
Ursprung, Deborah Lynn special education educator

### Dallas
Berkeley, Marvin H. management educator, former university dean
†Bonelli, Anthony Eugene former university dean
Cirilo, Amelia Medina educational consultant, supervisor
Cook, Gary Raymond university president, clergyman
Davis, Patricia Ann school system administrator
Davis, Patricia M. literacy educator
DePaola, Dominick Philip academic administrator
Friedheim, Jan V. education administrator
Haayen, Richard Jan university official, insurance company executive
Harbaugh, Lois Jensen secondary education educator
Harrison, Frank former university president
Hester, Linda Hunt university dean, counselor
Hopkins, Zora Clemons training and development specialist
Lindsey, Tanya Jamil secondary education administrator
Lopez, Francisca Uy elementary education educator
McNeely, Patricia Morse middle school educator, poet, writer
Phillips, Bettie Mae elementary school educator
Qualls, June Carol elementary education educator
Smith, Valerie Gay school counselor
Thomas, Sarah Elaine elementary music educator
Turner, Robert Gerald university president
Walvoord, John Flipse academic administrator, theologian
Walwer, Frank Kurt dean, legal educator
Wenrich, John William college president
Williams, Bryan university dean, medical educator

### De Soto
Judah, Frank Marvin retired school system administrator

### Decatur
Jordan, Linda Susan Darnell elementary school educator

### Denison
Farr, Reeta Rae special education administrator

### Denton
Baier, John Leonard university educator
Brownell, Blaine Allison university administrator, history educator
Carlson, William Dwight college president emeritus
Crocker, Betty Charlotte education educator
Elder, Mark Lee university research administrator, writer
Greenlaw, Marilyn Jean education educator, consultant, writer
Hurley, Alfred Francis retired military officer, university administrator
McDonald-West, Sandi M. headmaster, consultant
Pickett, Stephen Wesley university official, lecturer and consultant
Smith, Howard Wellington education educator, dean
Swigger, Keith dean
Thompson, Leslie Melvin college dean, educator
Toulouse, Robert Bartell retired college administrator
Turner, Philip Michael university official and dean, author

### Denver City
Taylor, Sharon Kay elementary school counselor

### Dilley
McMillian, Marilyn Lindsey elementary educator, health, home economics

### Edinburg
Esparza, Thomas, Sr. academic athletics administrator

### El Paso
Coleman, Edmund Benedict university dean
Grimes, William Gaylord adult education educator
Heger, Herbert Krueger education educator
Jaraba, Martha E. (Betty Jaraba) secondary school educator
Natalicio, Diana Siedhoff academic administrator
Riter, Stephen university administrator, electrical engineer
Tackett, Stephen Douglas education services specialist
von Tungeln, George Robert retired university administrator, economics consultant
Ward DiDio, Patty special education educator, educational diagnostician

### Euless
Warwick, Sharon Brenda elementary art educator

### Farwell
Franse, Jean Lucille secondary school educator

### Floresville
Alvarez, Olga Mendoza elementary school educator

### Fort Worth
Bickerstaff, Mina March Clark university administrator
Braudaway, Gary Wayne secondary school educator
Desha, Doris Hollingsworth retired elementary education educator
Jones, Evelene Manns principal, minister
Killingsworth, Maxine Armatha special education educator
Mays, Glenda Sue retired education educator
McKimmey, Martha Anne elementary education educator
Randle, Rolinda Carol elementary education educator
Saenz, Michael college president
Schrum, Jake Bennett university administrator
Scott-Wabbington, Vera V. elementary school educator
Tade, George Thomas university dean
Tucker, William Edward academic administrator, minister
Von Rosenberg, Gary Marcus, Jr. parochial school educator
Wilson-Webb, Nancy Lou adult educational administrator

### Freeport
Baskin, William Gresham counselor, music educator, vocalist

### Galveston
Banet, Charles Henry academic administrator, clergyman
Carrier, Warren Pendleton retired university chancellor, writer
Clayton, William Howard retired university president
Goodwin, Sharon Ann academic administrator
Johnson, Howard Eugene (Stretch Johnson) educator, consultant

### Garland
Foster, Rebecca Anne Hodges secondary school educator
Michaels, Cindy Whitfill (Cynthia G. Michaels) educational consultant, telecommunications representative
Shugart, Jill school system administrator

### Georgetown
Davis, O. L., Jr. education educator, researcher
Shilling, Roy Bryant, Jr. academic administrator

### Gladewater
Cox-Beaird, Dian Sanders middle school educator

### Granbury
Ketron, Carrie Sue secondary school educator
McWilliams, Chris Pater Elissa elementary school educator

### Grapevine
Hirsh, Cristy J. school counselor
Kraft, Karen Ann secondary school educator

### Hale Center
Courtney, Carolyn Ann school librarian

### Haltom City
Deering, Brenda Florine secondary education educator

### Harlingen
Zaslavsky, Robert secondary school educator

### Hawkins
Lewis, Annice Moore middle school language arts educator

### Hearne
Williams, Mary Lee elementary school educator

### Hillsboro
Auvenshine, William Robert academic administrator

### Houston
Auston, David Henry university administrator, educator
Bailar, Benjamin Franklin academic administrator, administration educator
Banks, Evelyn Yvonne middle school educator
Beckingham, Kathleen Mary education educator, researcher
Bui, Khoi Tien college counselor
Butler, William Thomas college chancellor, physician, educator
Crenshaw, Corinne Burrowes kindergarten educator
Darby, Anita Loyce secondary school educator
Davis, Bruce Gordon retired principal
DiRosa, Linda Mary education specialist, diagnostic company executive
Douglass, James academic administrator
Doyle, Joseph Francis, III art educator
Feigin, Ralph David medical school president, pediatrician, educator
Friedrich, Katherine Rose educational researcher
Fuller, Theodore, Jr. elementary education educator
Georgiades, William Den Hartog educational administrator
Gillis, (Stephen) Malcolm academic administrator, economics educator
†Goerke, Glenn Allen university administrator
Hamilton, Lorraine Rebekah adult education consultant
Hammack, Gladys Lorene Mann reading specialist, educator
Hitchman, Cal McDonald, Sr. secondary education educator
Ho, Yhi-Min university dean, economics educator
Hodo, Edward Douglas university president
Hoffman, Philip Guthrie former university president
Johnson, Judy Dianne elementary education educator
Kinnaird, Susan Marie special education educator
Lankford, Olga Juanita gifted and talented and elementary educator
Lindner, Kenneth Edward academic administrator and chemistry educator emeritus
Mansell, Joyce Marilyn special education educator
May, Beverly elementary school educator
Mc Fadden, Joseph Michael academic administrator
Meddleton, Francis Charles elementary and secondary school educator
Meyer, Dianne Scott Wilson secondary school educator, librarian
O'Neil, Sharon Lund educator
Pasternak, Joanna Murray special education and gifted and talented educator
Pennell, Linda Bennett secondary school educator
Pickering, James Henry, III academic administrator
Pinson, Artie Frances elementary school educator
Pittman, Katherine Anne Atherton elementary education educator
Rice, Emily Joy retired secondary school and adult educator
Robinson, Esther Martin secondary school educator
Sharp, Douglas Andrew secondary school educator
Sheehan, Linda Suzanne educational administrator
Shirley, Dennis Lynn education educator
Smith, Arthur Kittredge, Jr. academic administrator, political science educator
Smythe, Cheves McCord dean, medical educator
Thorne, Joye Holley special education administrator
Wagner, Paul Anthony, Jr. education educator
Walker, Sammie Lee retired elementary education educator
Webb, Marty Fox principal
Whitaker, Gilbert Riley, Jr. academic administrator, business economist
Wilhelm, Marilyn private school administrator
Wilks, William Lee retired educator, dean
Woods, Donna Sue education educator, reading consultant, state agency administrator
Woodward, Katherine Anne secondary education educator

**Huntsville**
Bowers, Elliott Toulmin *university president*
Warner, Laverne *education educator*

**Hurst**
Dodd, Sylvia Bliss *special education educator*

**Irving**
Cannon, Francis V., Jr. *academic administrator, electrical engineer, economist*
Clark, Priscilla Alden *elementary school educator*
Martin, Thomas Lyle, Jr. *university president*
Sasseen, Robert Francis *university educator*

**Johnson City**
Pollock, Margaret Landau Peggy *elementary school educator*

**Kerrville**
Holloway, Leonard Leveine *former university president*

**Killeen**
Harvey, Hilda Ruth *special education educator*
Reid, Sharon Lea *educational facilitator*

**Kingsville**
Ibanez, Manuel Luis *university official, biological sciences educator*
Robins, Gerald Burns *education educator*

**Klein**
Slater, Joan Elizabeth *secondary education educator*

**Lake Dallas**
Coleman, Brenda Forbis *gifted and talented educator*

**Laredo**
Black, Clifford Merwyn *academic administrator, sociologist, educator*
Condon, Maria del Carmen *retired elementary school educator*
Heimes, Charmaine Marie *elementary school educator*

**Lewisville**
Whiteley, Harold Lee *director*

**Littlefield**
Driskell, Charles Mark *principal*

**Livingston**
Oliver, Debbie Edge *elementary education educator*

**Longview**
Anderson, Linda Kay *elementary education educator*

**Lubbock**
Askins, Billy Earl *education educator, consultant*
Haragan, Donald Robert *university administrator, geosciences educator*
McManigal, Shirley Ann *university dean*
Pike, Douglas Eugene *educator*
Schmidly, David J. *university official and dean, biology educator*

**Mabank**
Beets, Hughla Fae *retired secondary school educator*

**Marshall**
Hawkins, Audrey Denise *academic administrator, educator*

**Mcallen**
Figgs, Linda Sue *principal*
Gonzalez, Rolando Noel *secondary school educator, religion educator, photographer*

**Mercedes**
Alaniz, Theodora Villarreal *elementary education educator*

**Mesquite**
Pratt, Sharon L. *secondary and elementary education educator*
Tabor, Beverly Ann *elementary school educator*
Vaughan, Joseph Lee, Jr. *education educator, consultant*

**Midland**
Hackler, Teri Cecilia *elementary education educator*

**Missouri City**
Trichel, Mary Lydia *middle school educator*

**Nacogdoches**
Schwei, Michael Allen *doctoral student*

**New Braunfels**
Oestreich, Charles Henry *president emeritus*

**Odessa**
Folsom, Hyta Prine *educational grant writer, consultant*
Sorber, Charles Arthur *academic administrator*

**Omaha**
Moos, Verna Vivian *special education educator*

**Pearland**
Smith, Annie Lee Northern *retired school system administrator*

**Plainview**
Porter, Joan Margaret *elementary education educator*

**Plano**
Fleming, Christina Samusson *special education educator*
Pointon, Mary Lou *special education educator*
Statman, Jackie C. *career consultant*

**Port Aransas**
Cook, Marilyn Jane *elementary school educator*
Goodwin, Mary McGinnis *secondary education educator*

**Prairie View**
Jones, Barbara Ann Posey *college dean*

**Ravenna**
Greene, Jennifer *elementary school counselor*

**Rhome**
Brammer, Barbara Rhudene *retired secondary education educator*

**Richardson**
Dunn, David E. *university dean*
Harp, Rose Marie *secondary education educator*
Kelly, Rita Mae *academic administrator, researcher*
Weaver, Jo Nell *elementary school educator*
Wildenthal, Bryan Hobson *university administrator*
Young, Malcolm Eugene, Jr. *social studies secondary educator*

**Round Rock**
Chavez, Dorothy Vaughan *elementary school educator, environmental educator*

**San Angelo**
Davison, Elizabeth Jane Linton *education educator*
Person, Ruth Janssen *academic administrator*

**San Antonio**
Ahart-Walls, Pamela *elementary school principal*
Arnold, Marie Collette *elementary school educator*
Barrow, Charles Wallace *university dean*
Boyers, John Martin *principal*
Calgaard, Ronald Keith *university president*
Dahl, Cathy Davenport *elementary educator*
Dickey, John Sloan, Jr. *dean, educator, geologist, researcher*
Garcia, Linda *secondary school principal*
Garcia, Yolanda Vasquez *educational services manager, educator*
Gibbons, Robert Ebbert *university official*
Goelz, Paul Cornelius *university dean*
Haggard, Victoria Marie *elementary education educator, secondary education educator*
Henderson, Dwight Franklin *dean, educator*
Hernandez, Christine *educational consultant*
Howell, Richard C. *secondary education educator*
Kalkwarf, Kenneth Lee *academic dean*
Kirkpatrick, Samuel Alexander *university president, social and policy sciences educator*
Koym, Zala Cox *elementary education educator*
Lloyd, Susan Elaine *middle school educator*
Madrid, Olga Hilda Gonzalez *retired elementary education educator, association executive*
Maxwell, Diana Kathleen *early childhood education educator*
Moder, John Joseph *academic administrator, priest*
Norwood, Carole Gene *middle school educator*
Robertson, Samuel Luther, Jr. *special education educator, therapist*
Salisbury, Margaret Mary *retired elementary school educator*
Senecal, Connie Montoya *special education educator*
Spears, Diane Shields *fine arts coordinator, educator*
Speer, Glenda O'Bryant *middle school educator*
Sueltenfuss, Sister Elizabeth Anne *academic administrator*
Tomkewitz, Marie Adele *elementary school educator*
Wimpee, Mary Elizabeth *elementary school educator*
Wood, Frank Preuit *educator, former air force officer*
Young, James Julius *university administrator, former army officer*

**San Juan**
Shelby, Nina Claire *special education educator*

**San Marcos**
Barragán, Celia Silguero *elementary education educator*
Bechtol, William Milton *education educator*
Clayton, Katy *elementary education educator*
Fite, Kathleen Elizabeth *education educator*
Moore, Betty Jean *retired education educator*
Supple, Jerome H. *academic administrator*

**Schulenburg**
Bauer, Laurie Koenig *principal*

**Sherman**
Page, Oscar Cletice *academic administrator*

**Stafford**
Brinkley, Elise Hoffman *academic administrator, biofeedback counselor, marriage and family therapist, nurse*

**Stephenville**
Sims, Larry Kyle *secondary school educator*

**Sugar Land**
Duvall, Cathleen Elaine *elementary school educator, consultant*
Ramos, Rose Mary *elementary education educator*
Thompson, Alice M. Broussard *special education administrator*

**Talpa**
Russell, Nedra Joan Bibby *secondary school educator*

**Temple**
Kreitz, Helen Marie *retired elementary education educator*
Staten, Donna Kay *elementary art educator*

**The Woodlands**
Topazio, Virgil William *university official*

**Trophy Club**
Melton, Lynda Gayle *reading specialist, educational diagnostician*

**Tyler**
Davidson, Jack Leroy *academic administrator*
Marsh, Owen Robert *education educator*
Sharpe, Aubrey Dean *college administrator*

**Uvalde**
Wilson, Benjamin Franklin, Jr. *education educator*

**Victoria**
Haynes, Karen Sue *university president, social work educator*

**Waco**
Belew, John Seymour *academic administrator, chemist*
Brooks, Roger Leon *university president*
Hillis, William Daniel *university administrator*
Lindsey, Jonathan Asmel *development executive, educator*
Moseley, Mary Prudence *educator*
Reynolds, Herbert Hal *academic administrator*
Stauber, Donna Beth *education educator*
Whaley, Carolyn Louise *primary school educator*

**Wharton**
Gonzalez, Antonio *academic administrator, mortgage company executive*

**Whiteface**
Lamb, Stacie Thompson *elementary school educator*

**Wichita Falls**
Harvill, Melba Sherwood *university librarian*
Rodriguez, Louis Joseph *university president, educator*

## UTAH

**Cedar City**
Sherratt, Gerald Robert *university president*

**Logan**
Gay, Charles W., Jr. *academic administrator*
Hunsaker, Scott Leslie *gifted and talented education educator*
McKell, Cyrus M. *college dean, plant physiologist, consultant*
Price, Susan Kay Lind *employment training organization administrator*
Shaver, James Porter *education educator, university dean*

**Mount Pleasant**
Schade, Wilbert Curtis *educational administrator*

**Murray**
Cannell, Cyndy Michelle *elementary school principal*

**Ogden**
Mecham, Steven Ray *school system administrator*
Smith, Robert Bruce *college administrator*
Thompson, Paul Harold *university president*

**Orem**
Green, John Alden *university director study abroad program*

**Provo**
Allred, Ruel Acord *education educator*
†Bateman, Merrill Joseph *university president*
Christensen, Bruce LeRoy *academic administrator, former public broadcasting executive*
Fleming, Joseph Clifton, Jr. *university dean, law educator*
Hansen, H. Reese *law school dean, educator*
Jensen, Clayne R. *university administrator*
Stahmann, Robert F. *education educator*
Stanford, Melvin Joseph *retired dean, educator*
Whatcott, Marsha Rasmussen *elementary education educator*

**Salt Lake City**
Chivers, Laurie Alice *state educational administrator*
Drew, Clifford James *university administrator, special education and educational psychology educator*
Fink, Kristin Danielson *secondary education educator*
Jarvis, Joseph Boyer *retired university administrator*
Kim, Sung Wan *educator*
Matsen, John Martin *academic administrator, pathologist*
McCleary, Lloyd E(verald) *education educator*
Miller, William Charles *college dean, architect*
Peterson, Chase N. *university president*
Simmons, Lynda Merrill Mills *educational administrator*
Stock, Peggy A(nn) *college president, educator*
Thatcher, Blythe Darlyn *assistant principal*

**Sandy**
Pierce, Ilona Lambson *educational administrator*
Sabey, J(ohn) Wayne *academic administrator, consultant*
Volpe, Ellen Marie *middle school educator*

**West Jordan**
Shepherd, Paul H. *elementary school educator*

## VERMONT

**Arlington**
Pentkowski, Raymond J. *superintendent*

**Bennington**
Coleman, Elizabeth *college president*
Glasser, William Arnold *academic administrator*

**Burlington**
Brandenburg, Richard George *university dean, management educator*
Della Santa, Laura *principal*
Frymayer, John W. *dean*
Son, Mun Shig *education educator*

**Ludlow**
Davis, Vera *elementary school educator*

**Manchester Center**
Waldinger Seff, Margaret *special elementary education educator*

**Middlebury**
O'Brien, George Dennis *retired university president*

**Saint Albans**
Johnson, Paula Bouchard *preschool administrator, educator, consultant*

**Saint Johnsbury**
Mayo, Bernier L. *secondary school principal*

**South Hero**
Bisson, Roger *middle school educator*

**South Royalton**
Kempner, Maximilian Walter *law school dean, lawyer*

**South Woodstock**
Kennan, Elizabeth Topham *university executive*

**Springfield**
Charest, Gabrielle Marya *educational administrator*

**Swanton**
Chaim, Linda Susan *school system administrator*

**Thetford**
Brown, Susan Elizabeth S. *secondary education educator*

**Waterbury**
Bunting, Charles I. *academic administrator*

**White River Junction**
Halperin, George Bennett *education educator, retired naval officer*

## VIRGINIA

**Alexandria**
Abernathy, Mary Gates *elementary school educator*
Anderson, Ann Davis *curriculum and staff development specialist*
Brown, Ann Herrell *secondary school educator*
Edgell, Karin Jane *reading specialist, special education educator*
Jarrard, James Paul *school program administrator*
Johnson, William David *retired university administrator*
Nekritz, Leah Kalish *dean, college administrator*
Wilson, Kathy *principal*

**Amherst**
Herbert, Amanda Kathryn *special education educator*

**Annandale**
Heyer, Laura Miriam *special education educator*
Wilhelmi, Mary Charlotte *education educator, college official*

**Arlington**
Bartlett, Elizabeth Susan *audio-visual specialist*
Berg, Sister Marie Majella *university chancellor*
Hartley, Craig Sheridan *dean, mechanical engineering educator*
Hill, Donald Wain *education accreditation commission executive*
Lane, Neal Francis *university provost, physics researcher, federal administrator*
Peterson, Paul Quayle *retired university dean, physician*
Sibley, William Arthur *academic administrator, physics educator, consultant*
Simms, Frances Bell *elementary education educator*
Violand-Sanchez, Emma Natividad *school administrator, educator*

**Ashland**
Henshaw, William Raleigh *middle school educator*
Martin, Roger Harry *college president*
Payne, Ladell *college president*
Stevenson, Carol Wells *secondary education educator*

**Blacksburg**
Brown, Gregory Neil *university administrator, forest physiology educator*
Campbell, Joan Virginia Loweke *secondary school educator, language educator*
Carlisle, Ervin Frederick *university provost, educator*
Edwards, Patricia K. *dean*
Smith, Robert McNeil *university dean*
Steger, Charles William *university administrator*
Torgersen, Paul Ernest *academic administrator, educator*
Wall, Robert Thompson *secondary school educator*

**Bridgewater**
Geisert, Wayne Frederick *educational consultant, retired administrator*
Richardson, John MacLaren, Jr. *school superintendent*

**Buena Vista**
Ripley, John Walter *academic administrator*

**Charlottesville**
Brandt, Richard Martin *education educator*
Breneman, David Worthy *dean, educator*
Bunker, Linda Kay *dean, physical education educator*
Campbell, Stephen Donald Peter *retired university administrator*
Carey, Robert Munson *university dean, physician*
Casteen, John Thomas, III *university president*
Cooper, James Michael *education educator*
Corse, John Doggett *university official, lawyer*
Fletcher, John Caldwell *bioethicist, educator*
Lancaster, B. Jeanette *dean, nursing educator*
Lankford, Francis Greenfield, Jr. *education educator emeritus*
Matson, Robert Edward *educator, leadership consultant*
McDonough, William Andrew *dean*
O'Neil, Robert Marchant *university administrator, law educator*
Reynolds, Robert Edgar *academic administrator, physician*
Thompson, Kenneth W(infred) *educational director, author, editor, administrator, social science educator*
Walker, Sharon Louise *gifted education educator*

Wang, Gwo Jaw *university educator*

**Chesapeake**
Clarkson, Phyllis Owens *early childhood educator*
Lewter, Helen Clark *elementary education educator*

**Chesterfield**
Copeland, Jean Parrish *school system administrator, school board executive*

**Clifton**
Latt, Pamela Yvonne *school system administrator*

**Cobbs Creek**
Lawson, Janice Rae *retired elementary education educator*

**Delaplane**
Harris, Charles Upchurch *seminary president, clergyman*

**Dumfries**
Hinnant, Hilari Anne *educator, educational consultant*

**Emporia**
Bottoms, Brenda Pinchbeck *elementary education educator*

**Evington**
Fortune, Laura Catherine Dawson *elementary school educator*

**Fairfax**
Graves, Dana Louise *elementary school educator*
Johnson, George William *university president emeritus*
Merten, Alan Gilbert *academic administrator*

**Falls Church**
Cleland, Sherrill *college president*
Todd, Shirley Ann *school system administrator*

**Fishersville**
Geiman, Stephen Royer *secondary school educator, coach*

**Fort Defiance**
Livick, Malcolm Harris *school administrator*

**Franklin**
Sprouse, Earlene Pentecost *educational diagnostician*

**Fredericksburg**
Jenks-Davies, Kathryn Ryburn *retired daycare provider and owner, civic worker*
Jones, Julia Pearl *elementary school educator*

**Hampden Sydney**
Wilson, Samuel V. *academic adminstrator*

**Hampton**
Harvey, William Robert *university president*
Hightower, John Brantley *arts administrator*

**Harrisonburg**
Carrier, Ronald Edwin *university administrator*
Slye, Carroll James *instructional supervisor*

**Haysi**
Deel, George Moses *elementary school educator*

**Heathsville**
Sisson, Jean Cralle *middle school educator*

**Lake Ridge**
Derrickson, Denise Ann *secondary school educator*

**Lexington**
Elrod, John William *university president, philosophy and religion educator*
Knapp, John Williams *retired college president*
Watt, William Joseph *academic administrator, chemistry educator*

**Lynchburg**
Marra, Anthony Tullio *audio visual specialist*
Sullivan, Gregory Paul *secondary education educator*

**Manassas**
Avella, Joseph Ralph *university dean*
Kettlewell, Gail Biery *academic administrator*
Young, Susan Eileen *elementary education educator*

**Marion**
Groseclose, Joanne Stowers *special education educator*

**Mc Dowell**
Harkleroad, Jo-Ann Decker *special education educator*

**Mc Lean**
Groennings, Sven Ole *academic administrator, higher education educator, corporate executive*
Laine, Elaine Frances *school system administrator*

**Mechanicsville**
Long, Patricia Gavigan *elementary education educator, English language educator*

**Melfa**
Harmon, Patricia Marie *special education educator*

**Midlothian**
Alligood, Mary Sale *special education educator*
Smith, Alma Davis *elementary education educator*
Williams, Dorothy Putney *middle school educator*

**Newport News**
Levy, Robin Carole *elementary guidance counselor*
Meade, Angela Kaye *special education educator*
Patty, Anna Christine *middle school educator*
Santoro, Anthony Richard *academic administrator*

**Norfolk**
Fox, Thomas George *academic adminstrator, health science educator*
Jones, Franklin Ross *education educator*
Koch, James Verch *academic administrator, economist*
Myers, Donald Allen *university dean*
Oberne, Sharon Brown *elementary education educator*
Proctor, Ronald Eugene *academic administrator, educator, consultant*
Russell, Susan Webb *elementary and middle school education educator*
Wheeler, Jock R. *dean*

**Norton**
Bowen, Bill Monroe *educational administrator*
Kendrick, Richard Lofton *university administrator, consultant*

**Orange**
Duncan, Douglas Allen *educator*
Mallison, N Daniele *elementary school educator*

**Palmyra**
Cawley, William Arthur *research educator*

**Petersburg**
Franklin, Virgil L. *school administrator, education educator*
Miles, Ruby Williams *secondary education educator*

**Poquoson**
Moore, Sandra Bucher *mathematics educator*
Parry, Thomas Herbert, Jr. *school system administrator, educational consultant*
Yard, Rix Nelson *former athletic director*

**Radford**
Hanna, Mary Ann *education educator*
Owens, Charles Wesley *university executive*

**Reston**
Keefe, James Washburn *educational researcher, consultant*

**Richmond**
Ackell, Edmund Ferris *university president*
Blank, Florence Weiss *literacy educator, editor*
Brush, Carey Wentworth *retired college administrator, history educator*
Hamel, Dana Bertrand *academic administrator*
Heilman, E. Bruce *academic administrator*
James, Allix Bledsoe *retired university president*
Jones, Jeanne Pitts *director early childhood school*
Kontos, Hermes *dean*
Leary, David Edward *university dean*
McGee, Henry Alexander, Jr. *university official*
Modlin, George Matthews *university chancellor emeritus*
Morrill, Richard Leslie *university administrator*
Rosenblum, John William *dean*
Sasser, Ellis A. *gifted and talented education educator*
Savage, William Woodrow *education educator*
Simmons, S. Dallas *university president*
Trani, Eugene Paul *academic administrator, educator*

**Roanoke**
Coleman, Sallye Terrell *retired social studies educator*
Denton, Judy Holley *elementary education educator*
King, Stephen Emmett *educational administrator*
Nickens, Harry Carl *academic administrator*

**Round Hill**
Bergeman, Clarissa Hellman *special education educator*

**Salem**
Gring, David M. *academic administrator*

**South Hill**
Taylor, Jean Mull *home economics educator, secondary educator*

**Springfield**
De Nigris, Anna Maria Theresa *middle school educator*
Leavitt, Mary Janice Deimel *special education educator, civic worker*
Sproul, Joan Heeney *elementary school educator*

**Stafford**
Lambert, Linda Margaret *reading specialist*

**Staunton**
Tyson, Cynthia Haldenby *academic administrator*

**Suffolk**
Matson, Virginia Mae Freeberg (Mrs. Edward J. Matson) *retired special education educator, author*
Parker, James Fletcher *middle school educator*

**Sweet Briar**
Baldwin, Nancy Godwin *program director*

**Urbanna**
Salley, John Jones *university administrator, oral pathologist*

**Virginia Beach**
Barriskill, Maudanne Kidd *primary school educator*
Corbat, Patricia Leslie *special education educator*
Jones, Robert Clair *middle school educator*
Richardson, Daniel Putnam *headmaster, history, economics and criminal law educator*
Selig, William George *university official*
Wiggins, Samuel Paul *education educator*

**Warrenton**
Haley, Jeanne Ackerman *preschool director*

**Waynesboro**
Tynes, Theodore Archibald *educational administrator*

**Williamsburg**
Birney, Robert Charles *retired academic administrator, psychologist*
Dittman, Duane Arthur *educational consultant*
Hess, Donald K. *academic administrator*
Mc Kean, John Rosseel Overton *university dean*
Polk-Matthews, Josephine Elsey *school psychologist*
Scholnick, Robert J. *college dean, English language educator*
Smith, James Brown, Jr. *secondary school educator*
Van Tassel-Baska, Joyce Lenore *education educator*
Williams, Ruth Elizabeth (Betty Williams) *retired secondary school educator*

**Winchester**
Engelage, James Roland *management and educational consultant*
Pleacher, David Henry *secondary school educator*
Tisinger, Catherine Anne *college dean*

**Wise**
Lemons, L. Jay *academic administrator*
Smiddy, Joseph Charles *retired college chancellor*

**Woodbridge**
Packard, Mildred Ruth *middle school educator*

## WASHINGTON

**Bainbridge Island**
Milander, Henry Martin *educational consultant*

**Bellevue**
Bergstrom, Marianne Elisabeth *program coordinator, special education educator*
Clark, Richard Walter *education consultant*
Mitchell, Gloria Jean *elementary school principal, educator*
Rice, Kay Diane *elementary education educator, consultant*
Wallentine, Mary Kathryn *secondary educator*

**Bellingham**
De Lorme, Roland L. *university provost and vice president*
Masland, Lynne S. *university official*
Morse, Karen Williams *academic administrator*
Pierce, George Adams *university administrator, educator*

**Bothell**
Banks, Cherry Ann McGee *education educator*
Fortier, Sharon Murphy *special education educator*
Icenhower, Rosalie B. *retired elementary school principal*

**Camas**
Howe, Robert Wilson *education educator*

**Centralia**
Kirk, Henry Port *academic administrator*

**Edmonds**
Walker, Doris Ann *education educator*

**Ellensburg**
Jones, Gail Kathleen *educational administrator*
Nelson, Ivory Vance *academic administrator*

**Enumclaw**
Goff, Thomas M. *secondary education educator*

**Everett**
Callaghan, Mary Anne *secondary school educator*

**Gig Harbor**
Minnerly, Robert Ward *retired headmaster*

**Issaquah**
Newbill, Karen Margaret *elementary school educator, education educator*

**Kennewick**
Fontana, Sharon Marie *early childhood education educator*

**Kent**
Irwin, Deborah Jo *secondary education educator, flutist*
Johnson, Dennis D. *elementary school principal*

**Kirkland**
Ayars, Albert Lee *retired school superintendent*
Davis, Dennis Albert *college president*

**Lacey**
Cosand, Joseph Parker, Jr. *education educator emeritus*
Kuniyasu, Keith Kazumi *secondary education educator*
Spangler, David Robert *college administrator, engineer*

**Lynnwood**
Benzel, Brian L. *superintendent*

**Mill Creek**
Larson, Mary Bea *elementary education educator*

**Nine Mile Falls**
Payne, Arlie Jean *parent education administrator*

**Olympia**
Humphrey, Camilla Marie *retired special education educator*
Jervis, Jane Lise *college official, science historian*
Ponder, William Stanley *university administrator*

**Port Angeles**
Chase, John David *university dean, physician*

**Prosser**
Boyle, Steven Leonard *secondary school educator*
Deffenbaugh, Kay Anne *secondary education art educator*

**Pullman**
Lewis, Norman G. *academic administrator, researcher, consultant*
Smith, Robert Victor *university administrator*
Smith, Samuel Howard *academic administrator, plant pathologist*

**Renton**
Tajon, Encarnacion Fontecha (Connie Tajon) *retired educator, association executive*

**Richland**
Piippo, Steve *educator*

**Seattle**
Abbott, Robert Dean *education scientist*
Banks, James Albert *educational research director, educator*
Bassett, Edward Powers *university official*
Brown, Kristi *principal*
Brown, Lillie McFall *elementary school principal*
Carlson, Dale Arvid *university dean*
Cook, Victor *physics educator, researcher*
Cox, Frederick Moreland *retired university dean, social worker*
Debro, Julius *university dean, sociology educator*
Denny, Brewster Castberg *retired university dean*
Drew, Jody Lynne *secondary education educator*
Fischer, Mary E. *special education educator*
Gerberding, William Passavant *retired university president*
Gibaldi, Milo *university dean*
Goodlad, John Inkster *education educator, author*
Halferty, Frank Joseph *middle school music educator*
Hampton, Shelley Lynn *hearing impaired educator*
Hart, Paul *retired dean and educator, poet*
Hegyvary, Sue Thomas *dean nursing school*
Hunkins, Francis Peter *education educator*
Jennerich, Edward John *university official and dean*
Omenn, Gilbert Stanley *university dean, physician*
Plotnick, Robert David *educator, economic consultant*
Ray, Charles Kendall *retired university dean*
Schulte, Henry Gustave *college administrator*
Silver, Michael *school superintendent*
Stringer, William Jeremy *academic administrator*
Terrell, W(illiam) Glenn *university president emeritus*

**Sequim**
Barton, Jay *university administrator, biologist*

**Spokane**
Coughlin, Bernard John *university chancellor*
Glynn, Edward *college administrator*
Linn, Diana Patricia *elementary education educator*
Matters, Clyde Burns *former college president*
McManus, Patrick Francis *educator, writer*
Nyman, Carl John, Jr. *university dean and official*
Robinson, William P. *academic administrator, consultant, speaker*

**Tacoma**
Jungkuntz, Richard Paul *university provost emeritus*
King, Gundar Julian *retired university dean*
Maloney, Patsy Loretta *university official, nursing educator*
Pierce, Susan Resneck *academic administrator, English educator*
Reisberg, Leon Elton *education educator*

**Toppenish**
Ross, Kathleen Anne *academic administrator*

**Vancouver**
Mangino, Kristin Mikalson *secondary education educator*

**Walla Walla**
Cronin, Thomas Edward *academic administrator*

## WEST VIRGINIA

**Athens**
†Beasley, Jerry L. *academic administrator*
Marsh, Joseph Franklin, Jr. *emeritus college president, educational consultant*

**Beckley**
Thompson, Novella Woodrum *college administrator, psychotherapist*

**Bethany**
Cummins, Delmer Duane *academic administrator, historian*
Krug, John Carleton (Tony Krug) *college administrator, library consultant*
Sandercox, Robert Allen *college official, clergyman*

**Bluefield**
Barsi, Louis Michael *college dean*

**Charleston**
Arrington, Carolyn Ruth *school system administrator*
Coe, Pam *educational researcher*
Hambrick, Arlene *school system administrator, minister*
Krotseng, Marsha Van Dyke *higher education administrator*
Manning, Charles W. *academic administrator*
Moore, Jeanne *arts educator and administrator*
Welch, Edwin Hugh *academic administrator*

**Clarksburg**
Murphy, Jeanne Ann *parochial school educator*

**Clay**
Gillespie, Larry *secondary school principal*

**Dellslow**
Allamong, Betty D. *academic administrator*

**Dunbar**
Russell, James Alvin, Jr. *college administrator*

**Elkins**
MacConkey, Dorothy I. *academic administrator*

**Fairmont**
Hardway, Wendell Gary *former college president*

Stalder, Florence Lucille *secondary education educator*

**Glen Jean**
Beverly, Laura Elizabeth *special education educator*

**Harpers Ferry**
Blue, Kathy Jo *elementary school educator*

**Huntington**
Gould, Alan Brant *academic administrator*
Hayes, Robert Bruce *former college president, educator*
Hooper, James William *educator*
Kent, Calvin Albert *university administrator*
McKown, Charles H. *dean*

**Martinsburg**
Bovey, Lisa Dawn *special education educator*

**Milton**
Roebuck, Judith Lynn *secondary school educator*

**Montgomery**
Keenan, Mary Elizabeth *vocational education educator*

**Morgantown**
Bajura, Richard Albert *university administrator, engineering educator*
Biddington, William Robert *university administrator, dental educator*
Brooks, Dana D. *dean*
Bucklew, Neil S. *educator, past university president*
D'Alessandri, Robert M. *dean*
Drvar, Margaret Adams *vocational education educator*
†Haggett, Rosemary R. *dean*
Jackson, Ruth Moore *academic administrator*
Stewart, Guy Harry *university dean emeritus, journalism educator*

**Mullens**
Lee, Debora Ann *elementary school educator, reading specialist*

**Nitro**
Lucas, Panola *elementary education educator*

**Parkersburg**
Meadows, Lois Annette *elementary education educator*

**Paw Paw**
Palmer, Robert Jeffrey *special education educator*

**Philippi**
Shearer, Richard Eugene *educational consultant*

**Ridgeley**
Unger, Roberta Marie *special education educator*

**Salem**
Ohl, Ronald Edward *academic administrator*

**Shady Spring**
Reed, Cathy Lorraine *elementary education educator*

**Shepherdstown**
Strasser, William Carl, Jr. *retired college president, educator*

**Spencer**
Parker, Theresa Ann *special education educator*

**Weston**
Sumpter, Sonja Kay *elementary school educator*

**Wheeling**
Campbell, Clyde Del *academic administrator*
Welker, William Andrew *reading specialist*

**Williamson**
Shaw, Laurie Jo *grant project director*

**WISCONSIN**

**Appleton**
Warch, Richard *academic administrator*

**Athelstane**
Outcalt, David Lewis *academic administrator, mathematician, educator*

**Bayfield**
Wilhelm, Sister Phyllis *principal*

**Belgium**
Murphy, Greta Werwath *retired academic administrator*

**Beloit**
Ferrall, Victor Eugene, Jr. *college administrator, lawyer*
Melvin, Charles Alfred, III *superintendent of schools*

**Brodhead**
O'Neil, J(ames) Peter *elementary education educator, computer software designer*

**Brookfield**
Gradeless, Donald Eugene *secondary education educator*
Jenkins, William Atwell *university chancellor*

**Cedarburg**
Mielke, Jon Alan *elementary school administrator*
Steffens, Donna Irene *gifted and talented education coordinator*

**De Pere**
Manion, Thomas A. *college president*

**Eagle River**
Nieuwendorp, Judy Lynell *special education educator*

**Eau Claire**
Dunlap, William Phillip *education educator*
Richards, Jerry Lee *academic administrator, religious educator*
Schnack, Larry Gene *university chancellor*

**Elkhorn**
Reinke, Doris Marie *retired elementary education educator*

**Elm Grove**
Barth, Karl Luther *retired seminary president*

**Elroy**
Gavin, Joan Elaine *special education educator*

**Exeland**
Engelhardt-Alvarez, Madeline *retired preschool administrator*

**Fish Creek**
Abegg, Martin Gerald *retired university president*

**Fond Du Lac**
Henken, Willard John *retired university dean*

**Glendale**
Moeser, Elliott *principal*

**Glidden**
Palecek, Sandra Marie *reading education specialist*

**Green Bay**
Martens, Lyle Charles *state education administrator*
Shebesta, Lynn Marie *school administrator*

**Greenwood**
Kern-Ystad, Carol Rae *special education educator*

**Hales Corners**
Michalski, (Żurowski) Wacław *adult education educator*

**Kenosha**
Campbell, F(enton) Gregory *college administrator, historian*
Levis, Richard George *middle school educator*
Smith, Eleanor Jane *university chancellor*
Zuhlke, Marybeth *elementary school curriculum consultant, educator*

**La Crosse**
Medland, William James *college president*
Novotney, Donald Francis *superintendent of schools*

**Lake Nebagamon**
Meyer, Karl William *retired university president*

**Madison**
Bell/Jackson, Marianne Jeanne *elementary education educator*
Busby, Edward Oliver *retired dean*
Ebben, James Adrian *college president*
Kreuter, Gretchen V. *academic administrator*
Lemberger, August Paul *university dean, pharmacy educator*
Lyall, Katharine C(ulbert) *academic administrator, economics educator*
McCarty, Donald James *retired education educator*
Mitby, Norman Peter *college president*
Nagy, Joanne Elizabeth Berg *associate dean university*
Netzer, Lanore A(gnes) *retired educational administration educator*
Odden, Allan Robert *education educator*
Policano, Andrew J. *university dean*
Sanders, Keith R. *university chancellor*
Taylor, Carolyn L. *principal*
Ward, David *academic administrator, educator*
Weiss, Mareda Ruth *dean*
Witiak, Donald Theodore *medicinal chemistry educator*
Yuill, Thomas MacKay *university administrator, microbiology educator*

**Markesan**
Jahns, Arthur William *retired educational administrator*

**Mayville**
Bell, Scott William *private school educator, principal*

**Menomonie**
Shaw, Dennis Lee *academic administrator*

**Mequon**
Dohmen, Mary Holgate *retired primary school educator*
Ellis, William Grenville *academic administrator, management consultant*
Watson-Boone, Rebecca A. *library & information studies educator, researcher*

**Middleton**
Conaway, Jane Ellen *elementary education educator*

**Milton**
Hosler, Russell John *retired education educator*

**Milwaukee**
Aman, Mohammed Mohammed *university dean, library and information science educator*
Armstrong, Leona May Bottrell *counselor, teacher*
Carter, Martha Eloise *retired curriculum specialist, reading consultant*
Coffman, Terrence J. *academic administrator*
Doehr-Blanck, Denise Louise *special education educator*
Dunn, Michael T. *dean*
Frank, Kristy Louise *English educator*
Fuller, Howard *education educator, academic administrator*
Keulks, George William *university dean, chemistry educator*
Lietz, Jeremy Jon *educational administrator, writer*

Raynor, John Patrick *university administrator*
Read, Sister Joel *academic administrator*
Reid, Robert Lelon *college dean, mechanical engineer*
Rheams, Annie Elizabeth *education educator*
Sankovitz, James Leo *development director, lobbyist*
Schaub, Theresa Marie *early childhood educator*
Schenker, Eric *university dean, economist*
Schroeder, John H. *university chancellor*
Szmanda, Lucille Marie *retired vocational school educator*
Viets, Hermann *college president, consultant*

**Neenah**
Talbot, John Dudley *college administrator*

**New Franken**
Weidner, Edward William *university chancellor, political scientist*

**New Holstein**
Tyunaitis, Patricia Ann *elementary school educator*

**New London**
Fitzgerald, Laurine Elisabeth *university dean, educator*

**Oconomowoc**
Reich, Rose Marie *retired art educator*

**Oconto Falls**
Schlieve, Hy C. J. *principal*

**Omro**
Turner, Mildred Edith *day care owner*

**Oshkosh**
Herzog, Barbara Jean *secondary school educator, administrator*
Kerrigan, John E. *academic administrator*

**Pewaukee**
Andacht, Herman William *retired educator and counselor*

**Platteville**
Lindahl, Thomas Jefferson *university dean*

**River Falls**
Thibodeau, Gary A. *academic administrator*

**Sheboygan**
Ladiges, Lori Jean *learning disabilities specialist*

**Solon Springs**
Kleven, Bruce Alan *academic administrator*

**Stevens Point**
Stevens, Dwight Marlyn *educational administrator*

**Stoddard**
Hollenbeck, Sue J. *elementary education educator*

**Three Lakes**
Bauknecht, Barbara Belle *educator*

**Twin Lakes**
Fleischer, John Richard *retired secondary education educator*

**Valders**
Fabian, Thomas Robert *superintentent of schools*

**Verona**
Hoffmeister, Ann Elizabeth *elementary education educator*

**Walworth**
Sissons, John Roger *educational administrator*

**Watertown**
Henry, Helga Irmgard *liberal arts educator*

**Waukesha**
Falcone, Frank S. *academic administrator*

**Wausau**
Plein, Kathryn Anne *secondary educator*

**West Bend**
Rodney, Joel Morris *dean*

**Whitewater**
Busse, Eileen E. *special education educator*
Greenhill, H. Gaylon *academic administrator*

**Wisconsin Rapids**
McGrath, Cheryl Julia *elementary education educator*
Olson-Hellerud, Linda Kathryn *elementary education educator*

**WYOMING**

**Casper**
Wilkes, Shar (Joan Charlene Wilkes) *elementary education educator*

**Cheyenne**
McDowell, Sherrie Lorraine *secondary education educator*
Robertson, Susan Joyce Coe *special education educator*

**Laramie**
Forster, Bruce Alexander *dean*
Meyer, Joseph B. *academic administrator, former state attorney general*

**Newcastle**
Sample, Bette Jeane *elementary educator*

**Riverton**
Mulholland, Barbara Ann *school director*

**Rock Springs**
Kathka, David Arlin *director educational services*

**Wheatland**
Morrison, Samuel Ferris *secondary school educator*

**TERRITORIES OF THE UNITED STATES**

**AMERICAN SAMOA**

**Pago Pago**
Ili, Esther Kaili *principal*
Varghese, Mary *secondary education educator*

**FEDERATED STATES OF MICRONESIA**

**Chuuk**
Marcus, Mariano Nakamura *secondary school principal*

**GUAM**

**Mangilao**
Lee, Chin-Tian *academic administrator, agricultural studies educator*

**Talofofo**
Taylor, James John *academic administrator*

**PUERTO RICO**

**Aguadilla**
Jaramillo, Juana Segarra *dean*

**Cabo Rojo**
Rivera-Martinez, Socorro *retired educator, assistant principal*

**Guayama**
Febres-Santiago, Samuel F. *university chancellor*

**Humacao**
Castrodad, Felix A. *university administrator*
Delgado-Rodriguez, Manuel *secondary school educator*

**Rio Piedras**
López de Mendez, Annette Giselda *education educator*
Medina-Diaz, Maria del Rosario *education educator*

**San German**
Mojica, Agnes *academic administrator*

**San Juan**
Basols, Jose Andres *school director, priest*
Carreras, Francisco José *retired university president, foundation executive*
Fernández-V., Juan Ramon *university chancellor*
Gonzalez, Jose Ramón *academic administrator*
Matheu, Federico Manuel *university chancellor*
Thompson, Annie Figueroa *academic director, educator*

**VIRGIN ISLANDS**

**Frederiksted**
Petrait, Brother James Anthony *secondary education educator, clergy member*

**Saint Thomas**
Ferguson, Glenn Walker *educational consultant, lecturer*
Henneman, Carol O'Bryan *secondary school educator*
Shuck, Annette Ulsh *education educator*

**MILITARY ADDRESSES OF THE UNITED STATES**

**EUROPE**

**FPO**
Chaiklin, Amy Lynn *childhood education program developer*

**CANADA**

**ALBERTA**

**Calgary**
Maher, Peter Michael *university dean*
Neale, E(rnest) R(ichard) Ward *retired university official, consultant*
Rasporich, Anthony Walter *university dean*
Smith, Eldon *dean*
Watanabe, Mamoru *former university dean, physician, researcher*
White, Terrence Harold *academic administrator, sociologist*

**Edmonton**
Adams, Peter Frederick *university president, civil engineer*
Tyrell, Lorne S. *dean*

### BRITISH COLUMBIA

**Cobble Hill**
Cox, Albert Reginald *academic administrator, physician, retired*

**Kelowna**
Muggeridge, Derek Brian *dean, engineering consultant*

**Sooke**
Booth, Andrew Donald *retired university administrator, scientist*

**Vancouver**
Andrews, John Hobart McLean *education educator*
Finnegan, Cyril Vincent *retired university dean, zoology educator*
Haycock, Kenneth Roy *education administrator*
Lusztig, Peter Alfred *university dean, educator*
McNeill, John Hugh *pharmaceutical sciences educator*
Webber, William Alexander *university administrator, physician*

**Victoria**
Strong, David F. *university administrator*
Welch, S(tephen) Anthony *university dean, Islamic studies and arts educator*

### MANITOBA

**Winnipeg**
Poettcker, Henry *retired seminary president*
Stalker, Jacqueline D'Aoust *academic administrator, educator*

### NEW BRUNSWICK

**Fredericton**
†McGreal, Rory Patrick *educational administrator*
Parr-Johnston, Elizabeth *academic administrator*

### NEWFOUNDLAND

**Saint John's**
May, Arthur W. *university president*

### NOVA SCOTIA

**Halifax**
Murray, Thomas John (Jock Murray) *medical humanities educator, medical researcher, neurologist*
Ozmon, Kenneth Lawrence *university president, educator*

**Timberlea**
Verma, Surjit K. *school system administrator*

**Truro**
Mac Rae, Herbert Farquhar *retired college president*

**Wolfville**
Ogilvie, Kelvin Kenneth *university president, chemistry educator*

### ONTARIO

**Hamilton**
Shaw, Denis Martin *university dean, former geology educator*

**London**
Davenport, Paul *university administrator, economics educator*
McMurty, Robert Y. *academic dean*

**North York**
Macdonald, Hugh Ian *university president emeritus, economist, educator*

**Ottawa**
Brombal, Douglas Nereo *retired university official, consultant*
Kroeger, Arthur *university chancellor, former government official*
Labarge, Margaret Wade *medieval history educator*
Malouin, Jean-Louis *university dean, educator*
Philogene, Bernard J. R. *academic administrator, science educator*
Seely, John F. *dean*

**Peterborough**
Theall, Donald Francis *retired university president*

**Thunder Bay**
Locker, J. Gary *university official, civil engineering educator*
Rosehart, Robert George *university president, chemical engineer*

**Toronto**
Aberman, Arnold *dean*
Armstrong, Robin Louis *university official, physicist*
Evans, John Robert *former university president, physician*
Hayhurst, James Frederick Palmer *career and business consultant, inspirational speaker, writer*
Korey-Krzeczowski, George J. M. Kniaz *university administrator, management consultant*
Kushner, Eva *academic administrator, educator, author*
Ostry, Sylvia *academic administrator, economist*
Prichard, John Robert Stobo *academic administrator, law educator*
Runte, Roseann *academic administrator*
Sessle, Barry John *university administrator, researcher*

**Waterloo**
Berczi, Andrew Stephen *academic administrator*
Downey, James *university president*
Kay, Jeanne *dean, educator*
Smith, Rowland James *educational administrator*
Wright, Douglas Tyndall *former university administrator, civil engineer*

**Windsor**
Ianni, Ronald William *university president and vice chancellor, lawyer*

### QUEBEC

**Brossard**
Allen, Harold Don *education educator, science writer, monetary historian*

**Montreal**
Belanger, Pierre Rolland *university dean, electrical engineering educator*
Cloutier, Gilles Georges *academic administrator, research executive*
Davidson, Colin Henry *university educator*
Freedman, Samuel Orkin *university official*
French, Stanley George *university dean, philosophy educator*
Granger, Luc Andre *university dean, psychologist*
Lajeunesse, Marcel *university administrator, educator*
Lowy, Frederick Hans *university president, psychiatrist*
Racine, Rene *academic administrator, astronomer*
Vinay, Patrick *university dean*

**Quebec**
Gervais, Michel *academic administrator*

**Sainte Anne de Bellevue**
Buckland, Roger Basil *university dean, educator, vice principal*

### SASKATCHEWAN

**Regina**
Barber, Lloyd Ingram *retired university president*

**Saskatoon**
Knight, Arthur Robert *technical institute administrator*
Knott, Douglas Ronald *college dean, agricultural sciences educator, researcher*
Nikiforuk, Peter N. *university dean*
Popkin, David Richard *academic dean, obstetrician, gynocologist*
Stewart, John Wray Black *college dean*

### MEXICO

**Mexico City**
Castillo Garcia, Luis Fernando *science and technology educator*

### CHILE

**Concepcion**
Trzebiatowski, Gregory L. *education educator*

### CHINA

**Guangzhou**
Mundorf, Nancy Knox *early childhood educator*

### EGYPT

**Cairo**
Miller, Harry George *education educator*

### ENGLAND

**Milton Keynes**
Daniel, Sir John Sagar *academic administrator, metallurgist*

**Surrey**
Petrek, William Joseph *college president emeritus*

### GERMANY

**Ingersheim**
Philippi, Dieter Rudolph *academic administrator*

### IRELAND

**Ballyvaughan**
Wicks, Eugene Claude *college president, art educator*

### JAPAN

**Gamagori**
Yamada, Toshikatsu Augustine *academic administrator, mechanical engineer*

**Kawasaki**
Hoshino, Yoshiro *industrial technology critic*

**Yokohama**
Inaba, Motokichi *organizational scientist*

### THE NETHERLANDS

**Amsterdam**
Armstrong-Law, Margaret *school administrator*

### SCOTLAND

**Aberdeen**
Rice, Charles Duncan *university official*

### SOUTH AFRICA

**Auckland Park**
Koekemoer, Carl Lodewicus *university official, business consultant*

### SPAIN

**Tacoronte**
Kardas, Sigmund Joseph, Jr. *secondary education educator*

### SWITZERLAND

**Geneva**
Kessinger, Tom G. *academic administrator*

### THAILAND

**Bangkok**
Kruck, Donna Jean *special education educator, consultant*

### UNITED ARAB EMIRATES

**Al Ain**
Voth, Douglas W. *academic dean*

### ADDRESS UNPUBLISHED

Aaslestad, Halvor Gunerius *university official*
Aladjem, Daniel *policy analyst*
Allen, Charles Eugene *college administrator, agriculturist*
Alligood, Elizabeth H. *retired special education educator*
Almeida, Evelyn *retired elementary education educator*
Almen, Louis Theodore *retired college president*
Altshuler, Alan Anthony *dean, political scientist*
Anderson, Iris Anita *retired secondary education educator*
Arkin, Mara J. *social studies educator*
Armacost, Mary-Linda Sorber Merriam *former college president*
Armstrong, Karen Lee *special education educator*
Armstrong, Lloyd, Jr. *university official, physics educator*
Armstrong, Warren Bruce *university president, historian, educator*
Arnold, P. A. *special education educator*
Babbitt, Samuel Fisher *retired university administrator*
Baghaei-Rad, Nancy Jane Bebb *elementary educator*
Bahre, Jeannette *education educator, librarian*
Ball, Howard Guy *education specialist educator*
Barnett, Linda Kay Smith *vocational guidance counselor*
Barone, John Anthony *university provost emeritus*
Barrett, Janet Tidd *academic administrator*
Barry, Janet Cecilia *retired elementary school educator*
Bassett, Carol Ann *journalism educator, freelance and writer, producer*
Baxter, Cecil William, Jr. *retired college president*
Becker, Richard Charles *retired college president*
Becker, Walter Heinrich *vocational educator, planner*
Bennett, Elsie Margaret *music school administrator*
Bergman, Hermas John (Jack Bergman) *retired college administrator*
Bernstein, I(rving) Melvin *university official and dean, materials scientist*
Beston, Rose Marie *college president*
Betts, Elaine Wiswall *retired headmistress*
Birman, Linda Lee *elementary education educator*
Bishop, Charles Edwin *university president emeritus, economist*
Black, David R. *superintendent*
Black, Rhonda Stout *special education educator*
Bloodworth, Gladys Leon *educator*
Boeker, Paul Harold *academic official, diplomat*
Bogue, Philip Roberts *consultant*
Bonner, Patricia J. *academic dean, educator*
Borchers, Mary Amelia *middle school educator*
Borst, Philip West *academic administrator*
Bost, Raymond Morris *retired college president*
Boucher, Laurence James *university dean, chemist*
Boyle, Betsy H. *educational administrator*
Brackenhoff, Lonnie Sue *principal*
Brain, George Bernard *university dean*
Branyan, Robert Lester *retired university administrator*
Brewer, Carey *retired academic administrator*
Bright, Harold Frederick *university provost emeritus, consultant*
Brown, Beulah Louise *retired elementary educator*
Brown-Whittington, Vanessa Elizabeth *educator*
Bryan, Lawrence Dow *college administrator*
Buckler, Marilyn Lebow *school psychologist, educational consultant*
Burbridge, Ann Arnold *elementary school educator*
Burke, Joseph C. *university administrator*
Burns, James Milton *retired educator*
Burns, Marie T. *retired secondary education educator*
Callan, Richard John *elementary school educator*
Cameron, J. Elliot *retired parochial educational system administrator*
Cameron, Lucille Wilson *retired dean of libraries*
Campbell, Sarah *elementary education educator, special education specialist*
Carlin, Betty *educator*
Carter, Herbert Edmund *former university official*
Carter, Ronald Gary *academic administrator*
Casler, Frederick Clair *academic administrator, law enforcement educator*
Casper, Gerhard *academic administrator, law educator*
Cassell, William Comyn *college president*
†Castor, Betty *academic administrator*
Castruita, Rudy *school system administrator*
Chajet, Lori Menschel *secondary education educator*
Chandler, Alice *university president, educator*
Chandler, John Herrick *college president*
Chase, James Richard *retired college president*
Chater, Shirley Sears *former vice chancellor, federal commissioner*
Clark, Claudia J. *educational administration, speech, language and learning disabilities professional*
Clark, James Milford *college president, retired*
Clarke, Lambuth McGeehee *academic administrator*
Clifford, Brother Peter *academic administrator, religious educator*
Cline, Linda Jean *reading educator*
Cobb, Millicent Amelia *special education educator*
Cochrane, Walter E. *education administrator, writer*
Coffee, Joseph Denis, Jr. *college chancellor emeritus*
Coleman, Barbara Helene *secondary education educator*
Coleman, Robert Elliott *retired secondary education educator*
Colgate-Lindberg, Catharine Pamella *educator*
Collier, Herman Edward, Jr. *retired college president*
Coluccio, Josephine Catherine *primary and elementary school educator*
Compton, Norma Haynes *retired university dean*
Connell, George Edward *former university president, scientist*
Conole, Clement Vincent *business administrator*
Conover, Nancy Anderson *secondary school counselor*
Copeland, Henry Jefferson, Jr. *former college president*
Cormican, M. Alma *elementary education educator*
Cramer, Robert Vern *retired college administrator, consultant*
Crawford, Kenneth Charles *educational institute executive, retired government official*
Crouse, Carol K. Mavromatis *elementary education educator*
Cummiskey, J. Kenneth *former college president*
Darke, Charles Bruce *academic administrator, dentist*
Davenport, Ernest Harold *university official, accountant*
Davenport, Lawrence Franklin *school system administrator*
Davis, Joseph Lloyd *educational administrator, consultant*
Davis, Robert Aldine *academic administrator*
Davison, Beaumont *retired university administrator*
Debs, Barbara Knowles *former college president, consultant*
DeFelice, Jonathan Peter *college president, priest*
De Jong, Arthur Jay *education consultant, former university president*
Delahanty, Rebecca Ann *school system administrator*
DeLuca, Angeline F. *elementary education educator, reading specialist*
Denton, David Edward *retired education educator*
Derucher, Kenneth Noel *university dean*
DeSpain, Ronald Leroy *retired academic administrator*
Dexter, Dallas-Lee *education administrator*
Diederich, Anne Marie *college president*
DiSalle, Michael Danny *secondary education educator*
Dobler, Donald William *retired college dean, consultant, corporate executive*
Dorsey, Rhoda Mary *retired academic administrator*
Drake, George Albert *college president, historian*
Dubois, Nancy Q. *elementary school educator*
Duff, John Bernard *college president, former city official*
Dunham, Rebecca Betty Beres *school administrator*
Dunworth, John *retired college president*
Dutson, Thayne R. *university dean*
Eaton, Dorel *elementary school educator*
Ebbert, Arthur, Jr. *retired university dean*
Edington, Robert Van *university official*
Edwards, Ardis Lavonne Quam *retired elementary education educator*
Eliot, Charles William John *former university president*
Elmen, Gary Warren *principal*
Endicott, Jennifer Jane *education educator*
Ertl, Rita Mae *elementary education educator*
Evans, Geraldine Ann *academic administrator*
Evans, Valerie Elaine *elementary education educator*
Fadum, Ralph Eigil *university dean*
Falk, Marshall Allen *retired university dean, physician*
Farquhar, Robin Hugh *former university president*
Faverty, Patrick William *principal*
Feldstein, Joshua *academic administrator*
Ferrera, Robert James *superintendent of schools*
Fields, Keith Allen *secondary education educator*
Fife, Jonathan Donald *higher education educator*
Filchock, Ethel *education educator, poet*
Fitzwater, Ivan W. *retired superintendant*
Foltiny, Stephen Vincent *special education educator*
Forney, Ronald Dean *elementary school educator, consultant*
Foster, Martha Tyahla *educational administrator*
Fox, Edward A. *retired college dean*
Franklin, Inga Sivills Knupp *special education educator*
Freeman, Meredith Norwin *former college president, education educator*
French, Earl Allan *principal*
Frey, Katie Manciet *educational administrator*
Frey, Margo Walther *career counselor, columnist*
Frick, Ivan Eugene *college president emeritus, education consultant*
Frierson, Jimmie Lou *retired vocational education educator*
Frost, Everett Lloyd *academic administrator*
Galdi-Weissman, Natalie Ann *secondary education educator*
Galliher, Clarice A. Andrews *secondary education educator*
Gates, Donna Marie *special education educator*
Genovese, Lawrence Matthew *secondary education educator*
Gentilcore, Eileen Marie Belsito *elementary school principal*
Gentilcore, John C. *school principal*
Gier, Patricia Chapman *elementary education educator*

Gillespie, Nellie Redd academic administrator, state official
Gladstone, Carol Lynn assistant principal
Glower, Donald Duane university executive, mechanical engineer
Goché, Joyce Priscilla Hughey special education and gifted education educator
Goewey, Gordon Ira university administrator
Golden, Beth Special Olympics administrator
Good, Linda Lou elementary education educator
Goode, Janet Weiss elementary school educator
Goodrich, Kenneth Paul retired college dean
Gordis, David Moses academic administrator, rabbi
Graupner, Sheryll Ann elementary education educator
Graves, Wallace Billingsley retired university executive
Grebstein, Sheldon Norman university administrator
Green, Nancy Loughridge academic administrator
Green, Patricia Pataky school system administrator, consultant
Groat, Pamela Ferne school media specialist
Guedri, Terry Tyrrell secondary education educator, educational consultant
Haas, Carolyn Buhai elementary education educator, publisher, writer, consultant
Haeberle, Rosamond Pauline retired music educator
Hammer, Joyce Mae gifted and talented education educator
Hankins, Mary Denman elementary school educator
Harader-Andrews, Dana special education consultant
Hardin, Clifford Morris retired university chancellor, cabinet member
Harrington, Jean Patrice college president
Harris, Merle Wiener college administrator, educator
Harville Smith, Martha Louise special education educator
Hasselmo, Nils university official, linguistics educator
Haug, Marilyn Ann reading and mathematics educator
Haynes, Michael Scott, Sr. resource specialist
Heaton-Marticorena, Jean early childhood educator
Heck, James Baker university official
Heestand, Diane Elissa educational technology educator, medical educator
Hegarty, George John university president, English educator
Heidt-Dunwell, Debra Sue vocational education educator
Helman, Alfred Blair retired college president, education consultant
Henkel, Cynthia Leigh preschool educator
Hermance, Betty Jean special education educator
Hitchcock, Walter Anson educational consultant, retired educational administrator
Hlywa, Jennifer Lyn secondary educator
Holtkamp, Susan Charlotte elementary education educator
Hood, Luann Sandra special education educator
Horner, Matina Souretis retired college president, corporate executive
Huff, Janet House special education educator
Huffman, Carol Koster retired middle school educator
Hughes, Eugene Morgan university president
Humphrey, Arthur Earl university administrator, retired
Huttenback, Robert Arthur academic administrator, educator
Jacobs, Linda Rotroff elementary school educator
Jakubauskas, Edward Benedict college president
Jerrytone, Samuel Joseph trade school executive
John, Ralph Candler retired college president, educator
Johnson, Charlene Elizabeth adult education educator
Johnson, Delores special education educator
Johnson, Kirsten Denise elementary education educator
Johnson, Sylvia Sue university administrator, educator
Jones, Lawrence Neale university dean, minister
Jontz, Polly retired college official, museum director
Karber, Johnnie Faye elementary education educator
Karlson, Dixie D. gifted and talented education educator
Kasberger-Mahoney, Elvera A. educational administrator
Kazmarek, Linda Adams secondary education educator
Keebler, Lois Marie elementary school educator
Keiper, Marilyn Morrison elementary education educator
Keith, Leroy, Jr. former college president
Kerins, Francis Joseph college president
Kersting, Edwin Joseph retired university dean
Kilmer, Joseph Charles secondary school educator
King, Annie Roberts elementary and secondary education educator
King, Frances education educator
Kirkpatrick, Dorothy Louise retired education educator, program coordinator
Kliebhan, Sister M(ary) Camille academic administrator
Klotzkin, Charles Edward secondary school educator
Kluge, Cheryle Darlene Jobe secondary education educator
Knabenshue, Catherine Sue special education educator
Knapp, Lonnie Troy elementary education educator
Knox, Ernest Rudder retired college president
Koenig, Allen Edward higher education consultant
Kolb, Dorothy Gong elementary education educator
Komisar, David Daniel retired university provost
Kormondy, Edward John university official, biology educator
Kraemer, Linda Gayle associate dean
Kraft, Arthur academic dean
Krey, Robert Dean education educator emeritus
Kristensen, Marlene early childhood education educator
Krueger, Eugene Rex academic program consultant
Kubiak, John Michael academic administrator
Laible, Jon Morse retired mathematics educator, dean
Langley, Joellen S. music educator
Langworthy, William Clayton college official
Lantz, Joanne Baldwin academic administrator emeritus
Lawrence, Linda Hiett retired school system administrator, writer
Leal, Herbert Allan Borden former university chancellor, former government official
Legington, Gloria R. middle school educator
Lennon, Joseph Luke college official, priest
leRoux, Betty Von Moore elementary education educator
Levering, Emma Gertrude special education educator
Lindegren, Jack Kenneth elementary and secondary education educator
Lipscomb-Brown, Edra Evadean retired childhood educator
Locklear, Brenda Louise mathematics educator
Lockwood, Theodore Davidge former academic administrator
Lomas, Bernard Tagg college president emeritus
Loser, Joseph Carlton, Jr. dean, retired judge
Lovinger, Warren Conrad emeritus university president
Lunde, Katherine LaMontagne educational consultant
Lundgren, Leonard, III retired secondary education educator
Lutz, Carl Freiheit academic administrator
Lynch, John Daniel secondary education educator, state legislator
Lyne, Dorothy-Arden educator
Lynn, Mark Wayne secondary school educator, assistant principal
Mack, Sandra Lee secondary school educator
Macmillan, William Hooper university dean, educator
MacPhee, Donald Albert academic administrator
Major, Patrick Webb, III principal
Mallory, Arthur Lee university dean, retired state official
Mañas, Rita educational administrator
Mandell, Arlene Linda writing and communications educator
Marshak, Robert Reuben former university dean, medical educator, veterinarian
Martin, Judy Brackin Hereford higher education administrator
Matera, Frances Lorine elementary educator
Maurer, Beverly Bennett school administrator
Mayfield, Robert Charles university official, geography educator
McCarthy, Joanne Mary reading specialist
McClaron, Louisianna Clardy retired secondary school educator
McGregor, F. Daniel education educator
McIntosh, Carolyn Meade retired educational administrator
McIntosh, Joyce Eubanks special education educator
McKenna, David Loren academic administrator, clergyman, consultant, author
McLoone, Eugene P. education educator
Mc Mahon, George Joseph academic administrator
McNully, Lynnette Larkin elementary education educator
Mc Pherson, Peter academic administrator
Medalie, Marjorie Lynn educational administrator, consultant
Medley, Donald Matthias retired education educator, consultant
Mehne, Paul Randolph associate dean, medical educator
Melady, Thomas Patrick academic administrator, ambassador, author, public policy expert, educator
Melton, Marie Frances retired university dean
Meyer, Frances Margaret Anthony elementary and secondary school educator, health education specialist
Meyer, Robert Lee secondary education educator
Miaskiewicz, Theresa Elizabeth secondary education educator
Miles, Elsie E. counselor, educator
Miles, Leland Weber university president
Miller, Arjay retired university dean
Miller, James Vince university president
Miller, Jerry Huber retired university chancellor
Mills, Eugene Sumner college president
Mills, Robert Lee president emeritus
Mindlin, Paula Rosalie retired reading educator
Miner, Mary Elizabeth Hubert retired secondary school educator
Moeckel, Bill Reid retired university dean
Monahan, Edward Charles academic administrator, marine science educator
Monson, David Carl school superintendent, farmer, state legislator
Moore, Thomas David academic administrator
Morgan, Mary Lou retired education educator, civic worker
Morgan, Ruth Prouse academic administrator, educator
Mortola, Edward Joseph academic administrator emeritus
Mosca, Christopher Patrick principal
Myers, Harold Mathews academic administrator
Nance, Mary Joe secondary education educator
Nelson, Edwin Clarence academic administrator, emeritus
Neunzig, Carolyn Miller elementary, middle and high school educator
Newman, Barbara Mae retired special education educator
Nichols, James Robbs university dean
Norman, Arlene Phyllis principal
Norris, Alfred Lloyd theological seminary president, clergyman
North, Anita secondary education educator
Null, Jack Elton schools superintendent
O'Connell, William Raymond, Jr. educational consultant
O'Donnell, Brother Frank Joseph principal
O'Driscoll, Marilyn Lutz elementary school educator
Oldham, Elaine Dorothea retired elementary and middle school educator
Oliveira, Mary Joyce middle school education educator
Olsen, John Richard education consultant
O'Malley, Thomas Patrick academic administrator
Orr, Kenneth Bradley academic administrator
Osnes, Pamela Grace special education educator
Palacio, Irene Elizabeth special education educator
Palmer, Irene Sabelberg university dean and educator emeritus, nurse, researcher, historian
Park, John Thornton academic administrator
Parrish, Alma Ellis elementary school educator
Patmos, Adrian Edward university dean emeritus
Patrick, John Franklin education educator
Patron, Nicholas Victor special education educator
Patterson, Mildred Lucas teaching specialist
Paulino, Sister Mary McAuley principal
Paulsen, Frank Robert college dean emeritus
Peavy, Sally Hudgins special education educator, diagnostician, school psychologist
Peebles, Ruth Addelle secondary education educator
Peoples, John Arthur, Jr. former university president, consultant
Perreault, Sister Jeanne college president
Perry, Raymond Carver education educator
Petoskey, Thomas W. secondary school educator
Pflaum, Susanna Whitney college dean
Pflueger, M(elba) Lee Counts academic administrator
Phelps, Deanne Elayne educational counselor, consultant
Pierce, Anne-Marie Bernheim private school administrator
Piper, Margarita Sherertz retired school administrator
Pippin, James Adrian, Jr. middle school educator
Pitrelli, Ellen Jane secondary school educator
Pizzuro, Salvatore Nicholas special education educator
Plane, Robert Allen academic administrator, chemistry educator, author
Platti, Rita Jane educator, draftsman, author, inventor
Polston, Barbara principal, educational psychologist
Potts, Sandra Dell elementary education educator
Pouncey, Peter Richard academic administrator, classics educator
Preston, Alda S. academic administrator, nursing educator
Preusser, Joseph William academic administrator
Prins, Robert Jack academic administrator
Pritchard, Claudius Hornby, Jr. retired university president
Prokasy, William Frederick academic administrator
Propst, Harold Dean retired academic administrator
Pryor, Harold S. retired college president
Quarles, Peggy Delores secondary school educator
Ramsey, Henry, Jr. university official, lawyer, retired judge
Ratcliff, James Lewis administrator
Ratliff, Lois L. secondary school educator
Rawdon, Cheryl Ann elementary school educator
Redmont, Bernard Sidney university dean, journalism educator
Reece, Geraldine Maxine elementary education educator
Reeves, Lucy Mary retired secondary school educator
Regn Fraher, Bonnie special education educator
Reid, Lorene Frances middle school educator
Reinke, Ralph Louis retired academic administrator
Remley, Audrey Wright retired educational administrator, psychologist
Renda, Rosa A. special education educator
Revor, Barbara Kay secondary school educator
Reynolds, Geneva B. special education educator
Reynolds, R. John university administrator
Rice, Gary Russell special education educator
Rice, Patricia Oppenheim Levin special education educator, consultant
Richardson, Elsie Helen retired elementary education educator
Riddle, Donald Husted former university chancellor
Riddle, James Douglass retired academic administrator
Riggs, Jacki Pieracci educational consultant
Riggs, Sonya Woicinski elementary school educator
Ritchie, Anne educational administrator
Roaden, Arliss Lloyd retired higher education executive director, former university president
Robbins, Frances Elaine educational administrator
Roberts, Francis Joy educational consultant
Roberts, Maura M. secondary school educator
Robertson, Mary Virginia retired elementary education educator
Robertson, Wyndham Gay university official
Robinson, James Arthur university president emeritus, political scientist
Rogers, Sharon J. education consultant
Roth, Evelyn Austin elementary school educator
Rotheim, Eleanor Sue elementary education specialist
Roulhac, Nellie Gordon retired special education educator
Russell, Attie Yvonne academic administrator, dean, pediatrics educator
Ryan, Daniel John university administrator
Ryan, Ione Jean Alohilani retired educator, counselor
Ryder, Georgia Atkins university dean, educator
Ryder, Jack McBride educational consultant
Rydz, John S. educator
Sanchez, Gilbert retired academic administrator, microbiologist, researcher
Scaffidi-Wilhelm, Gloria Angelamarie elementary education educator
Scandary, E. Jane special education educator, consultant
Schieffelin, George Richard educational consultant
Schleede, Lori Geraine primary education educator
Schmidt, Ruth Ann college president emerita
Schneider, Carolyn Alice Brauch elementary education educator
Scholl, Allan Henry retired school system administrator, education consultant
Schrage, Rose educational administrator
Schure, Alexander university chancellor
Schwartz, Eleanor Brantley academic administrator
Scollard, Diane Louise retired elementary school educator
Sessoms, Allen Lee academic administrator, former diplomat, physicist
Sestini, Virgil Andrew secondary education educator
Shagam, Marvin Hückel-Berri private school educator
Shanahan, Eileen Frances secondary education educator
Sharwell, William Gay retired university president and company executive
Shaw, Helen Lester Anderson university dean
Shearer, Charles Livingston academic administrator
Shelan, Debbie Levin travel agency administrator, school system administrator
Shellman-Lucas, Elizabeth C. special education educator, researcher
Sherman, Richard H. education educator
Shernoff, Elise Rubin special education educator
Shields, Rana Colleen special education educator
Shin, Edward Sung-Shik bilingual education educator
Sicuro, Natale Anthony academic and financial administrator, consultant
Silvius, Donald Joe educational consultant
Sinining, Vicente C. education educator
Siper, Cynthia Dawn special education educator
Skaggs, Bebe Rebecca Patten college dean, clergywoman
Snortland, Howard Jerome educational financial consultant
Snow, W. Sterling secondary education educator, retired sports coach
Sommer, Barbara school administrator
Sonnenschein, Hugo Freund academic administrator, economics educator
Southworth, Jamie MacIntyre education educator
Spain, Steve Randall secondary school educator
Speer, Max Michael special education educator
Spiesicke, Margrit Herma counselor
Spingola, Jeannie Saundra college, special education and adult educator, counselor
Stabile, Benedict Louis retired academic administrator, retired coast guard officer
Stacy, Bill Wayne academic administrator
Stark, Helen Morton secondary education educator
Starnes, Susan Smith elementary education educator
Stein, Dale Franklin retired university president
Steinberg, Joan Emily retired middle school educator
Stewart, Clinton Eugene adult education educator
Stewart, Dorothy K. educator, librarian
Stewart, John Ezell educational and business consultant
Stoddard, Edward John retired school superintendent
Stoker, Howard W. former education educator, educational administrator, consultant
Strangway, David William university president, geophysicist
Stuckey, Helenjean Lauterbach counselor educator
Stuckwisch, Clarence George retired university administrator
Surles, Carol D. university president
Sweetland, Annette Florence (Annie Sweetland) special education educator
Szelenyi, Ivan educator
Tanner, Laurel Nan education educator
Tarbi, William Rheinlander secondary education educator, curriculum consultant, educational technology researcher
Tenhoeve, Thomas academic administrator
Thompson, Raymond Eugene, Jr. education educator
Thorne, Barbara Lockwood guidance counselor, secondary education educator
Tonjes, Marian Jeannette Benton education educator
Tracanna, Kim elementary and secondary physical education educator
Trow, Jo Anne Johnson retired university official
Tuck, Russell R., Jr. former college president
Vandevender, Barbara Jewell elementary education educator, farmer
Van Solkema-Waitz, Terese Ellen special education educator, consultant
Volpe, Edmond L(oris) college president
Vorous, Margaret Estelle primary and secondary school educator
Wagner, Marilyn Faith elementary school educator
Wagoner, Geraldine Vander Pol music educator
Walker, Leroy Tashreau university chancellor, coach
Wallen, Lina Hambali educator, consultant
Ward, Lynda Sue Scoville special education educator, writer
Warder, Richard Currey, Jr. dean, mechanical aerospace engineering educator
Washington, Walter retired academic administrator
Waters, Donald Eugene academic administrator
Watkins, Cheryl Denise special education educator
Weaver, Charles Horace educator
Weimer, Gary W. academic administrator, consultant
Weiss, Bruce Jordan academic administrator
Weiss, Kenneth Jay education educator, reading specialist, administrator
Wendt, Marilynn Suzann elementary school educator, principal
West, Kathleen Shea special education educator, reading specialist
Wheeler, David Laurie university dean
White, Leslie Miles parochial school educator
Whitten, Dolphus, Jr. former university administrator, educational consortium executive
Wilks, Duffy Jean counselor, educator
Williams, James Orrin university administrator, educator
Williams-Monegain, Louise Joel science educator, administrator, retired
Wilson, Robin Scott university president, writer
Wittich, John Jacob retired college president, corporation consultant
Wong, David Yue academic administrator, physics educator
Woods, Phyllis Michalik elementary school educator
Workman, Kayleen Marie special education educator
Worthen, John Edward academic administrator
Wright, Connie Sue special education educator
Wrucke-Nelson, Ann C. elementary school educator
Wulf, Janie Scott McIlwaine gifted and talented education educator
Young, Margaret Chong elementary education educator
Young, Virgil M. education educator
Youngs, Diane Campfield learning disabilities specialist, educator
Zarzour, Robin Ann special education educator
Zeilinger, Elna Rae elementary educator, gifted-talented education educator
†Zilbert, Allen Bruce education educator, computer consultant
Zufryden, Fred S. academic administrator, marketing educator, researcher
Zuiches, James Joseph academic administrator

## ENGINEERING

### UNITED STATES

### ALABAMA

**Auburn**

Aldridge, Melvin Dayne electrical engineering educator
Cochran, John Euell, Jr. aerospace engineer, educator, lawyer
Irwin, John David electrical engineering educator
Jaeger, Richard Charles electrical engineer, educator, science center director
Rainer, Rex Kelly civil engineer, educator
Siginer, Dennis Aydeniz mechanical engineering educator, researcher
Turnquist, Paul Kenneth agricultural engineer, educator

**Birmingham**

Appleton, Joseph Hayne civil engineer, educator
Edmonds, William Fleming retired engineering and construction company executive
Goodrich, Thomas Michael engineering and construction executive, lawyer
Hidy, George Martel chemical engineer, executive

PROFESSIONAL INDEX 5159 ENGINEERING


MacKay, Jack Whiting *civil engineer*
Pitt, Robert Ervin *environmental engineer, educator*
Sain, Charles Haskell *civil engineer, surveyor*
Scott, Owen Myers, Jr. *nuclear engineer*
Szygenda, Stephen A. *electrical and computer engineering educator, researcher*

**Daphne**
Jeffreys, Elystan Geoffrey *geological engineer, petroleum consultant and appraiser*

**Elberta**
Brennan, Lawrence Edward *electronics engineer*

**Huntsville**
Adams, Gary Lee *engineering manager*
Balint, David Lee *engineering company executive*
Bramon, Christopher John *aerospace engineer*
Bridwell, G. Porter *aerospace engineer*
Buddington, Patricia Arrington *engineer*
Costes, Nicholas Constantine *aerospace technologist, government official*
Daussman, Grover Frederick *electrical engineer, consultant*
Douillard, Paul Arthur *engineering and financial executive, consultant*
Emerson, William Kary *engineering company executive*
Garriott, Owen Kay *astronaut, scientist*
Imtiaz, Kauser Syed *aerospace engineer*
Kim, Young Kil *aerospace engineer*
Kowel, Stephen Thomas *electrical engineer, educator*
Mc Donough, George Francis, Jr. *retired aerospace engineer, consultant*
Moore, Fletcher Brooks *engineering company executive*
Pastrick, Harold Lee *aeronautical engineer*
Pittman, William Claude *electrical engineer*
Polites, Michael Edward *aerospace engineer*
Potate, John Spencer, Sr. *engineering company executive, consultant*
Reddy, Thikkavarapu Ramachandra *electrical engineer*
Ritter, Alfred *aerospace consultant*
Russell, Lynn Darnell *engineering educator*
Schonberg, William Peter *aerospace, mechanical, civil engineering educator*
Schroer, Bernard Jon *industrial engineering educator*
Theisen, Russell Eugene *electrical engineer*
Watson, Raymond Coke, Jr. *engineering executive, academic administrator*
Wieland, Paul Otto *environmental control systems engineer*

**Loachapoka**
Schafer, Robert Louis *agricultural engineer, researcher*

**Madison**
Dannenberg, Konrad K. *aeronautical engineer*
Hawk, Clark Wiliams *mechanical engineering educator*

**Meridianville**
Hongsermeier, Martin Karl *software and systems architect, consultant*

**Mobile**
Hamid, Michael *electrical engineering educator, consultant*

**Montgomery**
Paddock, Austin Joseph *engineering executive*

**Pelham**
Miller, Edmond Trowbridge *civil engineer, educator, consultant*

**Point Clear**
Ferguson, Joseph Gantt *chemical engineer*

**Sheffield**
Badger, Phillip Charles *engineer*

**Shelby**
Jackson, Jimmy Lynn *engineer, consulting spectroscopist*

**Tuscaloosa**
Barfield, Robert F. *retired mechanical engineer, educator, dean*
Bryan, Colgan Hobson *aerospace engineering educator*
Doughty, Julian Orus *mechanical engineer, educator*
Frye, John H., Jr. *metallurgical engineering educator*
Griffin, Marvin Anthony *industrial engineer, educator*
Morley, Lloyd Albert *mining engineering educator*
Moynihan, Gary Peter *industrial engineering educator*

**Vernon**
Newell, Harold Joe *quality assurance engineer*

## ALASKA

**Anchorage**
Leman, Loren Dwight *civil engineer*
Thomas, Howard Paul *civil engineer, consultant*

**Fairbanks**
Behlke, Charles Edward *civil engineer, former university dean*
Bennett, Fred Lawrence *engineering educator*
Tilsworth, Timothy *retired environmental/civil engineering educator*

## ARIZONA

**Carefree**
Bergstrom, Richard Norman *civil engineer*

**Chandler**
Ratkowski, Donald J. *mechanical engineer, consultant*

**Flagstaff**
Somerville, Mason Harold *mechanical engineering educator, university dean*

**Fort Huachuca**
Weeks, Robert Lee *electronic engineer, program manager*

**Glendale**
Harris, Warren Lynn *development engineer*

**Mesa**
Backus, Charles Edward *engineering educator, researcher*
Baxter, Gene Kenneth *mechanical engineer, company executive*
Fairbanks, Harold Vincent *metallurgical engineer, educator*
Jackson, Andrew Edwin *engineering educator, researcher, aviator*
Joardar, Kuntal *electrical engineer*
Rummel, Robert Wiland *aeronautical engineer, author*
Tidwell, Joseph Paul, Jr. *systems safety engineer*

**Paradise Valley**
Russell, Paul Edgar *electrical engineering educator*

**Phoenix**
Bachus, Benson Floyd *mechanical engineer, consultant*
Burchard, John Kenneth *chemical engineer*
Chisholm, Tom Shepherd *environmental engineer*
Freyermuth, Clifford L. *structural engineering consultant*
Fullmer, Steven Mark *systems engineer*
Jorgensen, Gordon David *engineering company executive*
Miller, Michael Jon *survey engineer, local government manager*
Sochacki, Andrzej *mechanical engineer, researcher*
Stephenson, Frank Alex *environmental engineer, consultant*
Stine, George Harry *consulting engineer, author*
Thomas, Harold William *avionics systems engineer, flight instructor*
Watson, Harold George *engineering executive, mechanical engineer*
Ybarra, Kathryn Watrous *systems engineer*
Zeilinger, Philip Thomas *aeronautical engineer*

**Prescott**
Bieniawski, Zdzislaw Tadeusz Richard *engineering educator emeritus, writer, consultant*
Chesson, Eugene, Jr. *civil engineering educator, consultant*
Hasbrook, A. Howard *aviation safety engineer, consultant*
Kahne, Stephen James *systems engineer, educator, academic administrator, engineering executive*

**Prescott Valley**
Wynn, Robert Raymond *retired engineer, consultant*

**Rio Verde**
Jordan, Richard Charles *engineering executive*

**Scottsdale**
Blackburn, Jack Bailey *retired civil engineering educator*
Bodensieck, Ernest Justus *mechanical engineer*
Fisher, John Richard *engineering consultant, former naval officer*
Gookin, Thomas Allen Jaudon *civil engineer*
Kline, Arthur Jonathan *retired electronics engineer*
Leeland, Steven Brian *electronics engineer*
Leeser, David O. *materials engineer, metallurgist*
Roberts, Peter Christopher Tudor *engineering executive*

**Sedona**
Silvern, Leonard Charles *retired engineering executive*

**Sun City**
Fitch, W. Chester *industrial engineer*

**Sun City West**
Woodruff, Neil Parker *agricultural engineer*

**Sun Lakes**
Richardson, Robert Carleton *engineering consultant*

**Tempe**
Akers, Lex A. *engineering educator*
Balanis, Constantine Apostle *electrical engineering educator*
Berman, Neil Sheldon *chemical engineering educator*
Carpenter, Ray Warren *materials scientist and engineer, educator*
Ferreira, Jay Michael *mechanical engineer*
Ferry, David Keane *electrical engineering educator*
Karady, George Gyorgy *electrical engineering educator, consultant*
Kaufman, Irving *retired engineering educator*
Laananen, David Horton *mechanical engineer, educator*
Mense, Allan Tate *research and development engineering executive*
Schroder, Dieter Karl *electrical engineering educator*
Shaw, Milton Clayton *mechanical engineering educator*
Singhal, Avinash Chandra *engineering administrator, educator*
Zhang, Yong-Hang *electrical engineering educator*

**Tonopah**
Brittingham, James Calvin *nuclear engineer*

**Tucson**
Arnell, Walter James William *mechanical engineering educator, consultant*
Bryan, Gordon Redman, Jr. *nuclear power engineering consultant*
Chen, Chuan Fang *mechanical engineering educator*
Desai, Chandrakant S. *civil engineering and engineering mechanics educator*
Ganapol, Barry Douglas *nuclear engineering educator, consultant*
Gross, Joseph Francis *retired bio-engineering educator*
Harrington, Roger Fuller *electrical engineering educator, consultant*
Hunt, Bobby Ray *electrical engineering educator, consultant*
Jones, Roger Clyde *retired electrical engineering educator*
Kececioglu, Dimitri Basil *reliability engineering educator, consultant*
Kerwin, William James *electrical engineering educator, consultant*
Kinney, Robert Bruce *mechanical engineering educator*
Mitchell, Robert Campbell *nuclear consultant*
Nordby, Gene Milo *engineering educator*
Post, Roy Grayson *nuclear engineering educator*
Prince, John Luther, III *engineering educator*
Renard, Kenneth George *civil engineer*
Sears, William Rees *engineering educator*
Slack, Donald Carl *agricultural engineer, educator*
Speas, Robert Dixon *aeronautical engineer, aviation company executive*
Tellington, Wentworth Jordan *engineer*
Wait, James Richard *electrical engineering educator, scientist*
Zeigler, Bernard Phillip *electrical and computer engineering educator*

**Youngtown**
Gross, Al *electrical engineer, consultant*

## ARKANSAS

**Bella Vista**
Thompson, William Dennison, Jr. *aeronautical consultant*

**Fayetteville**
Andrews, John Frank *civil and environmental engineering educator*
Gaddy, James Leoma *chemical engineer, educator*
LeFevre, Elbert Walter, Jr. *civil engineering educator*

**Hot Springs Village**
Wennerstrom, Arthur John *aeronautical engineer*

**Little Rock**
Hocott, Joe Bill *chemical engineer*

## CALIFORNIA

**Alamo**
More, Vishwas *engineering laboratory administrator*

**Alpine**
Roberts, Dwight Loren *engineering consultant*

**Alta Loma**
Cooper, George Robert *electrical engineer, educator*

**Altadena**
Coles, Donald Earl *aeronautics educator, retired*

**Anaheim**
Brofman, Woody *astronautical engineer, educator*
Uyehara, Otto Arthur *mechanical engineering educator emeritus, consultant*

**Arcadia**
Barney, Kline Porter, Jr. *retired engineering company executive, consultant*
Broderick, Donald Leland *electronics engineer*
Massier, Paul Ferdinand *mechanical engineer*

**Atherton**
Rosen, Charles Abraham *electrical engineer, consultant*

**Belmont**
Hollis, Mary Frances *aerospace educator*

**Berkeley**
Angelakos, Diogenes James *electrical engineering educator*
Berger, Stanley Allan *mechanical engineering educator*
Birdsall, Charles Kennedy *electrical engineer*
Bogy, David B(eauregard) *mechanical engineering educator*
Cairns, Elton James *chemical engineering educator*
Chopra, Anil Kumar *civil engineering educator*
Denn, Morton Mace *chemical engineering educator*
Desoer, Charles Auguste *electrical engineer*
Dornfeld, David Alan *engineering educator*
Finnie, Iain *mechanical engineer, educator*
Frisch, Joseph *mechanical engineer, educator, consultant*
Fuerstenau, Douglas Winston *mineral engineering educator*
Garrison, William Louis *civil engineering educator*
Goldsmith, Werner *mechanical engineering educator*
Grossman, Lawrence Morton *nuclear engineering educator*
Harris, Guy Hendrickson *chemical research engineer*
Hodges, David Albert *electrical engineering educator*
Hsu, Chieh Su *applied mechanics engineering educator, researcher*
Hu, Chenming *electrical engineering educator*
Jewell, William Sylvester *engineering educator*
Kastenberg, William Edward *engineering and applied science educator*
Koshland, Catherine Preston *mechanical engineer, educator*
Kuh, Ernest Shiu-Jen *electrical engineering educator*
Laitone, Edmund Victor *mechanical engineer*
Leitmann, George *mechanical engineering educator*
Lewis, Edwin Reynolds *biomedical engineering educator*
Lieberman, Michael A. *electrical engineer, educator*
Maron, Melvin Earl *engineer, philosopher, educator*
Monismith, Carl Leroy *civil engineering educator*
Mote, Clayton Daniel, Jr. *mechanical engineer, educator, administrator*
Muller, Richard Stephen *electrical engineer, educator*
Newman, John Scott *chemical engineer, educator*
Ott, David Michael *engineering company executive*
Pagni, Patrick John *mechanical and fire safety engineering science educator*
Pask, Joseph Adam *ceramic engineering educator*
Penzien, Joseph *structural engineering educator*
Polak, Elijah *engineering educator, computer scientist*
Popov, Egor Paul *engineering educator*
Prausnitz, John Michael *chemical engineer, educator*
Schlueter, Erika Manriquez *civil engineer research scientist*
Schwarz, Steven E. *electrical engineering educator, administrator*
Scordelis, Alexander Costicas *civil engineering educator*
Susskind, Charles *engineering educator, author, publishing executive*
Whinnery, John Roy *electrical engineering educator*
White, Richard Manning *electrical engineering educator*
Wiegel, Robert Louis *consulting engineering executive*
Zwoyer, Eugene Milton *consulting engineering executive*

**Calabasas**
Chiang, Albert Chin-Liang *electrical engineer*

**Camarillo**
Lam, Cheung-Wei *electrical engineer*

**Cambria**
DuFresne, Armand Frederick *retired management and engineering consultant*

**Campbell**
Ross, Hugh Courtney *electrical engineer*
Wu, William Lung-Shen (You-Ming Wu) *aerospace medical engineering design specialist, foreign intelligence analyst*

**Canoga Park**
Olson, Paul S. *nuclear engineer*

**Capitola**
Barna, Arpad Alex *electrical engineering consultant*

**Carmel**
Alsberg, Dietrich Anselm *electrical engineer*

**Carmichael**
Zickel, John *mechanical engineering educator*

**Carson**
Karkia, Mohammad Reza *energy engineer, educator*

**Cayucos**
Theurer, Byron W. *aerospace engineer, business owner*

**Chatsworth**
Levine, Arnold Milton *retired electrical engineer, documentary filmmaker*

**Chico**
Allen, Charles William *mechanical engineering educator*

**Chula Vista**
Wolk, Martin *electronic engineer, physicist*

**Claremont**
Dym, Clive Lionel *engineering educator*
Molinder, John Irving *engineering educator, consultant*
Monson, James Edward *electrical engineer, educator*
Phillips, John Richard *engineering educator*
Tanenbaum, Basil Samuel *engineering educator*

**Concord**
Cassidy, John Joseph *hydraulic and hydrologic engineer*
Lee, Low Kee *electronics engineer, consultant*

**Corona**
Tillman, Joseph Nathaniel *engineering executive*

**Corona Del Mar**
Richmond, Ronald LeRoy *aerospace engineer*

**Coronado**
Crilly, Eugene Richard *engineering consultant*

**Costa Mesa**
Buchtel, Michael Eugene *optical mechanical engineer*

**Culver City**
Sensiper, Samuel *consulting electrical engineer*

**Cupertino**
Fenn, Raymond Wolcott, Jr. *retired metallurgical engineer*
Lindsay, Leslie *packaging engineer*

**Dana Point**
Furst, Raymond Bruce *engineer, consultant*

**Danville**
Maninger, R(alph) Carroll *engineering executive, consultant*
Trezek, George James *mechanical engineer*

**Davis**
Akesson, Norman Berndt *agricultural engineer, emeritus educator*
Beadle, Charles Wilson *retired mechanical engineering educator*
Brandt, Harry *mechanical engineering educator*
Chancellor, William Joseph *agricultural engineering educator*
Cheney, James Addison *civil engineering educator*
Dorf, Richard Carl *electrical engineering and management educator*
Fridley, Robert Bruce *agricultural engineering educator*
Gardner, William Allen *electrical engineering educator*
Gates, Bruce Clark *chemical engineer, educator*
Ghausi, Mohammed Shuaib *electrical engineering educator, university dean*
Hakimi, S. Louis *electrical and computer engineering educator*
Kepner, Robert Allen *agricultural engineering researcher, educator*

Krener, Arthur J. *systems engineering educator*
Krone, Ray Beyers *civil and environmental engineering educator, consultant*
Larock, Bruce Edward *civil engineering educator*
Laub, Alan John *engineering educator*
Levy, Bernard C. *electrical engineer, educator*
Tchobanoglous, George *civil engineering educator*
Wang, Shih-Ho *electrical engineer, educator*

**Del Mar**
Wilkinson, Eugene Parks *nuclear engineer*

**Diamond Bar**
Mirisola, Lisa Heinemann *air quality engineer*

**Dinuba**
Leps, Thomas MacMaster *civil engineer, consultant*

**Downey**
Baumann, Theodore Robert *aerospace engineer, consultant, army officer*
Demarchi, Ernest Nicholas *aerospace engineering executive*

**Duarte**
Chou, Chung-Kwang *bio-engineer*

**Edwards**
Elkins, Thomas Arthur *computer engineer*
Garcia, Andrew B. *chemical engineer*

**El Dorado Hills**
Huppert, Merle Cecil *mechanical engineer*

**El Segundo**
Chang, I-Shih *aerospace engineer*
Lantz, Norman Foster *electrical engineer*
Lotrick, Joseph *aeronautical engineer*
Mackey, Wayne Allison *electrical engineer*
Mitchell, John Noyes, Jr. *electrical engineer*
Mo, Roger Shih-Yah *electronics engineering manager*
Nguyen, Tien Manh *communications systems engineer*

**Encinitas**
Coler, Myron A(braham) *chemical engineer, educator*
Frank, Michael Victor *risk assessment engineer*
Morrow, Charles Tabor *aerospace consulting engineer*

**Encino**
Acheson, Louis Kruzan, Jr. *aerospace engineer and systems analyst*
Friedman, George Jerry *aerospace company executive, engineer*
Knuth, Eldon Luverne *engineering educator*

**Escondido**
Ghandhi, Sorab Khushro *electrical engineering educator*
Grew, Raymond Edward *mechanical engineer*

**Fair Oaks**
Agerbek, Sven *mechanical engineer*
Smiley, Robert William *industrial engineer*

**Folsom**
Ettlich, William F. *electrical engineer*

**Foster City**
Ham, Lee Edward *civil engineer*

**Fremont**
Le, Thuy Trong *research and development engineer, educator*
Wu, James Chen-Yuan *aerospace engineering educator*

**Fresno**
Brahma, Chandra Sekhar *civil engineering educator*

**Fullerton**
Lieberman, Paul *aeronautical engineer, engineering research company executive*
Tehrani, Fleur Taher *electrical engineer, educator, researcher*
Tuazon, Jesus Ocampo *electrical engineer, educator, consultant*

**Glendale**
Knoop, Vern Thomas *civil engineer, consultant*

**Glendora**
Ahern, John Edward *mechanical engineer, consultant*

**Greenbrae**
Elder, Rex Alfred *civil engineer*

**Hacienda Heights**
Love, Daniel Joseph *consulting engineer*

**Hawthorne**
Burns, Brent Emil *electrical engineer*
McRuer, Duane Torrance *aerospace engineering executive*

**Hayward**
Hunnicutt, Richard Pearce *metallurgical engineer*

**Hercules**
Emmanuel, Jorge Agustin *chemical engineer, environmental consultant*

**Hermosa Beach**
McDowell, Edward R. H. *chemical engineer*

**Huntington Beach**
Hildebrant, Andy McClellan *retired electrical engineer*
Nowlan, Daniel Ralph *engineering executive*

**Irvine**
Ang, Alfredo Hua-Sing *civil engineering educator*
Bershad, Neil Jeremy *electrical engineering educator*
Guymon, Gary LeRoy *civil engineering educator, consultant*
Hess, Cecil Fernando *engineering executive*
Kinsman, Robert Preston *biomedical plastics engineer*
McCraw, Leslie G. *engineering and construction company executive*
Orme, Melissa Emily *mechanical engineering educator*
Pluta, Stanley John *manufacturing project engineer*
Samueli, Henry *electrical engineering educator*
Sirignano, William Alfonso *aerospace and mechanical engineer, educator*
Sklansky, Jack *electrical and computer engineering educator, researcher*
Stubberud, Allen Roger *electrical engineering educator*
Walen, James Robert *engineering specialist*

**Kensington**
Oppenheim, Antoni Kazimierz *mechanical engineer*

**La Jolla**
Chang, William Shen Chie *electrical engineering educator*
Chien, Shu *physiology and bioengineering educator*
Conn, Robert William *engineering science educator*
Counts, Stanley Thomas *aerospace consultant, retired naval officer, retired electronics company executive*
Fung, Yuan-Cheng Bertram *bioengineering educator, author*
Helstrom, Carl Wilhelm *electrical engineering educator*
Levy, Ralph *engineering executive, consultant*
Milstein, Laurence Bennett *electrical engineering educator, researcher*
Penner, Stanford Solomon *engineering educator*
Rudee, Mervyn Lea *engineering educator, researcher*
Schmid-Schoenbein, Geert Wilfried *biomedical engineer, educator*
Simnad, Massoud T. *engineering educator*
Skalak, Richard *engineering mechanics educator, researcher*
Streichler, Jerry *industrial engineer, consultant company executive*
Sung, Kuo-Li Paul *bioengineering educator*
Williams, Forman Arthur *engineering science educator, combustion theorist*

**Lafayette**
Peirano, Lawrence Edward *civil engineer*

**Laguna Beach**
Kramarsic, Roman Joseph *engineering consultant*
Lurie, Harold *engineer, lawyer*

**Laguna Hills**
Green, Leon, Jr. *mechanical engineer*
Larson, Harry Thomas *electronics engineer, executive, consultant*
Lederer, Jerome *aerospace safety engineer, educator*

**Laguna Niguel**
Born, Robert Heywood *consulting civil engineer*

**Lake Forest**
Sheehy, Jerome Joseph *electrical engineer*

**Lancaster**
Hodges, Vernon Wray *mechanical engineer*

**Livermore**
Carley, James French *chemical and plastics engineer*
Jarnagan, Harry William, Jr. *project control manager*
Johnson, Roy Ragnar *electrical engineer*
King, Ray John *electrical engineer*
Sebasco, Salvador Monastra *safety engineer*
Sheem, Sang Keun *fiber optics engineering professional*

**Long Beach**
Brent, Paul Leslie *mechanical engineering educator*
de Soto, Simon *mechanical engineer*
Dillon, Michael Earl *engineering executive, mechanical engineer, educator*
Donald, Eric Paul *aeronautical engineer, inventor*
Kumar, Rajendra *electrical engineering educator*
Pugay, Jeffrey Ibanez *mechanical engineer*
Raiklen, Harold *aerospace engineering consultant*
Thorn, James Douglas *safety engineer*
Wiberg, Donald Martin *electrical engineering educator, consultant*

**Los Altos**
Bell, Chester Gordon *computer engineering company executive*
Bergrun, Norman Riley *aerospace executive*
Fondahl, John Walker *civil engineering educator*
Hecker, Michael Hanns Louis *electrical engineer, speech scientist*
Kazan, Benjamin *research engineer*
Moll, John Lewis *electronics engineer, retired*
Peterson, Victor Lowell *aerospace engineer, management consultant*
Sharpe, Roland Leonard *engineering company executive, earthquake and structural engineering consultant*

**Los Angeles**
Abdou, Mohamed A. *mechanical, aerospace, and nuclear engineering educator*
Alwan, Abeer Abdul-Hussain *electrical engineering educator*
Ayres, James Marx *mechanical engineer*
Blackwelder, Ron Forest *engineering educator, consultant, researcher*
Breuer, Melvin Allen *electrical engineering educator*
Bucy, Richard Snowden *aerospace engineering and mathematics educator, consultant*
Charwat, Andrew Franciszek *engineering educator*
Cheng, Hsien Kei *aeronautics educator*
Cheng, Tsen-Chung *electrical engineering educator*
Chobotov, Vladimir Alexander *aerospace engineer, educator*
Crombie, Douglass Darnill *aerospace communications system engineer*
Cross, Glenn Laban *engineering executive, development planner*
Delnik, Alexander *engineering executive, business consultant*
Dhir, Vijay K. *mechanical engineering educator*
†Dorman, Albert A. *consulting engineer executive, architect*
Dougherty, Elmer Lloyd, Jr. *retired chemical engineering educator, consultant*
Friedlander, Sheldon Kay *chemical engineering educator*
Friedmann, Peretz Peter *aerospace engineer, educator*
Ghil, Michael *atmospheric scientist, geophysicist*
Handy, Lyman Lee *petroleum engineer, chemist, educator*
Holman, Tomlinson *engineer, film educator*
Hovanessian, Shahen Alexander *electrical engineer, educator*
Incaudo, Joseph August *engineering company executive*
Itoh, Tatsuo *engineering educator*
Johnston, Roy G. *consulting structural engineer*
Karplus, Walter J. *engineering educator*
Kuehl, Hans Henry *electrical engineering educator*
Kumar, Anil *nuclear engineer*
Leal, George D. *engineering company executive*
Lehovec, Kurt *electrical engineering educator*
Li, Victor On-Kwok *electrical engineering educator*
Lin, Tung Hua *civil engineering educator*
MacKenzie, John Douglas *engineering educator*
Marmarelis, Vasilis Zissis *engineering educator, author, consultant*
Martin, J(ohn) Edward *architectural engineer*
Maxworthy, Tony *mechanical and aerospace engineering educator*
Meecham, William Coryell *engineering educator*
Mendel, Jerry Marc *electrical engineering educator*
Mortensen, Richard Edgar *engineering educator*
Muntz, Eric Phillip *aerospace engineering and radiology educator, consultant*
Nadler, Gerald *engineering educator, management consultant*
Nobe, Ken *chemical engineering educator*
Okrent, David *engineering educator*
Orchard, Henry John *electrical engineer*
Perkins, Gladys Patricia *retired aerospace engineer*
Perrine, Richard Leroy *environmental engineering educator*
Perry, Robert Michael *consulting engineering company executive*
Philpott, Lindsey *civil engineer, researcher, educator*
Portenier, Walter James *aerospace engineer*
Ramo, Simon *engineering executive*
Rauch, Lawrence Lee *aerospace and electrical engineer, educator*
Raymond, Arthur Emmons *aerospace engineer*
Rubinstein, Moshe Fajwel *engineering educator*
Safonov, Michael George *electrical engineering educator, consultant*
Scholtz, Robert Arno *electrical engineering educator*
Schumacher, Joseph Charles *chemical engineer*
Seide, Paul *civil engineering educator*
Wagner, Christian Nikolaus Johann *materials engineering educator*
Weber, Charles L. *electrical engineering educator*
Welch, Lloyd Richard *electrical engineering educator, communications consultant*
Willner, Alan Eli *electrical engineer, educator*
Yeh, William Wen-Gong *civil engineering educator*
Yen, Teh Fu *civil and environmental engineering educator*

**Los Gatos**
Naymark, Sherman *consulting nuclear engineer*
Rosenheim, Donald Edwin *electrical engineer*

**Los Osos**
Cloonan, Clifford B. *electrical engineer, educator*

**Manhattan Beach**
Bradburn, David Denison *engineer, retired air force officer*
Ricardi, Leon Joseph *electrical engineer*

**Menlo Park**
Edson, William Alden *electrical engineer*
Honey, Richard Churchill *retired electrical engineer*
Kohne, Richard Edward *retired engineering executive*
McCarthy, Roger Lee *mechanical engineer*
Nell, Janine Marie *metallurgical and materials engineer*
Ross, Bernard *engineering consultant, educator*

**Milpitas**
McDonald, Mark Douglas *electrical engineer*
Mian, Guo *electrical engineer*
Mittal, Manmohan *electronic design automation engineer*
Wang, Huai-Liang William *mechanical engineer*

**Mission Hills**
Cramer, Frank Brown *engineering executive, combustion engineer, systems consultant*

**Mission Viejo**
Pohl, John Henning *chemical engineer, consultant*

**Moffett Field**
Kerr, Andrew W. *aerodynamics researcher*
McCroskey, William James *aeronautical engineer*
Statler, Irving Carl *aerospace engineer*

**Monterey**
Butler, Jon Terry *computer engineering educator, researcher*
Marto, Paul James *retired mechanical engineering educator, consultant, researcher*
Newberry, Conrad Floyde *aerospace engineering educator*
Newton, Robert Eugene *mechanical engineering educator*

**Monterey Park**
Waiter, Serge-Albert *retired civil engineer*

**Moorpark**
Bahn, Gilbert Schuyler *retired mechanical engineer, researcher*

**Morgan Hill**
Johnson, Noel Lars *biomedical engineer*

**Newport Beach**
Sheppard, William Vernon *engineering and construction executive*

**Norco**
Lu, Guiyang *electrical engineer*

**Northridge**
Bekir, Nagwa Esmat *electrical engineer, educator, consultant*
Bradshaw, Richard Rotherwood *engineering executive*
Jakobsen, Jakob Knudsen *mechanical engineer*
Kiddoo, Robert James *engineering service company executive*
Rengarajan, Sembiam Rajagopal *electrical engineering educator, researcher, consultant*
Stout, Thomas Melville *control systems engineer*
Torgow, Eugene N. *electrical engineer*

**Oakland**
Brown, Stephen Lawrence *environmental consultant*
King, Cary Judson, III *chemical engineer, educator, university official*
Liang, Junxiang *aeronautics and astronautics engineer, educator*
Tsztoo, David Fong *civil engineer*

**Occidental**
Rumsey, Victor Henry *electrical engineering educator emeritus*

**Ontario**
Johnson, Maurice Verner, Jr. *agricultural research and development executive*

**Orange**
Fisk, Edward Ray *civil engineer, author, educator*
Vasudevan, Ramaswami *engineering consultant*

**Pacific Palisades**
Herman, Elvin E. *retired consulting electronic engineer*

**Palmdale**
Moule, William Nelson *electrical engineer*
Weiss, Richard Ronald *rocket propulsion technology executive*

**Palo Alto**
Brown, David Randolph *electrical engineer*
Cohen, Karl Paley *nuclear energy consultant*
Culler, Floyd LeRoy, Jr. *chemical engineer*
Eliassen, Rolf *environmental engineer, emeritus educator*
Hodge, Philip Gibson, Jr. *mechanical and aerospace engineering educator*
Johnson, Conor Deane *mechanical engineer*
Kino, Gordon Stanley *electrical engineering educator*
Lender, Adam *electrical engineer*
Partain, Larry Dean *solar research engineer*
Szczerba, Victor Bogdan *electrical engineer, sales engineer*
Taylor, John Joseph *nuclear engineer*
Thompson, David Alfred *industrial engineer*
Wilson, Frank Henry *electrical engineer*
Wong, Patrick Seck Lai *chemical engineer*

**Palos Verdes Peninsula**
Mirels, Harold *aerospace engineer*
Raue, Jorg Emil *electrical engineer*
Rechtin, Eberhardt *retired aerospace executive, retired educator*
Spinks, John Lee *retired engineering executive*
Waaland, Irving Theodore *retired aerospace design executive*
Weiss, Herbert Klemm *retired aeronautical engineer*

**Paradise**
Learned, Vincent Roy *electrical engineer , educator*

**Pasadena**
Boulos, Paul Fares *civil and environmental engineer*
Breckinridge, James Bernard *optical science engineer*
Bridges, William Bruce *electrical engineer, researcher, educator*
Carroll, William Jerome *civil engineer*
Cass, Glen Rowan *environmental engineer*
Dallas, Saterios (Sam ) *aerospace engineer, researcher, consultant*
Farr, Donald Eugene *engineering scientist*
Flagan, Richard Charles *chemical engineering educator*
Gavalas, George R. *chemical engineering educator*
Gould, Roy Walter *engineering educator*
Hatheway, Alson Earle *mechanical engineer*
Hemann, Raymond Glenn *research company executive*
Hilbert, Robert S(aul) *optical engineer*
Hirsch, Robert W. *engineering and construction company executive*
Hornung, Hans Georg *aeronautical engineering educator, science facility administrator*
Housner, George William *civil engineering educator, consultant*
Hudson, Donald Ellis *engineering educator*
Jacobs, Joseph John *engineering company executive*
Jennings, Paul Christian *civil engineering educator, academic administrator*
Knauss, Wolfgang Gustav *engineering educator*
Knowles, James Kenyon *applied mechanics educator*
List, Ericson John *environmental engineering science educator, engineering consultant*
Losh, Samuel Johnston *engineering administrator*
Martin, Craig Lee *engineering company executive*
McLaughlin, William Irving *aerospace engineer*
Otoshi, Tom Yasuo *electrical engineer, consultant*
Poon, Peter Tin-Yau *engineer, physicist*
Presecan, Nicholas Lee *environmental and civil engineer, consultant*
Sabersky, Rolf Heinrich *mechanical engineer*
Schlinger, Warren Gleason *retired chemical engineer*
Schober, Robert Charles *electrical engineer*
Seinfeld, John Hersh *chemical engineering educator*
Simon, Marvin Kenneth *electrical engineer, consultant*
Stewart, Homer Joseph *engineering educator*
Trussell, R(obert) Rhodes *environmental engineer*
Vanoni, Vito August *hydraulic engineer*
Weisbin, Charles Richard *nuclear engineer*
Wood, Lincoln Jackson *aerospace engineer*
Yamarone, Charles Anthony, Jr. *aerospace engineer, consultant*
Yariv, Amnon *electrical engineering educator, scientist*
Yeh, Paul Pao *electrical and electronics engineer, educator*

**Penn Valley**
Throner, Guy Charles, Jr. *engineering executive, scientist, engineer, inventor, consultant*

**Pismo Beach**
Saveker, David Richard naval and marine architectural engineering executive

**Placerville**
Morrin, Thomas Harvey engineering research company executive

**Playa Del Rey**
Tai, Frank aerospace engineering consultant

**Pleasanton**
Murthy, Srinivasa K. engineering corporation executive

**Pomona**
Armstrong, Bruce Irving mechanical engineer
Teague, Lavette Cox, Jr. systems educator, consultant

**Rancho Mirage**
Copperman, William H. value engineer, consultant

**Rancho Santa Fe**
Gunness, Robert Charles chemical engineer

**Redondo Beach**
Buchta, Edmund engineering executive
Chazen, Melvin Leonard chemical engineer
Cohen, Clarence Budd aerospace engineer
Hughes, James Arthur electrical engineer
Sackheim, Robert Lewis aerospace engineer, educator

**Ridgecrest**
Pearson, John mechanical engineer

**Riverside**
Allan, David R. safety engineer
Beni, Gerardo electrical and computer engineering educator, robotics scientist
Miskus, Michael Anthony electrical engineer
Mohanty, Binayak Prasad environmental engineer, hydrologist

**Rohnert Park**
Lord, Harold Wilbur electrical engineer, electronics consultant

**Rolling Hills Estates**
Wong, Sun Yet engineering consultant

**Roseville**
Folsom, Richard Gilman retired mechanical engineer and academic administrator, consultant

**Ross**
Scott, John Walter chemical engineer, research management executive

**Sacramento**
Bezzone, Albert Paul structural engineer
Cavigli, Henry James petroleum engineer
Collins, William Leroy telecommunications engineer
Crimmins, Philip Patrick metallurgical engineer, lawyer
Forsyth, Raymond Arthur civil engineer
Lathi, Bhagawandas Pannalal electrical engineering educator
Mujumdar, Vilas Sitaram structural engineer, management executive
Simeroth, Dean Conrad chemical engineer
Unde, Madhavji Anant (Mark Unde) welding specialist

**San Bernardino**
Bauer, Steven Michael cost containment engineer
French, Kirby Allan transportation engineer, computer programmer
Holtz, Tobenette aerospace engineer

**San Carlos**
Symons, Robert Spencer electronics engineer
True, Richard Brownell electrical engineer

**San Clemente**
White, Stanley Archibald research electrical engineer

**San Diego**
Airst, Malcolm Jeffrey electronics engineer
Anderson, Karl Richard aerospace engineer, consultant
Anderson, Paul Maurice electrical engineering educator, researcher, consultant
Beyster, John Robert engineering company executive
†Brown, Alan J. electrical engineer
Burke, Arthur Thomas engineering consultant
Butler, Geoffrey Scott systems engineer, educator, consultant
†Chang, Daniel Haiming engineering executive
Chen, Kao consulting electrical engineer
Conly, John Franklin engineering educator, researcher
Dabiri, Ali mechanical engineer, researcher
Dean, Richard Anthony mechanical engineer, engineering executive
Fernandez, Fernando Lawrence aeronautical engineer, research company executive
Gray, Gavin Campbell, II computer information engineer, computer consultant
Gross, Jeffrey software engineer
Hanson, Wendy Karen chemical engineer
Hills, Linda Launey advisory systems engineer
Hoyt, Jack Wallace engineering educator
Inoue, Michael Shigeru industrial engineer, electrical engineer
Lin, Yeou-Lin engineer, consultant
Marple, Stanley Lawrence, Jr. electrical engineer, signal processing researcher
Paget, John Arthur mechanical engineer
St. Clair, Hal Kay electrical engineer
Schaefer, Michael Jude industrial control systems engineer
Sell, Robert Emerson electrical engineer
Sesonske, Alexander nuclear and chemical engineer
Slate, John Butler biomedical engineer
Smith, Steven Cole engineering process consultant
Tricoles, Gus Peter electromagnetics engineer, physicist, consultant
Viterbi, Andrew James electrical engineering and computer science educator, business executive
Youngs, Jack Marvin cost engineer

**San Dimas**
Lau, Henry mechanical engineer, consultant

**San Fernando**
Yuan, Sidney Wei Kwun cryogenic engineer, consultant

**San Francisco**
Angell, James Browne electrical engineering educator
Bechtel, Riley Peart engineering company executive
Bechtel, Stephen Davison, Jr. engineering company executive
Brooks, William George aeronautical engineer
Cheng, Kwong Man structural engineer
Cheng, Wan-Lee mechanical engineer, industrial technology educator
Chu, Kuang-Han structural engineer, educator
Danziger, Bruce Edward structural engineer
Dolby, Ray Milton engineering company executive, electrical engineer
Gerwick, Ben Clifford, Jr. construction engineer, educator
Gulbenkian, Paul civil engineer, inventor
Keller, Edward Lowell electrical engineer, educator
Koffel, Martin M. engineering company executive
Lin, Tung Yen civil engineer, educator
Lolli, Andrew Ralph industrial engineer, retired army officer
Luft, Rene Wilfred civil engineer
Marshall, John Paul broadcast engineer
Mattern, Douglas James electronics reliability engineer
Park, U. Young nuclear engineer
Shor, Samuel Wendell Williston naval engineer
Shushkewich, Kenneth Wayne structural engineer
Smith, Bernard Joseph Connolly civil engineer
Wrona, Peter Alexander structural engineer
Yuan, Shao Wen aerospace engineer, educator

**San Jose**
Adams, William John, Jr. mechanical engineer
Huang, Francis Fu-Tse mechanical engineering educator
Israel, Paul Neal computer design engineer, author
Jacobson, Albert Herman, Jr. industrial and systems engineer, educator
Kirk, Donald Evan electrical engineering educator, dean
Montgomery, Leslie David biomedical engineer, cardiovascular physiologist
Moody, Frederick Jerome mechanical engineer, consultant thermal hydraulics
Morimoto, Carl Noboru computer system engineer, crystallographer
Parruck, Bidyut electrical engineer
Shaw, Charles Alden engineering executive
Valentine, Ralph Schuyler chemical engineer, research director
Woytowitz, Peter John mechanical engineer

**San Juan Capistrano**
Chang, Zhao Hua biomedical engineer

**San Luis Obispo**
Cummings, Russell Mark aerospace engineer, educator
Hasslein, George Johann architectural educator
Hoffmann, Jon Arnold aeronautical engineer, educator

**San Marcos**
Jeffredo, John Victor aerospace engineer, manufacturing company executive, inventor
Maggay, Isidore, III engineering executive, food processing engineer

**San Marino**
Smith, Apollo Milton Olin retired aerodynamics engineer

**San Pedro**
Ellis, George Edwin, Jr. chemical engineer
McCarty, Frederick Briggs electrical engineer

**San Ramon**
Schlitt, William Joseph, III metallurgical engineer

**Santa Ana**
Amoroso, Frank retired communication system engineer, consultant
Bauer, Bruce F. aerospace engineer
Kelly, James Patrick, Jr. retired engineering and construction executive
Schuller, Eddie engineering executive
Tu, John engineering executive
Zabsky, John Mitchell engineering executive

**Santa Barbara**
Chmelka, Bradley Floyd chemical engineering educator
Coldren, Larry Allen engineering educator, consultant
Crispin, James Hewes engineering and construction company executive
Fredrickson, Glenn Harold chemical engineering and materials educator
Gilbert, Paul Thomas chemical development engineer
Hedgepeth, John M(ills) aerospace engineer, mathematician, engineering executive
Iselin, Donald Grote civil engineering and management consultant
Kokotovic, Petar V. electrical and computer engineer, educator
Kramer, Edward John materials science and engineering educator
Kroemer, Herbert electrical engineer, educator, computer engineer, educator
Lawrance, Charles Holway civil and sanitary engineer
Leal, Leslie Gary chemical engineering educator
Lee, Hua electrical engineering educator
Mitra, Sanjit Kumar electrical and computer engineering educator
Russell, Charles Roberts chemical engineer
Wade, Glen electrical engineer, educator
Weinberg, William Henry chemical engineer, chemical physicist, educator
Wooldridge, Dean Everett engineering executive, scientist

**Santa Clara**
Chan, Shu-Park electrical engineering educator
Chen, James Jen-Chuan electrical engineer
Falgiano, Victor Joseph electrical engineer, consultant
Hoagland, Albert Smiley electrical engineer
Kershaw, David Joseph process engineer
Parden, Robert James engineering educator, management consultant
Yin, Gerald Zheyao technology and business executive
Zhang, Xiao-Feng power system engineer, researcher

**Santa Clarita**
Abbott, John Rodger electrical engineer
Granlund, Thomas Arthur engineering executive, consultant

**Santa Cruz**
Langdon, Glen George, Jr. electrical engineer

**Santa Monica**
Bedrosian, Edward electrical engineer
Crain, Cullen Malone electrical engineer
Gritton, Eugene Charles nuclear engineer
Hammond, R. Philip chemical engineer
Kayton, Myron engineering company executive
Kummer, Wolfgang H. electrical engineer
Mc Guire, Michael John environmental engineering executive
Roney, Robert Kenneth retired aerospace company executive

**Santa Rosa**
Apfel, Joseph H. optical engineer, research scientist
Rancourt, James Daniel optical engineer

**Santa Ynez**
Ellion, M. Edmund engineering executive

**Saratoga**
Cooper, George Emery aerospace consultant
Rawson, Eric Gordon optical engineer
Syvertson, Clarence Alfred engineering and research management consultant
Wenzel, James Gottlieb ocean engineering executive, consultant

**Sausalito**
Green, Joanta Hermion electrical engineer

**Seal Beach**
Harsha, Philip Thomas aerospace engineer
Robinson, Michael R. aeronautical engineer

**Sebastopol**
Norman, Arnold McCallum, Jr. engineer

**Sonoma**
Muchmore, Robert Boyer engineering consultant executive

**South Pasadena**
Glad, Dain Sturgis retired aerospace engineer, consultant
Kopp, Eugene Howard electrical engineer

**Stanford**
Aziz, Khalid petroleum engineering educator
Boudart, Michel chemical engineer, chemist, educator
Bracewell, Ronald Newbold electrical engineering educator
Bradshaw, Peter engineering educator
Cannon, Robert Hamilton, Jr. aerospace engineering educator
Carlson, Robert Codner industrial engineering educator
Cox, Donald Clyde electrical engineering educator
Eustis, Robert Henry mechanical engineer
Franklin, Gene Farthing engineering educator, consultant
Gere, James Monroe civil engineering educator
Goodman, Joseph Wilfred electrical engineering educator
Gray, Robert M(olten) electrical engineering educator
Hesselink, Lambertus electrical engineering and physics educator
Hewett, Thomas Avery petroleum engineer, educator
Hughes, Thomas J.R. mechanical engineering educator, consultant
Kailath, Thomas electrical engineer, educator
Kane, Thomas Reif engineering educator
Kline, Stephen Jay mechanical engineer, educator
Kruger, Charles Herman, Jr. mechanical engineering educator
Levitt, Raymond Elliot civil engineering educator
Linvill, John Grimes engineering educator
Macovski, Albert electrical engineering educator
Madix, Robert James chemical engineer, educator
Mc Carty, Perry Lee civil engineering educator, research director
McCluskey, Edward Joseph engineering educator
Nelson, Drew Vernon mechanical engineering educator
Orr, Franklin Mattes, Jr. petroleum engineering educator
Ortolano, Leonard civil engineering educator, water resources planner
Ott, Wayne Robert environmental engineer
Parkinson, Bradford Wells astronautical engineer, educator
Paté-Cornell, Marie-Elisabeth Lucienne industrial engineering educator
Pease, Roger Fabian Wedgwood electrical engineering educator
Pierce, John Robinson electrical engineer, educator
Quate, Calvin Forrest engineering educator
Reynolds, William Craig mechanical engineer, educator
Roth, Bernard mechanical engineering educator, researcher
Rott, Nicholas fluid mechanics educator
Shah, Haresh C. civil engineering educator
Siegman, Anthony Edward electrical engineer, educator
Spreiter, John Robert engineering educator, space physics scientist
Springer, George Stephen mechanical engineering educator
Steele, Charles Richard biomedical and mechanical engineering educator
Street, Robert Lynnwood civil and mechanical engineer
Sweeney, James Lee engineering and economic systems educator
Tsai, Stephen Wei-Lun aeronautical educator
Van Dyke, Milton Denman aeronautical engineering educator
Vincenti, Walter Guido aeronautical engineer, emeritus educator
White, Robert Lee electrical engineer, educator

**Sugarloaf**
Kind, Anne Wilson engineer

**Sunnyvale**
Antweiler, Dennis Francis mechanical engineer
Kim, Wan Hee electrical engineering educator, business executive
Laurance, Mark Rodney applications engineer, entrepreneur
Ma, Fengchow Clarence agricultural engineering consultant
Saluja, Sundar S. international engineering consultant
Schubert, Ronald Hayward retired aerospace engineer
Zebroski, Edwin Leopold consulting engineer

**Sylmar**
Madni, Asad Mohamed engineering executive

**Tarzana**
Hansen, Robert Clinton electrical engineering consultant
Macmillan, Robert Smith electronics engineer

**Temecula**
Minogue, Robert Brophy retired nuclear engineer

**Thousand Oaks**
Deisenroth, Clinton Wilbur electrical engineer
Krumm, Charles Ferdinand electrical engineer

**Torrance**
Brodsky, Robert Fox aerospace engineer
Kucij, Timothy Michael engineer, musician, minister
Mende, Howard Shigeharu mechanical engineer
Yoon, Sewang engineering executive

**Valencia**
Windsor, William Earl consulting engineer, sales representative

**Vallejo**
Hudak, Paul Alexander retired engineer

**Van Nuys**
Freiberg, Robert Jerry physicist, engineer, technology administrator

**Ventura**
Gaynor, Joseph chemical engineer, management consultant
Matley, Benvenuto Gilbert (Ben Matley) computer engineer, educator, consultant

**Victorville**
Syed, Moinuddin electrical engineer

**Walnut Creek**
Burgarino, Anthony Emanuel environmental engineer, consultant
Crandall, Ira Carlton consulting electrical engineer
Gentry, James Frederick chemical engineer, consultant
Lagarias, John Samuel engineering executive
Lee, William Chien-Yeh electrical engineer

**Watsonville**
Brown, Alan Charlton retired aeronautical engineer

**Westlake Village**
Caligiuri, Joseph Frank retired engineering executive

**Westminster**
Armstrong, Gene Lee systems engineering consultant, retired aerospace company executive

**Whittier**
Hartling, Earle Charles environmental engineer
Lillevang, Omar Johansen civil engineer
Winter, Foster, III environmental engineer

**Woodland Hills**
Amerine, Anne Follette aerospace engineer
Brozowski, Laura Adrienne mechanical engineer
Higginbotham, Lloyd William mechanical engineer
Portney, Joseph Nathaniel aerospace executive
Yackle, Albert Reustle aeronautical engineer

**Yorba Linda**
Porcello, Leonard Joseph engineering research and development executive

## COLORADO

**Boulder**
Barnes, Frank Stephenson electrical engineer, educator
Born, George H. aerospace engineer, educator
Cathey, Wade Thomas electrical engineering educator
Corotis, Ross Barry civil engineering educator, academic administrator
Fuller, Jackson Franklin electrical engineering educator
Gerstle, Kurt Herman retired civil engineering educator, consultant
Gupta, Kuldip Chand electrical and computer engineering educator, researcher
Hanna, William Johnson electrical engineering educator
Hauser, Ray Louis research engineer, entrepreneur
Hill, David Allan electrical engineer
Kanda, Motohisa electronics engineer
Lewin, Leonard electrical engineering educator
Maley, Samuel Wayne electrical engineering educator
Reitsema, Harold James aerospace engineer

Rodriguez, Juan Alfonso *technology corporation executive*
Sani, Robert LeRoy *chemical engineering educator*
Seebass, Alfred Richard, III *aerospace engineer, educator, university dean*
Shanahan, Eugene Miles *flow measurement instrumentation company executive*
Shang, Er-Chang *acoustician*
Smith, Ernest Ketcham *electrical engineer*
Sodal, Ingvar Edmund *electrical engineer, scientist*
Timmerhaus, Klaus Dieter *chemical engineering educator*
Uberoi, Mahinder Singh *aerospace engineering educator*
Utlaut, William Frederick *electrical engineer*
Waters, M. Bruce *engineering technician*

**Canon City**
McBride, John Alexander *retired chemical engineer*

**Colorado Springs**
Adnet, Jacques Jim Pierre *astronautical and electrical engineer, consultant*
Kohlman, David Leslie *engineering executive, consultant*
Watts, Oliver Edward *engineering consultancy company executive*
Ziemer, Rodger Edmund *electrical engineering educator, consultant*

**Denver**
Colvis, John Paris *aerospace engineer, mathematician, scientist*
East, Donald Robert *civil engineer*
Ferguson, Lloyd Elbert *manufacturing engineer*
Haddon, Timothy John *mining engineer*
Hinch, William Harry *retired consulting engineer*
Krill, Arthur Melvin *engineering, architectural and planning company executive*
Long, Francis Mark *retired electrical engineer, educator*
McCandless, Bruce, II *aerospace engineer, former astronaut*
Mehring, Clinton Warren *engineering executive*
Perez, Jean-Yves *engineering company executive*
Poirot, James Wesley *engineering company executive*

**Englewood**
Aguirre, Vukoslav Eneas *environmental engineer*
Bingham, Paris Edward, Jr. *electrical engineer, computer consultant*

**Estes Park**
Ojalvo, Morris *civil engineer, educator*
Webb, Richard C. *engineering company executive*

**Evergreen**
Jesser, Roger Franklyn *former brewing company engineering executive, consultant*
Newkirk, John Burt *metallurgical engineer, administrator*

**Fort Collins**
Boyd, Landis Lee *agricultural engineer, educator*
Cermak, Jack Edward *engineer, educator*
Criswell, Marvin Eugene *civil engineering educator, consultant*
Emslie, William Arthur *electrical engineer*
Garvey, Daniel Cyril *mechanical engineer*
†Grigg, Neil S. *civil engineering educator*
Heermann, Dale Frank *agricultural engineer*
Jacobs, Harold Robert *mechanical engineering educator*
Kaufman, Harold Richard *mechanical engineer and physics educator*
Medearis, Kenneth Gordon *engineering research consultant, educator*
Mesloh, Warren Henry *civil and environmental engineer*
Richardson, Everett Vern *hydraulic engineer, educator, administrator, consultant*
Winn, C(olman) Byron *mechanical engineering educator*
Woolhiser, David Arthur *hydraulic engineer*

**Glenwood Springs**
Violette, Glenn Phillip *construction engineer*

**Golden**
Ansell, George Stephen *metallurgical engineering educator, academic administrator*
Ervin, Patrick Franklin *nuclear engineer*
Hager, John Patrick *metallurgy engineering educator*
Johnstone, James George *engineering educator*
Patino, Hugo *food science research engineer*
Salamon, Miklos Dezso Gyorgy *mining engineer, educator*
Sloan, Earle Dendy, Jr. *chemical engineering educator*
Yarar, Baki *metallurgical engineering educator*

**Grand Junction**
Rybak, James Patrick *engineering educator*

**Greenwood Village**
Peterson, Ralph R. *engineering executive*

**Highlands Ranch**
McLellon, Richard Steven *aerospace engineer, consultant*

**Lakewood**
Danzberger, Alexander Harris *chemical engineer, consultant*
Lu, Paul Haihsing *mining engineer, geotechnical consultant*

**Littleton**
Ballard, Jack Stokes *engineering educator*
Kazemi, Hossein *petroleum engineer*
Kullas, Albert John *management and systems engineering consultant*
Ulrich, John Ross Gerald *aerospace engineer*

**Longmont**
Rueckert, Ronald Frank *engineering executive*

**Louisville**
Donze, Jerry Lynn *electrical engineer*

**Olathe**
Shriver, Allen Keith *electrical engineer, contractor, executive*

**Pueblo**
Giffin, Walter Charles *retired industrial engineer, educator, consultant*

**U S A F Academy**
Wright, Cameron Harrold Greene *electrical engineer*

**Wheat Ridge**
Barrett, Michael Henry *civil engineer*
Scherich, Erwin Thomas *civil engineer, consultant*

## CONNECTICUT

**Avon**
Mc Ilveen, Walter *mechanical engineer*
von Kutzleben, Bernd Eberhard *nuclear engineer*

**Bethel**
DeLugo, Ernest Mario, Jr. *electrical engineer*

**Bloomfield**
Kissa, Karl Martin *electrical engineer*
Leonberger, Frederick John *electrical engineer, photonics manager*

**Branford**
Cohen, Myron Leslie *mechanical engineer, business executive*
Izenour, George Charles *mechanical, electrical engineering educator*

**Bridgeport**
Brunale, Vito John *aerospace engineer*
Jiang, John Jianzhong *materials engineer*

**Cheshire**
Fuller, Jack Glendon, Jr. *retired plastics engineer*

**Darien**
Bays, John Theophanis *consulting engineering executive*
Forman, J(oseph) Charles *chemical engineer, consultant, writer*
Glenn, Roland Douglas *chemical engineer*
McCurdy, Richard Clark *engineering consultant*

**East Granby**
Pfeifer, Howard M(elford) *mechanical engineer*

**East Hartford**
Cassidy, John Francis, Jr. *industrial research center executive*
Day, William Hudson *mechanical engineer, turbomachinery company executive*
Foyt, Arthur George *electronics research administrator*
Hanson, Donald Burnett *mechanical engineer, researcher*

**Ellington**
Setzer, Herbert John *chemical engineer*

**Greenwich**
Nadel, Norman Allen *civil engineer*
Snowdon, Jane Louise *industrial engineer*

**Groton**
Boissevain, Matthijs Gideon Jan *mechanical engineer*
Lincoln, Walter Butler, Jr. *marine engineer, educator*
Sheets, Herman Ernest *marine engineer*

**Hamden**
†Theroux, Dennis Robert *engineering executive*
Walker, Charles Allen *chemical engineer, educator*

**Hartford**
Bronzino, Joseph Daniel *electrical engineer*
Cornell, Robert Witherspoon *engineering consultant*
Smith, Donald Arthur *mechanical engineer, researcher*

**Manchester**
Slaiby, Theodore George *aeronautical engineer, consultant*

**Mansfield Center**
Aldrich, Robert Adams *agricultural engineer*

**New Canaan**
Halverstadt, Robert Dale *mechanical engineer, metals manufacturing company executive*
O'Neill, Patrick Henry *consulting mining engineer*

**New Fairfield**
Daukshus, A. Joseph *systems engineer*

**New Hartford**
Hall, Newman A. *retired mechanical engineer*

**New Haven**
Apfel, Robert Edmund *mechanical engineering educator, applied physicist, research scientist*
Cunningham, Walter Jack *electrical engineering educator*
Haller, Gary Lee *chemical engineering educator*
Horváth, Csaba *chemical engineering educator, researcher*
Ma, Tso-Ping *electrical engineering educator, researcher, consultant*
Ricard, Thomas Armand *electrical engineer*
Wegener, Peter Paul *engineering educator, author*

**Old Saybrook**
Elrod, Harold Glenn *retired engineering science educator, consultant*

**Rocky Hill**
Chuang, Frank Shiunn-Jea *engineering executive, consultant*

**South Windsor**
Hobbs, David Ellis *mechanical engineer*

**Stamford**
Friedmann, Paul Garson *control engineer*
Rodriguez, J. Louis *civil engineer, land surveyor*

**Storrs Mansfield**
De Maria, Anthony John *electrical engineer*
DiBenedetto, Anthony Thomas *engineering educator*
Long, Richard Paul *civil engineering educator, geotechnical engineering consultant*
Marcus, Harris Leon *mechanical engineering and materials science educator*
McFadden, Peter William *mechanical engineering educator*
Pitkin, Edward Thaddeus *aerospace engineer, consultant*
Shaw, Montgomery Throop *chemical engineering educator*

**Tariffville**
Johnson, Loering M. *design engineer, historian, consultant*

**Tolland**
Wilde, Daniel Underwood *computer engineering educator*

**Trumbull**
Garelick, Melvin Stewart *engineering educator*
Gladki, Hanna Zofia *civil engineer, hydraulic mixer specialist*

**Waterford**
Hinkle, Muriel Ruth Nelson *naval warfare analysis company executive*

**West Mystic**
Hoagland, Porter, Jr. *electrical and mechanical engineer, consultant*

**Weston**
Offenhartz, Edward *aerospace executive*

**Wilton**
Juran, Joseph Moses *engineer*

## DELAWARE

**Dover**
Jones, Jay Paul *professional environmental engineer*

**Hockessin**
Bischoff, Kenneth Bruce *chemical engineer, educator*

**New Castle**
Rangan, Chakravarthi Ravi *environmental engineer*

**Newark**
Adams, Joseph Brian *operations research engineer, mathematics educator*
Allen, Herbert Ellis *environmental chemistry educator*
Barteau, Mark Alan *chemical engineering and chemistry educator*
Beris, Antony Nicolas *chemical engineer, educator*
Cheng, Alexander Hung-Darh *engineering educator, consultant*
Christy, Charles Wesley, III *industrial engineering educator*
Cooper, Stuart Leonard *chemical engineering educator, researcher, consultant*
Ih, Charles Chung Sen *electrical engineering educator, consultant*
Kennedy, Christopher Robin *ceramist*
Klein, Michael Tully *chemical engineering educator, consultant*
Kleinman, R. E. *computer engineering educator*
Lomax, Kenneth Mitchell *agricultural engineering educator*
McCullough, Roy Lynn *chemical engineering educator*
Nye, John Calvin *agricultural engineer, educator*
Russell, Thomas William Fraser *chemical engineering educator*
Sandler, Stanley Irving *chemical engineering educator*
Szeri, Andras Z. *engineering educator*
Urquhart, Andrew Willard *engineering and business executive*

**Wilmington**
Kutemeyer, Peter Martin *industrial engineering executive*
Murphy, Arthur Thomas *systems engineer*
Salzstein, Richard Alan *biomedical engineer, researcher*

## DISTRICT OF COLUMBIA

**Washington**
Aggarwal, Satish Kumar *electrical engineer, government official*
Arkilic, Galip Mehmet *mechanical engineer, educator*
Bainum, Peter Montgomery *aerospace engineer, consultant*
Blanchard, Bruce *environmental engineer, government official*
Brahms, Thomas Walter *engineering institute executive*
Briskman, Robert David *engineering executive*
Carioti, Bruno M. *civil engineer*
Chalmers, Franklin Stevens, Jr. *engineering consultant*
Chen, Ho-Hong H. H. *industrial engineering executive, educator*
Deason, Jonathan P. *environmental engineer, federal agency administrator*
Diaz, Nils Juan *nuclear engineer, consultant*
Dinberg, Michael David *industrial engineer, uniformed services officer*
Dinneen, Gerald Paul *electrical engineer, former government official*
Divone, Louis Vincent *aerospace engineer, educator, author, government official*
†Durocher, Cort Louis *aerospace engineer, association executive*
Eisner, Howard *engineering educator, engineering executive*
Freund, Deborah Miriam *transportation engineer*
Friedman, Arthur Daniel *electrical engineering and computer science educator, investment management company executive*
Giallorenzi, Thomas Gaetano *optical engineer*
Hershey, Robert Lewis *mechanical engineer, management consultant*
Jones, Howard St. Claire, Jr. *electronics engineering executive*
Kahn, Walter Kurt *engineering and applied science educator*
Kappaz, Michael H. *engineering company executive*
Kaufman, John Gilbert, Jr. *materials engineer*
Kim, John Chan Kyu *electrical engineer*
Kiper, Ali Muhlis *mechanical engineering educator, consultant*
Kitchens, Clarence Wesley, Jr. *physical science administrator*
Lee, Charlyn Yvonne *chemical engineer*
MacDonald, Paul Edward *electrical engineer*
McKay, Jack Alexander *electronics engineer, physicist*
Menendez, Adolfo *engineering company executive*
Monroe, Robert Rawson *engineering construction executive*
Nichols, Kenneth David *consulting engineer*
Page, Robert Wesley *engineering and construction company executive, federal official*
Pickholtz, Raymond Lee *electrical engineering educator, consultant*
Quinn, Pat Maloy *engineering company executive*
Reis, Victor H. *mechanical engineer, government official*
Salmon, William Cooper *mechanical engineer, engineering academy executive*
Shalowitz, Erwin Emmanuel *civil engineer*
Shapiro, Paul Sauveur *chemical engineer, researcher*
Shon, Frederick John *nuclear engineer*
†Singley, George T., III *mechanical engineer, federal agency administrator*
Skinner, Robert Earle, Jr. *civil engineer, engineering executive*
Skolnik, Merrill I. *electrical engineer*
Sorensen, John Noble *mechanical and nuclear engineer*
Stanwick, Tad *retired systems engineer*
Townsend, Marjorie Rhodes *aerospace engineer, business executive*
Walters, John Linton *electronics engineer, consultant*
Wang, John Cheng Hwai *communications engineer*
Warnick, Walter Lee *mechanical engineer*
Webb, David Owen *petroleum engineer, association executive*
White, Robert Roy *chemical engineer*
White, Roy Martin *engineering manager*
Xue, Lan *engineering educator*

## FLORIDA

**Alachua**
Dinculescu, Antonie *chemical engineer, researcher*

**Atlantic Beach**
Engelmann, Rudolph Herman *electronics consultant*

**Boca Raton**
Arockiasamy, Madasamy *engineering educator*
Han, Chingping Jim *industrial engineer, educator*
Johnson, James Robert *ceramic engineer, educator*
Lin, Y. K. *engineer, educator*
Reynolds, George Anthony, Jr. *engineering executive*

**Bradenton**
Friedrich, Robert Edmund *retired electrical engineer, corporate consultant*

**Cape Coral**
Purdy, Alan Harris *biomedical engineer*
Smith, Bruce William *safety engineer*

**Chuluota**
McClintic, Fred Frazier *simulation engineer*

**Clearwater**
Benavente, Javier Edgar *engineering executive*

**Cocoa Beach**
Gunn, Kenneth David *explosives safety specialist, consultant*

**Coral Gables**
Baddour, Raymond Frederick *chemical engineer, educator, entrepreneur*
Jury, Eliahu Ibraham *electrical engineer, research educator*
Kline, Jacob *biomedical engineering educator*
Saffir, Herbert Seymour *structural engineer, consultant*
Sumanth, David Jonnakoty *industrial engineer, educator*
Young, Tzay Y. *electrical and computer engineering educator*

**Coral Springs**
Elmore, Walter A. *electrical engineer, consultant*
Valasquez, Joseph Louis *industrial engineer*

**Crystal River**
Black, Charles Alvin *consulting engineering executive*

**Daytona Beach**
Geier, George *optical engineering consultant*
Millar, Gordon Halstead *mechanical engineer, agricultural machinery manufacturing executive*

**Delray Beach**
Smith, Charles Oliver *engineer*

**Dundee**
Johnson, Gordon Selby *consulting electrical engineer*

**Eglin AFB**
Franzen, Larry William *aerospace electronics engineer*
Gal, Richard John *industrial engineer*

**Fernandina Beach**
Lilly, Wesley Cooper *marine engineer, ship surveyor*

**Fort Lauderdale**
Meditz, Walter Joseph *engineering consultant*

### Fort Myers
Callanan, Kathleen Joan *retired electrical engineer*
Kareh, Ahmad Ragheb *civil engineer*
Mergler, Harry Winston *engineering educator*
Moeschl, Stanley Francis *electrical engineer, management consultant*
Ölling, Edward Henry *aerospace engineer, consulting firm executive*
Scott, Kenneth Elsner *mechanical engineering educator*
Sechrist, Chalmers Franklin, Jr. *electrical engineering educator*

### Gainesville
Abbaschian, Reza *materials science and engineering educator*
Anderson, Timothy J. *chemical engineering educator*
Anghaie, Samim *nuclear engineer, educator*
Balabanian, Norman *electrical engineering educator*
Block, Seymour Stanton *chemical engineering educator, consultant, writer*
Capehart, Barney Lee *industrial and systems engineer*
Cooper, James Ralph *engineering executive*
Cristescu, Nicolaie D. *engineering educator*
Delfino, Joseph John *environmental engineering sciences educator*
Drucker, Daniel Charles *engineer, educator*
Elzinga, Donald Jack *industrial engineering researcher, educator*
Fossum, Jerry George *electrical engineering educator*
Fournier, Donald Joseph, Jr. *mechanical engineer, consultant*
Holloway, Wade Justin *civil engineer*
Isaacs, Gerald William *agricultural engineer, educator*
Issacs, Gerald William *retired agricultural engineering educator, consultant*
Kurzweg, Ulrich Hermann *engineering science educator*
Law, Mark Edward *electrical engineer, educator*
Lindholm, Fredrik Arthur *electrical engineering educator*
Malvern, Lawrence Earl *engineering educator, researcher*
Neugroschel, Arnost *electrical engineering educator*
Ohanian, Mihran Jacob *nuclear engineering educator, research dean*
†Pearce, Joseph Huske *industrial engineer*
Pearton, Stephen John *materials science and engineering educator*
Peebles, Peyton Zimmerman, Jr. *electrical engineer, educator*
Schaub, James Hamilton *engineering educator*
Schmertmann, John Henry *civil engineer, educator, consultant*
Sheng, Yea-Yi Peter *oceanographic engineer, educator, researcher*
Sherif, S. A. *mechanical engineering educator*
Shyy, Wei *aerospace, mechanical engineering researcher, educator*
Singley, John Edward, Jr. *environmental scientist, consultant*
Verink, Ellis Daniel, Jr. *metallurgical engineering educator, consultant*
Wethington, John Abner, Jr. *retired nuclear engineering educator*

### Grove City
Suiter, John William *industrial engineer, consultant*

### Hollywood
Nusim, Stanley Herbert *chemical engineer, consultant*

### Indialantic
Davenport, Fountain St. Clair *electronic engineer*

### Jacksonville
Hawkins, James Douglas, Jr. *structural engineer, architect*
Joyce, Edward Rowen *retired chemical engineer, educator*
Lawrence, Christopher *engineering executive*
Liebtag, Benford Gustav, III (Ben Liebtag) *engineer, consultant*
Mueller, Edward Albert *retired transportation engineer executive*
Russell, David Emerson *mechanical engineer, consultant*
Shivler, James Fletcher, Jr. *retired civil engineer*

### Jaxville Beach
Garza, Nora *systems engineer*

### Jensen Beach
Kirjassoff, Gordon Louis *consulting civil engineer*

### Juno Beach
Migliaro, Marco William *electrical engineer*

### Jupiter
Callahan, Edward William *chemical engineer, retired manufacturing executive*
Nahavandi, Amir Nezameddin *retired engineering firm executive*

### Kennedy Space Center
Fussell, Ronald Moi *aerospace engineer*

### Lady Lake
Dore, Stephen Edward, Jr. *retired civil engineer*

### Lighthouse Point
Farho, James Henry, Jr. *mechanical engineer, consultant*

### Longboat Key
Workman, George Henry *engineer, consultant*

### Longwood
Tiblier, Fernand Joseph, Jr. *municipal engineering administrator*

### Maitland
Roesner, Larry August *civil engineer*

### Melbourne
Baylis, William Thomas *senior systems logistics engineer*
Denaburg, Charles Robert *metallurgical engineer, retired government official*
Lewis, Bernard Leroy *electronic scientist, consultant*

### Miami
Barthel, William Frederick, Jr. *engineer, electronics company executive*
de la Guardia, Mario Francisco *electrical engineer*
Ehrlich, Richard *electrical engineer, researcher*
Kidder, Benjamin Roger *safety engineer, consultant, educator*
Lindquist, Claude S. *electrical and computer engineering educator*
Milne, Edward Lawrence *biomedical engineer*
Polo, Richard Joseph *engineering executive*
Sanchez, Javier Alberto *industrial engineer*
Schuetzenduebel, Wolfram Gerhard *engineering executive*
Torres, Milton John *industrial engineering educator*
Ural, Oktay *civil engineering educator*
Veziroglu, Turhan Nejat *mechanical engineering educator, energy researcher*
Wolfenson, Azi U. *electrical engineer*

### Naples
Benedict, Manson *chemical engineer, educator*
Leverenz, Humboldt Walter *retired chemical research engineer*
Montone, Liber Joseph *engineering consultant*
Suziedelis, Vytautas A. *engineering corporation executive*
Tanner, Robert Hugh *engineer, consultant*
Widman, Richard Gustave *engineering and construction company executive*
Williams, George Earnest *engineer, retired business executive*

### Nokomis
Cather, Donald Warren *civil engineer*
Novak, Robert Louis *civil engineer, pavement management consultant*

### Orange Park
Rodgers, Billy Russell *chemical engineer, research scientist*

### Orlando
Davis, Gene *civil engineer*
Rattman, William John *electronics and eletro-optic engineer*
Rosenbach, Leopold *engineer, consultant*
Schroeter, Dirk Joachim *mechanical engineer*
Soileau, Marion Joseph *engineering and physics educator*

### Ormond Beach
Jacobson, Ira David *aerospace engineer, educator, researcher*
Wild, Harry E. *engineering company executive*

### Osprey
Boldt, Heinz *aerospace engineer*
Coates, Clarence Leroy, Jr. *research engineer, educator*

### Palm Beach
Turner, William Benjamin *electrical engineer*

### Palm Beach Gardens
Koff, Bernard Louis *retired engineering executive*

### Palm Harbor
McIlveen, Walter Ronald *architectural engineer*

### Panama City
D'Arcy, Gerald Paul *engineering executive, consultant*

### Pensacola
McSwain, Richard Horace *materials engineer, consultant*
Watt, Stuart George *engineering contracting company executive*

### Port Charlotte
Kok, Hans Gebhard *consulting engineer*
Munger, Elmer Lewis *civil engineer, educator*

### Port Saint Lucie
Huang, Denis Kuo Ying *chemical engineer, consultant*

### Punta Gorda
Olson, James Robert *consulting engineer*

### Saint Cloud
Everett, Woodrow Wilson *electrical engineer, educator*

### Saint Marks
Labitzke, Dale Russell *chemical processing engineer*

### Saint Petersburg
Collins, Carl Russell, Jr. *corporate services*
Donaldson, Merle Richard *electrical engineering educator, consultant*

### Sarasota
Beck, George William *retired industrial engineer*
Hrones, John Anthony *mechanical engineering educator*
Long, Robert Radcliffe *fluid mechanics educator*
Ross, Gerald Fred *engineering executive, researcher*
Veinott, Cyril George *electrical engineer, consultant*

### Satellite Beach
Clark, John F. *aerospace research and engineering educator*
Van Arsdall, Robert Armes *engineer, retired air force officer*

### Stuart
Morena, John Joseph *manufacturing engineer, executive*

### Sun City Center
Jeffries, Robert Joseph *retired engineering educator, business executive*

### Tallahassee
Arce, Pedro Edgardo *chemical engineering educator*
Braswell, Robert Neil *scientist, engineer, educator*
Chen, Ching Jen *mechanical engineering educator, research scientist*
Coloney, Wayne Herndon *civil engineer*
De Forest, Sherwood Searle *agricultural engineer, agribusiness services executive*
Gupta, Madhu Sudan *electrical engineering educator*
Hall, Houghton Alexander *electrical engineering*
Harrison, Thomas James *electrical engineer, educator*

### Tampa
Aguinaldo, Jorge Tansingco *chemical engineer, water treatment consultant*
Carnahan, Robert Paul *civil engineer, educator, researcher, consultant*
Deutsch, Sid *bioengineer, educator*
Givens, Paul Edward *industrial engineer, educator*
Henning, Rudolf Ernst *electrical engineer, educator, consultant*
Kaw, Autar Krishen *mechanical engineer, educator*
Kovac, Michael G. *engineering educator*
Miller, Charles Leslie *civil engineer, planner, consultant*
Wade, Thomas Edward *electrical engineering educator, university research administrator*
Zelinski, Joseph John *engineering educator, consultant*

### Tarpon Springs
Scala, Sinclaire Maximilian *retired aerospace engineer*

### Venice
Concordia, Charles *consulting engineer*
Hays, Herschel Martin *electrical engineer*
Przemieniecki, Janusz Stanislaw *engineering executive, former government senior executive and college dean*

### Vero Beach
Daly, John Francis *engineering company executive*
Haywood, Oliver Garfield *engineer*

### West Palm Beach
Aaron, M. Robert *electrical engineer*
Coar, Richard John *mechanical engineer, aerospace consultant*
Gillette, Frank C., Jr. *mechanical engineer*
Olsak, Ivan Karel *civil engineer*

### Winter Park
Johannes, Virgil Ivancich *electrical engineer*
Kerr, James Wilson *engineer*

### Winter Springs
Tran, Toan Vu *electronics engineer*

## GEORGIA

### Adrian
McCord, James Richard, III *chemical engineer, mathematician*

### Albany
Marbury, Ritchey McGuire, III *engineering executive, surveyor*

### Alpharetta
Barker, Michael Dean *nuclear engineer, internet engineer*
Miller, Robert Allen *software engineer, consultant*

### Athens
Grayson, Richard Andrew *aerospace engineer*
Kraszewski, Andrzej Wojciech *electrical engineer, researcher*
McCutcheon, Steven Clifton *environmental engineer, hydrologist*
Nelson, Stuart Owen *agricultural engineer, researcher, educator*
Tollner, Ernest William *agricultural engineering educator, agricultural radiology consultant*

### Atlanta
Abdel-Khalik, Said Ibrahim *nuclear and mechanical engineering educator*
Armanios, Erian Abdelmessih *aerospace engineer, educator*
Bacon, Louis Albert *retired consulting civil engineer*
Baldwin, Daniel Flanagan *mechanical engineer, researcher, educator*
Barksdale, Richard Dillon *civil engineer, educator*
Bellanca, Joseph Paul *engineering/construction executive*
Bourne, Henry Clark, Jr. *electrical engineering educator, former academic official*
Calise, Anthony John *aerospace engineering educator*
Carlson, Robert Lee *engineering educator*
Dalrymple, Gordon Bennett *former engineering company executive*
Draper, Stephen Elliot *engineer, lawyer*
†Drewry, Joe Samuel Jr. *design engineer*
Eckert, Charles Alan *chemical engineering educator*
Fitzgerald, John Edmund *civil engineering educator*
Ford, Edward Francis *process engineer*
Griffin, Clayton Houstoun *retired power company engineer, lecturer*
Haddad, Wassim Michael *aerospace engineer, educator*
Hess, Dennis William *chemical engineering educator*
Hodges, Dewey Harper *aerospace engineer, educator*
Hurley, John Steven *electrical engineering educator, research scientist*
Joy, Edward Bennett *electrical engineer, educator*
Komerath, Narayanan Menon *aerospace engineer*
Lebow, Jeffrey Albert *manufacturing engineer*
Loewy, Robert Gustav *engineering educator, aeronautical engineering executive*
Ludovice, Peter John *chemical engineer*
McClellan, James Harold *electrical engineering educator*
Moore, Henry Rogers *consulting engineer, retired railroad executive*
Nemhauser, George L. *industrial, systems engineer, operations research educator*
Nerem, Robert Michael *engineering educator, consultant*
Paris, Demetrius Theodore *electrical engineering educator*
Pence, Ira Wilson, Jr. *material handling research executive, engineer*
Porter, Alan Leslie *industrial and systems engineering educator*
Reedy, Edward K. *research operations administrator*
Richards, Robert Wadsworth *civil engineer, consultant*
Rodenbeck, Sven E. *environmental engineer, consultant*
Schafer, Ronald William *electrical engineering educator*
Scovil, Roger Morris *engineering company executive*
Smith, Glenn Stanley *electrical engineering educator*
Stacey, Weston Monroe, Jr. *nuclear engineer, educator*
Su, Kendall Ling-Chiao *engineering educator*
Tedder, Daniel William *chemical engineering educator*
Teja, Amyn Sadrudin *chemical engineering educator, consultant*
Thuesen, Gerald Jorgen *industrial engineer, educator*
Tomeh, Amin Adnan *geotechnical engineer, consultant*
Tucker, Robert Arnold *electrical engineer*
Vanegas, Jorge Alberto *civil engineering educator*
White, John Austin, Jr. *engineering educator, dean, consultant*
Wiedeman, John Herman *civil engineer*
Winer, Ward Otis *mechanical engineer, educator*
Wyvill, J. Craig *research engineer, program director*
Yoganathan, Ajit Prithiviraj *biomedical engineer, educator*
Zinn, Ben T. *engineer, educator, consultant*

### Baxley
Reddy, Yenemala Jaysimha *mechanical engineer*

### Dahlonega
Jones, William Benjamin, Jr. *electrical engineering educator*

### Doraville
Wempner, Gerald Arthur *engineering educator*

### Douglasville
Hubbard, Charles Ronald *engineering executive*

### Duluth
Cooke, Steven John *chemical engineer, consultant, scientist*

### Jersey
Batchelor, Joseph Brooklyn, Jr. *electronics engineer, consultant*

### Lilburn
Bristow, Preston Abner, Jr. *civil engineer, environmental engineer*

### Marietta
Miles, Thomas Caswell *aerospace engineer*
Pounds, Gerald Autry *aerospace engineer*
Ranu, Harcharan Singh *biomedical scientist, administrator, orthopaedic biomechanics educator*

### Norcross
Adams, Dee Briane *hydrologist, civil engineer*
Harrison, Gordon Ray *engineering executive, consultant, research scientist*
Rouse, William Bradford *systems engineering executive, researcher, educator*
Storey, Bobby Eugene, Jr. *electrical engineer, engineering consultant*

### Robins AFB
Christian, Thomas Franklin, Jr. *aerospace engineer, educator*
Hedden, Kenneth Forsythe *chemical engineer*

### Saint Simons Island
Hicks, Harold Eugene *chemical engineer*

### Savannah
Belles, Martin Russel *manufacturing engineer*
Haywood, John William, Jr. *engineering consultant*
Hsu, Ming-Yu *engineer, educator*
Seedlock, Robert Francis *engineering and construction company executive*

### Stone Mountain
Boothe, Edward Milton *aeronautical engineer, pilot*

### Thomaston
Beohm, Richard Thomas *fire protection/safety and loss control consultant*

### Woodstock
Webb, Edsel Philip *retired textile engineer*

## HAWAII

### Honolulu
Chiu, Arthur Nang Lick *engineering educator*
Cotlar, Morton *organizational scientist, educator*
Cox, Richard Horton *civil engineering executive*
Feher, Steve Joseph Kent *design engineer, research developer*
Kohloss, Frederick Henry *consulting engineer*
Koide, Frank Takayuki *electrical engineering educator*
Lin, Shu *electrical engineering educator*
Sato, Richard Michio *consulting engineering company executive*
Saxena, Narendra K. *marine research educator*
Wang, Jaw-Kai *agricultural engineering educator*
Wataru, Weston Yasuo *civil engineer*
Yee, Alfred Alphonse *structural engineer, consultant*

### Kapaau
McFee, Richard *electrical engineer, physicist*

## IDAHO

### Boise
Lee, Roger Ruojia *semiconductor engineer*
McKee, Joseph Fulton *engineering and construction executive*
Nuttall, Michael Lee *engineer, educator*
Slavich, Denis Michael *engineering and construction company executive*

### Idaho Falls
Riemke, Richard Allan *mechanical engineer*

**Inkom**
Ambrose, Tommy W. *chemical engineer, executive*

**Island Park**
Stratford, Ray Paul *electrical engineer, consultant*

**Moscow**
DeShazer, James Arthur *agricultural engineer, educator, administrator*
Jackson, Melbourne Leslie *chemical engineering educator and administrator, consultant*
Jacobsen, Richard T. *mechanical engineering educator*
Johnson, Brian Keith *electrical engineering educator*
Peterson, Charles Loren *agricultural engineer, educator*
Woodall, David Monroe *research engineer, dean*

**Pocatello**
Bennion, John Stradling *engineering educator, consultant*

**Rigby**
Peterson, Erle Vidaillet *retired metallurgical engineer*

## ILLINOIS

**Argonne**
Chang, Yoon Il *nuclear engineer*
Kumar, Romesh *chemical engineer*
Miller, Shelby Alexander *chemical engineer, educator*
Myles, Kevin Michael *metallurgical engineer*

**Aurora**
Ramirez, Martin Ruben *engineer, educator, administrator, consultant*

**Bannockburn**
Kotynek, George Roy *mechanical engineer, educator, marketing executive*

**Barrington**
Francis, Philip Hamilton *engineering executive, mechanical engineer*

**Bourbonnais**
Schwark, Howard Edward *civil engineer*

**Buffalo Grove**
Kaplan, Mitchell Philip *consulting engineer, marketing executive*

**Carbondale**
Chugh, Yoginder Paul *mining engineering educator*
Khonsari, Michael M. *mechanical engineering educator*
Orthwein, William Coe *mechanical engineer*
Smith, James Gilbert *electrical engineer*

**Carthage**
Erbes, John Robert *engineering executive*

**Champaign**
Cal, Mark Patrick *chemical engineer, researcher*
Korst, Helmut Hans *mechanical engineer, educator*
Kruger, William Arnold *consulting civil engineer*
May, Linda Karen Cardiff *safety engineer, nurse*
O'Connor, John T. *civil engineering educator*
Puckett, Hoyle Brooks *agricultural engineer, research scientist, consultant*
Sohn, Chang Wook *energy systems researcher, educator*
Sundy, George Joseph, Jr. *engineering executive*

**Chicago**
Acs, Joseph Steven *transportation engineering consultant*
Agarwal, Gyan Chand *engineering educator*
Aggarwal, Suresh Kumar *mechanical and aerospace engineering educator*
Babcock, Lyndon Ross, Jr. *environmental engineer, educator*
Banerjee, Prashant *industrial engineering educator*
Blanchard, James Arthur *engineer and computer systems specialist*
Breyer, Norman Nathan *metallurgical engineering educator, consultant*
Chen, Wai-Kai *electrical engineering and computer science educator, consultant*
Chung, Paul Myungha *mechanical engineer, educator*
Datta, Rathin *chemical engineer*
†Davis, DeForest P., Jr. *architectural engineer*
Dix, Rollin C(umming) *mechanical engineering educator, consultant*
Epstein, Raymond *engineering and architectural executive*
Fabisch, Gale Warren *civil engineer*
Fahnestock, Jean Howe *retired civil engineer*
Gerstner, Robert William *structural engineering educator, consultant*
Graupe, Daniel *electrical and computer engineering educator, systems and biomedical engineer*
Gupta, Krishna Chandra *mechanical engineering educator*
Guralnick, Sidney Aaron *civil engineering educator*
Hartnett, James Patrick *engineering educator*
Hobbs, Marvin *engineering executive*
Jaramillo, Carlos Alberto *civil engineer*
Kim, H. J. (Shaun Kim) *engineering company executive*
Lin, James Chih-I *biomedical and electrical engineer, educator*
Linden, Henry Robert *chemical engineering research executive*
Minkowycz, W. J. *mechanical engineering educator*
Munoz, Mario Alejandro *civil engineer, consultant*
Murata, Tadao *engineering and computer science educator*
Nickel, Melvin Edwin *metallurgical engineer*
Rikoski, Richard Anthony *engineering executive, electrical engineer*
Russo, Gilberto *engineering educator*
Rymer, Randal Eugene *chemical engineer*
Shah, Manu Hirachand *civil and structural engineer*
Shieh, Ching-Long *structural engineering executive*
Stoller, Patricia Sypher *structural engineer*
Swanson, Bernet Steven *consulting engineer, former educator*
Todd Copley, Judith Ann *materials and metallurgical engineering educator*
Wadden, Richard Albert *environmental engineer, educator, consultant, research director*

**Clarendon Hills**
Moritz, Donald Brooks *mechanical engineer, consultant*

**Clinton**
Ramanuja, Teralandur Krishnaswamy *structural engineer*

**Crystal Lake**
Dabkowski, John *electrical engineering executive*

**Darien**
Hanson, Martin Philip *mechanical engineer, farmer*

**De Kalb**
Kostic, Milivoje *mechanical engineering educator*

**Decatur**
Graf, Karl Rockwell *nuclear engineer*
Koucky, John Richard *metallurgical engineer, manufacturing executive*

**Des Plaines**
Bartoo, Richard Kieth *chemical engineer, consultant*
Dlouhy, Phillip Edward *engineering, construction executive*
Lyu, Seung Won *metallurgical engineer, environmental scientist*
Ripp, Bryan Jerome *geological engineer*
Winfield, Michael D. *engineering company executive*

**Dunlap**
Bailey, John Maxwell *retired mechanical engineer, consultant*

**East Saint Louis**
Baltz, Richard Arthur *chemical engineer*

**Elmhurst**
Burton, Darrell Irvin *engineering executive*
Grisim, J. Terrence *safety consulting company executive*

**Evanston**
Achenbach, Jan Drewes *engineering educator, scientist*
Bankoff, Seymour George *chemical engineer, educator*
Bazant, Zdenek Pavel *structural engineering educator, scientist, consultant*
Belytschko, Ted Bohdan *civil, mechanical engineering educator*
Brazelton, William Thomas *chemical engineering educator*
Butt, John Baecher *chemical engineering educator*
Carr, Stephen Howard *materials engineer, educator*
Cheng, Herbert Su-Yuen *mechanical engineering educator*
Chung, Yip-Wah *engineering educator*
Daniel, Isaac Mordochai *mechanical engineering educator*
Daskin, Mark Stephen *civil engineering educator*
Fessler, Raymond R. *metallurgical engineering consultant*
Fine, Morris Eugene *materials engineer, educator*
Fourer, Robert H. *industrial engineering educator, consultant*
Frey, Donald Nelson *industrial engineer, educator, manufacturing company executive*
Goldstick, Thomas Karl *biomedical engineering educator*
Haddad, Abraham Herzl *electrical engineering educator, researcher*
Keer, Leon Morris *engineering educator*
Kistler, Alan Lee *engineering educator*
Kliphardt, Raymond A. *engineering educator*
Krizek, Raymond John *civil engineering educator, consultant*
Kung, Harold Hing-Chuen *engineering educator*
Lee, Der-Tsai *electrical engineering and computer science educator, researcher, consultant*
Liu, Shu Qian *biomedical engineer, researcher, educator*
Liu, Wing Kam *mechanical and civil engineering educator*
Mah, Richard Sze Hao *chemical engineering educator*
Marhic, Michel Edmond *engineering educator, entrepreneur, consultant*
Murphy, Gordon John *engineering educator*
Ottino, Julio Mario *chemical engineering educator, scientist*
Rubenstein, Albert Harold *industrial engineering and management sciences educator*
Shah, Surendra Poonamchand *engineering educator, researcher*
Smith, Spencer Bailey *engineering and business educator*
Sobel, Alan *electrical engineer, physicist*
Taflove, Allen *electrical engineer, educator, researcher, consultant*
Tankin, Richard Samuel *fluid dynamics engineer, educator*
Van Ness, James Edward *electrical engineering educator*
Zhang, Jianping *electrical engineering educator, researcher*

**Evergreen Park**
Ephraim, Max, Jr. *mechanical engineer*

**Fairview Heights**
Moses, Daniel David *civil engineer*

**Gilman**
Ireland, Herbert Orin *engineering educator*

**Glenview**
Harris, Ronald David *chemical engineer*
Panarese, William C. *civil engineer*
Russell, Henry George *structural engineer*
Van Zelst, Theodore William *civil engineer, natural resource exploration company executive*

**Gurnee**
Sommerlad, Robert Edward *environmental research engineer*
Theis, Peter Frank *engineering executive, inventor*

**Itasca**
Mockus, Joseph Frank *electrical engineer*

**La Grange**
Mehlenbacher, Dohn Harlow *civil engineer, consultant*

**Lake Bluff**
Fortuna, William Frank *architectural engineer, architect*

**Lake Forest**
Bell, Charles Eugene, Jr. *industrial engineer*
Lambert, John Boyd *chemical engineer, consultant*

**Lemont**
Chen, Shoei-Sheng *mechanical engineer*

**Lisle**
Vora, Manu Kishandas *chemical engineer, quality consultant*

**Lombard**
Branum, William Howell *engineering company executive*

**Mattoon**
Simonelli, Michael Tarquin *chemical engineer*

**Moline**
Harrington, Roy Edwards *agricultural engineer, author*
Malicki, Gregg Hillard *engineer*

**Mount Prospect**
Kilian, Mark Kenneth *engineering executive*
Scott, Norman Laurence *engineering consultant*

**Mount Vernon**
Knight, Brenda Lee *quality engineer*

**Naperville**
Crawford, Raymond Maxwell, Jr. *nuclear engineer*

**Niles**
Bates, William Richie *electrical engineer*

**North Chicago**
Chu, Alexander Hang-Torng *chemical engineer*

**Northbrook**
Polsky, Michael Peter *mechanical engineer*

**Northfield**
Adler, Robert *electronics engineer*

**Oak Park**
Clark, John Peter, III *engineering consultant*
Goetz, Thomas *systems engineer, consultant*
Relwani, Nirmalkumar Murlidhar (Nick Relwani) *mechanical engineer*

**Oakbrook Terrace**
Samet, Dean Henry *safety engineer*

**Orland Park**
Dyott, Richard Burnaby *research engineering executive*
Knop, Charles Milton *electrical engineer*

**Park Ridge**
Bridges, Jack Edgar *electronics engineer*

**Peoria**
Kroll, Dennis Edwards *industrial engineering educator*
Polanin, W. Richard *engineering educator*

**Plainfield**
Chakrabarti, Subrata Kumar *marine research engineer*

**Rock Island**
Osborn, David Lee *engineer*

**Rockford**
Eliason, Jon Tate *electrical engineer*
Hornby, Robert Ray *mechanical engineer*
Vincenti-Brown, Crispin Rufus William *engineering executive*

**Schaumburg**
Wyslotsky, Ihor *engineering company executive*

**Skokie**
Corley, William Gene *engineering research executive*
Siegal, Rita Goran *engineering company executive*

**Springfield**
Chen, Eden Hsien-chang *engineering consultant*
Fleck, Gabriel Alton *electrical engineer*
Hahin, Christopher *metallurgical engineer, corrosion engineer*
Hanson, Walter Edmund *consulting civil engineer*
Lyons, J. Rolland *civil engineer*

**Sullivan**
Holder, Lonnie Edward *engineering administrator, design engineer*

**Urbana**
Addy, Alva Leroy *mechanical engineer*
Alkire, Richard Collin *chemical engineering educator*
Axford, Roy Arthur *nuclear engineering educator*
Basar, Tamer *electrical engineering educator*
Beck, Paul Adams *metallurgist, educator*
Benekohal, Rahim Farahnak *civil engineering educator, researcher, consultant*
Bergeron, Clifton George *ceramic engineer, educator*
Blahut, Richard Edward *electrical and computer engineering educator*
Chao, Bei Tse *mechanical engineering educator*
Chato, John Clark *mechanical and bioengineering educator*
Clausing, Arthur M. *mechanical engineering educator*
Coleman, Paul Dare *electrical engineering educator*
Conry, Thomas Francis *mechanical engineering educator, consultant*
Cusano, Cristino *mechanical engineer, educator*
Davis, Wayne Joseph *engineering educator*
Dobrovolny, Jerry Stanley *engineering educator*
Eden, James Gary *electrical engineering and physics educator, researcher*
Gaddy, Oscar Lee *electrical engineering educator*
Goering, Carroll E. *agricultural engineering educator*
Hall, William Joel *civil engineer, educator*
Hannon, Bruce Michael *engineer, educator*
Hanratty, Thomas Joseph *chemical engineer, educator*
Herrin, Moreland *civil engineering educator, consultant*
Hess, Karl *electrical and computer engineering educator*
Holonyak, Nick, Jr. *electrical engineering educator*
Huang, Thomas Shi-Tao *electrical engineering educator, researcher*
Jenkins, William Kenneth *electrical engineering educator*
Jones, Benjamin Angus, Jr. *retired agricultural engineering educator, administrator*
Kang, Sung-Mo (Steve Kang) *electrical engineering educator*
Kesler, Clyde Ervin *engineering educator*
Kumar, Panganamala Ramana *electrical and computer engineering educator*
Liu, Chung Laung *computer engineer, educator*
Maxwell, William Hall Christie *civil engineering educator*
May, Walter Grant *chemical engineer*
Mayes, Paul Eugene *engineering educator, technical consultant*
Miley, George Hunter *nuclear engineering educator*
Miller, Robert Earl *engineer, educator*
Pai, Anantha Mangalore *electrical engineering educator, consultant*
Rao, Nannapaneni Narayana *electrical engineer*
Siess, Chester Paul *civil engineering educator*
Socie, Darrell Frederick *mechanical engineering educator*
Soo, Shao Lee *mechanical engineer, educator*
Stallmeyer, James Edward *engineer, educator*
Swenson, George Warner, Jr. *electronics engineer, radio astronomer, educator*
Trick, Timothy Noel *electrical and computer engineering educator, researcher*
Trigger, Kenneth James *manufacturing engineering educator*
Wert, Charles Allen *metallurgical and mining engineering educator*
Westwater, James William *chemical engineering educator*
Yoerger, Roger Raymond *agricultural engineer, educator*

**Vernon Hills**
Jensen, Rolf H. *fire protection engineer, company executive*

**Washington**
Hallinan, John Cornelius *mechanical engineering consultant*

**Waukegan**
Srinivasa, Venkataramaniah *engineer*

**West Chicago**
Kieft, Gerald Nelson *mechanical engineer*

**Westchester**
Barrett, Robert David *engineering executive*

**Wilmette**
Barnett, Ralph Lipsey *engineering educator*
Muhlenbruch, Carl W. *civil engineer*

**Winnetka**
Fraenkel, Stephen Joseph *engineering and research executive*

**Wood Dale**
Smith, Michael William *biomedical engineer, consultant*

## INDIANA

**Batesville**
Myers, Daniel Lee *manufacturing engineer*

**Bloomington**
Harder, John E. *electrical engineer*

**Carmel**
Monical, Robert Duane *consulting structural engineer*

**Chesterfield**
Fry, Meredith Warren *civil engineer, consultant*

**Columbus**
Hercamp, Richard Dean *chemical engineer*
Kubo, Isoroku *mechanical engineer*

**Crane**
Waggoner, Susan Marie *electronics engineer*

**Elkhart**
McCarty, Richard Joseph *consulting engineer*

**Evansville**
Bennett, Paul Edmond *engineering educator*
Gerhart, Philip Mark *engineering educator*
Hartsaw, William O. *mechanical engineering educator*

**Fort Wayne**
Hwang, Santai *electrical engineering educator*
Lyons, Harvey Isaac *mechanical engineering educator*
Lyons, Jerry Lee *mechanical engineer*
Mahmoud, Aly Ahmed *electrical engineering educator*
Weatherford, George Edward *civil engineer*
Williams, Walter Jackson, Jr. *electrical engineer, consultant*

**Hammond**
Neff, Gregory Pall *manufacturing engineering educator, consultant*
Pierson, Edward Samuel *engineering educator, consultant*

**Indianapolis**
Austin, Robert Brendon *civil engineer*
Brannon-Peppas, Lisa *chemical engineer, researcher*
Cones, Van Buren *electronics engineer, consultant*
Evans, Richard James *mechanical engineer*
Fer, Ahmet F. *electrical engineer, educator*
Ott, Carl Neil *environmental engineer*

**Kokomo**
Miller, Robert Frank *retired electronics engineer, educator*

**Lafayette**
Bement, Arden Lee, Jr. *engineering educator*
Etzel, James Edward *environmental engineering educator*
Fox, Robert William *mechanical engineering educator*
Geddes, Leslie Alexander *bioengineer, physiologist, educator*
Gustafson, Winthrop Adolph *aeronautical and astronautical engineering educator*
Lindenlaub, J.C. *electrical engineer, educator*
Ott, Karl Otto *nuclear engineering educator, consultant*

**Muncie**
Bennon, Saul *electrical engineer, transformer consultant*
Seymour, Richard Deming *technology educator*

**Notre Dame**
Gray, William Guerin *civil engineering educator*
Jerger, Edward William *mechanical engineer, university dean*
Kohn, James Paul *engineering educator*
Michel, Anthony Nikolaus *electrical engineering educator, researcher*
Sain, Michael Kent *electrical engineering educator*
Schmitz, Roger Anthony *chemical engineering educator, academic administrator*
Szewczyk, Albin Anthony *engineering educator*
Varma, Arvind *chemical engineering educator, researcher*

**Owensville**
Snow, Jeffrey Scott *fuels engineer*

**Princeton**
Mullins, Richard Austin *chemical engineer*

**Purdue University**
Liley, Peter Edward *mechanical engineering educator*

**South Bend**
Jorgensen, Robert William *product engineer*

**Terre Haute**
Wheelock, Larry Arthur *engineer, consultant*

**West Lafayette**
Albright, Lyle Frederick *chemical engineering educator*
Altschaeffl, Adolph George *civil engineering educator*
Andres, Ronald Paul *chemical engineer, educator*
Bernhard, Robert James *mechanical engineer, educator*
Bogdanoff, John Lee *aeronautical engineering educator*
Chao, Kwang-Chu *chemical engineer, educator*
Chen, Wai-Fah *civil engineering educator*
Cohen, Raymond *mechanical engineer, educator*
Cooper, James Albert, Jr. *electrical engineering educator*
Dayananda, Mysore Ananthamurthy *materials engineering educator*
Delleur, Jacques William *civil engineering educator*
Dolch, William Lee *retired engineering materials educator*
Drnevich, Vincent Paul *civil engineering educator*
Eckert, Roger E(arl) *chemical engineering educator*
Friedlaender, Fritz Josef *electrical engineering educator*
Fukunaga, Keinosuke *engineering educator*
Grace, Richard Edward *engineering educator*
Greenkorn, Robert Albert *chemical engineering educator*
Hinkle, Charles Nelson *retired agricultural engineering educator*
Hoffman, Larry Dean *engineering educator*
Incropera, Frank Paul *mechanical engineering educator*
Kashyap, Rangasami Lakshmi Narayan *electrical engineering educator*
Koivo, Antti Jaakko *electrical engineering educator, researcher*
Landgrebe, David Allen *electrical engineer*
Leimkuhler, Ferdinand Francis *industrial engineering educator*
Lin, Pen-Min *electrical engineer, educator*
Marshall, Francis Joseph *aerospace engineer*
Mc Gillem, Clare Duane *electrical engineering educator*
Mc Laughlin, John Francis *civil engineer, educator*
Michael, Harold Louis *civil engineering educator*
Neudeck, Gerold Walter *electrical engineering educator*
Ong, Chee-Mun *engineering educator*
Peppas, Nikolaos Athanassiou *chemical engineering educator, consultant*
Pritsker, A. Alan B. *engineering executive, educator*
Ramadhyani, Satish *mechanical engineering educator*
Richey, Clarence Bentley *agricultural engineering educator*
Salvendy, Gavriel *industrial engineer*
Schuhmann, Reinhardt, Jr. *metallurgical engineering educator, consultant*
Schwartz, Richard John *electrical engineering educator, researcher*
Sozen, Mete Avni *civil engineering educator*
Stevenson, Warren Howard *mechanical engineering educator*
Taber, Margaret Ruth *electrical engineering technology educator, electrical engineer*
Taylor, Raymond Ellory *engineering executive*
Thomas, Marlin Uluess *industrial engineering educator, academic administrator*
Tomovic, Mileta Milos *mechanical engineer, educator*
Tsao, George T. *chemical engineer, educator*
Viskanta, Raymond *mechanical engineering educator*
Wankat, Phillip Charles *chemical engineering educator*
Weiner, Andrew Marc *electrical engineering educator*
Williams, Theodore Joseph *engineering educator*
Wright, Jeff Regan *civil engineering educator*

## IOWA

**Ames**
Anderson, Robert Morris, Jr. *electrical engineer*
Basart, John Philip *electrical engineering and radio astronomy researcher, educator*
Baumann, Edward Robert *sanitary engineering educator*
Boylan, David Ray *retired chemical engineer, educator*
Brown, Robert Grover *engineering educator*
Buchele, Wesley Fisher *retired agricultural engineering educator*
Burnet, George, Jr. *engineering educator*
Cleasby, John LeRoy *civil engineer, educator*
Colvin, Thomas Stuart *agricultural engineer, farmer*
Ekberg, Carl Edwin, Jr. *civil engineering educator*
Huston, Jeffrey Charles *mechanical engineer, educator*
Inger, George Roe *aerospace engineering educator*
Johnson, Howard Paul *agricultural engineering educator*
Jones, Edwin Channing, Jr. *electrical engineering educator*
Larsen, William Lawrence *materials science and engineering educator*
Larson, Maurice Allen *chemical engineer, educator*
Maze, Thomas H. *engineering educator*
Mischke, Charles Russell *mechanical engineering educator*
Okiishi, Theodore Hisao *mechanical engineering educator*
Riley, William Franklin *mechanical engineering educator*
Sanders, Wallace Wolfred, Jr. *civil engineer*
Tannehill, John C. *aerospace engineer, educator*
Venkata, Subrahmanyam Saraswati *electrical engineering educator, electric energy and power researcher*
Wilder, David Randolph *materials engineer, consultant*
Young, Donald Fredrick *engineering educator*

**Bettendorf**
Heyderman, Arthur Jerome *engineer, civilian military employee*

**Cedar Falls**
Johnson, Curtis Scott *engineer*

**Cedar Rapids**
Lewis, Daniel Edward *systems engineer, computer company executive*

**Cherokee**
Clark, Larry Dalton *civil engineer*

**Decorah**
Erdman, Lowell Paul *civil engineer, land surveyor*

**Iowa City**
Arora, Jasbir Singh *engineering educator*
Carmichael, Gregory Richard *chemical engineering educator*
Eyman, Earl Duane *electrical science educator, consultant*
Haug, Edward Joseph, Jr. *mechanical engineering educator, simulation research engineer*
Hering, Robert Gustave *mechanical engineer, educator, university administrator*
Kusiak, Andrew *manufacturing engineer, educator*
Lance, George Milward *mechanical engineering educator*
Lonngren, Karl Erik *electrical and computer engineering educator*
Marshall, Jeffrey Scott *mechanical engineer, educator*
Miller, Richard Keith *engineering educator*
Patel, Virendra Chaturbhai *mechanical engineering educator*

**Madrid**
Handy, Richard Lincoln *civil engineer, educator*

**Muscatine**
Fosholt, Sanford Kenneth *consulting engineer*
Stanley, Richard Holt *consulting engineer*
Thomopulos, Gregs G. *consulting engineering company executive*

**New Hampton**
Yared, Linda S. *mechanical engineer*

**Orange City**
Hancock, Albert Sidney, Jr. *engineering executive*

**Sioux City**
Walker, Jimmie Kent *mechanical engineer*

## KANSAS

**Lawrence**
Benjamin, Bezaleel Solomon *architecture and architectural engineering educator*
Darwin, David *civil engineering educator, researcher, consultant*
Green, Don Wesley *chemical and petroleum engineering educator*
Leonard, Roy Junior *civil engineering educator*
Lucas, William Max, Jr. *structural engineer, university dean*
McCabe, Steven Lee *structural engineer*
Moore, Richard Kerr *electrical engineering educator*
Muirhead, Vincent Uriel *aerospace engineer*
Rolfe, Stanley Theodore *civil engineer, educator*
Roskam, Jan *aerospace engineer*
Rowland, James Richard *electrical engineering educator*

**Leavenworth**
Hamilton, Mark Alan *electrical engineer*

**Leawood**
Karmeier, Delbert Fred *consulting engineer, realtor*

**Lenexa**
Herbel, LeRoy Alec, Jr. *telecommunications engineer*

**Manhattan**
Appl, Fredric Carl *retired mechanical engineering educator*
Erickson, Larry Eugene *chemical engineering educator*
Hagen, Lawrence Jacob *agricultural engineer*
Johnson, William Howard *agricultural engineer, educator*
Kirmser, Philip George *engineering educator*
Lee, E(ugene) Stanley *engineer, mathematician, educator*
Madanshetty, Sameer Ishwar *mechanical engineer*
Russell, Eugene Robert, Sr. *engineering educator, administrator*
Simons, Gale Gene *nuclear and electrical engineer, educator*

**Overland Park**
Bennett, Richard Douglas *electrical engineer*
Kutscher, Thomas Alan *electrical engineer*
Zhan, Steve Q. *optical engineer, researcher*

**Salina**
Crawford, Lewis Cleaver *engineering executive*
Reh, John W. *engineer, consultant*

**Shawnee Mission**
Callahan, Harry Leslie *civil engineer*
Cassidy, John Lemont *engineering executive*

**Topeka**
Comstock, Glen David *civil engineer*
Metzler, Dwight Fox *civil engineer, retired state official*

**Wichita**
Adegbola, Sikiru Kolawole *aerospace engineer, educator*
Egbert, Robert Iman *electrical engineering educator, academic administrator*
Gosman, Albert Louis *retired mechanical engineering educator*
Mc Kee, George Moffitt, Jr. *civil engineer, consultant*
Wentz, William Henry, Jr. *aerospace engineer, educator*
Wilhelm, William Jean *civil engineering educator*

## KENTUCKY

**Bowling Green**
Russell, Josette Renee *industrial engineer*

**Covington**
Middendorf, William Henry *electrical engineering educator*

**Fort Campbell**
Oakes, Thomas Wyatt *environmental engineer*

**Lexington**
Caroland, William Bourne *structural engineer*
Cremers, Clifford John *mechanical engineering educator*
Drake, David Lee *electronics engineer*
Drake, Vaughn Paris, Jr. *electrical engineer*
Foree, Edward Golden *environmental engineer, consultant*
Grimes, Craig Alan *electrical engineering educator*
Grimes, Dale Mills *physics and electrical engineering educator*
Hanson, Mark Tod *engineering mechanics educator*
Nasar, Syed Abu *electrical engineering educator*
Shah, Ramesh Keshavlal *engineering educator, researcher*
Steele, Earl Larsen *electrical engineering educator*
Tauchert, Theodore Richmond *mechanical engineer, educator*

**Louisville**
Clark, John Hallett, III *consulting engineering executive*
Cornelius, Wayne Anderson *electrical and computer engineering consultant*
Garcia, Rafael Jorge *chemical engineer*
Hanley, Thomas Richard *engineering educator*
Moll, Joseph Eugene *chemical engineer, chemical company executive*
Mueller, Robert William *process and instrument engineer*
Reinbold, Darrel William *energy engineering specialist*
Smith, Robert F., Jr. *civil engineer*
Tran, Long Trieu *industrial engineer*
Ward, Thomas Leon *engineering educator*

**Wickliffe**
Gray, Carol Hickson *chemical engineer*

## LOUISIANA

**Baker**
Moody, Lamon Lamar, Jr. *retired civil engineer*

**Baton Rouge**
Aghazadeh, Fereydoun *industrial engineer, educator*
Arman, Ara *civil engineering educator*
Chen, Peter Pin-Shan *electrical engineering and computer science educator, data processing executive*
Constant, William David *chemical engineer, educator*
Corripio, Armando Benito *chemical engineering educator*
Gernon, Clarke Joseph, Sr. *mechanical and forensic engineering consultant*
Ikossi-Anastasiou, Kiki *electrical and computer engineer*
Marshak, Alan Howard *electrical engineer, educator*
Moody, Gene Byron *engineering executive, small business owner*
Pike, Ralph Webster *chemical engineer, educator, university administrator*
Stopher, Peter Robert *civil and transportation engineering educator, consultant*
Tipton, Kenneth Warren *agricultural administrator, researcher*
Triantaphyllou, Evangelos *industrial engineering educator*
Tumay, Mehmet Taner *geotechnical consultant, educator, research administrator*
Valsaraj, Kalliat Thazhathuveetil *chemical engineering educator*

**Dubach**
Straughan, William Thomas *engineering educator*

**Hammond**
Parish, Richard Lee *engineer, consultant*

**Kenner**
Siebel, Mathias Paul *mechanical engineer*

**Lafayette**
Domingue, Emery *consulting engineering company executive*
Fang, Cheng-Shen *chemical engineering educator*
Liang, Qingjian Jim *petroleum engineer*

**Metairie**
N'Vietson, Tung Thanh *civil engineer*

**Monroe**
Khan, Khalid Saifullah *engineering executive*

**New Orleans**
Angelides, Demosthenes Constantinos *civil engineer*
Lannes, William Joseph, III *electrical engineer*
Lee, Griff Calicutt *civil engineer*
Nelson, Waldemar Stanley *civil engineer, consultant*
Quirk, Peter Richard *engineering company executive*

**Plaquemine**
Goodwin, Billy Wayne *chemical engineer*

**Ruston**
Barron, Randall Franklin *mechanical engineer, educator, consultant*
Hale, Paul Nolen, Jr. *engineering administrator, educator*
Painter, Jack Timberlake *civil engineer*
Sterling, Raymond Leslie *civil engineering educator, researcher, consultant*

**Saint Gabriel**
Das, Dilip Kumar *chemical engineer*

**Shreveport**
Burch, Paul Michael *financial consultant*

**Slidell**
Grantham, Donald James *engineer, educator, author*
Sullivan, Daniel Thomas *electrical engineer, consultant*
Tewell, Joseph Robert, Jr. *electrical engineer*

## MAINE

**Auburn**
Bastow, Richard Frederick *civil engineer, educator, surveyor*

**Bangor**
Hsu, Yu Kao *aerospace scientist, mathematician, educator*

**Bowdoin**
Watts, Helen Caswell *civil engineer*

**Brownfield**
Ellison, Thorleif *consulting engineer*

**East Boothbay**
Smith, Merlin Gale *engineering executive, researcher*

**Eastport**
Kennedy, Robert Spayde *electrical engineering educator*

**Gray**
Durgin, Scott Benjamin *radio frequency engineer*

**Greenville**
Pepin, John Nelson *materials research and design engineer*

**Oakland**
Poulin, Thomas Edward *marine engineer, state legislator, retail business owner*

**Oquossoc**
Hughes, William Frank *mechanical and electrical engineering educator*

**Orono**
Rivard, William Charles *mechanical engineering educator*
Ruthven, Douglas Morris *chemical engineering educator*

**Portland**
Raisbeck, Gordon *systems engineer*

**Prospect Harbor**
Shipman, Charles William *chemical engineer*

## MARYLAND

**Aberdeen Proving Ground**
Cozby, Richard Scott *electronics engineer, reserve army officer*

**Annapolis**
DiAiso, Robert Joseph *civil engineer*

Granger, Robert Alan *aerospace engineer*
Heller, Austin Norman *chemical and environmental engineer*
Johnson, Bruce *engineering educator*
Kapland, Mitchell Arthur *engineering firm executive*
Rapkin, Jerome *marine engineer, defense industry executive*

## Baltimore
Broadbent, J. Streett *engineering executive*
Carmi, Shlomo *mechanical engineering educator, scientist*
Corn, Morton *environmental engineer, educator*
Degenford, James Edward *electrical engineer, educator*
Ellingwood, Bruce Russell *structural engineering researcher, educator*
Fisher, Jack Carrington *environmental engineering educator*
Giddens, Don Peyton *engineering educator, researcher*
Hirsch, Richard Arthur *retired mechanical engineer*
Jelinek, Frederick *electrical engineer, educator*
Katz, Joseph Louis *chemical engineer, educator*
Kelman, Gary F. *environmental engineer*
Knoedler, Elmer L. *retired chemical engineer*
Lerner, Andrew Charles *engineer, economist*
Mc Cord, Kenneth Armstrong *consulting engineer*
O'Melia, Charles Richard *environmental engineering educator*
Popel, Aleksander S. *engineering educator*
Prince, Jerry Ladd *engineering educator*
ReVelle, Charles S. *environmental engineer, geophysicist, systems analysis and economics educator*
Sharpe, William Norman, Jr. *mechanical engineer, educator*
Wagner, James Warren *engineering educator*

## Bel Air
Powers, Doris Hurt *retired engineering company executive*

## Bethesda
Ballhaus, William Francis, Jr. *aerospace industry executive, research scientist*
Burdeshaw, William Brooksbank *engineering executive*
Di Marzo, Marino *engineering researcher, educator*
Eden, Murray *electrical engineer, emeritus educator*
Freedman, Joseph *sanitary and public health engineering consultant*
Koltnow, Peter Gregory *engineering consultant*
Pritchard, Wilbur Louis *telecommunications engineering executive*
Saville, Thorndike, Jr. *coastal engineer, consultant*
Sevik, Maurice *acoustical engineer, researcher*

## Brooklandville
Azola, Martin Peter *civil engineer, construction manager*

## California
Reagan, Lawrence Paul, Jr. *systems engineer*

## Chevy Chase
Edelson, Burton Irving *electrical engineer*
Mayers, Jean *aeronautical engineering educator*
Rockwell, Theodore *nuclear engineer*

## Clarksville
Brancato, Emanuel Leonard *electrical engineering consultant*

## Cockeysville Hunt Valley
Barr, Irwin Robert *retired aeronautical engineer*
Kinstlinger, Jack *engineering executive, consultant*

## College Park
†Ayyub, Bilal Mohammed *civil engineering educator, researcher, executive*
Barbe, David Franklin *electrical engineer, educator*
Blankenship, Gilmer Leroy *electrical engineering educator, engineering company executive*
Cunniff, Patrick Francis *mechanical engineer*
Ephremides, Anthony *electrical engineering educator*
Gentry, James Walter *chemical engineer, educator*
Gessow, Alfred *aerospace engineer, educator*
Granatstein, Victor Lawrence *electrical engineer, educator*
Gupta, Ashwani Kumar *mechanical engineering educator*
Kirk, James Allen *mechanical engineering educator*
Lee, Chi Hsiang *electrical engineer, educator*
Levine, William Silver *electrical engineering educator*
Lin, Hung C. *electrical engineer educator*
Marcus, Steven Irl *electrical engineering educator*
Nakayama, Wataru *engineering educator*
Newcomb, Robert Wayne *electrical engineer*
Taylor, Leonard Stuart *engineering educator, consultant*

## Columbia
Bremerman, Michael Vance *reliability engineer*

## Easton
Buescher, Adolph Ernst (Dolph Buescher) *aerospace company executive*
Gipe, Albert Bondsfield *electrical engineering consultant*

## Elkton
Chen, Oliver Tsung-Yu *chemical engineer, researcher*

## Ellicott City
Gagnon, Robert Michael *engineering executive, educator*

## Finksburg
Konigsberg, Robert Lee *electrical engineer*

## Fort Washington
Caveny, Leonard Hugh *mechanical engineer*

## Frederick
Bryan, John Leland *retired engineering educator*
Wolf, Donald Joseph *industrial engineer*

## Gaithersburg
Cookson, Alan Howard *electrical engineer, researcher*
Fuhrman, Ralph Edward *civil and environmental engineer*
Hoppes, Harrison Neil *chemical engineer, corporate executive*
Jahanmir, Said *materials scientist, mechanical engineer*
Levine, Robert Sidney *chemical engineer*
Mathias, Joseph Simon *metallurgical engineer, consultant*
Nayyar, Mohinder Lal *mechanical engineer*
Rabinow, Jacob *electrical engineer, consultant*
Stever, Horton Guyford *aerospace scientist and engineer, educator, consultant*
Tesk, John Aloysius *materials scientist*
Wisniewski, John William *mining engineer, bank engineering executive*
Wright, Richard Newport, III *civil engineer, government official*

## Germantown
Lee, Lin-Nan *communications engineer, engineering executive*
Pridmore, Charles Franklin, Jr. *mechanical engineer*

## Glen Arm
Harris, Benjamin Louis *chemical engineer, consultant*

## Greenbelt
Bryant, Paul T. *electronics engineering manager*
Cooper, Robert Shanklin *engineering executive, former government official*
Vranish, John Michael *electrical engineer, researcher*

## Hampstead
Jones, Bruce Edward, Jr. *electronic design engineer*

## Kingsville
Pullen, Keats A., Jr. *electronics engineer*

## Lanham
Durrani, Sajjad Haidar *space communications engineer*
Laurenson, Robert Mark *mechanical engineer*
Tadikonda, Sivakumara Sarma Kedara *mechanical and aerospace engineer*

## Largo
Freeman, Ernest Robert *engineering executive*

## Laurel
Dallman, Paul Jerald *engineer, writer*
Dolecek, Quentin Edward *electronic engineer*
Eaton, Alvin Ralph *aeronautical and systems engineer, research and development administrator*
Lombardo, Joseph Samuel *acoustical engineer*
Sherwood, Aaron Wiley *aerodynamics educator*
Westhaver, Lawrence Albert *electronics engineer, consultant*

## Linthicum Heights
Skillman, William Alfred *consulting engineering executive*

## New Market
Billig, Frederick Stucky *mechanical engineer*

## Potomac
Peters, Frank Albert *retired chemical engineer*

## Rockville
Burdick, William MacDonald *biomedical engineer*
Chakravarty, Dipto *computer performance engineer*
Chang, Kung-Li (Charlie) *engineering consulting firm executive*
Davies-Venn, Christian *environmental engineer*
Finch, Frank Robert *environmental engineer*
Lee, Fred Steven *telecommunications engineer*
McDonald, Capers Walter *biomedical engineer, corporate executive*
McMahon, Edward Peter *systems engineer, consultant*
Motayed, Asok K. *engineering company executive*
Seagle, Edgar Franklin *environmental engineer, consultant*
Ulbrecht, Jaromir Josef *chemical engineer*

## Severna Park
Davis, John Adams, Jr. *electrical engineer, roboticist, corporate research executive*
Retterer, Bernard Lee *electronic engineering consultant*

## Silver Spring
Benz, Carl Arvell *nuclear engineer, physics educator*
Blake, Lamont Vincent *electronics consultant*
Eades, James Beverly, Jr. *aeronautical engineer*
Foresti, Roy, Jr. *chemical engineer*
Hermach, Francis Lewis *consulting engineer*
Husemann, Robert William *retired mechanical engineer*
LaSala, Kenneth Paul *engineer, consultant*
Mok, Carson Kwok-Chi *structural engineer*
Shames, Irving Herman *engineering educator*
Short, Steve Eugene *engineer*
White, Edmund William *chemical engineer*

## Stevensville
Trescott, Sara Lou *water resources engineer*

## West River
Patermaster, John Joseph *inventor, consultant*

# MASSACHUSETTS

## Acton
Aldwinckle, Joseph George *electronic engineer*

## Amherst
Abbott, Douglas Eugene *engineering educator*
Berger, Bernard Ben *environmental and civil engineer, former educator and public health officer*
Franks, Lewis E. *electrical and computer engineering educator, researcher*
Haensel, Vladimir *chemical engineering educator*
Koren, Israel *electrical and computer engineering educator*
Laurence, Robert Lionel *chemical engineering educator*
McIntosh, Robert Edward, Jr. *electrical engineering educator, consultant, electronics executive*
Nash, William Arthur *civil engineer, educator*
Swift, Calvin Thomas *electrical and computer engineering educator*
Vogl, Otto *polymer science and engineering educator*

## Andover
Jakes, William Chester *electrical engineer*
Marsh, Robert Buford *chemical engineer, consultant*
Schlecker, James Henry *sales and engineering executive*

## Arlington
Casagrande, Dirk Rainer *civil engineer*
Gumpertz, Werner Herbert *structural engineering company executive*

## Ashfield
Nye, Edwin Packard *mechanical engineering educator*

## Bedford
Cronson, Harry Marvin *electronics engineer*
Fante, Ronald Louis *engineering scientist*
Hicks, Walter Joseph *electrical engineer*
Jelalian, Albert V. *electrical engineer*
Klobuchar, John A. *research engineer*
Winter, David Louis *systems engineer, human factors scientist, retired*

## Belmont
Haralampu, George Stelios *electric power engineer, former engineering executive electric utility company*
Merrill, Edward Wilson *chemical engineering educator*
Ognibene, Edward John *research and development mechanical engineer*

## Boston
Caisse, Thomas Louis *safety engineer*
De Luca, Carlo John *biomedical engineer*
Fine, Samuel *biomedical engineering educator, consultant*
Harrington, Joseph John *environmental engineering educator*
Heimann, David Isidore *software quality/reliability engineer, mathematical analyst*
Hines, Marion Ernest *electronic engineering consultant*
Langer, Robert Martin *retired chemical engineering company executive, consultant*
Levitin, Lev Berovich *engineering educator*
McCluskey, Jean Louise *civil and consulting engineer*
Moore, Richard Lawrence *structural engineer, consultant*
Pedersen, Karen Sue *electrical engineer*
Pierce, Allan Dale *engineering educator, researcher*
Raemer, Harold Roy *electrical engineering educator*
Saleh, Bahaa E. A. *electrical engineering educator*
Schubert, Fred Eric *electrical engineer, educator*
Teich, Malvin Carl *electrical engineering educator*
Zaldastani, Othar *consulting engineer*

## Boxboro
Lee, Shih-Ying *mechanical engineering educator*

## Braintree
Davis, Robert Jocelyn *engineering executive*
Foster, Arthur Rowe *mechanical engineering educator*

## Brewster
Fowle, Arthur Adams *mechanical engineer*

## Brighton
Megherbi, Dalila *electrical and computer engineer, researcher*

## Brockton
Wiegner, Allen Walter *biomedical engineering educator, researcher*

## Brookline
Katz, Israel *retired engineering educator*

## Cambridge
Abelson, Harold *electrical engineer, educator*
Abernathy, Frederick Henry *mechanical engineering educator*
Akylas, Triantaphyllos R. *mechanical engineering educator*
Argon, Ali Suphi *mechanical engineering educator*
Athans, Michael *electrical engineering educator, consultant*
Baggeroer, Arthur B. *electrical engineering educator*
Baron, Judson Richard *aerospace educator*
Baron, Sheldon *research and development company executive*
Battin, Richard Horace *astronautical engineer*
Beér, János Miklós *engineering educator*
Ben-Akiva, Moshe Emanuel *civil engineering educator*
Beranek, Leo Leroy *acoustical consultant*
Bras, Rafael Luis *engineering educator*
Brown, Robert Arthur *chemical engineering educator*
Budiansky, Bernard *engineering educator*
Carmichael, Alexander Douglas *engineering educator*
Chen, Sow-Hsin *nuclear engineering educator, researcher*
Cohen, Morris *engineering educator*
Cohen, Robert Edward *chemical engineering educator, consultant*
Colton, Clark Kenneth *chemical engineering educator*
Corbato, Fernando Jose *electrical engineer and computer science educator*
Counselman, Charles Claude, III *electrical engineering educator*
Crandall, Stephen Harry *engineering educator*
Crawley, Edward Francis *aerospace engineering educator*
Cummings-Saxton, James *chemical engineer, consultant, educator*
Davidson, Frank Paul *macroengineer, lawyer*
de Neufville, Richard Lawrence *engineering educator*
Dewey, Clarence Forbes, Jr. *engineering educator*
Drake, Elisabeth Mertz *chemical engineer*
Dubowsky, Steven *mechanical engineering educator*
Duffy, Robert Aloysius *aeronautical engineer*
Dugundji, John *aeronautical engineer*
Elias, Peter *electrical engineering educator*
Emmons, Howard Wilson *engineer, educator, consultant, researcher*
Fano, Robert Mario *electrical engineering educator*
Fay, James Alan *mechanical engineering educator*
Flemings, Merton Corson *engineering educator, materials scientist*
Fortmann, Thomas Edward *research and development company executive*
Fujimoto, James G. *electrical engineering educator*
Furman, Thomas D., Jr. *engineering company executive*
Gallager, Robert Gray *electrical engineering educator*
Gatos, Harry Constantine *engineering educator*
Glaser, Peter Edward *mechanical engineer, consultant*
Golay, Michael Warren *nuclear engineering educator*
Greitzer, Edward Marc *aeronautical engineering educator, consultant*
Griffith, Peter *mechanical engineering educator, researcher*
Guerra, John Michael *optical engineer*
Gyftopoulos, Elias Panayiotis *mechanical and nuclear engineering educator*
Hansen, Kent Forrest *nuclear engineering educator*
Hansman, Robert John, Jr. *aeronautics and astronautics educator*
Harleman, Donald Robert Fergusson *environmental engineering educator*
Harris, Wesley L. *aeronautics engineering educator*
Haus, Hermann Anton *electrical engineering educator*
Heney, Joseph Edward *environmental engineer*
Heywood, John Benjamin *mechanical engineering educator*
Ho, Yu-Chi *electrical engineering educator*
Howard, Jack Benny *chemical engineer, educator, researcher*
Jensen, Klavs Flemming *chemical engineering educator*
Kamm, Roger Dale *biomedical engineer, educator*
Kassakian, John Gabriel *research electrical engineer, engineering director*
Kazimi, Mujid Suliman *nuclear engineer, educator*
Kerrebrock, Jack Leo *aeronautics and astronautics engineering educator*
Kong, Jin Au *electrical engineering educator*
Kung, H. T. *computer science and engineering educator, consultant*
Kyhl, Robert Louis *electrical engineering educator*
Ladd, Charles Cushing, III *civil engineering educator*
Laibinis, Paul Edward *chemical engineering educator*
Lala, Jaynarayan Hotchand *computer engineer*
Langer, Robert Samuel *chemical, biomedical engineering educator*
Latanision, Ronald Michael *materials science and engineering educator, consultant*
Leehey, Patrick *mechanical and ocean engineering educator*
Lim, Jae Soo *engineering educator, information systems*
Longwell, John Ploeger *chemical engineering educator*
Makhoul, John Ibrahim *electrical engineer, researcher*
Mann, Robert Wellesley *biomedical engineer, educator*
Marini, Robert Charles *environmental engineering executive*
Markey, Winston Roscoe *aeronautical engineering educator*
Masubuchi, Koichi *marine engineer, educator*
McGarry, Frederick Jerome *civil engineering educator*
Meyer, John Edward *nuclear engineering educator*
Milgram, Jerome H. *marine and ocean engineer, educator*
Miller, Rene Harcourt *aerospace engineer, educator*
Mitter, Sanjoy K. *electrical engineering educator*
Ogilvie, T(homas) Francis *engineer, educator*
Oppenheim, Alan Victor *electrical engineering educator*
Parthum, Charles Albert *civil engineer*
Penfield, Paul Livingstone, Jr. *electrical engineering educator*
Pian, Theodore Hsueh-Huang *engineering educator, consultant*
Powers, Michael Kevin *architectural and engineering executive*
Probstein, Ronald Filmore *mechanical engineering educator*
Reid, Robert Clark *chemical engineering educator*
Remington, Paul James *mechanical engineer, educator*
Rogers, Peter Philips *environmental engineering educator, city planner*
Rohsenow, Warren Max *retired mechanical engineer, educator*
Roos, Daniel *civil engineering educator*
Rosenof, Howard Paul *electrical engineer*
Ruina, Jack Philip *electrical engineer, educator*
Russell, Kenneth Calvin *metallurgical engineer, educator*
Saltzer, Jerome Howard *computer science educator*
Satterfield, Charles Nelson *chemical engineer, educator*
Schreiber, William Francis *electrical engineer*
Sheridan, Thomas Brown *mechanical engineering and applied psychology educator, researcher, consultant*
Siebert, William McConway *electrical engineering educator*
Smith, Kenneth Alan *chemical engineer, educator*
Sonin, Ain A. *mechanical engineering educator, consultant*
Staelin, David Hudson *electrical engineering educator, consultant*
Stephanopoulos, Gregory *chemical engineering educator, consultant, researcher*
Stevens, Kenneth Noble *electrical engineering educator*
Thomas, Harold Allen, Jr. *civil engineer, educator*
Todreas, Neil Emmanuel *nuclear engineering educator*
Triantafyllou, Michael Stefanos *ocean engineering educator*
Trilling, Leon *aeronautical engineering educator*
Troxel, Donald Eugene *electrical engineering educator*
Tuller, Harry Louis *materials science and engineering educator*
Ungar, Eric Edward *mechanical engineer*
Vander Velde, Wallace Earl *aeronautical and astronautical educator*
Vér, István László *noise control consultant*
Wang, Daniel I-Chyau *biochemical engineering educator*

**Lansing**
Roberts, Calvin *materials engineer*
Shirtum, Earl Edward *retired civil engineer*

**Midland**
Carson, Gordon Bloom *engineering executive*
Meister, Bernard John *chemical engineer*
Robbins, Lanny Arnold *chemical engineer*

**Muskegon**
Anderson, Harvey Gregg *pattern company executive*

**Newport**
Riches, Kenneth William *nuclear regulatory engineer*

**North Branch**
Stevenson, James Laraway *communications engineer, consulting*

**Okemos**
Giacoletto, Lawrence Joseph *electronics engineering educator, researcher, consultant*

**Plymouth**
Grannan, William Stephen *safety engineer, consultant*

**Rochester**
Hovanesian, Joseph Der *mechanical engineering educator*

**Rochester Hills**
Hicks, George William *automotive and mechanical engineer*

**Saint Joseph**
Maley, Wayne Allen *engineering consultant*

**Shelby Township**
Jaeger, David Leonard *chemical engineer*

**South Lyon**
Guthrie, Michael Steele *magnetic circuit design engineer*

**Southfield**
Ellis, Robert William *engineering educator*
Gleichman, John Alan *safety and loss control executive*

**Tecumseh**
Savoia, Michael Anthony *engineer*

**Three Rivers**
Mackay, Edward *engineer*

**Troy**
Bautz, Jeffrey Emerson *mechanical engineer, educator, researcher*
Drebus, John Richard *systems engineer*
Helmle, Ralph Peter *computer systems developer, manager*
Ross, Eric Alan *civil engineer*
Widmann, Glenn Roger *electrical engineer*

**Warren**
Gallopoulos, Nicholas Efstratios *chemical engineer*
Jacovides, Linos Jacovou *electrical engineering research manager*
Lau, Ian Van *safety research engineer, biomechanics expert*
Nagy, Louis Leonard *engineering executive, researcher*

**Waterford**
Hampton, Phillip Michael *consulting engineering company executive*

**Ypsilanti**
Lou, Zheng (David) *mechanical engineer, biomedical engineer*

## MINNESOTA

**Aitkin**
Prickett, Gordon Odin *mining, mineral and energy engineer*

**Bloomington**
Beckwith, Larry Edward *mechanical engineer*

**Burnsville**
Lai, Juey Hong *chemical engineer*

**Chanhassen**
Thorson, John Martin, Jr. *electrical engineer, consultant*

**East Grand Forks**
Schmitz, Daniel Dean *mechanical engineer*

**Eden Prairie**
Higgins, Robert Arthur *electrical engineer, educator, consultant*

**Hopkins**
Karls, Nicholas James *engineering executive*

**Lutsen**
Napadensky, Hyla Sarane *engineering consultant*

**Madison**
Husby, Donald Evans *engineering company executive*

**Minneapolis**
Albertson, Vernon Duane *electrical engineering educator*
Anderson, John Edward *mechanical engineering educator*
Baker, Michael Harry *chemical engineer*
Cohen, Arnold A. *electrical engineer*
Eckert, Ernst R. G. *mechanical engineering educator*
Fairhurst, Charles *civil and mining engineering educator*
Fletcher, Edward Abraham *engineering educator*
Galambos, Theodore Victor *civil engineer, educator*
Gerberich, William Warren *engineering educator*
Goldstein, Richard Jay *mechanical engineer, educator*
Hillstrom, Thomas Peter *engineering executive*
Isbin, Herbert Stanford *chemical engineering educator*
Johnson, Walter Kline *civil engineer*
Joseph, Daniel Donald *aeronautical engineer, educator*
Kain, Richard Yerkes *electrical engineer, researcher, educator*
Keller, Kenneth Harrison *engineering educator, science policy analyst*
Kvalseth, Tarald Oddvar *mechanical engineer, educator*
Lambert, Robert Frank *electrical engineer, consultant*
Liu, Benjamin Young-hwai *engineering educator*
Mulich, Steve Francis *safety engineer*
Ogata, Katsuhiko *engineering educator*
Oriani, Richard Anthony *metallurgical engineering educator*
Persson, Erland Karl *electrical engineer*
Pfender, Emil *mechanical engineering educator*
Scriven, L. E.(dward), II *chemical engineering educator, scientist*
Sheikh, Suneel Ismail *aerospace engineer, researcher*
Shulman, Yechiel *engineering educator*
Sparrow, Ephraim Maurice *mechanical engineering scientist, educator*
Tirrell, Matthew *chemical engineering/materials science educator*

**Plymouth**
Peterson, Donn Neal *forensic engineer*
Quinn, Richard Kendall *environmental engineer*
Setterholm, Jeffrey Miles *systems engineer*

**Rochester**
Huffine, Coy Lee *retired chemical engineer, consultant*

**Saint Paul**
Fingerson, Leroy Malvin *engineering executive, mechanical engineer*
Goodman, Lawrence Eugene *structural analyst, educator*
Schlentz, Robert Joseph *reliability engineer*

**Spring Park**
Porter, William L. *electrical engineer*

**Stillwater**
Sowman, Harold Gene *ceramic engineer, researcher*

**Thief River Falls**
Gouin, Warner Peter *project engineer*

**Woodbury**
Benforado, David M. *environmental engineer*

## MISSISSIPPI

**Bay Saint Louis**
Corbin, James H. *executive engineer, meteorologist, oceanographer*

**Biloxi**
Ransom, Perry Sylvester *civil engineer*

**Brandon**
Mitchell, Roy Devoy *industrial engineer*

**Jackson**
Pearce, David Harry *biomedical engineer*

**Lorman**
Hylander, Walter Raymond, Jr. *retired civil engineer*

**Mississippi State**
Cliett, Charles Buren *aeronautical engineer, educator, academic administrator*
Jacob, Paul Bernard, Jr. *electrical engineering educator*
Taylor, Clayborne Dudley *engineering educator*
Thompson, Joe Floyd *aerospace engineer, educator*

**Pascagoula**
Chapel, Theron Theodore *quality assurance engineer*

**Ridgeland**
Brady, Michael Jay *environmental engineer, geologist*

**Starkville**
Carley, Charles Team, Jr. *mechanical engineer*
Priest, Melville Stanton *retired consulting hydraulic engineer*

**University**
Horton, Thomas Edward, Jr. *mechanical engineering educator*
Uddin, Waheed *civil engineer, educator*

**Waynesboro**
Brashier, Edward Martin *environmental consultant*

## MISSOURI

**Ballwin**
Cornell, William Daniel *mechanical engineer*

**Branson**
Hamon, Christopher Lloyd *electrical engineer*

**Centralia**
Harmon, Robert Wayne *electrical engineering executive*

**Chesterfield**
Smith, Ronald Earl *aircraft design engineer*
Yardley, John Finley *aerospace engineer*

**Columbia**
Day, Cecil LeRoy *agricultural engineering educator*
Frisby, James Curtis *agricultural engineering educator*
Heldman, Dennis Ray *engineering educator*
Pringle, Oran Allan *mechanical and aerospace engineering educator*
Viswanath, Dabir Srikantiah *chemical engineer*
Yasuda, Hirotsugu Koge *chemical engineering professor*

**Fenton**
Bubash, James Edward *engineering executive, entrepreneur, inventor*

**Florissant**
Martin, Edward Brian *electrical engineer*

**Fortuna**
Ramer, James LeRoy *civil engineer*

**Kansas City**
Acheson, Allen Morrow *retired engineering executive*
Adam, Paul James *engineering company executive, mechanical engineer*
Boyd, John Addison, Jr. *civil engineer*
Davis, F(rancis) Keith *civil engineer*
Nelson, Carlon Justine *engineering and operations executive*
Nofsinger, William Morris *engineering executive*
Stewart, Albert Elisha *safety engineer, industrial hygienist*
Wade, Robert Glenn *engineering executive*

**Kirkwood**
Holsen, James Noble, Jr. *retired chemical engineer*

**Lake Lotawana**
Heineman, Paul Lowe *consulting civil engineer*

**Lake Saint Louis**
Czarnik, Marvin Ray *retired aerospace engineer*

**Maryland Heights**
Beumer, Richard Eugene *engineer, architect, construction firm executive*
Uselton, James Clayton *engineering executive*

**Rolla**
Babcock, Daniel Lawrence *chemical engineer, educator*
Barr, David John *civil, geological engineering educator*
Crosbie, Alfred Linden *mechanical engineering educator*
Dagli, Cihan Hayreddin *engineering educator*
Day, Delbert Edwin *ceramic engineering educator*
Finaish, Fathi Ali *aeronautical engineering educator*
Grayson, Robert Larry *educator mining engineering educator*
Johnson, James Winston *chemical engineering educator*
Munger, Paul R. *civil engineering educator*
Numbere, Daopu Thompson *petroleum engineer, educator*
Saperstein, Lee Waldo *mining engineering educator*
Sarchet, Bernard Reginald *retired chemical engineering educator*
Sauer, Harry John, Jr. *mechanical engineering educator, university administrator*
Scott, James J. *retired mining engineer*
Tsoulfanidis, Nicholas *nuclear engineering educator, university official*

**Saint Charles**
Woods, Marvin *project controls engineer*

**Saint Joseph**
†Nassar, Ahmed Hassan *engineering educator, department head*

**Saint Louis**
Brasunas, Anton de Sales *metallurgical engineering educator*
Breihan, Erwin Robert *civil engineer, consultant*
Briggs, William Benajah *aeronautical engineer*
Cairns, Donald Fredrick *engineering educator, management consultant*
Cox, Jerome Rockhold, Jr. *electrical engineer*
Craig, Jerry Walker *engineering graphics educator*
Dreifke, Gerald Edmond *electrical engineering educator*
Dudukovic, Milorad P. *chemical engineering educator, consultant*
Erickson, Robert Anders *optical engineer, physicist*
Gould, Phillip Louis *civil engineering educator, consultant*
Howard, Walter Burke *chemical engineer*
McKelvey, James Morgan *chemical engineering educator*
Morgan, Robert Peter *engineering educator*
Muller, Marcel W(ettstein) *electrical engineering educator*
Orton, George Frederick *aerospace engineer*
Peters, David Allen *mechanical engineering educator, consultant*
Richardson, Thomas Hampton *design consulting engineer*
Ross, Donald Kenneth *consulting engineering executive*
Ross, Monte *electrical engineer*
Ryckman, DeVere Wellington *consulting environmental engineer*
Shrauner, Barbara Wayne Abraham *electrical engineering educator*
Sutera, Salvatore Philip *mechanical engineering educator*
Szabo, Barna Aladar *mechanical engineering educator, mining engineer*
Winter, David Ferdinand *electrical engineering educator, consultant*
Wolfe, Charles Morgan *electrical engineering educator*
Zurheide, Charles Henry *consulting electrical engineer*

**Saint Peters**
Lynch, Mark Bradley *electrical engineer, biomechanical researcher*

**Springfield**
Hansen, John Paul *metallurgical engineer*
Rogers, Roddy *civil and geotechnical engineer*

**Webb City**
Nichols, Robert Leighton *civil engineer*

## MONTANA

**Bozeman**
Berg, Lloyd *chemical engineering educator*
Cundy, Vic Arnold *mechanical engineer, educator*
Sanks, Robert Leland *environmental engineer, emeritus educator*
Stanislao, Joseph *consulting engineer, educator*

**Great Falls**
Walker, Leland Jasper *civil engineer*

**Helena**
Johnson, David Sellie *civil engineer*

## NEBRASKA

**Brownsville**
Fidler, Charles Robert *electrical engineer*

**Clay Center**
Hahn, George LeRoy *agricultural engineer, biometeorologist*

**Lincoln**
Bahar, Ezekiel *electrical engineering educator*
Edison, Allen Ray *electrical engineer, educator*
Edwards, Donald Mervin *biological systems engineering educator, university dean*
Elias, Samy E. G. *engineering executive*
Nelson, Don Jerome *electrical engineering and computer science educator*
Splinter, William Eldon *agricultural engineering educator*
Ullman, Frank Gordon *electrical engineering educator*
Woollam, John Arthur *electrical engineering educator*

**Omaha**
Coy, William Raymond *civil engineer*
Hultquist, Paul Fredrick *electrical engineer, educator*
Lenz, Charles Eldon *electrical engineering consultant, author*
Matthies, Frederick John *architectural engineer*
Puglisi, Philip James *electrical engineer*
Tunnicliff, David George *civil engineer*
Zerbs, Stephen Taylor *telecommunications development engineer*

## NEVADA

**Boulder City**
Wyman, Richard Vaughn *engineering educator, exploration company executive*

**Carson City**
James, Daryl Norman *environmental engineer*

**Incline Village**
Merdinger, Charles John *civil engineer, naval officer, academic adminstrator*

**Las Vegas**
Boehm, Robert Foty *mechanical engineer, educator, researcher*
Grace, John William *retired electrical company executive*
Haas, Robert John *aerospace engineer*
Herzlich, Harold J. *chemical engineer*
Messenger, George Clement *engineering executive, consultant*
Peng, Zhong *electrical engineer*
Ramos, Albert A. *electrical engineer*
Su, Shiaw-Der *nuclear engineer*

**Minden**
Bently, Donald Emery *electrical engineer*

**Reno**
Bautista, Renato Go *chemical engineer, educator*
Danko, George *engineering educator*
Krenkel, Peter Ashton *engineer, educator*
Lee, David DeWitt *industrial hygienist*
Middlebrooks, Eddie Joe *environmental engineer*
Weinbrenner, George Ryan *aeronautical engineer*

**Silver City**
Bloyd, Stephen Roy *environmental manager, educator, consultant*

**Sparks**
Byrd, Ronald Dallas *civil engineer*
Kleppe, John Arthur *electrical engineering educator, business executive*

## NEW HAMPSHIRE

**Center Sandwich**
Simmons, Alan Jay *electrical engineer, consultant*

**Durham**
Zarrow, Philip M. *electronic assembly process consultant*

**Hanover**
Browning, James Alexander *engineering company executive,inventor*
Dean, Robert Charles, Jr. *mechanical engineer, entrepreneur, innovator*
Ermenc, Joseph John *mechanical engineering educator*
Garmire, Elsa Meints *electrical engineering educator, consultant*
Hutchinson, Charles Edgar *engineering educator, dean emeritus*
Long, Carl Ferdinand *engineering educator*
Stearns, Stephen Russell *civil engineer, forensic engineer, educator*
Wallis, Graham Blair *engineer, educator*

PROFESSIONAL INDEX 5169 ENGINEERING


**Hillsboro**
Pearson, William Rowland *retired nuclear engineer*

**Merrimack**
Drobny, Jiri George *chemical engineer*
Hower, Philip Leland *semiconductor device engineer*
Malley, James Henry Michael *industrial engineer*

**Nashua**
Rotithor, Hemant Govind *electrical engineer*
Woodruff, Thomas Ellis *electronics consulting executive*

**Peterborough**
Farnham, Sherman Brett *retired electrical engineer*

**Warner**
Hunt, Everett Clair *engineering educator, researcher, consultant*

**West Lebanon**
MacAdam, Walter Kavanagh *consulting engineering executive*

## NEW JERSEY

**Aberdeen**
Smith, Marvin Frederick, Jr. *chemical engineer, consultant*

**Allendale**
Birdsall, Blair *consulting engineering executive*

**Barnegat**
Hawk, Frank Carkhuff, Sr. *industrial engineer*

**Basking Ridge**
Kurkjian, Charles R(obert) *ceramic engineer, researcher*

**Bedminster**
David, Edward Emil, Jr. *electrical engineer, business executive*

**Belle Mead**
Singley, Mark Eldridge *agricultural engineering educator*

**Berkeley Heights**
Klüver, Johan Wilhelm (Billy Klüver) *electrical engineer, writer*
Rabiner, Lawrence Richard *electrical engineer*

**Bloomfield**
Dohr, Donald R. *metallurgical engineer, researcher*
Hutcheon, Forbes Clifford Robert *engineer, company executive*

**Bloomsbury**
Danjczek, William Emil *engineering supplies manufacturing executive*

**Caldwell**
Stanton, George Basil, Jr. *engineering executive, chemical engineer*
Stevens, William Dollard *consulting mechanical engineer*

**Cherry Hill**
Melick, George Fleury *mechanical engineer, educator*

**Clifton**
Srinivasachari, Samavedam *chemical engineer*

**Clinton**
Swift, Richard J. *engineering company executive*

**Closter**
Hillman, Leon *electrical engineer*

**Columbus**
Litman, Bernard *electrical engineer, consultant*

**Cranbury**
Hochreiter, Joseph Christian, Jr. *engineering company executive*
Schoenfeld, Theodore Mark *industrial engineer*
Sorensen, Henrik Vittrup *electrical engineering educator*

**Cranford**
Schink, Frank Edward *electrical engineer*

**Denville**
Price, Robert Edmunds *civil engineer*

**Dunellen**
Richmond, Ernest Leon *research engineer, consultant*

**East Orange**
Shea, Gerald Patrick *engineering executive*

**Edison**
Pruden, Ann Lorette *chemical engineer, researcher*

**Elmwood Park**
Semeraro, Michael Archangel, Jr. *civil engineer*

**Englewood**
Deresiewicz, Herbert *mechanical engineering educator*

**Fairfield**
Finn, James Francis *consulting engineering executive*

**Florham Park**
Bhagat, Phiroz Maneck *mechanical engineer*

**Fort Lee**
Screpetis, Dennis *nuclear engineer, consultant*

**Fort Monmouth**
Perlman, Barry Stuart *electrical engineering executive, researcher*

**Franklin Lakes**
Neglia, John Peter *chemical engineer, environmental scientist*

**Freehold**
Schwartz, Perry Lester *information systems engineer, consultant*
Stirrat, William Albert *electronics engineer*

**Green Village**
Castenschiold, René *engineering company executive, author, consultant*

**Hackensack**
Mavrovic, Ivo *chemical engineer*
Michel, Robert Charles *retired engineering company executive*
Yagoda, Harry Nathan *system engineering executive*
Zimmerman, Marlin U., Jr. *chemical engineer*

**Haddonfield**
Siskin, Edward Joseph *engineering and construction company executive*

**Hewitt**
Selwyn, Donald *engineering administrator, researcher, inventor, educator*

**Hoboken**
Biesenberger, Joseph A. *chemical engineer*
Boesch, Francis Theodore *electrical engineer, educator*
Bruno, Michael Stephen *ocean engineering educator, researcher*
Griskey, Richard George *chemical engineering educator*
Savitsky, Daniel *engineer, educator*
Sisto, Fernando *mechanical engineering educator*
Swern, Frederic Lee *engineering educator*
Talimcioglu, Nazmi Mete *civil and environmental engineer, educator*

**Holmdel**
Abate, John E. *electrical and electronic engineer, communications consultant*
Boyd, Gary Delane *electro-optical engineer, researcher*
Erfani, Shervin *electrical engineer, educator, scientist*
Lang, Howard Lawrence *electrical engineer*
Linker, Kerrie Lynn *systems engineer*
Meadors, Howard Clarence, Jr. *electrical engineer*
Opie, William Robert *retired metallurgical engineer*
Ross, Ian Munro *electrical engineer*
Schmidt, Barnet Michael *communications and electronic engineer*
Tien, Ping King *electronics engineer*

**Jamesburg**
Karol, Reuben Hirsh *civil engineer, sculptor*
Maxwell, Bryce *engineer,educator*

**Jersey City**
Chatterjee, Amit *structural engineer*

**Kinnelon**
Haller, Charles Edward *engineering consultant*

**Lawrenceville**
Kihn, Harry *electronics engineer, manufacturing company executive*

**Livingston**
Daman, Ernest Ludwig *mechanical engineer*
Lieberman, Lester Zane *engineering company executive*

**Maplewood**
Lev, Alexander Shulim *mechanical engineer*

**Marlton**
Singh, Krishna Pal *mechanical engineer*
Zurick, Jack *electrical engineer*

**Mendham**
Kaprelian, Edward K. *mechanical engineer, physicist*

**Middletown**
O'Neill, Eugene Francis *communications engineer*

**Millburn**
Schiavello, Bruno *mechanical engineer*

**Monmouth Junction**
Ellerbusch, Fred *environmental engineer*

**Montclair**
Aronson, David *chemical and mechanical engineer*
Clech, Jean Paul Marie *mechanical engineer*
Eager, George Sidney, Jr. *electrical engineer, business executive*
Hutchins, Carleen Maley *acoustical engineer, violin maker, consultant*

**Montvale**
Schindler, Donald Warren *biopharmaceutical engineer, consultant*

**Morris Plains**
Townsend, Palmer Wilson *chemical engineer, consultant*

**Morristown**
Heilmeier, George Harry *electrical engineer, researcher*
Personick, Stewart David *electrical engineer*
Urban, John S. *engineering company executive*

**Mount Arlington**
Jacobs, Richard Moss *consulting engineer*

**Mount Laurel**
Vidas, Vincent George *engineering executive*

**New Brunswick**
Jaluria, Yogesh *mechanical engineering educator*
Katz, Carlos *electrical engineer*
Nawy, Edward George *civil engineer, educator*
Smith, Fredric Charles *electronic technician, consultant*
Vieth, Wolf Randolph *chemical engineering educator*
Wolfe, Robert Richard *bioresource engineer, educator*

**New Providence**
Cho, Alfred Yi *electrical engineer*
Dodabalapur, Ananth *electrical engineer*
Krishnamurthy, Ramachandran (Krish) *chemical engineer, researcher*
Mostello, Robert Anthony *chemical engineer*

**Newark**
Bar-Ness, Yeheskel *electrical engineer, educator*
Bigley, William Joseph, Jr. *control engineer*
Friedland, Bernard *engineer, educator*
Guenzel, Frank Bernhard *chemical engineer*
Hanesian, Deran *chemical engineer, chemistry and environmental science educator, consultant*
Hernon, Richard Francis *civil engineer*
Hrycak, Peter *mechanical engineer, educator*
Hsu, Cheng-Tzu Thomas *civil engineering educator*
Leu, Ming Chuan *engineering educator*
Misra, Raj Pratap *engineering educator, electrical engineer*
Pfeffer, Robert *chemical engineer, academic administrator, educator*
Pignataro, Louis James *engineering educator*
Rosato, Anthony Dominick *mechanical engineer, educator*
Spillers, William Russell *civil engineering educator*
Yu, Yi-Yuan *mechanical engineering educator*
Ziavras, Sotirios George *computer and electrical engineer, educator*

**Newfoundland**
Van Winkle, Edgar Walling *electrical engineer, computer consultant*

**North Brunswick**
Awan, Ahmad Noor *civil engineer*

**Norwood**
Barbini, Richard John *chemical engineer, marketing manager*

**Oakland**
Bacaloglu, Radu *chemical engineer*

**Ocean City**
Speitel, Gerald Eugene *consulting environmental engineer*

**Paramus**
Samuels, Reuben *engineering consultant*

**Passaic**
Lindholm, Clifford Falstrom, II *engineering executive, mayor*

**Pennsauken**
Alday, Paul Stackhouse, Jr. *mechanical engineer*
Bareford, William John *chemical engineer*

**Phillipsburg**
Cooper, Paul *mechanical engineer, research director*

**Picatinny Arsenal**
Janow, Chris *mechanical engineer*

**Piscataway**
Flanagan, James Loton *electrical engineer, educator*
Freeman, Herbert *computer engineering educator*
Frenkiel, Richard Henry *systems engineer, consultant*
Salkind, Alvin J. *electrochemical engineer, educator*
Sannuti, Peddapullaiah *electrical engineering educator*
Shanefield, Daniel Jay *ceramics engineering educator*
Welkowitz, Walter *biomedical engineer, educator*
Zhao, Jian Hui *electrical and computer engineering educator*

**Plainfield**
Granstrom, Marvin Leroy *civil and sanitary engineering educator*

**Princeton**
Ayers, William McLean *electrochemical engineering company executive*
Bartolini, Robert Alfred *electrical engineer, researcher*
Bergman, Richard Isaac *engineering executive, consultant*
Billington, David Perkins *civil engineering educator*
Bogdonoff, Seymour Moses *aeronautical engineer*
Cakmak, Ahmet Sefik *civil engineering educator*
Cinlar, Erhan *engineering educator*
Curtiss, Howard Crosby, Jr. *mechanical engineer, educator*
Debenedetti, Pablo Gaston *chemical engineering educator*
Denlinger, Edgar Jacob *electronics engineering research executive*
Dickinson, Bradley William *electrical engineering educator*
Durbin, Enoch Job *aeronautical engineering educator*
File, Joseph *research physics engineer*
Gibson, James John *electronics engineer, consultant*
Gillham, John Kinsey *chemical engineering educator*
Glassman, Irvin *mechanical and aeronautical engineering educator, consultant*
Graessley, William Walter *chemical engineering educator*
Hough, Robert Alan *civil engineer*
Jackson, Roy *chemical engineering educator*
Johnson, Ernest Frederick *chemical engineer, educator*
Johnson, Walter Curtis *electrical engineering educator*
Lechner, Bernard Joseph *consulting electrical engineer*
Linke, Richard A. *systems engineer, researcher*
Lo, Arthur Wu-nien *electrical engineering educator*
Miles, Richard Bryant *mechanical and aerospace engineering educator*
Nikain, Reza *civil engineer*
Poor, Harold Vincent *electrical engineering educator*
Prud'homme, Robert Krafft *chemical engineering educator*
Saville, Dudley Albert *chemical engineering educator*
Schroeder, Alfred Christian *electronics research engineer*
Socolow, Robert Harry *engineering educator, scientist*
Stengel, Robert Frank *mechanical and aerospace engineering educator*
Torquato, Salvatore *civil engineering educator*
Vahaviolos, Sotirios John *electrical engineer, scientist, corporate executive*
Vanmarcke, Erik Hector *civil engineering educator*
Walton, Clifford Wayne *chemical engineer, researcher*
Wei, James *chemical engineering educator, academic dean*
Weinstein, Norman Jacob *chemical engineer, consultant*
Wolf, Wayne Hendrix *electrical engineering educator*

**Princeton Junction**
Haddad, James Henry *chemical engineering consultant*
Lull, William Paul *engineering consultant*

**Raritan**
Hammonds, Elizabeth Ann *environmental engineer*

**Red Bank**
Li, Tingye *electrical engineer*
Schneider, Sol *electronic engineer, consultant, researcher*

**Ridgewood**
Abplanalp, Glen Harold *civil engineer*

**Riverside**
Gouda, Moustafa Abdel-Hamid *geotechnical engineer consultant*

**Robbinsville**
Goldstein, Norman Robert *safety engineer*

**Rumson**
Rosen, Bernard H. *chemical engineer*
Rowe, Harrison Edward *electrical engineer*

**Sea Bright**
Plummer, Dirk Arnold *professional engineer*

**Short Hills**
Kaye, Jerome R. *retired engineering and construction company executive*
Moore, Robert Condit *civil engineer*
Wharton, Lennard *engineering company executive*

**Shrewsbury**
Reich, Bernard *telecommunications engineer*

**Skillman**
Brill, Yvonne Claeys *engineer, consultant*
Schoen, Alvin E., Jr. *environmental engineer, consultant*

**South Plainfield**
Kennedy, John William *engineering company executive*

**Sparta**
Truran, William Richard *electrical engineer*

**Springfield**
Goldstein, Irving Robert *mechanical and industrial engineer, educator, consultant*
Perilstein, Fred Michael *electrical engineer, consultant*

**Stanton**
Jagel, Kenneth Irwin, Jr. *chemical engineer, consultant*

**Summit**
Fukui, Hatsuaki *electrical engineer, art historian*

**Swedesboro**
Lovell, Theodore *electrical engineer, consultant*

**Teaneck**
Borg, Sidney Fred *mechanical engineer, educator*
Ehrlich, Ira Robert *mechanical engineering consultant*

**Tenafly**
Lang, Hans Joachim *engineering company executive*

**Teterboro**
Ficalora, Joseph Paul *aeronautical engineering supervisor*

**Toms River**
Fanuele, Michael Anthony *electronics engineer, research engineer*

**Upper Saddle River**
Wallace, William, III *engineering executive*

**Warren**
Sartor, Anthony Joseph *environmental engineer*

**Watchung**
Tornqvist, Erik Gustav Markus *chemical engineer, research scientist*

**Wayne**
Benjamin, James Anthony *electrical engineer, educator*
Cheng, David Hong *mechanical engineering educator*
Friedman, Michael Lazar *chemical engineer*

**West New York**
Gruenberg, Elliot Lewis *electronics engineer and company executive*

**West Trenton**
Woods, Howard James, Jr. *civil engineer*

**Whippany**
Michaelis, Paul Charles *engineering physicist executive*

**Willingboro**
Schnapf, Abraham *aerospace engineer, consultant*

**Woodbridge**
Moran, Jeffrey William *safety engineer*
Morris, David *retired electrical engineer*

**Wyckoff**
Mirza, Muhammad Zubair *product development company executive, researcher, engineering consultant, inventor*

## NEW MEXICO

**Albuquerque**
Anderson, Lawrence Keith *electrical engineer*
Arvizu, Dan Eliab *mechanical engineer*
Austin, Edward Marvin *retired mechanical engineer, researcher*
Bolie, Victor Wayne *science and engineering consultant*
Brown, James Randall *mechanical engineer*
Clark, Arthur Joseph, Jr. *retired mechanical and electrical engineer*
Dorato, Peter *electrical and computer engineering educator*
Eaton, George Wesley, Jr. *petroleum engineer, oil company executive*
Haddad, Edward Raouf *civil engineer, consultant*
Hall, Jerome William *research engineering educator*
Howard, William Jack *mechanical engineer, retired*
Johnson, Daniel Leon *aeronautical engineer*
Karni, Shlomo *engineering and religious studies educator*
Land, Cecil E. *electrical engineer*
Lynch, Paul Vincent *safety engineer, consultant*
McKiernan, John William *mechanical engineer*
Molzen, Dayton Frank *consulting engineering executive*
Peck, Ralph Brazelton *civil engineering educator, consultant*
Plough, Charles Tobias, Jr. *retired electronics engineering executive*
Prinja, Anil Kant *nuclear engineering educator*
Robinett, Rush Daleth, III *robotics research manager*
Westwood, Albert Ronald Clifton *engineer*
Wildin, Maurice Wilbert *mechanical engineering educator*

**Belen**
Toliver, Lee *mechanical engineer*

**Carlsbad**
Wayman, Cooper Harry *environmental legal counsel*

**Farmington**
Caldwell, John Winston, III *petroleum engineer*
Garretson, Owen Loren *petroleum engineer*

**Kirtland AFB**
Anderson, Christine Marlene *software engineer*
Baum, Carl Edward *electromagnetic theorist*
Voelz, David George *electrical engineer*

**Las Cruces**
Colbaugh, Richard Donald *mechanical engineer, educator, researcher*
Ford, Clarence Quentin *mechanical engineer, educator*
Matthews, Larryl Kent *mechanical engineering educator*
Morgan, John Derald *electrical engineer*
Thode, Edward Frederick *chemical engineer, educator*

**Los Alamos**
Andrews, Andrew Edward *nuclear engineer*
Jackson, James F. *nuclear engineer*
Nunz, Gregory Joseph *aerospace engineer, program manager, educator, entrepreneur*
Stoddard, Stephen Davidson *ceramic engineer, former state senator*

**Mayhill**
Carter, Joy Eaton *electrical engineer, consultant*

**Santa Fe**
Miller, Edmund Kenneth *retired electrical engineer, educator*
Phister, Montgomery, Jr. *computer engineering consultant, writer*

**Socorro**
Lyons, William Claypool *engineering educator and consultant*

**White Sands Missile Range**
Arthur, Paul Keith *electronic engineer*

## NEW YORK

**Afton**
Church, Richard Dwight *electrical engineer, scientist*

**Akron**
Greatbatch, Wilson *biomedical engineer*

**Albany**
Happ, Harvey Heinz *electrical engineer, educator*
Roy, Rob J. *biomedical engineer, anesthesiologist*

**Alfred**
Frechette, Van Derck *ceramic engineer*
Spriggs, Richard Moore *ceramic engineer, research center administrator*

**Amherst**
Ashgriz, Nasser *mechanical and aerospace engineer, educator*
Reinhorn, Andrei M. *civil engineering educator, consultant*

**Ballston Lake**
Fiedler, Harold Joseph *electrical engineer, consultant*

**Bethpage**
Melnik, Robert Edward *aeronautical engineer*
Rockensies, John William *mechanical engineer*

**Big Flats**
Orsillo, James Edward *computer systems engineer, company executive*

**Binghamton**
Cornacchio, Joseph Vincent *engineering educator, computer researcher, consultant*
Jennings, Frank Louis *engineering company executive, engineer*
Lowen, Walter *mechanical engineering educator*
Schwartz, Richard Frederick *electrical engineering educator*

**Briarcliff Manor**
Cugnini, Aldo Godfrey *electrical engineer*

**Bronx**
Berger, Frederick Jerome *electrical engineer, educator*
Hovnanian, H. Philip *biomedical engineer, physicist*
Ignat, Ana *chemical engineer*

**Bronxville**
Leonard, Edward F. *chemical engineer, educator*

**Brooklyn**
Armenakas, Anthony Emmanuel *aerospace educator*
Bertoni, Henry Louis *electrical engineering educator*
El-Choum, Mohammed Kassem *civil engineer, educator*
Goodman, Alvin S. *engineering educator, consultant*
Helly, Walter Sigmund *engineering educator*
Kempner, Joseph *aerospace engineering educator*
McLean, William Ronald *electrical engineer, consultant*
Pan, Huo-Hsi *mechanical engineer, educator*
Rice, John Thomas *architecture educator*
Roess, Roger Peter *engineering educator*
Shaw, Leonard Glazer *electrical engineering educator, consultant*

**Buffalo**
Anderson, Wayne Arthur *electrical engineering educator*
Benenson, David Maurice *engineering educator*
Drury, Colin Gordon *engineering consultant, educator*
Hida, George T. *chemical and ceramic engineer*
Karwan, Mark Henry *engineering educator, dean*
Kinzly, Robert Edward *engineering company executive*
Kiser, Kenneth M(aynard) *chemical engineering educator*
Landi, Dale Michael *industrial engineer, academic administrator*
Lee, George C. *civil engineer, university administrator*
Mates, Robert Edward *mechanical engineering educator*
Meredith, Dale Dean *civil engineering educator*
Metzger, Ernest Hugh *aerospace engineer, scientist*
Reismann, Herbert *engineer, educator*
Ruckenstein, Eli *chemical engineering educator*
Rumer, Ralph Raymond, Jr. *civil engineer, educator*
Sarjeant, Walter James *electrical and computer engineering educator*
Shaw, David Tai-Ko *electrical and computer engineering educator, university administrator*
Weber, Thomas William *chemical engineering educator*
Weller, Sol William *chemical engineering educator*

**Central Islip**
Cordle, Kevin Gerard *electronic engineer*

**Chappaqua**
O'Neill, Robert Charles *inventor, consultant*
Pomerene, James Herbert *retired computer engineer*

**Clarence**
Muffoletto, Barry Charles *engineering executive*

**Clifton Park**
Panek, Jan *electrical power engineer, consultant*

**Clinton**
Pagani, Albert Louis *aerospace system engineer*

**Cold Spring**
Pugh, Emerson William *electrical engineer*

**Corning**
†Ackerman, Roger G. *ceramic engineer*

**Corona**
Miele, Joel Arthur, Sr. *civil engineer*

**Deer Park**
Taub, Jesse J. *electrical engineering researcher*

**Delmar**
Shen, Thomas To *environmental engineer*
Ting, Joseph K. *mechanical engineer*

**East Amherst**
Soong, Tsu-Teh *engineering science educator*

**East Syracuse**
Wiley, Richard Gordon *electrical engineer*

**Endwell**
Del Bianco, Kenneth Louis *civil engineer, house designer*

**Fairport**
Oldshue, James Y. *chemical engineering consultant*

**Farmingdale**
Bolle, Donald Martin *engineering educator*
Bongiorno, Joseph John, Jr. *electrical engineering educator*
Klosner, Jerome Martin *mechanical engineer, educator*
LaTourrette, James Thomas *retired electrical engineering and computer science educator*

**Fayetteville**
Dosanjh, Darshan S(ingh) *aeronautical engineer, educator*

**Flushing**
Birnstiel, Charles *consulting engineer*
Milone, James Michael *occupational health-safety engineering executive, environmental engineer*
Stahl, Frank Ludwig *civil engineer*

**Garden City**
Fleisig, Ross *aeronautical engineer, engineering manager*

**Glen Cove**
Conti, James Joseph *chemical engineer, educator*

**Glenham**
Douglas, Fred Robert *cost engineering consultant*

**Glens Falls**
Fawcett, Christopher Babcock *civil engineer, construction and water resources company executive*

**Glenville**
Anderson, Roy Everett *electrical engineering consultant*

**Great Neck**
Gillin, John F. *quality engineer*
Shaffer, Bernard William *mechanical and aerospace engineering educator*

**Greenlawn**
Bachman, Henry Lee *electrical engineer, engineering executive*
Newman, Edward Morris *engineering executive*

**Harrison**
†Schulz, Helmut Wilhelm *chemical engineer, environmental executive*

**Hauppauge**
Costa, Pat Vincent *automation sciences executive*
Uy, Philip M. *aeronautical engineer*

**Hawthorne**
McConnell, John Edward *electrical engineer, company executive*

**Hempstead**
Goldstein, Stanley Philip *engineering educator*
Maier, Henry B. *environmental engineer*

**Hicksville**
Rubano, Richard Frank *civil engineer*

**Holtsville**
†Musteric, Peter *engineering manager*

**Huntington**
Christiansen, Donald David *electrical engineer, editor, publishing consultant*

**Huntington Station**
Agosta, Vito *mechanical/aerospace engineering educator*
Lanzano, Ralph Eugene *civil engineer*

**Ithaca**
Berger, Toby *electrical engineer*
Booker, John Franklin *mechanical engineer, educator*
Carlin, Herbert J. *electrical engineering educator, researcher*
Caughey, David Alan *engineering educator, researcher*
Dalman, Gisli Conrad *electrical engineering educator*
De Boer, Pieter Cornelis Tobias *mechanical and aerospace engineering educator*
Dick, Richard Irwin *environmental engineer, educator*
Eastman, Lester Fuess *electrical engineer, educator*
Jenkins, James Thomas *mechanical engineering researcher*
Leibovich, Sidney *engineering educator*
Loucks, Daniel Peter *environmental systems engineer*
Lynn, Walter Royal *civil engineering educator, university administrator*
Maxwell, William Laughlin *industrial engineering educator*
Mc Guire, William *civil engineer, educator*
McIsaac, Paul Rowley *electrical engineer, educator*
Meyburg, Arnim Hans *transportation engineer, educator, consultant*
Nation, John Arthur *electrical engineering educator, researcher*
O'Rourke, Thomas Denis *civil engineer, educator*
Phelan, Richard Magruder *mechanical engineer*
Pope, Stephen Bailey *engineering educator*
Rodríguez, Ferdinand *chemical engineer, educator*
Shuler, Michael Louis *biochemical engineering educator, consultant*
Smith, Julian Cleveland, Jr. *chemical engineering educator*
Sudan, Ravindra Nath *electrical engineer, physicist, educator*
Thorp, James Shelby *electrical engineering educator*
Wang, Kuo-King *manufacturing engineer, educator*
White, Richard Norman *civil and environmental engineering educator*

**Jericho**
Shinners, Stanley Marvin *electrical engineer*

**Katonah**
Bashkow, Theodore Robert *electrical engineering consultant, former educator*

**Lakewood**
Brown, Melvin Henry *retired chemical engineer*

**Larchmont**
Margolin, Harold *metallurgical educator*

**Levittown**
Rubin, Arnold Jesse *aeronautical engineer*

**Locust Valley**
Schaffner, Charles Etzel *consulting engineering executive*

**Long Beach**
Sherman, Zachary *civil and aerospace engineer, consultant*

**Long Island City**
Barbanel, Sidney William *engineering consulting firm executive*
Theodoru, Stefan Gheorghe *civil engineer, writer*

**Massapequa Park**
Plotkin, Martin *retired electrical engineer*

**Melville**
Marchesano, John Edward *electro-optical engineer*
Scire, Frank Jackson *retired radar scientist*

**Millbrook**
Johnston, Robert Cossin *consulting engineer executive*

**Mineola**
Abraham, Carl Joel *executive, safety specialist, inventor, consultant*
Newman, Malcolm *civil engineering consultant*
Rosen, Meyer Robert *chemical engineer*

**Mount Kisco**
Moore, J. Scott *materials engineer*

**New Hartford**
Maurer, Gernant Elmer *metallurgical executive, consultant*

**New Hyde Park**
Hyman, Abraham *electrical engineer*

**New York**
Acrivos, Andreas *chemical engineering educator*
Ahmad, Jameel *civil engineer, researcher, educator*
Amster, Gerald Stanley *electrical engineer*
Baron, Melvin Leon *civil engineer, consultant*
Baum, Richard Theodore *engineering executive*
Bendelius, Arthur George *engineering firm executive*
Binger, Wilson Valentine *civil engineer*
Boley, Bruno Adrian *engineering educator*
Boshkov, Stefan Hristov *mining engineer, educator*
Bove, John Louis *chemistry and environmental engineering educator, researcher*
Brazinsky, Irv(ing) *chemical engineering educator*
Cantilli, Edmund Joseph *safety engineering educator, writer*
Cheh, Huk Yuk *engineering educator, electrochemist*
Cowin, Stephen Corteen *biomedical engineering educator, consultant*
De Gaster, Zachary *engineering company executive*
DiMaggio, Frank Louis *civil engineering educator*
Fogel, Irving Martin *consulting engineer*
Freudenstein, Ferdinand *mechanical engineering educator*
Galanopoulos, Kelly *biomedical engineer*
Goldfarb, Donald *industrial engineering educator*
Greenfield, Seymour Stephen *mechanical engineer*
Grunes, Robert Lewis *consulting engineer company executive*
Happel, John *chemical engineer, researcher*
Harris, Colin Cyril *mineral engineer, educator*
Hennessy, John Francis, III *engineering executive, mechanical engineer*
Jaffe, William J(ulian) *industrial engineer, educator*
Kim, Se Jung *civil engineer*
Klein, Morton *industrial engineer, educator*
Knobler, Alfred Everett *ceramic engineer, manufacturing company executive, publisher*
Koshar, Louis David *civil engineer*
Lai, W(ei) Michael *mechanical engineer, educator*
Lazar, Aurel A. *electrical engineer, educator*
Lee, Martin Yongho (Kyung-Joo Lee) *mechanical engineer*
Lee, Sidney Phillip *chemical engineer, state senator*
Lenton, Roberto Leonardo *research facility and environmental administrator*
Lowen, Gerard Gunther *mechanical engineering educator*
Michel, Henry Ludwig *civil engineer*
Morfopoulos, V. *metallurgical engineer, materials engineer*
Mow, Van C. *engineering educator, researcher*
Ozero, Brian John *chemical engineer*
Paaswell, Robert Emil *civil engineer, educator*
Robertson, Leslie Earl *structural engineer*
Ross, Donald Edward *engineering company executive*
Sadegh, Ali M. *mechanical engineering educator, researcher, consultant*
Salvadori, Mario *mathematical physicist, structural engineer*
Schoenfeld, Robert Louis *biomedical engineer*
Schwartz, Mischa *electrical engineering educator*
Schwarz, Ralph Jacques *engineering educator*
See, Saw-Teen *structural engineer*
Shapiro, Murray *structural engineer*
Shinnar, Reuel *chemical engineering educator, industrial consultant*
Simkhovich, Semen Lasarevich *cryogenic engineer, researcher, educator*
Smith, Gordon H. *civil engineer*
Sobel, Kenneth Mark *electrical engineer, educator*
Soejima, Daisuke *international trade engineer, economist*
Subak-Sharpe, Gerald Emil *electrical engineer, educator*
Themelis, Nickolas John *metallurgical and chemical engineering educator*
Tsividis, Yannis P. *electrical engineering educator*
Unger, Stephen Herbert *electrical engineer, computer scientist*
Vergilis, Joseph Semyon *mechanical engineering educator*
Vogelman, Joseph Herbert *scientific engineering company executive*
Watkins, Charles Booker, Jr. *mechanical engineering educator*
Weidlinger, Paul *civil engineer*
Weinbaum, Sheldon *biomedical engineer*
Weinstein, Herbert *chemical engineer, educator*
Yang, Edward S. *electrical engineering educator*
Yao, David Da-Wei *engineering educator*

PROFESSIONAL INDEX 5171 ENGINEERING


Yegulalp, Tuncel M. *mining engineer, educator*
Zakkay, Victor *aeronautical engineering educator, scientist*
Zuck, Alfred Christian *consulting mechanical engineer*

**Newburgh**
Wilcox, David Eric *electrical engineer, educational consultant*

**Newton Falls**
Hunter, William Schmidt *engineering executive, environmental engineer*

**Niagara Falls**
Dojka, Edwin Sigmund *civil engineer*

**Niskayuna**
Huening, Walter Carl, Jr. *retired consulting application engineer*
Johnson, Ingolf Birger *retired electrical engineer*

**Northport**
Litchford, George B. *aeronautical engineer*
Weber, Ray Everett *engineering executive, consultant*

**Old Bethpage**
Buzzelli, Dennis Kevin *mechanical engineer*

**Old Westbury**
Katz, Roger Martin *infosystems engineer*

**Owego**
Smoral, Vincent J. *electrical engineer*

**Oyster Bay**
Urdea, John *electromechanical engineer*

**Pelham**
Fayon, Abram Miko *chemical engineer*

**Pittsford**
Marshall, Joseph Frank *electronic engineer*

**Plattsburgh**
Treacy, William Joseph *electrical and environmental engineer*

**Pleasantville**
Pike, John Nazarian *optical engineering consultant*

**Port Chester**
Rubin, Jacob Carl *mechanical research engineer*
Whaley, Christopher David *manufacturing engineer*

**Potsdam**
Carroll, James Joseph *electrical and computer engineering educator*
Chin, Der-Tau *chemical engineer, educator*
Cotellessa, Robert Francis *retired electrical engineering educator, academic administrator*
Mochel, Myron George *mechanical engineer, educator*
Sathyamoorthy, Muthukrishnan *engineering researcher, educator*
Shen, Hung Tao *hydraulic engineering educator*

**Poughkeepsie**
Chu, Richard Chao-Fan *mechanical engineer*
Logue, Joseph Carl *electronics engineer, consultant*

**Purchase**
Daniel, Charles Timothy *transportation engineer, consultant*

**Remsenburg**
Edwards, Arthur Anderson *retired mechanical engineer*

**Riverdale**
Hollein, Helen Conway *chemical engineer, educator*

**Rochester**
Bouyoucos, John Vinton *research and development company executive*
Burns, Stephen James *engineering educator, materials science researcher*
Carstensen, Edwin Lorenz *biomedical engineer, biophysicist*
Cokelet, Giles Roy *biomedical engineering educator*
Freckleton, Jon Edward *engineering educator, consultant, retired military officer*
Gans, Roger Frederick *mechanical engineering educator*
Kinnen, Edwin *electrical engineer, educator*
Lessen, Martin *engineering educator, consulting engineer*
Loewen, Erwin G. *precision engineer, educator, consultant*
Loui, Alexander Chan Pong *electrical engineer, researcher*
Palmer, Harvey John *chemical engineering educator, consultant*
Parker, Kevin James *electrical engineer educator*
Schmidhammer, Robert Howard *environmental executive, engineering consultant*

**Rome**
Coppola, Anthony *electrical engineer*
Gabelman, Irving Jacob *consulting engineering executive, retired government official*
Pflug, Donald Ralph *electrical engineer*

**Roslyn**
Cohen, Edward *civil engineer*

**Rye**
Lehman, Lawrence Herbert *consulting engineering executive*

**Rye Brook**
Landegger, George F. *engineering executive*

**Saint James**
Irvine, Thomas Francis, Jr. *mechanical engineering educator*

**Scarsdale**
Florman, Samuel Charles *civil engineer*

**Schenectady**
Barthold, Lionel Olav *engineering executive*
Bucinell, Ronald Blaise *mechanical engineer*
Hedman, Dale Eugene *consulting electrical engineer*
Kliman, Gerald Burt *electrical engineer*
Lambert, Stephen R. *electrical engineer, consultant*
Matta, Ram Kumar *aeronautical engineer*
Ringlee, Robert James *consulting engineering executive*
Walsh, George William *engineering executive*

**Setauket**
Irving, A. Marshall *marine engineer*
Levine, Sumner Norton *industrial engineer, educator, editor, author, financial consultant*

**Slate Hill**
Reber, Raymond Andrew *chemical engineer*

**Slingerlands**
Wilcock, Donald Frederick *mechanical engineer*

**Somers**
Jacob, Alethea Marie *enterprise engineering consultant*

**Stafford**
Moran, John Henry, Jr. *electrical engineer, consultant*

**Staten Island**
Johansen, Robert John *electrical engineer*
Rajakaruna, Lalith Asoka *civil engineer*

**Stony Brook**
Cope, Randolph Howard, Jr. *electronic research and development executive, educator*
Truxal, John Groff *electrical engineering educator*
Zemanian, Armen Humpartsoum *electrical engineer, mathematician*

**Syracuse**
Brennan, Paul Joseph *civil engineer, educator*
Cheng, David Keun *engineering educator*
Drucker, Alan Steven *mechanical engineer*
Hamlett, James Gordon *electronics engineer, management consultant, educator*
Jefferies, Michael John *retired electrical engineer*
Konski, James Louis *civil engineer*
Pennock, Donald William *retired mechanical engineer*
Sargent, Robert George *engineering educator*

**Tarrytown**
Anderson, John Erling *chemical engineer*

**Tonawanda**
Rovison, John Michael, Jr. *chemical engineer*

**Troy**
Abetti, Pier Antonio *consulting electrical engineer, technology management and entrepreneurship educator*
Belfort, Georges *chemical engineering educator, consultant*
Bergles, Arthur Edward *mechanical engineering educator*
Block, Robert Charles *nuclear engineering and engineering physics educator*
Desrochers, Alan Alfred *electrical engineer*
Duquette, David Joseph *materials science and engineering educator*
Dvorak, George J. *mechanics and materials engineering educator*
Gerhardt, Lester A. *engineering educator, dean*
Gill, William Nelson *chemical engineering educator*
Glicksman, Martin Eden *materials engineering educator*
Graves, Robert John *industrial engineering educator*
Gutmann, Ronald J. *electrical engineering educator*
Jones, Owen Craven, Jr. *nuclear and mechanical engineer, educator*
Jordan, Mark Henry *consulting civil engineer*
Krempl, Erhard *mechanics educator, consultant*
Lahey, Richard Thomas, Jr. *nuclear engineer, fluid mechanics engineer*
Lemnios, Andrew Zachery *aerospace engineer, educator, researcher*
Littman, Howard *chemical engineer, educator*
McDonald, John Francis Patrick *electrical engineering educator*
Modestino, James William *electrical engineering educator*
Nelson, John Keith *electrical engineer*
Sanderson, Arthur Clark *engineering educator*
Saridis, George Nicholas *electrical engineer*
Shephard, Mark Scott *civil and mechanical engineering educator*
Stoloff, Norman Stanley *materials engineering educator, researcher*
Woods, John William *electrical, computer and systems engineering educator, consultant*
Zimmie, Thomas Frank *civil engineer, educator*

**Trumansburg**
Wolf, Edward Dean *electrical engineering educator*

**Upton**
Fthenakis, Vasilis *chemical engineer, consultant, educator*
Radeka, Veljko *electronics engineer*
Steinberg, Meyer *chemical engineer*
Susskind, Herbert *biomedical engineer, educator*
Van Tuyle, Gregory Jay *nuclear engineer*

**Valhalla**
Paik, John Kee *structural engineer*

**Vestal**
Wagner, Peter Ewing *physics and electrical engineering educator*

**Victor**
Drummond, Malcolm McAllister *electronics engineer*

**Washingtonville**
Guarino, Louis Joseph *mechanical engineer, consultant*

**Webster**
McWilliams, C. Paul, Jr. *engineering executive*

Zirilli, Francesco *mechanical engineer, engineering educator*

**West Islip**
Young, Morris *electrical engineering consultant*

**West Nyack**
Hornik, Joseph William *civil engineer*

**West Valley**
Itzo, Ralph Francis *chemical engineer*

**White Plains**
Dent, Robert Alan *electrical engineer*
Foster, John Horace *consulting environmental engineer*
Mitchell, Robert Dale *consulting engineer*
Westerhoff, Garret Peter *environmental engineer, executive*

**Woodbury**
McGovern, Thomas John *environmental engineer*

**Woodstock**
Smith, Albert Aloysius, Jr. *electrical engineer, consultant*

**Yorktown Heights**
Dennard, Robert Heath *engineering executive, scientist*
Henle, Robert Athanasius *engineer*
Hong, Se June *computer engineer*
Lavenberg, Stephen S. *electrical engineer, researcher*
Romankiw, Lubomyr Taras *materials engineer*
Terman, Lewis Madison *electrical engineer, researcher*
Troutman, Ronald R. *electrical engineer*

**NORTH CAROLINA**

**Boonville**
Reece, Joe Wilson *engineering company executive*

**Candler**
Boggs, William Brady *quality engineering and applied statistics consultant*

**Cary**
Conrad, Hans *materials engineering educator*
Khan, Masrur Ali *nuclear and chemical engineer, physicist*
Miranda, Constancio Fernandes *civil engineering educator*
Smith, Walter Sage *environmental engineer, consultant*
Vick, Columbus Edwin, Jr. *civil engineering design firm executive*

**Chapel Hill**
Baker, Charles Ray *engineering and mathematics educator, researcher*
Coulter, Norman Arthur, Jr. *biomedical engineering educator emeritus*
Eisenbud, Merril *engineer, scientist*
Kuhn, Matthew *engineering company executive*
Kusy, Robert Peter *biomedical engineering and orthodontics educator*
Lucas, Carol Lee *biomedical engineer*
Okun, Daniel Alexander *environmental engineering educator*
Singer, Philip C. *environmental engineer, educator*
Stidham, Shaler, Jr. *operations research educator*

**Charlotte**
Foss, Ralph Scot *mechanical engineer*
Keanini, Russell Guy *mechanical engineering educator, researcher*
Kim, Rhyn Hyun *engineering educator*
King, L. Ellis *civil engineer, educator, consultant*
Phibbs, Garnett Ersiel *engineer, educator, minister, religious organization administrator*
Rodite, Robert R.R. *engineering scientist*

**Clayton**
Amy, James Borden *mechanical engineer*

**Durham**
Bejan, Adrian *mechanical engineering educator*
Casey, H(orace) Craig, Jr. *electrical engineering educator*
Chaddock, Jack Bartley *mechanical engineering educator*
Fisher, Charles Page, Jr. *consulting geotechnical engineer*
Garg, Devendra Prakash *mechanical engineer, educator*
Goodwin, Frank Erik *materials engineer*
Harman, Charles Morgan *mechanical engineer*
Hochmuth, Robert Milo *mechanical and biomedical engineer, educator*
Mc Kinney, Ross Erwin *civil engineering educator*
Plonsey, Robert *electrical and biomedical engineer*
Strohbehn, John Walter *engineering science educator*
Utku, Senol *civil engineer, computer science educator*

**Flat Rock**
Davidson, Clayton Leslie *chemical engineer*

**Fuquay Varina**
Hairston, William Michael *manufacturing engineer*

**Granite Falls**
Humphreys, Kenneth King *engineer, educator, association executive*

**Greensboro**
Bailey, William Nathan *systems engineer*
Cazel, Hugh Allen *industrial engineer, educator*

**Hendersonville**
Schooley, Charles Earl *electrical engineer, consultant*

**High Point**
Huston, Fred John *retired automotive engineer*

**Highlands**
Sandor, George Nason *mechanical engineer, educator*
Watt, John Reid *retired mechanical engineering educator*

**Louisburg**
Boblett, Mark Anthony *civil engineering technician*

**Mebane**
Davidson, Lacinda Susan *materials engineer, chemist*

**Morehead City**
Williams, Winton Hugh *civil engineer*

**Mount Airy**
Ratliff, Robert Barns, Jr. *mechanical engineer*

**New Bern**
Baughman, Fred Hubbard *aeronautical engineer, former naval officer*
Moeller, Dade William *environmental engineer, educator*

**Raleigh**
Agrawal, Dharma Prakash *engineering educator*
Baliga, Bantval Jayant *electrical engineering educator, research administrator*
Beatty, Kenneth Orion, Jr. *chemical engineer*
Bitzer, Donald Lester *electrical engineering educator, retired research laboratory administrator*
Bourham, Mohamed Abdelhay *electrical and nuclear engineering educator*
DeJarnette, Fred Roark *aerospace engineer*
Dudziak, Donald John *nuclear engineer, educator*
Fang, Shu-Cherng *industrial engineering and operations research educator*
Foley, Gary J. *research chemical engineer, computer scientist, federal agency administrator*
Gardner, Robin Pierce *engineering educator*
Hanson, John M. *civil engineering and construction educator*
Hauser, John Reid *electrical engineering educator*
Havner, Kerry Shuford *civil engineering and solid mechanics educator*
Holton, William Coffeen *electrical engineering executive*
Kriz, George James *agricultural research administrator, educator*
Meier, Wilbur Leroy, Jr. *industrial engineer, educator, former university chancellor*
Murray, Raymond Le Roy *nuclear engineering educator*
Phillips, Oliverio Michelsen *chemical engineer*
Rohrbach, Roger Phillip *agricultural engineer, educator*
Skaggs, Richard Wayne *agricultural engineering educator*
Sneed, Ronald Ernest *engineering educator emeritus*
Stannett, Vivian Thomas *chemical engineering educator*
Turinsky, Paul Josef *nuclear engineer, educator*
Williams, Hugh Alexander, Jr. *retired mechanical engineer, consultant*
Woodland, N. Joseph *optical engineer, mechanical engineer*
Zorowski, Carl Frank *engineering educator, university administrator*

**Research Triangle Park**
Henschel, D. Bruce *chemical engineer, environmental researcher*
Larsen, Ralph Irving *environmental research engineer*

**Salisbury**
Reilly, Michael Thomas *chemical engineer*

**Supply**
Webb, Thomas George *aircraft manufacturing engineer*

**Thomasville**
Hinkle, William Paul *mechanical and electrical engineer, consultant*

**Washington**
Hackney, James Acra, III *industrial engineer, manufacturing company executive*

**Weaverville**
Weng, Chuan *mechanical engineer*

**Wilmington**
Sims, David Bryson, Jr. *engineer*

**NORTH DAKOTA**

**Bismarck**
Carmichael, Virgil Wesly *mining, civil and geological engineer, former coal company executive*

**OHIO**

**Akron**
Brown, David Rupert *engineering executive*
Isayev, Avraam Isayevich *polymer engineer, educator*
Mettler, Gerald Phillip *reliability engineer*
Miller, Irving Franklin *chemical engineering educator, biomedical engineering educator, academic administrator*
Sancaktar, Erol *engineering educator*

**Alliance**
Kitto, John Buck, Jr. *mechanical engineer*

**Athens**
Beale, William Taylor *engineering company executive*
Dinos, Nicholas *engineering educator, administrator*
Robe, Thurlow Richard *engineering educator, university dean*

**Barberton**
Zbacnik, Raymond Eric *process engineer*

**Batavia**
Bower, Kenneth Francis *electrical engineer*
McDonough, James Francis *civil engineer, educator*

**Beavercreek**
Sturgess, Geoffrey J. *aeronautical research engineer*
Tan, Seng C. *research scientist, materials research executive*

### Broadview Heights
Barth, Charles Fredrik *aerospace engineer*

### Brookpark
Bluford, Guion Stewart, Jr. *engineering company executive*
Lee, Jinho *research engineer, consultant*
Wilson, Jack *aeronautical engineer*

### Canton
Hoecker, David *engineering executive*
Hummell, Donna Grisoglio *metallurgical engineer*

### Chagrin Falls
Gilding, Ronald Edwin *electrical engineer*
Pauly, Bruce Henry *engineering consultant*

### Chandlersville
Herron, Janet Irene *industrial manufacturing engineer*

### Cincinnati
Anno, James Nelson *nuclear engineering scientist, educator*
Arantes, José Carlos *industrial engineer, educator*
Arnold, Lynn Ellis *metallurgist, consultant*
Bahr, Donald Walter *chemical engineer*
Bluestein, Paul Harold *management engineer*
Fried, Joel Robert *chemical engineering educator*
Gardner, Leonard Burton, II *retired industrial automation engineer*
Greenberg, David Bernard *chemical engineering educator*
Hersman, Fernando William (Ferd Hersman) *retired engineer*
Isaacs, S. Ted *engineering executive*
Johnson, K(enneth) O(dell) *aerospace engineer*
Katzen, Raphael *consulting chemical engineer*
Kenkel, Jerome Bernard *civil engineer*
Kroll, Robert James *aerospace engineering educator*
LaBath, Octave Aaron *mechanical engineer*
Martin, John Bruce *chemical engineer*
Morgan, William Richard *mechanical engineer*
Pancheri, Eugene Joseph *chemical engineer*
Rubin, Stanley Gerald *aerospace engineering educator*
Sansbury, Blake Edward *product development engineer*
Smith, Leroy Harrington, Jr. *mechanical engineer, aerodynamics consultant*
Smith, Stephen Dale *safety engineer*
Toftner, Richard Orville *engineering executive*
Weisman, Joel *nuclear engineering educator, engineering consultant*

### Cleveland
Angus, John Cotton *chemical engineering educator*
Baer, Eric *engineering and science educator*
Bahniuk, Eugene *mechanical engineering educator*
Brosilow, Coleman Bernard *chemical engineering educator*
Burghart, James Henry *electrical engineer, educator*
Collin, Robert Emanuel *electrical engineering educator*
Coulman, George Albert *chemical engineer, educator*
Dy Liacco, Tomas Enciso *engineering consulting executive*
Fernandez, René *aerospace engineer*
Goldstein, Marvin Emanuel *aerospace scientist, research center administrator*
Gyekenyesi, John Paul *mechanical engineer*
Heuer, Arthur Harold *ceramics engineer, educator*
Holcombe, Homer Wayne *nuclear quality assurance professional*
Ko, Wen-Hsiung *electrical engineering educator*
Lefkowitz, Irving *engineering educator*
Liu, Chung-Chiun *chemical engineering educator*
Madden, James Desmond *forensic engineer*
Merat, Francis Lawrence *engineering educator*
Ono, Cheryl Eiko *senior controls engineer*
Ostrach, Simon *engineering educator*
Reisman, Arnold *retired management science educator*
Reshotko, Eli *aerospace engineer, educator*
Saada, Adel Selim *civil engineer, educator*
Salkind, Michael Jay *technology administrator*
Sargent, Noel Boyd *electrical engineer*
Savinell, Robert Francis *engineering educator*
Siegel, Robert *heat transfer engineer*
Wessel, Dennis James *mechanical engineering administrator*
Yurko, Joseph Andrew *chemical engineer*

### Columbus
Alexander, Carl Albert *ceramic engineer*
Antler, Morton *consulting engineering executive, author, educator*
Arps, David Foster *electronics engineer*
Bailey, Cecil Dewitt *aerospace engineer, educator*
Bechtel, Stephen E. *mechanical engineer, educator*
Bedford, Keith Wilson *civil engineer, atmospheric science educator*
Bhushan, Bharat *mechanical engineer*
Boulger, Francis William *metallurgical engineer*
Brodkey, Robert Stanley *chemical engineering educator*
Chovan, John David *biomedical engineer*
Cruz, Jose Bejar, Jr. *engineering educator*
Duckworth, Winston Howard *retired ceramic engineer*
Dwon, Larry *retired electrical engineer, educator, consultant*
Ensminger, Dale *mechanical engineer, electrical engineer*
Fenton, Robert Earl *electrical engineering educator*
Gatewood, Buford Echols *retired educator, aeronautical and astronautical engineer*
Gozon, Jozsef Stephan *engineering educator*
Grant, Michael Peter *electrical engineer*
Houser, Donald Russell *mechanical engineering educator, consultant*
Hsu, Hsiung *engineering educator*
Hughes, James Sinclair *electronic engineer, writer*
Keaney, William Regis *engineering and construction services executive, consultant*
Kolcio, Nestor *electrical engineer*
Kouyoumjian, Robert G. *electrical engineering educator*
Ksienski, Aharon Arthur *electrical engineer*
Leissa, Arthur William *mechanical engineering educator*
Liu, Ming-Tsan *computer engineering educator*
Miller, Don Wilson *nuclear engineering educator*
Moulton, Edward Quentin *civil engineer, educator*
Ozkan, Umit Sivrioglu *chemical engineering educator*
Peters, Leon, Jr. *electrical engineering educator, research administrator*
Rapp, Robert Anthony *metallurgical engineering educator, consultant*
Redmond, Robert Francis *nuclear engineering educator*
Rubin, Alan J. *environmental engineer, chemist*
Sahai, Yogeshwar *engineering educator*
St. Pierre, George Roland, Jr. *materials science and engineering administrator, educator*
Singh, Rajendra *mechanical engineering educator*
Smith, George Leonard *industrial engineering educator*
Smith, Philip John *industrial and systems engineering educator*
Taiganides, E. Paul *agricultural and environmental engineer, consultant*
Turchi, Peter John *aerospace and electrical engineer, educator, scientist*
Uotila, Urho Antti Kalevi *geodesist, educator*
von Recum, Andreas F. *bioengineer*
Wagoner, Robert Hall *engineering educator, researcher*
Waldron, Kenneth John *mechanical engineering educator, researcher*
Ware, Brendan John *retired electrical engineer and utility executive*
Zakin, Jacques Louis *chemical engineering educator*
Zande, Richard Dominic *civil engineering firm executive*
Zapp, Robert Louis *electronic test engineer*

### Dayton
Ballal, Dilip Ramchandra *mechanical engineering educator*
Brown, William Milton *electrical engineering educator*
Cowden, Roger Hugh, II *systems engineer*
Glasgow, D. Gerald *polymer engineering researcher*
Houpis, Constantine Harry *electrical engineering educator*
Kazimierczuk, Marian Kazimierz *electrical engineer, educator*
Mitchell, Philip Michael *aerospace engineer, consultant*
Rowe, Joseph Everett *electrical engineering educator, administrator*
Schmitt, George Frederick, Jr. *materials engineer*
Shaw, George Bernard *consulting engineer, educator*

### Delphos
Staup, John Gary *safety engineer*

### Dublin
Major, Coleman Joseph *chemical engineer*

### Fairport Harbor
Kirchner, James William *retired electrical engineer*

### Gates Mills
Enyedy, Gustav, Jr. *chemical engineer*
Pace, Stanley Carter *retired aeronautical engineer*

### Kent
Anderson, William John, II *engineering and business management consultant*

### Lancaster
Huston, John Timothy *electrical engineer*

### Logan
Carmean, Jerry Richard *broadcast engineer*

### Loveland
Anderson, Roy Alan *chemical engineer*

### Mansfield
Sheridan, Mark William *mechanical engineer, strategic planner*

### Marblehead
Haering, Edwin Raymond *chemical engineering educator, consultant*

### Marysville
Baik-Kromalic, Sue S. *metallurgical engineer*

### Mentor
Barna, Kenneth James *design engineer*

### Middletown
Gilby, Steve *metallurgical engineering researcher*
Newby, John Robert *metallurgical engineer*

### North Olmsted
Lundin, Bruce Theodore *engineering and management consultant*

### Norwood
Wilson, William Alexander *manufacturing engineer*

### Oxford
Ward, Roscoe Fredrick *engineering educator*

### Painesville
Jayne, Theodore Douglas *technical research and development company executive*

### Perrysburg
Khan, Amir U. *agricultural engineering consultant*

### Powell
Schwab, Glenn Orville *retired agricultural engineering educator, consultant*

### Shelby
Moore Moif, Florian Howard *electronics engineer*

### Springboro
Saxer, Richard Karl *metallurgical engineer, retired air force officer*

### Strongsville
Mills, S. Loren *product safety manager, engineer*

### Toledo
Farison, James Blair *electrical biomedical engineer, educator*
Hauenstein, Henry William *civil engineer*
Oh, Keytack Henry *industrial engineering educator*
Schultz, Warren Robert *manufacturing administrator*
Wolff, Edwin Ray *construction engineer*

### Westlake
Bisson, Edmond Emile *mechanical engineer*
Huff, Ronald Garland *mechanical engineer*

### Wickliffe
Anthony, Donald Barrett *engineering executive*
Bardasz, Ewa Alice *chemical engineer*

### Worthington
Compton, Ralph Theodore, Jr. *electrical engineering educator*
Giannamore, David Michael *electronics engineer*

### Wright Patterson AFB
†Adams, Wade *materials engineer, researcher*
D'Azzo, John Joachim *electrical engineer, educator*
Haritos, George Konstantinos *engineering educator, military officer*
King, Paul Irvin *aerospace engineering educator*

### Yellow Springs
Jensen, Roger Christian *industrial engineer*
Trolander, Hardy Wilcox *engineering executive, consultant*

### Youngstown
Fok, Thomas Dso Yun *civil engineer*
Kenner, Marilyn Sferra *civil engineer*
Lacivita, Michael John *safety engineer*

## OKLAHOMA

### Bartlesville
Clay, Harris Aubrey *chemical engineer*
Gao, Hong Wen *chemical engineer*
Johnson, Marvin Merrill *chemical engineer, chemist*
Mihm, John Clifford *chemical engineer*

### Bethany
Arnold, Donald Smith *chemical engineer, consultant*

### Buffalo
Anthony, Jack Ramon *mechanical engineer, retired*

### Cushing
†Kyker, James Charles *engineering executive, computer programmer*

### Duncan
Surjaatmadja, Jim Basuki *research engineer*

### Eucha
Cole, Harold Spencer *engineer*

### Midwest City
Smith, Wayne Calvin *chemical engineer*

### Norman
Altan, M(ustafa) Cengiz *mechanical engineering educator*
Bert, Charles Wesley *mechanical and aerospace engineer, educator*
Campbell, John Morgan *retired chemical engineer*
Crane, Robert Kendall *engineering educator, researcher, consultant*
Egle, Davis Max *mechanical engineering educator*
Menzie, Donald E. *petroleum engineer, educator*
†O'Rear, Edgar Allen, III *chemical engineering educator*
Scamehorn, John Frederick *chemical engineer*
Zaman, Musharraf *civil engineering educator*
Zelby, Leon Wolf *electrical engineering educator, consulting engineer*

### Oklahoma City
Allen, James Harmon, Jr. *civil engineer*
Hofener, Steven David *civil engineer*
Mikkelson, Dean Harold *geological engineer*
Miller, Herbert Dell *petroleum engineer*
Wickens, Donald Lee *engineer executive, consultant, rancher*

### Oologah
Knight, Gary Charles *mechanical engineer*

### Stillwater
Barfield, Billy Joe *agricultural engineer, educator*
Bell, Kenneth John *chemical engineer*
Brusewitz, Gerald Henry *agricultural engineering educator, researcher*
Case, Kenneth Eugene *industrial engineering educator*
Hughes, Michael *civil engineer*
Maddox, Robert Nott *chemical engineer, educator*
Maule, Charles Gough *retired industrial engineer, educator*
Mize, Joe Henry *industrial engineer, educator*
Noyes, Ronald Tacie *agricultural engineering educator*
Thompson, David Russell *engineering educator, academic dean*

### Tulsa
Blanton, Roger Edmund *mechanical engineer*
Earlougher, Robert Charles, Sr. *petroleum engineer*
Elkins, Lloyd Edwin, Sr. *petroleum engineer, energy consultant*
Parker, Robert Lee, Sr. *petroleum engineer, drilling company executive*
Prayson, Alex Stephen *drafting and mechanical design educator*
Tubbs, David Eugene *mechanical engineer, marketing professional*
Williams, David Rogerson, Jr. *engineer, business executive*
Williams, John Horter *civil engineer, oil, gas, telecommunications and allied products distribution company executive*

### Washington
Sliepcevich, Cedomir M. *engineering educator*

### Yale
Berger, Billie David *corrosion engineer*

### Yukon
Morgan, Robert Steve *mechanical engineer*

## OREGON

### Albany
Yau, Te-Lin *corrosion engineer*

### Aloha
Rojhantalab, Hossein Mohammad *chemical engineer, researcher*

### Beaverton
Chartier, Vernon Lee *electrical engineer*

### Cloverdale
Jortner, Julius *materials engineer, consultant*

### Corvallis
Engelbrecht, Rudolf *electrical engineering educator*
Forbes, Leonard *engineering educator*
Hansen, Hugh Justin *agricultural engineer*
Knudsen, James George *chemical engineer, educator*
Miner, John Ronald *bioresource engineer*
Mohler, Ronald Rutt *electrical engineering educator*
Olleman, Roger Dean *industry consultant, former metallurgical engineering educator*
Rapier, Pascal Moran *chemical engineer, physicist*
Temes, Gabor Charles *electrical engineering educator*
Yim, Solomon Chik-Sing *civil engineering educator, consultant*

### Florence
Ericksen, Jerald Laverne *educator, engineering scientist*

### Klamath Falls
Buchanan, Walter Woolwine *electrical engineer, educator and administrator*

### Lincoln City
Gehrig, Edward Harry *electrical engineer, consultant*

### Medford
Davenport, Wilbur Bayley, Jr. *electrical engineering educator*

### Myrtle Point
Walsh, Don *marine consultant, executive*

### Portland
Becker, Bruce Douglas *mechanical engineer*
Chrzanowska-Jeske, Malgorzata Ewa *electrical engineering educator, consultant*
Daly, Donald F. *engineering company executive*
Dryden, Robert D. *engineering educator*
Grappe, Harold Hugo *civil engineer*
Khalil, Mohammad Aslam Khan *environmental science and engineering educator*
Kocaoglu, Dundar F. *engineering management educator, industrial and civil engineer*
Lall, B. Kent *civil engineering educator*
Li, Fu *electrical engineering educator, editor*
Perkowski, Marek Andrzej *electrical engineering educator*
Taylor, Carson William *electrical engineer*
Van Valkenburg, Mac Elwyn *retired electrical engineering educator*
Yamayee, Zia Ahmad *engineering educator, dean*

### Redmond
Rychetsky, Steve *civil and environmental engineer, consultant*

### Roseburg
Amnéus, John Sigfrid *retired research mechanical engineer*

### Salem
Butts, Edward Perry *civil engineer, environmental consultant*

### Sunriver
Clough, Ray William, Jr. *civil engineering educator*

### Tualatin
Webster, Merlyn Hugh, Jr. *manufacturing engineer, information systems consultant*

## PENNSYLVANIA

### Alcoa Center
Stol, Israel *welding engineer*

### Allentown
Gewartowski, James Walter *electrical engineer*
Hansel, James Gordon *engineer, educator*
Lesak, David Michael *safety engineer, educator, consultant*
Singhal, Kishore *engineering administrator*
Wu, Pan *electrical engineer*

### Berwyn
Lund, George Edward *retired electrical engineer*

### Bethel Park
Korchynsky, Michael *metallurgical engineer*
O'Donnell, William James *engineering executive*

### Bethlehem
Anderson, David Martin *environmental engineer*
Beedle, Lynn Simpson *civil engineering educator*
Chen, John C. *chemical engineering educator*
Durkee, Jackson Leland *civil engineer*
Fisher, John William *civil engineering educator*
Gardiner, Keith Mattinson *engineering educator*
Geffe, Philip Reinhold *electrical engineer, consultant*
Georgakis, Christos *chemical engineer educator, consultant, researcher*
Karakash, John J. *engineering educator*
Levy, Edward Kenneth *mechanical engineering educator*
Neti, Sudhakar *mechanical engineering educator*
Pense, Alan Wiggins *metallurgical engineer, academic administrator*
Roberts, Richard *mechanical engineering educator*
Tuzla, Kemal *mechanical engineer, scientist*

Wenzel, Leonard Andrew *engineering educator*

**Birdsboro**
Mengle, Tobi Dara *mechanical engineer, consultant*

**Blue Bell**
Vollmar, John Raymond *electrical engineer*

**Boyertown**
Novak, Darwin Albert, Jr. *engineering company executive, chemical engineer*

**Bridgeville**
Pearlman, Seth Leonard *civil engineer*

**Broomall**
Lerner, Julius *mechanical engineer*

**Butler**
Kay, George Paul *environmental engineer*

**Camp Hill**
Scheiner, James Ira *engineering company executive*

**Chadds Ford**
Isakoff, Sheldon Erwin *chemical engineer*

**Cheltenham**
Weinstock, Walter Wolfe *systems engineer*

**Chester**
Kornfield, Nathaniel Richard *computer engineer educator*

**Collegeville**
Kelly, Jeffrey Charles *materials engineer*

**Conshohocken**
Rippel, Harry Conrad *mechanical engineer, consultant*

**Coopersburg**
Peserik, James E. *electrical, controls and computer engineer, consultant, forensics and safety engineer, fire cause and origin investigator*
Siess, Alfred Albert, Jr. *engineering executive, management consultant*

**Douglassville**
Haratunian, Michael *engineering company executive*

**Easton**
Belyea, Robert Combs *electrical engineer*
Wimmer, Maureen Kathryn *chemical engineer*

**Ebensburg**
Ramsdell, Richard Adoniram *marine engineer*

**Ellwood City**
Rorquist, Ivor Carl *mechanical engineer*

**Erie**
Gray, Robert Beckwith *electrical engineer, consultant*
Hsu, Bertrand Dahung *mechanical engineer*

**Erwinna**
Geldmacher, Robert Carl *engineering educator*

**Export**
Colborn, Harry Walter *electrical engineering consultant*
Wagner, Charles Leonard *electrical engineer, consultant*

**Exton**
Falcone, Anthony *mechanical engineer*

**Fairview**
Gorski, Brian C. *engineer, consultant*

**Fort Washington**
Pillai, Raviraj Sukumar *chemical engineer, researcher*

**Gibsonia**
Shoub, Earle Phelps *chemical engineer, educator*

**Glen Mills**
Churchill, Stuart Winston *chemical engineering educator*

**Glenside**
Forman, Edgar Ross *mechanical engineer*
Hargens, Charles William, III *electrical engineer, consultant*

**Greensburg**
Guyker, William Charles, Jr. *electrical engineer, researcher*

**Harrisburg**
Cate, Donald James *mechanical engineer, consultant*
Dietz, John Raphael *consulting engineer executive*

**Hatboro**
Marshall, Trevor John *engineering professional*

**Havertown**
Sheppard, Walter Lee, Jr. *chemical engineer, consultant*

**Hellertown**
Viest, Ivan M(iroslav) *consulting structural engineer*

**Hershey**
McInerney, Joseph John *biomedical engineer, educator*

**Horsham**
Goff, Kenneth Wade *electrical engineer*
Landberg, George Gustaf *mechanical engineer*

**Huntingdon Valley**
West, A(rnold) Sumner *chemical engineer*

**Indiana**
Soule, Robert D. *safety and health educator, administrator*

**Jenkintown**
Cohen, Alan *civil engineer*
Haythornthwaite, Robert Morphet *civil engineer, educator*
Klock, Fred William *materials engineer*

**Johnstown**
Kuhn, Howard Arthur *engineering executive, educator*

**King Of Prussia**
Ghorpade, Ajit Kisanrao *chemical and environmental engineer*

**Lake Ariel**
Tague, Charles Francis *retired engineering, construction and real estate development company executive*

**Lansdale**
Cartlidge, Edward Sutterley *mechanical engineer*

**Lansdowne**
Popovics, Sandor *civil engineer, educator, researcher*

**Latrobe**
Conley, Edward Vincent, Jr. *metallurgical engineering researcher*

**Lewisburg**
Rich, Thomas Paul *engineering educator, administrator*

**Monroeville**
Jacobi, William Mallett *nuclear engineer, consultant*
Mandel, Herbert Maurice *civil engineer*

**Mont Alto**
Wagaman, James Brian *environmentalist*

**Moon Township**
Rabosky, Joseph George *engineering consulting company executive*

**Murrysville**
McWhirter, James Herman *consulting engineering business executive, financial planner*

**New Galilee**
Randza, Jason Michael *engineer*

**New Kensington**
Jarrett, Noel *chemical engineer*
Li, Nai-Yi *mechanical engineer, researcher*
Pien, Shyh-Jye John *mechanical engineer*

**Newtown Square**
Perrone, Nicholas *mechanical engineer, business executive*
Yeh, George Chiayou *engineering company executive*

**Philadelphia**
Awani, Alfred Owumi *aerospace engineer*
Batterman, Steven Charles *engineering mechanics and bioengineering educator*
Chance, Henry Martyn, II *engineering executive*
Cohen, Ira Myron *aeronautical and mechanical engineering educator*
Eisenstein, Bruce Allan *electrical engineering educator*
Falkie, Thomas Victor *mining engineer, natural resources company executive*
Fegley, Kenneth Allen *systems engineering educator*
Ferber, Arthur Henry *engineering executive*
Gaither, William Samuel *civil engineering executive, consultant*
Haas, Charles Nathan *environmental engineering educator*
Jaron, Dov *biomedical engineer, educator*
Joner, Bruno *aeronautical engineer*
Kritikos, Haralambos N. *electrical engineering educator*
Lawley, Alan *materials engineering educator*
Lewin, Peter Andrew *electrical engineer, educator*
Litt, Mitchell *chemical engineer, educator, bioengineer*
Mc Mahon, Charles Joseph, Jr. *materials science educator*
Morlok, Edward Karl *engineering educator, consultant*
Mortimer, Richard Walter *mechanical engineering educator*
Pipes, Wesley O'Feral *civil engineering educator*
Quinn, John Albert *chemical engineering educator*
Rothwarf, Allen *electrical engineering educator*
Rumpf, John Louis *civil engineer, consultant*
Schwan, Herman Paul *electrical engineering and physical science educator, research scientist*
Showers, Ralph Morris *electrical engineer educator*
Sun, Hun H. *electrical engineering and biomedical engineering educator*
Thomson, Robert Gordon, Jr. *environmental engineer*
Tomiyasu, Kiyo *consulting engineer*
Van der Spiegel, Jan *engineering educator*
Zemel, Jay Norman *electrical engineer, educator*

**Pittsburgh**
Amon Parisi, Cristina Hortensia *mechanical engineering educator, researcher*
Behrend, William Louis *electrical engineer*
Birks, Neil *metallurgical engineering educator, consultant*
Bjorhovde, Reidar *civil engineer, educator, researcher, consultant*
Bloom, William Millard *furnace design engineer*
Boczkaj, Bohdan Karol *structural engineer*
Brubaker, James Edward *engineer*
Casasent, David Paul *electrical engineering educator, data processing executive*
Charap, Stanley Harvey *electrical engineering educator*
Chiang, Shiao-Hung *chemical engineering educator*
Chigier, Norman *mechanical engineering educator*
Conti, Ronald Samuel *electronics engineer, fire prevention engineer*
Fenves, Steven Joseph *civil engineer*
Freudenrich, David Robert *civil engineer, traffic engineer*
Geiger, Gene Edward *engineer, educator*
Gottfried, Byron Stuart *engineering educator*
Griffin, Donald Spray *mechanical engineer, consultant*
Grossman, Ignacio E. *chemical engineering educator*
Grossmann, Ignacio Emilio *chemical engineering educator*
Hamilton, Howard Britton *electrical engineer, educator*
Hendrickson, Chris Thompson *civil and environmental engineering educator, researcher*
Hoburg, James Frederick *electrical engineering educator*
Hung, Tin-Kan *engineering educator, researcher*
Jordan, Angel Goni *electrical and computer engineering educator*
Krutz, Ronald L. *computer engineer*
Li, Ching-Chung *electrical engineering, computer science educator*
Luthy, Richard Godfrey *environmental engineering educator*
McAvoy, Bruce Ronald *engineer, consultant*
McMichael, Francis Clay *civil engineering educator, environmental engineering consultant*
Meiksin, Zvi H. *electrical engineering educator*
Milnes, Arthur George *electrical engineer, educator*
Moura, José Manuel Fonseca *electrical engineer*
Nathanson, Harvey Charles *electrical engineer*
Neuman, Charles P. *electrical and computer engineering educator*
Pettit, Frederick Sidney *metallurgical engineering educator, researcher*
Pohland, Frederick George *environmental engineering educator, researcher*
Raimondi, Albert Anthony *mechanical engineer*
Reznik, Alan A. *petroleum engineering educator*
Schultz, Jerome Samson *biochemical engineer, educator*
Simaan, Marwan A. *electrical engineering educator*
Sinclair, Glenn Bruce *mechanical engineering educator, researcher*
Spanovich, Milan *civil engineer*
Stahl, Laddie L. *electrical engineer, manufacturing company executive*
Stuckeman, Herman Campbell *architectural engineer*
Tierney, John William *chemical engineering educator*
Touhill, C. Joseph *environmental engineer*
Turbeville, Robert Morris *engineering executive*
Vogeley, Clyde Eicher, Jr. *engineering educator, artist, consultant*
Wallace, William Edward *engineering educator, scientist*
Westerberg, Arthur William *chemical engineering educator*
Williams, Lisle Edward *civil and structural engineer*
Woo, Savio Lau-Yuen *bioengineering educator*
Yang, Wen-Ching *chemical engineer*

**Plymouth Meeting**
Kostinsky, Harvey *clinical and electrical engineer*
Suydam, Peter R. *clinical engineer, consultant*

**Reading**
Hollander, Herbert I. *consulting engineer*

**Springfield**
Gordon, Robert Bruce *mechanical engineer*
Parmiter, James Darlin *safety engineer*

**Star Junction**
Baldwin, Clarence Jones, Jr. *electrical engineer, manufacturing company executive*

**State College**
Barnoff, Robert Mark *civil engineering educator*
Foderaro, Anthony Harolde *nuclear engineering educator*
Kulakowski, Bohdan Tadeusz *mechanical engineering educator*
Maneval, David Richard *mineral engineering consultant*
Olson, Donald Richard *mechanical engineering educator*
Thompson, Fred Clayton *engineering executive, consultant*
Wysk, Richard A. *engineering educator, researcher*

**Swarthmore**
Krendel, Ezra Simon *systems and human factors engineering consultant*

**University Park**
Aplan, Frank Fulton *metallurgical engineering educator*
Bose, Nirmal Kumar *electrical engineering, mathematics educator*
Brown, John Lawrence, Jr. *electrical engineering educator*
Davids, Norman *engineering science and mechanics educator, researcher*
Duda, John Larry *chemical engineering educator*
†Elliott, Herschel *agricultural engineer, educator*
Feng, Tse-yun *computer engineer, educator*
Ham, Inyong *industrial engineering educator*
Helfferich, Friedrich G. *chemical engineer, educator*
Holl, John William *engineering educator*
Kabel, Robert Lynn *chemical engineering educator*
Knott, Kenneth *engineering educator, consultant*
Lakshminarayana, Budugur *aerospace engineering educator*
Macdonald, Digby Donald *scientist, science administrator*
Mathews, John David *electrical engineering educator, research director, consultant*
McCormick, Barnes Warnock *aerospace engineering educator*
McDonnell, Archie Joseph *environmental engineer*
McWhirter, John Ruben *chemical engineering educator*
Mentzer, John Raymond *electrical engineer, educator*
Morris, Philip John *aerospace engineering educator*
Nisbet, John Stirling *electrical engineering educator*
Ramani, Raja Venkat *mining engineering educator*
Reed, Joseph Raymond *civil engineering educator, academic administrator*
Ruud, Clayton Olaf *engineering educator*
Scanlon, Andrew *structural engineering educator*
Thompson, William, Jr. *engineering educator*
Thuering, George Lewis *industrial engineering educator*
Tittmann, Bernhard Rainer *engineering science and mechanics educator*
Vannice, M. Albert *chemical engineering educator, researcher*
Webb, Ralph Lee *mechanical engineering educator*
Witzig, Warren Frank *nuclear engineer, educator*

**Valley Forge**
Atilgan, Timur Faik *structural engineer*

**Villanova**
McLaughlin, Philip VanDoren, Jr. *mechanical engineering educator, researcher, consultant*
Tomlinson, J. Richard *engineering services company executive*
Whitman, Alan Morris *mechanical engineering educator*

**Wallingford**
Parker, Jennifer Ware *chemical engineer, researcher*

**Warminster**
Tatnall, George Jacob *aeronautical engineer*

**Warrendale**
Hartwig, Thomas Leo *civil engineer*

**Wayne**
Grigg, William Clyde *electrical engineer*
Warshell, Jay *systems engineer*

**West Chester**
Bartlett, Desmond William *engineering company executive*
Dwyer, Francis Gerard *chemical engineer, researcher*
Murphy, Stephan David *electrical engineer*
Weston, Roy Francis *environmental consultant*

**West Mifflin**
Ardash, Garin *mechanical engineer*

**West Point**
Teltser, Michael *chemical engineer*

**Wexford**
DoVale, Fern Louise *civil engineer*

**Yardley**
Patel, Mukund Ranchhodlal *electrical engineer, researcher*

**York**
Horn, Russell Eugene *engineering executive, consultant*

## RHODE ISLAND

**Cranston**
Thielsch, Helmut John *engineering company executive*

**East Greenwich**
†Juechter, John William *retired mechanical engineer, consultant*

**Greenville**
Calo, Joseph Manuel *chemical engineering educator*

**Kingston**
Lee, Kang-Won Wayne *engineer, educator*
Polk, Charles *electrical engineer, educator, biophysicist*
Tufts, Donald Winston *electrical engineering educator*

**North Kingstown**
Apostal, Michael Christopher *structural engineer*

**Portsmouth**
Baker, Walter Louis *engineering company executive*
Becken, Bradford Albert *engineering executive*

**Providence**
Freund, Lambert Ben *engineering educator, researcher, consultant*
Glicksman, Maurice *engineering educator, former dean and provost*
Gurland, Joseph *engineering educator*
Hazeltine, Barrett *electrical engineer, educator*
Needleman, Alan *mechanical engineering educator*
Preparata, Franco Paolo *computer science and engineering educator*
Richardson, Peter Damian *mechanical engineering educator*
Richman, Marc Herbert *forensic engineer, educator*
Suuberg, Eric Michael *chemical engineering educator*
Symonds, Paul Southworth *mechanical engineering educator, researcher*
Weiner, Jerome Harris *mechanical engineering educator*

**Rumford**
Findley, William Nichols *mechanical engineering educator*

**Wakefield**
Boothroyd, Geoffrey *industrial and manufacturing engineering educator*

**Warwick**
Baffoni, Frank Anthony *biomedical engineer, consultant*

## SOUTH CAROLINA

**Aiken**
Hootman, Harry Edward *retired nuclear engineer, consultant*
Williamson, Thomas Garnett *nuclear engineering and engineering physics educator*

**Anderson**
Bergmann, Warren Clarence *mechanical engineer*
Goodner, Homer Wade *process systems failure risk consultant*

**Beaufort**
Pinkerton, Robert Bruce *mechanical engineer*

### Charleston
Baron, Seymour *engineering and research executive*
Bolin, Edmund Mike *electrical engineer, franchise engineering consultant*

### Clemson
Adams, John Quincy, III *nuclear engineer*
Bunn, Joe Millard *agricultural engineering educator*
Chisman, James Allan *industrial engineering educator, consultant*
Couch, James Houston *industrial engineer, educator*
Han, Young Jo *agricultural engineer, educator*
Leonard, Michael Steven *industrial engineering educator*
Paul, Frank Waters *mechanical engineer, educator, consultant*
Pursley, Michael Bader *electrical engineering educator, communications systems research and consulting*
Williamson, Robert Elmore *agricultural engineering educator*
Zumbrunnen, David Arnold *mechanical engineering educator, consultant*

### Columbia
Ernst, Edward Willis *electrical engineering educator*
Willoughby, William, II *retired nuclear engineer*

### Fort Mill
Brooks, Jerry Claude *safety engineer, educator*
Hodge, Bobby Lynn *mechanical engineer, bearing company executive*

### Goose Creek
Floss, Mark Thaddeus *civil engineer, computer scientist*
Sullivan, James *consultant*

### Greenville
Carlay, Ronald Leon *mechanical engineer*
Plumstead, William Charles *quality engineer, consultant*

### Hampton
Platts, Francis Holbrook *plastics engineer*

### Hartsville
Menius, Espie Flynn, Jr. *electrical engineer*

### Hilton Head Island
Davis, Milton Wickers, Jr. *chemical engineer, educator*
Huckins, Harold Aaron *chemical engineer*
Windman, Arnold Lewis *retired mechanical engineer*

### North Charleston
Fei, James Robert *engineer*
Mc Aleece, Donald John *mechanical engineering educator*

### Orangeburg
Graule, Raymond (Siegfried) *metallurgical engineer*

### Pawleys Island
Alexander, William D., III *civil engineer, consultant, former army air force officer*

### Rock Hill
Hardin, William Beamon, Jr. *electrical engineer*

### Salem
Jones, Charles Edward *mechanical engineer*

## SOUTH DAKOTA

### Brookings
Storry, Junis Oliver *retired engineering educator*

### Rapid City
Gowen, Richard Joseph *electrical engineering educator, academic administrator*
Ramakrishnan, Venkataswamy *civil engineer, educator*
Riemenschneider, Albert Louis *engineering educator*
Scofield, Gordon Lloyd *mechanical engineer, educator*

## TENNESSEE

### Arnold AFB
Chapman, Randall Allen *research engineer*
Davis, John William *government science and engineering executive*

### Chattanooga
Arndt, Steven Andrew *nuclear engineer*
Baker, Merl *engineering educator*
Cox, Ronald Baker *engineering and management consultant, university dean*
Duckworth, Jerrell James *electrical engineer*
Gore, Barry Maurice *electrical engineer*
Kittlitz, Rudolf Gottlieb, Jr. *chemical engineer*

### Cookeville
Chowdhuri, Pritindra *electrical engineer, educator*
Sissom, Leighton Esten *engineering educator, dean, consultant*
Smaili, Ahmad *mechanical engineering educator*

### Elizabethton
Claussen, Lisa Renee *engineering executive*

### Greenbrier
Newell, Paul Haynes, Jr. *engineering educator, former college president*

### Kingsport
Reasor, Roderick Jackson *industrial engineer*
Rex, David Lawrence *project manager*
Scott, H(erbert) Andrew *retired chemical engineer*
Siirola, Jeffrey John *chemical engineer*

### Knoxville
Bailey, John Milton *electrical engineering educator*
Bose, Bimal Kumar *electrical engineering educator*
Bressler, Marcus N. *consulting engineer*
Garrison, Arlene Allen *engineering executive, engineering educator*
Gonzalez, Rafael Ceferino *electrical engineering educator*
Hung, James Chen *engineer, educator, consultant*
Laroussi, Mounir *electrical engineer*
LeVert, Francis Edward *nuclear engineer*
Mc Dow, John Jett *agricultural engineering educator*
Richards, Stephen Harold *engineering educator*
Richardson, Don Orland *agricultural educator*
Roth, J(ohn) Reece *electrical engineer, educator, researcher-inventor*
Schuler, Theodore Anthony *retired civil engineer, retired city official*
Sorrells, Frank Douglas *mechanical engineer, consultant*
Tschantz, Bruce Allen *civil engineer, educator*
Uhrig, Robert Eugene *nuclear engineer, educator*

### Lenoir City
Brown, Donald Vaughn *technical educator, engineering consultant*

### Luttrell
Milligan, Mancil Wood *mechanical and aerospace engineering educator*

### Maryville
Mosher, Donald Raymond *chemical engineer, consultant*
Oakes, Lester Cornelius *retired electrical engineer, consultant*

### Memphis
French, Louis Bertrand *engineering educator*
Kellogg, Frederic Hartwell *civil engineer, educator*

### Nashville
Brodersen, Arthur James *electrical engineer*
Cadzow, James Archie *engineering educator, researcher*
Cook, George Edward *electrical engineering educator, consultant*
Galloway, Kenneth Franklin *electrical engineering educator*
Hahn, George Thomas *materials engineering educator, researcher*
Harrawood, Paul *civil engineering educator*
Harris, Thomas Raymond *biomedical engineer, educator*
House, Robert William *technology management educator*
Hughes, Gayle Womack *civil engineer, educator*
McClanahan, Larry Duncan *civil engineer, consultant*
Parker, Frank Leon *environmental engineering educator, consultant*
Potter, John Leith *mechanical and aerospace engineer, educator, consultant*
Schnelle, Karl Benjamin, Jr. *chemical engineering educator, consultant, researcher*
Speece, Richard Eugene *civil engineer, educator*
Thackston, Edward Lee *engineer, educator*

### Oak Ridge
Cain, Victor Ralph *nuclear engineer*
Kasten, Paul Rudolph *nuclear engineer, educator*
Mulkey, Charles Eric *environmental engineer*
Rivera, Angel Luis *chemical engineer*
Rosenthal, Murray Wilford *chemical engineer, science administrator*
Trauger, Donald Byron *nuclear engineering laboratory administrator*

### Shelbyville
White, James Claiborne *manufacturing engineer executive*

### Summertown
Emanuel, William Gilbert *electrical engineer*

### Tullahoma
Antar, Basil Niman *engineering educator*
Butler, R. W. *engineering company executive*
Wu, Ying Chu Lin Susan *engineering company executive, engineer*

### Vonore
Lownsdale, Gary Richard *mechanical engineer*

## TEXAS

### Allen
Dawes, Robert Leo *research company executive*

### Amarillo
Keaton, Lawrence Cluer *safety engineer, consultant*

### Arlington
Anderson, Dale Arden *aerospace engineer, educator*
Boyer, Vincent Lee *engineering executive*
Chen, Mo-Shing *electrical engineering educator*
Clark, Dayle Meritt *civil engineer*
Deaver, Pete Eugene *civil and aeronautical engineer*
Fung, Adrian Kin-Chiu *electrical engineering educator, researcher*
Mc Elroy, John Harley *electrical engineering educator*
Payne, Fred R(ay) *aerospace engineering educator, researcher*
Ptaszkowski, Stanley Edward, Jr. *civil engineer, structural engineer*
Qasim, Syed Reazul *civil engineering educator, researcher*
Stevens, Gladstone Taylor, Jr. *industrial engineer*

### Austin
Adcock, Willis Alfred *electrical engineer, educator*
Aggarwal, Jagdishkumar Keshoram *electrical and computer engineering educator, research administrator*
Armstrong, Neal Earl *civil engineering educator*
Baker, Lee Edward *biomedical engineering educator*
Beard, Leo Roy *civil engineer*
Breen, John Edward *civil engineer, educator*
Brock, James Rush *chemical engineering educator*
Bronaugh, Edwin Lee *electromagnetic compatibility engineer, consultant*
Brown, Stephen Neal *computer engineer*
Burns, Ned Hamilton *civil engineering educator*
Carey, Graham Francis *engineering educator*
Carlton, Donald Morrill *research, development and engineering executive*
Castaldi, Frank James *environmental engineer, consultant*
Dougal, Arwin Adelbert *electrical engineer, educator*
Evans, Walter Reed *engineering executive, consultant*
Fair, James Rutherford, Jr. *chemical engineering educator, consultant*
Fowler, David Wayne *architectural engineering educator*
Fults, Kenneth Wyatt *civil engineer, surveyor*
Gloyna, Earnest Frederick *environmental engineer, educator*
Goodenough, John Bannister *engineering educator, research physicist*
Grimm, Clayford Thomas *architectural engineer, consultant*
Harris, Richard Lee *engineering executive, retired army officer*
Himmelblau, David Mautner *chemical engineer*
Hixson, Elmer L. *engineering educator*
Howell, John Reid *mechanical engineering educator*
Hull, David George *aerospace engineering educator, researcher*
Juricic, Davor *mechanical engineering educator*
Koen, Billy Vaughn *mechanical engineering educator*
Koepsel, Wellington Wesley *electrical engineering educator*
Kopp, Debra Lynn *manufacturing engineer, consultant*
Koros, William John *chemical engineering educator*
Krishna, Hari J. *engineer*
LaGrone, Alfred Hall *electrical engineering educator*
Lamb, Jamie Parker, Jr. *mechanical engineer, educator*
Luedecke, William Henry *mechanical engineer, company executive*
Mark, Hans Michael *aerospace engineering educator, physicist*
Mautz, Karl Emerson *engineering executive*
McGinnis, Charles Irving *civil engineer*
Mc Ketta, John J., Jr. *chemical engineering educator*
Metcalfe, Tom Brooks *chemical engineering educator*
Nichols, Steven Parks *mechanical engineer, university official*
Paul, Donald Ross *chemical engineer, educator*
Perkins, Richard Burle, II *chemical engineer, international consultant*
Raina, Rajesh *computer engineer*
Rhyne, Vernon Thomas, III *electrical engineer, consultant*
Richards-Kortum, Rebecca Rae *biomedical engineering educator*
Rylander, Henry Grady, Jr. *mechanical engineering educator*
Sanchez, Isaac Cornelius *chemical engineer, educator*
Sandberg, Irwin Walter *electrical and computer engineering educator*
Schapery, Richard Allan *engineering educator*
Schechter, Robert Samuel *chemical engineer, educator*
Schmidt, Philip S. *mechanical engineering educator*
Sciance, Carroll Thomas *chemical engineer*
Steinfink, Hugo *chemical engineering educator*
Stice, James Edward *chemical engineer, educator*
Straiton, Archie Waugh *electrical engineering educator*
Streetman, Ben Garland *electrical engineering educator*
Swartzlander, Earl Eugene, Jr. *engineering educator, former electronics company executive*
Szebehely, Victor G. *aeronautical engineer*
Tapley, Byron Dean *aerospace engineer, educator*
Tesar, Delbert *machine systems and robotics educator, researcher, manufacturing consultant*
Thurston, George Butte *mechanical and biomedical engineering educator*
Tucker, Richard Lee *civil engineer, educator*
Vliet, Gary Clark *mechanical engineering educator*
Walton, Charles Michael *civil engineering educator*
Wehring, Bernard William *nuclear engineering educator*
Welch, Ashley James *engineering educator*
Woodson, Herbert Horace *retired electrical engineering educator*
Wright, Stephen Gailord *civil engineering educator, consultant*

### Baird
Rodenberger, Charles Alvard *aerospace engineer, consultant*

### Bedford
Lewis, Frank Leroy *electrical engineer, educator, researcher*

### Bellaire
Moore, Pat Howard *engineering and construction company executive*
Wisch, David John *structural engineer*

### Big Spring
Fryrear, Donald William *agricultural engineer*

### Boerne
Mitchelhill, James Moffat *civil engineer*

### Brooks AFB
Olsen, Richard Galen *biomedical engineer, researcher*

### Bryan
Samson, Charles Harold, Jr. (Car Samson) *retired engineering educator, consultant*

### Burnet
Gomes, Norman Vincent *retired industrial engineer*

### Bushland
Howell, Terry Allen *agricultural engineer*

### Carrollton
Schulz, Richard Burkart *electrical engineer, consultant*

### College Station
Baskharone, Erian Aziz *mechanical and aerospace engineering educator*
Bhattacharyya, Shankar Prashad *electrical engineer, educator*
Buth, Carl Eugene *civil engineer*
Cochran, Robert Glenn *nuclear engineering educator*
Ehsani, Mehrdad (Mark Ehsani) *electrical engineering educator, consultant*
Fletcher, Leroy Stevenson *mechanical engineer, educator*
Godbey, Luther David *architectural and engineering executive*
Hall, Kenneth Richard *chemical engineering educator, consultant*
Herbich, John Bronislaw *engineering educator*
Holland, Charles Donald *chemical engineer, educator*
Isdale, Charles Edwin *chemical engineer*
Kunze, Otto Robert *retired agricultural engineering educator*
Kuo, Way *industrial engineer, researcher*
Lee, William John *petroleum engineering educator, consultant*
Lowery, Lee Leon, Jr. *civil engineer*
Lytton, Robert Leonard *civil engineer, educator*
Mathewson, Christopher Colville *engineering geologist, educator*
Neff, Ray Quinn *electric power educator, consultant*
Page, Robert Henry *engineer, educator, researcher*
Painter, John Hoyt *electrical engineer*
Patton, Alton DeWitt *electrical engineering educator, consultant, research administrator*
Pitt, Woodrow Wilson, Jr. *engineering educator*
Rabins, Michael Jerome *mechanical engineer, educator*
Reddell, Donald Lee *agricultural engineer*
Richardson, Herbert Heath *mechanical engineer, educator, institute director*
Urbanik, Thomas, II *research civil engineer*
Weese, John Augustus *mechanical engineer, educator*
Yao, James Tsu-Ping *civil engineer*
Yeung, Albert Tak-Chung *civil engineering educator*

### Corpus Christi
Umfleet, Lloyd Truman *electrical engineering technology educator*

### Crosby
Ohsol, Ernest Osborne *consulting chemical engineer*

### Dallas
Brown, A.C., Jr. *electrical engineer*
Bruene, Warren Benz *electronic engineer*
Cruikshank, Thomas Henry *energy services and engineering executive*
Fix, Douglas Martin *electrical engineer*
Fontana, Robert Edward *electrical engineering educator, retired air force officer*
Honkanen, Jari Olavi *electrical engineer*
Huang, Yen Ti *civil engineer*
Johnson, Richard Clayton *engineer, physicist*
Kilby, Jack St. Clair *electrical engineer*
Le, Can *mechanical engineer, inventor, author*
McCall, Clyde Samuel, Jr. *petroleum engineer*
Schulze, Richard Hans *engineering executive, environmental engineer*
Skaggs, Merton Melvin, Jr. *environmental engineer*

### Deer Park
Mujica, Mary Bernadette *mechanical engineer*

### Edinburg
Diong, Billy Ming *control engineering researcher*

### El Paso
Friedkin, Joseph Frank *consulting engineering executive*
Grieves, Robert Belanger *engineering educator*
Heide, John Wesley *engineering executive*

### Fair Oaks Ranch
Dixon, Robert James *aerospace consultant, former air force officer, former aerospace company executive*

### Fort Worth
Al-Shakhshir, Ragheb Hilmi *pharmaceutical engineer*
Cunningham, Atlee Marion, Jr. *aeronautical engineer*
Kenderdine, John Marshall *petroleum engineer, retired army officer*
McLane, William Delano *mechanical engineer*
Nichols, James Richard *civil engineer, consultant*
Pray, Donald George *aerospace engineer*
Romine, Thomas Beeson, Jr. *consulting engineering executive*

### Freeport
Tsai, Tom Chunghu *chemical engineer*

### Friendswood
Lampton, Robert Donald, Jr. *chemical engineer, consultant*

### Galveston
Otis, John James *civil engineer*
Sheppard, Louis Clarke *biomedical engineer, educator*

### Garland
Christensen, Allan Robert *electrical engineer, enrolled agent*

### Grapevine
Killebrew, James Robert *architectural engineering firm executive*

### Greenville
White, William Dudley *safety engineer*

### Houston
Akers, William Walter *chemical engineering educator*
Allen, John Timothy *mechanical engineer*
Allman, Mark C. *engineer, physicist*
Amundson, Neal Russell *chemical engineer, mathematician, educator*
Antalffy, Leslie Peter *mechanical engineer*
Billingsley, David Stuart *chemical engineer, researcher*
Bishop, David Nolan *electrical engineer*
Bishop, Thomas Ray *retired mechanical engineer*
Bovay, Harry Elmo, Jr. *retired engineering company executive*
Bozeman, Ross Elliot *engineering executive*
Brandl, Ernest David *civil engineer*
Brouse, Michael *petroleum engineer, management consultant*
Carlson, Warren Ore *civil engineer*
Chapman, Alan Jesse *mechanical engineering educator*
Chavez, Victor Manuel *process engineer*

Cheatham, John Bane, Jr. *retired mechanical engineering educator*
Cizek, John Gary *safety and fire engineer*
Clark, John William, Jr. *electrical engineer, educator*
Collipp, Bruce Garfield *ocean engineer, consultant*
Cui, Michael Minqin *mechanical engineer*
David, Yadin B. *biomedical engineer, health care technology consultant*
Davis, Michael Jordan *civil engineer, natural gas company executive*
Dawn, Frederic Samuel *chemical and textile engineer*
Duerr, David *civil engineer*
Duke, Michael B. *aerospace scientist*
Dwight, Kenneth Harlan *metallurgical engineer*
Edwards, Victor Henry *chemical engineer*
Eichberger, LeRoy Carl *mechanical engineer, consultant, stress analyst*
Focht, John Arnold, Jr. *geotechnical engineer*
Frankhouser, Homer Sheldon, Jr. *engineering and construction company executive*
Gattis, James Ralph *engineering company executive*
Geer, Ronald Lamar *mechanical engineering consultant, retired oil company executive*
Gibson, Michael Addison *chemical engineering company executive*
Gidley, John Lynn *engineering executive*
Goldman, William Alexander *computer engineer*
Guinn, David Crittenden *petroleum engineer, drilling and exploration company executive*
Heit, Raymond Anthony *civil engineer*
Hellums, Jesse David *chemical engineering educator and researcher*
Hightower, Joe Walter *chemical engineering educator, consultant*
Hsu, Thomas Tseng-Chuang *civil engineer, educator*
Ivins, Marsha S. *aerospace engineer, astronaut*
King, Robert Augustin *engineering executive*
Kirby, Sarah Ann Van Deventer *aerospace engineer*
Kobayashi, Riki *chemical engineer, educator*
Kobs, Alfred W. *engineer*
Krause, William Austin *engineering executive*
Krishen, Kumar *aerospace research technologist*
Larks, Jack *forensic engineer, consultant*
Lienhard, John Henry, IV *mechanical engineering educator*
Lopez-Nakazono, Benito *chemical and industrial engineer*
Luss, Dan *chemical engineering educator*
Maligas, Manuel Nick *metallurgical engineer*
Matney, William Brooks, VII *electrical engineer, marine engineer*
Matthews, Charles Sedwick *petroleum engineering consultant, research advisor*
McEvilly, Michael James *civil engineer*
McIntire, Larry Vern *chemical engineering educator*
Meinke, Roy Walter *electrical engineer, consultant*
Menzies, John Alexander *mechanical and chemical engineer*
Mian, Farouk Aslam *chemical engineer, educator*
Miele, Angelo *engineering educator, researcher, consultant, author*
Miller, Charles Rickie *thermal and fluid systems analyst, engineering manager*
Moore, Walter Parker, Jr. *civil engineering company executive*
Morris, Owen Glenn *engineering corporation executive*
Nordgren, Ronald Paul *engineering educator, researcher*
Ostrofsky, Benjamin *business and engineering management educator, industrial engineer*
Oxer, John Paul Daniell *civil engineer*
Pearson, James Boyd, Jr. *electrical engineering educator*
Powell, Alan *mechanical engineer, scientist*
Prats, Michael *petroleum engineer, educator*
Rypien, David Vincent *welding engineer*
Schulze, Arthur Edward *biomedical engineer, researcher*
Shen, Liang Chi *electrical engineer, educator, researcher*
Skov, Arlie Mason *petroleum engineer, consultant*
Sloan, Harold David *chemical engineering consultant*
Smalley, Arthur Louis, Jr. *engineering and construction company executive*
Spanos, Pol Dimitrios *engineering educator*
Symons, James Martin *environmental engineer, educator*
Tucker, Randolph Wadsworth *engineering executive*
Walker, Esper Lafayette, Jr. *civil engineer*
Wong, Daniel On-Cheong *geotechnical and environmental engineer*
Wren, Robert James *aerospace engineering manager*
Wu, Gary G. *petroleum engineer, consultant*
Yu, Aiting Tobey *engineering executive*

### Humble
Brown, Samuel Joseph, Jr. *scientist, engineer*
Fortney, Thomas Kent *cost and petroleum engineer, management consultant*

### Hurst
Bishara, Amin Tawadros *mechanical engineer, technical services executive*

### Irving
Longwell, H.J. *petroleum engineer*
Potter, Robert Joseph *technical and business executive*
Rainwater, R. Steven *systems engineer*
Robinson, Charles Emanuel *systems engineer, consultant*

### Kerrville
Matlock, (Lee) Hudson *civil engineer, educator*
Sinninger, Dwight Virgil *engineer*

### Lake Jackson
McCutchen, Charles William *chemical engineer*

### League City
Faget, Maxime A(llan) *aeronautical engineer*

### Lindale
Bockhop, Clarence William *retired agricultural engineer*
Wilson, Leland Earl *petroleum engineering consultant*

### Lubbock
Archer, James Elson *engineering educator*
Dudek, Richard Albert *engineering educator*
Heath, Brent Alan *electrical engineer*
Ishihara, Osamu *electrical engineer, physicist, educator*
Kristiansen, Magne *electrical engineer, educator*
Portnoy, William Manos *electrical engineering educator*

### Mc Kinney
Gill, David Brian *electrical engineer, educator*

### Pearland
Jones, Lionel Troy, Jr. *electronic engineer*

### Plano
Clement, Clarence Clark, Jr. *petroleum engineer*

### Port Aransas
Lehmann, William Leonardo *electrical engineer, educator*

### Richardson
Biard, James Robert *electrical engineer*
Lutz, Raymond Price *industrial engineer, educator*
Witherspoon, W(illiam) Tom *engineering consultant*

### Rockport
Minor, Joseph Edward *civil engineer, educator*

### Rockwall
Griffith, James William *engineer, consultant*

### San Antonio
Abramson, Hyman Norman *engineering and science research executive*
Akujuobi, Cajetan Maduabuchukwu *research engineer, electrical engineering educator*
Belzung, Paul Edward *engineering executive*
Buster, Alan Adair *control engineer*
Chan, Kwai Shing *materials engineer, researcher*
Lindholm, Ulric Svante *engineering research institute executive, retired*
Smith, Richard Thomas *electrical engineer*
Stebbins, Richard Henderson *electronics engineer, peace officer, security consultant*

### Spring
Cross, Carole Ann *plastics engineer*
Szymczak, Edward Joseph *mechanical engineer*

### Temple
Patureau, Arthur Mitchell *chemical engineer, consultant*

### Texas City
Lamar, James Lewis, Jr. *chemical engineer*

### The Woodlands
Lanclos, Ritchie Paul *petroleum engineer*
Norton, David Jerry *mechanical research engineer*

### Tyler
Trent, Warren C. *mechanical engineer*

### Universal City
Atchley, Curtis Leon *mechanical engineer*

### Webster
Stephens, Douglas Kimble *chemical engineer*
Terry, Reese *engineering executive*

### Woodsboro
Rooke, Allen Driscoll, Jr. *civil engineer*

## UTAH

### Bingham Canyon
Callender, Jonathan Ferris *environmental engineer, consultant*

### Fort Duchesne
Cameron, Charles Henry *petroleum engineer*

### Logan
Hargreaves, George Henry *civil and agricultural engineer, researcher*
Keller, Jack *agricultural engineering educator, consultant*

### Murray
Volberg, Herman William *electronics engineer, consultant*

### Ogden
Davidson, Thomas Ferguson *chemical engineer*
Ritchey, Harold W. *retired chemical engineer*

### Orem
Harris, Michael James *software engineer*

### Provo
Barker, Dee H. *chemical engineering educator*
Jonsson, Jens Johannes *electrical engineering educator*
Merritt, LaVere Barrus *engineering educator, civil engineer*
Pope, Bill Jordan *chemical engineering educator, business executive*
Smoot, Leon Douglas *chemical engineering educator, research director, former university dean*

### Salt Lake City
Anderson, Charles Ross *civil engineer*
Bhayani, Kiran Lilachand *environmental engineer, programs manager*
Dahlstrom, Donald Albert *chemical and metallurgical engineering educator, former equipment manufacturing company executive*
De Vries, Kenneth Lawrence *mechanical engineer, educator*
Epperson, Vaughn Elmo *civil engineer*
Gandhi, Om Parkash *electrical engineer*
Gutzman, Philip Charles *aerospace executive, logistician*
Hogan, Mervin Booth *mechanical engineer, educator*
Iskander, Magdy Fahmy *electrical engineering educator, consultant*
Pershing, David Walter *chemical engineering educator, researcher*
Rogers, Vern Child *engineering company executive*
Sandquist, Gary Marlin *engineering educator*
Seader, Junior DeVere *chemical engineering educator*
Sohn, Hong Yong *metallurgical and chemical engineering educator*
Stringfellow, Gerald B. *engineering educator*
Zeamer, Richard Jere *engineer, executive*

### Sandy
Jorgensen, Leland Howard *aerospace research engineer*

### West Valley City
Bertoch, Richard Keith *electrical engineer, consultant*

## VERMONT

### Burlington
Anderson, Richard Louis *electrical engineer*
Pinder, George Francis *engineering educator, scientist*

### Essex Junction
Pricer, Wilbur David *electrical engineer*

### Underhill
Panner, Jeannie Harrigan *electrical engineer*

### White River Junction
Linnell, Robert Hartley *environment, safety consultant*

## VIRGINIA

### Afton
Anderson, Donald Norton, Jr. *retired electrical engineer*

### Alexandria
Ackerman, Roy Alan *research and development executive*
Brackett, James Vincent *electrical engineer*
Brandell, Sol Richard *electrical power and control system engineer, research mathematician*
Cook, Charles William *aerospace consultant, educator*
Coyne, James Kitchenman, III *engineering executive*
Darling, Thomas, Jr. *retired rural electrification specialist*
Dobson, Donald Alfred *electrical engineer*
Doeppner, Thomas Walter *electrical engineer, consultant*
Eckhart, Myron, Jr. (Max Myron) *marine engineer*
Gray, John Edmund *chemical engineer*
Heacock, Phillip Kaga *aerospace executive*
Jokl, Alois Louis *electrical engineer*
Jones, Russel Cameron *civil engineer*
Kemble, James Richard *engineering services executive, retired*
Lasser, Howard Gilbert *chemical engineer, consultant*
Mandil, I. Harry *nuclear engineer*
Murray, Russell, II *aeronautical engineer, defense analyst, consultant*
Rall, Lloyd Louis *civil engineer*
Scurlock, Arch Chilton *chemical engineer*
Studebaker, John Milton *utilities engineer, consultant, educator*
Thompson, LeRoy, Jr. *radio engineer, military reserve officer*
Weiner, Robert Michael *engineering design company executive, consulting engineer*

### Annandale
Geiger, Richard Bernard *engineer, retired federal agency administrator*

### Arlington
Arndt, Roger Edward Anthony *hydraulic engineer, educator*
Bordogna, Joseph *engineer, educator*
Cohen, Eliot Dorsey *electrical engineer*
Cox, Geraldine Vang *engineering executive*
Davis, Michael *engineering company executive*
†Denman, Gary L. *mechanical engineer*
Dillaway, Robert Beacham *engineering and management consultant*
Flowers, Harold Lee *aerospace engineer, consultant*
Gilbert, Arthur Charles *aerospace engineer, consulting engineer*
Hagn, George Hubert *electrical engineer, researcher*
Hall, Carl William *agricultural and mechanical engineer*
Heineken, Frederick George *biochemical engineer*
Henderson, Robert Earl *mechanical engineer, educator, consultant*
Katona, Peter Geza *biomedical engineer, educator*
Larsen-Basse, Jorn *mechanical and materials engineering educator, researcher, consultant*
Lau, Clifford *electrical engineer, researcher*
Lynn, Larry (Verne Lauriston Lynn) *engineering executive*
Meyers, Sheldon *engineering company executive*
Milburn, Richard Allan *aerospace company executive*
Murray, Arthur Joseph *engineering executive, lecturer*
Nickle, Dennis Edwin *electronics engineer, church deacon*
Poehlein, Gary Wayne *chemical engineering educator*
Rahman, Muhammad Abdur *mechanical engineer*
Reynik, Robert J. *materials scientist, research and education administrator*
Roco, Mihail Constantin *mechanical engineer, educator*
Stevens, Donald King *aeronautical engineer*
Stuart, Charles Edward *electrical engineer, oceanographer*
Sutton, George Walter *research laboratory executive, mechanical engineer*

### Blacksburg
Batra, Romesh Chander *engineering mechanics educator, researcher*
Blackwell, William Allen *electrical engineering educator*
Boardman, Gregory Dale *environmental engineer, educator*
Brown, Gary Sandy *electrical engineering educator*
de Wolf, David Alter *electrical engineer, educator*
Fabrycky, Wolter Joseph *engineering educator, author, industrial and systems engineer*
Glasser, Wolfgang Gerhard *wood science and chemical engineering researcher, educator*
Haugh, Clarence Gene *agricultural engineering educator*
Hibbard, Walter Rollo, Jr. *retired engineering educator*
Inman, Daniel John *mechanical engineer, educator*
Jones, James Beverly *retired mechanical engineering educator, consultant*
Lee, Fred C. *electrical engineering educator*
Lucas, J. Richard *retired mining engineering educator*
Meirovitch, Leonard *engineering educator*
Mitchell, James Kenneth *civil engineer, educator*
Moore, James Mendon *industrial engineering educator, consultant*
Murray, Thomas Michael *civil engineering educator, consultant*
Price, Dennis Lee *industrial engineer, educator*
Randall, Clifford Wendell *civil engineer*
Smith, Charles William *engineering educator*
Squires, Arthur Morton *chemical engineer, educator*
Stutzman, Warren Lee *electrical engineer, educator*

### Burke
Lynch, Charles Theodore, Sr. *materials science engineering researcher, consultant, educator*

### Centreville
Bucciero, Joseph Mario, Jr. *executive engineering firm*

### Chantilly
Evans, Richard Taylor *aerospace engineer, consultant*

### Charlottesville
Aylor, James Hiram *electrical engineering educator, department chair*
Bly, Charles Albert *nuclear engineer, research scientist*
Dorning, John Joseph *nuclear engineering, engineering physics and applied mathematics educator*
Edlich, Richard French *biomedical engineering educator*
Flack, Ronald Dumont *mechanical engineering educator*
Gaden, Elmer Lewis, Jr. *chemical engineering educator*
Gilruth, Robert Rowe *aerospace consultant*
Haimes, Yacov Yosseph *systems and civil engineering educator, consultant*
Herakovich, Carl Thomas *civil engineering, applied mechanics educator*
Hoel, Lester A. *civil engineering educator*
Hudson, John Lester *chemical engineering educator*
Inigo, Rafael Madrigal *electrical engineering educator*
Johnson, W(alker) Reed *nuclear engineering educator*
Krzysztofowicz, Roman *systems engineering and statistical science educator, consultant*
Morton, Jeffrey Bruce *aerospace engineering educator*
Reynolds, Albert Barnett *nuclear engineer, educator*
Theodoridis, George Constantin *biomedical engineering educator, researcher*
Thompson, Anthony Richard *electrical engineer, astronomer*
Townsend, Miles Averill *aerospace and mechanical engineering educator*
Waxman, Ronald *computer engineer*

### Chesapeake
Bockwoldt, Todd Shane *nuclear engineer*
Donohue, David Patrick *engineering executive, retired navy rear admiral*

### Fairfax
Beale, Guy Otis *engineering educator, consultant*
Boone, James Virgil *retired engineering executive, researcher*
†Burklew, Donald R. *engineering company executive*
Cook, Gerald *electrical engineering educator*
Coulter, David Creswell *research engineer*
Gollobin, Leonard Paul *chemical engineer*
Jamieson, John Anthony *engineering consulting company executive*
Khan, Mohammad Shamim *civil engineer*
Langley, Rolland Ament, Jr. *engineering technology company executive*
Larsen, Phillip Nelson *electrical engineer*
Levis, Alexander Henry *systems engineer educator, consultant*
Lott, Wayne Thomas *systems engineer*
Pedersen, George J. *engineering company executive, computer support company executive*
Schilling, William Richard *aerospace engineer, research and development company executive*
Snyder, Thomas Daniel *retired electronics engineer, consultant*
Ward, Charles Raymond *systems engineer*
Warfield, John Nelson *engineering educator, consultant*
Wolff, Edward A. *electronics engineer*

### Falls Church
Dodd, Steven Louis *systems engineer*
Lorenzo, Michael *engineer, government official, real estate broker*
Villarreal, Carlos Castaneda *engineering executive*

### Fort Belvoir
Barnholdt, Terry Joseph *chemical, industrial, and general engineer*

### Fredericksburg
Anderson, Roberta June *computer engineer*
Medding, Walter Sherman *environmental engineer*

### Great Falls
Litton, Robert Clifton *marine engineer, consultant*

### Hampton
Bartels, Robert Edwin *aerospace engineer*
Duberg, John Edward *retired aeronautical engineer, educator*
Dwoyer, Douglas Leon *engineering executive*
Joshi, Suresh Meghashyam *research engineering executive*
Kelly, Jeffrey Jennings *mechanical engineer*
Looges, Peter John *systems engineer, architect*
Mehrotra, Sudhir C. *engineering company executive*
Noblitt, Nancy Anne *aerospace engineer*

Pandey, Dhirendra Kumar *mechanical engineer, scientist*
Sobieski, Jaroslaw *aerospace engineer*
Whitesides, John Lindsey, Jr. *aerospace engineering educator, researcher*

**Hartfield**
Lovell, Robert R(oland) *engineering executive*

**Herndon**
Larson, Arvid Gunnar *electrical engineer*

**Huddleston**
Kopp, Richard Edgar *electrical engineer*

**King George**
Hoglund, Richard Frank *research and technical executive*

**Lynchburg**
Latimer, Paul Jerry *non-destructive testing engineer*

**Mc Lean**
Beene, Kirk D. *systems engineer*
Bivins, Susan Steinbach *systems engineer*
Carnicero, Jorge Emilio *aeronautical engineer, business executive*
Enger, Walter Melvin *consulting engineer, former navy officer*
Hollister, Cullen Agur *engineer*
Kimmel, H. Steven *engineering and information systems executive*
Klopfenstein, Rex Carter *electrical engineer*
Klotz, John Wesley *electronics consultant*
Loven, Andrew Witherspoon *environmental engineering company executive*
McCambridge, John James *civil engineer*
Mohleji, Satish Chandra *electrical engineer*
Rosenbaum, David Mark *engineering executive, consultant, educator*
Schmeidler, Neal Francis *engineering executive*
Shanklin, Richard Vair, III *mechanical engineer*
Snyder, Franklin Farison *hydrologic engineering consultant*
Sonnemann, Harry *electrical engineer, consultant*
Stasior, William F. *engineering company executive*
Walsh, John Breffni *aerospace consultant*

**Newington**
Chase, Emery John, Jr. *nuclear engineer, researcher*
Foster, Eugene Lewis *engineering executive*

**Newport News**
Corlett, William Albert *retired aerospace engineer*
Donaldson, Coleman duPont *aerodynamics and aerospace consulting engineer*
Hubbard, Harvey Hart *aeroacoustician, noise control engineer, consultant*
Young, Maurice Isaac *mechanical and aerospace engineering educator*

**Norfolk**
Mc Gaughy, John Bell *civil engineer*
Wei, Benjamin Min *engineering educator*
Wiltse, James Clark *civil engineer*

**Oakton**
Curry, Thomas Fortson *electronics engineer, defense industry executive*

**Palmyra**
Leslie, William Cairns *metallurgical engineering educator*
Ramsey, Forrest Gladstone, Jr. *engineering company executive*

**Reston**
Harvey, Aubrey Eaton, III *industrial engineer*
Hutchin, Nancy Lee *reengineering process business consultant*
Kramish, Arnold *technical consultant, historian, author*

**Richmond**
Compton, Olin Randall *consulting electrical engineer, researcher*
Cox, Edwin, III *chemical engineer*
Hanneman, Rodney Elton *metallurgical engineer*
Mattauch, Robert Joseph *electrical engineering educator*
Palik, Robert Richard *mechanical engineer*
Sprinkle, William Melvin *engineering administrator, audio-acoustical engineer*
Wist, Abund Ottokar *biomedical engineer, radiation physicist, educator*

**Roanoke**
Hamrick, Joseph Thomas *mechanical engineer, aerospace company executive*
Jackson, Daniel Wyer *electrical engineer*
McKenna, John Dennis *environmental testing engineer*
Shaffner, Patrick Noel *architectural engineering executive*
Sowers, William Armand *civil engineer*

**Springfield**
Broome, Paul Wallace *engineering research and development executive*
Casazza, John Andrew *electrical engineer, business executive*
Duff, William Grierson *electrical engineer*
Fowler, Ray Harland *engineering consultant*

**Stafford**
Tallent, Robert Glenn *chemical and environmental engineer, entrepreneur*

**Sterling**
McPherson, John Barkley *aerospace consultant, retired military officer*

**Vienna**
Dodson, Louis Raymond *computer systems engineer*
Keiser, Bernhard Edward *engineering company executive, consulting telecommunications engineer*
Meisinger, Henry Peter *electronics engineer*
Salah, Sagid *retired nuclear engineer*
Woodward, Kenneth Emerson *retired mechanical engineer*

**Virginia Beach**
Stephan, Charles Robert *retired ocean engineering educator, consultant*
Yurso, Joseph Francis *engineering manager*

**Warrenton**
Andresen, Mark Nils *electrical engineer*

**Waynesboro**
Aronson, Mark Theodore *chemical engineer*
Lane, Lawrence Jubin *retired electrical engineer, consultant*
McNair, John William, Jr. *civil engineer*

**Williamsburg**
Hughes, George Farant, Jr. *retired safety engineer*
Spitzer, Cary Redford *avionics consultant, electrical engineer*

**Wise**
Gibson, David Allen *civil engineer*

## WASHINGTON

**Auburn**
Westbo, Leonard Archibald, Jr. *electronics engineer, educator*
Whitmore, Donald Clark *retired engineer*

**Bainbridge Island**
Fox, Kenneth *naval engineer, shipbuilder, water transit consultant*

**Bellevue**
Dow, Daniel Gould *electrical engineering educator*
Edde, Howard Jasper *retired engineering executive*
Faris, Charles Oren *civil engineer*
Liang, Jeffrey Der-Shing *retired electrical engineer, civil worker, diplomat*
Parks, Donald Lee *mechanical engineer, human factors engineer*
Schairer, George Swift *aeronautical engineer*
Szablya, John Francis *electrical engineer, consultant*
Wright, Theodore Otis *forensic engineer*

**Bellingham**
Albrecht, Albert Pearson *electronics engineer, consultant*
Jansen, Robert Bruce *consulting civil engineer*

**Bothell**
Sengupta, Mritunjoy *mining engineer, educator*

**Bremerton**
Joseph, James Edward *engineering technician*

**Cathlamet**
Torget, Arne Odmund *retired electrical engineer*

**Dupont**
Pettit, Ghery St. John *electronics engineer*

**Edmonds**
Landau, Henry Groh *geoenvironmental consulting engineer*
Peckol, James Kenneth *consulting engineer*
Schmit, Lucien André, Jr. *structural engineer*
Terrel, Ronald Lee *civil engineer, business executive, educator*

**Federal Way**
Studebaker, Irving Glen *mining engineering consultant*

**Issaquah**
Reid, John Mitchell *biomedical engineer, researcher*

**Kennewick**
Cobb, William Thompson *environmental consultant*
Gates, Thomas Edward *civil engineer, waste management administrator*

**Kent**
Williams, Max Lea, Jr. *engineer, educator*

**Kingston**
Pichal, Henri Thomas *electronics engineer, physicist, consultant*

**Kirkland**
Forsen, Harold Kay *retired engineering executive*
Wenk, Edward, Jr. *civil engineer, policy analyst, educator, writer*

**Lake Forest Park**
Polonis, Douglas Hugh *engineering educator*

**Lummi Island**
Ewing, Benjamin Baugh *environmental engineering educator, consultant*

**Mercer Island**
Bridgforth, Robert Moore, Jr. *aerospace engineer*

**Olympia**
Loftness, Marvin O. *electrical engineer*
Mylroie, Willa Wilcox *transportation engineer, regional planner*
Nichols, James Raymond, Jr. *civil engineer*

**Pullman**
Crowe, Clayton T. *engineering educator*
Funk, William Henry *environmental engineering educator*
Hirth, John Price *metallurgical engineering educator*
Stock, David Earl *mechanical engineering educator*

**Redmond**
Rossano, August Thomas *environmental engineering educator*

**Richland**
Albaugh, Fred William *nuclear engineer, retired research and development executive*
Evans, Ersel Arthur *consulting engineer executive*
Liu, Yosen *nuclear engineer*
Schwinkendorf, Kevin Neil *nuclear engineer*
Trent, Donald Stephen *thermo fluids engineer*

**Seattle**
Babb, Albert Leslie *biomedical engineer, educator*
Blake, Robert Wallace *aeronautical engineer, consultant*
Bowen, Jewell Ray *chemical engineering educator*
Christiansen, Walter Henry *aeronautics educator*
Clark, Robert Newhall *electrical and aeronautical engineering educator*
Culp, Gordon Louis *consulting engineer*
Davis, Earl James *chemical engineering educator*
Finlayson, Bruce Alan *chemical engineering educator*
Gartz, Paul Ebner *systems engineer*
Gilbert, Paul H. *engineering executive, consultant*
Guy, Arthur William *electrical engineering educator, researcher*
Haralick, Robert Martin *electrical engineering educator*
Hertzberg, Abraham *aeronautical engineering educator, university research scientist*
Hoffman, Allan Sachs *chemical engineer, educator*
Ishimaru, Akira *electrical engineering educator*
Joppa, Robert Glenn *aeronautics educator*
Kapur, Kailash Chander *industrial engineering educator*
Kim, Yongmin *electrical engineering educator*
Kippenhan, Charles Jacob *mechanical engineer, retired educator*
Kobayashi, Albert Satoshi *mechanical engineering educator*
Lauritzen, Peter Owen *electrical engineering educator*
Martin, George Coleman *aeronautical engineer*
Mc Feron, Dean Earl *mechanical engineer*
Meditch, James Stephen *electrical engineering educator*
Oman, Henry *retired electrical engineer, engineering executive*
Pollack, Gerald Harvey *bioengineering educator*
Raisbeck, James David *engineering company executive*
Rubbert, Paul Edward *engineering executive*
Simcox, Craig Dennis *aeronautical engineer*
Skilling, John Bower *structural and civil engineer*
Sleicher, Charles Albert *chemical engineer*
Spindel, Robert Charles *electrical engineering educator*
Sutter, Joseph F. *aeronautical engineer, consultant, retired aircraft company executive*
Vesper, Karl Hampton *business and mechanical engineering educator*
Weissman, Eugene Yehuda *chemical engineer*
Wood, Stuart Kee *retired engineering manager*
Woodruff, Gene Lowry *nuclear engineer, university dean*

**South Bend**
Heinz, Roney Allen *civil engineering consultant*

**Spokane**
Maus, John Andrew *computer systems engineer*

**Tacoma**
Holman, Kermit Layton *chemical engineer*

**Wenatchee**
Bennett, Grover Bryce *engineering consultant*

**Woodinville**
Pihl, James Melvin *electrical engineer*

## WEST VIRGINIA

**Berkeley Springs**
Weinberger, Leon Walter *sanitary engineer*

**Charleston**
Koleske, Joseph Victor *chemical engineer, consultant*
Sterling, Donald Eugene *retired civil engineer*
Whittington, Bernard Wiley *electrical engineer, consultant*

**Fairmont**
Brizendine, Anthony Lewis *civil engineering educator*

**Huntington**
deBarbadillo, John Joseph *metallurgist, management executive*

**Morgantown**
Adler, Lawrence *mining engineering consultant*
Cogley, Allen C. *mechanical engineering educator, administrator*
Dadyburjor, Dady B. *chemical engineering educator, researcher*
Eck, Ronald Warren *civil engineer, educator*
Guthrie, Hugh Delmar *chemical engineer*
Kent, James A. *consulting chemical engineer, author, consultant*
Klein, Ronald Lloyd *electrical engineer, educator*
Schroder, John L., Jr. *retired mining engineer*

**Point Pleasant**
Vance, Thomas Ray *engineer*

**South Charleston**
Nielsen, Kenneth Andrew *chemical engineer*

**Washington**
Pace, John Edward, III *chemical engineer*

**Weirton**
Adamczyk, Edmond David *metallurgical engineer*

## WISCONSIN

**Appleton**
Kolbe-Mims, Margie Loretta *safety and health engineer*

**Brookfield**
Curfman, Floyd Edwin *engineering educator, retired*

**Edgerton**
Peck, David Blackman *electrical engineer*

**Frederic**
Rudell, Milton Wesley *aerospace engineer*

**Green Bay**
Heaster, Arlene L. *chemical engineer*

**Madison**
Beachley, Norman Henry *mechanical engineer, educator*
Berthouex, Paul Mac *civil and environmental engineer, educator*
Bird, Robert Byron *chemical engineering educator, author*
Bohnhoff, David Roy *agricultural engineer, educator*
Boyle, William Charles *civil engineering educator*
Bruhn, Hjalmar Diehl *retired agricultural engineer, educator*
Bubenzer, Gary Dean *agricultural engineering educator, researcher*
Caldwell, Barrett Scott *industrial engineering educator*
Carbon, Max William *nuclear engineering educator*
Chang, Y. Austin *materials engineer, educator*
Coberly, Camden Arthur *chemical engineering educator*
Converse, James Clarence *agricultural engineering educator*
Crandall, Lee Walter *civil and structural engineer*
DeVries, Marvin Frank *mechanical engineering educator*
Dietmeyer, Donald Leo *electrical engineer*
Duffie, John Atwater *chemical engineer, educator*
Emmert, Gilbert Arthur *engineer, educator*
Eriksson, Larry John *electrical engineer*
Foell, Wesley Kay *engineer, energy and environmental scientist, educator, consultant*
Gustafson, David Harold *industrial engineering and preventive medicine educator*
Hill, Charles Graham, Jr. *chemical engineering educator*
Kulcinski, Gerald LaVerne *nuclear engineer, educator*
Lasseter, Robert Haygood *electrical engineering educator, consultant*
Lipo, Thomas A. *electrical engineer, educator*
Long, Willis Franklin *electrical engineering educator, researcher*
Loper, Carl Richard, Jr. *metallurgical engineer, educator*
Lovell, Edward George *mechanical engineering educator*
Malkus, David Starr *mechanics educator, applied mathematician*
Novotny, Donald Wayne *electrical engineering educator*
Rowlands, Robert Edward *engineering educator*
Seireg, Ali A(bdel Hay) *mechanical engineer*
Skiles, James Jean *electrical and computer engineering educator*
Smith, Michael James *industrial engineering educator*
Stewart, Warren Earl *chemical engineer, educator*
Thesen, Arne *industrial engineering educator*
Webster, John Goodwin *biomedical engineering educator, researcher*

**Manitowoc**
Sfat, Michael Rudolph *retired biochemical engineer*

**Milwaukee**
Bacon, John Stuart *biochemical engineer*
Bartel, Fred Frank *consulting engineer executive*
Battocletti, Joseph Henry *electrical engineer, biomedical engineer, educator*
Boettcher, Harold Paul *engineer, educator*
Chan, Shih Hung *mechanical engineering educator, consultant*
Demerdash, Nabeel Aly Omar *electrical engineer*
Fournelle, Raymond Albert *engineering educator*
Gaggioli, Richard Arnold *mechanical engineering educator*
Graef, Luther William *civil engineer*
Heinen, James Albin *electrical engineering educator*
James, Charles Franklin, Jr. *engineering educator*
Landis, Fred *mechanical engineering educator*
Renner, Richard Henry *industrial engineer*
Widera, Georg Ernst Otto *materials engineering educator, consultant*
Wilsdon, Thomas Arthur *product development engineer, administrator*
Zelazo, Nathaniel K. *engineering executive*

**Pewaukee**
Dupies, Donald Albert *retired civil engineer*

**Racine**
Stephens, James Linton *mechanical engineer*

**Saint Croix Falls**
Rimmereide, Arne Magnar *engineering executive*

**Spooner**
Frey, Paul Howard *chemical engineer, engineering consultants company executive*

**Sussex**
Dantzman, Gregory Peter *design engineer*

**Waukesha**
Mielke, William John *civil engineer*

**West Bend**
Styve, Orloff Wendell, Jr. *electrical engineer*

**Woodruff**
Polasek, Edward John *electrical engineer, consultant*

## WYOMING

**Casper**
Hinchey, Bruce Alan *environmental engineering company executive*

**Laramie**
Bellamy, John Cary *civil engineer, meteorologist*
Mingle, John Orville *engineer, educator, lawyer, consultant*
Rechard, Paul Albert *civil engineering consulting company executive*
Sutherland, Robert L. *engineering company executive, educator*

**Wilson**
Lawroski, Harry *nuclear engineer*

## TERRITORIES OF THE UNITED STATES

### PUERTO RICO

**Mayaguez**
Deliz-Alvarez, Jose Rinaldo *industrial engineering educator, consultant*
Rodríguez-Arias, Jorge Herminio *retired agricultural engineering educator*
Romaguera, Mariano Antonio *consulting engineer*

## CANADA

### ALBERTA

**Calgary**
Glockner, Peter G. *civil and mechanical engineering educator*
Heidemann, Robert Albert *chemical engineering educator, researcher*
Kentfield, John Alan *mechanical engineering educator*
Malik, Om Parkash *electrical engineering educator, researcher*
McDaniel, Roderick Rogers *petroleum engineer*

**Edmonton**
Koval, Don O. *electrical engineering educator*
Lock, Gerald Seymour Hunter *retired mechanical engineering educator*
McDougall, John Roland *civil engineer*
Offenberger, Allan Anthony *electrical engineering educator*
Otto, Fred Douglas *chemical engineering educator*
Rajotte, Ray V. *biomedical engineer, researcher*

### BRITISH COLUMBIA

**North Vancouver**
Wedepohl, Leonhard Martin *electrical engineering educator*

**Vancouver**
Bennett, Winslow Wood *mechanical engineer*
Crawford, Carl Benson *retired civil engineer, government research administrator*
Grace, John Ross *chemical engineering educator*
Jull, Edward V. *electrical engineer, radio scientist, educator*
Klohn, Earle Jardine *engineering company executive, consultant*
Meisen, Axel *chemical engineering educator, university dean*
Peters, Ernest *metallurgy educator, consultant*
Salcudean, Martha Eva *mechanical engineer, educator*
Young, Lawrence *electrical engineering educator*

**Victoria**
Antoniou, Andreas *electrical engineering educator*
Lind, Niels Christian *civil engineering educator*

### MANITOBA

**Winnipeg**
Cohen, Harley *civil engineer, science educator*
Kuffel, Edmund *electrical engineering educator*
Morrish, Allan Henry *electrical engineering educator*

### NEW BRUNSWICK

**Fredericton**
Faig, Wolfgang *survey engineer, engineering educator*

### NEWFOUNDLAND

**Saint John's**
Clark, Jack I. *civil engineer, researcher*

### NOVA SCOTIA

**Kentville**
Baker, George Chisholm *engineering executive, consultant*

### ONTARIO

**Burlington**
Harris, Philip John *engineering educator*

**Downsview**
Bakht, Baidar *civil engineer, researcher, educator*

**Etobicoke**
Stojanowski, Wiktor J. *mechanical engineer*

**Hamilton**
Bandler, John William *electrical engineering educator, consultant*
Campbell, Colin Kydd *electrical and computer engineering educator, researcher*
Crowe, Cameron Macmillan *chemical engineering educator*

**Islington**
Foster, John Stanton *nuclear engineer*

**Kingston**
Bacon, David Walter *chemical engineering educator*
Batchelor, Barrington de Vere *civil engineer, educator*
Furter, William Frederick *chemical engineer, educator, university dean*
Sen, Paresh Chandra *electrical engineering educator*

**London**
Davenport, Alan Garnett *civil engineer, educator*
Inculet, Ion I. *electrical engineering educator, research director, consultant*
Wilson, Gerald Einar *mechanical and industrial engineer, business executive*

**Mississauga**
Hornby-Anderson, Sara Ann *metallurgical engineer, marketing professional*

**North York**
Buzacott, John Alan *engineering educator*

**Ottawa**
Cockshutt, E(ric) Philip *engineering executive, research scientist*
Georganas, Nicolas D. *electrical engineering educator*
Gussow, William Carruthers *petroleum engineer, geologist*
Moore, William John Myles *electrical engineer, researcher*
Seaden, George *civil engineer*

**Saint Catharines**
Picken, Harry Belfrage *aerospace engineer*

**Toronto**
Balmain, Keith George *electrical engineering educator, researcher*
Davison, Edward Joseph *electrical engineering educator*
Endrenyi, Janos *research engineer*
Ganczarczyk, Jerzy Jozef *civil engineering educator, wastewater treatment consultant*
Goring, David Arthur Ingham *chemical engineering educator, scientist*
Ham, James Milton *engineering educator*
Janischewskyj, Wasyl *electrical engineering educator*
Kunov, Hans *biomedical and electrical engineering educator*
Mackiw, Vladimir Nicholaus *metallurgical consultant*
Meagher, George Vincent *mechanical engineer*
Rimrott, Friedrich Paul Johannes *engineer, educator*
Runnalls, (Oliver) John (Clyve) *nuclear engineering educator*
Salama, C. Andre Tewfik *electrical engineering educator*
Sedra, Adel Shafeek *electrical engineering educator, university administrator*
Semlyen, Adam *electrical engineering educator*
Slemon, Gordon Richard *electrical engineering educator*
Smith, Peter William Ebblewhite *electrical engineering educator, scientist*
Venetsanopoulos, Anastasios Nicolaos *electrical engineer, educator*
Wonham, Walter Murray *electrical engineer, educator*

**Waterloo**
Penlidis, Alexander *chemical engineering educator*
Pindera, Jerzy Tadeusz *mechanical and aeronautical engineer*
Rempel, Garry Llewellyn *chemical engineering educator, consultant*
Sherbourne, Archibald Norbert *civil engineering educator*
Vlach, Jiri *electrical engineering educator, researcher*

**Windsor**
Hackam, Reuben *electrical engineering educator*

### QUEBEC

**Boucherville**
Martel, Jacques G. *engineer, adminstrator*

**Montreal**
Alepian, Taro *engineering and construction executive*
Cameron, Alastair Duncan *engineering consultant*
Carreau, Pierre *chemical engineering educator*
Corinthios, Michael Jean George *electrical engineering educator*
Dealy, John Michael *chemical engineer, educator*
Haccoun, David *electrical engineering educator*
Jonas, John Joseph *metallurgical engineering educator*
Kearney, Robert Edward *biomedical engineering educator*
Ladanyi, Branko *civil engineer*
Lamarre, Bernard *engineering, contracting and manufacturing advisor*
Paidoussis, Michael Pandeli *mechanical engineering educator*
Ramachandran, Venkatanarayana Deekshit *electrical engineering educator*
Saint-Pierre, Guy *engineering executive*
Selvadurai, Antony Patrick Sinnappa *civil engineering educator, applied mathematician, consultant*
Shaw, Robert Fletcher *retired civil engineer*
Stangel, Ivan *biomaterials scientist, educator*
Tavenas, François *civil engineer, educator*
Yong, Raymond Nen-Yiu *civil engineering educator*
Zames, George David *electrical engineer, educator*

**Quebec**
Lecours, Michel *electrical engineering educator*

**Saint Lambert**
Terreault, R. Charles *engineer, management educator, researcher*

**Sainte Anne de Bellevue**
Broughton, Robert Stephen *irrigation and drainage engineering educator, consultant*

**Sillery**
La Rochelle, Pierre-Louis *civil engineering educator*

**Trois Rivieres**
Lavallee, H.-Claude *chemical engineering educator, researcher*

**Varennes**
Bartnikas, Raymond *electrical engineer, educator*
Maruvada, Pereswara Sarma *engineering executive, researcher*

### SASKATCHEWAN

**Regina**
Mollard, John Douglas *engineering and geology executive*

**Saskatoon**
Billinton, Roy *engineering educator*
Gupta, Madan Mohan *engineering educator, researcher*
Kumar, Surinder *electrical engineering educator, consultant*
Sachdev, Mohindar Singh *engineering educator*

## BRAZIL

**Santa Maria**
Radharamanan, Ramachandran *mechanical and industrial engineering educator*

## CHINA

**Beijing**
Shu, Wenlong *environmental engineer, educator*

**Chengdu**
Zeng, Xuegang *telecommunications enginer, engineering educator*

**Nanjing**
Wang, Xinwei *aeronautics educator*

**Shanghai**
Li, Guosong *mechanical engineering educator*

## DENMARK

**Vedbaek**
Rasmussen, Gunnar *engineer*

## ENGLAND

**London**
Baxendell, Sir Peter (Brian) *petroleum engineer*

## FRANCE

**Paris**
Goupy, Jacques Louis *chemiometrics engineer*

## GERMANY

**Bonn**
Wohlleben, Rudolf *microwave and antenna researcher*

**Dortmund**
Freund, Eckhard *electrical engineering educator*

**Erlangen**
Lips, H. Peter *systems engineer director*

**Stuttgart**
Nagel, Joachim Hans *biomedical engineer, educator*

## GREECE

**Athens**
Arnis, Efstathios Constatine *space naval designer*
Halkias, Christos Constantine *electronics educator*
Hatzakis, Michael *retired electrical engineer, research executive*
Ligomenides, Panos Aristides *electrical and computer engineering educator, consultant*

**Patras**
Makios, Vasilios *electronics educator*

## HONG KONG

**Clear Water Bay**
Tang, Wilson Hon-chung *engineering educator*

**Hong Kong**
Wang, Jun *engineering educator*

**Kowloon**
Liou, Ming-Lei *electrical engineer*

**Sha Tin**
Kao, Charles Kuen *electrical engineer, educator*

## INDONESIA

**Palembang**
Saputra, Daniel *agricultural engineering educator*

## JAPAN

**Ebetsu**
Saito, Shuzo *electrical engineering educator*

**Funabashi**
Sakuta, Masaaki *engineering educator, consultant*

**Kanagawa**
Shimazaki, Yoji *civil engineering educator*

**Kita-Kyushu**
Mine, Katsutoshi *instrumentation educator*

**Kobe**
Masai, Mitsuo *chemical engineer, educator*

**Kurume**
Koga, Tosiro *electrical engineering educator*

**Kyoto**
Ohnami, Masateru *mechanical engineering educator*

**Nagoya**
Abe, Yoshihiro *ceramic engineering educator, materials scientist*
Sendo, Takeshi *mechanical engineering educator, researcher, author*
Tasaka, Shuji *engineering educator*

**Oita**
Ishibashi, Eiichi *engineering researcher and educator*

**Osaka**
Ishii, Junya *engineering educator*

**Sagamihara**
Taniuchi, Kiyoshi *retired mechanical engineering educator*

**Shimizu**
Anma, So *engineering consultant*

**Tokyo**
Aoyama, Hiroyuki *structural engineering educator*
Hori, Yukio *engineering educator, scientific association administrator*
Ohe, Shuzo *chemical engineer, educator*
Yasufuku, Sachio *electrical engineer, educator*

## THE NETHERLANDS

**Roosendaal**
van Deventer, Arie Pieter *agricultural engineer*

## THE PHILIPPINES

**Manila**
Stepanich, Fred Charles *civil and water resources engineer*

## PORTUGAL

**Vila Nova de Gaia**
Moura-Relvas, Joaquim M.M.A. *electrical engineer, educator*

## REPUBLIC OF KOREA

**Pusan**
Ha, Chang Sik *polymer science educator*

**Taejon**
Kim, Sung Chul *polymer engineering educator*

## SAUDI ARABIA

**Jeddah**
Hussain, Kazi Fareeduddin *engineering executive*

**Riyadh**
Uygur, Mustafa Eti *materials and mechanical engineering educator*

## SWITZERLAND

**Burgdorf**
Haeberlin, Heinrich Rudolf *electrical engineering educator*

**Zurich**
Bailey, James Edwin *chemical engineer*

## TAIWAN

**Chung Li**
Hong, Zuu-Chang *engineering educator*

**Tainan**
Huang, Ting-Chia *chemical engineering educator, researcher*
Shih, Tso Min *mining engineering educator*

**Taipei**
Young, Der-Liang Frank *civil engineering educator, researcher*

## VENEZUELA

**Caracas**
Chang-Mota, Roberto *electrical engineer*

## WALES

**Gwynedd**
Owen, Walter Shepherd *materials science and engineering educator*

## ADDRESS UNPUBLISHED

Allison, John McComb *retired aeronautical engineer*
Al-Qadi, Imad Lutfi *civil engineering educator, researcher*
Altan, Taylan *engineering educator, mechanical engineer, consultant*
Amann, Charles Albert *mechanical engineer*

Anderson, John Gaston *electrical engineer*
Anderson, Thomas Patrick *mechanical engineer, educator*
Au, Tung *civil engineer, educator, consultant*
Baltazzi, Evan Serge *engineering research consulting company executive*
Bar-Cohen, Avram *mechanical engineering educator*
Bartholomew, Donald Dekle *engineering executive, inventor*
Bascom, Willard Newell *engineer, scientist, underwater archaeologist*
Bauer, Richard Carlton *nuclear engineer*
Becerra-Fernandez, Irma *electrical engineer, researcher, educator*
Beck, John Roland *environmental consultant*
Beckjord, Eric Stephen *nuclear engineering educator, energy researcher*
Bellow, Donald Grant *mechanical engineering educator*
Bergfield, Gene Raymond *engineering educator*
Berkholtz, Nicholas Evald *engineering manager, consultant*
Bers, Abraham *electrical engineering and physics educator*
Bertin, John Joseph *aeronautical engineer, educator, researcher*
Bertolett, Craig Randolph *mechanical engineer consultant*
Biljetina, Richard *chemical engineering researcher*
Bissell, Allen Morris *engineer, consultant*
Bjorndahl, David Lee *electrical engineer*
Blanchard, David Lawrence *aerospace executive, real estate developer*
Bloch, Erich *retired electrical engineer, former science foundation administrator*
Bornhorst, Kenneth Frank *electrical and systems engineer*
Bose, Anjan *electrical engineering educator, academic administrator*
Bowen, Douglas Glenn *electrical engineer, consultant*
Boyle, Bryan Douglas *computer and network systems architect*
Brickell, Charles Hennessey, Jr. *marine engineer, retired military officer*
Bridger, Baldwin, Jr. *electrical engineer*
Brimacombe, James Keith *metallurgical engineering educator, researcher, consultant*
Brooks, Mark Hunter *systems engineering manager, consultant*
Bunch, Jennings Bryan, Jr. *electrical engineer*
Burke, Mona *sales engineer*
Burns, Richard Francis *mechanical engineer*
Bussgang, Julian Jakob *electronics engineer*
Byrd, Lloyd Garland *civil engineer*
Carreker, John Russell *retired agricultural engineer*
Carrier, W(illiam) David, III *geotechnical engineer*
Carter, Hugh Clendenin *mechanical consulting engineer*
Cerny, Louis Thomas *civil engineer, association executive*
Chance, Kenneth Donald *engineer*
Chandra, Abhijit *engineering educator*
Chapanis, Alphonse *human factors engineer, ergonomist*
Chastain, Denise Jean *process improvement engineer*
Chawla, Krishan Kumar *materials engineer, educator, consultant*
Cheston, Theodore C. *electrical engineer*
Chryssis, George Christopher *engineering executive*
Clarke, W. Hall *engineer*
Conway, Richard Ashley *environmental engineer*
Cook, Charles Emerson *electrical engineer*
Cooper, Austin Morris *chemist, chemical engineer, consultant, researcher*
Cooper, David Wayne *aerospace engineer*
Crossley, Francis Rendel Erskine *engineering educator*
Crowley, Joseph Michael *electrical engineer, educator*
Curtis, James Richard *flight engineer*
Dally, James William *mechanical engineering educator, consultant*
Diamond, Fred I. *electronic engineer*
Di Cicco, Joseph Nicholas, Jr. *chemical engineer*
Dix, Samuel Morman *industrial engineer, physical economist, apprasier*
Donahoo, Melvin Lawrence *aerospace management consultant, industrial engineer*
Donohue, Marc David *chemical engineering educator*
Dransite, Brian Robert *electrical engineer*
Drew, Richard Allen *electrical and instrument engineer*
Dull, William Martin *engineering executive*
Dyer, Ira *ocean engineering educator, consultant*
Eaglet, Robert Danton *electrical engineer, aerospace consultant, retired military officer*
East, Don Gaylord *computer engineer, archaeologist, writer*
Eberstein, Arthur *former biomedical engineering educator, researcher*
Edgar, Thomas Flynn *chemical engineering educator*
Edmundson, Charles Wayne *mechanical engineer, communications executive*
Eissmann, Robert Fred *manufacturing engineer*
Ellis, Harold Bernard *civil engineer*
Ellis, Michael David *aerospace engineer*
Eschenbrenner, Gunther Paul *engineering consultant*
Ettinger, Harry Joseph *industrial hygiene engineer, project manager*
Farnsworth, Michael Edward *mechanical engineer*
Faruqui, G. Ahmad *engineering consultant*
Felix, Richard James *engineering executive, consultant*
Fetrow, George Lawrence *retired plans engineer*
Fiala, Dennison Fairchild *technical consultant*
Field, Charles William *metallurgical engineer, small business owner, consultant*
Finger, Harold B. *energy, space, nuclear energy and urban affairs consultant*
Fishman, Bernard *mechanical engineer*
Fleischer, Gerald Albert *industrial engineer, educator*
Flick, Carl *electrical engineer, consultant*
Gangriwala, Huned Ahmedi *engineering executive*
Gens, Ralph Samuel *electrical engineering consultant*
Gerhardt, Heinz Adolf August *aircraft design engineer*
Gerhardt, Jon Stuart *mechanical engineer, engineering educator*
Germany, Daniel Monroe *aerospace engineer*
Giardina, Paul Anthony *environmental nuclear engineer, thoroughbred horse investment specialist*
Godo, Einar *computer engineer*
Goetzel, Claus Guenter *metallurgical engineer*
Goldberger, Arthur Earl, Jr. *industrial engineer, executive*
Gordon, Michael D. *electronics engineer and nurse, air force officer*
Gouse, S. William, Jr. *engineering executive, scientist*
Grandi, Attilio *engineering consultant*
Gray, Harry Joshua *electrical engineer, educator*
Gregersen, Max A. *structural, earthquake and civil engineer*
Groenier, James Scott *civil engineer*
Hallett, William Jared *nuclear engineer*
Halpin, Daniel William *civil engineering educator, consultant*
Halushynsky, George Dobroslav *systems engineer*
Hammam, M. Shawky *electrical engineer, educator*
Harris, Roy Hartley *electrical engineer*
Henderson, Charles Brooke *research company executive*
Herman, William Arthur *physics and engineering laboratory administrator*
Herriott, David Neil *aerospace engineer*
Herz, George Peter *chemical engineer, industrial consultant*
Hess, Ulrich Edward *electrical engineer*
Hetfeld, Elizabeth Ann *industrial engineer*
Higby, Edward Julian *safety engineer*
Hinderliter, Richard Glenn *electrical engineer*
Ho, Louis Ting *retired mechanical engineer*
Hoag, Kevin Lane *engineering education administrator*
Hoeppner, David William *mechanical engineering educator*
Hoffer, Roy Daniel *electrical engineer*
Hogan, Neville John *mechanical engineering educator, consultant*
Howard, Dean Denton *electrical engineer, researcher, consultant*
Hunt, Donald Edward *planning and engineering executive*
Hunt, Donnell Ray *retired agricultural engineering educator*
Hutchinson, John Woodside *applied mechanics educator, consultant*
Jensen, Marvin Eli *retired agricultural engineer*
Johnson, Arnold Ivan *civil engineer*
Johnson, Joe William *engineering educator, consultant*
Johnson, Mary Elizabeth Susan *consulting engineer*
Johnson, Robert Walter *marine engineer, priest*
Johnson, Stewart Willard *civil engineer*
Johnston, Ralph Kennedy, Sr. *aerospace engineer*
Jordan, Howard Emerson *retired engineering executive, consultant*
Kahn, Irwin William *industrial engineer*
Karp, Sherman *aerospace consultant*
Keigler, John E. *aerospace engineer*
Kemper, John Dustin *mechanical engineering educator*
Kennedy, Keith Clyde *mechanical engineer, entrepreneur, administrator*
Kennedy, Leo Raymond *engineering executive*
Ketchum, Milo Smith *civil engineer*
Kinsman, Frank Ellwood *engineering executive*
Kisak, Paul Francis *engineering company executive*
Kleckner, Willard Richards *electrical engineer, consultant, educator*
Klein, Martin *ocean engineering consultant*
Klink, Robert Michael *consulting engineer, management consultant, financial consultant, property developer*
Kodali, Hari Prasad *electrical engineer*
Koltai, Stephen Miklos *mechanical engineer, consultant, economist, writer, educator*
Korab, Arnold Alva *engineering executive*
Kretschmer, Frank Frederick, Jr. *electrical engineer, researcher, consultant*
Kryder, Mark Howard *computer and electrical engineering educator, consultant*
Kuesel, Thomas Robert *civil engineer*
Kurfess, Thomas Roland *mechanical engineering educator*
Lancaster, John Howard *civil engineer*
Landgren, George Lawrence *electrical engineer, consultant*
Lee, Jen-shih *biomedical engineering educator*
Lee, Thomas Henry *electrical engineer, educator*
Le Mehaute, Bernard Jean *marine physics educator*
Letcher, Naomi Jewell *quality engineer, educator, counselor*
Levinson, Herbert Sherman *civil and transportation engineer*
Levinson, Stephen Eliot *electrical engineer*
Levy, Robert Edward *engineering consultant*
Libertiny, Thomas Gabor *mechanical engineer, administrator*
Lindsley, John Martin *chemical engineer*
Lipsky, Stephen Edward *engineering executive, electronic warfare engineer*
Liu, Young King *biomedical engineering educator*
Lodge, Arthur Scott *mechanical engineering educator*
Longobardo, Anna Kazanjian *engineering executive*
Lovell, Walter Carl *engineer, inventor*
Lowe, John, III *consulting civil engineer*
Loy, Richard Franklin *civil engineer*
Luger, Donald R. *engineering company executive*
Magnabosco, Louis Mario *chemical engineer, researcher, consultant*
Mahle, Christoph Erhard *electrical engineer*
Mai, Chao Chen *engineer*
†Mak, Ben Bohdan *engineer*
Maksymowicz, John *electrical engineer*
Marshall, Gerald Francis *optical engineer, consultant, physicist*
Marshall, Julie W. Gregovich *engineering executive*
Martin, Lee *mechanical engineer*
Masnari, Nino Antonio *electrical engineer, educator*
Mason, John Latimer *engineering executive*
McDermott, Kevin J. *engineering educator, consultant*
McGonigle, John Leo, Jr. *civil engineer*
†Merriam, Robert W. *engineering executive, educator*
Merritt, Joshua Levering, Jr. *retired engineering executive, consultant*
Meyer, L. Donald *retired agricultural engineer, researcher, educator*
Miah, Abdul Malek *electrical engineer, educator*
Mike, Deborah Denise *systems engineering consultant*
Mitzner, Kenneth Martin *electrical engineering consultant*
Mortimer, David William *communications engineer*
Mulvihill, Peter James *fire protection engineer*
Myers, Phillip Samuel *mechanical engineering educator*
Nahman, Norris Stanley *electrical engineer*
Neshyba, Victor Peter *retired aerophysics engineer*
Norris, James Arnold *engineering company executive*
Obaidat, Mohammad Salameh *electrical and computer engineering educator*
Olstowski, Franciszek *chemical engineer, consultant*
Ortiz-Quiñones, Carlos Ruben *electronics engineer, educator*
Ortolano, Ralph J. *engineering consultant*
Pai, Shih I. *aeronautical engineer*
Palladino, Nunzio Joseph *retired nuclear engineer*
Parker, William Elbridge *consulting civil engineer*
Peck, Joan Kay *systems engineer*
Peltier, Eugene Joseph *civil engineer, former naval officer, business executive*
Perrenod, Douglas Arthur *astronautical engineer*
Pezeshki, Kambiz A. *metallurgical engineer*
Pickering, Howard William *metallurgy engineer, educator*
Pierce, Robert Raymond *materials engineer, consultant*
Pniakowski, Andrew Frank *structural engineer*
Pomraning, Gerald Carlton *engineering educator*
Porter, Philip Thomas *retired electrical engineer*
Potvin, Alfred Raoul *engineering executive*
Pratt, David Terry *mechanical engineering educator, combustion researcher*
Rappaport, Theodore Scott *electrical engineering educator*
Reaves, Ray Donald *civil engineer*
Rees, Morgan Rowlands *engineer, educator*
Rehm, Leo Frank *civil engineer*
Reifsnider, Kenneth Leonard *metallurgist, educator*
Reitan, Daniel Kinseth *electrical and computer engineering educator*
Remer, Donald Sherwood *engineering economist, cost estimator, educator*
Reppen, Norbjorn Dag *electrical engineer, consultant*
Roetman, Orvil M. *aerospace company executive*
Rogo, Kathleen *safety engineer*
Rohr, Davis Charles *aerospace consultant, business executive, retired air force officer*
Rosenkoetter, Gerald Edwin *engineering and construction company executive*
Rudzki, Eugeniusz Maciej *chemical engineer, consultant*
Russo, Roy Lawrence *electronic design automation engineer, retired*
Ryan, Carl Ray *electrical engineer*
Saeks, Richard Ephraim *engineering executive*
Salvatorelli, Joseph J. *civil engineer, consultant*
Sandry, Karla Kay Foreman *industrial engineering educator*
Schachter, Max *retired engineering services company executive*
Schell, Allan Carter *retired electrical engineer*
Scherer, A. Edward *nuclear engineering executive*
Schey, John Anthony *metallurgical engineering educator*
Schoeffmann, Rudolf *consulting engineer*
Schoeppel, John Frederick *mechanical and electrical engineer, consultant*
Schrader, Henry Carl *civil engineer, consultant*
Schwartz, Michael Alan *engineering executive*
Scott, Charles David *chemical engineer*
Seamans, Robert Channing, Jr. *astronautical engineering educator*
Sears, Robert Louis *industrial engineer*
Seldner, Betty Jane *environmental engineer, consultant, aerospace company executive*
Shank, Maurice Edwin *aerospace engineering executive, consultant*
Sheh, Robert Bardhyl *environmental management company executive*
Shur, Michael *electrical engineer, educator, consultant*
Shuster, John A. *civil engineer*
Siljak, Dragoslav D. *engineering educator*
Simpson, Murray *engineer, consultant*
Skromme, Lawrence H. *consulting agricultural engineer*
Smally, Donald Jay *consulting engineering executive*
Somasundaran, Ponisseril *surface and colloid engineer, applied science educator*
Sreenivasan, Katepalli Raju *mechanical engineering educator*
Sten, Johannes Walter *control systems engineer, consultant*
Stroud, John Franklin *engineering educator, scientist*
Stumpe, Warren Robert *scientific, engineering and technical services company executive*
Swalm, Thomas Sterling *aerospace executive, retired military officer*
Swift, Jill Anne *industrial engineer, educator*
Tachmindji, Alexander John *systems engineering consultant*
Tamaro, George John *consulting engineer*
Templeton, Carson Howard *engineering executive, policy analyst*
Thal, Herbert Ludwig, Jr. *electrical engineer, engineering consultant*
Ting, Albert Chia *bioengineering researcher*
Toor, Herbert Lawrence *chemical engineering educator, researcher*
Turner, Lee S., Jr. *civil engineer, consultant, former utilities executive*
Uman, Martin Allan *electrical engineering educator, researcher, consultant*
Urban, Joseph Jaroslav *engineer, consultant*
Van Dreser, Merton Lawrence *ceramic engineer*
Varon, Dan *electrical engineer*
Vega, J. William *aerospace engineering executive, consultant*
Velzy, Charles O. *mechanical engineer*
Wagner, Sigurd *electrical engineering educator, researcher*
Walker, John Neal *agricultural engineering educator*
Walker, Loren Haines *electrical engineer*
Walton, Harold Vincent *former agricultural engineering educator, academic administrator*
Weigle, Robert Edward *civil engineer, research director*
Weinberger, Arnold *retired electrical engineer*
Weingarten, Joseph Leonard *aerospace engineer*
Weinschel, Bruno Oscar *engineering executive, physicist*
Weinsier, Philip David *electronics educator*
Weldon, William Forrest *electrical and mechanical engineer, educator*
Wetzel, Donald Truman *engineering company executive*
Wheeler, George Charles *materials and processes engineer*
White, Charles Olds *aeronautical engineer*
Williams, Charles Wesley *technical executive, researcher*
Williams, Ronald Oscar *systems engineer*
Willis, Selene Lowe *electrical engineer, software consultant*
Wilson, Melvin Edmond *civil engineer*
Wintle, Rosemarie *bio-medical electronic engineer*
Wood, Allen John *electrical engineer, consultant*
Woodward, Clinton Benjamin, Jr. *civil engineering educator*
Young, Leo *electrical engineer*
Yovicich, George Steven Jones *civil engineer*
Yue, Alfred Shui-choh *metallurgical engineer, educator*
Yun, James Kyoon *electrical engineer*

## FINANCE: BANKING SERVICES. *See also* FINANCE: INVESTMENT SERVICES.

### UNITED STATES

#### ALABAMA

**Birmingham**
Horsley, Richard David *banker*
Jones, D. Paul, Jr. *banker, lawyer*
Morgan, Hugh Jackson, Jr. *bank executive*
Northen, Charles Swift, III *banker*
Powell, William Arnold, Jr. *retired banker*
Rainer, James W., Jr. *bank executive*
Sellers, Fred Wilson *banker*
Stone, Edmund Crispen, III *banker*
Weatherly, Robert Stone, Jr. *banker*

**Huntsville**
Boykin, Betty Ruth Carroll *mortgage loan officer, bank executive*

**Mobile**
Coker, Donald William *economic banker, valuation & healthcare consultant*
Crow, James Sylvester *retired banker, railway executive*

**Montgomery**
Hoffman, Richard William *banker*

#### ALASKA

**Anchorage**
Cuddy, Daniel Hon *bank executive*
Harris, Roger J. *mortgage company executive, entrepreneur*
Rasmuson, Elmer Edwin *banker, former mayor*
Reed, Frank Metcalf *bank executive*

#### ARIZONA

**Carefree**
Craft, Robert Homan *banker, corporate executive*

**Green Valley**
Miner, Earl Howard *retired trust banker*

**Phoenix**
Bradley, Gilbert Francis *retired banker*
Housewort h, Richard Court *banker*
Wallace, Kenneth Alan *investor*

**Scottsdale**
Carpenter, Peter Rockefeller *bank executive*
Gray, Walter Franklin *retired banker*
Howe, H(ugh) Philip *banker*

**Tubac**
Miller, Frederick Robeson *banker*

#### ARKANSAS

**Barling**
Francis, Darryl Robert *former banker*

**Conway**
Daugherty, Billy Joe *banker*

**Little Rock**
Bohlken, Deborah Kay *information services/banking consultant, lobbyist*
Bowen, William Harvey *banker, lawyer*
Butler, Richard Colburn *banker, lawyer*
Gulley, Wilbur Paul, Jr. *former savings and loan executive*
McAdams, Herbert Hall, II *banker*

#### CALIFORNIA

**Aptos**
Dobey, James Kenneth *banker*

**Arcadia**
Baillie, Charles Douglas *banker*

**Baldwin Park**
Swartz, Stephen Arthur *banker, lawyer*

**Beverly Hills**
Goldsmith, Bram *banker*

**Burbank**
DeMieri, Joseph L. *bank executive*
Miller, Clifford Albert *merchant banker, business consultant*

**Calistoga**
Dillon, James McNulty *retired banker*

**Carpinteria**
Montgomery, Parker Gilbert *investment banker*

**Chatsworth**
Montgomery, James Fischer *savings and loan association executive*

**Corona Del Mar**
Ripper, Rita Jo (Jody Ripper) *strategic planner, researcher*

**Escondido**
Newman, Barry Ingalls *retired banker, lawyer*

**Fairfax**
Delaney, Marion Patricia *bank executive*

**Fresno**
Smith, Richard Howard *banker*

**Glendale**
Cross, Richard John *banker*
Trafton, Stephen J. *bank executive*

**Hillsborough**
Souter, Robert Taylor *retired banker*

**Huntington Beach**
MacCauley, Hugh Bournonville *banker*

**Irvine**
Jamshidipour, Yousef *bank executive, economist, financial planner*

**Irwindale**
Rinehart, Charles R. *savings and loan association executive*

**La Jolla**
Angotti, Antonio Mario *international merchant, banker*

**La Mesa**
Schmidt, James Craig *retired bank executive, bankruptcy examiner*

**Lafayette**
Dethero, J. Hambright *banker*

**Long Beach**
Hancock, John Walker, III *banker*
Keller, J(ames) Wesley *credit union executive*

**Los Angeles**
Badie, Ronald Peter *banker*
Buchman, Mark Edward *banker*
Lenard, Michael Barry *merchant banker, lawyer*
McLarnan, Donald Edward *banker, corporation executive*
Riordan, George Nickerson *investment banker*
Van Asperen, Morris Earl *banker*
Wu, Li-Pei *banker*

**Menlo Park**
Schmidt, Chauncey Everett *banker*

**Mill Valley**
Flynn, Thomas Charles *banker*

**Monterey**
Spitler, Lee William *banker*

**Monterey Park**
Crawford, Philip Stanley *bank executive*

**Napa**
Hill, Orion Alvah, Jr. *retired banker*

**Newport Beach**
Frederick, Dolliver H. *merchant banker*

**Oakland**
Sandler, Herbert M. *savings and loan association executive*
Sandler, Marion Osher *savings and loan association executive*

**Orange**
Floyd, Brett Alden *mortgage banker*
Starr, Richard William *retired banker*

**Pasadena**
Patton, Richard Weston *retired mortgage company executive*
Ulrich, Peter Henry *banker*
Vaughn, John Vernon *banker, industrialist*

**Pebble Beach**
Burkett, William Andrew *banker*

**Piedmont**
Hoover, Robert Cleary *retired bank executive*

**Playa Del Rey**
Blomquist, Carl Arthur *medical and trust company executive, insurance executive*

**Rancho Cordova**
Ling, Robert Malcolm *banker, publishing executive*

**Rancho Cucamonga**
Horton, Michael L. *mortgage company executive, publishing executive*

**Redwood City**
Jurdana, Ernest J. *banker, accountant*

**San Diego**
Blakemore, Claude Coulehan *banker*
Kendrick, Ronald H. *banker*
Lindh, Patricia Sullivan *banker, former government official*
Reinhard, Christopher John *merchant banking, venture capital executive*
Wiesler, James Ballard *retired banker*

**San Dimas**
Sawyer, Nelson Baldwin, Jr. *credit union executive*

**San Francisco**
August-deWilde, Katherine *banker*
Baumhefner, Clarence Herman *banker*
Bee, Robert Norman *banker*
Braasch, Barbara Lynn *banker*
Demarest, David Franklin, Jr. *banker, former government official*
Eckersley, Norman Chadwick *banker*
Gillette, Frankie Jacobs *retired savings and loan executive, social worker, government administrator*
Hazen, Paul Mandeville *banker*
Luikart, John Ford *investment banker*
Meyer, Donald Robert *banker, lawyer*
Peterson, Rudolph A. *banker*
Rosenberg, Richard Morris *banker*
Saavedra, Charles James *banker*
Trowbridge, Thomas, Jr. *mortgage banking company executive*
Tyran, Garry Keith *banker*
Vogt, Evon Zartman, III (Terry Vogt) *merchant banker*
Warner, Harold Clay, Jr. *banker, investment management executive*
Williams, Morgan Lloyd *retired investment banker*
Yao, Hilda Maria Hsiang *banker, strategic planner*

**San Jose**
Myer, Warren Hitesh *mortgage broker, internet advertising executive*

**Santa Barbara**
Anderson, Donald Meredith *bank executive*
Tilton, David Lloyd *savings and loan association executive*

**Santa Monica**
Morgan, Monroe *retired savings and loan executive*
Mortensen, William S. *banking executive*
Weil, Leonard *banker*

**Walnut Creek**
McGrath, Don John *banker*
Rhody, Ronald Edward *banker, communications executive*

## COLORADO

**Boulder**
Martin, Phillip Dwight *bank consulting company executive, mayor*

**Colorado Springs**
Olin, Kent Oliver *banker*

**Denver**
Childears, Linda *banker*
Davidson, John Robert (Jay) *banking executive*
Grant, William West, III *banker*
Krane, Robert Alan *banker*
Levinson, Shauna T. *financial services executive*
Malone, Robert Joseph *bank executive*
Nicholson, Will Faust, Jr. *bank holding company executive*
Rockwell, Bruce McKee *retired banker, retired foundation executive*

**Englewood**
Rosser, Edwin Michael *mortgage company executive*
Sims, Douglas D. *bank executive*

**Fort Collins**
Koessel, Donald Ray *retired banker*

**Greeley**
Smith, Jack Lee *bank executive*

**Lakewood**
Orullian, B. LaRae *bank executive*

## CONNECTICUT

**Bridgeport**
Freeman, Richard Francis *banker*

**Brookfield**
Petrusky, John W. *banker, consultant*

**Darien**
Mapel, William Marlen Raines *retired banking executive*

**Essex**
Miller, Elliott Cairns *retired bank executive, lawyer*

**Fairfield**
Brett, Arthur Cushman, Jr. *banker*
DeCarlo, Deena M. *mortgage company executive*
Jewitt, David Willard Pennock *retired banker*

**Greenwich**
Birle, James Robb *investment banker*
Caruso, Victor Guy *investment banker*
Egbert, Richard Cook *retired banker*
Prouty, Norman R. *investment banker*
Shanks, Eugene Baylis, Jr. *banker*
Spaeh, Winfried Heinrich *retired banker*

**Hamden**
Williams, Edward Gilman *retired banker*

**Hartford**
Kraus, Eileen S. *bank executive*
Krauss, Eileen S. *bank executive*
Newell, Robert Lincoln *retired banker*

**Middletown**
Stevens, Robert Edwin *bank executive, former insurance company executive*

**Monroe**
Verano, Anthony Frank *retired banker*

**New Canaan**
MacEwan, Nigel Savage *merchant banker*

**Norfolk**
Vagliano, Alexander Marino *banker*

**Stamford**
Baylis, Robert Montague *investment banker*
Philipps, Edward William *banker, real estate appraiser*

**Weston**
Lindsay, Charles Joseph *banker*

## DELAWARE

**New Castle**
Freytag, Richard Arthur *banker*

**Wilmington**
Porter, John Francis, III *banker*
St. Clair, Jesse Walton, Jr. *retired savings and loan executive*
Wright, Vernon Hugh Carroll *bank executive*

## DISTRICT OF COLUMBIA

**Washington**
Aguirre-Sacasa, Francisco Xavier *international banker*
Applegarth, Paul Vollmer *investment and finance executive*
Baxter, Nevins Dennis *bank consultant*
Bibby, Douglas Martin *mortgage association executive*
†Birdsall, Nancy *banking administrator*
Coreth, Joseph Herman *bank executive*
Coughlin, Timothy Crathorne *bank executive*
Dame, William Page, III *bank executive, educational administrator*
D'Aniello, Daniel *merchant banker*
DuCran, Claudette Deloris *bank officer*
Fitts, C. Austin *investment banker, former federal agency administrator*
Fitz-Hugh, Glassell Slaughter, Jr. *bank executive*
Frank, Richard *bank executive*
Greenspan, Alan *banker*
Higgins, Mark C. *development banker*
Kesterman, Frank Raymond *investment banker*
Kimmitt, Robert Michael *banker, lawyer, diplomat*
Lasko, Warren Anthony *mortgage banker, economist*
Marsh, Quinton Neely *banker*
Mathias, Edward Joseph *merchant banker*
Mc Namara, Robert Strange *former banking executive, cabinet member*
Miller, G(eorge) William *merchant banker, business executive*
Murphy, Shaun Edward *bank executive*
Newton, Leilani L. *bank executive*
Palmer, R(obie Marcus Hooker) Mark *banker*
Raines, Franklin Delano *investment banker*
Robinson, Daniel Baruch *banker*
Rodriguez, Rita Maria *banker*
Roley, Jerry L. *bank executive*
Rotberg, Eugene Harvey *investment banker, lawyer*
Shihata, Ibrahim Fahmy Ibrahim *development banker, lawyer*
Stevenson, Eric Van Cortlandt *mortgage banker, real estate executive, lawyer*
Tanous, Peter Joseph *banker*

## FLORIDA

**Boca Raton**
Barnes, Donald Winfree *financial services executive*
Cannon, Herbert Seth *investment banker*

**Bonita Springs**
Birky, John Edward *banker, consultant, financial advisor*

**Boynton Beach**
Jacobs, C. Bernard *banker*

**Dunedin**
Rosa, Raymond Ulric *retired banker*

**Fort Lauderdale**
Levi, Kurt *retired banker*

**Holmes Beach**
Browning, Henry Prentice *banker*

**Jacksonville**
Graham, Cynthia Armstrong *banker*
Lane, Edward Wood, Jr. *retired banker*
Mitchell, John Adam, III *banker*
Rice, Charles Edward *bank executive*
Rishel, Richard Clinton *banker*

**Jupiter**
Cotter, Joseph Francis *retired bank officer*

**Lantana**
Shanahan, Robert B. *banker*

**Maitland**
Fichthorn, Luke Eberly, III *investment banker*

**Marco Island**
Cooper, Thomas Astley *banking executive*

**Miami**
Brownell, Edwin Rowland *banker, civil engineer, land surveyor and mapper*
Giller, Norman Myer *banker, architect, author*
Kanter, Joseph Hyman *banker, community developer*
Smathers, Frank, Jr. *banker, horticulturist*
Weiner, Morton David *banker, insurance agent*

**Naples**
Craighead, Rodkey *banker*
Hooper, John Allen *retired banker*
Kley, John Arthur *banker*
Lange, George Willard, Jr. *trust banker, lawyer*
Martinuzzi, Leo Sergio, Jr. *banker*
Rigor, Bradley Glenn *bank executive*

**New Smyrna Beach**
Howard, Stanley Louis *investment banker*

**Palm Beach**
Callaway, Trowbridge *banker*
Curry, Bernard Francis *former banker, consultant*
Levine, Laurence Brandt *investment banker*
Lickle, William Cauffiel *banker*

**Pensacola**
Nickelsen, Eric J. *bank executive*

**Pompano Beach**
Kester, Stewart Randolph *banker*

**Ponte Vedra Beach**
de Selding, Edward Bertrand *retired banker*
O'Brien, Raymond Vincent, Jr. *banker*

**Punta Gorda**
Haswell, Carleton Radley *banker*

**Saint Petersburg**
Kruse, James Joseph *merchant banker*

**Santa Rosa Beach**
Wright, John Peale *retired banker*

**Sarasota**
Page, George Keith *banker*

**Temple Terrace**
Rink, Wesley Winfred *banker*

**Tequesta**
Turrell, Richard Horton, Sr. *retired banker*

**Venice**
O'Keefe, Robert James *retired banker*

**West Palm Beach**
Corley, Leslie M. *investment banker*
Lynch, William Walker *savings and loan association executive*
O'Brien, Robert Brownell, Jr. *investment banker, consultant, yacht broker, opera company executive*

## GEORGIA

**Atlanta**
Barron, Patrick Kenneth *bank executive*
†Carlisle, Patricia Kinley *mortgage company executive, paralegal*
Chapman, Hugh McMaster *banker*
Forrestal, Robert Patrick *banker, lawyer*
Halwig, Nancy Diane *banker*
Spiegel, John William *banker*
Williams, James Bryan *banker*
Williams, John Young *merchant banker*

**Flowery Branch**
Monroe, Melrose *retired banker*

**Savannah**
Bell, William Henry, Jr. *banker*
Giblin, Patrick David *retired banker*

**Sea Island**
LaWare, John Patrick *retired banker, federal official*

**Snellville**
Carlson, Roy Perry Merritt *retired banker*

## HAWAII

**Honolulu**
Dods, Walter Arthur, Jr. *bank executive*
Hoag, John Arthur *retired bank executive*
Johnson, Lawrence M. *banker*
Keir, Gerald Janes *banker*
Midkiff, Robert Richards *financial and trust company executive, consultant*
Stephenson, Herman Howard *retired banker*
Wolff, Herbert Eric *banker, former army officer*
Wong, Henry Li-Nan *bank executive, economist*

## IDAHO

**Boise**
Speer, William Thomas, Jr. *banker, investor, consultant, rancher*

## ILLINOIS

**Batavia**
Schilling, Arlo Leonard *bank executive*

**Belleville**
Badgley, William S. *retired multi-bank holding company executive*

**Blue Island**
Yager, Vincent Cook *banker*

**Champaign**
Froom, William Watkins *banker*

**Chicago**
Bakwin, Edward Morris *banker*
Barrow, Charles Herbert *investment banker*
Bartter, Brit Jeffrey *investment banker*
Bobins, Norman R. *banker*
Dancewicz, John Edward *investment banker*
Darr, Milton Freeman, Jr. *banker*
De Leonardis, Nicholas John *banker*
Eddy, David Latimer *banker*
Fabian, Larry Louis *bank executive*
Finley, Harold Marshall *investment banker*
Franke, Richard James *investment banker*
Ginley, Thomas J. *banker*
Heagy, Thomas Charles *banker*
Hollis, Donald Roger *banking consultant*
Istock, Verne George *banker*
Kearney, Michael John *banker*
Kinzie, Raymond Wyant *banker, lawyer*
Klapperich, Frank Lawrence, Jr. *investment banker*
Kramer, Ferdinand *mortgage banker*

Lecker, Abraham *former banker*
Lorenz, Katherine Mary *banker*
McKay, Neil *banker*
Montgomery, Charles Howard *retired bank executive*
O'Connell, Harold Patrick, Jr. *banker*
Osborn, William A. *trust company executive*
Pollock, Alexander John *banker*
Rahe, Maribeth Sembach *bank executive*
Roberts, Theodore Harris *banker*
Robinson, Gwendolyn Powell *savings and loan executive, church executive*
Schroeder, Charles Edgar *banker, investment management executive*
Socolofsky, Jon Edward *banker*
Stevens, Mark *banker*
Stirling, James Paulman *investment banker*
Theobald, Thomas Charles *banker*
Thomas, Richard Lee *banker*
Vander Wilt, Carl Eugene *banker*
Williams, Edward Joseph *banker*

**Deerfield**
Chiozzi, Richard Emilio *financial planner, investment advisor*

**Evanston**
Scholten, Menno Nico *mortgage banker*

**Fox River Grove**
Abboud, Alfred Robert *banker, consultant, investor*

**Golf**
Fellingham, Warren Luther, Jr. *retired banker*

**Highwood**
Brown, Lawrence Haas *banker*

**Hinsdale**
Kinney, Kenneth Parrish *banker, retired*

**Hoffman Estates**
Weston, Roger Lance *banker*

**Joliet**
Barber, Andrew Bollons *bank executive*

**Kenilworth**
Corrigan, John Edward, Jr. *banker, lawyer*

**Lake Bluff**
Anderson, Roger E. *bank executive*

**Lake Forest**
Ross, Robert Evan *bank executive*

**Northbrook**
Edelson, Ira J. *venture banker*
Keehn, Silas *retired bank executive*

**Palatine**
Fitzgerald, Gerald Francis *retired banker*

**Springfield**
Ferguson, Mark Harmon *banker, lawyer*
Lohman, Walter Rearick *banker*

**West Frankfort**
Lindsey, Steven Frank *banker*

## INDIANA

**Columbus**
Abts, Henry William *banker*
Nash, John Arthur *bank executive*

**Fort Wayne**
Bender, Linda Arlene *bank officer*
Kirkwood, Maurice Richard *banker*
Shaffer, Paul E. *retired banker*

**Indianapolis**
Dietz, William Ronald *financial services executive*
Meyer, William Michael *mortgage banking executive*

**Monticello**
Howarth, David H. *retired bank executive*

**Muncie**
Anderson, Stefan Stolen *bank executive*
Sursa, Charles David *banker*

**Ogden Dunes**
Gasser, Wilbert (Warner), Jr. *retired banker*

**South Bend**
Raclin, Ernestine Morris *banker*

**Terre Haute**
Smith, Donald E. *banker*

**Vincennes**
Rose, Robert Carlisle *retired banker*

## IOWA

**Adel**
Garst, Elizabeth *bank executive*

**Cedar Rapids**
Nebergall, Donald Charles *investment consultant*
Wax, Nadine Virginia *retired banker*

**Clinton**
Weil, Myron *retired banker*

**Des Moines**
Bucksbaum, Matthew *real estate investment trust company executive*

**Oskaloosa**
Steele, Betty Louise *retired banker*

**Schaller**
Currie, James Morton *bank executive*

## KANSAS

**Leawood**
Ballard, John William, Jr. *banker*

**Manhattan**
Stolzer, Leo William *bank executive*

**Overland Park**
Dore, James Francis *financial services executive*
Linn, James Herbert *retired banker*
Murdock, Stuart Laird *banker, investment adviser*

**Pratt**
Loomis, Howard Krey *banker*

**Shawnee Mission**
McEachen, Richard Edward *banker, lawyer*

**Topeka**
Dicus, John Carmack *savings and loan association executive*
Johnson, Arnold William *mortgage company executive*

**Wichita**
Jabara, Francis Dwight *merchant banker, educator, entrepreneur*

## KENTUCKY

**Inez**
Duncan, Robert Michael *banker, lawyer, Republican national committeeman*

**Lexington**
Nyere, Robert Alan *banker*

**Louisa**
Burton, John Lee, Sr. *banker*

**Louisville**
Guillaume, Raymond Kendrick *banker*
Hower, Frank Beard, Jr. *retired banker*
Tyrrell, Gerald Gettys *banker*

**Marrowbone**
Clark, Betty Pace *banking executive*

## LOUISIANA

**Alexandria**
Bolton, Robert Harvey *banker*

**Baton Rouge**
Moyse, Hermann, Jr. *banker*
Moyse, Hermann, III *banker*

**Covington**
Blossman, Alfred Rhody, Jr. *banker*

**Lafayette**
Stuart, Walter Bynum, III *banker*

**New Orleans**
Shofstahl, Robert Maxwell *savings and loan executive*
Wakefield, Benton McMillin, Jr. *banker*

## MAINE

**Andover**
Ellis, George Hathaway *retired banker and utility company executive*

**Bangor**
Bullock, William Clapp, Jr. *banker*

**Bristol**
Schmidt, Thomas Carson *international development banker*

**Cumberland Foreside**
Harper, Ralph Champlin *retired banker*

**Portland**
Grosset, Alexander Donald, Jr. *banker*
Saufley, William Edward *banker, lawyer*

## MARYLAND

**Annapolis**
Schleicher, Nora Elizabeth *banker, treasurer, accountant*

**Baltimore**
Baldwin, Henry Furlong *banker*
Couper, William *banker*
DeGroff, Ralph Lynn, Jr. *investment banker*
Graham, Jerry Fisher *bank executive, accountant*
Liberto, Joseph Salvatore *banker*
McGuirk, Ronald Charles *banker*
Morrel, William Griffin, Jr. *banker*
Murray, Joseph William *banker*
Schaefer, Robert Wayne *banker*
Shattuck, Mayo Adams, III *investment bank executive*
Wood, Howard Graham *banker*

**Bethesda**
Comings, William Daniel, Jr. *mortgage banker, housing development executive*
Petty, John Robert *banker*
Veniard, Jose M. *bank officer*

**Chestertown**
Williams, Henry Thomas *retired banker, real estate agent*

**Chevy Chase**
Saul, B. Francis, II *bank executive*

**Cockeysville Hunt Valley**
Schnering, Philip Blessed *investment banker*

**Crownsville**
Wright, Harry Forrest, Jr. *retired banker*

**Elkton**
Harrington, Benjamin Franklin, III *business consultant*

**Ellicott City**
Faulstich, Albert Joseph *banking consultant*

**Frederick**
Hoff, Charles Worthington, III *banker*

**Potomac**
Schonholtz, Joan Sondra Hirsch *banker, civic worker*

**Rockville**
Meyer, F. Weller *bank executive*

**Sparks Glencoe**
Swackhamer, Gene L. *bank executive*

## MASSACHUSETTS

**Boston**
Alden, Vernon Roger *corporate director, trustee*
Beinhocker, Gilbert David *investment banker*
Brown, William L. *banker*
Comeau, Susan *bank executive*
Costellese, Linda E. Grace *banker*
Crozier, William Marshall, Jr. *bank holding company executive*
Donahue, Douglas Aidan, Jr. *bank executive*
Driver, William Raymond, Jr. *banker*
Finnegan, Neal Francis *banker*
Gulley, Joan Long *banker*
Hamill, John P. *bank executive*
Little, Arthur Dehon *investment banker*
McCann, Edward *investment banker*
Monrad, Ernest Ejner *trust company executive*
Phillips, Daniel Anthony *trust company executive*
Ray, William F. *banker*
Rines, S. Melvin *investment banker*
Safe, Kenneth Shaw, Jr. *fiduciary firm executive*
Sheehan, Monica Mary *banker*
Stepanian, Ira *banking executive*
Vermilye, Peter Hoagland *banker*
Vestner, Eliot N., Jr. *bank executive*
Vineburgh, James Hollander *banking executive*
Williams, Charles Marvin *commercial banking educator*

**Cambridge**
Edgerly, William Skelton *banker*

**Dover**
Aldrich, Frank Nathan *bank executive*
Crittenden, Gazaway Lamar *retired banker*
Stockwell, Ernest Farnham, Jr. *banker*

**Longmeadow**
Lo Bello, Joseph David *bank executive*

**Marstons Mills**
Wheeler, Richard Warren *banker*

**Medford**
Sloane, Marshall M. *banker*

**Newburyport**
MacWilliams, Kenneth Edward *investment banker*

**Norwood**
Carpenter, Pamela Prisco *bank officer, foreign language educator*

**Waltham**
Fallon, John Golden *banker*
Riley, Henry Charles *banker*

**West Bridgewater**
Worrell, Cynthia Lee *bank executive*

**Weston**
Aquilino, Daniel *banker*

**Winchester**
Brennan, Francis Patrick *banker*

**Worcester**
Hunt, John David *retired banker*
Spencer, Harry Irving, Jr. *retired banker*

## MICHIGAN

**Bay City**
Van Dyke, Clifford Craig *retired banker*

**Bloomfield Hills**
Colladay, Robert S. *trust company executive, consultant*
Davis-Cartey, Catherine Bernice *bank executive*
Houston, E. James, Jr. *bank officer*

**Detroit**
Babb, Ralph Wheeler, Jr. *banker*
Jeffs, Thomas Hamilton, II *banker*
Miller, Eugene Albert *bank executive*
†Piper, William Howard *banker*
Ransom, Kevin Renard Dortch *investment banker*

**Elk Rapids**
Briggs, Robert Peter *banker*

**Farmington Hills**
Gladchun, Lawrence L. *banker, lawyer*
Heiss, Richard Walter *former bank executive, consultant, lawyer*

**Flint**
Piper, Mark Harry *retired banker*
Taeckens, Pamela Webb *bank executive*

**Frankfort**
Foster, Robert Carmichael *banker*

**Grand Rapids**
Canepa, John Charles *banking consultant*
Sadler, Robert Livingston *banker*

**Grosse Pointe**
Richardson, Dean Eugene *retired banker*
Surdam, Robert McClellan *retired banker*
Thurber, Cleveland, Jr. *trust banker*

**Kalamazoo**
Holland, Harold Herbert *banker*

**Litchfield**
Edwards, E. Dean *banking, building and real estate executive*

**Saginaw**
Evans, Harold Edward *banker*

**Southfield**
Shields, Robert Emmet *merchant banker, lawyer*

**Suttons Bay**
Whitney, William Chowning *retired banker, financial consultant*

**Troy**
Leach, Ralph F. *banker*

## MINNESOTA

**Chanhassen**
Severson, Roger Allan *bank executive*

**Eden Prairie**
Hanson, Dale S. *banker*

**Excelsior**
Rich, Willis Frank, Jr. *banker*

**Minneapolis**
Andreas, David Lowell *banker*
Campbell, James Robert *banker*
Deming, Frederick Lewis *banker*
Grundhofer, John F. *banking executive*
Hetland, James Lyman, Jr. *banker, lawyer, educator*
Huston, Beatrice Louise *banker*
Keller, Darla Lynn *financial manager, organization consultant*
Kovacevich, Richard M. *banking executive*
Morrison, Clinton *banker*
Rahn, Alvin Albert *former banker*
Swanson, Lloyd Oscar *former savings and loan association executive*
Walters, Glen Robert *banker*

**Saint Paul**
Rothmeier, Steven George *merchant banker, investment manager*

## MISSISSIPPI

**Gulfport**
Thatcher, George Robert *banker*

**Hattiesburg**
Moore, Henderson Alfred, Jr. *retired savings and loan executive*

**Jackson**
Sewell, Charles Haslett *banker*
Tullos, John Baxter *banker*

**Monticello**
Allen, Frank Carroll *retired banker*

**Tupelo**
Patterson, Aubrey Burns, Jr. *banker*
Ramage, Martis Donald, Jr. *banker*

## MISSOURI

**Kansas City**
Brown, John O. *banker*
Green, Jerry Howard *investment banker*
Kemper, David Woods, II *banker*
Reiter, Robert Edward *banker*
Vaughan, Kirk William *banker*

**Saint Louis**
Barksdale, Clarence Caulfield *banker*
Bealke, Linn Hemingway *bank executive*
Bryant, Ruth Alyne *banker*
Craig, Andrew Billings, III *bank holding company executive*
Jacobsen, Thomas H(erbert) *banker*
James, William W. *banker*
Kling, S(tephen) Lee *banker*
Leonard, Eugene Albert *banker*
Shell, Owen G., Jr. *banker*
Stann, John Anthony *investment banker*
Stoecker, David Thomas *banker*

**Springfield**
Archibald, Charles Arnold *holding company executive*
McCartney, N. L. *investment banker*

## NEBRASKA

**Lincoln**
Lundstrom, Gilbert Gene *banker, lawyer*
Stuart, James *banker, broadcaster*
Young, Dale Lee *banker*

## NEVADA

### Henderson
Campbell, David Martin *bank executive*

### Las Vegas
Troidl, Richard John *banker*

### Reno
Binns, James Edward *retired banker*
Day, Kevin Thomas *banker, community services director*

## NEW HAMPSHIRE

### Hanover
Paganucci, Paul Donnelly *banker, lawyer, former college official*

### Lancaster
Drapeau, Phillip David *banking executive*

### Sanbornville
Berg, Warren Stanley *retired banker*

## NEW JERSEY

### Basking Ridge
Schneider, Donald Frederic *banker*

### Burlington
†Denbo, Alexander *retired bank executive*

### Cinnaminson
Johnson, Victor Lawrence *banker*

### Clifton
Magnus, Frederick Samuel *investment banker*

### Colts Neck
French, Charles Ferris, Jr. *banker*

### Elizabeth
Leonett, Anthony Arthur *banker*

### Glen Rock
Lewis, Donald Emerson *banker*

### Jamesburg
Penny, Josephine B. *retired banker*

### Jersey City
Gibson, William Francis *investment banking executive*
Goldberg, Arthur Abba *merchant banker, financial advisor*
Nash, Lee J. *banker*

### Montclair
Pierson, Robert David *banker*

### Montvale
Sbarbaro, Robert Arthur *banker*

### Morristown
Moore, Milo Anderson *banker*
Simon, William Edward *investment banker, former secretary of treasury*

### Mountain Lakes
Turnheim, Palmer *banker*

### Ocean City
Dittenhafer, Brian Douglas *banker, economist*

### Parsippany
Singleterry, Gary Lee *investment banker*

### Perth Amboy
Gemmell, Joseph Paul *banker*

### Point Pleasant
Feeks, J. Michael *bank executive*

### Princeton
Feeney, John Robert *banker*
Ganoe, Charles Stratford *banker*
Haggerty, John Richard *banker*
Mills, Bradford *merchant banker*
Semrod, T. Joseph *banker*

### Red Bank
Dale, Madeline Houston McWhinney *banker*

### Roseland
Costanzo, Hilda Alba *retired banker*

### Short Hills
Klemme, Carl William *banker*
Lohse, Austin Webb *banker*

### Shrewsbury
Jones, Charles Hill, Jr. *banker*

### Spring Lake
D'Luhy, John James *investment banker*

### Summit
Mueller, Paul Henry *retired banker*
Sayles, Thomas Dyke, Jr. *banker*
Terracciano, Anthony Patrick *banker*

### Tenafly
Levy, Norman Jay *investment banker, financial consultant*

### Totowa
Jelliffe, Charles Gordon *banker*

### Windsor
Phelan, Richard Paul *bank executive*

## NEW MEXICO

### Alamogordo
Dewey, David Lawrence *banker, business consultant, author*

### Albuquerque
Frost, W. Gregory *mortgage company executive*

## NEW YORK

### Albany
Brown, Albert Joseph, Jr. *banker*
Murray, Terrence *banker*
Robinson, John Bowers, Jr. *bank holding company executive*

### Babylon
Keane, Daniel J. *banker*

### Bedford
Chia, Pei-Yuan *banker*
Philip, Peter Van Ness *former trust company executive*

### Briarcliff Manor
Carey, James Henry *banker*

### Bronxville
Arndt, Kenneth Eugene *banker*
Wilson, John Donald *banker, economist*

### Brooklyn
Hamm, Charles John *banker*
Hohenrath, William Edward *retired banker*
Pollack, Bruce *banker, real estate consultant*

### Buffalo
Knox, Northrup Rand *banker*
Stainrook, Harry Richard *banker*
Wilmers, Robert George *banker*

### Cold Spring Harbor
Hargraves, Gordon Sellers *banker*

### Elmont
Cusack, Thomas Joseph *banker*

### Flushing
Lee, Paul Ching-Lai *banker, real estate developer*

### Garden City
Desch, Carl William *banker, consultant*
Lovely, Thomas Dixon *banker*

### Geneseo
Hickman, John Hampton, III *entrepreneurial investment banker, industrialist, educator*

### Great Neck
Katz, Edward Morris *banker*

### Hicksville
Walsh, Charles Richard *banker*

### Ithaca
Smith, Robert Samuel *banker, former agricultural finance educator*

### Larchmont
Aburdene, Odeh Felix *banker*
Kaufmann, Henry Mark *mortgage banker*

### Long Island City
Kane Hittner, Marcia Susan *bank executive*

### Melville
Olson, Gary Robert *banker*

### Mohegan Lake
Galleno, Anthony Massimo *retired bank executive, consultant*

### New York
Aisenbrey, Stuart Keith *trust company official*
Altschul, Arthur Goodhart *investment banker*
Bacot, John Carter *banking executive*
Bains, Leslie Elizabeth *banker*
Barbeosch, William Peter *banker, lawyer*
Barkhorn, Henry Charles, III *investment banker*
Beale, Christopher William *banker*
Beim, David Odell *investment banker, educator*
Bellanger, Serge René *banker*
Benedetto, M. William *investment banker*
Bermudez, Jorge Alberto *bank executive*
Bernstein, William Robert *banker*
Biggs, Jeremy Hunt *trust company executive*
Bisno, Alison Peck *investment banker*
Bloom, Jack Sandler *investment banker*
Boothby, Willard Sands, III *bank executive*
Bottiglia, Frank Robert *bank executive*
Brennan, Donald P. *merchant banker*
Brenner, Howard Martin *banker*
Brown, Robert Mott, III *investment banker*
Bruckmann, Donald John *investment banker*
Calise, Ronald Jan *investment banking executive*
Campbell, Douglass *banker*
Cardew, William Joseph *bank executive*
Carey, Francis James *investment banker*
Casey, Karen Anne *banker*
Castle, John Krob *merchant banker*
Cayne, James E. *investment banker*
Childs, John Farnsworth *investment banker*
Clark, Thomas Carlyle *banker*
Clayton, Jonathan Alan *banker*
Clifford, Stewart Burnett *banker*
Comfort, William Twyman, Jr. *banker*
Conway Carey, Allison *banker*
Corrigan, E. Gerald *investment banker*
Cromwell, Oliver Dean *investment banker*
Darst, David Martin *investment banking company executive, writer, educator*
David-Weill, Michel Alexandre *investment banker*
Davis, Stephen Edward Folwell *banker*
Davison, Daniel Pomeroy *retired banker*
Debs, Richard A. *investment banker, government official*
Djeddah, Richard Nissim *investment banker*
Douglass, Robert Royal *banker, lawyer*
Doyle, L. F. Boker *trust company executive*
Druker, Henry Leo *investment banker*
Dwek, Cyril S. *banker*
Enders, Anthony Talcott *banker*
Farley, Terrence Michael *banker*
Feder, Harry Simon *bank executive*
Feldberg, Chester Ben *banker, lawyer*
Fisher, Bennett Lawson *investment executive*
Flugger, Penelope Ann *banker*
Frangopoulos, Zissimos A. *banker*
Franz, Donald Eugene, Jr. *merchant banker, security analyst*
Friedberg, Barry Sewell *investment banker*
Fruitman, Frederick Howard *investment banker*
Gallagher, Thomas Joseph *banker*
Gamble, Theodore Robert, Jr. *investment banker*
Georgantas, Aristides William *banking executive*
Goldmark, Peter Francis *banker*
Goodwin, Todd *banker*
Gossett, Robert Francis, Jr. *merchant banker*
Grant, William Packer, Jr. *banker*
Greenstein, Abraham Jacob *mortgage company executive, accountant*
Griffith, Alan Richard *banker*
Gruver, William Rolfe *investment banker*
Guenther, Jack Donald *banker*
Hartman, Stephen Jennings, Jr. *banker*
Heard, Edwin Anthony *banker*
Hellmold, Ralph O. *investment banker*
Herregat, Guy-Georges Jacques *banker*
Hilliard, Landon *banker*
Hover, John Calvin, II *banker*
Hughes, Norah Ann O'Brien *bank securities executive*
Huntington, Lawrence Smith *investment banker*
Ingraham, John Wright *banker*
Johnson, Thomas Stephen *banker*
Joseph, Frederick Harold *investment banker*
Kane, Jay Brassler *banker*
Kaufmann, Mark Steiner *banker*
Keilin, Eugene Jacob *investment banker, lawyer*
Kilburn, H(enry) T(homas), Jr. *investment banker*
Kopech, Robert Irving *banker*
Koppelman, Murray *investment banker*
Labrecque, Thomas G. *bank executive*
Lattin, Albert Floyd *banker*
Lear, Robert William *holding company executive*
LeBlond, Richard Knight, II *banker*
Lincoln, Edmond Lynch *investment banker*
Lomas, Eric James *investment banker*
Magdol, Michael Orin *bank executive*
Mailer-Howat, Patrick Lindsay Macalpine *investment banker*
Manges, James Horace *investment banker*
McCree, Donald Hanna, Jr. *banker*
McDonough, William J. *banker*
Mc Gillicuddy, John Francis *retired banker*
Meachin, David James Percy *investment banker*
Menaker, Ronald Herbert *bank executive*
Mendell, Oliver M. *banking executive*
Menschel, Robert Benjamin *investment banker*
Merriss, Philip Ramsay, Jr. *banker*
Mesznik, Joel R. *investment banker*
Meyer, Sandra W(asserstein) *bank executive, management consultant*
Miller, Edward Daniel *banker*
Miller, Richard Jerome *bank executive*
Mintz, Norman Nelson *investment banker, educator*
Moore, Andrew Given Tobias, II *investment banker, educator*
Murphy, Charles Joseph *investment banker*
Myerberg, Marcia *investment banker*
Newman, Frank Neil *bank executive*
Nuzum, John M., Jr. *banker*
olan, William Joseph, III *banker*
Olds, John Theodore *banker*
Oliver, Steven Wiles *banker*
Ostergard, Paul Michael *bank executive*
Pados, Frank John, Jr. *investment company executive*
Palmer, Edward Lewis *banker*
Patterson, Ellmore Clark *banker*
Peterson, M. Roger *international banker, retired manufacturing executive, retired air force officer*
Peterson, Peter G. *banker*
Petrie, Donald Joseph *banker*
Pettus, Barbara Wyper *bank executive*
Pincus, Lionel I. *venture banker*
Poll, Robert Eugene, Jr. *bank executive*
Prizzi, Jack Anthony *investment banking executive*
Ramsey, Peter Christie *bank executive*
Reed, John Shepard *bank executive*
Reese, William Willis *banker*
Rhodes, William Reginald *banker*
Rimerman, Ira Stephen *banker*
Roach, John Hendee, Jr. *bank executive, investment banker, financial service executive*
Roberts, Donald Munier *retired banker, trust company executive*
Rockefeller, David *banker*
Ruding, Herman Onno *banker, former Dutch government official*
Salmans, Charles Gardiner *banker*
Sanford, Charles Steadman, Jr. *banker*
Schumacher, Robert Denison *banker*
Segalas, Hercules Anthony *investment banker*
Shipley, L. Parks, Jr. *banker*
Shipley, Walter Vincent *banker*
Shuman, Stanley S. *investment banker*
Silberstein, Alan Mark *financial services executive*
Sim, Craig Stephen *investment banker*
Simmons, John Derek *investment banker*
Singer, Eric T. *investment banker*
Slusser, William Peter *investment banker*
Smith, Kathleen Tener *bank executive*
Smith, Phillips Guy *banker*
Solar, Richard Leon *banker*
Spangler, Arnold Eugene *investment banker*
Speciale, Richard *bank executive*
Stein, Howard S. *banker*
Stewart, James Montgomery *banker*
Strong, Robert S. *banker*
Tarnopol, Michael Lazar *bank executive*
Trachtenberg, Matthew J. *bank holding company executive*
Urkowitz, Michael *banker*
van Hengel, Maarten *banker*
Von Fraunhofer-Kosinski, Katherina *bank executive*
Wainwright, Cynthia Crawford *banker*
Warner, Douglas Alexander, III *banker*
Warner, Scott Dennis *investment banker*
Wasserman, Charles *banker*
Weil, Frank A. *investment banker, lawyer*
Weill, Sanford I. *bank executive*
Weiner, Walter Herman *banker, lawyer*
Whitcraft, Edward C. R. *investment banker*
Whittemore, Laurence Frederick *private banker*

Wirz, Pascal Francois *trust company executive*
Wolff, William F., III *investment banker*
Wriston, Walter Bigelow *retired banker*
Zwerling, Gary Leslie *investment bank executive*

### Niskayuna
Whittingham, Harry Edward, Jr. *retired banker*

### Oyster Bay
Schwab, Hermann Caspar *banker*

### Pittsford
Biklen, Stephen Clinton *student loan company executive*
Schubert, John Edward *former banker*

### Port Kent
Mc Kee, James, Jr. *retired bank executive*

### Queensbury
Mead, John Milton *banker*

### Ridgewood
Jones, Harold Antony *banker*

### Rochester
Hargrave, Alexander Davidson *banker, lawyer*
Simon, Leonard Samuel *banker*
Wayland-Smith, Robert Dean *banker*

### Saratoga Springs
Wait, Charles Valentine *banker*

### Scarsdale
Hines, William Eugene *banker*

### Shelter Island
Dowd, David Joseph *banker, builder*

### Stamford
Bergleitner, George Charles, Jr. *investment banker*

### Staten Island
Chapin, Elliott Lowell *retired bank executive*

### Syracuse
Gray, Charles Augustus *banker*
Meyers, Peter L. *banker*
O'Day, Royal Lewis *former banker*

### Tonawanda
Haller, Calvin John *banker*

### Utica
Schrauth, William Lawrence *banker, lawyer*

### Valley Cottage
Atha, Stuart Kimball, Jr. *retired banker*

### Westbury
Tulchin, Stanley *banker, lecturer, author, business reorganization consultant*

### White Plains
Bober, Lawrence Harold *retired banker*

### Whitesboro
Raymonda, James Earl *retired banker*

## NORTH CAROLINA

### Asheville
Everett, Durward R., Jr. *retired banker*

### Burnsville
Snelling, George Arthur *banker*

### Charlotte
Browning, Roy Wilson, III *mortgage banking executive*
Crutchfield, Edward Elliott, Jr. *banking executive*
Georgius, John R. *bank executive*
McColl, Hugh Leon, Jr. *bank executive*

### Fairmont
Byrne, James Frederick *banker*

### Gastonia
Teem, Paul Lloyd, Jr. *savings and loan executive*

### Highlands
Sheehan, Charles Vincent *investment banker*

### Huntersville
Wilson, Milner Bradley, III *retired banker*

### Pilot Mountain
Ross, Norman Alexander *retired banker*

### Pinehurst
Henderson, Paul Audine *banker, consultant*

### Raleigh
Hardin, Eugene Brooks, Jr. *retired banker*
Holding, Lewis R. *banker*

### Rocky Mount
Mauldin, Robert Ray *banker*
Wilkerson, William Holton *banker*

### Wilson
Stewart, Burton Gloyden, Jr. *banker*

### Winston Salem
Austell, Edward Callaway *banker*
Baker, Leslie Mayo, Jr. *banker*
Cramer, John Scott *retired banker*
McNair, John Franklin, III *banker*
Medlin, John Grimes, Jr. *banker*
Runnion, Howard J., Jr. *banker*
Wanders, Hans Walter *banker*
Watlington, John Francis, Jr. *banker*
Worley, Bland Wallace *banker*

## OHIO

**Akron**
Showalter, Robert Earl *banker*

**Canton**
Carpenter, Noble Olds *banker*

**Chagrin Falls**
Obert, Charles Frank *banker*

**Cincinnati**
Brumm, Paul Michael *banker*
McKenny, Collin Grad *banker*
Schaefer, George A., Jr. *bank executive*
Thiemann, Charles Lee *banker*

**Cleveland**
Blackstone, Patricia Clark *bank officer, psychotherapist*
Brandon, Edward Bermetz *retired banking executive*
Gillespie, Robert Wayne *banker*
Glickman, Carl David *banker*
Koch, Charles Joseph *banker*
Powers, Richard Daniel *bank executive*
Robertson, William Richard *banker, holding company executive*
Rupert, John Edward *retired savings and loan executive, business and civic affairs consultant*
Schaut, Joseph William *banker*
Schutter, David John *banker*
Siefers, Robert George *banker*
Simonson, John Alexander *banking executive*

**Columbus**
Leiter, William C. *banking executive*
Mc Coy, John Bonnet *banker*
O'Donnell, F. Scott *banker*
Page, Linda Kay *banking executive*

**Dublin**
Gores, Gary Gene *credit union executive*

**Elyria**
Kreighbaum, John Scott *banker*

**Hamilton**
Pontius, Stanley N. *bank holding company executive*

**Newark**
McConnell, William Thompson *commercial banker*

**Pepper Pike**
Mc Call, Julien Lachicotte *banker*

**Perrysburg**
Yager, John Warren *retired banker, lawyer*

**Sylvania**
Bergsmark, Edwin Martin *mortgage bank executive*

**Toledo**
Carson, Samuel Goodman *retired banker, company director*
Kunze, Ralph Carl *savings and loan executive*

**Washington Court House**
Fultz, Clair Ervin *former banker*

**Willoughby**
Abelt, Ralph William *bank executive*

## OKLAHOMA

**Bartlesville**
Doty, Donald D. *retired banker*

**Konawa**
Rains, Mary Jo *banker*

**Oklahoma City**
Brown, Kenneth Ray *banker*
Browne, John Robinson *banker*
Danforth, Louis Fremont *banker, educator*
Hammons, Royce Mitchell *bank executive*
Williams, William Ralston *retired bank and trust company executive*

**Tulsa**
Eaton, Leonard James, Jr. *banker*
Hawkins, Francis Glenn *banker, lawyer*

## OREGON

**Milwaukie**
McKay, Laura L. *banker, consultant*

**Portland**
Cameron, Gerry B. *banking executive*
Jensen, Edmund Paul *bank holding company executive*
†Pierson, Wayne George *trust company executive*
Staver, Leroy Baldwin *banker*

**Salem**
Weight, George Dale *banker, educator*

## PENNSYLVANIA

**Bala Cynwyd**
Bausher, Verne C(harles) *banker*
Potamkin, Meyer P. *mortgage banker*

**Bryn Mawr**
Clark, George Roberts *retired trust company executive*

**Conshohocken**
Boenning, Henry Dorr, Jr. *investment banker*
Tily, Stephen Bromley, III *bank executive*

**Easton**
Ashby, Richard James, Jr. *bank executive, lawyer*

**Erie**
Bracken, Charles Herbert *banker*

**Fort Washington**
Shah, Bipin Chandra *banker*

**Gratz**
Herb, Jane Elizabeth *banker*

**Harleysville**
Daller, Walter E., Jr. *banking executive*

**Harrisburg**
Campbell, Carl Lester *banker*

**Indiana**
Rocco, Domenic Patrick, Jr. *trust company executive, retired army officer*

**Kennett Square**
Taylor, Bernard J., II *banker*

**Lansdale**
Fawley, John Jones *retired banker*

**Lebanon**
Parrott, Charles Norman *bank executive*

**Leola**
McElhinny, Wilson Dunbar *banker*

**Lititz**
Bolinger, Robert Stevens *banker*

**Malvern**
Eagleson, William Boal, Jr. *banker*

**Media**
Cooke, M(erritt) Todd *banker*

**Philadelphia**
Boehne, Edward George *banker*
Foulke, William Green *banker*
Hailey, Jacob Joseph *bank executive*
Haskin, Donald Lee *bank executive*
Kardon, Robert *mortgage company executive*
Larsen, Terrance A. *bank holding company executive*
Murdoch, Lawrence Corlies, Jr. *retired banker, economist*
Ross, George Martin *investment banker*
Spolan, Harmon Samuel *banker*

**Pittsburgh**
Cahouet, Frank Vondell *banking executive*
Clyde, Larry Forbes *banker*
Higgins, James Henry *retired banker*
McGuinn, Martin Gregory *banker, lawyer*
Milsom, Robert Cortlandt *banker*
O'Brien, Thomas Henry *bank holding company executive*
Ostern, Wilhelm Curt *retired holding company executive*
Pearson, Nathan Williams *investment management executive*

**Reading**
Erdman, Carl L. N. *retired banker*
Mengel, Philip R(ichard) *investment banker*
Roesch, Clarence Henry *banker*
Snyder, Clair Allison *banker*

**Saint Davids**
Sheftel, Roger Terry *merchant bank executive*

**Scranton**
Janoski, Henry Valentine *banker, former investment counselor, realtor*
Newman, Samuel *trust company executive*

**Souderton**
Hoeflich, Charles Hitschler *banker*

**Spring House**
Hart, Alex Way *banker*

**Telford**
Hagey, Walter Rex *retired banker*

**West Chester**
Swope, Charles Evans *banker, lawyer*

**Wyomissing**
Moll, Lloyd Henry *banker*

## RHODE ISLAND

**Cranston**
Stark, Dennis Edwin *banker*

**Providence**
Burns, Robert E. *bank executive*
Gardner, Thomas Earle *investment banker, managment/financial consultant*
Johnson, Maxine Frahm *bank executive*

## SOUTH CAROLINA

**Columbia**
Boggs, Jack Aaron *banker, municipal government official*
Lumpkin, John Henderson *retired banker*

## SOUTH DAKOTA

**Centerville**
Thomson, John Wanamaker *bank executive*

**Freeman**
Waltner, John Randolph *banker*

**Hartford**
Murray, Barbara Ann *bank officer*

**Rapid City**
Undlin, Charles Thomas *banker*

## TENNESSEE

**Clinton**
Birdwell, James Edwin, Jr. *retired banker*

**Harrogate**
Robertson, Edwin Oscar *banker*

**Kingsport**
Meyerrose, Sarah Louise *bank holding company executive*

**Knoxville**
Blake, Gerald Rutherford *banker*
Mikels, J(ames) Ronald *bank executive*

**Maryville**
Lawson, Fred Raulston *banker*

**Memphis**
Booth, Robert Lee, Jr. *banker*
Horn, Ralph *bank executive*
Terry, Ronald Anderson *bank holding company executive*

**Murfreesboro**
Ford, William F. *banker*

**Nashville**
Bottorff, Dennis C. *banker*
Cook, Charles Wilkerson, Jr. *banker, former county official*
Daane, James Dewey *banker*
Fleming, Samuel M. *banker*
Harrison, Clifford Joy, Jr. *banker*
Johnson, Albert William *mortgage banker, real estate broker*
Maihafer, Harry James *retired banker, former army officer, writer*
Overton, Stanley Dixon *banking executive*

## TEXAS

**Austin**
Bunten, William Daniel *retired banker*
Deal, Ernest Linwood, Jr. *banker*
Stone, Leon *banker*

**Carrollton**
Bentley, Clarence Edward *savings and loan executive*

**Dallas**
Bishop, Gene Herbert *corporate executive*
Brown, Gloria Vasquez *banker*
Cochran, George Calloway, III *retired banker*
Mason, Barry Jean *retired banker*
McTeer, Robert D., Jr. *banker*
Pistor, Charles Herman, Jr. *former banker, academic administrator*
Reid, Langhorne, III *merchant banker*

**Hearne**
Moore, Loretta Westbrook *banker*

**Houston**
Elkins, James Anderson, Jr. *banker*
Elkins, James Anderson, III *banker*
Ellis, Rodney Glenn *investment banking firm director*
Geis, Duane Virgil *retired investment banker*
Knapp, David Hebard *banker*

**Irving**
Hughes, Keith William *banking and finance company executive*

**New Braunfels**
Pharis, Ruth McCalister *retired banker*

**Pasadena**
Moon, John Henry, Sr. *banker*

**San Antonio**
McClane, Robert Sanford *bank holding company executive*
Post, Gerald Joseph *retired banker, retired air force officer*

**Tyler**
Bell, Henry Marsh, Jr. *banking executive*
Blasingame, Donald Ray (Don Blasingame) *banker*
Juneau, Stafford Gerard, III *bank officer*

**Victoria**
Stubblefield, Page Kindred *banker*

## UTAH

**Ogden**
Browning, Roderick Hanson *banker*

**Saint George**
Beesley, H(orace) Brent *savings and loan executive*

**Salt Lake City**
Eccles, Spencer Fox *banker*
Simmons, Roy William *banker*

## VIRGINIA

**Alexandria**
Birely, William Cramer *investment banker*
Woelflein, Kevin Gerard *banker*

**Arlington**
Graham, William Pierson *investment banker, entrepreneur*
Leland, Marc Ernest *trust advisor, lawyer*
Rogers, James Frederick *banker, management consultant*

**Charlottesville**
Bull, George Albert *retired banker*

**Danville**
Goodson, Louie Aubrey, Jr. *retired bank executive*

**Falls Church**
Geithner, Paul Herman, Jr. *banker*

**Great Falls**
Foryst, Carole *mortgage broker*

**Lynchburg**
Quillian, William Fletcher, Jr. *retired banker, former college president*

**Mc Lean**
Brendsel, Leland C. *federal mortgage company executive*
Kimberly, William Essick *investment banker*
Ramsey, Lloyd Brinkley *retired savings and loan executive, retired army officer*
Ring, James Edward Patrick *mortgage banking consulting executive*
Schools, Charles Hughlette *banker, lawyer*

**Norfolk**
Cutchins, Clifford Armstrong, III *banker*

**Richmond**
Ashworth, Lawrence Nelson *bank executive*
Black, Robert Perry *retired banker, executive*
Broaddus, John Alfred, Jr. *bank executive, economist*
Harris, Henry Hiter, Jr. *banker*
Hatch, Robert Norris *banker*
Henley, Vernard William *banker*
Jones, Catesby Brooke *retired banker*
Miller, Lewis Nelson, Jr. *banker*
Millner, Wallace B., III *banker*
Moore, Andrew Taylor, Jr. *banker*
Talley, Charles Richmond *commercial banking executive*
Tilghman, Richard Granville *banker*

**Roanoke**
Deppen, Douglas *bank executive*

**Vienna**
Hood, William Clarence *international banking official*

**Virginia Beach**
Harrison, William Wright *retired banker*

**Williamsburg**
Bernhardt, John Bowman *banker*

**Winchester**
Pavsek, Daniel Allan *banker, educator*

## WASHINGTON

**Bellevue**
Davidson, Robert William *merchant banker*
Melby, Orville Erling *retired banker*
Metz, Marilyn Joyce *bank executive*

**Friday Harbor**
Buck, Robert Follette *retired banker, lawyer*

**Mercer Island**
Spitzer, Jack J. *banker*

**Oak Harbor**
Piercy, Gordon Clayton *bank executive*

**Olympia**
Alfers, Gerald Junior *bank executive, retired*

**Seattle**
Andrew, Lucius Archibald David, III *bank executive*
Arnold, Robert Morris *banker*
Berg, Margarete Claire *banker*
Campbell, Robert Hedgcock *investment banker*
Cockburn, John F. *retired banker*
Cullen, James Douglas *banker, finance company executive*
Faulstich, James R. *bank executive*
Gilchrist, James Beardslee *banker*
Green, Joshua, III *banker*
Greenwood, Wilbur R., III *investment banker*
Hampton, Philip McCune *banker*
Killinger, Kerry Kent *bank executive*
Porter, Walter Thomas, Jr. *bank executive*
Williams, Walter Baker *mortgage banker*
Winnowski, Thaddeus Richard (Ted Winnowski) *bank executive*

**Sequim**
Laube, Roger Gustav *retired trust officer, financial consultant*

**Silverdale**
Horn, Thomas Carl *retired banker*

**Spokane**
Lindsay, Donald Parker *former savings bank executive*
McWilliams, Edwin Joseph *banker*

**Tacoma**
Fetters, Norman Craig, II *banker*
Kaltinick, Paul R. *trust company executive*
Odlin, Richard Bingham *retired banker*
Owen, Thomas Walker *banker, broker*

**Vancouver**
Firstenburg, Edward William *banker*

### Yakima
Aldridge, Geanie Black *bank executive*

## WEST VIRGINIA

### Princeton
†Spracher, John C. *banking executive*

## WISCONSIN

### Kaukauna
Janssen, Gail Edwin *banking executive*

### Marinette
Staudenmaier, Mary Louise *banker, lawyer*

### Milwaukee
Bauer, Chris Michael *banker*
Fitzsimonds, Roger Leon *bank holding company executive*
Long, Robert Eugene *banker*
Murphy, Judith Chisholm *trust company executive*
Samson, Allen Lawrence *bank executive*

### Nekoosa
Sigler, LeRoy Walter *banker, lawyer, entrepreneur*

## WYOMING

### Cheyenne
Knight, Robert Edward *banker*

## CANADA

## BRITISH COLUMBIA

### Vancouver
Gardiner, William Douglas Haig *bank executive*

## ONTARIO

### Ottawa
Bonin, Bernard *bank executive*
Freedman, Charles *bank executive*

### Toronto
Augustine, Jerome Samuel *merchant banker*
Baillie, Alexander Charles, Jr. *banker*
Barrett, Matthew W. *banker*
Bickford, James Gordon *banker*
Brooks, Robert Leslie *bank executive*
Cleghorn, John Edward *bank executive*
Flood, A. L. (Al Flood) *bank executive*
Fullerton, R. Donald *banker*
Godsoe, Peter Cowperthwaite *banker*
Greenwood, Lawrence George *banker*
Grosland, Emery Layton *banker*
Hayes, Derek Cumberland *banking executive, lawyer*
Johnston, Malcolm Carlyle *bank executive*
Kluge, Holger *bank executive*
MacDougall, Hartland Molson *corporate director, retired bank executive*
Styles, Richard Geoffrey Pentland *retired banker*
Taylor, Allan Richard *retired banker*
Taylor, Paul Albert *banker*
Thomson, Richard Murray *banker*
Webb, Anthony Allan *banker*

## QUEBEC

### Laval
Pichette, Claude *former banking executive, university rector, research executive*

### Montreal
Beaudoin, François *financial company president, chief executive bank officer*
Bérard, André *bank executive*
Lawson, Jane Elizabeth *bank executive*
Turmel, Jean Bernard *banker*

## MEXICO

### Mexico City
de Brun, Shauna Doyle *investment banker, industrialist*

## ARGENTINA

### Buenos Aires
Cascales, José María *bank executive*
Sacerdote, Manuel Ricardo *banker*

## CHINA

### Hong Kong
Magarity, Russell Lynn *banker*

## DENMARK

### Copenhagen
Massolo, Arthur James *banker*

## ENGLAND

### Berryhill
Barlow, Matthew Blaise Joseph *merchant banker*

### London
Barren, Bruce Willard *merchant banker*
Billings, Donald Franklin *international banking consultant*
Binney, Robert Harry *bank executive*
Bischoff, Winfried Franz Wilhelm *merchant banker*
Catto of Cairncatto, Baron Stephen Gordon *banker*
Chappell, Anthony Gordon *banker*
Collins, Paul John *banker*
Mallinckrodt, George W. *bank executive*
Moreno, Glen Richard *banker*
Pennant-Rea, Rupert Lascelles *banker*

## FRANCE

### La Couture Boussey
Karnath, Lorie Mary Lorraine *bank officer, consultant*

## HONG KONG

### Hong Kong
Rowe, Kevin S. *banker*
Torres, Cynthia Ann *banker*

### Sha Tin
Larr, Peter *banker*

## SINGAPORE

### Singapore
Enlow, Fred Clark *banker*

## SWITZERLAND

### Geneva
Agostinelli, Robert Francesco *investment banker*
Hedstrom, Mitchell Warren *banker*

### Zurich
Gut, Rainer Emil *banker*

## TAIWAN

### Taipei
Yeh, K. H. *bank executive*

## ADDRESS UNPUBLISHED

Ackerman, Jack Rossin *investment banker*
Almgren, Herbert Philip *bank executive*
Alvord, Joel Barnes *bank executive*
Baker, Henry S., Jr. *retired banker*
Beck, Jeffrey Dengler *banking executive*
Blum, Barbara Davis *banker*
Bowen, James Ronald *banker*
Boykin, Robert Heath *banker*
Boyles, James Kenneth *retired banker*
Britt, John Roy *banker*
Brown, Sandra Jean *banker*
Browning, Colin Arrott *retired banker*
Buckels, Marvin Wayne *savings and loan executive*
Burden, Ordway Partridge *investment banker*
Busse, Leonard Wayne *banker, financial consultant*
Christenson, Gregg Andrew *bank executive*
Clifton, Russell B. *banking and mortgage lending consultant, retired mortgage company executive*
Coleman, Lewis Waldo *bank executive*
Cooney, John Thomas *retired banker*
Costello, Daniel Walter *retired bank executive*
Cottrell, Mary-Patricia Tross *banker*
Crooks, Bruce Philip *retired bank executive*
Crosby, John Griffith *investment banker*
Davis, George Linn *banker*
Dodson, Samuel Robinette, III *investment banker*
Eaton, Curtis Howarth *banker, state agency administrator*
Fahey, Joseph Francis, Jr. *banker, financial consultant*
Fahringer, Catherine Hewson *retired savings and loan executive*
Fellingham, David Andrew *retired mortgage banker*
Fielding, Harold Preston *bank executive*
Finocchiaro, Alfonso G. *bank executive*
Fix, John Neilson *banker*
Flanagan, William Stanley, Jr. *banker, lawyer*
Ford, William Francis *retired bank holding company executive*
Foster, Stephen Kent *banker*
Gaffney, Thomas *banker*
Gainor, Thomas Edward *banker*
Gibbons, Michael Eugene *investment banker*
Grant, James Colin *banker*
Greene, Richard Thaddeus *bank executive*
Greer, K. Gordon *banker*
Gros, Francisco Roberto André *banker*
Groves, Michael *banker*
Hall, Jesse Seaborn *retired banker*
Harrison, William Burwell, Jr. *banker*
Higginson, Jerry Alden, Jr. *bank executive*
Hogan, Robert Henry *trust company executive, investment strategist*
Howard, Donald Searcy *banker*
Iles, Eileen Marie *bank executive, controller*
Ingersoll, Paul Mills *banker*
Jennings, Joseph Ashby *banker*
Jones, Richard Melvin *bank executive, former retail executive*
Keehner, Michael Arthur Miller *banker*
Klett, Gordon A. *retired savings and loan association executive*
Kooken, John Frederick *retired bank holding company executive*
Korpal, Eugene Stanley *banker, former army officer*
Lafley, Alan Frederick *retired banker*
Lankford, Duane Gail *investment banker, mountaineer*
Leigh, Margie *mortgage company originator*
Liu, Ernest K. H. *international banking executive, international financial consultant*
Mayo, Robert Porter *banker*
Meeker, Guy Bentley *banker*
Meyer, Henry Lewis, III *banker*
Milligan, Arthur Achille *banker*
Miracle, Robert Warren *retired banker*
Moriarty, Donald William, Jr. *banker*
Morris, Frank Eugene *banker*
Morrison, James R. *retired banker*
Mortensen, Peter *banker*
Muñoz, Carlos Ramón *bank executive*
†Newman, Denis *fund executive*
Nichols, C. Walter, III *retired trust company executive*
Nicholson, Richard Joseph *trust banking executive*
North, Phil Record *retired banker*
Odell, Frank Harold *banker*
Ortiz, Paulina Patricia *banker, research analyst*
Osborn, William George *savings and loan executive*
Otto, Ingolf Helgi Elfried *banking institute fellow*
Owen, Suzanne *retired savings and loan executive*
Palmer, Langdon *banker*
Paquin, Paul Peter *corporate finance executive*
Pendleton, Barbara Jean *retired banker*
Porretta, Emanuele Peter *retired bank executive*
Reuber, Grant Louis *banking insurance company executive*
Rice, Joseph Albert *banker*
Richardson, Richard Thomas *retired banker*
Risk, John Fred *banker, investment banker*
Rogers, Nathaniel Sims *banker*
Rundquist, Howard Irving *investment banker*
Salony, John, III *banker*
Searle, Philip Ford *banker*
Simonet, John Thomas *banker*
Smith, Richard Anthony *investment banker*
Smith, Wilburn Jackson, Jr. *retired bank executive*
Stanton, Robert John *corporate bank executive, lawyer*
Stephens, Donald R(ichards) *banker*
Stephens, Elton Bryson *bank executive, service and manufacturing company executive*
Stewart, Carleton M. *banker, corporate director*
Stotter, Harry Shelton *banker, lawyer*
Sweet, Philip W. K., Jr. *former banker*
Swope, Donald Downey *retired banker*
Taylor, David George *retired banker*
Thiessen, Gordon George *banker*
Thompson, J. Andy *bank executive*
Thurmond, John Peter, II *bank executive, rancher, archaeologist*
Tobin, Michael Edward *banker*
Tyson, H. Michael *retired bank executive*
Vachon, Serge Jean *bank executive*
Weatherstone, Sir Dennis *bank executive*
Weir, Thomas Charles *banker*
West, Rexford Leon *banker*
Womach, Emily Hitch *retired banker and marketing and public relations executive*
Woodard, Nina Elizabeth *banker*

# FINANCE: FINANCIAL SERVICES

## UNITED STATES

## ALABAMA

### Auburn
Solomon, Michael Robert *marketing educator*

### Birmingham
Morris, Florence Henderson *auditor*
Powers, Edward Latell *accountant*
Raabe, William Alan *tax author and educator*

### Huntsville
Graves, Benjamin Barnes *business administration educator*
Michelini, Sylvia Hamilton *auditor*
Morgan, Ethel Branman *accountant, retired electronics engineer*

### Montgomery
Frazer, Nimrod Thompson *financial services company executive*

### Point Clear
Hart, Eric Mullins *finance company executive*
Salter, LaNora Jeanette *corporate financial officer*

### Tuscaloosa
Gilliland, Terri Kirby *accountant*
Gup, Benton Eugene *banking educator*
Lee, Thomas Alexander *accountant, educator*
Mayer, Morris Lehman *marketing educator*
Penz, Anton Jacob *retired accounting educator*

## ALASKA

### Anchorage
Illk, Serena Pearl *accountant*
Swalling, John Christian *accountant, president*

## ARIZONA

### Avondale
Rosztoczy, Ferenc Erno *business executive*

### Fort Huachuca
Kelly, Maureen Ann *management accountant*

### Mc Neal
Smith, Clifford Neal *business educator, writer*

### Mesa
Markey, Thomas Adam *financial officer*

### Peoria
Molinsky, Bert *tax consultant*

### Phoenix
Chrisman, William Herring *property tax consultant*
Daniel, James Richard *accountant, computer company financial executive*
Fitzsimmons, Robert James *finance company executive*
Fulk, Roscoe Neal *retired accountant*
Hardy, Gary Wayne *financial planner*
Holloway, Edgar Austin *retired diversified business executive*
Khan, Ahmed Mohiuddin *finance, insurance executive*
Linxwiler, Louis Major, Jr. *retired finance company executive*
Mullen, Daniel Robert *finance executive*
Naylor, Franklin Llewellyn, Jr. *financial advisor*
Norton, Douglas Ray *auditor general*
Stern, Richard David *investment company executive*

### Prescott
Harris, Earl Edward *business educator*

### Scottsdale
Hansen, Donald W. *insurance and financial services executive*
Huizingh, William *former accounting educator*

### Sun City
Cortright, Inga Ann *accountant*
Feldman, Allan Jay *financial planner, stockbroker*
Roberts, Anna Ruth *financial consultant*

### Sun City West
Person, Robert John *financial management consultant*
Schrag, Adele Frisbie *business education educator*

### Tempe
Gwinner, Robert Fred, Jr. *marketing educator*
Kaufman, Herbert Mark *finance educator*
Manz, Charles C. *management educator*
Pany, Kurt Joseph *accounting educator, consultant*
Poe, Jerry B. *financial educator*
Upson, Donald V. *financial executive*

### Tucson
Braswel, Kerry *tax accountant, horsewoman*
Koons, Stephen Eugene *accountant, real estate developer*
Nixon, Robert Obey, Sr. *business educator*
Toland, Florence Winifred *printing company executive*

## ARKANSAS

### Arkadelphia
Webster, Robert Lee *accounting educator, researcher*

### Fayetteville
Cook, Doris Marie *accountant, educator*
Hay, Robert Dean *retired management educator*
Orr, Betsy *business education educator*
Rosenberg, Leon Joseph *marketing educator*

### Hot Springs National Park
Mayhugh, Joel Ogden, Jr. *financial executive*
Wallace, William Hall *economic and financial consultant*

### Little Rock
Adkins, Fredrick Earl, III *financial consultant, educator*
Bethea, William C. *financial administrator, lawyer*
Flournoy, Jacob Wesley *internal audit director*

### Siloam Springs
Hill, James Robert *accountant*

### State University
Ruby, Ralph, Jr. *vocational business educator*

## CALIFORNIA

### Alameda
Taveggia, Thomas Charles *management educator*

### Alhambra
Siler, Walter Orlando, Jr. *retired business executive*

### Alta Loma
Currie, Madeline Ashburn *business administration educator*
Wu, Seng-Chai *financial planner, life insurance agency official*

### Anaheim
Barbas, Jeffrey Lawrence *finance company executive*
Lano, Charles Jack *retired financial executive*

### Atherton
Barker, Robert Jeffery *financial executive*
Chetkovich, Michael N. *accountant*

### Belvedere Tiburon
Cook, Robert Donald *financial service executive*

### Berkeley
Blume, James Beryl *financial advisor*
Bucklin, Louis Pierre *business educator, consultant*
Holton, Richard Henry *business educator*
Staubus, George Joseph *accounting educator*

### Beverly Hills
McGagh, William Gilbert *financial consultant*

### Burbank
Gold, Stanley P. *diversified investments executive*
Marinace, Kenneth Anthony *financial advisor*
Thornton, Cameron Mitchell *financial planner*

### Carlsbad
Billingsley, William Scott *accountant, controller*
Peasland, Bruce Randall *financial executive*

### Carmel
Steele, Charles Glen *retired accountant*

### Carmichael
Areen, Gordon E. *finance company executive*

### Chatsworth
Erikson, J. Lance *financial corporation executive*

### Chico
Olsen, Robert Arthur *finance educator*

O'Neill, Michael Foy *business educator*

**Claremont**
Christian, Suzanne Hall *financial planner*

**Compton**
Bogdan, Carolyn Louetta *financial specialist*

**Concord**
Gregory, Leslie Finlayson *tax accountant, financial consultant, realtor*
Lhotka, Sidney Bruno *tax accountant*

**Corona Del Mar**
Helphand, Ben J. *actuary*

**Coronado**
Allen, Charles Richard *retired financial executive*

**Costa Mesa**
Patterson, Joseph Cromwell *financial company executive*

**Culver City**
Buskirk, Bruce David *marketing educator*
Eckel, James Robert, Jr. *financial planner*
Richardson, John Edmon *marketing educator*

**Cypress**
Freedman, Gail *financial analyst*

**Dana Point**
Kesselhaut, Arthur Melvyn *financial consultant*

**Del Mar**
Jeub, Michael Leonard *financial executive*

**Emeryville**
Chason, Lloyd Ralph *corporate educator*

**Encino**
Dor, Yoram *accountant, firm executive*
Fuld, Steven Alan *financial advisor, insurance specialist*

**Escondido**
Strong, James Thompson *management, security, human resources consultant*

**Fair Oaks**
Doyel, Cindy M. *controller*

**Fairfax**
Ackerman, Arlene Alice *accountant, business consultant, artist, writer*

**Fallbrook**
Freeman, Harry Lynwood *accountant*

**Foster City**
MacNaughton, Angus Athole *finance company executive*
Paterson, Richard Denis *financial executive*

**Fountain Valley**
Penderghast, Thomas Frederick *business educator*

**Fresno**
Emrick, Terry Lamar *financial business consultant*
Pinkerton, Richard LaDoyt *management educator*
Shanafelt, Nancy Sue *quality consultant, career consultant*
Tellier, Richard Davis *management educator*

**Fullerton**
Oh, Tai Keun *business educator*

**Glendale**
Tookey, Robert Clarence *consulting actuary*
Tripoli, Masumi Hiroyasu *financial consultant and diplomat*

**Glendora**
Christofi, Andreas Charalambos *finance educator*

**Hayward**
Kam, Vernon Tam Siu *accounting educator*

**Irvine**
Feldstein, Paul Joseph *management educator*
Finestone, Sandra Agnes *accountant*
Olofson, Roy Leonard *retail executive*

**La Jolla**
Dorsey, Dolores Florence *corporate treasurer, business executive*
Purdy, Kevin M. *estate planner*

**La Mesa**
Bailey, Brenda Marie *accountant*

**Lafayette**
Yarlagadda, Rambabu Venkata *financial manager*

**Laguna Beach**
Garfin, Louis *actuary*
Indiek, Victor Henry *finance corporation executive*
Warner, Robert S. *company director, former accountant*

**Lake Sherwood**
Pollak, Norman L. *retired accountant*

**Long Beach**
Lewis, Ralph Jay, III *management and human resources educator*
Metzger, Vernon Arthur *management educator, consultant*
Valek, Bernard Michael *accounting executive*
Walker, Linda Ann *financial planner*

**Los Altos**
Halverson, George Clarence *business administration educator*
Hinckley, Gregory Keith *financial executive*

**Los Angeles**
Bennis, Warren Gameliel *business administration educator, author, consultant*
Borsting, Jack Raymond *business administration educator*
Broad, Eli *financial services executive*
Chan, David Ronald *tax specialist*
Chavez, Albert Blas *financial executive*
Cohen, William Alan *marketing educator, author, consultant*
Coombs, John Wendell *financial service executive*
Engler, George Nichols *financial consultant, educator*
Frisch, Robert A. *financial planning company executive*
Gooch, Lawrence Boyd *accounting executive*
Hein, Leonard William *accounting educator*
Knapp, Cleon Talboys *business executive*
Larson, Karin Louise *financial analyst*
Meloan, Taylor Wells *marketing educator*
Mock, Theodore Jaye *accounting educator*
Morrison, Donald Graham *business educator, consultant*
Morrow, Winston Vaughan *financial executive*
Mosich, Anelis Nick *accountant, author, educator, consultant*
Ross, Stan *accounting firm executive*
Roussey, Robert Stanley *accountant, educator*
Stancill, James McNeill *finance educator, consultant*
Weston, John Frederick *business educator, consultant*
Williams, Julie Ford *mutual fund officer*

**Malibu**
Baskin, Otis Wayne *business educator*
Yates, Jere Eugene *business educator, management consultant*

**Manhattan Beach**
Anderson, Charles Michael *accountant*

**Menlo Park**
Love, Amy Dundon *business executive, marketing and sales executive*
McDonald, Warren George *accountant, former savings and loan executive*
Wolfson, Mark Alan *investor, business educator*

**Mill Valley**
Isslieb, Lutz *finance company executive*

**Mission Viejo**
Rodrigues, Mark *financial executive, manpower consultant*

**Modesto**
Dunbar, Sharon Kay *controller, accountant*

**Montebello**
Orr, Stanley Chi-Hung *financial executive*

**Monterey Park**
Tseng, Felix Hing-Fai *accountant*

**Mountain View**
North, Daniel Warner *consulting analyst*

**Napa**
Harrison, E(rnest) Frank(lin) *management educator, consultant, author, former university president and chancellor*
Schunke, Hildegard Heidel *accountant*

**Newbury Park**
Kocen, Lorraine Ayral *accountant*

**Newport Beach**
Harris, Brent Richard *investment company executive*
Masotti, Louis Henry *management educator, consultant*
Mc Guire, Joseph William *business educator*
Panetti, Ramon Stanley *investment company executive, consultant, lawyer*
Plat, Richard Vertin *corporate finance executive*
Tracy, James Jared, Jr. *accountant, law firm administrator*
Wood, George H. *investment executive*

**North Hollywood**
Baker, Richard Eugene *controller, corporate executive*
Boulanger, Donald Richard *financial services executive*

**Northridge**
Lehtihalme, Larry (Lauri) K. *financial planner*

**Oakland**
Barlow, William Pusey, Jr. *accountant*
Helvey, Julius Louis, II *finance company executive*
Lee, Jong Hyuk *accountant*
Schwyn, Charles Edward *accountant*
Tyndall, David Gordon *business educator*

**Oceanside**
McIntyre, Louise S. *income tax consultant*

**Orange**
Peralta, Joseph Soriano *financial planner*

**Palo Alto**
Herrick, Tracy Grant *fiduciary*
Ivy, Benjamin Franklin, III *financial and real estate investment advisor*

**Pasadena**
Axelson, Charles Frederic *retired accounting educator*
Caldwell, William Mackay, III *business executive*

**Petaluma**
Cuggino, Michael Joseph *financial executive*

**Piedmont**
Cole, Peter William *financial executive*

**Pleasant Hill**
Marshall, Carol Sydney *labor market analyst, employment counselor*

**Pollock Pines**
Johnson, Stanford Leland *marketing educator*

**Pomona**
Patten, Thomas Henry, Jr. *management, human resources educator*
†Swartz, James Eugene *international business educator, army officer*

**Redlands**
Barnes, A. Keith *management educator*

**Redwood City**
Eaton, Mark Rayner *financial executive*
Elkus, Richard J. *finance and industrial company executive*
Larson, Mark Allan *financial executive*

**Riverside**
Harrison, Ethel Mae *financial executive*

**Salinas**
Stevens, Wilbur Hunt *accountant*

**San Diego**
Bateman, Giles Hirst Litton *finance executive*
Brimble, Alan *business executive*
Bruggeman, Terrance John *financial corporate executive*
Gee, Roger Allan *accounting educator, writer*
Markowitz, Harry M. *finance and economics educator*
Pierson, Albert Chadwick *business management educator*
Riedy, Mark Joseph *finance educator*
Tennent, Valentine Leslie *accountant*
West, James Harold *accounting company executive*

**San Francisco**
Buckner, John Knowles *pension administrator*
Carniglia, Stephen Davis *accountant, real estate consultant, lawyer*
Duff, James George *financial services executive*
Entriken, Robert Kersey *management educator*
Fuller, James William *financial director*
Gruber, George Michael *accountant, business management and financial systems consultant*
Hallstrom, Robert Chris *government actuary*
Herringer, Frank Casper *diversified financial services company executive*
Jimenez, Josephine Santos *portfolio manager*
Kahn, Paul Markham *actuary*
Kuhns, Craig Shaffer *business educator*
Maginn, Stephen Arthur *financial company executive*
Mayer, Patricia Jayne *financial officer, management accountant*
Mumford, Christopher Greene *corporate financial executive*
Nord, Paul Elliott *accountant*
O'Toole, James Joseph *business educator*
Palmer, William Joseph *accountant*
Peterson, Harries-Clichy *financial adviser*
Quiban, Estelita Cabrera *controller*
Simini, Joseph Peter *accountant, financial consultant, author, former educator*
Trone, Donald Burnell *investment company executive*
Uri, George Wolfsohn *accountant*
Weihrich, Heinz *management educator*

**San Gabriel**
Tadian, Luanne F. B. *financial analyst, consultant, researcher*

**San Jose**
Delucchi, George Paul *accountant*
Kertz, Marsha Helene *accountant, educator*
Smith, David Eugene *business administration educator*

**San Mateo**
Hopkins, Cecilia Ann *business educator*
Johnson, Charles Bartlett *mutual fund executive*
†Johnson, Rupert Harris, Jr. *finance company executive*

**San Rafael**
Heller, H(einz) Robert *financial executive*
Purcell, Stuart McLeod, III *financial planner*

**Santa Ana**
Pratt, Paul Bernard *financial services executive*

**Santa Barbara**
Mehra, Rajnish *finance educator*

**Santa Clara**
Beebe, Naomi Marie *financial consultant, accountant*
Martin, Joseph Robert *financial executive*

**Santa Monica**
Markoff, Steven C. *finance company executive*
Taylor, Nigel Brian *financial planner*

**Sherman Oaks**
Tsiros, John Andreas *accountant*

**Simi Valley**
Rehart, Margaret Lee *controller*

**Stanford**
Beaver, William Henry *accounting educator*
Holloway, Charles Arthur *public and private management educator*
Horngren, Charles Thomas *accounting educator*
Leavitt, Harold Jack *management educator*
Martin, Joanne *business educator*
McDonald, John Gregory *financial investment educator*
Miller, James Rumrill, III *finance educator*
Montgomery, David Bruce *marketing educator*
Pfeffer, Jeffrey *business educator*
Porterfield, James Temple Starke *business administration educator*
Saloner, Garth *management educator*
Serbein, Oscar Nicholas *business educator, consultant*

**Stockton**
Vargo, Richard Joseph *accounting educator, writer*

**Torrance**
Young, Aline Patrice *controller*

**Upland**
Jones, Nancy Langdon *financial planning practitioner*

**Ventura**
Cammalleri, Joseph Anthony *financial planner, retired air force officer*

**Vista**
Ferguson, Margaret Ann *tax consultant*
Helmuth, Philip Alan *tax consultant*

**Walnut Creek**
Hamilton, Allen Philip *financial advisor*
McCauley, Bruce Gordon *financial consultant*
Midanek, Deborah Hicks *portfolio manager, director*

**West Hollywood**
Santillan, Antonio *financial company executive*

**Westlake Village**
Robison, Frederick Mason *financial executive*

**Whittier**
Maxwell, Raymond Roger *accountant*

**Willits**
Akins, George Charles *accountant*

**Woodland Hills**
Anaya, Richard Alfred, Jr. *accountant, investment banker*
Harmon, David *finance company executive*
Labbett, John Edgar *senior financial executive*
Taubitz, Fredricka *financial executive*

## COLORADO

**Boulder**
Bangs, F(rank) Kendrick *former business educator*
Baughn, William Hubert *former business educator and academic administrator*
Buchanan, Dodds Ireton *business educator, consultant*
Goeldner, Charles Raymond *business educator*
Mason, Leon Verne *financial planner*
Melicher, Ronald William *finance educator*
Richardson, Donn Charles *business and marketing educator*
Stanton, William John, Jr. *marketing educator, author*

**Castle Rock**
Eppler, Jerome Cannon *private financial advisor*

**Colorado Springs**
Bressan, Robert R. *accountant*
Peiser, Robert Alan *financial executive*

**Columbine Valley**
Wittbrodt, Edwin Stanley *consultant, former bank executive, former air force officer*

**Denver**
Clark, Suzanne *accountant*
Cook, Albert Thomas Thornton, Jr. *financial advisor*
Herz, Leonard *financial consultant*
Lee, Kate Leary *financial adviser*
Sandler, Thomas R. *accountant*
Sullivan, Claire Ferguson *marketing educator*

**Englewood**
Bondi, Bert Roger *accountant, financial planner*
Sprincz, Keith Steven *financial services company professional*

**Fort Collins**
Ewing, Jack Robert *accountant*

**Greenwood Village**
Barnard, Rollin Dwight *retired financial executive*

**Jefferson**
Maatsch, Deborah Joan *former paralegal, tax specialist, tax advisor, controller*

**Lakewood**
Finnie, Doris Gould *investment company executive*
Keller, Shirley Inez *accountant*

**Littleton**
Bass, Charles Morris *financial and systems consultant*
Hadley, Marlin LeRoy *direct sales financial consultant*
Snyder, William Harry *financial advisor*

**Niwot**
Sliker, Todd Richard *accountant, lawyer*

**Wheat Ridge**
Gerlick, Helen J. *tax practitioner, accountant*

## CONNECTICUT

**Bridgeport**
Marcus, Norman *tax and financial consultant*
Watson, David Scott *financial services executive*

**Bristol**
Jabs, Jennifer *financial planner*

**Danbury**
Bailey, Robert Elliott *financial executive*
Goldstein, Joel *management science educator, researcher*
Proctor, Richard Jerome, Jr. *business educator, accountant, expert witness*

**Darien**
Nava, Eloy Luis *financial consultant*
Owen, Robert Vaughan *financial company executive*

Schell, James Munson *financial executive*

**East Hartford**
Barredo, Rita M. *auditor*

**Fairfield**
Golub, Stephen Bruce *accountant, consultant, educator*
Leask, John McPhearson, II *accountant*
McCain, Arthur Williamson, Jr. *retired pension investment consultant*

**Farmington**
Rabuska, Michèle Joanne *valuation analyst*

**Greenwich**
Glick, Steven Lawrence *financial consultant*
Higgins, Jay Francis *financial service executive*
Horton, Jared Churchill *retired corporation executive*
Howard, John Arnold *marketing educator*
Loh, Arthur Tsung Yuan *finance company executive*
Maroni, Paul L. *finance executive*
McLaughlin, Michael John *financial executive*
Miles, Jesse Mc Lane *retired accounting company executive*
Moonie, Clyde Wickliffe *financial consultant*
Moskowitz, Stanley Alan *financial executive*
Smith, Rodger Field *financial executive*

**Hamden**
Tomasko, Edward A. *financial planner*

**Hartford**
Centofanti, Joseph *accountant*
Generas, George Paul, Jr. *finance educator, lawyer*
Kramer, Karen Lee Van Brunt *business administration educator*
Mason, George Henry *business educator, consultant*

**New Canaan**
Flaschen, Joyce Davies *business consultant*

**New Haven**
Abdelsayed, Wafeek Hakim *accounting educator*
French, Kenneth Ronald *finance educator*
Fried, Charles A. *accountant, financial executive*
Malkin, Moses Montefiore *employee benefits administration company executive*
Vroom, Victor Harold *management consultant, educator*

**North Stonington**
Nolf, David Manstan *financial executive*

**Norwalk**
Foster, John McNeely *accounting standards executive*
Mueller, Gerhard G(ottlob) *financial accounting standard setter*
Schmalzried, Marvin Eugene *financial consultant*

**Riverside**
Lupia, David Thomas *corporate financial advisor, management consultant*

**Stamford**
Fillet, Mitchell Harris *financial services executive*
Frank, Charles Raphael, Jr. *financial executive*
Godfrey, Robert R. *financial services executive*
James, John Whitaker, Sr. *financial services executive*
Jason, J. Julie *money manager, author, lawyer*
Marsden, Charles Joseph *financial executive*
McNear, Barbara Baxter *financial communications executive, consultant*
Morgan, William J. *accounting company executive*
Norman, Geoffrey Robert *financial executive*
Pansini, Michael Samuel *tax and financial consultant*
Pollack, Gerald J. *financial executive*
Popelyukhin, Aleksey *actuary, researcher*
Siegel, Arthur Herbert *accounting company executive*
Wendt, Gary Carl *finance company executive*

**Stonington**
Rees, Charles H. G. *retired financial officer, investor, consultant*

**Thompson**
Fisher, William Thomas *business administration educator*

**Torrington**
Adorno, Monica S. *taxpayer representative*

**Westport**
Deese, James LaMotte *financial executive*
Ready, Robert James *financial company executive*

**Wilton**
Billings, Edward Robert *accountant*
Campbell, Robert Ayerst *accounting company executive*
Cook, Jay Michael *accounting company executive*
Kangas, Edward A. *accounting firm executive*

**DELAWARE**

**Claymont**
Doto, Paul Jerome *accountant*

**Wilmington**
Caspersen, Finn Michael Westby *diversified financial services company executive*
Rogoski, Patricia Diana *financial executive*
Schofield, Paul Michael *finance company executive*

**DISTRICT OF COLUMBIA**

**Washington**
Allbritton, Joe Lewis *diversified holding company executive*
†Armstrong, Alexandra *financial advisor*
Arnold, G. Dewey, Jr. *accountant*
Arundel, John Howard *financial consultant*
Byron, William James *management educator, former university president*
Campbell, Ruth Ann *budget analyst*

---

Dacey, Robert Frank *accountant, executive*
De La Torre-Leano, Jose Adolfo *financial advisor, lawyer*
de Saint Phalle, Thibaut *investment banker, educator, lawyer, financial consultant*
Droms, William George *finance educator*
Edwards, Bert Tvedt *accountant*
Fischetti, Michael Joseph *accounting educator*
Frankel, Michael Henry *accountant, lawyer*
Gordon, Arnold Barry *tax specialist*
Hough, Lawrence A. *financial organization executive*
Johnson, James A. *financial organization executive*
Kanter, Arnold Lee *policy analyst*
Larsen, Richard Gary *accounting firm executive*
Levy, Michael B. *business educator*
Litke, Arthur Ludwig *business executive*
MacLaury, Bruce King *research institution executive*
Malek, Frederic Vincent *finance company executive*
Masri, Jane Martyn *finance and operations administrator*
Mosso, David *accountant*
Nason, Charles Tuckey *financial services executive*
O'Leary, Kathleen A. *financial advisor, legal assistant*
Page, Harry Robert *business administration educator*
Parrish, Edgar Lee *financial services executive*
Seale, William Edward *finance educator*
Silver, David *financial executive, lawyer*
Slate, Martin Ira *pension benefit executive*
Stowe, Alexis Mariani *accountant, consultant*
Taylor, David Kerr *international business educator, consultant*
Tuggle, Francis Douglas *management educator*
Walker, David A(lan) *finance educator*
Wesberry, James Pickett, Jr. *financial management consultant, auditor, international organization executive*
West, E. Joseph *financial analyst, investment portfolio manager*

**FLORIDA**

**Apopka**
Rufenacht, Roger Allen *accounting educator*

**Arcadia**
Davis, Bruce Livingston, Jr. *retired accountant*

**Aventura**
Kliger, Milton Richard *financial services executive*

**Boca Raton**
Jaffe, Leonard Sigmund *financial executive*
Jessup, Joe Lee *business educator, management consultant*
Kelley, Eugene John *business educator*
Nolan, Lone Kirsten *financial advisor*
Shane, Ronald *financial company executive*
Sigel, Marshall Elliot *financial consultant*

**Boynton Beach**
Bartholomew, Arthur Peck, Jr. *accountant*

**Clearwater**
Jenkins, Linda Diane *accountant*
Leeds, Robert Lewis, Jr. *marketing and management educator*
Loos, Randolph Meade *financial planner*
Pendleton, Sumner Alden *financial consultant*

**Coral Gables**
Lampert, Wayne Morris *corporate financier*

**Coral Springs**
Luing, Gary Alan *financial management educator*
Sommerer, John *accountant*

**Deland**
Horton, Thomas R. *business advisor*

**Delray Beach**
Bryan, Robert Fessler *former investment analyst*
Gatewood, Robert Payne *financial planning executive*

**Englewood**
Defliese, Philip Leroy *accountant, educator*

**Fort Lauderdale**
Bamberg, Louis Mark *estate planning specialist*
Becker, Edward A. *accounting educator, consultant*
†Cobb, David Keith *business executive*
Holtzman, Gary Yale *administrative and financial executive*
Pohlman, Randolph A. *business administration educator, dean*
Shoemaker, William Edward *financial executive*

**Gainesville**
Stone, Williard Everard *accountant, educator*

**Gotha**
Powell, Thomas Ervin *consultant, accountant, small business owner*

**Hallandale**
Boyce, Henry Worth, III *portfolio manager, financial consultant*

**Hernando**
Bell, Philip Wilkes *accounting and economics educator*

**Hialeah**
Shaw, Steven John *retired marketing educator, academic administrator*

**Hobe Sound**
Vanderbilt, Oliver Degray *financier*

**Hollywood**
Harkin, Daniel John *controller*
Sim, Robert Wilson *accountant*

**Jacksonville**
Edwards, Marvin Raymond *investment counselor, economic consultant*
Febel, Joel William *mergers and acquisitions intermediary executive, international consultant*

---

Lindner, Carl Henry, Jr. *financial holding company executive*
Tomlinson, William Holmes *management educator, retired army officer*
Vane, Terence G., Jr. *finance and insurance company executive, lawyer*

**Jupiter**
Danforth, Arthur Edwards *finance executive*

**Lake Worth**
Lineberry, Sandra Beech *accountant*

**Lighthouse Point**
Shein, Jay Lesing *financial planner*

**Longwood**
Smith, Barry Merton *financial planner, consultant*

**Melbourne**
Canfield, Constance Dale *accountant, nurse*
Roub, Bryan R(oger) *financial executive*
Suojanen, Waino W. *management educator*

**Miami**
Berkman, Harold William *marketing educator*
Capraro, Franz *accountant*
Coton, Carlos David *finance manager*
Dahlfues, Donald Michael *accountant*
Ehrlich, Morton *international finance executive*
Esteves, Vernon Xavier *financial consultant, investment advisor*
Garcia, Isa *accountant*
Hendrickson, Harvey Sigbert *accounting educator*
Hodgetts, Richard Michael *business management educator*
Kregg, Judith Lynne *accountant*
Pomeranz, Felix *accounting educator*
Satuloff, Barth *accounting executive, dispute resolution professional*
Wolper, Marshall *insurance and financial consultant*

**Miami Lakes**
Weldon, Norman Ross *financial company executive*

**Naples**
Fess, Philip Eugene *accountant, educator*
Handy, Charles Brooks *accountant, educator*
Ordway, John Danton *retired pension administrator, lawyer, accountant*
Thomas, Gary Lynn *financial executive*
Weeks, Richard Ralph *marketing educator*

**New Smyrna Beach**
Thomson, John Christian *financial analyst, portfolio manager*

**Nokomis**
Meyerhoff, Jack Fulton *financial executive*

**North Miami Beach**
Fishel, Peter Livingston *accounting business executive*

**North Palm Beach**
Frevert, James Wilmot *financial planner, investment advisor*

**Ocala**
Clayton, Robert Beville *insurance and financial services professional*

**Orlando**
Abbott, Edward Leroy *finance executive*
Armacost, Robert Leo *management educator*
Gray, Anthony Rollin *capital management company executive*
Martin, William Robert *accountant*
Pelton, Charles R. *financial institution executive*
Van Sickle, Paul Brunton *financial executive*

**Palm Beach**
Barness, Amnon Shemaya *financial service executive*
Bishop, Warner Bader *finance company executive*
Cook, Edward Willingham *diversified industry executive*
Fitilis, Theodore Nicholas *portfolio manager*
Robertson, Sara Stewart *portfolio manager*

**Palm Beach Gardens**
Herrick, John Dennis *financial consultant, former law firm executive, retired food products executive*

**Panama City**
Miller, Robert William *personal property appraiser, writer*

**Plantation**
Garrett, Linda Silverstein *financial planner*
Tobias, Benjamin Alan *portfolio manager, financial planner*

**Pompano Beach**
Heir, Kal M. *financial executive*
Mulvey, John Thomas, Jr. *financial consultant*

**Punta Gorda**
Bulzacchelli, John G. *financial executive*

**Saint Petersburg**
Blumenthal, Herman Bertram *accountant*
Freeman, Corinne *financial services, former mayor*
†McMurray, Joseph Patrick Brendan *financial consultant*
Putnam, J. Stephen *financial executive*
Shuck, Robert F. *financial executive*
Wasserman, Susan Valesky *accountant*

**Sarasota**
Arreola, John Bradley *diversified financial service company executive, financial planner*
Lambert, John Phillip *financial executive, consultant*
Miles, Arthur J. *financial planner, consultant*
Pesut, Timothy S. *investment advisor, professional speaker, consultant*
Vestal, Lucian LaRoe *financier*

**Stuart**
O'Connor, Francis X. *financial executive*

---

White, Donald Francis *financial planner, insurance agent*

**Tallahassee**
Anthony, William Philip *management educator*

**Tampa**
Alexander, William Olin *finance company executive*
Hanford, Agnes Rutledge *financial adviser*
Hernandez, Gilberto Juan *accountant, auditor, management consultant*
Holder, Anna Maria *holding company executive*
Nord, Walter Robert *business administration educator, researcher, consultant*

**Tarpon Springs**
Hubbs, Arden Perry, II *financial services company executive, consultant*

**Venice**
Buckley, John William *financial company executive*

**Vero Beach**
Conway, Earl Cranston *business educator, retired manufacturing company executive*
Fetter, Robert Barclay *retired administrative sciences educator*
Koontz, Alfred Joseph, Jr. *financial and operating management executive, consultant*
Riefler, Donald Brown *financial consultant*

**Wesley Chapel**
Mendelsohn, Louis Benjamin *financial analyst*

**West Palm Beach**
Eppley, Roland Raymond, Jr. *retired financial services executive*
Livingstone, John Leslie *accountant, management consultant, business economist, educator*

**Winter Haven**
Goodman, Karen Lacerte *financial services executive*

**Winter Park**
Plane, Donald Ray *management science educator*
Richards, Max De Voe *management educator, consultant, researcher, author*
Rogers, Donald Patrick *business administration educator*
Starr, Martin Kenneth *management educator*

**GEORGIA**

**Alpharetta**
Zimmermann, John *financial consultant*

**Athens**
Bamber, Linda Smith *accounting educator*
Miller, Herbert Elmer *accountant*
Zinkhan, George Martin, III *marketing educator*

**Atlanta**
Assunto, Richard Anthony *payroll executive*
Baxter, Arthur Pearce *financial services marketing company executive*
Benston, George James *accountant, economist*
Dykes, John Henry, Jr. *retired finance executive*
Frank, Ronald Edward *marketing educator*
Hanna, Frank Joseph *credit company executive*
Hawkins, Robert Garvin *management educator, consultant*
Henry, William Ray *business administration educator*
Hiller, George Mew *financial advisor, investment manager, lawyer*
Hites, Becky E. *financial executive*
Jones, Dorothy Clement *accountant*
Lobb, William Atkinson *financial services executive*
Manners, George Emanuel *business educator, emeritus dean*
Nelson, Robert Earl, Jr. *financial services company executive*
Parsons, Leonard Jon *marketing educator, consultant*
Seto, William Roderick *public accounting company executive*
Sheth, Jagdish Nanchand *business administration educator*
Stubbs, Thomas Hubert *company executive*
Walker, David Michael *human capital consultant, accountant*
Whittington, Frederick Brown, Jr. *business administration educator*
Winter, Wilburn Jackson, Jr. *financial executive*

**Augusta**
Powell, James Kevin *financial planner*

**College Park**
Williams, Mattie Pearl *accounting educator*

**Dalton**
Winter, Larry Eugene *accountant*

**Decatur**
Hollis, Charles Eugene, Jr. *accountant, financial consultant*
Myers, Clark Everett *retired business administration educator*
Rodgers, Richard Malcolm *management accountant*

**Duluth**
Rogers, William Brookins *financial consultant, business appraiser*

**Kennesaw**
Aronoff, Craig Ellis *management educator, consultant*

**Lula**
Suggs, Josephine Greenway *controller*

**Marietta**
Kiger, Ronald Lee *price analyst*
North, John Adna, Jr. *accountant, real estate appraiser*
O'Haren, Thomas Joseph *financial services executive*

**Milledgeville**
Engerrand, Doris Dieskow *business educator*

**Norcross**
Wagner, Harvey Alan *finance executive*

**Riverdale**
Minter, Jimmie Ruth *accountant*

**Roswell**
Richkin, Barry Elliott *financial services executive*

**Savannah**
Sortor, Harold Edward *financial executive*

**Statesboro**
Murkison, Eugene Cox *business educator*

**Suwanee**
Harvey, Rebecca Suzanne *accountant, business analyst*

**Washington**
Mansfield, Norman Connie *bookkeeper*

**Watkinsville**
Tate, Curtis E. *management educator*

**Woodstock**
Austin, John David *financial executive*

## HAWAII

**Honolulu**
Betts, James William, Jr. *financial analyst*
Cassiday, Paul Richard *estate administrator*
Hook, Ralph Clifford, Jr. *business educator*
Palia, Aspy Phiroze *marketing educator, researcher, consultant*
Solidum, James *finance and insurance executive*
Sterrett, James Melville *accountant, business consultant*

**Laie**
Bradshaw, James R. *business educator*

## IDAHO

**Boise**
Mock, Stanley Clyde *financial planner, investment advisor*
Pomeroy, Horace Burton, III *accountant, corporate executive*

**Burley**
Westfall, Stephen Donald *accountant, small business owner*

**Caldwell**
Allen, Edward Raymond *retired business educator, accountant*

## ILLINOIS

**Aurora**
Halloran, Kathleen L. *financial executive, accountant*

**Belleville**
Fietsam, Robert Charles *accountant*

**Bloomington**
Friedman, Joan M. *accounting educator*

**Buffalo Grove**
Johnson, Craig Theodore *portfolio manager*

**Calumet City**
Edwards, James Clifford *finance company executive*

**Carbondale**
Vance, David Alvin *management educator*
Wills, Walter Joe *agricultural marketing educator*

**Champaign**
Bailey, Andrew Dewey, Jr. *accounting educator*
Brighton, Gerald David *accounting educator*
Neumann, Frederick Loomis *accounting educator, academic administrator, consultant*
Perry, Kenneth Wilbur *accounting educator*
Schoenfeld, Hanns-Martin Walter *accounting educator*
Spice, Dennis Dean *investment banking and financial consultant*

**Chicago**
Aguilera, Gloria Patricia *financial executive*
Almeida, Richard Joseph *finance company administrator*
Bell, Jason Cameron *accountant*
Bott, Harold Sheldon *accountant, management consultant*
Bryan, William Royal *finance educator*
Caccamo, Nicholas James *financial executive*
Chapman, Alger Baldwin *finance executive, lawyer*
Chlebowski, John Francis, Jr. *financial executive*
Chookaszian, Dennis Haig *financial executive*
Eppen, Gary Dean *business educator*
Fensin, Daniel *diversified financial service company executive*
Fiorentino, Leon Francis *holding company executive*
Fitzgerald, Robert Maurice *financial executive*
Fleming, Richard H. *finance executive*
Forbes, John Edward *financial consultant*
Garrigan, Richard Thomas *finance educator, consultant, editor*
Hanna, James Leanord *financial consultant*
Hansen, Claire V. *financial executive*
Harding, James Warren *finance company executive*
Hassan, M. Zia *management educator*
Hicks, Cadmus Metcalf, Jr. *financial analyst*
Hogarth, Robin Miles *business educator, university official*
Kleckner, Robert A. *accounting firm executive*
Krupnik, Vee M. *financial company executive*

Kudish, David J. *financial executive*
Kullberg, Duane Reuben *accounting firm executive*
Lindskog, Norbert F. *business and health administration educator, consultant*
Longman, Gary Lee *accountant*
Lorie, James Hirsch *business administration educator*
Lyman, Arthur Joseph *financial executive*
Mallory, Robert Mark *controller, finance executive*
Masek, Barry Michael *accountant*
Mayer, Raymond Richard *business administration educator*
McCormack, Robert Cornelius *investment banker*
Moor, Roy Edward *finance educator*
Morisato, Susan Cay *actuary*
Nason, Robert E. *accountant*
Neuhausen, Benjamin Simon *auditor, accountant*
O'Connell, Edward Joseph, III *financial executive, accountant*
Rachwalski, Frank Joseph, Jr. *financial executive*
Reiss, Dale Anne *accounting executive*
Rigsbee, Stephen Reese *risk management executive*
Rosenbaum, Michael A. *investor relations consultant*
Schornack, John James *accountant*
Smith, Freddye L(ee) *financial planner*
Stelzel, Walter Tell, Jr. *accountant, financial company executive*
Sullivan, Bernard James *accountant*
Thornton, Theodore Kean *investment advisor*
Timbers, Stephen Bryan *financial services company executive*
Velisaris, Chris Nicholas *financial analyst*
Verbockel Rogers, Jolene Mary *auditor*
Verschoor, Curtis Carl *business educator, consultant*
Ward, James Frank *pension fund administrator*
Weil, Roman Lee *accounting educator*
Wishner, Maynard Ira *finance company executive, lawyer*
Yacktman, Donald Arthur *financial executive, investment counselor*
Zimmerman, Martin E. *financial executive*

**Crestwood**
Cowie, Norman Edwin *credit manager*

**Crystal Lake**
Haas, Jonathan Stuart *financial company executive*

**De Kalb**
Hanna, Nessim *marketing educator*

**Decatur**
Decker, Charles Richard *business educator*

**Deerfield**
Boyd, Joseph Don *financial services executive*
Chromizky, William Rudolph *accountant*
Fulrath, Andrew Wesley *financial planner, charitable gift planner*
Heiman, Marvin Stewart *financial services company executive*
Kessler, Paula Gail *controller*
Russell, William Steven *finance executive*

**Dolton**
Lucas, Patricia Lynn *financial executive*

**Elgin**
Wiese, Dorothy Jean *business educator*

**Elk Grove Village**
Bandel, David Brian *accountant*
Epstein, Stephen Roger *financial executive*

**Evanston**
Cassell, Frank Hyde *business educator*
Catlett, George Roudebush *accountant*
Corey, Gordon Richard *financial advisor, former utilities executive*
Duncan, Robert Bannerman *strategy and organizations educator*
Jacobs, Donald P. *banking and finance educator*
Lavengood, Lawrence Gene *management educator, historian*
Meyer, Stuart Lloyd *management educator*
Prince, Thomas Richard *accountant, educator*
Revsine, Lawrence *accounting educator, consultant*
Scott, Walter Dill *management educator*
Stern, Louis William *marketing educator, consultant*

**Evergreen Park**
Bak, Diann Lee *accountant*

**Gays**
Finley, Gary Roger *financial company executive*

**Geneva**
Young, Jack Allison *financial executive*

**Glen Ellyn**
Drafke, Michael Walter *business educator, consultant*

**Glencoe**
Lifschultz, Phillip *financial and tax consultant, accountant, lawyer*

**Hanover Park**
Gale, Neil Jan *finance company executive, computer consultant*

**Hinsdale**
Urbik, Jerome Anthony *financial consultant*

**La Grange**
Norby, William Charles *financial consultant*

**Lake Forest**
Reichert, Norman Vernon *financial services consultant*
Van Gorkom, Jerome William *financial executive*

**Lincolnshire**
Pappano, Robert Daniel *financial company executive*

**Lombard**
Williams, Ronald Boal, Jr. *financial consulting company executive, software designer, consultant*

**Loves Park**
Zaksheske, Mark Richard *treasurer*

**Mount Prospect**
Zorko, Mark A. *financial executive*

**Naperville**
Tan, Li-Su Lin *accountant, insurance executive*

**Northbrook**
Afterman, Allan B. *accountant, educator, researcher, consultant*
Hill, Thomas Clarke, IX *accountant, systems specialist, entrepreneur*
Newman, Lawrence William *financial executive*
Roehl, Kathleen Ann *financial executive*
Stearns, Neele Edward, Jr. *diversified holding company executive*

**Northfield**
Seaman, Jerome Francis *actuary*

**Oak Brook**
Stonich, Timothy Whitman *financial executive*

**Oakbrook Terrace**
Ciccarone, Richard Anthony *financial executive*

**Okawville**
Schmale, Allen Lee *financial services company executive*

**Palatine**
Butler, John Musgrave *business financial consultant*

**Riverdale**
Hoekwater, James Warren *treasurer*

**Riverside**
Perkins, William H., Jr. *finance company executive*

**Rock Island**
Kruse, Rosalee Evelyn *accountant, auditor*

**Rockford**
Albert, Christine Lynnette *accountant*
DeLuca, August Frank, Jr. *financial executive*
Schmerse, Traci Jo *financial services company executive*

**Rosemont**
Macioch, James Edward *investment consultant, financial planner*
Zorio, John William *financial services executive*

**Skokie**
Forman, Linda Helaine *accountant*

**Springfield**
Travis, Lawrence Allan *accountant*

**Tuscola**
Kirchhoff, Michael Kent *economic development executive*

**Urbana**
Bedford, Norton Moore *accounting educator*
Mayer, Robert Wallace *emeritus finance educator*

**Villa Park**
Tang, George Chickchee *financial consultant*

**Waukegan**
Schueppert, George Louis *financial executive*

**Wheaton**
Holman, James Lewis *financial and management consultant*

**Winnetka**
Bohne, Carl John, Jr. *accountant*

## INDIANA

**Beech Grove**
Clapper, George Raymond *accountant, computer consultant*

**Bloomington**
Belth, Joseph Morton *retired business educator*
DeHayes, Daniel Wesley *management executive, educator*
Dieterle, Donald Lyle *accountant, educator*
Gordon, Paul John *management educator*
Swanson, Robert Mclean *retired business educator*
Wentworth, Jack Roberts *business educator, consultant*

**Carmel**
Pickens, Robert Bruce *accountant*

**Columbus**
Berman, Lewis Paul *financial executive*
Kidwell, Mary F. *accountant*
Sales, A. R. *financial executive*

**Danville**
Wean, Blanche McNeely *accountant*

**Evansville**
Gaither, John Francis *accountant, consultant*
Luckett, John Mills, III *construction company financial executive*

**Fort Wayne**
Graf, Robert Arlan *financial services executive*

**Goshen**
Lehman, Karl Franklyn *accountant*

**Indianapolis**
Brinkerhoff, Tom J. *financial services executive*
Carey, Edward Marshel, Jr. *accounting company executive*
Fisher, Gene Lawrence *financial executive*
Furlow, Mack Vernon, Jr. *retired financial executive, treasurer*
Goodwin, William Maxwell *financial executive*

Isaac, Stanley Eugene *accountant*
Israelov, Rhoda *financial planner, writer, entrepreneur*
Kaufman, Barton Lowell *financial services company executive*
Khalil, Michael O. *actuary*
Long, Clarence William *accountant*
Ritz, Stephen Mark *financial advisor, lawyer*

**Notre Dame**
Bella, Salvatore Joseph *management educator*
Reilly, Frank Kelly *business educator*
Shannon, William Norman, III *marketing and international business educator, food service executive*
Vecchio, Robert Peter *business management educator*

**Portage**
Cunningham, R. John *retired financial consultant*

**South Bend**
Cohen, Ronald S. *accountant*
Harriman, Gerald Eugene *retired business administrator, economics educator*
Murphy, Christopher Joseph, III *financial executive*

**Terre Haute**
Carraher, Shawn Michael *management educator*

**West Lafayette**
Cooper, Arnold Cook *management educator, researcher*
Lewellen, Wilbur Garrett *management educator, consultant*

## IOWA

**Ankeny**
Boelens, Patricia Ann *accountant, nurse*

**Cedar Falls**
Greer, Willis Roswell, Jr. *accounting educator*

**Cedar Rapids**
Knapp, Barbara Allison *financial services, oncological nurse consultant*

**Davenport**
Brocka, M. Suzanne *controller*

**Iowa City**
Collins, Daniel W. *accountant, educator*
Riesz, Peter Charles *marketing educator, consultant*

**Keokuk**
Atterberg, Douglas Keith *financial planner*

**Muscatine**
Dvorchak, Thomas Edward *financial executive*
McMains, Melvin L(ee) *controller*

**Pacific Junction**
Krogstad, Jack Lynn *accounting educator*

**Sioux City**
Silverberg, David S. *financial consultant*

**Storm Lake**
Shafer, Everett Earl *business administration educator*

**Waterloo**
Taylor, Lyle Dewey *economic development company executive*

**West Des Moines**
Sather, Everett Norman *accountant*

## KANSAS

**Emporia**
Hashmi, Sajjad Ahmad *business educator, university dean*

**Lawrence**
Beedles, William LeRoy *finance educator, financial consultant*

**Lecompton**
Conard, John Joseph *financial official*

**Mc Pherson**
Hull, Robert Glenn *retired financial administrator*

**Shawnee**
Cashman, William Elliott *investment manager, consultant*

**Shawnee Mission**
Dyches, Kevin James *investment analyst*
Hechler, Robert Lee *financial services company executive*
Hoffman, Alfred John *retired mutual fund executive*

**Topeka**
McCandless, Barbara J. *auditor*
Miller, Gary Allen *financial planner*

## KENTUCKY

**Frankfort**
Hatchett, Edward Bryan, Jr. *auditor, lawyer*

**Goshen**
Mc Clinton, Donald G. *diversified holding company executive*

**Louisville**
Daulton, David Coleman *actuary*
Hampton, Martin Justus *financial planner*

## LOUISIANA

### Baton Rouge
Bedeian, Arthur George *business educator*
Booth, George Geoffrey *finance educator*
Crumbley, Donald Larry *accounting educator, writer, consultant*
D'Souza, Alan S. *tax consultant, real estate agent, pianist, writer*
Redman, Dale E. *diversified financial services company executive*

### Covington
Files, Mark Willard *business and financial consultant*

### Crowley
Martin, Edythe Louviere *business educator*

### Kenner
Scherich, Edward Baptiste *retired diversified company executive*

### Lafayette
Burnam, Paul Wayne *accountant, educator*
Castellini, Patricia Bennett *business management educator*

### Metairie
Janis, Donald Emil *corporate controller*
McShan, Clyde Griffin, II *financial executive*

### New Orleans
Fisk, Raymond Paul *marketing educator*
Hansel, Stephen Arthur *holding company executive*
Ingraham, Joseph Edwin *financial officer*
Wild, Dirk Jonathan *accountant*
Wright, Clifford Sidney *accounting educator*

### Pineville
Beall, Grace Carter *business educator*

### Ruston
Posey, Clyde Lee *business administration and accounting educator*

### Thibodaux
Delozier, Maynard Wayne *marketing educator*

## MAINE

### Bangor
Albrecht, Ronald Lewis *financial services executive*

### Friendship
MacIlvaine, Chalmers Acheson *retired financial executive, former association executive*

### Topsham
Palesky, Carol East *tax accountant*

## MARYLAND

### Baltimore
Ambler, Bruce Melville *finance company executive*
Beasley, Robert Scott *financial executive*
Blake, Norman Perkins, Jr. *finance company executive*
Colhoun, Howard Post *financial executive*
Cook, Joseph Daniel *finance executive, accountant*
Eanes, Joseph Cabel, Jr. *surety company executive*
Fontanazza, Franklin Joseph *accountant*
Gray, Dahli *accounting educator and administrator*
Hale, Danny Lyman *financial executive*
Jacobs, Richard James *banker, educator*
Killebrew, Robert Sterling, Jr. *investment manager*
Kues, Irvin William *health care financial executive*
Miller, Carl Frank *business appraiser*
Ourednik, Patricia Ann *accountant*
Quinn, Michael Desmond *diversified financial services executive*
Roupe, James Paul *accountant*
Smith, Robert Luther *management educator*
Tringali, Joseph *financial planner, accountant*

### Berlin
Howarth, Thomas *tax consultant*

### Bethesda
Castelli, Alexander Gerard *accountant*
Stroesenreuther, George Dale *financial executive*

### Bozman
Wyatt, Wilson Watkins, Jr. *finance association and public relations executive*

### College Park
Gordon, Lawrence Allan *accounting educator*
Kolodny, Richard *finance educator*
Lamone, Rudolph Philip *business educator*
Sims, Henry P., Jr. *management educator*

### Columbia
Hotchkies, Barry *financial executive*

### Elkridge
Calton, Sandra Jeane *accountant*

### Frederick
Orzechowski, Alice Louise *accountant*

### Frostburg
Groer, Connie Jean *accounting educator*

### Gaithersburg
†Johnson, George H. *financial services company executive*
Ruth, James Perry *financial planning executive*

### Hanover
Schmidt, Sandra Jean *financial analyst*

### Mitchellville
Hagans, Robert Reginald, Jr. *financial executive*

### Owings Mills
Leibtag, Bernard *accountant*

### Potomac
Gowda, Narasimhan Ramaiah *financial consultant*

### Rockville
Graff, Stuart Leslie *accounting executive*
Milan, Thomas Lawrence *accountant*

### Silver Spring
Abdelrahman, Talaat Ahmad Mohammad *financial executive*
Brodie, Norman *retired financial actuary*
Grubbs, Donald Shaw, Jr. *retired actuary*
Luo, Jessica Chaoying *actuary*
Moore, Shirley Throckmorton (Mrs. Elmer Lee Moore) *accountant*
Simon, Donald John *financial planner, insurance and investment broker*
Yasher, Michael *accountant*

### Upper Marlboro
McClelland, W. Clark *retail company financial executive*

### Woodstock
Price, John Roy, Jr. *financial executive*

### Wye Mills
Schnaitman, William Kenneth *finance company executive*

## MASSACHUSETTS

### Allston
Mills, Daniel Quinn *business educator, consultant, author*

### Bedford
Kouyoumjian, Charles H. *diversified financial services company executive*

### Belmont
Rich, Sharon Lee *financial planner*

### Boston
Akin, Steven Paul *financial company executive*
Baker, Charles Duane *business administration educator, former management executive*
Berg, Norman Asplund *management educator*
Bower, Joseph Lyon *business administration educator*
Boyd, David Preston *business educator*
Bruns, William John, Jr. *business administration educator*
Christensen, Carl Roland *business administration educator*
Christenson, Charles John *business educator*
Cohen, Daniel Booth *financial executive*
Crook, Robert Wayne *mutual funds executive*
D'Alessandro, David Francis *financial services company executive*
DiStasio, James Shannon *accountant*
Dooley, Arch Richard *retired business administration educator*
Eastman, Thomas George *investment management executive*
Elfner, Albert Henry, III *mutual fund management company executive*
Gifford, Nelson Sage *financial company executive*
Gould, James Spencer *financial consultant*
Hayes, Robert Herrick *technology management educator*
Hayes, Samuel Linton, III *business educator*
Hjerpe, Edward Alfred, III *finance and banking executive*
Johnson, Edward Crosby, III *financial company executive*
Kanter, Rosabeth Moss *management educator, consultant, writer*
Karelitz, Richard Alan *financial executive, lawyer*
Kingman, William Lockwood *financial consultant*
Lawrence, Paul Roger *retired organizational behavior educator*
Lee, Jonathan Owen *financial services company executive, lawyer*
Lodge, George C(abot) *business administration educator*
Lovett, Miller Currier *management educator, clergyman*
Marshall, Martin Vivan *business administration educator, business consultant*
Maxwell, J.B. *financial and marketing consultant*
McArthur, John Hector *business educator*
McCraw, Thomas Kincaid *business history educator, editor, author*
McFarlan, Franklin Warren *business administration educator*
Monaghan, William Edward, II *financial services company executive*
Park, William H(erron) *financial executive*
Pitts, James Atwater *financial executive*
Pratt, Albert *financial consultant, trustee*
Reiling, Henry Bernard *business educator*
Schnitzer, Iris Taymore *financial management executive, lawyer*
Silk, Alvin John *business educator*
Skinner, Wickham *business administration educator*
Sloane, Carl Stuart *business educator, management consultant*
Smith, Anders Downey *financial services company executive*
Stevenson, Howard Higginbotham *business educator*
Stobaugh, Robert Blair *business educator, business executive*
Temkin, Robert Harvey *accountant*
Toomey, Paula Kathleen *financial analyst, consultant*
Tucker, Richard Lee *financial executive*
Uyterhoeven, Hugo Emil Robert *business educator and consultant*
Vatter, Paul August *business administration educator, dean*
Walton, Richard Eugene *business educator*
Weiss, James Michael *financial analyst, portfolio manager*
Wheatland, Richard, II *fiduciary services executive, museum executive*
Young, David William *accounting educator*

### Brockton
Clark, Carleton Earl *tax consultant*

### Burlington
Pettinella, Nicholas Anthony *financial executive*
Scogno, Stacie Joy *financial services company executive*

### Cambridge
Deshpandé, Rohit *marketing educator*
Hauser, John Richard *marketing and management science educator*
Hax, Arnoldo Cubillos *management educator, industrial engineer*
Kelley, Albert Joseph *global management strategy consultant*
Leonard, Herman Beukema (Dutch Leonard) *public finance and management educator*
Little, John Dutton Conant *management scientist, educator*
Pounds, William Frank *management educator*
Safran, Edward Myron *financial service company executive*
Schein, Edgar Henry *management educator*
Scott Morton, Michael Stewart *business management educator*
Tofias, Allan *accountant*
Urban, Glen L. *management educator*

### Canton
Tockman, Ronald Chester *accountant*

### Chestnut Hill
Fouraker, Lawrence Edward *retired business administration educator*
Glynn, Arthur Lawrence *business administration and accounting educator*

### Concord
Smith, Peter Walker *finance executive*

### Dartmouth
Kahalas, Harvey *business educator*

### Everett
Jenkins, Alexander, III *financial business executive*

### Falmouth
Mitchell, Charles Archie *financial planning consultant, engineer*

### Foxboro
Bush, Raymond T. *accountant, corporate professional*

### Gloucester
Means, Elizabeth Rose Thayer *financial consultant, lawyer*

### Hingham
Hart, Richard Nevel, Jr. *financial exective, consultant*

### Hopkinton
McGuire, Frank Joseph *accountant*

### Hyannis Port
Ludtke, James Buren *business and finance educator*

### Lexington
Colburn, Kenneth Hersey *financial executive*
Deitcher, Herbert *financial executive*
Farb, Thomas Forest *financial executive*
Wyss, David Alen *financial service executive*

### Longmeadow
Skelton, Don Richard *consulting actuary, retired insurance company executive*

### Millbury
Noonan, Stephen Joseph *accounting firm executive*

### Monson
Krach, Mitchell Peter *retired financial services executive*

### Needham
Tarsky, Eugene Stanley *accountant, management and systems consultant*

### Peabody
Bernstein, Emil S. *financial executive*

### Randolph
Cammarata, Richard John *financial advisor*

### Salisbury
Camacho, Henry Francis *accountant*

### South Orleans
Hickok, Richard Sanford *accountant*

### South Yarmouth
Arthur, George Roland *accountant, engineer, mathematician*

### Southborough
Astill, Robert Michael *credit manager*

### Stoughton
Bestgen, William Henry, Jr. *financial planner*

### Sudbury
Meltzer, Donald Richard *treasurer*

### Waltham
Pantazelos, Peter George *financial executive*

### Wellesley
Klein, Lawrence Allen *accounting educator*
Papageorgiou, John Constantine *management science educator*

### Westborough
Drees, Stephen Daniel *financial services executive, strategy, marketing and product development consultant*

### Weston
Clayton, Richard Reese *holding company executive*
Ives, J. Atwood *financial executive*
Rockwell, George Barcus *financial consultant*
Valente, Louis Patrick (Dan Valente) *business and financial consultant*

### Wilmington
Bartlett, John Bruen *financial executive*
Hartford, Ann Marie *accountant, controller*

### Woburn
Caplitz, Gregg D. *financial planner*

### Worcester
Britt, Margaret Mary *financial services educator*
Greenberg, Nathan *accountant*

## MICHIGAN

### Ada
Van Andel, Steve Alan *business executive*

### Ann Arbor
Cornelius, Kenneth Cremer, Jr. *finance executive*
Crawford, Charles Merle *business administration educator*
Elger, William Robert, Jr. *accountant*
Foster, Alan Herbert *financial consultant*
Huntington, Curtis Edward *actuary*
Kim, E. Han *finance and business administration educator*
Pierpont, Wilbur K. *retired administrator, accounting educator*
Terpstra, Vern *marketing educator*
Warshaw, Martin Richard *marketing educator*

### Auburn Hills
Trebing, David Martin *corporate finance manager*

### Battle Creek
Dillard, Joan Helen *financial executive*

### Benton Harbor
LeBlanc, James E. *financial services company executive*

### Birmingham
McDonald, Alonzo Lowry, Jr. *business and financial executive*
Van Dyke-Cooper, Anny Marion *retired financial company executive*

### Bloomfield Hills
Gulati, Vipin *accountant*
Marks, Craig *management educator, consultant, engineer*
Poth, Stefan Michael *retired sales financing company executive*

### Dearborn
Jeffries Ashford, Alecia *accounting analyst*

### Detroit
Adams, William Johnston *financial and tax consultant*
Massura, Edward Anthony *accountant*

### East Lansing
Arens, Alvin Armond *accountant, educator*
Hollander, Stanley Charles *marketing educator*
Melnyk, Steven Alexander *business management educator*

### Farmington Hills
Fox, Dean Frederick *coporate executive*
Helppie, Charles Everett, III *financial consultant*
Michlin, Arnold Sidney *finance executive*

### Flint
Rappleye, Richard Kent *financial executive, consultant, educator*

### Grosse Pointe
Fromm, Joseph L. *financial consultant*
Nicholson, George Albert, Jr. *financial analyst*

### Holland
Zick, Leonard Otto *accountant, manufacturing executive, financial consultant*

### Lansing
DeHaven, Clark Edwin *business educator*
Feight, Theodore J. *financial planner*

### Livonia
McCuen, John Joachim *building company and financial company executive*

### Marquette
Camerius, James Walter *marketing educator, corporate researcher*

### Midland
Hall, David McKenzie *marketing and management educator*

### Monroe
Mlocek, Sister Frances Angeline *financial executive*

### Mount Pleasant
Zimmerman, Helene Loretta *business educator*

### Muskegon
Delong, Donald R. *accountant*

### Okemos
Oberg, Roger Winston *management educator*

### Plymouth
Garpow, James Edward *financial executive*

### Port Huron
Ragle, George Ann *accountant*

### Portage
Zhang, Charles C. *financial planner*

**Rochester**
Horwitz, Ronald M. *business administration educator*

**Romeo**
Rose, Mary Philomena *business educator*

**Saginaw**
Kern, Franklin Lorenz *auditor*

**Saint Joseph**
De Long, Dale Ray *financing executive*

**Southfield**
Boyce, Daniel Hobbs *financial planning company executive*
Cantwell, Dennis Michael *finance company executive*

**Stanwood**
Cawthorne, Kenneth Clifford *retired financial planner*

**Sylvan Lake**
Wood, Barbara Ann *financial executive*

**Traverse City**
Taylor, Donald Arthur *marketing educator*

**Troy**
Pott, Sandra Kay *finance company executive*

**Warren**
Valerio, Michael Anthony *financial executive*

**Ypsilanti**
Duncan, Charles Howard *business education educator*

## MINNESOTA

**Duluth**
Fryberger, Elizabeth Ann *financial consultant*

**Mankato**
Janavaras, Basil John *university business educator, consultant*
Lee, Chan H. *finance educator*

**Minneapolis**
Berry, David J. *financial services company executive*
Berryman, Robert Glen *accounting educator, consultant*
Diracles, John Michael, Jr. *financial executive*
Goldberg, Luella Gross *corporation executive*
Hoffmann, Thomas Russell *business management educator*
King, Richard Harding *financial consultant, retired food processing company executive*
Kinney, Earl Robert *mutual funds company executive*
Martens, Roy Michael *commercial loan broker*
Montgomery, Andrew Stuart *financial advisor*
Montgomery, Henry Irving *financial planner*
Pillsbury, George Sturgis *investment adviser*
Rudelius, William *marketing educator*
Sidders, Patrick Michael *financial executive*
Viera, James Joseph *financial executive*

**Nisswa**
Marmas, James Gust *retired businees educator, retired college dean*

**Ottertail**
Hanson, Al *financial newsletter editor and publisher*

**Red Wing**
Sorensen, Peter Alan *employee benefits consultant*

**Saint Paul**
Dalton, Howard Edward *accounting executive*
Eames, Earl Ward, Jr. *management educator, development specialist*
Halverson, Richard Paul *investment management company executive*
Palmer, Roger Raymond *accounting educator*
Vaughn, John Rolland *auditor*

**Woodbury**
Bretz, Kelly Jean Rydel *actuary*

## MISSISSIPPI

**Clarksdale**
Walters, William Lee *accountant*

**Mississippi State**
Nash, Henry Warren *marketing educator*

**Ocean Springs**
Morrison, Mable Johnson *business technology educator*

**Starkville**
George, Ernest Thornton, III *financial consultant*

## MISSOURI

**Blue Springs**
Foudree, Charles M. *financial executive*

**Cape Girardeau**
Farrington, Thomas Richard *financial executive, investment advisor*

**Chesterfield**
Armstrong, Theodore Morelock *financial executive*
Henry, Roy Monroe *financial planner*
Liggett, Hiram Shaw, Jr. *retired diversified industry financial executive*

**Columbia**
Cunningham, Billie M. *accounting educator*
Nikolai, Loren Alfred *accounting educator, author*

Silvoso, Joseph Anton *accounting educator*
Stockglausner, William George *accountant*
Wagner, William Burdette *business educator*

**Kansas City**
Bloch, Henry Wollman *tax preparation company executive*
Boysen, Melicent Pearl *finance company executive*
James, Claudia Ann *business educator and trainer, motivational speaker*
Lancaster, Ruth Vysoky *tax training manager*
Latza, Beverly Ann *accountant*
Mustard, Mary Carolyn *financial executive*
Sexton, Donald Lee *business administration educator*
Shaw, Richard David *marketing and management educator*
Stevens, James Hervey, Jr. *retired financial advisor*

**Saint Louis**
Baloff, Nicholas *business educator, consultant*
Brockhaus, Robert Herold, Sr. *business educator, consultant*
Brown, Melvin F. *corporate executive*
Butler, James Lawrence *financial planner*
Carlson, Arthur Eugene *accounting educator*
Crider, Robert Agustine *international financier, law enforcement official*
Dill, Virginia S. *accountant*
Hewitt, Thomas Edward *financial executive*
Jones, Wilbur Boardman, Jr. *trust company executive*
Kniffen, Jan Rogers *finance executive*
Petru, Suzanne Mitton *health care finance executive*
Roberts, Hugh Evan *business investment services company executive*
Schmidt, Clarence Anton *financial consultant*
Schmidt, Robert Charles, Jr. *finance executive*
Sharkey, Kathleen *accountant*
Shepperd, Thomas Eugene *accountant*
Wallis, Michael Van *financial consultant, insurance agent*
Walsh, John E., Jr. *business educator, consultant*
Wildhaber, Michael Rene *accountant*
Winter, Richard Lawrence *financial and health care consulting company executive*

**Springfield**
Abraham, Yohannan *management educator*

## MONTANA

**Billings**
Elser, Danny Ray *financial planner*

**Bozeman**
Davis, Nicholas Homans Clark *finance company executive*

**Troy**
Sherman, Signe Lidfeldt *portfolio manager, former research chemist*

## NEBRASKA

**Fremont**
Dunklau, Rupert Louis *personal investments consultant*

**Hastings**
Nelson, Ricky Eugene *financial executive*

**Hershey**
Rausch, Paul Matthew *financial executive*

**Lincoln**
Broman, Keith Leroy *finance educator, financial planner*
Digman, Lester Aloysius *management educator*
Foy, Edward Donald *financial planner*
Johnson, Margaret Kathleen *business educator*
Lienemann, Delmar Arthur, Sr. *accountant, real estate developer*

**Norfolk**
Wehrer, Charles Siecke *business and education educator*

**Omaha**
Andreski, Raymond John *financial planner*
Drummer, Donald Raymond *financial services executive*
Erickson, James Paul *retired financial service company executive*
†Munger, Charles T. *diversified company executive*
Murphy-Barstow, Holly Ann *financial consultant*
Pitts, Robert Eugene, Jr. *marketing educator, consultant*

## NEVADA

**Carson City**
Larson, Gerald Lee *auditor*
Reid, Belmont Mervyn *brokerage house executive*

**Incline Village**
Henderson, Paul Bargas, Jr. *economic development consultant*

**Las Vegas**
Hobbs, Guy Stephen *financial executive*
Rodgers, Steven Edward *tax practitioner, educator*
Rogers, David Hughes *finance executive*
Samuels, Simon J. *finance, insurance company executive*
Sevalstad, Suzanne Ada *accounting educator*

**Reno**
Neidert, Kalo Edward *accountant, educator*

**Sparks**
Vandergriff, Christina Rai *controller*

## NEW HAMPSHIRE

**Concord**
Currie, Glenn Kenneth *financial consultant*

**Gilmanton**
Osler, Howard Lloyd *controller*

**Grantham**
Springsteen, David Folger *retired financial consultant*

**Hanover**
Anthony, Robert Newton *management educator emeritus*

**Keene**
Stearns, Lloyd Worthington *investment adviser, Oriental artifact consultant*

**Laconia**
Grow, Philip William *accountant*

**Nashua**
Hemming, Walter William *business financial consultant*
Perkins, George William, II *financial services executive, film producer*

**Portsmouth**
Barr, Jane Kay *investment advisor*
Levin, Harvey Jay *financial institution design and construction specialist, developer, auctioneer*

## NEW JERSEY

**Annandale**
Appelbaum, Michael Arthur *finance company executive*

**Avon By The Sea**
Bruno, Grace Angelia *accountant, educator*

**Bay Head**
Benning, Joseph Francis, Jr. *portfolio manager, financial analyst*

**Bloomingdale**
Wanamaker, Ellen Ponce *tax specialist*

**Carlstadt**
Cooke, Edward Francis, Jr. *accountant*

**Cherry Hill**
Newell, Eric James *financial planner, tax consultant, former insurance executive*

**Convent Station**
Healy, Gwendoline Frances *controller*

**Cranbury**
Kemmerer, Peter Ream *financial executive*

**East Brunswick**
Wheeler, Valerie A. Syslo *credit analyst*

**Eatontown**
Dalton, John Joseph *healthcare financial consultant*
Van Winkle, William *certified financial planner*

**Edison**
Cangemi, Michael Paul *accountant, financial executive, author*
Hecht, William David *accountant*

**Elmwood Park**
Nadzick, Judith Ann *accountant*

**Fairfield**
Byer, Theodore Scott *accountant*

**Fort Lee**
Forson, Norman Ray *controller*

**Glen Rock**
Fine, Seymour Howard *marketing educator, lecturer, author, consultant*

**Hackensack**
Mehta, Jay *financial executive*

**Hoboken**
Jurkat, Martin Peter *management educator*
Mankin, Robert Stephen *financial executive*

**Holmdel**
Ayub, Yacub *financial consultant*

**Jackson**
Hagberg, Carl Thomas *financial executive*

**Jersey City**
Dubin, Michael *financial services executive*
Fortune, Robert Russell *financial consultant*

**Lawrenceville**
Farrar, Donald Keith *financial executive*

**Lincroft**
Keenan, Robert Anthony *financial services company executive, educator, consultant*

**Little Falls**
Armellino, Michael Ralph *retired asset management executive*

**Maplewood**
Kusnetz, Hyman *investment advisor*

**Marlton**
Mann, Louis Eugene *financial planner*

**Middletown**
Meyler, William Anthony *financial executive*

**Milltown**
Holland, Joseph John *financial manager*

**Monmouth Beach**
Herbert, LeRoy James *retired accounting firm executive*

**Montvale**
Brecht, Warren Frederick *business executive*

**Montville**
Klapper, Byron D. *financial company executive*

**Morristown**
Cregan, Frank Robert *financial executive, consultant*
Flynn, Marie Cosgrove *portfolio manager*
Hesselink, Ann Patrice *financial executive, lawyer*
Sangiuliano, Barbara Ann *tax manager*

**Mount Laurel**
Gorenberg, Charles Lloyd *financial services executive*
Laubach, Roger Alvin *accountant*

**Netcong**
Sekula, Edward Joseph, Jr. *financial executive*

**New Brunswick**
Mills, George Marshall *insurance and financial consultant*

**New Providence**
Bopp, William Clarence *financial executive*
Symanski, Robert Anthony *treasurer*

**Newark**
Arabie, Phipps *marketing educator, researcher*
Contractor, Farok *business and management educator*
Kelleher, Kathleen *financial services marketing specialist*
Rosenberg, Jerry Martin *business administration educator*

**Paramus**
Balter, Leslie Marvin *business communications educator*

**Parsippany**
Ross, Thomas J., Jr. *personal finanical adviser*
Wechter, Ira Martin *tax specialist, financial planner*

**Phillipsburg**
Burkhart, Glenn Randall *corporate internal auditor*

**Point Pleasant**
Albano, Pasquale Charles *management educator, management and organization development consultant*

**Princeton**
Darr, Walter Robert *financial analyst*
Goldfarb, Irene Dale *financial planner*
Goldman, Clifford Alan *financial advisor*
Harvey, Norman Ronald *finance company executive*
Henkel, William *financial services executive*
Osei, Edward Kofi *financial analyst, educator, strategic planner*
Pimley, Kim Jensen *financial training consultant*
Tabell, Anthony *financial analyst*

**Raritan**
Licetti, Mary Elizabeth *business analysis director*

**Red Bank**
McCann, John Francis *financial services company executive*

**Ridgewood**
Geraghty, Margaret Karl *financial consultant, portfolio manager*
McBride, William Bernard *treasurer*

**River Edge**
Gass, Manus M. *accountant, business executive*

**Rockaway**
Reeves, Marylou *financial planner*

**Saddlebrook**
Donahoe, Maureen Alice *accounting consultant*

**Secaucus**
Rothman, Martin *finance company executive, accountant*

**Short Hills**
Mebane, William Black *controller, financial consultant*
†Price, Michael F. *money management executive*

**Skillman**
Wheelock, Keith Ward *retired consulting company executive, educator*

**Somerville**
Cohen, Walter Stanley *accountant, financial consultant*

**Southampton**
Knortz, Walter Robert *accountant, former insurance company executive*

**Spring Lake**
Perkowski, Paul James *accountant*

**Summit**
Batzer, R. Kirk *accountant*
Vogel, Julius *consulting actuary, former insurance company executive*

**Tenafly**
Lilley, Theodore Robert *financial executive*

**Union**
Soni, Maria Habib *controller, treasurer*

**Waldwick**
Surdoval, Donald James *accounting and management consulting company executive*

**Warren**
Hartman, David Gardiner *actuary*

**Wayne**
Hamill, A(llen) William *finance executive*

**Westfield**
Boutillier, Robert John *accountant*
Lipkin, William Joel *controller, history educator*

**Whitehouse Station**
Atieh, Michael Gerard *accountant*

## NEW MEXICO

**Albuquerque**
Bencke, Ronald *financial executive*
D'Anza, Lawrence Martin *marketing educator*
Kaehele, Bettie Louise *accountant*

**Las Cruces**
Bell, M. Joy Miller *financial planner, real estate broker*
Peterson, Robin Tucker *marketing educator*

**Portales**
Morris, Donald *tax specialist*

**Santa Fe**
Watkins, Stephen Edward *accountant*

## NEW YORK

**Albany**
Alexander, Clark Everts *accountant*
Blount, Stanley Freeman *marketing educator*
Culp, Margaret Geralyn *tax administrator*
Hancox, David Robert *audit administrator, educator*
Holstein, William Kurt *business administration educator*

**Amherst**
Jen, Frank Chifeng *finance and management educator*

**Amityville**
Hughes, Spencer Edward, Jr. *retired financial executive, consultant*
Linehan, Patrick Francis, Jr. *financial planner*

**Binghamton**
Shillestad, John Gardner *financial services company executive*

**Bridgehampton**
Needham, James Joseph *retired financial services executive*

**Bronx**
Aiken, William *accountant*
Hamilton, John Ross *financial consultant, educator*
Sedacca, Angelo Anthony *financial executive*
Stuhr, David Paul *business educator, consultant*

**Bronxville**
Martin, R. Keith *business and information systems educator, consultant*
Sharp, Donald Eugene *bank consultant*

**Brooklyn**
Abrams, Roni *business education educator, communications consultant, trainer*
DeBock, Florent Alphonse *controller*
DeLustro, Frank Joseph *financial executive, consultant*
Gordon, Conrad J. *financial executive*
Lebouitz, Martin Frederick *financial services industry executive, consultant*
Sands, Edith Sylvia Abeloff (Mrs. Abraham M. Sands) *retired finance educator, author*

**Buffalo**
Draper, Verden Rolland *accountant*
Gruen, David Henry *financial executive, consultant*
Jacobs, Jeremy M. *diversified holding company executive, hockey team owner*
Koontz, Eldon Ray *management and financial consultant*
Layton, Rodney Eugene *controller, newspaper executive*
Southwick, Lawrence, Jr. *management educator*

**Canandaigua**
Read, Eleanor May *financial analyst*

**Canton**
Pollard, Fred Don *finance company executive*

**Cedarhurst**
Cohen, Philip Herman *accountant*

**Central Islip**
McCrain, Michael William *accountant, consultant*

**Chittenango**
Cassell, William Walter *retired accounting operations consultant*

**Cold Spring**
Powell, Carol Ann *accountant*

**Commack**
Nelson, Marvin Bernard *financial executive*
Rakower, Joel A. *business appraiser, litigation consultant*

**East Greenbush**
Mucci, Patrick John *financial consultant, realtor, commercial loan broker*

**East Hampton**
Dalzell, Fred Briggs *financial consultant*

**East Rochester**
Murray, James Doyle *accountant*

**Elmsford**
Kroner, Arnold Friedrich *financial consultant, economist*
Urbanas, Alban William *financial planner*

**Far Rockaway**
Epstein, Samuel Abraham *stock and bond broker, petroleum consultant*

**Garden City**
Baker, J. A., II *monetary architect, financial engineer, coordination consultant*
Kurlander, Neale *accounting and law educator, lawyer*
Smith, Paul Thomas *financial services company executive*
Vitale, Paul *accountant*

**Glens Falls**
Tenne, Donald Paul *financial planner*
Wright, Stephen Charles *financial planner*

**Hampton Bays**
Yavitz, Boris *business educator and dean emeritus*

**Harrison**
Serenbetz, Warren Lewis *financial management company executive*

**Hartsdale**
Gillingham, Stephen Thomas *financial planner*

**Hastings On Hudson**
Shillinglaw, Gordon *accounting educator, consultant, writer*

**Hauppauge**
Harrington, Carolyn Marie *accountant, artist*
Malaga, Stanley *accounting educator*

**Hawthorne**
Kiamie, Don Albert Najeeb *accountant*

**Hempstead**
Lee, Keun Sok *business educator, consultant*
Montana, Patrick Joseph *management educator*

**Horseheads**
Huffman, Patricia Joan *retired accounting coordinator*

**Ithaca**
Dyckman, Thomas Richard *accounting educator*
Elliott, John *accountant, educator*
Lesser, William Henri *marketing educator*
Van Houtte, Raymond A. *financial executive*

**Jamaica**
Angerville, Edwin Duvanel *accountant, educator*

**Mamaroneck**
Fletcher, Denise Koen *strategic and financial consultant*

**Melville**
McCusker, John *financial executive*

**Merrick**
Beckman, Judith Kalb *financial counselor and planner, educator, writer*
Kaplan, Steven Mark *accountant*

**Millwood**
Doyle, John McCormick *actuary, pension plan consultant*

**Mineola**
McGonigle, James Gregory *financial consultant*

**Mount Kisco**
Keesee, Thomas Woodfin, Jr. *financial consultant*

**New Hyde Park**
Dalal, Mayur Thakorbhai *estate planner*

**New York**
Alexander, Barbara Toll *investment banker*
Alper, Merlin Lionel *financial executive*
Altfest, Karen Caplan *financial planning executive*
Altfest, Lewis Jay *financial and investment advisor*
Anderson, Theodore Wellington *portfolio strategist*
Assael, Henry *marketing educator*
Atwater, Verne Stafford *finance educator*
Auriemmo, Frank Joseph, Jr. *financial holding company executive*
Bains, Harrison MacKellar, Jr. *financial executive*
Banks, Russell *financial planner, consultant*
Barnett, Bernard *accountant*
Barrett, Martin Jay *financial executive*
Baumann, Gary Joseph *accountant*
Becker-Roukas, Helane Renée *securities analyst, financial executive*
Berger, Stephen *financial services company executive*
Bernstein, Zalman C. *research and money management executive*
Bloomberg, R. Michael *finance and information services company executive*
Bolter, Eugene P. *investment counselor*
Brofman, Lance Mark *portfolio manager, mutual fund executive*
Brooke, Paul Alan *finance company executive*
Brown, G(lenn) William, Jr. *financial services executive*
Brown, James Nelson, Jr. *accountant*
Brustein, Lawrence *financial executive*
†Butler, Stephen G. *financial planner*
Byington, Homer Morrison, III *financial consultant*
Campbell, Timothy Reid *financial services company executive*
Canes, Brian Dennis *professional services company official*
Carthaus, James Arthur *financial service company executive*
Chang, Ryan Chih-Kang *financial planner and analyst, researcher*
Chenault, Kenneth Irvine *financial services company executive*
Claire, Thomas Andrew *educator, writer*
Clark, Charles Alan *financial analyst*
Clark, Howard Longstreth, Jr. *finance company executive*
Clauson, James Wilson *accountant*
Cohen-Sabban, Nessim *auditor, accountant*
Connor, Joseph E. *accountant*
Conta, Richard Vincent *actuary*
Conway, E. Virgil *financial consultant, banker, lawyer*
Craig, Charles Samuel *marketing educator*
Das, T. K. *management educator, consultant*
Dawson, Thomas Cleland, II *financial executive*
de St. Paer, Jerry Michael *insurance executive*
Deupree, Marvin Mattox *accountant, business consultant*
Dewing, Merlin Eugene *diversified financial services company executive*
DeWitt, Eula *accountant*
Donaldson, William Henry *financial executive*
Edwards, James D. *accounting company executive*
Efrat, Isaac *financial analyst, mathematician*
Eig, Norman *investment company executive*
Eimicke, William Brewster *management and finance educator, consultant*
Eisner, Richard Alan *accountant*
Emmerman, Michael N *financial analyst*
Erosh, William Daniel *financial services company executive*
Eveillard, Jean-Marie *financial company executive*
Fahey, James Edward *financial executive*
Farley, Peggy Ann *finance company executive*
Fontana, John Arthur *employee benefits specialist*
Freiberg, Lowell Carl *financial executive*
Frimerman, Leslie *financial services company executive*
Froewiss, Kenneth Clark *corporate finance executive*
Frommer, Henry *financial executive*
Frye, Clayton Wesley, Jr. *financial executive*
Garba, Edward Aloysius *financial executive*
Garrett, Robert *financial advisory executive*
Gaughan, Eugene Francis *accountant*
Geraghty, Kenneth George *financial services company executive*
Gill, Ardian C. *actuary, photographer*
Gladstone, William Louis *accountant*
Glynn, Gary Allen *pension fund executive*
Goldberg, Edward L. *financial services executive*
Golden, William Theodore *trustee, corporate director*
Goldman, Robert Irving *financial services company executive*
Goldschmidt, Robert Alphonse *financial executive*
Goldstein, Fred *accountant*
Golub, Gerald Leonard *accounting company executive*
Golub, Harvey *financial services company executive*
Gorewitz, Rubin Leon *accountant, financial consultant*
Gowens, Walter, II *financial and business services executive*
Graf, Peter Gustav *accountant, lawyer*
Green, David O. *accounting educator, educational administrator*
Grisi, Jeanmarie Conte *finance executive*
Groves, Ray John *accountant*
Halloran, Leo Augustine *retired financial executive*
Harrison, John Alexander *financial executive*
Hazen, William Harris *finance executive*
Heintz, Joseph E. *financial services company executive*
Henning, Michael Anthony *diversified financial company executive*
Herrera, Paul Fredrick *accountant*
Hewitt, Dennis Edwin *financial executive*
Hibel, Bernard *financial consultant, former apparel company executive*
Hickman, J. Kenneth *accounting company executive*
Hoffman, Philip Joseph *financial executive*
Insardi, Nina Elizabeth *benefits administrator*
Jacey, Charles Frederick, Jr. *accounting company executive, consultant*
Jacobs, Mark Neil *financial services corporation executive, lawyer*
Johnson, Christian Carl *equity analyst*
Johnson, Clarke Courtney *finance educator*
Johnson, Freda S. *public finance consultant*
Johnson, J. Chester *financial executive, poet*
Joseph, Michael Sarkies *accountant*
Kaye, Walter *financial executive*
Kirk, Donald James *accounting educator, consultant*
Kirsch, Donald *financial consultant, author*
Kirschenbaum, Lisa L. *portfolio manager, financial advisor*
Koeppel, Noel Immanuel *financial planner, securities and real estate broker*
Kolesar, Peter John *business and engineering educator*
Komansky, David H. *financial services executive*
Kopelman, Richard Eric *management educator*
Kotecha, Mahesh Kanjibhai *financial guarantee insurance company executive*
Kovalcik, Kenneth John *accountant*
Krat, Gary Walden *financial services company executive*
†Kravis, Henry R. *venture financier*
Lammie, James L. *financial planner, consultant*
Langford, Laura Sue *ratings analyst*
Laskawy, Philip A. *accounting and management consulting firm executive*
Leaf, Roger Warren *business consultant*
Lee, Victor Ho *lawyer*
Lessing, Brian Reid *actuary*
†Levin, Robert E. *financial management company executive*
Lewins, Steven *security analyst, investment advisor, corporate executive, diplomaticadvisor*
Libby, John Kelway *financial services company executive*
Lindquist, Richard James *portfolio manager*
Loeb, Peter Kenneth *money manager*
Loss, Stuart Harold *financial executive*
Lowenthal, Jacob *finance executive*
Lust, Herbert Cohnfeldt, II *finance executive*
Madden, Michael Daniel *finance company executive*
Madonna, Jon C. *accounting firm executive*
Martinez, Ronan, IV *investment banker*
Matthews, Westina Lomax *finance and banking executive*
Maurer, Jeffrey Stuart *finance executive*
McCaffrey, William Thomas *financial services company executive*
McDonald, Thomas Paul *controller*
†McGraw, Harold Whittlesey, III (Terry McGraw) *financial services company executive*
Mc Gruder, Stephen Jones *portfolio manager*
Miller, John R. *accountant*
Miller, Neil Stuart *financial officer, advertising executive*
Misthal, Howard Joseph *accountant, lawyer*
Moore, Nicholas G. *finance company executive*
Mosse, Peter John Charles *financial services executive*
Nagle, Arthur Joseph *investment banker*
Neff, Robert Arthur *business and financial executive*
Nichols, Edie Diane *executive recruiter*
Norman, Stephen Peckham *financial services company executive*
Paddock, Anthony Conaway *financial consultant*
Palitz, Bernard G. *finance company executive*
†Pappas, Michael *financial services company executive*
Peppet, Russell Frederick *accountant*
Peritz, Abraham Daniel *business executive*
Posner, Roy Edward *finance executive*
Potter, Delcour S. *finance company executive*
Prehle, Tricia A. *accountant*
Presby, J. Thomas *financial advisor*
Prestia, Michael Anthony *accounting executive*
Purcell, Philip James *financial services company executive*
Pyle, Robert Milner, Jr. *financial services company executive*
Rein, Catherine Amelia *financial services executive, lawyer*
Rinaldini, Luis Emilio *investment banker*
Ritch, Herald LaVern *finance company executive*
Ritch, Kathleen *diversified company executive*
Robinson, James D., III *corporate executive*
Robinson, Robert Armstrong *pension fund executive*
Rockefeller, Laurance S. *business executive, conservationist*
Roethenmund, Otto Emil *financial and banking executive*
Rosenberg, Alan David *accountant*
Rosenberg, Michael Joseph *financial executive*
Rosenthal, Charles Michael *financial executive*
Ross, Coleman DeVane *accountant, insurance company consultant*
Salzman, Robert Jay *accountant*
Sandor, Richard Laurence *financial company executive*
Scanlon, Peter Redmond *accountant*
Segal, Martin Eli *retired actuarial and consulting company executive*
Shapoff, Stephen H. *financial executive*
Sharp, J(ames) Franklin *finance educator, academic administrator*
Shaw, Alan Roger *financial executive, educator*
Short, George William *financial executive*
Siguler, George William *financial services executive*
Silber, William Leo *finance educator*
Silverman, Herbert R. *corporate financial executive*
Skomorowsky, Peter P. *accounting company executive, lawyer*
Skwiersky, Paul *accountant*
Smith, Harold Charles *private pension fund executive*
Soros, George *fund management executive*
Sorter, George Hans *accounting and law educator, consultant*
Sparkes, Cheryl Flowers *accountant*
Stockman, David Allen *former federal official, congressman, financier*
Stone, David Kendall *financial executive*
Stovall, Robert H(enry) *money management company executive*
Stux, Ivan Ernest *financial executive*
Tarantino, Dominic A. *accounting firm executive*
Tavel, Mark Kivey *money management company executive, economist*
Tisch, Preston Robert *finance executive*
Tognino, John Nicholas *financial services executive*
Treuhold, Charles Richard *retired investment banker*
Tully, Daniel Patrick *financial services executive*
Valles, Jean-Paul *finance company executive*
Walker, Dale Rush *financial company executive*
Walsh, Thomas Gerard *actuary*
Weinbach, Lawrence Allen *financial executive*
Weiner, Ronald Gary *accounting firm executive*
Weingrow, Howard L. *financial executive, investor*
†Weinstein, Mark S. *finance company executive*
Weiss, Myrna Grace *business consultant*
Wiener, Robert Alvin *accountant*
Wilby, William Langfitt *global mutual fund manager, economist*
Wright, Richard John *business executive*
Young, George H., III *investment banker*
Zand, Dale Ezra *business management educator*

**Newburgh**
Apuzzo, Gloria Isabel *retired accountant*

**Niagara Falls**
Shaghoian, Cynthia Lynne *accountant*
Stirling, Michelle Dianne *tax specialist, accountant*

**Old Bethpage**
Dryce, H. David *accountant, consultant*

**Orangeburg**
Frommelt, John Banta *financial executive*

**Ossining**
Finnegan, George Bernard, III *financial advisor*

**Palenville**
Coletti, Louis Roland *financial planner, realtor*

**Pittsford**
Herge, Henry Curtis, Jr. *consulting firm executive*

**Plainview**
Feller, Benjamin E. *actuary*

**Plattsburgh**
Dossin, Ernest Joseph, III *credit consulting company executive*

**Pleasantville**
Reps, David Nathan *finance educator*

**Pomona**
Landau, Lauri Beth *accountant, tax consultant*

**Port Washington**
Phelan, Arthur Joseph *financial executive*

**Poughkeepsie**
Handel, Bernard *accountant, actuarial and insurance consultant, lawyer*
Hansen, Karen Thornley *accountant*
McFadden, John Thomas *financial planner, insurance agent, investor*

**Pound Ridge**
Webb, Richard Gilbert *financial executive*

**Purchase**
Noonan, Frank R. *business executive*
Panaro, Joseph *financial services company executive*

**Queensbury**
Bitner, William Lawrence, III *retired banker, educator*
Borgos, Stephen John *business educator, consultant, municipal administrator, real estate broker*
Lake, William Thomas *financial consultant*

**Rochester**
Balderston, William, III *retired banker*
Garg, Devendra *financial executive*
Golisano, B. Thomas *finance company director, human resources director*
Olson, Russell L. *pension fund administrator*
Watts, Ross Leslie *accounting educator, consultant*

**Rye**
Beldock, Donald Travis *financial executive*
Finnerty, John Dudley *investment banker, financial educator*

**Rye Brook**
FitzSimons, Sharon Russell *international financial and treasury executive*

**Saratoga Springs**
Colangelo, Jayne Anne Parker *accountant, auditor*

**Scarsdale**
Eforo, John Francis *financial officer*
Gollin, Stuart Allen *accountant*
Paige, Susanne Lynn *financial consultant*

**Sleepy Hollow**
Hyman, Leonard Stephen *finanical consultant, economist, author*

**Smithtown**
Kreimer, Michael Walter *financial planner*

**South Salem**
Cronin, Raymond Valentine *financial executive*

**Southold**
Curcuru, Edmond Harvey *management educator*

**Staten Island**
Fung, Amy Shu-Fong *accountant*

**Sunnyside**
Privo, Alexander *finance educator, department chairman*

**Syosset**
Kendric, Deborah Ann *controller*

**Syracuse**
Marcoccia, Louis Gary *accountant, university administrator*
Ortiz, Fernando, Jr. *small business consultant*

**Tarrytown**
Ferrari, Robert Joseph *business educator, former banker*

**Valley Stream**
Grassi, Louis C. *accountant*

**Vestal**
Piaker, Philip Martin *accountant, educator*

**Wappingers Falls**
Hogan, Edward Robert *financial services executive*

**Webster**
McCormack, Stanley Eugene *financial consultant*
Nicholson, Douglas Robert *accountant*

**White Plains**
Ladjevardi, Hamid *fund manager*
Sacco, John Michael *accountant*

**Whitestone**
Brill, Steven Charles *financial advisor, lawyer*

**York**
Coleman, David Cecil *financial executive*

**Yorktown Heights**
Donovan, Andrew Joseph *financial analyst*

**NORTH CAROLINA**

**Advance**
Herpel, George Lloyd *marketing educator*

**Asheville**
Banks, James Barber *financial consultant*

**Benson**
Doyle, Sally A. *controller*

**Bolivia**
Horne, Lithia Brooks *finance executive*

**Boone**
Bowden, Elbert Victor *banking, finance and economics educator, author*

**Cary**
Hagan, John Aubrey *financial executive*

**Cashiers**
DeHority, Edward Havens, Jr. *retired accountant, lawyer*

**Chapel Hill**
Barnhill, Cynthia Diane *accountant*
Brummet, Richard Lee *accounting educator*
Langenderfer, Harold Quentin *accountant, educator*
Perreault, William Daniel, Jr. *business administration educator*
Rondinelli, Dennis A(ugust) *business administration educator, research center director*
Rosen, Benson *business administration educator*
Roth, Aleda Vender *business educator*

**Charlotte**
Anderson, Gerald Leslie *financial executive*
Cornick, Michael F(rederick) *accounting educator*
Halas, Paul Anthony, Jr. *business appraisal and valuation specialist, consultant*
Mazze, Edward Mark *marketing educator, consultant*
Rajani, Prem Rajaram *transportation company financial executive*
Wentz, Billy Melvin, Jr. *finance educator*
Williford, Donald Bratton *accounting company executive*

**Clemmons**
Cawood, Merton Campbell *investment management executive*

**Durham**
Bettman, James Ross *management educator*
Staelin, Richard *business administration educator*

**Greensboro**
Compton, John Carroll *accountant*
Mecimore, Charles Douglas *accounting educator*

**Greenville**
Hines, Danny Ray *accountant, educator*
Schellenberger, Robert Earl *management educator and department chairman*

**High Point**
Foscue, James E. *commercial finance company executive*

**Hillsborough**
Pagano, Filippo Frank *financial broker, commercial loan consultant*

**Jacksonville**
Hutto, James Calhoun *retired financial executive*

**Manteo**
Miller, Judith Ann *retired financial executive*

**Morrisville**
Richardson, Arline Annette *accountant, comptroller*

**Raleigh**
Homick, Daniel John *financial executive, lawyer*
Jessen, David Wayne *accountant*
Ward, Edith Burnette *business educator*

**Wilkesboro**
Waller, Jim D. *holding company executive*

**NORTH DAKOTA**

**Fargo**
Risher, Stephan Olaf *investment officer*

**Grand Forks**
Zahrly, Janice Honea *management educator*

**OHIO**

**Ada**
Cooper, Ken Errol *management educator*

**Amelia**
Hayden, Joseph Page, Jr. *company executive*

**Andover**
Mole, Richard Jay *accounting company executive*

**Athens**
Miller, Peggy McLaren *management educator*
Patterson, Harlan Ray *finance educator*
Rakes, Ganas Kaye *finance and banking educator*

**Bowling Green**
Guthrie, Mearl Raymond, Jr. *business administration educator*
Lunde, Harold Irving *management educator*

**Canton**
Warner, E. John *manufacturing financial executive*

**Chagrin Falls**
Poza, Ernesto J. *business consultant, educator*
Strachan, Donald M. *financial executive*

**Cincinnati**
Black, David deLaine *investment consultant*
Conaton, Michael Joseph *financial service executive*
DeBrunner, Gerald Joseph *accounting firm executive*
De Stefano, John Joseph *accountant*
Evans, Barry Craig *financial services company executive*
Gyuro, Paula Candice *financial planner*
Lindner, Robert David *finance company executive*
Lintz, Robert Carroll *financial holding company executive*
Mantel, Samuel Joseph, Jr. *management educator, consultant*
Peters, Ann Louise *accounting manager*
Sedgwick-Hirsch, Carol Elizabeth *financial executive*
Siekmann, Donald Charles *accountant*
Walker, Michael Claude *finance educator*

**Cleveland**
Arlen, Mark Dale *financial planner*
Dossey, Richard L. *accountant*
Gelfand, Ivan *investment advisor*
Hartley, Robert Frank *business educator, author*
Key, Helen Elaine *accountant, consulting company executive, educator*
Krulitz, Leo Morrion *financial executive*
Mayne, Lucille Stringer *finance educator*
Pierson, Marilyn Ehle *financial planner*
Roberts, James Owen *financial planning executive*
Seaton, Robert Finlayson *retired planned giving consultant*
Stratton-Crooke, Thomas Edward *financial consultant*

**Columbus**
Aldridge, Mark Donald *financial advisor, investment counselor*
Berry, William Lee *business administration educator*
Collier, David Alan *management educator*
Dunham, Frank L. *accounting and consulting company executive*
Eaton, Michael Christopher *accounting technician*
Grapski, Ladd Raymond *accountant*
Gunnels, Lee O. *retired finance and management educator, manufacturing company executive*
Kasper, Larry John *accountant, litigation support consultant*
Knisely, Douglas Charles *accountant*
LaLonde, Bernard Joseph *educator*
Leong, G. Keong *operations management educator*
McMaster, Robert Raymond *accountant*
Schilling, David August *management educator*

**Concord**
Hanzak, Janice Chrisman *accountant*

**Cuyahoga Falls**
Moses, Abe Joseph *international financial consultant*

**Dayton**
Hoge, Franz Joseph *accounting firm executive*
McCutcheon, Holly Marie *accountant*
Singhvi, Surendra Singh *finance and strategy consultant*
Walden, James William *accountant, educator*
Wilson, Robert M. *financial executive*

**Dublin**
Heneman, Robert Lloyd *management educator*
Madigan, Joseph Edward *financial executive, consultant, director*

**Harrison**
Kocher, Juanita Fay *retired auditor*

**Holland**
Kennedy, James L. *accountant*

**Lancaster**
Voss, Jack Donald *international business consultant, lawyer*

**Mansfield**
Haldar, Frances Louise *business educator, accountant, treasurer*
Shah, James M. *actuarial consultant*

**Maumee**
Tigges, Kenneth Edwin *retired financial executive*

**North Canton**
Lynham, C(harles) Richard *foundry company executive*

**North Olmsted**
Brady, Michael Cameron *investment consultant*

**Oxford**
Wilson, James Ray *international business educator*

**Painesville**
Clement, Daniel Roy, III *accountant, assistant nurse, small business owner*

**Perrysburg**
Barbe, Betty Catherine *financial analyst*

**Saint Clairsville**
Bearce, Peter James *accountant*

**Sandusky**
Duttera, Brian Cleve *financial consultant and sales manager*

**Shaker Heights**
Donnem, Sarah Lund *financial analyst, non-profit and political organization consultant*

**Sylvania**
Sampson, Wesley Claude *auditor*

**Toledo**
Brockmeyer, Ann Hartmann *financial planner*

**Youngstown**
Bartlett, Shirley Anne *accountant*

**OKLAHOMA**

**Enid**
Rider, John Allen, II *business educator, paralegal*

**Lawton**
Davis, Ellen Marie *business educator*

**Moore**
Harrington, Gary Burnes *retired controller*

**Norman**
Cosier, Richard A. *business educator, consultant*
Evans, Rodney Earl *business educator*
Lis, Anthony Stanley *business administration educator*
McGuckin, Wendy Michelle Blassingame *accounting specialist*

**Oklahoma City**
Petito, Victor Thomas, Jr. *credit bureau executive*
Tolbert, James R., III *financial executive*

**Stillwater**
Trennepohl, Gary Lee *finance educator*

**Tulsa**
Bowen, William Augustus *financial consultant*
Gaddis, Richard William *management educator*

**OREGON**

**Albany**
Bianchi, Charles Paul *technical and business executive, money manager, financial consultant*

**Ashland**
Farrimond, George Francis, Jr. *management educator*

**Clackamas**
Luchterhand, Ralph Edward *financial advisor*

**Corvallis**
Nielson, Norma Lee *business educator*

**Eugene**
Lindholm, Richard Theodore *economics and finance educator*
Mowday, Richard Thomas *management educator*

**Grants Pass**
Smith, Barnard Elliot *management educator*

**Lake Oswego**
Mylnechuk, Larry Herbert *financial executive*

**Portland**
Gren, Conrad Roger *accountant*
Weber, George Richard *financial consultant, writer*
Workman, Norman Allan *accountant, graphic arts consultant*

**PENNSYLVANIA**

**Allentown**
Balog, Ibolya *accountant*
Heitmann, George Joseph *business educator, consultant*

**Allison Park**
LaDow, C. Stuart *consultant financial services*

**Ardmore**
Giese, William Herbert *tax accountant*

**Bala Cynwyd**
McGill, Dan Mays *insurance business educator*
Miller, L. Martin *accountant, financial planning specialist*

**Bethlehem**
Barsness, Richard Webster *management educator, administrator*
Hobbs, James Beverly *business administration educator, writer*

**Braddock**
Slack, Edward Dorsey, III *financial systems professional, consultant*

**Broomall**
Dibianca, Joseph Philip *finance and tax executive*

**Bryn Mawr**
Moyer, F. Stanton *financial executive, advisor*

**Butler**
Kendall, George Jason *accountant, financial planner, computer consultant*

**Camp Hill**
Robinson, Ronald Michael *health care financial executive, financial consultant*

**Coraopolis**
Giliberti, Michael Richard *financial planner*

**Dunmore**
Pencek, Carolyn Carlson *treasurer, educator*

**Enola**
Baumann, Matthew Louis *business education educator, elementary school educator*

**Flourtown**
Christy, John Gilray *financial company executive*

**Fort Washington**
Blumberg, Judith Toplin *international consulting firm executive*

**Gladwyne**
Booth, Harold Waverly *finance and investment company executive, lawyer*

**Harrisburg**
Crall, Dale Eugene *accountant*

**Haverford**
Merrill, Arthur Alexander *financial analyst*

**Havertown**
Brinker, Thomas Michael *finance executive*

**Horsham**
Wesselink, David Duwayne *finance company executive*

**Indiana**
Stevenson, Charles Beman *business educator*

**Jenkintown**
Smith, Francis Xavier *accountant*

**Johnstown**
Smiach, Deborah *accountant, educator, consultant*

**Kutztown**
Ogden, James Russell *marketing educator, consultant, lecturer, trainer*

**Lafayette Hill**
King, Leon *financial services executive*

**Lancaster**
Freeman, Clarence Calvin *financial executive*
Hendrix, Stephen C. *financial executive*

**Lincoln University**
Dadson, William Kwame *economics and business administration educator*

**Loretto**
Benham, Philip Owen, Jr. *business marketing educator, consultant*

**Malvern**
Fredrick, Susan Walker *tax company manager*

**Mc Donald**
Tannehill, Norman Bruce, Jr. *consultant, educator*

**Media**
Hemphill, James S. *investment management executive, financial advisor*

**Mercer**
Inman, Thomas Leroy *county auditor*

**Middletown**
Kaynak, Erdener *marketing educator, consultant editor*

**Morrisville**
Marsh, Frederick William *accountant*

**Nazareth**
Rayner, Robert Martin *financial executive*

**Newfoundland**
Sked, Marie Josephine *financial service owner, nurse*

**Newtown Square**
Graf, Arnold Harold *employee benefits executive, financial planner*
Steinman, Robert Cleeton *accountant*

**Philadelphia**
Abel, Andrew Bruce *finance and economics educator*
Alexander, William Herbert *business educator, former construction executive*
Anderson, Rolph Ely *marketing educator*
Andrisani, Paul *business educator, management consultant*
Babbel, David Frederick *finance educator*
Blume, Marshall Edward *finance educator*
Bowman, Edward Harry *business science educator*
Cox, Douglas Lynn *financial service executive*
Daly, Donald Francis *investment counsel*
Fisher, Marshall Lee *operations management educator*
Friedman, Sidney A. *financial services executive*
Goldsmith, Nancy Carrol *business and health services management educator*
Goodman, Charles Schaffner *marketing educator*
Kelley, William Thomas *marketing educator*
Kimberly, John Robert *management educator, consultant*
Kozlowski, Bette Marie *accountant*
Krebs, Hope Paula *tax consultant, lawyer*
Ksansnak, James E. *service management company executive*
La Blanc, Charles Wesley, Jr. *financial consultant*
Lodish, Leonard Melvin *marketing educator, entrepreneur*
Malhotra, Davinder Kumar *finance educator, consultant, researcher*
Mazzarella, James Kevin *business administration educator*
Micko, Alexander S. *financial executive*
Nadley, Harris Jerome *accountant, educator, writer*
Robinson, Robert L. *financial service company executive, lawyer*
Root, Franklin Russell *business educator*
Rose, Robert Lawrence *financial services company executive*
Rosenbloom, Bert *marketing educator*
Rowan, Richard Lamar *business management educator*
Saks, Stephen Howard *accountant*
Santomero, Anthony M. *business educator*
Sanyour, Michael Louis, Jr. *financial services company executive*
Saul, Ralph Southey *financial service executive*
Savitz, Samuel J. *actuarial consulting firm executive*
Selles, Robert Hendrikus *actuary, consultant*
Spivak, Robert Elliot *financial consultant*
Staloff, Arnold Fred *financial executive*
Taylor, Wilson H. *diversified financial company executive*
Webber, Ross Arkell *management educator*
Woods, Richard Seavey *accountant, educator*
Ziegler, Donald Robert *accountant*
Zucker, William *retired business educator*

**Pittsburgh**
Bernt, Benno Anthony *financial executive, entrepreneur and investor*
Bly, James Charles, Jr. *financial services executive*
Foreman, John Daniel *financial executive*
Franklin, Kenneth Ronald *franchise company executive, consultant*
Grady, James Stran *financial planner*
Haley, Roy W. *financial services executive*
Herrington, Donald Francis *financial services executive*
Ijiri, Yuji *accounting and economics educator*
Junker, Edward P., III *diversified financial services company executive*
Kilmann, Ralph Herman *business educator*
King, William Richard *business educator, consultant*
Kraus, John Delbert *investment advisor*
Kriebel, Charles Hosey *management sciences educator*
Lewis, Richard Allan *financial planner, business consultant*
Murray, Davina Ann *financial analyst, accounting officer*
Thorne, John Reinecke *business educator, venture capitalist*
Zoffer, H. Jerome *business educator, university dean*

**Plymouth Meeting**
Litman, Raymond Stephen *financial services consultant*

**Radnor**
Mestre, Oscar Luis *financial consultant*
Stearns, Milton Sprague, Jr. *financial executive*

**Reading**
Gebbia, Robert James *tax executive*

**Saint Davids**
Bertsch, Frederick Charles, III *business executive*
Rogers, James Gardiner *accountant, educator*

**Scranton**
Volk, Thomas *accountant*

**Sewickley**
Jehle, Michael Edward *financial executive*

**Troy**
Hulslander, Marjorie Diane *auditor*

**University Park**
Bennett, Peter Dunne *marketing educator*
Jaffe, Austin Jay *business administration educator*
Lusht, Kenneth Michael *business administration educator*
McKeown, James Charles *accounting educator, consultant*
Rigby, Paul Herbert *management educator, college dean*
Schrader, William Joseph *accountant, educator*

**Valley Forge**
Cuzzolina, Michael Joseph *financial executive*

**Villanova**
Dorian, Harry Aram *financial consultant, former bank executive*

**Wayne**
Mudry, Michael *pension and benefit consultant*

**West Chester**
Handzel, Steven Jeffrey *accountant*
McMeen, Albert Ralph, Jr. *investment advisor*

**West Conshohocken**
Richard, Scott F. *portfolio manager*

**Wilkes Barre**
Bevevino, Frank *finance company executive*

**Williamsport**
Bellmore, Lawrence Robert, Jr. *financial planner*
Facey, Karlyle Frank *financial executive, consultant*

**Wynnewood**
Frankl, Razelle *management educator*

**Wyomissing**
Stephen, Dennis John *financial planner*

## RHODE ISLAND

**East Providence**
Tripp, Michael Windsor *accountant*

**Lincoln**
Carter, Wilfred Wilson *financial executive, controller*

**Pawtucket**
Davison, Charles Hamilton *financial executive*

**Providence**
Harris, Richard John *diversified holding company executive*
Satterthwaite, Franklin Bache, Jr. *management educator, consultant*
Tillinghast, Charles Carpenter, Jr. *aviation and financial consultant*

**Tiverton**
Constance, Barbara Ann *financial planner, small business owner, consultant*

## SOUTH CAROLINA

**Batesburg**
Drafts, James Pickens, III *financial and actuarial examiner*

**Cayce**
Byars, Merlene Hutto *accountant, visual artist, writer, publisher*

**Charleston**
Adelson, Gloria Ann *financial executive*
Franklin, Paul Deane *financial consultant, financial planner*
Hogan, Arthur James *portfolio manager*
Rustin, Dowse Bradwell, III *credit union executive*

**Clemson**
Hicks, Edwin Hugh *accountant*
Sheriff, Jimmy Don *accounting educator, academic dean*

**Columbia**
Davis, Barbara Langford *financial advisor*
Edwards, James Benjamin *accountant, educator*
Gasque, Diane Phillips *funding specialist*
Hand, Herbert Hensley *management educator, executive, consultant, inventor*
Patterson, Grady Leslie, Jr. *financial advisor*
Pritchett, Samuel Travis *finance and insurance educator, researcher*

**Georgetown**
McGrath, James Charles, III *financial services company executive, lawyer, consultant*

**Greenville**
Fayonsky, James Leon *financial planner*

**Hilton Head Island**
Kaley, Arthur Warren *financial consulting company executive*

**Sumter**
Blakely, Delores Phinella *financial consultant, business advisor*

## SOUTH DAKOTA

**Burbank**
Simmons, Joseph Thomas *accountant, educator*

**Platte**
Pennington, Beverly Melcher *financial services company executive*

**Spearfish**
Anderson, Thomas Caryl *financial and administrative systems professional*

## TENNESSEE

**Alamo**
Finch, Evelyn Vorise *financial planner*

**Bristol**
Sessoms, Stephanie Thompson *accountant*

**Chattanooga**
Smith, David Yarnell *financial consultant*

**Elizabethton**
Taylor, Wesley Alan *accountant, consultant*

**Georgetown**
Geren, Brenda L. *business educator*

**Hendersonville**
Gregory, Sandra K. *accountant, consultant*

**Knoxville**
Vance, Stanley Charles *management educator*

**Memphis**
Forell, David Charles *financial executive*

**Murfreesboro**
Lee, John Thomas *finance educator, financial planner*

**Nashville**
Brophy, Jeremiah Joseph *financial company official, former army officer*
Dykes, Archie Reece *financial services executive*
Holsen, Robert Charles *accountant*
Richmond, Samuel Bernard *management educator*
Ullestad, Merwin Allan *tax services executive*
Van, George Paul *international money management consultant*
Weingartner, H(ans) Martin *finance educator*

## TEXAS

**Addison**
McElvain, David Plowman *retired manufacturing company financial executive*

**Amarillo**
Streu, Raymond Oliver *financial planner, securities executive*
Strickland, Anita Maurine *retired business educator, librarian*

**Arlington**
Dickinson, Roger Allyn *business administration educator*
Quant, Harold Edward *financial services company executive, rancher*
Swanson, Peggy Eubanks *finance educator*

**Austin**
Alpert, Mark Ira *marketing educator*
Anderson, Urton Liggett *accounting educator*
Blair, Calvin Patton *retired business administration educator*
Crum, Lawrence Lee *banking educator*
Cundiff, Edward William *marketing educator*
Doenges, Rudolph Conrad *finance educator*
Granof, Michael H. *accounting educator*
Graydon, Frank Drake *retired accounting educator, university administrator*
Kimberlin, Sam Owen, Jr. *financial institutions consultant*
Larson, Kermit Dean *accounting educator*
Montgomery, William J. *finance company executive*
Peterson, Robert Allen *marketing educator*
Robertson, Jack Clark *accounting educator*
Welsch, Glenn Albert *accounting educator*
Wolf, Harold Arthur *finance educator*

**Brownsville**
Cohen, Barry Mendel *financial executive, educator*

**Brownwood**
DeHay, Jerry Marvin *business educator*

**College Station**
Manning, Walter Scott *accountant, former educator, consultant*
Plum, Charles Walden *retired business executive and educator*
Wichern, Dean William *business educator*

**Colleyville**
Johnson, Zoe Ann *accounting executive*

**Dallas**
Blakeley, Kellie Elder *accountant, small business owner*
Coldwell, Philip Edward *financial consultant*
Eads, John A. *accountant*
Hay, Jess Thomas *retired finance company executive*
Howland, Grafton Dulany *financial counselor*
Jobe, Larry Alton *financial company executive*
Lomax, John H. *financial service company executive*
Mahr, George Joseph *financial service executive, real estate developer*
McElyea, Jacquelyn Suzanne *accountant, real estate consultant*
Moore, Thomas Joseph *financial company executive*
Murray, Suzanne Marie *accountant*
Owen, Robert Randolph *accountant*
Peiser, John George *accountant, consultant*
Shimer, Daniel Lewis *corporate executive*
Shower, Robert Wesley *financial executive*
Smiles, Ronald *management educator*
Solender, Robert Lawrence *financial, newsprint manufacturing executive*
Stratton, Robert *financial company executive*
Zammit, John P. *financial planner*

**Denton**
Brock, Horace Rhea *accounting educator*
Taylor, Sherrill Ruth *management educator*

**El Paso**
Hoagland, Jennifer Hope *accountant*
Kelley, Sylvia Johnson *financial services firm executive*
Showery, Charles George, Jr. *financial services company executive, consultant*

**Fort Worth**
Clark, Emory Eugene *financial planning executive*
Dominiak, Geraldine Florence *accounting educator*
†Rainwater, Richard *financial consultant, investor*
Yarbro, James Wesley *financial executive*

**Galveston**
Welch, Ronald J. *actuary*

**Garland**
McGill, Maurice Leon *financial executive*

**Georgetown**
Lord, William Grogan *financial holding company executive*

**Houston**
Arnold, Daniel Calmes *finance company executive*
D'Agostino, James Samuel, Jr. *financial executive*
Daily, James L., Jr. *retired financial executive*
Dunn, James Randolph *chief financial officer*
Goldberg, William Jeffrey *accountant*
Gomez, Lucas *assistant treasurer, credit manager*
Hargrove, James Ward *financial consultant*
Horvitz, Paul Michael *finance educator*
Janssens, Joe Lee *controller*
Jenkins, Judith Alexander *bank consultant*
Knauss, Robert Lynn *international business educator, corporate executive*
Mermelstein, Isabel Mae Rosenberg *financial consultant*
Miller, Kenneth William *holding company executive, financier*
Pluff, Stearns Charles, III *investment banker*
Quick, Lisa R. *accountant, scheduler*
Rockwell, Elizabeth Dennis *retirement specialist, financial planner*
Sims, Rebecca Gibbs *accountant, certified fraud examiner*
Van Caspel, Venita Walker *retired financial planner*
Wells, Damon, Jr. *investment company executive*
Wilkinson, Harry Edward *management educator and consultant*
Williams, James Lee *financial industries executive*
Young, Jeanette Cochran *corporate planner, reporter, analyst*
Zeff, Stephen Addam *accounting educator*

**Irving**
Mobley, William Hodges *management educator, researcher*
Pickett, Edwin Gerald *financial executive*
Serverian, Heidi Sue Whitaker *accountant, systems developer*

**Kingsville**
Stanford, Jane Herring *business administration educator*

**League City**
Lawson, Randall Clayton, II *financial executive*

**Lubbock**
Sears, Robert Stephen *finance educator*
Stem, Carl Herbert *business educator*
Wolfe, Verda Nell *pension consultant, financial planner*

**Marshall**
Thames, Earl Glenn *accounting educator*

**Mc Kinney**
Brewer, Ricky Lee *investment broker, estate planner*

**Midland**
Groce, James Freelan *financial consultant*

**Plano**
Bode, Richard Albert *retired financial executive*
Grant, Joseph Moorman *finance executive*

**Richardson**
Burke, Thomas William *executive benefits consulting company official*

Schrimsher, Jerry James *diversified financial services company executive*
Thomas, Robert Lee *financial services company executive, consultant*

**San Antonio**
Carroll, William Marion *financial services executive*
Fawcett, Leslie Clarence, Jr. *accountant*
Fuhrmann, Charles John, II *strategic and finance consultant*
Jones, James Richard *business administration educator*
Little, Mark McKenna *financial management executive*
Wills, Irene Young *accountant*

**Southlake**
Norris, Richard Anthony *accountant*

**Spring**
Griffith Fries, Martha *controller*

**Stephenville**
Collier, Boyd Dean *finance educator, management consultant*

**Sugar Land**
Keefe, Carolyn Joan *tax accountant*

**Texarkana**
Mitcham, Julius Jerome *accountant*

**Universal City**
Smith, James Earlie, Jr. *accountant*

**Waco**
Henke, Emerson Overbeck *accountant, educator*
Miller, Carl Chet *business educator*
Rose, John Thomas *finance educator*

**Wichita Falls**
Silverman, Gary William *financial planner*

**Wimberley**
Skaggs, Wayne Gerard *financial services company executive, retired*

**UTAH**

**Cedar City**
Hamlin, Alan Russell *financial educator*

**Ogden**
Paralez, Linda Lee *technology management consultant*

**Provo**
Hunt, H(arold) Keith *business management educator, marketing consultant*

**Saint George**
†Day, Steven M. *accounting educator, accountant*

**Salt Lake City**
Burdette, Robert Soelberg *accountant*
Creer, James Read *financial officer*
Dibb, Roger Alan *accountant*
Joseph, Kevin Mark *financial services executive*
Marsh, Scott Clyde *financial consultant, writer, lecturer*
Monson, David Smith *accountant, former congressman*
Nelson, Roger Hugh *management educator, business executive*
Snell, Ned Colwell *financial planner*
Young, Scott Thomas *business management educator*

**VERMONT**

**Burlington**
Thimm, Alfred Louis *management educator*

**Chittenden**
Haley, John Charles *financial executive*

**Manchester**
Mills, Gordon Lawrence *financial executive*

**Perkinsville**
Freeburg, Richard Gorman *financial derivatives company executive*

**Rutland**
Wright, William Bigelow *financial executive*

**Weston**
Neff, Walter Perry *financial consultant*

**VIRGINIA**

**Alexandria**
Brickhill, William Lee *international finance consultant*
†Hammad, Alam E. *international business consultant, educator*
Kyprios, Tina Slocum *auditor*
Le, Thuy Xuan *financial control systems developer, consultant, metaphysics scientist*

**Annandale**
Connair, Stephen Michael *financial analyst*

**Arlington**
Drake, Diana Ashley *financial planner*
Fulton, Diann Marie *financial consultant*
Lewis, Hunter *financial advisor, publisher*
Merrifield, Dudley Bruce *business educator, former government official*
Thomas, Jimmy Lynn *financial executive*

**Blacksburg**
Brozovsky, John A. *accounting educator*
Killough, Larry Neil *accounting educator*
Moore, Laurence John *business educator*

Ross, James Barrett *finance and insurance educator*

**Bristol**
Creger, David L. *financial planner, insurance executive*

**Broad Run**
Kube, Harold Deming *retired financial executive*

**Charlottesville**
Broome, Oscar Whitfield, Jr. *accounting educator, administrator*
Davis, Edward Wilson *business administration educator*
DeMong, Richard Francis *finance and investments educator*
Dickman, James Earl *financial services executive*
Dunn, Wendell Earl, III *business educator*
Horton, Madeline Mary *financial planner, consultant*
Mc Kinney, George Wesley, Jr. *banking educator*
Scott, Charlotte H. *business educator*
Shenkir, William Gary *business educator*
Sihler, William Wooding *finance educator*
Sorensen, Thomas Chaikin *retired financial executive*
Thompson, David William *business educator*
Trent, Robert Harold *business educator*

**Fairfax**
Bowden, Howard Kent *accountant*
Buzzell, Robert Dow *management educator*
Clive, Craig N. *compensation executive*
Sisodia, Rajendra Singh *business educator, researcher, consultant*

**Falls Church**
Hahn, Thomas Joonghi *accountant*
McVay, Mary Frances *portfolio manager*
Rosenberg, Theodore Roy *financial executive*

**Floyd**
McBroom, Diane Craun *accountant, horse trainer*

**Fort Belvoir**
Gould, Jay William, III *management development educator, lecturer, author, international consultant*

**Glen Allen**
Fairbank, Richard *diversified financial services company executive*

**Hampton**
Wiedman, Timothy Gerard *management educator*

**Harrisonburg**
Ramsey, Jackson Eugene *management educator*

**Lexington**
DeVogt, John Frederick *management science and business ethics educator, consultant*
Warner, Harry Hathaway *financial consultant*

**Mc Lean**
Halaby, Najeeb E. *financier, lawyer*
Hazlett, David C. *controller*
Maul, Kevin Jay *financial consultant*

**Newport News**
Le Mons, Kathleen Ann *portfolio manager, investment broker*

**Norfolk**
Haug, James Charles *business and management educator*
McKee, Timothy Carlton *taxation educator*

**Palmyra**
Sahr, Morris Gallup *financial planner*

**Reston**
Polemitou, Olga Andrea *accountant*

**Richmond**
Capps, Thos E. *diversified financial services company executive*
Coffman, Edward Nathaniel *accounting educator*
†Gottwald, Bruce Cobb, Jr. *treasurer analyst*
Hull, Rita Prizler *accounting educator*
King, Robert Leroy *business administration educator*
McDermott, William Thomas *accountant, lawyer*
Thompson, Francis Neal *financial services consultant*
Trumble, Robert Roy *business educator*

**Sterling**
Murchie, Edward Michael *accountant*

**Upperville**
Smart, Stephen Bruce, Jr. *business and government executive*

**Urbanna**
Hudson, Jesse Tucker, Jr. *financial executive*

**Vienna**
Bauer, Karen Mary *accountant, consultant*
Kautt, Glenn Gregory *financial planner*
Kumar, Verinder *accountant, financial executive*
Vreeland, Russell Glenn *accountant, consultant*
Zoeller, Jack Carl *financial executive*

**Virginia Beach**
O'Brien, Robert James *financial consultant, business owner*

**Waterford**
Harper, James Weldon, III *finance executive, consultant*

**Williamsburg**
Fulmer, Robert M. *business educator, management consultant*
Kottas, John Frederick *business administration educator*
Messmer, Donald Joseph *business management educator, marketing consultant*
O'Connell, William Edward, Jr. *finance educator*
Parkany, John *business educator, international financial consultant*
Regan, Donald Thomas *financier, writer, lecturer*
Ruppel, George Robert *accountant*

Strong, John Scott *finance educator*
Warren, William Herbert *business administration educator*

**Winchester**
Proe, John David *business educator, consultant, administrator*

**Woodbridge**
Dillaber, Philip Arthur *budget and resource analyst, economist, consultant*
Rose, Marianne Hunt *business educator*

**WASHINGTON**

**Bellevue**
Graham, John Robert, Jr. *financial executive*

**Bellingham**
Self, Charles Edwin *financial consultant, retail company executive*

**Cheney**
Drummond, Marshall Edward *business educator, university administrator*

**Everett**
Toyer, Richard Henry *accountant*

**Medical Lake**
Grub, Phillip Donald *business educator*

**Olympia**
Myers, Sharon Diane *auditor*

**Seattle**
Allen, Thomas Joseph *treasurer*
Bunting, Robert Louis *accounting firm executive, management consultant*
Collett, Robert Lee *financial company executive*
Etcheson, Warren Wade *business administration educator*
Feiss, George James, III *financial services company executive*
Gorans, Gerald Elmer *accountant*
Hanson, Kermit Osmond *business administration educator, university dean emeritus*
Harder, Virgil Eugene *business administration educator*
Johnson, Janice Susan Gallik *finance executive*
Kasama, Hideto Peter *accountant, advisor, real estate consultant*
MacLachlan, Douglas Lee *marketing educator*
Pitts, Barbara Towle *accountant, painter*
Ramanathan, Kavasseri Vaidianatha *accounting educator, researcher, consultant*
Saunders, William Lockwood *financial consultant*
Saxberg, Borje Osvald *management educator*
Tollett, Glenna Belle *accountant, mobile home park operator*

**Spokane**
Burton, Robert Lyle *accounting firm executive*

**Yakima**
Bruenn, Ronald Sherman *financial company executive*

**WEST VIRGINIA**

**Charleston**
Lamb, Patrick John *research associate, accountant*
Seiber, William Joseph *financial and insurance consultant*

**Elkins**
Payne, Gloria Marquette *business educator*

**Inwood**
Cloyd, Helen Mary *accountant, educator*

**Weirton**
Robinson, Charles Warren *controller*

**WISCONSIN**

**Belgium**
Slater, John Greenleaf *financial consultant*

**Brookfield**
Roder, Ronald Ernest *accountant*

**Eau Claire**
Weil, D(onald) Wallace *business administration educator*

**Greenfield**
Neal, Jon C(harles) *accountant, consultant*

**Madison**
Aldag, Ramon John *management and organization educator*
Baron, Alma Fay S. *management educator*
Googins, Louise Paulson *financial planner*
Keenan, John Paul *management educator, consultant, psychologist*
Nevin, John Robert *business educator, consultant*
Prieve, E. Arthur *arts administration educator*
Reuschlein, Robert William *accountant, researcher*
Thompson, Howard Elliott *business educator*
Wade, Royce Allen *financial services representative*

**Menomonee Falls**
Walters, Ronald Ogden *finance company executive*

**Mequon**
Berry, William Martin *financial consultant*

**Middleton**
Foss, Karl Robert *auditor*

**Milwaukee**
Goldin, Martin Bruce *financial executive, consultant*

Kendall, Leon Thomas *finance and real estate educator, retired insurance company executive*
Manko, Wesley Daniel *financial advisor*
Panenka, James Brian Joseph *financial company executive*

**Muskego**
Stefaniak, Norbert John *business administration educator*

**Oconomowoc**
Kneiser, Richard John *accountant*

**Pewaukee**
Tessmann, Cary Annette *controller*

**Solon Springs**
Robek, Mary Frances *business education educator*

**Wisconsin Rapids**
Kenney, Richard John *paper company finance executive*

**WYOMING**

**Afton**
Hunsaker, Floyd B. *accountant*

**Cody**
Riley, Victor J., Jr. *financial services company executive*

**Green River**
Thoman, Mary E. *business and marketing educator, rancher*

**Laramie**
Spiegelberg, Emma Jo *business education educator*

**Riverton**
Clark, Stanford E. *accountant*

**Wheatland**
Whitney, Ralph Royal, Jr. *financial executive*

**TERRITORIES OF THE UNITED STATES**

**GUAM**

**Tamuning**
Camacho, Eduardo Garcia *finance company executive, insurance agent*

**NORTHERN MARIANA ISLANDS**

**Saipan**
Aldan, Tomas Benavente *pension fund administrator*

**CANADA**

**BRITISH COLUMBIA**

**Burnaby**
Tung, Rosalie Lam *business educator, consultant*

**Powell River**
Carsten, Arlene Desmet *financial executive*

**Vancouver**
Mahler, Richard T. *finance executive*
Mattessich, Richard Victor (Alvarus) *business administration educator*
Stone, Robert Ryrie *financial executive*

**NEW BRUNSWICK**

**Saint Andrews**
Anderson, John Murray *operations executive, former university president*

**ONTARIO**

**Islington**
White, Adrian Michael Stephen *financial executive*

**London**
Osbaldeston, Gordon Francis *business educator, former government official*

**Mississauga**
Turnbull, Adam Michael Gordon *financial executive, accountant*

**Toronto**
Cockwell, Jack Lynn *financial executive*
Cunningham, Gordon Ross *financial executive*
Greig, Thomas Currie *retired financial executive*
Hirst, Peter Christopher *consulting actuary*
Jagt, Jack *trading company executive*
Lowe, Robert Edward *financial company executive*
Mann, George Stanley *real estate and financial services corporation executive*
Payton, Thomas William *corporate finance consultant executive*
†Poprawa, Andrew *financial services executive, accountant*
Ronald, Thomas Iain *financial services executive*
Silk, Frederick C.Z. *financial consultant*
Skinner, Alastair *accountant*
Sloan, David Edward *retired corporate executive*
Weldon, David Black *financial executive*

**Welland**
Wintermans, Joseph Jack Gerard Francis *financial services executive*

## QUEBEC

**Montreal**
Crowston, Wallace Bruce Stewart *management educator*
Daly, Gerald *accountant*
Desmarais, Paul *holding company executive*
Laurin, Pierre *finance company executive*
Marcoux, Yvon *financial executive, lawyer*
Mintzberg, Henry *management educator, researcher, writer*
Olivella, Barry James *financial executive*
Picard, Laurent A(ugustin) *management educator, administrator, consultant*
Pike, Charles James *employee benefits consultant, financial planner*
Saumier, Andre *finance executive*
Speirs, Derek James *diversified corporation financial executive*
Thompson, John Douglas *financier*
Weir, Stephen James *financial executive*

**Sainte Foy**
†Saint-Pierre, Michael R. *financial services executive*

**Verdun**
Lessard, Michel M. *finance company executive*

## SASKATCHEWAN

**Saskatoon**
Irvine, Vernon Bruce *accounting educator, administrator*

## ENGLAND

**London**
Berger, Thomas Jan *financial company executive*
Gyllenhammar, Pehr Gustaf *finance company executive, retired automobile company executive, writer*
Hallissey, Michael *accounting company executive*
MacHale, Joseph P. *financial executive*
Pacter, Paul Allan *accounting standards researcher*

## FINLAND

**Helsinki**
Siimestö, Orvo Kalervo *financial executive*

## FRANCE

**Paris**
Bourdais de Charbonn, Eric *financial executive*

## INDONESIA

**Jakarta**
Hamidjaja, Wiriadi (Willy Hamidjaja) *finance executive*

## JAPAN

**Irumagun**
Kobayashi, Noritake *business educator*

**Kyoto**
Shima, Hiromu *management educator*

**Suita**
Ohashi, Shoichi *business administration educator*

**Tokyo**
Reich, Pauline Carole *international business consultant, educator, author*

## SAUDI ARABIA

**Riyadh**
Olayan, Suliman Saleh *finance company executive*

## SWEDEN

**Hasselby**
Wasell, Gösta *retired auditor*

**Lund**
Welin, Walter *financial advisor*

## SWITZERLAND

**Geneva**
Farman-Farmaian, Ghaffar *investment company executive*

**Lugano**
Ricci, Giovanni Mario *finance company executive*

## ADDRESS UNPUBLISHED

Adam, Orval Michael *retired financial executive, lawyer*
Amdahl, Byrdelle John *business consulting executive*
Anderson, Michael L. *financial planning manager*
Arenberg, Julius Theodore, Jr. *retired accounting company executive*
Barbee, George E. L. *financial services and business executive*

Barcenas, Jude R. L. *financial services company executive*
Barney, Austin Cornelius Dunham, II *estate planner*
Barton, Ann Elizabeth *retired financial executive*
Beebe, John Eldridge *financial service executive*
Beller, Luanne Evelyn *accountant*
Belluomini, Frank Stephen *accountant*
Beltz, Herbert Allison *retired financial consultant*
Benjamin, James Cover *controller, manufacturing company executive*
Benson, James Carl *retired accountant*
Blasco, Alfred Joseph *business and financial consultant*
Blausey, Jeanne Martha *accountant, financial systems analyst, fraud examiner*
Bliss, William Stanley, Jr. *corporate financial and marketing consultant*
Borum, Rodney Lee *financial business executive*
Bowne, Shirlee Pearson *credit union executive, real estate executive*
Boyd, Edward Lee *financial executive*
Boyd, Francis Virgil *retired accounting educator*
Branson, Harley Kenneth *finance executive, motion picture producer*
Brennan, Ciaran Brendan *accountant, independent oil producer, real estate developer*
Brink, John William *financial corporation executive*
Brown, Henry Bedinger Rust *financial management company executive*
Brune, David Hamilton *financial corporation executive, lawyer*
Burns, Mary Ferris *finance executive*
Campbell, Alan Keith *business educator*
Campbell, Alice Shaw *retired accountant, poet*
Carroll, Karen Jeorgianna *fund administrator*
Carter, Richard Duane *business educator*
Castiglione, Kathie Anne *accountant*
Charlton, Jesse Melvin, Jr. *management educator, lawyer*
Chelberg, Bruce Stanley *holding company executive*
Chia, Felipe Humberto *management marketing educator, author, consultant*
†Christen, Paul Richert *financial company executive*
Contillo, Lawrence Joseph *financial and computer company executive*
Covington, Gary Wayne *accountant*
Cox, David Brummal *accounting firm executive*
Crooker, Diane Kay *accountant*
Darany, Michael Anthony *financial executive*
Davidson, John *financial advisory executive*
Delany, Logan Drummond, Jr. *financial consultant, investor*
†Deli, Steven Frank *finance company executive*
Derchin, Michael Wayne *financial analyst*
Doherty, Thomas Joseph *financial services industry consultant*
Doty, Philip Edward *accountant*
Eggan, Hugh Melford *accountant*
Ernstthal, Henry L. *management educator*
Estrin, Herbert Alvin *financial consultant, entertainment company executive*
Everett, Donna Raney *business educator*
Fagerberg, Dixon, Jr. *retired accountant, weather observer*
Falker, John Richard *financial and securities market consultant*
Farrall, Harold John *retired accountant*
Ferguson, Robert *financial services executive, educator, writer*
Fowler, Raymond David *financial executive*
Fowler, Robert Joseph *financial company executive, consultant*
Frank, Edgar Gerald *retired financial executive*
Franklin, Barbara Kipp *financial advisor*
Fuller, Stephen Herbert *business administration educator*
Garfinkel, Fran Sylvia *professional business coach, financial planner*
Garten, Wayne Philip *financial executive*
Gierlasinski, Kathy Lynn *accountant*
Gleijeses, Mario *holding company executive*
Gray, Margaret Ann *management educator, consultant*
Griffin, Carleton Hadlock *accountant, educator*
Gruber, Fredric Francis *financial planning and investment research executive*
Guimond, John Patrick *retired financial consultant*
Haddock, Harold, Jr. *retired accounting firm executive*
Hall, Terry Lee *accountant*
Hamlin, Dan William *accountant, management consultant*
Handy, Edward Otis, Jr. *financial services executive*
Hanson, Carl Malmrose *financial company executive*
Harper, W(alter) Joseph *financial consultant*
Harper-Arens, Rebecca Coleman *accountant*
Hershberger, Steven Kaye *controller*
Hickson, Ernest Charles *financial executive*
Holloran, Thomas Edward *business educator*
Holton, Grace Holland *accountant*
Hoy, Harold Joseph *marketing educator, retail executive, management consultant, author, military officer*
Hubbe, Henry Ernest *financial forecaster, funds manager*
Hudak, Thomas F(rancis) *finance company executive*
Huddleston, Marilyn Anne *international financier, merchant banker, educator, author*
Hudson, Sharon Marie *credit and collections specialist*
Hutner, Herbert L. *financial consultant, lawyer*
Jacques, Andre Charles *financial consultant*
Jamison, John Callison *business educator, investment banker*
Jeansonne, Angela Lynne *senior analyst*
Johnson, Philip *investment banking executive*
Kaplan, Leonard Eugene *accountant*
Keegan, Kenneth Donald *financial consultant, retired oil company executive*
Kennedy, Thomas Patrick *financial executive*
Kidd, Robert Hugh *financial executive, accountant*
King, Algin Braddy *marketing educator*
Kingsbery, Walton Waits, Jr. *retired accountant*
Kolton, Paul *business executive*
Korgaonkar, Pradeep Kashinath *marketing educator*
Kreitzer, Lois Helen *personal investor*
Kryza, E(lmer) Gregory *financial planner, international affairs advisor, former ambassador*
La Blanc, Robert Edmund *consulting company executive*
Larizadeh, M(ohammed) R(eza) *business educator*
Lavin, Roxanna Marie *finance executive*
Lesher, John Lee, Jr. *consulting services company executive*
Leventhal, Ellen Iris *portfolio manager, financial services executive*
Levy, Louis Edward *retired accounting firm executive*

Lewis, Charles Arlen *financial services company executive*
Lewis, Gordon Carter *auditor*
Lewis, James Lee, Jr. *actuary*
Litow, Joel David *strategic planning and financial analyst*
Longo, Kathryn Milani *pension consultant*
Loren, Mary Rooney *controller*
Madison, T. Jerome *business executive*
Magnano, Salvatore Paul *retired financial executive, treasurer*
Mahoney, Donald Scott *financial industry marketing executive*
Malone, Edward H. *financial executive*
Mand, Martin G. *financial executive*
Martin, LeRoy E. *finance company executive*
Martin, Preston *financial services executive*
Massachi, Albert (David Massachi) *financial strategist*
May, Phyllis Jean *financial executive*
Mayoras, Donald Eugene *corporate executive, speaker, consultant, educator*
Mc Gowan, James Atkinson *business executive, financial consultant*
McVey, Diane Elaine *accountant*
Mednick, Robert *accountant*
Miller, Donald Muxlow *accountant, administrator*
Miller, Kenneth William, II *business consultant, educator*
Miller, Robert Stevens, Jr. *finance professional*
Morgan, Robert Arthur *accountant*
Mosler, John *retired financial planner*
Muller, Margie Hellman *financial services consultant*
Nair, Raghavan D. *accountant, educator*
Nank, Lois Rae *financial executive*
Needles, Belverd Earl, Jr. *accountant, educator*
Neelankavil, James Paul *international business educator, researcher and consultant*
Nehrt, Lee Charles *management educator*
Neimark, Philip John *financial consultant, editor*
Newman, Dennis Collins, Sr. *accountant*
Nichols, John David *insurance and financial services broker*
Palmer, Gary Andrew *portfolio manager*
Park, Charles Donald, Sr. *financial executive*
Parr, Harry Edward, Jr. *financial executive*
Paul, Gordon Wilbur *marketing educator*
Pefley, Norman Gordon *financial analyst*
Phillips, Charles Alan *accounting firm executive*
Pick, James Block *management and sociology educator*
Puryear, Alvin Nelson *management educator*
Quirk, Kenneth Paul *accountant*
Reeves, Peggy Lois Zeigler *accountant*
Reynolds, Billie Iles *financial representative and counselor, former association executive*
Robertson, A. Haeworth *actuary, benefit consultant, foundation executive*
Rodriguez, Elena Garcia *retired pension fund administrator*
Rosenkrans, Kenneth Ray *financial services*
Roth, Suzanne Allen *financial services agent*
Roveto, Connie Ida *financial services executive*
Rowe, William Davis *financial services company executive*
Ruggles, Rudy Lamont, Jr. *investment banker, consultant*
Rush, Richard Henry *financial executive, writer, lecturer*
Ryan, Leo Vincent *business educator*
Said, Kamal E. *accounting educator*
Sayles, Leonard Robert *management educator, consultant*
Scheel, Nels Earl *financial executive, accountant*
Schoen, William Jack *financier*
Schulz, Marianne *accountant*
Sefcik, John Delbert *financial services executive*
Shaw, David Elliot *financial executive*
Shelet, Dawn Ardelle *financial analyst*
Shepherd, Steven Stewart *auditor, consultant*
Sheridan, Patrick Michael *finance company executive*
Shields, H. Richard *tax consultant,business executive*
Shoop, Glenn Powell *investment consultant*
Shore, Harvey Harris *business educator*
Shultis, Robert Lynn *finance educator, cost systems consultant, retired professional association executive*
Smith, Kenneth Blose *former financial executive*
Smith, Seymour Maslin *financial advisor, investment banker*
Snelling, Robert Orren, Sr. *franchising executive*
Srinivasan, Venkataraman *marketing and management educator*
Swanson, Rune E. *financial executive*
Tongue, Paul Graham *financial executive*
Treynor, Jack Lawrence *financial advisor, educator*
Turner, Henry Brown *finance executive*
Tyler, Richard James *personal and professional development educator*
†Udvar-Hazy, Steven F. *leasing company financial executive*
Ulrich, Richard William *finance executive*
van Hengel, Maarten R. *financial executive*
Wain, Christopher Henry Fairfax Moresby *actuary, insurance and investment consultant*
Wall, M. Danny *finance company executive*
Waters, Cheryl Diane *accountant*
Watson, W(allace) Robert *financial executive*
Watt, John H. *financial executive*
Wells, Toni Lynn *accountant*
Whalen-Blaauwgeers, Herma-Jozé *financial analyst*
Wilhelmsen, Harold John *accountant, operations controller*
Williams Jones, Elizabeth *financial planner, business consultant*
Wolf, Rosalie Joyce *financial executive*
Zick, John Walter *retired accounting company executive*

---

## FINANCE: INSURANCE

### UNITED STATES

### ALABAMA

**Birmingham**
Currie, Larry Lamar *insurance company executive*
Rushton, William James, III *insurance company executive*

**Montgomery**
Owens, Doris Jerkins *insurance underwriter*

### ARIZONA

**Carefree**
Wise, Paul Schuyler *insurance company executive*

**Flagstaff**
Mullens, William Reese *retired insurance company executive*

**Green Valley**
Brissman, Bernard Gustave *insurance company executive*

**Lake Havasu City**
Shervheim, Lloyd Oliver *insurance company executive, lawyer*

**Paradise Valley**
Day, Richard Putnam *marketing, strategic planning and employee benefits consultant*

**Phoenix**
Barbanell, Alexander Stanley *insurance marketing company executive*
Hacker, Kenneth Russell *insurance executive*
Melner, Sinclair Lewis *insurance company executive, retired*

**Prescott**
Osborn, DeVerle Ross *insurance company executive*

**Scottsdale**
Burr, Edward Benjamin *life insurance company executive, financial executive*
Prisbrey, Rex Prince *retired insurance agent, underwriter, consultant*
Tyner, Neal Edward *retired insurance company executive*
Vairo, Robert John *insurance company executive*

**Tempe**
Oxford, Sharon M. *insurance company executive*

**Tubac**
Fey, John Theodore *retired insurance company executive*

**Tucson**
Martin, Paul Edward *retired insurance company executive*
Ziehler, Tony Joseph *insurance agent*

### ARKANSAS

**Fayetteville**
Dulan, Harold Andrew *former insurance company executive, educator*

**Pine Bluff**
Bradford, Jay Turner *insurance executive, state legislator*

### CALIFORNIA

**Agoura Hills**
Koff, Robert Louis *insurance executive*

**Auburn**
Jeske, Howard Leigh *retired life insurance company executive, lawyer*

**Burlingame**
Bell, Herbert Aubrey Frederick *life insurance company executive*

**Danville**
Frederickson, John Marcus *insurance executive*

**Encino**
Webster, David Arthur *life insurance company executive*

**Garden Grove**
Williams, J(ohn) Tilman *insurance executive, real estate broker, city official*

**Gold River**
Gray, Myles McClure *retired insurance company executive*

**Irvine**
Bañuelos, Robert Alexander *insurance company executive*

**Los Angeles**
Baker, Lawrence Colby, Jr. *insurance company executive*
Decaminada, Joseph Pio *insurance company executive, educator*
Faulwell, Gerald Edward *insurance company executive*
Gurash, John Thomas *insurance company executive*
Houston, Ivan James *insurance company executive*
Johnson, E. Eric *insurance executive*
Rinsch, Charles Emil *insurance company executive*

**Newport Beach**
Fries, Arthur Lawrence *life health insurance broker, disability claim consultant*
Gerken, Walter Bland *insurance company executive*
Grager, Steven Paul *insurance consultant*
Marcoux, Carl Henry *former insurance executive, writer, historian*

**Novato**
Grove, Douglas David *insurance company executive*

**Orange**
Boynton, Donald Arthur *retired title insurance company executive*

**Palm Springs**
Fromm, Erwin Frederick *retired insurance company executive, health facility executive*

**Rancho Cordova**
Alenius, John Todd *insurance executive*
Crowley, Daniel D. *health insurance executive*

**Redlands**
Treece, Joseph Charles *insurance broker*

**San Diego**
Hayes, Robert Emmet *retired insurance company executive*
Jeffers, Donald E. *retired insurance executive, consultant*
McBroom, Nancy Lee *insurance executive*
Purcifull, Robert Otis *insurance company executive*
Ross, Vonia Pearl *insurance agent, small business owner*
Rotter, Paul Talbott *retired insurance executive*

**San Francisco**
Bow, Stephen Tyler, Jr. *insurance company executive*
Broome, Burton Edward *insurance company executive*
Clark, Edgar Sanderford *insurance broker, consultant*
Djordjevich, Michael *insurance company executive*
Drexler, Fred *insurance executive*
Enfield, D(onald) Michael *insurance executive*
Hatfield, Dale Charles *insurance company executive, banker*
Lamberson, John Roger *insurance company executive*
Levine, Norman Gene *insurance company executive*
Murrin, Thomas Edward *insurance company executive*

**San Jose**
Jackson, Patrick Joseph *insurance executive*

**Santa Barbara**
Reis, Edward Thomas, Jr. *insurance executive, educator*

**Santa Rosa**
Farrell, Thomas Joseph *insurance company executive, consultant*

**Spring Valley**
Peterson, Donald Curtis *life care executive, consultant*

**Thousand Oaks**
Gregory, Calvin *insurance service executive*

**Tustin**
Evans, Thomas Edgar, Jr. *title insurance agency executive*

**Woodland Hills**
Greaves, Roger F. *health maintenance organization executive*
Southam, Arthur M. *insurance company executive*

## COLORADO

**Denver**
Axley, Hartman *underwriter*
Conroy, Thomas Francis *insurance company executive*
Robinson-Petersen, Carole Ann *insurance executive, retired*

**Englewood**
†Engleberg, David *health insurance company executive*
Hardy, Wayne Russell *insurance broker*
Manley, Richard Walter *insurance executive*
O'Bryan, William Hall *insurance executive*

**Lakewood**
Lewis, Charles D. *insurance executive, rancher, consultant*

**Littleton**
Moore, Dan Sterling *insurance executive, sales trainer*

**Parker**
Nelson, Marvin Ray *retired life insurance company executive*

**Pueblo**
Kelly, William Bret *insurance executive*

## CONNECTICUT

**Collinsville**
Ford, Dexter *retired insurance company executive*

**Cos Cob**
Woodman, Harry Andrews *retired life insurance company executive, consultant*

**Danbury**
Gogliettino, John Carmine *insurance broker*

**Fairfield**
O'Connell, Robert John *insurance company executive*

**Farmington**
Hickey, Kevin Francis *healthcare executive*

**Glastonbury**
Randall, Gerald J. *insurance company executive*

**Greenwich**
Berkley, William Robert *insurance holding company executive*
Clements, Robert *insurance executive*
Fuller, Theodore *retired insurance executive*
Heer, Edwin LeRoy *insurance executive*

**Hartford**
Abbot, Quincy Sewall *retired insurance executive*
Budd, Edward Hey *retired insurance company executive*
Compton, Ronald E. *insurance and financial services executive*
Fiondella, Robert William *insurance company executive*
Gingold, George Norman *insurance company executive, lawyer*
Herman, Joan Elizabeth *insurance company executive*
Holt, Timothy Arthur *insurance company executive*
Jones, Thomas Chester *insurance company executive*
Mullane, Denis Francis *insurance executive*
Sargent, Joseph Denny *insurance executive*
Scully, John Carroll *life insurance marketing research company executive*
Westervelt, James Joseph *insurance company executive*
Wilde, Wilson *insurance company executive*
Wilder, Michael Stephen *insurance company executive*

**New Canaan**
Cohen, Richard Norman *insurance executive*

**Simsbury**
Krisher, William K. *former insurance company executive*
Vander Putten, LeRoy Andrew *insurance company executive*

**Stamford**
Block, Ruth *retired insurance company executive*
Ferguson, Ronald Eugene *reinsurance company executive*
Hudson, Harold Jordon, Jr. *retired insurance executive*
Kellogg, Tommy Nason *reinsurance corporation executive*
Schofield, Herbert Spencer, III *insurance executive*

**Weston**
Thompson, N(orman) David *insurance company executive*

## DELAWARE

**Greenville**
Dombeck, Harold Arthur *insurance company executive*

**Wilmington**
Nottingham, Robinson Kendall *life insurance company executive*
Pell, Jane Eileen *insurance executive*

## DISTRICT OF COLUMBIA

**Washington**
Browne, Ray *insurance broker*
Conrad, Donald Glover *insurance executive*
Freeman, Robert Turner, Jr. *insurance executive*
Howes, Theodore Clark *claims examiner*
Lewin, George Forest *former insurance company executive*
Lynn, James Thomas *investment banker, insurance company executive, government executive, lawyer*
Nicely, Olza M. (Tony) *insurance company executive*
Oakley, Diane *insurance executive, benefit consultant*
†Parde, Duane Arthur *insurance company executive*
Poulin, Claude *actuarial consultant*
Simpson, Louis A. *insurance company executive*

## FLORIDA

**Boca Raton**
Deppe, Henry A. *insurance company executive*
Knudsen, Rudolph Edgar, Jr. *insurance company executive*
Leahy, William F. *insurance company executive, lawyer*
Lipsey, John C. (Jack Lipsey) *insurance company executive*
Lynn, Eugene Matthew *insurance company executive*
Richardson, R(oss) Fred(erick) *insurance executive*
Sena, John Michael *insurance agent*

**Boynton Beach**
Bryant, Donald Loyd *insurance company executive*
Caras, Joseph Sheldon *life insurance company executive*

**Bradenton**
Phelan, John Densmore *insurance executive, consultant*

**Clearwater**
Caronis, George John *insurance executive*

**Fort Lauderdale**
Donoho, Tim Mark *insurance and publishing executive*
McIntyre, Charles Earl *insurance executive*

**Fort Myers**
Cooke, Joan Ellen *healthcare executive, consultant*

**Hollywood**
Napsky, Martin Ben *insurance executive*

**Jacksonville**
Howell, John Floyd *insurance company executive*
Lyon, Wilford Charles, Jr. *insurance executive*
McCullough, Ray Daniel, Jr. *insurance company executive*
Morehead, Charles Richard *insurance company executive*

**Key Largo**
Daenzer, Bernard John *insurance company executive, legal consultant*

**Largo**
Guthrie, John Craver *insurance agency owner*

**Longwood**
Brown, Donald James, Jr. *insurance company executive*

**Miami**
Denison, Floyd Gene *insurance executive*
George, Stephen Carl *insurance company executive, educator, consultant, author*
Heggen, Arthur William *insurance company executive*
Johnson, Glendon E. *insurance company executive*
Landon, Robert Kirkwood *insurance company executive*
Van Wyck, George Richard *insurance company executive*

**Naples**
Duff, Daniel Vincent *former insurance company executive, former mayor*
Kennedy, Donald Davidson, Jr. *retired insurance company executive*
Mc Queen, Robert Charles *retired insurance executive*
Parish, John Cook *insurance executive*

**Orlando**
Vaughn, E(lbert) Hardy *insurance and financial company executive*

**Osprey**
Woodall, William Leon *retired insurance executive*

**Oviedo**
Brethauer, William Russell, Jr. *claim investigator*

**Palatka**
Ginn, John Arthur, Jr. *insurance agent*

**Palm Beach**
Becker, John Lionel, Jr. *insurance company executive, marketing company executive*

**Palm Beach Gardens**
†Sigel, Jay *insurance company executive*

**Pensacola**
DeBardeleben, John Thomas, Jr. *retired insurance company executive*

**Pompano Beach**
Zinman, Jacques *former insurance agency executive*

**Port Saint Lucie**
Rhodes, Alfred William *former insurance company executive*

**Saint Petersburg**
Alpert, Barry Mark *insurance company and banking executive*

**Seminole**
Hoche, Philip Anthony *life insurance company executive*

**Tallahassee**
Gunter, William Dawson, Jr. (Bill Gunter) *insurance company executive*
Hunt, John Edwin *insurance company executive, consultant*

**Tampa**
Dodds, Linda Carol *insurance company executive*
Poe, William Frederick *insurance agency executive, former mayor*
Tutwiler, Charles Richard (Dick Tutwiler) *insurance company executive*

**Tequesta**
Holmes, Melvin Almont *insurance company executive*

**Vero Beach**
Burton, Arthur Henry, Jr. *insurance company executive*
Feagles, Robert West *insurance company executive*

**Village Of Golf**
Bates, Edward Brill *retired insurance company executive*

**Winter Park**
Conrad, Judy L. *insurance company executive*

## GEORGIA

**Atlanta**
Atkinson, A. Kelley *insurance company executive*
Baxter, Robert Hampton, III *insurance executive*
Black, Kenneth, Jr. *insurance executive, educator, author*
Buck, Lee Albert *retired insurance company executive, evangelist*
Fowler, Vivian Delores *insurance company executive*
†Garner, Thomas Emory, Jr. *health insurance executive*
Gregory, Mel Hyatt, Jr. *retired insurance company executive*
Huntley, William Thomas, III *investor, consultant*
Peacock, George Rowatt *retired life insurance company executive*
Smith, Dennis A. *insurance company executive*
Waggoner, Leland Tate *insurance company executive*

**Columbus**
Amos, Daniel Paul *insurance executive*
Cloninger, Kriss, III *insurance company executive*

**Duluth**
Burns, Carroll Dean *insurance company executive*

**Macon**
Hartman, Alan Frazier *estate planning specialist*

**Savannah**
Dodge, William Douglas *insurance company consultant*

Innes, John Phythian, II *insurance company executive*
Standbridge, Peter Thomas *retired insurance company executive*

**Smyrna**
Cressey, Douglas B. *insurance company executive*

**Statesboro**
Parrish, Benjamin Emmitt, II *insurance executive*

## HAWAII

**Honolulu**
Kanehiro, Kenneth Kenji *insurance educator, risk analyst, consultant*
Lee, Marcia Ellen *insurance agent*
Okada, Ronald Masaki *insurance agent*
Ronsman, Wayne John *insurance company executive*

## ILLINOIS

**Bloomington**
Callis, Bruce *insurance company executive*
Curry, Alan Chester *insurance company executive*
Engelkes, Donald John *insurance company executive*
Johnson, Earle Bertrand *insurance executive*
Joslin, Roger Scott *insurance company executive*
Miller, Duane Leon *insurance company executive*
Rust, Edward Barry, Jr. *insurance company executive, lawyer*
Shelley, Edward Herman, Jr. *retired insurance company executive*

**Burr Ridge**
Greulich, Robert Charles *insurance company marketing executive*

**Champaign**
Peterson, Roger Lyman *insurance company executive*

**Chicago**
Bartholomay, William C. *insurance brokerage company executive, professional baseball team executive*
Berkery, Michael John *insurance company executive*
Bolnick, Howard Jeffrey *insurance consultant, educator, private investor*
Chang, Yi-Cheng *insurance agent*
Cizza, John Anthony *insurance executive*
DeMoss, Jon W. *insurance company executive, lawyer*
Desch, Theodore Edward *health insurance company executive, lawyer*
†Engel, Philip L. *insurance company executive*
Hinkelman, Ruth Amidon *insurance company executive*
Ingram, Donald *insurance company executive*
Jerome, Jerrold V. *insurance company executive*
Kendrick, William Monroe *insurance company executive*
Lee, William Kendall, Jr. *insurance industry executive*
Lorenz, Hugo Albert *retired insurance executive, consultant*
Manning, Frederick James *insurance company executive*
Parcells, Frederick R. *product management*
Ryan, Patrick G. *insurance company executive*
Rycroft, Donald Cahill *insurance executive*
Tocklin, Adrian Martha *insurance company executive, lawyer*
Vie, Richard Carl *insurance company executive*
Zucaro, Aldo Charles *insurance company executive*

**Decatur**
Braun, William Joseph *life insurance underwriter*
Strong, John David *insurance company executive*

**Deerfield**
Cruikshank, John W., III *life insurance underwriter*

**Des Plaines**
Pannke, Peggy M. *long term care insurance agency executive*

**Evanston**
Pabst, Edmund G. *retired insurance company executive, lawyer*
Peponis, Harold Arthur *insurance agent, broker*

**Galena**
Crandall, John Lynn *insurance consultant, retired insurance company executive*

**Geneva**
Goulet, Charles Ryan *retired insurance company executive*

**Glencoe**
Webb, James Okrum, Jr. *insurance company executive*

**Highland Park**
Boruszak, James Martin *insurance company executive*

**Hinsdale**
Denton, Ray Douglas *insurance company executive*

**Lake Forest**
Brown, Cameron *insurance company consultant*
Eckert, Ralph John *insurance company executive*
Ford, Donald James *retired insurance company executive, consultant, lawyer*
O'Loughlin, John Kirby *retired insurance executive*
Peterson, Donald Matthew *insurance company executive*

**Lake Zurich**
Fachet, William F., Jr. *insurance company executive*

**Morrison**
French, Raymond Douglas *insurance agent, realtor*

**Northbrook**
Choate, Jerry D. *insurance company executive*

McFadden, Joseph Patrick *insurance company executive*
Pike, Robert William *insurance company executive, lawyer*
Saunders, Kenneth D. *insurance company executive, consultant, arbitrator*
Wilson, Rita P. *insurance company executive*

**Northfield**
Hoopis, Harry Peter *insurance executive, entrepreneur*

**Oakbrook Terrace**
Shalek, James Arthur, Jr. *insurance agent, financial consultant*

**Orland Park**
Schultz, Barbara Marie *insurance company executive*

**Peoria**
Michael, Jonathan Edward *insurance company executive*

**Prospect Heights**
Clark, Donald Robert *retired insurance company executive*

**Rock Island**
Cheney, Thomas Ward *insurance company executive*
Lardner, Henry Petersen (Peter Lardner) *insurance company executive*

**Schaumburg**
Fitzpatrick, John Henry *insurance company executive*

**Skokie**
Hedien, Wayne Evans *retired insurance company executive*

**Springfield**
Budinger, Charles Jude *state agency insurance analyst*

**Wheaton**
Flynn, James Rourke *retired insurance company executive*

## INDIANA

**Bloomington**
Long, John D. *retired insurance educator*

**Carmel**
Hilbert, Stephen C. *insurance company executive*

**Fort Wayne**
Clarke, Kenneth Stevens *insurance company executive*
Dunsire, P(eter) Kenneth *insurance company executive*
Lupke, Duane Eugene *insurance company executive*
Robertson, Richard Stuart *insurance holding company executive*
Rolland, Ian McKenzie *insurance executive*
Steiner, Paul Andrew *retired insurance executive*
Vachon, Marilyn Ann *retired insurance company executive*
West, Thomas Meade *financial services strategic consultant*

**Greenwood**
Daniel, Michael Edwin *insurance agency executive*

**Indianapolis**
Baxter, Carla Louise Chaney *insurance product specialist*
Christenson, Le Roy Howard *insurance company officer*
Cramer, Betty F. *life insurance company executive*
Gagel, Barbara Jean *health insurance administrator*
Gaunce, Michael Paul *insurance company executive*
Heard, William Robert *retired insurance company executive*
Henderson, Bruce Wingrove *insurance executive*
Husman, Catherine Bigot *insurance company executive, actuary*
Lytle, L(arry) Ben *insurance company executive, lawyer*
McCarthy, Harold Charles *retired insurance company executive*
McKinney, E. Kirk, Jr. *retired insurance company executive*
Norman, LaLander Stadig *insurance company executive*
Prible, Larry R. *insurance company executive*
Robinson, Larry Robert *insurance company executive*
Wolsiffer, Patricia Rae *insurance company executive*

**Jasper**
Fleck, Albert Henry, Jr. *insurance agency executive*

**Lafayette**
Whitsel, Robert Malcolm *retired insurance company executive*

**Leo**
Worman, Richard W. *insurance company executive, state senator*

**Pendleton**
Kischuk, Richard Karl *insurance company executive*

**Valparaiso**
Anderson, William August *insurance agency executive*
Messer, Allen *insurance consultant, trainer, educator*

## IOWA

**Cedar Rapids**
Fick, E(arl) Dean *insurance executive*
Mitchell, Beverly Ann Bales *insurance agency owner, women's rights advocate*

**Council Bluffs**
Johnson, Michael Randy *insurance company executive*
Nelson, H. H. Red *insurance company executive*

**Des Moines**
Brooks, Roger Kay *insurance company executive*
Drury, David J. *insurance company executive*
Ellis, Mary Louise Helgeson *insurance company executive*
Hutchison, Theodore Murtagh *insurance company executive*
Kalainov, Sam Charles *insurance company executive*
Kelley, Bruce Gunn *insurance company executive, lawyer*
Kelley, Robb Beardsley *retired insurance company executive*
Richards, Riley Harry *insurance company executive*
Schneider, William George *former life insurance company executive*
Speas, Raymond Aaron *retired insurance company executive*
Stauffer, William Albert *insurance company executive*

**West Des Moines**
Davis, Ronald Arthur *life insurance brokerage executive*
Westerbeck, Kenneth Edward *retired insurance company executive*

## KANSAS

**Lenexa**
Oldham, Dale Ralph *life insurance company executive, actuary*

**Overland Park**
Jones, Charles Calhoun *estate and business planning consultant*
Loepp, Herman Albert *subrogation examiner*
Neal, Louise Kathleen *life insurance company executive, accountant*

**Shawnee Mission**
Barton, C. Robert *insurance company executive*
Holliday, John Moffitt *insurance company executive*
Landau, Mason Stephen *business broker, insurance professional*
Miller, Stanford *reinsurance exeuctive, arbitrator, lawyer*

**Topeka**
Morris, Michael Allen *insurance executive*
Zientara, Suzannah Dockstader *insurance company executive*

**Wichita**
Van Milligen, James M. *health care administrator*

## KENTUCKY

**Lexington**
Johnson, Lizabeth Lettie *insurance agent*

**Louisville**
Bailey, Irving Widmer, II *insurance holding company executive*
Baxter, James William, III *insurance and investment executive*
Haddaway, James David *retired insurance company official*
McCormick, Steven Thomas *insurance company executive*
Rosky, Theodore Samuel *insurance company executive*

**Whitesburg**
Smith, Roger Keith *insurance agent*

## LOUISIANA

**Baton Rouge**
Greer, Robert Stephenson *insurance company executive*

**New Orleans**
Marks, Charles Dennery *insurance salesman*
Purvis, George Frank, Jr. *life insurance company executive*
Trapolin, Frank Winter *retired insurance executive*

## MAINE

**Cape Elizabeth**
Dalbeck, Richard Bruce *insurance executive*

**Portland**
Freilinger, James Edward *insurance and investments company executive*
Orr, James F., III *insurance company executive*

## MARYLAND

**Annapolis**
Drury, Paul Eugene *life insurance manager*

**Baltimore**
Bradley, Thomas Andrew *insurance company executive*
Dishon, Cramer Steven *sales executive*
Hecht, Alan Dannenberg *insurance executive*
†Paine, Ruth M. *medical insurance company administrator*
Schoenfeld, Henry F. *insurance executive*
Williams, Richard Francis *insurance executive*

**Brandywine**
Jaffe, Morris Edward *insurance executive*

**Chester**
Dabich, Eli, Jr. *insurance company executive*

**Cockeysville Hunt Valley**
Mather, Dennis Bryan *wholesale insurance company executive*
Spinella, J(oseph) John *insurance company executive*

**Columbia**
Hayes, Charles Lawton *insurance company executive, holding company executive*

**Gaithersburg**
Boddiger, George Cyrus *insurance corporate executive, consultant*

**Lutherville Timonium**
Kolker, Roger Russell *insurance executive*

**Mount Airy**
Collins, Henry James, III *insurance company executive*

**Owings Mills**
Disharoon, Leslie Benjamin *retired insurance executive*
Walsh, Semmes Guest *retired insurance company executive*

**Oxford**
Radcliffe, George Grove *retired life insurance company executive*

**Severna Park**
Ebersberger, Arthur Darryl *insurance company executive, consultant*

**Silver Spring**
Jaskot, John Joseph *insurance company executive*

## MASSACHUSETTS

**Andover**
Fitzgerald, Michael Anthony *insurance company executive*

**Boston**
Aborn, Foster Litchfield *insurance company executive*
Brown, Michael *information technology executive*
Brown, Stephen Lee *insurance company executive*
Buckley, Joseph W. *insurance company executive*
Chilvers, Derek *insurance company executive*
Countryman, Gary Lee *insurance company executive*
Kamer, Joel Victor *insurance company executive, actuary*
Kelley, Kevin H. *insurance company executive*
King, Richard David *insurance company executive*
Lykins, Marshall Herbert *insurance company executive*
Mansfield, Christopher Charles *insurance company legal executive*
Morton, Edward James *insurance company executive*
Nashe, Carol *association executive, public relations consultant*
Rosensteel, John William *insurance company executive*
Schneider, Robert Edward *insurance company executive, actuary*
Scipione, Richard Stephen *insurance company executive, lawyer*
Shafto, Robert Austin *insurance company executive*
Shemin, Barry L. *insurance company executive*
Taylor, Edward Michael *insurance and risk management consultant*

**Brookline**
Shaw, Samuel Ervine, II *retired insurance company executive, consultant*

**Duxbury**
Wangler, William Clarence *retired insurance company executive*

**Eastham**
McLaughlin, Richard Warren *retired insurance company executive*

**Framingham**
Oleskiewicz, Francis Stanley *retired insurance executive*

**Great Barrington**
Schenck, Benjamin Robinson *insurance consultant*

**Lynnfield**
Gianino, John Joseph *former insurance executive*

**Needham**
Carey, Robert Williams *retired insurance company executive*

**Newton**
Rodman, Sumner *insurance executive*

**North Dighton**
Silvia, David Alan *insurance broker*

**Pittsfield**
Cornelio, Albert Carmen *insurance executive*

**Salem**
O'Brien, Robert Kenneth *insurance company executive*

**Sandwich**
Pearson, Paul Holding *insurance company executive*

**Springfield**
Bixby, Allan Barton *retired insurance company executive*
Clark, William James *retired insurance company executive*
Finnegan, Thomas Joseph, Jr. *insurance company executive, lawyer*
Johnson, Robert Allison *life insurance company executive*
Wheeler, Thomas Beardsley *insurance company executive*

**Waltham**
Yancey, Wallace Glenn *retired insurance company executive*

**Weston**
Conners, John Brendan *insurance company executive*
Fish, David Earl *insurance company executive*
Mc Elwee, John Gerard *retired life insurance company executive*

**Winchester**
Cowgill, F(rank) Brooks *retired insurance company executive*

**Worcester**
Davidson, Lee David *insurance executive*
O'Brien, John F. *insurance company executive*
Olson, Robert Leonard *retired insurance company executive*

## MICHIGAN

**Bloomfield Hills**
Pero, Joseph John *retired insurance company executive*

**Detroit**
Buselmeier, Bernard Joseph *insurance company executive*

**Lansing**
Saltzman, Robert Paul *insurance company executive*

**Naubinway**
Smith, Richard Ernest *retired insurance company executive*

**Port Huron**
Haynes, Marcia Margaret *insurance agent*

**Redford**
Hemminger, Allen Edward *retired insurance consultant*

**Southgate**
Torok, Margaret Louise *insurance company executive*

**Tecumseh**
Taylor, Robert Lee *financial services and sales executive, information systems account executive, educator*

**Traverse City**
Chang, Ching-I Eugene *insurance executive*

## MINNESOTA

**Arden Hills**
Van Houten, James Forester *insurance company executive*

**Bemidji**
Bridston, Paul Joseph *strategic consultant*

**Hopkins**
Johnson, James Erling *insurance executive*

**Minneapolis**
Blomquist, Robert Oscar *insurance company executive*
Eitingon, Daniel Benjamin *insurance executive*
Gandrud, Robert P. *fraternal insurance executive*
McErlane, Joseph James *insurance company executive*
Mitchell, James Austin *insurance company executive*

**Minnetonka**
Robbins, Orem Olford *insurance company executive*

**Saint Paul**
Boudreau, James Lawton *insurance company executive*
Kane, Stanley Phillip *insurance company executive*
Leatherdale, Douglas West *insurance company executive*
Oswald, Eva Sue Aden *insurance executive*
Sinklar, Robert *insurance company executive*
Williams, Chester Arthur, Jr. *insurance educator*

## MISSISSIPPI

**Carrollton**
McConnell, David Stuart *insurance agent, retired federal executive*

**Clinton**
Montgomery, Keith Norris, Sr. *insurance executive, state legislator*

**Gulfport**
Hewes, William Gardner, III *insurance executive, real estate agent, legislator*

**Jackson**
Dean, Jack Pearce *retired insurance company executive*
Stovall, Jerry (Coleman Stovall) *insurance company executive*

**Summit**
Jones, Lawrence David *insurance and medical consultant*

## MISSOURI

**Jefferson City**
Decker, Malcolm Doyle *insurance executive*

**Kansas City**
Bixby, Walter E. *insurance company executive*

Hazlett, James Arthur *insurance administrator*
Malacarne, C. John *insurance company executive, lawyer*
Mc Gee, Joseph John, Jr. *former insurance company executive*
Yates, Dan Charles *insurance company official*

**Saint Louis**
Haberstroh, Richard David *insurance agent*
Winer, Warren James *insurance executive*

**Springfield**
Ostergren, Gregory Victor *insurance company executive*
Rowan, Gerald Burdette *insurance company executive, lawyer*

## MONTANA

**Whitefish**
Hemp, Ralph Clyde *retired reinsurance company executive, consultant, arbitrator, umpire*

## NEBRASKA

**Holdrege**
Hendrickson, Bruce Carl *life insurance company executive*

**Lincoln**
Angle, John Charles *retired life insurance company executive*
Arth, Lawrence Joseph *insurance executive*

**Omaha**
Ames, George Ronald *insurance executive*
Barrett, Frank Joseph *insurance company executive*
Bookout, John G. *insurance company executive*
Conley, Eugene Allen *retired insurance company executive*
Haney, J. Terrence *insurance consultant*
Jay, Burton Dean *insurance actuary*
Jetter, Arthur Carl, Jr. *insurance company executive*
Skutt, Thomas James *insurance company executive*
Weekly, John William *insurance company executive*

## NEVADA

**Carson City**
Marangi, Vito Anthony, Sr. *claim administrator*
Rankin, Teresa P. Froncek *insurance educator, consultant, former state agency administrator*

**Reno**
Delaney, William Francis, Jr. *reinsurance broker*

## NEW HAMPSHIRE

**Grantham**
Boothroyd, Herbert J. *insurance company executive*
Smith, Dudley Renwick *retired insurance company executive*

**Hanover**
Kemp, Karl Thomas *insurance company executive*

**Nashua**
Barton, Carl P. *retired insurance company executive*

**Rochester**
Dworkin, Gary Steven *insurance company executive*

## NEW JERSEY

**Berkeley Heights**
Gottheimer, George Malcolm, Jr. *insurance executive, educator*

**Florham Park**
Bossen, Wendell John *insurance company executive*
Erickson, Charles Edward *insurance company executive*
Marshall, Philips Williamson *insurance agency executive*
Smith, Robert William *former insurance company executive, lawyer*

**Glen Rock**
Mc Elrath, Richard Elsworth *retired insurance company executive*

**Holmdel**
Meyer, Robert Alan *insurance company executive*

**Jersey City**
Sanders, Franklin D. *insurance company executive*

**Madison**
Calligan, William Dennis *retired life insurance company executive*
Leak, Margaret Elizabeth *insurance company executive*

**Marlton**
Hayes, Michele Thelma *insurance professional*

**Morristown**
Munson, William Leslie *insurance company executive*

**Mountain Lakes**
Cook, Charles Francis *insurance executive*

**Newark**
Gerathy, E. Carroll *former insurance executive, real estate developer*
Gillen, James Robert *insurance company executive, lawyer*
Latini, Anthony A. *financial services company executive*
†Light, Dorothy Kaplan *insurance executive, lawyer*
Ryan, Arthur Frederick *insurance company executive*

**Parsippany**
Ostroff, Allen J. *insurance company executive*

**Pitman**
Beebe, Leo Clair *industrial equipment executive, former educator*

**Princeton**
Wentz, Sidney Frederick *insurance company executive, foundation executive*

**Ridgewood**
Knies, Paul Henry *former life insurance company executive*

**Rumson**
Creamer, William Henry, III *insurance company executive*

**Short Hills**
MacKinnon, Malcolm D(avid) *retired insurance company executive*

**Somerset**
Brophy, Joseph Thomas *information company executive*

**Summit**
Keith, Garnett Lee, Jr. *insurance company investment executive*

**Warren**
Chubb, Percy, III *insurance company executive*
O'Hare, Dean Raymond *insurance company executive*

**Wyckoff**
Miller, Walter Neal *insurance company consultant*

## NEW MEXICO

**Albuquerque**
Rotherham, Larry Charles *insurance executive*

**Las Cruces**
Cochrun, John Wesley *chartered financial consultant*

## NEW YORK

**Albany**
Cole, John Adam *insurance executive*

**Armonk**
Elliott, David H. *insurance company executive*

**Binghamton**
Best, Robert Mulvane *insurance company executive*

**Bronx**
Lewis, Harold Alexander *insurance company executive*
†Mullender, Barton *insurance company executive*

**Bronxville**
Knapp, George Griff Prather *insurance consultant, arbitrator*

**Brooklyn**
Faison, Seth Shepard *retired insurance broker*

**Buffalo**
Deasy, Jacqueline Hildegard *insurance consultant*

**Cohocton**
Sarfaty, Wayne Allen *insurance agent, financial planner*

**Dryden**
Baxter, Robert Banning *insurance company executive*

**Fayetteville**
Sager, Roderick Cooper *retired life insurance company executive*

**Flushing**
Sanborn, Anna Lucille *pension and insurance consultant*

**Jericho**
Spivack, Henry Archer *life insurance company executive*

**Locust Valley**
Sunderland, Ray, Jr. *retired insurance company executive*

**Malverne**
Knight, John Francis *insurance company executive*

**Melville**
Olivero, Gary *insurance company executive, financial planner*

**Merrick**
Cherry, Harold *insurance company executive*
O'Brien, Kenneth Robert *life insurance company executive*

**New York**
Athanassiades, Ted *insurance company executive*
Benjamin, George David *retired insurance company executive, risk consultant*
Biggs, John Herron *insurance company executive*
Briggs, Philip *insurance company executive*
Bushey, Alan Scott *insurance holding company executive*
Caouette, John Bernard *insurance company executive*
Conklin, Thomas J. *insurance company executive*
Crane, Stephen Andrew *insurance company executive*
Creedon, John J. *insurance company executive*
Crosby, Gordon Eugene, Jr. *insurance company executive*
Crystal, James William *insurance company executive*
Dolan, Raymond Bernard *insurance executive*
Earls, Kevin Gerard *insurance company executive*
Forte, Wesley Elbert *insurance company executive, lawyer*
Gammill, Lee Morgan, Jr. *insurance company executive*
Gavrity, John Decker *insurance company executive*
Gibson, William Shepard *insurance executive*
Gilmore, Robert Gordon *retired insurance company executive*
Goodstone, Edward Harold *retired insurance company executive*
Greenberg, Maurice Raymond *insurance company executive*
Hansen, Richard Arthur *insurance company executive, psychologist*
Harris, David Henry *retired life insurance company executive*
Henderson, Greer F. *insurance company executive*
Henry, Catherine Theresa *insurance company executive*
Hill, Patricia Lispenard *insurance educator*
Hohn, Harry George *retired insurance company executive, lawyer*
Hutchings, Peter Lounsbery *insurance company executive*
Impellizzeri, Anne Elmendorf *insurance company executive, social services executive*
Jibaja, Gilbert *insurance company executive*
Kamen, Harry Paul *life insurance company executive, lawyer*
Kaplan, Keith Eugene *insurance company executive, lawyer*
Kavee, Robert Charles *insurance company executive*
Leaf, Robert Jay *dental insurance consultant*
Lowry, William Ketchin, Jr. *insurance company executive*
Manton, Edwin Alfred Grenville *insurance company executive*
Martin, Richard L. *insurance executive*
Matthews, Edward E. *insurance company executive*
McCormack, John Joseph, Jr. *insurance executive*
McLaughlin, Michael John *insurance company executive*
Melone, Joseph James *insurance company executive*
Milton, Christian Michel *insurance executive*
Murray, Richard Maximilian *insurance executive*
Nagler, Stewart Gordon *insurance company executive*
Noren-Iacovino, Mary-Jo Patricia *insurance company executive*
Olsen, David Alexander *insurance executive*
Papa, Vincent T. *insurance company executive*
Paul, Douglas Allan *insurance executive*
Putney, John Alden, Jr. *insurance company executive*
Reuter, Carol Joan *insurance company executive*
Ross, Donald Keith *retired insurance company executive*
Sandler, Robert Michael *insurance company executive, actuary*
Sargent, Joseph Dudley *insurance executive*
Schwartz, Robert George *retired insurance company executive*
Shinn, Richard Randolph *former insurance executive, former stock exchange executive*
Smith, Alexander John Court *insurance executive*
Smith, John Matthew *insurance company executive*
Somers, John Arthur *insurance company executive*
Staniar, Linda Burton *insurance company executive*
Sullivan, Joseph Peter *risk and insurance management consultant*
Underhill, Jacob Berry, III *retired insurance company executive*
Vidal, David Jonathan *insurance company executive, journalist*
Washington, Clarence Edward, Jr. *insurance company executive*
Wolf, James Anthony *insurance company executive*
Woodbury, Marion A. *insurance company executive*
Yalen, Gary N. *insurance company executive*

**North Salem**
Gruber, Alan Richard *insurance company executive*

**Point Lookout**
Stack, Maurice Daniel *retired insurance company executive*

**Poughkeepsie**
O'Shea, John P. *insurance executive*

**Rock Hill**
Lombardi, Kent Bailey *insurance company administrator*

**Schenectady**
Lawrence, Albert Weaver *insurance company executive*
Murray, Edward Rock *insurance broker*

**Searingtown**
Entmacher, Paul Sidney *insurance company executive, physician, educator*

**Syosset**
Barry, Richard Francis *retired life insurance company executive*

**Utica**
Ehre, Victor Tyndall *insurance company executive*

**White Plains**
Blumstein, William A. *insurance company executive*

**Yonkers**
Wolfson, Irwin M. *insurance company executive*

## NORTH CAROLINA

**Camden**
Hammond, Roy Joseph *reinsurance company executive*

**Chapel Hill**
Fine, J(ames) Allen *insurance company executive*
Kittredge, John Kendall *retired insurance company executive*
Stewart, Richard Edwin *insurance consulting company executive*

**Charlotte**
Maday, Clifford Ronald *insurance professional*
Mendelsohn, Robert Victor *insurance company executive*
Pehl, Glen Eugene *risk and insurance consultant*

**Durham**
Clark, Arthur Watts *insurance company executive*
Collins, Bert *insurance executive*

**Greensboro**
Carr, Howard Ernest *retired insurance agency executive*
Hall, William Edward, Jr. *insurance agency executive*
Macon, Seth Craven *retired insurance company executive*
Reid, Charles Murry *insurance company executive*
Soles, William Roger *insurance company executive*

**Raleigh**
Coggin, Michael Wright *insurance marketing and training executive*
Pendleton, Gary H(erman) *life insurance agent*
Whitehead, Ian *insurance company executive*

**Winston Salem**
Beardsley, Charles Mitchell *retired insurance company executive*

## OHIO

**Akron**
Arnett, James Edward *retired insurance company executive, retired secondary school educator*

**Bedford**
Moore, Dianne J. Hall *insurance claims administrator*

**Blacklick**
Doyle, Patrick Lee *retired insurance company executive*

**Canton**
Malcolm, Douglas Raymond *insurance agent, real estate developer*
Repp, Ronald Stewart *insurance company executive*

**Cincinnati**
Addison, Harry Metcalf *insurance executive*
Byers, Kenneth Vernon *insurance company executive*
Clark, James Norman *insurance executive*
Horrell, Karen Holley *insurance company executive, lawyer*
Klinedinst, Thomas John, Jr. *insurance agency executive*
Krohn, Claus Dankertsen *insurance company executive*
Puthoff, Francis Urban *insurance salesman*
Schiff, John Jefferson *insurance company executive*
Vasholz, Lothar Alfred *retired insurance company executive*
Weed, Ithamar Dryden *life insurance company executive*
Zimmer, William Homer, Jr. *retired insurance company executive*

**Cleveland**
Lewis, Peter Benjamin *insurance company executive*

**Columbus**
Duryee, Harold Taylor *insurance executive*
Emanuelson, James Robert *retired insurance company executive*
Frenzer, Peter Frederick *retired insurance company executive*
Fullerton, Charles William *retired insurance company executive*
Galloway, Harvey Scott, Jr. *insurance company executive*
McCutchan, Gordon Eugene *lawyer, insurance company executive*
McFerson, Diamond Richard *insurance company executive*
Neckermann, Peter Josef *insurance company executive*
Shook, Robert Louis *business writer*
Sokol, Saul *insurance agency executive*
Wells, Richard Lewis *insurance company executive*
Wilhelmy, Odin, Jr. *insurance agent*

**Grove City**
Purdy, Dennis Gene *insurance company executive, education consultant*

**Hamilton**
Marcum, Joseph LaRue *insurance company executive*
Patch, Lauren Nelson *insurance company, chief executive officer*

**Independence**
Riedthaler, William Allen *risk management professional*

**Westfield Center**
Blair, Cary *insurance company executive*

**Youngstown**
Carlomagno, Stephen Guido *insurance company executive*

## OKLAHOMA

**Norman**
Williams, David Samuel *insurance company executive*

**Oklahoma City**
Ille, Bernard Glenn *insurance company executive*

**Perry**
Doughty, Michael Dean *insurance agent*

**Tulsa**
Abbott, William Thomas *claim specialist*

Bryant, Dennis Michael *insurance executive*

## OREGON

**Hillsboro**
Yates, Keith Lamar *retired insurance company executive*

**Portland**
Galbraith, John Robert *insurance company exeuctive*
Lang, Philip David *former state legislator, insurance company executive*
Whiteley, Benjamin Robert *insurance company executive*

**Salem**
Rasmussen, Neil Woodland *insurance agent*

## PENNSYLVANIA

**Bala Cynwyd**
Shepard, Geoffrey Carroll *insurance executive*

**Berwyn**
McIntyre, James Owen *insurance executive*

**Bushkill**
Garretto, Leonard Anthony, Jr. *insurance company executive*

**Camp Hill**
Mead, James Matthew *insurance company executive*
Robertson, James Colvert *insurance company executive*

**Erie**
Hagen, Thomas Bailey *business owner, former state official, former insurance company executive*

**Hatboro**
Quigley, Robert Charles *insurance industry consultant*

**Haverford**
Zalinski, Edmund Louis Gray *insurance executive, mutual funds and real estate executive, investor*

**Hummelstown**
Moffitt, Charles William *insurance sales executive*

**Jenkintown**
Silver, Leonard J. *insurance and risk management company executive*

**King Of Prussia**
Volpe, Ralph Pasquale *insurance company executive*

**Media**
Hart, William C. *insurance underwriter, educator, writer*

**Newtown Square**
Staats, Dean Roy *retired reinsurance executive*

**Norristown**
Clemens, Alvin Honey *insurance company executive*

**Philadelphia**
Coyne, Frank J. *insurance company executive*
Farnam, Walter Edward *insurance company executive*
Frohlich, Kenneth R. *insurance executive*
Mella, Arthur John *insurance company executive*
O'Connor, John Joseph *insurance company executive*
Parker, Grace Patrice *insurance specialist*
Ross, Roderic Henry *insurance company executive*
Snider, Harold Wayne *risk and insurance educator*

**Pittsburgh**
Duval, Robert *leasing company executive*

**Plymouth Meeting**
Guckes, William Ruhland, Jr. *insurance executive*

**Shippensburg**
Fogelsonger, Ned Raymond *insurance agency executive*

**Spring House**
van Steenwyk, John Joseph *health care plan consultant, educator*

**Wayne**
Yoskin, Jon William, II *insurance company executive*

## RHODE ISLAND

**Little Compton**
MacKowski, John Joseph *retired insurance company executive*

## SOUTH CAROLINA

**Columbia**
Averyt, Gayle Owen *insurance executive*
Smith, Franklin Sumner, Jr. *retired insurance executive*

**Greenville**
Hipp, William Hayne *insurance and broadcasting executive*

## SOUTH DAKOTA

**Mitchell**
Widman, Paul Joseph *insurance agent*

## TENNESSEE

**Chattanooga**
Chandler, J. Harold *insurance company executive*

**Lookout Mountain**
Hardy, Thomas Cresson *insurance company executive*

**Nashville**
Davis, James Verlin *insurance brokerage executive*
Dedman, Bertram Cottingham *retired insurance company executive*
Elberry, Zainab Abdelhaliem *insurance company executive*
Gaultney, John Orton *life insurance agent, consultant*
Lazenby, Fred Wiehl *insurance company executive*
Sutton, Barrett Boulware *former insurance company executive*

**Seymour**
Steele, Ernest Clyde *retired insurance company executive*

## TEXAS

**Austin**
Caldwell, William McNeilly *insurance agent*
Golden, Edwin Harold *insurance company executive*
Grace, James Martin *insurance company executive*
Mullen, Ron *insurance company executive*
Payne, Eugene Edgar *insurance company executive*
Payne, Tyson Elliott, Jr. *retired insurance executive*

**Dallas**
Beck, Luke Ferrell Wilson *insurance specialist*
Cline, Bobby James *insurance company executive*
Guthrie, M. Philip *insurance company executive*
Hardy, Tom Charles, Jr. *medical equipment company*
Head, Mark D. *insurance and employee benefit broker*
Langston, Roy A. *insurance company consultant*
Madden, Teresa Darleen *insurance agency owner*
Rinne, Austin Dean *insurance company executive*

**Fort Worth**
Brannon, Treva Lee (Wood) *insurance company executive*
Faherty, John Kevin *insurance broker, consultant*

**Greenville**
Peters, Ted Hopkins *insurance company executive*

**Houston**
Bailey, Charles Lyle *insurance company executive*
Bickel, Stephen Douglas *insurance company executive*
Couch, Jesse Wadsworth *retired insurance company executive*
Davenport, Joseph Dale *insurance executive*
Davis, Rex Lloyd *insurance company executive*
Dean, Robert Franklin *insurance company executive*
Devlin, Robert Manning *financial services company executive*
Farr, Walter Emil, Jr. *insurance agent*
†Gonzalez, Georgina S. *insurance executive, actuary*
Harris, Richard Foster, Jr. *insurance company executive*
Hook, Harold Swanson *insurance company executive*
Kellison, Stephen George *insurance executive*
Lindsey, John Horace *insurance executive, museum official*
Poulos, Michael James *insurance company executive*
Skalla, John Lionell *insurance agent*
Thomas, Marilyn Jane *insurance company executive*
West, Thomas Lowell, Jr. *insurance company executive*
Woodson, Benjamin Nelson, III *insurance executive*

**Lake Jackson**
Elbert, James Peak *independent insurance agent, minister*

**Lubbock**
Allison, Cecil Wayne *insurance company executive*

**Odessa**
Bailey, Keith Stewart *insurance company executive*

**San Antonio**
Colyer, Kirk Klein *insurance executive, real estate investment executive*
Cook, John Roscoe, Jr. *insurance company executive*
Herres, Robert Tralles *insurance company executive*
Mawhinney, King *insurance company executive*
Wellberg, Edward Louis, Jr. *insurance company executive*

**Stafford**
Friedberg, Thomas Harold *insurance company executive*

**The Woodlands**
Connell, Joseph Edward *retired insurance executive*

**Tyler**
Guin, Don Lester *insurance company executive*

**Waco**
Rapoport, Bernard *life insurance company executive*

## UTAH

**Ogden**
Buckner, Elmer La Mar *insurance executive*

**Salt Lake City**
Engar, Richard Charles *insurance executive, dentist, educator*
Poulton, Craig Kidd *insurance broker, consultant*

## VERMONT

**Montpelier**
Bertrand, Frederic Howard *insurance company executive*
Leland, Lawrence *insurance executive*

**Moscow**
Kende, Stephen James *insurance sales executive*

**Plainfield**
Harding, John Hibbard *retired insurance company executive*

**Quechee**
Baney, John Edward *insurance company executive*

**South Burlington**
Hackett, Luther Frederick *insurance company executive*

**Woodstock**
Blackwell, David Jefferson *insurance company executive*

## VIRGINIA

**Abingdon**
Graham, Howard Lee, Sr. *corporate executive*

**Alexandria**
Casey, Michael Kirkland *business executive, lawyer*

**Arlington**
Clarke, Frederic B., III *risk analysis consultant*
DeHarde, William M. *business consultant, pension plan administrator*

**Chesterfield**
Jacobs, James A. *insurance professional*

**Huddleston**
Saunders, Dorothy Ann *insurance company executive, sales management*

**Lynchburg**
McRorie, William Edward *life insurance company executive*
Stewart, George Taylor *insurance executive*

**Mc Lean**
Creedon, Mary Alice *insurance company executive*

**Newport News**
Miller, W. Marshall, II *insurance consultant*

**Richmond**
Coleman, Ronald Lee *insurance claims executive*
Jacobs, James Paul *retired insurance executive*

**Roanoke**
Berry, John Coltrin *insurance executive*

**Vienna**
Sirpis, Andrew Paul *insurance company executive*

**Williamsburg**
Herrmann, Benjamin Edward *former insurance executive*
Webster, Robert Louis *insurance company executive*

**Woodstock**
Walker, Charles Norman *retired insurance company executive*

## WASHINGTON

**Bellevue**
Clay, Orson C. *insurance company executive*
Eigsti, Roger Harry *insurance company executive*
Roddis, Richard Stiles Law *insurance company executive, consultant, legal educator*

**Bellingham**
Fullmer, Donald Kitchen *insurance executive*

**Edmonds**
Eisenzimmer, Betty Wenner *insurance agency executive*
Holcomb, M. Staser *insurance executive*

**Kennewick**
Stevens, Henry August *insurance agent, educator*

**Kirkland**
McDonald, Joseph Lee *insurance broker*

**Seattle**
Dubes, Michael John *insurance company executive*
Duckworth, Tara Ann *insurance company executive*
Dyer, Philip E. *insurance company executive*
Johnson, Mildred Grace Mash *investment company executive*
LaPoe, Wayne Gilpin *retired business executive*
Phillips, Josef Clayton *insurance and investment company executive*
Robb, Bruce *former insurance company executive*
Zunker, Richard E. *insurance company executive*

**Walla Walla**
Perry, Louis Barnes *retired insurance company executive*

## WISCONSIN

**Appleton**
Gunderson, Richard L. *insurance company executive*

**Brookfield**
Payne, Howard James *insurance company executive*
Trytek, David Douglas *insurance company executive*

**Fontana**
Kummer, Daniel William *insurance executive*

**Hartland**
Wilson, Peter Michael *insurance company executive*

**Madison**
DuRose, Stanley Charles, Jr. *insurance executive*
Herndon, Terry Eugene *insurance executive*
Larson, John David *life insurance company executive, lawyer*
Mathwich, Dale F. *insurance company executive*
McKinnon, Robert Harold *retired insurance company executive*
Waldo, Robert Leland *retired insurance company executive*

**Merrill**
Whitburn, Gerald *insurance company executive*

**Milwaukee**
Tolan, David J. *insurance corporation executive*
Van Antwerpen, Regina Lane *underwriter, insurance company executive*
Zore, Edward John *insurance company investment executive*

**Nashotah**
Vincent, Norman L. *retired insurance company executive*

**Stevens Point**
Dougherty, Daniel Allan *insurance claims manager*

**Wausau**
Huebner, Suzanne M. *insurance company executive*

## CANADA

## ONTARIO

**Etobicoke**
Howe, James Tarsicius *retired insurance company executive*
Wykes, Edmund Harold *retired insurance company executive*

**London**
Allan, Ralph Thomas Mackinnon *insurance company executive*
Creighton, Dale Edward *retired insurance company executive*
Orser, Earl Herbert *insurance company executive*

**Toronto**
Nesbitt, Mark *management consultant*

**Waterloo**
Masterman, Jack Verner *insurance company executive*

## QUEBEC

**Saint Hyacinthe**
Brouillette, Yves *insurance company executive*

## AUSTRALIA

**Sydney**
Melkonian, Harry G. *insurance executive, rancher*

## BERMUDA

**Hamilton**
Kramer, Donald *insurance executive*
Stempel, Ernest Edward *insurance executive*

**Pembroke**
Wiedemann, Joseph Robert *insurance company executive*

## FRANCE

**Paris**
Blondeau, Jacques Patrick Adrien *reinsurance company executive*
Peugeot, Patrick *insurance executive*

## HONG KONG

**Hong Kong**
Tse, Edmund Sze-Wing *insurance company executive*

## SWITZERLAND

**Basel**
Gerber, Fritz *insurance company executive, diversified financial services company executive*

## ADDRESS UNPUBLISHED

Adam, John, Jr. *insurance company executive emeritus*
Adams, Gregory James *insurance company executive*
Allen, Kenneth Dale *insurance executive, corporate counsel*
Alpert, Ann Sharon *insurance claims examiner*
Alvernaz, Rodrigo *insurance company executive*
Anker, Robert Alvin *insurance company executive*
Armstrong, F(redric) Michael *insurance company executive, consultant*
Bare, Bruce *retired life insurance company executive*
Barnhill, Howard Eugene *insurance company executive*

Beattie, Nora Maureen *insurance company executive, actuary*
Becker, JoAnn Elizabeth *insurance company executive*
Bellamy, James Carl *insurance company executive*
Bumpus, Frederick Joseph *retired insurance company executive*
Bundschuh, George August William *retired insurance company executive*
Carver, Kendall Lynn *insurance company executive*
Clemens, Charles Joseph *insurance agent*
Cooper, Charles Gordon *insurance consultant, former executive*
Culp, William Newton *retired insurance executive*
Dackow, Orest Taras *insurance company executive*
Dannenberg, Martin Ernest *retired insurance company executive*
DeAlessandro, Joseph Paul *insurance company executive*
Deering, Fred Arthur *retired insurance company executive*
Denn, Cyril Joseph *insurance agent*
Fibiger, John Andrew *life insurance company executive*
Goldsholle, Gerry H(arvey) *insurance executive, lawyer*
Gummere, John *insurance company executive*
Gundelfinger, Ralph Mellow *retired insurance company executive*
Hartsell, Samuel David *insurance agent*
Hawk, Carole Lynn *insurance company executive, research/analyst*
Hinds, Edward Dee *insurance and investment professional, financial planner*
Hirst, Heston Stillings *former insurance company executive*
Ipsen, Grant Ruel *insurance and investments professional*
Jacobson, James Bassett *insurance executive*
Kerns, Stephen Rimmer *insurance executive*
Knittel, Diane Lynne *insurance marketing executive*
Lacey, Cloyd Eugene *retired insurance company executive*
Ladd, Joseph Carroll *retired insurance company executive*
Lamel, Linda Helen *insurance company executive, former college president, lawyer, consultant*
Lee, J. Daniel, Jr. *retired insurance company executive*
Long, Alvin William *title insurance company executive*
Ludlam, James Edward, III *insurance company executive*
Maatman, Gerald Leonard *insurance company executive*
Maloney, Therese Adele *insurance company executive*
McCarty, Dennis L. *insurance executive*
McKenna, Terence Patrick *insurance company executive*
Merk, Elizabeth Thole *sales representative*
Moore, Robert Henry *insurance company executive*
Morrill, Thomas Clyde *insurance company executive*
Moynahan, John Daniel, Jr. *retired insurance executive*
Nelson, Walter Gerald *retired insurance company executive*
Newman, Steven Harvey *insurance company executive*
Norris, Darell Forest *retired insurance company executive*
Plummer, Daniel Clarence, III *insurance consultant*
Powers, Thomas Edward *managed care executive*
Resnick, Myron J. *retired insurance company executive, lawyer*
Reynolds, John Francis *insurance company executive*
Rondepierre, Edmond Francois *insurance executive*
Rowell, Lester John, Jr. *retired insurance company executive*
Ryan, James *insurance company executive*
Scott, John Burt *life insurance executive*
Sharick, Merle Dayton, Jr. *mortgage insurance company executive*
Smith, Floyd Leslie *insurance company executive*
Snyder, Alan Carhart *insurance company executive*
Snyder, William Burton *insurance executive*
Stewart, Gordon Curran *insurance information association executive*
Stitt, Frederick Hesse *insurance broker*
Todd, John Odell *insurance company sales professional*
Tresnowski, Bernard Richard *retired health insurance company executive*
Vanderhoof, Irwin Thomas *life insurance company executive*
Weber, John Walter *insurance company executive*
Wilkins, Roger Carson *retired insurance company executive*
Wills, William Ridley, II *former insurance company executive, historian*
Zarb, Frank Gustave *insurance brokerage executive*
Zupsic, Matthew Michael *insurance company executive*

## FINANCE: INVESTMENT SERVICES

### UNITED STATES

### ALABAMA

#### Birmingham
Comer, Donald, III *investment company executive*
Culp, Charles Allen *financial executive*
Haworth, Michael Elliott, Jr. *investor, former aerospace company executive*
Marks, Charles Caldwell *retired investment banker, retired industrial distribution company executive*
Massey, Richard Walter, Jr. *investment counselor*
Tucker, Thomas James *investment manager*

#### Montgomery
Blount, Winton Malcolm, III *investment executive*
Taylor, Watson Robbins, Jr. *investment banker*

### ALASKA

#### Anchorage
Hickel, Walter Joseph *investment firm executive, forum administrator*
Jay, Christopher Edward *stockbroker*
Rose, David Allan *investment manager*

#### Juneau
Bushre, Peter Alvin *investment company executive*

### ARIZONA

#### Phoenix
Quinsler, William Thomson *retired investment advisor*
Salmonson, Marty Lee *stockbroker, consulting engineer*
Tribble, Richard Walter *brokerage executive*

#### Scottsdale
Budge, Hamer Harold *mutual fund company executive*
Cormie, Donald Mercer *investment company executive*

#### Sierra Vista
Hasney, Christopher William *retired investment company executive, educator*

#### Tucson
Schannep, John Dwight *brokerage firm executive*

#### Yuma
Stuart, Gerard William, Jr. *investment company executive, city official*

### ARKANSAS

#### Fort Smith
Hembree, Hugh Lawson, III *diversified holding company executive*

#### Little Rock
Light, Jo Knight *stockbroker*
McGowan, Michael Benedict *investment banker*
Reeves, Rosser Scott, III *retired investment company executive*
Stephens, Jackson Thomas *investment executive*

#### Newport
Holmes, Paul Kinloch, Jr. *private investor*

### CALIFORNIA

#### Alamo
†Morgan, Joe Leonard *investment company executive, former professional baseball player*

#### Arcadia
Kalm, Arne *investment banker*

#### Benicia
Szabo, Peter John *investment company executive, financial planner, mining engineer, lawyer*

#### Beverly Hills
Evans, Louise *investor, retired psychologist, philanthropist*
Haller, Howard Edward *investment banker, real estate developer, film writer and producer*
Israel, Richard Stanley *investment banker*
Mc Kenna, William Edward *business executive*
Walker, William Tidd, Jr. *investment banker*
Winthrop, John *business executive*

#### Burlingame
Heath, Richard Raymond *investment executive*
Most, Nathan *mutual fund executive*

#### Carmel
Jordan, Edward George *business investor, former college president, former railroad executive*
Stratton, Thomas Oliver *investment banker*

#### Century City
Feiman, Thomas E. *investment manager*

#### Coronado
Grant, Alan J. *business executive, educator*

#### Cupertino
Horn, Christian Friedrich *venture capital company executive*
Perkins, Thomas James *venture capital company executive*

#### Del Mar
Koehler, John Edget *venture capitalist*

#### Escondido
Allen, Donald Vail *investment executive, author, concert pianist*

#### Foster City
Turner, Ross James *investment corporation executive*

#### Fresno
Buzick, William Alonson, Jr. *investor, lawyer, educator*
Dauer, Donald Dean *investment executive*

#### Goleta
Bartlett, James Lowell, III *investment company executive*

#### Hollywood
Marshall, Conrad Joseph *entrepreneur*

#### Irvine
Le Bon, Douglas Kent *investment manager*

#### Larkspur
Kirk, Gary Vincent *investment advisor*

#### Long Beach
Schinnerer, Alan John *entrepreneur*

#### Los Altos
Carsten, Jack Craig *venture capitalist*

#### Los Angeles
Angeloff, Dann Valentino *investment banking executive*
Bernstein, Arthur Harold *venture capital executive*
Bradshaw, Carl John *investor, lawyer, consultant*
DeBard, Roger *investment executive*
Drew, Paul *entrepreneur*
Emmeluth, Bruce Palmer *investment banker, venture capitalist*
Gebhart, Carl Grant *security broker*
Gordy, Berry *entrepreneur, record company executive, motion picture executive*
Greenstadt, Melvin *investor, retired educator*
Hamilton, Beverly Lannquist *investment management professional*
Horning, Robert Alan *securities broker*
Hurt, William Holman *investment management company executive*
Hurwitz, Lawrence Neal *investment banking company executive*
Kaye, Barry *investment company executive*
Kim, Ke Bom *stockbroker, financial planner*
Koffler, Stephen Alexander *investment banker*
Mann, Nancy Louise (Nancy Louise Robbins) *entrepreneur*
Ogle, Edward Proctor, Jr. *investment counseling executive*
Perry, Donald Lester, II *venture capitalist*
Reed, George Ford, Jr. *investment executive*
Winkler, Howard Leslie *investment banker, business and financial consultant*

#### Menlo Park
Hoagland, Laurance Redington, Jr. *investment executive*
†Kaufman, Robert J. *investment company executive*
Lucas, Donald Leo *private investor*
Roberts, George R. *investment banking company executive*
Walsh, William Desmond *investor*

#### Mountain View
Crowley, Jerome Joseph, Jr. *investment company executive*
Guldimann, Till Markus *financial company executive*

#### Napa
Strock, David Randolph *brokerage house executive*

#### Newport Beach
Albright, Archie Earl, Jr. *investment banker*
Fletcher, Douglas Baden *investment company executive*
Giannini, Valerio Louis *investment banker*
Hinshaw, Ernest Theodore, Jr. *private investor, former Olympics executive, former financial executive*

#### Northridge
Lauter, James Donald *retired stockbroker*

#### Oakland
Al Malek, Amir Isa *entrepreneur, business consultant, actor, musician*

#### Palm Desert
Krallinger, Joseph Charles *entrepreneur, business advisor, author*

#### Palo Alto
Cirigliano, John J(oseph) *investment company executive*

#### Palos Verdes Peninsula
Mennis, Edmund Addi *investment management consultant*

#### Pasadena
Arnott, Robert Douglas *investment company executive*
Baum, Dwight Crouse *investment banking executive*

#### Placentia
Frank, Judith Ann (Jann Frank) *entrepreneur, small business owner*

#### Riverside
Rosenzweig, Herbert Stephen *stockbroker*

#### Ross
Rosenbaum, Michael Francis *securities dealer*

#### San Diego
Dunn, David Joseph *financial executive*
Smith, Benjamin Eric *venture capitalist, executive*

#### San Francisco
Apatoff, Michael John *finance executive*
Bertelsen, Thomas Elwood, Jr. *investment banker*
Colwell, Kent Leigh *venture capitalist*
Dachs, Alan Mark *investment company executive*
Dellas, Robert Dennis *investment banker*
De Lutis, Donald Conse *investment manager, consultant*
deWilde, David Michael *executive search consultant, financial services executive, lawyer*
Dunn, Richard Joseph *investment counselor*
Gardner, James Harkins *venture capitalist*
Greber, Robert Martin *financial investments executive*
Gund, George, III *financier, professional sports team executive*
†Hagenbuch, John Jacob *investment banker*
Halliday, John Meech *investment company executive*
Hambrecht, William R. *venture capitalist*
Hellman, F(rederick) Warren *investment advisor*
Latzer, Richard Neal *investment company executive*
Mahoney, Michael James *investment executive*
Matthews, Gilbert Elliott *investment banker*
McGettigan, Charles Carroll, Jr. *investment banker*
Miller, Corbin Russell *financial executive*
Pfau, George Harold, Jr. *stockbroker*
Pottruck, David Steven *brokerage house executive*
Redo, David Lucien *investment company executive*
Rock, Arthur *venture capitalist*
Rosenberg, Claude Newman, Jr. *investment adviser*
Ross, Sue *entrepreneur, author, fundraising executive*
Schwab, Charles R. *brokerage house executive*
Turner, Marshall Chittenden, Jr. *venture capitalist, consultant*
Veitch, Stephen William *investment counselor*
Wiley, Thomas Glen *retired investment company executive*

#### San Jose
Hall, Robert Emmett, Jr. *investment banker, realtor*

#### San Juan Capistrano
Robinson, Daniel Thomas *brokerage company executive*

#### San Marino
Zimmerman, William Robert *entrepreneur, engineering based manufacturing company executive*

#### San Mateo
Fenton, Noel John *venture capitalist*

#### Santa Barbara
Rasher, George Joseph *entrepreneur, business owner*
Vos, Hubert Daniel *private investor*

#### Santa Clara
Lynch, Charles Allen *investment executive, corporate director*

#### Santa Monica
Richards, David Kimball *investor*

#### Sausalito
Lamoreaux, Phillip Addison *investment management company executive*

#### Sherman Oaks
Hagenbuch, Rodney Dale *stock brokerage house executive*

#### Solana Beach
Beare, Bruce Riley *trading company and sales executive*

#### South San Francisco
Leylegian, Jack H., II *investment management company executive*

#### Tarzana
Smuckler, Harvey Glasgow *financial consultant*

#### West Sacramento
Lipscomb, Jeffrey Jon *fund specialist, insurance agent*

#### Westlake Village
Fredericks, Ward Arthur *venture capitalist, food industry consultant*
Valentine, Gene C. *securities dealer*

### COLORADO

#### Aurora
Ericson, Mark Frederick *investment analyst*

#### Boulder
Mehalchin, John Joseph *entrepreneur, finance company executive*

#### Colorado Springs
Ramsay, Robert Henry *investment manager*

#### Denver
Berger, William Merriam Bart *investment management company executive*
Butler, Owen Bradford *securities advisor*
Holte, Debra Leah *investment executive, financial analyst*
Imhoff, Walter Francis *investment banker*
Stephenson, Arthur Emmet, Jr. *investment company executive, banker*
Wagner, Judith Buck *investment firm executive*

#### Englewood
Larkin, Edward Colby *securities analyst, financial services company executive*
Van Loucks, Mark Louis *venture capitalist, business advisor*

#### Evergreen
Jackson, William Richard *entrepreneur*

#### Grand Junction
Sewell, Ralph Byron *investment broker, financial planner, manager*

#### Placerville
Kickert, Juliana Arlene *private investor*

#### Snowmass Village
Bancroft, Paul, III *investment company executive, venture capitalist*
Le Buhn, Robert *investment executive*

### CONNECTICUT

#### Bridgeport
Wetzel, Edward Thomas *investment company executive*

#### Darien
Alderman, Rhenus Hoffard, III *investment company executive*
Moltz, James Edward *brokerage company executive*
Morse, Edmond Northrop *investment management executive*

#### Farmington
Bigler, Harold Edwin, Jr. *investment company executive*
Flynn, Daniel Francis *investment company executive*
Halligan, Howard Ansel *investment management company executive*

**Greenwich**
Baker, Charles Ernest *stockbroker*
Lewis, Perry Joshua *investment banker*
Miller, Donald Keith *venture capitalist, asset management executive*
Nevin, Crocker *investment banker*
Schneider, John Arnold *business investor*
Tournillon, Nicholas Brady *trade finance, international investments company executive*

**Hartford**
Anderson, James Brent *venture capitalist*
Carpenter, Michael Alan *financial services executive*
Fiszel, Geoffrey Lynn *investment banker, investment adviser*

**Litchfield**
Booth, John Thomas *investment banker*

**Lyme**
Friday, John Ernest, Jr. *retired securities company executive*

**Mystic**
Starks, William Edward (Skip Starks) *investment consultant*

**New Canaan**
Gilbert, Steven Jeffrey *venture capitalist, screenwriter, lawyer*
Grace, Julianne Alice *investor relations firm executive*
Pike, William Edward *business executive*
Snyder, Nathan *entrepreneur*

**Norwalk**
Feskoe, Gaffney Jon *investment banker, management consultant*
Hathaway, Carl Emil *investment management company executive*

**Southbury**
Fabiani, Dante Carl *industrialist*

**Southport**
Sheppard, William Stevens *investment banker*
Wilbur, E. Packer *investment company executive*

**Stamford**
Beyman, Jonathan Eric *information officer*
Ekernas, Sven Anders *investment company executive*
Frey, Dale Franklin *financial investment company executive, manufacturing company executive*
Hawley, Frank Jordan, Jr. *venture capital executive*

**Weston**
Zimmerman, Bernard *investment banker*

**Westport**
Kelly, Paul Knox *investment banker*
O'Keefe, John David *investment specialist*
Walton, Alan George *venture capitalist*
Weissman, Robert Evan *information services company executive*

**Wilton**
Scheinman, Stanley Bruce *venture capital executive, lawyer*

**DELAWARE**

**Greenville**
Dewees, Donald Charles *securities company executive*
Hindes, Gary Eugene *securities executive*

**Wilmington**
Kalil, James, Sr. *investment executive*
Laird, Walter Jones, Jr. *investment professional*

**DISTRICT OF COLUMBIA**

**Washington**
Ansary, Cyrus A. *investment company executive, lawyer*
Bonde, Count Peder Carlsson *investment company executive*
Brody, Kenneth David *investment banker*
Caldwell, John L. *investment company executive*
Countryman, John Russell *business executive, former ambassador*
Cusick, Ralph A., Jr. *investment banking company executive*
Darman, Richard G. *investor, former government official, former investment banker, former educator*
Douglas, Leslie *investment banker*
Ellsworth, Robert Fred *investment executive, former government official*
Ferris, George Mallette, Jr. *investment banker*
Fisher, Robert Dale *stockbroker, retired naval officer*
Fleming, Robert Wright *investment banker*
Galvin, Michael Paul *venture capital executive*
Gibson, Paul Raymond *international trade and investment development executive*
Hartwell, Stephen *investment company executive*
Hirsch, Robert Louis *energy research and development consultant*
Kelly, Charles J., Jr. *investment company executive*
Lister, Harry Joseph *financial company executive, consultant*
Lurton, Horace VanDeventer *brokerage house executive*
Macomber, John D. *industrialist*
Middendorf, J. William, II *investment banker*
Selin, Ivan *entrepreneur*
Sethness, Charles Olin *international financial official*
Shrier, Adam Louis *investment firm executive*
Silby, Donald Wayne *investment executive, entrepreneur*
Silver, Jonathan Moses *investment management executive*
Spangler, Scott Michael *private investor*
Stearns, James Gerry *retired securities company executive*
Thompson, Bruce Edward, Jr. *brokerage house executive, former government official*
Tomlinson, Alexander Cooper *investment banker, consultant*

Tucker, Howard McKeldin *investment banker, consultant*
Winslow, James David *international trade analyst*
Wortley, George Cornelius *government affairs consultant, investor*

**FLORIDA**

**Boca Raton**
Landry, Michael Gerard *investment company executive*
Ohlman, Douglas Ronald *commodities and securities trader, investment consultant, lawyer*

**Boynton Beach**
Allison, Dwight Leonard, Jr. *investor*

**Coral Gables**
Nunez-Portuondo, Ricardo *investment company executive*

**Daytona Beach**
Locke, Edwin Allen, Jr. *investment banker*

**Destin**
Horne, Thomas Lee, III *entrepreneur*

**Englewood**
Simis, Theodore Luckey *investment banker, information technology executive*

**Fort Lauderdale**
Garvin, Glenn *venture capitalist*
Huizenga, Harry Wayne *entrepreneur, entertainment corporation executive, professional sports team executive*
Niehaus, Robert James *investment banking executive*
Sanders, Howard *investment company executive*
Sands, Roberta Alyse *real estate investor*
Shaw, Bryan P. H. *retired investment company executive*
Thayer, Charles J. *investment banker*
Vladem, Paul Jay *investment advisor, broker*

**Hobe Sound**
Fiske, Guy Wilbur *investment company executive*
Hotchkiss, Winchester Fitch *retired investment banker*
Parker, H. Lawrence *investor, rancher, retired investment banker*

**Jacksonville**
Monsky, John Bertrand *investment banking executive*
Schultz, Frederick Henry *investor, former government official*

**Jupiter**
Kulok, William Allan *entrepreneur, venture capitalist*

**Key Biscayne**
Wilson, Robert Gordon *investment banker*

**Longboat Key**
Levitt, Irving Francis *investment company executive*
Phillips, Howard William *investment banker*

**Marco Island**
Pettersen, Kjell Will *stockbroker, consultant*

**Miami**
Babun, Teo Abraham *venture capital executive*
Bishopric, Karl *investment banker, real estate executive, advertising executive*
Dorion, Robert Charles *entrepreneur, investor*
Gittlin, Arthur Sam *industrialist, banker*
Steinberg, Alan Wolfe *investment company executive*

**Naples**
Elliott, Edward *investment executive, financial planner*
Guarino, Roger Charles *consulting company executive*
Oliver, Robert Bruce *retired investment company executive*
Osias, Richard Allen *international financier, investor, real estate investment executive, corporate investor*

**North Palm Beach**
Doede, John Henry *investment company executive*
Gray, Harry Jack *investment executive*

**Palm Beach**
Adduci, Vincent James *investment company executive*
Bagby, Joseph Rigsby *financial investor*
Gundlach, Heinz Ludwig *investment banker, lawyer*
Halmos, Peter *investment company executive*
Korn, David *investment company executive*
Lede, Richard *investment company executive*
Rudolph, Malcolm Rome *investment banker*

**Palm Beach Gardens**
Hannon, John Robert *investment company executive*
Mergler, H. Kent *investment counselor*

**Pompano Beach**
Presley, Brian *investment company executive*
Rifenburgh, Richard Philip *investment company executive*

**Ponte Vedra**
Garner, John Michael *investment company executive*

**Ponte Vedra Beach**
Thorndike, Richard King *former brokerage company executive*

**Port Saint Lucie**
Olson, Edward Charles *entrepreneur, conservationist, film industry executive, writer, environmental consultant, business consultant*

**Saint Petersburg**
Emerson, William Allen *retired investment company executive*

Galbraith, John William *securities company executive*
Godbold, Francis Stanley *investment banker, real estate executive*
Scott, Lee Hansen *retired holding company executive*

**Sarasota**
Cox, Houston Abraham, Jr. *financial and futures markets consultant*

**Surfside**
Batcheller, Joseph Ann *entrepreneur*

**Tampa**
Ault, Jeffrey Michael *investment banker*
Holder, Harold Douglas, Sr. *investor, industrialist*
Sigety, Charles Birge *investment company executive*

**Tequesta**
Kraft, Otto Fritz *investment advisor, artist*

**Tierra Verde**
Gaffney, Thomas Francis *investment company executive*

**Vero Beach**
Clawson, John Addison *financier, investor*
Glassmeyer, Edward *investment banker*
Thompson, William David *investment banking executive*

**West Palm Beach**
Cano, Marta Mendendez *securities company executive, financial consultant*
Price, William James, IV *investment banker*

**Winter Park**
Maher, William James *investment executive*

**GEORGIA**

**Atlanta**
Averitt, Richard Garland, III *securities executive*
Blackwell, Michael Sidney *broker, financial services executive*
Dowling, Roderick Anthony *investment banker*
Keough, Donald Raymond *investment company executive*
McMahon, Donald Aylward *investor, corporate director*
McNabb, Dianne Leigh *investment banker, accountant*
Roberts, Cassandra Fendley *investment company executive*
Thomas, James Edward, Jr. *brokerage house executive*
Whitman, Homer William, Jr. *investment counseling company executive*
Williams, Ralph Watson, Jr. *retired securities company executive*
Winship, Wadleigh Chichester *holding company executive*

**Cleveland**
Lewis, Richard, Sr. *securities broker, consultant*

**Lawrenceville**
Greene, William Joshua, III *investment executive and consultant*

**Saute Nacoche**
Warren, Edus Houston, Jr. *investment management executive*

**Sea Island**
Brown, Ann Catherine *investment company executive*
Brown, George Hay *investment counselor*

**HAWAII**

**Honolulu**
Behnke, Richard Frederick *investment banking executive*
Haight, Warren Gazzam *investor*
Ho, Stuart Tse Kong *investment company executive*
Mau, William Koon-Hee *financier*

**Kailua**
Amos, Wally *entrepreneur*

**Kaneohe**
Fukumoto, Geal S. *investment representative*

**IDAHO**

**Boise**
Hendren, Merlyn Churchill *investment company executive*

**ILLINOIS**

**Alton**
Greenwood, John E. *stock brokerage executive*

**Chicago**
Bergonia, Raymond David *venture capitalist*
Blair, Bowen *investment banker*
Blair, Edward McCormick *investment banker*
Block, Philip Dee, III *investment counselor*
Brodsky, William J. *futures options exchange executive*
Buckle, Frederick Tarifero *international holding company executive, political and business intelligence analyst*
†Case, Donni Marie *investment company executive*
Chaleff, Carl Thomas *brokerage house executive*
Clarke, Philip Ream, Jr. *investment banker*
Cloonan, James Brian *investment executive*
Crown, James Schine *investment executive*
Ender, Jon T. *investment management executive, banker*
Fenton, Clifton Lucien *investment banker*
Foster, James Reuben *investment company executive*

Freehling, Stanley Maxwell *investment banker*
Gorter, James Polk *investment banker*
Harris, Ronald William *commodities trader*
Hawkinson, John *former investment management company executive*
Hickey, Jerome Edward *investment company executive*
Kahn, Herta Hess (Mrs. Howard Kahn) *retired stockbroker*
Kelly, Arthur Lloyd *management and investment company executive*
Knox, Lance Lethbridge *venture capital executive*
Lewis, Charles A. *investment company executive*
Loucks, Ralph Bruce, Jr. *investment company executive*
McCausland, Thomas James, Jr. *brokerage house executive*
McConahey, Stephen George *securities company executive*
Meers, Henry W. *investment banker*
Melamed, Leo *investment company executive*
Miner, Thomas Hawley *international entrepreneur*
Mukoyama, James Hidefumi, Jr. *securities executive*
Mulvihill, Terence Joseph *investment banking executive*
Nash, Donald Gene *commodities specialist*
Oliver, Harry Maynard, Jr. *retired brokerage house executive*
Porter, Stuart Williams *investment company executive*
Rasin, Rudolph Stephen *corporate executive*
Rogers, John Washington, Jr. *investment management company executive*
Schulte, David Michael *investment banker*
Slansky, Jerry William *investment company executive*
Stead, James Joseph, Jr. *securities company executive*
Swift, Edward Foster, III *investment banker*
Underwood, Robert Leigh *venture capitalist*
Waite, Dennis Vernon *investor relations consultant*
Weitzman, Robert Harold *investment company executive*
Wilmouth, Robert K. *commodities executive*
Woods, Robert Archer *investment counsel*
Young, Ronald Faris *commodity trader*

**Danville**
Burnside, William Charles *investment company executive*

**Deerfield**
Howell, George Bedell *equity investing and managing executive*
Leatham, John Tonkin *business executive*

**Elgin**
Freeman, Corwin Stuart, Jr. *investment adviser*

**Elk Grove Village**
Lombardo, Gaetano (Guy Lombardo) *venture capitalist*

**Evanston**
Downen, David Earl *investment banking executive*

**Glenview**
Gillis, Marvin Bob *investor, consultant*

**Highland Park**
Uhlmann, Frederick Godfrey *commodity and securities broker*

**Lincolnshire**
Caballero, Mario Gustavo *investment company executive*

**Naperville**
Penisten, Gary Dean *entrepreneur*

**Oak Brook**
Kelly, Donald Philip *entrepreneur*

**Princeton**
Schultz, Robert Vernon *entrepreneur*

**Quincy**
Taylor, Judith Caroline *entrepreneur*

**River Forest**
Wirsching, Charles Philipp, Jr. *brokerage house executive, investor*

**Schaumburg**
Balasa, Mark Edward *investment consultant*

**Springfield**
Newtson, Richard Evan *stockbroker*

**Western Springs**
Lynn, Phyllis Jean *entrepreneur*

**Willow Springs**
Jashel, Larry Steven (L. Steven Rose) *entrepreneur, consultant*

**Wilmette**
Albright, Townsend Shaul *investment banker, government benefits consultant*

**Winnetka**
Mathers, Thomas Nesbit *financial consultant*
Sick, William Norman, Jr. *investment company executive*

**INDIANA**

**Columbus**
Hollansky, Bert Voyta *stock brokerage executive*

**Evansville**
Brill, Alan Richard *entrepreneur*
Justice, Phillip Howard *securities broker*

**Greensburg**
Moore, Albert Lawrence *investment company executive, investment broker*

## Indianapolis
Baker, R. Kent *entrepreneur*
Fritz, Cecil Morgan *investment company executive*
Holland, George Frank, II *investment company executive*
King, Kay Sue *investment company executive*

## Richmond
Passmore, Jan William *private investor*

# KANSAS

## Shawnee Mission
Van Tuyl, Cecil L. *investment company executive*

## Wichita
Barry, Donald Lee *investment broker*

# KENTUCKY

## Harrods Creek
Chandler, James Williams *retired securities company executive*

## Lexington
Wagner, Alan Burton *entrepreneur*

## Louisville
Lomicka, William Henry *investor*
Porter, Henry Homes, Jr. *investor*

## Murray
Boston, Betty Lee *investment broker, financial planner*

# LOUISIANA

## Mandeville
Mackenzie-Wood, Melody *entrepreneur*

## New Orleans
Fischer, Ashton John, Jr. *investor*
Flower, Walter Chew, III *investment counselor*
Levert, John Bertels, Jr. *investment executive*

# MAINE

## Augusta
Moody, Stanley Alton *entrepreneur, financial consultant*

## Bryant Pond
Conary, David Arlan *investment company executive*

## Portland
Harte, Christopher McCutcheon *investment manager*

## Topsham
Skolnik, Barnet David *entrepreneur*

# MARYLAND

## Baltimore
Bacigalupo, Charles Anthony *brokerage company executive*
Brinkley, James Wellons *investment company executive*
Cashman, Edmund Joseph, Jr. *investment banker*
Collins, George Joseph *investment counselor*
Curley, John Francis, Jr. *securities company executive*
DeRouchey, Beverly Jean *investment company executive*
Hardiman, Joseph Raymond *securities industry executive*
Harvey, Curran Whitthorne, Jr. *investment management executive*
Himelfarb, Richard Jay *securities firm executive*
Hopkins, Samuel *retired investment banker*
Kent, Edgar Robert, Jr. *investment banker*
Krongard, Alvin B. *corporation executive*
McManus, Walter Leonard *investment executive*
Preston, Mark I. *investment company executive*
Semans, Truman Thomas *investment company executive*
Shaeffer, Charles Wayne *investment counselor*

## Bethesda
Freedman, Marc Allan *investment company executive*
Johnson, Theodore Mebane *investment executive*

## Chestertown
Sener, Joseph Ward, Jr. *securities company executive*

## Chevy Chase
Freeman, Harry Louis *investment executive*

## College Park
Mayer, William Emilio *investor*

## Hagerstown
Baer, John Metz *entrepreneur*

## Lutherville Timonium
Cappiello, Frank Anthony, Jr. *investment advisor*

## Randallstown
Torgerson, Richard Warren *investment broker*

## Riverdale
Guetzkow, Daniel Steere *technology company entrepreneur*

## Rockville
Proffitt, John Richard *business executive, educator*
Tripp, Frederick Gerald *investment advisor*

# MASSACHUSETTS

## Boston
Bailey, Richard Briggs *investment company executive*
Bennett, George Frederick *investment manager*
Calderwood, Stanford Matson *investment management executive*
Cantella, Vincent Michele *stockbroker*
Cole, Carolyn Jo *brokerage company executive*
Conrad, Jeffrey Alan *investment company executive*
Cox, Howard Ellis, Jr. *venture capitalist*
de Burlo, Comegys Russell, Jr. *investment advisor, educator*
Elfers, William *retired investment company director*
Estin, Hans Howard *investment executive*
Fitzgerald, Daniel Louis *securities dealer*
Hagler, Jon Lewis *investment executive*
Hale, Martin de Mora *investor*
Hart, Douglas Edward *investment company executive*
Hobbs, Matthew Hallock *investment banker*
Langermann, John W. R. *institutional equity salesperson*
Lieberman, Gail Forman *investment company executive*
Loring, Caleb, Jr. *investment company executive*
Lovell, Francis Joseph *investment company executive*
McCullen, Joseph T., Jr. *venture capitalist*
Mc Neice, John Ambrose, Jr. *retired investment company executive*
Meister, Doris Powers *investment management executive*
Morby, Jacqueline *venture capitalist*
Morrison, Gordon Mackay, Jr. *investment company executive*
Morton, William Gilbert, Jr. *stock exchange executive*
Oates, William Armstrong, Jr. *investment company executive*
Peckham, John Munroe, III *investment executive, author, lecturer*
Piret, Marguerite Alice *investment banker*
Rice, William Phipps *investment counselor*
Sobin, Julian Melvin *international consultant*
Stone, David Barnes *investment advisor*
Tempel, Jean Curtin *venture capitalist*
Thorndike, John Lowell *investment executive*
Webb, Alexander, III *investment company executive*
Weinstein, David Carl *investment company executive, lawyer*

## Cambridge
Babson, David Leveau *retired investment counsel*
Bedrosian, Edward Robert *investment management company executive*

## Carlisle
Fohl, Timothy *consulting and investment company executive*

## Concord
Schiller, Pieter Jon *venture capital executive*
Wickfield, Eric Nelson *investment company executive*

## Lincoln
Holberton, Philip Vaughan *entrepreneur, educator, professional speaker*

## Milton
Kennedy, Thomas Leo *investment management company executive*

## Newton
Glazer, Donald Wayne *business executive, lawyer, educator*
Henderson, Kenneth Atwood *investment counseling executive*

## Otis
Wampler, Barbara Bedford *entrepreneur*

## Quincy
Edelman, Raymond Howard *investment company executive*

## Reading
Burbank, Nelson Stone *investment banker*

## Scituate
Keating, Margaret Mary *entrepreneur, business consultant*

## Stoneham
Mc Donald, Andrew Jewett *securities firm executive*

## Taunton
Ricciardi, Louis Michael *brokerage house executive*

## Wakefield
Spaulding, William Rowe *investment consultant*

## Wellesley
Anthony, Edward Lovell, II *retired investments executive*
Rowe, Stephen Cooper *venture capitalist, entrepreneur*

## Westwood
Gillette, Hyde *investment banker*

## Wilbraham
Gaudreau, Jules Oscar, Jr. *insurance and financial services company executive*

## Woburn
Eddison, Elizabeth Bole *entrepreneur, information specialist*

# MICHIGAN

## Beulah
Auch, Walter Edward *securities company executive*

## Bloomfield Hills
Benton, Robert Austin, Jr. *investment banker, broker*
Rom, (Melvin) Martin *securities executive*

## Detroit
Brown, William Paul *investment executive*
Openshaw, Helena Marie *investment company executive, portfolio manager*

## Farmington Hills
Ellmann, Sheila Frenkel *investment company executive*

## Grosse Pointe
Lane, James McConkey *investment executive*
Mengden, Joseph Michael *investment banker*

## Oak Park
Novick, Marvin *investment company executive, former automotive supplier executive, accountant*

## Southgate
Richart, John Douglas *investment banker*

## Traverse City
LeJeune, Dennis Edward *investment counsel*

# MINNESOTA

## Minneapolis
Dale, John Sorensen *investment company executive, portfolio manager*
Gallagher, Gerald Raphael *venture capitalist*
Horsch, Lawrence Leonard *venture capitalist, corporate revitalization executive*
Lindau, James H. *grain exchange executive*
Piper, Addison Lewis *securities executive*

## Savage
Bean, Glen Atherton *entrepreneur*

## Waubun
Christensen, Marvin Nelson *venture capitalist*

# MISSISSIPPI

## Jackson
Roehm, MacDonell, Jr. *retail executive*

# MISSOURI

## Bowling Green
Galloway, Daniel Lee *investment executive*

## Jefferson City
Beatty, Grover Douglas *stockbroker*

## Kansas City
Braude, Michael *commodity exchange executive*
Stowers, James Evans, Jr. *investment company executive*

## Lees Summit
Korschot, Benjamin Calvin *investment executive*

## Saint Louis
Avis, Robert Grier *investment company executive, civil engineer*
Bachmann, John William *securities firm executive*
Bernstein, Donald Chester *brokerage company executive, lawyer*
Bickel, Floyd Gilbert, III *investment counselor*
Clement, Richard Francis *retired investment company executive*
Costigan, Edward John *investment banker*
Jackson, Gayle Pendleton White *venture capitalist, international energy specialist*
Maguire, John Patrick *investment company executive*
Newton, George Addison *investment banker, lawyer*
O'Neill, Eugene Milton *mergers and acquisitions consultant*

# NEBRASKA

## Lincoln
Knox, Arthur Lloyd *investor*

## Omaha
Buffett, Warren Edward *entrepreneur*
Cross, W. Thomas *investment company executive*
Greer, Randall Dewey *investment company executive*
Johnson, Richard Walter *investment executive*
Sawtell, Stephen M. *private investor, lawyer*
Sokolof, Phil *industrialist, consumer advocate*
Soshnik, Joseph *investment banking consultant*
Velde, John Ernest, Jr. *business executive*

# NEVADA

## Glenbrook
Jabara, Michael Dean *investment banker*

## Incline Village
Dale, Martin Albert *investment banking executive*
Johnson, James Arnold *business consultant, venture capitalist*

## Logandale
Smiley, Robert William, Jr. *investment banker*

## Smith
Weaver, William Merritt, Jr. *investment banker*

# NEW HAMPSHIRE

## Concord
Levins, John Raymond *investment advisor, management consultant, educator*

## Portsmouth
Morin, Carlton Paul *private investments executive*

# NEW JERSEY

## Atlantic City
Geary, William John *entrepreneur, researcher*

## Avenel
Berg, Louis Leslie *investment executive*

## Cliffside Park
Goldstein, Howard Bernard *investment banker, advertising and marketing executive*

## Cranford
Bardwil, Joseph Anthony *investments consultant*

## East Orange
Howe, James Everett *investment company executive*

## Florham Park
Clayton, William L. *investment banking executive*
Lovell, Robert Marlow, Jr. *retired investment company executive*

## Fort Lee
Lippman, William Jennings *investment company executive*

## Gladstone
Detwiler, Peter Mead *investment banker*

## Haddonfield
Carter, Joan Pauline *investment company executive*

## Jersey City
Smith, James Frederick *securities executive*

## Little Silver
Turbidy, John Berry *investor, management consultant*

## Madison
Johnson, William Joseph *stockbroker*

## Marlboro
Friedman, Howard Martin *financial executive*

## Mendham
Kirby, Allan Price, Jr. *investment company executive*

## Montclair
Kidde, John Lyon *investment manager*

## Morganville
Sternfeld, Marc Howard *investment banker*

## Morristown
Booth, Albert Edward, II *investment executive*
Kearns, William Michael, Jr. *investment banker*

## New Brunswick
Mills, Dorothy Allen *investor*

## Newark
O'Leary, Paul Gerard *investment executive*

## Parsippany
McGirr, David William John *investment banker*
Winograd, Bernard *financial adviser*

## Plainfield
Stella, John Anthony *investment company executive*

## Plainsboro
Schreyer, William Allen *retired investment firm executive*
Urciuoli, J. Arthur *investment executive*

## Princeton
Burns, Patrick Owen *venture capital company executive*
Chamberlin, John Stephen *investor, former cosmetics company executive*
Dilworth, Joseph Richardson *investment banker*
Ehrenberg, Edward *executive, consultant*
Johnston, Robert Fowler *venture capitalist*
Schafer, Carl Walter *investment executive*
Treu, Jesse Isaiah *venture capitalist*

## Red Bank
Dreman, David Nasaniel *investment counselor, security analyst*
Hertz, Daniel Leroy, Jr. *entrepreneur*
Weiant, William Morrow *investment banking executive*

## Ridgewood
Ege, Hans Alsnes *securities company executive*

## Saddle River
Giovannoli, Joseph Louis *entrepreneur*

## Scotch Plains
Bishop, Robert Milton *former stock exchange official*

## Somerset
Hall, Edwin Huddleston, Jr. *investment company executive*

## Summit
Malin, Robert Abernethy *investment management executive*

## Teaneck
Palitz, Clarence Yale, Jr. *commercial finance executive*

## Tuckerton
Dinges, Richard Allen *entrepreneur*

## Upper Saddle River
Oolie, Sam *manufacturing and investment company executive*

## Weehawken
Hess, Dennis John *investment banker*

Weathersby, George Byron *investment management executive*
Webster, John Kimball *investment executive*
Weinberg, John Livingston *investment banker*
Weintz, Jacob Frederick, Jr. *retired investment banker*
Wellin, Keith Sears *investment banker*
Whitehead, John Cunningham *investment executive*
Whitman, Martin J. *investment banker*
Whitney, Edward Bonner *investment banker*
Wigmore, Barrie Atherton *investment banker*
Wilkinson, Donald McLean *investment counsel*
Williams, Dave Harrell *investment executive*
Williamson, Robert Webster *brokerage house executive*
Wit, Harold Maurice *investment banker, lawyer, investor*
Wolcott, Samuel H., III *investment banker*
Wolitzer, Steven Barry *investment banker*
Woods, Ward Wilson, Jr. *investment company executive*
Wruble, Brian Frederick *investment firm executive*
Yancey, Richard Charles *investment banker*
Yeager, George Michael *investment counsel executive*
Zeisler, Richard Spiro *investor*
Zeuschner, Erwin Arnold *investment advisory company executive*
Zuckerberg, Roy J. *investment banking executive*

**Ridgewood**
Meehan, Richard Andrew *investment banker*

**Rochester**
Lewis, A. Duff, Jr. *investment executive*
Rulison, Joseph Richard *investment advisor*
Spurrier, Mary Eileen *investment advisor, financial planner*

**Roslyn Heights**
Jaffe, Melvin *securities company executive*

**Rye**
Wagner, Edward Frederick, Jr. *investment management company executive*

**Scarsdale**
Abbe, Colman *investment banker*

**Southampton**
Atkins, Victor Kennicott, Jr. *investment banker*
Brokaw, Clifford Vail, III *investment banker, business executive*

**Syosset**
Kantor, Edwin *investment company executive*

**Uniondale**
Brustein, Martin *investment executive*

**Wainscott**
Dubow, Arthur Myron *investor, lawyer*

**Wantagh**
Zinder, Newton Donald *stock market analyst, consultant*

**Westbury**
Fogg, Joseph Graham, III *investment banking executive*

**White Plains**
†Slaughter, James C. *trading company executive*
Wahaab, Jay *entrepreneur*

**Williamsville**
Alexander, Theodore William, III *venture capitalist*

**Woodstock**
Ober, Stuart Alan *investment consultant, book publisher*

**Yonkers**
Smith, Aldo Ralston, Jr. *brokerage house executive*

**NORTH CAROLINA**

**Efland**
Efland, Simpson Lindsay *entrepreneur*

**Greensboro**
Johnson, Marshall Hardy *investment company executive*

**High Point**
Gay, David Braxton *stockbroker*
Phillips, Earl Norfleet, Jr. *financial services executive*

**North Wilkesboro**
Pardue, Dwight Edward *venture capitalist*

**Pinehurst**
Lebeck, Warren Wells *commodities consultant*

**Raleigh**
Anderson, Glenn Elwood *investment banker*
McKinney, Charles Cecil *investment company executive*
Tucker, Garland Scott, III *investment banker*

**Winston Salem**
Strickland, Robert Louis *business executive*
Sullivan, Richard Leo *brokerage house executive*

**NORTH DAKOTA**

**Fargo**
Tallman, Robert Hall *investment company executive*

**OHIO**

**Alpha**
James, Francis Edward, Jr. *investment counselor*

**Cincinnati**
Anning, Robert Doan Hopkins *brokerage company executive*
Joseph, David J., Jr. *trading company executive*
Lucke, Robert Vito *merger and acquisition executive*
Niehoff, Karl Richard Besuden *financial executive*
Street, David Hargett *investment company executive*

**Cleveland**
Brentlinger, Paul Smith *venture capital executive*
Hook, John Burney *investment company executive*
O'Brien, John Feighan *investment banker*
O'Donnell, Thomas Michael *brokerage firm executive*
Roulston, Thomas Henry *investment adviser*
Warren, Russell James *investment banking executive, consultant*

**Columbus**
Barthelmas, Ned Kelton *investment and commercial real estate banker*
Pointer, Peter Leon *investment executive*

**Galion**
Cobey, Ralph *industrialist*

**Hudson**
Kempe, Robert Aron *venture management executive*

**Lancaster**
Hurley, Samuel Clay, III *investment management company executive*

**Martins Ferry**
Gracey, Robert William *account executive, minister*

**Westerville**
Barr, John Michael *investment adviser, training and management consultant*

**Westlake**
Barker, Keith Rene *investment banker*

**OKLAHOMA**

**Oklahoma City**
Frager, Norman *stockbroker*
Painton, Ira Wayne *retired securities executive*
Sulc, Dwight George *investment advisor*

**Tulsa**
Sanditen, Edgar Richard *investment company executive*

**OREGON**

**Chiloquin**
Reed, David George *entrepreneur*

**Depoe Bay**
Fish, Barbara Joan *investor, small business owner*

**Medford**
Cutler, Kenneth Ross *investment company and mutual fund executive*

**Portland**
Hay, Andrew Mackenzie *merchant banking and commodities company executive*
Myers, Clay *retired investment management company executive*
Olsen, Kurt *investment company executive, adviser*
Rutherford, William Drake *investment executive, lawyer*
Silver, Stephen Hal *stockbroker, financial planner*

**PENNSYLVANIA**

**Bensalem**
Graf, William J. *entrepreneur*

**Blue Bell**
Gleklen, Donald Morse *investment company executive*

**Bryn Mawr**
Lewis, James Earl *investment banker*

**Canonsburg**
Prado, Gerald M. *investment banker*

**Conshohocken**
Cheung, Peter Pak Lun *investment company executive, chemistry educator*

**Dover**
Hayek, William Edward *investment advisor, counsel*

**Doylestown**
Holstrom, Carleton Arthur *brokerage house executive*

**Erie**
Ryan, Gerald Anthony *financial advisor, venture capitalist*

**Gladwyne**
Geisel, Cameron Meade, Jr. *investment professional*

**Havertown**
Godwin, Pamela June *financial services executive*

**Hummelstown**
Custer, John Charles *investment broker*

**Jenkintown**
Newburger, Frank L., Jr. *retired investment broker*

**King Of Prussia**
Pope, Dale Allen *investment company executive*

**Ligonier**
Mellon, Seward Prosser *investment executive*

**Malvern**
Bogle, John Clifton *investment company executive*

**Newtown Square**
Turner, George Pearce *consulting company executive*

**Philadelphia**
Borer, Edward Turner *investment banker*
Bowditch, Nathaniel Rantoul *brokerage house executive*
Giordano, Nicholas Anthony *stock exchange executive*
Johnson, Craig Norman *investment banker*
McGinley, Joseph Patrick *brokerage house executive*
Palmer, Russell Eugene *investment executive*
Wilde, Norman Taylor, Jr. *investment banking company executive*
Wolitarsky, James William *securities industry executive*

**Pittsburgh**
Casturo, Don James *venture capitalist*
Curtis, Gregory Dyer *investment company executive, foundation administrator, lawyer, author, poet*
Donahue, John Francis *investment company executive*
Fisher, Henry *investment banker*
Hillman, Henry L. *investment company executive*
Hunter, David Wittmer *security brokerage executive*
Hyman, Lewis Neil *investment company executive, investment advisor*
Knapp, George Robert *investment executive, business advisor, lawyer*
Mathieson, Andrew Wray *investment management executive*
Maurer, Richard Michael *investment company executive*
Walton, James M. *investment company executive*

**Plymouth Meeting**
Yarnall, D. Robert, Jr. *entrepreneur, investor*

**Quarryville**
Bird, L. Raymond *investor*

**Radnor**
†Buck, James Mahlon, Jr. *venture capital executive*
Humes, Graham *investment banker*

**Reading**
White, Timothy Paul *brokerage house executive*

**Sewickley**
Chaplin, James Crossan, IV *securities firm executive*

**West Conshohocken**
Miller, Paul Fetterolf, Jr. *retired investment company executive*

**York**
Thornton, George Whiteley *investment company executive*

**RHODE ISLAND**

**East Greenwich**
Hunter, Garrett Bell *investment banker*

**Providence**
Joukowsky, Artemis A. W. *private investor*
Manchester, Robert D. *venture capitalist*

**Wakefield**
Mason, Scott MacGregor *entrepreneur, inventor, consultant*

**SOUTH CAROLINA**

**Aiken**
Hanna, Carey McConnell *securities and investments executive*

**Charleston**
Winthrop, John *investment company executive*

**Hilton Head Island**
Batten, William Milfred *retired stock exchange executive*
Urato, Barbra Casale *entrepreneur*

**Johns Island**
Cameron, Thomas William Lane *investment company executive*

**Sullivans Island**
Romaine, Henry Simmons *investment consultant*

**TENNESSEE**

**Chattanooga**
Corey, Charles William *investment banker*
Witherspoon, John Knox, Jr. *investment banking executive*

**Knoxville**
Penn, Dawn Tamara *entrepreneur*
Springer, John K. *securities representative*

**Nashville**
Bradford, James C., Jr. *brokerage house executive*
Hanselman, Richard Wilson *entrepreneur*
Kuhn, Paul Hubert, Jr. *investment counsel*
Nelson, Edward Gage *merchant banking investment company executive*
Roberts, Kenneth Lewis *investor, lawyer, foundation administrator*
Sullivan, Allen Trousdale *securities company executive*

**Parsons**
Franks, Hollis Berry *retired investment executive*

**Shelbyville**
Cooper, James Hayes Shofner (Jim Cooper) *investment company executive, former congressman, lawyer*

**TEXAS**

**Austin**
Boswell, Gary Taggart *investor, former electronics company executive*
Davis, Tony Robert *investment company executive*
Inman, Bobby Ray *investor, former electronics executive*
Spertus, Philip *investment company executive*

**Borger**
Schneck, Gary Alan *securities broker*

**Corpus Christi**
Bateman, John Roger *investment holding company executive*

**Corsicana**
Dyer, James Mason, Jr. *investment company executive*

**Dallas**
Collins, Michael James *investment company executive*
Hillis, Robert Gregory *investment executive*
Lynch, William Wright, Jr. *investment executive, engineer*
McClure, Frederick Donald *public affairs consultant, lawyer*
Parent, David Hill *investment company executive*
Philipson, Herman Louis, Jr. *investment banker*
Reed, Jesse Francis *entrepreneur, artist, inventor, theologian, business consultant*
Smith, Cece *venture capitalist*
Whitson, James Norfleet, Jr. *diversified company executive*

**El Paso**
Prendergast, Thomas A. *investments and management consultant*

**Fort Worth**
Asher, Garland Parker *investment holding company executive*

**Friendswood**
Arnaud, Sandra *financial advisor*

**Garland**
McGrath, James Thomas *real estate investment company executive*

**Houston**
Anderson, William (Albion), Jr. *investment banker*
Claiborn, Stephen Allan *investment banker*
Cunningham, R. Walter *venture capitalist*
Currie, John Thornton (Jack Currie) *retired investment banker*
Dantone, W. Bryan *real estate investor, principal*
Duncan, Charles William, Jr. *investor, former government official*
Dworsky, Clara Weiner *merchandise brokerage executive, lawyer*
Glassell, Alfred Curry, Jr. *investor*
Mackey, William Sturges, Jr. *investor, consultant*
Montle, Paul Joseph *entrepreneur*
Neuhaus, Philip Ross *investment banker*
O'Connor, Ralph Sturges *investment company executive*
Parsons, Edmund Morris *investment company executive*
Riesser, Gregor Hans *arbitrage investment advisor*
Stralem, Pierre *retired stockbroker*
Taylor, James B. *securities trader, financial planner*
Williams, Edward Earl, Jr. *entrepreneur, educator*

**San Antonio**
Arnold, Stephen Paul *investment professional*
Duncan, A. Baker *investment banker*

**Stafford**
Franks, Charles Leslie *investments executive*

**Texas City**
Legan, Robert William *securities analyst*

**Wichita Falls**
Jones, William Houston *stock brokerage executive, financial consultant*

**UTAH**

**Salt Lake City**
†Ballard, Melvin Russell, Jr. *investment executive, church official*
Meldrum, Peter Durkee *venture capital/biotechnology company executive*

**VIRGINIA**

**Alexandria**
Pabarcius, Algis *investment executive*
Richards, Darrie Hewitt *investment company executive*

**Annandale**
Khim, Jay Wook *high technology systems integration executive*

**Arlington**
Gregg, David, III *investment banker*
Sands, Frank Melville *investment manager*

**Charlottesville**
Monroe, Brooks *investment banker*
Newman, James Wilson *business executive*

**Fairfax**
Jiang, Hubin *entrepreneur, software engineer*

**Falls Church**
Isaac, William Michael *investment firm executive, former government official*

**Keswick**
Markman, Sherman *investment banker, venture capitalist, corporate financier*

**Mc Lean**
Bisbee, Gerald Elftman, Jr. *investment company executive*
Searles, Dewitt Richard *retired investment firm executive, retired air force officer*
Smith, Thomas Eugene *investment company executive, financial consultant*
Urquhart, Glen Taylor *investment and development executive*

**Petersburg**
Ryan, James Herbert *security and retail services company executive*

**Richmond**
Dahlenburg, Lyle Marion *investment company executive*
Fields, William Jay *investment banker*
Gorr, Louis Frederick *investment consultant*
Hong, James Ming *industrialist, venture capitalist*
Phillips, Thomas Edworth, Jr. *investment executive, senior consultant*
Powell, Kenneth Edward *investment banker*

**Stanardsville**
Anns, Philip Harold *international trading executive, former pharmaceutical company executive*

**Stanleytown**
Stanley, Thomas Bahnson, Jr. *investor*

**Virginia Beach**
Lawson, Beth Ann Reid *strategic planner*

**Warrenton**
Watkins, Birge Swift *real estate investment executive*

**Williamsburg**
Gordon, Baron Jack *stockbroker*
Roberson, Robert S. *investment company executive*

**WASHINGTON**

**Bellevue**
Arnold, Robert Lloyd *investment broker*
McAleer, William Harrison *software venture capitalist*
Ryles, Gerald Fay *private investor, business executive*

**Olympia**
Foley, Thomas Michael *financial executive*

**Redmond**
Pacholski, Richard Francis *retired securities company executive, financial advisor, consultant*

**Seattle**
Bayley, Christopher T. *public affairs consultant*

**Tacoma**
Habedank, Gary L. *brokerage house executive*

**WISCONSIN**

**Mequon**
Bloom, James Edward *commodity trading and financial executive*

**Milwaukee**
Kaiser, George Chapin *investment company executive*
Samson, Richard Max *investments and real estate executive*
Schnoll, Howard Manuel *investment banking and managed asset consultant*

**Oak Creek**
Giblin, Louis *stockbroker*

**Wauwatosa**
Ladd, Louise Elizabeth *investments company executive*

**WYOMING**

**Casper**
True, Jean Durland *entrepreneur, oil company executive*

**Jackson**
Hirschfield, Alan J. *entrepreneur*

**Wilson**
Chrystie, Thomas Ludlow *investor*
Sage, Andrew Gregg Curtin, II *corporate investor, manager*

**TERRITORIES OF THE UNITED STATES**

**PUERTO RICO**

**Hato Rey**
Ferrer, Miguel Antonio *brokerage firm and investment bank executive*

**CANADA**

**ALBERTA**

**Calgary**
Cumming, Thomas Alexander *stock exchange executive*
King, Frank *investment company executive*
Seaman, Donald Roy *investment company executive*

**Edmonton**
†Pocklington, Peter H. *business executive*

**BRITISH COLUMBIA**

**Vancouver**
Budzinsky, Armin Alexander *investment banker*
Harwood, Brian Dennis *securities industry executive*
Johnson, Michael E. *stock exchange executive*
Saunders, Peter Paul *investor*

**MANITOBA**

**Winnipeg**
Alexander, Norman James *investment consultant*

**NOVA SCOTIA**

**Bedford**
Hennigar, David J. *investment broker*

**ONTARIO**

**Chatham**
McKeough, William Darcy *investment company executive*

**Oakville**
Holmes, James *investment company executive*

**Ottawa**
Morand, Peter *investment company executive*

**Toronto**
Bloomberg, Lawrence S. *securities executive, art collector*
Hore, John Edward *commodity futures educator*
Lindsay, Roger Alexander *investment executive*
Petrillo, Leonard Philip *corporate securities executive, lawyer*
Weston, W. Galen *diversified holdings executive*

**QUEBEC**

**Montreal**
Cedraschi, Tullio *investment management company executive*
Elie, Jean André *investment banker*
Schwartz, Roy Richard *holding company executive*
Torrey, David Leonard *investment banker*

**SASKATCHEWAN**

**Regina**
†Stengler, Ron Joseph *gaming corporation executive*

**BAHAMAS**

**Grand Cayman**
McIntire, Jerald Gene *investment executive, former municipal official*

**Nassau**
Templeton, John Marks *investment counsel, financial analyst*

**BERMUDA**

**Tuckers Town**
Heizer, Edgar Francis, Jr. *venture capitalist*

**CHINA**

**Beijing**
Melville, Richard Allen *investment company executive*

**ENGLAND**

**London**
Berger, Andrew L. *investment banker, lawyer*
Downing, Danielle Santander *brokerage house executive*
Hale, Charles Martin *stockbroker*
Hayden, Richard Michael *investment banker*
Jourdren, Marc Henri *investment banking company executive*
Mulford, David Campbell *finance company executive*

**FRANCE**

**Paris**
Masurel, Jean-Louis Antoine Nicolas *investment company executive*

**GERMANY**

**Moglingen**
Meyberg, Bernhard Ulrich *entrepreneur*

**HONG KONG**

**Hong Kong**
Chun, Wendy Sau Wan *investment company executive*
Solberg, Ronald Louis *investment banker, fixed-income strategist*

**ISRAEL**

**Jerusalem**
Arnon, Michael *finance company executive*

**PAKISTAN**

**Karachi**
Shroff, Firoz Sardar *merger and acquisition professional*

**SOUTH AFRICA**

**Marshalltown**
Chen, Philip Minkang *investment banker, corporate executive, lawyer, engineer*

**SWITZERLAND**

**Lausanne**
Bloemsma, Marco Paul *investor*

**ADDRESS UNPUBLISHED**

Ackerman, Melvin *investment company executive*
Aljian, James Donovan *investment company executive*
Anderson, Kenneth Ward *investor, consultant*
Anderson, Mary Theresa *investment manager*
Anker, Peter Louis *retired securities executive*
Apel-Brueggeman, Myrna L. *entrepreneur*
Aurin, Robert James *entrepreneur*
Bacharach, Melvin Lewis *retired venture capitalist*
Bacon, Caroline Sharfman *investor relations consultant*
Bagwill, John Williams, Jr. *retired pension fund company executive*
Bailey, Rita Maria *investment advisor, psychologist*
Bansak, Stephen A., Jr. *investment banker, financial consultant*
Bantry, Bryan *entrepreneur*
Bell, David Eugene *investment company executive*
Black, Richard Bruce *business executive, consultant*
Bogosian, Mark Jerome *investment company executive*
Bratt, Nicholas *investment management and research company executive*
Brodkin, Alan Keith *investment company executive*
Brown, Herbert Graham *entrepreneur*
Browning, Jesse Harrison *entrepreneur*
Bruzda, Francis Joseph *investment executive, former banker*
Caldwell, Warren Frederick *investment company executive*
Callard, David Jacobus *investment banker*
Carr, Harold Noflet *investment corporation executive*
Cockrum, William Monroe, III *investment banker, consultant, educator*
Czarnecki, Gerald Milton *investment banking and venture capital*
DeVries, Richard *entrepreneur*
Doherty, Charles Vincent *investment counsel executive*
Drake, Rodman Leland *investment executive, consultant*
Duval, Michael Raoul *investment banker*
Dwyer, Charles Breen *arbitrage and Eurobond specialist*
Frankenberger, Bertram, Jr. *investor, consultant*
Friedlander, Charles Douglas *investment company executive, space consultant*
Froehlke, Robert Frederick *financial services executive*
Fuld, Richard Severin, Jr. *investment banker*
Garcia-Granados, Sergio Eduardo *brokerage house executive*
Geissinger, Frederick Wallace *investment banker*
Gelles, Harry P. *investment banker, land investor*
Glasberg, Laurence Brian *private investor, business executive*
Goldberg, Arthur H. *brokerage services company executive*
Goldman, Alan Ira *investment banking executive*
Good, Walter Raymond *investment executive*
Goyan, Michael Donovan *stockbroker, investment executive*
Grant, Frederick Anthony *investment banker*
Greene, Frank Sullivan, Jr. *investment management executive*
Haber, Warren H. *investment company executive*
Hapner, Mary Lou *securities trader/dealer*
Hays, Thomas Chandler *holding company executive*
Headley, Anne Renouf *technology commercialization financier*
Heckler, John Maguire *stockbroker, investment company executive*
Henkel, Arthur John, Jr. *investment banker*
Hentic, Yves Frank Mao *investment banker, industrial engineer*
Hickey, Joseph Michael *investment banker*
Hill, John Edward, Jr. *investment banker, small business owner*
Hogan, Mark *investment company executive*
Howard, James Webb *investment banker, lawyer, engineer*
Hudson, Donald J. *retired stock exchange executive*
Iasiello, Dorothy Barbara *brokerage company executive*
Jacobs, Herbert Howard *investor*
Jepson, Robert Scott, Jr. *international investment banking specialist*
Johnson, Michael Warren *international relations specialist*
Kotler, Steven *investment banker*
Lee, David Stoddart *investment counselor*
Lewis, Brock *investment company executive*
Lipton, Susan Lytle *investment banker, lawyer*
Lohrer, Richard Baker *investment consultant*

Luke, Douglas Sigler *business executive*
Lynch, Phyllis Anne *stockbroker*
Lynch, Thomas Peter *securities executive*
Marks, Leonard, Jr. *retired corporate executive*
Marler, Larry John *private investor*
Mascheroni, Eleanor Earle *investment company executive*
Mc Gill, Archie Joseph *venture capitalist*
McNeill, Robert Patrick *investment counselor*
McRae, Thomas Kenneth *retired investment company executive*
Mendez, Albert Orlando *industrialist, financier*
Mikitka, Gerald Peter *investment banker, financial consultant*
Miller, Alan Jay *financial consultant, author*
Millsaps, Fred Ray *investor*
Moran, Charles A. *securities executive*
Morgenroth, Earl Eugene *entrepreneur*
Myers, John Herman *investment management executive*
Nilsson, A. Kenneth *investor*
O'Sullivan, Lawrence Joseph *retired investment counselor*
Peters, Ralph Frew *investment banker*
Pilkington, Mary Ellen *stockbroker, trader*
Pinkney, D. Timothy *investment company executive*
Pool, Philip Bemis, Jr. *investment banker*
Prince, Milton S. *investment company executive*
Robertson, Mark Wayne *investment specialist*
Robinson, Bob Leo *international investment services executive*
Sells, Boake Anthony *private investor*
Servison, Roger Theodore *investment executive*
Smoot, Wendell McMeans, Jr. *investment counselor*
Stanfill, Dennis Carothers *business executive*
Stansell, Ronald Bruce *investment banker*
Steen, Carlton Duane *private investor, former food company executive*
Swanberg, Edmund Raymond *investment counselor*
Taber, Edward Albert, III *investment executive*
Tansor, Robert Henry *investor*
Taylor, Linda Rathbun *investment banker*
Weisman, Lorenzo David *investment banker*
Wilson, Robert James Montgomery *investment company executive*

---

**FINANCE: REAL ESTATE**

**UNITED STATES**

**ALABAMA**

**Arab**
Hammond, Ralph Charles *real estate executive*

**Birmingham**
Copeland, Hunter Armstrong *real estate executive*

**Florence**
Mullins, Betty Johnson *realtor*

**Huntsville**
Dembowski, Fannie Ruth *real estate brokerage executive*

**Tuscaloosa**
McFarland, James William *real estate development company executive*

**ALASKA**

**Anchorage**
Faulkner, Sewell Ford *real estate executive*

**ARIZONA**

**Bullhead City**
Jones, Vernon Quentin *surveyor*

**Mesa**
Bell, Daniel Carroll *realtor, community association, ranch and land manager*
McCollum, Alvin August *real estate company executive*

**Peoria**
Morrison, Manley Glenn *real estate investor, former army officer*

**Phoenix**
Donaldson, Wilburn Lester *property management corporation executive*
Lewis, Orme, Jr. *investment company executive, land use advisor*
Mounes, Janice Rose Moore *real estate broker*
Rau, David Edward *real estate company executive*
Wilson, Carl Arthur *real estate broker, contractor*

**Sedona**
Copeland, Suzanne Johnson *real estate executive*

**Tempe**
Berg, Linda Thoms *real estate broker*

**Tucson**
Best, Gary Thorman *real estate broker*
Broce, Dorothy Diane *real estate broker, interior designer*
Irvin, Mark Christopher *real estate consultant, broker and developer*
Longan, George Baker, III *real estate executive*
Swihart, H. Gregg *real estate company executive*
Taylor, William Malcolm *environmentalist, educator*

**West Sedona**
Lane, Margaret Anna Smith *property manager developer*

## ARKANSAS

**Bella Vista**
Cooper, John Alfred, Jr. *community development company executive*
McMennamy, Roger Neal *community development company executive*

**Fayetteville**
Jackson, Robert Lee *real estate agent*

**Hot Springs National Park**
Craft, Kay Stark *real estate broker*

**Little Rock**
McConnell, John Wesley *real estate-resort developer, corporate executive*
Shults, Robert Lee *real estate executive, airline executive*

## CALIFORNIA

**Agoura Hills**
Scardina, Frank Joseph *real estate executive*

**Apple Valley**
Ledford, Gary Alan *real estate developer*

**Atherton**
Holvick, Patricia Valerie Jean *property manager, financial planner*

**Belvedere Tiburon**
Caselli, Virgil P. *real estate executive*

**Berkeley**
Wachs, Martin *urban planning educator*

**Beverly Hills**
Bergman, Nancy Palm *real estate investment company executive*
Glazer, Guilford *real estate developer*
Shapell, Nathan *financial and real estate executive*
Victor, Robert Eugene *real estate corporation executive, lawyer*

**Big Sur**
Cross, Robert Louis *realtor, land use planner, writer*
Owings, Margaret Wentworth *conservationist, artist*

**Burlingame**
Berwick, Andrew Struthers, Jr. *real estate executive*

**Campbell**
Nicholson, Joseph Bruce *real estate developer*

**Coronado**
Stames, William Alexander *realtor, cost management executive*

**Danville**
Plummer, Marcie Stern *real estate broker*

**El Macero**
Wheeler, Douglas Paul *conservationist, government official, lawyer*

**Fontana**
Atkinson, Donald D., Sr. *real estate broker*
Poulsen, Dennis Robert *environmentalist*

**Glendale**
Nelson, James Augustus, II *real estate executive, architect, banker*
Yegian, Richard *real estate executive*

**Goleta**
Koart, Nellie Hart *real estate investor and executive*

**Idyllwild**
Acheson, Barbara *real estate broker, small business owner*

**Inglewood**
†Buss, Jerry Hatten *real estate executive, sports team owner*

**Irvine**
Chronley, James Andrew *real estate executive*
Stack, Geoffrey Lawrence *real estate developer*

**La Jolla**
Anthony, Harry Antoniades *city planner, architect, educator*
Foley, L(ewis) Michael *real estate executive*

**Laguna Beach**
Hanauer, Joe Franklin *real estate executive*

**Laguna Niguel**
Hough, J. Marie *real estate company official*
York, James Orison *real estate executive*

**Larkspur**
Roulac, Stephen E. *real estate consultant*

**Long Beach**
Rosenberg, Jill *realtor, civic leader*

**Los Alamitos**
Spiegel, Marilyn Harriet *real estate executive*

**Los Altos**
Bracken, Thomas Robert James *real estate investment executive*
Getreu, Sanford *city planner*

**Los Angeles**
Abernethy, Robert John *real estate developer*
Beban, Gary Joseph *real estate corporation officer*
Farhat, Vince Lee *lawyer*
Furlotti, Alexander Amato *real estate development company executive*
†Gilchrist, Richard Irwin *real estate developer*
Gordon, Milton G. *real estate counselor, consultant*

Levy, Alan David *real estate executive*
Linsk, Michael Stephen *real estate executive*
Montgomery, Robin Vera *realtor*
Osgood, Frank William *urban and economic planner, writer*
Swartz, Roslyn Holt *real estate investment executive*
Tornek, Terry E. *real estate executive*
Truman, Edward Crane *real estate manager, consultant, composer*

**Lynwood**
Dove, Donald Augustine *city planner, educator*

**Manhattan Beach**
Krienke, Carol Belle Manikowske (Mrs. Oliver Kenneth Krienke) *realtor*

**Mission Viejo**
Smith, William K. *real estate developer*

**National City**
Potter, J(effrey) Stewart *property manager*

**Newbury Park**
Fredericks, Patricia Ann *real estate executive*
Guggenheim-Boucard, Alan Andre Albert Paul Edouard *business executive, international consultant*

**Newport Beach**
Bren, Donald L. *real estate company executive*
Kenney, William John, Jr. *real estate development executive*
Matteucci, Dominick Vincent *real estate developer*

**North Hollywood**
Milner, Howard M. *real estate developer, international real estate financier*

**Oakland**
Anthony, Elaine Margaret *real estate executive, interior designer*
Fischer, Michael Ludwig *environmental executive*

**Palm Desert**
Wiedle, Gary Eugene *real estate management company executive*

**Palmdale**
Anderson, R(obert) Gregg *real estate company executive*

**Pasadena**
Crowley, John Crane *real estate developer*

**Placerville**
Craib, Kenneth Bryden *resource development executive, physicist, economist*

**Rancho Mirage**
Gardner, Donald LaVere *development company executive*

**Rancho Santa Fe**
DeMarco, Ralph John *real estate developer*

**Riverside**
Davis, JoAn *business manager, general contractor, tax preparer, vocational business educator*

**Sacramento**
Lukenbill, Gregg *real estate developer, sports promoter*

**San Bernardino**
Willis, Harold Wendt, Sr. *real estate developer*

**San Diego**
Mc Comic, Robert Barry *real estate development company executive, lawyer*
Munson, Lucille Marguerite (Mrs. Arthur E. Munson) *real estate broker*
Oldham, Maxine Jernigan *real estate broker*

**San Francisco**
Brower, David Ross *conservationist*
Freund, Fredric S. *real estate broker, property manager*
Frush, James Carroll, Jr. *real estate development company executive*
Shorenstein, Walter Herbert *commercial real estate development company executive*

**San Jose**
Rothblatt, Donald Noah *urban and regional planner, educator*

**San Marino**
Grantham, Richard Robert *real estate company consultant*

**Santa Cruz**
Dilbeck, Charles Stevens, Jr. *real estate company executive*

**Santa Rosa**
Brunner, Howard William *professional land surveyor*

**Sausalito**
Klingensmith, Arthur Paul *business and personal development consultant*
Klotsche, Charles Martin *real estate development company executive, writer*

**Seal Beach**
Nesmith, Audrey Marie *military housing manager (retired), writer*

**Simi Valley**
Glindeman, Henry Peter, Jr. *real estate developer*

**Torrance**
Alter, Gerald L. *real estate executive*

**Twain Harte**
Kinsinger, Robert Earl *property company executive, educational consultant*

**Upland**
Lewis, Goldy Sarah *real estate developer, corporation executive*
Lewis, Ralph Milton *real estate developer*

**Valencia**
Hunter, Diana Lynn *real estate consultant*

**Venice**
Rosenthal, Richard Jay *real estate consultant, mediator, educator*

**Vista**
Cavanaugh, Kenneth Clinton *retired housing consultant*

## COLORADO

**Aurora**
Bobrick, Steven Aaron *property manager*
Lochmiller, Kurtis L. *real estate entrepreneur*

**Boulder**
Clifford, Lawrence M. *real estate company executive*

**Colorado Springs**
Ansorge, Iona Marie *retired real estate agent, musician, high school and college instructor*
Leonard, George Edmund *real estate, bank, and consulting executive*

**Denver**
Antonoff, Gary L. *real estate executive*
Barnes, William Anderson *real estate investment manager*
Norman, John Edward *petroleum landman*
Smyth, David Shannon *real estate investor, commercial and retail builder and developer*

**Fort Collins**
Driscoll, Richard Stark *land use planner*
Frink, Eugene Hudson, Jr. *business and real estate consultant*

**Golden**
Sacks, Arthur Bruce *environmental and liberal arts educator*

**Grand Junction**
Nelson, Paul William *real estate broker*

**Lakewood**
Penwell, Jones Clark *real estate appraiser, consultant*

**Vail**
Kelton, Arthur Marvin, Jr. *real estate developer*

## CONNECTICUT

**Bethel**
Kurfehs, Harold Charles *real estate executive*

**Danbury**
Anderson, Alan Reinold *real estate executive, communications consultant*

**Darien**
Wood, Christopher L. J. *real estate consulting firm executive*

**East Hartford**
Pudlo, Frances Theresa *real estate company administrator*

**Greenwich**
†Badman, John, III *real estate developer, architect*
Urstadt, Charles J. *real estate executive*

**New Britain**
Adams, John Francis, Jr. *real estate executive*

**New Haven**
Harrison, Henry Starin *real estate educator, appraiser, entrepreneur*

**North Haven**
Pearce, Herbert Henry *real estate company executive*

**Old Lyme**
LeBoutillier, Janet Ela *real estate investment asset manager, writer*

## DELAWARE

**Dover**
Cohen, William John *urban and environmental planner, educator, photographer*

**Newark**
Byrne, John Michael *energy and environmental policy educator, researcher*

**Wilmington**
Gilman, Marvin Stanley *real estate developer, educator*
Maley, Patricia Ann *preservation planner*

## DISTRICT OF COLUMBIA

**Washington**
Berg, Norman Alf *conservation consultant*
Blackwelder, Brent Francis *environmentalist*
Blair, William Draper, Jr. *conservationist*
Hollander, Richard Edward *real estate executive*
McMahon, Neil Michael *real estate executive*
Meyer, Alden Merrill *environmental association executive*
†Oge, Margo Tsirigotis *environmentalist*
Rosan, Richard Marshall *real estate executive, architect, non-profit research executive*

Stegman, Michael Allen *city and regional planning educator*
Stollman, Israel *city planner*
Stone, Roger David *environmentalist*

## FLORIDA

**Arcadia**
Schmidt, Harold Eugene *real estate company executive*

**Boca Raton**
Lagin, Neil *property management executive, landscape designer, consultant*
Natkin, Alvin Martin *environmental company executive*

**Cedar Key**
Starnes, Earl Maxwell *urban and regional planner, architect*

**Coral Gables**
Blumberg, David *builder, developer*

**Deland**
Tedros, Theodore Zaki *educator, real estate broker, appraiser*

**Fort Lauderdale**
Bird, Linda W. *realtor*
Cummings, Virginia (Jeanne) *retired real estate company executive*
Paulauskas, Edmund Walter *real estate broker, retired*
Van Howe, Annette Evelyn *retired real estate agent*

**Fort Walton Beach**
Cooke, Fred Charles *real estate broker*

**Gainesville**
May, Jackson Campbell *real estate developer, writer*
Stein, Jay M. *planning and design educator, consultant*
York, Vermelle Cardwell *real estate broker and developer*

**Gulf Breeze**
Jenkins, Robert Berryman *real estate developer*

**Hollywood**
Burton, John Jacob *retired real estate company executive appraiser*

**Jacksonville**
Clarkson, Charles Andrew *real estate investment executive*
Lovett, Radford Dow *real estate and investment company executive*
Parker, David Forster *real estate development consultant*

**Lake Park**
Totten, Gloria Jean (Dolly Totten) *real estate executive, financial consultant*

**Lakeland**
Smith, Levie David, Jr. *real estate appraiser, consultant*

**Longwood**
Gasperoni, Emil, Sr. *realtor, developer*

**Maitland**
Vallee, Judith Delaney *environmentalist, writer, fundraiser*

**Marco Island**
Genrich, Judith Ann *real estate executive*
Llewellyn, Leonard Frank *real estate broker*

**Melbourne**
Evans, Arthur Forte *real estate developer*
Michalski, Thomas Joseph *city planner, developer*

**Miami**
Esslinger, Anna Mae Linthicum *realtor*
Kunz, Margaret McCarthy *realtor*
Mozian, Gerard Paul *real estate company executive, business consultant*
Nestor Castellano, Brenda Diana *real estate executive*
Raffel, Leroy B. *real estate development company executive*
Roemer, Elaine Sloane *real estate broker*
Salvaneschi, Luigi *real estate and development executive, business educator*
Stover, James Howard *real estate executive*

**Mount Dora**
Adams, Carl Morgan, Jr. *real estate appraiser, mortgage banker*

**Naples**
Corkran, Virginia Bowman *real estate associate*
Evans, Elizabeth Ann West *realtor*
Stratton, John Caryl *real estate executive*

**Ocala**
Booth, Jane Schuele *real estate broker, executive*

**Palm Beach**
Bagby, Martha L. Green *real estate holding company, novelist, publisher*
Dillard, Rodney Jefferson *real estate executive*

**Palm Beach Gardens**
Freeman, Donald Wilford *real estate developer, horse breeder*

**Palmetto**
Rains, Gloria Cann *environmentalist company executive*

**Plantation**
Lehman, Joan Alice *real estate executive*

**Ponte Vedra**
Moore, Philip Walsh *appraisal company executive*

**Ponte Vedra Beach**
Berry, Clare Gebert *real estate broker*

**Punta Gorda**
Beever, Lisa Britt-Dodd *transportation and environmental planner, researcher*

**Saint Petersburg**
Rummel, Harold Edwin *real estate development executive*

**Saint Petersburg Beach**
Hurley, Frank Thomas, Jr. *realtor*

**Sanibel**
Courtney, James Edmond *real estate development*

**Sebastian**
Muller, Henry John *real estate developer*

**Sebring**
Sherrick, Daniel Noah *real estate broker*

**Tallahassee**
Avant, David Alonzo, Jr. *realty company executive, photographer*
Johnson, Benjamin F., VI *real estate developer, consulting economist*
Lisenby, Dorrece Edenfield *realtor*

**Tampa**
Blomgren, Bruce Holmes *real estate developer, motivational speaker*
Corbitt, Doris Orene *real estate agent, dietitian*

**Titusville**
Kirchman, Budagail Simms *realtor*

**Winter Park**
Strawn, Frances Freeland *real estate executive*

## GEORGIA

**Atlanta**
Charania, Barkat *real estate consultant*
Cupp, Robert Erhard *golf course designer, land use planner*
Curtis, Philip Kerry *real estate developer*
Glover, John Trapnell *real estate executive*
Grady, Joseph Patrick *real estate professional*
Murphy, James Gregory *real estate executive*
Regenstein, Lewis Graham *conservationist, author, lecturer, speech writer*
Simpson, Allan Boyd *real estate company executive*
Wolbrink, James Francis *real estate investor*

**Augusta**
Mayberry, Julius Eugene *realty company owner, investor*

**Folkston**
Crumbley, Esther Helen Kendrick *realtor, retired secondary education educator*

**Macon**
Jones, John Ellis *real estate broker*

**Scottdale**
Borochoff, Ida Sloan *real estate executive, artist*

**Toccoa**
Maypole, John Floyd *real estate holding company executive*

## HAWAII

**Honolulu**
Albano, Andres, Jr. *real estate developer, real estate broker*
Chiu, Margaret Chi Yuan Liu *real estate broker*
Gillmar, Jack Notley Scudder *real estate company executive*
Glogower, Michael Howard *public housing revitalization specialist*
Kwok, Reginald Yin-Wang *urban planning and development educator, architect*
Lum, Jody Mae Kam Quon *real property appraiser*
Olsen, Harris Leland *real estate and international business executive, educator, diplomat*
Walker, Margaret Smith *real estate company executive*

**Kailua**
Sullivan, Karen Lau *real estate company executive, campaign consultant, federal commissioner*

**Waianae**
Kunewa-Armitage, Carinthia Urbanette *realtor*

## IDAHO

**Idaho Falls**
Thorsen, Nancy Dain *real estate broker*
Williams, Phyllis Cutforth *retired realtor*

**Payette**
Jones, Donna Marilyn *real estate broker, legislator*

**Stanley**
Kimpton, David Raymond *natural resource consultant, writer*

**Sun Valley**
Gray, James Edward *real estate broker*

**Troy**
Hepler, Merlin Judson, Jr. *real estate broker*

## ILLINOIS

**Addison**
Kachiroubas, Christopher *assessor, real estate appraiser*

**Champaign**
Guttenberg, Albert Ziskind *planning educator*

**Chicago**
Amato, Isabella Antonia *real estate executive*
Berger, Miles Lee *land economist*
Bynoe, Peter Charles Bernard *real estate developer, lawyer*
Campbell, Gavin Elliott *real estate investor and developer*
Daly, Patrick F. *real estate executive, architect*
Eubanks-Pope, Sharon G. *real estate entrepreneur*
Gerst, C(ornelius) Gary *real estate executive*
Grabowski, Roger J. *business, intangible assets, real estate appraiser*
Pappas, Philip James *real estate company executive*
Pezzella, Jerry James, Jr. *investment and real estate corporation executive*
Prince, Oliver Gilbert, Jr. *human resources professional*
Reschke, Michael W. *real estate executive*
Rowe, Randall Keith *real estate executive*
Sahler, Christy Lee *real estate manager*
Schwab, James Charles *urban planner*
Sen, Ashish Kumar *urban planner, educator*
Stein, Paula Jean Anne Barton *hotel real estate consultant*
Totlis, Gust John *title insurance company executive*
Travis, Dempsey Jerome *real estate executive, mortgage banker*
Utigard, Philip Richard *real estate executive*
Wirtz, William Wadsworth *real estate and sports executive*

**Edwardsville**
Ottwein, Merrill William George *real estate company executive, veterinarian*
Wentz, Charles Alvin, Jr. *environmentalist, chemical engineer*

**Granite City**
Kaegel, Ray Martin *real estate and insurance broker*

**Lake Bluff**
Hiestand, Sharon DiLorenzo *real estate professional, architect*

**Lake Zurich**
Schultz, Carl Herbert *real estate management and development company executive*

**Macomb**
Maguire, Dave *real estate manager*

**Northbrook**
Levy, Arnold S(tuart) *real estate company executive*
Michna, Andrea Stephanie *real estate agent and developer*

**O'Fallon**
Cecil, Dorcas Ann *property management executive*

**Oak Brook**
Goodwin, Daniel L. *real estate company executive*
Wheeler, Paul James *real estate executive*

**Oswego**
Stephens, Steve Arnold *real estate broker*

**Saint Charles**
Urhausen, James Nicholas *real estate developer, construction executive*

**Urbana**
Blair, Lachlan Ferguson *urban planner, educator*

## INDIANA

**Bloomington**
Ellis, Lucille Lorraine Laughlin (Mrs. Wallace Iverson Ellis) *realtor*

**Indianapolis**
Borns, Robert Aaron *real estate developer*
Jewett, John Rhodes *real estate executive*
Mullen, Thomas Edgar *real estate consultant*

**Jeffersonville**
McMichael, Jeane Casey *real estate corporation executive, educator*
Reisert, Charles Edward, Jr. *real estate executive*

**Montpelier**
Neff, Kenneth D. *realtor*

**Newburgh**
Tierney, Gordon Paul *real estate broker, genealogist*

**Terre Haute**
Perry, Eston Lee *real estate and equipment leasing company executive*

## IOWA

**Ankeny**
†Kleine, Douglas *soil and water conservation society administrator*

**Spencer**
Lemke, Alan James *environmental specialist*

## KANSAS

**Westwood**
Buckner, William Claiborne *real estate broker*

**Wichita**
Lusk, William Edward *real estate and oil company executive*

## KENTUCKY

**Bowling Green**
Stewart, Harold Sanford *real estate investment and supply executive*

**Lexington**
Gable, Robert Elledy *real estate investment company executive*
Tyson, Rosendo Felicito, Jr. *urban planner*

**Louisville**
Gott, Marjorie Eda Crosby *conservationist, former educator*

## LOUISIANA

**Baton Rouge**
Marvin, Wilbur *real estate executive*
Siegel, Lawrence Iver *real estate development company executive*

**Metairie**
Derbes, Max Joseph, Jr. *real estate appraiser*
Myers, Iona Raymer *real estate and property manager*

**New Orleans**
Lupo, Robert Edward Smith *real estate developer and investor*
Villavaso, Stephen Donald *urban planner, lawyer*

## MAINE

**Lincolnville**
Williams, Robert Luther *city planning consultant*

**Portland**
Melanson, Susan C. *property manager*

**Rockport**
Duarte, Patricia M. *real estate and insurance broker*

## MARYLAND

**Baltimore**
Briscoe, Marian Denise *real estate agent, lyricist*
DeVito, Mathias Joseph *retired real estate executive*
Mierzwicki, Anthony Joseph *real estate executive*

**Berlin**
Passwater, Barbara Gayhart *real estate broker*

**Bethesda**
Clark, A. James *real estate company executive*
John, Frank Herbert, Jr. *real estate appraiser, real estate investor*
†Kibbe, James William *real estate broker*
Sams, James Farid *real estate development company executive*
Walker, Mallory *real estate executive*

**Chevy Chase**
Lee, Edward Brooke, Jr. *real estate executive, fund raiser*

**Columbia**
Alexander, Bruce Donald *real estate executive*
Cook, Stephen Bernard *homebuilding company executive*
Hilderbrandt, Donald Franklin, II *urban designer, landscape architect, artist*
McCuan, William Patrick *real estate company executive*
Millspaugh, Martin Laurence *real estate developer, urban development consultant*

**Lutherville Timonium**
Kerr, Patrick Corbitt *real estate appraiser, consultant*

**Port Republic**
Hanke, Byron Reidt *residential land planning and community associations consultant*

**Potomac**
Eaves, Maria Perry *realtor*

**Rockville**
Kusterer, Thomas *environmental planner*
Lee, James Jieh *environmental educator, computer specialist*

**Silver Spring**
Humphries, Weldon R. *real estate/hotel executive*
Kronstadt, Arnold Mayo *regional and architectual planner*
Ventre, Francis Thomas *environmental design and policy educator*

## MASSACHUSETTS

**Amherst**
Bentley, Richard Norcross *regional planner, educator*
Larson, Joseph Stanley *environmentalist, educator, researcher*

**Arlington**
Braithwaite, John Michael *title company executive*

**Boston**
Beal, Robert Lawrence *real estate executive*
Gerrity, Daniel Wallace *real estate developer*
Imperato, Robert Edward *real estate company executive*

Lovejoy, George Montgomery, Jr. *real estate executive*
Radloff, Robert Albert *real estate executive*
Thibedeau, Richard Herbert *environmental planner, administrator*

**Braintree**
Fantozzi, Peggy Ryone *environmental planner*

**Cambridge**
Fagans, Karl Preston *real estate facilities administration executive*
Spunt, Shepard Armin *real estate executive, management and financial consultant*
Susskind, Lawrence Elliott *urban and environmental planner, educator, mediator*
Vigier, François Claude Denis *city planning educator*

**Fairhaven**
Hotchkiss, Henry Washington *real estate broker and financial consultant*

**Franklin**
Bonin, Paul Joseph *real estate and banking executive*

**Gloucester**
Sallah, Majeed (Jim Sallah) *real estate developer*

**Longmeadow**
Louargand, Marc Andrew *real estate executive, financial consultant*

**Natick**
Strauss, Harlee Sue *environmental consultant*

**Newton**
Bernard, Michael Mark *city planning consultant, lawyer*

**North Reading**
Dolan, Edward Corcoran *real estate developer and investor*

**Peabody**
Wood, Richard Robinson *real estate executive*

**Springfield**
†Thurmond, Nathaniel *retired basketball player*

**Topsfield**
Brady, James Robert, Jr. *real estate developer*

**Waltham**
Nelson, Arthur Hunt *real estate management development company executive*

**Wenham**
Whittemore, Frank Bowen *environmental, energy and management consultant*

**West Newton**
Frieden, Bernard Joel *urban studies educator*

**West Tisbury**
Logue, Edward Joseph *development company executive*

**Winchester**
Blackham, Ann Rosemary (Mrs. J. W. Blackham) *realtor*

## MICHIGAN

**Ann Arbor**
Clark, Thomas B., Sr. *real estate broker*
Duke, Richard De La Barre *urban planner, educator*
Gooch, Nancy Jane *realtor, mortgage executive*
Rycus, Mitchell Julian *urban planning educator, urban security and energy planning consultant*
Schenk, John Erwin *environmental engineer*
Surovell, Edward David *real estate company executive*

**Berkley**
Arroyo, Rodney Lee *city planning and transportation executive*

**Charlevoix**
Lobenherz, Richard Ernest *real estate developer*

**Dearborn**
Werling, Donn Paul *environmental educator*

**Detroit**
Topey, Ishmael Aloysius *urban planner*

**Grosse Ile**
Smith, Veronica Latta *real estate corporation officer*

**Kalamazoo**
Taborn, Jeannette Ann *real estate investor*

**Rogers City**
Heidemann, Mary Ann *community planner*

**Saginaw**
Cline, Thomas William *real estate leasing company executive, management consultant*

**Saint Clair Shores**
Field, Thomas Lee *business executive, politician*

**Traverse City**
McCafferty, John Martin *real estate executive, commodities trader*

**White Lake**
Clyburn, Luther Linn *real estate broker, appraiser, ship captain*

## MINNESOTA

**Bloomington**
Dahlberg, Burton Francis *real estate corporation executive*

**Duluth**
Bowman, Roger Manwaring *real estate executive*

**Minneapolis**
Bolan, Richard Stuart *urban planner, educator, researcher*
Stuebner, James Cloyd *real estate developer, contractor*

**Rochester**
Gilbertson, Steven E(dward) Satyaki *real estate broker, guidance counselor*

**Saint Peter**
Turnbull, Charles Vincent *real estate broker*

## MISSISSIPPI

**Meridian**
Church, George Millord *real estate executive*

## MISSOURI

**Chesterfield**
Schierholz, William Francis, Jr. *real estate developer*
Williams, John Franklin *real estate broker*

**Kansas City**
Dumovich, Loretta *real estate and transportation company executive*
Shutz, Byron Christopher *real estate executive*

**Saint Joseph**
Miller, Lloyd Daniel *real estate agent*
Rachow, Sharon Dianne *realtor*

**Saint Louis**
Koehler, Harry George *real estate executive*
Loomstein, Arthur *real estate company executive*
Meissner, Edwin Benjamin, Jr. *real estate broker*
Morley, Harry Thomas, Jr. *real estate executive*

**Springfield**
Condellone, Trent Peter *real estate developer*

**Stockton**
Jackson, Betty L. Deason *real estate developer*

## MONTANA

**Darby**
Brandborg, Stewart Monroe *conservationist, government official*

**Great Falls**
Stevens, George Alexander *realtor*

## NEBRASKA

**Madison**
Wozniak, Richard Michael, Sr. *retired city and regional planner*

**Omaha**
Gallagher, Paula Marie *real estate appraiser*

## NEVADA

**Carson City**
McLain, John Lowell *resource specialist, consultant*

**Henderson**
McKinney, Sally Vitkus *state official*

**Las Vegas**
Jeske, Keith William *real estate and mortgage executive*
Thomas, Peter M. *real estate developer*

**Reno**
Dulgar, Pam *real estate agent*
Fore, Richard Lewis *real estate company executive, entrepreneur*

**Winnemucca**
Clemons, Lynn Allan *land use planner*

## NEW JERSEY

**Butler**
Wingert, Hannelore Christiane *real estate sales executive, chemical company executive*

**Chatham**
Lax, Philip *land developer, space planner*

**Clifton**
Kessler, Carolyn Joan *industrial and commercial real estate developer*

**Colts Neck**
Rode, Leif *real estate personal computer consultant*

**East Orange**
Moese, Mark Douglas *environmental consultant*

**Flemington**
Salamon, Renay *real estate broker*

**Green Brook**
Elias, Donald Francis *environmental consultant*

**Haddon Heights**
Luste, Joseph Francis, Jr. *land use, environmental transportation and planning specialist*

**Haworth**
Stokvis, Jack Raphael *urban planner, entrepreneur computer consultnt and developer, government agency administrator*

**Mount Laurel**
Buchan, Alan Bradley *land planner, consultant, civil engineer*

**New Brunswick**
Chiapperini, Patricia Bignoli *real estate appraiser, consultant*

**Newark**
Simmons, Peter *law and urban planning educator*

**Paramus**
Gingras, Paul Joseph *real estate management company executive*

**Princeton**
Baker, Richard Wheeler, Jr. *real estate executive*

**Red Bank**
Schimpf, John Joseph *real estate developer*

**Short Hills**
Good, Allen Hovey *acquisitions broker, real estate broker, business consultant*

## NEW MEXICO

**Albuquerque**
Stahl, Jack Leland *real estate company executive*

**Mora**
Hanks, Eugene Ralph *land developer, cattle rancher, retired naval officer*

**Santa Fe**
Harding, Marie *ecological executive, artist*
Pearson, Margit Linnea *development company executive*

## NEW YORK

**Albany**
Matuszek, John Michael, Jr. *environmental scientist, educator, consultant*

**Briarcliff Manor**
Pasquarelli, Joseph J. *real estate, engineering and construction executive*

**Bronx**
Robinson, John Gwilym *conservationist*

**Brooklyn**
Balbi, Kenneth Emilio *environmental lead specialist, researcher*
Blackman, Robert Irwin *real estate developer and investor, lawyer, accountant*

**Central Islip**
McGowan, Harold *real estate developer, investor, scientist, author, philanthropist*

**Elizabethtown**
Davis, George Donald *executive land use policy specialist*

**Flushing**
†Wilpon, Fred *real estate developer, baseball team executive*

**Goshen**
Ward, William Francis, Jr. *real estate investment banker*

**Great Neck**
Zirinsky, Daniel *real estate investor and photographer*

**Ithaca**
Goldsmith, William Woodbridge *city and regional planning educator*

**Jericho**
Axinn, Donald Everett *real estate investor, developer*

**Larchmont**
Levi, James Harry *real estate executive, investment banker*

**Locust Valley**
Devendorf, Barbara Lancaster (Bonnie Lancaster Devendorf) *real estate broker*

**Mill Neck**
von Briesen, Edward Fuller *builder, real estate developer*

**Monsey**
Zeisel, Gloria *real estate company executive*

**Mount Vernon**
Rossini, Joseph *contracting and development corporate executive*

**New Hyde Park**
Cooper, Milton *real estate investment trust executive*

**New York**
Benenson, Edward Hartley *realty company executive*
Berliner, Ruth Shirley *real estate company executive*
Cohen, Irving Elias *real estate executive*
Cuneo, Jack Alfred *real estate investment executive*
Fox-Freund, Barbara Susan *real estate executive*
Gochberg, Thomas *real estate investor, financial executive*
Goddess, Lynn Barbara *commercial real estate broker*
Goldenberg, Charles Lawrence *real estate company executive*
Hemmerdinger, H. Dale *real estate executive*
Hernstadt, Judith Filenbaum *city planner, real estate executive, broadcasting executive*
Howell, William Page *real estate developer*
Hutton, Ernest Watson, Jr. *urban designer, city planner*
Kalikow, Peter Stephen *real estate developer, former newspaper owner, publisher*
Katz, Daniel Roger *conservation executive*
Keith, John Pirie *urban planner*
Kiley, Bruce Edward *real estate financing executive*
Lachman, Marguerite Leanne *real estate investment advisor*
Lee, Lloyd Eng-Meng *real estate consultant*
Malino, John Gray *real estate executive*
Marder, John G. *real estate investor, marketing consultant, corporate director*
Marshall, Alton Garwood *real estate counselor*
Mirante, Arthur J., II *real estate company executive*
Muller, Alexandra Lida *real estate management director*
Nichols, Carol D. *real estate professional, association executive*
Perry-Widney, Marilyn (Marilyn Perry) *international finance and real estate executive, television producer*
Petz, Edwin V. *real estate executive, lawyer*
Purse, Charles Roe *real estate investment company executive*
Rogers, Elizabeth Barlow *urban planner, municipal park administrator*
Rose, Daniel *real estate company executive, consultant*
Rose, Elihu *real estate executive*
Rose, Frederick Phineas *builder and real estate executive*
Roskind, E. Robert *real estate company executive*
Ruben, Lawrence *real estate developer, building company executive, lawyer*
Scott, Stanley DeForest *real estate executive, former lithography company executive*
Scurry, Richardson Gano, Jr. *investment management company financial executive*
Smith, Andrew Alfred, Jr. *urban planner*
Strum, Brian J. *real estate executive*
Thomas, Violeta de los Angeles *real estate broker*
Tishman, John L. *realty and construction company executive*
Toote, Gloria E. A. *developer, lawyer, columnist*
Warsawer, Harold Newton *real estate appraiser and consultant*
Weston, M. Moran, II *real estate developer, banker, clergyman, educator*
Wolf, Peter Michael *investment management and land planning consultant, educator, author*

**Newburgh**
Koskella, Lucretia C. *real estate broker, appraiser*

**Oakdale**
Bragdon, Clifford Richardson *city planner, educator*

**Palisades**
Anderson, Margaret Tayler *real estate broker, career consultant*

**Purchase**
Schwerin, Warren Lyons *real estate developer*

**Rochester**
Nutter, David George *urban planner*
Walker, Michael Charles, Sr. *retirement services executive*

**Rye**
Mintz, Stephen Allan *real estate company executive, lawyer*

**Scarsdale**
Goldberg, Harriet David *urban planner*

**Smithtown**
Aleschus, Justine Lawrence *real estate broker*

**Stony Brook**
Koppelman, Lee Edward *regional planner, educator*

**Tarrytown**
Raymond, George Marc *city planner, educator*

**Washingtonville**
Guarino, Iris Cooper *realtor, appraiser*

**Woodhaven**
Krohley, Patricia Anne *realtor, artist, writer*

**Woodsburgh**
Cohen, Lawrence Alan *real estate executive*

**Wyandanch**
Barnett, Peter John *property development executive, educator*

## NORTH CAROLINA

**Asheville**
Morosani, George Warrington *real estate developer, realtor*

**Chapel Hill**
Rohe, William Michael *urban planning educator*
Weiss, Shirley F. *urban and regional planner, economist, educator*

**Charlotte**
Wiggins, Nancy Bowen *real estate broker, market research consultant*

**Fayetteville**
Kendrick, Mark C. *real estate executive*

**Greensboro**
Conrad, David Paul *business broker/retired restaurant chain executive*

## RALEIGH

**Raleigh**
Anderson, Amy Lee *realtor*
Redman, William Walter, Jr. *realtor, public utilities commissioner*

**Winston Salem**
Doggett, Aubrey Clayton, Jr. *real estate executive, consultant*

## OHIO

**Akron**
Peavy, Homer Louis, Jr. *real estate executive, accountant*

**Athens**
Smith, Robert John, Jr. *real estate executive*

**Beachwood**
Lerner, Alfred *real estate and financial executive*

**Canton**
Wolanin, John Charles *realtor*

**Cincinnati**
Chatterjee, Jayanta *educator, urban designer*
Dunigan, Dennis Wayne *real estate executive*
Randman, Barry I. *real estate developer*
Schuler, Robert Leo *appraiser, consultant*
Shenk, Richard Lawrence *real estate developer, photographer, artist*
Weiskittel, Ralph Joseph *real estate executive*
Winchell, Margaret Webster St. Clair *realtor*

**Cleveland**
†Cleary, Martin Joseph *real estate company executive*
Eski, John Robert *residential appraiser, real estate consultant*
Gould, Bonnie Marincic *realtor*
Jacobs, Richard E. *real estate executive, sports team owner*
Markos, Chris *real estate company executive*
Sulik, Dorie *realtor, marketing professional*

**Columbus**
Merwin, Harmon Turner *retired regional planner*
Pyatt, Leo Anthony *real estate broker*
Voss, Jerrold Richard *city planner, educator, university official*

**Dayton**
Wertz, Kenneth Dean *real estate executive*

**Gates Mills**
Schanfarber, Richard Carl *real estate broker*

**Hudson**
Stec, John Zygmunt *real estate executive*

**Lancaster**
Wagonseller, James Myrl *real estate executive*

**New Albany**
Kessler, John Whitaker *real estate developer*

**Rocky River**
Slaby, Lillian Frances *home finance counselor, real estate professional*

**Salem**
Barcey, Harold Edward Dean (Hal Barcey) *real estate counselor*

**Shaker Heights**
Ellett, Alan Sidney *real estate development company executive*

**South Euclid**
Adler, Naomi Samuel *real estate counselor*

**Toledo**
Batt, Nick *property and investment executive*

**Twinsburg**
Solganik, Marvin *real estate executive*

**Wintersville**
Becker, William A(lbert) *real estate developer*

**Youngstown**
Sokolov, Richard Saul *real estate company executive*

## OKLAHOMA

**Ada**
Davison, Victoria Dillon *real estate executive*

**Miami**
Taylor, Vesta Fisk *real estate broker, educator*

**Norman**
Zelby, Rachel *realtor*

**Tulsa**
Cardwell, Sandra Gayle Bavido *real estate broker*
Henderson, James Ronald *industrial real estate developer*
Hill, Josephine Carmela *realtor*
Matthews, Dane Dikeman *urban planner*

**Wagoner**
Semore, Mary Margie *abstractor*

**Watonga**
Hoberecht, Earnest *abstract company executive, former newspaper executive*

## OREGON

**Bend**
Kozak, Michael *real estate counselor, seminar instructor*

**Eugene**
Dasso, Jerome Joseph *real estate educator, consultant*

**Gladstone**
Lavigne, Peter Marshall *environmentalist, lawyer, consultant*

**Lake Oswego**
Morse, Lowell Wesley *real estate executive, banking executive*

**Portland**
Abbott, Carl John *urban studies and planning educator*
Lilly, Elizabeth Giles *mobile park executive*
Robbins, Donald Kenneth *real estate investment advisor, consultant*
Standring, James Douglas *real estate developer*

## PENNSYLVANIA

**Bloomsburg**
Loncosky, Walter Beugger *real estate manager*

**Doylestown**
Carson, John Thompson, Jr. *environmental consultant*
Long, Ronald Alex *real estate and financial consultant, educator*

**Leesport**
Otterman, Kenneth James *real estate investor, author, consultant*

**Milton**
Ellis, Jane Marie *real estate manager*

**Philadelphia**
Bacon, Edmund Norwood *city planner*
Henry, Rene Arthur, Jr. *environmental agency administrator*
Mellman, Leonard *real estate investor and advisor*
Peck, Robert McCracken *naturalist, science historian, writer*
Pew, Robert Anderson *retired real estate corporation officer*
Tomazinis, Anthony Rodoflos *city planning educator*
Wender, Herbert *title company executive*

**Pittsburgh**
Stephenson, Robert Clay *real estate company executive*
Thorpe, Leon Ferber *real estate investment company executive*
Wilson, Charles Reginald *real estate executive*

**University Park**
Golany, Gideon Salomon *urban designer*

## RHODE ISLAND

**East Greenwich**
Deutsch, Stephen R. *real estate development executive, retired state senator*

**Providence**
Hitt, Mary Frances Lyster *environmentalist, deacon*

**Wakefield**
Morrison, Fred Beverly *real estate consultant*

**Warwick**
Lachapelle, Cleo Edward *real estate broker*

## SOUTH CAROLINA

**Aiken**
Neiswander, Linda Carol *realtor, interior decorator*

**Charleston**
Evans, Allen Donald *investment real estate company executive*

**Greenville**
Wyche, Marguerite Ramage *realtor*

**Hilton Head Island**
Gruchacz, Robert S. *real estate executive*

**Lexington**
Love, Kenneth Edward *real estate, investment and business consultant*

**Spartanburg**
Gray, Gwen Cash *real estate broker*

## SOUTH DAKOTA

**Sioux Falls**
Kilian, Thomas Randolph *rural economic developer, consultant*

## TENNESSEE

**Brentwood**
Raskin, Edwin Berner *real estate executive*

**Chattanooga**
Porter, Dudley, Jr. *environmentalist, foundation executive, lawyer*

**Hampton**
McClendon, Fred Vernon *real estate professional, business consultant, equine and realty appraiser, financial consultant*

**Knoxville**
Brown, Kevin James *real estate broker*

**Memphis**
Connolly, Matthew B., Jr. *conservationist*
Cooper, Irby *real estate development company executive*
Haizlip, Henry Hardin, Jr. *real estate consultant, former banker*

**Nashville**
Beck, Robert Beryl *real estate executive*
Driscoll, Joseph Francis *real estate executive*

## TEXAS

**Austin**
Boeker, Herbert Ralph, Jr. *urban planner*
Mathias, Reuben Victor (Vic Mathias) *real estate executive, investor*

**Bay City**
Aylin, Elizabeth Twist Pabst *real estate broker, developer*

**Brenham**
Moorman, Robert Lawson *real estate appraiser and broker*

**Bullard**
Buckner, John Hugh *retired real estate broker, retired construction company executive, retired air force officer*

**College Station**
Roeseler, Wolfgang Guenther Joachim *city planner*

**Dallas**
Behrens, Richard John *real estate executive*
Cansler, Denise Ann *real estate executive*
Doran, Mark Richard *real estate financial executive*
Gidel, Robert Hugh *real estate investor*
Hamilton, David Lee *retired environmental company executive*
Hewett, Arthur Edward *real estate developer, lawyer*
Yeslow, Rosemarie *real estate professional*

**Denton**
Owen, William Michael *real estate developer*

**El Paso**
Lyle, James Arthur *real estate broker*

**Elgin**
Osborne, Michael James *real estate executive, energy executive, author*

**Galveston**
McLeod, E. Douglas *real estate developer, lawyer*

**Georgetown**
Comola, James Paul *legislative and environmental consultant*

**Houston**
Goldsmith, Billy Joe *real estate broker*
Holcomb, William A. *retired oil and gas exploration, pipeline executive, retired real estate broker, consultant*
Kollaer, Jim C. *real estate executive, architect*
Lehrer, Kenneth Eugene *real estate advisor, economic consultant*
Morris, Malcolm Stewart *title company executive, lawyer*
Peck, Edwin Russell *real estate management executive*
Strudler, Robert Jacob *real estate development executive*
Weekley, David *real estate developer*

**Mico**
Shockey, Thomas Edward *real estate executive, engineer*

**Montgomery**
Brown, Lewis Arnold *realtor*

**Plano**
Wilke, Chet *real estate executive*

**Salado**
Mackie, Donald John, Jr. *real estate developer*

**San Antonio**
Bryan, Richard Ray *real estate development executive, construction executive*

## VERMONT

**Shelburne**
Carpenter, Donald Blodgett *real estate appraiser*

## VIRGINIA

**Alexandria**
Holland, Dianna Gwin *real estate broker*
Marino, Ann Dozier *real estate broker*
Palma, Dolores Patricia *urban planner*

**Arlington**
Koury, Agnes Lillian *real estate property manager*
Sawhill, John Crittenden *conservationist, economist, university president, government official*

**Fairfax**
Eppink, Jeffrey Francis *energy and environmental specialist*

**Falls Church**
Frazier, Walter Ronald *real estate investment company executive*

**Haymarket**
Crafton-Masterson, Adrienne *real estate executive, writer, poet*

**Mc Lean**
McLean, Robert, III *real estate company executive*
Wilbur, Mark *environmental executive*

**Norfolk**
Goode, Stacy J. *real estate broker*

**Oakton**
Brauer, Gwendolyn Gail *real estate broker*

**Palmyra**
Mulckhuyse, Jacob John *energy conservation and environmental consultant*

**Richmond**
Dickinson, Alfred James *realtor*
Goff, Stephen Charles *retail and franchise executive*
Plaisted, Harris Merrill, III *real estate executive*
Tuck, Grayson Edwin *real estate agent, former natural gas transmission executive*

**Vienna**
†Van Patten, Mark *environmentalist*

**Virginia Beach**
Markson, Daniel Ben *real estate developer, consultant, syndicator*

## WASHINGTON

**Bothell**
Cothern, Barbara Shick *real estate investor*

**Lynnwood**
Edwards, Kirk Lewis *real estate company executive*

**Olympia**
Stewart, Jeffree Robert *environmental planner, artist*

**Puyallup**
DeBock, Ronald Gene *real estate company executive*

**Seattle**
Dillard, Marilyn Dianne *property manager*
Gerrodette, Charles Everett *real estate company executive, consultant*
McKinnon, James Buckner *real estate sales executive, writer, researcher*
Painter, Diana Jean *urban designer, consultant*
Stevens, Clyde Benjamin, Jr. *property manager, retired naval officer*

**Spokane**
Kirschbaum, James Louis *real estate company administrator*

## WISCONSIN

**Beaver Dam**
Butterbrodt, John Ervin *real estate executive*

**Madison**
Ring, Gerald J. *real estate developer, insurance executive*
Vandell, Kerry Dean *real estate and urban economics educator*

**Mequon**
Ryan, Mary Nell H. *training consultant*

**Milwaukee**
Machulak, Edward Leon *real estate, mining and advertising company executive*
Smith, Lois Ann *real estate executive*

**Minocqua**
Utt, Glenn S., Jr. *motel investments and biotech industry company executive*

**Wauwatosa**
Jasiorkowski, Robert Lee *real estate broker, computer consultant*

## WYOMING

**Jackson**
Thulin, Walter Willis *real estate company executive*

## TERRITORIES OF THE UNITED STATES

## PUERTO RICO

**San Juan**
†Ocasio Belén, Félix E. *real estate development company executive*

## CANADA

## ALBERTA

**Calgary**
McEwen, Alexander Campbell *cadastral studies educator, former Canadian government official, surveying consultant*
Milavsky, Harold Phillip *real estate executive*

## BRITISH COLUMBIA

**Vancouver**
Belzberg, Samuel *real estate investment professional*
Goldberg, Michael Arthur *land policy and planning educator*

## NOVA SCOTIA

**Stellarton**
Sobey, Donald Creighton Rae *real estate developer*

## ONTARIO

**London**
Pearson, Norman *urban and regional planner, administrator, academic and planning consultant, writer*

**Newmarket**
Wood, Neil Roderick *real estate development company executive*

**North York**
Carrothers, Gerald Arthur Patrick *environmental and city planning educator*

**Ottawa**
MacNeill, James William *international environment consultant*

**Toronto**
Braithwaite, J(oseph) Lorne *real estate executive*
Cullingworth, Larry Ross *residential and real estate development company executive*
Dimma, William Andrew *real estate executive*
Goring, Peter Allan Elliott *real estate executive*
Grier, Ruth *environmentalist*

**Weston**
McIntyre, John George Wallace *real estate development and management consultant*

## QUEBEC

**Montreal**
Gabbour, Iskandar *city and regional planning educator*

**Rimouski**
Larivée, Jacques *conservationist*

## ENGLAND

**London**
Hall, Peter Geoffrey *urban and regional planning educator*

## JAPAN

**Tokyo**
Sakai, Akiyoshi *urban redevelopment consultant*

## SWITZERLAND

**Geneva**
Polunin, Nicholas *environmentalist, author, editor*

## ADDRESS UNPUBLISHED

Aulbach, George Louis *property investment company executive*
Beal, Merrill David *conservationist, museum director*
Bergau, Frank Conrad *real estate, commercial and investment properties executive*
Bernhardt, Arthur Dieter *building industry executive and consultant*
Berzin, Russell Frank *land and housing developer*
Brady, George Moore *real estate executive, mortgage banker*
Brooks, Michael Paul *urban planning educator*
Burk, Sylvia Joan *petroleum landman, freelance writer*
Colton, Victor Robert *real estate developer, investor, planning educator, researcher*
Corey, Kenneth Edward *geography and urban planning educator, researcher*
Danielson, Patricia Rochelle Frank *urban planner*
deButts, Robert Edward Lee *corporate development and real estate executive*
Denney, Talbert Lorrine *real estate investment executive, antique automobile dealer*
DeWitt, Sallie Lee *realtor*
†Ellis, William Ben *environmental educator, retired utility executive*
Fellman, Barry L. *real estate developer*
Fetterly, Lynn Lawrence *real estate broker, developer*
Fleming, Ronald Lee *urban designer, administrator, preservation planner, environmental educator*
Friedman, Howard W. *retired real estate company executive*
Frost, Anne *real estate broker, author, publisher*
Gellman, Isaiah *environmental consultant*
Gilbert, Frederick E. *international development planner, consultant*
Heinsman, Raymond Edward *land surveyor*
Hodson, Nancy Perry *real estate agent*
Holleb, Doris B. *urban planner, economist*
Houstoun, Lawrence Orson, Jr. *development consultant*
Hufschmidt, Maynard Michael *resources planning educator*
Johnson, Kay Durbahn *real estate manager, consultant*
Kaiser, Jean Morgan *real estate broker*
Kendrick, Daniel Frederick, III *real estate executive*
Kirk, Judd *real estate development executive*
Kremer, Honor Frances (Noreen Kremer) *real estate broker, small business owner*

Ledford, Janet Marie Smalley *real estate appraiser, consultant*
Maguire, Robert Francis, III *real estate investor*
Mann, Clarence Charles *real estate company official*
Mercurio, Renard Michael *real estate corporation executive*
Messenkopf, Eugene John *real estate and business consultant*
Meyer, Daniel Kramer *real estate executive*
Mitchell, Robert Edward *urban planner, international development specialist, educator*
Mohamed, Joseph *real estate broker*
Newsome, Edward Baldwin *retired real estate broker, retired insurance agent*
Perkins, Charles Theodore *real estate developer, consultant*
Rassman, Joel H. *real estate company executive, accountant*
Richman, Marvin Jordan *real estate developer, investor, educator*
Ridloff, Richard *real estate executive, lawyer, consultant*
Riss, Robert Bailey *real estate investor*
Saunders, Alexander Hall *real estate executive*
Senerchia, Dorothy Sylvia *urban planner, author*
Sherf, Sandee Croft *real estate corporation executive*
Simon, Melvin *real estate developer, professional basketball executive*
Slayton, William Larew *planning consultant, former government official*
Sullivan, Ben Frank, Jr. *real estate broker*
Taubman, A. Alfred *real estate developer*
Trump, Donald John *real estate developer*
VanButsel, Michael R. *real estate developer, healthcare consultant*
Wadsworth, Jacqueline Dorèt *private investor*
Weisinger, Ronald Jay *economic development consultant, real estate developer*
Williamson, Fletcher Phillips *real estate executive*

## GOVERNMENT: AGENCY ADMINISTRATION

### UNITED STATES

#### ALABAMA

**Athens**
Wilson, Lucy Lynn Willmarth *postal service administrator*

**Birmingham**
Brennan, Oscar A. *protective services official*

**Clanton**
Williams, Paulette W. *state agency administrator*

**Kimberly**
Howell, Pamela Ann *federal agency professional*

**Mobile**
Lager, Robert John *state agency administrator*

**Montgomery**
Gainous, Fred Jerome *state agency administrator*
Richardson, Edward R. *state agency administrator*

#### ALASKA

**Fairbanks**
Davis, Charles Lee *fire marshal*

**Juneau**
Holloway, Shirley J. *state agency administrator*

#### ARIZONA

**Phoenix**
Bishop, C. Diane *state agency administrator, educator*
Brunacini, Alan Vincent *fire chief*
Garrett, Dennis Andrew *police official*
Nielson, Theo Gilbert *law enforcement official, university official*
North, Warren James *government official*
Wilson, Stephen Rip *public policy consultant*

**Scottsdale**
Hill, Robert Martin *police detective, consultant, lecturer*

**Sun City West**
De Layo, Leonard Joseph *former state education official*

**Tucson**
Isenhower, Eleanor Anne Hexamer *state government administrator*

#### ARKANSAS

**Little Rock**
Tudor, Jim Patrick *law enforcement officer, photographer*
Wilhoit, Gene *state agency administrator*

**Mountain Home**
Saltzman, Benjamin Nathan *retired state health administrator, physician*

#### CALIFORNIA

**Anaheim**
Bowman, Jeffrey R. *protective services official*

**Benicia**
von Studnitz, Gilbert Alfred *state official*

**Bonita**
Yokley, Richard Clarence *fire department administrator*

**Burbank**
Chaffee, James Albert *protective services official*

**Castro Valley**
Palmer, James Daniel *inspector*

**Coronado**
Straley, Ruth A. Stewart *federal agency administrator, small business owner*

**Cupertino**
Compton, Dale Leonard *retired space agency executive, consultant*

**El Centro**
Steensgaard, Anthony Harvey *federal agent*

**Fremont**
Eastin, Delaine Andree *state agency administrator*

**Fresno**
Rank, Everett George *government official*

**Indio**
Hare, Paul DeHaven *public safety director*

**La Jolla**
Knauss, John Atkinson *federal agency administrator, oceanographer, educator, former university dean*

**Laguna Beach**
Johnson, Roger W. *former federal official, computer manufacturing company executive*

**Long Beach**
Jeffery, James Nels *protective services official*

**Los Angeles**
Montoya, Velma *federal agency administrator*
Williams, Willie *protective services official*

**Menlo Park**
Prabhakar, Arati *federal administration research director, electrical engineer*

**Mountain View**
Spencer, Carol Brown *association executive*

**Palm Springs**
Borders, Karen Lynn *police officer*

**Palos Verdes Estates**
Basnight, Arvin Odell *public administrator, aviation consultant*

**Pasadena**
Schander, Mary Lea *police official*

**Rocklin**
Ha, Chong Wan *state government executive*

**Roseville**
Simms, Thomas Haskell *police chief*

**Sacramento**
Drown, Eugene Ardent *federal agency administrator*
Gentry, James William *retired state official*
Muehleisen, Gene Sylvester *retired law enforcement officer, state official*
Pettite, William Clinton *public affairs consultant*
Strock, James Martin *state agency administrator, lawyer, conservationist*

**San Bruno**
Kell-Smith, Carla Sue *federal agency administrator*

**San Diego**
Osby, Robert Edward *protective services official*

**San Francisco**
Costello, Marcelle Welling *federal agency administrator, marketing consultant*

**Sonora**
Efford, Michael Robert *police administrator, educator*

**Stockton**
Jackson, Jewel *state youth authority executive*

**Vacaville**
Martinez, Gayle Frances *protective services official*

**Westlake Village**
Rogge, Richard Daniel *former government executive, security consultant, investigator*

#### COLORADO

**Boulder**
Gilman, Peter Augustus *national science laboratory administrator*

**Colorado Springs**
Leuver, Robert Joseph *former government official, association executive*

**Denver**
Berger, John Milton *state agency administrator*
Logan, James Scott, Sr. *federal agency administrator, emergency analyst*
McGraw, Jack Wilson *government official*
Nash, Stella B. *government nutrition administrator*
Simons, Lynn Osborn *federal education official*
Smith, Waldo Gregorius *former government official*

**Golden**
Baumgart, Norbert K. *retired government official*
Olson, Marian Katherine *emergency management executive, consultant, publisher*

Stewart, Frank Maurice, Jr. *federal agency administrator*

**Littleton**
Hayes, Roger Matthew *deputy sheriff*

**Longmont**
Kaminsky, Glenn Francis *deputy chief of police retired, business owner, teacher*

**Monument**
Miele, Alfonse Ralph *former government official*

**Vail**
McGee, Michael Jay *fire marshal, educator*

**Wheat Ridge**
Larson, Kurt Paul *fire chief*

#### CONNECTICUT

**Cheshire**
McKee, Margaret Jean *federal agency executive*

**Hartford**
Piotrowski, Richard Francis *state agency administrator, council chairman*
Recchia, Christopher *state agency environmental administrator*

**Meriden**
Cardona, Hector Manuel *police officer*

**Norwich**
LeClair, Peter R. *state agency supervisor, mental retardation services professional*

**Riverside**
Powers, Claudia McKenna *state government official*

**Stratford**
Chase, J. Vincent *state agency official, shopping center executive, justice of the peace*

**Suffield**
Hanzalek, Astrid Teicher *public policy consultant*

#### DELAWARE

**Dover**
Barrett, Marihelen Eggert *public health administrator, pediatrics nurse*
Britt, Maisha Dorrah *protective services official*
Lowell, Howard Parsons *government records administrator*
Williams, Donna Lee H. *state agency adminstrator*

**Newark**
Keene, William Blair *state education official*

**Smyrna**
Pippin, Kathryn Ann *state agency administrator*

**Wilmington**
Benson, Barbara Ellen *state agency administrator*
delTufo, Theresa Lallana Izon *state official*
Eichler, Thomas P. *state agency administrator*

#### DISTRICT OF COLUMBIA

**Washington**
Adams, Gordon Merritt *federal agency administrator*
Aikens, Joan Deacon *government official*
Akey, Steven John *federal agency administrator*
Alberts, Bruce Michael *federal agency administrator, foundation administrator, biochemist*
Alexander, Jane *federal agency administrator, actress, producer*
Allen, Frederick Warner *federal agency executive*
Alvarez, Aida *federal agency administrator*
Anderson, David Turpeau *government official, judge*
Anfinson, Thomas Elmer *government financial administrator*
Apfel, Kenneth S. *federal government official*
Armstrong, David Andrew *federal agency official, retired army officer*
Armstrong, Robert *federal agency administrator*
Attaway, David Henry *retired federal research administrator, oceanographer*
Atwood, John Brian *federal agency administrator*
Bacon, Kenneth H. *federal agency administrator, editor, journalist*
†Bailey, Betty L. *federal agency administrator*
Bailey, John E. *federal agency administrator*
Bailey, Vicky A. *federal agency administrator*
Baker, D(onald) James *government official, oceanographer*
Baquet, Charles R., III *federal agency administrator*
Barnicle, Timothy *federal agency administrator*
†Barolo, Daniel M. *government official*
Barram, David J. *federal agency administrator*
Barton, William Russell *government official*
Bateman, Paul William *government official, business executive*
Bauerlein, Robert D. *federal agency administrator*
Beebe, Cora Prifold *government official*
Beecher, William Manuel *government official*
Beneke, Patricia Jane *fedeal agency administrator*
Benton, Marjorie Craig *federal agency administrator*
Berry, Mary Frances *federal agency administrator, history and law educator*
Berube, Raymond P. *federal agency administrator*
Biddle, Livingston Ludlow, Jr. *former government official, author, consultant*
Biechman, John Charles *federal agency official*
Bigelow, Donald Nevius *educational administrator, historian, consultant*
†Bobbitt, Jane *federal agency administrator*
Bowen, Jerry Wayne *federal agency administrator, retired army officer*
Bowron, Eljay B. *federal agency administrator*
†Brenner, Robert David *federal agency administrator*
Bresee, James Collins *federal agency administrator*
Brickhouse, Eugene Avon *federal agency administrator*

Brown, Dale Susan *government administrator, educational program director, writer*
Brown, Harold *former secretary of defense, corporate director*
Browner, Carol *federal agency administrator*
Buck, Jennifer Cooney *government administrator*
Bullard, John Kilburn *federal agency administrator*
Burnett, Michael A. *federal agency administrator*
†Campbell, Arthur C. *federal agency adminstrator*
†Cannon, Jonathan Z. *government official*
†Chamberlin, John Charlton *federal agency administrator*
†Chavers, Kevin G. *federal agency adminstrator*
Chesser, Judy Lee *federal agency administrator, lawyer*
Childress, Kerri J. *federal agency administrator*
Christie, Deborah P. *federal agency administrator*
Clarke, Richard A. *national security specialist*
Claussen, Eileen Barbara *federal agency administrator*
Coleman, Rodney Albert *government official*
Congel, Frank Joseph *federal agency administrator, physicist*
Constantine, Thomas A. *federal agency administrator*
Conway, John Thomas *government official, lawyer, engineer*
Corlett, Cleve Edward *government administrator*
Costiglio, Lawrence U. *federal agency administrator*
Cotruvo, Joseph Alfred *federal agency administrator*
Coyle, Philip E. *federal agency administrator, engineer*
Creel, Harold Jennings, Jr. *federal commission administrator, lawyer*
Cremona, Vincent Anthony *federal agency administrator*
Cunningham, George Woody *federal official, metallurgical engineer*
Cuomo, Andrew *federal agency administrator*
†Curtis, Charles B. *federal agency administrator*
Danaher, James William *federal government executive*
†Daniels, Legree S. *federal agency administrator*
Daniels, Stephen M. *government official*
Dawson, Robert Kent *government relations expert*
†DeCell, Hal C. *federal agency administrator*
Deer, Ada E. *federal agency official, social worker, educator*
delJunco, Tirso *federal agency administrator*
Denniston, Scott F. *federal agency administrator*
Derby, Adele *government agency administrator*
Detchon, Bryan Reid *federal agency administrator*
DiMario, Michael Francis *federal agency official, lawyer*
Donahue, Agnes H. *federal agency administrator*
Dorn, Edwin *educator, federal agency administrator*
Duffey, Joseph Daniel *federal agency administrator*
Duffy, Dennis M. *federal agency administrator*
Early, James Counts *federal ageny administrator*
Eggenberger, Andrew Jon *federal agency administrator*
Erdreich, Ben Leader *federal agency executive*
Ervin, Christine A. *government official*
Esserman, Susan Gayle *government official*
Etheridge, Bob *state agency superintendant*
Fair, Rita I. *federal agency administrator*
†Farland, William H. *government official*
Farmer, Greg *former federal agency administrator*
Fell, James Carlton *traffic safety research and evaluation executive, consultant*
Finch, Johnny Charles *government agency executive*
Fingerhut, Marilyn Ann *federal agency administrator*
Fischer, Dennis James *government official*
Fitz-Pegado, Lauri Joy *federal agency administrator*
Flynn, Nancy Marie *government executive*
Fox, Claude Earl *state health officer*
Fox, Lynn Smith *federal government official*
Freeh, Louis J. *federal agency administrator*
Freeman, Chas. W., Jr. *government official, ambassador, author*
Fried, Edward R. *government official*
Friedlander, Bernice *federal agency administrator*
Gardiner, David *federal agency administrator*
Gearan, Mark D. *federal agency administrator*
Gibson, Thomas Fenner, III *public affairs consultant, political cartoonist*
Gillingham, Robert Fenton *federal agency administrator, economist*
Gilliom, Judith Carr *government official*
Gleiman, Edward Jay *federal agency administrator*
Glickman, Daniel Robert *federal agency administrator*
Gober, Hershel W. *government official*
Goldin, Daniel S. *federal agency administrator*
Goldman, Lynn Rose *assistant administrator*
Good, Mary Lowe (Mrs. Billy Jewel Good) *government official*
Goodman, Margaret Gertrude *government administrator*
Goodwin, Larry Kenneth *federal government official*
Gorn, Janet Marie *government official*
Gottlieb, James Rubel *federal agency administrator, lawyer*
Grayson, Lawrence Peter *federal educational administrator*
Greaux, Cheryl Prejean *federal agency administrator*
Gulya, Brigitta Rianna *federal government official*
Haass, Richard Nathan *federal agency administrator, educator*
Hackney, Sheldon *federal agency administrator, academic administrator*
Hagenstad, M. Thomas *federal government administrator*
Hakes, Jay E. *federal agency administrator*
Hale, Robert Fargo *government official*
Hall, James Evan *federal agency administrator, lawyer*
Hammond, Jerome Jerald *government program administrator, agricultural economist*
Hannigan, Vera Simmons *federal agency administrator*
Hansen, Frederic J. *state environmental agency director*
Harkin, Ruth R. *federal agency administrator, lawyer*
Hayashi, Dennis W. *federal agency administrator, lawyer*
Hayes, Paula Freda *governmental official*
Helfer, Ricki Tigert *federal agency administrator*
†Henry, Katherine L. *government official*
Herberger, Albert J. *federal agency administrator, retired naval officer*
Hervey, Homer Vaughan *federal agency administrator*
Heumann, Judith *federal agency administrator*
Higgins, Kathryn O'Leary *government official*
Hill, Jimmie Dale *retired government official*

Sprott, Richard Lawrence *government official, researcher*
Twiss, John Russell, Jr. *federal government agency executive*
Varmus, Harold Eliot *government health institutes administrator, educator*
Whaley, Storm Hammond *retired government official, consultant*
Young, Frank Edward *former federal agency administrator, religious organization administrator*

**Chevy Chase**
Hudson, Anthony Webster *retired federal agency administrator, minister*
Mulligan, James Kenneth *government official*
Quinn, Eugene Frederick *government official, clergyman*
Weiss, Ernest *federal agency administrator*

**Clinton**
Harrison, Virginia M. *federal government agency employee*
Kennedy, G. Alfred *retired federal agency administrator*

**Fort Washington**
Stiver, William Earl *retired government administrator*

**Gaithersburg**
Cassidy, Esther Christmas *government official*
Hertz, Harry Steven *government official*
Kammer, Raymond Gerard, Jr. *government official*
Snell, Jack Eastlake *federal agency administrator*

**Greenbelt**
Rothenberg, Joseph Howard *federal agency administrator*

**Ijamsville**
Chen, Philip S., Jr. *government official*

**Kensington**
Suraci, Charles Xavier, Jr. *retired federal agency administrator, aerospace education consultant*

**Laurel**
Chrismer, Ronald Michael *federal agency administrator*

**Oxon Hill**
Boerrigter, Glenn Charles *educational administrator*

**Potomac**
Frey, James McKnight *government official*
Rotberg, Iris Comens *social scientist*
Tomlinson, John Edward *secret service agent*

**Rockville**
Aamodt, Roger Louis *federal agency administrator*
Chavez, Nelba *federal agency administrator*
Fouchard, Joseph James *retired government agency administrator*
†Friedman, Michael A. *federal agency administrator*
Galaty, Carol Popper *health policy administrator*
Gaus, Clifton R. *federal agency administrator*
Ink, Dwight A. *government agency administrator*
Kawazoe, Robin Inada *federal official*
Kelsey, Frances Oldham (Mrs. Fremont Ellis Kelsey) *government official*
Kessler, David A. *health services commissioner*
Keston, Joan Balboul *government agency administrator*
Rheinstein, Peter Howard *government official, physician, lawyer*
Simpson, Lisa Ann *government agency administrator, physician*
Stoiber, Carlton Ray *government agency official*
†Vogel, Linda Ann *federal agency administrator*

**Saint Inigoes**
Swanson, Norma Frances *federal agency administrator*

**Silver Spring**
Carnell, Paul Herbert *federal education official*
Day, Daniel Edgar *government information officer*
Friday, Elbert Walter, Jr. *federal agency administrator, meteorologist*
Hall, J. Michael *federal agency administrator, oceanographer*
Haynes, Leonard L., III *former government official, consultant, educator*
Maas, Joe (Melvin Joseph Maas) *retired federal agency administrator*
Manheimer, Bernard Henry *federal agency administrator, consultant*
Sahli, Nancy Ann *retired federal agency administrator, consultant*
Telesetsky, Walter *government official*

**Sykesville**
Enoff, Louis D. *international consultant*

**Woodbine**
Brush, Peter Norman *federal agency administrator, lawyer*

## MASSACHUSETTS

**Amesbury**
DeLucia, Gene Anthony *government administrator, computer company executive*

**Bedford**
Ferrandino, Vincent L. *stage agency administrator*

**Beverly**
Golin, Joyce Arlene *public information officer*

**Boston**
Evans, Paul F. *protective services official*
Kamarck, Martin Alexander *federal agency administrator, lawyer*
Mason, Nancy Tolman *state agency director*
Pierce, Martin E., Jr. *fire commissioner*

**Cambridge**
Bane, Mary Jo *federal agency administrator*

Deutch, John Mark *federal agency administrator, chemist, academic administrator*
Donahue, John David *public official, educator*

**Dorchester**
Garrison, Althea *government official*

**Everett**
Shedden, Kenneth Charles *fire department official, business owner*

**Malden**
Antonucci, Robert V. *state agency administrator*

**Medfield**
Heffernan, Peter John *state official*

**New Bedford**
Benoit, Richard Armand *retired police chief, lawyer*

**Plymouth**
Forman, Peter *sheriff, former state legislator*

## MICHIGAN

**Ann Arbor**
Schmitt, Mary Elizabeth *postal supervisor*

**Bloomfield Hills**
Jones, John Paul *probation officer, psychologist*

**Detroit**
Forbes-Richardson, Helen Hilda *state agency administrator*
McKinnon, Isaiah *police chief*
Moss, Leslie Otha *criminal justice administrator, philanthropist*

**East Lansing**
Montgomery, James Huey *state government administrator, consultant*
Perrin, Robert *federal agency consultant, writer*

**Farmington Hills**
Ryan, Earl M. *public affairs analyst*

**Lansing**
Beardmore, Dorothy *state education official*

**New Haven**
Shaw, Charles Rusanda *government investigator*

## MINNESOTA

**Arden Hills**
Lindmark, Ronald Dorance *retired federal agency administrator*

**Minneapolis**
Carlson, Norman A. *government official*
Stark, Matthew *higher education and civil rights administrator*

**Saint Paul**
Hall, Beverly Joy *police officer*

## MISSISSIPPI

**Jackson**
Johnson, Joyce Thedford *state agency administrator*
Mitchell, Jackie Williams *state agency administrator, consultant*

## MISSOURI

**Jefferson City**
Bartman, Robert E. *state education official*
Karll, Jo Ann *state agency administrator, lawyer*
Mahfood, Stephen Michael *governmental agency executive*
Parr, Lloyd Byron *state official*
Peeno, Larry Noyle *state agency administrator, consultant*

**Kansas City**
English, R(obert) Bradford *marshal*
Parker, Dennis Gene *former sheriff, karate instructor*
Walker, Thomas H. *federal agency administrator*

**Lambert Airport**
Griggs, Leonard LeRoy, Jr. *federal agency administrator*

**Liberty**
Orth-Aikmus, Gail Marie *police chief*

**Springfield**
Gruhn, Robert Stephen *parole officer*
Luttrull, Shirley JoAnn *protective services official*

## NEBRASKA

**Lincoln**
Christiensen, Douglas *state agency administrator*

**O'Neill**
Hedren, Paul Leslie *national park administrator, historian*

**Omaha**
Humphries, Roger Lee *postal service administrator*

## NEVADA

**Carson City**
Peterson, Mary L. *state agency official*

**Las Vegas**
Chevers, Wilda Anita Yarde *probation officer*
Lally, Norma Ross *federal agency administrator, retired*

**North Las Vegas**
Marchand, Russell David, II *fire chief*

## NEW HAMPSHIRE

**Concord**
Brunelle, Robert L. *retired state education director*
Day, Russell Clover *state agency administrator*
Mevers, Frank Clement *state archivist, historian*

**Exeter**
Boggess, Jerry Reid *protective services official*

**Jaffrey**
Coffin, Lori Ann *police officer*

## NEW JERSEY

**Absecon**
Byrne, Shaun Patrick *law enforcement officer*

**Atlantic City**
Tucci, Mark A. *state agency administrator*

**Barrington**
Florio, Maryanne J. *state health research scientist*

**Cherry Hill**
Iglewicz, Raja *state agency administrator, researcher, industrial hygienist*

**Fort Monmouth**
Kalwinsky, Charles Knowlton *government official*

**Lawrenceville**
Hunt, Wayne Robert, Sr. *state government official*

**Morristown**
Kubas, Christine *retired law enforcement officer*

**Mountainside**
Weigele, Richard Sayre *police officer*

**New Brunswick**
Stewart, Ruth Ann *public policy analyst, library administrator*

**Trenton**
Wolfe, Albert J. *state agency researcher*
Wolfe, Deborah Cannon Partridge *government education consultant*

**Weehawken**
Murphy, Barbara Ann *protective services official*

**Willingboro**
Greene, Natalie Constance *protective services official*

## NEW MEXICO

**Albuquerque**
Gordon, Larry Jean *public health administrator and educator*
Jaramillo, Mari-Luci *federal agency administrator*

**Roswell**
Lewis, George Raymond *state agency administrator, clinical social worker*

**Santa Fe**
Knapp, Edward Alan *government administrator, scientist*
Morgan, Alan Douglas *state education official*
Rogers, Jerry L. *federal agency administrator*

## NEW YORK

**Albany**
Cross, Robert Francis *city official*
Meader, John Daniel *state agency administrator, judge*
Mills, Richard P. *state agency administrator*

**Angola**
Meno, Lionel R. *state agency administrator*

**Centereach**
Buggé, Brian Keith *police supervisor, educator*

**Fredonia**
Strauser, Jeffrey Arthur *public safety official*

**Great Neck**
Blumberg, Barbara Salmanson (Mrs. Arnold G. Blumberg) *retired state housing official, housing consultant*

**Hartsdale**
Jones, Donald Kelly *state agency executive*

**Islip**
Muuss, John *public safety and emergency management director*

**Ithaca**
Murphy, Eugene Francis *retired government official, consultant*

**Latham**
Standfast, Susan J(ane) *state official, research, consultant, educator*

**New York**
Beausoleil, Doris Mae *federal agency administrator, housing specialist*

FitzGerald, Gerald P. *state agency executive*
Forbes, John Francis *federal government executive*
Gelb, Bruce S. *city commissioner*
Gregg, Donald Phinney *federal agency administrator, lecturer*
Holzer, Harold *public information officer, historian, writer*
Rothkopf, David Jochanan *federal official*
Sorensen, Gillian Martin *United Nations official*
Talbot, Phillips *Asian affairs specialist*

**Niagara Falls**
May, David A. *protective services official, public official*

**Rochester**
Meloni, Andrew P. *protective services official*

**Stony Point**
Ricci, Daniel Michael *protective services official*

**Syracuse**
Naum, Christopher John *fire protection management and training consultant, educator*

**Woodbury**
Zirkel, Don *public information official*

## NORTH CAROLINA

**Asheville**
Roberts, Bill Glen *retired fire chief, investor, consultant*

**Burlington**
Kee, Walter Andrew *former government official*

**Corolla**
Schrote, John Ellis *retired government executive*

**Greensboro**
Daughtry, Sylvester *protective services official*
Reed, William Edward *government official, educator*

**Hope Mills**
Windham, Cuyler LaRue *police official*

**Mooresville**
Dausman, George Erwin *retired federal official, aeronautical engineer, consultant*

**Raleigh**
Freeman, Franklin Edward, Jr. *state agency administrator*

## NORTH DAKOTA

**Bismarck**
Isaak, Larry A. *state agency administrator*
Sanstead, Wayne Godfrey *state superintendent, former lieutenant governor*

## OHIO

**Columbus**
Anderson, John Robert *state agency administrator*
Goff, John *state agency administrator*
Jackson, G. James *protective services official*
Ray, Frank David *government agency official*
Taylor, Calvin Lee *public administrator*

**Cuyahoga Falls**
Shane, Sandra Kuli *postal service administrator*

**Toledo**
Smith, Robert Nelson *former government official, anesthesiologist*

**Zanesville**
O'Sullivan, Christine *executive director social service agency*

## OKLAHOMA

**Chickasha**
Beets, Freeman Haley *retired government official*

**Oklahoma City**
Collins, William Edward *aeromedical administrator, researcher*
Harbour, Robert Randall *state agency administrator*

**Tulsa**
Deihl, Michael Allen *federal agency administrator*
Palmer, Ron *police chief*

**Wanette**
Thompson, Joyce Elizabeth *retired state education official*

## OREGON

**Portland**
Adams, Hilda Chaski *public health administrator, epidemiologist*
Brockley, John P. *state agency executive, airport executive*

## PENNSYLVANIA

**Allentown**
McElroy, Janice Helen *government agency executive*
Tredinnick, Arthur Fred *private detective*

**Castle Shannon**
Selkowitz, Lucy Ann *security officer*

**Gettysburg**
Roach, James Clark *government official*

**Harrisburg**
Glass, Brent D. *state commission administrator*
Megargee, Kathleen Anne *state public information officer, producer*
Peechatka, Walter Norman *government official*

**Mont Alto**
Sourbier, James Henry, IV *police chief*

**Philadelphia**
Brown, Betty Marie *government agency administrator*
Hairston, Harold B. *protective services official*

**Reading**
Williams, Sandra Keller *postal service executive*

**Stewartstown**
Kandra, Joseph *retired federal agency administrator*

**University Park**
Lee, Robert Dorwin *public affairs educator*

**RHODE ISLAND**

**Providence**
McWalters, Peter *state agency administrator*
Sapinsley, Lila Manfield *state official*

**SOUTH CAROLINA**

**Charleston**
Gaillard, John Palmer, Jr. *former government official, former mayor*

**Columbia**
Duffie, Virgil Whatley, Jr. *state agency administrator*
Inkley, Scott Russell, Jr. *state agency administrator*
LeFever, Michael Grant *state agency administrator*

**Hilton Head Island**
Ambler, Ernest *government official*

**North**
Moran, John Bernard *government official*

**TENNESSEE**

**Brighton**
King, James Andrew *protective services educator and administrator*

**Gatlinburg**
†Wade, Karen *national parks administrator*

**Knoxville**
Crowell, Craven H., Jr. *federal agency administrator*

**Memphis**
Knight, H. Stuart *law enforcement official, consultant*
Smith, Charles E. *protective services official*

**Nashville**
Guy, Sharon Kaye *state agency executive*
Mathews, Robert C.H. *state agency executive*
Smith, Charles Edward *state agency administrator*
Walters, Jane *state agency administrator*

**TEXAS**

**Amarillo**
Bull, Walter Stephen *police officer*

**Austin**
Martin, David Hugh *private investigator, business executive, writer*
Sansom, Andrew *federal agency administrator*
Watson, Elizabeth Marion *protective services official*

**Baytown**
Leiper, Robert Duncan *protective services official*

**Bryan**
Owens, Harold B. *former state agency consultant*

**Carrollton**
Varner, Bruce H., Jr. *fire department official, educator*

**Dallas**
Click, Bennie R. *protective services official*

**Denton**
Jackson, Stephen Eric *police official*

**Fort Worth**
Sasser, William Jack *retired federal agency administrator, consultant*

**Granbury**
Scogin, Martha Aduddell *public information officer*

**Houston**
Corral, Edward Anthony *fire marshal*
Faison, Holly *state agency administrator*
Holloway, Tommy W. *government agency administrator*
McCollum, Gary Wayne *government official*

**Richardson**
Garreans, Leonard Lansford *protective services official, criminal justice professional*

**San Antonio**
Philippus, Al A. *protective services official*
Sessions, William Steele *former government official*

**UTAH**

**Provo**
Porter, Bruce Douglas *federal agency administrator, educator, writer*

**Salt Lake City**
Gold, Rick L. *federal government executive*

**Springdale**
†Falvey, Donald *government official*

**VERMONT**

**Springfield**
Putnam, Paul Adin *retired government agency official*

**VIRGINIA**

**Alexandria**
Brockert, Joseph Paul *government administrator, writer, editor, design consultant*
Chamberlain, Adrian Ramond *trade association executive*
Christie, Thomas Philip *federal agency administrator, research manager*
Clinkscales, William Abner, Jr. *government administrator*
Connally, Ernest Allen *retired federal agency administrator*
Connell, John Gibbs, Jr. *former government official*
Entzminger, John Nelson, Jr. *federal agency administrator, electronic engineer, researcher*
Hughes, Grace-Flores *former federal agency administrator, management consulting executive*
Johnson, Robert Gerald *federal agency consultant*
Kelso, John Hodgson *former government official*
Martinez, Ricardo *federal agency administrator*
Naylor, Kenneth Glen *federal agency administrator*
Senese, Donald Joseph *former government official*
Williams, Justin W. *government official*

**Annandale**
Hedrick, Floyd Dudley *government official, author*

**Arlington**
Alford, Paula N. *federal agency administrator*
Bardon, Marcel *government official*
Beggs, James Montgomery *former government official*
Boyle, Robert Patrick *retired government agency consultant, lawyer*
Brandt, Werner William *federal agency official*
Ehrman, Madeline Elizabeth *federal agency administrator*
Fisher, Farley *federal agency administrator, chemist*
Gonzalez, Eduardo Bernard *federal agency administrator*
†Luftig, Stephen D. *federal agency administrator*
Marzetti, Loretta A. *government agency executive, policy analyst*
McDonald, Bernard Robert *federal agency administrator*
Moore, Julia Alice *federal government executive*
Nalen, Craig Anthony *government official*
Nielsen, Aldon Dale *retired government agency official, economist*
†Pippen, Harvey G. *government official*
Reeder, Franklin S. *retired federal agency administrator*
Secular, Sidney *federal agency administrator, procurement analyst*
Tarbell, David S. *federal agency administrator*
Verburg, Edwin Arnold *federal agency administrator*

**Burgess**
Towle, Leland Hill *retired government official*

**Burke**
Daski, Robert Steven *federal agency executive*

**Chantilly**
Rowe, Audrey *postal service administrator*

**Charlottesville**
Cowles, Roger William *federal agency administrator*
Handy, Alice Warner *state agency administrator*
Smith, Curtis Johnston *government executive*

**Fairfax**
Fisher, Mary Maurine *federal agency official*

**Fairfax Station**
Taylor, Eldon Donivan *government official*

**Fort Belvoir**
Molholm, Kurt Nelson *federal agency administrator*
Reed, William H. *federal agency administrator*
†Richbourg, Donna S. *federal agency administrator*

**Herndon**
Sherwin, Michael Dennis *government official*

**Lorton**
Francis, Richard Haudiomont *government administrator*

**Manassas**
Webb, Dennis Wayne *protective services official*

**Mc Lean**
Duncan, Robert Clifton *retired government official*
Hathaway, William Dodd *federal agency administrator*
Mahan, Clarence *retired government official, writer*
Martin, Marsha Pyle *federal agency administrator*
Mater, Maud *federal agency administrator, lawyer*
Reswick, James Bigelow *former government official, rehabilitation engineer, educator*
Svahn, John Alfred *government official*
Turner, Stansfield *former government official, lecturer, writer, teacher*
Verhalen, Robert Donald *consultant*
Yancik, Joseph John *government official*

**Mineral**
Donald, James Robert *federal agency official, economist, outdoors writer*

**Norfolk**
Melvin C., High *protective services official*

**Oakton**
Mosemann, Lloyd Kenneth, II *government official*

**Reston**
Calio, Anthony John *scientist, business executive*

**Richmond**
Kyle, Penelope Ward *state administrator, lawyer*
Pollard, Overton Price *state agency executive, lawyer*

**Roanoke**
Hooper, M. David *protective services official*

**Roseland**
Arey, William Griffin, Jr. *former government official*

**Springfield**
Meikle, Philip G. *retired government agency executive*
Patterson, Veda Malia *equal opportunity specialist*

**Sterling**
Port, Arthur Tyler *retired government administrator, lawyer*

**Virginia Beach**
Wootten, Thomas Franklin *criminal justice administrator*

**Williamsburg**
Davis, Emma-Jo Levey *retired government executive, publishing executive*
Petersen, Richard Herman *government executive, aeronautical engineer*

**WASHINGTON**

**Ashford**
Briggle, William James *federal agency administrator*

**Bellevue**
O'Keefe, Kathleen Mary *state government official*

**Greenbank**
Grant, Robert Yearington *former government official*

**Seattle**
Davis, Patricia *state agency executive*

**Sequim**
Meacham, Charles Harding *government official*

**Tacoma**
Arreola, Philip *police officer*

**Vancouver**
Howsley, Richard Thornton *regional government administrator, lawyer*

**WEST VIRGINIA**

**Charleston**
Douglass, Gus Ruben *state agency administrator*
Marockie, Henry R. *state school system administrator*

**Parkersburg**
Miller, Steven Douglas *federal agency executive*

**WISCONSIN**

**Madison**
Benson, John T. *state agency administrator*
Cronin, Patti Adrienne Wright *state agency administrator*
Parrino, Cheryl Lynn *state agency administrator*

**Mequon**
Wray, Gail Miller *government agency administrator, environmentalist*

**WYOMING**

**Casper**
Reed, James Earl *fire department commander*

**Cheyenne**
Catchpole, Judy *state agency administrator*

**MILITARY ADDRESSES OF THE UNITED STATES**

**ATLANTIC**

**APO**
Dyal, William M., Jr. *federal agency administrator*
Kadunc, Edward Louis, Jr. *federal government official*

**CANADA**

**BRITISH COLUMBIA**

**Victoria**
†MacPhail, Joy K. *provincial agency administrator*

**MANITOBA**

**Winnipeg**
†Ernst, James Arthur *cabinet minister*

**NEW BRUNSWICK**

**Fredericton**
Blanchard, Edmond P. *Canadian government official*
McKenna, Frank Joseph *Canadian government official, lawyer*

**NOVA SCOTIA**

**Lawrencetown**
Pottie, Roswell Francis *Canadian federal science and technology consultant*

**ONTARIO**

**Mississauga**
Morden, John Reid *Canadian government corporation administrator*

**Nepean**
†Pokotylo, August Elmer *government official*

**Orillia**
O'Grady, Thomas B. *Canadian provincial official*

**Ottawa**
Cashin, Richard *Canadian federal official*
De Cotret, Robert Rene *former Canadian government official*
Gibbs, Willie *national parole board administrator*
Gusella, Mary Margaret *commissioner*
†Harvie, James Duncan *nuclear regulator*
Ingstrup, Ole Michaelsen *Canadian government agency official*
†Lapointe, Lucie *government agency executive*
MacFarlane, John Alexander *former federal housing agency administrator*
Minaker, George *Canadian provincial official*
Murray, J. P. R. *Canadian protective services official*
Penner, Keith *Canadian government official*

**Toronto**
Fraser, William Neil *government official*
Gillespie, Alastair William *former Canadian government official*
Hodgson, Chris *Canadian provincial official*
Saunderson, William *Canadian provincial official*
Tsubouchi, David H. *Canadian provincial official*

**PRINCE EDWARD ISLAND**

**Charlottetown**
†Beck, Rory *government agency administrator*

**QUEBEC**

**Hull**
†Isenberg, Seymour *government agency administrator*
†Ostry, Adam Knelman *public information office*

**Quebec**
†Tardif, Jean *federal agency administrator*

**Saint Hubert**
†McNally, Joseph Lawrence *space agency executive*

**Sainte Foy**
†Cote, Pierre F. *chief electoral officer*

**SASKATCHEWAN**

**Regina**
Nuttall, Richard Norris *state agency administrator*
Teichrob, Carol *Canadian provincial official*
†Warriner, William Ernest *government official*

**ENGLAND**

**London**
Russell, Thomas *British government official*

**SWITZERLAND**

**Signy**
Murphy, Edmund Michael *federal agency administrator, demographer*

**ADDRESS UNPUBLISHED**

Anderson, Wayne Carl *public information officer*
Argun, Fatima Hatice *international business and marketing consultant*
Bayer, Robert Edward *retired defense department official*
Benjaminson, James Albert *protective services official*
Boozer, Howard Rai *retired state education official*
Boysen, Thomas Cyril *state school system administrator*
Brinkley, Fred Sinclair, Jr. *state agency administrator, pharmacist*
Brogan, Frank T. *state agency administrator*
Brubaker, Crawford Francis, Jr. *government official, aerospace consultant*
Burgess, Marjorie Laura *protective services official*
Camdessus, Michel (Jean) *federal agency administrator, international organization executive*
Campbell, Arthur Andrews *retired government official*
Campbell, Donald Alfred *retired government official*

Claytor, Richard Anderson *retired federal agency executive, consultant*
Conway, James Valentine Patrick *forensic document examiner, former postal service executive*
Crawford, Carol Tallman *government executive*
†Curtis, Peter J. *government official*
De Leon, Rudy *government official*
Dorman, Hattie Lawrence *former federal agency official, management consultant*
Fasullo, Eugene Jack *state official*
Frazier, Henry Bowen, III *retired government official, lawyer*
Golding, Carolyn May *former government senior executive, consultant*
Gorden, Phillip *federal agency administrator*
Gordon, Peter Lowell *immigration administrator*
Griffith, Carl Leslie *protective services official*
Guild, Nelson Prescott *retired state education official*
Harder, Robert Clarence *state official*
Harding, Jessica Rose *public affairs specialist, journalist*
Healton, Donald Carney *retired government official*
Hedrick, Basil Calvin *state agency administrator, ethnohistorian, educator, museum and multicultural institutions consultant*
Helms, J. Lynn *former government agency administrator*
Heyman, Ira Michael *federal agency administrator, museum executive, law educator*
Johnson, Ralph Raymond *ambassador, federal agency administrator*
Klagholz, Leo F. *state agency administrator*
Kusserow, Richard Phillip *government official, business consultant*
LaBarre, Carl Anthony *retired government official*
Lewis, Samuel Winfield *retired government official, former ambassador*
Mancher, Rhoda Ross *federal agency administrator, strategic planner*
McCoy, Mary Ann *state official*
Mc Coy, Tidal Windham *former government official*
Mc Fee, Thomas Stuart *retired government agency administrator*
Murr, James Coleman *federal government official*
Myers, Ann Margaret *state agency supervisor*
Passmore, Michael Forrest *environmental research administrator*
Patino, Isidro Frank *law enforcement educator*
Ray, Gayle Elrod *sheriff*
Reilly, Edward Francis, Jr. *former state senator, federal agency administrator*
Rhett, John Taylor, Jr. *government official, civil engineer*
Rivkind, Perry Abbot *federal railroad agency administrator*
Robson, Marian Lorraine *Canadian federal official*
Saddler, George Floyd *government economic adviser*
Schuster, Charles Roberts *federal government scientist*
Scott, William Herbert *state agency administrator*
Shanahan, Michael George *police officer*
Shasteen, Donald Eugene *government official*
Shelton, Philip Anderson *criminal investigator, writer*
Shute, Richard Emil *government official, engineer*
Skaff, Joseph John *state agency administrator, retired army officer*
Smith, Doris Victoria *educational agency administrator*
Smith, Elmer W. *retired federal government administrator*
Sobczak, Darlene Marie *police officer*
Soderberg, Nancy *federal agency administrator*
Sorter, Bruce Wilbur *federal program administrator, educator, consultant*
Tanguay, Norbert Arthur *retired municipal police training officer*
Trodden, Stephen Anthony *federal agency administrator*
Walsh, Edward Patrick *federal agency administrator*
White, Thomas Edward *retired government park official*
Young, Edwin S. W. *federal agency official*

## GOVERNMENT: EXECUTIVE ADMINISTRATION

### UNITED STATES

### ALABAMA

**Bessemer**
Bains, Lee Edmundson *state official*

**Birmingham**
Arrington, Richard, Jr. *mayor*
Boomershine, Donald Eugene *bureau executive, development official*
Dentiste, Paul George *city and regional planning executive*

**Mobile**
Delaney, Thomas Caldwell, Jr. *city official*

**Montgomery**
Bennett, James Ronald *secretary of state*
James, Fob, Jr. (Forrest Hood James) *governor*
Latham, Larry Lee *state administrator, psychologist*
Siegelman, Don Eugene *state official*
Wallace, George Corley *former governor*
Williamson, Donald E. *state official*

### ALASKA

**Delta Junction**
Holland, Bernard George *pipeline security officer*

**Fairbanks**
Smith, Robert London *commissioner, retired air force officer, political scientist, educator*
Wolting, Robert Roy *city official*

**Juneau**
Botelho, Bruce Manuel *state official, mayor*
Knowles, Tony *governor*
Meacham, Charles P. *president, capital consulting*
Twomley, Bruce Clarke *commissioner, lawyer*
Ulmer, Frances Ann *state official*

**Kodiak**
Selby, Jerome M. *mayor*

**Ninilchik**
Oskolkoff, Grassim *Native American Indian tribal chief*

**Seward**
Kincheloe, Lawrence Ray *state official*

### ARIZONA

**Florence**
Griffis, Stanley Douglas *county manager*

**Gilbert**
Carrico, Donald Jefferson *public transit system manager*

**Green Valley**
Egger, Roscoe L., Jr. *consultant, former IRS commissioner*

**Mesa**
Wong, Willie *former mayor, automotive executive*

**Phoenix**
Cordova, Alexander M. *city clerk*
Curcio, Christopher Frank *city official*
Hull, Jane Dee *state official, former state legislator*
Rimsza, Skip *mayor*
Skinner, Nancy Jo *municipal recreation executive*
Symington, J. Fife, III *governor*
Welsh, John Richard *state official*
Woods, Grant *state attorney general*

**Prescott**
Daly, Paul Sylvester *mayor, retired academic administrator*

**Scottsdale**
Quayle, James Danforth *former vice president United States, entrepreneur*

**Sun City**
Farwell, Albert Edmond *retired government official, consultant*

**Tempe**
Tambs, Lewis Arthur *diplomat, historian, educator*

**Tucson**
Hutchinson, Edward Paul *city official*
Miller, George *mayor*
Partridge, William Russell *retired federal executive*
Williams, Ben Franklin, Jr. *mayor, lawyer*

**Yuma**
Young, Marilyn Rae *mayor, former school system adminstrative secretary*

### ARKANSAS

**Bella Vista**
Medin, Myron James, Jr. *city manager*

**Heber Springs**
Rawlings, Paul C. *retired government official*

**Little Rock**
Ahlen, John William, III *state official, scientist, educator*
Barton, Kay G. *state official*
Bryant, Winston *state attorney general*
Cheek, James Richard *ambassador*
Fisher, Jimmie Lou *state official*
Huckabee, Michael Dale *governor*
Priest, Sharon Devlin *state official*

### CALIFORNIA

**Anaheim**
Daly, Tom *mayor*

**Berkeley**
Rice, Edward Earl *former government official, author*

**Beverly Hills**
Covitz, Carl D. *state official, real estate and investment executive*

**Brea**
Georgino, Susan Martha *city redevelopment services administrator*

**Claremont**
Pedersen, Richard Foote *diplomat and academic administrator*

**Concord**
Davis, Robert Leach *retired government official, consultant*

**Coronado**
Hostler, Charles Warren *international affairs consultant*

**Costa Mesa**
Hugo, Nancy *county official, alcohol and drug addiction professional*

**Downey**
Schoettger, Theodore Leo *city official*

**El Monte**
Wallach, Patricia *mayor*

**Fall River Mills**
Reed, Eva Silver Star *chieftain*

**Fallbrook**
†Shaver, Carl A. *government official*

**Felicity**
Istel, Jacques Andre *mayor*

**Fresno**
Patterson, James *mayor*

**La Jolla**
Klein, David *foreign service officer*
Shakespeare, Frank *ambassador*

**Laguna Hills**
Hussey, William Bertrand *retired foreign service officer*

**Long Beach**
O'Neill, Beverly Lewis *mayor, former college president*
Sato, Eunice Noda *former mayor, consultant*

**Los Altos**
Gray, Robert Donald *municipal government official*

**Los Angeles**
Brown, Kathleen *state treasurer, lawyer*
Buichl, Anna Elizabeth *city official*
Christopher, Warren *lawyer, former government official*
Cisneros, Henry G. *former federal official, broadcast executive*
Hwang, John Dzen *municipal official*
Peters, Aulana Louise *government agency commissioner, lawyer*
Reagan, Ronald Wilson *former President of United States*
Riordan, Richard J. *mayor*
Schnabel, Rockwell Anthony *ambassador*
Toman, Mary Ann *federal official*
Young, Caprice Yvonne *municipal official*

**Marina**
Myers, James David *municipal government official*

**Martinez**
Uilkema, Gayle Burns *mayor, councilwoman, business educator*

**Mckinleyville**
Kulstad, Guy Charles *public works official*

**Menlo Park**
Lane, Laurence William, Jr. *retired ambassador, publisher*

**Monterey Park**
Smith, Betty Denny *county official, administrator, fashion executive*

**Napa**
Battisti, Paul Oreste *county supervisor*

**Norwalk**
Drant, Sandra Elizabeth *court reporter, educator*

**Oakland**
Harris, Elihu Mason *mayor*

**Oceanside**
Lyon, Richard *mayor, retired naval officer*

**Palm Springs**
Parrish, Jeanne Elaine *former mayor, city councilwoman, former health services administrator, nurse*

**Pasadena**
Bean, Maurice Darrow *retired diplomat*

**Rancho Mirage**
Ford, Gerald Rudolph, Jr. *former President of United States*

**Rancho Santa Fe**
Capen, Richard Goodwin, Jr. *ambassador*

**Redlands**
Hanson, Gerald Warner *retired county official*

**Richmond**
Corbin, Rosemary Mac Gowan *mayor*

**Riverside**
Steckel, Barbara Jean *city financial officer*

**Sacramento**
Betts, Bert A. *former state treasurer, accountant*
Cozad, Lyman Howard *city manager*
Davis, Gray *lieutenant governor*
Fong, Matthew Kipling *state official*
Grissom, Lee Alan *state official*
Lungren, Daniel Edward *state attorney general*
Nelson, Alan Curtis *government official, lawyer*
Peck, Ellie Enriquez *retired state administrator*
Serna, Joe, Jr. *mayor*
Takasugi, Nao *state official, business developer*
Walston, Roderick Eugene *state government official*
Whiteside, Carol Gordon *state official, former mayor*
Wilson, Pete *governor*

**San Bernardino**
Lenz, Philip Joseph *municipal administrator*
Stark, S. Daniel, Jr. *convention and visitors bureau executive*

**San Diego**
Bliesner, James Douglas *municipal/county official, consultant*
Freeman, Myrna Faye *county schools official*
Golding, Susan *mayor*
Partida, Gilbert A. *chamber of commerce executive*

**San Francisco**
Brown, Willie Lewis, Jr. *mayor, former state legislator, lawyer*
Frank, Anthony Melchior *federal official, former financial executive*
Taylor, John Lockhart *city official*

**San Jose**
Hammer, Susan W. *mayor*

**San Pedro**
Main, Betty Jo *management analyst*

**Santa Monica**
Rice, Donald Blessing *business executive, former secretary of air force*

**Santa Rosa**
Frowick, Robert Holmes *retired diplomat*

**Solana Beach**
Ernst, Roger Charles *former government official, natural resources consultant, association executive*
Gildred, Theodore Edmonds *ambassador*

**Stanford**
Shultz, George Pratt *former government executive, economics educator*

**Union City**
Lewis, Mark Earldon *city manager*

**Yuba City**
Kemmerly, Jack Dale *retired state official, aviation consultant*

### COLORADO

**Bayfield**
Giller, Edward Bonfoy *retired government official, retired air force officer*

**Boulder**
Bolen, David B. *ambassador, former corporation executive*

**Colorado Springs**
Isaac, Robert Michael *former mayor*
Milton, Richard Henry *retired diplomat, children's advocate*

**Denver**
Brown, Keith Lapham *retired ambassador*
Buckley, Vikki *state official*
Gallagher, Dennis Joseph *city councilman, former state senator, educator*
Hackworth, Theodore James, Jr. *city official*
Howlett, John David *government relations*
Minger, Terrell John *public administration institute executive*
Norton, Gale A. *state attorney general*
Romer, Roy R. *governor*
Webb, Wellington E. *mayor*

**Grand Junction**
Achen, Mark Kennedy *city manager*

**Lakewood**
Morton, Linda *mayor*

**Littleton**
Cismaru, Pat Klein *municipal official*

**Pueblo**
Casey, William Robert, Jr. *ambassador, mining engineer*
Occhiato, Michael Anthony *city official*

### CONNECTICUT

**Bridgeport**
†Ganim, Joseph P. *mayor*

**Bristol**
Moffitt, George, Jr. *retired foreign service officer*

**Canton**
Humphrey, Samuel Stockwell *former town official, physicist*

**Easton**
Meyer, Alice Virginia *state official*

**Hartford**
Blumenthal, Richard *state attorney general*
Burnham, Christopher Bancroft *state treasurer, investment banker*
De Rocco, Andrew Gabriel *state commissioner, scientist, educator*
Harriman, Stephen A. *state public health commissioner*
Harris, James George, Jr. *social services administrator, consultant*
Killian, Robert Kenneth *former lieutenant governor*
Noonan, John G(erard) *state financial management specialist*
Rapoport, Miles S. *state official*
Rell, M. Jodi *state official*
Rowland, John G. *governor, former congressman*

**Kent**
Ober, Robert Fairchild, Jr. *retired government official, school administrator*

**Manchester**
Precourt, George Augustine *government official*

**New Britain**
Polinsky, Janet Naboicheck *state official, former state legislator*

**Northford**
James, William Hall *former state official, educator*

**Stamford**
Joondeph, Marcia *diplomat*
Malloy, Dannel Patrick *mayor*

## DELAWARE

### Dover
Bookhammer, Eugene Donald *state government official*
Carper, Thomas Richard *governor*
Freel, Edward J. *state official*
Minner, Ruth Ann *state official*

### Newark
Woo, S. B. (Shien-Biau Woo) *former lieutenant governor, physics educator*

### Wilmington
Brady, M. Jane *state official*
Ianni, Francis Alphonse *state official, former army officer*
Morris, Ronald Anthony *county official*

## DISTRICT OF COLUMBIA

### Washington
Abramowitz, Morton I. *former ambassador*
Abshire, David Manker *diplomat, research executive*
Acheson, Eleanor Dean *federal government official*
Achtenberg, Roberta *federal official*
†Albright, Madeleine Korbel *federal official, diplomat, political scientist*
Alexander, Dawn Alicia *public relations executive*
Andersen, Robert Allen *retired government official*
Anderson, J. Brady *ambassador*
Angula, Helmut Kangulohi *Namibian government official*
Anschuetz, Norbert Lee *retired diplomat, banker*
Anthony, Sheila Foster *government official*
Argrett, Loretta Collins *assistant attorney general, educator*
Atherton, Charles Henry *federal commission administrator*
Auten, John Harold *government official*
Ayres, Mary Ellen *government official*
Azcuenaga, Mary Laurie *government official*
Babbitt, Bruce Edward *federal official*
Bachula, Gary R. *federal official*
Baer, Donald Aaron *federal official*
Baldyga, Leonard J. *diplomat, international consultant, retired*
Ballantyne, Robert Jadwin *former foreign service officer, consultant*
Barnes, Shirley Elizabeth *foreign service officer*
Barnett, Robert Warren *diplomat, author*
Barrett, Archie Don *federal official*
Barringer, Philip E. *government official*
Barry, Marion Shepilov, Jr. *mayor*
†Barshefsky, Charlene *diplomat*
Bartholomew, Reginald *diplomat*
Bassin, Jules *foreign service officer*
Bauer, Gary Lee *government official*
Bell, Robert G. *federal agency official*
Bellinger, John B., Jr. *federal official*
Bellows, Michael Donald *foreign service officer*
Benedick, Richard Elliot *diplomat*
Benedict, Lawrence Neal *foreign service officer*
Berg, Olena *federal official*
Berger, Samuel R. *federal official*
Bissell, Richard Etter *international finance agency executive*
Blanchard, James Johnston *ambassador, former governor of Michigan*
†Boswell, Eric J. *federal official*
Bowles, Erskine *White House staff member*
Bowsher, Charles Arthur *government official*
Bragg, Lynn Munroe *commissioner*
Brazeal, Aurelia Erskine *ambassador*
Brewster, Robert Charles *diplomat, consultant*
Bromwich, Michael Ray *federal official*
Brotzman, Donald Glenn *government official, lawyer*
Brown, Elizabeth Ann *foreign service officer*
Brown, Janet Huidekoper *foundation executive*
Brown, Jesse *federal official*
Brown, June Gibbs *government official*
Browning, Stephen Carroll *government official*
Bruno, Marilyn Joan *foreign service officer, management consultant, trade specialist*
Brynn, Edward Paul *ambassador*
Burleigh, A. Peter *ambassador*
†Burns, R. Nicholas *federal official*
Calderhead, William Dickson *former foreign service officer*
†Callahan, John J. *federal official*
Cantú, Norma V. *federal official*
Carlucci, Frank Charles, III *former secretary of defense*
Carnell, Richard Scott *federal official*
Carrington, Walter C. *ambassador*
Carson, Johnnie *ambassador*
Casstevens, Kay L. *federal official*
†Castro, Ida *federal official*
Catlett, D. Mark *federal official*
Chaveas, Peter R. *ambassador*
Chrétien, Raymond A. J. *ambassador*
Christensen, Claude Jay *federal official*
Christensen, Sally Hayden *government executive*
Clarke, Henry Lee *ambassador, foreign service officer*
Cleland, Joseph Maxwell (Max Cleland) *state official*
Clinton, Bill (William Jefferson Clinton) *President of the United States*
Clinton, Hillary Rodham *First Lady of United States, lawyer*
Cohen, Bonnie R. *government official*
Cole, Kenneth J. *federal commissioner*
Coleman, William Thaddeus, III *federal official*
Collins, James Franklin *ambassador*
Collins, Keith *federal executive*
Cook, Michael Blanchard *government executive*
Cooke, David Ohlmer *government official*
Copps, Michael Joseph *commerce administrator*
Courtney, William Harrison *diplomat*
Crawford, William Rex, Jr. *former ambassador*
Crocker, Chester Arthur *diplomat, scholar, federal agency administrator*
Cutler, Walter Leon *diplomat, foundation executive*
†Daley, William M. *federal government official*
Dalton, John Howard *Secretary of the Navy, financial consultant*
Danvers, William *federal official*
Danzig, Richard Jeffrey *government official, lawyer*
†Davidow, Jeffrey *ambassador*
Davis, Marilynn A. *housing agency administrator*
Davis, Ruth A. *ambassador*
Deal, Timothy *diplomat, government association executive*
Dean, Edwin Robinson *government official, economist*
Dean, Leslie Alan (Cap Dean) *foreign service officer*
DeGeorge, Francis Donald *federal official*
Deitering, Randy Wayne *intelligence official*
DeSeve, G. Edward *federal official*
Despres, John *government executive, economist*
Dewhurst, Stephen B. *government official, lawyer*
Dhanapala, Jayantha *diplomat*
Dickey, George Edward *federal government executive*
Dobbins, James Francis, Jr. *foreign service officer*
Dodd, Thomas J. *ambassador, educator*
Doggett, Leslie *federal government official*
Donilon, Thomas E. *federal official*
Dreyer, David E. *federal official*
Duemling, Robert Werner *diplomat, museum director*
Durham, Archer L. *federal official, retired career officer*
Ebbitt, James Roger *government official*
Eddy, John Joseph *diplomat*
Ehrlich, Everett Michael *federal official, computer company executive*
Eizenstat, Stuart E. *ambassador, lawyer*
Elliott, Lee Ann *federal official*
Ely-Raphel, Nancy *diplomat*
†Emmanuel, Rahm *federal official*
Ferrara, Peter Joseph *federal official, lawyer, author, educator*
†Fishman, Paul J. *federal official*
FitzGerald, William Henry G. *diplomat, corporation executive*
Flanigan, Alan H. *ambassador*
Fleisher, Eric Wilfrid *retired foreign service officer*
Fleming, Patricia Stubbs *federal official*
Fowler, Mary Emily *federal agency administrator*
Franklin, Barbara Hackman *former goverment official*
Fried, Daniel *federal official*
Gaffney, Susan *federal official*
Galloway, William Jefferson *former foreign service officer*
†Garthoff, Raymond Leonard *diplomat, diplomatic historian and researcher*
Gati, Toby T. *federal official*
Gatons, Anna-Marie Kilmade *government manager*
Gaviria Trujillo, César *international organization administrator, former president of Colombia, economist*
Geisel, Harold Walter *diplomat*
Gelbard, Robert Sidney *ambassador*
Gessaman, Donald Eugene *consultant, former government official*
Gibbons, John Howard (Jack Gibbons) *government official, physicist*
Glassman, Jon David *diplomat*
Glauthier, T. James *federal official*
Godley, Patricia Fry *government official, lawyer*
Gore, Albert, Jr. *Vice President of the United States*
Green, Marshall *former ambassador, consultant*
Grimmett, Richard Fieldon *government official, analyst*
Grove, Brandon Hambright, Jr. *diplomat, public and international affairs consultant*
Haas, Lawrence Jay *federal official*
Haig, Alexander Meigs, Jr. *former government official, former army officer, business executive*
Hale, Marcia L. *federal official*
Harrop, William Caldwell *retired ambassador, foreign service officer*
Hauser, Timothy J. *federal official*
Hawk, Kathleen M. *federal official*
Hawkins, Wilbur *federal official*
Herman, Alexis M. *federal official*
High, George Borman *executive director, research organization*
Hillman, Jennifer Anne *ambassador, trade negotiator*
†Holbrooke, Richard Charles Albert *former ambassador, government official*
Holliday, Carolyn Pamela *government agency administrator*
Holmes, Henry Allen *government official*
Houdek, Robert G. *diplomat*
Hrinak, Donna Jean *ambassador*
Huddle, Franklin Pierce, Jr. *diplomat*
Huddleston, Vicki Jean *diplomat*
Hunger, Frank Watson *federal official*
Hunt, Robert Gayle *government official*
Huntress, Wesley Theodore, Jr. *government official*
Irving, Clarence L., Jr. (Larry Irving) *federal official*
Jackson, Karl Dion *government official business executive, scholar*
Janis, Michael B. *federal official*
Jeter, Howard F. *diplomat*
Johnson, Mark *ambassador*
Johnson, Paul W. *federal executive*
Jordan, Mary Lucille *commissioner*
Joseph, James Alfred *ambassador*
Kalnay, Eugenia *government official, meteorologist*
Kalnins, Ojars Eriks *Latvian diplomat*
Karelis, Charles Howard *government official*
Kauzlarich, Richard Dale *ambassador, foreign service officer*
Keating, Robert B. *ambassador*
Kelley, Wayne Plumbley, Jr. *federal official*
Kelman, Steven Jay *government official*
Kennedy, Patrick F. *federal official*
Kennedy, Richard Thomas *government official*
Kerber, Frank John *diplomat*
Kidd, Charles Vincent *former civil servant, educator*
Klosson, Michael *foreign service officer*
Komer, Robert William *government official, consultant*
Kornblum, John Christian *foreign service officer*
Korth, Penne Percy *ambassador*
Koskinen, John Andrew *federal government executive*
Kovach, Eugene George *government official, consultant*
Kraemer, Sylvia Katharine *government official, historian*
Kyle, Robert D. *federal agency official*
Laird, Melvin Robert *former secretary of defense*
Lake, Joseph Edward *ambassador*
Lalley, Frank Edward *federal government official*
Lanza, Kenneth Anthony *foreign service officer*
La Rocque, Gene Robert *retired naval officer, government official, author*
†Larson, Alan Philip *federal official*
Lastowka, James Anthony *former federal agency executive, lawyer*
Le Baron, Joseph Evan *diplomat*
Lilly, William Eldridge *government official*
Longanecker, David A. *federal official*
Longstreet, Victor Mendell *government official*
Longuemare, R. Noel, Jr. *federal official*
Lovell, Malcolm Read, Jr. *public policy institute executive, educator, former government official, former trade association executive*
Lowe, Mary Frances *federal government official*
Lowenstein, James Gordon *former diplomat, international consultant*
Lucas, James Walter *federal government official*
Ludwig, Eugene Allan *United States comptroller of the currency, lawyer*
Lyman, Princeton Nathan *ambassador*
Lyons, James Robert *federal official*
Magaw, John W. *federal law enforcement official*
Magaziner, Ira *federal official*
Maldon, Alphonso, Jr. *federal official, retired military officer*
Malloy, Eileen Anne *ambassador*
Martin, William Edwin *government official*
†Matheson, Michael J. *federal official*
Mathews, Jessica Tuchman *policy researcher, columnist*
McAdams, James Glen () *federal official*
McCaffrey, Barry Richard *federal official, retired army officer*
McCargar, James Goodrich *diplomat, writer*
McCurry, Michael Demaree *government spokesman, press secretary*
Mc Donald, John Warlick *diplomat, global strategist*
McGinty, Kathleen *federal official*
McGue, Christie *federal official*
McKee, Alan Reel *foreign service officer*
McKinley, Brunson *diplomat*
McLarty, Thomas F., III (Mack McLarty) *federal official*
McMichael, Guy H., III *federal official*
†McNamara, Thomas Edmund *diplomat*
McNicol, David Leon *federal official*
Meissner, Doris *federal commissioner*
Merrill, David Nathan *ambassador*
Messenger, Jon Carleton *government project manager*
Meyer, Armin Henry *retired diplomat, author, educator*
Michaud, Michael Alan George *diplomat, writer*
Milam, William Bryant *diplomat, economist*
Miles, Richard *diplomat*
Miller, Marcia E. *federal government official*
Mintz, Richard I. *federal official*
Mitchell, Graham Richard *government engineering executive*
Montgomery, William D. *ambassador*
†Morningstar, Richard L. *diplomat*
Murphy, Gerald *government official*
Myrick, Bismarck *diplomat*
Negroponte, John Dimitri *diplomat*
Nemfakos, Charles Panagiotis *federal official*
Neumann, Ronald Eldredge *diplomat*
Newton, David George *diplomat*
Norland, Donald Richard *retired foreign service officer*
Norris, Genie M. *senior government official*
Oakley, Phyllis Elliott *diplomat*
O'Bryon, James Fredrick *defense executive*
Ochmanek, David Alan *defense analyst*
Oleksiw, Daniel Philip *consultant, former foreign service officer*
O'Toole, Tara J. *federal official*
Owen, Henry *former ambassador, consultant*
Palmer, Ronald DeWayne Faisal *retired diplomat, educator, consultant*
Palmer, Steven O. *federal official*
Parker, Robert Allan Ridley *government administrator, astronaut*
Pashayev, Hafiz Mir Jalal *diplomat, physics educator*
Passage, David *diplomat*
Pelletreau, Robert Halsey *diplomat*
Peña, Federico Fabian *federal official*
Pendleton, Miles Stevens, Jr. *diplomat*
Perle, Richard Norman *government official*
Petric, Ernest *Slovenian ambassador*
Phillips, Christopher Hallowell *diplomat*
Phillips, James D. *retired diplomat*
Pickering, Thomas Reeve *diplomat*
Pierce, Margaret Hunter *government official*
Placke, James A(nthony) *foreign service officer, international affairs consultant*
Prince, Garnett B., Jr. *business executive*
Pringle, Robert Maxwell *diplomat*
Pryce, William Thornton *ambassador, executive*
Quainton, Anthony Cecil Eden *diplomat*
Raiser, Mary M. *chief of protocol*
Rankin, Haywood Forney *diplomat*
Raphel, Robin *federal official*
Ray, Charles Aaron *foreign service officer*
Reed, John Hathaway *former ambassador*
Reeder, Joe Robert *federal official*
Render, Arlene *ambassador*
Reno, Janet *federal official, lawyer*
Retsinas, Nicolas P. *federal official*
Rice, Susan Elizabeth *federal agency official*
Richard, Mark M. *government official, lawyer*
Ridgway, Rozanne LeJeanne *former diplomat, executive*
Riley, Michael Joseph *government official*
Riley, Richard Wilson *federal official*
Robinson, Laurie Overby *assistant attorney general*
Rogowsky, Robert Arthur *trade commission director*
Romani, Paul Nicholas *government official*
Romero-Barceló, Carlos Antonio *governor of Puerto Rico*
Rosewater, Ann *federal official*
Ross, Christopher Wade Stelyan *diplomat*
Rostker, Bernard *federal official*
Roth, Kathryn Gaie *government executive*
Rubin, Robert E. *federal official*
Rugh, William Arthur *diplomat*
Runyon, Marvin Travis *postmaster general*
Ryan, Mary A. *diplomat*
Sacksteder, Frederick Henry *former foreign service officer*
Saloom, Joseph A., III *diplomat*
Samaniego Breach, Norma *Mexican government official*
Samet, Andrew *government official*
Sampas, Dorothy M. *government official*
San Martin, Robert L. *federal official*
Sayre, Robert Marion *ambassador*
Scarbrough, Frank Edward *government official*
Schneiter, George Robert *government executive*
Schroeder, Fredric Kauffmann *federal commissioner*
Scott-Finan, Nancy Isabella *government administrator*
Seck, Mamadou Mansour *ambassador, career officer*
Sellin, Theodore *foreign service officer, consultant*
Shalala, Donna Edna *federal official, political scientist, educator, university chancellor*
Shattuck, John *federal official*
Shinn, David Hamilton *diplomat*
Shlaudeman, Harry Walter *retired ambassador*
Shumate, John Page *diplomat*
Simmons, Anne L. *federal official*
Simon, Jeanne Hurley *federal commissioner*
Skolfield, Melissa T. *government official*
Slater, Rodney E. *federal official*
Smith, Dallas R. *federal official*
Smith, Elaine Diana *foreign service officer*
Smith, Marshall Savidge *government official, academic dean, educator*
Smith, Patricia Grace *government official*
Somerville, Walter Raleigh, Jr. *government official*
Sommerfelt, Soren Christian *foreign affairs, international trade consultant, former Norwegian diplomat, lawyer*
Sonnenfeldt, Helmut *former government official, educator, consultant, author*
Southwick, E. Michael *diplomat*
Sprott, John T. *ambassador*
Stearn, Todd *federal government official*
Steele, Howard Loucks *government official*
Steiger, Janet Dempsey *government official*
Stephanopoulos, George Robert *federal official*
Stoll, Louise Frankel *federal official*
Storing, Paul Edward *foreign service officer*
Strauss, David *federal official*
Street, Stephanie *federal official*
Stuart, Sandra Kaplan *federal official*
Sutter, Eleanor Bly *diplomat*
Swihart, James W., Jr. *diplomat*
Swing, William Lacy *ambassador*
Taylor, Lawrence Palmer *diplomat*
Taylor, William James, III *federal official*
Thomas, Scott E. *federal government executive, lawyer*
Thomasson, Patsy *federal official*
Tomasky, Susan *federal officer*
Torkelson, Jodie Rae *executive branch staff member*
Trezise, Philip Harold *government official*
Tucker, Alvin Leroy *government official*
Tuthill, John Wills *former diplomat, educator*
Twining, Charles Haile *ambassador*
Underwood, Robert Anacletus *congressional delegate, university official*
Varney, Christine A. *federal official*
Verville, Elizabeth Giavani *federal official*
Viadero, Roger C. *government official*
Wachtmeister, Count Wilhelm H. F. *diplomat*
Walter, Judith Anne *government executive*
Ward, George Frank, Jr. *foreign service officer*
Ware, Thaddeus Van *government official*
Watson, Arthur Dennis *government official*
Wayne, Stephen J. *government educator, academic director, writer*
Weise, George James *commissioner*
Welch, Charles David *diplomat*
West, Togo Dennis, Jr. *secretary of Army, former aerospace executive*
Wexler, Anne *government relations and public affairs consultant*
Widnall, Sheila Evans *secreatry of the airforce, former aeronautical educator, former university official*
Williams, Anthony A. *federal official*
Williams, Margaret *federal official*
Williams-Bridgers, Jacquelyn *federal government official*
Winter, Harvey John *government official*
Wirth, Timothy Endicott *federal official, former senator*
Wisner, Frank George *ambassador*
Withrow, Mary Ellen *treasurer of United States*
Wolters, Curt Cornelis Frederik *foreign service officer*
Woodward, Robert Forbes *retired government official, consultant*
Worthy, Patricia Morris *municipal official, lawyer*
Yalowitz, Kenneth Spencer *ambassador*
Yates, John Melvin *ambassador*
Yellen, Janet Louise *government official, economics educator*
Young, Johnny *foreign service officer*
Ziglar, James W. *former federal official, lawyer, investment banker*
Zirschky, John H. *federal government official*

## FLORIDA

### Bal Harbour
Horton, Jeanette *municipal government official*

### Brooksville
Anderson, Richard Edmund *city manager, management consultant*
Hetrick, Charles Brady *county official*

### Clearwater
Campolettano, Thomas Alfred *government contract manager*

### Coral Gables
Arcos, Cresencio S. *ambassador*

### Daytona Beach
Keene, Douglas Ralph *diplomat*

### Fort Lauderdale
Gunzburger, Suzanne Nathan *county commissioner, social worker*
Hanbury, George Lafayette, II *city manager*

### Fort Pierce
Dusanek, Linda Sue *municipal housing official*

### Gainesville
Heflin, Martin Ganier *foreign service officer, international political economist*
Jones, Elizabeth Nordwall *county government official*

### Hialeah
Martinez, Raul L. *mayor, publisher*

### Hollywood
Giulianti, Mara Selena *mayor, civic worker*

### Jacksonville
Austin, T. Edward (Ed Austin) *former mayor*
Delaney, John Adrian *mayor*

### Kennedy Space Center
Banks, Lisa Jean *government official*

### Lakeland
Hollis, Mark D. *federal official*

**Leesburg**
Houston, John Coates, Jr. *consultant*

**Miami**
León, Eduardo A. *diplomat, business executive*
†Lichacz, Sheila Enit *diplomat, artist*
Moorman, Rose Drunell *county administrator, systems analyst*
Redruello, Rosa Inchaustegui *municipal official*

**Ocala**
Lewis, Richard Knox *city official*

**Ormond Beach**
Burton, Alan Harvey *city official*

**Palm City**
Henry, David Howe, II *retired diplomat*

**Punta Gorda**
Brenner, Jane Segrest *city council member*
Piacitelli, John Joseph *county official, educator, pediatrician*

**Redington Beach**
McConnell, Robert Chalmers *former city official*

**Saint Augustine**
Borchardt, Duke *federal labor relations professional*

**Sarasota**
Connor, Robert T. *former government official*
Hennemeyer, Robert Thomas *diplomat*
Twentyman, Lee *foreign service officer, economist*
Yordan, Carlos Manuel *foreign service officer*

**Tallahassee**
Butterworth, Robert A. *state attorney general*
Chiles, Lawton Mainor *governor, former senator*
Crawford, Bob *state commissioner*
Lindner, William H. *state official*
MacKay, Kenneth Hood, Jr. (Buddy MacKay) *state official, former congressman*
Mortham, Sandra Barringer *state official*
Parker, Herbert Gerald *state official*

**Tampa**
Freedman, Sandra Warshaw *former mayor*
Greco, Dick A. *mayor, hardware company executive*
Platt, Jan Kaminis *county official*
Studer, William Allen *county official*

**West Palm Beach**
Roberts, Carol Antonia *county commissioner, real estate associate*

**Winter Park**
Hawkins, Paula *federal official, former senator*

## GEORGIA

**Athens**
Hillenbrand, Martin Joseph *diplomat, educator*

**Atlanta**
Bell, Griffin B. *lawyer, former attorney general*
Bowers, Michael Joseph *state attorney general*
Campbell, Bill *mayor, broadcasting executive*
Carter, Jimmy (James Earl Carter, Jr.) *former President of United States*
Durden, Robert J. *state commissioner, lawyer*
Griffith, Linda Marie *county government official*
Howard, Pierre *state official*
Laney, James Thomas *ambassador, educator*
Malone, Perrillah Atkinson (Pat Malone) *retired state official*
Massey, Lewis *state official*
Miller, Zell Bryan *governor*
Nethercut, Philip Edwin *honorary consul, retired*
Poythress, David Bryan *state commissioner, lawyer*
Rogers, Werner *state superintendent schools*
Schwartz, William B., Jr. *ambassador*
Streeb, Gordon Lee *diplomat, economist*
Sullivan, Louis Wade *former secretary health and human services, physician*

**Bowdon**
Henson, Diana Jean *county official*

**Cartersville**
Harris, Joe Frank *former governor*

**Conyers**
Kelly, John Hubert *diplomat, business executive*

**Decatur**
Gay, Robert Derril *public agency director*

**Midland**
Hadden, Mayo Addison *chamber of commerce executive, military officer, educator*

**Saint Simons Island**
Douglas, William Ernest *retired government official*

**Savannah**
Rousakis, John Paul *former mayor*

## HAWAII

**Camp Smith**
Teare, Richard Wallace *ambassador*

**Honolulu**
Anderson, John Wynn *attorney general*
†Bronster, Margery S *attorney general*
Cayetano, Benjamin Jerome *governor, former state senator and representative*
Harris, Jeremy *mayor*
Hirono, Mazie Keiko *state official*

## IDAHO

**Boise**
Batt, Philip E. *governor*
Cenarrusa, Pete T. *secretary of state*
Edwards, Lydia Justice *state official*
Hawkins, James Victor *state official*
Otter, Clement Leroy *lieutenant governor*
Wilson, Jack Fredrick *retired federal government official*

## ILLINOIS

**Champaign**
Semonin, Richard Gerard *retired state official*

**Chicago**
Bishop, Oliver Richard *state official*
Cherry, Robert Steven, III *municipal agency administrator*
Chun, Shinae *state official*
Daley, Richard Michael *mayor*
Holowinski, John Joseph *state executive*
Silins, Ints M. *ambassador*
Topinka, Judy Baar *state official*

**Decatur**
Rockefeller, Margaretta Fitler Murphy (Happy Rockefeller) *widow of former vice president of U.S.*

**Elk Grove Village**
Yiannias, Nancy Magas *municipal official*

**Evanston**
Ingersoll, Robert Stephen *former diplomat, federal agency administrator*

**Joliet**
O'Connell, James Joseph *port official*

**Normal**
Edwards, Marianne *city clerk*

**Peoria**
Maloof, James A. *mayor, real estate company executive*

**Quincy**
Points, Roy Wilson *municipal official*

**Springfield**
Edgar, Jim *governor*
Kustra, Robert W. (Bob Kustra) *state official, educator*
Ryan, James E. *attorney general*
Schmidt, Mark James *state public health official*

**Urbana**
Prussing, Laurel Lunt *state official, economist*

**Wheaton**
Bellock, Patricia Rigney *county government official*

## INDIANA

**Fishers**
Christie, Walter Scott *retired state official*

**Fort Wayne**
Helmke, (Walter) Paul, Jr. *mayor, lawyer*
Lee, Timothy Earl *international agency executive, paralegal*

**Indianapolis**
Bayh, Evan *former governor*
Carter, Pamela Lynn *former state attorney general*
Gilroy, Sue Anne *state official*
Goldsmith, Stephen *mayor*
O'Bannon, Frank Lewis *governor, lawyer*
Usher, Phyllis Land *state official*
Zeller, Kenneth J. *state official*

**Notre Dame**
Wadsworth, Michael A. *athletic director, former ambassador*

**Tell City**
Gebhard, Diane Kay *county administrator, political advisor*

## IOWA

**Cedar Rapids**
Novetzke, Sally Johnson *former ambassador*

**Council Bluffs**
Boone, Dorothy Mae *county official*

**Des Moines**
Branstad, Terry Edward *governor, lawyer*
Corning, Joy Cole *state official*
Fitzgerald, Michael Lee *state official*
Miller, Thomas J. *state attorney general*

**Johnston**
Odell, Mary Jane *former state official*

**Oelwein**
McFarlane, Beth Lucetta Troester *former mayor*

**Steamboat Rock**
Taylor, Ray *state senator*

## KANSAS

**Kansas City**
Hollenbeck, Marynell *municipal government official*

**Mc Pherson**
Steffes, Don Clarence *state senator*

**Overland Park**
Jekel, Joseph Frank *government official*

**Shawnee Mission**
Kemp, John Bernard *retired state secretary of transportation*

**Topeka**
Freden, Sharon Elsie Christman *state education assistant commissioner*
Graves, William Preston *governor*
Sebelius, Kathleen Gilligan *state commissioner*
Stovall, Carla Jo *state official, lawyer*
Thompson, Sally Engstrom *state official*
Thornburgh, Ron E. *state official*

**Wichita**
Knight, Robert G. *mayor, investment banker*

## KENTUCKY

**Burkesville**
Smith, Paul Traylor *mayor, former business executive, former army officer*

**Frankfort**
Brown, John Y., III *state official*
Chandler, Albert Benjamin III *attorney general*
Henry, Stephen Lewis *state official, orthopedic surgeon, educator*
Palmore, Carol M. *state official*
Patton, Paul E. *governor*
Sonego, Ian G. *state assistant attorney general*
Strong, Marvin E., Jr. *state official*

**Lexington**
Miller, Pamela Gundersen *mayor*
Yates, Isabel McCants *city council member*

**Louisville**
Freund, Adrian Paul *county official*

**Shelbyville**
Miller, Mary Helen *retired public administrator*

## LOUISIANA

**Baton Rouge**
Blanco, Kathleen Babineaux *lieutenant governor*
Foster, Murphy J., Jr. (Mike Foster) *governor*
Ieyoub, Richard Phillip *state attorney general*
McKeithen, Walter Fox *secretary of state*

**Boyce**
Chilton, Alice Pleasance Hunter (Mrs. St. John Poindexter Chilton) *former state official, vocational counselor*

**Lake Charles**
Mount, Willie Landry *mayor*

**Metairie**
Stansbury, Harry Case *state commissioner*

**New Orleans**
Hunter, Sue Persons *former state official*
Levell, Edward, Jr. *city official*
Morial, Marc Haydel *mayor*
Ortique, Revius Oliver, Jr. *city official*
Roesler, Robert Harry *city official*
Simms, Ellenese Brooks *civic leader, retired school system administrator*

## MAINE

**Augusta**
Butland, Jeffrey H. *president of senate, customer service representative*
Gwadosky, Dan A. *secretary of state*
King, Angus S., Jr. *governor of Maine*
Scribner, Rodney Latham *state official*

**Belfast**
Worth, Mary Page *mayor*

**Springvale**
Eastman, Harland Horace *former foreign service officer*

**Topsham**
Tierney, James Edward *attorney general*

**Windham**
Diamond, G. William *former secretary of state*

## MARYLAND

**Annapolis**
Coulter, James Bennett *state official*
Glendening, Parris Nelson *governor, political science educator*
Goldstein, Louis Lazarus *state official*
Townsend, Kathleen Kennedy *state official*
Willis, John T. *state official*

**Baltimore**
Curran, J. Joseph, Jr. *state attorney general*
Jones, Raymond Moylan *strategy and public policy educator*
Phillips, Carla *county official*
Schmoke, Kurt L. *mayor*

**Bethesda**
Clark, William Doran *former government official*
Gallagher, Hubert Randall *government consultant*
Green, Jerome George *federal government official*
Hempstone, Smith, Jr. *diplomat, journalist*
Ingraham, Edward Clarke, Jr. *foreign service officer*
Kirby, Harmon E. *ambassador*
Laingen, Lowell Bruce *diplomat*
Lewis, James Histed *retired foreign service officer*
Morgan, John Davis *consultant*

Neill, Denis Michael *government relations consulting executive*
Neumann, Robert Gerhard *ambassador, consultant*
Newsom, David Dunlop *foreign service officer, educator*
North, William Haven *foreign service officer*
Peck, Edward Lionel *retired foreign service officer, corporate executive*
Rowell, Edward Morgan *retired foreign service officer, lecturer*
Sweasy, Joyce Elizabeth *government official, military reserve officer*
Vest, George Southall *diplomat*

**Braddock Heights**
Wirths, Theodore William *public policy consultant*

**Chevy Chase**
Albright, Raymond Jacob *government official*
Bush, Frederick Morris *federal official*
Lukens, Alan Wood *retired ambassador and foreign service officer*
Pancoast, Edwin C. *retired senior foreign service officer, writer, researcher*

**College Park**
Broadnax, Walter D. *public policy educator*
Peterson, David Frederick *government agency executive*

**Columbia**
Meima, Ralph Chester, Jr. *corporate execuitve, former foreign service officer*

**Crownsville**
Hanna, James Curtis *state official*

**Dunkirk**
Ewing, Richard Tucker *diplomat, educator, publisher*

**Ellicott City**
Galinsky, Deborah Jean *county official*

**Gaithersburg**
French, Judson Cull *government official*
Warshaw, Stanley Irving *government official*

**Grasonville**
Andrews, Archie Moulton *government official*

**Hyattsville**
Fisher, Gail Feimster *government official*

**Kensington**
Root, William Alden *export control consultant*
Rosenthal, Alan Sayre *former government official*

**Laurel**
Harris, Marion Hopkins *business educator, management consultant*
Sharpless, Joseph Benjamin *former county official*

**Potomac**
Newhouse, Alan Russell *retired federal government executive*
Shepard, William Seth *government official, diplomat, writer*

**Rockville**
Chiogioji, Melvin Hiroaki *government official*
Holston, Sharon Smith *government official*
Hoobler, James Ferguson *federal executive*
Hubbard, William Keith *government executive*
Krahnke, Betty Ann *county official*
Pagan Martinez, Juan *administrative corps officer*
Rechcigl, Miloslav, Jr. *government official*
Sacchet, Edward M. *foreign service officer*
Szabo, Daniel *government official*
Woodcock, Janet *federal official*

**Silver Spring**
Goott, Daniel *government official, consultant*
Schmitten, Rolland Arthur *government official*

**Westminster**
Cronin, Susan Gayle *county official*
Cueman, Edmund Robert *county official*

## MASSACHUSETTS

**Belchertown**
Russell, Joseph William *regional planner, emergency planner*

**Boston**
Allukian, Myron, Jr. *government administrator, public health educator, dental educator*
Cellucci, Argeo Paul *state official*
Connolly, Michael Joseph *state official*
Galvin, William Francis *secretary of state, lawyer*
Harshbarger, Scott *state attorney general*
†Linsky, Martin Alan *state official*
Malone, Joseph D. *state treasurer*
Markel, Robert Thomas *mayor*
Menino, Thomas M. *mayor*
Merrill, Stephen *former governor*
Weld, William Floyd *governor, lawyer*

**Cambridge**
Porter, Roger Blaine *government official, educator*

**Concord**
Rathore, Naeem Gul *retired United Nations official*

**Duxbury**
McAuliffe, Eugene Vincent *retired diplomat and business executive*

**Falmouth**
Brewer, William Dodd *former ambassador, political science educator emeritus*

**Lowell**
Natsios, Nicholas Andrew *retired foreign service officer*

**Lynn**
McManus, Patrick J. *mayor, lawyer, accountant*

**Marlborough**
Petrin, John Donald *town administrator*

**Sherborn**
Kennedy, Chester Ralph, Jr. *former state official, art director*

**Springfield**
Albano, Michael J. *mayor*

**Taunton**
Lopes, Maria Fernandina *commissioner*

**Waltham**
Fuchs, Lawrence Howard *government official, educator*

**Wellesley**
Parker, William H., III *federal official*

## MICHIGAN

**Ann Arbor**
Sheldon, Ingrid Kristina *mayor*

**Bloomfield Hills**
Fauver, John William *mayor, retired business executive*

**Detroit**
Archer, Dennis Wayne *mayor, lawyer*
Martin, Fred *retired municipal official*
McNamara, Edward Howard *county official, former mayor*
Worden, William Michael *city agency administrator, preservation consultant*

**Flint**
Stanley, Woodrow *mayor*

**Grand Rapids**
Logie, John Hoult *mayor, lawyer*

**Lansing**
Bell Wilson, Carlotta A. *state official, consultant*
Binsfeld, Connie Berube *state official*
Kelley, Frank Joseph *state attorney general*
Miller, Candice S. *state official*
Muchmore, Dennis C. *governmental affairs consultant*

**Mount Clemens**
Kolakowski, Diana Jean *county commissioner*

**Muskegon**
Roy, Paul Emile, Jr. *county official*

**Negaunee**
Friggens, Thomas George *state official, historian*

**Saint Clair Shores**
Weis, Lawrence Frederick *city official*

**Taylor**
Pitoniak, Gregory Edward *mayor*

**Tecumseh**
Sackett, Dianne Marie *city treasurer, accountant*

**Traverse City**
Rundio, Joan Peters (Jo Rundio) *public administrator*

**Trenton**
Smith, Linda Lou *city official*

**Warren**
Omelenchuk, Jeanne *mayor pro tem, owner*

**West Bloomfield**
Ho, Leo Chi Chien *Chinese government official*

## MINNESOTA

**Minneapolis**
Belton, Sharon Sayles *mayor*
Fellner, Michael Joseph *government executive, educator*
Fraser, Arvonne Skelton *former United Nations ambassador*
Hilary, Sandra Marie *county commissioner*
Joseph, Geri Mack (Geraldine Joseph) *former ambassador, educator*
Rietow, Dottie Miller *government and public relations consultant*

**Northfield**
Flaten, Robert Arnold *retired ambassador*
Levin, Burton *diplomat*

**Saint Paul**
Benson, Joanne E. *lieutenant governor of Minnesota*
Carlson, Arne Helge *governor*
Carruthers, Philip Charles *public official, lawyer*
Coleman, Norm *mayor*
Denn, James N. *commissioner*
Growe, Joan Anderson *state official*
Humphrey, Hubert Horatio, III *state attorney general*
McGrath, Michael Alan *state government officer*

## MISSISSIPPI

**Jackson**
Clark, Eric C. *state official*
Ditto, (John) Kane *mayor*
Fordice, Kirk (Daniel Kirkwood Fordice, Jr.) *governor, construction company executive, engineer*
Moore, Mike *state attorney general*
Musgrove, Ronnie *state official*
Winter, William Forrest *former governor, lawyer*

**Madison**
Hays, Donald Osborne *retired government official*

**Natchez**
Parker, Mary Evelyn *former state treasurer*

**Stennis Space Center**
Mc Call, Jerry Chalmers *government official*

## MISSOURI

**Columbia**
Lubensky, Earl Henry *diplomat, anthropologist*
Northup, Beverly A. Baker *principal chief*

**Jefferson City**
Carnahan, Mel *governor, lawyer*
Cook, Rebecca McDowell *state official*
Holden, Bob *state official*
Maxwell, Joe *state senator*
Nixon, Jeremiah W. (Jay Nixon) *state attorney general*
Stroup, Kala Mays *state higher education commissioner*
Wilks, R(alph) Kenneth, Jr. *state official*
Wilson, Roger Byron *lieutenant governor, school administrator*

**Kansas City**
Cleaver, Emanuel, II *mayor, minister*
Danner, Kathleen Frances Steele *federal official*
Davis, Richard Francis *city government official*
Edwards, Horace Burton *former state official, former oil pipeline company executive, management consultant*
Price, Charles H., II *former ambassador*

**Saint Louis**
Bosley, Freeman Robertson, Jr. *former mayor*
Pon-Salazar, Francisco Demetrio *diplomat, educator, deacon, counselor*
Wagner, Raymond Thomas, Jr. *lawyer*
Winter, William Earl *mayor, retired beverage company executive*

**Springfield**
Montgomery, Linda Stroupe *county official*

## MONTANA

**Billings**
Larsen, Richard Lee *former mayor and city manager, business, municipal and labor relations consultant, arbitrator*

**Helena**
Cooney, Mike *state official*
Ekanger, Laurie *state official*
Mazurek, Joseph P. *state attorney general, former state legislator*
Racicot, Marc F. *governor*

## NEBRASKA

**Lincoln**
Beermann, Allen J. *former state official*
Moore, Scott *state official*
Moul, Maxine Burnett *state official*
Nelson, E. Benjamin *governor*
Robak, Kim M. *state official*
Stenberg, Donald B. *state attorney general*

**North Bend**
Johnson, Lowell C. *state commissioner*

**North Platte**
Hawks, James Wade *county highway superintendent, county surveyor*

**Omaha**
Cunningham, Glenn Clarence *government official*
Daub, Hal *mayor of Omaha, former congressman*

**Wood River**
Bish, Milan David *former ambassador, consultant*

## NEVADA

**Carson City**
Del Papa, Frankie Sue *state attorney general*
Heller, Dean *state official*
Miller, Robert Joseph *governor, lawyer*
Seale, Robert L. *state treasurer*

**Las Vegas**
Hammargren, Lonnie *lieutenant governor*
Jones, Jan Laverty *mayor*
Regan, John Bernard (Jack Regan) *community relations executive, senator*

## NEW HAMPSHIRE

**Concord**
Gardner, William Michael *state official*
Howard, Jeffrey R. *state attorney general*
Twomey, Elizabeth Molloy *education commissioner*

**Grantham**
Feldman, Roger Bruce *government official*

**Manchester**
Wieczorek, Raymond J. *mayor*

## NEW JERSEY

**Eastampton**
Holloway, William Raymond, Jr. *state official*

**Egg Harbor Township**
Blee, Francis J. *municipal official*

**Irvington**
Paden, Harry *municipal official*

**Marmora**
Camp, Barbara Ann *municipal government official*

**Moonachie**
Malley, Raymond Charles *retired foreign service officer, industrial executive*

**Newark**
Huhn, Darlene Marie *county official, poet*
James, Sharpe *mayor*
Martin, James Hanley *deputy state attorney general*

**Princeton**
Matlock, Jack Foust, Jr. *diplomat*

**Sea Isle City**
Tull, Theresa Anne *retired ambassador*

**Trenton**
Clymer, Brian William *state official*
Fishman, Len *state commissioner*
Hooks, Lonna R. *state official*
Verniero, Peter *state attorney general*
Whitman, Christine Todd *governor*

**West Trenton**
D'Anna, Vincent P. *federal commissioner*

## NEW MEXICO

**Albuquerque**
Chavez, Martin Joseph *mayor, attorney*
Clark, Alan Barthwell *city administrator*

**Las Cruces**
Shepard, Earl Alden *retired government official*

**Placitas**
Reade, Lewis Pollock *retired diplomat, engineer*

**Santa Fe**
Bradley, Walter D. *lieutenant governor, real estate broker*
Gonzales, Stephanie *state official*
Johnson, Gary Earl *governor*
Udall, Thomas *state attorney general*

## NEW YORK

**Albany**
Berman, Carol *commissioner*
Bruno, Cathy Eileen *state official*
Clarey, Donald Alexander *government affairs consultant*
Herman, Robert S. *former state official, economist, educator*
McCaughey Ross, Elizabeth P. (Betsy McCaughey) *state official*
Pataki, George E. *governor*
Treadwell, Alexander F. *state official*
Vacco, Dennis C. *state attorney general*

**Baliston Lake**
Cotter, William Donald *state commissioner, former newspaper editor*

**Briarcliff Manor**
Bates, Barbara J. Neuner *retired municipal official*

**Buffalo**
Marinelli, Lynn M. *county official*
Masiello, Anthony M. (Tony Masiello) *mayor*
Rochwarger, Leonard *former ambassador*

**Chappaqua**
Laun, Louis Frederick *government official*

**Floral Park**
Corbett, William John *government and public relations consultant, lawyer*

**Hoosick Falls**
Morris, Margretta Elizabeth *government official*

**Levittown**
Cohen, Max *retired government official*

**Long Island City**
Trent, James Alfred *city official*

**Mineola**
Salten, David George *county agency administrator, academic administrator*

**Mount Vernon**
Ben-Dak, Joseph David *United Nations official, educator*

**New York**
†Annan, Kofi A. *diplomat*
Baker, James Estes *foreign service officer*
Barbera, Jose Eduardo *international trade diplomat*
Baumanis, Aivars *Latvian diplomat*
Brown, Carroll *diplomat, association executive*
Bushnell, John Alden *diplomat, economist*
Carlson, Mitchell Lans *international technical advisor*
Chaves, Jose Maria *diplomat, foundation administrator, lawyer, educator*
Clark, William, Jr. *political advisor*
Cohn, David Herc *retired foreign service officer*
Curley, Walter Joseph Patrick *diplomat, investment banker*
Dayson, Diane Harris *superintendent, park ranger*
Dunham, Donald Carl *diplomat*
Eisenstadt, G. Michael *diplomat, author, lecturer, research scholar*
Ertur, Omer Selcukhan *United Nations official, educator*
Fowler, Robert Ramsay *Canadian government official*
Gardner, Richard Newton *diplomat, lawyer, educator*
Giuliani, Rudolph W. *mayor, former lawyer*
Gnehm, Edward W., Jr. *ambassador*
†Green, Rosario *United Nations official*
Guillot, Cyril Etienne *international organization administrator*
Katz, Abraham *retired foreign service officer*
Koch, Edward I. *former mayor, lawyer*
Lehman, Orin *retired state official*
Levin, Herbert *diplomat, foundation executive*
Macais, Tello Manuel *diplomat*
Manz, Johannes Jakob *Swiss diplomat*
Murphy, Richard William *retired foreign service officer, Middle East specialist, consultant*
Ney, Edward N. *ambassador, advertising and public relations company executive*
Noble, Ronald Kenneth *government official, lawyer*
Okun, Herbert Stuart *ambassador, international executive*
Platt, Nicholas *Asian affairs specialist, retired ambassador*
Ranald, Ralph Arthur *goverment official*
Rao, Sethuramiah Lakshminarayana *demographer, United Nations official*
Reed, Joseph Verner, Jr. *diplomat*
Schweitzer, Melvin L. *commissioner, lawyer*
Segesváry, Victor Gyözö *retired diplomat*
Shafer, Jeffrey Richard *federal official, investment banker*
Sobol, Thomas *state education commissioner*
Speth, James Gustave *United Nations executive, lawyer*
Tomka, Peter *diplomat*
Townsend, Alair Ane *municipal official*
Weil, Leon Jerome *diplomat*
Werthein, Jorge R. *diplomat*

**Plainview**
Fulton, Richard *lecture bureau executive*

**Rochester**
Johnson, William A., Jr. *mayor*

**Staten Island**
Vu, Ha Manh *city official*

**Syosset**
Swenson, Eric David *town official, lawyer*

**Syracuse**
Sullivan, Michael Joachim *financial executive*

**Voorheesville**
Haydock, Michael Damean *building and code consultant, writer*

**Watertown**
Coe, Benjamin Plaisted *retired state official*

**Williamsville**
Danni, F. Robert *municipal official*

## NORTH CAROLINA

**Advance**
Legere, Laurence Joseph *government official*

**Apex**
Ellington, John David *retired state official*

**Chapel Hill**
Bolick, Ernest Bernard, Jr. *housing administrator*

**Charlotte**
Edwards, Harold Mills *government official, lawyer*
McCrory, Patrick *mayor*

**Greensboro**
Nussbaum, V. M., Jr. *former mayor*

**Jackson Springs**
Krebs, Max Vance *retired foreign service officer, educator*

**Raleigh**
Boyles, Harlan Edward *state official*
Cameron, John Lansing *retired government official*
Easley, Michael F. *state attorney general*
Hunt, James Baxter, Jr. *governor, lawyer*
†Marshall, Elaine F. *state official*
Payne, Harry Eugene, Jr. *state labor commissioner*
Wicker, Dennis A. *state official*

**Southern Pines**
Toon, Malcolm *former ambassador*

**Waynesville**
Matlock, Clifford Charles *retired foreign service officer*

**Wilmington**
Nichol, Henry Ferris *former government official, environment consultant*

**Wilson**
Wyatt, Edward Avery, V *city manager*

## NORTH DAKOTA

**Bismarck**
Gilmore, Kathi *state treasurer*
Heitkamp, Heidi *state attorney general*
Jaeger, Alvin A. (Al Jaeger) *secretary of state*
Myrdal, Rosemarie Caryle *state official, former state legislator*
Rice, Jon Richard *state health officer, physician*
Schafer, Edward T. *governor*

**Grand Forks**
Glassheim, Eliot Alan *grants officer*

**Minot**
Turner, Jane Ann *federal agent*

## OHIO

**Akron**
Schrader, Helen Maye *retired municipal worker*

**Alliance**
Woods, Rose Mary *former presidential assistant, consultant*

**Cincinnati**
Holscher, Robert F. *county official*
Qualls, Roxanne *mayor*

**Cleveland**
Chema, Thomas V. *government official, lawyer*
Robiner, Donald Maxwell *federal official, lawyer*
Smercina, Charles Joseph *mayor, accountant*
White, Michael Reed *mayor*

**Columbus**
Hollister, Nancy *state official*
Jackson, Sally A(nn) *state official*
Lashutka, Gregory S. *mayor, lawyer*
Montgomery, Betty Dee *state official, former state legislator*
Taft, Bob *state official*
Teater, Dorothy Seath *county official*
Voinovich, George V. *governor*

**Dayton**
Lashley, William Bartholomew *county official*

**Gahanna**
Sherman, Ruth Todd *government advisor, counselor, consultant*

**Indian Springs**
Earley, Kathleen Sanders *municipal official*

**Portsmouth**
Davis, Donald W. *government official*

**Toledo**
Finkbeiner, Carlton S. (Carty Finkbeiner) *mayor*

**University Heights**
Rothschild, Beryl Elaine *mayor*

**Wilmington**
Hackney, Howard Smith *retired county official*

## OKLAHOMA

**Ada**
Anoatubby, Bill *governor*

**Norman**
Corr, Edwin Gharst *ambassador*
Perkins, Edward J. *diplomat*

**Oklahoma City**
Anthony, Robert Holland *state official*
Cole, Tom *state official*
Edmondson, Drew *attorney general*
Edmondson, W. A. Drew *state attorney general*
Fallin, Mary Copeland *state official*
Keating, Francis Anthony, II *governor, lawyer*
Kennedy, John H., Jr. *former state official*
McKenzie, Clif Allen *Indian tribe official, accountant*
Norick, Ronald J. *mayor*
Rush, Richard P. *chamber of commerce executive*

**Park Hill**
Mankiller, Wilma Pearl *tribal leader*

**Tulsa**
Savage, M. Susan *mayor*

## OREGON

**Dayton**
Williams, Kenneth James *retired county official*

**Eugene**
Bascom, Ruth F. *former mayor*

**Florence**
Day, John Francis *city official, former savings and loan executive, former mayor*

**Lake Oswego**
Gawf, John Lee *foreign service officer*

**Portland**
Katz, Vera *mayor, former college administrator, state legislator*

**Salem**
Keisling, Phillip Andrew *state official*
Kitzhaber, John Albert *governor, physician, former state senator*
Kulongoski, Theodore R. *state supreme court justice*
†Myers, William Hardy *attorney general*
Tetzlaff, Karen Marie *state official*

## PENNSYLVANIA

**Allentown**
Smith, Robert G., Jr. *public official, retired hotel executive*

**Boiling Springs**
Clarke, Walter Sheldon *retired federal government official, educator*

**Bristol**
Hutton, Ann Hawkes *state official*

**Carlisle**
Russell, Theodore Emery *diplomat*

**Coatesville**
DiBona, Margaret Rose *state official*

**Donora**
Todd, Norma Jean Ross *retired government official*

**Erie**
Savocchio, Joyce A. *mayor*

**Gettysburg**
Hill, Hugh Kenneth *retired diplomat, former ambassador*

**Glen Riddle**
Dunion, Celeste Mogab *township official, consultant*

**Harrisburg**
Cauley, Alvin Paul *state government administrator*
Kaiser, Linda Susan *state commissioner, lawyer*
Kane, Yvette *state official, lawyer*
Lourie, Norman Victor *government official, social worker*
Newsome, William Roy, Jr. *state official*
Ridge, Thomas Joseph *governor, former congressman*
Schweiker, Mark S. *lieutenant governor*

**Ligonier**
Schmidt, Adolph William *retired ambassador*

**Lititz**
Koch, Bruce R. *diplomat*

**New Florence**
Olson, Clinton Louis *foreign service officer, former ambassador*

**Newtown**
Cohen, Myer *former international organization official*

**Newtown Square**
Strausz-Hupé, Robert *ambassador, author*

**Philadelphia**
Basora, Adrian A. *ambassador*
Corrigan, John Edward *government official*
Harris, Raymond Jesse *retired government official*
Knapton, David Robert *city planner*
Long, Mary Louise *retired government official*
Rendell, Edward Gene *mayor*
Uhler, Walter Charles *government official, writer, reviewer*

**Pittsburgh**
Donahoe, David Lawrence *state and city official*
Murphy, Thomas J., Jr. *mayor*

**State College**
Lamb, Robert Edward *diplomat*

**University Park**
Chang, Parris Hsu-cheng *government official, political science educator, writer*

**West Chester**
Dinniman, Andrew Eric *county commissioner, history educator, academic program director, international studies educator*

## RHODE ISLAND

**Newport**
Peters, Lauralee Milberg *diplomat*
Sundlun, Bruce *former governor*

**Pawtucket**
Metivier, Robert Emmett *mayor*

**Providence**
Almond, Lincoln *governor*
Langevin, James R. *state official*
Mayer, Nancy J. *state official*
Pine, Jeffrey Barry *state attorney general*
Sanderson, Edward French *state official*

## SOUTH CAROLINA

**Columbia**
Adams, Weston *diplomat, lawyer*
Beasley, David Muldrow *governor*
Condon, Charles Molony *state attorney general*
Miles, Jim *state official*
Morris, Earle Elias, Jr. *state official, business executive*
Peeler, Bob *state official*
Waites, Candy Yaghjian *former state official*
Walker, Richard Louis *former ambassador, educator, author*

**Greenville**
Workman, William Douglas, III *former mayor*

**Hilton Head Island**
West, John Carl *lawyer, former ambassador, former governor*

## SOUTH DAKOTA

**Pierre**
Barnett, Mark William *state attorney general*
Hazeltine, Joyce *state official*
Hillard, Carole *state official*
Janklow, William John *governor*
Moser, Jeffery Richard *state official*

**Rapid City**
Strand, Neal Arnold *retired county government official*

## TENNESSEE

**Columbia**
Chafin, William Vernon, Jr. *retired public housing manager*

**Memphis**
Herenton, Willie W. *mayor*

**Nashville**
Bredesen, Philip Norman *mayor*
Burson, Charles W. *state attorney general*
Darnell, Riley Carlisle *state government executive, lawyer*
Palmer-Hass, Lisa Michelle *state official*
Sundquist, Donald *governor, former congressman, sales corporation executive*
Wadley, Fredia Stovall *state commissioner*
†Walkup, John Knox *state official*
Wilder, John Shelton *state official, state legislator*

**Sparta**
Pearson, Margaret Donovan *former mayor*

**Springfield**
Nutting, Paul John *city official*

## TEXAS

**Austin**
Ashworth, Kenneth Hayden *state educational commissioner*
Buerschinger, Charles Albert *state commissioner*
Bush, George W. *governor*
Cooke, Carlton Lee, Jr. *mayor*
Franke, Wayne Thomas *government affairs director, lobbyist*
Garza, Antonio O. *state official*
Gates, Charles W., Sr. *city official*
Jeffords, Edward Alan *former state attorney general*
Johnson, Lady Bird (Mrs. Lyndon Baines Johnson) *widow of former President of United States*
Morales, Dan *state attorney general*
Moses, Mike *commissioner*
Richards, Ann Willis *former governor*
Todd, Bruce M. *mayor*

**Beaumont**
Gray, Enid Maurine *city official, director of libraries*
Lord, Evelyn Marlin *former mayor*

**Brenham**
Pipes, Paul Ray *county commissioner*

**Brooks AFB**
Monk, Richard Francis *air force officer, health care administrator*

**Corpus Christi**
Rhodes, Mary *mayor*

**Dallas**
Cheney, Dick (Richard Bruce Cheney) *former secretary of defense, former congressman*
Cottingham, Jennifer Jane *city official*
Kirk, Ron *mayor, lawyer*
Rubottom, Roy Richard, Jr. *retired diplomat and educator, consultant*

**El Paso**
Dyer, Travis Neal *defense consultant, retired army officer*
Francis, Larry *mayor*

**Fort Worth**
Barr, Kenneth L. *mayor*
Shosid, Joseph Lewis *government official*

**Houston**
Brown, Lee Patrick *federal official, law enforcement educator*
Bush, George Herbert Walker *former President of the United States*
Flack, Joe Fenley *county and municipal official, former insurance executive*
Fowler, Robert Asa *diplomat, consultant, business director*
†Lanier, Bob *mayor*
Lanier, Robert C. (Bob Lanier) *mayor*

**Irving**
Card, Hugh Cleveland, III *city official*

**La Feria**
Philip, Sunny Koipurathu *municipal official*

**Laredo**
Colón, Phyllis Janet *city official*
Jones, James Robert *ambassador, former congressman, lawyer*

**Lubbock**
Cooke, Alex "Ty", Jr. *mayor*
Stuart, Frank Adell *county official*

**Missouri City**
Mathur, Rupa Ajwani *former state official, risk management consultant*

**New Braunfels**
Krueger, Robert Charles *ambassador, former senator, former congressman*

**North Richland Hills**
Cunningham, Larry J. *city official*

**San Antonio**
Catto, Henry Edward *former government official, former ambassador*
Henderson, Connie Chorlton *city planner, artist and writer*
Thornton, William E. *mayor, oral surgeon*

## UTAH

**Bountiful**
Oveson, W(ilford) Val *state official, accountant*

**Ogden**
Evans, Keith Edward *government official, researcher*
Schow, Terry D. *state official*

**Salt Lake City**
Alter, Edward T. *state treasurer*
Corradini, Deedee *mayor*
Graham, Jan *state attorney general*
Hilbert, Robert Backus *county water utility administrator*
Leavitt, Michael Okerlund *governor, insurance executive*
†Racine, Doug *state official*
Walker, Olene S. *lieutenant governor*
White, Constance Burnham *state official*

**West Valley City**
Wright, Gearld Lewis *mayor, retired educator*

## VERMONT

**Barre**
Milne, James *secretary of state*

**Montpelier**
Dean, Howard *governor*
Klinck, Patricia Ewasco *state official*
†Sorrell, William H. *state official*

**Peacham**
Engle, James Bruce *ambassador*

**South Londonderry**
Spiers, Ronald Ian *diplomat*

## VIRGINIA

**Alexandria**
Costagliola, Francesco *former government official, macro operations analyst*
Ensslin, Robert Frank, Jr. *retired association executive and military officer*
Fitton, Harvey Nelson, Jr. *former government official, publishing consultant*
Hampton, E. Lynn *municipal finance administrator*
Havens, Harry Stewart *former federal assistant comptroller general, government consultant*
Helman, Gerald Bernard *government official*
Hilton, Robert Parker, Sr. *national security affairs consultant, retired naval officer*
Justesen, Benjamin Ray, II *foreign service officer*
Kennedy, Mary Virginia *diplomat*
Mathews, Mary Kathryn *retired government official*
Rose, Susan Porter *federal commissioner*
Scheupelein, Robert John *government official*

**Amelia Court House**
Wallace, John Robert *county administrator*

**Annandale**
Christianson, Geryld B. *government relations consultant*
Freitag, Robert Frederick *retired government official*
Rogers, Stephen Hitchcock *former ambassador*
Tontz, Robert L. *government official*

**Arlington**
Aggrey, Orison Rudolph *former ambassador, university administrator*
Allen, David *government official*
Banister, G. Huntington *federal official*
Bolster, Archie Milburn *retired foreign service officer*
Busby, Morris D. *ambassador*
Cargo, William Ira *ambassador, retired*
Conger, Clement Ellis *foreign service officer, curator*
Coronado, Gil *federal official*
Covington, James Edwin *government agency administrator, psychologist*
Edmondson, William Brockway *retired foreign service officer*
Everett, Warren Sylvester *consultant, former government official*
Gergen, David Richmond *federal official, magazine editor*
Hall, Douglas K. *conservation official*
Kaiser, Philip Mayer *diplomat*
Keel, Alton Gold, Jr. *ambassador*
Krys, Sheldon Jack *retired foreign service officer, career minister*
Kull, Joseph *government administrator*
Pyatt, Everett Arno *government official*
†Schaffer, Teresita Currie *federal official*
Smalley, Robert Manning *government official*
Taggart, G. Bruce *government program executive*
Umminger, Bruce Lynn *government official, scientist, educator*

**Burke**
Pfister, Cloyd Harry *consultant, former career officer*

**Chesapeake**
Ward, William E. *mayor*

**Dumfries**
Wolle, William Down *foreign service officer*

**Fairfax**
Beckler, David Zander *government official, science administrator*

**Falls Church**
Block, John Rusling *former secretary of agriculture*
Moscato, Anthony Charles *federal official*
Nach, James Peter *foreign service officer*

**Fort Belvoir**
Diercks, Frederick Otto *government official*

**Great Falls**
Savage, Michael Thomas *federal executive*
Zimmermann, Warren *former foreign service officer*

**Haymarket**
Doolittle, Warren T. *retired federal official*

**Herndon**
Vogel, Frederick John *diplomat*

**King George**
Newhall, David, III *former federal government official*
Storke, Dwight Clifton, Jr. *government official*

**Ladysmith**
Provencher, Roger Arthur *international consultant*

**Leesburg**
Brown, William Holmes *government official, parliamentary consultant*

**Lexington**
Cash, Frank Errette, Jr. *foreign service officer*

**Lynchburg**
Dodge, Lynn Louise *municipal official, librarian*
Stephens, Bart Nelson *former foreign service officer*

**Markham**
Katzen, Jay Kenneth *consultant, former foreign service officer*

**Mc Lean**
Cahill, Harry Amory *diplomat, educator*
Cannon, Mark Wilcox *government official, business executive*
Frostic, Frederick Lee *government official*
Healy, Theresa Ann *former ambassador*
McCormack, Richard Thomas Fox *government official, former ambassador*
Smith, Russell Jack *former intelligence official*
Sollenberger, Howard Edwin *retired government official*
Trout, Maurice Elmore *foreign service officer*

**Morattico**
Dawson, Carol Gene *former commissioner, writer, consultant*

**Norfolk**
Andrews, Mason Cooke *mayor, obstetrician, gynecologist, educator*
Bullington, James R. *ambassador*
Cason, James Caldwell *diplomat*

**Orange**
Cortada, James N. *mayor, former diplomat*

**Reston**
Sherman, William Courtney *foreign service officer*

**Richmond**
Allen, George Felix *governor*
Beamer, Betsy Davis *state official*
Beyer, Donald Sternoff, Jr. *state official*
Chavis, Larry Eugene *mayor*
Gilmore, James Stuart, III *state attorney general*
Henderson, Bernard Levie, Jr. *former state official, funeral service executive*
Holcomb, Richard D. *state commissioner*
Sgro, Beverly Huston *state official, educator*

**Springfield**
Stottlemyer, David Lee *government official*

**Suffolk**
Hope, James Franklin *mayor, civil engineer, consultant*

**Susan**
Ambach, Dwight Russell *retired foreign service officer*

**Vienna**
DeWitt, Charles Barbour *federal government official*
Palmer, Stephen Eugene, Jr. *government official*
Sanbrailo, John A. *mission director*

**Virginia Beach**
Oberndorf, Meyera E. *mayor*

**Williamsburg**
Mouser, Grant Earl, III *retired foreign service officer*

**WASHINGTON**

**Bainbridge Island**
Huntley, James Robert *government official, international affairs scholar and consultant*

**Dayton**
McFarland, Jon Weldon *retired county commissioner*

**Edmonds**
Thyden, James Eskel *diplomat, educator*

**Lacey**
Felger, Ralph William *educator, retired military officer*

**Olympia**
†Locke, Gary *governor*
Munro, Ralph Davies *state government official*
O'Brien, Robert S. *state official*
†Owen, Bradley Scott *lieutenant governor*

**Pullman**
Halvorson, Alfred Rubin *retired mayor, consultant, education educator*

**Seattle**
Lowry, Mike *former governor, former congressman*
Rice, Norman B. *mayor*
Skidmore, Donald Earl, Jr. *government official*
Voget, Jane J. *city official, lawyer*

**Sequim**
McMahon, Terrence John *retired foriegn service officer*

**Sumas**
Hemry, Larry Harold *former federal agency official, writer*

**Vancouver**
Ogden, Daniel Miller, Jr. *government official, educator*

**Yakima**
Sveinsson, Johannes *former city and county government official*

**WEST VIRGINIA**

**Charleston**
Clark, Hanley C. *state insurance commissioner*
Hechler, Ken *state official, former congressman, political science educator, author*
Mc Graw, Darrell Vivian, Jr. *state attorney general*
Melton, G. Kemp *mayor*
Tomblin, Earl Ray *state official*
Underwood, Cecil H. *governor, company executive*

**WISCONSIN**

**Juneau**
Carpenter, David Erwin *county planner*

**Madison**
Doyle, James E(dward) *state attorney general*
Earl, Anthony Scully *former governor of Wisconsin, lawyer*
La Follette, Douglas J. *secretary of state*
McCallum, James Scott *lieutenant governor, former state senator*
McCallum, Scott *state official*
Thompson, Tommy George *governor*
Tracy, Alan Thomas *government official*
Voight, Jack C. *state official*
Wynn, Robert Louis, II *state government official, business owner*
Zobel, Robert Leonard *state government official*

**Milwaukee**
Norquist, John Olof *mayor*
Schmitz, Francis David *lawyer*

**WYOMING**

**Cheyenne**
Geringer, James E. *governor*
Ohman, Diana J. *state official, former school system administrator*
Smith, Stanford Sidney *state treasurer*
Thomson, Thyra Godfrey *former state official*
Wittler, Shirley Joyce *former state official, state commissioner*

**Laramie**
Dickman, Francois Moussiegt *former foreign service officer, educator*

**TERRITORIES OF THE UNITED STATES**

**AMERICAN SAMOA**

**Pago Pago**
Lutali, A. P. *governor of American Samoa*
Sunia, Tausese *governor*

**FEDERATED STATES OF MICRONESIA**

**Pohnpei**
Eu, March Fong *ambassador, former California state official*

**GUAM**

**Agana**
Bordallo, Madeleine Mary (Mrs. Ricardo Jerome Bordallo) *lieutenant governor of Guam, wife of former governor of Guam*
Gutierrez, Carl T. C. *Guamanian government official*

**PUERTO RICO**

**San Juan**
Corrada del Río, Baltasar *state official, lawyer, former mayor, former congressman*
Fajardo, Victor *state commissioner*

**REPUBLIC OF MARSHALL ISLAND**

**Majuro**
Plaisted, Joan M. *diplomat*
Zackhras, Ruben *Marshallese government official*

**VIRGIN ISLANDS**

**Charlotte Amalie**
Aubain, Joseph F. *municipal official*
Mapp, Kenneth E. *lieutenant governor of Virgin Islands*

**Saint Thomas**
Schneider, Roy *United States Virgin Islands government official*

**MILITARY ADDRESSES OF THE UNITED STATES**

**ATLANTIC**

**APO**
Alexander, Leslie M. *ambassador*
Baltimore, Richard Lewis, III *foreign service officer*
Bracete, Juan Manuel *diplomat, lawyer*
Bruno, George C. *ambassador*
Carner, George *foreign service executive, economic strategist*
Creagan, James Francis *diplomat*
de Vos, Peter Jon *ambassador*
Frechette, Myles Robert Rene *ambassador*
Gutierrez, Lino *diplomat*
Jett, Dennis Coleman *foreign service officer*
Kamman, Curtis Warren *ambassador*
Maisto, John F. *ambassador*
Service, Robert E. *ambassador*

**FPO**
Hyde, Jeanette W. *ambassador*

**EUROPE**

**APO**
Aaron, David L. *diplomat*
Archard, Douglas Bruce *foreign service officer*
Bindenagel, James Dale *diplomat*
Blinken, Alan John *ambassador*
Carney, Timothy Michael *diplomat*
Connell, Mary Ellen *diplomat*
Cook, Frances D. *diplomat*
Crocker, Ryan C. *ambassador*
Cunningham, James Blair *foreign service officer*
Dornbush, K. Terry *ambassador*
Eastham, Alan Walter, Jr. *foreign service officer, lawyer*
Elson, Edward Elliott *diplomat*
Evans, John Marshall *diplomat*
Flynn, Raymond Leo *ambassador to the Holy See, former mayor*
†Fowler, Wyche, Jr. *ambassador*
Frawley-Bagley, Elizabeth *ambassador*
Ginsberg, Marc C. *ambassador*
Harriman, Pamela Digby Churchill *diplomat, philanthropist*
Indyk, Martin S. *ambassador*
Kunin, Madeleine May *ambassador to Switzerland, former governor*
Loftus, Thomas Adolph *ambassador*
Niles, Thomas Michael Tolliver *ambassador*
Simpson, Daniel H. *ambassador*
Tompkins, Tain Pendleton *foreign service official*
Walker, Edward S., Jr. *diplomat*
Westley, John Richard *foreign service officer*
Wilson, Joseph Charles, IV *ambassador*
Wood, Roberta Susan *foreign service officer*

**FPO**
Ransom, David Michael *diplomat*

**PACIFIC**

**APO**
Harvey, Barbara Sillars *foreign service officer*
†Holmes, Genta Hawkins *diplomat*
Itoh, William H. *ambassador*
McGuire, Roger Alan *foreign service officer*
Mondale, Joan Adams *wife of former vice president of United States*

**FPO**
Beeman, Josiah Horton *diplomat*
Burghardt, Raymond Francis, Jr. *foreign service officer*
Chorba, Timothy A. *ambassador to Singapore*
Sasser, James Ralph (Jim Sasser) *ambassador, former senator*

**CANADA**

**ALBERTA**

**Calgary**
†Clark, Charles Joseph (Joe Clark) *Canadian government official, former prime minister*
†Duerr, Alfred *mayor*

**Edmonton**
†Cardinal, Melvin Percy Joseph *government official*
Day, Stockwell Burt *government official*
†Ekelund, Michael William *government official*
Forsyth, Joseph *Canadian government official*
†McCrank, Michael Neil *government official*
Reimer, Jan Rhea *former mayor*
†Ward Neville, Johanna (Anne) *government official*

**BRITISH COLUMBIA**

**Kaleden**
Siddon, Thomas Edward *Canadian government official, environmental consultant*

**Richmond**
Halsey-Brandt, Greg *mayor*

**Vancouver**
†Duncan, Mark *government official*

**Victoria**
Gardom, Garde Basil *lieutenant governor of British Columbia*
†Maloney, Maureen *government official*
†McIntosh, Gordon Andrew *local government official*

**MANITOBA**

**Headingley**
Gerrard, Jon *Canadian government official*

**Winnipeg**
Curtis, Charles Edward *Canadian government official*
Downey, James Erwin *government official*
Dumont, W. Yvon *provincial official*
Filmon, Gary Albert *Canadian provincial premier, civil engineer*
†Forand, Liseanne *government official*
†Praznik, Darren Thomas *provincial legislator*
Thompson, Susan A. *mayor*

**NEW BRUNSWICK**

**Fredericton**
†LeBreton, Paul M. *government official*
†Loughrey, Carol Elaine Ashfield *government official*
McCain, Margaret *province official*

**NEWFOUNDLAND**

**Saint John's**
†Gibbons, Rex Vincent *government official*
†Matthews, Lloyd *government official*
Murphy, John Joseph *city official, retail executive*
Russell, Frederick William *Canadian provincial official*
†Wells, Clyde Kirby *Canadian provincial government official*

**NOVA SCOTIA**

**Dartmouth**
†Norrie, Eleanor E. *government official*

**Halifax**
Cosman, Francene Jen *government official*
Kinley, John James *government official*
Savage, John Patrick *provincial official*

**Waverley**
†Grady, Wayne J. *government official*

**ONTARIO**

**Brampton**
Robertson, Peter Barrie *mayor*

**Etobicoke**
Holyday, Douglas Charles *mayor*

**London**
Haskett, Dianne Louise *mayor, lawyer*

**Maberly**
Kennett, William Alexander *retired Canadian government official, consultant*

**Manotick**
Prince, Alan Theodore *former government official, engineering consultant*

**Mississauga**
†McCallion, Hazel *mayor*

**Nepean**
Stanford, Joseph Stephen *diplomat, lawyer, educator*

**Nobleton**
Embleton, Tony Frederick Wallace *retired Canadian government official*

**North York**
Lastman, Melvin D. *mayor*

**Ottawa**
Anderson, David *Canadian government official*
Armstrong, Henry Conner *former Canadian government official, consultant*
Axworthy, Chris *Canadian government official*
Axworthy, Lloyd *Canadian government official*
Beehan, Cathy *government official, lawyer*
Bélisle, Paul *Canadian government official*
†Bennett, Ian Edward *government official*
†Cameron, Christina *government official*
Campbell, Avril Kim *Canadian legislator, justice official*
Chan, Raymond *parliamentarian, secretary of state*
Charest, Jean J. *Canadian government official, legislator*
Chrétien, (Joseph Jacques) Jean *prime minister of Canada, lawyer*
Collenette, David M. *Canadian government official*
Copps, Sheila *Canadian government official*
†Dawson, Mary E. *government official*
Desautels, L. Denis *Canadian government official, auditor*
Dingwall, David C. *Canadian government official*
Dodge, David A. *Canadian government official*
Eggleton, Arthur C. *Canadian government official, member of Parliament*
Fairbairn, Joyce *Canadian government official*
Finestone, Sheila *Canadian government official*
†Finn, Gerard *federal government official*
Giroux, Robert-Jean-Yvon *retired Canadian government official*
Gold, Lorne W. *Canadian government official*
Goldbloom, Victor Charles *commissioner, pediatrician*
Goodale, Ralph E. *Canadian government minister*
Gray, Herbert Eser *Canadian government official*
Halstead, John G. H. *educator, diplomat, consultant*
Harder, V. Peter *government official*
†Harper, Stephen J. *government official, economist*
Hays, Dan *federal officer*
†Hubbard, M. Ruth *government official*
Kingsley, Jean-Pierre *government official*
Kirkwood, David Herbert Waddington *Canadian government official*
†Kohler, L. Richard *government official*

LaRocque, Judith Anne *federal official*
LeBlanc, Roméo *Canadian government official*
MacDonald, Flora Isabel *Canadian government official*
Manley, John *Canadian government official*
†Martin, James Kay *government official*
Martin, Paul *Canadian government official*
Massé, Marcel *Canadian government minister*
McLellan, A. Anne *Canadian government official*
†McLure, John Douglas *government official*
Mifflin, Fred J. *Canadian government official*
Molgat, Gildas L. *Canadian government official*
†Nicholson-O'Brien, Dawn *government official*
Peters, Douglas Dennison *Canadian government official, member of Parliament*
Robertson, Robert Gordon *retired Canadian government official*
†Robichaud, Fernand *Canadian government official*
Robillard, Lucienne *federal official*
Rock, Allan Michael *Canadian government official*
Roland, Anne *registrar Supreme Court of Canada*
†St-Pierre, Jean-Claude *federal government official*
Shelly, Christine Deborah *foreign service officer*
†Silverman, Ozzie *Canadian government official*
Smith, Wilfred Irvin *former Canadian government official*
Stewart, Christine Susan *Canadian government official*
Tait, John Charles *Canadian government official*
Withers, Ramsey Muir *government consultant, former government official*
Yalden, Maxwell Freeman *Canadian diplomat*
Yeomans, Donald Ralph *Canadian government official, consultant*
Young, Douglas *Canadian government official*

**Scarborough**
Faubert, Frank *mayor*

**Toronto**
Evans, Gregory Thomas *commissioner, retired justice*
Gotlieb, Allan E. *former ambassador*
†Hall, Barbara *mayor*
Jackman, Henry Newton Rowell *former Canadian provincial official*
Redway, Alan Arthur Sydney *Canadian legislator, lawyer*
Taman, Larry *Canadian provincial official*
Todres, Elaine Meller *foundation administrator*
Turner, John Napier *former prime minister of Canada, legislator*
Wilson, Jim *Canadian provincial official*

**PRINCE EDWARD ISLAND**

**Charlottetown**
†Hicken, Barry W. *environmental legislator*
MacAulay, Lawrence A. *Canadian government official*

**QUEBEC**

**Chelsea**
Warren, Jack Hamilton *former diplomat and trade policy advisor*

**Hull**
Blondin-Andrew, Ethel *Canadian government official*
Gagliano, Alfonso *Canadian government official*
Gruchy, Charles George *Canadian government official*
Irwin, Ronald A. *Canadian government official*
Marchi, Sergio Sisto *Canadian government official*
Marleau, Diane *Canadian government official*

**Montreal**
Bourque, Pierre *mayor*
†Crête, Michel *government agency administrator*
†Giroux, Jean *government official*
Mulroney, (Martin) Brian *former prime minister of Canada*

**Nemaska**
Coon Come, Matthew *Native American tribal chief*

**Quebec**
Bouchard, Lucien *Canadian government official*
†O'Bready, Jacques *city administrator*
Parizeau, Jacques *former Canadian government official*
†Pronovost, Jean *government official*
†Rochon, Jean *government official*

**Trois Rivieres**
†Landry, Roger *government official*

**SASKATCHEWAN**

**Regina**
†Atkinson, Patricia *minister of education*
†Kuziak, Myron A. *government official, lawyer*
Penikett, Antony David John *Canadian government official*
Romanow, Roy John *provincial government official, barrister, solicitor*
Shillington, Edward Blain *government official*
Wiebe, J. E. N. *province official*
†Zukowsky, Ronald James *environmental regulator*

**Saskatoon**
Blakeney, Allan Emrys *Canadian government official, lawyer*

**MEXICO**

**Mexico City**
Aspe, Pedro *former Mexican government official*
Blanco, Herminio *Mexican government official*
Cervantes Aguirre, Enrique *Mexican government official*
de la Fuente Ramirez, Juan Ramon *Mexican government official*
Hernandez, Silvia *Mexican government official*
Limón Rojas, Miguel *Mexican government official*
Rojas Gutierrez, Carlos *Mexican government official*

Ruiz Sacristán, Carlos *Mexican government official*
Warman, Arturo Gryj *Mexican government official*
Zedillo Ponce de León, Ernesto *president of Mexico*

**ARMENIA**

**Yerevan**
Gilmore, Harry J. *ambassador*

**AUSTRIA**

**Vienna**
†de Maria y Campos, Mauricio *United Nations official*
Hunt, Swanee G. *ambassador*

**BAHAMAS**

**Nassau**
Cates, Nelia Barletta de *diplomat*
Ford, John Seabury *diplomat*

**BELGIUM**

**Brussels**
Hunter, Robert Edwards *ambassador, scholar*
Pendleton, Mary Catherine *foreign service officer*
†Solana Madariaga, Javier *Spanish government official*

**CAPE VERDE**

**Praia**
McNamara, Francis T. *ambassador*

**CHILE**

**Santiago**
Wilkey, Malcolm Richard *retired ambassador, former federal judge*

**CROATIA**

**Zagreb**
Galbraith, Peter W. *ambassador*

**EGYPT**

**Cairo**
Boutros-Ghali, Boutros *former United Nations official*

**ENGLAND**

**London**
Crowe, William James, Jr. *diplomat, think tank executive*
Elizabeth, Her Majesty II (Elizabeth Alexandra Mary) *Queen of United Kingdom of Great Britain and Northern Ireland, and her other Realms and Territories, head of the Commonwealth, defender of the faith*
MacLaren, Roy *Canadian government official, publisher*
Marsden, William *government official*
Orr, Bobette Kay *diplomat*
Streator, Edward *diplomat*

**ETHIOPIA**

**Addis Ababa**
Hicks, Irvin *ambassador*

**FRANCE**

**Aveyron**
Roudybush, Franklin *diplomat, educator*

**Beduer**
Ezelle, Robert Eugene *diplomat*

**Paris**
Dean, John Gunther *diplomat*
Ferriter, John Pierce *diplomat*
Michel, James H. *ambassador, lawyer*
Myerson, Jacob Myer *former foreign service officer*
Roussel, Lee Dennison *economist*

**Sannois**
Cornell, Robert Arthur *retired international government official, consultant*

**GERMANY**

**Berlin**
Anderson, David *former ambassador*

**HONG KONG**

**Hong Kong**
Mueller, Richard Walter *foreign service officer*

**INDONESIA**

**Jakarta**
Roy, J(ames) Stapleton *ambassador*

**IRELAND**

**Dublin**
Smith, Jean Kennedy *ambassador*

**ITALY**

**Rome**
Bertini, Catherine Ann *United Nations world food program administrator*
Cassiers, Juan *diplomat*

**JAMAICA**

**Kingston**
Cooper, Jerome Gary *ambassador*

**MALAYSIA**

**Kuala Lumpur**
Malott, John Raymond *foreign service officer*

**MOROCCO**

**Rabat**
Sundquist, Maria Alexandra *diplomat*

**SCOTLAND**

**Edinburgh**
Singer, Norman A. *government official, former diplomat*

**SINGAPORE**

**Singapore**
Skodon, Emil Mark *diplomat*

**SOUTH AFRICA**

**Arcadia**
Berry, Ann Roper *diplomat*

**SRI LANKA**

**Colombo**
Smyth, Richard Henry *foreign service officer*

**SWEDEN**

**Stockholm**
Siebert, Thomas L. *ambassador*

**SWITZERLAND**

**Geneva**
Bogsch, Arpad *diplomat*
Brown, Kent Newville *ambassador*
Ledogar, Stephen J. *diplomat*

**UKRAINE**

**Kiev**
Miller, William Green *ambassador*

**VIETNAM**

**Hanoi**
Peterson, Douglas Pete (Pete Peterson) *ambassador, former congressman*
†Peterson, Pete *ambassador, former congressman*

**WESTERN SAMOA**

**Apia**
†Alesana, Tofilau Eti *Samoan prime minister*

**ZAIRE**

**Kinshasa**
†Seko, Mobutu Sese *President Zaire*

**ADDRESS UNPUBLISHED**

Adams, Edwin Melville *former foreign service officer, actor, author, lecturer*
Adams, James Blackburn *former state government official, former federal government official, lawyer*
Adams, Michael John *air force non-commissioned officer*
Allegra, Francis *federal government official*
Anderson, Glen Robert *federal official*
Anderson, John Rogers *Canadian diplomat*
Anderson, Ned, Sr. *Apache tribal chairman*
Anderson, Nils, Jr. *former government official, retired business executive, industrial historian*
Anderson, Ollie Palmer, Jr. *former diplomat*
Armstrong, Anne Legendre (Mrs. Tobin Armstrong) *former ambassador, corporate director*
Barkley, Richard Clark *ambassador*
Barreda, William Eloy *retired government official*
Beck, John Ryder *ambassador*
Bentsen, Lloyd *former government official, former senator*

Berlincourt, Marjorie Alkins *government official, retired*
Betti, John Anso *federal official, former automobile manufacturing company executive*
Beyer, Gordon Robert *foreign service officer*
Blood, Archer Kent *retired foreign service officer*
Boyatt, Thomas David *former ambassador*
Brawn, Linda Curtis *political consultant, former state legislator*
Brown, Kay (Mary Kathryn Brown) *former state official, talk radio host*
Buchanan, John MacLennan *Canadian provincial official*
Burchman, Leonard *government official*
Cannon, Isabella Walton *mayor*
†Carollo, Joe *mayor*
Carter, Rosalynn Smith *wife of former President of United States*
Cary, Anne O. *diplomat*
†Cohen, Roberta Jane *government executive*
Condayan, John *retired foreign service officer, consultant*
Coop, Frederick Robert *retired city manager*
Coppie, Comer Swift *state official*
Corkery, James Caldwell *retired Canadian government executive, mechanical engineer*
Cougill, Roscoe McDaniel *mayor, retired air force officer*
Dawson, Horace Greeley, Jr. *former diplomat, government official*
†Dona, Christina *Canadian government official*
Donohue, George L. *government official, mechanical engineer*
Drennen, William Miller, Jr. *cultural administrator, film executive, producer, director, mineral resource executive*
Dunford, David Joseph *foreign service officer, ambassador*
Dyrstad, Joanell M. *former lieutenant governor, consultant*
Egan, Wesley William, Jr. *ambassador*
Emmons, Robert Duncan *diplomat*
Engler, John *governor*
Evatt, Parker *former state commissioner, former state legislator*
Ewing, Raymond Charles *retired ambassador*
Ford, Ford Barney *retired government official*
Fraser, Donald MacKay *former mayor, former congressman, educator*
Gallucci, Robert Louis *diplomat, federal government official*
Gregoire, Christine O. *state attorney general*
Grossman, Marc *ambassador*
Hall, Keith R. *federal official*
†Hammergren, Lonnie *state official*
Hanmer, Stephen Read, Jr. *government executive*
Harcourt, Michael Franklin *retired premier of Province of British Columbia, lawyer, educator*
Hecht, Chic *ambassador, former senator*
Hester, Nancy Elizabeth *county government official*
Hilsman, Roger *government educator*
Hockeimer, Henry Eric *business executive*
Holiday, Edith Elizabeth *former presidential adviser, cabinet secretary*
Howard, Robert Elliott *former federal official, consultant, educator*
Isom, Harriet Winsar *ambassador*
Jacobson, Herbert Laurence *diplomat*
Jarvis, William Esmond *retired Canadian government official*
Jones, Donna Marie *public administrator, lawyer, consultant*
Joseph, Shirley Troyan *retired executive*
Kendig, William L. *retired government official, accountant*
Kendrick, Joseph Trotwood *former foreign service officer, writer, consultant*
Kernan, Barbara Desind *senior government executive*
†Kernan, Joseph E. *state official*
King, James B. *federal official*
Kissinger, Henry Alfred *former secretary of state, international consulting company executive*
Korn, Peter A. *city manager, public administration educator*
Lader, Philip *government official, business executive*
Lafontant-Mankarious, Jewel (Mrs. Naguib S. Mankarious) *diplomat, lawyer*
Lee, Chester Maurice *government official*
Lee, James Matthew *Canadian politician*
Lenahan, Walter Clair *retired foreign service officer*
Levitsky, Melvyn *ambassador*
Levy, Leah Garrigan *federal official*
Lindsay, John Vliet *former mayor, former congressman, author, lawyer*
Lorenzo Franco, José Ramón *Mexican government official*
Luche, Thomas Clifford *foreign service officer*
Lyng, Richard Edmund *former secretary of agriculture*
MacLean, John Angus *former premier of Prince Edward Island*
Maestrone, Frank Eusebio *diplomat*
Maradona, Remigio Martin *international diplomat*
†Martz, Judy *state official*
Marvin, William Glenn, Jr. *former foreign service officer*
Mattingly, Mack F. *former ambassador, former senator, entrepreneur*
Mazankowski, Donald Frank *Canadian government official*
McBee, Robert Levi *retired federal government official, writer, consultant*
McClinton, James Leroy *city administrator*
McLean, Walter Franklin *international consultant, pastor, former Canadian government official*
Mendonsa, Arthur Adonel *retired city official*
Millane, Lynn *town official*
Miller, Judith *federal official*
Mills, Kevin Lee *government executive*
Mohler, Brian Jeffery *diplomat*
Mondale, Walter Frederick *former vice president of United States, diplomat, lawyer*
Monfils-Clark, Maud Ellen *analyst*
Moore, Powell Allen *former government official, consultant*
Morris, Robert G(emmill) *retired foreign service officer*
Myatt, Clifford E. *federal official*
Neff, Francine Irving (Mrs. Edward John Neff) *former federal government official*
Nelson, Harvey Frans, Jr. *retired foreign service officer*
Nelson, Norman Daniel *government official*
Nielsen, Glade Benjamin *mayor, former state senator*
Nightingale, Retha Lee *federal agency administrator*
Obermann, Richard Michael *governmental technology and policy analyst*
Ogg, George Wesley *retired foreign service officer*

Ortiz, Francis Vincent, Jr. *retired ambassador*
Page, Marcus William *federal official*
Papet, Louis M. *retired federal official, civil engineer*
Petrequin, Harry Joseph, Jr. *foreign service officer*
Pierce, Samuel Riley, Jr. *government official, lawyer*
Pridmore, Roy Davis *government official*
Pritts, Kim Derek *state conservation officer, writer*
†Pryor, Bill *attorney general*
Rattley, Jessie Menifield *former mayor, educator*
Raynolds, Harold, Jr. *retired state education commissioner*
Reich, Robert Bernard *federal official, political economics educator*
Reinhardt, John Edward *former international affairs specialist*
Rey, Nicholas Andrew *ambassador*
Reynolds, Carl Christiansen *government official*
Rice, Richard Campbell *retired state official, retired army officer*
Rich, David Barry *city official, auditor, accountant, entertainer*
Rickert, Jonathan Bradley *foreign service officer*
Roberts, Thomas Morgan *former government official*
†Rockefeller, Winthrop P. *state official*
Rosenthal, Helen Nagelberg *county official, advocate*
Rosenthal, James D. *former federal official, former ambassador, government and foundation executive*
Rosselló, Pedro *governor of Puerto Rico*
Rothing, Frank John *government official*
Rudin, Anne Noto *former mayor, nurse*
Ryan, George H. *state government official, pharmacist*
Sabatini, Nelson John *government official*
†Savage, Susan, 1953 *mayor*
Scanlan, John Douglas *foreign service officer, former ambassador*
Schoettler, Gail Sinton *state official*
Schwartz, Carol Levitt *government official*
Sentenne, Justine *corporate ombudsman consultant*
†Sherrer, Gary *state official*
Simons, Thomas W., Jr. *ambassador*
Smith, Robert Powell *former ambassador, former foundation executive*
Snider, L. Britt *government executive*
Sotirhos, Michael *ambassador*
Soule, Sallie Thompson *retired state official*
Steinberg, Melvin Allen *lieutenant governor, lawyer*
Taylor, Barbara Jo Anne Harris *government official, librarian, educator, civic and political worker*
Thomas, Charles Howard, II *federal official*
Thomas, Richard Emery *federal government official*
Tienken, Arthur T. *retired foreign service officer*
†Valaskakis, Kimon P. *ambassador, economics educator*
Walker, Lannon *foreign service officer*
Watkins, James David *government official, naval officer*
Whitney, Jane *foreign service officer*
Wolf, Dale Edward *state official*
Wright, Sir (John) Oliver *retired diplomat*
Zischke, Douglas Arthur *foreign service officer*

## GOVERNMENT: LEGISLATIVE ADMINISTRATION

### UNITED STATES

#### ALABAMA

**Mobile**
Callahan, Sonny (H.L. Callahan) *congressman*
Edwards, Jack *former congressman, lawyer*

**Montgomery**
Dixon, Larry Dean *state legislator*
Langford, Charles Douglas *state legislator, lawyer*

**Tuscumbia**
Heflin, Howell Thomas *former senator, lawyer, former state supreme court chief justice*

#### ALASKA

**Anchorage**
Rieger, Steven Arthur *state legislator, business consultant*

**Eagle River**
Cotten, Samuel Richard *former state legislator, fisherman*

**Juneau**
Hensley, William Lynn (Willie Hensley) *state senator, corporate executive*
Kelly, Timothy Donahue *state senator*
Pearce, Drue *state legislator*

**North Pole**
James, Jeannette Adeline *state legislator, accountant*

#### ARIZONA

**Glendale**
Brewer, Janice Kay *state legislator, property and investment firm executive*

**Phoenix**
Preble, Lou-Ann M. *state legislator*

**Scottsdale**
Rudd, Eldon *retired congressman, political consultant*

**Tucson**
Bartlett, David Carson *state legislator*

**Waddell**
Turner, Warren Austin *state legislator*

#### ARKANSAS

**Dumas**
Schexnayder, Charlotte Tillar *state legislator*

**Fayetteville**
Malone, David Roy *state senator, university administrator*

**Fort Smith**
Miles, Travis Anthony *state senator*
Pollan, Carolyn Joan *state legislator, job research administrator*

**Greenwood**
Walters, Bill *state senator, lawyer*

**Hughes**
Lambert Lincoln, Blanche M. *former congresswoman*

**Little Rock**
Thornton, Ray *former congressman*

**Malvern**
Hopkins, George *senator*

**Searcy**
Beebe, Mike *state senator, lawyer*

**Sherwood**
Wood, Marion Douglas *state legislator, lawyer*

#### CALIFORNIA

**Danville**
Baker, William P. (Bill Baker) *former congressman*

**Garden Grove**
Dornan, Robert Kenneth *former congressman*

**Glendale**
Moorhead, Carlos J. *former congressman*
Russell, Newton Requa *retired state senator*

**Inglewood**
Dymally, Mervyn Malcolm *retired congressman, international business executive*

**Los Altos**
Cranston, Alan *former senator*

**Newport Beach**
Cox, Christopher *congressman*

**Sacramento**
Alpert, Deirdre Whittleton *state legislator*
Holmes, Robert Eugene *state legislative consultant, journalist*
Hughes, Teresa P. *state legislator*
Jones, William Leon *state legislator, rancher*
Knight, William J. (Pete Knight) *state senator, retired air force officer*
Leslie, (Robert) Tim *state legislator*
Napolitano, Grace F. *state legislator*
Presley, Robert Buel *state senator*

**Sanger**
Haddix, Charles E. *legislative and regulatory consultant*

#### COLORADO

**Aurora**
Kerns, Peggy Shoup *former state legislator*

**Denver**
Bishop, Tilman Malcolm *state senator, retired college administrator*
Brown, Hank *former senator*
Faatz, Jeanne Ryan *state legislator*
Meiklejohn, Alvin J., Jr. *state senator, lawyer, accountant*
Morrison, Marcy *state legislator*
Wham, Dorothy Stonecipher *state legislator*

**Golden**
Hopper, Sally *state legislator*

#### CONNECTICUT

**Glastonbury**
Googins, Sonya Forbes *state legislator, retired banker*

**Hartford**
Bysiewicz, Susan *state legislator*
Cook, Cathy Welles *state senator*
Flaherty, Patrick John *state legislator, economist*
Gunther, George Lackman *state senator, natureopathic physician, retired*
Hess, Marilyn Ann *state legislator*
McGrattan, Mary K. *state legislator*
Simmons, Robert Ruhl *state legislator, educator*
Upson, Thomas Fisher *state legislator, lawyer*

**New Haven**
Stolberg, Irving J. *state legislator, international consultant*

**Stamford**
Aveni, Beverly A. *executive aide*

**Vernon Rockville**
Herbst, Marie Antoinette *former state senator*

**Westport**
Freedman, Judith Greenberg *state senator, importer*

#### DELAWARE

**Newark**
Amick, Steven Hammond *senator, lawyer*
Neal, James Preston *state senator, project engineer*

#### DISTRICT OF COLUMBIA

**Washington**
Abercrombie, Neil *congressman*
Abraham, Spencer *senator*
Ackerman, Gary Leonard *congressman*
Akaka, Daniel Kahikina *senator*
Allard, A. Wayne *senator, veterinarian*
†Allen, Thomas H. *congressman, lawyer*
Andrews, Robert E. *congressman*
Archer, William Reynolds, Jr. (Bill Reynolds) *congressman*
Ashcroft, John David *senator*
Bachus, Spencer T., III *congressman, lawyer*
Baesler, Scotty *congressman*
Baldacci, John Elias *congressman*
Ballenger, Thomas Cass *congressman*
Barcia, James A. *congressman*
Barr, Robert Laurence, Jr. *congressman, lawyer*
Barrett, Thomas M. *congressman*
Barrett, William E. *congressman*
Bartlett, Roscoe G. *congressman*
Bass, Charles F. *congressman*
Bateman, Herbert Harvell *congressman*
Baucus, Max S. *senator*
Baumgartner, Eileen Mary *government official*
Becerra, Xavier *congressman, lawyer*
Bennett, Robert F. *senator*
Bentsen, Kenneth E., Jr. *congressman*
Bereuter, Douglas Kent *congressman*
Berman, Howard Lawrence *congressman*
†Berry, Marion *congressman*
Biden, Joseph Robinette, Jr. *senator*
Bilbray, Brian P. *congressman*
Bilirakis, Michael *congressman, lawyer, business executive*
Bingaman, Jeff *senator*
Bishop, Sanford Dixon, Jr. *congressman*
†Blagojevich, Rod R. *state legislator, congressman*
†Blumenauer, Earl *congressman*
†Blunt, Roy D. *congressman*
Boehlert, Sherwood Louis *congressman*
Boehner, John A. *congressman*
Bond, Christopher Samuel (Kit Bond) *senator, lawyer*
Bonilla, Henry *congressman, broadcast executive*
Bonior, David Edward *congressman*
Borski, Robert Anthony *congressman*
Boucher, Frederick C. *congressman, lawyer*
Boxer, Barbara *senator*
Breaux, John B. *senator, former congressman*
Browder, John Glen *congressman, educator*
Brown, Corrine *congresswoman*
Brown, George Edward, Jr. *congressman*
Brown, Sherrod *congressman, former state official*
Brownback, Sam *senator*
Bryan, Richard H. *senator*
Bryant, Edward *congressman*
Bryant, John Wiley *former congressman*
Bumpers, Dale L. *senator, former governor*
Burns, Conrad Ray *senator*
Burr, Richard M. *congressman*
Burton, Dan L. *congressman*
Buyer, Steve E. *congressman, lawyer*
Byrd, Robert Carlyle *senator*
†Byrne, Leslie Larkin *congresswoman*
Calvert, Ken *congressman*
Camp, Dave *congressman*
Campbell, Ben Nighthorse *senator*
†Campbell, Thomas J. *congressman*
Canady, Charles T. *congressman, lawyer*
†Cannon, Christopher B. *congressman*
Cardin, Benjamin Lewis *congressman*
Carlisle, Margo Duer Black *chief senatorial staff*
Carr, Bob (Bob Carr) *former congressman, lawyer*
Castle, Michael N. *congressman, former governor, lawyer*
Chabot, Steven J. *congressman*
Chafee, John Hubbard *senator*
Chambliss, Saxby *congressman*
Chapman, James L. (Jim Chapman) *former congressman*
Chenoweth, Helen *congresswoman*
Christensen, Jon *congressman*
Clark, Dick *former senator, ambassador, foreign affairs specialist*
Clay, William Lacy *congressman*
Clayton, Eva M. *congresswoman, former county commissioner*
†Cleland, Max *senator*
Clement, Bob *congressman*
Clyburn, James E. *congressman*
Coats, Daniel Ray *senator*
Cobb, Jane Overton *legislative staff member*
Coburn, Tom A. *congressman*
Cochran, Jill Teague *legislative staff member*
Cohen, William Sebastian *senator*
Collins, Barbara-Rose *former congresswoman*
Collins, Michael A. (Mac Collins) *congressman*
†Collins, Susan M. *senator*
Combest, Larry Ed *congressman*
Condit, Gary A. *congressman*
Conrad, Kent *senator*
Conyers, John, Jr. *congressman*
Costello, Jerry F., Jr. *congressman, former county official*
Coverdell, Paul Douglas *senator*
Coyne, William Joseph *congressman*
Craig, Larry Edwin *senator*
Cramer, Robert E., Jr. (Bud Cramer) *congressman*
Crane, Philip Miller *congressman*
Crapo, Michael Dean *congressman, lawyer*
Cremeans, Frank A. *former congressman*
Cubin, Barbara Lynn *congresswoman, former state legislator, public relations consultant*
Cummings, Elijah E. *state legislator*
Cunningham, Randy *congressman*
D'Amato, Alfonse M. *senator*
Danner, Patsy Ann (Mrs. C. M. Meyer) *congresswoman*
Daschle, Thomas Andrew *senator*
Davis, Thomas M., III *congressman*
Deal, Nathan J. *congressman, lawyer*
DeFazio, Peter A. *congressman*
†Degette, Diana *congresswoman*
†Delahunt, William D. *congressman*
DeLauro, Rosa L. *congresswoman*
DeLay, Thomas D. (Tom DeLay) *congressman*
Dellums, Ronald V. *congressman*
Deutsch, Peter R. *congressman, lawyer*
DeWine, R. Michael *senator, lawyer*
Diaz-Balart, Lincoln *congressman*
Dickey, Jay W., Jr. *congressman, lawyer*
Dicks, Norman De Valois *congressman*
Dingell, John David, Jr. *congressman*
Dixon, Julian Carey *congressman*
Dodd, Christopher J. *senator*
Doggett, Lloyd *congressman, former state supreme court justice*
Dole, Robert J. *senator*
Domenici, Pete (Vichi Domenici) *senator*
Dooley, Calvin Millard *congressman*
Doolittle, John Taylor *congressman*
Dorgan, Byron Leslie *senator*
Doyle, Michael F. *congressman*
Dreier, David Timothy *congressman*
Duncan, John J., Jr. *congressman*
Dunn, Jennifer Blackburn *congresswoman*
Durbin, Richard Joseph *senator*
Edwards, Chet *congressman*
Ehrlich, Robert L., Jr. *congressman*
†Emerson, Jo Ann *congresswoman*
Engel, Eliot L. *congressman*
English, Philip Sheridan *congressman*
Ensign, John E. *congressman*
Enzi, Michael Bradley *senator, accountant*
Eshoo, Anna Georges *congresswoman*
Evans, Lane *congressman*
Everett, R. Terry *congressman, farmer, newspaper executive, bank executive*
Everett, Terry *congressman*
Ewing, Thomas William *congressman, lawyer*
Faircloth, Duncan McLauchlin (Lauch Faircloth) *senator, businessman, farmer*
Faleomavaega, Eni F. H. *congressman*
Farr, Sam *congressman*
Fattah, Chaka *congressman, former state legislator*
Fawell, Harris W. *congressman*
Fazio, Vic *congressman*
Feingold, Russell Dana *senator*
Feinstein, Dianne *senator*
Feltus, William James *legislative staff member*
Fields, Cleo *former congressman*
Filner, Bob *congressman*
Fisher, Joseph A. *legislative official*
Flake, Floyd Harold *congressman*
Flanagan, Michael Patrick *former congressman, lawyer*
Foley, Mark Adam *congressman*
Forbes, Michael P. *congressman*
Ford, Harold Eugene *congressman*
Fowler, Tillie Kidd *congresswoman*
Fox, Jon D. *congressman*
Frahm, Sheila *senator, lieutenant governor, former state legislator*
Frank, Barney *congressman*
Frelinghuysen, Rodney P. *congressman*
Frisa, Daniel *former congressman*
Frist, William H. *senator, surgeon*
Frost, Jonas Martin, III *congressman*
Funderburk, David B. *congressman, history educator, former ambassador*
Furse, Elizabeth *congresswoman, small business owner*
Ganske, J. Greg *congressman, plastic surgeon*
Gejdenson, Sam *congressman*
Gekas, George William *congressman*
Gephardt, Richard Andrew *congressman*
Gest, Kathryn Waters *press secretary*
†Gibbons, James Arthur *congressman*
Gilchrest, Wayne Thomas *congressman, former high school educator*
Gillmor, Paul E. *congressman, lawyer*
Gilman, Benjamin Arthur *congressman*
Gingrich, Newt(on Leroy) *congressman*
Glenn, John Herschel, Jr. *senator*
Gonzalez, Henry Barbosa *congressman*
†Goode, Virgil H., Jr. *congressman*
Goodlatte, Robert William *congressman, lawyer*
Goodling, William F. *congressman*
Gordon, Barton Jennings (Bart Gordon) *congressman, lawyer*
Gorton, Slade *senator*
Graham, D. Robert (Bob Graham) *senator, former governor*
Graham, Lindsey O. *congressman*
Gramm, William Philip (Phil Gramm) *senator, economist*
Grams, Rodney D. *senator, former congressman*
Grassley, Charles Ernest *senator*
Greenwood, James Charles *congressman*
Gregg, Judd *senator, former governor*
Gutierrez, Luis V. *congressman, elementary education educator*
Gutknecht, Gilbert William, Jr. *congressman, former state legislator, auctioneer*
†Hagel, Charles *senator*
Hall, Ralph Moody *congressman*
Hall, Tony P. *congressman*
Hamilton, Lee Herbert *congressman*
Hamre, John J. *financial officer*
Harkin, Thomas Richard *senator*
Harman, Jane Frank *congresswoman, lawyer*
Hastert, (J.) Dennis *congressman*
Hastings, Alcee Lamar *congressman, former federal judge*
Hastings, Richard (Doc Hastings) *congressman*
Hattan, Susan K. *legislative staff member*
Hayworth, John David, Jr. *congressman, sportscaster, commentator, broadcaster*
Hefley, Joel M. *congressman*
Hefner, W. G. (Bill Hefner) *congressman*
Helms, Jesse *senator*
Herger, Wally W. *congressman*
†Hill, Rick Allan *congressman*
Hilleary, Van *congressman*
Hilliard, Earl Frederick *congressman, lawyer*
Hinchey, Maurice D., Jr. *congressman*
Hobson, David Lee *congressman, lawyer*
Hoekstra, Peter *congressman, manufacturing executive*
Hoke, Martin Rossiter *former congressman*
Holden, Tim *congressman, protective official*
Hollings, Ernest Frederick *senator*
Horn, (John) Stephen *congressman, political science educator*
Hostettler, John N. *congressman*
Houghton, Amory, Jr. *congressman*
Hoyer, Steny Hamilton *congressman*
†Hulshof, Kenny *congressman*
Hutchinson, Tim *senator*
Hyde, Henry John *congressman*
Inglis, Robert D. (Bob Inglis) *congressman, lawyer*
Inhofe, James M. *senator*
Inouye, Daniel Ken *senator*
Istook, Ernest James, Jr. (Jim Istook) *congressman, lawyer*

†Jackson, Jesse, Jr. *congressman*
Jackson Lee, Sheila *congresswoman*
James, Julie Ann *congressional staff member*
Jefferson, William L. (Jeff Jefferson) *congressman*
Jeffords, James Merrill *senator*
†Jenkins, William L. (Bill Jenkins) *congressman*
†John, Chris *congressman*
Johnson, Eddie Bernice *congresswoman*
†Johnson, Jay Withington *congressman*
Johnson, Nancy Lee *congresswoman*
Johnson, Samuel (Sam Johnson) *congressman*
Johnson, Timothy Peter *senator*
Johnston, John Bennett, Jr. *former senator*
Jones, Walter Beaman, Jr. *congressman*
Kanjorski, Paul Edmund *congressman, lawyer*
Kaptur, Marcia Carolyn *congresswoman*
Kasich, John R. *congressman*
Kassebaum, Nancy Landon *former senator*
Kasten, Robert W., Jr. *former senator*
Kelly, Sue W. *congresswoman*
Kempthorne, Dirk Arthur *senator*
Kennedy, Edward Moore *senator*
Kennedy, Joseph Patrick, II *congressman*
Kennedy, Patrick J. *congressman*
Kennelly, Barbara B. *congresswoman*
Kerrey, Bob (J. Robert Kerrey) *senator*
Kerry, John Forbes *senator*
Kildee, Dale Edward *congressman*
Kim, Jay *congressman*
King, Peter T. *congressman, lawyer*
Kingston, Jack *congressman*
Kleczka, Gerald D. *congressman*
Klink, Ron *congressman, reporter, newscaster*
Knollenberg, Joseph (Joe Knollenberg) *congressman*
Kohl, Herbert *senator, professional sports team owner*
Kolbe, James Thomas *congressman*
†Kucinich, Dennis J. *congressman*
Kundanis, George *congressional aide*
Kyl, Jon *senator*
La Falce, John Joseph *congressman, lawyer*
LaHood, Ray *congressman*
†Lampson, Nick *congressman*
Lancaster, H(arold) Martin *former congressman, former advisor to the President*
†Landrieu, Mary L. *senator*
Lantos, Thomas Peter *congressman*
Largent, Steve *congressman, former professional football player*
Latham, Tom *congressman*
LaTourette, Steven C. *congressman*
Laughlin, Gregory H. (Greg Laughlin) *congressman*
Lautenberg, Frank R. *senator*
Lazio, Rick A. *congressman, lawyer*
Leach, James Albert Smith *congressman*
Leahy, Patrick Joseph *senator*
Lent, Norman Frederick, Jr. *former congressman*
Levin, Carl *senator*
Levin, Sander M. *congressman*
Lewis, Jerry *congressman*
Lewis, John R. *congressman*
Lewis, Ron *congressman*
Lieberman, Joseph I. *senator*
Lincoln, Blanche Lambert *congresswoman*
Linder, John E. *congressman, dentist*
Lipinski, William Oliver *congressman*
Livingston, Robert Linlithgow, Jr. (Bob Livingston, Jr.) *congressman*
LoBiondo, Frank A. *congressman*
Lofgren, Zoe *congresswoman*
Lott, Trent *senator*
Lowey, Nita M. *congresswoman*
Lucas, Frank D. *congressman*
Lugar, Richard Green *senator*
Luther, William P. *congressman*
Mack, Connie, III (Cornelius Mack) *senator*
Maloney, Carolyn Bosher *congresswoman*
Maloney, James Henry *congressman*
Manton, Thomas Joseph *congressman*
Manzullo, Donald A *congressman, lawyer*
Markey, Edward John *congressman*
Martinez, Matthew Gilbert *congressman*
Mascara, Frank *congressman*
Matsui, Robert Takeo *congressman*
May, Edgar *former state legislator, nonprofit administrator*
McCain, John Sidney, III *senator*
McCarthy, Karen P. *congresswoman, former state representative*
Mc Collum, Ira William, Jr. (Bill Mc Collum) *congressman*
McConnell, Addison Mitchell, Jr. (Mitch McConnell, Jr.) *senator, lawyer*
McCrery, James (Jim McCrery) *congressman*
McDade, Joseph Michael *congressman*
McDermott, James A. *congressman, psychiatrist*
†McGovern, James P. *congressman*
McHugh, John Michael *congressman, former state senator*
McInnis, Scott Steve *congressman, lawyer*
McIntosh, David M. *congressman*
McKeon, Howard P. (Buck McKeon) *congressman, former mayor*
McKinney, Cynthia Ann *congresswoman*
McNulty, Michael Robert *congressman*
Meehan, Martin Thomas *congressman, lawyer*
Meek, Carrie P. *congresswoman*
Menendez, Robert *congressman, lawyer*
†Merrill, Cook *congressman*
Metcalf, Jack *congressman, retired state senator*
Metz, Craig Huseman *legislative administrator*
Metzenbaum, Howard Morton *former senator*
Meyers, Jan *former congresswoman*
†Millender-McDonald, Juanita *congresswoman, former school system administrator*
Miller, Dan *congressman*
Miller, George *congressman*
Minge, David *congressman, lawyer, law educator*
Mink, Patsy Takemoto *congresswoman*
Moakley, John Joseph *congressman*
Molinari, Susan *congresswoman*
Mollohan, Alan B. *congressman, lawyer*
Moran, James Patrick, Jr. *congressman, stockbroker*
†Moran, Jerry *congressman*
Morella, Constance Albanese *congresswoman*
Morrison, Bruce Andrew *government executive, former congressman*
Moseley-Braun, Carol *senator*
Moynihan, Daniel Patrick *senator, educator*
Murkowski, Frank Hughes *senator*
Murray, Patty *senator*
Murtha, John Patrick *congressman*
Myrick, Sue *congresswoman, former mayor*
Nadler, Jerrold Lewis *congressman, lawyer*
Neal, Richard Edmund *congressman, former mayor*
Nelson, Gaylord Anton *former senator, association executive*
Nethercutt, George Rector, Jr. *congressman, lawyer*
Neumann, Mark W. *congressman*
Ney, Robert W. *congressman*
Nickles, Donald (Don Nickles) *senator*
Nintemann, Terri *legislative staff member*
†Northup, Anne Meagher *state legislator*
Norton, Eleanor Holmes *congresswoman, lawyer, educator*
Norwood, Charles W., Jr. *congressman*
Oberstar, James L. *congressman*
Obey, David Ross *congressman*
Olver, John Walter *congressman*
Ortiz, Solomon P. *congressman*
Orton, William H. (Bill Orton) *former congressman, lawyer*
Owens, Major Robert Odell *congressman*
Oxley, Michael Garver *congressman*
Packard, Ronald *congressman*
Packwood, Bob *retired senator*
Pallone, Frank, Jr. *congressman*
†Pappas, Michael *congressman*
Parker, Michael (Mike Parker) *congressman*
†Pascrell, William J., Jr. *congressman*
Pastor, Ed *congressman*
Paxon, L. William *congressman*
Payne, Donald M. *congressman*
Pease, Edward Allan *congressman*
Pell, Claiborne *former senator*
Pelosi, Nancy *congresswoman*
Peterson, Collin C. *congressman*
†Peterson, John E. *congressman*
Petri, Thomas Evert *congressman*
†Pickering, Charles W., Jr. *congressman*
Pickett, Owen B. *congressman*
†Pitts, Joseph R. *congressman*
Pombo, Richard *congressman, rancher, farmer*
Pomeroy, Earl R. *congressman, former state insurance commissioner*
Porter, John Edward *congressman*
Portman, Rob *congressman*
Poshard, Glenn W. *congressman*
Pressler, Larry *senator*
Pryor, David Hampton *former senator*
Quillen, James Henry (Jimmy Quillen) *former congressman*
Quinn, Jack *congressman, English language educator, sports coach*
Radanovich, George P. *congressman*
Rahall, Nick Joe, II (Nick Rahall) *congressman*
Ramstad, Jim *congressman, lawyer*
Rangel, Charles Bernard *congressman*
Reed, John Francis (Jack Reed) *senator*
Regula, Ralph *congressman, lawyer*
Riggs, Frank *congressman*
†Riley, Bob *congressman*
Rivers, Lynn N. *congresswoman*
Robb, Charles Spittal *senator, lawyer*
Roberts, Charles Patrick *senator*
Rockefeller, John Davison, IV (Jay Rockefeller) *senator, former governor*
Roemer, Timothy J. *congressman*
Rogers, Harold Dallas (Hal Rogers) *congressman*
Rohrabacher, Dana *congressman*
Ros-Lehtinen, Ileana *congresswoman*
Roth, William V., Jr. *senator*
Roukema, Margaret Scafati *congresswoman*
Roybal-Allard, Lucille *congresswoman*
Royce, Edward R. (Ed Royce) *congressman*
Rudman, Warren Bruce *former senator, lawyer, think tank executive*
Rush, Bobby L. *congressman*
Sabo, Martin Olav *congressman*
Salmon, Matt *congressman*
†Sanchez, Loretta *congresswoman*
Sanders, Bernard (Bernie Sanders) *congressman*
†Sandlin, Max Allen, Jr. *congressman*
Sanford, Marshall (Mark Sanford) *congressman*
Santorum, Rick *senator*
Sarbanes, Paul Spyros *senator*
Sawyer, Thomas C. *congressman*
Saxton, H. James *congressman*
Saxton, James *congressman*
Scarborough, Joe *congressman*
Schaefer, Dan L. *congressman*
Schaffer, Robert (Bob Schaffer) *congressman*
Schiff, Steven Harvey *congressman, lawyer*
Schroeder, Patricia Scott (Mrs. James White Schroeder) *former congresswoman*
Schumer, Charles Ellis *congressman*
Scott, Robert Cortez *congressman, lawyer*
Sensenbrenner, Frank James, Jr. *congressman, lawyer*
Serrano, Jose E. *congressman*
Sessions, Jefferson Beauregard, III *senator*
Shadegg, John B. *congressman*
Shaw, E. Clay, Jr. (Clay Shaw) *congressman*
Shays, Christopher *congressman*
Shelby, Richard Craig *senator, former congressman*
†Sherman, Bradley James *congressman*
†Shimkus, John Mondy *congressman*
Shuster, Bud *congressman*
Sisisky, Norman *congressman, soft drink bottler*
Skaggs, David E. *congressman*
Skeen, Joseph Richard *congressman*
Skelton, Isaac Newton, IV (Ike Skelton) *congressman*
Slaughter, Louise McIntosh *congresswoman*
Smith, Christopher Henry *congressman*
†Smith, D. Adam *congressman*
†Smith, Gordon Harold *senator*
Smith, Lamar Seeligson *congressman*
Smith, Linda A. *congresswoman, former state legislator*
Smith, Nick *congressman, farmer*
Smith, Robert Clinton *senator*
Snowbarger, Vincent Keith *congressman*
Snowe, Olympia J. *senator*
Solomon, Gerald Brooks Hunt *congressman*
Souder, Mark Edward *congressman*
Specter, Arlen *senator*
Spence, Floyd Davidson *congressman*
Spratt, John McKee, Jr. *congressman, lawyer*
†Stabenow, Deborah Ann *congresswoman*
Stark, Fortney Hillman (Pete Stark) *congressman*
Stearns, Clifford Bundy *congressman, business executive*
Stenholm, Charles W. *congressman*
Stevens, Theodore Fulton *senator*
Stokes, Louis *congressman*
†Strickland, Ted *congressman, clergyman, psychology educator, psychologist*
Studds, Gerry Eastman *former congressman*
Stump, Bob *congressman*
Stupak, Bart T. *congressman, lawyer*
Talent, James M. *congressman, lawyer*
Tanner, John S. *congressman, lawyer*
Tauzin, W. J. Billy, II (Wilbert J. Tauzin) *congressman*
Taylor, Charles H. *congressman*
Taylor, Gene *congressman*
Thomas, Craig *senator*
Thomas, William Marshall *congressman*
Thompson, Bennie G. *congressman*
Thompson, Fred *senator*
Thompson, Jill Lynette Long *congresswoman*
Thornberry, William M. (Mac Thornberry) *congressman*
Thurman, Karen L. *congresswoman*
Thurmond, Strom *senator*
Tiahrt, W. Todd *congressman, former state senator*
Torres, Esteban Edward *congressman, business executive*
Torricelli, Robert G. *senator*
Towns, Edolphus *congressman*
Traficant, James A., Jr. *congressman*
†Turner, Jim *congressman*
Upton, Frederick Stephen *congressman*
Vazirani-Fales, Heea *legislative staff member, lawyer*
Velazquez, Nydia M. *congresswoman*
Vento, Bruce Frank *congressman*
Visclosky, Peter John *congressman, lawyer*
Vucanovich, Barbara Farrell *former congresswoman*
Walker, Robert Smith *former congressman*
Walsh, James Thomas *congressman*
Wamp, Zach P. *congressman*
Warner, John William *senator*
Waters, Maxine *congresswoman*
†Watkins, Wesley Wade *congressman*
Watt, Melvin L. *congressman, lawyer*
Watts, J. C., Jr. *congressman*
Waxman, Henry Arnold *congressman*
Weiss, Gail Ellen *legislative staff director*
Weiss, Leonard *senate staff director, mathematician, engineer*
Weldon, David Joseph, Jr. *congressman, physician*
Weldon, W(ayne) Curtis *congressman*
Weller, Gerald C. *congressman*
Wellstone, Paul *senator*
†Wexler, Robert *congressman*
White, Richard A. *congressman*
Whitfield, Edward (Wayne Whitfield) *congressman*
Wicker, Roger F. *congressman*
Wilson, Charles (Charlie Wilson) *former congressman*
Wise, Robert Ellsworth, Jr. (Bob Ellsworth) *congressman*
Wofford, Harris Llewellyn *former senator, national service executive*
Wolf, Frank R. *congressman, lawyer*
Woolsey, Lynn *congresswoman*
Wyden, Ron *senator*
Wynn, Albert Russell *congressman*
Yates, Sidney Richard *congressman, lawyer*
Young, C. W. (Bill Young) *congressman*
Young, Donald E. *congressman*

## FLORIDA

### Bradenton
Woodson-Howard, Marlene Erdley *former state legislator*

### Jacksonville
Bennett, Charles Edward *former congressman, educator*

### Miami
Cosgrove, John Francis *state legislator, lawyer*
Fascell, Dante B. *congressman, lawyer*
Gordon, Jack David *senator, foundation executive*

### Pensacola
Hutto, Earl *retired congressman*

### Tampa
Davis, Helen Gordon *former state senator*
Glickman, Ronnie Carl *state official, lawyer*

### West Palm Beach
Johnston, Harry A., II *former congressman*

### Winter Park
Mica, John L. *congressman*

## GEORGIA

### Americus
Hooks, George Bardin *state senator, insurance and real estate company executive*

### Atlanta
Henson, Michele *state legislator*
Martin, James Francis *state legislator, lawyer*
McBee, Mary Louise *state legislator, former academic administrator*
Murphy, Thomas Bailey *state legislator*
Nunn, Samuel (Sam Nunn) *former senator*
Purcell, Ann Rushing *state legislator, office manager medical business*

### Augusta
Barnard, Druie Douglas, Jr. *former congressman, former bank executive*

### Jonesboro
King, Glynda B. *state legislator*

### Lawrenceville
Wall, Clarence Vinson *state legislator*

### Smyrna
Atkins, William Austin (Bill ) *state legislator*

## HAWAII

### Hilo
Ushijima, John Takeji *state senator, lawyer*

### Honolulu
Baker, Rosalyn Hester *state legislator*
Cachola, Romy Munoz *state representative*
Chun Oakland, Suzanne Nyuk Jun *state legislator*
Fasi, Frank Francis *state senator*
Fong, Hiram Leong *former senator*
Takumi, Roy Mitsuo *state representative*

### Kailua
George, Mary Shannon *state senator*
Young, Jacqueline Eurn Hai *state legislator*

## IDAHO

### Boise
Black, Pete *state legislator, educator*
Stone, Ruby Rocker *state legislator*
Taylor, W. O. (Bill Taylor) *state legislator, business consultant*

### Pocatello
Hofman, Elaine D. *state legislator*

## ILLINOIS

### Aurora
Etheredge, Forest DeRoyce *former state senator, university administrator*

### Belleville
Holbrook, Thomas Aldredge *state legislator*

### Buffalo Grove
Clayton, Verna Lewis *state legislator*

### Carbondale
Simon, Paul *former senator, educator, author*

### Chicago
Berman, Arthur Leonard *state senator*
Bugielski, Robert Joseph *state legislator*
Dunea, Mary Mills *protocal consultant*
Stevenson, Adlai Ewing, III *lawyer, former senator*

### Jacksonville
Findley, Paul *former congressman, author, educator*

### Lake Forest
Frederick, Virginia Fiester *state legislator*

### Naperville
Cowlishaw, Mary Lou *state legislator*

### Palatine
Fitzgerald, Peter Gosselin *state senator, lawyer*

### Springfield
Carroll, Howard William *state senator, lawyer*
Currie, Barbara Flynn *state legislator*
Geo-Karis, Adeline Jay *state senator*
Hughes, Ann *state legislator*
Madigan, Michael Joseph *state legislator*
Moore, Andrea S. *state legislator*
Philip, James (Pate Philip) *state senator*
Ronen, Carol *state legislator*
Severns, Penny L. *state legislator*

### Sterling
von Bergen Wessels, Pennie Lea *state legislator*

### Wheaton
Fawell, Beverly Jean *state legislator*
Roskam, Peter James *state legislator, lawyer*

## INDIANA

### Attica
Harrison, Joseph William *state senator*

### Columbus
Garton, Robert Dean *state senator*

### Fort Wayne
Goeglein, Gloria J. *state legislator*
Moses, Winfield C., Jr. *state legislator, construction company executive*

### Indianapolis
†Carson, Julia M. *congresswoman*
Clark, James Murray *state legislator*
Jacobs, Andrew, Jr. *former congressman*
Klinker, Sheila Ann J. *state legislator, middle school educator*
Scholer, Sue Wyant *state legislator*

## IOWA

### Cedar Rapids
Chapman, Kathleen Halloran *state legislator, lawyer*

### Davis City
Boswell, Leonard L. *congressman*

### Des Moines
Daggett, Horace Clinton *retired state legislator*
Deluhery, Patrick John *state senator*
Drake, Richard Francis *state senator*
Harper, Patricia M. *state legislator*
Murphy, Patrick Joseph *state representative*
Pate, Paul Danny *state senator, business executive, entrepreneur*
Rittmer, Sheldon *state senator, farmer*
Rosenberg, Ralph *former state senator, lawyer, consultant, educator*
Szymoniak, Elaine Eisfelder *state senator*

### Johnston
Churchill, Steven Wayne *state legislator, fund-raising consultant*

### Saint Ansgar
Koenigs, Deo Aloysius *state representative*

### Sioux City
Andersen, Leonard Christian *former state legislator, real estate investor*

## KANSAS

**Clay Center**
Braden, James Dale *former state legislator*

**Coffeyville**
Garner, Jim D. *state legislator, lawyer*

**Hutchinson**
Kerr, David Mills *state legislator*
O'Neal, Michael Ralph *state legislator, lawyer*

**Iola**
Talkington, Robert Van *state senator*

**Kansas City**
Spangler, Douglas Frank *state legislator*

**Lawrence**
Winter, Winton Allen, Jr. *state senator, lawyer*

**Lenexa**
Parkinson, Mark Vincent *state legislator, lawyer*

**Mc Pherson**
Nichols, Richard Dale *former congressman, banker*

**Olathe**
Burke, Paul E., Jr. *state senator, business consultant, public government affairs*
O'Connor, Kay *state legislator*

**Prairie Village**
Langworthy, Audrey Hansen *state legislator*

**Salina**
Horst, Deena Louise *state legislator*

**Shawnee Mission**
Sader, Carol Hope *former state legislator*

**Topeka**
Ballard, Barbara W. *state legislator*
Mays, M. Douglas *state legislator, financial consultant*
Salisbury, Alicia Laing *state legislator*
Wagnon, Joan *former state legislator, association executive*

**Wichita**
Pottorff, Jo Ann *state legislator*

## KENTUCKY

**Covington**
Celella, Jan Gerding *legislative staff member*
Harper, Kenneth Franklin *retired state legislator, real estate broker*

## LOUISIANA

**La Place**
Landry, Ronald Jude *lawyer, state senator*

**Marksville**
Riddle, Charles Addison, III *state legislator, lawyer*

**Shreveport**
Nelson, Sydney B. *state senator, lawyer*

## MAINE

**Augusta**
Amero, Jane Adams *state legislator*
Barth, Alvin Ludwig, Jr. *state legislator*
Daggett, Beverly Clark *state legislator*
Desmond, Mabel Jeannette *state legislator, educator*
Kilkelly, Marjorie Lee *state legislator*
Martin, John L. *state legislator*

**Brunswick**
Pfeiffer, Sophia Douglass *state legislator, lawyer*

**Cape Elizabeth**
Simonds, Stephen Paige *former state legislator*

**Fort Fairfield**
Donnelly, James Owen *state legislator, bank executive*

## MARYLAND

**Aberdeen**
Bonsack, Rose Mary Hatem *state legislator, physician*

**Annapolis**
Forehand, Jennie Meador *state legislator*
Hixson, Sheila Ellis *state legislator*
Hollinger, Paula Colodny *state senator*
Kelley, Delores Goodwin *state legislator*
Klima, Martha Scanlan *state senator*
Madden, Martin Gerard *state legislator, insurance agent*
Menes, Pauline H. *state legislator*
Morgan, John Stephen *state legislator, materials science researcher*
Roesser, Jean Wolberg *state legislator*
Ruben, Ida Gass *state senator*

**Baltimore**
Marriot, Salima Siler *state legislator, social work educator*
Mfume, Kweisi *former congressman*

**Bethesda**
Gude, Gilbert *former state and federal legislator, nurseryman, writer*

**Chevy Chase**
Beilenson, Anthony Charles *former congressman*

**Frederick**
Byron, Beverly Butcher *congresswoman*
Horton, Frank *former congressman, lawyer*

**Rockville**
Petzold, Carol Stoker *state legislator*

## MASSACHUSETTS

**Boston**
Bertonazzi, Louis Peter *state agency administrator*
Canavan, Christine Estelle *state legislator*
Cleven, Carol Chapman *state legislator*
Cronin, Bonnie Kathryn Lamb *legislative staff executive*
Durand, Robert Alan *state senator*
Hawke, Robert Douglas *state legislator*
Melconian, Linda Jean *state senator, lawyer*
Moore, Richard Thomas *state legislator*
Rogeness, Mary Speer *state legislator*
Sprague, Jo Ann *state senator*
Swift, Jane Maria *former state senator*
Walrath, Patricia A. *state legislator*

**Fall River**
Correia, Robert *state legislator*

**Peabody**
Torkildsen, Peter G. *congressman*

**Quincy**
Harold, Paul Dennis *state senator*

## MICHIGAN

**Brighton**
Chrysler, Richard R. *former congressman*

**Farmington Hills**
Dolan, Jan Clark *former state legislator*

**Grand Rapids**
Ehlers, Vernon James *congressman*

**Kalamazoo**
Welborn, John Alva *former state senator, small business owner*

**Lansing**
Bullard, Willis Clare, Jr. *state legislator*
Cisky, Jon Ayres *state senator*
Dobronski, Agnes Marie *state legislator*
Emmons, Joanne *state senator*
Geake, Raymond Robert *state legislator*
Geiger, Terry *state legislator*
Hammerstrom, Beverly Swoish *state legislator*
Hoffman, Philip Edward *state senator*
Jellema, Jon *state legislator*
Kaza, Greg John *state representative, economist*
LaForge, Edward *state legislator*
McManus, George Alvin, Jr. *state senator, cherry farmer*
Perricone, Charles *state legislator*
Posthumus, Richard Earl *state senator, farmer*
Schuette, Bill *state senator*
Schwarz, John J.H. *state senator, surgeon*
Sikkema, Kenneth R. *state legislator*
Vaughn, Jackie, III *state legislator*

**Mount Pleasant**
McBryde, James Edward *state legislator*

**Rochester**
Peters, Gary Charles *state senator, lawyer, educator*

## MINNESOTA

**Austin**
Leighton, Robert Joseph *state legislator*

**Lakeville**
Krueger, Richard Arnold *state legislator*

**Mankato**
Hottinger, John Creighton *state legislator, lawyer*

**Minneapolis**
Oliver, Edward Carl *state senator, retired investment executive*
Reichgott Junge, Ember D. *state legislator, lawyer*

**New Brighton**
Pellow, Richard Maurice *state legislator*

**Saint Paul**
Carlson, Lyndon Richard Selvig *state legislator, educator*
Frederickson, Dennis Russel *senator, farmer*
Greenfield, Lee *state legislator*
Haukoos, Melvin Robert *state representative*
Johnson, Janet B. *state legislator*
Kiscaden, Sheila M. *state legislator*
Leppik, Margaret White *state legislator*
Luther, Darlene *state legislator*
McCollum, Betty *state legislator*
McGuire, Mary Jo *state legislator*
Molnau, Carol *state legislator*
Orfield, Myron Willard, Jr. *state legislator, educator*
Seagren, Alice *state legislator*
Solberg, Loren Albin *state legislator, secondary education educator*
Spear, Allan Henry *state senator, historian, educator*
Vellenga, Kathleen Osborne *former state legislator*

## MISSISSIPPI

**Amory**
Bryan, Hob *state senator, lawyer*

**Columbia**
Simmons, Miriam Quinn *state legislator*

**Hattiesburg**
Saucier, Gene Duane *state legislator, import/export company executive*

**Mendenhall**
Rotenberry, Clinton Grice *state representative, real estate broker*

## MISSOURI

**Chesterfield**
Hale, David Clovis *former state representative*

**Harrisonville**
Hartzler, Vicky J. *state legislator*

**Jefferson City**
Bray, Joan *state legislator*
Clay, William Lacy, Jr. *state legislator*
Lumpe, Sheila *state legislator*
McClelland, Emma L. *state legislator*
Pouche, Fredrick *state legislator*
Richardson, Mark *state legislator*
Westfall, Morris *state legislator*

**Saint Joseph**
Kelly, Glenda Marie *state legislator*

**Saint Louis**
Danforth, John Claggett *senator, lawyer, clergyman*
Hoblitzelle, George Knapp *former state legislator*

**Springfield**
Hancock, Mel *former congressman*

## MONTANA

**Dutton**
De Bruycker, Jane Crystal *state legislator*

**Great Falls**
Ryan, William Matthew *state legislator, safety educator*

**Hardin**
Russell, Angela Veta *state legislator, social worker*

**Helena**
Swanson, Emily *state legislator*

**Missoula**
Williams, Pat *former congressman*

## NEBRASKA

**Lincoln**
Curtis, Carl Thomas *former senator*
Engel, L. Patrick *state legislator*
Exon, J(ohn) James *former senator*
Johnson, Cindy Coble *councilwoman, marketing executive*
Landis, David Morrison *state legislator*
Marsh, Frank (Irving) *former state official*
Pirsch, Carol McBride *county official, community relations manager*
Schimek, DiAnna Ruth Rebman *state legislator*
Stuhr, Elaine Ruth *state legislator*
Wesely, Donald Raymond *state senator*
Will, Eric John *state senator*

## NEVADA

**Carson City**
O'Connell, Mary Ann *state senator, business owner*
Tiffany, Sandra L. *state legislator*
Titus, Alice Cestandina (Dina Titus) *state legislator*

**Reno**
Raggio, William John *state senator*

**Yerington**
Dini, Joseph Edward, Jr. *state legislator*

## NEW HAMPSHIRE

**Berlin**
Bradley, Paula E. *state legislator*

**Concord**
Arnold, Thomas Ivan, Jr. *legislator*
Bagley, Amy L. *state legislator*
Clay, Susan Jose *legislator*
Cote, David Edward *state legislator*
Delahunty, Joseph Lawrence *state senator, business investor*
Hager, Elizabeth Sears *state legislator, social services organization administrator*
Holley, Sylvia A. *state legislator*
Lozeau, Donnalee M. *state legislator*
Merritt, Deborah Foote *state legislator, vocational coordinator*
Packard, Bonnie Bennett *former state legislator*
Pignatelli, Debora Becker *state legislator*
Richardson, Barbara Hull *state legislator, social worker*
Teschner, Douglass Paul *state legislator*

**Derry**
Aranda, Mary Kathryn *state legislator*
Katsakiores, George Nicholas *state legislator, retired restauranteur*

**Dover**
Parks, Joe Benjamin *state legislator*
Pelletier, Arthur Joseph *state legislator, industrial arts and computer programming educator*
Pelletier, Marsha Lynn *state legislator, secondary school educator*

**Durham**
Wheeler, Katherine Wells *state legislator*

**Etna**
Copenhaver, Marion Lamson *state legislator*

**Hanover**
Crory, Elizabeth L. *state legislator*
Guest, Robert Henry *state legislator, management educator*

**Jackson**
Zeliff, William H., Jr. *former congressman*

**Lancaster**
Pratt, Leighton Calvin *state legislator*

**Loudon**
Heath, Roger Charles *state senator, writer*

**Manchester**
Arnold, Barbara Eileen *state legislator*
Nardi, Theodora P. *former state legislator*

**Newport**
Stamatakis, Carol Marie *state legislator, lawyer*

**Plaistow**
Senter, Merilyn P(atricia) *former state legislator and freelance reporter*

**Rindge**
White, Jean Tillinghast *former state senator*

**Rumney**
King, Wayne Douglas *state senator*

## NEW JERSEY

**Cedar Grove**
Martini, William J. *former congressman*

**Flemington**
Lance, Leonard *assemblyman*

**New Brunswick**
Lynch, John A. *state senator, lawyer*

**Newark**
Bradley, Bill *former senator*

**Short Hills**
Ogden, Maureen Black *retired state legislator*

**Trenton**
DiFrancesco, Donald T. *state senator*

**Union**
Franks, Robert D. (Bob Franks) *congressman*

**Woodbury**
Zane, Raymond J. *state senator, lawyer*

## NEW MEXICO

**Albuquerque**
Hall, Lois Riggs *former state senator, former symphony orchestra administrator*
Riley, Ann J. *former state legislator, technology specialist*
Rutherford, Thomas Truxtun, II *state senator, lawyer*

**Hobbs**
Reagan, Gary Don *state legislator, lawyer*

**Los Alamos**
Wallace, Jeannette Owens *state legislator*

**Roswell**
Casey, Barbara A. Perea *state representative, school superintendent*
Jennings, Timothy Zeph *state senator, rancher*

**Santa Fe**
Nava, Cynthia D. *state legislator*
Stefanics, Elizabeth T. (Liz Stefanics) *state legislator*

## NEW YORK

**Albany**
Bruno, Joseph L. *state legislator*
Calhoun, Nancy *state legislator*
Farley, Hugh T. *state senator, law educator*
Harenberg, Paul E. *state legislator*
Hill, Earlene Hooper *state legislator*
Lack, James J. *state senator, lawyer*
Matusow, Naomi C. *state legislator*
O'Neil, Chloe Ann *state legislator*
Proskin, Arnold W. *state assemblyman, lawyer*
Smith, Ada L. *state legislator*
Stachowski, William T. *state senator*
Vitaliano, Eric Nicholas *state legislator, lawyer*
Volker, Dale Martin *state senator, lawyer*

**Binghamton**
Libous, Thomas William *state senator*

**Bronx**
Greene, Aurelia *state legislator*

**Glen Head**
Savinetti, Louis Gerard *town councilperson*

**Glendale**
Maltese, Serphin Ralph *state senator, lawyer*

**Herkimer**
Mitchell, Donald J. *former congressman*

**New City**
Gromack, Alexander Joseph *state legislator*

## New York

**Byrnes**, Robert Charles, Jr. *state legislative staff director*
**Coelho**, Tony *former congressman*
**Richardson**, William Blaine *former congressman, ambassador*
**Silver**, Sheldon *state legislator, lawyer*

### Pearl River
**Colman**, Samuel *assemblyman*

### Port Chester
**Oppenheimer**, Suzi *state senator*

### Roslyn Heights
**Tully**, Michael J., Jr. *state senator*

### Staten Island
**Connelly**, Elizabeth Ann *state legislator*

### Yonkers
**Singer**, Cecile Doris *state legislator*

## NORTH CAROLINA

### Advance
**Cochrane**, Betsy Lane *state senator*

### Burlington
**Holt**, Bertha Merrill *state legislator*

### Chapel Hill
†**Price**, David Eugene *congressman, educator*

### Fayetteville
**Tyson-Autry**, Carrie Eula *legislative consultant, researcher, small business owner*

### New Bern
**Perdue**, Beverly Moore *state legislator, geriatric consultant*

### Raleigh
**Cauthen**, Carmen Wimberley *legislative staff member, jewelry designer*
**Sutton**, Ronnie Neal *state legislator, lawyer*
**Tally**, Lura Self *state legislator*

### Winston Salem
**Ward**, Marvin Martin *retired state senator*

## NORTH DAKOTA

### Ashley
**Kretschmar**, William Edward *state legislator, lawyer*

### Bismarck
**Clark**, Tony *state legislator*
**Schobinger**, Randy Arthur *state legislator*

### Crosby
**Andrist**, John M. *state senator*

### Edgeley
**Schimke**, Dennis J. *state legislator*

### Fargo
**Berg**, Rick Alan *state legislator, real estate investor*
**Mathern**, Tim *state senator, social worker*

### Fessenden
**Streibel**, Bryce *state senator*

### Grand Forks
**DeMers**, Judy Lee *state legislator, university dean*
**Poolman**, Jim *state legislator*
**Stenehjem**, Wayne Kevin *state senator, lawyer*

### Minot
**Mickelson**, Stacey *state legislator*
**Watne**, Darlene Claire *state legislator*

### Saint Anthony
**Tomac**, Steven Wayne *state senator, farmer*

### Valley City
**Sabby**, Leland *state legislator*

### Williston
**Rennerfeldt**, Earl Ronald *state legislator, farmer, rancher*
**Wenstrom**, Frank Augustus *state senator*
**Yockim**, James Craig *state senator, oil and gas executive*

## OHIO

### Akron
**Seiberling**, John Frederick *former congressman, law educator, lawyer*

### Cincinnati
**Sterne**, Bobbie Lynn *city council member*

### Cleveland
**Pringle**, Barbara Carroll *state legislator*

### Columbus
**Boyd**, Barbara H. *state legislator*
**Drake**, Grace L. *state senator*
**Furney**, Linda Jeanne *state legislator*
**Gillmor**, Karen Lako *state legislator, strategic planner*
**Hottinger**, Jay *state legislator*
**Kearns**, Merle Grace *state senator*
**McLin**, Rhine Lana *state senator, funeral service executive, educator*
**Mead**, Priscilla *state legislator*

### Dayton
**Reid**, Marilyn Joanne *state legislator, lawyer*

### Hillsboro
**Snyder**, Harry Cooper *retired state senator*

### Kettering
**Horn**, Charles F. *state senator, lawyer, electrical engineer*

### Lima
**Cupp**, Robert Richard *state senator, attorney*

### Parma
**Mottl**, Ronald M. *state legislator, lawyer*

## OKLAHOMA

### Oklahoma City
**Boyd**, Laura Wooldridge *state legislator*
**Fair**, Michael Edward *state senator*
**Ford**, Charles Reed *state senator*
**Garrett**, Kathryn Ann (Kitty Garrett) *legislative clerk*
**Pope**, Tim Lane *state legislator, consultant*

## OREGON

### Bend
**Cooley**, Wes *former congressman*

### Gladstone
**Bradbury**, William Chapman, III *former state senator*

### Portland
**Hatfield**, Mark O. *former senator*

### Salem
**Brown**, Kate *state legislator*
**Gold**, Shirley Jeanne *state legislator, labor relations specialist*
**Taylor**, Jacqueline Self *state legislator*
**VanLeeuwen**, Liz Susan (Elizabeth VanLeeuwen) *state legislator, farmer*

## PENNSYLVANIA

### Allentown
**DeFiore**, Anthony Edward *administrative aide*

### Centre Hall
**Rudy**, Ruth Corman *former state legislator*

### Easton
**Reibman**, Jeanette Fichman *retired state senator*

### Erie
**Boyes**, Karl W. *state legislator*

### Harrisburg
**Armstrong**, Gibson E. *state senator*
**Armstrong**, Thomas Errol *state legislator*
**Gruitza**, Michael *state legislator, lawyer*
**Hart**, Melissa A. *state senator*
**Itkin**, Ivan *state legislator*
**Josephs**, Babette *state legislator*
**Loeper**, F. Joseph *state senator*
**Nyce**, Robert Eugene *state legislator, tax accountant*

### North Huntingdon
**Kukovich**, Allen Gale *legislator, lawyer*

### Oil City
**Hutchinson**, Scott Edward *state legislator*

### Philadelphia
**Foglietta**, Thomas Michael *congressman*

### Pittsburgh
**Fisher**, D. Michael *state senator, lawyer*

### Wayne
**Rubley**, Carole A. *state legislator*

### Wellsboro
**Baker**, Matthew Edward *state legislator*

## RHODE ISLAND

### Lincoln
**Lyle**, John William, Jr. *former state senator, lawyer, social studies educator*

### Providence
**Algiere**, Dennis L. *state senator*
**Coffey**, Sean Owen *former state senator, lawyer*
**Fogarty**, Charles Joseph *state senator*
**Gibbs**, June Nesbitt *state senator*
**Weygand**, Robert A. *congressman*

### Warwick
**Carlin**, David R., Jr. *state senator*
**Revens**, John Cosgrove, Jr. *state senator, lawyer*

## SOUTH CAROLINA

### Columbia
**Cork**, Holly A. *state legislator*
**Courson**, John Edward *state senator, insurance company executive*
**Harvin**, Charles Alexander, III *state legislator*
**Leatherman**, Hugh Kenneth, Sr. *state senator, business executive*
**Smith**, James Roland *state legislator*

### Greenville
**Manly**, Sarah Letitia *state legislator, ophthalmic photographer, angiographer*
**Mann**, James Robert *congressman*

### Spartanburg
**Patterson**, Elizabeth Johnston *former congresswoman*

### West Columbia
**Wilson**, Addison Graves (Joe Wilson) *state senator, lawyer*

## SOUTH DAKOTA

### Bison
**Wishard**, Della Mae *state legislator*

### Black Hawk
**Maicki**, G. Carol *former state senator, consultant*

### Brookings
**McClure-Bibby**, Mary Anne *former state legislator*

### Miller
**Morford-Burg**, JoAnn *state senator, investment company executive*

### Pierre
**Pederson**, Gordon Roy *state legislator, retired military officer*

### Sioux Falls
**Paisley**, Keith Watkins *state senator, small business owner*

### Sturgis
**Ingalls**, Marie Cecelie *former state legislator, retail executive*

## TENNESSEE

### Maryville
**Koella**, Carl Ohm, Jr. *retired state senator, lawyer*

### Nashville
**Bragg**, John Thomas *state legislator, retired businessman*
**Kisber**, Matthew Harris *state legislator*
**Person**, Curtis S., Jr. *state senator, lawyer*

## TEXAS

### Abilene
**Hunter**, Robert Dean (Bob Hunter) *state legislator, retired university official*

### Austin
**Brown**, J. E. (Buster Brown) *state senator, lawyer*
**Bullock**, Robert D. (Bob Bullock) *state legislator, lieutenant governor, lawyer*
**Denny**, Mary Craver *state legislator, rancher*
**Kilgore**, Joe Madison *former congressman, lawyer*
**Turner**, Sylvester *state legislator, lawyer*

### Beaumont
**Brooks**, Jack Bascom *congressman*

### Dallas
**Cain**, David *state senator, lawyer*
**Leedom**, John Nesbett *state senator, distribution company executive*

### El Paso
**Vowell**, Jack C. *former state legislator, investor*

### Fort Worth
**Geren**, Pete (Preston Geren) *former congressman*
**Mowery**, Anna Renshaw *state legislator*
**Shannon**, Larry Redding *administrative assistant*
**Willis**, Doyle Henry *state legislator, lawyer*

### Garland
**Driver**, Joe L. *state legislator, insurance agent*

### Houston
**Green**, Gene *congressman*

### Humble
**Fields**, Jack Milton, Jr. *former congressman*

### Irving
**Armey**, Richard Keith (Dick Armey) *congressman*

### Laredo
**Zaffirini**, Judith *state senator*

### Lubbock
**Montford**, John Thomas *state legislator, academic administrator, lawyer*

### Midland
**Craddick**, Thomas Russell *state representative, investor*

## UTAH

### Bountiful
**Burningham**, Kim Richard *former state legislator*

### Cedar City
**Hunter**, R. Haze *former state legislator*

### Corinne
**Ferry**, Miles Yeoman *state official*

### Ogden
**Montgomery**, Robert F. *state legislator, retired surgeon, cattle rancher*

### Provo
**Valentine**, John Lester *state legislator, lawyer*

### Salt Lake City
**Bennett**, Janet Huff *legislative staff member*

**Black**, Wilford Rex, Jr. *state senator*
**Carnahan**, Orville Darrell *state legislator, retired college president*
**Garn**, Edwin Jacob (Jake Garn) *former senator*
**Greene**, Enid *former congresswoman*
**Shepherd**, Karen *former congresswoman*

### Tremonton
**Kerr**, Kleon Harding *former state senator, educator*

## VERMONT

### Burlington
**Carroll**, John Marcus Conlon *state senator, banker*

### Montpelier
**Paquin**, Edward H., Jr. *state legislator*
**Steele**, Karen Kiarsis *state legislator*
**Wood**, Barbara Louise Champion *state legislator, retired*

### Saint Johnsbury
**Crosby**, George Miner *state legislator*

## VIRGINIA

### Alexandria
**Clinger**, William Floyd, Jr. *former congressman*
**Collins**, Cardiss *former congresswoman*
**Montgomery**, Gillespie V. (Sonny Montgomery) *former congressman*
**Ticer**, Patricia *state senator*

### Arlington
**Bevill**, Tom *retired congressman, lawyer*
**Rose**, Charles Grandison, III (Charlie Rose) *former congressman*
**Volkmer**, Harold L. *former congressman*

### Burke
**Smeeton**, Thomas Rooney *governmental affairs consultant*

### Charlottesville
**Payne**, Lewis Franklin, Jr. (L.F. Payne) *former congressman*

### Danville
**Moorefield**, Jennifer Mary *legislative staff member*

### Fairfax
**Johns**, Michael Douglas *legislative staff member, public policy analyst*
**Miller**, Emilie F. *former state senator, consultant*

### Franconia
**Keating**, Gladys Brown *state legislator*

### Halifax
**Anderson**, Howard Palmer *former state senator*

### Leesburg
**Mims**, William Cleveland *state legislator, lawyer*

### Mc Lean
**Burke**, Sheila P. *legislative staff member*
**Callahan**, Vincent Francis, Jr. *state legislator, publisher*
**Hirst**, Nancy Hand *retired legislative staff member*
**St. Germain**, Fernand Joseph *congressman*

### Merrifield
**Scott**, James Martin *state legislator, healthcare system executive*

### Newport News
**Trible**, Paul Seward, Jr. *former United States senator*

### Norfolk
**Miller**, Yvonne Bond *state senator, educator*

### Richmond
**Schaar**, Susan Clarke *state legislative staff member*

### Vienna
**Higginbotham**, Wendy Jacobson *political adviser, writer*

### Woodbridge
**Garon**, Richard Joseph, Jr. *chief of staff, political worker*

## WASHINGTON

### Everett
**Nelson**, Gary *county councilman, engineer*

### Olympia
**Kessler**, Lynn Elizabeth *state legislator*
**Kohl**, Jeanne Elizabeth *state senator, sociologist, educator*
**Long**, Jeanine Hundley *state legislator*
**Spanel**, Harriet Rosa Albertsen *state senator*

### Puyallup
**Tate**, Randall J. (Randy Tate) *former congressman*

### Ritzville
**Schoesler**, Mark Gerald *state legislator, farmer*

### Seattle
**Evans**, Daniel Jackson *former senator*

### Spokane
**Dellwo**, Dennis A. *state legislator*

## WEST VIRGINIA

### Elkins
**Spears**, Jae *state legislator*

**Parkersburg**
Brum, Brenda *state legislator, librarian*

### WISCONSIN

**Green Bay**
Green, Mark Andrew *state legislator, lawyer*

**Janesville**
Wood, Wayne W. *state legislator*

**Juneau**
Fitzgerald, Scott *state legislator*

**Madison**
Barish, Lawrence Stephen *nonpartisan legislative staff administrator*
Burke, Brian B. *state senator, lawyer*
Darling, Alberta Statkus *state legislator, marketing executive, former art museum executive*
Farrow, Margaret Ann *state legislator*
Klug, Scott Leo *congressman*
Krusick, Margaret Ann *state legislator*
Moen, Rodney Charles *state senator, retired naval officer*
Panzer, Mary E. *state legislator*
Porter, Cloyd Allen *state representative*
Roessler, Carol Ann *state senator*
Rude, Brian David *state legislator*
Rutkowski, James Anthony *state legislator*
Schultz, Dale Walter *state senator*
Swoboda, Lary Joseph *state legislator*
Turner, Robert Lloyd *state legislator*
Young, Rebecca Mary Conrad *state legislator*

**Waterford**
Gunderson, Scott L. *state legislator*

### WYOMING

**Casper**
Donley, Russell Lee, III *former state representative*
Meenan, Patrick Henry *state legislator*

**Cody**
Shreve, Peg *state legislator, retired elementary educator*

**Gillette**
Gilbertz, Larry E. *state legislator, entrepreneur*

**Jackson**
LaLonde, Robert Frederick *state senator, retired*

**Lander**
Tipton, Harry Basil, Jr. *state legislator, physician*

**Laramie**
Maxfield, Peter C. *state legislator, law educator, lawyer*

**Rock Springs**
Blackwell, Samuel Eugene *state legislator*

## TERRITORIES OF THE UNITED STATES

### AMERICAN SAMOA

**Pago Pago**
Lutu, Afoa Moega *legislator, lawyer*
Tulafono, Togiola T.A. *senator*

### PUERTO RICO

**San Juan**
Acevedo-Vilá, Aníbal *state legislator, lawyer*

## MILITARY ADDRESSES OF THE UNITED STATES

### ATLANTIC

**APO**
Hughes, William John *former congressman, diplomat*

## CANADA

### ALBERTA

**Edmonton**
Klein, Ralph *premier of Alberta*

### BRITISH COLUMBIA

**Vancouver**
McWhinney, Edward Watson *Canadian government legislator*

**Victoria**
Boone, Lois Ruth *legislator*
Weisgerber, John Sylvester *provincial legislator*

### MANITOBA

**Winnipeg**
Roblin, Duff *former Canadian senator, health facility administrator*

### ONTARIO

**Ottawa**
Austin, Jacob (Jack Austin) *Canadian senator*
Boudria, Don *Canadian government official*
†Collenette, Penny *legislative aide*
Doyle, Richard James *Canadian senator, former editor*
Foster, Maurice Brydon *Canadian legislator*
Kilgour, David *Canadian member of parliament*
Lynch-Staunton, John *Canadian senator*
MacEachen, Allan Joseph *retired senator*
Maheu, Shirley *Canadian legislator*
Marleau, Robert *parliamentary clerk*
Murray, Lowell *Canadian senator*
Parent, Gilbert *member Canadian House of Commons*
Robichaud, Louis Joseph *Canadian senator*

### QUEBEC

**Montreal**
Castonguay, Claude *former senator, corporate director, actuary*

## ADDRESS UNPUBLISHED

Arnold, Sheila *former state legislator*
Baker, Howard Henry, Jr. *former senator, lawyer*
Baker, Richard Hugh *congressman*
Barnhart, Jo Anne B. *government official*
Barton, Joe Linus *congressman*
Beals, Nancy Farwell *state legislator*
Bell, Clarence Deshong *state senator, lawyer*
Bell, Clarence Elmo *former state senator*
Berman, Lori Beth *legislative staff member*
Bilbray, James Hubert *former congressman, lawyer, consultant*
Bliley, Thomas Jerome, Jr. *congressman*
Bluechel, Alan *state senator, wood structural components manufacturing company executive*
Bono, Sonny Salvatore *congressman, singer, composer, former mayor*
Brodsky, Richard Louis *state legislator*
Bunning, Jim *congressman, former professional baseball player*
Burton, Joseph Alfred *state legislator*
Charlton, Betty Jo *retired state legislator*
Churchill, Robert Wilson *state legislator, lawyer*
Coble, Howard *congressman, lawyer*
Cochran, Thad *senator*
Coleman, Ronald D. (Ron Coleman) *former congressman*
de la Garza, Kika (Eligio de la Garza) *former congressman*
Doderer, Minnette Frerichs *state legislator*
Drake, Robert Alan *state legislator, animal nutritionist, mayor*
Farmer, Elaine Frazier *state legislator*
Findley, Troy Ray *state legislator*
Ford, Wendell Hampton *senator*
Franks, Gary Alvin *former congressman, real estate professional*
Gallegly, Elton William *congressman*
Gordly, Avel Louise *state legislator, community activist*
Goss, Porter J. *congressman*
Granger, Kay *state legislator*
Gullatt, Jane *state legislator*
Hammerschmidt, John Paul *retired congressman, lumber company executive*
Hansen, James Vear *congressman*
Hatch, Orrin Grant *senator*
Hawkins, Mary Ellen Higgins (Mary Ellen Higgins) *former state legislator, public relations consultant*
Hearn, Joyce Camp *retired state legislator, educator*
Hichens, Walter Wilson *former state senator*
Hickey, Winifred E(spy) *former state senator, social worker*
Hill, Anita Carraway *retired state legislator*
†Hinojosa, Rubén *congressman*
Holliday, Robert Kelvin *retired state senator, former newspaper executive*
Humphrey, Shirley Joy *state education administrator*
Hunter, Duncan Lee *congressman*
Hutchison, Kay Bailey *senator*
Johnson, Bruce *state legislator*
Kindness, Thomas Norman *former congressman, lawyer, consultant*
Kleven, Marguerite *state senator*
Knight, Alice Dorothy Tirrell *state legislator*
Konnyu, Ernest Leslie *former congressman*
Lazechko, D. M. (Molly Lazechko) *former state legislator*
Lightfoot, James Ross *former congressman*
Marty, John *state senator, writer*
†McCarthy, Carolyn *congresswoman*
Mc Govern, George Stanley *former senator*
McHale, Paul *congressman, lawyer*
†McIntyre, Mike *congressman*
Meshel, Harry *state senator, political party official*
Mikulski, Barbara Ann *senator*
Myers, John Thomas *retired congressman*
Nielson, Howard Curtis *former congressman, retired educator*
Nussle, James Allen *congressman*
Osler, Dorothy K. *state legislator*
Parry, Atwell J., Jr. *state senator, retailer*
Pascoe, Patricia Hill *state senator, writer*
†Paul, Ron *congressman*
Pena, Manuel, Jr. *retired state senator*
Penny, Timothy Joseph *congressman*
Pettis-Roberson, Shirley McCumber *former congresswoman*
Pond, Phyllis Joan Ruble *state legislator*
Proxmire, William *former senator*
Pryce, Deborah D. *congresswoman*
Reid, Harry *senator*
†Reyes, Silvestre *congressman*
Roth, Toby *former congressman, political consultant*
Satterthwaite, Helen Foster *retired state legislator*
Searle, Rodney Newell *state legislator, farmer, insurance agent*
Seastrand, Andrea H. *former congresswoman*
†Sessions, Pete *congressman*
Simpson, Alan Kooi *former senator*
Skinner, Patricia Morag *state legislator*
Soles, Ada Leigh *former state legislator, government advisor*
Sorensen, Sheila *state senator*
Stallings, Henry E., II *state legislator*
Stickney, Jessica *former state legislator*
Stockman, Stephen E. *former congressman*
†Sununu, John E. *congressman*
Sykora, Barbara Zwach *state legislator*
†Tauscher, Ellen O. *congresswoman*
†Thune, John *congressman*
Treppler, Irene Esther *retired state senator*
Valentine, I. T., Jr. (Tim Valentine) *former congressman*
Vancrum, Robert James *retired state senator, lawyer*
Van Engen, Thomas Lee *state legislator*
Viverito, Louis S. *state legislator*
Waldon, Alton Ronald, Jr. *state senator*
Zimmerman, Harold Samuel *retired state senator, state administrator, newspaper executive*

# HEALTHCARE: DENTISTRY

## UNITED STATES

### ALABAMA

**Birmingham**
Alling, Charles Calvin, III *oral-maxillofacial surgeon, educator, writer*
Davidson, Roy Grady, Jr. *dentist*
Fullmer, Harold Milton *dentist, educator*
Manson-Hing, Lincoln Roy *dental educator*

**Lillian**
Shory, Naseeb Lein *dentist, retired state official*

### ARIZONA

**Flagstaff**
Ririe, Craig Martin *periodontist*

**Oro Valley**
Haas-Oro, Debra Ann *dentist*

**Phoenix**
Fournier, Donald Frederick *dentist*
Sullivan, George Anerson *orthodontist*

**Tucson**
†Davis, Richard Calhoun *dentist*
Geistfeld, Ronald Elwood *retired dental educator*
Hawke, Robert Francis *dentist*
Nadler, George L. *orthodontist*

### CALIFORNIA

**Arcadia**
Gamboa, George Charles *oral surgeon, educator*

**Arcata**
Hise, Mark Allen *dentist*

**Burlingame**
Donlon, William Christopher *maxillofacial surgeon, educator, author, editor*
Truta, Marianne Patricia *oral and maxillofacial surgeon, educator, author*

**Concord**
Chiappone, Robert Carl *orthodontist*

**La Jolla**
Silverstone, Leon Martin *dental research cariologist, neuroscientist, educator, researcher*

**La Verne**
Huigens, Daniel Dean *dentist*

**Loma Linda**
Feller, Ralph Paul *dentist, educator*

**Long Beach**
Gehring, George Joseph, Jr. *dentist*

**Los Angeles**
Dummett, Clifton Orrin *dentist, educator*
Evans, Caswell Alves, Jr. *dentist*
Yagiela, John Allen *dental educator*

**Manteca**
Tonn, Elverne Meryl *pediatric dentist, dental benefits consultant*

**Orange**
Martin, Michael Lee *orthodontist*

**Pasadena**
Mc Carthy, Frank Martin *oral surgeon, surgical sciences educator*

**Pebble Beach**
Rossing, Catherine Barrett Schwab *dental hygienist*

**San Diego**
Barsan, Richard Emil *oral and maxillofacial surgeon*

**San Francisco**
Bensinger, David August *dentist, university dean*
Dugoni, Arthur A. *orthodontics educator, university dean*
Greene, John Clifford *dentist, former university dean*
Greenspan, Deborah *oral medicine educator*
Greenspan, John S. *dentistry educator, educator and administrator*
Khosla, Ved Mitter *oral and maxillofacial surgeon, educator*
Wirthlin, Milton Robert, Jr. *periodontist*

**San Jose**
Higgins, James Bradley *dentist*
Yoshizumi, Donald Tetsuro *dentist*

**San Rafael**
Gryson, Joseph Anthony *orthodontist*

**Thousand Palms**
Smith, Charles Thomas *retired dentist, educator*

**Torrance**
Leake, Donald Lewis *oral and maxillofacial surgeon, oboist*

**Vacaville**
Dedeaux, Paul J. *orthodontist*

**West Hollywood**
Etessami, Rambod *endonontist*

### COLORADO

**Boulder**
Colbert, Elbert Lynn *dentist, recording artist*

**Englewood**
Eames, Wilmer Ballou *dental educator*

**Golden**
Christensen, Robert Wayne *oral maxillofacial surgeon, minister*

**U S A F Academy**
Linehan, Allan Douglas *prosthodontist*

### CONNECTICUT

**Brookfield**
Cohen, Mark Steven *dentist*

**Farmington**
Löe, Harald *dentist, educator, researcher*

**New Haven**
Dileone, Carmel Montano *dental hygienist*

**Norwalk**
Brod, Morton Shlevin *oral surgeon*

**Old Greenwich**
Strait, Almuth Vandiveer *dentist*

### DISTRICT OF COLUMBIA

**Washington**
Calhoun, Noah Robert *oral maxillofacial surgeon, educator*
Gardner, Alvin Frederick *oral pathologist, government official*
Lorton, Lewis *dentist, researcher, computer scientist*
Sazima, Henry John *oral and maxillofacial surgery educator*
Sinkford, Jeanne Craig *dentist, educator*

### FLORIDA

**Aventura**
Hyman, Milton *dental educator*

**Bay Harbor Island**
Rosenbluth, Morton *periodontist, educator*

**Boca Raton**
Lerner, Theodore Raphael *dentist*

**Boynton Beach**
Kronman, Joseph Henry *orthodontist*

**Fort Lauderdale**
Dorn, Samuel O. *endodontist*

**Fort Myers**
Laboda, Gerald *oral and maxillofacial surgeon*

**Gainesville**
Javid, Nikzad Sabet *dentist, prosthodontist educator*
Medina, Jose Enrique *dentist, educator*
Widmer, Charles Glenn *dentist, researcher*

**Jupiter**
Nessmith, H(erbert) Alva *dentist*

**Miami**
Gittess, Ronald Marvin *dentist*
Glenn, Frances Bonde *dentist*
Haas, Charles David *dentist*
Higley, Bruce Wadsworth *orthodontist*
Iver, Robert Drew *dentist*
Leeds, Robert *dentist*

**Pensacola**
Hooley, James Robert *oral and maxillofacial surgeon, educator, dean*

**West Palm Beach**
Elder, Stewart Taylor *dentist, retired naval officer*

**Winter Park**
Counts, Christine Gay *dental hygienist*
McKean, Thomas Wayne *dentist, retired naval officer*

### GEORGIA

**Atlanta**
Freedman, Louis Martin *dentist*

**Augusta**
Hammer, Wade Burke *oral and maxillofacial surgeon, educator*

**Evans**
Beaudreau, David Eugene *dentist, educator*

## HAWAII

**Honolulu**
George, Peter T. *orthodontist*
Nishimura, Pete Hideo *oral surgeon*
Scheerer, Ernest William *dentist*

**Pearl City**
Sue, Alan Kwai Keong *dentist*

## ILLINOIS

**Alton**
Dickey, Keith Winfield *dentist, dental educator*

**Chicago**
Bogert, John Alden, II *dental association executive*
Buckner, James Lowell *dentist*
Diefenbach, Viron Leroy *dental, public health educator, university dean*
Eisenmann, Dale Richard *dental educator*
Glenner, Richard Allen *dentist, dental historian*
Goepp, Robert August *dental educator, oral pathologist*
Graber, Thomas M. *orthodontist*
Hardaway, Ernest, II *oral and maxillofacial surgeon, public health official*
Horowitz, Fred L. *dentist, administrator, consultant*
Liu, Khang-Lee *dentist, educator*
Santangelo, Mario Vincent *dentist*
Weclew, Victor T. *dentist*
Yale, Seymour Hershel *dental radiologist, educator, university dean, gerontologist*
Zaki, Abdelmoneim Emam *dental educator*

**Elburn**
Willey, James Lee *dentist*

**Elgin**
Perry, Harold Tyner *dentist, educator*

**Geneva**
Kallstrom, Charles Clark *dentist*

**Godfrey**
King, Ordie Herbert, Jr. *oral pathologist*

**Naperville**
Grimley, Jeffrey Michael *dentist*

**Pekin**
Bell, John Richard *dentist*

**Riverwoods**
Douglas, Bruce Lee *oral and maxillofacial surgeon, educator, health consultant, gerontology consultant*

**Schaumburg**
Colvard, Michael David *periodontist, oral medicine and laser surgery specialist*

**Taylorville**
Gardner, Jerry Dean *dentist, military officer*

## INDIANA

**Carmel**
Roche, James Richard *pediatric dentist, university dean*

**Columbus**
Arthur, Jewell Kathleen *dental hygienist*

**Dyer**
Teuscher, George William *dental educator*

**Evansville**
Brown, Randall Keith *orthodontist*
Fritz, Edward Lane *dentist*

**Indianapolis**
Christen, Arden Gale *dental educator, researcher, consultant*
Kemper, Walker Warder, Jr. *dentist, educator*
Sarbinoff, James Adair *periodontist, consultant*
Standish, Samuel Miles *oral pathologist, college dean*

**Peru**
Davidson, John Robert *dentist*

**Terre Haute**
Roshel, John Albert, Jr. *orthodontist*

## IOWA

**City**
Bjorndal, Arne Magne *endodontist*

**Iowa City**
Bishara, Samir Edward *orthodontist*
Jacobs, Richard Matthew *dentist, orthodontics educator*
Olin, William Harold *orthodontist, educator*

## KANSAS

**Overland Park**
Eshelman, Enos Grant, Jr. *prosthodontist*

**Wellington**
Willis, Robert Addison *dentist*

## KENTUCKY

**Brandenburg**
Bowen, Patricia Lederer *dental educator*

**Lexington**
Mink, John Robert *dental educator*
Wesley, Robert Cook *dental educator*

**Louisville**
Crim, Gary Allen *dental educator*
Parkins, Frederick Milton *dental educator, university dean*
Stewart, Arthur Van *dental educator, geriatric health administrator*

## LOUISIANA

**New Orleans**
Misiek, Dale Joseph *oral and maxillofacial surgeon*

**Shreveport**
Lloyd, Cecil Rhodes *pediatric dentist*

## MARYLAND

**Bethesda**
Kruger, Gustav Otto, Jr. *oral surgeon, educator*

**Potomac**
Cotton, William Robert *dentist*

## MASSACHUSETTS

**Boston**
Frankl, Spencer Nelson *dentist, university dean*
Goldhaber, Paul *dental educator*
Shklar, Gerald *oral pathologist, periodontist, educator*
White, George Edward *pedodontist, educator*

**Brewster**
Gumpright, Herbert Lawrence, Jr. *dentist*

**Brockton**
Hodge-Spencer, Cheryl Ann *orthodontist*

**Dorchester**
Lee, June Warren *dentist*

**Hanover**
Lonborg, James Reynold *dentist, former professional baseball player*

**Medfield**
Hein, John William *dentist, educator*

**North Quincy**
Segelman, Allyn Evan *dentist, researcher*

**Wellesley**
Doku, Hristo Chris *dental educator*

## MICHIGAN

**Ann Arbor**
Asgar, Kamal *dentistry educator*
Ash, Major McKinley, Jr. *dentist, educator*
Avery, James Knuckey *dental educator*
Christiansen, Richard Louis *orthodontics educator, research director, former dean*
Craig, Robert George *dental science educator*
Reese, James W. *orthodontist*

**Detroit**
Dziuba, Henry Frank *dental school administrator*

## MINNESOTA

**Mankato**
Dumke, Melvin Philip *dentist*

**Minneapolis**
Elzay, Richard Paul *dental school administrator*
Shapiro, Burton Leonard *oral pathologist, geneticist, educator*
Wolff, Larry F. *dental educator, researcher*

**Saint Paul**
Jensen, James Robert *dentist, educator*

## MISSOURI

**Kansas City**
Burk, Norman *oral surgeon*
Moore, David Lowell *dentist*
Moore, Dorsey Jerome *dentistry educator, maxillofacial prosthetist*
Scott, Ruth Lois *dental hygiene educator*

**Lees Summit**
Waite, Daniel Elmer *retired oral surgeon*

**Saint Louis**
Isselhard, Donald Edward *dentist*
Selfridge, George Dever *dentist, retired naval officer*

## MONTANA

**Hardin**
MacClean, Walter Lee *dentist*

## NEBRASKA

**Omaha**
Lynch, Benjamin Leo *oral surgeon educator*
Zaiman, K. Robert *dentist*

## NEW JERSEY

**Barrington**
Fanelle, Carmella *dentist*

**Chatham**
Hurley, Allyson Kingsley *dentist*

**Eatontown**
Furman, Samuel Elliott *dentist*

**Englewood**
Schwartz, Howard Alan *periodontist*

**Fort Lee**
Kiriakopoulos, George Constantine *dentist*

**Hammonton**
Stephanick, Carol Ann *dentist, consultant*

**Ho Ho Kus**
Van Slooten, Ronald Henry Joseph *dentist*

**Leonia**
Armstrong, Edward Bradford, Jr. *oral and maxillofacial surgeon, educator*

**Montclair**
Bolden, Theodore Edward *denist, educator, dental research consultant*

**Morris Plains**
Picozzi, Anthony *dentistry educator, educational administrator*

**Mountainside**
Ricciardi, Antonio *prosthodontist, implantologist, educator*

**Newark**
Kantor, Mel Lewis *dental educator, researcher*

**Ridgewood**
Lucca, John James *retired dental educator*

**Sparta**
Alberto, Pamela Louise *oral and maxillofacial surgeon, educator*

**Westfield**
Feret, Adam Edward, Jr. *dentist*

**Woodbridge**
Galkin, Samuel Bernard *orthodontist*

## NEW YORK

**Albertson**
Goodstein, Daniel Bela *oral and maxillofacial surgeon, educator, consultant*

**Bayside**
Lewkowitz, Karen Helene *orthodontist*

**Bronx**
Andreen, Aviva Louise *dentist, researcher, academic administrator, educator*
Friedman, Joel Matthew *oral and maxillofacial surgeon, educator*

**Brooklyn**
Cranin, Abraham Norman *oral and maxillofacial surgeon, researcher*
Ivanhoe, Herman *dentist*

**Buffalo**
Ciancio, Sebastian Gene *periodontist, educator*
Drinnan, Alan John *oral pathologist*
Machtei, Eli E. *periodontist*

**Camillus**
Caryl, William R., Jr. *orthodontist*

**Elmira**
Bellohusen, Ronald Michael *orthodontist, educator*

**Great Neck**
Elkowitz, Lloyd Kent *dental anesthesiologist, dentist, pharmacist*
Wank, Gerald Sidney *periodontist*

**Jamaica**
Zambito, Raymond Francis *oral surgeon, educator*

**New York**
Arvystas, Michael Geciauskas *orthodontist, educator*
Brzustowicz, Stanislaw Henry *clinical dentistry educator*
Di Salvo, Nicholas Armand *dental educator, orthodontist*
Joskow, Renee W. *dentist, educator*
Kaslick, Ralph Sidney *dentist, educator*
Klatell, Jack *dentist*
Kulik, Lewis Tashrak *dentist*
Mandel, Irwin Daniel *dentist*
Marder, Michael Zachary *dentist, researcher, educator*
McCabe, John Charles *oral surgeon*
Mulvihill, James Edward *periodontist*
Scarola, John Michael *dentist, educator*
Sendax, Victor Irven *dentist, educator, dental implant researcher*

**Oakdale**
Sherman, Jeffrey Alan *dentist*

**Port Jefferson**
Boucher, Louis Jack *retired dentist, educator*

**Rochester**
Billings, Ronald J. *dental research administrator*
Bowen, William Henry *dental researcher, dental educator*

**Rye**
Hopf, Frank Rudolph *dentist*

**Stony Brook**
Sreebny, Leo M. *oral biology and pathology educator*

**Tarrytown**
Zegarelli, Edward Victor *retired dental educator, researcher*

**Wantagh**
Ross, Sheldon Jules *dentist*

**Wappingers Falls**
Engelman, Melvin Alkon *retired dentist, business executive, scientist*

## NORTH CAROLINA

**Chapel Hill**
Arnold, Roland R. *dental educator and researcher*
Baker, Ronald Dale *dental educator, surgeon, university administrator*
Barker, Ben D. *dentist, educator*
Bawden, James Wyatt *dental educator, dental scientist*
Hershey, H(oward) Garland, Jr. *university administrator, orthodontist*
Kula, Katherine Sue *dentist*
Proffit, William Robert *orthodontics educator*
Stamm, John William Rudolph *dentist, educator, academic dean*
White, Raymond Petrie, Jr. *dentist, educator*

**Charlotte**
Twisdale, Harold Winfred *dentist*

## OHIO

**Canton**
Osborne, Harry Alan *orthodontist*

**Cleveland**
De Marco, Thomas Joseph *periodontist, educator*

**Columbus**
Buchsieb, Walter Charles *orthodontist*
Goorey, Nancy Jane *dentist*
Horton, John Edward *periodontist, educator*
Jolly, Daniel Ehs *dental educator*
Stevenson, Robert Benjamin, III *prosthodontist, writer*

**Cuyahoga Falls**
Barsan, Robert Blake *dentist*

**Hubbard**
Rose, Ernst *dentist*

**Lancaster**
Burns, Glenn Richard *dentist*

**Uniontown**
Naugle, Robert Paul *dentist*

**Willoughby**
Stern, Michael David *dentist*

## OKLAHOMA

**Edmond**
Brown, William Ernest *dentist*

**Tulsa**
Kelly, Vincent Michael, Jr. *orthodontist*

## OREGON

**Medford**
Barnum, William Laird *pedodontist*

**Newport**
Richardson, Bruce LeVoyle *dentist*

**Portland**
Bates, Richard Mather *dentist*
Clarke, J(oseph) Henry *dental educator, dentist*
Van Hassel, Henry John *dentist, educator, university dean*

**Tualatin**
Barnett, Baron Gale *prosthodontist*

## PENNSYLVANIA

**Allison Park**
Soxman, Jane Ann *pediatric dentist*

**Clarion**
Foreman, Thomas Alexander *dentist*

**Danville**
Kleponis, Jerome Albert *dentist*
Lessin, Michael Edward *oral-maxillofacial surgeon*

**Lansdale**
Strohecker, Leon Harry, Jr. *orthodontist*

**New Holland**
Amor, James Michael *dentist*

**Norristown**
Steinberg, Arthur Irwin *periodontist, educator*

**Philadelphia**
Fielding, Allen Fred *oral and maxillofacial surgeon, educator*
Listgarten, Max Albert *periodontics educator*

Winkler, Sheldon *dentist, educator*

**Pittsburgh**
Ismail, Yahia Hassan *dentist, educator*
Stiff, Robert Henry *dentist, educator*
Thompson, Kay Francis *dentist*

**Radnor**
Vanarsdall, Robert Lee, Jr. *orthodontist, educator*

**Wayne**
Guernsey, Louis Harold *retired oral and maxillofacial surgeon, educator*

## RHODE ISLAND

**Providence**
Mehlman, Edwin Stephen *endodontist*

## SOUTH CAROLINA

**Charleston**
Salinas, Carlos Francisco *dentist, educator*

**Lake City**
TruLuck, James Paul, Jr. *dentist, vintner*

## TENNESSEE

**Knoxville**
Gotcher, Jack Everett, Jr. *oral and maxillofacial surgeon*

**Memphis**
Butts, Herbert Clell *dentist, educator*
Fields, W(ade) Thomas *dental educator*
Harris, Edward Frederick *orthodontics educator, physical anthropologist*
Huget, Eugene Floyd *dental educator, researcher*
Jurand, Jerry George *periodontology educator, researcher*
Spitznagel, John Keith *periodontist, researcher*

## TEXAS

**Dallas**
Farris, Edward Thompson *dentist, medical researcher, real estate developer and broker*
Goodwin, Joel Franklin, Sr. *dentist*
Lambert, Joseph Parker *dentist*
McWhorter, Kathleen *orthodontist*

**Flower Mound**
Kolodny, Stanley Charles *oral surgeon, air force officer*

**Houston**
Allen, Don Lee *dentistry educator*
Masters, Ronald G. *dentist, educator*
Sweet, James Brooks *oral and maxillofacial surgeon*

**Plano**
Taylor, Paul Peak *pediatric dentist, educator*

**Richardson**
Brady, Vicki Lee *dental assistant*

**San Antonio**
Pigno, Mark Anthony *prosthodontist, educator, researcher*

## VERMONT

**Essex Junction**
Lampert, S. Henry *dentist*

**Shelburne**
Sawabini, Wadi Issa *retired dentist*

## VIRGINIA

**Falls Church**
Imburg, Irving Jerome *dentist*

**Richmond**
Laskin, Daniel M. *oral and maxillofacial surgeon, educator*

**Sterling**
Block, Robert Michael *endodontist, researcher*

**Virginia Beach**
Farrell, Paul Edward *dentist, retired naval officer, educator*

**Yorktown**
Edwards, Richard Charles *oral and maxillofacial surgeon*

## WASHINGTON

**Ashford**
Ingle, John Ide *dental educator*

**Bellevue**
Carlson, Curtis Eugene *orthodontist, periodontist*

**Everett**
Oliver, William Donald *orthodontist*

**Seattle**
Dworkin, Samuel Franklin *dentist, psychologist*
Herring, Susan Weller *dental educator, oral anatomist*
Page, Roy Christopher *periodontist, educator*

**Spokane**
Foster, Ruth Mary *dental association administrator*

## WISCONSIN

**Green Bay**
Swetlik, William Philip *orthodontist*

**Milwaukee**
Scrabeck, Jon Gilmen *dental eductor*

**Racine**
Moles, Randall Carl *orthodontist*

**Wausau**
Derwinski, Dennis Anthony *dentist*

## WYOMING

**Casper**
Keim, Michael Ray *dentist*

## CANADA

### ALBERTA

**Edmonton**
Thompson, Gordon William *dentist, educator, administrator*

### BRITISH COLUMBIA

**Vancouver**
Beagrie, George Simpson *dentist, educator, dean emeritus*

### ONTARIO

**London**
Dunn, Wesley John *dental educator*

**Toronto**
Ten Cate, Arnold Richard *dentistry educator*

### QUEBEC

**Montreal**
Bentley, Kenneth Chessar *oral and maxillofacial surgeon, educator*

**Sainte Foy**
Maranda, Guy *oral maxillofacial surgeon, Canadian health facility executive, educator*

**Westmount**
Lussier, Jean-Paul *dentistry educator*

## GERMANY

**Witten**
Gaengler, Peter Wolfgang *dentist, researcher*

## SWEDEN

**Goteborg**
Bona, Christian M. *dentist, psychotherapist*

## ADDRESS UNPUBLISHED

Adisman, I. Kenneth *prosthodontist*
Brooke, Ralph Ian *dental educator, vice provost, university dean*
Coval-Apel, Naomi Miller *dentist*
Grewe, John Mitchell *orthodontist, educator*
Herman, David Jay *orthodontist*
Hoffman, Jerry Irwin *dental educator*
Johnson, Dewey E(dward), Jr. *dentist*
Lippert, Christopher Nelson *dentist, consultant*
McHugh, Earl Stephen *dentist*
Nelson, Dennis George Anthony *dental researcher, life scientist*
Newbrun, Ernest *oral biology and periodontology educator*
Scopp, Irwin Walter *periodontist, educator*

---

# HEALTHCARE: HEALTH SERVICES

## UNITED STATES

## ALABAMA

**Auburn**
Barker, Kenneth Neil *pharmacy administration educator*

**Birmingham**
Booth, Rachel Zonelle *nursing educator*
Caplan, Lester *optometrist, educator*
Cooper, Karen René *health facility administration nurse*
Devane, Denis James *health care company executive*
Gibbs, Sydney Royston *health facility administrator*
Holmes, Suzanne McRae *nursing supervisor*
Loftin, Sister Mary Frances *religious organization administrator*
Loftin, Kevin Eugene *medical facility administrator*
Miller, Dennis Edward *health medical executive*

Musacchio, Marilyn Jean *nurse midwife, educator*
Nesbitt, Carol Kelley *health services administrator*
Pedersen, Paul Bodholdt *psychologist, educator*
Peters, Henry Buckland *optometrist, educator*
Quintana, Jose Booth *health care executive*
Ramey, Craig T. *psychology educator*
Richards, J. Scott *rehabilitation medicine professional*
Roth, William Stanley *hospital foundation executive*
Smith, John Stephen *retired educational administrator, consultant*
Taub, Edward *psychology researcher*
Thorson-Houck, Janice Hargreaves *speech, language pathologist*
Weinsier, Roland Louis *nutrition educator and director*

**Daphne**
Gettig, Carl William *optometrist*

**Dothan**
Inscho, Jean Anderson *social worker*

**Fairhope**
Brumback Patterson, Cathy Jean *psychologist*

**Fort Rucker**
Caldwell, John Alvis, Jr. *experimental psychologist*

**Fultondale**
Moss, Betty Smith *social worker*

**Gadsden**
Bangham, Robert Arthur *orthotist*
Lefelhocz, Irene Hanzak *nurse, business owner*

**Hartselle**
Penn, Hugh Franklin, Jr. *psychology educator*
Slate, Joe Hutson *psychologist, educator*

**Huntsville**
Noble, Ronald Mark *sports medicine facility administrator*
O'Reilly, Patty Mollett *psychometrist, consultant*

**Lillian**
Moyer, Kenneth Evan *psychologist, educator*

**Mobile**
Clark, Jack *retired hospital company executive, accountant*
McElhaney, Richard Franklin *quality assurance nursing coordinator*
Suess, James Francis *clinical psychologist*

**Montgomery**
Keaton, Charles Howard *health care administrator*
Myers, Ira Lee *physician*
Rowan, John Robert *retired medical center director*

**Normal**
Okezie, B. Onuma *food scientist, nutritionist, educator*

**Opelika**
Knecht, Charles Daniel *veterinarian*

**Ozark**
DuBose, Elizabeth *community health nurse*

**Pelham**
Lee, James A. *health facility finance executive*

**Pell City**
Passey, George Edward *psychology educator*

**Sylacauga**
Bledsoe, Mary Louise *medical, surgical nurse*

**Tuscaloosa**
Bills, Robert E(dgar) *emeritus psychology educator*
Cooper, Eugene Bruce *speech, language pathologist, educator*
Doerr, Robert Wayne *nursing administrator*
Shellhase, Leslie John *social work educator*
Thomas, Jerry *pharmacist*

**Valley**
Striblin, Lori Ann *critical care nurse, medicare coordinator, nursing educator*

**Woodville**
Wells, Robin Denise *nurse*

## ALASKA

**Anchorage**
Erickson, Merlyn K. *anesthesia nurse*
Henderson-Dixon, Karen Sue *psychologist*
Kuehnert, Deborah Anne *medical center administrator*
Meddleton, Daniel Joseph *health facility administrator*
Risley, Todd Robert *psychologist, educator*

**Kotzebue**
Harris, Jan C. *health care administrator*

**Sitka**
Carlson, Susan Spevack *hospital administrator, family physician*

**Soldotna**
Franzmann, Albert Wilhelm *wildlife veterinarian, consultant*

## ARIZONA

**Bisbee**
Behney, Charles Augustus, Jr. *veterinarian*

**Casa Grande**
McGillicuddy, Joan Marie *psychotherapist, consultant*

**Chandler**
Graham, Anita Louise *correctional and community health nurse*

**Glendale**
Boettcher, Nancy Biondolillo *nurse*
Cassidy, Barry Allen *physician assistant, clinical medical ethicist*
Chan, Michael Chiu-Hon *chiropractor*

**Mesa**
Beck, Jerome Joseph *health care administrator, biomedical technologist*
Boyd, Leona Potter *retired social worker*
Evans, Don A. *healthcare company executive*

**Phoenix**
Cheifetz, Lorna Gale *psychologist*
Dillenberg, Jack *public health officer*
Fitzgerald-Verbonitz, Dianne Elizabeth *nursing educator*
Levin, Linda Rose *mental health counselor*
Manning-Weber, Claudia Joy *medical radiography administrator, consultant*
Marker, Loretta Irene *medical/surgical cardiac nurse*
Marshall, Margaret Elizabeth *psychologist-therapist*
McWhorter, Ruth Alice *counselor, marriage and family therapist*
Mitchell, Wayne Lee *health care administrator*
†Piatt, Malcolm Keith, Jr. *medical center administrator*
Richardson, Mary Lou *psychotherapist*
Roe, William Thomas *psychology educator, researcher*
Seiler, Steven Lawrence *health facility administrator*
Van Kilsdonk, Cecelia Ann *retired nursing administrator, volunteer*
Welliver, Charles Harold *hospital administrator*

**Prescott**
Longfellow, Layne Allen *psychologist, educator, author, musician*
Mc Cormack, Fred Allen *state social services administrator*
Samples, Martina *nursing home administrator*

**Rio Verde**
Ramsey, David Selmer *retired hospital executive*

**Scottsdale**
Cohn, Michael Jay *psychologist, consultant, educator*
Cordingley, Mary Jeanette Bowles (Mrs. William Andrew Cordingley) *social worker, psychologist, artist, writer*
Ellensohn, Karol Kaye *psychotherapist*
Kizziar, Janet Wright *psychologist, author, lecturer*
Richie, Sharon I. *army nursing educator, retired*
Timmons, Evelyn Deering *pharmacist*

**Sedona**
Catterton, Marianne Rose *occupational therapist*

**Sells**
Enas, Lena Mae *research coordinator, consultant*

**Sonoita**
Scott, William Coryell *medical executive*

**Sun City West**
Becker, Wesley Clemence *psychology educator emeritus*

**Tempe**
Anchie, Toby Levine *health facility administrator*
Uttal, William R(eichenstein) *psychology and engineering educator, research scientist*
Wesbury, Stuart Arnold, Jr. *health administration and policy educator*

**Tucson**
Beach, Lee Roy *psychologist, educator*
Blue, James Guthrie *veterinarian*
Brainerd, Charles J(on) *experimental psychologist, applied mathematician, educator*
Kmet, Rebecca Eugenia Patterson *pharmacist*
Nation, James Edward *retired speech pathologist*
Rumler, Diana Gale *geriatrics nurse*
Sampliner, Linda Hodes *psychologist, consultant*
Shropshire, Donald Gray *hospital executive*
Smith, David Wayne *psychologist, educator*
Tang, Esther Don *development consultant, retired social worker*
Weber, Charles Walter *nutrition educator*

**Whiteriver**
Murphey, Margaret Janice *marriage and family therapist*

## ARKANSAS

**Forrest City**
Glover, Deborah Joyce *school psychologist, consultant*

**Fort Smith**
Banks, David Russell *health care executive*

**Harrison**
McKelvy, Nikki Kay *nurse*

**Hot Springs National Park**
Farley, Roy C. *rehabilitation researcher, educator*
Kirksey, Laura Elizabeth *medical, surgical nurse*
McDaniel, Ola Jo Peterson *social worker, educator*

**Little Rock**
Hueter, Diana T. *health facility executive*
Lewis, Delbert O'Neal *disability consultant, former state official*
Nichols, Sandra B. *public health service officer*
Pierson, Richard Allen *hospital administrator*
Van Arsdale, Stephanie Kay Lorenz *cardiovascular clinical specialist, nursing educator, researcher*
Wepfer, Julia M. *psychologist*

**Lonoke**
Adams, Mary Raprich *retired nursing education administrator*

**North Little Rock**
Funk, Dorothea *public health nurse*

**State University**
Whitis, Grace Ruth *nursing educator*

**Walnut Ridge**
Nodine, Loren L. *critical care nurse, consultant*

## CALIFORNIA

**Agoura Hills**
Merchant, Roland Samuel, Sr. *hospital administrator, educator*

**Alameda**
Herrick, Sylvia Anne *health service administrator*
Yeaw, Marion Esther *retired nurse*

**Albany**
Daniels, Lydia M. *health care administrator*

**Alhambra**
Obert, Jessie Craig *nutritionist, consultant*

**Aliso Viejo**
Davidson, Melody Kay *critical care nurse, educator*

**Anaheim**
Lee, Donna Jean *retired hospice and respite nurse*

**Arcadia**
Anderson, Holly Geis *women's health facility administrator, commentator, educator*
Sloane, Robert Malcolm *healthcare consultant*

**Arcata**
Janssen-Pellatz, Eunice Charlene *healthcare facility administrator*

**Atherton**
Alexander, Theron *behavioral scientist, psychologist, writer*

**Bakersfield**
McMillan, Leonard David *family life specialist, consultant, lecturer*
Murillo, Velda Jean *social worker, counselor*
Osterkamp, Dalene May *psychology educator, artist*

**Berkeley**
Calloway, Doris Howes *nutrition educator*
Cohn, Theodore Elliot *optometry educator, vision scientist*
Day, Lucille Lang *health facility administrator, educator, author*
Emery, Marcia Rose *psychologist, consultant*
Enoch, Jay Martin *vision scientist, educator*
Freedman, Mervin Burton *psychologist, educator*
†Friedman, Mendel *hospital administration executive*
Gilbert, Neil Robin *social work educator, author, consultant*
Gough, Harrison Gould *psychologist, educator*
Greene, Albert Lawrence *hospital administrator*
Hafey, Joseph Michael *health association executive*
Hancock, Emily Stone *psychologist*
Hill, Lorie Elizabeth *psychotherapist*
Jensen, Arthur Robert *psychology educator*
Lambert, Nadine Murphy *psychologist, educator*
Lashof, Joyce Cohen *public health educator*
Lazarus, Richard Stanley *psychology educator*
Margen, Sheldon *public health educator, nutritionist emeritus*
Maslach, Christina *psychology educator*
Maurer, Adah Electra *psychologist*
Rosenzweig, Mark Richard *psychology educator*
Silva, Joanna Kontaxis *dietitian*
Staw, Barry Martin *business and psychology educator*
Westheimer, Gerald *optometrist, educator*

**Beverly Hills**
Aguilera, Donna Conant *psychologist, researcher*
Mindell, Earl Lawrence *nutritionist, author*
Yaryan, Ruby Bell *psychologist*

**Bishop**
Haber, Ralph Norman *psychology consultant, researcher, educator*

**Brea**
Dyer, Alice Mildred *psychotherapist*

**Burlingame**
Pemberton, Bobette Marie (Harman) *nursing administrator*

**Camarillo**
Tarnow, Malva May Wescoe *post-anesthesia care nurse*

**Canoga Park**
Taylor, Edna Jane *employment program representative*

**Capitola**
Crawford, George Truett *health facility executive, minister*

**Carmel**
Parker, Donald Henry *psychologist, author*
Reese, William Albert, III *psychologist*

**Carmichael**
Edgar, Marilyn Ruth *marriage and family therapist, counselor*

**Carpinteria**
Lipinski, Barbara Janina *psychotherapist, psychology educator*

**Cayucos**
Hedlund, James Lane *retired psychologist, educator*

**Cedar Ridge**
Bruno, Judyth Ann *chiropractor*

**Cerritos**
Bovitz, Carole Jones *psychotherapist*

**Chatsworth**
Boswell, Dan Alan *health maintenance organization executive, health care consultant*
Stephenson, Irene Hamlen *biorhythm analyst, consultant, editor, educator*

**Chico**
Ward, Chester Lawrence *physician, retired county health official, retired military officer*

**Chowchilla**
Von Prince, Kilulu Magdalena *occupational therapist, sculptor, retired*

**Chula Vista**
Kemery, William Elsworth *psychotherapist, hypnotherapist*
Schorr, Martin Mark *forensic psychologist, educator, writer*

**Claremont**
Martin, Jay Herbert *psychoanalysis and English educator*

**Corona**
Callender, Lorna Ophelia *nurse administrator*

**Corte Madera**
Kratka-Schneider, Dorothy Maryjohanna *psychotherapist*

**Costa Mesa**
Gardin, John George, II *psychologist*

**Culver City**
Edwards, Marie Babare *psychologist*
Maltzman, Irving Myron *psychology educator*

**Cupertino**
Norman, Donald Arthur *cognitive scientist*

**Danville**
Nothern, Marjorie Carol *nursing administrator*

**Davis**
Ardans, Alexander Andrew *veterinarian, laboratory director, educator*
Biberstein, Ernst Ludwig *veterinary medicine educator*
Fowler, William Mayo, Jr. *rehabilitation medicine physician*
Harper, Lawrence Vernon *human development educator*
Hawkes, Glenn Rogers *psychology educator*
†Lewis, Jonathan *health care association administrator*
Mason, William A(lvin) *psychologist, educator, researcher*
Owings, Donald Henry *psychology educator*
Rhode, Edward Albert *veterinary medicine educator, veterinary cardiologist*
Schwabe, Calvin Walter *veterinarian, medical historian, medical educator*
Steffey, Eugene Paul *veterinary medicine educator*
Theilen, Gordon Henry *veterinary surgery educator*

**Duarte**
Sollenberger, Donna Kay Fitzpatrick *hospital and clinics executive*

**El Cajon**
Brown, Marilynne Joyce *emergency nurse*
Schenk, Susan Kirkpatrick *geriatric psychiatry nurse, educator, consultant*

**El Cerrito**
Conti, Isabella *psychologist, consultant*
Cooper, William Clark *physician*
Schilling, Janet Naomi *nutritionist, consultant*

**El Monte**
Glass, Jean Ann *special education services professional*

**Emeryville**
Finney, Lee *negotiator, social worker*

**Encino**
Bekey, Shirley White *psychotherapist*
House-Hendrick, Karen Sue *nursing consultant*
Johnson, Patricia Diane *psychotherapist, consultant*
Vogel, Susan Carol *nursing administrator*

**Escondido**
Damsbo, Ann Marie *psychologist*
Gentile, Robert Dale *optometrist, consultant*
Rich, Elizabeth Marie *nursing educator*

**Eureka**
Kriger, Peter Wilson *healthcare administrator*

**Fairfax**
Neuharth, Daniel J., II *psychotherapist*

**Fairfield**
Datta, Purna Chandra *clinical psychologist, educator*

**Foster City**
Nugent, Denise Smith *holistic nurse*

**Fountain Valley**
Jessup, R. Judd *managed care executive*

**Fremont**
Loarie, Thomas Merritt *healthcare executive*
Sahatjian, Manik *nurse, psychologist*

**Fresno**
Huddleston, Forest Willis *mental healing counselor*
O'Connor, Kevin John *psychologist*
Ryan, Charlotte Muriel *oncology nurse*
Stude, Everett Wilson, Jr. *rehabilitation counselor, educator*

**Fullerton**
Cole, Sherwood Orison *psychologist*
Griffin, Kirsten Bertelsen *nursing educator*
Hershey, Gerald Lee *psychologist*
Kaisch, Kenneth Burton *psychologist, priest*

**Gardena**
Kronenberg, Jacalyn (Jacki Kronenberg) *nurse administrator*

**Granada Hills**
Aller, Wayne Kendall *psychology educator, researcher, computer education company executive, property manager*
Pappas, Maria Eleni *nurse*

**Grass Valley**
Cartwright, Mary Lou *laboratory scientist*

**Hayward**
Whalen, Thomas Earl *psychology educator*

**Hemet**
Minnie, Mary Virginia *social worker, educator*

**Hermosa Beach**
Wickwire, Patricia Joanne Nellor *psychologist, educator*

**Huntington Beach**
Carey, Shirley Anne *nursing consultant*
Dolan, Vikki Aldrich *healthcare nurse executive*
Kanode, Carolyn Kerrigan *school nurse, pediatric nurse practitioner*
Martin, Wilfred Wesley Finny *psychologist, property owner and manager*
Olsen, Greg Scott *chiropractor*

**Inglewood**
Epstein, Marsha Ann *public health administrator, physician*

**Irvine**
Greenberger, Ellen *psychologist, educator*
Jones, Joie Pierce *acoustician, educator, writer, scientist*
Luce, R(obert) Duncan *psychology educator*
Mc Gaugh, James Lafayette *psychobiologist*
Ryan, Julie Mae *optometrist, educator, researcher*
Sperling, George *cognitive scientist, educator*

**La Jolla**
Cain, William Stanley *psychologist, educator*
Castleman, Breaux Ballard *health management company executive*
Coburn, Marjorie Foster *psychologist, educator*
Farson, Richard Evans *psychologist*
Harris, Philip Robert *management and space psychologist*
Lakier, Nancy S. *health care consultant*
Mandler, George *psychologist*
Mandler, Jean Matter *psychologist, educator*
Marshall, Sharon Bowers *nursing educator, director clinical trials*
Randolph, Harry Franklin, III *health facility administrator, physician assistant*

**La Mirada**
Pike, Patricia Louise *psychology educator*

**La Quinta**
Hartley, Celia Love *nursing educator, nursing administrator*

**Lafayette**
Cotton, Barbara Lynn *correctional health systems management consultant*

**Laguna Beach**
Banuelos, Betty Lou *rehabilitation nurse*

**Laguna Hills**
Lindsay, Helen Mills *psychotherapist*

**Laguna Niguel**
Carr, Bernard Francis *hospital administrator*
Freeland, Darryl Creighton *psychologist, educator*
Milunas, J. Robert *health care organization executive*
Smith, Leslie Roper *hospital and healthcare administrator*

**Larkspur**
Saxton, Lloyd *psychologist, author*

**Lodi**
Bernhoft, Franklin Otto *psychotherapist, psychologist*

**Long Beach**
Carlton-Adams, Dana Georgia Marie Anne *psychotherapist*
Ferreri, Michael Victor *optometrist*
Hall, Phyllis Charlene *therapist, counselor*
Kohn, Gerhard *psychologist, educator*
Kokaska, Charles James *educational psychologist*
Mullins, Ruth Gladys *pediatrics nurse*

**Los Alamitos**
Abrams, Lois Marcia *psychotherapist*

**Los Angeles**
Andersen, Ronald Max *health services educator, researcher*
Baron, Melvin Farrell *pharmacy educator*
Blitz-Weisz, Sally *speech pathologist*
Bloland, Paul Anson *psychology educator emeritus*
Boswell, James Douglas *medical research executive*
Brown, Gay West *school psychologist*
Feshbach, Seymour *psychology educator*
Forness, Steven Robert *educational psychologist*
Goldberg, Herb *psychologist, educator*
Greenberg, Ira Arthur *psychologist*
Gunn, Karen Sue *psychologist, educator*
Henry, Richard Joseph, Jr. *nursing home management executive*
Holt, Susan Lynne *mental health counselor*
Hopkins, Carl Edward *public health educator*
Horowitz, Ben *medical center executive*
Hummel, Joseph William *hospital administrator*
Ilanit, Tamar *psychologist*
Jacobs, Marilyn Susan *clinical psychologist*
Johns, Karen Louise *nurse, psychotherapist*
Katchur, Marlene Martha *nursing administrator*
Kelley, Harold Harding *psychology educator*
Lasswell, Marcia Lee *psychologist, educator*
Lien, Eric Jung-chi *pharmacist, educator*
Lopez-Navarro, Eduardo Luis *family therapist*
Lyman, John *psychology and engineering educator*
McRae, Marion Eleanor *critical care nurse*
Michael, William Burton *psychologist, educator*
Morales, Cynthia Torres *clinical psychologist, consultant*
Noce, Walter William, Jr. *hospital administrator*
Okeh, Samson Ewruje *psychiatric nurse*
Phinney, Jean Swift *psychology educator*
Raven, Bertram H(erbert) *psychology educator*
Reichenthal, Jay Jeffrey *health facility administrator*
Roberts, Robert Winston *social work educator, dean*
Rodnick, Eliot Herman *psychologist, educator*
Scanlon, Deralee Rose *dietitian, educator, author*
Shneidman, Edwin S. *psychologist, educator, thanatologist, suicidologist*
Silberman, Irwin Alan *public health physician*
Sokolov, Jacque Jenning *health care executive, nuclear cardiologist*
Storms, Lester (C Storms) *retired veterinarian*
Strack, Stephen Naylor *psychologist*
Territo, Mary C. *health facility administrator, oncologist*
Thompson, Richard Frederick *psychologist, neuroscientist, educator*
Troispoux, Christianne Valerie Ann *psychologist*
van Dam, Heiman *psychoanalyst*
Ver Steeg, Donna Lorraine Frank *nurse, sociologist, educator*
Watson, Sharon Gitin *psychologist, executive*
Whybrow, Peter Charles *psychiatrist, educator*
Wittrock, Merlin Carl *educational psychologist*
Wood, Nancy Elizabeth *psychologist, educator*

**Los Gatos**
Asher, James John *psychology educator*

**Los Osos**
Thomas, Robert Murray *educational psychology educator*

**Malibu**
Aiken, Lewis Roscoe, Jr. *psychologist, educator*
Palacio, June Rose Payne *nutritional science educator*

**Marina**
Cornell, Annie Aiko *nurse, administrator, retired army officer*

**Menlo Park**
Clair, Theodore Nat *educational psychologist*
Salmon, Vincent *acoustical consultant*
Speidel, John Joseph *physician, foundation officer*

**Mill Valley**
Benezet, Louis Tomlinson *retired psychology educator, former college president*
Taylor, Rose Perrin *social worker*

**Millbrae**
Koleniak Gignoux, Barbara Donna *nurse*

**Mission Viejo**
Henderson, Marsha Roslyn Thaw *clinical social worker*

**Modesto**
Berry, John Charles *psychologist*
Moe, Andrew Irving *veterinarian*

**Moffett Field**
Cohen, Malcolm Martin *psychologist, researcher*
Haines, Richard Foster *psychologist*

**Monrovia**
Salaman, Maureen Kennedy *nutritionist*

**Monte Sereno**
Jackson, Suzanne Elise *health education coordinator*

**Montecito**
Bell, Donald William *experimental psychologist*

**Monterey**
Finnberg, Elaine Agnes *psychologist, editor*

**Monterey Park**
Chan, Daniel Siu-Kwong *psychologist*
Ramsey, Nancy Lockwood *nursing educator*

**Moraga**
Allen, Richard Garrett *health care and education consultant*

**Mountain View**
Heaney, Dorothy Phelps *nurse, nursing administrator*

**Murrieta**
Spangler, Lorna Carrie *pharmacy technician*

**Newhall**
Stone, Susan Foster *mental health services professional, psychologist*

**Newport Beach**
Green, Melanie Jane *speech-language pathologist*
Hansen, Mark H. *retired speech pathologist, consultant*
Stephens, Michael Dean *hospital administrator*
Whittemore, Paul Baxter *psychologist*

**Norco**
Parmer, Dan Gerald *veterinarian*

**Northridge**
Reagan, Janet Thompson *psychologist, educator*

**Oakhurst**
Bonham, Clifford Vernon *retired social work educator*

**Oakland**
Caulfield, W. Harry *health care industry executive, physician*
Lawrence, David M. *health facility administrator*
Lusby, Grace Irene *infection control nurse practitioner*
Nebelkopf, Ethan *psychologist*

**Oceanside**
Hertweck, E. Romayne *psychology educator*

**Orange**
Montgomery, Thom Mathew *health program administrator, counselor*
Price, Gail J. Goodman *marriage family, and child therapist, deaf and hearing impaired specialist*
Schlose, William Timothy *health care executive*

**Orinda**
Spraings, Violet Evelyn *psychologist*

**Oroville**
Strawn, Susan Heathcote *medical administrator*

**Oxnard**
Dimitriadis, Andre C. *health care executive*
Herlinger, Daniel Robert *hospital administrator*

**Palm Springs**
Boyajian, Timothy Edward *public health officer, educator, consultant*

**Palmdale**
Kinzell, La Moyne B. *school health services administrator, educator*

**Palo Alto**
Gordon, Marc Stewart *pharmacist, scientist*
Hammett, Benjamin Cowles *psychologist*
Kohn, Jean Gatewood *medical facility administrator, physician*
Lindzey, Gardner *psychologist, educator*
Maiden, Eva Wenkart *psychotherapist, school psychologist*
Pauling, Linus Carl, Jr. *health science administrator*
Saksen, Louis Carl *hospital administrator, architect*
Skeff, Kelley Michael *health facility administrator*

**Panorama City**
Henrickson, Mark *social worker, priest*

**Pasadena**
Cole, Roberta Carley *nursing educator*
Horner, Althea Jane *psychologist*
Messenger, Ron J. *health facility administrator*
Nackel, John George *health care consulting director*
Sharp, Sharon Lee *gerontology nurse*

**Paso Robles**
Rocha, Marilyn Eva *clinical psychologist*

**Pauma Valley**
Dooley, George Elijah *health facility administrator*

**Pebble Beach**
Keene, Clifford Henry *medical administrator*

**Petaluma**
Carr, Les *psychologist, educator*

**Placentia**
Linnan, Judith Ann *psychologist*

**Pleasant Hill**
Gomez, Edward Casimiro *physician, educator*
Stevenson, James D(onald), Jr. *psychologist, counselor*

**Pleasanton**
Shen, Mason Ming-Sun *medical center administrator*

**Rancho Mirage**
Deiter, Newton Elliott *clinical psychologist*
Ford, Betty Bloomer (Elizabeth Ford) *health facility executive, wife of former President of United States*
Hegarty, William Kevin *medical center executive*
Lacey, John Irving *psychologist, physiologist, educator*
Overby, Monessa Mary *clinical supervisor, counselor*

**Rancho Palos Verdes**
Keenan, Retha Ellen Vornholt *retired nursing educator*

**Rancho Santa Fe**
Trout, Monroe Eugene *hospital systems executive*

**Redding**
Wilson, David Lee *clinical psychologist*

**Redondo Beach**
Cardin, Suzette *nurse manager*

**Reseda**
Hoover, Pearl Rollings *nurse*
Pearson, Susan Rose *psychotherapist, fine arts educator, artist*

**Riverside**
Brandt, Blanch Marie *health care facility administrator*
Chang, Sylvia Tan *health facility administrator, educator*
Eyman, Richard Kenneth *psychologist, educator*
Ham, Gary Martin *psychologist*
Nieves, Carmen *emergency services coordinator*
Petrinovich, Lewis F. *psychology educator*
Smith, Jeffry Alan *health administrator, physician, consultant*
Warren, David Hardy *psychology educator*

**Rohnert Park**
Criswell, Eleanor Camp *psychologist*

**Rosemead**
Gibson, Frances *nurse*

**Sacramento**
†Atkins, Thomas N. *medical administrator*
Bennett, Lawrence Allen *psychologist, criminal justice researcher*
Bohnen, Mollyn Villareal *nurse, educator*
Chapman, Loring *psychology educator, neuroscientist*
Childress, Dori Elizabeth *nursing consultant*
Farrell, Francine Annette *psychotherapist, educator, author*
Greenfield, Carol Nathan *psychotherapist*
Kelley, Lisa Stone *public guardian, conservator*
Majesty, Melvin Sidney *psychologist, consultant*
Merwin, Edwin Preston *health care consultant, educator*
Roberts, Paul Dale *health services administrator*
Sato-Viacrucis, Kiyo *nurse, inventor, entrepreneur, consultant*
von Friederichs-Fitzwater, Marlene Marie *health communication educator*
Whitaker, Cynthia Ellen *nurse*

**Salinas**
Eifler, Carl Frederick *retired psychologist*
Francis, Alexandria Stephanie *psychologist*
Quick, Valerie Anne *sonographer*

**San Bernardino**
Tacal, Jose Vega, Jr. *public health official, veterinarian*
Timmreck, Thomas C. *health sciences and health administration educator*
Turpin, Joseph Ovila *counselor, educator*

**San Diego**
Bakko, Orville Edwin *retired health care executive, consultant*
Callahan, LeeAnn Lucille *psychologist*
Christiansen, David K. *healthcare administrator*
Colling, Kenneth Frank *hospital administrator*
Cooper, James Melvin *healthcare executive, consultant*
Dwyer, Lauraine Theresa *ambulatory care administrator, rehabilitation nurse*
Early, Ames S. *healthcare system executive*
Johnson, Kenneth Owen *retired audiologist*
Kent, Theodore Charles *psychologist*
Klausmeier, Herbert John *psychologist, educator*
Litrownik, Alan Jay *psychologist, educator*
McGuigan, Frank Joseph *psychologist, educator*
Murray, Colette Morgan *healthcare executive, fundraising consultant*
Nenner, Victoria Corich *nurse, educator*
Prsha, Marie Alice *administrator, educator*
Rezin, Joyce June *pediatric nurse practitioner*
Sabatella, Elizabeth Maria *clinical therapist, educator, mental health facility administrator*
Schmidt, Patricia Fain *nurse educator*
Schmidt, Terry Lane *health care executive*
Springer, Wayne Richard *medical center safety director*
Weisman, Irving *social worker, educator*

**San Dimas**
Flores, Frank Cortez *health sciences administrator, public health educator*

**San Francisco**
Adler, Nancy Elinor *psychologist, educator*
Anargyros, Nedra Harrison *cytotechnologist*
Calvin, Allen David *psychologist, educator*
Chin, Jennifer Young *public health educator*
Collins, Fuji *mental health professional*
Dibble, Suzanne Louise *nurse, researcher*
Eng, Catherine *health care facility administrator, physician, medical educator*
Gortner, Susan Reichert *nursing educator*
Green, Robert Leonard *hospital management company executive*
Howatt, Sister Helen Clare *human services director, former college library director*
Johnson, Herman Leonall *research nutritionist*
King, Janet Carlson *nutrition educator, researcher*
Krippner, Stanley Curtis *psychologist*
Leone, Lucile P. *retired health administrator*
Martinson, Ida Marie *nursing educator, nurse, physiologist*
McCormick, Donna Lynn *social worker*
Meleis, Afaf Ibrahim *nurse sociologist, educator, clinician, researcher*
Norbeck, Jane S. *nursing educator*
Rosales, Suzanne Marie *hospital coordinator*
Silverman, Mervyn F. *health science association administrator, consultant*
Turnlund, Judith Rae *nutrition scientist*

**San Jose**
Cedoline, Anthony John *psychologist*
Oak, Ronald Stuart *health and safety administrator*
Smith, Joan Petersen *nursing administrator, educator*
Supan, Richard Matthew *health facility administrator*

**San Luis Obispo**
Smith, Joey Spauls *mental health nurse, biofeedback therapist, bodyworker, hypnotist*

**San Marcos**
Knight, Edward Howden *retired hospital administrator*

**San Mateo**
Hospy, Patricia L. *chiropractor*
Richens, Muriel Whittaker *AIDS therapist, counselor and educator*
Steiner, Mary Ann *nursing administrator, consultant*

**San Rafael**
Friesecke, Raymond Francis *health company executive*

**Santa Ana**
Oberstein, Marydale *geriatric specialist*
Rockoff, Sheila G. *nursing and health facility administrator, nursing and health occupations educator*

**Santa Barbara**
Barbakow, Jeffrey *health facility administrator*
Beutler, Larry Edward *psychology educator*
Blum, Gerald Saul *psychologist, educator*
Brown, Baillie Russell *health services administrator*

**Davis**, James Ivey *company president, laboratory associate*
Donnerstein, Edward Irving *communications and psychology educator, researcher, author*
Duarte, Ramon Gonzalez *nurse, educator, researcher*
Focht, Michael Harrison *health care industry executive*
Kendler, Howard H(arvard) *psychologist, educator*
Mayer, Richard Edwin *psychology educator*
Narayanamurti, Venkatesh *research administrator*
Sherman, Alan Robert *psychologist, educator*

**Santa Cruz**
Pettigrew, Thomas Fraser *social psychologist, educator*
Rorer, Leonard George *psychologist, writer*
Smith, M(ahlon) B(rewster) *psychologist, educator*
Tharp, Roland George *psychology, education educator*
Tonay, Veronica Katherine *psychology educator*

**Santa Monica**
Brook, Robert Henry *physician, educator, health services researcher*
Carder, Kathy Young *critical care nurse*
Kahan, James Paul *psychologist*
Levine, Peggy Aylsworth *psychotherapist, writer, poet*
Lindsley, Donald Benjamin *physiological psychologist, educator*
Nizze, Judith Anne *physician assistant*
Pettit, John W. *administrator*
Veit, Clairice Gene Tipton *measurement psychologist*

**Santa Rosa**
Nickens, Catherine Arlene *retired nurse, freelance writer*

**Sausalito**
Seymour, Richard Burt *health educator*

**Seal Beach**
Stillwell, Kathleen Ann Swanger *healthcare consultant*

**Sherman Oaks**
Azpeitia, Lynne Marie *psychotherapist, educator, trainer, consultant*
Peplau, Hildegard Elizabeth *nursing educator*

**Sonoma**
Markey, William Alan *health care administrator*

**Soquel**
Murray, Barbara Olivia *psychologist*

**South San Francisco**
Westerdahl, John Brian *nutritionist, health educator*

**Stanford**
Bandura, Albert *psychologist*
Basch, Paul Frederick *international health educator, parasitologist*
Calfee, Robert Chilton *psychologist, educational researcher*
Carlsmith, James Merrill *psychologist, educator*
Gage, Nathaniel Lees *psychologist, educator*
Hilgard, Ernest Ropiequet *psychologist*
Krumboltz, John Dwight *psychologist, educator*
Lepper, Mark Roger *psychology educator*
Maccoby, Eleanor Emmons *psychology educator*
Mc Namara, Joseph Donald *researcher, retired police chief, novelist*
Shepard, Roger Newland *psychologist, educator*
Van Etten, Peter Walbridge *hospital administrator*
Zajonc, Robert B(oleslaw) *psychology educator*
Zimbardo, Philip George *psychologist, educator, writer*

**Stockton**
Matuszak, Alice Jean Boyer *pharmacy educator*

**Studio City**
Weiner, Sandra Samuel *critical care nurse, nursing consultant*

**Tarzana**
Michaelson, Richard Aaron *health science facility administrator*
Rinsch, Maryann Elizabeth *occupational therapist*

**Thousand Oaks**
Mulkey, Sharon Renee *gerontology nurse*

**Tiburon**
Harary, Keith *psychologist*

**Torrance**
Harmon Brown, Valarie Jean *hospital laboratory director, information systems executive*
Prell, Joel James *medical group administrator*
Todd, Frances Eileen *pediatrics nurse*

**Turlock**
Ahlem, Lloyd Harold *psychologist*

**Ukiah**
Nugent, Constance Marie Julie *health facility administrator*

**Union City**
Glueck, Mary A. *psychiatric and mental health nurse, administrator*

**Upland**
Rice, Sharon Margaret *clinical psychologist*

**Vacaville**
Zaleski, Brian William *chiropractor*

**Valley Center**
Harper, Lilah Marie *health science administrator, consultant*

**Van Nuys**
Rosen, Alexander Carl *psychologist, consultant*

**Ventura**
Bircher, Andrea Ursula *psychiatric mental health nurse, educator, clinical nurse specialist*

**Visalia**
Madden, Wanda Lois *nurse*

**Walnut**
Martin, George *psychologist, educator*

**Walnut Creek**
Du Bois, Philip Hunter *psychologist, educator*
Williams, Michael James *health care services consultant*
Zander, Alvin Frederick *social psychologist*

**West Hills**
Levine, Howard Harris *health facility executive*

**Westlake Village**
Derr, John Frederick *health care products company executive*

**Winters**
Low, Donald Gottlob *retired veterinary medicine educator*

**Woodlake**
Lippmann, Bruce Allan *rehabilitative services professional*

**Woodland**
Clement, Katherine Robinson *social worker*

**Woodland Hills**
Hasan, Malik M. *health maintenance organization executive*
Schaeffer, Leonard David *health care executive*

**Yountville**
Helzer, James Dennis *hospital executive*

## COLORADO

**Aurora**
Babel, Deborah Jean *social worker, accountant*
Dunn, Karen K. *mental health center executive, psychotherapist*

**Boulder**
†Borysenko, Joan *psychologist, biologist*
Bourne, Lyle Eugene, Jr. *psychology educator*
Chan, Peter Wing Kwong *pharmacist*
Healy, Alice Fenvessy *psychology educator, researcher*
Holdsworth, Janet Nott *women's health nurse*
Jessor, Richard *psychologist, educator*
Kelley, Bruce Dutton *pharmacist*
Kintsch, Walter *psychology educator, director*
Middleton-Downing, Laura *psychiatric social worker, artist, small business owner*

**Canon City**
Romano, Rebecca Kay *counselor*

**Colorado Springs**
Cameron, Paul Drummond *research facility administrator*
Hamilton, James Milton *veterinarian*
West, Ralph Leland *veterinarian*
Williams, Ruth Lee *clinical social worker*

**Denver**
Allen, Robert Edward, Jr. *physician assistant*
Anderson, Paula D.J. *pharmacist*
Berland, Karen Ina *psychologist*
Burnett, Elizabeth (Betsy Burnett) *counselor*
Clough, Nadine Doerr *school psychologist, psychotherapist*
Conger, John Janeway *psychologist, educator*
Edelman, Joel *medical center executive*
Hill, Diane Seldon *corporate psychologist*
Jennett, Shirley Shimmick *home care management executive, nurse*
Kirkpatrick, Charles Harvey *physician, immunology researcher*
Lefly, Dianne Louise *research psychologist*
Markman, Howard J. *psychology educator*
McDonnell, Barbara *health facility administrator*
Nett, Louise Mary *nursing educator, consultant*
Plummer, Ora Beatrice *nursing educator, trainer*
Purcell, Kenneth *psychology educator, university dean*
Rael, Henry Sylvester *retired health administrator, financial and management consultant*
Rizzi, Teresa Marie *bilingual speech and language pathologist*
Schaubman, Averi Lyn *social worker*
Shepard, Thomas Akers *physician assistant*
Taussig, Lynn Max *healthcare administrator, pulmonologist, pediatrician, educator*
Witt, Catherine Lewis *neonatal nurse practitioner, writer*
Yamamoto, Kaoru *psychology and education educator*
Zimet, Carl Norman *psychologist, educator*

**Englewood**
Albrecht, Duane Taylor *veterinarian*
Busse, Lu Ann *audiologist*
Haupenthal, Laura Ann *clinical psychologist*

**Fort Collins**
Benjamin, Stephen Alfred *veterinary medicine educator, environmental pathologist, researcher*
Bennett, Thomas LeRoy, Jr. *clinical neuropsychology educator*
Charney, Michael *science laboratory administrator*
Gubler, Duane J. *research scientist, administrator*
Guest, Richard Eugene *psychologist*
Hu, Edna Gertrude Fenske *pediatrics nurse*
Lumb, William Valjean *veterinarian*
Schatz, Mona Claire Struhsaker *social worker, educator, consultant, researcher*
Suinn, Richard Michael *psychologist*
Thies, Margaret Diane *nurse*

**Golden**
Wellisch, William Jeremiah *social psychology educator*

**Grand Junction**
Pantenburg, Michel *hospital administrator, health educator, holistic health coordinator*
Zumwalt, Roger Carl *hospital administrator*

**Greeley**
Hart, Milford E. *psychotherapist, counselor*
Linde, Lucille Mae (Jacobson) *motor-perceptual specialist*

**Idledale**
Brown, Gerri Ann *physical therapist*

**Littleton**
Anderson, Darrell Edward *psychologist, educator*
Cabell, Elizabeth Arlisse *psychologist*
Vail, Charles Daniel *veterinarian, consultant*

**Longmont**
Dierks, Richard Ernest *veterinarian, educational administrator*
Jones, Beverly Ann Miller *nursing administrator, patient services administrator*
Melendez, Joaquin *orthopedic assistant*

**Louisville**
Billings, Becky Leigh *nurse*
Shively, Merrick Lee *pharmaceutical scientist, consultant*

**Monument**
Ahlgren, Aleda Joan *nursing administrator, career officer*

**Pueblo**
Hawkins, Robert Lee *health facility administrator*
Kulkosky, Paul Joseph *psychology educator*

**Westminster**
DiPasquale-Lehnerz, Pamela Ann *occupational therapist*

**Wheat Ridge**
LaMendola, Walter Franklin *human services, information technology consultant*

## CONNECTICUT

**Avon**
O'Malley, Marjorie Glaubach *health care executive*

**Bridgeport**
Fuller, Doris Elizabeth *nurse*
Trefry, Robert J. *healthcare administrator*

**Bristol**
Pope, Preston Carleton *anesthetist, nurse*

**Brookfield**
Sartori, Bridget Ann *home health care nurse*

**Canterbury**
Brown, Philip Henry *psychiatric social worker*

**Clinton**
Douglas, Hope M. *psychotherapist, forensic hypnotist*

**Cromwell**
Darius, Franklin Alexander, Jr. (Chip Darius) *health administrator, educator, consultant*

**Danbury**
Burns, Jacqueline Mary *laboratory administrator*
Tolor, Alexander *psychologist, educator*
Weinstein, Sidney *neuropsychologist*

**Derby**
Brassil, Jean Ella *psychologist*

**Durham**
Russell, Thomas J. *critical care supervisor*

**Fairfield**
Mead, Philomena *mental health nurse*
Meyer, Goldye W. *psychologist, educator*
Oberg, Muriel Curnin *community health nurse, health facility manager*
Obrig, Alice Marie *nursing educator*

**Farmington**
Buncher, James Edward *healthcare management executive*
Kegeles, S. Stephen *behavioral science educator*

**Greenwich**
Gagnon, John Harvey *psychotherapist, educator*
Langley, Patricia Coffroth *psychiatric social worker*
Sheppard, Posy (Mrs. Jeremiah Milbank) *social worker*

**Guilford**
Eustice, David C. *pharmaceutical researcher*
Hayes, Michael Ernest *psychotherapist, educator*
Rotnem, Diane Louise *clinical social worker, educator, researcher*

**Haddam**
Twachtman-Cullen, Diane *communication disorders and autism specialist*

**Hamden**
Spodick, Pearl Blegen *counselor, medical psychotherapist*

**Hartford**
Bruner, Robert B. *hospital consultant*
Gillmor, Rogene Godding *medical technologist*
Hamilton, Thomas Stewart *physician, hospital administrator*
Moy, Samuel Yew *psychologist*

**Kensington**
Bailey, Debra Sue *psychologist, neuropsychologist*

**Manchester**
Chung, Douglas Chu *pharmacist, consultant*
Ogedegbe, Henry *medical technologist, clinical laboratory scientist, chemist, consultant*
Richard, Ann Bertha *nursing administrator*

**Mansfield Center**
Liberman, Alvin Meyer *psychology educator*

**Meriden**
Gaj, Stanley Thomas *pharmacist, computer business consultant*
Smits, Helen Lida *physician, administrator, educator*

**Middletown**
Harris, Dale Benner *psychologist, educator*
Scheibe, Karl Edward *psychology educator*

**Milford**
Muth, Eric Peter *ophthalmic optician, consultant*
Taylor, Charles Henry *psychoanalyst, educator*

**New Britain**
Cline, John Carroll *clinical psychologist*

**New Canaan**
Thomas, Marianne Gregory *school psychologist*

**New Haven**
Abelson, Robert Paul *psychologist, educator*
Blatt, Sidney Jules *psychology educator, psychoanalyst*
Brownell, Kelly David *psychologist, educator*
†Cadman, Edwin C. *health facility administrator, medical educator*
Child, Irvin Long *psychologist, educator*
Clark, Susan Atkinson *clinical social worker, educator*
Clizbe, John Anthony *psychologist*
Cohen, Jane A. *social worker*
Condon, Thomas Brian (Brian Condon) *hospital executive*
Crowder, Robert George *psychology educator*
Diers, Donna Kaye *nurse educator*
Doob, Leonard William *psychology educator, academic administrator*
Garner, Wendell Richard *psychology educator*
Griffith, Ezra Edward Holman *health facility administrator, educator*
Hoge, Michael Alan *psychologist*
Jekel, James Franklin *physician, public health educator*
Kessen, William *psychologist, educator*
Krauss, Judith Belliveau *nursing educator*
Marks, Lawrence Edward *psychologist*
Mc Guire, William James *social psychology educator*
Miller, Neal Elgar *psychologist, emeritus educator*
Savin, Abby Luria *social worker*
Sternberg, Robert Jeffrey *psychology educator*
Stevens, Joseph Charles *psychology educator*
Vicenzi, Angela Elizabeth *nursing educator*
Wagner, Allan Ray *psychology educator, experimental psychologist*
Zigler, Edward Frank *psychologist, educator*

**North Haven**
†Bradow, Barbara G. *health care executive*
Mahl, George Franklin *psychoanalyst, psychologist, educator*
Phillips, Elizabeth Vellom *social worker, educator*
Wohlert, Earl Ross *health care analyst*

**Norwalk**
Baez, Manuel *health care executive*
Boles, Lenore Utal *nurse psychotherapist, educator*
Hackett, Linda Lepley *nurse psychotherapist, consultant*
Potluri, Venkateswara Rao *medical facility administrator*

**Old Greenwich**
Nelson, Norma Randy deKadt *psychotherapist, consultant*

**Old Lyme**
Johnson, James Myron *psychologist, educator*

**Putnam**
Desaulniers, Rene Gerard Lesieur *optometrist*

**Redding**
Benyei, Candace Reed *psychotherapist*

**Ridgefield**
Phelps, Judson Hewett *therapist, counselor, marketing sales executive*

**Riverside**
Otto, Charles Edward *health care administrator*

**Shelton**
Eichhorst, Gerda Irene *geriatrics nurse*

**Southbury**
Wilson, Geraldine O'Connor *psychologist*

**Southport**
Singer, Henry A. *behavioral scientist, institute director*

**Stamford**
Haber, Judith Ellen *nursing educator*
Penachio, Anthony Joseph, Jr. *psychotherapist, hypnotherapist, behavioral therapist*
Schechter, Audrey *medical, surgical nurse*

**Storrs Mansfield**
Anderson, Stephen Alan *family psychology educator*
Chinn, Peggy Lois *nursing educator, editor*
Denenberg, Victor Hugo *psychology educator*
Katz, Leonard *psychology educator*
Kerr, Kirklyn M. *veterinary pathologist, researcher*
Redman, Barbara Klug *nursing educator*
Schwarz, J(ames) Conrad *psychology educator*

**Wallingford**
Spero, Barry Melvin *medical center executive*

**Waterbury**
Fischbein, Charles Alan *pediatrician*
Oliver, Eugene Alex *speech and language pathologist*

**Waterford**
Hinerfeld, Lee Ann *veterinarian*

**Weatogue**
Dumais, Arlene *psychiatric mental health and critical care nurse*

**Willimantic**
De Rose, Sandra Michele *psychotherapist, educator, supervisor, administrator*

**Wilton**
Paulson, Loretta Nancy *psychoanalyst*

**Woodbridge**
Womer, Charles Berry *retired hospital executive, management consultant*

## DELAWARE

**Camden Wyoming**
Porterfield, Craig Allen *psychologist, consultant*

**Delmar**
Tasker, John Baker *veterinary medical educator, college dean*

**Dover**
Richman, Joseph Herbert *public health services official*
Wisneski, Sharon M. *critical care nurse, educator*

**Lewes**
Fried, Jeffrey Michael *health care administrator*

**Newark**
Corballis, Ben Charles *health facility administrator*
Doberenz, Alexander R. *nutrition educator, chemist*
Graham, Frances Keesler (Mrs. David Tredway Graham) *psychologist, educator*
Grimaldi, Polly Nan *wellness consultant and educator*
Gulick, Walter Lawrence *psychologist, former college president*
Hurst, Christina Marie *respiratory therapist*
Sheer, Barbara Lee *nursing educator*

**Wilmington**
Adams, Wayne Verdun *pediatric psychologist, educator*
Burton, Robert Jones *psychologist*
Drudy, Patrick *psychologist, human relations consultant*
Kneavel, Thomas Charles, Jr. *psychologist, educator*
Kohler, Frederick William, Jr. *pharmacist*
Manz, Betty Ann *nurse, consultant*
McDonough, Kenneth Lee *disease management company executive*

## DISTRICT OF COLUMBIA

**Washington**
Ackerman, F. Kenneth, Jr. *health facility administrator*
Alward, Ruth Rosendall *nursing consultant*
Arling, Donna Dickson *social worker*
Barton, Jean Marie *psychologist, educator*
Beale, Susan Yates *social worker*
Bentley, James Daniel *medical association executive*
Caldwell, Willard E. *psychologist, educator*
Chilman, Catherine Earles Street *social welfare educator, author*
Cotter, Dennis Joseph *health services company executive*
Crawford, Lester Mills, Jr. *veterinarian*
Eckenhoff, Edward Alvin *health care administrator*
Falter, Robert Gary *correctional health care administrator, educator*
Gehlmann, Sheila Cathleen *psychologist, research analyst*
Green, Edward Crocker *international health organization consultant*
Grob, George F. *health services association administrator*
Hannett, Frederick James *healthcare consulting company executive*
Harper, Robert Allan *consulting psychologist, retired*
Hudec, Mary Suzanne *nursing and patient services administrator*
Hurd, Shirley Dyer *health care administrator*
Jones, Stanley Boyd *health policy analyst, priest*
Joseph, Stephen C. *health sciences administrator*
Koch, Barbara Louise *foreign service family nurse*
Korniewicz, Denise M. *nursing educator*
Lash, Myles Perry *hospital administrator, consultant*
Lee, Shew Kuhn *retired optometrist, consultant*
Levin, Peter J. *hospital administrator, public health professor*
Littig, Lawrence William *psychologist, educator*
LLubién, Joseph Herman *psychotherapist, counselor*
Masi, Dale A. *research company executive, social work educator*
McDaniel, John Perry *health care company executive*
McGeein, Mary Martha *health care organization executive*
McGinnies, Elliott Morse *psychologist, educator*
McShane, Franklin John, III *nurse anesthetist, army officer*
Miller, Margery Silberman *psychologist, speech and language pathologist*
Muldrow, Tressie Wright *psychologist*
Nef, Evelyn Stefansson *psychotherapist, author, editor, specialist polar regions*
O'Connell, Daniel Craig *psychology educator*
Peele, Roger *hospital administrator*
Raphael-Howell, Frances Jayne *clinical psychologist*
Raslear, Thomas Gregory *psychologist*
Rheintgen, Laura Dale *research center official*
Rizzo, Joanne T. *family nurse practitioner*
Robinson, Daniel N. *psychology educator*
Samet, Kenneth Alan *hospital administrator*
Schorr, Lisbeth Bamberger *child and family policy analyst, author, educator*
Stark, Nathan J. *medical administrator, consultant, lawyer*
Tracy, Thomas Miles *international health organization official*
VandenBos, Gary Roger *psychologist, publisher*
Wager, Deborah Miller *researcher, consultant*
Wagner, William Charles *veterinarian*
Wallace, Joan Scott *psychologist, social worker, international consultant*
Wargo, Andrea Ann *public health official, commissioned officer*
Weinhold, Linda Lillian *psychologist, researcher*
Wells, Samuel Fogle, Jr. *research center administrator*
Wilford, Bonnie Baird *health policy specialist*
†Žužul, Miomir *government official, psychologist, educator*

## FLORIDA

**Apopka**
Webb, Erma Lee *nurse educator*

**Arcadia**
Kurtz, Myers Richard *hospital administrator*

**Archer**
Lockwood, Rhonda J. *mental health services professional*

**Bal Harbour**
Radford, Linda Robertson *psychologist*

**Boca Raton**
Fels, Robert Alan *psychotherapist*
Goldman, Lisa Eachus *health facility administrator*
Greenfield-Moore, Wilma Louise *social worker, educator*
Guillama-Alvarez, Noel Jesus *healthcare company executive*
Latané, Bibb *social psychologist*
Perlick, Lillian *counselor, therapist*
Rothberg, June Simmonds *retired nursing educator, psychotherapist, psychoanalyst*
Wolgin, David Lewis *psychology educator*

**Boynton Beach**
Peltzie, Kenneth Gerald *hospital administrator, educator*

**Brandon**
Mussenden, Gerald *psychologist*

**Chattahoochee**
Ivory, Peter B. C. B. *medical administrator*

**Clearwater**
Fenderson, Caroline Houston *psychotherapist*
Gibson, Barbara Arlene *nurse, writer*
Houtz, Duane Talbott *hospital administrator*
Peterson, James Robert *retired engineering psychologist*
Whedon, George Donald *medical administrator, researcher*

**Coral Springs**
Bartolotti, Jossif Peter *nutritionist, psychoanalyst, research scientist, educator*
Wilson, Arthur Jess *psychologist, educator*

**Daytona Beach**
Cardwell, Harold Douglas, Sr. *rehabilitation specialist*
Elliott, Carol Harris *nutrition counselor, dietitian*
McCoy, Edward Fitzgerald *social services facility administrator*
Salter, Leo Guilford *mental health services professional*
Wehner, Henry Otto, III *pharmacist, consultant*

**Deerfield Beach**
Areskog, Donald Clinton *retired chiropractor*
Solomon, Barry Jason *healthcare administrator, consultant*

**Delray Beach**
Erenstein, Alan *emergency room nurse, medical education consultant, aeromedical specialist*
Levinson, Harry *psychologist, educator*

**Dunedin**
McIntosh, Roberta Eads *retired social worker*
Weber, Ellen Schmoyer *pediatric speech pathologist*

**Dunnellon**
Dixon, W(illiam) Robert *retired educational psychology educator*

**Eglin AFB**
Smith, Sheila Diane *medical transcriptionist*

**Englewood**
Lahiff, Marilyn J. *nursing administrator*

**Fort Lauderdale**
Alpert, Martin Jeffrey *chiropractic physician*
Andrews, John Harold *health care administrator*
Appel, Antoinette Ruth *neuropsychologist*
Azrin, Nathan Harold *psychologist*
Cash, Ralph Eugene *psychologist*
Costa, Robin Leueen *psychologist, counselor*
Forsyth, George Lionel *psychotherapist, author*
Kurzenberger, Dick *health services executive*
Lister, Mark Wayne *clinical laboratory scientist*
Maxwell, Sara Elizabeth *psychologist, educator, speech pathologist, director*
McGinnis, Patrick Bryan *mental health counselor*
Rentoumis, Ann Mastroianni *psychotherapist*

**Fort Myers**
Harmer, Rose *marriage and family therapist, mental health counselor*
Newland, Jane Lou *nursing educator*
Rachman, Bradley Scott *chiropractic physician*

**Fort Pierce**
Wohlford, James Gregory *pharmacist*

**Fort Walton Beach**
Villecco, Judy Diana *substance abuse, mental health counselor, director*

Wyatt, Russell Scott optician

### Gainesville
Baker, Bonnie Barbara mental health and school counselor, educator
Burridge, Michael John veterinarian, educator, research administrator
Bzoch, Kenneth Rudolph speech and language educator, department chairman
Capaldi, Elizabeth Ann Deutsch psychological sciences educator
Catasus, Jose Magin Perez school psychologist
Crane, Beverly Rose counselor
Dewsbury, Donald Allen historian of psychology, comparative psychologist
Eyler, Fonda Davis developmental psychologist
Green, Eleanor Myers veterinarian, educator
Himes, James Albert veterinary medicine educator emeritus
Hornberger, Robert Howard psychologist
Malasanos, Lois Julanne Fosse nursing educator
Nicoletti, Paul Lee veterinarian, educator
Randall, Malcom health care administrator
Severy, Lawrence James psychologist, educator
Small, Natalie Settimelli pediatric mental health counselor
Sutton, Douglas Hoyt nurse
Teitelbaum, Philip psychologist
Thompson, Neal Philip food science and nutrition educator
Wass, Hannelore Lina educational psychology educator
Watson, Robert Joe hospital administrator, retired career officer

### Gulf Breeze
Lankton, Stephen Ryan family therapist, management consultant

### Havana
Whitehead, Lucy Grace health facility administrator

### Holiday
Jones, Vaughn Paul healthcare administrator

### Hollywood
†Tucker, Nina Angella hospital administrator

### Homosassa
Acton, Norman international organization executive

### Inverness
Lewis, Christina Lynn human services administrator
Mavros, George S. clinical laboratory director
Nichols, Sally Jo geriatrics nurse

### Jacksonville
Akers, James Eric medical practice marketing executive
Gregg, Andrea Marie nursing administrator, educator, researcher
Helganz, Beverly Buzhardt counselor
Kespohl, Elizabeth Kiser lead radiology special procedures nurse
Mason, William Cordell, III hospital administrator
Monroe, Helen Leola nurse, consultant, educator
Rubens, Linda Marcia home health services administrator
Wilson, C. Nick health educator, consultant, researcher, lecturer
Yamane, Stanley Joel optometrist

### Jensen Beach
Gamble, Raymond Wesley marriage and family therapist, clergyman

### Jupiter
Buck-Moore, Joanne Rose nursing administrator, mental health educator
Mc Call, Charles Barnard health facility executive, educator

### Lake City
Norman, Alline L. health facility administrator

### Lake Wales
Rynear, Nina Cox retired registered nurse, author, artist

### Lakeland
Campbell, Doris Klein retired psychology educator
Smith, Sherwood Draughon retired hospital administrator
Zucco, Ronda Kay health facility administrator

### Largo
Beck, Donald James veterinarian, educator
Mandelker, Lester veterinarian

### Lauderhill
†Schultz, Howard Michael registered nurse

### Longboat Key
Albee, George Wilson psychology educator

### Maitland
†Radi, Dorinda Rudy health facility administrator
Von Hilsheimer, George Edwin, III neuropsychologist

### Mango
Spencer, Francis Montgomery James pharmacist

### Melbourne
Hughes, Ann Nolen psychotherapist
Lyon, Isolda Yvette dietitian

### Miami
Albright, John D. emergency room and telemetry nurse
Barkley, Marlene A. Nyhuis nursing administrator
Barritt, Evelyn Ruth Berryman nurse, educator, university dean
Boyle, Judith Pullen clinical psychologist, educator
Burkett, Marjorie Theresa nursing educator, gerontology nurse
Cherry, Andrew Lawrence, Jr. social work educator, researcher
Fairchild, Susan S. nursing educator, consultant
Fitzgerald, Lynne Marie Leslie family therapist
Huysman, Arlene Weiss psychologist, educator
Johnson, Lisa Ann mental health counselor
Kunce, Avon Estes vocational rehabilitation counselor
Lazowick, Andrea Lee pharmacist
Mezey, Judith Paul social worker
Nadeau, Joseph Eugene health care management consultant, information systems consultant
Noriega, Rudy Jorge hospital administrator
Perry, E. Elizabeth social worker, real estate manager
Routh, Donald K(ent) psychology educator
Russell, Elbert Winslow neuropsychologist
†Sonenreich, Steven Douglas hospital administrator
Stuchins, Carol Mayberry nursing executive
Sundel, Martin social work educator, psychologist
Teicher, Morton Irving social worker, anthropologist, educator
Ugwu, Martin Cornelius pharmacist
†Yaffa, Jack Ber healthcare administrator, educator

### Miami Lakes
Getz, Morton Ernest medical facility director, gastroenterologist

### Micanopy
Cripe, Wyland Snyder veterinary medicine educator, consultant

### Naples
Clark, Kenneth Edwin psychologist, former university dean
Conrad, Kelley Allen industrial and organizational psychologist
Dion, Nancy Logan health care administrator, management consultant
Eggland, Ellen Thomas community health nurse, consultant
Gilman, John Richard, Jr. organization behavior consultant
Johnson, Sally A. nursing educator
Lewis, Marianne H. psychiatric nurse practitioner
Megee, Geraldine Hess social worker
Terenzio, Peter Bernard hospital administrator

### New Port Richey
Charters, Karen Ann Elliott critical care nurse, health facility administrator

### North Miami Beach
†Gare, Fran nutritionist

### Ocala
Lamon, Kathy Lynn nursing administrator

### Orange Park
Rice, Ronald James hospital administrator

### Orlando
Bittle, Polly Ann nephrology nurse, researcher
Mallette, Phyllis Spencer Cooper medical/surgical nurse
Osborne-Popp, Glenna Jean health services administrator
White, Susan Victoria nursing administrator
Woodard, Clara Veronica nursing home official

### Palm Bay
Jones, Mary Ann geriatrics nurse

### Palm Coast
Brumback, Gary Bruce industrial and organizational psychologist

### Palm Harbor
Smith, W. James health facility administrator

### Panama City
Childers, Perry Robert psychology educator
Nelson, Edith Ellen dietitian

### Pembroke Pines
Gordon, Lori Heyman therapist, writer, educator
Jones, Janet Louise health services administrator

### Pensacola
Caton, Betty Ann health science administrator
Loesch, Mabel Lorraine social worker
†Serangeli, Deborah S. health care facility administrator
Taggart, Linda Diane women's health nurse
Yoder, Ronda Elaine nursing educator

### Pineland
Donlon, Josephine A. diagnostic and evaluation counseling therapist, educator

### Plantation
Collins, Ronald William psychologist, educator
Louck, Lori Ann speech-language pathologist

### Pompano Beach
Hoffman, Susan E. Sladen medical nurse, case manager
Kimberly, Ann Geyer nursing administrator, medical, surgical nurse
Valdes, Jacqueline C. neuropsychologist, consultant, researcher

### Port Charlotte
Gendzwill, Joyce Annette retired health officer

### Port Richey
Mueller, Lois M. psychologist

### Port Saint Lucie
Arnold, Roxanne post-anesthesia nurse
McBride, Wanda Lee psychiatric nurse

### Punta Gorda
Herum, Jane Lentz psychology educator, consultant
Varney, Suzanne Glaab health facility administrator
Wood, Emma S. nurse practitioner

### Saint Petersburg
Bailey, Robin Keith physician assistant, perfusionist
Clark, Carolyn Chambers nurse, author, educator
Keyes, Benjamin B. therapist
McIntyre, Deborah psychotherapist, author
Weaver, Thomas Harold health facility administrator
Wisler, Willard Eugene health care management executive

### Sanford
San Miguel, Sandra Bonilla social worker

### Sarasota
Borsos, Erika cardiac care, medical/surgical nurse
Byron, H. Thomas, Jr. veterinarian, educator
Covert, Michael Henri healthcare facility administrator
Dearden, Robert James retired pharmacist
Gurvitz, Milton Solomon psychologist
Middleton, Norman Graham social worker, psychotherapist
Tucci, Steven Michael health facility administrator, physician, recording industry executive

### Seminole
Dubel, Doris Geraldine Cottrell gerontology nurse

### Stuart
Petzold, Anita Marie psychotherapist

### Sun City Center
Hall, John Fry psychologist, educator
Parsons, George Williams retired medical center administrator, cattle rancher

### Sunrise
Symon-Gutierrez, Patricia Paulette dietitian

### Tallahassee
Ford, Ann Suter family nurse practitioner, health planner
Hedstrom, Susan Lynne maternal women's health nurse
Kenshalo, Daniel Ralph psychologist, educator
Mustian, Middleton Truett hospital administrator
Rhodes, Roberta Ann dietitian
Rice, Nancy Marie nursing consultant
Tuckman, Bruce Wayne educational psychologist, educator, researcher

### Tamarac
Bekoff, Oscar psychotherapist
Krause, John L. optometrist

### Tampa
Fagan, Mildred B. (Mitzi Fagan) occupational health nurse
Ferlita, Theresa Ann clinical social worker
Hedrick, Steve Brian psychotherapist
Kimmel, Ellen Bishop psychologist, educator
Mahan, Charles Samuel public health service officer
Parker, Carol Jean psychotherapist, consultant
Plawecki, Judith Ann nursing educator
Scott, Charles Francis health facility administrator
Solomon, Eldra Pearl Brod psychologist, educator, biologist, author
Van Matre, Joyce Dianne rehabilitation nurse

### Tarpon Springs
Georgiou, Ruth Schwab retired social worker

### Titusville
Hartung, Patricia McEntee therapist
Roath-Algera, Kathleen Marie massage therapist

### Treasure Island
Meisner, Judith Anne clinical social worker, marital and sex therapist, psychotherapist

### Venice
Baga, Margaret Fitzpatrick nurse, medical office manager
Ward, Jacqueline Ann Beas nurse, healthcare administrator

### Vero Beach
McCrystal, Ann Marie community health nurse, administrator

### West Palm Beach
Davis, Shirley Harriet social worker, editor
Glinski, Helen Elizabeth operating room nurse
Green, Linda Gail international healthcare and management consultant
Holloway, Edward Olin human services manager
Kaslow, Florence W. psychologist
Katz, William David psychologist, psychoanalytic psychotherapist, educator, mental health consultant
Lewter, Billy Ray psychology educator

### Weston
Seelin, Judith Lee rehabilitation specialist

### Winter Garden
Clifford, Margaret Louise psychologist

### Winter Haven
West, Mary Elizabeth psychiatric management professional

### Winter Park
Blair, Mardian John hospital management executive
Granzig, William Walker clinical sexologist, educator

## GEORGIA

### Albany
Cox, Lynetta Frances neonatal nurse practitioner

### Alpharetta
Mock, Melinda Smith orthopedic nurse specialist, consultant
Rettig, Terry veterinarian, wildlife consultant
White, Carl Edward, Jr. pharmaceutical adminstrator

### Americus
Thomas, Paul Louis health services administrator
Worrell, Billy Frank health facility administrator

### Athens
Barry, John Reagan psychology educator
Pavlik, William Bruce psychologist, educator
Peacock, Lelon James psychologist, educator
Posey, Loran Michael pharmacist, editor
Swayne, David Eugene avian pathologist, researcher
Tesser, Abraham social psychologist
Tyler, David Earl veterinary medical educator

### Atlanta
†Anderson, Gail Victor health science association administrator, educator
Bales, Virginia S. healthcare administration
Banks, Bettie Sheppard psychologist
Barker, William Daniel hospital administrator
Baron, Linda psychotherapist, consultant
Bockwitz, Cynthia Lee psychologist, psychology/women's studies educator
Butte, Anthony Jeffrey healthcare executive
Chandler, Robert Charles healthcare consultant
Crutchfield, Carolyn Ann physical therapy educator
Eber, Herbert Wolfgang psychologist
Finley, Sarah Maude Merritt social worker
Foerster, David Wendel, Jr. counselor, consultant, human resources specialist
Honaman, J. Craig health facility administrator
Hopkins, Donald Roswell public health physician
Iodice, Joanna DiMeno (Jody Iodice) psychotherapist
Johnson, Carl Frederick marriage and family therapist
Kerr, Nancy Helen psychology educator
Koplan, Jeffrey Powell physician
Levine, Susan Michelle social worker
Marks, James S. public health service administrator
Martin, David Edward health sciences educator
Martin, Virve Paul licensed professional counselor
Meehan, Patrick John public health officer
Nichols, William Curtis psychologist, family therapist, consultant
Oakley, Godfrey Porter, Jr. health facility administrator, medical educator
Orenstein, Walter A. health facility administrator
Panlilio, Adelisa Lorna public health physician
Payne, Maxwell Carr, Jr. retired psychology educator
Pontius, Priscilla Floyd nursing administrator
Rosenberg, Mark L. health facility administrator
Satcher, David public health service officer, federal official
Seffrin, John Reese health science association administrator, educator
Smith, Anderson Dodd psychologist
Tkaczuk, Nancy Anne cardiovascular services administrator
Walton, Carole Lorraine clinical social worker
Weed, Roger Oren rehabilitation services professional, educator
Weiss, Jay M(ichael) psychologist, educator
Whitehead, John Jed healthcare and biotech company executive
Woody, Mary Florence nursing educator, university administrator

### Augusta
Barab, Patsy Lee nutritionist, consultant, realtor
Feldman, Elaine Bossak medical nutritionist, educator
Gillespie, Edward Malcolm hospital administrator
Zachert, Virginia psychologist, educator

### Ball Ground
McGhee, Vicki Gunter home health nurse, pediatrics psychiatry, alcohol and Drug rehabilitation

### Brunswick
Crowe, Hal Scott chiropractor
Shockley, Carol Frances psychologist, psychotherapist

### Canton
Williams, Sally Broadrick infection control nurse and consultant

### Carrollton
Barron, Purificacion Capulong nursing administrator, educator
Driver, Judy Anne home health consultant

### Clayton
English, Cheryl Ann medical technologist

### College Park
Hood, Ollie Ruth health facilities executive

### Columbus
Brabson, Max LaFayette health care executive
Kerr, Allen Stewart psychologist

### Conyers
Kemp, Gina Christine social services provider

### Dahlonega
Frank, Mary Lou Bryant psychologist, educator

### Decatur
Dame, Laureen Eva nursing administrator
Hinman, Alan Richard public health administrator, epidemiologist

### Demorest
Vance, Cynthia Lynn psychology educator

### Doraville
Yancey, Eleanor Garrett retired crisis intervention clinician

### Douglasville
Henley, Lila Jo school social worker, consultant, retired

### Dublin
Joyner, Jo Ann geriatrics nurse

### Dunwoody
Bartolo, Donna Marie hospital administrator, nurse

### Evans
Fournier, Joseph Andre Alphonse nurse, social worker, psychotherapist

### Gracewood
Whittemore, Ronald P. hospital administrator, retired army officer, nursing educator

HEALTHCARE: HEALTH SERVICES 5230 WHO'S WHO IN AMERICA


**Grayson**
Hollinger, Charlotte Elizabeth *medical technologist, tree farmer*
Wilson, Barbara Mitchell *nurse*

**Jonesboro**
Frey, Bob Henry *psychotherapist, sociologist, educator, poet*

**Kennesaw**
Munoz, Steven Michael *physician associate*

**La Grange**
Naglee, Elfriede Kurz *retired medical nurse*
Rhodes, Eddie, Jr. *medical technologist, phlebotomy technician, educator*

**Macon**
Fickling, William Arthur, Jr. *health care manager*
Murdoch, Bernard Constantine *psychology educator*

**Marietta**
Petit, Parker Holmes *health care corporation executive*

**Milledgeville**
Peterson, Dave Leonard *psychologist*

**Morrow**
Samson, Linda Forrest *nursing educator and administrator*

**Norcross**
Adams, Belinda Jeanette Spain *nursing administrator*
van Reenen, Jane Smith *speech and language pathologist*

**Richmond Hill**
McCormack, Dennis K. *clinical psychologist*

**Ringgold**
Hayes, Laura Joanna *psychologist*

**Rome**
Papp, Leann Ilse Kline *respiratory therapy educator*
Wynn, Bruce *physician assistant*

**Saint Simons Island**
Edwards, Brenda Faye *rehabilitation services professional, counselor*

**Savannah**
Barnette, Candice Lewis *speech/language pathologist*
†Boone, James Latham *healthcare executive*
DiClaudio, Janet Alberta *health information administrator*
Strauser, Edward B. *psychologist, educator*
Whitaker, Von Best *nursing educator*

**Tifton**
Thomas, Adrian Wesley *laboratory director*

**Toccoa**
Scott, Louyse Hulsey *school social worker*

**Valdosta**
Branan, John Maury *psychology educator, counselor*
Waldrop, Mary Louise *nursing educator*

**Young Harris**
Jones, Mary Emma B. *counselor, therapist, educator*

## HAWAII

**Hilo**
Dixon, Paul William *psychology educator*
Werner, Marlin Spike *speech pathologist and audiologist*

**Honolulu**
Ardolf, Deborah Ann *speech pathologist*
Bitterman, Morton Edward *psychologist, educator*
Corsini, Raymond Joseph *psychologist*
Fischer, Joel *social work educator*
Flannelly, Kevin J. *psychologist, research analyst*
Flannelly, Laura T. *mental health nurse, nursing educator, researcher*
Fullmer, Daniel Warren *psychologist, educator, retired*
Hanson, Dennis Michael *medical imaging executive*
Hatfield, Elaine Catherine *psychology educator*
Katz, Alan Roy *public health educator*
Lum, Jean Loui Jin *nurse educator*
Marsella, Anthony Joseph *psychologist, educator*
Miike, Lawrence Hiroshi *public health officer*
Moccia, Mary Kathryn *social worker*
Nakamoto, Fay *public health officer*
Shotwell, Cherrie Leigh *speech and language pathologist*
Thompson, Henry Nainoa *hospital administrator*
Weiner, Ferne *psychologist*

**Kahului**
Shaw, Virginia Ruth *clinical psychologist*

**Kailua Kona**
Ashley, Darlene Joy *psychologist*
Scarr, Sandra Wood *psychology educator, researcher*

**Kula**
Miguel deSousa, Linda J. *critical care nurse, nursing educator*

**Mililani**
Kiley, Thomas *rehabilitation counselor*
Kiyota, Heide Pauline *clinical psychologist*

**Waianae**
Pinckney, Neal Theodore *psychologist, educator*

**Waipahu**
Kuwabara, Dennis Matsuichi *optometrist*

## IDAHO

**Boise**
Blonshine, Sheena Kay *medical, surgical nurse*
Brown, Christopher Patrick *health care administrator, educator*
Langenfeld, Mary Lucille *healthcare facility administrator*
Nelson, Willard Gregory *veterinarian, mayor*

**Bonners Ferry**
McClintock, William Thomas *health care administrator*

**Payette**
Bragg, Darrell Brent *nutritionist, consultant*

## ILLINOIS

**Argonne**
Masek, Mark Joseph *laboratory administrator*

**Arlington Heights**
Kennedy, Sandra Anne *physical therapist*

**Bedford Park**
Spiegel-Hopkins, Phyllis Marie *psychotherapist*

**Bensenville**
Pippin, James Rex *health care company executive, educator*

**Bolingbrook**
Price, Theodora Hadzisteliou *individual and family therapist*

**Carbondale**
Buckley, John Joseph, Jr. *health care executive*
Lit, Alfred *experimental psychologist, vision science educator, engineering psychology consultant*
Rubin, Harris B. *psychology educator*

**Champaign**
Davis, James Henry *psychology educator*
Donchin, Emanuel *psychologist, educator*
Eriksen, Charles Walter *psychologist, educator*
Humphreys, Lloyd Girton *research psychologist, educator*
Kelly, Gay Anne *social worker, educator*
Taylor, James David *health care executive*
Triandis, Harry Charalambos *psychology educator*

**Chatham**
Chew, Keith Elvin *healthcare services administrator*
Powell, Carol Sue *pediatric special education educator, nursing consultant*

**Chicago**
Andreoli, Kathleen Gainor *nurse, educator, administrator*
Anthony-Perez, Bobbie Cotton Murphy *psychology educator, researcher*
Arekapudi, Kumar Vijaya Vasantha *sanitarian, real estate agent*
Bailar, John Christian, III *public health educator, physician, statistician*
Baptist, Allwyn J. *health care consultant*
Beser, Roberta Ruth (Bobbie Beser) *physical therapy company executive*
Burger, Mary Louise *psychologist, educator*
Butler, Robert Allan *psychologist, educator*
Campbell, Bruce Crichton *hospital administrator*
Carlson, Rolland S. *healthcare system administrator*
Carney, Jean Kathryn *psychologist*
Cohen, Jerome *psychology educator, electrophysiologist*
Conibear, Shirley Ann *occupational health consultant, physician*
Connors, Mary Eileen *psychologist*
Csikszentmihalyi, Mihaly *psychology educator*
†Davis, Danny K. *healthcare consultant, educator*
Edelsberg, Sally C. *physical therapy educator and administrator*
Feldman, Edwin *health care executive, internist, cardiologist*
†Franklin, Cory Michael *medical administrator, educator*
Fromm, Erika (Mrs. Paul Fromm) *clinical psychologist*
Getzels, Jacob Warren *psychologist, educator*
Goldmann, James Allen *healthcare consultant*
Goldsmith, Ethel Frank *medical social worker*
Gutmann, David Leo *psychology educator*
Hartman, David Elliott *neuropsychologist*
Kalina, Christine Marie *occupational health nurse*
Kennedy, Eugene Cullen *psychology educator, writer*
Kidd, Lynden Louise *healthcare consultant*
Levin, Arnold Murray *social worker, psychotherapist*
Logemann, Jerilyn Ann *speech pathologist, educator*
Lopatka, Susana Beaird *maternal, child health nurse consultant*
Lubawski, James Lawrence *health care consultant*
Marsh, Jeanne Cay *social welfare educator, researcher*
Marston-Scott, Mary Vesta *nurse, educator*
McKinney, William T. *psychiatrist, educator*
McNeill, G. David *psychology educator*
Mecklenburg, Gary Alan *hospital executive*
Mugnaini, Enrico *neuroscience educator*
Muthuswamy, Petham Padayatchi *pulmonary medicine and critical care specialist*
Osowiec, Darlene Ann *clinical psychologist, educator, consultant*
Palmer, Martha H. *counseling educator*
Pisciotta, Vivian Virginia *psychotherapist*
Preisler, Harvey D. *medical facility administrator, medical educator*
Pugh, Roderick Wellington *psychologist, educator*
Reed, Vastina Kathryn (Tina Reed) *child psychotherapist*
Rogalski, Carol Jean *clinical psychologist, educator*
Rosenheim, Margaret Keeney *social welfare policy educator*
Rothstein, Ruth M. *hospital adminstrator*
Russell, Lillian *medical, surgical nurse*
Rychlak, Joseph Frank *psychology educator, theoretician*
Sanders, Jacquelyn Seevak *psychologist, educator*
Schuerman, John Richard *social work educator*
Schwartz, John Norman *health care executive*
Simon, Bernece Kern *social work educator*
Simons, Helen *school psychologist, psychotherapist*
Spivey, Bruce E. *integrated healthcare delivery systems management executive*
Tipp, Karen Lynn Wagner *school psychologist*
Walberg, Herbert John *psychologist, educator, consultant*
Walker, Ronald Edward *psychologist, educator*
Watanabe, Mark David *pharmacist, educator*
Weimer, Jean Elaine *nursing educator*
Zoloto, Jerrold Albert *psychologist, consultant*

**Chicago Heights**
Patton, Sharlene Darlage *nurse*

**Cicero**
Cichowicz, Wayne Richard *health commissioner, dean*

**Danville**
Evans, Austin James *hospital administrator*
Kettling, Virginia *health facility administrator*

**De Kalb**
Eineke, Alvina Marie *public health nurse*

**Decatur**
Perry, Anthony John *retired hospital executive*

**Deerfield**
Sanner, John Harper *retired pharmacologist*

**Dixon**
Belcher-Redebaugh-Levi, Caroline Louise *nursing home administrator, nurse*

**Downers Grove**
Feeney, Don Joseph, Jr. *psychologist*
Gioioso, Joseph Vincent *psychologist*
Gruen, Dolores Colen *psychologist consultant*
Soder-Alderfer, Kay Christie *counseling administrator*

**East Saint Louis**
Martin, Betty J. *speech, language pathologist*

**Edwardsville**
Adkerson, Donya Lynn *clinical counselor*

**Effingham**
Shetler, Christopher David *chiropractor*

**Elgin**
Hoeft, Elizabeth Bayless *speech and language pathologist*
Nelson, John Thilgen *retired hospital administrator, physician*

**Evanston**
Alak, Ala Mohammed *health facility administrator, pharmaceutical researcher*
Eagly, Alice Hendrickson *social psychology educator*
Howard, Kenneth Irwin *psychology educator*
Rosenbaum, James Edward *psychologist, educator*
White, Sylvia Frances *gerontology home care nurse, consultant*

**Forest Park**
Hatch, Edward William (Ted Hatch) *health care executive*

**Galesburg**
Kowalski, Richard Sheldon *hospital administrator*

**Geneva**
Shapiro, Joan Isabelle *laboratory administrator, nurse*

**Glen Ellyn**
Kaleba, Richard Joseph *healthcare consultant*

**Glencoe**
Grabow, Beverly *learning disability therapist*

**Glenview**
Coulson, Elizabeth Anne *physical therapy educator*

**Godfrey**
Harner, Linda Jeane *allied health educator*

**Granite City**
Raczkiewicz, Paul Edward *hospital administrator*

**Grayslake**
Devney, Anne Marie *nursing educator*

**Harrisburg**
Endsley, Jane Ruth *nursing educator*
Rushing, Philip Dale *retired social worker*

**Highland Park**
Kravets, Barbara Zeitlin *clinical nutritionist*
Liebow, Phoebe Augusta Recht *nursing educator, school nurse*

**Hillsboro**
Herrmann, Jane Marie *physical therapist*

**Hines**
Nosek, Laura J. *health facility administrator*

**Hinsdale**
Caron, Theresa Lynn White *health facility administrator, medical educator*

**Homewood**
Bultema, Janice Kay *mental health and skilled nursing administrator*

**Joliet**
Benfer, David William *hospital administrator*
Cochran, Mary Ann *nurse educator*
Lynch, Priscilla A. *nursing educator, therapist*

**Kampsville**
Schumann, Alice Melcher *medical technologist, educator, sheep farmer*

**Kankakee**
Schroeder, David Harold *health care facility executive*

**Lake Forest**
Strauss, Jeffrey Lewis *healthcare executive*

**Libertyville**
Treanor, Helen June *nursing administrator, geriatrics professional*

**Litchfield**
Deaton, Beverly Jean *nursing administrator, educator*

**Lombard**
Beideman, Ronald Paul *chiropractor, college dean*

**Macomb**
Hopper, Stephen Rodger *hospital administrator*

**Marion**
Livengood, Joanne Desler *healthcare administrator*

**Maryville**
Stark, Patricia Ann *psychologist, educator*

**Maywood**
Cera, Lee Marie *veterinarian*
Flores, Susan M. *health facility administrator*

**Mc Henry**
Duel, Ward Calvin *health care consultant*

**Moline**
Larson, Sandra Mae *nursing educator*

**Morton Grove**
Farber, Isadore E. *psychologist, educator*

**Mount Carroll**
Hayes, Randy Alan *family therapist*

**Mount Prospect**
Kuffel, Joan Elizabeth *school nurse*

**Mundelein**
Meehan, Jean Marie Ross *occupational health and safety management consultant*

**North Aurora**
†Hillberg, Owen Eugene *pharmacist*

**North Chicago**
Hui, Ho-Wah *pharmaceutical scientist*
Kringel, John G. *health products company executive*

**Northbrook**
Hecker, Lawrence Harris *industrial hygienist*
Kahn, Sandra S. *psychotherapist*
Lever, Alvin *health science association administrator*
Rudnick, Ellen Ava *health care executive*

**Oak Brook**
Baker, Robert J(ohn) *hospital administrator*
Bower, Barbara Jean *nurse*
Risk, Richard Robert *health care executive*
Schultz, Karen Rose *clinical social worker, author, publisher, speaker*

**Oak Park**
Edwards, Linda H. *public health professional*
Fiorella, Beverly Jean *medical technologist, educator*
Varchmin, Thomas Edward *environmental health administrator*

**Olympia Fields**
Haley, David Alan *preferred provider organization executive*

**Orland Park**
Rasmason, Frederick C., III *emergency nurse*

**Palatine**
Benzies, Bonnie Jeanne *clinical and industrial psychologist*

**Park Forest**
McDonald, Stanford Laurel *clinical psychologist*
Steinmetz, Jon David *mental health executive, psychologist*

**Park Ridge**
Boe, Gerard Patrick *health science association administrator, educator*
McCarthy, Michael Shawn *health care company executive, lawyer*
Rojek, Kenneth J. *health facility administrator, hospital*

**Peoria**
Hungate, Carolyn Wolf *nursing administrator*
McCollum, Jean Hubble *medical assistant*
Walker, Philip Chamberlain, II *health care executive*

**Peru**
Lane, Patricia Peyton *nursing consultant*
Powell, Robert Charles *marriage and family counselor*

**Philo**
Martin, Earl Dean *physical therapist*

**Plainfield**
Schinderle, Robert Frank *retired hospital administrator*

**River Forest**
Puthenveetil, Jos Anthony *laboratory executive*

**River Grove**
Hill-Hulslander, Jacquelyne L. *nursing educator and consultant*

**Riverwoods**
Kirby, Emily Baruch *psychologist, writer*

**Owensboro**
Derstadt, Ronald Theodore *health care administrator*

**Russellville**
Harper, Shirley Fay *nutritionist, educator, consultant*

**Whitesburg**
Williams, Debbie Kaye *optometrist*

## LOUISIANA

**Alexandria**
Bradford, Louise Mathilde *social services administrator*
Sneed, Ellouise Bruce *nursing educator*

**Baton Rouge**
Berg, Irwin August *psychology educator*
Besch, Everett Dickman *veterinarian, university dean emeritus*
†Chastant, Ledoux J., III *medical clinic administrator*
Cox, Hollis Utah *veterinarian*
Davidge, Robert Cunninghame, Jr. *hospital administrator*
Geiselman, Paula Jeanne *psychologist, educator*
Riopelle, Arthur Jean *psychologist*
Timmons, Edwin O'Neal *psychologist*
Vaeth, Agatha Min-Chun Fang *clinical nurse*

**Bossier City**
Fry, Randy Dale *emergency medical technician, paramedic*
Winham, George Keeth *retired mental health nurse*

**Cut Off**
Adams, Laura Ann *critical care nurse*

**Hall Summit**
Wimberly, Evelyn Louise Russell *nursing coordinator*

**Harahan**
Ryan, Teresa Weaver *obstetrical and clinical nurse specialist*

**Haughton**
Ivy, Berrynell Baker *critical care nurse*
†Turner, Robert J. *health facility administrator*

**Jackson**
Payne, Mary Alice McGill *mental health quality consultant*

**Lake Charles**
Briggs, Arleen Frances *mental health nurse, educator*
Middleton, George, Jr. *clinical child psychologist*

**Leesville**
Gutman, Lucy Toni *school social worker, educator, counselor*

**Mandeville**
Treuting, Edna Gannon *retired nursing administrator*

**Metairie**
Brisolara, Ashton *substance abuse and employee assistance programs consultant*
Evans, Carol Rockwell *nursing administrator*

**Natchitoches**
Egan, Shirley Anne *nursing educator, retired*

**New Orleans**
Barone, Carol Parker *director quality management*
Grace, Marcellus *pharmacy educator, university dean*
Hudzinski, Leonard Gerard *social worker*
Moely, Barbara E. *psychology educator*
Oliver, Ronald *retired medical technologist*
Olson, Richard David *psychology educator*
O'Neal, Edgar Carl *psychology educator*
Paradise, Louis Vincent *educational psychology educator, university official*
Pickett, Stephen Alan *hospital executive*
Remley, Theodore Phant, Jr. *counseling educator, lawyer*
Rigby, Perry Gardner *medical center administrator, educator, former university dean, physician*
Wakeman, Richard John *psychologist, neuropsychologist*

**Reserve**
Hanson, Clarence Francis *home health nurse, retired firefighter*

**Shreveport**
Angermeier, Ingo *hospital administrator, educator*
Heacock, Donald Dee *social worker*
Preston, Loyce Elaine *retired social work educator*
St. Aubyn, Ronald Anthony *pediatrics nurse*
Schneider, Thomas Richard *hospital administrator*
Staats, Thomas Elwyn *neuropsychologist*
Vestal, Judith Carson *occupational therapist*

**Slaughter**
Gremillion, Curtis Lionel, Jr. *psychologist, hospital administrator, musician*

**Slidell**
Hall, Ogden Henderson *allied health educator*

**West Monroe**
Costello, Elizabeth Ann *home health nurse*
Houchin, John Frederick, Sr. *human services administrator*

## MAINE

**Augusta**
Brown, Arnold *health science facility administrator*
Fiori, Michael J. *pharmacist*
Kany, Judy C(asperson) *health policy analyst, former state senator*
Lewis, Jacquelyn Rochelle *quality administrator*
Sotir, Thomas Alfred *healthcare executive, retired shipbuilder*

**Bangor**
Ballesteros, Paula M. *nurse*
Johnson, Sharon Marguerite *social worker, clinical hypnotherapist*
McGuigan, Charles James *rehabilitation therapist*

**Blue Hill**
Mills, David Harlow *psychologist, association executive*

**Brunswick**
Fuchs, Alfred Herman *psychologist, college dean, educator*

**Caribou**
Swanson, Shirley June *registered nurse, adult education educator*

**Cumberland Center**
Brewster, Linda Jean *family nurse practitioner*

**East Boothbay**
Eldred, Kenneth McKechnie *acoustical consultant*

**Kittery**
Clark, Sandra Ann *clinical social worker*

**Mount Desert**
Straus, Donald Blun *retired company executive*

**Orono**
Goldstone, Sanford *psychology educator*

**Surry**
Pickett, Betty Horenstein *psychologist*

**Waterville**
Tormollan, Gary Gordon *health facility administrator, physical therapist*

## MARYLAND

**Abingdon**
Bonsack, Karen Nancy *physical therapist*

**Andrews AFB**
Morris, Dorothea Louise *nurse midwife*
Wong, Ruth Ann *nursing administrator*

**Annapolis**
Core, Mary Carolyn W. Parsons *radiologic technologist*

**Baltimore**
Abeloff, Martin David *medical administrator, educator, researcher*
Applebaum, Gary E. *medical director, executive*
Bellack, Alan Scott *clinical psychologist*
Brieger, Gert Henry *medical historian, educator*
Catania, A(nthony) Charles *psychology educator*
Crawford, Edward E. *psychologist*
Cunningham, Terence Thomas, III *hospital administrator*
Davis, Ada Romaine *nursing educator*
DeTolla, Louis James *veterinarian, researcher*
Ebinger, Mary Ritzman *pastoral counselor*
Feldman, Deborah Karpoff *nursing education consultant*
Fox, Madeline Joan *speech and language pathologist*
Gaber, Robert *psychologist*
Gimbel, Michael Marc *alcohol and drug abuse services professional*
Green, Bert Franklin, Jr. *psychologist*
Groenheim, Henri Arnold *psychologist, consultant*
Hansen, Jeanne Bodine *retired counselor*
Heyssel, Robert Morris *physician, retired hospital executive*
Hill, Barbara Benton *healthcare executive*
Howard, Bettie Jean *surgical nurse*
Hulse, Stewart Harding, Jr. *educator, experimental psychologist*
Jenkins, Louise Sherman *nursing researcher*
Knapp, David Allan *pharmaceutical educator, researcher*
Kumin, Libby Barbara *speech language pathologist, educator*
Larch, Sara Margaret *medical administrator*
Lee, Carlton K. K. *clinical pharmacist, consultant, educator*
Lefko, Jeffrey Jay *hospital administrator*
Money, John William *psychologist*
Nelson, Randy J. *psychology educator*
Palumbo, Francis Xavier Bernard *pharmacy educator*
Peters, Douglas Alan *neurology nurse*
Pigott, Karen Gray *community health nurse, geriatrics nurse*
Piotrow, Phyllis Tilson *public health educator, international development specialist*
Sachs, Murray B. *audiologist, educator*
Shapiro, Sam *health care analyst, biostatistician*
Sharfstein, Steven Samuel *health care executive, medical director*
Stanley, Julian Cecil, Jr. *psychology educator*
Steinwachs, Donald Michael *public health educator*
Vasile, Gennaro James *health care executive*
Wallace, Paul Edward, Jr. *health services management*
Washington, Vivian Edwards *social worker, former government official*
Wasserman, Martin P. *human health administrator*
Weller, Jane Kathleen *emergency nurse*

**Beltsville**
Levin, Gilbert Victor *health information, services and products*

**Bethesda**
Atwell, Constance Woodruff *health services executive, researcher*
Banik, Sambhu Nath *psychologist*
Coelho, Anthony Mendes, Jr. *health science administrator*
Cooper, Merri-Ann *psychologist*
Cornette, William Magnus *scientist, technical advisor*
Dogoloff, Lee Israel *clinical social worker, psychotherapist, consultant*
Duncan, Constance Catharine *psychologist, researcher*
Fauci, Anthony Stephen *health facility administrator, physician*
Feingold, S. Norman *psychologist*
Gaarder, Marie *speech pathologist*
Gaston, Marilyn Hughes *health facility administrator*
Geller, Ronald Gene *health administrator*
Hairstone, Marcus Alexander *health science administrator*
Hall, Zach Winter *medical institute executive, researcher*
Haugan, Gertrude M. *clinical psychologist*
Hoyer, Mary Louise *social worker, educator*
Hurd, Suzanne Sheldon *federal agency health science director*
Irving, George Washington, Jr. *health science association administrator*
Jonas, Gary Fred *health care center executive*
Kimzey, Lorene Miller *endocrinology nurse*
Malone, Winfred Francis *health scientist*
Malouff, Frank Joseph *health care association executive*
Marino, Pamela Anne *health sciences administrator*
Metzger, Henry *federal research institution administrator*
Milligan, Glenn Ellis *retired psychologist*
Mirsky, Allan Franklin *psychologist, researcher*
Mishkin, Mortimer *neuropsychologist*
Nee, Linda Elizabeth *social science analyst*
Obrams, Gunta Iris *research administrator*
O'Donnell, James Francis *health science administrator*
Onufrock, Richard Shade *pharmacist, researcher*
Ory, Marcia Gail *social science researcher*
Quraishi, Mohammed Sayeed *health scientist, administrator*
Snyder, Marvin *neuropsychologist*
Swinson, Angela Anthony *physician*
Talbot, Bernard *government medical research facility official, physician*
Trumbull, Richard *psychologist*
Vaitukaitis, Judith Louise *medical research administrator*
Varricchio, Claudette Goulet *nursing educator, researcher*
Wheeler, Beverly (Barnes) *cardiology nurse specialist*
Woolery-Antill, Myra Jo *pediatric clinical nurse specialist*
Wurtz, Robert Henry *neuroscientist*

**Bowie**
Boland, Gerald Lee *health facility financial executive*
Newhouse, Quentin, Jr. *social psychologist, educator, researcher*

**Chevy Chase**
Crawford, Meredith Pullen *research psychologist*
Schneider, John Hoke *health science administrator*
Walk, Richard David *retired psychology educator*

**Clinton**
Sizemore, Carolyn Lee *nuclear medicine technologist*

**College Park**
Gaylin, Ned L. *psychology educator*
Greenberg, Jerrold Selig *health education educator*
Hill, Clara Edith *psychology educator*
Locke, Edwin Allen, III *psychologist, educator*
Schneider, Benjamin *psychology educator*
Sigall, Harold Fred *psychology educator*

**Columbia**
Alexander, Nancy J. *psychotherapist, educator*
Margolis, Vivienne O. *psychotherapist*
May, John Raymond *clinical psychologist*
Moore, Sheryl Stansil *medical nurse*
Queen, Sandy (Sandra Jane Queen) *psychologist, trainer, small business owner*
Radinsky, Allan Michael *human services administrator, behavior consultant, mental health services professional*

**Cumberland**
Mazzocco, Gail O'Sullivan *nursing educator*
Wolford, Nancy Lou *medical and surgical nurse*

**Delmar**
Cugler, Carol Marie Miller *retired mental health services professional*

**Elkridge**
Szilagyi, Sherry Ann *psychotherapist, lawyer*

**Ellicott City**
Becker, Shawn Coniff *community health professional*
Robison, Susan Miller *psychologist, educator, consultant*
Tillman, Elizabeth Carlotta *nurse, educator*

**Fallston**
Lewis, Howard Franklin *chiropractor*

**Gaithersburg**
Feinendegen, Ludwig Emil *retired hospital and research institute director*
Ross, Sherman *psychologist, educator*
Tenney, Lisa Christine Gray *healthcare administrator*

**Germantown**
Norcross, Marvin Augustus *veterinarian, retired government agency official*

**Glen Burnie**
Dawson, Marcia Ann *nurse administrator*
Sprabery, Carol Ann *mental health service professional*

**Greenbelt**
Morris, Joseph Anthony *health science association administrator*
Nevans-Palmer, Laurel Suzanne *rehabilitation counselor*

**Hagerstown**
Harrison, Lois Smith *hospital executive, educator*

**Hyattsville**
Bender, Randi Laine *occupational therapist*
Feldman, Jacob J. *health facility administrator*

**Ijamsville**
Vickers, James Hudson *veterinarian, research pathologist*

**Kensington**
Schmerling, Erwin Robert *counselor, retired physicist*

**La Plata**
Galvin, Noreen Ann *nurse, educator*

**Largo**
Isom, Virginia Annette Veazey *nursing educator*

**Laurel**
Landis, Donna Marie *nursing administrator, women's health nurse*

**Linthicum Heights**
Ryan, Judith W. *geriatrics nurse, adult nurse practitioner, educator, researcher*

**Lutherville**
Goodman, Valerie Dawson *psychiatric social worker*

**Lutherville Timonium**
Muuss, Rolf Eduard *retired psychologist, educator*

**Millersville**
Kunsman, Cynthia Louise Mullen *critical care nurse*
Spoeri, Randall Keith *healthcare company executive*

**Monkton**
O'Neill, Catherine R. *emergency nurse, nurse manager*

**Oakland**
McClintock, Donna Mae *social worker*

**Olney**
Michael, Jerrold Mark *public health specialist, former university dean, educator*

**Owings Mills**
Casper, Mary Lee *speech and language pathologist*
†Yen, Sherman *applied behavior analyst, educator, substance abuse treatment specialist*

**Perry Point**
Yackley, Luke Eugene *head nurse, mental health nurse*

**Potomac**
Brewer, Nathan Ronald *veterinarian, consultant*
Evans, Christine Burnett *healthcare management executive*
Heller, Peggy Osna *psychotherapist*
Higgins, Dr. Nancy Branscome *management and counseling educator*
Leva, Neil Irwin *psychotherapist, hypnotherapist*
Reynolds, Frank Miller *retired government administrator*

**Rockville**
Gabelnick, Henry Lewis *medical research director*
Gleich, Carol S. *health professions education executive*
Gluckstein, Fritz Paul *veterinarian, biomedical information specialist*
Howard, Lee Milton *international health consultant*
Johnston, Linda Louise Hanna *public health analyst*
Koslow, Stephen Hugh *science administrator, pharmacologist*
Long, Cedric William *health research facility executive*
McCormick, Kathleen Ann Krym *geriatrics nurse, computer information specialist, federal agency administrator*
Mealy, J. Burke () *psychological services administrator*
Milner, Max *food and nutrition consultant*
Nightingale, Stuart Lester *physician, public health officer*
Nora, Audrey Hart *physician*
Robinson, William Andrew *health service executive, physician*
Scully, Martha Seebach *speech and language pathologist*
Stover, Ellen Simon *health scientist, psychologist*
Uppoor, Rajendra *pharmaceutical scientist, educator, researcher*

**Silver Spring**
Colyer, Sheryl Lynn *psychologist*
Gilbert, Arthur Charles Francis *psychologist*
Mashin, Jacqueline Ann Cook *medical sciences adminstrator*
Munson, John Christian *acoustician*
Rayburn, Carole (Mary Aida) Ann *psychologist, researcher, writer*

**Towson**
Wurmser, Leon *psychiatry educator*

**Upper Marlboro**
Elwood, Patricia Cowan *school hearing therapist, political consultant*

**Wheaton**
Goode, Margaret Nighan *nurse*

## MASSACHUSETTS

**Acton**
Brody, Leslie Gary *social worker, sociologist*

**Agawam**
Ashley, Cynthia Elizabeth *psychotherapist, human service administrator*

**Amherst**
Averill, James Reed *psychology educator*
Berger, Seymour Maurice *social psychologist*
Fox, Thomas Walton *veterinary science educator*
Grose, Robert Freeman *psychology educator*
Strickland, Bonnie Ruth *psychologist, educator*

PROFESSIONAL INDEX 5233 HEALTHCARE: HEALTH SERVICES


**Andover**
Anderson, Amelia E. *nursing administrator, geriatrics nurse*
Whidden, Robert Lee, Jr. *health care consultant*

**Arlington**
Horn, Roberta Claire *psychotherapist, photographer*

**Bedford**
†Steinberg, James Jonah *medical administrator, educator*

**Belmont**
Benyo, Joanne *critical care nurse*
Levendusky, Philip George *clinical psychologist, administrator*
Pollack, William Shelley *psychologist, organizational consultant*
Ronningstam, Elsa Frideborg *psychologist*
Youngberg, Robert Lovett *psychologist*

**Beverly**
Carlson, Sandra Anne *nursing educator, consultant*

**Billerica**
Ahern, Barbara Ann *nursing educator, vocational school educator*

**Bolton**
Dyer-Cole, Pauline *school psychologist, educator*

**Boston**
Bacigalupe, Gonzalo Manuel *family therapist, educator*
Blendon, Robert Jay *health policy educator*
Carton, Lonnie Caming *educational psychologist*
Coffey, Joanne Christine *dietitian*
Copeland, Anne Pitcairn *psychologist*
Drought, James Henry *healthcare business owner, exercise physiologist*
Fein, Rashi *health sciences educator*
Gleason, Jean Berko *psychology educator*
Goldman, Peter *nutrition and clinical pharmacology educator*
Grabauskas, Patricia Anne *nurse midwife*
Grossman, Frances Kaplan *psychologist*
Jackson, Earl, Jr. *medical technologist*
Kubzansky, Philip Eugene *environmental and organizational psychologist*
Liang, Matthew H. *medical director*
McIntyre, Mildred Jean *clinical psychologist, writer, neuroscientist*
Millar, Sally Gray *nurse*
Murphy, Evelyn Frances *healthcare administrator, former lieutenant governor*
Norman, Dennis Keith *psychologist, educator*
O'Hern, Jane Susan *psychologist, educator*
Otten, Jeffrey *health facility administrator*
Reinherz, Helen Zarsky *social services educator*
Righter, Anne Robinson *clinical social worker, psychotherapist*
Robinson, William J. *health facility adminstrator*
Scrimshaw, Nevin Stewart *physician, nutrition and health educator*
Stare, Fredrick John *nutritionist, biochemist, physician*
Strange, Donald Ernest *health care company executive*
Upshur, Carole Christofk *psychologist, educator*
Wechsler, Henry *research psychologist*
Weinstein, Milton Charles *health policy educator*
Winkelman, James Warren *hospital administrator, pathology educator*
Wirth, Dyann Fergus *public health educator, microbiologist*

**Boxford**
Siegert, Barbara (Marie) *health care administrator*

**Brookline**
Buchin, Jacqueline Chase *clinical psychologist*
Gewirtz, Mindy L. *organizational and human relations consultant*
Kibrick, Anne *nursing educator, university dean*

**Burlington**
Anaebonam, Aloysius Onyeabo *pharmacist*

**Cambridge**
Appley, Mortimer Herbert *psychologist, university president emeritus*
Bailyn, Lotte *psychology and management educator*
Brown, Roger William *psychologist, educator*
Burlage, Dorothy Dawson *clinical psychologist*
Chall, Jeanne Sternlicht *psychologist, educator*
†Clifton, Anne Rutenber *psychotherapist*
Colby, Anne *psychologist*
Collins, Allan Meakin *cognitive scientist, psychologist, educator*
Davis, Edgar Glenn *science and health policy executive*
Drago-Severson, Eleanor Elizabeth *developmental psychologist, educator, researcher*
Estes, William Kaye *psychologist, educator*
Gardner, Howard Earl *psychologist, author*
†Gilligan, Carol F. *psychologist, writer*
Henninger, Polly *neuropsychologist, researcher and clinician*
Holzman, Philip Seidman *psychologist, educator*
Kagan, Jerome *psychologist, educator*
Keniston, Kenneth *psychologist, educator*
Kosslyn, Stephen M. *psychologist educator*
Langer, Ellen Jane *psychologist, educator, writer*
Loew, Franklin Martin *medical and biological scientist, business entrepreneur*
Maher, Brendan Arnold *psychology educator, editor*
Pinker, Steven A. *cognitive science educator*
Rosenthal, Robert *psychology educator*
Swets, John Arthur *psychologist, researcher*
Young, Vernon Robert *nutrition, biochemistry educator*

**Canton**
Bihldorff, John Pearson *hospital director*
Sawtelle, Carl S. *psychiatric social worker*

**Charlestown**
Murphy-Lind, Karen Marie *health educator, dermatology nurse*

**Chatham**
Bianchi-Bigelow, Cheryl Ann *mental health facility director*

**Cheshire**
Frye-Moquin, Marsha Marie *social worker*

**Chestnut Hill**
Hawkins, Joellen Margaret Beck *nursing educator*
Munro, Barbara Hazard *nursing educator, college dean, researcher*
Wysocki, Boleslaw A(ntoni) *psychologist, educator*

**Chicopee**
Dame, Catherine Elaine *acupuncturist*

**Danvers**
Baures, Mary Margaret *psychotherapist, author*
Manganello, James Angelo *psychologist*

**Dedham**
Winder, Alvin Eliot *public health educator, clinical psychologist*

**Eastham**
Thompson, Cheryl Ann *special education educator*

**Feeding Hills**
Bianchi, Maria *critical care nurse, adult nurse practitioner*

**Framingham**
Dube, Beatrice Dorothy *psychologist*
Paul, Nancy Elizabeth *psychiatric-mental health nurse*
Vermette, Raymond Edward *clinical laboratories administrator*

**Great Barrington**
Berryhill, Mary Finley *emergency nurse*

**Greenfield**
Curtiss, Carol Perry *nursing consultant*

**Hanson**
Norris, John Anthony *health sciences executive, lawyer, educator*

**Harvard**
Larson, Roland Elmer *health care executive*

**Haverhill**
Ruiz, Eduardo Antonio *psychology and sociology educator*

**Holyoke**
Chapdelaine, Lorraine Elder *gerontology nurse*

**Hopkinton**
Main, Martha Lane Hughes *medical/surgical nurse*

**Hyannis**
White, Allen Jordan *nursing home adminstrator, consultant*

**Jamaica Plain**
Manzo, David William *human services administrator*

**Lancaster**
McDowell, David Jamison *clinical psychologist*

**Lexington**
Bombardieri, Merle Ann *psychotherapist*
Chaskelson, Marsha Ina *neuropsychologist*
Powers, Martha Mary *nursing consultant, education specialist*
Shapiro, Marian Kaplun *psychologist*

**Lincoln**
Barrett, Beatrice Helene *psychologist*

**Longmeadow**
Donoghue, Linda *nursing administrator, community health nurse*

**Lowell**
Sakellarios, Gertrude Edith *retired office nurse*
Sutter, Linda Diane *health services administrator*

**Ludlow**
Budnick, Thomas Peter *social worker*

**Lynn**
Loftis, Rebecca Hope *psychotherapist*

**Marblehead**
Plakans, Shelley Swift *social worker, psychotherapist*

**Marion**
McPartland, Patricia Ann *health educator*

**Marlborough**
Bethel, Tamara Ann *psychiatric nurse, consultant*

**Marshfield**
French, Frederic Rawson, Jr. *psychotherapist*

**Mattapoisett**
Busher, Penelope Chace-Squire *school psychologist*

**Medford**
DeBold, Joseph Francis *psychology educator*
Elkind, David *psychology educator*
Junger, Miguel Chapero *acoustics researcher*
Luria, Zella Hurwitz *psychology educator*
Miczek, Klaus Alexander *psychology educator*

**Melrose**
Henken, Bernard Samuel *clinical psychologist, speech pathologist*

**Middleboro**
Castaldi, David Lawrence *health care company executive*

**Milton**
Berzon, Faye Clark *retired nursing educator*
Desmond, Patricia Lorraine *psychotherapist, writer, publisher*

**Nantucket**
Murray, Caroline Fish *psychologist*

**Natick**
Bensel, Carolyn Kirkbride *psychologist*
Bower, Kathleen Anne *nurse consultant*
Swanson, Karin *hospital administrator, consultant*

**Needham**
Cantor, Pamela Corliss *psychologist*

**New Bedford**
Merolla, Michele Edward *chiropractor, broadcaster*

**Newton**
Sheehy, Joan Mary *nurse*
White, Burton Leonard *educational psychologist, author*

**North Attleboro**
Bordeleau, Lisa Marie *human services professional, consultant*
Williams, Ruth L. *rehabilitation counselor, consultant*

**North Easton**
Paul, Donald W. *therapist, audiologist*

**North Grafton**
Ross, James Neil, Jr. *veterinary educator*
Schwartz, Anthony *veterinary surgeon, educator*

**Northampton**
Volkmann, Frances Cooper *psychologist, educator*

**Osterville**
Weber, Adelheid Lisa *former nurse, chemist*

**Pepperell**
Scholefield, Adeline Peggy *therapist*

**Quincy**
O'Brien, John Steininger *clinical psychologist*
Spangler, Arthur Stephenson, Jr. *psychologist*

**Raynham**
Kaplan, Kenneth Barry *psychologist*

**Revere**
Chesna-Serino, Edna Mae *nurse*

**Roxbury**
Kelley, Ruth M. *nurse, alcohol, drug abuse services professional*

**Sagamore Beach**
Martin, Dale *vocational rehabilitation executive*

**Salem**
Wathne, Carl Norman *hospital administrator*

**Sandwich**
Terrill, Robert Carl *hospital administrator*

**South Dennis**
Stiefvater, Pamela Jean *chiropractor*

**Southbridge**
Anderson, Ross Barrett *healthcare environmental services manager*
Mangion, Richard Michael *health care executive*

**Springfield**
Ciak, Brenda Susan *nurse*
Miranda, Michele Renee *optometrist*
Rivest, Anne-Marie Therese *post-anesthesia nurse*

**Stoneham**
Dalimonte, Josephine Ann (Jo-Ann Dalimonte) *school nurse practitioner*

**Swampscott**
Smith, Carl Dean, Jr. *counselor, child advocate, business broker*

**Taunton**
Tenney, Patricia Ann *psychotherapist, nurse*

**Waltham**
Cotter, Douglas Adrian *healthcare executive*
Gibbons, Patrice Ellen *critical care nurse*
Mitchell, Janet Brew *health services researcher*
Morant, Ricardo Bernardino *psychology educator*
Nogelo, Anthony Miles *retired health care company executive*
Sekuler, Robert William *psychology educator, scientist*
Zebrowitz, Leslie Ann *psychology educator*

**Watertown**
Pellegrom, Daniel Earl *international health and development executive*

**Wayland**
Wolf, Irving *clinical psychologist*

**Wellesley**
Giddon, Donald B(ernard) *psychologist, educator*

**West Tisbury**
Smith, Henry Clay *retired psychology educator*

**Westborough**
Staffier, Pamela Moorman *psychologist*
Tobias, Lester Lee *psychological consultant*

**Weston**
Bales, Robert Freed *social psychologist, educator*
Fine, Bernard J. *retired psychologist, consultant*

**Williamstown**
Conklin, Susan Joan *psychotherapist, educator, corporate staff development*
Cramer, Phebe *psychologist*
Crider, Andrew Blake *psychologist*
Hastings, Philip Kay *psychology educator*
McGill, Thomas Emerson *psychology educator*

Solomon, Paul Robert *neuropsychologist, educator*

**Wilmington**
Freeman, Donald Chester, Jr. *health care company executive*

**Woburn**
Goela, Jitendra Singh *researcher, consultant*
†Tramonte, Michael Robert *school psychologist*

**Worcester**
Joshi, Harihar S. *medical laboratory executive*
Latham, Eleanor Ruth Earthrowl *neuropsychology therapist*
Micklitsch, Christine Nocchi *health care administrator*
Wapner, Seymour *psychologist, educator, administrator*

## MICHIGAN

**Ada**
Bandemer, Norman John *healthcare consulting executive*

**Addison**
Durant, Charles Edward, Jr. *medical facility administrator*

**Allegan**
Krause, Liz Young *community health nurse*

**Allendale**
Haller, Kathleen *nursing educator, family nurse practitioner*

**Alpena**
Fraleigh, John Walter *psychotherapist, social worker*

**Ann Arbor**
Apperson, Jean *psychologist*
Barbarin, Oscar Anthony *psychologist*
Behling, Charles Frederick *psychology educator*
Brown, Donald Robert *psychology educator*
Cain, Albert Clifford *psychology educator*
Cannell, Charles Frederick *psychologist, educator*
Clark, Noreen Morrison *behavioral science educator, researcher*
Douvan, Elizabeth *social psychologist, educator*
Eron, Leonard David *psychology educator*
Gaston, Hugh Philip *marriage counselor, educator*
Gomberg, Edith S. Lisansky *psychologist, educator*
Gordinier, Terri Klein *speech-language pathologist*
Griffith, John Randall *health services administrator, educator*
Hagen, John William *psychology educator*
House, James Stephen *social psychologist, educator*
Jackson, James Sidney *psychology educator*
Kalisch, Beatrice Jean *nursing educator, consultant*
Ketefian, Shaké *nursing educator*
Leong, Sue *retired community health and pediatrics nurse*
Manis, Melvin *psychologist, educator*
McKeachie, Wilbert James *psychologist, educator*
Nisbett, Richard Eugene *psychology educator*
Oakley, Deborah Jane *researcher, educator*
Powell, Linda Rae *educational healthcare consultant*
Romani, John Henry *health administration educator*
Rupp, Ralph Russell *audiologist, educator, author*
Simms, Lillian Miller *nursing educator*
Smith, J(ames) E(verett) Keith *psychologist, educator*
Stevenson, Harold William *psychology educator*
Warner, Kenneth E. *public health educator, consultant*
Zucker, Robert A(lpert) *psychologist*

**Benton Harbor**
Rasmussen, Alice Call *nursing educator*

**Big Rapids**
Weinlander, Max Martin *retired psychologist*

**Birmingham**
Denes, Michel Janet *physical therapist, consultant in rehabilitation*

**Brighton**
Lamson, Evonne Viola *counselor, computer software company executive, consultant, pastor, Christian education administrator*

**Buchanan**
Paustian, Bonita Joyce *school health administrator*

**Conklin**
Kelly, Josephine Kaye *social worker*

**Dearborn**
Good, Cheryl Denise *veterinarian*
Montgomery, Martha M. *nursing educator*
Suchy, Susanne N. *nursing educator*

**Detroit**
Banks, Lois Michelle *nurse*
Bennett, Margaret Ethel Booker *psychotherapist*
Birdsong, Emil Ardell *psychologist*
Cantoni, Louis Joseph *psychologist, poet, sculptor*
Garriott, Lois Jean *clinical social worker, educator*
Hamilton, Jonnie Mae *pediatric nurse practitioner, educator*
Heppner, Gloria Hill *medical science administrator, educator*
Jacox, Ada Kathryn *nurse, educator*
Klosinski, Deanna Dupree *medical laboratory sciences educator*
Lee, André Lafayette *hospital administrator*
Mack, Robert Emmet *hospital administrator*
Miller Davis, Mary-Agnes *social worker*
Prasad, Ananda Shiva *medical educator*
Warden, Gail Lee *health care executive*
Wittrup, Richard Derald *health care executive*

**East Lansing**
Abeles, Norman *psychologist, educator*
Ilgen, Daniel Richard *psychology educator*
Majors, Richard George *psychology educator*
Overton, Sarita Rosa *psychologist*
Winder, Clarence Leland *psychologist, educator*
Witter, Richard Lawrence *veterinarian, educator*

**Farmington**
Baker, Edward Martin *engineering and industrial psychologist*
Burns, Sister Elizabeth Mary *hospital administrator*

**Farmington Hills**
McNamara, Ann Dowd *medical technologist*
Sobczak, Judy Marie *clinical psychologist*

**Flint**
Alarie, Peggy Sue *physician assistant*
Cawood, Thomas Fred *music therapist*
Marx, Sharon Rose *health facility administrator*
Palinsky, Constance Genevieve *hypnotherapist, educator*

**Fowlerville**
Edwards, Nelson Grey *optometrist*

**Fruitport**
Anderson, Frances Swem *nuclear medical technologist*

**Grand Haven**
Anderson, Cynthia Finkbeiner Sjoberg *speech and language pathologist*

**Grand Ledge**
Evert, Sandra Florence *medical/surgical nurse*

**Grand Rapids**
Brent, Helen Teressa *health planner/evaluator*
Gemmell-Akalis, Bonni Jean *psychotherapist*
Kramer, Carol Gertrude *marriage and family counselor*
MacDonald, David Richard *industrial psychologist*

**Grosse Pointe**
Cartmill, George Edwin, Jr. *retired hospital administrator*
Hudson, Marlene Mary *speech and language pathologist*

**Hastings**
Adrounie, V. Harry *public health administrator, scientist, educator, environmentalist*

**Holland**
Hountras, Peter Timothy *psychologist, educator*

**Holt**
Ribby, Alice Marie *nurse*

**Hopkins**
Ludlam, Heather Jo *veterinarian*

**Howell**
Korsgren, Mary Louise *home care nurse*

**Jackson**
Genyk, Ruth Bel *psychotherapist*

**Kalamazoo**
Bennett, Arlie Joyce *clinical social worker emeritus*
Campbell, Raymond William *surgical nurse*
Fredericks, Sharon Kay *nurses aide*
Hamilton, Diane Bronkema *nursing educator*
Lander, Joyce Ann *nursing educator, medical/surgical nurse*
Shah, Shirish Anantlal *pharmacist*
Slager, Joan K. *nurse midwife*
Walcott, Delores Deborah *psychologist, educator*

**Lansing**
Liebler, Edward Charles *veterinarian, construction company executive*
Muneio, Patricia Anne *public health nurse*

**Lincoln Park**
Russell, Harriet Shaw *social worker*

**Livonia**
Needham, Kathleen Ann *gerontology educator, consultant*

**Marquette**
Hill, Betty Jean *nursing educator, academic administrator*
Poindexter, Kathleen A. Krause *nursing educator, critical care nurse*

**Middleville**
Miller, Stephen Bryan *social worker, marriage counselor*

**Monroe**
Knezevich, Janice A. *critical care nurse*

**Mount Pleasant**
Lovinger, Sophie Lehner *child psychologist*

**Novi**
Crane, Patricia Sue *probation services administrator, social worker*

**Ortonville**
Coffel, Patricia K. *retired clinical social worker*

**Plainwell**
Ortiz-Button, Olga *social worker*

**Plymouth**
McClendon, Edwin James *health science educator*

**Portage**
Elliott, George Algimon *pathologist, toxicologist, veterinarian*

**Rapid River**
Olson, Marian Edna *nursing consultant, social psychologist*

**Reed City**
Creede, Michael David (Woodman Mike ) *nursing supervisor*

**Royal Oak**
Lechner, Jon Robert *nursing administrator, educator*

**Saginaw**
Brown, Alice Mary *pharmacist*
Shackelford, Martin Robert *social worker*

**Saint Clair Shores**
Neal-Vittiglio, Cynthia Karen *clinical psychologist*

**Southfield**
Beuerlein, Sister Juliana *hospital administrator*
†Swartz, William John *managed care company executive*
Thimotheose, Kadakampallil George *psychologist*
Wagner, Muriel Ginsberg *nutrition therapist*

**Spring Arbor**
Richard, Lyle Elmore *retired school social worker, consultant*

**Troy**
Kulich, Roman Theodore *healthcare administrator*
Potts, Anthony Vincent *optometrist, orthokeratologist*

**University Center**
May, Margrethe *allied health educator*

**West Bloomfield**
Barr, Martin *health care and higher education adminstrator*
Dvorkin, Louis *neuropsychologist*
Myers, Kenneth Ellis *hospital administrator*
Sugintas, Nora Maria *veterinarian, scientist, medical company executive, performing arts dancer*

**Westland**
Gaipa, Nancy Christine *pharmacist*
Shaw, Randy Lee *human services administrator*

**Whitmore Lake**
Ely, JoAnn Denice *health science facility administrator*

**Ypsilanti**
deSouza, Joan Melanie *psychologist*
Holland, Joy *health care facility executive*
Wilson, Lorraine M. *medical and surgical nurse, nursing educator*

## MINNESOTA

**Albert Lea**
Jensen, Annette M. *mental health nurse, administrator*

**Brooklyn Park**
Frank, Paul Wilbur *social worker*

**Cottage Grove**
Glazebrook, Rita Susan *nursing educator*

**Duluth**
Gallinger, Lois Mae *medical technologist*

**Elysian**
Thayer, Edna Louise *medical facility administrator, nurse*

**Fairmont**
Hillestad, Donna Dawn *nurse*

**Golden Valley**
Van Hauer, Robert *former health care company executive*

**Hastings**
Blackie, Spencer David *physical therapist, administrator*

**International Falls**
Stevens, Linda Louise Halbur *addiction counselor*

**Mankato**
Erickson-Weerts, Sally Annette *dietetics educator*
Zeller, Michael James *psychologist, educator*

**Minneapolis**
Appel, William Frank *pharmacist*
Bouchard, Thomas Joseph, Jr. *psychology educator, researcher*
Cummings, Larry Lee *psychologist, educator*
Dahl, Gerald LuVern *psychotherapist, educator, consultant, writer*
Dawis, René V. *psychology educator, research consultant*
Farr, Leonard Alfred *hospital administrator*
Garmezy, Norman *psychology educator*
Grant, David James William *pharmacy educator*
Hansen, Jo-Ida Charlotte *psychology educator, researcher*
Hanson, A. Stuart *health facility administrator, physician*
Johnson, David Wolcott *psychologist, educator*
Kanfer, Frederick H. *psychologist, educator*
Kennon, Rozmond Herron *physical therapist*
Konopka, Gisela Peiper (Mrs. Erhardt Paul Konopka) *social worker, author, lecturer, educator*
Kralewski, John Edward *health service administration educator*
Marks, Florence Carlin Elliott *retired nursing informaticist*
Meehl, Paul Everett *psychologist, educator*
Morehead, Annette Marie *disabled children's facility administrator, child advocate*
Schwartz, Howard Wyn *health facility administrator*
Suryanarayanan, Raj Gopalan *researcher, consultant, educator*
Toscano, James Vincent *medical institute administration*
Travis, Marlene O. *healthcare management executive*
Weinberg, Richard Alan *psychologist*
Wiener, Daniel Norman *psychologist*
Ysseldyke, James Edward *psychology educator, research center administrator*
Ziegenhagen, David Mackenzie *healthcare company executive*

**Morris**
Dee, Scott Allen *veterinarian*

**Palisade**
Kilde, Sandra Jean *nurse anesthetist, educator, consultant*

**Plainview**
Reincke, Rhonda *nursing educator*

**Plymouth**
†Barden, Robert Christopher *psychologist, educator, lawyer, public policy consultant*

**Redlake**
Ceterski, Dorothy *nutritionist*

**Robbinsdale**
Anderson, Scott Robbins *hospital administrator*

**Rochester**
Gervais, Sister Generose *hospital consultant*
Goodman, Julie *nurse midwife*
Marttila, James Konstantin *pharmacy administrator*
Stewart, Karen Meyer *pediatrics nurse, nursing manager*
Verbout, James Paul *recreational therapist*

**Saint Louis Park**
Gerike, Ann Elizabeth *psychologist*

**Saint Paul**
Ashton, Sister Mary Madonna *healthcare administrator*
Brozek, Josef *psychology educator, scientist*
Charmoli, Margaret Charity *psychologist*
Czarnecki, Caroline MaryAnne *veterinary anatomy educator*
Diesch, Stanley La Verne *veterinarian, educator*
†Feldman, Nancy Jane *health organization executive*
Johnson, Kenneth Harvey *veterinary pathologist*
Newman, Margaret Ann *nursing educator*
Pomeroy, Benjamin Sherwood *veterinary medicine educator*
Rossmann, Jack Eugene *psychology educator*
Victor, Lorraine Carol *critical care nurse*

**Stillwater**
Francis, D. Max *healthcare management executive*

**White Bear Lake**
Williams, Julie Belle *psychiatric social worker*

**Winona**
Holm, Joy Alice *psychology educator, art educator, artist, goldsmith*

## MISSISSIPPI

**Carriere**
Wilson, Raymond Clark *former hospital executive*

**Cleveland**
Thornton, Larry Lee *psychotherapist, author, educator*

**Clinton**
Sanders, Barbara Boyles *health services director*

**Hattiesburg**
Noblin, Charles Donald *clinical psychologist, educator*

**Horn Lake**
Golliver, Cheryl Rena *nurse*

**Jackson**
Baltz, Richard Jay *health care company executive*
Dubbert, Patricia Marie *psychologist, educator*
Malloy, James Matthew *managed care executive, health care consultant*
Patterson, Helen Crosby *clinical psychologist*
Stubbs, James Carlton *retired hospital administrator*
Tchounwou, Paul Bernard *environmental health specialist, educator*

**Mississippi State**
Arnizaut de Mattos, Ana Beatriz *veterinarian*

**Nesbit**
Berti, Phyllis Mae *health information management specialist*

**Newton**
Hagan, Lynn Purnell *social worker, recreation therapist*

**Ocean Springs**
McNulty, Matthew Francis, Jr. *health sciences and health services administrator, educator, university administrator, consultant, horse and cattle breeder*

**Pascagoula**
McIlwain, Thomas David *fishery administrator, marine biologist, educator*

**Ridgeland**
O'Neill, Paul John *retired psychology educator*

**Southaven**
Utroska, William Robert *veterinarian*

**Tupelo**
Brown, Betty Harrison *mental health counselor*
Zurawski, Jeanette *rehabilitation services professional*

**Walls**
Jones, Yvonne Dolores *social worker*

**Waynesboro**
Dickerson, Marie Harvison *nurse anesthetist*

**Whitfield**
Morton, James Irwin *hospital administrator*

## MISSOURI

**Ballwin**
Meiner, Sue Ellen Thompson *gerontologist, nursing educator and researcher*
Stevens, Julie Ann *peri-operative nurse*

**Belton**
Shymanski, Catherine Mary *health facility administrator, nursing education administrator*

**Bois D Arc**
Westphal, Leonard Wyrick *health care executive, consultant*

**Camdenton**
DeShazo, Marjorie White *occupational therapist*

**Canton**
Glover, Albert Downing *retired veterinarian*

**Cape Girardeau**
Nicholson, Gerald Lee *medical facilities administrator*
Southard-Ritter, Marcia *nursing administrator*

**Carthage**
Coffield, Mary Eleanor *speech clinician, educator*

**Chesterfield**
Robinson, Patricia Elaine *women's health nurse practitioner*

**Clayton**
McCann-Turner, Robin Lee *child, adolescent analyst*

**Columbia**
Biddle, Bruce Jesse *social psychologist, educator*
Blaine, Edward H. *health science administrator, educator*
Dolliver, Robert Henry *psychology educator*
Hensley, Elizabeth Catherine *nutritionist, educator*
Kausler, Donald Harvey *psychology educator*
Kiesler, Charles Adolphus *psychologist, academic administrator*
Kilgore, Randall Freeman *health information services administrator*
Longo, Daniel Robert *health services researcher, medical educator*
LoPiccolo, Joseph *psychologist, educator, author*
Morehouse, Lawrence Glen *veterinarian, emeritus professor*
Wagner, Joseph Edward *veterinarian, educator*

**Dexter**
Owens, Debra Ann *chiropractor*

**Fayette**
Stewart, Bobby Gene *laboratory director*

**Florissant**
Betts, Warren Romeo *retired health facility administrator*

**Grandview**
Justesen, Don Robert *psychologist*

**Hamilton**
Esry, Cordelia Cochran *community health nurse, emeritus educator*

**Imperial**
Hughes, Barbara Bradford *nurse*

**Independence**
Scott, Helen Cecile *critical care nurse*
Vigen, Kathryn L. Voss *nursing administrator, educator*

**Jefferson City**
Dey, Charlotte Jane *retired community health nurse*

**Kansas City**
Bonci, Andrew S. *chiropractor*
Couch, Daniel Michael *healthcare executive*
Dahl, Andrew Wilbur *health services executive*
Eddy, William Bahret *psychology educator, university dean*
Graham, Charles *psychologist*
Kingsley, James Gordon *healthcare executive*
Lubin, Bernard *psychologist, educator*
Piepho, Robert Walter *pharmacy educator, researcher*
Samuel, Robert Thompson *optometrist*
Stolov, Jerry Franklin *healthcare executive*
Tansey, Robert Paul, Sr. *pharmaceutical chemist*
Tunley, Naomi Louise *retired nurse administrator*
Williams, Thelma Jean *social worker*
†Zechman, David Mark *hospital administrator, educator*

**Lebanon**
Caplinger, Patricia E. *family nurse practitioner*

**Nevada**
Studer, Patricia S. *psychologist*

**Raytown**
Smith, Robert Francis *psychologist, consultant, investment advisor*

**Rolla**
Irion, Arthur Lloyd *psychologist, educator*

**Saint Joseph**
Boor, Myron Vernon *psychologist, educator*
†Johnson, Robert Charles *medical administrator*

**Saint Louis**
Briggs, John James *nuclear pharmacist, clinical specialist*
Farrell, John Timothy *hospital administrator*
Fitch, Rachel Farr *health policy analyst*
Folk, Roger Maurice *laboratory director*
Herzfeld-Kimbrough, Ciby *mental health educator*
Hirsh, Ira Jean *psychology educator, researcher*
Ihde, Daniel Carlyle *health science executive*
Johnson, Gloria Jean *counseling professional*

Kiser, Karen Maureen *medical technologist, educator*
Koesterer, Larry J. *pharmacist*
LaBruyere, Thomas Edward *health facility administrator*
Meiners, Ginny *clinical psychologist, nurse consultant*
Merbaum, Michael *psychology educator, clinical psychologist*
Molloff, Florence Jeanine *speech and language therapist*
Myers, Raymond Irvin *optometrist, researcher*
Ozawa, Martha Naoko *social work educator*
Rhodes, Marlene Rutherford *counseling educator, educational consultant*
Rosenzweig, Saul *psychologist, educator, administrator*
Schoenhard, William Charles, Jr. *health care executive*
Storandt, Martha *psychologist*
Stretch, John Joseph *social work educator, management and evaluation consultant*
Swiener, Rita Rochelle *psychologist, educator*
Thompson, Vetta Lynn Sanders *psychologist, educator*

**Sparta**
Madore, Joyce Louise *gerontology nurse*

**Springfield**
McCullough, V. Beth *pharmacist, educator*

**Warrensburg**
Kemp, Arthur Derek *psychology educator*

## MONTANA

**Bozeman**
Gray, Philip Howard *retired psychologist, educator*

**Glendive**
Bruno, Peter Jackson *counselor, consultant, pastor*

**Great Falls**
Downer, William John, Jr. *retired hospital administrator*

**Missoula**
Watkins, John Goodrich *psychologist, educator*
Wemple, James Robert *psychotherapist*
Wollersheim, Janet Puccinelli *psychology educator*
Yee, Albert Hoy *retired psychologist, educator*

## NEBRASKA

**Grand Island**
Etheridge, Margaret Dwyer *medical center director*

**Lincoln**
Auld, James S. *educational psychologist*
Bleich, Michael Robert *nursing administrator and consultant*
Donkin, Scott William *chiropractor*
Hamilton, David Wendell *medical services executive*
Rohren, Brenda Marie Anderson *therapist, educator*
Travis, Shirley Louise *nursing administrator*

**Omaha**
Dash, Alekha K. *pharmaceutical scientist, educator*
Hachten, Richard Arthur, II *health system administrator*
Jackson, Mary Teresa *critical care nurse*
Lee, Carla Ann Bouska *nursing educator*
Leininger, Madeleine Monica *nurse, anthropologist, administrator, consultant, editor, author*
Omer, Robert Wendell *hospital administrator*
Parker, Carol Tommie *psychotherapist, educator*
Vallery, Janet Alane *industrial hygienist*

**Papillion**
Rees, Patricia Glines *occupational health nurse, consultant, educator*

**South Sioux City**
Graves, Maureen Ann *counselor*

**Superior**
Drullinger, Leona Pearl *obstetrics nurse*

## NEVADA

**Carson City**
Kwalick, Donald S. *human services manager*

**East Ely**
Alderman, Minnis Amelia *psychologist, educator, small business owner*

**Hawthorne**
Sortland, Trudith Ann *speech and language therapist, educator*

**Henderson**
Byleckie, Scott Andrew, Sr. *health facility coordinator*

**Las Vegas**
Francis, Timothy Duane *chiropractor*
Gowdy, Miriam Betts *nutritionist*
Hallas, Evelyn Margaret *physical therapist*
Jagodzinski, Ruth Clark *nursing administrator*
Kowalski, Susan Dolores *critical care nurse, educator*
Law, Flora Elizabeth (Libby Law) *retired community health and pediatrics nurse*
Michel, Mary Ann Kedzuf *nursing educator*
Ogren, Carroll Woodrow *retired hospital administrator*
Pearson, Robert Allen *optometrist*
Schultz, Gregory Paul *health center official*
Wilson, Warner Rushing *psychology educator*

**Reno**
Baird, Charles Finley, Jr. *oncology nurse*
Bijou, Sidney William *psychology educator*
Bramwell, Marvel Lynnette *nurse, social worker*

Cummings, Nicholas Andrew *psychologist*
Guinn, Janet Martin *psychologist, consultant*
Larwood, Laurie *psychologist*
May, Jerry Russell *psychologist*
McGary, Rita Rose *social worker*
Pinson, Larry Lee *pharmacist*
Smith, Aaron *clinical psychologist, research director*
Webster, Michael Anderson *experimental psychologist*

## NEW HAMPSHIRE

**Bedford**
Collins, Diana Josephine *psychologist*
Patti, Sister Josephine Marie *health science facility administrator*

**Claremont**
Demers, Nancy Kae *nursing educator*

**Concord**
Kalipolites, June E. Turner *rehabilitation professional*
Mac Kay, James Robert *psychiatric social worker, mayor*

**Dover**
Boyle, Nancy Reynolds *home health agency administrator*

**Greenfield**
Wheelock, Major William, Jr. *health care adminstrator*

**Hampstead**
Sewitch, Deborah E. *health science association administrator, educator, sleep researcher*

**Hanover**
Kleck, Robert Eldon *psychology educator*
Riggs, Lorrin Andrews *psychologist, educator*

**Hudson**
Rice, Annie L. Kempton *medical, surgical and rehabilitation nurse*

**Keene**
Baldwin, Peter Arthur *psychologist, educator, author, minister*

**Lebanon**
Emery, Virginia Olga Beattie *psychologist, researcher*
Silberfarb, Peter Michael *psychiatrist, educator*
Varnum, James William *hospital administrator*

**Manchester**
Ehlers, Eileen Spratt *family therapist*
Mailloux, Raymond Victor *health services administrator*

**Meredith**
Hamlin, Robert Henry *public health educator, management consultant*

**Nashua**
Flynn, William Berchman, Jr. *psychology educator, clinical psychologist*

**Sandown**
Densen, Paul Maximillian *former health administrator, educator*

**Tilton**
Wolf, Sharon Ann *psychotherapist*

**Windham**
Hurst, Michael William *psychologist*

## NEW JERSEY

**Atlantic Highlands**
Royce, Paul Chadwick *medical administrator*

**Avalon**
Beatrice, Ruth Hadfield *hypnotherapist, retired educator*

**Basking Ridge**
Manda, Joseph Alexander, III *veterinary consulting executive*

**Belford**
Bauer, Linda P. *nurse*

**Belle Mead**
Sarle, Charles Richard *health facility executive*
Wilson, Nancy Jeanne *laboratory director, medical technologist*

**Belmar**
De Santo, Donald James *psychologist*

**Bergenfield**
Mango-Hurdman, Christina Rose *psychiatric art therapist*

**Blairstown**
Horn-Alsberge, Michele Maryann *school psychologist*

**Bordentown**
Blackson, Benjamin F(ranklin) *clinical social worker*

**Bound Brook**
Borah, Kripanath *pharmacist*

**Branchville**
Johanson, Gregory John *psychotherapy trainer, minister*

**Brick**
Rusoff, Irving Isadore *industrial food scientist, consultant*

**Bridgewater**
Colline, Marguerite Richnavsky *maternal, women's health and pediatrics nurse*
Hillegass, Christine Ann *psychologist*
Weingast, Marvin *laboratory executive*

**Burlington**
Rowlette, Henry Allen, Jr. *social worker*

**Camden**
Abbott, Ann Augustine *social worker, educator*
Weeks, Sandra Kenney *healthcare facilitator*

**Chatham**
Murphy, Joseph James *chiropractic physician*

**Cherry Hill**
Grado-Wolynies, Evelyn (Evelyn Wolynies) *clinical nurse specialist, educator*
Israelsky, Roberta Schwartz *speech pathologist, audiologist*

**Clark**
Kinley, David *physical therapist, acupuncturist*

**Clifton**
Adelsberg, Harvey *hospital administrator*
Epstein, William Eric *health care executive*

**Cranford**
Herz, Sylvia Beatrice *clinical and community psychologist*
Nasta, Marilyn Jean *speech and language pathologist, consultant*

**Dumont**
Davidson, Grace Evelyn *nursing educator, retired administrator*

**East Brunswick**
Johnson, Edward Elemuel *psychologist, educator*

**Elizabeth**
Blecher, Carol Stein *oncology clinical nurse specialist*

**Englewood**
Farrell, Patricia Ann *psychologist, educator*
Mc Mullan, Dorothy *nurse educator*

**Florham Park**
Oths, Richard Philip *health systems administrator*
Sniffen, Michael Joseph *hospital administrator*

**Fort Lee**
Cohen, Judith Lynne *healthcare administrator*
Kadish, Lori Gail *clinical psychologist*
Welfeld, Joseph Alan *healthcare consultant*

**Franklin Lakes**
Hegelmann, Julius *retired pharmacy educator*

**Glassboro**
Fails, Donna Gail *mental health services professional*

**Hackensack**
Baker, Andrew Hartill *clinical laboratory executive*
Ferguson, John Patrick *medical center executive*

**Hammonton**
Proll, George Simon *psychologist*

**Hightstown**
Hart, Patricia A. *public health officer*

**Holmdel**
Tambaro, Marie Grace *health specialist, nursing educator*

**Hopatcong**
Wolahan, Caryle Goldsack *nursing educator*

**Iselin**
Cruz, Nelson Xavier *healthcare executive*

**Jersey City**
Giuffra, Lawrence John *hospital administrator, medical educator*
Moore-Szepesy, Mariann Lydia *health care executive*
Mortensen, Eugene Phillips *hospital administrator*

**Kinnelon**
Preston, Andrew Joseph *pharmacist, drug company executive*
Richardson, Irene M. *health facility administrator*

**Lafayette**
Mitchell, Peter William *addictions counselor*

**Lakewood**
Shawl, S. Nicole *hypnobehavioral scientist*

**Lawrenceville**
Griffith, Barbara E. *social worker, political activist*
Moser, Rosemarie Scolaro *psychologist*

**Ledgewood**
Smith, Sally Elaine Beckley *veterinary technician*

**Linden**
Banda, Geraldine Marie *chiropractic physician*

**Linwood**
Cohen, Diana Louise *mental health administrator, psychology, educator, psychotherapist*

**Livingston**
Brenner, Betty Esther Bilgray *social worker*
Francavilla, Barbara Jean *human services administrator*
Friedman, Merton Hirsch *retired psychologist, educator*
Machlin, Lawrence J. *nutritionist, biochemist, educator*

**Lodi**
Force, Herman Edgar *psychologist*

**Madison**
Ellenbogen, Leon *nutritionist, pharmaceutical company executive*
Marquis, Harriet Hill *social worker*

**Magnolia**
Holt, James Theodore *nursing educator*

**Marlton**
Misiorek, Mary Madelyn *social worker*

**Medford**
Katzell, Raymond A. *psychologist, educator*
Wallis, Robert Ray *psychologist, entrepreneur*

**Mendham**
Shrader, William Keating *clinical psychologist, consultant*

**Middlesex**
Colanduoni, Bernadette Louise *school nurse*

**Montclair**
Tonges, Mary Crabtree *patient care executive*

**Morristown**
Gearhart, Marguerite Theresa *school nurse, health educator, nurse, counselor*
Hager, Mary Hastings *nutritionist, educator, consultant*

**Mount Ephraim**
Nusbaum, Geoffrey Dean *psychotherapist*

**Mount Holly**
Losse, Catherine Ann *pediatric nurse, critical care nurse, educator, clinical nurse specialist, family nurse practitioner*

**Mountainside**
Kozberg, Donna Walters *rehabilitation administration executive*

**Netcong**
Davis, Dorinne Sue Taylor Lovas *audiologist*

**New Brunswick**
Boehm, Werner William *social work educator*
Dinerman, Miriam *social work educator*
Greenberg, Michael Richard *urban studies and community health educator*
Kovach, Barbara Ellen *management and psychology educator*
Momah, Ethel Chukwuekwe *women's health nurse*
†Pallone, Nathaniel John *psychologist, educator*
Peterson, Donald Robert *psychologist, educator, university administrator*
Rosenberg, Seymour *psychologist, educator*
Terrill, Thomas Edward *health facility administrator*
Wilkinson, Louise Cherry *psychology educator, dean*

**New Providence**
Atal, Bishnu Saroop *speech research executive*

**Newark**
Carroll, John Douglas *mathematical and statistical psychologist*
Cheng, Mei-Fang *psychobiology educator, neuroethology researcher*
Pagán, Gilberto, Jr. *clinical psychologist*

**Newton**
Worman, Linda Kay *nursing administrator*

**Nutley**
Drews, Jürgen *pharmaceutical researcher*

**Ocean Gate**
Campbell, Edward Wallace *nutritionist*

**Paramus**
Adams, Eda Ann Fischer *nursing educator*

**Paterson**
†McEvoy, Lorraine K. *oncology nurse*

**Pennsauken**
Daly, Charles Arthur *health services administrator*

**Pequannock**
MacMurren, Harold Henry, Jr. *psychologist, lawyer*

**Piscataway**
Alderfer, Clayton Paul *organizational psychologist, educator, author, consultant, administrator*
Goldstein, Bernard David *physician, educator*
Julesz, Bela *experimental psychologist, educator, electrical engineer*
Lazarus, Arnold Allan *psychologist, educator*
Pandina, Robert John *neuropsychologist*
Schwebel, Milton *psychologist, educator*

**Pomona**
Bukowski, Elaine Louise *physical therapist*

**Port Monmouth**
Lechtanski, Cheryl Lee *chiropractor*

**Princeton**
Cooper, Joel *psychology educator*
Ekstrom, Ruth Burt *psychologist*
Elliott-Moskwa, Elaine Sally *psychologist, researcher*
Emmerich, Walter *psychologist*
Fried, Eleanor Reingold *psychologist, educator*
Girgus, Joan Stern *psychologist, university administrator*
Glucksberg, Sam *psychology educator*
Gross, Charles Gordon *psychology educator, neuroscientist*
Hawver, Dennis Arthur *psychological consultant*
Manning, Winton Howard *psychologist, educational administrator*
Meade, Dale Michael *laboratory director*
Miller, George Armitage *psychologist, educator*
Parry, Scott Brink *psychologist*
Spence, Donald Pond *psychologist, psychoanalyst*
Vallet, Jean-Marie P. *health care company executive*
Willingham, Warren Willcox *psychologist, testing service executive*

**Ramsey**
Vogel, Mary Ellen Virginia *psychologist, learning consultant*

**Randolph**
Allen, B. Marc *managed care executive*

**Raritan**
Goldstein, Jack *health science executive, microbiologist*

**Red Bank**
Fred, Rogers Murray, III *veterinary oncologist*
Gutentag, Patricia Richmand *social worker, family counselor, occupational therapist*
Jones, Nancy Patricia *addictions therapist, consultant*

**Ridgewood**
Clements, Lynne Fleming *family therapist, programmer*

**Roseland**
Malafronte, Donald *health executive*

**Rutherford**
Aberman, Harold Mark *veterinarian*

**Saddle River**
Peters, Eleanor White *retired mental health nurse*

**Scotch Plains**
Sweeney, Lucy Graham *psychologist*

**Secaucus**
Newton, V. Miller *medical psychotherapist, neuropsychologist, writer*

**Shrewsbury**
Alburtus, Mary Jo *social worker, consultant, trainer*

**Somerset**
Bieber, Mark Allan *nutrition scientist, researcher*
DeVaris, Jeannette Mary *psychologist*
Kwetkauskie, John A. *medical technologist*

**Somerville**
Weidenfeller, Geraldine Carney *speech and language pathologist*

**Sparta**
Buist, Jean Mackerley *veterinarian*

**Summit**
Hall, Pamela Elizabeth *psychologist*

**Teaneck**
Alperin, Richard Martin *clinical social worker, psychoanalyst*
Fairfield, Betty Elaine Smith *psychologist*
Fanshel, David *social worker*
Gordon, Jonathan David *psychologist*
Hollman, Barbara Carol *psychoanalyst, psychotherapist, consultant*

**Tenafly**
Blank, Marion Sue *psychologist*

**Toms River**
Chambers, Elizabeth Donan *neonatal nurse, administrator*

**Trenton**
DeMontigney, James Morgan *health services administrator*
Peroni, Peter A., II *psychologist, educator*
Saraf, Komal C. *psychologist*
Schirber, Annamarie Riddering *speech and language pathologist, educator*

**Turnersville**
Cammarota, Marie Elizabeth *health services administration/nursing educator*

**Union**
Kaplan, Doris Weiler *social worker*
Muller, Gregory Alan *health facilities administrator, mayor*
Williams, Carol Jorgensen *social work educator*

**Vineland**
Hunt, Howard F(rancis) *psychologist, educator*
Popp, Charlotte Louise *health development center administrator, nurse*

**Wall**
Cobb, Lorene Pozyc *physical therapist*

**Warren**
Cohen, Bertram David *psychologist, educator*

**Wayne**
†Silverman-Dresner, Toby Roslyn *psychologist*
Tanzman-Bock, Maxine M. *psychotherapist, hypnotherapist, consultant*

**West Caldwell**
Schiff, Robert *health care consultancy company executive*

**West New York**
Kelly, Lucie Stirm Young *nursing educator*

**West Orange**
Bornstein, Lester Milton *retired medical center executive*
De Lisa, Joel Alan *rehabilitation physician, rehabilitation facility executive*

**Westfield**
Mc Fadden, G. Bruce *hospital administrator*

**Whitehouse Station**
Gilmartin, Raymond V. *health care products company executive*

**Wyckoff**
Cropper, Susan Peggy *veterinarian*

## NEW MEXICO

**Albuquerque**
Clark, Teresa Watkins *psychotherapist, clinical counselor*
Cofer, Charles Norval *psychologist, educator*
Elliott, Charles Harold *clinical psychologist*
Exner, Jane Frances *nursing administrator*
Johnson, William Hugh, Jr. *hospital administrator*
Koffler, Herbert *health facility administrator, educator*
Kroken, Patricia Ann *health science association administrator*
Mateju, Joseph Frank *hospital administrator*
Moody, Patricia Ann *psychiatric nurse, artist*
Sanderlin, Terry Keith *counselor*
Solomon, Arthur Charles *pharmacist*

**Carlsbad**
Moore, Bobbie Fay *geriatrics nurse practitioner, nurse administrator*

**Clovis**
Rehorn, Lois M(arie) *nursing administrator*

**Cordova**
Kazmierski, Susan Hedwig *family nurse practitioner, nurse midwife*

**Corrales**
Adams, James Frederick *psychologist, educational administrator*

**Espanola**
Abeyta, Santiago Audoro (Jim Abeyta) *human services administrator*

**Las Cruces**
McElyea, Ulysses, Jr. *veterinarian*
Roscoe, Stanley Nelson *psychologist, aeronautical engineer*
Sims, James Larry *hospital administrator, healthcare consultant*

**Los Alamos**
Bame, Samuel Jarvis, Jr. *research scientist*
†Moore, Tom O. *program administrator*
Thompson, Lois Jean Heidke Ore *psychologist*

**Milan**
Kanesta, Nellie Rose *chemical dependency counselor*

**Raton**
Carter, Kathryn Ann *home health nurse, mental health counselor*

**Roswell**
Johnston, Mary Ellen *nursing educator*
MacKellar, Keith Robert *hospital administrator*

**Ruidoso**
Wade, Pamela Sue *women's health nurse*

**Santa Fe**
Noble, Merrill Emmett *retired psychology educator, psychologist*
Nuckolls, Leonard Arnold *retired hospital administrator*
Phipps, Claude Raymond *research scientist*
Wilson, Tish *children's services administrator*

**Taos**
Pasternack, Robert Harry *school psychologist*

**Truth Or Consequences**
Rush, Domenica Marie *health facilities administrator*

**Wagon Mound**
Abeyta, Jose Reynato *retired pharmacist, state legislator, cattle rancher*

## NEW YORK

**Albany**
Clark, Janet *retired health services executive*
Csiza, Charles Karoly *veterinarian, microbiologist*
DeNuzzo, Rinaldo Vincent *pharmacy educator*
Durovic, Jerry John *psychologist, state official*
Genshaft, Judy Lynn *psychologist, educator*
Giblin, Mary Ellen *mental health professional*
Hill, Valerie Charlotte *nurse*
Kelley, Sister Helen *hospital executive*
†Kim, Paul David *emergency medical administrator*
Ley, Ronald *psychologist, educator*
Reid, William James *social work educator*
Stone, James Lester *mental health administrator*
Teevan, Richard Collier *psychology educator*

**Albertson**
Michaels, Craig Adam *psychologist*

**Alfred**
Keith, Timothy Zook *psychology educator*
Rand, Joella Mae *nursing educator, counselor*

**Amherst**
Cramer, Stanley Howard *psychology educator, author*

**Amityville**
Degrassi, David John *physical therapist*

**Ardsley**
Mohl, Allan S. *social worker*

**Babylon**
Wilkes, David Ross *therapist, social worker*

**Bayside**
Helfat, Lucille Podell *social services professional*

**Beacon**
Moreno, Zerka Toeman *psychodrama educator*

**Bethpage**
Barnathan, Jack Martin *chiropractor*

**Binghamton**
Babb, Harold *psychology educator*
Isaacson, Robert Lee *psychology educator, researcher*
Levis, Donald James *psychologist, educator*

**Brockport**
Herrmann, Kenneth John, Jr. *social work educator*

**Bronx**
Connor, Paul Eugene *social worker*
Dickens, Joan Wright *hospital administrator*
Gootzeit, Jack Michael *rehabilitation institute executive*
Hooker, Olivia J. *psychologist, educator*
Joseph, Stephen *nephrology, dialysis nurse*
Martinez-Tabone, Raquel *school psychologist supervisor*
Ottenberg, James Simon *hospital executive*
†Shine, Daniel I. *hospital administrator*
Sylvester, John Edward *social worker*

**Bronxville**
Broas, Donald Sanford *hospital executive*
Dvorak, Roger Gran *health facility executive*
Franklin, Margery Bodansky *psychology educator, researcher*

**Brooklyn**
Adasko, Mary Hardy *speech pathologist*
Agard, Emma Estornel *psychotherapist*
Allen, George Desmond *epidemiology nurse, surgical nurse*
Boloker, Rose L. *school psychologist*
Brillhart, Susan J. *pediatric nurse, nursing educator*
Ebanks, Marlon Udel *health paraprofessional*
Eisenberg, Karen Sue Byer *nurse*
Fratianni, Margaret Moroney *critical care nurse*
Gross, Stephen Mark *pharmacist, academic dean*
Gustin, Mark Douglas *hospital administrator*
Harris, Fred *orthotist, prosthetist*
Jimenez, Kathryn Fisher *nurse, patient educator*
Kippel, Gary M. *psychologist*
Klainberg, Marilyn Blau *community health educator*
†LaCosta, Cosmo Joseph *medical center executive*
Marcus, Harold *physician, health facility administrator*
Marsala-Cervasio, Kathleen Ann *medical/surgical nurse*
Martinez-Pons, Manuel *psychology educator*
Murillo-Rohde, Ildaura Maria *marriage and family therapist, consultant, educator, dean*
Peters, Mercedes *psychoanalyst*
Phillips, Gretchen *clinical social worker*
Reinisch, June Machover *psychologist, educator*
Rothenberg, Mira Kowarski *clinical psychologist and psychotherapist*
Spivack, Frieda Kugler *psychologist, administrator, educator, researcher*
Steiner, Robert S. *psychologist*
Strauss, Dorothy Brandfon *marital, family, and sex therapist*
Twining, Lynne Dianne *psychotherapist, writer*
Yeaton, Cecelia E(mma) *healthcare administration executive*
Zukowski, Barbara Wanda *clinical social work psychotherapist*

**Brookville**
Araoz, Daniel Leon *psychologist, educator*

**Buffalo**
Blane, Howard Thomas *research institute administrator*
Chiaravalloti, Mary Frances *nurse, educator*
Katz, Jack *audiology educator*
Keem, Michael Dennis *veterinarian*
Levy, Kenneth Jay *psychology educator, academic administrator*
Perry, J. Warren *health sciences educator, administrator*
Pruitt, Dean Garner *psychologist, educator*
Segarra, Tyrone Marcus *pharmacist, medicinal chemist*
Solo, Alan Jere *medicinal chemistry educator, consultant*
Zatko, Patricia Ann *nursing administrator, geriatrics nurse*

**Carmel**
Huckabee, Carol Brooks *psychologist*

**Castle Point**
Laubscher, Leeann *medical and surgical nurse*

**Central Islip**
Piemontese, David Stefano *pharmaceutical scientist*

**Chappaqua**
Boal, Lyndall Elizabeth *social worker*

**Cheektowaga**
Freedman, Anne Maureen *nurse, consultant*

**Cohoes**
Kennedy, Kathleen Ann *faculty/nursing consultant*

**Commack**
Landau, Dorothy *psychotherapist, consultant*
Nilson, Patricia *clinical psychologist*

**Coram**
Helmer, Carol A. *psychologist, school psychologist*

**Cornwall On Hudson**
Holstein, David *psychotherapist, management consultant*

**Delmar**
Pember, John Bartlett *social worker, educator*

**Dobbs Ferry**
Perelle, Ira B. *psychologist, educator*

**Dunkirk**
Huels, Steven Mark *laboratory analyst*

**East Meadow**
Albert, Gerald *clinical psychologist*

**Fairport**
Badenhop, Sharon Lynn *psychologist, educator, entrepreneur*

**Fayetteville**
Dall, Jane Vollbrecht *psychotherapist*
Paul, Linda Baum *geriatrics nurse, toy business owner*

**Fishkill**
Dixon, Linda *child, adolescent and adult therapist*
Stein, Paula Nancy *psychologist, educator*

**Floral Park**
Brancaleone, Laurie Ann *social worker*
Weinrib, Sidney *retired optometric and optical products and services executive*

**Flushing**
Kaufman, Michele Beth *clinical pharmacist, educator*

**Forest Hills**
O'Brien, Margaret Josephine *retired community health nurse*

**Fresh Meadows**
Watson, Joseph Gartrell *medical facility administrator*

**Garden City**
Nicklin, George Leslie, Jr. *psychoanalyst, educator, physician*

**Germantown**
Geistfeld, James Gordon *veterinarian*

**Glen Head**
Cohen, Lawrence N. *health care management consultant*

**Goshen**
Hall, Wanda Jean *mental health professional, consultant*
Hawkins, Barry Tyler *author, mental health services professional*

**Great Neck**
Haber, Diane Lois *psychotherapist, clinical specialist*
Harris, Rosalie *psychotherapist, clinical counselor, Spanish language professional and multi-linguist, English as second language educator*

**Greenfield Center**
Templin, John Leon, Jr. *healthcare consulting executive*

**Guilderland**
Byrne, Donn Erwin *psychologist, educator*
Gordon, Leonard Victor *psychologist, educator emeritus*

**Hampton Bays**
Allmen, Robert Joseph *psychotherapist, priest*

**Hempstead**
Block, Jules Richard *psychologist, educator, university official*
Smith, June Ann *counseling educator*

**Hicksville**
Calabrese, Alphonse Francis Xavier *psychotherapist*

**Holbrook**
Lissman, Barry Alan *veterinarian*

**Howard Beach**
Berliner, Patricia Mary *psychologist*

**Huntington Station**
Williams, Una Joyce *psychiatric social worker*

**Ithaca**
Darlington, Richard Benjamin *psychology educator*
Dobson, Alan *veterinary physiology educator*
Fox, Francis Henry *veterinarian*
Gillespie, James Howard *veterinary microbiologist, educator*
Glock, Marvin David *retired psychology educator*
Haas, Jere Douglas *nutritional sciences educator, researcher*
Haltom, Cristen Eddy *psychologist*
Kallfelz, Francis A. *veterinary medicine educator*
Lust, Barbara C. *psychology and linguistics educator*
Mueller, Betty Jeanne *social work educator*
Neisser, Ulric *psychology educator*
Pagliarulo, Michael Anthony *physical therapy educator*
Phemister, Robert David *veterinary medical educator*
Poppensiek, George Charles *veterinary scientist, educator*
Rasmussen, Kathleen Maher *nutritional sciences educator*
Schlafer, Donald Hughes *veterinary pathologist*
Scott, Fredric Winthrop *veterinarian*
Williams, David Vandergrift *organizational psychologist*
Zall, Robert Rouben *food scientist, educator*

**Jamaica**
Carrington, Betty Watts *nurse midwife, educator*
Etzel, Joseph Vincent *pharmacy educator*
Geffner, Donna Sue *speech pathologist, audiologist*
Kahn, Faith-Hope *nurse, administrator, writer*
Lassiter, Katrina Ann *medical/surgical nurse*
McGuire, William Dennis *health care system executive*
†Sossi, Anthony *medical administrator*

**Jamaica Estates**
Morrill, Joyce Marie *social worker*

**Kingston**
Petruski, Jennifer Andrea *speech and language pathologist*
Soltanoff, Jack *nutritionist, chiropractor*

**Lake Placid**
Caguiat, Carlos Jose *health care administrator, episcopal priest*
Fava, Donald Anthony *clinical psychologist*

**Lake Ronkonkoma**
Halper, Evelyn Ann *occupational therapist*

**Latham**
Agard, Nancey Patricia *nursing administrator*

**Lewiston**
O'Neil, Mary Agnes *health science facility administrator*

**Little Falls**
Feeney, Mary Katherine O'Shea *retired public health nurse*

**Liverpool**
Emmert, Roberta Rita *health facility administrator*

**Livingston Manor**
Zagoren, Joy Carroll *health facility director, researcher*

**Mahopac**
Richards, Edgar Lester *psychologist, educator*

**Malverne**
Ryan, Suzanne Irene *nursing educator*

**Massapequa**
Margulies, Andrew Michael *chiropractor*

**Massapequa Park**
Johnson, Jeanne Marie *nurse psychotherapist, clinical nurse specialist*

**Medford**
Brower, Robert Charles *rehabilitation counselor, small business owner*

**Melville**
Graziani, Jeanne Patricia *health facility administrator*
Reich, Paula Judy *nursing educator*

**Middle Village**
Chang, Lydia Liang-Hwa *school social worker, educator*

**Mill Neck**
Grieve, William Roy *psychologist, educator, researcher, consultant*

**Millbrook**
Turndorf, Jamie *clinical psychologist*

**Mineola**
Hinson, Gale Mitchell *social worker*

**Monsey**
Schore, Robert *social worker, educator*

**Mount Kisco**
Gudanek, Lois Bassolino *clinical social worker*
Schwarz, Wolfgang *psychologist*

**Narrowsburg**
Kunkel, Barbara *psychotherapist, consultant, educator*

**Nesconset**
Feldman, Gary Marc *nutritionist, consultant*

**New Hartford**
Benzo-Bonacci, Rosemary Anne *health facility administrator*

**New Hyde Park**
Dantzker, David Roy *health facility administrator*
Gagnon, Bruce Alan *child psychiatry nurse*

**New Rochelle**
Golub, Sharon Bramson *psychologist, educator*
Thornton, Elaine Seretha *oncology nurse*
Wolf, Robert Irwin *psychoanalyst, art and art therapy educator*

**New York**
Allison, David Bradley *psychologist*
Asperilla, Purita Falgui *retired nursing administrator*
Baker, Elmer Elias, Jr. *speech pathology and communication educator*
Bardach, Joan Lucile *clinical psychologist*
Barnum, Barbara Stevens *nursing educator*
Bernard, Viola Wertheim *psychiatrist*
Bernstein, Anne Elayne *psychoanalyst*
Binkert, Alvin John *hospital administrator*
Bird, Sharlene *clinical psychologist*
Botvin, Gilbert Joseph *psychologist, educator*
Brown, Linda *psychotherapist, psychoanalyst*
Browne, Joy *psychologist*
Buck, Louise Zierdt *psychologist*
Buehler, Thomas *psychotherapist, expressive therapist*
Cardinale, Kathleen Carmel *medical center administrator*
Caroff, Phyllis M. *social work educator*
Carr, Arthur Charles *psychologist, educator*
Castro, José Luis *public health administrator, educator*
Catalano, James Anthony *social worker*
Chamson, Sandra Potkorony *psychologist*
Channing, Alan Harold *hospital administrator*
Clamar, Aphrodite J. *psychologist*
Cloward, Richard Andrew *social work educator*
Cohen, Michael *psychologist*
Cole, Ann Harriet *psychologist, communications consultant*
Congett, Sylvia Monica *psychologist*
Connolly, John Joseph *health care company executive*
Costa, Max *health facility administrator, pharmacology educator, environmental medicine educator*
Cutler, Rhoda *psychologist*
Davis, Samuel *hospital administrator, educator, consultant*
De Gregorio, Jorge Eduardo *psychoanalyst, educator*
deMause, Lloyd *psychohistorian*
Dimen, Muriel Vera *psychoanalyst*
Dobrof, Rose Wiesman *geriatrics services professional*
Dorn, Sue Bricker *hospital and medical school administrator*
Eagan, Marie T. (Ria Eagan) *chiropractor*
Edelstein, Joan Erback *physical therapy educator*
Ellis, Albert *clinical psychologist, educator, author*
Ethan, Carol Baehr *psychotherapist*
Farkas, Carol Garner *nurse, administrator*
Feinberg, Mortimer Robert *psychologist, educator*
Feldman, Ronald Arthur *social work educator, researcher*
Feldmann, Shirley Clark *psychology educator*
Fenchel, Gerd H(erman) *psychoanalyst*
Fewell, Christine Huff *psychoanalyst, alchohol counselor*
Fiorillo, John A(nthony) *health care executive*
Freudenberger, Herbert Justin *psychoanalyst*
Frost, Ellen Elizabeth *psychologist*
Galanter, Eugene *psychologist, educator*
Garvey, Michael Steven *veterinarian, educator*
Gitterman, Alex *social work educator*
Glass, David Carter *psychology educator*
Glassman, Urania Ernest *social worker, educator*
Gold, William Elliott *health care management consultant*
Goldberg, Harold Howard *psychologist, educator*
Goldberg, Jane G. *psychoanalyst*
Goldman, Leo *psychologist, educator*
Goldrich, Stanley Gilbert *optometrist*
†Goodwill, George Walton *hospital administrator*
Grant, James Deneale *health care company executive*
Gray, Bradford Hitch *health policy researcher*
Green, Miriam Blau *psychologist*
Greene, Kay C. *psychologist, author*
Haber, Pierre-Claude *psychologist*
Hammer, Emanuel Frederick *clinical psychologist, psychoanalyst*
Haywood, H(erbert) Carl(ton) *psychologist, educator*
Hershcopf, Berta Ruth *psychotherapist, writer*
Heyde, Martha Bennett (Mrs. Ernest R. Heyde) *psychologist*
Hirsch, Joseph Allen *neuropsychologist/psychologist/neuropharmacologist*
Hoffman, Martin Leon *psychology educator*
Hollander, Edwin Paul *psychologist, educator*
Howard, Clifton Merton *psychiatrist*
Jacoby, Jacob *consumer psychology educator*
Jonas, Ruth Haber *psychologist*
Kamerman, Sheila Brody *social worker, educator*
Kassel, Catherine M. *community and maternal-women's health nurse*
Kent, Deborah Warren *hypnotherapist, consultant, lecturer*
King, Sheldon Selig *medical center administrator, educator*
Koppenaal, Richard John *psychology educator*
Kramer, Marc B. *forensic audiologist*
Krauss, Herbert Harris *psychologist*
Labovitz, Deborah Rose Rubin *occupational therapist, educator*
Lantay, George Charles (Wagner) *psychologist, psychotherapist, environmental consultant*
Lawrence, Lauren *psychoanalytical theorist, psychoanalyst*
Lawry, Sylvia (Mrs. Stanley Englander) *health association administrator*
Lederman, Sally Ann *nutrition educator and researcher*
Lee, Robert Sanford *psychologist*
Liebmann, Martha *psychotherapist*
†Maiale, Nicholas F. *healthcare communications executive*
Mandracchia, Violet Ann Palermo *psychotherapist, educator*
Markle, Cheri Virginia Cummins *nurse*
Marshak, Hilary Wallach *psychotherapist, owner*
Mattson, Joy Louise *oncological nurse*
Mc Cullough, J. Lee *industrial psychologist*
McGivern, Diane *nursing educator*
Meyer-Bahlburg, Heino F. L. *psychologist, educator*
Mintz, Donald Edward *psychologist, educator*
Monegro, Francisco *psychology educator, alternative medicine consultant*
Morris, Thomas Quinlan *hospital administrator, physician*
Neubauer, Peter Bela *psychoanalyst*
O'Neill, Mary Jane *health agency executive*
Pakter, Jean *medical consultant*
Papalia, Diane Ellen *human development educator*
Parker, Susan Brooks *healthcare executive*
Pelli, Denis Guillermo *visual perception, psychology educator*
Piemonte, Robert Victor *association executive*
Pilcz, Maleta *psychotherapist*
Piombino, Nicholas *psychotherapist*
Pulitzer, Roslyn K. *social worker, psychotherapist*
Ringler, Lenore *educational psychologist*
Riss, Eric *psychologist*
Roglieri, John Louis *health facility administrator*
Rudan, Vincent Thaddeus *nursing administrator*
Sackeim, Harold *psychologist, educator*
Saxe, Leonard *social psychologist, educator*
Scott, Adrienne *social worker, psychotherapist*
Scott, Mimi Koblenz *psychotherapist, actress, publicist, journalist*
Shohen, Saundra Anne *health care communications and public relations executive*
†Sigety, Cornelius Edward *office manager*
Simon, Norma Plavnick *psychologist*
Solender, Sanford *social worker*
†Spriggs, David *healthcare administrator, educator*
Stark, Robin Caryl *psychotherapist, consultant*
Suraci, Patrick Joseph *clinical psychologist*
Tallmer, Margot Sallop *psychologist, psychoanalyst, gerontologist*
Turo, Joann K. *psychoanalyst, psychotherapist, consultant*
Vitz, Paul Clayton *psychologist, educator*
Walman, Jerome *psychotherapist, publisher, consultant, critic*
Weiner, Max *educational psychology educator*
Wessler, Sheenah Hankin *psychotherapist, consultant*
Witkin, Mildred Hope Fisher *psychotherapist, educator*
Wolfert, Ruth *Gestalt therapist*
Wood, Paul F. *national health agency executive*
Yousef, Mona Lee *psychotherapist*
Zawistowski, Stephen Louis *psychologist, educator*
Zazula, Bernard Meyer *physician administrator*
Zucker-Franklin, Dorothea *medical scientist, educator*

**Newburgh**
Fallon, Rae Mary *psychology educator, early childhood consultant*

**Newtonville**
Apostle, Christos Nicholas *social psychologist*

**Niagara Falls**
Smeal, Carolyn A. *community health nurse, educator*

**Niagara University**
Osberg, Timothy M. *psychologist, educator, researcher*

**North Hartford**
Fellone, Christina Kates *oncology nurse*

**North Syracuse**
Brophy, Mary O'Reilly *industrial hygienist*

**Norwich**
Garzione, John Edward *physical therapist*

**Oneonta**
Bergstein, Harry Benjamin *psychology educator*
Diehl, Lesley Ann *psychologist*
Grappone, William Eugene *clinical social worker, gerontologist, consultant*

**Orangeburg**
Furlong, Patrick Louis *health science association administrator*

**Ossining**
Beard, Janet Marie *health care administrator*

**Oswego**
Gooding, Charles Thomas *psychology educator, college provost*
Gordon, Norman Botnick *psychology educator*

**Painted Post**
Ogden, Anita Bushey *nursing educator*

**Pittsford**
Taub, Aaron Myron *healthcare administrator, consultant*

**Plattsburgh**
Smith, Noel Wilson *psychology educator*

**Pleasantville**
Black, Percy *psychology educator*

**Pomona**
Gordon, Edmund Wyatt *psychologist, educator*

**Poughkeepsie**
Barker, Richard Alexander *organizational psychologist*
Carino, Aurora Lao *psychiatrist, hospital administrator*
Gardenier, Edna Frances *nursing educator*
Heller, Mary Bernita *psychotherapist*
Henley, Richard James *healthcare institution administrator and financial officer*

**Purchase**
Berman, Richard Angel *health and educational administrator*

**Rhinebeck**
Barker, Barbara Yvonne *respiratory care administrator*

**Riverdale**
De La Cancela, Victor *psychologist*

**Rochester**
Alpert-Gillis, Linda Jayne *clinical psychologist*
Brideau, Leo Paul *healthcare executive*
Deci, Edward Lewis *psychologist, educator*
DuBrin, Andrew John *behavioral sciences, management educator, author*
Geertsma, Robert Henry *psychologist, educator*
Hunt, Roger Schermerhorn *hospital administrator*
Johns, J.C. *health facility administrator, internist*
Johnson, Jean Elaine *nursing educator*
Johnston, Frank C. *psychologist*
Laties, Victor Gregory *psychology educator*
Lipman, Jane Crawford *school nurse*
Marriott, Marcia Ann *human resources administrator, educator, consultant*
Moore, Duncan Thomas *optics educator*
Schaffner, Robert Jay, Jr. *nurse practitioner*
Thomas, Garth Johnson *psychology educator emeritus*
Von Holden, Martin Harvey *psychologist*
Wey, Jong-Shinn *research laboratory manager*
Zax, Melvin *psychologist, educator*

**Rome**
Campbell, Joann Cavo *social worker*

**Roslyn**
Epstein, Arthur Barry *optometrist*
Freedman, Joseph Mark *optometrist*
Scollard, Patrick John *hospital executive*

**Rye**
Newburger, Howard Martin *psychoanalyst*

**Saratoga Springs**
Higgins, Marika O'Baire *nurse, educator, designer, writer, entrepreneur*

**Scarsdale**
Glickenhaus, Sarah Brody *speech therapist*
Liston, Mary Frances *retired nursing educator*
Rogalski, Lois Ann *speech and language pathologist*

**Schenectady**
Duncan, Stanley Forbes *health care executive*
Oliker, David William *healthcare management administrator*
Terry, Richard Allan *consulting psychologist, former college president*

**Scottsville**
Dwyer, Ann Elizabeth *equine veterinarian*

**Seneca Falls**
Norman, Mary Marshall *counselor, therapist, educator*

**Sleepy Hollow**
Safian, Keith Franklin *hospital administrator*

**Somers**
Joerger, Jay Herman *psychologist, entrepreneur*

**Southold**
Callis, Jerry Jackson *veterinarian*

**Springville**
Balling, Louise Mary *social worker*

**Staten Island**
Gokarn, Vijay Murlidhar *pharmacist, consultant*
Johnson, Frank Corliss *criminal psychologist*
Popler, Kenneth *behavioral healthcare executive, psychologist*
Toliver, Maxwell Doel *hypnotherapist*

**Stony Brook**
Katkin, Edward Samuel *psychology educator*

**Suffern**
Longberg, Debra Lynn *dietitian, nutrition consultant*
Monahan, Frances Donovan *nursing educator*

**Syracuse**
Black, Lois Mae *clinical psychologist, educator*
Fitzgerald, Harold Kenneth *social work educator, consultant*
Pearl, Harvey *psychologist*
Shedlock, Kathleen Joan Petrouskie *community health/research nurse*

**Troy**
Baron, Robert Alan *psychology and business educator, author*
Caruso, Aileen Smith *managed care consultant*

**Valhalla**
Radeboldt-Daly, Karen Elaine *medical nurse*

**Wantagh**
Kushner, Aileen *medical/surgical nurse*

**Warwick**
Altman, Eileen Shea *psychotherapist*

**Webster**
Liebert, Arthur Edgar *retired hospital administrator*

**West Bloomfield**
Charron, Helene Kay Shetler *nursing educator*

**West Henrietta**
Doty, Dale Vance *psychotherapist, hypnotherapist*

**White Plains**
Bostin, Marvin Jay *hospital and health services consultant*
Fowlkes, Nancy Lanetta Pinkard *social worker*
Nauert, Roger Charles *health care executive*

**Williamsville**
Paladino, Joseph Anthony *clinical pharmacist*

**Woodbury**
Agresti, Miriam Monell *psychologist*

**Woodmere**
Natow, Annette Baum *nutritionist, author, consultant*

**Wyandanch**
Hodges-Robinson, Chettina M. *nursing administrator*

**Yonkers**
Drisko, Elliot Hillman *marriage and family therapist*
Lupiani, Donald Anthony *psychologist*

## NORTH CAROLINA

**Arden**
Adams, Pamela Jeanne *nurse, flight nurse*
Dowdell, Michael Francis *critical care and anesthesia nurse practitioner*

**Asheville**
Korb, Elizabeth Grace *nurse midwife*
Weil, Thomas P. *health services consultant*

**Beaufort**
Hardee, Luellen Carroll Hooks *school psychologist*

**Boone**
Jones, Dan Lewis *psychologist*
Singleton, Stella Wood *educator and habilitation assistant*

**Burlington**
Mason, James Michael *biomedical laboratories executive*
Powell, James Bobbitt *biomedical laboratories executive, pathologist*

**Calabash**
Strunk, Orlo Christopher, Jr. *psychology educator*

**Carolina Beach**
Brown, Barry Stephen *research psychologist*

**Cashiers**
O'Connell, Edward James, Jr. *psychology educator, computer applications and data analysis consultant*

**Chapel Hill**
Baroff, George Stanley *psychologist, educator*
Carroll, John Bissell *psychologist, educator*
Cobb, Henry Van Zandt *psychologist*
Dahlstrom, William Grant *psychologist, educator*
Fox, Ronald Ernest *psychologist*
Gottlieb, Gilbert *psychobiologist, educator*
Gray-Little, Bernadette *psychologist*
Hochbaum, Godfrey Martin *retired behavioral scientist*
Jones, Lyle Vincent *psychology educator*
Lowman, Robert Paul *psychology educator, academic administrator*
Mc Curdy, Harold Grier *psychologist*
Palmer, Gary Stephen *health services administrator*
Schopler, John Henry *psychologist, educator*
Tolley, Aubrey Granville *hospital administrator*
Upshaw, Harry Stephan *psychology educator*
Zeisel, Steven H. *nutritionist, educator*

**Charlotte**
Brazeal, Donna Smith *psychologist*
Carper, Barbara Anne *nursing educator*
Doyle, Esther Piazza *critical care nurse, educator*
Goolkasian, Paula A. *psychologist, educator*
Hinson, Jane Pardee Henderson *lactation consultant*
Kidda, Michael Lamont, Jr. *psychologist, educator*
Latimer, Ben William *healthcare executive*
Martin, James Grubbs *medical research executive, former governor*
Shaul, Roger Louis, Jr. *health care consultant, executive, researcher*
Smith, Elizabeth Hegeman *mental health therapist, hypnotherapist*

**Concord**
O'Toole, Michael Doran *psychologist*

**Davidson**
Palmer, Edward L. *social psychology educator, television researcher, writer*
Plyler, John Laney, Jr. *healthcare management professional*

**Durham**
Colvin, O. Michael *medical director, medical educator*
Copeland, Betty Marable *psychotherapist*
Dunteman, George Henry *psychologist*
Gratz, Pauline *former nursing science educator*
†Israel, Michael David *healthcare executive*
Lifton, Walter M. *psychology and education consultant*
Lockhead, Gregory Roger *psychology educator*
Page, Ellis Batten *behavioral scientist, educator, corporate officer*
Schiffman, Susan Stolte *medical psychologist, educator*
Staddon, John Eric Rayner *psychology, zoology, neurobiology educator*
Surwit, Richard Samuel *psychology educator*
Wilson, Ruby Leila *nurse, educator*

**Elizabeth City**
Griffin, Gladys Bogues *critical care nurse, educator*

**Elon College**
Knesel, Ernest Arthur, Jr. *diagnostic company executive*

**Fayetteville**
Mayrose, Mona Pearl *critical care nurse, flight nurse, educator*
Schaefer, Lewis George *physicians assistant*

**Greensboro**
Coltrane, Tamara Carleane *intravenous therapy nurse*
Eason, Robert Gaston *psychology educator*
Gill, Diane Louise *psychology educator, university official*
Goldman, Bert Arthur *psychologist, educator*
Harris-Offutt, Rosalyn Marie *counselor, therapist, nurse, anesthetist, educator, writer*
Johnson, Willie Spoon *hospital administrator*
Ritter, Sandra Helen *psychotherapist, counselor*
Rosser, Rhonda LaNae *psychotherapist*
Schwenn, Lee William *retired medical center executive*
Smith, Rebecca McCulloch *human relations educator*

**Greenville**
Griffin, Linner Ward *social work educator*
Moseley, Sheryl Buck *nursing administrator*

**Hickory**
Gingrich-Petersen, Carolyn Ashcraft *psychologist*
Loehr, Arthur William, Jr. *healthcare executive, nurse*

**Hillsborough**
†Taylor, Martha Croll *nursing adminstrator*

**Kinston**
†Woodall, Jim S. *hospital administrator*

**Raleigh**
Aronson, Arthur Lawrence *veterinary pharmacology and toxicology educator*
Berry, Joni Ingram *hospice pharmacist, educator*
Geller, Janice Grace *nurse*
Hughes, Barbara Ann *dietitian, public health administrator*
Johnson, Charles Lavon, Jr. *clinical neuropsychologist, consultant*
Johnson, Janet Gray Andrews *clinical social worker*
Newman, Slater Edmund *psychologist, educator*
Slaton, Joseph Guilford *social worker*
†Stokes, George Clive *healthcare administrator*

**Research Triangle Park**
Olden, Kenneth *science administrator, researcher*

**Roxboro**
Broyles, Bonita Eileen *nursing educator*

**Salisbury**
Logan, David Bruce *health care administrator*

**Tarboro**
Andrews, Claude Leonard *psychotherapist*

**Weaverville**
Hauschild, Douglas Carey *optometrist*

**Wilmington**
Dixon, N(orman) Rex *speech and hearing scientist, educator*
Israel, Margie Olanoff *psychotherapist*

**Wilson**
Batchelor, Ruby Stephens *retired nurse*

**Winston Salem**
Dodd, Virginia Marilyn *veterinarian*
Moskowitz, Jay *public health sciences educator*
Walters, Doris Lavonne *pastoral counselor, counseling services facility administrator*

## NORTH DAKOTA

**Dickinson**
Kessel, Lloyd R. *acute care nursing director, educator*

**Fargo**
Nickel, Janet Marlene Milton *geriatrics nurse*
Orr, Steven R. *health facility administrator*
Revell, Dorothy Evangeline Tompkins *dietitian*

**Grand Forks**
Nielsen, Forrest Harold *research nutritionist*
Penland, James Granville *psychologist*
Plaud, Joseph Julian *psychology educator*

**Minot**
Danielson, David Gordon *health science facility administrator, general legal counsel*
Mohler, Marie Elaine *nurse educator*

## OHIO

**Akron**
Considine, William Howard *health care administrator*
Coz, Mary Kathleen *respiratory therapist*
Hale, Beverlee Ann *home care nurse*
Schlichting, Nancy Margaret *hospital administrator*
Smithkey, John, III *public health nurse, consultant*
West, Michael Alan *hospital administrator*

**Ashtabula**
Hornbeck, Harold Douglas *psychotherapist*

**Athens**
Brehm, Sharon Stephens *psychology educator, university administrator*
Klare, George Roger *psychology educator*

**Bay Village**
Daly-Mattio, Barbara Ann *counselor, nurse*
Hiller, Deborah Lewis *long term care and retirement facility executive*

**Beachwood**
Tolchinsky, Paul Dean *organization design psychologist*

**Bellbrook**
Anderson, Mary Elizabeth (Beth Anderson) *nursing administrator*

**Berea**
Anders, Claudia Dee *occupational therapist*
Bersin, Susan Joyce-Heather (Reignbeaux Joyce-Heather Bersin) *critical care nurse, police officer*

**Bowling Green**
Guion, Robert Morgan *psychologist, educator*
Hakel, Milton Daniel, Jr. *psychology educator, consultant, publisher*
Scherer, Ronald Callaway *voice scientist, educator*

**Canfield**
Itts, Elizabeth Ann Dunham *psychotherapist, consultant, designer*

**Canton**
Crossland, Ann Elizabeth *psychotherapist*

**Centerville**
Fulk, Paul Frederick *chiropractor*

**Cincinnati**
Bieliauskas, Vytautas Joseph *clinical psychologist, educator*
Bluestein, Venus Weller *retired psychologist, educator*
Boggs, Robert Wayne *healthcare administrator*
Bradley, Sister Myra James *health science facility executive*
Carney, Robert Alfred *health care administrator*
Curtin, Leah Louise *nurse, consultant, editor, author, ethician*
Dember, William Norton *psychologist, educator*
Frazier, Todd Mearl *retired health science administrator, epidemiologist*
Gault, Patricia Ann *nursing home administrator*
Goldstein, Sidney *pharmaceutical scientist*
Hensgen, Herbert Thomas *medical technologist*
Jackobs, Miriam Ann *dietitian*
Kaplan, Stanley Meisel *psychoanalyst*
Koebel, Sister Celestia *health care system executive*
Lichtin, (Judah) Leon *pharmacist*
Lippincott, Jonathan Ramsay *healthcare executive*
Morgan, John Bruce *hospital care consultant*
Reeb, Patricia A. *nursing educator, administrator*
Spraley, Judith Ann *nursing educator, administrator*
†Streck, Richard James *medical administrator*
Warm, Joel Seymour *psychology educator*
Weinrich, Alan Jeffrey *occupational hygienist*
Zierolf, Mary Louise *nurse anesthetist*

**Cleveland**
Beamer, Yvonne Marie *psychotherapist, counselor*
Blum, Arthur *social work educator*
Boyle, Kammer *management psychologist*
Cartier, Charles Ernest *alcohol and drug abuse services professional*
Dadley, Arlene Jeanne *sleep technologist*
Davidson, James Wilson *clinical psychologist*
Dylag, Helen Marie *healthcare administrator*
Giesser, Nancy Lynne *nursing educator*
Hokenstad, Merl Clifford, Jr. *social work educator*
Huston, Samuel Richard *health facility executive*
Johnson, Mattiedna *nurse, retired diaconal minister*
Kohn, Mary Louise Beatrice *nurse*
Kolb, David Allen *psychology educator*
Manley, Norlee K. *nurse, chemical dependence program administrator*
Neuhauser, Duncan von Briesen *health services educator*
Nicolini, Francesca Antonia *health science association administrator*
Schlotfeldt, Rozella May *nursing educator*
Schorr, Alvin Louis *social worker, educator*
Shakno, Robert Julian *hospital administrator*
Spottsville, Sharon Ann *counselor*
Waters, Gwendolyn *human services administrator*

**Cleveland Heights**
Banks, Melanie Anne *nutritionist, biochemist, educator*

**Columbus**
Anderson, Carole Ann *nursing educator*
Arnold, Kevin David *psychologist, educational researcher*
Becker, Ralph Leonard *psychologist*
Beckholt, Alice *public health nurse*
Blickenstaff, Kathleen Mary *mental health nurse, nursing educator*
Cacioppo, John Terrance *psychology educator*
Capen, Charles Chabert *veterinary pathology educator, researcher*
Carter, Cheryl A. *medical/surgical nurse*
Hobson, Harry E., Jr. *health care administrator*
Leland, Henry *psychology educator*
Lince, John Alan *pharmacist*
Meyer, Donald Ray *psychologist, brain researcher*
Meyer, Patricia Morgan *neuropsychologist, educator*
Naylor, James Charles *psychologist, educator*
Newman, Barbara Miller *psychologist, educator*
Osipow, Samuel Herman *psychology educator*
Petty, Richard Edward *psychologist, educator, researcher*
Rowland, Robert Charles *writer, clinical psychotherapist, researcher*
Rudmann, Sally Vander Linden *medical technology educator*
Schuller, David Edward *cancer center administrator, otolaryngology*
Sims, Richard Lee *hospital administrator*
Somani, Peter *human service administrator*

**Copley**
Smith, Joan H. *women's health nurse, educator*

**Cuyahoga Falls**
Hahn, David Bennett *hospital administrator, marketing professional*

**Dayton**
Christensen, Julien Martin *psychologist, educator*
Fridrick, M. Rogene *gerontology educator, retired social worker*
Miller, Tamara Dedra *psychologist*
Nixon, Charles William *bioacoustician*
O'Malley, Patricia *critical care nurse*
Versic, Linda Joan *nurse educator, research company executive*
Williams, Michael Alan *psychologist*

**Duncan Falls**
Cooper, April Helen *nurse*

**Fairborn**
Leffler, Carole Elizabeth *mental health nurse, women's health nurse*

**Fairfield**
Goodman, Myrna Marcia *school nurse*

**Findlay**
Stephani, Nancy Jean *social worker, journalist*

**Gallipolis**
Niehm, Bernard Frank *mental health center administrator*

**Georgetown**
Rose, Beverly Anne *pharmacist*

**Hamilton**
Erbe, Janet Sue *medical surgical, orthopedics and pediatrics nurse*
Johnson, Pauline Benge *nurse, anesthetist*
Sebastian, Sandra Mary Thompson *mental health counselor, social worker*

**Highland**
Taylor, Theresa Evereth *registered nurse, artist*

**Hinckley**
Sprungl, Katherine Louise *nurse*

**Hudson**
Wooldredge, William Dunbar *health facility administrator*

**Lakewood**
O'Hara, Tamara Lynn *public health nurse, consultant*

**Lancaster**
Varney, Richard Alan *medical office manager*

**Lorain**
†Buzas, John William *hospital administrator, surgical nurse*

**Lyndhurst**
Dellas, Marie C. *retired psychology educator and consultant*

**Mansfield**
Reese, Wina Harner *speech pathologist, consultant*

**Marysville**
Covault, LLoyd R., Jr. *hospital administrator, psychiatrist*

**Mason**
Clements, Michael Craig *health services consulting executive, retired renal dialysis technician*

**Massillon**
Barr, Dixie Lou *geriatrics nurse*
Fogle, Marilyn Louise Kiplinger *hospital administrator*

**Medina**
Walcott, Robert *healthcare executive, priest*

**Mentor**
Core, Harry Michael *psychiatric social worker, mental health therapist/administrator*

**Middleburg Heights**
Hartman, Lenore Anne *physical therapist*

**Middletown**
Gilmore, June Ellen *psychologist*
Redding, Barbara J. *nursing administrator, occupational health nurse*

**Mogadore**
Sonnhalter, Carolyn Therese *physical therapist, consultant*

**New Carlisle**
Peters, Elizabeth Ann Hampton *nursing educator*

**North Royalton**
Michak, Helen Barbara *nurse, educator*

**Northfield**
Gupta, Kishan Chand *psychologist*

**Oberlin**
Friedman, William John *psychology educator*
Layman, Emma McCloy (Mrs. James W. Layman) *psychologist, educator*

**Painesville**
Lemr, James Charles *geriatrics nurse*

**Parma**
Bate, Brian R. *psychologist*

**Portsmouth**
Christensen, Margaret Anna *nursing educator, consultant*

**Saint Clairsville**
Sidon, Claudia Marie *psychiatric and mental health nursing educator*

**Salem**
Moss, Susan *nurse, retail store owner*

**Sandusky**
Riedy, Virginia Kathleen *nursing educator*
Round, Alice Faye Bruce *school psychologist*

**Springfield**
Maki, Jerrold Alan *health system executive*

**Sylvania**
Verhesen, Anna Maria Hubertina *counselor*

**Terrace Park**
Madewell, Mary Ann *nursing educator*

**Toledo**
Depew, Charles Gardner *research company executive*
Kneen, James Russell *health care administrator*
Riseley, Martha Suzannah Heater (Mrs. Charles Riseley) *psychologist, educator*
†Talmage, Lance Allen *obstetrician/gynecologist, career military officer*
Weikel, Malcolm Keith *health care company executive*
West, Ann Lee *clinical nurse specialist, educator, trauma nurse coordinator*

**Toronto**
Hoffman, Janet N. *psychic counselor*

**University Heights**
Bloch, Andrea Lynn *physical therapist*

**Valley View**
Van Kirk, Robert John *nursing case manager, educator*

**Vandalia**
Davis, Pamela J. *nursing educator*

**Warren**
VanAuker, Lana Lee *recreational therapist, educator*

**Westerville**
Thompson, Claire Louisa *nurse, educator, administrator*
Williams, John Michael *physical therapist, sports medicine educator*

**Wooster**
Loess, Henry Bernard *psychology educator*

**Worthington**
Bernhagen, Lillian Flickinger *school health consultant*
Bilderback, George Garrison, III *human services manager*
Castner, Linda Jane *instructional technologist, nurse educator*
Lentz, Edward Allen *consultant, retired health administrator*

**Wright Patterson AFB**
Boff, Kenneth Richard *engineering research psychologist*
Rinta, Christine Evelyn *nurse, air force officer*

**Youngstown**
Biehl, Jane M. *rehabilitation services professional*

## OKLAHOMA

**Broken Arrow**
Westerman, Rosemary Matzzie *nurse, administrator*

**Claremore**
Cesario, Sandra Kay *women's health nurse, educator*
Marshall, Linda Lantow *pediatrics nurse*

**Durant**
Kennedy, Elizabeth Carol *psychologist, educator*

**Edmond**
Lewis, Gladys Sherman *nurse, educator*
Necco, E(dna) Joanne *school psychologist*

**El Reno**
Buendia, Imelda Bernardo *clinical director, physician*

**Enid**
Lopez, Francisco, IV *health care administrator*

**Lawton**
Cooke, Wanda (Cookie Cooke) *hearing aid specialist*
Hooper, Roy B. *hospital administrator, insurance broker*
Mayes, Glenn *social worker*

**Mangum**
Ford, Linda Lou *dietitian*

**Norman**
Donahue, Hayden Hackney *mental health institute administrator, medical educator, psychiatric consultant*
Hiner, Gladys Webber *psychologist*
Tackwell, Elizabeth Miller *social worker*
Weber, Jerome Charles *education and human relations educator, former academic dean and provost*

**Oklahoma City**
Allbright, Karan Elizabeth *psychologist, consultant*
Forni, Patricia Rose *nursing educator, university dean*
†Johnson-Bailey, Marquita P. *nursing administrator, consultant*
Keeth, Betty Louise *geriatrics nursing director*
Lynn, Thomas Neil, Jr. *retired medical center administrator, physician*
Macer, Dan Johnstone *retired hospital administrator*
McClellan, Mary Ann *pediatrics nurse, educator*
Pishkin, Vladimir *psychologist, educator*
Rundell, Orvis Herman, Jr. *psychologist*
Sanders, Gilbert Otis *health and addictions psychologist, consultant*
Sookne, Herman Solomon (Hank Sookne) *human services executive*
Spencer, Melvin Joe *hospital administrator, lawyer*
Stephen, Michael *psychologist*
Walker, Clarence Eugene *psychology educator*

**Pawhuska**
Strahm, Samuel Edward *veterinarian*

**Ponca City**
Newport, L. Joan *clinical social worker, psychotherapist*

**Stillwater**
Confer, Anthony Wayne *veterinary pathologist, educator*
Ewing, Sidney Alton *veterinary medical educator, parasitologist*
Monlux, Andrew W. *educator, veterinarian*
Qualls, Charles Wayne, Jr. *veterinary pathology educator*
Quinn, Art Jay *veterinarian, retired educator*

**Tahlequah**
Edmondson, Linda Louise *optometrist*
Wickham, M(arvin) Gary *optometry educator*

**Tulsa**
Alexander, John Robert *hospital administrator, internist*
Davis, Annalee C. *clinical social worker*
Ginn, Connie Mardean *nurse*
Hannah, Barbara Ann *nurse, educator*
Horvath, Carol Mitchell *home health administrator*
Mattocks-Whisman, Frances *nursing administrator, educator*
Thompson, Harold Jerome *counselor, mental retardation professional*

**Woodward**
Billings, Letha Marguerite *nurse*

## OREGON

**Albany**
Chowning, Orr-Lyda Brown *dietitian*

**Beaverton**
Mersereau, Susan S. *clinical psychologist*

**Brookings**
Cross, Lynda Lee *health facility administrator, nurse*

**Chiloquin**
Mead, Terry Eileen *clinic administrator, consultant*

**Corvallis**
Cerklewski, Florian Lee *human nutrition educator, nutritional biochemistry researcher*
Gillis, John Simon *psychologist, educator*
Oldfield, James Edmund *nutrition educator*
Storvick, Clara Amanda *nutrition educator emerita*

**Cove**
Kerper, Meike *family violence, sex abuse and addictions abuse rehabilitation educator, consultant*

**Dexter**
Myhre, Kathleen Randi *nurse*

**Eugene**
Acker, Martin Herbert *psychotherapist, educator*
Freyd, Jennifer Joy *psychology educator*
Littman, Richard Anton *psychologist, educator*
Phelps, Kathryn Annette *mental health counseling executive, consultant*
Watson, Mary Ellen *ophthalmic technologist*

**Florence**
Corless, Dorothy Alice *nurse educator*

**Forest Grove**
Gibby-Smith, Barbara *psychologist, nurse*

**Klamath Falls**
Klepper, Carol Herdman *mental health therapist*

**Lake Oswego**
Loveless, Peggy Ann *social work administrator*
Salibello, Cosmo *optometrist, medical products executive*

**Lebanon**
Pearson, Dennis Lee *optometrist*

**Medford**
Roy, Catherine Elizabeth *physical therapist*

**Portland**
Baldwin-Halvorsen, Lisa Rogene *community health and critical care nurse*
Commerford, Kathleen Anne *psychologist*
†Giffin, Sandra Lee *nursing administrator*
Goldfarb, Timothy Moore *hospital administrator*
Greenlick, Merwyn Ronald *health services researcher*
Kupel, Frederick John *counselor*
Matarazzo, Joseph Dominic *psychologist, educator*
McDaniel, Rickey David *senior living executive*
Meighan, Stuart Spence *hospital consultant, internist, writer*
Olson, Roger Norman *health service administrator*
Pfeifer, Larry Alan *public health service coordinator*
Rooks, Judith Pence *family planning, maternal health care, midwifery consultant*
Shireman, Joan Foster *social work educator*
Wiens, Arthur Nicholai *psychology educator*

**Saint Helens**
Van Horn, O. Frank *retired counselor, consultant*

**Salem**
Edge, James Edward *health care administrator*
Warnath, Maxine Ammer *organizational psychologist, mediator*

**West Linn**
Vinyard, Roy George, II *hospital administrator*

**White City**
Moore, Charles August, Jr. *psychologist*

## PENNSYLVANIA

**Abington**
Pilla, Felix Mario *hospital administrator*
†Roediger, Paul M. *hospital administrator*
Schwartz, Lita Linzer *psychologist, educator*

**Acme**
Babcock, Marguerite Lockwood *addictions treatment therapist, writer*

**Allensville**
Yoder, Sara Ann *emergency nurse*

**Allentown**
Berman, Muriel Mallin *optometrist, humanities lecturer*
Graham, Kenneth Robert *psychologist, educator*
Spering, Mark Andrew *optometrist*
†Wastak, John Rudolph *health care executive, educator*

**Altoona**
Arbitell, Michelle Reneé *clinical psychologist, clinical neuropsychologist*
Clark, Threese Anne *occupational therapist, disability analyst*
Meadors, Allen Coats *health administrator, educator*

**Berwick**
Smith, Clara Jean *retired nursing home administrator*

**Bethel Park**
DeMay, Helen Louise *nursing services administrator*

**Bethlehem**
Scanlon, Edward Charles *clinical psychologist*

**Blakeslee**
Hayes, Alberta Phyllis Wildrick *retired health service executive*

**Blue Bell**
Baine, Richard Joseph *vocational rehabilitation counselor*
Cherry, John Paul *science research association director, researcher*

**Brodbecks**
McMenamin, Helen Marie Foran *home health care, pediatric, maternal nurse*

**Bryn Mawr**
Hoffman, Howard Stanley *experimental psychologist, educator*
Hoopes, Janet Louise *educator, psychologist*

**Buffalo Mills**
Braendel, Douglas Arthur *healthcare executive*

**Camp Hill**
Crider, Rudyard Lee *psychotherapist*
Nowak, Jacquelyn Louise *administrative officer, realtor, consultant*
Williams, Marie Cloney *rehabilitation nurse administrator, business owner*
Winberry, Joseph Paul, Jr. *optometrist*

**Clarks Summit**
Firmin, Michael Wayne *counselor, educator*

**Coatesville**
Giancola, Mary Ann *school nurse*

**Collegeville**
Cawthorn, Robert Elston *health care executive*

**Coudersport**
Kysor, Daniel Francis *psychologist*

**Cranberry Township**
Birch, Jack Willard *psychologist, educator*
St. John, Maria Ann *nurse anesthetist*

**Dallas**
Baltimore, Ruth Betty *social worker*
Moran, Michael Lee *physical therapist, computer consultant*

**Dickson City**
Carluccio, Sheila Cook *psychologist*

**Doylestown**
Cathcart, Harold Robert *hospital administrator*
Davis, Carole Joan *psychologist*
Haines, Bonnie Nadine *psychiatric nurse, visiting nurse*
King, Robert Edward *retired pharmacy educator*
Miller, Lynne Marie *critical care nurse, administrator*

**Drexel Hill**
Baessler, Christina A. *medical/surgical nurse*

**Duncannon**
Roach, Ralph Lee *human services and rehabilitation consultant*

**Easton**
DiMatteo, Rhonda Lynn *speech-language pathologist, audiologist*

**Edinboro**
Paul, Charlotte P. *nursing educator*

**Erie**
Moore, Christine Helen *critical care nurse*
Nash, Mary Alice *nursing educator*

**Fairless Hills**
Rosella, John Daniel *psychologist*

**Fleetwood**
Buckalew, Robert Joseph *psychologist, consultant*

**Gettysburg**
Schein, Virginia Ellen *psychologist, educator*

**Gouldsboro**
West, Daniel Jones, Jr. *hospital administrator, rehabilitaton counselor, health care consultant, educator*

**Gwynedd Valley**
Giordano, Patricia J. *radiation therapist*

**Hamburg**
Schappell, Abigail Susan *speech, language and hearing therapist*

**Harrisburg**
Comoss, Patricia B. *cardiac rehabilitation nurse, consultant*
Gallaher, William Marshall *dental laboratory technician*
Hyle, Jack Otto *orthomolecular psychologist*
Krobath, Krista Ann *pharmacist*
O'Donnell, John Joseph, Jr. *optometrist*
Ozereko-deCoen, Mary Therese *therapeutic recreation specialist and therapist*
Stuckey, Susan Jane *perioperative nurse, consultant*
Trexler, Suzanne Frances *geriatrics nurse*
Tyson, Gail L. *health federation administrator*
†Weiss, Stephen Max *health care administrator, surgeon, educator*

**Harveys Lake**
Wolensky, Joan *occupational therapist, interfaith minister*

**Haverford**
Perloe, Sidney Irwin *psychologist, primatologist, educator*

**Hershey**
Anderson, Allan Crosby *hospital executive*
†Hamory, Bruce Hill *health facility administrator*
Lang, Carol Max *veterinarian, educator*
Lindenberg, Steven Phillip *counselor, consultant*
Little, Rhoda Smeltzer *nursing administrator*

**Honesdale**
Campbell, Linda Sue *guidance counselor*

**Horsham**
Logue, John J(oseph) *psychologist*
Neff, P. Sherrill *health care executive*

**Huntingdon**
Buzminsky, David Andrew *school psychologist*

**Indiana**
Nelson, Linda Shearer *child development and family relations educator*

**Jenkintown**
Hankin, Elaine Krieger *psychologist, researcher*

**Johnstown**
Hull, Patricia Ann *nursing administrator*

**Kennett Square**
Allam, Mark Whittier *veterinarian, former university administrator*
Beck, Dorothy Fahs *social researcher*

**King Of Prussia**
Doniger, Irene G. *psychologist, business owner*
Miller, Alan B. *hospital management executive*
Stoughton, W. Vickery *healthcare executive*

**Lake Ariel**
Caldwell, Nancy Ann *social worker, nurse*

**Lancaster**
Brunner, Lillian Sholtis *nurse, author*
Gingerich, Naomi R. *emergency room nurse*
McCollom, Herbert Forrest, Jr. *audiologist*

**Lansdale**
Lovelace, Robert Frank *health facility administrator, researcher*
Reast, Deborah Stanek *ophthalmology center administrator*
Wittreich, Warren James *psychologist, consultant*

**Latrobe**
Zanotti, Marie Louise *hospital admininstrator*

**Lebanon**
Marshall, Marilyn Jean *social services director, consultant*

**Leola**
Wedel, Paul George *retired hospital administrator*

**Loretto**
Sackin, Claire *social work educator*

**Meadville**
Wharton, William Polk *psychologist, consultant*

**Media**
Heilig, Margaret Cramer *nurse, educator*
Lewandowski, Theodore Charles *psychology educator*
Salo, Harry A. *health care executive*

**Mercersburg**
Coffman, Patricia JoAnne *school nurse, counselor*

**Monaca**
Jaskiewicz, David Walter *optometrist*

**Narberth**
Knapp, Nancy Hay *mental health administrator*
Pedersen, Darlene Delcourt *health science publishing consultant*

**New Castle**
Flannery, Wilbur Eugene *health science association administrator, internist*
Grzebieniak, John Francis *psychologist*

**New Kensington**
Blair, Karen Elaine *respiratory care practitioner, health educator*
Hahn, William Orr *psychologist, consultant*

**Newtown Square**
Tipka, Karen *obstetric and women's health nurse*

**Norristown**
Quinn-Kerins, Catherine *psychologist*
Seiderman, Arthur Stanley *optometrist, consultant, author*

**North East**
Ayrault, Evelyn West *psychologist, writer*

**Perkasie**
Laincz, Betsy Ann *nurse*

**Philadelphia**
Abrams, Jules Clinton *psychologist*
Aiken, Linda Harman *nurse, sociologist, educator*
Anyanwu, Chukwukre *alcohol and drug abuse facility administrator*
Burgess, Ann Wolbert *nursing educator*
Byrd, Malcolm Todd *public health administrator*
Casey, Rita Jo Ann *nursing administrator*
Chase, Sandra Lee *pharmacist, consultant*
†Coché, Judith *psychologist, educator*
Collier-Evans, Demetra Frances *veterans benefits counselor*
Coltoff, Beth Jamie *psychologist, small business owner*
Cramp, Donald Arthur *hospital executive*
Dean-Zubritsky, Cynthia Marian *psychologist, reseacher*
Denenberg, Herbert Sidney *journalist, lawyer, former state official*
Detweiler, David Kenneth *veterinary physiologist, educator*
Ems, Christine Marie *chiropractor*
Fagin, Claire Mintzer *nursing educator, administrator*
Ferraro, Ronald Louis *health facility administrator*
Gable, Fred Burnard *pharmacist, author*
Harvey, Colin Edwin *veterinary medicine educator*
Harvey, John Adriance *psychology and pharmacology educator, researcher, consultant*
Hurvich, Leo Maurice *experimental psychologist, educator, vision researcher*
Hussar, Daniel Alexander *pharmacy educator*
Kaufman, Denise Norma *psychologist, addictions counselor, educator*
Kaye, Janet Miriam *psychologist*
Lawton, Lois *health facility administrator*
Manganiello, Janice Marie *peri-operative nurse*
Maratea, James Michael *healthcare administrator, editor, consultant*
Maschak-Carey, Barbara Jean *clinical nurse specialist*
Micozzi, Marc Stephen *health executive, physician, educator*

Newman, Cory Frank *clinical psychologist*
Orne, Emily Carota *psychologist*
Piccolo, Joseph Anthony *hospital administrator*
Pilborough, Barbara Jean *healthcare consultant*
Pino, H. Eduardo *clinical psychologist*
Potter, Alice Catherine *clinical laboratory scientist*
Premack, David *psychologist*
Rescorla, Robert Arthur *psychology educator*
Rosenberg, Robert Allen *psychologist, educator, optometrist*
Schaffner, Roberta Irene *medical, surgical nurse*
Seligman, Martin E. P. *psychologist*
Solomon, Phyllis Linda *social work educator, researcher*
Sovie, Margaret Doe *nursing administrator, educator*
Wadden, Thomas Antony *psychologist, educator*
Weber, Janet M. *nurse*
Welhan, Beverly Jean Lutz *nursing educator, administrator*
Williams, Sankey Vaughan *health services researcher, internist*

**Pittsburgh**
Abdelhak, Sherif Samy *health science executive*
Anderson, John Robert *psychology and computer science educator*
Barry, Herbert, III *psychologist*
Bell, Lori Jo *psychiatric nurse, mental health counselor, infectious disease education specialist*
Berman, Malcolm Frank *health facility administrator*
Buyny, Marianne Jo *eating disorders therapist, addictions counselor*
Cagney, William Robert *psychologist*
Connolly, Ruth Carol *critical care nurse*
Dawes, Robyn Mason *psychology educator*
Doerfler, Leo G. *audiology educator*
Evey, Lois Reed *psychiatric nurse*
Fischhoff, Baruch *psychologist, educator*
Friday, Paul J(ohn) *psychologist*
Goldstein, Gerald *research psychologist*
Harper, Gladys Coffey *health services adviser*
Longest, Beaufort Brown *health services administration educator, research director*
Lundquist, Dana R. *health insurance executive*
Matchett, Janet Reedy *psychologist*
Matzke, Gary Roger *pharmacist*
McCall, Dorothy Kay *social worker, psychotherapist*
McClelland, James Lloyd *psychology educator, cognitive scientist*
Missiriotis, Irene *recreational activities director, artist*
Moore, Daniel Edmund *psychologist, educator, retired educational administrator*
Moore, Pearl B. *nurse*
Mulvihill, John Joseph *medical geneticist*
Omiros, George James *medical foundation executive*
Pacifico, Diane Alane *ophthalmic nurse*
Perloff, Robert *psychologist, educator*
Ramm, Douglas Robert *psychologist*
Ramsey, David Allen *psychologist*
Romoff, Jeffrey Alan *university officer, health care executive*
Sanzo, Anthony Michael *health care executive*
Schmeler, Mark Raymond *occupational therapist*
Schorr-Ribera, Hilda Keren *psychologist*
Voss, James Frederick *psychologist, educator*
Wallman, George *hospital and food services administrator*
Zanardelli, John Joseph *healthcare services executive*

**Polk**
Hall, Richard Clayton *retired psychologist*

**Pottsville**
Walsh, James William *mental health professional*

**Quakertown**
Ambrus, Lorna *medical, surgical and geriatrics nurse*
Wartella, Rosanne Karen *occupational therapy assistant*

**Reading**
Bell, Frances Louise *medical technologist*
Blue, John James *psychotherapist, consultant*
Hedegard, Victor Christian, III *clinical psychologist*
Sauer, Elissa Swisher *nursing educator*

**Reedsville**
Miller, Mary Lois *retired nurse midwife*

**Rosemont**
Kline, Harriet Dennis *psychologist, school psychologist*

**Scranton**
Lepore, Marie Ann *home care nurse*
Maislin, Isidore *hospital administrator*
Narsavage, Georgia Roberts *nursing educator, researcher*
Sebastianelli, Carl Thomas *clinical psychologist*
Shovlin, Joseph Patrick *optometrist*
Wood, Kathleen Marie *physical therapist*

**Sharon**
Ullrich, Linda J. *medical technologist*

**Shrewsbury**
Martin, Debra Michele *nurse*

**State College**
Chiswick, Nancy Rose *psychologist*
Farr, Jo-Ann Hunter *psychologist*
Morrow, David Austin, III *veterinary medical educator*

**Transfer**
Miller, Gayle D. *health facility administrator, nurse, health educator*

**Tyrone**
Stoner, Philip James *hospital administrator*

**Uniontown**
Prescott, Janelle *medical and surgical nurse*

**University Park**
Cavanagh, Peter Robert *science educator, researcher*
Ford, Donald Herbert *psychologist, educator*
Guthrie, Helen A. *nutrition educator, registered dietitian*
Mayers, Stanley Penrose, Jr. *public health educator*
Ray, William Jackson *psychologist*

Schaie, K(laus) Warner *human development and psychology educator*

**Verona**
Matthews, Jack *psychologist, speech pathologist, educator*

**Villanova**
Beletz, Elaine Ethel *nurse, educator*
Fitzpatrick, M. Louise *nursing educator*

**Warrendale**
Friede, Samuel A(rnold) *health care executive*

**Waymart**
Giambrone, Angela C. *psychologist*

**Wayne**
Crofford, Bonnie Ann *rehabilitation clinical specialist*

**Waynesboro**
Swartz, William Rick *school psychologist*

**West Chester**
Gibson, JoAnn Marie *psychotherapist, consultant, personal mentor*
Hajcak, Frank *psychologist, cartoonist, writer, photographer, consultant*

**West Point**
Chen, I-Wu *pharmaceutical researcher*

**Wilkes Barre**
Van Scoy, Gary *social services administrator*

**Wyncote**
Bersh, Philip Joseph *psychologist, educator*

**Wyndmoor**
Uemura, Teruki *child brain developmentalist*

**Yardley**
Kaska, Charles Powers *psychologist*

**York**
Bartels, Bruce Michael *health care executive*
Chronister, Virginia Ann *school nurse, educator*
†Greisler, David Scott *healthcare executive*
Hamilton, Shirley Ann *nursing administrator*
Keiser, Paul Harold *hospital administrator*
Nau, Douglas Scott *psychotherapist*
Page, Sean Edward *emergency medical care provider, educator*
Rosen, Raymond *health facility executive*

## RHODE ISLAND

**Barrington**
Paolino, Ronald Mario *clinical psychologist, consultant, psychopharmacologist, pharmacist*

**Cranston**
Gardner, Ann Jeannette *family and child therapist*
Terry, Brian R. *counselor, academic administrator*
Vavala, Domenic Anthony *medical scientist, educator, retired air force officer*

**East Providence**
McGee, Mary Alice *health science research administrator*

**Johnston**
D'Ambra, Diane M. *nursing educator*

**Kingston**
Berman, Allan *psychologist, educator*
Biller, Henry Burt *psychologist, educator*
Seifer, Marc Jeffrey *psychology educator*

**Newport**
Graziano, Catherine Elizabeth *nursing educator*

**Pawtucket**
Holden, Raymond Henry *clinical psychologist*
Tarpy, Eleanor Kathleen *social worker*

**Providence**
Anderson, James Alfred *psychology educator*
Blough, Donald S. *psychology educator*
Boekelheide, Kim *pathologist*
Church, Russell Miller *psychology educator*
Damon, William Van Buren *developmental psychologist, educator, writer*
Edens, Myra Jim *health facility nursing administrator*
Jones, Ferdinand Taylor, Jr. *psychologist, educator*
Metrey, George David *social work educator, academic administrator*
Monteiro, Lois Ann *medical science educator*
Parris, Thomas Godfrey, Jr. *medical facility administrator*
Pomerantz, James Robert *psychology educator, academic admininstrator*
Schottland, Edward Morrow *hospital adminstrator*
Shepp, Bryan Eugene *psychologist, educator*
Siqueland, Einar *psychology educator*

## SOUTH CAROLINA

**Anderson**
Campbell, Susan Rebecca *psychotherapist, educator*
Harllee, Mary Beth *social worker, educator*

**Camden**
Barker, Martha Smith *retired mental health nurse*

**Cayce**
Paynter, Vesta Lucas *pharmacist*

**Charleston**
Austin, Charles John *health services educator*
Barclay, James Ralph *psychologist, educator*
Bowman, Daniel Oliver *psychologist*
Cheng, Kenneth Tat-Chiu *pharmacy educator*

Hollis, Bruce Warren *experimental nutritionist, industrial consultant*
Kirschner-Bromley, Victoria Ann *clinical counselor*
Richburg, W. Edward *nurse educator*
Robinson, Jakie Lee *human services administrator*
Smith, W. Stuart *strategic planning director*

**Columbia**
Amidon, Roger Lyman *health administration educator*
Bland, Annie Ruth (Ann Bland) *nursing educator*
Bryant, Douglas E. *public health service official*
Cooper, William Allen, Jr. *audiologist*
Coursey, Joy Hammond *critical care nurse*
Davis, Keith Eugene *psychologist, educator, consultant*
Ginsberg, Leon Herman *social work educator*
Madden, Arthur Allen *nuclear pharmacist, educator*
Manwill, Diane Rachel *counselor*
Melton, Gary Bentley *psychology and law educator*

**Conway**
Nale, Julia Ann *nursing educator*

**Dillon**
Labbe, Patrick Charles *legal nursing consultant*

**Easley**
Spearman, David Hagood *veterinarian*

**Georgetown**
Rogers, Rynn Mobley *community health nurse*

**Greenville**
Armstrong, Joanne Marie *clinical and consulting psychologist, business advisor, mediator*
Pate, Frances Valerie *psychotherapist, clinical social worker*
Steed, Connie Mantle *nurse*

**Greer**
Howell, Maxine Dill *women's health nurse*

**Hartsville**
Edson, Herbert Robbins *foundation and hospital executive*

**Hilton Head Island**
Patton, Susan Oertel *clinical social worker, educator*
Stockard, Joe Lee *public health service officer, consultant*
Wesselmann, Glenn Allen *retired hospital executive*

**Hopkins**
Clarkson, Jocelyn Adrene *medical technologist*

**Inman**
Kunze, Dolores Johanna *veterinarian*

**Mauldin**
Harris, Daniel Frederick *biomechanical analyst, educator*

**Moncks Corner**
Deavers, James Frederick *optometrist*

**Myrtle Beach**
Dail, Hilda Lee *psychotherapist*
Madory, James Richard *hospital administrator, former air force officer*

**Orangeburg**
Benson, Sarah D. *rehabilitation services professional*
Grimes, Tresmaine Judith Rubain *psychology educator*

**Rock Hill**
Stewart, Lyn Varn *critical care nurse*

**Saint Helena Island**
Austin-Long, Jean Audrey *psychiatric department administrator*

**Summerville**
Duffy, Margaret McLaughlin *nephrology nurse, educator*
Stasiukaitis, Brenda Hodge *physical therapist*
Young, Margaret Aletha McMullen (Mrs. Herbert Wilson Young) *social worker*

**Ware Shoals**
Webb, Patricia Dyan W. *speech and language pathologist, sign language educator*

**West Columbia**
Brown, Opal Diann *medical technologist, nurse*

## SOUTH DAKOTA

**Aberdeen**
Hahnemann, Barbara K. *family nurse practitioner*

**Brookings**
Spease, Loren William *chiropractor*

**Chamberlain**
Gregg, Robert Lee *pharmacist*

**Huron**
Kuhler, Deborah Gail *grief counselor, former state legislator*

**Lake Andes**
Dolliver, Mary Gwen *medical, surgical nurse*

**North Sioux City**
Grant, Judith Iversen *family health nurse, nursing administrator*

**Rapid City**
Corwin, Bert Clark *optometrist*

**Sioux Falls**
Brendtro, Larry Kay *psychologist, educator*
Richards, LaClaire Lissetta Jones (Mrs. George A. Richards) *social worker*

Williams, W. Vail *psychologist*

**Sturgis**
Daane, Kathryn D. *retired nursing administrator*

**Vermillion**
Rotert, Denise Anne *occupational therapist, army officer, educator*

## TENNESSEE

**Brentwood**
Dalton, James Edgar, Jr. *health facility administrator*
Ragsdale, Richard Elliot *healthcare management executive*
†Stow, Gerald Lynn *human services executive, speaker*
†White, Steve Allen *health facility administrator*

**Chattanooga**
Bechtel, Sherrell Jean *psychotherapist*
Bush, Patricia Ann *occupational health nurse*
Pinkerton, Helen Jeanette *health care executive*
Scott, Mark Alden *hospital network executive*
Waring, Mary Louise *social work administrator*
Weinmann, Judy Munger *nurse*

**Cookeville**
Nash, Sheena Ann Hargis *flight nurse*

**Franklin**
Woodside, Donna J. *nursing educator*

**Hartsville**
Todd, Mary Patricia *nursing administrator*

**Hendersonville**
Davis, Robert Norman *hospital administrator*
Thomas, Roberta Will *home care agency administrator*

**Huntsville**
Boardman, Maureen Bell *community health nurse*

**Jackson**
Mitchell, Elizabeth Marelle *nursing educator, medical, surgical nurse*
Smith, Geri Garrett *nurse educator*
Woodall, Gilbert Earl, Jr. *medical administrator*

**Jellico**
Hausman, Keith Lynn *hospital administrator, physical therapist*

**Johnson City**
Isaac, Walter Lon *psychology educator*
Larkin, Donald Wayne *clinical psychologist*

**Kingsport**
Bremer, Louis Henry, Jr. *health care administrator*
Moore, Marilyn Patricia *community counselor*

**Knoxville**
Bateman, Veda Mae *industrial psychologist, management consultant*
Bell (Jarratt), Corinne *psychologist*
Swanson, Lorna Ellen *physical therapist, athletic trainer, researcher*

**La Follette**
Williams, Jane Crouch *mental health counselor, social worker*

**Lawrenceburg**
Calvert, Lois Prince *nursing home administrator, registered nurse*

**Loudon**
Morton, Jerome Holdren *school psychologist*

**Maynardville**
Smith, Fred Doyle *nurse*

**Memphis**
Battle, Allen Overton, Jr. *psychologist, educator*
Byrd, Paula Strickland *mental health nurse clinician, educator*
Diggs, Walter Whitley *health science faclty administrator*
Elfervig, Lucie Theresa Savoie *ophthalmic nursing consultant*
Jarvis, Daphne Eloise *laboratory administrator*
Johnson, Johnny *research psychologist, consultant*
Kahane, Joel Carl *speech pathologist*
McNabb, Darcy LaFountain *medical management company executive*
Mendel, Maurice *audiologist, educator*
Mirvis, David Marc *health administrator, cardiologist, educator*
Mulholland, Kenneth Leo, Jr. *health care facility administrator*
Nolly, Robert J. *hospital administrator, pharmaceutical science educator*
Ward, Jeannette Poole *psychologist, educator*

**Millington**
Melcher, Jerry William Cooper *clinical psychologist, army officer*

**Morristown**
Harmon, David Eugene *optometrist, geneticist*

**Mount Juliet**
Masters, John Christopher *psychologist, educator, writer*

**Murfreesboro**
Westwick, Carmen Rose *retired nursing educator, consultant*

**Nashville**
Aubrey, Roger Frederick *psychology and education educator*
†Betts, Virginia Trotter *nursing educator, policy researcher*
Bolian, George Clement *health care executive, physician*

Dale, Kathy Gail *rehabilitation rheumatology nurse*
Fenner, Catherine Munro *association administrator*
Graves, Rebecca O. *public health nurse, consultant*
Guinsburg, Philip Fried *psychologist*
Johnson, David *medical administrator*
Kaas, Jon H. *psychology educator*
Land, Rebekah Ruth *marriage and family therapist*
Manning, David Lee *health care executive*
Sanders, Jay William *audiology educator*
Schoggen, Phil H(oward) *psychologist, educator*
Sloan, Reba Faye *dietitian, consultant*
Spinella, Judy Lynn *healthcare administrator*
Stone, Robert Edward, Jr. *speech pathologist*
Stringfield, Charles David *hospital administrator*
Strupp, Hans Hermann *psychologist, educator*
Weiss, Judith Miriam *psychologist*
Wilson, Sheryl A. *pharmacist*
Young, Tommie Morton *social psychology educator, writer*

**Oak Ridge**
Jones, Virginia McClurkin *social worker*

**Oliver Springs**
Davis, Sara Lea *pharmacist*

**Sevierville**
Witucki, Janet Marie *nursing educator, geriatric researcher*

**Signal Mountain**
Reading, Sadie Ethel *retired public health nurse*

**Trenton**
McCullough, Kathryn T. Baker *social worker, utility commissioner*

**Wartburg**
Freytag, Addie Lou *nurse*

## TEXAS

**Abilene**
Calvert, Linda Darnell *women's health nurse, educator*
Crowell, Sherry Diegel *clinical psychologist*
Fryer, William Neal *retired psychologist*
Hennig, Charles William *psychology educator*
Morrison, Shirley Marie *nursing educator*

**Allen**
Garner, Julie Lowrey *occupational therapist*
Gilliland, Mary Margarett *healthcare consultant*

**Amarillo**
Ayad, Joseph Magdy *psychologist*
Bowling, Joyce Blankenchip *retired critical care nurse*
Jones, Michael Wayne *health services administrator*
Sprowls, Robert Wayne *veterinarian, laboratory administrator*

**Anson**
Kilpatrick, Martha Sue *speech-language pathologist*

**Arlington**
Bunten, Brenda Arlene *geriatrics nurse*
Gelinas, Marc Adrien *healthcare administrator*
Glisson, Melissa Ann *dietitian*
Goelden-Bowen, Michelle Marie *occupational therapist*
Grzesiak, Robert Charles *therapist*
McCall, Tina *critical care nurse*
McCuistion, Peg Orem *hospice administrator*
McCuistion, Robert Wiley *lawyer, hospital administrator, management consultant*
McNairn, Peggi Jean *speech pathologist, educator*
Watkins, Ted Ross *social work educator*
Wiig, Elisabeth Hemmersam *audiologist, educator*

**Austin**
Austin, David Mayo *social work educator*
Blake, Robert Rogers *psychologist, behavioral science company executive*
Cleland, Charles Carr *psychologist, educator*
Dalton, Caryl *school psychologist*
Davis, Donald Robert *nutritionist, researcher, consultant*
Doluisio, James Thomas *pharmacy educator*
Drake, Stephen Douglas *clinical psychologist, health facility administrator*
Durbin, Richard Louis, Sr. *healthcare admnistration consultant*
Elder, Patricia Anne *nursing educator, nurse midwife*
Eldredge, Linda Gaile *psychologist*
Gardner, Joan *medical, surgical nurse*
Gilbert, Lucia Albino *psychology educator*
Girling, Bettie Joyce Moore *home health executive*
Golden, Kimberly Kay *critical care, flight nurse*
Grangaard, Daniel Robert *psychologist*
Hall, Beverly Adele *nursing educator*
Heffley, James Dickey *nutrition counselor*
Holtzman, Wayne Harold *psychologist, educator*
Hurley, Laurence Harold *medicinal chemistry educator*
Huston, Ted Laird *psychology educator*
Hutchins, Karen Leslie *psychotherapist*
Iscoe, Ira *psychology educator*
Johnson, Mildred Snowden *retired nursing educator*
Kirk, Lynda Pounds *biofeedback therapist, neurotherapist*
Loehlin, John Clinton *psychologist, educator*
Manosevitz, Martin *psychologist*
Martin, Frederick Noel *audiology educator*
McFadden, Dennis *experimental psychology educator*
Prentice, Norman Macdonald *clinical psychologist*
Ragsdale, Keith Ellen *nurse, educator, administrator*
Reid, Jackson Brock *psychologist, educator*
Thiessen, Delbert Duane *psychologist*

**Baytown**
Percoco, Thelma Ann *nurse, educator*

**Beaumont**
Tucker, Gary Wilson *nurse educator*

**Bedford**
Harrison, Jerry Ann *nursing administration*

**Bellaire**
Mayo, Clyde Calvin *organizational psychologist, educator*
Smeal, Janis Lea *operating room nurse, health facility administrator*

**Brooks AFB**
Patterson, John C. *clinical psychology researcher*

**Brownsville**
French, Bertha Doris *medical, surgical and geriatrics nurse*

**Bryan**
Sulik, Edwin (Pete Sulik) *health care administrator*

**Carrollton**
Nichols, Gerry Lynn *occupational therapist*
Withrow, Lucille Monnot *nursing home administrator*

**Castroville**
Strickland, Sandra Jean Heinrich *nursing educator*

**Cedar Park**
Koop, Tobey Kent *research consultant, educational psychologist*

**Chillicothe**
Brock, Helen Rachel McCoy *retired mental health and community health nurse*

**College Station**
Beaver, Bonnie Veryle *veterinarian, educator*
Harvey, Roger Bruce *veterinary toxicologist, researcher*
Heidelbaugh, Norman Dale *veterinary medicine educator, consultant, author, inventor*
Luepnitz, Roy Robert *psychologist, consultant, small business owner, entrepreneur*
McCrady, James David *veterinarian, educator*
Ogburn, Wayne Lee *health science facility administrator*
Pierce, Kenneth Ray *veterinary medicine educator*
Sis, Raymond Francis *veterinarian, educator*

**Colleyville**
Driscoll, Diana Sanderson *optometrist, consultant*

**Conroe**
Bruce, Rachel Mary Condon *nurse practitioner*

**Converse**
Droneburg, Nancy Marie *geriatrics nurse*

**Copperas Cove**
Townsend, Linda Ladd *mental health nurse*

**Corpus Christi**
Clark, Joyce Naomi Johnson *nurse*
Cole, June Robertson *psychotherapist*
Cutlip, Randall Brower *retired psychologist, college president emeritus*
Hamilton, Paul Martin *psychologist*
Long, Ralph Stewart *clinical psychologist*
†Shook, Donald Ray *health care administrator*

**Crosby**
Cole, Edith Fae *dietitian, consultant*

**Dallas**
Anderson, Ron Joe *hospital administrator, physician, educator*
Barnett, Peter Ralph *health science facility administrator, dentist*
Bell-Tolliver, LaVerne *social worker*
Bradley, John Andrew *hospital management company executive*
Brand, Julia Marie *occupational health nurse*
Bryant, L. Gerald *health care administrator*
Bunker, Anthony Louis *health science executive*
Champion, Michael Ray *health facility administrator*
Dudley, George William *behavioral scientist, writer*
Dykes, Virginia Chandler *occupational therapist*
Fleming, Jon Hugh *psychology educator, business executive, educational consultant*
France, Newell Edwin *former hospital administrator, consultant*
Fritze, Julius Arnold *marriage counselor*
Gibby, Mabel Enid Kunce *psychologist*
Goodson, Shannon Lorayn *behavioral scientist, author*
Gouge, Betty Merle *family therapist*
Greenstone, James Lynn *psychotherapist, police psychologist, mediator, consultant, author, educator*
Hafner, Dudley H. *health agency executive*
Heileman, Sandra Marie *health facility administrator, educator*
Hitt, David Hamilton *hospital executive*
Holl, Dee Lynn *career counselor, psychotherapist, management consultant*
Howe, Beverly Jeanne *nurse*
Johnson, Murray H. *optometrist, researcher, consultant, lecturer*
†King, C(larence) Carleton, II *health care executive*
Le Vieux, Jane Stuart *pediatrics nurse*
†Monserrate, Jennifer Kratzer *healthcare administrator*
Powell, Boone, Jr. *hospital administrator*
Semmler, Caryl J. *occupational therapist*
Sims, Konstanze Olevia *social worker, case manager*
Smith, William Randolph (Randy Smith) *health care management association executive*
Talley, Linda Jean *food scientist, dietitian*
Williams, Martha Spring *psychologist*

**Denton**
Cissell, William Bernard *health studies educator*
Lawhon, Tommie Collins Montgomery *child development and family living educator*
Schumacker, Randall Ernest *educational psychology educator*

**Edinburg**
Nieto, Beatriz Chavez *nursing educator*
Wilson, Bruce Keith *men's health nurse*

**El Paso**
Adams, Nancy R. *nurse, military officer*
Bartlett, Janet Sanford (Walz) *school nurse*
Cuevas, David *psychologist*
Hedrick, Wyatt Smith *pharmacist*
Juarez, Antonio *psychotherapist, consultant, counselor, educator*
Kimmel, Herbert David *psychology educator*
Mitchell, Paula Rae *nursing educator*
Roark, Charles Elvis *healthcare executive*
Salewski, Ruby Marie Graf *nursing educator*
Simon, Doris Marie Tyler *nurse*

**Floydada**
Hinton, Sharon Tonya Curtis *nursing educator*

**Fort Worth**
Brockman, Leslie Richard *social worker*
Byas, Teresa Ann Uranga *healthcare professional*
Dees, Sandra Kay Martin *psychologist, research consultant*
Ford, Kathleen Marie *home health nurse, trainer*
Hurley, Linda Kay *psychologist*
Jensen, Harlan Ellsworth *veterinarian, educator*
Robinson, Nell Bryant *nutrition educator*
Simpson, Dennis Dwayne *psychologist, educator*
Strength, Danna Elliott *nursing educator*
Zeigler, Vicki Lynn *pediatrics nurse*

**Galveston**
Barratt, Ernest Stoelting *psychologist, educator*
Fisher, Seymour *psychologist, educator*
Shannon, Mary Lou *adult health nursing educator*
Thomas, Leelamma Koshy *women's health care nurse*

**Graham**
Ritchlin, Martha Ann *occupational therapist*

**Grand Prairie**
Frost, James Hamner *health facility administrator*

**Grapevine**
Arnott, Ellen Marie *medical case management and occupational health executive*

**Henderson**
McDonald, Benna J. *nursing educator, critical care nurse*

**Hereford**
Langford, Karen Soltis *counselor, family therapist*

**Hermleigh**
Barnes, Maggie Lue Shifflett (Mrs. Lawrence Barnes) *nurse*

**Highland Village**
Wiedemann, Ramona Diane *occupational therapist*

**Hondo**
Swort, Arlowayne *retired nursing educator and administrator*

**Houston**
Bahl, Saroj Mehta *nutritionist, educator*
Baranowski, Tom *public health educator, researcher*
Becker, Frederick Fenimore *cancer center administrator, pathologist*
†Booker, Ronald Joseph *physician practice management*
Burdine, John A. *hospital administrator, nuclear medicine educator*
Cadwalder, Hugh Maurice *psychology educator*
Callender, Norma Anne *psychology educator, counselor*
Crisp, Jennifer Ann Clair *neurosurgical nurse*
DeVilla, Lucena M. *home healthcare nurse, administrator, business owner*
Frenger, Paul Fred *medical computer consultant, physician*
Grossett, Deborah Lou *psychologist, behavior analyst, consultant*
Gunn, Joan Marie *health care administrator*
Hansen, Paula Renee *healthcare administrator*
Haymond, Paula J. *psychologist, diagnostician, hypnotherapist*
†Hodge, Etta Lee *director of surgical services, nurse*
Holmes, Harry Dadisman *health facility administrator*
Jhin, Michael Kontien *health care executive*
Johnston, Ben Earl *veterinarian*
Justice, (David) Blair *psychology educator, author*
Kershaw, Carol Jean *psychologist*
Kuntz, Edward Lawrence *health care executive*
Lenox, Angela Cousineau *healthcare consultant*
Martin, Randi Christine *psychology educator*
McGuire, Dianne Marie *psychotherapist*
Miller, Janel Howell *psychologist*
Moore, Lois Jean *health science facility administrator*
Patterson, Ronald R(oy) *health care systems executive*
Paul, Gordon Lee *behavioral scientist, psychologist*
Phillips, Linda Lou *pharmacist*
†Raber, Martin *health facility administrator, medical educator*
Reed, Kathlyn Louise *occupational therapist, educator*
Schiflett, Mary Fletcher Cavender *health facility executive, researcher, educator*
Schneider, David J. *psychology educator, academic administrator*
Schneider, Karen Lee *psychotherapist*
Simmons, Lawrence William *health care company executive*
Steele, James Harlan *former public health veterinarian, educator*
Turner, William Wilson *hospital administrator*
Wagner, Donald Bert *health care consultant*
Wainerdi, Richard Elliott *medical center executive*
Wolinsky, Ira *nutritionist*
Wong-Liang, Eirene Ming *psychologist*

**Hughes Springs**
Koelker, Gail *family nurse practitioner*

**Hunt**
Price, Donald Albert *veterinarian, consultant*

**Irving**
Collins, Stephen Barksdale *health care executive*
Donnelly, Barbara Schettler *medical technologist*

**Katy**
†Thorne, Melvin Quentin *managed healthcare executive*

**Kerrville**
Rhodes, James Devers *psychotherapist*

**Kilgore**
Wilcox, Nancy Diane *nurse, administrator*

**Lago Vista**
Kinsey, Julia Catherine *medical records coding specialist*

**Laredo**
Cavazos, Hilda Valdez *nursing administrator, educator*
Wood, Jack Calvin *health care consultant, lawyer*

**Llano**
Anderson, Janet Ann *women's health care nurse practitioner*
Walter, Virginia Lee *psychologist, educator*

**Lockhart**
Williams, Margaret Lu Wertha Hiett *nurse*

**Lubbock**
Broselow, Linda Latt *medical office technician, aviculturist*
Reeves, A. Sue Windsor *healthcare administrator*
Rose, Sharon Marie *critical care nurse*
Smith, Doris Corinne Kemp *retired nurse*

**Marshall**
Weathers, Melba Rose *hospital utilization review coordinator*

**Midland**
Best, Alynda Kay *conflict resolution mediator*
Sullivan, Patricia G. *maternal, child and women's health nursing educator*

**Montgomery**
Gooch, Carol Ann *psychotherapist consultant*

**Nacogdoches**
Cart-Rogers, Katherine Cooper *emergency nurse*
Clagett, Arthur F(rank) *psychologist, sociologist, qualitative research writer, retired sociology educator*
Migl, Donald Raymond *therapeutic optometrist, pharmacist*

**Newton**
Hopkins, Sallye F. *women's health nurse*

**Odessa**
Jackson, Dorothy Faye Greene *nursing educator*
Miller, Margaret Joanne *pediatrics nurse*

**Pampa**
Lane, Jerry Ross *alcohol and drug abuse service counselor*

**Panhandle**
Sherrod, Lloyd B. *nutritionist*

**Paris**
Proctor, Richard Owen *public health administrator, army officer*
Sawyer, Mary Catherine *hospital administrator*

**Plano**
Carmicle, Linda Harper *psychotherapist*

**Richardson**
Brown, Ollie Dawkins *marriage, family and child therapist, scientific researcher*

**Roanoke**
Kleinkort, Joseph Alexius *physical therapist, consultant*

**Round Rock**
Bruce-Juhlke, Debbie *nursing consultant, social worker*

**Rowlett**
Ogden, LouAnn Marie *dietitian, consultant*

**Rusk**
Jones, Janet Valeria *psychiatric nurse*

**San Angelo**
Tillery-Tate, Johnnie Lea *mental health and geriatrics nurse*

**San Antonio**
Celmer, Virginia *psychologist*
Crabtree, Tania Oylan *home health nurse, administrator, consultant*
Eaves, Sandra Austra *social worker*
Fisher, Dierdre Denise *mental health nurse, administrator, educator*
Flaherty, Sergina Maria *ophthalmic medical technologist*
Gonzalez, Hector Hugo *nurse, educator, consultant*
Hawken, Patty Lynn *nursing educator, dean of faculty*
Holguin, Alfonso Hudson *physician, educator*
Irving, George Washington, III *veterinarian, research director, consultant*
Klepac, Robert Karl *psychologist, consultant*
Martin, Suzanne Carole *health facility administrator*
McIntosh, Dennis Keith *veterinary practitioner, consultant*
Nisbett, Dorothea Jo *nursing educator*
Parks, Madelyn N. *nurse, retired army officer, university official*
Reyes, Rose Marie *nursing educator*
Ribble, Ronald George *psychologist, educator, writer*
Rogers, William *psychologist, consultant, writer, lecturer, journalist*
Swansburg, Russell Chester *medical administrator educator*
Todd, Jan Theresa *counselor*

Tucker, Stephen Lawrence *health administration educator, consultant*
Vermersch-Douglass, Susan Marie *nurse*
Wilson, Janie Menchaca *nursing educator, researcher*

**Shiner**
Wendtland, Mona Bohlmann *dietitian, consultant*

**Temple**
Frost, Juanita Corbitt *hospital foundation coordinator*
Oliver, Sandra Kay *nursing researcher*
Swartz, Jon David *psychologist, educator*
Trujillo, Sandra Sue *nurse*

**The Woodlands**
Frison, Paul Maurice *health care executive*
Martineau, Julie Peperone *social worker*

**Tyler**
Deardorff, Kathleen Umbeck *nursing educator, researcher*

**Universal City**
Lamoureux, Gloria Kathleen *nurse, air force officer*

**Uvalde**
Ramsey, Frank Allen *veterinarian, retired army officer*

**Waco**
Achor, Louis Joseph Merlin *psychology and neuroscience educator*
Hynan, Linda Susan *psychology educator*
Lamkin, Bill Dan *psychologist, educator, consultant*

**Weatherford**
Buckner-Reitman, Joyce *psychologist, educator*

**Wichita Falls**
Cagle, Paulette Bernice *mental health administrator and psychologist*

## UTAH

**Logan**
Van Dusen, Lani Marie *psychologist*

**Provo**
Bergin, Allen Eric *clinical psychologist, educator*

**Richfield**
Murphy, Millene Freeman *psychiatric rehabilitation nurse, business executive*

**Saint George**
Chilow, Barbara Gail *social worker*

**Salt Lake City**
Benjamin, Lorna Smith *psychologist*
Benson, Joan Ellen *dietetics educator, researcher*
Giles, Gerald Lynn *psychology,learning enhancement,computer educator*
Good, Rebecca Mae Wertman *learning and behavior disorder counselor, grief and loss counselor, hospice nurse*
Goodey, Ila Marie *psychologist*
Grabarz, Donald Francis *pharmacist*
Gunnell, Dale Ray *hospital administrator*
Johanson, Orin William *social worker, consultant*
Jorgensen, Lou Ann Birkbeck *social worker*
Lee, Glenn Richard *medical administrator, educator*
Mason, James Ostermann *public health administrator*
Morris, Elizabeth Treat *physical therapist*
Reeves, Bruce *social worker*
Rigdon, Imogene Stewart *nursing educator, associate dean*
Sinclair, Sara Voris *health facility administrator, nurse*
Skidmore, Rex Austin *social work educator*
Wolf, Harold Herbert *pharmacy educator*
Zaharia, Eric Stafford *developmental disabilities program administrator*

## VERMONT

**Brattleboro**
Gregg, Michael B. *health science association administrator, epidemiologist*

**Burlington**
Blomfield, Muriel May *medical technologist*
Lawson, Robert Bernard *psychology educator*
Mead, Philip Bartlett *healthcare administrator, physician*
Milliard, Aline *social worker*

**Charlotte**
Melby, Edward Carlos, Jr. *veterinarian*

**Colchester**
Kiszka, Sonia Ann *nurse practictioner, educator*

**Essex Junction**
Dietzel, Louise A. *psychologist*

**Middlebury**
Gibson, Eleanor Jack (Mrs. James J. Gibson) *retired psychology educator*

**Thetford**
Cummings Rockwell, Patricia Guilbault *psychiatric nurse*

## VIRGINIA

**Accomac**
Reid-Roberts, Dayl Helen *mental health counselor*

**Alexandria**
Abbott, Preston Sargent *psychologist*
Black, Beverly Holstun *psychiatric social worker*
Chatelier, Paul Richard *aviation psychologist, training company officer*
Fisher, Donald Wayne *medical association executive*
Girouard, Shirley Ann *nurse, policy analyst*
Hanft, Ruth S. Samuels (Mrs. Herbert Hanft) *health care consultant, educator, economist*
Johnson, Edgar McCarthy *psychologist*
Krueger, Gerald Peter *psychologist*
Parsons, Henry McIlvaine *psychologist*
Revere, Virginia Lehr *clinical psychologist*

**Altavista**
Jones, Susan Renee *counselor, mental health services professional*

**Annandale**
Abdellah, Faye Glenn *retired public health service executive*

**Arlington**
Adreon, Beatrice Marie Rice *pharmacist*
Behney, Clyde Joseph *health services researcher*
Chipman, Susan Elizabeth *psychologist*
Contis, George *medical services company executive*
Held, Joe Roger *veterinarian, epidemiologist*
Kuwamoto, Roderick Dean, Jr. *physician assistant, perfusionist, educator*
Rabun, John Brewton, Jr. *social services agency administrator*

**Ashburn**
Walsh, Geraldine Frances *nursing administrator*

**Beaumont**
Jackson, Hermoine Prestine *psychologist*

**Berryville**
White, Eugene Vaden *pharmacist*

**Blacksburg**
Ash, Philip *psychologist*
Purswell, Beverly Jean *veterinary medicine educator, theriogenologist*
Sgro, Joseph Anthony *psychologist, educator*

**Burke**
Bayer, Ada-Helen *industrial and organizational psychologist, educator*

**Charlottesville**
†Bouchard, Ronald A. *health care administrator*
Chalam, Ann *healthcare administrator*
Deese, James Earle *psychologist, educator*
Gold, Paul Ernest *psychology educator, behavioral neuroscience educator*
Hetherington, Eileen Mavis *psychologist, educator*
Hinnant, Clarence Henry, III *health care executive*
McCarty, Richard Charles *psychology educator*
Menaker, Shirley Ann Lasch *psychology educator, academic administrator*
Mesinger, John Frederick *psychologist, special education educator*
Novak, Julie Cowan *nursing educator, researcher, clinician*
Pate, Robert Hewitt, Jr. *counselor educator*
Reppucci, Nicholas Dickon *psychologist, educator*

**Chesapeake**
Skrip, Linda Jean *nursing administrator*

**Elliston**
Murray, Lynda Beran *counselor*

**Fairfax**
Boneau, C. Alan *psychology educator, researcher*
Knee, Ruth Irelan (Mrs. Junior K. Knee) *social worker, health care consultant*
Levitt, Serena Farr *nursing administrator*
Marohn, Ann Elizabeth *health information professional*
Priesman, Elinor Lee Soll *family dynamics administrator, mediator, educator*

**Fairfax Station**
Johansen, Eivind Herbert *special education services executive, former army officer*

**Falls Church**
Blanck, Ronald Ray *hospital administrator, internist, career officer*
†Cuddy, John James *deputy surgeon general*
Dunton, James Gerald *association executive*
Fink, Charles Augustin *behavioral systems scientist*

**Lancaster**
Beane, Judith Mae *psychologist*

**Leesburg**
Ecker, G. T. Dunlop *hospital administration executive*

**Lexington**
Elmes, David Gordon *psychologist, educator*
Jarrard, Leonard Everett *psychologist, educator*

**Low Moor**
Loudermilk, Peggy Joyce *pediatrics nurse, public health nurse*

**Lynchburg**
Weimar, Robert Henry *counselor, clinical hypnotherapist*

**Manassas**
Bass-Rubenstein, Deborah Sue *social worker, educator, consultant*

**Mc Lean**
Dean, Lydia Margaret Carter (Mrs. Halsey Albert Dean) *nutrition coordinator, author, consultant*
Filerman, Gary Lewis *health education executive*
Gavazzi, Aladino A. *retired medical center administrator*
Gladeck, Susan Odell *social worker*
Harmon, Robert Gerald *health company administrator, educator*
Obrien, Barbara Ann *speech and language pathologist*
Smith, Carey Daniel *acoustician, undersea warfare technologist*
Walsh, Marie Leclerc *nurse*
Zeleny, Marjorie Pfeiffer (Mrs. Charles Ellingson Zeleny) *psychologist*

**Newport News**
Phillips, Denise *critical care nurse*

**Norfolk**
Glickman, Albert Seymour *psychologist, educator*
Green, Janice Strickland *emergency services nurse*
Knox, Richard Douglas, Jr. *healthcare executive*

**Oakton**
Trifoli-Cunniff, Laura Catherine *psychologist, consultant*

**Palmyra**
Chapin, Suzanne Phillips *retired psychologist*

**Petersburg**
Edmunds, Cecelia Powers *health facility administrator*
Northrop, Mary Ruth *mental retardation nurse*
Spangler, Vera Mae *mental health nurse*

**Powhatan**
Huff, Cynthia Fae *medical and orthopedic nurse*

**Radford**
Henderson, Nancy Carr *dietitian, medical transcriber, writer*
Pribram, Karl Harry *psychology educator, brain researcher*
Reed, Helen I. *medical, surgical nurse*

**Reston**
Kader, Nancy Stowe *nurse, consultant*

**Richmond**
Barker, Thomas Carl *retired health care administration educator, executive*
Fischer, Carl Robert *health care facility administrator*
Freund, Emma Frances *medical technologist*
Gandy, Gerald Larmon *rehabilitation counseling educator, psychologist, writer*
Geraghty, Patrick James *organ recovery coordinator*
Hardage, Page Taylor *health care administrator*
Hardy, Richard Earl *rehabilitation counseling educator, clinical psychologist*
McMurray, Carol Dolber *human services administrator*
Simpson, John Noel *healthcare administrator*
White, Kenneth Ray *health administration educator, consultant*

**Roanoke**
Duff, Doris Eileen (Shull) *critical care nurse*
Word, Eliza Switzer *critical care nurse, administrator*

**Salem**
Dagenhart, Betty Jane Mahaffey *nursing educator, administrator*

**Spotsylvania**
Arnhoff, Franklyn Nathaniel *psychologist, sociologist, educator*

**Stafford**
Woldt, Gerald D. (Jay Woldt) *nurse anesthetist*

**Staunton**
Sweetman, Beverly Yarroll *physical therapist*

**Sterling**
Finn, Gloria Inez *geriatrics nurse*
Gunberg, Edwin Woodrow, Jr. *counseling psychologist, consultant, researcher*

**Vienna**
Chamberlain, Diane *psychotherapist, author, clinical social worker*
Rovis, Christopher Patrick *clinical social worker, psychotherapist*

**Virginia Beach**
Abbott, Regina A. *neurodiagnostic technologist, consultant, business owner*

**Williamsburg**
Austin, Sigrid Linnevold *counselor*
Johnston, Robert Atkinson *psychologist, educator*
Kelly, William E. *psychoanalyst*
Lange, Carl James *psychology educator*
Refinetti, Roberto *physiological psychologist*
Rosen, Ellen Freda *psychologist, educator*
Shaver, Kelly G. *psychology educator*

**Winchester**
Billeter, Marianne *pharmacy educator*

**Woodbridge**
Carvalho, Julie Ann *psychologist*
Flori, Anna Marie DiBlasi *nurse anesthetist, educational administrator*

## WASHINGTON

**Anacortes**
Kuure, Bojan Marlena *operating room nurse*

**Bellevue**
Akutagawa, Donald *psychologist, educator*
Gosslee, Mary June *chiropractor*
Lipkin, Mary Castleman Davis (Mrs. Arthur Bennett Lipkin) *retired psychiatric social worker*

**Bellingham**
Diers, Carol Jean *psychology educator*
Haensly, Patricia A. *psychology educator*
Johnson, Jennifer Lucky *psychotherapist*

**Bothell**
McDonald, Michael Lee *clinic administrator, retired naval officer*

**Chehalis**
Burrows, Robert Paul *optometrist*

**Cheney**
Gerber, Sanford Edwin *audiologist*

**Clarkston**
Ramsden, Norma La Vonne Huber *nurse*

**Colfax**
Young, Joann Elizabeth *veterinarian*

**Des Moines**
Harper, Vera Jean *retirement home activity director, music therapist*

**Everett**
Sandahl, Bonnie Beardsley *pediatric nurse practitioner, clinical nurse specialist, nurse manager*
Van Ry, Ginger Lee *school psychologist*

**Freeland**
Freehill, Maurice F. *retired educational psychology educator*

**Friday Harbor**
MacGinitie, Walter Harold *psychologist*

**Gig Harbor**
Canter, Ralph Raymond *psychology educator, research director*

**Kirkland**
Look, Janet K. *psychologist*

**Medical Lake**
Taylor, Eldon *psychologist researcher*

**Mount Vernon**
Garcia, John *psychologist, educator*
Poppe, Patricia Lee *clinical social worker, consultant*

**Napavine**
Morgan-Fadness, Corrina May *staff charge nurse*

**Oak Harbor**
Miller, Robert Scott *mental health administrator, social worker*

**Olympia**
Blake, Ann Beth *psychologist*
Boruchowitz, Stephen Alan *health policy analyst*
Inverso, Marlene Joy *optometrist*
Reilly, Robert Joseph *counselor*

**Pullman**
Baugh, Bradford Hamilton *occupational and environmental health advisor*
Bustad, Leo Kenneth *veterinary educator, college administrator*
Gustafsson, Borje Karl *veterinarian, educator*
Henson, James Bond *veterinary pathologist*
McSweeney, Frances Kaye *psychology educator*
Mitchell, Madeleine Enid *nutritionist, educator*
Warner, Dennis Allan *psychology educator*
Wilson, Robert Burton *veterinary and medical educator*
Young, Francis Allan *psychologist*

**Puyallup**
Brandner, (Mary Ann) Joyce *retired nurse educator*
Veatch, John William *Reiki educator, educational administrator*
Walize, Reuben Thompson, III *health research administrator*

**Redmond**
Oaks, Lucy Moberley *retired social worker*
Sasenick, Joseph Anthony *health care company executive*

**Rollingbay**
Young, Jeffry *psychologist, gerontologist, educator, statistician*

**Seattle**
Adams, Julie Karen *clinical psychologist*
Boaz, Doniella Chaves *psychotherapist, consultant*
Brammer, Lawrence Martin *psychology educator*
Burns, Robert Carter *psychologist, author*
Carlyon, Diane Claire *nurse*
Coffman, Sandra Jeanne *psychologist*
Day, Robert Winsor *cancer research administrator*
Dear, Ronald Bruce *social work educator*
de Tornyay, Rheba *nurse, former university dean, educator*
Dorpat, Theodore Lorenz *psychoanalyst*
Duncan, Elizabeth Charlotte *marriage and family therapist, educator*
Evans, Ellis Dale *psychologist, educator*
Fiedler, Fred Edward *organizational psychology educator, consultant*
Green, G. Dorsey *psychologist, author*
Gunter, Laurie M. *retired nurse educator*
Huey, Constance Anne Berner *mental health counselor*
Johnston, William Frederick *emergency services administrator*
Kolbeson, Marilyn Hopf *holistic practioner, educator, artist, retired organization and management consultant*
Monsen, Elaine Ranker *nutritionist, educator, editor*
Muilenburg, Robert Henry *hospital administrator*
Perkin, Gordon Wesley *international health agency executive*
Perrin, Edward Burton *health services researcher, biostatistician, public health educator*
Peterson, Jane White *nursing educator, anthropologist*
Prins, David *speech pathologist, educator*
Sarason, Irwin G. *psychology educator*
Schaller, Joanne F. *nursing consultant*
Thompson, Arlene Rita *nursing educator*
Woods, Nancy Fugate *women's health nurse, educator*

**Shoreline**
Treseler, Kathleen Morrison *retired nursing educator*

**Spanaway**
Campbell, Thomas J. *chiropractor, former legislator*

**Spokane**
Evoy, John Joseph *psychology educator*
Hendershot, Carol Miller *physical therapist*
Robinson, Herbert Henry, III *educator, psychotherapist*
Vaux, Dora Louise *sperm bank official, consultant*

**Tacoma**
Ernst, John Allan *clinical neuropsychologist*
Ingram, Artonyon S. *mental health professional, therapist*
Mohler, Georgia Ann *geriatrics nurse practitioner*
Smith, Leo Gilbert *hospital administrator*
Taylor, Mary D. *counselor*

**Vancouver**
†Fishman, Neill Timothy *medical services administrator*
Lollar, Katherine Louise *social worker, therapist*
Simontacchi, Carol Nadine *nutritionist, retail store executive*

**Yakima**
Simonson, Susan Kay *hospital administrator*
Tanner, Patricia Ruth *gerontology nurse*

## WEST VIRGINIA

**Bluefield**
Davenport, Dorothy Dean *nurse*
Scott, Nina Ogle *nurse*

**Charleston**
Goodwin, Phillip Hugh *hospital administrator*

**Hurricane**
Nance, Martha McGhee *rehabilitation nurse*

**Kingwood**
Rock, Gail Ann *obstetrical/gynecological nurse*

**Lewisburg**
Byrd, Julie Anderson *nurse*
Seifer, Judith Huffman *sex therapist, educator*

**Martinsburg**
†Farrar, John Thruston *health facility administrator*

**Morgantown**
Barba, Roberta Ashburn *retired social worker*
McAvoy, Rogers *educational psychology educator, consultant*
Reese, Hayne Waring *psychologist*

**Pratt**
Terrell-McDaniel, Robin F. *cardiac rehabilitation and critical care nurse*

**Rainelle**
Scott, Pamela Moyers *physician assistant*

**Ridgeley**
Hammond, Anna Josephine *nurse practitioner*

**Saint Albans**
Alderson, Gloria Frances Dale *rehabilitation specialist*

**Wheeling**
Ritz, Lorraine Isaacs *nursing administrator*
Stidd, Linda Marie *rehabilitation nurse*
Urval, Krishna Raj *health facility administrator, educator*

## WISCONSIN

**Brookfield**
Zander, Gaillienne Glashow *psychologist*

**Burlington**
Oestmann, Mary Jane *retired senior radiation specialist*

**Chippewa Falls**
Copeland, Christine Susan *therapist*

**De Pere**
Ngo, Paul Y.L. *psychology educator*

**Eau Claire**
Dick, Raymond Dale *psychology educator*
Schenk, Quentin Frederick *retired social work educator, mayor*
Thompson, Lynn Renee *chiropractor*

**Ellison Bay**
MacKinney, Arthur Clinton, Jr. *retired university official, psychologist*

**Elm Grove**
Headlee, Raymond *psychoanalyst, educator*

**Fond Du Lac**
Bespalec, Dale Anthony *clinical psychologist*
Kaufman, Harvey Isidore *neuropsychology consultant*

**Fort Atkinson**
Albaugh, John Charles *hospital executive*

**Green Bay**
Butler, Robert Andrews *clinical psychologist*
McIntosh, Elaine Virginia *nutrition educator*

**La Crosse**
Anderson, Mary Ann *hospital nursing administrator*
Morehouse, Richard Edward *psychology educator*

**Madison**
Chapman, Loren J. *psychology educator*
Coe, Christopher Lane *psychology researcher*

---

Derzon, Gordon M. *hospital administrator*
Dunham, Michael Herman *managed care executive*
Easterday, Bernard Carlyle *veterinary medicine educator*
Epstein, William *experimental psychologist*
Gavin, Mary Jane *medical, surgical nurse*
Greenfield, Norman Samuel *psychologist, educator*
Littlefield, Vivian Moore *nursing educator, administrator*
Marlett, Judith Ann *nutritional sciences educator, researcher*
Merrick, William Andrew *neuropsychologist*
Piliavin, Jane Allyn *social psychologist*
Rice, Joy Katharine *psychologist, educational policy studies and women's studies educator*
Schoeller, Dale Alan *nutrition research educator*
Szymanski, Edna Mora *rehabilitation psychology and special education educator*
Vandell, Deborah Lowe *educational psychology educator*

**Marshfield**
Jaye, David Robert, Jr. *retired hospital administrator*

**Milwaukee**
Bartels, Jean Ellen *nursing educator*
Blum, Lawrence Philip *educational psychology educator*
Brown, Edith *social worker*
Cohn, Lucile *psychotherapist, nurse*
Coogan, Frank Neil *health and social services administrator*
Falconer, Judith Ann *public health and occupational therapist, educator*
Gengler, Sister M. Jeanne *hospital administrator*
Grochowski, Mary Ann *psychotherapist*
Harvieux, Anne Marie *psychotherapist*
Humber, Wilbur James *psychologist*
King, Guadalupe Vasquez *psychology and social work educator*
Kupst, Mary Jo *psychologist, researcher*
Lange, Marilyn *social worker*
Shields, James Richard *alcohol and drug counselor, consultant*
Silverman, Franklin Harold *speech pathologist, educator*
Vice, Jon Earl *hospital executive*
Wake, Madeline Musante *nursing educator*
Warren, Richard M. *experimental psychologist, educator*
†Weifbecker, Robert T. *healthcare administrator*
Wells, Carolyn Cressy *social work educator*

**New Berlin**
Nelson, Kay Ellen *speech and language pathologist*
Winkler, Dolores Eugenia *retired hospital administrator*

**Oconomowoc**
Morgan, Donna Jean *psychotherapist*

**Park Falls**
Westphal, William Henry *staff nurse*

**Plymouth**
Woythal, Constance Lee *psychologist*

**River Falls**
LeCapitaine, John Edward *counseling psychology educator, researcher*

**Spooner**
Schaeffer, Brenda Mae *psychologist, author*

**Watertown**
Leitzke, Jacque Herbert *psychologist, corporate executive*

**Wauwatosa**
Janzen, Norine Madelyn Quinlan *medical technologist*

**Whitewater**
Culbertson, Frances Mitchell *psychology educator*

**Woodruff**
Rosenberg, Douglas Owen *healthcare management executive*

## WYOMING

**Basin**
Kennette, Jennie Laura Fakes *medical and surgical nurse*

**Cheyenne**
Hardway, James Edward *vocational and rehabilitative specialist*
Hirst, Wilma Elizabeth *psychologist*

**Green River**
Thompson, Josie *nurse*

**Laramie**
Nord, Thomas Allison *hospital administrator*

**Powell**
Brophy, Dennis Richard *psychology and philosophy educator*

**Saratoga**
Collamer, Sonja Mae Soreide *veterinary facility administrator*

**Teton Village**
Ellwood, Paul Murdock, Jr. *health policy analyst, consultant*

**Wilson**
Breitenbach, Mary Louise McGraw *psychologist, chemical dependency counselor*

## TERRITORIES OF THE UNITED STATES

---

## GUAM

**Agana**
Hardin, Ann *marriage and family therapist*

**Perez Acres**
Duenas, Laurent Flores *health and nursing consultant*

**Sinajana**
Toves, Jo Ann Villamor *nursing supervisor*

## PUERTO RICO

**Bayamon**
Herrans-Perez, Laura Leticia *psychologist, educator, research consultant*

**Ponce**
Figueroa-Roman, Betsy *medical records administrator*

**Rio Piedras**
Davila, Norma *developmental psychologist and program evaluator*

**San Juan**
Muñoz Dones Carrascal, Eloisa *hospital administrator, pediatrician, consultant, educator*
Prevor, Ruth Claire *psychologist*

**Trujillo Alto**
Antoun, Mikhail *medicinal chemistry and pharmacognosy educator*

## MILITARY ADDRESSES OF THE UNITED STATES

## EUROPE

**APO**
Gresham, Dorothy Ann *operating room nurse, educator*
Terry, Wayne Gilbert *healthcare executive, hospital administrator*

## PACIFIC

**FPO**
Murray, Julia Kaoru (Mrs. Joseph E. Murray) *occupational therapist*

## CANADA

## ALBERTA

**Calgary**
Calkin, Joy Durfée *healthcare consultant, educator*
Meyers, Marlene O. *hospital administrator*

**Edmonton**
Fields, Anthony Lindsay Austin *health facility administrator, oncologist, educator*
Hislop, Mervyn Warren *health advocate administrator, psychologist*
Lechelt, Eugene Carl *psychology educator*

**Lethbridge**
Cho, Hyun Ju *veterinary research scientist*

## BRITISH COLUMBIA

**New Westminster**
Fair, James Stanley *hospital administrator*

**Vancouver**
Collins, Mary *health association executive, former Canadian legislator*
Craig, Kenneth Denton *psychologist, educator, researcher*
Cynader, Max Sigmund *psychology, physiology, brain research educator, researcher*
Gilbert, John Humphrey Victor *audiologist, speech scientist, educator*
Klonoff, Harry *psychologist*
Riedel, Bernard Edward *retired pharmaceutical sciences educator*
Splane, Richard Beverley *social work educator*
Suedfeld, Peter *psychologist, educator*
Tees, Richard Chisholm *psychology educator, researcher*

**Victoria**
Payne, Robert Walter *psychologist, educator*

## MANITOBA

**Winnipeg**
Hogan, Terrence Patrick *psychologist, university administrator*
Seifert, Blair Wayne *clinical pharmacist*
Thorfinnson, A. Rodney *hospital administrator*

## NEW BRUNSWICK

**Charters Settlement**
Easterbrook, James Arthur *psychology educator*

**Moncton**
McGeorge, Ronald Kenneth *hospital executive*

**Mouth of Keswick**
†Hoyt-Hallett, Bonny *health facility administrator*

---

**Sussex**
Secord, Lloyd Douglas *healthcare administrator*

## ONTARIO

**Brantford**
Inns, Harry Douglas Ellis *optometrist*
Woodcock, Richard Beverley *health facility administrator*

**Downsview**
Endler, Norman Solomon *psychology educator*

**Elgin**
Lafave, Hugh Gordon John *medical association executive, psychiatrist, educator, consultant*

**Guelph**
Benn, Denna M. *veterinarian*

**Hamilton**
Ryan, Ellen Bouchard *psychology educator, gerontologist*

**Keswick**
Macdonald, John Barfoot *research foundation executive*

**Kingston**
Berry, John Widdup *psychologist*
Glynn, Peter Alexander Richard *hospital administrator*
McGeer, James Peter *research executive, consultant*

**London**
Kimura, Doreen *psychology educator, researcher*

**North York**
MacKenzie, Donald Murray *hospital administrator*
Tulving, Endel *psychologist, educator*

**Ottawa**
Langill, George Francis *hospital administrator, educator*

**Owen Sound**
Jones, Phyllis Edith *nursing educator*

**Ridgeway**
Jacobs, Eleanor Alice *retired clinical psychologist, educator*

**Toronto**
Ferguson, Kingsley George *psychologist*
Freedman, Theodore Jarrell *healthcare executive*
Herbert, Stephen W. *hospital executive*
Scholefield, Peter Gordon *health agency executive*
Turner, Gerald Phillip *hospital administrator*

**Windsor**
Auld, Frank *psychologist, educator*

## QUEBEC

**Montreal**
Chevrier, Jean-Marc *psychologist, publisher, author*
Dudek, Stephanie Zuperko *psychology educator*
Gallagher, Tanya Marie *speech pathologist, educator*
Melzack, Ronald *psychology educator*
Messing, Karen *occupational health researcher*
Milner, Brenda Atkinson Langford *neuropsychologist*
Milner, Peter Marshall *psychology educator*
Scriver, Charles Robert *medical scientist, human geneticist*
Sirois, Gerard *pharmacy educator*
Stewart, Jane *psychology educator*
Vikis-Freibergs, Vaira *psychologist, educator*

**Saint Nicolas**
Blanchet, Madeleine *research executive*

## SASKATCHEWAN

**Saskatoon**
Belovanoff, Olga *retired health care facility administrator*
Randhawa, Bikkar Singh *psychologist, educator*

## MEXICO

**Mexico City**
Baer, George Martin *veterinarian, researcher*
Weber, Ernesto Juan *counselor, educator, industrialist*

## BRAZIL

**São Paulo**
Fernicola, Nilda Alicia Gallego Gándara de *pharmacist, biochemist*

## DENMARK

**Copenhagen**
Bundesen, Claus Mogens *psychologist, educator*

## ENGLAND

**London**
Pickle, James C. *hospital administrator*

## JAMAICA

**Kingston**
Ferguson, Marjorie Delores *nursing educator*

## JAPAN

**Otawara**
Imai, Shiro *psychology educator*

**Shibuya**
Torii, Shuko *psychology educator*

## THE PHILIPPINES

**Manila**
Llamanzares, Magda Carolina Go Vera *nurse, clinical child psychologist*

## SINGAPORE

**Henderson Industrial Park**
Shima, Larry Mitsuru *health facility administrator*

## SOUTH AFRICA

**Medunsa**
Walubo, Andrew *clinical pharmacologist, researcher*

## SWITZERLAND

**Cologny**
Maglacas, A. Mangay *nursing researcher, educator*

**Versoix**
Mahler, Halfdan Theodor *physician, health organization executive*

## TURKEY

**Istanbul**
Rountree, George Denton *health services managemtent consultant*

## ZAMBIA

**Mumbwa**
Hansen, Florence Marie Congiolosi (Mrs. James S. Hansen) *social worker*

## ADDRESS UNPUBLISHED

Abdoo, Raymond Thomas *preventive health consultant*
Abel, Harold *psychologist, educator, academic administrator*
Abernathy, Vicki Marie *nurse*
Addiss, Susan Silliman *public health consultant*
Aehlert, Barbara June *health services executive*
Altman, Irwin *psychology educator*
Anaple, Elsie Mae *medical, surgical and geriatrics nurse*
Anderson, Dianne Jean *nursing administrator*
Anderson, Dorothy Fisher *social worker, psychotherapist*
Angus, Robert Carlyle, Jr. *health facility administrator*
Armas, Jennifer Villareal *nurse*
Arnold, Deborrah Ann *human services director*
Autorino, Anne Turnbull *retired social worker*
Ayres, Jayne Lynn Ankrum *community health nurse*
Babao, Donna Marie *community health, psychiatric nurse, educator*
Babitzke, Theresa Angeline *health facility administrator*
Baier, Edward John *former public health official, industrial hygiene engineer, consultant*
Bailey-Jones, Carla Lynn *nursing administrator*
Baker, Ginger Lee *oncological and cardiac nurse*
Baldwin, Deanna Louise *dietitian*
Baldwin, William Russell *optometrist, foundation executive*
Barker, Virginia Lee *nursing educator*
Barnhouse, Lillian May Palmer *retired medical surgical nurse, researcher, civic worker*
Basham-Tooker, Janet Brooks *retired geropsychologist, educator*
Bass, Lynda D. *medical/surgical nurse, educator*
Batalden, Paul Bennett *pediatrician, health care educator*
Baumann-Sinacore, Patricia Lynn *nursing administrator*
Becich, Raymond Brice *healthcare consultant, mediator, trainer, educator*
Bell, Susan Jane *nurse*
Belles, Donald Arnold *pastoral therapist, mental health counselor*
Belmont, Larry Miller *health association executive*
Bender, James Frederick *psychologist, educator, university dean*
Benenson, Esther Siev (Mrs. William Benenson) *nursing home administrator, gerontologist*
Berdanier, Carolyn Dawson *nutrition educator, researcher*
Berger, Anita Hazel *psychotherapist, adult educator, organizational consultant*
Berger-Kraemer, Nancy *speech and language pathologist, artist*
Bern, Lynda Kaplan *women's health and pediatric nurse*
Bernfield, Lynne *psychotherapist*
Berry, Laurie Ann *critical care nurse*
Berzon, Betty *psychotherapist*
Betsinger, Peggy Ann *oncological nurse*
Biegel, David Eli *social worker, educator*
Bishop, (Ina) Sue Marquis *psychiatric and mental health nurse educator, researcher, administrator*
Blacher, Joan Helen *psychotherapist, educator*
Blumberg, Mark Stuart *health care researcher*
Blumengold, Jeffrey Gene *health care financial reimbursement expert*
Bolla, Karen Irene *neuropsychologist, educator*
Borg, Ruth I. *home nursing care provider*
Borgstahl, Kaylene Denise *health facility administrator*
Bottone, JoAnn *health services executive*
Braden, Joan Kay *mental health counselor*
Bradley, Carol Ann *nursing administrator*
Braen, Bernard Benjamin *psychology educator*
Braswell, Jackie Terry *medical, surgical nurse*
Braun, Mary Lucile Dekle (Lucy Braun) *therapist, consultant, counselor*
Breen, Janice DeYoung *health services executive, community health nurse*
Breslin, Evalynne L. W. *retired psychiatric nurse*
Brosz, Margaret Headley *pediatrics nurse*
Brower, Forrest Allen *retired health facility administrator*
Brown, Barbara June *hospital and nursing administrator*
Brown, Carol Rentiers *health facility administrator*
Brown, Geraldine *nurse, freelance writer*
Bruno, Barbara Altman *social worker*
Bryant, Bertha Estelle *retired nurse*
Bryant, Gail Annette Grippen *nurse, educator*
Buchbinder, Sharon Bell *health science educator*
Buchin, Jean *psychologist*
Buckley, Linda Anne *critical care and psychiatric-mental health, chemical dependency nurse*
Bugella, Barbara Ann *psychiatric nurse therapist*
Bullough, Vern LeRoy *nursing educator, historian, sexologist, researcher*
Bundy, Mary Lothrop *retired social worker*
Burney, Mary Ann *mental health nurse*
Burns, James F. *social work therapist*
Büsch, Annemarie *mental health nurse*
Busho, Elizabeth Mary *nurse, consultant, educator*
Buzard, James Albert *healthcare management consultant*
Caddeo, Maria Elizabeth *critical care nurse*
Calamita, Kathryn Elizabeth *nursing administrator*
Calvert, Marilyn Rose Stewart *nursing consultant*
Camayd-Freixas, Yoel *management, strategy & planning consultant*
Cameron, David Brian *health service administrator*
Campbell, Margaret M. *retired social work educator*
Carlsen, Mary Baird *clinical psychologist*
Carlson, Janet Frances *psychologist, educator*
Carpenter, Kenneth John *nutrition educator*
Carruthers, Claudelle Ann *occupational and physical therapist*
Carson, Regina Edwards *healthcare administrator, pharmacist, educator*
Cason, Nica Virginia *nursing educator*
Castro, Amuerfina Tantiongco *geriatrics nurse*
Cauthorne-Burnette, Tamera Dianne *family nurse practitioner, healthcare consultant*
Cecil, Maxine *critical care nurse*
Chalfant, Richard Dewey *hypnotherapist, composer, insurance consultant*
Chambers, Judith Tarnpoll *speech pathologist, audiologist*
Chapman, Hope Horan *psychologist*
Chase, Clinton Irvin *psychologist, educator, business executive*
Child, Carroll Cadell *research nursing administrator*
Chojnowski, Donna A. *cardiac transplant nurse, administrator*
Chow, Rita Kathleen *nurse consultant*
Clanon, Thomas Lawrence *retired hospital administrator*
†Clark, Richard Harry Jr. *clinic administrator*
Clauser, Angela Frances *medical surgical, pediatrics and geriatrics nurse*
Cleveland, Charlene S. *community health nurse*
Clover-Lee, Shevonne Jones *geriatrics nurse*
Colangelo, James Joseph *psychotherapist*
Coleman, Arlene Florence *nurse practitioner*
Colosimo, Mary Lynn Sukurs *psychology educator*
Condie, Vicki Cook *nurse, educator*
Condry, Robert Stewart *retired hospital administrator*
Cook, Quentin LaMar *healthcare executive, lawyer*
Cooper, Sarah Jean *nursing educator*
Cooper, Signe Skott *retired nurse educator*
Cooper-Lewter, Nicholas Charles *psychotherapist, educator, minister, author*
Copeland, Terrilyn Denise *speech pathologist*
Cornell, David Roger *health care executive*
Coté, Kathryn Marie *psychotherapist, stress management educator*
Couchman, Robert George James *human services consultant*
Coven, Berdeen *psychotherapist*
Cox, J. William *retired physician, health services administrator*
Cox, John Curtis *healthcare and educational administrator*
Cozan, Lee *clinical research psychologist*
Craig, Carol Mills *marriage, family and child counselor*
Crawford, Pamela J. *critical care nurse*
Cromwell, Florence Stevens *occupational therapist*
Crowder, Eleanor Louise McElheny *nursing educator*
Dake, Marcia Allene *retired nursing educator, university dean*
Dale Riikonen, Charlene Boothe *international health administrator*
Daniels, Kurt R. *speech and language pathologist*
Davidow, Jenny Jean *counselor, writer*
Davis, Alphonse *health facility administrator, special education counselor*
Davis, Carolyne Kahle *health care consultant*
Davis, Gay Ruth *psychotherapist, social welfare educator, author, researcher, consultant*
Davis, Sandra Bernice *nurse anesthetist*
Dawes, Carol J. *retired psychologist*
Dawkins, Marva Phyllis *psychologist*
Deely, Maureen Cecelia *community health nurse*
Deidan, Cecilia Theresa *neuropsychologist*
Dempsey, Barbara Matthea *medical, surgical and critical care nurse*
Dennis, Marcia Lynn *speech and language pathologist*
Dolan, June Ann *health facility administrator*
Dole, Arthur Alexander *psychology educator*
Dumler, Patricia Ann *critical care nurse*
Durham, Mary Ann *pharmacist, pharmacy owner*
Dyer, Wayne Walter *psychologist, author, radio and television personality*
Eddy, Esther Dewitz *retired pharmacist*
Edmonds, Velma McInnis *nursing educator*
Edwards, Ward Dennis *psychology and industrial engineering educator*
Eisen, Henry *retired pharmacy educator*
Eitel, Dolores J. *healthcare consultant, educator*
Elliott-Zahorik, Bonnie *nurse, administrator*
Emerson, Ann Parker *dietitian, educator*
Engel, Bernard Theodore *psychologist, educator*
English, Jujuan Bondman *women's health nurse, educator*
Evans, Frederick John *psychologist*
Ewell, Charles Muse *health care industry executive, consultant, educator*
Fail, Joyce Ann *critical care nurse*
Fairburn, Sandra Jean *nursing educator*
Falbe, Maryann Christine *nursing administrator*
Farrington, Bertha Louise *nursing administrator*
Faub, Kenneth James *school nurse practitioner*
Fehr, Lola Mae *nursing association director*
Fein, Adrienne Myra *nursing educator*
Fischer, Linda Marie *nursing educator*
Fisherman, Nina Yarlovsky *nursing administrator*
Fitzpatrick, William Allen *pharmacist*
Flanagan, Mary Haley *nursing administrator, mental health nurse*
Fletcher, J. Sue *health educator*
Forest, Eva Brown *nurse, supervisor and paralegal*
Forman-Mason, Monica N. *speech and language pathologist*
Foulkes, William David *psychologist, educator*
Fox, Michael Wilson *veterinarian, animal behaviorist*
Franciosa, Joseph Anthony *health care consultant*
Frank-Fitzner, Fontaine Lynne *geriatrics nurse, health insurance utilization reviewer*
Franklin-Griffin, Cathy Lou Hinson *nursing educator*
Freeman, Arthur *veterinarian, retired association administrator*
Frost, Carolyn Dean *critical care nurse, nursing administrator*
Fuller, Gayle Barnes *psychotherapist*
Fuller, Margaret Jane *medical technologist*
Fullwood, Altburg Marie *women's health nurse*
Fusciardi, Katherine *nursing administrator*
Garber, Sharon N. *medical/surgical nurse*
Gardner, Kathryn Johanna *nursing educator, community health nurse*
Garnett, Linda Kopec *nurse, researcher*
Garrett, Shirley Gene *nuclear medicine technologist*
Garvey, Evelyn Jewel *retired mental health nurse*
Gay, William Ingalls *veterinarian, health science administrator*
Geitgey, Doris Arlene *retired nursing educator, dean*
Gerald, Michael Charles *pharmacy educator, college dean*
Gerry, Debra Prue *psychotherapist*
Gerstner, Mary Jane *nurse*
Giancaterino, Linda DeMarsico *social worker*
Giles, Susan Michele *medical/surgical nurse*
Giles, Walter Edmund *alcohol and drug treatment executive*
Goetzke, Gloria Louise *social worker, income tax specialist*
Goldston, Stephen Eugene *community psychologist, educator, consultant*
Gordon, Rena Joyce *health services researcher, educator*
Goslawski, Violet Ann *nurse, substance abuse counselor*
Govan, Gladys Vernita Mosley *retired critical care and medical/surgical nurse*
Grant, Richard Earl *medical and legal consultant*
Graver, Mary Kathryn *medical, surgical nurse*
Gray, Margaret Edna *retired nursing educator, dean*
Green, Barbara Strawn *psychotherapist*
Green, Beth Ingber *intuitive practitioner, counselor, musician, composer*
Green, Karen Danielle *psychotherapist*
Greenfield, Linda Sue *nursing educator*
Greenwood, Janet Kae Daly *psychologist, educational administrator*
Griffin, Christopher Oakley *hospital professional*
Griffin, Suzanne Marie *medical and surgical nurse*
Grolli, Frank Thomas *retired pharmacist*
Grossman, Audrey Marie *medical/surgical nurse*
Gundersen, Allison Maureen *consultant*
Guthrie, Robert Val *psychologist*
Hadley, Jane Byington *psychotherapist*
Hagelston, Karman Weatherly *speech pathologist*
Hagen, Edna Mae *retired medical nurse*
Haining, Jeane *psychologist*
Hall, Ella Taylor *clinical school psychologist*
Hall, Jay *social psychologist*
Hanks, Gary Arlin *psychology educator*
Hanni, Geraldine Marie *therapist*
Hanrahan, Lawrence Martin *healthcare consultant*
Hardy, Beth Benita *nurse*
Harrigan, Rosanne Carol *nursing educator*
Harrington, Michael Ballou *health economist, systems engineer*
Hasselmeyer, Eileen Grace *medical research administrator*
Hawryluk, Christine Joanne *school nurse*
Hayes, Judith *psychotherapist, educator*
Healy, Sonya Ainslie *health facility administrator*
Heath, Richard Murray *retired hospital administrator*
Held, Nancy B. *perinatal nurse, lactation consultant*
Helfrich, Wauneta Meyne *retired school social worker*
Heris, Toni *psychologist, psychotherapist*
Herkner, Bernadette Kay *occupational health nurse*
Herrmann, Walter *retired laboratory administrator*
Hertz, Kenneth Theodore *health care executive*
Heywood, Elizabeth Z. *nurse educator, nurse manager*
Hickcox, Leslie Kay *health educator, consultant, counselor*
Hille, Robert Arthur *healthcare executive*
Hiner, Elizabeth Ellen *pharmacist*
Hires, William Leland *psychologist, consultant*
Hoffer, Alma Jeanne *nursing educator*
Hofmann, Paul Bernard *health care consultant*
Hollis, Mary Fern Caudill *community health nurse*
Holloway, Richard Lawrence *marriage-family therapist, college official*
Holmes, Wilhelmina Kent *community health nurse*
Holtsberg, Philip *gerontologist, lawyer, psychologist*
Homestead, Susan E. (Susan Freedlender) *psychotherapist*
Horton, James David *critical care and emergency nurse*
Howe, John Prentice, III *health science center executive, physician*
Howe, Virginia Hoffman *nurse administrator*
Howell, Embry Martin *researcher*
Huber, Vida S. *nursing educator*
Hufferd, Linda M. *nurse*
Hukins-Rodrigue, Dana Ann *community health nurse*
Hunt, Ronald Duncan *veterinarian, educator, pathologist*
Hutzler, Lisa Ann *mental health nurse, adult clinical psychologist*
Isaacs, Kenneth S(idney) *psychoanalyst, educator*
Jacobs, Marion Kramer *psychologist*
Jebsen, Joan Helene *medical senior secretary*
Jennings, Elizabeth Moomaw *social worker*
Jensen, Mogens Reimer *psychologist*
Jobe, Muriel Ida *medical technologist, educator*
Jones, Shirley Ann *psychiatric nurse*
Juenemann, Sister Jean *hospital executive*
Kaiser, Nina Irene *health facility administrator*
Kapitan, Mary L. *retired nursing administrator, educator*
Karson, Samuel *psychologist, educator*
Katz, Phyllis Alberts *developmental research psychologist*
Kaye, Jennifer Lynn *healthcare executive*
Kellam, Norma Dawn *medical, surgical nurse*
Kendrick, Budd Leroy *psychologist*
Kidd, A. Paul *hospital administrator, government official*
Kieffer, Joyce Loretta *health science facility administrator, educator*
King, Imogene M. *nurse, educator*
Klein, Fay Magid *health administrator*
Klinetob, Carson Wayne *physical therapist*
Klivington, Kenneth Albert *research administrator*
Kolasa, Kathryn Marianne *food and nutrition educator, consultant*
Koller, Loren D. *veterinary medicine educator*
Labins, Deborah Lynne *maternal women's health nurse*
Ladly, Frederick Bernard *health services and financial services company executive*
Lamb, Joann Isabel *adult nurse practitioner*
Lamb, Katie A. *nursing educator*
Lamberg, Stanley Lawrence *medical technologist, educator*
Lane, Debra Ann *critical care nurse*
LaRock, Terrance Edmond *health facility administrator*
Lauber, John K. *research psychologist*
Lay, Elizabeth Marian *health association administrator*
Leach, Kay T. *critical care nurse, administrator*
Leddy, Susan *nursing educator*
L'Eplattenier, Nora Sweeny Hickey *nursing educator*
Lewis, Charles Leonard *psychologist*
Lewis, Lois A. *health services administrator*
Lewis, Russell Carl, Jr. *family nurse practitioner*
Lilly-Hersley, Jane Anne Feeley *nursing researcher*
Lindgren, Kermit Lyle *nurse*
Lipsitt, Lewis Paeff *psychology educator*
Localio, Marcia Judith *medical/surgical nurse*
†Looney, John G. *mental health services administrator*
Lyman, Ruth Ann *psychologist*
Lynch, Michael Edward *medical facility administrator*
Lynch, Virginia Anne (Virginia A. Red Hawk) *forensic nurse, educator, consultant*
Lyngbye, Jørgen *hospital administrator, researcher*
Lyons, Natalie Beller *family counselor*
MacLennan, Beryce Winifred *psychologist*
Maehr, Martin Louis *psychology educator*
Magafas, Diania Lee *geriatrics nurse consultant, administrator*
Magnuson, Robert Martin *retired hospital administrator*
Majors, Nelda Faye *physical therapist*
Maloney, Diane Marie *legal nurse consultant*
Marcinek, Margaret Ann *nursing educator*
Marcoux, Julia A. *midwife*
Marshall, Donald Thomas *medical technologist*
Marshall, L. B. *clinical lab scientist*
Marvel, Wanda Faye *home health clinical consultant*
Massa, Salvatore Peter *psychologist*
Matheny, Adam Pence, Jr. *child psychologist, educator, consultant, researcher*
Matherlee, Thomas Ray *health care consultant*
Matsuda, Fujio *technology research center administrator*
Matthews, Wendy Schempp *psychologist, researcher*
Mayer, Patricia Lynn Sorci *mental health nurse, educator*
Maynard, E. Rose *retired school health services coordinator*
McCann, Michael F. *industrial hygienist*
McCartt, Susan Stockton *medical, surgical nurse*
McCoy, Patricia A. *psychology educator, writer, art critic*
McDaniel, Geraldine Howell *nursing adminsitrator*
McKenna, Richard Henry *healthcare management consultant*
McLaren, Susan Smith *therapist, healing touch practitioner, instructor*
McLendon, Dorothy *school psychologist*
Meahl, Barbara *occupational health nurse*
Meehan, John Joseph, Jr. *hospital administrator*
Meo, Roxanne Marie *critical care nurse*
Merenbloom, Robert Barry *hospital and medical school administrator*
Meyer, Harry Martin, Jr. *retired health science facility administrator*
Mich, Connie Rita *mental health nurse, educator*
Michalski, Carol Ann *medical, surgical and psychiatric nurse, writer, poet*
Mikel, Thomas Kelly, Jr. *laboratory administrator*
Milewski, Barbara Anne *pediatrics nurse, neonatal intensive care nurse*
Miller, Lillie M. *nursing educator*
Miller, Patricia Anne *speech and language pathologist*
Mills, Celeste Louise *hypnotherapist, professional magician*
Mitchell, Carol Ann *nursing educator*
Moffatt, Hugh McCulloch, Jr. *hospital administrator, physical therapist*
Mogielski, Phyllis Ann *health association administrator, psychotherapist*
Morandi, John Arthur, Jr. *nursing administrator, educator, nurse*
Moreland, Alvin Franklin *veterinarian*
Mueller, Barbara Stewart (Bobbie Mueller) *youth drug use prevention specialist, volunteer*
Muller, Frederica Daniela *psychology educator*
Munic, Rachelle Ethel *health services administrator*
Munier, William Boss *medical service executive*
Murphy, Mary Kathleen *nursing educator*
Nabholz, Mary Vaughan *rehabilitation nurse*
Nakagawa, Allen Donald *radiologic technologist*
Nangle, Carole Folz *counselor*
Nara, Bonnie A. *psychologist*
Natale, Laurel A. *nursing case manager*
Nattras, Ruth A(nn) *school nurse*
Naughton, Patricia J. *gerontological nurse, administrator, consultant*
Nearine, Robert James *educational psychologist*

Nedelman, Dorothy O'Flaherty primary care nurse
Nelson, Kaye Lynn healthcare consultant
Neumann, Forrest Karl retired hospital administrator
Newell, Miyako De Lige medical/surgical nurse
Newell, William Talman, Jr. hospital administrator
Nichols, Elizabeth Grace nursing educator, administrator
Noffsinger, Anne-Russell L. former nursing administrator, educator
Nolde, Shari Ann pediatrics, critical care nurse
Nordel, Patricia A. Olmstead medical/surgical, critical care, and obstetrical nurse
Norkin, Cynthia Clair physical therapist
Norman, Dudley Kent hospital administrator, nurse
Okolski, Cynthia Antonia psychotherapist, social worker
O'Neal, Harriet Roberts psychologist, psycholegal consultant
O'Neill, Donald Edmund health science executive
Orem, Cassandra Elizabeth health systems administrator, educator, author, holistic health practitioner, entrepreneur
Otis, Jack social work educator
Owens, Flora Concepcion critical care nurse
Oxhandler, Myra mental health nurse
Pace, Charles Robert psychologist, educator
Palermo, David Stuart retired psychology educator and administrator
Palisi, Anthony Thomas psychologist, educator
Pandya, Deanna Mears mental health counselor
Paquette, Elise Goossen rehabilitation nurse
Parham, Ellen Speiden nutrition educator
Parker, Harry John retired psychologist, educator
Patrick, Brenda Jean educational consultant
Paul, Evelyn Rose critical care nurse
Pearlmutter, Florence Nichols psychologist, therapist
Pepper, Dorothy Mae nurse
Pettit, Ghery DeWitt retired veterinary medicine educator
Pilisuk, Marc community psychology educator
Pilous, Betty Scheibel medical, surgical nurse
Pine, Charles Joseph clinical psychologist
Pinilla, Ana Rita neuropsychologist, researcher
Plaskonos, Anne school nurse
Pohlman, Janet Elizabeth healthcare executive, consultant
Porter, Marie Ann neonatal nurse, labor and delivery nurse
Poser, Ernest George psychologist, educator
Pracht, Drenda Kay psychologist
Preszler, Sharon Marie psychiatric home health nurse
Price, Annie Laurie senior health program manager
Price, Jeannine Alleenica clinical psychologist, retired computer consultant
Principe, Helen Mary medical case manager
Prisco, Frank J. psychotherapist
Przybylski, Sandra Marie speech pathologist
Quaife, Marjorie Clift nursing educator
Quattrone-Carroll, Diane Rose clinical social worker
Ragland, Terry Eugene emergency physician
Ragusea, Stephen Anthony psychologist, educator
Rainey, Claude Gladwin retired health care executive
Ramsey, Sandra Lynn psychotherapist
Randolph, Nancy Adele nutritionist, consultant
Rankin, Elizabeth Anne DeSalvo nurse, psychotherapist, educator, consultant
Rappach, Norma Jeanne health occupations educator
Rasmussen, Gail Maureen critical care nurse
Rathmell, Sandra Lee women's health nurse
Recine, Judy Ann surgical nurse
Reed, Adam Victor psychologist, engineer
Reed, Diane Marie psychologist
Reeves, Nancy Alice critical care nurse
Reisch, Michael Stewart social work educator
Reynolds, Louise Maxine Kruse retired school nurse
Ricards, June Elaine nursing consultant, administrator
Richardson, Kenneth T., Jr. psychotherapist, consultant, educator, author
Richardson, Wanda Louise Gibson family practice nurse
Richstone, Beverly June psychologist
Richter, Susan Mary medical and surgical nurse
Rickel, Annette Urso psychology educator
Riecken, Henry William psychologist, research director
Ries, Barbara Ellen alcohol and drug abuse services professional
Roberts, Joan I. social psychologist, educator
Robertson, R(ita) Kae nurse, administrator
Robinson, Angela Tomei clinical laboratory scientist
Robinson, Gail Patricia mental health counselor
Rodriguez, Nora social worker
Roubik, Charlene Mary nursing administrator
Rouw, Carla Sue Roberts medical nurse
Rubell, Bonnie Levine occupational therapist
Rubin, Zick psychology educator, lawyer, writer
Saari, Joy Ann family nurse practitioner, geriatrics medical and surgical nurse
Sadler, Sallie Inglis psychotherapist
Sameroff, Arnold Joshua developmental psychologist, educator, research scientist
Sanders, Augusta Swann retired nurse
Santos, Lisa Wells critical care nurse
Sardeson, Lynda Schultz nursing, diabetes educator
Sauvage, Lester Rosaire health facility administrator, cardiovascular surgeon
Savoy, Suzanne Marie critical care nurse
Scala, James health care industry consultant, author
Scheinblum, Anita Franusiszin pediatrics nurse
Schoenberg, April Mindy nursing administrator
Schwartz, Doris Ruhbel nursing educator, consultant
Schwartz, Ilene psychotherapist, educator
Schwartz, Michael Robinson health administrator
Seaver, Frank Alexander, III retired medical center administrator
Sewer, Doris E. critical care nurse, educator
Shaffer, Deborah nurse
Shanks, Kathryn Mary health care administrator
Shannon, Margaret T. nursing administrator, educator
Shapiro, Marcia Haskel speech and language pathologist
Shemansky, Cindy Ann nursing educator
Shure, Myrna Beth psychologist, educator
Simms, Maria Ester health services administrator
Simpson, Madeline Louisa psychologist
Smith, Ann C. nursing educator
Smith, Barbara Anne healthcare management company consultant
Smith, Leonard, Jr. medical/surgical and oncology nurse
Smith, Paula Marion urology and medical/surgical nurse
Smith, Ronald Lynn health system executive
Soeth, Sarah Laverne Reedy McMillan psychiatric nurse
Sollon, Phillip Benedict pharmacist, computer specialist
Solomon, Julius Oscar Lee pharmacist, hypnotherapist
Sonderegger, Theo Brown psychology educator
Soper, Anne Marie psychologist
Spagnuolo, Pasqualina Marie rehabilitation nurse
Spencer-Dahlem, Anita Joyce medical, surgical and critical care nurse
Splitstone, George Dale retired hospital administrator
Sprinthall, Norman Arthur psychology educator
Stallone, Thomas Michael clinical psychologist
Stancil, Irene Mack family counselor
Stewart, Barbara Lynne geriatrics nursing educator
Stewart, Cindy Kathleen school social worker, educator
Stillings, Dennis Otto research association administrator, consultant
Stockwell, Vivian Ann nursing educator
Stohlman, Connie Suzanne obstetrical gynecological nurse
Stratton, Mariann retired naval nursing administrator
Stratton-Whitcraft, Cathleen Sue critical care, pediatrics nurse
Strong, Sara Dougherty psychologist, family and custody mediator
Stump, John Edward veterinary anatomy educator, ethologist
Stundza, William Anthony mental health and retardation nurse
Suber, Robin Hall former medical and surgical nurse
Suhr, Geraldine M. medical/surgical nurse
Swan, Beth Ann nursing administrator
Swist, Marian Irene emergency nurse
Szantai, Linda Marie speech and language therapist
Tack, Theresa Rose women's health nurse
Talingdan, Arsenio Preza health science administrator
Taylor, Karen Annette mental health nurse
Tenney, Ruth Dawn medical/surgical nurse
Thomas, Cynthia Elizabeth advanced practice nurse
Thomassen, Pauline F. medical and surgical nurse
Thompson, Janice M. women's health, pediatrics nurse, educator
Thrasher, Rose Marie critical care and community health nurse
Tinner, Franziska Paula social worker, artist, designer, educator
Tourtillott, Eleanor Alice nurse, educational consultant
Tran, Henry Bang Q. social work case manager
Travers, Rose Elaine nursing supervisor
Trippet, Susan Elaine nursing educator
Tuck, Mary Beth nutritionist, educator
Tyler, Gail Madeleine nurse
Uhrich, Richard Beckley hospital executive, physician
Uzsoy, Patricia J. nursing educator and administrator
Van Blaricum, Amy Joan perioperative nurse
VanDemark, Michelle Volin critical care, neuroscience nurse
Vecchione, Jane Frances school nurse
Verney, Judith La Baie health program administrator
Verplanck, William Samuel psychologist, educator
Voelker, Margaret Irene (Meg Voelker) gerontology, medical, surgical nurse
Vogel, H. Victoria psychotherapist, educator
Vohs, James Arthur health care program executive
von Schwarz, Carolyn M. Geiger psychotherapist, educator
Vosburgh, Margaret Murphy hospital administrator
Wademan, Patsy Ann psychiatric, geriatrics nurse
Waldrop, Linda McGill medical administrator
Warner, Heidi C. clinical research nurse
Wasseen, Marjorie rehabilitation nurse, administrator
Weaver, Esther Ruth medical and surgical, geriatrics and oncology nurse
Webster, John Kingsley Ohl, II health administrator, rehabilitation manager
Wedeen, Marvin Meyer hospital executive
Weichler, Nancy Karen pediatric nurse
Weightman, Esther Lynn emergency trauma nurse
Wenzel, Sandra Lee Ann pediatrics nurse
Werner-Jacobsen, Emmy Elisabeth developmental psychologist
Wessler, Richard Lee psychology educator, psychotherapist
Whaley-Buckel, Marnie social service administrator
Wheatley, George Milholland medical administrator
Wiebe, Leonard Irving radiopharmacist, educator
Wiese, Neva critical care nurse
Wiley, Myra mental health nurse, educator
Wilson, Geneva June gerontology nurse, consultant
Wing, Lilly Kelly Raynor health services administrator
Winton, Howard Phillip optometrist
Witte, Raymond Henry psychologist, educator
Wolfberg, Melvin Donald optometrist, educational administrator, consultant
Woodruff, Martha Joyce home health agency executive
Woods, Geraldine Pittman health education consultant, educational consultant
Yoshiuchi, Ellen Haven childbirth educator
Yost, William Albert psychology educator, hearing researcher
Yother, Anthony Wayne critical care nurse, nurse manager
Younger, Betty Nichols social worker
Zimet, Lloyd psychologist, health planner, educator
Zimmerman, Lydia community health nurse, retired
Zucker, Jean Maxson nurse
Zweck, Ruth Edna Feeney human services administrator, psychiatric nurse

## HEALTHCARE: MEDICINE

### UNITED STATES

### ALABAMA

#### Auburn
McEldowney, Rene health care educator, consultant
Parsons, Daniel Lankester pharmaceutics educator

#### Birmingham
Allman, Richard Mark physician, gerontologist
Avent, Charles Kirk medical educator
Bridgers, William Frank physician, educator
Briggs, Dick Dowling, Jr. physician, educator
Bueschen, Anton Joslyn physician, educator
Caulfield, James Benjamin pathologist, educator
Cooper, John Allen Dicks medical educator
Cooper, Max Dale physician, medical educator, researcher
Crenshaw, James Faulkner physician
Curtis, John J. medical educator
Diethelm, Arnold Gillespie surgeon
Dubovsky, Eva Vitkova nuclear medicine physician, educator
Eby, Thomas Lee neuro-otologist, educator
Fallon, Harold Joseph physician, pharmacology and biochemistry educator
Finley, Wayne House medical educator
Foft, John William physician, educator
Fraser, Robert Gordon diagnostic radiologist
Frenette, Luc anesthesiologist, educator
Friedel, Robert Oliver physician
Friedlander, Michael J. neuroscientist, animal physiologist, medical educator
Granger, Wesley Miles medical educator
Hill, Samuel Richardson, Jr. medical educator
Hirschowitz, Basil Isaac physician
Kelly, David Reid pathologist
Kirklin, John Webster surgeon
Kochakian, Charles Daniel endocrinologist, educator
Koopman, William James medical educator, internist, immunologist
Lloyd, Lewis Keith, Jr. surgery and urology educator
McLain, David Andrew internist, rheumatologist, health facility administrator
Meezan, Elias pharmacologist, educator
Mowry, Robert Wilbur pathologist, educator
Nepomuceno, Cecil Santos physician
Nielsen, Leonard Maurice physician assistant
Nuckols, Frank Joseph psychiatrist
Oakes, Walter Jerry pediatric neurosurgeon
Omura, George Adolf medical oncologist
Oparil, Suzanne cardiologist, educator, researcher
Pacifico, Albert Dominick cardiovascular surgeon
Pfister, Roswell Robert ophthalmologist
Phillips, Michael Gray physician assistant, medical association administrator
Pittman, Constance Shen physician, educator
Pittman, James Allen, Jr. physician, educator
Pohost, Gerald Michael cardiologist, medical educator
Russell, Richard Olney, Jr. cardiologist, educator
Sams, W(iley) Mitchell, Jr. dermatologist
Schroeder, Harry William, Jr. physician, scientist
Skalka, Harold Walter ophthalmologist, educator
Strickler, Howard Martin physician
Tieszen, Ralph Leland, Sr. internist
Warnock, David Gene nephrologist
Zeiger, Herbert Evan, Jr. neurosurgeon

#### Daphne
Rinderknecht, Robert Eugene internist

#### Fairfield
Hamrick, Leon Columbus surgeon, medical director

#### Florence
Burford, Alexander Mitchell, Jr. physician, pathologist

#### Gadsden
Hanson, Ronald Windell cardiologist, lawyer, physicist

#### Huntsville
Huber, Donald Simon physician
Loux, Peter Charles anesthesiologist
Nuessle, William Raymond surgeon

#### Mobile
Anderson, Lewis Daniel medical educator, orthopaedic surgeon
Atkinson, William James, Jr. retired cardiologist
Barik, Sailen biomedical scientist, educator
Brogdon, Byron Gilliam physician, radiology educator
Conrad, Marcel Edward hematologist, educator
Durizch, Mary Lou radiology educator
Eichold, Samuel medical educator, medical museum curator
Gardner, William Albert, Jr. pathologist, medical foundation executive
Goodin, Julia C. medical investigator, state official, educator
Guarino, Anthony Michael pharmacologist, educator, consultant, counselor
Littleton, Jesse Talbot, III radiology educator
Parmley, Loren Francis, Jr. medical educator
Pitcock, James Kent head and neck surgical oncologist
Raider, Louis physician, radiologist
Rodning, Charles Bernard surgeon
Smith, Jesse Graham, Jr. dermatologist, educator
Thomas, Joseph Paul psychiatrist
White, Lowell E., Jr. medical educator

#### Montgomery
Boyd, Billy Willard internist
Frazer, David Hugh, Jr. allergist
Hunker, Fred Dominic internist, medical educator

#### Opelika
Brown, Robert Glenn plastic surgeon

#### Pelham
Allen, James Madison family practice physician, lawyer, consultant

#### Phenix City
Greene, Ernest Rinaldo, Jr. anesthesiologist, chemical engineer

#### Piedmont
Ulrich, Russell Dean osteopathic physician

#### Sylacauga
Poole, William Lannon, Jr. dermatologist

#### Talladega
Cooper, Suzane physician

#### Tuscaloosa
Mozley, Paul David obstetrics and gynecology educator
Pieroni, Robert Edward internist, educator
Umakantha, Kaggal V. physiatrist

### ALASKA

#### Anchorage
Archer, Gary William cardiologist
Chen, Barbara Marie anesthesiologist
Mala, Theodore Anthony physician, consultant

#### Fairbanks
Doolittle, William Hotchkiss internist

#### Valdez
Todd, Kathleen Gail physician

### ARIZONA

#### Casa Grande
Hopple, Janet Lynette medical technologist

#### Flagstaff
Reno, Joseph Harry retired orthopedic surgeon

#### Fountain Hills
Herzberger, Eugene E. retired neurosurgeon

#### Green Valley
Furman, Robert Howard physician, educator
Wasmuth, Carl Erwin physician, lawyer

#### Mesa
Boren, Kenneth Ray endocrinologist
Hagen, Nicholas Stewart medical educator, consultant
Sanders, Aaron Perry radiation biophysics educator
Thompson, Ronald MacKinnon family physician, artist, writer
Verschoor, John, IV physician assistant

#### Peoria
Palmer, Alice Eugenia retired physician, educator

#### Phoenix
Bower, Willis Herman retired psychiatrist, former medical administrator
Butler, Byron Clinton obstetrician, gynecologist
Calkins, Jerry Milan anesthesiologist, educator, administrator, biomedical engineer
Charlton, John Kipp pediatrician
Cozzi, Hugo Louis psychiatrist
Desser, Kenneth Barry cardiologist, educator
Fink, Joel Charles dermatologist
Goldenthal, Nathan David physician
Kail, Konrad physician
Kandell, Howard Noel pediatrician
Karpman, Robert Ronald orthopedic surgeon
Kurtz, Joan Helene pediatrician
Laufer, Nathan cardiologist
Lawrence, William Doran physician
Lee, Gilbert Brooks retired ophthalmology engineer
Lorenzen, Robert Frederick ophthalmologist
†Lovett, William Lee physician
Reed, Wallace Allison physician
Roth, Sanford Harold rheumatologist, health care administrator, educator
Rowley, Beverley Davies medical sociologist
Schiller, William Richard surgeon
Steward, Lester Howard psychiatrist, academic administrator, educator
Targovnik, Selma E. Kaplan physician
Tour, Robert Louis ophthalmologist
Wright, Richard Oscar, III pathologist, educator
Zerella, Joseph T. pediatric surgeon

#### Prescott
Alegre, Jose Alberto family practice physician

#### Scottsdale
Clement, Richard William plastic and reconstructive surgeon
DeHaven, Kenneth Le Moyne retired physician
Evans, Tommy Nicholas physician, educator
Friedman, Shelly Arnold cosmetic surgeon
Harrison, Harold Henry physician, scientist, educator
Kübler-Ross, Elisabeth physician
Lillo, Joseph Leonard osteopath, family practice physician
Nadler, Henry Louis pediatrician, geneticist, medical educator
Orford, Robert Raymond consulting physician
Reznick, Richard Howard pediatrician
Sanderson, David R. physician
Scherzer, Joseph Martin dermatologist

#### Sedona
Hawkins, David Ramon psychiatrist, writer, researcher
Shors, Clayton Marion cardiologist

#### Sun City
Pallin, Irving M. anesthesiologist
Pallin, Samuel Lear ophthalmologist

#### Sun City West
Forbes, Kenneth Albert Faucher urological surgeon

#### Sun Lakes
Houser, Harold Byron epidemiologist

#### Tempe
Anand, Suresh Chandra physician
Levin, Hal Alan psychiatrist

#### Tucson
Abrams, Herbert Kerman physician, educator
Ahern, Geoffrey Lawrence behavioral neurologist
Alberts, David Samuel physician, pharmacologist, educator
Alpert, Joseph Stephen physician, educator
Ben-Asher, M. David physician
Boyse, Edward Arthur research physician
Brosin, Henry Walter psychiatrist, educator
Burrows, Benjamin retired physician, educator
Capp, Michael Paul physician, educator
Carter, L. Philip neurosurgeon, consultant
Cisler, Theresa Ann osteopath, former nurse

Dalen, James Eugene *physician, educator*
David, Ronald Sigmund *psychiatrist*
Deluca, Dominick *medical educator, researcher*
Ewy, Gordon Allen *cardiologist, educator*
†Fernandez, Jose J. *cardiologist*
Giesser, Barbara Susan *neurologist, educator*
Graham, Anna Regina *pathologist, educator*
Harris, David Thomas *immunology educator*
Hildebrand, John G(rant) *neurobiologist, educator*
Hutter, John Joseph, Jr. *pediatric hematologist and oncologist, educator*
Kaszniak, Alfred Wayne *neuropsychologist*
Kischer, Clayton Ward *embryologist, educator*
Kotin, Paul *pathologist*
Krasner, Scott Allan *physician, health facility administrator*
†Labelle, James William *pediatrician*
Lebowitz, Michael David *epidemiologist*
Levenson, Alan Ira *psychiatrist, physician, educator*
Marchalonis, John Jacob *immunologist, educator*
Marcus, Frank Isadore *physician, educator*
†Marks, Sheldon Harris Feiler *urologist*
Martinez, Maria Dolores *pediatrician*
Masters, William Howell *physician, educator*
McCuskey, Robert Scott *anatomy and cell biology educator, researcher*
Nugent, Charles Arter *physician*
Reinmuth, Oscar MacNaughton *physician, educator*
Salmon, Sydney Elias *medical educator, director*
Sibley, William Austin *neurologist, educator*
Smith, Josef Riley *internist*
Stearns, Elliott Edmund, Jr. *retired surgeon*
†Weil, Andrew Thomas *physician*
Weinstein, Ronald S. *physician, pathologist, educator*
Witte, Marlys Hearst *internist, educator*
Woolfenden, James Manning *nuclear medicine physician, educator*
Yan, Chong Chao *pharmacology, toxicology and nutrition researcher*
Zukoski, Charles Frederick *surgeon, educator*

### Vail
Reichlin, Seymour *physician, educator*

### Yuma
Johnston, Gessica T. *emergency physician*
Martin, James Franklin *physician, lawyer*

## ARKANSAS

### Bella Vista
Rose, Donald L. *physician, educator*

### Clarksville
Pennington, Donald Harris *physician*

### Conway
McCarron, Robert Frederick, II *orthopedic surgeon*

### De Valls Bluff
Jones, Robert Eugene *physician*

### El Dorado
Tommey, Charles Eldon *retired surgeon*

### Fort Smith
Coleman, Michael Dortch *nephrologist*
Hoge, Marlin Boyd *surgeon*
Howell, James Tennyson *allergist, immunologist, pediatrician*
Snider, James Rhodes *radiologist*

### Jefferson
Hart, Ronald Wilson *radiobiologist, toxicologist, government research executive*

### Little Rock
Bates, Joseph Henry *physician, educator*
†Brodsky, Michael Carroll *ophthalmologist, educator*
Campbell, Gilbert Sadler *surgery educator, surgeon*
Cave, Mac Donald *anatomy educator*
Deer, Philip James, Jr. *ophthalmologist*
Diner, Wilma Canada *radiologist, educator*
Doherty, James Edward, III *physician, educator*
Elbein, Alan David *medical science educator*
Ferris, Ernest Joseph *radiology educator*
Garcia-Rill, Edgar Enrique *neuroscientist*
Guggenheim, Frederick Gibson *psychiatry educator*
Hough, Aubrey Johnston, Jr. *pathologist, physician, educator*
Jansen, G. Thomas *dermatologist*
Kemp, Stephen Frank *pediatric endocrinologist, educator, composer*
†Lang, Nicholas Paul *surgeon*
Lucy, Dennis Durwood, Jr. *neurologist*
Maloney, Francis Patrick *physiatrist, educator*
McMillan, Donald Edgar *pharmacologist*
Ramaprasad, Subbaraya *medical educator*
Sotomora-von Ahn, Ricardo Federico *pediatrician, educator*
Stead, William White *physician, educator, public health administrator*
Suen, James Yee *otolaryngologist, educator*
Ward, Harry Pfeffer *physician, university chancellor*
Yousuff, Sarah Safia *physician*

### North Little Rock
Griffith, Jack William *medical librarian*

### Rogers
Summerlin, William Talley *allergist, immunologist, dermatologist*

### Scranton
Uzman, Betty Geren *pathologist, retired educator*

## CALIFORNIA

### Agoura Hills
deCiutiis, Alfred Charles Maria *medical oncologist, television producer*

### Alameda
Whorton, M. Donald *occupational and environmental health physician, epidemiologist*

### Alamo
Burchell, Mary Cecilia *surgeon*

### Anaheim
Carvajal, Jorge Armando *endocrinologist, internist*

### Apple Valley
Win, Khin Swe *anesthesiologist*

### Atascadero
†Knapp, Robert S. *psychiatrist*

### Bakersfield
Izenstark, Joseph Louis *radiologist, physician, educator*
Rahal, Paramvir Singh *physician*
Rice, Frances Mae *pediatrician*

### Belvedere Tiburon
Behrman, Richard Elliot *pediatrician, neonatologist, university dean*

### Berkeley
Abel, Carlos Alberto *immunologist*
Budinger, Thomas Francis *radiologist, educator*
Caetano, Raul *psychiatrist, educator*
Castro, Joseph Ronald *physician, oncology researcher, educator*
Diamond, Marian Cleeves *anatomy educator*
Duhl, Leonard *psychiatrist, educator*
Falkner, Frank Tardrew *physician, educator*
Goodman, Corey Scott *neurobiology educator, researcher*
Grossman, Elmer Roy *pediatrician*
Hurst, Deborah *pediatric hematologist*
Koshland, Marian Elliott *immunologist, educator*
Patterson, Lloyd Clifford *psychiatrist*
Policoff, Leonard David *physician, educator*
Poor, Clarence Alexander *retired physician*
Roller, Robert Douglas, III *psychiatrist*
Seitz, Walter Stanley *cardiovascular research consultant*
Syme, Sherman Leonard *epidemiology educator*
Tempelis, Constantine Harry *immunologist, educator*
†Thygeson, Nels Marcus *physician*

### Beverly Hills
Allen, Howard Norman *cardiologist, educator*
Catz, Boris *endocrinologist, educator*
Fein, William *ophthalmologist*
Gilberg, Arnold L. *psychiatrist and psychoanalyst*
Giorgi, Elsie Agnes *physician*
Karpman, Harold Lew *cardiologist, educator, author*
Klein, Arnold William *dermatologist*
Lesser, Gershon Melvin *physician, lawyer, medical and legal media commentator*
Menkes, John Hans *pediatric neurologist*
Stein, Myron *internist, educator*
Towers, Bernard Leonard *medical educator*

### Brawley
Jaquith, George Oakes *ophthalmologist*

### Burbank
Casey, William Carleton *physician, urologist*
†Renner, Andrew Ihor *surgeon*

### Burlingame
Beattie, George Chapin *orthopedic surgeon*
Gradinger, Gilbert Paul *plastic surgeon*

### Camarillo
Street, Dana Morris *orthopedic surgeon*

### Camp Pendleton
Edwards, Bruce George *ophthalmologist, naval officer*

### Capo Beach
Roemer, Edward Pier *neurologist*

### Carmel
Felch, William Campbell *internist, editor*

### Carmichael
Wagner, Carruth John *physician*

### Chatsworth
Chernof, David *internist*

### Chico
Ritter, Dale William *obstetrician, gynecologist*

### Chula Vista
Allen, Henry Wesley *biomedical researcher*
Cohen, Elaine Helena *pediatrician, pediatric cardiologist*

### Claremont
Gabriel, Earl A. *osteopathic physician*

### Coronado
Mock, David Clinton, Jr. *internist*

### Corte Madera
Epstein, William Louis *dermatologist, educator*

### Covina
Schneider, Calvin *physician*
Takei, Toshihisa *otolaryngologist*

### Culver City
Rose, Margarete Erika *pathologist*

### Daly City
Shaw, Richard Eugene *cardiovascular researcher*

### Davis
Cardiff, Robert Darrell *pathology educator*
Enders, Allen Coffin *anatomy educator*
Gardner, Murray Briggs *pathologist, educator*
Hance, Anthony James *retired pharmacologist, educator*
Hendrickx, Andrew George *anatomy educator*
Hollinger, Mannfred Alan *pharmacologist, educator, toxicologist*
Lazarus, Gerald Sylvan *physician, university dean*
Lipscomb, Paul Rogers *orthopedic surgeon, educator*
Palmer, Philip Edward Stephen *radiologist*
Plopper, Charles George *anatomist, cell biologist*
Richman, David Paul *neurologist, researcher*
Schenker, Marc Benet *preventive medicine educator*
Stowell, Robert Eugene *pathologist, retired educator*
Tupper, Charles John *physician, educator*
Williams, Hibbard Earl *medical educator, physician*
Youmans, Julian Ray *neurosurgeon, educator*

### Deer Park
Hodgkin, John E. *pulmonologist*

### Del Mar
Lesko, Ronald Michael *osteopathic physician*

### Downey
Gong, Henry, Jr. *physician, researcher*
Hackney, Jack Dean *physician*
Magnes, Harry Alan *physician*
Redeker, Allan Grant *physician, medical educator*
Sapico, Francisco Lejano *internist, educator*
Shapiro, Richard Stanley *physician*

### Duarte
Balch, Charles M. *surgeon, educator*
Comings, David Edward *physician, medical genetics scientist*
Kovach, John Stephen *oncologist, research center administrator*
Levine, Rachmiel *physician*

### El Cajon
Turk, Robert Louis *radiologist*

### El Macero
Raventos, Antolin *radiology educator*

### Encinitas
Satur, Nancy Marlene *dermatologist*

### Encino
Costea, Nicolas Vincent *physician, researcher*

### Escondido
Everton, Marta Ve *ophthalmologist*

### Fairfield
Martin, Clyde Verne *psychiatrist*
Munn, William Charles, II *psychiatrist*

### Fontana
Barry(-Branks), Diane Dolores *podiatrist*

### Fremont
Steinmetz, Seymour *pediatrician*

### Fresno
Falcone, Alfonso Benjamin *physician and biochemist*
Holmes, Albert William, Jr. *physician*
Leigh, Hoyle *psychiatrist, educator, writer*
Patton, Jack Thomas *family practice physician*
Smith, V. Roy *neurosurgeon*
Thompson, Leonard Russell *pediatrician*

### Fullerton
Aston, Edward Ernest, IV *dermatologist*
†Sugarman, Michael *physician, rheumatologist*

### Garden Grove
Wong, Michael Henry *anesthesiologist*

### Glendale
Dent, Ernest DuBose, Jr. *pathologist*
Kernen, Jules Alfred *pathologist*

### Greenbrae
Levy, S. William *dermatologist*
Parnell, Francis William, Jr. *physician*

### Half Moon Bay
Robertson, Abel L., Jr. *pathologist*

### Hemet
Galletta, Joseph Leo *physician*
Kopiloff, George *psychiatrist*

### Hillsborough
Kraft, Robert Arnold *retired medical educator, physician*

### Huntington Beach
Desai, Veena Balvantrai *obstetrician and gynecologist, educator*

### Indian Wells
Carter, Paul Richard *physician*

### Indio
Fischer, Craig Leland *physician*

### Inglewood
Jobe, Frank Wilson *orthopedic surgeon*
Zemel, Norman Paul *orthopedic surgeon*

### Irvine
Connolly, John Earle *surgeon, educator*
Felton, Jean Spencer *physician*
Friou, George Jacob *immunologist, physician, educator*
Gottschalk, Louis August *neuropsychiatrist, psychoanalyst*
Gupta, Sudhir *immunologist, educator*
Hubbell, Floyd Allan *physician, educator*
Jones, Edward George *anatomy and neurobiology professor, department chairman*
Korc, Murray *endocrinologist*
Miledi, Ricardo *neurobiologist*
Tobis, Jerome Sanford *physician*
van-den-Noort, Stanley *physician, educator*
Weinstein, Gerald D. *dermatology educator*

### La Canada Flintridge
Byrne, George Melvin *physician*

### La Jolla
Anderson, Richard William *retired psychiatrist, educator*
Barrett-Connor, Elizabeth Louise *epidemiologist, educator*
Bergan, John Jerome *vascular surgeon*
Beutler, Ernest *physician, research scientist*
Block, Melvin August *surgeon, educator*
Brown, Stuart I. *ophthalmologist, educator*
Carmichael, David Burton *physician*
Churg, Jacob *pathologist*
Covell, Ruth Marie *medical educator, medical school administrator*
Dalessio, Donald John *physician, neurologist, educator*
Dixon, Frank James *medical scientist, educator*
Edwards, Charles Cornell *physician, research administrator*
Fosburg, Richard Garrison *cardiothoracic surgeon*
Friedmann, Theodore *physician*
Garland, Cedric Frank *epidemiologist, educator*
Gill, Gordon N. *medical educator*
Gittes, Ruben Foster *urological surgeon*
Hamburger, Robert N. *pediatrics educator, consultant*
Hench, Philip Kahler *physician*
Hofmann, Alan Frederick *biomedical educator, researcher*
Johnson, Allen Dress *cardiologist*
Jorgensen, Judith Ann *psychiatrist*
Katzman, Robert *medical educator, neurologist*
Keeney, Edmund Ludlow *physician*
Klinman, Norman Ralph *immunologist, medical educator*
Lele, Padmakar Pratap *physician, educator*
Mathews, Kenneth Pine *physician, educator*
Nakamura, Robert Motoharu *pathologist*
Nyhan, William Leo *pediatrician, educator*
Rearden, Carole Ann *clinical pathologist, educator*
Resnik, Robert *medical educator*
Rosenfeld, Michael G. *medical educator*
Spiegelberg, Hans Leonhard *medical educator*
Squire, Larry Ryan *neuroscientist, psychologist, educator*
Steinberg, Daniel *preventive medicine physician, educator*
Tan, Eng Meng *immunologist, rheumatologist, biomedical scientist*
Teirstein, Paul Shepherd *physician, health facility administrator*
Terry, Robert Davis *neuropathologist, educator*
Thal, Leon Joel *neuroscientist*
Weigle, William Oliver *immunologist, educator*
Yen, Samuel S(how)-C(hih) *obstetrics and gynecology educator, reproductive endocrinologist*

### La Mesa
Wohl, Armand Jeffrey *cardiologist*

### Laguna Hills
Ierardi, Stephen John *physician*
Ross, Mathew *psychiatry educator*
Widyolar, Sheila Gayle *dermatologist*

### Laguna Niguel
Sturdevant, Charles Oliver *physician, neuropsychiatrist*

### Lake Isabella
Fraser, Eleanor Ruth *radiologist, administrator*

### Larkspur
Shepard, James Edward *physician*

### Lodi
Albert, N. Erick *urologist*

### Loma Linda
Adey, William Ross *physician*
Aloia, Roland Craig *scientist, administrator, educator*
Alvarez, Ofelia Amparo *medical educator*
Ashwal, Stephen *pediatrician, child neurologist, educator*
Behrens, Berel Lyn *physician, academic administrator*
Brandstater, Murray Everett *physiatrist*
Buchholz, John Nicholas *pharmacology educator*
Bull, Brian Stanley *pathology educator, medical consultant, business executive*
Chan, Philip J. *medical educator*
Coggin, Charlotte Joan *cardiologist, educator*
Condon, Stanley Charles *gastroenterologist*
Hardesty, Robert Alan *plastic surgeon*
Hinshaw, David B., Jr. *radiologist*
Johns, Varner Jay, Jr. *medical educator*
Kirk, Gerald Arthur *nuclear radiologist*
Kuhn, Irvin Nelson *hematologist, oncologist*
Llaurado, Josep G. *nuclear medicine physician, scientist*
Mace, John Weldon *pediatrician*
Peterson, John Eric *physician, educator*
Rendell-Baker, Leslie *anesthesiologist, educator*
Roberts, Walter Herbert Beatty *anatomist*
Sewell, Robert Dalton *pediatrician*
Slater, James Munro *radiation oncologist*
Strother, Allen *biochemical pharmacologist, researcher*
Young, Lionel Wesley *radiologist*

### Long Beach
Alkon, Ellen Skillen *physician*
Anderson, Garry Michael *diagnostic radiologist*
Fagan, Frederic *neurosurgeon*
Kurnick, Nathaniel Bertrand *oncologist-hematologist, educator, researcher*
Kwaan, Jack Hau Ming *retired physician*
Loganbill, G. Bruce *logopedic pathologist*
Looney, Gerald Lee *medical educator, administrator*
Macer, George Armen, Jr. *orthopedic hand surgeon*
Mills, Don Harper *pathology and psychiatry educator, lawyer*
†Moran, Edgar M. *physician, educator*
†Stemmer, Edward Alan *surgeon, educator*
Todd, Malcolm Clifford *surgeon*
White, Katherine Elizabeth *retired pediatrician*

### Los Altos
Abrams, Arthur Jay *physician*

### Los Angeles
Ahn, Samuel Seunghae *vascular surgeon, researcher, consultant*
Anderson, Kathryn Duncan *surgeon*
Apt, Leonard *physician*
Archie, Carol Louise *obstetrician and gynecologist, educator*
Ashley, Sharon Anita *pediatric anesthesiologist*
Askanas-Engel, Valerie *neurologist, educator, researcher*
Bao, Joseph Yue-Se *orthopaedist, microsurgeon, educator*

Barker, Wiley Franklin *surgeon, educator*
†Barrett, Cynthia Townsend *neonatologist*
Beart, Robert W., Jr. *surgeon, educator*
Beck, John Christian *physician, educator*
Becker, Donald Paul *surgeon, neurosurgeon*
Berglund, Robin G. *psychiatrist, former corporate executive*
Bernstein, Sol *cardiologist, educator*
Bessman, Samuel Paul *pediatrician, biochemist*
Biles, John Alexander *pharmacology educator, chemistry educator*
Blahd, William Henry *physician*
Bluestone, David Allan *pediatrician*
Boak, Ruth Alice *physician, educator*
Bodey, Bela *immunomorphologist*
Bondareff, William *psychiatry educator*
Borenstein, Daniel Bernard *physician, educator*
Bowman, C. Michael *physician*
Braunstein, Glenn David *physician, educator*
Breslow, Lester *physician, educator*
Brunell, Philip A. *physician*
Burgess, J. Wesley *neuropsychiatrist*
Chandor, Stebbins Bryant *pathologist*
Cherry, James Donald *physician*
Cicciarelli, James Carl *immunology educator*
Clemente, Carmine Domenic *anatomist, educator*
Cochran, Sachiko Tomie *radiologist*
Cook, Ian Ainsworth *psychiatrist, researcher, educator*
Cooper, Edwin Lowell *anatomy educator*
Corman, Marvin Leonard *surgeon*
Dai, Jing Chu Ling *medical writer, researcher*
Dann, Francis Joseph *dermatologist, educator*
Danoff, Dudley Seth *surgeon, urologist*
Davidson, Ezra C., Jr. *physician, educator*
De Cherney, Alan Hersh *obstetrics and gynecology educator*
Detels, Roger *epidemiologist, physician, former university dean*
Dignam, William Joseph *obstetrician, gynecologist, educator*
Edgerton, Bradford Wheatly *plastic surgeon*
Engel, William King *neurologist, educator*
Enstrom, James Eugene *cancer epidemiologist*
Ettenger, Robert Bruce *physician, nephrologist*
Feig, Stephen Arthur *pediatrics educator, hematologist, oncologist*
Fish, Barbara *psychiatrist, educator*
Fleming, Arthur Wallace *physician, surgeon*
Fogelman, Alan Marcus *internist*
Fonkalsrud, Eric Walter *pediatric surgeon, educator*
Fowler, Vincent R. *dermatologist*
Fox, Saul Lourie *physician, researcher*
Frasier, S. Douglas *medical educator*
Fricker, John Arthur *pediatrician, educator*
Friedman, Nathan Baruch *physician*
Fyfe, Alistair Ian *cardiologist, scientist, educator*
Gale, Robert Peter *physician, scientist, researcher*
Geller, Stephen Arthur *pathologist, educator*
Giannotta, Steven Louis *neurosurgery educator*
Gold, Richard Horace *radiologist*
Gonick, Harvey Craig *nephrologist, educator*
Gorney, Roderic *psychiatry educator*
Gorski, Roger Anthony *neuroendocrinologist, educator*
Grinnell, Alan Dale *neurobiologist, educator, researcher*
Guze, Phyllis Arlene *internist, educator, academic administrator*
Harold, John Gordon *cardiologist, internist*
Haskell, Charles Mortimer *medical oncologist, educator*
Haywood, L. Julian *physician, educator*
Henriksen MacLean, Eva Hansine *former anesthesiology educator*
Hoang, Duc Van *theoretical pathologist, educator*
Holland, Gary Norman *ophthalmologist, educator*
Horwitz, David A. *physician, scientist, educator*
House, John W. *otologist*
Hsiao, Chie-Fang *neuroscientist*
Hughes, Everett Clark *otolaryngology educator*
Jalali, Behnaz *psychiatrist, educator*
Jelliffe, Roger Woodham *cardiologist, clinical pharmacologist*
Johnson, Cage Saul *hematologist, educator*
Kambara, George Kiyoshi *retired ophthalmologist, educator*
Kamil, Elaine Scheiner *physician, educator*
Kaplan, Samuel *pediatric cardiologist*
Katz, Roger *pediatrician, educator*
Katz, Ronald Lewis *physician, educator*
Kelly, Arthur Paul *physician*
Kerman, Barry Martin *ophthalmologist, educator*
Kilburn, Kaye Hatch *medical educator*
Koch, Richard *pediatrician, educator*
Korsch, Barbara M. *pediatrician*
Kramer, Barry Alan *psychiatrist*
Landing, Benjamin Harrison *pathologist, educator*
Lawrence, Sanford Hull *physician, immunochemist*
Levey, Gerald Saul *physician, educator*
Lewin, Klaus J. *pathologist, educator*
Lewis, Charles Edwin *physician, educator*
Liberman, Robert Paul *psychiatry educator, researcher, writer*
Lim, David Jong-Jai *otolaryngology educator, researcher*
Liu, Don *ophthalmologist, medical researcher*
Longmire, William Polk, Jr. *physician, surgeon*
Mabee, John Richard *physician assistant, educator*
Makowka, Leonard *medical educator, surgeon*
Malcolm, Dawn Grace *family physician*
Maloney, Robert Keller *ophthalmologist, medical educator*
Marmor, Judd *psychiatrist, educator*
Maronde, Robert Francis *internist, clinical pharmacologist, educator*
Mellinkoff, Sherman Mussoff *medical educator*
Mihan, Richard *retired dermatologist*
Miles, Samuel Israel *psychiatrist, educator*
Mishell, Daniel R., Jr. *physician, educator*
Moxley, John Howard, III *physician*
Moy, Ronald Leonard *dermatologist, surgeon*
Nathwani, Bharat Narottam *pathologist, consultant*
Neufeld, Naomi Das *pediatric endocrinologist*
Noble, Ernest Pascal *physician, biochemist, educator*
Ourieff, Arthur Jacob *psychiatrist*
Parker, John William *pathology educator, investigator*
Parker, Robert George *radiation oncology educator, academic administrator*
Parmelee, Arthur Hawley, Jr. *pediatric medical educator*
†Passaro, Edward, Jr. *surgeon, educator*
Perloff, Joseph Kayle *cardiologist*
Pitkin, Roy Macbeth *retired medical educator*
Rachelefsky, Gary S. *medical educator*
Rangell, Leo *psychiatrist, psychoanalyst*
Rimoin, David Lawrence *physician, geneticist*
Ritvo, Edward Ross *psychiatrist*
Roemer, Milton Irwin *physician, educator*
Ross, Joseph Foster *physician, educator*
Ryan, Stephen Joseph, Jr. *ophthalmology educator, university dean*
Sadun, Alfredo Arrigo *neuro-ophthalmologist, scientist, educator*
Sager, Philip Travis *academic physician, cardiac electrophysiologist*
Sarian, Jirair Nerses *radiologist*
Sarnat, Bernard George *plastic surgeon, educator, researcher*
Savage, Edward Warren, Jr. *physician*
Sawyer, Charles Henry *anatomist, educator*
Scheibel, Arnold Bernard *psychiatrist, educator, research director*
Schelbert, Heinrich Ruediger *nuclear medicine physician*
Schiff, Martin *physician, surgeon*
Schneider, Edward Lewis *medicine educator, research administrator*
Schwabe, Arthur David *physician, educator*
Siegel, Michael Elliot *nuclear medicine physician, educator*
Siegel, Sheldon C. *physician*
Solomon, David Harris *physician, educator*
Solomon, George Freeman *academic psychiatrist*
Sprague, Norman Frederick, Jr. *surgeon, educator*
Steckel, Richard J. *radiologist, academic administrator*
Stern, Walter Eugene *neurosurgeon, educator*
Straatsma, Bradley Ralph *ophthalmologist, educator*
Sullivan, Stuart Francis *anesthesiologist, educator*
†Tabachnick, Norman Donald *psychiatrist, educator*
Titus, Edward Depue *psychiatrist, administrator*
Tompkins, Ronald K. *surgeon*
Tourtellotte, Wallace William *neurologist*
Tranquada, Robert Ernest *medical educator, physician*
Urist, Marshall Raymond *orthopedic surgeon, educator, researcher*
Van Der Meulen, Joseph Pierre *neurologist*
Villablanca, Jaime Rolando *medical scientist, educator*
Vredevoe, Donna Lou *research immunologist, microbiologist, educator*
Walsh, John Harley *medical educator*
Weiner, Leslie Philip *neurology educator, researcher*
Weinstein, Irwin Marshall *internist, hematologist*
Weiss, Martin Harvey *neurosurgeon, educator*
Wilkinson, Alan Herbert *nephrologist, medical educator*
Wilson, M. Roy *medical educator*
Wilson, Miriam Geisendorfer *retired physician, educator*
Wincor, Michael Z. *psychopharmacology educator, clinician, researcher*
Withers, Hubert Rodney *radiotherapist, radiobiologist, educator*
Woolf, Nancy Jean *neuroscientist, educator*
Wright, Kenneth Weston *pediatric ophthalmologist*
Yamamoto, Joe *psychiatrist, educator*
Zawacki, Bruce Edwin *surgeon, ethicist*

### Los Gatos
Cohen, James Robert *oncologist, hematologist*

### Malibu
Jenden, Donald James *pharmacologist, educator*
Morgenstern, Leon *surgeon*

### Martinez
Efron, Robert *neurology educator, research institute administrator*
Love, Gordon Lee *pathologist, researcher*
McKnight, Lenore Ravin *child psychiatrist*

### Menlo Park
Glaser, Robert Joy *physician, foundation executive*
Hoffman, Thomas Edward *dermatologist*
Kovachy, Edward Miklos, Jr. *psychiatrist*

### Mill Valley
Wallerstein, Robert Solomon *psychiatrist*

### Milpitas
Chiu, Peter Yee-Chew *physician*

### Modesto
Goldberg, Robert Lewis *preventive and occupational medicine physician*

### Monterey
Black, Robert Lincoln *pediatrician*

### Moraga
Frey, William Rayburn *healthcare educator, consultant*

### Morro Bay
Eggertsen, Paul Fred *psychiatrist*

### Mountain View
Gelpi, Armand Philippe *internist*
Warren, Richard Wayne *obstetrician, gynecologist*

### Napa
Francis, Marc Baruch *pediatrician*
Zimmermann, John Paul *plastic surgeon*

### National City
Morgan, Jacob Richard *cardiologist*

### Newport Beach
Kahn, Douglas Gerard *psychiatrist*
Zalta, Edward *otorhinolaryngologist, physician*

### Northridge
Davidson, Sheldon Jerome *hematologist*

### Novato
Franklin, Robert Blair *cardiologist*
Reed, Dwayne Milton *medical epidemiologist, educator*

### Oakland
Barricks, Michael Eli *retinal surgeon*
Collen, Morris Frank *physician*
Friedman, Gary David *epidemiologist, research facility administrator*
Johnson, Leonard Morris *pediatric surgeon*
Ng, Lawrence Ming-Loy *pediatric cardiologist*
Weinmann, Robert Lewis *neurologist*

### Oceanside
Haley, Thomas John *retired pharmacologist*

### Orange
Achauer, Bruce Michael *plastic surgeon*
Anzel, Sanford Harold *orthopedic surgeon*
Armentrout, Steven Alexander *oncologist*
Barr, Ronald Jeffrey *dermatologist, pathologist*
Berk, Jack Edward *physician, educator*
Crumley, Roger Lee *surgeon, educator*
Dana, Edward Runkle *physician, educator*
†Eagan, Robert T. *oncologist*
Furnas, David William *plastic surgeon*
Gardin, Julius Markus *cardiologist, educator*
Lott, Ira Totz *pediatric neurologist*
MacArthur, Carol Jeanne *pediatric otolaryngology educator*
Morgan, Beverly Carver *physician, educator*
Mosier, Harry David, Jr. *physician, educator*
Quilligan, Edward James *obstetrician, gynecologist, educator*
Rowen, Marshall *radiologist*
Skinner, Harry Bryant *orthopaedic surgery educator*
Thompson, William Benbow, Jr. *obstetrician, gynecologist, educator*
Vaziri, Nosratola Dabir *internist, nephrologist, educator*
Wilson, Archie Fredric *medical educator*
Yu, Jen *medical educator*

### Oxnard
Walker, Lorenzo Giles *surgeon, educator*

### Pacific Palisades
Claes, Daniel John *physician*
Dignam, Robert Joseph *retired orthopaedic surgeon*

### Palm Desert
McKissock, Paul Kendrick *plastic surgeon*

### Palm Springs
Weil, Max Harry *physician, medical educator, medical scientist*

### Palo Alto
Adamson, Geoffrey David *reproductive endocrinologist, surgeon*
Amylon, Michael David *physician, educator*
Bhatt, Kiran *physician, educator*
Blaschke, Terrence Francis *medicine and molecular pharmacology educator*
Britton, M(elvin) C(reed), Jr. *physician, rheumatologist*
Charlton, Randolph Seville *psychiatrist, educator*
Chase, Robert Arthur *surgeon, educator*
Chen, Stephen Shi-hua *pathologist, biochemist*
Date, Elaine Satomi *physician*
Dement, William Charles *sleep researcher, medical educator*
Desai, Karvin Hirendra *pediatrician*
Donaldson, Sarah Susan *radiologist*
Farber, Eugene Mark *psoriasis research institute administrator*
Farquhar, John William *physician, educator*
Fries, James Franklin *internal medicine educator*
Goldstein, Avram *pharmacology educator*
Goldstein, Mary Kane *physician*
Harris, Edward D., Jr. *physician*
Hays, Marguerite Thompson *physician*
Holman, Halsted Reid *medical educator*
Jadvar, Hossein *physician, biomedical engineer*
Jamison, Rex Lindsay *medical educator*
Jamplis, Robert Warren *surgeon, medical foundation executive*
Kundu, Smriti Kana *biomedical scientist*
Lane, Alfred Thomas *medical educator*
Lane, William Kenneth *physician*
Linna, Timo Juhani *immunologist, researcher, educator*
Litt, Iris Figarsky *pediatrics educator*
Mansour, Tag Eldin *pharmacologist, educator*
Michie, Sara H. *pathologist, educator*
Polan, Mary Lake *obstetrics and gynecology educator*
Robinson, Thomas Nathaniel *pediatrician, educator, researcher*
Salvatierra, Oscar, Jr. *physician*
Sawyer, Wilbur Henderson *pharmacologist, educator*
Schrier, Stanley Leonard *physician, educator*
Schurman, David Jay *orthopedic surgeon, educator*
Shortliffe, Edward Hance *internist, medical informatics educator*
Shuer, Lawrence Mendel *neurosurgery educator*
Strober, Samuel *immunologist, educator*
Tune, Bruce Malcolm *pediatrics educator, renal toxicologist*
Urquhart, John *medical researcher, educator*
Wong, Nancy L. *dermatologist*

### Palos Verdes Peninsula
Haynes, Moses Alfred *physician*
Thomas, Claudewell Sidney *psychiatry educator*

### Panorama City
Bass, Harold Neal *pediatrician, medical geneticist*

### Pasadena
Cailleouette, James Clyde *physician*
Harvey, Joseph Paul, Jr. *orthopedist, educator*
Helsper, James T. *surgical oncologist, researcher, educator*
Lake, Kevin Bruce *medical association administrator*
Mathies, Allen Wray, Jr. *physician, hospital administrator*
Opel, William *medical research administrator*
Yeager, Caroline Hale *radiologist, consultant*

### Piedmont
Cuttle, Tracy Donald *physician, former naval officer*
Hughes, James Paul *physician*
Montgomery, Theodore Ashton *physician*
Sharpton, Thomas *physician*

### Pinole
Harvey, Elinor B. *child psychiatrist*
Naughton, James Lee *internist*

### Placerville
Bonser, Quentin *retired surgeon*

### Portola Valley
Creevy, Donald Charles *obstetrician-gynecologist*
Fogarty, Thomas James *surgery educator*

### Rancho Mirage
Cone, Lawrence Arthur *research medicine educator*
Lacey, Beatrice Cates *psychophysiologist*

### Rancho Santa Fe
Affeldt, John Ellsworth *physician*
Rockoff, S. David *radiologist, physician, educator*

### Redlands
Flores, John A. *internist*
Richardson, A(rthur) Leslie *former medical group consultant*
Skoog, William Arthur *retired oncologist*

### Redwood City
Seltzer, Ronald Anthony *radiologist, educator*
Strauss, Judith Feigin *physician*

### Richmond
Rubanyi, Gabor Michael *medical research company executive*

### Riverside
Childs, Donald Richard *pediatric endocrinologist*
Jukkola, George Duane *obstetrician, gynecologist*
Jung, Timothy Tae Kun *otolaryngologist*
Linaweaver, Walter Ellsworth, Jr. *physician*

### Rolling Hills Estates
Bellis, Carroll Joseph *surgeon*
Kline, Frank Menefee *psychiatrist*

### Ross
Way, Walter Lee *anesthetist, pharmacologist, educator*

### Rowland Heights
Allen, Delmas James *anatomist, educator, university administrator*

### Sacramento
Benfield, John Richard *surgeon*
Chapman, Michael William *orthopedist, educator*
Chole, Richard Arthur *otolaryngologist, educator*
Cunningham, Mary Elizabeth *physician*
Dorn, Robert Murray *physician, psychiatrist, educator, psychoanalyst*
Evrigenis, John Basil *obstetrician-gynecologist*
Frey, Charles Frederick *surgeon, educator*
Lynch, Peter John *dermatologist*
Rounds, Barbara Lynn *psychiatrist*
Shapero, Harris Joel *pediatrician*
Sharma, Arjun Dutta *cardiologist*
Stevenson, Thomas Ray *plastic surgeon*
Styne, Dennis Michael *physician*
Wolfman, Earl Frank, Jr. *surgeon, educator*

### Salinas
Leighton, Henry Alexander *physician, consultant*
Phillips, John P(aul) *retired neurosurgeon*

### San Bernardino
De Haas, David Dana *emergency physician*
Nies, Boyd Arthur *hematologist, oncologist*
Weis, Edmund Bernard, Jr. *orthopaedist, educator, engineer, lawyer*

### San Bruno
Bradley, Charles William *podiatrist, educator*

### San Diego
Akeson, Wayne Henry *orthopedic surgeon, educator*
Bailey, David Nelson *pathologist, educator*
Benirschke, Kurt *pathologist, educator*
Blum, John Alan *urologist, educator*
Brookler, Harry Aaron *retired physician*
Buchbinder, Maurice *cardiologist*
Chambers, Henry George *orthopedic surgeon*
Convery, F. Richard *surgeon, orthopedist*
Crutchfield, Susan Ramsey *neurophysiologist*
DeMaria, Anthony Nicholas *cardiologist, educator*
Demeter, Steven *neurologist, publishing company executive*
Dziewanowska, Zofia Elizabeth *neuropsychiatrist, pharmaceutical executive, researcher, educator*
Friedenberg, Richard Myron *radiology educator, physician*
Friedman, Paul Jay *radiologist, chest radiologist, educator*
Goltz, Robert William *physician, educator*
Griffin, Herschel Emmett *retired epidemiology educator*
Halasz, Nicholas Alexis *surgeon*
Hamburg, Marian Virginia *health science educator*
Harwood, Ivan Richmond *pediatric pulmonologist*
Hourani, Laurel Lockwood *epidemiologist*
Hunt, Robert Gary *medical consultant, oral and maxillofacial surgeon*
Intriere, Anthony Donald *physician*
Jacoby, Irving *physician*
Jamieson, Stuart William *surgeon, educator*
Jones, Clyde William *anesthesiologist*
Kaback, Michael *medical educator*
Kaplan, George Willard *urologist*
Levy, Jerome *dermatologist, retired naval officer*
Lewis, Gregory Williams *scientist*
Magnuson, Harold Joseph *physician*
Mendoza, Stanley Atran *pediatric nephrologist, educator*
Moossa, A. R. *surgery educator*
Moser, Kenneth Miles *physician, educator*
Neuman, Tom S. *emergency medical physician, educator*
Oliphant, Charles Romig *physician*
O'Malley, Edward *physician, consultant*
Owsia, Nasrin Akbarnia *pediatrician*
Parthemore, Jacqueline G. *physician, educator*
Ranney, Helen Margaret *physician, educator*
Ray, Albert *family physician*
Rodin, Alvin Eli *retired pathologist, medical educator, author*
Ross, John, Jr. *physician, educator*
Scherger, Joseph E. *family physician, educator*
Schmidt, Joseph David *urologist*
Seagren, Stephen Linner *oncologist*
Shirer, Bruce Edward *pathologist*
Teguh, Collin *osteopathic physician, educator*
Wallace, Helen Margaret *physician, educator*
Wasserman, Stephen Ira *physician, educator*

Welch, Arnold DeMerritt *pharmacologist, biochemist*
Whitehill, Jules Leonard *surgeon, educator*
Wight, Nancy Elizabeth *neonatologist*
Wong-Staal, Flossie *geneticist, medical educator*

**San Fernando**
Chiu, Dorothy *pediatrician*

**San Francisco**
Aird, Robert Burns *neurologist, educator*
Amend, William John Conrad, Jr. *physician, educator*
Bainton, Dorothy Ford *pathology educator, researcher*
Barondes, Samuel Herbert *psychiatrist, educator*
Benet, Leslie Zachary *pharmacokineticist*
Biglieri, Edward George *physician*
Bishop, John Michael *biomedical research scientist, educator*
Boles, Roger *otolaryngologist*
Caputo, Gary Richard *radiology educator*
Carson, Jay Wilmer *pathologist, educator*
Cheitlin, Melvin Donald *physician, educator*
Clever, Linda Hawes *physician*
Curtis, David Lambert *rheumatologist, educator*
Dawson, Chandler Robert *ophthalmologist, educator*
Debas, Haile T. *gastrointestinal surgeon, physiologist, educator*
Embry, Ronald Lee *physician, diagnostic radiologist*
Engleman, Ephraim Philip *rheumatologist*
Epstein, Charles Joseph *physician, medical geneticist, pediatrics and biochemistry educator*
Epstein, John Howard *dermatologist*
Epstein, Leon Joseph *psychiatrist*
Erskine, John Morse *surgeon*
Finberg, Laurence *pediatrician, educator, dean*
Fishman, Robert Allen *neurologist, educator*
Foye, Laurance Vincent *physician, hospital administrator*
Frick, Oscar Lionel *physician, educator*
Friedman, Meyer *physician*
Fu, Karen King-Wah *radiation oncologist*
Gellin, Gerald Alan *dermatologist*
Glassberg, Alan Burnett *physician*
Goode, Erica Tucker *internist*
Gooding, Charles Arthur *radiologist, physician, educator*
Gooding, Gretchen Ann Wagner *physician, educator*
Gottfried, Eugene Leslie *physician, educator*
Greenspan, Francis S. *physician*
Greyson, Clifford Russell *internist*
Grumbach, Melvin Malcolm *physician, educator*
Harris, Jeffrey Saul *physician executive*
Havel, Richard Joseph *physician, educator*
Herbert, Chesley C. *psychiatrist, educator*
Heyman, Melvin Bernard *pediatric gastroenterologist*
Hinman, Frank, Jr. *urologist, educator*
Hoffman, Julien Ivor Ellis *pediatric cardiologist, educator*
Hollander, Daniel *gastroenterologist, medical educator*
Hsu, John Chao-Chun *retired pediatrician*
Jacobs, Edwin Max *oncologist, consultant*
Jaffe, Robert Benton *obstetrician, gynecologist, reproductive endocrinologist*
Jensen, Ronald H. *medical educator*
Kan, Yuet Wai *physician, investigator*
Katz, Hilliard Joel *physician*
Kiefer, Renata Gertrud *pediatrician, epidemiologist, economist, international health consultant*
Kolb, Felix Oscar *physician*
Kramer, Steven G. *ophthalmologist*
Lee, Philip Randolph *medical educator*
Levin, Alan Scott *pathologist, allergist, immunologist, lawyer*
Lidofsky, Steven David *medical educator*
Lim, Robert Cheong, Jr. *surgeon, educator*
†Low, Randall *internist, cardiologist*
Lucia, Marilyn Reed *physician*
Maibach, Howard I. *dermatologist*
Margulis, Alexander Rafailo *physician, educator*
Martin, Joseph Boyd *neurologist, educator*
Mason, Dean Towle *cardiologist*
Mathes, Stephen John *plastic and reconstructive surgeon, educator*
McAninch, Jack Weldon *urological surgeon, educator*
McCorkle, Horace Jackson *physician, educator*
Mills, Thomas Cooke *psychiatrist*
Mohr, Selby *retired ophthalmologist*
Mustacchi, Piero *physician, educator*
Myers, Howard Milton *pharmacologist, educator*
O'Connor, G(eorge) Richard *ophthalmologist*
Perkins, Herbert Asa *physician*
Petrakis, Nicholas Louis *physician, medical researcher, educator*
Phillips, Theodore Locke *radiation oncologist, educator*
Piel, Carolyn Forman *pediatrician, educator*
Ralston, Henry James, III *neurobiologist, anatomist, educator*
Risse, Guenter Bernhard *physician, historian, educator*
Roe, Benson Bertheau *surgeon, educator*
Rosinski, Edwin Francis *health sciences educator*
Rudolph, Abraham Morris *physician, educator*
Schiller, Francis *neurologist, medical historian*
Schmid, Rudi (Rudolf Schmid) *internist, educator, academic administrator, scientist*
Schmidt, Robert Milton *physician, scientist, educator*
Scholten, Paul *obstetrician, gynecologist, educator*
†Schrock, Theodore R. *surgeon*
Seebach, Lydia Marie *physician*
Shapiro, Larry Jay *pediatrician, scientist, educator*
Shinefield, Henry Robert *pediatrician*
Shumate, Charles Albert *retired dermatologist*
Smith, David Elvin *physician*
Smith, Lloyd Hollingsworth *physician*
Sokolow, Maurice *physician, educator*
Sparks, Robert Dean *medical administrator, physician*
Stamper, Robert Lewis *ophthalmologist, educator*
Szabo, Zoltan *medical science educator, medical institute director*
Terr, Abba Israel *allergist, immunologist*
Terr, Lenore Cagen *psychiatrist, writer*
Thompson, Charlotte Ellis *pediatrician, educator, author*
Trejo, JoAnn *medical researcher*
Trigiano, Lucien Lewis *physician*
Van Dyke, Craig *psychiatrist*
Veith, Ilza *historian of psychiatric and Oriental medicine*
†Volberding, Paul Arthur *academic physician*
Volpe, Peter Anthony *surgeon*
Wallerstein, Ralph Oliver *physician*
Watts, Malcolm S(tuart) M(cNeal) *physician, medical educator*
Way, E(dward) Leong *pharmacologist, toxicologist, educator*
Wescott, William Burnham *oral pathologist, educator*
Wilbur, Dwight Locke *physician*
Wilson, Charles B. *neurosurgeon, educator*
Wintroub, Bruce Urich *dermatologist, educator, researcher*
Wolff, Sheldon *radiobiologist, educator*
Zippin, Calvin *epidemiologist, educator*

**San Gabriel**
Chen, John Calvin *child and adolescent psychiatrist*
Terry, Roger *pathologist, consultant*

**San Jose**
Boldrey, Edwin Eastland *retinal surgeon, educator*
Johnson, Allen Halbert *surgeon*
Kramer, Richard Jay *gastroenterologist*
Lippe, Philipp Maria *physician, surgeon, neurosurgeon, educator, administrator*
Malish, David Marc *physician*
Nguyen, Thinh Van *physician*
Okita, George Torao *pharmacologist educator*
Weeker, Ellis *emergency physician*

**San Juan Capistrano**
Fisher, Delbert Arthur *physician, educator*

**San Leandro**
Leighton, Joseph *pathologist*

**San Marcos**
Billing, Ronald James *immunologist, researcher*

**San Marino**
Benzer, Seymour *neuroscience educator*

**San Mateo**
Adams, Robert Monroe *retired dermatologist, educator*
Kidera, George Jerome *physician*
Van Kirk, John Ellsworth *cardiologist*

**San Pablo**
Bristow, Lonnie Robert *physician*
Woodruff, Kay Herrin *pathologist, educator*

**San Rafael**
Bruyn, Henry Bicker *physician*
Danse, Ilene Homnick Raisfeld *physician, educator, toxicologist*
Hinshaw, Horton Corwin *physician*
Meecham, William James *ophthalmologist*

**San Ramon**
Litman, Robert Barry *physician, author, television and radio commentator*
Novales-Li, Philipp *neuropharmacologist*

**Santa Ana**
Abbruzzese, Carlo Enrico *physician, writer, educator*
Myers, Marilyn Gladys *pediatric hematologist and oncologist*
Pratt, Lawrence Arthur *thoracic surgeon, foreign service officer*

**Santa Barbara**
Bischel, Margaret DeMeritt *physician, managed care consultant*
Enelow, Allen Jay *psychiatrist, educator*
Fisher, Steven Kay *neurobiology eductor*
Kohn, Roger Alan *surgeon*
Mathews, Barbara Edith *gynecologist*
Peterson, Charles Marquis *medical educator*
Prager, Elliot David *surgeon, educator*
Riemenschneider, Paul Arthur *physician, radiologist*
Rockwell, Don Arthur *psychiatrist*
Shackman, Daniel Robert *psychiatrist*

**Santa Clara**
Fernbach, Stephen Alton *pediatrician*

**Santa Cruz**
Magid, Gail Avrum *neurosurgeon, neurosurgery educator*
Schwartz, Arthur Alan *surgeon*
Shorenstein, Rosalind Greenberg *physician*

**Santa Monica**
Bohn, Paul Bradley *psychiatrist, psychoanalyst*
McGuire, Michael Francis *plastic and reconstructive surgeon*
Mitchell, Thomas Soren *urologist*
Rand, Robert Wheeler *neurosurgeon, educator*
Schultz, Victor M. *physician*
Singer, Frederick Raphael *medical researcher, educator*
Thompson, Dennis Peters *plastic surgeon*

**Santa Rosa**
Bozdech, Marek Jiri *physician*
Leuty, Gerald Johnston *osteopathic physician and surgeon*
Resch, Joseph Anthony *neurologist*

**Sausalito**
Arieff, Allen Ives *physician*

**Sepulveda**
Wasterlain, Claude Guy *neurologist*

**Sherman Oaks**
King, Peter D. *psychiatrist, educator, real estate developer*
Zemplenyi, Tibor Karol *cardiologist*

**Sierra Madre**
Nation, Earl F. *retired urologist, educator*

**Sonora**
Erich, Louis Richard *physician*

**South San Francisco**
Blethen, Sandra Lee *pediatric endocrinologist*
Spitzer, Walter Oswald *epidemiologist, educator*

**Spring Valley**
Long, David Michael, Jr. *biomedical researcher, cardiothoracic surgeon*

**Stanford**
Abrams, Herbert LeRoy *radiologist, educator*
Bauer, Eugene Andrew *dermatologist, educator*
Baylor, Denis Aristide *neurobiology educator*
Beard, Rodney Rau *physician, educator*
Bensch, Klaus George *pathology educator*
Blumenkranz, Mark Scott *surgeon, researcher, educator*
Carlson, Robert Wells *physician, educator*
Cohen, Harvey Joel *pediatric hematology and oncology educator*
Dafoe, Donald Cameron *surgeon, educator*
Fee, Willard Edward, Jr. *otolaryngologist*
Gibson, Count Dillon, Jr. *physician, educator*
Glazer, Gary Mark *radiology educator*
Goldstein, Dora Benedict *pharmacologist, educator*
Hentz, Vincent R. *surgeon*
Hlatky, Mark Andrew *cardiologist, health services researcher*
Hubert, Helen Betty *epidemiologist*
Jardetzky, Oleg *medical educator, scientist*
Kendig, Joan Johnston *neurobiology educator*
Maffly, Roy Herrick *medical educator*
Mark, James B. D. *surgeon*
Marmor, Michael Franklin *ophthalmologist, educator*
McDevitt, Hugh O'Neill *immunology educator, physician*
McDougall, Iain Ross *nuclear medicine educator*
Melmon, Kenneth Lloyd *physician, biologist, pharmacologist, consultant*
Merigan, Thomas Charles, Jr. *physician, medical researcher, educator*
Moss, Richard B. *pediatrician*
Niederhuber, John Edward *surgical oncologist and molecular immunologist, university educator and administrator*
Oberhelman, Harry Alvin, Jr. *surgeon, educator*
Paffenbarger, Ralph Seal, Jr. *epidemiologist, educator*
Payne, Anita Hart *reproductive endocrinologist, researcher*
Raffin, Thomas A. *physician*
Reitz, Bruce Arnold *cardiac surgeon, educator*
Rosenberg, Saul Allen *oncologist, educator*
Rosenthal, Myer H. *anesthesiologist*
Rubenstein, Edward *physician, educator*
†Rudd, Peter *physician, medical educator*
Schatzberg, Alan Frederic *psychiatrist, researcher*
Schendel, Stephen Alfred *plastic surgery educator, craniofacial surgeon*
Silverman, Frederic Noah *physician*
Stamey, Thomas Alexander *physician, urology educator*
Warnke, Roger Allen *pathology educator*
Weissman, Irving L. *medical scientist*
Zarins, Christopher Kristaps *surgery educator, vascular surgeon*

**Stockton**
Talley, Robert Boyd *physician*

**Studio City**
Shekhar, Stephen S. *obstetrician, gynecologist*

**Sylmar**
Corry, Dalila Boudjellal *internist*
Shaw, Anthony *physician, pediatric surgeon*
Tully, Susan Balsley *pediatrician, educator*
Ziment, Irwin *medical educator*

**Tehachapi**
Badgley, Theodore McBride *psychiatrist, neurologist*

**Thousand Oaks**
Klein, Jeffrey Howard *oncologist, internist*

**Torrance**
Brasel, Jo Anne *physician*
Emmanouilides, George Christos *physician, educator*
Goldberg, Mark Arthur *neurologist*
Itabashi, Hideo Henry *neuropathologist, neurologist*
Krout, Boyd Merrill *psychiatrist*
Leake, Rosemary Dobson *physician*
Mehringer, Charles Mark *medical educator*
Myhre, Byron Arnold *pathologist, educator*
Narasimhan, Padma Mandyam *physician*
†Stabile, Bruce Edward *surgeon*
Tanaka, Kouichi Robert *physician, educator*

**Ukiah**
McClintock, Richard Polson *dermatologist*

**Vallejo**
Kleinrock, Robert Allen *physician*

**Van Nuys**
Fox, James Michael *orthopedic surgeon*

**Ventura**
Abul-Haj, Suleiman Kahil *pathologist*
Villaveces, James Walter *allergist, immunologist*

**Visalia**
Riegel, Byron William *ophthalmologist*

**Volcano**
Prout, Ralph Eugene *physician*

**Walnut Creek**
Acosta, Julio Bernard *obstetrician, gynecologist*
Farr, Lee Edward *nuclear medicine physician*

**West Hollywood**
†LeVay, Simon *neurologist, writer, educator*
Wilson, Myron Robert, Jr. *retired psychiatrist*

**Whittier**
Arcadi, John Albert *urologist*
Arenowitz, Albert Harold *psychiatrist*
Briney, Allan King *radiologist*
Prickett, David Clinton *physician*
Welsh, William Daniel *family practitioner,*

**Woodland Hills**
Herdeg, Howard Brian *physician*

**Woodside**
Blum, Richard Hosmer Adams *gynecology and obstetrics educator, writer*

## COLORADO

**Aspen**
Evans, William Thomas *physician*
Oden, Robert Rudolph *surgeon*

**Aurora**
Bennion, Scott Desmond *physician*

**Boulder**
Dubin, Mark William *educator, neuroscientist*

**Canon City**
Mohr, Gary Alan *physician*

**Castle Rock**
Thornbury, John Rousseau *radiologist, physician*

**Colorado Springs**
Anderson, Paul Nathaniel *oncologist, educator*
Halling, Leonard William *retired pathologist, laboratory administrator*
Todd, Harold Wade *association executive, retired air force officer*
†Watz, Hallet N. *emergency physician*

**Denver**
Adler, Charles Spencer *psychiatrist*
Aikawa, Jerry Kazuo *physician, educator*
Atkins, Dale Morrell *physician*
Barkin, Roger Michael *pediatrician, emergency physician, educator*
Battaglia, Frederick Camillo *physician*
Bies, Roger David *cardiologist*
Brantigan, Charles Otto *surgeon*
Bunn, Paul A., Jr. *oncologist, educator*
Campbell, David Neil *physician, educator*
Clayton, Mack Louis *surgery professor, educator*
Cochran, John Howard *plastic and reconstructive surgeon*
Deitrich, Richard Adam *pharmacology educator*
Eickhoff, Theodore Carl *physician*
Fennessey, Paul Vincent *pediatrics and pharmacology, educator, research administrator*
Filley, Christopher Mark *neurologist*
Friedman, H. Harold *cardiologist, internist*
Gibbs, Ronald Steven *obstetrician-gynecologist*
Golitz, Loren Eugene *dermatologist, pathologist, clinical administrator, educator*
Green, Larry Alton *physician, educator*
Harken, Alden Hood *surgeon, thoracic surgeon*
Imber, Richard Joseph *physician, dermatologist*
Jafek, Bruce William *otolaryngologist, educator*
Johnson, Candice Elaine Brown *pediatrics educator*
Jones, Melvin Douglas, Jr. *pediatrician, educator, academic administrator*
Kauvar, Abraham J. *gastroenterologist, medical administrator*
Kern, Fred, Jr. *physician, educator*
Kinzie, Jeannie Jones *radiation oncologist*
Krikos, George Alexander *pathologist, educator*
Krugman, Richard David *physician, university administrator, educator*
Larsen, Gary Loy *physician, researcher*
Lubeck, Marvin Jay *ophthalmologist*
Martin, Richard Jay *medical educator*
McAtee, Patricia Anne Rooney *medical educator*
Meldrum, Daniel Richard *general surgeon, physician*
Moore, Ernest Eugene, Jr. *surgeon, educator*
Moore, George Eugene *surgeon*
Nakakuki, Masafumi *physician, psychiatry educator*
Nelson, Nancy Eleanor *pediatrician, educator*
Nutting, Paul A. *medical educator, medical science administrator*
Petty, Thomas Lee *physician, educator*
Pomerantz, Marvin *thoracic surgeon*
Rainer, William Gerald *cardiac surgeon*
Repine, John E. *internist, educator*
Rosenwasser, Lanny Jeffrey *allergist, immunologist*
Ruge, Daniel August *retired neurosurgeon, educator*
Schiff, Donald Wilfred *pediatrician, educator*
Schrier, Robert William *physician, educator*
Shore, James H(enry) *psychiatrist*
Silverman, Arnold *physician*
Sondheimer, Judith McConnell *pediatrician, educator*
Sujansky, Eva Borska *physician, educator*
Szefler, Stanley James *pediatrics and pharmacology educator*
Talbott, Richard David *retired physician*
Taylor, Edward Stewart *physician, educator*
Wachtel, Thomas Lee *surgeon*
Washington, Reginald Louis *pediatric cardiologist*
Weatherley-White, Roy Christopher Anthony *surgeon, consultant*
Weston, William Lee *dermatologist*
Wiggs, Eugene Overbey *ophthalmologist, educator*
Zisman, Lawrence S. *internist*

**Dillon**
Becker, Quinn Henderson *orthopedic surgeon, army officer*

**Durango**
Moore, John George, Jr. *medical educator*

**Englewood**
Arenberg, Irving Kaufman *ear surgeon, educator*
Pearlman, David Samuel *allergist*
Rumack, Barry H. *physician, toxicologist, pediatrician*

**Fort Carson**
Lewey, Scot Michael *gastroenterologist, army officer*

**Fort Collins**
Gillette, Edward LeRoy *radiation oncology educator*

**Fort Garland**
Leighninger, David Scott *cardiovascular surgeon*

**Fort Morgan**
Gibbs, Denis Laurel *radiologist*

**Grand Junction**
Sadler, Theodore R., Jr. *thoracic and cardiovascular surgeon*

**Greeley**
Cook, Donald E. *pediatrician*

**Highlands Ranch**
Bublitz, Deborah Keirstead *pediatrician*

**Lakewood**
Bettinghaus, Erwin Paul *cancer research center administrator*
Karlin, Joel Marvin *allergist*
Swan, Henry *retired surgeon*

**Littleton**
Bachman, David Christian *orthopedic surgeon*
Forstot, S. Lance *ophthalmologist*
Palmer, Madelyn Stewart Silver *family practice physician*

**Pueblo**
Lewallen, William M., Jr. *ophthalmologist*

**Silverthorne**
Rutherford, Robert Barry *surgeon*

**Vail**
Bevan, William Arnold, Jr. *emergency physician*

**Wheat Ridge**
Hashimoto, Christine L. *physician*

## CONNECTICUT

**Ansonia**
Yale, Jeffrey Franklin *podiatrist*

**Cos Cob**
Duncalf, Deryck *retired anesthesiologist*

**East Haven**
Conn, Harold O. *physician, educator*

**Essex**
Burris, Harriet Louise *emergency physician*
Goff, Christopher Wallick *pediatrician*

**Fairfield**
Burd, Robert Meyer *hematologist, oncologist, educator*
Richard, Patricia Antoinette *physician, dentist*
Rosenman, Stephen David *physician, obstetrics, gynecology*

**Farmington**
Besdine, Richard William *medical educator, scientist*
Cooperstein, Sherwin Jerome *medical educator*
Donaldson, James Oswell, III *neurology educator*
Gossling, Harry Robert *orthopaedic surgeon, educator*
Grunnet, Margaret Louise *pathology educator*
Hinz, Carl Frederick, Jr. *physician, educator*
Katz, Arnold Martin *medical educator*
Liebowitz, Neil Robert *psychiatrist*
Massey, Robert Unruh *physician, university dean*
Maulik, Nilanjana *medical educator*
Raisz, Lawrence Gideon *medical educator, consultant*
Rothfield, Naomi Fox *physician*
Schenkman, John Boris *pharmacologist, educator*
Walker, James Elliot Cabot *physician*

**Glastonbury**
Singer, Paul Richard *ophthalmologist*

**Greenwich**
Brennan, Edward Noel *psychiatrist, educator*
Foraste, Roland *psychiatrist*
Kopenhaver, Patricia Ellsworth *podiatrist*

**Groton**
Holt, Edward Thomas Robert *physician, retired*
Martin, Jeffrey Allen *anesthesiologist*
Perotti, Beatrice Yee-wa Tam *pharmacokineticist, research scientist*

**Guilford**
Springgate, Clark Franklin *physician, researcher*

**Hamden**
Nuland, Sherwin *surgeon, author*

**Hartford**
Brauer, Rima Lois *psychiatrist*
Donnelly, John *psychiatrist, educator*
†Dworkin, Paul Howard *pediatrician*
Ergin, M.T. *physician and surgeon*
Gibbons, John Martin, Jr. *physician, educator*
Gillam, Linda Dawn *cardiologist, researcher*
Hickcox, Curtiss Bronson *anesthesiologist*
Humphrey, Chester Bowden *cardio-thoracic surgeon*
Jung, Betty Chin *epidemiologist, educator*
McCawley, Austin *psychiatrist, educator*
†Painter, Robert Lowell *surgeon, educator*
Pangilinan, Danilo Manalese *internist*
Pirro, Alfred Anthony, Jr. *physician*
Powers, Robert David *physician*
Roberts, Melville Parker, Jr. *neurosurgeon, educator*
†Sanders, William Michael *emergency physician*
Silver, Herbert *physician*
Trowbridge, Phillip Edmund *surgeon, educator*

**Lyme**
Bloom, Barry Malcolm *pharmaceutical consultant*

**Madison**
Langdon, Robert Colin *dermatologist, educator*
Snell, Richard Saxon *anatomist*

**Manchester**
Milewski, Stanislaw Antoni *ophthalmologist, educator*

**Milford**
Fink, Howard David *pediatrician*

**New Canaan**
Coughlin, Francis Raymond, Jr. *surgeon, educator, lawyer*

**New Haven**
Aghajanian, George Kevork *medical educator*
Askenase, Philip William *medicine and pathology educator*
Barash, Paul George *anesthesiologist, educator*
Beardsley, G(eorge) Peter *pediatric oncologist, biochemical pharmacologist*
Behrman, Harold Richard *endocrinologist, physiologist, educator*
Berliner, Robert William *physician, medical educator*
Bolognia, Jean Lynn *academic dermatologist*
Boyer, James Lorenzen *physician, educator*
Braverman, Irwin Merton *dermatologist, educator*
Brown, Thomas Huntington *neuroscientist*
Bunney, Benjamin Stephenson *psychiatrist*
Burrow, Gerard Noel *physician, educator*
Byck, Robert Samuel *psychiatrist, educator*
Caprioli, Joseph *ophthalmologist*
Cohen, Donald Jay *pediatrics, psychiatry and psychology educator, administrator*
Cohen, Lawrence Sorel *physician, educator*
Collins, William F., Jr. *neurosurgery educator*
Comer, James Pierpont *psychiatrist, educator*
Cooney, Leo Mathias, Jr. *geriatrician, educator*
Cooper, Dennis Lawrence *oncologist, educator*
Cooper, Jack Ross *pharmacology educator, researcher*
Davey, Lycurgus Michael *neurosurgeon*
Davis, Michael *medical educator*
Donaldson, Robert Macartney, Jr. *physician*
Edelson, Marshall *psychiatry educator, psychoanalyst*
Feinstein, Alvan Richard *physician, educator*
Ferholt, J. Deborah Lott *pediatrician*
Fikrig, Erol *rheumatologist, medical educator*
Fleck, Stephen *psychiatrist*
Freedman, Gerald Stanley *radiologist, healthcare administrator*
Friedlaender, Gary Elliott *orthopedist, educator*
Genel, Myron *pediatrician, educator*
Glaser, Gilbert Herbert *neuroscientist, physician, educator*
Goldman-Rakic, Patricia Shoer *neuroscience educator*
Goodrich, Isaac *neurosurgeon, educator*
Gross, Ian *academic pediatrician, neonatologist*
Heninger, George Robert *psychiatry educator, researcher*
Herbert, Peter Noel *physician, medical educator*
Hines, Roberta L. *medical educator*
Hoffer, Paul B. *nuclear medicine physician, educator*
Horstmann, Dorothy Millicent *physician, educator*
Horwitz, Ralph Irving *internist, medical educator, epidemiologist*
Igarashi, Peter *nephrologist, educator, researcher*
Jackson, Stanley Webber *psychiatrist, medical historian*
Jacoby, Robert Ottinger *comparative medicine educator*
Jatlow, Peter I. *pathologist, medical educator, researcher*
Kashgarian, Michael *pathologist, physician*
Katz, Jay *psychiatry and law educator*
Kirchner, John Albert *retired otolaryngology educator*
Komp, Diane Marilyn *pediatric oncologist, hematologist, writer*
Kushlan, Samuel Daniel *physician, educator, hospital administrator*
Leffell, David Joel *surgeon, medical administrator, dermatologist, educator, researcher*
Lentz, Thomas Lawrence *biomedical educator, dean, researcher*
Levine, Robert John *physician, educator*
Lewis, Melvin *psychiatrist, pediatrician, psychoanalyst*
Mark, Harry Horst *ophthalmologist, researcher*
McCarthy, Paul Louis *pediatrics educator*
Mermann, Alan Cameron *pediatrics educator, chaplain*
Merrell, Ronald Clifton *surgeon, educator*
Merritt, John Augustus *geriatrician, educator*
Musto, David Franklin *physician, educator, historian, consultant*
Nadel, Ethan Richard *epidemiology educator*
Naftolin, Frederick *physician, reproductive biologist educator*
Newman, Harry Rudolph *urologist, educator*
Niederman, James Corson *physician, educator*
Nwangwu, John Tochukwu *epidemiologist, public health educator*
Ostfeld, Adrian Michael *physician*
Pruett, Kyle Dean *psychiatrist, writer, educator*
Prusoff, William Herman *biochemical pharmacologist, educator*
Rakic, Pasko *neuroscientist, educator*
Redmond, Donald Eugene, Jr. *neuroscientist, educator*
Reiser, Morton Francis *psychiatrist, educator*
Ritchie, J. Murdoch *pharmacologist, educator*
Sartorelli, Alan Clayton *pharmacology educator*
Sasaki, Clarence Takashi *surgeon, medical educator*
Schowalter, John Erwin *psychiatrist, educator*
†Schriver, John Allen *emergency medicine physician*
Schwartz, Peter Edward *physician, gynecologic oncology educator*
Sears, Marvin *ophthalmologist, educator*
Seashore, Margretta Reed *physician*
Shulman, Gerald I. *clinical investigator*
Siegel, Norman Joseph *pediatrician, educator*
Silver, George Albert *physician, educator*
Silverstone, David Edward *ophthalmologist*
Solimena, Michele *endocrinologist, educator, researcher*
Solnit, Albert Jay *physician, commissioner, educator*
Spiro, Howard Marget *physician, educator*
Tamborlane, William V., Jr. *physician, biomedical researcher, pediatrics educator*
Taylor, Kenneth J. *diagnostic sonologist*
Warshaw, Joseph Bennett *pediatrician, educator*
Waxman, Stephen George *neurologist, neuroscientist*
Wright, Hastings Kemper *surgeon, educator*
Zaret, Barry Lewis *cardiologist, medical educator*

**New London**
Bobruff, Jerome *physician*
Schoenberger, Steven Harris *physician, research consultant*
Urbanetti, John Sutherland *internist, consultant*

**New Milford**
Pendagast, Edward Leslie Jr. *physician*

**Norwalk**
Floch, Martin Herbert *physician*
†Huskins, Dennis G. *internist*
Kam, Frederick Anthony *internist, physician*

**Reder**, Robert Frank *physician*
Tracey, Edward John *physician, surgeon*

**Old Lyme**
Cook, Charles Davenport *pediatrician, educator*

**Old Saybrook**
Kaplan, Bernard Joseph *surgeon*

**Orange**
†Fasanella, Rocko Michael *ophthalmologist*

**Ridgefield**
Byrne, Daniel William *biomedical research consultant, biostatistician, computer specialist, educator*

**Sharon**
Gottlieb, Richard Matthew *psychiatrist, consultant*

**Stamford**
Cook, Colin Burford *psychiatrist*
Epstein, Simon Jules *psychiatrist*
Gagnon, Monique Francine *pediatrician*
Gefter, William Irvin *physician, educator*
Goodhue, Peter Ames *obstetrician and gynecologist, educator*
Klein, Neil Charles *physician*
Klenk, Rosemary Ellen *pediatrician*
Rosenberg, Charles Harvey *otorhinolaryngologist*
Sheftell, Fred David *psychiatrist, educator, writer*
Walsh, Thomas Joseph *neuro-ophthalmologist*

**Storrs Mansfield**
Dardick, Kenneth Regen *physician, educator*
Skauen, Donald Matthew *retired pharmaceutical educator*

**Stratford**
Feinberg, Dennis Lowell *dermatologist*

**Vernon Rockville**
Marmer, Ellen Lucille *pediatrician*

**Waterbury**
Dudrick, Stanley John *surgeon, scientist, educator*
Ostrov, Melvyn R. *physician*
Sherwood, James Alan *physician, scientist, educator*

**West Haven**
†Ezekowitz, Michael David *physician*
Janis, Ronald Allen *pharmacologist*
Perlmutter, Lynn Susan *neuroscientist*

**West Simsbury**
Morest, Donald Kent *neuroscientist*

**Weston**
Meinke, Alan Kurt *surgeon*

**Westport**
Burns, John Joseph *pharmacology educator*
Clausman, Gilbert Joseph *medical librarian*
Lopker, Anita Mae *psychiatrist*
Sacks, Herbert Simeon *psychiatrist, educator, consultant*
Satinover, Jeffrey B. *psychiatrist, health science facility administrator, lecturer, author*

**Wilton**
Rogers, Mark Charles *physician, educator*

**Woodbridge**
Bondy, Philip Kramer *physician, educator*
Russell, Cynthia Pincus *social worker, educator*

## DELAWARE

**Dover**
Wilson, Samuel Mayhew *surgeon*

**Lewes**
Adams, John Pletch *orthopaedic surgeon*

**Newark**
Graff, Harold *psychiatrist, psychoanalyst, medical administrator*
Lemole, Gerald Michael *surgeon*
Reider, Martha Crawford *industrial immunologist*

**Rockland**
Levinson, John Milton *obstetrician, gynecologist*

**Seaford**
Cosgrove, Martin Joseph *radiologist*

**Wilmington**
Cornelison, Floyd Shovington, Jr. *retired psychiatrist, former educator*
Frelick, Robert W. *physician*
Goldberg, Morton Edward *pharmacologist*
Harley, Robison Dooling *physician, educator*
Ikeda, Satoshi *thoracic and cardiovascular surgeon*
Inselman, Laura Sue *pediatrician*
Kay, Jerome *retired psychiatrist, educator*
Nelson, Dewey Allen *neurologist, educator*
Pan, Henry Yue-Ming *clinical pharmacologist*
Pell, Sidney *epidemiologist*
Schwartz, Marshall Zane *pediatric surgeon*
Smith, S(tewart) Gregory *ophthalmologist, inventor, product developer, consultant, author*
Stein, Robert Benjamin *biomedical researcher, physician*

## DISTRICT OF COLUMBIA

**Washington**
Adamson, Richard Henry *pharmacologist*
Akhter, Mohammad Nasir *physician, government public health administrator*
Anthony, Virginia Quinn Bausch *medical association executive*
Arling, Bryan Jeremy *internist*
Armaly, Mansour F(arid) *ophthalmologist, educator*
Bachman, Leonard *physician, retired federal official*

Banta, James Elmer *physician, epidemiologist, university dean*
Beard, Lillian B. McLean *physician, consultant*
Beary, John Francis, III *physician, pharmaceutical executive*
Belman, A. Barry *pediatric urologist*
Berman, Sidney *psychiatrist*
Blumenthal, Susan Jane *physician*
Bourne, Peter Geoffrey *physician, educator, author*
Bryant, Thomas Edward *physician, lawyer*
Callaway, Clifford Wayne *physician*
Callender, Clive Orville *surgeon*
Canter, Jerome Wolf *surgeon, educator*
Carlo, George Louis *epidemiologist*
Catoe, Bette Lorrina *physician, health educator*
Cheng, Tsung O. *cardiologist, educator*
Chester, Alexander Campbell, III *physician*
Cohen, Jordan Jay *medical association executive*
Coleman, Roy Melvin *psychiatrist*
Collins, Robert Ellwood *surgeon*
Cornely, Paul Bertau *physician, educator*
Cox, James Lewis *surgeon*
Crisp, Elizabeth Amanda *retired physician*
Cummings, Martin Marc *medical educator, physician, scientific administrator*
Curfman, David Ralph *neurological surgeon, musician*
Curry, Sadye Beatryce *gastroenterologist, educator*
Cytowic, Richard Edmund *neurologist*
Davis, David Oliver *radiologist, educator*
Dawson, Nancy Ann *hematologist, oncologist*
Deutsch, Stanley *anesthesiologist, educator*
Dey, Radheshyam Chandra *cytologist*
Dhanireddy, Ramasubbareddy *neonatologist, researcher*
Dublin, Thomas David *physician*
Dym, Martin *medical educator*
Earll, Jerry Miller *internist, educator*
†Edwards, Maureen Crittenden *neonatologist, educator*
Ein, Daniel *allergist*
Elgart, Mervyn L. *dermatologist, educator*
Elliott, Larry Paul *cardiac radiologist, educator*
Epps, Charles Harry, Jr. *orthopaedic surgery educator*
Fairbanks, David Nathaniel Fox *physician, surgeon, educator*
Feldman, Bruce Allen *otolaryngologist*
Felts, William Robert, Jr. *physician*
Finkelstein, James David *physician*
Fromm, Hans *gastroenterologist, educator, researcher*
Gay-Bryant, Claudine Moss *retired physician*
Gehrig, Leo Joseph *surgeon*
Gelmann, Edward Paul *oncologist, educator*
Gerson, Elliot Francis *health care executive*
Gilbert, Charles Richard Alsop *physician, medical educator*
Goldson, Alfred Lloyd *oncologist, educator*
Gottlieb, H. David *podiatrist*
Gray, Sheila Hafter *psychiatrist, psychoanalyst*
Grigsby, Margaret Elizabeth *physician*
Grossman, John Henry, III *obstetrician, gynecologist, educator*
Grundfast, Kenneth Martin *otolaryngologist*
†Hark, William Henry *medical executive, retired military officer*
Harvey, John Collins *physician, educator*
†Hein, Karen Kramer *pediatrician, epidemiologist*
Henry, Walter Lester, Jr. *physician, educator*
Herman, Mary Margaret *neuropathologist*
Holden, Raymond Thomas *physician, educator*
Hollinshead, Ariel Cahill *research oncologist*
Hussain, Syed Taseer *biomedical educator, researcher*
Irey, Nelson Sumner *pathologist*
Johnston, Gerald Samuel *physician, educator*
Kant, Gloria Jean *neuroscientist, researcher*
Karcher, Donald Steven *medical educator*
Katz, Sol *physician*
Kizer, Kenneth Wayne *physician, educator*
Koering, Marilyn Jean *anatomy educator, researcher*
Korn, David *educator, pathologist*
Kurtzke, John Francis, Sr. *neurologist, epidemiologist*
Landau, Emanuel *epidemiologist*
Lessin, Lawrence Stephen *hematologist, oncologist, educator*
Little, John William *plastic surgeon, educator*
Luhrs, Caro Elise *internal medicine physician, administrator, educator*
Lynn, D. Joanne *physician, ethicist, health services researcher*
MacLean, Paul Donald *government institute medical research official*
Majd, Massoud *radiology and nuclear medicine educator*
Mann, Marion *physician, educator*
Mann, Oscar *physician, internist, educator*
Marcus, Devra Joy Cohen *internist*
Martuza, Robert L. *neurosurgeon*
McGinnis, James Michael *physician*
McGrath, Mary Helena *plastic surgeon, educator*
Meyerhoff, James Lester *medical researcher*
Mitchell, John David *ophthalmologist*
Moritsugu, Kenneth Paul *physician, government official*
Mrazek, David Allen *pediatric psychiatrist*
Murray, Robert Fulton, Jr. *physician*
Nelson, Alan Ray *internist, medical association executive*
Neviaser, Robert Jon *orthopaedic surgeon, educator*
Novitch, Mark *physician, educator, retired pharmaceutical executive*
Nowak, Judith Ann *psychiatrist*
Oertel, Yolanda Castillo *pathologist, educator, diagnostician*
†O'Toole, Tara Jeanne *physician*
Packer, Roger Joseph *neurologist, neuro-oncologist*
Parker, Gerald William *physician, medical center administrator, retired air force officer*
Parrott, Robert Harold *pediatrician, educator*
Paulson, Jerome Avrom *pediatrician*
Pawlson, Leonard Gregory *physician*
Pearse, Warren Harland *obstetrician and gynecologist, association executive*
Pellegrino, Edmund Daniel *physician, educator, former university president*
Perlin, Seymour *psychiatrist, educator*
Perry, Seymour Monroe *physician*
Piemme, Thomas E. *medical educator*
Pincus, Jonathan Henry *neurologist, educator*
Pollack, Murray Michael *physician, medical services administrator*
Potter, John Francis *surgical oncologist, educator*
Queenan, John Thomas *obstetrician, gynecologist, educator*
Rall, David Platt *pharmacologist, environmentalist*

Reaman, Gregory Harold *pediatric hematologist, oncologist*
Rennert, Owen Murray *physician, educator*
Robertson, William Wright, Jr. *orthopedic surgeon educator*
Robinowitz, Carolyn Bauer *psychiatrist, educator*
Rodriguez, William Julio *physician*
Ross, Allan Michael *physician, medical educator*
Ruckman, Roger Norris *pediatric cardiologist*
Sabshin, Melvin *psychiatrist, educator, medical association administrator*
Samman, George *obstetrician, gynecologist*
Sandler, Sumner Gerald *medical educator*
Schechter, Geraldine Poppa *hematologist*
†Seneff, Michael Geren *anesthesiologist*
Sessions, Roy Brumby *otolaryngologist, educator*
Shanahan, Sheila Ann *pediatrician, educator*
Shine, Kenneth Irwin *cardiologist, educator*
Shrier, Diane Kesler *psychiatrist*
Sidransky, Herschel *pathologist*
Simon, Gary Leonard *internist, educator*
Simopoulos, Artemis Panageotis *physician, educator*
Sivasubramanian, Kolinjavadi Nagarajan *neonatologist, educator*
Sly, Ridge Michael *physician, educator*
Smith, Lee Elton *surgery educator, retired military officer*
Smyth, Nicholas Patrick D. *surgeon*
†Snyder, Vic *physician, congressman*
Spagnolo, Samuel Vincent *internist, pulmonary specialist, educator*
Sweeney, Rosemarie *medical association administrator*
Telford, Ira Rockwood *anatomist, educator*
Tosi, Laura Lowe *orthopaedic surgeon*
Wartofsky, Leonard *medical educator*
Webster, Thomas Glenn *psychiatrist*
Weingold, Allan B. *obstetrician, gynecologist, educator*
Werkman, Sidney Lee *psychiatry educator*
White, Martha Vetter *allergy and immunology physician, researcher*
Wiener, Jerry M. *psychiatrist*
Willis, Arnold Jay *urologic surgeon, educator*
Wilson, Norman Louis *psychiatrist, educator*
Woosley, Raymond *pharmacology and medical educator*
Wyatt, Richard Jed *psychiatrist, educator*
Young, Donald Alan *physician*
Zaloznik, Arlene Joyce *oncologist, army officer*
Zimmerman, Hyman Joseph *internist, educator*

## FLORIDA

### Alachua
Gifford, George E. *immunology and medical microbiology educator*

### Altamonte Springs
Dotts, Randall James *physician associate*

### Atlantic Beach
Walker, Richard Harold *pathologist, educator*

### Bay Pines
Johnson, David Porter *infectious diseases physician*
Keskiner, Ali *psychiatrist*
Law, David Hillis *physician*
Robson, Martin Cecil *surgery educator, plastic surgeon*
Stewart, Jonathan Taylor *psychiatrist, educator*
Wasserman, Fred, III *internist*

### Belleair
Lasley, Charles Haden *cardiovascular surgeon, health and fitness consultant*

### Boca Grande
VanItallie, Theodore Bertus *physician*

### Boca Raton
Cohn, Jess Victor *psychiatrist*
Friend, Harold Charles *neurologist*
Kramer, Cecile E. *retired medical librarian*
Mirkin, Abraham Jonathan *surgeon*
Stein, Irvin *orthopedic surgeon, educator*
Zuckerman, Sidney *retired allergist, immunologist*

### Boynton Beach
Pataky, Paul Eric *ophthalmologist*

### Bradenton
Mandell, Marshall *physician, allergist, consultant*

### Brandon
Lafferty, Beverly Lou Brookover *retired physician, consultant*

### Cape Coral
Martin, Benjamin Gaufman *ophthalmologist*

### Clearwater
Dexter, Helen Louise *dermatologist, consultant*
Fromhagen, Carl, Jr. *obstetrician, gynecologist*
Greengold, Julian Bart *physician*
Horowitz, Harry I. *podiatrist*
Lokys, Linda J. *dermatologist*
McAllister, Charles John *nephrologist, medical administrator*
Wheat, Myron William, Jr. *cardiothoracic surgeon*

### Coral Gables
Perez, Josephine *psychiatrist, educator*
Quillian, Warren Wilson, II *pediatrician, educator*

### Coral Springs
Andrews, George Andreas *cardiologist*

### Dade City
†Feld, Harvey Joel *pathologist*
McBath, Donald Linus *osteopathic physician*

### Davie
Wong, Antonio Ham *family physician*

### Daytona Beach
Di Nicolo, Roberto *allergist*
Goldberg, Paul Bernard *gastroenterologist, clinical researcher*

### Delray Beach
Rosenfeld, Steven Ira *ophthalmologist*

### Dunedin
Bradley, Robert Lee *surgeon*
Gambone, Victor Emmanuel, Jr. *physician*

### Fernandina Beach
Barlow, Anne Louise *pediatrician, medical research administrator*

### Fort Lauderdale
Adams, Kelly Lynn *emergency physician*
Daniel, Gerard Lucian *physician, pharmaceutical company executive*
Gill, Carl Carter *cardiothoracic surgeon*
Lipkin, David Lawrence *physician*
Lodwick, Gwilym Savage *radiologist, educator*
Maulion, Richard Peter *psychiatrist*
Raybeck, Michael Joseph *surgeon*
Rendon-Pellerano, Marta Ines *dermatologist*
Swiller, Randolph Jacob *internist*
†Whitmore, Douglas Michael *physician*

### Fort Myers
Aleo, Joseph John *pathology scientist, educator, academic research administrator*
†Arnall, Robert Esric *physician, medical administrator*
Grove, William Johnson *physician, surgery educator*
Simmons, Vaughan Pippen *medical consultant*
Steier, Michael Edward *cardiac surgeon*

### Fort Walton Beach
Gates, Philip Don *anesthesiologist*

### Gainesville
Anderson, Richard McLemore *internist*
Behnke, Marylou *neonatologist, educator*
Cluff, Leighton Eggertsen *physician*
Gravenstein, Joachim Stefan *anesthesiologist, educator*
Greer, Melvin *medical educator*
Heuer, Marvin Arthur *physician, research and industry consultant*
Limacher, Marian Cecile *cardiologist*
Modell, Jerome Herbert *anesthesiologist, educator*
Neiberger, Richard Eugene *pediatrician, nephrologist, educator*
Palovcik, Reinhard Anton *research neurophysiologist*
Pfaff, William Wallace *medical educator*
Reynolds, Richard Clyde *physician, educator*
Rhoton, Albert Loren, Jr. *neurological surgery educator*
Rosenbloom, Arlan Lee *physician, educator*
Rubin, Melvin Lynne *ophthalmologist, educator*
Schiebler, Gerold Ludwig *physician, educator*
Small, Parker Adams, Jr. *pediatrician, educator*
Suzuki, Howard Kazuro *retired anatomist, educator*
Talbert, James Lewis *pediatric surgeon, educator*
Taylor, William Jape *physician*
Uthman, Basim Mohammad *neurologist, epileptologist, consultant*
Vaughen, Justine L. *rehabilitation hospital medical professional*
Walker, Robert Dixon, III *surgeon, urologist, educator*
Williams, Ralph Chester, Jr. *physician, educator*

### Hallandale
Haspel, Arthur Carl *podiatrist, surgeon*

### Hawthorne
Fackler, Martin L(uther) *surgeon*

### Hialeah
Economides, Christopher George *pathologist*
Iribar, Manuel R. *internist, health facility administrator*
Koreman, Dorothy Goldstein *physician, dermatologist*

### Hollywood
Bergman, Harry *urologist*
Duffner, Lee R. *ophthalmologist*
Weinberg, Harry Bernard *cardiologist*

### Jacksonville
Amornmarn, Rumpa *physician*
Boylan, Kevin Bernard *neurologist*
Carithers, Hugh Alfred *physician*
Groom, Dale *physician, educator*
Hecht, Frederick *physician, researcher, author, educator, consultant*
†Johnson, Douglas William *physician, radiologist-oncologist*
Kelalis, Panayotis *pediatric urologist*
Lewis, Richard Harlow *urologist*
Mandia, Stephen Ernest *urologist*
Mass, M. F. *allergist, immunologist*
Mizrahi, Edward Alan *allergist*
Paryani, Shyam Bhojraj *radiologist*
†Siegel, Steven Douglas *oncologist*
Stephenson, Samuel Edward, Jr. *physician*
Thorsteinsson, Gudni *physiatrist*
Toker, Karen Harkavy *physician*

### Key Biscayne
Palmer, Roger Farley *pharmacology educator*

### Key Largo
Manning, John Warren, III *retired surgeon, medical educator*

### Key West
Stein, Michael Alan *cardiologist*

### Lake Worth
Freund, Norman Lawrence *colon and rectal surgeon*
Newmark, Emanuel *ophthalmologist*
Stone, Ross Gluck *orthopaedic surgeon*

### Lakeland
Roberts, William Smithson *gynecologic oncologist*
Spoto, Angelo Peter, Jr. *internist, allergist*

### Largo
Brown, Warren Joseph *physician*
Grove, Jeffrey Scott *family practice physician*

### Longboat Key
Kabara, Jon Joseph *biochemical pharmacology educator*

### Maitland
Hall, Richard C. Winton *psychiatrist*

### Marathon
Calvert, William Preston *radiologist*

### Marco Island
Sundberg, R. Dorothy *physician, educator*

### Margate
Glick, Brad Peter *dermatologist, family physician*

### Melbourne
Baney, Richard Neil *physician, internist*
Minor, Mark William *allergist*
Pocoski, David John *cardiologist*

### Miami
Alvarez, Raul Alberto *physician*
Anderson, Douglas Richard *ophthalmologist, educator, scientist, researcher*
Bahadue, George Paul *general, family physician*
Beck, Morris *allergist*
Bolooki, Hooshang *cardiac surgeon*
Casariego, Jorge Isaac *psychiatrist, psychoanalyst, educator*
Cassel, John Michael *plastic surgeon*
Cassileth, Peter Anthony *internist*
Cohen, Sanford Irwin *physician, educator*
Daughtry, DeWitt Cornell *surgeon, physician*
Davis, Richard Edmund *facial plastic surgeon*
Dean, Stanley Rochelle *psychiatrist*
Eaglstein, William Howard *dermatologist, educator*
Eftekhari, Nasser *physiatrist*
Eisdorfer, Carl *psychiatrist, health care executive*
Engle, Howard A. *pediatrician*
Freshwater, Michael Felix *surgeon, educator*
Ganz, William I. *radiology educator, researcher*
Gelband, Henry *pediatric cardiologist*
Ginsberg, Myron David *neurologist*
Gittelson, George *physician*
Goldstein, Burton Jack *psychiatrist*
Goodnick, Paul Joel *psychiatrist*
Hicks, Dorothy Jane *obstetrician and gynecologist, educator*
Howell, Ralph Rodney *pediatrician, educator*
Jude, James Roderick *cardiac surgeon*
Karl, Robert Harry *cardiologist*
Ketcham, Alfred Schutt *surgeon, educator*
Kirton, Orlando Cecilio *surgeon, educator*
Lasseter, Kenneth Carlyle *pharmacologist*
Lemberg, Louis *cardiologist, educator*
Mc Kenzie, John Maxwell *physician*
Mettinger, Karl Lennart *neurologist*
Mintz, Daniel Harvey *diabetologist, educator, academic administrator*
Nisonson, Ian *urologist*
Page, Larry Keith *neurosurgeon, educator*
Papper, Emanuel Martin *anesthesiologist*
Patarca, Roberto *immunologist, molecular biologist, physician*
Poblete, Rita Maria Bautista *physician, educator*
Potter, James Douglas *pharmacology educator*
Prineas, Ronald James *epidemiologist, educator*
Quencer, Robert Moore *neuroradiologist, researcher*
Raines, Jeff *biomedical scientist, medical research director*
Reik, Rita Ann Fitzpatrick *pathologist*
Ricordi, Camillo *surgeon, transplant and diabetes researcher*
Ripstein, Charles Benjamin *surgeon*
Sackner, Marvin Arthur *physician*
Scerpella, Ernesto Guillermo *physician researcher*
Scheinberg, Peritz *neurologist*
Schiff, Eugene Roger *medical educator, hepatologist*
Smith, Stanley Bertram *clinical pathologist, allergist, immunologist, anatomic pathologist*
Sturge, Karl *surgeon*
Sussex, James Neil *psychiatrist, educator*
Tejada, Francisco *physician, educator*
Valdes-Dapena, Marie Agnes *pediatric pathologist, educator*
Wheeler, Steve Dereal *neurologist*
Wolff, Grace Susan *pediatrician*
Wolfson, Aaron Howard *radiation oncologist, educator*

### Miami Beach
†Krieger, Bruce Phillip *medical educator*
†Nixon, Daniel David. *physician*
†Ratzan, Kenneth Roy *physician*

### Miami Lakes
Rodriguez, Manuel Alvarez *pathologist*

### Naples
Brooks, Joae Graham *psychiatrist, educator*
Gahagan, Thomas Gail *obstetrician, gynecologist*
Gaskins, William Darrell *ophthalmologist*
Gray, Seymour *medical educator, author*
Harvey, Walter H(ayden) *hematologist, medical oncologist*
Levitt, LeRoy Paul *psychiatrist, psychoanalyst*

### New Port Richey
Hauber, Frederick August *ophthalmologist*
Hu, Chen-Sien *surgeon*

### North Miami Beach
Shuster, Frederick *internist*

### North Palm Beach
Fierer, Joshua Allan *pathology educator*
Stein, Mark Rodger *allergist*

### Ocala
Altenburger, Karl Marion *allergist, immunologist*
Corwin, William *psychiatrist*
Hunter, Oregon K., Jr. *physiatrist*

### Orlando
Cary, Freeman Hamilton *physician*
Hornick, Richard Bernard *physician*
Norris, Franklin Gray *thoracic and cardiovascular surgeon*
Okun, Neil Jeffrey *vitreoretinal surgeon*
Shub, Harvey Allen *surgeon*
Willis, William Harris *internist, cardiologist*

### Ormond Beach
Cromartie, Robert Samuel, III *thoracic surgeon*
Raimondo, Louis John *psychiatrist*

### Osprey
Gross, James Dehnert *pathologist*

### Palm Beach
Alpert, Seymour *anesthesiologist, educator*
Tiecke, Richard William *pathologist, educator, association executive*
Unger, Gere Nathan *physician, lawyer*

### Palm Beach Gardens
Shapiro, Steven David *dermatologist*
Small, Melvin D. *physician, educator*

### Pensacola
Dillard, Robert Perkins *pediatrician, educator*
†Hanline, Manning Harold *internist*
Love, Robert William, Jr. *retired physician, government administrator*
Sharp, Elaine Cecile *obstetrician, gynecologist*
Vuksta, Michael Joseph *surgeon*

### Plantation
Gewirtzman, Garry Bruce *dermatologist*
Ramos, Manuel Antonio, Jr. *pulmonologist*
Tingley, Floyd Warren *physician*

### Pompano Beach
Bliznakov, Emile George *biomedical research scientist*

### Ponte Vedra Beach
Nadler, Sigmond Harold *physician, surgeon*
ReMine, William Hervey, Jr. *surgeon*
Weinstein, George William *ophthalmology educator*

### Saint Petersburg
Bercu, Barry B. *pediatric endocrinologist*
Betzer, Susan Elizabeth Beers *family physician, geriatrician*
Clarke, Kit Hansen *radiologist*
Collins, Paul Steven *vascular surgeon*
Donovan, Denis Miller *psychiatrist, author, lecturer*
Good, Robert Alan *physician, educator*
Marsalisi, Frank Bernard *obstetrician-gynecologist*
Pardoll, Peter Michael *gastroenterologist*
Root, Allen William *pediatrician, educator*
Williams, Larry Ross *surgeon*

### Sanibel
Adair, Charles Valloyd *retired physician*

### Sarasota
Aull, Susan *physician*
Friedberg, Harold David *cardiologist*
Jelks, Mary Larson *retired pediatrician*
Kiplinger, Glenn Francis *pharmacologist, medical-legal consultant*
Klutzow, Friedrich Wilhelm *neuropathologist*
Magenheim, Mark Joseph *physician, epidemiologist, educator*
O'Malley, Thomas Anthony *gastroenterologist, internist*
Sturtevant, Ruthann Patterson *anatomy educator*
Welch, John Dana *urologist, performing arts association executive*
Yonker, Richard Aaron *rheumatologist*

### Seminole
Christ, Philip William *orthopaedic surgeon, osteopath*
Nesbitt, Robert Edward Lee, Jr. *physician, educator, scientific researcher, writer*

### South Miami
†Zwerling, Leonard Joseph *physician, educator*

### Spring Hill
Finney, Roy Pelham, Jr. *urologist, surgeon, inventor*

### Stuart
Delagi, Edward Francis *physician, retired educator*
Haserick, John Roger *retired dermatologist*
Patterson, Robert Arthur *physician, health care consultant, retired health care company executive, retired air force officer*
Pisani, Joseph Michael *physician*
Westlake, Robert Elmer, Sr. *physician*

### Surfside
Prystowsky, Harry *physician, educator*

### Tallahassee
Maguire, Charlotte Edwards *retired physician*
Penrod, Kenneth Earl *medical education consultant, retired*

### Tampa
Afield, Walter Edward *psychiatrist, service executive*
Barness, Lewis Abraham *physician*
Bedford, Robert Forrest *anesthesiologist*
Behnke, Roy Herbert *physician, educator*
Bowen, Thomas Edwin *cardiothoracic surgeon, retired army officer*
Branch, William Terrell *urologist, educator*
Bukantz, Samuel Charles *physician, educator*
Bunker-Soler, Antonio Luis *physician*
Cavanagh, Denis *physician, educator*
del Regato, Juan Angel *radiotherapeutist, oncologist, educator*
Donelan, Peter Andrew *dermatologist*
†Flynn, Michael Patrick *radiologist*
Frias, Jaime Luis *pediatrician, educator*
Gilbert-Barness, Enid F. *pathologist, pathology and pediatrics educator*
Glasser, Stephen Paul *cardiologist*
Greenfield, George B. *radiologist*
Hadden, John Winthrop *immunopharmacology educator*
Hartmann, William Herman *pathologist, educator*
†Hillman, James V. *pediatrician*
Holfelder, Lawrence Andrew *pediatrician, allergist*
Hulls, James Robert *emergency physician*
Jacobs, Timothy Andrew *epidemiologist, international health consultant*
Jacobson, Howard Newman *obstetrics and gynecology educator, researcher*
Kaufman, Ronald Paul *physician, school official*

PROFESSIONAL INDEX 5251 HEALTHCARE: MEDICINE

Krzanowski, Joseph John, Jr. *pharmacology educator*
Lakdawala, Sharad R. *psychiatrist*
Lockey, Richard Funk *allergist, educator*
Lozner, Eugene Leonard *internal medicine educator, consultant*
Lyman, Gary Herbert *epidemiologist, cancer researcher, educator*
Martin, Robert Leslie *physician*
McIntosh, Henry Deane *cardiologist*
Melendez, Edwin Manuel *orthopaedic hand surgeon*
Muroff, Lawrence Ross *nuclear medicine physician*
Murtagh, Frederick Reed *neuroradiologist, educator*
Nagera, Humberto *psychiatrist, psychoanalyst, educator, author*
Olson, Robert Eugene *physician, biochemist, educator*
Pfeiffer, Eric Armin *psychiatrist, gerontologist*
Pollara, Bernard *immunologist, educator, pediatrician*
Powers, Pauline Smith *psychiatrist, educator, researcher*
†Pupello, Dennis Frank *cardiac surgeon, educator*
Reading, Anthony John *physician*
Richardson, Sylvia Onesti *physician*
Rogal, Philip James *physician*
Rowlands, David Thomas *pathology educator*
Schmidt, Paul Joseph *physician, educator*
Schnitzlein, Harold Norman *anatomy educator*
Schonwetter, Ronald Scott *physician, educator*
Shively, John Adrian *pathologist*
Shons, Alan Rance *plastic surgeon, educator*
Siegel, Richard Lawrence *allergist, immunologist, pediatrician*
Silbiger, Martin L. *radiologist, medical educator, college dean*
†Sinnott, John Thomas *internist, educator*
Spellacy, William Nelson *obstetrician, gynecologist, educator*
Watkins, Joan Marie *osteopath, occupational medicine physician*

### Tarpon Springs
Gills, James Pitzer, Jr. *surgeon, educator, philanthropist*

### Tequesta
Seaman, William Bernard *physician, radiology educator*

### Venice
Hrachovina, Frederick Vincent *osteopathic physician and surgeon*
Kinney, Michael James *physician*

### Vero Beach
Lawrence, Merle *medical educator*
Schulman, Harold *obstetrician, gynecologist, perinatologist*
Schwarz, Berthold Eric *psychiatrist*

### West Palm Beach
Brumback, Clarence Landen *physician*
Cox, Linda Susan *allergist, immunologist*
Craft, Jerome Walter *plastic surgeon, health facility administrator*
Darby, Bonnie Mae Hanson *anesthetist*
Kapnick, S. Jason *oncologist*
Khouri, George George *ophthalmologist*
Pottash, A. Carter *psychiatrist, hospital executive*
Roberts, Hyman Jacob *internist, researcher, author, historian, publisher*
Upledger, John Edwin *osteopath, physician*
†Wisnicki, Jeffrey Leonard *plastic surgeon*

### Winter Haven
Honer, Richard Joseph *surgeon*

### Winter Park
Pineless, Hal Steven *neurologist*

## GEORGIA

### Athens
Gregory, John Michael *urologist*

### Atlanta
Alexander, Robert Wayne *medical educator*
Ambrose, Samuel Sheridan, Jr. *urologist*
Bakay, Roy Arpad Earle *neurosurgeon, educator*
Baker, Edward L., Jr. *physician, science facility executive*
Barnett, Crawford Fannin, Jr. *internist, educator, cardiologist, travel medicine specialist*
Barrow, Daniel Louis *neurosurgeon*
Brandenburg, David Saul *gastroenterologist, educator*
Broome, Claire Veronica *epidemiologist, researcher*
Byrd, Larry Donald *behavioral pharmacologist*
Casarella, William Joseph *physician*
Clements, James David *retired psychiatry educator, physician*
Cooper, Gerald Rice *clinical pathologist*
Curran, James W. *epidemiologist, educator*
Davis, Lawrence William *radiation oncologist*
Dean, Andrew Griswold *epidemiologist*
Dobes, William Lamar, Jr. *dermatologist*
Dowda, William F. *internist*
Dutt, Kamla *medical educator*
Edelhauser, Henry F. *physiologist, ophthalmic researcher, educator*
Elsas, Louis Jacob, II *medical educator*
Elsner, Carlene W. *reproductive endocrinologist*
Evans, Edwin Curtis *internist, educator, geriatrician*
Foster, Roger Sherman, Jr. *surgeon, educator, health facility administrator*
Frank, Erica *preventive medicine physician*
Galambos, John Thomas *medical educator, internist*
Gayles, Joseph Nathan, Jr. *adminstrator, fund raising consultant*
Goldman, John Abner *rheumatologist, immunologist, educator*
Gonzalez, Emilio Bustamante *rheumatologist, educator*
Gordon, Frank Jeffrey *medical educator*
Gordon, Robert Dana *transplant surgeon*
Hall, Wilbur Dallas, Jr. *medical educator*
Hanson, Victor Arthur *surgeon*
Harris, Econ Nigel *rheumatologist, internist*
Hatcher, Charles Ross, Jr. *cardiothoracic surgeon, medical center executive*
Haverty, John Rhodes *physician, former university dean*
Houpt, Jeffrey Lyle *psychiatrist, educator*
Hug, Carl Casimir, Jr. *pharmacology and anesthesiology educator*
Hughes, James Mitchell *epidemiologist*
Ingram, Roland Harrison, Jr. *physician, educator*
Israili, Zafar Hasan *scientist, clinical pharmacologist, educator*
Jackson, Richard Joseph *epidemiologist, public health physician, educator*
Jann, Brigitte *physiatrist, educator*
Jarrett, William Hope *ophthalmologist*
Johns, Michael Marieb Edward *otolaryngologist, academic administrator*
Jurkiewicz, Maurice John *surgeon, educator*
Karp, Herbert Rubin *neurologist, educator*
Kaufmann, James A. *internist, educator*
King, Frederick Alexander *neuroscientist, educator*
Klein, Luella Voogd *obstetrics-gynecology educator*
Kokko, Juha Pekka *physician, educator*
Lee, John Everett *physician*
Lipman, Bernard *internist, cardiologist*
Lubin, Michael Frederick *physician, educator*
Lybarger, Jeffrey Allen *epidemiology research administrator*
Margolis, Harold Stephen *epidemiologist*
McDuffie, Frederic Clement *physician*
Meyer, George Wilbur *internist, health facility administrator*
Mitch, William Evans *nephrologist*
Nemeroff, Charles Barnet *neurobiology and psychiatry educator*
Nichols, Joseph J., Sr. *surgeon*
O'Brien, Mark Stephen *pediatric neurosurgeon*
O'Shea, Patricia A. *physician, educator*
Owings, Francis Barre *surgeon*
Parks, John Scott *pediatric endocrinologist*
Peacock, Lamar Batts *retired physician*
Pratt, Michael Francis *physician and surgeon, otolaryngologist*
Reed, James Whitfield *physician, educator*
Rock, John Aubrey *gynecologist and obstetrician, educator*
Schoborg, Thomas William *urologist*
Schwartz, David Alan *infectious diseases and placental pathologist, educator*
†Sexson, William R. *pediatrician, educator*
Sherman, Roger Talbot *surgeon, educator*
Smith, Michael Vincent *surgeon*
Smith, Robert Boulware, III *vascular surgeon, educator*
Spangler, Dennis Lee *physician*
Steinhaus, John Edward *physician, medical educator*
Thacker, Stephen Brady *medical association administrator, epidemiologist*
Thomas, Kenneth Eastman *cardiothoracic surgeon*
Turner, John Sidney, Jr. *otolaryngologist, educator*
Tyler, Carl Walter, Jr. *physician, health research administrator*
Van Assendelft, Onno Willem *hematologist*
Waller, John Louis *anesthesiology educator*
Watne, Alvin L. *surgeon, educator*
Wertheim, Steven Blake *orthopedist*
White, Perry Merrill, Jr. *orthopedic surgeon*
Willis, Isaac *dermatologist, educator*
Wilson, Frank Lyndall *surgeon*
Woodard, John Roger *urologist*
Yancey, Asa Greenwood, Sr. *physician*
Yeargin-Allsopp, Marshalyn *epidemiologist, pediatrician*

### Augusta
Chandler, Arthur Bleakley *pathologist, educator*
Colborn, Gene Louis *anatomy educator, researcher*
Dolen, William Kennedy *allergist, immunologist, pediatrician, educator*
†Gadacz, Thomas Roman *surgery educator*
Gambrell, Richard Donald, Jr. *endocrinologist, educator*
Given, Kenna Sidney *surgeon, educator*
Guill, Margaret Frank *pediatrics educator, medical researcher*
Hooks, Vendie Hudson, III *surgeon*
Loomis, Earl Alfred, Jr. *psychiatrist*
Luxenberg, Malcolm Neuwahl *ophthalmologist, educator*
Mahesh, Virendra Bhushan *endocrinologist*
Mansberger, Arlie Roland, Jr. *surgeon*
Merin, Robert Gillespie *anesthesiology educator*
Meyer, Carol Frances *pediatrician, allergist*
Miller, Jerry Allan, Jr. *pediatrician*
Parrish, Robert Alton *retired pediatric surgeon, educator*
Prisant, L(ouis) Michael *cardiologist*
Pryor, Carol Graham *obstetrician, gynecologist*
Puchtler, Holde *histochemist, pathologist, educator*
Rasmussen, Howard *medical educator, medical institute executive*
Rausch, Jeffrey Lynn *psychiatrist, psychopharmacologist*
Rivner, Michael Harvey *neurologist*
Ryan, James Walter *physician, medical researcher*
Solursh, Lionel Paul *psychiatrist*
Wray, Betty Beasley *allergist, immunologist, pediatrician*

### Austell
Halwig, J. Michael *allergist*

### Clarkston
Thatcher, Sharon Louise *medical educator*

### Decatur
Bain, James Arthur *pharmacologist, educator*
Hill, Thomas Glenn, III *dermatologist*
Martinez-Maldonado, Manuel *medical service administrator, physician*
Mirra, Suzanne Samuels *neuropathologist, researcher*
Rausher, David Benjamin *internist, gastroenterologist*

### Evans
Hartlage, Lawrence Clifton *neuropsychologist, educator*

### Fort Benning
Chan, Philip *dermatologist, army officer*

### Fort Gordon
Xenakis, Stephen Nicholas *psychiatrist, army officer*

### Fort Valley
Swartwout, Joseph Rodolph *obstetrics and gynecology educator, administrator*

### Griffin
Carter, Edward Fenton, III *pathologist, medical examiner*

### La Grange
Copeland, Robert Bodine *internist, cardiologist*
West, John Thomas *surgeon*

### Lawrenceville
Fetner, Robert Henry *radiation biologist*

### Macon
†Robinson, Joe Sam *neurosurgeon*
Skelton, William Douglas *physician*
Young, Henry E. *medical educator*

### Marietta
†Biggs, Barbara Conner *internist*
Hagood, M. Felton *surgeon*
Krug, Douglas Edward *emergency physician*
Thomas, Pamella Delores *medical director, physician, educator*
Tissue, Mike *medical educator, respiratory therapist*
Wheatley, Joseph Kevin *physician, urologist*

### Martinez
McKenzie, Harry James *surgeon, surgical researcher*

### Monroe
Adams, Lamar Taft *physician*

### Norcross
Nardelli-Olkowska, Krystyna Maria *ophthalmologist, educator*

### Quitman
Baum, Joseph Herman *retired biomedical educator*

### Roswell
Udoff, Eric Joel *diagnostic radiologist*

### Savannah
Hemphill, John Michael *neurologist*
Horan, Leo Gallaspy *physician, educator*
Krahl, Enzo *retired surgeon*
†Ramage, James Everett, Jr. *respiratory and critical care physician, educator*
Shields, Richard Owen, Jr. *emergency physician*
Stonnington, Henry Herbert *physician, medical executive, educator*
Wirth, Fremont Philip *neurosurgeon, educator*
Woodhouse, Bernard Lawrence *pharmacologist, educator*
Zoller, Michael *otolaryngologist, head and neck surgeon, educator*

### Snellville
Brueckner, Lawrence Terence *orthopedic surgeon*

### Stone Mountain
Gotlieb, Jaquelin Smith *pediatrician*

### Thomaston
Zimmerman, James Robert *radiologist, engineer*

### Thomasville
Watt, William Vance *surgeon*

### Tifton
Dorminey, Henry Clayton, Jr. *allergist*

### Valdosta
Beal, John M. *surgeon, medical educator*
Von Taaffe-Rossmann, Cosima T. *physician, writer, inventor*

### Warm Springs
Knowles, James Barron *rehabilitative medicine physician*
Peach, Paul E. *physician, medical facility administrator*

### Watkinsville
Johnson, Norman James *physician, lawyer*

## HAWAII

### Hilo
Taniguchi, Tokuso *surgeon*

### Honolulu
Brady, Stephen R.P.K. *physician*
Chee, Percival Hon Yin *ophthalmologist*
†Chesne, Edward Leonard *physician*
Chock, Clifford Yet-Chong *family practice physician*
Fong, Bernard W. D. *physician, educator*
Goldstein, Sir Norman *dermatologist*
Goodhue, William Walter, Jr. *pathologist, military officer, medical educator*
Ho, Reginald Chi Shing *medical educator*
Hollison, Robert Victor, Jr. *physician, executive, army officer*
Hundahl, Scott Alfred *oncologic surgeon*
Kane, Thomas Jay, III *orthopaedic surgeon, educator*
Kolonel, Laurence Norman *epidemiologist, public health educator*
Lee, Yeu-Tsu Margaret *surgeon, educator*
Linman, James William *retired physician, educator*
Marvit, Robert Charles *psychiatrist*
†Mc Dermott, John Francis, Jr. *psychiatrist, physician*
Meagher, Michael *radiologist*
Moreno-Cabral, Carlos Eduardo *cardiac surgeon*
Pang, Herbert George *ophthalmologist*
Pien, Francis D. *internist, microbiologist*
Schatz, Irwin Jacob *cardiologist*
Sharma, Santosh Devraj *obstetrician, gynecologist, educator*
Shen, Edward Nin-Da *cardiologist, educator*
Smith, Thomas Kent *radiologist*
Stevens, Stephen Edward *psychiatrist*
Sugiki, Shigemi *ophthalmologist, educator*
Terminella, Luigi *critical care physician, educator*
†Wallach, Stephen Joseph *cardiologist*

### Koloa
Donohugh, Donald Lee *physician*

### Lahaina
Ard, James George *family physician*

### Mililani
Gardner, Sheryl Paige *gynecologist*

### Tripler Army Medical Center
Person, Donald Ames, Sr. *pediatrician, rheumatologist*

### Waianae
Kakugawa, Terri Etsumi *osteopath*

### Waikoloa
Copman, Louis *radiologist*

### Wailuku
Savona, Michael Richard *physician*

## IDAHO

### Coeur D Alene
Strimas, John Howard *allergist, immunologist, pediatrician*
West, Robert Sumner *surgeon*

### Nampa
Botimer, Allen Ray *retired surgeon, retirement center owner*

### Pocatello
Hillyard, Ira William *pharmacologist, educator*

## ILLINOIS

### Abbott Park
Bush, Eugene Nyle *pharmacologist, research scientist*

### Arlington Heights
Pochyly, Donald Frederick *physician, hospital administrator*
Shetty, Mulki Radhakrishna *oncologist, consultant*

### Aurora
Ball, William James *pediatrician*
Bleck, Phyllis Claire *surgeon, musician*

### Belleville
Cagas, Cosme Ralota *pediatrician, endocrinologist*

### Berwyn
Rossof, Arthur Harold *internal medicine educator*

### Carbondale
Pelton, Sharon Janice *emergency physician*

### Carol Stream
Schmerold, Wilfried Lothar *dermatologist*

### Champaign
Rosenblatt, Karin Ann *community health educator*

### Chicago
Abcarian, Herand *surgeon, educator*
Abelson, Herbert Traub *pediatrician, educator*
Albrecht, Ronald Frank *anesthesiologist*
Andersen, Burton Robert *physician, educator*
Applebaum, Edward Leon *otolaryngologist, educator*
Arekapudi, Vijayalakshmi *obstetrician-gynecologist*
Astrachan, Boris Morton *psychiatry educator, consultant*
Baffes, Thomas Gus *cardiac surgeon, lawyer*
Bailey, Orville Taylor *neuropathologist*
Balsam, Theodore *physician*
Barker, Walter Lee *thoracic surgeon*
†Barton, John Joseph *obstetrician-gynecologist, educator*
Bassiouny, Hishan Salah *surgeon, educator*
Batle, Daniel *nephrologist*
Beaty, Harry Nelson *internist, educator, university dean*
Beck, Robert N. *nuclear medicine educator*
Becker, Michael Allen *physician, educator*
Beigl, William *physician, naturopath, hypnotist, acupuncturist, consultant*
Berendi, Erlinda Bayaua *surgeon*
Betts, Henry Brognard *physician, health facility administrator, educator*
Boggs, Joseph Dodridge *pediatric pathologist, educator*
Bonow, Robert Ogden *medical educator*
Boshes, Louis D. *physician, scientist, educator*
Bowman, James Edward *physician, educator*
Bransfield, James Joseph *surgeon*
Bresnahan, James Francis *medical ethics educator*
Brueschke, Erich Edward *physician, researcher, educator*
Calenoff, Leonid *radiologist*
Caro, William Allan *physician*
Charles, Allan G. *physician, educator*
Chatterton, Robert Treat, Jr. *reproductive endocrinology educator*
Cho, Wonhwa *biomedical researcher*
Clark, John Whitcomb *diagnostic radiologist*
Coe, Fredric L. *physician, educator, researcher*
Cohen, Melvin R. *physician, educator*
Colley, Karen J. *medical educator, medical researcher*
Colten, Harvey Radin *pediatrician, educator*
Conway, James Joseph *physician*
Coopersmith, Bernard Ira *obstetrician, gynecologist, educator*
Costa, Erminio *pharmacologist, cell biology educator*
Cui, Ke-hui *embryologist, obstetrician, gynecologist*
Datta, Syamal Kumar *medical educator, researcher*
†Davidson, Richard J. *medical association administrator*
Davison, Richard *physician, educator*
Degroot, Leslie Jacob *medical educator*
Deorio, Anthony Joseph *surgeon*
Derlacki, Eugene L(ubin) *otolaryngologist, physician*
Deutsch, Thomas Alan *ophthalmologist, educator*
Diamond, Seymour *physician*
Diamond, Shari Seidman *psychology educator, law researcher*
Diaz-Franco, Carlos *surgeon, anatomist, anesthesiologist*
Dunea, George *nephrologist, educator*

Dyrud, Jarl Edvard psychiatrist
Ebert, Paul Allen surgeon, educator
Eisenman, Trudy Fox dermatologist
Erdös, Ervin George pharmacology and biochemistry educator
Espinosa, Gustavo Adolfo radiologist, educator
Evans, Thelma Jean Mathis internist
Feingold, Daniel Leon anesthesiologist
Fennessy, John James radiologist, educator
Ferguson, Donald John surgeon, educator
Ferguson, Mark Kendric physician, educator, researcher
Fitch, Frank Wesley pathologist educator, immunologist, educator, administrator
Flaherty, Emalee Gottbrath pediatrician
Frederiksen, Marilynn Elizabeth Conners physician
Frohman, Lawrence Asher endocrinology educator, scientist
Gartner, Lawrence Mitchel pediatrician, medical college educator
Gecht, Martin Louis physician, bank executive
Gerbie, Albert Bernard obstetrician, gynecologist, educator
Gewertz, Bruce Labe surgeon, educator
Giovacchini, Peter Louis psychoanalyst
Goldberg, Arnold Irving psychoanalyst, educator
Golomb, Harvey Morris oncologist, educator
Gould, Samuel Halpert pediatrics educator
Grayhack, John Thomas urologist, educator
Grimes, Hugh Gavin physician
Haber, Meryl Harold physician, educator, author
Hambrick, Ernestine colon and rectal surgeon
Hand, Roger physician, educator
Haring, Olga Munk medical educator, physician
Harris, Jules Eli medical educator, physician, clinical scientist, administrator
Hartz, Renee Semo cardiothoracic surgeon
Hast, Malcolm Howard medical educator, biomedical scientist
Heller, Paul medical educator
Hellman, Samuel radiologist, physician, educator
Herbolsheimer, Henrietta physician, consultant
Herbst, Arthur Lee obstetrician, gynecologist
Hier, Daniel Barnet neurologist
Hines, James Rodger surgeon
Hinojosa, Raul physician, ear pathology researcher
Honig, George Raymond pediatrician
Horwitz, Irwin Daniel otolaryngologist, educator
Huckman, Michael Saul neuroradiologist, educator
Hughes, John Russell physician, educator
Hunter, James Alexander surgeon, educator
Joehl, Raymond Joseph surgeon, educator
Jonasson, Olga surgeon, educator
Jones, Richard Jeffery physician, educator
Kahrilas, Peter James medical educator, researcher
Katz, Adrian Izhack physician, educator
Katz, Robert Stephen rheumatologist, educator
Kirschner, Barbara Starrels pediatric gastroenterologist
Kirsner, Joseph Barnett physician, educator
Kittle, Charles Frederick surgeon
Kohrman, Arthur Fisher pediatric educator
Kraft, Sumner Charles physician, educator
Kumar, Anand medical educator, researcher
Landau, Richard L. physician, educator
Laumann, Anne Elizabeth dermatologist
LaVelle, Arthur anatomy educator
Lazar, Richard Beck physician, medical administrator
Lee, Raphael Carl plastic surgeon, biomedical engineer
Leff, Alan Richard medical educator
Leventhal, Bennett Lee psychiatry and pediatrics educator, administrator
Levy, Robert Michael neurosurgeon, researcher
Lichter, Edward Arthur physician, educator
Lin, Chin-Chu physician, educator, researcher
Loomis, Salora Dale psychiatrist
†Lurain, John Robert, III gynecologic oncologist
Marcus, Joseph child psychiatrist
Martin, Gary Joseph medical educator
Mayer, Robert Samuel physician
Mets, Marilyn Baird pediatric ophthalmologist
Metz, Charles Edgar radiology educator
Millichap, Joseph Gordon neurologist, educator
Mirkin, Bernard Leo clinical pharmacologist, pediatrician
Mittendorf, Robert physician, epidemiologist
Moawad, Atef obstetrician, gynecologist, educator
Morris, Naomi Carolyn Minner medical educator, administrator, researcher, consultant
Morris, Ralph William chronopharmacologist
Mullan, John Francis (Sean Mullan) neurosurgeon, educator
Mullen, Charles Frederick health educator
Mustoe, Thomas Anthony physician, plastic surgeon
Naclerio, Robert Michael otolaryngologist, educator
Nahrwold, David Lange surgeon, educator
Narahashi, Toshio pharmacology educator
Nemickas, Rimgaudas cardiologist, educator
Newell, Frank William ophthalmologist, educator
Nyhus, Lloyd Milton surgeon, educator
Offer, Daniel psychiatrist
Oryshkevich, Roman Sviatoslav physician, physiatrist, dentist, educator
Osiyoye, Adekunle obstetrician, attorney medical and legal consultant, gynecologist, educator
Pachman, Daniel J. physician, educator
Page, Ernest medical educator
Pappas, George Demetrios anatomy and cell biology educator, scientist
Patterson, Roy physician, educator
Pinsky, Steven Michael radiologist, educator
Pollak, Raymond general and transplant surgeon
Polley, Edward Herman anatomist, educator
Pollock, George Howard psychiatrist, psychoanalyst
Pope, Richard M. rheumatologist
Poznanski, Andrew Karol pediatric radiologist
Prinz, Richard Allen surgeon
Ramsey-Goldman, Rosalind physician
Reddy, Janardan K. medical educator
Rhone, Douglas Pierce pathologist, educator
Rice, Charles Lane surgical educator
Robinson, June Kerswell dermatologist, educator
Roizen, Nancy J. physician, educator
Rosen, Steven Terry oncologist, hematologist
Rosenfield, Robert Lee pediatric endocrinologist, educator
Rosenthal, Ira Maurice pediatrician, educator
Roth, Sanford Irwin pathologist, educator
Rotman, Carlotta J.H. Hill physician
Rowley, Janet Davison physician
Rubenstein, Arthur Harold physician, educator
Rudy, Lester Howard psychiatrist
Sabbagha, Rudy E. obstetrician, gynecologist, educator
Sandlow, Leslie Jordan physician, educator
Scarse, Olivia Marie cardiologist, consultant
Schade, Stanley Greinert, Jr. hematologist, educator
Schafer, Michael Frederick orthopedic surgeon
Schilsky, Richard Lewis oncologist, researcher
Schuler, James Joseph vascular surgeon
Schulman, Sidney neurologist, educator
Schumer, William surgeon, educator
Sciarra, John J. physician, educator
Scommegna, Antonio physician, educator
Scotti, Michael John, Jr. medical association executive
Seeler, Ruth Andrea pediatrician, educator
Shambaugh, George Elmer, III internist
Shields, Thomas William surgeon, educator
Short, Marion Priscilla neurology educator
Siegler, Mark internist, educator
Singh, Manmohan orthopedic surgeon, educator
Smith, David Waldo Edward pathology and gerontology educator, physician
Socol, Michael Lee obstetrician, gynecologist, educator
Sorensen, Leif Boge physician, educator
Sparberg, Marshall Stuart gastroenterologist, educator
Spargo, Benjamin H. educator, renal pathologist
Steele, Glenn Daniel, Jr. surgical oncologist
Sternberg, Paul retired ophthalmologist
Storb, Ursula Beate molecular genetics and cell biology educator
Strange, Gary R. medical educator
Strauch, Gerald Otto surgeon
Stumpf, David Allen pediatric neurologist
Svanborg, Alvar geriatrics educator, researcher
Swerdlow, Martin Abraham physician, pathologist, educator
Tardy, Medney Eugene, Jr. otolaryngologist, facial plastic surgeon
Telfer, Margaret Clare internist, hematologist
Thomas, Leona Marlene health information educator
Todd, James S. surgeon, educator, medical association administrator
Tulsky, Alex Sol physician
Ultmann, John Ernest physician, educator
Vanecko, Robert Michael surgeon, educator
Visotsky, Harold Meryle psychiatrist, educator
Waldstein, Sheldon Saul physician, educator
Walton, Robert Lee, Jr. plastic surgeon
Waxler, Beverly Jean anesthesiologist, physician
Webster, James Randolph, Jr. physician
Weir, Bryce Keith Alexander neurosurgeon, neurology educator
Weis, Mervyn J. physician, gastroenterologist
Wetzel, Franklin Todd spinal surgeon, educator, researcher
Wied, George Ludwig physician
Wilber, David James cardiologist
Wilbur, Andrew Clayton radiologist
Willoughby, William Franklin, II physician, researcher
Winnie, Alon Palm anesthesiologist, educator
Wolpert, Edward Alan psychiatrist
Woodle, E. Steve transplant surgeon
Woodley, David Timothy dermatology educator
Yao, Tito Go pediatrician
Yarkony, Gary Michael physician, researcher
Zatuchni, Gerald Irving physician, educator

### Columbia
Megahy, Diane Alaire physician

### Danville
Prabhudesai, Mukund M. pathology educator, laboratory director, researcher, administrator

### Decatur
Requarth, William Henry surgeon

### Deerfield
Kingdon, Henry Shannon physician, biochemist, educator, executive
Scheiber, Stephen Carl psychiatrist

### Des Plaines
Cucco, Ulisse P. obstetrician, gynecologist

### Dixon
Polascik, Mary Ann ophthalmologist

### Downers Grove
Colbert, Marvin Jay retired internist, educator
Henkin, Robert Elliott nuclear medicine physician

### Elk Grove Village
Herrerias, Carla Trevette epidemiologist, program manager

### Elmhurst
Blain, Charlotte Marie physician, educator
Fornatto, Elio Joseph otolaryngologist, educator

### Evanston
Adelson, Bernard Henry physician
Bashook, Philip G. medical association executive, educator
Beatty, William Kaye medical bibliography educator
Crawford, James Weldon psychiatrist, educator, administrator
Dockery, J. Lee medical school administrator
Enroth-Cugell, Christina Alma Elisabeth neurophysiologist, educator
Hughes, Edward physician, educator
Khandekar, Janardan Dinkar oncologist, educator
Langsley, Donald Gene psychiatrist, medical board executive
Langsley, Pauline Royal psychiatrist
Plaut, Eric Alfred retired psychiatrist, educator
Samter, Max physician, educator
Schwartz, Neena Betty endocrinologist, educator
Schwartz, Theodore B. physician, educator
Shortell, Stephen M. medical educator
Sprang, Milton LeRoy obstetrician, gynecologist, educator
Takahashi, Joseph S. neuroscientist
Traisman, Howard Sevin pediatrician
Vick, Nicholas A. neurologist

### Flossmoor
Lis, Edward Francis pediatrician, consultant

### Galesburg
Tourlentes, Thomas Theodore psychiatrist

### Glen Ellyn
Dieter, Raymond Andrew, Jr. physician, surgeon
Egan, Richard Leo retired medical educator
Temple, Donald allergist, dermatologist

### Glencoe
Fenninger, Leonard Davis medical educator, consultant
Milloy, Frank Joseph, Jr. surgeon

### Glendale Heights
Pimental, Patricia Ann neuropsychologist, consulting company executive, author

### Glenview
Freedman, Philip physician, educator

### Greenville
Junod, Daniel August podiatrist

### Harvey
Heilicser, Bernard Jay emergency physician
Jensen, Harold Leroy physician
Replogle, Robert L. cardiovascular and thoracic surgeon

### Highland Park
Bluefarb, Samuel Mitchell physician
Hirsch, Jay G. psychiatrist, educator
Saltzberg, Eugene Ernest physician, educator

### Hillsboro
Mulch, Robert F., Jr. physician

### Hines
Best, William Robert physician, educator, university official
†Folk, Frank Anton surgeon, educator
Green, Joseph Barnet neurologist, educator
Zvetina, James Raymond pulmonary physician

### Hinsdale
Beatty, Robert Alfred surgeon
Paloyan, Edward physician, educator, researcher

### Homewood
Schumacher, Gebhard Friederich Bernhard obstetrician-gynecologist

### Jacksonville
Scott, Fred Dacon surgeon

### Joliet
Layman, Dale Pierre medical educator, author, researcher
Ring, Alvin Manuel pathologist

### Lake Bluff
Kelly, Daniel John physician

### Lake Forest
Levy, Nelson Louis physician, scientist, corporate executive
Murad, Ferid physician
Salter, Edwin Carroll physician
Wilbur, Richard Sloan physician, foundation executive

### Lincolnshire
Hughes, William Franklin, Jr. ophthalmologist, emeritus educator

### Lockport
Musa, Mahmoud Nimir psychiatry educator

### Lombard
Bachop, William Earl, Jr. retired anatomist, zoologist
Kasprow, Barbara Anne biomedical scientist, writer

### Long Grove
Ausman, Robert K. surgeon, research executive

### Macomb
Dexter, Donald Harvey surgeon

### Marshall
Mitchell, George Trice physician

### Maywood
Canning, John Rafton urologist
Celesia, Gastone Guglielmo neurologist, neurophysiologist, researcher
Freeark, Robert James surgeon, educator
Greenlee, Herbert Breckenridge surgeon, educator
Hanin, Israel pharmacologist, educator
Hart, Cecil William Joseph otolaryngologist, head and neck surgeon
Light, Terry Richard orthopedic hand surgeon
Mason, George Robert surgeon, educator
Newman, Barry Marc pediatric surgeon
Picklemann, Jack R. surgeon
Slogoff, Stephen anesthesiologist, educator

### Moline
Arnell, Richard Anthony radiologist
Banas, John Stanley obstetrician, gynecologist
†Bradley, Walter James emergency physician

### Naperville
Schwab, Paul Josiah psychiatrist, educator

### Niles
Chertack, Melvin M. internist

### Normal
Cooley, William Emory, Jr. radiologist

### North Chicago
Beer, Alan Earl physician, medical educator
Ehrenpreis, Seymour pharmacology educator
Freese, Uwe Ernest physician, educator
Gall, Eric Papineau physician, educator
Hawkins, Richard Albert medical educator, administrator
Kim, Yoon Berm immunologist, educator
Kyncl, John Jaroslav pharmacologist
Morris, Charles Elliot neurologist
Nair, Velayudhan pharmacologist, medical educator
Rogers, Eugene Jack medical educator
Rudy, David Robert physician, educator
Schlager, Seymour Irving physician
Schneider, Arthur Sanford physician, educator
Sierles, Frederick Stephen psychiatrist, educator
Taylor, Michael Alan psychiatrist

### Northbrook
Day, Emerson physician
Hirsch, Lawrence Leonard physician, retired educator
Mc Laren, John Alexander retired physician
Rodriguez-Erdmann, Franz physician
Scanlon, Edward F. surgeon, educator

### Northfield
Cutler, Robert Porter psychiatrist, psychoanalyst
Giffin, Mary Elizabeth psychiatrist, educator

### Oak Brook
Christian, Joseph Ralph physician
Dmowski, W. Paul obstetrician, gynecologist

### Oak Lawn
†Earle, Richard H. medical educator
Rathi, Manohar Lal pediatrician, neonatologist

### Oak Park
Brackett, Edward Boone, III orthopedic surgeon

### Oakbrook Terrace
Becker, Robert Jerome allergist, health care consultant

### Olney
Edwards, Ian Keith retired obstetrician, gynecologist

### Olympia Fields
Kasimos, John Nicholas pathologist
Webster, Douglas Peter emergency physician

### Palos Heights
McInerney, John Vincent obstetrician and gynecologist

### Park Ridge
Bitran, Jacob David internist
Fried, Walter hematologist, educator
Mangun, Clarke Wilson, Jr. public health physician, consultant
Weinberg, Milton, Jr. cardiovascular, thoracic surgeon

### Peoria
Gross, Thomas Lester obstetrician, gynecologist, researcher
Meriden, Terry physician
†Miller, Rick Frey emergency physician
Stine, Robert Howard pediatrician
Traina, Jeffrey Francis orthopedic surgeon

### Pinckneyville
Cawvey, Clarence Eugene physician

### Rock Island
Forlini, Frank John, Jr. cardiologist

### Rockford
Frakes, James Terry physician, gastroenterologist, educator
Heerens, Robert Edward physician
Olson, Stanley William physician, educator, medical school dean

### Saint Charles
McCartney, Charles Price retired obstetrician-gynecologist

### Schaumburg
Kitt, Walter psychiatrist

### Schiller Park
†Canella, Joseph M. preventive medicine physician
Ring, Alice Ruth Bishop physician

### Skokie
Bellows, Randall Trueblood ophthalmologist, educator
Olwin, John Hurst surgeon

### Springfield
Dodd, Robert Bruce physician, educator
Feldman, Bruce Alan psychiatrist
Frank, Stuart cardiologist
Holland, John Madison family practice physician
Lucore, Charles Lee cardiologist
Myers, Phillip Ward otolaryngologist
Rabinovich, Sergio physician, educator
Rockey, Paul Henry physician, medical educator, university official
Sumner, David Spurgeon surgery educator
Yaffe, Stuart Allen physician
Zaricznyj, Basilius orthopedic surgeon
Zook, Elvin Glenn plastic surgeon, educator

### Urbana
Austin, Jean Philippe medical educator, radiologist
Churchill, Mair Elisa Annabelle medical educator
Greenwold, Warren Eldon retired physician, medical educator
Kocheril, Abraham George physician, educator
Krock, Curtis Josselyn pulmonologist
Nelson, Ralph Alfred physician
O'Morchoe, Charles Christopher Creagh administrator, anatomical sciences educator
O'Morchoe, Patricia Jean pathologist, educator
Voss, Edward William, Jr. immunologist, educator
Welch, William Ben emergency physician

### Villa Grove
Moss Bower, Phylis Dawn medical researcher

### West Chicago
Paulissen, James Peter retired physician, county official

### Wheaton
Bogdonoff, Maurice Lambert physician
Haenszel, William Manning epidemiologist, educator
Maibenco, Helen Craig anatomist, educator

Karibo, John Michael *allergist, immunologist, pediatrician*
†King, William Bradley *emergency medicine physician*
Kleinert, Harold Earl *plastic surgery educator*
Neustadt, David Harold *physician*
Olson, William Henry *neurology educator, administrator*
Parker, Joseph Corbin, Jr. *pathologist*
Pence, Hobert Lee *physician*
Polk, Hiram Carey, Jr. *surgeon, educator*
Sanfilippo, Joseph Salvatore *physician, reproductive endocrinologist, educator*
Schwab, John Joseph *psychiatrist, educator*
Scott, Ralph Mason *physician, radiation oncology educator*
Slung, Hilton B. *surgeon*
Spinnato, Joseph Anthony, II *obstetrician*
Spratt, John Stricklin *surgeon, educator, researcher*
Tasman, Allan *psychiatry educator*
Tsai, Tsu-Min *surgeon*
Uhde, George Irvin *physician*
Waddell, William Joseph *pharmacologist, toxicologist*
Weisskopf, Bernard *pediatrician, child behavior, development and genetics specialist, educator*
Wright, Jesse Hartzell *psychiatrist, educator*
Zimmerman, Thom Jay *ophthalmologist, educator*

### Madisonville
Stulc, Jaroslav Peter *surgeon, educator*

### Morehead
Miller, Jon William *emergency physician*

### Russellville
Hattem, Albert Worth *physician*

## LOUISIANA

### Baton Rouge
Bray, George August *physician, scientist, educator*
Cherry, William Ashley *surgeon, state health officer*
Dunlap, Wallace Hart *pediatrician*
Kidd, James Marion, III *allergist, immunologist, educator*
Krotoski, Wojciech Antoni *physician, educator*
Le Vine, Jerome Edward *retired ophthalmologist, educator*
Lovejoy, Jennifer Carole *medical educator*
Lucas, Fred Vance *pathology educator, university administrator*
Parra, Pamela Ann *physician, educator*
Romero, Jorge Antonio *neurologist, educator*

### Benton
Dunnihoo, Dale Russell *physician, medical educator*

### Covington
Roberts, James Allen *urologist*

### Gretna
Lupin, Ellis Ralph *physician, lawyer, coroner*

### Hammond
Hejtmancik, Milton Rudolph *medical educator*

### Houma
Conrad, Harold Theodore *psychiatrist*

### Kenner
White, Charles Albert, Jr. *medical educator, obstetrician-gynecologist*

### Lafayette
Cade, Toni Marie *medical educator*

### Lake Charles
Drez, David Jacob, Jr. *orthopedic surgeon, educator*
Yadalam, Kashinath Gangadhara *psychiatrist*

### Mandeville
Ray, Charles Jackson *retired surgeon*

### Metairie
Bower, Philip Jeffrey *cardiologist, administrator*
Carter, Rebecca Davilene *general surgeon, surgical oncology educator*
Conway, James Donald *internist, educator*
DiBenedetto, Robert Lawrence *obstetrician, gynecologist, insurance company executive*
Edisen, Clayton Byron *physician*
Lake, Wesley Wayne, Jr. *internist, allergist, educator*
Ochsner, Seymour Fiske *radiologist, editor*
Spruiell, Vann *psychoanalyst, educator, editor, researcher*
Young, Lucy Cleaver *physician*

### Monroe
†Cooksey, John Charles *ophthalmic surgeon*

### New Orleans
Agrawal, Krishna Chandra *pharmacology educator*
Arshad, M. Kaleem *psychiatrist*
Bautista, Abraham Parana *immunologist*
Beck, David Edward *surgeon*
Bertrand, William Ellis *public health educator, academic administrator*
Boudreaux, J. Philip *transplant surgeon, educator*
Burch, Robert Emmett *physician, educator*
Caldwell, Delmar Ray *ophthalmologist, educator*
Cohn, Isidore, Jr. *surgeon, educator*
Connolly, Edward S. *neurological surgeon*
Corrigan, James John, Jr. *pediatrician, dean*
Daniels, Robert Sanford *psychiatrist, administrator*
Domer, Floyd Ray *pharmacologist, educator*
Domingue, Gerald James *medical scientist, microbiology, immunology and urology educator, researcher, clinical bacteriologist*
Duffy, John Charles *psychiatric educator*
Duncan, Margaret Caroline *physician*
Easson, William McAlpine *psychiatrist*
Eichberg, Rodolfo David *physician, educator*
England, John David *neurologist*
Ensenat, Louis Albert *surgeon*
Epstein, Arthur William *physician, educator*
Espinoza, Luis Rolan *rheumatologist*
Ewin, Dabney Minor *surgeon*
Fisch, Bruce Jeffrey *physician, educator*
Fisher, James William *medical educator, pharmacologist*
Friedlander, Miles Herbert *ophthalmologist*
Frohlich, Edward David *medical educator*
†Fuselier, Harold Anthony, Jr. *physician, urologist*
García Oller, José Luis *neurosurgeon*
Gathright, John Byron, Jr. *colon and rectal surgeon, educator*
Gatipon, Betty Becker *medical educator, consultant*
Gottlieb, A(braham) Arthur *medical educator*
Hewitt, Robert Lee *surgeon, educator*
Hicks, Terrell Cohlman *surgeon*
Howard, Richard Ralston, II *medical health advisor, researcher, financier*
Hyman, Albert Lewis *cardiologist*
Hyman, Edward Sidney *physician, researcher*
Hyslop, Newton Everett, Jr. *infectious disease specialist*
Imig, John David *medical educator*
Incaprera, Frank Philip *internist, medical educator, health facility administrator*
Jaffe, Bernard Michael *surgeon*
Jung, Rodney C. *internist, academic administrator*
Kewalramani, Laxman Sunderdas *surgeon, consultant*
Kline, David Gellinger *neurosurgery educator*
Kolinsky, Michael Allen *emergency physician*
Krementz, Edward Thomas *surgeon*
Lang, Erich Karl *physician, radiologist*
Le Jeune, Francis Ernest, Jr. *otolaryngologist*
Lewy, John Edwin *pediatric nephrologist*
Litwin, Martin Stanley *surgeon*
Locke, William *endocrinologist*
Lopez, Manuel *immunology and allergy educator*
Low, Frank Norman *anatomist, educator*
Martin, David Hubert *physician, educator*
Massare, John Steve *medical association administrator, educator*
Miller, Robert Harold *otolaryngologist, educator*
Millikan, Larry Edward *dermatologist*
Mogabgab, William Joseph *epidemiologist, educator*
Nelson, James Smith *pathologist, educator*
Nice, Charles Monroe, Jr. *physician, educator*
Nichols, Ronald Lee *surgeon, educator*
Norman, Edward Cobb *retired psychiatrist, educator*
Ochsner, John Lockwood *thoracic-cardiovascular surgeon*
O'Quinn, April Gale *physician, educator*
Paddison, Richard Milton *neurologist, educator*
Pankey, George Atkinson *physician, educator*
Pfister, Richard Charles *physician, radiology educator*
Phelps, Carol Jo *neuroendocrinologist*
Plavsic, Branko Milenko *radiology educator*
Puschett, Jules B. *medical educator, neprhrologist, researcher*
Puyau, Francis Albert *physician, radiology educator*
Re, Richard Noel *endocrinologist*
Reisin, Efrain *nephrologist, researcher, educator*
Riddick, Frank Adams, Jr. *physician, health care facility administrator*
Rietschel, Robert Louis *dermatologist*
Salatich, John Smyth *cardiologist*
Schally, Andrew Victor *endocrinologist, researcher*
Schneider, George T. *obstetrician-gynecologist*
Stewart, Gregory Wallace *physician*
Straumanis, John Janis, Jr. *psychiatry educator*
Timmcke, Alan Edward *physician and surgeon*
Turkish, Lance *physician, ophthalmologist*
Usdin, Gene Leonard *physician, psychiatrist*
Ventura, Hector Osvaldo *cardiologist*
Waring, William Winburn *pediatric pulmonologist, educator*
Webb, Watts Rankin *surgeon*
Weill, Hans *physician, educator*
Weiss, Thomas Edward *physician*
Welsh, Ronald Arthur *physician, educator*
Winstead, Daniel Keith *psychiatrist*
Yates, Robert Doyle *anatomy educator*
Zimny, Marilyn Lucile *anatomist, educator*

### Opelousas
Pinac, André Louis, III *obstetrician, gynecologist*

### Pineville
Hirsch, Joe Elbe *surgeon*
Swearingen, David Clarke *physician, musician*

### Scott
Bergeron, Wilton Lee *physician*

### Shreveport
Bradley, Ronald James *neuroscientist*
Breffeilh, Louis Andrew *ophthalmologist, educator*
Conrad, Steven Allen *physician, biomedical engineer, educator, researcher*
Dilworth, Edwin Earle *retired obstetrician, gynecologist*
Fort, Arthur Tomlinson, III *physician, educator*
Freeman, Arthur Merrimon, III *psychiatry educator, dean*
Ganley, James Powell *ophthalmologist, educator*
†George, Ronald Baylis *physician, educator*
Griffith, Robert Charles *allergist, educator, planter*
Huot, Rachel Irene *biomedical educator, research scientist*
Levy, Harold Bernard *pediatrician*
Linhart, Joseph Wayland *cardiologist, educational administrator*
Mancini, Mary Catherine *cardiothoracic surgeon, researcher*
McDonald, John Clifton *surgeon*
Misra, Raghunath Prasad *physician, educator*
Reddy, Pratap Chandupatla *cardiologist, educator, researcher*
Rush, Benjamin McGraw *surgeon*
Shelby, James Stanford *cardiovascular surgeon*
Thurmon, Theodore Francis *medical educator*

### Slidell
McBurney, Elizabeth Innes *physician, educator*
Muller, Robert Joseph *gynecologist*

### Thibodaux
Hebert, Leo Placide *physician*

## MAINE

### Augusta
Cheng, Hsueh Ching *physician*
Hussey, John Francis *physician, geriatrician*

### Bangor
Watt, Thomas Lorne *dermatologist*

### Biddeford
Ally, Ahmmed *neuroscientist, researcher, educator*

### Camden
Spock, Benjamin McLane *physician, educator*

### Chebeague Island
Middleton, Elliott, Jr. *physician*

### Friendship
Walker, Douglass Willey *retired pediatrician, medical center administrator*

### Hampden
Brown, Robert Horatio, Sr. *retired orthopedic surgeon*

### Kennebunk
Sholl, John Gurney, III *physician*

### Orono
Weiss, Robert Jerome *psychiatrist, educator*

### Oxford
Bensen, Pamela Parke *emergency medicine physician, educator, researcher*

### Portland
Brigham, Christopher Roy *occupational medicine physician*
Clark, Gordon Hostetter, Jr. *physician*

### Rockport
Swenson, Orvar *surgeon*

### South Portland
Katz, Steven Edward *psychiatrist, state health official*

### Union
Buchan, Ronald Forbes *preventive medicine physician*

### York
Lauter, M. David *family physician*

## MARYLAND

### Annapolis
Brown-Christopher, Cheryl Denise *physician*
Calabrese, Anthony Joseph *gastroenterologist*
Halpern, Joseph Alan *physician*
Holtgrewe, Henry Logan *urologist*

### Baltimore
Adkinson, N. Franklin, Jr. *clinical immunologist*
Albuquerque, Edson Xavier *pharmacology educator*
Andres, Reubin *gerontologist*
Bachur, Nicholas Robert, Sr. *research physician*
Baker, R. Robinson *surgeon*
Baker, Susan P. *public health educator*
Baker, Timothy Danforth *physician, educator*
Bartlett, John Gill *infectious disease physician*
Baughman, Kenneth Lee *cardiologist, educator*
Baumgartner, William Anthony *cardiac surgeon*
Bayless, Theodore M(orris) *gastroenterologist, educator, researcher*
Benz, Edward J., Jr. *physician, educator*
Bereston, Eugene Sydney *retired dermatologist*
Berlin, Fred Saul *psychiatrist, educator*
Berman, Barnett *internist, educator*
Bhardwaj, Anish *neuroscientist, medical educator*
Bigelow, George E. *psychology and pharmacology scientist*
Breitenecker, Rudiger *pathologist*
Brody, Eugene B. *psychiatrist, educator*
Brody, William R. *radiologist, educator*
Brusilow, Saul *pediatrics researcher*
Bundick, William Ross *retired dermatologist*
Cameron, Duke Edward *cardiac surgeon, educator*
Campazzi, Earl James *physician*
†Carson, Benjamin Solomon *neurosurgeon*
Chernow, Bart *critical care physician*
Childs, Barton *retired, physician, educator*
Conley, Carroll Lockard *physician, emeritus educator*
Connaughton, James Patrick *psychiatrist*
Cornblath, Marvin *pediatrician, educator*
Cummings, Charles William *physician, educator*
Dang, Chi Van *hematology and oncology educator*
Daniels, Worth B., Jr. *retired internist*
Dannenberg, Arthur Milton, Jr. *experimental pathologist, immunologist, educator*
DeAngelis, Catherine D. *pediatrics educator*
DeLateur, Barbara Jane *medical educator*
Dembo, Donald Howard *cardiologist, medical administrator, educator*
Dorst, John Phillips *physician, radiology and pediatrics educator*
Drachman, Daniel Bruce *neurologist*
Eisenberg, Howard Michael *neurosurgeon*
Eldefrawi, Amira Toppozada *medical educator*
Faden, Ruth R. *medical educator, ethicist, researcher*
Felsenthal, Gerald *physiatrist, educator*
Ferencz, Charlotte *pediatrician, epidemiology and preventive medicine educator*
Fishman, Jacob Robert *psychiatrist, administrator, educator, corporate executive, investor*
Fox, Harold Edward *obstetrician, gynecologist, educator, researcher*
Freeman, John Mark *pediatric neurologist*
Friedman, Marion *internist, family physician, medical administrator, medical editor*
Gimenez, Luis Fernando *physician, educator*
Godenne, Ghislaine Dudley *physician, psychoanalyst, educator*
Goldberg, Morton Falk *ophthalmologist, educator*
Gordis, Leon *physician*
Graham, George Gordon *physician*
Greenough, William Bates, III *medical educator*
Griffin, Diane Edmund *research physician, virologist, educator*
Griffith, Lawrence Stacey Cameron *cardiologist*
Handelsman, Jacob Charles *surgeon*
Hart, John, Jr. *behavioral neurologist, neuroscientist, educator*
Harvey, Abner McGehee *physician, educator*
Hellmann, David Bruce *medical educator*
Helrich, Martin *anesthesiologist, educator*
Henderson, Donald Ainslie *public health educator*
Hofkin, Gerald Alan *gastroenterologist*
Hungerford, David Samuel *orthopedic surgeon, educator*
Hutchins, Grover MacGregor *pathologist, educator*
Imboden, John Baskerville *psychiatry educator*
Jani, Sushma Niranjan *pediatrics and child and adolescent psychiatrist*
Jastreboff, Pawel Jerzy *neuroscientist, educator*
Johns, Carol Johnson *physician, educator*
Johns, Richard James *physician, educator*
Johnson, Kenneth Peter *neurologist, medical researcher*
Kastor, John Alfred *cardiologist, educator*
Kern, David Evans *physician*
Kinnard, William James, Jr. *retired pharmacy educator*
Kowarski, Allen Avinoam *endocrinologist, educator*
Kuppusamy, Periannan *medical educator, medical researcher*
Kwiterovich, Peter Oscar, Jr. *medical science educator, researcher, physician*
Lakatta, Edward Gerard *biomedical researcher*
Lawrence, Robert Swan *physician, educator, academic administrator*
Lewison, Edward Frederick *surgeon*
Lichtenstein, Lawrence Mark *allergy, immunology educator, physician*
Litrenta, Frances Marie *psychiatrist*
Long, Donlin Martin *surgeon, educator*
Manson, Paul Nellis *plastic surgeon*
Markowska, Alicja Lidia *neuroscientist, researcher*
Massof, Robert William *neuroscientist, educator*
Matheson, Nina W. *medical researcher*
Matjasko, M. Jane *anesthesiologist, educator*
Maumenee Hussels, Irene E. *ophthalmology educator*
McDowell, Elizabeth Mary *retired pathology educator*
Mc Hugh, Paul R. *psychiatrist, neurologist, educator*
McKhann, Guy Mead *physician, educator*
Meny, Robert *medical research administrator*
Migeon, Barbara Ruben *pediatrician, geneticist*
Migeon, Claude Jean *pediatrics educator*
Miller, Edward Doring, Jr. *anesthesiologist*
Milnor, William Robert *physician*
Mizel, Mark Stuart *orthopedic surgeon*
Monroe, Russell Ronald *psychiatrist, educator*
Moser, Hugo Wolfgang *physician*
†Mosley, W. Henry *medical educator*
Munster, Andrew Michael *surgery educator*
Mysko, William Keifer *emergency physician, educator*
Nagey, David Augustus *physician, researcher*
Norman, Philip Sidney *physician*
North, Richard Boydston *neurological surgery educator*
Patz, Arnall *physician*
Platt, William Rady *pathology educator*
Proctor, Donald Frederick *otolaryngology educator, physician*
Provost, Thomas Taylor *dermatology educator, researcher*
Rayson, Glendon Ennes *internist, preventive medicine specialist, writer*
Rennels, Marshall Leigh *neuroanatomist, biomedical scientist, educator*
Rose, Noel Richard *immunologist, microbiologist, educator*
Rosenstein, Beryl Joel *physician*
Samet, Jonathan Michael *epidemiologist, educator*
Sanfilippo, Alfred Paul *pathologist, educator*
Schimpff, Stephen Callender *internist, oncologist*
Schuster, Marvin Meier *physician, educator*
Shuldiner, Alan Rodney *physician, endocrinologist, educator*
Silbergeld, Ellen Kovner *environmental epidemiologist and toxicologist*
Silverstein, Arthur Matthew *ophthalmic immunologist, educator, historian*
Simpson, Thomas William *physician*
Smith, Gardner Watkins *physician*
Smith, Julian Payne *gynecological oncologist, educator*
Snyder, Solomon Halbert *psychiatrist, pharmacologist*
Sommer, Alfred *medical educator, scientist, ophthalmologist*
Stair, Thomas Osborne *physician, educator*
Starfield, Barbara Helen *physician, educator*
Stobo, John David *physician, educator*
Stolley, Paul David *medical educator, researcher*
Strickland, George Thomas, Jr. *physician, researcher, educator*
Tabatznik, Bernard *physician, educator*
Talalay, Paul *pharmacologist, physician*
Tamminga, Carol Ann *neuroscientist*
Taylor, Carl Ernest *physician, educator*
Udvarhelyi, George Bela *neurosurgery educator emeritus, cultural affairs administrator*
Vogelstein, Bert *oncology educator*
Waalkes, T. Phillip *physician, educator*
Wagner, Henry Nicholas, Jr. *physician*
Wallach, Edward Eliot *physician, educator*
Walser, Mackenzie *physician, educator*
Walsh, Patrick Craig *urologist*
†Waterbury, Larry *physician, educator*
Weiss, James Lloyd *cardiology educator*
Welch, Robert Bond *ophthalmologist, educator*
Williams, G(eorge) Melville *surgeon, medical educator*
Wilson, Donald Edward *physician, educator*
Woodward, Theodore Englar *medical educator, internist*
Young, Barbara *psychiatrist, psychoanalyst, psychiatry educator, photographer*
Young, Grace May-En *pediatrician*
Yuan, Xiao-Jian *medical researcher, educator*
Zassenhaus, Hiltgunt Margret *physician*
Zizic, Thomas Michael *physician, educator*

### Bethesda
Abbrecht, Peter Herman *medical educator*
Alexander, Duane Frederick *pediatrician, research administrator*
Axelrod, Julius *pharmacologist, biochemist*
Barter, Robert Henry *physician, retired educator*
Berendes, Heinz Werner *medical epidemiologist, pediatrician*
Breggin, Peter Roger *psychiatrist, author*
Brodine, Charles Edward *physician*
Brown, Dudley Earl, Jr. *psychiatrist, educator, health executive, former federal agency administrator, former naval officer*
Carney, William Patrick *medical educator*
Cath, Stanley Howard *psychiatrist, psychoanalyst*
Chanock, Robert Merritt *pediatrician*

Maher, Timothy John pharmacologist, educator
Malt, Ronald A. surgeon, educator
Mankin, Henry Jay physician, educator
Mannick, John Anthony surgeon
Maynard, Kenneth Irwin medical educator, researcher
Mc Arthur, Janet Ward endocrinologist, educator
McCormick, Marie Clare pediatrician, educator
Mc Dermott, William Vincent, Jr. physician, educator
McDougal, William Scott urology educator
McNeil, Barbara Joyce radiologist, educator
Medearis, Donald Norman, Jr. physician, educator
Mellins, Harry Zachary radiologist, educator
Merk, Frederick Bannister biomedical educator, medical researcher
Messerle, Judith Rose medical librarian, public relations director
Michel, Thomas Mark internal medicine educator, scientist, physician
Moellering, Robert Charles, Jr. internist, educator
Monaco, Anthony Peter surgery educator, medical institute administrator
Mongan, James John physician, hospital administrator
Montgomery, William Wayne surgeon
Morgan, James Philip pharmacologist, cardiologist, educator
Morgentaler, Abraham urologist, researcher
Nadas, Alexander Sandor pediatric cardiologist, educator
Naimi, Shapur cardiologist, educator
Nathan, David Gordon physician, educator
Nichols, David Harry gynecologic surgeon, obstetrics and gynecology educator, author
O'Donnell, Thomas Francis vascular surgeon, health facility administrator
Oxenkrug, Gregory Fayva psychopharmacologist
Papageorgiou, Panagiotis medical educator
Paul, Oglesby cardiologist
Payne, Douglas DeFrees cardiothoracic surgeon, educator
Petersen, Robert Allen pediatric ophthalmologist
Pochi, Peter Ernest physician
Poser, Charles Marcel neurology educator
Potts, John Thomas, Jr. physician, educator
Poussaint, Alvin Francis psychiatrist, educator
Prout, Curtis physician
Puliafito, Carmen Anthony ophthalmologist, laser researcher
Rabkin, Mitchell Thornton physician, hospital administrator, educator
Ransil, Bernard J(erome) research physician, methodologist, consultant, educator
Reid, Lynne McArthur pathologist
Relman, Arnold Seymour physician, educator, editor
Reppert, Steven Marion scientist, educator, pediatrician
Richie, Jerome Paul surgeon, educator
Rockoff, Mark Alan pediatric anesthesiologist
Rohrer, Richard Jeffrey surgeon, educator
Rosen, Fred Saul pediatrics educator
Rosenblatt, Michael medical researcher, educator
Rush, David medical investigator, epidemiologist
Russell, Paul Snowden surgeon, educator
Ryan, Kenneth John physician, educator
Ryser, Hugues Jean-Paul pharmacologist, medical educator, cell biologist
Sadeghi-Nejad, Abdollah pediatrician, educator
Sallan, Stephen E. pediatrician
Salzman, Edwin William surgery educator
Sandson, John I. physician, educator, retired university dean
Saper, Clifford Baird neurobiology and neurology educator
Schaller, Jane Green pediatrician
Schlossman, Stuart Franklin physician, educator, researcher
Schnitzer, Jan Eugeniusz medical educator, scientist
Schwartz, Bernard physician
Schwartz, Carl Robert Emden psychiatrist and educator
Scott, James Arthur radiologist, educator
Seddon, Johanna Margaret ophthalmologist, epidemiologist
Seely, Ellen Wells endocrinologist
Selkoe, Dennis Jesse neurologist, researcher, educator
Shader, Richard Irwin psychiatrist, educator
Shapiro, Jerome Herbert radiologist, educator
Shields, Lawrence Thornton orthopedic surgeon, educator
Silen, William physician, surgery educator
Sledge, Clement Blount orthopedic surgeon, educator
Smith, Thomas Woodward cardiologist, educator
Snydman, David Richard infectious diseases specialist, educator
Solomon, Caren Grossbard internist
Steere, Allen Caruthers, Jr. physician, educator
Swartz, Morton Norman medical educator
Tauber, Alfred Imre hematologist, immunologist, philosopher of science
Taubman, Martin Arnold immunologist
Taveras, Juan Manuel physician, educator
Theoharides, Theoharis Constantin pharmacologist, physician, educator
Thorn, George Widmer physician, educator
Tilney, Nicholas Lechmere surgery educator
Trichopoulos, Dimitrios Vassilios epidemiologist, educator
Trier, Jerry Steven gastroenterologist, educator
Tsuang, Ming Tso psychiatrist, educator
Vachon, Louis psychiatrist, educator
Vaillant, George Eman psychiatrist
†Walls, Ron M. emergency medicine physician, educator, health facility administrator
Warshaw, Andrew Louis surgeon, researcher
Weber, Georg Franz immunologist
Weiss, Earle Burton physician
Williams, Gordon Harold internist, medical educator, researcher
Wood, Lawrence Crane medical association administrator, educator
Woog, John J. eye plastic surgeon
Yuan, Junying medical educator, researcher
Zaleznik, Abraham psychoanalyst, management specialist, educator
Zarins, Bertram orthopaedic surgeon
Zervas, Nicholas Themistocles neurosurgeon
Zinner, Michael Jeffrey surgeon, educator

### Brockton
Carlson, Desiree Anice pathologist
†Kligler, Roger Michael physician

### Brookline
Blom, Gaston Eugene psychiatrist
Jakab, Irene psychiatrist
Jordan, Ruth Ann physician
Kraut, Joel Arthur ophthalmologist
Lown, Bernard cardiologist, educator
Nadelson, Carol Cooperman psychiatrist, educator
Rachlin, William Selig surgeon
Sarfaty, Suzanne internist and educator
Spellman, Mitchell Wright surgeon, academic administrator
Sweet, William Herbert neurosurgeon
Tyler, H. Richard physician

### Burlington
Clerkin, Eugene Patrick physician
Fager, Charles Anthony physician, neurosurgeon
McAlpine, Frederick Sennett anesthesiologist
Moschella, Samuel L. dermatology educator
Schoetz, David John, Jr. colon and rectal surgeon
Wise, Robert Edward radiologist

### Cambridge
Anderson, William Henry psychobiologist, educator
Bartus, Raymond Thomas neuroscientist, pharmaceutical executive, writer
Bizzi, Emilio neurophysiologist, educator
Brusch, John Lynch physician
Buchanan, John Robert physician, educator
Buchwald, Jed Zachary environmental health researcher, science history educator
Coles, Robert child psychiatrist, educator, author
Davidson, Charles Sprecher physician
Davie, Joseph Myrten physician, pathology and immunology educator, science administrator
†Dorwart, Robert Alan psychiatrist
Eisen, Herman Nathaniel immunology researcher, medical educator
Eisenberg, Carola psychiatry educator
Havens, Leston Laycock psychiatrist, educator
Homburger, Freddy physician, scientist, artist
Johnson, Michael Lewis psychiatrist
London, Irving Myer physician, educator
Mathews, Joan Helene pediatrician
Platika, Doros neurologist
Shore, Miles Frederick psychiatrist, educator
Wacker, Warren Ernest Clyde physician, educator
Wilson, Mary Elizabeth physician, educator
Wurtman, Richard Jay physician, educator, inventor

### Charlestown
Bonventre, Joseph Vincent physician, scientist, medical educator
Isselbacher, Kurt Julius physician, educator
Lamont-Havers, Ronald William physician, research administrator
Moskowitz, Michael Arthur neuroscientist, neurologist

### Chelmsford
Howard, Terry Thomas obstetrician/gynecologist

### Chelsea
Ablow, Keith Russell psychiatrist, journalist, author

### Chestnut Hill
Baum, Jules Leonard ophthalmologist, educator
Cohen, David Joel medical educator
Courtiss, Eugene Howard plastic surgeon, educator
Franklin, Morton Jerome emergency physician
Knapp, Robert Charles retired obstetrics and gynecology educator
Kosasky, Harold Jack gynecologic researcher
Meissner, William Walter psychiatrist, clergyman
Simon, Harold radiologist
Stanbury, John Bruton physician, educator
Thier, Samuel Osiah physician, educator

### Concord
Meistas, Mary Therese endocrinologist, diabetes researcher
Palay, Sanford Louis retired scientist, educator

### Danvers
Rubinstein, Sidney Jacob orthopedic technologist

### Dartmouth
Leclair, Susan Jean hematologist, clinical laboratory scientist, educator

### Dover
Buyse, Marylou pediatrician, clinical geneticist, medical administrator

### Falmouth
Litterer, William Edward, III physician
Sato, Kazuyoshi pathologist

### Fitchburg
Bogdasarian, John Robert otolaryngologist
Price, Malcolm Ivan podiatrist

### Gloucester
White, Harold Jack pathologist

### Harwich
Rigg, Charles Andrew pediatrician

### Haverhill
Ehrig, Ulrich physician
MacMillan, Francis Philip physician
Niccolini, Drew George gastroenterologist

### Jamaica Plain
Arbeit, Robert David physician
Pierce, Chester Middlebrook psychiatrist, educator
Snider, Gordon Lloyd physician

### Lexington
Paul, Norman Leo psychiatrist, educator

### Lincoln
Cannon, Bradford surgeon
Kulka, J(ohannes) Peter retired physician, pathologist

### Lowell
Dubner, Daniel William pediatrician

### Marlborough
Birk, Lee (Carl Birk) psychiatrist, educator

### Medfield
Woolston-Catlin, Marian psychiatrist

### Medford
Burke, Edward Newell radiologist

### Milton
Gaffey, Virginia Anne anesthetist
Lucek, Donald Walter surgeon

### Needham
MacMahon, Brian epidemiologist, educator
Weller, Thomas Huckle physician, former educator

### New Bedford
Shapiro, Gilbert Lawrence orthopedist

### New Salem
Lenherr, Frederick Keith neurophysiologist, computer scientist

### Newton
Bassuk, Ellen Linda psychiatrist
Blacher, Richard Stanley psychiatrist
Gill, Benjamin Franklin physician
Levine, Barry William internist
Ravnikar, Veronika A. medical educator
Rogoff, Jerome Howard psychiatrist, psychoanalyst, forensic expert

### North Andover
Scully, Stephen J. plastic surgeon

### North Attleboro
Friend, Dale Gilbert retired medical educator

### North Billerica
Witover, Stephen Barry pediatrician

### North Dighton
Cserr, Robert psychiatrist, physician, hospital administrator

### North Falmouth
Bass, Norman Herbert physician, scientist, university and hospital administrator, health care executive

### Northampton
Dashef, Stephen Sewell psychiatrist

### Northborough
Fulmer, Hugh Scott physician, educator

### Norwood
Berliner, Allen Irwin dermatologist
Florian, Agustin Max thoracic and cardiovascular surgeon

### Petersham
Chivian, Eric Seth psychiatrist, educator

### Pittsfield
Fanelli, Robert Drew surgeon

### Roxbury
Berman, Marlene Oscar neuropsychologist, educator
Meenan, Robert Francis academician, rheumatologist, researcher
Peters, Alan anatomy educator
Resnick, Oscar neuroscientist

### Salem
Piro, Anthony John radiologist

### Sharon
Honikman, Larry Howard pediatrician

### Sherborn
Kasser, James R. medical educator

### Shrewsbury
Lanza, Robert Paul medical scientist
Magee, Bernard Dale obstetrician, gynecologist
Zamecnik, Paul Charles oncologist, medical research scientist

### South Weymouth
Greineder, Juergen Kurt surgeon
Young, Michael C. allergist, immunologist, pediatrician

### Southborough
Dews, P(eter) B(ooth) medical scientist, educator
Sidman, Richard Leon neuroscientist

### Springfield
Dastgeer, Ghulam Mohammad surgeon
Farkas, Paul Stephen gastroenterologist
Frankel, Kenneth Mark thoracic surgeon
Friedmann, Paul surgeon, educator
Liptzin, Benjamin psychiatrist
McGee, William Tobin intensive care physician
Navab, Farhad medical educator
Smith, James Almer, Jr. psychiatrist

### Stockbridge
Shapiro, Edward Robert psychiatrist, educator, psychoanalyst

### Stoneham
Igou, Raymond Alvin, Jr. orthopedic surgeon

### Taunton
Bornstein, Myer Sidney obstetrician, gynecologist

### Vineyard Haven
Jacobs, Gretchen Huntley psychiatrist

### Waban
Aisner, Mark internist

### Walpole
Warthin, Thomas Angell physician, educator

### Waltham
Lackner, James Robert aerospace medicine educator
Leach, Robert Ellis physician, educator
Reilly, Philip Raymond medical research administrator

### Wellesley
Coyne, Mary Downey biologist, endocrinologist, educator
Jovanovic, Miodrag Stevana surgeon, educator

### Wellesley Hills
Spierings, Egilius Leonardus Hendricus neurologist, headache specialist, pharmacologist

### West Falmouth
Holz, George G., IV research scientist, medicine educator

### West Newton
Sasahara, Arthur Asao cardiologist, educator, researcher

### West Roxbury
Goyal, Raj Kumar medical educator
Hedley-Whyte, John anesthesiologist, educator

### Weston
Wells, Lionelle Dudley psychiatrist

### Westwood
Brooks, John Robinson surgeon, educator

### Williamstown
Payne, Michael Clarence gastroenterologist
Wilkins, Earle Wayne, Jr. surgery educator emeritus

### Winchester
Smith, Robert Moors anesthesiologist

### Woods Hole
Rafferty, Nancy Schwarz anatomy educator

### Worcester
Appelbaum, Paul Stuart psychiatrist, educator
Bernhard, Jeffrey David dermatologist, educator
Brill, A. Bertrand nuclear medicine educator
Charney, Evan pediatrician, educator
Drachman, David Alexander neurologist
Dunlop, George Rodgers retired surgeon
Hanshaw, James Barry physician, educator
Hunter, Richard Edward physician
Kaplan, Melvin Hyman immunology, rheumatology, medical educator
Kotilainen, Helen Jean Rosen infection control epidemiologist, researcher
Laster, Leonard physician, consultant, author
Lawrence, Walter Thomas plastic surgeon
Levine, Peter Hughes physician, health facility administrator
Ludlum, David Blodgett pharmacologist, educator
Maini, Baltej S. surgeon
Menon, Mani urological surgeon, educator
Och, Mohamad Rachid psychiatrist, consultant
Smith, Edward Herbert radiologist, educator
Townes, Philip Leonard pediatrician, educator
Wheeler, Hewitt Brownell surgeon, educator
Wilkinson, Harold Arthur neurosurgeon
Yankauer, Alfred physician, educator
Zurier, Robert Burton medical educator, clinical investigator

### Yarmouth Port
Gordon, Benjamin Dichter medical executive, pediatrician

## MICHIGAN

### Allen Park
Victor, Jay dermatologist

### Alma
Sanders, Jack Ford physician

### Ann Arbor
Abrams, Gerald David physician, educator
Akil, Huda neuroscientist, educator, researcher
Ansbacher, Rudi physician
Bacon, George Edgar pediatrician, educator
Bloom, David Alan pediatric urology educator
Bloom, Jane Maginnis emergency physician
Bole, Giles G. physician, researcher, medical educator
Burdi, Alphonse Rocco anatomist
Burke, Robert Harry surgeon, educator
Cameron, Oliver Gene psychiatrist, educator psychobiology reseacher
Carlson, Bruce Martin anatomist
Casey, Kenneth Lyman neurologist
Christensen, A(lbert) Kent anatomy educator
Coran, Arnold Gerald pediatric surgeon
Counsell, Raymond Ernest pharmacology educator
Curtis, George Clifton psychiatry educator, clinical research investigator
De La Iglesia, Felix Alberto pathologist, toxicologist
DeWeese, Marion Spencer educator, surgeon
Domino, Edward Felix clinical pharmacologist, educator
Donabedian, Avedis physician
Dubin, Howard Victor dermatologist
Fajans, Stefan Stanislaus internist, retired educator
Fekety, Robert physician, educator
Feldman, Eva Lucille neurology educator
Fox, David Alan rheumatologist, immunologist
Frueh, Bartley Richard surgeon
Gikas, Paul William medical educator
Gilman, Sid neurologist
Goldstein, Irwin Joseph medical research executive
Goldstein, Steven Alan medical and engineering educator
Gray, Michael William osteopathic, general and aesthetic plastic and bariatric surgeon
Greden, John Francis psychiatrist, educator
Greene, Douglas A. internist, educator
Halter, Jeffrey B. internal medicine educator, geriatrician
Hawthorne, Victor Morrison epidemiologist, educator
Heidelberger, Kathleen Patricia physician
Henderson, John Woodworth ophthalmologist, educator
Hiss, Roland Graham physician, medical educator
Hoff, Julian Theodore physician, educator
Hollenberg, Paul Frederick pharmacology educator

Humes, H(arvey) David nephrologist, educator
Kimbrough, William Walter, III psychiatrist
Kramer, Charles Henry psychiatrist
Krause, Charles Joseph otolaryngologist
Kronfol, Ziad Anis psychiatrist, educator, researcher
Kuhl, David Edmund physician, nuclear medicine educator
La Du, Bert Nichols, Jr. pharmacology educator, physician
Lichter, Paul Richard ophthalmology educator
Lockwood, Dean H. physician, pharmaceutical executive
Lopatin, Dennis Edward immunologist, educator
Lozoff, Betsy pediatrician
Margolis, Philip Marcus psychiatrist, educator
Martel, William radiologist, educator
Midgley, A(lvin) Rees, Jr. reproductive endocrinology educator, researcher
Monto, Arnold Simon epidemiology educator
Morley, George William gynecologist
Nelson, Virginia Simson pediatrician, physiatrist, educator
Oliver, William John pediatrician, educator
Orringer, Mark Burton surgeon, educator
Owyang, Chung gastroenterologist, researcher
Pitt, Bertram cardiologist, educator, consultant
Rosenthal, Amnon pediatric cardiologist
Schnitzer, Bertram hematopathologist
Schottenfeld, David epidemiologist, educator
Schteingart, David Eduardo internist
Shayman, James Alan nephrologist, educator
Silverman, Albert Jack psychiatrist, educator
Sloan, Herbert Elias physician, surgeon
Smith, David John, Jr. plastic surgeon
Smith, Donald Cameron physician, educator
Strang, Ruth Hancock pediatric educator, pediatric cardiologist, priest
Stross, Jeoffrey Knight physician, educator
Tandon, Rajiv psychiatrist, educator
Taren, James Arthur neurosurgeon, educator
Thompson, Norman Winslow surgeon, educator
Todd, Robert Franklin, III oncologist, educator
Turcotte, Jeremiah George physician, surgery educator
Ward, Peter Allan pathologist, educator
Watson, Andrew Samuel psychiatry and law educator
Weber, Wendell William pharmacologist
Weg, John Gerard physician
Wegman, Myron Ezra physician, educator
Wiggins, Roger C. internist, educator, researcher
Zuidema, George Dale surgeon

**Battle Creek**
Bruce, Thomas Allen physician, philanthropic administrator, educator

**Bloomfield Hills**
Ball, Patricia Ann physician
Chason, Jacob (Leon Chason) retired neuropathologist
Rosenfeld, Joel ophthalmologist, lawyer
Wydra, Frank Thomas healthcare executive

**Clinton Township**
Brown, Ronald Delano endocrinologist
Waldmann, Robert hematologist

**Copemish**
Wells, Herschel James physician, former hospital administrator

**Dearborn**
Coburn, Ronald Murray ophthalmic surgeon, researcher
Fordyce, James George physician
Hirsch, Lore psychiatrist
Katz, Sidney Franklin obstetrician, gynecologist
Myers, Woodrow Augustus, Jr. physician, health care management director
Schulz, Karen Alice medical and vocational case manager

**Detroit**
Abramson, Hanley Norman pharmacy educator
Anderson, John Albert physician
Balon, Richard psychiatrist, educator
Berkelhamer, Jay Ellis pediatrician
Blain, Alexander, III surgeon, educator
Brown, Eli Matthew anesthesiologist
Cerny, Joseph Charles urologist, educator
Cohen, Sanford Ned pediatrics educator, academic administrator
Dombrowski, Mitchell Paul physician, inventor, researcher
Enam, Syed Ather neurosurgeon, researcher
Ernst, Calvin Bradley vascular surgeon, surgery educator
Evans, Mark Ira obstetrician, geneticist
Fromm, David surgeon
Gonzalez, Ricardo surgeon, educator
Hashimoto, Ken dermatology educator
Hayashi, Hajime immunologist
Johnson, Mark Paul obstetrics and gynecology educator, geneticist
Kantrowitz, Adrian surgeon, educator
Kaplan, Joseph pediatrician
Krull, Edward Alexander dermatologist
Lesch, Michael cardiologist
†Lewis, Frank R., Jr. surgeon, hospital administrator
Li, Yi staff investigator
†Lim, Henry Wan-Peng physician
Livingood, Clarence S. dermatologist
Lupulescu, Aurel Peter medical educator, researcher, physician
Lusher, Jeanne Marie pediatric hematologist, educator
Maiese, Kenneth neurologist
Mayes, Maureen Davidica physician, educator
McCarroll, Kathleen Ann radiologist, educator
Miller, Orlando Jack physician, educator
Moghissi, Kamran S. obstetrician/gynecologist, educator
Ownby, Dennis Randall pediatrician, allergist, educator, researcher
Perry, Burton Lars pediatrician
Peters, William P. oncologist, science administrator, educator
Phillips, Eduardo surgeon, educator
Porter, Arthur T. oncologist, educator
Schaffler, Mitchell Barry research scientist, anatomist, educator
Silverman, Norman Alan cardiac surgeon
Sokol, Robert James obstetrician, gynecologist, educator
Stein, Paul David cardiologist
Szilagyi, D(esiderius) Emerick surgeon, researcher, educator
Tolia, Vasundhara K. pediatric gastroenterologist, educator
Tse, Harley Y. immunologist, educator
Uhde, Thomas Whitley psychiatry educator, psychiatrist
Whitehouse, Fred Waite endocrinologist, researcher
Wiener, Joseph pathologist

**East Lansing**
Beckmeyer, Henry Ernest anesthesiologist, medical educator
Brody, Theodore Meyer pharmacologist, educator
Gottschalk, Alexander radiologist, diagnostic radiology educator
Hoffman, Gwendolyn Leah emergency medicine physician, educator
Johnson, John Irwin, Jr. neuroscientist
Moore, Kenneth Edwin pharmacology educator
Murray, Raymond Harold physician
Netzloff, Michael Lawrence pediatric educator, endocrinologist, geneticist
Reinhart, Mary Ann medical board executive
Ristow, George Edward neurologist, educator
Rosenman, Kenneth D. medical educator
Rovner, David Richard endocrinology educator
Sato, Paul Hisashi pharmacologist
Waite, Donald Eugene medical educator, consultant
Walker, Bruce Edward anatomy educator

**Escanaba**
Cooper, Janelle Lunette neurologist, educator

**Farmington Hills**
Bahr, Sheila Kay physician
Blum, Jon H. dermatologist
Gordon, Craig Jeffrey oncologist, educator

**Flint**
Farrehi, Cyrus cardiologist, educator
Jayabalan, Vemblaserry nuclear medicine physician, radiologist
Soderstrom, Robert Merriner dermatologist
Tauscher, John Walter retired pediatrician, emeritus educator

**Flushing**
Himes, George Elliott pathologist

**Franklin**
Adler, Philip osteopathic physician

**Grand Blanc**
Wasfie, Tarik Jawad surgeon, educator

**Grand Rapids**
Bartek, Gordon Luke radiologist
Daniels, Joseph neuropsychiatrist
†Maurer, John Raymond internist, educator
Wilt, Jeffrey Lynn pulmonary and critical care physician

**Grosse Pointe**
Beierwaltes, William Henry physician, educator
Perez-Borja, Carlos M. neurologist, hospital executive
Powsner, Edward Raphael physician
Sphire, Raymond Daniel anesthesiologist

**Harper Woods**
DeGiusti, Dominic Lawrence medical science educator, academic administrator

**Indian River**
Knecht, Richard Arden family practitioner

**Ithaca**
Craig, Zane Grant obstetrician, gynecologist

**Kalamazoo**
Aladjem, Silvio obstetrician, gynecologist, educator
Chodos, Dale David Jerome physician, consumer advocate
Gladstone, William Sheldon, Jr. radiologist
Taylor, Duncan Paul research neuropharmacologist

**Kalkaska**
Batsakis, John George pathology educator

**Lake Angelus**
Kresge, Bruce Anderson retired physician

**Lansing**
†Herman, James George radiation oncologist
Vincent, Frederick Michael, Sr. neurologist, electromyographer, educational administrator
Wiegenstein, John Gerald physician

**Livonia**
Sobel, Howard Bernard osteopath

**Mancelona**
Whelan, Joseph L. neurologist

**Midland**
McCarty, Leslie Paul pharmacologist, chemist

**Northport**
Schultz, Richard Carlton plastic surgeon

**Northville**
Abbasi, Tariq Afzal psychiatrist, educator

**Oak Park**
Borovoy, Marc Allen podiatrist

**Okemos**
Monson, Carol Lynn osteopath, psychotherapist
Ochberg, Frank Martin psychiatrist, foundation administrator

**Pleasant Ridge**
Krabbenhoft, Kenneth Lester radiologist, educator

**Portage**
Berkowitz, Marvin transplant consultant

**Richland**
Atkinson, Arthur John, Jr. clinical pharmacologist, educator

**Rochester**
Reddy, Venkat Narsimha ophthalmalogist, researcher

**Rochester Hills**
Badalament, Robert Anthony urologic oncologist
Bartunek, James Scott psychiatrist

**Royal Oak**
Bernstein, Jay pathologist, researcher, educator
Dworkin, Howard Jerry nuclear physician, educator
LaBan, Myron Miles physician, administrator
†O'Neill, William Walter physician, educator
Proctor, Conrad Arnold physician
Ryan, Jack physician, retired hospital corporation executive

**Saginaw**
Ferlinz, Jack cardiologist, medical educator
La Londe, Lawrence Lee family practice physician

**Saint Clair Shores**
Walker, Frank Banghart pathologist

**Southfield**
Green, Henry Leonard physician
Hammel, Ernest Martin medical educator, academic administrator
Mathog, Robert Henry otolaryngologist, educator
McQuiggan, Mark Corbeille urologist
O'Hara, John Paul, III orthopaedic surgeon
Rosenzweig, Norman psychiatry educator
Zubroff, Leonard Saul surgeon

**Sterling Heights**
Frank, Michael Sanford dermatologist

**Sturgis**
Cabansag, Vicente Dacanay, Jr. medical association administrator

**Troy**
Golusin, Millard R. obstetrician and gynecologist
Schafer, Sharon Marie anesthesiologist

**Warren**
Miller, Aileen Etta Martha medical association administrator, consultant, metabolic nutritionist

**Waterford**
Chodorkoff, Bernard psychoanalyst, psychiatrist

**West Bloomfield**
Joseph, Ramon Rafael physician, educator
Sarwer-Foner, Gerald Jacob physician, educator
Sawyer, Howard Jerome physician

**Ypsilanti**
Ritter, Frank Nicholas otolaryngologist, educator

## MINNESOTA

**Apple Valley**
Doyle, O'Brien John, Jr. emergency medical services consultant, lobbyist, writer

**Bloomington**
Lakin, James Dennis allergist, immunologist, director

**Crosslake**
Kettleson, David Noel retired orthopaedic surgeon, timber manager

**Detroit Lakes**
Eginton, Charles Theodore surgeon, educator

**Duluth**
Aufderheide, Arthur Carl pathologist
Eisenberg, Richard Martin pharmacology educator

**Excelsior**
Bilka, Paul Joseph physician
French, Lyle Albert surgeon

**Mendota Heights**
Dennis, Clarence surgeon, educator

**Minneapolis**
Anderson, Geraldine Louise medical researcher
Balfour, Henry Hallowell, Jr. medical educator, researcher, physician, writer
Blackburn, Henry Webster, Jr. retired physician
†Bolman, Ralph Morton (Chip), III cardiac surgeon
Boudreau, Robert James nuclear medicine physician, researcher
Brown, David M. physician, educator, dean
Buchwald, Henry surgeon, educator, researcher
Burton, Charles Victor physician, surgeon, inventor
Cavert, Henry Mead physician, retired educator
Chavers, Blanche Marie pediatrician, educator, reseacher
Chester, Thomas J. physician
Chisholm, Tague Clement pediatric surgeon, educator
Chou, Shelley Nien-chun neurosurgeon, university official, educator
Ciriacy, Edward Walter physician, educator
Craig, James Lynn physician, consumer products company executive
Dykstra, Dennis Dale physiatrist
Etzwiler, Donnell Dencil pediatrician
Fisch, Robert Otto medical educator
Foreman, Harry obstetrician, gynecologist, educator
Gajl-Peczalska, Kazimiera J. surgical pathologist, pathology educator
Gedgaudas, Eugene radiologist, educator
Gorlin, Robert James medical educator
Gullickson, Glenn, Jr. physician, educator
Hardten, David Ronald ophthalmologist
Holter, Arlen Rolf cardiothoracic surgeon
Horns, Howard Lowell physician, educator
Kane, Robert Lewis public health educator
Kaplan, Manuel E. physician, educator
Keane, William Francis nephrology educator, research foundation executive
Kennedy, B(yrl) J(ames) medicine and oncology educator
Knopman, David S. neurologist
Langer, Leonard O., Jr. radiologist, educator
Leon, Arthur Sol research cardiologist, exercise physiologist
Levitt, Seymour Herbert physician, radiology educator
Loh, Horace H. pharmacology educator
Luepker, Russell Vincent epidemiology educator
Mazze, Roger Steven medical educator, researcher
McQuarrie, Donald Gray surgeon, educator
Michael, Alfred Frederick, Jr. physician, medical educator
Najarian, John Sarkis surgeon, educator
Oppenheimer, Jack Hans internist, scientist, educator
Palahniuk, Richard John anesthesiology educator, researcher
Paparella, Michael M. otolaryngologist
Payne, Elizabeth Eleanore surgeon, otolaryngologist
Peterson, Douglas Arthur physician
Phibbs, Clifford Matthew surgeon, educator
Prem, Konald Arthur physician, educator
Quie, Paul Gerhardt physician, educator
Rothenberger, David Albert surgeon
Sawchuk, Ronald John pharmaceutical sciences educator
Schultz, Alvin Leroy retired internist, retired endocrinologist, retired university health science facility administrator
Shapiro, Fred Louis physician, educator
Staba, Emil John pharmacognosy and medicinal chemistry educator
Steinberg, Paul allergist, immunologist
Stenwick, Michael William internist, geriatric medicine consultant
Tagatz, George Elmo obstetrician, gynecologist, educator
Thompson, Roby Calvin, Jr. orthopedic surgeon, educator
Thompson, Theodore Robert pediatric educator
Thompson, William Moreau radiologist, educator
Weir, Edward Kenneth cardiologist
Wild, John Julian surgeon, director medical research institute
Wilson, Leonard Gilchrist history of medicine educator
Wirtschafter, Jonathan Dine neuro-ophthalmology educator, scientist

**Olivia**
Cosgriff, James Arthur physician

**Rochester**
Bartholomew, Lloyd Gibson physician
Beahrs, Oliver Howard surgeon, educator
Beckett, Victoria Ling physician
Berge, Kenneth George retired internist, educator
Brimijoin, William Stephen pharmacology educator, neuroscience researcher
Butt, Hugh Roland gastroenterologist, educator
†Cascino, Terrence neurologist
Corbin, Kendall Brooks physician, scientist
Danielson, Gordon Kenneth, Jr. cardiovascular surgeon, educator
DeRemee, Richard Arthur physician, educator, researcher
Dickson, Edgar Rolland gastroenterologist
Douglass, Bruce E. physician
Du Shane, James William physician, educator
Engel, Andrew George neurologist
Feldt, Robert Hewitt pediatric cardiologist, educator
Gilchrist, Gerald Seymour pediatric hematologist, oncologist, educator
Gleich, Gerald Joseph immunologist, medical scientist
Gomez, Manuel Rodriguez physician
Gracey, Douglas Robert physician, physiologist, educator
Hattery, Robert R. radiologist, educator
Hunder, Gene Gerald physician, educator
Kempers, Roger Dyke obstetrics and gynecology educator
Krom, Ruud Arne Finco surgeon
Kurland, Leonard Terry epidemiologist educator
Kyle, Robert Arthur medical educator, oncologist
LaRusso, Nicholas F. gastroenterologist, educator, scientist
Lofgren, Karl Adolph surgeon
Lucas, Alexander Ralph child psychiatrist, educator
Mackenzie, Ronald Alexander anesthesiologist
Malkasian, George Durand, Jr. physician, educator
Martin, Maurice John psychiatrist
Mc Conahey, William McConnell, Jr. physician, educator
Mc Goon, Dwight Charles retired surgeon, educator
Michenfelder, John Donahue anesthesiology educator
Morlock, Carl Grismore physician, medical educator
Mulder, Donald William physician, educator
Neel, Harry Bryan, III surgeon, scientist, educator
Nichols, Donald Richardson medical educator
Oesterling, Joseph Edwin urologic surgeon
Olsen, Arthur Martin physician, educator
Payne, W(illiam) Spencer retired surgeon
Perry, Harold Otto dermatologist
Phillips, Sidney Frederick gastroenterologist
Pittelkow, Mark Robert physician, dermatology educator, researcher
Pratt, Joseph Hyde, Jr. surgeon
Reitemeier, Richard Joseph physician
Rogers, Roy Steele, III dermatology educator, dean
Rosenow, Edward Carl, III medical educator
Siekert, Robert George neurologist
Stillwell, G(eorge) Keith physician
Symmonds, Richard Earl gynecologist
Unni, Chandra Sheila psychiatrist
Waller, Robert Rex ophthalmologist, educator, foundation executive
Whisnant, Jack Page neurologist
Woods, John Elmer plastic surgeon

**Saint Cloud**
Gruys, Robert Irving physician, surgeon
Olson, Barbara Ford physician

**Saint Louis Park**
Galbraith, Richard Frederick physician, neurologist
Knighton, David Reed vascular surgeon, educator

**Saint Paul**
Burchell, Howard Bertram retired physician, educator
Crabb, Kenneth Wayne obstetrician, gynecologist
Edwards, Jesse Efrem physician, educator

Fuller, Benjamin Franklin *physician, educator*
Hays, Thomas S. *medical educator, medical researcher*
Hodgson, Jane Elizabeth *obstetrician and gynecologist, consultant*
Lillehei, C. Walton *surgeon*
Sher, Phyllis Kammerman *pediatric neurology educator*
Swaiman, Kenneth Fred *pediatric neurologist, educator*
Titus, Jack L. *pathologist, educator*
Wang, Zeng-Yu *neurologist, immunologist*
Yeh, John *reproductive endocrinologist*
Zander, Janet Adele *psychiatrist*

### Spicer
Wescoe, W(illiam) Clarke *physician*

### Spring Grove
Roverud, Eleanor *pathologist, neuropathologist*

### Stillwater
Asch, Susan McClellan *pediatrician*

### Virginia
Knabe, George William, Jr. *pathologist, educator*

### Willmar
Vander Aarde, Stanley Bernard *retired otolaryngologist*

## MISSISSIPPI

### Biloxi
Ozolek, John Anthony *pediatrician, neonatologist*

### Gautier
Egerton, Charles Pickford *anatomy and physiology educator*

### Gulfport
Kaufman-Derbes, Linda Ruth *physician*

### Hattiesburg
Brinson, Ralph Alan *physician, pediatrician, neonatologist*

### Jackson
Achord, James Lee *gastroenterologist, educator*
Ball, Carroll Raybourne *anatomist, medical educator, researcher*
Bloom, Sherman *pathologist, educator*
Brooks, Thomas Joseph, Jr. *preventive medicine educator*
Burrow, William Hollis, II *dermatologist*
Conwill, David E. *preventive medicine educator, emergency physician*
Cruse, Julius Major, Jr. *pathologist, educator*
Currier, Robert David *neurologist*
Das, Suman Kumar *plastic surgeon, researcher*
Draper, Edgar *psychiatrist*
Eigenbrodt, Edwin Hixson *physician, pathologist, educator*
Eigenbrodt, Marsha Lillian *internal medicine educator, epidemologist*
Freeland, Alan Edward *orthopedic surgery educator, physician*
Guyton, Arthur Clifton *physician, educator*
Halaris, Angelos *psychiatrist, educator*
Houston, Gerry Ann *oncologist*
Howard, William Percy *physician*
Kermode, John Cotterill *pharmacology educator, researcher*
Lewis, Robert Edwin, Jr. *pathology immunology educator, researcher*
Poole, Galen Vincent *surgeon, educator, researcher*
Shirley, Aaron *pediatrician*
Sneed, Raphael Corcoran *physiatrist, pediatrician*
Suess, James Francis *retired psychiatry educator*
Tourney, Garfield *psychiatrist, educator*
Vance, Ralph Brooks *oncologist and educator*
Walcott, Dexter Winn *allergist*

### Ridgeland
Morrison, Francis Secrest *physician*

### Tupelo
Bullard, Rickey Howard *podiatric physician, surgeon*

## MISSOURI

### Bridgeton
†Johnson, Kevin Todd *physician*

### Chesterfield
Berland, David I. *psychiatrist, educator*
Frawley, Thomas Francis *physician*
Hunter, Harlen Charles *orthopedic surgeon*
Levin, Marvin Edgar *physician*
Payne, Meredith Jorstad *physician*

### Columbia
Allen, William Cecil *physician, educator*
Barbero, Giulio John *physician, educator*
Boedeker, Ben Harold *anesthesiologist, educator*
Bryant, Lester R. *surgeon, educator*
Colwill, Jack Marshall *physician, educator*
Cunningham, Milamari Antoinella *anesthesiologist*
Eaton, Gary David *physician*
Eggers, George William Nordholtz, Jr. *anesthesiologist, educator*
Griffing, George Thomas *medical educator, endocrinologist*
Hardin, Christopher D. *medical educator*
Heimburger, Elizabeth Morgan *psychiatrist*
Hess, Darla Bakersmith *cardiologist, educator*
Hess, Leonard Wayne *obstetrician gynecologist, perinatologist*
Hillman, Richard Ephraim *pediatrician, educator*
James, Elizabeth Joan Plogsted *pediatrician, educator*
Kashani, Javad Hassan-Nejad *physician*
Khojasteh, Ali *medical oncologist, hematologist*
Perkoff, Gerald Thomas *physician, educator*
Perry, Michael Clinton *physician, medical educator, academic administrator*
Puckett, C. Lin *plastic surgeon, educator*
Silver, Donald *surgeon, educator*
Weiss, James Moses Aaron *psychiatrist, educator*
Witten, David Melvin *radiology educator*

### Florissant
Tanphaichitr, Kongsak *rheumatologist, allergist, immunologist, internist*

### Fulton
Gish, Edward Rutledge *surgeon*

### Independence
Smith, Wallace Bunnell *physician, church official*

### Jefferson City
Forks, Thomas Paul *osteopathic physician*
Giffen, Lawrence Everett, Sr. *family physician, anesthesiologist, historian*

### Joplin
Daus, Arthur Steven *neurological surgeon*
Singleton, Marvin Ayers *otolaryngologist, senator*

### Kansas City
Abdou, Nabih I. *physician, educator*
Blim, Richard Don *pediatrician*
Cronkleton, Thomas Eugene *physician*
Dimond, Edmunds Grey *medical educator*
Ellfeldt, Howard James *orthopedic surgeon*
Graham, Robert *medical association executive*
Hagan, John Charles, III *ophthalmologist*
Hunzicker, Warren John *research consultant, physician, cardiologist*
Huston, Kent Allen *rheumatologist*
Johnson, Vincent Gregory *anesthesiologist*
Kagan, Stuart Michael *pediatrician*
Lofland, Gary Kenneth *cardiac surgeon*
Long, Edwin Tutt *surgeon*
Massey, Vickie Lea *radiologist*
Mc Coy, Frederick John *retired plastic surgeon*
†McPhee, Mark Steven *medical educator, physician, gastroenterologist*
Mebust, Winston Keith *surgeon, educator*
Noback, Richardson Kilbourne *medical educator*
Sauer, Gordon Chenoweth *physician, educator*
Schoolman, Arnold *neurological surgeon*

### Moberly
Noel, Larry Kenneth *family physician*

### Osage Beach
East, Mark David *physician*

### Poplar Bluff
Piland, Donald Spencer *internist*

### Saint Charles
Schneider, Thomas Aquinas *surgeon, educator*

### Saint Joseph
Heizer, David Eugene *health information management educator*

### Saint Louis
Agrawal, Harish Chandra *neurobiologist, researcher, educator*
Alpers, David Hershel *physician, educator*
Anderhub, Beth Marie *medical educator*
Arrington, Barbara *public health educator*
Backer, Matthias, Jr. *obstetrician-gynecologist*
Bacon, Bruce Raymond *physician*
Ballinger, Walter Francis *surgeon, educator*
Baue, Arthur Edward *surgeon, educator, administrator*
Berg, Leonard *neurologist, educator, researcher*
Blumenthal, Herman Theodore *physician, educator*
Bowen, Stephen Francis, Jr. *ophthalmic surgeon*
Brodeur, Armand Edward *pediatric radiologist*
Brown, Eric Joel *biomedical researcher*
Brown, Wendy Weinstock *nephrologist*
Cabbabe, Edmond Bechir *plastic and hand surgeon*
Chaplin, David Dunbar *medical research specialist, medical educator*
Chaplin, Hugh, Jr. *physician, educator*
Cloninger, Claude Robert *psychiatric researcher, educator, genetic epdemiologist*
Coe, Rodney Michael *medical educator*
Cole, Barbara Ruth *pediatrician, nephrologist*
Contis, John Chris *surgeon, educator*
Cryer, Philip Eugene *medical educator, scientist, endocrinologist*
Cummings, James M. *urology educator*
Dewald, Paul Adolph *psychiatrist*
Dodge, Philip Rogers *physician, educator*
Dougherty, Charles Hamilton *pediatrician*
Drews, Robert Carrel *physician*
†Eisenberg, Paul Richard *cardiologist, consultant, educator*
Evens, Ronald Gene *radiologist, medical center administrator*
Fitch, Coy Dean *physician, educator*
Flanagan, Fidelma Louise *radiologist*
Fletcher, James Warren *physician*
Flye, M. Wayne *surgeon, immunologist, educator*
Fogarty, William Martin, Jr. *physician*
Friedman, William Hersh *otolaryngologist, educator*
Gay, William Arthur, Jr. *thoracic surgeon, educator*
Goldberg, Anne Carol *physician, educator*
Goodenberger, Daniel Marvin *medical educator*
Grossberg, George Thomas *psychiatrist, educator*
Grubb, Robert L., Jr. *neurosurgeon*
Guze, Samuel Barry *psychiatrist, educator, university official*
Hammerman, Marc Randall *nephrologist, educator*
Hanley, Thomas Patrick *obstetrician, gynecologist*
Hofstatter, Leopold *psychiatrist, researcher*
Holmes, Nancy Elizabeth *pediatrician*
Hsu, Chung Yi *neurologist*
Hudgens, Richard Watts *psychiatry educator*
Hyers, Thomas Morgan *physician*
Johnston, Marilyn Frances-Meyers *physician, medical educator*
Kaiser, George Charles *surgeon*
Kaminski, Donald Leon *medical educator, surgeon, gastrointestinal physiologist*
Kang, Juan *pathologist*
Kaplan, Henry Jerrold *ophthalmologist, educator*
Kelly, Daniel P. *cardiologist, molecular biologist*
Keltner, Raymond Marion, Jr. *surgeon, educator*
Kimmey, James Richard, Jr. *medical educator, consultant*
Kincaid, Marilyn Coburn *medical educator*
Kinsella, Ralph Aloysius, Jr. *physician*
Kipnis, David Morris *physician, educator*
Kirsch, Jeffrey Philip *otolaryngologist*
Klahr, Saulo *physician, educator*
Knutsen, Alan Paul *pediatrician, allergist, immunologist*
Kolker, Allan Erwin *ophthalmologist*
Kornfeld, Stuart A. *hematology educator*
Kouchoukos, Nicholas Thomas *surgeon*
Lacy, Paul Eston *pathologist*
Lagunoff, David *physician, educator*
Lewis, Robert David *ophthalmologist, educator*
Loeb, Virgil, Jr. *oncologist, hematologist*
Lustman, Patrick J. *psychiatrist*
Luther, George Aubrey *orthopedic surgeon*
Majerus, Philip Warren *physician*
Mangelsdorf, Thomas Kelly *psychiatrist, consultant*
Manske, Paul Robert *orthopedic hand surgeon, educator*
Mantovani, John Francis *neurologist, educator*
Martin, Kevin John *nephrologist, educator*
Middelkamp, John Neal *pediatrician, educator*
Mooradian, Arshag Dertad *physician, educator*
Morales-Galarreta, Julio *psychiatrist, child psychoanalyst*
Morley, John Edward *physician*
Murphy, George Earl *psychiatrist, educator*
Myerson, Robert J. *radiation oncologist, educator*
Owens, William Don *anesthesiology educator*
Peck, William Arno *physician, educator, university official and dean*
Perez, Carlos A. *radiation oncologist, educator*
Perlmutter, David H. *physician, educator*
Prensky, Arthur Lawrence *pediatric neurologist, educator*
Purkerson, Mabel Louise *physician, physiologist, educator*
Radford, Diane Mary *surgeon, surgical oncologist*
Rao, Dabeeru C. *genetic epidemiologist*
Robins, Lee Nelken *medical educator*
Royal, Henry Duval *nuclear medicine physician*
Ryall, Jo-Ellyn M. *psychiatrist*
Santiago, Julio Victor *medical educator, researcher, administrator*
Schonfeld, Gustav *medical educator, researcher*
Schreiber, James Ralph *obstetrics, gynecology researcher*
Schwartz, Alan Leigh *pediatrician, educator*
Schwartz, Henry Gerard *surgeon, educator*
Shank, Robert Ely *physician, preventive medicine educator emeritus*
Shehadi, Sameer Ibrahim *plastic surgeon*
Siegel, Barry Alan *nuclear radiologist*
Slavin, Raymond Granam *allergist, immunologist*
Spector, Gershon Jerry *physician, educator, researcher*
Steigman, Carmen Kay *pathologist*
Stoneman, William, III *physician, educator*
Strunk, Robert Charles *physician*
Suba, Antonio Ronquillo *retired surgeon*
Sutter, Richard Anthony *physician*
Teitelbaum, Steven Lazarus *pathology educator*
Ternberg, Jessie Lamoin *pediatric surgeon*
Thomas, James Lewis *biomedical research scientist*
Tolan, Robert Warren *pediatric infectious disease specialist*
Ulett, George Andrew *psychiatrist*
Walentik, Corinne Anne *pediatrician*
Wells, Samuel Alonzo, Jr. *surgeon, educator*
Whyte, Michael Peter *medicine and pediatrics educator, research director*
Wickline, Samuel Alan *cardiologist, educator*
Willman, Vallee Louis *physician, surgery educator*
Young, Paul Andrew *anatomist*

### Springfield
Coscia, Robert Lingua *surgeon, educator*
Geter, Rodney Keith *plastic surgeon*
Hackett, Earl Randolph *neurologist*
H'Doubler, Francis Todd, Jr. *surgeon*
Shealy, Clyde Norman *neurosurgeon*

## MONTANA

### Billings
Hylton, Robert Ralph *anesthesiologist*
Kohler, William Curtis *sleep specialist, neurologist*

### Helena
Strickler, Jeffrey Harold *pediatrician*

### Missoula
Fawcett, Don Wayne *anatomist*

### Whitefish
Miller, Ronald Alfred *family physician*

### Wolf Point
Listerud, Mark Boyd *retired surgeon*

## NEBRASKA

### Grand Island
Francis, Gordon Dean *physician*

### Hastings
Dungan, John Russell, Jr. (Viscount Dungan of Clane) *anesthesiologist*

### Lincoln
Clyne, Dianna Marie *psychiatrist*
Hirai, Denitsu *surgeon*
Koszewski, Bohdan Julius *internist, medical educator*

### Omaha
Brody, Alfred Walter *pulmonologist*
Davis, John Byron *surgeon*
Fusaro, Ramon Michael *dermatologist, researcher*
Girouard, Gail Patricia *family practice physician*
Harned, Roger Kent *radiology educator*
Heaney, Robert Proulx *physician, educator*
Hodgson, Paul Edmund *surgeon*
Howard, Thomas Clement *surgeon*
Imray, Thomas John *radiologist, educator*
Kessinger, Margaret Anne *medical educator*
Korbitz, Bernard Carl *retired oncologist, hematologist, educator, consultant*
Lackner, Rudy Paul *cardiothoracic surgeon*
Lemon, Henry Martyn *physician, educator*
Mardis, Hal Kennedy *urological surgeon, educator, researcher*
Maurer, Harold Maurice *pediatrician*
Mohiuddin, Syed Maqdoom *cardiologist, educator*
Monaghan, Michael Sean *pharmacist*
O'Donohue, Walter John, Jr. *medical educator*
Pearson, Paul Hammond *physician*
Rakowicz-Szulczynska, Eva Maria *molecular oncologist*
Rogan, Eleanor Groeniger *cancer researcher, educator*
Rupp, Mark Edmund *medical educator*
Sanders, W(illiam) Eugene, Jr. *physician, educator*
Scott, David Michael *pharmacy educator*
Sheehan, John Francis *cytopathologist, educator*
Skoog, Donald Paul *retired physician, educator*
Tinker, John Heath *anesthesiologist, educator*
Townley, Robert Gordon *medical educator*
Truhlsen, Stanley Marshall *physician, educator*
Waggener, Ronald Edgar *radiologist*
Ward, Vernon Graves *internist*

### Papillion
Casale, Thomas Bruce *medical educator*
Dvorak, Allen Dale *radiologist*

## NEVADA

### Carson City
Fischer, Michael John *ophthalmologist, physician*

### Glenbrook
Goldsmith, Harry Sawyer *surgeon, educator*

### Henderson
Perel, Michael Joseph *dermatologist, inventor*

### Las Vegas
Amirana, M. T. *surgeon*
Bandt, Paul Douglas *physician*
Barger, James Daniel *physician*
Capanna, Albert Howard *neurosurgeon, neuroscientist*
Herte, Mary Charlotte *plastic surgeon*
Kurlinski, John Parker *physician*
Lazerson, Jack *pediatrician, educator*
Merkin, Albert Charles *pediatrician, allergist*
Moritz, Timothy Bovie *psychiatrist*
Muller, Sigfrid Augustine *dermatologist, educator*
Records, Raymond Edwin *ophthalmologist*
Sabanas-Wells, Alvina Olga *orthopedic surgeon*
Shettles, Landrum Brewer *obstetrician-gynecologist*
Shires, George Thomas *surgeon, educator*
Speck, Eugene Lewis *internist*
Wax, Arnold *physician*

### Reno
Barnet, Robert Joseph *cardiologist, ethicist*
†Johns, Joseph Peter *medical educator*
MacKintosh, Frederick Roy *oncologist*
Rahe, Richard Henry *psychiatrist, educator*
Shapiro, Leonard *immunologist, allergist*
Small, Elisabeth Chan *psychiatrist, educator*

### Sparks
Lee, Richard Scott *neurologist*

## NEW HAMPSHIRE

### Barrington
Castro, Robert R. *surgeon*

### Bedford
Khazei, Amir Mohsen *surgeon, oncologist*

### Canterbury
Chamberlin, Robert West *medical educator*

### Concord
Davis, Sybil Alicia *obstetrician gynecologist*

### Etna
Ferm, Vergil Harkness *anatomist, embryologist*

### Grantham
Behrle, Franklin Charles *retired pediatrician and educator*
Knights, Edwin Munroe *pathologist*
MacNeill, Arthur Edson *physician, science consultant*
Wells, Edward Phillips *radiologist*

### Hanover
Almy, Thomas Pattison *physician, educator*
Koop, Charles Everett *surgeon, educator, former surgeon general*
Moeschler, John Boyer *physician, educator*
Rawnsley, Howard Melody *physician, educator*
Rueckert, Frederic *plastic surgeon*
Sporn, Michael Benjamin *cancer researcher*
Staples, O. Sherwin *orthopedic surgeon*
Wallace, Andrew Grover *physician, educator, medical school dean*
Zubkoff, Michael *medical educator*

### Hooksett
Bagan, Merwyn *neurological surgeon*

### Keene
Fachada, Ederito Paul *podiatrist, surgeon*
Fuld, Gilbert Lloyd *pediatrician*

### Lebanon
Barney, Christine Anne *psychiatrist, educator*
Clendenning, William Edmund *dermatologist*
Cornwell, Gibbons Gray, III *physician, medical educator*
Cronenwett, Jack LeMoyne *vascular surgeon educator*
Fanger, Michael W. *medical educator*
Foote, Robert Stephens *physician*
Galton, Valerie Anne *endocrinology educator*
Kelley, Maurice Leslie, Jr. *gastroenterologist, educator*
McCollum, Robert Wayne *physician, educator*
Rolett, Ellis Lawrence *medical educator, cardiologist*
Rous, Stephen Norman *urologist, educator*
Shorter, Nicholas Andrew *pediatric surgeon*
Smith, Barry David *obstetrician-gynecologist, educator*
Sox, Harold Carleton, Jr. *physician, educator*
von Reyn, C. Fordham *infectious disease physician*

PROFESSIONAL INDEX 5259 HEALTHCARE: MEDICINE


**Lee**
Young, James Morningstar *physician, naval officer*

**Lyme**
McIntyre, Oswald Ross *physician*

**Manchester**
Angoff, Gerald Harvey *cardiologist*
DesRochers, Gerard Camille *surgeon*
Emery, Paul Emile *psychiatrist*

**Newport**
Hickey, William Francis *retired surgeon, medical consultant*

## NEW JERSEY

**Belleville**
Caputo, Wayne James *surgeon, podiatrist*
Goldenberg, David Milton *experimental pathologist, oncologist*

**Bernardsville**
Dixon, Rosina Berry *physician, pharmaceutical development consultant*

**Brick**
Abel, Mark *dermatologist*

**Bridgewater**
Bernson, Marcella Shelley *psychiatrist*
Hirsch, Paul J. *orthopedic surgeon, educator*

**Browns Mills**
Cha, Se Do *internist*
Lumia, Francis James *internist*

**Camden**
Ances, I. G(eorge) *obstetrician, gynecologist, educator*
Camishion, Rudolph Carmen *physician*
†Goldberg, Jack *hematologist*
Stahl, Gary Edward *neonatologist*

**Cherry Hill**
Amsterdam, Jay D. *psychiatrist, educator*
Kahn, Sigmund Benham *retired internist and dean*
Olearchyk, Andrew *cardiothoracic surgeon, educator*
Robinson, Mary Jo *pathologist*
Werbitt, Warren *gastroenterologist, educator*

**Clifton**
Kirrer, Ernest Douglas *physician*
Silber, Judy G. *dermatologist*

**Cranbury**
Sofia, R. D. *pharmacologist*

**Cresskill**
Gardner, Richard Alan *psychiatrist, writer*

**Denville**
Greer, Robert Bruce, III *orthopedic surgeon, educator*

**East Brunswick**
Elias, Harry *medical educator*
Rosenberg, Norman *surgeon*

**East Hanover**
Finkel, Marion Judith *physician*
Salans, Lester Barry *physician, scientist, educator*

**East Orange**
Cunningham, Robert Marcus *ophthalmologist*
Husar, Walter Gene *neurologist, neuroscientist, educator*
Yoo, James H. *radiation oncologist, nuclear medicine physician*

**Eatontown**
Granet, Kenneth M. *internist*
Orlando, Carl *medical research and development executive*

**Edison**
Jacobey, John Arthur, III *surgeon, educator*

**Elizabeth**
Berger, Harold Richard *physician*
Gutfreund, Donald E. *internist, hematologist, oncologist*
†Rosenstein, Neil *surgeon, genealogical researcher*

**Englewood**
Wuhl, Charles Michael *psychiatrist*

**Fair Lawn**
Infantino, Salvatore *physician*

**Flanders**
Huang, Jacob Chen-ya *physician*

**Flemington**
Katcher, Avrum L. *pediatrician*

**Forked River**
Novak, Dennis E. *family practice physician*

**Fort Lee**
Chessler, Richard Kenneth *gastroenterologist, endoscopist*

**Franklin Lakes**
Ginsberg, Barry Howard *physician, researcher*

**Franklin Park**
Perry, Arthur William *plastic surgeon*

**Glen Ridge**
Clemente, Celestino *physician, surgeon*

**Green Village**
Roper, William Lee *physician, health care executive*

**Hackensack**
De Groote, Robert David *general and vascular surgeon*
Gross, Peter Alan *epidemiologist, researcher*
Riegel, Norman *physician*
Spackman, Thomas James *radiologist*

**Haddonfield**
Capelli, John Placido *nephrologist*
Lee, Young Bin *psychiatrist, neurologist*

**Hamilton**
Kane, Michael Joel *physician*

**Hammonton**
Pellegrino, Peter *surgeon*

**Hawthorne**
Lozito, Deborah Ann *osteopathic internist*

**Hillsdale**
Copeland, Lois Jacqueline (Mrs. Richard A. Sperling) *physician*

**Hillside**
Fox, Sheldon *retired radiologist, medical educator*

**Jamesburg**
Miller, Theodore Robert *surgeon, educator*

**Jersey City**
Demos, Nicholas John *physician, surgeon, researcher*

**Kendall Park**
Berger, Richard Stanton *dermatologist*

**Kenilworth**
Scott, Mary Celine *pharmacologist*

**Lakewood**
Bowers, John Zimmerman *physician, educator*
Hurlbut, Terry Allison *pathologist*

**Lawrenceville**
Pouleur, Hubert Gustave *cardiologist*

**Livingston**
Caballes, Romeo Lopez *pathologist, bone tumor researcher*
Cohn, Joseph David *surgeon*
Eisenstein, Theodore Donald *pediatrician*
Krieger, Abbott Joel *neurosurgeon*
Maron, Arthur *pediatrician, medical administrator*
Rickert, Robert Richard *pathologist, educator*
Rommer, James Andrew *physician*
Samojlik, Eugeniusz *medical educator, retired researcher*

**Long Branch**
Barnett, Lester Alfred *surgeon*
Fox, Howard Alan *physician, medical educator*
Kristan, Ronald Wayne *physician, consultant*
Makhija, Mohan *nuclear medicine physician*
Poch, Herbert Edward *pediatrician, educator*

**Lyons**
Zimering, Mark Bernard *endocrinologist, researcher*

**Manalapan**
Harrison-Johnson, Yvonne Elois *pharmacologist*

**Manasquan**
Topilow, Arthur Alan *internist*

**Maplewood**
Shuttleworth, Anne Margaret *psychiatrist*

**Margate City**
Videll, Jared Steven *cardiologist*

**Mendham**
Desjardins, Raoul *medical association administrator, financial consultant*
Winters, Robert W. *medical educator, pediatrician*

**Middletown**
Anania, William Christian *podiatrist*

**Midland Park**
Rosin, Henry David *physician*

**Millburn**
Corwin, Andrew David *physician*

**Montclair**
Fleming, Thomas Crawley *physician, medical director, former editor*

**Montville**
Leeson, Lewis Joseph *research pharmacist, scientist*

**Moorestown**
Cervantes, Luis Augusto *neurosurgeon*
Margolis, Gerald Joseph *psychiatrist, educator*

**Morris Plains**
Fielding, Stuart *psychopharmacologist*

**Morristown**
Casale, Alfred Stanley *thoracic and cardiovascular surgeon*
Granet, Roger B. *psychiatrist, educator*
Parr, Grant Van Siclen *surgeon*
Scher, Allan Joseph *oncologist, consultant*
†Smith, Thomas J. *surgeon, educator*
Thornton, Yvonne Shirley *physician, author, musician*

**Mountainside**
Lissenden, Carolkay *pediatrician*

**Neptune**
Boak, Joseph Gordon *cardiologist*
Harrigan, John Thomas, Jr. *physician, obstetrician-gynecologist*
Rice, Stephen Gary *medical educator*

**New Brunswick**
Aisner, Joseph *oncologist, physician*
Eisinger, Robert Peter *nephrologist, educator*
Ettinger, Lawrence Jay *pediatric hematologist and oncologist, educator*
Gocke, David Joseph *immunology educator, physician, medical scientist*
Graham, Alan Morrison *surgeon*
Greco, Ralph Steven *surgeon, researcher, medical educator*
Laraya-Cuasay, Lourdes Redublo *pediatric pulmonologist, educator*
Nosko, Michael Gerrik *neurosurgeon*
Paz, Harold Louis *internist and educator*
Scully, John Thomas *obstetrician, gynecologist, educator*
Seibold, James Richard *physician, researcher*
Walters, Arthur Scott *neurologist, educator, clinical research scientist*

**Newark**
Baker, Herman *vitaminologist*
Cherniack, Neil Stanley *physician, medical educator*
Cinotti, Alfonse Anthony *ophthalmologist, educator*
Cohen, Stanley *pathologist, educator*
Cook, Stuart Donald *physician, educator*
Deitch, Edwin Alan *surgeon*
Donahoo, James Saunders *cardiothoracic surgeon*
Eslami, Hossein Hojatol *surgeon, educator*
Evans, Hugh E. *pediatrician*
Feldman, Susan Carol *neurobiologist, anatomy educator*
Gambert, Steven Ross *geriatrician*
Gardner, Bernard *surgeon, educator*
Herman, Steven Douglas *cardiothoracic surgeon, educator*
Hobson, Robert Wayne, II *surgeon*
Hutcheon, Duncan Elliot *physician, educator*
Iffy, Leslie *medical educator*
Layman, William Arthur *psychiatrist, educator*
Ledeen, Robert Wagner *neurochemist, educator*
Leevy, Carroll Moton *medical educator, hepatology researcher*
Lourenco, Ruy Valentim *physician, educator*
Materna, Thomas Walter *ophthalmologist*
Reichman, Lee Brodersohn *physician*
Shain-Alvaro, Judith Carol *physician assistant*
Weiss, Gerson *physician, educator*

**Nutley**
Mostillo, Ralph *medical association executive*
Weber, Paul Frederick *physician, pharmacist, educator*

**Ocean**
Kreider, Clement Horst, Jr. *neurosurgeon*

**Paramus**
Bagli, Vincent Joseph *plastic surgeon*
DeVita, Marie N. *physician*
Greenberg, William Michael *psychiatrist*
Liva, Edward Louis *eye surgeon*

**Parlin**
Flick, Ferdinand Herman *surgeon, prevention medicine physician*

**Passaic**
Haddad, Jamil Raouf *physician*
Pino, Robert Salvatore *radiologist*

**Paterson**
DeBari, Vincent Anthony *medical researcher, educator*
Dicovsky, Carlos Jose *physician*

**Phillipsburg**
Rosenthal, Marvin Bernard *pediatrician, educator*

**Piscataway**
Bretschneider, Ann Margery *histotechnologist*
Conney, Allan Howard *pharmacologist*
Escobar, Javier Ignacio *psychiatrist*
Mehlman, Myron A. *environmental and occupational medicine educator, environmental toxicologist*
Murphree, Henry Bernard Scott *psychiatry and pharmacology educator, consultant*
Pollack, Irwin William *psychiatrist, educator*
Rhoads, George Grant *medical epidemiologist*
Shea, Stephen Michael *physician, educator*
Upton, Arthur Canfield *experimental pathologist, educator*

**Plainfield**
Eisenstat, Theodore Ellis *colon and rectal surgeon, educator*
Winell, Marvin *orthopaedic surgeon*
Yood, Harold Stanley *internist*

**Plainsboro**
Royds, Robert Bruce *physician*

**Point Pleasant**
Monaco, Robert Anthony *radiologist*

**Point Pleasant Beach**
Motley, John Paul *psychiatrist, consultant*

**Princeton**
Bunn, William Bernice, III *physician, lawyer, epidemiologist*
Carver, David Harold *physician, educator*
Chandler, James John *surgeon*
Conn, Hadley Lewis, Jr. *physician, educator*
Corbett, Siobhan Aiden *surgeon*
Gomoll, Allen Warren *cardiovascular pharmacologist*
Hathaway, David Roger *physician, medical educator, scientist*
Haynes, William Forby, Jr. *internist, cardiologist, educator*
Mayhew, Eric George *cancer researcher, educator*
Napoliello, Michael John *psychiatrist*
Rosen, Arye *microwave, optoelectronics and medicine researcher*
Sandy, Lewis Gordon *physician, foundation administrator*
Schroeder, Steven Alfred *medical educator, researcher, foundation executive*
Sugerman, Abraham Arthur *psychiatrist*
Wei, Fong *nephrologist*

**Rahway**
Regenthal, Jeanine A. *immunologist, researcher*

**Ridgewood**
Baddoura, Rashid Joseph *emergency medicine physician*
Bristow, William Harvey, Jr. *psychiatrist*
Sumers, Anne Ricks *ophthalmologist, museum director*

**Roseland**
Schneider, George *internist, endocrinologist*

**Roselle Park**
Wilchins, Sidney A. *gynecologist*

**Rumson**
Pflum, William John *physician*

**Secaucus**
Rachlin, Stephen Leonard *psychiatrist*

**Short Hills**
Aviado, Domingo M. *pharmacologist, toxicologist*
Chaiken, Bernard Henry *internist, gastroenterologist*

**Shrewsbury**
†Shagan, Bernard Pellman *endocrinologist, educator*

**Somerset**
De Salva, Salvatore Joseph *pharmacologist, toxicologist*

**Springfield**
Duberstein, Joel Lawrence *physician*

**Stratford**
Mendels, Joseph *psychiatrist, educator*

**Summit**
Avery, Christine Ann *pediatrician*
Carniol, Paul J. *plastic and reconstructive surgeon, otolaryngologist*
O'Byrne, Elizabeth Milikin *pharmacologist, researcher, endocrinologist*
Panzarino, Saverio Joseph *physician*

**Teaneck**
Ngai, Shih Hsun *physician*
Scotti, Dennis Joseph *educator, researcher, consultant*
Wiseman, Gloria Diana *medical educator, physician*

**Tenafly**
Cosgriff, Stuart Worcester *internist, consultant, medical educator*
Katzman, Merle Hershel *orthopaedic surgeon*

**Titusville**
Conway, Paul Gary *neuropharmacologist*
Hassell, Alan Edward *pharmaceutical administrator, researcher*

**Toms River**
†Clancy, Kevin F. *cardiologist*
Marchese, Michael James, Jr. *radiation oncologist*

**Trenton**
Dimasi, Linda Grace *epidemiologist*
Rubin, Bernard *pharmacologist, biomedical writer, consultant*
Weinberg, Martin Herbert *retired psychiatrist*
Zanna, Martin Thomas *physician*

**Turnersville**
DePace, Nicholas Louis *physician*

**Union**
Rokosz, Gregory Joseph *emergency medicine physician, educator*

**Ventnor City**
Zuckerman, Stuart *psychiatrist, educator*

**Voorhees**
Barone, Donald Anthony *neurologist, educator*
Swiecicki, Martin *neurosurgeon*

**Washington**
Drago, Joseph Rosario *urologist, educator*

**Wayne**
Gollance, Robert Barnett *ophthalmologist*
Siepser, Stuart Lewis *cardiologist, internist*

**West Long Branch**
Herman, Martin Neal *neurologist, educator*

**West Orange**
Brodkin, Roger Harrison *dermatologist, educator*
Ghali, Anwar Youssef *psychiatrist, educator*
Langsner, Alan Michael *pediatrician*
Panagides, John *pharmacologist*

**Whitehouse Station**
Douglas, Robert Gordon, Jr. *physician*

**Whiting**
Williams, Roger Wright *public health educator*

**Woodbury**
Gehring, David Austin *physician, adminstrator, cardiologist*
Stambaugh, John Edgar *oncologist, hematologist, pharmacologist, educator*

**Wyckoff**
Bauer, Theodore James *physician*
Marcus, Linda Susan *dermatologist*
Stahl, Alice Slater *psychiatrist*

## NEW MEXICO

**Alamogordo**
Lindley, Norman Dale *physician*

Stapp, John Paul *flight surgeon, retired air force officer*

**Albuquerque**
†Auger, Tamara M. *psychotherapist*
Ballard, David Eugene *anesthesiologist*
Barbo, Dorothy Marie *obstetrician, gynecologist, educator*
Dixon, George Lane, Jr. *orthopedic surgeon*
Edwards, William Sterling, III *cardiovascular surgeon*
Kelley, Robert Otis *medical science educator*
Knospe, William Herbert *medical educator*
McCarty, W(illard) Duane *obstetrician, gynecologist, physician executive*
Mora, Federico *neurosurgeon*
Napolitano, Leonard Michael *anatomist, university administrator*
Omer, George Elbert, Jr. *orthopaedic surgeon, hand surgeon, educator*
Ottensmeyer, David Joseph *healthcare consultant, retired neurosurgeon*
Reyes, Edward *pharmacology educator*
Saland, Linda Carol *anatomy educator*
Stevenson, James Richard *radiologist, lawyer*
Summers, William Koopmans *neuropsychiatrist, researcher*
Tatum, Ronald Winston *physician, endocrinologist*
Uhlenhuth, Eberhard Henry *psychiatrist, educator*
Waitzkin, Howard Bruce *physician, sociologist, educator*
Winslow, Walter William *psychiatrist*
Wong, Phillip Allen *osteopathic physician*
Worrell, Richard Vernon *orthopedic surgeon, educator, academic administrator*
Zumwalt, Ross Eugene *forensic pathologist, educator*

**Carlsbad**
Markle, George Bushar, IV *surgeon*

**Chama**
Moser, Robert Harlan *physician, educator, writer*

**Clovis**
Goodwin, Martin Brune *radiologist*

**Corrales**
Cobb, John Candler *medical educator*

**Farmington**
Neidhart, James Allen *physician, educator*

**Las Cruces**
Jacobs, Kent Frederick *dermatologist*
Talamantes, Roberto *developmental pediatrican*

**Los Alamos**
Smith, Fredrica Emrich *rheumatologist, internist*

**Roswell**
Jennings, Emmit M. *surgeon*

**Santa Fe**
Gilmour, Edward Ellis *psychiatrist*

## NEW YORK

**Albany**
Ambros, Robert Andrew *pathologist, educator*
Arseneau, James Charles *physician*
Beebe, Richard Townsend *physician*
Bennett, Edward Virdell, Jr. *surgeon*
Bradley, Wesley Holmes *physician*
†Burkart, Peter Thomas *hematologist*
†Capone, Robert Joseph *physician, educator*
Davis, Paul Joseph *endocrinologist*
DeFelice, Eugene Anthony *physician, medical educator, consultant, magician*
Dougherty, James *orthopedic surgeon, educator*
Doyle, Joseph Theobald *physician, educator*
Han, Jaok *cardiologist, researcher, educator*
Hoffmeister, Jana Marie *cardiologist*
Howard, Lyn Jennifer *medical educator*
Kaye, Gordon Israel *pathologist, anatomist, educator*
Lumpkin, Lee Roy *dermatologist, educator*
Macario, Alberto Juan Lorenzo *physician*
Spooner, Eric Warbasse *pediatric cardiologist*
Sturman, Lawrence Stuart *health research administrator*
Swartz, Donald Percy *physician*
Yunich, Albert Mansfeld *physician*

**Amherst**
Katz, Leonard Allen *medical director, educator*
Levy, Gerhard *pharmacologist*
Wiesenberg, Jacqueline Leonardi *medical lecturer*

**Amityville**
Upadhyay, Yogendra Nath *physician, educator*

**Ardsley**
Kuntzman, Ronald *pharmacology research executive*

**Argyle**
Bruce, David Lionel *retired anesthesiologist, educator*

**Armonk**
Mellors, Robert Charles *physician, scientist*

**Bay Shore**
Killian, Edward James *pediatrician*
Pinsker, Walter *allergist, immunologist*

**Bayside**
Gavencak, John Richard *pediatrician, allergist*

**Beacon**
Garell, Paul Charles *physician, family practice*

**Bedford**
Lord, Jere Williams, Jr. *retired surgeon*

**Bellmore**
Crouch, Howard Earle *health service organization executive*

**Bethpage**
Brodie, Sheldon J. *physician*
Budoff, Penny Wise *physician, author, researcher*
De Santis, Mark *osteopathic physician*

**Binghamton**
Bethje, Robert *general surgeon, retired*
Michael, Sandra Dale *reproductive endocrinology educator, researcher*
Peterson, Alfred Edward *family physician*
Schecter, Arnold Joel *preventive medicine educator*

**Briarcliff Manor**
Glassman, Jerome Martin *clinical pharmacologist, educator*
Weintraub, Michael Ira *neurologist*

**Bronx**
†Balsano, Nicholas A. *surgeon, educator*
Bhalodkar, Narendra Chandrakant *cardiologist*
Blaufox, Morton Donald *physician, educator*
Burde, Ronald Marshall *neuro-ophthalmologist*
Buschke, Herman *neurologist*
Cherkasky, Martin *physician*
†Chiaramida, Salvatore *cardiologist, educator, health facility adminstrator*
Cimino, James Ernest *physician*
Cohen, Herbert Jesse *physician, educator*
Cohen, Michael I. *pediatrician*
Coupey, Susan McGuire *pediatrician, educator*
DeMartino, Anthony Gabriel *cardiologist, internist*
Diamond, Betty Ann *internist, educator*
Dutcher, Janice Jean Phillips *oncologist*
Edelmann, Chester Monroe, Jr. *pediatrician, medical school dean*
Eder, Howard Abram *physician*
Eliasoph, Joan *radiologist, educator*
Elkin, Milton *radiologist, physician, educator*
†Eng, Calvin *cardiologist, researcher*
Fishman, Glenn I. *medical educator*
Fleischer, Norman *director of endocrinology, medical educator*
Foreman, Spencer *pulmonary specialist, hospital executive*
Freeman, Leonard Murray *radiologist, nuclear medicine physician, educator*
Frishman, William Howard *cardiology educator, cardiovasular pharmacologist, gerontologist*
Fulop, Milford *physician*
Gerst, Paul Howard *physician*
Gillman, Arthur Emanuel *psychiatrist*
Gliedman, Marvin L. *surgeon, educator*
Goldberg, Marcia B. *medical educator*
Gross, Ludwik *physician*
Herbert, Victor Daniel *medical educator*
Hirano, Asao *neuropathologist*
Hirschy, James Conrad *radiologist*
Jacobson, Harold Gordon *radiologist, educator*
Jaffé, Ernst Richard *medical educator and administrator*
Kadish, Anna Stein *pathologist, educator, researcher*
Kahn, Thomas *medical educator*
Karasu, T(oksoz) Byram *psychiatry educator*
Karkanias, George B. *neurologist, educator*
Koss, Leopold G. *physician, pathologist, educator*
Lieber, Charles Saul *physician, educator*
Marx, Gertie Florentine *anesthesiologist*
Michelsen, W(olfgang) Jost *neurosurgeon, educator*
Muschel, Louis Henry *immunologist, educator*
Nagler, Arnold Leon *pathologist, scientist, educator*
Nanna, Michele *cardiologist, educator*
Nitowsky, Harold Martin *physician, educator*
Orkin, Louis Richard *physician, educator*
Pitchumoni, Capecomorin Sankar *gastroenterologist, educator*
Plimpton, Calvin Hastings *physician, university president*
Purpura, Dominick P. *neuroscientist, university dean*
Radel, Eva *pediatrician, hematologist*
Rapin, Isabelle *physician*
Reynolds, Benedict Michael *surgeon*
Romney, Seymour Leonard *physician, educator*
Ruben, Robert Joel *physician, educator*
Rubinstein, Arye *pediatrician, microbiology and immunology educator*
Sable, Robert Allen *gastroenterologist*
Scharff, Matthew Daniel *immunologist, cell biologist, educator*
Schaumburg, Herbert Howard *neurology educator*
†Scheuer, James *physician, educator, researcher*
Senturia, Yvonne Dreyfus *pediatrician, epidemiologist*
Shafritz, David Andrew *physician, research scientist*
Shapiro, Nella Irene *surgeon*
Shatin, Harry *medical educator, dermatologist*
Shinnar, Shlomo *child neurologist, educator*
Spitzer, Adrian *pediatrician, medical educator*
Stein, Ruth Elizabeth Klein *physician*
Surks, Martin I. *medical educator, endocrinologist*
Wiernik, Peter Harris *oncologist, educator*
Williams, Marshall Henry, Jr. *physician, educator*

**Bronxville**
Kaplan, Sanford Allen *internist, allergist*
Levitt, Miriam *pediatrician*
Perez, Louis Anthony *radiologist*
Rizzo, Thomas Dignan *orthopedic surgeon*

**Brooklyn**
Alfonso, Antonio Escolar *surgeon*
Barth, Robert Henry *nephrologist, educator*
Baumgarten, Stephen Robert *physician, urologist*
Bergeron, R. Thomas *radiologist, educator*
Berman, David Hirsh *physician*
Biro, Laszlo *dermatologist*
Clark, Luther Theopolis *physician, educator, researcher*
Cracco, Roger Quinlan *medical educator, neurologist*
Davidson, Steven J. *emergency physician*
Duffoo, Frantz Michel *nephrologist, director of medicine*
Edemeka, Udo Edemeka *surgeon*
El Kodsi, Baroukh *gastroenterologist, educator*
Erber, William Franklin *gastroenterologist*
Feit, Alan *cardiologist, internist, medical educator*
Fodstad, Harald *neurosurgeon*
Friedman, Eli Arnold *nephrologist*
Furchgott, Robert Francis *pharmacologist, educator*
Gintautas, Jonas *physician, scientist, administrator*
Gotta, Alexander Walter *anesthesiologist, educator*
Holden, David Morgan *medical educator*
Kamholz, Stephan L. *physician*
Kravath, Richard Elliot *pediatrician, educator*
†Leff, Sanford Erwin *cardiologist*
Levendoglu, Hulya *gastroenterologist*
Levere, Richard David *physician, academic administrator, educator*
†Levowitz, Bernard Samuel *surgeon, administrator*
Levy, Norman B. *psychiatrist, educator*
Lindo, J. Trevor *psychiatrist, consultant*
Malach, Monte *physician*
Mark, Richard Kushakow *internist*
Mayer, Ira Edward *gastroenterologist*
Mendez, Hermann Armando *pediatrician, educator*
Milhorat, Thomas Herrick *neurosurgeon*
Milman, Doris Hope *pediatrics educator, psychiatrist*
Mohaideen, A. Hassan *surgeon, healthcare executive*
Mydlo, Jack Henry *surgeon, researcher*
Namba, Tatsuji *physician, medical researcher*
Naqvi, Shehla Hasnain *pediatric infectious disease specialist, pediatrician*
Norstrand, Iris Fletcher *psychiatrist, neurologist, educator*
Pertschuk, Louis Philip *pathologist*
Peter, Sebastian Augustine *endocrinologist*
Plotz, Charles Mindell *physician*
Price, Ely *dermatologist*
Qiao, Liang *physician*
Ravitz, Leonard, Jr. *physician, scientist, consultant*
Reich, Nathaniel Edwin *physician, poet, author, artist, educator*
Ricca, Joseph John *internist, gastroenterologist*
†Savits, Barry Sorrel *surgeon*
Sawyer, Philip Nicholas *surgeon, educator, health science facility administrator*
Schwarz, Richard Howard *obstetrician, gynecologist, educator*
Shalita, Alan Remi *dermatologist*
Sullivan, Colleen Anne *physician, educator*
Weiner, Irwin M. *medical educator, college dean, researcher*
Wolintz, Arthur Harry *physician, neuro-ophthalmologist*
Wollman, Leo *physician*

**Buffalo**
Ambrus, Clara Maria *physician*
Ambrus, Julian L. *physician, medical educator*
Aquilina, Alan T. *physician*
Bakay, Louis *neurosurgeon*
Brody, Harold *neuroanatomist, gerontologist*
Calkins, Evan *physician, educator*
Chu, Tsann Ming *immunochemist, educator*
Chutkow, Jerry Grant *neurologist, educator*
Coles, William Henry *ophthalmologist, educator*
Creaven, Patrick Joseph *physician, research oncologist*
Enhorning, Goran *obstetrician, gynecologist, educator*
Fallavollita, James A. *cardiologist, educator, researcher*
Genco, Robert Joseph *scientist, immunologist, periodontist, educator*
Glasauer, Franz Ernst *neurosurgeon*
Graham, (Lloyd) Saxon *epidemiology educator*
Gresham, Glen Edward *physician*
Halbreich, Uriel Morav *psychiatrist, educator*
Henderson, Edward Shelton *oncologist*
Hershey, Linda Ann *neurology and pharmacology educator*
Hohn, David *physician*
Hoover, Eddie Lee *cardiothoracic surgeon, educator*
Horoszewicz, Juliusz Stanislaw *oncologist, cancer researcher, laboratory administrator*
Krackow, Kenneth Alan *orthopaedic surgeon, educator, inventor*
Kurlan, Marvin Zeft *surgeon, educator*
Lele, Amol Shashikant *obstetrician and gynecologist*
Levy, Harold James *physician, psychiatrist*
†Logue, Gerald L. *hematologist*
Mendelow, Gary N. *physician, emergency consultant*
Mihich, Enrico *medical researcher*
Milgrom, Felix *immunologist, educator*
Mindell, Eugene Robert *surgeon, educator*
Mirand, Edwin Albert *medical scientist*
Naughton, John Patrick *cardiologist*
Nolan, James Paul *medical educator, scientist*
Panaro, Victor Anthony *radiologist*
Pentney, Roberta Jean *neuroanatomist, educator*
Pincus, Stephanie Hoyer *dermatologist, educator*
Piver, M. Steven *gynecologic oncologist*
Raghavan, Derek *oncology and medical educator*
Regan, Peter Francis, III *physician, psychiatry educator*
Rekate, Albert C. *physician*
Richmond, Allen Martin *speech pathologist, educator*
Seller, Robert Herman *cardiologist, family physician*
Shedd, Donald Pomroy *surgeon*
Simpson, George True *surgeon, educator*
Stoll, Howard Lester, Jr. *dermatologist*
Trevisan, Maurizio *epidemiologist, researcher*
Voorhess, Mary Louise *pediatric endocrinologist*
Wright, John Robert *pathologist*

**Canaan**
Rothenberg, Albert *psychiatrist, educator*

**Carle Place**
Linchitz, Richard Michael *psychiatrist, pain medicine specialist, physician*

**Cedarhurst**
Cohen, Harris L. *diagnostic radiologist, consultant*

**Centerport**
Fischel, Edward Elliot *physician*

**Cheektowaga**
Woldman, Sherman *pediatrician*

**Chestnut Ridge**
Day, Stacey Biswas *physician, educator*

**Clinton**
Stowens, Daniel *pathologist*

**Cohocton**
Frame, Paul Sutherland *medical educator, physician*

**Cooperstown**
Bordley, James, IV *surgeon*
Franck, Walter Alfred *rheumatologist, medical administrator, educator*

**Corning**
Lin, Min-Chung *obstetrician-gynecologist*

**Dix Hills**
Sampino, Anthony F. *physician, obstetrician and gynecologist*

**East Islip**
Delman, Michael Robert *physician*
Fleishman, Philip Robert *internist*

**Eastchester**
Liebert, Peter S. *pediatric surgeon, consultant*

**Eatons Neck**
Altner, Peter Christian *orthopedic surgeon, medical educator*

**Edmeston**
Price, James Melford *physician*

**Elmhurst**
Barron, Charles Thomas *psychiatrist*
Cheng, Alexander Lim *internist*
Masci, Joseph Richard *medical educator, physician*
Shanies, Harvey Michael *pulmonologist, medical educator*

**Elmira**
Graham, David Richard *orthopedic surgeon*
Quintos, Elias Rilloraza *cardiac surgeon, thoracic surgeon*

**Fairport**
Kelly, Francis W. *retired psychiatrist*

**Far Rockaway**
Madhusoodanan, Subramoniam *psychiatrist, educator*

**Fayetteville**
Pirodsky, Donald Max *psychiatrist, educator*

**Fishkill**
Brocks, Eric Randy *ophthalmologist, surgeon*

**Flushing**
Dubov, Spencer Floyd *podiatrist, educator*
Eden, Alvin Noam *pediatrician, author*
Ellis, John Taylor *pathologist, retired educator*
Hon, John Wingsun *physician*
Kaplan, Barry Hubert *physician*
Kornhauser, Stanley Henry *medical administrator, educator, consultant*
Kresic, Eva *pediatrician*
Nussbaum, Michel Ernest *physician*
Stark, Joel *speech language pathologist*

**Fort Drum**
Ebbels, Bruce Jeffery *physician, health facility administrator*

**Garden City**
Deane, Leland Marc *plastic surgeon*
Good, Larry Irwin *physician, consultant*

**Glenmont**
Kolb, Lawrence Coleman *psychiatrist*

**Glens Falls**
Wurzberger, Bezalel *psychiatrist*

**Great Neck**
Arlow, Jacob A. *psychiatrist, educator*
Gross, Lillian *psychiatrist*
Kechijian, Paul *dermatologist, educator*
Kodsi, Sylvia Rose *ophthalmologist*
Ratner, Harold *pediatrician, educator*
Rosenberg, Richard F. *physician, radiologist*
Simon, Arthur *pharmacologist, research laboratory executive*
Wolff, Edward *physician*

**Hartsdale**
Chait, Maxwell Mani *physician*

**Hastings Hdsn**
Rosch, Paul John *physician, educator*

**Hauppauge**
Graham, David Gregory *preventive medicine physician, psychiatrist*

**Hempstead**
Laano, Archie Bienvenido Maaño *cardiologist*

**Hewlett**
Cohen, David Leon *physician*
Steinfeld, Philip S. *pediatrician*

**Hollis**
Malis, Leonard Irving *neurosurgeon*

**Hudson**
Mustapha, Tamton *gastroenterologist*

**Huntington**
Joseph, Richard Saul *cardiologist*
Vale, Margo Rose *physician*

**Huntington Station**
Zingale, Robert G. *surgeon*

**Ithaca**
Dietert, Rodney Reynolds *immunology and toxicology educator*
Pickett, Lawrence Kimball *physician, educator*
Quimby, Fred William *pathology educator, veterinarian*
Whitaker, Susanne Kanis *veterinary medical librarian*

**Jackson Heights**
Fischbarg, Zulema F. *pediatrician, educator*

**Jamaica**
Boal, Bernard Harvey *cardiologist, educator, author*
Rosner, Fred *physician, educator*
Walker, Sonia Evadne *osteopath*

Rainer, John David *psychiatrist, educator*
Rainess, Alan Edward *psychiatrist*
Ramirez, Gloria Maria *physician*
Ramsay, David Leslie *physician, dermatologist, medical educator*
Raskin, Noel Michael *thoracic surgeon*
Raynor, Richard Benjamin *neurosurgeon, educator*
Redo, S(averio) Frank *surgeon*
Reemtsma, Keith *surgeon, educator*
Reidenberg, Marcus Milton *physician, educator*
Reis, Donald Jeffery *neurologist, neurobiologist, educator*
Reisberg, Barry *geropsychiatrist, neuropsychopharmacologist*
Reisner, Milton *psychiatrist, psychoanalyst*
†Reiss, Robert Francis *physician*
Rifkin, Harold *physician, educator*
Rifkind, Arleen B. *physician, researcher*
Robinson, Bernard Pahl *thoracic surgeon, educator*
Rodriguez-Sains, Rene S. *ophthalmologist, surgeon, educator*
Roen, Philip Ruben *urologist, surgeon, medical educator*
Rom, William Nicholas *physician*
Roman, Stanford Augustus, Jr. *medical educator, dean*
Romano, John Francis *physician*
Rosendorff, Clive *cardiologist*
Rosenfield, Allan *physician*
Rothenberg, Robert Edward *physician, surgeon, author*
Roufa, Arnold *gynecologist, obstetrician*
Rovit, Richard Lee *neurological surgeon*
Rowland, Lewis Phillip *neurologist, medical editor, educator*
Rubin, Albert Louis *physician, educator*
Rubin, Gustav *orthopedic surgeon, consultant, researcher*
Rubin, Theodore Isaac *psychiatrist*
Saadeh, Peter Boutros *physiatrist, educator*
Sachar, David Bernard *gastroenterologist, medical educator*
Sachdev, Ved Parkash *neurosurgeon*
Sacks, Oliver Wolf *neurologist, writer*
Sadock, Benjamin James *psychiatrist, educator*
Sager, Clifford J(ulius) *psychiatrist, educator*
Samman, Juan M. *prosthodontist*
Sanchez, Miguel Ramon *dermatologist, educator*
Santulli, Thomas Vincent *surgeon*
Saphir, Richard Louis *pediatrician*
Sawyer, William Dale *physician, educator, university dean, foundation administrator*
Schaffner, Bertram Henry *psychiatrist*
Schiff, Andrew Newman *physician, venture capitalist*
Schlesinger, Edward Bruce *neurological surgeon*
Schley, William Shain *otorhinolaryngologist*
Schneck, Jerome M. *psychiatrist, medical historian, educator*
Schuster, Carlotta Lief *psychiatrist*
Schwartz, Irving Leon *physician, scientist, educator*
Schwartz, Miles Joseph *cardiologist*
Schwartz, Roselind Shirley Grant *podiatrist*
Sedlin, Elias David *physician, orthopedic researcher, educator*
Seely, Robert Daniel *physician, medical educator*
Shainess, Natalie *psychiatrist, educator*
Shapiro, Theodore *psychiatrist, educator*
Shatan, Chaim Felix *psychiatrist, medical educator, expert on Vietnam veterans, traumatic stress pioneer*
Shepherd, Gillian Mary *physician*
Siffert, Robert Spencer *orthopedic surgeon*
Silver, Richard Tobias *physician, educator*
Siris, Ethel Silverman *endocrinologist*
Sitarz, Anneliese Lotte *pediatrics educator, physician*
Skinner, David Bernt *surgeon, educator, administrator*
Snyderman, Selma Eleanore *pediatrician, educator*
Soave, Rosemary *internist*
Socarides, Charles William *psychiatrist, psychoanalyst, educator, writer*
Solomon, Gail Ellen *physician*
Sorrel, William Edwin *psychiatrist, educator, psychoanalyst*
Spaide, Richard Frederick *ophthalmologist*
Spencer, Frank Cole *medical educator*
Spiegel, Herbert *psychiatrist, educator*
Stark, Richard Boies *surgeon, artist*
Stein, Bennett Mueller *neurosurgeon*
Stein, Marvin *psychiatrist, historian*
Steinglass, Peter Joseph *psychiatrist, educator*
Steinherz, Laurel Judith *pediatric cardiologist*
Stenzel, Kurt Hodgson *physician, nephrologist, educator*
Stern, Claudio Daniel *medical educator, embryological researcher*
Stern, Marvin *psychiatrist, educator*
Stevens, Jerome Hebert *management consultant*
Stevenson, Nikolai *medical association executive*
Stimmel, Barry *cardiologist, internist, educator, university dean*
Susser, Mervyn Wilfred *epidemiologist, educator*
Thomas, Stephen J. *anesthesiologist*
Thomashow, Byron Martin *pulmonary physician*
Thomson, Gerald Edmund *physician, educator*
Tilson, M(artin) David *surgeon, scientist, educator*
Tolchin, Joan Gubin *psychiatrist, educator*
Tourlitsas, John Constantine *radiologist*
Turino, Gerard Michael *physician, medical scientist, educator*
Turndorf, Herman *anesthesiologist, educator*
Tzimas, Nicholas Achilles *orthopedic surgeon, educator*
Vaughan, Edwin Darracott, Jr. *urologist, surgeon*
Vilcek, Jan Tomas *medical educator*
Waksman, Byron Halsted *neuroimmunologist, experimental pathologist, educator, medical association administrator*
Wallace, Joyce Irene Malakoff *internist*
Wallach, Stanley *medical educator, consultant, administrator*
Walsh, Joseph Brennan *ophthalmologist*
Waltz, Joseph McKendree *neurosurgeon, educator*
Wang, Frederick Mark *pediatric ophthalmologist, medical educator*
Warshaw, Leon J(oseph) *physician*
Wasserman, Louis Robert *physician, educator*
Waugh, Theodore Rogers *orthopedic surgeon*
Weber, Carol Martinez *physician*
Wecker, William A. *preventive medicine physician, neuropsychiatrist*
Weinstein, I. Bernard *oncologist, geneticist, research administrator*
Weisfeldt, Myron Lee *physician, educator*
Weissmann, Gerald *medical educator, researcher, writer, editor*
Weksler, Marc Edward *physician, educator*
Whelan, Elizabeth Ann Murphy *epidemiologist*
Whitehead, E. Douglas *urology educator*
Whitsell, John Crawford, II *general surgeon*
Wiesel, Torsten Nils *neurobiologist, educator*
Wilson, Philip Duncan, Jr. *orthopedic surgeon*
Winawer, Sidney Jerome *physician, clinical investigator, educator*
Wishnick, Marcia Margolis *pediatrician, geneticist, educator*
Wood-Smith, Donald *plastic surgeon*
Worman, Howard Jay *physician, educator*
Worner, Theresa Marie *physician*
Wright, Irving Sherwood *physician, retired educator*
Wright, Jane Cooke *physician, educator, consultant*
Wysocki, Annette B. *nurse scientist, educator*
Yahr, Melvin David *physician*
Yin, Beatrice Wei-Tze *medical researcher*
Yurt, Roger William *surgeon, educator*
Zatlin, Gabriel Stanley *physician*
Zimmerman, Sol Shea *pediatrician*
Zitrin, Arthur *physician*
Zonszein, Joel *endocrinologist*
Zucker, Howard Alan *pediatric cardiologist, intensivist, anesthesiologist*

### Niskayuna
De Jesus-McCarthy, Fe Teresa *physician*

### Nyack
Rossi, Harald Hermann *retired radiation biophysicist, educator, administrator*

### Olean
Catalano, Robert Anthony *ophthalmologist, physician, hospital administrator, writer*
Godfrey, John *internist*

### Oneida
Muschenheim, Frederick *pathologist*

### Orangeburg
Levine, Jerome *psychiatrist, educator*

### Orchard Park
Lee, Richard Vaille *physician, educator*

### Ossining
Wolfe, Mary Joan *physician*

### Pearl River
Rasch, Stuart Gary *emergency physician*

### Pittsford
Faloon, William Wassell *physician, educator*
Schwartz, Ruth Wainer *physician*

### Plainview
Kelemen, John *neurologist, educator*
Krauss, Leo *urologist, educator*
Lieberman, Elliott *urologist*

### Plattsburgh
Rech, Susan Anita *obstetrician, gynecologist*

### Pleasantville
Waletsky, Lucy Rockefeller *psychiatrist*

### Pomona
Glassman, Lawrence S. *plastic surgeon*

### Port Jefferson
Dranitzke, Richard J. *thoracic surgeon*

### Port Jefferson Station
Kaplan, Martin Paul *pediatrician, educator*

### Port Washington
Brownstein, Martin Herbert *dermatopathologist*

### Poughkeepsie
Berlin, Doris Ada *psychiatrist*
Kanwit, Bert Alfred *retired surgeon*

### Rego Park
Gudeon, Arthur *podiatrist*

### Rochester
†Afifi, Alaa Youssef *cardiothoracic surgeon*
Barton, Russell William *psychiatrist, author*
Baum, John *physician*
Bennett, John Morrison *medical oncologist*
Berg, Robert Lewis *physician, educator*
Bessey, Palmer Quintard *surgeon*
Bonfiglio, Thomas Albert *pathologist, educator*
Borch, Richard Frederic *pharmacology and chemistry educator*
Brody, Bernard B. *physician, educator*
Brooks, Walter S. *dermatologist*
Brzustowicz, Richard John *neurosurgeon, educator*
Burgener, Francis André *radiology educator*
Burton, Richard Irving *orthopedist, educator*
Bushinsky, David Allen *nephrologist, educator, researcher*
Cain, Russell M. *psychiatrist*
Ciccone, J. Richard *psychiatrist*
Cohen, Nicholas *immunologist, educator*
Crino, Marjanne Helen *anesthesiologist*
de Papp, Elise Wachenfeld *pathologist*
Doty, Robert William *neurophysiologist, educator*
Dreyfuss, Eric Martin *allergist*
Forbes, Gilbert Burnett *physician, educator*
Frank, Irwin Norman *urologist, educator*
Frazer, John Paul *surgeon*
Frisina, Robert Dana *sensory neuroscientist, educator*
Goldstein, Marvin Norman *physician*
Griggs, Robert Charles *physician*
Halpern, Werner Israel *psychiatrist, educator*
Haywood, Anne Mowbray *pediatrics, virology, and biochemistry educator*
Heinle, Robert Alan *physician*
Herz, Marvin Ira *psychiatrist*
Hood, William Boyd, Jr. *cardiologist, educator*
Hoskin, William Dickel *physician*
Jacobs, Laurence Stanton *physician, educator*
Lawrence, Ruth Anderson *pediatrician, clinical toxicologist*
Lichtman, Marshall Albert *medical educator*
McClure, Lucretia Walker *medical librarian*
Mc Donald, Joseph Valentine *neurosurgeon*
McMeekin, Thomas Owen *dermatologist*
Mc Quillen, Michael Paul *physician*
Menguy, Rene *surgeon, educator*
Morgan, William Lionel, Jr. *physician, educator*
Morton, John H. *surgeon, educator*
Moss, Arthur Jay *physician*
Nazarian, Lawrence Fred *pediatrician*
O'Mara, Robert Edmund George *radiologist, educator*
Panner, Bernard J. *pathologist, educator*
Paterson, Eileen *radiation oncologist, educator*
Pearson, Thomas Arthur *epidemiologist, educator*
Pettee, Daniel Starr *neurologist*
Powers, James Matthew *neuropathologist*
Reifler, Clifford Bruce *psychiatrist, educator*
Risher, William Henry *cardiothoracic surgeon*
Rowley, Peter Templeton *physician, educator*
Schwartz, Seymour Ira *surgeon, educator*
Sherman, Charles Daniel, Jr. *surgeon*
Smith, Julia Ladd *medical oncologist, hospice physician*
Toribara, Taft Yutaka *radiation biologist, biophysicist, chemist, toxicologist*
Utell, Mark Jeffrey *medical educator*
Wiley, Jason LaRue, Jr. *neurosurgeon*
Williams, Thomas Franklin *physician, educator*
Wynne, Lyman Carroll *psychiatrist*

### Roslyn
Damus, Paul Shibli *cardiac surgeon*

### Roslyn Heights
Glickman, Franklin Sheldon *dermatologist, educator*
Rogatz, Peter *physician*

### Rye
Barker, Harold Grant *surgeon, educator*
Marcus, Joel David *pediatrician*
Reader, George Gordon *physician, educator*
Wessler, Stanford *physician, educator*
Wilmot, Irvin Gorsage *former hospital administrator, educator, consultant*

### Sands Point
Goodman, Edmund Nathan *surgeon*
Lear, Erwin *anesthesiologist, educator*

### Sayville
Blume, Sheila Bierman *psychiatrist*

### Scarsdale
Buttinger-Fedeli, Catharine Sarina Caroline *psychiatrist*
Moser, Marvin *physician, educator, author*
Newman, Fredric Alan *plastic surgeon, educator*
Rivlin, Richard Saul *physician, educator*
Scheinberg, Labe Charles *physician, educator*

### Schenectady
Jarrett, Steven Ronald *physician, physical medicine and rehabilitation*
Schenck, John Frederic *physician*

### Silver Creek
Schenk, Worthington George, Jr. *surgeon, educator*

### Smithtown
Dvorkin, Ronald Alan *emergency physician*

### Somers
Rubin, Samuel Harold *physician, consultant*

### Staten Island
Banner, Burton *pediatrician*
Bruckstein, Alex Harry *internist, gastroenterologist, geriatrician*
Campbell, Craig John *podiatrist*
Mirsepassi-Toloui, Shirley Shirin *pathologist, educator*
O'Connor, Robert James *gynecologist, consultant*
Worth, Melvin H. *surgeon, educator*

### Stony Brook
Bilfinger, Thomas Victor *surgeon, educator*
Cesa, Michael Peter *cardiologist, consultant*
Cottrell, Thomas Sylvester *pathology educator, university dean*
Davis, James Norman *neurologist, neurobiology researcher*
Dervan, John Patrick *cardiologist*
Edelman, Norman Herman *medical educator, university dean and official*
Fritts, Harry Washington, Jr. *physician, educator*
Jonas, Steven *public health physician, medical educator, writer*
Kuchner, Eugene Frederick *neurosurgeon, educator*
Lane, Dorothy Spiegel *physician*
Liang, Jerome Zhengrong *radiology educator*
Meyers, Morton Allen *physician, radiology educator*
Miller, Frederick *pathologist*
Poppers, Paul Jules *anesthesiologist, educator*
Priebe, Cedric Joseph, Jr. *pediatric surgeon*
Rapaport, Felix Theodosius *surgeon, researcher, educator*
Sokoloff, Leon *pathology educator*
Steigbigel, Roy Theodore *infectious disease physician and scientist, educator*
Steinberg, Amy Wishner *dermatologist*

### Suffern
Codispoti, Andre John *allergist, immunologist*
Marcus, Janet Carol *cytotechnologist*
Schachter, Michael Ben *psychiatrist, complementary physician*

### Syracuse
Baker, Bruce Edward *orthopedic surgeon, consultant*
Bellanger, Barbara Doris Hoysak *biomedical research technologist*
Clausen, Jerry Lee *psychiatrist*
Cohen, William Nathan *radiologist*
Daly, Robert W. *psychiatrist, medical educator*
Gold, Joseph *medical researcher*
Horst, Pamela Sue *medical educator, family physician*
Irwin, Martin *psychiatrist*
Kieffer, Stephen Aaron *radiologist, educator*
Landaw, Stephen Arthur *physician, educator*
Lemanski, Larry Fredrick *medical educator*
McGraw, James L. *retired ophthalmologist, educator*
Murray, David George *orthopedic surgeon, educator*
Nast, Edward Paul *cardiac surgeon*
Perl, Andras *immunologist, educator, scientist*
Phillips, Richard Hart *psychiatrist*
Rabuzzi, Daniel D. *medical educator*
Rogers, Sherry Anne *physician*
Rosenbaum, Arthur Elihu *neuroradiologist, educator*
Scheinman, Steven Jay *medical educator*
Smith, Robert L. *medical research administrator*
Szasz, Thomas Stephen *psychiatrist, educator, writer*
Verrillo, Ronald Thomas *neuroscientist*
Williams, William Joseph *physician, educator*

### Tarrytown
Chu, Foo *physician*
Field, Barry Elliot *internist, gastroenterologist*

### Tuxedo Park
Regan, Ellen Frances (Mrs. Walston Shepard Brown) *ophthalmologist*

### Upton
Cronkite, Eugene Pitcher *physician*
Hamilton, Leonard Derwent *physician, molecular biologist*

### Utica
Bowers, Roger Paul *radiologist*

### Valhalla
Carter, Anne Cohen *physician*
Cimino, Joseph Anthony *physician, educator*
Couldwell, William Tupper *neurosurgeon, educator*
Del Guercio, Louis Richard Maurice *surgeon, educator, company executive*
Fink, Raymond *medical educator*
Frost, Elizabeth Ann McArthur *physician*
Hodgson, W(alter) John B(arry) *surgeon*
Kline, Susan Anderson *medical school administrator, internist*
Levin, Aaron Reuben *pediatrician, educator*
Madden, Robert Edward *surgeon, educator*
McGiff, John C(harles) *pharmacologist*
Niguidula, Faustino Nazario *pediatric cardiothoracic surgeon*
Reed, George Elliott *surgery educator*
Weisburger, John Hans *medical researcher*
Williams, Gary Murray *medical researcher, pathology educator*

### Vestal
†Kuehl, Alexander *emergency physician, health facility administrator, medical educator, writer*

### Warsaw
Dy-Ang, Anita C. *pediatrician*

### West Haverstraw
Cochran, George Van Brunt *physician, surgery educator, researcher*

### West Islip
Cokinos, Stephan George *cardiologist*

### Westbury
Ente, Gerald *pediatrician*

### Westfield
Brown, Kent Louis, Sr. *surgeon*

### White Plains
Baum, Carol Grossman *physician*
Biers, Martin Henry *physician*
Blank, H. Robert *psychiatrist*
Blass, John Paul *medical educator, physician*
Johnston, Richard Boles, Jr. *pediatrician, educator, biomedical researcher*
Katz, Michael *pediatrician, educator*
Marano, Anthony Joseph *cardiologist*
McDowell, Fletcher Hughes *physician, educator*
Monteferrante, Judith Catherine *cardiologist*
Morris, Robert Warren *physician assistant*
Samii, Abdol Hossein *physician, educator*
Smith, Gerard Peter *neuroscientist*
Soley, Robert Lawrence *plastic surgeon*

### Whitestone
Rosmarin, Leonard Alan *dermatologist*

### Williamsville
Jasiewicz, Ronald Clarence *physician*
Reisman, Robert E. *physician, educator*

### Woodbury
Bleicher, Sheldon Joseph *endocrinologist, medical educator*

### Woodstock
Dolamore, Michael John *physician*

### Yonkers
DeAngelis, Roger Thomas *surgeon*

### Yorktown Heights
Klein, Richard Stephen *internist*

## NORTH CAROLINA

### Advance
Meschan, Isadore *radiologist, educator*
Meschan, Rachel Farrer (Mrs. Isadore Meschan) *obstetrics and gynecology educator*

### Apex
Knapp, Richard Bruce *anesthesiologist*

### Asheboro
Helsabeck, Eric H. *emergency physician*

### Asheville
Astler, Vernon Benson *surgeon*
Enriquez, Manuel Hipolito *physician*
Powell, Norborne Berkeley *urologist*
White, Terry Edward *physician*

### Bahama
Epstein, David Lee *ophthalmologist, surgeon, educator*

### Belhaven
Boyette, Charles Otis *family physician*

**Burlington**
Wilson, William Preston *psychiatrist, emeritus educator*

**Chapel Hill**
Azar, Henry Amin *medical historian, educator*
Barnett, Thomas Buchanan *physician, medical educator*
Bondurant, Stuart *physician, educational administrator*
Boone, Franklin Delanor Roosevelt, Sr. *cardiovascular perfusionist, realtor*
Briggaman, Robert Alan *dermatologist, medical educator*
Brinkhous, Kenneth Merle *pathologist, educator*
Bromberg, Philip Allan *internist, educator*
Brownlee, Robert Calvin *pediatrician, educator*
Cance, William George *surgeon*
Carson, Culley Clyde, III *urologist*
Cefalo, Robert Charles *obstetrician, gynecologist*
Clark, Richard Lee *radiologist*
Clemmons, David Robert *internist, educator*
Clyde, Wallace Alexander, Jr. *pediatrics and microbiology educator*
Collier, Albert M. *pediatric educator, child development center director*
Cromartie, William James *medical educator, researcher*
De Friese, Gordon H. *health services researcher*
Denny, Floyd Wolfe, Jr. *pediatrician*
De Rosa, Guy Paul *orthopedic surgery educator*
Earley, Laurence Elliott *medical educator*
Easterling, William Ewart, Jr. *obstetrician, gynecologist*
Eifrig, David Eric *ophthalmologist, educator*
Ellis, Fred Wilson *retired pharmacology educator*
Farmer, Thomas Wohlsen *neurologist, educator*
Fowler, Wesley C., Jr. *obstetrician, gynecologist*
Frelinger, Jeffrey Allen *immunologist, educator*
Gottschalk, Carl William *physician, educator*
Goyer, Robert Andrew *pathology educator*
Graham, John Borden *pathologist, writer, educator*
Greganti, Mac Andrew *physician, medical educator*
Grisham, Joe Wheeler *pathologist, educator*
Hawkins, David Rollo, Sr. *psychiatrist*
Hendricks, Charles Henning *retired obstetrics and gynecology educator*
Henson, Anna Miriam *otolaryngology researcher, medical educator*
Henson, O'Dell Williams, Jr. *anatomy educator*
Hirsch, Philip Francis *pharmacologist, educator*
Hollister, William Gray *psychiatrist*
Howell, James Theodore *medical consultant, internist*
Hulka, Barbara Sorenson *epidemiology educator*
Hulka, Jaroslav Fabian *obstetrician, gynecologist*
Johnson, George, Jr. *physician, educator*
Juliano, Rudolph L. *medical educator*
Keagy, Blair Allen *surgery educator*
Langdell, Robert Dana *medical educator*
Lawson, Edward Earle *neonatologist*
McMillan, Campbell White *pediatric hematologist*
Miller, C. Arden *physician, educator*
Ontjes, David Ainsworth *medicine and pharmacology educator*
Pagano, Joseph Stephen *physician, researcher, educator*
Palmer, Jeffress Gary *hematologist, educator*
Pillsbury, Harold Crockett *otolaryngologist*
Pollitzer, William Sprott *anatomy educator*
Prange, Arthur Jergen, Jr. *psychiatrist, neurobiologist, educator*
Prather, Donna Lynn *psychiatrist*
Sanders, Charles Addison *physician*
Sheldon, George F. *medical educator*
Sorenson, James Roger *public health educator*
Spencer, Roger Felix *psychiatrist, psychoanalyst, medical educator*
Stockman, James Anthony, III *pediatrician*
Sugioka, Kenneth *anesthesiologist educator*
Suzuki, Kunihiko *biomedical educator, researcher*
Thomas, Colin Gordon, Jr. *surgeon, medical educator*
Tunnessen, Walter William, Jr. *pediatrician*
Van Wyk, Judson John *endocrinologist, pediatric educator*
Wheeler, Clayton Eugene, Jr. *dermatologist, educator*
Wilcox, Benson Reid *cardiothoracic surgeon, educator*
Williams, Roberta Gay *pediatric cardiologist, educator*
Winfield, John Buckner *rheumatologist, educator*
Wood, Robert Emerson *pediatrics educator*

**Charlotte**
†Bosse, Michael Joseph *orthopedic trauma surgeon, retired medical officer*
Citron, David Sanford *physician*
Edwards, Irene Elizabeth (Libby Edwards) *dermatologist, educator, researcher*
Freeman, Tyler Ira *physician*
Hutcheson, J. Sterling *allergist, immunologist, physician*
Lapp, Charles Warren *internal medicine physician, pediatrician*
McLanahan, Charles Scott *neurosurgeon*
Nicholson, Henry Hale, Jr. *surgeon*
Saikevych, Irene A. *pathologist*
Shah, Nandlal Chimanlal *physiatrist*
Short, Earl de Grey, Jr. *psychiatrist, consultant*
Thompson, John Albert, Jr. *dermatologist*
Tillett, Grace Montana *ophthalmologist, real estate developer*
Visser, Valya Elizabeth *physician*
Watkins, Carlton Gunter *retired pediatrician*

**Concord**
Campbell, Paul Thomas *cardiologist*

**Davidson**
Ramirez, Julio Jesus *neuroscientist*

**Durham**
Alexander, C. Alex *physician*
Amos, Dennis B. *immunologist*
Anderson, William Banks, Jr. *ophthalmology educator*
Anlyan, William George *surgeon, university administrator*
Baerg, Richard Henry *podiatric physician, surgeon*
Barry, David Walter *infectious diseases physician, researcher*
Bennett, Peter Brian *researcher, anesthesiology educator*
Blazer, Dan German *psychiatrist, epidemiologist*
Blazing, Michael August *internist*
Bradford, William Dalton *pathologist, educator*
Brahen, Leonard S. *psychiatrist*
Brodie, Harlow Keith Hammond *psychiatrist, educator, past university president*
Buckley, Charles Edward, III *physician, educator*
Buckley, Rebecca Hatcher *physician, educator*
Busse, Ewald William *psychiatrist, educator*
Carlson, Alan Neil *ophthalmologist*
Carter, James Harvey *psychiatrist, educator*
Cartmill, Matt *anthropologist, anatomy educator*
Christmas, William Anthony *internist, educator*
Cohen, Harvey Jay *physician, educator*
Coleman, Ralph Edward *nuclear medicine physician*
Davis, James Evans *general and thoracic surgeon, parliamentarian, author*
Dawson, Robert Edward, Sr. *ophthalmologist*
Elion, Gertrude Belle *research scientist, pharmacology educator*
Estes, Edward Harvey, Jr. *medical educator*
Falletta, John Matthew *pediatrician, educator*
Feldman, Jerome Myron *physician*
Foreman, John William *pediatrician, educator*
Freemark, Michael Scott *pediatric endocrinologist and educator*
Frothingham, Thomas Eliot *pediatrician*
Gaede, Jane Taylor *pathologist*
Georgiade, Nicholas George *physician*
Greenfield, Joseph Cholmondeley, Jr. *physician, educator*
Hamilton, Michael A. *medical educator*
Hammond, Charles Bessellieu *obstetrician, gynecologist, educator*
Harmel, Merel Hilber *anesthesiologist, educator*
Harris, Jerome Sylvan *pediatrician, pediatrics and biochemistry educator*
Jennings, Robert Burgess *experimental pathologist, medical educator*
Johnson, Victoria Susan Kaprielian *medical educator*
Johnston, William Webb *pathologist, educator*
Katz, Samuel Lawrence *pediatrician, scientist*
Kaufman, Russell Eugene *hematologist, oncologist*
King, Lowell Restell *pediatric urologist*
Kirshner, Norman *pharmacologist, researcher, educator*
Klitzman, Bruce *physiologist, plastic surgery educator, researcher*
Koepke, John Arthur *hematologist, clinical pathologist*
Krishnan, Krishnaswamy Ranga Rama *psychiatrist*
Kylstra, Johannes Arnold *physician*
Lack, Leon *pharmacology and biochemistry educator*
Layish, Daniel T. *internist*
Lefkowitz, Robert Joseph *physician, educator*
Llewellyn, Charles Elroy, Jr. *psychiatrist*
London, William Lord *pediatrician*
Lyerly, Herbert Kim *surgical oncology educator, researcher*
Marchuk, Douglas Alan *medical educator*
Michener, James Lloyd *medical educator*
Miller, David Edmond *physician*
Moon, Samuel David *medical educator*
Moore, John Wilson *neurophysiologist, educator*
Murphy, Barbara Anne *emergency physician, surgery educator*
Murphy, Thomas Miles *pediatrician*
Murray, William James *anesthesiology educator, clinical pharmacologist*
Nevins, Joseph Roy *medical educator*
Odom, Guy Leary *retired physician*
Osterhout, Suydam *physician, educator*
Parker, Joseph B., Jr. *psychiatrist, educator*
Pinnell, Sheldon Richard *physician, medical educator*
Pizzo, Salvatore Vincent *pathologist*
Pratt, Philip Chase *pathologist, educator*
Reves, Joseph Gerald *anesthesiology educator*
Ritter, Frederick Edmond *plastic surgeon, educator*
Roses, Allen David *neurologist, educator*
Sabiston, David Coston, Jr. *surgeon, educator*
Schanberg, Saul Murray *pharmacology educator*
Serafin, Donald *plastic surgeon*
Sessoms, Stuart McGuire *physician, educator, retired insurance company executive*
Severance, Harry Wells *emergency medicine educator*
Shelburne, John Daniel *pathologist*
Snyderman, Ralph *medical educator, physician*
Spach, Madison Stockton *cardiologist*
Spock, Alexander *pediatrician, professor*
Stead, Eugene Anson, Jr. *physician*
Stiles, Gary Lester *cardiologist, molecular pharmacologist, educator*
Tedder, Thomas Fletcher *immunology educator, researcher*
Watts, Charles DeWitt *retired surgeon, corporate medical director*
Weiner, Richard David *psychiatrist, researcher*
Werman, David Sanford *psychiatrist, psychoanalyst, educator*
Wilkins, Robert Henry *neurosurgeon, editor*
Williams, Redford Brown *medical educator*
Yancy, William Samuel *pediatrician*

**Fairview**
Gaffney, Thomas Edward *retired physician*

**Fayetteville**
Chipman, Martin *neurologist, retired army officer*

**Gastonia**
Prince, George Edward *pediatrician*

**Greensboro**
Baird, Haynes Wallace *pathologist*
Houston, Frank Matt *dermatologist*
Johnson, Andrew Myron *pediatric immunologist, educator*
Stevens, Elliott Walker, Jr. *allergist, pulmonologist*

**Greenville**
Bolande, Robert Paul *pathologist, scientist, educator*
Furth, Eugene David *physician, educator*
Hallock, James Anthony *pediatrician, school dean*
Laupus, William Edward *physician, educator*
Lee, Kenneth Stuart *neurosurgeon, educator*
Mattsson, Ake *psychiatrist, physician*
Meggs, William Joel *internist, emergency physician, educator*
Metzger, W. James, Jr. *physician, researcher, educator*
Norris, H. Thomas *pathologist, academic administrator*
Pories, Walter Julius *surgeon, educator*
Sanchez, Rafael Camilo *physician*
Tingelstad, Jon Bunde *physician*
Waugh, William Howard *biomedical educator*
Wortmann, Dorothy Woodward *physician*

**Hampstead**
Solomon, Robert Douglas *pathology educator*

**Hendersonville**
Reinhart, John Belvin *child and adolescent psychiatrist, educator*

**Hickory**
Crouch, Fred Michael *physician, surgeon*
Lefler, Wade Hampton, Jr. *ophthalmologist*

**High Point**
Bardelas, Jose Antonio *allergist*
Draelos, Zoe D. *dermatologist, consultant*

**Hillsborough**
Marzluff, William F. *medical educator*

**Indian Beach**
Wiley, Albert Lee, Jr. *physician, engineer, educator*

**Lenoir**
Carswell, Jane Triplett *family physician*

**Mebane**
Langley, Ricky Lee *occupational medicine physician*

**Mooresville**
Davis, Courtland Harwell, Jr. *neurosurgeon*

**Morganton**
Baden, Thomas James *dermatologist*

**Mount Airy**
Thoppil, Cecil Koshey *pediatrician, educator*

**Nags Head**
Crow, Harold Eugene *physician, family medicine educator*

**New Bern**
Finnerty, Frances Martin *medical administrator*
Hunt, William B. *cardiopulmonary physician*
Sinning, Mark Alan *thoracic and vascular surgeon*

**Pinehurst**
Jacobson, Peter Lars *neurologist, educator*

**Raleigh**
Barish, Charles Franklin *internist, gastroenterologist, educator*
Boone, Stephen Christopher *neurosurgeon*
Garrett, Leland Earl *nephrologist, educator*
†Hughes, Francis P. *medical researcher*
Kimbrell, Odell Culp, Jr. *physician*
Levine, Ronald H. *physician, state official*
Peacock, Erle Ewart, Jr. *surgeon, lawyer, educator*
Stratas, Nicholas Emanuel *psychiatrist*
Wilkinson, James Spencer *general physician*

**Research Triangle Park**
Barrett, J. Carl *cancer researcher, molecular biologist*
Golden, Carole Ann *immunologist, microbiologist*
Wilsnack, Roger E. *retired medical association administrator*

**Rocky Mount**
Zipf, Robert Eugene, Jr. *pathologist, legal medicine consultant*

**Salisbury**
Kiser, Glenn Augustus *retired pediatrician, philanthropist, investor*
Lomax, Donald Henry *physician*

**Thomasville**
Sprinkle, Robert Lee, Jr. *podiatrist*

**Waynesville**
McKinney, Alexander Stuart *neurologist, retired*

**Whisper Pines**
Enlow, Donald Hugh *anatomist, educator, university dean*

**Wilmington**
Donahue, Michael J. *dermatologist*
Gillen, Howard William *neurologist, medical historian*
Kesler, James L(ester) *ophthalmologist*
Penick, George Dial *pathologistst*
Wilkins, Lucien Sanders *gastroenterologist*

**Wilson**
Kushner, Michael James *neurologist, consultant*
Ladwig, Harold Allen *neurologist*

**Winston Salem**
Alexander, Eben, Jr. *neurological surgeon*
Bittinger, Isabel *orthopedic surgeon, retired, photographer*
Cheng, Che Ping *cardiologist, researcher, educator*
Clarkson, Thomas Boston *comparative medicine educator*
Cowan, Robert Jenkins *radiologist, educator*
Crandall, Sonia Jane *medical educator*
Dean, Richard Henry *surgeon, educator*
Donofrio, Peter Daniel *neurology educator*
Ferree, Carolyn Ruth *radiation oncologist, educator*
Georgitis, John *allergist, educator*
Hazzard, William Russell *geriatrician, educator*
Henrichs, W(alter) Dean *dermatologist*
Hopkins, Judith Owen *oncologist*
Howell, Charles Maitland *dermatologist*
Howell, Julius Ammons *plastic surgeon*
James, Francis Marshall, III *anesthesiologist*
Jorizzo, Joseph L. *dermatology educator*
Kandt, Raymond S. *neurologist*
Kaufman, William *internist*
Kelly, David Lee, Jr. *neurosurgeon, educator*
Kohut, Robert Irwin *otolaryngologist, educator*
Lawless, Michael Rhodes *pediatrics educator*
Little, William Campbell *cardiologist, physiologist*
Lorentz, William Beall *pediatrician*
Maynard, Charles Douglas *radiologist*
Meis, Paul Jean *obstetrics and gynecology educator*
Mueller-Heubach, Eberhard August *obstetrician gynecologist, medical researcher*
O'Steen, Wendall Keith *neurobiology and anatomy educator*
Podgorny, George *emergency physician*
Rogers, Lee Frank *radiologist*
Simon, Jimmy Louis *pediatrician, educator*
Stein, Barry Edward *medical educator*
Toole, James Francis *medical educator*
Veille, Jean-Claude *maternal-fetal medicine physician, educator*
Woods, James Watson, Jr. *cardiologist*

## NORTH DAKOTA

**Bismarck**
Hook, William Franklin *radiologist*

**Grand Forks**
Carlson, Edward C. *anatomy educator*
Sobus, Kerstin MaryLouise *physician, physical therapist*

**Williston**
Adducci, Joseph Edward *obstetrician, gynecologist*

## OHIO

**Akron**
Dorsett, Roswell Branson, III *neurologist*
Evans, Douglas McCullough *surgeon, educator*
Levy, Richard Philip *physician, educator*
Milsted, Amy *medical educator*
Rothmann, Bruce Franklin *pediatric surgeon*
†Tan, James *physician*
Timmons, Gerald Dean *pediatric neurologist*

**Athens**
Chila, Anthony George *osteopathic educator*
Hedges, Richard H. *epidemiologist, lawyer*
Palmer, Brent David *environmental physiology educator, biologist*

**Beachwood**
Morris, Jeffrey Selman *orthopedic surgeon*

**Boardman**
Butterworth, Jane Rogers Fitch *physician*

**Bryan**
Carrico, Virgil Norman *physician*

**Bucyrus**
Solt, Robert Lee, Jr. *surgeon*

**Canal Winchester**
Burrier, Gail Warren *physician*

**Canton**
Di Simone, Robert Nicholas *radiologist, educator*
Howland, Willard J. *radiologist, educator*
Maioriello, Richard Patrick *otolaryngologist*
Ognibene, Andre J(ohn) *physician, army officer, educator*

**Centerville**
Kelso, Harold Glen *family practice physician*

**Chagrin Falls**
Lingl, Friedrich Albert *psychiatrist*
Weckesser, Elden Christian *surgery educator*

**Chardon**
Dobyns, Brown McIlvaine *surgeon, educator*

**Cincinnati**
Adolph, Robert J. *physician, medical educator*
Alexander, James Wesley *surgeon, educator*
Balistreri, William Francis *physician, pediatric gastroenterologist*
Biddinger, Paul Williams *pathologist, educator*
Boat, Thomas Frederick *physician, educator, researcher*
Bower, Robert Hewitt *surgeon, educator, researcher*
Bridenbaugh, Phillip Owen *anesthesiologist, physician*
Buchman, Elwood *physician, pharmaceutical company medical director*
Buncher, Charles Ralph *epidemiologist, educator*
Carothers, Charles Omsted *orthopedic surgeon*
Chin, Nee Oo Wong *reproductive endocrinologist*
Fenoglio-Preiser, Cecilia Mettler *pathologist, educator*
Fischer, Carl G. *anesthesiologist*
Fowler, Noble Owen *physician, university administrator*
Gesteland, Robert Charles *neurophysiologist*
Greenwalt, Tibor Jack *physician, educator*
Harshman, Morton Leonard *physician, business executive*
Heimlich, Henry Jay *physician, surgeon*
Hess, Evelyn Victorine (Mrs. Michael Howett) *medical educator*
Hollerman, Charles Edward *pediatrician*
Hutton, John James *medical researcher, medical educator*
Kereiakes, Dean James *cardiologist*
Loggie, Jennifer Mary Hildreth *medical educator, physician*
Lucas, Stanley Jerome *radiologist, physician*
Luchette, Frederick A. *surgeon*
Macpherson, Colin R(obertson) *pathologist, educator*
Neale, Henry Whitehead *plastic surgery educator*
Rapoport, Robert Morton *medical educator*
†Rashkin, Mitchell Carl *internist, pulmonary medicine specialist*
Saenger, Eugene Lange *radiology educator, laboratory director*
Schneider, Harold Joel *radiologist*
Schreiner, Albert William *physician, educator*
Smith, Roger Dean *pathologist*
Sodd, Vincent Joseph *nuclear medicine researcher, educator*
Suskind, Raymond Robert *physician, educator*
Toltzis, Robert Joshua *cardiologist*
Vilter, Richard William *physician, educator*
Weber, Fredrick Louis, Jr. *hepatologist, medical researcher*
West, Clark Darwin *pediatric nephrologist, educator*
Wilson, James Miller, IV *cardiovascular surgeon, educator*

Wiot, Jerome Francis *radiologist*
Woodward, James Kenneth *pharmacologist*

### Cleveland
Alfidi, Ralph Joseph *radiologist, educator*
†Altose, Murray David *physician*
Awais, George Musa *obstetrician, gynecologist*
Badal, Daniel Walter *psychiatrist, educator*
Baker, Saul Phillip *geriatrician, cardiologist, internist*
Bambakidis, Peter *neurologist, educator*
Bass, Jonathan *dermatologist*
Berger, Melvin *allergist, immunologist*
Bowerfind, Edgar Sihler, Jr. *physician, medical administrator*
†Bronson, David Leigh *physician, educator*
Budd, John Henry *physician*
Carter, James Rose, Jr. *medical educator*
Carter, John Robert *physician*
Cascorbi, Helmut Freimund *anesthesiologist, educator*
Castele, Theodore John *radiologist*
Cole, Monroe *neurologist, educator*
Daroff, Robert Barry *neurologist*
Davis, Pamela Bowes *pediatric pulmonologist*
Dell'Osso, Louis Frank *neuroscience educator*
Denko, Joanne D. *psychiatrist, writer*
Doershuk, Carl Frederick *physician, professor of pediatrics*
Eastwood, Douglas William *anesthesiologist*
Eiben, Robert Michael *pediatric neurologist, educator*
Elewski, Boni Elizabeth *dermatologist, educator*
Ellis, Lloyd H., Jr. *emergency physician*
Fazio, Victor Warren *physician, colon and rectal surgeon*
Geha, Alexander Salim *cardiothoracic surgeon, educator*
Gifford, Ray Wallace, Jr. *physician, educator*
Hardesty, Hiram Haines *ophthalmologist, educator*
Harris, John William *physician, educator*
Hermann, Robert Ewald *surgeon*
Herndon, Charles Harbison *retired orthopaedic surgeon*
Holzbach, Raymond Thomas *gastroenterologist, author, educator*
Izant, Robert James, Jr. *pediatric surgeon*
Jackson, Edgar B., Jr. *medical educator*
†Judge, Nancy E. *obstetrician, gynecologist*
Kass, Lawrence *hematologist, oncologist, hematopathologist*
Katzman, Richard A. *cardiologist, consultant*
Kellermeyer, Robert William *physician, educator*
Lamm, Michael Emanuel *pathologist, immunologist, educator*
Lazo, John, Jr. *physician*
Lee, Te Gyu *neurologist*
Lefferts, William Geoffrey *physician, educator*
Lenkoski, Leo Douglas *psychiatrist, educator*
Mahmoud, Adel *infectious diseases, tropical medicine physician*
McFadden, Edward Regis, Jr. *pulmonary educator*
Mc Henry, Martin Christopher *physician, educator*
Medalie, Jack Harvey *physician*
Montague, Drogo K. *urologist*
Moskowitz, Roland Wallace *internist*
Novick, Andrew Carl *urologist*
Olness, Karen Norma *pediatrics and international health educator*
Perez, Dianne M. *medical researcher*
Perry, George *neuroscience researcher*
Pretlow, Thomas Garrett *physician, pathology educator, researcher*
Rakita, Louis *cardiologist, educator*
Ransohoff, Richard Milton *neurologist, researcher*
Ratnoff, Oscar Davis *physician, educator*
Reydman, Melvin Maxwell *thoracic surgeon*
Robbins, Frederick Chapman *physician, medical school dean emeritus*
Ruff, Robert Louis *neurologist, physiology researcher*
Scarpa, Antonio *medicine educator, biomedical scientist*
Schneider, Edward Martin *retired physician*
Schwartz, Howard Julius *allergy educator*
Schwartz, Michael Alan *physician*
Shuck, Jerry Mark *surgeon, educator*
Spirnak, John Patrick *urologist, educator*
Stanton-Hicks, Michael D'Arcy *anesthesiologist, educator*
Stavitsky, Abram Benjamin *immunologist, educator*
Straffon, Ralph Atwood *urologist*
Strome, Marshall *otolaryngologist, educator*
Utian, Wulf Hessel *gynecologist, endocrinologist*
Washington, John Augustine *physician, pathologist*
Webster, Leslie Tillotson, Jr. *pharmacologist, educator*
West, Burton Carey *physician*
†Whittlesey, Diana *surgeon*
Wiedemann, Herbert Pfeil *physician*
Wish, Jay Barry *nephrologist, specialist*
Wolfman, Alan *medical educator, researcher*
Wolinsky, Emanuel *physician, educator*
Young, Jess R. *physician*

### Columbus
Ackerman, John Henry *health services consultant, physician*
Bachman, Sister Janice *health care executive*
Barth, Rolf Frederick *pathologist, educator*
Bell, George Edwin *retired physician, insurance company executive*
Berggren, Ronald Bernard *surgeon, emeritus educator*
Berntson, Gary Glen *psychiatry, psychology and pediatrics educator*
Billings, Charles Edgar *physician*
Boudoulas, Harisios *physician*
Bowman, Louis L. *emergency physician*
Bullock, Joseph Daniel *pediatrician, educator*
Christoforidis, A. John *radiologist, educator*
Copeland, William Edgar, Sr. *physician*
Cramblett, Henry Gaylord *pediatrician, virologist, educator*
Ellison, Edwin Christopher *physician, surgeon*
Falcone, Robert Edward *surgeon*
Ferguson, Ronald Morris *surgeon, educator*
Furste, Wesley Leonard, II *surgeon, educator*
Goodman, Hubert Thorman *psychiatrist, consultant*
Hansen, Thomas Nanastad *pediatrician, health facility administrator*
Haque, Malika Hakim *pediatrician*
Healy, Bernadine P. *physician, educator, federal agency administrator, scientist*
Huheey, Marilyn Jane *ophthalmologist*
†Kakos, Gerard Stephen *thoracic and cardiovascular surgeon*
Kim, Moon Hyun *physician, educator*
Lander, Ruth A. *medical group and association administrator*
Laufman, Leslie Rodgers *hematologist, oncologist*
Leier, Carl Victor *internist, cardiologist*
Lewis, Richard Phelps *physician, educator*
Lim, Shun Ping *cardiologist*
Long, Sarah Elizabeth Brackney *physician*
Mazzaferri, Ernest Louis *physician, educator*
Morrow, Grant, III *medical research director, physician*
Moser, Debra Kay *medical educator*
Mueller, Charles Frederick *radiologist, educator*
Myerowitz, P. David *cardiologist, cardiac surgeon*
Nasrallah, Henry Ata *psychiatry researcher, educator*
Newton, William Allen, Jr. *pediatric pathologist*
Pacht, Eric Reed *pulmonary and critical care physician*
Robbins, Darryl Andrew *pediatrician*
Ruberg, Robert Lionel *surgery educator*
Rund, Douglas Andrew *emergency physician, educator*
St. Pierre, Ronald Leslie *anatomy educator, university administrator*
Sayers, Martin Peter *pediatric neurosurgeon*
Senhauser, Donald A(lbert) *pathologist, educator*
Skillman, Thomas Grant *endocrinology consultant, former educator*
Speicher, Carl Eugene *pathologist*
Stoner, Gary David *pathology educator*
Tzagournis, Manuel *physician, educator, university administrator*
Vogel, Thomas Timothy *surgeon, health care consultant, lay church worker*
Whitacre, Caroline Clement *immunologist, researcher*
Yashon, David *neurosurgeon, educator*
Zuspan, Frederick Paul *obstetrician, gynecologist, educator*

### Dayton
Arn, Kenneth Dale *physician, city official*
Bohanon, Kathleen Sue *neonatologist, educator*
Chabali, Raul *pediatrician*
†Cohen, Steven Michael *internist, health facility administrator*
†Cruikshank, Stephen Herrick *physician, consultant*
DeWall, Richard Allison *retired surgeon*
†Dunn, Margaret Mary *general surgeon*
Elliott, Daniel Whitacre *surgeon, retired educator*
Gardner, Charles Clifford, Jr. *colorectal surgeon*
Heller, Abraham *psychiatrist, educator*
Kogut, Maurice David *pediatric endocrinologist*
Loughead, Jeffrey Lee *physician*
Mandal, Anil Kumar *nephrologist, medical educator*
Mohler, Stanley Ross *physician, educator*
Monk, Susan Marie *physician, pediatrician*
Nanagas, Maria Teresita Cruz *pediatrician, educator*
Pflum, Barbara Ann *pediatric allergist*
Savage, Joseph Scott *physician, career officer*
Von Gierke, Henning Edgar *biomedical science educator, former government official, researcher*
Weinberg, Sylvan Lee *cardiologist, educator, author, editor*
†Wilson, William C.M. *gastroenterologist*

### Defiance
Kane, Jack Allison *physician, county administrator*

### Dublin
Graham, Bruce Douglas *pediatrician*

### Elyria
Eady, Carol Murphy (Mrs. Karl Ernest Eady) *medical association administrator*
Kuchynski, Marie *physician*

### Gahanna
Penn, Gerald Melville *pathologist*

### Gallipolis
Clarke, Oscar Withers *physician*

### Girard
Gaylord, Sanford Fred *physician*

### Grove City
Kilman, James William *surgeon, educator*

### Huber Heights
Lee, Daniel Andrew *osteopathic physician, ophthalmologist*

### Kent
Rubin, Patricia *internist*

### Kettering
Mantil, Joseph Chacko *nuclear medicine physician, researcher*

### Lancaster
Gogate, Shashi Anand *pathologist*
Snider, Gordon B. *retired medical educator*

### Lebanon
Holtkamp, Dorsey Emil *medical research scientist*

### Lima
Becker, Dwight Lowell *physician*
Collins, William Thomas *retired pathologist*
Wangler, Mark Adrian *anesthesiologist*

### Mansfield
Houston, William Robert Montgomery *ophthalmic surgeon*

### Marietta
Tipton, Jon Paul *allergist*

### Massillon
Lin, Edward Daniel *anesthesiologist, inventor*

### Medina
Noreika, Joseph Casimir *ophthalmologist*

### New Richmond
Reynolds, Ronald Davison *family physician*

### Norwalk
Burrell, Joel Brion *neuroimmunologist, researcher, clinician*
Gutowicz, Matthew Francis, Jr. *radiologist*

### Oregon
Culver, Robert Elroy *osteopathic physician*

### Pepper Pike
Froelich, Wolfgang Andreas *neurologist*

### Rocky River
De Long, Erika Venta *psychiatrist*

### Rootstown
Blacklow, Robert Stanley *physician, medical college administrator*
Campbell, Colin *obstetrician, gynecologist, school dean*

### Shaker Heights
Boyd, Arthur Bernette, Jr. *surgeon, clergyman, beverage company executive*

### Springfield
Kurian, Pius *physician*
Wood, Dirk Gregory *surgeon, physician, forensic consultant*

### Tipp City
Dallura, Sal Anthony *physician*

### Toledo
Barrett, Michael John *anesthesiologist*
Bedell, Archie William *family physician, educator*
Lawrence, Edmund P., Jr. *neurosurgeon*
Martin, John Thomas *physician, author, educator*
Mayhew, Harry Eugene *physician, educator*
Mulrow, Patrick Joseph *medical educator*
Rejent, Marian Magdalen *pediatrician*
Rubin, Allan Maier *physician, surgeon*
Shelley, Walter Brown *physician, educator*
Zrull, Joel Peter *psychiatry educator*

### Troy
Davies, Alfred Robert *physician, educator*

### Warren
Brodell, Robert Thomas *internal medicine educator*
Rizer, Franklin Morris *physician, otolarynogologist*

### Westerville
Dadmehr, Nahid *neurologist*

### Whitehouse
Howard, John Malone *surgeon, educator*

### Willoughby
Combs, Steven Paul *orthopedic surgeon*
Pazirandeh, Mahmood *rheumatologist, consultant*

### Wooster
Geho, Walter Blair *biomedical research executive*
Kuffner, George Henry *dermatologist*

### Worthington
Stone, Linda Chapman *physician, consultant, medical educator*
Winter, Chester Caldwell *physician, surgery educator*

### Wright Patterson AFB
Scriggins, Alan Lee *developmental pediatrician*

### Xenia
Morrison, Robert Townsend *nephrologist*

### Yellow Springs
Webb, Paul *physician, researcher, consultant, educator*

### Youngstown
†Rubin, Jeffrey Reed *vascular surgeon*
Walton, Ralph Gerald *psychiatrist, educator*

### Zanesville
Ray, John Walker *otolaryngologist, educator, broadcast commentator*

## OKLAHOMA

### Ada
Van Burkleo, Bill Ben *osteopath, emergency physician*

### Ardmore
Mynatt, Cecil Ferrell *psychiatrist*

### Edmond
Nelson, John Woolard *neurology educator, physician*

### Enid
Dandridge, William Shelton *orthopedic surgeon*

### Jenks
Wootan, Gerald Don *osteopathic physician, educator*

### Kingfisher
Buswell, Arthur Wilcox *physician, surgeon*

### Lawton
Hensley, Ross Charles *dermatologist*
Webb, O(rville) Lynn *physician, pharmacologist, educator*

### Mc Loud
Whinery, Michael Albert *physician*

### Midwest City
Bogardus, Carl Robert, Jr. *radiologist, educator*

### Muskogee
Kent, Bartis Milton *physician*

### Norman
Cochran, Gloria Grimes *pediatrician, retired*
Dille, John Robert *physician*

### Oklahoma City
Bahr, Carman Bloedow *internist*
Bozalis, John Russell *physician*
Brandt, Edward Newman, Jr. *physician, educator*
Cameron, Charles Metz, Jr. *physician, medical educator*
Chan, Peter P. *osteopathic physician*
Claflin, James Robert *pediatrician, allergist*
Comp, Philip Cinnamon *medical researcher*
Couch, James Russell, Jr. *neurology educator*
Ellis, Robert Smith *allergist, immunologist*
Everett, Mark Allen *dermatologist, educator*
Felton, Warren Locker, II *surgeon*
Filley, Warren Vernon *allergist, immunologist*
Fishburne, John Ingram, Jr. *obstetrician-gynecologist, educator*
Gavaler, Judith Ann Stohr Van Thiel *bio-epidemiologist*
George, James Noel *hematologist-oncologist, educator*
Halverstadt, Donald Bruce *urologist, educator*
Haywood, B(etty) J(ean) *anesthesiologist*
Horton, Donald *neurosurgeon*
Hough, Jack Van Doren *otologist*
Kimerer, Neil Banard, Sr. *psychiatrist, educator*
Kinasewitz, Gary Theodore *medical educator*
Lambird, Perry Albert *pathologist*
Lewis, Wilbur Curtis *surgeon*
Massion, Walter Herbert *anesthesiologist, educator*
McFadden, Robert Stetson *hepatologist*
Minocha, Anil *physician, educator, researcher*
Moore, Joanne Iweita *pharmacologist, educator*
Neuenschwander, Pierre Fernand *medical educator*
Oehlert, William Herbert, Jr. *cardiologist, administrator, educator*
Parke, David Wilkin, II *ophthalmologist, educator, healthcare executive*
Perez-Cruet, Jorge *psychiatrist, psychopharmacologist, psychophysiologist, educator*
Rahhal, Donald K. *obstetrician, gynecologist*
Rayburn, William Frazier *obstetrician, gynecologist, educator*
Robinson, Malcolm *gastroenterologist*
Robison, Clarence, Jr. *surgeon*
Rossavik, Ivar Kristian *obstetrician, gynecologist*
Thadani, Udho *physician, cardiologist*
Thurman, William Gentry *medical research foundation executive, pediatric hematology and oncology physician, educator*
Williams, George Rainey *retired surgeon, educator*
Worsham, Bertrand Ray *psychiatrist*
Zuhdi, Nazih *surgeon, administrator*

### Shawnee
Wilson, Robert Godfrey *radiologist*

### Stillwater
Cooper, Donald Lee *physician*
Hooper, Billy Ernest *medical association administrator*

### Tulsa
Allen, Thomas Wesley *medical educator, dean*
Brunk, Samuel Frederick *oncologist*
Calvert, Jon Channing *family practice physician*
Gregg, Lawrence J. *physician*
Hayes, Sharon LaRue (Shari Hayes) *clinical medical assistant, travel agent*
Kalbfleisch, John McDowell *cardiologist, educator*
Lewis, Ceylon Smith, Jr. *physician, educator*
Lhevine, Dave Bernard *radiologist, educator*
Lindsay, Patricia Mae *physician, medical administrator*
Miller, Gerald Cecil *immunologist, laboratory administrator, educator*
Nebergall, Robert William *orthopedic surgeon, educator*
Nettles, John Barnwell *obstetrics and gynecology educator*
Pippin, John Joseph *cardiologist*
Plunket, Daniel Clark *pediatrician*
Say, Burhan *physician*
Shane, John Marder *endocrinologist*
Stone, William Charles *surgeon*
Tompkins, Robert George *physician*

### Vinita
Neer, Charles Sumner, II *orthopedic surgeon, educator*

### Woodward
Keith, Howard Barton *surgeon*

## OREGON

### Beaverton
Conn, P. Michael *pharmacologist, educator*
Swank, Roy Laver *physician, educator, inventor*

### Corvallis
Hafner-Eaton, Chris *health services researcher, educator*
Steele, Robert Edwin *orthopedic surgeon*
Willis, David Lee *radiation biology educator*

### Eugene
Biglan, Anthony *medical educator*
Flanagan, Latham, Jr. *surgeon*
Loescher, Richard Alvin *gastroenterologist*
Nissel, Martin *radiologist, consultant*
Roe, Thomas Leroy Willis *pediatrician*
Schroeder, Donald J. *orthopedic surgeon*

### Grants Pass
Petersen, Michael Kevin *internist, osteopathic physician*

### Klamath Falls
Bohnen, Robert Frank *hematologist, oncologist, educator*

### Lake Oswego
Thong, Tran *biomedical company executive*

### Lebanon
Girod, Frank Paul *retired surgeon*

### Ontario
Tyler, Donald Earl *urologist*

### Portland
Amon, Robert Bickford *physician, consultant*
†Bagby, Grover Carlton *medical educator*

Baker, Diane R.H. *dermatologist*
Barmack, Neal Herbert *neuroscientist*
Bennett, William Michael *physician*
Benson, John Alexander, Jr. *physician, educator*
Berthelsdorf, Siegfried *psychiatrist*
Brummett, Robert Eddie *pharmacology educator*
Campbell, John Richard *pediatric surgeon*
Connor, William Elliott *physician, educator*
Crawshaw, Ralph *psychiatrist*
†DeMots, Henry *cardiologist*
Fraunfelder, Frederick Theodore *ophthalmologist, educator*
Greer, Monte Arnold *physician, educator*
Harrison, Howard F. *psychiatrist*
Hutchens, Tyra Thornton *physician, educator*
Jacob, Stanley Wallace *surgeon, educator*
Julien, Robert Michael *anesthesiologist, author*
Kendall, John Walker, Jr. *medical educator, researcher, university dean*
Lees, Martin Henry *pediatrician, educator*
Lobitz, Walter Charles, Jr. *physician, educator*
†Palmer, Earl A. *ophthalmologist, educator*
Patterson, James Randolph *physician*
Press, Edward *consulting physician*
Riker, William Kay *pharmacologist, educator*
Saslow, George *psychiatrist, educator*
Schmidt, Waldemar Adrian *pathologist, educator*
Seil, Fredrick John *neuroscientist, neurologist*
Sklovsky, Robert Joel *naturopathic physician, pharmacist, educator*
Stalnaker, John Hulbert *physician*
Stevens, Wendell Claire *anesthesiology educator*
Sutherland, Donald Wood *cardiologist*
Swan, Kenneth Carl *surgeon*
Taylor, Robert Brown *medical educator*
Zerzan, Charles Joseph, Jr. *gastroenterologist*
Zimmerman, Earl Abram *physician, scientist, educator, neuroendocrinology researcher*
Zimmerman, Gail Marie *medical foundation executive*

**Roseburg**
Jones, Henry Earl *dermatologist, direct patient care educator*

**Springfield**
Kimball, Reid Roberts *psychiatrist*

**Tigard**
Heatherington, J. Scott *retired osteopathic physician and surgeon*

**Wilsonville**
Bernard, Richard Montgomery *physician*

## PENNSYLVANIA

**Abington**
Bell, H. Craig *psychiatrist*
†Redmond, John *oncologist*

**Allentown**
Chang, Chris C.N. *physician, pediatric surgeon*
Fitzgibbons, John P. *nephrologist*
Gaylor, Donald Hughes *surgeon, educator*
Tepper, Lloyd Barton *physician*

**Bala Cynwyd**
Alter, Milton *neurologist, educator*
Burland, J(ohn) Alexis *psychoanalyst*
Cander, Leon *physician, educator*
Chiusano, Michael Augustus *urologic surgeon, mechanical engineer*
Lefton, Harvey Bennett *gastroenterologist, educator, author*
Marden, Philip Ayer *physician, educator*
Newman, Andrew *physician*

**Bangor**
Wolf, Stewart George, Jr. *physician, medical educator*

**Berwick**
Crake, Roger F. *general surgeon*

**Bethlehem**
Benz, Edward John *retired clinical pathologist*
Cole, Jack Eli *physician*

**Blue Bell**
Flaherty, Lois Talbot *psychiatrist, educator*

**Boothwyn**
McLaughlin, Edward David *surgeon, medical educator*

**Bradford**
Laroche, Roger Renan *psychiatrist*

**Bryn Mawr**
Brunt, Manly Yates, Jr. *psychiatrist*
Friedman, Arnold Carl *diagnostic radiologist*
Grossman, William *medical researcher, educator*
Harkins, Herbert Perrin *otolaryngologist, educator*
Huth, Edward Janavel *physician, editor*
Levitt, Robert E. *gastroenterologist*
Noone, Robert Barrett *plastic surgeon*
Widzer, Steven J. *pediatric gastroenterologist*

**Carlisle**
Gorby, William Guy *anesthesiologist*
Graham, William Patton, III *plastic surgeon, educator*

**Chalfont**
Clifford, Maurice Cecil *physician, former college president, foundation executive*

**Chester Springs**
Scheer, R. Scott *physician*

**Coatesville**
Ainslie, George William *psychiatrist, behavioral economist*

**Conshohocken**
Schein, Philip Samuel *physician, educator, pharmaceutical executive*

**Danville**
Cochran, William John *physician, pediatrician, gastroenterologist, nutritionist, consultant*
Kazem, Ismail *radiation oncologist, educator, health science facility administrator*
Pierce, James Clarence *surgeon*
Randall, Neil Warren *gastroenterologist*

**Devon**
Burget, Dean Edwin, Jr. *plastic surgeon*

**Dillsburg**
Jackson, George Lyman *nuclear medicine physician*

**Doylestown**
Blewitt, George Augustine *physician, consultant*

**Drexel Hill**
Bomberger, John Henry Augustus *pediatrician*
Heilig, David *osteopathic physician*

**Easton**
Grunberg, Robert Leon Willy *nephrologist*
Rohatgi, Rajeev *cardiologist*

**Elkins Park**
Check, Jerome Harvey *reproductive endocrinologist*
Glijansky, Alex *psychiatrist, psychoanalyst*
Kolansky, Harold *physician, psychiatrist, psychoanalyst*
Rosen, Rhoda *obstetrician and gynecologist*
Yun, Daniel Duwhan *physician, foundation administrator*

**Erie**
Kalkhof, Thomas Corrigan *physician*
Kish, George Franklin *thoracic and cardiovascular surgeon*
Mason, Gregg C. *orthopedic surgeon, researcher*
Upton, Thomas Vernon *medical educator*

**Fort Washington**
Pappas, Charles Engelos *plastic surgeon*
Urbach, Frederick *physician, educator*

**Gaines**
Beller, Martin Leonard *retired orthopaedic surgeon*

**Gibsonia**
Cauna, Nikolajs *physician, medical educator*

**Gladwyne**
Gonick, Paul *urologist*

**Glenside**
Johnson, Waine Cecil *dermatologist*
Reiss, George Russell, Jr. *physician*

**Greensburg**
Lisowitz, Gerald Myron *neuropsychiatrist*

**Greenville**
Sakkal, Saad *endocrinologist, geriatrician*

**Harrisburg**
Cadieux, Roger Joseph *physician, mental health care executive*
Chernicoff, David Paul *osteopath, educator*
Jeffries, Richard Haley *physician, broadcasting company executive*
Logue, James Nicholas *epidemiologist*
Margo, Katherine Lane *physician*
†Rudy, Frank R. *pathologist*

**Haverford**
Rosefsky, Jonathan Benensohn *pediatrician*

**Havertown**
Prevoznik, Stephen Joseph *anesthesiologist, retired*

**Hershey**
Berlin, Cheston Milton, Jr. *pediatrician, educator*
Biebuyck, Julien Francois *anesthesiologist, educator*
†Caputo, Gregory Michael *physician, educator*
Cary, Gene Leonard *psychiatrist*
Davis, Dwight *cardiologist, educator*
Eyster, Mary Elaine *hematologist, educator*
Kauffman, Gordon Lee, Jr. *surgeon, educator*
Leaman, David Martin *cardiologist*
Madewell, John Edward *radiologist*
Marks, James Garfield, Jr. *dermatologist*
Naeye, Richard L. *pathologist, educator*
Pierce, William Schuler *cardiac surgeon, educator*
Reynolds, Herbert Young *physician, internist*
Rohner, Thomas John, Jr. *urologist*
Schuller, Diane Ethel *allergist, immunologist, educator*
Severs, Walter Bruce *pharmacology educator, researcher*
Tan, Tjiauw-Ling *psychiatrist, educator*
Vesell, Elliot Saul *pharmacologist, educator*
Waldhausen, John Anton *surgeon, editor*
Wassner, Steven Joel *pediatric nephrologist, educator*
Zelis, Robert Felix *cardiologist, educator*

**Huntingdon**
Schock, William Wallace *pediatrician*

**Huntingdon Valley**
Altman, Brian David *pediatric ophthalmologist*

**Jenkintown**
Greenspan-Margolis, June E. *psychiatrist*
Sadoff, Robert Leslie *psychiatrist*

**Johnstown**
McNiesh, Lawrence Melvin *radiologist*
Untracht, Steven Harris *surgeon*

**Kennett Square**
Leymaster, Glen R. *former medical association executive*
Perera, George A. *physician*

**Lafayette Hill**
Sehn, Susan Cleary *psychiatrist*

**Lancaster**
Brod, Roy David *ophthalmologist, educator*
Eshleman, Silas Kendrick, III *psychiatrist*

**Langhorne**
Byrne, Jeffrey Edward *pharmacology researcher, educator, consultant*
Lamonsoff, Norman Charles *psychiatrist*

**Lansdale**
Schwartz, Louis Winn *ophthalmologist*

**Latrobe**
Berardi, Ronald Stephen *pathologist, educator*

**Lower Gwynedd**
Pendleton, Robert Grubb *pharmacologist*

**Meadowbrook**
Kiesel, Harry Alexander *physician*

**Media**
Behbehanian, Mahin Fazeli *surgeon*
Bosacco, David N. *orthopedic surgeon*
Klinefelter, Hylda Catharine *obstetrician and gynecologist*
Schuller, Edwin Arthur *osteopathic physician*

**Merion Station**
Lewis, Paul Le Roy *pathology educator*

**Monongahela**
Brandon, John Mitchell *physician*

**Monroeville**
Lin, Ming Shek *allergist, immunologist*
Marasco, Joseph A., Jr. *radiologist*

**Mount Gretna**
Newman, Richard August *psychiatrist, educator*

**Narberth**
Madow, Leo *psychiatrist, educator*
Strom, Brian Leslie *internist, educator*

**Natrona Heights**
Stanger, Robert Henry *psychiatrist, educator*

**New Hope**
Lee, Robert Earl *retired physician*

**Newtown**
Somers, Anne Ramsay *medical educator*

**Norristown**
Hunter, Patricia Phelps *physician assistant*
Tsou, Walter Hai-tze *physician*

**Old Forge**
Korényi-Both, András Levente *pathologist, educator*

**Palmyra**
Moyer, John Henry, III *physician, educator*

**Paoli**
LeWitt, Michael Herman *physician, educator*

**Pennsburg**
Shuhler, Phyllis Marie *physician*

**Philadelphia**
Abrahm, Janet Lee *hematologist, oncologist, educator*
Abrams, Charles S. *oncologist, hematologist, educator*
Adom, Edwin Nii Amalai *psychiatrist*
Agus, Zalman S. *physician, educator*
Alexander, John Dewey *internist*
Allen, Julian Lewis *medical educator, researcher*
Arce, A. Anthony *psychiatrist*
Aronson, Carl Edward *pharmacology and toxicology educator*
Asbury, Arthur Knight *neurologist, educator*
Atkinson, Barbara Frajola *pathologist*
Austrian, Robert *physician, educator*
Baker, Lester *physician, educator, research administrator*
Ball, John Robert *healthcare executive*
Barchi, Robert Lawrence *neuroscience educator, clinical neurologist, neuroscientist*
Barker, Clyde Frederick *surgeon, educator*
Beck, Aaron Temkin *psychiatrist*
Bianchi, Carmine Paul *pharmacologist*
Bibbo, Marluce *physician, educator*
Bilaniuk, Larissa Tetiana *neuroradiologist, educator*
Bishop, Harry Craden *surgeon*
Black, Perry *neurological surgeon, educator*
Boden, Guenther *endocrinologist*
Bove, Alfred Anthony *medical educator*
Bowles, L. Thompson *medical executive*
Brady, John Paul *psychiatrist*
Brady, Luther W., Jr. *physician, radiation oncology educator*
Bridger, Wagner H. *psychiatrist, educator*
Brighton, Carl Theodore *orthopedic surgery educator*
Buerk, Donald Gene *medical educator, biomedical engineer*
Burns, Rosalie Annette *neurologist, educator*
Capizzi, Robert Lawrence *physician*
Chait, Arnold *radiologist*
Christman, Robert Alan *podiatric radiologist*
Chung, Edward Kooyoung *cardiologist, educator, author*
Clearfield, Harris Reynold *physician*
†Cohen, Marc *cardiologist*
Cohen, Sidney *medical educator*
Colman, Robert Wolf *physician, medical educator, researcher*
Comer, Nathan Lawrence *psychiatrist, educator*
Comerota, Anthony James *vascular surgeon, biomedical researcher*
Conn, Rex Boland, Jr. *physician, educator*
Copeland, Adrian Dennis *psychiatrist*
Cortner, Jean Alexander *physician, educator*
Cowchock, Frances Susan *geneticist, endocrinologist*
Dalinka, Murray Kenneth *radiologist, educator*
D'Angio, Giulio John *radiologist, educator*
DeHoratius, Raphael Joseph *rheumatologist*
De La Cadena, Raul Alvarez *physician, pathology and thrombosis educator*
Depp, (O.) Richard, III *obstetrician-gynecologist, educator*
Dinoso, Vicente Pescador, Jr. *physician, educator*
DiPalma, Joseph Rupert *pharmacology educator*
Djerassi, Isaac *physician, medical researcher*
Doty, Richard Leroy *medical researcher*
Dunn, Linda Kay *physician*
Ehrlich, George Edward *rheumatologist, international pharmaceutical consultant*
Eichelman, Burr Simmons, Jr. *psychiatrist, researcher, educator*
Eisenberg, Ted Steven *plastic and reconstructive surgeon*
Evans, Audrey Elizabeth *physician, educator*
Fisher, Robert *gastroenterologist, health facility administrator*
Fishman, Alfred Paul *physician*
FitzGerald, Garret Adare *medical educator*
Fitzgerald, Robert Hannon, Jr. *orthopedic surgeon*
Frankl, William Stewart *cardiologist, educator*
Fraser, David William *epidemiologist*
Freed, Edmond Lee *podiatrist*
Freese, Andrew *neurosurgeon*
Freiman, David Burl *radiologist*
Friedman, Harvey Michael *infectious diseases educator*
Gabrielson, Ira Wilson *physician, educator*
García, Celso-Ramón *obstetrician and gynecologist*
Gardiner, Geoffrey Alexander, Jr. *radiologist, educator*
Gartland, John Joseph *physician, writer*
Gary, Nancy Elizabeth *nephrologist, academic administrator*
Gerner, Edward William *medical educator*
Ginsberg, Phillip Carl *physician*
Glick, John H. *oncologist, medical educator*
Goldberg, Martin *physician, educator*
Golden, Gerald Samuel *national medical board executive*
Goldfarb, Stanley *internist, educator*
Goldsmith, Sidney *physician, scientist, inventor*
Goodman, David Barry Poliakoff *physician, educator*
Graessle, William Rudolf *physician, educator*
Graziani, Leonard Joseph *pediatric neurologist, researcher*
Greene, Ronald Barry *orthopedic surgeon*
Greenfield, Val Shea *ophthalmologist*
Greenstein, Jeffrey Ian *neurologist*
Gueson, Emerita Torres *obstetrician, gynecologist*
Hansen-Flaschen, John Hyman *medical educator, researcher*
Hanuschak, Lee Nicholas *physician*
Haugaard, Niels *pharmacologist*
Helfand, Arthur E. *podiatrist*
Holzbaur, Erika L. *medical educator*
Hussain, M. Mahmood *medical educator*
Iannotti, Joseph Patrick *orthopedic surgeon*
Jackson, Laird Gray *physician, educator*
Jacobson, Sheldon *emergency medicine physician, medical administrator*
Jameson, Dorothea *sensory neuroscientist*
Jensh, Ronald Paul *anatomist, educator*
Jimenez, Sergio A. *physician*
Johnson, Joseph Eggleston, III *physician, educator*
Joseph, Rosaline Resnick *hematologist and oncologist*
Kaji, Hideko Katayama *pharmacology educator*
Kantner, Theodore Robert *family physician*
Katz, Julian *gastroenterologist, educator*
Kauffman, Leon A. *internist, educator*
Kaye, Donald *physician, educator*
Kaye, Robert *pediatrics educator*
Kazazian, Haig Hagop, Jr. *medical scientist, physician, educator*
Keenan, Mary Ann *orthopedic surgeon, researcher*
Kefalides, Nicholas Alexander *physician, educator*
Kelley, Mark Albert *internal medicine educator, university official*
Kelley, William Nimmons *physician, educator*
Kennedy, David William *otolaryngologist, educator*
Kimball, Harry Raymond *medical association executive, educator*
Kligerman, Morton M. *radiologist*
Klinghoffer, June Florence *physician, educator*
Koelle, George Brampton *university pharmacologist, educator*
Kotler, Ronald Lee *physician, educator*
Kurtz, Alfred Bernard *radiologist*
Ladman, A(aron) J(ulius) *anatomist, educator*
Lambertsen, Christian James *environmental physiologist, physician, educator*
Lanza, Donald Charles *otolaryngologist, rhinologist*
Legido, Agustin *pediatric neurologist*
Leventhal, Lawrence Jay *rheumatologist, educator*
Levine, Rhea Joy Cottler *anatomy educator*
Levinson, Arnold Irving *allergist, immunologist*
Levit, Edithe Judith *physician, medical association administrator*
Levitt, Jerry David *medical educator*
Levy, Robert Isaac *physician, educator, research director*
Little, Brian W. *pathology educator, administrator*
Long, Sarah S. *pediatrician, educator*
Longnecker, David Eugene *anesthesiologist, educator*
Lotsch, Richard Charles *osteopath*
Luscombe, Herbert Alfred *physician, educator*
Macdonald, John Stephen *oncologist, educator*
Mac Ewen, George Dean *physician, medical institute executive*
Madaio, Michael P. *medical educator, investigator, physician*
Mancall, Elliott Lee *neurologist, educator*
Marino, Paul Lawrence *physician, researcher*
Marshall, Bryan Edward *anesthesiologist, educator*
Mastroianni, Luigi, Jr. *physician, educator*
Matsumoto, Teruo *surgeon, educator*
Mayock, Robert Lee *internist*
McCrae, Keith R. *medical educator, researcher*
Miller, Leonard David *surgeon*
Ming, Si-Chun *pathologist, educator*
Miyamoto, Curtis Trent *medical educator*
Monos, Dimitrios *medical educator, researcher*
Mulholland, S. Grant *urologist*
Murphey, Sheila Ann *infectious diseases physician, educator, researcher*
Myers, Allen Richard *rheumatologist*
Neilson, Eric Grant *physician, educator, health facility administrator*
Nimoityn, Philip *cardiologist*
Nowell, Peter Carey *pathologist, educator*
O'Brien, Charles P. *psychiatrist, educator*
Olenginski, Jan Anthony *surgeon*
Parish, Lawrence Charles *physician, editor*
Pietra, Giuseppe Giovanni *pathology educator*
Platsoucas, Chris Dimitrios *immunologist*
Potsic, William Paul *physician, educator*
Pugliese, Maria Alessandra *psychiatrist*
Rabinowitz, Howard K. *physician, educator*
Reece, E. Albert *obstetrician, gynecologist, perinatologist*
Reinecke, Robert Dale *ophthalmologist*

Rhoads, Jonathan Evans *surgeon*
Rickels, Karl *psychiatrist, physician, educator*
Ritchie, Wallace Parks, Jr. *surgeon, educator*
Ritter, Deborah Elizabeth *anesthesiologist, educator*
Roberts, Jay *pharmacologist, educator*
Rogers, Fred Baker *medical educator*
Rorke, Lucy Balian *neuropathologist*
Ross, Leonard Lester *anatomist*
Rovera, Giovanni Aurelio *medical educator, scientist*
Rubin, Emanuel *pathologist, educator*
Rubin, Stephen Curtis *gynecologic oncologist, educator*
Rudley, Lloyd Dave *psychiatrist*
Russo, Irma Haydee Alvarez de *pathologist*
Salganicoff, Leon *pharmacology educator*
Salzberg, Brian Matthew *neuroscience and physiology educator*
Saunders, James C. *neuroscientist, educator*
Savage, Michael Paul *medicine educator, interventional cardiologist*
Schidlow, Daniel *pediatrician, medical association administrator*
Schimmer, Barry Michael *rheumatologist*
Schneider, Jan *obstetrics and gynecology educator*
Schotland, Donald Lewis *neurologist, educator*
Schumacher, H(arry) Ralph *internist, researcher, medical educator*
Schwartz, Gordon Francis *surgeon, educator*
Segal, Bernard Louis *physician, educator*
Seri, Istvan *physician, researcher*
Sevy, Roger Warren *retired pharmacology educator*
Shapiro, Sandor Solomon *hematologist*
Silberberg, Donald H. *neurologist*
Simeone, Frederick Anthony *neurosurgeon, researcher*
Simpkins, Henry *medical educator*
Sloviter, Henry Allan *medical educator*
Smith, David Stuart *anesthesiology educator, physician*
Smith, Randall Norman *orthopedist*
Soloff, Louis Alexander *physician, educator*
Spaeth, George Link *physician, ophthalmology educator*
Spector, Harvey M. *osteopathic physician*
Sprague, James Mather *medical scientist, educator*
Steel, Howard Haldeman *pediatric orthopedic surgeon*
Steinberg, Marvin Edward *orthopaedic surgeon, educator*
Strauss, Jerome Frank, III *physician, educator*
Stuart, Marie Jean *physician, hematologist, researcher*
Stunkard, Albert James *psychiatrist, educator*
Sudak, Howard Stanley *physician, psychiatry educator*
Sunderman, Frederick William *physician, educator, author, musician*
Taichman, Norton Stanley *pathology educator*
Tasman, William Samuel *ophthalmologist, medical association executive*
Thomas, Carmen Christine *physician, consultant administrator*
Thomas, Patrick Robert Maxwell *oncology educator, academic administrator*
Torg, Joseph Steven *orthopaedic surgeon, educator*
Tourtellotte, Charles Dee *physician, educator*
Van Decker, William Arthur *cardiologist*
Walinsky, Paul *cardiology educator*
Webber, John Bentley *orthopedic surgeon*
Wein, Alan Jerome *urologist, educator, researcher*
Weiss, William *retired pulmonary medicine and epidemiology educator*
Weller, Elizabeth Boghossian *child and adolescent psychiatrist*
Whitaker, Linton Andin *plastic surgeon*
Yanoff, Myron *ophthalmologist*
Young, Donald Stirling *clinical pathology educator*
†Yunginger, John W. *allergist*
Zweiman, Burton *physician, scientist, educator*

**Pittsburgh**
Allen, Thomas E. *obstetrician, gynecologist*
Beachley, Michael Charles *radiologist*
Benitez, John Griswold *medical toxicologist, emergency physician*
Berga, Sarah Lee *women's health physician, educator*
Broussard, Elsie Rita *physician, educator, researcher*
Burke, Leah Weyerts *physician*
Cooper, William Marion *physician*
Cressman, Michael David *internist, researcher*
Culhane, M. Bridget *nursing society executive, oncology clinical nurse specialist*
Culyba, Michael John *physician, medical administrator*
Cutler, John Charles *physician, educator*
Dameshek, H(arold) Lee *physician*
deGroat, William Chesney *pharmacology educator*
DeKosky, Steven Trent *neurologist*
Delaney, John Francis *neurologist, psychiatrist*
Detre, Thomas *psychiatrist, educator*
Dixit, Balwant Narayan *pharmacology and toxicology educator*
Donaldson, William Fielding, Jr. *orthopedic surgeon*
Ferguson, Donald Guffey *radiologist*
Fireman, Philip *pediatrician, allergist, immunologist, medical association executive*
Fisher, Bernard *surgeon, educator*
Friday, Gilbert Anthony, Jr. *pediatrician*
Gaffney, Paul Cotter *retired physician*
Gill, Thomas James, III *physician, educator*
Hardesty, Robert Lynch *surgeon, educator*
Harrold, Ronald Thomas *research scientist*
Heckler, Frederick Roger *plastic surgeon*
Herndon, James Henry *orthopedic surgeon, educator*
Hingson, Robert Andrew *physician, educator, inventor, farmer, poet*
Jannetta, Peter Joseph *neurosurgeon*
Joyner, Claude Reuben, Jr. *physician, medical educator*
Kalnicki, Shalom *radiologist, educator*
Kang, Yoogoo *anesthesiologist*
Karol, Meryl Helene *immunologist, educator*
Keshavan, Matcheri *psychiatrist*
Kochanek, Patrick Michael *pediatrician, educator*
Krause, Helen Fox *physician, otolaryngologist*
Kupfer, David J. *psychiatry educator*
Levine, Macy Irving *physician*
Lewis, Jessica Helen (Mrs. Jack D. Myers) *physician, educator*
Lotze, Michael Thomas *surgeon*
Lowery, Willa Dean *obstetrician-gynecologist*
Ludwig, Karl David *psychiatrist*
Lyjak Chorazy, Anna Julia *pediatrician, medical administrator, educator*
MacLeod, Gordon Kenneth *physician, educator*
Marino, Ignazio Roberto *transplant surgeon, researcher*
Mc Kenzie, Ray *anesthesiologist, educator*
Moore, Robert Yates *neuroscience educator*
Moriarty, Richard William *pediatrician*
Myers, Eugene Nicholas *otolaryngologist, otolaryngology educator*
Myers, Jack Duane *physician*
Needleman, Herbert Leroy *psychiatrist, pediatrician*
†Pepe, Paul Ernest *emergency physician, educator*
Pham, Si Mai *cadiothoracic surgeon, medical educator*
Pollock, Bruce Godfrey *psychiatrist, educator*
Price, Fredric Victor *physician, educator, researcher*
Price, Trevor Robert Pryce *psychiatrist, educator*
Pyeritz, Reed Edwin *medical geneticist, educator, research director*
Rabin, Bruce Stuart *immunologist, physician, educator*
Rao, Abdul Sohail *transplant immunologist, researcher*
Rogers, Robert Mark *physician*
Roth, Loren H. *psychiatrist*
Rubin, Robert Terry *physician, researcher*
Shapiro, Alvin Philip *physician, educator*
Siker, Ephraim S. *anesthesiologist*
Simmons, Richard L. *surgeon*
Spina, Horacio Anselmo *physician*
Troen, Philip *physician, educator*
Vidovich, Danko Victor *neurosurgeon, researcher*
Vogel, Victor Gerald *medical educator, researcher*
Wald, Niel *medical educator*
Walsh, Arthur Campbell *psychiatrist*
Winnie, Glenna Barbara *pediatric pulmonologist*
Winter, Peter Michael *physician, anesthesiologist, educator*
Wylie, Mary Evelyn *psychiatrist, retired anesthesiologist, educator*
Yu, Victor Lin-Kai *physician, educator*

**Plymouth Meeting**
Nobel, Joel J. *biomedical researcher*

**Pottsville**
Boran, Robert Paul, Jr. *orthopedic surgeon*
Garloff, Samuel John *psychiatrist*

**Radnor**
Rothrock, Robert William *physician assistant*
Templeton, John Marks, Jr. *pediatric surgeon, foundation executive*

**Reading**
Alexander, Robert William *radiologist*
Hildreth, Eugene A. *physician, educator*
Lusch, Charles Jack *physician*

**Sayre**
Moody, Robert Adams *neurosurgeon*

**Scranton**
Culliney, John James *radiologist, educator*
Rhiew, Francis Changnam *radiologist*

**Sellersville**
Loux, Norman Landis *psychiatrist*
Rilling, David Carl *surgeon*

**Somerset**
Nair, Velupillai Krishnan *cardiologist*

**State College**
Yoder, Stanley Jonas *orthopedic surgeon*

**Swarthmore**
Carey, William Bacon *pediatrician, educator*
Sing, Robert Fong *physician*

**Thorndale**
Hodess, Arthur Bart *cardiologist*

**Tyrone**
Lewis, Kathryn Huxtable *pediatrician*

**University Park**
Fedoroff, Nina Vsevolod *research scientist, consultant*

**Upland**
Ridout, Daniel Lyman, III *physician, educator*

**Upper Darby**
Hurley, Harry James, Jr. *dermatologist*

**Vandergrift**
Bullard, Ray Elva, Jr. *retired psychiatrist, hospital administrator*

**Wayne**
de Rivas, Carmela Foderaro *psychiatrist, hospital administrator*
Horwitz, Orville *cardiologist, educator*
Lief, Harold Isaiah *psychiatrist*

**Waynesboro**
Kirk, Daniel Lee *physician, consultant*
Stefenelli, George Edward *physician*

**Wescosville**
Rienzo, Robert James *radiologist*

**West Chester**
Flood, Dorothy Garnett *neuroscientist*
Harrington, Anne Wilson *medical librarian*

**West Point**
Sherwood, Louis Maier *physician, scientist, pharmaceutical company executive*
Vickers, Stanley *biochemical pharmacologist*

**Wilkes Barre**
Denaro, Anthony Thomas *psychiatrist*
Ru Dusky, Basil Michael *cardiologist, consultant*

**Williamsport**
Lattimer, Gary Lee *physician*

**Windber**
Furigay, Rodolfo Lazo *surgeon*

**Wynnewood**
Doherty, Henry Joseph *anesthesiologist, medical hypnotist*
Flanagan, Joseph Charles *ophthalmologist*
Hodges, John Hendricks *physician, educator*
Koprowska, Irena *cytopathologist, cancer researcher*

**Wyomissing**
Smith, Raymond Leigh *plastic surgeon*

**Yardley**
Somma, Beverly Kathleen *medical and marriage educator*

## RHODE ISLAND

**Barrington**
Carpenter, Charles Colcock Jones *physician, educator*

**Block Island**
Gasner, Walter Gilbert *retired dermatologist*

**Middletown**
Ning, John Tse-Tso *urologic surgeon*

**Pawtucket**
Carleton, Richard Allyn *cardiologist*
Herman, Steven David *cardiologist, educator, researcher*
Plotz, Richard Douglas *pathologist*

**Providence**
Amaral, Joseph Ferreira *surgeon*
Aronson, Stanley Maynard *physician, educator*
Biron, Christine Anne *medical science educator, researcher*
Block, Stanley Hoyt *pediatrician, allergist*
Breda, John Alexander *physician, musician*
Calabresi, Paul *pharmacologist, oncologist, educator*
Crowley, James Patrick *hematologist*
Davis, Robert Paul *physician, educator*
Dowben, Robert Morris *physician, scientist*
Easton, J(ohn) Donald *neurologist, educator*
Erikson, G(eorge) E(mil) (Erik Erikson) *anatomist, archivist, historian, educator, information specialist*
Galletti, Pierre Marie *medical science educator, artificial organ scientist*
Gilmore, Judith Marie *physician*
Glicksman, Arvin S(igmund) *radiologist, physician*
Hamolsky, Milton William *physician*
Jackson, Benjamin Taylor *surgeon, educator, medical facility administrator*
Kane, Agnes Brezak *pathologist, educator*
Lekas, Mary Despina *retired otolaryngologist*
Lewis, David Carleton *medical educator, university center director*
Mates, Susan Onthank *physician, medical educator, writer, violinist*
McCartney, James Robert *psychiatrist*
Mc Donald, Charles J. *physician, educator*
Merlino, Anthony Frank *orthopedic surgeon*
Oh, William *physician*
Parks, Robert Emmett, Jr. *medical science educator*
Patinkin, Terry Allan *physician*
Pueschel, Siegfried M. *pediatrician, educator*
Souney, Paul Frederick *pharmacist*
Vezeridis, Michael Panagiotis *surgeon, educator*

**Westerly**
Bachmann, William Thompson *dermatologist*
Christy, Nicholas Pierson *physician*

## SOUTH CAROLINA

**Aiken**
von Buedingen, Richard Paul *urologist*

**Charleston**
Anderson, Marion Cornelius *surgeon, medical educator*
Bell, Norman Howard *physician, endocrinologist, educator*
Bissada, Nabil Kaddis *urologist, educator, researcher, author*
Brewerton, Timothy David *psychiatrist*
Carabello, Blase Anthony *cardiology educator*
Carek, Donald J(ohn) *child psychiatry educator*
Crawford, Fred Allen, Jr. *cardiothoracic surgeon, educator*
Cuddy, Brian Gerard *neurosurgeon*
Daniell, Herman Burch *pharmacologist*
Dobson, Richard Lawrence *dermatologist, educator*
Favaro, Mary Kaye Asperheim (Mrs. Biagino Philip Favaro) *pediatrician*
Finn, Albert Frank, Jr. *physician*
Gettys, Thomas Wigington *medical researcher*
Haines, Stephen John *neurological surgeon*
Hogan, Edward Leo *neurologist*
Jaffa, Ayad A. *medical educator, medical researcher*
Jaffe, Murray Sherwood *surgeon, retired*
Jenrette, Joseph Malphus, III *radiation oncologist*
Kaplan, Allen P. *physician, educator, researcher*
Key, Janice Dixon *physician, medical educator*
Langdale, Emory Lawrence *physician*
La Via, Mariano Francis *physician, pathology and laboratory medicine educator*
LeRoy, Edward Carwile *rheumatologist*
Lutz, Myron Howard *obstetrician, gynecologist, surgeon, educator*
Margolius, Harry Stephen *pharmacologist, physician*
McCurdy, Layton *medical educator*
Mohr, Lawrence Charles *physician*
O'Brien, Paul Herbert *surgeon*
Ogawa, Makio *physician*
Othersen, Henry Biemann, Jr. *pediatric surgeon, physician, educator*
Roof, Betty Sams *internist*
Rustin, Rudolph Byrd, III *physician*
Schuman, Stanley H. *epidemiologist, educator*
†Shealy, Ralph McKeetha *emergency physician, educator*
Simson, Jo Anne *anatomy and cell biology educator*
Swift, Steven Edward *gynecologist, educator*
Warrick, Kenneth Ray *dermatologist, cosmetic surgeon*
Wilson, Frederick Allen *medical educator, medical center administrator, gastroenterologist*

**Columbia**
Abel, Anne Elizabeth Sutherland *pediatrician*
Adcock, David Filmore *radiologist, educator*
Almond, Carl Herman *surgeon, physician, educator*
Brooker, Jeff Zeigler *cardiologist*
da Silva, Ercio Mario *physician*
Donald, Alexander Grant *psychiatrist, educator*
Flanagan, Clyde Harvey, Jr. *psychiatist, psychoanalyst, educator*
Horger, Edgar Olin, III *obstetrics and gynecology educator*
Humphries, John O'Neal *physician, educator, university dean*
Jervey, Harold Edward, Jr. *medical education consultant, retired*
List, Noel David *medical educator*
Sheppe, Joseph Andrew *surgeon*
Shmunes, Edward *dermatologist*
†Stewart, Nathaniel Johnson *emergency medicine physician*
Still, Charles Neal *neurologist, consultant*
Waldron, Robert Leroy, II *radiologist, educator*

**Florence**
Imbeau, Stephen Alan *allergist*
Wagner, John Garnet *pharmacologist, educator*

**Gaffney**
Wheeler, William Earl *general surgeon*

**Greenville**
Bonner, Jack Wilbur, III *psychiatrist, educator, administrator*
DeLoache, William Redding *pediatrician*
Kilgore, Donald Gibson, Jr. *pathologist*

**Greenwood**
Abercrombie, Stoney Alton *family physician*

**Hilton Head Island**
Birk, Robert Eugene *retired physician, educator*
Engelman, Karl *physician*
Humphrey, Edward William *surgeon, medical educator*
Lindner, Joseph, Jr. *physician, medical administrator*
Margileth, Andrew Menges *physician, former naval officer*
Santos, George Wesley *physician, educator*

**Isle Of Palms**
Wohltmann, Hulda Justine *pediatric endocrinologist*

**Myrtle Beach**
Naumoff, Philip *physician*

**Orangeburg**
Babb, Julius Wistar, III *cardiovascular surgeon*

**Seneca**
Uden, David Elliott *cardiologist, educator*

**Spartanburg**
Fowler, Paul Raymond *physician, lawyer*
Sovenyhazy, Gabor Ferenc *surgeon*

**West Columbia**
Carter, Saralee Lessman *immunologist, microbiologist*

## SOUTH DAKOTA

**Mitchell**
Gaede, James Ernest *physician, medical educator*

**Rapid City**
Quinn, Robert Henry *surgeon, medical school administrator*

**Sioux Falls**
Fenton, Lawrence Jules *pediatric educator*
Flora, George Claude *retired neurology educator, neurologist*
Hoskins, John H. *urologist, educator*
Jaqua, Richard Allen *pathologist*
Morse, Peter Hodges *ophthalmologist, educator*
Trujillo, Angelina *endocrinologist*
Wegner, Karl Heinrich *physician, educator*
Witzke, David John *plastic surgeon, educator*
Zawada, Edward Thaddeus, Jr. *physician, educator*

**Vermillion**
Hagen, Arthur Ainsworth *pharmacologist*

## TENNESSEE

**Bolivar**
Morson, Philip Hull, III *psychiatrist, osteopath*
Wingate, Robert Lee, Jr. *internist*

**Brentwood**
Bates, George William *obstetrician, gynecologist, educator*

**Bristol**
Harkrader, Charles Johnston, Jr. *surgeon*
McIlwain, William Anthony *orthopedic surgeon*

**Chattanooga**
Feinberg, Edward Burton *ophthalmologist, educator*
Fody, Edward Paul *pathologist*
Kaplan, Hyman M. *internist*
Shuck, Edwin Haywood, III *surgeon*
Thow, George Bruce *surgeon*

**Clarksville**
Tsambassis, Nicholas Alexander *pediatrician*

**Franklin**
Moessner, Harold Frederic *allergist*

**Germantown**
Tutko, Robert Joseph *radiology administrator, educator*

**Jackson**
Hazlehurst, George Edward *physician*

Taylor, Ronald Fulford *physician*

### Jefferson City
Muncy, Estle Pershing *physician*

### Johnson City
Adebonojo, Festus O. *medical educator*
Coogan, Philip Shields *pathologist*
Dyer, Allen Ralph *psychiatrist*
Fukuda, Aisaku (Isaac Fukuda) *reproductive endocrinologist*
Hamdy, Ronald Charles *geriatrician*
Kostrzewa, Richard Michael *pharmacology educator*
Schueller, William Alan *dermatologist*
Shurbaji, M. Salah *pathologist*
Skalko, Richard Gallant *anatomist, educator*
Wiebe, Richard Herbert *reproductive endocrinologist, educator*

### Jonesborough
Weaver, Kenneth *gynecologist, researcher*

### Knoxville
Acker, Joseph Edington *retired cardiology educator*
Adams, Linas Jonas *gastroenterologist*
Brott, Walter Howard *cardiac surgeon, educator, retired army officer*
Burkhart, John Henry *physician*
Coulson, Patricia Bunker *endocrinologist*
DePersio, Richard John *otolaryngologist, plastic surgeon*
Diamond, Daniel Lloyd *surgeon*
Filston, Howard Church *pediatric surgeon, educator*
Kliefoth, A(rthur) Bernhard, III *neurosurgeon*
Lange, Robert Dale *internist, educator, medical researcher*
Natelson, Stephen Ellis *neurosurgeon*

### Maryville
Howard, Cecil Byron *pediatrician*
Lucas, Melinda Ann *pediatrician, educator*

### Memphis
Babin, Richard Weyro *surgeon, educator*
Chesney, Russell Wallace *pediatrician*
Christopher, Robert Paul *physician*
Cicala, Roger Stephen *physician, educator*
Cowan, George Sheppard Marshall, Jr. *surgeon, educator, research administrator*
Cox, Clair Edward, II *urologist, medical educator*
Doherty, Peter Charles *immunologist*
Gerald, Barry *radiology educator, neuroradiologist*
Godsey, William Cole *physician*
Hall, Johnnie Cameron *pathologist*
Heimberg, Murray *pharmacologist, biochemist, physician, educator*
Herrod, Henry Grady, III *allergist, immunologist*
Hughes, Walter Thompson *physician, pediatrics educator*
Ingram, Alvin John *surgeon*
†Korones, Sheldon Bernarr *physician, educator*
Latta, George Haworth, III *neonatologist*
Lazar, Rande Harris *otolaryngologist*
Martin, Daniel C. *surgeon, educator*
Mauer, Alvin Marx *physician, medical educator*
McMahan, Gary Lynn *medical foundation executive*
Neely, Charles Lea, Jr. *retired physician*
Nienhuis, Arthur Wesley *physician, researcher*
Riely, Caroline Armistead *physician, medical educator*
Runyan, John William, Jr. *medical educator*
Shanklin, Douglas Radford *physician*
Shochat, Stephen Jay *pediatric surgeon*
Solomon, Solomon Sidney *endocrinologist, pharmacologist, scientist*
Sullivan, Jay Michael *medical educator*
Summitt, Robert Layman *pediatrician, educator*
Wilcox, Harry Hammond *retired medical educator*
Woodson, Gayle Ellen *otolaryngologist*

### Mountain Home
McCoy, Sue *surgeon*

### Murfreesboro
Eckles, George Love, Jr. *surgeon*

### Nashville
Allen, George Sewell *neurosurgery educator*
Allison, Fred, Jr. *physician, educator*
Barnett, Joey Victor *pharmacologist, educator, researcher*
Bender, Harvey W., Jr. *cardiac and thoracic surgeon*
Bernard, Louis Joseph *surgeon, educator*
Brigham, Kenneth Larry *medical educator*
Burk, Raymond Franklin, Jr. *physician, educator, researcher*
Burnett, Lonnie Sheldon *obstetrics and gynecology educator*
Burt, Alvin Miller, III *anatomist, cell biologist, educator, writer*
Butler, Javed *internist*
Butler, Merlin Gene *physician, medical geneticist, educator*
Byrd, Benjamin Franklin, Jr. *surgeon, educator*
Clinton, Mary Ellen *neurologist*
Elam, Lloyd Charles *psychiatrist*
Fazio, Sergio *medical educator, researcher*
Fenichel, Gerald Mervin *neurologist, educator*
Fields, James Perry *dermatologist, dermatopathologist, allergist*
Foster, Henry Wendell *medical educator*
Fowinkle, Eugene W. *physician, medical center administrator*
Franks, John Julian *anesthesiology educator, medical investigator*
George, Alfred L., Jr. *medical educator, researcher*
Graham, Thomas Pegram, Jr. *pediatric cardiologist*
Hardman, Joel Griffeth *pharmacologist*
Holmquest, Donald Lee *physician, astronaut, lawyer*
Huffman, William Raymond *emergency physician*
Jennings, Henry Smith, III *cardiologist*
†Kaplan, Peter Robert *cardiologist*
Kenner, William Davis, III *psychiatrist*
Krantz, Sanford Burton *physician*
Lawton, Alexander Robert, III *immunologist, educator*
Leftwich, Russell Bryant *allergist, immunologist, consultant*
Lynch, John Brown *plastic surgeon, educator*
Marney, Samuel Rowe *physician, educator*
Martin, Peter Robert *psychiatrist, pharmacologist*
May, James M. *medical educator, medical researcher*
Meltzer, Herbert Yale *psychiatry educator*
Morrow, Jason Drew *medical and pharmacology educator*
Oates, John Alexander, III *medical educator*
O'Day, Denis Michael *ophthalmologist, educator*
O'Neill, James Anthony, Jr. *pediatric surgeon, educator*
Ossoff, Robert Henry *otolaryngological surgeon*
Partain, Clarence Leon *radiologist, nuclear medicine physician, educator, administrator*
Pendergrass, Henry Pancoast *physician, radiology educator*
Pinson, Charles Wright *transplant surgeon, educator*
Ray, Wayne Allen *epidemiologist*
Riley, Harris DeWitt, Jr. *pediatrician, educator*
Robertson, David *pharmacologist, physician, educator*
Robinson, Roscoe Ross *nephrologist, educator*
Roden, Dan Mark *cardiologist, medical educator*
Ross, Joseph Comer *physician, educator, academic administrator*
Sawyers, John Lazelle *surgeon*
†Shack, R. Bruce *plastic surgeon*
Sharp, Vernon Hibbett *psychiatrist*
†Smith, Joseph A. *urologic surgeon*
Smith, William Barney *allergist*
South, Mary Ann *pediatrics educator*
Spengler, Dan Michael *orthopedic surgery educator, researcher, surgeon*
Stahlman, Mildred Thornton *pediatrics and pathology educator, researcher*
†Strupp, John Allen *oncologist*
Thornton, Spencer P. *ophthalmologist, educator*
van Eys, Jan *retired pediatrician, educator, administrator*
Wasserman, David H. *medical educator, researcher*
†Whitworth, Thomas C. *neonatologist*
Wilkinson, Grant Robert *pharmacology educator*
Williams, Lester Frederick, Jr. *general surgeon*
Wolraich, Mark Lee *pediatrician*

### Oak Ridge
Clapp, Neal Keith *experimental pathologist*
Spray, Paul Elsworth *surgeon*
Stevens, George M., III *surgeon*
Wise, Edmund Joseph *physician assistant, industrial hygienist*

### Williamsport
Dysinger, Paul William *physician, educator, health consultant*

## TEXAS

### Abilene
Morgan, Clyde Nathaniel *dermatologist*
Richert, Harvey Miller, II *ophthalmologist*
Russell, Byron Edward *physical therapy educator*

### Amarillo
Berry, Rita Kay *medical technologist*
Laur, William Edward *retired dermatologist*
Marupudi, Sambasiva Rao *surgeon, educator*
Norrid, Henry Gail *osteopath, surgeon, researcher*
Parker, Lynda Michele *psychiatrist*
Pratt, Donald George *physician*
Saadeh, Constantine Khalil *internist, health facility administrator, educator*

### Aransas Pass
Stehn, Lorraine Strelnick *physician*

### Arlington
Chong, Vernon *surgeon, physician, Air Force officer*

### Austin
Austin, John Riley *surgeon, educator*
Bernstein, Robert *retired physician, state official, former army officer*
Brender, Jean Diane *epidemiologist, nurse*
Dorsen, Michael *physician*
Elequin, Cleto, Jr. *retired physician*
Ersek, Robert Allen *plastic surgeon, inventor*
Fleeger, David Clark *colon and rectal surgeon*
Le Maistre, Charles Aubrey *internist, epidemiologist, educator*
Mullins, Charles Brown *physician, academic administrator*
Painter, Theophilus Shickel, Jr. *physician*
Werner, Gerhard *pharmacologist, psychoanalyst, educator*

### Bastrop
Shurley, Jay Talmadge *psychiatrist, medical educator, administrator, behavioral sciences researcher, polar explorer, author, genealogist*

### Baytown
Williams, Drew Davis *surgeon*

### Beaumont
Allums, James A. *retired cardiovascular surgeon*
Lee, Shung-Man *nephrologist*
Lozano, Jose *nephrologist*
Phan, Tâm Thanh *medical educator, psychotherapist, consultant, researcher*

### Bellaire
Haywood, Theodore Joseph *physician, educator*
Thorne, Lawrence George *allergist, immunologist, pediatrician*
Weyandt, Linda Jane *anesthetist*

### Boerne
Wittmer, James Frederick *preventive medicine physician, educator*

### Bryan
Dirks, Kenneth Ray *pathologist, medical educator, army officer*

### Carrollton
Kelly, Ralph Whitley *emergency physician, health facility administrator*

### College Station
Chiou, George Chung-Yih *pharmacologist, educator*
Knight, James Allen *psychiatrist, educator*
Kuo, Lih *medical educator*
Way, James Leong *pharmacology and toxicology educator*

### Corpus Christi
Appel, Truman Frank *surgeon*
Cox, William Andrew *cardiovascular thoracic surgeon*
Lim, Alexander Rufasta *neurologist, clinical investigator, educator, writer*
Morales, John Mark *cardiac surgeon*
Pinkel, Donald Paul *pediatrician*
Sisley, Nina Mae *physician, public health officer*
Ward, Harold William Cowper *oncologist, educator*

### Dallas
Allen, Terry Devereux *urologist, educator*
Bashour, Fouad Anis *cardiology educator*
Blomquist, Carl Gunnar *cardiologist*
Bonte, Frederick James *radiology educator, physician*
Burnside, John Wayne *medical educator, university official*
Carman, George Henry *retired physician*
Cavanagh, Harrison Dwight *ophthalmic surgeon*
Cloud, Robert Royce *surgeon*
Cox, Rody P(owell) *medical educator, internist*
Cullum, Colin Munro *psychiatry and neurology educator*
Drach, George Wisse *urology educator*
Dutta, Paritosh Chandra *immunologist*
Edwards, George Alva *physician, educator*
Eichenwald, Heinz Felix *physician*
Einspruch, Burton Cyril *psychiatrist*
Emmett, Michael *physician*
Ericson, Ruth Ann *psychiatrist*
Feiner, Joel S. *psychiatrist*
Flatt, Adrian Ede *surgeon*
Fogelman, Morris Joseph *physician*
Frenkel, Eugene Phillip *physician*
Friedberg, Errol Clive *pathology educator, researcher*
Gage, Tommy Wilton *pharmacologist, dentist, pharmacist, educator*
Gant, Norman Ferrell, Jr. *obstetrician, gynecologist*
Gantt, James Raiford *thoracic surgeon*
Gilman, Alfred Goodman *pharmacologist, educator*
Goldstein, Joseph Leonard *physician, medical educator, molecular genetics scientist*
Gonwa, Thomas Arthur *nephrologist, transplant physician*
†Grant, Lester Howard *retired physician*
†Griffith, Rachel *neonatologist*
Gross, Gary Neil *allergist, physician*
Gruebel, Barbara Jane *internist, pulmonologist*
Harrington, Marion Ray *ophthalmologist*
Helm, Phala Aniece *physiatrist*
Hilgemann, Donald William *medical educator*
Holman, James *allergist, immunologist*
Hurd, Eric Ray *rheumatologist, internist, educator*
Jialal, Ishwarlal *medical educator*
Johnson, Robert Lee, Jr. *physician, educator, researcher*
Kindberg, Shirley Jane *pediatrician*
Kollmeyer, Kenneth Robert *surgeon*
Kramer, Robert Ivan *pediatrician*
Lewis, Jerry M. *psychiatrist, educator*
Lichliter, Warren Eugene *surgeon, educator*
Lumry, William Raymond *physician, allergist*
Maddrey, Willis Crocker *medical educator, internist, academic administrator, consultant, researcher*
Margolin, Solomon Begelfor *pharmacologist*
Marks, James Frederic *pediatric endocrinologist, educator*
Martin, Jack *physician*
Mc Clelland, Robert Nelson *surgeon, educator*
McCord, Don Lewis *surgeon*
McCracken, Alexander Walker *pathologist*
Mickey, Bruce Edward *neurosurgeon*
Mitchell, Teddy Lee *physician*
Mueller, James Bernhard *anesthesiologist, pain managememt consultant*
New, William Neil *physician, retired naval officer*
Odom, Floyd Clark *surgeon*
Olinger, Sheff Daniel *neurologist, educator*
Page, Richard Leighton *cardiologist, medical educator, researcher*
Parkey, Robert Wayne *radiology and nuclear medicine educator, research radiologist*
Perry, Malcolm Oliver *vascular surgeon*
Petty, Charles Sutherland *pathologist*
Phillips, Margaret A. *pharmacology educator*
Race, George Justice *pathology educator*
Rainey, William E., II *medical educator*
Ram, Chitta Venkata *physician*
Roberts, Lynne Jeanine *physician*
Rosenberg, Roger Newman *neurologist, educator*
Salyer, Kenneth E. *surgeon*
Simon, Theodore Ronald *physician, medical educator*
Smith, Barry Samuel *physiatrist*
Smith, Edwin Ide *medical educator*
Sparkman, Robert Satterfield *retired surgeon, educator*
Sprague, Charles Cameron *medical foundation president*
Stembridge, Vernie A(lbert) *pathologist, educator*
Stone, Marvin Jules *physician, educator*
Thompson, Jesse Eldon *vascular surgeon*
Tong, Alex Waiming *immunologist*
Unger, Roger Harold *physician, scientist*
Wasserman, Richard Lawrence *pediatrician, educator*
Weiner, Myron Frederick *psychiatrist, educator, clinical investigator*
Wheeler, Clarence Joseph, Jr. *physician*
Wildenthal, C(laud) Kern *physician, educator*
Wilson, Jean Donald *endocrinologist, educator*
Ziff, Morris *internist, rheumatologist, educator*

### Eden
Boyd, John Hamilton *osteopath*

### El Paso
Crossen, John Jacob *radiologist, educator*
Foley, John Donald *physician*
Gainer, Barbara Jeanne *radiology educator*
Huchton, Paul Joseph, Jr. *pediatrician*
Mrochek, Michael J. *physician*
Pazmiño, Patricio Augusto *physician, scientist, consultant*
Simpson, Michael Homer *dermatologist*
Verghese, Abraham Cheeran *internist, writer, educator*
Williams, Darryl Marlowe *medical educator*

### Fort Sam Houston
Cohen, David John *cardiothoracic surgeon*

### Fort Worth
Ahmed, M. Basheer *psychiatrist, educator*
Brooks, Lloyd William, Jr. *osteopath, interventional cardiologist, educator*
Cox, James Sidney *physician*
†Dewar, Thomas Norman *gastroenterologist*
Gillette, Paul Crawford *pediatric cardiologist*
Joe, George Washington *clinical researcher, quantitative methodologist*
Jurgensen, Warren Peter *retired psychiatrist, educator*
Lorenzetti, Ole John *pharmaceutical research executive, ophthalmic research and development executive*
Smith, Thomas Hunter *ophthalmologist, ophthalmic plastic and orbital surgeon*
Tobey, Martin Alan *cardiologist*
Treviño, Fernando Manuel *medical educator*
Wynn, Susan Rudd *physician*
Yanni, John Michael *pharmacologist*

### Galveston
Arens, James F. *anesthesiologist, educator*
Bailey, Byron James *otolaryngologist, medical association executive*
Bernier, George Matthew, Jr. *physician, medical educator, medical school dean*
Brasier, Allan R. *medical educator*
Bungo, Michael William *physician, educator, science administrator*
Burns, Chester Ray *medical history educator*
Calverley, John Robert *physician, educator*
Chonmaitree, Tasnee *pediatrician, educator, infectious disease specialist*
Dawson, Earl Bliss *obstetrician/gynecologist, educator*
Felthous, Alan Robert *psychiatrist*
Gold, Daniel Howard *ophthalmologist, educator*
Goodwin, Jean McClung *psychiatrist*
Grant, J(ohn) Andrew, Jr. *medical educator, allergist*
Herndon, David N. *surgeon*
Hillman, Gilbert Rothschild *medical educator*
Hilton, James Gorton *pharmacologist*
Jahadi, Mohammad Reza *surgeon*
James, Thomas Naum *cardiologist, educator*
Levin, William Cohn *hematologist, former university president*
Mader, Jon Terry *physician*
Ogra, Pearay L. *physician, educator*
Pearl, William Richard Emden *pediatric cardiologist*
Phillips, Linda Goluch *plastic surgeon, educator, researcher*
Powell, Don Watson *medical educator, physician, physiology researcher*
Powell, Leslie Charles, Jr. *obstetrics and gynecology educator*
Sandstead, Harold Hilton *medical educator*
Schreiber, Melvyn Hirsh *radiologist*
Shope, Robert Ellis *epidemiology educator*
Smith, David English *physician, educator*
Smith, Edgar Benton *physician*
Smith, Jerome Hazen *pathologist*
Tyson, Kenneth Robert Thomas *surgeon, educator*
White, Robert Brown *medical educator*
Willis, William Darrell, Jr. *neurophysiologist, educator*

### Garland
Duren, Michael *cardiologist*
Hockett, Sheri Lynn *radiologist*

### Harlingen
†Klein, Garner Franklin *cardiologist, internist*

### Houston
†Abbruzzese, James Lewis *medical oncologist*
Able, Luke William *retired pediatric surgeon, consultant*
Alexanian, Raymond *hematologist*
Alford, Bobby Ray *physician, educator, university official*
Appel, Stanley Hersh *neurologist*
†Bailey, Harold Randolph *surgeon*
Ballantyne, Christie Mitchell *medical educator*
Barcenas, Camilo Gustavo *internist, educator*
Baskin, David Stuart *neurosurgeon*
Bast, Robert Clinton, Jr. *medical researcher, medical educator*
Beasley, Robert Palmer *epidemiologist, dean, educator*
Beck, John Robert *pathologist, information scientist*
Berry, Michael A. *physician, consultant*
Bethea, Louise Huffman *allergist*
Blacklock, Jerry Bob *neurosurgeon*
Blanco, Jorge Desiderio *physician, medical educator, researcher*
Bodey, Gerald Paul *medical educator, physician*
Bonilla-Felix, Melvin A. *pediatrician, educator*
Bowman, Jeffrey Neil *podiatrist*
†Brown, Dale, Jr. *obstetrician, educator, health facility adminstrator*
Burdette, Walter James *surgeon, educator*
Burzynski, Stanislaw Rajmund *internist*
Busch, Harris *medical educator*
Buster, John Edmond *gynecologist, medical researcher*
Butler, Ian John *neurologist*
Campbell, Andrew William *immunotoxicology physician*
Cantrell, William Allen *psychiatrist, educator*
Cardus, David *physician*
Casscells, Samuel Ward, III *cardiologist, educator*
Catlin, Francis Irving *physician*
Collins, Vincent Patrick *radiologist, physician, educator*
Cooley, Denton Arthur *surgeon, educator*
Corriere, Joseph N., Jr. *urologist, educator*
Couch, Robert Barnard *physician, educator*
Daily, Louis *ophthalmologist*
DeBakey, Michael Ellis *cardiovascular surgeon, educator, scientist*
Donnelly, Edward James, Jr. *medical services company executive*
Doubleday, Charles William *dermatologist, educator*
Drutz, Jan Edwin *pediatrics educator*
DuPont, Herbert Lancashire *medical educator, researcher*
Eisner, Diana *pediatrician*
Elwood, William Norelli *medical researcher*
Engelhardt, Hugo Tristram, Jr. *physician, educator*
Evans, Harry Launius *pathology educator*
Feigon, Judith Tova *ophthalmologist, surgeon, educator*
Ferrendelli, James Anthony *neurologist, educator*
Fishman, Marvin Allen *pediatrician, neurologist, educator*
Freireich, Emil J *hematologist, educator*
Fritsch, Derek Adrian *nurse anesthetist*

Gibson, Kathleen Rita *anatomy and anthropology educator*
Gigli, Irma *physician, educator, academic administrator*
Gildenberg, Philip Leon *neurosurgeon*
Glassman, Armand Barry *physician, pathologist, scientist, educator, administrator*
Goldman, Stanford Milton *medical educator*
Gorry, G. Anthony *medical educator*
Gould, Kenneth Lance *physician, educator*
Graham, David Yates *gastroenterologist*
Grossman, Herbert Barton *urologist, researcher*
Grossman, Robert George *physician, educator*
Gunn, Albert Edward, Jr. *internist, educator, lawyer, hospital and university administrator*
Gupta, Kaushal Kumar *internist*
Guynn, Robert William *psychiatrist, educator*
Hall, Robert Joseph *physician, medical educator*
Hanania, Nicola Alexander *physician*
Harle, Thomas Stanley *radiologist*
Harrell, James Earl, Sr. *radiologist, educator*
Haynie, Thomas Powell, III *physician*
Henning, Susan June *biomedical researcher*
Hollister, Leo Edward *physician, educator*
Hong, Waun Ki *medical oncologist, clinical investigator*
Hsu, Katharine Han Kuang *pediatrics educator*
Ibrahim, Nuhad Khalil *oncologist*
Jackson, Gilchrist L. *surgeon*
Jankovic, Joseph *neurologist, educator, scientist*
Jenkins, Daniel Edwards, Jr. *physician, educator*
Johnson, Thomas David *pharmacologist*
Jones, Dan B. *ophthalmologist, educator*
Jones, Edith Irby *physician*
Jones, James Wilson *physician, cell biologist*
Jordon, Robert Earl *physician*
Kahan, Barry Donald *surgeon, educator*
Katrana, David John *plastic and reconstructive surgeon*
Kaufman, Raymond Henry *physician*
Kellaway, Peter *neurophysiologist, researcher*
Key, James Everett *ophthalmologist*
Kitowski, Vincent Joseph *medical consultant, former physical medicine and rehabilitation physician*
Knight, J. Vernon *medicine and microbiology educator*
Kraft, Irvin Alan *psychiatrist*
Kutka, Nicholas *nuclear medicine physician*
Lane, Montague *physician, educator*
Letsou, George Vasilios *cardiothoracic surgeon*
Levin, Bernard *physician*
Low, Morton David *physician, educator*
Marshall, Gailen Daugherty, Jr. *physician, scientist, educator*
Mattox, Kenneth Leon *surgeon, educator, medical scientist*
Max, Ernest *surgeon*
Mc Pherson, Alice Ruth *ophthalmologist*
Mendelsohn, John *oncologist, hematologist, educator*
Meyer, John Stirling *neurologist, educator*
Milam, John Daniel *pathologist, educator*
Miller, Gary Evan *psychiatrist, mental health services administrator*
Miner, Michael E. *neurosurgery educator*
Morgenstern, Lewis B. *medical educator*
Munk, Zev Moshe *allergist, researcher*
Murphy, William Alexander, Jr. *diagnostic radiologist, educator*
Musher, Daniel Michael *physician*
Ordonez, Nelson Gonzalo *pathologist*
Owsley, William Clinton, Jr. *radiologist*
Phung, Nguyen Dinh *medical educator*
Poston, Walker Seward, II *medical educator, researcher*
Radke, Jan Rodger *pulmonologist, hospital program administrator*
Raijman, Isaac *gastroenterologist, endoscopist, educator*
Rakel, Robert Edwin *physician, educator*
Raymer, Warren Joseph *retired allergist*
Redmon, Agile Hugh, Jr. *allergist*
Ribble, John Charles *medical educator*
Rich, Robert Regier *immunology educator, physician*
Riley, William John *neurologist*
Ro, Jae Yun *pathologist*
Romsdahl, Marvin Magnus *surgeon, educator*
Ross, Patti Jayne *obstetrics and gynecology educator*
Roth, Jack Alan *thoracic surgeon*
Rudolph, Andrew Henry *dermatologist, educator*
Scharold, Mary Louise *psychoanalyst, educator*
Scheuerle, Angela Elizabeth *geneticist*
Schoolar, Joseph Clayton *psychiatrist, pharmacologist, educator*
Selke, Oscar O., Jr. *physiatrist, educator*
Shearer, William Thomas *pediatrician, educator*
Shulman, Robert Jay *physician*
Simpson, Joe Leigh *obstetrics and gynecology educator*
Spencer, William A. *physician, educational administrator*
Spira, Melvin *plastic surgeon*
Stehlin, John Sebastian, Jr. *surgeon*
Thomas, Orville C. *physician*
Tulloch, Brian Robert *endocrinologist*
Tullos, Hugh Simpson *orthopedic surgeon, educator*
Vallbona, Carlos *physician*
Vanderploeg, James M. *preventive medicine physician*
Vassilopoulou-Sellin, Rena *medical educator*
Vogel, Susan Michelle *physician*
Walker, William Easton *surgeon, educator, lawyer*
†Wall, Matthew J., Jr. *surgeon, scientist*
Wheless, James Warren *neurologist*
Wiemer, David Robert *plastic surgeon*
Williams, Temple Weatherly, Jr. *internist, educator*
Zhang, Jingwu *immunologist*

### Humble
Trowbridge, John Parks *physician*

### Irving
Wood, Joseph George *neurobiologist, educator*

### Kemp
Wurlitzer, Fred Pabst *physician, surgeon*

### Killeen
Vancura, Stephen Joseph *radiologist*

### Lubbock
Beck, George Preston *anesthesiologist, educator*
Bricker, Donald Lee *surgeon*
Buesseler, John Aure *ophthalmologist, management consultant*
Illner-Canizaro, Hana *physician, oral surgeon, researcher*
Jackson, Francis Charles *physician, surgeon*
Kimbrough, Robert Cooke, III *infectious diseases physician*
Kurtzman, Neil A. *medical educator*
May, Donald Robert Lee *ophthalmologist, retina and vitreous surgeon, educator, academic administrator*
Mittemeyer, Bernhard Theodore *urology and surgery educator*
Way, Barbara Haight *dermatologist*
Woolam, Gerald Lynn *surgeon*

### Lufkin
Perry, Lewis Charles *emergency medicine physician, osteopath*

### Marshall
Sudhivoraseth, Niphon *pediatrician, allergist, immunologist*

### Mcallen
Ramirez, Mario Efrain *physician*

### Midland
Lohmann, George Young, Jr. *neurosurgeon, hospital executive*
Rebik, James Michael *otolaryngologist*

### Nacogdoches
Fish, Stewart Allison *retired obstetrician and gynecologist*
Mallot, Michael E. *gastroenterologist*

### Odessa
Lane, Daniel McNeel *pediatric hematologist, lipidologist*

### Pasadena
D'Andrea, Mark *radiation oncologist*
Shapiro, Edward Muray *dermatologist*

### Plano
Ahmad, Syeda Sultana *physician*
Vengrow, Michael Ian *neurologist*

### Randolph AFB
Carroll, Robert Eugene *senior flight surgeon*

### Richmond
Hay, Richard Carman *retired anesthesiologist*

### San Antonio
Aust, Joe Bradley *surgeon, educator*
Baker, Floyd Wilmer *surgeon, retired army officer*
Beckmann, Charles Henry *cardiologist, educator*
Croft, Harry Allen *psychiatrist*
Davis, Steven Andrew *dermatologist*
Dobie, Robert Alan *otologist*
†Fornos, Peter S. *pulmonary medicine physician*
Freeman, Theodore Monroe *physician*
Hall, Brad Bailey *orthopaedic surgeon, educator*
Huff, Robert Whitley *obstetrician, gynecologist, educator*
James, Vernon Lester *pediatrician, educator*
Jorgensen, James H. *pathologist, educator, microbiologist*
Kamada-Cole, Mika M. *allergist, immunologist, medical educator*
Kniker, William Theodore *pediatrician, allergist, educator, researcher, immunologist*
Kotas, Robert Vincent *research physician, educator*
Leon, Robert Leonard *psychiatrist, educator*
Martin, Bryan Leslie *allergist, immunologist*
Martinez-O'Ferrall, José A. *public health physician, retired air force officer*
McAnelly, Robert D. *physiatrist, researcher*
Mc Fee, Arthur Storer *physician*
McGill, Henry Coleman, Jr. *physician, educator, researcher*
Mitchell, George Washington, Jr. *physician, educator*
Neel, Spurgeon Hart, Jr. *physician, retired army officer*
New, Pamela Zyman *neurologist*
Nguyen, Vung Duy *radiologist, educator*
Persellin, Robert Harold *physician*
Pestana, Carlos *physician, educator*
Pruitt, Basil Arthur, Jr. *surgeon, army officer, retired*
Ramos, Raul *surgeon*
Reuter, Stewart Ralston *radiologist, lawyer, educator*
Rhodes, Linda Jane *psychiatrist*
Rosoff, Leonard, Sr. *retired surgeon, medical educator*
Schenker, Steven *physician, educator*
Smith, Reginald Brian Furness *anesthesiologist, educator*
Townsend, Frank Marion *pathology educator*
Wiedeman, Geoffrey Paul *physician, air force officer*
Zilveti, Carlos Benjamin *preventive medicine physician, pediatrician*

### Sanger
Perry, Richard Jay *physician*

### Seabrook
Patten, Bernard Michael *neurologist, writer, educator*

### Stafford
Polinger, Iris Sandra *dermatologist*

### Temple
†Bailey, William Harold *medical educator*
Brasher, George Walter *physician*
Dyck, Walter Peter *gastroenterologist, educator, university official*
Holleman, Vernon Daughty *physician, internist*
Knudsen, Kermit Bruce *physician*
Rohack, John James *cardiologist*
Wadenberg, Marie-Louise Gertrud *psychopharmacologist, researcher*

### Texarkana
Selby, Roy Clifton, Jr. *neurosurgeon*

### Tyler
Kronenberg, Richard Samuel *physician, educator*

### Waco
Dow, David Sontag *retired ophthalmologist*
Richie, Rodney Charles *critical care and pulmonary medicine physician*

### Webster
Farnam, Jafar *allergist, immunologist, pediatrician*
Rappaport, Martin Paul *internist, nephrologist, educator*

### West
Eisma, Jose Albarracin *pulmonary physician*

## UTAH

### Layton
†Yates, Jay Reese *physician*

### Ogden
Maughan, Willard Zinn *dermatologist*
Spencer, LaVal Wing *physician*

### Park City
Wardell, Joe Russell, Jr. *pharmacologist*

### Salt Lake City
Abildskov, J. A. *cardiologist, educator*
Bauer, A(ugust) Robert, Jr. *surgeon, educator*
Bragg, David Gordon *physician, radiology educator*
Brandon, Kathryn Elizabeth Beck *pediatrician*
Carey, John Clayton *pediatrician*
Davis, Brian Adam *physician*
Davis, Roy Kim *otolaryngologist, health facility administrator*
Evanega, George Ronald *medical company executive*
Fujinami, Robert Shin *neurology educator*
Goates, Delbert Tolton *child psychiatrist*
Goldstein, Michael L. *neurologist*
Goodman, Louis Sanford *pharmacologist*
Grosser, Bernard Irving *psychiatry educator*
Hammond, M(ary) Elizabeth Hale *pathologist*
Iverius, Per-Henrik *physician, biochemist, educator*
Knight, Joseph Adams *pathologist*
Kolff, Willem Johan *internist, educator*
Lloyd, Ray Dix *health physicist, consultant*
Matsuo, Fumisuke *physician, educator*
Middleton, Anthony Wayne, Jr. *urologist, educator*
Moser, Royce, Jr. *physician, medical educator*
Nelson, Russell Marion *surgeon, educator*
Odell, William Douglas *physician, scientist, educator*
Overall, James Carney, Jr. *pediatrics laboratory medicine educator*
Renzetti, Attilio David *physician*
Smart, Charles Rich *retired surgeon*
Swensen, Laird S. *orthopedic surgeon*
Ward, John Robert *physician, educator*
Wong, Kuang Chung *anesthesiologist*

## VERMONT

### Bellows Falls
Cole, Stephen Adams *psychiatrist*

### Bennington
Wallace, Harold James, Jr. *physician*

### Bradford
Kaplow, Leonard Samuel *pathologist, educator*

### Brattleboro
Agallianos, Dennis Dionysios *psychiatrist*
Ames, Adelbert, III *neurophysiologist, educator*

### Burlington
Ciongoli, Alfred Kenneth *neurologist*
Cooper, Sheldon Mark *medical educator, immunology researcher, rheumatologist*
Craighead, John Edward *pathology educator*
Davis, John Herschel *surgeon, educator*
Galbraith, Richard Anthony *physician, hospital administrator*
Incavo, Stephen Joseph *orthopaedic surgeon*
†LeWinter, Martin M. *cardiologist*
Lucey, Jerold Francis *pediatrician*
Muss, Hyman Bernard *oncologist, educator*
Riddick, Daniel Howison *obstetrics and gynecology educator, priest*
Sobel, Burton Elias *physician, educator*
Weed, Lawrence L. *pharmacology educator*

### Dorset
Bamford, Joseph Charles, Jr. *gynecologist, obstetrician, educator, medical missionary*

### Essex Junction
Dustan, Harriet Pearson *former physician, educator*

### Middlebury
Patterson, William Bradford *surgical oncologist*

### Saint Johnsbury
Toll, David *pediatrician*

### South Burlington
Terris, Milton *physician, educator*

### Swanton
Wooding, William Minor *medical statistics consultant*

### Underhill
Danforth, Elliot, Jr. *medical educator*

### Waitsfield
Clark, Samuel Smith *urologist*

### West Dover
Humphreys, George H., II *surgery educator*

### White River Junction
Myers, Warren Powers Laird *physician, educator*

### Woodstock
Lash, James William (Jay Lash) *embryology educator*
Wollman, Harry *health care and executive search consultant*

## VIRGINIA

### Alexandria
Buhain, Wilfrido Javier *medical educator*
Chapman, Anthony Bradley *psychiatrist*
Hurtado, Rodrigo Claudio *allergist, immunologist*
Maves, Michael Donald *medical association executive*
Mosely, Linda Hays *surgeon*

### Annandale
Binder, Richard Allen *hematologist, oncologist*
Kaufmanas, Petras G. *biomedical researcher, psychologist*
†Lefrak, Edward Arthur *cardiovascular surgeon*
Scott, Hugh Patrick *physician, naval officer*
Shamburek, Roland Howard *physician*
Simonian, Simon John *surgeon, scientist, educator*

### Arlington
Ascunce, Gil *physician*
Brown, James Harvey *neuroscientist, government research administrator*
Dolan, William David, Jr. *physician*
Harper, Michael John Kennedy *obstetrics and gynecology educator*
Kaufman, Paul *physician, former naval officer, association executive*
Werbos, Paul John *neural net research director*

### Blackstone
Walton, G. Clifford *family practice physician*

### Charlottesville
Barnett, Benjamin Lewis, Jr. *physician*
Beller, George Allan *medical educator*
Cantrell, Robert Wendell *otolaryngologist, head and neck surgeon, educator*
Chevalier, Robert Louis *pediatric nephrologist, educator, researcher*
Conway, Brian Peter *ophthalmologist, educator*
Craig, James William *physician, educator, university dean*
Dalton, Claudette Ellis Harloe *anesthesiologist, educator, university official*
DeSilvey, Dennis Lee *cardiologist, educator, university administrator*
Detmer, Don Eugene *medical educator, health policy researcher, surgeon*
Dreifuss, Fritz Emanuel *neurologist, educator*
Epstein, Robert Marvin *anesthesiologist, educator*
Fechner, Robert Eugene *pathology educator*
Ferguson, James Edward, II *obstetrician, gynecologist*
Fernbach, Louise Oftedal *psychiatrist*
Flickinger, Charles John *anatomist, educator*
Gillenwater, Jay Young *urologist, educator*
Gross, Charles Wayne *physician, educator*
Hambrick, George Walter, Jr. *dermatologist, educator*
Harbert, Guy Morley, Jr. *retired obstetrician, gynecologist*
Hook, Edward Watson, Jr. *physician, educator*
Howards, Stuart S. *physician, educator*
Jane, John Anthony *neurosurgeon, educator*
Jones, Rayford Scott *surgeon, medical educator*
Kassell, Neal Frederic *neurosurgery educator*
Kattwinkel, John *physician, pediatrics educator*
Keats, Theodore Eliot *physician, radiology educator*
Kitchin, James D., III *obstetrician-gynecologist, educator*
Mandell, Gerald Lee *physician, medicine educator*
†Marshall, Barry James *gastroenterologist*
Marshall, Victor Fray *physician, educator*
McDuffie, Marcia Jensen *pediatrics educator, researcher*
Morgan, Raymond F. *plastic surgeon*
Muller, William Henry, Jr. *surgeon, educator*
Nolan, Stanton Peelle *surgeon, educator*
Owen, John Atkinson, Jr. *physician, educator*
Peterson, Kent Wright *physician*
Phillips, Lawrence H., II *neurologist, educator*
Platts-Mills, Thomas Alexander E. *immunologist, educator, researcher*
Pullen, Edwin Wesley *anatomist, university dean*
Rowlingson, John Clyde *anesthesiologist, educator, physician*
Roy, Raymond Clyde *anesthesiologist*
Sarembock, Ian Joseph *internist*
Stevenson, Ian *psychiatrist, educator*
Steward, Oswald *neuroscience educator, researcher*
Taylor, Peyton Troy, Jr. *gynecologic oncologist, educator*
Teates, Charles David *radiologist, educator*
Thorner, Michael Oliver *medical educator, research center administrator*
Tillack, Thomas Warner *pathologist*
Tuttle, Jeremy Ballou *neurobiologist*
Underwood, Paul Benjamin *obstetrician, educator*
Villar-Palasi, Carlos *pharmacology educator*
Weary, Peyton Edwin *medical educator*
Wilhelm, Morton *surgery educator*
Wills, Michael Ralph *medical educator*
Woode, Moses Kwamena Annan *scientist, medical and chemistry educator*

### Chesapeake
Kovalcik, Paul Jerome *surgeon*

### Culpeper
Broman, George Ellis, Jr. *surgeon*

### Danville
Moore, Richard Carroll, Jr. *family physician*

### Fairfax
Dettinger, Garth Bryant *surgeon, physician, retired air force officer, county health officer*
DuRocher, Frances Antoinette *physician, educator*
Galioto, Frank Martin, Jr. *pediatric cardiologist, educator*
Rubin, Robert Joseph *physician, health care consultant*
Stage, Thomas Benton *psychiatrist*
Strauch, Barry Stuart *physician, educator*

### Falls Church
Bucur, John Charles *neurological surgeon*
Ehrlich, S(aul) Paul, Jr. *physician, consultant, former government official*
Evans, Peter Yoshio *ophthalmologist, educator*
Harrison, Virginia Florence *retired anatomist and educator, investment advisor, publisher, philanthropist*

### Fond Du Lac
Lambert, Eugene Kent *oncologist, hematologist*
Treffert, Darold Allen *psychiatrist, author, hospital director*

### Green Bay
Finesilver, Alan George *rheumatologist*

### Hales Corners
Kuwayama, S. Paul *physician, allergist, immunologist*

### Hartford
Babbitt, Donald Patrick *radiologist*

### La Crosse
Corser, David Hewson *pediatrician*
Lindesmith, Larry Alan *physician, administrator*
Webster, Stephen Burtis *physician, educator*

### Madison
Albert, Daniel Myron *ophthalmologist, educator*
Atkinson, Richard Lee, Jr. *internal medicine educator*
Bass, Paul *pharmacology educator*
Bloodworth, J(ames) M(organ) Bartow, Jr. *physician, educator*
Boutwell, Roswell Knight *oncology educator*
Brown, Arnold Lanehart, Jr. *pathologist, educator, university dean*
Burgess, Richard Ray *oncology educator, molecular biology researcher, biotechnology consultant*
Carbone, Paul Peter *oncologist, educator, administrator*
Cohen, Marcus *allergist*
Colás, Antonio Espada *medical educator*
DeMets, David L. *medical educator, biomedical researcher*
Dodson, Vernon Nathan *physician, educator*
Fahien, Leonard August *physician, educator*
Farrell, Philip M. *physician, educator, researcher*
Ford, Charles Nathaniel *otolaryngologist, educator*
Forster, Francis Michael *physician, educator*
Graziano, Frank Michael *medical educator, researcher*
Guillery, Rainer Walter *anatomy educator*
Harkness, Donald Richard *hematologist, educator*
Hetsko, Cyril Michael *physician*
Javid, Manucher J. *neurosurgery educator*
Kepecs, Joseph Goodman *physician, educator*
Laessig, Ronald Harold *pathology educator, state official*
Leavitt, Lewis A. *pediatrician, educator*
Lemanske, Robert F., Jr. *allergist, immunologist*
Lobeck, Charles Champlin, Jr. *pediatrics educator*
Mac Kinney, Archie Allen, Jr. *physician*
Maki, Dennis G. *medical educator, researcher, clinician*
Malter, James Samuel *pathologist, educator*
Marton, Laurence Jay *clinical pathologist, educator, researcher*
McBeath, Andrew Alan *orthopedic surgery educator*
Miller, James Alexander *oncologist, educator*
Nordby, Eugene Jorgen *orthopedic surgeon*
Peters, Henry Augustus *neuropsychiatrist*
Pitot, Henry Clement, III *physician, educator*
Reynolds, Ernest West *physician, educator*
Roberts, Leigh Milton *psychiatrist*
Robins, H(enry) Ian *medical oncologist*
Rowe, George Giles *cardiologist, educator*
Sackett, Joseph Frederic *radiologist, educator, administrator*
Schutta, Henry Szczesny *neurologist, educator*
Smith, Morton Edward *ophthalmology educator, dean*
Sobkowicz, Hanna Maria *neurology researcher*
Sondel, Paul Mark *pediatric oncologist, educator*
Sonnedecker, Glenn Allen *historian of pharmacy*
Tomar, Russell Herman *pathologist, educator, researcher*
Valdivia, Hector Horacio *medical educator*
Westman, Jack Conrad *child psychiatrist, educator*
Whiffen, James Douglass *surgeon, educator*
Wilson, Pamela Aird *physician*

### Manitowoc
Trader, Joseph Edgar *orthopedic surgeon*

### Marshfield
Fye, W. Bruce, III *cardiologist*
Stueland, Dean Theodore *emergency physician*

### Middleton
Jefferson, James Walter *psychiatry educator*

### Milwaukee
Alexander, Janice Hoehner *physician, educator*
Bhore, Jay Narayan *psychiatrist*
Browning, Carol Anne *pediatrician, educator*
Condon, Robert Edward *surgeon, educator*
Cooper, Richard Alan *hematologist, college dean, health policy analyst*
Esterly, Nancy Burton *physician*
Feinsilver, Donald Lee *psychiatry educator*
Goblirsch, Dean Edmund *otolaryngologist*
Gonnering, Russell Stephen *ophthalmic plastic surgeon*
Grim, Clarence Ezra *medical educator, internist, researcher*
†Hosenpud, Jeffrey *cardiovascular physician*
Kampine, John P. *anesthesiologist*
Kao, Sue Fei *ophthalmologist*
Kochar, Mahendr Singh *physician, educator, administrator, scientist, writer, consultant*
Krausen, Anthony Sharnik *surgeon*
†Larson, David Lee *surgeon*
McCormick, Kenneth L. *pediatrics educator, researcher*
Meyer, Jon Keith *psychiatrist, psychoanalyst, educator*
Montgomery, Robert Renwick *medical association administrator, educator*
Namdari, Bahram *surgeon*
Pisciotta, Anthony Vito *physician, educator*
Schultz, Richard Otto *ophthalmologist, educator*
Shindell, Sidney *medical educator, physician*
Siegesmund, Kenneth August *forensic anatomist, consultant, educator*
Soergel, Konrad Hermann *physician*
Stokes, Kathleen Sarah *dermatologist*
Terry, Leon Cass *neurologist, educator*
†Towne, Jonathan Baker *vascular surgeon*

### Onalaska
Waite, Lawrence Wesley *osteopathic physician*

### Pewaukee
Loteyro, Corazon Bigata *physician*

### Racine
Stewart, Richard Donald *internist, educator*

### Tomah
†Due, James M. *pharmacist*

### Verona
Kieser, Randall John *family practice, addiction medicine and emergency medicine physician*

### Wauwatosa
Hollister, Winston Ned *pathologist*
White, Herbert Charles *psychiatrist*

### West Bend
Gardner, Robert Joseph *general and thoracic surgeon*

### Woodruff
Agre, James Courtland *physical medicine and rehabilitation educator*

## WYOMING

### Cheyenne
Hunton, Donald Bothen *retired internist*

### Gillette
Naramore, James Joseph *family practice physician, educator*

# TERRITORIES OF THE UNITED STATES

## PUERTO RICO

### Caparra Terrace
León, Felix Ivan *pulmonologist*

### Gurabo
Morales-Borges, Raul Hector *physician*

### Mayaguez
Sahai, Hardeo *medical statistics educator*

### Ponce
Cummings, Luis Emilio *anesthesiologist, consultant*
Sala, Luis Francisco *surgeon, educator*
Torres-Aybar, Francisco Gualberto *medical educator*

### San Juan
Ghaly, Evone Shehata *pharmaceutics and industrial pharmacy educator*
Piovanetti, Simon *pediatrician*
Ramirez-Rivera, Jose *physician*
Rodriguez, Agustin Antonio *surgeon*
Soltero-Harrington, Luis Rubén *surgeon, educator*

### Santurce
Fleisher, T. Lawrence *dermatologist*

# CANADA

## ALBERTA

### Calgary
Lederis, Karolis Paul (Karl Lederis) *pharmacologist, educator, researcher*
Melvill-Jones, Geoffrey *physician, educator*
Rewcastle, Neill Barry *neuropathology educator*
Stell, William Kenyon *neuroscientist, educator*

### Edmonton
Cook, David Alastair *pharmacology educator*
Dewhurst, William George *psychiatrist, educator, research director*
Miller, Jack David R. *radiologist, physician, educator*

## BRITISH COLUMBIA

### Vancouver
Baird, Patricia Ann *physician, educator*
Bates, David Vincent *physician, medical educator*
Chow, Anthony Wei-Chik *physician*
Doyle, Patrick John *otolaryngologist*
Eaves, Allen Charles Edward *hematologist, medical agency administrator*
Freeman, Hugh James *gastroenterology educator*
Friedman, Sydney M. *anatomy educator, medical researcher*
Hardwick, David Francis *pathologist*
Knobloch, Ferdinand J. *psychiatrist, educator*
McGeer, Edith Graef *neurological science educator emerita*
Mizgala, Henry F. *physician*
Paty, Donald Winston *neurologist*
Rootman, Jack *ophthalmologist, surgeon, pathologist, oncologist, artist*
Roy, Chunilal *psychiatrist*
Slonecker, Charles Edward *anatomist, medical educator, author*
Sutter, Morley Carman *medical scientist*
Thurlbeck, William Michael *retired pathologist, retired medical educator*
Tingle, Aubrey James *pediatric immunologist, research administrator*
Tyers, Geddes Frank Owen *surgeon*

### Victoria
Mac Diarmid, William Donald *physician*

## MANITOBA

### Winnipeg
Angel, Aubie *physician, academic administrator*
Haworth, James Chilton *pediatrics educator*
Israels, Lyonel Garry *hematologist, medical educator*
Naimark, Arnold *medical educator, physiologist, educator*
Persaud, Trivedi Vidhya Nandan *anatomy educator, researcher, consultant*
Ronald, Allan Ross *internal medicine and medical microbiology educator, researcher*
Ross, Robert Thomas *neurologist, educator*
Schacter, Brent Allan *oncologist, health facility administrator*

## NOVA SCOTIA

### Halifax
Gold, Judith Hammerling *psychiatrist*
Goldbloom, Richard Ballon *pediatrics educator*
Langley, George Ross *medical educator*
Stewart, Ronald Daniel *medical educator, government official*
Tonks, Robert Stanley *pharmacology and therapeutics educator, former university dean*

## ONTARIO

### Hamilton
Basmajian, John Varoujan *medical scientist, educator, physician*
Bienenstock, John *physician, educator*
Collins, John Alfred *obstetrician-gynecologist, educator*
Mueller, Charles Barber *surgeon, educator*
Roland, Charles Gordon *physician, medical historian, educator*
Smith, Stuart Lyon *psychiatrist, corporate executive*
Uchida, Irene Ayako *cytogenetics educator, researcher*

### Kingston
Boag, Thomas Johnson *physician*
Kaufman, Nathan *pathology educator, physician*
Low, James A. *physician*

### London
Brooks, Vernon Bernard *neuroscientist, educator, author*
Buck, Carol Kathleen *medical educator*
Carruthers, S. George *medical educator, physician*
Lala, Peeyush Kanti *medical scientist, educator*
Marotta, Joseph Thomas *medical educator*
McWhinney, Ian Renwick *physician, medical educator*
Valberg, Leslie Stephen *medical educator, physician, researcher*

### North York
Regan, David *brain researcher, educator*
Turnbull, John Cameron *pharmacist, consultant*

### Ottawa
de Bold, Adolfo J. *pathology and physiology educator, research scientist*
Friesen, Henry George *endocrinologist, educator*
Hagen, Paul Beo *physician, medical scientist*
Hurteau, Gilles David *retired obstetrician, gynecologist, educator, dean*
Jackson, W. Bruce *ophthalmology educator, researcher*
Lavoie, Lionel A. *physician, medical executive*
†Losos, Joseph Zbigniew *epidemiologist*
Waugh, Douglas Oliver William *pathology educator*

### Sault Sainte Marie
Banerjee, Samarendranath *orthopedic surgeon*

### Toronto
Alberti, Peter William *otolaryngologist*
Brown, Gregory Michael *psychiatrist, educator, researcher*
Bruce, William Robert *physician, educator*
Carlen, Peter Louis *neuroscientist educator, science administrator*
Cinader, Bernhard *immunologist, gerontologist, scientist, educator*
Goldenberg, Gerald Joseph *physician, educator*
Greben, Stanley Edward *psychiatrist, educator, author, editor*
Hudson, Alan Roy *neurosurgeon, medical educator, hospital administrator*
Kalant, Harold *pharmacology educator, physician*
Kalow, Werner *pharmacologist, toxicologist*
Lindsay, William Kerr *surgeon*
Mc Culloch, Ernest Armstrong *physician, educator*
Miller, Anthony Bernard *physician, medical researcher*
Nesbitt, Lloyd Ivan *podiatrist*
Ogilvie, Richard Ian *clinical pharmacologist*
Rakoff, Vivian Morris *psychiatrist, writer*
Rothstein, Aser *radiation biology educator*
Silver, Malcolm David *pathologist, educator*
Silverman, Melvin *medical research administrator*
Sole, Michael Joseph *cardiologist*
Till, James Edgar *medical educator, researcher*
Turner, Robert Edward *psychiatrist, educator*
Volpé, Robert *endocrinologist, researcher, educator*

## QUEBEC

### Beauport
Parent, André *neurobiology educator, researcher*

### Montpellier
Poirier, Louis Joseph *neurology educator*

### Montreal
Aguayo, Albert Juan *neuroscientist*
Baxter, Donald William *physician, educator, retired*
Beardmore, Harvey Ernest *retired physician, educator*
Becklake, Margaret Rigsby *physician, educator*
Burgess, John Herbert *physician, educator*
Clermont, Yves Wilfrid *anatomy educator, researcher*
Cruess, Richard Leigh *surgeon, university dean*
Cuello, Augusto Claudio Guillermo *medical research scientist, author*
Feindel, William Howard *neurosurgeon, consultant*
Freeman, Carolyn Ruth *radiation oncologist*
Genest, Jacques *physician, researcher, administrator*
Gold, Phil *physician, educator*
Goltzman, David *endocrinologist, educator, researcher*
Jasmin, Gaetan *pathologist, educator*
Karpati, George *neurologist, neuroscientist*
Kramer, Michael Stuart *pediatric epidemiologist*
Leblond, Charles Philippe *anatomy educator, researcher*
Lehmann, Heinz Edgar *psychiatrist, consultant, researcher*
Little, Alan Brian *obstetrician, gynecologist, educator*
MacDonald, R(onald Angus) Neil *physician, educator*
Mac Lean, Lloyd Douglas *surgeon*
Mc Gregor, Maurice *cardiologist, medical educator*
Milic-Emili, Joseph *physician, educator*
Moore, Sean *pathologist, educator*
Mulder, David S. *cardiovascular surgeon*
Nadeau, Reginald Antoine *medical educator*
Nattel, Stanley *cardiologist, research scientist*
Osmond, Dennis Gordon *medical educator, researcher*
Pelletier, Louis Conrad *surgeon, educator*

### Quebec
Couture, Jean G. *surgeon, educator*
Labrie, Fernand *physician*

### Sainte Foy
Dussault, Jean H. *endocrinologist, medical educator*

### Sherbrooke
Bureau, Michel André *pediatrician, pulmonologist*

### Verdun
Gauthier, Serge Gaston *neurologist*

### Westmount
Jasper, Herbert Henri *neuroscience researcher, consultant, writer*
Kessler, Jacques Isaac *gastroenterologist, educator*

## SASKATCHEWAN

### Saskatoon
Houston, C(larence) Stuart *radiologist, educator*
Jaques, Louis Barker *pharmacologist*

# MEXICO

### Mexico City
Martinez de la Escalera, Gonzalo *neuroendocrinologist*

### Zapopan
Garibay-Gutierrez, Luis *physician, educator*

# ARGENTINA

### Buenos Aires
Bergel, Meny *physician, researcher*

# AUSTRALIA

### Nedlands
Oxnard, Charles Ernest *anatomist, anthropologist, human biologist, educator*

# AUSTRIA

### Maria Enzersdorf
Vetter, Herbert *physician, educator*

### Vienna
Frankl, Viktor E. *psychiatrist, author*

# BRAZIL

### São Paulo
Marino, Raul, Jr. *neurosurgeon*

# CHINA

### Beijing
†Li, Gong-song *cardiac surgeon, educator*

# COSTA RICA

### Nicoya
Brunson, Joel Garrett *retired pathologist, educator*

# DENMARK

### Copenhagen
Skylv, Grethe Krogh *rheumatologist, anthropologist*

# ENGLAND

### Birmingham
Casson, Alan Graham *thoracic surgeon, researcher*

### Cambridge
Acheson, Roy Malcolm *epidemiologist, educator*

### Carshalton
Das, Sankar Kumar *cardiopulmonologist*

Levin, Jack *physician, educator, biomedical investigator*
Liard, Jean-Francois *cardiovascular physiologist, researcher, educator*
Lindburg, Daytha Eileen *physician assistant*
Linz, Anthony James *osteopathic physician, consultant, educator*
Lipowski, Zbigniew Jerzy *retired psychiatrist, educator*
Livezey, Mark Douglas *physician*
LoIudice, Thomas Anthony *gastroenterologist, researcher*
Long, Charles William *child and adolescent psychiatrist*
Loube, Samuel Dennis *physician*
Lutz, Lawrence Joseph *family practice physician*
Maas, Anthony Ernst *pathologist*
Maclaren, Noel Keith *pathologist, pediatrician, educator*
Maier, Alfred *neuroscientist*
Mair, Douglas Dean *medical educator, consultant*
Maitra, Subir Ranjan *medical educator*
Makowski, Edgar Leonard *obstetrician and gynecologist*
Malkinson, Frederick David *dermatologist*
Malloy, Craig Riggs *physician, educator*
Malluche, Hartmut Horst *nephrologist, medical educator*
Manning, Deborah A. *physician*
Marshall, John Crook *internal medicine educator*
Materson, Richard Stephen *physician, educator*
Mattson, Richard Henry *neurologist, educator*
McCauley, Floyce Reid *psychiatrist*
McCullough, David L. *urologist*
McDonagh, Thomas Joseph *physician*
†McGuire, Hunter Holmes, Jr. *surgeon, educator*
McLarnon, Mary Frances *neurologist*
McLeskey, Charles Hamilton *anesthesiology educator*
Mead, Beverley Tupper *physician, educator*
Meilman, Edward *physician*
Meister, Steven Gerard *cardiologist, educator*
Metzner, Richard Joel *psychiatrist, psychopharmacologist, educator*
Meyer, Greg Charles *psychiatrist*
Miller, Ross Hays *retired neurosurgeon*
Millikan, Clark Harold *physician*
Moffet, Hugh Lamson *pediatrician*
Monninger, Robert Harold George *ophthalmologist, educator*
Montgomery, John Richard *pediatrician, educator*
Moore, Emily Allyn *pharmacologist*
Moossy, John *neuropathologist, neurologist, consultant*
Morgan, Elizabeth *plastic and reconstructive surgeon*
Moser, Robert Lawrence *pathologist, health facility administrator*
Motto, Jerome Arthur *psychiatry educator*
Mountain, Clifton Fletcher *surgeon, educator*
Munger, Bryce L. *physician, educator*
Mutafova-Yambolieva, Violeta Nikolova *pharmacologist*
Nabrit, Samuel Milton *retired embryologist*
Napodano, Rudolph Joseph *internist, medical educator*
Needleman, Philip *cardiologist, pharmacologist*
Nelson, William Rankin *surgeon, educator*
Nicholas, Peter *medical educator*
Nissenbaum, Gerald *physician, educator*
Noda, Mitsuhiko *diabetologist, medical educator*
Nora, James Jackson *physician, author, educator*
Novack, Alvin John *physician*
Oates, Joyce Marie *psychiatrist*
Olds, Jacqueline *psychiatrist, educator*
O'Leary, Denis Joseph *retired physician, insurance company executive*
O'Leary, Dennis Sophian *medical organization executive*
Ornston, Darius Gray, Jr. *psychiatrist*
Packard, John Mallory *physician*
Paine, Robert Edward, Jr. *internist*
Palmer, Raymond A. *administrator, librarian*
Parker, Brent Mershon *retired medical educator, internist, cardiologist*
Parrish, Matthew Denwood *psychiatrist*
Parsons, Harry Glenwood *retired surgeon*
Patterson, James Willis *pathology and dermatology educator*
Paul, Frank Allen *physician*
Pauly, John Edward *anatomist*
Peete, William Pettway Jones *surgeon*
Peixoto, Jose Ulysses *internist, researcher*
Peterson, Ann Sullivan *physician, health care consultant*
Pick, Robert Yehuda *orthopedic surgeon, consultant*
Pomeroy, Kent Lytle *physical medicine and rehabilitation physician*
Potts, Douglas Gordon *neuroradiologist*
Powell, Clinton Cobb *radiologist, physician, former university administrator*
Prange, Hilmar Walter *neurology educator*
Pritz, Michael Burton *neurological surgeon*
Prusiner, Stanley Ben *neurology and biochemistry educator, researcher*
Quetglas, Moll Juan *plastic and maxillofacial surgeon*
Ragucci, John Albert *family practice physician*
Raichle, Marcus Edward *radiology, neurology educator*
Ramos, Eleanor Lacson *transplant nephrologist*
Randolph, Judson Graves *pediatric surgeon*
Renson, Jean Felix *psychiatry educator*
Richmond, Julius Benjamin *retired physician, health policy educator emeritus*
Riker, Walter F., Jr. *pharmacologist, physician*
Rimpila, Charles Robert *physician*
Robinson, David Adair *neurophysiologist*
Rodgers, Lawrence Rodney *physician, educator*
Roehrig, C(harles) Burns *internist, health policy consultant, editor*
Rollins, Arlen Jeffery *osteopathic physician*
Rosemberg, Eugenia *physician, educator, medical research administrator*
Rosenblum, Mindy Fleischer *pediatrician*
Rosenow, John Henry *surgeon, educator*
Rubnitz, Myron Ethan *pathologist, educator*
Rui, Hallgeir *cancer researcher*
Ruoho, Arnold Eino *pharmacology educator*
Russo, Jose *pathologist*
Rutecki, Gregory William *physician, educator*
Sacha, Robert Frank *osteopathic physician*
St. Cyr, John Albert, II *cardiovascular and thoracic surgeon*
Sandt, John Joseph *psychiatrist, educator*
Saneto, Russell Patrick *pediatrician, neurobiologist*
Sanfelippo, Peter Michael *cardiac, thoracic and vascular surgeon*

Saravolatz, Louis Donald *epidemiologist, physician educator*
Sargent, William Winston *anesthesiologist*
Schauf, Victoria *pediatrician, educator, infectious diseases consultant*
Schecter, William Palmer *surgeon*
Schell, Catherine Louise *family practice physician*
Schiavi, Raul Constante *psychiatrist, educator, researcher*
Schmid, Lynette Sue *child and adolescent psychiatrist*
Schneck, Stuart Austin *retired neurologist, educator*
Sekitani, Toru *otolaryngologist, educator*
Sever, John Louis *medical researcher and educator*
Shaw, Ronald Ahrend *physician, educator*
Sher, Paul Phillip *physician, pathologist*
Sherman, John Foord *biomedical consultant*
Sherman, Joseph Owen *pediatric surgeon*
Shils, Maurice Edward *physician, educator*
Shumacker, Harris B., Jr. *surgeon, educator, author*
Sifontes, Jose E. *pediatrics educator*
Silberberg, Inga *dermatologist*
Silva, Omega Logan *physician*
Silverberg, Stuart Owen *obstetrician, gynecologist*
Silverstein, Martin Elliot *surgeon, author, consultant*
Simone, Regina *family practice physician*
†Skolnick, Lawrence *neonatologist, medical administrator*
Smith, Gregory Scott *medical researcher, educator*
Smith, Jonathan David *medical educator*
Smith, Martin Henry *pediatrician*
Smith, Martin Lane *biomedical researcher*
Soyke, Jennifer Mae *emergency and family physician*
Spinner, Robert Jay *orthopedic surgeon*
Steiner, Michael Louis *pediatrician*
Stephenson, Bette Mildred *physician, former Canadian legislator*
Stickler, Gunnar Brynolf *pediatrician*
Stoken, Jacqueline Marie *physician*
Stollerman, Gene Howard *physician, educator*
Stone, David Deaderick *physician, educator*
Stone, James Robert *surgeon*
Strain, James Ellsworth *pediatrician, retired association administrator*
Stringham, Renée *physician*
Sultana, Najma *psychiatrist*
Surbone, Antonella *medical oncologist, bioethics researcher*
Svensson, Lars Georg *cardiovascular and thoracic surgeon*
Swick, Herbert Morris *medical educator, neurologist*
Tagiuri, Consuelo Keller *child psychiatrist, educator*
Takasaki, Etsuji *urology educator*
Tan, Veronica Y. *psychiatrist*
Terris, Susan *physician, cardiologist*
Thorsen, Marie Kristin *radiologist, educator*
Threefoot, Sam Abraham *physician, educator*
Todd, James Stiles *surgeon, professional association executive*
Toledo-Pereyra, Luis Horacio *transplant surgeon, researcher, historian educator*
Toy, Pearl Tak-Chu Yau *transfusion medicine physician*
Troost, Bradley Todd *neurologist, educator*
Turk, Richard Errington *retired psychiatrist*
Turner, William Joseph *retired psychiatrist*
Turrill, Fred Lovejoy *surgeon*
Unger, Albert Howard *allergist, immunologist*
Valentine, William Newton *physician, educator*
Van Brunt, Edmund Ewing *physician*
Vittetoe, Marie Clare *retired clinical laboratory science educator*
Walenga, Jeanine Marie *medical educator, researcher*
Warfel, John Hiatt *medical educator, retired*
Watring, Watson Glenn *gynecologic oncologist, educator*
Wechsler, Arnold *osteopathic obstetrician, gynecologist*
Weiss, Robert M. *urologist, educator*
Wenzel, Richard Putnam *internist*
Wessel, Morris Arthur *pediatrics educator*
West, Gregory Alan *physician*
Westmoreland, Barbara Fenn *neurologist, electroencephalographer, educator*
White, Augustus Aaron, III *orthopedic surgeon*
White, Kerr Lachlan *retired physician, foundation director*
Whitley, Nancy O'Neil *retired radiology educator*
Williams, Henry Stratton *radiologist, educator*
Williams, Robert Leon *psychiatrist, neurologist, educator*
Williams, Roger Stewart *physician*
Williams, Ronald Lee *pharmacologist*
Williams, Thomas Lloyd *psychiatrist*
Wilmore, Douglas Wayne *physician, surgeon*
Wilson, Almon Chapman *surgeon, physician, retired naval officer*
Winter, Harland Steven *pediatric gastroenterologist*
†Wolfgang, Gary L. *orthopaedic surgeon*
Wood, Margaret Gray *dermatologist, educator*
Woodhouse, Derrick Fergus *ophthalmologist*
Worrell, Audrey Martiny *geriatric psychiatrist*
Wyer, Peter Charles *emergency physician*
Wyngaarden, James Barnes *physician*
Yamane, George Mitsuyoshi *oral diagnosis and radiology educator*
Yielding, K. Lemone *physician*
Yodaiken, Ralph E. *pathologist, occupational medicine physician*
Yollick, Bernard Lawrence *otolaryngologic surgeon*
Zacks, Sumner Irwin *pathologist*
Zukin, Paul *retired health research educator*
Zwislocki, Jozef John *neuroscience educator, researcher*

# HUMANITIES: LIBERAL STUDIES

## UNITED STATES

### ALABAMA

**Auburn**
Amacher, Richard Earl *literature educator*
Andelson, Robert Vernon *social philosopher, educator*
Lewis, Walter David *historian*
Littleton, Taylor Dowe *humanities educator*

**Birmingham**
Allen, Lee Norcross *historian, educator*
Benditt, Theodore Matthew *humanities educator*

Hamilton, Virginia Van der Veer *historian, educator*
Irons, George Vernon *history educator*
Morton, Marilyn Miller *genealogy and history educator, lecturer, researcher, travel executive, director*

**Huntsville**
Mercieca, Charles *history, philosophy and political science educator*
Robb, David Metheny, Jr. *art historian*
Roberts, Frances Cabaniss *history educator*
White, John Charles *historian*

**Lillian**
Burnette, Ollen Lawrence, Jr. *historian*

**Montgomery**
Cornett, Lloyd Harvey, Jr. *retired historian*
Futrell, Robert Frank *military historian, consultant*
Gribben, Alan *English language educator, research consultant*
Napier, Cameron Mayson Freeman *historic preservationist*
Whitt, Mary F. *reading educator, consultant*

**Tuscaloosa**
Bell, Robert Fred *German language educator*
Hocutt, Max Oliver *philosophy educator*
McDonald, Forrest *historian, educator*
Mills, Gary Bernard *history educator*

### ALASKA

**Fairbanks**
Krauss, Michael Edward *linguist*

**Juneau**
Ruotsala, James Alfred *historian, writer*

### ARIZONA

**Apache Junction**
Bracken, Harry McFarland *philosophy educator*
Ransom, Evelyn Naill *language educator, linguist*

**Flagstaff**
Hallowell, Robert Edward *French language educator*
Marcus, Karen Melissa *foreign language educator*
Poen, Monte M. *history educator, researcher*

**Glendale**
Galletti, Marie Ann *English language and linguistics educator*
Tuman, Walter Vladimir *Russian language educator, researcher*

**Green Valley**
Dmytryshyn, Basil *historian, educator*

**Peoria**
Bergmann, Fredrick Louis *English language educator, theater historian*

**Phoenix**
Land, George A. *philosopher, writer, educator, consultant*
Socwell, Margaret Gertrude Osborn Harris *reading and language arts educator, consultant*

**Prescott**
†Brown, James Isaac *rhetoric educator*
Moses, Elbert Raymond, Jr. *speech and dramatic arts educator*

**Scottsdale**
Donaldson, Scott *English language educator, writer*

**Sun City**
Oppenheimer, Max, Jr. *foreign language educator, consultant*

**Surprise**
Clark, Lloyd *historian, educator*

**Tempe**
Adelson, Roger Dean *history educator, editor, historian*
Brack, O. M., Jr. *English language educator*
Harris, Mark *English educator, author*
Iverson, Peter James *historian, educator*
MacKinnon, Stephen R. *Asian studies administrator, educator*
Ney, James Walter Edward Colby *English language educator*
Rios, Alberto Alvaro *English educator*
Ruiz, Vicki Lynn *history educator*

**Tucson**
Austin, John Norman *classics educator*
Birkinbine, John, II *philatelist*
Briggs, Peter Stromme *art historian, curator*
Dinnerstein, Leonard *historian, educator*
Dufner, Max *retired German language educator*
Herrnstadt, Richard Lawrence *American literature educator*
Kellogg, Frederick *historian, educator*
Langendoen, Donald Terence *linguistics educator*
Milton, Corinne Holm *art history educator*
Rabuck, Donna Fontanarose *English educator*
Tao, Chia-lin Pao *humanities educator*

### ARKANSAS

**Arkadelphia**
Bass, Carol Ann (Mitzi) *English language educator*
Graves, John William *historian*

**Conway**
Kearns, Terrance Brophy *English language educator*

**Fayetteville**
Faulkner, Claude Winston *language professional*
Gatewood, Willard Badgett, Jr. *historian*
Levine, Daniel Blank *classical studies educator*

**Jonesboro**
Elkins, Francis Clark *history educator, university official*

**Little Rock**
Ferguson, John Lewis *state historian*
Williams, C(harles) Fred *history professor*

**Magnolia**
Davis, Elizabeth Hawk *English language educator*

**Monticello**
Babin, Claude Hunter *history educator*

**Mountain Home**
Easley, June Ellen Price *genealogist*

**State University**
Schichler, Robert Lawrence *English language educator*

### CALIFORNIA

**Atherton**
Bales, Royal Eugene *philosophy educator*

**Bakersfield**
Boyd, William Harland *historian*
Kegley, Jacquelyn Ann *philosophy educator*

**Berkeley**
Alter, Robert B. *comparative literature educator and critic*
Anderson, William Scovil *classics educator*
Baas, Jacquelynn *art historian, museum administrator*
Barish, Jonas Alexander *English language educator*
Bouwsma, William James *history educator*
Bronstein, Arthur J. *linguistics educator*
Costa, Gustavo *Italian language educator*
Crews, Frederick Campbell *humanities educator, writer*
Davidson, Donald Herbert *philosophy educator*
Greenblatt, Stephen J. *English language educator*
Herr, Richard *history educator*
Jordan, John Emory *language professional, educator*
Karlinsky, Simon *language educator, author*
Kay, Paul de Young *linguist*
Kerman, Joseph Wilfred *musicologist, critic*
Lichterman, Martin *history educator*
Litwack, Leon Frank *historian, educator*
Long, Anthony Arthur *classics educator*
Mc Cullough, Helen Craig *Oriental languages educator*
Middlekauff, Robert Lawrence *history educator, administrator*
Morton, Eric *liberal arts educator*
Muscatine, Charles *English educator, author*
Rauch, Irmengard *linguist, educator*
Selz, Peter Howard *art historian, educator*
Shannon, Thomas Frederic *German language educator*
Sloane, Thomas O. *speech educator*
Tracy, Robert (Edward) *English language educator, poetry translator*
Wakeman, Frederic Evans, Jr. *historian educator*
Wang, William Shi-Yuan *linguistics educator*
Zwerdling, Alex *English educator*

**Beverly Hills**
Kravitz, Ellen King *musicologist, educator*

**Cambria**
Salaverria, Helena Clara *educator*

**Carmel**
Chung, Kyung Cho *Korean specialist, scholar, educator, author*
McGlynn, Betty Hoag *art historian*

**Chatsworth**
Schneider, Duane Bernard *English literature educator, publisher*

**Chico**
Moore, Brooke Noel *philosophy educator*

**Claremont**
Ackerman, Gerald Martin *art historian, consultant*
Atlas, Jay David *philosopher, consultant, linguist*
Barnes, Richard Gordon *English literature educator, poet*
Burns, Richard Dean *history educator, publisher, author*
Davis, Nathaniel *humanities educator*
Dunbar, John Raine *retired English educator*
Elsbree, Langdon *English language educator*
Goodrich, Norma Lorre (Mrs. John H. Howard) *French and comparative literature educator*
Lofgren, Charles Augustin *legal and constitutional historian, history educator*
Macaulay, Ronald Kerr Steven *linguistics educator, former college dean*
McKirahan, Richard Duncan, Jr. *classics and philosophy educator*
Moss, Myra Ellen (Myra Moss Rolle) *philosophy educator*
Neumann, Harry *philosophy educator*
Pinney, Thomas Clive *English language educator*
Post, Gaines, Jr. *history educator, dean, administrator*
Roth, John King *philosopher, educator*
Sellery, J'nan Morse *English, Canadian and American literature educator*
Smith, Steven Albert *philosophy educator*
Sontag, Frederick Earl *philosophy educator*
Young, Howard Thomas *foreign language educator*

**Culver City**
Clodius, Albert Howard *history educator*

**Cupertino**
Dunbar, Maurice Victor *English language educator*

**Davis**
Hayden, John Olin *English literature educator, author*
Hays, Peter L. *English language and literature educator*
Hoffman, Michael Jerome *humanities educator*

Jackson, William Turrentine *history educator*
Manoliu, Maria *linguist*
Rothstein, Morton *historian, retired educator*
Waddington, Raymond Bruce, Jr. *English language educator*
Williamson, Alan Bacher *English literature educator, poet, writer*
Willis, Frank Roy *history educator*
Woodress, James Leslie, Jr. *English language educator*

### El Cerrito
Kuo, Ping-chia *historian, educator*

### Fallbrook
Burns, Louis Francis *retired history educator*

### Flintridge
Dales, Richard Clark *history educator*

### Fresno
Genini, Ronald Walter *history educator, historian*
Kouymjian, Dickran *art historian, Orientalist, educator*

### Gualala
Gaustad, Edwin Scott *historian*

### Hayward
Mayers, Eugene David *philosopher, educator*

### Imperial
Montenegro, Jean Baker *English language educator*

### Irvine
Clark, Michael Phillip *English educator*
Hine, Robert Van Norden, Jr. *historian, educator*
Key, Mary Ritchie (Mrs. Audley E. Patton) *linguist, author, educator*
Kluger, Ruth *German language educator, editor*
Krieger, Murray *English language educator, author*
Lee, Meredith *German literature and language educator*
Lehnert, Herbert Hermann *foreign language educator*
Lillyman, William John *German language educator*
Maddy, Penelope Jo *philosopher*
Mc Culloch, Samuel Clyde *history educator*
Sutton, Dana Ferrin *classics educator*
Wiener, Jon *history educator*

### Kensington
Malkiel, Yakov *linguistics educator*

### Kingsburg
Garrigus, Charles Byford *retired literature educator*

### La Jolla
Bernstein, Michael Alan *history educator, department chairman*
Langacker, Ronald Wayne *linguistics educator*
McDonald, Marianne *classicist*
Newmark, Leonard Daniel *linguistics educator*
Olafson, Frederick Arlan *philosophy educator*
Wesling, Donald Truman *English literature educator*
Wright, Andrew *English literature educator*

### Laguna Beach
Calderwood, James Lee *former English literature educator, writer*

### Long Beach
Beebe, Sandra E. *retired English language educator, artist, writer*
Tang, Paul Chi Lung *philosophy educator*

### Los Angeles
Alkon, Paul Kent *English language educator*
Allen, Michael John Bridgman *English educator*
Alpers, Edward Alter *history educator*
Amneus, D. A. *English language educator*
Andersen, Henning *linguistics educator*
Appleby, Joyce Oldham *historian*
Bahr, Ehrhard *Germanic languages and literature educator*
Bauml, Franz Heinrich *German language educator*
Birnbaum, Henrik *Slavic languages and literature educator*
Boime, Albert Isaac *art history educator*
Bradshaw, Murray Charles *musicologist*
Burns, Robert Ignatius *historian, educator, clergyman*
Cherkin, Adina *interpreter, translator*
Cohen, S(tephen) Marshall *philosophy educator*
Cortinez, Veronica *literature educator*
Darby, Joanne Tyndale (Jaye Darby) *arts and humanities educator*
Davidson, Herbert Alan *Near Eastern languages and cultures educator*
Dearing, Vinton Adams *retired English language educator*
De Jong-Hawley, Cherie *reading and language arts educator*
Dyck, Andrew Roy *philologist, educator*
Fromkin, Victoria Alexandra *linguist, phonetician, educator*
Fry, Michael Graham *historian, educator*
Geary, Patrick Joseph *history educator*
Göllner, Marie Louise *musicologist, educator*
Greene, Donald Johnson *retired English language educator, author*
Hadda, Janet Ruth *Yiddish language educator, lay psychoanalyst*
Hospers, John *philosophy educator*
Hovannisian, Richard G. *Armenian and Near East history educator*
Hundley, Norris Cecil, Jr. *history educator*
Jorgensen, Paul Alfred *English language educator emeritus*
Kelly, Henry Ansgar *English language educator*
Kolve, V. A. *English literature educator*
Laird, David *humanities educator emeritus*
Lehan, Richard D'Aubin *English language educator, writer*
Levine, Philip *classics educator*
Löfstedt, Bengt Torkel Magnus *classics educator*
Mellor, Ronald John *history educator*
Miles, Richard Robert *art historian, writer*
Nakanishi, Don Toshiaki *Asian American studies educator, writer*
Nunis, Doyce Blackman, Jr. *historian, educator*
Rabinovitz, Jason *film and television consultant*
Rathbun, John Wilbert *American studies educator*
Rogger, Hans Jack *history educator*
Rouse, Richard Hunter *historian, educator*
Schaefer, William David *English language educator*
Schipper, Merle *art historian and critic, exhibition curator*
Schutz, John Adolph *historian, educator, former university dean*
Schwartz, Leon *foreign language educator*
See, Carolyn *English language educator, novelist, book critic*
Shideler, Ross Patrick *foreign language and comparative literature educator, author, translator, poet*
Stockwell, Robert Paul *linguist, educator*
Tennyson, G(eorg) B(ernhard) *English educator*
Toulmin, Stephen Edelston *humanities educator*
Wills, John Elliot, Jr. *history educator, writer*
Winterowd, Walter Ross *English educator*
Wortham, Thomas Richard *English language educator*

### Los Gatos
Tinsley, Barbara Sher *historian, educator, writer*

### Menlo Park
Craig, Gordon Alexander *historian, educator*

### Montclair
Haage, Robert Mitchell *retired history educator, organization leader*

### Montecito
Atkins, Stuart (Pratt) *German language and literature educator*
Rose, Mark Allen *humanities educator*

### Monterey
Kennedy-Minott, Rodney *international relations educator, former ambassador*
Peet, Phyllis Irene *women's studies educator*

### Newport Beach
Brown, Giles Tyler *history educator, lecturer*

### Northridge
Chen, Joseph Tao *historian, educator*
Flores, William Vincent *Latin American studies educator*

### Orange
Yeager, Myron Dean *English language educator, business writing consultant*

### Oxnard
Cathcart, Linda *art historian*
Hill, Alice Lorraine *history, genealogy and social researcher, educator*

### Pacific Grove
Elinson, Henry David *artist, language educator*
Voss, Ali Annelies *history of art educator, antique dealer*

### Pacific Palisades
Garwood, Victor Paul *retired speech communication educator*
Georges, Robert Augustus *emeritus professor, researcher, writer*
Nash, Gary Baring *historian, educator*

### Palo Alto
Buss, Claude Albert *history educator*
Dallin, Alexander *history and political science educator*
Knoles, George Harmon *history educator*
Mommsen, Katharina *retired German language and literature educator*
Walker, Carolyn Peyton *English language educator*

### Palos Verdes Peninsula
Thomas, Pearl Elizabeth *English educator*

### Pasadena
Elliot, David Clephan *historian, educator*
Fay, Peter Ward *history educator*
Kevles, Daniel Jerome *history educator, writer*
Kousser, J(oseph) Morgan *history educator*
Mandel, Oscar *literature educator, writer*
Searle, Eleanor Millard *history educator*

### Piedmont
Putter, Irving *French language educator*

### Pleasant Hill
Ashby, Denise Stewart *speech educator, communication consultant*

### Pleasanton
Anderson-Imbert, Enrique *retired Hispanic literature educator, author*

### Rancho Santa Fe
Ruiz, Ramon Eduardo *history educator*

### Riverside
Elliott, Emory Bernard *English language educator, educational adminstrator*
Fagundo, Ana Maria *creative writing and Spanish literature educator*
Ross, Delmer Gerrard *historian, educator*
Snyder, Henry Leonard *history educator, bibliographer*

### Sacramento
Meindl, Robert James *English language educator*
Nesbitt, Paul Edward *historian, author, educator*
Reed, Nancy Boyd *English language and elementary education educator*
Schmitz, Dennis Mathew *English language educator*

### San Diego
Brandes, Raymond Stewart *history educator*
Coox, Alvin David *history educator*
Daley, Arthur Stuart *retired humanities educator*
Feinberg, Leonard *English language educator*
Vanderbilt, Kermit *English language educator*
Velasquez, Ana Maria *languages educator*

### San Francisco
Cherny, Robert Wallace *history educator*
Costa-Zalessow, Natalia *foreign language educator*
Gregory, Michael Strietmann *English literature and science educator, editor*
Henderson, Horace Edward *World War II historian, peace activist*
Needleman, Jacob *philosophy educator, writer*
Satin, Joseph *language professional, university administrator*
Wilczek, John Franklin *history educator*

### San Jose
Hodgson, Peter John *music educator, musician*

### San Luis Obispo
Riedlsperger, Max Ernst *history educator*

### San Marcos
Christman, Albert Bernard *historian*

### San Marino
Karlstrom, Paul Johnson *art historian*
Ridge, Martin *historian, educator*
Rolle, Andrew F. *historian, educator, author*
Steadman, John Marcellus, III *English educator*
Zall, Paul Maxwell *retired English language educator, consultant*

### San Rafael
Eekman, Thomas Adam *Slavic languages educator*

### Santa Barbara
Brownlee, Wilson Elliot, Jr. *history educator*
Chafe, Wallace LeSeur *linguist, educator*
Collins, Robert Oakley *history educator*
Crawford, Donald Wesley *philosophy educator, university official*
Dauer, Francis Watanabe *philosophy educator*
Del Chiaro, Mario Aldo *art historian, archeologist, etruscologist, educator*
Fingarette, Herbert *philosopher, educator*
Fleming, Brice Noel *retired philosophy educator*
Gunn, Giles Buckingham *English educator, religion educator*
Helgerson, Richard *English literature educator*
Hollister, Charles Warren *history educator, author*
Hsu, Immanuel Chung Yueh *history educator*
Martinez-López, Enrique *Spanish educator*
McGee, James Sears *historian*
Moir, Alfred Kummer *art history educator*
Renehan, Robert Francis Xavier *Greek and Latin educator*
Russell, Jeffrey Burton *historian, educator*
Wilkins, Burleigh Taylor *philosophy educator*
Zimmerman, Everett Lee *English educator, academic administrator*

### Santa Clara
Meier, Matthias S(ebastian) *historian*

### Santa Cruz
Ellis, John Martin *German literature educator*
Lieberman, Fredric *ethnomusicologist, educator*
Stevens, Stanley David *local history researcher, retired librarian*
Suckiel, Ellen Kappy *philosophy educator*

### Santa Monica
Heimann-Hast, Sybil Dorothea *language arts and literature educator*

### Santa Rosa
Aman, Reinhold Albert *philologist, publisher*

### Stanford
Baker, Keith Michael *history educator*
Carnochan, Walter Bliss *retired English educator*
Degler, Carl Neumann *history educator*
Dekker, George Gilbert *literature educator, literary scholar, writer*
Dunlop, John Barrett *foreign language educator, research institution scholar*
Duus, Peter *history educator*
Eitner, Lorenz Edwin Alfred *art historian, educator*
Fehrenbacher, Don Edward *retired history educator*
Frank, Joseph Nathaniel *comparative literature educator*
Fredrickson, George Marsh *history educator*
Gelpi, Albert Joseph *English educator, literary critic*
Gelpi, Barbara Charlesworth *English literature and women's studies educator*
Giraud, Raymond Dorner *retired language professional*
Guerard, Albert Joseph *retired modern literature educator, author*
Johnson, John J. *historian, educator*
Kennedy, David Michael *historian, educator*
L'Heureux, John Clarke *English language educator*
Loftis, John (Clyde), Jr. *English language educator*
Lohnes, Walter F. W. *German language and literature educator*
Middlebrook, Diane Wood *English language educator*
Moravcsik, Julius Matthew *philosophy educator*
Newman-Gordon, Pauline *French language and literature educator*
Nivison, David Shepherd *Chinese and philosophy educator*
Perloff, Marjorie Gabrielle *English and comparative literature educator*
Perry, John Richard *philosophy educator*
Robinson, Paul Arnold *historian, educator, author*
Sheehan, James John *historian, educator*
Sorrentino, Gilbert *English language educator, novelist, poet*
Spitz, Lewis William *historian, educator*
Stansky, Peter David Lyman *historian*
Traugott, Elizabeth Closs *linguistics educator and researcher*

### Stockton
Limbaugh, Ronald Hadley *history educator, history center director*

### Van Nuys
Zucker, Alfred John *English educator, academic administrator*

### Walnut
Lane, David Christopher *humanities educator, author, researcher*

### Walnut Creek
Bardy, Sharon Davis *language educator*

### Wilmington
Smith, June Burlingame *English educator*

### Woodland Hills
Pickard, Dean *philosophy and humanities educator*

### Yorba Linda
Keating, Norma Storrs *professional genealogist, small business owner*

## COLORADO

### Aurora
Johnson, Geraldine Esch *language specialist*

### Boulder
Frey, Julia Bloch *French language educator*
Gonzalez-del-Valle, Luis Tomas *Spanish language educator*
Hawkins, David *philosophy and history of science, educator*
Hill, Boyd H., Jr. *medieval history educator*
Limerick, Patricia Nelson *history educator*
Main, Jackson Turner *history educator*
Rood, David S. *linguistics educator*
Taylor, Allan Ross *linguist, educator*

### Colorado Springs
Cramer, Owen Carver *classics educator*
Hallenbeck, Kenneth Luster *numismatist*
Stavig, Mark Luther *English language educator*
Watkins, Lois Irene *English educator*

### Denver
Breck, Allen du Pont *historian, educator*
Pfnister, Allan Orel *humanities educator*
Storey, Brit Allan *historian*
Wetzel, Jodi (Joy Lynn Wetzel) *history and women's studies educator*

### Dolores
Kreyche, Gerald Francis *retired philosophy educator*

### Englewood
Bardsley, Kay *historian, archivist, dance professional*
Bonnet, Beatriz Alicia *interpreter, translator, flutist*

### Fort Collins
Gilderhus, Mark Theodore *historian, educator*
Kennedy, George Alexander *classicist, educator*
Rock, Kenneth Willett *history educator*
Rollin, Bernard Elliot *philosophy educator, consultant on animal ethics*

### Glenwood Springs
Walker, Robert Harris *historian, author, editor*

### Golden
Eckley, Wilton Earl, Jr. *humanities educator*
Pegis, Anton George *English educator*
Sneed, Joseph Donald *philosophy educator, author*

### Greeley
Worley, Lloyd Douglas *English language educator*

### Gunnison
Myers, Rex Charles *history educator, retired college dean*

### Lakewood
Joy, Carla Marie *history educator*
Woodruff, Kathryn Elaine *English educator*

### Littleton
Champney, Linda Lucas *reading educator*
Elrick, Billy Lee *English language educator*

### Pueblo
Farwell, Hermon Waldo, Jr. *parliamentarian, educator, former speech communication educator*

## CONNECTICUT

### Bridgeport
Allen, Richard Stanley (Dick Allen) *English language educator, author*

### Brooklyn
Meigs, Joseph Carl, Jr. *retired English language educator*

### Colebrook
Mc Neill, William Hardy *retired history educator, writer*

### Danbury
Edelstein, David Simeon *historian, educator*
Toland, John Willard *historian, writer*

### Deep River
Hieatt, Allen Kent *language professional, educator*
Hieatt, Constance Bartlett *English language educator*

### East Granby
Scanlon, Lawrence Eugene *English language educator*

### Fairfield
Newton, Lisa Haenlein *philosophy educator*

### Guilford
Whitaker, Thomas Russell *English literature educator*

### Hamden
Gay, Peter *history educator, author*
McClellan, Edwin *Japanese literature educator*
Pelikan, Jaroslav Jan *history educator*
Rosenthal, Franz *language educator*
Woodward, C. Vann *historian*

### Hartford
Chiarenza, Frank John *English language educator*
Decker, Robert Owen *history educator, clergyman*

Mahoney, Michael Robert Taylor *art historian, educator*

### Ivoryton
Osborne, John Walter *historian, educator, author*

### Middletown
Arnold, Herbert Anton *German language educator*
Briggs, Morton Winfield *Romance language educator*
Buel, Richard Van Wyck, Jr. *history educator, writer, editor*
Gillmor, Charles Stewart *history and science educator, researcher*
Gourevitch, Victor *philosophy educator*
Meyer, Priscilla Ann *Russian language and literature educator*
Pomper, Philip *history educator*
Reed, Joseph Wayne *American studies educator, artist*
Rose, Phyllis *English language professional, author*
Shapiro, Norman Richard *Romance languages and literatures educator*
Slotkin, Richard Sidney *American studies educator, writer*
Wensinger, Arthur Stevens *language and literature educator, author*
Winston, Krishna Ricarda *foreign language professional*

### New Britain
Emeagwali, Gloria Thomas *humanities educator*
Gallo, Donald Robert *English educator*

### New Haven
Alexandrov, Vladimir Eugene *Russian literature educator*
Andreopoulos, George J. *history educator, lawyer, political science educator*
Bers, Victor *classics educator*
Bloom, Harold *humanities educator*
Blum, John Morton *historian*
Borroff, Marie *English language educator*
Brooks, Peter (Preston) *French and comparative literature educator, writer*
Davis, David Brion *historian, educator*
Demos, John Putnam *history educator, writer, consultant*
Dupré, Louis *philosopher, educator*
Erlich, Victor *Slavic languages educator*
Gaddis, John Lewis *history educator*
Gilbert, Creighton Eddy *art historian*
Glier, Ingeborg Johanna *German language and literature educator*
Górniak-Kocikowska, Krystyna Stefania *philosopher, educator*
Greene, Liliane *French educator, editor*
Greene, Thomas McLernon *language professional, educator*
Hallo, William Wolfgang *Assyriologist*
Harries, Karsten *philosophy educator, researcher*
Hartman, Geoffrey H. *language professional, educator*
Hersey, George Leonard *art history educator*
Hollander, John *humanities educator, poet*
Holmes, Frederic Lawrence *science historian*
Holquist, James Michael *Russian and comparative literature educator*
Hyman, Paula E(llen) *history educator*
Insler, Stanley *philologist, educator*
Kagan, Donald *historian, educator*
Kennedy, Paul Michael *history educator*
Kleiner, Diana Elizabeth Edelman *art history educator, administrator*
Lord, George deForest *English educator*
MacMullen, Ramsay *retired history educator*
Martz, Louis Lohr *English literature educator*
Outka, Gene Harold *philosophy and Christian ethics educator*
Palisca, Claude Victor *musicologist, educator*
Peterson, Linda H. *English language and literature educator*
Pollitt, Jerome Jordan *art history educator*
Prown, Jules David *art historian educator*
Rawson, Claude Julien *English educator*
Robinson, Fred Colson *English language educator*
Sammons, Jeffrey Leonard *foreign language educator*
Schenker, Alexander Marian *Slavic linguistics educator*
Smith, John Edwin *philosophy educator*
Spence, Jonathan Dermot *historian, educator*
Totman, Conrad Davis *history educator*
Turner, Frank Miller *historian, educator*
Underdown, David Edward *historian, educator*
van Altena, Alicia Mora *language educator*
Wandycz, Piotr Stefan *history educator*
Winks, Robin William *history educator*
Yeazell, Ruth Bernard *English language educator*

### New London
Mulvey, Helen Frances *retired history educator*
Rice, Argyll Pryor *Hispanic studies and Spanish language educator*
Taranow, Gerda *English language educator, researcher, author*

### North Haven
Culler, Arthur Dwight *English language educator*

### Old Greenwich
Baritz, Loren *history educator*

### Ridgefield
Norman, Richard Arthur *humanities educator*

### Storrs Mansfield
Abramson, Arthur Seymour *linguistics educator, researcher*
Charters, Ann *biographer, editor, educator*
Coons, Ronald Edward *historian, educator*
Greene, John Colton *retired history educator*
Reed, Howard Alexander *historian, educator*
Rosen, William *English language educator*
Shaffer, Jerome Arthur *philosophy educator*

### Washington
Leab, Daniel Joseph *history educator*

### Waterbury
Meyer, Judith Chandler Pugh *history educator*

### Willimantic
Philips, David Evan *English language educator*

### Windsor
Auten, Arthur Herbert *history educator*

### Woodbridge
Ecklund, Constance Cryer *French language educator*

## DELAWARE

### Dover
Angstadt, F. V. *language arts and theatre arts educator*

### Newark
Allmendinger, David Frederick, Jr. *history educator*
Day, Robert Androus *English language educator, former library director, editor, publisher*
Halio, Jay Leon *language professional, educator*
Homer, William Innes *art history educator, art expert, author*
McLaren, James Clark *French educator*
Roselle, David Paul *university president, mathematics educator*
Steiner, Roger Jacob *linguistics educator, author, researcher*
Tolles, Bryant Franklin, Jr. *history and art history educator*
Valbuena-Briones, Angel Julian *language educator, author*
Venezky, Richard Lawrence *English educator*
Wolters, Raymond *historian, educator*

### Wilmington
Kneavel, Ann Callanan *humanities educator, communications consultant*
Lahvis, Sylvia Leistyna *art historian, educator, curator*

## DISTRICT OF COLUMBIA

### Fort Mcnair
Marr, Phebe Ann *historian, educator*

### Washington
Ashkenazi, Elliott Uriel *historian, lawyer*
†Bader, William Banks *historian, foundation executive, former corporate executive*
Beauchamp, Tom L. *philosophy educator*
Bedini, Silvio A. *historian, author*
Bennett, Betty T. *English language educator, university dean, writer*
Billington, James Hadley *historian, librarian*
Bloomfield, Maxwell Herron, III *history and law educator*
Boorstin, Daniel Joseph *historian, lecturer, educator, author, editor*
Bowen, Margareta Maria *interpretation and translation educator*
Broun, Elizabeth *art historian, museum administrator*
Burgan, Mary Alice *English language educator*
Cafritz, Robert Conrad *art historian, critic, consultant*
Caws, Peter James *philosopher, educator*
Cheney, Lynne V. *humanities educator, writer*
Cook, Walter Anthony *linguist, educator*
Craig, Peter Stebbins *historian*
Cua, Antonio S. *philosophy educator*
Dallek, Robert *history educator*
Davidson, Dan Eugene *Russian educator and scholar, administrator*
De Pauw, Linda Grant *history educator, publisher*
Durfee, Harold Allen *philosophy educator*
Farr, Judith Banzer *writer, literature educator*
Fern, Alan Maxwell *art historian, museum director*
Fink, Lois Marie *art historian*
Goode, James Moore *historian*
Hallion, Richard Paul *aerospace historian, museum consultant*
Hamarneh, Sami Khalaf *historian of pharmacy, medicine and science, author*
Hammond, Deanna Lindberg *linguist*
Heelan, Patrick Aidan *philosophy educator*
†Howland, Richard Hubbard *architectural historian*
Irizarry, Estelle Diane *foreign language educator, author, editor*
Kennedy, Robert Emmet, Jr. *history educator*
Kreidler, Charles W(illiam) *linguist, educator*
Kreinheder, Hazel Fuller *genealogist, historian*
Laiou, Angeliki Evangelos *history educator*
Langan, John Patrick *philosophy educator*
Laqueur, Walter *history educator*
Lewis, Douglas *art historian*
Lichtman, Allan Jay *historian, educator, consultant*
Menard, Edith *English language educator, artist, poet, actress*
Miles, Ellen Gross *art historian, museum curator*
Miller, Jeanne-Marie Anderson (Mrs. Nathan J. Miller) *English language educator, academic administrator*
Minnich, Nelson Hubert Joseph *historian, educator*
Morse, Richard McGee *historian*
Myers, Robert Manson *English educator, author*
Park, Alice Mary Crandall *genealogist*
Pinkett, Harold Thomas *archivist, historian*
Raaflaub, Kurt Arnold *classics educator*
Rand, Harry Zvi *art historian, poet*
Reed, Berenice Anne *art historian, artist, government official*
Reingold, Nathan *historian*
Robb, James Willis *Romance languages educator*
Roberts, Jeanne Addison *literature educator*
Rosenblatt, Jason Philip *English language educator*
Schlagel, Richard H. *philosophy educator*
Schwartz, Richard Brenton *English language educator, university dean, writer*
Scott, Gary Thomas *historian*
Severino, Roberto *foreign language educator, academic administration executive*
Simko, Jan *English and foreign language literature educator*
Smith, Bruce R. *English language educator*
Snowden, Frank Martin, Jr. *classics educator*
Taylor, Estelle Wormley *English educator, college dean*
Taylor, Henry Splawn *literature educator, poet, writer*
Thompson, Wayne Wray *historian*
Van Cleve, John Vickrey *history educator, university official*
Vaslef, Irene *historian, librarian*
Veatch, Robert Marlin *philosophy educator, medical ethics researcher*
Ver Eecke, Wilfried Camiel *philosopher, educator*
Voll, John Obert *history educator*
Washburn, Wilcomb Edward *historian, educator*
Webb, Robert Kiefer *history educator*
Weiss, Paul *philosopher, educator*
Wheelock, Arthur Kingsland, Jr. *art historian*
Wippel, John Francis *philosophy educator*

## FLORIDA

### Beverly Hills
Larsen, Erik *art history educator*

### Boca Raton
Collins, Robert Arnold *English language educator*

### Bonita Springs
Payne, Alma Jeanette *English language educator, author*

### Bradenton
Lengyel, Alfonz *art history, archeology and museology educator*

### Coral Gables
Chabrow, Sheila Sue *English language educator*
Kirsner, Robert *language educator*
Lemos, Ramon Marcelino *philosophy educator*
McCarthy, Patrick A. *English language educator*
Speiller-Morris, Joyce *English composition educator*

### Daytona Beach
Carmona, José Antonio *Spanish language educator, English language educator*
Osterholm, J(ohn) Roger *humanities educator*

### Deland
García, Mary Elizabeth *Spanish and English as second language educator*

### Dunedin
Espy, Charles Clifford *English language educator, author, consultant, lecturer, administrator*

### Englewood
Marchand, Leslie Alexis *language educator, writer*

### Fort Lauderdale
Van Alstyne, Judith Sturges *English language educator, writer*

### Fort Myers
Brown, Earl Kent *historian, clergyman*
Fernandez, Laura Bove *retired language educator*

### Fort Pierce
Bynum, Henri Sue *education and French educator*

### Gainesville
Abbott, Thomas Benjamin *speech educator*
Brown, William Samuel, Jr. *communication processes and disorders educator*
Der-Houssikian, Haig *linguistics educator*
Emch-Dériaz, Antoinette Suzanne *historian, educator*
Goldhurst, William *retired humanities and English educator, writer*
Haring, Ellen Stone (Mrs. E. S. Haring) *philosophy educator*
Kushner, David Zakeri *musicologist, educator*
Proctor, Samuel *history educator*
Schmeling, Gareth *classics educator*
Stephan, Alexander F. *German language and literature educator*
Wyatt-Brown, Bertram *historian, educator*

### Green Cove Springs
Norton, Joan Jennings *English language educator*

### Highland Beach
Stimson, Frederick Sparks *Hispanist, educator*

### Hillsboro Beach
McGarry, Carmen Racine *historian, artist*

### Homestead
Reeder, Cecelia Painter *English educator*

### Jacksonville
Joos, Olga Martín-Ballestero de *language educator*
Lloyd, Jacqueline *English language educator*
Stanton, Robert John, Jr. *English language educator*

### Key Biscayne
Markell, Alan William *linguistic company executive*

### Lakeland
Fadley, Ann Miller *English language and literature educator, writer*
Peeler, Scott Loomis, Jr. *foreign language educator*

### Leesburg
Fletcher, Mary H. *English language educator*
Gaeng, Paul Ami *foreign language educator*

### Maitland
Nash, Ronald Herman *philosophy educator*

### Marathon
Mc Cormick, Edward Allen *foreign language educator*
Wiecha, Joseph Augustine *linguist, educator*

### Melbourne
Jones, Elaine Hancock *humanities educator*

### Miami
Johnson-Cousin, Danielle *French literature educator*
Jones y Diez Arguelles, Gastón Roberto *language educator*
Leeder, Ellen Lismore *language and literature educator, literary critic*
Mendez, Jesus *history educator, education administrator*
Schwartz, Kessel *modern language educator*

### Mount Dora
Laux, James Michael *historian, educator*

### Naples
Griffin, Linda Louise *English language and speech educator*
Waller, George Macgregor *historian, educator*

### New Port Richey
McCabe, Sharon *humanities and art educator*

### New Smyrna
Little, W(illia)m A(lfred) *foreign language educator, researcher*

### Oldsmar
Thompson, Mack Eugene *history educator*

### Palm Beach
Artinian, Artine *French literature scholar, collector*

### Pensacola
Maddock, Lawrence Hill *language educator, writer*

### Port Saint Lucie
Wedzicha, Walter *foreign language educator*

### Saint Augustine
Adams, William Roger *historian*

### Saint Petersburg
Davis, Ann Caldwell *history educator*
Sherburne, Donald Wynne *philosopher, educator*
Walker, Brigitte Maria *translator, linguistic consultant*

### Sarasota
Ebitz, David MacKinnon *art historian, museum director*
Hoover, Dwight Wesley *history educator*
Noether, Emiliana Pasca *historian, educator*

### Tallahassee
Bartlett, Richard Adams *American historian, educator*
Beck, Earl Ray *historian, educator*
Burroway, Janet G. *English language educator, novelist*
Davis, Bertram Hylton *retired English educator*
Dillingham, Marjorie Carter *foreign language educator*
Dorn, Charles Meeker *art education educator*
Frechette, Ernest Albert *foreign language educator emeritus*
Golden, Leon *classicist, educator*
Harper, George Mills *English language educator*
Hunt, Mary Alice *library science educator*
Kaelin, Eugene Francis *philosophy educator*
McCrimmon, James McNab *language educator*
Moore, John Hebron *history educator*
Oldson, William Orville *history educator*

### Tampa
Anton, John Peter *philosopher, educator*
Cundiff, Paul Arthur *English language educator*
Perry, James Frederic *philosophy educator, author*
Preto-Rodas, Richard A. *foreign language educator*

### Winter Park
Seymour, Thaddeus *English educator*

## GEORGIA

### Americus
Isaacs, Harold *history educator*

### Andersonville
Boyles, Frederick Holdren *historian*

### Athens
Dickie, Margaret McKenzie *English language educator*
Fallows, Noel *foreign language educator*
Freer, Coburn *English language educator*
Kretzschmar, William Addison, Jr. *English language educator*
Mamatey, Victor Samuel *history educator*
Miller, Ronald Baxter *English language educator, author*
Moore, Margaret Bear *American literature educator*
Moore, Rayburn Sabatzky *American literature educator*
Nute, Donald E., Jr. *philosophy educator*
Steer, Alfred Gilbert, Jr. *foreign language educator*
Wall, Bennett Harrison *history educator*

### Atlanta
Benario, Herbert William *classics educator*
Benario, Janice Martin *classics educator*
Burns, Thomas Samuel *history educator*
Carter, Dan T. *history educator*
Fox-Genovese, Elizabeth Ann Teresa *humanities educator*
Garrow, David Jeffries *historian, author*
Genovese, Eugene Dominick *historian, educator*
Hartle, Robert Wyman *retired foreign language and literature educator*
Kuntz, Marion Lucile Leathers *classicist, historian, educator*
Manley, Frank *English language educator*
Puckett, James Manuel, Jr. *genealogist*
Rojas, Carlos *Spanish literature educator*
Sitter, John Edward *English literature educator*
Spivey, Ted Ray *English educator*

### Augusta
Cashin, Edward Joseph *history educator*
Puryear, Joan Copeland *English language educator*
Yaworski, JoAnn *reading skills educator*

### Clarkston
Foster, Dorothy Jean Peck *English for speakers of other languages educator*

### Decatur
Dillingham, William Byron *literature educator, author*
Major, James Russell Richards *historian, educator*
Pepperdene, Margaret Williams *English educator*
Young, James Harvey *historian, educator*

### Griffin
Canup, Sherrie Margaret *foreign languages educator*

### Kennesaw
Corley, Florence Fleming *history educator*

### Marietta
Rainey, Kenneth Tyler *English language educator*

### Moody AFB
Kennedy, Kimberly Kaye *history educator, bookkeeper*

### Robins AFB
Head, William Pace *historian, educator*

### Tucker
Twining, Henrietta Stover *retired English language educator*

### Valdosta
Adler, Brian Ungar *English language educator, program director*
McClain, Benjamin Richard *music educator, educational administrator*

## HAWAII

### Honolulu
Aung-Thwin, Michael Arthur *history educator*
Bender, Byron Wilbur *linguistics educator*
Copi, Irving Marmer *philosophy educator*
Dyen, Isidore *linguistic scientist, educator*
Hoffmann, Kathryn Ann *humanities educator*
Knowlton, Edgar Colby, Jr. *linguist, educator*
Moore, Willis Henry Allphin *history and geography educator*
Nagtalon-Miller, Helen Rosete *humanities educator*
Nunn, G. Raymond *history educator*
Pagotto, Louise *English language educator*
Rapson, Richard L. *history educator*
Stephan, John Jason *historian, educator*
Topping, Donald M. *English language professional, educaor*
Varley, Herbert Paul *Japanese language and cultural history educator*

### Keaau
Bailey, Charles-James Nice *linguistics educator*

## IDAHO

### Boise
Nguyen, King Xuan *language educator*
Wells, Merle William *historian, state archivist*

### Caldwell
Attebery, Louie Wayne *English language educator, folklorist*

### Emmett
Farnham, Wallace Dean *historian*

### Moscow
Greever, William St. Clair *educator, historian*

## ILLINOIS

### Carbondale
Ammon, Harry *history educator*
Fladeland, Betty *historian, educator*
Gilbert, Glenn Gordon *linguistics educator*
Hahn, Lewis Edwin *philosopher, retired educator*
Webb, Howard William, Jr. *retired humanities educator, university official*
Woodbridge, Hensley Charles *retired foreign languages educator, librarian*

### Champaign
Friedberg, Maurice *Russian literature educator*
Koenker, Diane P. *history educator*
Love, Joseph L. *history educator, cultural studies center administrator*
O'Neill, John Joseph *speech educator*
Smith, Ralph Alexander *cultural and educational policy educator*
Spence, Clark Christian *history educator*

### Chicago
Adler, Mortimer Jerome *philosopher, author*
Aronson, Howard Isaac *linguist, educator*
Bevington, David Martin *English literature educator*
Biggs, Robert Dale *Near Eastern studies educator*
Booth, Wayne Clayson *English literature and rhetoric educator, author*
Brinkman, John Anthony *historian, educator*
Chappell, Sally *art historian*
Cohen, Ted *philosophy educator*
Cullen, Charles Thomas *historian, librarian*
Debus, Allen George *history educator*
Dembowski, Peter Florian *foreign language educator*
Erlebacher, Albert *history educator*
Fleischer, Cornell Hugh *history educator*
Gannon, Sister Ann Ida *retired philosophy educator, former college administrator*
Garber, Daniel Elliot *philosophy educator*
Gilman, Sander Lawrence *German language educator*
Goldsmith, John Anton *linguist, educator*
Gossett, Philip *musicologist*
Grant, Robert McQueen *humanities educator*
Gray, Hanna Holborn *history educator*
Haley, George *Romance languages educator*
Hamp, Eric Pratt *linguist*
Harris, Neil *history educator*
Headrick, Daniel Richard *history and social sciences educator*
Heller, Reinhold August *art educator, consultant*
Hellie, Richard *Russian history educator, researcher*
Helmbold, Nancy Pearce *classical languages educator*
Holt, Thomas Cleveland *history educator, consultant, writer, lecturer*
Hunter, J(ames) Paul *English language educator, literary critic, historian*
Ingham, Norman William *Russian literature educator, genealogist*
Karanikas, Alexander *English language educator, author, actor*
Karl, Barry Dean *historian, educator*
Keenan, James George *classics educator*
Kolb, Gwin Jackson *language professional, educator*
Lawler, James Ronald *French language educator*
Lieb, Michael *English educator, humanities educator*
Ma, Yuanxi *Chinese and English language and literature educator, translator*
Marshall, Donald Glenn *English language and literature educator*
Miller, James Edwin, Jr. *English language educator*
Najita, Tetsuo *history educator*
Newman, Ralph Geoffrey *literary scholar historian*
Nussbaum, Martha Craven *philosophy and classics educator*
Pestureau, Pierre Gilbert *literature educator, literary critic, editor*
Pollock, Sheldon Ivan *language professional, educator*
Rosenheim, Edward Weil *English educator*
Roy, David Tod *Chinese literature educator*
Saller, Richard Paul *classics educator*
Shaughnessy, Edward Louis *Chinese language educator*
Sochen, June *history educator*
Tanner, Helen Hornbeck *historian*
Thaden, Edward Carl *history educator*
Weinberg, Meyer *humanities educator*
Weintraub, Karl Joachim *history educator*

### Des Plaines
Krupa, John Henry *English language educator*

### Dorsey
Hinkle, Jo Ann *English language educator*

### Edwardsville
Going, William Thornbury *English educator*

### Elgin
Duffy, John Lewis *Latin, English and reading educator*

### Evanston
Buchbinder-Green, Barbara Joyce *art and architectural historian*
Cole, Douglas *English literature educator*
De Coster, Cyrus Cole *Spanish language and literature educator*
Fine, Arthur I. *philosopher*
Fox, Edward Inman *education administrator and Spanish educator*
Greenberg, Douglas Stuart *history educator*
Sheridan, James Edward *history educator*
Sundquist, Eric John *American studies educator*
Ver Steeg, Clarence Lester *historian, educator*
Weil, Irwin *Slavic languages and literature educator*
Weil, Irwin *language educator*
Werckmeister, Otto Karl *art historian and educator*
Wright, John *classics educator*

### Galesburg
Hane, Mikiso *history educator*

### Glenview
Levine, Edwin Burton *retired classics educator*

### Itasca
Bradshaw, Linda Jean *English language educator*

### Macomb
Brown, Spencer Hunter *historian*
Hallwas, John Edward *English language educator*
Spencer, Donald Spurgeon *historian, academic administrator*
Vos, Morris *foreign languages educator, language services consultant*

### Mount Prospect
Stamper, James M. *retired English language educator*

### Palatine
Hull, Elizabeth Anne *English language educator*

### Palos Heights
Higgins, Francis Edward *history educator*

### Peoria
Ballowe, James *English educator, author*

### River Grove
ZeLeVas, Sharon Rose *art history educator, lawyer*

### Rockford
Hoshaw, Lloyd *historian, educator*

### Romeoville
Lifka, Mary Lauranne *history educator*

### Schaumburg
Smith-Pierce, Patricia A. *speech professional*

### Springfield
Davis, George Cullom *historian*
Fischoff, Ephraim *humanities educator, sociologist, social worker*
Temple, Wayne Calhoun *historian*

### Urbana
Aldridge, Alfred Owen *English language educator*
Antonsen, Elmer Harold *Germanic languages and literature educator*
Arnstein, Walter Leonard *historian, educator*
Bateman, John Jay *classics educator*
Baym, Nina *English educator*
Broudy, Harry Samuel *retired philosophy educator*
Cheng, Chin-Chuan *linguistics educator*
Davidson, Fred *education educator*
Dawn, Clarence Ernest *history educator*
Haile, H. G. *German language and literature educator*
Hendrick, George *English language educator*
Hurt, James Riggins *English language educator*
Jacobson, Howard *classics educator*
Kachru, Braj Behari *linguist*
Kachru, Yamuna *linguist*
Kaufmann, Urlin Milo *English literature educator*
Mainous, Bruce Hale *foreign language educator*
Manning, Sylvia *English studies educator*
Marcovich, Miroslav *classics educator*
McColley, Robert McNair *history educator*
McGlathery, James Melville *foreign language educator*
Newman, John Kevin *classics educator*
Scanlan, Richard Thomas *classics educator*
Schacht, Richard Lawrence *philosopher, educator*
Solberg, Winton Udell *history educator*
Spence, Mary Lee *historian*
Stillinger, Jack Clifford *English educator*
Talbot, Emile Joseph *French language educator*
Watts, Emily Stipes *English language educator*

### Westchester
Masterson, John Patrick *retired English language educator*

### Wilmette
Fries, Robert Francis *historian, educator*

## INDIANA

### Bloomington
Anderson, Judith Helena *English language educator*
Barnstone, Willis (Robert Barnstone) *language literature educator, poet, scholar*
Baxter, Maurice Glen *historian, educator*
Boerner, Peter *language and literature educator*
Bonser, Charles Franklin *public administration educator*
Brantlinger, Patrick *English educator*
Buelow, George John *musicologist, educator*
Byrnes, Robert Francis *history educator*
Cohen, William Benjamin *historian, educator*
Cole, Bruce Milan *art historian*
Dunn, Jon Michael *philosophy educator*
Edgerton, William B. *foreign language educator*
Ferrell, Robert Hugh *historian, educator*
Hanson, Karen *philosopher, educator*
Hodge, Carleton Taylor *linguist, educator*
Johnson, Sidney Malcolm *foreign language educator*
Juergens, George Ivar *history educator*
Lebano, Edoardo Antonio *foreign language educator*
Martins, Heitor Miranda *foreign language educator*
Mickel, Emanuel John *foreign language educator*
Pletcher, David Mitchell *history educator*
Rosenberg, Samuel Nathan *French and Italian language educator*
Sebeok, Thomas Albert *linguistics educator*
Simmons, Merle Edwin *foreign language educator*
Sinor, Denis *Orientalist, educator*
Sperling, Elliot Harris *history educator*

### Carmel
Hayashi, Tetsumaro *English and American literature educator, author*

### Centerville
Wendeln, Darlene Doris *English language educator*

### Charlestown
Schmidt, Jakob Edward *medical and medicolegal lexicographer, physician, author, inventor*

### Crawfordsville
Barnes, James John *history educator*

### Culver
Holaday, Allan Gibson *English educator*

### Fort Wayne
Fairchild, David Lawrence *philosophy educator*
Scheetz, Sister Mary JoEllen *English language educator*

### Greencastle
DiLillo, Leonard Michael *Spanish language educator, researcher, academic administrator*
Dittmer, John Avery *history educator*
Phillips, Clifton J. *history educator*
Weiss, Robert Orr *speech educator*

### Indianapolis
Baetzhold, Howard George *English language educator*
Davis, Kenneth Wayne *English language educator, business communication consultant*
Gooldy, Walter Raymond *genealogist*
Krasean, Thomas Karl *historian*
Mason, Thomas Alexander *historian, educator, author*
Plater, William Marmaduke *English language educator, academic administrator*

### Muncie
Rippy, Frances Marguerite Mayhew *English language educator*

### Notre Dame
Bruns, Gerald L. *English literature educator*
Delaney, Cornelius Francis *philosophy educator*
De Santis, Vincent Paul *historian, educator*
Gabriel, Astrik Ladislas *medieval studies educator, scholar*
Gutting, Gary Michael *philosophy educator*
Jemielity, Thomas John *English educator*
Lanzinger, Klaus *language educator*
Matthias, John Edward *English literature educator*
McInerny, Ralph Matthew *philosophy educator, author*
Mc Mullin, Ernan Vincent *philosophy educator*
Nugent, Walter Terry King *historian*
Quinn, Philip Lawrence *philosophy educator*
Roche, Mark William *German language educator*
Rosenberg, Charles Michael *art historian, educator*
Sayre, Kenneth Malcolm *philosophy educator*
Walicki, Andrzej Stanislaw *history of ideas educator*

### South Bend
van Inwagen, Peter Jan *philosophy educator*

### Terre Haute
Baker, Ronald Lee *English educator*
Brennan, Matthew Cannon *English literature educator, poet*
Carmony, Marvin Dale *linguist, educator*
De Marr, Mary Jean *English language educator*

### Valparaiso
Peters, Howard Nevin *foreign language educator*

### West Lafayette
Bertolet, Rodney Jay *philosophy educator*
Broden, Thomas Francis, III *French language educator*
Contreni, John Joseph, Jr. *humanities educator*
Garfinkel, Alan *Spanish language and education educator*
Gottfried, Leon Albert *English language educator*
Leitch, Vincent Barry *literary and cultural studies educator*
Mc Bride, William Leon *philosopher, educator*
Reichard, Hugo Manley *English literature educator*
Rothenberg, Gunther Erich *history educator*
Woodman, Harold David *historian*

## IOWA

### Ames
Bruner, Charlotte Hughes *French language educator*

### Avoca
Hardisty, William Lee *English language educator*

### Cedar Falls
Clohesy, William Warren *philosophy educator*
Maier, Donna Jane-Ellen *history educator*
Thompson, Thomas Henry *philosophy educator*
Wilson, Robley Conant, Jr. *English educator, editor, author*

### Cedar Rapids
Lisio, Donald John *historian, educator*

### Davenport
Luzkow, Jack Lawrence *history educator, writer, consultant*
Weinberg, Marylin Lynn *foreign language educator*

### Grinnell
Kaiser, Daniel Hugh *historian, educator*
Kintner, Philip L. *history educator*
Kissane, James Donald *English literature educator*
Leggett, Glenn *former English language educator, academic administrator*
Michaels, Jennifer Tonks *foreign language educator*

### Iowa City
Addis, Laird Clark, Jr. *philosopher, educator, musician*
Butchvarov, Panayot Krustev *philosophy educator*
Cox, Jeffrey Lee *history educator*
Dettmer, Helena R. *classics educator*
Ertl, Wolfgang *German language and literature educator*
Folsom, Lowell Edwin *English language educator*
Fumerton, Richard Anthony *philosopher educator*
Gelfand, Lawrence Emerson *historian, educator*
Gerber, John Christian *English language educator*
Goldstein, Jonathan Amos *ancient history and classics educator*
Hawley, Ellis Wayne *historian, educator*
Hornsby, Roger Allen *classics educator*
Kerber, Linda Kaufman *historian, educator*
Percas de Ponseti, Helena *foreign language and literature educator*
Persons, Stow Spaulding *historian, educator*
Raeburn, John Hay *English language educator*
Ringen, Catherine Oleson *linguistics educator*
Sayre, Robert Freeman *English language educator*
Schoenbaum, David Leon *historian*
Solbrig, Ingeborg Hildegard *German literature educator, author*
Steele, Oliver *English educator*
Trank, Douglas Monty *rhetoric and speech communications educator*
Wachal, Robert Stanley *linguistics educator, consultant*

### Lamoni
Wight, Darlene *retired speech educator*

## KANSAS

### Chanute
Dillard, Dean Innes *English language educator*

### Dighton
Stanley, Ellen May *historian, consultant*

### Lawrence
Alexander, John Thorndike *historian, educator*
Debicki, Andrew Peter *foreign language educator*
De George, Richard Thomas *philosophy educator*
Eldredge, Charles Child, III *art history educator*
Gunn, James E. *English language educator*
Li, Chu-Tsing *art history educator*
Quinn, Dennis B. *English language and literature educator*
Robinson, Walter Stitt, Jr. *historian*
Saul, Norman Eugene *history educator*
Schoeck, Richard J(oseph) *English and humanities scholar*
Seaver, James Everett *historian, educator*
Spires, Robert Cecil *foreign language educator*
Tuttle, William McCullough, Jr. *history educator*
Vincent, Jon Stephen *foreign language educator*
Woelfel, James Warren *philosophy educator*
Worth, George John *English literature educator*

### Manhattan
Higham, Robin *historian, editor, publisher*
McCulloh, John Marshall *historian*

### Ottawa
Tyler, Priscilla *retired English language and education educator*

### Topeka
Saeed, Mohammed *Islamic historian, eqyptologist, educator*

## KENTUCKY

### Bowling Green
Minton, John Dean *historian, educator*

**Danville**
Newhall, David Sowle *history educator*

**Lexington**
Bryant, Joseph Allen, Jr. *English language educator*
Coffman, Edward McKenzie *history educator*
Madden, Edward Harry *philosopher, educator*
Warth, Robert Douglas *history educator*

**Louisville**
Brockwell, Charles Wilbur, Jr. *history educator*
Ford, Gordon Buell, Jr. *English language, linguistics, and medieval studies educator, author, retired hospital industry accounting financial management executive*
Garcia-Varela, Jesus *language educator, literature educator*
Kearney, Anna Rose *history educator*

**Midway**
Minister, Kristina *speech communication educator*

**Radcliff**
Cranston, John Welch *historian, educator*

**Richmond**
Shearon, Forrest Bedford *humanities educator*
Witt, Robert Wayne *English educator*

**Southgate**
Glenn, Jerry Hosmer, Jr. *foreign language educator*

**Versailles**
Freehling, William Wilhartz *historian, educator*

## LOUISIANA

**Baton Rouge**
Arceneaux, William *historian, educator, association official*
Cooper, William James, Jr. *history educator*
Edgeworth, Robert Joseph *classical languages educator*
Hardy, John Edward *English language educator, author*
Olney, James *English language educator*
Smith, David Jeddie *American literature educator*
Stanford, Donald Elwin *English educator, editor, poet, critic*

**Eunice**
Rogers, Donald Onis *language educator*

**Hammond**
Thorburn, James Alexander *humanities educator*

**Lafayette**
Nicassio, Susan Vandiver *history and humanities educator*

**New Orleans**
Ambrose, Stephen Edward *history educator, author*
Cohen, Joseph *English literature educator, writer, business owner*
Cummings, Anthony Michael *music historian, educator, academic administrator*
Greenleaf, Richard Edward *Latin American history educator*
Kukla, Jon (Keith) *historian, museum director*
Luza, Radomir Vaclav *historian, educator*
Paolini, Gilberto *literature and science educator*
Pindle, Arthur Jackson, Jr. *philosopher, researcher*
Poesch, Jessie Jean *art historian*
Reck, Andrew Joseph *philosophy educator*
Roberts, Louise Nisbet *philosopher*
Sellin, Eric *linguist, poet, educator*
Thompson, Annie Laura *foreign language educator*
Woodward, Ralph Lee, Jr. *historian, educator*

**Pineville**
Howell, Thomas *history educator*
Tapley, Philip Allen *English language and literature educator*

**Ruston**
Halliburton, Lloyd *Romance philology educator*

**Thibodaux**
Swetman, Glenn Robert *English language educator, poet*

## MAINE

**Brunswick**
Hodge, James Lee *German language educator*

**Castine**
Berleant, Arnold *philosopher*

**Dresden**
Turco, Lewis Putnam *English educator*

**Orono**
Hatlen, Burton Norval *English educator*
Ives, Edward Dawson *folklore educator*

**Portland**
Schwanauer, Francis *philosopher, educator*

**Scarborough**
Martin, Harold Clark *humanities educator*
Sadik, Marvin Sherwood *art consultant, former museum director*

**Waterville**
Bassett, Charles Walker *English language educator*
Hudson, Yeager *philosophy educator, minister*

## MARYLAND

**Baltimore**
Achinstein, Peter Jacob *philosopher, educator*
Baldwin, John Wesley *history educator*
Barker, Stephen Francis *philosophy educator*
Cacossa, Anthony Alexander *Romance languages educator*
Castro-Klaren, Sara *Latin American literature educator*
Cohen, Warren I. *history educator*
Cooper, Jerrold Stephen *historian, educator*
Cropper, M. Elizabeth *art history educator*
DeLuna, D.N. *literary educator*
Dempsey, Charles Gates *art historian, educator*
Fleishman, Avrom Hirsch *English educator*
Forster, Robert *history educator*
Greene, Jack Phillip *historian, educator*
Higham, John *history educator*
Hillers, Delbert Roy *Near East language educator*
Irwin, John Thomas *humanities educator*
Johnson, Michael Paul *history educator*
Judson, Horace Freeland *history of science, writer, educator*
Kagan, Richard Lauren *history educator*
Kessler, Herbert Leon *art historian, educator*
Knight, Franklin W. *history educator*
Kurth, Lieselotte *foreign language educator*
Lidtke, Vernon LeRoy *history educator*
Luck, Georg Hans Bhawani *classics educator*
McCarter, P(ete) Kyle, Jr. *Near Eastern studies educator*
McKinney, Richard Ishmael *philosophy educator*
Nichols, Stephen George *Romance languages educator*
Paulson, Ronald Howard *English and humanities educator*
Peirce, Carol Marshall *English educator*
Ranum, Orest Allen *historian, educator*
Ross, Dorothy Rabin *history educator*
Russell-Wood, Anthony John R. *history educator*
Schneewind, Jerome Borges *philosophy educator*
Sedlak, Valerie Frances *English language educator, university administrator*
Thompson-Cager, Chezia Brenda *literature educator, writer, performance artist*
Walker, Mack *historian, educator*
Ziff, Larzer *English language educator*

**Bel Air**
Lu, David John *history educator, writer*

**Bethesda**
Benson, Elizabeth Polk *Pre-Columbian art specialist*
Briend-Walker, Monique Marie *French and Spanish language educator*
Duncan, Francis *historian, government official*
Highfill, Philip Henry, Jr. *retired language educator*

**Bowie**
McManus, Mary Hairston *English language educator*
Sterling, Richard Leroy *English and foreign language educator*

**Catonsville**
Loerke, William Carl *art history educator*

**Chestertown**
Trout, Charles Hathaway *historian, educator*

**Chevy Chase**
Durant, Frederick Clark, III *aerospace history and space art consultant*
Goodwin, Ralph Roger *historian, editor*

**Cockeysville Hunt Valley**
Peirce, Brooke *English language educator*

**College Park**
Brown, Peter Gilbert *philosopher, educator, tree farmer*
Fuegi, John *comparative literature educator, author, filmmaker*
Harlan, Louis Rudolph *history educator, writer*
Holton, William Milne *English language and literature educator*
Lightfoot, David William *linguistics educator*
Olson, Keith Waldemar *history educator*
Oster, Rose Marie Gunhild *foreign language professional, educator*
Panichas, George Andrew *English language educator, critic, editor*
Pasch, Alan *philosopher, educator*
Weart, Spencer Richard *historian*
Yaney, George *history educator*

**Columbia**
Butcher, (Charles) Philip *English language educator, author*
Collins, Grace Elizabeth *English educator, writer*

**Darnestown**
Knox, Bernard MacGregor Walker *retired classics educator*

**Frederick**
Pyne, Frederick Wallace *genealogist, clergyman, retired civil engineer, retired mathematics educator*

**Kingsville**
Clark, Wilma Jean Marshall *English language educator*

**Largo**
LeValley, Guy Glenn *speech communication educator*

**Lusby**
Eshelman, Ralph Ellsworth *maritime historian, educator, consultant*

**Myersville**
Blake, John Ballard *retired historian*

**Rockville**
Brown, David Harry *speech educator*
Cantelon, Philip Louis *historian*
Hewlett, Richard Greening *historian*

**Saint Michaels**
Marshall, Robert Gerald *language educator*

**Severna Park**
Schick, Edgar Brehob *German literature educator*

**Silver Spring**
Borkovec, Vera Z. *Russian studies educator*
Calinger, Ronald Steve *historian*
Cole, Wayne Stanley *historian, educator*
Doherty, William Thomas, Jr. *historian, retired educator*
Dowd, Mary-Jane Martin *historian*
Pacuska, Alison Brandi *Russian studies professional*
Papas, Irene Kalandros *English language educator, writer, poet*

**Sparks**
Suarez-Murias, Marguerite C. *retired language and literature educator*

**Towson**
Baker, Jean Harvey *history educator*

**Upper Marlboro**
Carroll, Cyril James *speech communication and theatre educator*

## MASSACHUSETTS

**Amesbury**
Labaree, Benjamin Woods *history educator*

**Amherst**
Baker, Lynne Rudder *philosophy educator*
Bezucha, Robert Joseph *history educator*
Chappell, Vere Claiborne *philosophy educator*
Creed, Robert Payson, Sr. *literature educator*
Gibson, Walker *retired English language educator, poet, writer*
Hernon, Joseph Martin, Jr. *history educator*
Kinney, Arthur Frederick *literary history educator, author, editor*
Oates, Stephen Baery *history educator*
Partee, Barbara Hall *linguist, educator*
Rosbottom, Ronald Carlisle *French, arts and humanities educator*
Tager, Jack *historian, educator*
Taubman, Jane Andelman *Russian literature educator*
Wideman, John Edgar *English literature educator, novelist*
Wolff, Robert Paul *philosophy educator*
Wyman, David Sword *historian, educator*

**Belmont**
Bloch, Herbert *retired foreign language and literature and history educator*
Buckley, Jerome Hamilton *English language educator*

**Boston**
Brandt, Allan M. *medical history educator*
Bromsen, Maury Austin *historian, bibliographer, antiquarian bookseller*
Cardona, Rodolfo *Spanish language and literature educator*
Collins, Martha *English language educator, writer*
Foss, Clive Frank Wilson *history educator*
Freeman, Robert Schofield *musicologist, educator, pianist*
Henry, DeWitt Pawling, II *creative writing educator, writer, arts administrator*
Hintikka, Jaakko *philosopher, educator*
Jones, Robert Emmet *French language educator*
Kleiner, Fred Scott *art history and archaeology educator, editor*
Langer, Lawrence Lee *English educator, writer*
Lowry, Bates *art historian, museum director*
Lyons, David Barry *philosophy and law educator*
Mc Carthy, Joseph Michael *historian*
Menyuk, Paula *developmental psycholinguistics educator*
Miller, Naomi *art historian*
Naeser, Margaret Ann *linguist, medical researcher*
Phillips, William *English language educator, editor, author*
Riley, Stephen Thomas *historian, librarian*
Rosen, Stanley Howard *humanities educator*
Sanborn, George Freeman, Jr. *genealogist*
Scanlon, Dorothy Therese *history educator*
Weitzman, Arthur Joshua *English educator*
Wermuth, Paul Charles *retired English educator*
Wiseman, James Richard *classicist, archaeologist, educator*

**Bridgewater**
Farrar, Ruth Doris *reading and literacy educator*

**Brookline**
Mc Cormick, Thomas Julian *art history educator*

**Cambridge**
Appiah, Kwame Anthony *philosophy educator*
Badian, Ernst *history educator*
Bailyn, Bernard *historian, educator*
Barnet, Sylvan *English literature educator*
Bate, Walter Jackson *English literature educator*
Bolster, Arthur Stanley, Jr. *history educator*
Brustein, Robert Sanford *English language educator, theatre director, author*
Chomsky, Avram Noam *linguistics and philosophy educator*
Chvany, Catherine Vakar *foreign language educator*
Clausen, Wendell Vernon *classics educator*
Conley, Tom Clark *literature educator*
Cross, Frank Moore, Jr. *foreign language educator*
Cushing, Steven *linguist, educator, researcher, consultant*
Della-Terza, Dante Michele *comparative literature educator*
Dunn, Charles William *Celtic languages and literature educator, author*
Dupree, Anderson Hunter *historian, educator*
Dyck, Arthur James *ethicist, educator*
Dyck, Martin *literary theorist, mathematics historian*
Engell, James Theodore *English educator*
Fanger, Donald Lee *Slavic language and literature educator*
Fisher, Philip J. *English language and literature educator*
Fleming, Donald Harnish *historian, educator*
Flier, Michael Stephen *Slavic languages educator*
Ford, Franklin Lewis *history educator, historian*
Ford, Patrick Kildea *Celtic studies educator*
Frye, Richard Nelson *historian, educator*
Gates, Henry Louis, Jr. *English language educator*
Gienapp, William Eugene *history educator*
Goldfarb, Warren (David) *philosophy educator*
Graham, Loren Raymond *historian, educator*
Graubard, Stephen Richards *history educator, editor*
Guthke, Karl Siegfried *foreign language educator*
Halle, Morris *linguist, educator*
Hanan, Patrick Dewes *foreign language professional, educator*
Handlin, Oscar *historian, educator*
Heimert, Alan Edward *humanities educator*
Henrichs, Albert Maximinus *classicist, educator*
Iriye, Akira *historian, educator*
Jones, Christopher Prestige *classicist, historian, educator, consultant*
†Kalb, Marvin *public policy and government educator*
Keenan, Edward Louis *history educator*
Keyser, Samuel Jay *linguistics educator, university official*
Ladjevardi, Habib *historian*
Lunt, Horace Gray *linguist, educator*
MacMaster, Robert Ellsworth *historian, educator*
Mahoney, Thomas Henry Donald *historian, educator, government official*
Maier, Charles Steven *history educator*
Maier, Pauline *history educator*
Malmstad, John Earl *Slavic languages and literatures, educator*
May, Ernest Richard *historian, educator*
Mazlish, Bruce *historian, educator*
McCormick, Michael *history educator*
Nozick, Robert *philosophy educator, author*
Nykrog, Per *French literature educator*
O'Neil, Wayne *linguist, educator*
Ozment, Steven *historian, educator*
Paradis, James Gardiner *historian*
Perkins, David *English language educator*
Pian, Rulan Chao *musicologist, scholar*
Pipes, Richard *historian, educator*
Preyer, Robert Otto *English literature educator*
Quine, Willard Van Orman *philosophy educator*
Ryan, Judith Lyndal *German language and literature educator*
Scheffler, Israel *philosopher, educator*
Segal, Charles Paul *classics educator, author*
Sevcenko, Ihor *history and literature educator*
Shinagel, Michael *English literature educator*
Simon, Eckehard (Peter) *foreign language educator*
Singer, Irving *philosophy educator*
Smith, Merritt Roe *history educator*
Sollors, Werner *English language, literature and American studies educator*
Southern, Eileen (Mrs. Joseph Southern) *music educator*
Striker, Gisela *philosophy educator*
Sulloway, Frank Jones *historian*
Tarrant, R(ichard) J(ohn) *classicist, educator*
Tayler, Irene *English literature educator*
Teeter, Karl van Duyn *retired linguistic scientist, educator*
Thernstrom, Stephan Albert *historian, educator*
Thorburn, David *literature educator*
Tu, Wei-Ming *historian, philosopher, writer*
Ulrich, Laurel Thatcher *historian, educator*
Vanger, Milton Isadore *history educator*
Vendler, Helen Hennessy *literature educator, poetry critic*
Ward, John Milton *music educator*
Winner, Thomas Gustav *foreign literature educator*
Wolff, Christoph Johannes *music historian, educator*
Wolff, Cynthia Griffin *humanities educator, author*
Ziolkowski, Jan Michael *medievalist educator*

**Centerville**
Embree, Ainslie Thomas *history educator*

**Chestnut Hill**
Barth, John Robert *English educator, priest*
Blanchette, Oliva *philosophy educator*
Casper, Leonard Ralph *American literature educator*
Duhamel, Pierre Albert *English language professional*
Mahoney, John L. *English literature educator*
McAleer, John Joseph *English literature educator*
Reed, James Eldin *historian, educator*
Valette, Rebecca Marianne *Romance languages educator*

**Framingham**
Lipton, Leah *art historian, educator, museum curator*

**Longmeadow**
Cobbs, Russell L(ewis) *English language educator*

**Medford**
Bedau, Hugo Adam *philosophy educator*
Brooke, John L. *history educator*
Dennett, Daniel Clement *philosopher, author, educator*
Fyler, John Morgan *English language educator*
Laurent, Pierre-Henri *history educator*
Marcopoulos, George John *history educator*
Simches, Seymour Oliver *language educator*

**Milton**
Frazier, Marie Dunn *speech educator, public relations and human resources specialist*

**Needham**
Bottiglia, William Filbert *humanities educator*

**North Andover**
Longsworth, Ellen Louise *art historian, consultant*

**North Dartmouth**
Yoken, Mel B(arton) *French language educator, author*

**Northampton**
Elkins, Stanley Maurice *historian, educator*
Ellis, Frank Hale *English literature educator*
Hoyt, Nelly Schargo (Mrs. N. Deming Hoyt) *history educator*
Little, Lester Knox *historian, educator*
Pickrel, Paul *English educator*
Smith, Malcolm Barry Estes *philosophy educator, lawyer*
Vaget, Hans Rudolf *language professional, educator*
von Klemperer, Klemens *historian, educator*

**Norton**
Dahl, Curtis *English literature educator*
Olson, Roberta Jeanne Marie *art historian, author, educator*

Taylor, Robert Sundling *English educator, art critic*

**Randolph**
Morrissey, Edmond Joseph *classical philologist*

**Rockport**
Delakas, Daniel Liudviko *retired foreign language educator*
Walen, Harry Leonard *historian, lecturer, author*

**Salem**
Gozemba, Patrica Andrea *women's studies and English language educator, writer*

**South Hadley**
Berek, Peter *English educator*
Brownlow, Frank Walsh *English language educator*
Ciruti, Joan Estelle *Spanish language and literature educator*
Doezema, Marianne *art historian*
Farnham, Anthony Edward *English language educator*
Herbert, Robert Louis *art history educator*
Johnson, Richard August *English language educator*
Mazzocco, Angelo *language educator*
Quinn, Betty Nye *former classics educator*
Robin, Richard Shale *philosophy educator*

**South Yarmouth**
Benoit, Leroy James *language educator*

**Springfield**
Porter, Burton Frederick *philosophy educator, author, dean*

**Swampscott**
Truog, Dean-Daniel Wesley *educator, consultant*

**Waltham**
Black, Eugene Charlton *historian, educator*
Harth, Erica *French language and comparative literature educator*
Jackendoff, Ray Saul *linguistics educator*
Marshall, Robert Lewis *musicologist, educator*
Staves, Susan *English educator*
Young, Dwight Wayne *ancient civilization educator*

**Watertown**
Goodheart, Eugene *English language educator*
Rivers, Wilga Marie *foreign language educator*

**Wayland**
Clogan, Paul Maurice *English language and literature educator*

**Webster**
Siddall, Patricia Ann *English language educator*

**Wellesley**
Bidart, Frank *English educator, poet*
Lefkowitz, Mary Rosenthal *Greek literature educator*
Mistacco, Vicki E. *foreign language educator*
Piper, Adrian Margaret Smith *philosopher, artist, educator*
Putnam, Ruth Anna *philosopher, educator*

**Wellfleet**
Mc Feely, William Shield *historian, writer*

**West Barnstable**
Corsa, Helen Storm *language professional*

**Weston**
Higgins, Sister Therese *English educator, former college president*

**Westwood**
Burrell, Sidney Alexander *history educator*

**Williamstown**
Bahlman, Dudley Ward Rhodes *history educator*
Bell-Villada, Gene H. *literature educator, writer*
Dalzell, Robert Fenton, Jr. *historian*
Dew, Charles Burgess *historian, educator*
Dickerson, Dennis Clark *history educator*
Edgerton, Samuel Youngs, Jr. *art historian, educator*
Filipczak, Zirka Zaremba *art historian, educator*
Fuqua, Charles John *classics educator*
Graver, Lawrence Stanley *English language professional*
Hyde, John Michael *history educator*
Norton, Glyn Peter *French literature educator*
Oakley, Francis Christopher *history educator, former college president*
Payne, Harry Charles *historian, educator*
Pistorius, George *language educator*
Raab, Lawrence Edward *English educator*
Rudolph, Frederick *history educator*
Stamelman, Richard Howard *French and humanities educator*
Waite, Robert George Leeson *history educator*

**Worcester**
Billias, George Athan *history educator*
Langevin, Edgar Louis *retired humanities educator*
Vaughan, Alden True *history educator*
Von Laue, Theodore Herman *historian, educator*
Zeugner, John Finn *history educator, writer*

**MICHIGAN**

**Ann Arbor**
Aldridge, John Watson *English language educator, author*
Arthos, John *English language educator*
Bailey, David Roy Shackleton *classics educator*
Bailey, Richard Weld *English language educator*
Baker, Sheridan *English educator, author*
Becker, Marvin Burton *historian*
Blouin, Francis Xavier, Jr. *history educator*
Bornstein, George Jay *literary educator*
Brandt, Richard Booker *former philosophy educator*
Brown, Deming Bronson *Slavic languages and literature educator*
Burbank, Jane Richardson *Russian and European studies educator*
Cole, Juan R.I. *history educator*
Cowen, Roy Chadwell, Jr. *German language educator*

Curley, Edwin Munson *philosophy educator*
Danly, Robert Lyons *Japanese studies educator, author, translator*
Dunnigan, Brian Leigh *military historian, curator*
Eisenberg, Marvin Julius *art history educator*
Eisenstein, Elizabeth Lewisohn *historian, educator*
Fader, Daniel Nelson *English language educator*
Feuerwerker, Albert *history educator*
Forsyth, Ilene Haering *art historian*
Gomez, Luis Oscar *Asian and religious studies educator*
Hackett, Roger Fleming *history educator*
Knott, John Ray, Jr. *language professional, educator*
Konigsberg, Ira *film and literature educator, writer*
Lewis, David Lanier *business history educator*
Lewis, Robert Enzer *lexicographer, educator*
McCarus, Ernest Nasseph *retired language educator*
McDougal, Stuart Yeatman *comparative literature educator, author*
Mersereau, John, Jr. *Slavic languages and literatures educator*
Morris, Phyllis Sutton *philosophy educator*
Munro, Donald Jacques *philosopher, educator*
Murphey, Rhoads *history educator*
Pulgram, Ernst *linguist, philologist, Romance and classical linguistics educator, writer*
Starr, Chester G. *history educator*
Steinhoff, William Richard *English literature educator*
Stolz, Benjamin Armond *foreign language educator*
Trautmann, Thomas Roger *history and anthropology educator*
Woodcock, Leonard *humanities educator, former ambassador*

**Berrien Springs**
Waller, John Oscar *English language educator*

**Big Rapids**
Mehler, Barry Alan *humanities educator, journalist, consultant*

**Bloomfield Hills**
Bonner, Thomas Neville *history and higher education educator*

**Detroit**
Abt, Jeffrey *art and art history educator, artist, writer*
Brill, Lesley *literature and film studies educator*
Finkenbine, Roy Eugene *history educator*
Kowalczyk, Richard Leon *English language educator, technical writing consultant*
Rashid, Harun Ur *philosopher, educational administrator*
Reide, Jerome L. *humanities educator, lawyer*
Schindler, Marvin Samuel *foreign language educator*
Small, Melvin *history educator*
van der Marck, Jan *art historian*
Williamson, Marilyn Lammert *English educator, university adminstrator*

**East Lansing**
Anderson, David Daniel *retired humanities educator, writer, editor*
Appel, John J. *history educator*
Eadie, John William *history educator*
Falk, Julia S. *linguist, educator*
Fisher, Alan Washburn *historian, educator*
Huzar, Eleanor Goltz *history educator*
Kronegger, Maria Elisabeth *French and comparative literature educator*
Mansour, George P. *Spanish language and literature educator*
Mead, Carl David *educator*
Paananen, Victor Niles *English educator*
Platt, Franklin Dewitt *history educator*
Pollack, Norman *history educator*
Silverman, Henry Jacob *history educator*
Whallon, William *literature educator*

**Grand Blanc**
Lemke, Laura Ann *foreign language educator, assistant principal*

**Grand Rapids**
Zuidervaart, Lambert Paul *philosophy educator*

**Grosse Pointe**
Peters, Thomas Robert *English language educator, writer*

**Harbert**
Morrissette, Bruce Archer *Romance languages educator*

**Harper Woods**
Havrilcsak, Gregory Michael *historian, educator*

**Hillsdale**
Castel, Albert Edward *history educator*

**Holland**
Quimby, Robert Sherman *retired humanities educator*

**Huntington Woods**
Gutmann, Joseph *art history educator*

**Jackson**
Feldmann, Judith Gail *language professional, educator*

**Kalamazoo**
Breisach, Ernst A. *historian, educator*
Dybek, Stuart *English educator, writer*
Gordon, Jaimy *English educator, writer*
Gregory, Ross *history educator, author*
Maier, Paul Luther *history educator, author, chaplain*
Moritz, Edward *historian, educator*
Ruoff, Cynthia Osowiec *foreign language educator*
Waring, Walter Weyler *English language educator*

**Lansing**
Harvey, Joanne H. *genealogist*

**Livonia**
Holtzman, Roberta Lee *French and Spanish language educator*

**Marquette**
Heldreth, Leonard Guy *English educator, university official*

**Mount Pleasant**
Steffel, Susan Elizabeth *English language and literature educator*

**Okemos**
Huddleston, Eugene Lee *retired American studies educator*

**Olivet**
Walker, Donald Edwin *history educator*

**Rochester**
Garcia, Wilma Thackston *English language and literature educator*
Thomas, S. Bernard *history educator*

**Rochester Hills**
Matthews, George Tennyson *history educator*

**Southfield**
Papazian, Dennis Richard *history educator, political commentator*
Stern, Guy *German language and literature educator, writer*

**Sterling Heights**
Ice, Orva Lee, Jr. *history educator*

**Ypsilanti**
Norton, Jody (John Douglas Norton) *English language educator*
Perkins, Bradford *history educator*

**MINNESOTA**

**Bemidji**
Bonner, Helen Ward *English language and literature educator*

**Coon Rapids**
Carlson, Linda Marie *language arts educator, consultant*

**Duluth**
Fischer, Roger Adrian *history educator*
Jankofsky, Klaus Peter *medieval studies educator*
Schroeder, Fred Erich Harald *humanities educator*

**Minneapolis**
Anderson, Chester Grant *English educator*
Bales, Kent Roslyn *English language educator*
Bashiri, Iraj *Central Asian studies educator*
Browne, Donald Roger *speech communication educator*
Campbell, Karlyn Kohrs *speech and communication educator*
Erickson, Gerald Meyer *classical studies educator*
Farah, Caesar Elie *Middle Eastern and Islamic studies educator*
Firchow, Evelyn Scherabon *German educator, author*
Firchow, Peter Edgerly *language professional, educator, author*
Good, David Franklin *economic historian, educator*
Hauch, Valerie Catherine *historian, educator, researcher*
Kohlstedt, Sally Gregory *history educator*
Lehmberg, Stanford Eugene *historian, educator*
Leppert, Richard David *humanities educator*
Marling, Karal Ann *art history and social sciences educator*
McDonald, William Andrew *classics educator*
Monson, Dianne Lynn *literacy educator*
Nagel, Paul Chester *historian, writer, lecturer*
Noonan, Thomas Schaub *history educator, Russian studies educator*
Norberg, Arthur Lawrence, Jr. *historian, physicist educator*
Pazandak, Carol Hendrickson *liberal arts educator*
Rath, R. John *historian, educator*
Ross, Donald, Jr. *English language educator, university administrator*
Scott, Robert Lee *speech educator*
Seidel, Robert Wayne *science historian, educator, institute administrator*
Sonkowsky, Robert Paul *classicist, educator, actor*
Tracy, James Donald *historian*
Vecoli, Rudolph John *history educator*
Weiss, Gerhard Hans *German language educator*

**Moorhead**
Anderson, Jerry Maynard *speech educator*

**Northfield**
Clark, Clifford Edward, Jr. *history educator*
Iseminger, Gary H. *philosophy educator*
Mason, Perry Carter *philosophy educator*
Sipfle, David Arthur *philosophy educator*
Soule, George Alan *literature educator*
Yandell, Cathy Marleen *foreign language educator*
Zelliot, Eleanor Mae *history educator*

**Saint Cloud**
Braun, Janice Larson *language arts educator*
Hofsommer, Donovan Lowell *history educator*

**Saint Paul**
Mather, Richard Burroughs *retired Chinese language and literature educator*
Murray, Peter Bryant *English language educator*
Stewart, James Brewer *historian, author, college administrator*
Weiner, Carl Dorian *historian*

**Vadnais Heights**
Polakiewicz, Leonard Anthony *foreign language and literature educator*

**Winona**
Adickes, Sandra Elaine *English language educator, writer*

**MISSISSIPPI**

**Biloxi**
Hagood, Annabel Dunham *speech communication educator, consultant*

**Cleveland**
Cash, William McKinley *history educator*

**Clinton**
Bigelow, Martha Mitchell *retired historian*

**Hattiesburg**
Gonzales, John Edmond *history educator*
Sims, James Hylbert *English educator, former university administrator*

**Jackson**
Curtis, Verna P. *reading educator*
Palmer, Dora Deen Pope *English and French language educator*

**Magnolia**
Coney, Elaine Marie *English and foreign languages educator*

**Mississippi State**
Chatham, James Ray *foreign language educator*
Crowell, Lorenzo Mayo *historian, educator*
Donaghy, Henry James *English literature educator, academic administrator*
Lowery, Charles Douglas *history educator, academic administrator*
Parrish, William Earl *history educator*
Wiltrout, Ann Elizabeth *foreign language educator*

**Starkville**
Wolverton, Robert Earl *classics educator*

**University**
Jordan, Winthrop Donaldson *historian, educator*
Kiger, Joseph Charles *history educator*
Landon, Michael de Laval *historian, educator*
Walton, Gerald Wayne *English educator, university officiala*

**MISSOURI**

**Chesterfield**
Matros, Larisa Grigoryevna *medical philosophy researcher*

**Columbia**
Alexander, Thomas Benjamin *history educator*
Anderson, Donald Kennedy, Jr. *English educator*
Bien, Joseph Julius *philosophy educator*
Fulweiler, Howard Wells *language professional*
Geiger, Louis George *historian*
Goodrich, James William *historian, association executive*
Horner, Winifred Bryan *humanities educator, researcher, consultant, writer*
Jones, William McKendrey *language professional, educator*
Lago, Mary McClelland *English language educator, author*
Mullen, Edward John, Jr. *Spanish language educator*
Overby, Osmund Rudolf *art historian, educator*
Reid, Loren Dudley *speech educator*
Strickland, Arvarh Eunice *history educator*
Timberlake, Charles Edward *history educator*

**Kansas City**
Hoffmann, Donald *architectural historian*
Miller, Patricia Elizabeth Cleary *American and British literature educator*

**Kirksville**
Schnucker, Robert Victor *history and religion educator*

**Marshall**
Gruber, Loren Charles *English language educator, writer*

**Maryville**
Heusel, Barbara Stevens *English scholar and educator*

**Rolla**
Allison, Sandy *genealogist, appraiser, political consultant*

**Saint Charles**
Barnett, Howard Albert *English language educator*

**Saint Louis**
Bagley, Mary Carol *literature educator, writer, broadcaster*
Barmann, Lawrence Francis *history educator*
Berthoff, Rowland Tappan *historian, educator*
Bourke, Vernon Joseph *philosophy educator*
Boyd, Robert Cotton *English language educator*
Heath, Peter *foreign language educator*
Herbert, Kevin Barry John *classics educator*
Krukowski, Lucian *philosophy educator, artist*
Ruland, Richard Eugene *English and American literature educator, critic, literary historian*
Sale, Merritt *classicist, comparatist, educator*
Schwarz, Egon *humanities and German language educator, author, literary critic*
Shea, Daniel Bartholomew, Jr. *English language educator, actor*
Smith, Jeffrey E. *historian, educator*
Spector, Stanley *historian, foreign language educator*
Ullian, Joseph Silbert *philosophy educator*
Watson, Richard Allan *philosophy educator, writer*
Wellman, Carl Pierce *philosophy educator*
Wu, Nelson Ikon *art history educator, author, artist*

**Springfield**
Burgess, Ruth Lenora Vassar *speech and language educator*

**Warrensburg**
Robbins, Dorothy Ann *foreign language educator*

## MONTANA

### Billings
Small, Lawrence Farnsworth *history educator*

## NEBRASKA

### Hastings
McEwen, Larry Burdette *retired English and theater arts educator, author*

### Kearney
Young, Ann Elizabeth O'Quinn *historian, educator*

### Lincoln
Bailey, Dudley *English educator*
Crompton, Louis William *English literature educator*
Leinieks, Valdis *classicist, educator*
Rawley, James Albert *history educator*
Sawyer, Robert McLaran *history educator*
Stover, John Ford *railroad historian, educator*

### Omaha
Dougherty, Charles John *philosophy and medical ethics educator*
Horning, Ross Charles, Jr. *historian, educator*
Kaspar, Victoria Ann *educator English*
Okhamafe, Imafedia *English literature and philosophy educator*

## NEVADA

### Las Vegas
Abramson, Albert *television historian, consultant*
Adams, Charles Lynford *English language educator*

### North Las Vegas
Schmitt, Paul John *history and geography educator*

## NEW HAMPSHIRE

### Alstead
Lyon, Bryce Dale *historian, educator*

### Center Sandwich
Folch-Pi, Willa Babcock *romance language educator*

### Durham
Hapgood, Robert Derry *English educator*
Rouman, John Christ *classics educator*

### Exeter
Dunleavy, Janet Frank Egleson *English language educator*

### Freedom
Kucera, Henry *linguistics educator*

### Hanover
Arndt, Walter W. *Slavic scholar, linguist, writer, translator*
Bien, Peter Adolph *English language educator, author*
Daniell, Jere Rogers, II *history educator, consultant, public lecturer*
Doenges, Norman Arthur *retired classics educator*
Doney, Willis Frederick *philosophy educator*
Garthwaite, Gene Ralph *historian, educator*
Gert, Bernard *philosopher, educator*
Green, Mary Jean Matthews *foreign language educator*
Heffernan, James Anthony Walsh *English language and literature educator*
Kritzman, Lawrence David *humanities educator*
Mansell, Darrel Lee, Jr. *English educator*
Oxenhandler, Neal *language educator, writer*
Parton, James *historian*
Penner, Hans Henry *historian*
Russell, Robert Hilton *Romance languages and literature educator*
Scher, Steven Paul *literature educator*
Scherr, Barry Paul *foreign language educator*
Sheldon, Richard Robert *Russian language and literature educator*
Shewmaker, Kenneth Earl *history educator*
Wood, Charles Tuttle *history educator*

### Madbury
Bruce, Robert Vance *historian, educator*

### Nashua
Light, James Forest *English educator*

### New Castle
Silva, Joseph Donald *English language educator*

### Portsmouth
Brage, Carl Willis *genealogist*

### Strafford
Simic, Charles *English language educator, poet*

## NEW JERSEY

### Avon By The Sea
Potter, Emma Josephine Hill *language educator*

### Burlington
Holmes-Baxter, Maureen Olivia *language arts educator*

### Caldwell
Jennings, Sister Vivien Ann *English language educator*

### Camden
Showalter, English, Jr. *French language educator*

### Cape May
Lassner, Franz George *educator*

### Englewood
Beer, Jeanette Mary Scott *foreign language educator*

### Ewing
Jenson, Pauline Marie *speech and hearing educator*

### Fort Monmouth
Ignoffo, Matthew Frederick *English language educator, writer, counselor*

### Highland Park
Pane, Remigio Ugo *Romance languages educator*

### Jamesburg
Finch, Jeremiah Stanton *English language educator*

### Jersey City
Lane, Ted *literacy education educator*

### Lincroft
Jones, Floresta D. *English educator*

### Livingston
Saffer, Amy Beth *foreign language educator*

### Madison
Knox, John, Jr. *philosopher, educator*
Mc Mullen, Edwin Wallace, Jr. *English language educator*
Mitsis, George *English language and literature educator*

### Mahwah
Weinberg, Sydney Stahl *historian*

### Morristown
Fredericks, Robert Joseph *language company executive*

### New Brunswick
Akinlabi, Akinbiyi *linguistics educator*
Derbyshire, William Wadleigh *language educator, translator*
Gardner, Lloyd Calvin, Jr. *history educator*
Gillette, William *historian, educator*
Grob, Gerald N. *historian, educator*
Hartman, Mary S. *historian*
Kelley, Donald Reed *historian*
Lawrence, Francis Leo *language educator, educational administrator*
Levine, George Lewis *English language educator, literature critic*
Lewis, David Levering *history educator*
O'Neill, William Lawrence *history educator*
Poirier, Richard *English educator, literary critic*
Reed, James Wesley *social historian, educator*
Stich, Stephen Peter *philosophy educator*
Stimpson, Catharine Roslyn *English language educator, writer*

### Newark
Estrin, Herman Albert *English language educator*
Schweizer, Karl Wolfgang *historian, writer*

### Newton
Ancona, Francesco Aristide *humanities and mythology educator, writer*

### Piscataway
Mc Cormick, Richard Patrick *history educator*

### Princeton
Aarsleff, Hans *linguistics educator*
Beeners, Wilbert John *speech professional, minister*
Bowersock, Glen Warren *historian*
Brombert, Victor Henri *literature educator, author*
Brown, Leon Carl *history educator*
Champlin, Edward James *classics educator*
Coffin, David Robbins *art historian, educator*
Cooper, John Madison *philosophy educator*
Corngold, Stanley Alan *German and comparative literature educator, writer*
Curschmann, Michael Johann Hendrik *German language and literature educator*
Darnton, Robert Choate *history educator*
Ermolaev, Herman Sergei *Slavic languages educator*
Goheen, Robert Francis *classicist, educator, former ambassador*
Grafton, Anthony Thomas *history educator*
Habicht, Christian Herbert *history educator*
Harman, Gilbert Helms *philosophy educator*
Hollander, Robert B., Jr. *Romance languages educator*
Hynes, Samuel *English language educator, author*
Itzkowitz, Norman *history educator*
Jansen, Marius Berthus *historian, educator*
Jeffery, Peter Grant *musicologist, fine arts educator*
Jeffrey, Richard Carl *philosophy educator*
Jordan, William Chester *history educator*
Kaufmann, Thomas DaCosta *art history educator*
Keaney, John Joseph *classics educator*
Keeley, Edmund LeRoy *English, creative writing and modern Greek studies educator, author*
Kennan, George Frost *historian, educator, former ambassador*
Knoepflmacher, Ulrich Camillus *literature educator*
Lewis, Bernard *Near Eastern studies educator*
Lewis, David Kellogg *philosopher, educator*
Litz, Arthur Walton, Jr. *English language educator*
Ludwig, Richard Milton *English literature educator, librarian*
Mahoney, Michael Sean *history educator*
Marks, John Henry *Near Eastern studies educator*
Mc Pherson, James Munro *history educator*
Miner, Earl Roy *literature educator*
Moote, A. Lloyd *history educator*
Moynahan, Julian Lane *English language educator, author*
Nehamas, Alexander *philosophy educator*
Paret, Peter *historian*
Peterson, Willard James *Chinese history educator*
Rabb, Theodore K. *historian, educator*
Rigolot, François *French literature educator, literary critic*
Rodgers, Daniel Tracy *history educator*
Schofield, Robert E(dwin) *history educator, academic administrator*
Schorske, Carl Emil *historian, educator*
Shimizu, Yoshiaki *art historian, educator*
Showalter, Elaine *humanities educator*
Stone, Lawrence *historian*
Townsend, Charles Edward *Slavic languages educator*
Uitti, Karl David *language educator*
White, Morton Gabriel *philosopher, author*
Wightman, Ludmilla G. Popova *language educator, foreign educator, translator*
Wilson, Margaret Dauler *philosophy educator*
Ziolkowski, Theodore Joseph *comparative literature educator*

### Ridgewood
Molnar, Thomas *philosophy of religion educator, author*

### River Edge
Haynes, Barbara Judith *language educator*

### River Vale
Ehrsam, Theodore George *English language educator*

### Scotch Plains
Edwards, Thomas Robert, Jr. *language professional, investment company executive*

### Short Hills
Broder, Patricia Janis *art historian, writer*

### Somerset
Wasson, Richard Howard *English language educator*

### Teaneck
Fatemi, Faramarz Saifpour *history and political science educator, consultant*
Gordon, Lois Goldfein *English language educator*
Rudy, Willis *historian*
Williams, John Alfred *educator, author*

### Trenton
George, Emery Edward *foreign language and studies educator*

### Wayne
†Dougherty, Mildred Swanson *English educator*
O'Connor, John Morris, III *philosophy educator*

### Westfield
McDevitt, Brian Peter *history educator, educational consultant*

## NEW MEXICO

### Albuquerque
Frings, Manfred Servatius *philosophy educator*
Frumkin, Gene *writer, educator*
Fuller, Anne Elizabeth Havens *English language and literature educator, consultant*
Hutton, Paul Andrew *history educator, writer*
Kutvirt, Duda Chytilova (Ruzena) *scientific translator*
Lind, Levi Robert *classics educator, author*
MacCurdy, Raymond Ralph, Jr. *modern language educator*
Nash, Gerald David *historian*
Peña, Juan José *interpreter*
Thorson, James Llewellyn *English language educator*

### Las Cruces
Bloom, John Porter *historian, editor, administrator, archivist*
Newman, Edgar Leon *historian, educator*

### Placitas
Forrest, Suzanne Sims *research historian*

### Santa Fe
Maehl, William Henry *historian, university administrator, educational consultant*

## NEW YORK

### Albany
Beharriell, Frederick John *German and comparative literature educator*
Creegan, Robert Francis *philosophy educator*
Donovan, Robert Alan *English educator*
Eckstein, Jerome *philosopher, educator*
Lenardon, Robert Joseph *classics educator*
Martland, T(homas) R(odolphe) *philosophy educator*
Moelleken, Wolfgang Wilfried *Germanic languages and literature educator*
Patterson, Rodney Lee *foreign language and literature educator, translator*
Pohlsander, Hans Achim *classics educator*
Reese, William Lewis *philosophy educator*
Zacek, Joseph Frederick *history educator, international studies consultant, East European culture and affairs specialist*

### Alfred
Potter, Barrett George *historian, educator*

### Amherst
Kibby, Michael William *reading educator*

### Annandale On Hudson
Ashbery, John Lawrence *language educator, poet, playwright*
Mullen, William Cocke *classics educator*

### Astoria
Chan, See Fong *retired linguist, composer*

### Bear Mountain
Smith, Andrew Josef *historian, publishing executive, naturalist, writer*

### Binghamton
Block, Haskell Mayer *humanities educator*
Gaddis Rose, Marilyn *comparative literature educator, translator*
Kessler, Milton *English language educator, poet*
Sklar, Kathryn Kish *historian, educator*
Stein, George Henry *historian, educator, administrator*

### Briarcliff Manor
Leiser, Burton Myron *philosophy and law educator*

### Brockport
Bucholz, Arden Kingsbury *historian, educator*
Leslie, William Bruce *history educator*
Marcus, Robert D. *historian, educator*

### Bronx
Asare, Karen Michelle Gilliam *reading and English educator*
Bowers, Francis Robert *literature educator*
Hallett, Charles Arthur, Jr. *English and humanities educator*
Hilfstein, Erna *science historian, educator*
Himmelberg, Robert Franklin *historian, educator*
Karp, Abraham Joseph *historian, rabbi, educator*
Macklin, Ruth *bioethics educator*
Sherman, Susan Jean *English language educator*
Ultan, Lloyd *historian*
Zeichner, Oscar *historian, educator*

### Bronxville
Forester, Erica Simms *decorative arts historian, consultant, educator*
Peters, Sarah Whitaker *art historian, writer, lecturer*
Randall, Francis Ballard *historian, educator, writer*

### Brookhaven
Reeves, John Drummond *English language professional, writer*

### Brooklyn
Ashley, Leonard Raymond Nelligan *English language educator*
Blasi, Alberto *Romance languages educator, writer*
Brownstone, Paul Lotan *retired speech communications and drama educator*
Everdell, William Romeyn *humanities educator*
Flam, Jack Donald *art historian, educator*
Hoogenboom, Ari Arthur *historian, educator*
Jofen, Jean *foreign language educator*
King, Margaret Leah *history educator*
Lobron, Barbara L. *speech educator, writer, editor, photographer*
Olson, Robert Goodwin *philosophy educator*
Spector, Robert Donald *language professional, educator*
Vidal, Maureen Eris *English educator, actress*

### Buffalo
Allen, William Sheridan *history educator*
Dewald, Jonathan Stewart *history educator*
Drew, Fraser Bragg Robert *English language educator*
Fiedler, Leslie Aaron *English educator, actor, author*
Garver, Newton *philosophy educator*
Gracia, Jorge Jesus Emiliano *philosopher, educator*
Hare, Peter Hewitt *philosophy educator*
Iggers, Georg Gerson *history educator*
LaHood, Marvin John *English educator*
Levine, George Richard *English language educator*
Merini, Rafika *foreign language and literature and women's studies educator*
Milligan, John Drane *historian, educator*
Payne, Frances Anne *literature educator, researcher*
Peradotto, John Joseph *classics educator, editor*
Richards, David Gleyre *German language educator*
Riepe, Dale Maurice *philosopher, writer, illustrator, educator, Asian art dealer*
Saveth, Edward Norman *history educator*
Siedlecki, Peter Anthony *English language and literature educator*
Wolck, Wolfgang Hans-Joachim *linguist, educator*

### Canton
Goldberg, Rita Maria *foreign language educator*

### Charlton
Kekes, John *philosopher, educator*

### Clifton Park
Hughes, Edward Thomas *English educator*

### Clinton
Blackwood, Russell Thorn, III *philosophy educator*
Rupprecht, Carol Schreier *comparative literature educator, dream researcher*
Wagner, Frederick Reese *language professional*

### Cortland
Anderson, Donna Kay *musicologist, educator*
Kaminsky, Alice Richkin *English language educator*

### East Berne
Grenander, M. E. *English language educator, critic*

### Farmingdale
Austin, William James *humanities educator, poet, literary critic*

### Flushing
Bird, Thomas Edward *foreign language and literature educator*
Hirshson, Stanley Philip *history educator*
Lamont, Rosette Clementine *Romance languages educator, theatre journalist, translator*
Rabassa, Gregory *Romance languages educator, translator, poet*
Ranald, Margaret Loftus *English literature educator, author*
Tytell, John *humanities educator, writer*

### Forest Hills
Kra, Pauline Skornicki *French language educator*

### Fredonia
Sonnenfeld, Marion *linguist, educator*

### Garden City
Diamandopoulos, Peter *philosopher, educator*
Jenkins, Kenneth Vincent *literature educator, writer*
Korshak, Yvonne *art historian*
Shneidman, J. Lee *historian, educator*

### Gardiner
Mabee, Carleton *historian, educator*

### Geneseo
Edgar, William John *philosophy educator*
Fausold, Martin Luther *history educator*

**Geneva**
Caponegro, Mary *English language educator*

**Hamilton**
Blackton, Charles S(tuart) *history educator*
Busch, Briton Cooper *historian, educator*
Garland, Robert Sandford John *classical studies educator*
Hathaway, Robert Lawton *Romance languages educator*
Jones, Frank William *language educator*
Levy, Jacques *educator, theater director, lyricist, writer*
Staley, Lynn *English educator*
Van Schaack, Eric *art historian, educator*

**Herkimer**
Martin, Lorraine B. *humanities educator*

**Highland**
Brady, Christine Ellen *language arts educator*

**Hillsdale**
Parmet, Herbert Samuel *historian, educator*

**Interlaken**
Taylor, Richard *philosopher, educator*

**Ithaca**
Abrams, Meyer Howard *English language educator*
Brown, Theodore Morey *art history educator*
Colby-Hall, Alice Mary *Romance studies educator*
Culler, Jonathan Dwight *English language educator*
Eddy, Donald Davis *English language educator*
Elledge, Scott Bowen *language professional, educator*
Gibian, George *Russian and comparative literature educator*
Groos, Arthur Bernhard, Jr. *German literature educator*
Hohendahl, Peter Uwe *German language and literature educator*
Kammen, Michael *historian, educator*
Koschmann, J. Victor *history educator, academic program director*
Kronik, John William *Romance studies educator*
LaCapra, Dominick Charles *historian*
LaFeber, Walter Frederick *history educator, author*
McConkey, James Rodney *English educator, writer*
Norton, Mary Beth *history educator, author*
Porte, Joel Miles *English educator*
Radzinowicz, Mary Ann *language educator*
Shoemaker, Sydney S. *philosophy educator*
Silbey, Joel Henry *history educator*
Williams, Leslie Pearce *history educator*

**Jamaica**
Dircks, Richard Joseph *English educator, writer*
Fay, Thomas A. *philosopher, educator*
Harmond, Richard Peter *historian, educator*
Wintergerst, Ann Charlotte *language educator*

**Jericho**
Astuto, Philip Louis *retired Spanish educator*

**Mount Vernon**
Fitch, Nancy Elizabeth *historian*

**New Paltz**
Hathaway, Richard Dean *language professional, educator*
Ryan, Marleigh Grayer *Japanese language educator*

**New York**
Abel, Reuben *humanities educator*
Alazraki, Jaime *Romance languages educator*
Anderson, Quentin *English language educator, critic*
Baker, Paul Raymond *history educator*
Balakian, Anna *foreign language educator, scholar, critic, writer*
Belknap, Robert Lamont *Slavic language educator*
Bender, Thomas *history and humanities educator, writer*
Bishop, Thomas Walter *French language and literature educator*
Block, Ned *philosophy educator*
Bonfante, Larissa *classics educator*
Brilliant, Richard *art history educator*
Brody, Saul Nathaniel *English literature educator*
Brook, Barry S. *musicologist, foundation administrator*
Brooks, Jerome Bernard *English and Afro-American literature educator*
Brown, Jonathan *art historian, fine arts educator*
Brown, Milton Wolf *art historian, educator*
Brush, Craig Balcombe *retired French language and computer educator*
Bulliet, Richard Williams *history educator, novelist*
Burrill, Kathleen R. F. (Kathleen R. F. Griffin-Burrill) *Turkologist, educator*
Cahn, Steven M. *philosopher, educator*
Cantor, Norman Frank *history educator, writer*
Castronovo, David *humanities educator*
Cavallo, Jo Ann *Italian language educator*
Caws, Mary Ann *French language and comparative literature educator, critic*
Colon, Elsie Flores *American and English literature educator*
Compagnon, Antoine Marcel *French language educator*
Cook, Blanche Wiesen *history educator, journalist*
Costello, John Robert *linguistics educator*
Cullen, Patrick Colborn *English educator*
Czerwinski, Edward Joseph *foreign language educator*
Dauben, Joseph Warren *history educator*
Davies, Jane B(adger) (Mrs. Lyn Davies) *architectural historian*
Deak, Istvan *historian, educator*
Dore, Anita Wilkes *English language educator*
Driver, Martha Westcott *English language educator, writer, researcher*
Duberman, Martin *historian*
Eisler, Colin Tobias *art historian, curator*
Ferrante, Joan Marguerite *English and comparative literature educator*
Foner, Eric *historian, educator*
Frank, Elizabeth *English literature, author*
Freedberg, David Adrian *art educator, historian*
Gallo, Pia *art historian*
Gerdts, William Henry *art history educator*
Ginter, Valerian Alexius *urban historian, educator*
Glissant, Edouard Mathieu *French language educator, writer*
Gluck, Carol *history educator*
Grinnell, Helen Dunn *musicologist, arts administrator*
Gromada, Thaddeus V. *historian, administrator*
Harris, Katherine Safford *speech and hearing educator*
Harris, William Vernon *history educator*
Harvey, Donald Joseph *history educator*
Heffner, Richard Douglas *historian, educator, communications consultant, television producer*
Heilbrun, Carolyn Gold *English literature educator*
Held, Virginia *philosophy educator*
Hoeflin, Ronald Kent *philosopher, test designer, newsletter publisher*
Hooks, Bell *English educator, writer*
Hovde, Carl Frederick *language professional, educator*
Howe, Florence *English educator, writer, publisher*
Hunter-Stiebel, Penelope *art historian, art dealer*
Jackson, Kenneth Terry *historian, educator*
Johnson, Samuel Frederick *English and literature educator emeritus*
Karsen, Sonja Petra *retired Spanish educator*
†Kastan, David S. *university professor, writer*
Kerz, Louise *historian*
Kivette, Ruth Montgomery *English language educator*
Kneller, John William *retired French language educator*
Krinsky, Carol Herselle *art history educator*
Kristeller, Paul Oskar *former philosophy educator*
Kroeber, Karl *English language educator*
La Rue, (Adrian) Jan (Pieters) *musicologist, educator, author*
Leavitt, Charles Loyal *English language educator, administrator*
Leibowitz, Herbert Akiba *English language educator, author*
Lencek, Rado L. *Slavic languages educator*
Levi, Isaac *philosophy educator*
London, Herbert Ira *humanities educator*
Lorch, Maristella De Panizza (Mrs. Inama von Brunnenwald) *Romance languages educator, writer, lecturer*
Low, Anthony *English language educator*
Lowenthal, Constance *art historian*
Maguire, Robert Alan *Slavic languages and literatures educator*
Malefakis, Edward E. *history educator*
Malin, Irving *English literature educator, literary critic*
Malone, Joseph Lawrence *linguistics educator*
Matthews, William Procter *English educator*
May, Gita *French language and literature educator*
Mayerson, Philip *classics educator*
Maynard, John Rogers *English educator*
Mc Kitrick, Eric Louis *historian, educator*
Meier, August *historian, educator*
Meisel, Martin *English and comparative literature educator*
Meisel, Perry *English educator*
Middendorf, John Harlan *English literature educator*
Miller, Walter James *English and humanities educator, writer*
Mundy, John Hine *history educator*
Myers, Gerald E. *humanities educator*
Novak, Barbara *art history educator*
Olivares, Rene Eugenio *translator*
Pan, Loretta Ren-Qiu *retired educator*
Paxton, Robert Owen *historian, educator*
Plottel, Jeanine Parisier *foreign language educator*
Posner, Donald *art historian*
Ravitch, Diane Silvers *historian, educator, author, government official*
Rebay, Luciano *Italian literature educator, literary critic*
Reiman, Donald Henry *English language educator*
Reiss, Timothy James *comparative literature educator, writer*
Reynolds, Donald Martin *art historian, foundation administrator, educator*
Rice, Eugene Franklin, Jr. *history educator*
Rosand, David *art history educator*
Rosenberg, John David *English educator, literary critic*
Rosenblum, Robert *art historian, educator*
Rothman, David J. *history and medical educator*
Rowen, Ruth Halle *musicologist, educator*
Sandler, Lucy Freeman *art history educator*
Scaglione, Aldo Domenico *literature educator*
Scammell, Michael *writer, translator*
Schama, Simon *historian, educator, author*
Scheindlin, Raymond Paul *Hebrew literature educator, translator*
Seigel, Jerrold Edward *historian, writer*
Selig, Karl-Ludwig *language and literature educator*
Silverman, Kenneth Eugene *English educator, writer*
Sisman, Elaine Rochelle *musicology educator*
Stade, George Gustav *humanities educator*
Steinberg, Leo *art historian, educator*
Stern, Fritz Richard *historian, educator*
Swerdlow, Amy *historian, educator, writer*
Tanselle, George Thomas *English language educator, foundation executive*
Taran, Leonardo *classicist, educator*
Thompson, William Irwin *humanities educator, author*
Tilly, Louise Audino *history and sociology educator*
Tison-Braun, Micheline Lucie *French language educator*
Turner, Almon Richard *art historian, educator*
Tusiani, Joseph *foreign language educator, author*
Tuttleton, James Wesley *English educator*
Unger, Irwin *historian, educator*
Unger, Peter Kenneth *philosophy educator*
Walkowitz, Daniel J. *historian, filmmaker, educator*
Wardwell, Allen *art historian*
Wasser, Henry *retired English educator*
Weil-Garris Brandt, Kathleen (Kathleen Brandt) *art historian*
Weinberg, H. Barbara *art historian, educator, curator paintings and sculpture*
Wheeler, Kenneth William *history educator*
Wixom, William David *art historian, museum administrator, educator*
Wortman, Richard S. *historian, educator*
Yerushalmi, Yosef Hayim *historian, educator*
Yurchenco, Henrietta Weiss *ethnomusicologist, writer*

**Old Westbury**
Rabil, Albert, Jr. *humanities educator*

**Oneonta**
Malhotra, Ashok Kumar *philsophy educator*

**Oswego**
Smiley, Marilynn Jean *musicologist*

**Oyster Bay**
Gable, John Allen *historian, association executive, educator*

**Plattsburgh**
Herod, Charles Carteret *Afro-American studies educator*
Myers, John Lytle *historian*

**Pleasantville**
Joseph, Harriet *English literature educator*

**Poestenkill**
Radley, Virginia Louise *humanities educator*

**Potsdam**
Cross, John William *foreign language educator*
Harder, Kelsie Brown *retired language professional, educator*

**Poughkeepsie**
Bartlett, Lynn Conant *English literature educator*
Daniels, Elizabeth Adams *English language educator*
Griffen, Clyde Chesterman *retired history educator*
Hytier, Adrienne Doris *French language educator*
Kelley, David Christopher *philosopher*
Kohl, Benjamin Gibbs *historian, educator*
Lipschutz, Ilse Hempel *language educator*

**Purchase**
Clark, Mary Twibill *philosopher, educator*

**Quogue**
Cooke, Robert John *history and law educator*

**Rensselaer**
Semowich, Charles John *art historian, art dealer and appraiser, curator, artist*

**Riverdale**
Cammarata, Joan Frances *Spanish language and literature educator*

**Rochester**
Annunziata, Frank *history educator*
Berman, Milton *history educator*
Carlton, Charles Merritt *linguistics educator*
Chiarenza, Carl *art historian, critic, artist, educator*
Dohanian, Diran Kavork *art historian, educator*
Eaves, Morris Emery *English language educator*
Gordon, Dane Rex *philosophy educator, minister*
Gustina, Donna Elizabeth *sign language educator, consultant*
Hauser, William Barry *history educator, historian*
Herminghouse, Patricia Anne *foreign language educator*
Howard, Hubert Wendell *English language educator, academic administrator, choral conductor*
Hoy, Cyrus Henry *language professional, educator*
Johnson, Bruce Marvin *English language educator*
Johnson, James William *English educator, author*
Joyce, John Joseph *English language educator*
Mann, Alfred *musicology educator, choral conductor*
Ramsey, Jarold William *English language educator, author*
Young, Mary Elizabeth *history educator*
Zagorin, Perez *historian, educator*

**Sanborn**
Michalak, Janet Carol *reading education educator*

**Sayville**
Lippman, Sharon Rochelle *art historian, curator, art therapist, writer*

**Scarsdale**
Graff, Henry Franklin *historian, educator*

**Schenectady**
Jonas, Manfred *historian, educator*
Morris, John Selwyn *philosophy educator, college president emeritus*
Murphy, William Michael *literature educator, biographer*

**Setauket**
Simpson, Louis Aston Marantz *English educator, author*

**Southampton**
Brophy, James David, Jr. *humanities educator*

**Spencerport**
Clarke, Stephan Paul *English language educator, writer*

**Staten Island**
Hartman, Joan Edna *English educator*

**Stony Brook**
Aronoff, Mark H. *linguistics educator, author, consultant*
Goldberg, Homer Beryl *English language educator*
Ihde, Don *philosophy educator, university administrator*
Kuspit, Donald Burton *art historian, art critic, educator*
Levin, Richard Louis *English language educator*
Mignone, Mario B. *Italian studies educator*
Semmel, Bernard *historian, educator*
Silverman, Hugh J. *philosophy educator*
Spector, Marshall *philosophy educator*

**Suffern**
Commanday, Sue Nancy Shair *English language educator*
Walsh, James Jerome *philosophy educator*

**Syracuse**
Alston, William Payne *philosophy educator*
Crowley, John W(illiam) *English language educator*
Denise, Theodore Cullom *philosophy educator*
Hoffman, Arthur Wolf *English language educator*
Ketcham, Ralph *history and political science educator*
Lichtblau, Myron Ivor *language educator*
Meiklejohn, Donald *philosophy educator*
Powell, James Matthew *history educator*
Sternlicht, Sanford *English and theater arts educator, writer*
Sutton, Walter *English educator*
Tatham, David Frederic *art historian, educator*

**Troy**
Ahlers, Rolf Willi *philosopher, theologian*
Whitburn, Merrill Duane *English literature educator*

**West Point**
Meschutt, David Randolph *historian, curator*

**Yonkers**
Agli, Stephen Michael *English language educator, literature educator*

## NORTH CAROLINA

**Asheville**
Hubbell, Elizabeth Wolfe *English language educator*

**Chapel Hill**
Andrews, William Leake *English educator*
Baron, Samuel Haskell *historian*
Calhoun, Richard James *English language educator*
Churchill, Larry Raymond *ethics educator*
Debreczeny, Paul *Slavic language educator, author*
Eaton, Charles Edward *English language educator, author*
Falk, Eugene Hannes *foreign language educator emeritus*
Flora, Joseph M(artin) *English language educator*
Furst, Lilian Renee *language professional, educator*
Hendrick, Randall *linguist*
Heninger, Simeon Kahn, Jr. *English language educator*
Jackson, Blyden *English language educator*
Jones, Houston Gwynne *history educator*
Kohn, Richard H. *historian, educator*
Lee, Sherman Emery *art historian, curator*
Levine, Madeline Geltman *Slavic literatures educator, translator*
Long, Douglas Clark *philosophy educator*
Ludington, Charles Townsend, Jr. *English and American studies educator*
Munsat, Stanley Morris *philosopher, educator*
Nelson, Philip Francis *musicology educator, consultant, choral conductor*
Rubin, Louis Decimus, Jr. *English language and literature educator, writer, publisher*
Schier, Donald Stephen *language educator*
Smith, Sidney Rufus, Jr. *linguist, educator*
Stadter, Philip Austin *classicist, educator*
Stanberry, Dosi Elaine *English literature educator, writer*
Stephens, Laurence David, Jr. *linguist, investor, oil industry executive*
Strauss, Albrecht Benno *English educator, editor*
Tindall, George Brown *historian, educator*
Vogler, Frederick Wright *French language educator*
Weinberg, Gerhard Ludwig *history educator*
Williamson, Joel Rudolph *humanities educator*
Ziff, Paul *philosophy educator*

**Charlotte**
Hill, Ruth Foell *language consultant*

**Cullowhee**
Blethen, Harold Tyler, III *history educator*
Farwell, Harold Frederick, Jr. *English language educator*

**Davidson**
Cole, Richard Cargill *English language educator*
Lester, Malcolm *historian, educator*
Mele, Alfred R. *philosophy educator*
Tong, Rosemarie *medical humanities and philosophy educator, consultant and researcher*
Williams, Robert Chadwell *history educator*
Zimmermann, T. C. Price *historian, educator*

**Durham**
Budd, Louis John *English language educator*
Butters, Ronald Richard *English language educator*
Cady, Edwin Harrison *English language educator, author*
Chafe, William Henry *history educator*
Colton, Joel *historian, educator*
Davis, Calvin De Armond *historian, educator*
Durden, Robert Franklin *history educator*
Fish, Stanley Eugene *English language and literature educator*
Franklin, John Hope *historian, educator, author*
Gleckner, Robert Francis *English language professional, educator*
Golding, Martin Philip *law and philosophy educator*
Holley, Irving Brinton, Jr. *historian, educator*
Lerner, Warren *historian*
Mauskopf, Seymour Harold *history educator*
Nygard, Holger Olof *English and folklore educator*
Oates, John Francis *classics educator*
Preston, Richard Arthur *historian*
Richardson, Lawrence, Jr. *Latin language educator, archeologist*
Ryals, Clyde de Loache *humanities educator*
Sanford, David Hawley *philosophy educator*
Scott, Anne Byrd Firor *history educator*
Smith, Grover Cleveland *English language educator*
Thompson, John Herd *history educator*
Wardropper, Bruce Wear *language educator*
Williams, George Walton *English educator*
Williams, Jocelyn Jones *reading educator*

**Fayetteville**
Bowman, Charles Harwood, Jr. *historian, educator*

**Greensboro**
Almeida, José Agustín *romance languages educator*
Bardolph, Richard *historian, educator*
Chappell, Fred Davis *English language educator, poet*
Gaines, Sarah Fore *retired foreign language educator*
Penninger, Frieda Elaine *retired English language educator*
Thompson, James Howard *historian, library administrator*

**Hendersonville**
Schwarz, Richard William *historian, educator*

**High Point**
McCaslin, Richard Bryan *history educator*

**Jacksonville**
†Kimball, Lynn Jerome *historian*

**Laurinburg**
Bayes, Ronald Homer *English language educator, author*

**Pope AFB**
Conley, Raymond Leslie *English language educator*

**Raleigh**
Rhodes, Donald Robert *musicologist, retired electrical engineer*

**Research Triangle Park**
Connor, Walter Robert *classics educator, humanities center administrator*

**Weldon**
Lewter, Alice Jenkins *history and political science educator*

**West End**
Moncure, James Ashby *historian*

**Wilmington**
Graham, Otis Livingston, Jr. *history educator*

**Winston Salem**
Barnett, Richard Chambers *historian, educator*
Covey, Cyclone *history educator*
Helm, Robert Meredith *philosophy educator*
Hendricks, J(ames) Edwin *historian, educator, consultant, author*
Scales, James Ralph *history educator, former university president*
Shapere, Dudley *philosophy educator*

## NORTH DAKOTA

**Bismarck**
Newborg, Gerald Gordon *historical agency administrator*

**Fargo**
Peet, Howard David *English language and literature educator, writer*

**Grand Forks**
Caldwell, Mary Ellen *English language educator*

**Rolla**
Jacobsen-Theel, Hazel M. *historian*

## OHIO

**Akron**
Bryant, Keith Lynn, Jr. *history educator*
Jones, Robert Huhn *history educator*
Knepper, George W. *history educator*

**Athens**
Booth, Alan Rundlett *history educator*
Borchert, Donald Marvin *philosopher, educator*
Crowl, Samuel Renninger *English language educator, author*
Eckes, Alfred Edward, Jr. *historian, international trade analyst*
Matthews, Jack (John Harold Matthews) *English educator, writer*
Perdreau, Cornelia Ruth Whitener (Connie Perdreau) *English as a second language educator, international exchange specialist*
Ping, Charles Jackson *philosophy educator, retired university president*
Whealey, Lois Deimel *humanities scholar*

**Berea**
Blumer, Frederick Elwin *philosophy educator*

**Bowling Green**
Browne, Ray Broadus *popular culture educator*
Lavezzi, John Charles *art history educator, archaeologist*
Middleton, Charles Ronald *history educator*

**Canton**
Dickens, Sheila Jeanne *family preservation educator*

**Chagrin Falls**
Rawski, Conrad H(enry) *humanities educator, medievalist*

**Cincinnati**
Bleznick, Donald William *Romance languages educator*
Ciani, Alfred Joseph *language professional, dean*
Huvos, Kornel *linguistics educator*
Lewis, Gene Dale *historian, educator*
Muntz, Ernest Gordon *historian, educator*
Peck, Abraham Joseph *historian*
Peterson, Gale Eugene *historian*
Schrier, Arnold *historian, educator*

**Cleveland**
Anderson, David Gaskill, Jr. *Spanish language educator*
Benseler, David Price *foreign language educator*
Buchanan, D(aniel) Harvey *art history educator*
Dancyger, Ruth *art historian*
Ferguson, Suzanne Carol *English educator*
Friedman, Barton Robert *English educator*
Greppin, John Aird Coutts *philologist, editor, educator*
Harper, Williard Flemmett *language educator*
Heald, Morrell *humanities educator*
Miller, Genevieve *retired medical historian*
Olszewski, Edward John *art history educator*
Pappas, Effie Vamis *English and business educator, writer*
Pursell, Carroll Wirth *history educator*
Roth, Jack Joseph *historian, educator*
Runyan, Timothy Jack *historian, educator*
Salomon, Roger Blaine *English language educator*
Spencer, James Calvin, Sr. *humanities educator*
Trawick, Leonard Moses *English educator*

Weinberg, Helen Arnstein *American art and literature educator*

**Columbus**
Babcock, Charles Luther *classics educator*
Battersby, James Lyons, Jr. *English language educator*
Beja, Morris *English literature educator*
Boh, Ivan *philosophy educator*
Brittin, Marie Eleanor *communications, psychology, speech and hearing science educator*
Brooks, Keith *retired speech communication educator*
Burnham, John Chynoweth *historian, educator*
DeSando, John Anthony *humanities educator*
Dillon, Merton Lynn *historian, educator*
Gribble, Charles Edward *Slavic languages educator, editor*
Hahm, David Edgar *classics educator*
Hare, Robert Yates *music history educator*
Hoffmann, Charles Wesley *retired foreign language educator*
Jarvis, Gilbert Andrew *humanities educator*
Kasulis, Thomas Patrick *humanities educator*
Kuhn, Albert Joseph *English educator*
Lehiste, Ilse *language educator*
Rule, John Corwin *history educator*
Scanlan, James Patrick *philosophy and Slavic studies educator*
Silbajoris, Frank Rimvydas *Slavic languages educator*

**Dayton**
Alexander, Roberta Sue *history educator*
Harden, Oleta Elizabeth *English educator, university administrator*

**Fremont**
Wethington, Norbert Anthony *medieval scholar*

**Galion**
Ross, Shirley S. *retired English educator*

**Gambier**
Sharp, Ronald Alan *English literature educator, author*

**Granville**
Santoni, Ronald Ernest *philosophy educator*

**Huron**
Ruble, Ronald Merlin *humanities and theater communications educator*

**Kent**
Beer, Barrett Lynn *historian, educator*
Byrne, Frank Loyola *history educator*
Dante, Harris Loy *history educator*
Harkness, Bruce *English language educator*
Hassler, Donald Mackey, II *English language educator, writer*
James, Patricia Ann *philosophy educator*
Reid, Sidney Webb *English educator*
Zornow, William Frank *historian, educator*

**Kirtland**
Skerry, Philip John *English educator*

**Marietta**
Wilbanks, Jan Joseph *philosopher*

**Mc Arthur**
Shuter, David Henry *foreign language educator*

**Medina**
Brown, Kathryn Lisbeth *secondary education educator*

**Niles**
Darlington, Oscar Gilpin *historian, educator*

**Oberlin**
Blodgett, Geoffrey Thomas *history educator*
Care, Norman Sydney *philosophy educator*
Colish, Marcia Lillian *history educator*
Spear, Richard Edmund *art history educator*
Young, David Pollock *humanities educator, author*

**Oxford**
Pratt, William Crouch, Jr. *English language educator, writer*
Siatra, Eleni *English educator*
Winkler, Allan Michael *history educator*

**Parma**
Cook, Jeanne Garn *historian, genealogist*

**Portsmouth**
Mirabello, Mark Linden *history educator*

**Tiffin**
Davison, Kenneth Edwin *American studies educator*
Kramer, Frank Raymond *classicist, educator*

**Toledo**
Hutton, William *art historian*
Smith, Robert Freeman *history educator*
Thompson, Gerald E. *historian, educator*

**Westerville**
Golladay, Loy Edgar *emeritus special educator*

**Yellow Springs**
Fogarty, Robert Stephen *historian, educator, editor*

**Youngstown**
Bell, Carol Willsey *genealogist*
Bowers, Bege K. *English educator*
Brothers, Barbara *English language educator*

## OKLAHOMA

**Bartlesville**
Austerman, Donna Lynne *Spanish language educator*

**Bethany**
Davis, Harrison Ransom Samuel, Jr. *English language educator*

**Norman**
Brown, Sidney DeVere *history educator*
Fears, Jesse Rufus *historian, educator, academic dean*
Glad, Paul Wilbur *history educator*
Hagan, William Thomas *history educator*
Lowitt, Richard *history educator*

**Oklahoma City**
Holt, Karen Anita Young *English educator*
Lestina, Roger Henry *English language educator*
Owens, Barbara Ann *English educator*
Todd, Joe Lee *historian*

**Stillwater**
Agnew, Theodore Lee, Jr. *historian, educator*
Fischer, LeRoy Henry *historian, educator*
Luebke, Neil Robert *philosophy educator*

**Tulsa**
Buckley, Thomas Hugh *historian, educator*
O'Brien, Darcy *English educator, writer*

## OREGON

**Ashland**
Bornet, Vaughn Davis *former history and social science educator, research historian*
Levy, Leonard Williams *history educator, author*

**Eugene**
Birn, Raymond Francis *historian, educator*
Donnelly, Marian Card *art historian, educator*
Lansdowne, Karen Myrtle *retired English language and literature educator*
Pascal, C(ecil) Bennett *classics educator*
Rendall, Steven Finlay *language educator, editor, translator, critic*
White, David Olds *researcher, former educator*
Wickes, George *English language educator, writer*

**Mcminnville**
Mc Kaughan, Howard Paul *linguistics educator*

**Netarts**
Hartman-Irwin, Mary Frances *retired language professional*

**Port Orford**
Drinnon, Richard *history educator*

**Portland**
Englert, Walter George *classics and humanities educator*
Harris, Frederick Philip *retired philosophy educator*
Kinzer, Donald Louis *retired historian, educator*
Schmidt, Stanley Eugene *retired speech educator*
Steinman, Lisa Malinowski *English literature educator, writer*
Vaughan, Thomas James Gregory *historian*

**Salem**
Trueblood, Paul Graham *retired English educator, author, editor*

**Seaside**
Andrews, Clarence Adelbert *historian, educator, writer, publisher*

## PENNSYLVANIA

**Allentown**
LoCicero, Donald *language educator, writer*

**Ardmore**
Gutwirth, Marcel Marc *French literature educator*

**Bala Cynwyd**
Michael, Gayle Granatir *English language educator, educational consultant*

**Bethlehem**
Beidler, Peter Grant *English educator*
Dowling, Joseph Albert *historian, educator*
Haynes, Thomas Morris *philosophy educator*
Lindgren, John Ralph *philosophy educator*
Smolansky, Oles M. *humanities educator*
Wolfgang, Lenora D. *foreign language educator*

**Bryn Mawr**
Brand, Charles Macy *history educator*
Dorian, Nancy Currier *linguistics educator*
Dudden, Arthur Power *historian, educator*
Gaisser, Julia Haig *classics educator*
King, Willard Fahrenkamp (Mrs. Edmund Ludwig King) *Spanish language educator*
Krausz, Michael *philosopher, educator*
Lane, Barbara Miller (Barbara Miller-Lane) *humanities educator*
Lang, Mabel Louise *classics educator*
Salmon, John Hearsey McMillan *historian, educator*
Stapleton, Katharine Laurence *English literature educator, writer*

**California**
Schwerdt, Lisa Mary *English language educator*

**Carlisle**
Fox, Arturo Angel *Spanish language educator*
Schiffman, Joseph Harris *literary historian, educator*
Shrader, Charles Reginald *historian*

**Chambersburg**
Gelbach, Martha Harvey *genealogist, writer, poet*

**Colmar**
Weber-Roochvarg, Lynn *English second language adult educator, communications consultant*

**East Stroudsburg**
Crackel, Theodore Joseph *historian*

**Easton**
Coleman, John Macdonald *historian*
Cooke, Jacob Ernest *history educator, author*

**Edinboro**
Kinch, Janet Carolyn Brozic *English and German language/literature educator*

**Elkins Park**
Davidson, Abraham Aba *art historian, photographer*

**Erie**
Allshouse, Robert Harold *history educator*

**Forty Fort**
Meeker, Robert Gardner *English language educator*

**Haverford**
Jorden, Eleanor Harz *linguist, educator*
Spielman, John Philip, Jr. *historian, educator*
Young-Bruehl, Elisabeth *philosophy educator, psychoanalyst*

**Johnstown**
Smith, William Raymond *history educator, philosophy educator*

**Kennett Square**
Beddall, Barbara Gould *science historian, writer*
Bronner, Edwin Blaine *history educator*

**Kutztown**
Meyer, Susan Moon *speech language pathologist, educator*

**Lancaster**
Steiner, Robert Lisle *language consultant, retired*

**Leesport**
Jackson, Eric Allen *philatelist*

**Lewisburg**
Edgerton, Mills Fox, Jr. *foreign language educator*
Little, Daniel Eastman *philosophy educator, university program director*
Payne, Michael David *English language educator*

**Lock Haven**
Congdon, Howard Krebs *philosopher, clergyman, educator*

**Meadville**
Hogan, James Charles *classicist, educator*
Katope, Christopher George *English language educator*

**Middletown**
Ross, Cheri Louise *English language educator*

**Millersville**
Miller, Steven Max *humanities educator*

**Mont Alto**
Russo, Peggy Anne *English language educator*

**Narberth**
Wagner, Frederick Balthas, Jr. *historian, retired surgery educator*

**Newtown**
Bohning, Elizabeth Edrop *foreign language educator*
Palmer, Robert Roswell *historian, educator*

**Philadelphia**
Bell, Whitfield Jenks, Jr. *historian*
Benson, Morton *Slavic languages educator, lexicographer*
Burke, Daniel William *retired English educator, college president*
Daemmrich, Horst Sigmund *German language and literature educator*
Davis, Allen Freeman *history educator, author*
DeLaura, David Joseph *English language educator*
Graham, Alexander John *classics educator*
Hoenigswald, Henry Max *linguist, educator*
Hoffman, Daniel (Gerard) *literature educator, poet*
Knauer, Georg Nicolaus *classical philologist*
Lee, Charles *retired English language and literature educator, arts critic*
Lewin, Moshe *historian, educator*
Lloyd, Albert Lawrence, Jr. *German language educator*
Logan, Marie-Rose van Stynvoort *literature educator, editor*
Lucid, Robert Francis *English educator*
Means, John Barkley *foreign language educator, association executive*
Morello, Celeste Anne *historian, educator, criminologist*
Moss, Roger William, Jr. *historian, writer, administrator*
Murphey, Murray Griffin *history educator*
Peters, Edward Murray *history educator*
Prince, Gerald Joseph *Romance languages educator*
Quann, Joan Louise *English language educator, real estate broker*
Rambo, Wayne Herbert *English language and education educator*
Regan, Robert Charles *English language educator*
Rocher, Ludo *humanities educator*
Rosenberg, Charles Ernest *historian, educator*
Schiffman, Harold Fosdick *Asian language educator*
Sebold, Russell Perry, III *Romance languages educator, author*
Sivin, Nathan *historian, educator*
Vitiello, Justin *language educator*
Weigley, Russell Frank *history educator*

**Phoenixville**
Lukacs, John Adalbert *historian, retired educator*

**Pittsburgh**
Anthony, Edward Mason *linguistics educator*
Buchanan, James Junkin *classics educator*
Clack, Jerry *classics educator*
Drescher, Seymour *history educator, writer*
Eskenazi, Maxine Solomon *speech researcher*
Ferguson, Mary Anne Heyward *language professional, educator*
Gale, Robert Lee *retired American literature educator and critic*
Goldstein, Donald Maurice *historian, educator*
Grunbaum, Adolf *philosophy educator, author*
Harris, Ann Birgitta Sutherland *art historian*

Hicks, Wendell Leon *history educator, publisher, political scientist*
Hsu, Cho-yun *history educator*
Miller, David William *historian, educator*
Modell, John *historian, educator*
Morice, Joseph Richard *history educator*
Paulston, Christina Bratt *linguistics educator*
Rawski, Evelyn Sakakida *history educator*
Rescher, Nicholas *philosophy educator*
Rimer, John Thomas *foreign language educator, academic administrator, writer, translator*
Seligson, Mitchell A. *Latin American studies educator*
Sheon, Aaron *art historian, educator*
Stearns, Peter Nathaniel *history educator*
Tarr, Joel Arthur *history and public policy educator*
Toker, Franklin K. *art history educator, archaeologist, foundation executive*
Udler, Rubin Yakovlevitch *linguist*
Weingartner, Rudolph Herbert *philosophy educator*

**Pottstown**
Ruth, Thomas Griswold *history educator*

**Rosemont**
Bolger, Stephen Garrett *English and American studies educator*

**Scranton**
Hoffman, Barbara Ann *English language educator*

**Selinsgrove**
Kolbert, Jack *foreign language educator, French literature educator, humanities educator*

**Sharpsville**
Durek, Dorothy Mary *retired English language educator*

**Springtown**
Hunt, John Wesley *English language educator*

**State College**
Johnstone, Henry Webb, Jr. *philosophy educator*
Kockelmans, Joseph J. *philosopher, educator*
Robinett, Betty Wallace *linguist*

**Swarthmore**
Bannister, Robert Corwin, Jr. *history educator*
Beeman, Richard Roy *historian, educator*
Blackburn, Thomas Harold *English language professional, educator*
Lacey, Hugh Matthew *philosophy educator*
North, Helen Florence *classicist, educator*
Ostwald, Martin *classics educator emeritus*
Pagliaro, Harold Emil *English language educator*

**Topton**
Haskell, Ellery Bickford *retired philosophy educator*

**University Park**
Ameringer, Charles D. *history educator*
Anderson, John Mueller *retired philosophy educator*
Brault, Gerard Joseph *French language educator*
De Armas, Frederick Alfred *foreign language educator*
Frank, Robert Worth, Jr. *English language educator*
Goldschmidt, Arthur Eduard, Jr. *historian, educator*
Hager, Hellmut Wilhelm *art history educator*
Lima, Robert *Hispanic studies and comparative literature educator*
Schmalstieg, William Riegel *Slavic languages educator*
Weintraub, Stanley *arts and humanities educator, author*
Williams, Edward Vinson *music history educator*

**Villanova**
Bergquist, James Manning *history educator*
Caputo, John David *philosophy educator*
Helmetag, Charles Hugh *foreign language educator*
Hunt, John Mortimer, Jr. *classical studies educator*
McDiarmid, Lucy *English educator, author*
Thomas, Deborah Allen *English educator*

**West Chester**
Dorchester, Jane Elizabeth *historic researcher*
Gougher, Ronald Lee *foreign language educator and administrator*
Hipple, Walter John *English language educator*

## RHODE ISLAND

**Kingston**
Kim, Yong Choon *philosopher, theologian, educator*
MacLaine, Allan Hugh *English language educator*

**Newport**
Brennan, Joseph Gerard *philosophy educator*
Haas, William Paul *humanities educator, former college president*

**Providence**
Ackerman, Felicia *philosophy educator, writer*
Anderson, James Arthur *humanities educator, academic director*
Arant, Patricia *Slavic languages and literature educator*
Bensmaia, Reda *French studies educator, researcher*
Berghahn, Volker Rolf *history educator*
Blasing, Mutlu Konuk *English language educator*
Boegehold, Alan Lindley *classics educator*
Cook, Albert Spaulding *comparative literature and classics educator, writer*
Donovan, Bruce Elliot *classics educator, university dean*
Enteman, Willard Finley *philosophy educator*
Fornara, Charles William *historian, classicist, educator*
Gleason, Abbott *history educator*
Harleman, Ann *English educator, writer*
Honig, Edwin *comparative literature educator, poet*
Jordy, William Henry *art history educator*
Kim, Jaegwon *philosophy educator*
Konstan, David *classics and comparative literature educator, researcher*
Lesko, Leonard Henry *Egyptologist, educator*
Monteiro, George *English educator, writer*
Neu, Charles Eric *historian, educator*
Putnam, Michael Courtney Jenkins *classics educator*
Ribbans, Geoffrey Wilfrid *Spanish educator*
Rohr, Donald Gerard *history educator*
Rosenberg, Bruce Alan *English language educator, author*
Saint-Amand, Pierre Nemours *humanities educator*
Scharf, Peter Mark *Sanskrit and Indian studies educator*
Schulz, Juergen *art history educator*
Sosa, Ernest *philosopher, educator*
Spilka, Mark *retired English language educator*
Terras, Victor *Slavic languages and comparative literature educator*
Trueblood, Alan Stubbs *former modern language educator*
Waldrop, Bernard Keith *English educator*
Williams, Lea Everard *history educator*
Wood, Gordon Stewart *historian, educator*
Wrenn, James Joseph *East Asian studies educator*

## SOUTH CAROLINA

**Beaufort**
†Rowland, Lawrence Sanders *history educator*

**Bluffton**
Brown, Dallas Coverdale, Jr. *retired army officer, retired history educator*

**Charleston**
Crout, Robert Rhodes *historian, educator*

**Clemson**
Riley, Helene Maria Kastinger *Germanist*

**Clinton**
Skinner, James Lister, III *English language educator*

**Columbia**
Ashley, Perry Jonathan *journalism educator*
Belasco, Simon *French language and linguistics educator*
Bruccoli, Matthew Joseph *English educator, publisher*
Edgar, Walter Bellingrath *historian*
Geckle, George Leo, III *English language educator*
Hardin, James Neal *German and comparative literature educator, publisher*
Hatch, Mary Gies *German language educator*
Howard-Hill, Trevor Howard *English language educator*
Johnson, Herbert Alan *history and law educator, lawyer, chaplain*
Kay, Carol McGinnis *literature educator*
Long, Eugene Thomas, III *philosophy educator, administrator*
Meriwether, James Babcock *retired English language educator*
Myerson, Joel Arthur *English language educator, researcher*
Nolte, William Henry *English language educator*
Reeves, George McMillan, Jr. *comparative literature educator, educational administrator*
Sproat, John Gerald *historian*
Synnott, Marcia Graham *history educator*

**Conway**
Talbert, Roy, Jr. *history educator*

**Darlington**
Holt, Robert LeRoi *philosophy educator*

**Greenville**
Crabtree, John Henry, Jr. *retired English educator*

**Hilton Head Island**
Male, Roy Raymond *English language educator*

**Mullins**
Stonesifer, Richard James *retired humanities and social science educator*

**Orangeburg**
Johnson, Alex Claudius *English language educator*

**Rock Hill**
Viault, Birdsall Scrymser *history educator*

**Spartanburg**
Deku, Afrikadzata *Afrikan-centric scholar, international speaker*

**West Columbia**
Ochs, Robert David *history educator*
Parker, Harold Talbot *history educator*

**York**
Lee, Joseph Edward *history educator*

## SOUTH DAKOTA

**Sioux Falls**
Carlson Aronson, Marilyn A. *English language educator*
Huseboe, Arthur Robert *American literature educator*
Staggers, Kermit LeMoyne, II *history and political science educator, state senator*

## TENNESSEE

**Big Sandy**
Chastain, Kenneth Duane *retired foreign language educator*

**Columbia**
Curry, Beatrice Chesrown *English educator*

**Cookeville**
Campana, Phillip Joseph *German language educator*

**Jefferson City**
Baumgardner, James Lewis *history educator*

**Johnson City**
Greninger, Edwin Thomas *former history educator*
Schneider, Valerie Lois *speech educator*
Wyatt, Doris Fay Chapman *English language educator*
Zayas-Bazan, Eduardo *foreign language educator*

**Kingsport**
Egan, Martha Avaleen *history educator, archivist*
Wolfe, Margaret Ripley *historian, educator, consultant*

**Knoxville**
Brady, Patrick *French literature educator, novelist*
Cutler, Everette Wayne *history educator*
Fisher, John Hurt *English language educator*
Klein, Milton Martin *history educator*
Moser, Harold Dean *historian*

**Memphis**
Copper, John Franklin *Asian studies educator, consultant*
Jolly, William Thomas *foreign language educator*
Jones, Marguerite Jackson *English language educator*
O'Donnell, William Hugh *English educator*
Stagg, Louis Charles *English language and literature educator*
Vest, James Murray *foreign language and literature educator*

**Murfreesboro**
Huhta, James Kenneth *historian, university administrator, educator, consultant*
Rupprecht, Nancy Ellen *historian, educator*

**Nashville**
Boorman, Howard Lyon *history educator*
Collier, Simon *history educator*
Compton, John Joseph *philosophy educator*
Conkin, Paul Keith *history educator*
Cook, Ann Jennalie *English language educator*
Doody, Margaret Anne *English language educator*
Doyle, Don Harrison *history educator*
Girgus, Sam B. *English literature educator*
Graham, Hugh Davis *history educator*
Grantham, Dewey Wesley *historian, educator*
Halperin, John William *English literature educator*
Harris, Alice Carmichael *linguist, educator*
Hassel, Rudolph Christopher *English language educator*
Jarman, Mark Foster *English language educator*
Lachs, John *philosopher, educator*
Neel, Jasper Phillip *English educator*
Perry, Lewis Curtis *historian, educator*
Pichois, Claude P. *classical studies educator*
Ransom, Nancy Alderman *sociology and women's studies educator, university administrator*
Smith, Samuel Boyd *history educator*
Stumpf, Samuel Enoch *philosophy educator*
Voegeli, Victor Jacque *history educator, dean*
von Raffler-Engel, Walburga (Walburga Engel) *linguist, lecturer, writer*

**Sewanee**
Spears, Monroe Kirk *English educator, author*
Williamson, Samuel Ruthven, Jr. *historian, university administrator*

**Shiloh**
Hawke, Paul Henry *historian*

**Tullahoma**
Moulton, Dawn G. *English language educator*

## TEXAS

**Abilene**
McWhiney, Grady *history educator*

**Arlington**
Kubecka, Ronna Denise *English language and art educator, psychotherapist*

**Austin**
Bonevac, Daniel Albert *philosopher, author*
Bordie, John George *linguistics educator*
Boyd, Carolyn Patricia *history educator*
Boyer, Mildred Vinson *retired foreign language educator*
Braybrooke, David *philosopher, educator*
Brown, Norman Donald *history educator*
Carleton, Don Edward *history center administrator, educator, writer*
Causey, Robert Louis *philosopher, educator, consultant*
Cline, Clarence Lee *language professional*
Crosby, Alfred Worcester *history educator*
Divine, Robert Alexander *history educator*
Dulles, John Watson Foster *history educator*
Farrell, Edmund James *English language educator, author*
Friedman, Alan Warren *humanities educator*
Galinsky, Gotthard Karl *classicist, educator*
Gould, Lewis Ludlow *historian*
Green, Peter Morris *classics educator, writer, translator*
Hancock, Ian Francis (O Yanko le Redžosko) *linguistics educator*
Harms, Robert Thomas *linguist, educator*
Hinojosa-Smith, Roland *English language educator, writer*
Hopper, Robert William *speech communication educator*
Jazayery, Mohammad Ali *foreign languages and literature educator emeritus*
Katz, Michael Ray *Slavic languages educator*
King, Robert D. *linguistics educator*
Lehmann, Ruth Preston Miller *literature educator*
Lehmann, Winfred Philipp *linguistics educator*
Louis, William Roger *historian, educator, editor*
Mackey, Louis Henry *philosophy educator*
Meacham, Standish *historian, educator*
Megaw, Robert Neill Ellison *English educator*
Middleton, Christopher *Germanic languages and literature educator*
Moag, Rodney Frank *language educator, country music singer*
Paredes, Americo *English language educator*
Phillips, Frances Marie *history educator*
Polomé, Edgar Charles *foreign language and linguistics educator*
Pope, Marvin Hoyle *language educator, writer*
Rich, John Martin *humanities educator, researcher*
Seung, Thomas Kaehao *philosophy educator*
Staley, Thomas Fabian *language professional, academic administrator*
Sutherland, William Owen Sheppard *English language educator*
Todd, William Burton *English language and literature educator*
Tyler, Ronnie Curtis *historian*
Velz, John William *literature educator*
Wadlington, Warwick Paul *English language educator*
Werbow, Stanley Newman *language educator*
Whitbread, Thomas Bacon *English educator, author*

**Burleson**
Robin, Clara Nell (Claire Robin) *English language educator*

**College Station**
Berthold, Dennis Alfred *English language educator*
Cannon, Garland *English language educator*
Davenport, Manuel Manson *philosophy educator*
Dethloff, Henry Clay *history educator*
Fedorchik, Bette Joy Winter *foreign language professional*
Nance, Joseph Milton *history educator*
Unterberger, Betty Miller *history educator, writer*

**Commerce**
Grimshaw, James Albert, Jr. *English language educator*
Linck, Charles Edward, Jr. *English language educator*
Perry, Thomas Amherst *English literature and language educator*

**Corpus Christi**
Snouffer, Nancy Kendall *English and reading educator*
Wooster, Robert *history educator*

**Dallas**
Britton, Wesley Alan *English language educator*
Comini, Alessandra *art historian, educator*
Countryman, Edward Francis *historian, educator*
Crain, John Walter *historian*
Hunter, Robert Grams *retired English language educator*
Lutz, Gretchen Kay *English language educator*
Martin, Carol Jacquelyn *educator, artist*
Pike, Kenneth Lee *linguist, educator*
Taylor, William Berley *history educator*
Terry, Marshall Northway, Jr. *English language educator, author*

**Denton**
Kamman, William *historian, educator*
Kesterson, David Bert *English language educator*
Palmer, Leslie Howard *literature educator*
Preston, Thomas Ronald *English language educator, researcher*
Rektorik-Sprinkle, Patricia Jean *Latin language educator*
Snapp, Harry Franklin *historian*
Vaughn, William Preston *historian, educator*

**Edinburg**
Barrera, Eduardo *Spanish language and literature educator*

**El Paso**
Bailey, Kenneth Kyle *history educator*
Lujan, Rosa Emma *bilingual specialist, trainer, consultant*

**Fort Worth**
Durham, Carolyn Richardson *foreign language and literature educator*
Erisman, Fred Raymond *English literature educator*
Reuter, Frank Theodore *history educator*
Wertz, Spencer K. *philosophy educator*
Worcester, Donald Emmet *history educator, author*

**Galveston**
Ryan, James Gilbert *historian, educator, writer*

**Georgetown**
Browning, Grayson Douglas *philosophy educator*

**Grapevine**
Stack, George Joseph *philosophy educator*

**Harlingen**
Martin, Leland Morris (Pappy Martin) *history educator*

**Houston**
Castañeda, James Agustín *Spanish language educator, university golf coach*
Chance, Jane *English literature educator*
Decker, Hannah Shulman *history educator*
Drew, Katherine Fischer *history educator*
Gruber, Ira Dempsey *historian, educator*
Haskell, Thomas Langdon *history educator*
Hult, Susan Freda *history educator*
Huston, John Dennis *English educator*
Hyman, Harold M. *history educator, consultant*
Lamb, Sydney MacDonald *linguistics and cognitive science educator*
Martin, James Kirby *historian, educator*
Minter, David Lee *English literature educator*
Patten, Robert Lowry *English language educator*
Pryor, William Daniel Lee *humanities educator*
Russman, Thomas Anthony *philosophy educator*
Sher, George Allen *philosophy educator*
Smith, Richard Joseph *history educator*
Temkin, Larry Scott *philosopher, educator*
Thompson, Ewa M. *foreign language educator*
Urbina, Manuel, II *legal research historian, history educator*
Vallbona, Rima-Gretel Rothe *Spanish language educator, writer*
Wiener, Martin Joel *historian*
Wyschogrod, Edith *philosophy educator*

**Huntsville**
Gutermuth, Mary Elizabeth *foreign language educator*
Raymond, Kay E(ngelmann) *Spanish language educator, consultant*

**Irving**
Sommerfeldt, John Robert *historian*

**Levelland**
Sears, Edward L. *English language educator*

**Lubbock**
Connor, Seymour Vaughan *historian, educator, writer*
Eddleman, Floyd Eugene *retired English language educator*
Kelsey, Clyde Eastman, Jr. *philosophy and psychology educator*
Ketner, Kenneth Laine *philosopher, educator*
Pearce, William Martin *history educator*
Walker, Warren Stanley *English educator*

**Nacogdoches**
Kallsen, Theodore John *retired English language educator*

**Prairie View**
Boyd-Brown, Lena Ernestine *history educator, education consultant*

**Ranger**
Jones, Roger Walton *English language educator, writer*

**Richardson**
Akmakjian, Alan Paul *English language, literature and creative writing educator*
Redman, Timothy Paul *English language educator, author, chess federation administrator*

**Round Top**
Lentz, Edwin Lamar *art historian*

**San Antonio**
Kellman, Steven G. *literature educator, author*
Leighton, Albert Chester *history educator*
Schulte, Josephine Helen *historian, educator*

**Seguin**
Hsu, Patrick Kuo-Heng *languages educator, librarian*
Moline, Jon Nelson *philosopher, educator, college president*

**Stephenville**
Christopher, Joe Randell *English language educator*

**Uvalde**
Wood, James Albert *foreign language educator*

**Waco**
Baird, Robert Malcolm *philosophy educator, researcher*
Collmer, Robert George *English language educator*
Cutter, Charles Richard, III *retired classics educator*
Goode, Clement Tyson *English language educator*
Herring, Jack William *English language educator*

**Wichita Falls**
Bourland, D(elphus) David, Jr. *linguist*

## UTAH

**Logan**
Ellsworth, Samuel George *historian, educator*
Lye, William Frank *history educator*
Milner, Clyde A., II *historian*

**Provo**
Alexander, Thomas Glen *history educator*
Arrington, Leonard James *history educator*
Clark, Bruce Budge *humanities educator*
Forster, Merlin Henry *foreign languages educator, author, researcher*
Lyon, James Karl *German language educator*
Peer, Larry Howard *literature educator*
Skinner, Andrew Charles *history educator, religious writer*

**Salt Lake City**
Bremer, Ronald Allan *geneologist, historian*
Eakle, Arlene H. *genealogist*
Hibbard, Charles Gustin *historian*
Madsen, Brigham Dwaine *history educator*
Olpin, Robert Spencer *art history educator*
Sanderson, Cathy Ann *histotechnician, researcher*
Sillars, Malcolm Osgood *communication educator*
Steensma, Robert Charles *English language educator*

## VERMONT

**Bennington**
Kaplan, Harold *humanities educator, author*

**Burlington**
Daniels, Robert Vincent *history educator, former state senator*
Hall, Robert William *philosophy and religion educator*
Scrase, David Anthony *German language educator*
Weiger, John George *foreign language educator*

**Middlebury**
Freeman, Stephen Albert *retired foreign language educator*
Jacobs, Travis Beal *historian, educator*
Lamberti, Marjorie *history educator*
Vail, Van Horn *German language educator*

**Stowe**
Taplin, Winn Lowell *historian, retired senior intelligence operations officer*

## VIRGINIA

**Alexandria**
Byrne, John Edward *writer, retired government official*
DeZarn, Guy David *English language educator*
Hixson, Stanley G. *speech, language and computer technology educator*
Myers, Denys Peter, Jr. *architectural historian*
White, Gordon Eliot *historian*

**Arlington**
Allard, Dean Conrad *historian, retired naval history center director*
Mills, Elizabeth Shown *genealogist editor, writer*

**Ashland**
Inge, Milton Thomas *American literature and culture educator, author*

**Blacksburg**
Baumgartner, Frederic Joseph *history educator*
Doswald, Herman Kenneth *German language educator, academic administrator*
Landen, Robert Geran *historian, university administrator*
Peacock, Markham Lovick, Jr. *English educator*
Pitt, Joseph Charles *philosophy educator*
Robertson, James Irvin, Jr. *historian, educator*
Ulloa, Justo Celso *Spanish educator*

**Charlottesville**
Abbot, William Wright *history educator*
Alden, Douglas William *French language educator*
Arnold, A. James *foreign language educator*
Barolsky, Paul *art history educator*
Battestin, Martin Carey *English language educator*
Blotner, Joseph Leo *English language educator*
Cano-Ballesta, Juan *Spanish language educator*
Cherno, Melvin *humanities educator*
Clay, Jenny Strauss *classics educator*
Colker, Marvin Leonard *classics educator*
Courtney, Edward *classics educator*
Denommé, Robert Thomas *foreign language educator*
Forbes, John Douglas *architectural and economic historian*
Garrett, George Palmer, Jr. *creative writing and English language educator, writer*
Gianniny, Omer Allan, Jr. *humanities educator*
Gies, David Thatcher *language educator*
Graebner, Norman Arthur *history educator*
Havran, Martin Joseph *historian, educator, author*
Heath, Peter Lauchlan *philosophy educator*
Hirsch, Eric Donald, Jr. *English language educator, educational reformer*
Hopkins, P. Jeffrey *Asian studies educator, author, translator*
Humphreys, Paul William *philosophy educator, consultant*
Kellogg, Robert Leland *English language educator*
Kett, Joseph Francis *historian, educator*
Kohler, Charlotte *language professional, educator*
Kolb, Harold Hutchinson, Jr. *English language educator*
Kraehe, Enno Edward *history educator*
Lang, Cecil Yelverton *English language educator*
Langbaum, Robert Woodrow *English language educator, author*
Leffler, Melvyn P. *history educator*
Levenson, Jacob Clavner *English language educator*
Lyons, John David *French, Italian and comparative literature educator*
McGann, Jerome John *English language educator*
McGrady, Donald Lee *retired Spanish language educator*
Megill, Allan D. *historian, educator*
Midelfort, Hans Christian Erik *history educator*
Mikalson, Jon Dennis *classics educator*
Nelson, Raymond John *English literature educator, university dean, author*
Nohrnberg, James Carson *English language educator*
Perkowski, Jan Louis *language and literature educator*
Peterson, Merrill Daniel *history educator*
Rubin, David Lee *French literature educator, critic, editor, publisher*
Sedgwick, Alexander *historian, educator*
Shackelford, George Green *historian*
Shannon, Edgar Finley, Jr. *English language educator*
Shaw, Donald Leslie *Spanish language educator*
Simmons, Alan John *philosophy educator*
Spacks, Patricia Meyer *English educator*
Spearing, Anthony Colin *English literature educator*
Stocker, Arthur Frederick *classics educator*
Vaughan, Joseph Lee *language educator*
Wagoner, Jennings Lee, Jr. *history educator*
Westfall, Carroll William *architectural historian*
Wright, Charles Penzel, Jr. *English language educator*
Zunz, Olivier Jean *history educator*

**Fairfax**
Bailey, Helen McShane *historian*
King, James Cecil *Medievalist, educator*
†Lavine, Thelma Zeno *philosophy educator*
Verheyen, Egon *art historian, educator*

**Fort Lee**
Sterling, Keir Brooks *historian, educator*

**Fredericksburg**
Dorman, John Frederick *genealogist*
Funk, Ella Frances *genealogist, author*

**Gloucester**
Fang, Joong *philosopher, mathematician, educator*

**Hampden Sydney**
Bagby, George Franklin, Jr. *English language educator*
Jagasich, Paul Anthony *language educator, translator*

**Hampton**
Knewstep, Nancy Gay *language educator*
Maher, Kim Leverton *museum administrator*

**Lexington**
Brooke, George Mercer, Jr. *historian, educator*
McAhren, Robert Willard *history educator*
Pemberton, Harrison Joseph *philosopher, educator*
Ray, George Washington, III *English language educator*
Ryan, Halford Ross *speech educator*
Sessions, William Lad *philosophy educator, administrator*
Simpson, Pamela Hemenway *art historian, educator*

**Mc Lean**
Davis, William Columbus *history educator, writer, lecturer*
Topping, Peter *historian, educator*

**Newport News**
Morris, James Matthew *history educator*

**Norfolk**
Brignoni, Gladys *foreign language educator*
Hund, Barbara Maurer *speech broadcasting and English educator*
Martin, Mary Coates *genealogist, writer, volunteer*

**Petersburg**
Smith, Paul Edmund, Jr. *philosophy and religion educator*

**Portsmouth**
Williams, Lena Harding *English language educator*

**Richmond**
Gordon, John L., Jr. *historian, educator*
Gray, Clarence Jones *foreign language educator, dean emeritus*
Rilling, John Robert *history educator*
Robert, Joseph Clarke *historian, consultant*
Shapiro, Gary Michael *philosophy educator*
Taylor, Welford Dunaway *English language educator*
Treadway, John David *history educator*
Urofsky, Melvin Irving *historian, educator, director*
White, Ann Stewart *language educator, consultant*

**Roanoke**
Dillard, Richard Henry Wilde *English language professional, educator, author*

**Springfield**
Gawalt, Gerard W(ilfred) *historian, writer*

**Surry**
Wachsmann, Elizabeth Rideout *reading specialist*

**University Of Richmond**
Hall, James H(errick), Jr. *philosophy educator, author*
Terry, Robert Meredith *foreign language educator*

**Williamsburg**
Axtell, James Lewis *history educator*
Ball, Donald Lewis *retired English language educator*
Becker, Lawrence Carlyle *philosopher, educator, author*
Cell, Gillian Townsend *historian, educator*
Chappell, Miles Linwood, Jr. *art history educator*
Crapol, Edward P. *history educator*
Esler, Anthony James *historian, novelist, educator*
Fraser, Howard Michael *foreign language educator, editor*
Gross, Robert Alan *history educator*
Kevelson, Roberta *philosopher, educator*
Maccubbin, Robert Purks *literature and culture educator*
McGiffert, Michael *history educator, editor*
McLane, Henry Earl, Jr. *philosophy educator*
Nettels, Elsa *English language educator*
Sherman, Richard Beatty *history educator*
Tate, Thaddeus W(ilbur), Jr. (Thad Tate) *history educator, historical institute executive, historian*
Wallach, Alan *art historian, educator*

**Woodbridge**
†Hood, Ronald Chalmers, III *historian, writer*

## WASHINGTON

**Auburn**
Sims, Marcie Lynne *English language educator, writer*

**Bellingham**
Whisenhunt, Donald Wayne *history educator*

**Des Moines**
Wilson, Donna Mae *foreign language educator, administrator*

**Enumclaw**
Vernier, Richard *educator, author*

**Federal Way**
Boling, Joseph Edward *numismatist, retired military officer*

**Olympia**
Beck, Gordon Eugene *art history educator, consultant*
Nesbit, Robert Carrington *historian*

**Pullman**
Bennett, Edward Moore *historian, educator*

**Seattle**
Adams, Hazard Simeon *English educator, author*
Brandauer, Frederick Paul *Asian language educator*
Burgess, Charles Orville *history educator*
Butow, Robert Joseph Charles *history educator*
Coburn, Robert Craig *philosopher*
Coldewey, John Christopher *English literature educator*
Ellison, Herbert Jay *history educator*
Gerstenberger, Donna Lorine *humanities educator*
Harmon, Daniel Patrick *classics educator*
Heer, Nicholas Lawson *Arabist and Islamist educator*
Jones, Edward Louis *historian, educator*
Keyt, David *philosophy and classics educator*
Kirkendall, Richard Stewart *historian, educator*
Korg, Jacob *English literature educator*
Matchett, William H(enry) *English literature educator*
Newmeyer, Frederick Jaret *linguist, educator*
Nostrand, Howard Lee *language and literature educator*
Potter, Karl Harrington *philosophy educator*
Pressly, Thomas James *history educator*
Pyle, Kenneth Birger *historian, educator*
Silbergeld, Jerome Leslie *art historian, educator*
Sugar, Peter Frigyes *historian*
Webb, Eugene *English language educator*
Ziadeh, Farhat J. *Middle Eastern studies educator*

**Spokane**
Carriker, Robert Charles *history educator*
Kossel, Clifford George *retired philosophy educator, clergyman*
Stackelberg, John Roderick *history educator*

**Tacoma**
Browning, Christopher R. *historian, educator*
Collier, Richard Bangs *philosopher, foundation executive*
Le Roy, Bruce Murdock *historian*

**Walla Walla**
Carlsen, James Caldwell *musicologist, educator*
Edwards, Glenn Thomas *history educator*

**Yakima**
Meshke, George Lewis *drama and humanities educator*

## WEST VIRGINIA

**Institute**
Wohl, David *humanities educator, college dean-theatre director*

**Morgantown**
Blaydes, Sophia Boyatzies *English language educator*
Davis, Leonard McCutchan *speech educator*
Singer, Armand Edwards *foreign language educator*

**West Liberty**
Hunter, John Alfred *English educator*

## WISCONSIN

**Appleton**
Chaney, William Albert *historian, educator*
Goldgar, Bertrand Alvin *literary historian, educator*
Herscher, Susan Kay *English language educator*

**Ferryville**
Tedeschi, John Alfred *historian, librarian*

**Iola**
Rulau, Russell *numismatist, consultant*

**La Crosse**
Rausch, Joan Mary *art historian*

**Lodi**
Schereck, William John *retired historian, consultant*

**Madison**
Ammerman, Robert Ray *philosopher, educator*
Berg, William James *French language educator, writer, translator*
Bogue, Allan G. *history educator*
Brembeck, Winston Lamont *retired speech communication educator*
Cassidy, Frederic Gomes *humanities educator*
Chow, Tse-Tsung *foreign language and literature educator, author, poet*
Ciplijauskaite, Birute *humanities educator*
Cronon, E(dmund) David, Jr. *history educator, historian*
Cronon, William *history educator*
Dembo, Lawrence Sanford *English educator*
DeNovo, John August *history educator*
Fowler, Barbara Hughes *classics educator*
Frykenberg, Robert Eric *historian*
Hamalainen, Pekka Kalevi *historian, educator*
Hamerow, Theodore Stephen *history educator*
Howe, Herbert Marshall *classics educator*
Ihde, Aaron John *history of science educator emeritus*
Kelly, Douglas *medieval and foreign literature educator*
Kingdon, Robert McCune *historian, educator*
Klein, Sheldon *computational linguist, educator*
Kleinhenz, Christopher *foreign language educator, researcher*
Knowles, Richard Alan John *English language educator*
Kutler, Stanley Ira *history and law educator, author*
MacKendrick, Paul Lachlan *classics educator*
Marks, Elaine *French language educator*
Mosse, George Lachmann *history educator, author*
Nicholas, Robert Leon *foreign language educator*
O'Brien, James Aloysius *foreign language educator*
Perkins, Merle Lester *French language educator*
Powell, Barry Bruce *classicist*
Rideout, Walter Bates *English educator*
Rosenshield, Gary *Russian literature educator*
Sewell, Richard Herbert *historian, educator*
Shaw, Joseph Thomas *Slavic languages educator*
Singer, Marcus George *philosopher, educator*
Spear, Thomas Turner *history educator*
Vowles, Richard Beckman *literature educator*
Weinbrot, Howard David *English educator*

**Milwaukee**
Bicha, Karel Denis *historian, educator*
Buck, David Douglas *historian*
Carozza, Davy Angelo *Italian language educator*
Dziewanowski, Marian Kamil *history educator*
Gallop, Jane (Anne) *women's studies educator, writer*
Hachey, Thomas Eugene *British and Irish history educator, consultant*
Halloran, William Frank *English educator*
Horsman, Reginald *history educator*
McCanles, Michael Frederick *English language educator*
Olson, Frederick Irving *retired history educator*
Roeming, Robert Frederick *foreign language educator*
Schwartz, Joseph *English language educator*
Stromberg, Roland Nelson *historian*
Swanson, Roy Arthur *classicist, educator*
Waldbaum, Jane Cohn *art history educator*

**Oshkosh**
Burr, John Roy *philosophy educator*

**Ripon**
Ashley, Robert Paul, Jr. *English literature educator*
Miller, George H. *historian, educator*

**River Falls**
Smith, Clyde Curry *historian, educator*

**Stevens Point**
Paul, Justus Fredrick *historian, educator*

**Superior**
Feldman, Egal *historian, educator*

**Watertown**
Wallman, Charles James *historian*

**Whitewater**
Gulgowski, Paul William *German language, social science, and history educator*

**WYOMING**

**Gillette**
Garry, James B. *historian, storyteller, researcher, writer*

**Laramie**
Chisum, Emmett Dewain *historian, archeologist, researcher*
Gressley, Gene Maurice *history educator*
Hardy, Deborah Welles *history educator*
Nye, Eric William *English language and literature educator*
Roberts, Philip John *history educator, editor*
Williams, Roger Lawrence *historian, educator*

**Sheridan**
Goodwin, Doris Helen Kearns *history educator, writer*

**TERRITORIES OF THE UNITED STATES**

**PUERTO RICO**

**San Juan**
Ocasio-Melendez, Marcial Enrique *history educator*

**CANADA**

**ALBERTA**

**Calgary**
Izzo, Herbert John *language and linguistics educator, researcher*

**Edmonton**
McMaster, Juliet Sylvia *English language educator*

**BRITISH COLUMBIA**

**Burnaby**
Buitenhuis, Peter Martinus *language professional, educator*
Kitchen, John Martin *historian, educator*

**Sidney**
Saddlemyer, Ann (Eleanor Saddlemyer) *educator, critic, theater historian*

**Vancouver**
Batts, Michael Stanley *German language educator*
Bentley, Thomas Roy *English educator, writer, consultant*
Conway, John S. *history educator*
Durrant, Geoffrey Hugh *retired English language educator*
Overmyer, Daniel Lee *Asian studies educator*
Pacheco-Ransanz, Arsenio *Hispanic and Italian studies educator*
Pulleyblank, Edwin George *history educator emeritus, linguist*
Saint-Jacques, Bernard *linguistics educator*
Unger, Richard Watson *history educator*

**Victoria**
Kroetsch, Robert Paul *English language educator, author*

**MANITOBA**

**Winnipeg**
Wolfart, H.C. *linguistics scholar, author, editor*

**NEW BRUNSWICK**

**Douglas**
Cogswell, Frederick William *English language educator, poet, editor, publisher*

**Fredericton**
Kennedy, Richard Frederick *English language educator*

**Saint John**
Condon, Thomas Joseph *university historian*

**NOVA SCOTIA**

**Halifax**
Carrigan, David Owen *history educator*
Gray, James *English literature educator*

**Liscomb**
Hemlow, Joyce *language and literature educator, author*

**Wolfville**
Zeman, Jarold Knox *history educator*

**ONTARIO**

**Downsview**
Thomas, Clara McCandless *retired English language educator, biographer*

**Hamilton**
Blewett, David Lambert *English literature educator*
Lee, Alvin A. *literary educator, scholar, author*
Mc Kay, Alexander Gordon *classics educator*

**Kingston**
Akenson, Donald Harman *historian, educator*
Dick, Susan Marie *English language educator*
Hamilton, Albert Charles *English language educator*
Mac Kenzie, Norman Hugh *retired English educator, writer*
Riley, Anthony William *German language and literature educator*

**London**
Collins, Thomas Joseph *English language educator*
Creighton, Douglas George *French language educator*
Gerber, Douglas Earl *classics educator*

**Mississauga**
Astington, John Harold *English educator*

**Nepean**
Kallmann, Helmut Max *music historian, retired music librarian*

**North York**
Adelman, Howard *philosophy educator*
Coles, Don Langdon *English literature educator*
Mann, Susan *history educator*

**Ottawa**
Dray, William Herbert *philosophy educator*
Hamelin, Marcel *historian, educator*
Staines, David McKenzie *English educator*

**Rockwood**
Eichner, Hans *German language and literature educator*

**Thornbury**
Keyes, Gordon Lincoln *history educator*

**Toronto**
Birnbaum, Eleazar *language professional, educator*
Blissett, William Frank *English literature educator*
Bouissac, Paul Antoine *language professional*
Conacher, Desmond John *classics educator*
Dryer, Douglas Poole *retired philosophy educator*
Elkhadem, Saad Eldin Amin *foreign language and literature educator, author, editor, publisher*
Frank, Roberta *English educator*
Goffart, Walter André *history educator*
Graham, Victor Ernest *French language educator*
Granatstein, Jack Lawrence *history educator*
Grendler, Paul Frederick *history educator*
Johnson, Robert Eugene *historian, academic administrator*
McAuliffe, Jane Dammen *Middle Eastern and Islamic studies educator*
Millgate, Jane *language professional*
Millgate, Michael (Henry) *retired English educator*
Morey, Carl Reginald *musicologist, academic administrator*
Redford, Donald Bruce *historian, archaeologist*
Schogt, Henry Gilius *foreign language educator*
Skvorecky, Josef Vaclav *English literature educator, novelist*
Webster, Jill Rosemary *historian, educator*
Wetzel, Heinz *foreign language educator*
Wevers, John William *retired Semitic languages educator*
Zemans, Joyce Pearl *art historian, arts administrator*

**Waterloo**
Cornell, Paul Grant *history educator*
Haworth, Lawrence Lindley *philosophy educator*
Suits, Bernard Herbert *philosophy educator*

**QUEBEC**

**Montreal**
Beugnot, Bernard Andre Henri *French literature educator*
Duquette, Jean-Pierre *French language and literature educator*
Hamel, Reginald *history educator*
Hoffmann, Peter Conrad Werner *history educator*
Kinsley, William Benton *literature educator*
Leblanc, Hugues *philosophy educator*
McLelland, Joseph Cumming *philosophy educator, former university dean*
Morin, Yves-Charles *linguistics educator, researcher*
Paikowsky, Sandra Roslyn *art historian*
Silverthorne, Michael James *classics educator*

**North Hatley**
Jones, Douglas Gordon *retired literature educator*

**Outremont**
Domaradzki, Theodore Felix *Slavic studies educator, editor*

**Quebec**
Porter, John Robert *art history educator, curator, writer*

**Sainte Foy**
Murray, Warren James *philosophy educator*

**SASKATCHEWAN**

**Saskatoon**
Brewster, Elizabeth Winifred *English language educator, poet, novelist*
Kent, Christopher Andrew *history educator*

**MEXICO**

**Cuernavaca**
Illich, Ivan *educator, researcher*

**Morelia**
Warren, J. Benedict *retired history educator*

**AUSTRALIA**

**Sydney**
Salsbury, Stephen Matthew *historian, educator*

**AUSTRIA**

**Graz**
Weisstein, Ulrich Werner *English literature educator*

**Salzburg**
Mueller, Ulrich *literature educator*

**Vienna**
Steinbruckner, Bruno Friedrich *foreign language educator*

**DENMARK**

**Copenhagen**
Hansen, Elisa Marie *art historian*

**ENGLAND**

**Coventry**
Trigg, Roger Hugh *philosophy educator*

**Eastbourne**
Baylen, Joseph O. *retired history educator*

**Hove**
Kitchin, Laurence Tyson *liberal arts and drama educator, author*

**Liverpool**
Reilly, Thomas *humanities educator*

**London**
Elson, Sarah Lee *art historian*
Martines, Lauro *historian, writer*
Perkin, Harold James *retired social historian, educator*

**Milford on Sea**
Styan, John Louis *English literature and theater educator*

**Oxford**
Carey, John *English language educator, literary critic*
Heilbron, John L. *historian*
Howe, Daniel Walker *historian, educator*

**FRANCE**

**Strasbourg**
Shea, William Rene *historian, science philosopher, educator*

**Toulouse**
Courtés, Joseph Jean-Marie *humanities educator, writer, semiotician*

**Vence**
Polk, William Roe *historian*

**Villeneuve d'Ascq**
Allain, Louis *literature educator, scientific advisor*

**GERMANY**

**Münster**
Spevack, Marvin *English educator*

**Nuremberg**
Doerries, Reinhard René *modern history educator*

**Stuttgart**
Bettisch, Johann *linguist, researcher*

**HONG KONG**

**Kowloon**
McNaughton, William Frank *translator, educator*

**ITALY**

**Florence**
Kaiser, Walter *English language educator*

**Milan**
Bolognesi, Giancarlo *linguist, orientalist, educator*

**JAPAN**

**Bunkyo**
Kobayashi, Seiei *English literature educator*

**Fukuoka**
Fukumoto, Yasunobu *American history educator*

**Hyogo**
Ozaki, Yoseharu *English literature educator*

**Ishinomaki**
Enomoto, Ryokichi *English literature educator*

**Izumi**
Hagiwara, Naoyuki *English language and literature educator*

**Kawasaki**
Fukatsu, Tanefusa *retired Chinese classics educator*

**Kumamoto**
Fukuda, Shohachi *English language educator*

**Mito**
Kobayashi, Susumu *translator, editor, supercomputer consultant*

**Nagasaki**
Lorenz, Loretta Rose *English language educator*

**Nago**
Senaha, Eiki *English literature educator, university dean*

**Nagoya**
Tanaka, Harumi *linguist, educator*

**Takasaki**
Ota, Takao *American literature and studies educator*

**THE NETHERLANDS**

**Amsterdam**
Kolko, Gabriel *historian, educator*

**SCOTLAND**

**Aberdeen**
Rousseau, George Sebastian *eighteenth century studies educator, chamber musician*

**Cellardyke**
Roff, William Robert *history educator, writer*

**Saint Andrews**
Lenman, Bruce Philip *historian, educator*

**SOUTH AFRICA**

**Mamelodi West**
Ntlola, Peter Makhwenkwe *retired translator*

**SPAIN**

**Barcelona**
Jackson, Gabriel *historian*

**Segovia**
Harter, Hugh Anthony *foreign language educator*

**SWEDEN**

**Lerum**
Borei, Sven Hans Emil *translator*

**TAIWAN**

**Taichung**
Lu, Shih-Peng *history educator*

**THAILAND**

**Bangkok**
Pahnichaputt, Momluang Ananchanok *English and American literature educator*

**TURKEY**

**Ankara**
Inalcik, Halil *historian, educator*

**ADDRESS UNPUBLISHED**

Ahl, Janyce Barnwell *historian, writer, speaker, retired educator*
Angell, Richard Bradshaw *philosophy educator*
Ansbro, John Joseph *philosophy educator*
Aptekar, Sheldon I. *speech and theatre educator*
Aptheker, Herbert *historian, lecturer*
Arbelbide, C(indy) L(ea) *historian, author*
Baeumer, Maximilian Lorenz *literature historian*
Baker, Ronald James *English language educator, university administrator*
Barrs, James Thomas *speech, language educator*
Baxter, Stephen Bartow *retired history educator*
Belnap, Nuel Dinsmore, Jr. *philosophy educator*
Blackbourn, David Gordon *history educator*
Bok, Sissela *philosopher, writer*
Bolsterli, Margaret Jones *English educator, farmer*
Bosmajian, Haig Aram *speech communication educator*
Bosse, Malcolm Joseph, Jr. *professional language educator, author*
Brettell, Richard Robson *art historian, museum consultant*
Cachia, Pierre Jacques *Middle East languages and culture educator, researcher*
Caldwell, Louise Phinney *historical researcher, community volunteer*
Cartwright, Talula Elizabeth *writing and career development educator, communication and leadership consultant*
Chandler, Alfred Dupont, Jr. *historian, educator*
Chandra, Pramod *art history educator*

Chellas, Brian Farrell *philosophy educator*
Chinoy, Helen Krich *theater historian*
Clark, Thomas Lloyd *English linguistics educator*
Coffman, Stanley Knight, Jr. *English educator, former college president*
Condit, Doris Elizabeth *historian*
Cooper, John Milton, Jr. *history educator, author*
Cooper, Rebecca *art dealer*
Culverwell, Albert Henry *historian*
Cunningham, William Francis, Jr. *English language educator, university administrator*
Curry, Richard Orr *history educator and freelance writer*
Defever, Susanna Ethel *English language educator*
de Grazia, Sebastian *political philosopher, author*
Deligiorgis, Stavros G. *retired literature educator*
Demenchonok, Edward Vasilevich *philosopher, linguist, researcher, educator*
Djordjevic, Dimitrije *historian, educator*
Eby, Cecil DeGrotte *English language educator, writer*
Edel, Abraham *philosophy educator*
Edmunds, (Arthur) Lowell *philology educator*
Flint, John E. *historian, educator*
Fong, Wen Chih *art historian, educator, author, museum curator*
Froberg, Brent Malcolm *classics educator*
Galbraith, John Semple *history educator*
Garza, Deborah Jane *bilingual education educator*
Gay, Carlo Teofilo Eberhard *art historian*
Geiselhart, Lorene Annetta *English language educator*
Gentry, Francis G. *German language educator*
Gilb, Corinne Lathrop *history educator*
Gillespie, Gerald Ernest Paul *comparative literature educator, writer*
Gillett, Mary Caperton *military historian*
Goldberg, Maxwell Henry *retired humanities educator*
Goldstein, Phyllis Ann *art historian, educator*
Gonzalez-Vales, Luis Ernesto *historian, educational administrator*
Gordon, Cyrus Herzl *Orientalist, educator*
Greene, Elinore Aschah *speech and drama professional, writer*
Gromen, Richard John *historian, educator*
Haag, Walter M(onroe), Jr. *philatelist*
Haber, Lynn Becker *English language educator*
Hansen, Carol Louise *English language educator*
Hart, Arthur Alvin *historian, author*
Haskins, James *English language educator, writer*
Hawkes, John *humanities educator, author*
Haworth, Dale Keith *art history educator, gallery director*
Herbst, Jurgen *history and education educator*
Hetzron, Robert *linguist, educator*
Holloway, Julia Bolton *professor emerita, theologian*
Howard, Michael Eliot *historian, educator*
Hughes, Thomas Parke *history educator*
Hutcheon, Linda Ann *English language educator*
Ivry, Alfred Lyon *foreign language and literature educator*
Jacobs, William Jay *historian, writer*
Johnson, Clifton Herman *historian, archivist, former research center director*
Johnson, John Prescott *philosophy educator*
Jones, Peter d'Alroy *history educator, author*
Jones, Suejette Albritton *basic skills educator*
Jordan, William Bryan, Jr. *art historian*
Jourdain, Alice Marie *philosopher, retired educator*
Kalish, Donald *philosophy educator*
Kane, Loana *foreign language educator*
Kane, Patricia Lanegran *language professional, educator*
Kaplan, Robert B. *linguistics educator, consultant, researcher*
Kastor, Frank Sullivan *English language educator*
Khalidi, Rashid Ismail *history educator*
Korsgaard, Christine Marion *philosophy educator*
Kramer, Dale Vernon *retired English language educator*
Kwiat, Joseph J. *English literature and American studies educator*
Lawson Donadio, Carolina Anna *foreign language educator, translator*
Lederman, Marie Jean *English language educator*
Lewis, Norman *English language educator, writer*
Lightburn, Faye Marie *genealogist*
Lindsey, Roberta Lewise *music researcher, historian*
Link, Arthur Stanley *history educator, editor*
Longsworth, Robert Morrow *English educator*
Loughran, James Newman *philosophy educator, college president*
MacDonald, Robert Alan *language educator*
Maehl, William Harvey *historian, educator*
Marcus, Ruth Barcan *philosopher, educator, writer, lecturer*
Marion, Marjorie Anne *English educator*
Marshall, Richard *art historian, curator*
McCormick, John Owen *retired comparative literature educator*
McDermott, Agnes Charlene Senape *philosophy educator*
McGann, Lisa B. Napoli *language educator*
McGrady, Stephanie Jill *speech communications educator*
Meyer, Kathleen Marie *English educator*
Molloy, Sylvia *Latin American literature educator, writer*
Morgan, Edmund Sears *history educator*
Morrissey, Charles Thomas *historian, educator*
Morrow, Ralph Ernest *historian, educator*
Murdock, Mary-Elizabeth *history educator*
Murphy, Francis *English language educator*
Nagel, Thomas *philosopher, educator*
Nebel, Henry Martin, Jr. *literature historian, educator*
Nelson-Humphries, Tessa (Tessa Unthank) *English language educator*
Niedzielski, Henri Zygmunt *French and English language educator*
Nochman, Lois Wood Kivi (Mrs. Marvin Nochman) *english language educator*
Olson, James Clifton *historian, university president*
Olson, Paul Richard *Spanish literature educator, editor*
Paige, Anita Parker *retired English language educator*
Palter, Robert Monroe *philosophy and history educator*
Peterson, Barbara Ann Bennett *history educator, television personality*
Peyser, Joseph Leonard *historical researcher, author, translator*
Pflanze, Otto Paul *history educator*
Porter, Marsha Kay *Language professional and educator, English*
Potter, William Blake *language professional, educator*
Ramos, Gerardo Ernesto *Spanish teacher*
Reuman, Robert Everett *philosophy educator*
Riasanovsky, Nicholas Valentine *historian, educator*
Richardson, Robert Dale, Jr. *English language educator*
Rickard, Ruth David *retired history and political science educator*
Ritcheson, Charles Ray *university administrator, history educator*
Rollins, Alfred Brooks, Jr. *historian, educator*
Romeo, Luigi *linguist, educator*
Rosenberg, David Alan *military historian, educator*
Sabat-Rivers, Georgina *Latin American literature educator*
Seidensticker, Edward George *Japanese language and literature educator*
Seymour, Richard Kellogg *linguist, educator*
Shillingsburg, Miriam Jones *English educator, academic administrator*
Sices, David *language educator, translator*
Smith, Charlotte Reed *retired music educator*
Smith, Jane Wardell *historian, philanthropist, entrepreneur*
Smither, Howard Elbert *musicologist*
Smock, Raymond William *historian*
Snyder, Susan Brooke *retired English literature educator*
Solomon, Robert Charles *philosopher, educator*
Stokstad, Marilyn Jane *art history educator, curator*
Stolarik, M. Mark *history educator*
Street, John Charles *linguistics educator*
Stringer, Mary Evelyn *art historian, educator*
Sullivan, Mary Rose *English language educator*
Sutton, Julia Sumberg *musicologist, dance historian*
Szoverffy, Joseph *educator, medieval scholar*
Tedesco, Paul Herbert *humanities educator*
Thackray, Arnold Wilfrid *historian, foundation executive*
Topik, Steven Curtis *history educator*
Trelease, Allen William *historian, educator*
Vermeule, Emily Townsend (Mrs. Cornelius C. Vermeule, III) *classicist, educator*
Vestal, Thelma Shaw *history educator*
Wallace, William Augustine *philosophy and history educator*
Waller, Gary Fredric *English language educator, administrator, poet*
Warlick, Roger Kinney *history educator, assistant dean*
Weber, Eugen *historian, educator, author*
Wheeler, Burton M. *literature educator, higher education consultant, college dean*
Wolters, Oliver William *history educator*
Wright, Beth Segal *art historian, educator*
Wruck, Erich-Oskar *retired German language educator*
Yolton, John William *philosopher, educator*
Zwerver, Peter John *linguistics educator*

## HUMANITIES: LIBRARIES

### UNITED STATES

#### ALABAMA

**Birmingham**
Bulow, Jack Faye *library director*
Murrell, Susan DeBrecht *librarian*
Spence, Paul Herbert *librarian*
Stephens, Jerry Wayne *librarian, library director*
Stewart, George Ray *librarian*

**Huntsville**
Miller, Carol Lynn *librarian*

**Jacksonville**
Hubbard, William James *library director*

**Montgomery**
Harris, Patricia Lea *librarian*

**Troy**
Thompson, Jean Tanner *retired librarian*

#### ALASKA

**Anchorage**
Rollins, Alden Milton *documents librarian*

**Juneau**
Schorr, Alan Edward *librarian, publisher*

#### ARIZONA

**Chandler**
Miller, Robert Carl *library director*

**Dewey**
Beck, Doris Olson *library media director*

**Green Valley**
White, Herbert Spencer *research library educator, university dean*

**Mesa**
Anderson, Herschel Vincent *librarian*

**Phoenix**
Fox, Frances Juanice *retired librarian, educator*
Hanley, Fred William *librarian, educator*
Landers, Teresa Price *librarian*

**Sun City West**
Williams, William Harrison *retired librarian*

**Tempe**
Matthews, Gertrude Ann Urch *retired librarian, writer*

**Tucson**
Anderson, Rachael Keller *library administrator*
Grams, Theodore Carl William *librarian, educator*
Griffen, Agnes Marthe *library administrator*
Hurt, Charlie Deuel, III *library school director, educator*
Skorupski, Diane Christine *school library media specialist*
Wolfe, William Jerome *librarian, English language educator*

#### ARKANSAS

**Fort Smith**
Larson, Larry *librarian*

**Little Rock**
Jones, Philip Lindsey *librarian*
Mulkey, Jack Clarendon *library director*

**Lonoke**
Ross, Philip Rowland *library director*

**Pine Bluff**
Burdick, David *library director*

#### CALIFORNIA

**Alhambra**
Harnsberger, Therese Coscarelli *librarian*

**Aptos**
Heron, David Winston *librarian*

**Bakersfield**
Duquette, Diane Rhea *library director*

**Belvedere**
Crockett, Ethel Stacy *librarian*

**Berkeley**
Buckland, Michael Keeble *librarian, educator*
Danton, Joseph Periam *librarian, educator*
Hanff, Peter Edward *librarian, bibliographer*
Harlan, Robert Dale *information studies educator, academic administrator*
Minudri, Regina Ursula *library director, consultant*

**Carlsbad**
Lange, Clifford E. *librarian*

**Commerce**
Conover, Robert Warren *librarian*

**Cupertino**
Fletcher, Homer Lee *librarian*

**Davis**
Grossman, George Stefan *library director, law eductor*
Sharrow, Marilyn Jane *library administrator*

**El Centro**
Gotti, Margaret Lynn *library administrator*

**El Cerrito**
Kao, Yasuko Watanabe *retired library administrator*
Smith, Eldred Reid *library educator*

**Encino**
Wood, Raymund Francis *retired librarian*

**Fresno**
Gorman, Michael Joseph *library director, educator*
Kallenberg, John Kenneth *librarian*

**Fullerton**
Ayala, John *librarian, dean*

**Huntington Beach**
Halvorsen, Jan La Rayne *library services manager*

**Inglewood**
Alaniz, Miguel José Castañeda *library director*

**Irvine**
Euster, Joanne Reed *librarian*
Laird, Wilbur David, Jr. *bookseller, editor*

**La Jolla**
Mirsky, Phyllis Simon *librarian*

**Long Beach**
Lathrop, Ann *librarian, educator*

**Los Angeles**
Bates, Marcia Jeanne *information scientist educator*
Borko, Harold *information scientist, psychologist, educator*
Brecht, Albert Odell *library and information technology administrator*
Chang, Henry Chung-Lien *library administrator*
Ciccone, Amy Navratil *art librarian*
Coolbaugh, Carrie Weaver *librarian*
Cuadra, Carlos Albert *information scientist, management executive*
Gilman, Nelson Jay *library director*
Helgeson, Duane Marcellus *retired librarian*
Kent, Susan Goldberg *library director, consultant*
O'Brian, Bonnie Jean *library services supervisor*
Patron, Susan Hall *librarian, writer*
Polan, Morris *librarian*
Richardson, John Vinson, Jr. *library science educator*
Shank, Russell *librarian, educator*
Steele, Victoria Lee *librarian*
Sutherland, Michael Cruise *librarian*
Werner, Gloria S. *librarian*

**Mill Valley**
Dillon, Richard Hugh *librarian, author*

**Monterey**
Reneker, Maxine Hohman *librarian*

**Monterey Park**
Wilson, Linda *librarian*

**Mountain View**
Di Muccio, Mary Jo *retired librarian*

**Newport Beach**
Kienitz, LaDonna Trapp *city librarian, city official*

**North Hollywood**
Schlosser, Anne Griffin *librarian*

**Oxnard**
Carroll, Carmal Edward *retired librarian, educator, clergyman*

**Palmdale**
Storsteen, Linda Lee *librarian*

**Pasadena**
Buck, Anne Marie *library director, consultant*
Harmsen, Tyrus George *librarian*

**Redlands**
Burgess, Larry Eugene *library director, history educator*

**Sacramento**
Burns, John Francis *archivist, state official, museum director*
†Starr, Kevin *librarian, educator*

**Salinas**
Spinks, Paul *retired library director*

**San Bernardino**
Burgess, Michael *library science educator, publisher*
Ewing, Robert Stirling *retired library administrator*

**San Diego**
Ling, David Chang *international book dealer*
Sannwald, William Walter *librarian*

**San Francisco**
Aldrich, Michael Ray *library curator, health educator*
Dowlin, Kenneth Everett *librarian*

**San Jose**
Schmidt, Cyril James *librarian*
Woolls, Esther Blanche *library science educator*

**San Marcos**
Ciurczak, Alexis *librarian*

**San Marino**
Robertson, Mary Louise *archivist, historian*
Thorpe, James *humanities researcher*

**Santa Ana**
Adams, John M. *library director*

**Santa Barbara**
Dougan, Robert Ormes *librarian*
Higgins, Isabelle Jeanette *librarian*
Keator, Carol Lynne *library director*
Lockett, Barbara Ann *librarian*

**Santa Clara**
Hopkinson, Shirley Lois *library science educator*

**Santa Clarita**
Gardner, Frederick Boyce *library director*

**Santa Cruz**
Dyson, Allan Judge *librarian*

**Santa Monica**
Ackerman, Helen Page *librarian, educator*

**Santa Rosa**
Pearson, Roger Lee *library director*

**Sausalito**
Glaser, Edwin Victor *rare book dealer*

**Sebastopol**
Sabsay, David *library consultant*

**Sherman Oaks**
Miller, Margaret Haigh *librarian*

**Stanford**
Derksen, Charlotte Ruth Meynink *librarian*
Keller, Michael Alan *librarian, educator, musicologist*

**Torrance**
Buckley, James W. *librarian*

**Yorba Linda**
Naulty, Susan Louise *archivist*

#### COLORADO

**Aurora**
Miller, Sarah Pearl *librarian*
Nicholas, Thomas Peter *library administrator, community television consultant, producer*

**Bellvue**
Carter, Laura Lee *academic librarian, psychotherapist*

**Boulder**
O'Brien, Elmer John *librarian, educator*

**Canon City**
Cochran, Susan Mills *librarian*

**Colorado Springs**
Budington, William Stone *retired librarian*
Chen, Lynn Chia-Ling *librarian*

**Denver**
Ahern, Arleen Fleming *retired librarian*
Ashton, Rick James *librarian*

**West Lafayette**
Andrews, Theodora Anne *retired librarian, educator*
Markee, Katherine Madigan *librarian, educator*
Mobley, Emily Ruth *library dean, educator*
Nixon, Judith May *librarian*
Tucker, John Mark *librarian, educator*

## IOWA

**Ames**
Hill, Fay Gish *librarian*

**Carlisle**
Berning, Robert William *librarian*

**Cedar Rapids**
Armitage, Thomas Edward *library director*

**Davenport**
Potter, Corinne Jean *librarian*
Runge, Kay Kretschmar *library director*

**Decorah**
Kalsow, Kathryn Ellen *library clerk*

**Des Moines**
Rittmer, Elaine Heneke *library media specialist*
Smith, Sharman Bridges *state librarian*

**Grinnell**
McKee, Christopher Fulton *librarian, naval historian, educator*

**Iowa City**
Bentz, Dale Monroe *librarian*

**West Branch**
Mather, Mildred Eunice *retired archivist*
Walch, Timothy George *library administrator*

## KANSAS

**Enterprise**
Wickman, John Edward *librarian, historian*

**Lawrence**
Craig, Susan Virginia *librarian*
Koepp, Donna Pauline Petersen *librarian*

**Olathe**
Dennis, Patricia Lyon *librarian*

**Topeka**
Marvin, James Conway *librarian, consultant*

**Wichita**
Berner, Cynthia Kay *librarian*
Rademacher, Richard Joseph *librarian*

## KENTUCKY

**Burlington**
Crouch, Arline Parks *librarian*

**Columbia**
Seufert, Edward Cecil *librarian, retired military officer*

**Danville**
Campbell, Stanley Richard *library services director*

**Frankfort**
Nelson, James Albert *librarian, state official*

**Lexington**
Mason, Ellsworth Goodwin *librarian*
Sineath, Timothy Wayne *library educator, university dean*
Steensland, Ronald Paul *librarian*
Willis, Paul Allen *librarian*

**Louisville**
Deering, Ronald Franklin *librarian, minister*
Henderson, Harriet *librarian*
VanMeter, Vandelia L. *library director*

**Morehead**
Besant, Larry Xon *librarian, administrator, consultant*

**Owensboro**
Eaton, Clara Barbour *retired librarian*

**Summer Shade**
Smith, Ruby Lucille *librarian*

## LOUISIANA

**Arnaudville**
LaGrange, Claire Mae *school librarian*

**Baton Rouge**
Jaques, Thomas Francis *librarian*
Patterson, Charles Darold *librarian, educator*

**Lacombe**
Hendricks, Donald Duane *librarian*

**Lafayette**
Branch, Sonya Meyer *library director*
Carstens, Jane Ellen *retired library science educator*

**New Orleans**
Craft, Carol Ann *librarian*
Leinbach, Philip Eaton *librarian*
Taylor, Kenneth Byron, Jr. *librarian, minister, religion educator*
Wilson, C. Daniel, Jr. *library director*

**Oakdale**
Johnson, Bess Orr *retired librarian*

**Shreveport**
Pelton, James Rodger *librarian*

## MAINE

**Bangor**
Rea, Ann W. *librarian*

**Bar Harbor**
Dworak, Marcia Lynn *library director, library building consultant*

**Damariscotta**
Haas, Warren James *librarian, consultant*

**Gardiner**
Nowell, Glenna Greely *librarian, consultant, city manager*

**Millinocket**
Mitchell, Charles Peter *library director*

**Orient**
Chenevert, Edward Valmore, Jr. *retired librarian, real estate broker*

**Portland**
Parks, George Richard *librarian*

**Presque Isle**
McGrath, Anna Fields *librarian*

**Waterville**
Muehlner, Suanne Wilson *library director*

## MARYLAND

**Annapolis**
Kozlowski, Ronald Stephan *librarian*
Papenfuse, Edward Carl, Jr. *archivist, state official*
Werking, Richard Hume *librarian, historian, academic administrator*

**Baltimore**
Liu, Rhonda Louise *librarian*
Magnuson, Nancy *librarian*

**Beltsville**
Andre, Pamela Q. J. *library director*

**Bethesda**
Knachel, Philip Atherton *librarian*
Lindberg, Donald Allan Bror *library administrator, pathologist, educator*
Smith, Ruth Lillian Schluchter *librarian*
Tilley, Carolyn Bittner *technical information specialist*

**California**
Avram, Henriette Davidson *librarian, government official*

**College Park**
Burke, Frank Gerard *archivist*
Kellogg, Betty L. *librarian*
Wasserman, Paul *library and information science educator*

**Columbia**
Wolter, John Amadeus *librarian, government official*

**Damascus**
Cockrell, Diane Elyse *librarian*

**Gaithersburg**
Klein, Sami Weiner *librarian*

**Hunt Valley**
Tull, Willis Clayton, Jr. *librarian*

**Kensington**
Rather, Lucia Porcher Johnson *library administrator*

**Laurel**
Brandhorst, Wesley Theodore *information manager*
Sweetland, Loraine Fern *librarian, educator*

**Oakland**
Ferren, Emily Holchin *public library director, consultant*

**Potomac**
Broderick, John Caruthers *retired librarian, educator*

**Rockville**
Kohlhorst, Gail Lewis *librarian*

**Savage**
Filby, Percy William *library consultant*

**Takoma Park**
von Hake, Margaret Joan *librarian*

**Towson**
Fish, James Henry *library director*

**Westminster**
McAdam, Paul Edward *library administrator*

## MASSACHUSETTS

**Amesbury**
Dowd, Frances Connelly *librarian*

**Amherst**
Bridegam, Willis Edward, Jr. *librarian*
Tenenbaum, Jeffrey Mark *academic librarian*

**Boston**
Armstrong, Rodney *librarian*
Chen, Ching-chih *information science educator, consultant*
Christopher, Irene *librarian, consultant*
Curley, Arthur *library director*
Desnoyers, Megan Floyd *archivist, educator*
Gerratt, Bradley Scott *presidential library director*
Kowal, Ruth Elizabeth *library administrator*
Lawrence, Mary Josephine (Josie Lawrence) *library official, artist*
Lucker, Jay K. *library education educator*
Margolis, Bernard Allen *library administrator, antique book appraiser*
†Peek, Robin Patricia *library and information science educator*
von Fettweis, Yvonne Caché *archivist, historian*
Wendorf, Richard Harold *library director, educator*

**Brookline**
Finkelstein, Norman Henry *librarian*
Tuchman, Maurice Simon *library director*
Wertsman, Vladimir Filip *librarian, information specialist, author, translator*

**Cambridge**
Bond, William Henry *librarian, educator*
Cole, Heather Ellen *librarian*
Collins, John William, III *librarian*
Dunn, Mary Maples *library director*
Flannery, Susan Marie *library administrator*
Hamilton, Malcolm Cowan *librarian, editor, indexer, personnel professional*
Horrell, Jeffrey Lanier *library administrator*
Stoddard, Roger Eliot *librarian*
Willard, Louis Charles *librarian*

**Carver**
Neubauer, Richard A. *library science educator, consultant*

**Chestnut Hill**
Mellins, Judith Weiss *retired archivist*

**Fall River**
Sullivan, Ruth Anne *librarian*

**Leominster**
Lambert, Lyn Dee *library media specialist, law librarian*

**Lexington**
Freitag, Wolfgang Martin *librarian, educator*

**Medford**
Tilger, Justine Tharp *research director*

**Milton**
Mills, Elizabeth Ann *librarian*

**Natick**
†Rendell, Kenneth William *rare and historical documents dealer, consultant*

**Newton**
Glick-Weil, Kathy *library director*

**Northampton**
Piccinino, Rocco Michael *librarian*

**Norton**
Deekle, Peter Van *library director*

**Paxton**
Kuklinski, Joan Lindsey *librarian*

**Roxbury**
McLaughlin, Garland Eutreé *librarian*

**Springfield**
Stack, May Elizabeth *library director*
Utley, F. Knowlton *library director, educator*

**Waltham**
Hahn, Bessie King *library administrator, lecturer*
Hayes, Sherman Lee *library director*

**Williamstown**
Erickson, Peter Brown *librarian, scholar, writer*
Wikander, Lawrence Einar *librarian*

**Worcester**
Dunlap, Ellen S. *library administrator*
Johnson, Penelope B. *librarian*
McCorison, Marcus Allen *librarian, cultural organization administrator*

## MICHIGAN

**Adrian**
Dombrowski, Mark Anthony *librarian*

**Allendale**
Murray, Diane Elizabeth *librarian*

**Ann Arbor**
Beaubien, Anne Kathleen *librarian*
Bidlack, Russell Eugene *librarian, educator, former dean*
Carlen, Sister Claudia *librarian*
Daub, Peggy Ellen *library administrator*
Dougherty, Richard Martin *library and information science educator*
Dunlap, Connie *librarian*
Hessler, David William *information and multimedia systems educator*
Hodel, Mary Anne *library director*
Slavens, Thomas Paul *library science educator*
Williams, John Troy *librarian, educator*

**Dearborn**
Coady, Reginald Patrick *library director*
Marquis, Rollin Park *retired librarian*

**Detroit**
Mika, Joseph John *library director, consultant*
Spyers-Duran, Peter *librarian, educator*

**Sutton, Lynn Sorensen** *librarian*
Tsai, Bor-sheng *educator*

**East Lansing**
Chapin, Richard Earl *librarian*
De Benko, Eugene *librarian, consultant*

**Farmington Hills**
Papai, Beverly Daffern *library director*

**Flint**
Heymoss, Jennifer Marie *librarian*

**Grand Rapids**
Jacobsen, Arnold *archivist*

**Houghton**
Krenitsky, Michael V. *librarian*

**Kalamazoo**
Amdursky, Saul Jack *library director*
Carlson, Andrew Raymond *archivist*
Grotzinger, Laurel Ann *university librarian*
Pinkham, Eleanor Humphrey *retired university librarian*

**Montague**
Gundy-Reed, Frances Darnell *librarian, healthcare manager*

**Owosso**
Bentley, Margaret Ann *librarian*

**Plymouth**
Berry, Charlene Helen *librarian, musician*
deBear, Richard Stephen *library planning consultant*

**Port Huron**
Wu, Harry Pao-Tung *librarian*

**Rochester**
Hage, Christine Lind *library administrator*

**Saint Clair Shores**
Woodford, Arthur MacKinnon *library director, historian*

**Thompsonville**
Perry, Margaret *librarian, writer*

## MINNESOTA

**Collegeville**
Haile, Getatchew *archivist, educator*

**Duluth**
Pearce, Donald Joslin *retired librarian*

**Mankato**
Descy, Don Edmond *library media technology educator, writer, editor*

**Minneapolis**
Asp, William George *librarian*
Johnson, Donald Clay *librarian, curator*
Johnson, Margaret Ann *library administrator*
Kukla, Edward Richard *librarian, lecturer*
Shaughnessy, Thomas William *librarian, consultant*

**Northfield**
Hong, Howard Vincent *library administrator, philosophy educator, editor, translator*
Metz, T(heodore) John *librarian, consultant*

**Rochester**
Key, Jack Dayton *librarian*
Leachman, Roger Mack *librarian*

**Saint Paul**
Brudvig, Glenn Lowell *retired library director*
Holbert, Sue Elisabeth *archivist, writer, consultant*
Jacob, Rosamond Tryon *librarian*
Kane, Lucile Marie *archivist, historian*
Magnuson, Norris Alden *librarian, history educator*
Wagner, Mary Margaret *library and information science educator*
†Zietlow, Ruth Ann *reference librarian*

**Saint Peter**
Haeuser, Michael John *library administrator*

## MISSISSIPPI

**Calhoun City**
Macon, Myra Faye *retired library director*

**Hattiesburg**
Boyd, William Douglas, Jr. *library science educator, clergyman*

**Tupelo**
Radojcsics, Anne Parsons *librarian*

## MISSOURI

**Columbia**
Alexander, Martha Sue *librarian*
Almony, Robert Allen, Jr. *librarian, businessman*

**Hannibal**
Dothager, Julie Ann *librarian*

**Independence**
Ferguson, John Wayne, Sr. *librarian*

**Jefferson City**
Parker, Sara Ann *librarian*
Winn, Kenneth Hugh *archivist, historian*

**Kansas City**
Bradbury, Daniel Joseph *library administrator*
Irvine, Robert Keith *librarian*

La Budde, Kenneth James *librarian*
Pedram, Marilyn Beth *reference librarian*
Sheldon, Ted Preston *library director*

**Lake Lotawana**
Zobrist, Benedict Karl *library director, historian*

**Nevada**
Hizer, Marlene Brown *library director*

**Pleasant Valley**
Nelson, Freda Nell Hein *librarian*

**Saint Louis**
Baker, Shirley Kistler *university library administrator*
Gaertner, Donell J. *library director*
Guenther, Charles John *librarian, writer*
Holt, Glen Edward *library administrator*
Holt, Leslie Edmonds *librarian*
Jackson, Paul Howard *librarian, educator*

**Springfield**
Bohnenkamper, Katherine Elizabeth *library science educator*
Busch, Annie *library director*

**MONTANA**

**Billings**
Cochran, William Michael *librarian*

**Helena**
Fitzpatrick, Lois Ann *library administrator*

**NEBRASKA**

**Lincoln**
Montag, John Joseph, II *librarian*
Robson, John Merritt *library and media administrator*
Wagner, Rod *library director*

**Omaha**
Tollman, Thomas Andrew *librarian*

**Rushville**
Plantz, Christine Marie *librarian, union officer*

**NEVADA**

**Carson City**
Rocha, Guy Louis *archivist, historian*

**Las Vegas**
Gordon, Lee Diane *librarian*
Gray, Phyllis Anne *librarian*
Hunsberger, Charles Wesley *library consultant*
Richardson, Jane *librarian*

**Reno**
Ross, Robert Donald *library administrator*

**NEW HAMPSHIRE**

**Berlin**
Doherty, Katherine Mann *librarian, writer*

**Concord**
Wajenberg, Arnold Sherman *retired librarian, educator*
Wiggin, Kendall French *state librarian*

**Exeter**
Thomas, Jacquelyn May *librarian*

**Hampton**
Morton, Donald John *librarian*

**Hanover**
Otto, Margaret Amelia *librarian*

**Keene**
Martin, Vernon Emil *librarian*

**New London**
York, Michael Charest *librarian*

**Newmarket**
Getchell, Sylvia Fitts *librarian*

**NEW JERSEY**

**Budd Lake**
Lustig, Joanne *librarian*

**Delran**
Hartman, Mary Louise *information services librarian*

**Demarest**
Ahr, Ernest Stephan *business archive executive*

**East Brunswick**
Karmazin, Sharon Elyse *library director*

**Garfield**
Nickles, I. MacArthur *librarian*

**Glassboro**
Martin, Marilyn Joan *library director*

**Haworth**
Biesel, Diane Jane *librarian*

**Highland Park**
Coughlin, Caroline Mary *library consultant, educator*

**Hightstown**
Brodman, Estelle *librarian, retired educator*

**Hoboken**
Mintz, Kenneth Andrew *librarian*
Widdicombe, Richard Palmer *librarian*

**Irvington**
McConnell, Lorelei Catherine *library director*

**Jersey City**
Patterson, Grace Limerick *library director*

**Laurel Springs**
Cleveland, Susan Elizabeth *library administrator, researcher*

**Livingston**
Sikora, Barbara Jean *library director*

**Lodi**
Karetzky, Joanne Louise *librarian*
Karetzky, Stephen *library director, educator, researcher*

**Long Branch**
Pachman, Frederic Charles *library director*

**Lyndhurst**
Sieger, Charles *librarian*

**Mendham**
Chatfield, Mary Van Abshoven *librarian*

**Montclair**
Fannin, Caroline Mather *library consultant*

**Montville**
Bizub, Johanna Catherine *library director*

**New Brunswick**
Becker, Ronald Leonard *archivist*
Bernstein, Adriana Bennett *library and information consultant*
Edelman, Hendrik *library and information science educator*
Turock, Betty Jane *library and information science educator*

**Princeton**
Fox, Mary Ann Williams *librarian*
Henneman, John Bell, Jr. *library bibliographer*
Joyce, William Leonard *librarian*
Woodward, Daniel Holt *librarian, researcher*

**Rockaway**
Kelsey, Ann Lee *library administrator*

**Roselle**
Riley-Scott, Barbara Polk *retired librarian*

**Sewell**
Wright, William Cook *archivist, historian, researcher*

**Teaneck**
Huang, Theresa C. *librarian*

**Trenton**
Butorac, Frank George *librarian, educator*
Russell, Joyce Anne Rogers *librarian*

**Union**
Darden-Simpson, Barbara L. *library director*

**NEW MEXICO**

**Albuquerque**
Snell, Patricia Poldervaart *librarian, consultant*
Wolf, Cynthia Tribelhorn *librarian, library educator*

**Carlsbad**
Regan, Muriel *librarian*

**Gallup**
Fellin, Octavia Antoinette *retired librarian*

**Las Cruces**
Myers, R. David *library director, dean*

**NEW YORK**

**Albany**
Aceto, Vincent John *librarian, educator*
Galvin, Thomas John *information science policy educator, librarian, information scientist*
Katz, William Armstrong *library science educator*
Paulson, Peter John *librarian, publishing company executive*
Shubert, Joseph Francis *librarian*

**Bellmore**
Andrews, Charles Rolland *library administrator*

**Bohemia**
Manley, Gertrude Ella *librarian, media specialist*

**Bronx**
Caffin, Louise Anne *library media educator*
Humphry, James, III *librarian, publishing executive*
McCabe, James Patrick *library director*
Skurdenis, Juliann Veronica *librarian, educator, writer, editor*

**Brooklyn**
Bostic, Mary Jones *librarian*
Ciolli, Antoinette *librarian, retired educator*
Corry, Emmett Brother *librarian, educator, researcher, archivist*
†Sharify, Nasser *educator, librarian, author*

**Buffalo**
Bobinski, George Sylvan *librarian, educator*

Chrisman, Diane J. *librarian*
Rooney, Paul Monroe *former library administrator*
Zimmerman, Nancy Picciano *library science educator*

**Chappaqua**
Whittingham, Charles Arthur *library administrator, publisher*

**Clifton Park**
Farley, John Joseph *library science educator emeritus*

**Clinton**
Anthony, Donald Charles *librarian, educator*

**Cornwall On Hudson**
Weiss, Egon Arthur *retired library administrator*

**Corona**
Jackson, Andrew Preston *library director*

**Delmar**
Nitecki, Joseph Zbigniew *librarian*

**East Setauket**
Thom, Joseph M. *librarian*

**East Williston**
Berman, Sara Jane *library director*

**Flushing**
Cooke, Constance Blandy *librarian*

**Great Neck**
Pohl, Gunther Erich *retired library administrator*

**Hamilton**
Noyes, Judith Gibson *library director*

**Hempstead**
Freese, Melanie Louise *librarian, professor*

**Huntington**
Rosar, Virginia Wiley *librarian*

**Hyde Park**
Newton, Verne Wester *library director*

**Ithaca**
Finch, C. Herbert *retired archivist, library administrator, historia*
Law, Gordon Theodore, Jr. *library director*

**Jamaica**
Hammer, Deborah Marie *librarian*
Lin, Shu-Fang Hsia *librarian*
Strong, Gary Eugene *librarian*

**Kings Point**
Billy, George John *library director*

**Lewiston**
†Domzella, Janet *library director*
Newlin, Lyman Wilbur *bookseller, consultant*

**New York**
Ashton, Jean Willoughby *library director*
Belliveau, Gerard Joseph, Jr. *librarian*
Berger, Pearl *library director*
Berliner, Barbara *librarian, consultant*
Berner, Andrew Jay *library director, writer*
Birnbaum, Henry *librarian*
Bourke, Thomas Anthony *librarian, writer*
Bowen, Jean *librarian, consultant*
Brewer, Karen *librarian*
Bristah, Pamela Jean *librarian*
Cassell, Kay Ann *librarian*
Cohen, Selma *reference librarian, researcher*
Colby, Robert Alan *retired library science educator*
De Medeiros, Melissa Brown *librarian, art researcher*
Ellenbogen, Rudolph Solomon *library curator*
Gatch, Milton McCormick, Jr. *library administrator, clergyman, educator*
Gold, Leonard Singer *librarian, translator*
Gossage, Wayne *library director, management consultant, entrepreneur, executive recruiter*
Graves, Fred Hill *librarian*
Green, David Edward *librarian, priest, translator*
Heinrich, Amy Vladeck *library director*
Hewitt, Vivian Ann Davidson (Mrs. John Hamilton Hewitt, Jr.) *librarian*
Isaacson, Melvin Stuart *library director*
Jones, Anne *librarian*
Kasinec, Edward Joseph *library administrator*
LeClerc, Paul *library director*
Lohf, Kenneth A. *librarian, writer*
LoSchiavo, Linda Bosco *library director*
Lubetski, Edith Esther *librarian*
Lundquist, John Milton *librarian, author, travel writer, photographer*
Mackey, Patricia Elaine *librarian*
Massis, Bruce Edward *library director, media executive, consultant*
Mattson, Francis Oscar *retired librarian and rare books curator*
McCormick, Donald E. *librarian, archivist*
Meyerhoff, Erich *librarian, administrator*
Miller, Philip Efrem *librarian*
Mirsky, Sonya Wohl *librarian, curator*
Moore, Jane Ross *librarian*
Osten, Margaret Esther *librarian*
Ostrow, Rona Lynn *librarian, educator*
Palmer, Paul Richard *librarian, archivist*
Palmer, Robert Baylis *librarian*
Pierce, Charles Eliot, Jr. *library director, educator*
Placzek, Adolf Kurt *librarian*
Rabinowitz, Mayer Elya *librarian, educator*
Rachow, Louis A(ugust) *librarian*
Root, Nina J. *librarian*
Siefert-Kazanjian, Donna *corporate librarian*
Stoops, Louise *information services administrator*

**Niagara Falls**
Jessiman, Marilynn R. *library media specialist*

**Ogdensburg**
Rusaw, Sally Ellen *librarian*

**Oneonta**
Johnson, Richard David *retired librarian*

**Patchogue**
Gibbard, Judith R. *library director*

**Plattsburgh**
Ransom, Christina Roxane *librarian*

**Port Washington**
Ciccariello, Priscilla Chloe *librarian*

**Poughkeepsie**
Van Zanten, Frank Veldhuyzen *retired library system director*

**Rochester**
Chu, Ellin Resnick *librarian, consultant*
Matzek, Richard Allan *library director*
Palvino, Nancy Mangin *librarian*
Swanton, Susan Irene *library director*

**Sherrill**
Rosendale, Suzanne Moore *library media specialist*

**Somers**
Lane, David Oliver *retired librarian*

**Staten Island**
Auh, Yang John *librarian, academic administrator*
Mayer, Andrew Mark *librarian, journalist*

**Syracuse**
Abbott, George Lindell *librarian*
Daniels, Bruce Eric *library director*
Eisenberg, Michael Bruce *information studies educator*
Stam, David Harry *librarian*

**Tarrytown**
Bowen, Christopher Edward *library director*

**Tuckahoe**
Silk, Eleana S. *librarian*

**Tuxedo Park**
Friedman, Rodger *antiquarian bookseller, consultant*

**Vails Gate**
Fife, Betty H. *librarian*

**West Point**
Watson, Georgianna *librarian*

**White Plains**
Manville, Stewart Roebling *archivist*

**Williamsville**
Cloudsley, Donald Hugh *library administrator*

**NORTH CAROLINA**

**Albemarle**
Ingram-Tinsley, Dorothy Catherine *library automation specialist, horse stables owner*

**Chapel Hill**
Carpenter, Raymond Leonard *information science educator*
Holley, Edward Gailon *library science educator, former university dean*
Kilgour, Frederick Gridley *librarian, educator*
Moran, Barbara Burns *librarian, educator*
Pruett, James Worrell *librarian, musicologist*
Scepanski, Jordan Michael *librarian, administrator*

**Charlotte**
Cannon, Robert Eugene *librarian, public administrator, fund raiser*
Sintz, Edward Francis *librarian*

**Cove City**
Hawkins, Elinor Dixon (Mrs. Carroll Woodard Hawkins) *retired librarian*

**Davidson**
Jones, Arthur Edwin, Jr. *library administrator, English and American literature educator*
Park, Leland Madison *librarian*

**Durham**
Canada, Mary Whitfield *librarian*

**Eden**
Williams, Sue Darden *library director*

**Elm City**
Smith, Sue Parker *media administrator*

**Greensboro**
Kovacs, Beatrice *library studies educator*
Wright, Kieth Carter *librarian, educator*

**Greenville**
Lennon, Donald Ray *archivist, historian*

**Pembroke**
Sexton, Jean Elizabeth *librarian*

**Raleigh**
Littleton, Isaac Thomas, III *retired university library administrator, consultant*
Moore, Thomas Lloyd *librarian*

**Washington**
Timour, John Arnold *retired librarian, medical bibliography and library science educator*

**Wilmington**
Mc Cabe, Gerard Benedict *retired library administrator*

**Winston Salem**
Berthrong, Merrill Gray *retired library director*

## NORTH DAKOTA

**Mayville**
Karaim, Betty June *librarian*

**Valley City**
Fischer, Mary Elizabeth *library director*

## OHIO

**Akron**
Friedman, Richard Everett *librarian*
Rebenack, John Henry *retired librarian*

**Alliance**
Clem, Harriet Frances *library director*

**Athens**
Lee, Hwa-Wei *librarian, educator*

**Bedford**
Parch, Grace Dolores *librarian*

**Bluffton**
Smucker, Barbara Claassen *former librarian, writer*

**Bucyrus**
Herold, Jeffrey Roy Martin *library director*

**Cincinnati**
Bestehorn, Ute Wiltrud *retired librarian*
Brestel, Mary Beth *librarian*
Proffitt, Kevin *archivist*
Stoms, Donna Sue *librarian*
Wellington, Jean Susorney *librarian*
Wilson, Lucy Jean *librarian*
Zafren, Herbert Cecil *librarian, educator*

**Cleveland**
Abid, Ann B. *art librarian*
Gardner, Richard Kent *retired librarian, educator, consultant*
Mason, Marilyn Gell *library administrator, writer, consultant*
Pike, Kermit Jerome *library director*
Smythe Zäjc, M. Catherine *library administrator, development officer*

**Columbus**
Black, Larry David *library director*
Branscomb, Lewis Capers, Jr. *librarian, educator*
Meredith, Meri Hill *reference librarian, educator*
Sawyers, Elizabeth Joan *librarian, administrator*
Studer, William Joseph *library director*
Tiefel, Virginia May *librarian*

**Dayton**
Chait, William *librarian, consultant*
Coulton, Martha Jean Glasscoe *library consultant*
Klinck, Cynthia Anne *library director*

**Delaware**
Schlichting, Catherine Fletcher Nicholson *librarian, educator*

**Eaton**
Kendall, Susan Haines *library director*

**Grove City**
Black, Frances Patterson *library administrator*

**Harrison**
Everett, Karen J. *librarian*

**Lima**
Dicke, Candice Edwards *library educator*

**Middleburg Heights**
Maciuszko, Kathleen Lynn *librarian, educator*

**Niles**
Yancura, Ann Joyce *library director*

**Oberlin**
English, Ray *library administrator*
Greenberg, Eva Mueller *librarian*

**Oxford**
Sessions, Judith Ann *librarian, university library dean*

**Steubenville**
Hall, Alan Craig *library director*

**Van Wert**
Duprey, Wilson Gilliland *retired librarian*

**Wooster**
Hickey, Damon Douglas *library director*

**Youngstown**
Trucksis, Theresa A. *retired library director*

## OKLAHOMA

**Ardmore**
Brennen, Patrick Wayne *library director*

**Bartlesville**
Funk, Vicki Jane *librarian*

**Hodgen**
Brower, Janice Kathleen *library technician*

**Norman**
Hodges, Thompson Gene *librarian, retired university dean*
Kemp, Betty Ruth *librarian*
Lee, Sul Hi *library administrator*
Leonhardt, Thomas Wilburn *librarian, technical services director*
Lester, June *library and information management educator*
Sherman, Mary Angus *public library administrator*

**Oklahoma City**
Brawner, Lee Basil *librarian*
Clark, Robert Lloyd, Jr. *librarian*

**Stillwater**
Johnson, Edward Roy *library director*

**Taft**
Varner, Joyce Ehrhardt *librarian*

**Tulsa**
Huttner, Sidney Frederick *librarian*
Saferite, Linda Lee *library director*
Woodrum, Patricia Ann *librarian*

## OREGON

**Astoria**
Foster, Michael William *librarian*

**Beaverton**
Pond, Patricia Brown *library science educator, university administrator*

**Corvallis**
Hunt, Donald R. *retired librarian*

**Eugene**
Edwards, Ralph M. *librarian*
Hildebrand, Carol Ilene *librarian*
Morrison, Perry David *librarian, educator*

**Portland**
Browne, Joseph Peter *retired librarian*
Cooper, Ginnie *library director*
Esheiman, William Robert *librarian, editor*
Morgan, James Earl *librarian, administrator*

**Salem**
Kenyon, Carleton Weller *librarian*
Oberg, Larry Reynold *librarian*
Turnbaugh, Roy Carroll *archivist*

## PENNSYLVANIA

**Allentown**
Huber, Carolyn Michelle *librarian*

**Allison Park**
Hadidian, Dikran Yenovk *librarian, clergyman*

**Altoona**
Kinney, Janis Marie *librarian, consultant, storyteller*

**Bethel Park**
Marrs, Sharon Carter *librarian*

**Bethlehem**
Sacks, Patricia Ann *librarian, consultant*

**Bryn Mawr**
Tanis, James Robert *library director, history educator, clergyman*

**Greencastle**
Dietrich, Joyce Diane *librarian*

**Greensburg**
Duck, Patricia Mary *librarian*

**Kennett Square**
Vainstein, Rose *librarian, educator*

**Meadville**
Thorson, Connie Capers *library educator*

**New Kensington**
Miller, Albert Jay *retired librarian, educator*

**Philadelphia**
Arnold, Lee *library director*
Axam, John Arthur *library consultant*
Gendron, Michèle Marguerite Madeleine *librarian*
Griswold, Idawease Johnson *librarian*
Hamlin, Arthur Tenney *librarian*
Soultoukis, Donna Zoccola *library director*
Warner, Elizabeth Rose *librarian, educator*

**Phoenixville**
Fanus, Pauline Rife *librarian*

**Pittsburgh**
Carbo, Toni (Toni Carbo Bearman) *information scientist, university dean*
Josey, E(lonnie) J(unius) *librarian, educator, former state administrator*
Minnigh, Joel Douglas *library director*
Wohleber, Lynne Farr *archivist, librarian*

**Punxsutawney**
Dinsmore, Roberta Joan Maier *library director*

**Riegelsville**
Banko, Ruth Caroline *library director*

**State College**
Forth, Stuart Oliver

**University Park**
Eaton, Nancy Ruth Linton *librarian, dean*

**Villanova**
Mullins, James Lee *library director*

**Wayne**
Carter, Edward Carlos, II *librarian, historian*
Garrison, Guy Grady *librarian, educator*
Townsend, Philip W., Jr. *library director*

**Wilkes Barre**
Mech, Terrence Francis *library director*

## RHODE ISLAND

**Jamestown**
Logan, Nancy Allen *library media specialist*

**Newport**
Schnare, Robert Edey, Jr. *library director*

**Providence**
Adams, Thomas Randolph *bibliographer, librarian, historian*
Caldwell-Wood, Naomi Rachel *library media specialist*
Lynden, Frederick Charles *librarian*
Weaver, Barbara Frances *librarian*

**Warwick**
Charette, Sharon Juliette *library administrator*

## SOUTH CAROLINA

**Charleston**
Basler, Thomas G. *librarian, administrator, educator*
Buvinger, Jan *library director*

**Clemson**
Boykin, Joseph Floyd, Jr. *librarian*

**Columbia**
Callaham, Betty Elgin *librarian*
Duggan, Carol Cook *library director*
Griffin, Mary Frances *retired library media consultant*
Helsley, Alexia Jones *archivist*
Johnson, James Bek, Jr. *library director*
Rawlinson, Helen Ann *librarian*
Toombs, Kenneth Eldridge *librarian*
Warren, Charles David *library administrator*

**Ridgeland**
Kadar, Karin Patricia *librarian*

**Rock Hill**
Du Bois, Paul Zinkhan *library director*

## SOUTH DAKOTA

**Brookings**
Marquardt, Steve Robert *library director*

**Pierre**
Kolbe, Jane Boegler *state librarian*

**Sioux Falls**
Dertien, James LeRoy *librarian*
Thompson, Ronelle Kay Hildebrandt *library director*

## TENNESSEE

**Chattanooga**
McFarland, Jane Elizabeth *librarian*

**Collegedale**
Bennett, Peggy Elizabeth *librarian, library director, educator*

**Greeneville**
Smith, Myron John, Jr. *librarian, author*

**Knoxville**
Cottrell, Jeannette Elizabeth *retired librarian*
Watson, Patricia L. *library director*

**Memphis**
Drescher, Judith Altman *library director*
Meredith, Donald Lloyd *librarian*
Pourciau, Lester John *librarian*
Wallis, Carlton Lamar *librarian*

**Nashville**
Gleaves, Edwin Sheffield *librarian*
Hester, Bruce Edward *library media specialist, lay worker*
Stewart, David Marshall *librarian*

**Sewanee**
Dunkly, James Warren *theological librarian*

## TEXAS

**Abilene**
Specht, Alice Wilson *library director*

**Aledo**
Rowe, Sheryl Ann *librarian*

**Arlington**
Burson, Betsy Lee *librarian*

**Austin**
Billings, Harold Wayne *librarian, editor*
Branch, Brenda Sue *library director*
Davis, Donald Gordon, Jr. *librarian, educator*
Gracy, David Bergen, II *archivist, information science educator, writer*
Jackson, Eugene Bernard *librarian*
Jackson, William Vernon *library science and Latin American studies educator*
Middleton, Harry Joseph *library administrator*
Oram, Robert W. *library administrator*
Rascoe, Paul Stephen *librarian, researcher*

**Baytown**
Gardner, Kerry Ann *librarian*

**Bellaire**
Mote, Marie Therese *reference librarian*

**Cedar Hill**
Hickman, Traphene Parramore *library director, storyteller, library and library building consultant*

**Cedar Park**
Lam, Pauline Poha *library director*

**College Station**
Wilson, Don Whitman *archivist, historian*

**Corsicana**
Roberts, Nancy Mize *retired librarian, composer, pianist*

**Dallas**
Bockstruck, Lloyd DeWitt *librarian*
Bradshaw, Lillian Moore *retired library director*
Howell, Bradley Sue *librarian*
Ibach, Robert Daniel, Jr. *library director*
Pastine, Maureen Diane *librarian*
Salazar, Ramiro S. *library administrator*
Witmer, John Albert *librarian*

**Denton**
Poole, Eva Duraine *librarian*
Snapp, Elizabeth *librarian, educator*

**Fort Worth**
Allmand, Linda F(aith) *library director*
Ard, Harold Jacob *library administrator*
de Tonnancour, Paul Roger Godefroy *library administrator*

**Gilmer**
Green, Douglas Alvin *retired library director*

**Grand Prairie**
Ritterhouse, Kathy Lee *librarian*

**Houston**
Chang, Robert Huei *library director*
Gubbin, Barbara Ashley Brendon *librarian*
Henington, David Mead *library director*
Hornak, Anna Frances *library administrator*
Liddell, Leon Morris *librarian, educator*
Newbold, Benjamin Millard, Jr. *library manager, education consultant*
Radoff, Leonard Irving Marvin *consultant*
Russell, John Francis *retired librarian*
Suter, Jon Michael *academic library director, educator*
Wilson, Patricia Potter *library science and reading educator, educational and library consultant*

**Lubbock**
Wood, Richard Courtney *library director, educator*

**Marshall**
Magrill, Rose Mary *library director*

**Mcallen**
McGee, William Howard John *library system coordinator*

**Midland**
Wegner, Sandra Sue *library director*

**Palestine**
Williams, Franklin Cadmus, Jr. *bibliographer*

**Richardson**
Lovelace, Julianne *library director*

**San Antonio**
Garcia, June Marie *library director*
Jones, Daniel Hare *librarian*
Kozuch, Julianna Bernadette *librarian, educator*
Kronick, David A. *librarian*
Nance, Betty Love *librarian*
Young, Olivia Knowles *retired librarian*

**Seguin**
Moline, Sandra Lois *librarian*

**Snyder**
Anderson, Larry Vance *academic librarian, livestock farmer*

**Tyler**
Albertson, Christopher Adam *librarian*
Cleveland, Mary Louise *librarian, media specialist*

**Waco**
Bonnell, Pamela Gay *library administrator*
Progar, Dorothy *retired library director*

## UTAH

**Orem**
Hall, Blaine Hill *retired librarian*

**Provo**
Jensen, Richard Dennis *librarian*
Marchant, Maurice Peterson *librarian, educator*
Smith, Nathan McKay *library and information sciences educator*

**Riverside**
Reveal, Arlene Hadfield *retired librarian, consultant*

**Salt Lake City**
Buttars, Gerald Anderson *librarian*
Morrison, David Lee *librarian, educator*

## VERMONT

**Burlington**
Martin, Rebecca Reist *librarian*

**Pownal**
Gibson, Sarah Ann Scott *art librarian*

**South Burlington**
Kebabian, Paul Blakeslee *librarian*

## VIRGINIA

**Alexandria**
Berger, Patricia Wilson *retired librarian*
Budde, Mitzi Marie Jarrett *librarian*
Gray, Dorothy Louise Allman Pollet *librarian*
Mulvihill, John Gary *information services administrator*
O'Brien, Patrick Michael *library administrator*
Strickland, Nellie B. *library program director*

**Arlington**
Bold, Frances Ann *librarian*
Nida, Jane Bolster (Mrs. Dow Hughes Nida) *retired librarian*

**Bristol**
Muller, William Albert, III *library director*

**Castleton**
Hahn, James Maglorie *former librarian, farmer*

**Charlottesville**
Berkeley, Edmund, Jr. *archivist, educator*
Berkeley, Francis Lewis, Jr. *retired archivist*
Frantz, Ray William, Jr. *retired librarian*
Frieden, Charles Leroy *university library administrator*
Self, James Reed *librarian*
Stubbs, Kendon Lee *librarian*
Watson, Linda Anne *library director*

**Dumfries**
Gaudet, Jean Ann *librarian, educator*

**Farmville**
Boyer, Calvin James *librarian*

**Fredericksburg**
Dennis, Donald Daly *retired librarian*

**Harrisonburg**
Gill, Gerald Lawson *librarian*
Palmer, Forrest Charles *librarian, educator*

**Lexington**
Gaines, James Edwin, Jr. *retired librarian*
Leach, Maurice Derby, Jr. *librarian*

**Mathews**
Story, Martha vanBeuren *librarian*

**Mc Lean**
Fling, Jacqueline Ann *library administrator*

**Rapidan**
Grimm, Ben Emmet *former library director and consultant*

**Richmond**
Ford, Barbara Jean *library studies educator*
Self, Phyllis C. *library director*

**Roanoke**
Henn, Shirley Emily *retired librarian*

**Williamsburg**
Marshall, Nancy Haig *library administrator*

**Winchester**
Hughes, Donna Jean *librarian*

## WASHINGTON

**Bellevue**
Mutschler, Herbert Frederick *retired librarian*

**Kirkland**
Rosett, Ann Doyle *librarian*

**Lacey**
Smith, Donald Evans *library consultant*

**Seattle**
Blase, Nancy Gross *librarian*
Boylan, Merle Nelson *librarian*
Chisholm, Margaret Elizabeth *retired library education administrator*
Greggs, Elizabeth May Bushnell (Mrs. Raymond John Greggs) *retired librarian*
Hiatt, Peter *library studies educator*
Kruse, Paul Robert *retired librarian, educator*
Stroup, Elizabeth Faye *librarian*

**Shoreline**
Privat, Jeannette Mary *bank librarian*

**Spokane**
Bender, Betty Wion *librarian*
Burr, Robert Lyndon *information services specialist*
Murray, James Michael *librarian, law librarian, legal educator, lawyer*
Wirt, Michael James *library director*

**Tacoma**
Crisman, Mary Frances Borden *librarian*

**Walla Walla**
Jonish, Arley Duane *retired bibliographer*
Yaple, Henry Mack *library director*

## WEST VIRGINIA

**Glenville**
Tubesing, Richard Lee *library director*

**Institute**
Scott, John Edward *librarian*

**Morgantown**
Pyles, Rodney Allen *archivist, county official*

**Shepherdstown**
Elliott, Jean Ann *library administrator*

## WISCONSIN

**Eau Claire**
Thompson, Glenn Judean *library science educator*

**Kenosha**
Baker, Douglas Finley *library director*

**Madison**
Bunge, Charles Albert *library science educator*

**Milwaukee**
Huston, Kathleen Marie *library administrator*
McKinney, Venora Ware *librarian*

**Oshkosh**
Jones, Norma Louise *librarian, educator*
Urch, Diane Sherman *librarian*

**Thiensville**
Roselle, William Charles *librarian*

## WYOMING

**Cheyenne**
Johnson, Wayne Harold *librarian, county official*

**Laramie**
Cottam, Keith M. *librarian, educator, administrator*

## TERRITORIES OF THE UNITED STATES

## GUAM

**Mangilao**
Hamerly, Michael T. *librarian*

## PUERTO RICO

**San Juan**
Muñoz-Solá, Haydeé Socorro *library administrator*

## CANADA

## ALBERTA

**Calgary**
MacDonald, Alan Hugh *librarian, university administrator*

**Edmonton**
McDougall, Donald Blake *retired librarian, government official*

**Lethbridge**
Rand, Duncan D. *librarian*

## BRITISH COLUMBIA

**Abbotsford**
Fredeman, Betty Coley (Betty Coley) *retired librarian*

**Nanaimo**
Meadows, Donald Frederick *librarian*

**Vancouver**
Aalto, Madeleine *library director*
Piternick, Anne Brearley *librarian, educator*
Rothstein, Samuel *librarian, educator*

**Victoria**
Richards, Vincent Philip Haslewood *librarian*

## MANITOBA

**Winnipeg**
Converse, William Rawson Mackenzie *librarian*
Weismiller, David R. *library administrator*

## NOVA SCOTIA

**Dartmouth**
Horrocks, Norman *library science educator, editor*

**Halifax**
Birdsall, William Forest *librarian*
Dykstra Lynch, Mary Elizabeth *library and information science educator*

## ONTARIO

**Guelph**
Land, Reginald Brian *library administrator*

**Hamilton**
Hill, Graham Roderick *librarian*

**Mississauga**
Mills, Donald McKenzie *librarian*
Ryan, Noel *librarian, consultant*

**North York**
Bryant, Josephine Harriet *library executive*

**Ottawa**
Scott, Marianne Florence *librarian, educator*
Sylvestre, Jean Guy *former national librarian*
Wallot, Jean-Pierre *archivist, historian*

**Peterborough**
Brown, Wendy Evelynn *library director*

**Scarborough**
Bassnett, Peter James *retired librarian*

**Toronto**
Moore, Carole Irene *librarian*
Packer, Katherine Helen *retired library educator*
Schwenger, Frances *library director*

## QUEBEC

**Charlesbourg**
Paradis, Andre *librarian*

**Hull**
Boyer, Denis *library director*

**Montreal**
Large, John Andrew *library and information service educator*
Ormsby, Eric Linn *educator, researcher, writer*
Panneton, Jacques *librarian*
Sauvageau, Philippe *library director*
Sykes, Stephanie Lynn *library director, archivist, museum director*

**Rosemere**
Adrian, Donna Jean *librarian*

## SASKATCHEWAN

**Regina**
Powell, Trevor John David *archivist*

**Saskatoon**
Kennedy, Marjorie Ellen *librarian*

## MEXICO

**Mexico City**
Rodriguez, Adolfo *library director, historian*

## AUSTRALIA

**Belair**
Briggs, Geoffrey Hugh *retired librarian*

**Kensington**
Rayward, Warden Boyd *librarian, educator*

## CZECH REPUBLIC

**Prague**
Kalkus, Stanley *librarian, administrator, consultant*

## DENMARK

**Birketinget**
†Larsen, Poul Steen *library educator*

## HUNGARY

**Budapest**
Peterson, Trudy Huskamp *archivist*

## THAILAND

**Pathum Thani**
Stueart, Robert D. *university information services director, educator*

## ADDRESS UNPUBLISHED

Adamovich, Shirley Gray *retired librarian, state official*
Baker, Zachary Moshe *librarian*
Bowden, Ann *bibliographer, educator*
Brady, Jean Stein *retired librarian*
Burcher, Hilda Beasley *librarian*
Callard, Carole Crawford *librarian, educator*
Campbell, Henry Cummings *librarian*
Cartier, Celine Paule *librarian, administrator, consultant*
Clement, Hope Elizabeth Anna *librarian*
Cluff, E. Dale *librarian, educator, administrator*
Cooke, Eileen Delores *retired librarian*
Curley, Elmer Frank *librarian*
Dickinson, Donald Charles *library science educator*
Dorb, Alice *library media specialist, technology information specialist*
Driver, Lottie Elizabeth *librarian*
Eaton, Katherine Girton *retired library educator*
Edmonds, Anne Carey *librarian*
Ellis, Kem Byron *public library administrator*
Else, Carolyn Joan *library system administrator*
Erickson, Alan Eric *librarian*
Estes, Elaine Rose Graham *retired librarian*
Fasick, Adele Mongan *information services consultant*
Fawcett, John Thomas *archivist*
Felts, Margaret Davis *librarian, bibliographer*
Flinner, Beatrice Eileen *retired library and media sciences educator*
Gauthier, Mary Elizabeth *librarian, researcher, secondary education educator*
Giebel, Miriam Catherine *librarian, genealogist*
Gilbert, Nancy Louise *librarian*
Gould, Martha Bernice *retired librarian*
Gration, Selby Upton *retired library director, consultant*
Greenberg, Hinda Feige *library director*
Gregor, Dorothy Deborah *librarian*
Henry, Charles Jay *library director*
Hoke, Sheila Wilder *retired librarian*

Howard, Joseph Harvey *retired librarian*
Hughes, Sue Margaret *retired librarian*
Jenkins, Darrell Lee *librarian*
Kaser, David *retired librarian, educator, consultant*
Kaufman, Paula T. *librarian*
Klatt, Melvin John *library consultant*
Komidar, Joseph Stanley *librarian*
Leather, Victoria Potts *college librarian*
Lewis, Emanuel Raymond *historian, psychologist, retired librarian*
Lindgren, William Dale *librarian*
Loder, Victoria Kosiorek *information broker*
Martin, Murray Simpson *librarian, writer, consultant*
McBurney, Margot B. *librarian*
Meyer, Ursula *librarian*
Miele, Anthony William *retired librarian*
Miller, Charles Edmond *library administrator*
Miller, Jacqueline Winslow *library director*
Miller, Marilyn Lea *library science educator*
Moody, Roland Herbert *retired librarian*
Morgan, Jane Hale *retired library director*
Nelson, Helen Martha *retired library director*
Patterson, Robert Hudson *library director*
Rafael, Ruth Kelson *archivist, librarian, consultant*
Rhoads, James Berton *archivist, former government official, consultant, educator*
Rohlf, Robert Henry *retired library director, library consultant*
Rouse, Roscoe, Jr. *librarian, educator*
Sadler, Graham Hydrick *library administrator*
Scoles, Clyde Sheldon *library director*
Scott, Catherine Dorothy *librarian, information consultant*
Segal, JoAn Smyth *library consultant, business owner*
Shultz, Linda Joyce *retired library director*
Smith, Dentye M. *library media specialist*
Smith, Howard McQueen *librarian*
Smith, Sallye Wrye *librarian*
Spaeth, C. Edmond *library media specialist*
Spaulding, Frank Henry *librarian*
Spencer, David Mills *library administrator*
Stallworth-Barron, Doris A. Carter *librarian, educator*
Stavely, Keith Williams Fitzgerald *librarian*
Suput, Ray Radoslav *librarian*
Teeple, Fiona Diane *librarian, lawyer*
Thorn, Rosemary Kost *former librarian*
Trenery, Mary Ellen *librarian*
Van Orden, Phyllis Jeanne *librarian, educator*
Williams, Richard Clarence *retired librarian*
Wingate, Bettye Faye *librarian, educator*
Yeo, Ronald Frederick *librarian*

---

## HUMANITIES: MUSEUMS

## UNITED STATES

## ALABAMA

**Anniston**
Quick, Edward Raymond *museum director, educator*

**Birmingham**
†Schloder, John E. *museum director*

**Florence**
Wright, Mildred Anne (Milly Wright) *conservator, researcher*

**Mc Calla**
Gentry, Vicki Paulette *museum director*

**Mobile**
Richelson, Paul William *curator*
Schenk, Joseph Bernard *museum director*

## ALASKA

**Fairbanks**
Jonaitis, Aldona Claire *museum administrator, art historian*

## ARIZONA

**Phoenix**
Grinell, Sheila *museum director*
Sullivan, Martin Edward *museum director*

**Portal**
Zweifel, Richard George *curator*

**Tempe**
Zeitlin, Marilyn Audrey *museum director*

**Tucson**
Hancocks, David Morgan *museum director, architect*
Lusk, Harlan Gilbert *national park superintendent*
Yassin, Robert Alan *museum administrator, curator*

## ARKANSAS

**Little Rock**
DuBois, Alan Beekman *art museum curator*
Wolfe, Townsend Durant, III *art museum director, curator*

**State University**
Jones, Charlott Ann *museum director, art educator*

## CALIFORNIA

**Bakersfield**
Enriquez, Carola Rupert *museum director*

**Berkeley**
Benedict, Burton *retired museum director, anthropology educator*

**Carmel Valley**
Wolfe, Maurice Raymond *retired museum director, educator*

**Coloma**
Sugarman, Matthew S. *historic site adminstrator*

**Costa Mesa**
Botello, Troy James *arts administrator, counselor*
Labbe, Armand Joseph *museum curator, anthropologist*

**Fresno**
Sobey, Edwin J. C. *museum director, oceanographer, consultant*

**Hollywood**
Byrnes, James Bernard *museum director emeritus*

**Irvine**
Botwinick, Michael *museum director*

**La Jolla**
Beebe, Mary Livingstone *curator*

**Long Beach**
Glenn, Constance White *art museum director, educator, consultant*
Nelson, Harold Bernhard *museum director*

**Los Angeles**
Cohen, Daniel Morris *museum administrator, marine biology researcher*
Holo, Selma Reuben *museum director, educator*
Hopkins, Henry Tyler *museum director, art educator*
Koshalek, Richard *museum director, consultant*
Kuwayama, George *curator*
Naef, Weston John *museum curator*
Rudolph, Jeffrey N. *museum director*
Wittmann, Otto *art museum executive*

**North Hollywood**
Bull, David *fine art conservator*

**Oakland**
Burns, Catherine Elizabeth *art dealer*
Caldwell, Carey Teresa *museum curator*
Power, Dennis Michael *museum director*

**Orinda**
Dorn, Virginia Alice *art gallery director*

**Pacific Grove**
Adams, Margaret Bernice *retired museum official*

**Redding**
Becker, Stephen Arnold *museum executive*

**Riverside**
Green, Jonathan William *museum administrator and educator, artist, author*

**Sacramento**
Gray, Walter P., III *museum director, consultant*
Mette, Joe *museum director*

**San Diego**
DiMattio, Terry *historic site administrator*
Petersen, Martin Eugene *museum curator*

**San Francisco**
Adler, Adrienne Edna-Lois *art dealer, gallery owner, publisher*
Berggruen, John Henry *art gallery executive*
Delacote, Goery *museum director*
Griggs, Theresa *historic site administrator*
Lane, John Rodger *art museum director*
Leviton, Alan Edward *museum curator*
Lindsay, George Edmund *museum director*
Sano, Emily Joy *museum director*
Thomas, William Geraint *museum administrator*

**San Jose**
Burkhart, Sandra Marie *art gallery director*
Callan, Josi Irene *museum director*

**San Marino**
Skotheim, Robert Allen *museum administrator*
Wark, Robert Rodger *art curator*

**Santa Barbara**
Breunig, Robert G. *natural history museum director*
Karpeles, David *museum director*

**Santa Clara**
Schapp, Rebecca Maria *museum director*

**Santa Monica**
Walsh, John *museum director*

**Sausalito**
Elliott, James Heyer *retired university art museum curator, fine arts consultant*

**Simi Valley**
Hunt, Mark Alan *museum director*

**Stanford**
Seligman, Thomas Knowles *museum administrator*

**Watsonville**
Hernandez, Jo Farb *museum consultant*

## COLORADO

**Boulder**
Danilov, Victor Joseph *museum management program director, consultant, writer, educator*
Lanham, Urless Norton *curator*

**Colorado Springs**
Hoge, Robert Wilson *museum curator*
LeMieux, Linda Dailey *museum director*

**Denver**
Maytham, Thomas Northrup *art and museum consultant*

## CONNECTICUT

**Greenwich**
Sturges, Hollister, III *museum director*

**Hartford**
Faude, Wilson Hinsdale *museum director*
White, David Oliver *museum executive*

**Mystic**
Carr, James Revell *museum executive, curator*
Johnston, Waldo Cory Melrose *museum director*

**New Haven**
Hickey, Leo J(oseph) *museum curator, educator*
Parks, Stephen Robert *curator*

**Norwich**
Gualtieri, Joseph Peter *museum director*

**Old Lyme**
Dangremond, David W. *museum administrator, educator*

**Stamford**
Kinsman, Robert Donald *art museum administrator, cartoonist*
Scribner, Barbara Colvin *museum administrator*

**Weston**
Daniel, James *curator, business executive, writer, former editor,*

**Woodbury**
†Duffy, Henry J. *museum director, consultant*

## DELAWARE

**Wilmington**
Bruni, Stephen Thomas *art museum director*
Otey, Orlando *music executive, educator, pianist, theorist*
Porter, Glenn *museum and library administrator*

**Winterthur**
Hummel, Charles Frederick *museum official*
Lanmon, Dwight Pierson *museum director*

## DISTRICT OF COLUMBIA

**Washington**
Abbott, Rebecca Phillips *museum director*
Benezra, Neal *curator*
Bier, Carol Manson *museum curator, writer*
Brannan, Beverly Wood *curator of photography*
Bretzfelder, Deborah May *museum exhibit designer, photographer*
Cikovsky, Nicolai, Jr. *curator, art history educator*
Crew, Spencer *museum administrator*
Demetrion, James Thomas *art museum director*
Evelyn, Douglas Everett *museum executive*
Fetters, J. Michael *museum administrator*
Frankel, Diane *museum institute administrator*
Furgol, Edward Mackie *museum curator, historian*
Grasselli, Margaret Morgan *curator*
Hand, John Oliver *museum curator*
Hoffmann, Robert Shaw *museum administrator, educator*
Ketchum, James Roe *curator*
Kornicker, Louis S. *museum curator*
Lawton, Thomas *art gallery director*
Lowe, Harry *museum director*
Marsh, Caryl Amsterdam *museum exhibitions curator, psychologist*
Mellon, Paul *retired art gallery executive*
Moffett, Charles Simonton *museum director, curator, writer*
Neufeld, Michael John *curator, historian*
Panzer, Mary Caroline *museum curator*
Phillips, Laughlin *museum president, former magazine editor*
Rahill, Margaret Fish *retired museum curator*
Robison, Andrew Cliffe, Jr. *museum curator*
Russell, H. Diane *museum curator, educator*
†Scouten, Rex W. *curator*
Sheehan, Michael Terrence *arts administrator, historian, consultant*
Shestack, Alan *museum administrator*
Sultan, Terrie Frances *curator*
Viola, Herman Joseph *museum director*
Weil, Stephen Edward *museum official*
West, W. Richard *museum director*
Withuhn, William Lawrence *museum curator, railroad economics and management consultant*
Wolanin, Barbara Ann Boese *art curator, art historian*

## FLORIDA

**Daytona Beach**
Libby, Gary Russell *museum director*

**Delray Beach**
Shute, Melodie Ann *museum director*

**Gainesville**
Bishop, Budd Harris *museum administrator*
Dickinson, Joshua Clifton, Jr. *museum director, educator*
Wing, Elizabeth Schwarz *museum curator, educator*

**Jacksonville**
Dundon, Margo Elaine *museum director*
Schlageter, Robert William *museum administrator*

**Lakeland**
Stetson, Daniel Everett *museum director*

**Miami**
Etling, Russell Hull *museum director, production company executive*

**Orlando**
Morrisey, Marena Grant *art museum administrator*

**Saint Petersburg**
Duval, Cynthia *museum curator, adminstrator*

**Tallahassee**
Palladino-Craig, Allys *museum director*

**Winter Park**
Ruggiero, Laurence Joseph *museum director*

## GEORGIA

**Atlanta**
Bibb, Daniel Roland *antique painting restorer and conservator*
Davis, Eleanor Kay *museum administrator*
Lissimore, Troy *historic site director*
Vigtel, Gudmund *museum director emeritus*

**Marietta**
Oliver, Ann Breeding *fine arts education curator*

**Roswell**
Forbes, John Ripley *museum executive, educator, naturalist*

**Saint Simons Island**
King, Linda Orr *museum director*

## HAWAII

**Honolulu**
Ellis, George Richard *museum administrator*
Klobe, Tom *art gallery director*

**Mililani**
Magee, Donald Edward *retired national park service administrator*

## IDAHO

**Pocatello**
Jackson, Allen Keith *museum administrator*

## ILLINOIS

**Carbondale**
Whitlock, John Joseph *museum director*

**Chicago**
Balzekas, Stanley, Jr. *museum director*
Boyd, Karen Johnson *art dealer*
Boyd, Willard Lee *museum administrator, educator, lawyer*
Consey, Kevin Edward *museum administrator*
Edelstein, Teri J. *museum administrator, educator*
Flynn, John J. *museum curator*
Heltne, Paul Gregory *museum executive*
Jakstas, Alfred John *museum conservator, consultant*
Kahn, James Steven *museum director*
Kamyszew, Christopher D. *museum curator, executive educator, art consultant*
Kubida, Judith Ann *museum administrator*
Lewis, Phillip Harold *museum curator*
Mc Carter, John Wilbur, Jr. *museum executive*
Nordland, Gerald *art museum administrator, historian, consultant*
Wardropper, Ian Bruce *museum curator, educator*
Weisberg, Lois *arts administrator, city official*
Wilson, Karen Lee *museum director*
Wood, James Nowell *museum director and executive*
Zukowsky, John Robert *curator*

**Homewood**
MacMaster, Daniel Miller *retired museum official*

**Springfield**
Hallmark, Donald Parker *museum director*
Mc Millan, R(obert) Bruce *museum executive, anthropologist*

## INDIANA

**Bloomington**
Calinescu, Adriana Gabriela *museum curator, art historian*
Gealt, Adelheid Maria *museum director*

**Evansville**
Streetman, John William, III *museum official*

**Goshen**
Morris, Robert Julian, Jr. *art gallery owner*

**Indianapolis**
Gantz, Richard Alan *museum administrator*

**Muncie**
Joyaux, Alain Georges *art museum director*

**Notre Dame**
Porter, Dean Allen *art museum director, art historian, educator*

## IOWA

**Davenport**
Bradley, William Steven *art museum director*

**Iowa City**
Prokopoff, Stephen Stephen *art museum director, educator*

## KANSAS

**Dodge City**
Clifton-Smith, Rhonda Darleen *art center director*

**Lawrence**
Norris, Andrea Spaulding *art museum director*

**Manhattan**
Walker, Kathrine L. *museum educational administrator, educator*

## KENTUCKY

**Lexington**
Fowler, Harriet Whittemore *art museum director*

**Louisville**
Becker, Gail Roselyn *museum director*
Morrin, Peter Patrick *museum director*

**Owensboro**
Hood, Mary Bryan *museum director, painter*

## LOUISIANA

**New Orleans**
Bullard, Edgar John, III *museum director*
Casellas, Joachim *art gallery executive*
Fagaly, William Arthur *curator*
Freeman, Montine McDaniel *museum trustee*
Glasgow, Vaughn Leslie *museum curator and administrator*

## MAINE

**Augusta**
Phillips, Joseph Robert *museum director*

**Brunswick**
Watson, Katharine Johnson *art museum director, art historian*

**Hancock**
Silvestro, Clement Mario *museum director, historian*

**Kennebunk**
Escalet, Frank Diaz *art gallery owner, artist, educator*

**Orono**
Hartgen, Vincent Andrew *museum director, educator, artist*

**Portland**
Hull, William Floyd, Jr. *former museum director, ceramic consultant*

## MARYLAND

**Baltimore**
Fishman, Bernard Philip *museum director*
Lamp, Frederick John *museum curator*
Lanier, Jacqueline Ruth *artist*
Ott, John Harlow *museum administrator*
Randall, Lilian Maria Charlotte *museum curator*
Reeder, Ellen Dryden *museum curator*
Somerville, Romaine Stec *arts administrator*

**Bethesda**
Fri, Robert Wheeler *museum director*

**Elkton**
Smith, James Morton *museum administrator, historian*

**Saint Marys City**
Matelic, Candace Tangorra *museum studies educator, consultant, museum director*

## MASSACHUSETTS

**Amherst**
Parkhurst, Charles *retired museum director, art historian*
Sandweiss, Martha A. *author, American studies and history educator*

**Ashburnham**
Timms, Peter Rowland *art museum administrator*

**Boston**
Curran, Emily Katherine *museum director*
Ellis, David Wertz *museum director*
Fairbanks, Jonathan Leo *museum curator*
Freed, Rita Evelyn *curator, Egyptologist, educator*
Hills, Patricia Gorton Schulze *curator*
Howlett, D(onald) Roger *art gallery executive, art historian*
Logan, Lox Albert, Jr. *museum director*
Meister, Mark Jay *museum director, professional society administrator*
Nylander, Jane Louise *museum director*
Rogers, Malcolm Austin *museum director, art historian*
Stebbins, Theodore Ellis, Jr. *museum curator*
Vermeule, Cornelius Clarkson, III *museum curator*
Washburn, Bradford (Henry B. Washburn, Jr.) *museum administrator, cartographer, photographer*
Wentworth, Michael Justin *curator*
Wu, Tung *curator, art historian, art educator, artist*
Zannieri, Nina *museum director*

**Cambridge**
Cohn, Marjorie Benedict *curator, art historian, educator*
Cuno, James *art museum director*
Gaskell, Ivan George Alexander De Wend *art museum curator*
Mowry, Robert Dean *art museum curator, educator*

PROFESSIONAL INDEX 5291 HUMANITIES: MUSEUMS

Rathbone, Perry Townsend *art museum director*
Seamans, Warren Arthur *museum director*
Slive, Seymour *museum director, fine arts educator*

**Deerfield**
Friary, Donald Richard *museum administrator*

**Duxbury**
Vose, Robert Churchill, Jr. *former art gallery executive*

**Jamaica Plain**
Zahn, Carl Frederick *museum publications director, designer, photographer*

**Lincoln**
Master-Karnik, Paul Joseph *art museum director*

**Marion**
Cederholm, Theresa Miriam Dickason *museum director*

**Salem**
Finamore, Daniel Robert *museum curator*

**Southfield**
Melvin, Ronald McKnight *retired museum director*

**Springfield**
Muhlberger, Richard Charles *former museum administrator, writer, educator*

**Waltham**
Arena, Albert A. *museum director*

**Wellesley**
Freeman, Judi H. *curator, art historian*

**Williamstown**
Conforti, Michael Peter *museum director, art historian*
Hamilton, George Heard *curator*

**Worcester**
Barnhill, Georgia Brady *print curator*
Jareckie, Stephen Barlow *museum curator*
King, Anthony Gabriel *museum administrator*
Welu, James A. *art museum director*

**MICHIGAN**

**Ann Arbor**
Bailey, Reeve Maclaren *museum curator*
Sawyer, Charles Henry *art educator, art museum director emeritus*

**Dearborn**
Skramstad, Harold Kenneth, Jr. *museum administrator, consultant*

**Detroit**
Camp, Kimberly N. *museum administrator, artist*
Darr, Alan Phipps *curator, historian*
Edwards, Esther G. *museum administrator, former record, film and entertainment company executive*
Parrish, Maurice Drue *museum executive*
Peck, William Henry *museum curator, art historian, archaeologist, author, lecturer*
Sachs, Samuel, II *museum director*
Shaw, Nancy Rivard *museum curator, art historian, educator*

**East Lansing**
Bandes, Susan Jane *museum director, educator*

**Flint**
Germann, Steven James *museum director*

**Grand Rapids**
Frankforter, Weldon DeLoss *retired museum administrator*

**Kalamazoo**
Norris, Richard Patrick *museum director, history educator*

**MINNESOTA**

**Minneapolis**
King, Lyndel Irene Saunders *art museum director*

**Saint Paul**
Nelson-Mayson, Linda Ruth *art museum curator*
Osman, Stephen Eugene *historic site administrator*
Peterson, James Lincoln *museum executive*

**MISSISSIPPI**

**Madison**
Hiatt, Jane Crater *arts agency administrator*

**MISSOURI**

**Fort Leonard Wood**
Combs, Robert Kimbal *museum director*

**Hannibal**
Sweets, Henry Hayes, III *museum director*

**Kansas City**
McKenna, George LaVerne *art museum curator*
Scott, Deborah Emont *curator*
Svadlenak, Jean Hayden *museum administrator, consultant*
Ucko, David Alan *museum director*
Wilson, Marc Fraser *art museum administrator and curator*

**Saint Joseph**
Chilcote, Gary M. *museum director, reporter*

**Saint Louis**
Burke, James Donald *museum administrator*
Crandell, Dwight Samuel *museum executive*
Ketner, Joseph Dale *museum director, art historian*
Owyoung, Steven David *curator*
†Schmidt, Wayne William *museum director, curator*

**Springfield**
Berger, Jerry Allen *museum director*

**MONTANA**

**Bozeman**
Wolf, Arthur Henry *museum administrator*

**Missoula**
Brown, Robert Munro *museum director*

**NEBRASKA**

**Boys Town**
Lynch, Thomas Joseph *museum manager*

**Chadron**
Hanson, Charles Easton, Jr. *museum director, consultant*

**Kearney**
Lund, Virginia Llego *museum director, curator, chemistry educator*

**NEW HAMPSHIRE**

**Portsmouth**
O'Toole, Dennis Allen *museum director*

**NEW JERSEY**

**Cape May**
Cadge, William Fleming *gallery owner, photographer*

**Cranbury**
Greenwald-Ward, Alice Marian *museum consultant*

**Farmingdale**
Smith, Sibley Judson, Jr. *historic site administrator*

**Morristown**
Klindt, Steven *art museum director*

**New Brunswick**
Cate, Phillip Dennis *art museum director*

**Newark**
Reynolds, Valrae *museum curator*

**Park Ridge**
Maurer, C(harles) F(rederick) William, III *museum curator*

**Princeton**
Ryskamp, Charles Andrew *museum executive, educator*

**Somerville**
Peterson, John Douglas *museum administrator*

**NEW MEXICO**

**Albuquerque**
Black, Craig Call *retired museum administrator*

**Las Cruces**
Way, Jacob Edson, III *museum director*

**Placitas**
Smith, Richard Bowen *retired national park superintendent*

**Roswell**
Ebie, William D. *museum director*

**Ruidoso Downs**
Eldredge, Bruce Beard *museum director*

**Santa Fe**
DiMaio, Virginia Sue *gallery owner*
Enyeart, James L. *museum director*
Hassrick, Peter Heyl *museum director*
Livesay, Thomas Andrew *museum administrator, lecturer*

**Silver City**
Bettison, Cynthia Ann *museum director, archaeologist*

**Taos**
McFadden, David Revere *museum director*
Witt, David L. *curator, writer*

**NEW YORK**

**Albany**
Levine, Louis David *museum director, archaeologist*

**Brooklyn**
Faunce, Sarah Cushing *museum curator*
Ferber, Linda S. *museum curator*
Lehman, Arnold Lester *museum official, art historian*
Madigan, Richard Allen *museum director*
Shubert, Gabrielle S. *museum executive director*

**Buffalo**
Bayles, Jennifer Lucene *museum education curator*
Schultz, Douglas George *art museum director*

**Cooperstown**
MacLeish, Archibald Bruce *museum director*

**Corning**
Spillman, Jane Shadel *curator, researcher, writer*
Whitehouse, David Bryn *museum director*

**East Hampton**
Vered, Ruth *art gallery director*

**Flushing**
Fauntleroy, Carma Cecil *arts administration executive*

**Hewlett**
Flomenhaft, Eleanor *art curator*

**Ithaca**
Green, Nancy Elizabeth *curator, writer*
Robinson, Franklin Westcott *museum director, art historian*

**Katonah**
Simpson, William Kelly *curator, Egyptologist, educator*

**New York**
Arnot, Andrew H. *art gallery director*
Bandy, Mary Lea *museum official*
Baragwanath, Albert Kingsmill *curator*
Barnett, Vivian Endicott *curator*
Bates, Michael Lawrence *curator*
Batscha, Robert Michael *museum executive*
Bellamy, Richard *art gallery owner, director*
Biddle, Flora Miller *art museum administrator*
Bothmer, Dietrich Felix von *museum curator, archaeologist*
Brooks, Diana B. *auction house executive*
Brown, Eric Lucasen *art gallery director, art dealer*
Burge, Christopher *auction house executive*
Cohen, Mildred Thaler *art gallery director*
De Ferrari, Gabriella *curator, writer*
de Montebello, Philippe Lannes *museum administrator*
Desai, Vishakha N. *gallery executive, society administrator*
Dinaburg, Mary Ellen *art education and curatorial consultant*
Draper, James David *art museum curator*
Elam, Leslie Albert *museum administrator*
Emmerich, Andre *art gallery executive, author*
Esman, Rosa Mencher *art gallery executive*
Feldman, Ronald *art gallery director*
Fletcher, Harry George, III *curator*
Foulke, William Green, Jr. *business executive*
Freed, Stanley Arthur *museum curator*
Freudenheim, Tom Lippmann *museum administrator*
Gaudieri, Alexander V. J. *museum director*
Ginsburg, Sigmund G. *museum administrator*
Globus, Dorothy Twining *museum director*
Hambrecht, Patricia G. *auction house administrator*
Haskell, Barbara *curator*
Hawkins, Ashton *museum executive, lawyer*
Hollander, Stacy Candice Foster *museum curator*
Hoving, Thomas *museum and cultural affairs consultant, author*
Howat, John Keith *museum executive*
Ives, Colta Feller *museum curator, educator*
Kallir, Jane Katherine *art gallery director, author*
Kardon, Janet *museum director, curator*
Kind, Phyllis *art gallery owner*
Kingsley, April *art critic, curator, historian, art educator*
Kramer, Linda Konheim *curator, art historian*
Kuchta, Ronald Andrew *art museum director, magazine editor*
Kujawski, Elizabeth Szancer *art curator, consultant*
Lerner, Martin *museum curator*
Lowry, Glenn David *art museum director*
Luers, William Henry *art museum administrator*
Macdonald, Robert Rigg, Jr. *museum director*
Martin, Mary-Anne *art gallery owner*
Martin, Richard Harrison *curator, art historian*
Mertens, Joan R. *museum curator, art historian*
Messer, Thomas Maria *museum director*
Metcalf, William Edwards *museum curator*
Moore Hutton, Anne *museum consultant*
Muller, Priscilla Elkow *art historian*
Munhall, Edgar *curator, art history educator*
Murdock, Robert Mead *art consultant, curator*
Oldenburg, Richard Erik *auction house executive*
Parker, James *retired curator*
Pesner, Carole Manishin *art gallery owner*
Pilgrim, Dianne Hauserman *art museum director*
Pisano, Ronald George *art consultant*
Platnick, Norman I. *curator, arachnologist*
Rosenbaum, Joan Hannah *museum director*
Rosenthal, Nan *curator, author*
Ross, David A. *art museum director*
Schuster, Karen Sutton *administrator*
Shadwell, Wendy Joan *curator, writer*
Sidamon-Eristoff, Anne Phipps *museum official*
Simon, Ronald Charles *curator*
Smith, Paul J. *museum adminstrator*
Sragow, Ellen *gallery owner*
Stahl, Alan Michael *curator*
Storr, Robert *curator painting and sculpture, artist, writer*
Tobach, Ethel *retired curator*
Varnedoe, John Kirk Train *museum curator*
Vuilleumier, François *curator*
Wright, Gwendolyn *art center director, writer, educator*

**Nyack**
Rodwell-Bell, Regina *museum director*

**Purchase**
Gedeon, Lucinda Heyel *museum director*

**Rochester**
Adams, G. Rollie *museum executive*
Bannon, Anthony Leo *museum director*
Hall, Donald S. *retired planetarium administrator, pottery expert*
Hayes, Charles Franklin, III *museum research consultant*
Holcomb, Grant, III *museum director*

**Sands Point**
Olian, JoAnne Constance *curator, art historian*

**Setauket**
MacKay, Robert Battin *museum director*

**Southampton**
Lerner, Abram *retired museum director, artist*

**Stuyvesant**
Tripp, Susan Gerwe *museum director*

**Ticonderoga**
Westbrook, Nicholas Kilmer *museum administrator, historian*

**Tupper Lake**
Welsh, Peter Corbett *museum consultant, historian*

**Utica**
Schweizer, Paul Douglas *museum director*

**Wantagh**
Smits, Edward John *museum consultant*

**Waterford**
Gold, James Paul *museum director*

**West Falls**
Lindemann, Edna Meibohm *museum director, art consultant*

**Willow**
Cox, James David *art gallery executive*

**Yonkers**
†Schnee, Alix Sandra *historic site administrator*

**NORTH CAROLINA**

**Chapel Hill**
Bolas, Gerald Douglas *art museum administrator, art history educator*
Riggs, Timothy Allan *museum curator*

**Charlotte**
Evans, Bruce Haselton *art museum director*
Wolf, Sara Hevia *art librarian*

**Durham**
Krakauer, Thomas Henry *museum director*

**Greensboro**
Jones, Fred T., Jr. *museum administrator*

**Manteo**
Berry, Russell W. *historic site administrator*

**Raleigh**
Kuhler, Renaldo Gillet *museum official, scientific illustrator*
Wheeler, Lawrence Jefferson *art museum administrator*

**Salisbury**
Shalkop, Robert Leroy *retired museum director*

**Wilmington**
Janson, Anthony Frederick *art educator, former museum curator*
Scheu, David Robert, Sr. *historic site director*
Seapker, Janet Kay *museum director*

**Winston Salem**
Cawood, Hobart Guy *historic site administrator*
Gray, James Alexander *historic preservation official*
Rauschenberg, Bradford Lee *museum research director*

**OHIO**

**Akron**
Kahan, Mitchell Douglas *art museum director*

**Ashtabula**
Koski, Elizabeth Mitchell *arts center administrator*

**Athens**
Ahrens, Kent *museum director, art historian*

**Cincinnati**
Desmarais, Charles Joseph *museum director, writer, editor*
Long, Phillip Clifford *museum director*
Rogers, Millard Foster, Jr. *retired art museum director*
Sambi, Margaret Ann *curator*
Timpano, Anne *museum director, art historian*

**Cleveland**
Bergman, Robert Paul *museum administrator, art historian, educator, lecturer*
King, James Edward *museum director*
Turner, Evan Hopkins *retired art museum director*

**Dayton**
Nyerges, Alexander Lee *museum director*
Ruffer, David Gray *museum director, former college president*

**Fremont**
Bridges, Roger Dean *historical agency administrator*

**Mentor**
Miller, Frances Suzanne *historic site curator*

**Toledo**
Steadman, David Wilton *museum official*

**Vandalia**
Smith, Marjorie Aileen Matthews *museum director*

## OKLAHOMA

**Beaver**
Kachel, Harold Stanley *museum curator*

**Norman**
Toperzer, Thomas Raymond *art museum director*

**Tulsa**
Manhart, Marcia Y(ockey) *art museum director*

## OREGON

**Portland**
Eichinger, Marilynne H. *museum administrator*
Gilkey, Gordon Waverly *curator, artist*
Jenkins, Donald John *art museum administrator*
McKinley, Loren Dhue *museum director*
Schnitzer, Arlene Director *art dealer*
Taylor, J(ocelyn) Mary *museum administrator, zoologist, educator*

## PENNSYLVANIA

**Allentown**
Blume, Peter Frederick *museum director*

**Chadds Ford**
Duff, James Henry *museum director, environmental administrator*

**Doylestown**
Purpura, Peter Joseph *museum curator, exhibition designer*

**Erie**
Vanco, John L. *art museum director*

**Fort Washington**
Hague, Stephen George *museum director*

**Gettysburg**
Latschar, John A. *historic site administrator*

**Glenside**
Hemenway, Aice Pearson *retired museum director*

**Kennett Square**
Naeve, Milo Merle *museum curator and trustee*

**Philadelphia**
Bantel, Linda Mae *art museum director, art consultant*
Carter, John Swain *museum administrator, consultant*
Dyson, Robert Harris *museum director emeritus, archaeologist, educator*
Hanle, Paul Arthur *museum administrator*
Laverty, Bruce *curator*
Lindsey, Jack Lee, III *curator*
Shoemaker, Innis Howe *art museum curator*

**Pittsburgh**
Dawson, Mary Ruth *curator*
King, Elaine A. *curator, art historian, critic*
McIntosh, DeCourcy Eyre *museum director*

**Reading**
Dietrich, Bruce Leinbach *planetarium and museum administrator, astronomer, educator*

**Springfield**
Wilkinson, William Durfee *museum director*

**Strasburg**
Lindsay, George Carroll *former museum director*

**University Park**
Willumson, Glenn Gardner *curator, art historian*

**Villanova**
Scott, Robert Montgomery *museum executive, lawyer*

**Wayne**
Andes, Charles Lovett *direct marketing executive*

**Wyndmoor**
Wint, Dennis Michael *museum director*

## RHODE ISLAND

**Providence**
Hay, Susan Stahr Heller *museum curator*

**Saunderstown**
Leavitt, Thomas Whittlesey *museum director, educator*

## SOUTH CAROLINA

**Camden**
Craig, Joanna Burbank *historic site director*

**Charleston**
Brumgardt, John Raymond *museum administrator*

**Columbia**
Cilella, Salvatore George, Jr. *museum director*

**Florence**
Burns, William A. *museum administrator, author*

**Greenville**
Davis, Joan Carroll *museum director*

**Murrells Inlet**
Noble, Joseph Veach *fine arts administrator*

---

**Pawleys Island**
Tarbox, Gurdon Lucius, Jr. *retired museum executive*

## TENNESSEE

**Chattanooga**
Scarbrough, Cleve Knox, Jr. *museum director*

**Gatlinburg**
Pope, Randall Ray *retired national park superintendent*

**Memphis**
Carmean, E. A., Jr. *art museum director, art historian*
Creel, Wesley S. *museum director*
Czestochowski, Joseph Stephen *museum administrator*
Lewin, Ann White *museum director, educator*
Noble, Douglas Ross *museum administrator*

**Nashville**
Kreyling, Christine Moorman *museum curator, writer*

## TEXAS

**Austin**
Crain, William Henry *retired curator*

**Beaumont**
Smith, David Ryan *museum director*

**Dallas**
Meadows, Patricia Blachly *art curator, civic worker*
Silcox, Frances Eleanor *museum and exhibits planning consultant*
Vogel, Donald Stanley *gallery executive, artist*

**El Paso**
Sipiora, Leonard Paul *retired museum director*

**Fort Worth**
Auping, Michael G. *curator*
Otto, Donald R. *museum director*
Pillsbury, Edmund Pennington *museum director*

**Gun Barrel City**
Smith, Thelma Tina Harriette *gallery owner, artist*

**Houston**
Bowron, Edgar Peters *art museum curator, administrator*
Latimer, Roy Truett *museum executive*
Lee, Janie C. *curator*
Marzio, Peter Cort *museum director*

**San Antonio**
Lane, Mark *museum director*
Parsons, Merribell Maddux *museum administrator*

**Tyler**
Ott, Wendell Lorenz *art museum director, artist*

## UTAH

**Salt Lake City**
Leonard, Glen M. *museum administrator*
Oman, Richard George *museum curator*

## VERMONT

**Bennington**
Miller, Steven H. *museum diector*

**Huntington**
Spear, Robert Newell, Jr. *museum director*

**Manchester**
Kouwenhoven, Gerrit Wolphertsen *museum director*

**Shaftsbury**
Williams, Robert Joseph *museum director, educator*

## VIRGINIA

**Alexandria**
Evans, Grose *former curator, retired educator*
Gaynor, Margaret Cryor *program director*
Kennedy, Roger George *museum director, park service executive*
Lundeberg, Philip Karl Boraas *curator*

**Arlington**
Friedheim, Jerry Warden *museum executive*

**Charles City**
Tyler, Payne Bouknight *museum executive*

**Louisa**
Lanyon, Wesley Edwin *retired museum curator, ornithologist*

**Mount Vernon**
Rees, James Conway, IV *historic site administrator*

**Norfolk**
Hennessey, William John *art museum director*
Martin, Roy Butler, Jr. *museum director, retired broker*

**Richmond**
Miller, Nan Louise *museum director*
Witschey, Walter Robert Thurmond *science museum administrator, archaeologist, computer systems consultant*

---

**Tazewell**
Weeks, Ross Leonard, Jr. *museum executive, consultant*

**Waynesboro**
Rippe, Peter Marquart *museum administrator*

**Williamsburg**
Emerson, Philip G. *museum director*
Garrison, George Hartranft Haley *curator*
Kelm, Bonnie G. *art museum director, educator*
Wegner, Samuel Joseph *museum executive*

## WASHINGTON

**Bellevue**
Douglas, Diane Miriam *museum director*
Warren, James Ronald *retired museum director, author, columnist*

**Olympia**
Lind, Carl Bradley *retired museum director*

**Port Townsend**
Harrington, LaMar *curator, museum director*

**Pullman**
Watkinson, Patricia Grieve *museum director*

**Seattle**
Andrews, Richard Otis *museum director*
Herman, Lloyd Eldred *curator, consultant, writer*
Warren, Patricia J. *arts association executive*
West, Richard Vincent *art museum official*

**Tacoma**
Noll, Anna Cecilia *curator*

## WISCONSIN

**Madison**
Fleischman, Stephen *art center director*
Garver, Thomas Haskell *curator, art consultant, writer*
Westphal, Klaus Wilhelm *university museum administrator*

**Milwaukee**
Basquin, Mary Smyth (Kit Basquin) *museum curator*
Green, Edward Anthony *museum director*
Moynihan, William J. *museum executive*

**Sheboygan**
Kohler, Ruth DeYoung *arts center executive*

## WYOMING

**Casper**
Mobley, Karen Ruth *art gallery director*

**Cody**
Price, B. Byron *museum director*

**Rock Springs**
Chadey, Henry F. *museum director*

---

## CANADA

## ALBERTA

**Calgary**
Janes, Robert Roy *museum executive, archaeologist*

**Drumheller**
Naylor, Bruce Gordon *museum director*

## BRITISH COLUMBIA

**Victoria**
Barkley, William Donald *museum executive director*
Finlay, James Campbell *retired museum director*
Segger, Martin Joseph *museum director, art history educator*

## MANITOBA

**Winnipeg**
Cheff, Michel Vincent *art museum executive*

## NEW BRUNSWICK

**Fredericton**
Lumsden, Ian Gordon *art gallery director*

## NEWFOUNDLAND

**Saint John's**
Grattan, Patricia Elizabeth *art gallery director*

## NOVA SCOTIA

**Halifax**
Stevenson, Candace J. *museum director*

## ONTARIO

**Kleinburg**
Tyler, Barbara A. *museum director*

---

**London**
Poole, Nancy Geddes *art gallery curator*

**North York**
Cumming, Glen Edward *art gallery director*
Yarlow, Loretta *art museum director*

**Ottawa**
Bell, Phillip Michael *curator*
McAvity, John Gillis *museum director, association executive, museologist*
Thomson, Shirley Lavinia *museum director*

**Richmond Hill**
Tushingham, (Arlotte) Douglas *museum administrator*

**Toronto**
Anderson, Maxwell L. *museum director*

## PRINCE EDWARD ISLAND

**Charlottetown**
Severance, Christopher Churchill *museum director*

## QUEBEC

**Montreal**
Brisebois, Marcel *museum director*
Rombout, Luke *museum designer, administrator*

## MEXICO

**Mexico City**
del Conde, Teresa *museum director, art historian, researcher*

## AUSTRIA

**Vienna**
Oberhuber, Konrad Johannes *art museum curator, educator*

## FRANCE

**Paris**
Rosenberg, Pierre Max *museum director*

## JAPAN

**Miyazaki**
Meyer, Ruth Krueger *museum administrator, educator, art historian*

## ADDRESS UNPUBLISHED

Brumberg, G. David *historical center administrator, history bibliographer*
Castile, Jesse Randolph (Rand) *retired museum director*
Chenhall, Robert Gene *former museum director, consultant, author*
Coke, Frank Van Deren *museum director, photographer*
Cook, Alexander Burns *museum curator, artist, educator*
Dressel, Barry *museum administrator*
Emery, Alan Roy *museum executive*
English, Bruce Vaughan *museum director and executive, environmental consultant*
Friedman, Martin *museum director, arts adviser*
Graves, Sid Foster, Jr. *retired library and museum director*
Greaves, James Louis *art conservator*
Grogan, Kevin *museum director*
Hellmers, Norman Donald *historic site director*
Houlihan, Patrick Thomas *museum director*
Jacobowitz, Ellen Sue *museum and temple administrator*
Knowles, Elizabeth Pringle *art museum director*
Kochta, Ruth Martha *art gallery owner*
Lane, Lilly Katherine *museum staff member*
Leff, Sandra H. *gallery director, consultant*
Lutts, Ralph Herbert *museum administrator, scholar, educator*
Mahey, John Andrew *museum director*
Mason, James Albert *museum director, former university dean*
McKinney, Donald *art gallery director, art dealer*
Meyer, Mary-Louise *art gallery executive*
Millard, Charles Warren, III *museum director, writer*
Moore, William Jason *museum director*
Nasgaard, Roald *museum curator*
†Newman, Constance Berry *museum administrator*
Nihart, Franklin Brooke *marine museum consultant, writer and editor*
Nold, Carl Richard *state historic parks and museums administrator*
Oko, Andrew Jan *art gallery director, curator*
Pal, Pratapaditya *museum curator*
Parris, Nina Gumpert *curator, writer, researcher*
Pennington, Mary Anne *art museum director, museum management consultant, art educator*
Perrot, Paul Norman *museum director*
Pisney, Raymond Frank *international consulting services executive*
Pitts, Terence Randolph *curator and museum director*
Platou, Joanne (Dode) *retired museum director*
Porter, Daniel Reed, III *museum director*
Powell, Earl Alexander, III *art museum director*
Prakapas, Eugene Joseph *art gallery director*
Radice, Anne-Imelda *museum director*
Randall, Richard Harding, Jr. *art gallery director*
Rifkin, Ned *museum director*
Schneider, Janet M. *arts administrator, curator, painter*
Sennema, David Carl *museum consultant*
Shapiro, Michael Edward *museum administrator, curator, art historian*

Shimoda, Jerry Yasutaka *retired national historic park superintendent*
Stearns, Robert Leland *curator*
Stewart, Robert Gordon *former museum curator*
Stuart, Joseph Martin *art museum administrator*
Summerfield, John Robert *textile curator*
Talbot, Howard Chase, Jr. *retired museum administrator*
Welles, John Galt *retired museum director*
Wieser, Siegfried *planetarium executive director*
Yates, Charles Richardson *former arts center executive*
Yochelson, Bonnie Ellen *museum curator, art historian*
Zusy, Catherine *curator*

## INDUSTRY: MANUFACTURING. *See also* FINANCE: FINANCIAL SERVICES.

### UNITED STATES

#### ALABAMA

**Alexander City**
Gade, Marvin Francis *retired paper company executive*

**Andalusia**
Taylor, James Marion, II *automotive wholesale executive*

**Birmingham**
Bennett, Joe Claude *pharmaceutical executive*
Bolton, William J. *food products executive*
Chrencik, Frank *chemical company executive*
Harbert, Bill Lebold *construction corporation executive*
Holton, J(erry) Thomas *concrete company executive*
McMahon, John J., Jr. *metal processing company executive*
Neal, Phil Hudson, Jr. *manufacturing company executive*
Sklenar, Herbert Anthony *industrial products manufacturing company executive*
Styslinger, Lee Joseph, Jr. *manufacturing company executive*

**Gulf Shores**
Wingard, Raymond Randolph *transportation products executive*

**Lanett**
Fowler, Conrad Murphree *retired manufacturing company executive*

**Montgomery**
Blount, Winton Malcolm, Jr. *manufacturing company executive*

**Opelika**
Jenkins, Richard Lee *manufacturing company executive*

**Selma**
LeBeau, Hector Alton, Jr. *confectionary company executive*

**Theodore**
Mc Coy, Lee Berard *paint company executive*

**Tuscaloosa**
†Phifer, J. Reese *manufacturing executive*
Williams, Ernest Going *retired paper company executive*

#### ALASKA

**Anchorage**
Easley, George Washington *construction executive*

#### ARIZONA

**Carefree**
Byrom, Fletcher Lauman *chemical manufacturing company executive*
Galda, Dwight William *financial company executive*
Menk, Louis Wilson *retired manufacturing company executive*
Trimble, George Simpson *industrial executive*

**Chandler**
Farley, James Newton *manufacturing executive, engineer*

**Gilbert**
Earnhardt, Hal J., III *automotive executive*

**Gold Canyon**
Nelson, William O. *pharmaceutical company executive*

**Green Valley**
Blickwede, Donald Johnson *retired steel company executive*
Ehrenfeld, John Henry *grocery company executive*

**Mesa**
DeRosa, Francis Dominic *chemical company executive*
Luth, William Clair *retired research manager*
McDonald, Thomas Robert *materials technologist, consultant, business owner*
Woods, Joe Eldon *general contractor*

**Phoenix**
Carter, Ronald Martin, Sr. *pharmaceutical company executive*
Dewane, John Richard *manufacturing company executive*
Franke, William Augustus *corporate executive*
Giedt, Bruce Alan *paper company executive*
Mardian, Daniel *construction company director*
McClelland, Norman P. *food products executive*
Paul, Elias *food company consultant*
†Solheim, Karsten *golf equipment company executive*
Thompson, Herbert Ernest *tool and die company executive*
Weinstein, Allan M. *medical device company executive*
White, Edward Allen *electronics company executive*

**Prescott**
Parkhurst, Charles Lloyd *electronics company executive*

**Scottsdale**
Freedman, Stanley Marvin *manufacturing company executive*
Grenell, James Henry *retired manufacturing company executive*
Malsack, James Thomas *retired manufacturing company executive*
Ruhlman, Terrell Louis *business executive*
Walsh, Edward Joseph *toiletries and food company executive*

**Sun City**
Moore, William Cullen *retired electronics company executive*

**Sun City West**
Anderson, Ernest Washington *manufacturing company executive*

**Tucson**
Albrecht, Edward Daniel *metals manufacturing company executive*
Eckdahl, Donald Edward *manufacturing company executive*
Maxon, Don Carlton *construction company executive, mining company executive*
Meeker, Robert Eldon *retired manufacturing company executive*
Mullikin, Vernon Eugene *aerospace executive*
Sundt, Harry Wilson *construction company executive*

#### ARKANSAS

**Bella Vista**
Sutherland, Gail Russell *retired industrial equipment manufacturing company executive*

**Fayetteville**
†Marquardt, Stephen Alan *ironworks company executive*

**Fort Smith**
Boreham, Roland Stanford, Jr. *electric motor company executive*
Campbell, Vernon Deene *wire products company executive*
Flanders, Donald Hargis *manufacturing company executive*
Qualls, Robert L. *manufacturing executive, banker, former state official, educator*

**Hot Springs Village**
Schroeder, Donald Perry *retired food products company executive*

**Little Rock**
Dyke, James Trester *building materials distributing company executive*
Givens, John Kenneth *manufacturing executive*
Hickingbotham, Frank D. *food product executive*
McMullin, Carleton Eugene *automotive business executive*

**North Little Rock**
Harrison, Stephen Earle *manufacturing executive*

**Paragould**
Toomey, Kent Edward *manufacturing company executive*

**Pine Bluff**
Lea, George A., Jr. *retail food executive*

**Springdale**
Tollett, Leland Edward *food company executive*
Tyson, Donald John *food company executive*

**Stuttgart**
Bell, Richard Eugene *grain and food company executive*

#### CALIFORNIA

**Agoura**
Laney, Michael L. *manufacturing executive*

**Alamo**
Pritchett, Thomas Ronald *retired metal and chemical company executive*

**Aliso Viejo**
Baumgartner, Anton Edward *automotive sales professional*

**Anaheim**
Price, Richard Taft, Jr. *manufacturing company executive*

**Aptos**
Mechlin, George Francis *electrical manufacturing company executive*

**Atherton**
Goodman, Sam Richard *electronics company executive*
Hogan, Clarence Lester *retired electronics executive*
Mc Intyre, Henry Langenberg *former business executive, lawyer*

**Bakersfield**
Akers, Tom, Jr. *cotton broker, consultant*
Hart, Donald Milton *automotive and ranching executive, former mayor*
Lundquist, Gene Alan *cotton company executive*

**Belmont**
Wang, Su Sun *chemical company executive, chemist*

**Berkeley**
Cutter, David Lee *pharmaceutical company executive*

**Beverly Hills**
Casey, Joseph T. *corporate executive*
Hoch, Orion Lindel *corporate executive*
Singleton, Henry Earl *industrialist*
Willson, James Douglas *aerospace executive*

**Brisbane**
Mulligan, Martin Frederick *clothing executive, professional tennis player*

**Burbank**
Joseff, Joan Castle *manufacturing executive*
Raulinaitis, Pranas Algis *electronics executive*

**Calabasas**
Iacobellis, Sam Frank *retired aerospace company executive*

**Calistoga**
Ogg, Robert Danforth *corporate executive*

**Camarillo**
Cleary, Thomas Charles *technology company executive*
Denmark, Bernhardt *manufacturing executive*
Weiss, Carl *aerospace company executive*

**Campbell**
Sack, Edgar Albert *electronics company executive*

**Carlsbad**
Anderson, Paul Irving *management executive*
Crooke, Stanley Thomas *pharmaceutical company executive*
Randall, William B. *manufacturing company executive*

**Carpinteria**
Ehrlich, Grant C(onklin) *business consultant*

**Chino**
Goodman, Lindsey Alan *furniture manufacturing executive, architect*

**Compton**
†Golleher, George *food company executive*

**Concord**
Thompson, Jeremiah Beiseker *international medical business executive*

**Coronado**
Brunton, Paul Edward *retired diversified industry executive*

**Costa Mesa**
Hazewinkel, Van *manufacturing executive*
Kay, Kenneth Jeffrey *toy company executive*

**Covina**
Fillius, Milton Franklin, Jr. *food products company executive*

**Culver City**
Leve, Alan Donald *electronic materials manufacturing company owner, executive*

**Cupertino**
Burg, John Parker *signal processing executive*
Mathias, Leslie Michael *electronic manufacturing company executive*
†Mishelevich, David Jacob *medical company executive, consultant*
Peltzer, Douglas Lea *semiconductor device manufacturing company executive*

**Cypress**
Baugh, Coy Franklin *corporate executive*
Hoops, Alan *health care company executive*

**Danville**
Amon, William Frederick, Jr. *biotechnology company executive*
Liggett, Lawrence Melvin *vacuum equipment manufacturing company executive*
Manghirmalani, Ramesh *international trade corporation executive*

**Del Mar**
Cooper, Martin *electronics company executive*

**Dublin**
Whetten, John D. *food products executive*

**El Cajon**
McClure, Donald Edwin *electrical construction executive, consultant*

**El Segundo**
Amerman, John W. *toy company executive*
Criss, William Sotelo *electronics company executive*

**Emeryville**
Penhoet, Edward *biochemicals company executive*

**Encino**
Roderick, Robert Lee *aerospace executive*

**Escalon**
Barton, Gerald Lee *farming company executive*

**Fair Oaks**
Chernev, Melvin *retired beverage company executive*

**Fremont**
Chan, Steven S. *electronics company executive*
Lahri, Rajeeva *electronics executive*
Rugge, Henry Ferdinand *medical products executive*
Torian, Henry *automotive executive*

**Fullerton**
Miller, Arnold *electronics executive*

**Gardena**
Kanner, Edwin Benjamin *electrical manufacturing company executive*
Winston, Morton Manuel *equipment executive*

**Glendora**
Cahn, David Stephen *cement company executive*

**Goleta**
Thom, Richard David *aerospace executive*

**Granite Bay**
Manzo, Salvatore Edward *retired business developer*

**Hesperia**
Butcher, Jack Robert (Jack Risin) *manufacturing executive*

**Hillsborough**
Evans, Bob Overton *electronics executive*
Keller, John Francis *retired wine company executive, mayor*

**Hollywood**
Parks, Robert Myers *appliance manufacturing company executive*

**Huntington Beach**
Licata, Paul James *health products executive*

**Indian Wells**
Harris, Milton M. *distributing company executive*
Reed, A(lfred) Byron *retired apparel and textile manufacturing company*

**Irvine**
Alspach, Philip Halliday *manufacturing company executive*
Click, James H. *automotive executive*
Haggerty, Charles A. *electronics executive*
Herbert, Gavin Shearer *health care products company executive*
Webb, Louis *automotive company executive*
Williams, James E. *food products manufacturing company executive*

**La Jolla**
Drell, William *chemical company executive*
Geckler, Richard Delph *metal products company executive*
Richey, Phil Horace *former manufacturing executive, consultant*
Stevens, Paul Irving *manufacturing company executive*
†Tajima, George Kazuo *electronics company executive*
Thueson, David Orel *pharmaceutical executive, researcher, educator, writer*
Todd, Harry Williams *aircraft propulsion system company executive*
Wallace, Robert George *retired construction company executive, civil engineer*

**La Puente**
Hitchcock, Fritz *automotive company executive*

**Lafayette**
Lewis, Sheldon Noah *technology consultant*

**Laguna Beach**
Bezar, Gilbert Edward *retired aerospace company executive, volunteer*
Wolf, Karl Everett *aerospace and communications corporation executive*

**Laguna Hills**
Rossiter, Bryant William *chemistry consultant*

**Laguna Niguel**
Hanson, Larry Keith *plastics company executive*
Nelson, Alfred John *retired pharmaceutical company executive*

**Livermore**
Bennett, Alan Jerome *electronics executive, physicist*

**Livingston**
Fox, Robert August *food company executive*

**Long Beach**
Hulsey, Neven C. *metal products executive*
McGuire, James Charles *aircraft company executive*
Rethore, Bernard Gabriel *diversified manufacturing company executive*

**Los Altos**
Beer, Clara Louise Johnson *retired electronics executive*
Mullaley, Robert Charles *manufacturing company executive*

**Los Angeles**
Ash, Roy Lawrence *business executive*
Campion, Robert Thomas *manufacturing company executive*
Currie, Malcolm Roderick *aerospace and automotive executive, scientist*
Dalton, James Edward *aerospace executive, retired air force officer*
Davidson, Robert C., Jr. *manufacturing executive*
Drake, Hudson Billings *aerospace and electronics company executive*
Forester, Bernard I. *recreational equipment company executive*
Godbold, Wilford Darrington, Jr. *enclosure manufacturing company executive, lawyer*
Grant, David Browne *manufacturing executive*
Handschumacher, Albert Gustave *retired corporate executive*
Howard, Murray *manufacturing, real estate property management executive, farmer, rancher*

Hutchins, Joan Morthland *manufacturing executive, farmer*
Irani, Ray R. *oil and gas and chemical company executive*
Karatz, Bruce E. *business executive*
Korn, Lester Bernard *business executive, diplomat*
Mager, Artur *retired aerospace company executive, consultant*
Mall, William John, Jr. *aerospace executive, retired air force officer*
Marciano, Maurice *apparel executive*
Perkins, William Clinton *company executive*
Perry, William Joseph *food processing company executive*
Ramer, Lawrence Jerome *corporation executive*
Rive, Sarelle Roselyn *manufacturing company executive*
Segil, Larraine Diane *materials company executive*
Settles, F. Stan, Jr. *manufacturing executive, educator*
Tamkin, S. Jerome *business executive, consultant*

**Malibu**
Smith, George Foster *retired aerospace company executive*

**Marina Del Rey**
Brown, Anthony B. *aerospace executive*
Dankanyin, Robert John *international business executive*

**Menlo Park**
Bremser, George, Jr. *electronics company executive*
Cook, Paul M. *technology company executive*
Fergason, James L. *optical company executive*
Frisco, Louis Joseph *retired materials science company executive, electrical engineer*
Saifer, Mark Gary Pierce *pharmaceutical executive*
Taft, David Dakin *chemical executive*
Westcott, Brian John *manufacturing executive*

**Mill Valley**
Winskill, Robert Wallace *manufacturing executive*

**Milpitas**
Berkley, Stephen Mark *computer peripherals manufacturing company executive*
Granchelli, Ralph S. *company executive*

**Modesto**
Shastid, Jon Barton *wine company executive*

**Montecito**
Meghreblian, Robert Vartan *manufacturing executive, physicist*

**Moorpark**
Kavli, Fred *manufacturing executive*

**Mountain View**
Cusumano, James Anthony *chemical company executive, former recording artist*

**Newport Beach**
Chihorek, John Paul *electronics company executive*
Trivelpiece, Craig Evan *computer electronics executive*

**Northridge**
dePaolis, Potito Umberto *food company executive*

**Novato**
Womack, Thomas Houston *manufacturing company executive*

**Oakland**
Saunders, Ward Bishop, Jr. *retired aluminum company executive*
Serenbetz, Robert *manufacturing executive*
Sidney, William Wright *retired aerospace company executive*
Sullivan, G. Craig *household products executive*

**Ojai**
Weill, Samuel, Jr. *automobile company executive*

**Orange**
Skilling, David van Diest *manufacturing executive*

**Palm Desert**
Brown, James Briggs *retired business forms company executive*

**Palo Alto**
Burke, Edmund Charles *retired aerospace company executive*
Chow, Winston *engineering research executive*
DeLustro, Frank Anthony *biomedical company executive, research immunologist*
Early, James Michael *electronics research consultant*
Goff, Harry Russell *retired manufacturing company executive*
Halperin, Robert Milton *retired electrical machinery company executive*
Hewlett, William (Redington) *manufacturing company executive, electrical engineer*
Hornak, Thomas *electronics company executive*
Kennedy, W(ilbert) Keith, Jr. *electronics company executive*
Kincaid, Judith Wells *electronics company executive*
Kung, Frank F. C. *medical products executive*
Mario, Ernest *pharmaceutical company executive*
Neil, Gary Lawrence *pharmaceutical company research executive, biochemical pharmacologist*
Platt, Lewis Emmett *electronics company executive*
Saldich, Robert Joseph *electronics company executive*
Staprans, Armand *electronics executive*
Watkins, Dean Allen *electronics executive, educator*

**Palos Verdes Estates**
Mackenbach, Frederick W. *welding products manufacturing company executive*

**Palos Verdes Peninsula**
Grant, Robert Ulysses *retired manufacturing company executive*
Leone, William Charles *retired manufacturing executive*
†Pfund, Edward Theodore, Jr. *electronics company executive*

Wilson, Theodore Henry *retired electronics company executive, aerospace engineer*

**Pasadena**
Adler, Fred Peter *electronics company executive*
Chamberlain, Willard Thomas *retired metals company executive*
Jenkins, Royal Gregory *manufacturing executive*
Marlen, James S. *chemical-plastics-building materials manufacturing company executive*
Miller, Charles Daly *self-adhesive materials company executive*
Neal, Philip Mark *diversified manufacturing executive*
Smith, Howard Russell *manufacturing company executive*
Sudarsky, Jerry M. *industrialist*
Tollenaere, Lawrence Robert *retired industrial products company executive*

**Pebble Beach**
Crossley, Randolph Allin *retired corporate executive*
Rivette, Gerard Bertram *manufacturing company executive*

**Perris**
Gonzales, Richard Daniel *manufacturing executive*

**Petaluma**
Samuel, George *healthcare information company executive*

**Pleasanton**
Stager, Donald K. *construction company executive*
Weiss, Robert Stephen *medical manufacturing and services company financial executive*

**Portola Valley**
Graham, William James *packaging company executive*
Millard, Stephens Fillmore *electronics company executive*
Purl, O. Thomas *retired electronics company executive*

**Poway**
Aschenbrenner, Frank Aloysious *former diversified manufacturing company executive*

**Ramona**
Vaughn, Robert Lockard *aerospace and astronautics company executive*

**Rancho Mirage**
Greenbaum, James Richard *liquor distributing company executive, real estate developer*

**Rancho Santa Fe**
Jordan, Charles Morrell *retired automotive designer*

**Redding**
Emmerson, Red *sawmill owner*

**Redlands**
Skomal, Edward Nelson *aerospace company executive, consultant*

**Redondo Beach**
Dockstader, Jack Lee *electronics executive*
Kagiwada, Reynold Shigeru *advanced technology manager*

**Redwood City**
Ellison, Lawrence J. *computer software company executive*
Swinerton, William Arthur *retired construction company executive*
Wang, Chen Chi *electronics company, real estate, finance company, investment services and international trade executive*

**Riverside**
Crean, John C. *housing and recreational vehicles manufacturing company executive*
DeTemple, William Charles *technology executive*
Kummer, Glenn F. *manufactured housing executive*
Weide, William Wolfe *housing and recreational vehicles manufacturer*

**Sacramento**
Aldrich, Thomas Albert *former brewing executive, consultant*
Baccigaluppi, Roger John *agricultural company executive*
Boekhoudt-Cannon, Gloria Lydia *business education educator*
Mack, Edward Gibson *retired business executive*

**Salinas**
Taylor, Steven Bruce *agriculture company executive*

**San Carlos**
Gutow, Bernard Sidney *packaging manufacturing company executive*

**San Clemente**
Clark, Earnest Hubert, Jr. *tool company executive*

**San Diego**
Anjard, Ronald Paul, Sr. *business and industry executive, consultant, educator, technologist, importer, author*
Boarman, Patrick Madigan *economics and business administration educator, public official*
Carver, Juanita Ash *plastic company executive*
Darmstandler, Harry Max *real estate executive, retired air force officer*
Devine, Brian Kiernan *pet food and supplies company executive*
Duddles, Charles Weller *food company executive*
Goode, John Martin *manufacturing company executive*
Harriett, Judy Anne *medical equipment company executive*
Howell, Thomas Edwin *manufacturing company executive*
Ivans, William Stanley *electronics company executive*
Lewis, Alan James *pharmaceutical executive, pharmacologist*
Maier, Paul Victor *pharmaceutical executive*

Mullane, John Francis *pharmaceutical company executive*
Nassif, Thomas Anthony *business executive, former ambassador*
Ray, Gene Wells *industrial executive*
Rice, Clare I. *electronics company executive*

**San Fernando**
Boeckmann, H. F. *automotive executive*

**San Francisco**
Chiaverini, John Edward *construction company executive*
Grubb, David H. *construction company president*
Haas, Robert Douglas *apparel manufacturing company executive*
Hull, Cordell William *business executive*
James, George Barker, II *apparel industry executive*
Jewett, George Frederick, Jr. *forest products company executive*
Kreitzberg, Fred Charles *construction management company executive*
Marcus, Robert *aluminum company executive*
Merrill, Harvie Martin *manufacturing executive*
Monson, Arch, Jr. *fire alarm manufacturing company executive*
Nicholson, William Joseph *forest products company executive*
Powell, Sandra Theresa *timber company executive*
Siegel, Louis Pendleton *forest products executive*
Solomon, Neal Edward *management consultant*
Thacher, Carter Pomeroy *diversified manufacturing company executive*
Tusher, Thomas William *retired apparel company executive*
Wertheimer, Robert E. *paper company executive*
Wilson, Ian Robert *food company executive*
Zellerbach, William Joseph *retired paper company executive*

**San Jose**
Faggin, Federico *electronics executive*
Jacobson, Raymond Earl *electronics company entrepreneur and executive*
Jarrat, Henri Aaron *semiconductor company executive*
Rosendin, Raymond Joseph *electrical contracting company executive*
Schroeder, William John *electronics executive*
Scifres, Donald R. *semiconductor laser, fiber optics and electronics company executive*

**San Juan Capistrano**
Wong, Wallace *medical supplies company executive, real estate investor*

**San Marcos**
Andersen, Robert *health products/business executive*
Page, Leslie Andrew *disinfectant manufacturing company executive*

**San Mateo**
Aadahl, Jorg *business executive*
Besse, Robert Gale *food technologist*
Graham, Howard Holmes *manufacturing executive*
Rollo, F. David *hospital management company executive, health care educator*

**San Rafael**
Dewey, Edward Allen *retired construction company executive*

**Santa Ana**
Buster, Edmond Bate *metal products company executive*
Ware, James Edwin *retired international company executive*

**Santa Barbara**
Blasingame, Benjamin Paul *electronics company executive*
Bongiorno, James William *electronics company executive*
Potter, David Samuel *former automotive company executive*
Prindle, William Roscoe *consultant, retired glass company executive*
Zaleski, James Vincent *electronics executive*

**Santa Clara**
Baird, Mellon Campbell, Jr. *electronics industry executive*
Dunlap, F. Thomas, Jr. *electronics company executive, engineer, lawyer*
Elkus, Richard J., Jr. *electronics company executive*
Grove, Andrew S. *electronics company executive*
House, David L. *electronics components company executive*
McEachern, Alexander *electronics company executive*
Moore, Gordon E. *electronics company executive*
Stockton, Anderson Berrian *electronics company executive, consultant, genealogist*

**Santa Maria**
Grames-Lyra, Judith Ellen *building engineering inspector, artist, educator*

**Santa Monica**
Elson, Peter Frederic Alan *manufacturing company executive*

**Santee**
Vanier, Kieran Francis *business forms printing company executive*

**Saratoga**
†Houston, Joseph Brantley, Jr. *optical instrument company executive*
Reagan, Joseph Bernard *retired aerospace executive, management consultant*

**Seal Beach**
Beall, Donald Ray *multi-industry high-technology company executive*
Merrick, George Boesch *aerospace company executive*

**Sherman Oaks**
Reiner, Thomas Karl *manufacturing company executive*

**Simi Valley**
Weiser, Paul David *manufacturing company executive*

**Solana Beach**
Arledge, Charles Stone *former aerospace executive, entrepreneur*
Brody, Arthur *industrial executive*
Derbes, Daniel William *manufacturing executive*

**South Pasadena**
White-Thomson, Ian Leonard *mining company executive*

**Sunnyvale**
Amelio, Gilbert Frank *electronics company executive*
Evans, Barton, Jr. *analytical instrument company executive*
Hind, Harry William *pharmaceutical company executive*
Lewis, John Clark, Jr. *manufacturing company executive*
Sanders, Walter Jeremiah, III *electronics company executive*
Simon, Ralph E. *electronics executive*

**Tarzana**
Broadhurst, Norman Neil *foods company executive*
Krueger, Kenneth John *corporate executive, nutritionist, educator*

**Temecula**
Roemmele, Brian Karl *electronics, publishing, internet, financial and real estate executive*

**Thousand Oaks**
Binder, Gordon M. *health and medical products executive*

**Torrance**
Greaser, Constance Udean *automotive industry executive*
Mann, Michael Martin *electronics company executive*
Perrish, Albert *steel company executive*
Woodhull, John Richard *electronics company executive*

**Tustin**
Hester, Norman Eric *chemical company technical executive, chemist*

**Ukiah**
McAllister, (Ronald) Eric *pharmaceutical executive, physician*

**Upland**
Goodman, John M. *construction executive*

**Vacaville**
Castro, David Alexander *construction executive*

**Walnut Creek**
Graham, Dee McDonald *food company executive*
Hamlin, Kenneth Eldred, Jr. *retired pharmaceutical company executive*

**Watsonville**
Costanzo, Patrick M. *constuction executive*
Solari, R. C. *heavy construction company executive*

**Westlake Village**
Alagem, Beny *electronics executive*
Colburn, Keith W. *electronics executive*
DeLorenzo, David A. *food products executive*
Ghose, Rabindra Nath *technology research company executive*

**Willits**
Handley, Margie Lee *business executive*

**Wilmington**
Hamai, James Yutaka *business executive*

**Woodland Hills**
Firestone, Morton H. *business management executive*
Halamandaris, Harry *aerospace executive*
Leonis, John Michael *aerospace executive*
Morishita, Akihiko *trading company executive*

**Woodside**
Gates, Milo Sedgwick *retired construction company executive*
Raab, G. Kirk *biotechnology company executive*

**Yorba Linda**
Eriksen, Otto Louis *retired manufacturing company executive*
Forth, Kevin Bernard *beverage distributing industry consultant*

**Yuba City**
Giacolini, Earl L. *agricultural products company executive*

## COLORADO

**Arvada**
Holden, George Fredric *brewing company executive, policy specialist, author, professional speaker*

**Boulder**
Bills, Daniel Granville *manufacturing company executive*
Clark, Melvin Eugene *chemical company executive*
Hoerig, Gerald Lee *chemical company executive*
Leipold, William Charles, Jr. *plastics company executive, consultant*
Malone, Michael William *electronics executive, software engineer*
Miller, Norman Richard *diversified manufacturing company executive*

**Clark**
Bartoe, Otto Edwin, Jr. *aircraft company executive*

**Colorado Springs**
Cimino, Jay *automotive company executive*
Ehrhorn, Richard William *electronics company executive*
Fields, Robert Charles *retired printing company executive*
Robinson, Robert James *retired manufacturing executive*
Robinson, Ronald Alan *manufacturing executive*

**Denver**
Barry, Henry Ford *chemical company executive*
Gates, Charles Cassius *rubber company executive*
Lee, Richard Kenneth *building products company executive*
Livingston, Johnston R. *manufacturing executive*
Marcum, Walter Phillip *manufacturing executive, heavy*
May, Francis Hart, Jr. *retired building materials manufacturing executive*

**Englewood**
†Bowlen, Patrick Dennis *holding company executive, lawyer, professional sports team executive*
Chavez, Lloyd G. *automotive executive*
Mahoney, Gerald Francis *manufacturing company executive*
Saliba, Jacob *manufacturing executive*

**Fort Collins**
Hafford, Patricia Ann *electronic company executive*
Watz, Martin Charles *brewery executive*

**Golden**
Coors, William K. *brewery executive*
Woods, Sandra Kay *manufacturing executive*

**Greeley**
Arnold, Leonard J. *construction executive*
Morgensen, Jerry Lynn *construction company executive*

**Lakewood**
Heath, Gary Brian *manufacturing firm executive, engineer*
Owen, Robert Roy *retired manufacturing company executive*
Rosa, Fredric David *construction company executive*

**Littleton**
Gertz, David Lee *homebuilding company executive*
Plusk, Ronald Frank *manufacturing company executive*
Price, Gayl Baader *residential construction company administrator*

**Longmont**
Hahn, Yubong *electro-optics company executive*
Hall, Kathryn O'Neil *photographic company official*

**Monument**
Karasa, Norman Lukas *home builder, developer, geologist*

**Parker**
Cummings, Roger David *powder coatings consultant, sales executive*

## CONNECTICUT

**Ansonia**
Nichols, Russell James *manufacturing company executive*

**Branford**
Krupp, James Arthur Gustave *manufacturing materials executive, consultant*
McCurdy, Larry Wayne *automotive parts company executive*

**Bridgeport**
Semple, Cecil Snowdon *retired manufacturing company executive*

**Bristol**
Barnes, Carlyle Fuller *manufacturing executive*
Barnes, Wallace *manufacturing executive*
Wells, Arthur Stanton *retired manufacturing company executive*

**Broad Brook**
Kement, Isabella Viniconis *retired construction company executive*

**Danbury**
Baker, Leonard Morton *manufacturing company executive*
Kennedy, Robert Delmont *chemical company executive*
Lichtenberger, H(orst) William *chemical company executive*
Soviero, Joseph C. *chemical company executive*

**Darien**
Bowling, James Chandler *retired executive, farmer, philanthropist*
Britton, Robert Austin *manufacturing company executive*
Sprole, Frank Arnott *retired pharmaceutical company executive, lawyer*
Ziegler, William, III *diversified industry executive*

**East Hartford**
Coburn, Richard Joseph *company executive, electrical engineer*

**Fairfield**
Bunt, James Richard *electric company executive*
Krueger, Kurt Edward *appliance manufacturing company official*
Sutphen, Harold Amerman, Jr. *retired paper company executive*
Welch, John Francis, Jr. (Jack Welch) *electrical manufacturing company executive*

**Greenwich**
Allain, Emery Edgar *retired paper company executive*
Barber, Charles Finch *retired metals company executive, financial services company executive*
Damon, Edmund Holcombe *plastics company executive*
Dettmer, Robert Gerhart *beverage company executive*
Dorme, Patrick John *electronic company executive*
Ix, Robert Edward *food company executive*
Kelly, David Austin *investment counselor*
Lozyniak, Andrew *manufacturing company executive*
Mead, Dana George *diversified industrial manufacturing company executive*
Pollak, Edward Barry *chemical manufacturing company executive*
†Squier, David Louis *manufacturing executive*
Wearly, William Levi *business executive*
Weyher, Harry Frederick, III *metals company executive*

**Groton**
Auerbach, Michael Howard *chemical company research executive*
Hinman, Richard Leslie *pharmaceutical company executive*

**Hartford**
Clear, Albert F., Jr. *retired hardware manufacturing company executive*
Daniell, Robert F. *diversified manufacturing company executive*
David, George Alfred Lawrence *industrial company executive*
Doran, James Martin *retired food products company executive*
Hermann, Robert Jay *manufacturing company engineering executive, consultant*
Krieble, Robert H. *corporation executive*
Raffay, Stephen Joseph *manufacturing company executive*

**Madison**
Golembeski, Jerome John *wire and cable company executive*

**Middlebury**
Galie, Louis Michael *electronics company executive*

**Middletown**
Gerber, Murray A. *molding manufacturing company executive*

**Milford**
Hanlon, James Allison *confectionery company executive*

**Naugatuck**
Flannery, Joseph Patrick *manufacturing company executive*

**New Britain**
Ayers, Richard H. *manufacturing company executive*

**New Canaan**
Bartlett, Dede Thompson *company executive*
Burns, Ivan Alfred *grocery products and industrial company executive*
Hodgson, Richard *electronics company executive*
Johnston, Douglas Frederick *industrial holding company executive*
Kennedy, John Raymond *pulp and paper company executive*
Rutledge, John William *former watch company executive*
Sachs, John Peter *carbon company executive*
Toumey, Hubert John (Hugh Toumey) *textile company executive*

**New Hartford**
Perry, Lansford Wilder *manufacturing executive, consultant*

**New Haven**
Grossi, Richard J. *electric utility company executive*
Jacob, Deirdre Ann Bradbury *manufacturing executive, business educator, consultant*
Keiser, David Wharton *biotechnology executive*

**Newtown**
Krauss, Steven James *clothing executive*

**North Branford**
Mead, Lawrence Myers, Jr. *retired aerospace executive*

**North Haven**
Seton, Fenmore Roger *manufacturing company executive, civic worker*

**Norwalk**
Griffin, Donald Wayne *diversified chemical company executive*
†Harris, Holton Edwin *plastics machinery manufacturing executive*
Johnstone, John William, Jr. *chemical company executive*
Maarbjerg, Mary Penzold *office equipment company executive*
McDonell, Horace George, Jr. *instrument company executive*
Peltz, Alan Howard *manufacturing company executive*
Vanderbilt, Hugh Bedford, Sr. *mineral and chemical company executive*

**Old Greenwich**
Mc Donough, Richard Doyle *retired paper company executive*
Mc Quinn, William P. *corporation executive*
Plancher, Robert Lawrence *manufacturing company executive*
Rukeyser, Robert James *manufacturing executive*

**Old Lyme**
Mangin, Charles-Henri *electronics company executive*

**Plainfield**
O'Connell, Francis V(incent) *textile printing company executive*

**Plainville**
Glassman, Gerald Seymour *metal finishing company executive*

**Ridgefield**
Knortz, Herbert Charles *retired conglomerate company executive*
Levine, Paul Michael *paper industry executive, consultant*
Malhotra, Surin M. *aerospace manufacturing executive*
McGovern, R(ichard) Gordon *food company executive*
Sadow, Harvey S. *health care company executive*

**Riverside**
McCullough, Robert Willis *former textile executive*

**Salisbury**
Blum, Robert Edward *business executive*

**Sandy Hook**
Karkut, Emil Joseph *manufacturing company executive*

**Shelton**
Smith, Craig Richards *manufacturing executive*

**Somers**
Blake, Stewart Prestley *retired ice cream company executive*

**South Windsor**
Gentile, George Michael *manufacturing company finance executive*

**Southport**
Perry, Vincent Aloysius *corporate executive*
Roache, Edward Francis *retired manufacturing company executive*
Wheeler, Wilmot Fitch, Jr. *diversified manufacturing company executive*

**Stamford**
Allaire, Paul Arthur *office equipment company executive*
Anderson, Susan Stuebing *business equipment company executive*
Calarco, Vincent Anthony *specialty chemicals company executive*
Carlin, Gabriel S. *corporate executive*
Coleman, Ernest Albert *plastics and materials consultant*
Evans, Robert Sheldon *manufacturing executive*
Fernandez, Nino Joseph *manufacturing company executive*
Fickenscher, Gerald H. *chemicals company executive*
Filter, Eunice Margie *business equipment manufacturing executive*
Fortune, Philip Robert *metal manufacturing company executive*
Gladstone, Herbert Jack *manufacturing company executive*
Gross, Ronald Martin *forest products executive*
Hedge, Arthur Joseph, Jr. *corporate executive*
Hollander, Milton Bernard *corporate executive*
Hood, Edward Exum, Jr. *retired electrical manufacturing company executive*
Kingsley, John McCall, Jr. *manufacturing company executive*
Martin, Patrick *business equipment company executive*
Oatway, Francis Carlyle *corporate executive*
O'Malley, Thomas D. *diversified company executive*
Owen, Nathan Richard *manufacturing company executive*
Parker, Jack Steele *retired manufacturing company executive*
Peterson, Carl Eric *metals company executive, banker*
Ryan, Raymond D. *retired steel company executive, insurance and marketing firm executive*
Silver, R. Philip *metal products executive*

**Stratford**
Salzberg, Emmett Russell *new product developer*

**Thomaston**
Mühlanger, Erich *ski manufacturing company executive*

**Trumbull**
Schmitt, William Howard *cosmetics company executive*

**Vernon Rockville**
McKeever, Brian Edward *general contractor*

**Wallingford**
Cohen, Gordon S. *health products executive*
De George, Lawrence Joseph *diversified company executive*
Fleming, James Stuart, Jr. *pharmaceutial company manager*

**Waterbury**
Leever, Harold *chemical company executive*
Zampiello, Richard Sidney *metals and trading company executive*

**West Simsbury**
Brinkerhoff, Peter John *manufacturing company executive*

**Weston**
Liberatore, Nicholas Alfred *business consultant*

**Westport**
Breitbarth, S. Robert *manufacturing company executive*
Gans, Eugene Howard *cosmetic and pharmaceutical company executive*
McKane, David Bennett *business executive*
Stashower, Michael David *retired manufacturing company executive*

**Wethersfield**
Moran, John Joseph *retired food and beverage company executive*

**Windsor**
Ferraro, John Francis *business executive, financier*
Mangold, John Frederic *manufacturing company executive, former naval officer*

**Woodbridge**
Alvine, Robert *industrialist, entrepreneur, international business leader*

**Woodbury**
Farrell, Edgar Henry *lawyer, building components manufacturing executive*

## DELAWARE

**Milford**
Konowitz, Herbert Henry *textile company executive*

**Millsboro**
Townsend, P(reston) Coleman *agricultural business executive*

**Montchanin**
Olney, Robert C. *diversified products manufacturing executive*

**Newark**
Giacco, Alexander Fortunatus *chemical industry executive*
Molz, Robert Joseph *manufacturing company executive*

**Rockland**
Rubin, Alan A. *pharmaceutical and biotechnology consultant*

**Seaford**
Slater, Charles James *construction company executive*
Slater, Kristie *construction company executive*

**Wilmington**
Arrington, Charles Hammond, Jr. *retired chemical company executive*
Aungst, Bruce Jeffrey *pharmaceutical company scientist*
Gadsby, Robin Edward *chemical company executive*
Gibson, Joseph Whitton, Jr. *retired chemical company executive*
Holtzman, Arnold Harold *chemical company executive*
Jaffe, Edward E(phraim) *retired research and development executive*
Kane, Edward Rynex *retired chemical company executive, corporate director*
Karrh, Bruce Wakefield *retired industrial company executive*
Knight, Kenneth George *retired aerospace and defense company executive*
†Krol, John A. *diversified chemicals executive*
Lange, James Braxton *chemical company executive*
Robertson, David Wayne *pharmaceutical company executive*
Rose, Selwyn H. *chemical company executive*
Sganga, John B. *furniture holding company executive*
Wallace, Jesse Wyatt *pharmaceutical company executive*
Woods, Robert A. *chemical company executive*
Woolard, Edgar S., Jr. *chemical company executive*

## DISTRICT OF COLUMBIA

**Washington**
Alexander, Benjamin Harold *professional services firm executive, past government official*
Blanchette, Robert Wilfred *business executive, lawyer*
Briggs, Harold Melvin *corporate executive*
Case, Richard Paul *electronics executive*
†Cook, Merrill A. *explosives company executive, congressman*
Davis, True *corporate executive*
Griffin, Robert Thomas *automotive company executive*
Grossi, Ralph Edward *agricultural conservation organization executive, farmer, rancher*
Juliana, James Nicholas *ordnance company executive*
Marshall, C. Travis *manufacturing executive, government relations specialist*
Moore, Robert Madison *food industry executive, lawyer*
Park, Frances Mihei *food products executive, author*
Peapples, George Alan *automotive executive*
Persavich, Warren Dale *diversified manufacturing company executive*
Samartini, James Rogers *retired appliance company executive*
Shepherd, Alan J. *construction executive, management consultant*
Slater, Doris Ernestine Wilke *business executive*
Thomas, W. Dennis *paper company executive, former government official*
Willauer, Whiting Russell *consultant*

## FLORIDA

**Anna Maria**
Kaiser, Albert Farr *diversified corporation executive*

**Atlantis**
Minshall, Drexel David *retired manufacturing company executive*

**Boca Grande**
Nimitz, Chester William, Jr. *manufacturing company executive*

**Boca Raton**
Alvarado, Ricardo Raphael *retired corporate executive, lawyer*
Breslauer, Charles S. *chemical company executive*
Costello, Albert Joseph *chemicals executive*
Fetter, Richard Elwood *retired industrial company executive*
Ingwersen, Martin Lewis *shipyard executive*
†Keil, Charles Emanuel *corporation executive*
Klein, Robert *manufacturing company executive*

Levitetz, Jeff *food wholesaler*
Wyatt, James Luther *drapery hardware company executive*

**Bonita Springs**
Sargent, Charles Lee *manufacturing company executive*

**Boynton Beach**
Jensen, Reuben Rolland *former automotive company executive*
Johnson, Edward A. *manufacturing executive*
Smith, Charles Henry, Jr. *industrial executive*

**Bradenton**
Feeley, John Paul *retired paper company executive*
Price, Edgar Hilleary, Jr. *business consultant*

**Cape Coral**
Peters, Donald Cameron *construction company executive*

**Clearwater**
Chamberlin, Terry McBride *sailing equipment company executive*
Hoel, Robert Fredrick, Jr. *construction executive, civil engineer*
Scarne, John *game company executive*
Smith, Marion Pafford *avionics company executive*

**Clermont**
Dyson, Raymond Clegg *building contractor, construction consultant*

**Coral Gables**
Burini, Sonia Montes de Oca *apparel manufacturing and public relations executive*
Higginbottom, Samuel Logan *retired aerospace company executive*

**Delray Beach**
Bottner, Irving Joseph *cosmetic company executive*
Fuente, D. I. *office supply manufacturing executive*
Goldenberg, George *retired pharmaceutical company executive*
Himmelright, Robert John, Jr. *rubber company executive*
Saffer, Alfred *retired chemical company executive*
Smith, John Joseph, Jr. *textile company executive, educator*

**Dunedin**
Tweedy, Robert Hugh *retired equipment company executive*

**Fort Lauderdale**
Bishop, George Williams, III *supply company executive*
Carney, Dennis Joseph *former steel company executive, consulting company executive*
Carter, James Thomas *contractor*
Devol, George Charles, Jr. *manufacturing executive*
Feld, Joseph *construction executive*
Hoefling, John Alan *corporation executive, former army officer*
Keats, Harold Alan *corporate executive*
Morse, Edward J. *automotive executive*
Reigrod, Robert Hull *manufacturing executive*
Sklar, Alexander *electric company executive*

**Fort Myers**
Hudson, Leonard Harlow *contractor*
O'Dell, William Francis *retired business executive, author*
Wendeborn, Richard Donald *retired manufacturing company executive*

**Gainesville**
Gordon, Richard M. Erik *retailing executive, educator*

**Green Cove Springs**
Watson, Thomas Campbell *economic development consulting company executive*

**Gulf Breeze**
Strength, Robert Samuel *manufacturing company executive*

**Gulf Stream**
Stone, Franz Theodore *retired fabricated metal products manufacturing executive*

**Hallandale**
Cornblatt, Max *automotive batteries manufacturing company executive*

**Hillsboro Beach**
Case, Manning Eugene, Jr. *food products executive*

**Hobe Sound**
Casey, Edward Paul *manufacturing company executive*
Craig, David Jeoffrey *retired manufacturing company executive*
McChristian, Joseph Alexander *international business executive*

**Jacksonville**
Belin, Jacob Chapman *paper company executive*
Haskell, Preston Hampton, III *construction company executive*
Jackson, Julian Ellis *food company executive*
McGehee, Frank Sutton *paper company executive*
McGehee, Thomas Rives *paper company executive*
Saltzman, Irene Cameron *perfume manufacturing executive, art gallery owner*
Welch, Philip Burland *electronics and office products company executive*

**Jupiter**
Wrist, Peter Ellis *pulp and paper company executive*

**Key Largo**
Brown, David *retired petrochemical corporation executive*
Davidson, Thomas Noel *business executive*

**Lake Mary**
Scott, Gary LeRoy *photographic manufacturing executive, photographer*

**Lakeland**
Hatten, William Seward *manufacturing company executive*

**Largo**
†Newman, Francis A. *medical device company executive*

**Leesburg**
Talley, William Giles, Jr. *manufacturing company executive*

**Longboat Key**
Prizer, Charles John *chemical company executive*

**Longwood**
Blumberg, Herbert Kurt *corporate executive*
St. John, John *food company executive*

**Marathon**
Janicki, Robert Stephen *retired pharmaceutical company executive*

**Marco Island**
Butler, Frederick George *retired drug company executive*
Guerrant, David Edward *retired food company executive*

**Melbourne**
Bush, Norman *research and development executive*
Hartley, John T., Jr. *electronic systems, semiconductor, communications and office equipment executive*
Lucier, Gregory Thomas *manufacturing executive*

**Merritt Island**
Deardoff, R. Bruce *automotive executive*

**Miami**
Anscher, Bernard *manufacturing executive, investor, management consultant*
Bauer, Peter Alexander *clothing executive*
Blackburn, James Ross, Jr. *business executive, retired airline pilot*
Coulter, Wallace Henry *medical products executive*
Frigo, James Peter Paul *industrial hardware company executive*
Potamkin, Robert *automotive executive*
Spencer, Richard Thomas, III *healthcare industry executive*
Thornburg, Frederick Fletcher *diversified business executive, lawyer*

**Naples**
Baldwin, Ralph Belknap *retired manufacturing company executive, astronomer*
Barth-Wehrenalp, Gerhard *chemical company executive*
Biondo, Michael Thomas *retired paper company executive*
Borman, Earle Kirkpatrick, Jr. *chemical company executive*
Frazer, John Howard *tennis association executive, retired manufacturing company executive*
Gushman, John Louis *former corporation executive, lawyer*
Jaffe, Marvin Eugene *pharmaceutical company executive, neurologist*
Kapnick, Harvey Edward, Jr. *retired corporate executive*
Mutz, Oscar Ulysses *manufacturing and distribution executive*
Price, Thomas Benjamin *former textile company executive*
Reed, John Franklin *instrument manufacturing company executive*
Sekowski, Cynthia Jean *corporate executive, contact lens specialist*
Sharpe, Robert Francis *equipment manufacturing company executive*
von Arx, Dolph William *food products executive*
Williams, Edson Poe *retired automotive company executive*

**New Smyrna Beach**
Skove, Thomas Malcolm *retired manufacturing company financial executive*

**Niceville**
Litke, Donald Paul *business executive, retired military officer*

**North Palm Beach**
Hushing, William Collins *retired corporate executive*
Staub, W. Arthur *health care products executive*

**Ocala**
Lincoln, Larry W. *automotive executive*

**Orlando**
Brownlee, Thomas Marshall *lighting manufacturing company executive*
Hughes, David Henry *manufacturing company executive*
Jones, Constance Irene *medical products executive*
Jones, Joseph Wayne *food and beverage company executive, entrepreneur*
Pierce, Jerry Earl *business executive*

**Oviedo**
Whitworth, Hall Baker *forest products company executive*

**Palm Beach**
Habicht, Frank Henry *industrial executive*
Isenberg, Abraham Charles *shoe manufacturing company executive*
Jackson, John Tillson *corporate executive*
Oder, Frederic Carl Emil *retired aerospace company executive, consultant*
Roberts, Margot Markels *business executive*
Rumbough, Stanley Maddox, Jr. *industrialist*

**Palm Beach Gardens**
Keppler, William Edmund *multinational company executive*

**Palm City**
Derrickson, William Borden *manufacturing executive*
Wishart, Ronald Sinclair *retired chemical company executive*

**Pinellas Park**
Hall, Charles Allen *aerospace and energy company executive*

**Pompano Beach**
Fritsch, Billy Dale, Jr. *construction company executive*
Schwartz, Joseph *retired container company executive*

**Ponte Vedra Beach**
Elston, William Steger *food products company executive*
Klacsmann, John Anthony *retired chemical company executive*
Phelan, Martin DuPont *retired film company executive*
Spence, Richard Dee *paper products company executive, former railroad executive*

**Reddick**
Corwin, Joyce Elizabeth Stedman *construction company executive*

**Royal Palm Beach**
Graham, Carl Francis *consultant, former chemical products company executive, chemist*

**Safety Harbor**
Dohnal, William Edward *retired steel company executive, consultant, accountant*

**Saint Petersburg**
Joyce, Walter Joseph *retired electronics company executive*
Mills, William Harold, Jr. *construction company executive*
Remke, Richard Edwin *lumber company executive*
Sheen, Robert Tilton *manufacturing company executive*

**Sarasota**
Berkoff, Charles Edward *pharmaceutical executive*
Dlesk, George *retired pulp and paper industry executive*
Hoffman, Oscar Allen *retired forest products company executive*
Miranda, Carlos Sa *food products company executive*
Pollack, Joseph *diversified company executive*
Roth, James Frank *manufacturing company executive, chemist*
Slocum, Donald Hillman *product development executive*
Wigton, Paul Norton *steel company consultant, former executive*

**Spring Hill**
Martin, Gary J. *retired business executive, mayor*

**Stuart**
Conklin, George Melville *retired food company executive*
Leibson, Irving *industrial executive*
McKenna, Sidney F. *technical company executive*
Wasiele, Harry W., Jr. *diversified electrical manufacturing company executive*

**Sunrise**
Epstein, Samuel D. *electronics executive*

**Tampa**
Brown, Troy Anderson, Jr. *electrical distributing company executive*
Cohen, Frank Burton *wholesale novelty company executive*
Flom, Edward Leonard *retired steel company executive*
Johnson, Ewell Calvin *research and engineering executive*
McNeel, Van Louis *chemical company executive*
Naimoli, Vincent Joseph *diversified operating and holding company executive*
Robinson, Charles E. *building materials executive*

**Tarpon Springs**
Jackel, Simon Samuel *food products company executive, technical marketing and business consultant*
Vajk, Hugo *manufacturing executive*
Wilson, Robert William *defense systems company executive*

**Tequesta**
Danly, Donald Robert *retired manufacturing company executive*
Milton, Robert Mitchell *chemical company executive*
Peterson, James Robert *retired writing instrument manufacturing executive*

**Vero Beach**
Allik, Michael *diversified industry executive*
Cochrane, William Henry *municipal administration executive*
Dragone, Allan R. *manufacturing company executive*
MacTaggart, Barry *retired corporate executive*
Reed, Sherman Kennedy *chemical consultant*
Ritterhoff, C(harles) William *retired steel company executive*

**Village Of Golf**
Boer, F. Peter *chemical company executive*

**West Palm Beach**
Davis, Robert Edwin *manufacturing executive*
Hudson, Alice Peterson *chemistry consulting laboratory executive*
Luckett, Paul Herbert, III *manufacturing executive*
Nelson, Richard Henry *manufacturing company executive*
Oppenheim, Justin Sable *business executive*
Saraf, Shevach *company executive*
Scheckner, Sy *former greeting card company executive*
Vecellio, Leo Arthur, Jr. *construction company executive*

**Windermere**
Alexander, Judd Harris *retired paper company executive*
Hylton, Hannelore Menke *retired manufacturing executive*

**Winter Haven**
O'Connor, R. D. *health care executive*

**Winter Park**
Crosby, Philip Bayard *consultant, author*
Kost, Wayne L. *business executive*

## GEORGIA

**Ashburn**
Harvey, J. Ernest, Jr. *agricultural company executive*

**Atlanta**
Abrams, Bernard William *construction manufacturing and property development executive*
Abrams, Edward Marvin *construction company executive*
Baran, William Lee *food company executive*
Benatar, Leo *packaging company executive*
Bevington, E(dmund) Milton *electrical machinery manufacturing company executive*
Biggers, William Joseph *retired manufacturing company executive*
Boeke, Eugene H., Jr. *construction executive*
Corr, James Vanis *furniture manufacturing executive, investor, lawyer, accountant*
Correll, Alston Dayton, Jr. *forest products company executive*
DeLashmet, Gordon Bartlett *newsprint executive*
Dennison, Stanley Scott *retired lumber company executive, consultant*
Edwards, Louis Ward, Jr. *diversified manufacturing company executive*
Emerson, James Larry *beverage company executive*
Ferebee, John Spencer, Jr. *corporate executive*
Goizueta, Roberto Crispulo *food and beverage company executive*
Ivester, Melvin Douglas *beverage company executive*
Johnston, Summerfield K., Jr. *food products executive*
Jones, Christine Massey *furniture company executive*
Kuse, James Russell *chemical company executive*
Lee, R(aymond) William, Jr. *apparel company executive*
Liebmann, Seymour W. *construction consultant*
Mc Kenzie, Harold Cantrell, Jr. *retired manufacturing executive*
Millikan, James Rolens *cleaning service executive, musician, composer*
Nie, Zenon Stanley *manufacturing company executive*
Petersen-Frey, Roland *manufacturing executive*
Prince, Larry L. *automotive parts and supplies company executive*
Reed, Grant *phamaceutical executive*
Reith, Carl Joseph *apparel industry executive*
Richardson, Maurice M. *manufacturing executive*
Rivera, Richard E. *food products executive*
Schimberg, Henry Aaron *soft drink company executive*
†Seretean, Martin B. (Bud Seretean) *carpet manufacturing company executive*
Sutton, Berrien Daniel *beverage company executive*

**Baxley**
Reddy, Yenamala Ramachandra *metal processing executive*

**Brunswick**
Brubaker, Robert Paul *food products executive*
Iannicelli, Joseph *chemical company executive, consultant*

**Carrollton**
Richards, Roy, Jr. *wire and cable manufacturing company executive*

**Columbus**
Andrews, Gerald Bruce *textile executive*
Heard, William T. *automotive executive*
Leebern, Donald M. *distilled beverage executive*

**Conyers**
Mc Clung, Jim Hill *light manufacturing company executive*
Morse, Richard Van Tuyl *manufacturing executive, consultant*

**Dalton**
Bouckaert, Carl *manufacturing executive*
Shaw, Robert E. *carpeting company executive*

**Duluth**
Brody, Aaron Leo *food and packaging consultant*

**Gainesville**
Kartzinel, Ronald *pharmaceutical company executive, neuroscientist*

**Mableton**
Brannon, Winona Eileen *electrical contractor*

**Marietta**
Diercks, Chester William, Jr. *capital goods manufacturing company executive*
Falk, John Robert *packaging company executive*
Lewis, William Headley, Jr. *manufacturing company executive*

**Monroe**
Felker, G(eorge) Stephen *textile company executive*

**Moultrie**
Vereen, William Jerome *uniform manufacturing company executive*

**Norcross**
Adams, Kenneth Francis *automobile executive*

**Roswell**
Brands, James Edwin *medical products executive*

Tucker, Robert Dennard *health care products executive*
Woon, Paul Sam *technical executive*

**Savannah**
Cartledge, Raymond Eugene *retired paper company executive*
†Davis, Chris *aerospace company executive*
Gillespie, Daniel Curtis, Sr. *retired non-profit company executive, consultant*
Granger, Harvey, Jr. *manufacturing company executive, retired*
Peer, George Joseph *metals company executive*
Scott, Walter Coke *retired sugar company executive, lawyer*
Spitz, Seymour James, Jr. *retired fragrance company executive*
Sprague, William Wallace, Jr. *retired food company executive*

**Sea Island**
Mattis, Louis Price *pharmaceutical and consumer products company executive*

**Smyrna**
Craig, Nadine Karamarkovich *pharmaceutical executive*

**Thomaston**
Hightower, Neil Hamilton *textile manufacturing company executive*

**Thomasville**
Flowers, Langdon Strong *foods company executive*
Flowers, William Howard, Jr. *food company executive*
Mc Mullian, Amos Ryals *food company executive*

**West Point**
Glover, Clifford Clarke *retired construction company executive*

## HAWAII

**Honolulu**
Andrasick, James Stephen *agribusiness company executive*
Buyers, John William Amerman *agribusiness and specialty foods company executive*
Ching, Larry Fong Chow *construction company executive*
Couch, John Charles *diversified company executive*
Finney, John Edgar, III *food products executive*
Gary, James Frederick *business and energy advising company executive*
Hughes, Robert Harrison *former agricultural products executive*
Loeffler, Richard Harlan *retail and technology company executive*
Schnack, Gayle Hemingway Jepson (Mrs. Harold Clifford Schnack) *corporate executive*

## IDAHO

**Boise**
Appleton, Steven R. *electronics executive*
Beebe, Stephen A. *agricultural products company executive*
Cleary, Edward William *retired diversified forest products company executive*
Harad, George Jay *manufacturing company executive*
Kemp, J. Robert *beef industry consultant, food company executive*
Littman, Irving *forest products company executive*
McClary, James Daly *retired contractor*
Sullivan, James Kirk *forest products company executive*
Tinstman, Robert Allen *construction company executive*

**Hayden Lake**
Wogsland, James Willard *retired heavy machinery manufacturing executive*

## ILLINOIS

**Abbott Park**
Burnham, Duane Lee *pharmaceutical company executive*
Coughlan, Gary Patrick *pharmaceutical company executive*
Hodgson, Thomas Richard *health care company executive*
Lussen, John Frederick *pharmaceutical laboratory executive*
Young, Jay Maitland *product manager health care products*

**Addison**
Brunken, Gerald Walter, Sr. *manufacturing company executive*

**Antioch**
Strang, Charles Daniel *marine engine manufacturing company executive*

**Arlington Heights**
Church, Herbert Stephen, Jr. *retired construction company executive*
Hughes, John *chemical company executive*
Li, Norman N. *chemicals executive*

**Aurora**
Candlish, Malcolm *manufacturing company executive*

**Barrington**
Furst, Warren Arthur *retired holding company executive*
Kroha, Bradford King *electronics manufacturing corporation executive*

**Bedford Park**
Wenstrup, H. Daniel *chemical company executive*

**Bellwood**
D'Souza, Austin *manufacturing executive*

**Bloomington**
Hoyt, Don, Sr. *home builder, former association executive*

**Bourbonnais**
Bahls, Gene Charles *agricultural products company executive*

**Broadview**
Hohage, Frederick William *automotive parts company executive*
Pang, Joshua Keun-Uk *trade company executive*

**Calumet City**
Self, Madison Allen *chemical company executive*

**Carol Stream**
Catone, Lucio *manufacturing executive*

**Champaign**
Lyon, James Cyril *chemical society executive*
Richards, Daniel Wells *company executive*

**Chester**
Welge, Donald Edward *food manufacturing executive*

**Chicago**
Appleton, Arthur Ivar *retired electric products manufacturing company executive, horse breeder*
Barber, Edward Bruce *medical products executive*
Bergere, Carleton Mallory *contractor*
Brake, Cecil Clifford *diversified manufacturing executive*
Brookstone, Arnold F. *retired paper packaging company executive*
Bryan, John Henry *food and consumer products company executive*
Burhoe, Brian W. *automotive service executive*
Burt, Robert Norcross *diversified manufacturing company executive*
Callahan, Michael J. *chemicals and manufacturing company executive*
Carl, John L. *petroleum industry executive*
Conant, Howard Rosset *steel company executive*
Cooper, Charles Gilbert *toiletries and cosmetics company executive*
Cotter, Daniel A. *diversified company executive*
Covalt, Robert Byron *chemicals executive*
Crawford, William F. *corporate executive, consultant*
Crown, Lester *manufacturing company executive*
Darnall, Robert J. *steel company executive*
†Debczek, Arnold *pharmaceutical company executive*
Donnelley, James Russell *printing company executive*
Drexler, Richard Allan *manufacturing company executive*
Eisenberg, James *food company executive*
Farley, William F. *corporation executive*
Francois, William Armand *packaging company executive, lawyer*
Friedland, Richard Stewart *electronics company executive*
Gidwitz, Ronald J. *personal care products company executive*
Giesen, Richard Allyn *business executive*
Goss, Howard S(imon) *manufacturing executive*
Haas, Howard Green *bedding manufacturing company executive*
Hall, William King *manufacturing company executive*
Hamister, Donald Bruce *retired electronics company executive*
Harris, Irving Brooks *cosmetics executive*
Holland, Eugene, Jr. *lumber company executive*
Horne, John R. *farm equipment company executive*
Jezuit, Leslie James *manufacturing company executive*
Jones, Dennis Paul *food and consumer goods company executive*
Kirby, William Joseph *corporation executive*
Klein, Michael Sherman *manufacturing executive*
Lannert, Robert Cornelius *manufacturing company executive*
Lappin, Richard C. *corporate executive*
Lennes, Gregory *manufacturing and financing company executive*
Light, Kenneth B. *manufacturing company executive*
Linde, Ronald Keith *corporate executive, private investor*
Lockwood, Frank James *manufacturing company executive*
Lohman, Gordon R. *manufacturing executive*
Marcuse, Manfred Joachim *paper products executive*
Mayes, Frank Gorr *management consultant*
McKee, Keith Earl *manufacturing technology executive*
McLaughlin, William F. *paper company executive*
Moore, John Ronald *manufacturing executive*
Murphy, Michael Emmett *food company executive*
Nichol, Norman J. *manufacturing executive*
Nicholas, Arthur Soterios *manufacturing company executive*
Parrish, Overton Burgin, Jr. *pharmaceutical corporation executive*
Patel, Homi Burjor *apparel company executive*
Pigott, Richard J. *food company executive*
Pritzker, Robert Alan *manufacturing company executive*
Renkar-Janda, Jarri J. *paint manufacturing executive*
Rollhaus, Philip Edward, Jr. *manufacturing company executive*
Rosenberg, Gary Aron *construction executive, lawyer*
Schwartz, Charles Phineas, Jr. *replacement auto parts company executive, lawyer*
Siegel, Arthur *corporate executive*
Smithburg, William Dean *food manufacturing company executive*
Solomonson, Charles D. *corporate executive*
Sopranos, Orpheus Javaras *manufacturing company executive*
Stack, Stephen S. *manufacturing company executive*
Steinfeld, Manfred *furniture manufacturing executive*
Stewart, S. Jay *chemical company executive*
Stone, Alan *container company executive*
Stone, Roger Warren *container company executive*
Stotler, Edith Ann *grain company executive*
Strubel, Richard Perry *manufacturing company executive*
Stuart, Robert *container manufacturing executive*
Toll, Daniel Roger *corporate executive, civic leader*
Wechter, Clari Ann *paint manufacturing company executive*
Wellington, Robert Hall *manufacturing company executive*
Williams, Richard Lucas, III *electronics company executive, lawyer*
Zeffren, Eugene *toiletries company executive*

**Crystal Lake**
Althoff, J(ames) L. *construction company executive*
Anderson, Lyle Arthur *manufacturing company executive*
Smyth, Joseph Vincent *manufacturing company executive*

**De Kalb**
Troyer, Alvah Forrest *seed corn company executive, plant breeder*

**Decatur**
Kraft, Burnell D. *agricultural products company executive*
Staley, Henry Mueller *manufacturing company executive*

**Deerfield**
Batts, Warren Leighton *diversified industry executive*
Graham, William B. *pharmaceutical company executive*
Kushner, Jeffrey L. *manufacturing company executive*
Larrimore, Randall Walter *manufacturing company executive*
Loucks, Vernon R., Jr. *medical technologies executive*
McCarthy, Gerald Michael *electronics executive*
Ringler, James M. *cookware company executive*
Weiss, Stanley C. *electrical and electronics products wholesale distribution executive*
Zywicki, Robert Albert *electrical distribution company executive*

**Des Plaines**
Carroll, Barry Joseph *manufacturing and real estate executive*
Cronin, Kathleen Anne *executive search consultant*
Frank, James S. *automotive executive*
Meinert, John Raymond *clothing manufacturing and retailing executive, investment banker*

**Elk Grove Village**
Field, Larry *paper company executive*
McLain, Roger Sette *electronics company executive*
Nadig, Gerald George *manufacturing executive*

**Elmhurst**
Duchossois, Richard Louis *manufacturing executive, racetrack executive*

**Franklin Park**
Dean, Howard M., Jr. *food company executive*
Simpson, Michael *metals service center executive*
Watts, Ernest Francis *manufacturing company executive*
Wilson, Steven J. *metal products executive*

**Geneseo**
Cherry, Robert Earl Patrick *retired food company executive*

**Glen Ellyn**
Cvengros, Joseph Michael *manufacturing company executive*

**Glencoe**
Hickey, John Thomas *retired electronics company executive*
Silver, Ralph David *distilling company director*

**Glenview**
Bible, Geoffrey Cyril *tobacco company executive*
Hudnut, Stewart Skinner *manufacturing company executive, lawyer*
Nichols, John Doane *diversified manufacturing corporation executive*
Ptak, Frank S. *manufacturing executive*
Sherman, Elaine C. *gourmet foods company executive, educator*
Smith, Harold B. *manufacturing executive*
Winett, Samuel Joseph *manufacturing company executive*

**Highland Park**
Rudo, Milton *retired manufacturing company executive, consultant*
Singer, Norman Sol *food products executive, inventor*
Smith, Malcolm Norman *manufacturing company executive*

**Hinsdale**
Gallagher, John Pirie *retired corporation executive*
Lowenstine, Maurice Richard, Jr. *retired steel executive*

**Hoffman Estates**
Dennis, Steven Pellowe *retail executive*

**Indianhead Park**
Frisque, Alvin Joseph *retired chemical company executive*

**Ingleside**
Propst, Catherine Lamb *biotechnology company executive*

**Island Lake**
Benson, John Earl *construction executive*
O'Day, Kathleen Louise *food products executive*

**Itasca**
Boler, John *manufacturing executive*
Floyd-Teniya, Kathleen *business services executive*
Garratt, Reginald George *electronics executive*

**Kenilworth**
Weiner, Joel David *retired consumer packaged goods products executive*

**Kildeer**
Harrod, Scott *consulting manufacturing executive*

**Lake Bluff**
Wacker, Frederick Glade, Jr. *manufacturing company executive*

**Lake Forest**
Bernthal, Harold George *health care company executive*
Brown, Sharon Gail *company executive, consultant*
Deters, James Raymond *retired manufacturing and services company executive*
Dur, Philip Alphonse *automotive executive, retired naval officer*
Goodrich, Maurice Keith *retired business forms, systems and services company executive*
Hammar, Lester Everett *health care manufacturing company executive*
Larsen, Peter N. *leisure products manufacturing executive*
O'Mara, Thomas Patrick *manufacturing company executive*
Reichert, Jack Frank *manufacturing company executive*

**Lake Villa**
Anderson, Milton Andrew *chemical executive*

**Libertyville**
Burrows, Brian William *research and development manufacturing executive*

**Lincolnshire**
Bayly, George V. *manufacturing executive*
Carmichael, Leonard Lawrence *manufacturing executive, accountant*
Freund, Charles Gibson *retired holding company executive*
Keyser, Richard Lee *distribution company executive*

**Lisle**
Birck, Michael John *manufacturing company executive, electrical engineer*
Krehbiel, Frederick August, II *electronics company executive*
Psaltis, John Costas *retired manufacturing company executive*
Reum, W. Robert *manufacturing executive*

**Long Grove**
Liuzzi, Robert C. *chemical company executive*

**Mc Henry**
Schultz, Richard Martin *electronics application engineering executive*

**Melrose Park**
Bernick, Howard Barry *manufacturing company executive*
Cernugel, William John *hair care and household products company financial executive*
Umans, Alvin Robert *manufacturing company executive*

**Mendota**
Hume, Horace Delbert *manufacturing company executive*

**Moline**
Becherer, Hans Walter *agricultural equipment manufacturing executive*
Hanson, Robert Arthur *retired agricultural equipment executive*

**Mount Prospect**
Rogers, Richard F. *construction company executive, architect, engineer*
Smith, Ora Everett *corporate executive, lawyer*

**Mundelein**
Mills, James Stephen *medical supply company executive*

**Naperville**
Katai, Andrew Andras *chemical company executive*
Schaack, Philip Anthony *retired beverage company executive*
Wake, Richard W. *food products executive*
Wake, Thomas G. *food products executive*
Wellek, Richard Lee *business executive*

**Niles**
†Herb, Marvin J. *food products executive*
Rastogi, Anil Kumar *medical device manufacturer executive*

**Normal**
Ohinouye, Tsuneo *automobile manufacturing executive*

**Northbrook**
Boyce, Donald Nelson *diversified industry executive*
Harris, Neison *manufacturing company executive*
Kasperson, Richard Willet *retired pharmaceutical company executive*
Lenon, Richard Allen *chemical corporation executive*
Nordman, Richard Dennis *chemical company executive*
Sayatovic, Wayne Peter *manufacturing company executive*
Tucker, Frederick Thomas *electronics company executive*

**Northfield**
Carlin, Donald Walter *retired food products executive, consultant*
Hough, Richard T. *chemical company executive*
Smeds, Edward William *retired food company executive*
Stepan, Frank Quinn *chemical company executive*

**Oak Brook**
Holsinger, Wayne Townsend *apparel manufacturing executive*

**Oak Park**
Douglas, Kenneth Jay *food products executive*

**Oregon**
Abbott, David Henry *manufacturing company executive*

**Orland Park**
Gittelman, Marc Jeffrey *manufacturing and financial executive*

**Palatine**
Makowski, M. Paul *electronics research executive*
Roe, Richard C. *industry consultant, former home furnishings manufacturing executive*

**Palos Park**
Nelson, Lawrence Evan *business consultant*

**Park Ridge**
Weber, Philip Joseph *retired manufacturing company executive*

**Peoria**
Fites, Donald Vester *tractor company executive*

**Plainfield**
Aldinger, Thomas Lee *construction executive*

**Prospect Heights**
Byrne, Michael Joseph *business executive*

**Quincy**
Liebig, Richard Arthur *retired manufacturing company executive*

**Rock Falls**
Bippus, David Paul *manufacturing company executive*

**Rockford**
Gann, Gregory Charles *manufacturing company executive*
Gloyd, Lawrence Eugene *diversified manufacturing company executive*
Gurnitz, Robert Ned *steel industry company executive*
Horst, Bruce Everett *manufacturing company executive*
Kimball, Donald Robert *food company executive*
O'Donnell, William David *construction firm executive*

**Rolling Meadows**
Brennan, Charles Martin, III *construction company executive*

**Romeoville**
DePaul, John Phil *construction company executive, firefighter*

**Rosemont**
Isenberg, Howard Lee *manufacturing company executive*

**Round Lake**
Johnston, William David *health care company executive*

**Saint Charles**
Stone, John McWilliams, Jr. *electronics executive*

**Savoy**
Bosworth, Douglas LeRoy *international company executive, educator*

**Schaumburg**
Buchanan, Richard Kent *electronics company executive*
Tooker, Gary Lamarr *electronics company executive*
Weisz, William Julius *electronics company executive*

**Skokie**
Alexander, John Charles *pharmaceutical company executive, physician*
Caldwell, Wiley North *retired distribution company executive*
Green, David *manufacturing company executive*
Herting, Robert Leslie *pharmaceutical executive*

**South Elgin**
Burdett, George Craig *plastics industry executive*

**Sterling**
Knight, Herbert Borwell *manufacturing company executive*

**Streator**
Williams, Jeffry Cephas *business executive*

**Sycamore**
Grace, John Eugene *business forms company executive*

**Tinley Park**
Vogt, John Henry *corporate executive*

**Union**
Perlick, Richard Allan *steel company executive*

**Villa Park**
Miczuga, Mark Norbert *metal products executive*

**Waukegan**
Cherry, Peter Ballard *electrical products corporation executive*

**Westmont**
Gottlander, Robert Jan Lars *dental company executive*

**Wheaton**
Spedale, Vincent John *manufacturing executive*

**Wheeling**
Keats, Glenn Arthur *manufacturing company executive*

**Wilmette**
Barth, David Keck *industrial distribution industry consultant*
Bro, Kenneth Arthur *plastic manufacturing company executive*
Egloff, Fred Robert *manufacturers representative, writer, historian*
Pearlman, Jerry Kent *electronics company executive*

**Winnetka**
Bartlett, William McGillivray *hospital and scientific products company executive*
Gavin, James John, Jr. *diversified company executive*
Hartman, Robert S. *retired paper company executive*
Kennedy, George Danner *chemical company executive*
Menke, Allen Carl *industrial corporation executive*
Puth, John Wells *consulting company executive*

## INDIANA

**Batesville**
Buettner, Michael Lewis *healthcare manufacturing executive*
Smith, Lonnie Max *diversified industries executive*

**Bluffton**
Lawson, William Hogan, III *electrical motor manufacturing executive*

**Brownstown**
Robertson, Joseph Edmond *grain processing company executive*

**Carmel**
Shoup, Charles Samuel, Jr. *chemicals and materials executive*
Walsh, John Charles *metallurgical company executive*

**Chesterton**
Blaschke, Lawrence Raymond *steel manufacturing executive, energy professional*
Brown, Gene W. *steel company executive*
Haines, Robert Earl *retired industrial construction executive*

**Columbus**
Boll, Charles Raymond *engine company executive*
Draeger, Wayne Harold *manufacturing company executive*
Henderson, James Alan *engine company executive*
Kendall, James William *retired manufacturing company executive*
Stoner, R(ichard) B(urkett) *manufacturing company executive*

**Elkhart**
Corson, Thomas Harold *manufacturing company executive*
Decio, Arthur Julius *manufacturing company executive*
Groom, Gary Lee *recreational vehicle manufacturing executive*
Hill, Thomas Stewart *electronics executive, consultant, engineer*
Holtz, Glenn Edward *band instrument manufacturing executive*
Kloska, Ronald Frank *manufacturing company executive*
Martin, Rex *manufacturing executive*
Mischke, Frederick Charles *manufacturing company executive*

**Evansville**
Koch, Robert Louis, II *manufacturing company executive, mechanical engineer*
Muehlbauer, James Herman *manufacturing executive*

**Fort Wayne**
Burns, Thagrus Asher *manufacturing company executive, former life insurance company executive*
Collins, Linda Lou Powell *manager of contracts*
Latz, G. Irving, II *manufacturing company executive*
Marine, Clyde Lockwood *agricultural business consultant*
Molfenter, David P. *electronics executive*
Rifkin, Leonard *metals company executive*

**Franklin**
Janis, F. Timothy *technology company executive*

**Goshen**
Schrock, Harold Arthur *manufacturing executive*

**Granger**
Brissey, Ruben Marion *retired container company executive*

**Hammond**
Ash, Frederick Melvin *manufacturing company executive*

**Indianapolis**
Bindley, William Edward *pharmaceutical executive*
Dollens, Ronald W. *pharmaceuticals company executive*
Hunt, Robert Chester *construction company executive*
Justice, Brady Richmond, Jr. *medical services executive*
King, J. B. *medical device company executive, lawyer*
Lacy, Andre Balz *industrial executive*
Lanford, Luke Dean *electronics company executive*
Lantz, George Benjamin, Jr. *business executive, college executive, consultant*
Long, William Allan *retired forest products company executive*
Mc Farland, H. Richard *food company executive*
Pettinga, Cornelius Wesley *pharmaceutical company executive*
Reeve, Ronald Cropper, Jr. *manufacturing executive*
Richmond, James Ellis *restaurant company executive*
Salentine, Thomas James *pharmaceutical company executive*
Schmidt, William C. *chemical company executive*
Step, Eugene Lee *retired pharmaceutical company executive*

Swanson, David Heath *agricultural company executive*
Tobias, Randall L. *pharmaceutical company executive*
Tomlinson, Joseph Ernest *manufacturing company executive*
Zapas, James Richard *pharmaceutical company executive*

**Jasper**
Kohler, Jeffrey Martin *office furniture manufacturing executive*

**Lafayette**
Meyer, Brud Richard *pharmaceutical company executive*

**Middlebury**
Guequierre, John Phillip *manufacturing company executive*

**Mishawaka**
Kapson, Jordan *automotive executive*
Silver, Neil Marvin *manufacturing executive*

**Muncie**
Fisher, John Wesley *manufacturing company executive*
Sissel, George Allen *manufacturing executive*
Smith, Van P. *airplane engine company executive*

**Munster**
Corsiglia, Robert Joseph *electrical construction company executive*
Luerssen, Frank Wonson *retired steel company executive*

**Nappanee**
Shea, James F. *manufacturing executive*

**Newburgh**
Reavis, Hubert Gray, Jr. *metal products executive*

**Noblesville**
Almquist, Donald John *retired electronics company executive*

**Peru**
Marburger, John Allen *food manufacturing company executive*

**Portage**
Murphy, Newton Jerome *steel company executive*

**Richmond**
†Rubenstein, David H. *media manufacturing executive*

**South Bend**
Altman, Arnold David *business executive*

**Warsaw**
Dalton, William Matthews *retired foundry executive*

**West Lafayette**
Feinberg, Richard Alan *consumer science educator, consultant*
McDonald, Robert Bond *chemical company executive*
St. John, Charles Virgil *retired pharmaceutical company executive*

## IOWA

**Birmingham**
Goudy, James Joseph Ralph *electronics executive, educator*

**Boone**
Beckwith, F. W. *food products executive*

**Davenport**
Juckem, Wilfred Philip *manufacturing company executive*

**Dubuque**
Bertsch, Frank Henry *furniture manufacturing company executive*
Crahan, Jack Bertsch *manufacturing company executive*
McDonald, Robert Delos *manufacturing company executive*
Tully, Thomas Alois *building materials executive, consultant, educator*

**Fairfield**
Schaefer, Jimmie Wayne, Jr. *agricultural company executive*

**Mason City**
MacNider, Jack *retired cement company executive*

**Muscatine**
Dahl, Arthur Ernest *former manufacturing executive, consultant*
Howe, Stanley Merrill *manufacturing company executive*
Johnson, Donald Lee *agricultural materials processing company executive*
Koll, Richard Leroy *retired chemical company executive*

**Newton**
Hadley, Leonard Anson *appliance manufacturing corporation executive*
Haines, Richard Joseph *appliance manufacturing executive*
†Ward, Lloyd D. *appliance company executive*

**Pella**
Farver, Mary Joan *building products company executive*

**Spencer**
Pearson, Gerald Leon *food company executive*

**Springville**
Nyquist, John Davis *retired radio manufacturing company executive*

**Waterloo**
Mast, Frederick William *construction company executive*

**West Branch**
Sulg, Madis *corporation executive*

**West Des Moines**
Pomerantz, Marvin Alvin *container corporation executive*

## KANSAS

**Colby**
Baldwin, Irene S. *corporate executive, real estate investor*

**DeSoto**
Marcy, Charles Frederick *food packaging company executive*

**Dodge City**
Chaffin, Gary Roger *business executive*

**Goddard**
Peterman, Bruce Edgar *aircraft company executive, retired*

**Hesston**
Yost, Lyle Edgar *farm equipment manufacturing company executive*

**Hutchinson**
Dick, Harold Latham *manufacturing executive*

**Kansas City**
Baker, Clarence Albert, Sr. *structural steel construction company executive*
Olofson, Tom William *electronics executive*

**Lenexa**
Ascher, James John *pharmaceutical executive*
Pierson, John Theodore, Jr. *manufacturer*

**Overland Park**
Randolph, Scott Howard *chemical company executive*

**Salina**
Cosco, John Anthony *health care executive, educator, consultant*

**Shawnee Mission**
Arneson, George Stephen *manufacturing company executive, management consultant*
Dougherty, Robert Anthony *manufacturing company executive*
Gamet, Donald Max *appliance company executive*
Strubbe, Thomas R. *diagnostic testing industry executive*
Sunderland, Robert *cement company executive*

**Silver Lake**
Rueck, Jon Michael *manufacturing executive*

**Topeka**
Fink, H. Bernerd *corporate professional*

**Wichita**
Eby, Martin Keller, Jr. *construction company executive*
Meyer, Russel William, Jr. *aircraft company executive*

## KENTUCKY

**Bowling Green**
Holland, John Ben *clothing manufacturing company executive*

**Erlanger**
Cuneo, Dennis Clifford *automotive company executive*

**Florence**
Griggs, Roger Dale *pharmaceutical company executive*

**Gilbertsville**
Mathues, Thomas Oliver *retired automobile company executive*

**Lexington**
Mann, Marvin L. *electronics executive*

**Louisville**
Bujake, John Edward, Jr. *beverage company executive*
Cook, Howard Ruskin *construction company executive*
Gorman, Chris *construction company executive*
Heiden, Charles Kenneth *former army officer, metals company executive*
Kinsey, William Charles *building materials company executive*
Mountz, Wade *retired health service management executive*
Netter, Virginia Thompson *produce company owner*
Niblock, William Robert *manufacturing executive*
Street, William May *beverage company executive*

**Owensboro**
Hulse, George Althouse *steel company executive*

**Paducah**
Frankel, Andrew Joel *manufacturing company executive*

**Princeton**
P'Pool, Gerald W. *retired manufacturing executive*

PROFESSIONAL INDEX 5299 INDUSTRY: MANUFACTURING


## LOUISIANA

**Baton Rouge**
Turner, Bert S. *construction executive*

**Calhoun**
Robbins, Marion LeRon *agricultural research executive*

**Mandeville**
Napier, William James, Jr. *marine oil and gas construction consultant*

**Metairie**
Newman, Claire Poe *corporate executive*

**New Orleans**
Allen, F(rank) C(linton), Jr. *manufacturing executive, lawyer*
Collins, Harry David *construction consultant, forensic engineering specialist, mechanical and nuclear engineer, retired army officer*
Cospolich, James Donald *electrical engineering executive, consultant*
Crumley, Martha Ann *company executive*
Deasy, William John *construction, marine dredging, engineering and mining company executive*

**Saint Rose**
Lennox, Edward Newman *holding company executive*

## MAINE

**Brunswick**
Porter, Richard Sterling *retired metal processing company executive, lawyer*

**Ellsworth**
Goodyear, Austin *electronics and retail company executive*

**Falmouth**
Cabot, Lewis Pickering *manufacturing company executive, art consultant*

**Madawaska**
Vollmann, John Jacob, Jr. *cosmetic packaging executive*

**Portland**
Nixon, Philip Andrews *diversified company executive*

## MARYLAND

**Annapolis**
Hyde, Lawrence Henry, Jr. *industrial company executive*

**Baltimore**
Batterden, James Edward *business executive*
Bowe, Peter Armistead *manufacturing executive*
Deoul, Neal *electronics company executive*
†D'Erasmo, Martha Jean *health company executive*
Glassgold, Israel Leon *construction company executive, engineer, consultant*
Goetze, Marian Engle *business executive*
Haysbert, Raymond Victor *food company executive*
Legum, Jeffrey Alfred *automobile company executive*
McCarty, Harry Downman *tool manufacturing company executive*
Reeder, Oliver Howard *paint products manufacturing executive*
Scheeler, Charles *construction company executive*
Slatkin, Murray *paint sundry distribution executive*
Strull, Gene *technology consultant, retired electrical manufacturing company executive*
Wilgis, Herbert E., Jr. *corporate executive*

**Bethesda**
Augustine, Norman Ralph *industrial executive, educator*
Bregman, Jacob Israel *environmental consulting company executive*
Egan, John Frederick *electronics executive*
Fowler, James D., Jr. *marketing and human resources consulant*
Weinberger, Alan David *corporate executive*

**Bozman**
Peterson, H(arry) William *chemicals executive, consultant*

**Chevy Chase**
Bissinger, Frederick Lewis *retired manufacturing executive, consultant*
Richards, Merlon Foss *retired diversified technical services company executive*
Roberts, Clyde Francis *business executive*

**Columbia**
Peck, Charles Edward *retired construction and mortgage executive*
van Remoortere, Francois Petrus *chemical company research and development executive*

**Easton**
Peterson, James Kenneth *manufacturing company executive*

**Elkridge**
Calton, Gary Jim *chemical company executive, medical educator*

**Ellicott City**
Weingarten, Murray *manufacturing executive*

**Gaithersburg**
Ewing, Frank Marion *lumber company executive, industrial land developer*
Schrenk, W(illi) Juergen *health care company executive*

**Hagerstown**
Moore, Malcolm Frederick *manufacturing executive*

**Huntingtown**
Mitchell, Robert Greene *industrial manufacturing executive, consultant*

**Jessup**
Rauscher, Tomlinson Gene *electronics company executive, management consultant*

**Laurel**
Abbagnaro, Louis Anthony *corporate executive*

**Potomac**
Karson, Emile *international business executive*

**Rockville**
Drzewiecki, Tadeusz Maria *corporate executive, defense consultant*
Goldenberg, Melvyn Joel *information management services company executive*
Halperin, Jerome Arthur *pharmaceutical executive*
Miller, Kenneth Michael *electronics executive*

**Saint Michaels**
Jones, Raymond Edward, Jr. *brewing executive*
Meendsen, Fred Charles *retired food company executive*

**Salisbury**
Madden, Heather Ann *aluminum company executive*
Perdue, Franklin P. *poultry products company executive*
Perdue, James *food products executive*

**Sandy Spring**
Gibian, Thomas George *chemical company executive*

**Severna Park**
Kumm, William Howard *energy products company executive*

**Silver Spring**
Coates, Robert Jay *retired electronic scientist*
Porter, Dwight Johnson *former electric company executive, foreign affairs consultant*
Schneider, William Charles *aerospace consultant*

**Towson**
Morris, Edwin Thaddeus *construction consultant*
Ryker, Norman J., Jr. *retired manufacturing company executive*

**Upper Marlboro**
Bowles, Liza K. *construction executive*
Hechinger, John W., Jr. *home improvement company executive*

**White Hall**
Radigan, Frank Xavier *pharmaceutical company executive*

## MASSACHUSETTS

**Acton**
Hoopes, Walter Ronald *chemical company executive, retired*
Wade, Samuel David *medical products company executive*

**Amherst**
Torras, Joseph Hill *pulp and paper company executive*

**Andover**
Butler, Fred Jay, Jr. *manufacturing company executive*
Gaut, Norman Eugene *electronics firm executive*

**Attleboro**
Hammerle, Fredric Joseph *metal processing executive*

**Belmont**
Lewis, Henry Rafalsky *manufacturing company executive*

**Billerica**
Gray, Charles Agustus *chemical company research executive*
Kronick, Barry *lumber company executive*
McCaffrey, Robert Henry, Jr. *retired manufacturing company executive*

**Boston**
Alie, Alleyn A. *construction and engineering company executive*
Bodman, Samuel Wright, III *specialty chemicals and materials company*
Burnes, Kennett Farrar *chemical company executive*
Clarkson, Cheryl Lee *surgical products executive*
Connell, William Francis *diversified company executive*
Glass, Milton Louis *retired manufacturing company executive*
Kames, Kenneth F. *manufacturing company executive*
Leaman, J. Richard, Jr. *paper company executive*
Macera, Salvatore *industrial executive*
Macomber, John D. *construction executive*
Metcalf, Arthur George Bradford *electronics company executive*
Parks, Paul *corporate executive*
Schorr, Marvin G. *technology company executive*
Skelly, Thomas Francis *manufacturing company executive*
Spilhaus, Karl Henry *textiles executive, lawyer*
Swift, Humphrey Hathaway *manufacturing executive*
Vanderslice, Thomas Aquinas *electronics executive*

**Braintree**
Latham, Allen, Jr. *manufacturing company consultant*

**Brockton**
Droukas, Ann Hantis *management executive*

**Brookline**
Perry, Frederick Sayward, Jr. *electronics company executive*

**Burlington**
Bright, Willard Mead *manufacturing company executive*
Hall, John Reginald, II *electronics company executive, retired army officer*

**Cambridge**
†Ancona, Henry *camera equipment company executive*
Berger, Harvey James *pharmaceutical company executive, physician, educator*
Bullock, Francis Jeremiah *pharmaceutical research executive*
DiCamillo, Gary Thomas *manufacturing executive*
Epstein, Henry David *electronics company executive*
Gerrish, Catherine Ruggles *food company executive*
Gerrish, Hollis G. *confectionery company executive*
Kalelkar, Ashok Satish *consulting company executive*
Mc Cune, William James, Jr. *manufacturing company executive*
Snider, Eliot I. *lumber company executive*
Termeer, Henricus Adrianus *biotechnology company executive*
Tobin, James Robert *biotechnology company executive*
Vincent, James Louis *biotechnology company executive*

**Canton**
Ferrera, Kenneth Grant *food distribution company executive*

**Charlestown**
Waldfogel, Morton Sumner *prefabricated housing/plywood company executive*

**Chelsea**
Dunn, Norman Samuel *plastics and textiles company executive*

**Chestnut Hill**
Bender, Harold *beverage company consultant*
Cook, John Rowland *publishing and retail company executive*

**Chicopee**
Collins, Donald Francis *electrical contractor*

**Danvers**
Langford, Dean Ted *lighting and precision materials company executive*
Waite, Charles Morrison *food company executive*

**Easthampton**
Perkins, Homer Guy *manufacturing company executive*

**Falmouth**
Litschgi, Richard John *computer manufacturing company executive*

**Framingham**
Merser, Francis Gerard *manufacturing company executive, consultant*
Silverman, Harold Irving *pharmaceutical executive*
Waters, James Logan *analytical instrument manufacturing executive*

**Gloucester**
Lanzkron, Rolf Wolfgang *manufacturing company executive*

**Greenfield**
Moylan, Jay Richard *medical products executive*

**Ipswich**
Barth, Elmer Ernest *wire and cable company executive*

**Lawrence**
McBride, Thomas Dwayne *manufacturing executive*

**Lexington**
Berstein, Irving Aaron *biotechnology and medical technology executive*
Bishop, Robert Calvin *pharmaceutical company executive*
Picard, Dennis J. *electronics company executive*
Smith, Robert Louis *construction company executive*
Wainberg, Alan *footwear company executive*

**Lincoln**
Green, David Henry *manufacturing company executive*

**Lowell**
†Clark, Richard Paul *electronics company executive*

**Mansfield**
Forney, G(eorge) David, Jr. *electronics company executive*

**Marblehead**
Zeo, Frank James *health products company professional*

**Marion**
Walsh, William Egan, Jr. *electronics executive*

**Methuen**
Pollack, Herbert William *electronics executive*

**Middleboro**
Llewellyn, John Schofield, Jr. *food company executive*

**Natick**
Deutsch, Marshall E(manuel) *medical products company executive, inventor*

**Needham**
Cohen, Lewis Cobrain *security products firm executive*
Kung, Patrick Chung-Shu *biotechnology executive*

**Newton**
Balsamo, Salvatore Anthony *technical and temporary employment companies executive*
Chubb, Stephen Darrow *medical corporation executive*
Gerrity, J(ames) Frank, II *building materials company executive*
Stein, Seymour *electronics executive, scientist*

**North Andover**
Jannini, Ralph Humbert, III *electronics executive*

**North Dartmouth**
Tuttle, Clifford Horace, Jr. *electronics manufacturing company executive*

**North Grafton**
Nelson, John Martin *corporate executive*

**North Reading**
O'Neil, John P(atrick) *athletic footwear company executive*

**Nutting Lake**
Furman, John Rockwell *wholesale lumber company executive*

**Pembroke**
Freitas, Jeffrey Anthony *textile design agency executive*

**Sharon**
Paolino, Richard Francis *manufacturing company executive*

**Siasconset**
Kreitler, Richard Rogers *company executive*

**Somerville**
Verderber, Joseph Anthony *capital equipment company executive*

**Springfield**
D'Amour, Donald H. *supermarket chain executive*
Gallup, John Gardiner *retired paper company executive*

**Stoughton**
Fireman, Paul B. *footwear and apparel company executive*

**Sturbridge**
Belforte, David Arthur *company president*
Flynn, Richard Jerome *manufacturing company executive*

**Tewksbury**
DeMoulas, Telemachus A. *retail grocery company executive*

**Topsfield**
Fubini, Eugene Ghiron *business consultant*

**Waltham**
Bernstein, Stanley Joseph *manufacturing executive*
Floyd, John Taylor *electronics executive*
Weinert, Henry M. *biomedical company executive*

**Wellesley**
Gailius, Gilbert Keistutis *manufacturing company executive*
Kucharski, John Michael *scientific instruments manufacturing company executive*
Marcus, William Michael *rubber and vinyl products manufacturing company executive*
Ritt, Paul Edward *communications and electronics company executive*

**West Bridgewater**
Wyner, Justin L. *laminating company executive*

**Westborough**
Skates, Ronald Louis *computer manufacturing executive*

**Weston**
Chu, Jeffrey Chuan *business executive, consultant*
Saad, Theodore Shafick *retired microwave company executive*
Safiol, George E. *electronics company executive*

**Williamsburg**
Healy, Robert Danforth *manufacturing executive*

**Williamstown**
Lee, Arthur Virgil, III *biotechnology company executive*
McGill, Robert Ernest, III *retired manufacturing company executive*

**Wilmington**
Altschuler, Samuel *electronics company executive*

**Winthrop**
Moses, Ronald Elliot *retired toiletries products executive*

**Wrentham**
Teplow, Theodore Herzl *valve company executive*

## MICHIGAN

**Addison**
Knight, V. C. *manufacturing executive*

**Ann Arbor**
Decker, Raymond Frank *scientist, technology transfer executive*
Eberbach, Steven John *consumer electronics company executive*
Herzig, David Jacob *pharmaceutical company executive, immunopharmacologist*
Moss, Cruse Watson *automobile company executive*
Musa, Samuel Albert *technology and manufacturing executive director*
Powers, William Francis *automobile manufacturing company executive*
Saussele, Charles William *marking systems company executive*

Winbury, Martin Maurice *pharmaceutical executive, educator*

**Auburn Hills**
Beeckmans, Johan Jan *automotive company executive*
Corace, Joseph Russell *automotive parts company executive*
Davidson, William M. *diversified company executive, professional basketball executive*
Eaton, Robert James *automotive company executive*
Farrar, Stephen Prescott *glass products manufacturing executive*
Lutz, Robert Anthony *automotive company executive*

**Battle Creek**
Knowlton, Thomas A. *food products executive*
Langbo, Arnold Gordon *food company executive*
McKay, Eugene Henry, Jr. *food company executive*

**Benton Harbor**
Hopp, Daniel Frederick *manufacturing company executive, lawyer*
Whitwam, David Ray *appliance manufacturing company executive*

**Beulah**
Edwards, Wallace Winfield *retired automotive company executive*

**Birmingham**
VanDeusen, Bruce Dudley *company executive*

**Bloomfield Hills**
Caldwell, Will M. *former automobile company executive*
Caplan, John David *retired automotive company executive, research director*
Frey, Stuart Macklin *automobile manufacturing company executive*
Knudsen, Semon Emil *manufacturing company executive*
Lauer, Clinton Dillman *automotive executive*
Leonard, Michael A. *automotive executive*
Marko, Harold Meyron *diversified industry executive*
Maxwell, Jack Erwin *manufacturing company executive*

**Cass City**
Althaver, Lambert Ewing *manufacturing company executive*
Walpole, Robert *heavy manufacturing executive*

**Center Line**
Johnson, John Jay *automotive company administrator*

**Dearborn**
Bixby, Harold Glenn *manufacturing company executive*
Ford, William Clay *automotive company executive*
Hagenlocker, Edward E. *automobile company executive*
Lundy, J(oseph) Edward *retired automobile company executive*
Mc Cammon, David Noel *retired automobile company executive*
McTague, John Paul *automobile manufacturing company executive, chemist*
Sagan, John *former automobile company executive*
Trotman, Alexander J. *automobile manufacturing company executive*

**Detroit**
Chapin, Roy Dikeman, Jr. *automobile company executive*
Dauch, Richard E. *automobile manufacturing company executive*
Ferguson, James Peter *distilling company executive*
Hanson, David Bigelow *construction company executive, engineer*
Kalman, Andrew *manufacturing company executive*
Kantrowitz, Jean Rosensaft *research program administrator medical products*
Levy, Edward Charles, Jr. *manufacturing company executive*
Mc Millan, James *manufacturing executive*
Meilgaard, Morten Christian *food products specialist, international educator*
Murphy, Thomas Aquinas *former automobile manufacturing company executive*
Rakolta, John *construction company executive*
Rines, John Randolph *automotive company executive*
Sax, Stanley Paul *manufacturing company executive*
Smith, John Francis, Jr. *automobile company executive*
Stella, Frank Dante *food service and dining equipment executive*

**Dundee**
Yhouse, Paul Alan *manufacturing executive*

**Farmington Hills**
Landry, Thomas Henry *construction executive*
Mackey, Robert Joseph *business executive*

**Ferndale**
Cole, Gretchen Bornor *distribution and service executive*

**Grand Rapids**
Baker, Hollis MacLure *furniture manufacturing company executive*
Dykstra, William Dwight *business executive, consultant*
Hackett, James P. *manufacturing executive*
Hooker, Robert *automotive executive*
Pew, Robert Cunningham, II *office equipment manufacturing company executive*
Rougier-Chapman, Alwyn Spencer Douglas *furniture manufacturing company executive*
Woodrick, Robert *food products executive*

**Grosse Pointe**
Allen, Lee Harrison *wholesale company executive, industrial consultant*
Krebs, William Hoyt *company executive, industrial hygienist*
Obolensky, Marilyn Wall (Mrs. Serge Obolensky) *metals company executive*
Valk, Robert Earl *corporate executive*

Wilkinson, Warren Scripps *manufacturing company executive*

**Hickory Corners**
Hubbard, William Neill, Jr. *pharmaceutical company executive*

**Holland**
Brooks, James W. *beverage manufacturing executive*
Haworth, Gerrard Wendell *office systems manufacturing company executive*
Haworth, Richard G. *office furniture manufacturer*
Johanneson, Gerald Benedict *office products company executive*

**Howell**
Cattani, Luis Carlos *manufacturing engineer*

**Jackson**
Kelly, Robert Vincent, Jr. *metal company executive*
Vischer, Harold Harry *manufacturing company executive*

**Kalamazoo**
Connable, Alfred Barnes *retired business executive*
Edmondson, Keith Henry *chemical company executive, retired*
Hudson, Roy Davage *retired pharmaceutical company executive*
Markin, David Robert *motor company executive*
Vescovi, Selvi *pharmaceutical company executive*

**Laingsburg**
Scripter, Frank C. *manufacturing company executive*

**Lansing**
Anderton, James Franklin, IV *holdings company executive*
Hines, Marshall *construction engineering company executive*

**Madison Heights**
Kafarski, Mitchell I. *chemical processing company executive*

**Midland**
Cuthbert, Robert Lowell *product specialist*
Hampton, Leroy *retired chemical company executive*
Hazleton, Richard A. *chemicals executive*
McCarty, Roger Leland *chemical company official*
Popoff, Frank Peter *chemical company executive*
Stavropoulos, William S. *chemical executive*
Weiler, Scott Michael *machine tool manufacturing company executive*

**Oak Park**
Moilanen, Thomas Alfred *construction equipment distributor*

**Plymouth**
Massey, Donald E. *automotive executiv*
Merrill, Kenneth Coleman *retired automobile company executive*
Vlcek, Donald Joseph, Jr. *food distribution company executive, consultant*

**Pontiac**
Mahone, Barbara Jean *automotive company executive*
Stryker, James William *automotive executive, former military officer*

**Port Huron**
Hills, Randolph Allen *contractor*

**Portage**
Dykstra, David Allen *corporate executive*
Riesenberger, John Richard *pharmaceutical company executive*

**Rochester**
Gouldey, Glenn Charles *manufacturing company executive*

**Rochester Hills**
Cook, Leonard Clarence *manufacturing company executive*

**Romulus**
Scannell, Thomas John *cold metal forming company executive*

**Saint Clair Shores**
Gordon, Steven Stanley *automotive parts company executive*

**South Haven**
Nequist, John Leonard *retired food company executive*

**Southfield**
Gulda, Edward James *automotive executive*
Jeffrey, Walter Leslie *automotive executive*
Maibach, Ben C., III *construction company executive*
Raden, Louis *tape and label corporation executive*
Tauber, Joel David *manufacturing company executive*
Way, Kenneth L. *seat company executive*
Wisne, Lawrence A. *metal products executive*
Witt, Ray *automotive manufacturing executive*

**Taylor**
Manoogian, Richard Alexander *manufacturing company executive*
Rosowski, Robert Bernard *manufacturing company executive*

**Tecumseh**
Herrick, Todd W. *manufacturing company executive*

**Troy**
Buschmann, Siegfried *manufacturing executive*
Martin, Raymond Bruce *plumbing equipment manufacturing company executive*
Parker, Richard E. *building products manufacturing company executive*
Sharf, Stephan *automotive company executive*
Sloan, Hugh Walter, Jr. *automotive industry executive*

Williams, David Perry *manufacturing company executive*

**Warren**
Foxworth, John Edwin, Jr. *automotive executive, philatelist*
Lett, Philip Wood, Jr. *defense consultant*
Viano, David Charles *automotive safety research scientist*

**Washington**
Gothard, Donald Lee *retired auto company executive, consultant*

**West Branch**
Weiss, Denis Anthony *manufacturing executive, mechanical engineer*

**Williamsburg**
Harlan, John Marshall *construction company executive*

## MINNESOTA

**Alexandria**
Templin, Kenneth Elwood *paper company executive*

**Austin**
Hodapp, Don Joseph *food company executive*
Johnson, Joel W. *food products executive*
Knowlton, Richard L. *retired food and meat processing company executive*

**Bayport**
Wulf, Jerold W. *manufacturing executive*

**Bloomington**
Jodsaas, Larry Elvin *computer components company executive*

**Brooklyn Park**
Rogers, David *apparel executive*

**Edina**
Brown, Charles Eugene *retired electronics company executive*
Prince, Robb Lincoln *manufacturing company executive*
Sampson, John Eugene *consulting company executive*

**Fairmont**
Rosen, Thomas J. *food and agricultural products executive*

**Hopkins**
Rappaport, Gary Burton *defense equipment and software company executive*

**Lindstrom**
Messin, Marlene Ann *plastics company executive*

**Marshall**
Schwan, Alfred *food products executive*

**Mendota Heights**
Frechette, Peter Loren *dental products executive*

**Minneapolis**
Asplin, Edward William *retired packaging company executive*
†Atwater, Horace Brewster, Jr. *retired food company executive*
Bazany, Le Roy Francis *manufacturing company executive, controller*
Benson, Donald Erick *holding company executive*
Bonsignore, Michael Robert *electronics company executive*
Bullock, Norma Kathryn Rice *chemical development and engineering professional*
Carlson, Curtis LeRoy *corporate executive*
Findorff, Robert Lewis *retired air filtration equipment company executive*
Flaten, Alfred N. *food and consumer products executive*
Gherty, John E. *food products and agricultural products company executive*
Goldberger, Robert D. *food products company executive*
Goldfus, Donald Wayne *glass company executive*
Grieve, Pierson MacDonald *retired specialty chemicals and services company executive*
Hale, Roger Loucks *manufacturing company executive*
Hodder, William Alan *fabricated metal products company executive*
Jacobs, Irwin Lawrence *diversified corporate executive*
Johnson, Clark Eugene, Jr. *electronics and computer company executive, magnetics physicist*
Johnson, Sankey Anton *manufacturing company executive*
Kramp, Richard William *biotechnology executive*
Lupient, James *automotive executive*
Luthringshauser, Daniel Rene *manufacturing company executive*
MacMillan, Whitney *food products and import/export company executive*
McCune, Thomas *construction executive contractor*
Micek, Ernest S. *food products executive*
Morris, Richard Jeffery *plastic extrusion company executive*
Nelson, Glen David *medical products executive, physician*
Rauenhorst, Gerald *design and construction company executive*
Scott, Andrew *retired corporate executive*
Spoor, William Howard *food company executive*
Sullivan, Austin Padraic, Jr. *diversified food company executive*
Toupin, Harold Ovid *chemical company executive*
Van Dyke, William Grant *manufacturing company executive*
Walsh, Paul S. *food products executive*
Wurtele, Christopher Angus *paint and coatings company executive*

**Minnetonka**
Henningsen, Peter, Jr. *diversified industry executive*
Macfarlane, Alastair Iain Robert *business executive*

Mc Guire, William W. *health service organization executive*

**Osseo**
Haun, James William *retired food company executive, consultant, chemical engineer*

**Plymouth**
Friswold, Fred Ravndahl *manufacturing executive*
Groves, Franklin Nelson *construction company executive*
Kahler, Herbert Frederick *diversified business executive*
Rusch, Thomas William *manufacturing executive*

**Princeton**
Maas, Duane Harris *distilling company executive*

**Rochester**
Carlson, Roger Allan *manufacturing company executive, accountant*

**Saint Paul**
Andersen, Elmer Lee *manufacturing and publishing executive, former governor of Minnesota*
Baukol, Ronald Oliver *manufacturing company executive*
Desimone, Livio Diego *diversified manufacturing company executive*
Garretson, Donald Everett *retired manufacturing company executive*
Jones, Thomas Neal *manufacturing executive, mechanical engineer*
Kuhrmeyer, Carl Albert *manufacturing company executive*
Lehr, Lewis Wylie *diversified manufacturing company executive*
Ostby, Ronald *dairy and food products company executive*
Shannon, Michael Edward *specialty chemical company executive*
Wollner, Thomas Edward *manufacturing company executive*

**Wayzata**
Blodgett, Frank Caleb *retired food company executive*
Hoffman, Gene D. *food company executive, consultant*
Swanson, Donald Frederick *retired food company executive*

**West Saint Paul**
Markwardt, Kenneth Marvin *former chemical company executive*

## MISSISSIPPI

**Brookhaven**
Perkins, Thomas Hayes, III *furniture company executive*

**Diamondhead**
Jaumot, Frank Edward, Jr. *automobile parts manufacturing company executive*

**Jackson**
Irby, Stuart Charles, Jr. *construction company executive*
Julian, Michael *grocery company executive*

**Yazoo City**
Arnold, David Walker *chemical company executive, engineer*

## MISSOURI

**Ballwin**
Altman, Jeannette Mehr *pharmaceutical sales specialist*

**Berkeley**
Stonecipher, Harry Curtis *manufacturing company executive*

**Blue Springs**
Olsson, Björn Eskil *railroad supply company executive*

**Bridgeton**
Brauer, Stephen Franklin *manufacturing company executive*
McSweeney, Michael Terrence *manufacturing executive*

**Carthage**
Glauber, Michael A. *manufacturing company executive*
Jefferies, Robert Aaron, Jr. *diversified manufacturing executive, lawyer*

**Chesterfield**
Biggerstaff, Randy Lee *medical products executive, sports medicine rehabilitation consultant*
Carpenter, Will Dockery *chemical company executive*
Cornelsen, Paul Frederick *manufacturing and engineering company executive*
Malvern, Donald *retired aircraft manufacturing company executive*
McCarthy, Paul Fenton *aerospace executive, former naval officer*
Palazzi, Joseph L(azarro) *manufacturing executive*
Pylipow, Stanley Ross *retired manufacturing company executive*

**Clayton**
Beracha, Barry Harris *food company executive*
Buechler, Bradley Bruce *plastic processing company executive, accountant*
Heininger, S(amuel) Allen *retired chemical company executive*
Keyes, Marion Alvah, IV *manufacturing company executive*

**Columbia**
Rothwell, Robert Clark *agricultural products executive*

**Eldon**
†Pelan, Alan D. *manufacturing company executive*

**Fulton**
Backer, William Earnest *food products executive*

**Kansas City**
Bartlett, Paul Dana, Jr. *agribusiness executive*
†Bass, Lee Marshall *food products company executive*
Berkley, Eugene Bertram (Bert Berkley) *envelope company executive*
Carr, Jack Richard *candy company executive*
Cleberg, Harry C. *food products company executive*
Dees, Stephen Phillip *petroleum, farm and food products company executive, lawyer*
Hebenstreit, James Bryant *agricultural products executive, bank and venture capital executive*
†Herman, Michael Edward *pharmaceutical company executive*
Hoskins, William Keller *pharmaceutical company executive, lawyer*
Kronschnabel, Robert James *manufacturing company executive*
Wiegner, Edward Alex *multi-industry executive*

**Maryland Heights**
Schultz, Daniel Joseph *manufacturing executive, writer*

**Mexico**
Hummer, Paul F., II *manufacturing company executive*
Stover, Harry M. *corporate executive*

**Neosho**
Mailes, Kim(ber Dean) *automotive executive*

**Saint Charles**
Brahmbhatt, Sudhirkumar *chemical company executive*

**Saint Louis**
Abelov, Stephen Lawrence *uniform clothing company executive, consultant*
Abrahamson, Barry *chemical company executive*
Adams, Albert Willie, Jr. *lubrication company executive*
Ball, Kenneth Leon *manufacturing company executive, organizational development consultant*
Beare, Gene Kerwin *electric company executive*
Bock, Edward John *retired chemical manufacturing company executive*
†Brock, Louis Clark *business executive, former professional baseball player*
Brodsky, Philip Hyman *chemical executive, research director*
Browde, Anatole *electronics company executive, consultant*
Brown, JoBeth Goode *food products executive, lawyer*
Busch, August Adolphus, III *brewery executive*
Cleary, Thomas John *aluminum products company executive*
Conerly, Richard Pugh *retired corporation executive*
Cunningham, Charles Baker, III *manufacturing company executive*
Davis, Christopher Kevin *equipment company executive*
Dill, Charles Anthony *manufacturing and computer company executive*
Faught, Harold Franklin *electrical equipment manufacturing company executive*
Frederick, William Sherrad *manufacturing and retailing company executive*
Gilbert, Allan Arthur *manufacturing executive*
Gomes, Edward Clayton, Jr. *construction company executive*
Graff, George Stephen *aerospace company executive*
Griffin, W(illiam) L(ester) Hadley *shoe company executive*
Groennert, Charles Willis *electric company executive*
Gupta, Surendra Kumar *chemical firm executive*
Hermann, Robert Ringen *conglomerate company executive*
Hirsch, Raymond Robert *chemical company executive, lawyer*
Kessler, Nathan *technology consultant*
King, William Terry *manufacturing company executive*
Knight, Charles Field *electrical equipment manufacturing company executive*
McDonnell, John Finney *aerospace and aircraft manufacturing company executive*
McKenna, William John *textile products executive*
Miller, Michael Everett *chemical company executive*
Monroe, Thomas Edward *industrial corporation executive*
Neville, James Morton *food company executive, lawyer*
Priestley, G. T. Eric *manufacturing company executive*
Proscino, Steven Vincent *food products company executive*
Rich, Harry E. *financial executive*
Sanders, Fred Joseph *aerospace company executive*
Sathe, Sharad Somnath *chemical company executive*
Shapiro, Robert B. *manufacturing executive*
Sonnino, Carlo Benvenuto *electrical manufacturing company executive*
Stearley, Robert Jay *retired packaging company executive*
Stiritz, William P. *food company executive*
Suter, Albert Edward *manufacturing company executive*
Throdahl, Monte Corden *former chemical company executive*
Tober, Lester Victor *shoe company executive*
Weldon, Virginia V. *corporate executive, physician*
Zienty, Ferdinand Benjamin *chemical company research executive, consultant*

**Washington**
Randolph, Joe Wayne *machine manufacturing executive, stock broker*

## MONTANA

**Deer Lodge**
Baehr, Robert E. *electrical contractor*

**Great Falls**
Sletten, John Robert *construction company executive*

**Helena**
Morrison, John Haddow, Jr. *engineering company executive*

**Missoula**
Washington, Dennis *construction executive*

## NEBRASKA

**Columbus**
Keller, Harry Allan *electronics technician*

**Dakota City**
Broyhill, Roy Franklin *manufacturing executive*
Grigsby, Lonnie Oscar *food company executive*
Peterson, Robert L. *meat processing executive*

**Lincoln**
Fisher, Calvin David *food manufacturing company executive*
Tinstman, Dale Clinton *food products company consultant*

**Omaha**
Brown, Bob Oliver *retired manufacturing company executive*
Faith, Marshall E. *grain company executive*
Fletcher, Philip B. *food products company executive*
Jugel, Richard Dennis *corporate executive, management consultant*
Lindsay, James Wiley *agricultural company executive*
Norton, Robert R., Jr. *food products executive*
Regan, Timothy James *grain company executive*
Scott, Walter, Jr. *construction company executive*

## NEVADA

**Carson City**
Burns, Dan W. *manufacturing company executive*
Noland, Robert LeRoy *retired manufacturing company executive*

**Incline Village**
Strack, Harold Arthur *retired electronics company executive, retired air force officer, planner, analyst, author, musician*
Wahl, Howard Wayne *retired construction company executive, engineer*
Yount, George Stuart *paper company executive*

**Las Vegas**
Bennett, Bruce W. *construction company executive, civil engineer*
Jones, Fletcher, Jr. *automotive company executive*
Kaiser, Glen David *construction company executive*
Regazzi, John Henry *retired corporate executive*
Root, Alan Charles *diversified manufacturing company executive*
Warthen, John Edward *construction, leasing and finance executive*

## NEW HAMPSHIRE

**Bennington**
Verney, Richard Greville *paper company executive*

**Concord**
Hosmer, Bradley Edwin *corporate executive*

**Exeter**
Beck, Albert *manufacturing company executive*
Kozlowski, L. Dennis *manufacturing company executive*

**Hampton**
Russell, Richard R. *chemicals executive*

**Hill**
Thierry, John Adams *heavy machinery manufacturing company executive, lawyer*

**Keene**
Burkart, Walter Mark *manufacturing company executive*

**Lisbon**
Trelfa, Richard Thomas *paper company executive*

**Meredith**
Hatch, Frederick Tasker *chemicals consultant*

**Milford**
Morison, John Hopkins *casting manufacturing company executive*

**Nashua**
Gregg, Hugh *former cabinet manufacturing company executive, former governor New Hampshire*

**New London**
Condict, Edgar Rhodes *medical electronics, aviation instrument manufacturing and medical health care executive, inventor, mediator, pastor*
Nye, Thomas Russell *retired drafting, reproduction and surveying company executive*

**Newport**
Ruger, William Batterman *firearms manufacturing company executive*

**North Hampton**
White, Ralph Paul *automotive executive, consultant*

**Spofford**
Szmit, Frederick Andrew *paper manufacturing company executive*

**Sunapee**
Rauh, John David *manufacturing company executive*

**Winchester**
MacKay, Neil Duncan *plastics company executive*

## NEW JERSEY

**Allendale**
Hollands, John Henry *electronics consultant*

**Alpine**
Yuelys, Alexander *former cosmetics company executive*

**Annandale**
Drakeman, Lisa N. *biotechnology company executive*

**Avenel**
Heller, Patricia Ann *container company executive*
Sansone, Paul J. *automotive executive*

**Basking Ridge**
Abeles, James David *manufacturing company executive*
Conklin, Donald Ransford *retired pharmaceutical company executive*
Darrow, William Richard *pharmaceutical company executive, consultant*
Munch, Douglas Francis *pharmaceutical and health industry consultant*

**Bound Brook**
Gould, Donald Everett *retired chemical company executive*
Marchishin, Daniel *construction executive*

**Bridgewater**
Grey, Ruthann E. *pharmaceutical company executive*
Iovine, Carmine P. *chemicals executive*
Kennedy, James Andrew *chemical company executive*
Wieschenberg, Klaus *chemical company executive*

**Budd Lake**
Havens, Edwin Wallace *manufacturing executive*
Pollack, Jordan Ellis *pharmaceutical company executive*

**Butler**
Klaas, Nicholas Paul *management and technical consultant*

**Camden**
Johnson, David Willis *food products executive*

**Carteret**
Goldberg, Arthur M. *gaming and fitness company executive, food products executive, lawyer*

**Cherry Hill**
Keele, Lyndon Alan *electronic company executive*
Marsh, Robert Harry *chemical company executive*

**Clinton**
Acerra, Michele (Mike Acerra) *engineering and construction company executive*
DeGhetto, Kenneth Anselm *engineering and construction company executive*
Hansen, Arthur Magne *engineering and manufacturing executive*

**Cranbury**
Bodin, Jerome I. *pharmaceutical company executive, pharmaceutical chemist*
Daoust, Donald Roger *pharmaceutical and toiletries company executive, microbiologist*
Perhach, James Lawrence *pharmaceutical company executive*

**Cranford**
Cleaver, William Pennington *retired sugar refining company executive, consultant*
Mullen, Edward K. *paper company executive*

**Denville**
Minter, Jerry Burnett *electronic component company executive, engineer*

**Dover**
Mc Donald, John Joseph *electronics executive*

**East Brunswick**
Marshall, Keith *pharmaceutical consultant*

**East Hanover**
Knight, Frank James *pharmaceutical marketing professional*
Traina, Vincent Michael *pharmaceutical company executive*

**East Rutherford**
Gerstein, David Brown *hardware manufacturing company executive, professional basketball team executive*

**Edison**
Carretta, Richard Louis *beverage company executive*
Cavanaugh, James Henry *medical corporate executive, former government official*
Jones, James Thomas, Jr. *tobacco company executive*

**Elmwood Park**
Wygod, Martin J. *pharmaceuticals executive*

**Englewood**
Neis, Arnold Hayward *pharmaceutical company executive*

**Englewood Cliffs**
Scott, John William *food processing executive*
Shoemate, Charles Richard *food company executive*
Shrem, Charles Joseph *metals corporation executive*

**Englishtown**
Rudins, Leonids (Lee Rudins) *retired chemical company executive, financial executive*

**Fair Haven**
McKissock, David Lee *retired manufacturing company executive*

**Fairfield**
Giambalvo, Vincent *manufacturing company executive*
Meilan, Celia *food products executive*
Stein, Robert Alan *electronics company executive*

**Fairview**
Anton, Harvey *textile company executive*

**Farmingdale**
Martin, Robert Francis *roof maintenance systems executive*
Schluter, Peter Mueller *electronics company executive*

**Flemington**
Slovikowski, Gerald Jude *manufacturing company executive*

**Florham Park**
Sperber, Martin *pharmaceutical company executive, pharmacist*
Whitley, Arthur Francis *retired international consulting company executive, engineer, lawyer*

**Fords**
Kaufman, Alex *chemicals executive*

**Fort Lee**
Vignolo, Biagio Nickolas, Jr. *chemical company executive*
Winkler, Joseph Conrad *former recreational products manufacturing executive*

**Fort Monmouth**
Schwering, Felix Karl *electronics engineer, researcher*
Thornton, Clarence Gould *electronics engineering executive*

**Franklin Lakes**
Castellini, Clateo *medical products manufacturing executive*
Friedman, Martin Burton *chemical company executive*
Howe, Wesley Jackson *medical supplies company executive*
Throdahl, Mark Crandall *medical technology company executive*

**Freehold**
Laden, Karl *toiletries company executive*
Shapiro, Michael *supermarket corporate officer*

**Hainesport**
Sylk, Leonard Allen *housing company executive, real estate developer*

**Hazlet**
Miller, Duane King *health and beauty care company executive*

**Highlands**
Hansen, Christian Andreas, Jr. *plastics and chemical company executive*

**Hoboken**
Bonsal, Richard Irving *textile marketing executive*
Sgaramella, Peter *chemical products executive, technical consultant*

**Holmdel**
Kogelnik, Herwig Werner *electronics company executive*

**Hopatcong**
Reese, Harry Edwin, Jr. *electronics executive*

**Iselin**
Clarke, David H. *industrial products executive*
Garfinkel, Harmon Mark *specialty chemicals company executive*
LaTorre, L. Donald *chemical company executive*
Smith, Orin Robert *chemical company executive*
Wolynic, Edward Thomas *specialty chemicals technology executive*

**Jamesburg**
Denton, John Joseph *retired pharmaceutical company executive*

**Jersey City**
Alfano, Michael Charles *pharmaceutical company executive*
Pietrini, Andrew Gabriel *automotive aftermarket executive*
Zuckerberg, David Alan *pharmaceutical company executive*

**Kendall Park**
Hershenov, Bernard Zion *electronics research and development company executive*

**Keyport**
Warren, Craig Bishop *flavor and fragrance company executive, researcher*

**Lawrenceville**
O'Brien, James Jerome *construction management consultant*

**Linden**
Covino, Charles Peter *metal products company executive*
Tamarelli, Alan Wayne *chemical company executive*

**Madison**
Hassan, Frederich *pharmaceutical executive*
†Kogan, Richard Jay *pharmaceutical company executive*
Luciano, Robert Peter *pharmaceutical company executive*
McCulloch, James Callahan *manufacturing company executive*
Stafford, John Rogers *pharmaceutical and household products company executive*

**Medford**
Kesty, Robert Edward *chemical manufacturing company executive*

**Middletown**
Roesner, Peter Lowell *manufacturing company executive*

**Montclair**
Dubrow, Marsha Ann *high technology company executive, composer*
Mc Carthy, Daniel Christopher, Jr. *manufacturing company executive*

**Montvale**
Corrado, Fred *food company executive*
Roob, Richard *manufacturing executive*
Steinberg, Charles Allan *electronics manufacturing company executive*

**Moorestown**
Springer, Douglas Hyde *retired food company executive, lawyer*

**Morris Plains**
Goodes, Melvin Russell *manufacturing company executive*
Williams, Joseph Dalton *pharmaceutical company executive*

**Morristown**
Azzato, Louis Enrico *manufacturing company executive*
Bickerton, John Thorburn *retired pharmaceutical executive*
Bossidy, Lawrence Arthur *industrial manufacturing executive*
Cameron, Nicholas Allen *diversified corporation executive*
Herman, Robert Lewis *cork company executive*
Hittinger, William Charles *electronics company executive*
Huck, John Lloyd *pharmaceutical company executive*
Isko, Irving David *corporate executive*
Kirby, Fred Morgan, II *corporation executive*
Tokar, Edward Thomas *manufacturing company executive*

**Mount Laurel**
Instone, John Clifford *manufacturing company executive*

**Mountain Lakes**
Mazur, Leonard L. *pharmaceutical company executive*

**New Brunswick**
Bern, Ronald Lawrence *consulting company executive*
Cheiten, Marvin Harold *writer, hardware manufacturing company executive*
Larsen, Ralph S(tanley) *health care company executive*
McGuire, John Lawrence *pharmaceuticals research executive*
Mondschein, Lawrence Geoffrey *medical products executive*
Stewart, Joseph Turner, Jr. *retired pharmaceutical company executive*
Szarka, Laslo Joseph *pharmaceutical company executive*

**New Providence**
Chatterji, Debajyoti *manufacturing company executive*
Longfield, William Herman *health care company executive*
Schacht, Henry Brewer *manufacturing executive*

**Newark**
Christodoulou, Aris Peter *pharmaceutical executive, investment banker*
Fink, Aaron Herman *box manufacturing executive*
Hermann, Steven Istvan *textile executive*
Norwood, Carolyn Virginia *business educator*
Riggs, Benjamin Clapp, Jr. *building products manufacturing company executive*
Salvador, Richard Anthony *pharmaceutical company executive*

**North Bergen**
Lanier, Thomas *chemical and export company executive*
Miller, Samuel Martin *apparel company finance executive*

**North Brunswick**
Barcus, Gilbert Martin *medical products executive, business educator*
Coslow, Richard David *electronics company executive*

**North Haledon**
Brown, James Joseph *manufacturing company executive*

**Northvale**
Barna, Richard Allen *lighting company executive, broadcasting executive*

**Nutley**
Bess, Alan L. *pharmaceutical executive, physician*
English, Robert Joseph *electronic corporation executive*
Seyffarth, Linda Jean Wilcox *corporate executive*

**Old Bridge**
Mount, Karl A. *manufacturing executive*

**Old Tappan**
Dubnick, Bernard *retired pharmaceutical company administrator*

**Paramus**
Maclin, Ernest *biomedical diagnostics company executive*

**Parsippany**
Deones, Jack E. *corporate executive*
Fleisher, Seymour *manufacturing company executive*

**Manfredi, John Frederick** *food products executive*

**Paterson**
Danziger, Glenn Norman *chemical sales company executive*
Welles, Ernest I. *chemical company executive*

**Phillipsburg**
Testa, Douglas *biotechnology company executive*

**Piscataway**
Goodwin, Douglas Ira *steel distribution company executive*
Kampouris, Emmanuel Andrew *corporate executive*

**Princeton**
Autera, Michael Edward *health care products company executive*
Barker, Richard Gordon *corporate research and development executive*
Carnes, James Edward *electronics executive*
Cryer, Dennis Robert *pharmaceutical company executive, researcher*
Dovey, Brian Hugh *health care products company executive, venture capitalist*
Hayes, Edwin Junius, Jr. *business executive*
Hendrickson, Robert Frederick *pharmaceutical company executive*
Jacobson, Herbert Leonard *electronics company executive*
Kuebler, Christopher Allen *pharmaceutical executive*
Lessem, Jan Norbert *pharmaceuticals executive*
Liao, Paul Foo-Hung *electronics executive*
Minton, Dwight Church *manufacturing company executive*
Sapoff, Meyer *electronics component manufacturer*
Wavle, James Edward, Jr. *pharmaceutical company executive, lawyer*
Zissman, Lorin *marketing research, consulting company executive*

**Rahway**
Mandel, Lewis Richard *pharmaceutical company executive*

**Ramsey**
Founds, Henry William *pharmaceutical executive, microbiologist*

**Raritan**
Lloyd, Eugene Walter *construction company executive*
Mittleberg, Eric Michael *pharmaceutical administrator*

**Ridgewood**
Healey, Frank Henry *retired research executive*

**Rochelle Park**
Laskey, Richard Anthony *medical device company executive*
Schapiro, Jerome Bentley *chemical company executive*

**Rumson**
Brennan, William Joseph *manufacturing company executive*

**Saddle River**
McClelland, William Craig *paper company executive*

**Salem**
Seabrook, John Martin *retired food products executive, chemical engineer*

**Scotch Plains**
Abramson, Clarence Allen *pharmaceutical company executive, lawyer*

**Secaucus**
Unanue, Joseph *food products executive*

**Short Hills**
Jackson, William Ward *chemical company executive*

**Skillman**
Goldblatt, Barry Lance *manufacturing executive*
Wang, Jonas Chia-Tsung *pharmaceutical executive*

**Somerset**
Aronson, Louis Vincent, II *manufacturing executive*

**South Hackensack**
Cohen, Brett I. *health products executive*

**South Plainfield**
Hunsinger, Doyle J. *electronics executive*

**Springfield**
Adams, James Mills *chemicals executive*
Toresco, Donald *automotive executive*

**Summit**
Pawelec, William John *retired electronics company executive*

**Teaneck**
Feinberg, Robert S. *plastics manufacturing company executive, marketing consultant*
Gordon, Maxwell *pharmaceutical company executive*

**Toms River**
Gottesman, Roy Tully *chemical company executive*
Gross, Leroy *sugar company executive*

**Trenton**
Brandinger, Jay Jerome *electronics executive, state official*
Roshon, George Kenneth *manufacturing company executive*

**Union**
Lapidus, Norman Israel *food broker*
Schiffman, Robert Stanley *environmental test equipment manufacturing executive*

**Vineland**
Howell, James Burt, III *agricultural products company sales consultant*

**Warren**
Jackson, John Wyant *medical products executive*

**Watchung**
Knudson, Harry Edward, Jr. *retired electrical manufacturing company executive*
Nadeau, Earl Raymond *electronics executive*

**Wayne**
Cordover, Ronald Harvey *business executive, venture capitalist*
Heyman, Samuel J. *chemicals and building materials manufacturing company executive*
Jeffrey, Robert George, Jr. *industrial company executive*
Nicastro, Francis Efisio *defense electronics and retailing executive*

**West Orange**
Eisenberg, R. Neal *restoration company executive*
Johnson, Clarice P. *materials procurement executive*

**Westfield**
Connell, Grover *food company executive*
Keyko, George John *electronics company executive*
McLean, Vincent Ronald *former manufacturing company financial executive*

**Westwood**
Black, Theodore Halsey *retired manufacturing company executive*
Nachtigal, Patricia *equipment manufacturing company executive, general counsel*

**Whippany**
Golden, John F. *packaging company executive*

**Whitehouse Station**
Lewent, Judy Carol *pharmaceutical executive*

**Woodbridge**
Amato, Vincent Vito *business executive*
Kull, Bryan Paul *food products executive, real estate investor*

**Woodcliff Lake**
Perrella, James Elbert *manufacturing company executive*
Travis, J(ames) Frank *manufacturing company executive*

## NEW MEXICO

**Albuquerque**
Friberg, George Joseph *electronics company executive*
King, James Nedwed *construction company executive, lawyer*
Korman, Nathaniel Irving *research and development company executive*
Minahan, Daniel Francis *manufacturing company executive, lawyer*
Rust, John Laurence *heavy equipment sales/service company executive*
Stamm, Robert Jenne *building contractor, construction company executive*
†Sullivan, Terry Brian *semiconductor plant executive*
Swenka, Arthur John *food products executive*

**Carlsbad**
Watts, Marvin Lee *minerals company executive, chemist, educator*

**Las Cruces**
Cowden, Louis Fredrick *electronics executive, engineer*

**Roswell**
Armstrong, Billie Bert *retired highway contractor*

**Santa Fe**
Odell, John H. *construction company executive*
Robinson, Charles Wesley *energy company executive*

## NEW YORK

**Albany**
Naumann, Hans Juergen *manufacturing company executive*
Standish, John Spencer *textile manufacturing company executive*

**Armonk**
Chin, Carolyn Sue *business executive*
Lynett, Lawrence Wilson *electronics company executive*

**Athens**
Lew, Roger Alan *manufacturing company executive*

**Bedford**
Barth, Richard *pharmaceutical executive*

**Blauvelt**
Citardi, Mattio H. *business analyst, project manager, researcher*

**Bohemia**
Hausman, Howard *electronics executive*

**Briarcliff Manor**
Bingham, J. Peter *electronics research executive*

**Bridgehampton**
Baird, Charles Fitz *retired mining and metals company executive*

**Bronx**
Barton, Lewis *food manufacturing company executive*
Revelle, Donald Gene *manufacturing and health care company executive, consultant*

**Brooklyn**
Hood, Ernest Alva, Sr. *pharmaceutical company executive*
Oussani, James John *stapling company executive*

**Buffalo**
Chapman, Frederick John *manufacturing executive*
Goodell, Joseph Edward *manufacturing executive*
Green, Martin Lincoln *medical instrumentation executive*
Larson, Wilfred Joseph *chemical company executive*
Rice, Victor Albert *manufacturing executive, heavy*
Rich, Robert E., Jr. *food products company executive*
Starks, Fred William *chemical company executive*

**Carmel**
Laporte, Cloyd, Jr. *retired manufacturing executive, lawyer*

**Cedarhurst**
Cohen, David B. *optical company executive*

**Clarence**
Mehaffy, Thomas N. *retired tire company executive*

**Clifton Park**
Favreau, Donald Francis *corporate executive*
Fell, Samuel Kennedy (Ken Fell) *infosystems executive*
Scher, Robert Sander *instrument design company executive*

**Cooperstown**
Reynolds, Jack Mason *manufacturing company executive*
Tilton, Webster, Jr. *contractor*

**Corning**
Behm, Forrest Edwin *glass manufacturing company executive*
Booth, C(hesley) Peter Washburn *manufacturing company executive*
Dulude, Richard *glass manufacturing company executive*
Houghton, James Richardson *retired glass manufacturing company executive*
†Luther, David Byron *glass company executive*
Peck, Arthur John, Jr. *diversified manufacturing executive, lawyer*

**Cortland**
Miller, John David *manufacturing company executive*

**Dix Hills**
Meyers, George Edward *plastics company executive*

**East Aurora**
Hawk, George Wayne *retired electronics company executive*

**East Hampton**
Karp, Harvey Lawrence *metal products manufacturing company executive*

**East Rochester**
Clendenin, Johann Alfred (John Clendenin) *office products company executive*

**Ellenville**
Baer, Albert Max *metal products executive*

**Falconer**
Ruhlman, Herman C(loyd), Jr. *manufacturing company executive*

**Far Rockaway**
†Re, Edward Domenic, Jr. *construction executive*

**Farmingdale**
Blum, Melvin *chemical company executive, researcher*
Dordelman, William Forsyth *food company executive*
Smith, Joseph Seton *electronics company executive, consultant*

**Fayetteville**
Pachter, Irwin Jacob *pharmaceutical consultant*

**Flushing**
Henshel, Harry Bulova *watch manufacturer*
Hsu, Charles Jui-cheng *manufacturing company executive, advertising agent*

**Garden City**
Louis-Cotton d'Englesqueville, Francois Pierre *automobile company executive*

**Geneva**
Howard, Rustin Ray *corporate executive*

**Glen Cove**
Burnham, Harold Arthur *pharmaceutical company executive, physician*
Maxwell, J. Douglas, Jr. *chemical service company executive*

**Glenwood Landing**
Tane, Susan Jaffe *retired manufacturing company executive*

**Great Neck**
Machiz, Leon *electronic equipment manufacturing executive*

**Hague**
Cartwright, Alton Stuart *electrical manufacturing company executive*

**Hastings On Hudson**
Barth, Katrine *chemical company executive*

**Hauppauge**
Arams, Frank Robert *electronics company executive*
Finke, Douglas Lane *electronics company executive*
Miller, Ronald M. *manufacturing executive*

### Hicksville
Tucci, Gerald Frank *manufacturing company executive*

### Honeoye
Stone, Alan John *manufacturing company executive, real estate executive*

### Hoosick Falls
Dodge, Cleveland Earl, Jr. *manufacturing executive*

### Horseheads
Tanner, David Harold *professional roof consultant*

### Ithaca
Moore, Charles Hewes, Jr. *industrial and engineered products executive*

### Jamestown
Anderson, R. Quintus *diversified company executive*
Leising, Mary Kathleen *manufacturing executive*
Wellman, Barclay Ormes *furniture company executive*

### Jamesville
Nuckols, William Marshall *electrical goods manufacturing executive*

### Jericho
Berger, Charles Martin *food company executive*

### Lindenhurst
Boltz, Mary Ann *aerospace materials company executive, travel agency executive*
Levy, (Alexandra) Susan *construction company executive*

### Liverpool
Green, Edward Francis *manufacturing executive*
Greenway, William Charles *electronics executive, design engineer*
Morabito, Bruno Paul *machinery manufacturing executive*

### Lockport
Hoyme, Chad Earl *packaging company executive*

### Locust Valley
Schor, Joseph Martin *pharmaceutical executive, biochemist*

### Mamaroneck
Holz, Harold A. *chemical and plastics manufacturing company executive*
Mizrahi, Abraham Mordechay *retired cosmetics and health care company executive, physician*

### Manhasset
Keen, Constantine *retired manufacturing company executive*

### Melville
Kaufman, Stephen P. *electronics company executive*
Kissinger, Walter Bernhard *automotive test and service equipment manufacturing executive*

### Mount Kisco
Laster, Richard *biotechnology executive*

### Mount Vernon
Stern, Harold Peter *business executive*

### New Hartford
Muzyka, Donald Richard *specialty metals executive, metallurgist*

### New Hyde Park
Frankel, Arnold J. *chemical company executive*

### New Rochelle
Miller, Rita *retired diecasting company personnel executive, consultant*
Tassone, Gelsomina (Gessie Tassone) *metal processing executive*

### New York
Arnot-Heaney, Susan Eileen *cosmetics executive*
Asch, Arthur Louis *apparel company executive*
Bagnoli, Vincent James, Jr. *construction company executive, engineer*
Bennett, Joel Herbert *construction company executive*
Bertuccioli, Bruno *petrochemical company executive*
Blinken, Robert James *manufacturing and communications company executive*
Bordiga, Benno *automotive parts manufacturing company executive*
Bresani, Federico Fernando *business executive*
Briess, Roger Charles *brewing and food industry executive*
Bronfman, Edgar M., Jr. *food products executive*
Bronfman, Edgar Miles *beverage company executive*
Burns, Ward *textile company executive*
Call, Neil Judson *corporate executive*
Charron, Paul Richard *apparel company executive*
Chernow, David A. *former distillery executive, consultant*
Clark, Robert Henry, Jr. *holding company executive*
Clarke, Kenneth Kingsley *electrical equipment company executive*
Coffin, Dwight Clay *grain company executive*
Colbert, Lester Lum, Jr. *technology products executive*
Coleman, Martin Stone *retired office furniture company executive*
Collamore, Thomas Jones *corporate executive*
Colville, William Warner *manufacturing executive, lawyer*
†Cripps, Kathy Hickey *public relations company official*
Daniel, Richard Nicholas *fabricated metals manufacturing company executive*
Diamondstone, Lawrence *paper company executive*
D'Lower, Del *manufacturing executive*
Farber, John J. *chemical company executive*
Flaherty, William E. *chemicals and metals company executive*
Fletcher, Mary Lee *business executive*
French, Harold Stanley *food company executive*
Fribourg, Michel *international agribusiness executive*
Gardner, James Richard *pharmaceutical company executive*
Gelb, Harold Seymour *industrial company executive, investor*
Gessner, Charles Herman *apparel company executive*
Goelet, Robert G. *corporate executive*
Gold, Christina A. *cosmetics company executive*
Goldstone, Steven F. *consumer products company executive*
Goodale, Toni Krissel *development consultant*
Gould, Harry Edward, Jr. *industrialist*
Greaney, Patrick Joseph *electronics industry executive*
Greenfield, Gordon Kraus *software company executive*
Gross, Lawrence Robert *manufacturing executive*
Haas, Frederick Carl *paper and chemical company executive*
Harder, Lewis Bradley *ore bodies development company executive*
Hardwick, Charles Leighton *pharmaceutical company executive, state legislator*
Harkrader, Milton Keene, Jr. *corporate executive*
Harper, Charles Michel *food company executive*
Heimbold, Charles Andreas, Jr. *pharmaceutical company executive*
Helpern, David Moses *shoe corporation executive*
Hinerfeld, Norman Martin *manufacturing company executive*
Isogai, Masaharu *women's apparel executive*
Juliber, Lois *manufacturing executive*
†Kahn, Peter R. *publishing executive*
Kahn, Walter *steel company executive*
Kempa, Gerald *manufacturing company executive*
Kito, Teruo *former international trading company executive*
†Koch, David Hamilton *chemical company executive*
Koplik, Michael R. *durable goods company executive*
Koplik, Perry H. *durable goods company executive*
Krominga, Lynn *cosmetic and health care company executive, lawyer*
Kropf, Susan J. *cosmetics company executive*
Lala, Dominick J. *manufacturing company executive*
Landegger, Carl Clement *machinery and pulp manufacturing executive*
Lang, Eugene Michael *technology development company executive*
Lauder, Estée *cosmetics company executive*
Lauder, Leonard Alan *cosmetic and fragrance company executive*
Levin, Michael Stuart *steel company executive*
Levinson, Robert Alan *textile company executive*
Lewis, Loida Nicolas *food products holding company executive*
Lifton, Robert Kenneth *diversified companies executive*
Lord, Marvin *apparel company executive*
Luftglass, Murray Arnold *manufacturing company executive*
Luke, John A., Jr. *paper, packaging and chemical company executive*
Mango, Wilfred Gilbert, Jr. *construction company executive*
Marcus, Hyman *business executive*
Margolin, Arthur Stanley *distillery company executive*
Margolis, David I(srael) *corporate executive*
May, William Frederick *manufacturing executive*
McFadden, Mary Josephine *fashion industry executive*
McKinnon, Floyd Wingfield *textile executive*
Meyaart, Paul Jan *distilling company executive*
Miller, Morgan Lincoln *textile manufacturing company executive*
Mouchly-Weiss, Harriet *business executive*
Munroe, George Barber *former metals company executive*
Murdolo, Frank Joseph *pharmaceutical company executive*
Murphy, John Arthur *tobacco, food and brewing company executive*
Natori, Josie Cruz *apparel executive*
Nelson, Merlin Edward *international business consultant, company director*
Nussbaumer, Gerhard Karl *metals company executive*
Opel, John R. *business machines company executive*
Ostberg, Henry Dean *corporate executive*
Paalz, Anthony L. *beverage company executive*
Philipp, Elizabeth R. *manufacturing company executive, lawyer*
Pierce, Marianne Louise *pharmaceutical and healthcare companies executive, consultant*
Pomerantz, John J. *manufacturing executive*
Preston, James E. *cosmetics company executive*
Puschel, Philip P. *textiles executive*
Raasch, Ernest Martin *company executive*
Reece, Thomas L. *manufacturing executive*
Reis, Arthur Robert, Jr. *men's furnishings manufacturer*
Rennert, Ira Leon *heavy manufacturing executive*
Riklis, Meshulam *manufacturing and retail executive*
Riley, William *corporate executive, writer*
Rochlis, James Joseph *manufacturing company executive*
Rosenberg, Robert Charles *housing corporation executive*
Rosenthal, Milton Frederick *minerals and chemical company executive*
Roubos, Gary Lynn *diversified manufacturing company executive*
Rubin, Joel Edward *consulting company executive*
†Russo, Michael Arnold *sales manager*
Ruthchild, Geraldine Quietlake *training and development consultant, writer, poet*
Ruvane, John Austin *pharmaceutical industry consultant*
Sacks, David G. *retired distilling company executive, lawyer*
Sarnelle, Joseph R. *electronic publishing specialist, magazine and newspaper editor*
Schmitter, Charles Harry *electronics manufacturing company executive, lawyer*
Schulhof, Michael Peter *entertainment, electronics company executive*
Schumacher, Hans H. *steel company executive*
Schwartz, Bernard L. *electronics company executive*
Shineman, Edward William, Jr. *retired pharmaceutical executive*
Silverman, Jeffrey Stuart *manufacturing executive*
Smolinski, Edward Albert *holding company executive, lawyer, accountant, deacon*
Solomon, Howard *pharmaceutical company executive*
Solomon, Zachary Leon *apparel manufacturing company executive*
Staheli, Donald L. *grain company executive*
Steere, William Campbell, Jr. *pharmaceutical company executive*
Steiner, Jeffrey Josef *industrial manufacturing company executive*
Stern, Leonard Norman *pet supply manufacturing company executive*
Sullivan, Eugene John Joseph *manufacturing company executive*
Tapella, Gary Louis *manufacturing company executive*
Tumminello, Stephen Charles *consumer electronics manufacturing executive*
Wachner, Linda Joy *apparel marketing and manufacturing executive*
Wacker, Susan Regina *cosmetic design director*
Walker, Sally Barbara *retired glass company executive*
Weinstein, Martin *aerospace manufacturing executive, materials scientist*
Weisenburger, Randall *company executive*
Wiener, Harry *pharmaceutical company executive, physician*
Zoss, Abraham Oscar *chemical company executive*

### Niagara Falls
Collins, Christopher Carl *manufacturing executive*
King, George Gerard *chemical company executive*

### Niskayuna
Mangan, John Leo *retired electrical manufacturing company executive, international trade and trade policy specialist*

### Northport
Brown, John Edward *textile company executive*
Reinertsen, Norman *retired aircraft systems company executive*

### Norwich
Hanna, Eduardo Zacarias *pharmaceutical company executive*

### Old Brookville
Feinberg, Irwin L. *retired manufacturing company executive*

### Oneonta
Smith, Geoffrey Adams *special purpose mobile unit manufacturing executive*

### Orchard Park
Franklin, Murray Joseph *retired steel foundry executive*

### Pittsford
Palermo, Peter M., Jr. *photography equipment company executive*

### Plattsburgh
Cooper, Richard Francis *computer company executive*

### Poughkeepsie
Slade, Bernard Newton *electronics company executive*

### Purchase
Deering, Allan Brooks *beverage company executive*
Dillon, John T. *paper company executive*
Enrico, Roger A. *soft drink company executive*
Finnerty, Louise Hoppe *beverage and food company executive*
Hunziker, Robert McKee *paper company executive*
Turk, Milan Joseph *chemical company executive*
von der Heyden, Karl Ingolf Mueller *manufacturing company executive*
Wright, David L. *food and beverage company executive*

### Rego Park
LeFrak, Samuel J. *housing and building corporation executive*

### Rochester
Corio, Mark Andrew *electronics executive*
Fisher, George Myles Cordell *electronics equipment company executive, mathematician, engineer*
Friauf, Katherine Elizabeth *metal company executive*
Gaudion, Donald Alfred *former diversified manufacturing executive*
Harvey, Douglass Coate *retired photographic company executive*
Kohrt, Carl Fredrick *manufacturing executive, scientist*
Oberlies, John William *physician organization executive*
Pollicove, Harvey Myles *manufacturing executive*
Przybylowicz, Edwin Paul *chemical company executive, research director*
Resnick, Alan Howard *eye care executive*
Sieg, Albert Louis *photographic company executive*

### Rye
Sonneborn, Henry, III *former chemical company executive, business consultant*

### Rye Brook
Cameron, Dort *electronics executive*
Masson, Robert Henry *paper company executive*

### Sands Point
Wurzel, Leonard *retired candy manufacturing company executive*

### Scarsdale
Blitman, Howard Norton *construction company executive*
Hayman, Seymour *former food company executive*
Johnson, Boine Theodore *instruments company executive, mayor*
Netter, Kurt Fred *retired building products company executive*

### Schenectady
Adler, Michael S. *control systems and electronic technologies executive*
Grant, Ian Stanley *engineering company executive*
Petersen, Kenneth Clarence *chemical company executive*
Wilson, Delano Dee *consultant*

### Seaford
Setzler, William Edward *chemical company executive*

### Smithtown
Sporn, Stanley Robert *retired electronic company executive*

### Somers
Casey, Gerard William *food products company executive, lawyer*
Sora, Sebastian Antony *business machines manufacturing executive, educator*

### Staten Island
Bocaya, Renato Biso *pharmaceutical sales and marketing executive*

### Suffern
Jaffe, Elliot S. *women's clothing retail chain executive*
Sutherland, George Leslie *retired chemical company executive*

### Syosset
Bainton, Donald J. *diversified manufacturing company executive*
Guthart, Leo A. *electronics executive*

### Syracuse
Dixon, John T. *food products company executive*
Frazier, J(ohn) Phillip *manufacturing company executive*

### Tarrytown
Corbett, Gerard Francis *electronics executive*
Jarrett, Eugene Lawrence *chemical company executive*
Kane, Stanley Bruce *food products executive*
Vagelos, Pindaros Roy *pharmaceutical company executive*

### Troy
Doremus, Robert Heward *glass and ceramics processing educator*

### Utica
Mortenson, Thomas Theodore *medical products executive, management consultant*

### Valley Stream
Robbins, Harvey Arnold *textile company executive*

### Walden
Hanau, Kenneth John, Jr. *packaging company executive*

### Webster
Duke, Charles Bryan *research and development manufacturing executive, physics educator*

### West Chazy
Cumiskey, Gerald John *radio communications technician*

### Westbury
Cullen, John B. *food products company executive*
Martin, Daniel Richard *pharmaceutical company executive*

### White Plains
Greene, Leonard Michael *aerospace manufacturing executive, institute executive*
Krasne, Charles A. *food products executive*
Lapidus, Herbert *medical products executive*
Riha, William Edwin *beverage company executive*

### Whitestone
Rahr, Stewart *health medical products executive*

### Woodbury
Guttenplan, Harold Esau *retired food company executive*

### Yorktown Heights
LaRussa, Joseph Anthony *optical company executive*

### Youngstown
Alpert, Norman *chemical company executive*

## NORTH CAROLINA

### Advance
Huber, Thomas Martin *container company executive*

### Asheboro
Davis, J. B. *furniture manufacturing executive*

### Asheville
Armstrong, Robert Baker *textile company executive*
Coli, Guido John *chemical company executive*
Vander Voort, Dale Gilbert *textile company executive*

### Beaufort
Cullman, Hugh *retired tobacco company executive*

### Belmont
Stowe, Robert Lee, III *textile company executive*

### Blowing Rock
Barnebey, Kenneth Alan *food company executive*

### Burlington
Flagg, Raymond Osbourn *biology executive*

### Cary
Nyce, David Scott *electronics company executive*

### Chapel Hill
Blasius, Donald Charles *retired appliance company executive*
Thakor, Haren Bhaskerrao *manufacturing company executive*

**Charlotte**
Belk, Thomas Milburn *apparel executive*
Bowden, James Alvin *construction company financial executive*
Daniels, William Carlton, Jr. *construction executive*
Diamond, Harvey Jerome *machinery manufacturing company executive*
Goryn, Sara *textiles executive, real estate developer, psychologist*
Hannah, Thomas E. *textiles executive*
Hendrick, J. R., III *automotive executive*
Iverson, Francis Kenneth *metals company executive*
Johnstone, Chauncey Olcott *pharmaceutical company executive*
Lea, Scott Carter *retired packaging company executive*
McVerry, Thomas Leo *manufacturing company executive*
Rathke, Dieter B. *construction company executive*
Regelbrugge, Roger Rafael *steel company executive*
Siegel, Samuel *metals company executive*
Walker, Kenneth Dale *automotive service company executive*

**Durham**
Burger, Robert Mercer *semiconductor device research executive*
Fair, Richard Barton *electronics executive, educator*
Ricci, Robert Ronald *manufacturing company executive*

**Eden**
Bishopric, Welsford Farrell *textile executive*
Staab, Thomas Robert *textile company financial executive*

**Fayetteville**
Richardson, Emilie White *manufacturing company executive, investment company executive, lecturer*

**Flat Rock**
Demartini, Robert John *textile company executive*

**Fremont**
Smith, Mark Eugene *architectural engineering service company executive*

**Gastonia**
Kimbrell, Willard Duke *textile company executive*
Lawson, William David, III *retired cotton company executive*

**Greensboro**
Englar, John David *textile company executive, lawyer*
Howard, Paul Noble, Jr. *retired construction company executive*
Howard, Richard Turner *construction company executive*
Korb, William Brown, Jr. *manufacturing company executive*
Mann, Lowell Kimsey *retired manufacturing executive*
Morris, Edwin Alexander *retired apparel manufacturing company executive*

**Hickory**
Shuford, Harley Ferguson, Jr. *furniture manufacturing executive*

**High Point**
Fenn, Ormon William, Jr. *furniture company executive*
Marsden, Lawrence Albert *retired textile company executive*

**Hillsborough**
†Moore, Edward Towson *electronics company executive, electrical engineer*

**Kannapolis**
Ridenhour, Joseph Conrad *textile company executive*

**Maiden**
Pruitt, Thomas P., Jr. *textiles executive*

**Mars Hill**
Lennon, A. Max *food products company executive*

**Morganton**
Jokinen, John Victor *furniture company executive*

**Morven**
Jones, Sheila McLendon *construction company executive*

**Mount Airy**
Woltz, Howard Osler, Jr. *steel and wire products company executive*

**Oriental**
Sutter, John Richard *manufacturer, investor*

**Pine Knoll Shores**
Benson, Kenneth Victor *manufacturing company executive, lawyer*

**Pinehurst**
O'Neill, John Joseph, Jr. *business consultant, former chemical company executive*

**Raleigh**
Cresimore, James Leonard *food broker*
Klein, Verle Wesley *corporate executive, retired naval officer*
Leddicotte, George Comer *business executive, consultant*
Prior, William Allen *electronics company executive*
Sloan, O. Temple, Jr. *automotive equipment executive*

**Research Triangle Park**
Maar, Rosina *medical organization executive*
Niedel, James E. *pharmaceuticals executive*

**Rocky Mount**
Simpson, Dennis Arden *lighting contracting company executive*

**Sanford**
Beckwith, Hugh Foster, Jr. *textile company executive*
Kilmartin, Joseph Francis, Jr. *business executive, consultant*
Walker, Gary Linn *materials and logistics executive, consultant*

**Southern Pines**
Lipton, Clifford Carwood *retired glass company executive*

**Tar Heel**
Baxter, Raoul *meat packing company executive*

**Thomasville**
Starr, Frederick Brown *furniture manufacturing executive*

**Weldon**
Barringer, Paul Brandon, II *lumber company executive*
Conger, Stephen Halsey *lumber company executive*

**Wilmington**
Andrews, Willard Douglas *retired medical products manufacturer, consultant*
Stone, Minnie Strange *retired automotive service company executive*
Thompson, Donald Charles *electronics company executive, former coast guard officer*

**Wilson**
Ross, Guy Matthews, Jr. *international leaf tobacco executive*

**Winston Salem**
Emken, Robert Allan *diversified company executive*
Hanes, Ralph Philip, Jr. *former textiles executive, arts patron, cattle farmer*
Maselli, John Anthony *food products company executive*
Smith, Zachary Taylor, II *retired tobacco company executive*
Sticht, J. Paul *retired food products and tobacco company executive*

## NORTH DAKOTA

**Fargo**
Ommodt, Donald Henry *dairy company executive*

**Grand Forks**
Gjovig, Bruce Quentin *manufacturing consultant*

## OHIO

**Akron**
Brock, James Robert *manufacturing company executive*
Gibara, Samir S. G. *manufacturing executive*
Hackbirth, David William *aluminum company executive*
Kaufman, Donald Leroy *building products executive*
Shaffer, Oren George *manufacturing company executive*

**Archbold**
Sauder, Erie Joseph *manufacturing executive*

**Athens**
Werner, R(ichard) Budd *retired business executive*

**Aurora**
Lefebvre, Gabriel Felicien *retired chemical company executive*

**Berea**
Soppelsa, John Joseph *decal manufacturing company executive*

**Bratenahl**
Jones, Trevor Owen *automobile supply company executive, management consultant*

**Broadview Heights**
Braude, Edwin Simon *manufacturing company executive*

**Brookville**
Juhl, Daniel Leo *manufacturing and marketing firm executive*

**Canton**
Birkholz, Raymond James *metal products manufacturing company executive*
Elsaesser, Robert James *retired manufacturing executive*

**Cedarville**
Gordin, Dean Lackey *retired agricultural products executive*

**Chagrin Falls**
Brophy, Jere Hall *manufacturing company executive*
Callahan, Francis Joseph *manufacturing company executive*
Gelb, Victor *manufacturing executive*
Heckman, Henry Trevennen Shick *steel company executive*
Smith, Craig Richey *machinery executive*

**Chardon**
Seidemann, Robert Simon *manufacturing company executive*

**Cincinnati**
Anderson, Jerry William, Jr. *technical and business consulting executive, educator*
Chase, William Rowell *manufacturing executive*
Christensen, Paul Walter, Jr. *gear manufacturing company executive*
Coombe, V. Anderson *valve manufacturing company executive*
†Farmer, Richard T. *uniform rental and sales executive*
Keener, C(harles) Richard *food company information systems executive*
Leyda, James Perkins *pharmaceutical company executive*
Meyer, Daniel Joseph *machinery company executive*
Meyer, Walter H. *retired food safety executive, consultant*
Moore, Alfred Anson *corporate executive*
Niesz, George Melvin *tool and die company executive*
Pichler, Joseph Anton *food products executive*
Smale, John Gray *diversified industry executive*
Smittle, Nelson Dean *electronics executive*
Stern, Joseph Smith, Jr. *former footwear manufacturing company executive*
Thompson, Morley Punshon *textile company executive*
Voet, Paul C. *specialty chemical company executive*
Walker, Ronald F. *corporate executive*
Wilson, Frederic Sandford *pharmaceutical company executive*

**Cleveland**
Anderson, Harold Albert *engineering and building executive*
Bersticker, Albert Charles *chemical company executive*
Breen, John Gerald *manufacturing company executive*
Butler, William E. *retired manufacturing company executive*
Callsen, Christian Edward *medical device company executive*
Collins, Duane E. *manufacturing executive*
Cutler, Alexander MacDonald *manufacturing company executive*
Diskin, Michael Edward *construction products company executive*
Goodger, John Verne *electronics and computer systems executive*
Gorman, Joseph Tolle *corporate executive*
Grabner, George John *manufacturing executive*
Hamilton, William Milton *manufacturing executive*
Hardis, Stephen Roger *manufacturing company executive*
Hart, Alvin Leroy *electric manufacturing company executive*
Hauserman, William Foley *manufacturing company executive*
Hayes, Scott Birchard *raw materials company executive*
Henning, George Thomas, Jr. *chemical company executive*
Hoag, David H. *steel company executive*
Hushen, John W. *manufacturing company executive*
Ivy, Conway Gayle *paint company executive*
Jameson, J(ames) Larry *chemical company executive*
Kamm, Christian Philip *manufacturing company executive*
Kerr, Thomas Adolphus *retired construction company executive*
Luke, Randall Dan *retired tire and rubber company executive, lawyer*
Mac Laren, David Sergeant *manufacturing corporation executive, inventor*
Mandel, Jack N. *manufacturing company executive*
McFadden, John Volney *retired manufacturing company executive*
Mendelson, Ralph Richard *water heater manufacturing executive*
Moll, Curtis E. *manufacturing executive*
Mullally, Pierce Harry *retired steel company executive*
Myers, David N. *construction executive*
Oesterling, Thomas Ovid *pharmaceutical company executive*
Parker, Patrick Streeter *manufacturing executive*
Reid, James Sims, Jr. *automobile parts manufacturer*
Reitman, Robert Stanley *manufacturing and marketing executive*
Renner, Simon Edward *steel company executive*
Rich, Lawrence Vincent *manufacturing and engineering company executive*
Rosenthal, Leighton A. *aviation company executive*
Sabo, Richard Steven *electrical company executive*
Stone, Harry H. *business executive*
Tinker, H(arold) Burnham *chemical company executive*
Tomsich, Robert J. *heavy machinery manufacturing executive*
Tracht, Allen Eric *electronics executive*
Wright, Marshall *retired manufacturing executive, former diplomat*

**Coldwater**
Kunz, Charles Alphonse *farm machinery manufacturing executive*

**Columbus**
Alban, Roger Charles *construction equipment distribution executive*
Coopersmith, Jeffrey Alan *distribution corporation executive*
Crane, Jameson *plastics manufacturing company executive*
Daab-Krzykowski, Andre *pharmaceutical and nutritional manufacturing company administrator*
Dieker, Lawrence L. *chemicals executive*
Eickelberg, John Edwin *process control company executive*
Heffner, Grover Chester *retired corporate executive, retired naval officer*
Jones, Danny Clyde *healthcare products executive*
Kidder, C. Robert *food products executive*
Knilans, Michael Jerome *supermarkets executive*
Kyees, John Edward *apparel company executive*
Lazar, Theodore Aaron *retired manufacturing company executive, lawyer*
Pfening, Frederic Denver, III *manufacturing company executive*
Wigington, Ronald Lee *retired chemical information services executive*
Wolf, John Steven *construction executive, land developer*
Yenkin, Bernard Kalman *coatings and resins company executive*

**Concord**
Whedon, Ralph Gibbs *manufacturing executive*

**Dayton**
Duval, Daniel Webster *manufacturing company executive*
Enouen, William Albert *paper corporation executive*
Harlan, Norman Ralph *construction executive*
Ladehoff, Leo William *metal products manufacturing executive*
Mason, Steven Charles *forest products company executive*
Mathile, Clayton Lee *corporate executive*
Mc Swiney, James Wilmer *retired pulp and paper manufacturing company executive*
Price, Harry Steele, Jr. *construction materials company executive*
Shuey, John Henry *diversified products company executive*

**Delaware**
Eells, William Hastings *retired automobile company executive*

**Dublin**
Clement, Henry Joseph, Jr. *diversified building products executive*
Heffron, Robert F. *manufacturing company executive*
Jolly, Barbara Lee *home healthcare professional*
Lamp, Benson J. *tractor company executive*

**Fairlawn**
Bonsky, Jack Alan *chemical company executive, lawyer*
Gibson, Charles Colmery *former rubber manufacturing executive*

**Findlay**
Gorr, Ivan William *retired rubber company executive*
Kremer, Fred, Jr. *manufacturing company executive*

**Gates Mills**
Veale, Tinkham, II *former chemical company executive, engineer*

**Geneva**
Gambill, Terry A. *manufacturing executive*

**Grove City**
Funk, John William *emergency vehicle manufacturing executive, packaging company executive, lawyer*

**Groveport**
Ricart, Fred *automotive company executive*

**Hamilton**
Belew, David Lee *retired paper manufacturing company executive*

**Hilliard**
Rahal, Robert W. *automotive company executive*

**Holmesville**
Bolender, James Henry *tire and rubber manufacturing executive*

**Hudson**
Galloway, Ethan Charles *technology development executive, former chemicals executive*

**Huron**
Clark, Thomas Garis *rubber products manufacturer*

**Jackson Center**
Thompson, Wade Francis Bruce *manufacturing company executive*

**Kettering**
Caldabaugh, Karl *paper company executive*

**Lakewood**
Bradley, J. F., Jr. *retired manufacturing company executive*
Cochran, Earl Vernon *retired manufacturing company executive*

**Lancaster**
Fox, Robert Kriegbaum *manufacturing company executive*

**Lima**
Pranses, Anthony Louis *retired electric company executive, organization executive*

**Mansfield**
Gorman, James Carvill *pump manufacturing company executive*

**Mantua**
Ray, James Allen *research consultant*

**Marysville**
Hines, Anthony Loring *automotive executive*

**Maumee**
Anderson, Richard Paul *agricultural company executive*

**Mayfield Heights**
O'Brien, Frank B. *manufacturing executive*
Rankin, Alfred Marshall, Jr. *business executive*

**Medina**
Smith, Richey *chemical company executive*
Sullivan, Thomas Christopher *coatings company executive*

**Miamisburg**
Northrop, Stuart Johnston *manufacturing company executive*

**Middletown**
Kemerling, James Lee *paper company executive*

**Milan**
Henry, Joseph Patrick *chemical company executive*

**Milford**
Donahue, John Lawrence, Jr. *paper company executive*
Kenton, James Alan *healthcare products executive*
Klosterman, Albert Leonard *technical development business executive, mechanical engineer*

PROFESSIONAL INDEX 5305 INDUSTRY: MANUFACTURING


**North Ridgeville**
Haddox, Arden Ruth Stewart *automotive aftermarket manufacturing executive*

**Painesville**
Humphrey, George Magoffin, II *plastic molding company executive*

**Perrysburg**
Eastman, John Richard *retired manufacturing company executive*

**Pickerington**
Zacks, Gordon Benjamin *manufacturing company executive*

**Randolph**
Pecano, Donald Carl *truck trailer manufacturing executive*

**Reynoldsburg**
Woodward, Greta Charmaine *construction company executive*

**Richfield**
Tobler, D. Lee *chemical and aerospace company executive*

**Solon**
Rosica, Gabriel Adam *corporate executive, engineer*

**Stow**
Hooper, Blake Howard *manufacturing executive*

**Streetsboro**
Kearns, Warren Kenneth *business executive*

**Sugar Grove**
Bonner, Herbert Dwight *construction management educator*

**Sylvania**
Lock, Richard William *packaging company executive*

**Tipp City**
Panayirci, Sharon Lorraine *textiles executive, design engineer*
Tighe-Moore, Barbara Jeanne *electronics executive*

**Toledo**
Boller, Ronald Cecil *glass company executive*
Hiner, Glen Harold, Jr. *materials company executive*
Hirsch, Carl Herbert *manufacturing company executive*
Lemieux, Joseph Henry *manufacturing company executive*
Morcott, Southwood J. *automotive parts manufacturing company executive*
Reins, Ralph Erich *automotive components supply company executive*
Romanoff, Milford Martin *building contractor*
Strobel, Martin Jack *motor vehicle and industrial component manufacturing and distribution company executive*

**Troy**
Deering, Joseph William *manufacturing executive*

**Twinsburg**
Novak, Harry R. *manufacturing company executive*

**University Heights**
Epstein, Marvin Morris *retired construction executive*

**Warren**
Alli, Richard James, Sr. *manufacturing executive*
Thompson, Eric Thomas *manufacturing company executive*

**West Chester**
Rishel, James Burton *manufacturing executive*

**Westerville**
Lawrence, Ralph Waldo *manufacturing company executive*
Smith, C. Kenneth *business executive*

**Westfield Center**
Nance, James Clifton *business consulting company executive*

**Willoughby**
Manning, William Dudley, Jr. *retired specialty chemical company executive*

**Wooster**
Degnan, Martin J. *rubber products corporation executive, lawyer*
Gates, Richard Daniel *manufacturing company executive*

**Worthington**
Trevor, Alexander Bruen *computer company executive*

**Youngstown**
Courtney, William Francis *food and vending service company executive*
Marks, Esther L. *metals company executive*
Powers, Paul J. *manufacturing company executive*

## OKLAHOMA

**Bartlesville**
Dunlap, James Robert *contractor, state legislator*

**Oklahoma City**
Griggy, Kenneth Joseph *food company executive*
Hennigan, George R. *chemicals executive*
Mc Pherson, Frank Alfred *manufacturing corporate executive*
Smith, Robert Walter *food company executive*
Turner, Eugene Andrew *manufacturing executive*

**Poteau**
†Edwards, William Harold *manufacturing executive*

**Quapaw**
Dawes, Charles Edward *retired manufacturing company executive*

**Sand Springs**
Ackerman, Robert Wallace *steel company executive*

**Tulsa**
Bynum, George T., III (Ted Bynum) *biomedical company executive*
Calvert, Delbert William *chemical company executive*
Narwold, Lewis Lammers *paper products manufacturer*
Primeaux, Henry, III *automotive executive, author, speaker*
Thomas, Robert Eggleston *former corporate executive*
Williams, Joseph Hill *retired diversified industry executive*

## OREGON

**Beaverton**
Barnes, Keith Lee *electronics executive*
Donahue, Richard King *athletic apparel executive, lawyer*
Knight, Philip H(ampson) *shoe manufacturing company executive*

**Eugene**
Chaney, James Alan *construction company executive*
Woolley, Donna Pearl *timber and lumber company executive*

**Gladstone**
Thomason, Scott *automobile executive*

**Klamath Falls**
Wendt, Richard L. *manufacturing executive*

**Portland**
Abbott, Robert Carl *management company executive*
Foehl, Edward Albert *chemical company executive*
Fronk, William Joseph *retired machinery company executive*
Gray, John Delton *retired manufacturing company executive*
Jones, Alan C. *grocery company executive*
Marvin, Roy Mack *metal products executive*
McKennon, Keith Robert *chemical company executive*
Pamplin, Robert Boisseau, Sr. *textile manufacturing executive, retired*
Pamplin, Robert Boisseau, Jr. *agricultural company executive, minister, writer*
Russell, Marjorie Rose *manufacturing company executive*
Steinfeld, Ray, Jr. *food products executive*
Swindells, William, Jr. *lumber and paper company executive*
Watkins, Charles Reynolds *medical equipment company executive*

**Roseburg**
†Ford, Kenneth *lumber, wood products company executive*

**Sisters**
Baxter, John Lincoln, Jr. *manufacturing company executive*

**Springfield**
Detlefsen, William David, Jr. *chemicals executive*

**Sunriver**
Fosmire, Fred Randall *retired forest products company executive*

**Tigard**
Berglund, Carl Neil *electronics company executive*

**Wilsonville**
Kimberley, A. G. *industrial products factory representative, management executive*
Meyer, Jerome J. *diversified technology company executive*

**Woodburn**
Bradley, Lester Eugene *retired steel and rubber products manufacturing executive*

## PENNSYLVANIA

**Allentown**
Armor, John N. *chemical company scientist and research manager*
Baker, Dexter Farrington *manufacturing company executive*
Baraket, Edmund S., Jr. *general contractor, contracting consultant*
Donley, Edward *manufacturing company executive*
Foster, Edward Paul (Ted Foster) *process industries executive*
Samuels, Abram *stage equipment manufacturing company executive*
Shire, Donald Thomas *retired air products and chemicals executive, lawyer*
Zeitlin, Bruce Allen *cryogenics technology executive*

**Allison Park**
Backus, John King *former chemical company research administrator*

**Ardmore**
Bozzelli, Andrew Joseph, Jr. *retired valve company executive*

**Avondale**
Friel, Daniel Denwood, Sr. *manufacturing executive*

**Bala Cynwyd**
Driscoll, Edward Carroll *construction management firm executive*

Furlong, Edward V., Jr. *paper company executive*
Lotman, Herbert *food processing executive*

**Belle Vernon**
Wapiennik, Carl Francis *manufacturing firm executive, planetarium and science institute executive*

**Berwyn**
Burch, John Walter *mining equipment company executive*
Silverman, Stanley Wayne *chemical company executive*

**Bethlehem**
Barnette, Curtis Handley *steel company executive, lawyer*
Church, Thomas Trowbridge *former steel company executive*
Hartmann, Robert Elliott *manufacturing company executive, retired*
Jordan, John Allen, Jr. *steel company executive*
Kerchner, Charles Frederick, Jr. *electronics executive, engineer*
Rushton, Brian Mandel *chemical company executive*

**Blue Bell**
Theis, Steven Thomas *executive safety director*
Unruh, James Arlen *business machines company executive*

**Bradford**
Rice, Lester *electronics company executive*

**Bryn Mawr**
Snider, Harlan Tanner *former manufacturing company executive*

**Canonsburg**
Harker, Joseph Edward *construction, industrial and steel company executive*

**Central City**
Brown, Robert Alan *retired construction materials company executive*

**Chambersburg**
Holzman, Howard Eugene *health services executive*
Rumler, Robert Hoke *agricultural consultant, retired association executive*

**Clairton**
Dick, Douglas Patrick *construction company executive*

**Clarks Summit**
Alperin, Irwin Ephraim *clothing company executive*
Ross, Adrian E. *retired drilling manufacturing company executive*

**Collegeville**
De Rosen, Michel *pharmaceutical company executive*
Kun, Kenneth A. *business executive*
Rothwell, Timothy Gordon *pharmaceutical company executive*

**Conshohocken**
Gibson, Thomas Richard *automobile import company executive*
Naples, Ronald James *manufacturing company executive*
Spaeth, Karl Henry *retired chemical company executive, lawyer*

**Coopersburg**
Spira, Joel Solon *electronics company executive*

**Corry**
Rathinavelu, Madi *manufacturing executive*

**Cranberry Township**
Hogberg, Carl Gustav *retired steel company executive*

**Devon**
Carroll, Albert *retired corporate executive*

**Doylestown**
McNulty, Carrell Stewart, Jr. *manufacturing company executive, architect*
McNutt, Richard Hunt *manufacturing company executive*

**East Springfield**
Vadzemnieks, Michael Lester *plastics company executive*

**Eighty Four**
Capone, Alphonse William *retired industrial executive*

**Emmaus**
Bowers, Klaus D(ieter) *retired electronics research development company executive*

**Erie**
Duval, Albert Frank *paper company executive*
Hey, John Charles *electronics company executive*

**Exton**
Lewis, Thomas B. *specialty chemical company executive*

**Feasterville Trevose**
Faulkner, Henry, III *automotive executive*
Sergey, John Michael, Jr. *manufacturing company executive*

**Fort Washington**
Keating, Frank J. *paper company executive*
Meyer, Andrew R. *manufacturing executive*

**Franklin Center**
Resnick, Stewart Allen *diversified company executive*

**Gladwyne**
Mc Donald, Robert Emmett *company executive*

**Greentown**
Forcheskie, Carl S. *former apparel company executive*

**Greenville**
Stuver, Francis Edward *former railway car company executive*

**Hanover**
Kline, Donald *food company executive*

**Harrisburg**
Goell, James Emanuel *electronics company executive*
Hudson, William Jeffrey, Jr. *manufacturing company executive*

**Hatboro**
Hull, Lewis Woodruff *manufacturing company executive*

**Haverford**
Bogash, Richard *retired pharmaceutical company executive*
Talucci, Samuel James *retired chemical company executive*

**Hershey**
Duncan, Charles Lee *food products company executive*
Wolfe, Kenneth L. *food products manufacturing company executive*
Zimmerman, Richard Anson *food company executive*

**Hollidaysburg**
Bloom, Lawrence Stephen *retired clothing company executive*

**Horsham**
Hook, Jerry B. *pharmaceutical company executive*

**Indiana**
Jones, Shelley Pryce *chemical company executive, writer*

**Jenkintown**
Beavers, Ellington McHenry *chemical company executive*
Coccagna, Fred Joseph, Jr. *flooring manufacturing executive*
Reese, Francis Edward *retired chemical company executive, consultant*
Wilkinson, Harry J. *retired technical company executive*

**Johnstown**
Straw, Gary Lee *construction company executive*

**Kennett Square**
May, Harold Edward *chemical company executive*

**Kimberton**
Douglas, Bryce *former pharmaceutical company executive*

**King Of Prussia**
Dee, Robert Forrest *retired pharmaceutical company executive*
McLane, James Woods *healthcare executive*
†Middleton, Herbert Hunter, Jr. *tobacco manufacturing company executive*
Poste, George Henry *pharmaceutical company executive*
Traynor, Sean Gabrial *manufacturing executive*
Wachs, David V. *retired apparel executive*
Webb, Richard Stephen *manufacturing executive*

**Lancaster**
Dodge, Arthur Byron, Jr. *business executive*
High, S. Dale *diversified company executive*
Liddell, W. Kirk *specialty contracting and distribution company executive, lawyer*
Lorch, George A. *manufacturing company executive*

**Lebanon**
McMindes, Roy James *aggregate company executive*
Paul, Herman Louis, Jr. *valve manufacturing company executive*

**Lemoyne**
Deeg, Emil Wolfgang *manufacturing company executive, physicist*
Kirkwood, James Mace *pharmaceutical benefit management company executive*

**Ligonier**
Pilz, Alfred Norman *manufacturing company executive*

**Lititz**
Smith, Thomas Clair *manufacturing company executive*

**Lyon Station**
Breidegam, DeLight Edgar, Jr. *battery company executive*

**Malvern**
Smalley, Christopher Joseph *pharmaceutical company professional*
Weisman, Harlan Frederick *pharmaceutical company executive*

**Meadville**
Foster, Catherine Rierson *manufacturing company executive*
Kilgallon, Robert Donald *company executive, author, screenwriter*

**Media**
Peabody, William Tyler, Jr. *retired paper manufacturing company executive*

**Mohnton**
Bowers, Richard Philip *manufacturing executive*

**Monroeville**
Maclay, William Nevin *retired manufacturing and construction company executive*

**New Hope**
Williamson, Frederick Beasley, III *rubber company executive*

**Newtown**
Henshaw, Jonathan Cook *manufacturing company executive*
Messerschmidt, Gerald Leigh *pharmaceutical industry executive, physician*
Muth, Robert James *metal company executive, lawyer*
Ross, Edwin William *rubber company executive*

**Newtown Square**
Benenson, James, Jr. *manufacturer*

**Norristown**
Bergmann, Donald Gerald *pharmaceutical company executive*

**Oakmont**
DeFazio, John Lorenzo *retired manufacturing executive*

**Paoli**
Blankley, Walter Elwood *manufacturing company executive*

**Peach Glen**
Carey, Dean Lavere *fruit canning company executive*

**Philadelphia**
Avery, William Joseph *packaging manufacturing company executive*
Azoulay, Bernard *chemicals company executive*
Berwind, C. G., Jr. *manufacturing executive*
Callé, Craig R.L. *packaging executive*
Driscoll, Lee Francis, Jr. *corporate director, lawyer*
Featherman, Bernard *steel company executive*
Garrison, Walter R. *corporate executive*
Jones, Loren Farquhar *electronics executive*
Katherine, Robert Andrew *chemical company executive*
Lewis, George Withrow *business executive*
Liberati, Maria Theresa *fashion production company executive*
Lien, Eric L. *pharmaceutical executive*
McKenna, Michael Joseph *manufacturing company executive*
Rost, Peter *pharmaceutical company executive*
Sorgenti, Harold Andrew *petroleum and chemical company executive*
Stetson, John Batterson, IV *construction executive*
Wilson, James Lawrence *chemical company executive*
Yoh, Harold Lionel, Jr. *engineering, construction and management company executive*

**Pittsburgh**
Agnew, Franklin Ernest, III *former food company executive*
Burnham, Donald Clemens *manufacturing company executive*
Courtsal, Donald Preston *manufacturing company executive, financial consultant*
Dick, David E. *construction company executive*
Dinman, Bertram David *consultant, retired aluminum company executive*
Edelman, Harry Rollings, III *engineering and construction company executive*
Fairbanks, Frank Bates *manufacturing company executive*
Fischer, Richard Lawrence *metal products executive*
Foxen, Richard William *manufacturing company executive*
Frank, Alan I. W. *manufacturing company executive*
Giel, James Arthur, Jr. *steel company executive*
Grefenstette, Carl G. *medical products and real estate executive*
Hoffman, Ronald Robert *aluminum company executive*
Holcomb, Philo *steel company executive*
Huntington, James Cantine, Jr. *equipment manufacturing company executive*
Jordan, Michael Hugh *electrical and electronics company executive*
Langenberg, Frederick Charles *business executive*
Lauterbach, Robert Emil *steel company executive*
LeBoeuf, Raymond Walter *manufacturing company executive*
Lego, Paul Edward *retired corporation executive*
Limbach, Walter F. *construction company executive*
McCullough, Lauren Fink *aluminum company manager*
Mueller, Gerd Dieter *financial and administrative executive*
Mulloney, Peter Black *steel, oil and gas executive*
O'Neill, Paul Henry *aluminum company executive*
O'Reilly, Anthony John Francis *food company executive*
Paul, Robert Arthur *steel company executive*
Phillips, James Macilduff *material handling company executive, engineering and manufacturing executive*
Puskar, Milan *pharmaceuticals executive*
Roth, William George *manufacturing company executive*
Rust, William James *retired steel company executive*
Ruttenberg, Harold Joseph *manufacturing executive*
Sante, William Arthur, II *electronics manufacturing executive*
Smith, Phillip Hartley *steel company executive*
Thomas, W(illiam) Bruce *retired steel, oil, gas company executive*
Usher, Thomas James *steel executive, energy executive*
Wehmeier, Helge H. *chemical, health care and imaging technologies company executive*
Will, James Fredrick *steel company executive*
Williams, Louis Stanton *glass and chemical manufacturing executive*

**Pocopson**
Mulligan, James Francis *retired business executive, lawyer*

**Reading**
Beaver, Howard Oscar, Jr. *wrought specialty alloys manufacturing company executive*
Cottrell, G. Walton *manufacturing executive*
Ehlerman, Paul Michael *industrial battery manufacturing company executive*
Fiore, Nicholas Francis *special alloys and materials company executive*
Roedel, Paul Robert *steel company executive*

**Saint Marys**
Johnson, J. M. Hamlin *manufacturing company executive*

**Sewickley**
Snyder, William Penn, III *manufacturing company executive*

**Shippensburg**
Collier, Duaine Alden *manufacturing, distribution company executive*
Luhrs, H. Ric *toy manufacturing company executive*

**Sinking Spring**
Wilson, Terrence Raymond *manufacturing executive*

**Souderton**
Delp, R. Lee *meat packing company executive*

**Southampton**
DaCosta, Edward Hoban *plastics and electronics manufacturing company executive*
Zocholl, Stanley Ernest *electronics executive*

**Spring City**
Blanchard, Norman Harris *retired pharmaceutical company executive*

**Spring House**
Payn, Clyde Francis *technology company executive, consultant*

**State College**
Luther, William Lee *construction company executive*

**Swarthmore**
Heaps, Marvin Dale *food services company executive*
Kaufman, Antoinette D. *business services company executive*

**Swiftwater**
Woods, Walter Earl *biomedical manufacturing executive*

**Unionville**
Forney, Robert Clyde *retired chemical industry executive*

**University Park**
Jordan, Bryce *corporate director, retired university president*

**Valley Forge**
Dachowski, Peter Richard *manufacturing executive*
Hilyard, James Emerson *manufacturing company executive*

**Washington**
Kastelic, Robert Frank *aerospace company executive*
Piatt, Jack Boyd *manufacturing executive*

**Wayne**
Agersborg, Helmer Pareli K. *pharmaceutical company executive, researcher*
Bartholdson, John Robert *industrial company executive*
Curry, Thomas James *manufacturers representative*
Wolcott, Robert Wilson, Jr. *consulting company executive*

**Waynesboro**
Benchoff, James Martin *manufacturing company executive*

**West Chester**
Aiken, Robert McCutchen *retired chemical company executive, management consultant*
Bogle, Hugh Andrew *chemical company executive*

**West Conshohocken**
Brenner, Ronald John *pharmaceutical industry executive*

**West Point**
Abrams, William Bernard *pharmaceutical company executive, physician*

**Wilkes Barre**
Hobbs, William Barton Rogers *company executive*

**Willow Grove**
Kulicke, C(harles) Scott *business executive*

**Worcester**
McAdam, Will *electronics consultant*

**Wynnewood**
Connor, James Edward, Jr. *retired chemical company executive*

**Wyomissing**
Garr, Carl Robert *manufacturing company executive*
Pugh, Lawrence R. *apparel executive*

**York**
Garner, Edward Markley, II *manufacturing and engineering executive*
Macdonald, Andrew *manufacturing company executive*
Pokelwaldt, Robert N. *manufacturing company executive*

**Zionsville**
Fleming, Richard *chemical company executive*

## RHODE ISLAND

**Bristol**
Wilcox, Harry Wilbur, Jr. *retired corporate executive*

**North Kingstown**
Sharpe, Henry Dexter, Jr. *retired manufacturing company executive*

**Pawtucket**
Neff, Edward August *manufacturing company executive*
Tracy, Allen Wayne *manufacturing company executive*

**Providence**
Ames, Robert San *retired manufacturing company executive*
Choquette, Paul Joseph, Jr. *construction company executive*
Cooper, Gordon Mayo *retired manufacturing company executive*
Geckle, Robert Alan *manufacturing company executive*
Gilbane, Jean Ann (Mrs. Thomas F. Gilbane) *construction company executive*
Hardymon, James Franklin *diversified products company executive*
McCard, Harold Kenneth *aerospace company executive*

**West Warwick**
Galkin, Robert Theodore *company executive*

## SOUTH CAROLINA

**Arcadia**
Dent, Frederick Baily *mill executive, former ambassador, former secretary of commerce*

**Beaufort**
Richards, Charlene Anna *computer manufacturing company executive*

**Camden**
Daniels, John Hancock *agricultural products company executive*

**Charleston**
Addlestone, Nathan Sidney *metals company executive*
Geentiens, Gaston Petrus, Jr. *former construction management consultant company executive*
Harding, Enoch, Jr. *clothing executive*
Kent, Harry Ross *construction executive, lay worker*
†Mahoney, John Joseph *business executive, educator*
Martin, Roblee Boettcher *retired cement manufacturing executive*
Thompson, W(ilmer) Leigh *pharmaceutical company executive, physician, pharmacologist*

**Clinton**
Cornelson, George Henry, IV *retired textile company executive*
Vance, Robert Mercer *textile manufacturing company executive, banker*

**Columbia**
Spector, Joseph Robert *retired diversified manufacturing executive*

**Florence**
Dixon, Gale Harllee *drug company executive*

**Fort Mill**
Horten, Carl Frank *textile manufacturing company executive*

**Greenville**
Friedman, Steven M. *textile company executive*
Kondra, Emil Paul *transportation components manufacturing executive*
Maguire, D.E. *electronics executive*
Nemirow, Arnold Myles *manufacturing executive*
Roe, Thomas Anderson *building supply company executive*
Varin, Roger Robert *textile executive*

**Greenwood**
Self, W. M. *textile company executive*

**Greer**
Gallman, Clarence Hunter *textile executive*
Lane, James Garland, Jr. *diversified industry executive*
Scruggs, Jack Gilbert *retired chemical executive*

**Hartsville**
Browning, Peter Crane *packaging company executive*
Coker, Charles Westfield *diversified manufacturing company executive*

**Hilton Head Island**
Cunningham, William Henry *retired food products executive*
Harty, James D. *former manufacturing company executive*
Mersereau, Hiram Stipe *wood products company consultant*
Ouellette, Bernard Charles *pharmaceutical company executive*
Pritchard, Dalton Harold *retired electronics research engineer*
Ranney, Maurice William *chemical company executive*
Rulis, Raymond Joseph *manufacturing company executive, consultant*
Russell, Allen Stevenson *retired aluminum company executive*
Stoll, Richard Edmund *retired manufacturing executive*

**Johns Island**
Mackaness, George Bellamy *retired pharmaceutical company executive*

**North Charleston**
Zucker, Jerry *polymer systems manufacturing executive*

**River Hills**
Peacock, A(lvin) Ward *textile company executive*

**Salem**
Van Buren, William Benjamin, III *retired pharmaceutical company executive*

**Spartanburg**
Milliken, Roger *textile company executive*

**Townville**
Wright, George Cullen *electronics company executive*

## SOUTH DAKOTA

**Sioux Falls**
Christensen, David Allen *manufacturing company executive*

## TENNESSEE

**Bartlett**
Huffman, Delton Cleon, Jr. *pharmaceuticals executive*

**Chattanooga**
St. Goar, Herbert *food corporation executive*

**Collegedale**
McKee, Ellsworth *food products executive*

**Cordova**
Bellantoni, Maureen Blanchfield *manufacturing executive*
Colbert, Robert B., Jr. *apparel company executive*
Cooke, Edward William *corporate executive, former naval officer*
Dean, Jimmy *meat processing company executive, entertainer*

**Dandridge**
Comer, Evan Philip *manufacturing company executive*

**Ducktown**
Hopkins, David Lee *medical manufacturing executive*

**Dyersburg**
Wiggins, Jerome Meyer *apparel textile industry financial executive*

**Jackson**
Katz, Norman *manufacturing company executive*

**Kingsport**
Adams, W. G. *chemicals executive*
Coover, Harry Wesley *manufacturing company executive*
Deavenport, Earnest W., Jr. *chemical executive*
Findley, Don Aaron *manufacturing company executive*
Head, William Iverson, Sr. *retired chemical company executive*
Lunsford, Marvin Carl *chemical company executive*

**Knoxville**
Faires, Ross N. *manufacturing company executive*
Martin, James Robert *identification company executive*
Olmstead, Francis Henry, Jr. *plastics industry executive*
Stegmayer, Joseph Henry *housing industry executive*
Stringfield, Hezz, Jr. *contractor, financial consultant*

**Lookout Mountain**
Rymer, S. Bradford, Jr. *retired appliance manufacturing company executive*

**Memphis**
Andrews, William Eugene *construction products manufacturing executive*
Buckman, Robert Henry *chemical company executive*
Dobbs, James K., III *automotive executive*
Dunavant, William Buchanan, Jr. *textiles executive*
Dunnigan, T. Kevin *electrical and electronics manufacturing company executive*
Jenkins, Ruben Lee *chemical company executive*

**Nashville**
Dohrmann, Richard Martin *high technology manufacturing and publishing executive*
Fitzgerald, Edmund Bacon *electronics industry executive*
Gulmi, James Singleton *apparel manufacturing company executive*
Harris, J(acob) George *health care company executive*
Hass, Joseph Monroe *automotive executive*
Hummell, Burton Howard *food distribution company executive*
Langstaff, George Quigley, Jr. *retired footwear company executive*
Mahanes, David James, Jr. *retired distillery executive*
Mizell, Andrew Hooper, III *concrete company executive*
Scott, Richard L. *health and medical products company executive*
Wire, William Shidaker, II *retired apparel and footwear manufacturing company executive*

**Oak Ridge**
Poutsma, Marvin L. *chemical research administrator*

## TEXAS

**Arlington**
Kemp, Thomas Joseph *electronics company executive*

**Austin**
Alich, John Arthur, Jr. *manufacturing company executive*
Argo, William Frank *automotive executive*
Brager, Walter S. *retired food products corporation executive*
Cook, Chauncey William Wallace *retired food products company executive*
Culp, Joe C(arl) *electronics executive*
Edwards, Wayne Forrest *paper company executive*
Nelson, Steven Douglas *construction company executive*

PROFESSIONAL INDEX 5307 INDUSTRY: MANUFACTURING


Vykukal, Eugene Lawrence *wholesale drug company executive*

**Barker**
Atchley, Daniel Gene *business executive*

**Bartonville**
Spies, Jacob John *health care executive*

**Bellaire**
Lancaster, Carroll Townes, Jr. *business executive*

**Bryan**
Lusas, Edmund William *food processing research executive*

**Carrollton**
Heath, Jinger L. *cosmetics executive*
Hulbert, Paul William, Jr. *paper, lumber company executive*
Miller, Marvin Edward *building materials company executive*

**College Station**
Kubacak, Lawrence Don *energy efficient design and construction company executive*

**Conroe**
Cabaret, Joseph Ronald *defense company executive*

**Coppell**
Minyard, Liz *food products executive*

**Corpus Christi**
Heinz, Walter Ernst Edward *retired chemical executive*
Kane, Sam *meat company executive*
Turner, Elizabeth Adams Noble (Betty Turner) *healthcare executive, former mayor*

**Dallas**
Ash, Mary Kay *cosmetics company executive*
Barnes, Robert Vertreese, Jr. *masonry contractor executive*
Bartlett, Richard Chalkley *cosmetics executive, writer*
Bell, John Lewis McCulloch *manufacturing executive*
†Bradford, William Edward *oil field equipment manufacturing company executive*
Bucy, J. Fred, Jr. *retired electronics company executive*
Cherryholmes, James Gilbert *construction consultant, real estate agent*
Contreras, Israel *manufacturing executive*
Dawson, Edward Joseph *merger and acquisition executive*
Dorris, Carlos Eugene *chemicals executive*
Eisenberg, David H. *automotive executive*
Engels, Lawrence Arthur *metals company executive*
Gifford, Porter William *retired construction materials manufacturing company executive*
Guerin, Dean Patrick *food products executive*
Hirsch, Laurence Eliot *construction executive, mortgage banker*
Hirsh, Bernard *supply company executive, consultant*
Hughes, Joe Kenneth *retired beverage company executive*
Humann, Walter Johann *corporation executive*
Kostas, Evans *manufacturing executive*
Lane, Marvin Maskall, Jr. *electronics company executive*
Margerison, Richard Wayne *diversified industrial company executive*
McCally, Charles Richard *construction company executive*
Miller, Clint *technology company executive*
Murphy, John Joseph *manufacturing company executive*
Norris, John Windsor, Jr. *manufacturing company executive*
Pearce, Ronald *retired cosmetic company executive*
Roach, John D. C. *manufacturing company executive*
Robbins, Ray Charles *manufacturing company executive*
Robertson, Beverly Carruth *steel company executive*
Rochon, John Philip *cosmetics company executive*
Rogers, Ralph B. *industrial business executive*
Rosson, Glenn Richard *building products and furniture company executive*
St. John, Bill Dean *diversified equipment and services company executive*
Sammons, Elaine D. *corporate executive*
Schenkel, Peter *food company executive*
Solomon, William Tarver *general construction company executive*
Termini, Deanne Lanoix *research company executive*
Thompson, Charles Kerry *company executive*
Yanagisawa, Samuel Tsuguo *electronics executive*
Zumwalt, Richard Dowling *flour mill executive*

**Diboll**
Grum, Clifford J. *manufacturing company executive*
Harbordt, Charles Michael *forest products executive*

**Fort Worth**
Arena, M. Scott *pharmaceutical company executive*
Leone, George Frank *pharmaceutical executive*
Roberts, Leonard H. *retail executive*
Roland, Billy Ray *electronics company executive*
Thornton, Charles Victor *metals executive*
Williamson, Philip *apparel executive*

**Georgetown**
Gerding, Thomas Graham *medical products company executive*

**Granbury**
Adams, Christopher Steve, Jr. *retired defense electronics corporation executive, former air force officer*
Wisler, Charles Clifton, Jr. *retired cotton oil company executive*

**Grand Prairie**
Wietholter, William James *automotive parts manufacturing company executive*

**Houston**
Ahart, Jan Fredrick *electrical manufacturing company executive*
Austin, Harry Guiden *engineering and construction company executive*
Black, Kent March *aerospace and electronics company executive*
Bonner, David Calhoun *chemical company executive*
Boren, William Meredith *manufacturing executive*
Buchanan, Dennis Michael *manufacturing and holding company executive*
Cizik, Robert *manufacturing company executive*
Crawford, David Coleman *retired diversified manufacturing company executive*
Dean, Warren Michael *construction company executive*
De Wree, Eugene Ernest *manufacturing company executive*
Dodson, D. Keith *engineering and construction company executive*
Fabricant, Jill Diane *technology company executive*
Fort, John Franklin, III *manufacturing company executive*
Friedkin, Thomas H. *automotive executive*
Goff, Robert Burnside *retired food company executive*
Gore, Thomas Jackson *construction executive*
Hafner, Joseph A., Jr. *food company executive*
Irelan, Robert Withers *metal products executive*
Johnson, Frederick Dean *former food company executive*
Kaptopodis, Louis *supermarket chain executive*
†Kenney, Belinda Jill Forseman *electronics executive*
Klausmeyer, David Michael *scientific instruments manufacturing company executive*
Martin, J. Landis *manufacturing company executive, lawyer*
Mason, Franklin Rogers *automotive executive*
McClung, J(ames) David *corporate executive, lawyer*
Menscher, Barnet Gary *steel company executive*
Munisteri, Joseph George *construction executive*
Nuss, Eldon Paul *casket manufacturer*
Peterkin, George Alexander, Jr. *marine transportation company executive*
Pyle, Jerry *automotive executive*
Riedel, Alan Ellis *manufacturing company executive, lawyer*
Rock, Douglas Lawrence *manufacturing executive*
Roorda, John Francis, Jr. *business consultant*
Sebastian, Michael James *retired manufacturing company executive*
Templeton, Robert Earl *engineering and construction company executive*
Waggoner, James Virgil *chemicals company executive*
Waycaster, Bill *chemicals executive*

**Hurst**
Mc Keen, Chester M., Jr. *business executive*

**Irving**
Andrews, Judy Coker *electronics company executive*

**Longview**
Mann, Jack Matthewson *bottling company executive*

**Midland**
Crawford, Roger Brentley *industrial executive, inventor, author*

**Montgomery**
Holman, Charles Richardson *chemical company executive*

**Plano**
Bain, Travis Whitsett, II *manufacturing and retail executive*
Crowley, Daniel Francis, Jr. *food products manufacturing executive*
Cumming, Marilee *apparel company executive*

**Richardson**
Hiegel, James Edward *apparel executive*

**Richmond**
Barratt, Cynthia Louise *pharmaceutical company executive*

**Rockwall**
Fisher, Gene Jordan *retired chemical company executive*

**Round Rock**
Dell, Michael S. *manufacturing executive*

**San Angelo**
Henry, William Charles *manufacturing company supervisor*

**San Antonio**
Berg, Thomas *manufacturing executive*
Brown, Robert *manufacturing executive*
Cloud, Bruce Benjamin, Sr. *construction company executive*
Lyles, Mark Bradley *advanced technology company executive, dentist*
Smith, Pat Everett *chemical company executive*
Terracina, Roy David *retired food executive*
Zachry, Henry Bartell, Jr. *construction company executive*

**Sugar Land**
Kempner, Isaac Herbert, III *sugar company executive*

**Tyler**
Blair, James Walter, Jr. *machinery company executive*
Lassiter, Charles Whitfield *construction executive*
Smith, Howard Thompson *business executive*
Warner, John Andrew *foundry executive*

**UTAH**

**Ogden**
Garrison, U. Edwin *military, space and defense products manufacturing company executive*
Nickerson, Guy Robert *lumber company executive*

**Salt Lake City**
Anderson, Joseph Andrew, Jr. *retired apparel company executive, retail consultant*
Clark, Jeffrey Raphiel *research and development company executive*
Cook, M(elvin) Garfield *chemical company executive*
Frary, Richard Spencer *international consulting company executive*
Gregory, Herold La Mar *chemical company administrator*
Hembree, James D. *retired chemical company executive*
Huntsman, Jon M. *chemical company executive*
Motter, Thomas Franklin *medical products executive*
Norton, Delmar Lynn *candy company executive, video executive*

**VERMONT**

**Arlington**
Nowicki, George Lucian *retired chemical company executive*

**Bennington**
Killen, Carroll Gorden *electronics company executive*

**Brattleboro**
Cohen, Richard B. *grocery company executive*

**Brownsville**
Olderman, Gerald *retired medical device company executive*

**Danby**
Mitchell, John McKearney *manufacturing company executive*

**South Burlington**
Pizzagalli, James *construction executive*

**Vergennes**
Grant, Edwin Randolph *retail and manufacturing executive*

**Williamstown**
Dickinson, Charles Arthur *manufacturing company executive*

**Windsor**
Furnas, Howard Earl *business executive, educator, retired government official*

**VIRGINIA**

**Alexandria**
Cooper, Kenneth Banks *business executive, former army officer*
Haas, Ward John *research and development executive*
Keith, Donald Raymond *business executive, retired army officer*
Lantz, Phillip Edward *corporate executive, consultant*
McKinney, James Clayton *electronics executive, electrical engineer*
Mc Lucas, John Luther *aerospace company executive*
Stempler, Jack Leon *government and aerospace company executive*
Vander Myde, Paul Arthur *technology and engineering services executive*
Womack, Joseph Donald, Sr. *manufacturing and telecommunications executive, consultant*

**Arlington**
Bennett, John Joseph *professional services company executive*
Brunson, Burlie Allen *aerospace executive*
Cox, Henry *research company executive, research engineer*
Gracey, James Steele *corporate director, retired coast guard officer, consultant*
Knowlton, William Allen *business executive, consultant*
Otstott, Charles Paddock *company executive, retired army officer*

**Belle Haven**
Ross, Charles Worthington, IV *metals company executive*

**Blacksburg**
Kincade, Doris Helsing *apparel marketing educator*

**Broad Run**
Hinkle, Barton Leslie *retired electronics company executive*

**Broadway**
Keeler, James Leonard *food products company executive*

**Catlett**
Scheer, Julian Weisel *business executive, author*

**Chantilly**
Miller, Donald Eugene *aerospace electronics executive*

**Charlottesville**
Haigh, Robert William *business administration educator*
MacAvoy, Thomas Coleman *glass manufacturing executive, educator*
Rader, Louis T. *corporation executive, educator*
Rotch, William *business administration educator*

**Deltaville**
Koedel, John Gilbert, Jr. *forge company executive, retired*

**Fairfax**
Cuteri, Frank *automotive executive*
Edwards, James Owen *engineering and construction company executive*
Sheehan, Edward James *technical consultant, former government official*
Sheehy, Vincent *automotive executive*
Sowder, Donald Dillard *chemicals executive*
Swenson, Harold Francis *crisis management consultant*
West, Bob *pharmaceutical company executive*

**Fairfax Station**
Starry, Donn Albert *former aerospace company executive, former army officer*

**Falls Church**
Mellor, James Robb *electronics executive*
Post, Howard Allen *forest industry specialist*
Salvatori, Vincent Louis *corporate executive*
Schaer, Werner *computer services executive*

**Glen Allen**
Fife, William Franklin *retired drug company executive*
Minor, George Gilmer, III *drug and hospital supply company executive*
Murphey, Robert Stafford *pharmaceutical company executive*

**Great Falls**
MacGowan, Charles Frederic *retired chemical company executive*

**Hayes**
Dixon, Thomas Francis *aviation company executive*

**Heathsville**
Winkel, Raymond Norman *avionics manufacturing executive, retired naval officer*

**Herndon**
Gorog, William Francis *corporate executive*
Guerreri, Carl Natale *electronic company executive*

**Hopewell**
Leake, Preston Hildebrand *tobacco research executive*

**Keswick**
Norgren, C. Neil *retired manufacturing company executive*

**Manassas**
Geerdes, James D(ivine) (Divine Geerdes) *chemical company executive*
Parrish, Frank Jennings *food company executive*

**Marion**
Hadley, Stanton Thomas *international manufacturing and marketing company executive, lawyer*

**Marshall**
Moore, Robert Edward *retired electronics executive*

**Mc Lean**
Dempsey, James Raymon *industrial executive*
Franklin, Jude Eric *electronics executive*
Mars, Forrest E., Jr. *candy company executive*
Mars, John F. *candy company executive*
Mehuron, William Otto *electronics company executive*
Ryan, John Franklin *multinational company executive*

**Newport News**
Banks, Charles Augustus, III *manufacturing executive*
Fricks, William Peavy *shipbuilding company executive*
Luke, James Phillip *manufacturing executive*

**Portsmouth**
Mintz, Susan Ashinoff *menswear manufacturing comapany executive*

**Reston**
Bannister, Dan R. *professional and technical services company executive*
Christ, Thomas Warren *electronics research and development company executive, sociologist*
Lewis, Gene Evans *retired medical equipment company executive*
Uffelman, Malcolm Rucj *electronics company executive, electrical engineer*

**Richmond**
Bourke, William Oliver *retired metal company executive*
Bunzl, Rudolph Hans *retired diversified manufacturing company executive*
Gottwald, Bruce Cobb *chemical company executive*
Gottwald, Floyd Dewey, Jr. *chemical company executive*
Hagan, Randall Lee *manufacturing executive*
Helwig, Arthur Woods *chemical company executive*
Lindholm, John Victor *business executive*
†Marsh, Miles L. *textile company executive*
Nielsen, Steven B. *medical products executive*
Pauley, Stanley Frank *manufacturing company executive*
Pendleton, Eugene Barbour, Jr. *business executive*
Reynolds, David Parham *metals company executive*
Rogers, James Edward *paper company executive*
Sweeney, Arthur Hamilton, Jr. *metal manufacturing executive, retired army officer*
Thorp, Benjamin A., III *paper manufacturing company executive*
Watts, Robert Glenn *retired pharmaceutical company executive*

**Spring Grove**
Daniel, Robert Williams, Jr. *business executive, former congressman*

**Springfield**
Shuster, Robert G. *electronics company executive, consultant*

**Suffolk**
Birdsong, George Yancy *manufacturing company executive*

**Vienna**
Bajpai, Sanjay Kumar *pharmaceutical executive, consultant*
Savoca, Antonio Litterio *technology company executive*

**Winchester**
Holland, James Tulley *plastic products company executive*
Jolly, Bruce Dwight *manufacturing company executive*
Murtagh, John Edward *alcohol production consultant*

## WASHINGTON

**Anacortes**
Randolph, Carl Lowell *chemical company executive*

**Bellevue**
Hovind, David J. *manufacturing company executive*
Pigott, Charles McGee *transportation equipment manufacturing executive*
Puckett, Allen Weare *health care information systems executive*

**Bellingham**
Bestwick, Warren William *retired construction company executive*
Haggen, Donald E. *food products executive*
Krmpotich, Frank Zvonko *fiberglass company executive, consultant*

**Eastsound**
Anders, William Alison *aerospace and defense manufacturing executive*

**Federal Way**
Creighton, John W., Jr. *forest products company executive*
Curtis, Arnold Bennett *lumber company executive*

**Friday Harbor**
Daum, David Ernest *machinery manufacturing company executive*

**Indianola**
Nelson, John Howard *food company research executive*

**Issaquah**
Tenenbaum, Michael *steel company executive*
Wainwright, Paul Edward Blech *construction company executive*

**Kennewick**
Wistisen, Martin J. *agricultural business executive*

**Kent**
Goo, Abraham Meu Sen *retired aircraft company executive*
Hebeler, Henry Koester *retired aerospace and electronics executive*

**Longview**
Wollenberg, Richard Peter *paper manufacturing company executive*

**Maple Valley**
Brown, Thomas Andrew *retired aircraft/weaponry manufacturing executive*

**Medina**
Schlotterbeck, Walter Albert *manufacturing company executive, lawyer*

**Mercer Island**
Gould, Alvin R. *international business executive*

**Pasco**
Yoshino, George *food products executive*

**Port Ludlow**
Gullander, Werner Paul *retired consultant, retired corporate executive*

**Richland**
Nolan, John Edward *retired electrical corporation executive*

**Seattle**
Albrecht, Richard Raymond *airplane manufacturing company executive, lawyer*
Behnke, Carl Gilbert *beverage franchise executive*
Ernst, Chadwick Ellsworth *fastener company executive*
Farrell, Anne Van Ness *foundation executive*
Holtby, Kenneth Fraser *manufacturing executive*
Parrish, John Brett *manufacturing executive*
Schoenfeld, Walter Edwin *manufacturing company executive*
Shrontz, Frank Anderson *airplane manufacturing executive*
Stear, Edwin Byron *corporate executive*
Whitacre, John *apparel executive*

**Spokane**
Fosseen, Neal Randolph *business executive, former banker, former mayor*

**Tacoma**
Carlson, Frederick Paul *electronics executive*
Franklin, William Emery *forest products company executive*
Hutchings, George Henry *food company executive*
Meyer, Richard Schlomer *food company executive*
Weyerhaeuser, George Hunt *forest products company executive*

**Vancouver**
Vogel, Ronald Bruce *food products executive*

**Woodland**
Brown, Alan Johnson *chemicals executive*

## WEST VIRGINIA

**Charleston**
Gunnoe, Nancy Lavenia *food executive, artist*

**Nitro**
Magaw, Roger Wayne *construction company executive*

**Parkersburg**
Wakley, James Turner *manufacturing company executive*

**Wheeling**
Exley, Ben, III *pharmaceutical company executive*
Good, Laurance Frederic *company executive*

## WISCONSIN

**Appleton**
Barlow, F(rank) John *mechanical contracting company executive*
Boldt, Oscar Charles *construction company executive*
Rankin, Arthur David *paper company executive*
Spiegelberg, Harry Lester *retired paper products company executive*

**Brookfield**
Corby, Francis Michael, Jr. *manufacturing company executive*
DeLuca, Donald Paul *manufacturing company executive*
Grove, Richard Charles *power tool company executive*

**Cedarburg**
Schaefer, Gordon Emory *food company executive*

**Eau Claire**
Menard, John R. *lumber company executive*

**Fond Du Lac**
Chamberlain, Robert Glenn *retired tool manfacturing executive*

**Fort Atkinson**
Nesbitt, Arthur Wallace *mail order and manufacturing executive*

**Green Bay**
Hempel, Kathleen Jane *paper company executive*
Kress, George F. *packaging company executive*
Kress, William F. *manufacturing company executive*
Kuehne, Carl W. *food products executive*
Meng, Jack *food products executive*
Vesta, Richard V. *meat packing company executive*

**Kenosha**
Huml, Donald Scott *manufacturing company executive*
Infusino, Achille Francis *construction company executive*
Morrone, Frank *electronic manufacturing executive*
Steigerwaldt, Donna Wolf *clothing manufacturing company executive*

**Kohler**
Kohler, Herbert Vollrath, Jr. *diversified manufacturing company executive*

**La Crosse**
Gelatt, Charles Daniel *manufacturing company executive*

**Madison**
Felten, Edward Joseph *business executive accountant*
Frautschi, Walter Albert *contract and publications printing company executive*
Lonnebotn, Trygve *battery company executive*
Shain, Irving *retired chemical company executive and university chancellor*

**Manitowish Waters**
Laidig, William Rupert *retired paper company executive*

**Marion**
Simpson, Vinson Raleigh *manufacturing company executive*

**Medford**
Sebold, Duane David *food manufacturing executive*

**Menasha**
Baird, Roger Allen *retired corporation executive*

**Mequon**
Dohmen, Frederick Hoeger *retired wholesale drug company executive*

**Milwaukee**
Beals, Vaughn Le Roy, Jr. *motorcycle and recreational vehicle manufacturing executive*
Bishop, Charles Joseph *manufacturing company executive*
Chapman, William Paul *retired automatic control manufacturing company executive*
Crowe-Hagans, Natonia *manufacturing executive, engineer*
Davis, Thomas William *steel industry executive*
Feitler, Robert *shoe company executive*
Hudson, Katherine Mary *manufacturing company executive*
Keuler, Roland Leo *retired shoe company executive*
Keyes, James Henry *manufacturing company executive*
Killian, William Paul *industrial corporate executive*
Manning, Kenneth Paul *food company executive*
Marringa, Jacques Louis *manufacturing company executive*
Martin, Vincent Lionel *manufacturing company executive*
Morris, G. Ronald *industrial executive*
Mosher, George Allan *manufacturing company executive*
Novak, Victor Anthony *semi-retired manufacturing company executive*
Parker, Charles Walter, Jr. *consultant, retired equipment company executive*
†Rader, I. A. *electronic components manufacturing company executive*
Rich, Robert C. *manufacturing executive*
Sterner, Frank Maurice *industrial executive*

Taylor, Donald *retired manufacturing company executive*
Yontz, Kenneth Fredric *medical and chemical company executive*

**Neenah**
Bergstrom, Dedric Waldemar *retired paper company executive*
Bero, R.D. *manufacturing executive*
Hanson, Charles R(ichard) *manufacturing company executive*

**Oshkosh**
Drebus, Richard William *pharmaceutical company executive*
Goodson, Raymond Eugene *automotive executive*
Hulsebosch, Charles Joseph *truck manufacturing company executive*

**Racine**
Campbell, Edward Joseph *retired machinery company executive*
Gunnerson, Robert Mark *manufacturing company executive, accountant, lawyer*
Henley, Joseph Oliver *manufacturing company executive*
Johnson, Samuel Curtis *wax company executive*
Konz, Gerald Keith *manufacturing company executive*

**Sussex**
Stromberg, Gregory *printing company executive*

**Waterloo**
Burke, Richard A. *manufacturing executive*

**Wausau**
Slayton, John Arthur *electric motor manufacturing executive*

**Wisconsin Rapids**
Engelhardt, LeRoy A. *retired paper company executive*
Mead, George Wilson, II *paper company executive*

## WYOMING

**Casper**
Jozwik, Francis Xavier *agricultural business executive*
Stroock, Thomas Frank *manufacturing company executive*

**Jackson**
Furrer, John Rudolf *retired manufacturing business executive*
Gordon, Stephen Maurice *manufacturing company executive, rancher*

## TERRITORIES OF THE UNITED STATES

## PUERTO RICO

**Dorado**
Spector, Michael Joseph *agribusiness executive*

## CANADA

## ALBERTA

**Calgary**
Holman, J(ohn) Leonard *retired manufacturing corporation executive*
Southern, Ronald D. *diversified corporation executive*

**Edmonton**
Bateman, William Maxwell *retired construction company executive*
Stollery, Robert *construction company executive*

## BRITISH COLUMBIA

**Burnaby**
Bender, Graham I. *forest products executive*

**North Vancouver**
Gibbs, David George *retired food processing company executive*
Grunder, Arthur Neil *forest products industry executive, retired*

**Vancouver**
Bentley, Peter John Gerald *forest industry company executive*
Solloway, C. Robert *forest products company executive*

## MANITOBA

**Winnipeg**
MacKenzie, George Allan *diversified company executive*
Watchorn, William Ernest *diversified manufacturing executive*

## NEW BRUNSWICK

**Fredericton**
Grotterod, Knut *retired paper company executive*

## NOVA SCOTIA

**Halifax**
MacIntosh, Charles William *property development company executive*
Pincock, Douglas George *electronics company executive*

**Lunenburg**
Morrow, James Benjamin *retired sea products company executive*

**North Sydney**
Nickerson, Jerry Edgar Alan *manufacturing executive*

**Stellarton**
Gogan, James Wilson *corporate executive*
Rowe, Allan Duncan *food products executive*
Sobey, David Frank *food company executive*

## ONTARIO

**Agincourt**
Lutgens, Harry Gerardus *food company executive*

**Aurora**
Lanthier, Ronald Ross *retired manufacturing company executive*

**Brampton**
Greenhough, John Hardman *business forms company executive*
Prevost, Edward James *paint manufacturing executive*
Toole, David George *pulp and paper products executive*

**Burlington**
McMulkin, Francis John *steel company executive*

**Cambridge**
Turnbull, Robert Scott *manufacturing company executive*
White, Joseph Charles *manufacturing and retailing company executive*

**Fort Erie**
Watson, Stewart Charles *construction company executive*

**Galt**
Dobbie, George Herbert *retired textile manufacturing executive*

**Hamilton**
Telmer, Frederick Harold *steel products manufacturing executive*

**Hanover**
Adams, John David Vessot *manufacturing company executive*

**Kitchener**
Pollock, John Albon *broadcasting and manufacturing company executive*

**Markham**
Burns, H. Michael *health care company executive*
Stronach, Frank *automobile parts manufacturing executive*

**Mississauga**
Barkin, Martin *pharmaceutical company executive, physician*
Lewis, William Leonard *food products executive*
Strachan, Graham *pharmaceutical company executive*

**North York**
Wleugel, John Peter *manufacturing company executive*

**Ottawa**
†Wetherup, Danielle V. *metal manufacturing executive*

**Toronto**
Blundell, William Richard Charles *electric company executive*
Connell, Philip Francis *food industry executive*
Dale, Robert Gordon *business executive*
Eagles, Stuart Ernest *business executive*
Eisen, Leonard *food and retail company executive*
Lowe, Donald Cameron *corporate executive*
Mercier, Eileen Ann *management consultant*
Seagram, Norman Meredith *corporate executive*
Thomas, Alan Richard *natural resources products executive*
Turner, Peter Merrick *retired manufacturing company executive*
Van Houten, Stephen H. *manufacturing company executive*

**Willowdale**
McDonald, William Henry *financial executive*

**Windsor**
Landry, G. Yves *automotive company executive*

## QUEBEC

**Athelstan**
Ness, Owen McGregor *retired aluminum company executive*

**Longueuil**
Caplan, L(azarus) David *manufacturing company executive*
Smith, Elvie Lawrence *corporate director*

**Montreal**
Beauchamp, Jacques *wood products executive*
Bougie, Jacques *aluminum company executive*
Gagné, Paul E. *paper company executive*

Herling, Michael *steel company executive*
Ivanier, Paul *steel products manufacturing company executive*
Molson, Eric H. *beverage company executive*
Nadeau, Bertin F. *diversified company executive*
Pal, Prabir Kumar *aluminium company executive*
Pinard, Raymond R. *pulp and paper consultant*
Plourde, Gerard *company executive*
Poissant, Charles-Albert *paper manufacturing company executive*
Redfern, John D. *manufacturing company executive*

**Outremont**
Gouin, Serge *corporate executive*
Larose, Roger *former pharmaceutical company executive, former university administrator*

**Saint Jerome**
Rolland, Lucien G. *paper company executive*

**Verdun**
Ferguson, Michael John *electronics and communications educator*

## SASKATCHEWAN

**Regina**
Dalla-Vicenza, Mario Joseph *steel company financial executive*
Phillips, Roger *steel company executive*

**Saskatoon**
Carr, Roy Arthur *agricultural products applied research, development and commercialization processing organization executive*
Steck, Warren Franklin *chemical company executive, former biochemistry researcher*

## MEXICO

**Mexico City**
Schinkel, Claus *chemical company executive*

## AUSTRALIA

**Melbourne**
Lawson, Francis Colin *chemical company executive*

## BAHAMAS

**Nassau**
Dingman, Michael David *industrial company executive, international investor*

## BARBADOS

**Christ Church**
Goodine, Isaac Thomas *development executive, educator*

## BERMUDA

**Flatts**
Smith, Wendell Murray *graphic arts control and equipment manufacturing executive*

## ENGLAND

**Ascot Berkshire**
Grubman, Wallace Karl *chemical company executive*

**Heathfield**
Wilson, Leroy *retired glass manufacturing company executive*

**London**
Bates, Malcolm Rowland *corporate director*
†Dupee, Paul Rich, Jr. *business executive*
Greener, Anthony *beverage company executive*
Shaw, Sir Neil McGowan *sugar, cereal and starch refining company executive*
Taylor, Jonathan Francis *agribusiness executive*

**Malmesbury**
Shober, Edward Wharton *bioscience company executive*

**Poole**
Stokes, Donald Gresham *vehicle company executive*

**Suffolk**
Clement, John *food products company executive*

**Windsor**
Hall, Sir Arnold Alexander *aeronautical, mechanical and electrical executive*
Zabriskie, John L. *healthcare and agricultural products manufacturing company executive*

## FRANCE

**Genlis**
van Raalte, John A. *research and engineering management executive*

**Paris**
Collomb, Bertrand Pierre *cement company executive*
Lecerf, Olivier Maurice Marie *construction company executive*

**Sevres**
Asscher, Jean Claude *electronic executive*

## GERMANY

**Frankfurt**
Fozzati, Aldo *automobile manufacturing company executive*

**Gethles**
Frank, Dieter *technical consultant, retired chemical company executive*

**Hannover**
Döhler, Klaus Dieter *pharmaceutical and development company executive*

## GREECE

**Athens**
Larounis, George Philip *manufacturing company executive*

## HONG KONG

**Hong Kong**
Wong, Wing Keung *trading, electronics company executive, physician*

## IRELAND

**Arklow**
Barber, Jerry Randel *medical device company executive*

## ITALY

**Turin**
Agnelli, Giovanni *industrial executive*

## JAPAN

**Chiba**
Wada, Yutaka *electronics executive*

**Tokyo**
Baba, Isamu *construction company executive*
Makino, Shojiro (Mike Makino) *chemicals executive*
Ohga, Norio *electronics executive*
Wakumoto, Yoshihiko *electronics company executive, grants executive*

## LUXEMBOURG

**Luxembourg**
Kasperczyk, Jürgen *business executive, government official, educator*

## NEW CALEDONIA

**Noumea**
Curlook, Walter *mining company executive*

## RUSSIA

**Moscow**
Knaus, Jonathan Charles *manufacturing executive*

## SCOTLAND

**Edinburgh**
Miller, James *construction company executive*

**Kinross**
Finlay, Robert Derek *food company executive*

## SINGAPORE

**Singapore**
Brown, Kenneth Charles *manufacturing company executive*

## SPAIN

**Madrid**
Feltenstein, Harry David, Jr. *chemical executive*

## SWEDEN

**Stockholm**
Schröder, Harald Bertel *aerospace industry executive*

## SWITZERLAND

**Basel**
Moret, Marc *chemicals executive*

**Zurich**
Barnevik, Percy Nils *electrical company executive*

## TAIWAN

**Taipei**
O'Hearn, James Francis *chemical company executive*

## ADDRESS UNPUBLISHED

Adams, Warren Sanford, II *retired food company executive, lawyer*
Adams, William White *retired manufacturing company executive*
Adelman, Robert Paul *retired construction company executive, lawyer*
Albino, George Robert *business executive*
Alig, Frank Douglas Stalnaker *construction company executive*
Anderer, Joseph Henry *textile company executive*
Anderson, Fletcher Neal *chemical executive*
Anderson, Joseph Norman *executive consultant, former food company executive, former college president*
Andersson, Craig Remington *retired chemical company executive*
Andreas, Dwayne Orville *business executive*
Andrews, William Frederick *manufacturing executive*
Anspach, Herbert Kephart *retired appliance company executive, patent attorney*
Archibald, Nolan D. *household and industrial products company executive*
Armstrong, John Allan *business machine company research executive*
Aschauer, Charles Joseph, Jr. *corporate director, former company executive*
Ashton, Harris John *business executive*
Askins, Wallace Boyd *manufacturing company executive*
Auriemma, Louis Francis *printing company executive*
Azarnoff, Daniel Lester *pharmaceutical company consultant*
Baker, Charles DeWitt *research and development company executive*
Ballhaus, William Francis *retired scientific instruments company executive*
Barca, George Gino *winery executive, finanial investor*
Barron, Charles Elliott *retired electronics executive*
Bass, Robert Olin *manufacturing executive*
Battistelli, Joseph John *electronics executive*
Bauman, Robert Patten *diversified company executive*
Beadle, John Grant *retired manufacturing company executive*
Beighey, Lawrence Jerome *packaging company executive*
Belle Isle, Albert Pierre *electronics company executive*
Bennett, Richard Thomas *retired manufacturing executive*
Berry, Robert Vaughan *retired electrical manufacturing company executive*
Bierwirth, John Cocks *retired aerospace manufacturing executive*
Biggs, Arthur Edward *retired chemical manufacturing company executive*
Birkenstock, James Warren *business machine manufacturing company executive*
Bixler, Margaret Triplett *former manufacturing executive*
Blair, Charles Melvin *manufacturing company executive, scientist*
Blanchard, Richard Frederick *construction executive*
Bloom, Frank *corporation executive, consultant*
Bodea, Andy S(orin) *financial services and manufacturing executive*
Borten, William H. *research company executive*
Boyle, R. Emmett *metal products executive*
Boylston, Benjamin Calvin *retired steel company executive*
Brancato, Leo John *manufacturing company executive*
Brinckerhoff, Richard Charles *retired manufacturing company executive*
Brodie, Theodore Hamilton *construction company executive*
Brooker, Robert Elton, Jr. *manufacturing company executive*
Bruinsma, Theodore August *retired business executive*
Bull, Bergen Ira *retired equipment manufacturing company executive*
Bundalo, Milan Richard *manufacturing executive*
Burkett, Thomas O. *manufacturing executive*
Burlant, William Jack *retired chemical company executive*
Butler, Jack Fairchild *semiconductors company executive*
Buxton, Winslow Hurlbert *diversified manufacturing company executive*
Calcaterra, Edward Lee *construction company executive*
Calvert, James Francis *manufacturing company executive, retired admiral*
Camisa, George Lincoln *beverage company executive*
Campbell, Richard Alden *electronics company executive*
Carmody, Thomas Roswell *business products company executive*
Carpenter, Myron Arthur *manufacturing company executive*
Carrell, Terry Eugene *manufacturing company executive*
Carter, Orwin L. *chemical executive*
Cassidy, James Mark *construction company executive*
Cates, Dalton Reede *electronics company official, consultant*
Chamberlain, George Arthur, III *manufacturing company executive, venture capitalist*
Chaykin, Robert Leroy *manufacturing and marketing executive*
Chen, Di *electro-optic company executive, consultant*
Chmielinski, Edward Alexander *electronics company executive*
Closset, Gerard Paul *forest products company executive*
Clouston, Ross Neal *retired food and related products company executive*
Cohn, Leonard Allan *retired chemical company executive*
†Connolly, Gerald E. *company executive*
Cooley, James William *retired executive researcher*
Cooper, Norton J. *liquor, wine and food company executive*
Costantino, Lorine Protzman *woodworking company executive*
Costello, James Joseph *retired electrical manufacturing company executive*
Costello, Thomas Patrick *manufacturing executive*
Cotting, James Charles *manufacturing company executive*
Cox, John Francis *retired cosmetic company executive*
Cox, Wilford Donald *retired food company executive*
Craft, Edmund Coleman *automotive parts manufacturing company executive*
Cross, Alexander Dennis *business consultant, former chemical and pharmaceutical executive*
Cull, Robert Robinette *electric products manufacturing company executive*
Culwell, Charles Louis *retired manufacturing company executive*
Cushwa, William Wallace *retired machinery parts company executive*
D'Agostino, Stephen I. *bottling company executive*
Daly, William James *retired health industry distributing company executive*
Davis, Darrell L. *automotive executive*
Decker, Gilbert Felton *manufacturing company executive*
Denise, Robert Phillips *craft company executive*
Diener, Royce *corporate director, retired healthcare services company executive*
Dobelis, George *manufacturing company executive*
Dohrmann, Russell William *manufacturing company executive*
Dolan, Peter Robert *company executive*
Dole, Robert Paul *retired appliance manufacturing company executive*
Doran, Charles Edward *textile manufacturing executive*
Doyle, John Laurence *manufacturing company executive*
Dragon, William, Jr. *footwear and apparel company executive*
Dressler, David Charles *retired aerospace company executive*
Drew, Walter Harlow *retired paper manufacturing company executive*
Driscoll, William Michael *corporation executive*
Durr, Robert Joseph *construction firm executive, mechanical engineer*
Dye, Robert Harris *retired manufacturing company executive*
Earle, Arthur Percival *textile company executive, airport executive*
Eberle, Charles Edward *paper and consumer products executive*
Elverum, Gerard William, Jr. *retired electronic and diversified company executive*
Ely, Paul C., Jr. *electronics company executive*
Erdeljac, Daniel Joseph *retired manufacturing company executive*
Ericson, Rolf Eric George *manufacturing company executive*
Evanoff, George C. *retired business executive*
Farley, John Michael *steel industry executive, consultant*
Fein, Seymour Howard *pharmaceutical executive*
Feinberg, Herbert *apparel and beverage executive*
Fenger, Manfred *retired manufacturing executive*
Fitch, Robert McLellan *business and technology consultant*
Flaschen, Steward Samuel *high technology company executive*
Flitcraft, Richard Kirby, II *former chemical company executive*
Fogg, Richard Lloyd *food products company executive*
Ford, Jerry Lee *service company executive*
Forest, Harvey *electronics executive*
Fossier, Mike Walter *consultant, retired electronics company executive*
Foster, Edson L. *retired mining and manufacturing company executive*
Frame, Russell William *retired electronics executive*
Franco, Alexander *construction company executive*
Fraser, Campbell *business consultant*
Frawley, Patrick Joseph, Jr. *health care executive*
French, Clarence Levi, Jr. *retired shipbuilding company executive*
Friedman, Richard Lee *lumberyard owner*
Frieling, Gerald Harvey, Jr. *specialty steel company executive*
Fries, Raymond Sebastian *manufacturing company executive*
Fritz, Rene Eugene, Jr. *manufacturing executive*
Fuller, James Chester Eedy *retired chemical company executive*
Gardner, Clyde Edward *health care executive, consultant, educator*
Gidwitz, Gerald *retired hair care company executive*
Gillespie, Robert James *manufacturing company executive*
Gillette, Stanley C. *apparel manufacturing company executive*
Gilreath, Warren Dean *retired packaging company executive*
Goldbach, Ray *food products executive*
Goldberg, Lee Winicki *furniture company executive*
Grandy, James Frederick *retired electronics business executive, consultant*
Grass, George Mitchell, IV *pharmaceutical executive*
Grauman, Robert A. *healthcare executive*
Gray, Donna Mae *former agricultural products executive, bookkeeper*
Gray, Richard Alexander, Jr. *retired chemical company executive*
Greenberg, Milton *corporation executive*
Griffith, Daniel Boyd *automotive products executive*
Guiliano, Francis James *office products manufacturing company executive*
Gulcher, Robert Harry *aircraft company executive*
Gurney, Daniel Sexton *race car manufacturing company executive, racing team executive*
Hager, Robert Worth *retired aerospace company executive*
Hakimoglu, Ayhan *electronics company executive*
Hammond, Robert Lee *retired feed company executive*
Hare, LeRoy, Jr. *pharmaceutical company executive*
Harrell, Henry Howze *tobacco company executive*
Hartmann, George Herman *retired manufacturing company executive*
Hausman, Arthur Herbert *electronics company executive*
Hayes, John Patrick *retired manufacturing company executive*
Heckel, John Louis (Jack Heckel) *aerospace company executive*
Heilmann, Christian Flemming *corporate executive*
Heit, Ivan *packaging equipment company executive*
Heller, Ronald Gary *manufacturing company executive, lawyer*
Hiatt, Arnold *shoe manufacturer, importer, retailer*
Hirsch, Horst Eberhard *business consultant*
Hofmeyr, Harold David *yacht construction company executive*
Holder, Richard Gibson *metal products executive*
Horovitz, Zola Philip *pharmaceutical company executive*

Hudson, Franklin Donald diversified company executive, consultant
Hurd, Richard Nelson pharmaceutical company executive
Irani, Raymond Reza electro-mechanical company executive
Jacoby, Stanley Arthur retired manufacturing executive
Jaicks, Frederick Gillies retired steel company executive
Jedenoff, George Alexander steel consultant
Jensen, Erik Hugo pharmaceutical quality control consultant
Johnson, Irving Stanley pharmaceutical company executive, scientist
Johnson, Keith Gilbert retired heavy equipment company executive
Johnson, Marlene M. furniture company executive
Johnson, Rogers Bruce retired chemical company executive
Johnson, Warren Donald retired pharmaceutical executive, former air force officer
Judelson, David N. company executive
Kapcsandy, Louis Endre building construction and manufacturing executive, chemical engineering consultant
Katz, Leon packaging company executive
Keith, Brian Thomas automobile executive
Kelly, Anthony Odrian flooring manufacturing company executive
Kenyhercz, Thomas Michael pharmaceutical company executive
Kerber, Ronald Lee industrial corporation executive
Kern, Irving John retired food company executive
Kerstetter, Michael James retired manufacturing company executive
Killhour, William Gherky paper company executive
King, Susan Bennett retired glass company executive
Kiselik, Paul Howard manufacturing company executive
Kleinberg, Lawrence H. food industry executive
Kondo, Masatoshi S. pharmaceutical executive, educator
Kongabel, H. Fred industrial construction company executive
Kooloian, Elizabeth construction company executive
Kostka, Janice Ellen automotive wholesale company administator
Krause, Werner William plastics company executive
Kulik, Rosalyn Franta food company executive, consultant
Labrecque, Richard Joseph industrial executive
Landon, Robert Gray retired manufacturing company executive
Lane, Bernard Bell furniture company executive
Lane, William W. electronics executive
Langdale, John Wesley timber executive
Langford, Walter Martin retired greeting card and gift wrap manufacturing executive
Lathlaen, Robert Frank retired construction company executive
Laurenzo, Vincent Dennis industrial management company executive
Lavington, Michael Richard venture capital company executive
Lazay, Paul Duane telecommunications manufacturing company executive
Leff, Joseph Norman yarn manufacturing company executive
Lehman, John F., Jr. industrialist
Lennox, Donald D(uane) automotive and housing components company executive
Leonard, Guy Meyers, Jr. international holding company executive
Leveille, Gilbert Antonio food products executive
Lewis, Arthur Dee corporation executive
Lewis, Martin R. paper company executive, consultant
Lewis, Rita Hoffman plastic products manufacturing company executive
†Liebler, Arthur C. automotive executive
Liffers, William Albert retired chemical company executive
Lindars, Laurence Edward retired health care products executive
Lindsay, Franklin Anthony business executive, author
Lippincott, Philip Edward retired paper products company executive
Logan, John Francis electronics company executive, management consultant
Long, Robert Livingston retired photographic equipment executive
Lopina, Lawrence Thomas retired manufacturing executive
Lovelace, Alan Mathieson aerospace company executive
Lovett, John Robert retired chemical company executive
Lowden, John L. retired corporate executive
Lucas, William Ray aerospace consultant
Luke, David Lincoln, III retired paper company executive
Lynch, Charles Andrew chemical industry consultant
Macek, Anna Michaella cosmetics executive
MacNaughton, John David Francis aerospace company executive
Madden, Richard Blaine forest products executive
Malson, Rex Richard drug and health care corporation executive
Manchester, Kenneth Edward electronics executive, consultant
Marrington, Bernard Harvey retired automotive company executive
Martin, Albert Charles manufacturing executive, lawyer
Maskell, Donald Andrew contracts administrator
Mason, Frank Henry, III automobile company executive, leasing company executive
Matasovic, Marilyn Estelle business executive
May, Kenneth Nathaniel food industry consultant
Mayhew, Lawrence Lee electronics company executive
McCabe, Charles Law retired manufacturing company executive, management consultant
McCann, Jack Arland former construction and mining equipment company executive, consultant
McGillivray, Donald Dean agricultural products executive
McKenzie, Herbert A(lonza) pharmaceutical company executive
McNeeley, Donald Robert steel company executive
McNeil, Steven Arthur food company executive
Messmore, David William construction executive, former psychologist
Miles, John Frederick retired manufacturing company executive
Miller, Harold Edward retired manufacturing conglomerate executive, consultant
Miller, Leland Bishop, Jr. food processing and financial consultant
Miller, Lowell Donald pharmaceutical company research executive
Mims, Edward Trow electronics industry executive
Miskowski, Lee R. retired automobile executive
Mitchel, F(rederick) Kent retired food company executive
Moore, Vernon Lee agricultural consultant, retired food products company executive
Morgenstein, William shoe company executive
Morita, Toshiyasu technical manager
Morris, Albert Jerome pest control company executive
Mott, Stewart Rawlings business executive, political activist
Mudd, Sidney Peter former beverage company executive
Mueller, Robert Louis business executive
Munera, Gerard Emmanuel manufacturing company executive
Myers, Albert G., Jr. textile manufacturer
Neff, Jack Kenneth apparel manufacturing company executive
Nesheim, Robert Olaf food products executive
Noe, Elnora (Ellie Noe) retired chemical company executive
Nord, Eric Thomas manufacturing executive
Nordlund, Donald Elmer manufacturing company executive
Norrie, K. Peter manufacturing executive
Nugent, Daniel Eugene business executive
Oaks, Maurice David retired pharmaceutical company executive
O'Donnell, Kevin retired metal working company executive
Oelman, Robert Schantz retired manufacturing executive
Ordal, Caspar Reuben business executive
Oster, Lewis Henry manufacturing executive, engineering consultant
Pariser, Rudolph chemicals company executive, consultant
Parker, George retired pen manufacturing company executive
Parker, Thomas Lee business executive
Pearce, Paul Francis retired aerospace electronics company executive
Peck, Daniel Farnum chemical company executive
Penske, Roger S. manufacturing and transportation executive
Perelman, Leon Joseph paper manufacturing executive, university president
Peterson, Robert Austin manufacturing company executive retired
Petok, Samuel retired manufacturing company executive
Phillips, George Michael food manufacturing company executive
Phinizy, Robert Burchall electronics company executive
Potts, Gerald Neal manufacturing company executive
Powell, Thomas Edward, III biological supply company executive
Precopio, Frank Mario chemical company executive
Preston, Seymour Stotler, III manufacturing company executive
Prezzano, Wilbur John retired photographic products company executive
Price, Robert electronics consultant
Pruis, John J. business executive
Raval, Dilip N. retired pharmaceutical executive
Redmond, Douglas Michael diversified company executive
Regan, Paul Jerome, Jr. manufacturing company executive, consultant
Rhodes, Peter Edward label company executive
Richard, Edward H. manufacturing company executive, former municipal government official
Richman, Paul semiconductor industry executive, educator
Richman, Peter electronics executive
Rodgers, Nancy Lucille corporate executive
Roller, Thomas Benjamin manufacturing company executive
Romanos, Nabil Elias business development manager
Romans, Donald Bishop corporate executive
Rooke, David Lee retired chemical company executive
Roper, John Lonsdale, III shipyard executive
Rosen, Ana Beatriz electronics executive
Roth, Herbert, Jr. corporate executive
Roudane, Charles metal and plastic products company executive
Rubinovitz, Samuel diversified manufacturing company executive
Rudy, Raymond Bruce, Jr. retired food company executive
Ryan, George William manufacturing executive
Rymar, Julian W. manufacturing company executive
Salathe, John, Jr. manufacturing company executive
Salbaing, Pierre Alcee retired chemical company executive
Samek, Michael Johann corporation executive
Samper, Joseph Phillip retired photographic products company executive
Sanders, Wayne R. manufacturing executive
Saute, Robert Emile drug and cosmetic consultant
Sauvey, Donald (Robert) retired musical instrument company executive
Savin, Ronald Richard chemical company executive, inventor
Saxby, Lewis Weyburn, Jr. retired glass fiber manufacturing executive
Scheele, Paul Drake former hospital supply corporate executive
Schlensker, Gary Chris landscaping company executive
Schultz, Robert J. retired automobile company executive
Schwartz, Robert automotive manufacturing company executive, marketing executive
Schwartz, Samuel business consultant, retired chemical company executive
Schwartzberg, Martin M. chemical company executive
Scully, Michael Andrew pharmaceutical company executive, writer, editor
Sharkey, Leonard Arthur automobile company executive
Shea, Bernard Charles retired pharmaceutical company executive
Shepherd, Mark, Jr. retired electronics company executive
Shipley, Lucia Helene retired chemical company executive
Siegel, Jack Morton retired biotechnology company executive
Silkett, Robert Tillson food business consultant
Silverman, Michael manufacturing company executive
Simeral, William Goodrich retired chemical company executive
Slagle, Jacob Winebrenner, Jr. food products executive
Smith, Charles Conard refractory company executive
Smith, Christine author, lecturer, former pharmaceutical executive
Smith, Frederick Coe manufacturing executive
Smith, Goff industrial equipment manufacturing executive
Smith, Robert Hugh engineering construction company executive
Snetsinger, David Clarence retired animal feed company executive
Somers, Louis Robert retired food company executive
Sommer, Howard Ellsworth textile executive
Southerland, S. Duane manufacturing company executive
Spliethoff, William Ludwig chemical company executive
Stamper, Malcolm Theodore aerospace company executive
Starr, Leon retired chemical research company executive
Stern, Arthur Paul electronics company executive, electrical engineer
Stern, Milton chemical company executive
Stewart, Daniel Robert retired glass company executive
Stewart, Joe J. manufacturing executive
Stewart, Peter Beaufort retired beverage company executive
Stickler, Fred Charles manufacturing company executive
Stivers, William Charles forest products company executive
Strauss, Simon David manufacturing executive
Suddick, Patrick Joseph defense systems company executive
Swaim, David Dee diversified company financial executive
Swanger, Sterling Orville appliance manufacturing company executive
Swihart, John Marion retired aircraft manufacturing company executive
Tagliattini, Maurizio construction executive, research historian, writer
Tallett, Elizabeth Edith biopharmaceutical company executive
Talley, Robert Morrell aerospace company executive
Tannenberg, Dieter E. A. retired manufacturing company executive
Taylor, Robert Morgan electronics executive
Temple, Joseph George, Jr. retired pharmaceutical company executive
Thomas, Leo J. retired imaging company executive
Thomas, Tom retired plastics company executive
Thompson, Ralph Newell former chemical corporation executive
Tippett, Willis Paul, Jr. automotive and textile company executive, retired
Tombros, Peter George pharmaceutical company executive
Trice, William Henry paper company executive
Trombino, Roger A. food products executive
Turnbull, John Neil retired chemical company executive
Valade, Robert Charles apparel company executive
Vanaltenburg, Betty Marie lumber company executive
Van Tassel, James Henry retired electronics executive
Vitt, David Aaron medical manufacturing company executive
Volkhardt, John Malcolm food company executive
Warner, Walter Duke corporate executive
Wasson, James Walter aircraft manufacturing company executive
Watkins, James David food products executive
Weaver, William Charles retired industrial executive
Weinberger, Siegbert Jacob food company executive
Weiss, Max Tibor retired aerospace company executive
Welch, Oliver Wendell retired pharmaceutical executive
White, Gerald Andrew retired chemical company executive
†White, John Kiernan lighting company executive
Wiesen, Donald Guy retired diversified manufacturing company executive
Wigdor, Lawrence Allen chemical company executive
Wiley, Carl Ross timber company executive
Will, Joanne Marie food and consumer services executive, communications consultant, writer
Williams, Carolyn Elizabeth manufacturing executive
Winters, Nola Frances food company executive
Witcher, Daniel Dougherty retired pharmaceutical company executive
Witt, Hugh Ernest technology consultant
Wolf, Hans Abraham retired pharmaceutical company executive
Wolff, Brian Richard metal manufacturing company executive
Wollert, Gerald Dale retired food company executive, investor
Wommack, W(illiam) W(alton) retired manufacturing company executive
Wood, Elwood Steven, III chemical company executive
Woodall, Jack David manufacturing company executive
Wright, Linda Jean manufacturing company executive
Ying, John L. manufacturing executive
Young, John Alan electronics company executive
Zanetti, Joseph Maurice, Jr. corporate executive

## INDUSTRY: SERVICE

## UNITED STATES

### ALABAMA

#### Birmingham
Axel, Bernard restaurant owner
Bruno, Ronald G. food service executive
Etterer, Sepp industrial relations consultant
Floyd, John Alex, Jr. editor, marketing executive, horticulturist
Gunter, John Richmond communications executive
Harris, Aaron management consultant
Henderson, Louis Clifton, Jr. management consultant
Parker, John Malcolm management and financial consultant

#### Cullman
Graves, Marie Maxine public relations executive, OSHA consultant

#### Eufaula
Dixon, Giles company executive

#### Fairhope
Kanter, L. Erick public relations executive

#### Guntersville
Lyons, Brian Wesley marketing professional

#### Heflin
Brady, Jennie M. wholesale and retail sales professional

#### Huntsville
Dayton, Deane Kraybill computer company executive
Gray, Ronald W. business executive
Richter, William, Jr. technical management consulting executive

#### Montgomery
Dillon, Jean Katherine executive secretary, small business owner
Robinson, Peter Clark general management executive
Schloss, Samuel Leopold, Jr. retired food service executive, consultant

#### Ohatchee
Ellis, Bernice Allred personnel executive

#### Point Clear
Williams, Willie John, II marketing consultant

#### Roanoke
McCarley, George David management executive

#### Tuscaloosa
Barban, Arnold Melvin advertising educator

### ALASKA

#### Anchorage
Brady, Carl Franklin retired aircraft charter company executive
Gottstein, Barnard Jacob retail and wholesale food company executive, real estate executive
Porcaro, Michael Francis advertising agency executive
Schmitt, Nancy Cain public and corporate relations executive, writer
Schneibel, Vicki Darlene public relations administrator

#### Ketchikan
Kraft, Richard Joe sales executive
Laurance, Leonard Clark marketing researcher, educator and consultant

### ARIZONA

#### Carefree
Giolito, Caesar Augustus public relations executive, consultant

#### Cave Creek
O'Reilly, Thomas Eugene human resources consultant

#### Chandler
Barrett, Craig R. computer company executive
Goyer, Robert Stanton communication educator

#### Flagstaff
Putnam, William Lowell science association administrator

#### Globe
Lee, Joyce Ann administrative assistant

#### Green Valley
Crystall, Joseph N. communications company executive

#### Mesa
Johnson, Doug advertising and public relations executive
Murphy, Edward Francis sales executive

#### Paradise Valley
Bergamo, Ron marketing executive
De Shazor, Ashley Dunn business consultant
Grimm, James R. (Ronald Grimm) multi-industry executive
Hazard, Robert Culver, Jr. hotel executive

#### Peoria
Schindler, William Stanley retired public relations executive

#### Phoenix
Armstrong, Nelson William, Jr. gaming company executive
Babinec, Gehl P. convenience store company executive
Brown, James Carrington, III (Bing Brown) public relations and communications executive
Drain, Albert Sterling business management consultant
DuMoulin, Diana Cristaudo marketing professional
Evans, Ronald Allen lodging chain executive
Gall, Donald Alan data processing executive

Grier, James Edward *hotel company executive, lawyer*
Hill, Edward G. *food marketing executive*
Hoyt, Monty *car purchase consultant*
Lemon, Leslie Gene *consumer services company executive*
Shelby, Ronald Van Dorn *information systems executive*
Simunich, Mary Elizabeth Hedrick (Mrs. William A. Simunich) *public relations executive*
Snell, Richard *holding company executive*
Stewart, Sally *public relations practitioner*
Sweet, Cynthia Kay *business administrator*
Teets, John William *retired diversifed company executive*
Turner, William Cochrane *international management consultant*
Ward, Yvette Hennig *advertising executive*

**Prescott**
Mayol, Richard Thomas *advertising executive, political consultant*

**Scottsdale**
Blinder, Martin S. *business consultant, art dealer*
Chryss, George *consulting company executive*
Doglione, Arthur George *data processing executive*
Donnelly, Charles Francis *management consultant, lawyer*
Garfield, Ernest *bank consultant*
Joaquim, Richard Ralph *hotel executive*
Lillestol, Jane Brush *career development company executive*
Pavlik, Nancy *convention services executive*
Peterson, Louis Robert *retired consumer products company executive*
Quigley, Jerome Harold *management consultant*
Ralston, Joanne Smoot *public relations counseling firm executive*
Schleifer, Thomas C. *management consultant, author, lecturer*
Sullivan, George Edmund *editorial and marketing company executive*
Swanson, Robert Killen *management consultant*

**Sedona**
Wolfe, Al *marketing and advertising consultant*

**Sierra Vista**
Bowen, Harry Ernest *management consultant*

**Sun City West**
Berkenkamp, Fred Julius *management consultant*
Curtin, Richard Daniel *management consultant, retired air force officer, space pioneer*
Stevens, George Richard *business consultant, public policy commentator*

**Tempe**
Arters, Linda Bromley *public relations consultant, writer, lecturer*
McKeever, Jeffrey D. *computer company executive*
Sackton, Frank Joseph *public affairs educator*
Williams, James Eugene *management consultant*

**Tucson**
Barton, Stanley Faulkner *management consultant*
Cook, Annis Jane *customer service executive*
Cox, Robert Gene *management consultant*
Jones, Frank Wyman *management consultant, mechanical engineer*
King, Marcia *management consultant*
Lewis, Wilbur H. *educational management consultant*
Paley, Alfred Irving *value engineering and consulting company executive, lecturer*
Rose, Hugh *management consultant*
Vanatta, Chester B. *business executive, educator*

## ARKANSAS

**Conway**
Hatcher, Joe Branch *executive search consulting company executive*

**Fort Smith**
Harper, S. Birnie *business brokerage company owner*

**Hot Springs National Park**
Dellow, Reginald Leonard *advertising executive*

**Jonesboro**
Tims, Robert Austin *data processing official, pilot*

**Little Rock**
Russell, Jerry Lewis *public relations counselor, political consultant*

**Monticello**
Webster, Linda Jean *communication educator, media consultant*

**Pine Bluff**
Long, Edward Arlo *business consultant, retired manufacturing company executive*

## CALIFORNIA

**Agoura Hills**
Gressak, Anthony Raymond, Jr. *sales executive*

**Alameda**
Billings, Thomas Neal *computer and publishing executive, management consultant*

**Alamo**
Whalen, John Sydney *management consultant*

**Altadena**
†Willans, Richard James *religious organization executive, human resources management consultant*

**Anaheim**
Jurczyk, Joanne Monica *price analyst*
Kallay, Michael Frank, II *medical devices company official*
Lefebvre, Peggy Anderson *advertising executive*

Noorda, Raymond J. *computer software company executive*

**Apple Valley**
Yochem, Barbara June *sales executive, lecturer*

**Arroyo Grande**
Edwards, Patrick Michael *sales consultant*

**Atherton**
Lowry, Larry Lorn *management consulting company executive*
Scandling, William Fredric *retired food service company executive*

**Atwater**
DeVoe, Kenneth Nickolas *food service executive, mayor*

**Belvedere Tiburon**
Denton, Charles Mandaville *corporate consultant*
Hudnut, David Beecher *retired leasing company executive, lawyer*

**Berkeley**
Dost, Janice E.H. Burrows *human resources director*
Poulos-Woolley, Paige M. *public relations executive*

**Beverly Hills**
Berg, Jeffrey Spencer *talent agency executive*
Carlson, Gary Lee *public relations executive, director, producer*
David, Clive *event planning executive*
Fenimore, George Wiley *management consultant*
Fickinger, Wayne Joseph *advertising executive*
Hilton, Barron *hotel executive*
Levine, Michael *public relations executive, author*
Litman, Brian David *communications executive*
Riess, Gordon Sanderson *management consultant*
Rowan, Keith Patterson *communications executive, consultant*
Shepard, Kathryn Irene *public relations executive*
Toffel, Alvin Eugene *corporate executive, business and governmental consultant*
Zarem, Abe Mordecai *management consulting executive*

**Bishop**
Naso, Valerie Joan *automotive dealership executive, travel company operator*

**Brea**
Herzing, Alfred Roy *computer executive*

**Burbank**
Mather, Ann *international entertainment company executive*
Nieto del Rio, Juan Carlos *marketing executive*

**Burlingame**
Riach, Douglas Alexander *marketing and sales executive, retired military officer*

**Calabasas**
Bartizal, Robert George *computer systems company executive, business consultant*

**Camarillo**
Frayssinet, Daniel Fernand *software company executive*
Sime, Donald Rae *retired business administration educator*

**Cambria**
Morse, Richard Jay *human resources and organizational development consultant, manufacturers' representative company executive*

**Carlsbad**
Moore, Terry Wayne *high technology venture management consultant*
Wilson, Donald Grey *management consultant*

**Carmel**
Creighton, John Wallis, Jr. *consultant, author, former management educator*
Epstein-Shepherd, Bee J. *professional speaker*
Krugman, Stanley Lee *international management consultant*
Skidmore, Howard Franklyn *public relations counsel*
Smith, Gordon Paul *management consulting company executive*

**Castro Valley**
Denning, Eileen Bonar *management consultant*

**Cerritos**
Madden, James Cooper, V *management consultant*

**Chatsworth**
Sklar, Louise Margaret *service executive*
Urmer, Diane Hedda *management firm executive, financial officer*

**Cloverdale**
Collins, John Wendler *consumer products company executive*

**Corona Del Mar**
Hobbs, Linder Charlie *computer company executive*

**Costa Mesa**
Damsky, Robert Philip *communications executive*
†Paine, David M. *public relations executive*
Steed, Emmett D. *hotel executive*

**Culver City**
Berland, James Fred *software company executive*
Boonshaft, Hope Judith *public relations executive*
Williams, Kenneth Scott *entertainment company executive*

**Cupertino**
Flynn, Ralph Melvin, Jr. *sales executive, marketing consultant*
Krambeck, Robert Harold *communications and computer executive, researcher*
Mattathil, George Paul *communications specialist, consultant*

Tesler, Lawrence Gordon *computer company executive*

**Daly City**
Hargrave, Sarah Quesenberry *marketing, public relations company executive*

**Dana Point**
Jelinek, Robert *advertising executive, writer*

**Danville**
Gorman, Russell William *marketing executive, consultant*
Mattoon, Henry Amasa, Jr. *advertising and marketing consultant, writer*
Randolph, Kevin H. *marketing executive*

**Del Mar**
Comrie, Sandra Melton *human resource executive*
Watkins, Carol Charles *hotel, timeshare, apartments and shopping center executive, fundraiser*

**Diablo**
Pelandini, Thomas Francis *marketing executive*

**Downey**
Huff, Ricky Wayne *sales executive*

**El Cajon**
Fagot, Joseph Burdell *corporate executive*
McInerney, Joseph Aloysius *hotel executive*

**El Segundo**
Armstrong, Wallace Dowan, Jr. *data processor*
Autolitano, Astrid *consumer products executive*
Barad, Jill Elikann *toy company executive*
Mehlman, Lon Douglas *information systems specialist*
Olson, Jeanne Innis *technology/technical management*

**Emeryville**
Smith, Christopher Allen *technology company executive, marketing professional*

**Escondido**
Packer, Russell Howard *business services company executive*
Pershing, Richard Wilson *communications company executive, consultant*

**Fair Oaks**
Nolan, Mark Gregory *advertising executive*

**Fallbrook**
Cralley, Lester Vincent *retired industrial hygienist, editor*

**Fontana**
Cory, Rolland Wayne *business administrator*

**Foster City**
Lutvak, Mark Allen *computer company executive*

**Fountain Valley**
Lonegan, Thomas Lee *retired restaurant corporation executive*

**Fresno**
Ganulin, Judy *public relations professional*
Levy, Joseph William *department stores executive*
Shmavonian, Gerald S. *entertainment executive*

**Fullerton**
Hollander, Gerhard Ludwig *computer company executive*
Sa, Julie *restaurant chain owner, former mayor*

**Gardena**
Crismond, Linda Fry *public relations executive*

**Glendale**
Herzer, Richard Kimball *franchising company executive*
Marr, Luther Reese *communications executive, lawyer*
Misa, Kenneth Franklin *management consultant*

**Glendora**
Barrett, Thomas Joseph *sales executive, computer systems consultant*

**Granada Hills**
O'Connor, Betty Lou *service executive*
Shoemaker, Harold Lloyd *infosystem specialist*

**Grass Valley**
Hutcherson, Christopher Alfred *marketing and recruiting and educational consultant*

**Half Moon Bay**
Fennell, Diane Marie *marketing executive, process engineer*
Hinthorn, Micky Terzagian *volunteer, retired*

**Hayward**
Tribus, Myron *quality counselor, engineer, educator*

**Healdsburg**
Canfield, Grant Wellington, Jr. *management consultant*

**Hillsborough**
West, Hugh Sterling *aircraft leasing company executive*

**Hollywood**
Lempert, Philip *advertising executive, author, consumerologist, syndicated columnist, broadcast journalist*

**Huntington Beach**
Carino, Linda Susan *business consultant*
Goldberg, David Charles *computer company executive*

**Indian Wells**
Kelley, John Paul *communications consultant*

**Inglewood**
Leiweke, Timothy *sales executive, marketing professional*

**Irvine**
Colino, Richard Ralph *communications consultant*
Leets, Peter John *outplacement consulting firm executive*
Maybay, Duane Charles *recycling systems executive*
Rollans, James O. *service company executive*
Spindler, Paul *public relations executive*

**La Habra**
Chase, Cochrane *advertising agency executive*

**La Jolla**
Bardwick, Judith Marcia *management consultant*
Fricke, Martin Paul *science company executive*
Karin, Sidney *research and development executive*
Kent, Paula *public relations, marketing and management consultant, lecturer*
La Bonté, C(larence) Joseph *weight management and lifestyle company executive*
McNamara, Tom *scientific consulting corporation executive*
Morse, Jack Hatton *management consultant*
Muniain, Javier P. *computer company executive, physicist, researcher*
†Palmer, Paul Edward *communications executive*
Thrower, F. Mitchell, III *advertising executive*
Wertheim, Robert Halley *security consultant*

**La Puente**
Sheridan, Christopher Frederick *human resources executive*

**La Quinta**
Houze, William Cunningham *executive recruiter, management consultant*

**Lafayette**
Kahn, Robert Irving *management consultant*

**Laguna Beach**
†Segard, Hubert J. *international marketing company executive, consultant*
Taylor, James Walter *marketing consultant*

**Laguna Hills**
Miller, Eldon Earl *corporate business publications consultant, retired manufacturing company executive*
Schulz, Raymond Alexander *medical marketing professional, consultant*

**Laguna Niguel**
Kursewicz, Lee Z. *marketing consultant*

**Lake Arrowhead**
Bauer, Ralph Leroy *business executive*

**Lake Sherwood**
Burke, Tamara Lynn *marketing professional*

**Larkspur**
Finkelstein, James Arthur *management consultant*

**Livermore**
Portway, Patrick Stephen *telecommunications consulting company executive, telecommunications educator*

**Loma Linda**
Maurice, Don *personal care industry executive*

**Long Beach**
Brown, (Jerene) Roxanne *sales executive*
Sosoka, John Richard *consulting firm executive, engineer*
Vejsicky, Cathleen Lynn *management executive, educator*

**Los Alamitos**
Weinberger, Frank *information management consultant*

**Los Altos**
Esber, Edward Michael, Jr. *software company executive*

**Los Angeles**
Altfeld, Sheldon Isaac *communications executive*
Armstrong, C. Michael *computer business executive*
Bakeman, Carol Ann *administrative services manager, singer*
Beerbohm, Elisa Newell *advertising professional*
†Bender, Dean *public relations executive*
Bloch, Paul *public relations executive*
Bohle, Sue *public relations executive*
†Brockman, Kevin Michael *public relations executive*
Burton, Ralph Joseph *international development consultant*
†Cerrell, Joseph R. *business executive*
Counts, James Curtis *management consultant*
Crosby, Peter Alan *management consultant*
†Dash, Hal *business executive*
Doll, Lynne Marie *public relations agency executive*
Edwards, William H., Sr. *retired hotel corporation executive*
Einstein, Clifford Jay *advertising executive*
Feidelson, Marc *advertising executive*
Ferry, Richard Michael *executive search firm executive*
Garland, G(arfield) Garrett *sales executive, golf professional*
†Goldman, Larry *public relations executive*
Gorman, Lillian R. *human resources executive*
Gottfried, Ira Sidney *management consulting executive*
Greene, Alvin *service company executive, management consultant*
Hale, Kaycee *research marketing professional*
Hartsough, Gayla Anne Kraetsch *management consultant*
Heinisch, Robert Craig *sales and marketing executive, consultant*
†Helper, Lee *public relations executive*
†Hodal, Melanie *public relations executive*
Holt, James Franklin *retired numerical analyst, scientific programmer analyst*

Hotchkiss, Vivian Evelyn *employment agency executive*
Humphreys, Robert Lee *advertising agency executive*
Irving, Jack Howard *technical consultant*
Jarc, Frank Robert *printing company executive*
Jordan, Michelle Henrietta *public relations company executive*
Klein, Elaine *advertising executive*
Kline, Richard Stephen *public relations executive*
Klinger, Allen *engineering and applied science educator*
Krueger, Robert William *management consultant*
Kupchick, Alan Charles *advertising executive*
Laba, Marvin *management consultant*
Lee, Burns Wells *public relations executive*
Leibert, Richard William *special events producer*
Lukasik, Stephen Joseph *information technology executive*
Margol, Irving *personnel consultant*
O'Brien, John William, Jr. *investment management company executive*
Olson, Dale C. *public relations executive*
Ovitz, Michael S. *communications executive*
Patel, Chandra Kumar Naranbhai *communications company executive, educator, researcher*
Perdigao, George Michael *advertising executive*
†Riedl, John Joseph *communications executive*
Rucker, Thomas Douglas *purchasing executive*
Shonk, Albert Davenport, Jr. *advertising executive*
Silverman, Bruce Gary *advertising executive*
Sitrick, Michael Steven *communications executive*
Somerville, Virginia Pauline Winters *executive assistant*
Spofford, Robert Houston *advertising agency executive*
Stern, James Coper *sales executive*
Stevens, Roy W. *sales and marketing executive*
Strawn, Judy C. *public relations professional*
Tardio, Thomas A. *public relations executive*
Tellem, Susan Mary *public relations executive*
Tennant, John Randall *management advisory company executive*
Tobia, Stephen Francis, Jr. *marketing professional, consultant*
Tomash, Erwin *retired computer equipment company executive*
Webster, Jeffery Norman *technology policy analyst*
Zelikow, Howard Monroe *management and financial consultant*

**Los Gatos**
Heymann, Stephen *marketing management consultant*

**Malibu**
Samuels, Cynthia Kalish *communications executive*

**Mammoth Lakes**
Buchanan, Lee Ann *public relations executive*

**Manhattan Beach**
Stern, Daniel Alan *business management consultant*
Weinstock, Herbert Frank *public relations executive*

**Marina Del Rey**
Gold, Carol Sapin *international management consultant, speaker*

**Menlo Park**
Carlick, David *communications executive*
Kurtzig, Sandra L. *software company executive*
Parker, Donn Blanchard *retired information security consultant*
Phipps, Allen Mayhew *management consultant*
Shows, Winnie M. *speaker, author, consultant*
Sommers, William Paul *management consultant, think tank executive*

**Mill Valley**
Jackson, Sharon Juanita *management consultant*

**Millbrae**
Mank, Edward Warren *marketing professional*

**Milpitas**
Corrigan, Wilfred J. *data processing and computer company executive*
Fenner, Peter David *communications executive, management consultant*

**Mission Viejo**
Harder, Wendy Wetzel *communications executive*
Linton, Frederick M. *strategic planning consultant*

**Moffett Field**
Baldwin, Betty Jo *computer specialist*
Bousquet, John Frederick *security firm executive, desktop publishing executive, locksmith*

**Monterey**
Cutino, Bert Paul *restaurant owner, chef*

**Monterey Park**
Kwong, Daniel Wai-Kin *business consultant, educator, songwriter, poet*

**Moraga**
Sonenshein, Nathan *marine consulting company executive, retired naval officer*

**Mountain View**
†Andreessen, Marc *communications company executive*
Barksdale, James Love *communications company executive*
†Boyd, Dean Weldon *management consultant*
Braun, Michael Alan *data processing executive*
Castor, Jon Stuart *management consultant*
de Urioste, George Adolfo, IV *software company executive*
Hamilton, Judith Hall *computer company executive*
Koo, George Ping Shan *business consultant*
Mc Nealy, Scott *computer company executive*
Qureishi, A. Salam *computer software and services company executive*
Rulifson, Johns Frederick *computer company executive, computer scientist*

**Napa**
Buchanan, Teri Bailey *communications executive*
LaRocque, Marilyn Ross Onderdonk *public relations consultant, writer*

**Newark**
Joyce, Stephen Francis *human resource executive*

**Newbury Park**
†Marshall, Trevor Gordon *computer company executive, editor*

**Newport Beach**
Allumbaugh, Byron *retired grocery company executive*
Gellman, Gloria Gae Seeburger Schick *marketing professional*
Lipson, Melvin Alan *technology and business management consultant*
Otero-Smart, Ingrid Amarillys *advertising executive*
Potocki, Joseph Edmund *marketing company executive*

**North Hollywood**
Costello, Richard Neumann *advertising agency executive*

**Oakland**
Crane, Robert Meredith *health care executive*
Dunn, David Cameron *entrepreneur, business executive*
Gardner, Robert Alexander *career counselor, career management consultant*
Potash, Jeremy Warner *public relations executive*
Potash, Stephen Jon *international public relations practitioner*

**Oildale**
Gallagher, Joseph Francis *marketing executive*

**Ontario**
Hawley, Nanci Elizabeth *public relations and communications professional*
Kahn, Mario Santamaria *international marketing executive*

**Orange**
Kelley, Robert Paul, Jr. *management consultation executive*
McNeil, David James *communications executive, marketing consultant*

**Orinda**
Somerset, Harold Richard *retired business executive*

**Palm Springs**
Arnold, Stanley Norman *manufacturing consultant*
Capps, Anthony Thomas (Capozzolo Capps) *international public relations executive*

**Palo Alto**
Allen, Louis Alexander *management consultant*
Cunningham, Andrea Lee *public relations executive*
Curry, William Sims *procurement executive*
Gilbert, David *computer company executive*
Hecht, Lee Martin *software company executive*
Kaufman, Michael David *management executive*
Lau, John Hon Shing *company executive*
Lawrence-Forrest, Lori Louise *restaurateur*
Merrin, Seymour *computer marketing company executive*
Morris, Arlene Myers *marketing professional*
†Polese, Kim *software company executive*
Quraishi, Marghoob A. *management consultant*

**Palos Verdes Peninsula**
Marlett, De Otis Loring *retired management consultant*

**Pasadena**
Caine, Stephen Howard *data processing executive*
Drutchas, Gerrick Gilbert *investigator*
Griesche, Robert Price *hospital purchasing executive*
Kaplan, Gary *executive recruiter*
Koenig, Marie Harriet King *public relations director, fund raising executive*
Ott, George William, Jr. *management consulting executive*
Watkins, John Francis *management consultant*

**Paso Robles**
Boxer, Jerome Harvey *computer and management consultant, vintner, accountant*

**Pebble Beach**
Harvie, J. Jason *administrative aide, private secretary*

**Piedmont**
Hurley, Morris Elmer, Jr. *management consultant*

**Pine Valley**
Collins, Frank Charles, Jr. *industrial and service quality specialist*

**Pleasant Hill**
Newkirk, Raymond Leslie *management consultant*

**Pleasanton**
Burd, Steve *food service executive*
Howard, Karen Lynn *marketing executive*
Ruppert, Paul Richard *telecommunications executive*
Stout-Pierce, Susan *clinical specialist*

**Portola Valley**
Berghold, Joseph Philip *marketing executive*
Moses, Franklin Maxwell *retired chemical marketing executive*

**Poway**
Remer, Vernon Ralph *travel consultant*

**Rancho Mirage**
Rotman, Morris Bernard *public relations consultant*

**Rancho Palos Verdes**
Rubenstein, Leonard Samuel *communications executive, ceramist, painter, sculptor, photographer*
Savage, Terry Richard *information systems executive*

**Rancho Santa Fe**
Baker, Charles Lynn *management consultant*
Best, Jacob Hilmer (Jerry), Jr. *hotel chain executive*

Gruenwald, George Henry *new products development management consultant*
Matthews, Leonard Sarver *advertising executive, consultant*
Rible, Morton *financial services and manufacturing executive*
Schirra, Walter Marty, Jr. *business consultant, former astronaut*

**Redwood City**
Bertram, Jack Renard *information systems company executive*
Gagarin, Dennis Paul *advertising agency executive*
Stone, Herbert Allen *management consultant*

**Reseda**
Leahy, T. Liam *marketing and management consultant*

**Riverside**
Chute, Phillip Bruce *management consultant*
Walker, Moira Kaye *sales executive*

**Rohnert Park**
Johnston, Edward Elliott *insurance and management consultant*

**Rutherford**
Staglin, Garen Kent *finance and computer service company executive*

**Sacramento**
Collings, Charles LeRoy *supermarket executive*
Fertig, Ted Brian O'Day *producer, public relations and association director*
Franz, Jennifer Danton *public opinion and marketing researcher*
Hunt, Dennis *public relations executive*
McElroy, Leo Francis *communications consultant, journalist*
Solone, Raymond Joseph *advertising executive*
Wilks-Owens, Dixie Rae *conference/meeting planner*

**Saint Helena**
Kamman, Alan Bertram *communications consulting company executive*
Spann, Katharine Doyle *marketing and communications executive*

**Salinas**
Martins, Evelyn Mae *theatre owner*

**San Carlos**
Eby, Michael John *marketing research and technology consultant*

**San Clemente**
Fall, John Robert *management and information technology consultant*
Stenzel, William A. *consulting services executive*

**San Diego**
Barr, Robert Edward *computer company executive*
Boyd, Robert Giddings, Jr. *continuing care facility administrator*
Cornett, William Forrest, Jr. *local government management consultant*
Fauchier, Dan R(ay) *construction management consultant*
Gilbertson, Oswald Irving *marketing executive*
Goodall, Jackson Wallace, Jr. *restaurant company executive*
Hartland, Nanci Jean *communications executive, educator*
Hooper, Jere Mann *retired hotel executive, consultant*
Kennedy, Peter Smithson *personnel consultant*
MacCracken, Peter James *marketing executive, communications executive*
Mitchell, Thomas Edward, Jr. *communications cabling executive*
Nelson, Craig Alan *management consultant*
Nugent, Robert J., Jr. *fast food company executive*
Rudolph, Charles Herman *computer software development executive*
Shevel, Wilbert Lee *information systems executive*
Silverberg, Lewis Henry *management consultant*
Stoorza Gill, Gail *corporate professional*
Taylor, George Allen *advertising agency executive*
Theis, James Edward *pastry chef, interior designer*
Tillinghast, Charles Carpenter, III *marketing company executive*
Vallbona, Marisa *public relations counselor*
Warner, John Hilliard, Jr. *technical services, military and commercial systems and software company executive*
Ziegaus, Alan James *public relations executive*

**San Francisco**
Amidei, L. Neal *public relations counselor*
Bancel, Marilyn *fund raising management consultant*
†Blanc, Maureen *public relations executive*
Boyle, Antonia Barnes *audio producer, writer*
Burkett, William Cleveland *management consultant*
Butenhoff, Susan *public relations executive*
Cavanagh, John Charles *advertising agency executive*
Colton, Roy Charles *management consultant*
Currier, Frederick Plumer *market research company executive*
Doan, Mary Frances *advertising executive*
†Dunn, Suzanne Lynne *media company executive*
Edgar, James Macmillan, Jr. *management consultant*
Farley, Leon Alex *executive search consultant*
Gertler, Alfred Martin *public relations executive, retired*
Goldberg, Fred Sellmann *advertising executive*
Goodby, Jeffrey *advertising agency executive*
Gordon, Judith *communications consultant, writer*
Haas, Peter E., Sr. *company executive*
Handlery, Paul Robert *hotel executive*
Harlan, Neil Eugene *retired healthcare company executive*
Hayes, Thomas Jay, III *management consultant, retired construction and engineering company executive, retired army officer*
Hindery, Leo Joseph, Jr. *media company executive*
Howley, Peter Anthony *communications executive*
Hurlbert, Roger William *information service industry executive*
Jandreau-Smith, Paul R. *communications executive, marketing consultant*
Jones, J. Gilbert *research consultant*
Kalt, Howard Michael *public relations executive*

Keeney, Ralph Lyons *information systems specialist, educator*
Kielarowski, Henry Edward *marketing executive*
Klammer, Joseph Francis *management consultant*
Lautz, Lindsay Allan *retained executive search consultant*
†Marshall, Scott *advertising agency executive*
McEvoy, Nan Tucker *publishing company executive*
Miller, Burton Leibsle *sales executive*
Miller, Phoebe Amelia *marketing professional*
Murphy, Kathleen Anne Foley *advertising agency executive*
†Nee, D. Y. Bob *think tank executive, engineering consultant*
Oppel, Andrew John *computer systems consultant*
†Otus, Simone *public relations executive*
Parker, Diana Lynne *restaurant manager, special events director*
†Probert, Colin *advertising executive*
†Riccardi, Robert *advertising executive*
Riney, Hal Patrick *advertising executive*
Rosmini, Gary David *financial marketing executive, consultant*
Russell, Carol Ann *personnel service company executive*
Selover, William Charlton *corporate communications and governmental affairs executive*
Siegel, Patricia Ann *association management consultant*
Silverstein, Richard *advertising agency executive*
Thompson, Gary W. *public relations executive*
Torme, Margaret Anne *public relations executive, communications consultant*
Walklet, Judith Kula *printing company executive*
Weaver, Sara Lee *sales executive*
Wentz, Jeffrey Lee *information systems consultant*
Wernick, Sandie Margot *advertising and public relations executive*
Westerfield, Putney *management consulting executive*
Whitaker, Clem, Jr. *advertising and public relations executive*
Wilbur, Brayton, Jr. *distribution company executive*
Willner, Jay R. *consulting company executive*
Winkler, Agnieszka M. *advertising executive*
Witherington, Jennifer Lee *sales and marketing executive*

**San Jose**
Burnside, Mary *software company executive*
Cade, Jack Carlton *marketing professional*
Dean, Burton Victor *management educator*
Dougherty, John James *computer software company executive, consultant*
Jordan, Thomas Vincent *advertising educator, consultant*
Kiggins, Mildred L. *marketing executive*
Ostrom, Philip Gardner *computer company executive*
Schofield, John Trevor *environmental management company executive*
Sollman, George Henry *telecommunications company executive*

**San Lorenzo**
Morrison, Martin (Earl) *computer systems analyst*

**San Mateo**
Helfert, Erich Anton *management consultant, author, educator*
Roberts, Lawrence Gilman *telecommunications company executive*

**San Pedro**
Price, Harrison Alan *business research company executive*

**San Rafael**
Kennedy, James Waite *management consultant, author*
Nelson, James Carmer, Jr. *advertising executive, writer*
Thompson, John William *international management consultant*
Wilson, Ian Holroyde *management consultant, futurist*

**San Ramon**
Gardner, Nord Arling *management consultant administrator*

**Santa Ana**
Boynton, William Lewis *electronic manufacturing company official*
Holtz, Joseph Norman *marketing executive*
Kenney, Patti Marlene *sales executive*
McKee, Kathryn Dian Grant *human resources consultant*
Nowel, David John *marketing professional*

**Santa Barbara**
Amory, Thomas Carhart *management consultant*
Boehm, Eric Hartzell *information management executive*
Boxer, Rubin *software company owner, former research and development company executive*
Emmons, Robert John *corporate executive*
Grayson, Robert Allen *marketing executive, educator*
Jacobson, Saul P. *consumer products company executive*
Levi, Ilan Mosche *computer and communications company consultant*
Montgomery, Michael Davis *hotelier, advanced technology consultant*
Morgan, Alfred Vance *management consulting company executive*
Schultz, Arthur Warren *communications company executive*

**Santa Clara**
Marken, Gideon Andrew, III *advertising and public relations executive*
Reavis, Liza Anne *semiconductor executive*
Rostoker, Michael David *micro-electronics company executive, lawyer*
Vincent, David Ridgely *management consulting executive*
Warmenhoven, Daniel John *communications equipment executive*

**Santa Cruz**
Corrick, Ann Marjorie *communications executive*
Stilwell, Belle Jean *record company executive, printing company owner*

PROFESSIONAL INDEX 5313 INDUSTRY: SERVICE


**Santa Fe Springs**
Butterworth, Edward Livingston *retail company executive*
Ittner, Perry Martin *sales and marketing consultant*
Morgan, Ronald William *sales executive*

**Santa Monica**
Janulaitis, M. Victor *consulting company executive*
Krakower, Bernard Hyman *management consultant*
†Price, David *recreational facilities executive*
Roberts, Kevin *recreational facility executive*
†Rubin, Gerrold Robert *advertising executive*
Salzer, John Michael *technical and management consultant*
Seymour, Jeffrey Alan *governmental relations consultant*

**Santa Rosa**
Schudel, Hansjoerg *international business consultant*

**Santa Ynez**
Stern, Marvin *management consultant*

**Saratoga**
Grubb, William Francis X. *consumer software executive, marketing executive*
Lynch, Milton Terrence *retired advertising agency executive*

**Sausalito**
McCarthy, Brian Nelson *marketing and distribution company executive*
Treat, John Elting *management consultant*

**Scotts Valley**
Brough, Bruce Alvin *public relations and communications executive*
Shugart, Alan F. *electronic computing equipment company executive*

**Seal Beach**
Burge, Willard, Jr. *software company executive*
Thompson, Craig Snover *corporate communications executive*

**Shell Beach**
Barca, Kathleen *marketing executive*

**Sherman Oaks**
Lindgren, Timothy Joseph *supply company executive*
Strauss, John *public relations executive*
Winkler, Lee B. *business consultant*

**Signal Hill**
Jarman, Donald Ray *retired public relations professional, minister*

**South Pasadena**
Lowe, Richard Gerald, Jr. *computer programming manager*

**South San Francisco**
Walsh, Gary L. *consumer products company executive*

**Stanford**
Hellyer, Constance Anne *communications executive, writer*
Miller, William Frederick *research company executive, educator, business consultant*

**Stockton**
Jacobs, Marian *advertising agency owner*
Viscovich, Andrew John *educational management consultant*

**Sunnyvale**
Amdahl, Gene Myron *computer company executive*
Armistead, Robert Ashby, Jr. *scientific research company executive*
Byers, Charles Frederick *public relations executive, marketing executive*
Charlton, (James) Paul(ett Jr.) *information systems architect*
Koomen, Cornelis Jan *telecommunication and micro electronics executive*
Michals, Lee Marie *retired travel agency executive*
Scott, Edward William, Jr. *computer software company executive*

**Surfside**
Sonne, Maggie Lee *travel company executive*

**Taft**
Smith, Lee L. *hotel executive*

**Tehachapi**
Smith-Thompson, Patricia Ann *public relations consultant, educator*

**Temecula**
Coram, David James *marketing professional*

**Thousand Oaks**
Lark, M. Ann *management consultant, strategic planner, naturalist*
†Shirilla, Robert M. *executive recruiter*

**Torrance**
Carey, Kathryn Ann *advertising and public relations executive, consultant*
Parady, John Edward *information systems executive, consultant*
Signorovitch, Dennis James *communications executive*

**Tustin**
Bartlett, Arthur Eugene *franchise executive*
LeBow, Bennett S. *communications executive*

**Twentynine Palms**
Fultz, Philip Nathaniel *management analyst*

**Universal City**
Biondi, Frank J., Jr. *entertainment company executive*

**Van Nuys**
Ghent, Peer *management consultant*
Kagan, Stephen Bruce (Sandy Kagan) *network marketing executive*
Simon, David Harold *retired public relations executive*

**Venice**
Chiat, Jay *advertising agency executive*
Smith, Yvonne Smart *advertising agency executive*

**Ventura**
Shultz, Emmet Lavel *marketing executive, commodities trader*

**Villa Park**
Britton, Thomas Warren, Jr. *management consultant*
Hawe, David Lee *consultant*

**Walnut**
Tan, Colleen Woo *communications educator*

**Walnut Creek**
Garlough, William Glenn *marketing executive*
Leftwich, James Stephen *management consultant*
Maslin, Harvey Lawrence *staffing service company executive*
Stover, W. Robert *temporary services executive*

**West Hollywood**
†Evans, David *communications executive*
Holt, Dennis F. *media buying company executive*
Kingsley, Patricia *public relations executive*
Sweeney, Vonny Hilton *promotion company executive*
Wald, Donna Gene *advertising executive*

**Westlake Village**
Doherty, Patrick Francis *communications executive, educator*
Murdock, David H. *diversified company executive*
Smyth, Glen Miller *management consultant*

**Woodland Hills**
Maeda, J. A. *data processing executive*

**Yountville**
Kay, Douglas Casey *leasing consultant*

## COLORADO

**Arvada**
Deere, Cyril Thomas *retired computer company executive*

**Aspen**
McDade, James Russell *management consultant*

**Bailey**
Van Dusen, Donna Bayne *communication consultant, educator, researcher*

**Berthoud**
Spence, Douglas Richard *educational consultant*

**Boulder**
Bryson, Gary Spath *cable television and telephone company executive*
Fleener, Terry Noel *marketing professional*
Fukae, Kensuke *information systems specialist*
Jerritts, Stephen G. *computer company executive*

**Broomfield**
Livesay, Valorie Ann *security analyst*
Lybarger, John Steven *business development consultant, trainer*

**Colorado Springs**
Guthrie, David Neal *marketing executive*
Lewis, Sheila Muriel O'Neil *retired communications management specialist*
May, Melvin Arthur *computer software company executive*
Midkiff, Donald Wayne *program manager*
Munro, Michael Donald *hotel industry executive, retired military officer*
Pool, Timothy Kevin *facilities management consultant*

**Delta**
Vanderheyden, Mirna-Mar *resort management and services executive*

**Denver**
†Bartholomew, Charles R. *advertising executive*
Baysinger, Stephen Michael *quality assurance professional*
Blatter, Frank Edward *travel agency executive*
Browne, Spencer I. *mortgage company executive*
Clinch, Nicholas Bayard, III *business executive*
Dolsen, David Horton *mortician*
Droullard, Steven Maurice *jewelry company executive*
Giesen, John William *advertising executive*
Greenberg, David Ethan *communications consultant*
Hughes, Bradley Richard *business executive*
†Isenberg, Walter L. *recreational facility executive*
Johnston, Gwinavere Adams *public relations consultant*
Karsh, Philip Howard *advertising executive*
Lazarus, Steven S. *management consultant, marketing consultant*
Mackinnon, Peggy Louise *public relations executive*
McGuire, Michael William *communications executive*
McKechnie, Margaret A. *public relations professional*
Mc Kinney, Alexis *public relations consultant*
Muftic, Felicia Anne Boillot *consumer relations professional*
Murdock, Pamela Ervilla *travel and advertising company executive*
Neu, Carl Herbert, Jr. *management consultant*
†Neumeyer, Zachary T. *hotel executive*
Notari, Paul Celestin *communications executive*
Walshe, Brian Francis *management consultant*
Welchert, Steven Joseph *public affairs consultant*
Wessler, Mary Hraha *marketing and management executive*

**Englewood**
Ames, A. Gary *communications company executive*
Hateley, Lynnette Sue *telecommunications, cable and multimedia analyst*
Joffe, Barbara Lynne *computer project manager*
Jones, Glenn Robert *cable systems executive*
Neiser, Brent Allen *public affairs consultant*
Reisinger, George Lambert *management consultant*
Rounds, Donald Michael *public relations executive*
Slater, Shelley *operations process manager*

**Golden**
Evans, David Lynn *management consultant, executive*

**Greeley**
Fry, Linda Sue *restaurant manager, hotel sales director, food products company executive*
Mader, Douglas Paul *quality engineering manager*
Miller, Diane Wilmarth *human resources director*

**Greenwood Village**
Shaddock, Paul Franklin, Sr. *human resources director*

**Lakewood**
Porter, Lael Frances *communication consultant, educator*
Spisak, John Francis *environmental company executive*
Walton, Roger Alan *public relations executive, mediator, writer*

**Littleton**
Fisher, Louis McLane, Jr. *management consultant*
Hopping, William Russell *hospitality industry consultant and appraiser*
Martinen, John A. *travel company executive*
Mercer, Margaret Teele *medical and film industry marketing executive*
Smith, Derrin Ray *information systems company executive*
Snyder, John Millard *recreation resources executive, educator*

**Louisville**
Williams, Marsha Kay *data processing executive*

**Parker**
Jankura, Donald Eugene *hotel executive, educator*
Pastore, Thomas Michael *telecommunications sales executive*
Roberts, James Carl *communications executive, engineer*

**Rollinsville**
Burandt, Gary Edward *advertising agency executive*

**Steamboat Springs**
Langstaff, Gary Lee *marketing executive*

**Sterling**
Jones, Daniel Lee *software development company executive*
Jones, Laurie Ganong *sales and marketing executive*

**Telluride**
Hadley, Paul Burrest, Jr. (Tabbit Hadley) *chef services manager, photographer*

**Woodland Park**
Stufano, Thomas Joseph *investigative firm executive*

## CONNECTICUT

**Andover**
Domagala, Richard Edward *mail marketing analyst*

**Bethel**
Webb, Theora Graves *public relations executive*

**Bloomfield**
Handel, Morton Emanuel *management consultation executive*
Mackey, William Arthur Godfrey *computer software company executive*

**Brookfield**
Gross, Kenneth Paul *management executive*
Williamson, Brian David *information systems executive, consultant*

**Danbury**
Baruch, Eduard *management consultant*

**Darien**
Buchanan, Robert Edgar *retired advertising agency executive*
Cowherd, Edwin Russell *management consultant*
Grace, John Kenneth *communications and marketing executive*
Hubner, Robert Wilmore *retired business machines company executive, consultant*
Mundt, Barry Maynard *management consultant*

**Deep River**
Healy, William Kent *environmental services executive*

**East Haddam**
Clarke, Cordelia Kay Knight Mazuy *managment executive*
Clarke, Logan, Jr. *management consultant*

**East Windsor**
Kaufmann, Sylvia Nadeau *office equipment sales company executive*

**Essex**
Winterer, Victoria Thompson *hospitality executive*

**Fairfield**
Ambrosino, Ralph Thomas, Jr. *retired telecommunications executive*
Blackburn, David Wheeler *management consultant, fundraiser*
Booth, George Keefer *finanical service executive*
Cole, Richard John *marketing executive*
Dean, George Alden *advertising executive*
Hergenhan, Joyce *public relations executive*
Hodgkinson, William James *marketing company executive*
Kantrowitz, Jonathan Daniel *educational software company executive, lawyer*
Urquhart, John Alexander *management consultant*

**Farmington**
O'Connor, Mary Scranton *public relations executive*

**Georgetown**
Duvivier, Jean Fernand *management consultant*

**Greens Farms**
McManus, John Francis, III *advertising executive*

**Greenwich**
Amen, Robert Anthony *investor and corporate relations consultant*
Ball, John Fleming *advertising and film production executive*
Bollman, Mark Brooks, Jr. *retired communications executive*
Burton, Robert Gene *printing and publishing executive*
Carmichael, William Daniel *consultant, educator*
Chisholm, William Hardenbergh *management consultant*
Coudert, Victor Raphael, Jr. *marketing and sales executive*
Davidson, Thomas Maxwell *international management company executive*
Donley, James Walton *management consultant*
†Flinn, Lawrence, Jr. *communications executive*
Keegan, Richard John *advertising agency executive*
Keeshan, William Francis, Jr. *advertising executive*
†Kerr, Ian *public relations executive*
Kestnbaum, Albert S. *advertising executive*
Lewis, Audrey Gersh *financial marketing/public relations consultant*
MacDonald, Gordon Chalmers *management consultant*
Pappas, Alceste Thetis *consulting company executive, educator*
Paulson, Paul Joseph *advertising executive*
†Rizzo, Raymond S. *advertising executive*
Schlafly, Hubert Joseph, Jr. *communications executive*
Scott, John Constante *marketing company executive*
Srere, Benson M. *communications company executive, consultant*
Wallach, Philip C(harles) *financial, public relations consultant*
Whitmore, George Merle, Jr. *management consulting company executive*
Wyman, Ralph Mark *corporate executive*

**Groton**
Hostetler, Dean Bryan *maritime industry professional consultant, towing, salvage, marine transportation and emergency response specialist*

**Guilford**
Kelley, Richard Everett *management consultant*
Ragan, James Thomas *communications executive*

**Hartford**
Coleman, Winifred Ellen *administrator*
Hertel, Suzanne Marie *personnel administrator*
Hudson, Jane Duclos *management consultant, writer*
Lovejoy, Ann Louise *organizational development consultant*

**Ivoryton**
LeCompte, Roger Burton *management consultant*

**Lakeville**
Bookman, George B. *public relations consultant*

**Madison**
Keim, Robert Phillip *retired advertising executive, consultant*

**Manchester**
Tanaka, Richard I. *computer products company executive*

**Mansfield Center**
Petrus, Robert Thomas *distribution executive, real estate executive*

**Marion**
Perkins, James Winslow *international business consultant, builder, contractor*

**Milford**
Khoury, Robert John *international leadership management consultant*

**New Canaan**
Crossman, William Whittard *retired wire cable and communications executive*
McClure, Grover Benjamin *management consultant*
Mc Mennamin, George Barry *advertising agency executive*
Means, David Hammond *retired advertising executive*
Oakley, Gary William *travel incentive executive*
Stack, J. William, Jr. *management consultant*
Ward, Richard Vance, Jr. *management executive*

**New Haven**
Waters, Donald Joseph *information services administrator*
Woody, Carol Clayman *data processing executive*

**Newtown**
Coates, John Peter *technical marketing executive*

**North Haven**
Bulyk, Spider J(ohn) C(onrad) (Romanyshyn) *corporate development executive*

**Norwalk**
Brandt, Richard Paul *communications and entertainment company executive*
Manning, James Forrest *computer executive*
Neuman, Curtis William *computer systems company executive*
Quittell, Frederic Charles *personnel and labor relations executive*

**Old Greenwich**
Fernous, Louis Ferdinand, Jr. *consumer products company executive*
Yoder, Patricia Doherty *public relations executive*

**Old Saybrook**
Phillips, William E. *advertising agency executive*

**Ridgefield**
Lodewick, Philip Hughes *equipment leasing company executive*

**Riverside**
Battat, Emile A. *management executive*
Geismar, Richard Lee *communications executive*
McSpadden, Peter Ford *retired advertising agency executive*
Pearson, Robert Greenlees *writing services company executive*

**Salisbury**
Block, Zenas *management consultant, educator*

**Shelton**
Lobsenz, Herbert Munter *data base company executive*
Storck, Herbert Evan *marketing professional*

**Sherman**
Cohn, Jane Shapiro *public relations executive*

**Simsbury**
Hildebrandt, Frederick Dean, Jr. *management consultant*
Nolan, Robert *management consulting company executive*

**Somers**
Hooper, Donald Robert *retired corporate executive*

**South Windsor**
Coullard, Chad *information systems specialist*

**Southbury**
Cassidy, James Joseph *public relations counsel*
Leonard, John Harry *advertising executive*

**Stamford**
Ast, Steven Todd *executive search firm executive*
Axelson, Linda Rae *recreational facility manager*
Breakstone, Robert Albert *consumer products/information technology/entertainment executive*
Cochran, David MacDuffie *management consultant*
Czajkowski-Barrett, Karen Angela *human resources management executive*
Dell, Warren Frank, II *management consultant*
Elkes, Terrence Allen *communications executive*
Goldstein, Frederick Arya *marketing executive*
Loeffel, Bruce *software company executive, consultant*
Lynch, John T. *management consultant*
Marlowe, Edward *research company executive*
Miklovic, Daniel Thomas *research director*
Miller, Wilbur Hobart *business diversification consultant*
Murphy, Robert Blair *management consulting company executive*
Nightingale, William Joslyn *management consultant*
Obernauer, Marne *corporate executive*
Ogden, Dayton *executive search consultant*
Palumbo, Matthew Aloysius *marketing executive*
Quest, James Howard *marketing executive*
Rapp, James Allen *marketing executive*
Sadove, Stephen Irving *consumer products company executive*
Sarbin, Hershel Benjamin *management consultant, business publisher, lawyer*
Silver, Charles Morton *communications company executive*
Sveda, Michael *management and research consultant*
Tierney, Patrick John *information services executive*
Trivisonno, Nicholas Louis *communications company executive, accountant*
Vos, Frank *advertising and marketing executive*
Wallfesh, Henry Maurice *business communications company executive, editor, writer*
Wallington, Patricia McDevitt *computer company executive*
White, Richard Booth *management consultant*
Wilson, Robert Albert *communications consultant*
Yardis, Pamela Hintz *computer consulting company executive*

**Storrs Mansfield**
Glasser, Joseph *manufacturing and marketing executive*

**Stratford**
Kaufman, Jess *communication, financial and marketing executive*

**Waterbury**
Clary, Alexia Barbara *management company executive*

**Weston**
Murray, Thomas Joseph *advertising executive*

**Westport**
Aasen, Lawrence Obert *public relations executive*
Allen, Robert Hugh *retired communications corporation executive*
Brandt, Kathy A. *public relations and events management executive, secondary school educator*
Dickson, Sally I. *retired public relations executive*
†Friedman, Ron *advertising executive*
Gallagher, Michael Robert *consumer products company executive*
Gold, Richard N. *management consultant*
Hambleton, George Blow Elliott *management consultant*
Logue-Kinder, Joan *alcoholic beverages company executive*
McFarland, Richard M. *executive recruiting consultant*
Muller, Frank B. *advertising executive*
Nathan, Irwin *business systems company executive*
Radigan, Joseph Richard *human resources executive*
Savage, Robert Heath *advertising executive*
Schriever, Fred Martin *energy, environmental and information technology, satellite systems executive*

**Wilton**
Bescherer, Edwin A., Jr. *business information services company executive*
Bishop, William Wade *advertising executive*
Black, Rita Ann *communications executive*
Caravatt, Paul Joseph, Jr. *communications company executive*
Cassidy, George Thomas *international business development consultant*
Kovak, Ellen B. *public relations firm executive*
Lewis, Margaret M. *marketing professional*
McCreight, John A. *management consultant*
Mc Dannald, Clyde Elliott, Jr. *management consultation company executive*
Nickel, Albert George *advertising agency executive*
Sideroff, Barry *advertising executive*

**Windsor**
Cowen, Bruce David *environmental services company executive*
Kamerschen, Robert Jerome *consumer products executive*

**Windsor Locks**
Heisler, Elwood Douglas *hotel executive*

**Woodbridge**
Ostfeld, Alexander Marion *advertising agency executive*
Van Sinderen, Alfred White *former telephone company executive*

**Woodstock**
Boote, Alfred Shepard *marketing researcher, educator*

## DELAWARE

**Hockessin**
Bischoff, Joyce Arlene *information systems consultant, lecturer*
Keenan, William Francis, Jr. *information and communications executive*

**Middletown**
Jackson, Donald Richard *marketing professional*

**Millsboro**
Jones, Lowell Robert *safety and industrial hygiene consultant*

**Wilmington**
Emanuel, Abraham Gabriel *photo processing company executive, consultant*
Kjellmark, Eric William, Jr. *management consultant, opera company director*
Perse, Aria Leon *international business advanced technologies executive*
Shipley, Samuel Lynn *advertising and public relations executive*

## DISTRICT OF COLUMBIA

**Washington**
Allen, Richard Vincent *international business consultant, bank executive*
Allnutt, Robert Frederick *management consultant*
†Alm, Alvin Leroy *technical services executive*
Ansley, Darlene H. *communications executive*
Baldwin, Velma Neville Wilson *personnel consultant*
Balfour, Ana Maria *office manager*
Baruch, Jordan Jay *management consultant*
Bauer, Robert Albert *public policy consultant*
Bell, Jeanne Viner *public relations counselor*
Bingman, Charles Franklin *public administration educator*
Bradley, Melvin LeRoy *communications company executive*
Braunstein, Diane Karen *government relations professional*
Brewster, Bill K. *business executive, former congressman*
Buben, Jeffray Alan *restaurant owner, chef*
Carberry, Michael Glen *public relations executive*
Clay, Don Richard *environmental consulting firm executive*
Coin, Sheila Regan *organization and management development consultant*
Coons, Barbara Lynn *public relations executive, librarian*
Cope, Jeannette Naylor *executive search consultant*
Craft, Mary Faye *public relations consultant, television producer*
Culley-Foster, Anthony Robert *international business consultant*
Cutter, Curtis Carly *consulting company executive*
Dach, Leslie Alan *public relations company executive*
Dawson, Mimi Weyforth *government affairs consultant*
Day, Melvin Sherman *information and telecommunications company executive*
Denysyk, Bohdan *marketing professional*
Dobriansky, Paula Jon *business and communications executive, consultant*
Dorsey, William Robert, III *computer company executive*
DuPlain, Jan *public relations executive*
Ellis, Steven George *public relations and international political consultant*
Erumsele, Andrew Akhigbe *development policy analyst*
Fahmy, Ibrahim Mounir *hotel executive*
Fairchild, Samuel Wilson *professional services company executive, former federal agency administrator*
Farrell, June Martinick *public relations executive*
Flanagan, Francis Dennis *retired corporate executive*
Foreman, Carol Lee Tucker *corporate executive*
Fuller, Edwin Daniel *hotel executive*
Furash, Edward E. *management consultant, author, lecturer*
Gibbons, Samuel Melville (Sam Gibbons) *business executive, former congressman*
Goldstein, Irving *communications company executive*
Gottlieb, Anita Faye *management consultant*
Grant, Carl N. *communications executive*
Gunderson, Steve Craig *consultant, former congressman*
Guzda, Henry Peter *industrial relations specialist*
Hanback, Hazel Marie Smallwood *management consultant*
Hannaford, Peter Dor *public relations executive*
Harrison, Emmett Bruce, Jr. *public relations counselor*
Havlicek, Franklin J. *communications executive*
Hayes, James Alison *business executive, former congressman*
Helms, Richard McGarrah *international consultant, former ambassador*
Higgins, James Henry, III *marketing executive*
Hoffmann, Melane Kinney *marketing and public relations executive, writer*
Holland, James Ricks *public relations executive, association executive*
Holmes, Bradley Paul *information technology management consultant*
Hoving, John Hannes Forester *consulting firm executive*
Howe, Fisher *management consultant, former government official*
Huberman, Benjamin *technology consultant*
Huggins, James Bernard *corporate executive*
Krejci, Stanley Leon *executive search consultant*
Kusnet, David *communications executive, speechwriter*
Lambert, Deborah Ketchum *public relations executive*
†Lasko, Joel *company executive*
Lee, Ronald Barry *marketing company executive, former army officer*
Leibach, Dale W. *public relations executive*
Leslie, John William *public relations and advertising executive*
Lewis, William Walker *management consultant*
Lilley, William, III *communications business consultant*
Lisboa-Farrow, Elizabeth Oliver *public and government relations consultant*
Lombard, Judith Marie *human resource policy specialist*
Luikart, Fordyce Whitney *management consultant*
Maddock, Jerome Torrence *information services specialist*
Mansfield, Edward Patrick, Jr. *advertising executive*
Mantyla, Karen *sales executive*
Marriott, John Willard, Jr. *hotel and food service chain executive*
Marumoto, William Hideo *management consultant*
McBride, Jonathan Evans *executive search company executive*
McLaughlin, John *broadcast executive, television producer, political commentator, journalist*
McLennan, Barbara Nancy *management consultant*
McMahon, Debra Brylawski *management consultant*
Medalie, Susan Diane *management consultant*
Miller, Robert Allen *hotel executive*
Millian, Kenneth Young *public policy consultant*
Moe, Ronald Chesney *public administration researcher*
Moore, Bob Stahly *communications executive*
Nelson, Larry Dean *telecommunications and computer systems company executive, consultant*
Newton, Hugh C. *public relations executive*
Nohe, Richard Edgar *telecommunications executive*
Norman, William Stanley *travel and tourism executive*
O'Connor, Tom *corporate executive, management consultant*
Oliver-Simon, Gloria Craig *human resources advisor, consultant, lawyer*
Olson, Walter Justus, Jr. *management consultant*
Orski, C. Kenneth *consulting company executive, lawyer*
Palumbo, Benjamin Lewis *public affairs consulting company executive*
Patrick, Janet Cline *personnel company executive*
Payne, Michael Lee *association management executive*
Pedersen, Wesley Niels *public relations and public affairs executive*
Petito, Margaret L. *public relations executive, consultant*
Pfeiffer, Leonard, IV *executive recruiter, consultant*
Pines, Wayne Lloyd *public relations counselor*
Powell, Joseph Lester (Jody Powell) *public relations executive*
Pucie, Charles R., Jr. *public affairs executive*
Pyle, Robert Noble *public relations executive*
Rafshoon, Gerald Monroe *communications executive*
Rainey, Jean Osgood *public relations executive*
Rausch, Howard *information service executive*
Reed, Travis Dean *public relations executive*
Rice, Lois Dickson *former computer company executive*
Rosebush, James Scott *international management and public affairs consultant, former government official*
Rosenthal, Aaron *management consultant*
Rotunda, Donald Theodore *public relations consultant*
Schick, Michael William *public relations consultant*
Schlossberg, Stephen I. *management consultant*
Schriever, Bernard Adolph *management consultant*
Seats, Peggy Chisolm *marketing executive*
Shaw, Anesther O(live) *university administrative staff member*
Sills, Hilary H. *public relations executive*
Silverman, Alvin Michaels *public relations consultant*
Silverman, Marcia *public relations executive*
Sisco, Joseph John *management consultant, corporation director, educator, government official*
Skol, Michael *management consultant*
Slagle, Larry B. *human resources specialist*
Sonnenfeldt, Marjorie Hecht *public relations executive, consultant*
Stringer, Dann Pollard *executive search firm executive*
Talley, Kevin David *public relations executive*
Tanham, George Kilpatrick *retired research company executive*
Tate, Sheila Burke *public relations executive*
Tiefel, William Reginald *hotel company executive*
Timmons, William Evan *corporate executive*
Timperlake, Edward Thomas *professional staff member of Congress*
Trowbridge, Alexander Buel, Jr. *business consultant*
Turner, Jean-Louise *special events manager*
Veblen, Thomas Clayton *management consultant*
Wade, Robert Hirsch Beard *international consultant, former government and educational association official*
Walker, Ronald Hugh *executive search company executive*
Walker, Savannah T. *executive assistant, legislative assistant*
Weiss, Paul Thomas *management consultant*
Welles, Judith *public affairs executive*
Wertheim, Mitzi Mallina *technology company executive*
Wheeler, Thomas Edgar *communications technology executive*
Whittlesey, Judith Holloway *public relations executive*
Yulish, Charles Barry *public affairs executive*
Zion, Roger H. *consulting firm executive, former congressman*

## FLORIDA

**Amelia Island**
Harman, John Robert, Jr. *management consultant*

**Atlantic Beach**
Buell, Victor Paul *marketing educator, author, editor*
Hayward, John Tucker *management consultant*

**Boca Grande**
Dyche, David Bennett, Jr. *management consultant*

**Boca Raton**
Albrecht, Arthur John *advertising agency executive*
†Beck, Louis S. *hotel executive*
Dorfman, Allen Bernard *international management consultant*
Dunhill, Robert W. *advertising direct mail executive*
Epstein, Barry R. *public relations counselor*
†Faust, Charles *hotel executive*
Finegold, Ronald *computer service executive*
Houraney, William George *marketing and public relations executive*
Langbort, Polly *retired advertising executive*
Miller, Kenneth Roy *management consultant*
Monroe, William Lewis *human resources executive*
Posner, Sidney *advertising executive*
Rosner, M. Norton *business systems and financial services company executive*
Rothbaum, Ira *retired advertising and marketing executive*
Saffir, Leonard *public relations executive*
Turner, Lisa Phillips *human resources executive*

**Bonita Springs**
St. Mary, Edward Sylvester *direct mail marketing company executive*
Snedden, James Douglas *retired health service management consultant*

**Boynton Beach**
Bloede, Victor Gustav *retired advertising executive*
Ganz, Samuel *human resource and management professional*
Geltner, Sharon *communications executive*
Koteen, Jack *management consultant, writer*
Oliveti, Susan Gail *sales promotion and public relations executive*

**Bradenton**
Jones, Horace Charles *former sales company executive*
Robinson, Hugh R. *retired marketing executive*

**Brandon**
Williamson, Robert Charles *marketing executive*

**Cape Coral**
Andert-Schmidt, Darlene *management consultant and trainer*

**Casselberry**
Medin, A. Louis *computer company executive*

**Clearwater**
Donahue, Katherine Mary *sales executive*
Eshenbaugh, William Arthur *sales executive*
Raymund, Steven A. *computer company executive*
Rose, Susan Carol *restaurant executive, chef, consultant*
Sontag, Peter Michael *travel management company executive*

**Cocoa**
Parker, Mary Patrice *management consultant*

**Cocoa Beach**
Pearson, Patricia Kelley *marketing representative*

**Coral Gables**
Bishopric, Susan Ehrlich *public relations executive*
Hammes, Therese Marie (Terry) *advertising, public relations and marketing executive*
Hertz, Arthur Herman *business executive*
Hertz, David Bendel *management consultant, educator, lawyer*
Ramsey, John Hansberry *executive search firm executive, investment banker*

**Daytona Beach**
Furstman, Shirley Elsie Daddow *advertising executive*

**Deerfield Beach**
Moran, James M. *automotive sales executive*
Van Arnem, Harold Louis *marketing professional*

**Defuniak Springs**
Karger, Delmar William *industrial engineering and management consultant*

**Delray Beach**
Gaffey, Thomas Michael, Jr. *consumer products executive*
Randall, Priscilla Richmond *travel executive*

**Deltona**
Zagnoli, Roland Candiano *management and marketing consultant, pharmacist*

**Fort Lauderdale**
Bimstein, Benjamin William *caterer, chef*
Cumerford, William Richard *fund raising and public relations executive*
Fine, Howard Alan *travel industry executive*
Flynn, Donald F. *entertainment company executive*
Gerbino, John *advertising executive*

Golnick, Leon Shaffer advertising and marketing executive
Goodstein, Richard George sales and management consultant
Honahan, H(enry) Robert motion picture theatre executive
Jotcham, Thomas Denis marketing communications consultant
Kobert, Norman Noah asset management consultant
Koch, Katherine Rose communications executive
Motes, Joseph Mark cruise and convention promotion company executive
Olen, Milton William, Jr. marketing executive
Russo, Thomas Joseph hospitality and consumer durables industry executive
Sorensen, Allan Chresten service company executive
Vasquez, William Leroy marketing professional, educator

### Fort Myers
Fromm, Winfield Eric retired corporate executive, engineering consultant and investor
Garside, Marlene Elizabeth advertising executive
Ranney, Mary Elizabeth business executive
Ryan, William Joseph communications company executive
Zupko, Arthur George consultant to drug industry, retired college administrator

### Fort Myers Beach
Caracciolo, Francis Samuel management consultant

### Fort Pierce
Hurley, William Joseph retired information systems executive
Thoma, Richard William chemical safety and waste management consultant

### Gainesville
Felton, John Walter public relations executive

### Gulf Breeze
Strength, Janis Grace management executive, educator

### Havana
Beare, Muriel Anita Nikki public relations executive, author

### Hialeah
Edelcup, Norman Scott management and financial consultant

### Highland Bch
Wegman, Harold Hugh management consultant

### Highland Beach
Karp, Richard M. advertising agency executive
Summers, James Irvin retired advertising executive

### Hollywood
Angstrom, Wayne Raymond communications executive
Cowan, Irving real estate owner, developer
Ladin, Eugene communications company executive
Singer, Saul food industry execurive, retired surgeon

### Hudson
Miller, Mary Jeannette office management specialist

### Indian Rocks Beach
Mortensen, James E. management consultant
Sullivan, Paul William communications specialist

### Jacksonville
Bodkin, Ruby Pate corporate executive, real estate broker, educator
Constantini, JoAnn M. information management consultant
Davis, A. Dano grocery store chain executive
Fahner, Harold Thomas marketing executive
Holmes, Ray Edward human resources specialist
Humm, Charles Allen sales and marketing professional
Kelly, Patrick Chastain sales executive
Lestinger, Alan company executive
Motsett, Charles Bourke sales and marketing executive
Schramm, Bernard Charles, Jr. advertising agency executive
Sederbaum, William marketing executive

### Jupiter
Taylor, Claude J. sales executive, consultant

### Key Biscayne
Duffy, Earl Gavin hotel executive
Navarro, Antonio (Luis) public relations executive

### Key Largo
Chevins, Anthony Charles retired advertising agency executive

### Lady Lake
Langevin, Thomas Harvey higher education consultant

### Lake Buena Vista
Lomonosoff, James Marc marketing executive
Nunis, Richard A. amusement parks executive
Parke, Robert Leon communications executive

### Lake Park
Anderson, Mark Stephen recovery company executive

### Lake Worth
Bell, Melvin management consultant
Gorman-Gordley, Marcie Sothern personal care industry franchise executive
Stevens, William John management consultant, former association executive

### Lakeland
Jenkins, Howard M. supermarket executive
Meads, Walter Frederick executive recruitment consultant
Siedle, Robert Douglas management consultant

### Largo
Ray, Roger Buchanan retired communications executive, lawyer

### Leesburg
Entorf, Richard Carl management consultant

### Longboat Key
Cook, James Winfield Clinton sales and marketing company executive
Sandy, William Haskell training and communications systems executive
Schoenberg, Lawrence Joseph computer services company executive

### Longwood
Bernabei, Raymond management consultant
Brooker, Robert Elton corporate executive
Faller, Donald E. marketing and operations executive
Walters, Philip Raymond foundation executive

### Lynn Haven
Goebert, Kimberly Mae information systems specialist

### Melbourne
Boyd, Joseph Aubrey communications company executive
Costa, Manuel Antone recreational facility manager
Farmer, Phillip W. company executive
Gabriel, Roger Eugene management consulting executive
Ott, James Forgan financial executive
Vilardebo, Angie Marie management consultant, parochial school educator

### Miami
Argibay, Jorge Luis information systems firm executive and founder
Cole, Todd Godwin management consultant transportation
Collins, Susan Ford leadership consultant
Cubas, Jose M(anuel) advertising agency executive
Daoud, Abraham Joseph, IV funeral director, former police officer
Dye, H. Michael marketing executive
Evans, Peter Kenneth advertising executive
Frost, Philip company executive
Le Duc, Albert Louis, Jr. management consultant
†Lefton, Donald E. hotel executive
Neuman, Susan Catherine public relations and marketing consultant
Porter, Charles King advertising executive
Rothchild, Howard Leslie advertising executive
Rubin, Bruce Stuart public relations executive
Schwartz, Gerald public relations and fundraising agency executive
Shapiro, Samuel Bernard management consultant
Silva, Felipe former tobacco company executive
Strong, Charles Robert waste management administrator
Strul, Gene M. communications executive
Weiser, Ralph Raphael business executive
Weiser, Sherwood Manuel hotel and corporation executive, lawyer
Whittington, Robert Wallace corporate professional, pianist

### Miami Beach
Marcus, Eileen public relations and advertising executive

### Mount Dora
Hensinger, Margaret Elizabeth horticultural and agricultural advertising and marketing executive

### Naples
Berman, Robert S. marketing consultant
Censits, Richard John business consultant
Hochschwender, Herman Karl international consultant
Hughes, Laura Elizabeth resort and recreational facility executive
Kleinrock, Virginia Barry public relations executive
Marshall, Charles communications company executive
Moore, Mechlin Dongan communications executive, marketing consultant
Quigley, Jack Allen service company executive
Smarg, Richard Michael insurance and employee benefits specialist

### New Port Richey
Miller-Chermely, Dorothy L. sales executive
Oliveto, Frank Louis recreation consultant

### Nokomis
Halladay, Laurie Ann public relations consultant, former franchise executive

### North Miami
Paul, Joseph B. information technology executive

### Ocala
Kaplan, Judith Helene company executive

### Okeechobee
Hedges, Bobette Lynn business administrator

### Oldsmar
Brunner, George Matthew management consultant, former business executive

### Orlando
†Brazell, Stanley Harold information systems specialist, Navy officer
Connolly, Joseph Francis, II defense company executive, government consultant
Davis, William Albert theme park director
Hwang, Miriam information technology specialist
Moltzon, Richard Francis manufacturing executive
Neiman, Norman aerospace business and marketing executive
Pantuso, Vincent Joseph food service consultant
Yesawich, Peter Charles advertising executive

### Ormond Beach
Coke, C(hauncey) Eugene consulting company executive, scientist, educator, author

### Palm Beach
Druck, Kalman Breschel public relations counselor
Robb, David Buzby, Jr. financial services company executive, lawyer
Tremain, Alan hotel executive

### Palm Beach Gardens
Mendelson, Richard Donald former communications company executive
Wackenhut, Richard Russell security company executive

### Palm City
Thompson, George Lee consulting company executive

### Palm Coast
Linnen, Thomas Francis international strategic management consulting firm executive

### Panama City
Dykes, James Edgar advertising educator, consultant

### Placida
Grissom, Joseph Carol retired leasing and investments business executive

### Pompano Beach
Crandell, K(enneth) James management and strategic planning consultant, entrepreneur

### Ponte Vedra Beach
Scheller, Sanford Gregory printing company executive

### Port Charlotte
Reynolds, Helen Elizabeth management services consultant

### Punta Gorda
Harrington, John Vincent retired communications company executive, engineer, educator

### Riverview
Till, Beatriz Maria international business consultant, translator

### Rockledge
Mitchell, Virginia Brinkman development associate

### Safety Harbor
Fay, Carolyn M. education marketing business owner

### Saint Augustine
Tuseo, Norbert Joseph John marketing executive, consultant

### Saint Petersburg
Kubiet, Leo Lawrence newspaper advertising and marketing executive
Lau, Michele Denise advertising consultant, sales trainer, television personality
Layton, William George computer company executive, management consultant, human resources executive
Naimoli, Raymond Anthony infosystems specialist, financial consultant
Pyle, William Carmody human resource management educator, researcher
Silver, Lawrence Alan marketing executive
Söderberg, Bo Sigfrid business executive
Stevens, Edward Ira information systems educator

### Sanibel
Brodbeck, William Jan marketing consultant, speaker
Lautenbach, Terry Robert information systems and communications executive
Sheldon, Nancy Way environmental management consultant

### Sarasota
Beck, Robert Alfred hotel administration educator
Blazon-Popper, Denise G. sales executive
Campbell, Donna Marie telecommunications executive
Feder, Allan Appel management executive, consultant
Fendrick, Alan Burton retired advertising executive
Gittelson, Bernard public relations consultant, author, lecturer
Honner Sutherland, B. Joan advertising executive
Mattran, Donald Albert management consultant, educator
Neeley, Delmar George human resources consultant
Poppel, Harvey Lee management consultant
Schersten, H. Donald management consultant, realtor, mortgage broker
Shulman, Arthur communications executive
Simon, Joseph Patrick food services executive
Skelton, Howard Clifton advertising and public relations executive
Stickler, Daniel Lee health care management consultant
White, Will Walter, III public relations consultant, writer

### Shalimar
Kelly, Kathleen Suzanne marketing professional

### Stuart
DeRubertis, Patricia Sandra software company executive

### Tallahassee
Boutwell, Wallace Kenneth, Jr. management consultant, health care executive
Marshall, Stanley former educator, business executive
Penson, Edward Martin management consulting company executive

### Tampa
†Callen, David H. hotel executive
Christopher, Wilford Scott public relations consultant
DeVine, B. Mack management consultant
Gamble, Mary G(race) marketing and quality professional
Heuer, Martin temporary services executive
Kessen, George William employment agency manager
Koopmann, Reta Collene sales executive
Mangiapane, Joseph Arthur consulting company executive, applied mechanics consultant
Silver, Paul Robert marketing executive, consultant
Williams, Yvonne G. corporate trainer

### Tarpon Springs
Dempster, Richard Vreeland environmental company executive

### Tavernier
Mabbs, Edward Carl retired management consultant

### Tequesta
Vollmer, James E. consulting company executive

### Venice
Bluhm, Barbara Jean communications agency executive
Christy, Audrey Meyer public relations consultant
Dodderidge, Richard William retired marketing executive
McEntee, Robert Edward management consultant
Ogan, Russell Griffith business executive, retired air force officer

### Vero Beach
Calevas, Harry Powell management consultant
Fisher, Andrew management consultant
Halan, John Paul human resources executive
McNamara, John J(oseph) advertising executive, writer
Nichols, Carl Wheeler retired advertising agency executive

### Wellington
Jankus, Alfred Peter international management and marketing consultant
Patterson, Lydia Ross industrial relations specialist, consulting company executive

### West Palm Beach
Alimanestianu, Calin retired hotel consultant
Diener, Bert former food broker, artist
Ronan, William John management consultant
Stauderman, Bruce Ford advertising executive, writer

### Winter Haven
Cover, Norman Bernard retired electronic data processing administrator

### Winter Springs
Monopoli, Daniel Marco computer company executive

## GEORGIA

### Acworth
Meyer, Mary Coeli management consultant

### Ailey
Windsor, James Thomas, Jr. printing company executive, newspaper publisher

### Albany
Ezeamii, Hyacinth Chinedum public administration educator

### Alpharetta
Bobo, Genelle Tant (Nell Bobo) office administrator
Esher, Brian Richard environmental company executive
Woodson, Al Curtis software company executive, software engineer

### Ashburn
Paulk, Anna Marie office manager

### Athens
Cutlip, Scott Munson public relations educator, former university dean
Hofer, Charles Warren strategic management, entrepreneurship educator, consultant
Lane, Walter Ronald, Jr. advertising executive, educator

### Atlanta
Allio, Robert John management consultant, educator
Ashley, John Bryan software executive, management consultant
Barnett, Elizabeth Hale organizational consultant
Boyle, Robert Daniel management consultant, business process reengineering
Brown-Olmstead, Amanda public relations executive
Buoch, William Thomas corporate executive
Burge, William Lee retired business information executive
Carlos, Michael C. wine, spirits and linen service wholesale executive
Chaiet, Alan Howard advertising agency executive
Chasen, Sylvan Herbert computer applications consultant, investment advisor
Choa, Walter Kong technical service professional
Cohn, Bob public relations executive
Cooper, Thomas Luther retired printing company executive
Darden, Claibourne Henry, Jr. marketing professional
Delahanty, Edward Lawrence management consultant
Duquette, Diana Marie company official
Dysart, Benjamin Clay, III environmental consultant, conservationist, engineer
Ehrlich, Jeffrey data processing company executive
Farley, Charles P. public relations executive
Fitzgerald, David Patrick advertising agency executive
Flinn, Michael Joseph marketing executive
Fuqua, John Brooks retired consumer products and services company executive
Gable, Carl Irwin business consultant, private investor, lawyer
Gelardi, Robert Charles trade association executive, consultant
Goldstein, Burton Benjamin, Jr. communications executive
Goodwin, George Evans public relations executive
Hoffman, Fred L. human resources professional

House, Donald Lee, Sr. *software executive, private investor, management consultant*
Invester, M. Douglas *consumer products company executive*
Jennings, Carol *marketing executive*
Johnston, Kevin Richard *marketing and customer service executive, consultant*
Jorgensen, Alfred H. *computer software and data communications executive*
Kaiser, Fred *computer leasing company executive*
Kent, Philip *communications executive*
Laubscher, Robert James *consumer products company executive*
Love, William Jenkins *sales and marketing executive*
Malhotra, Naresh Kumar *management educator*
Massey, Charles Knox, Jr. *advertising agency executive*
McKenzie, Kay Branch *public relations executive*
McLean, Ephraim Rankin *information systems educator*
Miles, John Karl *marketing executive*
Mills, Stephen Nathaniel *computer software company executive*
Moore, Linda Kathleen *personnel agency executive*
Mullenix, Kathy Ann *relocation company executive*
Overstreet, Jim *public relations executive*
Pace, Wayne H. *communications executive*
Parr, Sandra Hardy *government affairs administrator*
Powers, Esther Safir *organizational consultant*
Raper, Charles Albert *retired management consultant*
Robbins, James O. *advertising executive*
Rosenberg, George A. *public relations company executive*
Ryan, J. Bruce *health care management consulting executive*
Shelton, Robert Warren *marketing executive*
Sherry, Henry Ivan *marketing consultant*
Shivers, Jane *corporate communications executive, director*
Simms, Arthur Benjamin *management consultant, financier*
Smith, David Doyle *international management consultant, consulting engineer*
Stormont, Richard Mansfield *hotel executive*
Strong-Tidman, Virginia Adele *marketing and advertising executive*
Summerlin, Glenn Wood *advertising executive*
Thomas, Mable *communications company executive, former state legislator*
Tomaszewski, Richard Paul *market representation specialist*
Turner, Michael Griswold *advertising executive, writer*
Verrill, F. Glenn *advertising executive*
Wells, Everett Clayton, Jr. *marketing professional*
White, Ronald Leon *financial management consultant*
Wittenstein, Michael David *marketing professional*
Yarnell, Jeffrey Alan *regional credit executive*
Zunde, Pranas *information science educator, researcher*

### Austell
Friedrich, Stephen Miro *credit bureau company executive*

### Columbus
Zallen, Harold *corporate executive, scientist, former university official*

### Dalton
Ashworth, Robert Vincent *data processing executive*

### Duluth
Galfas, Timothy, II *franchising and turnaround administrator*
Milaski, John Joseph *business transformation industry consultant*

### Fort Benning
Alles, Rodney Neal, Sr. *information management executive*

### Hazlehurst
Welsh, Michael Louis *business executive*

### Macon
Smith, Michael Charles *personnel director, human resources specialist*

### Marietta
Bradshaw, Rod Eric *personnel consultant*
Johnson, Herbert Frederick *sales executive, former university administrator, librarian*
Overton, Bruce *personnel executive, consultant*
Smith, Baker Armstrong *management executive, lawyer*
Smith, Beverly Ann Evans *performance management consultant*
Spann, George William *management consultant*

### Newnan
Andrews, Rowena *public relations executive*

### Norcross
Cole, David Winslow *personal care industry executive*
Emanuele, R.M. *business executive*
Manoukian, Rita Chake *sales executive*
Sherwood, Kenneth Wesley *information systems executive, consultant*
Young, Andrea C. *communications executive*

### Pine Mountain
Callaway, Howard Hollis *business executive*

### Robins AFB
Corley, Rose Ann McAfee *customer service representative*

### Roswell
Burgess, John Frank *management consultant, former utility executive, former army officer*
Jordan, DuPree, Jr. *management consultant, educator, journalist, publisher, business executive*

### Saint Simons Island
Riedeburg, Theodore *management consultant*
Sullivan, Barbara Boyle *management consultant*

### Savannah
Highsmith, Anna Bizzell *executive secretary*
Otter, John Martin, III *television advertising consultant, retired*
Priester, Horace Richard, Jr. *quality assurance professional*
Schafer, Thomas Wilson *advertising agency executive*
†Sheehy, Barry M. *management consultant*
Theis, Francis William *business executive*

### Smyrna
Wilding, Diane *marketing, financial and information systems executive*

### Suwanee
Tucker, George Maxwell, Sr. *interactive distribution company executive, business and political consultant*

### Tucker
Baker, Russ *executive search firm owner*
†Owens, W. Larry *hotel executive*

### Union City
Graham, John Hamilton, II *customer service specialist*

### Warm Springs
Barnes, Charles Gerald *historic site administrator*

## HAWAII

### Fort Shafter
Maruoka, Jo Ann Elizabeth *information systems manager*

### Hilo
Evans, Franklin Bachelder *marketing educator emeritus*

### Honolulu
Bossert, Philip Joseph *information systems executive*
Devenot, David Charles *human resource executive*
Kelley, Richard Roy *hotel executive*
Keogh, Richard John *firearms consultant*
Klink, Paul Leo *business executive*
O'Neill, Charles Kelly *marketing executive, former advertising agency executive*
Rho, Edward *information systems professional*
Shirai, Scott *communications executive*
Shoemaker, Forrest Hilton, Jr. *marketing and sales executive, consultant*
Simpson, Andrea Lynn *energy communications executive*
Smales, Fred Benson *corporate executive*
†Sorenson, Perry *resort facility executive*
Yamato, Kei C. *international business consultant*

### Kailua Kona
Causey, Gill Terry *recreation company executive*

### Kealakekua
Patton, David Wayne *health care executive*

### Kula
Rohlfing, Frederick William *travel executive, consultant, retired judge*

## IDAHO

### Boise
Beaumont, Pamela Jo *marketing professional*
Luthy, John Frederick *management consultant*
Pon-Brown, Kay Migyoku *technical marketing engineer*
Poore, Ralph Ezra, Jr. *public relations professional*
Wang, Xiaodong *corporate executive, consultant*
Wilson, Barbara Louise *communications executive*

### Driggs
Nelson, Robert E. *public relations executive, political consultant*

### Ketchum
Ziebarth, Robert Charles *management consultant*

## ILLINOIS

### Addison
Philipps, Louis Edward *data systems manufacturing company executive*

### Alton
Minsker, Robert Stanley *consultant, former industrial relations executive*

### Antioch
Dahl, Laurel Jean *human services administrator*

### Arlington Heights
Gabrielsen, Carol Ann *employment consulting company executive*
Leahigh, Alan Kent *association executive*
Morgan, David Ernest *computer and communications research executive*

### Barrington
Andler, Donald Andrew *marketing executive*
Edwards, Wilbur Shields *communications company executive*
Mathis, Jack David *advertising executive*
Smith, William Lewis *hotel executive*

### Barrington Hills
†Koten, John A. *retired communications executive*

### Bartlett
Miller, Kevin D. *corporate services executive*

### Bloomingdale
Konopinski, Virgil James *industrial hygienist*

### Bloomington
Daily, Jean A. *marketing executive, spokesperson*

### Blue Island
Friedrich, Charles William *corporate executive*

### Bolingbrook
Long, Charles Franklin *corporate communications executive*
Willadsen, Michael Chris *marketing professional, sales executive*

### Calumet City
Kovach, Joseph William *management consultant, psychologist, educator*

### Carbondale
Jugenheimer, Donald Wayne *advertising and communications educator, university administrator*

### Carmi
Edwards, Judith Elizabeth *advertising executive*

### Champaign
Knox, Charles Milton *purchasing agent, consultant*

### Chicago
Allen, Belle *management consulting firm executive, communications company executive*
Amberg, Thomas L. *public relations executive*
†Baglivo, Mary L. *client services administrator*
Bailey, Robert, Jr. *advertising executive*
Bard, John Franklin *consumer products executive*
Barnette, Dennis Arthur *management consultant*
Bayer, Gary Richard *advertising executive*
Beattie, Janet Holtzman *accounting firm executive*
Bechina, Melvin Jeremiah *leasing company executive*
Bensinger, Peter Benjamin *consulting firm executive*
Bergstrom, Betty Howard *consulting executive, foundation administrator*
Bernatowicz, Frank Allen *management consultant, expert witness*
Beugen, Joan Beth *communications company executive*
Biggles, Richard Robert *marketing executive*
†Black, James *advertising executive*
Borleis, Melvin William *management consultant*
Bowen, William Joseph *management consultant*
†Boyda, Debora *advertising executive*
Brandt, William Arthur, Jr. *consulting executive*
Brown, Faith A. *communications manager*
Buckley, Joseph Paul, III *polygraph specialist*
Bueschel, David Alan *management consultant*
Burack, Elmer Howard *management educator*
Case, Clyde Willard, Jr. *sales and marketing executive*
†Cass, Edward Roberts (Peter) *hotel and travel marketing professional*
Castorino, Sue *communications executive*
Choyke, Phyllis May Ford (Mrs. Arthur Davis Choyke, Jr.) *management executive, editor, poet*
†Clark, Erin M. *advertising executive*
Connelly, Kathleen Fitzgerald *public relations executive*
†Cornell, Rob *hotel executive*
Cox, Allan James *management consultant and sports executive*
Cushman, Aaron D. *public relations executive*
De Francesco, John Blaze, Jr. *public relations company executive*
Di Spigno, Guy Joseph *international management consultant, industrial psychologist*
Donovan, John Vincent *consulting company executive*
†Draft, Howard *advertising executive*
†Eastham, Dennis Michael *advertising executive*
Echols, M(ary) Evelyn *travel consultant*
Edelman, Daniel Joseph *public relations executive*
Feldman, Burton Gordon *printing company executive*
Fisher, Eugene *marketing executive*
Fisher, Lawrence Edgar *market research executive, anthropologist*
Fizdale, Richard *advertising agency executive*
Flagg, Michael James *communications and graphics company executive*
Foley, Joseph Lawrence *sales executive*
Freedman, Walter G. *corporate services executive*
Freidheim, Cyrus F., Jr. *management consultant*
Fullmer, Paul *public relations counselor*
Furcon, John Edward *management and organizational consultant*
Gardner, Howard Alan *travel marketing executive, travel writer and editor*
†Ginsburg, Dan *marketing company executive*
Gladden, Robert Wiley *corporate executive*
Glasser, James J. *leasing company executive, retired*
Goldring, Norman Max *advertising executive*
Gordon, Howard Lyon *advertising and marketing executive*
Grant, Paul Bernard *industrial relations educator*
Gray, Dawn Plambeck *public relations executive*
Greifenstein, Frederick John *software company executive*
Gross, Wendy S. *public relations consultant*
Grosso, James Alan *sales executive*
Haffner, Charles Christian, III *retired printing company executive*
†Hanika, Stephen D. *advertising executive*
Hansen, Carl R. *management consultant*
Harkna, Eric *advertising executive*
Haupt, Roger A. *advertising executive*
Hayden, Harrold Harrison *information company executive*
Heidrick, Gardner Wilson *management consultant*
Heidrick, Robert Lindsay *management consultant*
Hermann, Edward Robert *health engineer, educator, writer, consultant, hygieologist*
Hoey, Rita Marie *public relations executive*
Hofrichter, David Alan *management consultant*
Holmes, Colgate Frederick *hotel executive*
Holzer, Edwin *advertising executive*
†Howard, Will George *advertising executive*
Hughes, Sarah Gillette *consulting company executive*
†Hurley, Brian Xavier *advertising executive*
Iltis, John Frederic *advertising and public relations company executive*
Isaacs, Roger David *public relations executive*
†Jirchman, Donna *advertising executive*
Johnson, Robert Bruce *public relations executive*
Katz, Marilyn Faye *communications consultant, political strategist*
Kelly, Robert Donald *management consultant*
Keroff, William B. *advertising agency executive*
Kindzred, Diana *communications company executive*
Kipper, Barbara Levy *corporate executive*
Kobs, James Fred *advertising agency executive*
Kraus, Herbert Myron *public relations executive*
Kuhn, James Paul *management consultant*
Lane, Kenneth Edwin *retired advertising agency executive*
Larson, Paul William *public relations executive*
Lehman, George Morgan *food sales executive*
Leigh, Sherren *communications executive, editor, publisher*
Lesly, Philip *public relations counsel*
Lewy, Ralph I. *hotel executive*
Lynch, William Thomas, Jr. *advertising agency executive*
Lynnes, R. Milton *advertising executive*
†Mach, Kenneth *advertising executive*
Mahaffey, John Christopher *association executive*
†Mason, Bruce *advertising agency executive*
McConnell, E. Hoy, II *advertising executive*
McCullough, Richard Lawrence *advertising agency executive*
Menchin, Robert Stanley *marketing executive*
Meyer, Edward Paul *advertising executive*
Miller, Bernard Joseph, Jr. *advertising executive*
Miller, Paul McGrath, Jr. *executive search consulting company executive*
Minkus, Raymond David *communications and public relations executive*
Mitchell, Lee Mark *communications executive, investment fund manager, lawyer*
Nachman, Frederick J. *public relations executive*
Nelson, H(arry) Donald *communications executive*
Oates, James G. *advertising executive*
O'Connor, William Michael *executive search company executive*
Olins, Robert Abbot *communications research executive*
†Olson, Curtis D. *advertising executive*
O'Shea, Lynne Edeen *marketing executive, educator*
Paul, Ronald Neale *management consultant*
Pincus, Theodore Henry *public relations executive*
Plank, Betsy Ann (Mrs. Sherman V. Rosenfield) *public relations counsel*
Plotkin, Manuel D. *management consultant, educator, former corporate executive and government official*
Pritzker, Jay *travel company executive , lawyer*
Pritzker, Thomas Jay *lawyer, business executive*
Proctor, Barbara Gardner *advertising agency executive*
Prosperi, David Philip *public relations executive*
Provus, Barbara Lee *executive search consultant*
Raphaelson, Joel *retired advertising agency executive*
Reggio, Vito Anthony *management consultant*
Reid, Daniel James *public relations executive*
Reilly, Robert Frederick *valuation consultant*
Reitman, Jerry Irving *advertising agency executive*
Rich, S. Judith *public relations executive*
Robbins, Henry Zane *public relations and marketing executive*
†Robinson, Michael R. *advertising executive*
Rosenthal, Albert Jay *advertising agency executive*
Rydholm, Ralph Williams *advertising agency executive*
Sampson, Ronald A. *advertising executive*
Schindler, Judi(th Kay) *public relations executive, marketing consultant*
Schubert, Helen Celia *public relations executive*
Scott, Louis Edward *advertising agency executive*
Seaman, Irving, Jr. *public relations consultant*
Seemann, Rosalie Mary *international business association executive*
Shepherd, Daniel Marston *executive recruiter*
Shirley, Virginia Lee *advertising executive*
Sive, Rebecca Anne *public affairs company executive*
Small, Bruce W. *sales and marketing executive*
Smith, Jeffrey Earl *management consulting executive*
Smith, Scott Clybourn *media company executive*
Steingraber, Frederick George *management consultant*
Stern, Carl William, Jr. *management consultant*
Stone, James Howard *management consultant*
Stotter, David W. *marketing executive*
Streeto, Joseph Michael *catering company official*
Strubel, Ella Doyle *advertising executive*
Struggles, John Edward *management consultant*
Sweet, Charles Wheeler *executive recruiter*
Talbot, Pamela *public relations executive*
Teichner, Lester *management consulting executive*
Thomas, John Thieme *management consultant*
Tobaccowala, Rishad *marketing professional*
Tomek, Laura Lindemann *marketing executive*
Tripp, Marian Barlow Loofe *retired public relations company executive*
Turner, Cristina Benitez *advertising professional*
Tyler, W(illiam) Ed *printing company executive*
Van Den Hende, Fred J(oseph) *human resources executive*
†Vanover, Neil *advertising executive*
Varchetta, Felix R. *advertising agency executive*
Vilim, Nancy Catherine *advertising agency executive*
Wackerle, Frederick William *management consultant*
†Walters, Lawrence Charles *advertising executive*
Wang, Gung H. *management consultant*
Weaver, Donna Rae *company executive*
Weber, Donald B. *advertising and marketing executive*
Webster, Ronald D. *communications company executive*
Wiecek, Barbara Harriet *advertising executive*
Williams, David Arthur *marketing professional*
Williams, Mark H. *marketing communications agency executive*
Wooldridge, Patrice Marie *marketing professional, martial arts and meditation educator*

### Crete
Langer, Steven *human resources management consultant and industrial psychologist*

### De Kalb
Wit, Daniel *international consultant*

### Decatur
Blake, William Henry *credit and public relations consultant*
Bluhm, Myron Dean *sales professional*

### Deerfield
Gaples, Harry Seraphim *computer service company executive*
Kinzelberg, Harvey *leasing company executive*
Nelson, Richard Lawrence *public relations executive*
Plamondon, William N. *rental company executive*
Slavin, Craig Steven *management and franchising consultant*

### Des Plaines
†Daniele, Dan *hotel executive*
†Dolan, C. Michael *hotel executive*

**Junction City**
Werts, Merrill Harmon *management consultant*

**Kansas City**
Freund, Ronald S. *management consultant, marketing company executive*

**Lawrence**
Mackenzie, Kenneth Donald *management consultant, educator*
Schilling, John Michael *golf course executive*

**Lenexa**
Rayburn, George Marvin *business executive, investment executive*
White, Dirk Bradford *printing company executive*

**Manhattan**
Streeter, John Willis *information systems manager*

**Overland Park**
Haas, Kelley Weyforth *marketing and communications company executive*
Mealman, Glenn *corporate marketing executive*
Voska, Kathryn Caples *consultant, facilitator*

**Salina**
Ryan, Stephen Collister *funeral director*

**Shawnee Mission**
Albright, Richard Scott *marketing executive*
Findlay, Theodore Bernard *management consultant, motivational speaker*
Grady, William Earl *marketing executive*
Herring, Raymond Mark *strategic planning and organizational development*
Mindlin, Richard Barnett *market research executive*
Putman, Dale Cornelius *management consultant, lawyer*
Sack, Burton Marshall *restaurant company executive*
Savage, Thomas Joseph *executive, governance and planning consultant, educator, priest*

**Topeka**
Bronson, Kenneth Caldean *consultant, retired newspaper company executive*
Franklin, Benjamin Barnum *dinner club executive*
Randall, Elizabeth Ellen *press clippings company executive*
Vidricksen, Ben Eugene *food service executive, state legislator*

**Wichita**
Herr, Peter Helmut Friederich *sales executive*
Lair, Robert Louis *catering company executive*

## KENTUCKY

**Ashland**
Carter, David Edward *communications executive*

**Bardstown**
Willett, A. L. Thompson *public relations executive, consultant*

**Covington**
Sampson, Susan J. *marketing communications consultant, writer*
Surber, David Francis *public affairs consultant, journalist, television producer*

**Hopkinsville**
Neville, Thomas Lee *food service company executive*

**Lexington**
Blanchard, Richard Emile, Sr. *management services executive, consultant*
Carney, Robert Arthur *restaurant executive*
Charley, Nancy Jean *communications professional*
Dorio, Martin Matthew *material handling company executive*
Mitchell, John Charles *business executive*
Nathan, Richard Arnold *technology company executive*

**Louisville**
Brown, Owsley, II *diversified consumer products company executive*
Peden, Katherine Graham *industrial consultant*
Pepples, Ernest *tobacco company executive*
Swann, Rande Nortof *public relations executive*

## LOUISIANA

**Baton Rouge**
Crusemann, F(rederick) Ross *advertising agency official*

**Lafayette**
†Barnidge, Jack R. *safety management administrator*
Baudoin, Peter *family business consultant*
Sides, Larry Eugene *advertising executive*

**Mandeville**
Klein, Bernard Joseph *management specialist*

**Metairie**
Gereighty, Andrea Saunders *polling company executive, poet*
Grimm, John Lloyd *business executive, marketing professional*

**New Orleans**
Allerton, William, III *public relations executive*
Cook, Victor Joseph, Jr. *marketing educator, consultant*
Fertel, Ruth U. *restaurant owner*
Johnson, Arnold Ray *public relations executive*
Lambert, Olaf Cecil *hotel executive*
Womack, Edgar Allen, Jr. *technology executive*

**Shreveport**
Tullis, John Ledbetter *retired wholesale distributing company executive*

## MAINE

**Brooklin**
Schmidt, Klaus Dieter *management consultant, university administrator, marketing and management educator*

**Camden**
Lavenson, James H. *hotel industry executive*
Lavenson, Susan Barker *hotel corporate executive, consultant*

**Center Lovell**
Adams, Herbert Ryan *management consultant, retired clergyman, actor, director, educator, publishing executive*

**Ellsworth**
Becker, Ray Everett *management consultant*
Eustice, Russell Clifford *consulting company executive*

**Hartland**
Larochelle, Richard Clement *tanning company executive*

**Orono**
Perkins, Ralph Linwood *business executive, public health administration specialist*

**Portland**
End, William Thomas *business executive*
Hall, Christopher George Longden *management consultant*
Kendrick, Peter Murray *communications executive, investor*
Potter, Lillian Florence *business executive secretary*
Shaffer, James Burgess *communications executive*

**Sedgwick**
Mc Millan, Brockway *former communications executive*

**South Portland**
Howard, Eric Sevan *conservationist, environmental manager*

**Waterville**
Zukowski, Walter Henry *administrative science educator*

**York**
Peterson, Karen Ida *marketing research company executive*

## MARYLAND

**Aberdeen**
Engel, James Harry *computer company executive*

**Accokeek**
Aguirre-Sacasa, Rafael Eugenio *marketing administrator*

**Annapolis**
Biddle, A.G.W., III (Jack Biddle) *computer industry executive*
Carman, Anne *management consultant*
†Erickson, Donald C. *executive*
Jefferson, Ralph Harvey *international affairs consultant*
Montague, Brian John *consulting company executive*

**Arnold**
Barrett, John Anthony *publishing and printing company financial executive*

**Baldwin**
Decker, James Ludlow *management consultant*

**Baltimore**
Brotman, Phyllis Block *advertising and public relations executive*
Brown, Gerald Curtis *retired army officer, engineering executive*
Dodge, Calvert Renaul *education and training executive, author, educator*
Eisner, Henry Wolfgang *advertising executive*
Fried, Herbert Daniel *advertising executive*
Friedman, Maria Andre *public relations executive*
Greenspan, Arnold Michael *computer company executive*
Hug, Richard Ernest *environmental company executive*
†Kleiner, Arnold Joel *television executive*
Lowenthal, Henry *retired greeting card company executive*
Messinger, Scott James *advertising executive*
Park, Mary Woodfill *information consultant*
Pollard, Shirley *employment training director, consultant*
†Robinson, Brooks Calbert, Jr. *former professional baseball player, TV commentator, business consultant*
Roland, Donald Edward *advertising executive*
Rolland, Donald F. *printing company executive*
Talbot, Donald Roy *consulting services executive*

**Beltsville**
Quirk, Frank Joseph *management consulting company executive*

**Bethesda**
Barber, Arthur Whiting *communications company executive*
Barquín, Ramón Carlos *consulting company executive*
Brown, Earle Palmer *advertising agency executive*
Cody, Thomas Gerald *management consultant, writer*
Cutting, Mary Dorothea *audio and audio-visual communications company executive*
Deane, Leon *retired company executive*
Estrin, Melvyn J. *computer products company executive*
Feldman, Valerie Michele *marketing professional*
Goldschmidt, Peter Graham *physician executive, business development consultant*
†Herrett, Richard Allison *agricultural research institute administrator*
Kriegsman, William Edwin *consulting firm executive*
Lauret, Curtis Bernard, Jr. *international marketing professional*
Levin, Carl *public and government relations consultant*
Liakos, James Christ *business manager*
McClure, Brooks *management consultant*
Mc Gurn, Barrett *communications executive, writer*
Moseley, Chris Rosser *marketing executive*
Shellow, Robert *management service company executive, consultant*
Southwick, Paul *retired public relations executive*
Spector, Melbourne Louis *management consultant*
Spivak, Alvin A. *retired public relations executive*
Van Dyke, Joseph Gary Owen *computer consulting executive*
Wertheimer, Franc *retired corporate executive*

**Bowie**
Purcell, Steven Richard *international management consultant, engineer, economist*

**Brooklandville**
Miller, Paul George *computer company executive*

**Catonsville**
Ahalt, Mary Jane *management consultant*

**Chestertown**
Gordon, James Braund *management consultant*
Schreiber, Harry, Jr. *management consultant*
Van Houten, Elizabeth Ann *corporate communications executive*

**Chevy Chase**
Corrigan, Robert Foster *business consultant, retired diplomat*
Michaelis, Michael *management and technical consultant*
Schlegel, John Frederick *management consultant, speaker, trainer*
Zurkowski, Paul George *information company executive*

**Cockeysville Hunt Valley**
Elkin, Lois Shanman *business systems company executive*
Simms, Charles Averill *environmental management company executive*
Whitehurst, William Wilfred, Jr. *management consultant*

**College Park**
Armstrong, William Francis *purchasing professional*
Greer, Thomas Vernon *business consultant and educator*
Holder, Sallie Lou *training and meeting management consultant*

**Columbia**
Bretz, Thurman Wilbur *corporate professional*
Letaw, Harry, Jr. *technology corporation executive*
Steele, Richard J. *management consultant*

**Easton**
Burns, Michael Joseph *operations and sales-marketing executive*

**Elkton**
Jasinski-Caldwell, Mary L. *company executive*

**Ellicott City**
Gleaves, Leon Rogers *marketing and sales executive*
Neil, Fred Applestein *public relations executive*

**Fort Washington**
Fielding, Elizabeth M(ay) *public relations executive, editor, writer*

**Gaithersburg**
Brown, Dorothea Williams *technology consulting company executive*
Carey, John Edward *information services executive*
Ehrlich, Clifford John *hotel executive*
Flickinger, Harry Harner *organization and business executive, management consultant*
Wohl, Ronald H. *management consultant, writing and editorial expert*

**Germantown**
Shaw, Jack Allen *communications company executive*

**Greenbelt**
Beach, Linda Marie *total quality management professional*

**Harwood**
Pratt, Katherine Merrick *environmental consulting company executive*

**Hunt Valley**
Wilson, Donald Hurst, III *computer training services executive*

**Indian Head**
Wamsley, Barbara Simborski *public administration educator*

**Kensington**
†Roberts, Charles A. *construction safety/accident prevention expert*

**Lutherville**
Donaho, John Albert *consultant*

**Lutherville Timonium**
Chapman, Robert Breckenridge, III *retired company executive, consultant*

**Mitchellville**
Lauer, Michael Thomas *software company executive*
Simpich, William Morris *public affairs consultant*

**Odenton**
Mucha, John Frank *information systems professional*

**Olney**
Brady, Anita Kelley *training and organizational development executive*

**Phoenix**
Byrd, Harvey Clifford, III *information management company executive*

**Potomac**
DeVaney, Carol Susan *management consultant*
Fink, Daniel Julien *management consultant*
Rhode, Alfred Shimon *business consultant, educator*
Terragno, Paul James *information industry executive*

**Riverdale**
Gonzalez Arias, Victor Hugo *management executive*

**Rockville**
Belak, Michael James *information systems executive*
Carlton, Patricia Paletsky *marketing and business professional*
Isbister, James David *pharmaceutical business executive*
Keillor, Sharon Ann *computer company executive*
Leslie, John Walter *development consultant*
Morrison, Howard Irwin *computer services executive*
Nash, Jonathon Michael *program manager, mechanical engineer*
Selby, Clark Linwood, Jr. *sales executive*
Shaw, Robert William, Jr. *management consultant, venture capitalist*
Shelton, Wayne Vernon *professional services and systems integration company executive*
†Snyder, Robert M. *communication company executive*

**Silver Spring**
Burke, Gerard Patrick *business executive, lawyer*
Compton, Mary Beatrice Brown (Mrs. Ralph Theodore Compton) *public relations executive, writer*
Hedgepeth, Leroy J. *retired park director*
Hersey, David Floyd *information resources management consultant, retired government official*
Kendrick, James Earl *business consultant*
Kolodny, Debra Ruth *labor management consultant*
Lett, Cynthia Ellen Wein *marketing executive*
Perlmutter, Jerome Herbert *communications specialist*
Raphael, Coleman *business consultant*
Weger, William John *public relations executive*

**Stevensville**
Kepley, Thomas Alvin *management consultant*

**Tall Timbers**
Jensen, Paul Erik *marketing executive*

**Timonium**
Orlando, Alexander Mariano *international marketing and trade consultant*

**West River**
Bower, Catherine Downes *communications and public relations executive*

## MASSACHUSETTS

**Acton**
Leighton, Charles Milton *specialty consumer products company executive*
Webber, Howard Rodney *computer company executive*

**Andover**
Schmidt-Nelson, Martha Alice *communications and training executive, ergonomist*
Sintros, James Lee *management consultant, arbitrator*

**Arlington**
Hefferon, Lauren Jeanine *tour operator, business owner*

**Attleboro**
DeWerth, Gordon Henry *management consultant*

**Auburndale**
Gulotta, Victor *public relations executive, writer*

**Belmont**
Glines, Stephen Ramey *software industry executive*
Klein, Martin Samuel *management consulting executive*

**Beverly**
Barger, Richard Wilson *hotel executive*

**Boston**
Andrews, Kenneth Richmond *business administration educator*
Arnold, John David *management counselor, catalyst*
Bacon, A(delaide) Smoki *public relations consultant, radio and television host*
Berenson, Paul Stewart *advertising executive*
†Bronner, Michael *advertising executive*
Buchin, Stanley Ira *management consultant, educator*
Chandler, Harriette Levy *management consultant, educator, legislator*
Clarke, Terence Michael *public relations and advertising executive*
Cornwall, Deborah Joyce *consulting firm executive, management consultant*
Dowd, Peter Jerome *public relations executive*
Eskandarian, Edward *advertising agency executive*
Farkas, Charles Michael *management consultant*
Farrar, Constance Mosher *marketing executive*
Fausch, David Arthur *public relations executive*
Fonvielle, William Harold *management consultant*
Gould, John Joseph *communications executive*
Hayes, Andrew Wallace, II *consumer products company executive*
Hillman, Carol Barbara *communications executive*
Hoffman, S. Joseph *advertising agency executive*
Hunter, Durant Adams *executive search company executive*
Hurd, J. Nicholas *executive recruiting consultant, former banker*

Judson, Arnold Sidney *management consultant*
Kapioltas, John *hotel company executive*
King, Diane Marie *creative services national manager*
Lagarde, Jacques Yves *metal products company executive*
†Lawner, Ron *advertising executive*
†Lawson, Thomas Elsworth *advertising agency executive*
Luongo, C. Paul *public relations executive*
McGovern, Patrick J. *communications executive*
McLennan, Bernice Claire *human resources professional*
†Morrissey, Peter A. *public relations executive*
O'Block, Robert Paul *management consultant*
Rhinesmith, Stephen Headley *international management consultant*
Riccelli, Richard Joseph *advertising agency executive*
Saunders, Roger Alfred *hotel group executive*
Schrager, Mindy Rae *business professional*
Shapiro, Eli *business consultant, educator, economist*
Singer, Thomas Eric *industrial company executive*
Skinger, Kenneth Robert *communications executive, engineer, lawyer*
Slosberg, Mike *advertising executive*
Sonnabend, Roger Philip *hotel company executive*
Sullivan, John Louis, Jr. *retired search company executive*
Teixeira, Joseph *advertising executive*
Turillo, Michael Joseph, Jr. *management consultant*
Volk, Kristin *advertising agency executive*
Wilkes, Brent Ames *management consultant*
Willens, Alan Rush *management consultant*
Wilson, Robert Gould *management consultant*
Zeien, Alfred M. *consumer products company executive*

**Bourne**
Roper, Burns Worthington *retired opinion research company executive*

**Braintree**
Harris, Jeffrey Sherman *direct marketing company executive*
Lane, Barbara Ann *environmental company official, systems analyst*

**Brookline**
Walter, Helen Joy *executive director, teacher*

**Cambridge**
†Altshuler, David T. *software company executive*
Aspinall, Mara Glickman *marketing and general management professional*
Bloom, Kathryn Ruth *public relations executive*
Boghani, Ashok Balvantrai *consulting firm executive*
Branscomb, Anne Wells *communications consultant*
Davis, James Spencer *temporary service executive*
Dennis, Jack Bonnell *computer consultant*
Forrester, Jay Wright *management specialist, educator*
Greeno, J(ohn) Ladd *consulting company executive*
Huppe, Alex *public relations executive*
Kerpelman, Larry Cyril *consulting firm executive*
Knickrehm, Glenn Allen *management executive*
LaMantia, Charles Robert *management consulting company executive*
Levy, Stephen Raymond *high technology company executive*
Littlefield, Paul Damon *management consultant*
Marolda, Anthony Joseph *management consulting company executive*
Martin, Roger Lloyd *management consultant*
Mueller, Robert Kirk *management consulting company executive*
Rowley, Geoffrey Herbert *management consultant*
Tritter, Richard Paul *strategic planning consulting executive*
†Weber, Larry *public relations executive*

**Canton**
Ferrera, Arthur Rocco *food distribution company executive*
Pitts, Virginia M. *human resources executive*

**Carlisle**
Tema-Lyn, Laurie *management consultant*

**Charlestown**
Dickerson, Frank Secor, III *computer company executive*

**Chatham**
Anderson, Barbara Graham *philanthropic resources development consultant*
Miles, Robert Henry *management consultant, educator*

**Cohasset**
Rabstejnek, George John *executive*

**Concord**
Bloom, Edwin John, Jr. *human resources consultant*
Daltas, Arthur John *management consultant*
Eberle, William Denman *international management consultant*
Hogan, Daniel Bolten *management consultant*
Rarich, Anne Lippitt *management and organizational development consultant*

**Dedham**
Magner, Jerome Allen *entertainment company executive*
Redstone, Sumner Murray *entertainment company executive*

**Dennis**
Weilbacher, William Manning *advertising and marketing consultant*

**Dover**
Bonis, Laszlo Joseph *business executive, scientist*
Borel, Richard Wilson *communications executive, consultant*

**Duxbury**
Albritton, William Hoyle *training and consulting executive, lecturer, writer*
Erickson, Phyllis Traver *marketing executive*

**Falmouth**
Nolan, Edmund Francis *management consultant*

**Florence**
Park, Beverly Goodman *public relations professional*

**Foxboro**
Martin, Peter Gerard *infosystems specialist, consultant, teacher*

**Framingham**
Meador, Charles Lawrence *management and systems consultant, educator*
†Merrell, Therese Elizabeth *trade show production executive*

**Gardner**
McCarthy, Albert Henry *human resources executive*

**Gloucester**
Hausman, William Ray *fund raising and management consultant*
Lauenstein, Milton Charles *management consultant*

**Hopkinton**
Nickerson, Richard Gorham *research company executive*
Preston, William Hubbard *consultant to specialty businesses*

**Hull**
Anderson, Timothy Christopher *consulting company executive*

**Lexington**
Brick, Donald Bernard *consulting company executive*
Duboff, Robert Samuel *marketing professional*
Fray, Lionel Louis *management consultant*
Golden, John Joseph, Jr. *information systems executive*
Risch, Martin Donald *marketing-management consulting company executive*
Ross, Douglas Taylor *retired software company executive*

**Longmeadow**
Locklin, Wilbert Edwin *management consultant*

**Lowell**
Korkin, Steven Arthur *research and development company executive, industrial engineer*

**Marlborough**
Monia, Joan *management consultant*

**Marshfield**
Sostilio, Robert Francis *office equipment marketing executive*

**Marstons Mills**
Martin, Vincent George *management consultant*

**Maynard**
Palmer, Robert B. *computer company executive*

**Milton**
Gerring, Clifton, III *corporate executive*
Sgarlat, Mary Anne E. A. *public relations professional, entrepreneur*

**Nantucket**
Mercer, Richard Joseph *retired advertising executive, freelance writer*

**Natick**
Donovan, R. Michael *management consultant*
Strayton, Robert Gerard *public communications executive*

**Needham**
Kaplan, Steven F. *business management executive*

**New Bedford**
Anderson, James Linwood *pharmaceutical sales official*

**Newton**
Chlamtac, Imrich *computer company executive, educator*
Kosowsky, David I. *retired biotechnical company executive*

**North Reading**
Day, Ronald Elwin *management consultant*

**Norwell**
Case, David Knowlton *management consultant*

**Orleans**
Hiscock, Richard Carson *marine safety investigator*

**Palmer**
Dupuis, Robert Simeon *sales executive*

**Quincy**
Bierman, George William *technical consulting executive, food technologist*
Hall, John Raymond, Jr. *fire protection executive*
Levin, Robert Joseph *retail grocery chain store executive*
Young, Richard William *corporate director*

**Reading**
Donald, John Hepburn, II *quality assurance professional, consultant*
Neville, Elisabeth *computer applications specialist*
White, Karen Ruth Jones *information systems executive*

**Rockport**
Wiberg, Lars-Erik *human resources consultant*

**Roslindale**
Blomquist, Cecile La Chance *quality assurance professional, technologist*

**Salem**
Ettinger, Mort *marketing educator*

**Sheffield**
Velmans, Loet Abraham *retired public relations executive*

**South Orleans**
Burton, Robert William *retired office products executive*

**Stoughton**
Snyder, Mark Irwin *marketing and public relations executive*

**Stow**
Kulas, Frederick John *computer company executive*
Langenwalter, Gary Allan *manufacturing and management consulting company executive*
Vrablik, Edward A. *computer company executive, management consultant*

**Sudbury**
McCree, Paul William, Jr. *systems design and engineering company executive*

**Swansea**
Holmes, Henry (Hank Holmes) *advertising and marketing executive, editor*

**Waban**
Rossolimo, Alexander Nicholas *management consultant*

**Walpole**
Coleman, John Joseph *telephone company executive*

**Waltham**
Kalba, Kas *international communications consultant*
Kasputys, Joseph Edward *corporate executive, economist*
Large, G. Gordon M. *computer software company executive*
Nahigian, Alma Louise *technical documentation administrator*
Poduska, John William, Sr. *computer company executive*
Rodiger, William King *telecommunications and media industry consultant*

**Wellesley**
Goldberg, Pamela Winer *strategic consultant*
Nagler, Leon Gregory *management consultant, business executive*

**Wellesley Hills**
Coco, Samuel Barbin *venture consultant*

**Westfield**
Tower, Horace Linwood, III *consumer products company executive*

**Westford**
Tuttle, David Bauman *data processing executive*
Weston, Joan Spencer *production director, communications executive*

**Weston**
Paresky, David S. *travel company executive*
Stambaugh, Armstrong A., Jr. *restaurant and hotel executive*

**Weymouth**
Boers, Celia Ann *public relations executive*

**Wilbraham**
Anderson, Eric William *retired food service company executive*
O'Shaughnessy, Joseph A. *restaurant company executive*

**Williamstown**
Sprague, John Louis *management consultant*

**Winchester**
Brown, David A.B. *strategy consultant*
Cecich, Donald Edward *business executive*
Taggart, Ganson Powers *management consultant*

**Woburn**
Mehra, Raman Kumar *data processing executive, automation and control engineering researcher*

**Worcester**
Candib, Murray A. *business executive, retail management consultant*
Ullrich, Robert Albert *business management educator*

## MICHIGAN

**Ada**
†DeVos, Douglas Lee *sales company executive*
Van Andel, Jay *direct selling company executive*

**Ann Arbor**
Agno, John G. *management consultant*
Belcher, Louis David *marketing and operations executive, former mayor*
Foley, Daniel Ronald *business and personnel executive*
Lindsay, June Campbell McKee *communications executive*
Martin, Claude Raymond, Jr. *marketing consultant, educator*
Monaghan, Thomas Stephen *restaurant chain executive*
Pritts, Bradley Arthur, Jr. *management systems consultant*
Riley-Davis, Shirley Merle *advertising agency executive, marketing consultant, writer*

**Auburn Hills**
Wagner, Bruce Stanley *marketing communications executive*

**Beaverton**
Glenn, James *sales executive*

**Benton Harbor**
Goldin, Sol *marketing consultant*

**Bloomfield Hills**
Adams, Charles Francis *advertising and real estate executive*
Adams, Thomas Brooks *advertising consultant*
Benton, William Pettigrew *advertising agency executive*
Berline, James H. *advertising executive, public relations agency executive*
Bissell, John Howard *marketing executive*
Casey, John Patrick (Jack Casey) *public relations executive, political analyst*
†Mills, Peter Richard *advertising executive*
Pingel, John Spencer *advertising executive*
Weil, John William *technology management consultant*

**Brighton**
Bitten, Mary Josephine *quality consultant, municipal official*

**Charlotte**
Young, Everett J. *management consultant, agricultural economist*

**Dearborn**
Cassady, Kenneth Edward *creative and marketing analyst, public relations specialist, graphic artist*
Jelinek, John Joseph *public relations executive*

**Dearborn Heights**
Darin, Frank Victor John *management consultant*

**Detroit**
Bassett, Tina *communications executive*
Caldwell, John Thomas, Jr. *communications executive*
Czarnecki, Walter P. *truck rental company executive*
Dixson, J. B. *communications executive*
Go, Robert A. *management consultant*
Henry, William Lockwood *sales and marketing executive*
McCracken, Caron Francis *computer company executive, consultant*
McCracken, Ina *business executive*
Roberts, Seymour M. (Skip Roberts) *advertising agency executive*
Salter, Linda Lee *security officer*
Stanalajczo, Greg C. *computer services executive*
Tallet, Margaret Anne *theatre executive*
Werba, Gabriel *public relations consultant*

**East Lansing**
Jones, Kensinger *advertising executive*
Miracle, Gordon Eldon *advertising educator*
Wilson, R. Dale *marketing educator, consultant*

**Eaton Rapids**
Hall, Rebecca Ann *executive secretary*

**Farmington Hills**
Frederick, Raymond Joseph *sales engineering executive*

**Ferndale**
Gienapp, Helen Fischer *jewelry company owner*

**Franklin**
Vanderlaan, Richard B. *marketing company executive*

**Fraser**
Cannon, Christopher Perry *human resource development executive*

**Grand Rapids**
Bissell, Mark *consumer products company executive*
Hakala, Judyth Ann *data processing executive*
Sadler, David Gary *management executive*
Schwartz, Garry Albert *advertising executive*

**Grosse Pointe**
Blevins, William Edward *management consultant*
Mecke, Theodore Hart McCalla, Jr. *management consultant*
Thurber, Donald MacDonald Dickinson *public relations counsel*
Wilson, Henry Arthur, Jr. *management consultant*

**Holland**
Nelson, David Leonard *process management systems company executive*
Spoelhof, John *consumer products company executive*

**Interlochen**
Stolley, Alexander *advertising executive*

**Kalamazoo**
Freed, Karl Francis *professional planner*
Lawrence, William Joseph, Jr. *retired corporate executive*
Tracy, Joel Dean *marketing researcher*

**Lansing**
Hilbert, Virginia Lois *computer consultant and training executive*
Lowe, William Daniel *automotive company research executive, consultant*

**Mattawan**
Lough, Rick Leo *sales and marketing professional*

**Midland**
Hanes, James Henry *consulting business executive, lawyer*
Maneri, Remo R. *management consultant*

**Monroe**
Sewell, Robert Terrell, Jr. *executive search company owner*

**Mount Clemens**
Robinson, Earl, Jr. *marketing and economic research executive, transportation executive, business educator, retired air force officer*

**Novi**
Kinsey, Charles John *industrial auctioneer, consultant, cattle breeder, farmer*

**Plymouth**
Moore, Joan Elizabeth *human resources executive, lawyer*

**Port Huron**
Finch, Samuel Thomas *management consultant*

**Rapid City**
Coulson, John Selden *retired marketing executive*
Hefty, Duane Seymore *management consultant*

**Redford**
Flint, H. Howard, II *printing company executive*

**Rochester Hills**
Pfister, Karl Anton *industrial company executive*

**Royal Oak**
Stephens, Martha Foster *advertising executive*

**Saginaw**
Jernigan, Alvin, Jr. *automobile sales executive*
Loster, Gary Lee *personnel director*

**Saline**
Kausek, Albert Joseph *quality consultant, educator, former naval officer*

**Southfield**
Barnett, Marilyn *advertising agency executive*
Considine, John Joseph *advertising executive*
†Decerchio, John *advertising company executive*
Franco, Anthony M. *public relations executive*
†Kalter, Alan *advertising agency executive*
Koch, Albert Acheson *management consultant*
Maibach, Ben C., Jr. *service executive*
Matthes, Gerald Stephen *advertising agency executive*
Neman, Thomas Edward *advertising and marketing executive*
Romanoff, Stanley M., Jr. *human resource specialist*
Smith, Nancy Hohendorf *sales and marketing executive*

**Sturgis**
Newbrough, Edgar Truett *retired management consultant*

**Troy**
Adderley, Terence E. *corporate executive*
Baker, Ernest Waldo, Jr. *advertising executive*
Carr, Robin *advertising executive*
Hill, Richard A. *advertising executive*
Nikoui, Hossein Reza *quality assurance professional*

**Warren**
Gilbert, Suzanne Harris *advertising executive*
Schultz, Louis Michael *advertising agency executive*
Wallace, Jack Harold *employee development specialist, educator*

**West Bloomfield**
Meyers, Gerald Carl *management consultant, author, educator, lecturer, former automobile company executive*

## MINNESOTA

**Eden Prairie**
Cervilla, Constance Marlene *marketing consultant*
Knotek, Robert Frank *management consultant, educator*
Roth, Thomas *marketing executive*
Schulze, Richard M. *consumer products executive*
Verdoorn, Sid *food service executive*

**Edina**
Burdick, Lou Brum *public relations executive*
Hunt, David Claude *sales and marketing executive*
Slocum, Rosemarie R. *physician management search consultant*

**Hutchinson**
Graf, Laurance James *communications executive*

**Le Roy**
Erickson, Larry Alvin *electronics sales and marketing executive*

**Long Lake**
Tomhave, Beverly Korstad *corporate executive*

**Minneapolis**
Alcott, James Arthur *communications executive*
Anderson, Ron *advertising executive*
Beardsley, John Ray *public relations firm executive*
Bileydi, Sumer *advertising agency executive*
Brooks, Phillip *advertising executive*
Burns, Neal Murray *advertising agency executive*
Cardozo, Richard Nunez *marketing, entrepreneurship and business educator*
Cowles, John, III *management consultant, investor*
Cox, David Carson *media company executive*
Dunlap, William DeWayne, Jr. *advertising agency executive*
†Fallon, Patrick R. *advertising executive*
Ferner, David Charles *non-profit management and development consultant*
Fossum, John Anthony *industrial relations educator*
Gavin, Sara *public relations executive*
Goldstein, Mark David *advertising agency executive*
Johnson, Lola Norine *advertising and public relations executive, educator*
Koutsky, Dean Roger *advertising executive*
Lobeck, William E. *rental company executive*
Olson, Clifford Larry *management consultant, entrepreneur*
Perlman, Lawrence *business executive*
Pile, Robert Bennett *advertising executive, writer, consultant*
Read, John Conyers *industrial management*
Retzler, Kurt Egon *diversified management company executive, hospitality, travel and marketing company executive*
Sanger, Stephen W. *consumer products company executive*
Schultz, Louis Edwin *management consultant*
Stauff, William James *commitment systems manager*
Stubbs, Jan Didra *retired travel industry executive, travel writer*
Sullivan, Michael Patrick *food service executive*
Swenson, Faye Lorene *executive and management development firm administrator*
Tree, David L. *advertising agency executive*
Walton, Gloria Jean *secretary*
†Westbrook, Bill *advertising executive*
Wickesberg, Albert Klumb *retired management educator*
Yourzak, Robert Joseph *management consultant, engineer, educator*

**Minnetonka**
Boubelik, Henry Fredrick, Jr. *travel company executive*
Gillies, Donald Richard *advertising agency and marketing consultant*
Gottier, Richard Chalmers *retired computer company executive*
Kostka, Ronald Wayne *marketing consultant*

**New Brighton**
Grieman, John Joseph *communications executive*

**Rochester**
Milner, Harold William *hotel executive*

**Saint Paul**
Althof, Jay Allen *marketing executive*
Boehnen, David Leo *grocery company executive, lawyer*
Esposito, Bonnie Lou *marketing professional*
Feinberg, David Erwin *publishing company executive*
Hill, James Stanley *computer consulting company executive*
Morgan, Carol Miró *marketing executive*

**Scandia**
Speer, David James *retired public relations executive*

**Victoria**
Courtney, Eugene Whitmal *computer company executive*

**Wayzata**
Mithun, Raymond O. *advertising agency executive, banker, real estate and insurance executive*
Waldera, Wayne Eugene *crisis management specialist*

## MISSISSIPPI

**Bay Saint Louis**
Sprouse, Susan Rae Moore *human resources specialist*

**Carriere**
Woodmansee, Glenn Edward *employee relations executive*

**Columbus**
Holt, Robert Ezel *data processing executive*
Hudnall, Jarrett, Jr. *management and marketing educator*

**Hattiesburg**
Watkins, Cathy Collins *corporate purchasing agent*

**Jackson**
Lewis, Larry Lisle *human resources specialist company executive*
†Palmer, John N. *communications executive*
Skelton, Gordon William *data processing executive, educator*

**Philadelphia**
Molpus, Dick H. *resource management company executive*

**Robinsville**
Buxton, Glenn *marketing professional, public relations executive*

**Vicksburg**
Bagby, Rose Mary *pollution control administrator, chemist*

## MISSOURI

**Bridgeton**
Campbell, Anita Joyce *computer company executive*
†Henderson, Gene M. *marketing executive*

**Cape Girardeau**
Smallwood, Glenn Walter, Jr. *utility marketing management executive*

**Chesterfield**
Kelly, James Joseph *printing company executive*
Welshans, Merle Talmadge *management consultant*

**Clayton**
Vecchiotti, Robert Anthony *management and organizational consultant*

**Columbia**
Denney, Arthur Hugh *management consultant*
Rutter, Elizabeth Jane *consulting firm executive*

**Fenton**
Maritz, William E. *communications company executive*

**Golden City**
Howard, Joanne Frances *marketing executive, funeral director, extended care coordinator*

**Kansas City**
Baker, Ronald Phillip *service company executive*
Barnes, Donald Gayle *management consultant*
Benner, Richard Edward, Jr. *management and marketing consultant, investor*
Buchanan, Carla Williams *data processing consultant*
Click, Marianne Jane *credit manager*
Courson, Marna B.P. *public relations executive*
Dillingham, John Allen *marketing professional*
Egan, Charles Joseph, Jr. *greeting card company executive, lawyer*
Evans, Margaret Ann *human resources administrator, business owner*
Gilbert, John R. *advertising and public relations agency executive*
Grossman, Jerome Barnett *retired service firm executive*
Hagans, Robert Frank *industrial clothing cleaning company executive*
Hall, Donald Joyce *greeting card company executive*
Hockaday, Irvine O., Jr. *greeting card company executive*
Robertson, Leon H. *management consultant, educator*

**Lake Saint Louis**
Dommermuth, William P. *marketing consultant, educator*

**Lees Summit**
Letterman, Ernest Eugene *manufacturers representative company executive*

**Rolla**
Datz, Israel Mortimer *information systems specialist*

**Saint Charles**
Gross, Charles Robert *personnel executive, legislator, appraiser*

**Saint Louis**
Barney, Steven Matthew *human resources executive*
Bateman, Sharon Louise *public relations executive*
Davis, Irvin *advertising, public relations, broadcast executive*
Devantier, Paul W. *communications executive, broadcaster*
Epner, Steven Arthur *computer consultant*
Finnigan, Joseph Townsend *public relations executive*
Foster, Scarlett Lee *public relations executive*
Graham, John Dalby *public relations executive*
Heck, Debra Upchurch *information technology professional*
Hilgert, Raymond Lewis *management and industrial relations educator, consultant, arbitrator*
Hillard, Robert Ellsworth *public relations consultant*
Johnson, Kennett Conrad *advertising agency executive*
Khoury, George Gilbert *printing company executive, baseball association executive*
Kornblet, Donald Ross *communications company executive*
Loynd, Richard Birkett *consumer products company executive*
Lucking, Peter Stephen *marketing consultant, industrial engineering consultant*
†Macauley, Edward C. *company executive*
Mills, Linda S. *public relations executive*
Moseley, Marc Robards *sales executive*
†Musial, Stan(ley) (Frank Musial) *hotel and restaurant executive, former baseball team executive, former baseball player*
Saligman, Harvey *consumer products and services company executive*
Schulte, Stephen Thomas *employee benefits director*
Sibbald, John Ristow *management consultant*
Siemer, Paul Jennings *public relations executive*
Snyder, Peter Larsen *public relations executive*
Stork, Donald Arthur *advertising executive*
Taylor, Andrew C. *rental leasing company executive*
Taylor, Dennis Del *marketing executive*
Taylor, Jack C. *rental and leasing company executive*
Tyler, William Howard, Jr. *advertising executive, educator*
Weaver, Charles Lyndell, Jr. *educational facilities administrator*
Weaver, William Clair, Jr. (Mike Weaver) *human resources development executive*
Willman, John Norman *management consultant*
Wilson, Harry B. *retired public relations company executive*

**Saint Peters**
Greene, Christopher William *marketing professional*

**Springfield**
Denton, D. Keith *management educator*
Hignite, Michael Anthony *computer information systems educator, researcher, writer*

**Warrenton**
Dapron, Elmer Joseph, Jr. *communications executive*

## MONTANA

**Helena**
Manuel, Vivian *public relations company executive*

## NEBRASKA

**Lincoln**
Fleharty, Mary Sue *secretary, receptionist*
Preister, Donald George *greeting card manufacturer, state senator*

**Nehawka**
Schlichtemeier-Nutzman, Sue Evelyn *training consultant*

**Omaha**
Cady, Mary Margaret *advertising agency executive*
Eggers, James Wesley *executive search consultant*
Frazier, Chet June *advertising agency executive*
Frederickson, Keith Alvin *advertising agency executive*
Lietzen, John Hervy *human resources executive, health agency volunteer*
Meyers, Louisa Ann *business and communications consultant*
Phares, Lynn Levisay *public relations communications executive*
Roskens, Ronald William *international business consultant*

**Scottsbluff**
Fisher, J. R. *marketing executive*

## NEVADA

**Carson City**
Patrie, Peter Hugo *gaming control board investigator*

**Henderson**
Cohan, George Sheldon *advertising and public relations executive*

**Las Vegas**
Arce, Phillip William *hotel and casino executive*
Barnes, Wesley Edward *energy and environmental executive*
Basile, Richard Emanuel *retired management consultant, educator*
Cummings, Leslie Edwards *hospitality management educator*
Goodwin, Nancy Lee *corporate executive*
Helm, George Neville, III *limousine company executive*
Landau, Ellis *gaming company executive*
Schaeffer, Glenn William *casino corporate financial executive*
Shively, Judith Carolyn (Judy Shively) *office assistant, contract administrator*
Wada, Harry Nobuyoshi *training company executive*
Welter, William Michael *marketing and advertising executive*
Wiener, Valerie *communications consultant, state senator*
Wilson, Betty May *resort company executive*

**Laughlin**
Petit, Ellen Jayne *casino supervisor*

**North Las Vegas**
Folden, Norman C. (Skip Folden) *information systems executive, consultant*

**Reno**
Ford, Victoria *public relations executive*
Howard, Christopher Philip *business consultant*
Perry, Anthony Frank *entertainment company executive, printing company executive, graphic designer*
Wells, Richard H. *gaming research executive*

**Sparks**
Adams, Ken R. *gaming analyst, writer, consultant, historian*

## NEW HAMPSHIRE

**Bedford**
Cronin, Timothy Cornelius, III *computer manufacturing executive*
Hall, Pamela S. *environmental consulting firm executive*
Steadman, David Rosslyn Ayton *business executive, corporate director*

**Claremont**
Middleton, John Albert *retired communications executive*

**Concord**
Roberts, George Bernard, Jr. *business and government affairs consultant, former state legislator*
White, Jeffrey George *healthcare consultant, educator*

**Dublin**
Biklen, Paul *retired advertising executive*

**Exeter**
Harmon, Richard Wingate *management consultant*
Jackson, Patrick John *public relations counsel*

**Gilmanton**
Daigle, Candace Jean *municipal services provider*

**Grantham**
Hansen, Herbert W. *management consultant*

**Hampton**
Rice, Frederick Colton *environmental management consultant*

**Hancock**
Brown, David Warfield *management educator*

**Jackson**
Synnott, William Raymond *retired management consultant*

**Jaffrey**
Schott, John (Robert) *international consultant, educator*

**Keene**
Lyon, Ronald Edward *management consultant, computer consultant*

**Manchester**
Roth, Pamela Jeanne *strategic marketing professional, web site developer and publisher*

**Nashua**
Garbacz, Gerald George *information services company executive*
Hargreaves, David William *communications company executive*
Weinstein, Jeffrey Allen *consumer products company executive, lawyer*

**New London**
Wheaton, Perry Lee *management consultant*
Zuehlke, Richard William *technical communications consultant, writer*

PROFESSIONAL INDEX 5321 INDUSTRY: SERVICE

**Portsmouth**
†Akridge, William David *hotel management company executive*
†Greene, Douglas E. *hotel executive*

**Rye**
MacRury, King *management counselor*

**Salem**
Snierson, Lynne Wendy *communications executive*

**Sunapee**
Chait, Lawrence G. *marketing consultant*

**Waterville Valley**
Grimes, Howard Ray *management consultant*

**Windham**
Arvai, Ernest Stephen *consulting executive*

## NEW JERSEY

**Absecon**
Steinruck, Charles Francis, Jr. *management consultant, lawyer*

**Allenhurst**
Hinson, Robert William *advertising executive, consultant*

**Atlantic City**
Harris, Paul Smith *human resources professional*

**Avalon**
Yochum, Philip Theodore *retired motel and cafeteria chain executive*

**Barnegat**
Berroa, David Allen *environmental services director*

**Basking Ridge**
Heckendorf, Glenn *sales and marketing executive*
†Laurie, Marilyn *communications company executive*

**Bedminster**
Hart, Terry Jonathan *communications executive*

**Bernardsville**
DiDomenico, Mauro, Jr. *communication executive*
Dixon, Richard Wayne *retired communications company executive*
Wiedenmayer, Christopher M. *writing instrument manufacturer, distributor*

**Boonton**
Bridges, Beryl Clarke *marketing executive*

**Brick**
Shortess, Edwin Steevin *marketing consultant*

**Bridgewater**
Cucco, Judith Elene *international marketing professional*
Hulse, Robert Douglas *high technology executive*
Pickett, Doyle Clay *employment and training counselor, consultant*
Skidmore, James Albert, Jr. *management, computer technology and engineering services company executive*

**Butler**
Ward, Robert Allen, Jr. *advertising executive*

**Caldwell**
Bentley, Alfred Young, Jr. *information technology and education consultant*
Chatlos, William Edward *management consultant*

**Camden**
Citron, Richard Ira *management consultant*
Gans, Samuel Myer *temporary employment service executive*

**Cedar Grove**
Carlozzi, Catherine Laurel *public relations, communications consultant, writer*

**Chatham**
Glatt, Mitchell Steven *consumer products company executive*
Lenz, Henry Paul *management consultant*
Rockwood, Thomas Julian *management services executive, information technolgy consultant*

**Cherry Hill**
Sax, Robert Edward *food service equipment company executive*
Schelm, Roger Leonard *information systems specialist*

**Chester**
Maddalena, Lucille Ann *management executive*

**Clark**
Orlando, Joseph Michael *sales executive*

**Cologne**
Hoffman, Maryhelen H. Paulick *communications company executive*

**Convent Station**
Weber, Joseph H. *communications company executive*

**Cranbury**
Cuthbert, Robert Allen *pet products company executive*

**Dayton**
Mencher, Stuart Alan *sales and marketing executive*

**East Brunswick**
Muro, Roy Alfred *retired media service corporation executive*

**East Hanover**
Elam, Karen Morgan *food company executive, consultant*

**East Rutherford**
Kluge, John Werner *broadcasting and advertising executive*
†Subotnick, Stuart *food service executive*

**Edison**
Austad, Vigdis *computer software company executive*
D'Agostino, Matthew Paul *bakery executive*
Marash, Stanley Albert *consulting company executive*

**Emerson**
Cheslik, Francis Edward *management consultant*

**Englewood**
Miles, Virginia (Mrs. Fred C. Miles) *marketing consultant*

**Ewing**
D'Antonio, Cynthia Maria *sales executive*

**Fair Lawn**
Hayden, Neil Steven *communications company executive*

**Fairfield**
Edwards, William Pearson *retail company executive*
†Hower, Paul H. *hotel executive*

**Far Hills**
Barnum, William Douglas *communications company executive*
Holt, Jonathan Turner *public relations executive*

**Florham Park**
Kovach, Andrew Louis *human resources executive*
Naimark, George Modell *marketing and management consultant*

**Fort Lee**
Seitel, Fraser Paul *public relations executive*

**Freehold**
Schockaert, Barbara Ann *operations executive*

**Glen Gardner**
Yates, Michael Francis *management consultant*

**Glen Ridge**
Agnew, Peter Tomlin *employee benefit consultant*

**Glen Rock**
Harper, Pamela Solvith *management consultant*

**Guttenberg**
Pozniakoff, Rita Oppenheim *education software consultant*

**Hackensack**
Borg, Malcolm Austin *communications company executive*
Carra, Andrew Joseph *advertising executive*
Timmins, Michael Joseph *communications services company executive*

**Hackettstown**
Passantino, Benjamin Arthur *marketing executive*

**Haddonfield**
Bauer, Raymond Gale *sales professional*

**Hamburg**
Buist, Richardson *corporate executive, retired banker*

**Harrington Park**
Rizzi, Deborah L. *public relations professional*

**Hazlet**
Morrison, James Frederick *management consultant*

**Holmdel**
Haskell, Barry Geoffry *communications company research administrator*
Hudson, Wendy Joy *software manager*

**Jersey City**
Christensen, Walter Frederick, Jr. *information, telecommunications and financial systems specialist*
Fields, Walter Lee, Jr. *public affairs executive, journalist*

**Lawrenceville**
Coleman, Wade Hampton, III *management consultant, mechanical engineer, former banker*
Cox, Teri P. *public relations executive*
Gideon, Richard Walter *broadcasting management consultant*

**Linden**
Foege, Rose Ann Scudiero *human resources professional*

**Little Falls**
†Maurer, Theodore A. *advertising executive*

**Little Silver**
Finch, Rogers Burton *association management consultant*

**Livingston**
Grant, Daniel Gordon *information services company executive*
Mandelbaum, Howard Arnold *marketing and management consultant*

**Madison**
Byrd, Stephen Fred *human resource consultant*
Goodman, Michael B(arry) *communications educator*
Markowski, John Joseph *human resources executive*
O'Brien, Mary Devon *communications executive, consultant*

Shelby, Bryan Rohrer *information systems consultant*
Siegel, George Henry *international business development consultant*

**Mahwah**
King, Lis Sonder *public relations executive, writer*

**Mantoloking**
Mehta, Narinder Kumar *marketing executive*

**Maple Shade**
Martin, Darris Lee *quality assurance executive*

**Maplewood**
Safian, Gail Robyn *public relations executive*

**Marlton**
Farwell, Nancy Larraine *public relations executive*
Klein, Anne Sceia *public relations executive*
Klein, Gerhart Leopold *public relations executive*

**Metuchen**
Rakov, Barbara Streem *marketing executive*

**Millington**
Donaldson, John Cecil, Jr. *consumer products company executive*

**Mine Hill**
Nadeau, Michael Joseph *college service assistant*

**Montvale**
Mackerodt, Fred *public relations specialist*
Smith, Kenneth David *performance technologist, musician*

**Moorestown**
Bennington, William Jay *public relations executive*
Schwerin, Horace S. *marketing research executive*

**Morris Plains**
†Goodman, Steve Edward *public relations executive*
Guarino, Walter Francis *advertising executive*

**Morristown**
McClung, Kenneth Austin, Jr. *training executive, performance consultant*
Miller, Hasbrouck Bailey *financial and travel services company executive*
Musa, John Davis *computer and infosystems executive, software reliability engineering researcher and expert, independent consultant*
Silberman, H. Lee *public relations executive*

**Mount Laurel**
Hart, Larry Edward *communications company executive*
Li, Pearl Nei-Chien Chu *information specialist, executive*
Taylor, Henry Roth *sales and marketing executive*

**Mountain Lakes**
Williams, Edward David *consulting executive*

**Mountainside**
DiPietro, Ralph Anthony *marketing and management consultant, educator*
Kozberg, Ronald Paul *health and human services administrator*
Lipton, Bronna Jane *marketing communications executive*
Stefanile, Lawrence Vincent *management counsulting company executive*

**New Brunswick**
Budd, Richard Wade *communications scientist, educator, lecturer, consultant, university dean*
Burke, James Edward *consumer products company executive*
Ruben, Brent David *communication educator*
Wilson, Robert Nathan *health care company executive*

**New Providence**
Bartels, Joachim Conrad *marketing and publishing corporation executive*
Stepanski, Anthony Francis, Jr. *computer company executive*
Sundberg, Carl-Erik Wilhelm *telecommunications executive, researcher*
Taylor, Volney *information company executive*

**Newark**
Kaltenbacher, Philip D(avid) *industrialist, former public official*
Lederman, Peter (Bernd) *environmental services executive, consultant, educator*
Lieberman, Leonard *retired supermarket executive*
Pedone, Joseph Lawrence *advertising executive*

**North Haledon**
Anstatt, Peter Jan *marketing services executive*

**Northvale**
Goodman, Stanley Leonard *advertising executive*

**Old Bridge**
Engel, John Jacob *communications executive*
Kesselman, Bruce Alan *marketing executive, consultant, composer, writer*

**Oldwick**
Griggs, Stephen Layng *management consultant*

**Palmyra**
Overholt, Miles Harvard, III *management consultant, family therapist*

**Paramus**
Forman, Beth Rosalyne *entertainment industry professional*

**Park Ridge**
Kaplan, Daniel I. *leasing company executive*
Kennedy, Brian James *marketing executive*
Olson, Frank Albert *car rental company executive*

**Parsippany**
Adams, Christine Hanson *advertising executive*
Belmonte, Steven Joseph *hotel chain executive*
Derr, Debra Hulse *advertising executive, publisher, editor*
†Ferguson, Thomas George *health care advertising agency executive*
†Gokal, Ramesh B. *hotel executive*
Haselmann, John Philip *marketing executive*
Nalewako, Mary Anne *corporate secretary*
†Seymour, Jeffrey L. *hotel executive*
Visocki, Nancy Gayle *data processing consultant*
Weller, Robert N(orman) *hotel executive*

**Pennsauken**
Holman, Joseph S. *automotive sales executive*

**Plainsboro**
Spiegel, Phyllis *public relations consultant, journalist*

**Port Liberte**
Frank, William Fielding *computer systems design executive, consultant*

**Princeton**
Boyd, John Howard *corporate location consultant*
Chlopak, Donna Gayle *marketing and management consultant*
Crespi, Irving *public opinion and market research consultant*
Devine, Hugh James, Jr. *marketing executive, consultant*
Fouss, James H. *marketing executive*
Greenberg, Joel S. *management consultant, engineer*
Hillier, James *technology management executive, researcher*
Lincoln, Anna *company executive, foreign languages educator*
Lovitt, George Harold *advertising executive*
Morris, Mac Glenn *advertising bureau executive*
O'Connor, Neal William *former advertising agency executive*
Sethi, Shyam Sunder *management consultant*
†Spitzer, T. Quinn *management consultant company executive*
Trenner, Nelson Richards, Jr. *communications executive, writer*
Weinstein, Stephen Brant *communications executive, researcher, writer*
Williams, Brown F *television media services company executive*

**Princeton Junction**
Dine, Paul Joseph *communications and training consultant*

**Randolph**
Stoskus, Joanna Jorzysta *computer information systems educator*

**Red Bank**
Reinhart, Peter Sargent *corporate executive, lawyer*

**Ridgefield Park**
Lorelli, Michael Kevin *consumer products and services executive*

**Ridgewood**
Makadok, Stanley *management consultant*

**Roseland**
Lafer, Fred Seymour *data processing company executive*
Weinbach, Arthur Frederic *computing services company executive*
Weston, Josh S. *data processing company executive*

**Rumson**
Christianson, Lloyd Fenton *management consultant*

**Rutherford**
†Donahue, Timothy M. *communications executive*
†McAuley, Brian D. *communications executive*

**Saddle River**
Ross, Martin Harris *advertising executive*

**Scotch Plains**
Barnard, Kurt *retail marketing forecaster, publisher*
Ehmann, Carl William *consumer products executive, researcher*

**Secaucus**
Marcus, Alan C. *public relations consultant*
Schenck, Frederick A. *business executive*

**Short Hills**
Harwood, Jerry *market research executive*
Schaefer, Charles James, III *advertising agency executive, consultant*
Schaffer, Edmund John *management consultant, retired engineering executive*

**Somerset**
Aronson, Dana Lynne *program/public relations executive*
Greenberg, Lenore *public relations professional*

**Somerville**
Dobrinsky, Susan Elizabeth *human resources director*
Plant, Maretta Moore *public relations and marketing executive*

**South Orange**
Lapinski, Frances Constance *data processing systems executive*
Long, Philip Lee *information systems executive*

**South Plainfield**
Janiak, Cathy Lynn *sales consultant*

**Spring Lake**
Ernst, John Louis *management consultant*

**Stanton**
Clayton, Raymond Arthur *purchasing executive*

**Summit**
Bostwick, Randell A. *retired retail food company executive*
Fuess, Billings Sibley, Jr. *advertising executive*
Nessen, Ward Henry *typographer, lawyer*
Pace, Leonard *retired management consultant*

**Teaneck**
Allen, Brenda Joyce *management consultant, editor in chief*

**Tenafly**
Gibbons, Robert Philip *management consultant*

**Three Bridges**
Lawrence, Gerald Graham *management consultant*

**Titusville**
Marden, Kenneth Allen *advertising executive*

**Toms River**
Kanarkowski, Edward Joseph *data processing company executive*

**Trenton**
Himm, Emilie Gina *records and information manager, consultant*
Losi, Maxim John *medical communications and regulatory executive*
Robinson, Susan Mittleman *data processing executive*

**Upper Montclair**
Morris, John Lunden *global logistics and communications executive*

**Ventnor City**
Bolton, Kenneth Albert *management consultant*

**Verona**
Greenwald, Robert *public relations executive*

**Voorhees**
Schmid, Patricia Jean *personnel professional*

**Warren**
Blass, Walter Paul *consultant, management educator*
Earle, Jean Buist *computer company executive*
Wightman, Glenn Charles *environmental, health and safety administrator*

**Watchung**
Reeves, Patricia Ruth *heavy machinery manufacturing company executive*

**Wayne**
Donald, Robert Graham *retail food chain human resources executive*
Freimark, Jeffrey Philip *retail supermarket executive*

**West Caldwell**
Page, Frederick West *business consultant*

**West Milford**
Ferguson, Harley Robert *service company executive*

**West Orange**
Kyle, Corinne Silverman *management consultant*

**Westfield**
Cushman, Helen Merle Baker *retired management consultant*
Ganz, Felix *marketing professional*
Mazzarese, Michael Louis *executive coach, consultant*

**Wharton**
Rodzianko, Paul *energy and environmental company executive*

**Whippany**
Scroggs, Debbie Lee *communications professional*

**Woodcliff Lake**
Morrione, Melchior S. *management consultant, accountant*

**Wyckoff**
Lavery, Daniel P. *marketing management consultant*

## NEW MEXICO

**Albuquerque**
Geary, David Leslie *communications executive, educator, consultant*
Golden, Julius *advertising and public relations executive, lobbyist, investor*
Goodman, Phyllis L. *public relations executive*
Hale, Bruce Donald *retired marketing professional*
Hancock, Don Ray *researcher*
Hayo, George Edward *management consultant*
Ivester, Vicky Jo *sales professional*
Ofte, Donald *retired environmental executive, consultant*
Oppedahl, Phillip Edward *computer company executive*
Ortiz, Kathleen Lucille *travel consultant*
O'Toole, Robert John, II *telemarketing consultant*
Tope, Dwight Harold *retired management consultant*
Wellborn, Charles Ivey *science and technology licensing company executive*
Young, Joan Crawford *advertising executive*

**Sandia Park**
Greenwell, Ronald Everett *communications executive*

**Santa Fe**
Graybeal, Sidney Norman *national security executive, former government official*
Taylor, Beverly Lacy *stringed instrument restorer, classical guitarist*

## NEW YORK

**Albany**
Murphy, Thomas Joseph *strategic communications consultant*
Quellmalz, Henry *printing company executive*

**Amherst**
Cohen, Herman Nathan *private investigator*

**Amityville**
Brennan, Patrick Thomas *meteorology company executive*

**Ardsley**
Barton, Joan Chi-Hung Lo *sales executive*

**Armonk**
Bolduc, Ernest Joseph *association management consultant*
Harreld, James Bruce *computer company executive*
Levy, Kenneth James *advertising executive*
Mc Groddy, James Cleary *retired computer company executive, consultant*
Thoman, G. Richard *computer company executive*

**Averill Park**
Traver, Robert William, Sr. *management consultant, author, lecturer, engineer*

**Babylon**
Meirowitz, Claire Cecile *public relations executive*

**Bellerose**
Paramekanthi, Srinivasan Mandayam *software services executive*

**Bellport**
Hendrie, Elaine *public relations executive*

**Bethpage**
Marrone, Daniel Scott *business, production and quality management educator*

**Binghamton**
Surgent, Susan Pearl *human resources specialist*

**Briarcliff Manor**
Dolmatch, Theodore Bieley *management consultant*
Driver, Sharon Humphreys *marketing executive*
Haddad, Jerrier Abdo *engineering management consultant*

**Brockport**
Fisher, Robert Joseph *marketing and corporate executive*

**Bronx**
Capodilupo, Jeanne Hatton *public relations executive*

**Bronxville**
Ellinghaus, William Maurice *communications executive*

**Brooklyn**
Ahrens, Thomas H. *production company executive*
De Lisi, Joanne *communications executive, educator*
Frisch, Ivan Thomas *computer and communications company executive*
Goldsmith, Clifford Henry *former tobacco company executive*
Hendra, Barbara Jane *public relations executive*
Moehring, Fred Adolf *fastener distribution company executive*
Ogden, Peggy A. *personnel director*
Olson, Harry Andrew, Jr. *communications consultant*
Rike, Susan *public relations executive*

**Buffalo**
Fryer, Appleton *publisher, sales executive, lecturer, diplomat*
Halt, James George *advertising executive, graphic designer*
Hudson, Stanton Harold, Jr. *public relations executive, educator*
Morgan, James Durward *computer company executive*
Pegels, C. Carl *management science and systems educator*

**Copake Falls**
Chalk, Howard Wolfe *marketing company executive*

**Croton On Hudson**
Plotch, Walter *management consultant, fund raising counselor*

**Delhi**
Needham, Nancy Jean *management consultant*

**Delmar**
Button, Rena Pritsker *public affairs executive*

**Dix Hills**
Fisher, Fenimore *business development consultant*

**Dundee**
Pfendt, Henry George *retired information systems executive, management consultant*

**East Hampton**
Munson, Lawrence Shipley *management consultant*

**East Meadow**
Fuchs, Jerome Herbert *management consultant*

**Elmsford**
Kucic, Joseph *management consultant, industrial engineer*
Shaviv, Eddie *marketing and sales executive*
Turk, Stanley Martin *advertising agency executive*

**Farmingdale**
Doucette, David Robert *computer systems company executive*

**Fayetteville**
Cantwell, John Dalzell, Jr. *management consultant*
Wallace, Spencer Miller, Jr. *hotel executive*

**Floral Park**
Heyderman, Mark Baron *sales and marketing company executive*

**Flushing**
Safadi-Psyllos, Gina Moni *administrative assistant, business owner*

**Forest Hills**
Dessylas, Ann Atsaves *human resources and office management executive*
Miller, Donald Ross *management consultant*
Van Westering, James Francis *management consultant, educator*

**Freeport**
Landsberg, Jerry *management and investment consultant, optical laboratory executive*

**Garden City**
Conlon, Thomas James *marketing executive*
Crom, James Oliver *professional training company executive*
Doucette, Mary-Alyce *computer company executive*

**Glen Cove**
Greenberg, Allan *advertising and marketing research consultant*

**Glen Head**
Vizza, Robert Francis *hospital executive, former university administrator, marketing educator*

**Glenwood Landing**
Hahn, Joan Marjorie *public relations consultant, marketing consultant*

**Great Neck**
Donenfeld, Kenneth Jay *management consultant*
Friedland, Louis N. *retired communications executive*
Goldberg, Melvin Arthur *communications executive*

**Hancock**
DeLuca, Ronald *former advertising agency executive, consultant*

**Harrison**
Fuchs, Hanno *communications consultant, lawyer*
Krantz, Melissa Marianne *public relations company executive*

**Hauppauge**
Reich, William Michael *advertising executive*
Stemple, Joel Gilbert *computer company executive*

**Haverstraw**
Motin, Revell Judith *retired data processing executive*

**Hempstead**
Evans, Joel Raymond *marketing educator*
Pell, Arthur Robert *human resources development consultant, author*

**Hewlett**
Kislik, Louis A. *marketing company executive*

**Honeoye Falls**
Hillabrandt, Larry Lee *service industry executive*

**Howard Beach**
Krein, Catherine Cecilia *public relations professional*

**Huntington**
Ruppert, Mary Frances *management consultant, school counselor*

**Huntington Station**
Liguori, Frank Nickolas *temporary personnel company executive*

**Hyde Park**
Metz, Ferdinand *chef, educator, academic administrator*

**Irvington**
Steinberg, James Ian *marketing executive*

**Islandia**
Wang, Charles B. *computer software company executive*

**Ithaca**
Farley, Jennie Tiffany Towle *industrial and labor relations educator*
Park, Roy Hampton, Jr. *advertising media executive*
Whyte, William Foote *industrial relations educator, author*
Windmuller, John Philip *industrial relations educator, consultant*

**Jamaica**
Crivelli, Joseph Louis *security specialist*

**Katonah**
White, Harold Tredway, III *management consultant*

**Kingston**
Lanitis, Tony Andrew *market researcher*

**Lake Luzerne**
Goldstein, Manfred *retired consultant*

**Lancaster**
Neumaier, Gerhard John *environment consulting company executive*

**Larchmont**
Greenwald, Carol Schiro *professional services marketing research executive*
Levy, Walter Kahn *management consultant executive*
Plumez, Jean Paul *advertising agency executive, consultant*
Silverstone, David *advertising executive*
Wielgus, Charles Joseph *information services company executive*
Wolfson, Harold *public relations consultant*

**Liverpool**
Harris, Dana Bound *software company executive*
Stefano, Ross William *business executive*

**Long Beach**
Siegel, Herbert Bernard *certified professional management consultant*

**Long Island City**
Craig, Elizabeth Coyne *marketing executive*

**Loudonville**
Ferguson, Henry *international management consultant*

**Malverne**
Freund, Richard L. *communications company executive, consultant, lawyer*

**Mamaroneck**
Drexler, Michael David *advertising agency executive*
New, Anne Latrobe *public relations, fund raising executive*

**Manhasset**
Chesney, Robert Henry *communications executive, consultant*

**Manlius**
Harriff, Suzanna Elizabeth Bahner *advertising consultant*

**Marietta**
Goyette, Geoffrey Robert *sales executive*

**Melville**
Jagoda, Donald Robert *sales promotion agency executive*
Krusos, Denis Angelo *communications company executive*
LaRocco, Elizabeth Anne *management information systems professional*

**Merrick**
Baron, Theodore *public relations executive*

**Middle Island**
Linick, Andrew S. *direct marketing executive*

**Mount Kisco**
Dangler, Richard Reiss *corporate service companies executive, entrepreneur*

**Nanuet**
Vamvaketis, Carole *health services administrator*

**New Hyde Park**
Anderson, Ronald Howard *consumer packaged goods company marketing executive*

**New Paltz**
Franco, Carole Ann *international consultant*
Nyquist, Thomas Eugene *consulting business executive, mayor*

**New Rochelle**
Vernon, Lillian *mail order company executive*

**New York**
Abernathy, James Logan *public relations executive*
Achenbaum, Alvin Allen *marketing and management consultant*
Agisim, Philip *advertising and marketing company executive*
Alexander, Roy *public relations executive, editor, author*
Allen, Alice *communications, public relations and marketing executive*
Allen, Alice Catherine Towsley *public relations professional, writer, consultant*
Allen, Robert Eugene *communications company executive*
Alschuler, Steven *public relations executive, communications consultant, writer, political consultant*
Alvarez, Paul Hubert *communications and public relations consultant*
Ancona, Barry *publishing and marketing consultant*
Anderson, Arthur Allan *management consultant*
Anderson, Gavin *public relations consultant*
Andolsen, Alan Anthony *management consultant*
Ankerson, Robert William *management consultant*
Antonuccio, Joseph Albert *hospitality industry executive*
Applebaum, Stuart S. *public relations executive*
Arlow, Arnold Jack *advertising agency executive*
Aronson, Donald Eric *professional services firms consultant, value added tax consultant*
Asensi, Gustavo *advertising executive*
Avrett, John Glenn *advertising executive*
Axelrod, Norman N(athan) *technical planning and technology application consultant*
Bacher, Judith St. George *executive search consultant*
Bachrach, Nancy *advertising executive*
Baer, Andrew Rudolf *public relations consultant*
Baker, Stephen *advertising executive, author*
†Baldwin, Beth *advertising executive*
Balick, Kenneth D. *international real estate finance executive*
Bara, Jean Marc *finance and communications executive*
Barkann, Jeremy *automotive advertising and marketing professional*
Baron, Sheri Colonel *advertising agency executive*
Barrett, Herbert *artists management executive*
Barrett, Paulette Singer *public relations executive*
Barrett, William Gary *advertising executive*
Bartlett, Thomas Foster *international management consultant*
Bartow, Diane Grace *marketing and sales executive*
Bartucci, Janet Evelyn *marketing communications executive*
Bates, Don *public relations and marketing executive*

Bauman, Martin Harold executive search firm executive
Beard, Eugene P. advertising agency executive
Beaumont, Richard Austin management consultant
Becker, Ivan advertising executive
Becker, Robert A. advertising executive
Beckwith, Rodney Fisk management consulting firm executive
Beers, Charlotte Lenore advertising agency executive
Beinecke, William Sperry corporate executive
Bell, David Arthur advertising agency executive
Bell, Theodore Augustus advertising executive
Bellows, Howard Arthur, Jr. marketing research executive
Bennett, Georgette communications and planning consultant
Bergen, Jack public relations company executive
Berlowe, Phyllis Harriette public relations counselor
Bernard, David George management consultant
Bernbach, John Lincoln consultant
Beyer, Charlotte Bishop investment management marketing executive, consultant
Biederman, Barron Zachary (Barry Biederman) advertising agency executive
Bishop, Susan Katharine executive search company executive
Black, Susan public relations executive
Blades, Carol Brady public relations executive
†Bloom, Robert H. advertising executive
Bloomgarden, Kathy Finn public relations executive
Boice, Craig Kendall management consultant
Bona, Frederick Emil public relations executive
Booth, Margaret A(nn) communications company executive
Bostock, Roy Jackson advertising agency executive
Boves, Joaquin Lorenzo marketing consultant
Bower, Marvin management consultant
Brady, Adelaide Burks public relations agency executive, giftware catalog executive
Braun, Neil S. communications executive
Braz, Evandro Freitas management consultant
Bronkesh, Annette Cylia public relations executive
Brooks, Anita Helen public relations executive
Brooks, Timothy H. media executive
Brown, Hobson, Jr. executive recruiting consultant
Brumback-Henry, Sarah Elizabeth industrial psychologist, management and corporate consultant
Bruzs, Boris Olgerd management consultant
Buchwald, Elias public relations executive
Bullen, Richard Hatch former corporate executive
Bungey, Michael advertising executive
Burg, Mitchell Marc advertising executive
Burger, Chester retired management consultant
Burke, Daniel Barnett retired communications corporation executive
Burkhardt, Ronald Robert advertising executive
Burson, Harold public relations executive
Cadwell, Franchellie Margaret advertising agency executive, writer
Caggiano, Joseph advertising executive
†Cairns, AnneMarie public relations executive
†Calio, Vincent S. public relations executive
Calvillo, Ricardo C. communications executive
Canaan, Lee public relations executive
Canter, Stanley D. retired marketing consulting company executive
Cappon, Andre Alfred management consultant
Carnella, Frank Thomas information executive
†Casey, Bart advertising executive
Cavanagh, Richard Edward business policy organization executive
Cavior, Warren Joseph communications executive
Chajet, Clive communications consultant
Chandler, Robert Leslie public relations executive
Chang, Ling Wei sales executive
†Chemla, Alexandre Hubert travel company executive
Cheney, Richard Eugene public relations executive, psychoanalyst
Churchill, Mary Carey public relations executive
Clarke, Frank William advertising agency executive
Cohen, Alan Norman business executive
Cohn, Theodore management consultant
Conroy, Catherine Martin public relations executive
Conway, David Antony management executive, marketing professional
Cooney, Lenore public relations executivechairman
†Corbin, Herbert Leonard public relations executive
Coyne, Nancy Carol advertising executive
Craig, Sandra Kay sales executive
Crawford, Bruce Edgar advertising executive
Crisci, Mathew G. marketing executive
Culligan, John William retired corporate executive
Cuming, Pamela marketing professional, author
Cutler, Laurel advertising agency executive
Czarnecki, Selina Michelle Snyder sales and marketing executive, artist
Daily, John Charles executive recruiting company executive
Dane, Maxwell former advertising executive
Daniel, David Ronald management consultant
Davidson, Donald William advertising executive
Davis, J. Steve advertising agency executive
Davis, Susan Lynn public relations executive
De Blasio, Michael Peter satellite company executive
DeBow, Jay Howard Camden public relations executive
DeBow, Thomas Joseph, Jr. advertising executive
De Deo, Joseph E. advertising executive
†De Gregorio, Anthony advertising executive
Delano, Lester Almy, Jr. advertising executive
de Margitay, Gedeon acquisitions and management consultant
Dent, V. Edward former advertising and communications company executive
†DeSimone, Glenn J. advertising executive
Dessi, Adrian Frank marketing, communications executive
†Deutsch, Donny advertising executive
Diamond, Harris corporate communications executive, lawyer
Dickie, Brian Norman management consultant
Diehl, Stephen Anthony human resources consultant
Dienstag, Eleanor Foa corporate communications consultant
Dimling, John Arthur marketing executive
Doner, Frederick Nathan advertising and communications executive
Drobis, David R. public relations company executive
Dubin, Morton Donald management consultant, film producer
Duke, Robin Chandler Tippett public relations executive
Dunst, Laurence David advertising executive
Dzodin, Harvey Cary communications executive
Eckstut, Michael Kauder management consultant
Edelman, Richard Winston public relations executive
Edson, Andrew Stephen public relations executive
Eisler, Susan Krawetz advertising executive
Ellig, Bruce Robert personnel executive
Elliott, John, Jr. advertising agency executive
Elliott, Tim advertising agency executive
Emerson, Andi (Mrs. Andi Emerson Weeks) sales and advertising executive
Epstein, Harriet Pike public relations executive
Eswein, Bruce James, II human resources executive
Evans, Alfred Lee, Jr. advertising executive
Evans, Thomas Chives Newton communications executive
Evans, Van Michael advertising agency executive, consultant
Faber, Neil advertising executive
Fairbairn, Ursula Farrell human resources executive
Falk, Edgar Alan public relations consulting executive, author
Faraone, Ted public relations executive, consultant
Farinelli, Jean L. public relations firm executive
Fay, Toni Georgette communications executive
Feinberg, Robert Edward advertising agency executive, writer
†Feintuch, Henry P. public relations executive
Ferrell, John Frederick advertising executive
Fields, Jennie advertising executive, writer
Finn, David public relations company executive, artist
Finn, Peter public relations executive
Fisher, Robert Abel advertising executive
Flaherty, Tina Santi corporate communications executive
Fogge, Len advertising executive
Ford, John Charles communications executive
Foster, James Henry advertising and public relations executive
Foxworth, Jo advertising agency executive
†Fragola, Joseph Ralph executive
Frank, Robert Allen advertising executive
Franken, Martin public relations company executive
Frantz, Jack Thomas advertising executive
†Friedman, Adam Issac public relations consultant
Friedman, Frances public relations executive
Fulrath, Irene corporate sales and marketing executive
Furman, Anthony Michael public relations executive
Fursland, Richard Curtis international business executive
Gantman, Geraldine Ann marketing executive, consultant
Gardiner, E. Nicholas P. executive search executive
Gardner, Ralph David advertising executive
†Garfinkel, Lee advertising agency executive
Garvin, Andrew Paul information company executive, author, consultant
Geier, Philip Henry, Jr. advertising executive
Geller, Robert James advertising agency executive
Geltzer, Sheila Simon public relations executive
Georgescu, Peter Andrew advertising executive
Gerard-Sharp, Monica Fleur communications executive
Gerson, Irwin Conrad advertising executive
Gilliatt, Neal advertising executive, consultant
Ginsberg, Frank Charles advertising executive
Gitelson, Susan Aurelia business executive, civic leader
Glos, Margaret Beach real estate company executive, developer
Gold, Jay D. broadcasting company executive
Gold, Mari S. public relations executive
Goldschmidt, Charles advertising agency executive
Goldstein, Gary S. executive recruiter
Gomez, Francis D(ean) corporate executive, former foreign service officer
Gordon, Janine M. advertising agency executive
Gorup, Gregory James marketing executive
Gossett, Oscar Milton advertising executive
Gottlieb, Jerrold Howard advertising executive
Grace, Jason Roy advertising agency executive
Greenawalt, Peggy Freed Tomarkin advertising executive
Greenberg, Jerome advertising executive
Greene, Adele S. management consultant
Greenland, Leo advertising executive
Griffin, Kelly Ann public relations executive, consultant
Griffith, Katherine Scott communications executive
Groberg, James Jay information sciences company executive
Grossman, Jack advertising agency executive
Gugel, Craig Thomas advertising and new media executive
Gumbinner, Paul S. advertising and executive recruitment agency executive
Gupta, Rajat management consultant
Haddock, Robert Lynn information services entrepreneur, writer
Halpern, Nathan Loren communications company executive
Hammond, Lou Rena Charlotte public relations executive
Hancock, William Marvin computer network engineering executive
Hart, Karen Ann advertising executive
Hatheway, John Harris advertising agency executive
Hauser, Joyce Roberta marketing professional
Hearle, Douglas Geoffrey public relations consultant
Heinzerling, Larry Edward communications executive
Heller, Arthur advertising agency executive
Henschel, Shirley Myra licensing agent
Hilton, Andrew Carson management consultant, former manufacturing company executive
Hochhauser, Richard Michael marketing professional
Hoog, Thomas W. public relations executive
Hooper, Ian (John Derek Glass) marketing communications executive
Hopple, Richard Van Tromp, Jr. advertising agency executive
Horowitz, David H. communications industry executive, lawyer, consultant
†Hosokawa, David advertising executive
Howard, Elizabeth corporate communications and marketing executive
Howes, Alfred S. business and insurance consultant
†Hudes, Nana Brenda marketing professional
Hunter, Barbara Way public relations executive
Ilson, Bernard public relations executive
Jackson, Richard George advertising agency executive
Jacoby, Robert Harold management consulting executive
James, Robert Leo advertising agency executive
Johnson, Harold Earl human resources specialist
Johnson, John William, Jr. executive recruiter
Jonas, Gilbert public relations and fund raising executive
Jones, Caroline Robinson advertising executive
Jones, Gwenyth Ellen director information systems
Jones, Thomas Owen computer industry executive
Josephs, Ray public relations and advertising executive, writer, international relations consultant
Josephson, Marvin talent and literary agency executive
Just, Gemma Rivoli retired advertising executive
Kahn, Laurence communications executive
Kahn, Leonard Richard communications and electronics company executive
†Kane, Thomas Patrick broadcast executive
Kanuk, Leslie Lazar management consultant, educator
Kaplan, Larry public relations executive
Karalekas, George Steven advertising agency executive, political consultant
Karp, Martin Everett management consultant
Katz, Marcia public relations company executive
Keenan, Michael Edgar advertising executive
Kelley, Sheila Seymour public relations executive, crisis consultant
Kelmenson, Leo-Arthur advertising executive
Kelne, Nathan editorial and public relations consultant, retired
Kennedy, Daniel John national and international public relations consultant, communications executive
Kenny, Roger Michael executive search consultant
Kiam, Victor Kermit, II consumer products company executive
Kiel, Catherine Ann public relations executive
†Kientz, Steven J. advertising executive
Kieren, Thomas Henry management consultant
Killeffer, Louis MacMillan advertising executive
Kinser, Richard Edward management consultant
Kinsolving, Charles McIlvaine, Jr. marketing executive
Kish, Joseph Laurence, Jr. management consultant
†Klores, Dan public relations executive
Knox, George L(evi), III consumer products company executive
Kogstad, Rolf Egil retired sales company executive
Kohlenberg, Stanley marketing executive
Kohut, John Walter corporate executive
Korman, Jess J. advertising executive, writer, producer
Kotcher, Raymond Lowell public relations executive
Kotuk, Andrea Mikotajuk public relations executive, writer
Kraus, Norma Jean industrial relations executive
Kraushar, Jonathan Pollack communications and media consultant
Kreisberg, Neil Ivan advertising executive
Kreston, Martin Howard advertising, marketing, public relations, and publishing executive
Krinsky, Robert Daniel consulting firm executive
Kroeger, Lin J. management consultant
Kubin, Michael Ernest advertising and marketing executive
Kullberg, Gary Walter advertising agency executive
Kurnit, Shepard advertising agency executive
Kurz, Mitchell Howard marketing communications executive
Lamont, Lee music management executive
Lang, George restaurateur
Langton, Cleve Swanson advertising executive
†LaNicca, Ellen public relations executive
Lannamann, Richard Stuart executive recruiting consultant
Larberg, John Frederick wine consultant, educator
Laughren, Terry marketing executive
Lawrence, James Bland marketing executive
Lawrence, Ruddick Carpenter public relations executive
Lazarus, Rochelle Braff advertising executive
†Lee, Bruce advertising executive
Lee, Jason Davis communications executive
Leeds, Douglas Brecker advertising agency executive, theatre producer
Leet, Mildred Robbins corporate executive, consultant
Leff, Ilene J(oan) management consultant, corporate and goverment executive
†Lelchuk, Howard advertising executive
Leslie, John Webster, Jr. communications company executive
Leslie, Seymour Marvin communications executive
Lesser, Lawrence J. advertising agency executive
Leubert, Alfred Otto Paul international business consultant, investor
Levenstein, Alan Peter advertising executive
†Levins, Ilyssa public relations executive
Levitt, Mitchell Alan management consultant
Levy, Matthew Degen consumer products executive, management consultant
Lewis, Richard Warren advertising executive
Lightman, Harold Allen marketing executive
Lindheim, James Bruce public relations executive
Lipscomb, Thomas Heber, III information technology executive
Lipton, Charles public relations executive
Lipton, Joan Elaine advertising executive
†Logan, Douglas George service company executive
Logan, Vicki advertising executive
Lois, George advertising agency executive
Lorber, Barbara Heyman communications executive
Lotas, Judith Patton advertising executive
†Lucca, Maria advertising executive
Lucht, John Charles management consultant, executive recruiter, writer
†Lyon, Patty advertising executive
MacKay, Malcolm executive search consultant
†Makovsky, Kenneth Dale public relations executive
Makrianes, James Konstantin, Jr. management consultant
Malgieri, Nick chef, author, educator
Mallozzi, Cos M. public relations executive
Manning, Burt advertising executive
Manoff, Richard Kalman advertising executive, public health consultant, author
Mansi, Joseph Anneillo public relations company executive
Marcosson, Thomas I. service company executive
Margaritis, John Paul public relations executive
Mark, Reuben consumer products company executive
Marlin, Kenneth Brian information and software company executive
Marsh, Cheryl Leppert marketing professional
Marshall, Daniel Stuart advertising executive
Marston, Robert Andrew public relations executive
McCartin, Thomas Joseph advertising executive
McCaslin, Teresa Eve human resources executive
McCoy, Millington F. management recruitment company executive
McDonough, Mamie public relations executive
McGarry, John Patrick, Jr. advertising agency executive
†McGrath, Patrick J. advertising agency executive
†McKelvey, Andrew J. advertising executive
McKenna, William Michael advertising executive
McNamara, John Jeffrey advertising executive
McNamee, Louise advertising agency executive
Meek, Phillip Joseph communications executive
Meigher, S. Christopher, III communications and media investor
†Meiner, Howard advertising executive
Menk, Carl William executive search company executive
Menninger, Edward Joseph public relations executive
Meranus, Arthur Richard advertising agency executive
Messner, Thomas G. advertising executive, copywriter
Meyer, Edward Henry advertising agency executive
Meyer, Fred Josef advertising executive
Meyer, Pearl executive compensation consultant
Miano, Louis Stephen advertising executive
Michenfelder, Joseph Francis public relations executive
Miller, Ernest Charles management consultant
Miller, Robert advertising executive
Milligan, Michael Edward insurance services company executive
Minasi, Anthony software company executive
Mines, Herbert Thomas executive recruiter
Minicucci, Robert A. business executive
Mitchell, Martin Morgan, Jr. advertising executive, educator
Mitchell, Richard Boyle advertising executive
Moreira, Marcio Martins advertising executive
Morgen, Lynn public relations executive
Morley, Michael B. public relations executive
Morris, Stephen Burritt marketing information executive
Mosbacher, Martin Bruce public relations executive
Moss, Charles advertising agency executive
Mulligan, David Keith consulting company executive
Murphy, James E. public relations and marketing executive
Nash, Edward L. advertising agency executive
Neff, Thomas Joseph executive search firm executive
Neft, David Samuel marketing professional
Nelson, Bruce Sherman advertising agency executive
Nesbit, Robert Grover management consultant
Newman, Geraldine Anne advertising executive, inventor
Nisenholtz, Martin Abram telecommunications executive, educator
Noonan, Susan Abert public relations counselor
Norcia, Stephen William advertising executive
†Novak, Christine Allison advertising agency executive
O'Brien, Richard Francis advertising agency executive
Ochman, B. L. public relations executive
Oldfield, Barney entertainment executive
Olinger, Carla D(ragan) medical advertising executive
†Olshan, Kenneth S. business executive, advisor
Olson, Thomas Francis, II communications company executive
O'Neill, Francis Xavier, III marketing executive
O'Neill, Harry William survey research company executive
Osnos, Gilbert Charles management consultant
Ostrow, Joseph W. advertising executive
O'Sullivan, Eugene Henry retired advertising executive
†Pagan, Hargot Owens public relations executive
†Paley, Norman advertising executive
Parrish, Thomas Kirkpatrick, III marketing consultant
Parsons, Andrew John management consultant
†Paseornek, Helene public relations executive
Paster, Howard G. public relations, public affairs company executive
Patton, Joanna advertising executive
Paul, Robert David management consultant
Paulus, Eleanor Bock professional speaker, author
Pazicky, Edward Paul human resources executive
Pearson, Clarence Edward management consultant
Peasback, David R. recruiting company executive
Peebler, Charles David, Jr. advertising executive
Perelman, Ronald Owen diversified holding company executive
Perless, Ellen advertising executive
Perlmutter, Diane F. communications executive
Perraud, Pamela Brooks human resources professional
Petrocelli, Anthony Joseph management executive, consultant
Pfenning, Arthur George social scientist
Phillips, Elizabeth Joan marketing executive
Phillips, John David management consultant
Phillips, Joyce Martha human resources executive
Pickholz, Jerome Walter advertising agency executive
Pittman, Preston Lawrence executive assistant
Pollak, Tim advertising agency executive
Pollock-O'Brien, Louise Mary public relations executive
Pompadur, I. Martin communications executive
Quinlan, Mary Lou advertising executive
Quintero, Ronald Gary management consultant
Rathke, Sheila Wells advertising and public relations executive
Rauch, Arthur Irving management consultant
Reda, James Francis business consultant
Reddy, Gerard Anthony corporate training executive
Reel, Shaun Delane institutional consultant, business executive
Reges, Marianna Alice marketing executive
Reichel, Walter Emil advertising executive
Reinhard, Keith Leon advertising executive
Reuben, Alvin Bernard entertainment executive
Reynolds, James management consultant
Rhodes, John Bower management consultant
Rice, Regina Kelly marketing executive
Rich, Kenneth Malcolm executive search and management consultant
Richardson, Grace Elizabeth consumer products company executive
†Riches, Wendy advertising executive
Rider, Joseph Kuntzman information systems specialist
Rindlaub, John Wade advertising agency executive
Riordan, James Quentin retired company executive
Ritchie, Richard Lee media company executive
Robbins, John Clapp management consultant
Roberts, Francis Stone advertising executive
Robinson, Hobart Krum management consulting company executive
Roche, Gerard Raymond management consultant
Roman, Kenneth, Jr. corporate communications executive

Romano, Joseph Anthony *marketing and consulting executive*
Rosenthal, Peter *public relations executive*
Ross, Thomas Bernard *communications company executive*
Rothenberg, Robert Philip *public relations counselor*
Rothholz, Peter Lutz *public relations executive*
†Rothstein, Richard *public relations executive*
Ruben, William Samuel *marketing consultant*
Rubenstein, Howard Joseph *public relations executive*
Rubenstein, Stanley Ellis *public relations consultant*
Rubin, Norman Julius *public relations consultant*
Rudd, Nicholas *marketing communications company executive*
Ruder, William *public relations executive*
Russo, Anthony Joseph *public relations professional*
Ruth, Carol A. *public relations executive*
Rutman, Mark Charles *public relations executive*
Ryle, Joseph Donald *public relations executive*
Sacks, Temi J. *public relations executive*
Sakai, Hiroko *trading company executive*
Santos, Eileen *management consultant*
Sarkis, J. Ziad *management consultant*
Sauerhaft, Stan *public relations executive, consultant*
Savas, Emanuel S. *public management educator*
Savory, Mark *management consultant, insurance company executive*
Sayre, Linda Damaris *human resources professional*
Schaffer, Kenneth B. *communications executive, satellite engineer, inventor, consultant*
Schaub, Sherwood Anhder, Jr. *management consultant*
†Schiekofer, Susan *advertising executive*
Schlaifer, Charles *advertising executive*
Schmertz, Herbert *public relations and advertising executive*
Schnall, David Jay *management and administration educator*
Schneider, Norman M. *business executive*
Schoonover, Jean Way *public relations consultant*
Schulman, Mark Allen *market research company executive*
Schupak, Leslie Allen *public relations company executive*
Schur, Jeffrey *advertising executive*
Schwab, Frank, Jr. *management consultant*
Schwartz, Alan Victor *advertising executive*
Schwartz, Lyle Victor *advertising executive*
Schweitzer, George *communications executive*
Scott, William Clement, III *entertainment industry executive*
Seadler, Stephen Edward *business and computer consultant, social scientist*
Seaman, Alfred Jarvis *retired advertising agency executive*
Secunda, Eugene *marketing communications executive, educator*
Segal, Joel Michael *advertising executive*
Seiden, Henry (Hank Seiden) *advertising executive*
Seiden, Steven Arnold *executive search consultant*
Seligson, Carl Harold *management consultant*
Selkowitz, Arthur *advertising agency executive*
Shaffer, Russell K. *advertising agency executive*
Shair, David Ira *human resources executive*
†Shapiro, Marvin Lincoln *communications company executive*
Sherman, Eugene Jay *marketing executive, economist, retired*
Sherman, Norman Mark *advertising agency executive*
Siegel, Herbert Jay *communications executive*
Siegel, Lucy Boswell *public relations executive*
Sikes, Alfred Calvin *communications executive*
Silverman, Marylin A. *advertising agency executive*
Simmons, J(ames) Gerald *management consultant*
Sinclair, Daisy *advertising executive, casting director*
Smith, George S., Jr. *communications financial executive*
Smith, Guy Lincoln, IV *strategic and crisis communications company executive*
Smith, Martin Jay *advertising and marketing executive*
Softness, John *public relations executive*
Soika, Helmut Emil *retirement plan executive*
†Solberg, Kathleen *advertising executive*
Sorensen, Robert C. *marketing executive, educator*
Soter, George Nicholas *advertising executive*
Souham, Gérard *communications executive*
Spector, Anita Frohmann *buyer*
Spirer, June Dale *marketing executive, clinical psychologist*
Spivak, Joan Carol *medical public relations specialist*
Sprague, Peter Julian *software company executive, lecturer*
Springer, John Shipman *public relations executive*
Stack, Edward William *business management and foundation executive*
Stautberg, Susan Schiffer *communications executive*
Stein, Elliot, Jr. *media executive*
Steinberg, Stephen Arthur *information systems executive*
†Stepanek, Daniel P. *public relations executive*
Stetler, Russell Dearnley, Jr. *private investigator*
Stevens, Art *public relations executive*
Stewart, Jeff *advertising agency executive*
Stewart, Kirk T. *public relations executive*
Stoddard, Laurence Ralph, Jr. *retired advertising executive*
Strand, Curt Robert *hotel executive*
†Stratigos, William Narge *computer company executive*
Strear, Joseph D. *public relations executive*
Stroock, Mark Edwin, II *public relations company executive*
Stuart, John McHugh, Jr. *public relations consultant, retired foreign service officer*
Stuart, Lori Ames *public relations executive*
Sturges, John Siebrand *management consultant*
Sulcer, Frederick Durham *advertising executive*
Sussman, Jeffrey Bruce *public relations and marketing executive*
Svinkelstin, Abraham Joshua *information technology executive*
Swanzey, Robert Joseph *data processing executive*
Swid, Stephen Claar *business executive*
Swift, John Francis *health care advertising company executive*
†Tanaka, Patrice Aiko *public relations executive*
Tarter, Fred Barry *advertising executive*
Tavon, Mary E. *public relations, marketing and communications executive*
†Tawaka, Patrice *public relations executive*
Taylor, Humphrey John Fausitt *information services executive*
Teran, Timothy Eric Alba *marketing professional*
Thrapp, Mark Stephen *executive search consultant*
Tilson, Dorothy Ruth *word processing executive*
Tisch, James S. *diversified holding company executive*
Tisch, Jonathan Mark *hotel company executive*
Tisch, Laurence Alan *diversified manufacturing and service executive*
Tofel, Richard Jeffrey *communication executive*
Torrenzano, Richard *public affairs executive*
Tortorello, Nicholas John *public opinion and market research company executive*
Tripodi, Louis Anthony *advertising agency executive*
Truesdell, Wesley Edwin *public relations and investor relations consultant*
Tumpowsky, Ira Bruce *advertising agency executive*
Turkel, Stanley *hotel consultant, management executive*
Turner, Hester Hill *management consultant*
Turso, Vito Anthony *public relations executive*
Ulrich, Max Marsh *executive search consultant*
Upson, Stuart Barnard *advertising agency executive*
Van Brunt, Albert Daniel *advertising agency executive*
Vermeer, Maureen Dorothy *sales executive*
Volpe, Thomas J. *advertising executive*
Wadsworth, Robert David *advertising agency executive*
Walke, David Michael *public relations executive*
Walsh, Annmarie Hauck *research firm executive*
Wanek, William Charles *public relations executive*
Warner, John Edward *advertising executive*
Weida, Lewis Dixon *marketing analyst, consultant*
Weiner, Richard *public relations executive*
Weinstein, Sharon Schlein *public relations executive, educator*
Weisberg, Jonathan Mark *public relations executive*
Weiss, Mark *public relations executive*
Weissman, Norman *public relations executive*
Wells, Victor Hugh, Jr. *advertising agency executive*
Wessinger, W. David *management consultant*
†Westover, Becke Karl *advertising executive*
Willett, Roslyn Leonore *public relations executive, food service consultant*
†Winston, Stanley S. *advertising executive*
†Wishner, Howard E. *public relations executive*
Wit, David Edmund *software and test preparation company executive*
Woit, Erik Peter *corporate executive, lawyer*
Wolff, Richard Joseph *public relations executive, consultant, historian*
Woodrum, Robert Lee *executive search consultant*
Woolsey, David Arthur *finance company executive*
Wright, Michael Kearney *public relations executive*
Wyse, Lois *advertising executive, author*
Zelnick, Strauss *entertainment company executive*
Zuckert, Donald Mack *marketing executive*

### Newtonville
Weber, Barbara M. *sales executive, consultant*

### Niskayuna
Sacklow, Stewart Irwin *advertising executive*

### North Salem
†Sloves, Marvin *advertising agency executive*

### North Tarrytown
Otten, Michael *data processing executive*

### Nyack
Karp, Peter Simon *marketing executive*
Keil, John Mullan *advertising agency executive*

### Orchard Park
Noll, John F. *sales and marketing executive, investment banker*

### Ossining
Eurell, Joseph Michael *marketing professional, municipal official*
Reynolds, Calvin *management consultant, business educator*

### Oyster Bay
Mooney, James David, Jr. *security consultant*

### Patterson
Winby, Mary Bernadette *marketing executive*

### Pearl River
Jackson, Phillip Ellis *cause-related marketing executive, writer*

### Pelham
Moore, Ellis Oglesby *retired public affairs consultant*

### Phillipsport
Hengesbach, Alice Ann *public relations consultant*

### Plattsburgh
Hanton, E(mile) Michael *public and personnel relations consultant*

### Pleasantville
Eschweiler, Peter Quintus *planning consultant*
Howard, Carole Margaret Munroe *public relations executive*
Keller, Mary Beth *advertising executive, researcher*
Schadt, James Phillip *consumer products executive*
Willis, William Henry *marketing executive*

### Port Chester
Ailloni-Charas, Dan *marketing executive*
†McKenna, John *computer company executive*

### Port Washington
Hackett, John Byron *advertising agency executive, lawyer*
Johnson, Tod Stuart *market research company executive*
Oromaner, Daniel Stuart *marketing consultant*
Sonnenfeldt, Richard Wolfgang *management consultant*

### Poughkeepsie
Agerwala, Tilak Krishna Mahesh *computer company executive*
Harris, Michael James *broadcasting executive*
Stridsberg, Albert Borden *advertising consultant, educator, editor*

### Pound Ridge
Rubino, John Anthony *management and human resources consultant*

Throckmorton, Joan Helen *direct marketing consultant*

### Ravena
Bower, Shelley Ann *business management consultant*

### Rhinebeck
Smith, Lewis Motter, Jr. *advertising and direct marketing executive*

### Rochester
Belgiorno, John *career consultant, educator*
DeToro, Irving John *management consultant*
Gartner, Joseph Charles *business systems administrator*
Harris, Diane Carol *merger and acquisition consulting firm executive*
Hart-Piper, Lauren *computer products professional*
Hutchins, Frank McAllister *advertising executive*
McCall, Thomas Donald *marketing communications company executive*
Mc Kelvey, Jean Trepp *industrial relations educator*
McKie, W. Gilmore *human resources executive*
Wegman, Robert B. *food service executive*
Wiedrick-Kozlowski, Jan Barbara *communications executive*

### Roosevelt
Wisner, Roscoe William, Jr. *retired human resources executive*

### Roslyn
Ulanoff, Stanley M. *communications executive*

### Rye
Kaulakis, Arnold Francis *management consultant*
Metzger, Frank *management consultant*
Mittelstadt, Charles Anthony *advertising executive*

### Saint Bonaventure
Khairullah, Zahid Yahya *management sciences and marketing educator, consultant*

### Saratoga Springs
Davis, John Eugene *restaurant owner*
Stanley, Karen Francine Mary Lesniewski *human resources professional*

### Scarsdale
Blinder, Abe Lionel *management consultant*
Celliers, Peter Joubert *public relations specialist*
Clark, Merrell Mays *management consultant*
Kaufman, Robert Jules *communications consultant, lawyer*
†Lehodey, John Francois *hotel company executive*
Oswald, George Charles *advertising executive, management and marketing consultant*
Rubin, A. Louis *advertising executive*

### Schenectady
Golub, Lewis *supermarket company executive*

### Shrub Oak
Roston, Arnold *information specialist, educator, advertising executive, artist, editor*

### Sleepy Hollow
Schmidt, Klaus Franz *advertising executive*

### Somers
Banik, Douglas Heil *marketing executive*
Cloudman, Francis Harold, III *computer company executive*
Estefan, Nabil *business and finance executive*
Miller, Alan *software executive, management specialist*
Sayers, Ken W(illiam) *writer and public relations executive*
Wahl, William Joseph, Jr. *information systems specialist*

### Southampton
Lieberman, Carol *healthcare marketing communications consultant*

### Stamford
Portland, Charles Denis *publishing executive*

### Staten Island
Fafian, Joseph, Jr. *management consultant*
Fernandes, Richard Louis *retired advertising agency executive*

### Stony Brook
Katz, Victoria Manuela *public relations executive, educator, consultant*

### Syosset
Roche, John Edward *human resources management consultant, educator*

### Syracuse
Cooper, John Ambrose *management coordinator, international marketer*
De Dell, Gary Jerome *printing company executive, consultant*
Higbee, Ann G. *public relations executive, consultant*
†Jabbour, John Jay *document product and services executive*
Mower, Eric Andrew *communications and marketing executive*

### Tappan
Fox, Muriel *public relations executive*

### Thornwood
Bassett, Lawrence C *management consultant*

### Troy
Bonney, William Lawless *data processing and telecommunications educator*
Schwartz, Robert William *management consultant*

### Tuckahoe
Brecher, Bernd *management consultant*
Elliott, Dennis Dawson *communications executive*

### Unadilla
Compton, John Robinson *printing company executive*

### Valley Stream
Greene, Howard Paul *communications executive*

### West Islip
Softness, Donald Gabriel *marketing and manufacturing executive*

### Westbury
DiFiglia, Constance Joan *professional ethics executive, consultant, physician, researcher, writer, poet*

### Westhampton Beach
Maas, Jane Brown *advertising executive*

### White Plains
Allen, Ralph Dean *diversified company corporate executive*
Colwell, Howard Otis *advertising executive*
Flesher, Margaret Covington *corporate communications executive*
Fortini, V(ictor) Scott *sales and marketing executive*
Fudge, Ann Marie *marketing executive*
Gill, Patricia Jane *human resources executive*
Mareth, Paul *communications consultant*
Roll, Irwin Clifford (Win Roll) *advertising, marketing and publishing executive*
Worboys, Roger Dick *communications executive*

### Woodbury
Stefancich, Donna Lee *information security specialist*

### Woodhaven
Bolster, Jacqueline Neben (Mrs. John A. Bolster) *communications consultant*

### Woodstock
Kugler, E(rnest) Richard *management consultant*

### Yaphank
Ahern, John James *software company executive*

### Yonkers
Miller, Karl A. *management counselor*
Pickover, Betty Abravanel *retired executive legal secretary, civic volunteer*

### Yorktown Heights
Rosenblatt, Stephen Paul *marketing and sales promotion company executive*

## NORTH CAROLINA

### Asheville
Etter, Robert Miller *retired consumer products executive, chemist*

### Burlington
Eddins, James William, Jr. *marketing executive*

### Carthage
Thomas, Carol Taylor *general services coordinator*

### Cary
Sussenguth, Edward Henry *computer company executive, computer network designer*

### Chapel Hill
Jerdee, Thomas Harlan *business administration educator, organization psychology researcher and consultant*
Lauterborn, Robert F. *advertising educator, consultant*
Swanson, Michael Alan *sales and marketing executive*

### Charlotte
Anoff, Jean Schoenstadt *advertising specialty company executive*
Bradshaw, Howard Holt *management consulting company executive*
†Eppes, Thomas Evans *advertising executive, public relations executive*
Glosson, Buster C. *venture capital, business development executive*
Hudgins, Catherine Harding *business executive*
Loeffler, William George, Jr. *advertising executive*
Lyerly, Elaine Myrick *advertising executive*
Risko, James Richard *business executive*
Sanford, James Kenneth *public relations executive*
Wenner, Gene Charles *arts management executive*

### Columbus
Lee, Wallace Williams, Jr. *retired hotel executive*

### Durham
Fogle, G. Lee *credit union executive, consultant*
Ladd, Marcia Lee *medical equipment and supplies company executive*
Otterbourg, Robert Kenneth *public relations consultant, writer*
Ryan, Gerard Spencer *inn executive*
Squire, Alexander *management consultant*

### Edenton
Rossman, Robert Harris *management consultant*

### Fremont
Ackerman, Lennis Campbell *management consultant retired*

### Goldsboro
Barkley, Monika Johanna *general contracting professional*

### Greensboro
Allen, Jesse Owen, III *management development and organizational behavior*
Formo, Brenda Terrell *travel company executive*
Sanders, William Eugene *marketing executive*
Spears, Alexander White, III *tobacco company executive*

### Hickory
George, Boyd Lee *consumer products company executive*

### Lake Toxaway
Morgan, Marianne *corporate professional*

### Matthews
Rivenbark, Jan Meredith *food service products corporate executive*

### Morganton
Sessa, Todd Raymond *marketing executive*

### New Bern
Mack, Clifford Glenn *investment banker, management consultant*

### North Wilkesboro
Herring, Leonard Gray *marketing company executive*
Parsons, Irene *management consultant*

### Pinehurst
Gilmore, Voit *travel executive*
Nuzzo, Salvatore Joseph *defense, electronics company executive*
Owings, Malcolm William *retired management consultant*
Paquette, Dean Richard *retired computer company executive, consultant*
Stingel, Donald Eugene *management consultant*

### Pinetops
Robertson, Richard Blake *management consultant*

### Raleigh
Doherty, Robert Cunningham *advertising executive*
Eberly, Harry Landis *retired communications company executive*
Grubb, Donald Hartman *paper industry company executive*
Holt, J. Darrin *corporate executive*
Howell-Drake, Mindy Anne *administrative assistant*
†Knutson, Gary Herbert *advertising company executive*
Leak, Robert E. *economic development consultant*
Ofner, J(ames) Alan *management consultant*
Rauch, Kathleen *computer executive*
Roisler, Glenn Harvey *quality assurance professional*
Shaw, Robert Gilbert *restaurant executive, senator*

### Research Triangle Park
Clark, Kevin Anthony *communications executive*
Hamner, Charles *company executive*

### Rural Hall
Wager, Michael *company executive*

### Sanford
Schneider, Steven L. *company executive*

### Statesville
Grogan, David R. *company executive*

### Supply
Jacobs, Richard Alan *management consultant*
Pollard, Joseph Augustine *advertising and public relations consultant*

### Vass
Glassman, Edward *public relations management creativity consultant*

### Weaverville
Parsons, Vinson Adair *retired computer software company executive*

### Wilmington
Flohr, Daniel P. *company executive*

### Wilson
Dean, Tad *research laboratory executive*

### Winston Salem
Atkinson, G. Douglas, Sr. *marketing executive, consultant*
Griswold, George *marketing, advertising and public relations executive*
Gunzenhauser, Gerard Ralph, Jr. *management consultant, investor*
Hamlin, Edwin Cliburn *sales consultant*
Johnston, James Wesley *retired tobacco company executive*
MacKinnon, Sally Anne *retired fast food company executive*

## NORTH DAKOTA

### Bismarck
Palmer, Richard Joseph *communications director*

### Bottineau
Gorder, Steven F. *business executive*

### Edinburg
Melsted, Marcella H. *retired administrative assistant, civic worker*

### Fargo
Koppelman, Kim Arden *advertising executive, public relations consultant*
Wallwork, William Wilson, III *automobile executive*

### Grand Forks
Rolshoven, Ross William *legal investigator, art photographer*

## OHIO

### Akron
Crawford, Robert John *credit company executive*
McCormick, William Edward *environmental consultant*
Sonnecken, Edwin Herbert *management consultant*

### Alliance
Rockhill, Jack Kerrigan *collections company executive*

### Avon Lake
Morton, David Ray *sales and marketing executive*

### Bay Village
Berger, James (Hank) *business broker*

### Beachwood
Seelbach, William Robert *management executive*

### Bedford
Baldassari, Jeffrey John *business executive*

### Broadview Heights
Sternlieb, Lawrence Jay *marketing professional*

### Chagrin Falls
Eastburn, Richard A. *consulting firm executive*
Fisher, Will Stratton *illumination consultant*

### Cincinnati
Artzt, Edwin Lewis *consumer products company executive*
Block, Janet Leven (Mrs. Joseph E. Rosen) *public relations consultant*
Brown, Dale Patrick *advertising executive*
Bull, Louis Antal (Tony) *sales executive*
†Christ, Iris Klein *healthcare sales executive*
Dillon, David Brian *retail grocery executive*
Eager, William Earl *information systems corporation executive*
Ferriss, David Platt *management consultant*
Groth, Jon Quentin *management consultant*
Henry, J(ohn) Porter, Jr. *sales consultant*
Hicks, Irle Raymond *retail food chain executive*
Howe, John Kingman *manufacturing, sales and marketing executive*
Hutton, Edward Luke *diversified public corporation executive*
Klein, Charles Henle *lithographing company executive*
Kollstedt, Paula Lubke *communications executive, writer*
Levy, Sam Malcolm *advertising executive*
Lockhart, John Mallery *management consultant*
Maier, Craig Frisch *restaurant executive*
McNulty, John William *retired public relations executive, automobile company executive*
Milligan, Lawrence Drake, Jr. *consumer products executive*
Million, Kenneth Rhea *management consultant*
Moler, James Clark *marketing research executive*
Pepper, John Ennis, Jr. *consumer products company executive*
Reitter, Charles Andrew *management consultant*
Sperzel, George E., Jr. *personal care industry executive*
Sullivan, Dennis James, Jr. *public relations executive*
†Wehling, Robert Louis *household products company executive*

### Cleveland
Alspaugh, Robert Odo *industrial management consultant*
Bailey, John Turner *public relations executive*
Clutter, Bertley Allen, III *management company executive*
Danco, Léon Antoine *management consultant, educator*
Dunbar, Mary Asmundson *communications executive, investor and public relations consultant*
Eaton, Henry Felix *public relations executive*
Fountain, Ronald Glenn *management consultant*
†Fusco, Diane Roman *public relations executive*
†Gallagher, Patrick Francis Xavier *public relations executive*
†Graham, John W. *advertising executive*
Hellman, Peter Stuart *corporate executive*
Henry, Edward Frank *computer accounting service executive*
Johnson, John Frank *professional recruitment executive*
†Juniewicz, Andrew M. *public relations executive*
Kenny, Raymond Patrick *greeting card company executive*
Liebow, Joanne Elisabeth *marketing communication coordinator*
Lowry, Dennis Martin *communications executive*
Marcus, Donald Howard *advertising agency executive*
Mason, Robert McSpadden *technology management educator, consultant*
McGinty, Thomas Edward *management consultant*
Mecredy, James R. *management consultant*
Miller, John Robert *environmental recycling company executive*
Newman, Joseph Herzl *advertising consultant*
Perkovic, Robert Branko *international management consultant*
Pollack, Florence K.Z. *management consultant*
Roop, James John *public relations executive*
Schonberg, Alan Robert *management recruiting executive*
†Silverman, William A. *public relations executive*
Skinner, Charles Scofield *technology management service executive, consultant, mechanical engineer*
Stashower, Sara Ellen *advertising executive*
Stevens, Edward *public relations executive*
Sudow, Thomas Nisan *marketing services company executive, broadcaster*
Taw, Dudley Joseph *sales executive*
Zimmerman, Michael Glenn *marketing and communications executive*

### Columbus
Ackerman, Kenneth Benjamin *management consultant, writer*
Brown, Rowland Chauncey Widrig *information systems, strategic planning and ethics consultant*
Burke, Kenneth Andrew *advertising executive*
McClain, Thomas E. *communications executive*
McCoy, William Earl, Jr. *economic development training consultant*
Muller, Mervin Edgar *information systems educator, consultant*
Ryan, Robert *consulting company executive*
Taylor, Celianna Isley *information systems specialist*
Tipton, Clyde Raymond, Jr. *communications and resources development consultant*

### Dayton
†Dalrymple, Cheryl *online information company executive*
†Davies, Tim *online information company executive*
Fulton, Darrell Nelson *information systems specialist*
Kegerreis, Robert James *management consultant, marketing educator*
Nevin, Robert Charles *information systems executive*
†Reading, Anthony John *business executive, accountant*
Schnier, David Christian *marketing executive, author*

### Dublin
Freytag, Donald Ashe *management consultant*
Smith, K(ermit) Wayne *computer company executive*

### Elyria
Patton, Thomas James *sales and marketing executive*
Pucko, Diane Bowles *public relations executive*

### Franklin
Murray, Thomas Dwight *advertising agency executive*

### Gates Mills
Abbott, James Samuel, III *marketing executive*

### Germantown
Lansaw, Charles Ray *sales industry executive*

### Hilliard
Cash, Francis Winford *hotel industry executive*
†Longerbone, Doug *hotel executive*

### Independence
Luciano, Gwendolyn Kaye *planning specialist, utility rates administrator*

### Kent
Bissler, Richard Thomas *mortician*
Stevenson, Thomas Herbert *management consultant, writer*

### Lancaster
Katlic, John Edward *management consultant*
Phillips, Edward John *consulting firm executive*

### Maineville
Collins, Larry Wayne *small business owner, information systems specialist*

### Mansfield
Ellison, Lorin Bruce *management consultant*
Pesec, David John *data systems executive*

### Maple Heights
Sargent, Liz Elaine (Elizabeth Sargent) *safety consulting executive*

### Marysville
Jones-Morton, Pamela *human resources specialist*
Rogula, James Leroy *consumer products company executive*

### Milford
Shipley, Tony L(ee) *software company executive*

### Niles
Travaglini, Raymond Dominic *corporate executive*

### North Olmsted
Galysh, Robert Alan *information systems analyst*

### Oberlin
Gladieux, Bernard Louis *management consultant*

### Oxford
Pringle, Lewis Gordon *marketing professional, educator*

### Painesville
Lucier, P. Jeffrey *publishing and computer company executive*

### Peninsula
Ludwig, Richard Joseph *ski resort executive*

### Port Clinton
Subler, Edward Pierre *advertising executive*

### Powell
Reed, Constance Louise *materials management and purchasing consultant*

### Saint Clairsville
Dankworth, Margaret Anne *management consultant*

### Salem
Fehr, Kenneth Manbeck *computer systems company executive*

### Solon
Stauffer, Thomas George *hotel executive*

### Streetsboro
Weiss, Joseph Joel *consulting company executive*

### Sylvania
Ring, Herbert Everett *management executive*

### Tipp City
Taylor, Robert Homer *quality assurance professional, pilot*

### Toledo
Block, Allan James *communications executive*
Carpenter, John Edward *marketing professional*
Cole, Jeffrey Clark *corporate public relations executive*
Loeffler, William Robert *quality productivity specialist, engineering educator*
Northup, John David *management consultant, inventor*
Paquette, Jack Kenneth *management consultant, antiques dealer*
Sanderson, David Alan *training and development administrator*

### Warren
Auchterlonie, David Thomas *quality assurance professional*

### West Alexandria
Scoville, George Richard *marketing professional*

### Westerville
Kollat, David Truman *management consultant*

### Westlake
†Wozniak, Donald Richard *information systems executive*

### Wooster
Schmitt, Wolfgang Rudolf *consumer products executive*

### Wright Patterson AFB
Szucs, Andrew Eric *training manager*

### Wyoming
Cooley, William Edward *regulatory affairs manager*

### Xenia
Nutter, Zoe Dell Lantis *retired public relations executive*

### Zanesville
Truby, John Louis *computer, management and trucking consultant*

## OKLAHOMA

### Ada
Mildren, Jack *legal services company executive, former state official*

### Broken Arrow
Everett, Carl Nicholas *management consulting executive*
Striegel, Peggy Simsarian *advertising executive*

### Edmond
Binning, Gene Barton *educator, management consultant*

### Miami
Dicharry, James Paul *company official, retired air force officer*

### Mustang
Laurent, J(erry) Suzanna *technical communications specialist*

### Norman
Carver, Charles Ray *retired information systems company executive*

### Oklahoma City
Ackerman, Raymond Basil *advertising agency executive*
Bailey, Clark Trammell, II *public relations/public affairs professional*
Blackwell, John Adrian, Jr. *computer company executive*
Burns, Marion G. *management consultant, retired council executive*
Hulseberg, Paul David *financial executive, educator*
Jones, Brenda Kaye *public relations executive*
Khaleeluddin, Mansoor *marketing professional*
LaMotte, Janet Allison *management specialist*
Ruhrup, Clifton Brown *sales executive*
Stauth, Robert Edward *food service executive*
Worthington, J.B. *business executive*

### Oktaha
Taylor, Clayton Charles *management and political legislative consultant*

### Stillwater
Matoy, Elizabeth Anne *personnel executive*

### Tulsa
Gentry, Bern Leon, Sr. *minority consulting company executive*
Mourton, J. Gary *communications executive*
Naumann, William Carl *consumer products company executive*
Robertson, Vicki Dawn *adminstrative secretary, writer*
Rubottom, Donald Julian *management consultant*

### Yukon
Ford, Yvonne Ardella *barber stylist, entrepreneur*

## OREGON

### Baker City
Graham, Beardsley *management consultant*

### Beaverton
Bosch, Samuel Henry *computer company executive*
Chang, David Ping-Chung *business consultant, architect*

### Eugene
Bennett, Robert Royce *engineering and management consultant*
Chambers, Carolyn Silva *communications company executive*
Miner, John Burnham *industrial relations educator, writer*

### Forest Grove
Carson, William Morris *manpower planning and development advisor*

### Grants Pass
Naylor, John Thomas *telephone company executive*

### Hillsboro
Masi, Edward A. *computer company executive*

**Mcminnville**
Naylor-Jackson, Jerry *public relations consultant, retired, entertainer, broadcaster*

**Medford**
Hennion, Reeve Lawrence *communications executive*
Keener, John Wesley *management consultant*

**Portland**
Anderegg, Karen Klok *marketing executive*
Butler, Leslie Ann *advertising executive, portrait artist, writer*
Conkling, Roger Linton *consultant, business administration educator, retired utility executive*
Linstone, Harold Adrian *management and systems science educator*
Maclean, Charles (Bernard Maclean) *public affairs and marketing consultant*
Martin, Lucy Z. *public relations executive*
Skiens, William Eugene *electrical interconnect systems scientist, polymer engineer*
Sugg, John Logan (Jack Sugg) *advertising executive*
Suwyn, Mark A. *building products executive*
†Van Sickle, Sharon *public relations executive*
†Wieden, Dan G. *advertising executive*

**Wilsonville**
McMahon, Paul Francis *international management consultant*

## PENNSYLVANIA

**Alcoa Center**
Kubisen, Steven Joseph, Jr. *marketing professional*

**Allentown**
Armstrong, W(illiam) Warren *advertising agency executive*
Craig, Douglas Warren *food service industry executive*

**Ambler**
Learnard, William Ewing *marketing executive*

**Ardmore**
Lockett-Egan, Marian Workman *advertising executive*
Scott, Bill *advertising agency executive*

**Bensalem**
Bishop, Howard Stuart *management consultant*

**Berwyn**
Guenther, George Carpenter *travel company executive, retired*

**Bethlehem**
Penny, Roger Pratt *management executive*
von Bernuth, Carl W. *diversified corporation executive, lawyer*

**Blue Bell**
Faden, Lee Jeffrey *technical advisory service executive*
Minter, Philip Clayton *retired communications company executive*

**Brentwood**
Swanson, Fred A. *communications designer, borough councilman*

**Bryn Mawr**
Kraftson, Raymond Harry *business executive*

**Buckingham**
Altier, William John *management consultant*

**Camp Hill**
Crist, Christine Myers *consulting executive*

**Chadds Ford**
Cantwell, John Walsh *advertising executive*

**Chambersburg**
Furr, Quint Eugene *marketing executive*

**Collegeville**
Galie, Frank D. *sales executive*

**Dallas**
Sutton, Royal Keith *marketing professional*

**Doylestown**
Thorne, John Watson, III *advertising and marketing executive*

**Evans City**
Salisbury, Judith Muriel *marketing consultant*

**Exton**
Burns, Richard James *marketing professional*
Sanford, Richard D. *computer company executive*
Walls, Thomas Francis *management consultant*

**Ferndale**
Folk, James *sales executive*

**Fort Washington**
Blumberg, Donald Freed *management consultant*
Deric, Arthur Joseph *management consultant, lawyer*

**Gettysburg**
Hallberg, Budd Jaye *management consulting firm executive*

**Gladwyne**
Stick, Alyce Cushing *information systems consultant*

**Grantville**
Sudor, Cynthia Ann *marketing and corporate sponsorship consultant*

**Greensburg**
Boyd, Robert Wright, III *lamp company executive*

**Greentown**
Hall, Cathy E. *sales professional*

**Gwynedd**
Chasins, Edward A. *communications company executive*

**Harrisburg**
Edwards, JoAnn Louise *human resources executive*
Moritz, Milton Edward *security consultant*
Neilson, Winthrop Cunningham, III *communications executive, financial communications consultant*
Stabler, Donald Billman *business executive*

**Haverford**
Gross, Stanley Carl *marketing consultant*

**Hummelstown**
Smedley, Elizabeth *researcher, codifier, consultant, historian, writer*

**Huntingdon Valley**
Vollum, Robert Boone *management consultant*

**Kennett Square**
Hennes, Robert Taft *former management consultant, investment executive*

**King Of Prussia**
Fitzgerald, Walter George *marketing executive*
Olson, Bob Moody *marketing executive*

**Lancaster**
Dunlap, Hallowell *data processing executive*
Kelly, Robert Lynn *advertising agency executive*
Veitch, Boyer Lewis *printing company executive*

**Langhorne**
Brennan, John James *marketing executive*

**Lebanon**
Deysher, Paul Evans *training consultant*

**Lewisburg**
Rote, Nelle Fairchild Hefty *business consultant*

**Lower Burrell**
Kinosz, Donald Lee *quality consultant*

**Mechanicsburg**
Bitner, Jerri Lynne *information systems professional*

**Media**
Barnett, Samuel Treutlen *international company executive*

**Mountainhome**
Buttz, Charles William *outdoor advertising executive*

**Narberth**
Newhall, John Harrison *management consultant*

**Nazareth**
Herrick, Robert Ford *personnel consultant*

**Newtown Square**
Bower, Ward Alan *management consultant, lawyer*

**Nineveh**
Quackenbush, Robert Dean *management consultant*

**Nottingham**
White, Richard Edmund *marketing executive*

**Oakmont**
Pruitt, Charles William, Jr. *long term health care executive, educator*

**Philadelphia**
†Albertini, Stephen A. *advertising executive*
Barrett, James Edward, Jr. *management consultant*
Blades, Herbert William *diversified consumer products company executive*
Burton, Richard Greene *retired marketing executive*
Coulson, Zoe Elizabeth *retired consumer marketing executive*
Dickerson, Rita M. *human resources professional*
DuBois, Ruth Harberg *human service agency executive*
Estrin, Deborah Perry *human resources executive*
Feninger, Claude *industry management services company executive*
Finney, Graham Stanley *management consultant*
Fuller, John Garsed Campbell *food and drug company executive*
Gemmill, Elizabeth H. *corporate executive*
Gilbert, Harry Ephraim, Jr. *hotel executive*
Goodchild, John Charles, Jr. *advertising and public relations executive*
Greenberg, Marshall Gary *marketing research consultant*
Jordan, Clifford Henry *management consultant*
Korsyn, Irene Hahne *marketing executive*
Landis, Edgar David *services business company executive*
McIntosh, L(orne) William *marketing executive*
Mitchell, Howard Estill *human resources educator, consultant*
Neubauer, Joseph *food services company executive*
Oliva, Terence Anthony *marketing educator*
Roberts, Brian Leon *communications executive*
Roberts, Ralph Joel *telecommunications, cable broadcast executive*
Schluth, Michael Vernon *advertising executive*
Seiders, Joseph Robert *service company corporate executive, lawyer*
Tierney, Brian Patrick *advertising and public relations executive*
Waite, Helen Eleanor *funeral director*
Wilder, Robert George *advertising and public relations executive*
Williams, Robert Benjamin *convention center executive*
Yaffe, Peter Marc *public policy consultant, gas industry executive*

**Phoenixville**
Brundage, Russell Archibald *retired data processing executive*

**Pittsburgh**
Aronson, Mark Berne *corporate executive, private consumer advocate*
Bender, Charles Christian *retail home center executive*
Bergen, John Donald *communications, public affairs executive*
Boyd, William, Jr. *business advisor, banker*
Burger, Herbert Francis *advertising agency executive*
Dempsey, Jerry Edward *service company executive*
Fine, Milton *hotel company executive, lawyer*
Fisher, James Aiken *industrial marketing executive*
Genge, William Harrison *advertising executive, writer*
Gerhard, Harry E., Jr. *counter trader, management and trade consultant*
Hershey, Colin Harry *management consultant*
Humphrey, Watts Sherman *technical executive, author*
Marts, Terri Louise *management executive*
Mason, Craig Watson *corporate planning executive*
Neel, John Dodd *memorial park executive*
Patten, Charles Anthony *management consultant, retired manufacturing company executive, author*
Reichblum, Audrey Rosenthal *public relations executive*
Shapira, David S. *food chain executive*
Simmermon, James Everett *credit bureau executive*
Wagner, Florence Zeleznik *telecommunications executive*
Walsh, Michael Francis *advertising executive*
Weaver, Charles Henry *business consulting executive*

**Plymouth Meeting**
Brownstone, Hugh Michael *technology executive*
Siegal, Jacob J. *management and financial consultant*
Thomsen, Thomas Richard *retired communications company executive*

**Port Royal**
Wert, Jonathan Maxwell, II *management consultant*

**Radnor**
Draeger, Kenneth W. *high technology company executive*
Harrison, Robert Drew *management consultant*
Marland, Alkis Joseph *leasing company executive, computer science educator, financial planner*
Paier, Adolf Arthur *computer software and services company executive*

**Reading**
Dersh, Rhoda E. *management consultant, business executive*

**Ridley Park**
Walls, William Walton, Jr. *management consultant*

**Rochester**
Goulait, John Joseph *aircraft maintenance specialist*

**Saint Marys**
Shobert, Erle Irwin, II *management consultant*

**Southampton**
Appell, Kathleen Marie *management consultant, legal administrator*

**Southeastern**
Hawley, Linda Donovan *advertising executive*

**Sunbury**
†Weis, Robert Freeman *supermarket company executive*

**Tannersville**
Moore, James Alfred *ski company executive, lawyer*

**Telford**
†Kamnitsis, Gus *electronic industry executive*

**Turtle Creek**
Collins, Carrie Linda Clark *administrative assistant*

**Unionville**
De Marino, Donald Nicholson *international business executive, former federal agency administrator*

**University Park**
Gouran, Dennis Stephen *communications educator*

**Valley Forge**
LaBoon, Lawrence Joseph *personnel consultant*
Rassbach, Herbert David *marketing executive*
Schaefer, Adolph Oscar, Jr. *advertising agency executive*

**Warrendale**
Buckley, Deborah Jeanne Morey *technical marketing specialist*
Snyder, Linda Ann *marketing specialist*

**Warrington**
Shaw, Milton Herbert *conglomerate executive*

**Wayne**
Carroll, Robert W. *retired business executive*
Coane, James Edwin, III *information technology executive*
Martino, Peter Dominic *software company executive, military officer*

**West Chester**
Dunlop, Edward Arthur *computer company executive*
Hurd-Graham, Robin J. *sales and marketing executive, consultant*
Tomlinson, Charles Wesley, Jr. *advertising executive*

**West Conshohocken**
Mullen, Eileen Anne *human resources executive*

**Willow Grove**
Asplundh, Christopher B. *tree service company executive*
Emory, Thomas Mercer, Jr. *data communications equipment manufacturing executive*
†Schiffman, Louis F. *management consultant*

**Wynnewood**
Belinger, Harry Robert *business executive, retired*

**Wyomissing**
Pellecchia, Eve Wassall *management consultant*

**Yardley**
Newsom, Carolyn Cardall *management consultant*

**York**
Horn, Russell Eugene, Jr. *business executive*
Snyder, Jan Louise *administrative aide, retired*

## RHODE ISLAND

**Barrington**
Mihaly, Eugene Bramer *corporate executive, consultant, writer, educator*

**Block Island**
Coxe, Weld *management consultant*

**Bristol**
Esty, David Cameron *marketing and communications executive*

**Cranston**
Cardi, Vincenzo *marketing professional, financial and investment consultant, pharmacist*

**Lincoln**
Burgdoerfer, Jerry J. *marketing and distribution executive*

**Pawtucket**
Davison, C. Hamilton *greeting card executive*
Hassenfeld, Alan Geoffrey *toy company executive*
O'Neill, John T. *toy company executive*

**Providence**
Eddy, Edward Danforth *academic administrator, educator*
†LaButti, Gerald Michael *company executive*

## SOUTH CAROLINA

**Anderson**
Vaughan, Dennis J. *business executive*

**Beaufort**
Day, John Sidney *management sciences educator*

**Charleston**
De Wolff, Louis *management consultant*
Perry, Evelyn Reis *communications company executive*

**Clemson**
Burch, Elmer Earl *management educator*

**Columbia**
Case, George Tilden, Jr. *marketing professional*
Ferillo, Charles Traynor, Jr. *public relations executive*
Floyd, Frank Albert, Jr. *management executive*
Jaco, Thomas Wright *hazardous materials administrator*
MacIlwinen, William Lee, Jr. *executive search consultant*
Martin, Charles Wallace *travel executive, retired university administrator*

**Easley**
Goldman, Joseph Elias *advertising executive*
Sundstrom, Harold Walter *public relations executive*

**Goose Creek**
Kershner, Jerry Wayne *human resources director*

**Green Pond**
Ittleson, H(enry) Anthony *bicycle vacation company executive*

**Greenville**
†Anderson, Greg Richard *broadcasting executive*
Fitzgerald, Eugene Francis *management consultant*
Gerretsen, Gilbert Wynand (Gil Gerretsen) *marketing and management consultant*
Morton, James Carnes, Jr. *public relations executive*
Taylor, John L. *communications executive*
Townes, Bobby Joe *travel agency executive*

**Hilton Head Island**
Klein, James Ronald *international consulting company executive*
Little, Thomas Mayer *public relations executive*
McKeldin, William Evans *management consultant*
Patton, Joseph Donald, Jr. *management consultant*
Perdunn, Richard Francis *management consultant*
Wood, Donald Craig *retired marketing professional*

**Mount Pleasant**
Hill, Larkin Payne *real estate company data processing executive*

**North Augusta**
Pritchard, Constance Jenkins *human resources/ organizion development trainer*

**Ridgeland**
Gardner, James *recreational management executive, personal care industry executive*
Smart, Jacob Edward *management consultant*

**Rock Hill**
Click, John William *communication educator*

**Saint Helena Island**
Herzbrun, David Joseph *retired advertising executive, consultant*

**Spartanburg**
Adamson, James *restaurant holding company executive*
Adamson, James B. *business executive*

## SOUTH DAKOTA

**Brookings**
Swiden, Ladell Ray *travel company executive*

**North Sioux City**
Waitt, Ted W. *computer company executive*

**Sioux Falls**
Johnson, Warren R. *marketing executive, consultant*
Taplett, Lloyd Melvin *human resources management consultant*

**Vermillion**
Clifford, Sylvester *retired communication educator*

## TENNESSEE

**Chattanooga**
Goodman, Michael Frederick *advertising executive*
Knight, Ralph H. *consumer products company executive*
Young, Sonia Winer *public relations director*

**Collierville**
†Ludwig, Charles T. *technical company executive*

**Dyersburg**
Baker, Kerry Allen *management consultant*

**Gallatin**
Bradley, Nolen Eugene, Jr. *personnel executive, educator*
Ellis, Joseph Newlin *retired distribution company executive*

**Knoxville**
Herndon, Anne Harkness *sales executive*
Mayfield, T. Brient, IV *media and computer executive*
Siler, Susan Reeder *communications educator*

**La Follette**
McDonald, Miller Baird *management consultant, columnist, historian*

**Maryville**
Davis, William Walter *recruiter, trainer*

**Memphis**
Abston, Dunbar, Jr. *management executive*
Granger, David Mason *broadcasting and communications executive*
Hyde, Joseph R., III *retail auto parts executive*
Krieger, Robert Lee, Jr. *management consultant, educator, writer, political analyst*
Ledsinger, Charles Albert, Jr. *hotel, gaming executive*
Pulido, Miguel Lazaro *marketing professional*
Sullivan, Eugene Joseph *food service company executive*

**Nashville**
Bolinger, John C., Jr. *management consultant*
Brown, Tony Ersic *record company executive*
Cawthon, William Connell *operations management consultant*
Clouse, Robert Wilburn *communication executive, educator*
Dobbs, George Albert *funeral director, embalmer*
Faust, A. Donovan *communications executive*
†Ingram, Martha R. *company executive*
James, Kay Louise *management consultant, healthcare executive*
Kaludis, George *management consultant, book company executive, educator*
Kephart, Floyd W. *corporate strategist*
Lawrence, Thomas Patterson *public relations executive*
Meredith, Owen Nichols *public relations executive, genealogist*
Moore, William Grover, Jr. *management consultant, former air freight executive, former air force officer*
Van Mol, Louis John, Jr. *public relations executive*
Wendell, Earl W. *entertainment company executive*

**Oak Ridge**
Whittle, Charles Edward, Jr. *consultant, lecturer*

**Shelbyville**
Yates, Patricia England *employment company executive*

**Tullahoma**
Gossick, Lee Van *consultant, executive, retired air force officer*

## TEXAS

**Amarillo**
Borchardt, Paul Douglas *recreational executive*

**Argyle**
Merritt, Joe Frank *industrial supply executive*

**Arlington**
Henderson, Arvis Burl *data processing executive, biochemist*
†Sawyer, Dolores *motel facility executive*
Spears, Georgann Wimbish *marketing executive*

**Austin**
Bredemeyer, Loretta Jeane *public relations, vocational and academic consultant*
Casey, James Francis *management consultant*
Chavarria, Ernest Montes, Jr. *international trade, business and finance consultant, lecturer*
Culp, George Hart *computer executive, consultant*
†Gurasich, Stephen William, Jr. *advertising executive*
Hammer, Katherine Gonet *software company executive*
Hart, Roderick P. *communications educator, researcher, author*
Hefner, Robert Eugene *technology management consultant*
Hodge, Ann F. *environmental company executive*

Johnson, Patrick D. *human resources executive*
Knapp, Mark Lane *communications educator, consultant*
Moore, Rebecca Ann Rucker *marketing executive*
Morgante, John-Paul *state government training administrator*
Pate, Jacqueline Hail *retired data processing company executive*
Payne, John Ross *rare books and archives appraisal consulting company executive, library science educator*
Shaw, James *computer systems analyst*
Shipley, George Corless *political consultant*
†Spence, Roy *advertising executive*
Vande Hey, James Michael *corporate executive, former air force officer*
Walls, Carl Edward, Jr. *communications company official*
Winegar, Albert Lee *computer systems company executive*
Young, Harrison, II *software development and marketing executive*

**Burleson**
Prior, Boyd Thelman *management consultant*

**College Station**
Gunn, Clare Alward *travel consultant, writer, retired educator*

**Colleyville**
Thompson, James Richard *human resources management consultant*

**Dallas**
Arnold, George Lawrence *advertising company executive*
Barnett, Patricia Ann *public relations professional*
Benn, Douglas Frank *information technology and computer science executive*
Buzzell, Barbara Feder *public relations executive*
Cave, Skip *company executive*
Cummings, Brian Thomas *public relations company executive*
Dalton, Harry Jirou, Jr. (Jerry Dalton) *public relations executive*
Dedman, Robert Henry *sales executive*
Dillon, Donald Ward *management consultant*
†Dobbs, James Frederick *marketing professional*
Dozier, David Charles, Jr. *marketing public relations and advertising executive*
Durham, Michael Jonathan *information technology company executive*
Dykeman, Alice Marie *public relations executive*
Elam, Andrew Gregory, II *convention and visitors bureau executive*
Ellis, June B. *human resource consultant*
Flores, Marion Thomas *advertising executive*
Friedheim, Stephen Bailey *public relations executive*
Gossen, Emmett Joseph, Jr. *motel chain executive, lawyer*
Grimes, David Lynn *communications company executive*
Halpin, James F. *business executive*
Halter, Kevin B. *communications executive*
Healy, Margaret Mary *retail marketing executive*
Heydrick, Linda Carol *consulting company executive, editor*
Hoffman, Harold Wayne *advertising agency executive*
Horchow, S(amuel) Roger *marketing consultant*
†Jorns, Steven D. *hotel executive*
Keith, Camille Tigert *airline marketing executive*
Korba, Robert W. *communications executive*
Lane, Alvin Huey, Jr. *management consultant*
Leigh-Manuell, Robert Allen *training executive, educator*
Lersch, DeLynden Rife *computer engineering executive*
Levenson, Stanley Richard *public relations and advertising executive*
Loveless, Kathy Lynne *client services executive*
Lucier, James Alfred *advertising executive*
MacMahon, Paul *advertising executive*
McCarthy, Michael Joseph *communications company executive*
Murphy, Randall Kent *training consultant*
Owens, Robin Maria *management consultant*
Robinson, Hugh Granville *consulting management company executive*
Rose, Charles David *consulting company executive*
Routman, Daniel Glenn *marketing and business development professional, lawyer*
Scott, Terry Lee *communications company executive*
Sheinberg, Israel *computer company executive*
Snead, Richard Thomas *restaurant company executive*
Solomon, Risa Greenberg *video software industry executive*
Spiegel, Lawrence Howard *advertising executive*
Taylor, Barbara Alden *public relations executive*
Thomas, Robert Ray *management consultant*
Vanderveld, John, Jr. *waste disposal company executive*
Warren, Thomas Paul *consulting executive*
Werner, Seth Mitchell *advertising executive*
Whitt, Robert Ampudia, III *advertising executive, marketing professional*
Wilber, Robert Edwin *corporate executive*
Wyly, Charles Joseph, Jr. *corporate executive*

**Del Rio**
Prather, Gerald Luther *management consultant, retired air force officer, judge*

**DeSoto**
Cupp, Marilyn Marie *sales executive*

**Dripping Springs**
Ballard, Mary Melinda *financial communications and investment banking firm executive*

**Dyess AFB**
Lawson, Melanie Kay *management administrator, early childhood consultant*

**Eastland**
Quinn, Janita Sue *city secretary*

**El Paso**
Cassidy, Richard Thomas *hotel executive, defense industry consultant, retired army officer*
Roberts, Ernst Edward *marketing consultant*

**Fort Worth**
Appel, Bernard Sidney *marketing consultant*
Bush, Alan Clifford *computer company executive*
Livengood, Charlotte Louise *employee development specialist*
Owens, Merle Wayne *executive search consultant*
Phillips, Robert James, Jr. *corporate executive*
Ray, Paul Richard, Jr. *executive search consultant*
Turner, Loyd Leonard *advertising executive, public relations executive*

**Grapevine**
Holley, Cyrus Helmer *management consulting service executive*
Smith, Lee Herman *business executive*

**Greenville**
Brown, Harley Mitchell *retired computer company executive, writer*

**Hico**
Blankenship, Jenny Mary *public relations executive, publisher, editor-in-chief*

**Horseshoe Bay**
Lesikar, Raymond Vincent *business administration educator*

**Houston**
Bostic, Jacqueline Whiting *management consultant, retired postmaster, association executive*
Cofran, George Lee *management consultant*
Cole, Aubrey Louis *management consultant, forest products company executive*
Dosher, John Rodney *consulting management consultant*
Finney, Clifton Donald *publishing executive*
Flato, William Roeder, Jr. *software development company executive*
Gilbert, Harold Stanley *warehousing company executive*
Hart, James Whitfield, Jr. *corporate public affairs executive, lawyer*
Heiker, Vincent Edward *information systems executive*
Helland, George Archibald, Jr. *management consultant, manufacturing executive, former government official*
Holmes, Darrell *tourism consultant*
Hutcheson, Thad Thomson, Jr. *international executive*
†Ifft, Lewis George, III *company administrator*
Jeanneret, Paul Richard *management consultant*
Kaye, Howard *business executive*
Kors, R. Paul *search company executive*
Larkin, William Vincent, Jr. *service company executive*
Levit, Max *food service executive*
Lowry, William Randall *executive recruiter*
Mampre, Virginia Elizabeth *communications executive*
†Marcus, Jerry *broadcasting executive*
Mauck, William M., Jr. *executive recruiter, small business owner*
McKim, Paul Arthur *management consultant, retired petroleum executive*
Morrison, Scott David *computer company executive*
Myers, James Clark *advertising and public relations executive*
Myers, Norman Allan *marketing professional*
Nesbitt, Vance Gordon *computer software company executive*
Newberry, Robert Curtis, Sr. *communications executive, newspaper editor*
Onstead, Randall *consumer goods company executive*
Onstead, Robert R. *consumer goods company executive*
Orr, Joseph Newton *recreational guide, outdoor educator*
Palmer, James Edward *public relations executive*
Pfeiffer, Eckhard *computer company executive*
Phillippi, Elmer Joseph, Jr. *data communications analyst*
Ribble, Anne Hoerner *communications executive*
Seaman, Roual Duane *data processing company executive*
Solymosy, Edmond Sigmond Albert *international marketing executive, retired army officer*
†Trimble, Eddie Don *television executive*
Watson, Max P., Jr. *computer software company executive*
Welch, Byron Eugene *communications educator*
Yuen, Benson Bolden *airline management consultant, software executive*

**Humble**
Hawk, Phillip Michael *service corporation executive*

**Huntsville**
Smyth, Joseph Philip *travel industry executive*

**Hurst**
Owen, Cynthia Carol *sales executive*

**Irving**
Dinicola, Robert *consumer products company executive*
Gretzinger, Ralph Edwin, III *management consultant*
Lifson, Kalman Alan *management consultant, retail executive*
†McClain, Dennis Douglas *advertising executive*
Tucker, Phyllis Anita *sales representative, guidance counselor*
Wicks, William Withington *retired public relations executive*

**Kerrville**
Cremer, Richard Eldon *marketing professional*

**Montgomery**
Snider, Robert Larry *management consultant*

**Plano**
Alberthal, Lester M., Jr. *information processing services executive*
Collumb, Peter John *communications company executive*
Grogan, Timothy James *information technology executive*

**Quinlan**
Gross, Paul Allan *health service executive*

**Randolph AFB**
Blankenbeker, Joan Winifred *communications computer/information management executive*

**Richardson**
Bick, David Greer *healthcare marketing executive*
Fahrlander, Henry William, Jr. *management consultant*
Hagan, Joseph Lawrence *communications executive*
Li, Shu *business executive*
Nugent, John Hilliard *communications executive*
Wyman, Richard Thomas *information services consultant*
†Yang, Yueh Sam *electronics company executive*

**Rosenberg**
Jaunal, Bridget Kennedy *energy and environmental company executive, consultant*

**San Angelo**
Coe, Robert Stanford *retired management educator*

**San Antonio**
Butt, Charles Clarence *food service executive*
†Conly, Michael J. *communications company executive, television executive*
Cory, William Eugene *retired consulting company executive*
Crowsey, Cheryl Ann *marketing professional*
Davis, Walter Barry *quality assurance professional*
Keck, James Moulton *retired advertising and marketing executive, retired air force officer*
Kehl, Randall Herman *executive, consultant, lawyer*
Leavitt, Audrey Faye Cox *television programming executive*
†Mead, Gary L. *hotel executive*
Montemayor, Carlos R. *advertising executive*
†Schultz, Steven T. *hotel executive*
Shirley, Graham Edward *management executive*
Wickstrom, Jon Alan *telecommunications executive, consultant*
Wimpress, Gordon Duncan, Jr. *corporate consultant, foundation executive*

**San Marcos**
Moore, Patsy Sites *food service consultant*

**Southlake**
Farquhar, Karen Lee *commercial printing company executive, consultant*
Friedman, Barry *financial marketing consultant*

**Spring**
Cooley, Andrew Lyman *corporation executive, former army officer*

**Sugar Land**
Preng, David Edward *management consultant*

**Temple**
Odem, Joyce Marie *human resources specialist*

**Trophy Club**
Caffee, Virginia Maureen *secretary*

**Tyler**
Resnik, Linda Ilene *marketing and information executive, consultant*

**Waco**
Garland, Meg *advertising executive*

**Weatherford**
McMahon, Robert Lee, Jr. (Bob McMahon) *information systems executive*

## UTAH

**Orem**
Morey, Robert Hardy *communications executive*
Sawyer, Thomas Edgar *management consultant*

**Park City**
Ebbs, George Heberling, Jr. *management consulting company executive*

**Provo**
Bartlett, Leonard Lee *communications educator, retired advertising agency executive, advertising historian*
Buck, William Fraser, II *marketing executive*
Clark, Loyal Frances *public affairs specialist*

**Riverdale**
Anderson, Byron Floyd *business and political consultant*

**Saint George**
Potwin, Juanita R. *marketing professional, dental hygienist*

**Salt Lake City**
Carlson, Ralph Jennings *communications executive*
Davis, Gene *public relations professional, state legislator*
Davis, Loyd Evan *defense industry marketing professional*
Elkins, Glen Ray *service company executive*
†Howell, Kevin L. *hotel executive*
†Jensen, Rodney H. *hotel executive*
†Johnson, Jon L. *advertising executive*
Lund, Victor L. *retail food company executive*
Maher, David L. *drug store company executive*
Mills, Carol Margaret *business consultant, public relations consultant*
Phillips, Ted Ray *advertising agency executive*
Scott, Howard Winfield, Jr. *temporary help services company executive*
Steiner, Richard Russell *linen supply company*

**Sandy**
Mitchell, David Campbell *inventor, corporate executive*
Skidmore, Joyce Thorum *public relations and communication executive*

York, Theodore Robert *consulting company executive*

**West Valley City**
Leibsla, Melvin Donald *data processing executive*

## VERMONT

**Burlington**
Williams, Linda Bergendahl *information specialist*

**Essex Junction**
Sweetser, Gene Gillman *quality assurance professional, state legislator*

**Gaysville**
Dawson, Wilfred Thomas *marketing executive, consultant*

**Londonderry**
Bigelow, David Skinner, III *management consultant*

**Manchester**
Yager, Hunter *advertising executive*

**Montpelier**
Serrani, Thom *contracting trade association executive*

**Norwich**
Fitzhugh, William Wyvill, Jr. *printing company executive*
Smith, Markwick Kern, Jr. *management consultant*

**Rutland**
Ferraro, Betty Ann *corporate administrator, state senator*

**Stowe**
Fiddler, Barbara Dillow *sales and marketing professional*

**Waterbury**
Pelton, Joan Elisabeth Mason *music company owner*

## VIRGINIA

**Abingdon**
Ramos-Cano, Hazel Balatero *caterer owner, innkeeper, entrepreneur*

**Alexandria**
Alloway, Robert Malcombe *computer consulting executive*
Bailey, Steven Scott *operations research analyst*
Broide, Mace Irwin *public affairs consultant*
Burch, Michael Ira *public relations executive, former government official*
Condrill, Jo Ellaresa *professional speaker*
Cooper, B. Jay *public relations executive*
Cooper, Roger Merlin *information technology executive, federal government official, educator*
Covone, James Michael *automotive parts manufacturer and distribution company executive*
Dawson, Samuel Cooper, Jr. *retired motel company executive*
Devine, Donald J. *management and political consultant*
Hagan, Robert Leslie *retired consulting company executive*
Hansan, Mary Anne *marketing professional*
Harris, David Ford *management consultant, retired government official*
Hartsock, Linda Sue *educational and management development executive*
Jagoda, Barry Lionel *media adviser, communications consultant*
Laurent, Lawrence Bell *communications executive, former journalist*
Locigno, Paul Robert *public affairs executive*
Loving, William Rush, Jr. *public relations company executive, consultant*
Mayo, Louis Allen *corporation executive*
McFarland, Janet Chapin *consulting company executive*
McMillan, Charles William *consulting company executive*
Reid, Ralph Waldo Emerson *management consultant*
Richardson, Robert Charlwood, III *management consultant, retired air force officer*
Simmons, Richard De Lacey *mass media executive*
Trent, Darrell M. *academic and corporate executive*
Widner, Ralph Randolph *civic executive*
Wilding, James Anthony *airport administrator*

**Annandale**
Gingrich, Lisa Cox *advertising and marketing executive, consultant*
Greinke, Everett Donald *corporate executive, international programs consultant*
Jarvis, Elbert, II (Jay Jarvis) *employee benefits specialist*
Osborn, Len *business executive*
Speakes, Larry Melvin *public relations executive*

**Arlington**
Allen, Harry Roulon, Jr. *data processing and storage company executive*
Bloomer, William Arthur *security industry executive*
Brehm, William Keith *information systems company executive*
Cocolis, Peter Konstantine *business development executive*
Erwin, Frank William *personnel research and publishing executive*
Faris, Frank Edgar *marketing executive*
†Feld, Donald H. *management consultant*
Freeman, Neal Blackwell *communications corporation executive*
Gianturco, Delio E. *management consultant*
Gormley, Dennis Michael *consulting company executive*
Hamor, Kathy Virginia *consultant*
Infosino, Iara Ciurria *management consultant*
Ingrassia, Anthony Frank *human resource specialist*
Johnson, John A. *communications company executive*
Kilduff, Bonnie Elizabeth *director of expositions*
Meyer, Richard Townsend *service company executive*
Morris, John Woodland, II *businessman, former army officer*
Newburger, Beth Weinstein *medical telecommunications company executive*
Oleson, Ray Jerome *computer service company executive*
Rimpel, Auguste Eugene, Jr. *management and technical consulting executive*
Samburg, A. Gene *security company executive*
Sowle, Donald Edgar *management consultant*
Widener, Peri Ann *business development executive*
Zorthian, Barry *communications executive*

**Berryville**
Croswell, Clyde Vernard, Jr. *human resources educator, researcher*

**Blacksburg**
Weaver, Pamela Ann *hospitality research professional*

**Boston**
Knoche, Douglas Andrew *marketing executive, consultant*

**Chantilly**
O'Brien, Robert John, Jr. *public relations executive, former government official, air force officer*

**Charlottesville**
Cohen, Helen Herz *camp owner, director*
Colley, John Leonard, Jr. *educator, author, management consultant*
Dunn, Mary Jarratt *public relations executive*
Warren, Mark Edward *shipping company executive, lawyer*
Wolcott, John Winthrop, III *corporate executive*

**Fairfax**
Anderson, Maynard Carlyle *national and international security executive*
Baker, Daniel Richard *computer company executive, consultant*
Gillette, Marcia Drucker *marketing executive*
Gross, Patrick Walter *business executive, management consultant*
Hess, Milton Siegmund *computer company executive*
Jones, Carleton Shaw *information systems company executive, lawyer*
Kieffer, Jarold Alan *policy and management consultant, writer, editor*
McCormick, Robert Junior *company executive, former government official*
Palmer, James Daniel *information technology educator*
Pitchell, Robert J. *business executive*
Rossotti, Charles Ossola *computer consulting company executive*
Saverot, Pierre-Michel *nuclear waste management company executive*
Walker, Betsy Ellen *consulting and systems integration company executive*
†Woodle, Roy V. *services company executive*

**Falls Church**
Beach, Robert Oliver, II *computer company executive*
Cain, David Lee *corporate executive*
Carney, Daniel L. *program and financial management consultant*
Cetron, Marvin Jerome *management executive*
Ehrlich, Geraldine Elizabeth *service management consultant*
Glass, Lawrence *business executive*
Harley, William Gardner *retired communications consultant*
Ibañez, Alvaro *patent design company executive, artist*
Nashman, Alvin Eli *computer company executive*
Nelson, Thomas William *former management consultant, government official*
Orkand, Donald Saul *management consultant*
Persinger, Judith Eileen *management plan clerk*
Webb, William John *public relations counsel*
Werner, Stuart Lloyd *computer services company executive*
Zirkle, William Vernon *philanthropist*

**Farnham**
Durham, James Michael, Sr. *marketing consultant*

**Fredericksburg**
Geary, Patrick Joseph *naval security administrator*
Hickman, Margaret Capellini *advertising executive*
Hickman, Richard Lonnie *advertising executive*

**Free Union**
Hart, Jean Hardy *international business operations systems specialist, consultant*

**Glasgow**
Riegel, Kurt Wetherhold *environmental protection executive*

**Goode**
Brown, John Robert, Jr. *international marketing executive, consultant*

**Great Falls**
Somers, James Wilford *information management company executive*

**Grundy**
Smith, Jack *food service executive*

**Hampton**
Drummond, James Everman *technology transfer company executive, former army officer*
Schauer, Catharine Guberman *public affairs specialist*

**Haymarket**
Douglas, Clarence James, Jr. *corporation executive, management consultant*

**Herndon**
Larese, Edward John *company executive*

**Kilmarnock**
Maxwell, W(ilbur) Richard *management consultant, retired*

**Lightfoot**
Morris, Robert Louis *management consultant*

**Lyndhurst**
Sidebottom, William George *communications executive*

**Mc Lean**
Adler, Larry *marketing executive*
Capone, Lucien, Jr. *management consultant, former naval officer*
Deal, George Edgar *management and industrial executive*
Estren, Mark James *business and media consultant, TV producer, author*
James, Daniel J. *management consultant*
Jennings, Jerry D. *communications company executive*
Johnson, Frank Stanley, Jr. *communications executive*
Kiviat, Philip Jay *computer services company executive*
Kolombatovic, Vadja Vadim *management consulting company executive*
McNichols, Gerald Robert *consulting company executive*
Miller, Christine Marie *marketing executive*
†O'Brien, Morgan Edward *communications executive*
Paschall, Lee McQuerter *retired communications consultant*
Pensmith, Sharyn Elaine *communications executive*
Steventon, Robert Wesley *marketing executive*
Tuttle, William G(ilbert) T(ownsend), Jr. *research executive*
Watson, Jerry Carroll *advertising executive*
Zimmerman, John H. *communications company executive*

**Moneta**
Ulmer, Walter Francis, Jr. *consultant, former army officer*

**Newport News**
Fisher, Denise Butterfield *marketing executive*
Guastaferro, Angelo *company executive*

**Norfolk**
Bernsen, Harold John *marketing executive, political affairs consultant, retired naval officer*
Blount, Robert Haddock *corporate executive, retired naval officer*
Valentine, Herman Edward *computer company executive*

**Reston**
Ackerson, Jeffrey Townsend *computer systems executive*
Blanchard, Townsend Eugene *service companies executive*
Brosseau, Irma Finn *management consultant*
Cerf, Vinton Gray *telecommunications company executive*
Cramer, James Perry *management consultant, publisher*
Easton, Glenn Hanson, Jr. *management and insurance consultant, federal official, naval officer*
Foster, William Anthony *management consultant, educator*
Johnson, Thea Jean *internet and intranet security service provider*
Sarreals, Sonia *data processing consultant*
Schleede, Glenn Roy *energy market and policy consultant*
Showalter-Keefe, Jean *data processing executive*
Wessner, Deborah Marie *telecommunications executive, computer consultant*

**Richmond**
Adams, John Buchanan, Jr. *advertising agency executive*
Altschul, B. J. *public relations counselor*
Barocci, Robert Louis *advertising agency executive*
Bohannon, Sarah Virginia *personnel assistant*
Jacobs, Harry Milburn, Jr. *advertising executive*
Lanahan, John Stevenson *management consultant*
Laverge, Jan *tobacco company executive*
Maneker, Deanna Marie *advertising executive*
Mc Grath, Lee Parr *public relations executive, author*
Moyne, Yves M. *water treatment executive*
Newbrand, Charles Michael *advertising firm executive*
Roop, Ralph Goodwin *retired oil marketing company executive*
Thornhill, Barbara Cole *marketing executive*
Toler, Ann Patrick *public relations executive*
Trott, Sabert Scott, II *marketing professional*
Williams, Robert C. *company executive*

**Roanoke**
Shaftman, Fredrick Krisch *telephone communications executive*

**Seaford**
Jenkins, Margaret Bunting *human resources executive*

**Springfield**
Bruen, John Dermot *business management consultant*
Fedewa, Lawrence John *information technology company executive*

**Staunton**
Farrell, Larry Charles *management consultant, author, speaker*

**Sterling**
Brewster-Walker, Sandra JoAnn *public relations executive, publishing executive, genealogist, historian, consultant*
Witek, James Eugene *public relations executive*

**Vienna**
Bartlett, John Wesley *consulting firm executive*
Brandel, Ralph Edward *management consultant*
Cantus, H. Hollister *government relations consultant*
†Case, Steve *business executive*
Clark, Katherine Karen *software company executive*
Hale, Thomas Morgan *professional services executive*
Hubbell, Katherine Jean *marketing consultant*
†Jayne, Edward Randolph, II *executive search consultant*
Leonsis, Ted *communications company executive, publishing company executive*
Rothery, Chet *business executive*
Sheinbaum, Gilbert Harold *international management consultant*
Smith, Esther Thomas *management consultant*
Van Stavoren, William David *management consultant, retired government official*
Veasey, Byron Keith *information systems consultant*
Walker, Edward Keith, Jr. *business executive, retired naval officer*

**Virginia Beach**
Alexander, William Powell *business advisor*
Burgess, Marvin Franklin *human resources specialist, consultant*
Goodwin, Robert *human resources specialist*
Kodis, Mary Caroline *marketing consultant*
Ratajski, Magda Anne *public relations executive*
Tarbutton, Lloyd Tilghman *motel executive, franchise consultant*
Wick, Robert Thomas *retired supermarket executive*

**White Stone**
Wroth, James Melvin *former army officer, computer company executive*

**Williamsburg**
Aaron, Bertram Donald *corporation executive*
Brackenridge, N. Lynn *public relations and development specialist*
Finn, A. Michael *public relations executive*

**Winchester**
Smith, Virginia A. *marketing communications professional*

**Woodbridge**
Cosner, David Dale *plastics industry executive, marketing executive*
Richardson, Sharon Young *marketing professional*

**Wytheville**
Hansen, B(obby) J. *management consultant, real estate investor and developer*

**Yorktown**
Behlmar, Cindy Lee *business manager, consultant*

## WASHINGTON

**Anacortes**
Spaulding, John Pierson *public relations executive, marine consultant*

**Bainbridge Island**
Schmidt, Karen Anne *travel company executive, state legislator*

**Bellevue**
Allen, Paul *computer executive, professional sports team owner*
Bates, Charles Walter *human resources executive, lawyer, internal auditor*
Dykstra, David Charles *management executive, consultant, accountant, author, educator*
Hall, Eleanor Williams *public relations executive*
Ladd, James Roger *international management consultant, accountant*
Otterholt, Barry L. *technology management consultant*

**Burlington**
Herbaugh, Roger Duane *computer and software company executive*

**Edmonds**
Sankovich, Joseph Bernard *cemetery management consultant*

**Federal Way**
Muzyka-McGuire, Amy *marketing professional, nutrition consultant*

**Gig Harbor**
Huyler, Jean Wiley *media and interpersonal communications consultant, hypnotherapist*
Robinson, James William *retired management consultant*

**Lacey**
Breytspraak, John, Jr. *management consultant*

**Langley**
Bitts, Todd Michael *sales and marketing consultant*

**Malaga**
Nanto, Roxanna Lynn *marketing professional, management consultant*

**Mercer Island**
Herres, Phillip Benjamin *computer software executive*

**Olympia**
Manning, Farley *retired public relations executive*
Ogden, Valeria Juan *management consultant, state representative*

**Puyallup**
Ruff, Lorraine Marie *public relations executive*

**Redmond**
Butler-Thomas, Jannette Sue *human resources professional*
Gates, William Henry, III *software company executive*
Gilmore, A. Douglas *retail sales executive*
Teeter, Rob R. *regulatory affairs specialist*

**Seattle**
Alberg, Tom Austin *communications executive, lawyer*
†Bartels, Juergen E. *hotel company executive*
Beetham, Stanley Williams *international management consultant*
Chang, Taiping *marketing executive, magazine publisher*

Dagnon, James Bernard *human resources executive*
Dederer, Michael Eugene *public relations company executive*
Duryee, David Anthony *management consultant*
Evans, Trevor Heiser *advertising executive*
Gist, Marilyn Elaine *organizational behavior and human resource management educator*
†Hartley, Robert *public relations executive*
†Hough, John *public relations executive*
Howard, Heather *corporate secretary*
Kane, Karen Marie *public affairs consultant*
†Kleisner, Fred *hotel executive*
†Kraft, Donald B. *advertising executive*
Leale, Olivia Mason *import marketing company executive*
MacDonald, Andrew Stephen *management consulting firm executive*
Marriott, David M. *public relations executive*
McConnell, J. Daniel *sports marketing professional*
McReynolds, Neil Lawrence *public affairs consultant*
O'Leary, Thomas Howard *resources executive*
Porad, Laurie Jo *jewelry company official*
Reis, Jean Stevenson *administrative secretary*
Ruckelshaus, William Doyle *investment group executive*
Scafe, Lincoln Robert, Jr. *retired sales executive*
Smith, Jeffrey L. (The Frugal Gourmet) *cook, writer*

**Spokane**
Higgins, Shaun O'Leary *media executive*
Nicolai, Eugene Ralph *public relations consultant, editor, writer*
Woodard, Alva Abe *business consultant*

**Tacoma**
Brevik, J. Albert *communications consultant*
Licens, Lila Louise *administrative assistant*
Taylor, Peter van Voorhees *advertising and public relations consultant*

**Vancouver**
Smith, Milton Ray *computer company executive, lawyer*

**Walla Walla**
Potts, Charles Aaron *management executive, writer*

**Winlock**
Brown, Stephan Mark *international fundraising and resource development executive, consultant*

**Yakima**
Vujovic, Mary Jane *education and employment training planner*

## WEST VIRGINIA

**Charleston**
Mc Gee, John Frampton *communications company executive*

**Huntington**
Barenklau, Keith Edward *safety services company executive*

**Parkersburg**
Crooks, Dorena May (Dee Crooks) *administrative assistant, social worker*
Fahlgren, H(erbert) Smoot *advertising agency executive*

**Summit Point**
Taylor, Harold Allen, Jr. *industrial mineral marketing consultant*

**Wellsburg**
Wellman, Gerald Edwin, Jr. *safety and fire inspector*

**Wheeling**
Kirkpatrick, Forrest Hunter *management consultant*

**White Sulphur Springs**
Kappa, Margaret McCaffrey *resort hotel consultant*

## WISCONSIN

**Algoma**
Golomski, William Arthur *consulting company executive*

**Appleton**
McManus, John Francis *association executive, writer*
Petinga, Charles Michael *business executive*

**Brookfield**
†Nickerson, Greg *public relations executive*
Welnetz, David Charles *human resources executive*

**Darien**
Miller, Malcolm Henry *manufacturing sales executive, real estate developer*

**Delavan**
Armstrong, Kevin William *marketing executive, researcher*

**Fond Du Lac**
Ingle, Sud Ranganath *management consultant*

**Fredonia**
Diesem, John Lawrence *business executive*

**Green Bay**
Bush, Robert G. *food service executive*

**Greendale**
Tucker, William Thomas, III *computer software company executive*

**Jefferson**
Morgan, Gaylin F. *public realtions executive*

**Kenosha**
Grover, Robert Lawrence *tool company executive*

**Kohler**
Brands, Robert Franciscus *marketing executive*

**Lake Geneva**
O'Hare, Linda Parsons *management consultant*
Weed, Edward Reilly *marketing executive*

**Lancaster**
Johnson, Hal Harold Gustav *marketing educator emeritus*

**Madison**
Garner, Jac Buford *management executive*
Johnson, Alton Cornelius *management educator*
Lee, Leslie Warren *marketing executive*
Moore, Judy Kay *media relations specialist*
Ray, Dennis Jay *utilities and business educator, researcher*
Scheidler, James Edward *business executive*
Stites, Susan Kay *human resources consultant*

**Mequon**
Elias, Paul S. *marketing executive*
Miller, Scott Joseph *software executive*

**Middleton**
Conklin, Charles D. *marketing executive*
Senn, Richard Allan *environmental safety professional*

**Milwaukee**
Arbit, Bruce *direct marketing executive, consultant*
Balbach, George Charles *technology company executive*
Bergmann, Linda J. *marketing professional*
Chait, Jon Frederick *corporate executive, lawyer*
Colbert, Virgis William *brewery company executive*
†Counsell, Paul S. *advertising executive*
Felde, Martin Lee *advertising agency executive, accountant*
Fromstein, Mitchell S. *temporary office services company executive*
Garnier, Robert Charles *management consultant*
Hill, Dennis P. *information technology executive*
Hunter, Victor Lee *marketing executive, consultant*
Joseph, Jules K. *retired public relations executive*
Kahlor, Robert A. *communications company executive*
Kerr, Dorothy Marie Burmeister *marketing executive, consultant*
Rabbat, Guy *electronics company executive, inventor*
Randall, William Seymour *leasing company executive*
Scheinfeld, James David *travel agency executive*
Shiely, John Stephen *company executive, lawyer*
Teuschler, Michael Alexander *computer company executive, consultant*

**Monroe**
Bishop, Carolyn Benkert *public relations counselor*

**Neenah**
Underhill, Robert Alan *consumer products company executive*

**Pewaukee**
Quadracci, Harry V. *printing company executive, lawyer*

**Plymouth**
Gentine, Lee Michael *marketing professional*

**Racine**
Klein, Gabriella Sonja *communications executive*

**River Falls**
DeLorenzo, David Joseph *retired public relations executive*

**South Milwaukee**
Kitzke, Eugene David *research management executive*

**Waukesha**
Burgess, William R. *food service executive*

**Waunakee**
Berthelsen, John Robert *printing company executive*

**West Bend**
Huff, Gayle Compton *advertising agency executive*

**Wisconsin Rapids**
Brennan, Patrick Francis *retired printing paper manufacturing executive*

## WYOMING

**Cheyenne**
Wagner, Samuel Albin Mar *records management executive, educator*

**Jackson**
Herrick, Gregory Evans *technology corporation executive*

**Mills**
Kennerknecht, Richard Eugene *marketing executive*

**Sheridan**
Taylor, Judith Ann *marketing and sales executive*

**Wilson**
Fritz, Jack Wayne *communications and marketing company executive*

## TERRITORIES OF THE UNITED STATES

## GUAM

**Mangilao**
Colfax, Richard Schuyler *business management and marketing educator*

## PUERTO RICO

**Guayama**
Flores-Nazario, Margarita *human resources director*

**San Juan**
†Callen, Tarquin M. *hotel executive*

## VIRGIN ISLANDS

**Christiansted**
Baar, James A. *public relations and corporate communications executive, author, consultant, internet publisher, software developer*

**Saint Thomas**
Miner, Robert Gordon *creative promotional consultant, auctioneer, writer, publisher, actor, educator*
Mitton, Michael Anthony *environmental technology company executive*

# CANADA

## ALBERTA

**Calgary**
Hume, James Borden *corporate professional, foundation executive*

**De Winton**
Shutiak, James *management consultant*

## BRITISH COLUMBIA

**Bowen Island**
Lambert, Michael Malet *investment and hospitality consultant*

**Richmond**
†Pfeifer, Joann *hotel executive*

**Vancouver**
Campbell, Bruce Alan *market research consultant*
Cormier, Jean G. *communications company executive*

**West Vancouver**
Rae, Barbara Joyce *former employee placement company executive*

## MANITOBA

**Winnipeg**
Fraser, John Foster *management company executive*
Liba, Peter Michael *communications executive*

## NEW BRUNSWICK

**Fredericton**
†Bourgeois, Maryanne *public administration executive*

## NOVA SCOTIA

**Dartmouth**
Callaghan, J. Clair *corporate executive*

**Halifax**
Gratwick, John *management consulting executive, writer, consultant*
†MacGillivray, Frederick Richard *executive*

## ONTARIO

**Downsview**
Burton, Ian *environmentalist, consultant, educator, writer*

**Gloucester**
Boisvert, Laurier J. *communications executive*

**Guelph**
Osen, Gregory Alan *water conditioning company executive*

**Kingston**
Stanley, James Paul *printing company executive*

**Markham**
Marshall, Donald Stewart *computer systems company executive*
Nelson, William George, IV *software company executive*
Wardell, David Joseph *travel industry specialist*

**Mississauga**
Beckley, Michael John *hotel executive*
†Farrell, Craig *hotel executive*
†Ortt, Terry *hotel executive*
Sonnenberg, Hardy *data processing company research and development executive, engineer*
Thibault, J(oseph) Laurent *service company executive*

**North York**
Denham, Frederick Ronald *management consultant*

**Oakville**
Barlow, Kenneth James *management consultant*

**Ottawa**
†Hoyles, John D.V. *company executive*
Kitchen, Paul Howard *government and association management consultant*
Ouellet, André *communication and distribution company executive*
†Pierce, Jonathan Leslie *planning commission executive*
Sharp, Mitchell William *advisor to prime minister*

**Palgrave**
Kieffer, Susan Werner *management consultant*

**Toronto**
Bandeen, Robert Angus *management corporation executive*
Bonnycastle, Lawrence Christopher *retired corporate director*
†Braun, Reto *computer systems company executive*
Clarkson, Max Boydell Elliott *printing company executive, business educator*
†Cooper, Simon F. *hotel executive*
DeMone, Robert Stephen *hotel company executive*
Fierheller, George Alfred *communications director*
Friendly, Lynda Estelle *theatre marketing and communications executive*
Godfrey, Paul Victor *communications company executive*
Graham, James Edmund *service management executive*
Gregor, Tibor Philip *management consultant*
Harvey, George Edwin *communications company executive*
Irwin, Samuel Macdonald *toy company executive*
Jacob, Ellis *entertainment company executive*
McCoubrey, R. James *advertising executive*
Meadows, George Lee *communications company executive*
Miller, Kenneth Merrill *computing services company executive*
Olsen, Richard W. *advertising executive*
Reid, Terence C. W. *corporation executive*
Rogers, Edward Samuel *communications company executive*
Ross, Henry Raymond *advertising executive and legal counsel*
Singleton-Wood, Allan James *communications executive*
†Tanaka, Ron S. *hotel executive*

**Unionville**
Nichols, Harold Neil *corporate executive, former pipeline company executive*

**Willowdale**
MacDonald, Brian Scott *management consultant*

## QUEBEC

**Leclercville**
Morin, Pierre Jean *retired management consultant*

**Montreal**
Audet, Henri *retired communications executive*
Beauregard, Luc *public relations executive*
Bouthillier, André *public relations executive, consultant*
Des Marais, Pierre, II *communications holding company executive*
Ducros, Pierre Y. *information technology consulting and systems management executive*
Ferrabee, (Francis) James *communications consultant*
Neveu, Jean *printing company executive*
Saint-Jacques, Madeleine *advertising agency executive*
Sirois, Charles *communications executive*
Tousignant, Jacques *human resources executive, lawyer*

**Mount Royal**
Chauvette, Claude R. *building materials company administrator*
Glezos, Matthews *consumer products and services company executive*

**Quebec**
Courtois, Bernard Andre *communications executive*

**Saint Sauveur**
Dunsky, Menahem *retired advertising agency executive, communications consultant, painter*

**Verdun**
Delisle, Gilles Yvan *telecommunications executive*

**Westmount**
Gordonsmith, John Arthur Harold *collection agency executive*

## SASKATCHEWAN

**Regina**
†Clayton, Raymond Edward *government official*

# MEXICO

**Coahuila**
Whelan, James Robert *communications executive, international trade and investment consultant, author, educator, mining executive, writer*

**Mexico City**
Arellano, Hector *telecommunications consulting company executive*
Dudley, Craig James *executive recruiter*

# BELGIUM

**Brussels**
Arion, Georges Julien *retired commercial organization executive*
Rose, Merrill *public relations counselor*

**Lens**
Peat, Randall Dean *defense analysis company executive, retired air force officer*

**Strombeek Bever**
Mancel, Claude Paul *household product company executive*

## CHILE

**Santiago**
Beshears, Charles Daniel *consultant, former insurance executive*

## CHINA

**Hong Kong**
Ligare, Kathleen Meredith *strategy and marketing executive*

## DENMARK

**Hoersholm**
Sørensen, Erik *international company executive*

## ENGLAND

**Coventry**
Monberg, Jay Peter *management consultant*

**Kettering**
Dellis, Frédy Michel *travel exchange company executive*

**London**
Ellis, Peter Hudson *management consultant*
Gummer, Baron Peter Selwyn *public relations executive*
Habgood, Anthony John *corporate executive*
Leaf, Robert Stephen *public relations executive*
McNulty, Dermot *public relations executive*
Montero, Fernan Gonzalo *advertising executive*
Sainsbury of Preston Candover, Lord (John Davan Sainsbury) *food retailer executive, art patron*
Sorrell, Martin Stuart *advertising and marketing executive*
Treasure, John Albert Penberthy *advertising executive*

**Stroud**
Robinson, John Beckwith *development management consultant*

## FRANCE

**Alpes Maritimes**
Morley, Roger Hubert *company executive, consultant*

**Levallois-Perret**
de Pouzilhac, Alain Duplessis *advertising executive*

**Paris**
Marcus, Claude *advertising executive*

## GERMANY

**Bonn**
Hutton, Winfield Travis *management consultant, educator*

**Gutersloh**
Wössner, Mark Matthias *business executive*

**Hemsbach**
Froessl, Horst Waldemar *business executive, data processing developer*

**Leipzig**
Hielscher, Udo Artur *business administration and finance educator*

## HONG KONG

**Hong Kong**
Pisanko, Henry Jonathan *command and control communications company executive*

## HUNGARY

**Budapest**
Rice, Kenneth Lloyd *environmental services executive, educator*

## IRELAND

**Dublin**
Voss, Katherine Evelyn *international management consultant*

## ISRAEL

**Herzliyya**
Warshavsky, Eli Samuel *media company chief executive*

## JAPAN

**Meguroku**
Miura, Akio *quality assurance professional*

## JORDAN

**Amman**
Jumean, Ayman Shafik *international business administrator*

## KUWAIT

**Jleed**
deJesus-Burgos, Sylvia Teresa *information systems specialist*

## SOUTH AFRICA

**Johannesburg**
Crockett, Phyllis Darlene *communications executive*

## SPAIN

**Santiago De Compostela**
Balseiro Gonzalez, Manuel *management executive, consultant*

## SWEDEN

**Stockholm**
Johnson, Antonia Axson *corporate executive*

## SWITZERLAND

**Basel**
†Rosenthal, David *media executive, publicist*

**Lyss**
Scheftner, Gerold *marketing executive*

## ADDRESS UNPUBLISHED

Aden, Arthur Laverne *retired office systems company executive*
Affatato, Joseph Frank *marketing professional*
Akbarian, Shah-Rokh *management consultant*
Albert, Margaret Cook *communications executive*
Allen, Theodore Earl *marketing consultant*
Alston, Eugene Benson *communications company executive*
Ambrose, James Richard *consultant, retired government official*
Anderson, Donald Lloyd *weapon systems consultant*
Anderson, Mark Robert *data processing executive, biochemist*
Anderson, Vernon Russell *technology company executive, entrepreneur*
Andriole, Stephen John *information systems executive*
Appell, Louise Sophia *consulting company executive*
Bainbridge, Dona Bardelli *international marketing executive*
Balaban-Perry, Eleanor *retired advertising executive*
Ballard, Marion Scattergood *software development professional*
Bamberger, Gerald Francis *plastics marketing consultant*
Barger, William James *management consultant*
Barro, Mary Helen *marketing professional, consultant*
Barton, Peter Richard, III *communications executive*
Bauer, Barbara Ann *marketing consultant*
Beasley, Barbara Starin *sales executive, marketing professional*
Bell, P. Jackson *computer executive*
†Benn, Caroline M. *public relations executive, advertising executive*
Bennett, John Roscoe *computer company executive*
Bennett, Saul *public relations agency executive*
Benney, Douglas Mabley *direct marketing executive, consultant*
Berger, Frank Stanley *management executive*
Bergstein, Stanley Francis *horse racing executive*
Berra, Robert Louis *human resources consultant*
Bigham, Cecilia Beth *retired communications and marketing professional*
Birk, John R. *marketing/financial services consultant*
Blacker, Harriet *public relations executive*
Blaine, Davis Robert *valuation consultant executive*
Blake, John Edward *retired car rental company executive*
Bogart, Judith Saunders *public relations executive*
Bonner, Jack *public relations company executive*
Booker, Nana Laurel *public relations executive*
Borda, Richard Joseph *management consultant*
Bouchey, L. Francis *publicist, diplomat*
Bower, Sandra Irwin *communications executive*
Braden, George Walter, II (Lord of Carrigaline) *company executive*
Bradford, Robert Edward *supermarket executive, retired*
Braithwaite, Ralph Rhey *organizational consultant*
Bray, Sharon Ann *management company executive*
Brennan, Donna Lesley *public relations company executive*
Brennan, Maryann *business consulting executive*
Brennen, Stephen Alfred *international business consultant*
Brickman, Ravelle *public relations writer and consultant*
Brody, Martin *food service company executive*
Broedling, Laurie Adele *human resources executive, psychologist, educator*
Buell, James Richard, Jr. *investment management company executive*
Bueno, Ana (Marie) *marketing executive, writer*
Bugbee, Joan Barthelme *retired corporate communications executive*
Burge, John Wesley, Jr. *management consultant*
Burnett, Iris Jacobson *corporate communications specialist*
Burnham, J. V. *sales executive*
Butler, Robert Leonard *sales executive*
Butler, Robert Thomas *retired advertising executive*
Butts, Virginia *corporate public relations executive*
Caine, Raymond William, Jr. *retired public relations executive*
Cantus, Jane Scott *management consultant*
Carder, Paul Charles *advertising executive*
Cardy, Andrew Gordon *hotel executive*
Carey, Dennis Clarke *executive search consultant*
Carter, Jaine M(arie) *human resources development company executive*
Casadesus, Penelope Ann *advertising executive, film producer*
Cashman, William James, Jr. *information processing marketing executive*
Castle, James Cameron *information systems executive*
Chaikin, A. Scott *public relations executive*
Chamberlain, William Edwin, Jr. *management consultant*
Chamblee, Mary Jane *management specialist*
Chapman, Kristin Heilig *public relations consultant*
Chinn, Thomas Wayne *typographic company executive*
Christy, Thomas Patrick *human resources executive, educator*
Cibbarelli, Pamela Ruth *information executive*
Cittone, Henry Aron *hotel and restaurant management educator*
Cohn, Martin *advertising executive, consultant*
Coleman, Claire Kohn *public relations executive*
Collins, William Michael *public relations executive*
Connell, Shirley Hudgins *public relations professional*
Conomikes, Melanie Remington *marketing consultant*
Cooper, Francis Loren *advertising executive*
Cork, Edwin Kendall *business and financial consultant*
Cortese, Richard Anthony *computer company executive*
Corwell, Ann Elizabeth *public relations executive*
Cotter, Richard Vern *management consultant, author, educator*
Courtheoux, Richard James *management consultant*
Crawford, William Walsh *retired consumer products company executive*
Croxton, Fred(erick) E(mory), Jr. *retired information specialist, consultant*
Dalziel, Robert David *telecommunications consultant*
Damaschino, Ann Toothman *development consultant*
Dangoor, David Ezra Ramsi *consumer goods company executive*
Darien, Steven Martin *technology company executive*
Deacon, David Emmerson *advertising executive*
Denneny, James Clinton, Jr. *business consultant*
Deoul, Kathleen Boardsen *executive*
Derzai, Matthew *retired telecommunications company executive*
Diamond, Susan Zee *management consultant*
Dilts, David Michael *management researcher, university facility director*
Dirks, Leslie Chant *communications and electronics company executive*
Dirvin, Gerald Vincent *retired consumer products company executive*
Dixon, Louis Frederick *information sciences and telecommunications consulting executive*
Dodson, Donald Mills *restaurant executive*
Doland, Judy Ann *administrative assistant, retired financial rating company associate*
Dolich, Andrew Bruce *sports marketing executive*
Doll, Patricia Marie *marketing and public relations consultant*
Dolman, John Phillips (Tim), Jr. (Tim Dolman) *communications company executive*
Doud, Wallace C. *retired information systems executive*
Dow, Peter Anthony *advertising agency executive*
Dowie, Ian James *management consultant*
Dudley, Elizabeth Hymer *retired security executive*
Duffy, Martin Edward *management consultant, economist*
Duke, William Edward *public affairs executive*
Dwan, Dennis Edwin *broadcast executive, photographer*
Dyckman, Suzanne Barbara *secretary, administrative assistant*
Ecton, Donna R. *business executive*
Eggleston, G(eorge) Dudley *management consultant, publisher*
Eisenberg, Lee B. *communications executive, author*
Elkind, Mort William *creative and business consultant*
Elliot, Jared *financial management consultant*
Ellis, Robert Harry *retired television executive, university administrator*
Eltringham, Thomas James Gyger *telecommunications professional*
Emerling, Carol G(reenbaum) *consultant*
Emerson, Daniel Everett *retired communications company executive, executive advisor*
Ennis, Thomas Michael *management consultant*
Erb, Richard Louis Lundin *resort and hotel executive*
Evangelista, Paula Lee *public affairs administrator*
Evans, Victor Miles *retired funeral home, cemetery company executive*
Farmer, Deborah Kiriluk *marketing professional*
Farrug, Jay (Eugene Joseph Farrug, Jr.) *technology executive, consultant*
Fay, Conner Martindale *management consultant*
Feld, Carole Leslie *marketing executive*
Feld, Kenneth J. *entertainment executive*
Feller, Robert William Andrew *baseball team public relations executive, retired baseball player*
Finkelstein, Seymour *business consultant*
Fischmar, Richard Mayer *resort executive, financial consultant*
Fleming, Charles Clifford, Jr. *retired airline and jet aircraft sales company executive*
Foote, William Chapin *executive officer*
Ford, E(mma) Jane *public relations executive*
Forester, Jean Martha Brouillette *innkeeper, retired librarian and educator*
Forster, Ann Dorothy *publicist*
Freeman, Ralph Carter *management consultant*
Freter, Mark Allen *marketing and public relations executive, consultant*
Gambrell, Luck Flanders *corporate executive*
Garahan, Peter Thomas *software company executive*
†Gardner, Meredith Lee *communication consultant*
Garrison, Richard Christopher *advertising agency executive*
Gendell, Gerald Stanleigh *retired public affairs executive*
George, William Douglas, Jr. *retired consumer products company executive*
Gerwin, Leslie Ellen *public affairs and community relations executive, lawyer*
Getchius, June Katherine *customer service administrator*
Gibson, Denice Yvonne *telecommunications, networking and computer executive*
Gilford, Leon *business executive and consultant*
Gillice, Sondra Jupin (Mrs. Gardner Russell Brown) *sales and marketing executive*
†Gilman, Steven A. *management consultant*
Glass, Kenneth Edward *management consultant*
Glazner, Raymond Charles *technical services consultant*
Gluys, Charles Byron *retired marketing management consultant*
Goldberg, Victor Joel *retired data processing company executive*
Goldin, Jacob Isaak *chemical software company executive*
Goldman, Alfred Emanuel *marketing research consultant*
Goldman, Sherry Robin *public relations executive*
Gorsline, Stephen Paul *detective, investigator*
Gottlieb, Alan Merril *advertising, fundraising and broadcasting executive, writer*
Grace, Marcia Bell *advertising executive*
Gray, John Lathrop, III *retired advertising agency executive*
Green, Bennett Donald *quality assurance specialist*
Griggs, Emma *management executive*
Grody, Mark Stephen *public relations executive*
Groome, Reginald Kehnroth *hotel executive, consultant*
Grundner, Thomas Michael *telecomputing educator*
Gschwind, Donald *management and engineering consultant*
Gumpert, Gustav *public relations executive*
Gunderson, John Davis *marketing professional*
Gunderson, Ted Lee *security consultant*
Gunst, Robert Allen *retail executive*
Gurwitch, Arnold Andrew *communications executive*
Haegele, John Ernest *business executive*
Hairston, James Christopher *airline catering and distribution executive*
Hamilton, Thomas Michael *marketing executive*
Hamlin, Sonya B. *communications specialist*
Hanneken, David William *advertising executive*
Hardy, Clarence Earl, Jr. *human resources executive*
Hargadon, Bernard Joseph, Jr. *retired consumer goods company executive*
Harris, David Philip *crisis management executive*
Harris, Gregory Scott *management services executive*
Harris, Robert Norman *advertising and communications educator*
Harris, William John *retired management holding company executive, consultant*
Hausdorfer, Gary Lee *management consultant*
Hawkins, Lawrence Charles *management consultant, educator*
Hayes, Janet Gray *retired business manager, former mayor*
Haynes, Thomas Joseph *marketing executive*
Helm, Lewis Marshall *public affairs executive*
Herbert, Carol Sellers *farming executive, lawyer*
Herrmann, Thomas Francis *database administrator*
Hersher, Richard Donald *management consultant*
Hess, Sidney Wayne *management consultant*
Hiatt, Robert Nelson *consumer products executive*
Hirsh, Norman Barry *management consultant*
Hite, Elinor Kirkland *oil company human resources manager*
Hock, Morton *entertainment advertising executive*
Holland, Henry Norman *marketing consultant*
Holmes, Robert Wayne *service executive, consultant, biological historian*
Hooper, Gerry Don *information systems specialist, consultant*
Hosea, Julia Hiller *communications executive, paralegal*
Houghtaling, Pamela Ann *public relations executive*
Hsin, Victor Jun-Kuan *information systems and telecommunications consultant*
Hunt, Martha *sales executive, researcher*
Ichaporia, Pallan R. *pharmaceutical marketing executive*
Irwin, Linda Belmore *marketing consultant*
Isaac, Steven Richard *communications executive*
Jarvis, Barbara Ann *conference planner, conference manager*
Jenkins, Anthony Curtis *sales executive*
Jernstedt, Richard Don *public relations executive*
Jewell, Florence Eva *telecommunications administrator*
Joanou, Phillip *advertising executive*
Jones, Gerre Lyle *marketing and public relations consultant*
Jones, Regina Nickerson *public relations executive*
Judge, Jean Frances *management consultant*
Kampmeier, Curt *management consultant*
Kaprielian, Walter *advertising executive*
Karalekas, Anne *media executive*
Karalis, John Peter *computer company executive, lawyer*
Karp, David *communications executive, writer*
Kasulka, Larry Herman *management consultant*
Keala, Francis Ahloy *security executive*
Kelleher, Richard Cornelius *marketing and communications executive*
Keller, Paul *advertising agency executive*
Kelley, Albert Benjamin *author, consultant*
Kennedy, Jerrie Ann Preston *public relations executive*
King, Philip Gordon *public relations consultant*
King, William Douglas *retired executive*
Kinney, Marjorie Sharon *marketing executive, artist*
Kirschenmann, Henry George, Jr. *management consultant, former government official, accountant*
Klauberg, William Joseph *technical services company executive*
Klein, Charlotte Conrad *public relations executive*
Knipp, Helmut *hospitality industry executive*
Koelmel, Lorna Lee *data processing executive*
Korwek, Alexander Donald *management consultant*
Kramer, Peter Robin *computer company executive*
Krisher, Patterson Howard *management consultant*
Krogius, Tristan Ernst Gunnar *international marketing consultant, lawyer*
Kushner, Harvey David *management consultant*
Lacey, John William Charles *management consultant*
Laczko, Robert Matthias *cook*
Lahourcade, John Brosius *retired service company executive*
Lakritz, Isaac *management consultant*
Lamalie, Robert Eugene *retired executive search company executive*
Lampert, Eleanor Verna *retired human resources specialist*
Lantz, Kenneth Eugene *consulting firm executive*
Latimer, Helen *information resource manager, writer, researcher*
Lavidge, Robert James *marketing research executive*
Lawrence, Margery H(ulings) *marketing consultant*

Lee, Joseph William *sales executive*
Lehman, Christopher M. *international business consultant*
Leizear, Charles William *retired information services executive*
Levine, Carl Morton *motion picture exhibition, real estate executive*
Levy, Arthur James *public relations executive, writer*
Lewis, Dennis Carroll *public relations executive*
Linda, Gerald *advertising and marketing executive*
Lindsey, Dottye Jean *marketing executive*
Littman, Earl *advertising and public relations executive*
Livingston, Alan Wendell *communications executive*
Locke, Norton *hotel management and construction company executive*
Lockhart, James Bicknell, III *company executive*
Lockwood, Robert W. *management consultant*
Loiello, John Peter *public affairs executive, consultant*
Lokmer, Stephanie Ann *public relations counselor*
Louison, Deborah Finley *public affairs consultant*
Lowrie, Walter Olin *management consultant*
Lubinsky, Menachem Yechiel *communications executive*
Luciano, Roselle Patricia *advertising executive, editor*
Luttner, Edward F. *consulting company executive*
Lynch, Charlotte Andrews *communications executive*
Lynn, Sheilah Ann *service executive, consultant*
Mackenzie, Malcolm Lewis *marketing executive*
Macon, Carol Ann Gloeckler *micro-computer data base management company executive*
Makepeace, Darryl Lee *consulting company executive*
Malakoff, James Leonard *management information executive*
Mallenbaum, Allan Eliyahu *marketing executive*
Malphurs, Roger Edward *biomedical marketing executive*
Manley, John Hugo *computing technology executive, educator*
Marinaccio, Paul John, Jr. *marketing professional*
Marple, Gary Andre *management consultant*
Marshall, Robert Charles *computer company executive*
Martin, Alan Edward *gasket company executive*
Martino, Rocco Leonard *computer systems executive*
Massey, William Walter, Jr. *sales executive*
Mathay, Mary Frances *marketing executive*
Mazzarella, Rosemary Louise *business administration executive*
McCarthy, Daniel William *management consultant*
McCullough, R. Michael *management consultant*
McGervey, Teresa Ann *technology information specialist*
Mc Kay, Dean Raymond *computer company executive*
McKinney, Elizabeth Anne *government purchasing professional*
McVeigh-Pettigrew, Sharon Christine *communications consultant*
McWilliams, Bruce Wayne *marketing professional*
Meads, Donald Edward *management services company executive*
Mekenney, C. Robert *management analyst, tax accountant*
Melsheimer, Mel P(owell) *consumer products business executive*
Mercoun, Dawn Denise *human resources executive*
Metz, Frank Andrew, Jr. *data processing executive*
Michael, Harold Kaye (Bud Michael) *sales and marketing executive*
Milanovich, Norma JoAnne *training company executive, occupational educator*
Miles, Laveda Ann *advertising executive*
Miller, Ellen S. *marketing communications executive*
Miller, Pamela Lynn *sales director*
Moeller, Robert John *management consultant*
Mogelever, Bernard *public relations executive*
Montgomery, James Morton *public relations, marketing executive, association executive*
Moore, George Elliott *management consultant*
Moore, Matthew Emerson *environmental program planning management specialist*
Moore, Richard Earl *communications creative director*
Moradi, Ahmad F. *software company executive, consultant*
Morin, William James *management consultant*
Moses, Jeffrey Michael *customer services executive*
Moszkowicz, Virginia Marie *quality administrator*
Mulcahy, Robert Edward *management consultant*
Myers, Phillip Fenton *financial services and technology company executive*
Myhren, Trygve Edward *communications company executive*
Naquin, Patricia Elizabeth *employee assistance consultant*
Newman, Sheldon Oscar *computer company executive*
Niemann, Lewis Keith *lamp manufacturing company executive*
Noolan, Julie Anne Carroll Virgo *management consultant*
Norris, Katharine Eileen *communications professional, educator*
Norton, Nathaniel Goodwin *marketing executive*
Novas, Joseph, Jr. *advertising agency executive*
O'Connor, John Joseph *operations executive*
Okada, Takuya *retail executive*
Olson, Kenneth Harvey *computer company executive*
O'Neil, Cleora Tanner *personnel specialist*
Opperman, Danny Gene *packaging professional, consultant*
Ortiz, James George *data information services company executive*
O'Shea, Catherine Large *marketing and public relations consultant*
O'Sullivan, Paul Kevin *business executive, management and instructional systems consultant*
Owens, Charles Vincent, Jr. *diagnostic company executive and consultant*
Parker, Scott Lane *management consultant*
Patterson, Dennis Joseph *management consultant*
Paul, Frank *retired consulting company executive*
Payne, Timothy E. *management consultant*
Peretti, Marilyn Gay Woerner *human services professional*
Perlov, Dadie *management consultant*
Perry, Donny Ray *electrician*
Peterman, Donna Cole *communications executive*
Pew, Thomas W., Jr. *advertising executive*
Philippi, Ervin William *mortician*
Phillips, Gabriel *travel marketing executive*
Phillips, John David *communications executive*
Pilette, Patricia Chehy *health care organizational/management consultant*
Post, Richard Bennett *retired human resources executive*
Potter, James Earl *retired international hotel management company executive*
Prokopis, Emmanuel Charles *computer company executive*
Pugliese, Karen Olsen *freelance public relations counsel*
Radkowsky, Karen *advertising/marketing research executive*
Rairdin, Craig Allen *software company executive, software developer*
Ramsey, Lynn Allison *public relations executive*
Rank, Larry Gene *management consultant*
Rasmussen, Dennis Loy *sales and marketing executive*
Rasor, Dina Lynn *investigator, journalist*
Reed, David Patrick *infosystems specialist*
Rhein, Murray Harold *management consultant*
Richard, Susan Mathis *communications executive*
Richards, Kenneth Edwin *management consultant*
Richardson, Roy *management consultant*
†Richey, Thomas Adam *advertising executive*
Robins, Norman Alan *strategic planning consultant, former steel company executive*
Robinson, Linda Gosden *communications executive*
Robison, James Everett *management consulting company executive*
Rodrigues, Alfred Benjamin Kameeiamoku *marketing consultant*
Rolof, Marcia Christine *sales executive*
Roseman, Jack *computer services company executive*
Rosen, Arthur Marvin *advertising executive*
Rosenfield, James Harold *communications executive*
Roy, Roland G. *information systems executive*
Salzman, Marilyn B. Wolfson *service company executive*
Sanders, William George *public relations executive*
Sands, I. Jay *corporate executive, business, marketing and real estate consultant, lecturer, realtor, analyst*
Satre, Philip Glen *casino entertainment executive, lawyer*
Saul, Ann *public relations executive*
Savage, Neve Richard *marketing executive*
Sawyer, Raymond Lee, Jr. *motel chain executive*
Sayer, John Samuel *retired information systems consultant*
Sceiford, Mary Elizabeth *retired public television administrator*
Schein, Harvey L. *communications executive*
Schmidt, Karen Lee *marketing consultant, management consultant*
Schmidt, Richard Alan *management company executive*
Schmutz, Charles Reid *university foundation executive*
Schreckinger, Sy Edward *advertising executive, consultant*
Schulberg, Jay William *advertising agency executive*
Schur, Susan Dorfman *public affairs consultant*
Schuster, Gary Francis *public relations executive*
Schwartz, Stephen Blair *retired information industry executive*
Schweickart, Jim *advertising executive, broadcast consultant*
Schweig, Margaret Berris *retired meeting and special events consultant*
Scutt, Cheryl Lynn *communications executive*
Sease, Gene Elwood *public relations company executive*
Seelig, Gerard Leo *management consultant*
Senske, Marlowe Orlyn *healthcare executive, hospital administrator*
Senter, Alan Zachary *communications company executive*
Shafran, Hank *public relations executive*
Shapiro, Richard Charles *sales and marketing executive*
Sheeline, Paul Cushing *hotel executive*
Shelton, Karl Mason *management consultant*
Sherman, Kathryn Ann *communication professional*
Shikuma, Eugene Yujin *travel agency executive*
Simecka, Betty Jean *marketing executive*
Simpson, Bob G. *retired quality assurance professional*
Sims, Albert Maurice *marketing professional*
Sincoff, Michael Z. *human resources and marketing professional*
Singer, David Michael *marketing and public relations company executive*
Singleton, Philip Arthur *corporate executive*
Sinicropi, Anthony Vincent *industrial relations and human resources educator*
Smith, Kathryn Ann *advertising executive*
Smith, Thomas Winston *cotton marketing executive*
†Snoddon, Larry Erle *public relations executive*
Sollender, Joel David *management consultant, financial executive*
Sorgi, Deborah Bernadette *educational software company executive*
Souveroff, Vernon William, Jr. *business executive, author*
Spain, Jayne Baker *corporate executive*
Spirn, Michele Sobel *communications professional, writer*
Sroge, Maxwell Harold *marketing consultant, publishing executive*
Stans, Maurice Hubert *retired business consultant, former government official*
Stark, Diana *public relations and promotion executive*
Stengel, Ronald Francis *management consultant*
Stephens, C. Michael *service executive*
Stevens, Berton Louis, Jr. *data processing manager*
Stewart, Arthur Irving, III (Art Stewart) *communications executive*
†Stewart, James Percy *safety and risk management consultant*
Stewart, Richard Alfred *business executive*
Stromberg, Arthur Harold *retired professional services company executive*
Strother, Patrick Joseph *public relations executive*
Strupp, Jacqueline Virginia *small business specialist, insurance professional*
Stults, Walter Black *management consultant, former trade organization executive*
Sturgeon, Charles Edwin *management consultant*
Sullivan, William Courtney *retired communications executive*
Tarar, Afzal Muhammad *management consultant*
Tarjan, Robert Wegg *retired information services executive*
Tarr, Curtis W. *business executive*
Temerlin, Liener *advertising agency executive*
Thomas, Joe Carroll *human resources director*
Thomas-Myers, Susan Jane *executive sales representatives group*
Thompson, Richard Stephen *management consultant*
Thongsak, Vajeeprasee Thomas *business planning executive*
Toevs, Alden Louis *management consultant*
Togerson, John Dennis *computer software company executive, retired*
Tomas, Jerold F. V. *business executive, management consultant*
Townsend, Jerrie Lynne *environmental services administrator*
Transou, Lynda Lew *advertising executive*
Travisano, Frank Peter *professional management consultant, business broker*
Triolo, Peter *advertising agency executive, marketing educator, consultant*
Tuft, Mary Ann *executive search firm executive*
Tytler, Linda Jean *communications and public affairs executive, retired state legislator*
Unger, Sonja Franz *package company executive, travel consultant, ceramist*
Ussery, Luanne *communications consultant*
Uvena, Frank John *retired printing company executive, lawyer*
Vallerand, Philippe Georges *sales executive*
Wadley, M. Richard *consumer products executive*
Wagner, Richard *business executive, former baseball team executive*
Wakeman, Olivia Van Horn *marketing professional*
Walash, Eileen Robin (Lee Walash) *promotions and public relations specialist*
Walsh, William Albert *management consultant, former naval officer*
Walter, John Robert *printing company executive*
†Wasserman, Anthony Ira *software company executive, educator*
Weismantel, Gregory Nelson *management consultant and software executive*
Werkman, Rosemarie Anne *past public relations professional, civic worker*
White, Erskine Norman, Jr. *management company executive*
White, Loray Betty *public relations executive, writer, actress, producer*
Whitmer, Joseph Morton *benefits consulting firm executive, retired*
Wikarski, Nancy Susan *information technology consultant*
Wilkinson, Rebecca Elaine *human resources application specialist*
Williams, Earle Carter *retired professional services company executive*
Williams, Louis Clair, Jr. *public relations executive*
Willig, Karl Victor *computer firm executive*
Wolf, William Martin *computer company executive, consultant*
Wolotkiewicz, Marian M. *program director*
Woods, Reginald Foster *management consulting executive*
Worth, Gary James *communications executive*
Wustenberg, Wendy Wiberg *public affairs specialist, consultant*
Wynne, Linda Marie *administrative assistant, artist*
Yancey, Jimmie Isaac *marketing professional*
Yocam, Delbert Wayne *software products company executive*
Young, Elizabeth Bell *consultant*
Zajas, J. Jonathan R. *management consulting company executive, principal*
Zehring, Karen *information executive*
Zeller, Joseph Paul *advertising executive*
Zinnen, Robert Oliver *general management executive*
Zizza, Salvatore J. *diversified company executive*
Zoellick, Robert Bruce *corporate executive, lawyer*
Zuckerman, Martin Harvey *personnel director*


## INDUSTRY: TRADE

### UNITED STATES

### ALABAMA

#### Birmingham


Bolton, William *retail executive*
George, Frank Wade *small business owner, antiquarian book dealer*
Hubbard, Kenneth Earl *retail executive*
Pizitz, Richard Alan *retail and real estate group executive*


#### Hartselle


Penn, Hugh Franklin *small business owner*


#### Pelham


Wabler, Robert Charles, II *retail and distribution executive*


#### Tuscaloosa


Blackburn, John Leslie *small business owner*


### ALASKA

#### Anchorage


Cairns, John J(oseph) *retail executive*
Vandergriff, Jerry Dodson *retired computer store executive*


### ARIZONA

#### Glendale


Covington, B(athild) June *business owner, advocate*


#### Scottsdale


Boat, Ronald Allen *business executive*
Cunningham, Gilbert Earl *business owner*


#### Tucson


Swanson, Cheryl Ann *small business owner, nurse*


### ARKANSAS

#### Bentonville


Bruce, Robert Thomas *retail executive*
Glass, David D. *department store company executive, professional baseball team executive*
White, Nick *retail executive*


#### Hot Springs National Park


Tanenbaum, Bernard Jerome, Jr. *corporate executive*


#### Little Rock


Dillard, William T. *department store chain executive*
Dwyer, Mary Elizabeth *retail executive*
Long, Walter Edward *international trade company executive, consultant*


### CALIFORNIA

#### Anaheim


Abramson, Norman *retail executive*
Brownhill, H. Bud *small business owner, canine behavior therapist*


#### Arcadia


Stangeland, Roger Earl *retail chain store executive*


#### Berkeley


Alpert, Norman Joseph *merchandising executive*


#### Beverly Hills


Orenstein, (Ian) Michael *philatelic dealer, columnist*


#### Brisbane


Orban, Kurt *foreign trade company executive*


#### Cathedral City


Jackman, Robert Alan *retail executive*


#### Cerritos


Webb, Lewis M. *retail executive*


#### Chula Vista


Austin, Mary Jane *small business owner*


#### Colton


Brown, Jack H. *supermarket company executive*


#### Dublin


Cope, Kenneth Wayne *chain store executive*


#### East Los Angeles


Tuthill, Walter Warren *retail executive*


#### Emeryville


Weaver, Velather Edwards *small business owner*


#### Encino


Vigdor, James Scott *distribution executive*


#### Fremont


†Wilson, Judy *small business owner*


#### Fresno


Blum, Gerald Henry *department store executive*


#### Garden Grove


Virgo, Muriel Agnes *swimming school owner*


#### Irwindale


Hughes, Roger K. *dairy and grocery store company executive*


#### Los Angeles


Blodgett, Julian Robert *small business owner*
Hawley, Philip Metschan *retired retail executive, consultant*
Roeder, Richard Kenneth *business owner, lawyer*
Sinay, Joseph *retail executive*
Williams, Theodore Earle *industrial distribution company executive*


#### Menlo Park


Katz, Robert Lee *business executive*


#### Modesto


Piccinini, Robert M. *grocery store chain executive*


#### Newark


Ferber, Norman Alan *retail executive*


#### Oakland


Hoopes, Lorenzo Neville *former retailing executive*


#### Orange


Underwood, Vernon O., Jr. *grocery stores executive*


#### Orinda


Hendler, Rosemary Nielsen *business owner, computer artist*


#### Pacific Palisades


Diehl, Richard Kurth *retail business consultant*


#### Palos Verdes Peninsula


Slayden, James Bragdon *retired department store executive*


#### Pasadena


Hecht, Harold Michael *retail executive*


#### Piedmont


Yep, Wallen Lai *import/export company executive, author*


#### Redding


Streiff, Arlyne Bastunas *business owner, educator*


#### San Bernardino


Sagmeister, Edward Frank *business owner, hospitality industry executive, civic official, retired consultant, fund raiser, career officer*


#### San Francisco


Bucherre, Veronique *environmental company executive*
Draper, William Henry, III *business executive*
Drexler, Millard S. *retail executive*

Fisher, Donald G. *casual apparel chain stores executive*
Fromm, Alfred *distributing company executive*
Nicolaï, Judithe *international business trade executive*
Seelenfreund, Alan *distribution company executive*
Ullman, Myron Edward, III *retail executive*

**San Jose**
Finnigan, Robert Emmet *business owner*
Mc Connell, John Douglas *retail corporation executive, owner*

**San Juan Capistrano**
Purdy, Alan MacGregor *financial executive*

**San Marino**
Meyer, William Danielson *retired department store executive*

**Santa Ana**
Shahin, Thomas John *dry cleaning wholesale supply company executive*

**Santa Rosa**
Furen, Shirley Ann *small business owner, art dealer*

**Stockton**
Dornbush, Vicky Jean *medical billing systems executive*

**Vernon**
Lynch, Martin Andrew *retail company executive*

**Walnut Creek**
Long, Robert Merrill *retail drug company executive*
Wolcott, Oliver Dwight *international trading company executive*

**West Sacramento**
Solomon, Russell *retail products executive*
Teel, James E. *supermarket and drug store retail executive*
Teel, Joyce *supermarket and drugstore retail executive*

## COLORADO

**Aurora**
Magalnick, Elliott Ben *retail medical supply company executive*
Reynolds, Robert Harrison *retired export company executive*

**Boulder**
Johnson, Maryanna Morse *business owner*

**Colorado Springs**
Noyes, Richard Hall *bookseller*

**Loveland**
Rodman, Alpine Clarence *arts and crafts company executive*
Rodman, Sue Arlene *wholesale Indian crafts company executive, artist, consultant*

## CONNECTICUT

**Avon**
Kling, Phradie (Phradie Kling Gold) *small business owner*

**Cheshire**
Bozzuto, Michael Adam *wholesale grocery company executive*

**Greenwich**
Pivirotto, Richard Roy *former retail executive*

**Hartford**
Goodwin, Rodney Keith Grove *international bank and trade company executive*
McNally, Alexander Campbell *wine authority, consultant*

**New Britain**
Davidson, Phillip Thomas *retail company executive*

**Norwalk**
Bennett, Carl *retired discount department store executive*

**Westport**
Wexler, Herbert Ira *retail company executive*

**Windsor**
Goldman, Ethan Harris *retail executive*

## DISTRICT OF COLUMBIA

**Washington**
Gordon, Shana *trade company executive*
McGraw, Lavinia Morgan *retired retail company executive*
Negron, Jaime *performing arts center sales director*
Smith, Jack Carl *foreign trade consultant*
Wurtzel, Alan Leon *retail company executive*

## FLORIDA

**Bradenton**
Beall, Robert Matthews, II *retail chain executive*

**Clearwater**
Hoornstra, Edward H. *retail company executive*
Maxwell, Richard Anthony *retail company executive*
Turley, Stewart *retired retail executive*

**Coral Gables**
Groover, Sandra Mae *retail executive*

**Daytona Beach**
St. James, Lyn *business owner, professional race car driver*

**Deerfield Beach**
Moran, Patricia Genevieve *corporate executive*

**Fort Lauderdale**
Palmer, Marcia Stibal *food and wine retailer, interior designer, real estate investor*
Wojcik, Cass *decorative supply company executive, former city official*

**Fort Myers**
Anthony, Susan Mae *entrepreneur*
Colgate, Doris Eleanor *retailer, sailing school owner and administrator*

**Gainesville**
DeSimone, Rory Jean *small business owner*

**Highland Beach**
Frager, Albert S. *retired retail food company executive*

**Hobe Sound**
Nuñez de, Maria Irene *small business owner, consultant*

**Homestead**
Risi, Louis J., Jr. *business executive*

**Jacksonville**
Mann, Timothy *corporate executive*
†Stein, Jay *retail executive*

**Lakeland**
Luther, George Albert *truck brokerage executive*

**Longboat Key**
Goldsmith, Jack Landman *former retail company executive*

**Marco Island**
Lesser, Joseph M. *retired business executive, retail store executive*

**Miami**
Chaplin, Harvey *wine and liquor wholesale executive*
Liebes, Raquel *import/export company executive, educator*
Newlin, Kimrey Dayton *international trade consultant, political consultant, personal computer analyst*
Tuttle, Toni Brodax *swimming pool company executive*

**Mount Dora**
Edgerton, Richard *restaurant and hotel owner*

**Orlando**
Hall-Kelly, Kathy B. *small business owner, columnist, speaker, consultant*
Kindlund, Newton C. *retail executive*

**Palm Bay**
Jurgevich, Nancy J. *retail executive, educator*

**Palm Beach**
Black, Leonard Julius *retail store consultant*

**Palm Harbor**
Stettner, Jerald W. *retail drugs stores executive*

**Sanibel**
Perkinson, Diana Agnes Zouzelka *import company executive*

**Sarasota**
Meyer, B. Fred *small business executive, home designer and builder, product designer*

**Sebastian**
Becker, Jim *small business owner*

**Tampa**
Crowder, Bonnie Walton *small business owner, composer*
Eddy, Colette Ann *aerial photography studio owner, photographer*

## GEORGIA

**Atlanta**
Allen, Ivan, Jr. *office products company owner*
Haverty, Rawson *retail furniture company executive*
Kalafut, George Wendell *distribution company executive, retired naval officer*
Marcus, Bernard *retail executive*
Moderow, Joseph Robert *package distribution company executive*
Roney, Shirley Fletcher *retail company executive*

**Covington**
Penland, John Thomas *import and export and development companies executive*

**Dalton**
Saul, Julian *retail executive*

**Smyrna**
Head, John Francis, Jr. *distributing company executive*

**Valdosta**
Halter, H(enry) James, Jr. (Diamond Jim Halter) *retail executive*

## HAWAII

**Hanalei**
Vogel, Richard Wiedemann *business owner, ichthyodynamicist, educator*

**Kailua Kona**
Luizzi, Ronald *wholesale distribution executive*

**Waipahu**
Matsui, Jiro *importer, wholesaler, small business owner*

## IDAHO

**Boise**
†Killebrew, Harmon Clayton *retail automobile executive, former baseball player, former insurance company executive*
Long, William D. *grocery store executive*
Michael, Gary G. *retail supermarket and drug chain executive*

**Coeur D Alene**
Chamberlain, Barbara Kaye *small business owner*

## ILLINOIS

**Auburn**
Burtle, Debra Ann *needlework and gift shop owner*

**Bensenville**
Lewis, Darrell L. *retail executive*

**Bloomingdale**
Corcoran, Philip E. *wholesale distribution executive*

**Burr Ridge**
Rinder, George Greer *retired retail company executive*

**Chicago**
Brennan, Bernard Francis *retail chain store executive*
Brodsky, Robert Jay *wholesale executive*
Christianson, Stanley David *corporate executive*
Doolittle, Sidney Newing *retail executive*
Dowling, Doris Anderson *business owner, educator, consultant*
Gingiss, Benjamin Jack *retired formal clothing stores executive*
Kroch, Carl Adolph *retail executive*
LeMonnier, Daniel Brian *small business owner, entertainer*
Telling, Edward Riggs *former retail, insurance, real estate and financial services executive*
Tomaino, Joseph Carmine *retail executive, retired postal inspector*
Vrablik, Edward Robert *import/export company executive*
Wood, Arthur MacDougall *retired retail executive*

**Chicago Heights**
Carpenter, Kenneth Russell *international trading executive*

**Deerfield**
Miller, James A. *wholesale grocery executive*
Walgreen, Charles Rudolph, III *retail store executive*

**Downers Grove**
Shea, John J. *catalog and retail company executive*

**Glen Ellyn**
Baloun, John Charles *wholesale grocery company executive, retired*

**Glencoe**
Nebenzahl, Kenneth *rare book and map dealer, author*

**Hoffman Estates**
Beitler, Stephen Seth *retail company executive*

**Morton Grove**
McKenna, Andrew James *paper distribution and printing company executive, baseball club executive*

**Naperville**
Wake, William S. *wholesale distribution executive*

**Northlake**
Jasper, Paul Tucker *food company executive*

**Oak Park**
Spartz, Alice Anne Lenore *retired retail executive*

**Vernon Hills**
Ferkenhoff, Robert J. *retail executive*

**Wilmette**
Mc Nitt, Willard Charles *business executive*
Williams, Emory *former retail company executive, banker*

**Winnetka**
Weldon, Theodore Tefft, Jr. *retail company executive*

## INDIANA

**Bicknell**
Risley, Gregory Byron *furniture company executive, interior designer*

**Elkhart**
Drexler, Rudy Matthew, Jr. *professional law enforcement dog trainer*

**Evansville**
Blesch, K(athy) Suzann *small business owner*

**Fort Wayne**
Curtis, Douglas Homer *small business owner*
Pathak, Sunit Rawly *business owner, consultant, journalist*

**Indianapolis**
Fredrickson, William Robert *trading company executive*

La Crosse, James *retail executive*
Seitz, Melvin Christian, Jr. *distributing company executive*
Seneff, Smiley Howard *business owner*
Stout, William Jewell *department store executive*

**New Albany**
Conway, William Frederick, Sr. *business founder*

## IOWA

**Chariton**
Vredenburg, Dwight Charles *retired supermarket chain executive*

**Creston**
Turner, Lula Mae Mansur *retail executive*

**Des Moines**
Westphal, Deborah Louise *retail executive, choreographer*

**Marshalltown**
Shawstad, Raymond Vernon *business owner, retired computer specialist*

**West Des Moines**
Pearson, Ronald Dale *retail food stores corporation executive*

**West Union**
Hansen, Ruth Lucille Hofer *business owner, consultant*

## KANSAS

**Atwood**
Gatlin, Fred *seed and feed business owner, state legislator*

**Great Bend**
Straub, Larry Gene *business executive*

**Kansas City**
Baska, James Louis *wholesale grocery company executive*
Carolan, Douglas *wholesale company executive*

**Overland Park**
Parker, Cheryl Jean *small business owner*

**Wichita**
Gates, Walter Edward *small business owner*

## KENTUCKY

**Glasgow**
Lessenberry, Robert Adams *retail executive*

**Olive Hill**
Rose, Melissa Eva Anderson *small business owner*

## LOUISIANA

**Bossier City**
Johnson, Ruby LaVerne *retail executive*

**Coushatta**
Wiggins, Mary Ann Wise *small business owner, educator*

**Lafayette**
Gossen, Renee Hebert *retail executive*

## MAINE

**Freeport**
Gorman, Leon A. *mail order company executive*

**Portland**
Moody, James L., Jr. *retail food distribution company executive*

**Scarborough**
Farrington, Hugh G. *wholesale food and retail drug company executive*

**Sedgwick**
Donnell, William Ray *small business owner, farmer, editor, author, lecturer*

## MARYLAND

**Baltimore**
Cain, Marcena Jean Beesley *retail store executive*
Hoffberger, Jerold Charles *corporation executive*
Stein, Bernard Alvin *business consultant*

**Childs**
Perkins, Esther Roberta *literary agent*

**Frederick**
Anderson, William Bert *import company executive*

**Gaithersburg**
Nemecek, Albert Duncan, Jr. *retail company executive, investment banker, management consultant*

**Lutherville Timonium**
Andrews, Charles *wholesale distribution executive*

**Potomac**
Shapiro, Richard Gerald *retired department store executive, consultant*

## Riva
Barto, Bradley Edward *small business owner, educator*

## Sykesville
Gubernatis, Thomas Frank, Sr. *electrical buyer*

## White Sands
Andrea, Elma Williams *retail executive*

## MASSACHUSETTS

### Auburn
Baker, David Arthur *small business owner, manufacturer*

### Boston
DeAmicis, Susan McNair *small business owner*
Kane, Louis Isaac *merchant*
Kwasnick, Paul Jack *retail executive*
Rosenberg, Manuel *retail company executive*
Rutstein, Stanley Harold *apparel retailing company executive*
Zaldastani, Guivy *business consultant*

### Cambridge
Lazarus, Maurice *retired retail executive*

### Canton
Bentas, Lily H. *retail executive*
Raven, Gregory Kurt *retail executive*

### Chelsea
Danckert, Stephen Christopher *retail executive*

### Cohasset
Lyne, Austin Francis *sporting goods business executive*

### Framingham
Cammarata, Bernard *retail company executive*
Feldberg, Sumner Lee *retired retail company executive*
Wishner, Steven R. *retail executive*

### Hingham
Cooke, Gordon Richard *retail executive*

### Holyoke
Radner, Sidney Hollis *retired rug company executive*

### Marlborough
Palihnich, Nicholas Joseph, Jr. *retail chain executive*

### Natick
Zarkin, Herbert *retail company executive*

### Needham
Reichman, Joel H. *retail executive*

### Newbury
Jones, Christopher Edward *manufacturing systems consultant*

### North Chatham
McCarthy, Joseph Harold *consultant, former retail food company executive*

### North Dartmouth
Hodgson, James Stanley *antiquarian bookseller*

### North Eastham
York, Elizabeth Jane *innkeeper*

### Quincy
McGlinchey, Joseph Dennis *retail corporation executive*
Tobin, Robert G. *supermarket chain executive*

### Taunton
Mosher, Wendy Jean *retail chain official*

### Wakefield
Irons, Diane Havelick *small business owner*

### Walpole
Morton, Robert Allen *small business owner*

### Worcester
Szaban, Marilyn C. *small business owner*

## MICHIGAN

### Ann Arbor
Quinnell, Bruce Andrew *retail book chain executive*

### Bad Axe
Sullivan, James Gerald *business owner, postal letter carrier*

### Bloomfield Hills
Robinson, Jack Albert *retail drug stores executive*

### Detroit
Tushman, J. Lawrence *wholesale distribution executive*

### Grand Blanc
Hicks, Susan Lynn Bowman *small business owner*

### Grand Rapids
DeLapa, Judith Anne *business owner*
Meijer, Douglas *retail company executive*
Meijer, Frederik *retail company executive*
Meijer, Hendrik *retail company executive*
Quinn, Patrick Michael *wholesale food executive*

### Lansing
LaHaine, Gilbert Eugene *retail lumber company executive*
Stanaway, Loretta Susan *small business owner*

## Royal Oak
Corwin, Vera-Anne Versfelt *small business owner, consultant*

## Saint Clair Shores
Seppala, Katherine Seaman (Mrs. Leslie W. Seppala) *retail company executive*

## Saint Joseph
Renwick, Ken *retail executive*

## Southfield
Primo, Joan Erwina *retail and real estate consulting business owner*

## Troy
Burken, Ruth Marie *retail company executive*
Hall, Floyd *retail executive*
Strome, Stephen *distribution company executive*

## Waterford
Lang, Catherine Lou *small business owner*

## MINNESOTA

### Edina
Emmerich, Karol Denise *former retail company executive, consultant*

### Minneapolis
Erickson, Ronald A. *retail executive*
Gilpin, Larry Vincent *retail executive*
Mammel, Russell Norman *retired food distribution company executive*
Trestman, Frank D. *distribution company executive*
Ulrich, Robert J. *retail discount chain stores executive*
Wright, Michael William *wholesale distribution, retailing executive*

### Plymouth
Froemming, Herbert Dean *retail executive*

### Saint Paul
Hart, Myrna Jean *art gallery and gift shop owner*
Nash, Nicholas David *retailing executive*

### Walker
Doughty, Anthony Rutgers *small business owner*

## MISSOURI

### Aurora
Goodman, Nancy Jane *small business owner*

### Buffalo
Louderback, Kevin Wayne *business owner*

### Clayton
Hall, Carl Loren *electrical distribution executive*
Ross, E. Earl *small business owner*

### Cuba
Work, Bruce Van Syoc *business consultant*

### Kansas City
Stanley, David *retail company executive*
Stueck, William Noble *small business owner*

### Maryland Heights
†Marcus, John *wholesale distribution executive*

### Richmond
Nordsieck, Karen Ann *custom design company owner*

### Rothville
Ginn, M. Stanly *retail executive, lawyer, bank executive*

### Saint Charles
Dauphinais, George Arthur *import company executive*

### Saint Louis
Battram, Richard L. *retail executive*
Bridgewater, Bernard Adolphus, Jr. *footwear company executive*
Edison, Bernard Alan *retired retail apparel company executive*
Farrell, David Coakley *department store executive*
Loeb, Jerome Thomas *retail executive*
Newman, Andrew Edison *restaurant executive*
Schnuck, Craig D. *grocery stores company executive*
Upbin, Hal Jay *consumer products executive*
Williams, Frank James, Jr. *department store chain executive, lawyer*

### Sibley
Morrow, Elizabeth Hostetter *business owner, sculptress, museum association administrator, educator*

## MONTANA

### Billings
Marcovitz, Leonard Edward *retail executive*

### Butte
†Gaiez, Riga *small business owner, artist*

### Helena
Brown, Jan Whitney *small business owner*

## NEBRASKA

### Lincoln
Rawley, Ann Keyser *small business owner, picture framer*

## Omaha
Inatome, Rick *retail computer company executive*

## NEVADA

### Henderson
Fehr, Gregory Paris *marketing and distribution company executive*

### Las Vegas
Fitch, Bonnie Lynn *music store owner*

## NEW HAMPSHIRE

### New Castle
Friese, George Ralph *retail executive*

### Rochester
Coviello, Robert Frank *retail executive*

## NEW JERSEY

### Barnegat
Lowe, Angela Maria *small business owner*

### Camden
Edgerton, Brenda Evans *soup company executive*

### Carteret
Jemal, Lawrence *retail executive*

### Chatham
Manning, Frederick William *retired retail executive*

### Elizabeth
Gellert, George Geza *food importing company executive*

### Englewood
Rawl, Arthur Julian (Lord of Cursons) *retail executive, accountant, consultant, author*

### Englewood Cliffs
Brandreth, John Breckenridge, II *chemical importer*
Solomon, Edward David *chain store executive*

### Freehold
Foster, Eric H., Jr. *retail executive*

### Haddonfield
White, Warren Wurtele *retired retailing executive*

### Mahwah
Inserra, Lawrence R. *retail executive*

### Montvale
O'Gorman, Peter Joseph *retail company executive*
Ulrich, Robert Gardner *retail food chain executive, lawyer*
Wood, James *supermarket executive*

### Morristown
Orlowsky, Martin L. *executive manager*

### New Milford
Walsh, Joseph Michael *magazine distribution executive*

### New Monmouth
Donnelly, Gerard Kevin *retail executive*

### North Bergen
Karp, Roberta S. *wholesale apparel and accessories executive*

### Oakhurst
Seltzer, Ronald *retail company executive*

### Paramus
Goldstein, Michael *retail executive*
Nakasone, Robert C. *retail toy and game company executive*

### Ridgefield
Toscano, Samuel, Jr. *wholesale distribution executive*

### Short Hills
Brous, Philip *retail consultant*

### Toms River
Tweed, John Louis *consultant, association executive, lecturer, small business owner*

### Verona
Brightman, Robert Lloyd *importer, textile company executive, consultant*

### Wayne
Lang, William Charles *retail executive*

## NEW YORK

### Appleton
Singer, Thomas Kenyon *international business consultant, farmer*

### Brooklyn
Magliocco, John *wholesale distribution executive*
Zelin, Jerome *retail executive*

### Chateaugay
Kanzler, Kathleen Patricia *kennel owner*

### Florida
Fisher, Joseph V. *retail executive*

### Hunter
Jaeckel, Christopher Carol *memorabilia company executive, antiquarian*

## Katonah
Levine, Pamela Gail *business owner*

## Mattituck
Marquardt, Ann Marie *small business administrator*

## Melville
Kett, Herbert Joseph *retail executive*

## New York
Becker, Isidore A. *business executive*
Bedi, Rahul *import and distribution company executive*
Bravo, Rose Marie *retail executive*
Brecker, Manfred *retail company executive*
†Brown, Andreas Le *book store and art gallery executive*
Brumm, James Earl *trading company executive*
Caputo, Lucio *trade company executive*
Catsimatidis, John Andreas *retail chain executive, airline executive*
Chung, Chia Mou (Charles Chung) *Oriental art business owner*
Farah, Roger *retail company executive*
Farkas, Robin Lewis *retail company executive*
Finkelstein, Edward Sydney *department store executive*
Fortgang, Charles *wholesale distribution executive*
Gilinsky, Stanley Ellis *department store executive*
Lachman, Lawrence *business consultant, former department store executive*
Mager, Ezra Pascal *automobile dealership executive*
Matthews, Norman Stuart *department store executive*
Michelson, Gertrude Geraldine *retired retail company executive*
Mondlin, Marvin *retail executive, antiquarian book dealer*
Pfeffer, Philip Maurice *book publishing executive*
Pressman, Robert *retail executive*
Quint, Ira *retail executive*
Regalmuto, Nancy Marie *small business owner, psychic consultant, therapist*
Roberti, William Vincent *manufacturing executive*
Sakin, Larry Albert *shop owner*
Seegal, Herbert Leonard *department store executive*
Stanton, Ronald P. *export company executive*
Stern, Madeleine Bettina *rare books dealer, author*
Strauss, Edward Robert *carpet company executive*
Tendler, David *international trade company executive*
Tutun, Edward H. *retired retail executive*

## Pelham
Bornand, Ruth Chaloux *small business owner*

## Purchase
Carleton, Robert L. *consumer products company executive*

## Rochester
McCurdy, Gilbert Geier *retired retailer*
Seager, Steven Albert *small business owner, accountant*

## Ronkonkoma
Nussdorf, Bernard *wholesale distribution executive*

## Sag Harbor
Barry, Nada Davies *retail business owner*

## Sands Point
Cohen, Ida Bogin (Mrs. Savin Cohen) *import and export executive*

## Scarsdale
Sandell, Richard Arnold *international trade executive, economist*

## West Islip
Carpenter, Angie M. *small business owner, editor*

## NORTH CAROLINA

### Charlotte
Belk, John M. *retail company executive*
Gambrell, Sarah Belk *retail executive*
Graham, Sylvia Angelenia *wholesale distributor, retail buyer*
Richards, Craig M. *wholesale distribution executive*

### Durham
Civello, Anthony Ned *retail drug company executive, pharmacist*

### Greensboro
Kennedy, Charles G. *wholesale distribution executive*

### Henderson
Church, John Trammell *retail stores company executive*

### Hendersonville
Heltman, Robert Fairchild *distribution executive*

### Hickory
Lynn, Tony Lee *import company executive*

### Huntersville
Evans, Trellany Victoria Thomas *entrepreneur*

### Rocky Mount
Rabon, Ronald Ray *retail jewelry store chain executive*
Wordsworth, Jerry L. *wholesale distribution executive*

### Salisbury
Ketner, Ralph Wright *retail food company executive*

## OHIO

### Beachwood
Charnas, Michael (Mannie Charnas) *packaging company executive*
Fufuka, Natika Njeri Yaa *retail executive*

**Chesterland**
Aster, Ruth Marie Rhydderch *business owner*

**Cincinnati**
Hodge, Robert Joseph *retail executive*
Lauck, A. Victoria *small business owner, volunteer*
Price, Thomas Emile *investment company executive*

**Cleveland**
Crosby, Fred McClellan *retail home and office furnishings executive*
Knisely Bonk, Helen *corporate customs broker*
Milgrim, Franklin Marshall *merchant*

**Columbus**
Callander, Kay Eileen Paisley *business owner, retired gifted talented education educator, writer*
Schottenstein, Jay L. *retail executive*
Wexner, Leslie Herbert *retail executive*

**Dayton**
Gray, Edman Lowell *metal distribution company executive*
Gutmann, Max *department store executive*
Jenefsky, Jack *wholesale company executive*

**Dublin**
Walter, Robert D. *wholesale pharmaceutical distribution executive*

**Fairfield**
Nichols, David L. *retail executive*

**Mansfield**
Benham, Lelia *small business owner, social/political activist*

**Maumee**
Walrod, David James *retail grocery chain executive*

**Oxford**
Paulin, Henry Sylvester *antiques dealer, emeritus educator*

**Shaker Heights**
Feuer, Michael *office supply store executive*

**Toledo**
Fuhrman, Charles Andrew *country club proprietor, real estate management executive, lawyer*

**Westerville**
Goh, Anthony Li-Shing *business owner, consultant*

**Youngstown**
Catoline, Pauline Dessie *small business owner*

## OKLAHOMA

**Oklahoma City**
Davis, Emery Stephen *wholesale food company executive*
Howeth, Lynda Carol *small business owner*
Werries, E. Dean *food distribution company executive*
Williams, Richard Donald *retired wholesale food company executive*

**Tulsa**
Brown, Connie Yates *business owner*
Rippley, Robert *wholesale distribution executive*

## OREGON

**Bend**
Nosler, Robert Amos *sports company executive*

**Eugene**
Gillespie, Penny Hannig *business owner*

**Portland**
Greenstein, Merle Edward *import and export company executive*
Hill, Ray Thomas, Jr. *import and export company executive*
Miller, Robert G. *retail company executive*
Tomjack, T.J. *wholesale distribution executive*

**Prineville**
Wick, Philip *wholesale distribution executive*

## PENNSYLVANIA

**Altoona**
Sheetz, Stanton R. *retail executive*

**Berwyn**
Fry, Clarence Herbert *retail executive*

**Butler**
Kane, Marilyn Elizabeth *small business owner*

**Camp Hill**
Grass, Alexander *retail company executive*

**Conshohocken**
Schumacher, Elizabeth Swisher *garden ornaments shop owner*

**Dallas**
Day, Maurice Jerome *automobile parts distributing company executive*

**Edgemont**
Armani, Aida Mary *small business executive*

**Fleetwood**
Lewis, Dana Kenneth *trading company executive, consultant, author*

**Lewisburg**
Ondrusek, David Francis *discount store chain executive*

**Littlestown**
Plunkert, Donna Mae *business owner*

**Media**
Wood, Richard D., Jr. *retail executive*

**Norristown**
Genuardi, Charles A. *retail executive*

**Parker**
Meixsell, Berrae Nevin (Mike Meixsell) *distribution executive*

**Pennsylvania Furnace**
LaBorde, Terrence Lee *small business owner, negotiator*

**Pittsburgh**
Hannan, Robert William *retail pharmaceutical company executive*
Heller, Lawrence Aaron *business owner, association executive*

**Reading**
Boscov, Albert *retail executive*

**Roaring Spring**
Smith, Larry Dennis *paper mill stores executive*

**Sharon**
Epstein, Louis Ralph *retired wholesale grocery executive*
Rosenblum, Harold Arthur *grocery distribution executive*

**Shippensburg**
Thompson, Elizabeth Jane *small business owner*

**Villanova**
Vander Veer, Suzanne *aupair business executive*

**Washington**
Erdner, Jon W. *small business owner, securities trader*

**Williamsport**
Largen, Joseph *retailer, furniture manufacturer, book wholesaler*

**Yardley**
Desai, Cawas Jal *distribution company executive*

## RHODE ISLAND

**Westerly**
Hirsch, Larry Joseph *retail executive, lawyer*

**Woonsocket**
Goldstein, Stanley P. *retail company executive*

## SOUTH CAROLINA

**Columbia**
Clark, David Randolph *wholesale grocer*

**Greenville**
Bauknight, Clarence Brock *wholesale and retail company executive*

## SOUTH DAKOTA

**Mitchell**
Randall, Ronald Fisher *grocery store chain executive*

## TENNESSEE

**Brentwood**
Zimmerman, Raymond *retail chain executive*

**Bristol**
Cauthen, Charles Edward, Jr. *retail executive, business consultant*

**Collierville**
Hendren, Gary E. *retail executive*

**Dandridge**
Trent, Wendell Campbell *business owner*

**Knoxville**
Harris, Charles Edgar *retired wholesale distribution company executive*
Jenkins, Roger Lane *retail executive, consultant*

**Memphis**
Clarkson, Andrew MacBeth *retail executive*

**Nashville**
Reid, Donna Joyce *small business owner*
Zibart, Michael Alan *wholesale book company executive*

## TEXAS

**Austin**
Girling, Robert George William, III *business owner*
Houston, Samuel Lee *computer software company executive*

**Boerne**
Morton, Michael Ray *retail company consultant*

**Colleyville**
Pavony, William H. *retail executive*

**Dallas**
Augur, Marilyn Hussman *distribution executive*
Beck, Abe Jack *retired business executive, retired air force officer*
Carter, Donald J. *wholesale distribution, manufacturing executive*
Hallam, Robert G. *wholesale distribution executive*
Halpin, James *retail computer stores executive*
Matthews, Clark J(io), II *retail executive, lawyer*
McDougall, Ronald Alexander *restaurant executive*
Shapiro, Robert Alan *retail executive*
Stone, Donald James *retired retail executive*

**El Paso**
Miller, Deane Guynes *salon and cosmetic studio owner*

**Fort Worth**
Herlihy, James Edward *retail executive*
Michero, William Henderson *retired retail trade executive*
Roach, John Vinson, II *retail company executive*
Thompson, Carson R. *retail, manufacturing company executive*

**Houston**
Baugh, John Frank *wholesale company executive*
Bjornson, Carroll Norman *business owner*
Levit, Milton *grocery supply company executive*
Lindig, Bill M. *food distribution company executive*
Orton, Stewart *retail company executive, merchant*
Tooker, Carl E. *department store executive*
Williams, Robert Lyle *corporate executive, consultant*
Woodhouse, John Frederick *food distribution company executive*

**Lubbock**
Snell, Robert *retail executive*
Willingham, Mary Maxine *retail store executive*

**Marble Falls**
Simpson, H. Richard (Dick Simpson) *retailer*

**Plano**
Neppl, Walter Joseph *retired retail store executive*
Oesterreicher, James E. *department stores executive*

**Seabrook**
Spears, James Grady *small business owner*

**Sulphur Springs**
McKenzie, Michael K. *wholesale executive*

**Tyler**
Hardin, James *retail food company executive*

**Wimberley**
Ellis, John *small business owner*

## UTAH

**Heber City**
Day, Gerald W. *wholesale grocery company executive*

**Logan**
Watterson, Scott *home fitness equipment manufacturer*

**Saint George**
Day, John Denton *retired company executive, cattle and horse rancher, trainer, wrangler, actor, educator*

**Salt Lake City**
Brewer, Stanley R. *wholesale grocery executive*
Miller, Lorraine *business owner*
Smith, Jeffrey P. *supermarket chain executive*

## VERMONT

**Brookfield**
Gerard, James Wilson *book distributor*

**Colchester**
Lawton, Lorilee Ann *pipeline supply company owner, accountant*

**Putney**
Loring, Honey *small business owner*

## VIRGINIA

**Alexandria**
Williams, Emma Crawford *business owner*

**Arlington**
Walker, Walter Gray, Jr. *small business owner, program statistician*

**Bristol**
McGlothlin, James W. *wholesale distribution executive*

**Fairfax**
Schrock, Simon *retail executive*

**Herndon**
Houston, Brian Christopher Michael *small business owner*

**Mc Lean**
Vandemark, Robert Goodyear *retired retail company executive*

**Purcellville**
Sharples, Winston Singleton *automobile importer and distributor*

**Richmond**
Cramer, Morgan Joseph, Jr. *international management executive*

Gresham, Ann Elizabeth *retailer, horticulturist executive, consultant*
Sharp, Richard L. *retail company executive*
Sniffin, John Harrison *retail executive*
Ukrop, James E. *retail executive*

**Roanoke**
Fulton, George Henry, Jr. *automobile and truck retail company executive*

**Salem**
Brand, Edward Cabell *retail executive*

**Staunton**
Hammaker, Paul M. *retail executive, business educator, author*

**Vienna**
Gardner, Joel Sylvanus *tempest products company executive*

**Virginia Beach**
DeVenny, Lillian Nickell *trophy company executive*

## WASHINGTON

**Bellingham**
Olsen, Mark Norman *small business owner*

**Federal Way**
Jemelian, John Nazar *retail and financial executive*

**Issaquah**
Brotman, Jeffrey H. *variety stores executive*
Sinegal, James D. *variety store wholesale business executive*

**Redmond**
Nagel, Daryl David *retail executive*

**Seattle**
Bridge, Herbert Marvin *jewelry executive*
Curley, Jonathan Edward *small business owner*
Fix, Wilbur James *department store executive*
McMillan, John A. *retail executive*
Mizrahi, Yves *retail executive*
Nordstrom, Bruce A. *department store executive*
Nordstrom, John N. *department store executive*
Stearns, Susan Tracey *lighting design company executive, lawyer*
†Stewart, Thomas J. *wholesale distribution executive*

**Spokane**
Wagner, Teresa Ann *business owner*

**Yakima**
Newland, Ruth Laura *small business owner*

## WEST VIRGINIA

**Charleston**
Lipton, Allen David *retail executive*

**Martinsburg**
Ayers, Anne Louise *small business owner, retired education specialist, consultant*

## WISCONSIN

**Beloit**
Hendricks, Kenneth *wholesale distribution executive*

**Hurley**
Nicholls, Thomas Maurice *business owner*

**Kenosha**
Tielke, James Clemens *retail and manufacturing management consultant*

**Madison**
Uselmann, Catherine Rose (Kit Uselmann) *small business owner, network marketer, behavioral researcher, financial independence consultant*

**Menomonee Falls**
Kellogg, William S. *retail executive*

**Pewaukee**
Lestina, Gerald F. *wholesale grocery executive*

**Stevens Point**
Copps, Michael William *retail and wholesale company executive*

**Sturgeon Bay**
Wallestad, Philip Weston *retired business owner*

**Wausau**
Builer, Dorothy Marion *business owner*

## WYOMING

**Douglas**
Harrop, Diane Glaser *shop owner, mayor*

**Jackson**
Law, Clarene Alta *innkeeper, state legislator*

## CANADA

## MANITOBA

**Winnipeg**
Cohen, Albert Diamond *retail executive*

### ONTARIO

**London**
Crncich, Tony Joseph *retired pharmacy chain executive*

**Ottawa**
Labbé, Paul *export corporation executive*

**Toronto**
Keenan, Anthony Harold Brian *catalog company executive*
Kosich, George John *retail executive*
Ryan, James Franklin *retail executive*
Smith, Stephen Alexander *retail and wholesale food distribution company executive*
Wolfe, Jonathan A. *food wholesaler, retailer*

**Willowdale**
Binder, Herbert R. *drug store chain executive*
Bloom, David Ronald *retail drug company executive*

### QUEBEC

**Pointe Claire**
Cohen, Charles Frank *retail executive*

## ITALY

**Bosisio Parini**
Buttram, Debra Doris *fashion vendor and consultant, English educator, assistance dog trainer*

## ADDRESS UNPUBLISHED

Aspen, Alfred William *agricultural import/export products, company executive*
Aved, Barry *retail executive, consultant*
Baker, Edward Kevin *retail executive*
Biagi, Richard Charles *retail executive, real estate consultant*
Bogart, Carol Lynn *small business owner, writer, talk show host, poet*
Campbell, Edward Clinton *small business owner, violin maker*
Cavnar, Margaret Mary (Peggy Cavnar) *business executive, former state legislator, nurse, consultant*
Chevalier, Paul Edward *retired retail executive, lawyer, art gallery executive*
Clark, Maxine *retail executive*
Colgate, Stephen *small business owner*
Conte, Andrea *retail executive, health care consultant*
Coons, Marion McDowell *retail food stores executive*
Crandall, Albert Earl *retail executive, accountant, entrepreneur*
Demme, James *retail executive*
Depkovich, Francis John *retired retail chain executive*
Dyer, Arlene Thelma *retail company owner*
Edwards, Patricia Burr *small business owner, counselor, consultant*
Edwards, Patrick Ross *former retail company executive, lawyer, management consultant*
Evans, Robert George, Jr. *retail and mail order executive*
Fields, Douglas Philip *building supply and home furnishings wholesale company executive*
Fields, Leo *former jewelry company executive, investor*
Folkman, David H. *retail, wholesale and consumer products consultant*
Franzetti, Lillian Angelina *former automobile dealership owner*
Galvao, Louis Alberto *import and export corporation executive, consultant*
Gartner, William Joseph *company executive, business owner*
Geoffroy, Charles Henry *retired business executive*
Goldman, Gerald Hillis *beverage distribution company executive*
Goldner, Sheldon Herbert *export-import company executive*
Goldstein, Alfred George *retail and consumer products executive*
Goldstein, Norman Ray *interntional trading company executive, consultant*
Guillemette, Gloria Vivian *small business owner, dressmaker, designer*
Haas, Edward Lee *business executive, consultant*
Hawk, Robert Dooley *wholesale grocery company executive*
Howell, William Robert *retail company executive*
Jensen, Barbara Wood *interior design business owner*
Jones, Robert Henry *automotive distribution executive*
Jordan, Sharie Cecilia *small business owner*
King, S(anford) MacCallum *business owner, consultant*
Kogut, John Anthony *retail/wholesale executive*
Lebor, John F(rancis) *retired department store executive*
Lee, Benny Y. C. *import and export company executive*
Lipsey, Joseph, Jr. *water bottling company executive, retail and wholesale corporation executive*
Lueke, Donna Mae *national retail company manager*
Marshall, George Dwire *retired supermarket chain executive*
Martini, Robert Edward *wholesale pharmaceutical and medical supplies company executive*
McGaw, Kenneth Roy *wholesale distribution executive*
Mench, John William *retail store executive, electrical engineer*
Metz, Steven William *small business owner*
Meyer, Lasker Marcel *retail executive*
Mrkonic, George Ralph, Jr. *retail executive*
Nicolas, Kenneth Lee *international financial business executive*
Nishimura, Joseph Yo *retired retail executive, accountant*
Paterson, Robert E. *trading stamp company executive*
Raab, Herbert Norman *retail executive*
Ransome, Ernest Leslie, III *retail company executive*
Raskin, Michael A. *retail company executive*
Rickard, Norman Edward *office equipment company executive*
Ring, Victoria A. *small business owner*
Rodbell, Clyde Armand *distribution executive*
Rohner, Bonnie-Jean *small business owner, computer consultant*
Rosenbaum, Irving M. *retail store executive*
Rosenfeld, Mark Kenneth *retired retail store executive*
Runge, Donald Edward *food wholesale company executive*
Samson, Alvin *former distributing company executive, consultant*
Sewell, Phyllis Shapiro *retail chain executive*
Sherwood, (Peter) Louis *retail executive*
Sprouse, Robert Allen, II *retail chain executive*
Stemberg, Thomas George *retail executive*
Stern, Charles *retired foreign trade company executive*
Tetro, Catherine Anne *shop owner*
Thayer, Martha Ann *small business owner*
Thomson, William Barry *retail company executive*
Trutter, John Thomas *consulting company executive*
Vernon, Carl Atlee, Jr. *retired wholesale food distributor executive*
Vila, Adis Maria *corporate executive, former government official, lawyer*
Waddle, John Frederick *former retail chain executive*
Wentworth, Malinda Ann Nachman *former small business owner, real estate broker*
Wien, Stuart Lewis *retired supermarket chain executive*
Wiesner, John Joseph *retail executive*
Worley, Gordon Roger *retail chain financial executive*

# INDUSTRY: TRANSPORTATION

## UNITED STATES

### ALABAMA

**Gulf Shores**
Wallace, John Loys *aviation services executive*

**Point Clear**
Elmer, William Morris *retired pipe line executive*

### ALASKA

**Anchorage**
Sullivan, George Murray *transportation consultant, former mayor*

### ARIZONA

**Flagstaff**
†Bryant, Leland Marshal *rail transportation executive, hotel executive*

**Phoenix**
Aybar, Charles Anton *aviation executive*
Bertholf, Neilson Allan, Jr. *aviation executive*
Elien, Mona Marie *air transportation professional*
Woods, Bobby Joe *transportation executive*

**Scottsdale**
Garelick, Martin *transportation executive*
Peyton, William Maupin *financial services executive, educator*

**Tucson**
Burg, Walter A. *airport terminal executive*
Gissing, Bruce *retired aerospace company executive*
Peete, Russell Fitch, Jr. *aircraft appraiser*

### ARKANSAS

**Conway**
†Petersen, Laddian Walter *flight operations director*

**Fort Smith**
Young, Robert A., III *freight systems executive*

**Harrison**
Garrison, F. Sheridan *transportation executive*

**Hindsville**
Pogue, William Reid *former astronaut, foundation executive, business and aerospace consultant*

**Huntsville**
Carr, Gerald Paul *former astronaut, business executive, former marine officer*

**Lowell**
Hunt, J. B. *transportation executive*

**Pine Bluff**
Seawell, William Thomas *former airline executive*

### CALIFORNIA

**Bayside**
Pierce, Lester Laurin *aviation consultant*

**Borrego Springs**
Scannell, William Edward *aerospace company executive, consultant, psychologist*

**Burbank**
Volk, Robert Harkins *aviations company executive*

**Calabasas**
Caren, Robert Poston *aerospace company executive*

**Corona Del Mar**
Tether, Anthony John *aerospace executive*

**Costa Mesa**
†Schooley, Otis Bryson, III *commercial airport executive*

**Edwards**
Brand, Vance Devoe *astronaut, government official*
Deets, Dwain Aaron *aerospace technology executive*

**Encino**
Cooper, Leroy Gordon, Jr. *former astronaut, business consultant*
Gasich, Welko Elton *retired aerospace executive, management consultant*

**Fremont**
Smith, Bernald Stephen *retired airline pilot, aviation consultant*

**Gilroy**
Borton, George Robert *airline captain*

**Glendale**
Aaronson, Robert Jay *aviation executive*
O'Donnell, Scott Richard *aviation administrator*

**Healdsburg**
Kamm, Thomas Allen *air transportation company executive*

**Hermosa Beach**
Kokalj, James Edward *retired aerospace administrator*

**La Mesa**
Hansen, Grant Lewis *retired aerospace and information systems executive*

**Lancaster**
Crew, Aubrey Torquil *aerospace inspector*

**Long Beach**
Anderson, Gerald Verne *retired aerospace company executive*
†Kunze, Chris *airport manager, educator*
Mandeville, Craig H. *aircraft company executive, retired military officer*
Myers, John Wescott *aviation executive*

**Los Angeles**
†Anderson, Roy A. *aerospace company executive*
Kresa, Kent *aerospace executive*
Park, Sam-Koo *transportation executive*
Williams, Walter David *aerospace executive, consultant*
Yee, Stephen *airport executive*

**Los Gatos**
Bortolussi, Michael Richard *aerospace human factors engineer*

**Malibu**
Ensign, Richard Papworth *transportation executive*

**Menlo Park**
Morrison, David Fred *freight company executive*
O'Brien, Raymond Francis *transportation executive*

**Mission Viejo**
Foulds, Donald Duane *aerospace executive*
LaRosa, Gianni *aerospace industry administrator*

**Moffett Field**
Dean, William Evans *aerospace agency executive*

**Oakland**
Crowley, Thomas B., Jr. *water transportation executive*
Haskell, Arthur Jacob *retired steamship company executive*
Reynolds, Kathleen Diane Foy (K.D.F. Reynolds) *transportation executive*

**Palo Alto**
Moffitt, Donald Eugene *transportation company executive*

**Palos Verdes Estates**
Smith, Stephen Randolph *aerospace executive*

**Palos Verdes Peninsula**
Ryker, Charles Edwin *former aerospace company executive*

**Ramona**
Hoffman, Wayne Melvin *retired airline official*

**Rancho Cucamonga**
Bucks, Charles Alan *airline industry consultant, former executive*

**Redondo Beach**
Krause, Kurth Werner *aerospace executive*
Wagemaker, David Isaac *human resources development executive*

**Redwood City**
Foley, Patrick *air courier company executive*
Waller, Stephen *air transportation executive*

**Rosamond**
Trippensee, Gary Alan *aerospace executive*

**Sacramento**
van Loben Sels, James W. *transportation executive*

**San Diego**
†Bogner, Jo L. *airport executive*
Reading, James Edward *transportation executive*

**San Francisco**
Hickerson, Glenn Lindsey *leasing company executive*
†Martin, John *airport executive*
Wood, Donald Frank *transportation educator, consultant*

**San Mateo**
Trabitz, Eugene Leonard *aerospace company executive*

**Stockton**
Biddle, Donald Ray *aerospace company executive*

**Sunnyvale**
Davis, Michael Chase *aerospace industry executive, consultant, retired naval officer*

**Torrance**
Savitz, Maxine Lazarus *aerospace company executive*

### COLORADO

**Aurora**
Minnich, Joseph Edward *tourist railway consultant*

**Colorado Springs**
†Davis, Richard Shermer, Jr. *aerospace defense consultant*
Freeman, J.P. Ladyhawk *underwater exploration, security and transportation executive, educator, fashion model*

**Denver**
Boulware, Richard Stark *airport administrator*
Burgess, Larry Lee *aerospace executive*
DeLong, James Clifford *air transportation executive*
McMorris, Jerry *transportation company executive*

**Englewood**
Claussen, Bonnie Addison, II *aerospace company executive*

**Evergreen**
Foret, Mickey Phillip *air transportation company executive*

**Golden**
Lindsay, Nathan James *aerospace company executive, retired career officer*

**Littleton**
Kleinknecht, Kenneth Samuel *retired aerospace company executive, former federal space agency official*
Strang, Sandra Lee *airline official*

**Trinidad**
Potter, William Bartlett *business executive*

### CONNECTICUT

**Darien**
Hartong, Hendrik J., Jr. *transportation company executive*

**Deep River**
Zack, Steven Jeffrey *master automotive instructor*

**Fairfield**
Peirce, George Leighton *airport administrator*

**Greenwich**
Roitsch, Paul Albert *pilot*

**Southport**
Taylor, James Blackstone *aviation company executive*

**Stamford**
Barker, James Rex *water transportation executive*
Tregurtha, Paul Richard *marine transportation and construction materials company executive*

### DELAWARE

**Dagsboro**
Lally, Richard Francis *aviation security consultant, former association executive, former government official*

**Wilmington**
†duPont, Edward B. *aviation service and sales company executive*

### DISTRICT OF COLUMBIA

**Washington**
Abrahamson, James Alan *transportation executive, retired military officer*
Altschul, Alfred Samuel *airline executive*
Burwell, David Gates *transportation executive*
Cocke, Erle, Jr. *international business consultant*
Del Balzo, Joseph Michael *aviation consulting company executive*
Donovan, George Joseph *industry executive, consultant*
Downey, Mortimer Leo, III *transportation executive*
Farrell, Joseph Michael *steamship company executive*
Hallett, Carol Boyd *air transportation executive*
Hinson, David Russell *airline company executive, federal agency administrator*
Kaufman, Irving N. *transportation executive*
Langstaff, David Hamilton *aerospace industry executive*
Luffsey, Walter Stith *transportation executive*
Mederos, Carolina Luisa *transportation policy consultant*
Melton, Augustus Allen, Jr. *airport executive*
Mineta, Norman Yoshio *aerospace transportation executive, former congressman*
Newman, William Bernard, Jr. *railroad executive*
Olcott, John Whiting *aviation executive*
Overbeck, Gene Edward *retired airline executive, lawyer*
Thayer, Russell, III *airlines executive*
Troutman, George Glenn *retired aerospace executive, retired military officer*

## FLORIDA

**Clearwater**
Howes, James Guerdon *airport director*

**Dania**
Vecci, Raymond Joseph *airline industry consultant*

**Daytona Beach**
Simatos, Nicholas Jerry *aerospace company executive, consultant*

**Fort Lauderdale**
Berwig, Newton Urbano *aerospace executive*

**Fort Myers**
Mc Grath, William Restore *transportation planner, traffic engineer*

**Jacksonville**
Aftoora, Patricia Joan *transportation executive*
Anderson, John Quentin *rail transportation executive*
Hamilton, William Berry, Jr. *shipping company executive*
Kilbourne, Krystal Hewett *rail transportation executive*

**Miami**
Bastian, James Harold *air transport company executive, lawyer*
Brock, James Daniel *retired airline executive, consultant*
Burns, Mitchel Anthony *transportation services company executive*
Dellapa, Gary J. *airport terminal executive*
Fain, Richard David *cruise line executive*
Trippe, Kenneth Alvin Battershill *shipping industry executive*

**Montverde**
Harris, Martin Harvey *aerospace company executive*

**Naples**
Bush, John William *federal transportation official*
Gresham, Robert Coleman *transportation consultant*
Johnson, Walter L. *transportation company executive*

**Oldsmar**
Burrows, William Claude *aerospace executive, retired air force officer*

**Orlando**
Pearlman, Louis Jay *aviation and promotion company executive*

**Pompano Beach**
Wright, Joseph Robert, Jr. *corporate executive*

**Ponte Vedra Beach**
Fiorentino, Thomas Martin *transportation executive, lawyer*

**Sanibel**
Hasselman, Richard B. *transportation company executive, retired*

**Sarasota**
Lindsay, David Breed, Jr. *aircraft company executive, former editor and publisher*

**Tampa**
Lykes, Joseph T., III *shipping company executive*

**Weston**
Durfey, Robert Walker *sea transportation consultant*

**Winter Park**
Cerbin, Carolyn McAtee *transportation executive, writer*

## GEORGIA

**Atlanta**
Allen, Ronald W. *retired airline company executive*
Callison, James W. *former airline executive, lawyer*
Gittens, Angela *airport executive*
Kelly, James P. *delivery service executive*
Nelson, Kent C. *delivery service executive*
Oppenlander, Robert *retired airline executive*
Robinson, Jeffery Herbert *transportation company executive*

**Macon**
Hails, Robert Emmet *aerospace consultant, business executive, former air force officer*

## HAWAII

**Honolulu**
†Fukunaga, Barry *airport executive*
Pfeiffer, Robert John *business executive*
†Zander, Glenn R. *airline company executive*

## IDAHO

**Boise**
DeVilbiss, Jonathan Frederick *aircraft sales engineer*
Ilett, Frank, Jr. *trucking company executive*

**Idaho Falls**
Thorsen, James Hugh *aviation director*

## ILLINOIS

**AMF Ohare**
†Loney, Mary Rose *airport administrator*

**Argonne**
Saricks, Christopher Lee *transportation analyst*

**Chicago**
Batory, Ronald Louis *rail transportation executive*
Burton, Raymond Charles, Jr. *transportation company executive*
Chartier, Janellen Olsen *airline service coordinator*
Heineman, Ben Walter *corporation executive*
Maher, Francesca Marciniak *air transportation executive, lawyer*
Nord, Henry J. *transportation executive*
Reed, John Shedd *former railway executive*
Ryan, Randel Edward, Jr. *airline pilot*

**Geneva**
Barney, Charles Richard *transportation company executive*

**Glen Ellyn**
Logan, Henry Vincent *transportation executive*

**Lake Forest**
Pope, John Charles *airline company executive*

**Lombard**
Yeager, Phillip Charles *transportation company exeuctive*

**Marion**
†Crane, Hugh W. *railroad executive*

**Oak Brook**
Duerinck, Louis T. *retired railroad executive, attorney*

**Park Ridge**
Carr, Gilbert Randle *retired railroad executive*

**Riverdale**
Szabo, Joseph Clark *labor lobbyist*

**Rosemont**
Burkhardt, Edward Arnold *transportation company executive*
Currie, Earl James *transportation company executive*

**Saint Charles**
Zito, James Anthony *retired railroad company executive*

## INDIANA

**Indianapolis**
†Mikelsons, J. George *air aerospace transportation executive*
†Roberts, David *airport executive*

**Noblesville**
Morrison, Joseph Young *transportation consultant*

**West Lafayette**
Drake, John Warren *aviation consultant*

## KANSAS

**Overland Park**
†Myers, A. Maurice *transportation executive*

**Shawnee Mission**
Henson, Paul Harry *transportation executive*

## KENTUCKY

**Franklin**
Clark, James Benton *railroad industry consultant, former executive*

## LOUISIANA

**New Orleans**
Amoss, W. James, Jr. *shipping company executive*
Chetta, Holly Ann *transportation executive*

**Shreveport**
Fish, Howard Math *aerospace industry executive*

## MARYLAND

**Annapolis**
Colussy, Dan Alfred *aviation executive*
Moellering, John Henry *aviation maintenance company executive*
†Wilson, Benjamin Franklin, Jr. *steamship agency executive*

**Baltimore**
Cunningham, M(urray) Hunt, Jr. *aerospace company executive, mechanical engineer, author*
†Harp, Solomon, III *airport executive*

**Bethesda**
Tellep, Daniel Michael *aerospace executive, mechanical engineer*

**Chevy Chase**
Coleman, Joseph Michael *truck lease and logistics consultant*

**College Park**
Keller, Samuel William *aerospace administrator*

**Monrovia**
Cooney, William Joseph, Jr. *transportation company owner*

**Rockville**
Fthenakis, Emanuel John *diversified aerospace company executive*
Porter, John Robert, Jr. *space technology company executive, geochemist*

**Stevensville**
Deen, Thomas Blackburn *retired transportation research executive*

## MASSACHUSETTS

**Boston**
Blute, Peter I. *transportation executive, former congressman*
Davis, David William *transportation consultant*
Doherty, Robert Francis, Jr. *aerospace industry professional*
Klotz, Charles Rodger *shipping company executive*

**Brookline**
Frankel, Ernst Gabriel *shipping and aviation business executive, educator*

**Cambridge**
John, Richard Rodda *transportation executive*

**Concord**
Smith, Eric Parkman *retired railroad executive*

**Framingham**
Ballou, Kenneth Walter *retired transportation executive, university dean*

**Lexington**
Baddour, Anne Bridge *aviatrix*

**Marlborough**
Birstein, Seymour Joseph *aerospace company executive*

**North Billerica**
Mellon, Timothy *transportation executive*

**Wilmington**
Buckley, Robert Paul *aerospace company executive*

## MICHIGAN

**Ann Arbor**
Waller, Patricia Fossum *transportation executive, researcher, psychologist*

**Detroit**
Braun, Robert C. *airport executive*
†Pobinson, Suzette E. *airport executive*

**Grand Rapids**
Auwers, Stanley John *motor carrier executive*

**Lansing**
†Schmidt, Thomas Walter *airport executive*

**Waterford**
†Randall, Karl W. *aviation executive, lawyer*

## MINNESOTA

**Minneapolis**
Anderson, Tim *airport terminal executive*
Harper, Donald Victor *transportation and logistics educator*
Nyrop, Donald William *airline executive*

**Saint Paul**
Checchi, Alfred A. *airline company executive*
Engle, Donald Edward *retired railway executive, lawyer*
Gehrz, Robert Gustave *retired railroad executive*
Mitchell, Pamela Ann *airline pilot*
Washburn, Donald Arthur *transportation executive*

## MISSISSIPPI

**Pass Christian**
Clark, John Walter, Jr. *shipping company executive*

## MISSOURI

**Blue Springs**
Reed, Tony Norman *aviation company executive*

**Bridgeton**
Delaney, Robert Vernon *logistics and transportation executive*

**Fenton**
Greenblatt, Maurice Theodore *transportation executive*

**Lake Saint Louis**
German, John George *transportation consultant*

**Saint Louis**
O'Neill, John Robert *airline executive*

## NEBRASKA

**Omaha**
Davis, Jerry Ray *railroad company executive*
Smithey, Donald Leon *airport authority director*

## NEVADA

**Las Vegas**
Di Palma, Joseph Alphonse *airline company executive, lawyer*
Hudgens, Sandra Lawler *retired state admnistrator*

**Reno**
Jordan, Joseph Rembert *airline pilot, captain*

## NEW HAMPSHIRE

**Dover**
Nelson, Michael Underhill *association executive*

**Sunapee**
Cary, Charles Oswald *aviation executive*

## NEW JERSEY

**Cedar Knolls**
†Dixon, Gerald Authur *aerospace manufacturing company executive*

**Cherry Hill**
Holfeld, Donald Rae *railroad consultant*

**Flemington**
Kettler, Carl Frederick *airline executive*

**Mount Arlington**
Krosser, Howard S. *aerospace company executive*

**Parsippany**
McNicholas, David Paul *automobile rental company executive*

**Peapack**
Weiss, Allan Joseph *transport company executive, lawyer*

**Raritan**
Alatzas, George *delivery service company executive*

**Short Hills**
Furst, E(rrol) Kenneth *transportation executive, accountant*

**Union**
White, Robert L. G., Jr. *aerospace company executive*

## NEW MEXICO

**Albuquerque**
Scott, Hanson Lee *airport executive*

**Holloman Air Force Base**
†Klause, Klaus J. *aircraft company executive*

**Las Cruces**
Borman, Frank *former astronaut, laser patent company executive*

**Santa Fe**
Swartz, William John *transportation resources company executive/retired*

## NEW YORK

**Babylon**
Collis, Charles *aircraft company executive*

**Brooklyn**
†Crawford, Robert Roy *rail company executive*
†Kiepper, Alan Frederick *rapid transit executive, educator*

**Carmel**
Shen, Chia Theng *former steamship company executive, religious institute official*

**Garden City**
Campbell, James R. *transportation executive*

**Great Neck**
Pollack, Paul Robert *airline service company executive*
Satinskas, Henry Anthony *airline services company executive*

**Huntington**
Jackson, Richard Montgomery *former airline executive*
Myers, Robert Jay *retired aerospace company executive*

**Jamaica**
Feldman, Arlene Butler *aviation industry executive*
Kelly, Robert *airport executive*
Mc Kinnon, Clinton Dan *aerospace transportation executive*
Prendergast, Thomas Francis *railroad executive*

**Latham**
Stallman, Donald Lee *corporate executive*

**Manhasset**
Frankum, James Edward *airlines company executive*

**New York**
Apostolakis, James John *shipping company executive*
Ascher, Michael Charles *transportation executive*
Chao, James S. C. *maritime executive*
Danaher, Frank Erwin *transportation technologist*
Davidson, Daniel P. *transportation executive*
Evans, James Hurlburt *retired transportation and natural resources executive*
Evans, Mary Johnston *transportation company director*
Gitner, Gerald L. *aviation and investment banking executive*
Hyman, Morton Peter *shipping company executive*
Johnsen, Niels Winchester *ocean shipping company executive*
Kondas, Nicholas Frank *shipping company executive*

**Peekskill**
Harte, Andrew Dennis *transportation company executive, travel agent*

**Syracuse**
†Carlson, William Clifford *defense company executive*
Everett, Charles R., Jr. *airport executive*

## NORTH CAROLINA

**Chapel Hill**
Bauer, Frederick Christian *motor carrier executive*

**Charlotte**
Murray, Peter William *airline executive, educator, college administrator*
Orr, T(homas) J(erome) (Jerry Orr) *airport terminal executive*

**Cherryville**
Huffstetler, Palmer Eugene *retired transportation executive, lawyer*
Mayhew, Kenneth Edwin, Jr. *transportation company executive*

**Durham**
Jacob, Jerry Rowland *airline executive*

**Kannapolis**
Thigpen, Alton Hill *motor transportation company executive*

**Winston Salem**
Davis, Thomas Henry *airline executive*
Miller, James (Jim) Alfred Locke, Jr. *aircraft maintenance technician*

## NORTH DAKOTA

**Grand Forks**
Lindseth, Paul Douglas *aerospace educator, flight instructor, farmer*

## OHIO

**Brecksville**
Worden, Alfred Merrill *former astronaut, research company executive*

**Cincinnati**
Murphy, Eugene F. *aerospace, communications and electronics executive*

**Cleveland**
Sheehan, Stephen Dennis *airport commissioner*

**Columbus**
Hedrick, Larry Willis *airport executive*
Hooper, Kelley Rae *delivery service executive*

**Oberlin**
Startup, Charles Harry *airline executive*
Williams, Eleanor Joyce *government air traffic control specialist*

**Xenia**
Bigelow, Daniel James *aerospace executive*

## OKLAHOMA

**Tulsa**
Collins, John Roger *transportation company executive*
Kruse, David Louis, II *transportation company executive*

## OREGON

**Oakland**
Smelt, Ronald *retired aircraft company executive*

## PENNSYLVANIA

**Bethlehem**
Lewis, Andrew Lindsay, Jr. (Drew Lewis) *transportation and natural resources executive*
Stuart, Gary Miller *railroad executive*

**Camp Hill**
Crowe, John Carl *aviation consultant, retired airline executive*

**Conshohocken**
Cunningham, James Gerald, Jr. *transportation company executive*

**Fairless Hills**
Decator, Carl James *transportation executive*

**Johnstown**
Manty, Brian Alan *high technology company executive*

**Macungie**
Billingsley, Charles Edward *retired transportation company executive*

**Philadelphia**
Fisher, Allan Campbell *railway executive*
Wilson, Bruce Brighton *transportation executive*

**Yardley**
Terry, John Joseph *transportation investor*

**York**
Grossman, Robert Allen *transportation executive*

## SOUTH CAROLINA

**Charleston**
Chapin, Fred *airport executive*

**Columbia**
Conrad, Paul Ernest *transportation consultant*

**Hilton Head Island**
Love, Richard Emerson *equipment manufacturing company executive*

## SOUTH DAKOTA

**Sioux Falls**
Smith, Murray Thomas *transportation company executive*

## TENNESSEE

**Chattanooga**
Quinn, Patrick *tranportation executive*

**Knoxville**
Igoe, Terence B. *airport terminal executive*

**Memphis**
†Cox, Larry D. *airport terminal executive*
Smith, Frederick Wallace *transportation company executive*

**Millington**
Lecuyer, Robert Raymond *aviation maintenance administrator*

**Morristown**
Johnson, Evelyn Bryan *flying service executive*

**Nashville**
Osborne, Charles William (Bill Osborne) *transportation executive*
Zierdt, John Graham, Jr. *transportation company executive*

## TEXAS

**Brownfield**
†Jany, Richard Wayne *railroad executive*

**Dallas**
Baker, Robert Woodward *airline executive*
†Carty, Donald J. *airline company executive*
Cleveland, Linda Joyce *delivery service executive*
Fegan, Jeffrey P. *airport executive*
Kelleher, Herbert David *airline executive, lawyer*
Miller, Brian Keith *airline executive*
Wallace, William C. *airline executive*

**Dickinson**
Bush, Robert Thomas *shipping company executive*

**El Paso**
Rankin, William Brown, II *airport administrator*

**Fort Worth**
Crandall, Robert Lloyd *airline executive*
Krebs, Robert Duncan *transportation company executive*
Shoemaker, Sandra Kaye *aerospace executive*

**Granbury**
†Mainord, William Ronald *pilot*

**Harlingen**
Farris, Robert Gene *transportation company executive*

**Houston**
†Acree, G. Handy *airport executive*
Barry, Allan Ronald *ship pilot, corporate executive*
Bean, Alan LaVern *retired astronaut, artist*
Bethune, Gordon *airline executive*
Bonderman, David *airline company executive*
Hartsfield, Henry Warren, Jr. *astronaut*
Kenley, Elizabeth Sue *commerce and transportation executive*
Musgrave, Story *astronaut, surgeon, pilot, physiologist, educator*
Thagard, Norman E. *astronaut, physician, engineer*
Young, John Watts *astronaut*

**Irving**
Plaskett, Thomas G. *transportation company executive*

**Lindale**
Carter, Thomas Smith, Jr. *retired railroad executive*

**McQueeney**
Gunter, Edwin Dale, Jr. *pilot*

**Roanoke**
Steward, Jerry Wayne *air transportation executive, consultant*

**Round Rock**
Aadnesen, Christopher *railroad company executive, consultant*

**San Antonio**
Gonzalez, Efren *airport executive*
Kutchins, Michael Joseph *aviation consultant, former airport executive*
Lowry, A. Robert *federal government railroad arbitrator*

## UTAH

**Bountiful**
Clement, Walter Hough *retired railroad executive*

**Ogden**
Dilley, William Gregory *aviation company executive*

**Orem**
Snow, Marlon O. *trucking executive, state agency administrator*

**Salt Lake City**
Bozich, Anthony Thomas *transportation industry consultant, retired motor freight company executive*

## VERMONT

**Burlington**
†Bergesen, Robert Nelson *transportation company executive*

**South Burlington**
Hamilton, John J., Jr. *airport executive*

**Woodstock**
Hoyt, Coleman Williams *postal consultant*

## VIRGINIA

**Alexandria**
Donohue, Thomas Joseph *transportation association executive*
Lund, Rita Pollard *aerospace consultant*
Matthews, Sir Stuart *aviation industry executive*
Pulling, Ronald Wilson, Sr. *aviation systems planner, civil engineer, consultant*

**Arlington**
Beyer, Barbara Lynn *aviation consultant*
Kirk, Robert L. *aerospace and transportation company executive*
Mason, Phillip Howard *aircraft company executive, retired army officer*
†Spooner, Richard Edward *aerospace company executive*
Stokes, B. R. *retired transportation consultant*

**Burke**
Forster, William Hull *aerospace executive*

**Cape Charles**
†Brookshire, James Knox, Jr. *transportation facility administrator*

**Catlett**
Broderick, Anthony James *air transportation executive*

**Chantilly**
Harris, Paul Lynwood *aerospace transportation executive*

**Chesterfield**
Congdon, John Rhodes *transportation executive*

**Fairfax**
†Whitcomb, Darrel Dean *pilot*

**Marshall**
Hayward, Charles Winthrop *retired railroad company executive*

**Midlothian**
Parsons, Robert Eugene *transportation consultant*

**Newport News**
Cox, Alvin Earl *shipbuilding executive*

**Norfolk**
Goode, David Ronald *transportation company executive*
McKinnon, Arnold Borden *transportation company executive*
Rump, Kendall E. *air transportation executive*
Scott, Kenneth R. *transportation executive*
Shannon, John Sanford *retired railway executive, lawyer*

**Poquoson**
Holloway, Paul Fayette *retired aerospace executive*

**Purcellville**
Mainwaring, Thomas Lloyd *motor freight company executive*

**Reston**
Crawford, Lawrence Robert *aviation and aerospace consultant*

**Richmond**
Aron, Mark G. *transportation executive, lawyer*
Hintz, Robert Louis *transportation company executive*
Watkins, Hays Thomas *retired railroad executive*

**Springfield**
Finkel, Karen Evans *school transportation association executive, lawyer*

**Virginia Beach**
Kreyling, Edward George, Jr. *railroad executive*

**Winchester**
Jamison, Richard Bryan *airport consultant*

## WASHINGTON

**Kirkland**
Brandenstein, Daniel Charles *astronaut, retired naval officer*

**Seattle**
†Bagley, George D. *aerospace transportation executive*
Beighle, Douglas Paul *business executive*
Brown, Janiece Alfreida *pilot*

Cella, John J. *freight company executive*
Clarkson, Lawrence William *airplane company executive*
Cline, Robert Stanley *air freight company executive*
Condit, Philip Murray *aerospace executive, engineer*
Elliott, Jeanne Marie Koreltz *transportation executive*
Givan, Boyd Eugene *aircraft company executive*
Grinstein, Gerald *transportation executive*
Jaeger, David Arnold *aerospace company executive*
Kelley, John F. *airline executive*
Lee, Ronald Eugene *international air transportation supply executive*
Liljebeck, Roy C. *transportation company executive*
Schmidt, Peter Gustav *shipbuilding industry executive*
Thornton, Dean Dickson *retired airplane company executive*

**Spanaway**
Loete, Steven Donald *pilot*

## WISCONSIN

**Appleton**
†Crowley, Geoffrey T. *airline executive*

**De Pere**
Schaupp, Joan Pomprowitz *trucking company executive, writer*

**Green Bay**
Olson, James Richard *transportation company executive*
Schneider, Donald J. *trucking company executive*

**Milwaukee**
†Bateman, C. Barry *airport terminal executive*
Mayer, Henry Michael *mass transit consultant*
Ziperski, James Richard *trucking company executive, lawyer*

**Neenah**
Fetzer, Edward Frank *transportation company executive*

## WYOMING

**Worland**
Woods, Lawrence Milton *airline company executive*

## CANADA

## ALBERTA

**Calgary**
McCaig, Jeffrey James *transportation company executive*
McCaig, John Robert *transportation executive*
Paquette, Richard *airport executive*

**Edmonton**
†Marcotte, Brian *transportation executive*

## NOVA SCOTIA

**Halifax**
Renouf, Harold Augustus *business consultant*

**Lower Sackville**
Ortlepp, Bruno *marine navigation educator, master mariner*

## ONTARIO

**Almonte**
Morrison, Angus Curran *aviation executive*

**Mississauga**
Tobias, Kal *transportation executive*

**Ottawa**
Coleman, John Morley *transportation research director*
Sheflin, Michael John Edward *environment and transportation official*

**Sault Sainte Marie**
Savoie, Leonard Norman *transportation company executive*

**Toronto**
Ansary, Hassan Jaber *transportation executive*
McCoomb, Lloyd Alexander *transportation executive*
Turpen, Louis A. *airport terminal executive*

## QUEBEC

**Dorval**
Brown, Robert Ellis *transportation company executive, former Canadian government official*

**Montreal**
Beaudoin, Laurent *industrial, recreational and transportation company executive*
Black, William Gordon *transportation executive*
Bourgeault, Jean-Jacques *air transportation executive*
Labelle, Eugene Jean-Marc *airport director general*
†Taddeo, Dominic *transportation executive*
Tellier, Paul M. *Canadian railway transportation executive*

**Pointe Claire**
Deegan, Derek James *transportation executive*

**Quebec**
Rochette, Louis *retired shipowner and shipbuilder*

**Saint Sauveur**
Hanigan, Lawrence *retired railway executive*

## MEXICO

**Mexico City**
†Martens, Ernesto *air, aerospace transportation executive*

## AUSTRALIA

**Canberra**
†Keith, Leroy Allen *aviation safety executive*

## DENMARK

**Vedbaek**
Nordqvist, Erik Askbo *shipping company executive*

## ENGLAND

**Burford**
Blackney, Arthur Bruce *Middle East defense and aviation consultant*

## GERMANY

**Munich**
Born, Gunthard Karl *aerospace executive*

## HONG KONG

**Hong Kong**
van Hoften, James Dougal Adrianus *business executive, former astronaut*

## THE PHILIPPINES

**Calookan City**
Dado, Jose Butial *railway company executive*

## ADDRESS UNPUBLISHED

Ames, Donald Paul *retired aerospace company executive, researcher*
Baer, Robert J. *transportation company executive*
Brazier, Don Roland *retired railroad executive*
Brown, Donald Douglas *transportation company executive, retired air force officer, consultant*
Butterfield, Alexander Porter *former business executive, government official*
Cheesman, John Michael *aeronautics company administrator, civic leader*
Collins, Eileen Marie *astronaut*
Culbertson, Philip Edgar *aerospace company executive, consultant*
Dasburg, John Harold *airline executive*
Davis, George Lynn *retired aerospace company executive*
Dely, Steven *aerospace company executive*
Eischen, Michael Hugh *retired railroad executive*
Falzone, Joseph Sam *retired airlines company crew chief*
†Flohr, Bruce M. *freight company executive*
Freitag, Peter Roy *transportation specialist*
Glennon, Harrison Randolph, Jr. *retired shipping company executive*
Goldstein, Bernard *transportation and casino gaming company executive*
Graebner, James Herbert *transportation executive*
Gray, Richard Arden *transportation executive*
Greenwald, Gerald *air transportation executive*
Hawkins, Willis Moore *aerospace and astronautical consultant*
Heitz, Edward Fred *freight traffic consultant*
Horton, Sir Robert Baynes (Sir ) *railroad company executive*
Howell, Saralee Fisher *pilot*
Hurst, John Emory, Jr. *retired airline executive*
King, Edward William *retired transportation executive*
Kish, Michael Louis *transportation executive*
Ledford, Jack Clarence *retired aircraft company executive, former air force officer*
Lerner-Lam, Eva I-Hwa *transportation executive*
Lesko, Harry Joseph *transportation company executive*
Lewis, Martin Edward *shipping company executive, foreign government concessionary*
Lillibridge, John Lee *retired airline executive*
Lloyd-Jones, Donald J. *transportation executive*
Marshall, Charles Noble *railroad consultant*
Masiello, Rocco Joseph *airlines and aerospace manufacturing executive*
Masson, Gayl Angela *airline pilot*
Mast, Stewart Dale *retired airport manager*
Matthews, L. White, III *railroad executive*
Morse, Leon William *traffic, physical distribution and transportation management executive, consultant*
Murray, Leonard Hugh *railroad executive*
Quesnel, Gregory L. *transportation company executive*
Regalado, Raul L. *airport parking executive*
Renda, Dominic Phillip *airline executive*
Rose, James Turner *aerospace consultant*
Ruegg, Donald George *retired railway company executive*
Schaefer, C. Barry *railroad executive, lawyer, investment banker*
Shepard, Alan Bartlett, Jr. *former astronaut, real estate developer*
Shockley, Edward Julian *aerospace company executive*
Smith, Russell Francis *transportation executive*
Snow, John William *railroad executive*
Snowden, Lawrence Fontaine *retired aircraft company executive, retired marine corps general officer*
Swanson, Ralph William *aerospace executive, consultant, engineer*

Voss, Omer Gerald *truck company executive*
Wallace, F. Blake *aerospace executive, mechanical engineer*
Watts, Dave Henry *retired corporate executive*
Wilson, Gary Lee *airline company executive*
Zenner, Nico *air transportation executive*

## INDUSTRY: UTILITIES, ENERGY, RESOURCES

### UNITED STATES

## ALABAMA

**Birmingham**
Barker, Thomas Watson, Jr. *energy company executive*
Bowron, Richard Anderson *retired utilities executive*
†Drummond, Garry N. *mining company executive*
Harris, Elmer Beseler *electric utility executive*
Hutchins, William Bruce, III *utility company executive*
Kuehn, Ronald L., Jr. *natural resources company executive*
Rubright, James Alfred *oil and gas company executive*

**Foley**
St. John, Henry Sewell, Jr. *utility company executive*

**Shoal Creek**
Ahearn, John Francis, Jr. *retired oil and gas company executive*

## ALASKA

**Anchorage**
Hopkins, Stephen Davis *mining company executive*

**Fairbanks**
Beistline, Earl Hoover *mining consultant*

**Nikiski**
Bumbaugh, Robert Warren, Sr. *oil industry executive*

## ARIZONA

**Carefree**
Birkelbach, Albert Ottmar *retired oil company executive*

**Cave Creek**
LeNeau, Thomas Ervin *gas company executive*

**Phoenix**
De Michele, O. Mark *utility company executive*
Hagerdon, Kathy Ann (Kay Hagerdon) *electric power industry executive*
Huffman, Edgar Joseph *oil company executive*
St. Clair, Thomas McBryar *mining and manufacturing company executive*
Yearley, Douglas Cain *mining and manufacturing company executive*

**Scottsdale**
Gillis, William Freeman *telecommunications executive*
Holliger, Fred Lee *oil company executive*
Swetnam, Monte Newton *petroleum exploration executive*

**Sun City West**
Black, Robert Frederick *former oil company executive*
O'Brien, Gerald James *utilities executive*

**Tempe**
Clevenger, Jeffrey Griswold *mining company executive*
Hickson, Robin Julian *mining company executive*

**Tucson**
Davis, James Luther *retired utilities executive, lawyer*
Heller, Frederick *retired mining company executive*
Osborne, Thomas Cramer *mineral industry consultant*
Peeler, Stuart Thorne *petroleum industry executive and independent oil operator*
Peters, Charles William *research and development company manager*

**Vail**
Saul, Kenneth Louis *retired utility company executive*

## ARKANSAS

**El Dorado**
McNutt, Jack Wray *oil company executive*
Vaughan, Odie Frank *oil company executive*
Watkins, Jerry West *retired oil company executive, lawyer*

**Fayetteville**
Scharlau, Charles Edward, III *natural gas company executive*

**Flippin**
Sanders, Steven Gill *telecommunications executive*

**Little Rock**
Gardner, Kathleen D. *gas company executive, lawyer*

**Russellville**
Jones, James Rees *retired oil company executive*

## CALIFORNIA

**Alamo**
Shiffer, James David *retired utility executive*

**Brea**
Stegemeier, Richard Joseph *oil company executive*

**Camarillo**
MacAlister, Robert Stuart *oil company executive*

**Carmel**
Loper, D. Roger *retired oil company executive*

**Corona Del Mar**
Hill, Melvin James *oil company executive*

**Downey**
Orden, Ted *gasoline service stations executive*

**Dublin**
Grady, Cheryl R. *telecommunications executive*

**El Segundo**
Beach, Roger C. *oil company executive*

**Flintridge**
Read, William McClain *retired oil company executive*

**Folsom**
Mine, Hilary Anne *telecommunications company executive, consultant*

**Fullerton**
Sadruddin, Moe *oil company executive, consultant*

**Hillsborough**
Willoughby, Rodney Erwin *retired oil company executive*

**Los Angeles**
Bowlin, Michael Ray *oil company executive*
Van Horne, R. Richard *oil company executive*
Wood, Willis Bowne, Jr. *utility holding company executive*
Wycoff, Robert E. *petroleum company executive*

**Mission Viejo**
Dergarabedian, Paul *energy and environmental company executive*

**Newport Beach**
Armstrong, Robert Arnold *petroleum company executive*

**Oxnard**
Parriott, James Deforis *retired oil company executive, consultant*

**Pacific Palisades**
Klein, Joseph Mark *retired mining company executive*
Middleton, James Arthur *oil and gas company executive*
Mulryan, Henry Trist *mineral company executive, consultant*

**Palo Alto**
Gouraud, Jackson S. *energy company executive*
Willrich, Mason *utilities executive, consultant*

**Palos Verdes Peninsula**
Christie, Hans Frederick *retired utility company subsidiaries executive, consultant*

**Pasadena**
Finnell, Michael Hartman *corporate executive*
Mc Duffie, Malcolm *oil company executive*
Van Amringe, John Howard *retired oil industry executive, geologist*

**Petaluma**
Frederickson, Arman Frederick *minerals company executive*

**Playa Del Rey**
Weir, Alexander, Jr. *utility consultant, inventor*

**Rosemead**
Allen, Howard Pfeiffer *electric utility executive, lawyer*
Bennett, Brian O'Leary *utilities executive*
Bryson, John E. *utilities company executive*
Bushey, Richard Kenneth *utility executive*

**Sacramento**
Crabbe, John Crozier *telecommunications consultant*
†Wickland, J. Al, Jr. *petroleum product executive, real estate executive*

**San Diego**
Cota, John Francis *utility executive*
Russel, Richard Allen *telecommunications consultant, aerospace engineer, nuclear engineer, electrical engineer, retired naval officer*

**San Francisco**
Brandin, Alf Elvin *retired mining and shipping company executive*
Bray, Arthur Philip *management science corporation executive*
Carter, George Kent *oil company executive*
Clarke, Richard Alan *electric and gas utility company executive, lawyer*
Derr, Kenneth T. *oil company executive*
Flittie, Clifford Gilliland *retired petroleum company executive*
Ginn, Sam L. *telephone company executive*
High, Thomas W. *utilities company executive*
Keller, George Matthew *retired oil company executive*
Kettel, Edward Joseph *oil company executive*
Kleeman, Michael Jeffrey *telecommunications and computer consultant*
Littlefield, Edmund Wattis *mining company executive*

Maneatis, George A. *retired utility company executive*
Premo, Paul Mark *oil company executive*
Quigley, Philip J. *telecommunications industry executive*
Renfrew, Charles Byron *oil company executive, lawyer*
†Saenger, Theodore Jerome *telephone company executive*
Savage, Michael John Kirkness *oil company and arts management executive*
Skinner, Stanley Thayer *utility company executive, lawyer*
Sproul, John Allan *retired public utility executive*
Sullivan, James N. *fuel company executive*
Wall, James Edward *telecommunications, petroleum and pharmaceutical executive*

**San Rafael**
Latno, Arthur Clement, Jr. *telephone company executive*

**Santa Cruz**
Cecil, Robert Salisbury *telecommunications company executive*

**Santa Ynez**
Byrne, Joseph *retired oil company executive*

**Stanford**
Brinegar, Claude Stout *retired oil company executive*

**Templeton**
Gandsey, Louis John *petroleum and environmental consultant*

**Thousand Oaks**
Monis, Antonio, Jr. (Tony Monis) *electric industry executive*

**Turlock**
Williams, Delwyn Charles *telephone company executive*

**Ventura**
Field, A. J. *former oil drilling company executive, engineering consultant*

**Walnut Creek**
Conger, Harry Milton *mining company executive*

**Woodland Hills**
Talbot, Matthew J. *oil company executive, rancher*

## COLORADO

**Boulder**
Thomas, Daniel Foley *telecommunications company executive*

**Broomfield**
Kober, Carl Leopold *exploration company executive*

**Colorado Springs**
King, Peter Joseph, Jr. *retired gas company executive*
O'Shields, Richard Lee *retired natural gas company executive*

**Denver**
†Dowdy, Andrea Lee *business development executive*
Fagin, David Kyle *natural resource company executive*
Fancher, George H., Jr. *oil company executive, petroleum engineer*
Lewis, Jerome A. *petroleum company executive, investment banker*
Macey, William Blackmore *oil company executive*
Owens, Marvin Franklin, Jr. *oil company executive*
Rendu, Jean-Michel Marie *mining executive*
Thompson, Lohren Matthew *oil company executive*
Timothy, Robert Keller *telephone company executive*
Trueblood, Harry Albert, Jr. *oil company executive*

**Englewood**
Le, Khanh Tuong *utility executive*
Malone, John C. *telecommunications executive*
McCormick, Richard *telecommunications company executive*
Ward, Milton Hawkins *mining company executive*

**Lakewood**
Hall, Larry D. *energy company executive, lawyer*

**Larkspur**
Bierbaum, J. Armin *petroleum company executive, consultant*

**Littleton**
Haley, John David *petroleum consulting company executive*
VanderLinden, Camilla Denice Dunn *telecommunications industry manager*

## CONNECTICUT

**Berlin**
Fox, Bernard Michael *utilities company executive, electrical engineer*

**Darien**
Kutz, Kenneth John *retired mining executive*
Smith, Elwin Earl *mining and oil company executive*

**Greenwich**
Bennett, Jack Franklin *oil company executive*
DeCrane, Alfred Charles, Jr. *petroleum company executive*
Lawi, David Steven *energy, agriservice and thermoplastic resins industries executive*
Nelson, Don Harris *gas and oil industry executive*
Schmidt, Herman J. *former oil company executive*

**Guilford**
Morgan, Leon Alford *retired utility executive*

**Hamden**
Gordon, Angus Neal, Jr. *retired electric company executive*

**Mystic**
Townsend, Thomas Perkins *former mining company executive*

**New Canaan**
McIvor, Donald Kenneth *retired petroleum company executive*

**New Haven**
Silvestri, Robert *electric company executive*

**Old Greenwich**
Hittle, Richard Howard *corporate executive, international affairs consultant*

**Orange**
Bowerman, Richard Henry *utility company executive, lawyer*

**Southport**
Damson, Barrie Morton *oil and gas exploration company executive*

**Stamford**
Donahue, Donald Jordan *mining company executive*
Gardiner, Hobart Clive *petroleum company executive*
Jacobson, Ishier *retired utility executive*
Kinnear, James Wesley, III *retired petroleum company executive*
Lee, Charles Robert *telecommunications company executive*
Mc Kinley, John Key *retired oil company executive*

**Waterford**
Sillin, Lelan Flor, Jr. *retired utility executive*

**Westport**
Nedom, H. Arthur *petroleum consultant*

**Wilton**
Hoefling, Rudolf Joachim *power generating company executive*

**DELAWARE**

**Wilmington**
Connelly, Donald Preston *electric and gas utility company executive*

**DISTRICT OF COLUMBIA**

**Washington**
Derrick, John Martin, Jr. *electric company executive*
Dreher, Richard Carl *wireless telecommunications executive, educator*
Lebow, Irwin Leon *communications engineering consultant*
Maher, Patrick Joseph *utility company executive*
McCollam, William, Jr. *utility company executive*
Modiano, Albert Louis *gas, oil industry executive*
Paige, Hilliard Wegner *corporate director, consultant*
Roberts, Bert C., Jr. *telecommunications company executive*
Thompson, William Reid *public utility executive, lawyer*
Wraase, Dennis Richard *utilities company executive, accountant*

**FLORIDA**

**Boca Raton**
Gralla, Eugene *natural gas company executive*

**Boynton Beach**
Babler, Wayne E. *retired telephone company executive, lawyer*

**Captiva**
Ronald, Peter *utility executive*

**Clearwater**
Soechtig, Jacqueline Elizabeth *telecommunications executive*

**Delray Beach**
Reef, Arthur *industry business consultant*

**Destin**
Cunningham, James Everett *retired energy services company executive*

**Eustis**
Pope, Theodore Campbell, Jr. *utilities executive, consultant*

**Jacksonville**
Francis, James Delbert *oil company executive*
Jelsma, Denny Gene *water company executive*

**Juno Beach**
Broadhead, James Lowell *electrical power industry executive*

**Largo**
Loader, Jay Gordon *retired utility company executive*

**Longwood**
Scoates, Wesley Marvin *mining company executive*

**Naples**
Ivancevic, Walter Charles *former gas distribution company executive*
Johnson, Zane Quentin *retired petroleum company executive*

**Kay**, Herbert *retired natural resources company executive*
Rowe, Jack Field *retired electric utility executive*

**Orlando**
Cirello, John *utility and engineering company executive*
Ispass, Alan Benjamin *utilities executive*

**Palm Beach**
Donnell, John Randolph *petroleum executive*

**Palm Beach Gardens**
Harnett, Joseph Durham *oil company executive*

**Panama City**
†Wimberly, Mark Vincent *utility executive*

**Pensacola**
Platz, Terrance Oscar *utilities company executive*

**Pinellas Park**
Perry, Paul Alverson *utility executive*

**Ponte Vedra Beach**
Green, Norman Kenneth *retired oil industry executive, former naval officer*
Milbrath, Robert Henry *retired petroleum executive*

**Quincy**
Laughlin, William Eugene *electric power industry executive*

**Saint Petersburg**
Critchfield, Jack Barron *utilities company executive*
Fassett, John D. *retired utility executive, consultant*
Hancock, John Allan *utility company executive*
Hines, Andrew Hampton, Jr. *utilities executive*

**Sun City Center**
McGrath, John Francis *utility executive*

**Tampa**
Campbell, David Ned *retired electric utility executive, business consultant*
Leavengood, Victor Price *telephone company executive*

**Venice**
Torrey, Richard Frank *utility executive*

**West Palm Beach**
Koch, William I. *energy company executive*

**Winter Park**
Spake, Ned Bernarr *energy company executive*

**GEORGIA**

**Atlanta**
Bolch, Carl Edward, Jr. *corporation executive, lawyer*
Born, Allen *mining executive*
Brinkley, Donald R. *oil industry executive*
Chilton, Horace Thomas *pipeline company executive*
Clendenin, John L. *telecommunications company executive*
Frost, Norman Cooper *retired telephone company executive*
Ramsey, Ira Clayton *retired pipeline company executive*
Voss, William Charles *retired oil company executive*

**Gainesville**
Leet, Richard Hale *oil company executive*

**Lithonia**
Keyes, David Taylor *telecommunications company administrator*

**Marietta**
Kagan, Jeffrey Allen *telecommunications analyst, consultant, author, columnist*

**Newnan**
McBroom, Thomas William, Sr. *utility manager*

**Roswell**
King, Jack L. *electric power industry executive*

**HAWAII**

**Honolulu**
Amioka, Wallace Shuzo *retired petroleum company executive*
Bates, George E. *oil industry executive*
Clarke, Robert F. *utilities company executive*
Williams, Carl Harwell *utilities executive*

**Kailua**
Engelbardt, Robert Miles *telecommunications executive*

**IDAHO**

**Coeur D Alene**
Griffith, William Alexander *former mining company executive*

**Idaho Falls**
Newman, Stanley Ray *oil refining company executive*

**ILLINOIS**

**Arlington Heights**
Wilson, Debra *oil, gas industry executive*

**Barrington**
Perry, I. Chet *petroleum company executive*

**Chicago**
Ban, Stephen Dennis *natural gas industry research institute executive*
Brooker, Thomas Kimball *oil company executive*
Carr, Robert Clifford *petroleum company executive*
Conrad, John R. *corporate executive*
Engel, Joel Stanley *telecommunications executive*
Fligg, James Edward *oil company executive*
Fuller, Harry Laurance *oil company executive*
Lowrie, William G. *oil company executive*
Morrow, Richard Martin *retired oil company executive*
Mullin, Leo Francis *utility company executive*
Notebaert, Richard C. *telecommunications industry executive*
O'Connor, James John *utility company executive*
Reeves, Michael Stanley *public utility executive*
Rogers, Desiree Glapion *utilities executive*
Rucker, Dennis Morton Arthur *telecommunications executive*
Williams, Carl Chanson *oil company executive*

**Decatur**
Dreyer, Alec Gilbert *independent power producer*
Womeldorff, Porter John *utilities executive*

**Geneva**
Pershing, Robert George *retired telecommunications company executive*

**Glen Ellyn**
Lischer, Ludwig Frederick *retired consultant, former utility company executive*

**Glenview**
Cozad, James William *retired oil company executive*

**Hinsdale**
Brandt, John Ashworth *fuel company executive*

**Lake Bluff**
Marino, William Francis *telecommunications industry executive, consultant*

**Naperville**
Many, Robert Todd *telecommunications executive*
Reuss, Robert Pershing *telecommunications executive, consultant*

**Northbrook**
Demaree, David Harry *utilities executive*

**Orland Park**
English, Floyd Leroy *telecommunications company executive*

**Peoria**
Viets, Robert O. *utilities executive*

**Rock Island**
Whitmore, Charles Horace *utility executive, lawyer, management consultant*

**INDIANA**

**Evansville**
Able, Warren Walter *natural resource company executive, physician*
Kiechlin, Robert Jerome *retired coal company executive, financial consultant*

**Frankfort**
Stonehill, Lloyd Herschel *gas company executive, mechanical engineer*

**Hammond**
Adik, Stephen Peter *energy company executive*
Schroer, Edmund Armin *utility company executive*

**Highland**
Purcell, James Francis *former utility executive, consultant*

**Indianapolis**
Ellerbrook, Niel Cochran *gas company executive*
Griffiths, David Neal *utility executive*
Husted, Ralph Waldo *former utility executive*
Krueger, Betty Jane *telecommunications company executive*
Todd, Zane Grey *retired utilities executive*

**Lawrenceburg**
Dautel, Charles Shreve *retired mining company executive*

**Michigan City**
Higgins, William Henry Clay, III *retired telecommunications consultant*

**Newburgh**
McGavic, Judy L. *coal company official*

**IOWA**

**Cedar Rapids**
Kucharski, Robert Joseph *power industry financial executive*

**Sioux City**
Wharton, Beverly Ann *utility company executive*

**KANSAS**

**Pittsburg**
Nettels, George Edward, Jr. *mining executive*

**Shawnee Mission**
Deaver, Darwin Holloway *former utility executive*

**Stilwell**
Keith, Dale Martin *utilities management consultant*

**Westwood**
Esrey, William Todd *telecommunications company executive*

**Wichita**
Cadman, Wilson Kennedy *retired utility company executive*
Koch, Charles de Ganahl *oil industry executive*
Varner, Sterling Verl *retired oil company executive*

**KENTUCKY**

**Ashland**
Boyd, James Robert *oil company executive*
Brothers, John Alfred *oil company executive*
Chellgren, Paul Wilbur *petroleum company executive*
Dansby, John Walter *oil company executive*
Hartl, William Parker *oil company executive*
Luellen, Charles J. *retired oil company executive*
Quin, Joseph Marvin *oil company executive*
Weaver, Carlton Davis *retired oil company executive*
Zachem, Harry M. *oil company executive*

**Louisville**
Royer, Robert Lewis *retired utility company executive*

**Owensboro**
Vickery, Robert Bruce *oil industry executive, consultant*

**Russell**
Crimmins, Sean T(homas) *oil company executive*
Gates, Deborah Wolin *petroleum company executive, lawyer*

**LOUISIANA**

**New Orleans**
Andrus, Gerald Louis *utilities holding company consultant*
Bachmann, Richard Arthur *oil company executive*
Kilanowski, Michael Charles, Jr. *oil, natural gas, minerals exploration company executive, lawyer*
Laborde, Alden James *oil company executive*
Lind, Thomas Otto *barge transportation company executive*
Murrish, Charles Howard *oil and gas exploration company executive, geologist*
Regan, William Joseph, Jr. *energy company executive*
Smith, John Webster *retired energy industry executive*
Stephens, Richard Bernard *natural resource company executive*
Williamson, Ernest Lavone *petroleum company executive*

**MAINE**

**Portland**
Haynes, Peter Lancaster *utility holding company executive*

**Surry**
Kilgore, John Edward, Jr. *former petroleum company executive*

**York Harbor**
Curtis, Edward Joseph, Jr. *gas industry executive, management consultant*

**MARYLAND**

**Annapolis**
Ellis, George Fitzallen, Jr. *energy services company executive*

**Baltimore**
Ihrie, Robert *oil, gas and real estate company executive*
McGowan, George Vincent *public utility executive*
Poindexter, Christian Herndon *utility company executive*
Rosenberg, Henry A., Jr. *petroleum executive*

**Bethesda**
Asbell, Fred Thomas *telecommunications company executive*
McMurphy, Michael Allen *energy company executive, lawyer*
Olmsted, Jerauld Lockwood *telephone company executive*

**Cabin John**
Dragoumis, Paul *electric utility company executive*

**Chevy Chase**
Bodman, Richard Stockwell *telecommunications executive*

**Easton**
Boutte, David Gray *oil industry executive, lawyer*

**Glen Arm**
Jackson, Theodore Marshall *retired oil company executive*

**Kensington**
Marienthal, George *telecommunications company executive*

**Rockville**
Cox, David Leon *telecommunications company executive*
Griffith, Jerry Dice *energy consultant*
Pollack, Louis *telecommunications company executive*

**Silver Spring**
Jacobs, George *broadcast engineering consulting company executive*

## MASSACHUSETTS

**Andover**
Maguire, Robert Edward *retired public utility executive*

**Boston**
Bok, Joan Toland *utility executive*
Burns, Richard Michael *public utility company executive*
Pardus, Donald Gene *utility executive*

**Burlington**
Reno, John F. *communications equipment company executive*

**Cambridge**
Buckler, Sheldon A. *energy company executive*

**Centerville**
Anderson, Gerald Edwin *utilities executive*
Scherer, Harold Nicholas, Jr. *electric utility company executive, engineer*

**Chelsea**
Kaneb, Gary *oil industry executive*

**Danvers**
Dolan, John Ralph *retired corporation executive*

**Harwich Port**
Staszesky, Francis Myron *electric company consultant*

**Marblehead**
Pruyn, William J. *energy industry executive*

**Melrose**
Brown, Ronald Osborne *telecommunications and computer systems consultant*

**Needham**
Cogswell, John Heyland *retired telecommunications executive, financial consultant*

**Norwood**
Smith, William Bridges *diversified company executive*

**Waltham**
Slifka, Alfred A. *oil corporation executive*

**West Bridgewater**
Gulvin, David Horner *electric company executive*

**Westborough**
Houston, Alfred Dearborn *energy company executive*
Rowe, John William *utility executive*
Young, Roger Austin *natural gas distribution company executive*

## MICHIGAN

**Dearborn**
Boulanger, Rodney Edmund *energy company executive*

**Detroit**
Garberding, Larry Gilbert *utilities companies executive*
Glancy, Alfred Robinson, III *public utility company executive*
Lobbia, John E. *utility company executive*
Schiffer, Daniel L. *gas company executive*
Wilkes, James E. *telecommunications industry executive*

**Jackson**
McCormick, William Thomas, Jr. *electric and gas company executive*
Patrick, Ueal Eugene *oil company executive*

**Lake Leelanau**
Shannahan, John Henry Kelly *energy consultant*

**Novi**
Simpkin, Lawrence James *utilities executive*

**Owosso**
Hoddy, George Warren *electric company executive, electrical engineer*

**Port Huron**
Thomson, Robert James *natural gas distribution company executive*

**Shelby Township**
Fillbrook, Thomas George *telephone company executive*

## MINNESOTA

**Eden Prairie**
Emison, James W. *petroleum company executive*

**Fergus Falls**
MacFarlane, John Charles *utility company executive*

**Minneapolis**
Gudorf, Kenneth Francis *business executive*
†Petersen, Gary N. *utility company executive*
Wyman, James Thomas *petroleum company executive*

**Saint Paul**
Estenson, Noel K. *refining and fertilizer company executive*
Frame, Clarence George *retired oil and gas refining company executive*
Robertson, Jerry Earl *retired manufacturing company executive*

## MISSISSIPPI

**Brandon**
Stampley, Norris Lochlen *former electric utility executive*

**Jackson**
Furrh, James Brooke, Jr. *oil company executive*

## MISSOURI

**Joplin**
Hadley, Debra Sue *electric company executive*
Lamb, Robert Lewis *electric utility executive*

**Kansas City**
Baker, John Russell *utilities executive*
Jennings, A. Drue *utility company executive*
Smith, Richard Conrad, Jr. *telecommunications company executive*

**Lebanon**
Beavers, Roy L. *retired utility executive, essayist, activist*

**Saint Louis**
Anderson, James Donald *mining company executive*
Dougherty, Charles Joseph *retired utility executive*
Elliott, Howard, Jr. *gas distribution company executive*
Lilly, Peter Byron *coal company executive*
Mueller, Charles William *electric utility executive*
Quenon, Robert Hagerty *retired mining consultant and holding company executive*
Thompson, James Clark *utilities executive*

**Springfield**
Boehm, Robert Kenneth *telecommunications consultant*
Jura, James J. *electric utility executive*

## MONTANA

**Bigfork**
Shennum, Robert Herman *retired telephone company executive*

**Billings**
Nance, Robert Lewis *oil company executive*
Reed, Kenneth G. *petroleum company executive*

**Butte**
Burke, John James *utility executive*
Mc Elwain, Joseph Arthur *retired power company executive*

**Missoula**
Brumit, Lawrence Edward, III *oil field service company executive*

## NEBRASKA

**Lincoln**
Tavlin, Michael John *telecommunications company executive*

## NEVADA

**Fallon**
Sanwick, James Arthur *mining executive*

**Las Vegas**
Laub, William Murray *retired utility executive*
Trimble, Thomas James *retired utility company executive, lawyer*

**Zephyr Cove**
Proctor, Robert Swope *retired petroleum company executive*

## NEW HAMPSHIRE

**Concord**
Tomajczyk, S(tephen) F(rancis) *communications company executive, author*

**Dover**
Tillinghast, John Avery *utilities executive*

**Portsmouth**
Powers, Henry Martin, Jr. *oil company executive*

**Rindge**
Emerson, Susan *oil company executive*

## NEW JERSEY

**Basking Ridge**
Collis, Sidney Robert *retired telephone company executive*
Perry, Matthew Edward, Jr. *telecommunications professional*

**Chatham**
Bast, Ray Roger *retired utility company executive*

**Chester**
Gurian, Mal *telecommunications executive*

**Collingswood**
Mohrfeld, Richard Gentel *heating oil distributing company executive*

**Edison**
Avery, James Stephen *oil company executive*
Francis, Peter T. *gas and oil industry executive*

**Fort Lee**
Schiessler, Robert Walter *retired chemical and oil company executive*
Weitzer, Bernard *telecommunications executive*

**Glen Ridge**
McGovern, Thomas Aquinas *retired utility executive*

**Hackensack**
Duques, Ric *information services executive*

**Hammonton**
Levitt, Gerald Steven *natural gas company executive*

**Holmdel**
Heirman, Donald Nestor *telecommunications engineering company manager*

**Lake Hopatcong**
Dowling, Robert Murray *oil company executive*

**Little Silver**
Gagnebin, Albert Paul *retired mining executive*

**Manahawkin**
Aurner, Robert Ray, II *oil company, auto diagnostic, restaurant franchise and company development executive*

**Morristown**
Everhart, Rodney Lee *telecommunications industry executive*

**New Providence**
Cohen, Melvin Irwin *communications systems and technology executive*

**Newark**
Ferland, E. James *electric utility executive*

**Nutley**
Mallard, Stephen Anthony *retired utility company executive*

**Parsippany**
Graham, John Gourlay *utility company executive*
Hafer, Frederick Douglass *utility executive*
Leva, James Robert *electric utility company executive*

**Paulsboro**
Wise, John James *oil company executive*

**Peapack**
Walsh, Philip Cornelius *retired mining executive*

**Piscataway**
Burke, Jacqueline Yvonne *telecommunications executive*
Lewis, Peter A. *energy consultant*

**Princeton**
Farley, Edward Raymond, Jr. *mining and manufacturing company executive*
Mc Cullough, John Price *retired oil company executive*

**Randolph**
Raber, Marvin *retired utility company executive, consultant*

**Red Bank**
Chynoweth, Alan Gerald *retired telecommunications executive, consultant*

**Ridgewood**
Dormire, Corwin Brooke *public utility business advisor, retired lawyer*

**Summit**
Pollak, Henry Otto *retired utility research executive, educator*

**Union**
Lewandowski, Andrew Anthony *utilities executive, consultant*

**Wall**
Colford, Francis Xavier *gas industry executive*

**Westfield**
Specht, Gordon Dean *retired petroleum executive*

**Wrightstown**
Drechsel, Edward Russell, Jr. *retired utility company executive*

## NEW MEXICO

**Albuquerque**
Gorham, Frank DeVore, Jr. *petroleum company executive*

**Farmington**
Macaluso, Frank Augustus *oil company executive*

**Hobbs**
Garey, Donald Lee *pipeline and oil company executive*

**Mora**
Mossavar-Rahmani, Bijan *oil and gas company executive*

**Roswell**
Anderson, Donald Bernard *oil company executive*

**Santa Fe**
Pickrell, Thomas Richard *retired oil company executive*
Reichman, Nanci Satin *oil company owner*

## NEW YORK

**Astoria**
Parascos, Edward Themistocles *utilities executive*

**Aurora**
Slocum, George Sigman *energy company executive*

**Babylon**
Lopez, Joseph Jack *oil company executive, consultant*

**Binghamton**
Carrigg, James A. *retired utility company executive*
Farley, Daniel W. *lawyer, utility company executive*
von Schack, Wesley W. *energy services company executive*

**Blauvelt**
Gillespie, John Fagan *mining executive*

**Bridgehampton**
Enstine, Raymond Wilton, Jr. *propane gas company executive*

**Brooklyn**
Bisbee, Joyce Evelyn *utility company manager*
Catell, Robert Barry *gas company executive*
Matthews, Craig Gerard *gas company executive*

**Buffalo**
Ackerman, Philip Charles *utility executive, lawyer*
Brown, John M. *gas company executive*
Kennedy, Bernard Joseph *utility executive*

**Huntington Station**
Pierce, Charles R. *electric company consultant*

**Jericho**
Fitteron, John Joseph *petroleum products company executive*

**Manhasset**
Anderson, Arthur N. *retired utility company executive*

**New York**
Alonzo, Martin Vincent *mining and aluminum company executive, investor, financial consultant*
Alpert, Warren *oil company executive, philanthropist*
Araskog, Rand Vincent *diversified telecommunications multinational company executive*
Baird, Dugald Euan *oil field service company executive*
Belknap, Norton *petroleum company consultant*
Bernstein, Alan Arthur *oil company executive*
Brown, Edward James, Sr. *utility executive*
Carey, Edward John *utility executive*
Case, Hadley *oil company executive*
Delaney, Robert Vincent *former gas company executive, economic development consultant*
Delz, William Ronald *petroleum company executive*
Douglas, Paul Wolff *retired mining executive*
Duke, Robert Dominick *mining executive, lawyer*
Geeslin, Bailey M. *telecommunications company executive*
Gelfand, Neal *oil company executive*
Hedley, Robert Peveril *retired petroleum and chemical company executive*
Hess, Leon *oil company executive*
Host, Stig *oil company executive*
Kramer, Philip *retired petroleum refining executive*
Levy, Walter James *oil consultant*
Luce, Charles Franklin *former utilities executive, lawyer*
Lyons, John Matthew *telecommunications executive, broadcasting executive*
Malozemoff, Plato *mining executive*
McGrath, Eugene R. *utility company executive*
Murray, Allen Edward *retired oil company executive*
Osborne, Richard de Jongh *mining and metals company executive*
†Paret, Dominique *petroleum company executive*
Passage, Stephen Scott *energy company executive*
Richards, Reuben Francis *natural resource company executive*
Smith, Stanton Kinnie, Jr. *utility company executive*
Staley, Delbert C. *telecommunications executive*
Underweiser, Irwin Philip *mining company executive, lawyer*
†Wakeham, Matthew S. *electronics marketing manager*
Warner, Rawleigh, Jr. *oil company executive*

**Niskayuna**
Fitzroy, Nancy deLoye *technology executive, engineer*

**Ossining**
Gilbert, Joan Stulman *public relations executive*

**Pearl River**
Caliendo, G. D. (Jerry Caliendo) *public utility*

**Poughkeepsie**
Mack, John Edward, III *utility company executive*

**Rochester**
Richards, Thomas Savidge *utility company executive*

**Schenectady**
Robb, Walter Lee *retired electric company executive, management company executive*

**Staten Island**
Barton, Jerry O'Donnell *telecommunications executive*

**Syosset**
Vermylen, Paul Anthony, Jr. *oil company executive*

**Syracuse**
Davis, William E. *utility executive*

**Tonawanda**
Dillman, Joseph John Thomas *electric utility executive*

**Houston**
†Adams, Kenneth Stanley, Jr. (Bud Adams) *energy company executive, football executive*
Barracano, Henry Ralph *retired oil company executive, consultant*
Barrow, Thomas Davies *oil and mining company executive*
Bartling, Phyllis McGinness *oil company executive*
Bonneville, Richard Briggs *retired petroleum exploration and production executive*
Bowen, W. J. *retired gas company executive*
Bryan, James Lee *oil field service company executive*
Burguieres, Philip *energy service and manufacturing company executive*
Campbell, Carl David *oil industry executive, landman*
Capps, Ethan LeRoy *oil company executive*
Carameros, George Demitrius, Jr. *natural gas company executive*
Carroll, Philip Joseph *oil company executive*
Carter, James Sumter *oil company executive, tree farmer*
Carter, John Boyd, Jr. *oil operator, bank executive*
Chalmers, David B. *petroleum executive*
Cox, Frank D. (Buddy Cox) *oil company executive, exploration consultant*
Danburg, Jerome Samuel *oil company executive*
Danos, Robert McClure *retired oil company executive*
Davis, Leon *oil company executive*
DeVault, John Lee *oil company executive, geophysicist*
de Vries, Douwe *oil company executive*
Dice, Bruce Burton *retired exploration company executive*
DiCorcia, Edward Thomas *oil industry executive*
Drury, Leonard Leroy *retired oil company executive*
Edens, Donald Keith *oil company executive*
Ferrand, Jean C. *oil company executive*
Foster, Joe B. *oil company executive*
Frost, John Elliott *minerals company executive*
Fulwiler, Robert Neal *oil company executive*
Giacalone, Frank Thomas *energy and environmental company executive*
Gibson, Jerry Leigh *oil company executive*
Gipson, Robert Malone *oil industry executive*
Goodman, Herbert Irwin *petroleum company executive*
Halbouty, Michel Thomas *geologist, petroleum engineer, petroleum operator*
Hardin, George Cecil, Jr. *petroleum consultant*
Hendrix, Dennis Ralph *energy company executive*
Hesse, Martha O. *natural gas company executive*
Hoglund, Forrest Eugene *petroleum company executive*
Honea, T. Milton *gas industry executive*
Howell, Paul Neilson *oil company execuitve*
Huff, John Rossman *oil service company executive*
Irwin, John Robert *oil and gas drilling executive*
Jamieson, John Kenneth *oil company executive*
Johnson, Kenneth Oscar *oil company executive*
Johnson, Wayne D. *gas industry executive*
Jones, Larry Leroy *oil company executive*
Jordan, Don D. *electric company executive*
Jorden, James Roy *retired oil company engineering executive*
Kerr, Baine Perkins *oil company executive*
Kirkland, John David *oil and gas company executive, lawyer*
Kuntz, Hal Goggan *petroleum exploration company executive*
Lay, Kenneth Lee *diversified energy company executive*
Leonard, Gilbert Stanley *oil company executive*
Long, William Everett *retired utility executive*
Loveland, Eugene Franklin *petroleum executive*
Luigs, Charles Russell *gas and oil drilling industry executive*
Martin, Jerry C. *oil company executive*
Matthews, Thomas Michael *energy company executive*
Monroe, L. A. J. *oil well drilling company executive*
Nanz, Robert Hamilton *petroleum consultant*
Nestvold, Elwood Olaf *oil and gas industry executive*
Nicandros, Constantine Stavros *business consultant, retired oil company executive*
Nyberg, Donald Arvid *oil company executive*
Pate, James Leonard *oil company executive*
Patin, Michael James *oil company executive*
Pester, Jack Cloyd *oil company executive*
Prentice, James Stuart *energy company executive, chemical engineer*
Reynolds, John Terrence *oil industry executive*
Richardson, Frank H. *retired oil industry executive*
Robbins, Earl L. *oil operator*
Roff, J(ohn) Hugh, Jr. *energy company executive*
Rossler, Willis Kenneth, Jr. *petroleum company executive*
Saizan, Paula Theresa *oil company executive*
Segner, Edmund Peter, III *natural gas company executive*
Smith, David Kingman *retired oil company executive, consultant*
Spincic, Wesley James *oil company executive, consultant*
Thorn, Terence Hastings *gas industry executive*
Williams, Robert Henry *oil company executive*
Wilson, Edward Converse, Jr. *oil and natural gas production company executive*
Wyatt, Oscar Sherman, Jr. *energy company executive*

**Ingram**
Hughes, David Michael *oil service company executive, rancher*

**Irving**
Baum, Herbert Merrill *motor oil company executive*
Bayne, James Elwood *oil company executive*
Helm, Terry Allen *telecommunications consultant*
Hess, Edwin John *oil company executive*
Le Vine, Duane Gilbert *petroleum company executive*
Lutz, Matthew Charles *oil company executive, geologist*
Nurenberg, David *oil company executive*
Robinson, Edgar Allen *oil company executive*

**Kingwood**
Ramsey, William Dale, Jr. *technology and regulatory consultant*

**Lewisville**
Bickel, Herbert Jacob, Jr. *corporation executive*

**Mc Kinney**
Dickinson, Richard Raymond *retired oil company executive*

**Midland**
Grover, Rosalind Redfern *oil and gas company executive*

**Plano**
Mackenzie, John *retired oil industry executive*
Schuh, Frank Joseph *drilling engineering company executive, consultant*

**Pottsboro**
Hanning, Gary William *utility executive, water company executive, consultant*

**Richardson**
McDaniel, Dolan Kenneth *oil exploration service company executive*

**Salado**
Parks, Lloyd Lee *oil company executive*

**San Antonio**
Benninger, Edward C., Jr. *petroleum and natural gas company executive*
Burke, Michael Donald *oil and gas company executive*
Gaulin, Jean *gas distribution company executive*
Hemminghaus, Roger Roy *energy company executive, chemical engineer*
Klaerner, Curtis Maurice *former oil company executive*
Whitacre, Edward E., Jr. *telecommunications executive*

**Sealy**
Young, Milton Earl *retired petroleum production company executive*

**The Woodlands**
Sharman, Richard Lee *telecommunications executive, consultant*
Thompson, John Kenton *energy company executive, natural gas engineer*

**Tyler**
Frankel, Donald Leon *retired oil service company executive*

**Winnsboro**
Fairchild, Raymond Eugene *oil company executive*

## UTAH

**Orem**
Jacobson, Alfred Thurl *petroleum executive*

**Park City**
Edwards, Howard Lee *retired petroleum company executive, lawyer*

**Salt Lake City**
Cash, R(oy) Don *gas and petroleum company executive*
Heiner, Clyde Mont *energy company executive*
Holding, R. Earl *oil company executive*
Joklik, Günther Franz *mining company executive*
Losse, John William, Jr. *mining company executive*
Scowcroft, John Major *petroleum refinery process development executive*

## VERMONT

**Barnard**
Larson, John Hyde *retired utilities executive*

**North Clarendon**
Freed, Walter Everett *petroleum company executive, state representative*

**Rutland**
Griffin, James Edwin *utilities executive*

**Springfield**
Guité, J. C. Michel *telephone company executive*

## VIRGINIA

**Alexandria**
Smith, Jeffrey Greenwood *industry executive, retired army officer*

**Arlington**
Endahl, Lowell Jerome *retired electrical cooperative executive*
Wakefield, Richard Alan *energy consulting firm executive*

**Fairfax**
Hoenmans, Paul John *oil company executive*
Noto, Lucio R. *gas and oil industry executive*
Smith, Robert Keith *exchange program associate*

**Glen Allen**
Farrell, Joseph Christopher *mining executive, services executive*

**Lexington**
Tyree, Lewis, Jr. *retired compressed gas company executive, inventor, technical consultant*

**Manassas Park**
Gray-Bussard, Dolly H. *energy company executive*

**Mc Lean**
Russo, Anthony Sebastian *telecommunications executive*

**Middleburg**
McGhee, George Crews *petroleum producer, former government official*

**Reston**
Richard, Oliver, III (Rick Richard) *gas company executive*
Schwolsky, Peter M. *gas industry executive, lawyer, partner*

**Richmond**
Berry, William Willis *retired utility executive*
Capps, Thomas Edward *utilities company executive, lawyer*
Clement, Alvis Macon *former utilities executive*

**Sterling**
Oller, William Maxwell *retired energy company executive, retired naval officer*

**Suffolk**
Hines, Angus Irving, Jr. *petroleum marketing executive*

**Upperville**
di Zerega, Thomas William *former energy company executive, lawyer*

**Williamsburg**
Baranowski, Frank Paul *energy consultant, former government official*

## WASHINGTON

**Bellevue**
Groten, Barnet *energy company executive*
Weaver, William Schildecker *electric power industry executive*

**Seattle**
Smith, Andrew Vaughn *telephone company executive*

**Sequim**
Beaton, Roy Howard *retired nuclear industry executive*

**Spokane**
Eliassen, Jon Eric *utility company executive*

## WEST VIRGINIA

**Charleston**
Bennett, Robert Menzies *retired gas pipeline company executive*
Maddox, Timothy Dwain *natural gas company manager*

**Elkview**
Banonis, Edward Joseph *gas industry executive*

**Huntington**
Justice, Franklin Pierce, Jr. *oil company executive*

## WISCONSIN

**Green Bay**
†Bollom, Daniel A. *energy executive*
†Weyers, Larry L. *energy executive*

**Madison**
Barr, Jim, III *telecommunications company executive*
Davis, Erroll Brown, Jr. *utility executive*
Gehl, Eugene O. *power company executive, lawyer*
Mackie, Frederick David *retired utility executive*

**Milwaukee**
Burstein, Sol *consultant, retired utility company executive, engineer*
Goetsch, John Hubert *consultant and retired utility company executive*
Schrader, Thomas F. *utilities executive*
Stephenson, Robert Baird *energy company executive*

**Thiensville**
Kostecke, B. William *utilities executive*

## WYOMING

**Casper**
Smith, Dick Martin *oil field service company executive, owner*

**Laramie**
Laman, Jerry Thomas *mining company executive*

**Riverton**
Bebout, Eli Daniel *oil executive*

# CANADA

## ALBERTA

**Calgary**
Furnival, George Mitchell *petroleum and mining consultant*
Gish, Norman Richard *oil industry executive*
Hagerman, Allen Reid *mining executive*
Haskayne, Richard Francis *petroleum company executive*
Hriskevich, Michael Edward *oil and gas consultant*
Little, Brian F. *oil company executive*
Maclagan, John Lyall *retired petroleum company executive*
Maier, Gerald James *natural gas transmission and marketing company executive*
McIntyre, Norman F. *petroleum industry executive*
Mc Kinnon, F(rancis) A(rthur) Richard *utility executive*
O'Brien, David Peter *oil company executive*
†Peltier, John Wayne (Jack ) *oil and gas industry executive*
Pick, Michael Claude *international exploration consultant*
Pierce, Robert Lorne *petrochemical, oil and gas company executive*
Reid, David Evans *pipeline company executive*
Seaman, Daryl Kenneth *oil company executive*
Travis, Vance Kenneth *petroleum business executive*
Wagner, Norman Ernest *corporate education executive*

**Edmonton**
Horton, William Russell *retired utility company executive*

**Red Deer**
Donald, Jack C. *oil company executive*

## BRITISH COLUMBIA

**Vancouver**
Birch, Murray Patrick *oil industry executive*
Keevil, Norman Bell *mining executive*
Petrina, Anthony J. *retired mining executive*
Phillips, Edwin Charles *gas transmission company executive*
Willson, John Michael *mining company executive*
Wilson, Graham McGregor *energy company executive*

**West Vancouver**
Kloepfer, Clarence Victor *oil company executive*

**White Rock**
Huntington, A. Ronald *retired coal terminal executive*

## MANITOBA

**Pinawa**
Allan, Colin James *research and development company manager*

**Winnipeg**
Brennan, Robert Bryan *utility company executive*
Lang, Otto E. *industry executive, former Canadian cabinet minister*

## NOVA SCOTIA

**Halifax**
Smith, Ronald Emory *telecommunications executive*

## ONTARIO

**Etobicoke**
Hyland, Geoffrey Fyfe *energy company executive*

**London**
Widdrington, Peter Nigel Tinling *environmental and energy company executive*

**Mississauga**
Pelley, Marvin Hugh *mining executive*

**Toronto**
Bone, Bruce Charles *mining and manufacturing executive*
Bush, John Arthur Henry *mining company executive, lawyer*
Cooper, Marsh Alexander *mining company executive*
Ediger, Nicholas Martin *energy resources company executive, consultant*
Leech, James William *technology company executive*
Martin, Robert William *corporate director*
Munk, Peter *mining executive*
Osler, Gordon Peter *retired utility company executive*
Peterson, Robert B. *petroleum company executive*
Shaw, Ian Alexander *mining company executive, accountant*
Sopko, Michael D. *mining company executive*
Thomas, Kenneth Glyndwr *mining executive*

## QUEBEC

**Brockville**
Spalding, James Stuart *retired telecommunications company executive*

**Montreal**
Andrew, Frederick James *telecommunications company executive*
Burns, James William *business executive*
Caillé, André *public service company executive*
Cyr, J. V. Raymond *telecommunications company executive*
Fridman, Josef Josel *telecommunications company executive*
Wilson, Lynton Ronald *telecommunications company executive*

**Rosemere**
Normand, Robert *utility industry executive*

**Varennes**
St. Jean, Guy *electric power industry executive*

## SASKATCHEWAN

**Saskatoon**
Childers, Charles Eugene *mining company executive*

# AUSTRALIA

**Melbourne**
Mc Gimpsey, Ronald Alan *oil company executive*

## ENGLAND

**London**
Gillam, Patrick John *oil company executive*
Smernoff, Richard Louis *oil company executive*

## FRANCE

**Paris**
Jaclot, Francois Charles *utility company executive*

## JAPAN

**Yokohama**
Ito, Noboru *electric power industry executive*

## THE NETHERLANDS

**The Hague**
Herkströter, Cornelius *oil industry executive*
Van Wachem, Lodewijk Christiaan *petroleum company executive*

## SPAIN

**Madrid**
De Reyna, Luis *oil drilling company executive*

## ADDRESS UNPUBLISHED

Addy, Frederick Seale *retired oil company executive*
Akel, Ollie James *oil company executive*
Anderson, Robert Orville *oil and gas company executive*
Arlidge, John Walter *utility company executive*
Arnold, William Howard *retired nuclear fuel executive*
Arthur, John Morrison *retired utility executive*
Barham, Charles Dewey, Jr. *electric utility executive, lawyer*
Barrack, William Sample, Jr. *petroleum company executive*
Barrow, Frank Pearson, Jr. *retired energy company executive*
Bartling, Theodore Charles *oil company executive*
Baumgartner, John H. *refining and petroleum products company executive*
Benediktson, Stephan Vilberg *oil company executive*
Bergman, Klaus *retired utility executive, lawyer*
Bowman, Charles Hay *petroleum company executive*
Braswell, Arnold Webb *retired military officer*
Brophy, Theodore Frederick *telephone company executive*
Browne, Edmund John Phillip *oil company executive*
Bruce, James Edmund *retired utility company executive*
Bumbery, Joseph Lawrence *diversified telecommunications company executive*
Bush, Charles Vernon *telecommunications executive*
Butler, Eugene L. *oil field equipment company executive*
Carr, David Robert *oil trading company executive*
Carver, Calvin Reeve *public utility company director*
Catacosinos, William James *utility company executive*
Clark, Philip Raymond *nuclear utility executive, engineer*
Cliff, Ronald Laird *energy company executive*
Cookson, Albert Ernest *telephone and telegraph company executive*
Counsil, William Glenn *electric utility executive*
Creigh, Thomas, Jr. *utility executive*
Crews, Esca Holmes, Jr. *utility company executive*
Cummer, William Jackson *former oil company executive, investor*
Di Giovanni, Anthony *retired coal mining company executive*
Dille, Earl Kaye *utility company executive*
Dorros, Irwin *consultant, retired telecommunications executive*
Driscoll, Garrett Bates *retired telecommunications executive*
†Engibous, Thomas J. *electronics company executive*
Ewing, Wayne Turner *coal company executive*
Fitzgeorge, Harold James *former oil and gas company executive*
Ford, Judith Ann Tudor *retired natural gas distribution company executive*
Gardner, Richard Hartwell *oil company executive*
Gerard, Roy Dupuy *oil company executive*
Gogarty, William Barney *oil company executive, consultant*
Greenberg, Arnold Elihu *water quality specialist*
Greer, Carl Crawford *petroleum company executive*
Gundersen, Wayne Campbell *oil and gas consultant, management consultant*
Hall, Milton Reese *retired oil company executive*
Hamilton, Allan Corning *retired oil company executive*
Hamilton, Lyman Critchfield, Jr. *telecommunications* industry executive
Hampton, Rex Herbert *former mining executive, director*
Hancock, John Coulter *telecommunications company executive*
Hansen, Shirley Jean *energy consulting executive, professional association administrator*
Harris, Howard Hunter *oil company executive*
Harton, John James *utility executive, consultant*
Heiney, John Weitzel *former utility executive*
Hesse, Christian August *mining and underground construction consultant*
Hinson, Howard Houston *petroleum company executive*
Hitchborn, James Brian *telecommunications executive*
Hogg, Karen Sue *telecommunications and information systems executive*
Houser, William Douglas *telecommunications company executive, former naval officer*
Howard, James Joseph, III *utility company executive*
Huffman, James Thomas William *oil exploration company executive*
Humke, Ramon L. *utility executive*
Hurst, Leland Lyle *natural gas company executive*
Hyde, Robert Burke, Jr. *retired oil industry executive*
Inglis, James *telecommunications company executive*
Inman, Cullen Langdon *telecommunications scientist*
Jackson, Robert William *utility company executive, retired*
Jones, Jack Dellis *oil company executive*
Judge, Rosemary Ann *oil company executive*
Kaufman, Raymond L. *energy company executive*
Kebblish, John Basil *retired coal company executive, consultant*
Kerr, James Winslow *pipe line company executive*
Kertz, Hubert Leonard *telephone company executive*
King, William Collins *oil company executive*
Kinzer, James Raymond *retired pipeline company executive*
Kirkby, Maurice Anthony *oil company executive*
Kousparis, Dimitrios *oil consulting company executive*
Kruizenga, Richard John *retired energy company executive*
Le Van, Daniel Hayden *retired gas industry executive*
Lewis, Alexander, Jr. *oil company executive*
Lewis, Floyd Wallace *former electric utility executive*
Lilly, Edward Guerrant, Jr. *retired utility company executive*
Lively, Edwin Lester *retired oil company executive*
Lordo, Phillip James *telecommunications professional*
Lupberger, Edwin Adolph *utility executive*
Macdonald, Sheila de Marillac *transaction management company executive*
Markle, Roger A(llan) *retired oil company executive*
Mc Carthy, Walter John, Jr. *retired utility executive*
McConnell, Elliott Bonnell, Jr. *oil company executive*
McCready, Kenneth Frank *past electric utility executive*
McSweeny, William Francis *petroleum company executive, author*
Meek, Forrest Burns *oil industry executive, trading company executive*
Melvin, Ben Watson, Jr. *petroleum and chemical manufacturing executive*
Mitchell, Claybourne, Jr. *retired utilities executive*
Montgomery, Roy Delbert *retired gas utility company executive*
Monty, Charles Embert *utility company executive*
Moran, John Arthur *oil company executive*
Morrell, Gene Paul *liquid terminal company executive*
Morrow, George Lester *retired oil and gas executive*
Munsey, Virdell Everard, Jr. *retired utility executive*
Murphy, Charles Haywood, Jr. *retired petroleum company executive*
Murrill, Paul Whitfield *former utility executive, former university administrator*
Nicholson, Leland Ross *retired utilities company executive, energy consultant*
Nugent, Jane Kay *retired utility executive*
O'Hare, James Raymond *energy company executive*
Osterhoff, James Marvin *retired telecommunications company executive*
Pack, Allen S. *retired coal company executive*
Peckham, Donald Eugene *retired utilities company executive*
Perkins, Frederick Myers *retired oil company executive*
Perkins, Thomas Keeble *oil company researcher*
Perry, Kenneth Walter *integrated oil company executive*
Portal, Gilbert Marcel Adrien *oil company executive*
Raymond, Lee R. *oil company executive*
Reynolds, Jack W. *retired utility company executive*
Roe, Thomas Coombe *former utility company executive*
Rogers, Justin Towner, Jr. *retired utility company executive*
Sadowski, John Stanley *utility executive*
Samuels, John Stockwell, III *mining company executive, financier*
Sanders, Charles Franklin *management and engineering consultant*
Schenck, Jack Lee *retired electric utility executive*
Schenker, Leo *retired utility company executive*
Schumacher, Robert Joseph *petroleum company executive*
Scott, Isadore Meyer *former energy company executive*
Seidenberg, Ivan G. *telecommunications company executive*
Skala, Gary Dennis *electric and gas utilities executive management consultant*
Smith, Paul Vergon, Jr. *corporate executive, retired oil company executive*
Smith, Richard Grant *retired telecommunications executive, electrical engineer*
Stratman, Joseph Lee *petroleum refining company executive, consultant, chemical engineer*
Sugarman, Samuel Louis *retired oil transportation and trading company executive, horse breeder*
Sutton, James Andrew *diversified utility company executive*
Templeton, John Alexander, II *coal company executive*
Thompson, Jack Edward *mining company executive*
Threet, Jack Curtis *oil company executive*
Tonkyn, Richard George *retired oil and gas company executive, researcher, consultant*
Tucker, H. Richard *oil company executive*
Turner, Thomas Marshall *telecommunications executive, consultant*
Ward, Edward Wells *telecommunications executive*
Werth, Andrew M. *telecommunications executive*
Wharton, Thomas William *mining executive*
White, Willis Sheridan, Jr. *retired utilities company executive*
Whitehouse, Alton Winslow, Jr. *retired oil company executive*
Williams, Joseph Theodore *oil and gas company executive*
Winzenried, Jesse David *retired petroleum executive*
Witte, Merlin Michael *oil company executive*
Wright, Randolph Earle *retired petroleum company executive*
Yates, Elton G. *retired petroleum industry executive*

# LAW: JUDICIAL ADMINISTRATION

## UNITED STATES

### ALABAMA

**Albertville**
Johnson, Clark Everette, Jr. *judge*

**Anniston**
Harwell, Edwin Whitley *judge*

**Ashland**
Ingram, Kenneth Frank *retired state supreme court justice*

**Birmingham**
Acker, William Marsh, Jr. *federal judge*
Blackburn, Sharon Lovelace *federal judge*
Clemon, U. W. *federal judge*
Goldstein, Debra Holly *judge*
Guin, Junius Foy, Jr. *federal judge*
Lynne, Seybourn Harris *federal judge*
Nelson, Edwin L. *federal judge*
Pointer, Sam Clyde, Jr. *federal judge*
Putnam, Terry Michael *federal judge*
Smith, Edward Samuel *federal judge*

**Florence**
Haltom, Elbert Bertram, Jr. *federal judge*
Tease, James Edward *judge*

**Gadsden**
Sledge, James Scott *judge*

**Mobile**
Butler, Charles Randolph, Jr. *federal judge*
Cox, Emmett Ripley *federal judge*
Hand, William Brevard *federal judge*
Howard, Alex T., Jr. *federal judge*
Kahn, Gordon Barry *retired federal bankruptcy judge*
McCall, Daniel Thompson, Jr. *retired judge*
Milling, Bert William, Jr. *federal judge*
Pittman, Virgil *federal judge*
Thomas, Daniel Holcombe *federal judge*

**Montgomery**
Albritton, William Harold, III *federal judge*
Almon, Reneau Pearson *state supreme court justice*
Black, Robert Coleman *judge, lawyer*
Butts, Terry Lucas *state supreme court justice*
Carnes, Edward E. *federal judge*
De Ment, Ira *judge*
Dubina, Joel Fredrick *federal judge*
Godbold, John Cooper *federal judge*
Hobbs, Truman McGill *federal judge, lawyer*
Houston, James Gorman, Jr. *state supreme court justice*
Johnson, Frank Minis, Jr. *federal judge*
Maddox, Alva Hugh *state supreme court justice*
Maddox, Hugh *state supreme court justice*
McPherson, Vanzetta Penn *federal judge*
Patterson, John Malcolm *judge*
Shores, Janie Ledlow *state supreme court justice*
Steele, Rodney Redfearn *judge*
Thompson, Myron H. *federal judge*
Torbert, Clement Clay, Jr. *state supreme court justice*
Varner, Robert Edward *federal judge*

**Selma**
Jackson, Michael Wayne *judge, lawyer*

### ALASKA

**Anchorage**
Branson, Albert Harold (Harry Branson) *magistrate judge, educator*
Fitzgerald, James Martin *federal judge*
Sedwick, John W. *judge*
Singleton, James Keith *federal judge*
von der Heydt, James Arnold *federal judge, lawyer*

**Fairbanks**
Kleinfeld, Andrew Jay *federal judge*

### ARIZONA

**Bisbee**
Holland, Robert Dale *retired magistrate, consultant*

**Phoenix**
Broomfield, Robert Cameron *federal judge*
Canby, William Cameron, Jr. *federal judge*
Carroll, Earl Hamblin *federal judge*
Copple, William Perry *federal judge*
Feldman, Stanley George *state supreme court justice*
Gerber, Rudolph Joseph *judge, educator*
Hardy, Charles Leach *federal judge*
Kaufman, Roger Wayne *state judge*
Martone, Frederick J. *judge*
McNamee, Stephen M. *federal judge*
Moeller, James *state supreme court justice*
Muecke, Charles Andrew (Carl Muecke) *federal judge*
Myers, Robert David *judge*
Rosenblatt, Paul Gerhardt *federal judge*
Schroeder, Mary Murphy *federal judge*
Strand, Roger Gordon *federal judge*

**Springerville**
Geisler, Sherry Lynn *justice of the peace, city magistrate*

**Tucson**
Bilby, Richard Mansfield *federal judge*
Browning, William Docker *federal judge*
Lacagnina, Michael Anthony *judge*
Livermore, Joseph McMaster *judge*
Marquez, Alfredo C. *federal judge*
Roll, John McCarthy *judge*

### ARKANSAS

**Batesville**
Harkey, John Norman *judge*

**Conway**
Hays, Steele *retired state supreme court judge*

**El Dorado**
Barnes, Harry F. *federal judge*

**Fayetteville**
Waters, H. Franklin *federal judge*

**Fort Smith**
Hendren, Jimm Larry *federal judge*
Jesson, Bradley Dean *state judge*

**Harrison**
Henley, J. Smith *federal judge*

**Little Rock**
Arnold, Morris Sheppard *federal judge*
Arnold, Richard Sheppard *federal judge*
Corbin, Donald L. *judge*
Eisele, Garnett Thomas *federal judge*
Glaze, Thomas A. *state supreme court justice*
Newbern, William David *state supreme court justice*
Reasoner, Stephen M. *federal judge*
Roaf, Andree Layton *judge*
Roy, Elsijane Trimble *federal judge*
Stroud, John Fred, Jr. *state supreme court justice, judge*
Wilson, William R., Jr. *judge*
Woods, Henry *federal judge*
Wright, Susan Webber *judge*

### CALIFORNIA

**Alameda**
Bartalini, C. Richard *judge*

**Berkeley**
Ogg, Wilson Reid *lawyer, poet, retired judge, lyricist, curator, publisher, educator, philospher, social scientist, parapsychologist*

**Beverly Hills**
Jaffe, F. Filmore *judge, retired*

**Downey**
Emerson, (Virgil) Leon *retired judge*
Tucker, Marcus Othello *judge*

**Fresno**
Beck, Dennis L. *magistrate judge*
Coyle, Robert Everett *federal judge*
Crocker, Myron Donovan *federal judge*
Price, Edward Dean *federal judge*
Wanger, Oliver Winston *federal judge*

**Long Beach**
Pokras, Sheila Frances *judge*

**Los Angeles**
Alarcon, Arthur Lawrence *federal judge*
Armstrong, Orville *judge*
Baird, Lourdes G. *federal judge*
Bufford, Samuel Lawrence *federal judge*
Byrne, William Matthew, Jr. *federal judge*
Chavez, Victor Edwin *judge*
Collins, Audrey B. *judge*
Curry, Daniel Arthur *superior court judge*
Davies, John G. *federal judge*
Fenning, Lisa Hill *federal judge*
Gold, Arnold Henry *judge*
Groh, Rupert James, Jr. *judge*
Hauk, A. Andrew *federal judge*
Hill, Irving *judge*
Hupp, Harry L. *federal judge*
Ideman, James M. *federal judge*
Ito, Lance Allan *judge*
Kelleher, Robert Joseph *federal judge*
Keller, William D. *federal judge*
Kenyon, David V. *federal judge*
Klein, Joan Dempsey *judge*
Letts, J. Spencer *federal judge*
Lew, Ronald S. W. *federal judge*
Marshall, Consuelo Bland *federal judge*
Masterson, William A. *judge*
Norris, William Albert *federal judge*
Pfaelzer, Mariana R. *federal judge*
Rafeedie, Edward *federal judge*
Rea, William J. *federal judge*
Real, Manuel Lawrence *federal judge*
Takasugi, Robert Mitsuhiro *federal judge*
Tevrizian, Dickran M., Jr. *federal judge*
Waters, Laughlin Edward *federal judge*
Williams, David Welford *federal judge*
Wilson, Stephen Victor *federal judge*

**Modesto**
Mayhew, William A. *judge*

**Newport Beach**
Curtis, Jesse William, Jr. *retired federal judge*
Kaufman, Marcus Maurice *retired judge, lawyer*

**Oakland**
Armstrong, Saundra Brown *federal judge*
Champlin, Malcolm McGregor *retired municipal judge*
Cline, Wilson Ettason *retired administrative law judge*
Jensen, D. Lowell *federal judge, lawyer, government official*
Newsome, Randall Jackson *judge*
Wilken, Claudia *judge*

**Pasadena**
Boochever, Robert *federal judge*
Fernandez, Ferdinand Francis *federal judge*
Goodwin, Alfred Theodore *federal judge*
Hall, Cynthia Holcomb *federal judge*
Kozinski, Alex *federal judge*
Nelson, Dorothy Wright (Mrs. James F. Nelson) *federal judge*
Rymer, Pamela Ann *federal judge*
Tashima, Atsushi Wallace *federal judge*

**Ramona**
Jordan, David Francis, Jr. *retired judge*

**Redwood City**
Harrington, Walter Howard, Jr. *judge*

**Richmond**
Herron, Ellen Patricia *retired judge*

**Sacramento**
Burrell, Garland E., Jr. *federal judge*
Dahl, Loren Silvester *retired federal judge*
Garcia, Edward J. *federal judge*
Karlton, Lawrence K. *federal judge*
Levi, David F. *federal judge*
MacBride, Thomas Jamison *federal judge*
Moulds, John F. *federal judge*
Russell, David E. *judge*
Schwartz, Milton Lewis *federal judge*
Shubb, William Barnet *federal judge*
Wilkins, Philip Charles *judge*

**San Diego**
Aaron, Cynthia G. *judge*
Brewster, Rudi Milton *federal judge*
Enright, William Benner *judge*
Gilliam, Earl B. *federal judge*
Gonzalez, Irma Elsa *federal judge*
Huff, Marilyn L. *federal judge*
Keep, Judith N. *federal judge*
Lewis, Gerald Jorgensen *judge*
McKee, Roger Curtis *federal magistrate judge*
Meyers, James William *federal judge*
Nielsen, Leland C. *federal judge*
Rhoades, John Skylstead, Sr. *federal judge*
Schwartz, Edward J. *federal judge*
Thompson, David Renwick *federal judge*
Thompson, Gordon, Jr. *federal judge*
Turrentine, Howard Boyd *federal judge*
Wallace, J. Clifford *federal judge*

**San Francisco**
Anderson, Carl West *judge*
Baxter, Marvin Ray *state supreme court judge*
Browning, James Robert *federal judge*
Conti, Samuel *federal judge*
Dail, Joseph Garner, Jr. *judge*
George, Ronald M. *judge*
Haerle, Paul Raymond *judge*
Henderson, Thelton Eugene *federal judge*
Jarvis, Donald Bertram *judge*
Kennard, Joyce L. *judge*
Legge, Charles Alexander *federal judge*
Lynch, Eugene F. *federal judge*
Mosk, Stanley *state supreme court justice*
Noonan, John T., Jr. *federal judge, legal educator*
Orrick, William Horsley, Jr. *federal judge*
Patel, Marilyn Hall *federal judge*
Poole, Cecil F. *circuit court judge*
Ramsey, Robert Lee *judge, lawyer*
Robertson, Armand James, II *judge*
Schwarzer, William W *federal judge*
Sneed, Joseph Tyree, III *federal judge*
Walker, Vaughn R. *federal judge*
Weigel, Stanley Alexander *judge*
Werdegar, Kathryn Mickle *judge*
Zimmerman, Bernard *judge*

**San Jose**
Ingram, William Austin *federal judge*
Morgan, Marilyn *federal judge*
†Panelli, Edward Alexander *retired state supreme court justice*
Stacy, Richard A. *administrative law judge*
Ware, James W. *federal judge*
Whyte, Ronald M. *federal judge*
Williams, Spencer Mortimer *federal judge*

**San Marino**
Mortimer, Wendell Reed, Jr. *superior court judge*

**Santa Ana**
Barr, James Norman *federal judge*
Ferguson, Warren John *federal judge*
McLaughlin, Linda Lee Hodge *federal judge*
Ryan, John Edward *federal judge*
Stotler, Alicemarie Huber *judge*
Taylor, Gary L. *federal judge*

**Santa Barbara**
Aldisert, Ruggero John *federal judge*

**Santa Monica**
Vega, Benjamin Urbizo *retired judge*

**Solana Beach**
Watson, Jack Crozier *retired state supreme court justice*

**South Pasadena**
Saeta, Philip Max *judge*

**Studio City**
Lasarow, William Julius *retired federal judge*

**Van Nuys**
Schwab, Howard Joel *judge*

**Woodland Hills**
Mund, Geraldine *bankruptcy judge*
Pregerson, Harry *federal judge*

## COLORADO

**Denver**
Abram, Donald Eugene *federal magistrate judge*
Babcock, Lewis Thornton *federal judge*
Ebel, David M. *federal judge*
Kane, John Lawrence, Jr. *federal judge*
Kirshbaum, Howard M. *arbiter, judge*
Kourlis, Rebecca Love *judge*
Lucero, Carlos *federal judge*
Matsch, Richard P. *judge*
McWilliams, Robert Hugh *federal judge*
Mullarkey, Mary J. *state supreme court justice*
Nottingham, Edward Willis, Jr. *federal judge*
Porfilio, John Carbone *federal judge*
Rovira, Luis Dario *state supreme court justice*
Sparr, Daniel Beattie *federal judge*
Weinshienk, Zita Leeson *federal judge*

**Englewood**
Erickson, William Hurt *retired state supreme court justice*

**Golden**
Rodgers, Frederic Barker *judge*

## CONNECTICUT

**Bridgeport**
Eginton, Warren William *federal judge*
Shiff, Alan Howard William *federal judge*

**Danbury**
Yamin, Dianne Elizabeth *judge*

**Fairfield**
Lumbard, Joseph Edward, Jr. *federal judge*

**Hartford**
Berdon, Robert Irwin *state supreme court justice*
Bieluch, William Charles *judge*
Borden, David M. *judge*
Callahan, Robert Jeremiah *state supreme court chief justice*
Covello, Alfred Vincent *federal judge*
Heiman, Maxwell *judge, lawyer*
Killian, Robert Kenneth, Jr. *judge, lawyer*
Newman, Jon O. *federal judge*
Palmer, Richard N. *judge*
Peters, Ellen Ash *state supreme court senior justice*
Shea, David Michael *state supreme court justice*
Wright, Douglass Brownell *judge, lawyer*

**Litchfield**
Sheldon, Michael Richard *judge, law educator*

**Madison**
Ross, Michael Frederick *magistrate, lawyer*

**New Britain**
Meskill, Thomas J. *federal judge*

**New Haven**
Burns, Ellen Bree *federal judge*
Cabranes, José Alberto *federal judge*
Calabresi, Guido *federal judge, law educator*
Dorsey, Peter Collins *federal judge*
Winter, Ralph Karl, Jr. *federal judge*

**New London**
Santaniello, Angelo Gary *retired state supreme court justice*

**Waterbury**
Glass, Robert Davis *judge*
Goettel, Gerard Louis *federal judge*

## DELAWARE

**Wilmington**
Balick, Helen Shaffer *judge*
Del Pesco, Susan Marie Carr *state judge*
Farnan, Joseph James, Jr. *federal judge*
Gebelein, Richard Stephen *judge, former state attorney general*
Latchum, James Levin *federal judge*
Longobardi, Joseph J. *federal judge*
McKelvie, Roderick R. *federal judge*
Robinson, Sue L(ewis) *federal judge*
Roth, Jane Richards *federal judge*
Schwartz, Murray Merle *federal judge*
Seitz, Collins Jacques *federal judge*
Stapleton, Walter King *federal judge*
Veasey, Eugene Norman *chief justice*
Walsh, Joseph Thomas *state supreme court justice*
Wright, Caleb Merrill *federal judge*

## DISTRICT OF COLUMBIA

**Washington**
Andewelt, Roger B. *federal judge*
Archer, Glenn LeRoy, Jr. *federal circuit judge*
Bacon, Sylvia *retired judge*
Bartnoff, Judith *judge*
Bayly, John Henry, Jr. *judge*
Beddow, Richard Harold *judge*
Beghe, Renato *federal judge*
Belson, James Anthony *judge*
Bennett, Marion Tinsley *federal circuit judge*
Bernstein, Edwin S. *judge*
Blair, Warren Emerson *federal judge*
Brennan, William Joseph, Jr. *retired United States supreme court justice*
Breyer, Stephen Gerald *United States supreme court justice*
Bruggink, Eric G. *federal judge*
Bryant, William B. *federal judge*
Bryson, William Curtis *federal judge*
Buckley, James Lane *federal judge*
Burg, Ruth Cooper (Thelma Breslauer) *administrative judge*
Burnett, Arthur Louis, Sr. *judge*
Chabot, Herbert L. *judge*
Chiechi, Carolyn Phyllis *federal judge*
Clapp, Charles E., II *federal judge*
Clevenger, Raymond C., III *federal judge*
Cohen, Mary Ann *judge*
Colvin, John O. *federal judge*
Conaboy, Richard Paul *federal judge*
Cooper, Jean Saralee *judge*
Cotter, B. Paul, Jr. *judge*
Couvillion, David Irvin *federal judge*
Cowen, Wilson *federal judge*
Cox, Walter Thompson, III *federal judge*
Crawford, Susan Jean *federal judge, lawyer*
Dawson, Howard Athalone, Jr. *federal judge*
Edwards, Harry T. *chief federal judge*
Everett, Robinson Oscar *federal judge, law educator*
Farley, John Joseph, III *federal judge*
Fay, William Michael *federal judge*
Ferren, John Maxwell *federal judge*
Friedman, Daniel Mortimer *federal judge*
Futey, Bohdan A. *federal judge*
Gale, Joseph H. *federal judge*
Garland, Merrick Brian *judge*
Gerber, Joel *federal judge*
Gibson, Reginald Walker *federal judge*
Gierke, Herman Fredrick, III *federal judge*
Ginsburg, Douglas Howard *federal judge, educator*
Ginsburg, Ruth Bader *United States supreme court justice*
Goldberg, Stanley Joshua *federal judge*
Goodrich, George Herbert *judge*
Green, Joyce Hens *federal judge*
Green, June Lazenby *federal judge*
Greene, Harold H. *federal judge*
Halpern, James S. *federal judge*
Hamblen, Lapsley Walker, Jr. *judge*
Harkins, Kenneth R. *federal judge*
Harris, Stanley S. *judge*
Heifetz, Alan William *federal judge*
Henderson, Karen LeCraft *federal judge*
Hodges, Robert H., Jr. *federal judge*
Holdaway, Ronald M. *federal judge*
Horn, Marian Blank *federal judge*
Ivers, Donald Louis *judge*
Jackson, Thomas Penfield *federal judge*
Jacobs, Julian I. *federal judge*
Johnson, Norma Holloway *federal judge*
Kennedy, Anthony McLeod *United States supreme court justice*
Kern, John Worth, III *judge*
Kessler, Gladys *federal judge*
Kline, Norman Douglas *federal judge*
Korner, Jules Gilmer, III *judge*
Kramer, Kenneth Bentley *federal judge, former congressman*
Lamberth, Royce C. *federal judge*
Laro, David *judge*
Lourie, Alan David *federal judge*
Lydon, Thomas J. *federal judge*
Mack, Julia Cooper *judge*
Margolis, Lawrence Stanley *federal judge*
Mayer, Haldane Robert *federal judge*
Mencher, Bruce Stephan *judge*
Merow, James F. *federal judge*
Michel, Paul Redmond *federal judge*
Miller, Christine Odell Cook *judge*
Nangle, John Francis *federal judge*
Nebeker, Frank Quill *federal judge*
Newman, Pauline *federal judge*
Nims, Arthur Lee, III *federal judge*
Oberdorfer, Louis F. *federal judge*
O'Connor, Sandra Day *United States supreme court justice*
Parr, Carolyn Miller *federal court judge*
Penn, John Garrett *federal judge*
Plager, S. Jay *federal judge*
Powell, Lewis Franklin, Jr. *retired United States supreme court justice*
Queen, Evelyn E. Crawford *judge, law educator*
Rader, Randall Ray *federal judge*
Randolph, Arthur Raymond *federal judge, lawyer*
Raum, Arnold *federal judge*
Rehnquist, William Hubbs *United States supreme court chief justice*
Rich, Giles Sutherland *federal judge*
Robertson, James *judge*
Robinson, Wilkes Coleman *federal judge*
Rogers, Judith W. *federal circuit judge*
Ruiz, Vanessa *judge*
Ruwe, Robert P. *federal judge*
Scalia, Antonin *United States supreme court justice*
Schall, Alvin Anthony *federal judge*
Schwelb, Frank Ernest *federal judge*
Scott, Irene Feagin *federal judge*
Sentelle, David Bryan *federal judge*
Simpson, Charles Reagan *retired judge*
Smith, Roy Philip *judge*
Sporkin, Stanley *federal judge*
Steadman, John Montague *judge*
Steinberg, Jonathan Robert *judge*
Stevens, John Paul *United States supreme court justice*
Sullivan, Emmet G. *judge*
Sullivan, Eugene Raymond *federal judge*
Swift, Stephen Jensen *federal judge*
Tannenwald, Theodore, Jr. *federal judge*
Tansill, Frederick Riker *retired judge*
Tatel, David Stephen *federal judge*
Terry, John Alfred *judge*
Thomas, Clarence *United States supreme court justice*
Tidwell, Moody Rudolph *federal judge*
Turner, James Thomas *judge*
Wagner, Curtis Lee, Jr. *judge*
Wald, Patricia McGowan *federal judge*
Weinstein, Diane Gilbert *federal judge, lawyer*
Wells, Thomas B. *federal judge*
Whalen, Laurence J. *federal judge*
White, Byron R. *former United States supreme court justice*
Wiese, John Paul *federal judge*
Williams, Stephen Fain *federal judge*
Wright, Lawrence A. *federal judge*
Yock, Robert John *federal judge*
Yoder, Ronnie A. *judge*
Zobel, Rya Weickert *federal judge*

## FLORIDA

**Coral Gables**
Davis, Mattie Belle Edwards *retired county judge*

**Delray Beach**
Cohen, Stephen M(artin) *judge*

**Fort Lauderdale**
Ferguson, Wilkie D., Jr. *federal judge*
Gonzalez, Jose Alejandro, Jr. *federal judge*
Zloch, William J. *federal judge*

**Fort Myers**
Shafer, Robert Tinsley, Jr. *judge*

**Gainesville**
Coleman, Mary Stallings *retired chief justice*
Paul, Maurice M. *federal judge*

**Jacksonville**
Black, Susan Harrell *federal judge*
Hill, James Clinkscales *federal judge*
Hodges, William Terrell *federal judge*
Melton, Howell Webster, Sr. *federal judge*
Schlesinger, Harvey Erwin *judge*
Tjoflat, Gerald Bard *federal judge*

**Key Biscayne**
Kraft, C. William, Jr. *federal judge*

**Lakeland**
Schoonover, Jack Ronald *judge*

**Miami**
Atkins, C(arl) Clyde *federal judge*
Barkett, Rosemary *federal judge*
Brown, Stephen Thomas *magistrate judge*
Cristol, A. Jay *federal judge*
Davis, Edward Bertrand *federal judge*
Dyer, David William *federal judge*
Fay, Peter Thorp *federal judge*
Fletcher, John Greenwood II *state judge*
Garber, Barry L. *judge*
Gold, Alan Stephen *judge, lawyer, educator*
Graham, Donald Lynn *federal judge*
Highsmith, Shelby *federal judge*
Hoeveler, William M. *federal judge*
Kehoe, James W. *federal judge*
King, James Lawrence *federal judge*
Marcus, Stanley *federal judge*
Moore, Kevin Michael *federal judge*
Moreno, Federico Antonio *federal judge*
Nesbitt, Lenore Carrero *federal judge*
Shevin, Robert Lewis *judge*
Ungaro-Benages, Ursula Mancusi *federal judge*

**Orlando**
Baker, David A. *federal judge*
Conway, Anne Callaghan *federal judge*
Fawsett, Patricia Combs *federal judge*
Sharp, George Kendall *federal judge*
Young, George Cressler *federal judge*

**Panama City**
Smith, Larry Glenn *retired state judge*

**Pensacola**
Collier, Lacey Alexander *federal judge*
Vinson, C. Roger *federal judge*

**Saint Petersburg**
Grube, Karl Bertram *judge*
Roney, Paul H(itch) *federal judge*

**Tallahassee**
Grimes, Stephen Henry *state supreme court justice*
Harding, Major Best *state supreme court justice*
Hatchett, Joseph Woodrow *federal judge*
Mc Cord, Guyte Pierce, Jr. *retired judge*
Overton, Benjamin Frederick *state supreme court justice*
Shaw, Leander Jerry, Jr. *state supreme court justice*
Stafford, William Henry, Jr. *federal judge*
Sundberg, Alan Carl *former state supreme court justice, lawyer*
Wells, Charles Talley *judge*

**Tampa**
Baynes, Thomas Edward, Jr. *judge, lawyer, educator*
Bucklew, Susan Cawthon *federal judge*
Corcoran, C. Timothy, III *judge*
Menendez, Manuel, Jr. *judge*
Merryday, Steven D. *federal judge*
Nimmons, Ralph Wilson, Jr. *federal judge*

**West Palm Beach**
Eschbach, Jesse Ernest *federal judge*
Hurley, Daniel T. K. *federal judge*
Paine, James Carriger *federal judge*
Ryskamp, Kenneth Lee *federal judge*

## GEORGIA

**Albany**
Sands, W. Louis *federal judge*

**Athens**
Brackett, Colquitt Prater, Jr. *judge*

**Atlanta**
Alexander, William Henry *senior judge*
Andrews, Gary Blaylock *state judge, lawyer*
Benham, Robert *state supreme court justice*
Birch, Stanley Francis, Jr. *federal judge*
Camp, Jack Tarpley, Jr. *federal judge*
Carley, George H. *judge*
Carnes, Julie E. *federal judge*
Clark, Thomas Alonzo *federal judge*
Dougherty, John Ernest *judge*
Edmondson, James Larry *federal judge*
Evans, Orinda D. *federal judge*
Feldman, Joel Martin *magistrate judge*
Fletcher, Norman S. *state supreme court justice*
Forrester, J. Owen *federal judge*
Freeman, Richard Cameron *federal judge*
Henderson, Albert John *federal judge*
Hull, Frank Mays *federal judge*
Hunt, Willis B., Jr. *federal judge*
Kravitch, Phyllis A. *federal judge*
Moye, Charles Allen, Jr. *federal judge*
Murphy, Margaret Hackett *federal bankruptcy judge*
Nichols, Horace Elmo *state justice*
O'Kelley, William Clark *federal judge*
Shoob, Marvin H. *federal judge*
Thompson, Hugh P *justice*
Tidwell, George Ernest *federal judge*
Vining, Robert Luke, Jr. *federal judge*
Ward, Horace Taliaferro *federal judge*

**Augusta**
Bowen, Dudley Hollingsworth, Jr. *federal judge*

**Brunswick**
Alaimo, Anthony A. *federal judge*

**Columbus**
Elliott, James Robert *federal judge*
Laney, John Thomas, III *federal judge*

**Decatur**
Shulman, Arnold *judge, lawyer*

**La Grange**
Morgan, Lewis Render *retired federal judge*

**Macon**
Anderson, Robert Lanier, III *federal judge*
Fitzpatrick, Duross *federal judge*
Gerson, Robert Walthall *judge, retired lawyer*
Hershner, Robert Franklin, Jr. *judge*

Owens, Wilbur Dawson, Jr. *federal judge*
Phillips, J(ohn) Taylor *judge*

### Marietta
Smith, George Thornewell *retired state supreme court justice*

### Rome
Murphy, Harold Loyd *federal judge*

### Savannah
Edenfield, Berry Avant *federal judge*
Moore, William Theodore, Jr. *judge*

## HAWAII

### Honolulu
Ashford, Clinton Rutledge *judge*
Choy, Herbert Young Cho *judge*
Ezra, David A. *federal judge*
Gillmor, Helen *federal judge*
Kay, Alan Cooke *federal judge*
King, Samuel Pailthorpe *federal judge*
Klein, Robert Gordon *judge*
Levinson, Steven Henry *judge*
Moon, Ronald T. Y. *state supreme court chief justice*
Nakayama, Paula Aiko *justice*
Pence, Martin *federal judge*

## IDAHO

### Boise
Boyle, Larry Monroe *federal judge*
Hagan, Alfred Chris *federal judge*
Johnson, Byron Jerald *state supreme court judge*
Lodge, Edward James *federal judge*
McDevitt, Charles Francis *state supreme court justice*
Mc Quade, Henry Ford *state justice*
Nelson, Thomas G. *federal judge*
Silak, Cathy R. *judge*
Trott, Stephen Spangler *federal judge, musician*

## ILLINOIS

### Barrington
Wynn, Thomas Joseph *judge, educator*

### Belleville
Ferguson, John Marshall *retired federal magistrate judge*
Stevens, C. Glenn *judge*

### Benton
Foreman, James Louis *retired judge*
Gilbert, J. Phil *federal judge*

### Chicago
Alesia, James H(enry) *judge*
Andersen, Wayne R. *federal judge*
Aspen, Marvin Edward *federal judge*
Bauer, William Joseph *federal judge*
Bilandic, Michael A. *state supreme court justice, former mayor*
Bowman, George Arthur, Jr. *judge*
Bua, Nicholas John *retired federal judge*
Bucklo, Elaine Edwards *federal judge*
Coar, David H. *federal judge*
Conlon, Suzanne B. *federal judge*
Cudahy, Richard D. *federal judge*
Cummings, Walter J. *federal judge*
Duff, Brian Barnett *federal judge*
Easterbrook, Frank Hoover *federal judge*
Fairchild, Thomas E. *federal judge*
Flaum, Joel Martin *federal judge*
Freeman, Charles E. *state supreme court chief justice*
Gettleman, Robert William *judge*
Hart, William Thomas *federal judge*
Holderman, James F., Jr. *federal judge*
Johnson, Glenn Thompson *judge*
Kanne, Michael Stephen *federal judge*
Lassers, Willard J. *judge*
Leighton, George Neves *retired federal judge*
Leinenweber, Harry D. *federal judge*
Lindberg, George W. *federal judge*
Manning, Blanche M. *federal judge*
Marovich, George M. *federal judge*
Marovitz, Abraham Lincoln *judge*
McGarr, Frank James *retired federal judge, dispute resolution consultant*
McMorrow, Mary Ann G. *judge*
Moran, James Byron *federal judge*
Nordberg, John Albert *senior federal judge*
Norgle, Charles Ronald, Sr. *federal judge*
†Palewicz, Richard Alfred *judge*
Pallmeyer, Rebecca Ruth *federal judge*
Pascale, Daniel Richard *circuit judge*
Pell, Wilbur Frank, Jr. *federal judge*
Plunkett, Paul Edward *federal judge*
Posner, Richard Allen *federal judge*
Rovner, Ilana Kara Diamond *federal judge*
Schmetterer, Jack Baer *federal judge*
Sonderby, Susan Pierson *federal bankruptcy judge*
Squires, John Henry *judge*
Williams, Ann Claire *federal judge*
Zagel, James Block *federal judge*

### East Saint Louis
Beatty, William Louis *federal judge*
Stiehl, William D. *federal judge*

### Elgin
Kirkland, Alfred Younges, Sr. *federal judge*

### Hennepin
Bumgarner, James McNabb *judge*

### Homewood
Dietch, Henry Xerxes *judge*

### Pekin
Heiple, James Dee *state supreme court chief justice*

### Peoria
McDade, Joe Billy *federal judge*
Mihm, Michael Martin *federal judge*

### Pontiac
Glennon, Charles Edward *judge, lawyer*

### Rock Island
Telleen, John Martin *retired judge*

### Rockford
Reinhard, Philip G. *federal judge*

### Springfield
Lessen, Larry Lee *federal judge*
Miller, Benjamin K. *state supreme court justice*
Mills, Richard Henry *federal judge*
Wood, Harlington, Jr. *federal judge*

### Tonica
Ryan, Howard Chris *retired state supreme court justice*

### Urbana
Baker, Harold Albert *federal judge*

### Waukegan
Brady, Terrence Joseph *judge*

### Wheaton
Leston, Patrick John *judge*

## INDIANA

### Evansville
Brooks, Gene Edward *federal judge*
Capshaw, Tommie Dean *judge*

### Fort Wayne
Lee, William Charles *judge*

### Hammond
Lozano, Rudolpho *federal judge*
Moody, James T(yne) *federal judge*
Rodovich, Andrew Paul *lawyer, federal magistrate*

### Indianapolis
Barker, Sarah Evans *judge*
Dickson, Brent E. *state supreme court justice*
Dillin, S. Hugh *federal judge*
Givan, Richard Martin *state supreme court justice, retired*
Godich, John Paul *federal magistrate judge*
McKinney, Larry J. *federal judge*
Shepard, Randall Terry *judge*
Sullivan, Frank, Jr. *state supreme court justice*

### Jeffersonville
Barthold, Clementine B. *retired judge*

### Lagrange
Brown, George E. *judge, educator*

### South Bend
Grant, Robert Allen *federal judge*
Manion, Daniel Anthony *federal judge*
Miller, Robert L., Jr. *federal judge*
Ripple, Kenneth Francis *federal judge*
Rodibaugh, Robert Kurtz *judge*
Sharp, Allen *chief federal judge*

## IOWA

### Cedar Rapids
Hansen, David Rasmussen *federal judge*
Mc Manus, Edward Joseph *federal judge*
Melloy, Michael J. *federal judge*

### Chariton
Stuart, William Corwin *federal judge*

### Council Bluffs
Peterson, Richard William *magistrate judge, lawyer*

### Des Moines
Andreasen, James Hallis *state supreme court judge*
Bremer, Celeste F. *judge*
Fagg, George Gardner *federal judge*
Harris, K. David *justice*
Larson, Jerry L. *state supreme court justice*
Lavorato, Louis A. *state supreme court justice*
Longstaff, Ronald E. *federal judge*
McGiverin, Arthur A. *state supreme court justice*
Snell, Bruce M., Jr. *state supreme court justice*
Vietor, Harold Duane *federal judge*
Wolle, Charles Robert *federal judge*

### Iowa City
Schultz, Louis William *judge*

### Osceola
Reynoldson, Walter Ward *state supreme court chief justice*

### Sioux City
Deck, Paul Wayne, Jr. *federal judge*
O'Brien, Donald Eugene *federal judge*

## KANSAS

### Kansas City
Lungstrum, John W. *federal judge*
O'Connor, Earl Eugene *federal judge*
Rushfelt, Gerald Lloyd *magistrate judge*
Van Bebber, George Thomas *federal judge*
Vratil, Kathryn Hoefer *federal judge*

### Lawrence
Tacha, Deanell Reece *federal judge*

### Leavenworth
Stanley, Arthur Jehu, Jr. *federal judge*

### Olathe
Chipman, Marion Walter *judge*

### Topeka
Abbott, Bob *justice*
Allegrucci, Donald Lee *state supreme court justice*
Briscoe, Mary Beck *federal judge*
Crow, Sam Alfred *federal judge*
Davis, Robert Edward *judge*
Herd, Harold Shields *state supreme court justice*
Holmes, Richard Winn *retired state supreme court justice, lawyer*
Lockett, Tyler Charles *state supreme court justice*
McFarland, Kay Eleanor *state supreme court chief justice*
Miller, Robert Haskins *retired state chief justice*
Pusateri, James Anthony *judge*
Rogers, Richard Dean *federal judge*
Saffels, Dale Emerson *federal judge*
Six, Fred N. *state supreme court justice*

### Wichita
Bell, Charles Robert, Jr. *judge*
Brown, Wesley Ernest *federal judge*
Pearson, John King *judge*
Theis, Frank Gordon *federal judge*

## KENTUCKY

### Ashland
Wilhoit, Henry Rupert, Jr. *federal judge*

### Bowling Green
Huddleston, Joseph Russell *judge*

### Danville
Lively, Pierce *federal judge*

### Fort Thomas
Pendery, Edward Stuart *deputy county judge*

### Frankfort
Hood, Joseph M. *federal judge*
Stephens, Robert F. *state supreme court chief justice*
Stumbo, Janet L. *justice*
Wintersheimer, Donald Carl *state supreme court justice*

### Lexington
Forester, Karl S. *federal judge*
Lee, Joe *federal judge*
Varellas, Sandra Motte *judge*

### London
Coffman, Jennifer B. *federal judge*
Siler, Eugene Edward, Jr. *federal judge*
Unthank, G. Wix *federal judge*

### Louisville
Allen, Charles Mengel *federal judge*
Boggs, Danny Julian *federal judge*
Heyburn, John Gilpin, II *federal judge*
Martin, Boyce Ficklen, Jr. *federal judge*
Roberts, J. Wendell *federal judge*

### Paducah
Johnstone, Edward Huggins *federal judge*

## LOUISIANA

### Baton Rouge
Cole, Luther Francis *former state supreme court associate justice*
Kelley, Timothy Edward *state judge*
Noland, Christine A. *magistrate judge*
Parker, John Victor *federal judge*
Polozola, Frank Joseph *federal judge*

### Crowley
Brunson, Hugh Ellis *judge*
Harrington, Thomas Barrett *judge*

### Denham Springs
Kuhn, James E. *judge*

### Gretna
McManus, Clarence Elburn *judge*
Wicker, Thomas Carey, Jr. *judge*

### Lafayette
Davis, William Eugene *federal judge*
Doherty, Rebecca Feeney *federal judge*
Duhe, John Malcolm, Jr. *federal judge*
Haik, Richard T., Sr. *federal judge*
Melançon, Tucker Lee *judge*
Putnam, Richard Johnson *federal judge*

### Lake Charles
Hunter, Edwin Ford, Jr. *federal judge*
McLeod, William Lasater, Jr. *retired judge, former state legislator*
Trimble, James T., Jr. *federal judge*

### Metairie
Thomas, Everette Earl *federal judge*

### New Orleans
Beer, Peter Hill *federal judge*
Berrigan, Helen Ginger *federal judge*
Calogero, Pascal Frank, Jr. *state supreme court chief justice*
Carr, Patrick E. *judge*
Clement, Edith Brown *federal judge*
Duplantier, Adrian Guy *federal judge*
Feldman, Martin L. C. *federal judge*
Livaudais, Marcel, Jr. *federal judge*
McNamara, A. J. *federal judge*
Mentz, Henry Alvan, Jr. *federal judge*
Mitchell, Lansing Leroy *federal judge*
Schwartz, Charles, Jr. *federal judge*
Sear, Morey Leonard *federal judge, educator*
Vance, Sarah S. *federal judge*
Wisdom, John Minor *federal judge*

### Shreveport
Payne, Roy Steven *judge*
Politz, Henry Anthony *federal judge*
Stagg, Tom *federal judge*
Stewart, Carl E. *federal judge*
Walter, Donald Ellsworth *federal judge*

Wiener, Jacques Loeb, Jr. *federal circuit judge*

## MAINE

### Auburn
Clifford, Robert William *judge*

### Bangor
Brody, Morton Aaron *federal judge*

### Portland
Bradford, Carl O. *judge*
Carter, Gene *federal judge*
Coffin, Frank Morey *federal judge*
Glassman, Caroline Duby *state supreme court justice*
Goodman, James A. *federal judge*
Hornby, David Brock *federal judge*
McKusick, Vincent Lee *former state supreme judicial court chief justice, lawyer*
Roberts, David Glendenning *state supreme court justice*

### Rockland
Collins, Samuel W., Jr. *judge*

## MARYLAND

### Annapolis
Eldridge, John Cole *judge*
Karwacki, Robert Lee *judge*

### Baltimore
Bell, Robert M. *judge*
Black, Walter Evan, Jr. *federal judge*
Blake, Catherine C. *judge*
Derby, Ernest Stephen *federal judge*
Garbis, Marvin Joseph *federal judge*
Gauvey, Susan K. *judge*
Goetz, Clarence Edward *magistrate, judge, retired*
Hargrove, John R. *federal judge*
Harvey, Alexander, II *federal judge*
Kaufman, Frank Albert *federal judge*
Legg, Benson Everett *federal judge*
Levin, Marshall Abbott *judge, educator*
Maletz, Herbert Naaman *federal judge*
Motz, Diana Gribbon *federal judge*
Motz, John Frederick *federal judge*
Murnaghan, Francis Dominic, Jr. *federal judge*
Nickerson, William Milnor *federal judge*
Niemeyer, Paul Victor *federal judge*
Northrop, Edward Skottowe *federal judge*
Rodowsky, Lawrence Francis *state judge*
Schneider, James Frederick *federal judge*
Smalkin, Frederic N. *federal judge*
Young, Joseph H. *federal judge*

### Greenbelt
Chasanow, Deborah K. *federal judge*
Mannes, Paul *judge*
Messitte, Peter Jo *judge*

### Rockville
McAuliffe, John F. *retired judge*
Megan, Thomas Ignatius *retired judge*

### Towson
Eyler, James R. *judge*

### Upper Marlboro
Chasanow, Howard Stuart *judge, lecturer*

## MASSACHUSETTS

### Boston
Aldrich, Bailey *federal judge*
Allard, David Henry *judge*
Boudin, Michael *federal judge*
Bowler, Marianne Bianca *judge*
Bownes, Hugh Henry *federal judge*
Campbell, Levin Hicks *federal judge*
Collings, Robert Biddlecombe *judge*
Connolly, Thomas Edward *judge*
Dacey, Kathleen Ryan *judge*
Dreben, Raya Spiegel *judge*
Fried, Charles *judge, educator*
Gertner, Nancy *federal judge, legal educator*
Harrington, Edward F. *federal judge*
Hillman, William Chernick *federal bankruptcy judge*
Keeton, Robert Ernest *federal judge*
Lasker, Morris E. *judge*
Lynch, Sandra Lea *federal judge*
Mazzone, A. David *federal judge*
O'Connor, Francis Patrick *state supreme court justice*
Saris, Patti B. *federal judge*
Skinner, Walter Jay *federal judge*
Stearns, Richard Gaylore *judge*
Tauro, Joseph Louis *federal judge*
Wilkins, Herbert Putnam *judge*
Wolf, Mark Lawrence *federal judge*
Woodlock, Douglas Preston *judge*
Young, William Glover *federal judge*
Zobel, Hiller Bellin *judge*

### Cambridge
Kaplan, Benjamin *judge*

### Hingham
Ford, Joseph *retired superior court judge*

### Longmeadow
Keady, George Cregan, Jr. *judge*

### Springfield
Freedman, Frank Harlan *federal judge*
Ponsor, Michael Adrian *federal judge*

### Worcester
Gorton, Nathaniel M. *federal judge, lawyer*

## MICHIGAN

### Ada
Engel, Albert Joseph *federal judge*

**Ann Arbor**
Guy, Ralph B., Jr. *federal judge*
Hackett, Barbara (Kloka) *federal judge*
Joiner, Charles Wycliffe *judge*
Pepe, Steven Douglas *federal magistrate judge*

**Bay City**
Spector, Arthur Jay *federal judge*

**Birmingham**
La Plata, George *federal judge*

**Bloomfield Hills**
Kaufman, Ira Gladstone *judge*

**Detroit**
Duggan, Patrick James *federal judge*
Edmunds, Nancy Garlock *federal judge*
Feikens, John *federal judge*
Friedman, Bernard Alvin *federal judge*
Gilmore, Horace Weldon *federal judge*
Graves, Ray Reynolds *judge*
Hood, Denise Page *federal judge*
Keith, Damon Jerome *federal judge*
Kennedy, Cornelia Groefsema *federal judge*
Levin, Charles Leonard *state supreme court justice*
Lombard, Arthur J. *judge*
Mallett, Conrad LeRoy, Jr. *state chief supreme court justice*
Morgan, Virginia *magistrate judge*
O'Meara, John Corbett *federal judge*
Riley, Dorothy Comstock *judge*
Rosen, Gerald Ellis *federal judge*
Ryan, James Leo *federal judge*
Sullivan, Joseph B. *retired judge*
Taylor, Anna Diggs *federal judge*
Woods, George Edward *judge*
Zatkoff, Lawrence P. *federal judge*

**Flint**
Newblatt, Stewart Albert *federal judge*

**Grand Rapids**
Bell, Robert Holmes *federal judge*
Brenneman, Hugh Warren, Jr. *judge*
Gibson, Benjamin F. *federal judge*
Hillman, Douglas Woodruff *federal judge*
Miles, Wendell A. *federal judge*
Quist, Gordon Jay *federal judge*

**Kalamazoo**
Enslen, Richard Alan *federal judge*
Rowland, Doyle Alfred *federal judge*

**Kentwood**
Kelly, William Garrett *judge*

**Lansing**
Boyle, Patricia Jean *judge*
Cavanagh, Michael Francis *state supreme court justice*
Harrison, Michael Gregory *judge*
McKeague, David William *district judge*
Suhrheinrich, Richard Fred *federal judge*
Weaver, Elizabeth A *judge*

**Pontiac**
Grant, Barry M(arvin) *judge*

**Port Huron**
DeMascio, Robert Edward *federal judge*

**Saint Clair Shores**
Stanczyk, Benjamin Conrad *judge*

**Southfield**
Doctoroff, Martin Myles *judge*

**Traverse City**
Brickley, James H. *state supreme court justice*

## MINNESOTA

**Duluth**
Heaney, Gerald William *federal judge*

**Minneapolis**
Amdahl, Douglas Kenneth *retired state supreme court justice*
Arthur, Lindsay Grier *retired judge, author, editor*
Doty, David Singleton *federal judge*
Kressel, Robert J. *federal judge*
Larson, Earl Richard *federal judge*
Lebedoff, Jonathan Galanter *federal judge*
MacLaughlin, Harry Hunter *federal judge*
Murphy, Diana E. *federal judge*
Noel, Franklin Linwood *federal chief magistrate judge*
Rosenbaum, James Michael *judge*
Simonett, John E. *state supreme court justice*

**Minnetonka**
Rogers, James Devitt *judge*

**Saint Paul**
Alsop, Donald Douglas *federal judge*
Anderson, Paul Holden *justice*
Gardebring, Sandra S. *judge*
Keith, Alexander Macdonald *state supreme court chief justice*
Kishel, Gregory Francis *federal judge*
Kyle, Richard House *federal judge*
Lay, Donald Pomeroy *federal judge*
Loken, James Burton *federal judge*
Magnuson, Paul Arthur *federal judge*
Mason, John Milton (Jack Mason) *judge*
Page, Alan Cedric *judge*
Rogosheske, Walter Frederick *lawyer, former state justice*
Tomljanovich, Esther M. *judge*

## MISSISSIPPI

**Aberdeen**
Davis, Jerry Arnold *judge*
Senter, Lyonel Thomas, Jr. *federal judge*

**Biloxi**
Bramlette, David C., III *federal judge*
Gex, Walter Joseph, III *federal judge*
Roper, John Marlin *federal magistrate judge*

**Gulfport**
Russell, Dan M., Jr. *federal judge*

**Hattiesburg**
Pickering, Charles W. *federal judge*

**Jackson**
Barbour, William H., Jr. *federal judge*
Barksdale, Rhesa Hawkins *federal judge*
Jolly, E. Grady *federal judge*
Lee, Tom Stewart *judge*
Payne, Mary Libby *judge*
Prather, Lenore Loving *state supreme court presiding justice*
Smith, James W., Jr. *judge*
Sugg, Robert Perkins *former state supreme court justice*
Sullivan, Michael David *state supreme court justice*
Wingate, Henry Travillion *federal judge*

**Oxford**
Biggers, Neal Brooks, Jr. *federal judge*

## MISSOURI

**Benton**
Heckemeyer, Anthony Joseph *circuit court judge*

**Jefferson City**
Benton, W. Duane *judge*
Covington, Ann K. *judge, lawyer*
Donnelly, Robert True *retired state supreme court justice*
Holstein, John Charles *state supreme court chief justice*
Limbaugh, Stephen Nathaniel, Jr. *judge*
Price, William Ray, Jr. *state supreme court judge*
Robertson, Edward D., Jr. *state supreme court chief justice*

**Kansas City**
Berrey, Robert Wilson, III *judge, lawyer*
Bowman, Pasco Middleton, II *federal judge*
Gaitan, Fernando J., Jr. *federal judge*
Gibson, Floyd Robert *federal judge*
Gibson, John Robert *federal judge*
Hunter, Elmo Bolton *federal judge*
Koger, Frank Williams *federal judge*
Larsen, Robert Emmett *federal judge*
Sachs, Howard F(rederic) *federal judge*
Stevens, Joseph Edward, Jr. *federal judge*
Ulrich, Robert Gene *judge*
Whipple, Dean *federal judge*
Wright, Scott Olin *federal judge*

**Moberly**
Blackmar, Charles Blakey *state supreme court justice*

**Saint Louis**
Barta, James Joseph *judge*
Filippine, Edward Louis *federal judge*
Gunn, George F., Jr. *federal judge*
Hamilton, Jean Constance *judge*
Jackson, Carol E. *federal judge*
Limbaugh, Stephen Nathaniel *federal judge*
McMillian, Theodore *federal judge*
Perry, Catherine D. *judge*
Reinhard, James Richard *judge*
Seiler, James Elmer *judge*
Shaw, Charles Alexander *judge*
Stohr, Donald J. *federal judge*

**Springfield**
Clark, Russell Gentry *federal judge*

## MONTANA

**Billings**
Fagg, Russell *judge, lawyer*
Shanstrom, Jack D. *federal judge*

**Great Falls**
Hatfield, Paul Gerhart *federal judge, lawyer*

**Helena**
Gray, Karla Marie *state supreme court justice*
Harrison, John Conway *state supreme court justice*
Hunt, William E., Sr. *state supreme court justice*
Lovell, Charles C. *federal judge*
McDonough, Russell Charles *retired state supreme court justice*
Trieweiler, Terry Nicholas *justice*
Turnage, Jean A. *state supreme court chief justice*

## NEBRASKA

**Columbus**
Whitehead, John C. *state judge*

**Lincoln**
Beam, Clarence Arlen *federal judge*
Caporale, D. Nick *state supreme court justice*
Hastings, William Charles *retired state supreme court chief justice*
Kopf, Richard G. *federal judge*
Minahan, John C., Jr. *federal judge*
Piester, David L(ee) *magistrate judge*
Urbom, Warren Keith *federal judge*
White, C. Thomas *state supreme court justice*

**Omaha**
Cambridge, William G. *federal judge*
Grant, John Thomas *retired state supreme court justice*
Shanahan, Thomas M. *judge*
Strom, Lyle Elmer *federal judge*

## NEVADA

**Carson City**
Gunderson, Elmer Millard *state supreme court justice, law educator*
Rose, Robert E(dgar) *state supreme court justice*
Springer, Charles Edward *state supreme court justice*
Young, C. Clifton *judge*

**Las Vegas**
George, Lloyd D. *federal judge*
Johnston, Robert Jake *federal magistrate judge*
Parraguirre, Ronald David *judge*
Pro, Philip Martin *judge*

**Reno**
Brunetti, Melvin T. *federal judge*
Hagen, David W. *judge*
Hug, Procter Ralph, Jr. *federal judge*
McKibben, Howard D. *federal judge*
Reed, Edward Cornelius, Jr. *federal judge*

## NEW HAMPSHIRE

**Concord**
Barbadoro, Paul J. *federal judge*
Brock, David Allen *state supreme court chief justice*
Cann, William Francis *judge*
Devine, Shane *federal judge*
DiClerico, Joseph Anthony, Jr. *federal judge*
Horton, Sherman D., Jr. *state supreme court justice*
McAuliffe, Steven James *federal judge*
Stahl, Norman H. *federal judge*
Thayer, W(alter) Stephen, III *state supreme court justice*

**Nashua**
Barry, William Henry, Jr. *federal judge*

## NEW JERSEY

**Atlantic City**
Knight, Edward R. *judge, lawyer, educator, psychologist*

**Belvidere**
Aaroe, Paul *superior court judge*

**Camden**
Brotman, Stanley Seymour *federal judge*
Irenas, Joseph Eron *judge*
Lashman, Shelley Bortin *judge*
Laskin, Lee B. *judge, laywer, former state senator*
Rodriguez, Joseph H. *federal judge*
Simandle, Jerome B. *federal judge*

**Elizabeth**
Beglin, Edward W., Jr. *judge*

**Freehold**
Fisher, Clarkson Sherman, Jr. *judge*

**Hackensack**
Kestin, Howard H. *judge*
Stein, Gary S. *state supreme court associate justice*

**Jersey City**
Connors, Richard F. *judge*

**Morristown**
Pollock, Stewart Glasson *state supreme court justice*

**Newark**
Ackerman, Harold A. *federal judge*
Alito, Samuel Anthony, Jr. *federal judge*
Barry, Maryanne Trump *federal judge*
Bassler, William G. *federal judge*
Bissell, John W. *federal judge*
Chesler, Stanley Richard *federal judge*
Debevoise, Dickinson Richards *federal judge*
Garth, Leonard I. *federal judge*
Lechner, Alfred James, Jr. *judge*
Lifland, John C. *federal judge*
Pisano, Joel A. *federal judge*
Politan, Nicholas H. *federal judge*
Walls, William Hamilton *judge*
Wolin, Alfred M. *federal judge*

**Red Bank**
O'Hern, Daniel Joseph *state supreme court justice*

**Springfield**
Coleman, James H., Jr. *state supreme court justice*

**Stockton**
Griffin, Bryant Wade *retired judge*

**Trenton**
Brown, Garrett Edward, Jr. *federal judge*
Cowen, Robert E. *federal judge*
Fisher, Clarkson Sherman *federal judge*
Gindin, William Howard *judge*
Greenberg, Morton Ira *federal judge*
Handler, Alan B. *state supreme court justice*
Parell, Mary Little *federal judge, former banking commissioner*
Thompson, Anne Elise *federal judge*

## NEW MEXICO

**Albuquerque**
Conway, John E. *federal judge*
Easley, Mack *retired state supreme court chief justice*
Hansen, Curtis LeRoy *federal judge*
Knowles, Richard John *judge*
Parker, James Aubrey *federal judge*
Ransom, Richard Edward *retired state supreme court justice*

**Las Cruces**
Bratton, Howard Calvin *federal judge*

**Roswell**
Baldock, Bobby Ray *federal judge*

**Santa Fe**
Baca, Joseph Francis *state supreme court justice*
Campos, Santiago E. *federal judge*
Franchini, Gene Edward *state supreme court chief justice*
Frost, Stanley *retired judge*
Kelly, Paul Joseph, Jr. *federal judge*
Vazquez, Martha Alicia *judge*
Yalman, Ann *magistrate, lawyer*

## NEW YORK

**Albany**
Bellacosa, Joseph W. *judge*
Kaye, Judith Smith *judge*
Miner, Roger Jeffrey *federal judge*
Smith, Ralph Wesley, Jr. *federal judge*
Titone, Vito Joseph *judge*

**Binghamton**
McAvoy, Thomas James *federal judge*

**Bronx**
Bamberger, Phylis Skloot *judge*
Roberts, Burton Bennett *administrative judge*

**Brooklyn**
Amon, Carol Bagley *federal judge*
Bartels, John Ries *federal judge*
Block, Frederic *judge*
Bramwell, Henry *federal judge*
Dearie, Raymond Joseph *federal judge*
Glasser, Israel Leo *federal judge*
Johnson, Sterling, Jr. *federal judge*
Korman, Edward R. *federal judge*
Raggi, Reena *federal judge*
Ross, Allyne R. *federal judge*
Ryan, Leonard Eames *administrative law judge*
Sifton, Charles Proctor *federal judge*
Solomon, Martin M. *judge, state senator*
Trager, David G. *federal judge*
Weinstein, Jack Bertrand *federal judge*

**Buffalo**
Arcara, Richard Joseph *federal judge*
Curtin, John T. *federal judge*
Elfvin, John Thomas *federal judge*
Heckman, Carol E. *judge*
Jasen, Matthew Joseph *state justice*
Joslin, Norman Earl *judge*
Skretny, William Marion *federal judge*

**Garden City**
Harwood, Stanley *retired judge, lawyer*

**Glens Falls**
Bacas, William Augustus *judge, lawyer*

**Hauppauge**
Hurley, Denis R. *federal judge*
Wexler, Leonard D. *federal judge*

**Manhasset**
Wachtler, Sol *retired judge, arbitration corporation executive, writer*

**Mineola**
Murphy, George Austin *justice*

**New York**
Aquilino, Thomas Joseph, Jr. *federal judge, law educator*
Baer, Harold, Jr. *judge*
Batts, Deborah A. *judge*
Beatty, Prudence Carter *federal judge*
Buchwald, Naomi Reice *judge*
Carman, Gregory Wright *federal judge*
Cedarbaum, Miriam Goldman *judge*
Ciparick, Carmen Beauchamp *judge*
Cote, Denise Louise *federal judge*
DiCarlo, Dominick L. *federal judge*
Duffy, Kevin Thomas *federal judge*
Edelstein, David Northon *federal judge*
Feinberg, Wilfred *federal judge*
Freedman, Helen Edelstein *justice*
Griesa, Thomas Poole *federal judge*
Haight, Charles Sherman, Jr. *federal judge*
Jacobs, Dennis *federal judge*
Kaplan, Lewis A. *judge*
Kearse, Amalya Lyle *federal judge*
Keenan, John Fontaine *federal judge*
Knapp, Whitman *federal judge*
Koeltl, John George *judge*
Kram, Shirley Wohl *federal judge*
Kupferman, Theodore R. *former state justice, laywer*
Leisure, Peter Keeton *federal judge*
Leval, Pierre Nelson *federal judge*
Lifland, Burton R. *federal judge*
Lowe, Mary Johnson *federal judge*
Martin, John S., Jr. *federal judge*
McKenna, Lawrence M. *federal judge*
McLaughlin, Joseph Michael *federal judge, law educator*
McMahon, Colleen *judge*
Motley, Constance Baker (Mrs. Joel Wilson Motley) *federal judge, former city official*
Mukasey, Michael B. *federal judge*
Musgrave, R. Kenton *federal judge*
Newman, Bernard *federal judge*
Owen, Richard *federal judge*
Patterson, Robert Porter, Jr. *federal judge*
Pollack, Milton *federal judge*
Preska, Loretta A. *federal judge*
Rakoff, Jed Saul *federal judge, author*
Restani, Jane A. *federal judge*
Rosenberger, Ernst Hey *judge*
Sand, Leonard B. *federal judge*
Scheindlin, Shira A. *federal judge*
Schwartz, Allen G. *federal judge*
Schwartz, Hilda G. *retired judge*
Sotomayor, Sonia *federal judge*
Sprizzo, John Emilio *federal judge*
Torres, Edwin *state judge, writer*
Tsoucalas, Nicholas *federal judge*
Walker, John Mercer, Jr. *federal judge*
Ward, Robert Joseph *federal judge*
Watson, James Lopez *federal judge*
Wood, Kimba M. *judge*

**Port Washington**
Jones, Farrell *judge*

Powers, John Y. *federal judge*
Summitt, Robert Murray *circuit judge*

**Greeneville**
Hull, Thomas Gray *federal judge*
Parsons, Marcia Phillips *judge*

**Jackson**
Todd, James Dale *federal judge*

**Knoxville**
Jarvis, James Howard, II *judge*
Jordan, Robert Leon *federal judge*
Murrian, Robert Phillip *magistrate, judge, educator*
Phillips, Thomas Wade *judge, lawyer*

**Memphis**
Allen, James Henry *magistrate*
Brown, Bailey *federal judge*
Gibbons, Julia Smith *federal judge*
Horton, Odell *federal judge*
McCalla, Jon P. *federal judge*
McRae, Robert Malcolm, Jr. *federal judge*
Turner, Jerome *federal judge*
Wellford, Harry Walker *federal judge*

**Nashville**
Anderson, Edward Riley *state supreme court justice*
Birch, Adolpho A., Jr. *judge*
Daughtrey, Martha Craig *federal judge*
Echols, Robert L. *federal judge*
Higgins, Thomas A. *federal judge*
Merritt, Gilbert Stroud *federal judge*
Nixon, John Trice *judge*
Reid, Lyle *judge*
Trauger, Aleta Arthur *judge*
Wiseman, Thomas Anderton, Jr. *federal judge*

**Signal Mountain**
Cooper, Robert Elbert *state supreme court justice*

## TEXAS

**Amarillo**
Robinson, Mary Lou *federal judge*

**Arlington**
Wright, James Edward *judge*

**Austin**
Baird, Charles F. *judge*
Benavides, Fortunato Pedro (Pete Benavides) *federal judge*
Clinton, Sam Houston *retired judge*
Derounian, Steven Boghos *retired judge, lawyer*
Enoch, Craig Trively *state supreme court justice*
Garwood, William Lockhart *federal judge*
Gonzalez, Raul A. *state supreme court justice*
Greenhill, Joe Robert *former chief justice state supreme, lawyer*
Hecht, Nathan Lincoln *state supreme court justice*
Johnson, Sam D. *federal judge*
Maloney, Frank *judge, lawyer*
Mansfield, Stephen W. *judge*
McCormick, Michael Jerry *judge*
Meyers, Lawrence Edward *judge*
Nowlin, James Robertson *federal judge*
Owen, Priscilla Richman *judge*
Phillips, Thomas Royal *judge*
Pope, Andrew Jackson, Jr. (Jack Pope) *retired judge*
Ray, Cread L., Jr. *retired state supreme court justice*
Reavley, Thomas Morrow *federal judge*
Sparks, Sam *federal judge*
Williams, Mary Pearl *judge, lawyer*

**Beaumont**
Cobb, Howell *federal judge*
Fisher, Joseph Jefferson *federal judge*

**Brownsville**
Garza, Reynaldo G. *federal judge*
Vela, Filemon B. *federal judge*

**Corpus Christi**
Head, Hayden Wilson, Jr. *district judge*
Jack, Janis Graham *judge*

**Dallas**
Buchmeyer, Jerry *federal judge*
Chae, Don B. *judge, educator, lawyer*
Fish, A. Joe *federal judge*
Fitzwater, Sidney Allen *federal judge*
Higginbotham, Patrick Errol *federal judge*
Kendall, Joe *federal judge*
Maloney, Robert B. *federal judge*
Price, Robert Eben *judge*
Robertson, Ted Zanderson *judge*
Sanders, Harold Barefoot, Jr. *federal judge*
Solis, Jorge Antonio *federal judge*

**Del Rio**
Thurmond, George Murat *judge*

**Edinburg**
Hinojosa, Federico Gustavo, Jr. *judge*

**El Paso**
Dinsmoor, Robert Davidson *judge*
Hudspeth, Harry Lee *federal judge*

**Fort Worth**
Mahon, Eldon Brooks *federal judge*
McBryde, John Henry *federal judge*
Means, Terry Robert *federal judge*

**Galveston**
Gibson, Hugh *federal judge*
Kent, Samuel B. *federal judge*

**Houston**
Atlas, Nancy Friedman *judge*
Black, Norman William *federal judge*
Bue, Carl Olaf, Jr. *retired federal judge*
Crone, Marcia Ann *judge*
DeMoss, Harold R., Jr. *federal judge*
Gilmore, Vanessa D. *federal judge*
Harmon, Melinda Furche *federal judge*
Hittner, David *federal judge*
Hoyt, Kenneth M. *federal judge*
Hughes, Lynn Nettleton *federal judge*
Jones, Edith Hollan *federal judge*
King, Carolyn Dineen *federal judge*
Lake, Simeon Timothy, III *federal judge*
Rainey, John David *federal judge*
Rosenthal, Lee H. *federal judge*
Schwarz, Paul Winston *judge, lawyer, business company executive*
Singleton, John Virgil, Jr. *retired federal judge, lawyer*
Smith, Jerry Edwin *federal judge*
Sondock, Ruby Kless *retired judge*
Steen, Wesley Wilson *former judge, lawyer*
Werlein, Ewing, Jr. *federal judge, lawyer*
York, James Martin *judge*

**Laredo**
Kazen, George Philip *federal judge*

**Levelland**
Walker, James Kenneth *judge*

**Lubbock**
Cummings, Sam R. *federal judge*

**Mc Kinney**
White, Nathan Emmett, Jr. *judge, lawyer*

**Mcallen**
Hinojosa, Ricardo H. *federal judge*

**Midland**
Furgeson, William Royal *federal judge*
Smith, Robin Doyle *judge*

**Pampa**
Cain, Donald Ezell *judge*

**San Angelo**
Sutton, John Ewing *judge*

**San Antonio**
Biery, Fred *judge*
Clark, Leif Michael *federal judge*
Garcia, Hipolito Frank (Hippo Garcia) *federal judge*
Garcia, Orlando Luis *judge*
Garza, Emilio M(iller) *federal judge*
Hardberger, Phillip Duane *judge, lawyer, journalist*
King, Ronald Baker *federal judge*
Nowak, Nancy Stein *judge*
Prado, Edward Charles *federal judge*
Suttle, Dorwin Wallace *federal judge*

**Sherman**
Brown, Paul Neeley *federal judge*

**Temple**
Skelton, Byron George *federal judge*

**Tyler**
Guthrie, Judith K. *federal judge*
Hannah, John Henry, Jr. *judge*
Justice, William Wayne *federal judge*
Parker, Robert M. *federal judge*
Steger, William Merritt *federal judge*

**Waco**
Smith, Walter S., Jr. *federal judge*

## UTAH

**Provo**
Schofield, Anthony Wayne *judge*

**Salt Lake City**
Anderson, Stephen Hale *federal judge*
Benson, Dee Vance *federal judge*
Durham, Christine Meaders *state supreme court justice*
Greene, John Thomas *judge*
Hall, Gordon R. *retired state supreme court chief justice*
Howe, Richard Cuddy *state supreme court justice*
Jenkins, Bruce Sterling *federal judge*
McKay, Monroe Gunn *federal judge*
Murphy, Michael R. *federal judge*
Sam, David *federal judge*
Stewart, Isaac Daniel, Jr. *judge*
Wilkins, Michael Jon *judge*
Winder, David Kent *federal judge*
Zimmerman, Michael David *state supreme court chief justice*

## VERMONT

**Brattleboro**
Oakes, James L. *federal judge*

**Burlington**
Parker, Fred I. *federal judge*

**Manchester**
Gagliardi, Lee Parsons *federal judge*

**Montpelier**
Morse, James L. *state supreme court justice*

**Waterbury Center**
Amestoy, Jeffrey Lee *judge*

**Woodstock**
Billings, Franklin Swift, Jr. *federal judge*

## VIRGINIA

**Abingdon**
Widener, Hiram Emory, Jr. *federal judge*
Williams, Glen Morgan *federal judge*

**Alexandria**
Bostetter, Martin V. B., Jr. *bankruptcy court judge*
Brinkema, Leonie Milhomme *federal judge*
Bryan, Albert V., Jr. *federal judge*
Cacheris, James C. *federal judge*
Ellis, Thomas Selby, III *federal judge*
Hilton, Claude Meredith *federal judge*

**Arlington**
Nejelski, Paul Arthur *judge*
Van Doren, Emerson Barclay *administrative judge*

**Charlottesville**
Crigler, B. Waugh *federal judge*
Michael, James Harry, Jr. *federal judge*
Wilkinson, James Harvie, III *federal judge*

**Clifton**
Gales, Robert Robinson *judge*

**Danville**
Kiser, Jackson L. *federal judge*

**Fairfax**
Stitt, David Tillman *judge*

**Falls Church**
†Gruggel, John Stuart, Jr. *judge*
Morse, Marvin Henry *judge*
Spector, Louis *retired federal judge, lawyer, arbitrator, consultant*

**Fredericksburg**
Jamison, John Ambler *retired circuit judge*

**Lynchburg**
Harris, Dale Hutter *judge, lecturer*

**Mc Lean**
Luttig, J. Michael *federal judge*

**Newport News**
Bateman, Fred Willom *retired judge*

**Norfolk**
Adams, David Huntington *judge*
Bonney, Hal James, Jr. *federal judge*
Clarke, J. Calvitt, Jr. *federal judge*
Doumar, Robert George *judge*
Jackson, Raymond A. *federal judge*
Morgan, Henry Coke, Jr. *judge*
Prince, William Taliaferro *federal judge*
Smith, Rebecca Beach *federal judge*

**Richmond**
Carrico, Harry Lee *state supreme court chief justice*
Compton, Asbury Christian *state supreme court justice*
Gordon, Thomas Christian, Jr. *former justice*
Hassell, Leroy Rountree, Sr. *state supreme court justice*
Lacy, Elizabeth Bermingham *state supreme court justice*
Merhige, Robert Reynold, Jr. *federal judge*
Payne, Robert E. *federal judge*
Poff, Richard Harding *state supreme court justice*
Spencer, James R. *federal judge*
Stephenson, Roscoe Bolar, Jr. *state supreme court justice*
Tice, Douglas Oscar, Jr. *federal judge*
Whiting, Henry H. *state supreme court justice*
Williams, Richard Leroy *federal judge*

**Roanoke**
Pearson, Henry Clyde *judge*
Turk, James Clinton *federal judge*
Wilson, Samuel Grayson *federal judge*

**Salem**
Koontz, Lawrence L., Jr. *judge*

**Staunton**
Cochran, George Moffett *retired judge*

## WASHINGTON

**Bellevue**
Andersen, James A. *retired state supreme court justice*

**Mercer Island**
Noe, James Alva *retired judge*

**Olympia**
Dolliver, James Morgan *state supreme court justice*
Durham, Barbara *state supreme court justice*
Guy, Richard P. *state supreme court justice*
Johnson, Charles William *justice*
Smith, Charles Z. *state supreme court justice*

**Seattle**
Beezer, Robert Renaut *federal judge*
Coughenour, John Clare *federal judge*
Dimmick, Carolyn Reaber *federal judge*
Dwyer, William L. *federal judge*
Farris, Jerome *federal judge*
Fletcher, Betty B. *federal judge*
Mc Govern, Walter T. *federal judge*
Overstreet, Hon. Karen A. *federal bankruptcy judge*
Rothstein, Barbara Jacobs *federal judge*
Weinberg, John Lee *federal judge*
Wilson, David Eugene *magistrate judge*
Wright, Eugene Allen *federal judge*
Zilly, Thomas Samuel *federal judge*

**Spokane**
Green, Dale Monte *retired judge*
Imbrogno, Cynthia *judge*
Nielsen, William Fremming *federal judge*
Quackenbush, Justin Lowe *federal judge*
Van Sickle, Frederick L. *federal judge*

**Tacoma**
Bryan, Robert J. *federal judge*
Tanner, Jack Edward *federal judge*

**Yakima**
Hovis, James Brunton *federal judge*
McDonald, Alan Angus *federal judge*
Suko, Lonny Ray *judge*

## WEST VIRGINIA

**Beckley**
Hallanan, Elizabeth V. *senior federal judge*

**Bluefield**
Faber, David Alan *federal judge*
Feinberg, Mary Stanley *judge*

**Charleston**
Cleckley, Franklin D. *judge*
Copenhaver, John Thomas, Jr. *federal judge*
Haden, Charles H., II *federal judge*
Hall, Kenneth Keller *federal judge*
Knapp, Dennis Raymond *federal judge*
Michael, M. Blane *federal judge*
Recht, Arthur *judge*
Workman, Margaret Lee *state supreme court justice, chief justice*

**Clarksburg**
Keeley, Irene Patricia Murphy *federal judge*

**Elkins**
Maxwell, Robert Earl *federal judge*

**Union**
Sprouse, James Marshall *retired federal judge*

## WISCONSIN

**Appleton**
Froehlich, Harold Vernon *judge, former congressman*

**Madison**
Abrahamson, Shirley Schlanger *state supreme court justice*
Bablitch, William A. *state supreme court justice*
Crabb, Barbara Brandriff *federal judge*
Day, Roland Bernard *retired chief justice state supreme court*
Deininger, David George *judge*
Fiedler, Patrick James *circuit court judge*
Heffernan, Nathan Stewart *retired state supreme court chief justice*
Martin, Robert David *judge, educator*
Wilcox, Jon P. *justice*

**Milwaukee**
Curran, Thomas J. *federal judge*
Evans, Terence Thomas *federal judge*
Goodstein, Aaron E. *federal magistrate judge*
Gordon, Myron L. *federal judge*
Randa, Rudolph Thomas *judge*
Reynolds, John W. *federal judge*
Shapiro, James Edward *judge*
Stadtmueller, Joseph Peter *federal judge*
Warren, Robert Willis *federal judge*

**Sheboygan**
Buchen, John Gustave *retired judge*

## WYOMING

**Cheyenne**
Barrett, James Emmett *federal judge*
Brimmer, Clarence Addison *federal judge*
Brorby, Wade *federal judge*
Brown, Charles Stuart *retired state supreme court justice*
Cardine, Godfrey Joseph *state supreme court justice*
Golden, Michael *state supreme court justice*
Johnson, Alan Bond *federal judge*
Macy, Richard J. *state judge*
Taylor, William Al *judge*

**Cody**
Patrick, H. Hunter *lawyer, judge*

**Green River**
Marty, Lawrence A. *magistrate*

**Story**
Mc Ewan, Leonard *former judge*

## TERRITORIES OF THE UNITED STATES

## GUAM

**Agana**
Maraman, Katherine Ann *judge*
Unpingco, John Walter Sablan *federal judge*

**Dededo**
Diaz, Ramon Valero *retired judge*

## NORTHERN MARIANA ISLANDS

**Saipan**
Dela Cruz, Jose Santos *retired state supreme court chief justice*
Munson, Alex Robert *judge*

## PUERTO RICO

**Hato Rey**
Acosta, Raymond Luis *federal judge*

**San Juan**
Andreu-Garcia, Jose Antonio *judge*
Cerezo, Carmen Consuelo *federal judge*
Fusté, José Antonio *federal judge*
Gierbolini-Ortiz, Gilberto *federal judge*
Hernandez-Denton, Federico *commonwealth supreme court justice*
Laffitte, Hector Manuel *federal judge*
Perez-Gimenez, Juan Manuel *federal judge*
Torruella, Juan R. *federal judge*

### VIRGIN ISLANDS

**Charlotte Amalie**
Moore, Thomas Kail *chief judge*

**Christiansted**
Finch, Raymond Lawrence *judge*
Resnick, Jeffrey Lance *federal magistrate judge*

**Saint Thomas**
Hodge, Verne Antonio *judge*

## CANADA

### ALBERTA

**Edmonton**
Fraser, Catherine Anne *Canadian chief justice*
Stevenson, William Alexander *retired justice of Supreme Court of Canada*

### BRITISH COLUMBIA

**Vancouver**
de Weerdt, Mark Murray *retired judge*
Lysyk, Kenneth Martin *judge*
McEachern, Allan *Canadian justice*

### MANITOBA

**Winnipeg**
Lyon, Sterling Rufus Webster *justice*

### NEW BRUNSWICK

**Oromocto**
Strange, Henry Hazen *judge*

**Westfield**
Logan, Rodman Emmason *retired jurist*

### NOVA SCOTIA

**Halifax**
Glube, Constance Rachelle *Canadian chief justice*

### ONTARIO

**Almonte**
Hugessen, James K. *judge*

**Dunrobin**
Dickson, Brian *retired chief justice of Canada*

**Lindsay**
Evans, John David Daniel *judge*

**North York**
Harris, Sydney Malcolm *retired judge*

**Ottawa**
†Archambault, Pierre Guy *judge*
Cory, Peter de Carteret *Canadian supreme court justice*
Couture, J. C. *Canadian federal judge*
Cullen, Jack Sydney George Bud *federal judge*
Décary, Robert *judge*
Gonthier, Charles Doherty *Canadian supreme court justice*
Heald, Darrel Verner *retired Canadian federal judge*
Jerome, James Alexander *Canadian federal justice*
†Joyal, L. Marcel *judge*
Lamer, Antonio *Canadian supreme court chief justice*
Letourneau, Gilles *judge*
L'Heureux-Dubé, Claire *judge*
MacGuigan, Mark Rudolph *judge*
MacKay, William Andrew *judge*
Mahoney, Patrick Morgan *retired judge*
Major, John Charles *judge*
†Margeson, Theodore Earl *judge*
†McKeown, William Philip *judge*
McLachlin, Beverley *supreme court judge*
Muldoon, Francis Creighton *Canadian federal judge*
Pratte, Louis *Canadian federal judge*
†Rip, Gerald J. *federal judge*
Sopinka, John *Canadian supreme court justice*
Stone, Arthur Joseph *judge*
Strayer, Barry Lee *federal judge*

**Toronto**
Boland, Janet Lang *judge*
McMurtry, R. Roy *chief justice*

### PRINCE EDWARD ISLAND

**Charlottetown**
Carruthers, Norman Harry *Canadian province supreme court justice*

### QUEBEC

**Montreal**
Bisson, Claude *retired chief justice of Quebec*
Gold, Alan B. *former Canadian chief justice*
Mailhot, Louise *judge*
Rothman, Melvin L. *judge*

**Quebec**
†Morin, Louis *judge*

### SASKATCHEWAN

**Regina**
Bayda, Edward Dmytro *judge*

## THE NETHERLANDS

**The Hague**
Allison, Richard Clark *judge*

## ADDRESS UNPUBLISHED

Adams, Arlin Marvin *retired judge, counsel to law firm*
Amundson, Robert A. *state supreme court justice*
Askey, William Hartman *federal judge, lawyer*
Bartunek, Joseph Wenceslaus *magistrate, judge*
Bertelsman, William Odis *federal judge*
Bierce, James Malcolm *retired judge*
Bistline, Stephen *retired state supreme court justice*
Blackmun, Harry Andrew *retired United States supreme court justice*
Bootle, William Augustus *retired federal judge*
Boslaugh, Leslie *retired judge*
Box, Dwain D. *former judge*
Brown, Robert Laidlaw *state supreme court justice*
Bunton, Lucius Desha, III *federal judge*
Burke, Edmond Wayne *retired judge, lawyer*
Callow, Keith McLean *judge*
Callow, William Grant *retired state supreme court justice*
Castagna, William John *federal judge*
Ceci, Louis J. *former state supreme court justice*
Coffey, John Louis *federal judge*
Cograve, John Edwin *retired judge*
Cohn, Avern Levin *federal judge*
Colaianni, Joseph Vincent *judge*
Cook, Julian Abele, Jr. *federal judge*
Cyr, Conrad Keefe *federal judge*
Daugherty, Frederick Alvin *federal judge*
Davis, Marguerite Herr *judge*
Eaton, Joe Oscar *federal judge*
Fahrnbruch, Dale E. *retired state supreme court justice*
Fisher, Ann L. *pro tem judge*
Foster, Robert Lawson *retired judge, deacon*
Fremont-Smith, Thayer *judge*
Garrity, Wendell Arthur, Jr. *federal judge*
Gorence, Patricia Josetta *judge*
Gotlib, Lorraine *retired justice, former lawyer*
Grant, Isabella Horton *retired judge*
Griffin, Robert Paul *former state supreme court justice and US senator*
Grimes, William Alvan *retired state supreme court chief justice*
Hall, Sophia Harriet *judge*
Hancock, James Hughes *federal judge*
Hawkins, Michael Daly *federal judge*
Hayek, Carolyn Jean *retired judge*
Hightower, Jack English *former state supreme court justice and congressman*
Hogan, Thomas Francis *federal judge*
Holland, Randy James *state supreme court justice*
Howard, George, Jr. *federal judge*
Hoyt, William Lloyd *chief justice*
Jones, Phyllis Gene *judge*
Kauger, Yvonne *state supreme court justice*
Kelly, Aurel Maxey *retired judge*
Krupansky, Blanche *retired judge*
Laycraft, James Herbert *judge*
Le Dain, Gerald Eric *retired Canadian Supreme Court justice*
Lee, Barbara A. *retired federal magistrate judge*
Lee, Dan M. *state supreme court justice*
Levine, Beryl Joyce *state supreme court justice*
Liacos, Paul Julian *retired state supreme judicial court chief justice*
Linde, Hans Arthur *state supreme court justice*
Logan, James Kenneth *federal judge*
Love, Miron Anderson *retired judge*
Low, Harry William *judge*
Mai, Harold Leverne *retired judge*
McClure, Ann Crawford *lawyer, judge*
McCown, Hale *retired judge*
Metzner, Charles Miller *federal judge*
Meyer, Louis B. *superior court judge, retired state supreme court justice*
Miles-LaGrange, Vicki Lynn *federal judge*
Montgomery, Seth David *retired state supreme court chief justice*
Murray, Florence Kerins *retired state supreme court justice*
Murray, Herbert Frazier *retired federal judge*
Mydland, Gordon James *judge*
Newman, Theodore Roosevelt, Jr. *judge*
Papadakos, Nicholas Peter *retired state supreme court justice*
Phillips, James Dickson, Jr. *federal judge*
Prager, David *retired state supreme court chief justice*
Quillen, William Tatem *judge, lawyer, educator*
Quirico, Francis Joseph *retired state supreme court justice*
Reinhardt, Stephen Roy *federal judge*
Rice, Walter Herbert *federal judge*
Rodriguez, Elias C. *judge*
Ross, Donald Roe *federal judge*
Royse, Mary Kay *judge*
Sarokin, H. Lee *retired federal judge*
Schroeder, Gerald F. *judge*
Schwebel, Stephen Myron *judge, arbitrator*
Scott, Gregory Kellam *state supreme court justice*
Shearing, Miriam *justice*
Sheedy, Patrick Thomas *judge*
Silberman, Laurence Hirsch *federal judge*
Sinclair, Virgil Lee, Jr. *judge, writer*
Smith, Fern M. *federal judge*
Smith, Loren Allan *federal judge*
Souter, David Hackett *United States supreme court justice*
Staker, Robert Jackson *senior federal judge*
Stamos, John James *judge*
Stamp, Frederick Pfarr, Jr. *federal judge*
Sweet, Robert Workman *federal judge*
Tillman, Massie Monroe *federal judge*
Trout, Linda Copple *judge*
Turnoff, William Charles *judge*
Utter, Robert French *retired state supreme court justice*
Vollmer, Richard Wade *federal judge*
Wathen, Daniel Everett *state supreme court chief justice*
Weber, Fred J. *retired state supreme court justice*
White, Renee Allyn *judge*
Wiggins, Charles Edward *federal judge*
Wood, Diane Pamela *federal judge*
Wyman, Louis Crosby *judge, former senator, former congressman*

# LAW: LAW PRACTICE AND ADMINISTRATION

## UNITED STATES

### ALABAMA

**Andalusia**
Albritton, William Harold, IV *lawyer*
Fuller, William Sidney *lawyer*

**Anniston**
Klinefelter, James Louis *lawyer*

**Auburn**
Samford, Thomas Drake, III *lawyer*

**Birmingham**
Akers, Ottie Clay *lawyer, publisher*
Alexander, James Patrick *lawyer*
Blan, Ollie Lionel, Jr. *lawyer*
Brown, Ephraim Taylor, Jr. *lawyer*
Carlton, Eric L. *lawyer*
Carmody, Richard Patrick *lawyer*
Carruthers, Thomas Neely, Jr. *lawyer*
Coleman, Brittin Turner *lawyer*
Coleman, John James, III *lawyer, educator*
Cooper, Jerome A. *lawyer*
Davis, Julian Mason, Jr. *lawyer*
Denson, William Frank, III *lawyer*
Farley, Joseph McConnell *lawyer*
Forman, James Ross, III *lawyer*
Friend, Edward Malcolm, III *lawyer, educator*
Gaede, Anton Henry, Jr. *lawyer*
Gale, Fournier Joseph, III *lawyer*
Gardner, William F. *lawyer*
Garner, Robert Edward Lee *lawyer*
Gewin, James W. *lawyer*
Givhan, Robert Marcus *lawyer*
Grant, Walter Matthews *lawyer, supermarket executive*
Greenwood, P. Nicholas *lawyer*
Hardin, Edward Lester, Jr. *lawyer*
Hinton, James Forrest, Jr. *lawyer*
Howell, William Ashley, III *lawyer*
Hunter, Robert Dean *lawyer*
Irons, William Lee *lawyer*
Johnson, Joseph H., Jr. *lawyer*
Lacy, Alexander Shelton *lawyer*
Logan, J. Patrick *lawyer*
Long, Thad Gladden *lawyer*
McFerrin, James Hamil *lawyer*
Mc Millan, George Duncan Hastie, Jr. *lawyer, former state official*
McWhorter, Hobart Amory, Jr. *lawyer*
Mills, William Hayes *lawyer*
Molen, John Klauminzer *lawyer*
Morgan, Carolyn F. *lawyer*
Norris, Robert Wheeler *lawyer, military officer*
Page, Lewis Wendell, Jr. *lawyer*
Pearson, Richard L. *lawyer*
Privett, Caryl Penney *lawyer*
Redden, Lawrence Drew *lawyer*
Riegert, Robert Adolf *law educator, consultant*
Rogers, Ernest Mabry *lawyer*
Rotch, James E. *lawyer*
Rountree, Asa *lawyer*
Scherf, John George, IV *lawyer*
Selfe, Edward Milton *lawyer*
Shanks, William Ennis, Jr. *lawyer*
Sinclair, Julie Moores Williams *consulting law librarian*
Small, Clarence Merilton, Jr. *lawyer*
Smith, John Joseph *lawyer*
Spotswood, Robert Keeling *lawyer*
Stabler, Lewis Vastine, Jr. *lawyer*
Sydnor, Edgar Starke *lawyer*
Timberlake, Marshall *lawyer*
Todd, Judith F. *lawyer*
Vinson, Laurence Duncan, Jr. *lawyer*
Weeks, Arthur Andrew *lawyer, law educator*
Wrinkle, John Newton *lawyer*

**Clanton**
Jackson, John Hollis, Jr. *lawyer*

**Clayton**
Jackson, Lynn Robertson *lawyer*

**Dadeville**
Adair, Charles Robert, Jr. *lawyer*

**Decatur**
Caddell, John A. *lawyer*

**Demopolis**
Dinning, Woodford Wyndham, Jr. *lawyer*
Lloyd, Hugh Adams *lawyer*

**Hoover**
Cole, Charles DuBose, II *law educator*

**Huntsville**
Huckaby, Gary Carlton *lawyer*
Potter, Ernest Luther *lawyer*
Smith, Robert Sellers *lawyer*

**Mobile**
Armbrecht, William Henry, III *lawyer*
Braswell, Louis Erskine *lawyer*
Coley, F(ranklin) Luke, Jr. *lawyer*
Harris, Benjamin Harte, Jr. *lawyer*
Helmsing, Frederick George *lawyer*
Holland, Lyman Faith, Jr. *lawyer*
Holmes, Broox Garrett *lawyer*
Johnston, Neil Chunn *lawyer*
Kimbrough, William Adams, Jr. *lawyer*
Lyons, Champ, Jr. *lawyer*
Lyons, George Sage *lawyer, oil industry executive, former state legislator*
Murchison, David Roderick *lawyer*
Reeves, William Boyd *lawyer*
Roedder, William Chapman, Jr. *lawyer*
Vulevich, Edward, Jr. *prosecutor*

**Montgomery**
Byars, Walter Ryland, Jr. *lawyer*
Eubanks, Ronald W. *lawyer, broadcaster*
Franco, Ralph Abraham *lawyer*
Graddick, Charles Allen *lawyer*
Hamner, Reginald Turner *lawyer*
Hawthorne, Frank Howard *lawyer*
Hester, Douglas Benjamin *lawyer, federal official*
Hill, Thomas Bowen, III *lawyer*
Howell, Allen Windsor *lawyer*
Kloess, Lawrence Herman, Jr. *lawyer*
Laurie, Robin Garrett *lawyer*
Leslie, Henry Arthur *lawyer, retired banker*
Lunt, Jennifer Lee *lawyer*
McFadden, Frank Hampton *lawyer, business executive, former judge*
Nachman, Merton Roland, Jr. *lawyer*
Pitt, Redding *lawyer*
Prestwood, Alvin Tennyson *lawyer*
Salmon, Joseph Thaddeus *lawyer*
Smith, Maury Drane *lawyer*
Volz, Charles Harvie, Jr. *lawyer*

**Opelika**
Samford, Yetta Glenn, Jr. *lawyer*

**Orange Beach**
Adams, Daniel Fenton *law educator*

**Selma**
Stewart, Edgar Allen *lawyer*

**Tuscaloosa**
Christopher, Thomas Weldon *legal educator, administrator*
Cook, Camille Wright *law educator*

### ALASKA

**Anchorage**
Butler, Rex Lamont *lawyer*
Cantor, James Elliot *lawyer*
De Lisio, Stephen Scott *lawyer*
Edwards, George Kent *lawyer*
Groh, Clifford J., Sr. *lawyer*
Hughes, Mary Katherine *lawyer*
Mason, Robert (Burt Mason) *lawyer*
Perkins, Joseph John, Jr. *lawyer*
Roberts, John Derham *lawyer*
Welch-McKay, Dawn Renee *legal assistant*
Wilson, Joseph Morris, III *lawyer*

**Fairbanks**
Rice, Julian Casavant *lawyer*

**Juneau**
Cole, Charles Edward *lawyer, former state attorney general*

**Kodiak**
Jamin, Matthew Daniel *lawyer, magistrate judge*

**Nondalton**
Gay, Sarah Elizabeth *lawyer*

### ARIZONA

**Carefree**
Hutchison, Stanley Philip *lawyer*

**Flagstaff**
Heitland, Ann Rae *lawyer*

**Green Valley**
Friedman, Edward David *lawyer, arbitrator*

**Mesa**
Allen, Merle Maeser, Jr. *lawyer*
Cameron, Janice Carol *legal regulatory administrator*
Gunderson, Brent Merrill *lawyer*
Shelley, James LaMar *lawyer*

**Nogales**
Castro, Raul Hector *lawyer, former ambassador, former governor*

**Peoria**
Degnan, Thomas Leonard *lawyer*
Keesling, Karen Ruth *lawyer*
Moshier, Mary Baluk *patent lawyer*

**Phoenix**
Allen, Robert Eugene Barton *lawyer*
Alsentzer, William James, Jr. *lawyer*
Bain, C. Randall *lawyer*
Baker, William Dunlap *lawyer*
Bakker, Thomas Gordon *lawyer*
Bauman, Frederick Carl *lawyer*
Begam, Robert George *lawyer*
Beggs, Harry Mark *lawyer*
Bergin, Daniel Timothy *lawyer, banker*
Blanchard, Charles Alan *lawyer, former state senator*
Bodney, David Jeremy *lawyer*
Bouma, John Jacob *lawyer*
Brockelman, Kent *lawyer*
Burke, Timothy John *lawyer*
Cabot, Howard Ross *lawyer*
Case, David Leon *lawyer*
Cohen, Jon Stephan *lawyer*
Colburn, Donald D. *lawyer*
Cole, George Thomas *lawyer*
Condo, James Robert *lawyer*
Cooledge, Richard Calvin *lawyer*
Coppersmith, Sam *lawyer*
Corson, Kimball Jay *lawyer*
Craig, Stephen Wright *lawyer*
Crockett, Clyll Webb *lawyer*
Daughton, Donald *lawyer*
Davies, David George *lawyer*
Deeny, Robert Joseph *lawyer*
Derdenger, Patrick *lawyer*
Derouin, James G. *lawyer*
Dunipace, Ian Douglas *lawyer*
Durrant, Dan Martin *lawyer*

Eaton, Berrien Clark *retired lawyer, author*
Ehmann, Anthony Valentine *lawyer*
Everett, James Joseph *lawyer*
Everroad, John David *lawyer*
Feinstein, Allen Lewis *lawyer*
Fennelly, Jane Corey *lawyer*
Fenzl, Terry Earle *lawyer*
Fine, Charles Leon *lawyer*
Flickinger, Don Jacob *patent agent*
Frank, John Paul *lawyer, author*
Gaffney, Donald Lee *lawyer*
Gaines, Francis Pendleton, III *lawyer*
Galbut, Martin Richard *lawyer*
Gilbert, Donald R. *lawyer*
Gladner, Marc Stefan *lawyer*
Goldstein, Stuart Wolf *lawyer*
Grant, Merwin Darwin *lawyer*
Griller, Gordon Moore *court administrator*
Halpern, Barry David *lawyer*
Harrison, Mark I. *lawyer*
Hay, John Leonard *lawyer*
Hayden, William Robert *lawyer*
Hendricks, Ed *lawyer*
Hicks, William Albert, III *lawyer*
Hoecker, Thomas Ralph *lawyer*
Hoxie, Joel P. *lawyer*
Huntwork, James R. *lawyer*
Inman, William Peter *lawyer*
Jacobson, (Julian) Edward *lawyer*
James, Charles E., Jr. *lawyer*
Jansen, Donald William *lawyer, legislative administrator*
Jirauch, Charles W. *lawyer*
Johnston, Logan Truax, III *lawyer*
Klausner, Jack Daniel *lawyer*
Koester, Berthold Karl *lawyer, retired honorary consul, educator*
Kreutzberg, David W. *lawyer*
Kurn, Neal *lawyer*
Lacey, Henry Bernard *lawyer*
Leonard, Jeffrey S. *lawyer*
Lowry, Edward Francis, Jr. *lawyer*
Madden, Paul Robert *lawyer*
Mangum, John K. *lawyer*
Marks, Merton Eleazer *lawyer*
Martori, Joseph Peter *lawyer*
Mc Clennen, Louis *lawyer, educator*
McDaniel, Joseph Chandler *lawyer*
McRae, Hamilton Eugene, III *lawyer*
Merritt, Nancy-Jo *lawyer*
Meyerson, Bruce Elliot *lawyer*
Miller, Louis Rice *lawyer*
Moya, Patrick Robert *lawyer*
Napolitano, Janet Ann *prosecutor*
North, Gerald David William *lawyer*
Olsen, Alfred Jon *lawyer*
Olsen, Gordon *retired lawyer*
Olson, Robert Howard *lawyer*
O'Steen, Van *lawyer*
Parrett, Sherman O. *lawyer*
Perry, Lee Rowan *lawyer*
Platt, Warren E. *lawyer*
Powers, Noyes Thompson *lawyer*
Price, Charles Steven *lawyer*
Pulaski, Charles Alexander, Jr. *lawyer*
Rathwell, Peter John *lawyer*
Refo, Patricia Lee *lawyer*
Richards, Charles Franklin, Jr. *lawyer*
Romley, Richard M. *lawyer*
Rose, David L. *lawyer*
Rudolph, Gilbert Lawrence *lawyer*
Salerno, Thomas James *lawyer*
Savage, Stephen Michael *lawyer*
Sherk, Kenneth John *lawyer*
Silverman, Alan H. *lawyer*
Smock, Timothy Robert *lawyer*
Stahl, Louis A. *lawyer*
Storey, Norman C. *lawyer*
Sutton, Samuel J. *lawyer, educator, engineer*
Terry, Peter Anthony *lawyer*
Udall, Calvin Hunt *lawyer*
Ulrich, Paul Graham *lawyer, author, publisher, editor*
Walker, Richard K. *lawyer*
Wall, Donald Arthur *lawyer*
Wheeler, Steven M. *lawyer*
Whisler, James Steven *lawyer, mining and manufacturing executive*
Williams, Quinn Patrick *lawyer*
Winthrop, Lawrence Fredrick *lawyer*
Wolf, G. Van Velsor, Jr. *lawyer*
Woolf, Michael E. *lawyer*
Yarnell, Michael Allan *lawyer*

### Prescott
Kleindienst, Richard Gordon *lawyer*

### Scottsdale
Kitchel, Denison *retired lawyer, writer*
Krupp, Clarence William *lawyer, personnel and hospital administrator*
Lisa, Isabelle O'Neill *law firm administrator, mergers and acquisitions executive*
Peshkin, Samuel David *lawyer*
Sears, Alan Edward *lawyer*
Starr, Isidore *law educator*

### Sierra Vista
Lowe, Robert Charles *lawyer, banker*

### Sun City
Hauer, James Albert *lawyer*
Treece, James Lyle *lawyer*
Woodside, Robert Elmer *lawyer, former judge*

### Sun City West
Burke, Richard Kitchens *lawyer, educator*

### Tempe
Evans, Lawrence Jack, Jr. *lawyer*
Matheson, Alan Adams *law educator*
Spritzer, Ralph Simon *lawyer, educator*
Vanderpoel, James Robert *lawyer*

### Tucson
Betteridge, Frances Carpenter *retired lawyer, mediator*
Dobbs, Dan Byron *lawyer, educator*
Dolph, Wilbert Emery *lawyer*
Eckhardt, August Gottlieb *law educator*
Franklin, John Orland *lawyer*
Froman, Sandra Sue *lawyer*
Gantz, David Alfred *lawyer, university official*
Gonzales, Richard Joseph *lawyer*
Grand, Richard D. *lawyer*
Henderson, Roger C. *law educator, former dean*
Kimble, William Earl *lawyer*
Lesher, Robert Overton *lawyer*
Mc Donald, John Richard *lawyer*
McNeill, Frederick Wallace *lawyer, educator, writer, federal government consultant, former military and commercial pilot*
Meehan, Michael Joseph *lawyer*
Morrow, James Franklin *lawyer*
Pace, Thomas M. *lawyer*
Robinson, Bernard Leo *retired lawyer*
Schorr, S. L. *lawyer*
Seligman, Joel *law educator*
Shultz, Silas Harold *lawyer*
Strong, John William *lawyer, educator*
Tindall, Robert Emmett *lawyer, educator*
Woods, Winton D. *law educator*

### Yuma
Hossler, David Joseph *lawyer, educator*

## ARKANSAS

### Blytheville
Fendler, Oscar *lawyer*

### Eureka Springs
Epley, Lewis Everett, Jr. *lawyer*

### Fayetteville
Ahlers, Glen-Peter, Sr. *law library director, educator, consultant*
Bassett, Woodson William, Jr. *lawyer*
Davis, Wylie Herman *lawyer, educator*
Niblock, Walter Raymond *lawyer*
Pearson, Charles Thomas, Jr. *lawyer*

### Fort Smith
Dotson, Donald L. *lawyer*
Holmes, Paul Kinloch, III *prosecutor*

### Harrison
Pinson, Jerry D. *lawyer*

### Helena
Roscopf, Charles Buford *lawyer*

### Jonesboro
Deacon, John C. *lawyer*

### Little Rock
Anderson, Philip Sidney *lawyer*
Bohannon, Charles Tad *lawyer*
Campbell, George Emerson *lawyer*
Casey, Paula Jean *prosecutor*
Cross, J. Bruce *lawyer*
Drummond, Winslow *lawyer*
Dumeny, Marcel Jacque *lawyer*
Fogleman, John Albert *lawyer, retired judge*
Gunter, Russell Allen *lawyer*
Haught, William Dixon *lawyer*
Jennings, Alston *lawyer*
Jones, Stephen Witsell *lawyer*
May, Ronald Alan *lawyer*
Murphey, Arthur Gage, Jr. *law educator*
Nelson, Edward Sheffield *lawyer, former utility company executive*
Shults, Robert Luther, Jr. *lawyer*
Stockburger, Jean Dawson *lawyer*
Warner, Cecil Randolph, Jr. *lawyer*
Witherspoon, Carolyn Brack *lawyer*
Wright, Robert Ross, III *law educator*

### Monticello
Ball, William Kenneth *lawyer*

### Newport
Thaxton, Marvin Dell *lawyer, farmer*

### North Little Rock
Hays, Patrick Henry *lawyer, mayor*
Patty, Claibourne Watkins, Jr. *lawyer*

### Osceola
Wilson, Ralph Edwin *lawyer, justice*

### Pine Bluff
Jones, John Harris *lawyer, banker*
Moon, Deborah Joan *paralegal*
Ramsay, Louis Lafayette, Jr. *lawyer, banker*

### Springdale
Cypert, Jimmy Dean *lawyer*

### Warren
Claycomb, Hugh Murray *lawyer, author*

### West Memphis
Fogleman, Julian Barton *lawyer*
Nance, Cecil Boone, Jr. *lawyer*

## CALIFORNIA

### Altadena
Vaughan, Audrey Judd *paralegal, musician*

### Anaheim
Faal, Edi M. O. *lawyer*

### Arcadia
Mc Cormack, Francis Xavier *lawyer, former oil company executive*

### Atherton
Surbeck, Leighton Homer *retired lawyer*

### Auburn
Henry, Karen Hawley *lawyer*

### Bakersfield
Martin, George Francis *lawyer*

### Barstow
Lundstrom, Thomas John *lawyer*

### Belvedere Tiburon
Widman, Gary Lee *lawyer, former government official*

### Berkeley
Barnes, Thomas G. *law educator*
Barton, Babette B. *lawyer, educator*
Buxbaum, Richard M. *law educator, lawyer*
Choper, Jesse Herbert *law educator, university dean*
Concepción, David Alden *arbitrator, educator*
De Goff, Victoria Joan *lawyer*
Eisenberg, Melvin A. *law educator*
Feeley, Malcolm M. *law educator, political scientist*
Feller, David E. *law educator, arbitrator*
Fleming, John Gunther *law educator*
Gordley, James Russell *law educator*
Halbach, Edward Christian, Jr. *legal educator*
Haley, George Patrick *lawyer*
Hetland, John Robert *lawyer, educator*
Kadish, Sanford Harold *law educator*
Kay, Herma Hill *law educator*
Kessler, Friedrich *retired law educator*
McNulty, John Kent *lawyer, educator*
Messinger, Sheldon L(eopold) *law educator*
Mishkin, Paul J. *lawyer, educator*
Moran, Rachel *lawyer, educator*
Nonet, Philippe *law educator*
Petty, George Oliver *lawyer*
Post, Robert Charles *law educator*
Scheiber, Harry N. *law educator*
Shapiro, Martin *law educator*
Van Winkle, Wesley Andrew *lawyer, educator*
Zimring, Franklin E. *law educator*

### Beverly Hills
Amado, Honey Kessler *lawyer*
Bloom, Jacob A. *lawyer*
Bordy, Michael Jeffrey *lawyer*
Brown, Hermione Kopp *lawyer*
Dickerson, William Roy *lawyer*
Haile, Lawrence Barclay *lawyer*
Hogan, Steven L. *lawyer*
Horwin, Leonard *lawyer*
Jessup, W. Edgar, Jr. *lawyer*
Kirkland, John C. *lawyer*
Nicholas, Frederick M. *lawyer*
Ramer, Bruce M. *lawyer*
Rondeau, Charles Reinhardt *lawyer*
Rosky, Burton Seymour *lawyer*
Schiff, Gunther Hans *lawyer*
Shacter, David Mervyn *lawyer*
Wainess, Marcia Watson *legal management consultant*

### Bishop
Buchanan, James Douglas *lawyer*

### Brea
Lounsbury, Steven Richard *lawyer*
Pearson, April Virginia *lawyer*

### Burbank
Ajalat, Sol Peter *lawyer*
Litvack, Sanford Martin *lawyer*
Noddings, Sarah Ellen *lawyer*
Seiden, Andy *lawyer*

### Burlingame
Cotchett, Joseph Winters *lawyer, author*
Narayan, Beverly Elaine *lawyer*
Ocheltree, Richard Lawrence *lawyer, retired forest products company executive*
Ziegler, R. W., Jr. *lawyer, consultant*

### California City
Friedl, Rick *lawyer, former academic administrator*

### Camarillo
Dunlevy, William Sargent *lawyer*

### Carlsbad
McCracken, Steven Carl *lawyer*

### Carmel
Blackstone, George Arthur *retired lawyer*
Robinson, John Minor *lawyer, retired business executive*

### Cerritos
Sarno, Maria Erlinda *lawyer, scientist*

### Chino
Determan, John David *lawyer*
Ofner, William Bernard *lawyer*

### Chula Vista
Allen, David Russell *lawyer*
Santee, Dale William *lawyer, air force officer*

### Claremont
Ansell, Edward Orin *lawyer, arbitrator/mediator*
Gray, Paul Bryan *lawyer, historian, arbitrator*

### Coalinga
Frame, Ted Ronald *lawyer*

### Concord
Lonnquist, George Eric *lawyer*
Williscroft, Beverly Ruth *lawyer*

### Corte Madera
Fawcett, F(rank) Conger *lawyer*

### Costa Mesa
Anderson, Jon David *lawyer*
Currie, Robert Emil *lawyer*
Daniels, James Walter *lawyer*
Frieden, Clifford E. *lawyer*
Gale, Mary Ellen *law educator*
Guilford, Andrew John *lawyer*
Hamilton, James William *lawyer*
Hay, Howard Clinton *lawyer*
Jansen, Allan W. *lawyer*
Jones, H(arold) Gilbert, Jr. *lawyer*
Lindstrom, Gregory P. *lawyer*
Reveal, Ernest Ira, III *lawyer*
Shallenberger, Garvin F. *lawyer*
Stone, Samuel Beckner *lawyer*
Tanner, R. Marshall *lawyer*
Tennyson, Peter Joseph *lawyer*
Thurston, Morris Ashcroft *lawyer*

### Culver City
von Kalinowski, Julian Onesime *lawyer*

### Cupertino
Maddux, Parker Ahrens *lawyer*
Simon, Nancy Ruth *lawyer*

### Cypress
Olschwang, Alan Paul *lawyer*

### Davis
Bartosic, Florian *lawyer, arbitrator, educator*
Bruch, Carol Sophie *lawyer, educator*
Dykstra, Daniel James *lawyer, educator*
Feeney, Floyd Fulton *legal educator*
Hackett, Nora Ann *patent agent*
Imwinkelried, Edward John *law educator*
Juenger, Friedrich Klaus *lawyer, educator*
Oakley, John Bilyeu *law educator, lawyer, judicial consultant*
Wolk, Bruce Alan *law educator*
Wydick, Richard Crews *lawyer, educator*

### El Centro
Albertson, Jack Aaron Paul *prosecutor*

### El Cerrito
Garbarino, Joseph William *labor arbitrator, economics and business educator*

### El Segundo
Willis, Judy Ann *lawyer*

### Elverta
Betts, Barbara Lang (Mrs. Bert A. Betts) *lawyer, rancher, realtor*

### Emeryville
Edginton, John Arthur *lawyer*

### Encino
Kaufman, Albert I. *lawyer*
Kuklin, Jeffrey Peter *lawyer, talent agency executive*
Lombardini, Carol Ann *lawyer*
Smith, Selma Moidel *lawyer, composer*

### Englewood
Fiske, Terry Noble *lawyer*

### Fairfield
Moore, Marianna Gay *law librarian, consultant*

### Felton
Kulzick, Kenneth Edmund *retired lawyer, writer*

### Flintridge
Hess, Robert Pratt *lawyer*

### Fresno
Ewell, A. Ben, Jr. *lawyer, businessman*
Jamison, Oliver Morton *retired lawyer*
Palmer, Samuel Copeland, III *lawyer*
Petrucelli, James Michael *lawyer*

### Fullerton
Frizell, Samuel *law educator*
Goldstein, Edward David *lawyer, former glass company executive*
Moerbeek, Stanley Leonard *lawyer*
Parsons, Rodney Hunter *lawyer*
Roberts, Mark Scott *lawyer*
Ruby, Charles Leroy *law educator, lawyer, civic leader*

### Glendale
Ball, James Herington *lawyer*
Boukidis, Constantine Michael *lawyer*
Hoffman, Donald M. *lawyer*
Kazanjian, Phillip Carl *lawyer, business executive*
Martin, John Hugh *lawyer, retired*
Martinetti, Ronald Anthony *lawyer*
O'Malley, Joseph James *lawyer*
Simpson, Allyson Bilich *lawyer*

### Grass Valley
Lawrence, Dean Grayson *retired lawyer*

### Hayward
Smith, John Kerwin *lawyer*
Stern, Ralph David *lawyer*

### Hillsborough
Zimmerman, Bryant Kable *retired lawyer*

### Imperial
O'Leary, Thomas Michael *lawyer*

### Imperial Beach
Merkin, William Leslie *lawyer*

### Indian Wells
Smith, Byron Owen *retired lawyer*

### Irvine
Bastiaanse, Gerard C. *lawyer*
Clark, Karen Heath *lawyer*
Hilker, Walter Robert, Jr. *lawyer*
Jeffers, Michael Bogue *lawyer*
Marshall, Ellen Ruth *lawyer*
Muller, Edward Robert *lawyer*
Puzder, Andrew F. *lawyer*
Ristau, Kenneth Eugene, Jr. *lawyer*
Williams, S. Linn *lawyer*
Wintrode, Ralph Charles *lawyer*

### Irwindale
Timmer, Barbara *lawyer*

### La Canada Flintridge
Costello, Francis William *lawyer*
Wallace, James Wendell *lawyer*

### La Jolla
Kirchheimer, Arthur E(dward) *lawyer, business executive*
Shannahan, William Paul *lawyer*
Siegan, Bernard Herbert *lawyer, educator*
Wilkins, Floyd, Jr. *retired lawyer, consultant*

### La Puente
Churchill, James Allen *lawyer*

### Laguna Beach
Reinglass, Michelle Annette *lawyer*
Simons, Barry Thomas *lawyer*

### Laguna Hills
Leydorf, Frederick Leroy *lawyer*

### Lancaster
Berg, Hans Fredrik *lawyer*

### Larkspur
Greenberg, Myron Silver *lawyer*
Maier, Peter Klaus *law educator, investment adviser*
Marker, Marc Linthacum *lawyer, investor*

### Loma Linda
Chang, Janice May *lawyer, law educator, naturopath, psychologist*

### Lompoc
Sabo, Ronald William *lawyer, financial consultant*

### Long Beach
Johnson, Philip Leslie *lawyer*
Roberts, James Donzil *lawyer*
Taylor, Reese Hale, Jr. *lawyer, former government administrator*
Wise, George Edward *lawyer*

### Los Altos
Weir, Robert H. *lawyer*

### Los Angeles
Aaron, Benjamin *law educator, arbitrator*
Abrams, Norman *law educator, university administrator*
Adamek, Charles Andrew *lawyer*
Adell, Hirsch *lawyer*
Adler, Erwin Ellery *lawyer*
Antin, Michael *lawyer*
Apfel, Gary *lawyer*
April, Rand Scott *lawyer*
Argue, John Clifford *lawyer*
Arnold, Dennis B. *lawyer*
Avery, Robert Dean *lawyer*
Barton, Alan Joel *lawyer*
Barza, Harold A. *lawyer*
Basile, Paul Louis, Jr. *lawyer*
Baum, Michael Lin *lawyer*
Bauman, John Andrew *law educator*
Baumann, Richard Gordon *lawyer*
Baumgarten, Ronald Neal *lawyer*
Beard, Ronald Stratton *lawyer*
Bell, Wayne Steven *lawyer*
Belleville, Philip Frederick *lawyer*
Bennett, Fred Gilbert *lawyer*
Berman, Myles Lee *lawyer*
Bernacchi, Richard Lloyd *lawyer*
Bernhard, Herbert Ashley *lawyer*
Bice, Scott Haas *lawyer, educator*
Biederman, Donald Ellis *lawyer*
Bierstedt, Peter Richard *lawyer, entertainment industry consultant*
Bishop, Sidney Willard *lawyer*
Black, Donna Ruth *lawyer*
Blackman, Lee L. *lawyer*
Blencowe, Paul Sherwood *lawyer*
Bloom, Alan *lawyer*
Blumberg, Grace Ganz *law educator, lawyer*
Bodkin, Henry Grattan, Jr. *lawyer*
Bogen, Andrew E. *lawyer*
Bomes, Stephen D. *lawyer*
Bonner, Robert Cleve *lawyer*
Borenstein, Mark A. *lawyer*
Bortman, David *lawyer*
Bosl, Phillip L. *lawyer*
Bower, Allan Maxwell *lawyer*
Bradley, Lawrence D., Jr. *lawyer*
Branca, John Gregory *lawyer, consultant*
Brandler, Jonathan M. *lawyer*
Brassell, Roselyn Strauss *lawyer*
Braun, David A(dlai) *lawyer*
Breidenbach, Francis Anthony *lawyer*
Bressan, Paul Louis *lawyer*
†Brittenham, Skip *lawyer*
Broussard, Thomas Rollins *lawyer*
Burch, Robert Dale *lawyer*
Burns, Marvin Gerald *lawyer*
Byrd, Christine Waterman Swent *lawyer*
Byrne, Jerome Camillus *lawyer*
Capron, Alexander Morgan *lawyer, educator*
Carlson, Robert E. *lawyer*
Carr, Willard Zeller, Jr. *lawyer*
Carroll, Raoul Lord *lawyer, investment banker*
Cartwright, Brian Grant *lawyer*
Castro, Leonard Edward *lawyer*
Cathcart, David Arthur *lawyer*
Cavanagh, John Edward *lawyer*
Chiate, Kenneth Reed *lawyer*
Chin, Kelvin Henry *legal association executive, mediator, consultant*
Christol, Carl Quimby *lawyer, political science educator*
Chu, Morgan *lawyer*
Clark, Marcia Rachel *prosecutor*
Clark, R. Bradbury *lawyer*
Cleary, William Joseph, Jr. *lawyer*
Cochran, Johnnie L., Jr. *lawyer*
Cohan, John Robert *retired lawyer*
Cohen, Cynthia Marylyn *lawyer*
Collier, Charles Arthur, Jr. *lawyer*
Collins, Charles Roland *lawyer*
Cooper, Leon Melvin *lawyer*
Curtiss, Thomas, Jr. *lawyer, educator*
Daniels, John Peter *lawyer*
Darby, G. Harrison *lawyer*
Davis, Edmond Ray *lawyer*
Davis, J. Alan *lawyer, producer, writer*
De Brier, Donald Paul *lawyer*
de Castro, Hugo Daniel *lawyer*
Decker, David R. *lawyer*
DeLuce, Richard David *lawyer*
Deukmejian, George *lawyer, former governor*
Diamond, Stanley Jay *lawyer*
Dickerson, Jaffe Dean *lawyer*
Donovan, John Arthur *lawyer*
Downey, William J., III *lawyer*
Dunham, Scott H. *lawyer*
Emanuel, William Joseph *lawyer*
English, Stephen Raymond *lawyer*
Etra, Donald *lawyer*
Eule, Julian Nathan *law educator*
Fairbank, Robert Harold *lawyer*
Farmer, Robert Lindsay *lawyer*
Field, Richard Clark *lawyer*
Fields, Bertram Harris *lawyer*
Fine, Richard Isaac *lawyer*
Fisher, Raymond Corley *lawyer*
Fisher, Richard N. *lawyer*
Fohrman, Burton H. *lawyer*
Follick, Edwin Duane *law educator, chiropractic physician*
Ford, Donald Hainline *lawyer*
Frackman, Russell Jay *lawyer*
Fragner, Matthew Charles *lawyer*
Francis, Merrill Richard *lawyer*
Fredman, Howard S *lawyer*
Friedman, Alan E. *lawyer*
Frimmer, Paul Norman *lawyer*
Fybel, Richard D. *lawyer*
Gallo, Jon Joseph *lawyer*
Garcetti, Gilbert I. *prosecutor*
Gebb, Sheldon Alexander *lawyer*
Gentile, Joseph F. *lawyer, educator*
Gest, Howard David *lawyer*
Geuss, Gary George *lawyer*
Gilbert, Judith Arlene *lawyer*
Gilbert, Robert Wolfe *lawyer*
Glazer, Michael *lawyer*
Glick, Earl A. *lawyer*
Goldman, Allan Bailey *lawyer*
Goldman, Benjamin Edward *lawyer*
Goodman, Max A. *lawyer, educator*
Gordon, David Eliot *lawyer*
Gorman, Joseph Gregory, Jr. *lawyer*
Gould, Charles Perry *lawyer*
Gould, David *lawyer*
Grausam, Jeffrey Leonard *lawyer*
Gray, Jan Charles *lawyer, business owner*
Greaves, John Allen *lawyer*
Green, William Porter *lawyer*
Griffey, Linda Boyd *lawyer*
Gross, Allen Jeffrey *lawyer*
Grosz, Philip J. *lawyer*
Gurfein, Peter J. *lawyer*
Halkett, Alan Neilson *lawyer*
Hall, Carlyle Washington, Jr. *lawyer*
Handzlik, Jan Lawrence *lawyer*
Hansell, Dean *lawyer*
Hanson, John J. *lawyer*
Hart, Larry Calvin *lawyer*
Havel, Richard W. *lawyer*
Hayes, Byron Jackson, Jr. *lawyer*
Hayutin, David Lionel *lawyer*
Hedlund, Paul James *lawyer*
Heinke, Rex S. *lawyer*
Hemminger, Pamela Lynn *lawyer*
Heyck, Theodore Daly *lawyer*
Heyler, Grover Ross *retired lawyer*
Hieronymus, Edward Whittlesey *lawyer*
Highberger, William Foster *lawyer*
Hight, B. Boyd *lawyer*
Hinerfeld, Robert Elliot *lawyer*
†Hirsch, Barry L. *lawyer*
Holliday, Thomas Edgar *lawyer*
Holtzman, Robert Arthur *lawyer*
Howard, Nancy E. *lawyer*
Hudson, Jeffrey Reid *lawyer*
Hufstedler, Seth Martin *lawyer*
Hufstedler, Shirley Mount (Mrs. Seth M. Hufstedler) *lawyer, former federal judge*
Hunter, Larry Dean *lawyer*
Hyman, Milton Bernard *lawyer*
Iamele, Richard Thomas *law librarian*
Irell, Lawrence E(lliott) *lawyer*
Irwin, Philip Donnan *lawyer*
James, William J. *lawyer*
Janofsky, Leonard S. *lawyer, association executive*
Johnson, Jonathan Edwin, II *lawyer*
Johnson, Michael Marion *lawyer*
Jordan, Robert Leon *lawyer, educator*
Kadison, Stuart L. *lawyer and educator*
Kamine, Bernard Samuel *lawyer*
Karst, Kenneth Leslie *legal educator*
Kay, Kelly W. *lawyer*
Kendig, Ellsworth Harold, Jr. *retired corporate lawyer*
Kiekhofer, William Henry *lawyer*
Kindel, James Horace, Jr. *lawyer*
Kirwan, Ralph DeWitt *lawyer*
Klee, Kenneth Nathan *lawyer*
Klein, Jeffrey S. *lawyer, newspaper executive*
Klein, Raymond Maurice *lawyer*
Kleinberg, Marvin H. *lawyer*
Klowden, Michael Louis *lawyer*
Koelzer, George Joseph *lawyer*
Kuechle, John Merrill *lawyer*
Kupietzky, Moshe J. *lawyer*
Kupperman, Henry John *lawyer*
Lane, Robert Gerhart *lawyer*
Lappen, Chester I. *lawyer*
Lashley, Lenore Clarisse *lawyer*
Latham, Joseph Al, Jr. *lawyer*
Lauchengco, Jose Yujuico, Jr. *lawyer*
Laybourne, Everett Broadstone *lawyer*
Leibow, Ronald Louis *lawyer*
Lesser, Joan L. *lawyer*
Letwin, Leon *legal educator*
Leung, Frankie Fook-Lun *lawyer*
Levine, C. Bruce *lawyer*
Liebeler, Wesley J. *law educator, lawyer*
Lindholm, Dwight Henry *lawyer*
Link, George Hamilton *lawyer*
Lipsig, Ethan *lawyer*
Loeb, Ronald Marvin *lawyer*
Logan, Francis Dummer *lawyer*
Long, Gregory Alan *lawyer*
Lublinski, Michael *lawyer*
Lurvey, Ira Harold *lawyer*
Lynch, Patrick *lawyer*
MacLaughlin, Francis Joseph *lawyer*
Manatt, Charles Taylor *lawyer*
Mancino, Douglas Michael *lawyer*
Marcus, Stephen Howard *lawyer*
Marshall, Arthur K. *lawyer, judge, arbitrator, educator, writer*
McAniff, Edward John *lawyer*
McBirney, Bruce Henry *lawyer*
McDermott, John E. *lawyer*
McDermott, Thomas John, Jr. *lawyer*
McKinzie, Carl Wayne *lawyer*
McKnight, Frederick L. *lawyer*
McLane, Frederick Berg *lawyer*
McLaughlin, Joseph Mailey *lawyer*
McLurkin, Thomas Cornelius, Jr. *lawyer*
Medearis, Miller *lawyer*
Mellinkoff, David *lawyer, educator*
Metzger, Robert Streicher *lawyer*
Meyer, Catherine Dieffenbach *lawyer*
Meyer, Michael Edwin *lawyer*
Millard, Neal Steven *lawyer*
Miller, Milton Allen *lawyer*
Mintz, Marshall Gary *lawyer*
Mintz, Ronald Steven *lawyer*
Moloney, Stephen Michael *lawyer*
Morganstern, Myrna Dorothy *lawyer*
Morgenthaler, Alisa Marie *lawyer*
Morris, Herbert *lawyer, educator*
Mosk, Richard Mitchell *lawyer*
Moskowitz, Joel Steven *lawyer*
Muhlbach, Robert Arthur *lawyer*
Munzer, Stephen R. *law educator*
Neely, Sally Schultz *lawyer*
Neiter, Gerald Irving *lawyer*
Nelson, Grant Steel *lawyer, educator*
Newman, David Wheeler *lawyer*
Newman, Michael Rodney *lawyer*
Nibley, Robert Ricks *retired lawyer*
Nicholas, William Richard *lawyer*
Niemeth, Charles Frederick *lawyer*
Niemiec, Peter Jude *lawyer*
Niles, John Gilbert *lawyer*
Noble, Richard Lloyd *lawyer*
Nocas, Andrew James *lawyer*
Nochimson, David *lawyer*
O'Connell, Kevin *lawyer*
O'Donnell, Pierce Henry *lawyer*
Ohlgren, Joel R. *lawyer*
Olsen, Frances Elisabeth *law educator, theorist*
Ordin, Andrea Sheridan *lawyer*
Orr, Ronald Stewart *lawyer*
Owen, Michael Lee *lawyer*
Packard, Robert Charles *lawyer*
Palazzo, Robert P. *lawyer, accountant*
Papiano, Neil Leo *lawyer*
Parsky, Gerald Lawrence *lawyer*
Pasich, Kirk Alan *lawyer*
Peck, Austin H., Jr. *lawyer*
Pedersen, Norman A. *lawyer*
Perlis, Michael Fredrick *lawyer*
Perry, Ralph Barton, III *lawyer*
Peters, Richard T. *lawyer*
Pieper, Darold D. *lawyer*
Pircher, Leo Joseph *lawyer*
Poindexter, William Mersereau *lawyer*
Pollock, John Phleger *lawyer*
Pope, Alexander H. *lawyer, former county official*
Porter, Verna Louise *lawyer*
Power, John Bruce *lawyer*
Preonas, George Elias *lawyer*
Presant, Sanford Calvin *lawyer*
Pugsley, Robert Adrian *legal educator*
Rabinovitz, Joel *lawyer, educator*
Rae, Matthew Sanderson, Jr. *lawyer*
Raeder, Myrna Sharon *lawyer, educator*
Rappeport, Ira J. *lawyer*
Rath, Howard Grant, Jr. *lawyer*
Ray, Gilbert T. *lawyer*
Reeves, Barbara Ann *lawyer*
Renwick, Edward S. *lawyer*
Richardson, Arthur Wilhelm *lawyer*
Richardson, Douglas Fielding *lawyer*
Ring, Michael Wilson *lawyer*
Robertson, Hugh Duff *lawyer*
Robinson, Martha Stewart *retired legal educator*
Roney, John Harvey *lawyer, consultant*
Rosendahl, Roger Wayne *lawyer*
Rosenthal, Sol *lawyer*
Rosett, Arthur Irwin *lawyer, educator*
Rothenberg, Alan I. *lawyer, professional sports association executive*
Rothman, Frank *lawyer, motion picture company executive*
Rothman, Michael Judah *lawyer*
Rutter, Marshall Anthony *lawyer*
Samet, Jack I. *lawyer*
Samuels, Donald L. *lawyer*
Saxe, Deborah Crandall *lawyer*
Scheifly, John Edward *retired lawyer*
Schmidt, Karl A. *lawyer*
Scott, A. Timothy *lawyer*
Scoular, Robert Frank *lawyer*
Selwood, Pierce Taylor *lawyer*
Shames, Henry Joseph *lawyer*
Shanks, Patricia L. *lawyer*
Shapiro, Marvin Seymour *lawyer*
Shapiro, Robert Leslie *lawyer*
Sheehan, Lawrence James *lawyer*
Sherwood, Allen Joseph *lawyer*
Sherwood, Arthur Lawrence *lawyer*
Shortz, Richard Alan *lawyer*
Shultz, John David *lawyer*
Silbergeld, Arthur F. *lawyer*
Slavitt, Earl Benton *lawyer*
Stamm, Alan *lawyer*
Stephens, George Edward, Jr. *lawyer*
Stone, Lawrence Maurice *lawyer, educator*
Stone, Richard James *lawyer*
Stromberg, Ross Ernest *lawyer*
Sumner, James DuPre, Jr. *lawyer, educator*
Tackowiak, Bruce Joseph *lawyer*
Tan, William Lew *lawyer*
Tarr, Ralph William *lawyer, former federal government official*
†Taylor, Minna *lawyer*
Teele, Cynthia Lombard *lawyer*
Thorpe, Douglas L. *lawyer*
Tinsley, Walton Eugene *lawyer*
Title, Gail Migdal *lawyer*
Tobisman, Stuart Paul *lawyer*
Treister, George Marvin *lawyer*
Trimble, Phillip Richard *law educator*
Troy, Joseph Freed *lawyer*
Trygstad, Lawrence Benson *lawyer*
Ukropina, James R. *lawyer*
Van de Kamp, John Kalar *lawyer*
Vanderet, Robert Charles *lawyer*
Vaughan, Joseph Robert *lawyer*
Vaughn, William Weaver *lawyer*
Volpert, Richard Sidney *lawyer*
Wagner, D. William *lawyer*
Walcher, Alan Ernest *lawyer*
Wayte, (Paul) Alan *lawyer*
Weinman, Glenn Alan *lawyer*
Weinstock, Harold *lawyer*
Weiss, Walter Stanley *lawyer*
Weissbard, Samuel Held *lawyer*
Weiswasser, Stephen Anthony *lawyer, broadcast executive*
Wessling, Robert Bruce *lawyer*
Wheat, Francis Millspaugh *retired lawyer*
White, Robert Joel *lawyer*
Wigmore, John Grant *lawyer*
Williams, Donald Clyde *lawyer*
Williams, Richard Thomas *lawyer*
Wine, Mark Philip *lawyer*
Wolas, Herbert *lawyer*
Wolfen, Werner F. *lawyer*
Wright, Kenneth Brooks *lawyer*
York, Gary Alan *lawyer*
Zelon, Laurie Dee *lawyer*
Ziffren, Kenneth *lawyer*

### Los Gatos
Seligmann, William Robert *lawyer, author*

### Malibu
Phillips, Ronald Frank *legal educator, academic administrator, dean*

### Manhattan Beach
Chettle, A(lvin) B(asil), Jr. *lawyer, educator*
Scott, Michael Dennis *lawyer*

### Marina Del Rey
Adams, Thomas Merritt *lawyer*
Davis, Donald G(lenn) *lawyer*
Grobe, Charles Stephen *lawyer, accountant*
Smolker, Gary Steven *lawyer*

### Martinez
Bray, Absalom Francis, Jr. *lawyer*

### Mendocino
Rappaport, Stuart R. *lawyer*

### Menlo Park
Bader, W(illiam) Reece *lawyer*
Borovoy, Roger Stuart *lawyer*
Dyer, Charles Arnold *lawyer*
Ferris, Robert Albert *lawyer, venture capitalist*
Gunderson, Robert Vernon, Jr. *lawyer*
Kirk, Cassius Lamb, Jr. *lawyer, investor*
Madison, James Raymond *lawyer*
Pooley, James Henry Anderson *lawyer, author*
Taylor, Robert P. *lawyer*

### Mill Valley
Nemir, Donald Philip *lawyer*

### Millbrae
Lande, James Avra *lawyer*

### Mission Viejo
Ruben, Robert Joseph *lawyer*

### Modesto
Owens, Jack Byron *lawyer*

### Monte Rio
Pemberton, John de Jarnette, Jr. *lawyer, educator*

### Monte Sereno
Allan, Lionel Manning *lawyer*

### Monterey
Bomberger, Russell Branson *lawyer, educator*
Fenton, Lewis Lowry *lawyer*
Haddad, Louis Nicholas *paralegal*
Stern, Gerald Daniel *lawyer*

### Mount Shasta
Armstrong, Kenneth *lawyer*

### Nevada City
Holtz, Sara *lawyer, consultant*

### Newport Beach
Adams, William Gillette *lawyer*
Allen, Russell G. *lawyer*
Baskin, Scott David *lawyer*
Bernauer, Thomas A. *lawyer*
Caldwell, Courtney Lynn *lawyer, real estate consultant*
Cano, Kristin Maria *lawyer*
Clark, Thomas P., Jr. *lawyer*
Dillion, Gregory Lee *lawyer*
Johnson, Thomas Webber, Jr. *lawyer*
Katayama, Arthur Shoji *lawyer*
Klein, Maurice J. *lawyer*
Mallory, Frank Linus *lawyer*
McEvers, Duff Steven *lawyer*
Millar, Richard William, Jr. *lawyer*
Mortensen, Arvid LeGrande *lawyer*
Pepe, Stephen Phillip *lawyer*
Phillips, Layn R. *lawyer*
Rooklidge, William Charles *lawyer*
Schnapp, Roger Herbert *lawyer*
Wentworth, Theodore Sumner *lawyer*
Willard, Robert Edgar *lawyer*

### North Hollywood
Kreger, Melvin Joseph *lawyer*
Peter, Arnold Philimon *lawyer*
Runquist, Lisa A. *lawyer*
Zimring, Stuart David *lawyer*

### Novato
Obninsky, Victor Peter *lawyer*

### Oakland
Allen, Jeffrey Michael *lawyer*
Burnison, Boyd Edward *lawyer*
Chilvers, Robert Merritt *lawyer*
Deming, Willis Riley *lawyer*
Fogel, Paul David *lawyer*
Heywood, Robert Gilmour *lawyer*
Johnson, Kenneth F. *lawyer*
Kaplan, Alvin Irving *lawyer, adjudicator, investigator*
Leslie, Robert Lorne *lawyer*
McLain, Christopher M. *lawyer*
Miller, Kirk Edward *lawyer, health foundation executive*
Miller, Thomas Robbins *lawyer, publisher*
O'Connor, Paul Daniel *lawyer*
Quinby, William Albert *lawyer, mediator, arbitrator*
Skaff, Andrew Joseph *lawyer, public utilities, energy and transportation executive*
Taylor, William James (Zak Taylor) *lawyer*
Wallis, Eric G. *lawyer*
Wick, William David *lawyer*
Wood, James Michael *lawyer*

### Oceanside
Robinson, William Franklin *retired legal consultant*

**Orange**
Batchelor, James Kent *lawyer*
Sawdei, Milan A. *lawyer*

**Orinda**
Brookes, Valentine *retired lawyer*
Medak, Walter Hans *lawyer*

**Oroville**
Chapman, Joyce Eileen *law educator, administrator*

**Oxnard**
O'Hearn, Michael John *lawyer*

**Pacific Palisades**
Cale, Charles Griffin *lawyer, investor*
Flattery, Thomas Long *lawyer, legal administrator*
Nothmann, Rudolf S. *legal researcher*
Rothenberg, Leslie Steven *lawyer, ethicist*
Schwartz, Murray Louis *lawyer, educator, academic administrator*
Sevilla, Stanley *lawyer*
Verrone, Patric Miller *lawyer, writer*

**Palm Desert**
Humphrey, Charles Edward, Jr. *lawyer*
Reinhardt, Benjamin Max *lawyer, arbitrator, mediator*
Singer, Gerald Michael *lawyer, educator, author, arbitrator and mediator*
Spirtos, Nicholas George *lawyer, financial company executive*

**Palm Springs**
Kimberling, John Farrell *retired lawyer*

**Palo Alto**
Adams, Marcia Howe *lawyer*
Bell, Richard G. *lawyer*
Bradley, Donald Edward *lawyer*
Brigham, Samuel Townsend Jack, III *lawyer*
Climan, Richard Elliot *lawyer*
Furbush, David Malcolm *lawyer*
Haslam, Robert Thomas, III *lawyer*
Hinckley, Robert Craig *lawyer*
Houpt, James Edward *lawyer*
Klotsche, John Chester *lawyer*
Massey, Henry P., Jr. *lawyer*
Mendelson, Alan Charles *lawyer*
Monroy, Gladys H. *lawyer*
Moretti, August Joseph *lawyer*
Nau, Charles John *lawyer*
Nicholson, Bradley James *lawyer*
Nordlund, Donald Craig *corporate lawyer*
Nycum, Susan Hubbell *lawyer*
Pasahow, Lynn H(arold) *lawyer*
Patterson, Robert Edward *lawyer*
Phair, Joseph Baschon *lawyer*
Rinsky, Arthur C. *lawyer*
Small, Jonathan Andrew *lawyer*
Smith, Glenn A. *lawyer*
Van Atta, David Murray *lawyer*
Walker, Ann Yvonne *lawyer*
Wheeler, Raymond Louis *lawyer*
Wunsch, Kathryn Sutherland *lawyer*

**Palos Verdes Peninsula**
Yeomans, Russell Allen *lawyer, translator*

**Paramount**
Hall, Howard Harry *lawyer*

**Pasadena**
Alschuler, Frederick Harold *lawyer*
Bakaly, Charles George, Jr. *lawyer, mediator*
Cahill, Richard Frederick *lawyer*
Calleton, Theodore Edward *lawyer*
D'Angelo, Robert William *lawyer*
Doyle, John C. *lawyer*
Epstein, Bruce Howard *lawyer, real estate broker*
Gillam, Max Lee *lawyer*
Haight, James Theron *lawyer, corporate executive*
Hale, Charles Russell *lawyer*
Hunt, Gordon *lawyer*
Koch, Albin Cooper *lawyer*
Mosher, Sally Ekenberg *lawyer*
Mueth, Joseph Edward *lawyer*
Myers, R(alph) Chandler *lawyer*
Pianko, Theodore A. *lawyer*
Tanner, Dee Boshard *retired lawyer*
Wyatt, Joseph Lucian, Jr. *lawyer, author*
Yohalem, Harry Morton *lawyer*
Zuetel, Kenneth Roy, Jr. *lawyer*

**Paso Robles**
Knecht, James Herbert *lawyer*

**Pebble Beach**
Maxeiner, Clarence William *lawyer, construction company executive*

**Piedmont**
McCormick, Timothy Brian Beer *lawyer*

**Pleasanton**
Staley, John Fredric *lawyer*

**Plymouth**
Andreason, John Christian *lawyer*

**Portola Valley**
Cooper, John Joseph *lawyer*

**Rancho Mirage**
Reuben, Don Harold *lawyer*

**Rancho Santa Fe**
Peterson, Nad A. *lawyer, retired corporate executive*

**Redding**
Ragland, Carroll Ann *law educator, judicial officer*

**Redlands**
Ely, Northcutt *lawyer*

**Redwood City**
Silvestri, Philip Salvatore *lawyer*
Tight, Dexter Corwin *lawyer*
Wilhelm, Robert Oscar *lawyer, civil engineer, developer*

**Richmond**
Kirk-Duggan, Michael Allan *retired law and computer sciences educator*
Quenneville, Kathleen *lawyer*

**Rio Linda**
Lebrato, Mary Theresa *lawyer, psychologist*

**Riverside**
Aderton, Jane Reynolds *lawyer*
Darling, Scott Edward *lawyer*

**Rolling Hills**
Rumbaugh, Charles Earl *lawyer, arbitrator/mediator*

**Roseville**
Robbins, Stephen J. M. *lawyer*

**Sacramento**
Albert-Sheridan, Lenore LuAnn *legal research fellow, business owner*
Andrew, John Henry *lawyer, retail corporation executive*
Blake, D. Steven *lawyer*
Bobrow, Susan Lukin *lawyer*
Brookman, Anthony Raymond *lawyer*
Callahan, Ronald *federal investigator, historian*
Day, James McAdam, Jr. *lawyer*
Friedman, Morton Lee *lawyer*
Goodart, Nan L. *lawyer, educator*
†James, Robert William *lawyer*
Janigian, Bruce Jasper *lawyer, educator*
Kolkey, Daniel Miles *lawyer*
Miller, Suzanne Marie *law librarian, educator*
Phillips, Dana Wayne *lawyer*
Plant, Forrest Albert *lawyer*
Root, Gerald Edward *courts resource manager*
Schaber, Gordon Duane *law educator, former judge*
Shirley, George Pfeiffer *lawyer, educational consultant*
Sullivan, Robert Joseph *lawyer*
Taylor, Walter Wallace *lawyer*
Twiss, Robert Manning *prosecutor*
Van Camp, Brian Ralph *lawyer*
Zeff, Ophelia Hope *lawyer*

**San Andreas**
Arkin, Michael Barry *lawyer, arbitrator*

**San Anselmo**
Murphy, Barry Ames *lawyer*

**San Diego**
Alpert, Michael Edward *lawyer*
Andreos, George Phillip *lawyer*
Bohrer, Robert Arnold *law educator*
Bowie, Peter Wentworth *lawyer, educator*
Brooks, John White *lawyer*
Chatroo, Arthur Jay *lawyer*
Copeland, Robert Glenn *lawyer*
Damoose, George Lynn *lawyer*
Estep, Arthur Lee *lawyer*
Gastwirth, Donald Edward *lawyer, literary agent*
Guinn, Stanley Willis *lawyer*
Guinn, Susan Lee *lawyer*
Hofflund, Paul *lawyer*
Huston, Kenneth Dale *lawyer*
Hutcheson, J(ames) Sterling *lawyer*
Kennerson, Paul *lawyer, author, educator*
Kripke, Kenneth Norman *lawyer*
Lathrop, Mitchell Lee *lawyer*
LeBeau, Charles Paul *lawyer*
Lory, Loran Steven *lawyer*
Mayer, James Hock *mediator, lawyer*
McGinnis, Robert E. *lawyer*
McManus, Richard Philip *lawyer, agricultural products company executive*
Meyer, Paul I. *lawyer*
Miller, William Charles *lawyer*
Mittermiller, James Joseph *lawyer*
Morris, Grant Harold *law educator*
Morris, Sandra Joan *lawyer*
Mulvaney, James Francis *lawyer*
O'Malley, James Terence *lawyer*
Patterson, Jamee Jordan *lawyer*
Pray, Ralph Marble, III *lawyer*
Pugh, Richard Crawford *lawyer*
Ross, Terry D. *lawyer*
St. George, William Ross *lawyer, retired naval officer, consultant*
Samuelson, Derrick William *lawyer*
Schuck, Carl Joseph *lawyer*
Seitman, John M. *lawyer*
Shaw, Lee Charles *lawyer*
Shaw, Richard Allan *lawyer*
Shearer, William Kennedy *lawyer, publisher*
Shelton, Dorothy Diehl Rees *lawyer*
Shippey, Sandra Lee *lawyer*
Smith, Steven Ray *law educator*
Snyder, David Richard *lawyer*
Sterrett, James Kelley, II *lawyer*
Stiska, John C. *lawyer*
Sullivan, William Francis *lawyer*
Weaver, Michael James *lawyer*
Whitmore, Sharp *lawyer*

**San Francisco**
Abbott, Barry Alexander *lawyer*
Adams, Lee Stephen *lawyer, banker*
Adams, Philip *lawyer*
Alexander, Robert C. *lawyer*
Allen, Jose R. *lawyer*
Alsup, William *lawyer*
Andrews, David Ralph *lawyer*
Arbuthnot, Robert Murray *lawyer*
Archer, Richard Joseph *lawyer*
Baker, Cameron *lawyer*
Bancroft, James Ramsey *lawyer, business executive*
Barbagelata, Robert Dominic *lawyer*
Barber, James P. *lawyer*
Bare, Joseph Edward, Jr. *retired lawyer*
Bates, John Burnham *lawyer*
Bates, William, III *lawyer*
Baxter, Ralph H., Jr. *lawyer*
Beck, Edward William *lawyer*
Bedford, Daniel Ross *lawyer*
Benvenutti, Peter J. *lawyer*
Berning, Paul Wilson *lawyer*
Berns, Philip Allan *lawyer*
Bertain, G(eorge) Joseph, Jr. *lawyer*
Bonapart, Alan David *lawyer*
Bookin, Daniel Henry *lawyer*
Booth, Forrest *lawyer*
Borowsky, Philip *lawyer*
Boucher, Harold Irving *lawyer*
Boutin, Peter Rucker *lawyer*
Boyd, William Sprott *lawyer*
Bridges, Robert Lysle *retired lawyer*
Briggs, Susan Shadinger *lawyer*
Briscoe, John *lawyer*
Bromley, Dennis Karl *lawyer*
Brown, Donald Wesley *lawyer*
Brown, Margaret deBeers *lawyer*
Bruen, James A. *lawyer*
Budge, Hamilton Whithed *lawyer*
Burns, Brian Patrick *lawyer, business executive*
Callan, Terrence A. *lawyer*
Campbell, Scott Robert *lawyer, former food company executive*
Carlson, John Earl *lawyer*
Carter, John Douglas *lawyer*
Cartmell, Nathaniel Madison, III *lawyer*
Casillas, Mark *lawyer*
Chao, Cedric C. *lawyer*
Cheatham, Robert William *lawyer*
Coblentz, William Kraemer *lawyer*
Coffin, Judy Sue *lawyer*
Coleman, Thomas Young *lawyer*
Collas, Juan Garduño, Jr. *lawyer*
Coombe, George William, Jr. *lawyer, retired banker*
Corcoran, Maureen Elizabeth *lawyer*
Crawford, Roy Edgington, III *lawyer*
Daggett, Robert Sherman *lawyer*
Davies, Paul Lewis, Jr. *retired lawyer*
Davis, Roger Lewis *lawyer*
De Benedictis, Dario *arbitrator, mediator*
Diamond, Philip Ernest *lawyer*
Diekmann, Gilmore Frederick, Jr. *lawyer*
Donnici, Peter Joseph *lawyer, law educator, consultant*
Doyle, Morris McKnight *lawyer*
Dryden, Robert Eugene *lawyer*
Dunne, Kevin Joseph *lawyer*
Dupree, Stanley M. *lawyer*
Edwards, Priscilla Ann *litigation support business owner*
Edwards, Robin Morse *lawyer*
Ehrlich, Thomas *law educator*
Elderkin, E(dwin) Judge *retired lawyer*
Ericson, Bruce Alan *lawyer*
Fergus, Gary Scott *lawyer*
Finberg, James Michael *lawyer*
Finck, Kevin William *lawyer*
Fine, Marjorie Lynn *lawyer*
Folberg, Harold Jay *lawyer, mediator, educator, university dean*
Foster, David Scott *lawyer*
Frankel, James Burton *lawyer*
Fredericks, Dale Edward *lawyer*
Freeman, Tom M. *lawyer*
Freud, Nicholas S. *lawyer*
Friedman, K. Bruce *lawyer*
Friese, Robert Charles *lawyer*
Furth, Frederick Paul *lawyer*
Gaither, James C. *lawyer*
Garvey, Joanne Marie *lawyer*
Gibson, Virginia Lee *lawyer*
Gowdy, Franklin Brockway *lawyer*
Gresham, Zane Oliver *lawyer*
Guggenhime, Richard Johnson *lawyer*
Hall, Paul J. *lawyer*
Halloran, Michael James *lawyer*
Hannawalt, Willis Dale *lawyer*
Hanschen, Peter Walter *lawyer*
Haven, Thomas Edward *lawyer*
Heafey, Edwin Austin, Jr. *lawyer*
Heilbron, David M(ichael) *lawyer*
Heng, Donald James, Jr. *lawyer*
Henson, Ray David *legal educator, consultant*
Hinman, Harvey DeForest *lawyer*
Hofmann, John Richard, Jr. *lawyer*
Holden, Frederick Douglass, Jr. *lawyer*
Homer, Barry Wayne *lawyer*
Howard, Carl (Michael) *lawyer*
Howe, Drayton Ford, Jr. *lawyer*
Hudner, Philip *lawyer, rancher*
Hudson, Mark Woodbridge *lawyer*
Hunt, James L. *lawyer*
Hunter, William Dennis *lawyer*
Irwin, William Rankin *lawyer*
James, David Lee *lawyer, international advisor, author*
Johnson, Martin Wayne *lawyer*
Johnson, Reverdy *lawyer*
Joseph, Allan Jay *lawyer*
Judson, Philip Livingston *lawyer*
Jung, David Joseph *law educator*
Kallgren, Edward Eugene *lawyer*
Kane, Mary Kay *law educator*
Kasanin, Mark Owen *lawyer*
Kaufman, Christopher Lee *lawyer*
Kelly, J. Michael *lawyer*
Kemp, Alson Remington, Jr. *lawyer, legal educator*
Kennedy, Raoul Dion *lawyer*
Kern, John McDougall *lawyer*
Kimport, David Lloyd *lawyer*
Klinger, Marilyn Sydney *lawyer*
Klott, David Lee *lawyer*
Knebel, Jack Gillen *lawyer*
Koeppel, John A. *lawyer*
Kuhl, Paul Beach *lawyer*
Ladar, Jerrold Morton *lawyer*
Ladd, John Curran *lawyer*
Lambert, Frederick William *lawyer, educator*
Lane, Fielding H. *lawyer*
Larson, John William *lawyer*
Lasky, Moses *lawyer*
Lathrope, Daniel John *law educator*
Laurie, Ronald Sheldon *lawyer*
Lee, John Jin *lawyer*
Lee, Richard Diebold *law educator, legal publisher*
Levit, Victor Bert *lawyer, foreign representative, civic worker*
Libbin, Anne Edna *lawyer*
Livsey, Robert Callister *lawyer*
Lotito, Michael Joseph *lawyer*
Lundquist, Weyman Ivan *lawyer*
Lynch, Timothy Jeremiah-Mahoney *lawyer, educator, theologian, realtor, writer*
MacGowan, Mary Eugenia *lawyer*
MacGuinness, Rosemary Anne *lawyer*
Mann, Bruce Alan *lawyer*
Manning, Jerome Alan *retired lawyer*
Marchant, David Judson *lawyer*
Marcus, Richard Leon *lawyer, educator*
Mason, Cheryl White *lawyer*
Mattes, Martin Anthony *lawyer*
McElhinny, Harold John *lawyer*
McGuckin, John H., Jr. *lawyer*
McKelvey, Judith Grant *lawyer, educator, university dean*
Mc Laughlin, Jerome Michael *lawyer, shipping company executive*
McLeod, Robert Macfarlan *lawyer, arbitrator*
McNally, Thomas Charles, III *lawyer*
McNamara, Thomas Neal *lawyer*
Mellor, Michael Lawton *lawyer*
Metzler, Roger James, Jr. *lawyer*
Miller, James Lynn *lawyer*
Miller, William Napier Cripps *lawyer*
Mills, Robert A. *lawyer*
Millstein, David J. *lawyer*
Minnick, Malcolm David *lawyer*
Mitchell, Bruce Tyson *lawyer*
Molligan, Peter Nicholas *lawyer*
Morrissey, John Carroll *lawyer*
Mosk, Susan Hines *lawyer*
Murphy, Arthur John, Jr. *lawyer*
Musfelt, Duane Clark *lawyer*
Musser, Sandra G. *lawyer*
Nelson, Paul Douglas *lawyer*
Offer, Stuart Jay *lawyer*
Olson, Walter Gilbert *lawyer*
Park, Roger Cook *law educator*
Parker, Harold Allen *lawyer, real estate executive*
Penskar, Mark Howard *lawyer*
Peritore, Laura *law librarian*
Peter, Laura Anne *lawyer*
Placier, Philip R. *lawyer*
Platt, Peter Godfrey *lawyer*
Plishner, Michael Jon *lawyer*
Poole, Gordon Leicester *lawyer*
Popofsky, Melvin Laurence *lawyer*
Prunty, Bert Sherman, Jr. *lawyer*
Ragan, Charles Ransom *lawyer*
Ramey, Drucilla Stender *legal association executive*
Ratner, David Louis *legal educator*
Raven, Robert Dunbar *lawyer*
Read, Gregory Charles *lawyer*
Reding, John A. *lawyer*
Reese, John Robert *lawyer*
Rembe, Toni *lawyer*
Renne, Louise Hornbeck *lawyer*
Rice, Denis Timlin *lawyer*
Richards, Norman Blanchard *lawyer*
Richardson, Daniel Ralph *lawyer*
Rockwell, Alvin John *lawyer*
Roethe, James Norton *lawyer*
Roman, Stan G. *lawyer*
Rosch, John Thomas *lawyer*
Rosen, Sanford Jay *lawyer*
Rosenthal, Herbert Marshall *legal association executive*
Rosston, Edward William *lawyer*
Rowland, John Arthur *lawyer*
Rubin, Michael *lawyer*
Russoniello, Joseph Pascal *lawyer*
Ryland, David Ronald *lawyer*
Salomon, Darrell Joseph *lawyer*
Schaffer, Jeffrey L. *lawyer*
Schwartz, Louis Brown *legal educator*
Seabolt, Richard L. *lawyer*
Sears, George Ames *lawyer*
†Seavey, William Arthur *lawyer, vintner*
Seegal, John Franklin *lawyer*
Selman, Roland Wooten, III *lawyer*
Seneker, Carl James, II (Kim Seneker) *lawyer*
Sevier, Ernest Youle *lawyer*
Shenk, George H. *lawyer*
Shepherd, John Michael *lawyer*
Sherry, Robert Joseph *lawyer*
Singer, Allen Morris *lawyer*
Small, Marshall Lee *lawyer*
Smegal, Thomas Frank, Jr. *lawyer*
Smith, Kerry Clark *lawyer*
Smith, Robert Michael *lawyer*
Snow, Tower Charles, Jr. *lawyer*
Sparks, John Edward *lawyer*
Sparks, Thomas E., Jr. *lawyer*
Spiegel, Hart Hunter *retired lawyer*
Stanzler, Jordan *lawyer*
Staples, John Norman, III *lawyer*
Staring, Graydon Shaw *lawyer*
Steer, Reginald David *lawyer*
Stotter, Lawrence Henry *lawyer*
Stratton, Richard James *lawyer*
Stuppi, Craig *lawyer*
Sugarman, Myron George *lawyer*
Sullivan, Robert Edward *lawyer*
Sutcliffe, Eric *lawyer*
Sutton, John Paul *lawyer*
Thompson, Robert Charles *lawyer*
Thompson, Roderick M. *lawyer*
Thornton, D. Whitney, II *lawyer*
Tiffany, Joseph Raymond, II *lawyer*
Tingle, James O'Malley *lawyer*
Tobin, James Michael *lawyer*
Trautman, William Ellsworth *lawyer*
Traynor, J. Michael *lawyer*
Truett, Harold Joseph, III (Tim Truett) *lawyer*
Tuttle, George D. *lawyer*
Veaco, Kristina *lawyer*
Venning, Robert Stanley *lawyer*
Walker, Ralph Clifford *lawyer*
Walker, Walter Herbert, III *lawyer, writer*
Walsh, Francis Richard *law educator*
Wang, William Kai-Sheng *law educator*
Warmer, Richard Craig *lawyer*
Weiner, Peter H. *lawyer*
Welch, Thomas Andrew *retire lawyer, arbitrator*
Whelan, John William *lawyer, law educator, consultant*
Wild, Nelson Hopkins *lawyer*
Willson, Prentiss, Jr. *lawyer*
Wingate, C. Keith *law educator*
Wolfe, Cameron Withgot, Jr. *lawyer*
Woods, James Robert *lawyer*
Wyle, Frederick S. *lawyer*
Yamaguchi, Michael Joseph *prosecutor*
Yamakawa, David Kiyoshi, Jr. *lawyer*
Yost, Nicholas Churchill *lawyer*
Young, Bryant Llewellyn *lawyer, business executive*
Young, Douglas Rea *lawyer*
Ziering, William Mark *lawyer*

**San Jose**
Alexander, Richard *lawyer*
Anderson, Edward Virgil *lawyer*
Gonzales, Daniel S. *lawyer*
Granneman, Vernon Henry *lawyer*
Greenstein, Martin Richard *lawyer*
Kennedy, George Wendell *lawyer*
Kraw, George Martin *lawyer, essayist*
Laskin, Barbara Virginia *legal association administrator*
Mitchell, David Walker *lawyer*
Smirni, Allan Desmond *lawyer*
Stutzman, Thomas Chase, Sr. *lawyer*
Towery, James E. *lawyer*

PROFESSIONAL INDEX 5353 LAW: LAW PRACTICE AND ADMINISTRATION

**San Juan Capistrano**
Black, William Rea *lawyer*
Curtis, John Joseph *lawyer*

**San Leandro**
Newacheck, David John *lawyer*

**San Luis Obispo**
Daly, John Paul *lawyer*

**San Marino**
Baldwin, James William *lawyer*
Galbraith, James Marshall *lawyer, business executive*
Tomich, Lillian *lawyer*

**San Mateo**
Bell, Frank Ouray, Jr. *lawyer*
Dworkin, Michael Leonard *lawyer*
Everett, Michael Thomas *lawyer*
Grill, Lawrence J. *lawyer, accountant, corporate/banking executive*

**San Rafael**
Roth, Hadden Wing *lawyer*
Stout, Gregory Stansbury *lawyer*

**San Ramon**
Kahane, Dennis Spencer *lawyer*
Pagter, Carl Richard *lawyer*

**Santa Ana**
Beasley, Oscar Homer *lawyer, educator*
Blaine, Dorothea Constance Ragetté *lawyer*
Capizzi, Michael Robert *lawyer*
Fay-Schmidt, Patricia Ann *paralegal*
Harley, Robison Dooling, Jr. *lawyer, educator*
Heckler, Gerard Vincent *lawyer*
Knox Rios, Delilah Jane *lawyer*
Storer, Maryruth *law librarian*
Zaenglein, William George, Jr. *lawyer*

**Santa Barbara**
Ah-Tye, Kirk Thomas *lawyer*
Bauer, Marvin Agather *lawyer*
Bridges, B. Ried *lawyer*
Carlson, Arthur W. *lawyer*
Gaines, Howard Clarke *retired lawyer*
Harris, James Dexter *lawyer*
Israel, Barry John *lawyer*
Metzinger, Timothy Edward *lawyer*
Moncharsh, Philip Isaac *lawyer*
Perloff, Jean Marcosson *lawyer*
Reed, Frank Fremont, II *retired lawyer*
Simpson, Curtis Chapman, III *lawyer*

**Santa Clara**
Alexander, George Jonathon *legal educator, former dean*
Glancy, Dorothy Jean *lawyer, educator*

**Santa Cruz**
Atchison, Rodney Raymond *lawyer, arbitrator*

**Santa Monica**
Boltz, Gerald Edmund *lawyer*
Bonesteel, Michael John *lawyer*
Dickson, Robert Lee *lawyer*
Hirsch, Richard G. *lawyer*
Jones, William Allen *lawyer, entertainment company executive*
Kanner, Gideon *lawyer*
Le Berthon, Adam *lawyer*
Loo, Thomas S. *lawyer*
McMillan, M. Sean *lawyer*
Prewoznik, Jerome Frank *lawyer*
Ringler, Jerome Lawrence *lawyer*
Risman, Michael *lawyer, business executive, securities company executive*
Roberts, Virgil Patrick *lawyer, business executive*
Sheller, John Willard *lawyer*
Sperling, George Elmer, Jr. *lawyer*
Walker, Charles Montgomery *lawyer*

**Sausalito**
Berkman, William Roger *lawyer, army reserve officer*
Trimmer, Harold Sharp, Jr. *lawyer, international telecommunications consultant*

**Seal Beach**
Calise, William Joseph, Jr. *lawyer*
O'Shaughnessy, James Patrick *lawyer*

**Seaside**
Weingarten, Saul Myer *lawyer*

**Sherman Oaks**
Crump, Gerald Franklin *retired lawyer*
Luna, Barbara Carole *expert witness, accountant, appraiser*

**Solvang**
Morrow, Richard Towson *lawyer*

**Stanford**
Babcock, Barbara Allen *lawyer, educator*
Bagley, Constance Elizabeth *lawyer, educator*
Barton, John Hays *law educator*
Baxter, William Francis *lawyer, educator*
Brest, Paul A. *law educator*
Cohen, William *law educator*
Donohue, John Joseph *law educator*
Franklin, Marc Adam *law educator*
Friedman, Lawrence M. *law educator*
Goldstein, Paul *lawyer, educator*
Gunther, Gerald *lawyer, educator*
Mann, J. Keith *arbitrator, law educator*
Mc Bride, Thomas Frederick *lawyer, former university dean, government official*
Rhode, Deborah Lynn *law educator*
Roster, Michael *lawyer*
Scott, Kenneth Eugene *lawyer, educator*
Sofaer, Abraham David *lawyer, legal advisor, federal judge, legal educator*
Williams, Howard Russell *lawyer, educator*

**Stockton**
Blewett, Robert Noall *lawyer*
Curtis, Orlie Lindsey, Jr. *lawyer*

**Studio City**
Miller, Charles Maurice *lawyer*

**Sunnyvale**
Ludgus, Nancy Lucke *lawyer*

**Temecula**
Rosenstein, Robert Bryce *lawyer*
Thompson, James Avery, Jr. *legal intern*
Thompson, Susannah Elizabeth *lawyer*

**Thousand Oaks**
Richelson, Harvey *lawyer, educator*

**Tiburon**
Bauch, Thomas Jay *lawyer, educator, former apparel company executive*

**Torrance**
Kaufman, Sanford Paul *lawyer*
Petillon, Lee Ritchey *lawyer*
Smith, Michael Cordon *lawyer*

**Van Nuys**
Arabian, Armand *arbitrator, mediator, lawyer*
Boyd, Harry Dalton *lawyer, former insurance company executive*
Mikesell, Richard Lyon *lawyer, financial counselor*

**Venice**
Annotico, Richard Anthony *legal scholar*

**Ventura**
Arant, Eugene Wesley *lawyer*
Bride, Robert Fairbanks *lawyer*
Clabaugh, Elmer Eugene, Jr. *lawyer*
Keister, Jean Clare *lawyer*

**Visalia**
Crowe, John T. *lawyer*

**Vista**
Patrick, Wendy Lynn *lawyer*

**Walnut Creek**
Curtin, Daniel Joseph, Jr. *lawyer*
Garrett, James Joseph *lawyer, partner*
Ginsburg, Gerald J. *lawyer, business executive*
Jones, Orlo Dow *lawyer, drug store executive*
Madden, Palmer Brown *lawyer*
Merritt, Robert Edward *lawyer, educator*
Mitgang, Iris Feldman *lawyer, educator*
Newmark, Milton Maxwell *lawyer*
Skaggs, Sanford Merle *lawyer*

**West Covina**
McHale, Edward Robertson *retired lawyer*

**West Hollywood**
Finstad, Suzanne Elaine *laywer, writer, producer*

**Westlake Village**
Jessup, Warren T. *retired lawyer*
Vinson, William Theodore *lawyer, diversified corporation executive*

**Woodland Hills**
Strote, Joel Richard *lawyer*

**Woodside**
Martin, Joseph, Jr. *retired lawyer, former ambassador*

**COLORADO**

**Aspen**
McGrath, J. Nicholas *lawyer*

**Aurora**
Halford, Sharon Lee *legal studies administrator, victimologist, educator*
Kaplan, Marc J. *lawyer*
McPherson, Gary Lee *lawyer, state representative*

**Boulder**
Bintliff, Barbara Ann *law librarian, educator*
Corbridge, James Noel, Jr. *law educator*
Dubofsky, Jean Eberhart *lawyer, former state supreme court justice*
Echohawk, John Ernest *lawyer*
Fiflis, Ted J. *lawyer, educator*
Moses, Raphael Jacob *lawyer*
Oesterle, Dale Arthur *law educator*
Peterson, Courtland Harry *law educator*
Porzak, Glenn E. *lawyer*
Purvis, John Anderson *lawyer*
Rieke, Elizabeth Ann *legal association administrator*
Steuben, Norton Leslie *lawyer, educator*
Tippit, John Harlow *lawyer*

**Cherry Hills Village**
Meyer, Milton Edward, Jr. *lawyer, artist*

**Colorado Springs**
Adams, Deborah Rowland *lawyer*
Buell, Bruce Temple *lawyer*
Campbell, Frederick Hollister *lawyer, historian*
Evans, Paul Vernon *lawyer*
Kendall, Phillip Alan *lawyer*
O'Rourke, Dennis *lawyer*
Pressman, Glenn Spencer *lawyer*
Rhodes, Eric Foster *arbitrator, employee relations consultant, insurance executive*
Rouss, Ruth *lawyer*

**Commerce City**
Trujillo, Lorenzo A. *lawyer, educator*

**Denver**
Alfers, Stephen Douglas *lawyer*
Atlass, Theodore Bruce *lawyer, educator*
Austin, H(arry) Gregory *lawyer*
Bain, Donald Knight *lawyer*
Bain, James William *lawyer*
Belitz, Paul Edward *lawyer*
Benson, Robert Eugene *lawyer*
Benson, Thomas Quentin *lawyer*
Benton, Auburn Edgar *lawyer*
Berardini, Jacqueline Hernandez *lawyer*
Blair, Andrew Lane, Jr. *lawyer, educator*
Blitz, Stephen M. *lawyer*
Blunk, Forrest Stewart *lawyer*
Breeskin, Michael Wayne *lawyer*
Brega, Charles Franklin *lawyer*
Burford, Anne McGill *lawyer*
Burke, Kenneth John *lawyer*
Butler, David *lawyer*
Bye, James Edward *lawyer*
Cain, Douglas Mylchreest *lawyer*
Campbell, Leonard Martin *lawyer*
Cantwell, William Patterson *lawyer*
Carr, James Francis *lawyer*
Carraher, John Bernard *lawyer*
Carrigan, Jim R. *arbitrator, mediator, retired federal judge*
Carver, Craig R. *lawyer*
Cheroutes, Michael Louis *lawyer*
Collins, Martha Traudt *lawyer*
Commander, Eugene R. *lawyer*
Conover, Frederic King *lawyer*
Cooper, Paul Douglas *lawyer*
Cope, Thomas Field *lawyer*
Cox, William Vaughan *lawyer*
Daniel, Wiley Y. *lawyer*
Dauer, Edward Arnold *law educator*
Dean, James Benwell *lawyer*
De Gette, Diana Louise *lawyer, state legislator*
de Marino, Thomas John *lawyer*
Dempsey, Howard Stanley *lawyer, mining executive, investment banker*
DeMuth, Alan Cornelius *lawyer*
Dolan, Brian Thomas *lawyer*
Downey, Arthur Harold, Jr. *lawyer, mediator*
Ehrlich, Stephen Richard *lawyer*
Eiberger, Carl Frederick *trial lawyer*
Eklund, Carl Andrew *lawyer*
Erisman, Frank *lawyer*
Farley, John Michael *lawyer*
Faxon, Thomas Baker *lawyer*
Featherstone, Bruce Alan *lawyer*
Flowers, William Harold, Jr. *lawyer*
Fognani, John Dennis *lawyer*
Grant, Patrick Alexander *lawyer, association administrator*
Green, Jersey Michael-Lee *lawyer*
Grissom, Garth Clyde *lawyer*
Halverson, Steven Thomas *lawyer, construction executive*
Harris, Dale Ray *lawyer*
Hartley, James Edward *lawyer*
Hendrix, Lynn Parker *lawyer*
Hilbert, Otto Karl, II *lawyer*
Hoagland, Donald Wright *lawyer*
Hobson, Harry Lee, Jr. *lawyer*
Hodges, Joseph Gilluly, Jr. *lawyer*
Hoffman, Daniel Steven *lawyer, legal educator*
Holleman, Paul Douglas *lawyer*
Holme, Richard Phillips *lawyer*
Hopfenbeck, George Martin, Jr. *lawyer*
Hopkins, Donald J. *lawyer*
Husband, John Michael *lawyer*
Imig, William Graff *lawyer, lobbyist*
Irwin, R. Robert *lawyer*
Jablonski, James Arthur *lawyer*
Jackson, Richard Brooke *lawyer*
Jacobs, Paul Alan *lawyer*
Jones, Richard Michael *lawyer*
Keatinge, Robert Reed *lawyer*
Keller, Glen Elven, Jr. *lawyer*
Keppler, Peter *lawyer*
Kerwin, Mary Ann Collins *lawyer*
Kintzele, John Alfred *lawyer*
Law, John Manning *retired lawyer*
Lerman, Eileen R. *lawyer*
Levy, Mark Ray *lawyer*
Lidstone, Herrick Kenley, Jr. *lawyer*
Low, John Wayland *lawyer*
Lutz, John Shafroth *lawyer*
Martz, Clyde Ollen *lawyer, educator*
Mauro, Richard Frank *lawyer, investment manager*
McCabe, John L. *lawyer*
McLain, William Allen *lawyer*
Merker, Steven Joseph *lawyer*
Miller, Gale Timothy *lawyer*
Miller, Robert Nolen *lawyer*
Moye, John Edward *lawyer*
Muldoon, Brian *lawyer*
Muller, Nicholas Guthrie *lawyer, business executive*
Murane, William Edward *lawyer*
Nanda, Ved Prakash *law educator, university official*
Nathan, J(ay) Andrew *lawyer*
Newton, James Quigg, Jr. *lawyer*
O'Keefe, Edward Franklin *lawyer*
Otten, Arthur Edward, Jr. *lawyer, corporate executive*
Owen, James Churchill, Jr. *lawyer*
Palmer, David Gilbert *lawyer*
Peloquin, Louis Omer *lawyer*
Petros, Raymond Louis, Jr. *lawyer*
Poulson, Robert Dean *lawyer*
Pringle, Edward E. *legal educator, former state supreme court chief justice*
Prochnow, James R. *lawyer*
Quail, Beverly J. *lawyer*
Quiat, Gerald M. *lawyer*
Rich, Ben Arthur *lawyer, educator*
Rich, Robert Stephen *lawyer*
Ris, William Krakow *lawyer*
Ritsema, Fredric A. *lawyer*
Rubright, Royal Cushing *lawyer*
Ruppert, John Lawrence *lawyer*
Sayre, John Marshall *lawyer, former government official*
Schmidt, L(ail) William, Jr. *lawyer*
Seaman, Peggy Jean *lawyer*
Shea, Kevin Michael *lawyer*
Shepherd, John Frederic *lawyer*
Speed, Leslie Bokee *lawyer*
Spencer, Margaret Gilliam *lawyer*
Stockmar, Ted P. *lawyer*
Sutton, Leonard von Bibra *lawyer*
Thomasch, Roger Paul *lawyer*
Tisdale, Douglas Michael *lawyer*
Tomlinson, Warren Leon *lawyer*
Tracey, Jay Walter, Jr. *retired lawyer*
Ulrich, Theodore Albert *lawyer*
Vigil, Charles S. *lawyer*
Walker, Timothy Blake *lawyer, educator*
Watson, William D. *lawyer*
Welch, Carol Mae *lawyer*
Welton, Charles Ephraim *lawyer*
Wheeler, Malcolm Edward *lawyer, law educator*
Williams, Michael Anthony *lawyer*
Williams, Wayne De Armond *lawyer*
Wohlgenant, Richard Glen *lawyer*
Woodward, Lester Ray *lawyer*
Wunnicke, Brooke *lawyer*
Yegge, Robert Bernard *lawyer, college dean emeritus, educator*
Young, Thomas Harlan *lawyer*

**Durango**
Burnham, Bryson Paine *retired lawyer*

**Eagle**
Sullivan, Selby William *lawyer, business executive*

**Englewood**
Burg, Michael S. *lawyer*
DeMuth, Laurence Wheeler, Jr. *lawyer, utility company executive*
Devine, Sharon Jean *lawyer*
Nixon, Scott Sherman *lawyer*
Poe, Robert Alan *lawyer*
Ramsey, John Arthur *lawyer*
Smead, Burton Armstrong, Jr. *lawyer, retired*
Steele, Elizabeth Meyer *lawyer*
Wagner, David James *lawyer*

**Fort Collins**
Rogers, Garth Winfield *lawyer*

**Frisco**
Helmer, David Alan *lawyer*

**Golden**
Cassidy, Samuel H. *lawyer, lieutenant governor, state legislator*
Wilson, James Robert *lawyer*

**Greeley**
Houtchens, Barnard *lawyer*

**Green Mountain Falls**
Faber, Michael Warren *lawyer*

**Greenwood Village**
Dymond, Lewis Wandell *lawyer, mediator, educator*
Katz, Michael Jeffery *lawyer*

**Lakewood**
Guyton, Samuel Percy *retired lawyer*
McElwee, Dennis John *lawyer, former parmaceutical company executive*
Purdy, Sherry Marie *lawyer*
Ulery, Shari Lee *lawyer*

**Littleton**
Keely, George Clayton *lawyer*
Spelts, Richard John *lawyer*
Truhlar, Doris Broaddus *lawyer*

**Louisville**
Raymond, Dorothy Gill *lawyer*

**Manassa**
Garcia, Castelar Medardo *lawyer*

**Pagosa Springs**
Kelly, Reid Browne *lawyer*

**Pueblo**
Altman, Leo Sidney *lawyer*
Kogovsek, Daniel Charles *lawyer*
O'Callaghan, Robert Patrick *lawyer*
O'Conner, Loretta Rae *lawyer*

**CONNECTICUT**

**Avon**
Wiechmann, Eric Watt *lawyer*

**Bloomfield**
Day, John G. *lawyer*
Mark, Henry Allen *lawyer*
Messemer, Glenn Matthew *lawyer*
Reid, Hoch *lawyer*

**Bridgeport**
Cederbaum, Eugene E. *lawyer*
Zeldes, Jacob Dean *lawyer*

**Brooklyn**
Dune, Steve Charles *lawyer*

**Clinton**
Hershatter, Richard Lawrence *lawyer, author*

**Danbury**
Chaifetz, David Harvey *lawyer*
Keenan, Linda Lee *paralegal*
Skolan-Logue, Amanda Nicole *lawyer, consultant*

**Darien**
Brown, James Shelly *lawyer*
Kaynor, Sanford Bull *lawyer*
Swiggart, Carolyn Clay *lawyer*

**Derby**
McEvoy, Sharlene Ann *business law educator*

**East Hartford**
Whiston, Richard Michael *lawyer*

**Enfield**
Berger, Robert Bertram *lawyer*

**Essex**
Riley, Georgianne Marie *lawyer*

**Fairfield**
Caruso, Daniel F. *lawyer, judge, former state legislator*
Daley, Pamela *lawyer*
Denniston, Brackett Badger, III *lawyer*
Frantz, Robert Wesley *lawyer*
Kenney, James Francis *lawyer*
Sealy, Albert Henry *lawyer*

**Farmington**
Anderson, Buist Murfee *lawyer*

**Glastonbury**
Schroth, Peter W(illiam) *lawyer, management and law educator*

**Greenwich**
Bam, Foster *lawyer*
Behren, Robert Alan *lawyer, accountant*
Bentley, Peter *lawyer*
Berk, Alan S. *law firm executive*
Cantor, Samuel C. *lawyer*
Cantwell, Robert *lawyer*
Close, Michael John *lawyer*
Coleman, Joel Clifford *lawyer*
Czajkowski, Frank Henry *lawyer*
Fisher, Everett *lawyer*
Forrow, Brian Derek *lawyer, corporation executive*
Gorin, Robert Seymour *lawyer, corporation executive*
Herbert, Kathy Lynne *lawyer*
Jones, Edwin Michael *lawyer, former insurance company executive*
Kurtz, Melvin H. *lawyer, cosmetics company executive*
Laudone, Anita Helene *lawyer*
Lowenstein, Peter David *lawyer*
Lynch, William Redington *lawyer*
Mendenhall, John Ryan *retired lawyer, transportation executive*
More, Douglas McLochlan *lawyer*
†Pascarella, Henry William *lawyer*
Paul, Roland Arthur *lawyer*
Rodenbach, Edward Francis *lawyer*
Schoonmaker, Samuel Vail, III *lawyer*
Steinmetz, Richard Bird, Jr. *lawyer*
Tetzlaff, Theodore R. *lawyer*
Trotta, Frank Paul, Jr. *lawyer*
Yonkman, Fredrick Albers *lawyer, management consultant*

**Hamden**
Margulies, Martin B. *lawyer, educator*
Peterson, George Emanuel, Jr. *lawyer, business executive*
Robinson, Toni *lawyer, educator*

**Hartford**
Alfano, Charles Thomas, Sr. *lawyer*
Anthony, J(ulian) Danford, Jr. *lawyer*
Asmar, Mark Abdon *lawyer*
Berall, Frank Stewart *lawyer*
Blumberg, Phillip Irvin *law educator*
Blumenthal, Jeffrey Michael *lawyer*
Bonee, John Leon, III *lawyer*
Buck, Gurdon Hall *lawyer, urban planner, real estate broker*
Buckingham, Harold Canute, Jr. *lawyer*
Cain, George Harvey *lawyer, business executive*
Cantor, Donald Jerome *lawyer*
Cole, William Kaufman *lawyer*
Conard, Frederick Underwood, Jr. *lawyer*
Coyle, Michael Lee *lawyer*
Cullina, William Michael *lawyer*
Del Negro, John Thomas *lawyer*
Dennis, Anthony James *lawyer*
Elliot, Ralph Gregory *lawyer*
Fain, Joel Maurice *lawyer*
Gale, John Quentin *lawyer*
Garfield, Gerald *lawyer*
Godfrey, Robert Douglas *lawyer*
Harrison, Thomas Flatley *lawyer*
Johnson, Dwight Alan *lawyer*
Karpe, Brian Stanley *lawyer*
Kennedy, Jack S. *lawyer*
Knickerbocker, Robert Platt, Jr. *lawyer*
Korzenik, Armand Alexander *lawyer*
Libassi, Frank Peter *lawyer*
Lyon, James Burroughs *lawyer*
Martocchio, Louis Joseph *lawyer, educator*
McCarthy, Patrice Ann *lawyer*
Merriam, Dwight Haines *lawyer, land use planner*
Metzler, Robert J., II *lawyer*
Middlebrook, Stephen Beach *lawyer*
Miller, Jeffrey Clark *lawyer*
Murtha, John Stephen *lawyer*
Nolan, John Blanchard *lawyer*
O'Connor, Richard Dennis *lawyer*
O'Donnell, Edward Francis, Jr. *lawyer*
Owen, H. Martyn *lawyer*
Pepe, Louis Robert *lawyer*
Pinney, Sidney Dillingham, Jr. *lawyer*
Quinn, Andrew Peter, Jr. *lawyer, insurance executive*
Richter, Donald Paul *lawyer*
Rome, Donald Lee *lawyer*
Ryan, David Thomas *lawyer*
Schatzki, George *law educator*
See, Edmund M. *lawyer*
Seidl, Jane Patricia *lawyer*
Space, Theodore Maxwell *lawyer*
Speziale, John Albert *lawyer*
Stravalle-Schmidt, Ann Roberta *lawyer*
Swerdloff, Mark Harris *lawyer*
Tancredi, James J. *lawyer*
Taylor, Allan Bert *lawyer*
Thomas, Calvert *lawyer*
Trachsel, William Henry *corporate lawyer*
Voigt, Richard *lawyer*
Webster, Arthur Edward *lawyer*
Wolfson, Nicholas *law educator*
Wolman, Martin *lawyer*
Yoskowitz, Irving Benjamin *lawyer, manufacturing company executive*
Young, Roland Frederic, III *lawyer*
Zakarian, Albert *lawyer*

**Lakeville**
Armstrong, John Kremer *lawyer, artist*
Jones, Ronald David *lawyer*

**Meriden**
Luby, Thomas Stewart *lawyer*

**Middlebury**
Davis, Joanne Fatse *lawyer*

**Mystic**
Antipas, Constantine George *lawyer, civil engineer*

**New Britain**
Pearl, Helen Zalkan *lawyer*

**New Canaan**
Wallace, Kenneth Donald *lawyer*

**New Haven**
Ackerman, Bruce Arnold *lawyer, educator*
Amar, Akhil Reed *law educator*
Belt, David Levin *lawyer*
Brown, Ralph Sharp *law educator*
Burt, Robert Amsterdam *lawyer, educator*
Carlson, Dale Lynn *lawyer*
Carty, Paul Vernon *lawyer*
Clark, Elias *law educator*
Clendenen, William Herbert, Jr. *lawyer*
Cohen, Morris Leo *retired law librarian and educator*
Craig, William Emerson *lawyer*
Damaska, Mirjan Radovan *law educator*
Days, Drew S., III *lawyer, law educator*
Dearington, Michael *lawyer*
Droney, Christopher F. *prosecutor*
Duke, Steven Barry *law educator*
Ellickson, Robert Chester *law educator*
Fiss, Owen M. *law educator*
Freed, Daniel Josef *law educator*
Gewirtz, Paul D. *lawyer, legal educator*
Goldstein, Abraham S. *lawyer, educator*
Goldstein, Joseph *law educator*
Greenfield, James Robert *lawyer*
Hansmann, Henry Baethke *law educator*
Holder, Angela Roddey *lawyer, educator*
Johnstone, Quintin *law educator*
Kronman, Anthony Townsend *lawyer, educator*
Langbein, John Harriss *lawyer, educator*
Logue, Frank *arbitrator, mediator, urban consultant, former mayor New Haven*
Marshall, Burke *law educator*
Murphy, William Robert *lawyer*
Priest, George L. *law educator*
Reisman, William M. *lawyer, educator*
Robinson, Dorothy K. *lawyer*
Rose-Ackerman, Susan *law and political economy educator*
Simon, John Gerald *law educator*
Stith-Cabranes, Kate *law educator*
Sullivan, Shaun S. *lawyer*
Tilson, John Quillin *lawyer*
Todd, Erica Weyer *lawyer*
†Wedgwood, Ruth *law educator, international affairs expert*
Wenig, Mary Moers *law educator*

**New London**
Clark, R. Thomas *lawyer*

**New Milford**
Edmondson, John Richard *lawyer, pharmaceutical manufacturing company executive*
Friedman, John Maxwell, Jr. *lawyer*

**Norfolk**
Lambros, Lambros John *lawyer, petroleum company executive*

**Norwalk**
Bermas, Stephen *lawyer*
Jacobs, Mark Randolph *lawyer*

**Old Lyme**
Crawford, Homer *retired lawyer, paper company executive*

**Redding**
Russell, Allan David *lawyer*

**Riverside**
Lovejoy, Allen Fraser *retired lawyer*

**Rowayton**
Raikes, Charles FitzGerald *retired lawyer*

**Shelton**
Asija, S(atya) Pal *lawyer*

**Sherman**
Piel, William, Jr. *lawyer, arbitrator*

**Simsbury**
Long, Michael Thomas *lawyer, manufacturing company executive*

**Southport**
Sanetti, Stephen Louis *lawyer*

**Stamford**
†Benedict, Peter Behrends *lawyer*
Birenbaum, Jonathan *lawyer*
Bowen, Patrick Harvey *lawyer, consultant*
Dederick, Ronald Osburn *lawyer*
Della Rocco, Kenneth Anthony *lawyer*
Dolian, Robert Paul *lawyer*
Gilman, Derek *lawyer*
Gold, Steven Michael *lawyer*
Huth, William Edward *lawyer*
Knag, Paul Everett *lawyer*
Krinsky, Mary McInerney *lawyer*
Kweskin, Edward Michael *lawyer*
Lowman, George Frederick *lawyer*
Margolis, Emanuel *lawyer, educator*
Masin, Michael Terry *lawyer*
McGrath, Richard Paul *lawyer*
Merritt, William Alfred, Jr. *lawyer, telecommunications company executive*
Nichols, Ralph Arthur *lawyer*
Padilla, James Earl *lawyer*
Paul, Richard Stanley *lawyer*
Perle, Eugene Gabriel *lawyer*
Rose, Richard Loomis *lawyer*
Sisley, G. William *lawyer*
Skidd, Thomas Patrick, Jr. *lawyer*
Spindler, John Frederick *lawyer*
Stapleton, James Francis *lawyer*
Strone, Michael Jonathan *lawyer*
Teitell, Conrad Laurence *lawyer, author*
Twardy, Stanley Albert, Jr. *lawyer*
Weitzel, William Conrad, Jr. *lawyer*
Wilhelm, Gayle Brian *lawyer*

**Stonington**
Dupont, Ralph Paul *lawyer, educator*
Van Rees, Cornelius S. *lawyer*

**Storrs Mansfield**
Tucker, Edwin Wallace *law educator*

**Stratford**
DiCicco, Margaret C. *lawyer*
O'Rourke, James Louis *lawyer*

**Torrington**
Leard, David Carl *lawyer*
Wall, Robert Anthony, Jr. *lawyer*

**Waterbury**
Dost, Mark W. *lawyer*
Marano, Richard Michael *lawyer*
Wolfe, Harriet Munrett *lawyer*

**Westport**
Albani, Suzanne Beardsley *lawyer*
Barton, James Miller *lawyer, international business consultant*
Dale, Erwin Randolph *lawyer, author*
Daw, Harold John *lawyer*
Razzano, Pasquale Angelo *lawyer*
Saxl, Richard Hildreth *lawyer*

**Willimantic**
Lombardo, Michael John *lawyer, educator*

**Wilton**
Adams, Thomas Tilley *lawyer*
Fricke, Richard John *lawyer*
Healy, James Casey *lawyer*
Lamb, Frederic Davis *lawyer*

**Windsor**
Molitor, Karen Ann *lawyer*
Saltman, Stuart Ivan *lawyer*

**Woodbridge**
Cousins, William Joseph *lawyer, litigation consultant*

**Woodbury**
Marsching, Ronald Lionel *lawyer, former precision instrument company executive*

## DELAWARE

**Dover**
Ennis, Bruce Clifford *lawyer*

**Wilmington**
Bader, John Merwin *lawyer*
Bartley, Brian James *lawyer*
Baumann, Julian Henry, Jr. *lawyer*
Carey, John Patrick, III *lawyer*
Carpenter, Edmund Nelson, II *retired lawyer*
Clark, Esther Frances *law educator*
Connolly, Arthur Guild *lawyer, partner emeritus*
Curran, Barbara Sanson *lawyer*
Devine, Donn *lawyer, archivist, former city official*
DiLiberto, Richard Anthony, Jr. *lawyer*
†Du Pont, Pierre Samuel, IV *lawyer, former governor of Delaware*
Fenton, Wendell *lawyer*
Frank, George Andrew *lawyer*
Green, James Samuel *lawyer*
Hannon, Leo Francis *retired lawyer, educator*
Herdeg, John Andrew *lawyer*
Holzman, James L(ouis) *lawyer*
Huntley, Donald Wayne *lawyer*
Joseph, Michael Brandes *lawyer*
Kimmel, Morton Richard *lawyer*
Kirk, Richard Dillon *lawyer*
Kirkpatrick, Andrew Booth, Jr. *lawyer*
Magee, Thomas Hugh *lawyer*
Meitner, Pamela *lawyer, educator*
Mekler, Arlen B. *lawyer, chemist*
Morris, Kenneth Donald *lawyer*
Mullen, Regina Marie *lawyer*
Patton, James Leeland, Jr. *lawyer*
Rich, Michael Joseph *lawyer*
Riegel, John Kent *corporate lawyer*
Rothschild, Steven James *lawyer*
Sawyer, H(arold) Murray, Jr. *lawyer*
Semple, James William *lawyer*
Shapiro, Irving Saul *lawyer*
Stone, F. L. Peter *lawyer*
Sutton, Richard Lauder *lawyer*
Turk, S. Maynard *lawyer*
Waisanen, Christine M. *lawyer, writer*
Ward, Rodman, Jr. *lawyer*
Wier, Richard Royal, Jr. *lawyer, inventor*

## DISTRICT OF COLUMBIA

**Washington**
Aaronson, David Ernest *lawyer, educator*
Abbott, Alden Francis *lawyer, government official, educator*
Abeles, Charles Calvert *retired lawyer*
Ablard, Charles David *lawyer*
Abrecht, Mary Ellen Benson *lawyer*
Acheson, David Campion *lawyer, author, policy analyst*
Acker, Lawrence G. *lawyer*
Ackerson, Nels J(ohn) *lawyer*
Adamson, Terrence Burdett *lawyer*
Adelman, Roger Mark *lawyer, educator*
Adler, Howard, Jr. *lawyer*
Adler, Howard Bruce *lawyer*
Adler, Robert Martin *lawyer*
Aisenberg, Irwin Morton *lawyer*
Alberger, William Relph *lawyer, government official*
Albertson, Terry L. *lawyer*
Alcorn, Wendell Bertram, Jr. *lawyer*
Alexander, Clifford Joseph *lawyer*
Alexander, Donald Crichton *lawyer*
†Allard, Nicholas W. *lawyer*
Allen, Toni K. *lawyer*
Allen, William Hayes *lawyer*
Ambrose, Myles Joseph *lawyer*
Anderson, Frederick Randolph, Jr. *lawyer, law educator*
Anderson, John Bayard *lawyer, educator, former congressman*
Andrews, Mark Joseph *lawyer*
Anthony, David Vincent *lawyer*
Applebaum, Harvey Milton *lawyer*
Arent, Albert Ezra *lawyer*
Ashton, Richard M. *federal lawyer*
Atwood, James R. *lawyer*
Aucutt, Ronald David *lawyer*
Austin, Page Insley *lawyer*
Avil, Richard D., Jr. *lawyer*
Axelrod, Jonathan Gans *lawyer*
Ayer, Donald Belton *lawyer*
Ayres, Richard Edward *lawyer*
Babby, Lon S. *lawyer*
Bachman, Kenneth Leroy, Jr. *lawyer*
Bachrach, Eve Elizabeth *lawyer*
Baer, William J. *lawyer*
Baird, Bruce Allen *lawyer*
Baker, David Harris *lawyer*
Ball, (Robert) Markham *lawyer*
Ballard, Frederic Lyman, Jr. *lawyer*
Baran, Jan Witold *lawyer, educator*
Bardin, David J. *lawyer*
Barnard, Robert C. *lawyer*
Barnes, Dennis Norman *lawyer*
Barnes, Donald Michael *lawyer*
Barnes, Mark James *lawyer*
Barnes, Michael Darr *lawyer, think tank executive*
Barnes, Peter *lawyer*
Barnett, Robert Bruce *lawyer*
Barr, Michael Blanton *lawyer*
Barron, Jerome Aure *law educator*
Bartlett, John Laurence *lawyer*
Bartlett, Michael John *lawyer*
Basseches, Robert Treinis *lawyer*
Bates, John Cecil, Jr. *lawyer*
Beatty, Richard Scrivener *lawyer*
Becker, Brandon *lawyer*
Becker, William Watters *lawyer*
Beckett, William Wade *lawyer*
Beckwith, Edward Jay *lawyer*
Beisner, John Herbert *lawyer*
Beizer, Richard L. *lawyer*
Beizer, Robert A. *lawyer*
Bell, James Frederick *lawyer*
Bell, Stephen Robert *lawyer*
Beller, Herbert N. *lawyer*
Bellinger, Edgar Thomson *lawyer*
Bello, Judith Hippler *lawyer*
Belman, Murray Joel *lawyer*
Belmar, Warren *lawyer*
Bennett, Alexander Elliot *lawyer*
Bennett, Joel P. *lawyer*
Ben-Veniste, Richard *lawyer*
Bercovici, Martin William *lawyer*
Berl, Joseph M. *lawyer*
Berlack, Evan Raden *lawyer*
Berman, Marshall Fox *lawyer*
Bernabei, Lynne Ann *lawyer*
Berner, Frederic George, Jr. *lawyer*
Bernhard, Berl *lawyer*
Bernstein, Mitchell Harris *lawyer*
Berryman, Richard Byron *lawyer*
Berz, David R. *lawyer*
Best, Judah *lawyer*
Biddle, Timothy Maurice *lawyer*
Bierman, James Norman *lawyer*
Birnbaum, S. Elizabeth *lawyer*
Bishop, Wayne Staton *lawyer*
Bittman, William Omar *lawyer*
Black, Stephen F. *lawyer*
Blair, William McCormick, Jr. *lawyer*
Blake, Jonathan Dewey *lawyer*
Blazek-White, Doris *lawyer*
Bleakley, Peter Kimberley *lawyer*
Bleicher, Samuel Abram *lawyer*
Bliss, Donald Tiffany, Jr. *lawyer*
Bloch, Richard Isaac *labor arbitrator*
Bloch, Stuart Marshall *lawyer*
Bloch, Susan Low *law educator*
Blumenfeld, Jeffrey *lawyer, educator*
Blumenthal, Ronnie *lawyer*
Bodner, John, Jr. *lawyer*
Boehm, Steven Bruce *lawyer*
Bogard, Lawrence Joseph *lawyer*
Boggs, George Trenholm *lawyer*
Boggs, Thomas Hale, Jr. *lawyer*
Bohlke, Gary Lee *lawyer*
Boland, Christopher Thomas, II *lawyer*
Bolton, John Robert *lawyer, former government official*
Bonner, Walter Joseph *lawyer*
Bonvillian, William Boone *lawyer*
Boone, Theodore Sebastian *lawyer*
Born, Brooksley Elizabeth *lawyer*
Born, Gary Brian *lawyer, educator*
Borsari, George Robert, Jr. *lawyer, broadcaster*
Boskey, Bennett *lawyer*
Boyd, Stephen Mather *arbitrator, mediator, lawyer*
Boyd, Thomas Marshall *lawyer*
Bradford, William Allen, Jr. *lawyer*
Bradford, William Hollis, Jr. *lawyer*
Brady, Phillip Donley *lawyer*
Brenner, Janet Maybin Walker *lawyer*
Bresnahan, Pamela Anne *lawyer*
Briggs, Alan Leonard *lawyer*
Britton, Katherine Lela Quainton *lawyer*
Broas, Timothy Michael *lawyer*
Broches, Aron *international lawyer, arbitrator*
Brockway, David Hunt *lawyer*
Bronstein, Alvin J. *lawyer*
Brooke, Edward William *lawyer, former senator*
Brooks, Daniel Townley *lawyer*
Brown, Charles Freeman *lawyer*
Brown, David Nelson *lawyer*
Brown, Donald Arthur *lawyer*
Brown, George Leslie *legislative affairs and business development consultant, former manufacturing company executive, former lieutenant governor*
Brown, Michael Arthur *lawyer*
Brown, Omer Forrest, II *lawyer*
Brown, Preston *lawyer*
Browne, Richard Cullen *lawyer*
Brownstein, Philip Nathan *lawyer*
Bruce, E(stel) Edward *lawyer*
Bruce, John Foster *lawyer*
Bruder, George Frederick *lawyer*
Brunsvold, Brian Garrett *lawyer, educator*
Bruton, James Asa, III *lawyer*
Bryant, Arthur H. *lawyer*
Buc, Nancy Lillian *lawyer*
Bucholtz, Harold Ronald *lawyer*
Buckley, Jeremiah Stephen *lawyer*
Buckley, John Joseph, Jr. *lawyer*
Buechner, Jack W(illiam) *lawyer, government affairs consultant*
Buergenthal, Thomas *lawyer, educator, international judge*
Buffon, Charles Edward *lawyer*
Burack, Michael Leonard *lawyer*
Burch, John Thomas, Jr. *lawyer*
Burchfield, Bobby Roy *lawyer*
Burdette, Robert Bruce *lawyer*
Burgess, David *lawyer*
Burk, Francis Lewis, Jr. *lawyer, federal*
Burka, Robert Alan *lawyer*
Burns, Stephen Gilbert *lawyer*
Burt, Jeffrey Amsterdam *lawyer*
Busby, David *lawyer*
Buscemi, Peter *lawyer*
Butler, J. Bradway *lawyer*
Butler, Michael Francis *lawyer*
Cabaniss, Thomas Edward *lawyer*
Calamaro, Raymond Stuart *lawyer*
Calderwood, James Albert *lawyer*
Calvani, Terry *lawyer, former government official*

Lichtenstein, Elissa Charlene *legal association executive*
Liebman, Ronald Stanley *lawyer*
Linn, Richard *lawyer*
Linowitz, Sol Myron *lawyer*
Lipstein, Robert A. *lawyer*
†Lister, Sara Elisabeth *lawyer*
Litan, Robert Eli *lawyer, economist*
Litman, Harry Peter *lawyer, educator*
Livingston, Donald Ray *lawyer*
Lockyer, Charles Warren, Jr. *lawyer*
Loeb, G. Hamilton *lawyer*
Loeffler, Robert Hugh *lawyer*
Loevinger, Lee *lawyer, science writer*
Long, Charles Thomas *lawyer*
Long, Clarence Dickinson, III *lawyer*
Lopatin, Alan G. *lawyer*
Love, Michael Kenneth *lawyer*
Lowe, Randall Brian *lawyer*
Lubic, Robert Bennett *lawyer, arbitrator, law educator*
Lubick, Donald Cyril *lawyer*
Lucas, Steven Mitchell *lawyer*
Luce, Gregory M. *lawyer*
Lupo, Raphael V. *lawyer*
Lurensky, Marcia Adele *lawyer*
Lybecker, Martin Earl *lawyer*
Lyons, Dennis Gerald *lawyer*
MacBeth, Angus *lawyer*
Macdonald, David Robert *lawyer, fund administrator*
Mackiewicz, Edward Robert *lawyer*
Macleod, John Amend *lawyer*
Madden, Murdaugh Stuart *lawyer*
Maechling, Charles, Jr. *lawyer, diplomat, educator, writer*
Magielnicki, Robert L. *lawyer*
Mahar, Ellen Patricia *law librarian*
Mailander, William Stephen *lawyer*
Maiwurm, James John *lawyer*
Majev, Howard Rudolph *lawyer*
Mann, Donegan *lawyer*
Manson, Joseph Lloyd, III *lawyer*
Marans, J. Eugene *lawyer*
Marcuss, Stanley Joseph *lawyer*
Margeton, Stephen George *law librarian*
Margolis, Daniel Herbert *lawyer*
Margolis, Eugene *lawyer, government official*
Marinaccio, Charles Lindbergh *lawyer*
Marks, Herbert Edward *lawyer*
†Marks, Jonathan Bowles *lawyer, mediator, arbitrator*
Marks, Leonard Harold *lawyer*
Marks, Richard Daniel *lawyer*
Markus, Kent Richard *lawyer*
Marquez, Joaquin Alfredo *lawyer*
Martin, David Alan *law educator, government official*
Martin, David Briton Hadden, Jr. *lawyer*
Martin, Guy *lawyer*
Martin, Keith *lawyer*
Martin, Ralph Drury *lawyer, educator*
Marvin, Charles Rodney, Jr. *lawyer*
Mathias, Charles McCurdy *lawyer, former senator*
Mathis, John Prentiss *lawyer*
Mattingly, J. Virgil, Jr. *federal lawyer*
May, Timothy James *lawyer*
Mayers, Daniel Kriegsman *lawyer*
Mayfield, Richard Heverin *lawyer*
Mayo, George Washington, Jr. *lawyer*
Mazo, Mark Elliott *lawyer*
Mazzaferri, Katherine Aquino *lawyer, bar association executive*
Mazzeo-Merkle, Linda L. *legal administrator*
McAvoy, John Joseph *lawyer*
McBride, Michael Flynn *lawyer*
McCarthy, David Jerome, Jr. *law educator*
Mc Carty, Robert Lee *lawyer*
McClain, William Thomas *lawyer*
McClure, William Pendleton *lawyer*
McCoy, Jerry Jack *lawyer*
McDaniels, William E. *lawyer*
McDavid, Janet Louise *lawyer*
Mc Dermott, Albert Leo *lawyer*
McDermott, Edward Aloysious *lawyer*
McElveen, Junius Carlisle, Jr. *lawyer*
Mc Giffert, David Eliot *lawyer, former government official*
McGovern, Michael Barbot *lawyer*
McGrath, Kathryn Bradley *lawyer*
McGuire, Patricia A. *lawyer, academic administrator*
McGuirl, Marlene Dana Callis *law librarian, educator*
McHugh, James Lenahan, Jr. *lawyer*
McKay, John *lawyer*
McLean, R. Bruce *lawyer*
McMahon, Joseph Einar *lawyer, consultant*
Mc Phee, Henry Roemer *lawyer*
Mc Pherson, Harry Cummings, Jr. *lawyer*
Means, Thomas Cornell *lawyer*
Medalie, Richard James *lawyer*
Melamed, Arthur Douglas *lawyer*
Melamed, Carol Drescher *lawyer*
Meloy, Sybil Piskur *lawyer*
Menkel-Meadow, Carrie Joan *law educator*
Mercer, Lee William *lawyer, corporate executive, former government agency administrator*
Meserve, Richard Andrew *lawyer*
Meyer, Dennis Irwin *lawyer*
Meyers, Tedson Jay *lawyer*
Michaelson, Martin *lawyer*
Miles, David Michael *lawyer*
Miller, Andrew Pickens *lawyer*
Miller, Charles A. *lawyer*
Miller, Gay Davis *lawyer*
Miller, H. Todd *lawyer*
Miller, Herbert John, Jr. *lawyer*
Miller, John T., Jr. *lawyer, educator*
Miller, Kerry Lee *lawyer*
Miller, Marshall Lee *lawyer*
Miller, Warren Lloyd *lawyer*
Mills, Kevin Paul *lawyer*
Milstein, Elliott Steven *legal educator, academic administrator*
Mintz, Seymour Stanley *lawyer*
Mitchell, Margery Hope *lawyer*
Mitchell, Roy Shaw *lawyer*
Moates, G. Paul *lawyer*
Mobbs, Michael Hall *lawyer*
Mode, Paul J., Jr. *lawyer*
Moe, Richard Palmer *lawyer*
Mogel, William Allen *lawyer*
Montgomery, George Cranwell *lawyer, former ambassador*
Mooney, Marilyn *lawyer*
Moore, Amy Norwood *lawyer*
More, John Herron *lawyer, classicist*
Morgan, Richard Greer *lawyer*

Moring, John Frederick *lawyer*
Mossinghoff, Gerald Joseph *patent lawyer, engineer*
Mostoff, Allan Samuel *lawyer, consultant*
Moyer, Homer Edward, Jr. *lawyer*
Muckenfuss, Cantwell Faulkner, III *lawyer*
Muir, J. Dapray *lawyer*
Munsell, Elsie Louise *lawyer*
Muntzing, L(ewis) Manning *lawyer*
Murchison, David Claudius *lawyer*
Murphy, Betty Jane Southard (Mrs. Cornelius F. Murphy) *lawyer*
Murphy, James Paul *lawyer*
Murphy, John Condron, Jr. *lawyer*
Murphy, Terence Roche *lawyer*
Murray, John Einar *lawyer, retired army officer, federal official*
Murry, Harold David, Jr. *lawyer*
Myers, James R. *lawyer*
Nace, Barry John *lawyer*
Namorato, Cono R. *lawyer*
Napier, John Light *lawyer*
Natalie, Ronald Bruce *lawyer*
Navarro, Bruce Charles *lawyer*
Neff, William L. *lawyer*
Neimark, Sheridan *lawyer*
Nelson, Robert Louis *lawyer*
Nemeroff, Michael Alan *lawyer*
Ness, Andrew David *lawyer*
Neuman, Robert Henry *lawyer*
Nichols, Henry Eliot *lawyer, savings and loan executive*
Nickel, Henry V. *lawyer*
Nolan, John Edward *lawyer*
Norberg, Charles Robert *lawyer*
Norcross, David Frank Armstrong *lawyer*
Nordhaus, Robert Riggs *lawyer*
Norton, Floyd Ligon, IV *lawyer*
Norton, Gerald Patrick *lawyer*
Nuland, Anthony C. J. *lawyer*
Nutter, Franklin Winston *lawyer*
Oakley, Robert Louis *law librarian, educator*
O'Connor, Charles P. *lawyer*
O'Connor, Jennifer *lawyer*
O'Connor, John Jay, III *lawyer*
Odle, Robert Charles, Jr. *lawyer*
O'Donnell, Terrence *lawyer*
O'Hara, James Thomas *lawyer*
Olender, Jack Harvey *lawyer*
Oliphant, Charles Frederick, III *lawyer*
Olmstead, Cecil Jay *lawyer*
Olson, Theodore Bevry *lawyer*
Oman, Ralph *lawyer*
O'Neill, Brian Dennis *lawyer*
O'Neill, John H., Jr. *lawyer*
O'Neill, William Patrick *lawyer*
Onek, Joseph Nathan *lawyer*
Ongman, John Will *lawyer*
Oppenheimer, Franz Martin *lawyer*
O'Rourke, C. Larry *lawyer*
Osnos, David Marvin *lawyer*
O'Sullivan, Lynda Troutman *lawyer*
O'Toole, Francis J. *lawyer*
Overman, Dean Lee *lawyer, investor, author*
Owen, Roberts Bishop *lawyer*
Oyewole, Godwin *lawyer*
Oyler, Gregory Kenneth *lawyer*
Padgett, Nancy Weeks *law librarian, consultant, lawyer*
Page, Joseph Anthony *law educator*
Painter, William Hall *law educator*
Paper, Lewis J. *lawyer*
Papkin, Robert David *lawyer*
Patchan, Joseph *lawyer*
Pate, Michael Lynn *lawyer*
Patten, Thomas Louis *lawyer*
Patton, Thomas Earl *lawyer*
Paul, William McCann *lawyer*
Payne, Kenneth Eugene *lawyer*
Pearlman, Ronald Alan *lawyer*
Peck, Robert Stephen *lawyer, educator*
Pedersen, William Francis, Jr. *lawyer*
Perkins, Nancy Leeds *lawyer*
Perlik, William R. *lawyer*
Perlman, Matthew Saul *lawyer*
Perry, B(illy) Dwight *lawyer*
Perry, Spence William *lawyer*
Peters, Frederick Whitten *lawyer*
Peterson, Charles Hayes *lawyer*
Petrash, Jeffrey Michael *lawyer*
Pettit, John Whitney *lawyer*
Pfeiffer, Margaret Kolodny *lawyer*
Pfeiffer, Steven Bernard *lawyer*
Pfunder, Malcolm R. *lawyer*
Phemister, Thomas Alexander *lawyer*
Phillips, Carter Glasgow *lawyer*
Pickering, John Harold *lawyer*
Pilecki, Paul Steven *lawyer*
Pipkin, James Harold, Jr. *lawyer*
Pitt, Harvey Lloyd *lawyer*
Pittman, Lisa *lawyer*
Pittman, Steuart Lansing *lawyer*
Plaine, Daniel J. *lawyer*
Plaine, Lloyd Leva *lawyer*
Plotkin, Harry Morris *lawyer*
Podberesky, Samuel *lawyer*
Poe, David Russell *lawyer*
Poe, Luke Harvey, Jr. *lawyer*
Pogue, Lloyd Welch *lawyer*
Polon, Ira H. *lawyer*
Pomeroy, Harlan *lawyer*
Poneman, Daniel Bruce *lawyer*
Poppler, Doris Swords *lawyer*
Postol, Lawrence Philip *lawyer*
Potenza, Joseph Michael *lawyer*
Potts, Ramsay Douglas *lawyer, aviator*
Potts, Stephen Deaderick *lawyer*
Poulson, Richard Jasper Metcalfe *lawyer*
Povich, David *lawyer*
Pozen, Walter *lawyer*
Preston, Richard McKim *lawyer*
Prettyman, Elijah Barrett, Jr. *lawyer*
Price, Daniel Martin *lawyer*
Price, Griffith Baley, Jr. *lawyer*
Price, Joseph Hubbard *lawyer*
Provorny, Frederick Alan *lawyer*
Provost, James H(arrison) *law educator*
Pugh, Keith E., Jr. *lawyer*
Pusey, William Anderson *lawyer*
Quale, John Carter *lawyer*
Quarles, James Linwood, III *lawyer*
†Quarterman, Cynthia Louise *lawyer*
Quigley, Thomas J. *lawyer*
Quint, Arnold Harris *lawyer*
Quintiere, Gary G. *lawyer*
Rabb, Harriet Schaffer *lawyer, educator*
Rademaker, Stephen Geoffrey *lawyer*
Rafferty, James Gerard *lawyer*
Raimo, Bernard, Jr. (Bernie Raimo) *lawyer*

Rainbolt, John Vernon, II *lawyer*
Ramey, Carl Robert *lawyer*
Rauh, Carl Stephen *lawyer*
Raul, Alan Charles *lawyer*
Raymond, David Walker *lawyer*
Reade, Claire Elizabeth *lawyer*
Reaves, John Daniel *lawyer, playwright, actor*
Reback, Joyce Ellen *lawyer*
Rehm, John Bartram *lawyer*
Reid, Inez Smith *lawyer, educator*
Reid, Robert Newton *retired lawyer, mortgage and financial consultant*
Rein, Bert Walter *lawyer*
Rezneck, Daniel Albert *lawyer*
Rhoades, Dennis Keith *legal foundation administrator*
Rice, Paul Jackson *lawyer, educator*
Rich, John Townsend *lawyer*
Richards, Suzanne V. *lawyer*
Richardson, Elliot Lee *lawyer*
Richmond, David Walker *lawyer*
Richmond, Marilyn Susan *lawyer*
Rieser, Joseph A., Jr. *lawyer*
Rill, James Franklin *lawyer*
Risher, John Robert, Jr. *lawyer*
Roach, Arvid Edward, II *lawyer*
Robbins, Frank Edward *lawyer*
Robbins, Robert B. *lawyer*
Roberts, James Harold, III *lawyer*
Roberts, Jared Ingersoll *lawyer*
Robinson, Davis Rowland *lawyer*
Robinson, Douglas George *lawyer*
Rockefeller, Edwin Shaffer *lawyer*
Rockler, Walter James *lawyer*
Rocque, Vincent Joseph *lawyer*
Rodemeyer, Michael Leonard, Jr. *lawyer*
Roetzel, Danny Nile *lawyer*
Rogers, James Albert *lawyer*
Rogers, Paul Grant *lawyer, former congressman*
Rogers, William Dill *lawyer*
Rogovin, John Andrew *lawyer*
Rohner, Ralph John *lawyer, educator, university dean*
Roll, David Lee *lawyer*
Romary, John M. *lawyer*
Romeo, Peter John *lawyer*
Rooney, Kevin Davitt *lawyer*
Rose, Henry *lawyer*
Rose, James McKinley, Jr. *lawyer, government official*
Rose, Jonathan Chapman *lawyer*
Rosenberg, Mark Louis *lawyer*
Rosenberg, Ruth Helen Borsuk *lawyer*
Rosenblatt, Peter Ronald *lawyer, former ambassador*
Rosenbloom, H. David *lawyer*
Rosenthal, Douglas Eurico *lawyer, author*
Rosenthal, Steven Siegmund *lawyer*
Ross, Douglas *lawyer, legal academic administrator*
Ross, Stanford G. *lawyer, former government official*
Rossides, Eugene Telemachus *lawyer, writer*
Rossotti, Barbara Jill Margulies *lawyer*
Rostow, Eugene Victor *lawyer, educator, economist*
Roth, Alan J. *lawyer*
†Rothman, Steven R. *lawyer*
Rothstein, Paul Frederick *lawyer, educator*
Rousselot, Peter Frese *lawyer*
Rouvelas, Emanuel Larry *lawyer*
Rowden, Marcus Aubrey *lawyer, former government official*
Rowe, Richard Holmes *lawyer*
Roycroft, Howard Francis *lawyer*
Rubin, Kenneth Allen *lawyer*
Rubin, Seymour Jeffrey *lawyer, judge, educator*
Ruddy, Frank S. *lawyer, former ambassador*
Rule, Charles Frederick (Rick Rule) *lawyer*
Russell, Michael James *lawyer*
Russin, Jonathan *lawyer, consultant*
Russo, Roy R. *lawyer*
Ruttenberg, Charles Byron *lawyer*
Ruttinger, George David *lawyer*
Ryan, Frederick Joseph, Jr. *lawyer, public official*
Ryan, Jerry William *lawyer*
Ryan, Joseph *lawyer*
Ryerson, Paul Sommer *lawyer*
Sacher, Steven Jay *lawyer*
Sachs, Stephen Howard *lawyer*
Sagalkin, Sanford *lawyer*
Sagawa, Shirley Sachi *lawyer*
Salem, George Richard *lawyer*
Saltzburg, Stephen Allan *law educator, consultant*
Samuelson, Kenneth Lee *lawyer*
Sanford, Bruce William *lawyer*
Santos, Leonard Ernest *lawyer*
Sapienza, John Thomas *lawyer*
Sauntry, Susan Schaefer *lawyer*
Schaller, James Patrick *lawyer*
Schenker, Carl Richard, Jr. *lawyer*
Schiffer, Lois Jane *lawyer*
Schifter, Richard *lawyer, government official*
Schmeltzer, Edward *lawyer*
Schmidt, Richard Marten, Jr. *lawyer*
Schmidt, William Arthur, Jr. *lawyer*
Schneider, Matthew Roger *lawyer*
Schropp, James Howard *lawyer*
Schwaab, Richard Lewis *lawyer, educator*
Schwartz, Daniel C. *lawyer*
Schwartz, Victor Elliot *lawyer*
Schwartzman, Andrew Jay *lawyer*
Scott, Edward Philip *lawyer*
Scott, Thomas Jefferson, Jr. *lawyer, electrical engineer*
Sczudlo, Raymond Stanley *lawyer*
Sears, John Patrick *lawyer*
Sears, Mary Helen *lawyer*
Segal, Donald E. *lawyer*
Seidman, Ellen Shapiro *lawyer, government official*
Seitz, Patricia Ann *lawyer*
Shafer, Raymond Philip *lawyer, business executive*
Shaffer, David James *lawyer*
Shaffer, Jay Christopher *lawyer*
Shaheen, Michael Edmund, Jr. *lawyer, government official*
Shapiro, George Howard *lawyer*
Shelley, Herbert Carl *lawyer*
Shenefield, John Hale *lawyer*
Shepard, Julian Leigh *lawyer, humanitarian*
Sherer, Samuel Ayers *lawyer, urban planning consultant*
Sherzer, Harvey Gerald *lawyer*
Shniderman, Harry Louis *lawyer*
Shrinsky, Jason Lee *lawyer*
Shriver, Robert Sargent, Jr. *lawyer*
Shulman, Stephen Neal *lawyer*
Shuman, Michael Harrison *lawyer, policy analyst*
Siegel, Allen George *lawyer*
Siegel, Richard David *lawyer, former government official*
Sierck, Alexander Wentworth *lawyer*

Silberg, Jay Eliot *lawyer*
Silver, Daniel B. *lawyer*
Silver, Harry R. *lawyer*
Simon, Kenneth Mark *lawyer*
Simons, Barbara M. *lawyer*
Simons, Lawrence Brook *lawyer*
Simpson, John M. *lawyer*
Sims, Joe *lawyer*
Singer, Daniel Morris *lawyer*
Singleton, Harry Michael *lawyer*
Smith, Brian William *lawyer, former government official*
Smith, Daniel Clifford *lawyer*
Smith, Dwight Chichester, III *lawyer*
Smoot, Oliver Reed, Jr. *lawyer, trade association executive*
Smyth, Paul Burton *lawyer*
Sneed, William R., III *lawyer*
Sohn, Louis Bruno *lawyer, educator*
Solomons, Mark Elliott *lawyer, art dealer*
Sommer, Alphonse Adam, Jr. *lawyer*
Sonde, Theodore Irwin *lawyer*
Spaeder, Roger Campbell *lawyer*
Spaeth, Steven Michael *lawyer*
Spencer, Samuel *lawyer*
Springer, James van Roden *lawyer*
Stahr, Elvis J(acob), Jr. *lawyer, conservationist, educator*
Stansbury, Philip Roger *lawyer*
Starrs, James Edward *law and forensics educator, consultant*
Stauffer, Ronald Eugene *lawyer*
Stayin, Randolph John *lawyer*
Steadman, Charles Walters *lawyer, corporate executive, writer*
Stern, Gerald Mann *lawyer*
Stern, Samuel Alan *lawyer*
Sterrett, Samuel Black *lawyer, former judge*
Stevens, Herbert Francis *lawyer, law educator*
Stevenson, John Reese *lawyer*
Stillman, Elinor Hadley *lawyer*
Stock, Stuart Chase *lawyer*
Stoll, Richard G(iles) *lawyer*
Stone, Donald Raymond *lawyer*
†Stout, Lynn Andrea *law educator*
Stranahan, Robert Paul, Jr. *lawyer*
Strauss, Stanley Robert *lawyer*
Stromberg, Clifford Douglas *lawyer*
Stromberg, Jean Wilbur Gleason *lawyer*
Stuart, Raymond Wallace *lawyer*
Stucky, Scott Wallace *lawyer*
Studley, Jamienne Shayne *lawyer*
Stumpf, Mark Howard *lawyer*
Sullivan, Brendan V., Jr. *lawyer*
Sullivan, Timothy *lawyer*
Sundermeyer, Michael S. *lawyer*
Susko, Carol Lynne *lawyer, accountant*
Sussman, Monica Hilton *lawyer*
Suter, William Kent *federal court administrator, former army officer, lawyer*
Sutherlund, David Arvid *lawyer*
Swankin, David Arnold *lawyer, consumer advocate*
Swidler, Joseph Charles *lawyer*
Tabackman, Steven Carl *lawyer*
Tabor, John Kaye *retired lawyer*
Tallent, Stephen Edison *lawyer, educator*
Tannenwald, Peter *lawyer*
Tauber, Mark J. *lawyer*
Taylor, James, Jr. *lawyer*
Taylor, Ralph Arthur, Jr. *lawyer*
Taylor, Richard Powell *lawyer*
Taylor, William Woodruff, III *lawyer*
Teague, Randal Cornell, Sr. *lawyer*
Tegtmeyer, Rene Desloge *lawyer*
Temko, Stanley Leonard *lawyer*
Terry, Gary A. *lawyer, former trade association executive*
Terwilliger, George James, III *lawyer*
Thaler, Paul Sanders *lawyer, mediator*
Theroux, Eugene *lawyer*
Thomas, Ritchie Tucker *lawyer*
Thompson, Mozelle Willmont *lawyer, federal agency administrator*
Thompson, Robert Thomas *lawyer*
Thornburgh, Dick (Richard L. Thornburgh) *lawyer, former United Nations official, former United States attorney general, former governor*
Thurm, Gil *lawyer*
Timberg, Sigmund *lawyer*
Tirana, Bardyl Rifat *lawyer*
Tompkins, Joseph Buford, Jr. *lawyer*
Topelius, Kathleen E. *lawyer*
Townsend, John Michael *lawyer*
Toy, Charles David *lawyer*
Trager, Michael David *lawyer*
Treanor, Gerard Francis, Jr. *lawyer*
Trooboff, Peter Dennis *lawyer*
Trosten, Leonard Morse *lawyer*
Troyer, Thomas Alfred *lawyer*
Tucker, Stefan Franklin *lawyer*
Tufaro, Richard Chase *lawyer*
Tuohey, Mark Henry, III *lawyer*
Turnage, Fred Douglas *lawyer*
Tushnet, Mark Victor *law educator*
Tuyakbaev, Zharmakhan Aitbajevich *prosecutor*
Tyner, Lee Reichelderfer *lawyer*
Uehlein, E(dward) Carl, Jr. *lawyer*
Unger, Laura S. *lawyer*
Unger, Peter Van Buren *lawyer*
Vacketta, Carl Lee *lawyer, educator*
Valentine, Steven Richards *lawyer*
Vander Clute, Norman Roland *lawyer*
Vanderstar, John *lawyer*
Vanderver, Timothy Arthur, Jr. *lawyer*
Vardaman, John Wesley *lawyer*
Verner, James Melton *lawyer*
Verrill, Charles Owen, Jr. *lawyer*
Vickery, Ann Morgan *lawyer*
Vieth, G. Duane *lawyer*
Villa, John Kazar *lawyer*
Vince, Clinton Andrew *lawyer*
Vodra, William W. *lawyer*
Wade, Robert Paul *lawyer*
Waits, John A. *lawyer*
Wallace, Don, Jr. *law educator*
Wallace, James Harold, Jr. *lawyer*
Wallison, Frieda K. *lawyer*
Wallman, Steven Mark Harte *lawyer*
Walsh, Michael J. *lawyer*
Walter, Sheryl Lynn *lawyer*
Walton, Morgan Lauck, III *lawyer*
Ward, Alan S. *lawyer*
Ward, Denitta Dawn *lawyer*
Warin, Roger E. *lawyer*
Warnke, Paul Culliton *lawyer*
Wasilewski, Vincent Thomas *retired lawyer*
Waters, Jennifer Nash *lawyer*
Watson, Jack H., Jr. *lawyer*

Watson, Thomas C. *lawyer*
Waxman, Seth Paul *lawyer*
Webber, Richard John *lawyer*
Webster, Robert Kenly *lawyer*
Webster, William Hedgcock *lawyer*
Wegener, Mark Douglas *lawyer*
Weidenfeld, Edward Lee *lawyer*
Weinman, Howard Mark *lawyer*
Weinstein, Harris *lawyer*
Weiss, Edith Brown *law educator*
Weiss, Ellyn Renee *lawyer*
Weiss, Mark Anschel *lawyer*
Weiss, Stephen J. *lawyer*
Weissman, William R. *lawyer*
Wellen, Robert Howard *lawyer*
Weller, Janet Louise *lawyer*
Wenner, Charles Roderick *lawyer*
West, Gail Berry *lawyer*
Westberg, John Augustin *lawyer*
Whelan, Roger Michael *lawyer, educator*
Whitaker, A(lbert) Duncan *lawyer*
White, Lee Calvin *lawyer*
Whiting, Richard Albert *lawyer*
Wides, Burton V. *lawyer*
Wilcher, Shirley J. *lawyer*
†Wilderotter, James Arthur *lawyer*
Wiley, Richard Emerson *lawyer*
Willard, Richard Kennon *lawyer*
Williams, B. John, Jr. *lawyer, former federal judge*
Williams, John Edward *lawyer*
Williams, Karen Hastie *lawyer, think tank executive*
Williams, Thomas Raymond *lawyer*
Williamson, Thomas Samuel, Jr. *lawyer*
Willmore, Robert Louis *lawyer*
Wilson, Charles Haven *lawyer*
Wilson, Gary Dean *lawyer*
Wine, L. Mark *lawyer*
Winston, Judith Ann *lawyer*
Winter, Douglas E. *lawyer, writer*
Wintrol, John Patrick *lawyer*
Wirtz, William Willard *lawyer*
Wise, Sandra Casber *lawyer*
Wiseman, Alan M(itchell) *lawyer*
Wiss, Marcia A. *lawyer*
Wolff, Alan William *lawyer*
Wolff, Elroy Harris *lawyer*
Wolff, Paul Martin *lawyer*
Wolin, Neal Steven *lawyer*
Wollenberg, J. Roger *lawyer*
Wood, John Martin *lawyer*
Woodworth, Ramsey Lloyd *lawyer*
Woolsey, R. James *lawyer*
Work, Charles Robert *lawyer*
Worsley, James Randolph, Jr. *lawyer*
Worthy, K(enneth) Martin *lawyer*
Wray, Robert *lawyer*
Wright, Wiley Reed, Jr. *lawyer, retired judge, mediator*
Wruble, Bernhardt Karp *lawyer*
Wyss, John Benedict *lawyer*
Yablon, Jeffery Lee *lawyer*
Yurow, John Jesse *lawyer*
Yuspeh, Alan Ralph *lawyer*
Zausner, L. Andrew *lawyer*
Zax, Leonard A. *lawyer*
Zeifang, Donald P. *lawyer*
Zimmerman, Edwin Morton *lawyer*
Zipp, Joel Frederick *lawyer*
Zuckman, Harvey Lyle *law educator*
Zweben, Murray *lawyer, consultant*

## FLORIDA

### Alachua
Gaines, Weaver Henderson *lawyer*

### Aventura
Fishman, Barry Stuart *lawyer*

### Bal Harbour
Hastings, Lawrence Vaeth *lawyer, physician, educator*

### Boca Grande
Baldwin, William Howard *lawyer, retired foundation executive*
Brock, Mitchell *lawyer*

### Boca Raton
Aranson, Michael J. *lawyer*
Barker, Charles Thomas *retired lawyer*
Barton, William Blackburn *retired lawyer*
Beber, Robert H. *lawyer, financial services executive*
Camilleri, Michael *lawyer, educator*
Erdman, Joseph *lawyer*
Hedrick, Frederic Cleveland, Jr. *lawyer*
Kassner, Herbert Seymore *lawyer*
MacFarland, Richard B. *lawyer*
Martin, Alvin Charles *lawyer*
Reinstein, Joel *lawyer*
Siegel, David Burton *lawyer*
Weitzman, Allan Harvey *lawyer*

### Bonita Springs
Olander, Ray Gunnar *retired lawyer*

### Boynton Beach
Armstrong, Jack Gilliland *lawyer*
Miller, Emanuel *retired lawyer, banker*
Saxbe, William Bart *lawyer, former government official*

### Bradenton
Barnebey, Mark Patrick *lawyer*

### Brandon
Curry, Clifton Conrad, Jr. *lawyer*

### Bushnell
Hagin, T. Richard *lawyer*

### Clearwater
Bairstow, Frances Kanevsky *labor arbitrator, mediator, educator*
Birmingham, Richard Gregory *lawyer*
Blakely, John T. *lawyer*
Bokor, Bruce H. *lawyer*
Conetta, Tami Foley *lawyer*
Falkner, William Carroll *lawyer*
Free, E. LeBron *lawyer*
Gassman, Alan Scott *lawyer*
Johnson, Timothy Augustin, Jr. *lawyer*

Pope, Fred Wallace, Jr. *lawyer*
Tragos, George Euripedes *lawyer*
Weidemeyer, Carleton Lloyd *lawyer*

### Coconut Creek
Godofsky, Stanley *lawyer*

### Coconut Grove
Arboleya, Carlos Joaquin *lawyer, broker*
Denaro, Gregory *lawyer*
McAmis, Edwin Earl *lawyer*

### Coral Gables
Ely, John Hart *lawyer, university dean*
Hoffman, Carl H(enry) *lawyer*
Kniskern, Joseph Warren *lawyer*
Lott, Leslie Jean *lawyer*
Rosenn, Keith Samuel *lawyer, educator*

### Coral Springs
Polin, Alan Jay *lawyer*

### Daytona Beach
Neitzke, Eric Karl *lawyer*

### Deerfield Beach
Brown, Colin W(egand) *lawyer, diversified company executive*
Rung, Richard Allen *lawyer, retired air force officer, retired educator*

### Delray Beach
Barlow, Joel *retired lawyer*
Groening, William Andrew, Jr. *lawyer, former chemical company executive*
Larry, R. Heath *lawyer*
Shister, Joseph *arbitrator, educator*

### Fernandina
Manson, Keith Alan Michael *lawyer*

### Fort Lauderdale
Adams, Daniel Lee *lawyer*
Anastasiou, Van E. *lawyer*
Bogenschutz, J. David *lawyer*
Buckstein, Mark Aaron *lawyer, educator*
Buell, Rodd Russell *lawyer*
Bunnell, George Eli *lawyer*
Bustamante, Nestor *lawyer*
Caulkins, Charles S. *lawyer*
Clark, Desmond Laverne *immigration legal secretary, editor, minister*
Colsky, Andrew Evan *lawyer, mediator, arbitrator*
Cooney, David Francis *lawyer*
Dressler, Robert A. *lawyer*
Gardner, Russell Menese *lawyer*
Hargrove, John Russell *lawyer*
Hirsch, Jeffrey Allan *lawyer*
Hoines, David Alan *lawyer*
Howard, William Matthew *lawyer, business executive, arbitrator, author*
James, Gordon, III *lawyer*
Joseph, Paul R *law educator*
Katz, Thomas Owen *lawyer*
Krathen, David Howard *lawyer*
Kubler, Frank Lawrence *lawyer*
Lataif, Lawrence P. *lawyer*
Meeks, William Herman, III *lawyer*
Moss, Stephen B. *lawyer*
Nussbaum, Howard Jay *lawyer*
O'Bryan, William Monteith *lawyer*
Richmond, Gail Levin *law educator*
Rodriguez, Carlos Augusto *lawyer*
Roselli, Richard Joseph *lawyer*
Schrader, Robert George *lawyer*
Schreiber, Alan Hickman *lawyer*
Sherman, Richard Allen *lawyer*
Turner, Hugh Joseph, Jr. *lawyer*
Walton, Rodney Earl *lawyer*

### Fort Myers
Allen, Richard Chester *retired lawyer, educator*
Medvecky, Robert Stephen *lawyer*
Morse, John Harleigh *lawyer*
Norton, Elizabeth Wychgel *lawyer*

### Fort Myers Beach
Cotter, Richard Timothy *lawyer*

### Fort Walton Beach
†Day, George Everette *lawyer, retired military officer*

### Gainesville
Boyes, Patrice Flinchbaugh *lawyer, environmental executive*
Eder, George Jackson *lawyer, economist*
Freeland, James M. Jackson *lawyer, educator*
Israel, Jerold Harvey *law educator*
Moberly, Robert Blakely *lawyer, educator*
Probert, Walter *lawyer, educator*
Quarles, James Cliv *law educator*
Smith, David Thornton *lawyer, educator*
Taylor, Grace Elizabeth Woodall (Betty Taylor) *lawyer, law educator, law library administrator*
Van Alstyne, W. Scott, Jr. *lawyer, educator*
Weyrauch, Walter Otto *law educator*
White, Jill Carolyn *lawyer*

### Hallandale
Solomon, Michael Bruce *lawyer*

### Hialeah
Dominik, Jack Edward *lawyer*

### Hobe Sound
Etherington, Edwin Deacon *lawyer, business executive, educator*
Havens, Oliver Hershman *lawyer, consultant*
Markoe, Frank, Jr. *lawyer, business and hospital executive*
Matheson, William Lyon *lawyer, farmer*
Simpson, Russell Gordon *lawyer, mayor, counselor to not-for-profit organizations*

### Hollywood
Cohen, Ronald J. *lawyer*

### Jacksonville
Ade, James L. *lawyer*
Ansbacher, Lewis *lawyer*

Braddock, Donald Layton, Sr. *lawyer, accountant, investor*
Bryan, Joseph Shepard, Jr. *lawyer*
Bullock, Bruce Stanley *lawyer*
Ceballos, M(ichael) Alan *lawyer*
Christian, Gary Irvin *lawyer*
Commander, Charles Edward *lawyer, real estate consultant*
Criser, Marshall M. *lawyer, retired university president*
Drew, Horace Rainsford, Jr. *lawyer*
Ehrlich, Raymond *lawyer*
Farmer, Guy Otto, II *lawyer*
Fawbush, Andrew Jackson *lawyer*
Fruit, Melvyn Herschel *lawyer, management consultant*
Gabel, George DeSaussure, Jr. *lawyer*
Getman, Willard Etheridge *lawyer, mediator*
Keefe, Kenneth M., Jr. *lawyer*
Kelso, Linda Yayoi *lawyer*
Korn, Michael Jeffrey *lawyer*
Legler, Mitchell Wooten *lawyer*
Link, Robert James *lawyer, educator*
McWilliams, John Lawrence, III *lawyer*
Milton, Joseph Payne *lawyer*
Moseley, James Francis *lawyer*
O'Neal, Michael Scott, Sr. *lawyer*
Pillans, Charles Palmer, III *lawyer*
Pope, Shawn Hideyoshi *lawyer*
Prom, Stephen George *lawyer*
Rinaman, James Curtis, Jr. *lawyer*
Sadler, Luther Fuller, Jr. *lawyer*
Slade, Thomas Bog, III *lawyer, investment banker*
Stone, Dennis J. *law educator, chief information officer, lawyer*
Wallis, Donald Wills *lawyer*
White, Edward Alfred *lawyer*
Zima, Michael David *lawyer*

### Jasper
McCormick, John Hoyle *lawyer*

### Jensen Beach
Stuart, Harold Cutliff *lawyer, business executive*

### Jupiter
Boykin, Lykes M. *lawyer, real estate company executive*
del Russo, Alessandra Luini *law educator*

### Key Largo
Mattson, James Stewart *lawyer, environmental scientist, educator*

### Key West
Coudert, Ferdinand Wilmerding *lawyer*

### Lake Wales
Adams, Paul Winfrey *lawyer, business executive*

### Lake Worth
Stafford, Shane Ludwig *lawyer*

### Lakeland
Artigliere, Ralph *lawyer, educator*
Dufoe, William Stewart *lawyer*
Henry, William Oscar Eugene *lawyer*
Kibler, David Burke, III *lawyer*
Kittleson, Henry Marshall *lawyer*
Knowlton, Kevin Charles *lawyer*
Koren, Edward Franz *lawyer*

### Leesburg
Austin, Robert Eugene, Jr. *lawyer*
Clement, Howard Wheeler *lawyer*
Fechtel, Vincent John *legal administrator*

### Longboat Key
Freeman, Richard Merrell *lawyer, corporate director*
Heitler, George *lawyer*

### Longwood
Tomasulo, Virginia Merrills *retired lawyer*

### Lutz
Hayes, Timothy George *lawyer, consultant*

### Melbourne
Cacciatore, S. Sammy, Jr. *lawyer*

### Miami
Alonso, Antonio Enrique *lawyer*
Amber, Laurie Kaufman *lawyer*
Astigarraga, Jose I(gnacio) *lawyer*
Barrett, John Richard *lawyer*
Bartel, Jeffrey Scott *lawyer*
Beckham, Walter Hull, Jr. *lawyer, educator*
Berley, David Richard *lawyer*
Berman, Bruce Judson *lawyer*
Blumberg, Edward Robert *lawyer*
Burnett, Henry *lawyer*
Chabrow, Penn Benjamin *lawyer*
Clark, James Kendall *lawyer*
Clarke, Mercer Kaye *lawyer*
Cole, Robert Bates *lawyer*
Crabtree, John Granville *lawyer*
Dady, Robert Edward *lawyer*
Deaktor, Darryl Barnett *lawyer*
de Leon, John Louis *lawyer*
Dribin, Michael A. *lawyer*
DuFresne, Elizabeth Jamison *lawyer*
Dyer, John Martin *lawyer, marketing educator*
England, Arthur Jay, Jr. *lawyer, former state justice*
Feingold, Laurence *lawyer*
Ferrell, Milton Morgan, Jr. *lawyer*
Fitzgerald, Joseph Michael, Jr. *lawyer*
Garrett, Richard G. *lawyer*
Godofsky, Lawrence *lawyer*
Gong, Edmond Joseph *lawyer*
Gonzalez-Pita, J. Alberto *lawyer*
Gragg, Karl Lawrence *lawyer*
Greer, Alan Graham *lawyer*
Grossman, Robert Louis *lawyer*
Hall, Andrew Clifford *lawyer*
Hartman, Douglas Cole *lawyer*
Hartz, Steven Edward Marshall *lawyer, educator*
Hector, Louis Julius *lawyer*
Hoffman, Larry J. *lawyer*
Houlihan, Gerald John *lawyer*
Hudson, Robert Franklin, Jr. *lawyer*
Kenin, David S. *lawyer*
Kleinfeld, Denis A. *lawyer*
Klock, Joseph Peter, Jr. *lawyer*

Korchin, Judith Miriam *lawyer*
Kuehne, Benedict P. *lawyer*
Lampen, Richard Jay *lawyer, investment banker*
Landy, Burton Aaron *lawyer*
Lipcon, Charles Roy *lawyer*
Long, Maxine Master *lawyer*
Louis, Paul Adolph *lawyer*
Mahnk, Karen *law librarian, legal assistant*
Marx, Richard Benjamin *lawyer*
Mehta, Eileen Rose *lawyer*
Merrill, George Vanderneth *lawyer, investment executive*
Milstein, Richard Craig *lawyer*
Mudd, John Philip *lawyer*
Munn, Janet Teresa *lawyer*
Murai, Rene Vicente *lawyer*
Myers, Kenneth M. *lawyer*
Nachwalter, Michael *lawyer*
Nuernberg, William R(ichard) *lawyer*
Osman, Edith Gabriella *lawyer*
Pallot, Joseph Wedeles *lawyer*
Paul, Robert *lawyer*
Payne, R.W., Jr. *lawyer*
Pearson, Daniel S. *lawyer*
Pearson, John Edward *lawyer*
Pfenniger, Richard Charles, Jr. *lawyer*
Poston, Rebekah Jane *lawyer*
Quirantes, Albert M. *lawyer*
Rashkind, Paul Michael *lawyer*
Roddenberry, Stephen Keith *lawyer*
Rosen, Howard Robert *lawyer*
Ruffner, Charles Louis *lawyer*
Rust, Robert Warren *retired lawyer*
Ryce, Donald Theodore *lawyer*
Sacher, Barton Stuart *lawyer*
Sarnoff, Marc David *lawyer*
Schuette, Charles A. *lawyer*
Schulman, Clifford A. *lawyer*
Silber, Norman Jules *lawyer*
Simmons, Sherwin Palmer *lawyer*
Smith, Samuel Stuart *lawyer*
Stein, Allan Mark *lawyer*
Steinberg, Marty *lawyer*
Stokes, Paul Mason *lawyer*
Suarez, Xavier Louis *lawyer, former mayor*
Tarkoff, Michael Harris *lawyer*
Touby, Kathleen Anita *lawyer*
Touby, Richard *lawyer*
Tumpson, Joan Berna *lawyer*
Valle, Laurence Francis *lawyer*
Vento, M. Thérèse *lawyer*
Walters, David McLean *lawyer*
Weiner, Lawrence *lawyer*
Weinstein, Alan Edward *lawyer*
Weinstein, Andrew H. *lawyer*
Whitlow, James Adams *lawyer*
Wright, Robert Thomas, Jr. *lawyer*

### Miami Lakes
Sharett, Alan Richard *lawyer, environmental litigator, mediator and arbitrator, law educator*

### Naples
Beam, Robert Thompson *retired lawyer*
Bornmann, Carl M(alcolm) *lawyer*
Budd, David Glenn *lawyer*
Cimino, Richard Dennis *lawyer*
Crehan, Joseph Edward *lawyer*
Davis, Sidney Fant *lawyer, author*
Doyle, Robert Eugene, Jr. *lawyer*
Dutton, Clarence Benjamin *lawyer*
Emerson, John Williams, II *lawyer*
Mac'Kie, Pamela S. *lawyer*
McCaffrey, Judith Elizabeth *lawyer*
Peck, Bernard Sidney *lawyer*
Putzell, Edwin Joseph, Jr. *lawyer, mayor*
Roberts, William B. *lawyer, business executive*
Schauer, Wilbert Edward, Jr. *lawyer, manufacturing company executive*
Smith, Numa Lamar, Jr. *lawyer*
Snyder, Marion Gene *lawyer, former congressman*
Stevens, William Kenneth *lawyer*
Strauss, Jerome Manfred *lawyer, banker*
Westman, Carl Edward *lawyer*

### New Port Richey
Focht, Theodore Harold *lawyer, educator*
Richardson, Richard Lewis *lawyer*

### New Smyrna
Henderson, Clay *lawyer*

### North Miami
Moreno, Christine Margaret *lawyer*

### North Miami Beach
Ballman, Donna Marie *lawyer*

### North Palm Beach
Boyden, Christopher Wayne *lawyer, divorce mediator*

### Ocala
Hatch, John D. *lawyer, consultant*

### Okeechobee
Selmi, William, Jr. *lawyer*

### Oldsmar
Hirschman, Sherman Joseph *lawyer, educator*

### Opa Locka
Light, Alfred Robert *lawyer, political scientist, educator*

### Orlando
Allen, William Riley *lawyer*
Arkin, J. Gordon *lawyer*
Bailey, Michael Keith *lawyer*
Blackford, Robert Newton *lawyer*
Blackwell, Bruce Beuford *lawyer*
Bussey, John W., III *lawyer*
Capouano, Albert D. *lawyer*
Chong, Stephen Chu Ling *lawyer*
Chotas, Elias Nicholas *lawyer*
Christiansen, Patrick T. *lawyer*
Conti, Louis Thomas Moore *lawyer*
deBeaubien, Hugo H. *lawyer*
Dietz, Robert Lee *lawyer*
Dunlap, Charles Leonard *lawyer*
Eidson, Frank M. *lawyer*
Feuvrel, Sidney Leo, Jr. *lawyer, educator*
Handley, Leon Hunter *lawyer*
Hartley, Carl William, Jr. *lawyer*

Higgins, Robert Frederick *lawyer*
Ioppolo, Frank S., Jr. *lawyer*
Jontz, Jeffry Robert *lawyer*
Leonhardt, Frederick Wayne *lawyer*
Mock, Frank Mackenzie *lawyer*
Nadeau, Robert Bertrand, Jr. *lawyer*
Nants, Bruce Arlington *lawyer*
Neff, A. Guy *lawyer*
Palmer, William D. *lawyer*
Reed, John Alton *lawyer*
Rolle, Christopher Davies *lawyer*
Rudolph, Wallace Morton *law educator*
Rush, Fletcher Grey, Jr. *lawyer*
Simmons, Cleatous J. *lawyer*
Simon, James Lowell *lawyer*
Sims, Roger W. *lawyer*
Skambis, Christopher Charles, Jr. *lawyer*
Snively, Stephen Wayne *lawyer*
Spoonhour, James Michael *lawyer*
Stewart, Harry A. *lawyer*
Turner, Thomas William *lawyer*
Urban, James Arthur *lawyer*
Weiss, Christopher John *lawyer*
Wilson, William Berry *lawyer*
Yates, Leighton Delevan, Jr. *lawyer*

**Ormond Beach**
Barker, Robert Osborne (Bob Barker) *mediator, property management and public relations executive*

**Osprey**
Fleming, William Harrison *retired lawyer*
Maddocks, Robert Allen *lawyer, manufacturing company executive*

**Palatka**
Baldwin, Allen Adail *lawyer, writer*

**Palm Beach**
Adler, Frederick Richard *lawyer, financier*
Bane, Charles Arthur *lawyer*
Chopin, L. Frank *lawyer*
Crawford, Sandra Kay *lawyer*
Fogelson, David *retired lawyer*
Ford, Thomas Patrick *lawyer*
Graubard, Seymour *lawyer*
Miller, Richard Jackson *lawyer*
Rauch, George Washington *lawyer*

**Palm Beach Gardens**
Desormier-Cartwright, Anné Maria *lawyer*
Lambert, George Robert *lawyer, insurance company executive, legal consultant, realtor*

**Palm City**
Burton, John Routh *lawyer*
Huntington, Earl Lloyd *lawyer, retired natural resources company executive*

**Palm Coast**
Patz, Edward Frank *retired lawyer*

**Palm Harbor**
Hoppensteadt, Jon Kirk *law librarian*

**Panama City**
Byrne, Robert William *lawyer*
Patterson, Christopher Nida *lawyer*

**Pensacola**
Adams, Joseph Peter *retired lawyer, consultant*
Bozeman, Frank Carmack *lawyer*
Geeker, Nicholas Peter *lawyer, judge*
George, Katie *lawyer, former city manager*
Johnson, Rodney Marcum *lawyer*
Kelly, John Barry, II *lawyer*
Marsh, William Douglas *lawyer*
Moulton, Wilbur Wright, Jr. *lawyer*
Soloway, Daniel Mark *lawyer*

**Plant City**
Buchman, Kenneth William *lawyer*

**Plantation**
Buck, Thomas Randolph *lawyer, financial services executive*
Ferris, Robert Edmund *lawyer*
Koltnow, H. Robert *lawyer*

**Pompano Beach**
Szilassy, Sandor *retired lawyer, library director, educator*

**Ponte Vedra Beach**
Kuhn, Bowie K. *lawyer, former professional baseball commissioner, consultant*

**River Ranch**
Swett, Albert Hersey *retired lawyer, business executive, consultant*

**Saint Petersburg**
Allen, John Thomas, Jr. *lawyer*
Battaglia, Anthony Sylvester *lawyer*
Brown, Jacqueline Ley White *lawyer*
Buchmann, Alan Paul *lawyer*
Elson, Charles Myer *law educator*
Escarraz, Enrique, III *lawyer*
Harrell, Roy G., Jr. *lawyer*
Mann, Sam Henry, Jr. *lawyer*
Moody, Lizabeth Ann *law educator*
Wilson, Darryl Cedric *lawyer, law educator, consultant*

**Sanibel**
Kiernan, Edwin A., Jr. *lawyer, corporation executive*

**Sarasota**
Christopher, William Garth *lawyer*
Goldsmith, Stanley Alan *lawyer*
Greenfield, Robert Kauffman *lawyer*
Herb, F(rank) Steven *lawyer*
Hull, J(ames) Richard *retired lawyer, business executive*
Ives, George Skinner *arbitrator, former government official*
Janney, Oliver James *lawyer, plastics and chemical company executive*
Kimbrough, Robert Averyt *lawyer*
Lawrence, George Durwood, Jr. *lawyer, corporate executive*

Lund, Wendell Luther *lawyer*
Mackey, Leonard Bruce *lawyer, former diversified manufacturing corporation executive*
Phillips, Elvin Willis *lawyer*
Raimi, Burton Louis *lawyer*
Schwartz, Norman L. *lawyer*
Wise, Warren Roberts *lawyer*

**Sebring**
McCollum, James Fountain *lawyer*

**Stuart**
Harvin, Wesley Reid *lawyer*

**Tallahassee**
Aurell, John Karl *lawyer*
Barley, John Alvin *lawyer*
Barnett, Martha Walters *lawyer*
Boyd, Joseph Arthur, Jr. *lawyer*
Carson, Leonard Allen *lawyer*
Clarkson, Julian Derieux *lawyer*
Curtin, Lawrence N. *lawyer*
Dariotis, Terrence Theodore *lawyer*
Ervin, Robert Marvin *lawyer*
Fonvielle, Charles David *lawyer*
Griffith, Elwin Jabez *lawyer, university administrator*
Manley, Walter Wilson, II *lawyer*
Miller, Gregory R. *prosecutor*
Miller, Morris Henry *lawyer*
Pelham, Thomas Gerald *lawyer*
Peterson, Rodney Delos *mediator, forensic economist*
Reid, Sue Titus *law educator*
Roland, Raymond William *lawyer, mediator*
Saunders, Ron *lawyer, former state legislator*
Schroeder, Edwin Maher *law educator*
Zaiser, Kent Ames *lawyer*

**Tamarac**
Weinstein, Peter M. *lawyer, state senator*

**Tampa**
Adkins, Edward Cleland *lawyer*
Aitken, Thomas Dean *lawyer*
Aye, Walter Edwards *lawyer*
Barkin, Marvin E. *lawyer*
Barton, Bernard Alan, Jr. *lawyer*
Bierley, John Charles *lawyer*
Burnette, Guy Ellington, Jr. *lawyer*
Butler, Paul Bascomb, Jr. *lawyer*
Campbell, Richard Bruce *lawyer*
Davis, Richard Earl *lawyer*
Doliner, Nathaniel Lee *lawyer*
Ellwanger, Thomas John *lawyer*
England, Lynne Lipton *lawyer, speech pathologist, audiologist*
Gassler, Frank Henry *lawyer*
Germany, John Fredrick *lawyer*
Gilbert, Leonard Harold *lawyer*
Gillen, William Albert *lawyer*
Hapner, Elizabeth Lynn *lawyer, writer*
Hoyt, Brooks Pettingill *lawyer*
Humphries, J. Bob *lawyer*
Jones, John Arthur *lawyer*
Kelly, Thomas Paine, Jr. *lawyer*
Kiernan, William Joseph, Jr. *lawyer, real estate investor*
Lane, Robin *lawyer*
LeFevre, David E. *lawyer, professional sports team executive*
Levine, Jack Anton *lawyer*
Litschgi, A. Byrne *lawyer*
MacDonald, Thomas Cook, Jr. *lawyer*
Mandelbaum, Samuel Robert *lawyer*
Martin, Gary Wayne *lawyer*
McAdams, John P. *lawyer*
McClurg, Douglas P. *lawyer*
McDevitt, Sheila Marie *lawyer, energy company executive*
McEnery, Janet Goldberg *lawyer*
†McKay, Richard James *lawyer*
Olson, John Karl *lawyer*
O'Neill, Albert Clarence, Jr. *lawyer*
O'Sullivan, Brendan Patrick *lawyer*
Pacheco, Felipe Ramon *lawyer*
Reyes, Lillian Jenny *lawyer*
Roberson, Bruce H. *lawyer*
Robinson, John William, IV *lawyer*
Rosenkranz, Stanley William *lawyer*
Schwenke, Roger Dean *lawyer*
Soble, James Barry *lawyer*
Sparkman, Steven Leonard *lawyer*
Stallings, (Charles) Norman *lawyer*
Stiles, Mary Ann *lawyer*
Sweet, Charles G. *paralegal school administrator, dean*
Taub, Theodore Calvin *lawyer*
Thomas, Wayne Lee *lawyer*
Vessel, Robert Leslie *lawyer*
Wagner, Frederick William (Bill Wagner) *lawyer*
Waller, Edward Martin, Jr. *lawyer*
Young, Gwynne A. *lawyer*

**Tierra Verde**
Garnett, Stanley Iredale, II *lawyer, utility company executive*

**Venice**
Miller, Allan John *lawyer*

**Vero Beach**
Anderson, Rudolph J., Jr. *lawyer*

**West Palm Beach**
Aron, Jerry E. *lawyer*
Baker, Bernard Robert, II *lawyer*
Brannon, Dave Lee *lawyer*
Dunston, Leigh Everett *lawyer*
Flanagan, L. Martin *lawyer*
Gildan, Phillip Clarke *lawyer*
Goetz, Cecelia Helen *lawyer, retired judge*
Hill, Thomas William, Jr. *lawyer, educator*
Holt, Richard Duane *lawyer*
Hudson, Lise Lyn *lawyer*
Kamen, Michael Andrew *lawyer*
Kiely, Dan Ray *lawyer, banking and real estate development executive*
Lampert, Michael Allen *lawyer*
Lane, Matthew Jay *lawyer*
McHale, Michael John *lawyer*
Montgomery, Robert Morel, Jr. *lawyer*
Moore, George Crawford Jackson *lawyer*
Mrachek, Lorin Louis *lawyer*
Norton, William Alan *lawyer*
O'Brien, Thomas George, III *lawyer*
O'Flarity, James P. *lawyer*

†Orlovsky, Donald Albert *lawyer*
Petersen, David L. *lawyer*
Porter, Jack A. *lawyer*
Royce, Raymond Watson *lawyer, rancher, citrus grower*
Sammond, John Stowell *lawyer*
Sklar, William Paul *lawyer, educator*
Smith, David Shiverick *lawyer, former ambassador*
Spillias, Kenneth George *lawyer*
Wagner, Arthur Ward, Jr. *lawyer*
Wroble, Arthur Gerard *lawyer*

**Weston**
Broder, Gail Steinmetz *lawyer*

**Winter Haven**
Chase, Lucius Peter *lawyer, retired corporate executive*

**Winter Park**
Brooten, Kenneth Edward, Jr. *lawyer*
Builder, J. Lindsay, Jr. *lawyer*
Fowler, Mark Stapleton *lawyer, corporation counsel*
Hadley, Ralph Vincent, III *lawyer*

# GEORGIA

**Alpharetta**
Feuss, Linda Anne Upsall *lawyer*

**Athens**
Beaird, James Ralph *legal educator*
Carlson, Ronald Lee *lawyer, educator*
Davis, Claude-Leonard *lawyer, educational administrator*
Elkins, Robert Neal *lawyer*
Ellington, Charles Ronald *lawyer, educator*
Huszagh, Fredrick Wickett *lawyer, educator, information management company executive*
Phillips, Walter Ray *lawyer, educator*
Puckett, Elizabeth Ann *law librarian, law educator*
Spurgeon, Edward Dutcher *law educator*
Tolley, Edward Donald *lawyer*
Wellman, Richard Vance *legal educator*

**Atlanta**
Abrams, Harold Eugene *lawyer*
Aldridge, John *lawyer*
Alexander, Miles Jordan *lawyer*
Anderson, Peter Joseph *lawyer*
Attridge, Richard Byron *lawyer*
Bankoff, Joseph R. *lawyer*
Barkoff, Rupert Mitchell *lawyer*
Bassett, Peter Q. *lawyer*
Batson, Richard Neal *lawyer*
Beckham, Walter Hull, III *lawyer*
Beckman, Gail McKnight *law educator*
Beller, Michael E. *lawyer*
Bennett, Jay D. *lawyer*
Bird, Francis Marion, Jr. *lawyer*
Bird, Wendell Raleigh *lawyer*
Blackburn, William Stanley *lawyer*
Blackstock, Jerry Byron *lawyer*
Blank, A(ndrew) Russell *lawyer*
Block, Mitchell Stern *lawyer*
Bloodworth, A(lbert) W(illiam) Franklin *lawyer*
Boisseau, Richard Robert *lawyer*
Boman, John Harris, Jr. *retired lawyer*
Bonds, John Wilfred, Jr. *lawyer*
Bondurant, Emmet Jopling, II *lawyer*
Boone, J. William *lawyer*
Booth, Gordon Dean, Jr. *lawyer*
Bowden, Henry Lumpkin, Jr. *lawyer*
Boynton, Frederick George *lawyer*
Bradley, William Hampton *lawyer*
Branch, Thomas Broughton, III *lawyer*
Brannon, Lester Travis, Jr. *lawyer*
Bratton, James Henry, Jr. *lawyer*
Brecher, Armin G. *lawyer*
Brown, John Robert *lawyer, priest, philanthropist*
Byrne, Granville Bland, III *lawyer*
Cadenhead, Alfred Paul *lawyer*
Calhoun, Scott Douglas *lawyer*
Candler, John Slaughter, II *retired lawyer*
Capron, John M. *lawyer*
Cargill, Robert Mason *lawyer*
Carpenter, David Allan *lawyer*
Carson, Christopher Leonard *lawyer*
Cheatham, Richard Reed *lawyer*
Chilivis, Nickolas Peter *lawyer*
Clarke, Thomas Hal *lawyer*
Cohen, Ezra Harry *lawyer*
Cohen, George Leon *lawyer*
Cohen, N. Jerold *lawyer*
Collins, Steven M. *lawyer*
Cook, Philip C. *lawyer*
Cooper, Frederick Eansor *lawyer*
Coxe, Tench Charles *lawyer*
Crews, William Edwin *lawyer*
Croft, Terrence Lee *lawyer*
Cutshaw, Kenneth Andrew *lawyer*
Dalton, John Joseph *lawyer*
Davis, Frank Tradewell, Jr. *lawyer*
Denny, Richard Alden, Jr. *lawyer*
Despriet, John G. *lawyer*
Douglas, John Lewis *lawyer*
Doyle, Michael Anthony *lawyer*
Driver, Walter W., Jr. *lawyer*
DuBose, Charles Wilson *lawyer*
Duffey, William Simon, Jr. *lawyer*
Durrett, James Frazer, Jr. *lawyer*
Eason, William Everette, Jr. *lawyer*
Egan, Michael Joseph *lawyer*
Ehrlichman, John Daniel *lawyer, company executive, author, former assistant to President of United States*
Epstein, David Gustav *lawyer*
Etheridge, Jack Paul *arbitrator, mediator, former judge*
Farnham, Clayton Henson *lawyer*
Fellows, Henry David, Jr. *lawyer*
Felton, Jule Wimberly, Jr. *lawyer*
Fleming, Julian Denver, Jr. *lawyer*
Forbes, Theodore McCoy, Jr. *retired lawyer, arbitrator, mediator*
Foreman, Edward Rawson *lawyer*
Franklin, Charles Scothern *lawyer*
Gambrell, David Henry *lawyer*
Genberg, Ira *lawyer*
Gertzman, Stephen F. *lawyer*
Girth, Marjorie Louisa *lawyer, educator*
Glaser, Arthur Henry *lawyer*
Goldstein, Elliott *lawyer*
González, Carlos A. *lawyer*

Greer, Bernard Lewis, Jr. *lawyer*
Grove, Russell Sinclair, Jr. *lawyer*
Haas, George Aaron *lawyer*
Hackett, Stanley Hailey *lawyer*
Hagan, James Walter *lawyer*
Harkey, Robert Shelton *lawyer*
Harlin, Robert Ray *lawyer*
Harney, Thomas C. *lawyer*
Hassett, Robert William *lawyer*
Hasson, James Keith, Jr. *lawyer*
Hill, Paul Drennen *lawyer, banker*
Hoff, Gerhardt Michael *lawyer, insurance company executive*
Hopkins, George Mathews Marks *lawyer, business executive*
Howard, Harry Clay *lawyer*
Hunter, Forrest Walker *lawyer*
Hunter, Howard Owen *law educator, dean*
Isaf, Fred Thomas *lawyer*
Izard, John *lawyer*
Janney, Donald Wayne *lawyer*
Jeffries, McChesney Hill *retired lawyer*
Jenkins, Albert Felton, Jr. *lawyer*
Jester, Carroll Gladstone *lawyer*
Johnson, Weyman Thompson, Jr. *lawyer*
Jones, Frank Cater *lawyer*
Jones, Glower Whitehead *lawyer*
Jordan, Hilary Peter *lawyer*
Katz, Joel Abraham *lawyer, music consultant*
Kaufman, Mark David *lawyer*
Kaufman, Mark Stuart *lawyer*
Kelley, James Francis *lawyer*
Kelly, James Michael *lawyer*
Kelly, James Patrick *lawyer*
Killorin, Edward Wylly *lawyer, tree farmer*
Kinzer, William Luther *lawyer*
Kitchens, William H. *lawyer*
Klamon, Lawrence Paine *lawyer*
Kneisel, Edmund M. *lawyer*
Knight, W. Donald, Jr. *lawyer*
Knowles, Marjorie Fine *lawyer, educator, dean*
Lackland, Theodore Howard *lawyer*
Lamon, Harry Vincent, Jr. *lawyer*
Landon, James Henry *lawyer*
Lanier, George H. *lawyer*
Leach, James Glover *lawyer*
Leonard, David Morse *lawyer*
Lester, Charles Turner, Jr. *lawyer*
Levy, David *lawyer*
Linkous, William Joseph, Jr. *lawyer*
Lipshutz, Robert Jerome *lawyer, former government official*
Lower, Robert Cassel *lawyer, educator*
Lunsford, Julius R(odgers), Jr. *lawyer*
Lurey, Alfred Saul *lawyer*
Macey, Morris William *lawyer*
Marshall, John Treutlen *lawyer*
Marshall, Thomas Oliver, Jr. *lawyer*
McNeill, Thomas Ray *lawyer*
Medlin, Charles McCall *lawyer*
Miller, Janise Luevenia Monica *lawyer*
Mobley, John Homer, II *lawyer*
Moeling, Walter Goos, IV *lawyer*
Mull, Gale W. *lawyer*
Murphy, Richard Patrick *lawyer*
Newman, Stuart *lawyer*
Newton, Floyd Childs, III *lawyer*
Oakley, Mary Ann Bryant *lawyer*
O'Day, Stephen Edward *lawyer*
Owen, Robert Hubert *lawyer, real estate broker*
Pannell, Robert D. *lawyer*
Partain, Eugene Gartly *lawyer*
Patterson, William Robert *lawyer*
Perry, Timothy Sewell *lawyer*
Persons, Oscar Newton *lawyer*
Phillips, Barry *lawyer*
Phillips, William Russell, Sr. *lawyer*
Piassick, Joel Bernard *lawyer*
Pike, Larry Samuel *lawyer*
Pless, Laurance Davidson *lawyer*
Poe, H. Sadler *lawyer*
Pratt, John Sherman *lawyer*
Price, Charles Eugene *lawyer, legal educator*
Reed, Glen Alfred *lawyer*
Rhodes, Thomas Willard *lawyer*
Richey, Thomas S. *lawyer*
Riggs, Gregory Lynn *lawyer*
Rogers, C. B. *lawyer*
Russell, Harold Louis *lawyer*
Saidman, Gary K. *lawyer*
Salo, Ann Sexton Distler *lawyer*
Sands, Robert O. *lawyer*
Savell, Edward Lupo *lawyer*
Schroder, Jack Spalding, Jr. *lawyer*
Schulte, Jeffrey Lewis *lawyer*
Schwartz, Arthur Jay *lawyer*
Schwartz, Dale Marvin *lawyer*
Sibley, Horace Holden *lawyer*
Sibley, James Malcolm *retired lawyer*
Skal, Debra Lynn *lawyer*
Smith, Alexander Wyly, Jr. *lawyer*
Smith, James Louis, III *lawyer*
Smith, Jeffrey Michael *lawyer*
Smith, Sidney Oslin, Jr. *lawyer*
Smith, Walton Napier *lawyer*
Stallings, Ronald Denis *lawyer*
Stamps, Thomas Paty *lawyer, consultant*
Stephenson, Mason Williams *lawyer*
Stewart, Jeffrey Bayrd *lawyer, commodity trading advisor*
Stokes, James Sewell *lawyer*
Strauss, Robert David *lawyer*
Swan, George Steven *law educator*
Swann, Jerre Bailey *lawyer*
Swift, Frank Meador *lawyer*
Tanner, W(alter) Rhett *lawyer*
Taylor, George Kimbrough, Jr. *lawyer*
Tennant, Thomas Michael *lawyer*
Thompson, Larry Dean *lawyer*
Varner, Chilton Davis *lawyer*
Veatch, J. William, III *lawyer*
Walsh, W. Terence *lawyer*
Weathersby, James Roy *lawyer*
Webb, Brainard Troutman, Jr. *lawyer, distribution company executive*
Wellon, Robert G. *lawyer*
Whitley, Joe Dally *lawyer*
Williams, David Howard *lawyer*
Williams, Neil, Jr. *lawyer*
Wilson, James Hargrove, Jr. *lawyer*
Withrow, William N., Jr. *lawyer*
Wolensky, Michael K. *lawyer*
Wright, Peter Meldrim *lawyer*
Zink, Charles Talbott *lawyer*

**Augusta**
Lee, Lansing Burrows, Jr. *lawyer, corporate executive*

Woods, Gerald Wayne *lawyer*

**Barnesville**
Kennedy, Harvey John, Jr. *lawyer*

**Cartersville**
Pope, Robert Daniel *lawyer*

**Columbus**
Brinkley, Jack Thomas *lawyer, former congressman*
Harp, John Anderson *lawyer*
Johnson, Walter Frank, Jr. *lawyer*
Lasseter, Earle Forrest *lawyer*
McGlamry, Max Reginald *lawyer*
Page, William Marion *lawyer*
Patrick, James Duvall, Jr. *lawyer*
Shelnutt, John Mark *lawyer*

**Conyers**
Polstra, Larry John *lawyer*

**Dalton**
Laughter, Bennie M. *corporate lawyer*

**Decatur**
Middleton, James Boland *lawyer*

**Dillard**
Wilkinson, Albert Mims, Jr. *lawyer*

**Douglas**
Hayes, Dewey Norman *lawyer*

**Dublin**
Greene, Jule Blounte *lawyer*

**Gainesville**
Schuder, Raymond Francis *lawyer*

**Lawrenceville**
Henson, Gene Ethridge *retired legal administrator*

**Lookout Mountain**
Hitching, Harry James *retired lawyer*

**Macon**
Cole, John Prince *lawyer*
Ennis, Edgar William, Jr. *lawyer*
Robinson, W. Lee *lawyer*
Rutledge, Ivan Cate *retired legal educator, arbitrator*
Sell, Edward Scott, Jr. *lawyer*
Snow, Cubbedge, Jr. *lawyer*

**Marietta**
Bentley, Fred Douglas, Sr. *lawyer*
Burkey, J(acob) Brent *lawyer, company executive*
Hammond, John William *lawyer*
Ingram, George Conley *lawyer*

**Metter**
Doremus, Ogden *lawyer*

**Norcross**
Gifford, Anita Sheree *lawyer*
Ramsay, Ernest Canaday *lawyer*

**Savannah**
Dickey, David Herschel *lawyer, accountant*
Forbes, Morton Gerald *lawyer*
Kenrich, John Lewis *lawyer*
Morrell, Diane Marie *lawyer*
Painter, Paul Wain, Jr. *lawyer*
Rawson, William Robert *lawyer, retired manufacturing company executive*
Stillwell, Walter Brooks, III *lawyer*

**Stone Mountain**
Weiman, Enrique Watson *lawyer*

**Valdosta**
Bass, Jay Michael *lawyer*

**Watkinsville**
Wright, Robert Joseph *lawyer*

## HAWAII

**Honolulu**
Akinaka, Asa Masayoshi *lawyer*
Bloede, Victor Carl *lawyer, academic executive*
Boas, Frank *lawyer*
Callies, David Lee *lawyer, educator*
Case, James Hebard *lawyer*
Char, Vernon Fook Leong *lawyer*
Chuck, Walter G(oonsun) *lawyer*
Crumpton, Charles Whitmarsh *lawyer*
Dang, Marvin S. C. *lawyer*
Devens, Paul *lawyer*
Dreher, Nicholas C. *lawyer*
Fong, Peter C. K. *lawyer, judge*
Gay, E(mil) Laurence *lawyer*
Gelber, Don Jeffrey *lawyer*
Gerson, Mervyn Stuart *lawyer*
Heller, Ronald Ian *lawyer*
Ingersoll, Richard King *lawyer*
Katayama, Robert Nobuichi *lawyer*
Kawachika, James Akio *lawyer*
Lilly, Michael Alexander *lawyer, author*
Lombardi, Dennis M. *lawyer*
Ma, Alan Wai-Chuen *lawyer*
Marks, Michael J. *lawyer, corporate executive*
Matayoshi, Coralie Chun *lawyer, bar association executive*
Miller, Clifford Joel *lawyer*
Miller, Richard Sherwin *legal educator*
Mirikitani, Andrew Kotaro *lawyer*
Miyasaki, Shuichi *lawyer*
Moore, Willson Carr, Jr. *lawyer*
Okinaga, Lawrence Shoji *lawyer*
Quinn, William Francis *lawyer*
Reber, David James *lawyer*
Roberti, Mario Andrew *lawyer, former energy company executive*
Sato, Glenn Kenji *lawyer*
Turbin, Richard *lawyer*
Umebayashi, Clyde Satoru *lawyer*
Weightman, Judy Mae *lawyer*
Wright, Harold Stanley *lawyer*
Zabanal, Eduardo Olegario *lawyer*

**Kahului**
Richardson, Robert Allen *lawyer, educator*

**Koloa**
Blair, Samuel Ray *lawyer*

**Paia**
Richman, Joel Eser *lawyer, mediator, arbitrator*

**Wailuku**
Kinaka, William Tatsuo *lawyer*

## IDAHO

**Boise**
Barber, Phillip Mark *lawyer*
Erickson, Robert Stanley *lawyer*
Graves, Ronald Norman *lawyer*
Klein, Edith Miller *lawyer, former state senator*
Lance, Alan George *lawyer, legislator, attorney general*
Leroy, David Henry *lawyer, state and federal official*
Marcus, Craig Brian *lawyer*
Minnich, Diane Kay *state bar executive*
Richardson, Betty H. *prosecutor*
Risch, James E. *lawyer*
Shurtliff, Marvin Karl *lawyer*
VanHole, William Remi *lawyer*

**Caldwell**
Kerrick, David Ellsworth *lawyer*

**Idaho Falls**
Whittier, Monte Ray *lawyer*

**Ketchum**
Hogue, Terry Glynn *lawyer*

**Lewiston**
Peterson, Philip Everett *legal educator*
Tait, John Reid *lawyer*

**Moscow**
Vincenti, Sheldon Arnold *law educator, lawyer*

**Pocatello**
Nye, W. Marcus W. *lawyer*

**Twin Falls**
Hohnhorst, John Charles *lawyer*
Tolman, Steven Kay *lawyer*

## ILLINOIS

**Aledo**
Heintz, Baron Strum *lawyer*

**Alton**
Hoagland, Karl King, Jr. *lawyer*

**Arlington Heights**
Wine-Banks, Jill Susan *lawyer*

**Aurora**
Alschuler, Sam *retired lawyer*
Lowe, Ralph Edward *lawyer*
Tyler, Lloyd John *lawyer*

**Barrington**
Tobin, Dennis Michael *lawyer*
Victor, Michael Gary *lawyer, physician*
Wyatt, James Frank, Jr. *lawyer*

**Belleville**
Bauman, John Duane *lawyer*
Boyle, Richard Edward *lawyer*
Coghill, William Thomas, Jr. *lawyer*
Heiligenstein, Christian E. *lawyer*
Hess, Frederick J. *lawyer*
Parham, James Robert *lawyer*

**Bloomington**
Bragg, Michael Ellis *lawyer, insurance company executive*
Goebel, William Mathers *lawyer*
Montgomery, William Adam *lawyer*
Sullivan, Laura Patricia *lawyer, insurance company executive*
Wozniak, Debra Gail *lawyer*

**Bridgeport**
Stout, James Dudley *lawyer*

**Carbondale**
Clemons, John Robert *lawyer*
Kionka, Edward James *lawyer*
Lesar, Hiram Henry *lawyer, educator*
Matthews, Elizabeth Woodfin *law librarian, law educator*

**Carrollton**
Strickland, Hugh Alfred *lawyer*

**Carthage**
Glidden, John Redmond *lawyer*

**Champaign**
Cribbet, John Edward *law educator, former university chancellor*
Frampton, George Thomas *legal educator*
Kindt, John Warren, Sr. *lawyer, educator, consultant*
Krause, Harry Dieter *law educator*
Maggs, Peter Blount *lawyer, educator*
Mamer, Stuart Mies *lawyer*
Miller, Harold Arthur *lawyer*
Nowak, John E. *law educator*
Rawles, Edward Hugh *lawyer*
Rotunda, Ronald Daniel *law educator, consultant*
Surles, Richard Hurlbut, Jr. *law librarian*

**Chicago**
Abrams, Lee Norman *lawyer*
Acker, Ann *lawyer*
Acker, Frederick George *lawyer*
Adair, Wendell Hinton, Jr. *lawyer*
Adelman, Stanley Joseph *lawyer*
Adelman, Steven Herbert *lawyer*
Aldrich, Thomas Lawrence *lawyer*
Alexander, William Henry *lawyer*
Alexis, Geraldine M. *lawyer*
Allard, Jean *lawyer, urban planner*
Allen, Ronald Jay *law educator*
Allen, Thomas Draper *lawyer*
Alschuler, Albert W. *law educator*
Altman, Louis *lawyer, author, educator*
Anderson, David A. *lawyer*
Anderson, J. Trent *lawyer*
Anderson, John Thomas *lawyer*
Anderson, Kimball Richard *lawyer*
Anderson, William Cornelius, III *lawyer*
Angst, Gerald L. *lawyer*
Anthony, Michael Francis *lawyer*
Antonio, Douglas John *lawyer*
Anvaripour, M. A. *lawyer*
Appel, Nina Schick *law educator, dean*
Armstrong, Edwin Richard *lawyer, publisher, editor*
Aronson, Virginia L. *lawyer*
Athas, Gus James *lawyer*
Auerbach, Marshall Jay *lawyer*
Axley, Frederick William *lawyer*
Badel, Julie *lawyer*
Baer, John Richard Frederick *lawyer*
Baetz, W. Timothy *lawyer*
Bailey, Robert Short *lawyer*
Baird, Douglas Gordon *law educator*
Baker, Bruce Jay *lawyer*
Baker, James Edward Sproul *retired lawyer*
Baker, Pamela *lawyer*
Baldwin, Shaun McParland *lawyer*
Banoff, Sheldon Irwin *lawyer*
Barker, William Thomas *lawyer*
Barnard, Robert N. *lawyer*
Barnes, James Garland, Jr. *lawyer*
Barr, John Robert *lawyer*
Barrett, Roger Watson *lawyer*
Barron, Howard Robert *lawyer*
Barry, Norman J., Jr. *lawyer*
Baruch, Hurd *lawyer*
Bashwiner, Steven Lacelle *lawyer*
Baugher, Peter V. *lawyer*
Beck, Philip S. *lawyer*
Beem, Jack Darrel *lawyer*
Bennett, Russell Odbert *lawyer*
Berens, Mark Harry *lawyer*
Berenzweig, Jack Charles *lawyer*
Berger, Robert Michael *lawyer*
Berland, Abel Edward *lawyer, realtor*
Berman, Bennett I. *lawyer*
Bernard, Frank Charles *lawyer*
Berner, Robert Lee, Jr. *lawyer*
Berning, Larry D. *lawyer*
Bernstein, H. Bruce *lawyer*
Berolzheimer, Karl *lawyer*
Biebel, Paul Philip, Jr. *lawyer*
Biederman, Jerry H. *lawyer*
Bierig, Jack R. *lawyer, educator*
Bitner, John Howard *lawyer*
Bixby, Frank Lyman *lawyer*
Blatt, Richard Lee *lawyer*
Block, Neal Jay *lawyer*
Blount, Michael Eugene *lawyer*
Blust, Larry D. *lawyer*
Bockelman, John Richard *lawyer*
Bodine, Laurence *lawyer, editor, marketer*
Boehnen, Daniel A. *lawyer*
Bosselman, Fred Paul *law educator*
Bowe, William John *lawyer*
Bowen, Stephen Stewart *lawyer*
Bower, Glen Landis *lawyer*
Bramnik, Robert Paul *lawyer*
Brand, Mark Allen *lawyer*
Brennan, James Joseph *lawyer, banking and financial services executive*
Brice, Roger Thomas *lawyer*
Bridewell, David Alexander *lawyer*
Bridgman, Thomas Francis *lawyer*
Bristol, Douglas *lawyer*
Brizzolara, Charles Anthony *lawyer*
Brown, Alan Crawford *lawyer*
Brown, Donald James, Jr. *lawyer*
Brown, Gregory K. *lawyer*
Bruner, Stephen C. *lawyer*
Bulger, Brian Wegg *lawyer*
Burditt, George Miller, Jr. *lawyer*
Burgdoerfer, Jerry *lawyer*
Burke, Edmund Patrick, Sr. *lawyer*
Burke, Thomas Joseph, Jr. *lawyer*
Burkey, Lee Melville *lawyer*
Burns, Terrence Michael *lawyer*
Busey, Roxane C. *lawyer*
Byrne, Katharine Crane *lawyer*
Carlin, Dennis J. *lawyer*
Carlson, Stephen Curtis *lawyer*
Carlson, Walter Carl *lawyer*
Carpenter, David William *lawyer*
Carren, Jeffrey P. *lawyer*
Carroll, James J. *lawyer*
Carroll, William Kenneth *law educator, psychologist, theologian*
Cederoth, Richard Alan *lawyer*
Chandler, Kent, Jr. *lawyer*
Chapman, Howard Stuart *lawyer, educator*
Cheely, Daniel Joseph *lawyer*
Chefitz, Joel Gerald *lawyer*
Chemers, Robert Marc *lawyer*
Cherney, James Alan *lawyer*
Chiles, Stephen Michael *lawyer*
Chin, Davis *lawyr*
Christian, John M. *lawyer*
Chudzinski, Mark Adam *lawyer*
Cicero, Frank, Jr. *lawyer*
Clark, James Allen *lawyer, educator*
Clemens, Richard Glenn *lawyer*
Closen, Michael Lee *law educator*
Cohen, Christopher B. *lawyer*
Cohen, Melanie Rovner *lawyer*
Collen, Sheldon Orrin *lawyer*
Comiskey, Michael Peter *lawyer*
Congalton, Susan Tichenor *lawyer*
Conklin, Thomas William *lawyer*
Connelly, Mary Jo *lawyer*
Conviser, Richard James *law educator, lawyer, publications company executive*
Conway, Michael Maurice *lawyer*
Cook, Catherine Coghlan *lawyer*
Coolley, Ronald B. *lawyer*
Copeland, Edward Jerome *lawyer*
Corcoran, James Martin, Jr. *lawyer, writer, lecturer*
Corwin, Sherman Phillip *lawyer*
Costello, John William *lawyer*
Cotton, Eugene *lawyer*
Coughlan, Kenneth Lewis *lawyer*
Coulson, William Roy *lawyer*
Crane, Mark *lawyer*
Craven, George W. *lawyer*
Crawford, Dewey Byers *lawyer*
Cremin, Susan Elizabeth *lawyer*
Cressey, Bryan Charles *lawyer*
Crihfield, Philip J. *lawyer*
Crisham, Thomas Michael *lawyer*
Crossan, John Robert *lawyer*
Csar, Michael F. *lawyer*
Cunningham, Robert James *lawyer*
Cunningham, Thomas Justin *lawyer*
Currie, David Park *lawyer, educator*
Custer, Charles Francis *lawyer*
Daley, Michael Joseph *lawyer*
Daley, Susan Jean *lawyer*
Dam, Kenneth W. *lawyer, law educator*
D'Amato, Anthony *law educator*
Daniels, Keith Byron, Jr. *lawyer*
Davidson, Stanley J. *lawyer*
Davis, G(eorge) Gordon *lawyer, international environmental policy consultant*
Davis, Michael W. *lawyer*
Davis, Muller *lawyer*
Davis, Scott Jonathan *lawyer*
DeCarlo, William S. *lawyer*
Dechene, James Charles *lawyer*
Decker, Richard Knore *lawyer*
Deitrick, William Edgar *lawyer*
Delp, Wilbur Charles, Jr. *lawyer*
Dent, Thomas G. *lawyer*
D'Esposito, Julian C., Jr. *lawyer*
Despres, Leon Mathis *lawyer, former city official*
Detuno, Joseph Edward *lawyer*
DeWolfe, John Chauncey, Jr. *lawyer*
Dilling, Kirkpatrick Wallwick *lawyer*
Dixon, Stewart Strawn *lawyer*
Dockterman, Michael *lawyer*
Dondanville, John Wallace *lawyer*
Donlevy, John Dearden *lawyer*
Donner, Ted A. *lawyer*
Donohoe, Jerome Francis *lawyer*
Dorman, Jeffrey Lawrence *lawyer*
Downing, Robert Allan *lawyer*
Doyle, John Robert *lawyer*
Dropkin, Allen Hodes *lawyer*
Drymalski, Raymond Hibner *lawyer, banker*
Duhl, Michael Foster *lawyer*
Duncan, John Patrick Cavanaugh *lawyer*
Durchslag, Stephen P. *lawyer*
Dykstra, Paul Hopkins *lawyer*
Early, Bert Hylton *lawyer, legal search consultant*
Ecker, Lori D. *lawyer*
Edelman, Alvin *lawyer*
Egan, Kevin James *lawyer*
Eggert, Russell Raymond *lawyer*
Eimer, Nathan Philip *lawyer*
Ekdahl, Jon Nels *lawyer, corporate secretary*
Elden, Gary Michael *lawyer*
Ellwood, Scott *lawyer*
Elson, Alex *lawyer, educator, arbitrator*
English, John Dwight *lawyer*
Ephraim, Donald Morley *lawyer*
Erens, Jay Allan *lawyer*
Esrick, Jerald Paul *lawyer*
Even, Francis Alphonse *lawyer*
Fahner, Tyrone C. *lawyer, former state attorney general*
Farber, Bernard John *lawyer*
Farrell, Thomas Dinan *lawyer*
Fazio, Peter Victor, Jr. *lawyer*
Fein, Roger Gary *lawyer*
Feinstein, Fred Ira *lawyer*
Feldman, Scott M. *lawyer*
Fellows, Jerry Kenneth *lawyer*
Felsenthal, Steven Altus *lawyer*
Ferencz, Robert Arnold *lawyer*
Ferguson, Bradford Lee *lawyer*
Ferrini, James Thomas *lawyer*
Field, Henry Frederick *lawyer*
Field, Robert Edward *lawyer*
Fina, Paul Joseph *lawyer*
Finke, Robert Forge *lawyer*
Fisher, Herbert Hirsh *lawyer*
Fitch, Morgan Lewis, Jr. *intellectual property lawyer*
Flanagin, Neil *lawyer*
Flynn, Peter Anthony *lawyer*
Formeller, Daniel Richard *lawyer*
Fort, Jeffrey C. *lawyer*
Foster, Teree E. *law educator, university dean*
Foudree, Bruce William *lawyer*
Fox, Elaine Saphier *lawyer*
Fox, Paul T. *lawyer*
Franch, Richard Thomas *lawyer*
Franklin, Richard Mark *lawyer*
Fraumann, Willard George *lawyer*
Frazen, Mitchell Hale *lawyer*
Freeborn, Michael D. *lawyer*
Freed, Mayer Goodman *law educator*
Freehling, Paul Edward *lawyer*
Freeman, Lee Allen, Jr. *lawyer*
Freeman, Louis S. *lawyer*
Friedman, Lawrence Milton *lawyer*
Friedman, Roselyn L. *lawyer*
Fross, Roger Raymond *lawyer*
Fullagar, William Watts *lawyer*
Fuller, Perry Lucian *lawyer*
Furlane, Mark Elliott *lawyer*
Gancer, Donald Charles *lawyer*
Garber, Samuel Baugh *lawyer, retail company executive*
Garth, Bryant Geoffrey *law educator, foundation executive*
Gates, Stephen Frye *lawyer*
Gearen, John J. *lawyer*
Geiman, J. Robert *lawyer*
Gelman, Andrew Richard *lawyer*
George, John Martin, Jr. *lawyer*
Geraldson, Raymond I. *lawyer*
Geraldson, Raymond I., Jr. *lawyer*
Gerlits, Francis Joseph *lawyer*
Gerstman, George Henry *lawyer*
Gertz, Elmer *lawyer, author, educator*
Getzendanner, Susan *lawyer, former federal judge*
Giampietro, Wayne Bruce *lawyer*
Gibbons, William John *lawyer*
Gilbert, Howard N(orman) *lawyer*
Gilford, Steven Ross *lawyer*
Gilson, Jerome *lawyer, writer*
Ginsberg, Lewis Robbins *lawyer*
Gladden, James Walter, Jr. *lawyer*
Gleeson, Paul Francis *lawyer*
Glieberman, Herbert Allen *lawyer*
Golan, Stephen Leonard *lawyer*
Goldblatt, Stanford Jay *lawyer*
Golden, Bruce Paul *lawyer*
Golden, William C. *lawyer*
Goldman, Louis Budwig *lawyer*
Goldschmidt, Lynn Harvey *lawyer*

Goodman, Gary Alan *lawyer*
Gordon, William A. *lawyer*
Gotfryd, William Ted *lawyer*
Gottlieb, Gidon Alain Guy *law educator*
Graham, David F. *lawyer*
Gralen, Donald John *lawyer*
Grant, Robert Nathan *lawyer*
Gray, Milton Hefter *lawyer*
Grayck, Marcus Daniel *lawyer*
Greenberger, Ernest *lawyer*
Griffith, Donald Kendall *lawyer*
Grossi, Francis Xavier, Jr. *lawyer, educator*
Grossman, Robert Mayer *lawyer*
Gustman, David Charles *lawyer*
Guthman, Jack *lawyer*
Hablutzel, Margo Lynn *lawyer*
Haderlein, Thomas M. *lawyer*
Hahn, Frederic Louis *lawyer*
Haines, Martha Mahan *lawyer*
Hales, Daniel B. *lawyer*
Hall, Joan M. *lawyer*
Halloran, Michael J. *lawyer*
Halprin, Rick *lawyer*
Hammesfahr, Robert Winter *lawyer*
Hannah, Wayne Robertson, Jr. *lawyer*
Hannay, William Mouat, III *lawyer*
Hanson, Ronald William *lawyer*
Hardgrove, James Alan *lawyer*
Harmon, Robert Lon *lawyer*
Harrington, Carol A. *lawyer*
Harrington, James Timothy *lawyer*
Harris, Donald Ray *lawyer*
Harrold, Bernard *lawyer*
Haskins, Charles Gregory, Jr. *lawyer*
Hayes, David John Arthur, Jr. *legal association executive*
Hayward, Thomas Zander, Jr. *lawyer*
Head, Patrick James *lawyer*
Heatwole, Mark M. *lawyer*
Hecht, Frank Thomas *lawyer*
Heindl, Warren Anton *law educator, retired*
Heinz, John Peter *lawyer, educator*
Heinz, William Denby *lawyer*
Heisler, Quentin George, Jr. *lawyer*
Heldrich, Gerard Charles, Jr. *lawyer*
Heller, Stanley J. *lawyer, physician, educator*
Helman, Robert Alan *lawyer*
Helmholz, R(ichard) H(enry) *law educator*
Henning, Joel Frank *lawyer, author, publisher, consultant*
Henry, Frederick Edward *lawyer*
Henry, Robert John *lawyer*
Herbert, William Carlisle *lawyer*
Herman, Sidney N. *lawyer*
Hermann, Donald Harold James *lawyer, educator*
Herpe, David A. *lawyer*
Herzel, Leo *lawyer*
Herzog, Fred F. *law educator*
Hess, Sidney J., Jr. *lawyer*
Hesse, Carolyn Sue *lawyer*
Hester, Thomas Patrick *lawyer*
Hickey, John Thomas, Jr. *lawyer*
Hickman, Frederic W. *lawyer*
Hilborn, Michael G. *lawyer, real estate development executive*
Hilliard, David Craig *lawyer*
Hillman, Jordan Jay *law educator*
Hirshman, Harold Carl *lawyer*
Hoban, George Savre *lawyer*
Hodes, Scott *lawyer*
Hofer, Roy Ellis *lawyer*
Hoff, John Scott *lawyer*
Hoffman, Richard Bruce *lawyer*
Hoffman, Valerie Jane *lawyer*
Hollins, Mitchell Leslie *lawyer*
Holmes, Stephen T. *political science and law educator*
Hooks, William Henry *lawyer*
Hopkins, Kevin L. *law educator, consultant*
Horwath, Leslie Kathleen *lawyer*
Horwich, Allan *lawyer*
Hoskins, Richard Jerold *lawyer*
Howe, Jonathan Thomas *lawyer*
Howell, R(obert) Thomas, Jr. *lawyer, former food company executive*
Huggins, Rollin Charles, Jr. *lawyer*
Hummel, Gregory William *lawyer*
Hunt, Lawrence Halley, Jr. *lawyer*
Hunter, James Galbraith, Jr. *lawyer*
Huston, DeVerille Anne *lawyer*
Huston, Steven Craig *lawyer*
Hyman, Michael Bruce *lawyer*
Inbau, Fred Edward *lawyer, educator, author*
Jacobson, Harold LeLand *lawyer*
Jacobson, Marian Slutz *lawyer*
Jacobson, Richard Joseph *lawyer*
Jacoby, John Primm *lawyer*
Jacover, Jerold Alan *lawyer*
Jager, Melvin Francis *lawyer*
Jahns, Jeffrey *lawyer*
Jambor, Robert Vernon *lawyer*
Jast, Raymond Joseph *lawyer*
Jersild, Thomas Nielsen *lawyer*
Jester, Jack D. *lawyer*
Jock, Paul F., II *lawyer*
Johnson, C. Richard *lawyer*
Johnson, Gary Thomas *lawyer*
Johnson, Lael Frederic *lawyer*
Johnson, Richard Fred *lawyer*
Johnston, Alan Rogers *lawyer*
Jones, Richard Cyrus *lawyer*
Jordan, Michelle Denise *lawyer*
Joseph, Robert Thomas *lawyer*
Joslin, Rodney Dean *lawyer*
Junewicz, James J. *lawyer*
Kallick, David A. *lawyer*
Kamin, Chester Thomas *lawyer*
Kaplan, Jared *lawyer*
Kaplan, Sidney Mountbatten *lawyer*
Karnes, Evan Burton, II *lawyer*
Kastel, Howard L. *lawyer*
Katz, Stuart Charles *lawyer, concert jazz musician*
Kaufman, Andrew Michael *lawyer*
Kelly, Charles Arthur *lawyer*
Kempf, Donald G., Jr. *lawyer*
Kenney, Frank Deming *lawyer*
Kenny, Edmund Joyce *lawyer*
Kikoler, Stephen Philip *lawyer*
Kim, Michael Charles *lawyer*
King, Clark Chapman, Jr. *lawyer*
King, Michael Howard *lawyer*
King, Sharon L. *lawyer*
Kins, Juris *lawyer*
Kirkland, John Leonard *lawyer*
Kissel, Richard John *lawyer*
Kite, Steven B. *lawyer*
Klenk, James Andrew *lawyer*
Klenk, Timothy Carver *lawyer*
Knepper, Thomas M. *lawyer*
Knight, Christopher Nichols *lawyer*
Knox, James Edwin *lawyer*
Kohn, Shalom L. *lawyer*
Kohn, William Irwin *lawyer*
Kolek, Robert Edward *lawyer*
Kopelman, Ian Stuart *lawyer*
Kravitt, Jason Harris Paperno *lawyer*
Kremin, David Keith *lawyer*
Kresse, William Joseph *lawyer, educator, accountant*
Kriss, Robert J. *lawyer*
Kroll, Barry Lewis *lawyer*
Krupka, Robert George *lawyer*
Kunkle, William Joseph, Jr. *lawyer*
Kuta, Jeffrey Theodore *lawyer*
Laidlaw, Andrew R. *lawyer*
Lampert, Steven A. *lawyer*
Landes, William M. *law educator*
Landow-Esser, Janine Marise *lawyer*
Landsberg, Jill Warren *lawyer, consultant to government agencies*
Lane, Ronald Alan *lawyer*
Laner, Richard Warren *lawyer*
Langhenry, John Godfred, Jr. *lawyer*
LaRue, Paul Hubert *lawyer*
Latimer, Kenneth Alan *lawyer*
Lauderdale, Katherine Sue *lawyer*
LeBaron, Charles Frederick, Jr. *lawyer*
Lee, William Marshall *lawyer*
Lefco, Kathy Nan *law librarian*
Leibowitz, David Perry *lawyer*
Leisten, Arthur Gaynor *lawyer*
Lemberis, Theodore Thomas *international law and law educator*
Levenfeld, Milton Arthur *lawyer*
Levi, John G. *lawyer*
Levin, Charles Edward *lawyer*
Levin, Jack S. *lawyer*
Levine, Laurence Harvey *lawyer*
Levy, Richard Herbert *lawyer*
Leyhane, Francis John, III *lawyer*
Liggio, Carl Donald *lawyer*
Lind, Jon Robert *lawyer*
Linklater, William Joseph *lawyer*
Lippe, Melvin Karl *lawyer*
Lipton, Lois Jean *lawyer*
Lipton, Richard M. *lawyer*
Litwin, Burton Howard *lawyer*
Lloyd, William F. *lawyer*
Lochbihler, Frederick Vincent *lawyer*
Lockwood, Gary Lee *lawyer*
Looman, James R. *lawyer*
Lorch, Kenneth F. *lawyer*
Loughnane, David J. *lawyer*
Lowry, Donald Michael *lawyer*
Lubin, Donald G. *lawyer*
Lucas, John Kenneth *lawyer*
Lundergan, Barbara Keough *lawyer*
Luning, Thomas P. *lawyer*
Lurie, Paul Michael *lawyer*
Lutter, Paul Allen *lawyer*
Lynch, John James *lawyer*
Lynch, John Peter *lawyer*
MacCarthy, Terence Francis *lawyer*
Maher, David Willard *lawyer*
Malkin, Cary Jay *lawyer*
Mancoff, Neal Alan *lawyer*
Mansfield, Karen Lee *lawyer*
Marks, Jerome *lawyer*
Marovitz, James Lee *lawyer*
Marshall, John David *lawyer*
Martin, Arthur Mead *lawyer*
Marwedel, Warren John *lawyer*
Marx, David, Jr. *lawyer*
Mason, Henry Lowell, III *lawyer*
Mason, Richard J. *lawyer*
Mattson, Stephen Joseph *lawyer*
Mayer, Frank D., Jr. *lawyer*
McCaleb, Malcolm, Jr. *lawyer*
McClain, Lee Bert *corporate lawyer, insurance executive*
Mc Clure, James J., Jr. *lawyer, former municipal executive*
McConnell, James Guy *lawyer*
McCracken, Thomas James, Jr. *lawyer*
McCrohon, Craig *lawyer*
McCue, Judith W. *lawyer*
McDermott, John H(enry) *lawyer*
McDermott, Robert B. *lawyer*
McDonald, Thomas Alexander *lawyer*
McDonough, John Michael *lawyer*
Mc Dougall, Dugald Stewart *retired lawyer*
McKenzie, Robert E. *lawyer*
McLaughlin, T. Mark *lawyer*
McLean, Robert David *lawyer*
McMenamin, John Robert *lawyer*
McNeill, Thomas B. *lawyer*
McVisk, William Kilburn *lawyer*
McWhirter, Bruce J. *lawyer*
McWilliams, Dennis Michael *lawyer*
Mehlman, Mark Franklin *lawyer*
Melbinger, Michael S. *lawyer*
Melton, David Reuben *lawyer*
Meltzer, Bernard David *legal educator*
Merrill, Thomas Wendell *lawyer, law educator*
Meyer, J. Theodore *lawyer*
Meyer, Michael Louis *lawyer*
Michalak, Edward Francis *lawyer*
Mikva, Abner Joseph *lawyer, retired federal judge*
Millard, Richard Steven *lawyer*
Miller, Douglas Andrew *lawyer*
Miller, Edward Boone *lawyer*
Miller, Maurice James *lawyer*
Miller, Paul J. *lawyer*
Miller, Stephen Ralph *lawyer*
Millner, Robert B. *lawyer*
Milnikel, Robert Saxon *lawyer*
Minichello, Dennis *lawyer*
Molo, Steven Francis *lawyer*
Moltz, Marshall Jerome *lawyer*
Momeyer, Douglas H. *lawyer*
Montgomery, Charles Barry *lawyer*
Moran, John Thomas, Jr. *lawyer*
Morency, Paula J. *lawyer*
Morgan, James Evan *lawyer*
Morrison, John Horton *lawyer*
Morrison, Portia Owen *lawyer*
Morsch, Thomas Harvey *lawyer*
Muchin, Allan B. *lawyer*
Mullen, J. Thomas *lawyer*
Mumford, Manly Whitman *lawyer*
Murdock, Charles William *lawyer, educator*
Murray, Daniel Richard *lawyer*
Murtaugh, Christopher David *lawyer*
Myers, Lonn William *lawyer*
Nachman, Norman Harry *lawyer*
Nechin, Herbert Benjamin *lawyer*
Nelson, Richard David *lawyer*
Neumeier, Matthew Michael *lawyer*
Newey, Paul Davis *lawyer*
Newlin, Charles Fremont *lawyer*
Nicolaides, Mary *lawyer*
Nissen, William John *lawyer*
Nitikman, Franklin W. *lawyer*
Nord, Robert Eamor *lawyer*
Norek, Joan I. *lawyer*
Notz, John Kranz, Jr. *arbitrator and mediator, retired lawyer*
Nowacki, James Nelson *lawyer*
Nugent, Lori S. *lawyer*
Null, Michael Elliot *lawyer*
Nussbaum, Bernard J. *lawyer*
O'Brien, James Phillip *lawyer*
O'Brien, Patrick William *lawyer*
Oesterle, Eric Adam *lawyer*
O'Flaherty, Paul Benedict *lawyer*
O'Hagan, James Joseph *lawyer*
O'Leary, Daniel Vincent, Jr. *lawyer*
Olian, Robert Martin *lawyer*
Oliver, Roseann *lawyer*
O'Malley, John Daniel *law educator, banker*
Ott, Gilbert Russell, Jr. *lawyer*
Overgaard, Mitchell Jersild *lawyer*
Overton, George Washington *lawyer*
Pallasch, B. Michael *lawyer*
Palm, Gary Howard *lawyer, educator*
Palmer, John Bernard, III *lawyer*
Palmer, Robert Towne *lawyer*
Panich, Danuta Bembenista *lawyer*
Paprocki, Thomas John *lawyer, priest*
Partridge, Mark Van Buren *lawyer*
Pascal, Roger *lawyer*
Pattishall, Beverly Wyckliffe *lawyer*
Pavalon, Eugene Irving *lawyer*
Pelton, Russell Meredith, Jr. *lawyer*
Perlberg, Jules Martin *lawyer*
Perlstadt, Sidney Morris *lawyer*
Petersen, Donald Sondergaard *lawyer*
Petersen, William Otto *lawyer*
Peterson, Ronald Roger *lawyer*
Piecewicz, Walter Michael *lawyer*
Piekarski, Victor J. *lawyer*
Pinsky, Michael S. *lawyer*
Pitt, George *lawyer*
Poe, Douglas Allan *lawyer*
Polaski, Anne Spencer *lawyer*
Pollock, Earl Edward *lawyer*
Pope, Daniel James *lawyer*
Pope, Michael Arthur *lawyer*
Pratt, Robert Windsor *lawyer*
Presser, Stephen Bruce *lawyer, educator*
Price, Paul L. *lawyer*
Price, William S. *lawyer*
Priess, Howard K., II *lawyer*
Prior, Gary L. *lawyer*
Pritikin, James B. *lawyer, employee benefits consultant*
Prochnow, Douglas Lee *lawyer*
Prochnow, Herbert Victor, Jr. *lawyer*
Ramseyer, J. Mark *law educator*
Rankin, James Winton *lawyer*
Rapoport, David E. *lawyer*
Ratner, Gerald *lawyer*
Rattner, William Edward *lawyer*
Reda, Robert Salvatore *lawyer*
Redman, Clarence Owen *lawyer*
Reed, Keith Allen *lawyer*
Reich, Allan J. *lawyer*
Reicin, Ronald Ian *lawyer*
Reiter, Michael A. *lawyer, educator*
Relias, John Alexis *lawyer*
Resnick, Donald Ira *lawyer*
Reum, James Michael *lawyer*
Rhind, James Thomas *lawyer*
Rhoads, Paul Kelly *lawyer*
Rhodes, Charles Harker, Jr. *lawyer*
Richardson, William F. *lawyer*
Richman, John Marshall *lawyer, business executive*
Richmond, James G. *lawyer*
Richmond, William Patrick *lawyer*
Rieger, Mitchell Sheridan *lawyer*
Riley, Jack T., Jr. *lawyer*
Rissman, Burton Richard *lawyer*
Ritchie, Albert *lawyer*
Rizzo, Ronald Stephen *lawyer*
Roberts, John Charles *law school educator*
Robin, Richard C. *lawyer*
Robinson, Theodore Curtis, Jr. *lawyer*
Roche, James McMillan *lawyer*
Rooney, Matthew A. *lawyer*
Ropski, Gary Melchior *lawyer*
Rosemarin, Carey Stephen *lawyer*
Rosenbloom, Lewis Stanley *lawyer*
Roston, David Charles *lawyer*
Rovner, Jack Alan *lawyer*
Rowder, William Louis *lawyer*
Rubin, E(rwin) Leonard *lawyer*
Ruder, David Sturtevant *lawyer, educator, government official*
Rudnick, Paul David *lawyer*
Rudstein, David Stewart *law educator*
Rundio, Louis Michael, Jr. *lawyer*
Rupert, Donald William *lawyer*
Russell, Paul Frederick *lawyer*
Rutkoff, Alan Stuart *lawyer*
Ruxin, Paul Theodore *lawyer*
Ryan, Thomas F. *lawyer*
Sabl, John J. *lawyer*
Sanders, David P. *lawyer*
Sanders, Richard Henry *lawyer*
Saunders, David Alan *lawyer*
Saunders, George Lawton, Jr. *lawyer*
Saunders, Terry Rose *lawyer*
Sawdey, Richard Marshall *lawyer*
Sawyier, David R. *lawyer*
Schar, Stephen L. *lawyer*
Schiller, Donald Charles *lawyer*
Schiller, Eric M. *lawyer*
Schimberg, A(rmand) Bruce *retired lawyer*
Schindel, Donald Marvin *lawyer*
Schink, James Harvey *lawyer*
Schippers, David Philip *lawyer*
Schlickman, J. Andrew *lawyer*
Schlitter, Stanley Allen *lawyer*
Schneider, Dan W. *lawyer, consultant*
Schneider, Robert Jerome *lawyer*
Schoonhoven, Ray James *retired lawyer*
Schoumacher, Bruce Herbert *lawyer*
Schreck, Robert A., Jr. *lawyer*
Schriver, John T., III *lawyer*
Schuette, Michael *lawyer*
Schulhofer, Stephen Joseph *law educator*
Schulte, Bruce John *lawyer*
Schulte, Stephen Charles *lawyer*
Schulz, Keith Donald *corporate lawyer*
Schuyler, Daniel Merrick *lawyer, educator*
Schwartz, Donald Lee *lawyer*
Scogland, William Lee *lawyer*
Scott, Theodore R. *lawyer*
Scullion, Annette Murphy *lawyer, educator*
Selfridge, Calvin *lawyer*
Sennet, Charles Joseph *lawyer*
Serritella, James Anthony *lawyer*
Serritella, William David *lawyer*
Serwer, Alan Michael *lawyer*
Sfikas, Peter Michael *lawyer, educator*
Shadur, Robert H. *lawyer*
Shank, William O. *lawyer*
Shannon, Peter Michael, Jr. *lawyer*
Shapiro, Harold David *lawyer, educator*
Shapiro, Stephen Michael *lawyer*
Shapo, Marshall Schambelan *lawyer, educator*
Shepherd, Stewart Robert *lawyer*
Shepro, Richard W. *lawyer*
Shields, Thomas Charles *lawyer*
Shindler, Donald A. *lawyer*
Shoenberger, Allen Edward *law educator*
Sido, Kevin Richard *lawyer*
Siegel, Howard Jerome *lawyer*
Sigal, Michael Stephen *lawyer*
Silberman, Alan Harvey *lawyer*
Silets, Harvey Marvin *lawyer*
Simon, John Bern *lawyer*
Simon, Seymour *lawyer, former state supreme court justice*
Siske, Roger Charles *lawyer*
Sklarsky, Charles B. *lawyer*
Smedinghoff, Thomas J. *lawyer*
Smith, Arthur B(everly), Jr. *lawyer*
Smith, Gordon Howell *lawyer*
Smith, James Barry *lawyer*
Smith, John Gelston *lawyer*
Smith, Lawrence R. *lawyer*
Smith, Leo Emmet *lawyer*
Smith, Michele *lawyer*
Smith, Stephen Edward *lawyer*
Smith, Tefft Weldon *lawyer*
Snider, Lawrence K. *lawyer*
Snyder, Jean Maclean *lawyer*
Solomon, Jack Avrum *lawyer, automotive distributor, art dealer*
Solovy, Jerold Sherwin *lawyer*
Spain, Richard Colby *lawyer*
Spector, David M. *lawyer*
Spellmire, George W. *lawyer*
Spencer, Lewis Douglas *lawyer*
Spiotto, James Ernest *lawyer*
Springer, David Edward *lawyer*
Sproger, Charles Edmund *lawyer*
Sprowl, Charles Riggs *lawyer*
Staab, Michael Joseph *lawyer*
Stack, John Wallace *lawyer*
Stack, Paul Francis *lawyer*
Starkman, Gary Lee *lawyer*
Stassen, John Henry *lawyer*
†Stein, Robert Allen *legal association executive, law educator*
Steinberg, Morton M. *lawyer*
Stephan, Edmund Anton *lawyer*
Sternstein, Allan J. *lawyer*
Stetler, David J. *lawyer*
Stillman, Nina Gidden *lawyer*
Stoll, John Robert *lawyer, educator*
Stone, Geoffrey Richard *law educator, lawyer*
Stone, Randolph Noel *law educator*
Strasburger, Joseph Julius *retired lawyer*
Streff, William Albert, Jr. *lawyer*
Streicker, James Richard *lawyer*
Sullivan, Marcia Waite *lawyer*
Sullivan, Thomas Patrick *lawyer*
Sussman, Arthur Melvin *law educator*
Sutter, William Paul *lawyer*
Swaney, Thomas Edward *lawyer*
Sweeney, James Raymond *lawyer*
Swibel, Howard Jay *lawyer, investment advisor*
Swibel, Steven Warren *lawyer*
Swiger, Elinor Porter *lawyer*
Szczepanski, Slawomir Zbigniew Steven *lawyer*
Tabin, Julius *patent lawyer, physicist*
Talbot, Earl Armour *lawyer*
Tarun, Robert Walter *lawyer*
Taylor, Roger Lee *lawyer*
Theobald, Edward Robert *lawyer*
Thies, Richard Brian *lawyer*
Thomas, Dale E. *lawyer*
Thomas, Frederick Bradley *lawyer*
Thomas, Stephen Paul *lawyer*
Thompson, James Robert, Jr. *lawyer, former governor*
Thomson, George Ronald *lawyer, educator*
Thorne-Thomsen, Thomas *lawyer*
Timmer, Stephen Blaine *lawyer*
Tobin, Craig Daniel *lawyer*
Tobin, Thomas F. *lawyer*
Tone, Philip Willis *lawyer, former federal judge*
Toohey, James Kevin *lawyer*
Torshen, Jerome Harold *lawyer*
Trapp, James McCreery *lawyer*
Trienens, Howard Joseph *lawyer*
Trost, Eileen Bannon *lawyer*
Truskowski, John Budd *lawyer*
Tucker, Bowen Hayward *lawyer*
Tucker, Watson Billopp *lawyer*
Turow, Scott F. *lawyer, author*
Ungaretti, Richard Anthony *lawyer*
Valukas, Anton Ronald *lawyer, former federal official*
Van Demark, Ruth Elaine *lawyer*
Vieregg, Robert Todd *lawyer*
Von Mandel, Michael Jacques *lawyer*
Vranicar, Michael Gregory *lawyer*
Vree, Roger Allen *lawyer*
Wahlen, Edwin Alfred *lawyer*
Waintroob, Andrea Ruth *lawyer*
Waite, Norman, Jr. *lawyer*
Wall, Robert F. *lawyer*
Walsh, Michael S. *lawyer*
Walter, Priscilla Anne *lawyer*
Waltz, Jon Richard *lawyer, educator, author*
Wander, Herbert Stanton *lawyer*
Wanke, Ronald Lee *lawyer*
Warnecke, Michael O. *lawyer*
Watson, Robert R. *lawyer*
Weaver, Timothy Allan *lawyer*
Webb, Dan K. *lawyer*
Weclew, Robert George *lawyer, educator*
Weinberg, David B. *lawyer, investor*
Weinkopf, Friedrich J. *lawyer*
Weinsheimer, William Cyrus *lawyer*
Weissman, Michael Lewis *lawyer*
Welsh, Kelly Raymond *lawyer, telecommunications company executive*
Wexler, Richard Lewis *lawyer*
Whalen, Wayne W. *lawyer*

White, Craig Mitchell *lawyer*
White, H. Blair *lawyer*
White, Linda Diane *lawyer*
White, R. Quincy *lawyer*
Wick, Lawrence Scott *lawyer*
Wiggins, Charles Henry, Jr. *lawyer*
Wilcox, Mark Dean *lawyer*
Wildman, Max Edward *lawyer*
Williams, George Howard *lawyer, association executive*
Williamson, Richard Salisbury *lawyer*
Wilson, Clarence Sylvester, Jr. *lawyer, educator*
Wilson, Roger Goodwin *lawyer*
Winkler, Charles Howard *lawyer, investment management company executive*
Winton, Jeffrey Blake *arbitrator*
Wise, William Jerrard *lawyer*
Witcoff, Sheldon William *lawyer*
Witwer, Samuel Weiler, Jr. *lawyer*
Wolf, Charles Benno *lawyer*
Wolfe, David Louis *lawyer*
Wolfson, Larry M. *lawyer*
Wood, Allison Lorraine *lawyer*
Wright, Judith Margaret *law librarian, educator*
Young, Keith Lawrence *lawyer*
Zabel, Sheldon Alter *lawyer, law educator*
Zaremski, Miles Jay *lawyer*
Zemm, Sandra Phyllis *lawyer*
Zenner, Sheldon Toby *lawyer*
Zolno, Mark S. *lawyer*

**Chicago Heights**
Cifelli, John Louis *lawyer*

**Clarendon Hills**
Walton, Stanley Anthony, III *lawyer*

**Crystal Lake**
Knox, Susan Marie *paralegal*
Thoms, Jeannine Aumond *lawyer*

**De Kalb**
Witmer, John Harper, Jr. *lawyer*

**Decatur**
Dunn, John Francis *lawyer, state representative*

**Deerfield**
Abbey, G(eorge) Marshall *lawyer, former health care company executive, general counsel*
Bartlett, Robert William *lawyer, publishing executive*
Dawson, Suzanne Stockus *lawyer*
Gaither, John F. *lawyer*
Hannafan, Kay H. Pierce *lawyer*
Oettinger, Julian Alan *lawyer, pharmacy company executive*
Staubitz, Arthur Frederick *lawyer, healthcare products company executive*
Vollen, Robert Jay *lawyer*
Williams, Robert Jene *lawyer, rail car company executive*

**Des Plaines**
Brodl, Raymond Frank *lawyer, former lumber company executive*
Demouth, Robin Madison *lawyer, corporate executive*
Jacobs, William Russell, II *lawyer*
May, Frank Brendan, Jr. *lawyer*
Munden, Robin Ghezzi *lawyer*

**Downers Grove**
Siedlecki, Nancy Therese *lawyer, funeral director*

**East Moline**
Silliman, Richard George *retired lawyer, retired farm machinery company executive*

**Edwardsville**
Carlson, Jon Gordon *lawyer*

**Elgin**
Juergensmeyer, John Eli *lawyer*

**Elmhurst**
Berry, James Frederick *lawyer, biology educator*
Mastandrea, Linda Lee *lawyer*

**Elmwood Park**
Spina, Anthony Ferdinand *lawyer*

**Evanston**
Gormley, R(obert) James *retired lawyer*
Polzin, John Theodore *lawyer*
Taronji, Jaime, Jr. *lawyer*
Vanneman, Edgar, Jr. *lawyer*
Warshaw, Roberta Sue *lawyer, financial specialist*
Weston, Michael C. *lawyer*

**Fairview Heights**
Grace, Walter Charles *lawyer*

**Galesburg**
McCrery, David Neil, III *lawyer*

**Genoa**
Cromley, Jon Lowell *lawyer*

**Glen Ellyn**
Larson, Ward Jerome *lawyer, retired banker*
Ulrich, Werner *patent lawyer*

**Glencoe**
Baer, Joseph Winslow *retired lawyer, mediator, arbitrator*
Stewart, Charles Leslie *lawyer*

**Glenview**
Berkman, Michael G. *lawyer, chemical consultant*

**Greenville**
Kelsey, John Walter *lawyer, business owner*

**Gurnee**
Southern, Robert Allen *lawyer*

**Highland Park**
Dolin, Albert Harry *lawyer*
Haight, Edward Allen *lawyer*
Karol, Nathaniel H. *lawyer, consultant*

**Hinsdale**
Bennett, Margaret Airola *lawyer*
Bishop, Linda Dilene *lawyer, small business owner*
Yastow, Shelby *lawyer*

**Joliet**
Boyer, Andrew Ben *lawyer*
Guzman, Matthew Lopez *lawyer*
Lenard, George Dean *lawyer*

**Kenilworth**
McKittrick, William Wood *lawyer*

**La Grange**
Kerr, Alexander Duncan, Jr. *lawyer*

**Lafox**
Seils, William George *lawyer*

**Lake Bluff**
Burns, Kenneth Jones, Jr. *lawyer, consultant*

**Lake Forest**
Covington, George Morse *lawyer*
Emerson, William Harry *lawyer, retired, oil company executive*
Everson, Leonard Charles *lawyer*
Hamilton, Peter Bannerman *lawyer, business executive*
Palmer, Ann Therese Darin *lawyer*
Sikorovsky, Eugene Frank *retired lawyer*

**Lansing**
Hill, Philip *retired lawyer*

**Lewistown**
Davis, William C., Jr. *lawyer*

**Libertyville**
Beeler, Thomas Joseph *lawyer, general management consultant*
Ranney, George Alfred *lawyer, former steel company executive*

**Lincolnshire**
Giza, David Alan *lawyer*
Prasil, Linda Ann *lawyer, writer*

**Lisle**
Myers, Daniel N. *lawyer, association executive*
Sandrok, Richard William *lawyer*

**Lombard**
Goodman, Elliott I(rvin) *lawyer*
Sheehan, Dennis William, Sr. *lawyer*
Willis, Douglas Alan *lawyer*

**Long Grove**
Conway, John K. *lawyer*
Obert, Paul Richard *lawyer, manufacturing company executive*

**Marengo**
Franks, Herbert Hoover *lawyer*

**Mattoon**
Horsley, Jack Everett *lawyer, author*

**Melrose Park**
Gass, Raymond William *lawyer, consumer products company executive*

**Mokena**
Sangmeister, George Edward *lawyer, consultant, former congressman*

**Moline**
Cottrell, Frank Stewart *lawyer, manufacturing executive*
Morrison, Deborah Jean *lawyer*

**Mount Carmel**
Rhine, John E. *lawyer*

**Mount Prospect**
Covey, Frank Michael, Jr. *lawyer, educator*

**Naperville**
Larson, Mark Edward, Jr. *lawyer, educator, financial advisor*
Shaw, Michael Allan *lawyer, mail order company executive*

**Niles**
Walker, A. Harris *lawyer, manufacturing executive, retired*

**Normal**
Bender, Paul Edward *lawyer*

**Northbrook**
Cohen, Seymour *lawyer*
Lapin, Harvey I. *lawyer*
McGinn, Mary Jovita *lawyer, insurance company executive*
Sernett, Richard Patrick *lawyer*
Wallace, Harry Leland *lawyer*
Weber, Merrill Evan *lawyer, business executive*

**Northfield**
Porter, Helen Viney (Mrs. Lewis M. Porter, Jr.) *lawyer*
Spear, Kathleen Kelly *lawyer*

**Northlake**
Roti, Thomas David *lawyer, food service executive*

**Oak Brook**
Barnes, Karen Kay *lawyer*
Johnson, Grant Lester *lawyer, retired manufacturing company executive*
La Petina, Gary Michael *lawyer*

**Oak Brook Mall**
Getz, Herbert A. *lawyer*

**Oak Park**
McNaney, Robert Trainor *retired lawyer*

**Oakbrook Terrace**
Fenech, Joseph C. *lawyer*
Kohlstedt, James August *lawyer*
Tibble, Douglas Clair *lawyer*

**Palos Heights**
Matug, Alexander Peter *lawyer*

**Park Forest**
Goodrich, John Bernard *lawyer, consultant*

**Park Ridge**
Curtis, Philip James *lawyer*

**Peoria**
Allen, Lyle Wallace *lawyer*
Atterbury, Robert Rennie, III *lawyer*
Christison, William Henry, III *lawyer*
Dabney, Seth Mason, III *lawyer*
Eissfeldt, Theodore L. *lawyer*
Ryan, Michael Beecher *lawyer, former government official*
Strodel, Robert Carl *lawyer*

**Princeton**
Johnson, Watts Carey *lawyer*

**Prospect Heights**
Leopold, Mark F. *lawyer*

**River Forest**
Li, Tze-chung *lawyer, educator*

**Rock Island**
Wallace, Franklin Sherwood *lawyer*

**Rockford**
Anderson, LaVerne Eric *lawyer*
Barrick, William Henry *lawyer*
Channick, Herbert S. *lawyer, arbitrator, mediator*
Johnson, Thomas Stuart *lawyer*
Reno, Roger *lawyer*
Schilling, Richard M. *lawyer, corporate executive*

**Rolling Meadows**
Moore, William B. *lawyer*

**Saint Charles**
Mc Kay, Thomas, Jr. *lawyer*

**Schaumburg**
Gardner, Caryn Sue *lawyer*
Meltzer, Brian *lawyer*

**Skokie**
Salit, Gary *lawyer*

**Springfield**
Bergschneider, David Philip *defender*
Cullen, Mark Kenneth *lawyer*
Dodge, James William *lawyer, educator*
Hanley, William Stanford *lawyer*
Hulin, Frances C. *prosecutor*
Kerr, Gary Enrico *lawyer, educator*
Larison, Brenda Irene *law librarian*
Mathewson, Mark Stuart *lawyer, editor*
Morse, Saul Julian *lawyer*
Mulligan, Rosemary Elizabeth *paralegal*
Narmont, John Stephen *lawyer*
Oxtoby, Robert Boynton *lawyer*
Reed, Robert Phillip *lawyer*
Rowe, Max L. *lawyer, corporate executive, management consultant, judge*
Van Meter, Abram DeBois *lawyer, retired banker*

**Streator**
Harrison, Frank Joseph *lawyer*

**Toledo**
Prather, William C. III *lawyer, writer*

**Urbana**
Balbach, Stanley Byron *lawyer*
Fitz-Gerald, Roger Miller *lawyer*
Moore, David Robert *lawyer*

**Warrenville**
McGurn, George William *lawyer*

**Waukegan**
Hall, Albert L. *lawyer, retired*
Henrick, Michael Francis *lawyer*

**Western Springs**
Hanson, Heidi Elizabeth *lawyer*

**Westmont**
Biggert, Judith Borg *lawyer, state representative*

**Wheaton**
Butt, Edward Thomas, Jr. *lawyer*
Landan, Henry Sinclair *lawyer, business consultant*
Roberts, Keith Edward, Sr. *lawyer*
Stein, Lawrence A. *lawyer*

**Winnetka**
Abell, David Robert *lawyer*
Crowe, Robert William *lawyer, mediator*
Davis, Britton Anthony *lawyer*
Fowle, Frank Fuller *retired lawyer*
Greenblatt, Ray Harris *lawyer*
Mc Millen, Thomas Roberts *lawyer, arbitrator, mediator, retired judge*

**Woodridge**
Conti, Lee Ann *lawyer*
Everett, C. Curtis *retired lawyer*

**INDIANA**

**Angola**
McAlhany, Toni Anne *lawyer*

**Bloomington**
Aman, Alfred Charles, Jr. *law educator*
Heidt, Robert Harold *law educator, consultant*

**Carmel**
Stein, Richard Paul *lawyer*

**Columbus**
Harrison, Patrick Woods *lawyer*
Perkins Senn, Karon Elaine *lawyer*

**Connersville**
Kuntz, William Henry *lawyer, mediator*

**Crawfordsville**
Donaldson, Steven Bryan *lawyer*

**Danville**
Baldwin, Jeffrey Kenton *lawyer, educator*

**Elkhart**
Bowers, Richard Stewart, Jr. *lawyer*
Gassere, Eugene Arthur *lawyer, business executive*
Harman, John Royden *lawyer*
Treckelo, Richard M. *lawyer*

**Evansville**
Clouse, John Daniel *lawyer*
Harrison, Joseph Heavrin *lawyer*

**Fort Wayne**
Baker, Carl Leroy *lawyer*
Fink, Thomas Michael *lawyer*
Gerberding, Miles Carston *lawyer*
Hunter, Jack Duval *lawyer*
Keefer, J(ames) Michael *lawyer*
Lawson, Jack Wayne *lawyer*
Niewyk, Anthony *lawyer*
Peebles, Carter David *lawyer*
Shoaff, Thomas Mitchell *lawyer*
Steinbronn, Richard Eugene *lawyer*

**Fowler**
Kepner, Rex William *lawyer*

**Gary**
Lewis, Robert Lee *lawyer*

**Hammond**
Diamond, Eugene Christopher *lawyer, hospital administrator*
Kohl, Jacquelyn Marie *lawyer*

**Hartford City**
Ford, David Clayton *lawyer, Indiana state senator*

**Highland**
Forsythe, Randall Newman *paralegal, educator*
Goodman, Samuel J. *lawyer*

**Indianapolis**
Albright, Terrill D. *lawyer*
Allen, David James *lawyer*
Aschleman, James Allan *lawyer*
Badger, David Harry *lawyer*
Beckwith, Lewis Daniel *lawyer*
Beeler, Virgil L. *lawyer*
Blackwell, Henry Barlow, II *lawyer*
Boldt, Michael Herbert *lawyer*
Born, Samuel Roydon, II *lawyer*
Buttrey, Donald Wayne *lawyer*
Carney, Joseph Buckingham *lawyer*
Carpenter, Susan Karen *lawyer*
Choplin, John M., II *lawyer*
Comer, Jerome Edward *lawyer*
Daniel, Melvin Randolph *lawyer*
Deer, Richard Elliott *lawyer*
Downs, Thomas K. *lawyer*
Dutton, Stephen James *lawyer*
Emerson, Andrew Craig *retired lawyer, insurance executive*
Evans, Daniel Fraley, Jr. *lawyer*
Ewbank, Thomas Peters *lawyer, retired banker*
Fisher, James R. *lawyer*
FitzGibbon, Daniel Harvey *lawyer*
Fruehwald, Kristin G. *lawyer*
Fuller, Samuel Ashby *lawyer, mining company executive*
Funk, David Albert *retired law educator*
Grayson, John Allan *lawyer*
Haycox, Rolanda Moore *lawyer, nurse*
Henderson, Eugene Leroy *lawyer*
Hovde, F. Boyd *lawyer*
Huston, Michael Joe *lawyer*
Jegen, Lawrence A., III *law educator*
Johnstone, Robert Philip *lawyer*
Kashani, Hamid Reza *lawyer, computer consultant*
Kemper, James Dee *lawyer*
Kerr, William Andrew *lawyer, educator*
Kirk, Carol *lawyer*
Klaper, Martin Jay *lawyer*
Kleiman, David Harold *lawyer*
Knebel, Donald Earl *lawyer*
Lee, Stephen W. *lawyer*
Lefstein, Norman *lawyer, educator*
Lisher, John Leonard *lawyer*
Lobley, Alan Haigh *retired lawyer*
Lofton, Thomas Milton *lawyer*
McCarthy, Kevin Bart *lawyer*
McKinney, Dennis Keith *lawyer*
McTurnan, Lee Bowes *lawyer*
Miller, David Anthony *lawyer*
Miller, David W. *lawyer*
†Modisett, Jeffrey A. *lawyer, consultant*
Moffatt, Michael Alan *lawyer*
Neff, Robert Matthew *lawyer, investment and insurance executive*
Nolan, Alan Tucker *retired lawyer*
Padgett, Gregory Lee *lawyer*
Patrick, William Bradshaw *lawyer*
Paul, Stephen Howard *lawyer*
Petersen, James L. *lawyer*
Ponder, Lester McConnico *lawyer, educator*
Powlen, David Michael *lawyer*
Quayle, Marilyn Tucker *lawyer, wife of former vice president of United States*
Reynolds, Robert Hugh *lawyer*
Roberts, William Everett *lawyer*
Russell, David Williams *lawyer*
Ryder, Henry C(lay) *lawyer*
Scaletta, Phillip Ralph, III *lawyer*
Scanlon, Thomas Michael *lawyer*
Schlegel, Fred Eugene *lawyer*

Schneider, Robert E., II *lawyer*
Scism, Daniel Reed *lawyer*
Shideler, Shirley Ann Williams *lawyer*
Shula, Robert Joseph *lawyer*
Smith, Stephen Kendall *lawyer*
Snyder, Jack Ralph *lawyer*
Stayton, Thomas George *lawyer*
Steger, Evan Evans, III *lawyer*
Stieff, John Joseph *legislative lawyer, educator*
Sutherland, Donald Gray *lawyer*
Swhier, Claudia Versfelt *lawyer*
Tabler, Bryan G. *lawyer*
Tabler, Norman Gardner, Jr. *lawyer*
Townsend, Earl C., Jr. *lawyer, writer*
Vandivier, Blair Robert *lawyer*
Wampler, Lloyd Charles *retired lawyer*
Wellnitz, Craig Otto *lawyer, English language educator*
Whale, Arthur Richard *lawyer*
White, James Patrick *law educator*
Wishard, Gordon Davis *lawyer*
Wood, William Jerome *lawyer*
Woodard, Harold Raymond *lawyer*
Yeager, Joseph Heizer, Jr. *lawyer*

**Jeffersonville**
Hoehn, Elmer Louis *lawyer, state and federal agency administrator, educator, consultant*

**Lafayette**
Layden, Lynn McVey *lawyer*
O'Callaghan, Patti Louise *court program administrator*
O'Connell, Lawrence B. *lawyer*

**Merrillville**
Brenman, Stephen Morris *lawyer*

**Mount Vernon**
Bach, Steve Crawford *lawyer*

**Muncie**
Kelly, Eric Damian *lawyer, educator*
Radcliff, William Franklin *lawyer*

**Nashville**
McDermott, James Alexander *retired lawyer*
McDermott, Renée R(assler) *lawyer*

**Notre Dame**
Grazin, Igor Nikolai *law educator, state official*
Gunn, Alan *law educator*

**Portage**
Henke, Robert John *lawyer*

**Sandborn**
Gregg, John Richard *lawyer, state legislator*

**Seymour**
Gill, W(alter) Brent *lawyer*

**Shelbyville**
Lisher, James Richard *lawyer*

**South Bend**
Carey, John Leo *lawyer*
Ford, George Burt *lawyer*
McGill, Warren Everett *lawyer, consultant*
Reinke, William John *lawyer*
Seall, Stephen Albert *lawyer*
Shaffer, Thomas Lindsay *lawyer, educator*
Sopko, Thomas Clement *lawyer*
Vogel, Nelson J., Jr. *lawyer*

**Terre Haute**
Bopp, James, Jr. *lawyer*

**Unionville**
Franklin, Frederick Russell *retired legal association executive*

**Valparaiso**
Gaffney, Edward McGlynn *law educator, university administrator*
Hires, Jack Merle *law educator*
Persyn, Mary Geraldine *law librarian, law educator*

**Vincennes**
Emison, Ewing Rabb, Jr. *lawyer*

**Zionsville**
Bruess, Charles Edward *lawyer*

## IOWA

**Algona**
Handsaker, Jerrold Lee *lawyer*

**Burlington**
Hoth, Steven Sergey *lawyer*

**Cedar Rapids**
Albright, Justin W. *lawyer*
Faches, William George *lawyer*
Nazette, Richard Follett *lawyer*
Riley, Tom Joseph *lawyer*
Wilson, Robert Foster *lawyer*

**Charles City**
Mc Cartney, Ralph Farnham *lawyer*

**Dallas Center**
McDonald, John Cecil *lawyer*

**Davenport**
Le Grand, Clay *lawyer, former state justice*
Shaw, Donald Hardy *lawyer*
Vorbrich, Lynn Karl *lawyer, utility executive*

**Decorah**
Belay, Stephen Joseph *lawyer*

**Des Moines**
Begleiter, Martin David *law educator, consultant*
Campbell, Bruce Irving *lawyer*
Carroll, Frank J. *lawyer, educator*

Clark, Beverly Ann *lawyer*
Claypool, David L. *lawyer*
Conlin, Roxanne Barton *lawyer*
Davis, James Casey *lawyer*
Edwards, John Duncan *law educator, librarian*
Fisher, Thomas George *lawyer, retired media company executive*
Fisher, Thomas George, Jr. *lawyer*
Gotsdiner, Murray Bennett *lawyer*
Grefe, Rolland Eugene *lawyer*
Hansell, Edgar Frank *lawyer*
Harris, Charles Elmer *lawyer*
Hill, Luther Lyons, Jr. *lawyer*
Hockenberg, Harlan David *lawyer*
Jensen, Dick Leroy *lawyer*
Langdon, Herschel Garrett *lawyer*
Narber, Gregg Ross *lawyer*
Peddicord, Roland Dale *lawyer*
Power, Joseph Edward *lawyer*
Shors, John D. *lawyer*
Slade, Llewellyn Eugene *lawyer, engineer*
Wine, Donald Arthur *lawyer*

**Dubuque**
Ernst, Daniel Pearson *lawyer*
Hammer, David Lindley *lawyer, author*

**Forest City**
Beebe, Raymond Mark *lawyer*

**Iowa City**
Bonfield, Arthur Earl *lawyer, educator*
Downer, Robert Nelson *lawyer*
Dudziak, Mary Louise *law educator, lecturer*
Hines, N. William *law educator, administrator*
Kurtz, Sheldon Francis *lawyer, educator*
McAndrew, Paul Joseph, Jr. *lawyer*
Saks, Michael Jay *law educator*
Tomkovicz, James Joseph *law educator*
Vernon, David Harvey *lawyer, educator*
Widiss, Alan I. *lawyer, educator*
Wing, Adrien Katherine *law educator*

**Johnston**
Leitner, David Larry *lawyer*

**Marshalltown**
Brennecke, Allen Eugene *lawyer*
Geffe, Kent Lyndon *lawyer, educator*

**Mason City**
Winston, Harold Ronald *lawyer*

**Muscatine**
Coulter, Charles Roy *lawyer*
Nepple, James Anthony *lawyer*

**Nevada**
Countryman, Dayton Wendell *lawyer*

**Newton**
Bennett, Edward James *lawyer*

**Ottumwa**
Krafka, Mary Baird *lawyer*

**Shenandoah**
Rose, Jennifer Joan *lawyer*

**Sioux City**
Madsen, George Frank *lawyer*
Marks, Bernard Bailin *lawyer*
Mayne, Wiley Edward *lawyer*
O'Brien, David A. *lawyer*

**Storm Lake**
Crippin, Byron Miles, Jr. *lawyer, religious organization professional, consultant*

**Stuart**
Bump, Wilbur Neil *retired lawyer*

**Waterloo**
Rapp, Stephen John *United States attorney*

**West Des Moines**
Neiman, John Hammond *lawyer*

**Windsor Heights**
Belin, David William *lawyer*

## KANSAS

**Dodge City**
Haviland, Camilla Klein *lawyer*

**Fairway**
Marquardt, Christel Elisabeth *lawyer*

**Hugoton**
Nordling, Bernard Erick *lawyer*

**Hutchinson**
Hayes, John Francis *lawyer*
Swearer, William Brooks *lawyer*

**Kansas City**
Cantwell, Sandra Lee *legal assistant*

**Lawrence**
Casad, Robert Clair *legal educator*
Hoeflich, Michael Harlan *law school dean*
Murray, Thomas Veatch *lawyer*
Smith, Glee Sidney, Jr. *lawyer*
Turnbull, H. Rutherford, III *law educator, lawyer*
Wilson, Paul Edwin *lawyer, educator*

**Leawood**
Carmody, Timothy James *lawyer, educator*
Snyder, Willard Breidenthal *lawyer*

**Mc Pherson**
Shriver, Garner Edward *lawyer, former congressman*

**Olathe**
Branham, Melanie J. *lawyer*
Haskin, J. Michael *lawyer*

**Overland Park**
Cole, Elsa Kircher *lawyer*
Gaar, Norman Edward *lawyer, former state senator*
Keim, Robert Bruce *lawyer*
Krauss, Carl F. *lawyer*
Sampson, William Roth *lawyer*
Semegen, Patrick William *lawyer*
Short, Joel Bradley *lawyer, consultant, software publisher*
Starrett, Frederick Kent *lawyer*
Steinkamp, Robert Theodore *lawyer*
Van Dyke, Thomas Wesley *lawyer*
Waxse, David John *lawyer*
Webb, William Duncan *lawyer, investment executive*

**Prairie Village**
Stanton, Roger D. *lawyer*

**Shawnee Mission**
Badgerow, John Nicholas *lawyer*
Bennett, Robert Frederick *lawyer, former governor*
Biggs, J. O. *lawyer, general industry company executive*
Bond, Richard Lee *lawyer, state senator*
Cahal, Mac Fullerton *lawyer, publisher*
Nulton, William Clements *lawyer*
Rubin, Charles Elliott *lawyer, sports agent*

**Topeka**
Elrod, Linda Diane Henry *lawyer, educator*
Kuether, John Frederick *law educator*
Marshall, Herbert A. *lawyer*
Rainey, William Joel *lawyer*
Rosenberg, John K. *lawyer*
Spring, Raymond Lewis *legal educator*

**Wellington**
Ferguson, William McDonald *retired lawyer, rancher, author, banker, former state official*

**Westwood**
Devlin, James Richard *lawyer*

**Wichita**
Ayres, Ted Dean *lawyer, academic counsel*
Bogart, Vincent LaVaughn *lawyer*
Bostwick, Donald W. *lawyer*
Curfman, Lawrence Everett *retired lawyer*
Davis, Robert Louis *lawyer*
Docking, Thomas Robert *lawyer, former state lieutenant governor*
Purtell, Lawrence Robert *lawyer*
Randels, Ed Lee *lawyer*
Thompson, M(orris) Lee *lawyer*

## KENTUCKY

**Ashland**
Compton, Robert H. *lawyer*
Rhodes, Alice Graham *lawyer*

**Bowling Green**
Russell, Joyce M. *lawyer, apparel executive*

**Covington**
Gilliland, John Campbell, II *lawyer*
Head, Joseph Henry, Jr. *lawyer*
Walker, H. Lawson *lawyer*

**Danville**
McClure, George Morris, III *lawyer*

**Eddyville**
Story, James Eddleman *lawyer*

**Frankfort**
Carroll, Julian Morton *lawyer, former governor*
Palmore, John Stanley, Jr. *retired lawyer*

**Glasgow**
Baker, Walter Arnold *lawyer*

**Harlan**
Lawson, Susan Coleman *lawyer*

**Highland Heights**
Jones, William Rex *law educator*

**Lexington**
Bagby, William Rardin *lawyer*
Beshear, Steven L. *lawyer*
Breathitt, Edward Thompson, Jr. *lawyer, railroad executive, former governor*
Campbell, Joe Bill *lawyer*
Daniel, Marilyn S. *lawyer*
Eberle, Todd Bailey *lawyer, educator*
Fryman, Virgil Thomas, Jr. *lawyer*
Goldman, Alvin Lee *lawyer, educator*
Hinkle, Buckner, Jr. *lawyer*
Lewis, Thomas Proctor *law educator*
Philpott, James Alvin, Jr. *lawyer*
Rogers, Lon B(rown) *lawyer*
Schaeffer, Edwin Frank, Jr. *lawyer*

**London**
Keller, John Warren *lawyer*

**Louisville**
Aberson, Leslie Donald *lawyer*
Allen, Charles Ethelbert, III *lawyer*
Ardery, Philip Pendleton *lawyer*
Ballantine, John Tilden *lawyer*
Bishop, Robert Whitsitt *lawyer*
Chauvin, Leonard Stanley, Jr. *lawyer*
Collins, James Francis *lawyer, financial consultant*
Conner, Stewart Edmund *lawyer*
Cowan, Frederic Joseph *lawyer*
Davidson, Gordon Byron *lawyer*
Dudley, George Ellsworth *lawyer*
Duffy, Martin Patrick *lawyer*
Ethridge, Larry Clayton *lawyer*
Ferguson, Jo McCown *lawyer*
Fuchs, Olivia Anne Morris *lawyer*
Hallenberg, Robert Lewis *lawyer*
Hopson, Edwin Sharp *lawyer*
Humphreys, Gene Lynn *lawyer*
Hunter, William Jay, Jr. *lawyer*
Klotter, John Charles *retired legal educator*
Lavelle, Charles Joseph *lawyer*

Lay, Norvie Lee *law educator*
Luber, Thomas J(ulian) *lawyer*
Lyndrup, Peggy B. *lawyer*
Macdonald, Lenna Ruth *lawyer*
Maddox, Robert Lytton *lawyer*
Maggiolo, Allison Joseph *lawyer*
Mellen, Francis Joseph, Jr. *lawyer*
Meuter, Maria Coolman *lawyer*
Morris, Benjamin Hume *lawyer*
Osborn, John Simcoe, Jr. *lawyer*
Pelfrey, D. Patton *lawyer*
Pettyjohn, Shirley Ellis *lawyer, real estate executive*
Reed, John Squires, II *lawyer*
Runyon, Keith Leslie *lawyer, newspaper editor*
Schuster, Stephen Fowler *lawyer*
Skees, William Leonard, Jr. *lawyer*
Straus, R(obert) James *lawyer*
Talbott, Ben Johnson, Jr. *lawyer*
Weinberg, Edward Brill *lawyer*
Welsh, Alfred John *lawyer, consultant*
Willenbrink, Rose Ann *lawyer*
Wren, Harold Gwyn *arbitrator, lawyer, legal educator*
Zingman, Edgar Alan *lawyer*

**Madisonville**
Monhollon, Leland *lawyer*

**Munfordville**
Lang, George Edward *lawyer*

**Newport**
Seaver, Robert Leslie *law educator*
Siverd, Robert Joseph *lawyer*

**Paducah**
Westberry, Billy Murry *lawyer*

**Scottsville**
Wilcher, Larry K. *lawyer*

**Somerset**
Prather, John Gideon, Jr. *lawyer*

## LOUISIANA

**Alexandria**
Gist, Howard Battle, Jr. *lawyer*

**Baton Rouge**
Blackman, John Calhoun, IV *lawyer*
Brady, James Joseph *lawyer*
Burland, James S. *lawyer, lobbyist*
Bybee, Jay Scott *lawyer, educator*
Byrd, Warren Edgar, II *lawyer*
Dixon, Jerome Wayne *lawyer*
Hawkland, William Dennis *law educator*
Hymel, L(ezin) J(oseph) *prosecutor*
Lamonica, P(aul) Raymond *lawyer, academic administrator, educator*
Leonard, Paul Haralson *retired lawyer*
Mc Clendon, William Hutchinson, III *lawyer*
Pugh, George Willard *law educator*
Ray, Betty Jean G. *lawyer*
Richards, Marta Alison *lawyer*
Wittenbrink, Jeffrey Scott *lawyer*

**Gretna**
Stumpf, Harry Charles *lawyer*

**Hammond**
Matheny, Tom Harrell *lawyer*

**Kenner**
Valvo, Barbara-Ann *lawyer, surgeon*

**Lafayette**
Boustany, Alfred Frem *lawyer*
Curtis, Lawrence Neil *lawyer*
Davidson, James Joseph, III *lawyer*
Durio, William Henry *lawyer*
Judice, Marc Wayne *lawyer*
Keaty, Robert Burke *lawyer*
Mickel, Joseph Thomas *lawyer*
Myers, Stephen Hawley *lawyer*
Revels, Richard W., Jr. *lawyer*
Saloom, Kaliste Joseph, Jr. *lawyer, retired judge*

**Lake Charles**
Clements, Robert W. *lawyer*
Davidson, Van Michael, Jr. *lawyer*
Everett, John Prentis, Jr. *lawyer*
McHale, Robert Michael *lawyer*
Parkerson, Hardy Martell *lawyer*
Shaddock, William Edward, Jr. *lawyer*
Watson, Wells *lawyer*

**Mandeville**
Christian, John Catlett, Jr. *lawyer*
Deano, Edward Joseph, Jr. *lawyer, state legislator*

**Metairie**
Ford, Robert David *lawyer*
Ostendorf, Lance Stephen *lawyer, investor, financial officer*
Perlis, Sharon A. *lawyer*

**Monroe**
Curry, Robert Lee, III *lawyer*
Sartor, Daniel Ryan, Jr. *lawyer*

**New Orleans**
Abaunza, Donald Richard *lawyer*
Abbott, Hirschel Theron, Jr. *lawyer*
Acomb, Robert Bailey, Jr. *lawyer, educator*
Album, Jerald Lewis *lawyer*
Alsobrook, Henry Bernis, Jr. *lawyer*
Ates, J. Robert *lawyer*
Backstrom, William M., Jr. *lawyer*
Barham, Mack Elwin *lawyer, educator*
Barry, Francis Julian, Jr. *lawyer*
Benjamin, Edward Bernard, Jr. *lawyer*
Bernstein, Joseph *lawyer*
Bieck, Robert Barton, Jr. *lawyer*
Bordelon, Alvin Joseph, Jr. *lawyer*
Cheatwood, Roy Clifton *lawyer*
Claverie, Philip deVilliers *lawyer*
Coleman, James Julian, Jr. *lawyer, industrialist, real estate executive*
Combe, John Clifford, Jr. *lawyer*

Correro, Anthony James, III *lawyer*
Crusto, Mitchell Ferdinand *lawyer, educator*
Denegre, George *lawyer*
Dennery, Moise Waldhorn *lawyer, educator*
Fallon, Eldon Edward *lawyer, educator*
Fantaci, James Michael *lawyer*
Fierke, Thomas Garner *lawyer*
Fishman, Louis Yarrut *lawyer*
Force, Robert *law educator*
Friedman, Joel William *law educator*
Garcia, Patricia A. *lawyer*
Gelpi, C. James (Jim Gelpi) *lawyer*
Grundmeyer, Douglas Lanaux *lawyer, editor*
Haygood, Paul M. *lawyer*
Healy, George William, III *lawyer, mediator*
Henderson, Helena Naughton *legal association administrator*
Hilbert, Peter Louis, Jr. *lawyer*
Johnson, Patrick, Jr. *lawyer*
Jones, Philip Kirkpatrick, Jr. *lawyer*
Keller, Thomas Clements *lawyer*
†Kemp, James Bradley, Jr. *lawyer*
Kupperman, Stephen Henry *lawyer*
Lavelle, Paul Michael *lawyer*
Lemann, Thomas Berthelot *lawyer*
Lovett, William Anthony *law and economics educator*
Lowe, Robert Charles *lawyer*
Marcus, Bernard *lawyer*
McDaniel, Donald Hamilton *lawyer*
McGlone, Michael Anthony *lawyer*
McMillan, Lee Richards, II *lawyer*
Mintz, Albert *lawyer*
Molony, Michael Janssens, Jr. *lawyer*
Morrell, Arthur Anthony *lawyer, state legislator*
Nehrbass, Seth Martin *patent lawyer*
Norwood, Colvin Gamble, Jr. *lawyer*
Nuzum, Robert Weston *lawyer*
Phelps, Esmond, II *lawyer*
Plaeger, Frederick Joseph, II *lawyer*
Poitevent, Edward Butts, II *lawyer*
Pugh, William Whitmell Hill *lawyer*
Rice, Winston Edward *lawyer*
Rodriguez, Antonio Jose *lawyer*
Rosen, Charles, II *lawyer*
Rosen, William Warren *lawyer*
Sarpy, Leon *lawyer*
Schoemann, Rudolph Robert *lawyer*
Shinn, Clinton Wesley *lawyer*
Simon, H(uey) Paul *lawyer*
Sims, John William *lawyer*
Sinor, Howard Earl, Jr. *lawyer*
†Slater, Benjamin Richard, Jr. *lawyer*
Snyder, Charles Aubrey *lawyer*
Stapp, Dan Ernest *retired lawyer, utility executive*
Tarver, Michael Keith *lawyer*
Terrell, Suzanne Haik *lawyer*
Title, Peter Stephen *lawyer*
Trostorff, Alexander Peter *lawyer*
Vance, Robert Patrick *lawyer*
Vaudry, J. William, Jr. *lawyer*
Waechter, Arthur Joseph, Jr. *lawyer*
Wax, George Louis *lawyer*
Weigel, John J. *lawyer*
Weinmann, John Giffen *lawyer, diplomat*
Weiss, Kenneth Andrew *lawyer, law educator*
Willems, Constance Charles *lawyer*

### Shreveport
Achee, Roland Joseph *lawyer*
Carmody, Arthur Roderick, Jr. *lawyer*
Hall, Pike, Jr. *lawyer*
Hetherwick, Gilbert Lewis *lawyer*
Jeter, Katherine Leslie Brash *lawyer*
Ramey, Cecil Edward, Jr. *lawyer*
Smith, Brian David *lawyer, educator*
Woodman, Walter James *lawyer*

### Sulphur
Sumpter, Dennis Ray *lawyer, construction company executive*

### Sunset
Brinkhaus, Armand J. *lawyer, former state senator*

## MAINE

### Augusta
Adelberg, Arthur William *lawyer*
Cohen, Richard Stockman *lawyer*
Davis, Virginia Estelle *lawyer*
Ketterer, Andrew *prosecutor*

### Bangor
Ervin, Spencer *lawyer*
Haddow, Jon Andrew *lawyer*
Woodcock, John Alden *lawyer*

### Camden
Barney, John Bradford *legal counsel*

### Castine
Wiswall, Frank Lawrence, Jr. *lawyer, educator*

### Lincolnville
Nichols, David Arthur *mediator, retired state justice*

### Portland
Allen, Charles William *lawyer*
Bennett, Jeffrey *lawyer*
Bohan, Thomas Lynch *lawyer, physicist*
Coggeshall, Bruce Amsden *lawyer*
Coughlan, Patrick Campbell *lawyer*
Culley, Peter William *lawyer*
Graffam, Ward Irving *lawyer*
Harvey, Charles Albert, Jr. *lawyer*
Hirshon, Robert Edward *lawyer*
Lancaster, Ralph Ivan, Jr. *lawyer*
LeBlanc, Richard Philip *lawyer*
McCloskey, Jay P. *prosecutor*
Monaghan, Matthew John *lawyer*
Philbrick, Donald Lockey *lawyer*
Quinn, Thomas Joseph *lawyer*
Schwartz, Stephen Jay *lawyer*
Smith, William Charles *lawyer*
Stauffer, Eric P. *lawyer*
White, Jeffrey M. *lawyer*
Whiting, Stephen Clyde *lawyer*
Zarr, Melvyn *lawyer, law educator*

### South Portland
Connell, Lawrence *lawyer*

### Waterville
Sandy, Robert Edward, Jr. *lawyer*

### Wells
Carleton, Joseph George, Jr. *lawyer, state legislator*

## MARYLAND

### Abingdon
Wolf, Martin Eugene *lawyer*

### Annapolis
Arlow, Allan Joseph *lawyer*
Duncan, Charles Tignor *lawyer*
Evans, William Davidson, Jr. *lawyer*
Jones, Sylvanus Benson *adjudicator, consultant*
Levin, David Alan *lawyer*
Levitan, Laurence *lawyer, former state senator*
Lillard, John Franklin, III *lawyer*
Michaelson, Benjamin, Jr. *lawyer*
Perkins, Roger Allan *lawyer*

### Arnold
Green, John Cawley *lawyer*

### Baltimore
Adkins, Edward James *lawyer*
Archibald, James Kenway *lawyer*
Arnick, John Stephen *lawyer, legislator*
Ayres, Jeffrey Peabody *lawyer*
Bair, Robert Rippel *lawyer*
Baker, William Parr *lawyer*
Baldwin, John Chandler *lawyer*
Barnhouse, Robert Bolon *lawyer*
Bartlett, James Wilson, III *lawyer*
Battaglia, Lynne Ann *prosecutor*
Beall, George *lawyer*
Bernhardt, Herbert Nelson *law educator*
Blanton, Edward Lee, Jr. *lawyer*
Boone, Harold Thomas *retired lawyer*
Bowen, Lowell Reed *lawyer*
Brewster, Gerry Leiper *lawyer*
Brumbaugh, John Maynard *lawyer, educator*
Burch, Francis Boucher, Jr. *lawyer*
Carbine, James Edmond *lawyer*
Carey, Anthony Morris *lawyer*
Carey, Jana Howard *lawyer*
Carlin, Paul Victor *legal association executive*
Chaplin, Peggy Fannon *lawyer*
Chiarello, Donald Frederick *lawyer*
Chiu, Hungdah *lawyer, legal educator*
Chriss, Timothy D. A. *lawyer*
Cook, Bryson Leitch *lawyer*
Devan, Deborah Hunt *lawyer*
Dilloff, Neil Joel *lawyer*
Doory, Robert Leonard, Jr. *lawyer*
Dunne, Richard Edwin, III *lawyer*
Engel, Paul Bernard *lawyer*
Eveleth, Janet Stidman *law association administrator*
†Fergenson, Arthur Friend *lawyer*
Finch, Walter Goss Gilchrist *lawyer, engineer, accountant, retired army officer*
Finnerty, Joseph Gregory, Jr. *lawyer*
Fisher, Morton Poe, Jr. *lawyer*
Fraser, Joan Catherine *lawyer*
Friedman, Louis Frank *lawyer*
Gately, Mark Donohue *lawyer*
Gillece, James Patrick, Jr. *lawyer*
Goldman, Brian Arthur *lawyer, accountant*
Goldscheider, Sidney *lawyer*
Graham, John Stuart, III *lawyer*
Gray, Frank Truan *lawyer*
Gray, Oscar Shalom *lawyer*
Hafets, Richard Jay *lawyer*
Haines, Thomas W. W. *lawyer*
Hanks, James Judge, Jr. *lawyer*
Herschman, Jeffrey D. *lawyer*
Hirsh, Theodore William *lawyer*
Hochberg, Bayard Zabdial *lawyer*
Honemann, Daniel Henry *lawyer*
Howell, Harley Thomas *lawyer*
Hubbard, Herbert Hendrix *lawyer*
Hughes, Harry Roe *lawyer*
Immelt, Stephen J. *lawyer*
Johnston, Edward Allan *lawyer*
Johnston, George W. *lawyer*
Jones, John Martin, Jr. *lawyer*
Kallina, Emanuel John, II *lawyer*
Kandel, Nelson Robert *lawyer*
Kandel, Peter Thomas *lawyer*
King, David Paul *lawyer*
Kramer, Paul R. *lawyer*
Lerch, Richard Heaphy *retired lawyer*
Levin, Edward Jesse *lawyer*
Levine, Richard E. *lawyer*
Lewis, Alexander Ingersoll, III *lawyer*
Liebmann, George W(illiam) *lawyer*
Lohr, Walter George, Jr. *lawyer*
Lundy, Audie Lee, Jr. *lawyer*
Marvel, L. Paige *lawyer*
McClung, A(lexander) Keith, Jr. *lawyer*
McPherson, Donald Paxton, III *lawyer*
McWilliams, John Michael *lawyer*
Melvin, Norman Cecil *lawyer*
Miller, Decatur Howard *lawyer*
Moser, M(artin) Peter *lawyer*
Nilson, George Albert *lawyer*
Orman, Leonard Arnold *lawyer*
Owen, Stephen Lee *lawyer*
Pappas, George Frank *lawyer*
Peacock, James Daniel *lawyer*
Plant, Albin MacDonough *lawyer*
Plummer, Risque Wilson *lawyer*
Pokempner, Joseph Kres *lawyer*
Pollak, Joanne E. *lawyer*
Pollak, Mark *lawyer*
Potts, Bernard *lawyer*
Priest, Troy Alfred-Wiley *lawyer*
Putzel, Constance Kellner *lawyer*
Radding, Andrew *lawyer*
Rafferty, William Bernard *lawyer*
Redden, Roger Duffey *lawyer*
Reed, Gregory *lawyer*
Reno, Russell Ronald, Jr. *lawyer*
Reynolds, William Leroy *lawyer, educator*
Ritzenthaler, Patty Parsons *lawyer*
Robinson, Zelig *lawyer*
Rose, Rudolph L. *lawyer*
Rosenthal, William J. *lawyer*
Sack, Sylvan Hanan *lawyer*
Sagett, Jan Jeffrey *lawyer, former government official*
Sampson, Richard Thomas *lawyer*
Schaefer, William G. *lawyer*
Schochor, Jonathan *lawyer*
Scott, Robert Edward, Jr. *lawyer*
Scriggins, Larry Palmer *lawyer*
Sfekas, Stephen James *lawyer*
Shapiro, Harry Dean *lawyer*
Sharkey, Robert Emmett *lawyer*
Sharpe, Donald Edward *lawyer*
Short, Alexander Campbell *lawyer*
Shortridge, Deborah Green *lawyer*
Silver, Michael Joel *lawyer*
Smith, Robert G. *lawyer*
Smouse, H(ervey) Russell *lawyer*
Stalfort, John Arthur *lawyer*
Stewart, C(ornelius) Van Leuven *lawyer*
Stiller, Shale David *lawyer, educator*
Summers, Thomas Carey *lawyer*
Sykes, Melvin Julius *lawyer*
Thomas, Daniel French *lawyer*
Trimble, William Cattell, Jr. *lawyer*
Vice, LaVonna Lee *lawyer*
Walker, Irving Edward *lawyer*
Wasserman, Richard Leo *lawyer*
White, Pamela Janice *lawyer*
White, William Nelson *lawyer*
Winn, James Julius, Jr. *lawyer*
Yarmolinsky, Adam *law educator*
Zimmerly, James Gregory *lawyer, physician*
Zinkham, W. Robert *lawyer*

### Bel Air
Crocker, Michael Pue *lawyer*
Miller, Max Dunham, Jr. *lawyer*

### Bethesda
Abrams, Samuel K. *lawyer*
Alper, Jerome Milton *lawyer*
Bauersfeld, Carl Frederick *lawyer*
Brickfield, Cyril Francis *lawyer, retired association executive*
Brown, Thomas Philip, III *lawyer*
Burton, Charles Henning *lawyer*
Calvert, Gordon Lee *retired legal association executive*
Cass, Millard *lawyer, arbitrator*
Elman, Philip *lawyer*
English, William deShay *lawyer*
Eule, Norman L. *lawyer*
Hall, William Darlington *lawyer*
Herman, Stephen Allen *lawyer*
Hill, Hugh Francis, III *lawyer, physician*
Inkellis, Barbara G. *lawyer*
Jayson, Lester Samuel *lawyer, educator*
Loewy, Steven A. *lawyer*
Mannix, Charles Raymond *law educator*
McKenna, Stephen James *lawyer, corporate executive*
Meier, Louis Leonard, Jr. *lawyer*
Moss, Stephen Edward *lawyer*
Pankopf, Arthur, Jr. *lawyer*
Pritchard Schoch, Teresa Noreen *lawyer, law librarian, executive*
Robertson, Paul Joseph *lawyer, educator*
Ross, William Warfield *lawyer*
Schmeltzer, David *lawyer*
Scully, Roger Tehan *lawyer*
Stetler, C. Joseph *retired lawyer*
Strandberg, Rebecca Newman *lawyer*
Strickler, Scott Michael *lawyer*
Toomey, Thomas Murray *lawyer*

### Bowie
Bagaria, Gail Farrell *lawyer*

### Brookeville
Johns, Warren LeRoi *lawyer*

### Burtonsville
Covington, Marlow Stanley *lawyer*

### Cambridge
Robbins, Vernon Earl *lawyer, accountant*

### Catonsville
Stowe, David Henry *arbitrator*
Zumbrun, Alvin John Thomas *law and criminology educator*

### Chevy Chase
Chase, Nicholas Joseph *lawyer, educator*
Elliott, R Lance *lawyer*
Groner, Beverly Anne *lawyer*
Harris, Judith Linda *lawyer*
Ikenberry, Henry Cephas, Jr. *lawyer*
Ketcham, Orman Weston *lawyer, former judge*
Klain, Ronald Alan *lawyer*
Lyons, Ellis *retired lawyer*
Mackall, Laidler Bowie *lawyer*
Paul, Carl Frederick *lawyer*

### Cockeysville Hunt Valley
Edgett, William Maloy *lawyer, labor arbitrator*

### Columbia
Crowe, Thomas Leonard *lawyer*
Ulman, Louis Jay *lawyer*

### Easton
Jacobs, Michael Joseph *lawyer*
Maffitt, James Strawbridge *lawyer*
Woods, William Ellis *lawyer, pharmacist, association executive*

### Ellicott City
Shatto, John Frederick *court administrator*
Wehland, Granville Warren Pearson *lawyer, consultant*

### Fort Washington
Alexander, Gary R. *lawyer, state legislator, lobbyist*

### Frederick
Hogan, Ilona Modly *lawyer*

### Gaithersburg
Phillips, Leo Harold, Jr. *lawyer*
Santa Maria, Philip Joseph, III *lawyer*

### Greenbelt
Ekstrand, Richard Edward *lawyer, educator*
Greenwald, Andrew Eric *lawyer*
Jascourt, Hugh D. *lawyer, arbitrator, mediator*

### Hagerstown
Berkson, Jacob Benjamin *lawyer, writer, conservationist*

### Hyattsville
Houle, Philip P. *lawyer*

### Keedysville
Doub, William Offutt *lawyer*

### Kensington
Daisley, William Prescott *lawyer*
Revoile, Charles Patrick *lawyer*

### Lanham
Brugger, George Albert *lawyer*
McCarthy, Kevin John *lawyer*

### Laytonsville
McDowell, Donna Schultz *lawyer*

### Lexington Park
Lacer, Alfred Antonio *lawyer, educator*

### Linthicum Heights
†Fanseen, James Foster *lawyer*

### Lutherville
Mc Kenney, Walter Gibbs, Jr. *lawyer, publishing company executive*

### New Market
Gabriel, Eberhard John *lawyer*

### North Potomac
Kehoe, Patrick Emmett *law librarian, educator*

### Ocean City
Wimbrow, Peter Ayers, III *lawyer*

### Potomac
Conner, Troy Blaine, Jr. *lawyer, writer*
DiSibio, Carol Lynn Kridler *lawyer*
Elisburg, Donald Earl *lawyer*
Latham, Patricia Horan *lawyer*
Meyer, Lawrence George *lawyer*
Peter, Phillips Smith *lawyer*
Reichart, Stuart Richard *lawyer*

### Rockville
Barkley, Brian Evan *lawyer, political consultant*
Byrne, Olivia Sherrill *lawyer*
De Jong, David Samuel *lawyer, educator*
Frye, Roland Mushat, Jr. *lawyer*
Gordon, Joan Irma *lawyer*
Kadish, Richard L. *lawyer*
Margulies, Laura Jacobs *lawyer*
Mitchell, Charles F. *lawyer*
Molitor, Graham Thomas Tate *lawyer*
Rachanow, Gerald Marvin *lawyer, pharmacist*
Shadoan, George Woodson *lawyer*
Titus, Roger Warren *lawyer*

### Silver Spring
Craig, Paul Max, Jr. *lawyer*
Hannan, Myles *lawyer, banker*
Mitchell, Milton *lawyer*
Pellerzi, Leo Maurice *lawyer*
Ryan, Miles Francis, III *lawyer*

### Solomons
Whitaker, Mary Fernan *lawyer*

### Sparks
Single, Richard Wayne, Sr. *lawyer*

### Towson
Carney, Bradford George Yost *lawyer, educator*
Levasseur, William Ryan *lawyer*
Proctor, Kenneth Donald *lawyer*

### Upper Marlboro
Lilly, John Richard, II *lawyer*

### Westminster
Bryson, Brady Oliver *lawyer*
Dulany, William Bevard *lawyer*

### Wheaton
Kirchman, Eric Hans *lawyer*

## MASSACHUSETTS

### Abington
Auton, Linda May Eisenschmidt *lawyer, nurse*

### Andover
Bucci, Kathleen Elizabeth *lawyer, nurse*
Lakin, John Francis *lawyer*
Thorn, Andrea Papp *lawyer*

### Ashfield
Pepyne, Edward Walter *lawyer, psychologist, former educator*

### Barnstable
Brown, Robert G. *lawyer*

### Bedford
Nunes, Geoffrey *lawyer, corporate executive*

### Belmont
Luick, Robert Burns *lawyer*

### Boston
Abraham, Nicholas Albert *lawyer, real estate developer*
Achatz, John *lawyer*
Ames, James Barr *lawyer*
Annas, George J. *health law educator*
Aresty, Jeffrey M. *lawyer*
Auerbach, Joseph *lawyer, educator*
Bae, Frank S. H. *law educator, law librarian*
Bangs, Will Johnston *lawyer*
Batchelder, Samuel Lawrence, Jr. *corporate lawyer*
Beard, Charles Julian *lawyer*

Becker, Fred Ronald *lawyer*
Belin, Gaspard d'Andelot *lawyer*
Benjamin, William Chase *lawyer*
Bergen, Kenneth William *lawyer*
Berlew, Frank Kingston *lawyer*
Bernhard, Alexander Alfred *lawyer*
Bines, Harvey Ernest *lawyer, educator, writer*
Blodgett, Mark Stephen *lawyer, legal studies educator, author*
Bohnen, Michael J. *lawyer*
Bok, John Fairfield *lawyer*
Borenstein, Milton Conrad *lawyer, manufacturing company executive*
Bornheimer, Allen Millard *lawyer*
Borod, Ronald Sam *lawyer*
Brody, Richard Eric *lawyer*
Brountas, Paul Peter *lawyer*
Brown, Judith Olans *lawyer, educator*
Brown, Matthew *lawyer*
Brown, Michael Robert *lawyer*
Browne, Kingsbury *lawyer*
Buchanan, Robert McLeod *lawyer*
Burgess, John Allen *lawyer*
Burleigh, Lewis Albert *lawyer*
Burns, Thomas David *lawyer*
Burr, Francis Hardon *lawyer*
Cabot, Charles Codman, Jr. *lawyer*
Campbell, Richard P. *lawyer*
Caner, George Colket, Jr. *lawyer*
Cantor, Stefanie Dara *lawyer*
Carr, Stephen W. *lawyer*
Carroll, James Edward *lawyer*
Carter, T(homas) Barton *law educator*
Casner, Truman Snell *lawyer*
Cass, Ronald Andrew *lawyer, educator*
Cekala, Chester *lawyer*
Chapin, Melville *lawyer*
Chaplin, Ansel Burt *lawyer*
Coffey, James Francis *lawyer*
Cogan, John Francis, Jr. *lawyer*
Cohn, Andrew Howard *lawyer*
Comegys, Walker Brockton *lawyer*
Cronin, Philip Mark *lawyer*
Crossen, Gary Charles *lawyer*
Curtin, John Joseph, Jr. *lawyer*
Cushing, George Littleton *lawyer*
Cutler, Arnold Robert *lawyer*
Daley, Paul Patrick *lawyer*
Daynard, Richard Alan *law educator*
Delaney, John White *lawyer*
de Rham, Casimir, Jr. *lawyer*
Dignan, Thomas Gregory, Jr. *lawyer*
Dillon, James Joseph *lawyer*
Dineen, John K. *lawyer*
Duffy, James Francis, III *lawyer*
Dusseault, C. Dean *lawyer*
Ehrlich, M. Gordon *lawyer*
Elfman, Eric Michael *lawyer*
Engel, David Lewis *lawyer*
Erickson, Kenneth W. *lawyer*
Eurich, Richard Rex *lawyer*
Everett, Jonathan Jubal *lawyer*
Fay, Michael Leo *lawyer*
Felter, John Kenneth *lawyer*
Finn, Terrence M. *lawyer*
Fischer, Eric Robert *lawyer, educator*
Fischer, Thomas Covell *law educator, consultant, writer, lawyer*
Fisher, Champe Andrews *lawyer*
Floor, Richard Earl *lawyer*
Fox, Francis Haney *lawyer*
Frankenheim, Samuel *lawyer*
Fraser, Robert Burchmore *lawyer*
Freehling, Daniel Joseph *law educator, law library director*
Fremont-Smith, Marion R. *lawyer*
Gad, Robert K., III *lawyer*
Galvani, Paul B. *lawyer*
Garcia, Adolfo Ramon *lawyer*
Gaudreau, Russell A., Jr. *lawyer*
Gault, Robert Mellor *lawyer*
Gerstmayr, John Wolfgang *lawyer*
Gesmer, Henry *lawyer*
Gill, Robert Tucker *lawyer*
Giso, Frank, III *lawyer*
Givelber, Daniel James *law educator*
Glosband, Daniel Martin *lawyer*
Goodman, Bruce Gerald *lawyer*
Goodman, Louis Allan *lawyer*
Graceffa, John Philip *lawyer*
Greer, Gordon Bruce *lawyer*
Gupta, Paul R. *lawyer*
Haddad, Ernest Mudarri *lawyer*
Haley, Paul Richard *lawyer, state legislator*
Hall, Henry Lyon, Jr. *lawyer*
Hamel, Louis H., Jr. *lawyer*
Hand, John *lawyer*
Harrington, John Michael, Jr. *lawyer*
Haussermann, Oscar William, Jr. *lawyer*
Hawkey, G. Michael *lawyer*
Hayes, Robert Francis *lawyer*
Heigham, James Crichton *lawyer*
Hester, Patrick Joseph *lawyer*
Hines, Edward Francis, Jr. *lawyer*
Hoffman, Christian Matthew *lawyer*
Hoffman, David Alan *lawyer*
Holland, Hubert Brian *lawyer*
Hoort, Steven Thomas *lawyer*
Hotchkiss, Andra Ruth *lawyer*
Howe, Jas. Murray *lawyer*
Johnston, Richard Alan *lawyer*
Jones, Jeffrey Foster *lawyer*
Jones, Sheldon Atwell *lawyer*
Jordan, Alexander Joseph, Jr. *lawyer*
Kanin, Dennis Roy *lawyer*
Kaplan, Lawrence Edward *lawyer*
Karelitz, Robert N(elson) *lawyer*
Katzmann, Gary Stephen *lawyer*
Kavanaugh, James Francis, Jr. *lawyer*
Keating, Michael Burns *lawyer*
Kehoe, William Francis *lawyer*
Keller, Stanley *lawyer*
Kelly, Thomas J. *lawyer*
Kenney, Raymond Joseph, Jr. *lawyer*
Kerry, Cameron F. *lawyer*
King, William Bruce *lawyer*
Kirchick, William Dean *lawyer*
Kirk, Paul Grattan, Jr. *lawyer, former political organization official*
Knight, Peter Carter *lawyer*
Koffel, William Barry *lawyer*
Kopelman, Leonard *lawyer*
Korb, Kenneth Allan *lawyer*
Krasnow, Jordan Philip *lawyer*
Lambert, Gary Ervery *lawyer*
Lane, Newton Alexander *retired lawyer*
Last, Michael P. *lawyer*
Latham, James David *lawyer*
Lewis, Scott P. *lawyer*
Licata, Arthur Frank *lawyer*
Lockwood, Rhodes Greene *retired lawyer*
Loeser, Hans Ferdinand *lawyer*
Looney, William Francis, Jr. *lawyer*
Loring, Arthur *lawyer, financial services company executive*
Lukey, Joan A. *lawyer*
Lynch, Francis Charles *lawyer*
Lyons, Paul Vincent *lawyer*
MacDougall, Peter *lawyer*
MacFarlane, Maureen Anne *lawyer*
Mandel, David Michael *lawyer*
Martin, Stanley A. *lawyer*
Matthews, Roger Hardin *lawyer*
McChesney, S. Elaine *lawyer*
McGivney, John Joseph *lawyer*
Mercer, Douglas *lawyer*
Meserve, William George *lawyer*
Metzer, Patricia Ann *lawyer*
Mikels, Richard Eliot *lawyer*
Miller, Alan Gershon *lawyer*
Minkel, Herbert Philip, Jr. *lawyer*
Mokriski, J. Charles *lawyer*
Moncreiff, Robert P. *lawyer*
Mone, Michael Edward *lawyer*
Mooney, Michael Edward *lawyer*
Moran, James J., Jr. *lawyer*
Moriarty, George Marshall *lawyer*
Muldoon, Robert Joseph, Jr. *lawyer*
Mullaney, Joseph E. *lawyer*
Mygatt, Susan Hall *lawyer*
Neely, Thomas Emerson *lawyer*
Neumeier, Richard L. *lawyer*
Notopoulos, Alexander Anastasios, Jr. *lawyer*
Nutt, Robert L. *lawyer*
O'Dell, Edward Thomas, Jr. *lawyer*
O'Donnell, Thomas Lawrence Patrick *lawyer*
O'Neill, Philip Daniel, Jr. *lawyer, educator*
O'Neill, Timothy P. *lawyer*
Osteen, Carolyn McCue *lawyer*
Packenham, Richard Daniel *lawyer*
Packer, Rekha Desai *lawyer*
Park, William Wynnewood *law educator*
Parker, Christopher William *lawyer*
Partan, Daniel Gordon *lawyer, educator*
Patterson, John de la Roche, Jr. *lawyer*
Pechilis, William John *lawyer*
Perera, Lawrence Thacher *lawyer*
Perkins, James Wood *lawyer*
Perkins, John Allen *lawyer*
Perkins, Samuel *lawyer*
Pomeroy, Robert Corttis *lawyer*
Raish, David Langdon *lawyer*
Ramsden, Linda Gisele *lawyer*
Reardon, Frank Emond *lawyer*
Remis, Shepard M. *lawyer*
Richmond, Alice Elenor *lawyer*
Ritt, Roger Merrill *lawyer*
Rivlin, Rachel *lawyer*
Rizzo, William Ober *lawyer*
Rose, Alan Douglas *lawyer*
Rostow, Charles Nicholas *lawyer, educator*
St. Clair, James Draper *lawyer*
Saparoff, Peter M. *lawyer*
Sapers, Carl Martin *lawyer*
Sargeant, Ernest James *lawyer*
Savrann, Richard Allen *lawyer*
Schmelzer, Henry Louis Phillip *lawyer, financial company executive*
Schram, Ronald Byard *lawyer*
Scott, A. Hugh *lawyer*
Segal, Robert Mandal *lawyer*
Shapiro, Sandra *lawyer*
Shepard, Henry Bradbury, Jr. *lawyer*
Silberman, Robert A. S. *lawyer*
Sirkin, Joel H. *lawyer*
Smith, Edwin Eric *lawyer*
Smith, Philip Jones *lawyer*
Snyder, John Gorvers *lawyer*
Soden, Richard Allan *lawyer*
Solet, Maxwell David *lawyer*
Sommerfeld, Nicholas Ulrich *lawyer*
Sonnenschein, Adam *lawyer*
Southard, William G. *lawyer*
Stein, Marshall David *lawyer*
Steinberg, Laura *lawyer*
Steinhauer, Gillian *lawyer*
Stevenson, Philip Davis *lawyer*
Stokes, James Christopher *lawyer*
Storer, Jeffrey B. *lawyer*
Storer, Thomas Perry *lawyer*
Storey, James Moorfield *lawyer*
Streeter, Henry Schofield *lawyer*
Sugarman, Paul Ronald *lawyer, educator, academic administrator*
Surkin, Elliot Mark *lawyer*
Swaim, Charles Hall *lawyer*
Swope, Jeffrey Peyton *lawyer*
Sykes, Tracy Allan *lawyer*
Taylor, Thomas William *lawyer*
Testa, Richard Joseph *lawyer*
Thibeault, George Walter *lawyer*
Trimmier, Roscoe, Jr. *lawyer*
Tuchmann, Robert *lawyer*
Van, Peter *lawyer*
Vance, Verne Widney, Jr. *lawyer*
Vaughan, Herbert Wiley *lawyer*
Walker, Gordon T. *lawyer*
Weiner, Stephen Mark *lawyer*
Weitzel, John Patterson *lawyer*
Wellington, Carol Strong *law librarian*
Weltman, David Lee *lawyer*
White, Barry Bennett *lawyer*
Whitlock, John L. *lawyer*
Whitters, James Payton, III *lawyer, university administrator*
Williams, John Taylor *lawyer*
Williams, Robert Dana *lawyer*
Winter, Donald Francis *lawyer*
Wolf, David *lawyer*
Woodburn, Ralph Robert, Jr. *lawyer*
Woolsey, John Munro, Jr. *lawyer*
Wright, Walter Augustine, III *business and corporate lawyer*
Young, Raymond Henry *lawyer*
Yurko, Richard John *lawyer*
Zack, Arnold Marshall *lawyer, mediator, arbitrator*
Zupcofska, Peter F. *lawyer*

**Braintree**
Segersten, Robert Hagy *lawyer, investment banker*

**Brookline**
Burnstein, Daniel *lawyer*
Nayor, Charles Francis *lawyer*

**Cambridge**
Alevizos, Susan Bamberger *lawyer, santouri player, author*
Alevizos, Theodore G. *lawyer, singer, author*
Andrews, William Dorey *lawyer, educator*
Bartholet, Elizabeth *law educator*
Bok, Derek *law educator, former university president*
Boyden, W(alter) Lincoln *lawyer*
Chapin, Richard *arbitrator, consultant*
Chayes, Abram *law educator, lawyer*
Cox, Archibald *lawyer, educator*
Dershowitz, Alan Morton *lawyer, educator*
Driscoll, Kimberlee Marie *lawyer*
Fallon, Richard H., Jr. *law educator*
Fisher, Roger Dummer *lawyer, educator, negotiation expert*
Frug, Gerald E. *law educator*
Glauner, Alfred William *lawyer, engineering company executive*
Glendon, Mary Ann *law educator*
Gonson, S. Donald *lawyer*
Howard, Susanne C. *lawyer*
†Kahin, Brian *lawyer, computer industry professional, consultant*
Kaplow, Louis *law educator*
Kassman, Herbert Seymour *lawyer, management consultant*
Kaufman, Andrew Lee *law educator*
Kennedy, David W. *law educator*
Loss, Louis *lawyer, retired educator*
Malme, Jane Hamlett *lawyer, educator, researcher*
Mansfield, John H. *lawyer, educator*
Meltzer, Daniel J. *law educator*
Michelman, Frank I. *lawyer, educator*
Miller, Arthur Raphael *legal educator*
Mnookin, Robert Harris *lawyer, educator*
Roche, John Jefferson *lawyer*
Ryan, Allan Andrew, Jr. *lawyer, author, lecturer*
Sander, Frank Ernest Arnold *law educator*
Schauer, Frederick Franklin *legal educator*
Scott, Hal S. *law educator*
Shapiro, David Louis *lawyer, educator*
Steiner, Henry Jacob *law and human rights educator*
Stone, Alan A. *law educator, psychiatry educator*
Ta, Tai Van *lawyer, researcher*
Vagts, Detlev Frederick *lawyer, educator*
von Mehren, Arthur Taylor *lawyer, educator*
Vorenberg, James *lawyer, educator, university dean*
Warren, Alvin Clifford, Jr. *lawyer*
Weinreb, Lloyd Lobell *law educator*
Westfall, David *lawyer, educator*
Wirth, Peter *lawyer*
Wolfman, Bernard *lawyer, educator*

**Canton**
Friend, William Kagay *lawyer*

**Chatham**
Pacun, Norman *lawyer*

**Chelmsford**
Grossman, Debra A. *lawyer, real estate manager, radio talk show host*
Lerer, Neal M. *lawyer*

**Chestnut Hill**
Bursley, Kathleen A. *lawyer*
Norris, Melvin *lawyer*

**Concord**
Berger, Raoul *law educator, violinist*
White, James Barr *lawyer, real estate investor, consultant*

**Dover**
Craver, James Bernard *lawyer*

**Framingham**
Hunt, Samuel Pancoast, III *lawyer, corporate executive*
Meltzer, Jay H. *lawyer, retail company executive*
Munro, Meredith Vance *lawyer*

**Gloucester**
Birchfield, John Kermit, Jr. *lawyer*

**Greenfield**
Lee, Marilyn (Irma) Modarelli *law librarian*

**Hingham**
Lane, Frederick Stanley *lawyer*

**Hyannis**
Paquin, Thomas Christopher *lawyer*

**Ipswich**
Getchell, Charles Willard, Jr. *lawyer, publisher*

**Lexington**
D'Avignon, Roy Joseph *lawyer*
Eaton, Allen Ober *lawyer*
Hoffmann, Christoph Ludwig *lawyer*

**Lincoln**
Gnichtel, William Van Orden *lawyer*
Schwartz, Edward Arthur *lawyer, foundation executive*

**Lowell**
Curtis, James Theodore *lawyer*

**Maynard**
Siekman, Thomas Clement *lawyer*

**Medford**
Berman, David *lawyer, poet*
Salacuse, Jeswald William *lawyer, educator*

**Middleboro**
Beeby, Kenneth Jack *lawyer, food products executive*

**Milford**
Murray, Brian William *lawyer*

**Milton**
Cooperstein, Paul Andrew *lawyer, business consultant*

**Nantucket**
Lobl, Herbert Max *lawyer*

**Natick**
Grassia, Thomas Charles *lawyer*
Savage, James Cathey, III *lawyer*

**Needham**
Bullard, Robert Oliver, Jr. *lawyer*

**Newton**
Baron, Charles Hillel *lawyer, educator*
Coquillette, Daniel Robert *lawyer, educator*
Hauser, Harry Raymond *lawyer*
Horbaczewski, Henry Zygmunt *lawyer, publishing executive*
Huber, Richard Gregory *lawyer, educator*
Hughes, George Michael *lawyer*
Messing, Arnold Philip *lawyer*

**North Reading**
Green, Jack Allen *lawyer*

**Norwell**
Mullare, T(homas) Kenwood, Jr. *lawyer*

**Plymouth**
Barreira, Brian Ernest *lawyer*

**Salem**
Del Vecchio, Debra Anne *lawyer*
Griffin, Thomas McLean *retired lawyer*
Moran, Philip David *lawyer*

**Sherborn**
Borgeson, Earl Charles *law librarian, educator*

**Somerset**
Sabra, Steven Peter *lawyer*

**South Hadley**
Sheridan, Daniel Joseph *lawyer*

**South Orleans**
Parker, Douglas Martin *writer, retired lawyer*

**Springfield**
Dunn, Donald Jack *law librarian, law educator, lawyer*
Maidman, Stephen Paul *lawyer*
Milstein, Richard Sherman *lawyer*
Oldershaw, Louis Frederick *lawyer*
Susse, Sandra Slone *lawyer*

**Stoughton**
Douglas, John Breed, III *lawyer*
Schepps, Victoria Hayward *lawyer*

**Tewksbury**
Dulchinos, Peter *lawyer*

**Waltham**
Barnes-Brown, Peter Newton *lawyer*
Touster, Saul *law educator*

**Wellesley**
Aldrich, Richard Orth *lawyer*
Carlson, Christopher Tapley *lawyer*
Goglia, Charles A., Jr. *lawyer*
Shea, Robert McConnell *lawyer*
Weiss, Andrew Richard *lawyer*

**West Chatham**
Rowley, Glenn Harry *lawyer*

**West Falmouth**
Carlson, David Bret *lawyer, consultant*

**Westborough**
Frank, Jacob *lawyer*

**Westfield**
Ettman, Philip *business law educator*

**Weston**
Haas, Jacqueline Crawford *lawyer*
Thomas, Roger Meriwether *lawyer*

**Westwood**
Galston, Clarence Elkus *lawyer*

**Winthrop**
O'Connell, Henry Francis *lawyer*

**Worcester**
Cowan, Fairman Chaffee *lawyer*
Erskine, Matthew Forbes *lawyer*
LeDoux, William John *lawyer*

**Worthington**
Hastings, Wilmot Reed *lawyer*

## MICHIGAN

**Ada**
Mc Callum, Charles Edward *lawyer*

**Adrian**
Kralick, Richard Louis *lawyer*

**Ann Arbor**
Allen, Layman Edward *law educator, research scientist*
Bogaard, William Joseph *lawyer*
Bollinger, Lee Carroll *law educator*
Britton, Clarold Lawrence *lawyer, consultant*
Browder, Olin Lorraine *legal educator*
Cole, Roland Jay *lawyer*
Cooper, Edward Hayes *lawyer, educator*
DeVine, Edmond Francis *lawyer*
Duquette, Donald Norman *law educator*
Ellmann, Douglas Stanley *lawyer*
Ellmann, William Marshall *lawyer, mediator, arbitrator, researcher*
†French, David A. *lawyer*
Frier, Bruce W. *law educator*
Gilbert, Robert Edward *lawyer*
Jackson, John Howard *lawyer, educator*
Joscelyn, Kent Buckley *lawyer, research scientist*

Kahn, Douglas Allen *legal educator*
Kamisar, Yale *lawyer, educator*
Kennedy, Frank Robert *lawyer*
Keppelman, Nancy *lawyer*
Krier, James Edward *law educator, author*
Lehman, Jeffrey Sean *law educator*
Lempert, Richard Owen *lawyer, educator*
MacKinnon, Catharine A. *lawyer, law educator, legal scholar, writer*
McHugh, Richard Walker *lawyer*
Phillips, Daniel Miller *lawyer*
Pierce, William James *law educator*
Reed, John Wesley *lawyer, educator*
Roach, Thomas Adair *lawyer*
St. Antoine, Theodore Joseph *law educator, arbitrator*
Sandalow, Terrance *law educator*
Schneider, Carl Edward *law educator*
Simpson, A. W. B. *law educator*
Southwick, Arthur Frederick *legal educator*
Stein, Eric *retired law educator*
Vining, (George) Joseph *law educator*
Waggoner, Lawrence William *law educator*
White, James Boyd *law educator*

**Bay City**
Greve, Guy Robert *lawyer*

**Berkley**
Linkner, Monica Farris *lawyer*

**Bingham Farms**
Moffitt, David Louis *lawyer, county and state official*

**Birmingham**
Bromberg, Stephen Aaron *lawyer*
Buesser, Anthony Carpenter *lawyer*
Elsman, James Leonard, Jr. *lawyer*
Gold, Edward David *lawyer*
Morganroth, Fred *lawyer*

**Bloomfield Hills**
Andrews, Frank Lewis *lawyer*
Baker, Robert Edward *lawyer, retired financial corporation executive*
Berlow, Robert Alan *lawyer*
Brodhead, William McNulty *lawyer, former congressman*
Bruegel, David Robert *lawyer*
Clippert, Charles Frederick *lawyer*
Cumbey, Constance Elizabeth *lawyer, author, lecturer*
Cunningham, Gary H. *lawyer*
Dawson, Stephen Everette *lawyer*
Gelder, John William *lawyer*
Googasian, George Ara *lawyer*
Gornick, Alan Lewis *lawyer*
Hurlbert, Robert P. *lawyer*
Kasischke, Louis Walter *lawyer*
LoPrete, James Hugh *lawyer*
Lower, Joyce Q. *lawyer*
McDonald, Patrick Allen *lawyer, arbitrator, educator*
Meyer, George Herbert *lawyer*
Nolte, Henry R., Jr. *lawyer, former automobile company executive*
Norris, John Hart *lawyer*
Pappas, Edward Harvey *lawyer*
Paul, Richard Wright *lawyer*
Rader, Ralph Terrance *lawyer*
Snyder, George Edward *lawyer*
Solomon, Mark Raymond *lawyer, educator*
Thurber, John Alexander *lawyer*
Weinstein, William Joseph *lawyer*
Williams, Walter Joseph *lawyer*

**Dearborn**
Gardner, Gary Edward *lawyer*
Martin, John William, Jr. *lawyer, automotive industry executive*
Simon, Evelyn *lawyer*
Taub, Robert Allan *lawyer*

**Detroit**
†Adamany, David Walter *law and political science educator*
Amsden, Ted Thomas *lawyer*
Andreoff, Christopher Andon *lawyer*
Babcock, Charles Witten, Jr. *lawyer*
Banas, C. Leslie *lawyer*
Brady, Edmund Matthew, Jr. *lawyer*
Brand, George Edward, Jr. *lawyer*
Braun, Richard Lane, II *lawyer*
Brown, Stratton Shartel *lawyer*
Brustad, Orin Daniel *lawyer*
Burstein, Richard Joel *lawyer*
Bushnell, George Edward, Jr. *lawyer*
Callahan, John William (Bill) *judge*
Candler, James Nall, Jr. *lawyer*
Charfoos, Lawrence Selig *lawyer*
Charla, Leonard Francis *lawyer*
Choate, Robert Alden *lawyer*
Cohan, Leon Sumner *lawyer, retired electric company executive*
Collier, James Warren *lawyer*
Connor, Laurence Davis *lawyer*
Corrigan, Maura Denise *lawyer, state judge*
Cothorn, John Arthur *lawyer*
Darlow, Julia Donovan *lawyer*
Draper, James Wilson *lawyer*
Driker, Eugene *lawyer*
Dudley, John Henry, Jr. *lawyer*
Dunn, William Bradley *lawyer*
Eggertsen, John Hale *lawyer*
Ettinger, David A. *lawyer*
Faison, W. Mack *lawyer*
Fromm, Frederick Andrew, Jr. *lawyer*
Garzia, Samuel Angelo *lawyer*
Getz, Ernest John *lawyer*
Gushee, Richard Bordley *lawyer*
Hampton, Verne Churchill, II *lawyer*
Hatie, George Daniel *lawyer*
Heaphy, John Merrill *lawyer*
Herstein, Carl William *lawyer*
Howbert, Edgar Charles *lawyer*
Kahn, Mark Leo *arbitrator, educator*
Kessler, Philip Joel *lawyer*
Krsul, John Aloysius, Jr. *lawyer*
Kuehn, George E. *lawyer, beverage company executive*
Lamborn, LeRoy Leslie *legal educator*
Lawrence, John Kidder *lawyer*
Ledwidge, Patrick Joseph *lawyer*
Lenga, J. Thomas *lawyer*
Lewand, F. Thomas *lawyer*
Lockman, Stuart M. *lawyer*
Longhofer, Ronald Stephen *lawyer*
Lucow, Milton *lawyer*
Majzoub, Mona Kathryne *lawyer*
Malone, Daniel Patrick *lawyer*
Mamat, Frank Trustick *lawyer*
Maurer, David L. *lawyer*
Maycock, Joseph Farwell, Jr. *lawyer*
McKim, Samuel John, III *lawyer*
McNair, Russell Arthur, Jr. *lawyer*
McNish, Susan Kirk *lawyer*
Mengel, Christopher Emile *lawyer, educator*
Miller, George DeWitt, Jr. *lawyer*
Mitseff, Carl *lawyer*
Nadeau, Steven C. *lawyer*
Nix, Robert Royal, II *lawyer*
Parker, George Edward, III *lawyer*
Pearce, Harry Jonathan *lawyer*
Phillips, Elliott Hunter *lawyer*
Richardson, Ralph Herman *lawyer*
Robinson, James Kenneth *lawyer, educator*
Roche, Douglas David *lawyer, bar examiner*
Rossen, Jordan *lawyer*
Rossman, Richard Alan *lawyer*
Rozof, Phyllis Claire *lawyer*
Russell, Robert Gilmore *lawyer*
Saxton, William Marvin *lawyer*
Saylor, Larry James *lawyer*
Schultz, Dennis Bernard *lawyer*
Schwartz, Alan E. *lawyer*
Schwartz, Jerome Merrill *lawyer*
Scott, John Edward Smith *lawyer*
Sedler, Robert Allen *law educator*
Semple, Lloyd Ashby *lawyer*
Shaevsky, Mark *lawyer*
Shannon, Margaret Anne *lawyer*
Shapiro, Michael B. *lawyer*
Smith, James Albert *lawyer*
Sott, Herbert *lawyer*
Sparrow, Herbert George, III *lawyer*
Thelen, Bruce Cyril *lawyer*
Thoms, David Moore *lawyer*
Thurber, Peter Palms *lawyer*
Timm, Roger K. *lawyer*
Toll, Sheldon Samuel *lawyer*
Volz, William Harry *law educator, administrator*
Weiss, Robert Benjamin *lawyer*
Williams, J. Bryan *lawyer*
Wise, John Augustus *lawyer*
Wittlinger, Timothy David *lawyer*
Ziegler, John Augustus, Jr. *lawyer*
Zuckerman, Richard Engle *lawyer, law educator*

**East Lansing**
Hackett, Wesley Phelps, Jr. *lawyer*
Wilkinson, William Sherwood *lawyer*

**Farmington Hills**
Birnkrant, Sherwin Maurice *lawyer*
Haliw, Andrew Jerome, III *lawyer, engineer*
Nathanson, Leonard Mark *lawyer*

**Flint**
Cooley, Richard Eugene *lawyer*
Lehman, Richard Leroy *lawyer*
Pelavin, Michael Allen *lawyer*

**Grand Rapids**
Barnes, Thomas John *lawyer*
Blackwell, Thomas Francis *lawyer*
Boyden, Joel Michael *lawyer*
Bradshaw, Conrad Allan *lawyer*
Bransdorfer, Stephen Christie *lawyer*
Curtin, Timothy John *lawyer*
Davis, Henry Barnard, Jr. *lawyer*
Deems, Nyal David *lawyer, mayor*
Jennette, Noble Stevenson, III *lawyer*
McGarry, John Everett *lawyer*
McNeil, John W. *lawyer*
Mears, Patrick Edward *lawyer*
Pestle, John William *lawyer*
Smith, H(arold) Lawrence *lawyer*
Sytsma, Fredric A. *lawyer*
Titley, Larry J. *lawyer*
Van Haren, W(illiam) Michael *lawyer*
Van't Hof, William Keith *lawyer*

**Grosse Pointe**
Avant, Grady, Jr. *lawyer*
Axe, John Randolph *lawyer, financial executive*
Brucker, Wilber Marion *lawyer*
Gilbride, William Donald *lawyer*
Goss, James William *lawyer*
King, John Lane *lawyer*
McIntyre, Anita Grace Jordan *lawyer*
Mogk, John Edward *law educator, association executive, consultant*
Pytell, Robert Henry *lawyer, former judge*

**Hickory Corners**
Bristol, Norman *lawyer, arbitrator, former food company executive*

**Holland**
Moritz, John Reid *lawyer*
Nelson, Helaine Queen *lawyer*

**Ishpeming**
Steward, James Brian *lawyer, pharmacist*

**Jackson**
Curtis, Philip James *lawyer*
Marcoux, William Joseph *lawyer*
Raduazo, Anthony F. *lawyer*

**Kalamazoo**
Brown, Eric Vandyke, Jr. *lawyer*
Gordon, Edgar George *lawyer, business executive*
Halpert, Richard L. *lawyer*
Hilboldt, James Sonnemann *lawyer, investment advisor*
Hooker, Richard Alfred *lawyer*
Ritter, Charles Edward *lawyer*

**Lansing**
Baker, Frederick Milton, Jr. *lawyer*
Demlow, Daniel J. *lawyer*
Fink, Joseph Allen *lawyer*
Fitzgerald, John Warner *law educator*
Foster, Joe C., Jr. *lawyer*
Gallagher, Byron Patrick, Jr. *lawyer*
Houston, David John *lawyer*
Kritselis, William Nicholas *lawyer*
Lindemer, Lawrence Boyd *lawyer, former utility executive, former state justice*
Rooney, John Philip *law educator*
Stackable, Frederick Lawrence *lawyer*
Stockmeyer, Norman Otto, Jr. *law educator, consultant*
Valade, Alan Michael *lawyer*
Winder, Richard Earnest *legal foundation administrator, writer, consultant*

**Livonia**
Hoffman, Barry Paul *lawyer*
McCuen, John Francis, Jr. *lawyer*

**Menominee**
Anuta, Michael Joseph *lawyer*

**Monroe**
Lipford, Rocque Edward *lawyer, corporate executive*

**Muskegon**
McKendry, John H., Jr. *lawyer, educator*
Nehra, Gerald Peter *lawyer*
Van Leuven, Robert Joseph *lawyer*

**Northville**
Hariri, V. M. *arbitrator, mediator, lawyer, educator*
Leavitt, Martin Jack *lawyer*
Liegl, Joseph Leslie *lawyer*

**Owosso**
Moorhead, Thomas Edward *lawyer*

**Petoskey**
Smith, Wayne Richard *lawyer*

**Plymouth**
Morgan, Donald Crane *lawyer*

**Rockford**
Sawyer, Harold S(amuel) *lawyer*

**Saginaw**
Zanot, Craig Allen *lawyer*

**Saint Clair Shores**
Caretti, Richard Louis *lawyer*
Danielson, Gary R. *lawyer*

**South Haven**
Waxman, Sheldon Robert *lawyer*

**Southfield**
Baumkel, Mark S. *lawyer*
Cohen, Norton Jacob *lawyer*
Dawson, Dennis Ray *lawyer, manufacturing company executive*
Gale, Connie R(uth) *lawyer*
Hanket, Mark John *lawyer*
Harbour, Nancy Caine *lawyer*
Hotelling, Harold *law and economics educator*
Jacobs, John Patrick *lawyer*
Labe, Robert Brian *lawyer*
Martin, J. Patrick *lawyer*
McClow, Roger James *lawyer*
Morganroth, Mayer *lawyer*
Satovsky, Abraham *lawyer*
Shillman, Jeffrey Nathaniel *lawyer*
Thurswell, Gerald Elliott *lawyer*

**Taylor**
Hirsch, David L. *lawyer, corporate executive*
Leekley, John Robert *lawyer*
Pirtle, H(arold) Edward *lawyer*

**Tecumseh**
McDonald, Daryl Patrick *lawyer*

**Traverse City**
Wolfe, Richard Ratcliffe *lawyer*

**Troy**
Alber, Phillip George *lawyer*
Alterman, Irwin Michael *lawyer*
Cantor, Bernard Jack *patent lawyer*
Crane, Louis Arthur *retired labor arbitrator*
Dillon, Joseph Francis *lawyer*
Gornbein, Henry Seidel *lawyer*
Gullen, Christopher Roy *lawyer*
Haron, David Lawrence *lawyer*
Hartwig, Eugene Lawrence *lawyer*
Hirschhorn, Austin *lawyer*
Kienbaum, Thomas Gerd *lawyer*
Kruse, John Alphonse *lawyer*
LaDuke, Nancie *lawyer, corporate executive*
Ponitz, John Allan *lawyer*
Tombers, Evelyn Charlotte *lawyer*

**MINNESOTA**

**Anoka**
Hicken, Jeffrey Price *lawyer*

**Bemidji**
Kief, Paul Allan *lawyer*

**Bloomington**
Wilson, Rebecca Lynn *lawyer*

**Brooklyn Center**
Brosnahan, Roger Paul *lawyer*

**Burnsville**
Knutson, David Lee *lawyer, state senator*

**Duluth**
Balmer, James Walter *lawyer*
Burns, Richard Ramsey *lawyer*
Johnson, Joseph Bernard *lawyer*

**Eagan**
Angle, Margaret Susan *lawyer*

**Eden Prairie**
Nilles, John Michael *lawyer*

**Edina**
Burk, Robert S. *lawyer*

**Fridley**
Savelkoul, Donald Charles *lawyer*

**Golden Valley**
Hagglund, Clarance Edward *lawyer, publishing company owner*

**Hopkins**
Hunter, Donald Forrest *lawyer*

**Mankato**
Gage, Fred Kelton *lawyer*

**Minneapolis**
Ackman, Lauress V. *lawyer*
Adamson, Oscar Charles, II *lawyer*
Anderson, Eric Scott *lawyer*
Anderson, Laurence Alexis *lawyer*
Anderson, Thomas Willman *lawyer*
Bearmon, Lee *lawyer*
Berens, William Joseph *lawyer*
Berg, Thomas Kenneth *lawyer*
Blanton, W. C. *lawyer*
Bleck, Michael John *lawyer*
Boelter, Philip Floyd *lawyer*
Bonvino, Frank W. *lawyer*
Borger, John Philip *lawyer*
Brand, Steve Aaron *lawyer*
Breimayer, Joseph Frederick *patent lawyer*
Bress, Michael E. *lawyer*
Brink, David Ryrie *lawyer*
Bruner, Philip Lane *lawyer*
Buratti, Dennis P. *lawyer*
Burke, Martin Nicholas *lawyer*
Burns, Robert Arthur *lawyer*
Busdicker, Gordon G. *lawyer*
Carlson, Thomas David *lawyer*
Carpenter, Norman Roblee *lawyer*
Champlin, Steven Kirk *lawyer*
Christiansen, Jay David *lawyer*
Ciresi, Michael Vincent *lawyer*
Clary, Bradley Grayson *lawyer, educator*
Cohen, Earl Harding *lawyer*
Cole, Phillip Allen *lawyer*
Comstock, Rebecca Ann *lawyer*
Conn, Gordon Brainard, Jr. *lawyer*
Corwin, Gregg Marlowe *lawyer*
Crosby, Thomas Manville, Jr. *lawyer*
Drawz, John Englund *lawyer*
Eck, George Gregory *lawyer*
Erstad, Leon Robert *lawyer*
Finzen, Bruce Arthur *lawyer*
Fisher, Michael Bruce *lawyer*
Flom, Gerald Trossen *lawyer*
Forneris, Jeanne M. *lawyer*
Frase, Richard Stockwell *law educator*
Frecon, Alain *lawyer*
Freeman, Gerald Russell *lawyer*
Freeman, Orville Lothrop *lawyer, former governor of Minnesota, think tank executive*
Freeman, Todd Ira *lawyer*
French, John Dwyer *lawyer*
Gagnon, Craig William *lawyer*
Garon, Philip Stephen *lawyer*
Garton, Thomas William *lawyer*
Gearty, Edward Joseph *lawyer*
Gifford, Daniel Joseph *lawyer, educator, antitrust consultant*
Gill, Richard Lawrence *lawyer*
Goodman, Elizabeth Ann *lawyer*
Gottschalk, Stephen Elmer *lawyer*
Greener, Ralph Bertram *lawyer*
Griffith, G. Larry *lawyer*
Harris, John Edward *lawyer*
Hayward, Edward Joseph *lawyer*
Heiberg, Robert Alan *lawyer*
Hendrixson, Peter S. *lawyer*
Henson, Robert Frank *lawyer*
Hibbs, John Stanley *lawyer*
Hippee, William H., Jr. *lawyer*
Hobbins, Robert Leo *lawyer*
Holman, Diane Rosalie *lawyer*
Howland, Joan Sidney *law librarian, law educator*
Hudec, Robert Emil *lawyer, educator*
Hvass, Sheryl Ramstad *lawyer*
Jarboe, Mark Alan *lawyer*
Johnson, Eugene Laurence *lawyer*
Johnson, Gary M. *lawyer*
Johnson, Larry Walter *lawyer*
Johnson, Paul Owen *lawyer*
Kampf, William Ira *lawyer*
Kaplan, Sheldon *lawyer*
Karan, Bradlee *lawyer, educator*
Kelly, A. David *lawyer*
Keppel, William James *lawyer, educator*
Keyes, Jeffrey J. *lawyer*
Kilbourn, William Douglas, Jr. *law educator*
Klaas, Paul Barry *lawyer*
Koeppen, Bart *law educator, consultant*
Koneck, John M. *lawyer*
Krohnke, Duane W. *lawyer*
Landry, Paul Leonard *lawyer*
Lareau, Richard George *lawyer*
Lazar, Raymond Michael *lawyer, educator*
Lebedoff, David M. *lawyer, author, investment advisor*
Lebedoff, Randy Miller *lawyer*
Lindgren, D(erbin) Kenneth, Jr. *retired lawyer*
Lofstrom, Mark D. *lawyer, educator, communications executive*
Magnuson, Roger James *lawyer*
Manning, William Henry *lawyer*
Manthey, Thomas Richard *lawyer*
Marshall, Siri Swenson *corporate lawyer*
Martin, Phillip Hammond *lawyer*
Matthews, James Shadley *lawyer*
McClintock, George Dunlap *lawyer*
McGuire, Timothy James *lawyer, editor*
McNamara, Michael John *lawyer*
Mellum, Gale Robert *lawyer*
Meshbesher, Ronald I. *lawyer*
Minish, Robert Arthur *lawyer*
Mooty, Bruce Wilson *lawyer*
Mooty, John William *lawyer*
Morrison, Fred LaMont *law educator*
Myers, Howard Sam *lawyer*
Neff, Fred Leonard *lawyer*
Nelson, Gary Michael *lawyer*
Nelson, Richard Arthur *lawyer*
Nelson, Steven Craig *lawyer*
Nemo, Anthony James *lawyer*
O'Neill, Brian Boru *lawyer*
Palmer, Brian Eugene *lawyer*

Palmer, Deborah Jean *lawyer*
Parsons, Charles Allan, Jr. *lawyer*
Pluimer, Edward J. *lawyer*
Potuznik, Charles Laddy *lawyer*
Pratte, Robert John *lawyer*
Price, Joseph Michael *lawyer*
Rachie, Cyrus *lawyer*
Radmer, Michael John *lawyer, educator*
Rebane, John T. *lawyer*
Rein, Stanley Michael *lawyer*
Reinhart, Robert Rountree, Jr. *lawyer*
Reister, Raymond Alex *retired lawyer*
Reske, Steven David *lawyer, writer*
Reuter, James William *lawyer*
Rockenstein, Walter Harrison, II *lawyer*
Rockwell, Winthrop Adams *lawyer*
Roe, Roger Rolland *lawyer*
Saeks, Allen Irving *lawyer*
Safley, James Robert *lawyer*
Sanner, Royce Norman *lawyer*
Sawicki, Zbigniew Peter *lawyer*
Schermer, Judith Kahn *lawyer*
Schnell, Robert Lee, Jr. *lawyer*
Schnobrich, Roger William *lawyer*
Schoettle, Ferdinand P. *lawyer, educator*
Shnider, Bruce Jay *lawyer*
Shulman, Daniel Rees *lawyer*
Silver, Alan Irving *lawyer*
Silverman, Robert Joseph *lawyer*
Soland, Norman R. *corporate lawyer*
Sortland, Paul Allan *lawyer*
Stageberg, Roger V. *lawyer*
Steilen, James R. *lawyer*
Stern, Leo G. *lawyer*
Stroup, Stanley Stephenson *lawyer, educator*
Struthers, Margo S. *lawyer*
Struyk, Robert John *lawyer*
Tanick, Marshall Howard *lawyer, law educator*
Todd, John Joseph *lawyer*
Trucano, Michael *lawyer*
Ueland, Sigurd, Jr. *lawyer*
Vander Molen, Thomas Dale *lawyer*
Wahoske, Michael James *lawyer*
Whelpley, Dennis Porter *lawyer*
Wille, Karin L. *lawyer*
Windhorst, John William, Jr. *lawyer*
Woods, Robert Edward *lawyer*
Younger, Judith Tess *lawyer, educator*
Zalk, Robert H. *lawyer*
Zotaley, Byron Leo *lawyer*

### Minnetonka Mills
Hoard, Heidi Marie *lawyer*

### North Saint Paul
O'Brien, Daniel William *lawyer, corporation executive*

### Pipestone
Scott, William Paul *lawyer*

### Plymouth
Bergerson, David Raymond *lawyer*

### Rochester
Orwoll, Gregg S. K. *lawyer*
Seeger, Ronald L. *lawyer*
Wicks, John R. *lawyer*

### Saint Cloud
Hughes, Kevin John *lawyer*
Lalor, Edward David Darrell *labor and employment arbitrator, lawyer*
Seifert, Luke Michael *lawyer*

### Saint Louis Park
Rothenberg, Elliot Calvin *lawyer, writer*

### Saint Paul
Allison, John Robert *lawyer*
Brehl, James William *lawyer*
Daly, Joseph Leo *law educator*
Devoy, Kimball John *lawyer*
Dietz, Charlton Henry *lawyer*
Ebert, Robert Alvin *retired lawyer, retired airline executive*
Failinger, Marie Anita *law educator, editor*
Fisk, Martin H. *lawyer*
Friel, Bernard Preston *lawyer*
Galvin, Michael John, Jr. *lawyer*
Geis, Jerome Arthur *lawyer, legal educator*
Goodrich, Leon Raymond *lawyer*
Halva, Allen Keith *legal publications consultant*
Hammond, Frank Joseph *lawyer*
Hansen, Robyn L. *lawyer*
Hasling, Robert J. *retired lawyer*
Haynsworth, Harry Jay, IV *lawyer, educator*
Heidenreich, Douglas Robert *lawyer*
Hirst, Richard B. *lawyer*
Johnson, Paul Oren *lawyer*
Jones, C. Paul *lawyer, educator*
Kane, Thomas Patrick *lawyer*
Kaner, Harvey Sheldon *lawyer, executive*
Kirwin, Kenneth Francis *law educator*
Maclin, Alan Hall *lawyer*
Martin, David George *lawyer*
McNeely, John J. *lawyer*
Seymour, Mary Frances *lawyer*
Seymour, McNeil Vernam *lawyer*
Sippel, William Leroy *lawyer*
Ursu, John Joseph *lawyer*

### Shoreview
Bertelsen, Michael William *lawyer*

### South Saint Paul
Pugh, Thomas Wilfred *lawyer*

### Wayzata
Alton, Howard Robert, Jr. *lawyer, real estate and food company executive*
Reutiman, Robert William, Jr. *lawyer*

## MISSISSIPPI

### Clarksdale
Curtis, Chester Harris *lawyer, retired bank executive*

### Cleveland
Alexander, William Brooks *lawyer, former state senator*

### Columbus
Gholson, Hunter Maurice *lawyer*
Pounds, Billy Dean *law educator*

### Greenville
Martin, Andrew Ayers *lawyer, physician, educator*

### Gulfport
Allen, Harry Roger *lawyer*
Harral, John Menteith *lawyer*
Hopkins, Alben Norris *lawyer*

### Jackson
Barnett, Robert Glenn *lawyer*
Butler, George Harrison *lawyer*
Chinn, Mark Allan *lawyer*
Clark, David Wright *lawyer*
Corlew, John Gordon *lawyer*
Fuselier, Louis Alfred *lawyer*
Hammond, Frank Jefferson, III *lawyer*
Henegan, John C(lark) *lawyer*
Hosemann, C. Delbert, Jr. *lawyer*
Hurt, Joseph Richard *law educator*
Langford, James Jerry *lawyer*
Lilly, Thomas Gerald *lawyer*
Moize, Jerry Dee *lawyer, government official*
Phillips, George Landon *prosecutor*
Pyle, Luther Arnold *lawyer*
Ray, H. M. *lawyer*

### Meridian
Eppes, Walter W., Jr. *lawyer*

### Ocean Springs
Lawson-Jowett, M. Juliet *lawyer*
Luckey, Alwyn Hall *lawyer*

### Oxford
Rayburn, S. T. *lawyer*

### Pascagoula
Krebs, Robert Preston *lawyer*
Roberts, David Ambrose *lawyer*

### Ridgeland
Dye, Bradford Johnson, Jr. *lawyer, former state official*

### Tupelo
Bush, Fred Marshall, Jr. *lawyer*
Lukas, Joseph Frank *paralegal*

## MISSOURI

### Ballwin
Banton, Stephen Chandler *lawyer*

### Camdenton
Clark, Mark Jeffrey *paralegal, researcher*

### Cape Girardeau
McManaman, Kenneth Charles *lawyer*

### Cassville
Melton, Emory Leon *lawyer, state legislator, publisher*

### Chesterfield
Hier, Marshall David *lawyer*
Pollihan, Thomas Henry *lawyer*

### Clayton
Belz, Mark *lawyer*
Klarich, David John *lawyer, state senator*
Livergood, Robert Frank *prosecutor*

### Columbia
Fisch, William Bales *lawyer, educator*
Parrigin, Elizabeth Ellington *lawyer*
Welliver, Warren Dee *lawyer, retired state supreme court justice*
Westbrook, James Edwin *lawyer, educator*

### Fenton
Stolar, Henry Samuel *lawyer*

### Grandview
Dietrich, William Gale *lawyer, real estate developer, consultant*

### Hannibal
Terrell, James Daniel *lawyer*
Welch, Joseph Daniel *lawyer*

### Independence
Cady, Elwyn Loomis, Jr. *medicolegal consultant, educator*
Lashley, Curtis Dale *lawyer*
Walsh, Rodger John *lawyer*

### Jefferson City
Bartlett, Alex *lawyer*
Deutsch, James Bernard *lawyer*
Gaw, Robert Steven *lawyer, state representative*
Tettlebaum, Harvey M. *lawyer*

### Joplin
Guillory, Jeffery Michael *lawyer*
Scott, Robert Haywood, Jr. *lawyer*

### Kansas City
Anderson, Christopher James *lawyer*
Ayers, Jeffrey David *lawyer*
Ball, Owen Keith, Jr. *lawyer*
Bates, William Hubert *lawyer*
Becker, Thomas Bain *lawyer*
Beckett, Theodore Charles *lawyer*
Beckett, Theodore Cornwall *lawyer*
Beihl, Frederick *lawyer*
Berkowitz, Lawrence M. *lawyer*
Bevan, Robert Lewis *lawyer*
Black, John Sheldon *lawyer*
Blackwell, Menefee Davis *lawyer*
Borel, Steven James *lawyer*
Bradshaw, Jean Paul, II *lawyer*
Brous, Thomas Richard *lawyer*
Bruening, Richard P(atrick) *lawyer*
Bryant, Richard Todd *lawyer*
Canfield, Robert Cleo *lawyer*
Cavitt, Bruce Edward *lawyer*
Chisholm, Donald Herbert *lawyer*
Clark, Charles Edward *arbitrator*
Clarke, Milton Charles *lawyer*
Cozad, John Condon *lawyer*
Crawford, Howard Allen *lawyer*
Cross, William Dennis *lawyer*
Davis, John Charles *lawyer*
Deacy, Thomas Edward, Jr. *lawyer*
Edgar, John M. *lawyer*
Eldridge, Truman Kermit, Jr. *lawyer*
Field, Lyman *lawyer*
Foster, Mark Stephen *lawyer*
Fremont, Ernest Hoar, Jr. *lawyer*
French, Linda Jean *lawyer*
Gardner, Brian E. *lawyer*
Giffin, Reggie Craig *lawyer*
Graham, Harold Steven *lawyer*
Greer, Norris E. *lawyer*
Helder, Jan Pleasant, Jr. *lawyer*
Hopkins, William Carlisle, II *lawyer*
Hubbell, Ernest *lawyer*
Johnson, Leonard James *lawyer*
Johnson, Mark Eugene *lawyer*
Joyce, Michael Patrick *lawyer*
Kaplan, Harvey L. *lawyer*
Kaufman, Michelle Stark *lawyer*
Kelley, Clarence Marion *retired lawyer*
Kilroy, John Muir *lawyer*
Kilroy, William Terrence *lawyer*
King, Richard Allen *lawyer*
Koelling, Thomas Winsor *lawyer*
Kroenert, Robert Morgan *lawyer*
Langworthy, Robert Burton *lawyer*
Levings, Theresa Lawrence *lawyer*
Lindsey, David Hosford *lawyer*
Lombardi, Cornelius Ennis, Jr. *lawyer*
Loudon, Donald Hoover *lawyer*
Manka, Ronald Eugene *lawyer*
Matheny, Edward Taylor, Jr. *lawyer*
Matzeder, Jean Marie Znidarsic *lawyer*
McManus, James William *lawyer*
Mick, Howard Harold *lawyer*
Milton, Chad Earl *lawyer*
Molzen, Christopher John *lawyer*
Moore, Stephen James *lawyer*
Mordy, James Calvin *lawyer*
Newcom, Jennings Jay *lawyer*
Newsom, James Thomas *lawyer*
Northrip, Robert Earl *lawyer*
Owen, Loyd Eugene, Jr. *lawyer*
Owens, Stephen J. *lawyer*
Palmer, Dennis Dale *lawyer*
Pearce, Margaret Tranne *law librarian*
Pelofsky, Joel *lawyer*
Popper, Robert *law educator, former dean*
Price, James Tucker *lawyer*
Prugh, William Byron *lawyer*
Ralston, Richard H. *lawyer*
Sanders, William Huggins *lawyer, rancher*
Satterlee, Terry Jean *lawyer*
Schult, Thomas Peter *lawyer*
Setzler, Edward Allan *lawyer*
Shaw, John W. *lawyer*
Shay, David E. *lawyer*
Smith, R(onald) Scott *lawyer*
Smithson, Lowell Lee *lawyer*
Spalty, Edward Robert *lawyer*
Spencer, Richard Henry *lawyer*
Stoup, Arthur Harry *lawyer*
Toll, Perry Mark *lawyer*
Vandever, William Dirk *lawyer*
Varner, Barton Douglas *lawyer*
Vering, John Albert *lawyer*
Viani, James L. *lawyer*
Whittaker, Judith Ann Cameron *lawyer*
Wirken, James Charles *lawyer*
Woods, Richard Dale *lawyer*
Wrobley, Ralph Gene *lawyer*
Wyrsch, James Robert *lawyer, educator, author*

### Kirkwood
Gibbons, Michael Randolph *lawyer*

### Lamar
Geddie, Rowland Hill, III *lawyer*

### Lebanon
Hutson, Don *lawyer*

### Maryland Heights
Sobol, Lawrence Raymond *lawyer*

### Nevada
Ewing, Lynn Moore, Jr. *lawyer*

### Saint Joseph
Kranitz, Theodore Mitchell *lawyer*
Taylor, Michael Leslie *lawyer*

### Saint Louis
Appleton, R. O., Jr. *lawyer*
Arnold, John Fox *lawyer*
Attanasio, John Baptist *law educator*
Atwood, Hollye Stolz *lawyer*
Aylward, Ronald Lee *lawyer*
Babington, Charles Martin, III *lawyer*
Baldwin, Edwin Steedman *lawyer*
Barken, Bernard Allen *lawyer*
Baum, Gordon Lee *lawyer, non-profit organization administrator*
Bean, Bourne *lawyer*
Becker, David Mandel *legal educator, author, consultant*
Berendt, Robert Tryon *lawyer*
Berger, John Torrey, Jr. *lawyer*
Bernstein, Merton Clay *lawyer, educator, arbitrator*
Bonacorsi, Mary Catherine *lawyer*
Boyarsky, Saul *lawyer, forensic urologist, physiologist, educator*
Breece, Robert William, Jr. *lawyer*
Brickey, Kathleen Fitzgerald *law educator*
Brickler, John Weise *lawyer*
Brickson, Richard Alan *lawyer*
Brody, Lawrence *lawyer, educator*
Brown, Paul Sherman *lawyer*
Brownlee, Robert Hammel *lawyer*
Bryan, Henry C(lark), Jr. *lawyer*
Carp, Richard Lawrence (Larry Carp) *lawyer*
Carr, Gary Thomas *lawyer*
Chestnut, Kathi Lynne *lawyer*
Clear, John Michael *lawyer*
Collins, James Slade, II *lawyer*
Conran, Joseph Palmer *lawyer*
Cornfeld, Dave Louis *lawyer*
Crebs, P(aul) Terence *lawyer*
Denneen, John Paul *lawyer*
DeWoskin, Alan Ellis *lawyer*
Donohue, Carroll John *lawyer*
Dorsey, Gray Lankford *law educator emeritus*
Dorwart, Donald Bruce *lawyer*
Dowd, Edward L., Jr. *prosecutor*
Duesenberg, Richard William *lawyer*
Erwin, James Walter *lawyer*
Falk, William James *lawyer*
Farnam, Thomas Campbell *lawyer, educator*
Farris, Clyde C. *lawyer*
Fogle, James Lee *lawyer*
Fryer, Edwin Samuel *lawyer*
Gerard, Jules Bernard *law educator*
Gershenson, Harry *lawyer*
Gianoulakis, John Louis *lawyer*
Gillis, John L., Jr. *lawyer*
Gladding, Nicholas C. *lawyer*
Godiner, Donald Leonard *lawyer*
Goebel, John J. *lawyer*
Goldstein, Michael Gerald *lawyer*
Goldstein, Steven *lawyer*
Goodman, Harold S. *lawyer*
Gray, Charles Elmer *lawyer, rancher, investor*
Green, Dennis Joseph *lawyer*
Greenfield, Milton, Jr. *lawyer*
Guerri, William Grant *lawyer*
Hansen, Charles *lawyer*
Harris, Whitney Robson *lawyer*
Hays, Ruth *lawyer*
Hecker, George Sprake *lawyer*
Hellmuth, Theodore Henning *lawyer*
Hetlage, Robert Owen *lawyer*
Hiles, Bradley Stephen *lawyer*
Immel, Vincent Clare *retired law educator*
Inkley, John James, Jr. *lawyer*
Jaudes, Richard Edward *lawyer*
Kauffman, William Ray *lawyer*
Keller, Juan Dane *lawyer*
Klobasa, John Anthony *lawyer*
Krehbiel, Robert J. *lawyer*
Lander, David Allan *lawyer*
Lane, Frank Joseph, Jr. *lawyer*
Lause, Michael Francis *lawyer*
Lebowitz, Albert *lawyer, author*
Lents, Don Glaude *lawyer*
Levin, Ronald Mark *law educator*
Lieberman, Edward Jay *lawyer*
Lipeles, Maxine Ina *lawyer*
Logan, Joseph Prescott *lawyer*
Lowenhaupt, Charles Abraham *lawyer*
Luberda, George Joseph *lawyer, educator*
Lucy, Robert Meredith *lawyer*
Mandelker, Daniel Robert *law educator*
Mandelstamm, Jerome Robert *lawyer*
McCarter, Charles Chase *lawyer*
Mc Daniel, James Edwin *lawyer*
McKinnis, Michael B. *lawyer*
McMullin, Kimball Ray *lawyer*
Meisel, George Vincent *lawyer*
Merrill, Charles Eugene *lawyer*
Metcalfe, Walter Lee, Jr. *lawyer*
Mohan, John J. *lawyer*
Moore, McPherson Dorsett *lawyer*
Mulligan, Michael Dennis *lawyer*
Newman, Charles A. *lawyer*
Newman, Joan Meskiel *lawyer*
Noel, Edwin Lawrence *lawyer*
O'Keefe, Michael Daniel *lawyer*
Olson, Robert Grant *lawyer*
O'Malley, Kevin Francis *lawyer, writer, educator*
Palans, Lloyd Alex *lawyer*
Peper, Christian Baird *lawyer*
Pickle, Robert Douglas *lawyer, footwear industry executive*
Poscover, Maury B. *lawyer*
Preuss, Ronald Stephen *lawyer, educator*
Rataj, Edward William *lawyer*
Ring, Lucile Wiley *lawyer*
Ritter, Robert Forcier *lawyer*
Ritterskamp, Douglas Dolvin *lawyer*
Rubenstein, Jerome Max *lawyer*
Sachs, Alan Arthur *lawyer, corporate executive*
Sale, Llewellyn, III *lawyer*
Sandberg, John Steven *lawyer*
Sant, John Talbot *lawyer*
Schoene, Kathleen Snyder *lawyer*
Schwabe, John Bennett, II *lawyer*
Searls, Eileen Haughey *lawyer, librarian, educator*
Sestric, Anthony James *lawyer*
Shands, Courtney, Jr. *lawyer*
Shaw, John Arthur *lawyer*
Sherby, Kathleen Reilly *lawyer*
Siegel, Sarah Ann *lawyer*
Smith, Arthur Lee *lawyer*
Suhre, Walter Anthony, Jr. *retired lawyer and brewery executive*
Teasdale, Kenneth Fulbright *lawyer*
Thomas, Rhonda Churchill *lawyer*
Tierney, Michael Edward *lawyer*
Turley, Michael Roy *lawyer*
Van Cleve, William Moore *lawyer*
Virtel, James John *lawyer*
Walsh, Joseph Leo, III *lawyer*
Walsh, Thomas Charles *lawyer*
Wang, Hengtao (Hank T. Wang) *lawyer*
Watters, Richard Donald *lawyer*
Weiss, Charles Andrew *lawyer*
Willard, Gregory Dale *lawyer*
Williams, Theodore Joseph, Jr. *lawyer*
Wilson, Margaret Bush *lawyer, civil rights leader*
Wilson, Michael E. *lawyer*
Winning, John Patrick *lawyer*
Wolff, Frank Pierce, Jr. *lawyer*
Woodruff, Bruce Emery *lawyer*
Young, Marvin Oscar *lawyer*

### Springfield
Carlson, Thomas Joseph *lawyer, real estate developer, former mayor*
FitzGerald, Kevin Michael *lawyer*
Hulston, John Kenton *lawyer*
Jones, Sheryl Leanne *paralegal*
Lowther, Gerald Halbert *lawyer*
McDonald, William Henry *lawyer*
Penninger, William Holt, Jr. *lawyer*
Roberts, Patrick Kent *lawyer*
Starnes, James Wright *lawyer*
Woody, Donald Eugene *lawyer*

### Wildwood
Nicely, Constance Marie *paralegal, physician recruiter, medical consultant*

## Princeton
Ackourey, Peter Paul *lawyer*
Anderson, Ellis Bernard *retired lawyer, pharmaceutical company executive*
Beidler, Marsha Wolf *lawyer*
Bergman, Edward Jonathan *lawyer*
Brennan, William Joseph, III *lawyer*
Carter, Jeanne Wilmot *lawyer, publisher*
Connor, Geoffrey Michael *lawyer*
Durst, Robert Joseph, II *lawyer*
Hill, James Scott *lawyer*
Judge, Marty M. *lawyer*
Katz, Stanley Nider *law history educator, association executive*
Katzenbach, Nicholas deBelleville *lawyer*
Savitsky, Thomas Robert *lawyer*
Wood, Joshua Warren, III *lawyer, foundation executive*
Zimmer, Richard Alan *lawyer*

## Red Bank
Auerbach, Philip Gary *lawyer*
Nucciarone, A. Patrick *lawyer*
Rogers, Lee Jasper *lawyer*
Warshaw, Michael Thomas *lawyer*

## Ridgewood
Harris, Micalyn Shafer *lawyer*
Trocano, Russell Peter *lawyer*

## Roseland
Berkowitz, Bernard Solomon *lawyer*
D'Avella, Bernard Johnson, Jr. *lawyer*
Dore, Michael *lawyer, educator*
Drasco, Dennis J. *lawyer*
Eakeley, Douglas Scott *lawyer*
Fleischman, Joseph Jacob *lawyer*
Foster, M. Joan *lawyer*
Goldstein, Marvin Mark *lawyer*
Greenberg, Stephen Michael *lawyer, businesss executive*
Kemph, Carleton Richard *lawyer*
Kohl, Benedict M. *lawyer*
Levithan, Allen B. *lawyer*
Lowenstein, Alan Victor *lawyer*
MacKay, John Robert, II *lawyer*
Saloman, Mark Andrew *lawyer*
Shoulson, Bruce Dove *lawyer*
Slutsky, Kenneth Joel *lawyer*
Stern, Herbert Jay *lawyer*
Tarino, Gary Edward *lawyer*
Vanderbilt, Arthur T., II *lawyer*
Wovsaniker, Alan *lawyer, educator*

## Salem
Petrin, Helen Fite *lawyer, consultant*

## Sayreville
Corman, Randy *lawyer*

## Scotch Plains
Klock, John Henry *lawyer*

## Secaucus
Endyke, Mary Beth *lawyer*
Fahy, John J. *lawyer*
Rosenblum, Edward G. *lawyer*

## Short Hills
Greenberg, Carl *lawyer*
Hazlehurst, Robert Purviance, Jr. *lawyer*
Siegfried, David Charles *lawyer*

## Shrewsbury
Hopkins, Charles Peter, II *lawyer*

## Somerset
Chaitman, Helen Davis *lawyer*
Kozlowski, Thomas Joseph, Jr. *lawyer, trust company executive*
Robinson, Patricia Snyder *lawyer*

## Somerville
Hutcheon, Peter David *lawyer*

## South Plainfield
Saltz, Ralph *corporate lawyer*

## Spring Lake
Anderson, James Francis *lawyer*

## Springfield
Grayson, Bette Rita *lawyer*

## Summit
Kenyon, Edward Tipton *lawyer*
McDonough, Patrick Joseph, Jr. *lawyer*
Mulreany, Robert Henry *retired lawyer*
Parsons, Judson Aspinwall, Jr. *lawyer*
Thompson, Robert L., Jr. *lawyer*
Woller, James Alan *lawyer*

## Tenafly
Badr, Gamal Moursi *Arab laws consultant*

## Toms River
Whitman, Russell Wilson *lawyer*

## Trenton
Bigham, William J. *lawyer*
Caldwell, Wesley Stuart, III *lawyer, lobbyist*
Hill, Robyn Marcella *lawyer*
Poritz, Deborah T. *former state attorney general, state judge*
Sterns, Joel Henry *lawyer*

## Verona
Ward, Roger Coursen *lawyer*

## Wanaque
Jordan, Leo John *lawyer*

## Warren
Kasper, Horst Manfred *lawyer*
Massler, Howard Arnold *lawyer, corporate executive*

## Weehawken
Hayden, Joseph A., Jr. *lawyer*

## West Orange
Askin, Marilyn *lawyer*
Haney, James Kevin *lawyer*
Kushen, Allan Stanford *retired lawyer*
Richmond, Harold Nicholas *lawyer*

## Westfield
†Decker, Mark Richard *lawyer*
Jacobson, Gary Steven *lawyer*

## Woodbridge
Becker, Frederic Kenneth *lawyer*
Brauth, Marvin Jeffrey *lawyer*
Brown, Morris *lawyer*
Buchsbaum, Peter A. *lawyer*
Cirafesi, Robert J. *lawyer*
Constantinou, Clay *lawyer*
Hoberman, Stuart A. *lawyer*
Jaffe, Sheldon Eugene *lawyer*
Lepelstat, Martin L. *lawyer*
McCarthy, G. Daniel *lawyer*

## Woodbury
White, John Lindsey *lawyer*

## Woodcliff Lake
Pollak, Cathy Jane *lawyer*
Sneirson, Marilyn *lawyer*

# NEW MEXICO

## Albuquerque
Addis, Richard Barton *lawyer*
Bardacke, Paul Gregory *lawyer, former attorney general*
Beach, Arthur O'Neal *lawyer*
Bova, Vincent Arthur, Jr. *lawyer, consultant, photographer*
Cargo, David Francis *lawyer*
Caruso, Mark John *lawyer*
Ellis, Willis Hill *lawyer, educator*
Haltom, B(illy) Reid *lawyer*
Harman, Wallace Patrick *lawyer*
Hart, Frederick Michael *law educator*
Lawit, John Walter *lawyer*
Loubet, Jeffrey W. *lawyer*
McCue, Stephen Patrick *lawyer*
Meiering, Mark C. *lawyer*
Paster, Janice D. *lawyer, former state legislator*
Roehl, Jerrald J(oseph) *lawyer*
Romero, Jeff *lawyer*
Schoen, Stevan Jay *lawyer*
Sisk, Daniel Arthur *lawyer*
Slade, Lynn Heyer *lawyer*
Stephenson, Barbera Wertz *lawyer*
Thompson, Rufus E. *lawyer*
Youngdahl, James Edward *lawyer*

## Carlsbad
Byers, Matthew T(odd) *lawyer, educator*

## Farmington
Morgan, Jack M. *lawyer*
Titus, Victor Allen *lawyer*

## Hobbs
Stout, Lowell *lawyer*

## Las Cruces
Lutz, William Lan *lawyer*
Sandenaw, Thomas Arthur, Jr. *lawyer*

## Roswell
Olson, Richard Earl *lawyer, state legislator*

## Santa Fe
Besing, Ray Gilbert *lawyer*
Burton, John Paul (Jack Burton) *lawyer*
Casey, Patrick Anthony *lawyer*
Citrin, Phillip Marshall *retired lawyer*
Coffield, Conrad Eugene *lawyer*
Cuming, George Scott *retired lawyer, retired gas company official*
Dodds, Robert James, III *lawyer*
Hickey, John Miller *lawyer*
Noland, Charles Donald *lawyer, educator*
Pound, John Bennett *lawyer*
Quintana, Sammy J. *lawyer*
Roesler, John Bruce *lawyer*
Schwarz, Michael *lawyer*
Stephenson, Donnan *lawyer, former state supreme court justice*
Stevens, Ron A. *lawyer, public interest organization administrator*

## Seneca
Monroe, Kendyl Kurth *retired lawyer*

## Silver City
Foy, Thomas Paul *lawyer, state legislator, banker*

## Tijeras
Berry, Dawn Bradley *lawyer, writer*

# NEW YORK

## Albany
Beach, John Arthur *lawyer*
Brown, Judith Anne *law librarian*
Case, Forrest N., Jr. *lawyer*
Catalano, Jane Donna *lawyer*
Couch, Mark Woodworth *lawyer*
Danziger, Peter *lawyer*
Ferris, Walter V. *retired lawyer*
Holt-Harris, John Evan, Jr. *lawyer*
Hyde, Carol Ann *lawyer*
Koff, Howard Michael *lawyer*
Lewis, Kirk McArthur *lawyer*
Rohan, Brian Patrick *lawyer*
Salkin, Patricia E. *law educator*
Siegel, David Donald *law educator*
Sprow, Howard Thomas *lawyer, educator*
Teitelbaum, Steven Usher *lawyer*

## Amagansett
Frankl, Kenneth Richard *retired lawyer*

## Ardsley On Hudson
Stein, Milton Michael *lawyer*

## Armonk
Quinn, James W. *lawyer*
Weill, Richard L. *lawyer*

## Auburn
Wolczyk, Joseph Michael *lawyer*

## Babylon
Hennelly, Edmund Paul *lawyer, oil company executive*

## Batavia
Litteer, Harold Hunter, Jr. *lawyer*

## Bedford
Atkins, Ronald Raymond *lawyer*

## Bethpage
Sanna, Richard Jeffrey *lawyer*

## Binghamton
Anderson, Warren Mattice *lawyer*
Gerhart, Eugene Clifton *lawyer*
Regenbogen, Adam *lawyer*

## Bronx
Adler, Nadia C. *lawyer*
Balka, Sigmund Ronell *lawyer*
Cornfield, Melvin *lawyer, university institute director*
Garance, Dominick (D. G. Garan) *lawyer, author*

## Bronxville
Cook, Charles David *international lawyer, arbitrator, consultant*
Falvey, Patrick Joseph *lawyer*
Recabo, Jaime Miguel *lawyer*

## Brooklyn
Fallek, Andrew Michael *lawyer*
Graham, Arnold Harold *lawyer, educator*
Karmel, Roberta Segal *lawyer, educator*
Landron, Michel John *lawyer*
Lewis, Felice Flanery *lawyer, educator*
Lizt, Sara Enid Vanefsky *lawyer, educator*
Onken, George Marcellus *lawyer*
Pinczower, Kenneth Ephraim *lawyer*
Poser, Norman Stanley *law educator*
Raskind, Leo Joseph *law educator*
Roth, Pamela Susan *lawyer*
Schussler, Theodore *lawyer, physician, educator*
†Skolnik, Miriam *lawyer*

## Buffalo
Barney, Thomas McNamee *lawyer*
Bean, Edwin Temple, Jr. *lawyer*
Blaine, Charles Gillespie *retired lawyer*
Brock, David George *lawyer*
Brydges, Thomas Eugene *lawyer*
Carmichael, Donald Scott *lawyer, business executive*
Clemens, David Allen *lawyer*
Cordes, Alexander Charles *lawyer*
Day, Donald Sheldon *lawyer*
Duke, Emanuel *lawyer*
Feuerstein, Alan Ricky *lawyer, consultant*
Floyd, David Kenneth *lawyer, judge*
Freedman, Maryann Saccomando *lawyer*
Fuzak, Victor Thaddeus *lawyer*
Gardner, Arnold Burton *lawyer*
Garvey, James Anthony *lawyer*
Gerstman, Sharon Stern *lawyer*
Glanville, Robert Edward *lawyer*
Goldberg, Neil A. *lawyer*
Grasser, George Robert *lawyer*
Gray, F(rederick) William, III *lawyer*
Hall, David Edward *lawyer*
Halpern, Ralph Lawrence *lawyer*
Hayes, J. Michael *lawyer*
Hazlewood, Olga Alicia *lawyer, educator*
Head, Christopher Alan *lawyer*
Headrick, Thomas Edward *lawyer, educator*
Heilman, Pamela Davis *lawyer*
Kieffer, James Marshall *lawyer*
Kristoff, Karl W. *lawyer*
Lippes, Gerald Sanford *lawyer, business executive*
MacLeod, Gordon Albert *retired lawyer*
Manning, Kenneth Alan *lawyer*
McElvein, Thomas I., Jr. *lawyer*
Mucci, Gary Louis *lawyer*
Murray, William Michael *lawyer*
Newman, Stephen Michael *lawyer*
Odza, Randall M. *lawyer*
O'Loughlin, Sandra S. *lawyer*
Pajak, David Joseph *lawyer, consultant*
Pearson, Paul David *lawyer, mediator*
Pitegoff, Peter Robert *lawyer, educator*
Rachlin, Lauren David *lawyer*
Ritchie, Stafford Duff, II *lawyer*
Salisbury, Eugene W. *lawyer, justice*
Sampson, John David *lawyer*
Schroeder, Harold Kenneth, Jr. *lawyer*
Sherwood, Arthur Morley *lawyer*
Stachowski, Michael Joseph *lawyer*
Toohey, Philip S. *lawyer*
Wickser, John Philip *lawyer*
Wisbaum, Wayne David *lawyer*

## Campbell Hall
Stone, Peter George *lawyer, publishing company executive*

## Canaan
Pennell, William Brooke *lawyer*

## Carle Place
Matturro, Anthony *lawyer*
Smolev, Terence Elliot *lawyer, educator*

## Carmel
Lowe, E(dwin) Nobles *lawyer*

## Cedarhurst
Taubenfeld, Harry Samuel *lawyer*

## Chappaqua
Howard, John Brigham *lawyer, foundation executive*

## Cheektowaga
LaForest, Lana Jean *lawyer, real estate broker*

## Corning
Becraft, Charles D., Jr. *lawyer*
Hauselt, Denise Ann *lawyer*
Ughetta, William Casper *lawyer, manufacturing company executive*

## Cutchogue
O'Connell, Francis Joseph *lawyer, arbitrator*

## Dobbs Ferry
Juettner, Diana D'Amico *lawyer, educator*
Maiocchi, Christine *lawyer*

## East Aurora
Brott, Irving Deerin, Jr. *lawyer, judge*

## East Meadow
Adler, Ira Jay *lawyer*

## Eastchester
Katz, Kenneth Arthur *lawyer, accountant*
Keeffe, John Arthur *lawyer, director*

## Fairport
Tomaino, Michael Thomas *lawyer*

## Farmingdale
Firetog, Theodore Warren *lawyer*

## Fayetteville
Evans, Nolly Seymour *lawyer*

## Floral Park
Chatoff, Michael Alan *lawyer*

## Flushing
Bohner, Robert Joseph *lawyer*
Schwartz, Estar Alma *lawyer*

## Garden City
Balkan, Kenneth J. *lawyer*
Caputo, Kathryn Mary *paralegal*
Cook, George Valentine *lawyer*
Corsi, Philip Donald *lawyer*
Fishberg, Gerard *lawyer*
Friedman, Sari Martin *lawyer*
Gordon, Jay F(isher) *lawyer*
Hand, Stephen Block *lawyer*
Kreger-Grella, Cheryl Leslie *lawyer*
Lioz, Lawrence Stephen *lawyer, accountant*
Minicucci, Richard Francis *lawyer, former hospital administrator*
Posch, Robert John, Jr. *lawyer*
Tucker, William P. *lawyer, writer*

## Glen Cove
Mills, Charles Gardner *lawyer*

## Glens Falls
Bartlett, Richard James *lawyer, former university dean*
McMillen, Robert Stewart *lawyer*

## Great Neck
Busner, Philip H. *lawyer*
Gellman, Yale H. *lawyer*
Glushien, Morris P. *lawyer, arbitrator*
Samanowitz, Ronald Arthur *lawyer*
Wachsman, Harvey Frederick *lawyer, neurosurgeon*

## Greene
Sternberg, Paul J. *lawyer*

## Greenvale
Halper, Emanuel B(arry) *real estate lawyer, developer, consultant, author*

## Guilderland
Sills, Nancy Mintz *lawyer*

## Hamburg
Gaughan, Dennis Charles *lawyer*

## Hammond
Musselman, Francis Haas *lawyer*

## Hastings Hdsn
Thornlow, Carolyn *law firm administrator, consultant*

## Hawthorne
Traub, Richard Kenneth *lawyer*

## Hempstead
Agata, Burton C. *lawyer, educator*
Freedman, Monroe Henry *lawyer, educator, columnist*
Mahon, Malachy Thomas *lawyer, educator*
Rabinowitz, Stuart *law educator, dean*

## Henrietta
Snyder, Donald Edward *corporate executive*

## Hicksville
Giuffré, John Joseph *lawyer*

## Hillsdale
Lunde, Asbjorn Rudolph *lawyer*

## Huntington
Augello, William Joseph *lawyer*
German, June Resnick *lawyer*
Glickstein, Howard Alan *law educator*
Munson, Nancy Kay *lawyer*
Pratt, George Cheney *law educator, retired federal judge*

## Huntington Station
Schoenfeld, Michael P. *lawyer*

## Irvington
Bonomi, John Gurnee *retired lawyer*
Sexter, Deborah Rae *lawyer*

## Ithaca
Alexander, Gregory Stewart *law educator*
Barcelo, John James, III *law educator*

Barney, John Charles *lawyer*
Clermont, Kevin Michael *law educator*
Court, Patricia Grace *law librarian*
Cramton, Roger Conant *lawyer, legal educator*
Eisenberg, Theodore *law educator*
Germain, Claire Madeleine *law librarian, educator*
Hay, George Alan *law and economics educator*
Hillman, Robert Andrew *law educator, former university dean*
Kent, Robert Brydon *law educator*
Macey, Jonathan R. *law educator*
Martin, Peter William *lawyer, educator*
Palmer, Larry Isaac *lawyer, educator*
Rossi, Faust F. *lawyer, educator*
Simson, Gary Joseph *law educator*
Stamp, Neal Roger *lawyer*
Summers, Robert Samuel *lawyer, author, educator*
Thoron, Gray *lawyer, educator*

**Jamaica**
Angione, Howard Francis *lawyer, editor*
Berman, Richard Miles *lawyer*
Reams, Bernard Dinsmore, Jr. *lawyer, educator*
Scheich, John F. *lawyer*
Tschinkel, Andrew Joseph, Jr. *law librarian*

**Jamestown**
DeAngelo, Charles Salvatore *lawyer*
Idzik, Martin Francis *lawyer*

**Jamesville**
DeCrow, Karen *lawyer, author, lecturer*

**Jericho**
Blau, Harvey Ronald *lawyer*
Friedman, David Samuel *lawyer, law review executive*

**Kew Gardens**
Adler, David Neil *lawyer*

**Kinderhook**
Benamati, Dennis Charles *law librarian, editor, consultant*

**Lancaster**
Walsh, J(ohn) B(ronson) *lawyer*

**Larchmont**
Berridge, George Bradford *retired lawyer*
Bloom, Lee Hurley *lawyer, public affairs consultant, retired household products manufacturing executive*
Engel, Ralph Manuel *lawyer*
Halket, Thomas D(aniel) *lawyer*
Lurie, Alvin David *lawyer*
Murphy, James Gilmartin *lawyer*
Pelton, Russell Gilbert *lawyer*
Seton, Charles B. *lawyer*
White, Thomas Edward *lawyer*

**Latham**
Conway, Robert George, Jr. *lawyer*

**Le Roy**
Harner, Timothy R. *lawyer*

**Lido Beach**
Billauer, Barbara Pfeffer *lawyer, educator*

**Lockport**
Penney, Charles Rand *lawyer, civic worker*

**Long Island City**
Barnholdt, Terry Joseph, Jr. *lawyer, real estate executive*
Cushing, Robert Hunter *lawyer, real estate investment executive*
Walker, Linda Lee *lawyer*

**Mamaroneck**
Nolletti, James Joseph *lawyer*

**Manchester**
Wells, Robert Alfred *lawyer*

**Manhasset**
Carucci, Samuel Anthony *lawyer*
Hayes, Arthur Michael *lawyer*

**Margaretville**
Barabash, Claire *lawyer, special education administrator, psychologist*

**Melville**
Green, Carol H. *lawyer, educator, journalist*
Klatell, Robert Edward *lawyer, electronics company executive*
McMillan, Robert Ralph *lawyer*

**Mineola**
Bartlett, Clifford Adams, Jr. *lawyer*
Bartol, Ernest Thomas *lawyer*
Braid, Frederick Donald *lawyer*
Jones, Lawrence Tunnicliffe *lawyer*
Klein, Arnold Spencer *lawyer*
Kral, William George *lawyer*
Lynn, Robert Patrick, Jr. *lawyer*
Meyer, Bernard Stern *lawyer, former judge*
Millman, Bruce Russell *lawyer*
Paterson, Basil Alexander *lawyer*
Rubine, Robert Samuel *lawyer*
Schaffer, David Irving *lawyer*
Stanisci, Thomas William *lawyer*
Tankoos, Sandra Maxine *court reporting services executive*

**Monticello**
Cooke, Lawrence Henry *lawyer, former state chief judge*

**Mount Kisco**
Goodhue, Mary Brier *lawyer, former state senator*

**Neponsit**
Re, Edward Domenic *law educator, retired federal judge*

**New Hartford**
Jones, Hugh Richard *lawyer*

**New Hyde Park**
Lee, Brian Edward *lawyer*
Offner, Eric Delmonte *lawyer*

**New Rochelle**
Blotner, Norman David *lawyer, real estate broker, corporate executive*
Frenkel, Michael *lawyer*
Gunning, Francis Patrick *lawyer, insurance association executive*

**New York**
Abberley, John J. *lawyer*
Abrams, Floyd *lawyer*
Abrams, Robert *lawyer, former state attorney general*
Adams, George Bell *lawyer*
Adams, John Hamilton *lawyer*
Adams, Roy M. *lawyer, writer*
Aibel, Howard J. *lawyer*
Aidinoff, M(erton) Bernard *lawyer*
Aksen, Gerald *lawyer, educator*
†Albert, Garett J. *lawyer*
Albert, Neale Malcolm *lawyer*
Alden, Steven Michael *lawyer*
Alessandroni, Venan Joseph *lawyer*
Allen, Leon Arthur, Jr. *lawyer*
Alter, David *lawyer*
Alter, Eleanor Breitel *lawyer*
Amabile, John Louis *lawyer*
Amdur, Martin Bennett *lawyer*
Amhowitz, Harris J. *lawyer, educator*
Amsterdam, Anthony Guy *law educator*
Anderson, Eugene Robert *lawyer*
Andrews, Gordon Clark *lawyer*
Andrus, Roger Douglas *lawyer*
Angland, Joseph *lawyer*
Anthoine, Robert *lawyer, educator*
Appel, Albert M. *lawyer*
Appelbaum, Ann Harriet *lawyer*
Arenson, Gregory K. *lawyer*
Arkin, Stanley S. *lawyer*
Armstrong, James Sinclair *foundation director, retired lawyer*
Aron, Roberto *lawyer, writer, educator*
Arouh, Jeffrey Alan *lawyer*
Arquit, Kevin James *lawyer*
Arther, Richard Oberlin *polygraphist, educator*
Ashton, Robert W. *lawyer, foundation administrator*
Atkins, Peter Allan *lawyer*
Auerbach, William *lawyer*
Axinn, Stephen Mark *lawyer*
Bachelder, Joseph Elmer, III *lawyer*
Backman, Gerald Stephen *lawyer*
Badertscher, David Glen *law librarian, consultant*
Bagger, Richard Hartvig *lawyer*
Bainton, J(ohn) Joseph *lawyer*
Baity, John Cooley *lawyer*
Baker, David Remember *lawyer*
Baker, Martin S. *lawyer*
Baker, Stuart David *lawyer*
Ball, John H(anstein) *lawyer*
Bamberger, Michael Albert *lawyer*
Bancroft, Alexander Clerihew *lawyer*
Bancroft, Margaret Armstrong *lawyer*
Bankston, Archie Moore, Jr. *lawyer*
Barandes, Robert *lawyer*
Barasch, Clarence Sylvan *lawyer*
Barasch, Mal Livingston *lawyer*
Barist, Jeffrey A. *lawyer*
Bar-Levav, Doron Mordecai *lawyer*
Barr, Thomas D. *lawyer*
Barron, Francis Patrick *lawyer*
Barry, David Earl *lawyer*
Barry, Desmond Thomas, Jr. *lawyer*
Barth, Mark Harold *lawyer*
Bartlett, Joseph Warren *lawyer*
Bason, George R., Jr. *lawyer*
Bassen, Ned Henry *lawyer*
Bauer, Douglas F. *lawyer*
Bauer, Ralph Glenn *lawyer, maritime arbitrator*
Baumgardner, John Ellwood, Jr. *lawyer*
Baumgarten, Paul Anthony *lawyer*
Baumrin, Bernard Stefan Herbert *lawyer, educator*
Bazerman, Steven Howard *lawyer*
Bear, Larry Alan *lawyer, educator*
Beatie, Russel Harrison, Jr. *lawyer*
Beck, Andrew James *lawyer*
Beerbower, Cynthia Gibson *lawyer*
Beerbower, John Edwin *lawyer*
Beha, James Joseph *lawyer*
Behr, Alan Andrew *lawyer*
Beinecke, Candace Krugman *lawyer*
Bell, Derrick Albert *legal educator, author, lecturer*
Bell, James Halsey *lawyer*
Bell, Jonathan Robert *lawyer*
Beller, Daniel J. *lawyer*
Belnick, Mark Alan *lawyer*
Bender, John Charles *lawyer*
Benedict, James Nelson *lawyer*
Benenson, Mark Keith *lawyer*
Benkard, James W. B. *lawyer*
Bennett, Scott Lawrence *lawyer*
Berg, Alan *lawyer, government official*
Bergan, Edmund Paul, Jr. *lawyer*
Bergan, Philip James *lawyer*
Berger, Curtis Jay *law educator*
Berger, George *lawyer*
Berger, Michael Gary *lawyer*
Bergreen, Morris Harvey *lawyer, business executive, private investor*
Bergstein, Daniel Gerard *lawyer*
Berman, Joshua Mordecai *lawyer, manufacturing company executive*
Berman, Keith *solicitor, lawyer*
Bernard, Richard Phillip *lawyer*
Bernstein, Bernard *lawyer, corporate executive*
Bernstein, Daniel Lewis *lawyer*
Bernstein, Donald Scott *lawyer*
Berry, Edna Janet *patent lawyer, chemist*
Beshar, Robert Peter *lawyer*
Bettman, Gary Bruce *lawyer*
Beuchert, Edward William *lawyer*
Bezanson, Thomas Edward *lawyer*
Bialkin, Kenneth Jules *lawyer*
Bialo, Kenneth Marc *lawyer*
Bicks, David Peter *lawyer*
Bicks, Peter Andrews *lawyer*
Bidwell, James Truman, Jr. *lawyer*
Birnbaum, Edward Lester *lawyer*
Birnbaum, Irwin Morton *lawyer*
Bizar, Irving *lawyer*
Black, Barbara Aronstein *legal history educator*
Black, James Isaac, III *lawyer*
Black, Jerry Bernard *lawyer*
Blackman, Kenneth Robert *lawyer*
Blakeslee, Edward Eaton *lawyer, insurance executive*

Blanc, Roger David *lawyer*
Blattmachr, Jonathan George *lawyer*
Blind, William Charles *lawyer*
Bliwise, Lester Martin *lawyer*
Block, Dennis Jeffrey *lawyer*
Block, William Kenneth *lawyer*
Bloom, Robert Avrum *lawyer*
Bloomer, Harold Franklin, Jr. *lawyer*
Bluestone, Andrew Lavoott *lawyer*
Blumberg, Gerald *lawyer*
Blume, Lawrence Dayton *lawyer*
Blumkin, Linda Ruth *lawyer*
Bockstein, Herbert *lawyer*
Bodovitz, James Philip *lawyer*
Boes, Lawrence William *lawyer*
Bolan, Thomas Anthony *lawyer*
Booth, Edgar Hirsch *lawyer*
Booth, Mitchell B. *lawyer*
Borchard, William Marshall *lawyer*
Borisoff, Richard Stuart *lawyer*
Boros, Jerome S. *lawyer*
Borsody, Robert Peter *lawyer*
Boshkov, Stefan Robert *lawyer*
Bowden, William P., Jr. *lawyer, banker*
Boxer, Leonard *lawyer*
Bozorth, Squire Newland *lawyer*
Bradley, E. Michael *lawyer*
Brandrup, Douglas Warren *lawyer*
Braun, Jeffrey Louis *lawyer*
Brecker, Jeffrey Ross *lawyer, educator*
Breglio, John F. *lawyer*
Brenner, Frank *lawyer, venture capitalist*
Bresler, Martin Isidore *lawyer*
Bressler, Bernard *lawyer*
Briggs, Taylor Rastrick *lawyer*
Bring, Murray H. *lawyer*
Broadwater, Douglas Dwight *lawyer*
Brock, Charles Lawrence *lawyer, business executive*
Broder, Douglas Fisher *lawyer*
Brodsky, Edward *lawyer*
Brodsky, Samuel *lawyer*
Brome, Thomas Reed *lawyer*
Bronstein, Richard J. *lawyer*
Brooks, Lorimer Page *patent lawyer*
Bross, Steward Richard, Jr. *lawyer*
Brosterman, Melvin A. *lawyer*
Broude, Richard Frederick *lawyer, educator*
Broughton, Phillip Charles *lawyer*
Browdy, Joseph Eugene *lawyer*
Brown, Charles Dodgson *lawyer*
Brown, Meredith M. *lawyer*
Brown, Paul M. *lawyer*
Brown, Peter Megargee *lawyer, writer, lecturer*
Brown, Ralph Sawyer, Jr. *lawyer, business executive*
Brown, Ronald Erik *lawyer*
Browne, Jeffrey Francis *lawyer*
Brundige, Robert William, Jr. *lawyer*
Bryan, Barry Richard *lawyer*
Burak, H(oward) Paul *lawyer*
Burgweger, Francis Joseph Dewes, Jr. *lawyer*
Burke, Kathleen Mary *lawyer*
Burns, Arnold Irwin *lawyer*
Burrows, Michael Donald *lawyer*
Bursky, Herman Aaron *lawyer*
Bushnell, George Edward, III *lawyer*
Butler, Samuel Coles *lawyer*
Butler, William Joseph *lawyer*
Butowsky, David Martin *lawyer*
Buttenwieser, Lawrence Benjamin *lawyer*
Butterklee, Neil Howard *lawyer*
Caginalp, Aydin S. *lawyer*
Cahn, Jeffrey Barton *lawyer*
Calder, Duncan Graham, III *lawyer*
Callahan, Joseph Patrick *lawyer*
Campbell, Maria Bouchelle *lawyer, church executive*
Cannell, John Redferne *lawyer*
Canoni, John David *lawyer*
Cantor, Melvyn Leon *lawyer*
Capel, Guy B. *lawyer, banker*
Carb, Stephen Ames *lawyer*
Cardinali, Albert John *lawyer*
Cardozo, Benjamin Mordecai *lawyer*
Carey, J. Edwin *lawyer*
Carling, Francis *lawyer*
Carlson, Theodore Joshua *lawyer, retired utility company executive*
Carroll, Joseph J(ohn) *lawyer*
Carter, James Hal, Jr. *lawyer*
Casey, Thomas J. *lawyer*
Castel, P. Kevin *lawyer*
Catuzzi, J. P., Jr. *lawyer*
Cayea, Donald Joseph *lawyer*
Caytas, Ivo George *lawyer*
Chapnick, David B. *lawyer*
Chappell, John Charles *lawyer*
Chave, Carolyn Margaret *lawyer, arbitrator*
Chazen, Hartley James *lawyer*
Chell, Beverly C. *lawyer*
Chen, Wesley *lawyer*
Cherovsky, Erwin Louis *lawyer, writer*
Chester, John Geoffrey *lawyer*
Chiarchiaro, Frank John *lawyer*
Chilstrom, Robert Meade *lawyer*
Chin, Sylvia Fung *lawyer*
Chirls, Richard *lawyer*
Christaldi, Brian *lawyer*
Christensen, Henry, III *lawyer*
Christy, Arthur Hill *lawyer*
Chromow, Sheri P. *lawyer*
Clark, Carolyn Cochran *lawyer*
Clark, Howard Longstreth *lawyer, business executive*
Clark, John Holley, III *retired lawyer*
Clark, Jonathan Montgomery *lawyer*
Clark, Merrell Edward, Jr. *lawyer*
Clary, Richard Wayland *lawyer*
Clayton, Joe Don *lawyer*
Clemente, Constantine Louis *lawyer, health care company executive*
Cliff, Walter Conway *lawyer*
Coffee, John Collins, Jr. *legal educator*
Cohen, Edmund Stephen *lawyer*
Cohen, Edward Herschel *lawyer*
Cohen, Henry Rodgin *lawyer*
Cohen, Joel J. *lawyer, investment banker*
Cohen, Marcy Sharon *lawyer, bank executive*
Cohen, Myron *lawyer, educator*
Cohen, Richard Gerard *lawyer*
Cole, Lewis George *lawyer*
Coll, John Peter, Jr. *lawyer*
Collins, William T. *lawyer*
Collinson, Dale Stanley *lawyer*
Collyer, Michael *lawyer*
Conboy, Kenneth *lawyer, former federal judge*
Connelly, Albert R. *lawyer*
Connor, John Thomas, Jr. *lawyer*
Conrad, Winthrop Brown, Jr. *lawyer*
Constance, Thomas Ernest *lawyer*
Constantine, Jan Friedman *lawyer*

Conston, Henry Siegismund *lawyer*
Cook, Michael Lewis *lawyer*
Cook, Robert S., Jr. *lawyer*
Cooney, John Patrick, Jr. *lawyer*
Cooper, Michael Anthony *lawyer*
Cooper, R. John, III *lawyer*
Cooper, Stephen Herbert *lawyer*
Corbin, Sol Neil *lawyer*
Corry, John Adams *lawyer*
Costikyan, Edward N. *lawyer*
Cotter, James Michael *lawyer*
Cotton, Richard *lawyer*
Cowan, Wallace Edgar *lawyer*
Cowen, Edward S. *lawyer*
Cowen, Robert Nathan *lawyer*
Cowles, Frederick Oliver *lawyer*
Cox, Marshall *lawyer*
Craft, Randal Robert, Jr. *lawyer*
Cramer, Edward Morton *lawyer, music company executive*
Crane, Benjamin Field *lawyer*
Cranney, Marilyn Kanrek *lawyer*
Crary, Miner Dunham, Jr. *lawyer*
Creel, Thomas Leonard *lawyer*
Crisona, James Joseph *lawyer*
Critchlow, Charles Howard *lawyer*
Cubitto, Robert J. *lawyer*
Cudd, Robert A. N. *lawyer*
Cuiffo, Frank Wayne *lawyer*
Cuneo, Donald Lane *lawyer, educator*
Cunha, Mark Geoffrey *lawyer*
Curtis, Frank R. *lawyer*
Curtis, Susan Grace *lawyer*
Cutler, Kenneth Burnett *lawyer, investment company executive*
Dacey, Eileen M. *lawyer*
Dallas, William Moffit, Jr. *lawyer*
Dankner, Jay Warren *lawyer*
Darrell, Norris, Jr. *lawyer*
Darrow, Jill E(llen) *lawyer*
Davidson, Clifford Marc *lawyer*
Davidson, George Allan *lawyer*
Davidson, Mark Edward *lawyer*
Davidson, Robert Bruce *lawyer*
Davis, Evan Anderson *lawyer*
Davis, Frederick Townsend *lawyer*
Davis, Richard Joel *lawyer, former government official*
Davis, Wendell, Jr. *lawyer*
Dean, Jay Douglas *lawyer*
Debo, Vincent Joseph *lawyer, manufacturing company executive*
Degener, Carol Marie-Laure *lawyer*
Delson, Robert *lawyer*
Demarest, Daniel Anthony *retired lawyer*
De Natale, Andrew Peter *lawyer*
Denham, Robert Edwin *lawyer, investment company executive*
DeOrchis, Vincent Moore *lawyer*
Derzaw, Richard Lawrence *lawyer*
de Saint Phalle, Pierre Claude *lawyer*
De Sear, Edward Marshall *lawyer*
DeWeil, Dawn Susan *lawyer*
Diamond, Bernard Robin *lawyer*
Diamond, David Howard *lawyer*
DiBlasi, Gandolfo Vincent *lawyer*
Dichter, Barry Joel *lawyer*
Diskant, Gregory L. *lawyer*
†Doman, Nicholas R. *lawyer*
Donald, Norman Henderson, III *lawyer*
Donnellan, Andrew B., Jr. *lawyer*
Dorsen, Norman *lawyer, educator*
Douchkess, George *lawyer*
Doyle, Joseph Anthony *lawyer*
Doyle, Paul Francis *lawyer*
Drebsky, Dennis Jay *lawyer*
Dreizen, Alison M. *lawyer*
Drucker, Jacquelin F. *lawyer, arbitrator, author*
Dubin, James Michael *lawyer*
Dundas, Philip Blair, Jr. *lawyer*
Dunham, Corydon Busnell *lawyer, broadcasting executive*
Dunham, Wolcott Balestier, Jr. *lawyer*
Dunn, M(orris) Douglas *lawyer*
Dworkin, Ronald Myles *legal educator*
Dykhouse, David Wayne *lawyer*
Earle, Victor Montagne, III *lawyer*
Edelman, Paul Sterling *lawyer*
Edelson, Gilbert Seymour *lawyer*
Edgar, Harold Simmons Hull *legal educator*
Effel, Laura *lawyer*
Ehrenkranz, Joel S. *lawyer*
Einhorn, Harold *lawyer, writer*
Eisert, Edward Gaver *lawyer*
Elicker, Gordon Leonard *lawyer*
Elkin, Jeffrey H. *lawyer*
Ellins, Howard A. *lawyer*
Elliott, Donald Harrison *lawyer*
Ellis, Carolyn Terry *lawyer*
Elsen, Sheldon Howard *lawyer*
Emil, Arthur D. *lawyer*
Epling, Richard Louis *lawyer*
Epstein, Jeremy G. *lawyer*
Epstein, Melvin *lawyer*
Epstein, Michael Alan *lawyer*
Ercklentz, Enno Wilhelm, Jr. *lawyer*
Ericson, Robert Walter *lawyer*
Estreicher, Samuel *lawyer, educator*
Etra, Aaron *lawyer*
Eustice, James Samuel *lawyer, educator*
Evans, Martin Frederic *lawyer*
Evans, Thomas William *lawyer*
†Evarts, William Maxwell, Jr. *lawyer*
Everett, James William, Jr. *lawyer*
Faber, Peter Lewis *lawyer*
Fales, Haliburton, II *lawyer*
Farley, Robert Donald *lawyer, business executive*
Farnsworth, E(dward) Allan *lawyer, educator*
Farr, Charles Sims *lawyer*
Fass, Peter Michael *lawyer, educator*
Faulkner, Walter Thomas *lawyer*
Feder, Saul E. *lawyer*
Feit, Glenn M. *lawyer*
Feld, Katherine Phoebe *lawyer*
Feldberg, Michael Svetkey *lawyer*
Felder, Raoul Lionel *lawyer*
Feldkamp, John Calvin *lawyer, educational administrator*
Feldman, Franklin *lawyer, printmaker*
Feldman, Jerome Ira *lawyer, patent development executive*
Fensterstock, Blair Courtney *lawyer*
Ferguson, Milton Carr, Jr. *lawyer*
Ferguson, Robert Harry Munro *lawyer*
Fernandez, Jose Walfredo *lawyer*
Fier, Elihu *lawyer*
Filler, Ronald Howard *lawyer*

Finch, Edward Ridley, Jr. *lawyer, diplomat, author, lecturer*
Fineman, Martha Albertson *law educator*
Fink, Robert Steven *lawyer, writer, educator*
Finkelstein, Allen Lewis *lawyer*
Finkelstein, Bernard *lawyer*
First, Harry *legal educator*
Fischman, Bernard D. *lawyer*
Fishbein, Peter Melvin *lawyer*
Fisher, Ann Bailen *lawyer*
Fisher, Robert I. *lawyer*
Fishman, Fred Norman *lawyer*
Fishman, Mitchell Steven *lawyer*
Fiske, Robert Bishop, Jr. *lawyer*
Fitzpatrick, Joseph Mark *lawyer*
Fleder, Robert Charles *lawyer*
Fleischer, Arthur, Jr. *lawyer*
Fleischman, Edward Hirsh *lawyer*
Fleming, Peter Emmet, Jr. *lawyer*
Fletcher, Anthony L. *lawyer*
Fletcher, George P. *law educator*
Fletcher, Raymond Russwald, Jr. *lawyer*
Fleur, Mary Louise *legal administrator*
Flint, George Squire *lawyer*
Flom, Joseph Harold *lawyer*
Flumenbaum, Martin *lawyer*
Fodor, Susanna Serena *lawyer*
Fogg, Blaine Viles *lawyer*
Fontana, Vincent Robert *lawyer*
Forstadt, Joseph Lawrence *lawyer*
Forster, Arnold *lawyer, author*
Fortenbaugh, Samuel Byrod, III *lawyer*
Foster, David Lee *lawyer*
Fox, Donald Thomas *lawyer*
Fox, Eleanor Mae Cohen *lawyer, educator, writer*
Fox, Jeanne Marie *lawyer*
Fraidin, Stephen *lawyer*
Fraiman, Genevieve Lam *lawyer*
Franck, Thomas Martin *law educator*
Frank, Lloyd *lawyer, retired chemical company executive*
Frankel, Benjamin Harrison *lawyer*
Frankel, Marvin E. *lawyer*
Franklin, Blake Timothy *lawyer*
Frazza, George S. *lawyer, business executive*
Fredericks, Wesley Charles, Jr. *lawyer*
Freedman, Gerald M. *lawyer*
Freeman, David John *lawyer*
Freilicher, Morton *lawyer*
Freitas, Elizabeth Frances *lawyer*
French, John, III *lawyer*
Freund, Fred A. *lawyer*
Frey, Andrew Lewis *lawyer*
Fricklas, Michael David *lawyer*
Fried, Burton Theodore *lawyer*
Fried, Donald David *lawyer*
Fried, Walter Jay *lawyer*
Friedman, Alan Roy *lawyer*
Friedman, Bart *lawyer*
Friedman, Elaine Florence *lawyer*
Friedman, Robert Laurence *lawyer*
Friedman, Samuel Selig *lawyer*
Friedman, Stephen James *lawyer*
Friedman, Victor Stanley *lawyer*
Friedman, Wilbur Harvey *lawyer*
Frischling, Carl *lawyer*
Frost, William Lee *lawyer*
Fry, Morton Harrison, II *lawyer*
Fryer, Judith Dorothy *lawyer*
Fuhrer, Arthur K. *lawyer*
Fuld, James Jeffrey *lawyer*
Fuld, Stanley Howells *lawyer*
Fuzesi, Stephen, Jr. *lawyer, communications executive*
Gabay, Donald David *lawyer*
Galant, Herbert Lewis *lawyer*
Gallagher, Terence Joseph *lawyer*
Gallantz, George Gerald *lawyer*
Gamboni, Ciro Anthony *lawyer*
Gambro, Michael S. *lawyer*
Gans, Walter Gideon *lawyer*
Ganz, Howard Laurence *lawyer*
Ganzi, Victor Frederick *lawyer*
Garber, Robert Edward *lawyer, insurance company executive*
Garfinkel, Barry Herbert *lawyer*
Garland, Sylvia Dillof *lawyer*
Gartner, Murray *lawyer*
Garvey, Richard Anthony *lawyer*
Gassel, Philip Michael *lawyer*
Gatting, Carlene J. *lawyer*
Gelb, Judith Anne *lawyer*
Gelfman, Robert William *lawyer*
Genova, Joseph Steven *lawyer*
Geoghegan, Patricia *lawyer*
George, Beauford James, Jr. *lawyer, educator*
Gerard, Whitney Ian *lawyer*
Gerber, Robert Evan *lawyer*
Getnick, Neil Victor *lawyer*
Giannetti, Thomas Leonard *lawyer*
Gibbs, L(ippman) Martin *lawyer*
Gifford, William C. *lawyer*
Gilbert, Phil Edward, Jr. *lawyer*
Gill, E. Ann *lawyer*
Gillers, Stephen *law educator*
Gillespie, George Joseph, III *lawyer*
Ginsberg, Ernest *lawyer, banker*
Girden, Eugene Lawrence *lawyer*
Gitter, Max *lawyer*
Glekel, Jeffrey Ives *lawyer*
Glicksman, Eugene Jay *lawyer*
Glickstein, Steven *lawyer*
Glynn, Robert *lawyer, foundation chairman*
Goetz, Maurice Harold *lawyer*
Gold, Martin Elliot *lawyer, educator*
Gold, Simeon *lawyer*
Goldberg, David *lawyer, law educator*
Goldberg, Victor Paul *law educator*
Goldblatt, David Ira *lawyer*
Golden, Arthur F. *lawyer*
Goldman, Donald Howard *lawyer*
Goldman, Lawrence Saul *lawyer*
Goldman, Marvin Gerald *lawyer*
Goldschmid, Harvey Jerome *law educator*
Goldsmith, Gerald P. *lawyer*
Goldsmith, Lee Selig *lawyer, physician*
Goldstein, Alvin *lawyer*
Goldstein, Bernard Herbert *lawyer*
Goldstein, Charles Arthur *lawyer*
Goldstein, Howard Warren *lawyer*
Goldstein, Marcia Landweber *lawyer*
Gooch, Anthony Cushing *lawyer*
Goodale, James Campbell *lawyer, media executive, television producer/host*
Goodfriend, Herbert Jay *lawyer*
Goodhartz, Gerald *law librarian*
Goodkind, Louis William *lawyer*
Goodman, Gary A. *lawyer*
Goodridge, Allan D. *lawyer*
Goodwin, Bernard *lawyer, executive, educator*
Goott, Alan F(ranklin) *lawyer*
Gordon, Jeffrey Neil *law educator*
Gordon, Michael Mackin *lawyer*
Gordon, Nicole Ann *lawyer*
Gotthoffer, Lance *lawyer*
Gottlieb, Paul Mitchel *lawyer*
Gotts, Ilene Knable *lawyer*
Gould, Milton Samuel *lawyer, business executive*
Grad, Frank Paul *lawyer*
Graff, George Leonard *lawyer*
Graham, Jesse Japhet, II *lawyer*
Graifman, Brian Dale *lawyer*
Granoff, Gary Charles *lawyer, investment company executive*
Grant, Stephen Allen *lawyer*
Grashof, August Edward *lawyer*
Green, Alvin *lawyer, consultant*
Green, Robert S. *lawyer*
Greenawalt, Robert Kent *lawyer, law educator*
Greenawalt, William Sloan *lawyer*
Greenbaum, Maurice Coleman *lawyer*
Greenberg, Daniel Herbert *lawyer*
Greenberg, Gary Howard *lawyer*
Greenberg, Ira George *lawyer*
Greenberg, Jack *lawyer, law educator*
Greenberg, Joshua F. *lawyer, educator*
Greenberg, Ronald David *lawyer, law educator*
Greenberger, Howard Leroy *lawyer, educator*
Greene, Bernard Harold *lawyer*
Greene, Ira S. *lawyer*
Greer, Allen Curtis, II *lawyer*
Greer, James Alexander, II *lawyer*
Greig, Robert Thomson *lawyer*
Greilsheimer, James Gans *lawyer*
Greiner, Stephen W. *lawyer*
Groban, Robert Sidney, Jr. *lawyer*
Gropper, Allan Louis *lawyer*
Gross, Ernest Arnold *lawyer*
Gross, Richard Benjamin *lawyer*
Gross, Steven Ross *lawyer*
Grossman, Dan Steven *lawyer*
Grossman, Sanford *lawyer*
Grunewald, Raymond Bernhard *lawyer*
Grunstein, Leonard *lawyer*
Gruson, Michael *lawyer*
Guggenheim, Martin Franklin *law educator*
Gunther, Jack Disbrow, Jr. *lawyer*
Guth, Paul C. *lawyer*
Hackett, Kevin R. *lawyer*
Haddad, Mark Anthony *lawyer*
Haffner, Alfred Loveland, Jr. *lawyer*
Hagendorn, William *lawyer*
Hager, Charles Read *lawyer*
Haggerty, Robert Henry *lawyer*
Haidt, Harold *lawyer*
Haig, Robert Leighton *lawyer*
Haims, Bruce David *lawyer*
Halberstam, Malvina *law educator, lawyer*
Halliday, Joseph William *lawyer*
Halperin, Richard E. *lawyer, holding company executive*
Hamburg, Charles Bruce *lawyer*
Hamel, Rodolphe *lawyer, pharmaceutical company executive*
Hamm, David Bernard *lawyer*
Handelsman, Lawrence Marc *lawyer*
Handler, Arthur M. *lawyer*
Handler, Milton *lawyer*
Hanson, Jean Elizabeth *lawyer*
Harbison, James Wesley, Jr. *lawyer*
Harnett, Thomas Aquinas *lawyer*
Harper, Conrad Kenneth *lawyer, former government official*
Harper, Emery Walter *lawyer*
Harper, Gerard Edward *lawyer*
Harris, Joel B(ruce) *lawyer*
Harrison, S. David *lawyer*
Hart, Kenneth Nelson *lawyer*
Hart, Robert M. *lawyer*
Hartzell, Andrew Cornelius, Jr. *lawyer*
Hauser, Rita Eleanore Abrams *lawyer*
Hawes, Douglas Wesson *lawyer*
Hawke, Roger Jewett *lawyer*
Hayden, Raymond Paul *lawyer*
Hayes, Gerald Joseph *lawyer*
Haynes, Jean Reed *lawyer*
Head, Elizabeth *lawyer*
Healy, Harold Harris, Jr. *lawyer*
Healy, Nicholas Joseph *lawyer, educator*
Hearn, George Henry *lawyer, steamship corporate executive*
Heftler, Thomas E. *lawyer*
Heineman, Andrew David *lawyer*
Heisler, Stanley Dean *lawyer*
Heitner, Kenneth Howard *lawyer*
Helander, Robert Charles *lawyer*
Hellawell, Robert *law educator*
Hellenbrand, Samuel Henry *lawyer, diversified industry executive*
Heller, Edwin *lawyer*
Heller, Robert Martin *lawyer*
Hellerstein, Alvin Kenneth *lawyer*
Heming, Charles E. *lawyer*
Henderson, Donald Bernard, Jr. *lawyer*
†Henderson, Harold Richard, Jr. *lawyer, labor relations executive*
Hendry, Andrew Delaney *lawyer, consumer products company executive*
Henkin, Louis *lawyer, law educator*
Herbst, Abbe Ilene *lawyer*
Herbst, Todd L. *lawyer*
Herman, Kenneth Beaumont *lawyer*
Herold, Karl Guenter *lawyer*
Herz, Andrew Lee *lawyer*
Herzeca, Lois Friedman *lawyer*
Hetherington, John Warner *lawyer*
Hiden, Robert Battaile, Jr. *lawyer*
Higginbotham, A. Leon, Jr. *lawyer, educator*
Higgs, John H. *lawyer*
Hill, Alfred *lawyer, educator*
Hirsch, Barry *lawyer*
Hirsch, Jerome S. *lawyer*
Hirschfeld, Michael *lawyer*
Hirshfield, Stuart *lawyer*
Hirshowitz, Melvin Stephen *lawyer*
Hoblin, Philip J., Jr. *securities lawyer*
Hodes, Robert Bernard *lawyer*
Hoff, Jonathan M(orind) *lawyer*
Hoffman, John Ernest, Jr. *retired lawyer*
Hoffman, Mathew *lawyer*
Holman, Bud George *lawyer*
Holtzman, Alexander *lawyer, consultant*
Holtzmann, Howard Marshall *lawyer, judge*
Hooker, Wade Stuart, Jr. *lawyer*
Hopper, Walter Everett *lawyer*
Horowitz, Raymond J. *lawyer*
Howe, Richard Rives *lawyer*
Hruska, Alan J. *lawyer*
Hudspeth, Stephen Mason *lawyer*
Huettner, Richard Alfred *lawyer*
Hughes, Kevin Peter *lawyer*
Huhs, John I. *international lawyer*
Hulbert, Richard Woodward *lawyer*
Hull, Philip Glasgow *lawyer*
Hunt, Franklin Griggs *lawyer*
Hupper, John Roscoe *lawyer*
Hurlock, James Bickford *lawyer*
Hyde, David Rowley *lawyer*
Hyman, Jerome Elliot *lawyer*
Iannuzzi, John Nicholas *lawyer, author, educator*
Ichel, David W. *lawyer*
Idzik, Daniel Ronald *lawyer*
Ingram, Samuel William, Jr. *lawyer*
Insel, Michael S. *lawyer*
Intriligator, Marc Steven *lawyer*
Iovenko, Michael *lawyer*
Isaacson, Allen Ira *lawyer*
Iseman, Joseph Seeman *lawyer*
Isenberg, Steven Lawrence *law educator*
Isquith, Fred Taylor *lawyer*
Issler, Harry *lawyer*
Ivanick, Carol W. Trencher *lawyer*
Jackson, Raymond Sidney, Jr. *lawyer*
Jackson, Thomas Gene *lawyer*
Jackson, William Eldred *lawyer*
Jacob, Edwin J. *lawyer*
Jacob, Marvin Eugene *lawyer*
Jacobowitz, Harold Saul *lawyer*
Jacobs, Arnold Stephen *lawyer*
Jacobs, Jane Brand *lawyer*
Jacobs, Marisa Frances *lawyer*
Jacobs, Robert Alan *lawyer*
Jacobson, Jerold Dennis *lawyer*
Jacobson, Sandra W. *lawyer*
Jacqueney, Stephanie A(lice) *lawyer*
Jaffe, Alan Steven *lawyer*
Jaffin, Charles Leonard *lawyer*
Jander, Klaus Heinrich *lawyer*
Jasper, Seymour *lawyer*
Jassy, Everett Lewis *lawyer*
Javits, Eric Moses *lawyer*
Jefferies, Jack P. *lawyer*
Jessup, John Baker *lawyer*
Jeydel, Richard K. *lawyer*
Jinnett, Robert Jefferson *lawyer*
Joffe, Robert David *lawyer*
Jones, Douglas W. *lawyer*
Joseph, Ellen R. *lawyer*
Joseph, Gregory Paul *lawyer*
Joseph, L. Anthony, Jr. *lawyer*
Joseph, Leonard *lawyer*
Josephson, William Howard *lawyer*
Juceam, Robert E. *lawyer*
Kaden, Ellen Oran *lawyer, broadcasting corporation executive*
Kaden, Lewis B. *law educator*
Kahen, Harold I. *lawyer*
Kahn, Alan Edwin *lawyer*
Kahn, Anthony F. *lawyer*
Kahn, Richard Dreyfus *lawyer*
Kailas, Leo George *lawyer*
Kalish, Arthur *lawyer*
Kalish, Myron *lawyer*
Kamin, Sherwin *lawyer*
Kaminer, Peter H. *lawyer*
Kaminsky, Arthur Charles *lawyer*
Kamm, Linda Heller *lawyer*
Kane, Daniel Hipwell *lawyer*
Kanner, Frederick W. *lawyer*
Kaplan, Carl Eliot *lawyer*
Kaplan, Helene Lois *lawyer*
Kaplan, Joseph Solte *lawyer*
Kaplan, Madeline *legal administrator*
Kaplan, Mark Norman *lawyer*
Kaplan, Peter James *lawyer*
Karatz, William Warren *lawyer*
Karls, John Spencer *lawyer, accountant*
Karmali, Rashida Alimahomed *lawyer*
Kasowitz, Marc Elliot *lawyer*
Kassebaum, John Philip *lawyer*
Katsh, Salem Michael *lawyer*
Katz, Gregory *lawyer*
Katz, Jerome Charles *lawyer*
Katz, Ronald S. *lawyer*
Kaufman, Arthur Stephen *lawyer*
Kaufman, Robert Max *lawyer*
Kaufmann, Ed *lawyer*
Kaufmann, Jack *lawyer*
Kavaler, Thomas J. *lawyer*
Kavoukjian, Michael Edward *lawyer*
Kaye, Stephen Rackow *lawyer*
Kazanjian, John Harold *lawyer*
Kean, Hamilton Fish *lawyer*
Keany, Sutton *lawyer*
Kelly, Daniel Grady, Jr. *lawyer*
Kende, Christopher Burgess *lawyer*
†Kennedy, John Fitzgerald, Jr. *lawyer, magazine editor*
Kennedy, Michael John *lawyer*
Kenney, John Joseph *lawyer*
Keogh, Kevin *lawyer*
Kern, George Calvin, Jr. *lawyer*
Kern, Jerome H. *lawyer*
Kernochan, John Marshall *lawyer, educator*
Kess, Sidney *lawyer, educator, accountant, author*
Kessel, Mark *lawyer*
Kessler, Jeffrey L. *lawyer*
Kessler, Ralph Kenneth *lawyer, manufacturing company executive*
Kevlin, Mary Louise *lawyer*
Kheel, Theodore Woodrow *arbitrator and mediator*
Kidd, John Edward *lawyer, corporate executive*
Kies, David M. *lawyer*
Kill, Lawrence *lawyer*
Kimball, Richard Arthur, Jr. *lawyer*
Kimm, Michael S. *lawyer*
King, Henry Lawrence *lawyer*
King, Lawrence Philip *lawyer, educator*
Kinney, Stephen Hoyt, Jr. *lawyer*
Kinsolving, Augustus Blagden *lawyer*
Kinzler, Thomas Benjamin *lawyer*
Kirby, John Joseph, Jr. *lawyer*
Kirschbaum, Myron *lawyer*
Klapper, Molly *lawyer, educator*
Kleckner, Robert George, Jr. *lawyer*
Klein, Martin I. *lawyer*
Klein, William, II *lawyer*
Kleinbard, Edward D. *lawyer*
Kleinberg, Norman Charles *lawyer*
Kline, Eugene Monroe *lawyer*
Klingsberg, David *lawyer*
Klink, Fredric J. *lawyer*
Kmiotek-Welsh, Jacqueline *lawyer*
Knapp, Charles Lincoln *law educator*
Knight, Robert Huntington *lawyer, bank executive*
Knight, Townsend Jones *lawyer*
Knutson, David Harry *retired lawyer, banker*
Kobak, James Benedict, Jr. *lawyer, educator*
Kober, Jane *lawyer*
Kobrin, Lawrence Alan *lawyer*
Koegel, William Fisher *lawyer*
Koenigsberg, I. Fred *lawyer*
Kolbe, Karl William, Jr. *lawyer*
Kolbert, Kathryn *lawyer, educator*
Komaroff, Stanley *lawyer*
Koob, Charles Edward *lawyer*
Koral, Alan M. *lawyer*
Kornberg, Alan William *lawyer*
Kornreich, Edward Scott *lawyer*
Korotkin, Michael Paul *lawyer*
Kostelanetz, Boris *lawyer*
Kourides, Peter Theologos *lawyer*
Kraemer, Lillian Elizabeth *lawyer*
Kramer, Alan Sharfsin *lawyer*
Kramer, George P. *lawyer*
Kranwinkle, Conrad Douglas *lawyer*
Krasner, Daniel Walter *lawyer*
Kreitzman, Ralph J. *lawyer*
Krieger, Sanford *lawyer*
Krinsly, Stuart Zalmy *lawyer, manufacturing company executive*
Kroll, Arthur Herbert *lawyer, educator, consultant*
Krouse, George Raymond, Jr. *lawyer*
Krupman, William Allan *lawyer*
Krupp, Fred(eric) D. *lawyer, environmental agency executive*
Kufeld, William Manuel *lawyer*
Kuh, Richard Henry *lawyer*
Kuklin, Anthony Bennett *lawyer*
Kumble, Steven Jay *lawyer*
Kuntz, Lee Allan *lawyer*
Kurtz, Jerome *lawyer, educator*
Kury, Bernard Edward *lawyer*
Kurzweil, Harvey *lawyer*
Lacovara, Philip Allen *lawyer*
Lacy, Robinson Burrell *lawyer*
Lambert, Judith A. Ungar *lawyer*
Lanchner, Bertrand Martin *lawyer, advertising executive*
Landa, Howard Martin *lawyer, business executive*
Landau, Walter Loeber *lawyer*
Lane, Alvin S. *lawyer*
Lane, Arthur Alan *lawyer*
Lang, John Francis *lawyer*
Lang, Robert Todd *lawyer*
Lange, Marvin Robert *lawyer*
Larkin, Leo Paul, Jr. *lawyer*
Larose, Lawrence Alfred *lawyer*
La Rossa, James M(ichael) *lawyer*
Larsen, Robert Dhu *lawyer*
Lascher, Alan Alfred *lawyer*
Lasker, Richard S. *lawyer*
Lauer, Eliot *lawyer*
Lebow, Mark Denis *lawyer*
Leckie, Gavin Frederick *lawyer*
Lederer, Peter David *lawyer*
Lederman, Lawrence *lawyer, writer, educator*
Lee, In-Young *lawyer*
Lee, Jerome G. *lawyer*
Lee, Paul Lawrence *lawyer*
Leebron, David Wayne *law educator*
Lefkowitz, Howard N. *lawyer*
Lefkowitz, Jerry *lawyer, accountant*
Leichtling, Michael Alfred *lawyer*
Leisure, George Stanley, Jr. *lawyer*
Leland, Richard G. *lawyer*
Leness, George Crawford *lawyer*
Leonard, Edwin Deane *lawyer*
Lesch, Michael Oscar *lawyer*
Lester, Pamela Robin *lawyer*
Levie, Joseph Henry *lawyer*
Levine, Alan *lawyer*
Levine, Laurence William *lawyer*
Levine, Lawrence Steven *lawyer*
Levine, Mark Leonard *lawyer*
Levine, Melvin Charles *lawyer*
Levine, Robert Jay *lawyer*
Levine, Ronald Jay *lawyer*
Levine, Seymour *lawyer*
Levitan, James A. *lawyer*
Levy, Herbert Monte *lawyer*
Levy, Stanley Herbert *lawyer*
Lewyn, Thomas Mark *lawyer*
Liebman, Lance Malcolm *law educator, lawyer*
Lifland, William Thomas *lawyer*
Liman, Arthur Lawrence *lawyer*
Lin, Maria C. H. *lawyer*
Lindenbaum, Sandford Richard *lawyer*
Lindsay, George Peter *lawyer*
Lindskog, David Richard *lawyer*
Linsenmeyer, John Michael *lawyer*
Lipton, Charles Jules *lawyer*
Lipton, Martin *lawyer*
Lipton, Robert Steven *lawyer*
Lochner, Philip Raymond, Jr. *lawyer*
Loengard, Richard Otto, Jr. *lawyer*
Longstreth, Bevis *lawyer*
Lorch, Ernest Henry *lawyer*
Lore, Martin Maxwell *lawyer*
Loss, Margaret Ruth *lawyer*
Lotwin, Stanford Gerald *lawyer*
Lowenfeld, Andreas Frank *law educator, arbitrator*
Lowenfels, Fred M. *lawyer*
Lowenfels, Lewis David *lawyer*
Lowenstein, Louis *legal educator*
Lowy, George Theodore *lawyer*
Lunding, Christopher Hanna *lawyer*
Lupert, Leslie Allan *lawyer*
Lupkin, Stanley Neil *lawyer*
Luria, Mary Mercer *lawyer*
Lusky, Louis *legal educator*
Lustenberger, Louis Charles, Jr. *lawyer*
Lustgarten, Ira Howard *lawyer*
Lutringer, Richard Emil *lawyer*
Lynch, Gerard E. *law educator*
Lynn, Theodore Stanley *lawyer*
Lynton, Harold Stephen *lawyer*
Lyon, Carl Francis, Jr. *lawyer*
Macan, William Alexander, IV *lawyer*
Macioce, Frank Michael *lawyer, financial services company executive*
Mack, Dennis Wayne *lawyer*
MacKinnon, John Alexander *lawyer*
MacRae, Cameron Farquhar, III *lawyer*
Macris, Michael *lawyer*
Madden, Donald Paul *lawyer*
Madden, John Patrick *lawyer*
Madsen, Stephen Stewart *lawyer*
Mahon, Arthur J. *lawyer*
Maidman, Richard Harvey Mortimer *lawyer*
Malina, Michael *lawyer*
Malkin, Peter Laurence *lawyer*

Maloney, Michael Patrick *lawyer, corporate executive*
Mandelstam, Charles Lawrence *lawyer*
Maneker, Morton M. *lawyer*
Maney, Michael Mason *lawyer*
Mann, Philip Roy *lawyer*
Manning, William Joseph *lawyer*
Mantle, Raymond Allan *lawyer*
Marcus, Eric Peter *lawyer*
Marcus, Maria Lenhoff *lawyer, law educator*
Marcus, Norman *lawyer*
Marcusa, Fred Haye *lawyer*
Marke, Julius Jay *law librarian, educator*
Marlin, Richard *lawyer*
Marshall, John Patrick *lawyer*
Marshall, Sheila Hermes *lawyer*
Martin, George J., Jr. *lawyer*
Martin, Malcolm Elliot *lawyer*
Martone, Patricia Ann *lawyer*
Marx, Owen Cox *lawyer*
Marzulli, John Anthony, Jr. *lawyer*
Maslow, Will *lawyer, association executive*
Masters, Jon Joseph *lawyer*
Materna, Joseph Anthony *lawyer*
Mathers, William Harris *lawyer*
Matteson, William Bleecker *lawyer*
Matthews, Edwin Spencer, Jr. *lawyer*
Matus, Wayne Charles *lawyer*
Maulsby, Allen Farish *lawyer*
Maxfield, Guy Budd *lawyer, educator*
Mayer, Carl Joseph *lawyer, town official*
Mayerson, Sandra Elaine *lawyer*
Mayesh, Jay Philip *lawyer*
Mazza, Thomas Carmen *lawyer*
McBryde, Thomas Henry *lawyer*
Mc Cann, John Joseph *lawyer*
McCarthy, Robert Emmett *lawyer*
McClimon, Timothy John *lawyer*
McClung, Richard Goehring *lawyer*
McCormick, Hugh Thomas *lawyer*
McDavid, William Henry *lawyer*
McDermott, Richard T. *lawyer, educator*
McGanney, Thomas *lawyer*
McGinnis, John Oldham *lawyer, educator*
Mc Goldrick, John Gardiner *lawyer*
McGrath, Thomas J. *lawyer, writer, film producer*
McHenry, Barnabas *lawyer*
Mc Inerney, Denis *lawyer*
McKenna, Peter Dennis *lawyer*
McLaughlin, Joseph *lawyer*
McMeen, Elmer Ellsworth, III *lawyer, guitarist*
McNally, John Joseph *lawyer*
Mc Namara, J(ohn) Donald *retired lawyer, business executive*
Mc Nicol, Donald Edward *lawyer*
McSherry, William John, Jr. *lawyer, consultant*
Medina, Standish Forde, Jr. *lawyer*
Meiklejohn, Donald Stuart *lawyer*
Menack, Steven Boyd *lawyer, mediator*
Mercorella, Anthony J. *lawyer, former state supreme court justice*
Meron, Theodor *law educator, researcher*
Merow, John Edward *lawyer*
Merritt, Bruce Gordon *lawyer*
Mestres, Ricardo Angelo, Jr. *lawyer*
Michaelson, Arthur M. *lawyer*
Michel, Clifford Lloyd *lawyer, investment executive*
Milgrim, Roger Michael *lawyer*
Miller, Charles Hampton *lawyer*
Miller, David *lawyer, advertising executive*
Miller, Harvey R. *lawyer, bankruptcy reorganization specialist*
Miller, Paul S(amuel) *lawyer*
Miller, Richard Steven *lawyer*
Miller, Sam Scott *lawyer*
Miller, Steven Scott *lawyer*
Millson, Rory Oliver *lawyer*
Millstein, Ira M. *lawyer, lecturer*
Minkowitz, Martin *lawyer, former state government official*
Minsky, Bruce William *lawyer*
Modlin, Howard S. *lawyer*
Moerdler, Charles Gerard *lawyer*
Molinaro, Valerie Ann *lawyer*
Moloney, Thomas Joseph *lawyer*
Monge, Jay Parry *lawyer*
Montgomery, Robert Humphrey, Jr. *lawyer*
Moore, Donald Francis *lawyer*
Moore, Franklin Hall, Jr. *lawyer*
Moore, John Joseph *lawyer*
Moore, Thomas Ronald (Lord Bridestowe ) *lawyer*
Moorhead, Thomas Burch *lawyer, pharmaceutical company executive*
Moran, Edward Kevin *lawyer, consultant*
Morgan, Frank Edward, II *lawyer*
Morgenthau, Robert Morris *lawyer*
Morphy, James Calvin *lawyer*
Morris, Eugene Jerome *lawyer*
Mortimer, Peter Michael *lawyer*
Moskin, Morton *lawyer*
Moskovitz, Stuart Jeffrey *lawyer*
Moss, William John *lawyer*
Most, Jack Lawrence *lawyer, consultant*
Mullen, Peter P. *lawyer*
Muller, Frank *mediator, arbitrator*
Mulligan, Jeremiah T. *lawyer*
Mullman, Michael S. *lawyer*
Mulroy, Richard E., Jr. *lawyer*
Mundheim, Robert Harry *law educator*
Munzer, Stephen Ira *lawyer*
Murase, Jiro *lawyer*
Murphy, Arthur William *lawyer, educator*
Murray, Archibald R. *lawyer*
Myerson, Toby Salter *lawyer*
Naftalis, Gary Philip *lawyer, educator*
Nance, Allan Taylor *lawyer*
Nash, Paul LeNoir *lawyer*
Nassau, Michael Jay *lawyer*
Nathan, Frederic Solis *lawyer*
Neidell, Martin H. *lawyer*
Nemser, Earl Harold *lawyer*
Neuwirth, Alan James *lawyer*
Neveloff, Jay A. *lawyer*
Newcomb, Danforth *lawyer*
Newcombe, George Michael *lawyer*
Newman, Fredric Samuel *lawyer, business executive*
Newman, Howard Neal *lawyer, educator*
Newman, Kenneth E. *lawyer*
Newman, Lawrence Walker *lawyer*
Nicholls, Richard H. *lawyer*
Nimetz, Matthew *lawyer*
Nimkin, Bernard William *retired lawyer*
Nonna, John Michael *lawyer*
Norfolk, William Ray *lawyer*
North, Steven Edward *lawyer*
Novikoff, Harold Stephen *lawyer*
Nusbacher, Gloria Weinberg *lawyer*
Oberly, Kathryn Anne *lawyer*
Oberman, Michael Stewart *lawyer*
O'Brien, Donal Clare, Jr. *lawyer*
O'Brien, Kevin J. *lawyer*
O'Brien, Thomas Ignatius *lawyer*
O'Brien, Timothy James *lawyer*
O'Dea, Dennis Michael *lawyer*
O'Dell, Charlene Anne Audrey *lawyer*
O'Donnell, John Logan *lawyer*
Oechler, Henry John, Jr. *lawyer*
Ogden, Alfred *lawyer*
O'Grady, John Joseph, III *lawyer*
O'Hara, Alfred Peck *lawyer*
Olick, Arthur Seymour *lawyer*
Olick, Philip Stewart *lawyer*
Oliensis, Sheldon *lawyer*
O'Neil, John Joseph *lawyer*
Oppenheimer, Martin J. *lawyer*
Ornitz, Richard Martin *lawyer, business executive*
O'Rorke, James Francis, Jr. *lawyer*
Osborn, Donald Robert *lawyer*
Oshima, Michael W. *lawyer*
Ostrager, Barry Robert *lawyer*
O'Sullivan, Thomas J. *lawyer*
Owen, Robert Dewit *lawyer*
Oxman, David Craig *lawyer*
Pack, Leonard Brecher *lawyer*
Paladino, Daniel R. *lawyer, beverage corporation executive*
Paley, Alan H. *lawyer*
Palladino, Vincent Neil *lawyer*
Palmieri, Victor Henry *lawyer, business executive*
Panken, Peter Michael *lawyer*
Papernik, Joel Ira *lawyer*
Parish, J. Michael *lawyer, writer*
Parver, Jane W. *lawyer*
Patrikis, Ernest T. *lawyer*
Paul, Eve W. *lawyer*
Paul, James William *lawyer*
Paul, Robert Carey *lawyer*
Peaslee, James M. *lawyer*
Peet, Charles D., Jr. *lawyer*
Peloso, John Francis Xavier *lawyer*
Pelster, William Charles *lawyer*
Pelz, Robert Leon *lawyer*
Pennoyer, Paul Geddes, Jr. *lawyer*
Pennoyer, Robert M. *lawyer*
Pepper, Allan Michael *lawyer*
Peppers, Jerry P. *lawyer*
Perkiel, Mitchel H. *lawyer*
Perkins, Roswell Burchard *lawyer*
Perlmuth, William Alan *lawyer*
Perschetz, Martin L. *lawyer*
Pershan, Richard Henry *lawyer*
Peters, Alton Emil *lawyer*
Peterson, Charles Gordon *retired lawyer*
Petkanics, Bryan G. *lawyer*
Pettibone, Peter John *lawyer*
Pfeffer, David H. *lawyer*
Phillips, Anthony Francis *lawyer*
Phillips, Barnet, IV *lawyer*
Phillips, Charles Gorham *lawyer*
Phillips, Pamela Kim *lawyer*
Pidot, Whitney Dean *lawyer*
Pierce, Morton Allen *lawyer*
Pierpoint, Powell *lawyer*
Pietrzak, Alfred Robert *lawyer*
Pike, Laurence Bruce *retired lawyer*
Plant, David William *lawyer*
Plevan, Bettina B. *lawyer*
Plum, Bernard Mark *lawyer*
Polak, Werner L. *lawyer*
Polevoy, Nancy Tally *lawyer, social worker, genealogist*
Pollack, Stanley P. *lawyer*
Pollak, Martin Marshall *lawyer, patent development company executive*
Posen, Susan Orzack *lawyer*
Posner, Louis Joseph *lawyer, accountant*
Powell, James Henry *lawyer*
Powell, Richard Gordon *retired lawyer*
Powers, Elizabeth Whitmel *lawyer*
Preble, Laurence George *lawyer*
Preiskel, Barbara Scott *lawyer, association executive*
Prem, F. Herbert, Jr. *lawyer*
Prentice, Eugene Miles, III *lawyer*
Price, Robert *lawyer, media executive, investment banker*
Prince, Kenneth Stephen *lawyer*
Puleo, Frank Charles *lawyer*
Qian, Jin *law librarian*
Queller, Fred *lawyer*
Quinlan, Guy Christian *lawyer*
Quinn, Timothy Charles, Jr. *lawyer*
Quinn, Yvonne Susan *lawyer*
Raab, Sheldon *lawyer*
Rabb, Bruce *lawyer*
Rabb, Maxwell M. *lawyer, former ambassador*
Rabin, Jack *lawyer*
Rabunski, Alan E. *lawyer*
Rahm, David Alan *lawyer*
Rahm, Susan Berkman *lawyer*
Raisler, Kenneth Mark *lawyer*
Ralli, Constantine Pandia *lawyer*
Rand, Harry Israel *lawyer*
Rand, William *lawyer, former state justice*
Rankin, Clyde Evan, III *lawyer*
Rapoport, Bernard Robert *lawyer*
Rappaport, Charles Owen *lawyer*
Raylesberg, Alan Ira *lawyer*
Redlich, Norman *lawyer, educator*
Reibstein, Richard Jay *lawyer*
Reid, Edward Snover, III *lawyer*
Reid, John Phillip *law educator*
Reid, Sarah Layfield *lawyer*
Reilly, Conor Desmond *lawyer*
Reilly, Edward Arthur *lawyer*
Reinhold, Richard Lawrence *lawyer*
Reiniger, Douglas Haigh *lawyer*
Reinthaler, Richard Walter *lawyer*
Reis, Muriel Henle *lawyer, broadcast executive/ television commentator*
Reiss, Steven Alan *lawyer, law educator*
Rembar, Charles (Isaiah) *lawyer, writer*
Resor, Stanley Rogers *lawyer*
Reverdin, Bernard J. *lawyer*
Ribicoff, Abraham A. *lawyer, former senator*
Rice, Donald Sands *lawyer, entrepreneur*
Rice, Joseph Lee, III *lawyer*
Rich, R(obert) Bruce *lawyer*
Richards, David Alan *lawyer*
Richman, Martin Franklin *lawyer*
Rifkind, Robert S(inger) *lawyer*
Rikon, Michael *lawyer*
Riley, Scott C. *lawyer*
Ring, Renee E. *lawyer*
Ringel, Dean *lawyer*
Ringer, James Milton *lawyer*
Ritter, Ann L. *lawyer*
Ritter, Robert Joseph *lawyer*
Roberts, Sidney I. *lawyer*
Robertson, Edwin David *lawyer*
Robinowitz, Stuart *lawyer*
Robinson, Barbara Paul *lawyer*
Robinson, Irwin Jay *lawyer*
Rocklen, Kathy Hellenbrand *lawyer, banker*
Rodman, Leroy Eli *lawyer*
Rodriguez, Vincent Angel *lawyer*
Roe, Mark J. *law educator*
Roessler, Ronald James *lawyer*
Rogers, Theodore Otto, Jr. *lawyer*
Rohrbach, Heidi A. *lawyer*
Rolfe, Ronald Stuart *lawyer*
Romans, John Niebrugge *lawyer*
Rooney, Paul C., Jr. *lawyer*
Rosa, Margarita *agency chief executive, lawyer*
Rosdeitcher, Sidney Samuel *lawyer*
Rosen, Richard Lewis *lawyer, real estate developer*
Rosenberg, Alan Stewart *lawyer*
Rosenberg, Jerome I. *lawyer*
Rosenberg, Stephen *lawyer*
Rosenblum, Scott S. *lawyer*
Rosenfeld, Arthur H. *lawyer, publisher*
Rosenfeld, Steven B. *lawyer*
Rosensaft, Menachem Zwi *lawyer, author, foundation executive, community activist*
Rosenzweig, Charles Leonard *lawyer*
Rosow, Stuart L. *lawyer*
Ross, Mary Riepma Cowell (Mrs. John O. Ross) *retired lawyer*
Ross, Matthew *lawyer*
Roth, Eric M. *lawyer*
Roth, Judith Shulman *lawyer*
Roth, Paul Norman *lawyer*
Rothman, Bernard *lawyer*
Rothman, Henry Isaac *lawyer*
Rothman, Howard Joel *lawyer*
Rover, Edward Frank *lawyer*
Rovine, Arthur William *lawyer*
Rowe, Elizabeth Webb *paralegal administrator*
Rozel, Samuel Joseph *lawyer*
Rubenfeld, Stanley Irwin *lawyer*
Rubenstein, Joshua Seth *lawyer*
Rubin, Herbert *lawyer*
Rubin, Richard Allan *lawyer*
Rubino, Victor Joseph *law institute executive*
Rubinstein, Frederic Armand *lawyer*
Rudoff, Sheldon *lawyer, former religious organization executive*
Ruebhausen, Oscar Melick *lawyer*
Ruegger, Philip T., III *lawyer*
Rusmisel, Stephen R. *lawyer*
Russell, John St. Clair, Jr. *lawyer*
Russo, Gregory Thomas *lawyer*
Russo, Thomas Anthony *lawyer*
Ryan, J. Richard *lawyer*
Sabel, Bradley Kent *lawyer*
Sachs, David *lawyer*
Sack, Robert David *lawyer*
Sacks, Ira Stephen *lawyer*
Safer, Jay Gerald *lawyer*
Saft, Stuart Mark *lawyer*
Sahid, Joseph Robert *lawyer*
Saiman, Martin S. *lawyer*
Salman, Robert Ronald *lawyer*
Salter, Kevin Thornton *lawyer*
Samuels, Leslie B. *lawyer*
Sandler, Ross *law educator*
Sanseverino, Raymond Anthony *lawyer*
Santana, Robert Rafael *lawyer*
Sargent, James Cunningham *lawyer*
Satine, Barry Roy *lawyer*
Saufer, Isaac Aaron *lawyer*
Saunders, Mark A. *lawyer*
Saunders, Paul Christopher *lawyer*
Savitt, Susan Schenkel *lawyer*
Savrin, Louis *lawyer*
Schaab, Arnold J. *lawyer*
Schacht, Ronald Stuart *lawyer*
Schachter, Oscar *lawyer, educator, arbitrator*
Schade, Malcolm Robert *lawyer*
Schaffer, Seth Andrew *lawyer*
Schallert, Edwin Glenn *lawyer*
Schapiro, Donald *lawyer*
Scheiman, Eugene R. *lawyer*
Scheler, Brad Eric *lawyer*
Scher, Irving *lawyer*
Schirmeister, Charles F. *lawyer*
Schizer, Zevie Baruch *lawyer*
Schlain, Barbara Ellen *lawyer*
Schlesinger, Sanford Joel *lawyer*
Schmertz, Eric Joseph *lawyer, educator*
Schmidt, Daniel Edward, IV *lawyer*
Schmidt, Joseph W. *lawyer*
Schmolka, Leo Louis *law educator*
Schneider, Howard *lawyer*
Schneider, Willys Hope *lawyer*
Schneiderman, Irwin *lawyer*
Schorr, Brian Lewis *lawyer, business executive*
Schreiber, Paul Solomon *lawyer*
Schroeder, Edmund R. *lawyer*
Schueller, Thomas George *lawyer*
Schulte, Stephen John *lawyer, educator*
Schuur, Robert George *lawyer*
Schwab, Harold Lee *lawyer*
Schwab, Terrance Walter *lawyer*
Schwartz, Barry Fredric *lawyer, diversified holding company executive*
Schwartz, Barry Steven *lawyer*
Schwartz, Herbert Frederick *lawyer*
Schwartz, Marvin *lawyer*
Schwartz, Renee Gerstler *lawyer*
Schwartz, William *lawyer, educator*
Schwind, Michael Angelo *law educator*
Sederbaum, Arthur David *lawyer*
Segall, Harold Abraham *lawyer*
Seidel, Selvyn *lawyer, educator*
Seifert, Thomas Lloyd *lawyer*
Seiff, Eric A. *lawyer*
Seigel, Stuart Evan *lawyer*
Seitelman, Mark Elias *lawyer*
Seligman, Frederick *lawyer*
Seltzer, Richard C. *lawyer*
Selver, Paul Darryl *lawyer*
Semaya, Francine L. *lawyer*
Senzel, Martin Lee *lawyer*
Serbaroli, Francis J. *lawyer, educator, writer*
Serota, Susan Perlstadt *lawyer*
Sesser, Gary Douglas *lawyer*
Setrakian, Berge *lawyer*
Severs, Charles A., III *lawyer*
Seward, George Chester *lawyer*
Shanman, James Alan *lawyer*
Shapiro, George M. *lawyer*
Shapiro, Howard Alan *lawyer*
Shapiro, Jerome Gerson *lawyer*
Shaw, L. Edward, Jr. *lawyer*
Shays, Rona Joyce *lawyer*
Shea, Edward Emmett *lawyer, educator, author*
Shea, James William *lawyer*
Shechtman, Ronald H. *lawyer*
Sheehan, Robert C. *lawyer*
Shelby, Jerome *lawyer*
Shen, Michael *lawyer*
Shepard, Robert M. *lawyer, investment banker, engineer*
Sheresky, Norman M. *lawyer*
Sherman, Jonathan Henry *lawyer*
Sherman, Randolph S. *lawyer*
Shientag, Florence Perlow *lawyer*
Shimer, Zachary *lawyer*
Shorter, James Russell, Jr. *lawyer*
Shoss, Cynthia Renée *lawyer*
Shulman, Max Rees *lawyer*
Shupack, Paul Martin *law educator*
Shyer, John D. *lawyer*
Sidamon-Eristoff, Constantine *lawyer*
Siegel, Jeffrey Norton *lawyer*
Siegel, Martin Jay *lawyer, investment advisor*
Siegel, Stanley *lawyer, educator*
Siegel, Sylvia *law librarian*
Silberberg, Michael Cousins *lawyer*
Silberberg, Richard Howard *lawyer*
Silberman, John Alan *lawyer*
Silkenat, James Robert *lawyer*
Silleck, Harry Garrison *lawyer*
Silverberg, Michael Joel *lawyer*
Silverman, Arthur Charles *lawyer*
Silverman, Moses *lawyer*
Silverman, Samuel Joshua *lawyer*
Silvers, Eileen S. *lawyer*
Simone, Joseph R. *lawyer*
Simons, Albert, III *lawyer*
Sinnott, John Patrick *lawyer, educator*
Sirkin, Michael S. *lawyer*
Siskind, Arthur *lawyer, director*
Siskind, Donald Henry *lawyer*
Sitrick, James Baker *lawyer*
Skigen, Patricia Sue *lawyer*
Skirnick, Robert Andrew *lawyer*
Sklaren, Cary Stewart *lawyer*
Skolnick, Jerome H. *law educator*
Slain, John Joseph *legal educator*
Slater, Jill Sherry *lawyer*
Slonaker, Norman Dale *lawyer*
Small, Jonathan Andrew *lawyer*
Smit, Hans *law educator, academic administrator, lawyer*
Smith, Bradley Youle *lawyer*
Smith, Edward Paul, Jr. *lawyer*
Smith, James Walker *lawyer*
Smith, Robert Everett *lawyer*
Smith, Stuart A. *lawyer*
Smith, Vincent Milton *lawyer, designer, consultant*
Snitow, Charles *lawyer*
Sommers, George R. *lawyer*
Sorensen, Theodore Chaikin *lawyer, former special counsel to President of United States*
Sorkin, Laurence Truman *lawyer*
Sovern, Michael Ira *law educator*
Soyster, Margaret Blair *lawyer*
Spear, Harvey M. *lawyer*
Sperling, Allan George *lawyer*
Spiegel, Jerrold Bruce *lawyer*
Spivack, Gordon Bernard *lawyer, lecturer*
Squire, Walter Charles *lawyer*
Stamm, Charles H. *lawyer*
Stanger, Abraham M. *lawyer*
Starer, Brian D. *lawyer*
Stathis, Nicholas John *lawyer*
Steele, Diana Alexander *lawyer*
Stein, Stephen William *lawyer*
Steinberg, Howard Eli *lawyer, holding company executive, public official*
Stephenson, Alan Clements *lawyer*
Sternman, Joel W. *lawyer*
Steuer, Richard Marc *lawyer*
Stewart, Charles Evan *lawyer*
Stewart, Duncan James *lawyer*
Stewart, Richard Burleson *lawyer, educator*
Steyer, Roy Henry *retired lawyer*
Stoll, Neal Richard *lawyer*
Stone, David Philip *lawyer*
Stone, Merrill Brent *lawyer*
Storette, Ronald Frank *lawyer*
Stratton, Walter Love *lawyer*
Straub, Chester John *lawyer*
Strauber, Donald I. *lawyer*
Strauss, Gary Joseph *lawyer*
Strauss, Peter L(ester) *law educator*
Strickon, Harvey Alan *lawyer*
Strom, Milton Gary *lawyer*
Strum, Jay Gerson *lawyer*
Struve, Guy Miller *lawyer*
Sugarman, Irwin J. *lawyer*
Sugarman, Robert Gary *lawyer*
Suhr, J. Nicholas *lawyer*
Sulger, Francis Xavier *lawyer*
Sullivan, Peter Meredith *lawyer*
Supino, Anthony Martin *lawyer*
Sussman, Alexander Ralph *lawyer*
†Sussman, David William *lawyer*
Sutter, Laurence Brener *lawyer*
Sweeney, Thomas Joseph, Jr. *lawyer*
Symmers, William Garth *international maritime lawyer*
Tancredi, Laurence Richard *law and psychiatry educator, administrator*
Taylor, Job, III *lawyer*
Taylor, John Chestnut, III *lawyer*
Taylor, Richard Trelore *retired lawyer*
Taylor, Telford *lawyer, educator*
Teclaff, Ludwik Andrzej *law educator, consultant, author, lawyer*
Teiman, Richard B. *lawyer*
Tengi, Frank R. *lawyer, insurance company executive*
Tenney, Dudley Bradstreet *lawyer*
Terrell, J. Anthony *lawyer*
Terry, James Joseph, Jr. *lawyer*
Testa, Michael Harold *lawyer*
Thackeray, Jonathan E. *lawyer*
Thal, Steven Henry *lawyer*
Thalacker, Arbie Robert *lawyer*
Thomas, Robert Morton, Jr. *lawyer*
Thomas, Roger Warren *lawyer*
Thoyer, Judith Reinhardt *lawyer*
Tillinghast, David Rollhaus *lawyer*
Todd, Ronald Gary *lawyer*
Tondel, Lawrence Chapman *lawyer*
Tract, Marc Mitchell *lawyer*
Tracy, Janet Ruth *legal educator, librarian*
Tramontine, John Orlando *lawyer*
Traum, Jerome S. *lawyer*
Tricarico, Joseph Archangelo *lawyer*

Trost, J. Ronald *lawyer*
Trubin, John *lawyer*
Tuck, Edward Hallam *lawyer*
Tulchin, David Bruce *lawyer*
Tung, Ko-Yung *lawyer*
Turner, E. Deane *lawyer*
Tyler, Harold Russell, Jr. *lawyer, former government official*
Udell, Richard *lawyer*
Ufford, Charles Wilbur, Jr. *lawyer*
Ullman, Leo Solomon *lawyer*
Underberg, Mark Alan *lawyer*
Uram, Gerald Robert *lawyer*
Urowsky, Richard J. *lawyer*
Valente, Peter Charles *lawyer*
Vance, Andrew Peter *lawyer*
Vance, Cyrus Roberts *lawyer, former government official*
Van Gundy, Gregory Frank *lawyer*
Varet, Michael A. *lawyer*
Vassallo, Edward E. *lawyer*
Vega, Matias Alfonso *lawyer*
Versfelt, David Scott *lawyer*
Viener, John D. *lawyer*
Vig, Vernon Edward *lawyer*
Vitkowsky, Vincent Joseph *lawyer*
Vogel, Eugene L. *lawyer*
Volckhausen, William Alexander *lawyer, banker*
Volk, Stephen Richard *lawyer*
von Mehren, Robert Brandt *lawyer, retired*
Wachtel, Norman Jay *lawyer*
Wadsworth, Dyer Seymour *lawyer*
Wailand, George *lawyer*
Wainwright, Carroll Livingston, Jr. *lawyer*
Waks, Jay Warren *lawyer*
Waksman, Ted Stewart *lawyer*
Wald, Bernard Joseph *lawyer*
Wales, Gwynne Huntington *lawyer*
Wallace, Nora Ann *lawyer*
Wallace, Walter C. *lawyer, government official*
Wallach, Eric Jean *lawyer*
Wallance, Gregory J. *lawyer*
Walpin, Gerald *lawyer*
Warden, John L. *lawyer*
Warner, Edward Waide, Jr. *lawyer*
Warren, Irwin Howard *lawyer*
Warren, William Bradford *lawyer*
Warren, William Clements *law educator*
Warshauer, Irene Conrad *lawyer*
Washburn, David Thacher *lawyer*
Watson, Solomon Brown, IV *lawyer, business executive*
Wattman, Malcolm Peter *lawyer*
Watts, David Eide *lawyer*
Wechsler, Herbert *retired legal educator*
Weiksner, Sandra S. *lawyer*
Weil, Gilbert Harry *lawyer*
Weinberg, Herschel Mayer *lawyer*
Weinberger, Harold Paul *lawyer*
Weiner, Andrew Jay *lawyer*
Weiner, Earl David *lawyer*
Weiner, Stephen Arthur *lawyer*
Weiner, Stephen L. *lawyer*
Weinschel, Alan Jay *lawyer*
Weinstein, Mark Michael *lawyer*
Weinstein, Ruth Joseph *lawyer*
Weinstock, Leonard *lawyer*
Weir, John Keeley *lawyer*
Weir, Peter Frank *lawyer*
Weisbrod, Carl Barry *lawyer, public official*
Weisburd, Steven I. *lawyer*
Weiss, Lawrence N. *lawyer*
Weld, Jonathan Minot *lawyer*
Welikson, Jeffrey Alan *lawyer*
Welles, James Bell, Jr. *lawyer*
Wellington, Harry Hillel *lawyer, educator*
Welt, Philip Stanley *lawyer, consultant*
Wemple, William *lawyer*
Wendel, Martin *lawyer*
Wender, Ira Tensard *lawyer*
Werner, Robert L. *lawyer*
Wesely, Edwin Joseph *lawyer*
Westin, David Lawrence *lawyer*
Wetzler, Monte Edwin *lawyer*
Wexelbaum, Michael *lawyer*
Weyher, Harry Frederick *lawyer*
Whelan, Stephen Thomas *lawyer*
Whelchel, Betty Anne *lawyer*
White, Harry Edward, Jr. *lawyer*
White, John Patrick *lawyer*
Whoriskey, Robert Donald *lawyer*
Wickes, R(ichard) Paul *lawyer*
Wilcox, John Caven *lawyer, corporate consultant*
Wilder, Charles Willoughby *lawyer, consultant*
Wildes, Leon *lawyer, educator*
Wilensky, Saul *lawyer*
Wilkinson, John Hart *lawyer*
Williams, Lowell Craig *lawyer, employee relations executive*
Williams, Omer S. J. *lawyer*
Williams, Thomas Allison *lawyer*
Williamson, Douglas Franklin, Jr. *lawyer*
Willis, Everett Irving *lawyer*
Willis, William Ervin *lawyer*
Willkie, Wendell Lewis, II *lawyer*
Wilson, Paul Holliday, Jr. *lawyer*
Wilson, Thomas William *lawyer*
Windels, Paul, Jr. *lawyer*
Wing, John Russell *lawyer*
Winger, Ralph O. *lawyer*
Winterer, Philip Steele *lawyer*
Witkin, Eric Douglas *lawyer*
Witmeyer, John Jacob, III *lawyer*
Woglom, Eric Cooke *lawyer*
Wolf, Gary Wickert *lawyer*
Wolfe, James Ronald *lawyer*
Wolff, Jesse David *lawyer*
Wolff, Kurt Jakob *lawyer*
Wolff, Sanford Irving *lawyer*
Wolfson, Michael George *lawyer*
Wolkoff, Eugene Arnold *lawyer*
Wolson, Craig Alan *lawyer*
Worenklein, Jacob Joshua *lawyer*
Worley, Robert William, Jr. *lawyer*
Wray, Cecil, Jr. *lawyer*
Wulf, Melvin Lawrence *lawyer*
Wyckoff, E. Lisk, Jr. *lawyer*
Wyser-Pratte, John Michael *lawyer*
Yamin, Michael Geoffrey *lawyer*
Yelenick, Mary Therese *lawyer*
Yerman, Fredric Warren *lawyer*
Yodowitz, Edward J. *lawyer*
Young, Alice *lawyer*
Young, John Edward *lawyer*
Young, Nancy *lawyer*
Young, William F. *legal educator*
Youngwood, Alfred Donald *lawyer*
Zaitzeff, Roger Michael *lawyer*
Zammit, Joseph Paul *lawyer*
Zedrosser, Joseph John *lawyer*
Zerin, Steven David *lawyer*
Ziegler, William Alexander *lawyer*
Zifchak, William C. *lawyer*
Zimand, Harvey Folks *lawyer*
Zimmerman, Jean *lawyer*
Zimmett, Mark Paul *lawyer*
Zirin, James David *lawyer*
Zirinsky, Bruce R. *lawyer*
Zoeller, Donald J. *lawyer*
Zonana, Victor *lawyer, educator*
Zoogman, Nicholas Jay *lawyer*
Zornow, David M. *lawyer*
Zukerman, Michael *lawyer*
Zweibel, Joel Burton *lawyer*
Zychick, Joel David *lawyer*

### Newburgh
Liberth, Richard Francis *lawyer*

### Niagara Falls
Anton, Ronald David *lawyer*

### Nyack
Seidler, B(ernard) Alan *lawyer*

### Oneida
Matthews, William D(oty) *lawyer, consumer products manufacturing company executive*

### Orangeburg
Rivet, Diana Wittmer *lawyer, developer*

### Orchard Park
Schulz, Lawrence A. *lawyer*
Sullivan, Mortimer Allen, Jr. *lawyer*

### Ossining
Daly, William Joseph *lawyer*

### Oyster Bay
Robinson, Edward T., III *lawyer*

### Pearl River
Meyer, Irwin Stephan *lawyer, accountant*

### Peconic
Mitchell, Robert Everitt *lawyer*

### Pelham
Simon, Robert G. *lawyer*

### Pittsford
Kieffer, James Milton *lawyer*
Williams, Henry Ward, Jr. *lawyer*

### Plattsburgh
Lewis, Clyde A. *lawyer*

### Pleasantville
Ahrensfeld, Thomas Frederick *lawyer*
Needleman, Harry *lawyer*

### Pomona
Zerin, Jay M. *lawyer*

### Port Washington
Feldman, Jay Newman *lawyer, telecommunications executive*
Read, Frederick Wilson, Jr. *lawyer, educator*
Saltzman, Ellen S. *mediator*

### Poughkeepsie
Millman, Jode Susan *lawyer*
Ostertag, Robert Louis *lawyer*

### Purchase
Gioffre, Bruno Joseph *lawyer*
Guedry, James Walter *lawyer, paper corporation executive*
Kelly, Edmund Joseph *lawyer, investment banker*
Melican, James Patrick, Jr. *lawyer*
Wallach, Ira David *lawyer, business executive*
Wallin, James Peter *lawyer*

### Riverdale
Itzkoff, Norman Jay *lawyer*

### Rochester
Andolina, Lawrence J. *lawyer*
Blyth, John E. *lawyer, educator*
Braunsdorf, Paul Raymond *lawyer*
Buckley, Michael Francis *lawyer*
Clement, Thomas Earl *lawyer*
Colby, William Michael *lawyer*
Donovan, Kreag *lawyer*
Doyle, Justin P *lawyer*
George, Richard Neill *lawyer*
Goldman, Joel J. *lawyer*
Gootnick, Margery Fischbein *lawyer*
Gumaer, Elliott Wilder, Jr. *lawyer*
Hampson, Thomas Meredith *lawyer*
Harris, Wayne Manley *lawyer*
Hoffberg, David Lawrence *lawyer*
Holmes, Jay Thorpe *lawyer*
Hood, John B. *lawyer*
Jesserer, Henry L., III *lawyer*
Kraus, Sherry Stokes *lawyer*
Kurland, Harold Arthur *lawyer*
Law, Michael R. *lawyer*
Lundback, Staffan Bengt Gunnar *lawyer*
McCrory, John Brooks *retired lawyer*
Morrison, Patrice B. *lawyer*
Palermo, Anthony Robert *lawyer*
Paley, Gerald Larry *lawyer*
Parsons, George Raymond, Jr. *lawyer*
Reed, James Alexander, Jr. *lawyer*
Robfogel, Susan Salitan *lawyer*
Rosenbaum, Richard Merrill *lawyer*
Rosner, Leonard Allen *lawyer*
Schumacher, Jon Lee *lawyer*
Scutt, Robert Carl *lawyer*
Smith, John Stuart *lawyer*
†Speranza, Paul Samuel, Jr. *lawyer*
Stewart, Sue S. *lawyer*
Stonehill, Eric *lawyer*
Trueheart, Harry Parker, III *lawyer*
Turner, Scott MacNeely *lawyer*
Turri, Joseph A. *lawyer*
Tyler, John Randolph *lawyer*
Underberg, Alan Jack *lawyer*
Waite, Stephen Holden *lawyer*
Wild, Robert Warren *lawyer*
Willett, Thomas Edward *lawyer*
Witmer, George Robert, Jr. *lawyer*
Zamboni, Helen Attena *lawyer, international telecommunications executive*

### Rockville Centre
Lerner, Steven Paul *lawyer*

### Rome
Griffith, Emlyn Irving *lawyer*
Simons, Richard Duncan *lawyer*

### Roslyn
Levitan, David M(aurice) *lawyer, educator*

### Rye
Dixon, Paul Edward *lawyer, metal products and manufacturing company executive*
Flanagan, Eugene John Thomas *retired lawyer*

### Rye Brook
Garcia C., Elisa Dolores *lawyer*

### Sands Point
Hoynes, Louis LeNoir, Jr. *lawyer*

### Scarsdale
Gerber, Roger Alan *lawyer, business consultant*
Hoffman, Richard M. *lawyer*
King, Robert Lucien *lawyer*
O'Brien, Edward Ignatius *lawyer, private investor*
Sheehan, Larry John *lawyer*

### Schenectady
Levine, Sanford Harold *lawyer*
Taub, Eli Irwin *lawyer, arbitrator*
Wickerham, Richard Dennis *lawyer*

### Schoharie
Duncombe, Raynor Bailey *lawyer*

### Shokan
Schwartzberg, Paul David *lawyer*

### Silver Bay
Parlin, Charles C., Jr. *retired lawyer*

### Smithtown
Goodman, Richard Shalem *lawyer, orthopedic surgeon*
Pruzansky, Joshua Murdock *lawyer*
Spellman, Thomas Joseph, Jr. *lawyer*

### Spencertown
Dunne, John Richard *lawyer*

### Staten Island
Harris, Allen *lawyer, educator, consultant*
Henry, Paul James *lawyer, health care administrator*
Paunov, Catherine Pennington *legal technology consultant*

### Syracuse
Barclay, H(ugh) Douglas *lawyer, former state senator*
Beeching, Charles Train, Jr. *lawyer*
Bogart, William Harry *lawyer*
Bottar, Anthony Samuel *lawyer*
Cirando, John Anthony *lawyer*
DiLorenzo, Louis Patrick *lawyer*
Ferguson, Tracy Heiman *lawyer, educational administrator*
Fitzpatrick, James David *lawyer*
Fraser, Henry S. *lawyer*
Gaal, John *lawyer*
Gilman, Karen Frenzel *legal assistant*
Hayes, David Michael *lawyer*
Herzog, Peter Emilius *legal educator*
Hole, Richard Douglas *lawyer*
King, Bernard T. *lawyer*
Kopp, Robert Walter *lawyer*
Lawton, Joseph J., Jr. *lawyer*
Mathewson, George Atterbury *lawyer*
Moses, Robert Edward *lawyer*
Regan, Paul Michael *lawyer*
Shattuck, George Clement *lawyer*
Strutin, Kennard Regan *lawyer, educator, law librarian*
Traylor, Robert Arthur *lawyer*
Wiecek, William Michael *law educator*
Zimmerman, Aaron Mark *lawyer*

### Tarrytown
Benjamin, Jeff *lawyer, pharmaceutical executive*
Oelbaum, Harold *lawyer, corporate executive*

### Troy
Jones, E. Stewart, Jr. *lawyer*

### Tupper Lake
Johnson, David Wesley *lawyer*

### Tuxedo Park
Brown, Walston Shepard *lawyer*

### Uniondale
Brown, Kenneth Lloyd *lawyer*
Cassidy, David Michael *lawyer*
Shapiro, Barry Robert *lawyer*

### Valley Stream
Blakeman, Royal Edwin *lawyer*

### Watertown
Militello, Samuel Philip *lawyer*

### White Plains
Alin, Robert David *lawyer*
Bader, Izaak Walton *lawyer*
Berlin, Alan Daniel *lawyer, international energy and legal consultant*
Carey, John *lawyer, judge*
Castrataro, Barbara Ann *lawyer*
Feder, Robert *lawyer*
Gjertsen, O. Gerard *lawyer*
Graham, Lawrence Otis *lawyer, writer, television personality*
Greenspan, Leon Joseph *lawyer*
Greenspan, Michael Evan *lawyer*
Halpern, Philip Morgan *lawyer*
Jensen, Eric Finn *lawyer*
Klein, Paul E. *lawyer*
Maffeo, Vincent Anthony *lawyer, executive*
McQuaid, John Gaffney *lawyer*
Munneke, Gary Arthur *law educator, consultant*
Mutz, Steven Herbert *lawyer*
O'Rourke, Richard Lynn *lawyer*
Payson, Martin Fred *lawyer*
Rosenberg, Michael *lawyer*
Serchuk, Ivan *lawyer*
Silverberg, Steven Mark *lawyer*
Sinsheimer, Warren Jack *lawyer*
Sive, David *lawyer*
Triffin, Nicholas *law librarian, law educator*
Vogel, Howard Stanley *lawyer*

### Wolcott
Bartlett, Cody Blake *lawyer, educator*

### Woodbury
Lemle, Robert Spencer *lawyer*

### Woodmere
Bobroff, Harold *lawyer*
Raab, Ira Jerry *lawyer, judge*

### Yorktown Heights
Samalin, Edwin *lawyer, educator*

## NORTH CAROLINA

### Asheville
Baldwin, Garza, Jr. *lawyer, manufacturing company executive*
Bissette, Winston Louis, Jr. *lawyer, mayor*
Davis, Roy Walton, Jr. *lawyer*
Dillard, John Robert *lawyer*
Hyde, Herbert Lee *lawyer*
Johnston, John Devereaux, Jr. *law educator, retired*
Lavelle, Brian Francis David *lawyer*
Pinkerton, Linda F. *lawyer*
Sharpe, Keith Yount *retired lawyer*

### Boone
Brown, Wade Edward *lawyer, retired*

### Buies Creek
Davis, Ferd Leary, Jr. *law educator, lawyer, consultant*

### Burnsville
Peterson, Allen Jay *lawyer, educator*

### Cary
Montgomery, Charles Harvey *lawyer*

### Chapel Hill
Broun, Kenneth Stanley *lawyer, educator*
Crassweller, Robert Doell *retired lawyer, writer*
Crohn, Max Henry, Jr. *lawyer*
Cummings, Anthony William *lawyer, educator*
Daye, Charles Edward *law educator*
Gasaway, Laura Nell *law librarian, educator*
Gressman, Eugene *lawyer*
Haskell, Paul Gershon *law educator*
Herman-Giddens, Gregory *lawyer*
Lawrence, David Michael *lawyer, educator*
Lilley, Albert Frederick *retired lawyer*
Loeb, Ben Fohl, Jr. *lawyer, educator*
Martin, Harry Corpening *lawyer, retired state supreme court justice*
Sharpless, Richard Kennedy *lawyer*
Wegner, Judith Welch *law educator, dean*

### Charlotte
Abelman, Henry Moss *lawyer*
Ayscue, Edwin Osborne, Jr. *lawyer*
Belthoff, Richard Charles, Jr. *lawyer*
Brackett, Martin Luther, Jr. *lawyer*
Buchan, Jonathan Edward, Jr. *lawyer*
Cogdell, Joe Bennett, Jr. *lawyer*
Dagenhart, Larry Jones *lawyer*
Davis, William Maxie, Jr. *lawyer*
Ferguson, James Elliot, II *lawyer*
Gage, Gaston Hemphill *lawyer*
Grier, Joseph Williamson, Jr. *lawyer*
Griffith, Steve Campbell, Jr. *lawyer*
Hanna, George Verner, III *lawyer*
McBryde, Neill Gregory *lawyer*
McConnell, David Moffatt *lawyer*
Orsbon, Richard Anthony *lawyer*
Preston, James Young *lawyer*
Raper, William Cranford *lawyer*
Shoemaker, Raleigh A. *lawyer*
Taylor, David Brooke *lawyer, banker*
Thigpen, Richard Elton, Jr. *lawyer*
Van Allen, William Kent *lawyer*
Van Alstyne, Vance Brownell *arbitration management consultant*
Waggoner, William Johnson *lawyer*
Walker, Clarence Wesley *lawyer*
Wood, William McBrayer *lawyer*
Woolard, William Leon *lawyer, electrical distributing company executive*
Zeller, Michael Eugene *lawyer*

### Durham
Bartlett, Katharine Tiffany *law educator*
Carrington, Paul DeWitt *lawyer, educator*
Christie, George Custis *lawyer, educator, author*
Cox, James D. *law educator*
Danner, Richard Allen *law educator, dean*
Demott, Deborah Ann *lawyer, educator*
Gann, Pamela Brooks *law educator*
Graham, William Thomas *lawyer*
Havighurst, Clark Canfield *law educator*
Horowitz, Donald Leonard *lawyer, educator, researcher, political scientist, arbitrator*
Lange, David L. *law educator*
Luney, Percy Robert, Jr. *law educator, dean, lawyer, consultant*
Markham, Charles Buchanan *lawyer*
Maxwell, Richard Callender *lawyer, educator*
McMahon, John Alexander *law educator*
Mosteller, Robert P. *law educator*
Robertson, Horace Bascomb, Jr. *law educator*
Rowe, Thomas Dudley, Jr. *law educator*
Schwarcz, Steven Lance *lawyer*
Shimm, Melvin Gerald *law educator*

Warren, David Grant *lawyer, educator*
Welborn, Reich Lee *lawyer*

### Fairview
Rhynedance, Harold Dexter, Jr. *lawyer, consultant*

### Fayetteville
Mitchell, Ronnie Monroe *lawyer*

### Gastonia
Alala, Joseph Basil, Jr. *lawyer, accountant*
Garland, James Boyce *lawyer*
Stott, Grady Bernell *lawyer*

### Gibsonville
Foster, C(harles) Allen *lawyer*

### Greensboro
Bell, Haney Hardy, III *lawyer*
Clark, David M. *lawyer*
Davidson, Gerard H., Jr. *lawyer*
Davis, Herbert Owen *lawyer*
Erwin, Martin Nesbitt *lawyer*
Floyd, Jack William *lawyer*
Gabriel, Richard Weisner *lawyer*
Gumbiner, Kenneth Jay *lawyer*
Harllee, JoAnn Towery *lawyer, educator*
Holton, Walter Clinton, Jr. *U.S. attorney*
Hopkins, John David *lawyer*
Hunter, Bynum Merritt *lawyer*
Koonce, Neil Wright *lawyer*
McGinn, Max Daniel *lawyer*
Melvin, Charles Edward, Jr. *lawyer*
Moore, Beverly Cooper *lawyer*
Rowlenson, Richard Charles *lawyer*
St. George, Nicholas James *lawyer, manufactured housing company executive*
Schell, Braxton *lawyer*
Smith, John McNeill, Jr. *lawyer*
Smith, Lanty L(loyd) *lawyer, business executive*

### Greenville
Flanagan, Michael Perkins *lawyer*

### High Point
Sheahan, Robert Emmett *lawyer, consultant*

### Horse Shoe
Howell, George Washington *lawyer, consultant*

### Lenoir
Flaherty, David Thomas, Jr. *lawyer*

### Marion
Burgin, Charles E. *lawyer*

### Morganton
Simpson, Daniel Reid *lawyer*

### Murphy
Bata, Rudolph Andrew, Jr. *lawyer*

### New Bern
Davis, James Lee *lawyer*
Kellum, Norman Bryant, Jr. *lawyer*
Overholt, Hugh Robert *lawyer, retired army officer*
Skipper, Nathan Richard, Jr. *lawyer*
Stoller, David Allen *lawyer*
Ward, Thomas Monroe *lawyer, law educator*

### Oxford
Burnette, James Thomas *lawyer*

### Raleigh
Carlton, Alfred Pershing, Jr. *lawyer*
Carter, Jean Gordon *lawyer*
Case, Charles Dixon *lawyer*
Collins, G. Bryan, Jr. *lawyer*
Dannelly, William David *lawyer*
Davis, Egbert Lawrence, III *lawyer*
Davis, Thomas Hill, Jr. *lawyer*
Dixon, Daniel Roberts, Jr. *tax lawyer*
Dixon, Wright Tracy, Jr. *lawyer*
Eason, Joseph W. *lawyer*
Edwards, Charles Archibald *lawyer*
Ellis, Lester Neal, Jr. *lawyer*
Ellis, Richard W. *lawyer*
Foley, Peter Michael *lawyer*
Graham, William Edgar, Jr. *lawyer, retired utility company executive*
Gwyn, William Blair, Jr. *lawyer*
Jolly, John Russell, Jr. *lawyer*
Joyner, Walton Kitchin *lawyer*
Kapp, Michael Keith *lawyer*
Kurz, Mary Elizabeth *lawyer*
Markoff, Brad Steven *lawyer*
Maupin, Armistead Jones *lawyer*
Millberg, John C. *lawyer*
Miller, Ralph Bradley *lawyer, state legislator*
Miller, Robert James *lawyer*
Neely, Charles B., Jr. *lawyer*
Poyner, James Marion *retired lawyer*
Ragsdale, George Robinson *lawyer*
Roach, Wesley Linville *lawyer, insurance executive*
Sanford, Terry *lawyer, educator, former United States Senator, former governor, former university president*
Shyllon, Prince E.N. *lawyer, law educator*
Simpson, Steven Drexell *lawyer*
Suhr, Paul Augustine *lawyer*

### Rocky Mount
Cooper, Roy Asberry, III *lawyer, state senator*

### Sanford
Raisig, Paul Jones, Jr. *lawyer*

### Tabor City
Jorgensen, Ralph Gubler *lawyer, accountant*

### Tarboro
Hopkins, Grover Prevatte *lawyer*

### Tryon
Stinson, George Arthur *lawyer, former steel company executive*

### Washington
Rader, Steven Palmer *lawyer*

### Waynesville
Cole, James Yeager *legal services associate, consultant*

### Wilkesboro
Gray, William Campbell *lawyer*

### Wilmington
Medlock, Donald Larson *lawyer*

### Winston Salem
Barnhardt, Zeb Elonzo, Jr. *lawyer*
Barnhill, Henry Grady, Jr. *lawyer*
Benfield, Marion Wilson, Jr. *law educator*
Blynn, Guy Marc *lawyer*
Copenhaver, W. Andrew *lawyer*
Davis, Linwood Layfield *lawyer*
Davis, William Allison, II *lawyer*
Farr, Henry Bartow, Jr. *lawyer*
Gitter, Allan Reinhold *lawyer*
Greason, Murray Crossley, Jr. *lawyer*
Gunter, Michael Donwell *lawyer*
Healy, Joseph Francis, Jr. *lawyer, arbitrator, retired airline executive*
Herring, Jerone Carson *lawyer, bank executive*
Leonard, R. Michael *lawyer*
Maready, William Frank *lawyer*
McAllister, Kenneth Wayne *lawyer*
Motsinger, John Kings *lawyer, mediator, arbitrator*
Petree, William Horton *lawyer*
Ray, Michael Edwin *lawyer*
Sandridge, William Pendleton, Jr. *lawyer*
Schollander, Wendell Leslie, Jr. *lawyer*
Strayhorn, Ralph Nichols, Jr. *lawyer*
Vance, Charles Fogle, Jr. *lawyer*
Walker, George Kontz *law educator*
Wells, Dewey Wallace *lawyer*
Womble, William Fletcher *lawyer*
Zagoria, Sam D(avid) *arbitrator, author, educator*

### Wrightsville Beach
Block, Franklin Lee *lawyer*

## NORTH DAKOTA

### Bismarck
Gilbertson, Joel Warren *lawyer*
Murry, Charles Emerson *lawyer, official*
Nelson, Keithe Eugene *lawyer, state court administrator*
Olson, John Michael *lawyer*
Strutz, William A. *lawyer*
Tabor, Sandra LaVonne *legal association administrator*

### Fargo
Spaeth, Nicholas John *lawyer, former state attorney general*

### Grand Forks
Anderson, Damon Ernest *lawyer*
Cilz, Douglas Arthur *lawyer*
Vogel, Robert *retired lawyer, educator*
Widdel, John Earl, Jr. *lawyer*

### Mandan
Bair, Bruce B. *lawyer*

### Minot
Armstrong, Phillip Dale *lawyer*

## OHIO

### Akron
Bartlo, Sam D. *lawyer*
Childs, James William *lawyer, legal educator*
Coleman, Malina *law educator*
Fisher, James Lee *lawyer*
Gippin, Robert Malcolm *lawyer*
Glinsek, Gerald John *lawyer*
Holloway, Donald Phillip *lawyer*
Lee, Brant Thomas *lawyer, federal official, educator*
Lombardi, Frederick McKean *lawyer*
Lynch, John Edward, Jr. *lawyer*
Moss, Robert Drexler *lawyer*
Richert, Paul *law educator*
Rooney, George Willard *lawyer*
Trotter, Thomas Robert *lawyer*

### Amelia
Thoman, Henry Nixon *lawyer*

### Aurora
Hermann, Philip J. *lawyer*

### Batavia
Rosenhoffer, Chris *lawyer*

### Beachwood
Donnem, Roland William *lawyer, real estate owner and manager*

### Berea
Jolles, Janet Kavanaugh Pilling *lawyer*

### Bowling Green
Hanna, Martin Shad *lawyer*
Holmes, Robert Allen *lawyer, educator, consultant, lecturer*

### Bucyrus
Neff, Robert Clark *lawyer*

### Canton
Bennington, Ronald Kent *lawyer*
Brown, Larry R. *lawyer*
Davila, Edwin *lawyer*
Lindamood, John Beyer *lawyer*
Mokodean, Michael John *lawyer, accountant*

### Chagrin Falls
Streicher, James Franklin *lawyer*

### Chesterland
Durn, Raymond Joseph *lawyer*
Kancelbaum, Joshua Jacob *lawyer*

### Cincinnati
Adams, Edmund John *lawyer*
Anderson, James Milton *lawyer*
Anderson, William Hopple *lawyer*
Anthony, Thomas Dale *lawyer*
Ashdown, Charles Coster *lawyer*
Bahlman, William Thorne, Jr. *retired lawyer*
Bissinger, Mark Christian *lawyer*
Black, Stephen L. *lawyer*
Bridgeland, James Ralph, Jr. *lawyer, mayor*
Bromberg, Barbara Schwartz *lawyer*
Bromberg, Robert Sheldon *lawyer*
Carpenter, James Willard *lawyer*
Carro, Jorge Luis *law educator, consultant*
Carson, Nolan Wendell *lawyer*
Chesley, Stanley Morris *lawyer*
Christenson, Gordon A. *law educator*
Cioffi, Michael Lawrence *lawyer*
Cissell, James Charles *lawyer*
Cody, Thomas Gerald *lawyer*
Covatta, Anthony Gallo, Jr. *lawyer*
Cowan, Jerry Louis *lawyer*
Craig, L. Clifford *lawyer*
Davis, Robert Lawrence *lawyer*
Dehner, Joseph Julnes *lawyer*
DeLong, Deborah *lawyer*
Desmond, William J. *lawyer*
Diller, Edward Dietrich *lawyer*
Dornette, W(illiam) Stuart *lawyer, educator*
Elleman, Lawrence Robert *lawyer*
Erickson, Richard J. *lawyer*
Faller, Susan Grogan *lawyer*
Fink, Jerold Albert *lawyer*
Flanagan, John Anthony *lawyer, educator*
Frank, William Nelson *lawyer, accountant*
Freedman, William Mark *lawyer*
Garfinkel, Jane E. *lawyer*
Gettler, Benjamin *lawyer, manufacturing company executive*
Goodman, Stanley *lawyer*
Greenberg, Gerald Stephen *lawyer*
Guggenheim, Richard E. *lawyer, shoe company executive*
Hardy, William Robinson *lawyer*
Harris, Irving *lawyer*
Heinlen, Ronald Eugene *lawyer*
Heldman, James Gardner *lawyer*
Hermanies, John Hans *lawyer*
Hill, Thomas Clark *lawyer*
Hoffheimer, Daniel Joseph *lawyer*
Hubschman, Henry Allan *lawyer*
Kelley, John Joseph, Jr. *lawyer*
Kiel, Frederick Orin *lawyer*
Kite, William McDougall *lawyer*
Kordons, Uldis *lawyer*
Lawrence, James Kaufman Lebensburger *lawyer*
Lemke, Judith A. *lawyer*
Lindberg, Charles David *lawyer*
Longenecker, Mark Hershey, Jr. *lawyer*
Lutz, James Gurney *lawyer*
Manley, Robert Edward *lawyer, economist*
Mann, David Scott *lawyer*
Maxwell, Robert Wallace, II *lawyer*
McClain, William Andrew *lawyer*
McCoy, John Joseph *lawyer*
McDowell, John Eugene *lawyer*
McGavran, Frederick Jaeger *lawyer*
Mc Henry, Powell *lawyer*
Meranus, Leonard Stanley *lawyer*
Meyers, Karen Diane *lawyer, educator, corporate officer*
Naylor, Paul Donald *lawyer*
Nechemias, Stephen Murray *lawyer*
Nelson, Frederick Dickson *lawyer*
Neltner, Michael Martin *lawyer*
Neumark, Michael Harry *lawyer*
Olson, Robert Wyrick *lawyer*
O'Reilly, James Thomas *lawyer, educator, author*
Parker, R. Joseph *lawyer*
Petrie, Bruce Inglis *lawyer*
Phillips, T. Stephen *lawyer*
Reed, D. Gary *lawyer*
Reichert, David *lawyer*
Rich, Robert Edward *lawyer*
Roe, Clifford Ashley, Jr. *lawyer*
Rose, Donald McGregor *lawyer*
Rubin, Robert Samuel *lawyer*
Ryan, James Joseph *lawyer*
Schmidt, Thomas Joseph, Jr. *lawyer*
Schmit, David E. *lawyer*
Schuck, Thomas Robert *lawyer, farmer*
Shore, Thomas Spencer, Jr. *lawyer*
Silbersack, Mark Louis *lawyer*
Strauss, William Victor *lawyer*
Streckfuss, James Arthur *lawyer, historian*
Swigert, James Mack *lawyer*
Terp, Thomas Thomsen *lawyer*
Tobias, Charles Harrison, Jr. *lawyer*
Tobias, Paul Henry *lawyer*
Townsend, Robert J. *lawyer*
Trauth, Joseph Louis, Jr. *lawyer*
Vander Laan, Mark Alan *lawyer*
Vogel, Cedric Wakelee *lawyer*
Wales, Ross Elliot *lawyer*
Watts, Barbara Gayle *law academic administrator*
Weeks, Steven Wiley *lawyer*
Weseli, Roger William *lawyer*
Whitaker, Glenn Virgil *lawyer*
Woodside, Frank C., III *lawyer*
Yund, George Edward *lawyer*
Yurchuck, Roger Alexander *lawyer*
Zavatsky, Michael Joseph *lawyer*

### Cleveland
Abram, Marian Christine *lawyer*
Adamo, Kenneth R. *lawyer*
Alfred, Stephen Jay *lawyer*
Andorka, Frank Henry *lawyer*
Andrews, Oakley V. *lawyer*
Ashmus, Keith Allen *lawyer*
Austin, Arthur Donald, II *lawyer, educator*
Bacon, Brett Kermit *lawyer*
Bamberger, Richard H. *lawyer*
Bates, Walter Alan *former lawyer*
Batt, John Paul *lawyer*
Baughman, R(obert) Patrick *lawyer*
Baxter, Howard H. *lawyer*
Berger, Sanford Jason *lawyer, securities dealer, real estate broker*
Berick, James Herschel *lawyer*
Berry, Dean Lester *lawyer*
Besse, Ralph Moore *lawyer*
Bilchik, Gary B. *lawyer*
Binford, Gregory Glenn *lawyer*
Bixenstine, Kim Fenton *lawyer*
Blattner, Robert A. *lawyer*
Braverman, Herbert Leslie *lawyer*
Bravo, Kenneth Allan *lawyer*
Brennan, Maureen *lawyer*
Brown, Seymour R. *lawyer*
Brucken, Robert Matthew *lawyer*
Burke, Kathleen B. *lawyer*
Cairns, James Donald *lawyer*
Calfee, John Beverly *retired lawyer*
Calfee, William Lewis *lawyer*
Campbell, Paul Barton *retired lawyer*
Canary, Nancy Halliday *lawyer*
Carrick, Kathleen Michele *law librarian*
Chandler, Everett Alfred *lawyer*
Clarke, Charles Fenton *lawyer*
Climaco, Michael Louis *lawyer*
Collin, Thomas James *lawyer*
Coquillette, William Hollis *lawyer*
Cornell, John Robert *lawyer*
Coyle, Martin Adolphus, Jr. *lawyer*
Crist, Paul Grant *lawyer*
Cudak, Gail Linda *lawyer*
Cunningham, Pierce Edward *lawyer, city planner*
Currivan, John Daniel *lawyer*
Dampeer, John Lyell *retired lawyer*
Doris, Alan S(anford) *lawyer*
Drinko, John Deaver *lawyer*
Duncan, Ed Eugene *lawyer*
Duvin, Robert Phillip *lawyer*
Dye, Sherman *retired lawyer*
Ekelman, Daniel Louis *lawyer*
Fabens, Andrew Lawrie, III *lawyer*
Falsgraf, William Wendell *lawyer*
Fay, Regan Joseph *lawyer*
Fay, Robert Jesse *lawyer*
Feinberg, Paul H. *lawyer*
Fisher, Thomas Edward *lawyer*
Fletcher, Robert *lawyer, horologist*
Friedman, Harold Edward *lawyer*
Friedman, James Moss *lawyer*
Gerhart, Peter Milton *law educator*
Gerlack, Lisa Marie *lawyer*
Gherlein, Gerald Lee *lawyer, diversified manufacturing company executive*
Glaser, Robert Edward *lawyer*
Goins, Frances Floriano *lawyer*
Gold, Gerald Seymour *lawyer*
Goldfarb, Bernard Sanford *lawyer*
Goler, Michael David *lawyer*
Groetzinger, Jon, Jr. *lawyer, consumer products executive*
Grossman, Theodore Martin *lawyer*
Grundstein, Nathan David *lawyer, management science educator, management consultant*
Haas, Douglas Eric *lawyer*
Haiman, Irwin Sanford *lawyer*
Hardy, Michael Lynn *lawyer*
Henes, Samuel Ernst *lawyer*
Hochman, Kenneth George *lawyer*
Hoerner, Robert Jack *lawyer*
Hollington, Richard Rings, Jr. *lawyer*
Horvitz, Michael John *lawyer*
Inglis, Patricia Marcus *lawyer*
Jacobs, Leslie William *lawyer*
Janke, Ronald Robert *lawyer*
Jeavons, Norman Stone *lawyer*
Jorgenson, Mary Ann *lawyer*
Kahrl, Robert Conley *lawyer*
Kapp, C. Terrence *lawyer*
Karch, George Frederick, Jr. *lawyer*
Katcher, Richard *lawyer*
Katz, Lewis Robert *law educator*
Kelly, Dennis Michael *lawyer*
Kilbane, Thomas Stanton *lawyer*
Kirchick, Calvin B. *lawyer*
Knerly, Stephen John, Jr. *lawyer*
Kola, Arthur Anthony *lawyer*
Kramer, Andrew Michael *lawyer*
Kramer, Eugene Leo *lawyer*
Kuhn, David Alan *lawyer*
Kundtz, John Andrew *lawyer*
Kurit, Neil *lawyer*
Lawniczak, James Michael *lawyer*
Lease, Robert K. *lawyer*
Leavitt, Jeffrey Stuart *lawyer*
Leech, John Dale *lawyer, health care/corporate consultant*
Leidner, Harold Edward *lawyer*
Leiken, Earl Murray *lawyer*
Lenn, Stephen Andrew *lawyer*
Lewis, John Bruce *lawyer*
Lewis, John Francis *lawyer*
Lewis, Robert Lawrence *lawyer, educator*
Madsen, H(enry) Stephen *retired lawyer*
Markey, Robert Guy *lawyer*
Markus, Richard M. *lawyer*
Marting, Michael G. *lawyer*
Mason, Thomas Albert *lawyer*
McAndrews, James Patrick *retired lawyer*
McCarthy, Mark Francis *lawyer*
McCormack, Mark Hume *lawyer, business management company executive*
Mc Elhaney, James Wilson *lawyer, educator*
McLaughlin, Patrick Michael *lawyer*
Mehlman, Maxwell Jonathan *law educator*
Melsher, Gary W. *lawyer*
Messinger, Donald Hathaway *lawyer*
Meyer, G. Christopher *lawyer*
Miller, Richard Hamilton *lawyer, broadcasting company executive*
Millstone, David J. *lawyer*
Moore, Kenneth Cameron *lawyer*
Morrison, Donald William *lawyer*
Newman, John M., Jr. *lawyer*
Nyerges, George Ladislaus *lawyer*
Oakar, Mary Rose *lawyer, former congresswoman*
Oberdank, Lawrence Mark *lawyer, arbitrator*
Ollinger, W. James *lawyer*
Orr, Parker Murray *former lawyer*
Pallam, John James *lawyer*
Pearlman, Samuel Segel *lawyer*
Perella, Marie Louise *lawyer*
Perris, Terrence George *lawyer*
Podboy, Alvin Michael, Jr. *lawyer, law library director*
Preston, Robert Bruce *retired lawyer*
Price, Charles T. *lawyer*
Putka, Andrew Charles *lawyer*
Pyke, John Secrest, Jr. *lawyer, polymers company executive*
Rains, Merritt Neal *lawyer*
Ransom, William Harrison *lawyer*
Rapp, Robert Neil *lawyer*
Rekstis, Walter J., III *lawyer*
Reppert, Richard Levi *lawyer*
Rosenbaum, Jacob I. *lawyer*
Ruben, Alan Miles *law educator*
Rydzel, James A. *lawyer*
Satola, James William *lawyer*
Sawyer, Raymond Terry *lawyer*

Schaefer, David Arnold *lawyer*
Schiller, James Joseph *lawyer*
Schneider, David Miller *lawyer*
Schnell, Carlton Bryce *lawyer*
Shanker, Morris Gerald *lawyer, educator*
Shapiro, Fred David *lawyer*
Sharp, Robert Weimer *lawyer*
Shaw, Russell Clyde *lawyer*
Sicherman, Marvin Allen *lawyer*
Skulina, Thomas Raymond *lawyer*
Slinger, Michael Jeffery *law library director*
Sloan, David W. *lawyer*
Smith, Barbara Jean *lawyer*
Sogg, Wilton Sherman *lawyer*
Solomon, Randall L. *lawyer*
Stanley, Hugh Monroe, Jr. *lawyer*
Steindler, Howard Allen *lawyer*
Stevens, Thomas Charles *lawyer*
Storey, Robert Davis *lawyer*
Strauch, John L. *lawyer*
Streeter, Richard Edward *lawyer*
Striefsky, Linda A(nn) *lawyer*
Strimbu, Victor, Jr. *lawyer*
Stuhan, Richard George *lawyer*
Swartzbaugh, Marc L. *lawyer*
Szaller, James Francis *lawyer*
Taft, Seth Chase *retired lawyer*
Toohey, Brian Frederick *lawyer*
Toomajian, William Martin *lawyer*
Traci, Donald Philip *retired lawyer*
Trevor, Leigh Barry *lawyer*
von Mehren, George M. *lawyer*
Waldeck, John Walter, Jr. *lawyer*
Wallach, Mark Irwin *lawyer*
Watson, Richard Thomas *lawyer*
Weber, Robert Carl *lawyer*
Weiler, Jeffry Louis *lawyer*
Whiteman, Joseph David *lawyer, manufacturing company executive*
Whitney, Richard Buckner *lawyer*
Williams, Clyde E., Jr. *lawyer*
Young, James Edward *lawyer*
Zambie, Allan John *lawyer*
Zangerle, John A. *lawyer*

### Cleveland Heights
Gutfeld, Norman E. *lawyer*

### Columbus
Adams, John Marshall *lawyer*
Anderson, Jon Mac *lawyer*
Ayers, James Cordon *lawyer*
Bahls, Steven Carl *law educator, university dean*
Bailey, Daniel Allen *lawyer*
Barnes, Wallace Ray *retired lawyer*
Beavers, John Parrish *lawyer*
Bennett, Steven Alan *lawyer*
Bibart, Richard L. *lawyer*
Binning, J. Boyd *lawyer*
Boardman, William Penniman *lawyer, banker*
Bridgman, G(eorge) Ross *lawyer*
Brinkman, Dale Thomas *lawyer*
Brooks, Richard Dickinson *lawyer*
Brown, Herbert Russell *lawyer, writer*
Brown, Philip Albert *lawyer*
Brubaker, Robert Loring *lawyer*
Buchenroth, Stephen Richard *lawyer*
Carnahan, John Anderson *lawyer*
Carpenter, Michael H. *lawyer*
Casey, John Frederick *lawyer*
Chester, John Jonas *lawyer*
Christensen, John William *lawyer*
Clovis, Albert Lee *lawyer, educator*
Conrad, David Keith *lawyer*
Cvetanovich, Danny L. *lawyer*
DeRousie, Charles Stuart *lawyer*
Di Lorenzo, John Florio, Jr. *lawyer*
Dreher, Darrell L. *lawyer*
Druen, William Sidney *lawyer*
Dugan, Charles Francis, II *lawyer*
Dunlay, Catherine Telles *lawyer*
Edwards, John White *lawyer*
Elam, John Carlton *lawyer*
Fahey, Richard Paul *lawyer*
Fay, Terrence Michael *lawyer*
Fisher, Lawrence L. *lawyer*
Fisher, Lloyd Edison, Jr. *lawyer*
Frasier, Ralph Kennedy *lawyer, banker*
Fu, Paul Shan *law librarian, consultant*
Gibson, Rankin MacDougal *lawyer*
Greek, Darold I. *lawyer*
Gross, James Howard *lawyer*
Hardymon, David Wayne *lawyer*
Hoberg, John William *lawyer*
Hollenbaugh, H(enry) Ritchey *lawyer*
Hughes, Donald Allen, Jr. *law librarian and educator*
Jenkins, George L. *lawyer, business executive*
Jenkins, John Anthony *lawyer*
Johnson, Mark Alan *lawyer*
Keller, John Kistler *lawyer*
Ketcham, Richard Scott *lawyer*
King, G. Roger *lawyer*
Knepper, William Edward *lawyer*
Kuehnle, Kenton Lee *lawyer*
Kurtz, Charles Jewett, III *lawyer*
Lehman, Harry Jac *lawyer*
Long, Thomas Leslie *lawyer*
Lopez, A. Ruben *lawyer*
Lowry, Bruce Roy *lawyer*
Maloon, Jerry L. *trial lawyer, physician, medicolegal consultant*
Martin, William Giese *lawyer*
Maser, Douglas James *lawyer*
Maynard, Robert Howell *lawyer*
Mayo, Elizabeth Broom *lawyer*
McAlister, Robert Beaton *lawyer*
McConnaughey, George Carlton, Jr. *lawyer*
McDermott, Kevin R. *lawyer*
McKenna, Alvin James *lawyer*
McMahon, John Patrick *lawyer*
McNealey, J. Jeffrey *lawyer, corporate executive*
Miller, Malcolm Lee *retired lawyer*
Miller, Terry Morrow *lawyer*
Minor, Charles Daniel *lawyer*
Minor, Robert Allen *lawyer*
Mirman, Joel Harvey *lawyer*
Moloney, Thomas E. *lawyer*
Mone, Robert Paul *lawyer*
Morgan, Dennis Richard *lawyer*
Moritz, Michael Everett *lawyer*
Moul, William Charles *lawyer*
Nathan, Jerry E. *lawyer*
Oliphant, James S. *lawyer*
Oman, Richard Heer *lawyer*
O'Reilly, Michael Joseph *lawyer, real estate investor*
Owsiany, David James *lawyer, lobbyist*
Petricoff, M. Howard *lawyer, educator*
Petro, James Michael *lawyer, politician*
Phillips, James Edgar *lawyer*
Pohlman, James Erwin *lawyer*
Pressley, Fred G., Jr. *lawyer*
Quigley, John Bernard *law educator*
Radnor, Alan T. *lawyer*
Ramey, Denny L. *bar association executive director*
Ray, Frank Allen *lawyer*
Reasoner, Willis Irl, III *lawyer*
Ridgley, Thomas Brennan *lawyer*
Robinson, Barry R. *lawyer*
Robol, Richard Thomas *lawyer*
Rose, Michael Dean *lawyer, educator*
Ryan, Joseph W., Jr. *lawyer*
Schrag, Edward A., Jr. *lawyer*
Scott, Thomas Clevenger *lawyer*
Shamansky, Robert Norton *lawyer*
Sidman, Robert John *lawyer*
Silverman, Perry Raynard *lawyer, consultant*
Sliger, Herbert Jacquemin, Jr. *lawyer*
Smith, Norman T. *lawyer*
Stedman, Richard Ralph *lawyer*
Stein, Jay Wobith *legal research and education consultant, mediator arbitrator*
Stern, Geoffrey *lawyer, disciplinary counsel*
Stinehart, Roger Ray *lawyer*
Swanson, Gillian Lee *law librarian*
Swetnam, Daniel Richard *lawyer*
Taft, Sheldon Ashley *lawyer*
Taggart, Thomas Michael *lawyer*
Tait, Robert E. *lawyer*
Tarpy, Thomas Michael *lawyer*
Taylor, Joel Sanford *lawyer*
Thomas, Duke Winston *lawyer*
Thompson, Harold Lee *lawyer*
Todd, William Michael *lawyer*
Turano, David A. *lawyer*
Vorys, Arthur Isaiah *lawyer*
Warner, Charles Collins *lawyer*
Wentworth, Andrew Stowell *lawyer*
Whipps, Edward Franklin *lawyer*
Wightman, Alec *lawyer*
Williams, Gregory Howard *lawyer, educator*
Wiseman, Randolph Carson *lawyer*
Wright, Harry, III *retired lawyer*
Yeazel, Keith Arthur *lawyer*

### Dayton
Berrey, Robert Forrest *lawyer*
Burick, Lawrence T. *lawyer*
Chernesky, Richard John *lawyer*
Conway, Mark Allyn *lawyer*
Finn, Chester Evans *lawyer*
Gottschlich, Gary William *lawyer*
Hadley, Robert James *lawyer*
Heyman, Ralph Edmond *lawyer*
Jacobs, Richard E. *lawyer*
Jenks, Thomas Edward *lawyer*
Johnson, C. Terry *lawyer*
Kinlin, Donald James *lawyer*
Lockhart, Gregory Gordon *lawyer*
Macklin, Crofford Johnson, Jr. *lawyer*
McSwiney, Charles Ronald *lawyer*
Randall, Vernellia *lawyer, nurse, educator*
Rapp, Gerald Duane *lawyer, manufacturing company executive*
Rogers, Richard Hunter *lawyer, business executive*

### Delphos
Clark, Edward Ferdnand *lawyer*

### Dresden
Reidy, Thomas Anthony *lawyer*

### Dublin
Powell, Ernestine Breisch *retired lawyer*

### Eaton
Thomas, James William *lawyer*

### Findlay
Jetton, Girard Reuel, Jr. *lawyer, retired oil company executive*

### Howard
Lee, William Johnson *lawyer*

### Hudson
Giffen, Daniel Harris *lawyer, educator*
Ong, John Doyle *lawyer*

### Jackson
Lewis, Richard M. *lawyer*

### Kent
Nome, William Andreas *lawyer*

### Lancaster
Libert, Donald Joseph *lawyer*

### Lima
Robenalt, John Alton *lawyer*

### Logan
Dillon, Neal Winfield *lawyer*

### Marietta
Fields, William Albert *lawyer*
Hausser, Robert Louis *lawyer*

### Maumee
Kline, James Edward *lawyer*
Marsh, Benjamin Franklin *lawyer*

### Medina
Ballard, John Stuart *retired law educator, former mayor*

### Mentor
Driggs, Charles Mulford *lawyer*

### Middletown
Rathman, William Ernest *lawyer, minister*

### Milford
Vorholt, Jeffrey Joseph *lawyer, software company executive*

### Mount Vernon
Turner, Harry Edward *lawyer*

### Newark
Mantonya, John Butcher *lawyer*

### North Canton
Dettinger, Warren Walter *lawyer*

### Norwalk
Carpenter, Paul Leonard *retired lawyer*

### Oak Harbor
Robertson, Jerry D. *lawyer*

### Oberlin
Jonesco, Jane Riggs *lawyer, development officer*

### Oxford
Brown, Edward Maurice *retired lawyer, business executive*

### Pepper Pike
Mc Innes, Robert Malcolm *lawyer, business consultant*

### Portsmouth
Horr, William Henry *lawyer*

### Reynoldsburg
Goostree, Robert Edward *political science and law educator*

### Richfield
Calise, Nicholas James *lawyer*
Heider, Jon Vinton *lawyer, corporate executive*
Schulz, Mary Elizabeth *lawyer*

### Springfield
Browne, William Bitner *lawyer*
Harkins, Daniel Conger *lawyer*
Lagos, James Harry *lawyer*

### Sylvania
Colasurd, Richard Michael *lawyer*

### Toledo
Anspach, Robert Michael *lawyer*
Baker, Richard Southworth *lawyer*
Boesel, Milton Charles, Jr. *lawyer, business executive*
Boggs, Ralph Stuart *lawyer*
Brown, Charles Earl *lawyer*
Craig, Harald Franklin *lawyer*
Dalrymple, Thomas Lawrence *retired lawyer*
Fisher, Donald Wiener *lawyer*
Hawkins, Donald Merton *lawyer*
Heywood, William H. *lawyer*
Hiett, Edward Emerson *retired lawyer, glass company executive*
Klein, James Martin *law educator, labor arbitrator*
La Rue, Carl Forman *lawyer*
Leech, Charles Russell, Jr. *lawyer*
Machin, Barbara E. *lawyer*
McCormick, Edward James, Jr. *lawyer*
Miller, Barbara Kaye *lawyer*
O'Connell, Maurice Daniel *lawyer*
Pletz, Thomas Gregory *lawyer*
Quick, Albert Thomas *law educator, university dean*
St. Clair, Donald David *lawyer*
Spitzer, John Brumback *lawyer*
Tuschman, James Marshall *lawyer*
Webb, Thomas Irwin, Jr. *lawyer*
Wicklund, David Wayne *lawyer*

### Twinsburg
Hill, Thomas Allen *lawyer*

### Warren
Dennison, David Short, Jr. *lawyer*
Rossi, Anthony Gerald *lawyer*
White, Martin Fred *lawyer*

### West Union
Carr, George Francis, Jr. *lawyer*

### Westerville
Lancione, Bernard Gabe *lawyer*

### Wickliffe
Crehore, Charles Aaron *lawyer*
Kidder, Fred Dockstater *lawyer*

### Wilmington
Schutt, Walter Eugene *lawyer*

### Wooster
Colclaser, H. Alberta *lawyer, retired government official*
Kennedy, Charles Allen *lawyer*

### Youngstown
Ausnehmer, John Edward *lawyer*
Messenger, James Louis *lawyer*
Mumaw, James Webster *lawyer*
Nadler, Myron Jay *lawyer*
Roth, Daniel Benjamin *lawyer, business executive*
Stevens, Paul Edward *lawyer*
Tucker, Don Eugene *retired lawyer*
Wellman, Thomas Peter *lawyer*

### Zanesville
Micheli, Frank James *lawyer*

## OKLAHOMA

### Anadarko
Pain, Charles Leslie *lawyer*

### Antlers
Stamper, Joe Allen *lawyer*

### Bartlesville
Roff, Alan Lee *lawyer, consultant*

### Chandler
Mather, Stephanie J. *lawyer*

### Cherokee
Mitchell, Allan Edwin *lawyer*

### Cushing
Draughon, Scott Wilson *lawyer, social worker*

### Edmond
Lester, Andrew William *lawyer*
Loving, Susan B. *lawyer, former state official*
Shadid, Randel Coy *lawyer*

### El Reno
Grantham, Robert Edward *lawyer, educator*

### Enid
Jones, Stephen *lawyer*
Musser, William Wesley, Jr. *lawyer*
Wyatt, Robert Lee, IV *lawyer*

### Fort Sill
Livingston, Douglas Mark *lawyer*

### Guthrie
Davis, Frank Wayne *lawyer*

### Guymon
Wood, Donald Euriah *lawyer*

### Mcalester
Cornish, Richard Pool *lawyer*

### Muskogee
Robinson, Adelbert Carl *lawyer, judge*
Ruby, Russell (Glenn) *lawyer*

### Norman
Elkouri, Frank *law educator*
Fairbanks, Robert Alvin *lawyer*
Hemingway, Richard William *law educator*
Pain, Betsy M. *lawyer*
Petersen, Catherine Holland *lawyer*

### Oklahoma City
Allen, Robert Dee *lawyer*
Almond, David Randolph *lawyer, company executive*
Angel, Arthur Ronald *lawyer, consultant*
Boston, William Clayton *lawyer*
Brooks, Norma Newton *legal assistant, secondary school educator*
Cantrell, Charles Leonard *lawyer, educator*
Champlin, Richard H. *lawyer, insurance company executive*
Christiansen, Mark D. *lawyer*
Coats, Andrew Montgomery *lawyer, former mayor, dean*
Court, Leonard *lawyer*
Cunningham, Stanley Lloyd *lawyer*
Denton, Michael David, Jr. *lawyer*
Durland, Jack Raymond *lawyer*
Elder, James Carl *lawyer*
Emerson, Marvin Chester *legal association administrator*
Epperson, Kraettli Quynton *lawyer, educator*
Fitch, Mark Keith *lawyer*
Ford, Michael Raye *lawyer*
Henry, Jerome Eldon *lawyer*
Hendrick, Howard H. *lawyer, state senator*
Johnson, Robert Max *lawyer*
Kaufman, James Mark *lawyer*
Kline, David Adam *lawyer, educator, writer*
Lambird, Mona Salyer *lawyer*
Larason, Timothy Manuel *lawyer*
Legg, William Jefferson *lawyer*
McBride, Kenneth Eugene *lawyer, title company executive*
Merritt, Kenni Barrett *lawyer*
Milsten, Robert B. *lawyer*
Moler, Edward Harold *lawyer*
Necco, Alexander David *lawyer, educator*
Nesbitt, Charles Rudolph *lawyer, energy consultant*
Paul, William George *lawyer*
Reynolds, Norman Eben *lawyer*
Rockett, D. Joe *lawyer*
Ross, William Jarboe *lawyer*
Ryan, Patrick M. *prosecutor*
Snider, John Joseph *lawyer*
Sowers, Wesley Hoyt *lawyer, management consultant*
Steinhorn, Irwin Harry *lawyer, educator, corporate executive*
Stringer, L.E. (Dean Stringer) *lawyer*
Taft, Richard George *lawyer*
Tompkins, Raymond Edgar *lawyer*
Towery, Curtis Kent *lawyer*
Tuck-Richmond, Doletta Sue *prosecutor*
Turpen, Michael Craig *lawyer*
Walsh, Lawrence Edward *lawyer*
Zevnik-Sawatzky, Donna Dee *litigation coordinator*

### Pauls Valley
Hope, Garland Howard *lawyer, retired judge*

### Ponca City
Northcutt, Clarence Dewey *lawyer*

### Stillwater
Fischer, Richard Samuel *lawyer*

### Tulsa
Arrington, John Leslie, Jr. *lawyer*
Atkinson, Michael Pearce *lawyer*
Belsky, Martin Henry *law educator, lawyer*
Biolchini, Robert Fredrick *lawyer*
Blackstock, LeRoy *lawyer*
Bryant, Hubert Hale *lawyer*
Clark, Gary Carl *lawyer*
Cooper, Richard Casey *lawyer*
Crawford, B(urnett) Hayden *lawyer*
Cremin, John Patrick *lawyer*
Daniel, Samuel Phillips *lawyer*
Davenport, Gerald Bruce *lawyer*
Doverspike, Terry Richard *lawyer*
Estill, John Staples, Jr. *lawyer*
Farrell, John L., Jr. *lawyer, business executive*
Frey, Martin Alan *lawyer, educator*
Gaberino, John Anthony, Jr. *lawyer*
Gable, G. Ellis *retired lawyer*
Graham, Tony M. *lawyer*
Howard, Gene Claude *lawyer, former state senator*
Imel, John Michael *lawyer*
Kihle, Donald Arthur *lawyer*
Killin, Charles Clark *lawyer*
Kothe, Charles Aloysius *lawyer*
Langholz, Robert Wayne *lawyer, investor*
Luthey, Graydon Dean, Jr. *lawyer*
McGonigle, Richard Thomas *lawyer*

Moffett, J. Denny *lawyer*
Quinn, Francis Xavier *arbitrator and mediator, author, lecturer*
Schwartz, Bernard *law educator*
Walker, Floyd Lee *lawyer*

### Vinita
Curnutte, Mark William *lawyer*
Johnston, Oscar Black, III *lawyer*

### Walters
Flanagan, Michael Charles *lawyer*

## OREGON

### Astoria
Haskell, Donald McMillan *lawyer*

### Beaverton
Robertson, Douglas Stuart *lawyer*

### Canby
Thalhofer, Paul Terrance *lawyer*

### Eugene
Clark, Chapin DeWitt *law educator*
Mumford, William Porter, II *lawyer*
Sahlstrom, E(lmer) B(ernard) *retired lawyer*
Scoles, Eugene Francis *law educator, lawyer*

### La Grande
Joseph, Steven Jay *lawyer*

### Lebanon
Kuntz, Joel Dubois *lawyer*

### Lincoln City
Elliott, Scott *lawyer*

### Medford
O'Connor, Karl William *lawyer*
Thierolf, Richard Burton, Jr. *lawyer*

### Milwaukie
Anderson, Mark Alexander *lawyer*

### Pendleton
Kottkamp, John Harlan *lawyer*

### Portland
Abravanel, Allan Ray *lawyer*
Achterman, Gail Louise *lawyer*
Anderson, Herbert H. *lawyer, farmer*
Arthur, Michael Elbert *lawyer*
Bakkensen, John Reser *lawyer*
Balmer, Thomas Ancil *lawyer*
Booth, Brian Geddes *lawyer*
Brenneman, Delbert Jay *lawyer*
Cable, John Franklin *lawyer*
Campbell, James, VII *patent lawyer*
Canaday, Richard A. *lawyer*
Carlsen, Clifford Norman, Jr. *lawyer*
Crowell, John B., Jr. *lawyer, former government official*
Dahl, Joyle Cochran *lawyer*
Dailey, Dianne K. *lawyer*
Dean, E. Joseph *lawyer*
DeChaine, Dean Dennis *lawyer*
Deering, Thomas Phillips *lawyer*
Dotten, Michael Chester *lawyer*
Drummond, Gerard Kasper *lawyer, retired minerals company executive*
DuBoff, Leonard David *lawyer*
Eakin, Margaretta Morgan *lawyer*
Edwards, Richard Alan *lawyer*
English, Stephen F. *lawyer*
Epstein, Edward Louis *lawyer*
Fell, James F. *lawyer*
Feuerstein, Howard M. *lawyer*
Foley, Ridgway Knight, Jr. *lawyer, writer*
Franzke, Richard Albert *lawyer*
Froebe, Gerald Allen *lawyer*
Georges, Maurice Ostrow *lawyer*
Glasgow, William Jacob *lawyer, venture capitalist*
Greene, Herbert Bruce *lawyer, merchant banker*
Hager, Orval O. *retired lawyer, consultant*
Hammer, Susan M. *lawyer*
Hanna, Harry Mitchell *lawyer*
Hart, John Edward *lawyer*
Haselton, Rick Thomas *lawyer*
Helmer, M. Christie *lawyer*
Hergenhan, Kenneth William *lawyer*
Hinkle, Charles Frederick *lawyer, clergyman, educator*
Hoffman, Jack Leroy *lawyer*
Holman, Donald Reid *lawyer*
Howorth, David Bishop *lawyer*
Hyatt, Dan Richard *lawyer*
Johnson, Alexander Charles *lawyer, electrical engineer*
Josephson, Richard Carl *lawyer*
Josselson, Frank *lawyer*
Kennedy, Jack Leland *lawyer*
Kester, Randall Blair *lawyer*
Knoll, James Lewis *lawyer*
Larpenteur, James Albert, Jr. *lawyer*
Leedy, Robert Allan, Sr. *retired lawyer*
Lindley, Thomas Ernest *environmental lawyer, law educator*
Livingston, Louis Bayer *lawyer*
Love, William Edward *lawyer*
Maloney, Robert E., Jr. *lawyer*
Miller, William Richey, Jr. *lawyer*
Moore, Thomas Scott *lawyer*
Mowe, Gregory Robert *lawyer*
Nash, Frank Erwin *lawyer*
Noonan, William Donald *lawyer*
Norby, Mark Alan *lawyer*
Nunn, Robert Warne *lawyer*
Olejko, Mitchell J. *lawyer*
Purcell, John F. *lawyer*
Rasmussen, Richard Robert *lawyer*
Rawlinson, Dennis Patrick *lawyer*
Richardson, Campbell *lawyer*
Richter, Peter Christian *lawyer*
Rosenbaum, Lois Omenn *lawyer*
Rubin, Bruce Alan *lawyer*
Rutzick, Mark Charles *lawyer*
Ryan, John Duncan *lawyer*
Sand, Thomas Charles *lawyer*
Schuster, Philip Frederick, II *lawyer, writer*
Simpson, Robert Glenn *lawyer*
Stewart, Milton Roy *lawyer*
Strader, Timothy Richards *lawyer*
Sullivan, Edward Joseph *lawyer, educator*
Troutwine, Gayle Leone *lawyer*
Van Valkenburg, Edgar Walter *lawyer*
Weaver, Delbert Allen *lawyer*
Webb, Jere Michael *lawyer*
Westwood, James Nicholson *lawyer*
Whinston, Arthur Lewis *lawyer*
White, Douglas James, Jr. *lawyer*
Wiener, Norman Joseph *lawyer*
Wilson, Owen Meredith, Jr. *lawyer*
Wood, Marcus Andrew *lawyer*
Wright, Charles Edward *lawyer*
Wyse, William Walker *lawyer, real estate executive*
Zalutsky, Morton Herman *lawyer*

### Salem
Bailey, Henry John, III *retired lawyer, educator*
Breen, Richard F., Jr. *law librarian, lawyer, educator*
Ferris, Evelyn Scott *lawyer*
Kulingoski, Theodore Ralph *lawyer*
Mannix, Kevin Leese *lawyer*
Tweedt, Anne Elizabeth *lawyer, legislative policy analyst*
Walsh, Richard Michael *lawyer*

### Wilsonville
Yacob, Yosef *lawyer, economist*

## PENNSYLVANIA

### Abington
Bildersee, Robert Alan *lawyer*

### Allentown
Agger, James H. *lawyer*
Brown, Robert Wayne *lawyer*
Frank, Bernard *lawyer*
Holt, Leon Conrad, Jr. *lawyer, business executive*
Nagel, Edward McCaul *lawyer, former utilities executive*

### Allison Park
Herrington, John David, III *lawyer*
Ries, William Campbell *lawyer*

### Bala Cynwyd
Cades, Stewart Russell *lawyer, communications company executive*
Ezold, Nancy O'Mara *lawyer*
Garrity, Vincent Francis, Jr. *lawyer*
Gerber, Albert B. *lawyer, former legal association executive*
Kane-Vanni, Patricia Ruth *lawyer, consultant*
Manko, Joseph Martin, Sr. *lawyer*
Odell, Herbert *lawyer*
Strazzella, James Anthony *law educator*
Wiener, Thomas Eli *lawyer*

### Bangor
Ceraul, David James *lawyer*

### Beaver
Ledebur, Linas Vockroth, Jr. *retired lawyer*

### Berwyn
Ewing, Joseph Neff, Jr. *lawyer*
Huffaker, John Boston *lawyer*
Markle, John, Jr. *lawyer*
Watters, Edward McLain, III *lawyer*
Wood, Thomas E. *lawyer*

### Blue Bell
Barron, Harold Sheldon *lawyer*
Elliott, John Michael *lawyer*
Lawrence, Gerald, Jr. *lawyer*
Simon, David Frederick *lawyer*
Swansen, Samuel Theodore *lawyer*

### Bradford
Hauser, Christopher George *lawyer*

### Carlisle
Turo, Ron *lawyer*

### Center Valley
Smillie, Douglas James *lawyer*

### Chadds Ford
Stewart, Allen Warren *lawyer*

### Chalfont
Breslin, Elvira Madden *lawyer, educator*

### Chester Springs
Quay, Thomas Emery *lawyer*

### Chesterbrook
Drake, William Frank, Jr. *lawyer*

### Clarks Summit
Beemer, John Barry *lawyer*

### Coatesville
Sprague, William Douglas *lawyer, company executive*

### Conshohocken
Bramson, Robert Sherman *lawyer*

### Doylestown
Elliott, Richard Howard *lawyer*
Hoopes, Robert Patrick *lawyer*

### Drexel Hill
West, Kenneth Edward *lawyer*

### Easton
Brown, Robert Carroll *lawyer*
Noel, Nicholas, III *lawyer*

### Erie
Eiben, Gary *lawyer*
Zamboldi, Richard Henry *lawyer*

### Exton
Ashton, Mark Randolph *lawyer*

### Feasterville Trevose
McEvilly, James Patrick, Jr. *lawyer*

### Fort Washington
Hess, Lawrence Eugene, Jr. *lawyer*

### Gibsonia
Heilman, Carl Edwin *lawyer*

### Gladwyne
Acton, David *lawyer*

### Greensburg
McDowell, Michael David *lawyer, utility executive*

### Harrisburg
Allen, Heath Ledward *lawyer*
Barto, Charles O., Jr. *lawyer*
Burcat, Joel Robin *lawyer*
Cline, Andrew Haley *lawyer*
Cramer, John McNaight *lawyer*
Diehm, James Warren *lawyer, educator*
Downey, Brian Patrick *lawyer*
Hanson, Robert DeLolle *lawyer*
Kelly, Robert Edward, Jr. *lawyer*
Klein, Michael D. *lawyer*
Kury, Franklin Leo *lawyer*
Lappas, Spero Thomas *lawyer*
Sadlock, Richard Alan *lawyer*
Schore, Niles *lawyer*
Settle, Eric Lawrence *lawyer*
Warshaw, Allen Charles *lawyer*
West, James Joseph *lawyer*

### Haverford
Frick, Benjamin Charles *lawyer*
McGlinn, Frank Cresson Potts *lawyer*
Stroud, James Stanley *lawyer*
Szabad, George Michael *lawyer, former mayor*

### Horsham
Rosoff, William A. *lawyer, executive*

### Huntingdon Valley
Forman, Howard Irving *lawyer, former government official*

### Jenkintown
Friedman, Ralph David *lawyer*
Nerenberg, Aaron *lawyer*

### Jersey Shore
Flayhart, Martin Albert *lawyer*
Nassberg, Richard T. *lawyer*

### Johnstown
Glock, Earl Ferdinand *lawyer*
Glosser, William Louis *lawyer*
Kaharick, Jerome John *lawyer*

### Jones Mills
Fish, Paul Waring *lawyer*

### Kennett Square
Judson, Franklyn Sylvanus *lawyer, consultant*
Partnoy, Ronald Allen *lawyer*

### King Of Prussia
Beausang, Michael Francis, Jr. *lawyer*
Noonan, Gregory Robert *lawyer*

### Lake Harmony
Polansky, Larry Paul *court administrator, consultant*

### Lancaster
Duroni, Charles Eugene *retired lawyer, food products executive*
Nast, Dianne Martha *lawyer*
Pyfer, John Frederick, Jr. *lawyer*
Whare, Wanda Snyder *lawyer*
Zimmerman, D(onald) Patrick *lawyer*

### Langhorne
Brafford, William Charles *lawyer*
Hillje, Barbara Brown *lawyer*

### Lansdale
Esterhai, John Louis *lawyer*

### Ligonier
Walters, Gomer Winston *lawyer*

### Lock Haven
Snowiss, Alvin L. *lawyer*

### Macungie
Gavin, Austin *retired lawyer*

### Malvern
Cameron, John Clifford *lawyer, health science facility administrator*
Churchill, Winston John *lawyer, investment firm executive*

### Mc Murray
Brzustowicz, John Cinq-Mars *lawyer*

### Media
Ackerman, Alvin S. *lawyer*
D'Amico, Andrew J. *lawyer*
Elman, Gerry Jay *lawyer*
Ewing, Robert Clark *lawyer*
Garrison, Susan Kay *lawyer*

### Mendenhall
Reinert, Norbert Frederick *patent lawyer, retired chemical company executive*

### Middletown
Pannebaker, James Boyd *lawyer*

### Moon Township
Alstadt, Lynn Jeffery *lawyer*

### Morrisville
Heefner, William Frederick *lawyer*

### Narberth
Mezvinsky, Edward M. *lawyer*

### New Castle
Flannery, Harry Audley *lawyer*
Mangino, Matthew Thomas *lawyer*

### New Kensington
Joseph, Daniel *lawyer*

### Norristown
Aman, George Matthias, III *lawyer*
Folmar, Larry John *lawyer*
Gregg, John Pennypacker *lawyer*
Mirabile, Carolyn Rose *lawyer*
Oliver, James John *lawyer*
Rounick, Jack A. *lawyer*
Wetherill, Eikins *lawyer, stock exchange executive*
Williamson, Ronald Thomas *lawyer*

### Philadelphia
Aaron, Kenneth Ellyot *lawyer*
Abbott, Frank Harry *lawyer*
Abrahams, Robert David *lawyer, author*
Abramowitz, Robert Leslie *lawyer*
Ake, John Notley *lawyer, former investment services executive*
Anders, Jerrold Paul *lawyer*
Aronstein, Martin Joseph *lawyer, educator*
Auten, David Charles *lawyer*
Baccini, Laurance Ellis *lawyer*
Bachman, Arthur *lawyer*
Bales, John Foster, III *lawyer*
Ballengee, James McMorrow *lawyer*
Barnum, Jeanne Schubert *lawyer*
Barrett, John J(ames), Jr. *lawyer*
Beasley, James Edwin *lawyer*
Beck, Stuart Edwin *lawyer*
Berger, David *lawyer*
Berger, Harold *lawyer, engineer*
Berkley, Emily Carolan *lawyer*
Berkman, Richard Lyle *lawyer*
Bernard, John Marley *lawyer, educator*
Bershad, Jack R. *lawyer*
Best, Franklin Luther, Jr. *lawyer*
Binder, David Franklin *lawyer, author*
Black, Allen Decatur *lawyer*
Black, Creed C., Jr. *lawyer*
Blackman, Murray Ivan *lawyer*
Bloom, Michael Anthony *lawyer*
Bochetto, George Alexander *lawyer*
Bogutz, Jerome Edwin *lawyer*
Boss, Amelia Helen *law educator, lawyer*
Bradley, Raymond Joseph *lawyer*
Bright, Joseph Coleman *lawyer*
Britt, Earl Thomas *lawyer*
Brown, Richard P., Jr. *lawyer*
Brown, Stephen D. *lawyer*
Brown, William Hill, III *lawyer*
Browne, Stanhope Stryker *lawyer*
Buccino, Ernest John, Jr. *lawyer*
Burbank, Stephen Bradner *law educator*
Calvert, Jay H., Jr. *lawyer*
Carnecchia, Baldo M., Jr. *lawyer*
Carroll, Mark Thomas *lawyer*
Carroll, Thomas Colas *lawyer, educator*
Carson, Timothy Joseph *lawyer*
Casper, Charles B. *lawyer*
Cherken, Harry Sarkis, Jr. *lawyer*
Cheston, George Morris *lawyer*
Child, John Sowden, Jr. *lawyer*
Chimples, George *lawyer*
Clark, John Arthur *lawyer*
Clauss, Peter Otto *lawyer*
Clothier, Isaac H., IV *lawyer*
Cloues, Edward Blanchard, II *lawyer*
Cohen, Felix Asher *lawyer*
Cohen, Frederick *lawyer*
Cohen, Sylvan M. *lawyer*
Collings, Robert L. *lawyer*
Comfort, Robert Dennis *lawyer*
Comisky, Hope A. *lawyer*
Comisky, Ian Michael *lawyer*
Comisky, Marvin *retired lawyer*
Connor, Joseph Patrick, III *lawyer*
Cooney, John Gordon *lawyer*
Cooney, John Gordon, Jr. *lawyer*
Cox, Roger Frazier *lawyer*
Coyne, Charles Cole *lawyer*
Cramer, Harold *lawyer*
Crawford, James Douglas *lawyer*
Cross, Milton H. *lawyer*
Dabrowski, Doris Jane *lawyer*
Damsgaard, Kell Marsh *lawyer*
D'Angelo, Christopher Scott *lawyer*
Darby, Karen Sue *legal education administrator*
Davis, Alan Jay *lawyer*
Davis, C. VanLeer, III *lawyer*
Dean, Michael M. *lawyer*
De Lone, H. Francis *lawyer*
Deming, Frank Stout *lawyer*
Denmark, William Adam *lawyer*
Dennis, Edward S(pencer) G(ale), Jr. *lawyer*
Denworth, Raymond K. *lawyer*
Diaz, Nelson Angel *federal government legal advisor*
Dichter, Mark S. *lawyer*
Dilks, Park Bankert, Jr. *lawyer*
Donner, Henry Jay *lawyer*
Donohue, James J. *lawyer*
Donohue, John Patrick *lawyer*
Doran, William Michael *lawyer*
Dorfman, John Charles *lawyer*
Dubin, Leonard *lawyer*
Dubin, Stephen Victor *lawyer*
Dworetzky, Joseph Anthony *lawyer, city official*
Efstratiades, Anastasius *lawyer*
Elkins, S. Gordon *lawyer*
Emerson, S. Jonathan *lawyer*
Esser, Carl Eric *lawyer*
Fader, Henry Conrad *lawyer*
Fala, Herman C. *lawyer*
Farage, Donald J. *lawyer, educator*
Feirson, Steven B. *lawyer*
Feldman, Albert Joseph *lawyer*
Ferst, Walter B. *lawyer*
Fickler, Arlene *lawyer*
Fiebach, H. Robert *lawyer*
Fineman, S. David *lawyer*
Finet, Scott *law librarian*
Fitts, Michael Andrew *law educator*
Flanagan, Joseph Patrick, Jr. *lawyer*
Fox, Reeder Rodman *lawyer*
Frank, Harvey *lawyer, writer*

Freedman, Robert Louis *lawyer*
Friedman, Frank Bennett *lawyer*
Fryman, Louis William *lawyer*
Gadsden, Christopher Henry *lawyer*
Garcia, Rudolph *lawyer*
Genkin, Barry Howard *lawyer*
Gillis, Richard Moffitt, Jr. *lawyer*
Glanton, Richard H. *lawyer*
Glassman, Howard Theodore *lawyer*
Glassmoyer, Thomas Parvin *lawyer*
Glazer, Ronald Barry *lawyer*
Goldberg, Jay Lenard *lawyer*
Goldberg, Marvin Allen *lawyer, business consultant*
Goldberg, Richard Robert *lawyer*
Goldman, Jerry Stephen *lawyer*
Goldsmith, Howard Michael *lawyer*
Goldstein, William Marks *lawyer*
Goodman, Stephen Murry *lawyer*
Goodrich, Herbert Funk, Jr. *lawyer*
Gordesky, Morton *lawyer*
Granoff, Gail Patricia *lawyer*
Grant, M. Duncan *lawyer*
Grant, Richard W. *lawyer*
Gray, Edward Anthony *lawyer*
Greenfield, Bruce Harold *lawyer, banker*
Grove, David Lavan *lawyer*
Hagan, Mary Ann *lawyer*
Haley, Vincent Peter *lawyer*
Hamilton, Stephen David Derwent *lawyer*
Hangley, William Thomas *lawyer*
Harkins, John Graham, Jr. *lawyer*
Hatoff, Howard Ira *retired labor lawyer*
Hauptfuhrer, George Jost, Jr. *lawyer*
Haviland, Bancroft Dawley *lawyer*
Haydanek, Ronald Edward *lawyer and consultant*
Hazard, Geoffrey Cornell, Jr. *law educator*
Henderson, J(oseph) Welles *lawyer*
Henrich, William Joseph, Jr. *lawyer*
Hess, Hans Ober *lawyer*
Hoelscher, Robert James *lawyer*
Hoffman, Alan Jay *lawyer*
Holloway, Hiliary Hamilton *lawyer, banker*
Humenuk, William Anzelm *lawyer*
Humes, James Calhoun *lawyer, communications consultant, author*
Hunter, James Austen, Jr. *lawyer*
Iskrant, John Dermot *lawyer*
Jellinek, Miles Andrew *lawyer*
Jones, Robert Jeffries *lawyer*
Jones, Robert Mead, Jr. *lawyer*
Justice, Jack Burton *retired lawyer*
Kahn, James Robert *lawyer*
Kane, Jonathan *lawyer*
Kauffman, Bruce William *lawyer, former state supreme court justice*
Kaufman, David Joseph *lawyer*
Keene, John Clark *lawyer, educator*
Kempin, Frederick Gustav, Jr. *lawyer, educator*
Kendall, Robert Louis, Jr. *lawyer*
Kessler, Alan Craig *lawyer*
King, David Roy *lawyer*
Klasko, Herbert Ronald *lawyer, law educator, writer*
Klaus, William Robert *lawyer*
Klayman, Barry Martin *lawyer*
Klein, Howard Bruce *lawyer, law educator*
Klein, Samuel Edwin *lawyer*
Kohn, Harold Elias *lawyer*
Kormes, John Winston *lawyer*
Kraemer, Michael Frederick *lawyer*
Kramer, Meyer *lawyer, editor, clergyman*
Krampf, John Edward *lawyer*
Krzyzanowski, Richard Lucien *lawyer, corporate executive*
Kupperman, Louis Brandeis *lawyer*
Laddon, Warren Milton *lawyer*
Ledwith, James Robb *lawyer*
Ledwith, John Francis *lawyer*
Leech, Noyes Elwood *lawyer, educator*
Leonard, Thomas Aloysius *lawyer*
Levin, A. Leo *law educator, retired government official*
Levin, Murray Simon *lawyer*
Levy, Dale Penneys *lawyer*
Lewis, John Hardy, Jr. *lawyer*
Libonati, Michael Ernest *lawyer, educator, writer*
Lichtenstein, Robert Jay *lawyer*
Lillie, Charisse Ranielle *lawyer, educator*
Lipman, Frederick D. *lawyer, writer, educator*
Loewenstein, Benjamin Steinberg *lawyer*
Lombard, John James, Jr. *lawyer*
Loveless, George Group *lawyer*
Lowery, William Herbert *lawyer*
Lucey, John David, Jr. *lawyer*
Lundy, Joseph E. *lawyer*
Mack, Wayne A. *lawyer*
Maclay, Donald Merle *lawyer*
Madeira, Edward W(alter), Jr. *lawyer*
Madva, Stephen Alan *lawyer*
Magargee, W(illiam) Scott, III *lawyer*
Magaziner, Fred Thomas *lawyer*
Mai, Elizabeth Hardy *lawyer*
Mann, Theodore R. *lawyer*
Mannino, Edward Francis *lawyer*
Mason, Theodore W. *lawyer*
Mathes, Stephen Jon *lawyer*
Mattoon, Peter Mills *lawyer*
McKeever, John Eugene *lawyer*
McMichael, Lawrence Grover *lawyer*
McQuiston, Robert Earl *lawyer*
Meigs, John Forsyth *lawyer*
Mellon, Thomas S. *lawyer*
Mesirov, Leon Isaac *lawyer*
Messa, Joseph Louis, Jr. *lawyer*
Meyers, Howard L. *lawyer*
Milbourne, Walter Robertson *lawyer*
Miller, Henry Franklin *lawyer*
Miller, Leslie Anne *lawyer*
Minisi, Anthony S. *lawyer*
Mirabello, Francis Joseph *lawyer*
Moss, Arthur Henshey *lawyer*
Mullinix, Edward Wingate *lawyer*
Narin, Stephen B. *lawyer*
Nofer, George Hancock *lawyer*
O'Brien, William Jerome, II *lawyer*
O'Connor, Joseph A., Jr. *lawyer*
O'Donnell, G. Daniel *lawyer*
O'Leary, Dennis Joseph *lawyer*
Ominsky, Alan Jay *lawyer, medical educator*
Ominsky, Harris *lawyer*
O'Reilly, Timothy Patrick *lawyer*
Oswald, Stanton S. *lawyer*
Pagliaro, James Domenic *lawyer*
Palmer, Richard Ware *lawyer*
Panzer, Mitchell Emanuel *lawyer*
Parry, William DeWitt *lawyer*
Phillips, Dorothy Kay *lawyer*
Phillips, Stephen S. *lawyer*
Pokotilow, Manny David *lawyer*
Pollack, Michael *lawyer*
Posner, Edward Martin *lawyer*
Poul, Franklin *lawyer*
Powell, Walter Hecht *labor arbitrator*
Pratter, Gene E. K. *lawyer*
Price, Robert Stanley *lawyer*
Promislo, Daniel *lawyer*
Putney, Paul William *lawyer*
Quinn, Charles Norman *lawyer*
Quinn, Francis F. *lawyer*
Rabinowitz, Samuel Nathan *lawyer*
Rachofsky, David J. *lawyer*
Rackow, Julian Paul *lawyer*
Rawdin, Grant *lawyer, financial planning company executive*
Reagan, Harry Edwin, III *lawyer*
Reed, Michael Haywood *lawyer*
Reich, Abraham Charles *lawyer*
Reiss, John Barlow *lawyer*
Reiter, Joseph Henry *lawyer, retired judge*
Reitz, Curtis Randall *lawyer, educator*
Rhoads, Nancy Glenn *lawyer*
Roberts, Carl Geoffrey *lawyer*
Roomberg, Lila Goldstein *lawyer*
Root, Stanley William, Jr. *lawyer*
Rosenbleeth, Richard Marvin *lawyer*
Rosenbloom, Sanford M. *lawyer*
Rosenfield, Bruce Alan *lawyer*
Rosenstein, James Alfred *lawyer*
Rosenthal, Brian David *lawyer*
Ross, Daniel R. *lawyer*
Ross, Murray Louis *lawyer, business executive*
Samuel, Ralph David *lawyer*
Satinsky, Barnett *lawyer*
Sax, Helen Spigel *lawyer*
Schaub, Harry Carl *lawyer*
Scher, Howard Dennis *lawyer*
Schneider, Carl William *lawyer*
Schneider, Pam Horvitz *lawyer*
Schneider, Richard Graham *lawyer*
Schorling, William Harrison *lawyer*
Schwartz, Robert M. *lawyer*
Scott, Donald Allison *lawyer*
Scott, William Proctor, III *lawyer*
Segal, Bernard Gerard *lawyer*
Segal, Irving Randall *lawyer*
Segal, Robert Martin *lawyer*
Shakow, David Joseph *law educator*
Shapiro, Raymond L. *lawyer*
Sharp, M. Rust *lawyer*
Sheils, Denis Francis *lawyer*
Shestack, Jerome Joseph *lawyer*
Shiekman, Laurence Zeid *lawyer*
Shipman, Lynn Karen *lawyer*
Siegel, Bernard Louis *lawyer*
Sigmond, Richard Brian *lawyer*
Siskind, Ralph Walter *lawyer*
Solano, Carl Anthony *lawyer*
Somers, Hans Peter *lawyer*
Spaeth, Edmund Benjamin, Jr. *lawyer, law educator, former judge*
Stakias, G. Michael *lawyer*
Steinberg, Robert Philip *lawyer*
Stern, Joan Naomi *lawyer*
Stewart, Robert Forrest, Jr. *lawyer*
Stiller, Jennifer Anne *lawyer*
Strasbaugh, Wayne Ralph *lawyer*
Strickler, Matthew M. *lawyer*
Stuntebeck, Clinton A. *lawyer*
Subak, John Thomas *lawyer*
Summers, Clyde Wilson *law educator*
Temin, Michael Lehman *lawyer*
Tiger, Ira Paul *lawyer*
Torregrossa, Joseph Anthony *lawyer*
Vaira, Peter Francis *lawyer*
†Vogel, Robert Philip *lawyer*
Wagner, Thomas Joseph *lawyer, insurance company executive*
Walker, Kent *lawyer*
Warner, Theodore Kugler, Jr. *lawyer*
Weil, Jeffrey George *lawyer*
Weisberg, Morris L. *retired lawyer*
White, John Joseph, III *lawyer*
Whiteside, William Anthony, Jr. *lawyer*
Wild, Richard P. *lawyer*
Wolf, Robert B. *lawyer*
Wolff, Deborah H(orowitz) *lawyer*
Wright, Minturn Tatum, III *lawyer*
Wrobleski, Jeanne Pauline *lawyer*
Young, Andrew Brodbeck *lawyer*
Zivitz, Stephen Charles *lawyer*

### Pipersville
Sigety, Charles Edward *lawyer, family business consultant*

### Pittsburgh
Aaron, Marcus, II *lawyer*
Acheson, Amy J. *lawyer*
Anderson, Edwyna Goodwin *lawyer*
Baier, George Patrick *lawyer, electrical engineer*
Baldauf, Kent Edward *lawyer*
Barnes, James Jerome *lawyer*
Bashline, Terry Lee Morgan *lawyer*
Basinski, Anthony Joseph *lawyer*
Beck, Paul Augustine *lawyer*
Bleier, Michael E. *lawyer*
Bleil, Walter G. *lawyer*
Blenko, Walter John, Jr. *lawyer*
Blum, Eva Tansky *lawyer*
Bonessa, Dennis R. *lawyer*
Botta, Frank Charles *lawyer*
Brennan, Carey M. *lawyer*
Brown, David Ronald *lawyer*
Brown, James Benton *lawyer*
Burke, Linda Beerbower *lawyer, aluminum manufacturing company executive, mining executive*
Burke, Timothy Francis, Jr. *lawyer*
Candris, Laura A. *lawyer*
Cheever, George Martin *lawyer*
Cohen, Henry C. *lawyer*
Colen, Frederick Haas *lawyer*
Colville, Robert E. *lawyer*
Coney, Aims C., Jr. *lawyer, labor-management negotiator*
Conley, Martha Richards *lawyer*
Connors, Eugene Kenneth *lawyer*
Conti, Joy Flowers *lawyer*
Cooper, Thomas Louis *lawyer*
Cowan, Barton Zalman *lawyer*
Daniel, Robert Michael *lawyer*
Davis, John Phillips, Jr. *lawyer*
DeForest, Walter Pattison, III *lawyer*
Demmler, John Henry *lawyer*
Donnelly, Thomas Joseph *lawyer*
Doty, Robert Walter *lawyer*
Dugan, John F. *lawyer*
Egler, Frederick Norton *lawyer*
Ehrenwerth, David Harry *lawyer*
Evans, Bruce Dwight *lawyer*
Ewalt, Henry Ward *lawyer*
Farley, Andrew Newell *lawyer*
Ferguson, Sanford Barnett *lawyer*
Fernsler, John Paul *lawyer*
Flatley, Lawrence Edward *lawyer*
Flinn, Michael James *lawyer*
Fort, James Tomlinson *lawyer*
Frank, Ronald W. *lawyer, financier*
Frolik, Lawrence Anton *law educator, lawyer, consultant*
Geeseman, Robert George *lawyer*
Geraghty, Andrea *lawyer*
Gerlach, G. Donald *lawyer*
Gold, Harold Arthur *lawyer*
Goldberg, Mark Joel *lawyer*
Graf, Edward Louis, Jr. *lawyer, finance executive*
Hackney, William Pendleton *lawyer*
Halpern, Richard I. *lawyer*
Hardie, James Hiller *lawyer*
Harff, Charles Henry *lawyer, retired diversified industrial company executive*
Harvey, Calvin Rea *lawyer*
Hellman, Arthur David *law educator, consultant*
Hershey, Dale *lawyer*
Hershey, Nathan *lawyer, educator*
Hickman, Leon Edward *lawyer, business executive*
Hill, John Howard *lawyer*
Hitt, Leo N. *lawyer, educator*
Hoffstot, Henry Phipps, Jr. *lawyer*
Hollinshead, Earl Darnell, Jr. *lawyer*
Johnson, Robert Alan *lawyer*
Jones, Craig Ward *lawyer*
Josephs, Eileen Sherle *mediator, financial consultant*
Kearns, John J., III *lawyer*
Kenrick, Charles William *lawyer*
Ketter, David Lee *lawyer*
Klett, Edwin Lee *lawyer*
Knox, Charles Graham *lawyer*
Leibowitz, Marvin *lawyer*
Lippard, Thomas Eugene *lawyer*
Litman, Roslyn Margolis *lawyer, educator*
Mansmann, J. Jerome *lawyer*
McCartney, Robert Charles *lawyer*
McConomy, James Herbert *lawyer*
McGough, Walter Thomas, Jr. *lawyer*
McKenna, J. Frank, III *lawyer*
McKenzie, Thomas James *lawyer, insurance consultant*
McLaughlin, John Sherman *lawyer*
Meisel, Alan *law educator*
Mendelson, Leonard M. *lawyer*
Messner, Robert Thomas *lawyer, banking executive*
Miller, Harbaugh *lawyer*
Miller, James Robert *lawyer*
Morton, James Davis *lawyer*
Mulvihill, David Brian *lawyer*
Murdoch, David Armor *lawyer*
Murray, John Edward, Jr. *lawyer, educator, university president*
Murray, Philip Joseph, III *lawyer*
Murrin, Regis Doubet *lawyer*
Nordenberg, Mark Alan *law educator, university official*
Norris, James Harold *lawyer*
Ober, Russell John, Jr. *lawyer*
O'Connor, Donald Thomas *lawyer*
O'Connor, Edward Gearing *lawyer*
O'Hare, Virginia Lewis *legal administrator*
Olson, Stephen M(ichael) *lawyer*
Patton, Robert Frederick *lawyer, banker*
Phillips, Larry Edward *lawyer*
Plowman, Jack Wesley *lawyer*
Pohl, Paul Michael *lawyer*
Pois, Joseph *lawyer, educator*
Powderly, William H., III *lawyer*
Prosperi, Louis Anthony *lawyer*
Pugliese, Robert Francis *lawyer, business executive*
Puhala, James Joseph *lawyer*
Purcupile, John Stephen *lawyer*
Pushinsky, Jon *lawyer*
Randolph, Robert DeWitt *lawyer*
Raynovich, George, Jr. *lawyer*
Reed, W. Franklin *lawyer*
Restivo, James John, Jr. *lawyer*
Ritchey, Patrick William *lawyer*
Roman, Andrew Michael *lawyer, educator*
Rosenberger, Bryan David *lawyer*
Scheinholtz, Leonard Louis *lawyer*
Schliebs, Charles Allan *lawyer*
Schmidt, Edward Craig *lawyer*
Schwab, Arthur James *lawyer*
Schwendeman, Paul William *lawyer*
Sell, William Edward *legal educator*
Shane, Peter Milo *law educator*
Silverman, Arnold Barry *lawyer*
Sokol, Stephen M. *lawyer*
Strader, James David *lawyer*
Stroyd, Arthur Heister *lawyer*
Swaim, Joseph Carter, Jr. *lawyer*
Sweeney, Clayton Anthony *lawyer, business executive*
Symons, Edward Leonard, Jr. *lawyer, educator, investment advisor*
Tarasi, Louis Michael, Jr. *lawyer*
Thomas, Richard Irwin *lawyer*
Thompson, Thomas Martin *lawyer*
Thurman, Andrew Edward *lawyer*
Tucker, Richard Blackburn, III *lawyer*
Turner, Harry Woodruff *lawyer*
Ubinger, John W., Jr. *lawyer*
Ummer, James Walter *lawyer*
Van Kirk, Thomas L. *lawyer*
Vater, Charles J. *lawyer*
Veeder, Peter Greig *lawyer*
von Waldow, Arnd N. *lawyer*
Walton, Jon David *lawyer*
Ward, Thomas Jerome *lawyer*
Williams, Robert Brickley *lawyer*
Woodward, Thomas Aiken *lawyer*
Wycoff, William Mortimer *lawyer*
Wynstra, Nancy Ann *lawyer*
Yorsz, Stanley *lawyer*
Zoghby, Guy Anthony *lawyer*

### Pottsville
Jones, Joseph Hayward *lawyer*

### Punxsutawney
Lorenzo, Nicholas Francis, Jr. *lawyer*

### Reading
Linton, Jack Arthur *lawyer*
Rothermel, Daniel Krott *lawyer, holding company executive*
Welty, John Rider *lawyer*

### Reynoldsville
Wheeler, Mark Andrew, Sr. *lawyer*

### Ridley Park
Clark, John H., Jr. *lawyer*

### Scranton
Cimini, Joseph Fedele *law educator, lawyer, former magistrate*
Haggerty, James Joseph *lawyer*
Howley, James McAndrew *lawyer*
Myers, Morey Mayer *lawyer*
Sposito, James A. *lawyer, consultant*

### Sewickley
Wilkinson, James Allan *lawyer, healthcare executive*

### Solebury
Valentine, H. Jeffrey *legal association executive*

### Spring City
Mayerson, Hy *lawyer*

### State College
Nollau, Lee Gordon *lawyer*

### Valley Forge
Bovaird, Brendan Peter *lawyer*
Corchin, Mark Alan *lawyer*
Simmons, James Charles *lawyer*
Walters, Bette Jean *lawyer*

### Villanova
Bersoff, Donald Neil *lawyer, psychologist*
Maule, James Edward *law educator, lawyer*
Mulroney, Michael *lawyer, law educator, graduate program director*
Perritt, Henry Hardy, Jr. *law educator*
Termini, Roseann Bridget *lawyer*

### Washington
Allison, Jonathan *retired lawyer*
Richman, Stephen I. *lawyer*

### Wayne
Baldwin, Frank Bruce, III *lawyer*
Emory, Hugh Mercer *lawyer*
Griffith, Edward, II *lawyer*
Woodbury, Alan Tenney *lawyer*

### Wernersville
Worley, Jane Ludwig *lawyer*

### West Chester
Osborn, John Edward *lawyer, former government official, writer*
Sommer, Jeffrey Robert *lawyer*

### West Conshohocken
Teillon, L. Pierre, Jr. *lawyer*

### Wilkes Barre
Harter, Robert Jackson, Jr. *lawyer*
Musto, Joseph John *lawyer*
Reilly, Michael James *law librarian*
Roth, Eugene *lawyer*

### Williamsport
Ertel, Allen Edward *lawyer, former congressman*
Kane, Joseph Patrick *lawyer, financial planner*

## RHODE ISLAND

### Cranston
Coletti, John Anthony *lawyer, furniture and realty company executive*
Ferguson, Christine C. *lawyer, state agency administrator*
Simonian, John S. *lawyer*

### East Greenwich
Dence, Edward William, Jr. *lawyer, banker*
Flynn, Richard James *lawyer*

### Newport
Cohen, Arthur Abram *lawyer*
Levie, Howard S(idney) *lawyer, educator, author*
Nelligan, Kenneth Egan *lawyer*

### Pawtucket
Kranseler, Lawrence Michael *lawyer*

### Providence
Almeida, Victoria Martin *lawyer*
Borod, Richard Melvin *lawyer*
Burrows, Richard Henry *lawyer*
Carlotti, Stephen Jon *lawyer*
Courage, Thomas Roberts *lawyer*
Curran, Joseph Patrick *lawyer*
Donnelly, Kevin William *lawyer*
Farrell, Margaret Dawson *lawyer*
Field, Noel Macdonald, Jr. *lawyer*
Gale, Edwin John *prosecutor*
Gasbarro, Pasco, Jr. *lawyer*
Germani, Elia *lawyer*
Gorham, Bradford *lawyer*
Jackvony, Bernard A. *lawyer*
Johnson, Vahe Duncan *lawyer*
Juchatz, Wayne Warren *lawyer*
Kacir, Barbara Brattin *lawyer*
Kean, John Vaughan *lawyer*
Kersh, DeWitte Talmadge, Jr. *lawyer*
Licht, Richard A. *lawyer*
Lipsey, Howard Irwin *law educator, justice, lawyer*
Long, Beverly Glenn *lawyer*
McCann, Gail Elizabeth *lawyer*
McIntyre, Jerry L. *lawyer*
Olsen, Hans Peter *lawyer*
Paster, Benjamin G. *lawyer*
Pendergast, John Joseph, III *lawyer*
Pierce, Richard Hilton *lawyer*
Resmini, Ronald Joseph *lawyer*
Robinson, William Philip, III *lawyer*
Salter, Lester Herbert *lawyer*
Sherman, Deming Eliot *lawyer*

Soutter, Thomas Douglas *retired lawyer*
Staples, Richard Farnsworth *lawyer*
Svengalis, Kendall Frayne *law librarian*
Walker, Howard Ernest *lawyer*
White, Benjamin Vroom, III *lawyer*

**Tiverton**
Davis, Stephen Edward *lawyer, educator*

**Wakefield**
Rothschild, Donald Phillip *lawyer, arbitrator*

**Warwick**
Knowles, Charles Timothy *lawyer, state legislator*
Reilly, John B. *lawyer*
Sholes, David Henry *lawyer, former state senator*

**West Warwick**
Pollock, Bruce Gerald *lawyer*

**Westerly**
Hennessy, Dean McDonald *lawyer, multinational corporation executive*

## SOUTH CAROLINA

**Aiken**
Rudnick, Irene Krugman *lawyer, former state legislator, educator*

**Anderson**
Watkins, William Law *retired lawyer*

**Barnwell**
Loadholt, Miles *lawyer*

**Beaufort**
Harvey, William Brantley, Jr. *lawyer, former lieutenant governor*

**Camden**
Jacobs, Rolly Warren *lawyer*

**Charleston**
Cannon, Hugh *lawyer*
Dominick, Paul Allen *lawyer*
Good, Joseph Cole, Jr. *lawyer*
Grimball, William Heyward *retired lawyer*
Groves, Stephen Peterson, Sr. *lawyer*
Kahn, Ellis Irvin *lawyer*
Patrick, Charles William, Jr. *lawyer*
Ray, Paul DuBose *lawyer*
Robinson, Neil Cibley, Jr. *lawyer*
Simons, Albert, Jr. *retired lawyer*

**Clemson**
Cox, Headley Morris, Jr. *lawyer, educator*

**Columbia**
Bailey, George Screven *lawyer*
Baum, Marsha Lynn *law educator*
Blanton, Hoover Clarence *lawyer*
Finkel, Gerald Michael *lawyer*
Foster, Robert Watson, Sr. *law educator*
Haimbaugh, George Dow, Jr. *lawyer, educator*
Jedziniak, Lee Peter *lawyer, educator, state insurance administrator*
Matthews, Steve Allen *lawyer*
Mc Cullough, Ralph Clayton, II *lawyer, educator*
Morrison, Stephen George *lawyer*
Nexsen, Julian Jacobs *lawyer*
Scott, Ronald Charles *lawyer*
Sheftman, Howard Stephen *lawyer*
Sloan, Frank Keenan *lawyer, writer*
Strom, J. Preston, Jr. *lawyer*
Tate, Harold Simmons, Jr. *lawyer*
Wells, Robert Steven *law association executive*
Wilson, Karen Wilkerson *paralegal*

**Conway**
Suggs, Michael Edward *lawyer*

**Georgetown**
Moore, Albert Cunningham *lawyer, insurance company executive*

**Greenville**
Barash, Anthony Harlan *lawyer*
Edwards, Harry LaFoy *lawyer*
Foulke, Edwin Gerhart, Jr. *lawyer*
Hagood, William Milliken, III *lawyer*
Horton, James Wright *retired lawyer*
Todd, John Dickerson, Jr. *lawyer*
Traxler, William Byrd *retired lawyer*
Walker, Wesley M. *lawyer*
Walters, Johnnie McKeiver *lawyer*
Wyche, Bradford Wheeler *lawyer*
Wyche, Cyril Thomas *lawyer*
Wyche, Madison Baker, III *lawyer*

**Hartsville**
DeLoach, Harris E(ugene), Jr. *lawyer, manufacturing company executive*

**Hilton Head Island**
Becker, Karl Martin *lawyer, investment company executive*
Hagoort, Thomas Henry *lawyer*
McKay, John Judson, Jr. *lawyer*
Rose, William Shepard, Jr. *lawyer*
Scarminach, Charles Anthony *lawyer*

**Landrum**
Hilton, Ordway *retired document examiner*

**Langley**
Bell, Robert Morrall *lawyer*

**Lexington**
Kelehear, Carole Marchbanks Spann *legal administrator*
Wilkins, Robert Pearce *lawyer*

**Mount Pleasant**
McConnell, John William, Jr. *lawyer*

**Newberry**
Pope, Thomas Harrington, Jr. *lawyer*

**Rock Hill**
Hardin, James Carlisle, III *lawyer, educator*

**Seneca**
Fleming, Mack Gerald *lawyer*

**Sheldon**
Goss, Richard Henry *lawyer*

**Spartanburg**
Williams, John Cornelius *lawyer*

**Summerville**
Mortimer, Rory Dixon *lawyer*

## SOUTH DAKOTA

**Britton**
Farrar, Frank Leroy *lawyer, former governor*

**Dakota Dunes**
Putney, Mark William *lawyer, utility executive*

**Parker**
Zimmer, John Herman *lawyer*

**Pierre**
Johnson, Julie Marie *lawyer/lobbyist*
Thompson, Charles Murray *lawyer*

**Rapid City**
Foye, Thomas Harold *lawyer*
Viken, Linda Lea Margaret *lawyer*

**Sioux Falls**
LaFave, LeAnn Larson *lawyer*

**Yankton**
Hirsch, Robert William *lawyer*

## TENNESSEE

**Brentwood**
Provine, John C. *lawyer*
Schreiber, Kurt Gilbert *lawyer*

**Chattanooga**
Collier, Curtis Lynn *lawyer*
Copeland, Floyd Dean *lawyer*
Durham, J(oseph) Porter, Jr. *lawyer, educator*
James, Stuart Fawcett *lawyer*
Proctor, John Franklin *lawyer*
Witt, Raymond Buckner, Jr. *lawyer*

**Cleveland**
Fisher, Richard Ashley *lawyer*

**Collierville**
Springfield, James Francis *retired lawyer, banker*

**Crossville**
Marlow, James Allen *lawyer*

**Erwin**
Shults-Davis, Lois Bunton *lawyer*

**Fayetteville**
Dickey, John Harwell *lawyer, public defender*

**Hendersonville**
McCaleb, Joe Wallace *lawyer*

**Hermitage**
Lockmiller, David Alexander *lawyer, educator*

**Jackson**
Drew, Gayden, IV *lawyer*

**Johnson City**
Jenkins, Ronald Wayne *lawyer*

**Kingsport**
Hull, E. Patrick *lawyer*

**Knoxville**
Ailor, Earl Starnes *lawyer*
Arnett, Foster Deaver *lawyer*
Bailey, Bridget *lawyer*
Bly, Robert Maurice *lawyer*
Christenbury, Edward Samuel *lawyer*
Dillard, W. Thomas *lawyer*
Hagood, Lewis Russell *lawyer*
Howard, Lewis Spilman *lawyer*
Murray, Rebecca Brake *lawyer*
Oberman, Steven *lawyer*
Ownby, Jere Franklin, III *lawyer*
Phillips, Jerry Juan *law educator*
Pollard, Dennis Bernard *lawyer, educator*
Rayson, Edwin Hope *lawyer*
Reynolds, Glenn Harlan *law educator*
Sanger, Herbert Shelton, Jr. *lawyer, former government official*
Smith, Leonard Ware *lawyer*
Wheeler, John Watson *lawyer*

**Lookout Mountain**
Leitner, Paul R. *lawyer*

**Mc Minnville**
Potter, Clement Dale *public defender*

**Memphis**
Allen, Newton Perkins *lawyer*
Bland, James Theodore, Jr. *lawyer*
Broadhurst, Jerome Anthony *lawyer*
Buchignani, Leo Joseph *lawyer*
Clark, Ross Bert, II *lawyer*
Cody, Walter James Michael *lawyer, former state official*
Coleman, Veronica Freeman *prosecutor*
Davis, Frederick Benjamin *law educator*
Gentry, Gavin Miller *lawyer*
Gilman, Ronald Lee *lawyer*
Haight, Scott Kerr *lawyer*
Harpster, James Erving *lawyer*
Harvey, Albert C. *lawyer*
Jerry, Robert Howard, II *law educator*
Manire, James McDonnell *lawyer*
Monypeny, David Murray *lawyer*
Noel, Randall Deane *lawyer*
Rice, George Lawrence, III (Larry Rice) *lawyer*
Russell, James Franklin *lawyer*
Smith, Joseph Philip *lawyer*
Spore, Richard Roland, III *lawyer, educator*
Streibich, Harold Cecil *lawyer*
Tate, Stonewall Shepherd *lawyer*
Walsh, Thomas James, Jr. *lawyer*

**Nashville**
Bass, James Orin *lawyer*
Belton, Robert *law educator*
Berry, William Wells *lawyer*
Bloch, Frank Samuel *law educator*
Blumstein, James Franklin *legal educator, lawyer, consultant*
Bostick, Charles Dent *lawyer, educator*
Bramlett, Paul Kent *lawyer*
Brown, Joe Blackburn *lawyer*
Carr, Davis Haden *lawyer*
Charney, Jonathan Isa *law educator, lawyer*
Cheek, James Howe, III *lawyer, educator*
Cobb, Stephen A. *lawyer*
Cooney, Charles Hayes *lawyer*
Covington, Robert Newman *law educator*
Culbertson, Katheryn Campbell *lawyer*
Doran, James Marion, Jr. *lawyer*
Ely, James Wallace, Jr. *law educator*
Gillmor, John Edward *lawyer*
Griffith, James Leigh *lawyer*
Hardin, Hal D. *lawyer, former United States attorney, former judge*
Hart, Richard Banner *lawyer*
Harwell, Aubrey Biggs *lawyer*
Hildebrand, Donald Dean *lawyer*
Hood, Howard Allison *law librarian*
Jackson, Kenneth Monroe *lawyer, actor*
Ledyard, Robins Heard *lawyer*
Levinson, L(eslie) Harold *lawyer, educator*
Lyon, Philip K(irkland) *lawyer*
Madu, Leonard Ekwugha *lawyer, human rights officer, newspaper columnist*
Maier, Harold Geistweit *law educator, lawyer*
Martin, Henry Alan *lawyer*
May, Joseph Leserman (Jack) *lawyer*
Mayden, Barbara Mendel *lawyer*
Mc Creary, James Franklin *lawyer, mediator*
Oldfield, Russell Miller *lawyer*
Partlett, David F. *law educator*
Ramsaur, Allan Fields *lawyer, lobbyist*
Sanders, Paul Hampton *lawyer, retired educator, arbitrator/mediator*
Sims, Wilson *lawyer*
Soderquist, Larry Dean *lawyer, educator*
Szarwark, Ernest John *lawyer*
Torrey, Claudia Olivia *lawyer*
Trautman, Herman Louis *lawyer, educator*
Tuke, Robert Dudley *lawyer, educator*
Winstead, George Alvis *law librarian, biochemist, educator, consultant*
Youngblood, Elaine Michele *lawyer*

**Newport**
Bunnell, John Blake *lawyer*

**Powell**
Hyman, Roger David *lawyer*

**Sevierville**
Waters, John B. *lawyer*

**Sewanee**
Pierce, Donna L. *lawyer*

**Springfield**
Wilks, Larry Dean *lawyer*

**Waverly**
Williams, John Lee *lawyer*

**White House**
Ruth, Bryce Clinton, Jr. *lawyer*

## TEXAS

**Abilene**
Boone, Billy Warren *lawyer, judge*
Boone, Celia Trimble *lawyer*
Wilson, Stanley P. *retired lawyer*

**Amarillo**
Madden, Wales Hendrix, Jr. *lawyer*
McDougall, Gerald Duane *lawyer*
Neal, A. Curtis *retired lawyer*
Smithee, John True *lawyer, state legislator*
White, Sharon Elizabeth *lawyer*
Woods, John William *retired lawyer*

**Angleton**
Panitz, Lawrence Herbert *lawyer*

**Arlington**
Moore, Tresi Lea *lawyer*
Rosenberry, William Kenneth *lawyer, educator*

**Austin**
Allday, Martin Lewis *lawyer*
Anderson, David Arnold *law educator*
Armbrust, David B. *lawyer*
Baade, Hans Wolfgang *legal educator, law expert*
Bobbitt, Philip Chase *lawyer, educator, writer*
Brown, Frank Beverly, IV *lawyer, accountant*
Byrd, Linward Tonnett *lawyer, rancher*
Calhoun, Frank Wayne *lawyer, former state legislator*
Cantilo, Patrick Herrera *lawyer*
Churgin, Michael Jay *law educator*
Cook, J. Rowland *lawyer*
Davis, Creswell Dean *lawyer, consultant*
Davis, David Murrel *lawyer*
Denius, Franklin Wofford *lawyer*
Dougherty, John Chrysostom, III *lawyer*
Gambrell, James Bruton, III *lawyer, educator*
Gammage, Robert Alton (Bob Gammage) *lawyer*
Gangstad, John Erik *lawyer*
Getman, Julius Gerson *law educator, lawyer*
Gibbins, Bob *lawyer*
Gibson, William Willard, Jr. *law educator*
Goldstein, E. Ernest *lawyer*
Golemon, Ronald Kinnan *lawyer*
Graglia, Lino Anthony *lawyer, educator*
Greene, John Joseph *lawyer*
Greig, Brian Strother *lawyer*
Hamilton, Dagmar Strandberg *lawyer, educator*
Hamilton, Robert Woodruff *law educator*
Hardin, Dale Wayne *retired law educator*
Harrison, Richard Wayne *lawyer*
Hazel, Joseph Patrick *law educator*
Helburn, Isadore B. *arbitrator, mediator, educator*
Helman, Stephen Jody *lawyer*
Henderson, George Ervin *lawyer*
Ikard, Frank Neville, Jr. *lawyer*
Ingram, Denny Ouzts, Jr. *lawyer, educator*
Jentz, Gaylord Adair *law educator*
Johnson, Corwin Waggoner *law educator*
Knight, Gary *lawyer, educator, publisher, trader*
Laycock, Harold Douglas *law educator, writer*
Lochridge, Lloyd Pampell, Jr. *lawyer*
Mauzy, Oscar Holcombe *lawyer, retired state supreme court justice*
McDaniel, Myra Atwell *lawyer, former state official*
Mersky, Roy Martin *law educator, librarian*
Miller, John Eddie *lawyer*
Moss, Bill Ralph *lawyer, publisher*
Mullenix, Linda Susan *lawyer, educator*
Nation, Floyd Reuben *lawyer*
Nevola, Roger Paul *lawyer*
Painton, Russell Elliott *lawyer, mechanical engineer*
Papadakis, Myron Philip *lawyer, educator, pilot*
Pickens, Franklin Ace *lawyer*
Probus, Michael Maurice, Jr. *lawyer*
Rabago, Karl Roger *lawyer*
Rider, Brian Clayton *lawyer*
Ruud, Millard Harrington *former legal association administrator, retired educator*
Schulze, Eric William *lawyer, legal publications editor, publisher*
Shapiro, David L. *lawyer*
Shapiro, Sander Wolf *lawyer*
Sims, Robert Barry *lawyer*
Stephen, John Erle *lawyer, consultant*
Strauser, Robert Wayne *lawyer*
Sturley, Michael F. *law educator*
Sullivan, Teresa Ann *law and sociology educator, academic administrator*
Sutton, John F., Jr. *law educator, university dean, lawyer*
Temple, Larry Eugene *lawyer*
Thomajan, Robert *lawyer, management and financial consultant*
Weddington, Sarah Ragle *lawyer, educator*
Weinberg, Louise *law educator, author*
Weintraub, Russell Jay *lawyer, educator*
Wellborn, Olin Guy, III *law educator*
Westbrook, Jay Lawrence *law educator*
White, Michael Lee *lawyer*
Wilson, James William *lawyer*
Winters, J. Sam *lawyer, federal government official*
Wright, Charles Alan *law educator, author*
Yudof, Mark G. *law educator, academic administrator*
Zimmerman, Louis Seymour *lawyer*

**Beaumont**
Scofield, Louis M., Jr. *lawyer*

**Bellaire**
Soffar, William Douglas *lawyer*

**Bellville**
Dittert, J. Lee, Jr. *lawyer*

**Big Spring**
Morrison, Walton Stephen *lawyer*

**Brownfield**
Moore, Bradford L. *lawyer*

**Bryan**
Steelman, Frank (Sitley) *lawyer*

**Burleson**
Johnstone, Deborah Blackmon *lawyer*

**Canton**
White, Jeffery Howell *lawyer*

**Cleburne**
MacLean, John Ronald *lawyer*
Urban, Carlyle Woodrow *retired lawyer*

**Coppell**
Auerbach, Ernest Sigmund *lawyer, company executive, writer*

**Corpus Christi**
Bonilla, Tony *lawyer*
Branscomb, Harvie, Jr. *lawyer*
Bucklin, Leonard Herbert *lawyer*
Fancher, Rick *lawyer*
Hall, Ralph Carr *lawyer, real estate consultant*
Miller, Carroll Gerard, Jr. (Gerry Miller) *lawyer*
Wood, James Allen *lawyer*

**Dallas**
Abney, Frederick Sherwood *lawyer*
Acker, Rodney *lawyer*
Agnich, Richard John *lawyer, electronics company executive*
Anderson, Barbara McComas *lawyer*
Anderson, E. Karl *lawyer*
Anglin, Michael Williams *lawyer*
Armour, James Lott *lawyer*
Austin, Ann Sheree *lawyer*
Babcock, Charles Lynde, IV *lawyer*
Baggett, W. Mike *lawyer*
Barbee, Linton E. *lawyer*
Barnett, Barry Craig *lawyer*
Bass, John Fred *lawyer*
Beuttenmuller, Rudolf William *lawyer*
Bickel, John W., II *lawyer*
Birkeland, Bryan Collier *lawyer*
Bishop, Bryan Edwards *lawyer*
Blachly, Jack Lee *lawyer*
Blau, Charles William *lawyer, former government official*
Bliss, Robert Harms *lawyer*
Blount, Charles William, III *lawyer*
Bonesio, Woodrow Michael *lawyer*
Bonney, Samuel Robert *lawyer*
Boone, Oliver Kiel *lawyer*

Travis, Andrew David *lawyer*
Tripp, Karen Bryant *lawyer*
Vaden, Frank Samuel, III *lawyer, engineer*
Vance, Carol Stoner *lawyer*
Van Fleet, George Allan *lawyer*
Vest, G. Waverly, Jr. *lawyer*
Wakefield, Stephen Alan *lawyer*
Watson, John Allen *lawyer*
Webb, Jack M. *lawyer*
Weber, Fredric Alan *lawyer*
Weberpal, Michael Andrew *lawyer*
Welch, Harry Scoville *lawyer, retired gas pipeline company executive*
Welch, Robert Morrow, Jr. *lawyer*
Wells, Benjamin Gladney *lawyer*
Westby, Timothy Scott *lawyer*
Wheelan, R(ichelieu) E(dward) *lawyer*
Wickliffe, Jerry L. *lawyer*
Wilde, Carlton D. *lawyer*
Wilde, William Key *lawyer*
Williamson, Peter David *lawyer*
Wray, Thomas Jefferson *lawyer*
Wright, Robert Payton *lawyer*
Yokubaitis, Roger T. *lawyer*

**Hurst**
Marling, Lynwood Bradley *lawyer*

**Irving**
Elliott, Frank Wallace *lawyer, educator*
Glober, George Edward, Jr. *lawyer*
Lieberman, Mark Joel *lawyer*
Zahn, Donald Jack *lawyer*

**Katy**
Fudge, Edward William *lawyer*

**Kaufman**
Legg, Reagan Houston *lawyer*

**Kerrville**
Tomlin, Linton *court reporter*

**Kilgore**
Rorschach, Richard Gordon *lawyer*

**Lampasas**
Harvey, Leigh Kathryn *lawyer*

**Lancaster**
Fewel, Harriett *lawyer*

**Lubbock**
Cochran, Joseph Wesley *law librarian, educator*
Crowson, James Lawrence *lawyer, financial company executive*
Duncan, Robert Lloyd *lawyer*
Glass, Carson McElyea *lawyer*
Nagy, Joe Howard *lawyer*
Purdom, Thomas James *lawyer*
Skillern, Frank Fletcher *law educator*

**Marshall**
Gilstrap, James Rodney *lawyer, judge*

**Mcallen**
Carrera, Victor Manuel *lawyer*
Connors, Joseph Aloysius, III *lawyer*

**Mesquite**
Zook, Bill *lawyer*

**Midland**
Bullock, Maurice Randolph *lawyer*
Estes, Andrew Harper *lawyer*
Frost, Wayne N. *lawyer*
Morrow, William Clarence *lawyer, mediator*

**Missouri City**
Hodges, Jot Holiver, Jr. *lawyer, business executive*

**Odessa**
Gilliland, William Elton *retired lawyer*

**Pecos**
Weinacht, John William *lawyer*

**Plano**
Bonet, Frank Joseph *lawyer*
Kranzow, Ronald Roy *lawyer*

**Pottsboro**
Thomas, Ann Van Wynen *law educator*

**Richardson**
DeBusk, Manuel Conrad *lawyer*
Douglas, John Paul *lawyer, commercial and family law mediator*
Edwards, Carl Elmo, Jr. *lawyer*
Ellwanger, J. David *lawyer*
Neely, Vicki Adele *legal assistant, poet*
Olson, Dennis Oliver *lawyer*
Standel, Richard Reynold, Jr. *lawyer, communications executive*

**Round Rock**
LaShelle, Charles Stanton *lawyer, insurance company executive*

**San Antonio**
Aldave, Barbara Bader *law educator, lawyer*
Allison, Stephen Philip *lawyer*
Anderson, Bruce Edwin *lawyer*
Armstrong, William Tucker, III *lawyer*
Barton, James Cary *lawyer*
Biery, Evelyn Hudson *lawyer*
Bramble, Ronald Lee *business and legal consultant*
Branton, James LaVoy *lawyer*
Castleberry, James Newton, Jr. *legal educator*
Cruse, Rex Beach, Jr. *lawyer*
Dazey, William Boyd *retired lawyer*
Durbin, Richard Louis, Jr. *lawyer*
Fagan, Wayne Irwin *lawyer*
Fox, Michael W. *lawyer*
Guenther, Jack Egon *lawyer*
Guess, James David *lawyer*
Hardy, Harvey Louchard *lawyer*
Henry, Peter York *lawyer, mediator*
Hollin, Shelby W. *lawyer*
Johnston, Murray Lloyd, Jr. *lawyer*

Labay, Eugene Benedict *lawyer*
Lynch, Robert Martin *lawyer, educator*
Macon, Jane Haun *lawyer*
Maloney, Marynell *lawyer*
Montgomery, James Edward, Jr. *lawyer*
Patrick, Dane Herman *lawyer*
Ross, James Ulric *lawyer, accountant, educator*
Ruttenberg, Frank Z. *lawyer*
Scalise, Celeste *lawyer*
Schlueter, David Arnold *law educator*
Spears, Sally *lawyer*
Steen, John Thomas, Jr. *lawyer*
West, Stephen Allan *lawyer*
Yates, Norris William, Jr. *lawyer*
Zepeda, Enrique E., V *lawyer*

**South Padre Island**
Yorty, Samuel *lawyer, former mayor*

**Sugar Land**
Greer, Raymond White *lawyer*

**Temple**
Pickle, Jerry Richard *lawyer*

**The Woodlands**
Kosut, Kenneth Paul *lawyer*

**Tyler**
Alworth, Charles Wesley *lawyer, engineer*
Ellis, Donald Lee *lawyer*

**Victoria**
Chapman, J. Milton *lawyer*

**Waco**
Denton, Betty *lawyer, state representative*
Smith, Cullen *lawyer*
Thomson, Basil Henry, Jr. *lawyer, university general counsel*
Wendorf, Hulen Dee *law educator, author, lecturer*
Wilson, John Ross *retired law educator*

**Westlake**
Pitts, Joe W., III (Chip Pitts) *lawyer, law educator*

**Wichita Falls**
Todd, Richard D. R. *lawyer*
Walker, Randall Wayne *lawyer*

**Yoakum**
Williams, Walter Waylon *lawyer, pecan grower*

## UTAH

**Brigham City**
McCullough, Edward Eugene *patent agent, inventor*

**Logan**
Hillyard, Lyle William *lawyer*
Honaker, Jimmie Joe *lawyer, ecologist*

**Manti**
Petersen, Benton Lauritz *paralegal*

**Ogden**
Kaufman, Steven Michael *lawyer*
Mecham, Glenn Jefferson *lawyer, mayor*

**Orem**
Abbott, Charles Favour, Jr. *lawyer*

**Park City**
Kennicott, James W. *lawyer*

**Provo**
Hill, Richard Lee *lawyer*
Kimball, Edward Lawrence *law educator, lawyer*
Smith, Maurice Edward *lawyer, business consultant*
Thomas, David Albert *law educator*
Whitman, Dale Alan *lawyer, educator*
Wilde, James L. *lawyer*

**Saint George**
Gallian, Russell Joseph *lawyer*

**Salt Lake City**
Adams, Joseph Keith *lawyer*
Anderson, Kent Taylor *lawyer*
Balthaser, Anita Young *legal assistant*
Barker, Ronald C. *lawyer*
Baucom, Sidney George *lawyer*
Berman, Daniel Lewis *lawyer*
Buchi, Mark Keith *lawyer*
Callister, Louis Henry, Jr. *lawyer*
Christensen, Ray Richards *lawyer*
Clark, Scott H. *lawyer*
Colessides, Nick John *lawyer*
Cornaby, Kay Sterling *lawyer, former state senator*
Curtis, LeGrand R., Jr. *lawyer*
Holbrook, Donald Benson *lawyer*
Holtkamp, James Arnold *lawyer, legal educator*
Kirkham, John Spencer *lawyer*
Lunt, Jack *lawyer*
Mabey, Ralph R. *lawyer*
Manning, Brent V. *lawyer*
Matsumori, Douglas *lawyer*
McIntosh, Terrie Tuckett *lawyer*
Melich, Mitchell *retired lawyer*
Mills, Lawrence *lawyer, business and transportation consultant*
Mock, Henry Byron *lawyer, writer, consultant*
Moore, Larry Gale *lawyer*
Nielsen, Greg Ross *lawyer*
Oaks, Dallin Harris *lawyer, church official*
Purser, Donald Joseph *lawyer*
Reeder, F. Robert *lawyer*
Roberts, Jack Earle *lawyer, ski resort operator, wood products company executive, real estate developer*
Scofield, David Willson *lawyer*
Teitelbaum, Lee E. *law educator*
Wadsworth, Harold Wayne *lawyer*
Weiss, Loren Elliot *lawyer, law educator*
Wikstrom, Francis M. *lawyer*

**Sandy**
Bush, Rex Curtis *lawyer*

**Snowbird**
Gardiner, Lester Raymond, Jr. *lawyer*

**Spanish Fork**
Ashworth, Brent Ferrin *lawyer*

## VERMONT

**Brattleboro**
Cummings, Charles Rogers *lawyer*

**Burlington**
Baker, Robert W., Jr. *lawyer*
Dinse, John Merrell *lawyer*
Hoff, Philip Henderson *lawyer, former state senator, former governor*
Kory, Marianne Greene *lawyer*
Martin, Allen *lawyer*
Sartore, John Thornton *lawyer*
Tetzlaff, Charles Robert *prosecutor*
Wick, Hilton Addison *lawyer*

**Middlebury**
Langrock, Peter Forbes *lawyer*

**Montpelier**
Brock, James Sidney *lawyer*
Diamond, M. Jerome *lawyer, former state official*
Guild, Alden *lawyer*

**Morrisville**
Simonds, Marshall *lawyer*

**Randolph**
Angell, Philip Alvin, Jr. *lawyer*

**Rutland**
Chalidze, Lisa Leah *lawyer*
Keyser, Frank Ray, Jr. *lawyer, former governor*
Stafford, Robert Theodore *lawyer, former senator*

**Shelburne**
Ross, Charles Robert *lawyer, consultant*

**South Royalton**
Wroth, L(awrence) Kinvin *lawyer, educator*

**Waitsfield**
Raphael, Albert Ash, Jr. *lawyer*

**Waterbury**
Adams, Charles Jairus *lawyer*

## VIRGINIA

**Abingdon**
Johnson, Janet Droke *legal secretary*

**Alexandria**
Abell, Richard Bender *lawyer, federal official*
Alexander, Fred Calvin, Jr. *lawyer*
Battle, Timothy Joseph *lawyer*
Brittigan, Robert Lee *lawyer*
Carlson, J(ohn) Philip *lawyer*
Carter, Richard Dennis *lawyer, educator*
Clubb, Bruce Edwin *retired lawyer*
Cohen, Bernard S. *lawyer*
Dietrich, Paul George *lawyer*
Evans, H(arold) Bradley, Jr. *lawyer*
Hathaway, Fred William *lawyer*
Hussey, Ward MacLean *lawyer, former government official*
Hutzelman, Martha Louise *lawyer*
Jameson, Paula Ann *lawyer*
Kopp, Eugene Paul *lawyer*
Krosin, Kenneth E. *lawyer*
†Mar, Eugene *lawyer*
Mathis, William Lowrey *lawyer*
McClure, Roger John *lawyer*
McDowell, Charles Eager *lawyer, retired military officer*
O'Hara, John Patrick *lawyer, accountant*
Schultz, Franklin M. *retired lawyer*
Straub, Peter Thornton *lawyer*
Sturtevant, Brereton *retired lawyer, former government official*
Swinburn, Charles *lawyer*
Thomas, William Griffith *lawyer*
Vance, Bernard Wayne *lawyer, government official*
Van Cleve, Ruth Gill *retired lawyer, government official*
Von Drehle, Ramon Arnold *lawyer*
Wegner, Helmuth Adalbert *lawyer, retired chemical company executive*
Wendel, Charles Allen *lawyer*
Wilner, Morton Harrison *retired lawyer*
Zarro, Janice Anne *lawyer*

**Annandale**
McGuire, Edward David, Jr. *lawyer*
Richstein, Abraham Richard *lawyer*
Yaffe, David Philip *lawyer*

**Arlington**
Anderson, David Lawrence *lawyer*
Anthony, Robert Armstrong *law educator*
Bader, Michael Haley *lawyer, telecommunications, broadcasting executive*
Belen, Frederick Christopher *lawyer*
Benzinger, Raymond Burdette *lawyer, educator*
Brenner, Edgar H. *legal administrator*
Chapple, Thomas Leslie *lawyer*
Collins, Philip Reilly *lawyer, educator*
Conklin, Kenneth Edward *lawyer, industry executive*
Damich, Edward John *law educator*
Drayton, William *lawyer, management consultant*
Dunham, Frank Willard *lawyer*
Dunn, Loretta Lynn *lawyer*
Eastin, Keith E. *lawyer*
Hansen, Kenneth D. *lawyer, ophthalmologist*
Hugler, Edward C. *lawyer, federal and state government*
Jackson, William Paul, Jr. *lawyer*
Kauffman, Thomas Richard *lawyer, consultant*
Kelly, John James *lawyer*
Korman, James William *lawyer*
Kosarin, Jonathan Henry *lawyer*
Kovacic, William Evan *law educator*

Kuelbs, John Thomas *lawyer*
Levinson, Lawrence Edward *lawyer, corporation executive*
Malone, William Grady *lawyer*
Mathis, Mark Jay *lawyer*
McDermott, Francis Owen *lawyer*
Muris, Timothy Joseph *law educator*
Parker, Jeffrey Scott *law educator, university official*
Smith, John Michael *lawyer*
Stover, David Frank *lawyer*
Van Landingham, Leander Shelton, Jr. *lawyer*
Van Lare, Wendell John *lawyer*
Wall, Barbara Wartelle *lawyer*

**Ashburn**
Gold, George Myron *lawyer, editor, writer, consultant*

**Blacksburg**
Jensen, Walter Edward *lawyer, educator*

**Charlottesville**
Abraham, Kenneth Samuel *law educator*
Bonnie, Richard Jeffrey *legal educator, lawyer*
Brame, Joseph Robert, III *lawyer*
Chandler, Lawrence Bradford, Jr. *lawyer*
Cohen, Edwin Samuel *lawyer, educator*
Conrad, Paul Edward *lawyer, army officer*
Dooley, Michael P. *law educator*
Edwards, James Edwin *lawyer*
Eustis, Albert Anthony *lawyer, diversified industry corporate executive*
Henderson, Stanley Dale *lawyer, educator*
Hodous, Robert Power *lawyer*
Howard, Arthur Ellsworth Dick *law educator*
Kitch, Edmund Wells *lawyer, educator, private investor*
Landess, Fred S. *lawyer*
McKay, John Douglas *lawyer*
Meador, Daniel John *law educator*
Menefee, Samuel Pyeatt *lawyer, anthropologist*
Middleditch, Leigh Benjamin, Jr. *lawyer, educator*
Monahan, John T. *law educator, psychologist*
Moore, John Norton *lawyer, diplomat, educator*
Mott, William Chamberlain *lawyer, retired naval officer*
O'Brien, David Michael *law educator*
O'Connell, Jeffrey *law educator*
Scott, Robert Edwin *law educator*
Sinclair, Kent *law educator*
Slaughter, Edward Ratliff, Jr. *lawyer*
Turner, Robert Foster *law educator, former government official, writer*
Wadlington, Walter James *law educator*
Wenger, Larry Bruce *law librarian, law educator*
White, George Edward *law educator, lawyer*
White, Thomas Raeburn, III *law educator, consultant*
Whitehead, John Wayne *law educator, organization administrator, author*

**Chesapeake**
Jones, John Lou *arbitrator, retired railroad executive*

**Chester**
Gray, Charles Robert *lawyer*

**Danville**
Conway, French Hoge *lawyer*
Goodman, Lewis Elton, Jr. *lawyer*
Talbott, Frank, III *lawyer*

**Earlysville**
Grattan, George Gilmer, IV *lawyer*

**Fairfax**
Arntson, Peter Andrew *lawyer*
Baird, Charles Bruce *lawyer, consultant*
Brown, Gary Wayne *lawyer*
Codding, Frederick Hayden *lawyer*
Folk, Thomas Robert *lawyer*
Groves, Hurst Kohler *lawyer, oil company executive*
Hopson, Everett George *retired lawyer*
Newsome, George Marvin *lawyer*
Sanderson, Douglas Jay *lawyer*
Spitzberg, Irving Joseph, Jr. *lawyer, corporate executive*

**Falls Church**
Becker, James Richard *lawyer*
Brady, Rupert Joseph *lawyer*
Calkins, Gary Nathan *lawyer, retired*
Christman, Bruce Lee *lawyer*
Diamond, Robert Michael *lawyer*
Duesenberg, Robert H. *lawyer*
Ehrlich, Bernard Herbert *lawyer, association executive*
Elderkin, Helaine Grace *lawyer*
Haynes, William J(ames), II *lawyer*
Honigberg, Carol Crossman *lawyer*
Jennings, Thomas Parks *lawyer*
O'Sullivan, Judith Roberta *lawyer, author*
Perkins, Jack Edwin *lawyer*
Schmidt, Paul Wickham *lawyer*
Winzer, P.J. *lawyer*
Young, John Hardin *lawyer*

**Franklin**
Cobb, G. Elliott, Jr. *lawyer*

**Fredericksburg**
Jones, Owaiian Maurice *lawyer*
Snapp, Roy Baker *lawyer*

**Galax**
Kapp, John Paul *lawyer, physician, educator*

**Glen Allen**
Batzli, Terrence Raymond *lawyer*
Weaver, Mollie Little *lawyer*

**Gloucester**
Powell, Bolling Raines, Jr. *lawyer, educator*

**Great Falls**
Jacobson, Richard Lee *lawyer, educator*
Neidich, George Arthur *lawyer*
Railton, William Scott *lawyer*

**Halifax**
Greenbacker, John Everett *retired lawyer*

**Hampton**
Schon, Alan Wallace *lawyer, actor*

**Harrisonburg**
Hodges, Ronald Dexter *lawyer*

**Heathsville**
McKerns, Charles Joseph *lawyer*

**Herndon**
Kunkel, David Nelson *lawyer*

**Ivy**
Wilcox, Harvey John *lawyer*

**Lanexa**
Kirk, Maurice Blake *retired lawyer, educator*

**Leesburg**
Mitchell, William Graham Champion *lawyer, business executive*

**Lexington**
Beveridge, Albert Jeremiah, III *lawyer*
Kirgis, Frederic Lee *law educator*
Massie, Ann MacLean *law educator*
Sullivan, Barry *lawyer, educator*
Sundby, Scott Edwin *law educator*
Wiant, Sarah Kirsten *law library director, educator*

**Lynchburg**
Angel, James Joseph *lawyer*
Burnette, Ralph Edwin, Jr. *lawyer*
Elliott, James Ward *lawyer*
Packert, G(ayla) Beth *lawyer*

**Manakin Sabot**
Bright, Craig Bartley *lawyer*

**Manassas**
Foote, John Holland *lawyer*

**Marshall**
Seder, Arthur Raymond, Jr. *lawyer*

**Mc Lean**
Appler, Thomas L. *lawyer*
Armstrong, C(harles) Torrence *lawyer*
Bingaman, Anne K. *lawyer*
Brown, Thomas C., Jr. *lawyer*
Church, Randolph Warner, Jr. *lawyer*
Cohn, Herbert B. *lawyer*
Corson, J. Jay, IV *lawyer*
Dicks, John G., III *lawyer*
Duncan, Stephen Mack *lawyer*
Gammon, James Alan *lawyer*
Herge, J. Curtis *lawyer*
Hicks, C. Thomas, III *lawyer*
Hoffman, Ira Eliot *lawyer*
Kennedy, Cornelius Bryant *lawyer*
Klinedinst, Duncan Stewart *lawyer*
Marino, Michael Frank, III *lawyer*
Morris, James Malachy *lawyer*
Murphy, Thomas Patrick *lawyer*
Nassikas, John Nicholas *lawyer*
Neel, Samuel Ellison *lawyer*
Ney, Robert Terrence *lawyer*
O'Brien, Francis Anthony *retired lawyer*
Olson, William Jeffrey *lawyer*
Pesner, Susan M. *lawyer*
Prichard, Edgar Allen *lawyer*
Rau, Lee Arthur *lawyer*
Rhyne, Charles Sylvanus *lawyer*
Stephens, Jay B. *lawyer*
Stephens, William Theodore *lawyer, business executive*
Stump, John Sutton *lawyer*
Tansill, Frederick Joseph *lawyer*
Titus, Bruce E. *lawyer*
Toole, John Harper *lawyer*
Traver, Courtland Lee *lawyer*
Trotter, Haynie Seay *lawyer*

**Middleburg**
Beddall, Thomas Henry *lawyer*

**Mineral**
Schelling, John Paul *lawyer, consultant*

**Mount Jackson**
Cohen, Lewis Isaac *lawyer*

**Nellysford**
Sims, John Rogers, Jr. *lawyer*

**Newport News**
Cuthrell, Carl Edward *lawyer, educator, clergyman*
Saunders, Bryan Leslie *lawyer*

**Norfolk**
Baird, Edward Rouzie, Jr. *lawyer*
Bishop, Bruce Taylor *lawyer*
Clark, Morton Hutchinson *lawyer*
Cooper, Charles Neilson *lawyer*
Cranford, Page Deronde *lawyer, educator, executive*
Crenshaw, Francis Nelson *lawyer*
Harrell, Charles Lydon, Jr. *lawyer*
Pearson, John Y., Jr. *lawyer*
Rephan, Jack *lawyer*
Russell, C. Edward, Jr. *lawyer*
Ryan, John M. *lawyer*
Ryan, Louis Farthing *lawyer*
Smith, Richard Muldrow *lawyer*
Tolmie, Donald McEachern *lawyer*
Wooldridge, William Charles *lawyer*

**Norton**
Jessee, Roy Mark *lawyer*
Shortridge, Judy Beth *lawyer*

**Orange**
Dunnington, Walter Grey, Jr. *lawyer, retired food and tobacco executive*

**Palmyra**
White, Luther Wesley *lawyer*

**Petersburg**
Burns, Cassandra Stroud *prosecutor*

**Portsmouth**
Moody, Willard James, Sr. *lawyer*
Spong, William Belser, Jr. *lawyer, educator*

**Radford**
Davis, Richard Waters *lawyer*

**Reston**
Bredehoft, Elaine Charlson *lawyer*
Bredehoft, John Michael *lawyer*
Humphreys, David John *lawyer, trade association executive*
Scharff, Joseph Laurent *lawyer*
Wiegley, Roger Douglas *lawyer*
Zollar, Carolyn Catherine *lawyer*

**Richmond**
Ackerly, Benjamin Clarkson *lawyer*
Addison, David Dunham *lawyer*
Anderson, Leonard Gustave *retired lawyer, retired business executive*
Baliles, Gerald L. *lawyer, former governor*
Bates, John Wythe, III *lawyer*
Belcher, Dennis Irl *lawyer*
Bing, Richard McPhail *lawyer*
Blanchard, Lawrence Eley, Jr. *lawyer, corporation executive*
Booker, Lewis Thomas *lawyer*
Brasfield, Evans Booker *lawyer*
Brissette, Martha Blevins *lawyer*
Brockenbrough, Henry Watkins *lawyer*
Brooks, Robert Franklin, Sr. *lawyer*
Buford, Robert Pegram *lawyer*
Burke, John K(irkland), Jr. *lawyer*
Burrus, Robert Lewis, Jr. *lawyer*
Bush, Thomas Norman *lawyer*
Carrell, Daniel Allan *lawyer*
Carter, Joseph Carlyle, Jr. *lawyer*
Catlett, Richard H., Jr. *retired lawyer*
Clinard, Robert Noel *lawyer*
Cohn, David Stephen *lawyer*
Dabney, H. Slayton, Jr. *lawyer*
Denny, Collins, III *lawyer*
Dray, Mark S. *lawyer*
Edmonds, Thomas Andrew *state bar executive director*
Ellis, Andrew Jackson, Jr. *lawyer*
Elmore, Edward Whitehead *lawyer*
Epps, Augustus Charles *lawyer*
Flannagan, Benjamin Collins, IV *lawyer*
Framme, Lawrence Henry, III *lawyer*
Gary, Richard David *lawyer*
Goodpasture, Philip Henry *lawyer*
Graves, H. Brice *lawyer*
Hackney, Virginia Howitz *lawyer*
Hall, Stephen Charles *lawyer*
Hettrick, George Harrison *lawyer*
Hicks, C. Flippo *lawyer*
Horsley, Waller Holladay *lawyer*
Howell, George Cook, III *lawyer*
Johnston, Francis Claiborne, Jr. *lawyer*
Kearfott, Joseph Conrad *lawyer*
Lanam, Linda Lee *lawyer*
Ledbetter, David Oscar *lawyer*
Levit, Jay J(oseph) *lawyer*
Mathews, Roderick Bell *lawyer*
McClard, Jack Edward *lawyer*
McElligott, James Patrick, Jr. *lawyer*
McFarlane, Walter Alexander *lawyer, educator*
McVey, Henry Hanna, III *lawyer*
Mezzullo, Louis Albert *lawyer*
Milmoe, Patrick Joseph *lawyer*
Minardi, Richard A., Jr. *lawyer*
Moore, Thurston Roach *lawyer*
Musick, Robert Lawrence, Jr. *lawyer*
Oakey, John Martin, Jr. *lawyer*
Palmore, Fred Wharton, III *lawyer*
Pasco, Hansell Merrill *retired lawyer*
Peters, David Frankman *lawyer*
Pinckney, C. Cotesworth *lawyer*
Pope, Robert Dean *lawyer*
Powell, Lewis Franklin, III *lawyer*
Rainey, Gordon Fryer, Jr. *lawyer*
Reveley, Walter Taylor, III *lawyer*
Rigsby, Linda Flory *lawyer*
Roach, Edgar Mayo, Jr. *lawyer*
Rolfe, Robert Martin *lawyer*
Rubinstein, Phyllis M. *lawyer*
Rudlin, David Alan *lawyer*
Shands, William Ridley, Jr. *lawyer*
Sharer, John Daniel *lawyer*
Slater, Thomas Glascock, Jr. *lawyer*
Slaughter, Alexander Hoke *lawyer*
Smith, R. Gordon *lawyer*
Spahn, Gary Joseph *lawyer*
Spain, Jack Holland, Jr. *lawyer*
Starke, Harold E., Jr. *lawyer*
Stoyko, William Nelson *lawyer*
Strickland, William Jesse *lawyer*
Thomas, John Charles *lawyer, former state supreme court justice*
Thompson, Paul Michael *lawyer*
Troy, Anthony Francis *lawyer*
Walsh, William Arthur, Jr. *lawyer*
Warthen, Harry Justice, III *lawyer*
Watts, Stephen Hurt, II *lawyer*
White, Hugh Vernon, Jr. *lawyer*
Witt, Walter Francis, Jr. *lawyer*

**Roanoke**
Bates, Harold Martin *lawyer*
Butler, Manley Caldwell *lawyer*
Densmore, Baron Douglas Warren *lawyer*
Fishwick, John Palmer *lawyer, retired railroad executive*
Hammond, Glenn Barry, Sr. *lawyer*
Woodrum, Clifton A., III *lawyer, state legislator*

**Springfield**
Chappell, Milton Leroy *lawyer*
Hughes, James Charles *lawyer*

**Stafford**
Brown, Harold Eugene *district chief magistrate*

**Sterling**
Padgett, Gail Blanchard *lawyer*

**Vienna**
Fasser, Paul James, Jr. *labor arbitrator*
Heller, John Roderick, III *lawyer, business executive*
Howard, Daggett Horton *lawyer*
McCabe, Thomas Edward *lawyer*
Molineaux, Charles Borromeo *lawyer, arbitrator, columnist, poet*
Peltz, Paulette Beatrice *corporate lawyer*
Price, Ilene Rosenberg *lawyer*
Razzano, Frank Charles *lawyer*
Whitaker, Thomas Patrick *lawyer*

**Virginia Beach**
Dumville, S(amuel) Lawrence *lawyer*
Happy, J. Nelson *legal educator, law school dean*
Sekulow, Jay Alan *lawyer*

**Warrenton**
vom Baur, Francis Trowbridge *retired lawyer*

**Washington**
Weinberg, Robert Lester *lawyer, law educator*

**Weems**
LaPrade, Carter *lawyer*

**Williamsburg**
Fisher, Chester Lewis, Jr. *retired lawyer*
Geddy, Vernon Meredith, Jr. *lawyer*
Marcus, Paul *lawyer, educator*
Smolla, Rodney Alan *lawyer, educator*
Sullivan, Timothy Jackson *law educator, academic administrator*
Whyte, James Primrose, Jr. *former law educator*

**Wytheville**
Baird, Thomas Bryan, Jr. *lawyer*

## WASHINGTON

**Bainbridge Island**
Nagle, James Francis *lawyer*
Otorowski, Christopher Lee *lawyer*

**Bellevue**
Boespflug, John Francis, Jr. *lawyer*
Hannah, Lawrence Burlison *lawyer*
Sebris, Robert, Jr. *lawyer*
Smith, George Lester *lawyer*
Treacy, Gerald Bernard *lawyer*

**Bellingham**
Packer, Mark Barry *lawyer, financial consultant, foundation official*

**Colfax**
Webster, Ronald B. *lawyer*

**Everett**
Bowden, George Newton *lawyer*

**Goldendale**
Maxwell, William Stirling *retired lawyer*

**Hoquiam**
Kessler, Keith Leon *lawyer*

**Issaquah**
Benoliel, Joel *lawyer*

**Kirkland**
Dorkin, Frederic Eugene *lawyer*

**Mount Vernon**
Moser, C. Thomas *lawyer*

**Olympia**
Allen, Robert Mark *lawyer*
Norwood, Deborah Anne *law librarian*
Walker, Francis Joseph *lawyer*

**Port Orchard**
Crawford, William Matterson *lawyer*

**Pullman**
Michaelis, Karen Lauree *law educator*

**Redmond**
Erxleben, William Charles *lawyer, data processing executive*

**Renton**
Barber, Mark Edward *lawyer*

**Richland**
Barr, Carlos Harvey *lawyer*

**Seattle**
Albright, Douglas Eaton *lawyer*
Alkire, John D. *lawyer*
Allen, Joanna Cowan *lawyer*
Anderson, Peter MacArthur *lawyer*
Andreasen, Steven W. *lawyer*
Andrews, J. David *lawyer*
Bagshaw, Bradley Holmes *lawyer*
Barnes, Susan Lewis *lawyer*
Birmingham, Richard Joseph *lawyer*
Black, W. L. Rivers, III *lawyer*
Blais, Robert Howard *lawyer*
Blom, Daniel Charles *lawyer, investor*
Blumenfeld, Charles Raban *lawyer*
Boeder, Thomas L. *lawyer*
Bowman, Patricia Lynn *lawyer*
Bringman, Joseph Edward *lawyer*
Burke, William Thomas *law educator, lawyer*
Burkhart, William Henry *lawyer*
Cavanaugh, Michael Everett *lawyer, arbitrator*
Char, Patricia Helen *lawyer*
Claflin, Arthur Cary *lawyer*
Clinton, Gordon Stanley *lawyer*
Clinton, Richard M. *lawyer*
Corker, Charles Edward *retired lawyer, educator*
Cross, Harry Maybury *retired law educator, consultant*
Cunningham, Joel Dean *lawyer*
Dahl, Lance Christopher *lawyer*
Dalton, Thomas George *paralegal, social worker, legal consultant*
Davis, John MacDougall *lawyer*
Derham, Richard Andrew *lawyer*
DeVore, Paul Cameron *lawyer*
Dickinson, Calhoun *lawyer*
Diggs, Bradley C. *lawyer*
Dolan, Andrew Kevin *lawyer*
Donohue, James Patrick *lawyer*
Ellis, James Reed *lawyer*
Emory, Meade *lawyer*
Fitzpatrick, Thomas Mark *lawyer*
Freedman, Bart Joseph *lawyer*
Freeman, Antoinette Rosefeldt *lawyer*
Gandara, Daniel *lawyer*
Giles, Robert Edward, Jr. *lawyer*
Gittinger, D. Wayne *lawyer*
Glover, Karen E. *lawyer*
Goeltz, Thomas A. *lawyer*
Gores, Thomas C. *lawyer*
Graham, Stephen Michael *lawyer*
Gray, Marvin Lee, Jr. *lawyer*
Greenan, Thomas J. *lawyer*
Greene, John Burkland *lawyer*
Gustafson, Alice Fairleigh *lawyer*
Guy, Andrew A. *lawyer*
Haggard, Joel Edward *lawyer*
Haman, Raymond William *lawyer*
Hansen, Wayne W. *lawyer*
Harwick, Dennis Patrick *lawyer*
Hazelton, Penny Ann *law librarian, educator*
Henderson, Dan Fenno *lawyer, law educator*
Hill, G. Richard *lawyer*
Hilpert, Edward Theodore, Jr. *lawyer*
Hofmann, Douglas Allan *lawyer*
Horton, Elliott Argue, Jr. *lawyer, business consultant*
Huff, Gary D. *lawyer*
Hunter, Theodore Paul *lawyer, energy consultant*
Huston, John Charles *law educator*
Hutcheson, Mark Andrew *lawyer*
Isaki, Lucy Power Slyngstad *lawyer*
Israel, Allen D. *lawyer*
Jackson, Dillon Edward *lawyer*
Jameson, Henry C. *lawyer*
Johnson, Bruce Edward Humble *lawyer*
Judson, C(harles) James (Jim Judson) *lawyer*
Kane, Alan Henry *lawyer*
Kane, Christopher *nonprofit organization executive, lawyer, legal consultant*
Kaplan, Barry Martin *lawyer*
Katz, Charles J., Jr. *lawyer*
Keegan, John E. *lawyer*
Kellogg, Kenyon P. *lawyer*
Klein, Otto G., III *lawyer*
Koehler, Reginald Stafford, III *lawyer*
Kuhrau, Edward W. *lawyer*
Leitzell, Terry Lee *lawyer*
Lemly, Thomas Adger *lawyer*
Loftus, Thomas Daniel *lawyer*
Lombard, David Norman *lawyer*
McCann, Richard Eugene *lawyer*
McKay, Michael Dennis *lawyer*
McKey, Thomas J. *lawyer*
Moch, Robert Gaston *lawyer*
Moore, James R. *lawyer*
Mussehl, Robert Clarence *lawyer*
Nellermoe, Leslie Carol *lawyer*
Niemi, Janice *lawyer, former state legislator*
Noble, Phillip D. *lawyer*
Oehler, Richard William *lawyer*
Oles, Stuart Gregory *lawyer*
Olsen, Harold Fremont *lawyer*
Olver, Michael Lynn *lawyer*
Palm, Gerald Albert *lawyer*
Palmer, Douglas S., Jr. *lawyer*
Parker, Omar Sigmund, Jr. *lawyer*
Parks, Patricia Jean *lawyer*
Parsons, A. Peter *lawyer*
Paul, Thomas Frank *lawyer*
Petrie, Gregory Steven *lawyer*
Pettigrew, Edward W. *lawyer*
Prentke, Richard Ottesen *lawyer*
Price, John Richard *lawyer, law educator*
Pritchard, Llewelyn G. *lawyer*
Pusch, William Gerard *lawyer*
Pym, Bruce Michael *lawyer*
Redman, Eric *lawyer*
Rieke, Paul Victor *lawyer*
Ritter, Daniel Benjamin *lawyer*
Rodin, Michael F. *lawyer, corporate*
Rosen, Jon Howard *lawyer*
Rummage, Stephen Michael *lawyer*
Sandman, Irvin W(illis) *lawyer*
Shulkin, Jerome *lawyer*
Soltys, John Joseph *lawyer*
Spitzer, Hugh D. *lawyer*
Squires, William Randolph, III *lawyer*
Steers, George W. *lawyer*
Steinberg, Jack *lawyer*
Stoebuck, William Brees *law educator*
Sweeney, David Brian *lawyer*
Tallman, Richard C. *lawyer*
Thorne, David W. *lawyer*
Thorson, Lee A. *lawyer*
Treiger, Irwin Louis *lawyer*
Veblen, John Elvidge *lawyer*
Vestal, Josephine Burnet *lawyer*
Voorhees, Lee R., Jr. *lawyer*
Wagner, Patricia Hamm *lawyer*
Waldman, Bart *lawyer*
Wallis, Richard James *lawyer*
Walters, Dennis H. *lawyer*
Wechsler, Mary Heyrman *lawyer*
Wells, Christopher Brian *lawyer*
Wells, Judee Ann *lawyer*
Whalen, Jerome Demaris *lawyer*
Whitehead, James Fred, III *lawyer*
Whitford, Joseph P. *lawyer*
Williams, J. Vernon *lawyer*
Wright, Willard Jurey *lawyer*

**Spokane**
Connolly, K. Thomas *lawyer*
Harbaugh, Daniel Paul *lawyer*
Koegen, Roy Jerome *lawyer*
Lamp, John Ernest *lawyer*
Sayre, Richard Layton *lawyer*
Symmes, William Daniel *lawyer*
Weatherhead, Leslie R. *lawyer*

**Tacoma**
Barcus, Benjamin Franklin *lawyer*
Gordon, Joseph Harold *lawyer*
Graves, Ray *lawyer*
Holt, William E. *lawyer*
Lane, Robert Casey *lawyer*
Miller, Judson Frederick *lawyer, former military officer*
Nance, John Joseph *lawyer, writer, air safety analyst, broadcaster, consultant*
Rudnick, Rebecca Sophie *lawyer, educator*
Steele, Anita Martin (Margaret Anne Martin) *law librarian, legal educator*
Thompson, Ronald Edward *lawyer*
Waldo, James Chandler *lawyer*

**Scarborough**
Krajicek, Mark Andrew *lawyer*

**Toronto**
Apple, B. Nixon *lawyer*
Bristow, David Ian *lawyer*
Chester, Robert Simon George *lawyer*
Cowan, Charles Gibbs *lawyer, corporate executive*
Davis, William Grenville *lawyer, former Canadian government official*
Dickens, Bernard Morris *law educator*
Donais, Gary Warren *lawyer*
Dubin, Charles Leonard *lawyer*
Elliott, R(oy) Fraser *lawyer, holding and management company executive*
Eyton, John Trevor *lawyer, business executive*
Farquharson, Gordon MacKay *lawyer*
Gee, Gregory Williams *lawyer*
Godfrey, John Morrow *lawyer, retired Canadian government official*
Graham, John Webb *lawyer*
Innanen, Larry John *lawyer, food products executive*
Macdonald, Donald Stovel *lawyer*
Peterson, David Robert *lawyer, former Canadian government official*
Wolfe, Harold Joel *lawyer, business executive*

## QUEBEC

**Charlesbourg**
†Gignac, Jean-Pierre *lawyer, judge*

**Montreal**
Brierley, John E. C. *legal educator, former university dean*
Gillespie, Thomas Stuart *lawyer*
Johnston, David Lloyd *law educator, lawyer*
Kirkpatrick, John Gildersleeve *lawyer*
Lacoste, Paul *lawyer, educator, university official*
Lalonde, Marc *lawyer, former Canadian government official*
Mercier, Francois *lawyer*
Messier, Pierre *lawyer, manufacturing company executive*
Montcalm, Norman Joseph *lawyer*
Normand, Robert *lawyer*
Popovici, Adrian *law educator*
Pound, Richard William Duncan *lawyer, accountant*
Régnier, Marc Charles *lawyer, corporate executive*
Robb, James Alexander *lawyer*
†Scraire, Jean-Claude *lawyer, investment company executive*
Sheppard, Claude-Armand *lawyer*
Somerville, Margaret Anne Ganley *law educator*
Tremblay, Andre Gabriel *lawyer, educator*
Trudeau, Pierre Elliott *lawyer, former Canadian prime minister*
Vennat, Michel *lawyer*

**Quebec**
LeMay, Jacques *lawyer*
Verge, Pierre *legal educator*

**Saint Jean Chrysostome**
†Rioux, Roch *lawyer, government official*

**Siclery**
†Bouchard, Pierre-Michel *lawyer*

**Sillery**
Dinan, Robert Michael *lawyer*

**Westmount**
Fortier, L. Yves *barrister*

## SASKATCHEWAN

**Regina**
Balfour, Reginald James *lawyer*
Laschuk, Roy Bogdan *lawyer*
MacKay, Harold Hugh *lawyer*

**Saskatoon**
Ish, Daniel Russell *law educator, academic adminstrator*

## AUSTRALIA

**Sydney**
Barusch, Ronald Charles *lawyer*

## BELGIUM

**Brussels**
Barnum, John Wallace *lawyer*
Bustin, George Leo *lawyer*
Glazer, Barry David *lawyer*
Hanotiau, Bernard Raoul *lawyer*
Liebman, Howard Mark *lawyer*
Oberreit, Walter William *lawyer*

## CHILE

**Zapallar**
Silbaugh, Preston Norwood *lawyer, consultant*

## DENMARK

**Copenhagen**
Alsted, Peter *lawyer*

## ENGLAND

**London**
Albert, Robert Alan *lawyer*
Batla, Raymond John, Jr. *lawyer*
Beharrell, Steven Roderic *lawyer*
Bigbie, John Taylor *lawyer, banker*
Brownwood, David Owen *lawyer*
Bruce, Robert Rockwell *lawyer*
Cole, Richard A. *lawyer*
Fabricant, Arthur E. *lawyer, corporate executive*
Fox, Hazel Mary *barrister, editor*
Gaines, Peter Mathew *lawyer*
Haubold, Samuel Allen *lawyer*
Hudson, Manley O., Jr. *lawyer*
Jalili, Mahir *lawyer*
Johnson, Thomas Edward *lawyer*
Kingham, Richard Frank *lawyer*
Markoski, Joseph Peter *lawyer*
Montgomery, John Warwick *law educator, theologian*
Morrison, William David *lawyer*
Nelson, Bernard Edward *lawyer*
Phocas, George John *international lawyer, business executive*
Smalley, David Vincent *lawyer*
Stevens, Robert Bocking *lawyer, educator*
Thomas, Allen Lloyd *lawyer, private investor*
Van Meter, John David *lawyer*

**London Bridge**
Nauheim, Stephen Alan *lawyer*

## FRANCE

**Paris**
Abboud, Ann Creelman *lawyer*
Baum, Axel Helmuth *lawyer*
Cochran, John M., III *lawyer*
Craig, William Laurence *lawyer*
Davidson, Alfred Edward *lawyer*
Herzog, Brigitte *lawyer*
Landers, Steven E. *lawyer*
MacCrindle, Robert Alexander *lawyer*
McGurn, William Barrett, III *lawyer*
Reeves, Van Kirk *lawyer*
Salans, Carl Fredric *lawyer*
Shapiro, Isaac *lawyer*

## GERMANY

**Duedenbuettel**
Pfennigstorf, Werner *lawyer*

**Finning**
English, Charles Brand *retired lawyer*

**Frankfurt**
Simitis, Spiros *legal educator*

**Kaiserslautern**
Immesberger, Helmut *lawyer*

**Wiesbaden**
Handy, Robert Maxwell *patent lawyer*

## GRENADA

**Saint George's**
Helgerson, John Walter *lawyer*

## GUATEMALA

**Guatemala City**
Mayora-Alvarado, Eduardo Rene *lawyer, law educator*

## HONG KONG

**Hong Kong**
Allen, Richard Marlow *lawyer*
Bleveans, John *lawyer*
Chu, Franklin Dean *lawyer*
Tanner, Douglas Alan *lawyer*

## ISRAEL

**Jerusalem**
Rosenne, Meir *lawyer, government agency administrator*

**Tel Aviv**
Gross, Joseph H. *lawyer, educator*

## ITALY

**Rome**
Alegi, Peter Claude *lawyer*

## JAPAN

**Hachioji**
Kojima, Takeshi *law educator, arbitrator, writer*

**Kyoto**
Miki, Arata *law educator*

**Musashino**
Makise, Yoshihiro *lawyer*

**Nagoya**
Kato, Masanobu *lawyer, educator*

**Osaka**
Solberg, Norman Robert *lawyer*

**Sapporo**
Kumamoto, Nobuo *law educator, university administrator*

**Tokyo**
Inoue, Akira *law educator*
Nakamura, Hideo *law educator*
Natori, Jeffrey Kazuo *lawyer*
Nishi, Osamu *law educator*
Shirai, Shun *law educator, lawyer*
Yamasaki, Yukuzo *lawyer*

## NORWAY

**Asker**
Fitzpatrick, Whitfield Westfeldt *lawyer*

**Oslo**
Fleischer, Carl August *law educator, consultant*

## THE PHILIPPINES

**Manila**
Metzger, Barry *lawyer*
Siguion-Reyna, Leonardo *lawyer, business executive*

## POLAND

**Warsaw**
Romney, Richard Bruce *lawyer*

## PORTUGAL

**Funchal**
Mayda, Jaro *lawyer, educator, author, consultant*

## REPUBLIC OF KOREA

**Seoul**
Rhi, Sang-Kyu *lawyer, educator*

## ROMANIA

**Bucharest**
Moses, Alfred Henry *lawyer*

## SAUDI ARABIA

**Riyadh**
Taylor, Frederick William, Jr. (Fritz Taylor) *lawyer*

## SCOTLAND

**Edinburgh**
Macneil, Ian Roderick *lawyer, educator*

## SINGAPORE

**Singapore**
Edwards, Stephen Allen *lawyer*

## SWITZERLAND

**Chambesy**
Spiegel, Daniel Leonard *lawyer*

**Fribourg**
Gurley, Franklin Louis *lawyer, military historian*

**Geneva**
Abram, Morris Berthold *lawyer, educator, diplomat*
De Pfyffer, Andre *lawyer*

**Lucerne**
Sherwin, James Terry *lawyer, window covering company executive*

## THAILAND

**Bangkok**
Lyman, David *lawyer*

## ADDRESS UNPUBLISHED

Aaron, Roy Henry *lawyer, arbitrator, business consultant*
Abzug, Bella Savitzky *lawyer, former congresswoman*
Adams, Thomas Lynch, Jr. *lawyer*
Adcock, Richard Paul *lawyer*
Alpern, Andrew *lawyer, architect, architectural historian*
Anastos, Anna Vedouras *federal lawyer*
Anderson, Geoffrey Allen *retired lawyer*
Anderson, Keith *retired lawyer, retired banker*
Areen, Judith Carol *law educator*
Arenella, Peter Lee *law educator*
Armstrong, William Henry *lawyer*
Arnold, Jerome Gilbert *lawyer*
Ashe, Bernard Flemming *lawyer, educator*
Axelrad, Irving Irmas *lawyer, motion picture producer*
Babb, Frank Edward *lawyer, executive*
Bagley, William Thompson *lawyer*
Bailey, Francis Lee *lawyer*
Bain, William Donald, Jr. *lawyer, chemical company executive*
Baker, Donald *lawyer*
Baker, Patricia (Jean) *lawyer, mediator*
Baker, William Thompson, Jr. *lawyer*
Bangs, John Kendrick *lawyer, foundation executive, former chemical company executive*
Banks, Robert Sherwood *lawyer*
Barrett, Jane Hayes *lawyer*
Baskin, Stuart Jay *lawyer*
Bates, Charles Turner *lawyer, educator*
Batson, David Warren *lawyer*
Battle, Frank Vincent, Jr. *lawyer*
Beasley, James W., Jr. *lawyer*
Beattie, Charles Robert, III *lawyer*
Beck, Mary Virginia *lawyer, public official*
Beldock, Myron *lawyer*
Bell, John William *lawyer*
Bellamy, Everett *law school administrator*
Bendix, Helen Irene *lawyer*
Benfield, Ann Kolb *lawyer*
Benjamin, Edward A. *lawyer*
Bergan, William Luke *lawyer*
Berger, Lawrence Douglas *lawyer*
Bergstrom, Robert William *lawyer*
Beringer, William Ernst *mediator, arbitrator, lawyer*
Berle, Peter Adolf Augustus *lawyer, media director*
Bernstein, George L. *lawyer, accountant*
Berry, Robert Worth *lawyer, educator, retired army officer*
Beukema, John Frederick *lawyer*
Bigelow, Robert P. *lawyer, arbitrator, mediator, journalist*
Blatt, Harold Geller *lawyer*
Blazzard, Norse Novar *lawyer*
Blount, David Laurence *lawyer*
Blow, George *lawyer*
Blumenthal, William *lawyer*
Boho, Dan L. *lawyer*
Bondi, Harry Gene *lawyer*
Booher, Alice Ann *lawyer*
Bork, Robert Heron *lawyer, author, educator, former federal judge*
Borow, Richard Henry *lawyer*
Borowitz, Albert Ira *lawyer, author*
Bost, Thomas Glen *lawyer*
Bower, Jean Ramsay *lawyer*
Bradford, Barbara Reed *lawyer*
Branagan, James Joseph *lawyer*
Brantz, George Murray *retired lawyer*
Brauer, Rhonda Lyn *lawyer*
Braun, Jerome Irwin *lawyer*
Brawner, Gerald Theodore *lawyer*
Brink, Richard Edward *lawyer*
Brodhead, David Crawmer *lawyer*
Brodsky, David M. *lawyer*
Brower, Charles Nelson *lawyer, judge*
Bryant, Cecil Farris *lawyer, retired insurance company executive*
Buechel, William Benjamin *retired lawyer*
Bujold, Tyrone Patrick *lawyer*
Burke, Thomas Edmund *retired lawyer*
Burlingame, James Montgomery, III *lawyer*
Burlingame, John Hunter *lawyer*
Burroughs, John Townsend *lawyer*
Califano, Joseph Anthony, Jr. *lawyer, public health policy educator, writer*
Cambrice, Robert Louis *lawyer*
Canan, Michael James *lawyer, author*
Capps, James Leigh, II *lawyer, military career officer*
Carmack, Mildred Jean *retired lawyer*
Carr, Jesse Metteau, III *lawyer, engineering executive*
Casey, Robert Reisch *lawyer*
Cashel, Thomas William *retired lawyer, educator*
Casselman, William E., II *lawyer*
Cassidy, John Harold *lawyer*
Cattani, Maryellen B. *lawyer*
Chamberlin, Michael Meade *lawyer*
Chase, Seymour M. *lawyer*
Clarke, Edward Owen, Jr. *lawyer*
Cobb, Miles Alan *retired lawyer*
Coleman, Robert Lee *retired lawyer*
Colodny, Edwin Irving *lawyer, retired airline executive*
Connell, William D. *lawyer*
Connelly, Sharon Rudolph *lawyer, federal official*
Cooke, Susan Marie *lawyer*
Cooper, Hal Dean *lawyer*
Coplin, Mark David *lawyer*
Crawford, Muriel Laura *lawyer, author, educator*
Criscuolo, Wendy Laura *lawyer, interior design consultant*
Cronson, Robert Granville *lawyer*
Crowe, James Joseph *lawyer*
David, Marilyn Hattie *lawyer, retired military officer*
Davis, Roger Edwin *lawyer, retired discount chain executive*
Davis, Wanda Rose *lawyer*
De Concini, Dennis *lawyer, former U.S. senator, consultant*
DeFoor, J. Allison, II *lawyer*
DeMitchell, Terri Ann *law educator*
Dennin, Timothy J. *lawyer*
Dewey, Anne Elizabeth Marie *lawyer*
Diakos, Maria Louise *lawyer*
Diamond, Stuart *law educator, lawyer, business executive, consultant*
Diehl, Deborah Hilda *lawyer*
Dietel, James Edwin *lawyer, consultant*
Dolan, Peter Brown *lawyer*
Dolce, Julia Wagner *lawyer*
Donlon, William James *lawyer*
Doty, James Robert *lawyer*
Drengler, William Allan John *lawyer*
Drost, Marianne *lawyer*
Duane, William Francis *lawyer*
Dubuc, Carroll Edward *lawyer*
Dunbar, Wylene Wisby *former lawyer, novelist*
Duncan, Donald William *lawyer*
Dunn, Thomas Tinsley *lawyer*
Dunn, Warren Howard *retired lawyer, brewery executive*
Dutile, Fernand Neville *law educator*
Eaton, Larry Ralph *lawyer*
Edwards, Jerome *lawyer*
Ehren, Charles Alexander, Jr. *lawyer, educator*
Eichhorn, Frederick Foltz, Jr. *retired lawyer*
Ellenberger, Jack Stuart *law librarian*
Ellingwood, Herbert Eugene *lawyer*
Embry, Stephen Creston *lawyer*
Emert, Timothy Ray *lawyer*
Enberg, Henry Winfield *retired law librarian*
Erlebacher, Arlene Cernik *retired lawyer*
Erlenborn, John Neal *lawyer, educator, former congressman*
Esposito, Amy Sklar *lawyer*
Ettinger, Joseph Alan *lawyer*
Everdell, William *lawyer*
Ewing, Robert *lawyer*
Fagin, Richard *litigation consultant*
Falkner, Robert Frank *lawyer*
Fanwick, Ernest *lawyer*
Farley, Barbara Suzanne *lawyer*
Farmakides, John Basil *lawyer*
Farren, Patricia *lawyer, producer*
Fenwick, William Augustus *lawyer*
Ferman, Irving *lawyer, educator*
Fernandez, Dennis Sunga *lawyer, electrical engineer, entrepreneur*
Ferraro, Geraldine Anne *lawyer, former congresswoman*
Fiala, David Marcus *lawyer*

PROFESSIONAL INDEX 5383 MILITARY

Field, Arthur Norman lawyer
Fiorito, Edward Gerald lawyer
Flaxman, Howard Richard lawyer
Fleischman, Herman Israel lawyer
Flick, John Edmond lawyer
Ford, Ashley Lloyd lawyer, retired consumer products company executive
Fowler, Donald Raymond retired lawyer, educator
Frank, James Stuart lawyer
Franklin, Michael Harold arbitrator, lawyer, consultant
Freeman, Russell Adams lawyer
Friedman, Paul Richard lawyer
Frost, Sterling Newell arbitrator, mediator, management consultant
Fryburger, Lawrence Bruce lawyer, mediator, writer
Fuller, Robert Ferrey lawyer, investor
Funnell, Kevin Joseph lawyer
Futter, Victor lawyer
Gamble, E. James lawyer, accountant
Gardner, Anne Lancaster lawyer
Gardner, Warner Winslow lawyer
George, Joyce Jackson lawyer, former judge
Gibb, Roberta Louise lawyer, artist
Gilbert, Ronald Rhea lawyer
Gingras, John Richard lawyer, consultant
Givens, Richard Ayres lawyer
Glosser, Jeffrey Mark lawyer
Gobel, John Henry lawyer
Goldman, Charles Norton retired corporate lawyer
Gordon, Kenneth Ira lawyer
Grabemann, Karl W. lawyer
Green, Mark Joseph lawyer, author
Griffin, Campbell Arthur, Jr. lawyer
Griffith, Steven Franklin, Sr. lawyer, real estate title insurance agent and investor
Grodsky, Jamie Anne lawyer
Grogan, Alice Washington lawyer
Grove, Kalvin M(yron) lawyer
Gudenberg, Harry Richard arbitrator, mediator
Guenette, Francoise lawyer, legal affairs executive
Guste, William Joseph, Jr. attorney general
Gutman, Richard Edward lawyer
Guttentag, Joseph Harris lawyer, educator
Hackel-Sims, Stella Bloomberg lawyer, former government official
Hackett, Robert John lawyer
Hafner, Thomas Mark lawyer
Hagerman, Michael Charles lawyer, arbitrator, mediator
Haley, George Brock, Jr. lawyer
Hall, Jack Gilbert lawyer, business executive
Hall, John Hopkins retired lawyer
Halleck, Charles White lawyer, former judge
Handler, Harold Robert lawyer
Hanzlik, Rayburn DeMara lawyer
Hardin, Paul, III law educator
Harnack, Don Steger lawyer
Harriman, John Howland lawyer
Harris, James T. lawyer
Harris, R. Robert lawyer
Harrison, Charles Maurice lawyer, former communications company executive
Hausman, Bruce lawyer
Hauver, Constance Longshore lawyer
Heath, Richard Eddy lawyer
Heffron, Howard A. lawyer
Helms, W. Richard lawyer
Hemmer, James Paul lawyer
Heppe, Karol Virginia lawyer, educator
Hewes, Laurence Ilsley, III lawyer, management, development, legal consultant
Heymann, Philip Benjamin law educator, academic director
Higginbotham, John Taylor lawyer
Hill, Harold Nelson, Jr. lawyer
Hinson, Sue Ann legal assistant, orthopedic nurse
†Ho, Geoffrey Bo Ning lawyer
Hoffman, Alan Craig lawyer, consultant
Hoffman, S. David lawyer, engineer, educator
Hoffmann, Malcolm Arthur lawyer
Hogan, Charles Marshall lawyer
Hogan, Richard Phillips lawyer
Holland, James Paul lawyer
Holmes, Michael Gene lawyer
Holt, Marjorie Sewell lawyer, retired congresswoman
Holtzschue, Karl Bressem lawyer, author, educator
Honeystein, Karl lawyer, entertainment company executive
Honnold, John Otis law educator
Hopkins, Jacques Vaughn lawyer, retired
Horn, Andrew Warren lawyer
Horwitz, Donald Paul lawyer
Howard, John Wayne lawyer
Howell, Donald Lee lawyer
Hughey, Richard Kohlman lawyer, author
Humphreys, Robert Russell lawyer, consultant, arbitrator
Hunt, Ronald Forrest lawyer
Huntley, Robert Edward Royall lawyer, business executive, former university president
Hybl, William Joseph lawyer, foundation executive
Hyman, Seymour C(harles) arbitrator
Iklé, Richard Adolph lawyer
Irvine, John Alexander lawyer
Jackson, Elmer Joseph lawyer, oil and gas company executive
Jamieson, Michael Lawrence lawyer
Jensen, Robert Trygve lawyer
Jochner, Michele Melina lawyer
Johnson, Daniel, Jr. lawyer
Jones, Keith Alden lawyer
Kahan, Rochelle Liebling lawyer, concert pianist
Kantrowitz, Susan Lee lawyer
Kapnick, Richard Bradshaw lawyer
Kaster, Laura A. lawyer
Katz, Martin Howard lawyer
Katz, Roberta R. lawyer
Katz, Sanford Noah lawyer, educator
Kennedy, Thomas J. lawyer
Keys, Jerry Malcom lawyer
Killeen, Michael John lawyer
Kippur, Merrie Margolin lawyer
Kirven, Gerald lawyer
Klafter, Cary Ira lawyer
Klaus, Charles retired lawyer
Kleiman, Bernard lawyer
Kleinberg, Judith G. lawyer, children's advocate
Kloze, Ida Iris lawyer
Knuth, Eric Joseph lawyer
Kratt, Peter George lawyer
Kreutzer, S. Stanley lawyer
Krongard, Howard J. lawyer
Kubo, Edward Hachiro, Jr. lawyer
Lackland, John lawyer
Lambert, Samuel Waldron, III lawyer
Lancaster, Robert Samuel lawyer, educator
Landy, Lisa Anne lawyer
Lawrence, Glenn Robert arbitrator, mediator
Layton, Robert lawyer
Lea, Lorenzo Bates lawyer
Leb, Arthur Stern lawyer
LeBaron, Edward Wayne, Jr. lawyer
Lecocke, Suzanne Elizabeth lawyer
Leibowitz, Ann Galperin lawyer
Levetown, Robert Alexander lawyer
Levine, Meldon Edises lawyer, former congressman
Levy, David lawyer, insurance company executive
Lewis, Dale Kenton retired lawyer, mediator
Lewis, John Furman retired lawyer, oil company executive
Lichtenstein, Sarah Carol lawyer
Liebeler, Susan Wittenberg lawyer
Liftin, John Matthew lawyer
Lightstone, Ronald lawyer
Linde, Maxine Helen lawyer, business executive, private investor
Ludwikowski, Rett Ryszard law educator, researcher
Lynch, Thomas Wimp lawyer
Magurno, Richard Peter lawyer
Maio, F. Anthony lawyer
Mallory, William Barton, III lawyer
Malloy, John Richard lawyer, chemical company executive
Maloney, John William lawyer, retired
Mangler, Robert James lawyer
Manne, Henry Girard lawyer, educator
Marden, Anne Elliott Roberts paralegal, estates and trusts specialist
Marinis, Thomas Paul, Jr. lawyer
Mark, Alan Samuel lawyer
Marks, Stanley Jacob lawyer, historian, lecturer, author
Marr, Carmel Carrington retired lawyer, retired state official
Marr, Jack Wayne lawyer
Marshall, Kathryn Sue lawyer
Matheson, Scott Milne, Jr. lawyer
Maulding, Barry Clifford lawyer
McCarthy, J. Thomas lawyer, educator
McCarthy, Vincent Paul lawyer
McCobb, John Bradford, Jr. lawyer
McConnell, Edward Bosworth legal organization administrator, lawyer
McCormick, David Arthur lawyer
McCormick, Robert William court reporting educator
McCue, Howard McDowell, III lawyer, educator
Mc Curley, Robert Lee, Jr. lawyer
Mc Donough, John Richard lawyer
McFadden, Nancy Elizabeth lawyer
McFarland, Robert Edwin lawyer
McGovern, Frances retired lawyer
McHugh, Edward Francis, Jr. lawyer
McKean, Robert Jackson, Jr. retired lawyer
McNeil, Heidi Loretta lawyer
Mc Pherson, Robert Donald retired lawyer
Mc Quade, Lawrence Carroll lawyer, corporate executive
McSorley, Cisco lawyer
Menhall, Dalton Winn lawyer, insurance executive, professional association administrator
Mercer, Edwin Wayne lawyer
Metcalfe, Robert Davis, III lawyer
Meyer, Max Earl lawyer
Miller, Frank William legal educator
Miller, Hainon Alfred lawyer, investor
Miller, Reed lawyer
Miller, Richard Alan lawyer, former merger and acquisition and forest products company executive
Miller, Thormund Aubrey lawyer
Millimet, Erwin lawyer
Milner, Irvin Myron lawyer
Mingle, James John lawyer
Mintz, M. J. lawyer
Missan, Richard Sherman lawyer
Mitchell, Ada Mae Boyd legal assistant
Mitchell, Briane Nelson lawyer
Mlyniec, Wallace John law educator, lawyer, consultant
Monroe, Murray Shipley lawyer
Monsma, Robbie Elizabeth lawyer, mediator, arbitrator, real estate executive
Moody, Graham Blair lawyer
Moore, John Cordell retired lawyer
†Morse, Robert Harry lawyer
Mossawir, Harve H., Jr. retired lawyer
Mugridge, David Raymond lawyer
Muller, Peter lawyer, entertainment company executive, retail company executive, consultant
Murphy, Lewis Curtis lawyer, former mayor
Murphy, Sandra Robison lawyer
Murray, Fred F. lawyer
Myers, Jesse Jerome lawyer
Myhand, Wanda Reshel paralegal, legal assistant
Natcher, Stephen Darlington lawyer, business executive
Negron, Carlos Daniel lawyer
Neilson, Benjamin Reath lawyer
Nelson, Carl Roger retired lawyer
Nelson, Ralph Stanley lawyer
Neuwirth, Jessica Anne lawyer
Newman, Carol L. lawyer
Nolen, William Giles lawyer, accountant
Norman, Albert George, Jr. lawyer
Norris, Martin Joseph lawyer
Oates, Carl Everette lawyer
O'Brien, Charles H. lawyer, retired state supreme court chief justice
O'Brien, J. Willard lawyer, educator
O'Connell, Philip Raymond retired lawyer, paper company executive
O'Connor, Gayle McCormick law librarian
Ogden, David William lawyer
Oliver, Samuel William, Jr. lawyer
O'Mahoney, Robert M. retired lawyer
Ordover, Abraham Philip lawyer, mediator
Orloff, Neil lawyer
Otis, Lee Liberman lawyer, educator
Parode, Ann lawyer
Patrick, Deval Laurdine lawyer
Patton, James Richard, Jr. lawyer
Paul, Herbert Morton lawyer, accountant, taxation educator
Paulus, Norma Jean Petersen lawyer, state school system administrator
Peccarelli, Anthony Marando lawyer, conflict resolutions company executive
Pennington, Richard Maier lawyer, retired insurance company executive
Penzer, Mark lawyer, editor, corporate trainer, former publisher
Pereyra-Suarez, Charles Albert lawyer
Perlstein, William James lawyer
Perry, George Williamson lawyer
Peters, R. Jonathan lawyer, chemical company executive
Peterson, Howard Cooper lawyer, accountant
Piga, Stephen Mulry lawyer
Pitcher, Griffith Fontaine lawyer
Pogue, Richard Welch lawyer
Poliakoff, Gary A. lawyer, educator
Polikoff, Benet, Jr. lawyer
Pollard, Henry lawyer
Pooley, Beverley John law educator, librarian
Porter, Michael Pell lawyer
Portnoy, Sara S. lawyer
Pratte, Lise lawyer, corporate secretary
Price, Alfred Lee lawyer, mining company executive
Prince, Andrew Steven lawyer, former government official
Pritikin, David T. lawyer
Protigal, Stanley Nathan lawyer
Prugh, George Shipley lawyer
Pullen, Richard Owen lawyer, communications company executive
Purtle, John Ingram lawyer, former state supreme court justice
Pusateri, Lawrence Xavier lawyer
Pustilnik, David Daniel lawyer
Quigley, Leonard Vincent lawyer
Quillen, Cecil Dyer, Jr. lawyer, consultant
Quinlan, J(oseph) Michael lawyer
Rae, John Joseph lawyer
Ramsey, Stephen Douglas lawyer, environmental manager
Rasmussen, Wayne Roger law educator, consultant
Raubicheck, Charles Joseph lawyer, educator
Ray, Jeanne Cullinan lawyer, insurance company executive
Reath, George, Jr. lawyer
Reeder, James Arthur lawyer
Reeder, Robert Harry retired lawyer
Regenstreif, Herbert lawyer
Rehmus, Charles Martin law educator, arbitrator
Reiche, Frank Perley lawyer, former federal commissioner
Reister, Ruth Alkema lawyer, business executive
Reiter, Glenn Mitchell lawyer
Reminger, Richard Thomas lawyer
Reynolds, William Bradford lawyer
Rhodes, John Jacob lawyer, former congressman
Richardson, John Carroll lawyer, tax legislative consultant
Rinzel, Daniel Francis lawyer
Rivers, Kenneth Jay judicial administrator, consultant
Roberts, Alfred Wheeler, III law firm executive
Roberts, John Glover, Jr. lawyer
Rock, Richard Rand lawyer, former state senator
Rodenberg-Roberts, Mary Patricia advocacy services administrator, lawyer
Rohrer, George John retired lawyer
Rosenn, Harold lawyer
Rosner, Seth lawyer, educator
Roth, Michael lawyer
Royalty, Kenneth Marvin lawyer
Ryan, Michael Lee lawyer
Saliterman, Richard Arlen lawyer, educator
Sampson, Ronald Gary lawyer
Sandefer, G(eorge) Larry lawyer
Santman, Leon Duane lawyer, former federal government executive
Savage, Charles Francis lawyer
Sax, Joseph Lawrence lawyer, educator
Saxon, John David lawyer, policy analyst, educator
Schild, Raymond Douglas lawyer
Schildhause, Sol lawyer
Schloss, Irving Steven lawyer
Schlueter, Linda Lee law educator
Schmults, Edward Charles lawyer, corporate and philanthropic administrator
Schor, Suzi lawyer, psychologist
Schrag, Philip Gordon law educator
Schuck, Peter Horner lawyer, educator
Schwab, Eileen Caulfield lawyer, educator
Schwartz, Harry Kane lawyer
Seeger, Leinaala Robinson law librarian, educator
Serota, James Ian lawyer
Shaffer, Richard James lawyer, former manufacturing company executive
Shapiro, Ivan lawyer
Shattuck, Cathie Ann lawyer, former government official
Sheldon, Terry Edwin lawyer, business consultant, advisor
Shook, Ann Jones lawyer
Shughart, Donald Louis lawyer
Shuman, Samuel Irving lawyer, law educator
Sigmond, Carol Ann lawyer
Silberman, Curt C. lawyer
Simmons, Raymond Hedelius lawyer
Skratek, Sylvia Paulette mediator, arbitrator, dispute systems designer
Slavitt, David Walton retired lawyer
Smith, Edward Reaugh retired lawyer, cemetery and funeral home consultant
Smith, George Patrick, II lawyer, educator
Smith, James A. lawyer
Smith, Lauren Ashley lawyer, journalist, clergyman, physicist
Smith, Ronald Ehlbert lawyer, referral-based distributor, public speaker, writer and motivator
Snyder, Stephen Edward lawyer, mediator
Sommers, Louise lawyer
Spanninger, Beth Anne lawyer
Spatta, Carolyn Davis mediator, consultant
Speaker, Susan Jane lawyer
Speers, Roland Root, II lawyer
Spence, William Allen lawyer
Spiekerman, James Frederick lawyer
Springer, Paul David lawyer, motion picture company executive
Steptoe, Mary Lou lawyer
Stevenson, Bryan Allen lawyer
Stone, Andrew Grover lawyer
Stream, Arnold Crager lawyer, writer
Sweeney, Deidre Ann lawyer
Tamen, Harriet lawyer
Tanenbaum, Jay Harvey lawyer
Tapley, James Leroy retired lawyer, railway corporation executive
Tatgenhorst, (Charles) Robert lawyer
Tavrow, Richard Lawrence lawyer, corporate executive
Terry, John Hart lawyer, former utility company executive, former congressman
Thiele, Howard Nellis, Jr. lawyer
Thomas, Ella Cooper lawyer
Thomas, Patricia Anne retired law librarian
Thompson, William Scott lawyer
Tigar, Michael Edward lawyer, educator
Titus, Christina Maria lawyer
Toensing, Victoria lawyer
Tolentino, Casimiro Urbano lawyer
Traeger, Charles Henry, III lawyer
Treacy, Vincent Edward lawyer
Trent, Clyde Nathaniel legal assistant
Trigg, Paul Reginald, Jr. lawyer
Trilling, Helen Regina lawyer
Tubman, William Charles lawyer
Turen, Barbara Ellen lawyer
Twitchell, E. Eugene lawyer
Urban, Lee Donald lawyer
Valcic, Susan Joan lawyer
Valois, Robert Arthur lawyer
van Gestel, Allan judge
Van Vleet, William Benjamin retired lawyer, life insurance company executive
Van Wagoner, Robert Louis lawyer
Varner, David Eugene lawyer
Vinroot, Richard Allen lawyer, mayor
Voight, Elizabeth Anne lawyer
Voorhees, James Dayton, Jr. lawyer
Vradenburg, George, III lawyer
Waldo, Burton Corlett lawyer
Walker, Craig Michael lawyer
Walker, John Sumpter, Jr. lawyer
Walker, Lawrence D. lawyer
Walker, Mark A. lawyer
Walker, Mary L. lawyer
Wallack, Rina Evelyn lawyer
Walner, Robert Joel lawyer
Watson, Keith Stuart lawyer
Weadon, Donald Alford, Jr. lawyer
Webb, John Gibbon, III lawyer
Weber, Julian L. lawyer, former publishing and entertainment company executive
Weil, Peter Henry lawyer
Weiland, Charles Hankes lawyer
Weldon, Jeffrey Alan lawyer
Wesely, Marissa Celeste lawyer
Wessel, Peter lawyer
Wheeler, R(ichard) Kenneth lawyer
White, Richard Clarence lawyer
Whitlock, William Abel retired lawyer
Whitman, Marland Hamilton, Jr. lawyer
Wigler, Andrew Jeffrey lawyer
Wilburn, Mary Nelson retired lawyer, writer
Wildhack, William August, Jr. lawyer
Wiley, Richard Arthur lawyer
Williams, William John, Jr. lawyer
Williamson, Edwin Dargan lawyer, former federal official
Wilner, Thomas Bernard lawyer
Wilson, Hugh Steven lawyer
Wilson, Paul W., Jr. lawyer, entrepreneur
Wimmer, Nancy T. lawyer
Wing, James David lawyer
Winslow, John Franklin lawyer
Wittebort, Robert John, Jr. lawyer, writer, business executive
Wittner, Loren Antonow lawyer, former public relations executive
Woodland, Irwin Francis lawyer
Wriston, Kathryn Dineen lawyer, business executive
Yarbro, Alan David lawyer
Yeager, Mark L. lawyer
Young, Michael Kent lawyer, educator
Zagorin, Janet Susan professional development director
Ziegenhorn, Eric Howard lawyer, legal writer
Ziegler, Richard Ferdinand lawyer
Zohn, Martin Steven lawyer

## MEDICINE. See HEALTHCARE: MEDICINE.

## MILITARY

### UNITED STATES

#### ALABAMA

**Alexander City**

Shuler, Ellie Givan, Jr. retired military officer, military museum administrator

**Enterprise**

Parker, Ellis D. retired career officer, electronics executive

**Fort Rucker**

Glushko, Gail M. military officer, physician

**Huntsville**

†Malkemes, William Charles career military officer

**Jacksonville**

Clarke, Mary Elizabeth retired army officer

**Madison**

Frakes, Lawrence Wright retired career officer, businessman
Jellett, James Morgan retired army officer, aerospace defense consultant

**Maxwell AFB**

Davis, Cindy Ann military officer, nursing educator
Henry, Gary Norman air force officer, astronautical engineer
Pendley, William Tyler naval officer, international relations educator

**Montgomery**

Boston, Hollis Buford, Jr. retired military officer
Hennies, Clyde Albert (Lou ) military officer, state official
Pickett, George Bibb, Jr. retired military officer

**Tuscaloosa**

Taber, Robert Clinton retired army officer

## ALASKA

**Anchorage**
Schnell, Roger Thomas *retired military officer, state official*

**Elmendorf AFB**
†Boese, Lawrence E. *air force officer*

## ARIZONA

**Peoria**
†Burke, Charlene B. *civilian military employee*

**Phoenix**
Beltrán, Anthony Natalicio *military non-commissioned officer, deacon*

**Scottsdale**
O'Berry, Carl Gerald *air force officer, electrical engineer*

**Tucson**
Guice, John Thompson *retired air force officer*
Running, Nels *air force officer*
Wickham, John Adams, Jr. *retired army officer*

**Yuma**
Hudson, John Irvin *retired marine officer*

## ARKANSAS

**Blytheville**
Slowik, Richard Andrew *air force officer, writer*

**Fort Smith**
Cameron, Richard Douglas *military officer, psychiatrist*

**Mountain Home**
Baker, Robert Leon *naval medical officer*

## CALIFORNIA

**Alameda**
Card, James Conrad *coast guard officer*

**Arroyo Grande**
Oseguera, Palma Marie *marine corps officer, reservist*

**Bonita**
Curtis, Richard Earl *former naval officer, former company executive, business consultant*

**Borrego Springs**
Shinn, Allen Mayhew *retired naval officer, business executive*

**Camp Pendleton**
†McKissock, Gary S. *non-commissioned officer*

**Carlsbad**
Kauderer, Bernard Marvin *retired naval officer*

**Carmichael**
McHugh, James Joseph *retired naval officer, retired associate dean*

**China Lake**
†Pendleton, Robert Leon *civilian military employee*

**Coronado**
Butcher, Bobby Gene *retired military officer*
Robinson, David Brooks *retired naval officer*
Worthington, George Rhodes *retired naval officer*

**Edwards**
Engel, Richard L. *career officer*

**El Segundo**
Dekok, Roger Gregory *air force officer*

**Escondido**
Briggs, Edward Samuel *naval officer*

**Folsom**
Aldridge, Donald O'Neal *military officer*
Meigel, David Walter *military officer, retired musician*

**Healdsburg**
Eade, George James *retired air force officer, research executive, defense consultant*

**La Jolla**
Greer, Howard Earl *former naval officer*

**Laguna Hills**
Faw, Duane Leslie *retired military officer, law educator, lay worker, author*

**Long Beach**
Higginson, John *retired military officer*

**Los Angeles**
Chernesky, John Joseph, Jr. *naval officer*

**Mcclellan AFB**
†Borland, Carter Allen *military career officer*

**Monterey**
Hoivik, Thomas Harry *military educator, international consultant*
Matthews, David Fort *military weapon system acquisition specialist*
Schrady, David Alan *operations research educator*

**Napa**
Smith, Robert Bruce *former security consultant, retired army officer*

**Oakland**
Patton, Warren Andre *non-commissioned officer, journalist*

**Paso Robles**
Smith, Helen Elizabeth *retired military officer*

**Pebble Beach**
Carns, Michael Patrick Chamberlain *air force officer*
Fergusson, Robert George *retired army officer*
Mauz, Henry Herrward, Jr. *retired naval officer*

**Riverside**
Mc Cormac, Weston Arthur *retired educator and army officer*
Wright, John MacNair, Jr. *retired army officer*

**Sacramento**
†Gibson, Daniel James *career military officer*

**San Carlos**
Schumacher, Henry Jerold *former career officer, business executive*

**San Diego**
Bennitt, Brent Martin *naval officer*
†Hayes, William Meredith *career officer*
†Osborne, Richard George *naval officer, cardiologist, educator*
Tedeschi, Ernest Francis, Jr. *retired naval officer, naval company executive*
Wachendorf, Miles Benton *naval officer*
Wagner, George Francis Adolf *naval officer*

**Santa Ana**
Izac, Suzette Marie *retired air force officer*

**Santa Barbara**
Conley, Philip James, Jr. *retired air force officer*

**Santa Rosa**
Andriano-Moore, Richard Graf *naval officer*
Bowen, James Thomas *military officer*

**Saratoga**
Henderson, William Darryl *army officer, writer*

**Seaside**
Gales, Samuel Joel *retired civilian military employee, counselor*

**Sonora**
Smith, Carlton Myles *military officer*

**South Dos Palos**
Hirohata, Derek Kazuyoshi *air force reserve officer*

## COLORADO

**Boulder**
Stone, John Helms, Jr. *admiralty advisor*

**Colorado Springs**
Barry, William Patrick *military officer*
Bowen, Clotilde Dent *retired army officer, psychiatrist*
Forgan, David Waller *retired air force officer*
Keen, Ronald Lee *career officer*
Mitchell, John Henderson *retired army officer, management consultant*
Porter, David Bruce *air force officer, behavioral scientist, educator*
Sawyer, Thomas William *air force officer*
Schaeffer, Reiner Horst *air force officer, retired librarian, foreign language professional*

**Denver**
Avrit, Richard Calvin *defense consultant*

**Englewood**
Nuce, Madonna Marie *military officer*

**Fort Collins**
Roberts, Archibald Edward *retired army officer, author*

**Golden**
†Frix, Robert Scott *career military officer*

**Littleton**
Allery, Kenneth Edward *air force officer*

**Monument**
Breckner, William John, Jr. *retired air force officer, corporate executive, consultant*
†Hindmarsh, George Ronald *air force officer*

**Peterson AFB**
†Ashy, Joseph W. *career officer*
Caruana, Patrick Peter *career officer*
†Dinerstein, Marc J. *career military officer*

**U S A F Academy**
Morris, Steven Lynn *career officer, aeronautical engineering educator*

**Woodland Park**
Stewart, Robert Lee *retired army officer, astronaut*

## CONNECTICUT

**Bloomfield**
Less, Anthony Albert *retired naval officer*
Schenkelbach, Leon *retired career officer, safety consultant*

**Niantic**
Hunt, Francis Howard *retired navy laboratory official*

**Rogers**
Boomer, Walter Eugene *marine officer*

## DISTRICT OF COLUMBIA

**Fort Mcnair**
Krise, Thomas Warren *military officer, English language educator*

**Washington**
†Adams, Patrick O. *career officer*
Adams, Ronald Emerson *army officer*
†Almquist, Theodore C. *career officer*
Aultman, William Robert *career officer*
†Baker, David E. *career officer*
Bates, Jared Lewis *army officer*
Becton, Julius Wesley, Jr. *army officer*
†Benken, Eric W. *career officer*
†Betsch, Keith Albert *airforce officer*
†Blair, Dennis Cutler *career officer*
Briggs, Steven Russell *naval officer*
Burr, Hiram Hale, Jr. *retired air force officer*
Burt, John Alan *naval officer*
Crawford, Hunt Dorn, Jr. *military officer, educator, diplomat*
†Davidson, William A. *career officer*
†DeFilippi, George *career military officer*
DeLuca, Anthony J. *director small and minority business program in United State Air Force*
†Donahue, Raymond Patrick *naval officer*
†Douglas, John W. *career officer*
Dubia, John Austin *army executive*
Dyke, Charles William *retired army officer*
†Fallon, William J. *career officer*
Falter, Vincent Eugene *retired army officer, consultant*
†Ferriter, Edward Chadwick *naval officer*
Finerty, Martin Joseph, Jr. *military officer, researcher, association management executive*
Fisher, Stephen Todd *naval officer*
Fogleman, Ronald Robert *military officer*
Frost, S. David *retired naval officer*
Fuller, Lawrence Joseph *military officer, lawyer*
Garner, Jay Montgomery *career officer*
Goodpaster, Andrew Jackson *retired army officer*
†Gravell, William *military career officer*
Graves, Ernest, Jr. *retired army officer, engineer*
Gray, Kenneth Darnell *career officer, judge*
Gregory, Frederick D. *career officer, space agency administrator*
Guenther, Otto J. *army officer*
†Habiger, Eugene E. *career officer*
Hancock, William John *career officer*
†Hudson, Joel B. *civilian military employee*
Huston, John Wilson *air force officer, historian*
†Johnson, Jay L. *career officer*
Kearns, Darien Lee *marine officer*
Klimp, Jack Wilbur *armed forces officer*
Koenig, Harold Martin *U.S. Navy surgeon general*
Kramek, Robert E. *U.S. coast guard officer*
Krulak, Charles Chandler *marine officer*
†Kuehn, Robert John Jr. *career military officer*
Leaf, Howard Westley *retired air force officer, military official*
Loren, Donald Patrick *naval officer*
Luti, William Joseph *career officer*
McGinty, Michael Dennis *air force officer*
McMiller, Anita Williams *army officer, transportation professional, educator*
Montelongo, Michael *career officer*
Moorer, Thomas Hinman *retired naval officer*
Murashige, Allen *defense analysis executive*
Navas, William Antonio, Jr. *military officer, civil engineer*
Nutting, Wallace Hall *army officer*
Odom, William Eldridge *army officer, educator*
O'Reilly, Kenneth William *military officer*
Orsini, Eric Andrew *army official*
Oster, Jeffrey Wayne *marine corps officer*
†Patterson, Albert Love III *career military officer*
Peterson, David Glenn *retired career officer*
Pirie, Robert Burns, Jr. *defense analyst*
†Ralston, Joseph W. *career officer*
†Reimer, Dennis J. *career military officer*
Riddell, Richard Anderson *naval officer*
Rokke, Ervin Jerome *air force officer, university president*
St. John, Adrian, II *retired army officer*
Schumaker, James Frederick *foreign service officer*
†Sconyers, Ronald T. *career officer*
Scowcroft, Brent *retired air force officer, government official*
Shea, Donald William *career officer*
†Sheehan, John J. *career officer*
Simmons, Edwin Howard *marine corps officer, historian*
†Story, Hugh Goodman, Jr. *non-commissioned officer*
Thomas, Clayton James *air force executive*
Thomas, Richard O. *civilian military employee*
Thornton, Wayne Allen *naval officer, engineer*
Tobin, Paul Edward, Jr. *naval officer*
Weiler, Todd Alan *army official*
†Wilkerson, Thomas L. *career military officer*
Williams, Kent Harlan *coast guard officer*
Yatsevitch, Gratian Michael *retired army officer, diplomat, engineer*

## FLORIDA

**Boynton Beach**
Leonard, Edward Paul *naval officer, dentist, educator*

**Daytona Beach**
Gauch, Eugene William, Jr. *former air force officer*

**Destin**
Carlton, Paul Kendall *retired air force officer, consultant*

**Eglin AFB**
Head, William Christopher *military officer, health care administrator*
Stewart, J. Daniel *air force development and test center administrator*

**Fernandina Beach**
Rogers, Robert Burnett *naval officer*

**Gainesville**
Parker, Harry Lee *retired military officer, counselor*

**Haines City**
Clement, Robert William *air force officer*

**Hurlburt Field**
Hobbs, Roy Jerry *military career officer, health services administrator*

**Jacksonville**
†Delaney, Kevin Francis *naval officer*
Lestage, Daniel Barfield *retired naval officer, physician*

**Lake Wales**
Mumma, Albert G. *retired naval officer, retired manufacturing company executive, management consultant*

**Longwood**
Smyth, Joseph Patrick *retired naval officer, physician*

**Lutz**
Bedke, Ernest Alford *retired air force officer*

**Niceville**
Phillips, Richard Wendell, Jr. *air force officer*

**Orange Park**
Enney, James Crowe *former air force officer, business executive*

**Orlando**
Laning, Richard Boyer *naval officer, writer, retired*
Smetheram, Herbert Edwin *government official*

**Ormond Beach**
Riley, Daniel Edward *air force officer*

**Palm City**
Senter, William Oscar *retired air force officer*

**Patrick A F B**
Haggis, Arthur George, Jr. *retired military officer, educator, publisher*

**Pensacola**
Johnson, Alfred Carl, Jr. *former navy officer*
Weisner, Maurice Franklin *former naval officer*

**Punta Gorda**
Hepfer, John William, Jr. *retired air force officer, consultant*

**Sarasota**
Loving, George Gilmer, Jr. *retired air force officer*

**Tallahassee**
Davis, Larry Michael *military officer, health-care consultant*

**Tampa**
†Bailey, Maxwell C. *career officer*
†Lionetti, Donald Michael *career military officer*
Matheny, Charles Woodburn, Jr. *retired army officer, retired civil engineer*
†Peay, J.H. Binford, III *career officer*

## GEORGIA

**Atlanta**
Champion, Charles Howell, Jr. *retired army officer*
Franks, Tommy Ray *army officer*
Hickerson, Patricia Parsons *military officer*
McGuinn, Michael Edward, III *retired army officer*

**Columbus**
Cavezza, Carmen James *career officer, cultural organization administrator*

**Duluth**
Holutiak-Hallick, Stephen Peter, Jr. *businessman, educator*

**Forest Park**
†Pulliam, James Michael *military career officer*

**Peachtree City**
Eichelberger, Charles Bell *retired career officer*
Yeosock, John John *army officer*

**Roswell**
Graham, Charles Passmore *retired army officer*

**Social Circle**
Malcom, Joseph Adams *retired military officer, project manager*

**Stockbridge**
Davis, Raymond Gilbert *retired career officer, real estate developer*

**Warner Robins**
DePriest, C(harles) David *engineer, retired air force officer*
Nugteren, Cornelius *air force officer*

## HAWAII

**Honolulu**
Hays, Ronald Jackson *naval officer*
Jenkins, Robert Gordon *air force officer*

## IDAHO

**Boise**
Manning, Darrell V. *national guard officer*

## ILLINOIS

**Chicago**
Borling, John Lorin *military officer*

**Hoffman Estates**
Pagonis, William Gus *retired army general*

**Mattoon**
Phipps, John Randolph *retired army officer*

**Scott AFB**
†Andrews, James E. *career officer*

**Springfield**
Herriford, Robert Levi, Sr. *army officer*

**Westmont**
Bajek, Frank Michael *career officer, retired, financial consultant*

## INDIANA

**Indianapolis**
Poel, Robert Walter *air force officer, physician*

**Indianpolis**
Abbott, Verlin Leroy *military career officer*

## IOWA

**Des Moines**
Durrenberger, William John *retired army general, educator, investor*

## KANSAS

**Fort Leavenworth**
Schneider, James Joseph *military theory educator, consultant*

## LOUISIANA

**Barksdale AFB**
Petters, Samuel Brian *air force officer*

**New Orleans**
Harness, Francis William *naval officer*

## MARYLAND

**Adelphi**
Lyons, John W(inship) *government official, chemist*

**Annapolis**
Barber, James Alden *military officer*
Larson, Charles Robert *naval officer*
Long, Robert Lyman John *naval officer*
McDonough, Joseph Corbett *former army officer, aviation consultant*
Whitford, Dennis James *naval officer, meteorologist, oceanographer*

**Baltimore**
Wilmot, Louise C. *retired naval commander, charitable organization executive*

**Bethesda**
†Contreras, Thomas J., Jr. *naval officer*
Cooper, William Ewing, Jr. *retired army officer*
Daniel, Charles Dwelle, Jr. *consultant, retired army officer*
Gallis, John Nicholas *naval officer, healthcare executive*
Hauck, Frederick Hamilton *retired naval officer, astronaut, business executive*
McNamee, Evelyn Haynes *civilian military employee*
O'Shaughnessy, Gary William *military officer*
Owen, Thomas Barron *retired naval officer, space company executive*
Schmidt, Raymond Paul *naval career officer, historian, government official*
Wishart, Leonard Plumer, III *army officer*

**Cascade**
Blickenstaff, Danny Jay *civilian military employee*

**Chevy Chase**
Delano, Victor *retired naval officer*

**Columbia**
Kime, J. William *career officer, engineer, ship management executiv*

**Edgewater**
Malley, Kenneth Cornelius *retired military officer, corporation executive*

**Ellicott City**
Scott, Richard Kevin *army officer*

**Fort Ritchie**
†Craig, Walter M., Jr. *army officer*

**Lanham**
Naylon, Michael Edward *military officer*

**Lutherville**
Sagerholm, James Alvin *retired naval officer*

**Patuxent River**
Watkiss, Eric John *naval flight officer*

**Rockville**
Harvey, Donald Phillips *retired naval officer*
Ramsey, William Edward *retired naval officer, space systems executive*
Trost, Carlisle Albert Herman *retired naval officer*

**Silver Spring**
Adams, Andrew Joseph *army officer*
Brog, David *consultant, former air force officer*

**Sykesville**
Weyandt, Daniel Scott *naval officer, engineer*

**Trappe**
Anderson, Andrew Herbert *retired army officer*

**Upper Marlboro**
Uzzell-Baggett, Karon Lynette *career officer*

## MASSACHUSETTS

**Boston**
Amirault, Richard B. *retired career officer, financial planner*
Doebler, James Carl *naval officer, engineering executive*
Holloway, Bruce Keener *former air force officer*

**Cambridge**
Trainor, Bernard Edmund *retired military officer*

**Dudley**
Carney, Roger Francis Xavier *retired army officer*

**Hanscom AFB**
Rollins, James Gregory *air force officer*

**Medford**
Galvin, John Rogers *educator, retired army officer*

**Nantucket**
Baldwin, John Ashby, Jr. *retired naval officer*

**North Dartmouth**
Cressy, Peter Hollon *naval officer, academic administrator*

**Osterville**
Schwarztrauber, Sayre Archie *former naval officer, maritime consultant*

**Quincy**
Miller, George David *retired air force officer, marketing consultant*

**South Hamilton**
Patton, George Smith *military officer*

**Westford**
Stansberry, James Wesley *air force officer*

## MICHIGAN

**Ann Arbor**
Ploger, Robert Riis *retired military officer, engineer*

**Plymouth**
Brown, Bruce Harding *naval officer*

## MINNESOTA

**Burnsville**
Larson, Doyle Eugene *retired air force officer, consultant*

**Minneapolis**
Chen, William Shao-Chang *retired army officer*

## MISSISSIPPI

**Bay Saint Louis**
Gaffney, Paul Golden, II *military officer*

**Keesler AFB**
Rigdon, David Tedrick *air force officer, geneticist, director*

**Madison**
Robinson, John David *retired army officer*

**Pass Christian**
McCardell, James Elton *retired naval officer*

**Vicksburg**
Howard, Bruce Kenneth *army officer, environmental engineer*

## MISSOURI

**Chesterfield**
Willis, Frank Edward *retired air force officer*

**Florissant**
Reese, Alferd George *retired army civilian logistics specialist*

**Kansas City**
Anderson, Edgar R., Jr. *career officer, hospital administrator, physician*

**Saint Louis**
Strevey, Tracy Elmer, Jr. *army officer, surgeon, physician executive*
Williamson, Donald Ray *retired career Army officer*

**Warrenton**
Roan, James Cortland, Jr. *air force officer*

## NEBRASKA

**Lincoln**
Heng, Stanley Mark *national guard officer*

**Offutt AFB**
Luckett, Byron Edward, Jr. *air force chaplain*

**Omaha**
Fowler, Stephen Eugene *retired military officer, human resources executive*

Nettles, Toni Olesco *non-commissioned officer*

## NEVADA

**Boulder City**
Heinlein, Oscar Allen *former air force officer*

**Henderson**
Creech, Wilbur Lyman *retired military officer*

**Las Vegas**
Alexander, John Bradfield *weaponry manager, retired army officer*

## NEW JERSEY

**Freehold**
Hooper, John David *career military officer*

**Moorestown**
†Cassidy, Richard Michael, Jr. *retired officer, defense company executive*

**Morristown**
Rogers, Alan Victor *former career officer*

## NEW MEXICO

**Albuquerque**
Flournoy, John Charles, Sr. *training specialist, retired military officer*
Gensler, Thomas Daniel *military officer, medical services executive*
Lucchetti, Lynn L. *career officer*

**Cedar Crest**
Sheppard, Jack W. *retired air force officer*

**Cerrillos**
Goodwin, Samuel McClure *officer*

**Kirtland AFB**
Harrison, George Brooks *career officer*
Heckathorn, William Gary *military officer*

**Santa Fe**
Fox, Jack Rex *military professional*
†Garcia, Alex R. *career military officer*
Sumner, Gordon, Jr. *retired military officer*

**Santa Teresa**
Leffler, Stacy Brent *retired government employee*

## NEW YORK

**Colton**
Bulger, Dennis Bernard *military officer, engineer*

**Fort Drum**
†Juskowiak, Terry Eugene *career military officer*

**Hamburg**
†Markulis, Henryk John *career military officer*

**New York**
Dugan, Michael J. *former air force officer, health agency executive*

**Orient**
Hanson, Thor *retired health agency executive and naval officer*

**West Point**
Christman, Daniel William *military officer*

## NORTH CAROLINA

**Camp Lejeune**
†Howard, Patrick Gene *marine corps officer*

**Fayetteville**
Kilgore, Joe Everett, Jr. *army officer*

**Pine Knoll Shores**
Lynn, Otis Clyde *former army officer*

**Pinehurst**
Carroll, Kent Jean *retired naval officer*
Ellis, William Harold *former naval officer*
Roberts, Francis Joseph *retired army officer, retired educational administrator, global economic advisor*

**Raleigh**
Robb, Nathaniel Heyward, Jr. *remote sensing company executive*

**Southern Pines**
Mataxis, Theodore Christopher *consultant, lecturer, writer, retired army officer, educator*

**Spring Hope**
Hildreth, James Robert *retired air force officer*

**Whisper Pines**
Blanchard, George Samuel *retired military officer, consultant*

## OHIO

**Columbus**
Elliot, Ernest Alexander *naval rear admiral*

**Dayton**
†Ardis, David G. *career officer*
Halki, John Joseph *retired military officer, physician*

Langford, Roland Everett *military officer, environmental scientist, author*
Miller, Kenneth Gregory *retired air force officer*
Whitlock, David C. *retired military officer*

**Fairborn**
Nowak, John Michael *retired air force officer, company executive*

**Tiffin**
Einsel, David William, Jr. *retired army officer and consultant*

**Wright Patterson AFB**
†Babbitt, George T. *career officer*
†Back, Donna J. *career officer*
†Batterman, Thomas W. *civilian military employee*
†Worthington, Walter Thomas *career military officer*

## OKLAHOMA

**Tinker AFB**
Goodman, Ernest Monroe *air force officer*

## OREGON

**Lake Oswego**
McPeak, Merrill Anthony *business executive, consultant, retired officer*

**Portland**
Blackwell, Garland Wayne *retired military officer*

## PENNSYLVANIA

**Gettysburg**
Coughenour, Kavin Luther *career officer, military historian*

**Mechanicsburg**
Chamberlin, Edward Robert *career officer, educator*
Kinney, Linford Nelson *retired army officer*
Pearsall, Gregory Howard *naval officer*

**Oakdale**
†Turnage, Larry *military career officer*

## RHODE ISLAND

**Narragansett**
Apperson, Jack Alfonso *retired army officer, business executive*

**Newport**
Bergstrom, Albion Andrew *army officer, federal official*
Jackson, John Edward *naval officer, educator, logistician*

## SOUTH CAROLINA

**Charleston**
Watts, Claudius Elmer, III *retired air force officer*

**Columbia**
Lander, James Albert *retired military officer, state senator*
Marchant, Trelawney Eston *retired national guard officer, lawyer*

**Fairfax**
McCarthy, Timothy Michael *career non-commissioned officer*

**Goose Creek**
†Lindquist, Michael Adrian *career military officer*

**Hilton Head Island**
Brown, Arthur Edmon, Jr. *retired army officer*

**Seneca**
Clausen, Hugh Joseph *retired army officer*

**Sumter**
Olsen, Thomas Richard, Sr. *air force officer*

**Wedgefield**
McLaurin, Hugh McFaddin, III *military officer, historian consultant*

**York**
Blackwell, Paul Eugene *army officer*

## SOUTH DAKOTA

**Rapid City**
†Murphy, Joseph Timothy *army officer*
Sykora, Harold James *military officer*

## TENNESSEE

**Clarksville**
Birdsong, William Herbert, Jr. *retired brigadier general*

**Knoxville**
Sullenberger, Donald Shields *air force officer, business executive*

**Memphis**
Cunningham, David Coleman *career officer*

**Oak Ridge**
Felton, Lewis A. *career officer*

## TEXAS

### Allen
Wynn, Robert E. *retired career officer, electronics executive*

### Amarillo
Taylor, Wesley Bayard, Jr. *retired army officer*

### Belton
Harrison, Benjamin Leslie *retired army officer*
Shoemaker, Robert Morin *retired army officer, county government official*

### Dallas
Campillo, Fred Grover *naval officer*
Cissik, John Henry *medical research director, consultant*

### El Paso
Shapiro, Stephen Richard *retired air force officer, physician*

### Fort Hood
Hughes, William Foster *career officer, surgeon, obstetrician, gynecologist*
Sprabary, Larry Drew *military analyst*

### Garland
Stimpson, Ritchie Ples *retired military officer*

### Georgetown
Weyrauch, Paul Turney *retired army officer*

### Grand Prairie
Loo, Maritta Louise *military officer, nurse*

### Houston
Jones, Lincoln, III *army officer*
Kline, John William *retired air force officer, management consultant*
Lichtman, David Michael *military officer, health care administrator, orthopedist, educator*
Loria, Christopher Joseph *marine officer*

### Kelly AFB
†Kelly, Gary Michael *career military officer*

### Lackland AFB
Carlton, Paul Kendall, Jr. *air force officer, physician*

### Mansfield
Rivera, Angel (Andy) Manuel *retired career officer, city official*

### Premont
Cisneros, Marc Anthony *military officer*

### Randolph AFB
†Anderson, Kurt B. *career officer*

### San Antonio
Ryder, Gene Ed *retired United States Air Force training administrator*

### San Marcos
Bullock, Jerry McKee *retired military officer, consultant, educator*

### Tyler
Gann, Benard Wayne *air force officer*

### Waco
Mitchell, William Allen *air force officer, political geography educator*

## UTAH

### Brigham City
Fife, Dennis Jensen *military officer, chemistry educator*

## VERMONT

### Burlington
Cram, Reginald Maurice *retired air force officer*

### Williston
†Cote, David Orman *career officer, health facility administrator*

## VIRGINIA

### Alexandria
Adams, Ranald Trevor, Jr. *retired air force officer*
Allen, Fred Cary *retired army officer*
Babcock, Jack Emerson *retired army officer, educator, corporate executive*
Boge, Walter Edward *retired army civilian official, private consultant*
Bowman, Richard Carl *defense consultant, retired air force officer*
Brown, Frederic Joseph *army officer*
Burke, Kelly Howard *former air force officer, business executive*
Curtin, Gary Lee *air force officer*
Dorsey, James Francis, Jr. *naval officer*
Downs, Michael Patrick *retired marine corps officer*
Dunn, Bernard Daniel *former naval officer, consultant*
Dyer, Joseph Wendell *career officer*
Gurke, Sharon McCue *naval officer*
Kingston, Robert Charles *retired army officer*
Lajoie, Roland *army officer*
†Lennon, Thomas John *retired air force officer, company executive*
Mc Mullen, Thomas Henry *retired air force officer*
McNair, Carl Herbert, Jr. *army officer, aeronautical engineer*
Minor, Mary Ellen *civilian military employee*
Powell, Colin Luther *retired military officer, author*
Rowden, William Henry *naval officer*
Saint, Crosbie Edgerton *retired army officer*
Stafford, Thomas Patten *retired military officer, former astronaut*
Strunz, Kim Carol *military officer*
Wagner, Louis Carson, Jr. *retired army officer*
Wolfe, Thad Allison *air force officer*

### Annandale
Guthrie, John Reiley *retired army officer, business executive*
Mandeville, Robert Clark, Jr. *former naval officer, business executive*
McCaffree, Burnham Clough, Jr. *retired naval officer*
McKee, Fran *retired naval officer*
Watts, Helena Roselle *military analyst*
Williams, James Arthur *retired army officer, information systems company executive*

### Arlington
Bradunas, John Joseph *marine corps officer*
Carr, Kenneth Monroe *naval officer*
Chapman, Donald D. *retired naval officer, lawyer*
Coady, Philip James, Jr. *naval officer*
Dillon, Francis Richard *air force officer, retired*
Edmonds, Albert J. *career officer*
Elam, Fred Eldon *career army officer, retired*
Forrester, Eugene Priest *former army officer, management marketing consultant*
Harrison, Jerry Calvin *retired army officer*
Kelley, Paul Xavier *retired marine corps officer*
Kem, Richard Samuel *retired army officer*
Kern, Paul John *army officer*
Lisanby, James Walker *retired naval officer*
Lockard, John Allen *naval officer*
†Maness, Stephen Ray *manufacturing engineer, retired army officer*
Marini, Elizabeth Ann *civilian military executive*
Merritt, Jack Neil *retired army officer*
Miller, Thomas Hulbert, Jr. *former marine corps officer*
†O'Connell, Patrick Michael *naval officer*
Putnam, George W., Jr. *army officer*
Quinn, William Wilson *army officer, manufacturing executive*
Rieken, Danny Michael *naval officer, aerospace and systems engineer*
Saalfeld, Fred Erich *naval researcher*
Scarborough, Robert Henry, Jr. *coast guard officer*
Seely, James Michael *defense consultant, retired naval officer, small business owner*
Singstock, David John *military officer*
Strean, Bernard M. *retired naval officer*
Thompson, Jonathan Sims *army officer*
Tice, Raphael Dean *army officer*
Zumwalt, Elmo Russell, Jr. *retired naval officer*

### Burke
O'Connor, Edward Cornelius *army officer*

### Centreville
Amerault, James F. *military officer*
Kelly, John Joseph, Jr. *career officer*

### Chantilly
Saunders, Norman Thomas *military officer*
Stone, Thomas Edward *defense consultant, retired rear admiral*

### Chesapeake
Picotte, Leonard Francis *naval officer*

### Fairfax
Allen, Gary Wayne *career officer, dentist*
Baer, Robert Jacob *retired army officer*
Clayton, William E. *naval officer*
Dawalt, Kenneth Francis *former army officer, former aerospace company executive*
Drenz, Charles Francis *retired army officer*
Ginn, Richard Van Ness *retired army officer, health care executive*
†Kerr, R. Dennis *career military officer*
Rosenkranz, Robert Bernard *military officer*
Scanlon, Charles Francis *army officer, retired, defense consultant*
Wood, C(harles) Norman *air force officer*

### Fairfax Station
Ross, Jimmy Douglas *army officer*

### Falls Church
Graves, Howard Dwayne *army officer, academic administrator, educator*
Gray, D'Wayne *retired marine corps officer*
Kalleres, Michael Peter *career officer*
Kroesen, Frederick James *retired army officer, consultant*
Layman, Lawrence *naval officer*
Pendleton, Elmer Dean, Jr. *retired military officer, international consultant*
Simokaitis, Frank Joseph *air force officer, lawyer*

### Fort Belvoir
Suycott, Mark Leland *naval flight officer*

### Fort Monroe
Miller, John Edward *army officer, educational administrator*

### Fort Myer
Hart, Herbert Michael *military officer*
Shalikashvili, John Malchase *military career officer*

### Hampton
Cravens, James J., Jr. *military officer*
Dula, Brett M. *military officer*
Goers, Melvin Armand *retired army officer*
Pulaski, Lori Jaye *career officer*

### Lynchburg
Snead, George Murrell, Jr. *army officer, scientist, consultant*

### Mc Lean
Cowhill, William Joseph *retired naval officer, consultant*
Davis, Bennie Luke *air force officer*
Fedorochko, William, Jr. *retired army officer, policy analyst*
Haddock, Raymond Earl *career officer*
Hopkins, Thomas Matthews *former naval officer*
Linville, Ray Pate *logistics analyst, editor*
†Molino, Thomas Michael *retired career military officer*
Oren, John Birdsell *retired coast guard officer*
Raymond, Dennis Kenneth *army officer*
Sullivan, Kenneth Joseph *strategic and intelligence programs analyst*

### Merrifield
Earner, William Anthony, Jr. *naval officer*

### Middleburg
Collins, James Lawton, Jr. *retired army officer*

### Mount Jackson
Sylvester, George Howard *retired air force officer*

### Newington
Miggins, Michael Denis *retired career officer, arms control analyst*

### Newport News
Otis, Glenn Kay *retired army officer*

### Norfolk
Garlette, William Henry Lee *army officer*
Katz, Douglas Jeffrey *naval officer*
Krantz, Kenneth Allan *military officer, judge*
Train, Harry Depue, II *retired naval officer*

### Oakton
Anderson, William Robert *career naval officer*

### Portsmouth
†Mason, Jon Donavon *military career officer, physician*

### Quantico
Van Riper, Paul Kent *marine corps officer*

### Reston
Brown, James Robert *retired air force officer*
Dantone, Joseph John, Jr. *naval officer*
Jaynes, Robert Henry, Jr. *retired military officer*
Seiberlich, Carl Joseph *retired naval officer*
Wilkinson, Edward Anderson, Jr. *retired naval officer, business executive*

### Richmond
Dilworth, Robert Lexow *career military officer, adult education educator*

### Springfield
Bond, William Jennings, Jr. *air force officer*

### Vienna
Chandler, Hubert Thomas *former army officer*
Davis, Cabell Seal, Jr. *naval officer*
Hatch, Harold Arthur *retired military officer*
Jackson, Dempster McKee *retired naval officer*
Phillips, Richard L(overidge) *marine corps officer*
Webb, William Loyd, Jr. *army officer*
Yarborough, William Glenn, Jr. *military officer, forest farmer, defense and international business executive*

### Virginia Beach
Halpin, Timothy Patrick *former air force officer*
Oldfield, Edward Charles, Jr. *retired naval officer, communications company executive*
Sanderson, James Richard *naval officer, planning and investment company consultant*

### Williamsburg
Cantlay, George Gordon *retired army officer*

### Woodbridge
†Scofield, Thomas Carey *retired army officer*

## WASHINGTON

### Anacortes
Higgins, Robert (Walter) *military officer, physician*

### Bellevue
Traister, Robert Edwin *naval officer, engineer*

### Fort Lewis
Davis, Harley Cleo *retired military officer*

### Lynnwood
Jenes, Theodore George, Jr. *retired military officer*

### Richland
McGinley, Edward Stillman, II *former naval officer, engineering executive*

### Washougal
†Davis, Paul Rick *military career officer*

## WISCONSIN

### Stone Lake
Kissinger, Harold Arthur *retired army officer*

## MILITARY ADDRESSES OF THE UNITED STATES

## ATLANTIC

### APO
Darnell, Susan Laura Browne *career officer*
Magruder, Lawson William, III *military officer*

## EUROPE

### APO
Astriab, Steven Michael *army officer*
Charlip, Ralph Blair *career officer*
Dickey, James Stuart *retired military officer*
Kinnan, Timothy Alan *air force officer*
Meigs, Montgomery Cunningham, Jr. *military officer*
Moloff, Alan Lawrence *army officer, physician*
Ray, Norman Wilson *career officer*
Scholes, Edison Earl *army officer*

### FPO
Griffin, Paul, Jr. *navy officer, engineer, educator*
Madison, Kenneth Edward *career officer*

## PACIFIC

### APO
Hicks, Robert Ruiz, Jr. *army officer*
McCarthy, Sean Michael *air force officer, pilot*
Mirick, Robert Allen *military officer*
Moser, Gregg Anthony *career officer*

### FPO
Haskins, Michael Donald *naval officer*
†Zacharias, David Alexander *career military officer*

## CANADA

## NORTHWEST TERRITORIES

### Yellowknife
†LeBlanc, Pierre Gabriel *military officer*

## ONTARIO

### Bracebridge
MacKenzie, Lewis Wharton *military officer*

### Ontario
†DeQuetteville, Allan M. *career officer*

### Ottawa
†Adams, John L. *retired career officer, federal agency administrator*
†Cox, James S. *career officer*
de Chastelain, A(lfred) John G(ardyne) D(rummond) *Canadian army officer, diplomat*
†Murray, Larry *Canadian Forces officer*

### Stittsville
Tellier, Henri *retired Canadian military officer*

## QUEBEC

### Montreal
Manson, Paul David *retired military officer, electronics executive*

### Saint Hubert
†Baril, Maurice *career officer*

## BELGIUM

### Brussels
Murdock, Robert McClellan *military officer*

## EGYPT

### Cairo
Callison, Charles Stuart *retired foreign service officer, development economist*

## ENGLAND

### London
Pletcher, John Harold, Jr. *career officer*

## LUXEMBOURG

### Strassen
Laposata, Joseph Samuel *army officer*

## ADDRESS UNPUBLISHED

Austin, Robert Clarke *naval officer*
†Bartrem, Duane Harvey *retired military officer, designer, building consultant*
Bauman, Richard Arnold *coast guard officer*
†Beale, Richard Ewing, Jr. *career military officer*
Block, Emil Nathaniel, Jr. *military officer*
Bridges, Roy Dubard, Jr. *career officer*
Brooks, James Sprague *retired national guard officer*
Brooks, Thomas Aloysius, III *retired naval officer, telecommunications company executive*
Buker, Robert Hutchinson, Sr. *army officer, thoracic surgeon*
Carter, William George, III *army officer*
Chelberg, Robert Douglas *army officer*
Cole, Brady Marshall *retired naval officer*
Davis, Henry Jefferson, Jr. *former naval officer*
Davis, James Richard *retired military officer*
Decker, Oscar Conrad, Jr. *retired army officer*
†Doleman, Edgar Collins *retired army officer*
Dozier, James Lee *former army officer*
Evans, Marsha Johnson *naval officer*
Faulkenberry, Virgil Thomas *retired naval officer, educator*
Fischer, Eugene H. *air force officer*
Fitzgerald, James Richard *naval officer*
Foote, Evelyn Patricia *retired army officer, consultant*
Foulk, David Wingerd *retired military civilian executive*
†Gaugler, Robert Walter *retired career military officer*
Gavin, Herbert James *consultant, retired air force officer*
Giordano, Andrew Anthony *retired naval officer*
Gray, David Lawrence *retired air force officer*
Guthrie, Wallace Nessler, Jr. *naval officer*
Halford, Elizabeth Nelle *army officer*
Hall, Thomas Forrest *naval officer*
Harper, Henry H. *military officer, retired*

Harris, Marcelite Jordan *retired air force officer*
Holloway, James Curtis *military officer*
Hoover, John Elwood *former military officer, consultant, writer*
Hostettler, Stephen John *naval officer*
Johnson, Silas R., Jr. *air force officer*
Johnston, James Monroe, III *air force officer*
Jones, David Charles *retired air force officer, former chairman Joint Chiefs of Staff*
†Joulwan, George A. *career military officer*
Kelley, Larry Dale *retired army officer*
Kelso, Frank Benton, II *naval officer*
Kempf, Cecil Joseph *naval officer*
Kutyna, Donald Joseph *air force officer*
Lautenbacher, Conrad Charles, Jr. *naval officer*
Lundin, Richard Allen *career military officer, federal government administrator, educator*
Manganaro, Francis Ferdinand *naval officer*
†McCoy, Helen Thomas *civilian military employee*
Mc Fadden, George Linus *retired army officer*
McKinnon, Daniel Wayne, Jr. *naval officer*
Minners, Howard Alyn *physician, research administrator*
Moore, William Leroy, Jr. *career officer, physician*
Morgan, Thomas Rowland *retired marine corps officer*
Mow, Douglas Farris *former naval officer, consultant*
Mullen, William Joseph, III *military analyst, retired army officer*
Neff, Diane Irene *naval officer*
Nelson, Ben, Jr. *retired air force officer*
Ninos, Nicholas Peter *retired miliatry officer, physician*
Olson, Phillip Roger *naval officer*
Palmer, Dave Richard *retired military officer, academic administrator*
Parent, Rodolphe Jean *Canadian air force official, pilot*
Partington, James Wood *naval officer*
Pearson, John Davis *retired naval officer*
Price, Robert Ira *coast guard officer*
Retz, William Andrew *retired naval officer*
Rhame, Thomas Gene *army officer*
Rogers, Bernard William *military officer*
Sagan, Stanley Daniel *career officer, retired*
Schrader, Harry Christian, Jr. *retired naval officer*
Schumacher, William Jacob *retired army officer*
Shapiro, Sumner *retired naval officer, business executive*
Shaw, John Frederick *retired naval officer*
Slewitzke, Connie Lee *retired army officer*
Smith, Leighton Warren, Jr. *naval officer*
Smith, Loretta Mae *contracting officer*
Springer, Robert Dale *retired air force officer, consultant, lecturer*
Stiner, Carl Wade *army officer*
Sullivan, Michael Patrick *marine officer*
Sunell, Robert John *retired army officer*
†Swanson, Dane Craig *naval officer, pilot*
Tuttle, Jerry Owen *retired naval officer, business executive*
Vessey, John William, Jr. *army officer*
Vincent, Hal Wellman *marine corps officer, investor*
Watts, Ronald Lester *retired military officer*
Weir, Kenneth Wynn *marine corps officer, experimental test pilot*
Wheeler, Albin Gray *U.S. Army career officer, educator, retail executive, law firm executive*
Wheeler, Jack Cox *army officer*
Williamson, Myrna Hennrich *retired army officer, lecturer, consultant*
Wilson, Dwight Liston *former military officer, investment advisor*
Wilson, Richard Alexander *career officer*

## RELIGION

### UNITED STATES

#### ALABAMA

**Andalusia**
Patterson, Edwin *minister*

**Birmingham**
Foley, David E. *bishop*
Hull, William Edward *theology educator*
†O'Brien, Dellanna West *religious organization administrator*
Roby, Jasper *bishop*
Threadcraft, Hal Law, III *pastor, counselor*
Zahl, Paul Francis Matthew *dean*

**Gadsden**
Arnold, Don Carl *pastor, religious organization executive*

**Helena**
Smith, John Lee, Jr. *minister, former association administrator*

**Mobile**
Lipscomb, Oscar Hugh *archbishop*

**Monroeville**
Adkisson, Randall Lynn *minister*

**Montgomery**
Bailey, Randall Charles *religious studies educator, consultant*
Oliver, John William Posegate *minister*

#### ALASKA

**Anchorage**
Hurley, Francis T. *archbishop*
Parsons, Donald D. *bishop*
Williams, Charles D. *bishop*

**Fairbanks**
Kaniecki, Michael Joseph *bishop*

**North Pole**
Fleming, Carolyn Elizabeth *religious organization administrator, interior designer*

#### ARIZONA

**Oro Valley**
Tinker, Robert Eugene *minister, educational consultant*

**Paradise Valley**
Sapp, Donald Gene *minister*

**Phoenix**
Dew, William Waldo, Jr. *bishop*
Hamilton, Ronald Ray *minister*
Harte, John Joseph Meakins *bishop*
King, Felton *bishop*
Kuzma, George Martin *bishop*
O'Brien, Thomas Joseph *bishop*

**Sun City**
Lapsley, James Norvell, Jr. *minister, pastoral theology educator*

**Sun City West**
Randall, Claire *church executive*
Schmitz, Charles Edison *evangelist*

**Tucson**
Moreno, Manuel D. *bishop*

#### ARKANSAS

**Conway**
Reddin, George *religious organization administrator*

**El Dorado**
Lee, Vernon Roy *minister*

**Hampton**
Copley, Stephen Jean *minister*

**Little Rock**
Mc Donald, Andrew J. *bishop*
Walker, L. T. *bishop*

**Mount Holly**
Mabson, Robert Langley *clergyman, librarian*

**North Little Rock**
Fitzpatrick, Joe Allen *music minister*
Holmes, James Frederick *minister*

**Russellville**
Chesnut, Franklin Gilmore *clergyman*
Inch, Morris Alton *theology educator*
Thompson, Robert Jaye *minister*

**Searcy**
Miller, Ken Leroy *religious studies educator, consultant, writer*

#### CALIFORNIA

**Altadena**
Willans, Jean Stone *religious organization executive*

**Anaheim**
Nguyen, Tai Anh *minister*

**Barstow**
Jones, Nathaniel *bishop*

**Berkeley**
Faulk, I. Carlton *religious organization executive*
Gall, Donald Arthur *minister*
Thomas, Owen Clark *clergyman, educator*
Welch, Claude (Raymond) *theology educator*

**Burbank**
Bower, Richard James *minister*

**Carmichael**
Probasco, Calvin Henry Charles *clergyman, college administrator*

**Century City**
Thomas, Issac David Ellis *clergy member*

**Chatsworth**
Dart, John Seward *religion news writer*

**Claremont**
Beardslee, William Armitage *religious organization administrator, educator*
Kucheman, Clark Arthur *religion educator*
Sanders, James Alvin *minister, biblical studies educator*

**Concord**
Jones, Gerald Edward *religion educator*

**Costa Mesa**
Williams, William Corey *theology educator, consultant*

**Cupertino**
Winslow, David Allen *chaplain, naval officer*

**Danville**
Davis, Ron Lee *clergyman, author*

**Del Mar**
Randall, Chandler Corydon *church rector*

**El Cerrito**
Dillenberger, John *theology educator emeritus, minister*

**Elk Grove**
Talbert, Melvin George *bishop*
Vang, Timothy Teng *church executive*

**Escondido**
Shanor, Clarence Richard *clergyman*

**Etna**
Auxentios, (Bishop Auxentios) *clergyman*

**Fillmore**
Guthrie, Harvey Henry, Jr. *clergyman*

**Fountain Valley**
Einstein, Stephen Jan *rabbi*

**Fresno**
Schofield, John-David Mercer *bishop*
Steinbock, John Thomas *bishop*
Wilson, Warren Samuel *clergyman, bishop*

**Fullerton**
Kim, Gil *minister*

**Glendale**
Courtney, Howard Perry *clergyman*

**Glendora**
Richey, Everett Eldon *religion educator*

**Hollywood**
Hovsepian, Vatche *clergyman*

**Irvine**
Lindquist, Raymond Irving *clergyman*

**La Jolla**
Freedman, David Noel *religion educator*
Wyle, Ewart Herbert *clergyman*

**Laguna Hills**
Wheatley, Melvin Ernest, Jr. *retired bishop*

**Long Beach**
Lowentrout, Peter Murray *religious studies educator*

**Los Alamitos**
Booth, John Nicholls *minister, magician, writer, photographer*

**Los Angeles**
Anderson, Robert Marshall *bishop*
Borsch, Frederick Houk *bishop*
Bowers, John William *church official*
Boyd, Malcolm *minister, religious author*
Breuer, Stephen Ernest *temple executive*
Burg, Gerald William *religious organization administrator*
Chedid, John G. *bishop*
Cravens, Virginia Lee *church official*
Fitzgerald, Tikhon (Lee R. H. Fitzgerald) *bishop*
Freehling, Allen Isaac *rabbi*
Helms, Harold Edwin *minister*
Holland, John Ray *minister*
†Jentzsch, Heber C. *church administrator*
Mahony, Roger M. Cardinal *archbishop*
Mc Pherson, Rolf Kennedy *clergyman, church official*
Milligan, Sister Mary *theology educator, religious consultant*
Neal, Joseph C., Jr. *church administrator*
Phillips, Keith Wendall *minister*
Rogers, James Wilson *church official*
Setian, Nerses Mikail *bishop, former apostolic exarchate*
Talton, Chester Lovelle *bishop*
Williams, Ronald Dean *minister, religious organization executive*
Wilson, Nancy Linda *church officer*
Wolf, Alfred *rabbi*
Wooten, Cecil Aaron *religious organization administrator*

**Malibu**
Wilson, John Francis *religion educator, educational institution administrator*

**Menlo Park**
Davis, William Emrys *religious organization official*

**Mill Valley**
Crews, William Odell, Jr. *seminary administrator*
DuBose, Francis Marquis *clergyman*

**Monrovia**
Huffey, Vinton Earl *clergyman*

**Monterey**
Ryan, Sylvester D. *bishop*
Shimpfky, Richard Lester *bishop*

**Napa**
†Trepp, Leo *rabbi*

**Oakland**
Benham, Priscilla Carla *religion educator, college president*
Crompton, Arnold *minister, educator*
Patten, Bebe Harrison *minister, chancellor*
Schomer, Howard *retired clergyman, educator, social policy consultant*

**Orange**
Janssen, Stephen Howard *clergyman*
Mc Farland, Norman Francis *bishop*

**Palm Desert**
Hunt, Barnabas John *priest, religious order administrator*
Ponder, Catherine *clergywoman*

**Palo Alto**
Brown, Robert McAfee *minister, religion educator*

**Pasadena**
Parker, Garry Otis *mission executive, missiologist*
Sano, Roy I. *bishop*
Torres, Ralph Chon *minister*

**Pittsburg**
Schmalenberger, Jerry Lew *pastor, seminary educator*

**Poway**
Dollen, Charles Joseph *clergyman, writer*

**Rancho Mirage**
Stenhouse, Everett Ray *clergy administrator*

**Redding**
Nicholas, David Robert *minister, college president*

**Redlands**
Hirsch, Charles Bronislaw *retired religion educator and administrator*

**Reedley**
Dick, Henry Henry *minister*

**Riverside**
Andersen, Frances Elizabeth Gold *religious leadership educator*

**Sacramento**
Cole, Glen David *minister*
Meier, George Karl, III *pastor, lawyer*
Quinn, Francis A. *bishop*
Venema, Jon Roger *educator, pastor*
Weigand, William Keith *bishop*

**San Anselmo**
Mudge, Lewis Seymour *theologian, educator, university dean*

**San Bernardino**
Barnes, Gerald R. *bishop*

**San Diego**
Brom, Robert H. *bishop*
Downing, David Charles *minister*
Fleischmann, Paul *youth minister*
Hughes, Gethin B. *bishop*
Owen-Towle, Carolyn Sheets *clergywoman*
Scorgie, Glen Given *religious organization leader*

**San Fernando**
Gosselin, Kenneth Stuart *minister*

**San Francisco**
Anthony, of Sourozh (Anthony Emmanuel Gergiannakis) *bishop*
Levada, William Joseph *archbishop*
Quinn, John R. *archbishop*
Rosen, Moishe *religious organization administrator*
Swing, William Edwin *bishop*

**San Jose**
Ratzlaff, Ruben Menno *religion educator, minister*

**Santa Barbara**
Campbell, Robert Charles *clergyman, religious organization administrator*
Moholy, Noel Francis *clergyman*

**Santa Clara**
DuMaine, R. Pierre *bishop*

**Santa Monica**
Hearn, Charles Virgil *minister*

**Santa Rosa**
Ziemann, G. Patrick *bishop*

**Sebastopol**
DeMartini, Rodney J. *executive director religious organization, priest*

**Simi Valley**
Witman, Frank McConnell *clergyman, educator*

**Solana Beach**
Friedman, Maurice Stanley *religious educator*
Gilliam, Vincent Carver *religion educator, minister, writer*

**Solvang**
Chandler, E(dwin) Russell *clergyman, author*

**South Lake Tahoe**
Null, Paul Bryan *minister*

**South Pasadena**
Castellano, Pasquale Allen *clergyman, marriage, family and child counselor*

**Stanford**
Harvey, Van Austin *religious studies educator*

**Stockton**
Montrose, Donald W. *bishop*

**Tustin**
Crouch, Paul Franklin *minister, church official*
Dearborn, Edwin Whittier *religious organization administrator, clergyman*

**Vallejo**
McGowan, Thomas Randolph *religious organization executive*

**Vista**
Rader, Paul Alexander *minister, administrator*

**West Hollywood**
Eastman, Donald *church officer*
Eger, Denise Leese *rabbi*
Perry, Troy D. *clergyman, church administrator*

**Whittier**
Connick, Charles Milo *retired religion educator, clergyman*

#### COLORADO

**Boulder**
Lester, Robert Carlton *religious studies educator*

**Colorado Springs**
Bishop, Leo Kenneth *clergyman, educator*
Fox, Douglas Allan *religion educator*
Hanifen, Richard Charles *bishop*

Mangham, R. Harold *church administrator*
Perkins, Floyd Jerry *retired theology educator*
Pickle, Joseph Wesley, Jr. *religion educator*
Sinclair, William Donald *church official, fundraising consultant, political activist, state legislator*
Wheeland, D. A. *church administrator*

**Crestone**
McNamara, William *priest*

**Denver**
Brownlee, Judith Marilyn *Wiccan priestess, psychotherapist*
Burrell, Calvin Archie *minister*
Chaput, Charles J. *archbishop*
Hayes, Edward Lee *religious organization administrator*
†Magnus, Kathy Jo *religious organization executive*
Morgan, David Forbes *minister*
Sheeran, Michael John Leo *priest, educational administrator*
Swenson, Mary Ann *bishop*
Winterrowd, William J. *bishop*

**Eaton**
Brown, Carl Mitchell *minister, engineer, geologist*

**Fort Collins**
Rolston, Holmes, III *theologian, educator, philosopher*

**Lafayette**
Short, Ray Everett *minister, sociology educator emeritus, author, lecturer*

**Lakewood**
Foster, David Mark *retired bishop*

**Louisville**
†Willette, Donald Corliss *reverend*

**Pueblo**
Tafoya, Arthur N. *bishop*

## CONNECTICUT

**Bethany**
Childs, Brevard Springs *religious educator*

**Bridgeport**
Agee, Kevin Jerome *minister*
Egan, Edward M. *bishop*
Rubenstein, Richard Lowell *theologian, educator*

**Danbury**
Malino, Jerome R. *rabbi*

**East Hartford**
Henry, Paul Eugene, Jr. *minister*
Scholsky, Martin Joseph *priest*

**Hamden**
Forman, Charles William *religious studies educator*

**Hartford**
Cronin, Daniel Anthony *archbishop*
Hart, Donald Purple *bishop*
Winter, Miriam Therese (Gloria Frances Winter) *nun, religious education educator*
Zikmund, Barbara Brown *minister, seminary president, church history educator*

**Middletown**
Crites, Stephen Decatur *religion educator*

**New Canaan**
Pickering, William Todd *minister*

**New Haven**
Brewer, Charles H., Jr. *bishop*
Dittes, James Edward *psychology of religion educator*
Kavanagh, Aidan Joseph *priest, university educator*
Keck, Leander Earl *theology educator*
Malherbe, Abraham Johannes, VI *religion educator, writer*
Meeks, Wayne A. *religious studies educator*
Sanneh, Lamin *religion educator*
Weinstein, Stanley *Buddhist studies educator*

**New Milford**
Johnson, Robert Clyde *theology educator*

**Newington**
Seddon, John Thomas, III *theologian, business consultant, educator*

**Norwich**
Hart, Daniel Anthony *bishop*

**Stamford**
Morse, Jonathan Kent *religious organization administrator*

**Torrington**
Kucharek, Wilma Samuella *minister*

**Woodstock**
Allaby, Stanley Reynolds *clergyman*

## DELAWARE

**New Castle**
Blackshear, L. T., Sr. *bishop*

**Newark**
Armour, Clifford Arnett, Jr. *minister*

**Wilmington**
Gewirtz, Leonard Benjamin *rabbi*
Grenz, Linda L. *Episcopal priest*
Harris, Robert Laird *minister, theology educator emeritus*
Linderman, Jeanne Herron *priest*
Tennis, Calvin Cabell *bishop*

## DISTRICT OF COLUMBIA

**Washington**
Allen, William Jere *minister*
Anderson, Carl Albert *theology school dean, lawyer*
Bentley, Carl *minister*
Burke, John *priest*
Cacciavillan, Agostino *archbishop*
Cenkner, William *religion educator, academic administrator*
†Clearfield, Sidney *religious organization executive*
Colson, Charles Wendell *lay minister, writer*
Di Lella, Alexander Anthony *biblical studies educator*
Dugan, Robert Perry, Jr. *minister, religious organization administrator*
Dunn, James Milton *religious organization administrator*
Fitzmyer, Joseph Augustine *theology educator, priest*
Godsey, John Drew *minister, theology educator emeritus*
Gros, Jeffrey *ecumenical theologian*
Haines, Ronald H. *bishop*
Harvey, Louis-Charles *minister, seminary president, religion educator*
Haught, John Francis *theology educator*
Hellwig, Monika Konrad *theology educator*
Hickey, James Aloysius Cardinal *archbishop*
Hicks, Sherman Gregory *pastor*
Hotchkin, John Francis *church official, priest*
Hug, James Edward *religious organization administrator*
Irwin, Paul Garfield *former minister, humane society executive*
Jansen, E. Harold *bishop*
Jensen, Joseph (Norman) *priest, educator*
Kane, Annette Pieslak *religious organization executive*
Lynn, Barry William *religious organization executive*
May, Felton Edwin *bishop*
Mc Lean, George Francis *philosophy of religion educator, clergyman*
Metz, Ronald Irwin *retired priest, addictions counselor*
Miller, Mary Hotchkiss *lay worker*
Moore, Jerry *religious organization administrator*
Novak, Michael (John) *religion educator, author, editor*
†Pitts, Tyrone S. *reverend*
Rabinowitz, Stanley Samuel *rabbi*
Saperstein, Marc Eli *religious history educator, rabbi*
Stookey, Laurence Hull *clergyman, theology educator*
Trisco, Robert Frederick *church historian, educator*
Wogaman, John Philip *minister, educator*

## FLORIDA

**Boca Raton**
Agler, Richard Dean *rabbi*
Sarna, Nahum Mattathias *biblical studies educator*
Silver, Samuel Manuel *rabbi, author*

**Clearwater**
Van Dine, Paul Edwin *clergyman*

**Daytona Beach**
Bronson, Oswald Perry *religious organization administrator, clergyman*

**Deland**
Fant, Clyde Edward, Jr. *religion educator*

**Fernandina Beach**
Hildebrand, Richard Allen *retired bishop*

**Fort Lauderdale**
Eynon, Steven Scott *minister*
Gerstner, Jonathan Neil *religious studies educator*
Skiddell, Elliot Lewis *rabbi*

**Fort Myers**
Koehler, Robert Brien *priest*
Massa, Conrad Harry *religious studies educator*

**Fort Pierce**
Garment, Robert James *clergyman*

**Gainesville**
Creel, Austin Bowman *religion educator*

**Jacksonville**
Bartholomew, John Niles *church administrator*
Blackburn, Robert McGrady *retired bishop*
Kensey, Calvin D. *bishop*
Reed, Loy Wayne *minister, ministry director*
Vines, Charles Jerry *minister*

**Jupiter**
McCall, Duke Kimbrough *clergyman*

**Longwood**
Dalles, John Allan *minister*
Hunter, Joel Carl *clergyman, educator*

**Miami**
Beatty, Robert Clinton *religious studies educator*
Cohen, Jacob *bishop*
Favalora, John Clement *bishop*
Fitzgerald, John Thomas, Jr. *religious studies educator*
Hoy, William Ivan *minister, religion educator*
Lehrman, Irving *rabbi*
Schofield, Calvin Onderdonk, Jr. *bishop*
Weeks, Marta Joan *priest*

**New Port Richey**
Sorensen, John Frederick *retired minister*

**New Smyrna Beach**
Hollis, Reginald *archbishop*

**Orlando**
Dorsey, Norbert M. *bishop*
Gokee, Donald LeRoy *clergyman, author*
Grady, Thomas J. *bishop*
Howe, John Wadsworth *bishop*
O'Farrell, Mark Theodore *religious organization administrator*

**Pace**
Sumrall, Kenneth Irvin *religious organization administrator*

**Palm Beach Gardens**
Symons, J. Keith *bishop*

**Penney Farms**
Bronkema, Frederick Hollander *retired minister and church official*

**Pensacola**
Duvall, Charles Farmer *bishop*
Mountcastle, William Wallace, Jr. *philosophy and religion educator*

**Plant City**
Patronelli, Raymond *church administrator*

**Plymouth**
Voelker, Charles Robert *archbishop, academic dean*

**Saint Petersburg**
Harris, Rogers S. *bishop*
Harris, Rogers Sanders *bishop*

**Sarasota**
Beal, Winona Roark *retired church administrator*

**Spring Hill**
Slaattè, Howard Alexander *minister, philosophy educator*

**Tampa**
Biles, (Lee) Thomas *religious organization executive, clergyman*
Davis, W. E. *clergyman, bishop*
Franzen, Lavern Gerhard *bishop*
Neusner, Jacob *humanities and religious studies educator*
Pope, Jesse Curtis *theology and religious studies educator*
Reeher, James Irwin *minister*

**Venice**
Nevins, John J. *bishop*

**Wellington**
Knudsen, Raymond Barnett *clergyman, association executive, author*

**West Palm Beach**
Nolan, Richard Thomas *clergyman, educator*

**Winter Park**
Armstrong, (Arthur) James *minister, religion educator, religious organization executive, consultant*
Britton, Erwin Adelbert *clergyman, college administrator*
Edge, Findley Bartow *clergyman, religious education educator*
Johnson, Constance Ann Trillich *minister, librarian, educator, internet service provider, small business owner, writer, researcher, lecturer*

**Zellwood**
Wallcraft, Mary Jane Louise *religious organization executive, songwriter, author*

## GEORGIA

**Atlanta**
Allan, Frank Kellog *bishop*
Cannon, William Ragsdale *bishop*
Donoghue, John Frances *archbishop*
Dunahoo, Charles *religious publisher, religious organization administrator, consultant, human resource director*
Gilchrist, Paul R. *religious organization administrator*
Hunter, Douglas Lee *religious organization administrator*
McMaster, Belle Miller *religious organization administrator*
Morris, Robert Renly *minister, clinical pastoral education supervisor*
Parks, R(obert) Keith *missionary, religious organization administrator*
Skillrud, Harold Clayton *minister*
Stokes, Mack (Marion) Boyd *bishop*
Sutherland, Raymond Carter *clergyman, English educator emeritus*
Westerhoff, John Henry, III *clergyman, theologian, educator*
White, Gayle Colquitt *religion writer, journalist*
Williams, W. Clyde *religious organization administrator*

**Brunswick**
Zbiegien, Andrea *religious education educator, consultant, educational administrator*

**Decatur**
Gericke, Paul William *minister, educator*
Hale, Cynthia Lynette *religious organization administrator*

**Macon**
Alexander, David Lee *clergyman*
Looney, Richard Carl *bishop*

**Metter**
Guido, Michael Anthony *evangelist*

**Norcross**
Kyle, John Emery *mission executive*

**Riverdale**
Waters, John W. *minister, educator*

**Roswell**
Sanks, Charles Randolph, Jr. *minister, psychotherapist*

**Savannah**
Boland, John K. *bishop*
Lessard, Raymond William *bishop*

**Woodstock**
Collins, David Browning *religious institution administrator*

## HAWAII

**Honolulu**
DiLorenzo, Francis X. *bishop*
Russi, John Joseph *priest, educational administrator*

**Ocean View**
Gilliam, Jackson Earle *bishop*

## IDAHO

**Boise**
Brown, Tod David *bishop*
Caufield, Marie Celine *religious organization administrator*
Thornton, John S., IV *bishop*

## ILLINOIS

**Arlington Heights**
Dickau, John C. *religious organization executive*
†Ricker, Robert S. *religious organization administrator*

**Bartlett**
Robinson, Jack F(ay) *clergyman*

**Belleville**
Gregory, Wilton D. *bishop*

**Bensenville**
Matera, Richard Ernest *minister*

**Bloomington**
Gerike, Ernest Luther *clergyman*

**Cairo**
Cobb, J. *bishop*

**Chicago**
Almen, Lowell Gordon *church official*
†Anderson, Hugh George *bishop*
Bacher, Robert Newell *church official*
Banks, Deirdre Margaret *church organization administrator*
Barbour, Claude Marie *minister*
Baumhart, Raymond Charles *Roman Catholic church administrator*
Betz, Hans Dieter *theology educator*
Bevan, Norman Edward *religious organization executive*
Browning, Don Spencer *religion educator*
Campbell, Edward Fay, Jr. *religion educator*
Doniger, Wendy *history of religions educator*
Farrakhan, Louis *religious leader*
Fortune, Michael Joseph *religion educator*
George, Francis *bishop*
Griswold, Frank Tracy, III *bishop*
Hefner, Philip James *theologian*
Homans, Peter *psychology and religious studies educator*
Inskeep, Kenneth W. *church administrator*
James, A. Lincoln, Sr. *minister, religious organization executive*
Larsen, Paul Emanuel *religious organization administrator*
LeFevre, Perry Deyo *minister, theology educator*
Lotocky, Innocent Hilarius *bishop*
Marshall, Cody *bishop*
Marty, Martin Emil *religion educator, editor*
McAuliffe, Richard L. *church official*
McCloskey, Guy Corbett *Buddhist religious leader*
McGinn, Bernard John *religious educator*
Miller, Charles S. *clergy member, church administrator*
Minnick, Malcolm L., Jr. *clergy member, church administrator*
Rajan, Fred E. N. *clergy member, church administrator*
Reynolds, Frank Everett *religious studies educator*
Rodriguez, David G., Jr. *art and religion educator, priest*
Schroeder, W(illiam) Widick *religion educator*
Schupp, Ronald Irving *clergyman, civil rights leader*
Shafer, Eric Christopher *minister*
Sherwin, Byron Lee *religion educator, college official*
Simon, Mordecai *religious association administrator, clergyman*
Sorensen, W. Robert *clergy member, church administrator*
Thurston, Stephen John *pastor*
Tracy, David *theology educator*
Trexler, Edgar Ray *minister, editor*
Wagner, Joseph M. *church administrator*
Wall, James McKendree *minister, editor*
Wiwchar, Michael *bishop*
Yu, Anthony C. *religion and literature educator*

**Decatur**
Morgan, E. A. *church administrator*

**Deerfield**
Larsen, Samuel Harry *minister, educator*

**Elburn**
Liechty, Eric *church administrator*

**Elgin**
Deeter, Joan G. *church administrator*
Miller, Donald Eugene *minister, educator*
Minnich, Dale E. *religious administrator*
Myers, Anne M. *church administrator*
Nolen, Wilfred E. *church administrator*
Ratthahao, Sisouphanh *minister*
Ziegler, Earl Keller *minister*

**Eureka**
Steffer, Robert Wesley *clergyman*

**Evanston**
Fisher, Neal Floyd *religious organization administrator*

Sisk, Mark Sean *priest, seminary dean, religious educator*
Walker, Harold Blake *minister*

**Evergreen Park**
Smith, Lawrence J. *bishop*

**Flossmoor**
Walker, George W. *bishop*

**Freeport**
Hunter, Georgia L. *clergywoman*

**Joliet**
Imesch, Joseph Leopold *bishop*
Kaffer, Roger Louis *bishop*

**Lincoln**
Wilson, Robert Allen *religion educator*

**Moline**
Johnson, Mary Lou *lay worker*

**Naperville**
Landwehr, Arthur John *minister*

**Oak Park**
Cary, William Sterling *retired church executive*
Hallstrand, Sarah Laymon *denomination executive*

**Palos Heights**
Nederhood, Joel H. *church organization executive, minister, retired*

**Peoria**
Myers, John Joseph *bishop*
Parsons, Donald James *retired bishop*

**Rock Island**
Bergendoff, Conrad John Immanuel *clergyman*

**Rockford**
Doran, Thomas George *bishop*
Hasley, Ronald K. *bishop*
Weissbard, David Raymond *minister*

**Springfield**
Ryan, Daniel Leo *bishop*

**Summit Argo**
Abramowicz, Alfred L. *retired bishop*

**Thornton**
Braico, Carmella Elizabeth Lofrano *clergy member*

**University Park**
McClellan, Larry Allen *educator, writer*

**Wheaton**
Estep, John Hayes *religious denomination executive, clergyman*
Pappas, Barbara E. *Biblical studies educator, author*

## INDIANA

**Anderson**
Conrad, Harold August *retired religious pension board executive*
Dale, Doris *religious organization executive*
Dye, Dwight Latimer *minister*
Grubbs, J. Perry *church administrator*
Hayes, Sherrill D. *religious organization administrator*
Lawson, David Lewis *religious organization administrator, minister*
Massey, James Earl *clergyman, educator*

**Elkhart**
Oltz, Richard John *minister, publishing executive*

**Evansville**
Hoy, George Philip *clergyman, food bank executive*

**Fort Wayne**
Bunkowske, Eugene Walter *religious studies educator*
D'Arcy, John Michael *bishop*
Fry, Charles George *theologian, educator*
Mann, David William *minister*
Mather, George Ross *clergy member*
Moran, John *religious organization administrator*
Stucky, Ken *clergy member, church organization administrator, foundation executive*

**Gary**
Gaughan, Norbert F. *bishop*

**Greencastle**
Lamar, Martha Lee *chaplain*

**Huntington**
Seilhamer, Ray A. *bishop*

**Indianapolis**
Austin, Spencer Peter *minister*
Bates, Gerald Earl *bishop*
Behar, Lucien E. *church administrator*
Brannon, Ronald Roy *minister*
Bray, Donald Lawrence *religious organization executive, minister*
Buechlein, Daniel Mark *archbishop*
Cassel, Herbert William *religion educator*
Castle, Howard Blaine *religious organization administrator*
Crow, Paul Abernathy, Jr. *clergyman, religious council executive, educator*
Dickinson, Richard Donald Nye *clergyman, educator, theological seminary administrator*
Ellis, Carollyn *religious organization administrator*
Ellis, Raymond W. *religious organization executive, consultant*
Foulkes, John R. *minister*
Grant, Claudia Ewing *minister*
Haines, Lee Mark, Jr. *religious denomination administrator*
Hamm, Richard L. *church administrator*
Johnson, James P. *religious organization executive*
Kempski, Ralph Aloisius *bishop*

Manworren, Donald B. *church administrator*
Nzeyimana, Noah *bishop*
Page, Curtis Matthewson *minister*
Plaster, George Francis *Roman Catholic priest*
Polston, Mark Franklin *minister*
Riemenschneider, Dan LaVerne *religious organization administrator*
Sindlinger, Verne E. *bishop*
Updegraff Spleth, Ann L. *church executive, pastor*
Watkins, Harold Robert *minister*
Welsh, Robert K. *relgious organization executive*
Wilson, Earle Lawrence *church administrator*
Woodring, DeWayne Stanley *religion association executive*

**Kokomo**
Hall, Milton L. *bishop*
Ungerer, Walter John *minister*

**Lafayette**
Higi, William L. *bishop*

**Marion**
McFarlane, Neil *church administrator*
McIntyre, Robert Walter *church official*

**Noblesville**
Wilson, Norman Glenn *church administrator, writer*

**Notre Dame**
Blenkinsopp, Joseph *biblical studies educator*
Hesburgh, Theodore Martin *clergyman, former university president*
Malloy, Edward Aloysius *priest, university administrator, educator*
McBrien, Richard Peter *theology educator*
McCormick, Richard Arthur *priest, religion educator, writer*
O'Meara, Thomas Franklin *priest, educator*
White, James Floyd *theology educator*

**Richmond**
Maurer, Johan Fredrik *religious denomination administrator*
Roop, Eugene Frederic *religion educator*

**Rochester**
Merrill, Arthur Lewis *retired theology educator*

**South Bend**
Gray, Francis Campbell *bishop*
Gray, Frank C. *bishop*

**Veedersburg**
Marshall, Carolyn Ann M. *church official, consultant*

**Winona Lake**
Ashman, Charles H. *retired minister*
Davis, John James *religion educator*
Julien, Thomas Theodore *religious denomination administrator*
Lewis, Edward Alan *religious organization adminstrator*

## IOWA

**Ankeny**
Hartog, John, II *theology educator, librarian*

**Cedar Rapids**
Barta, James Omer *priest, psychology educator, church administrator*

**Davenport**
O'Keefe, Gerald Francis *bishop, retired*

**Decorah**
Farwell, Elwin D. *minister, educational consultant*

**Des Moines**
Charron, Joseph L. *bishop*
Epting, C. Christopher *bishop*
Jordan, Charles Wesley *bishop*

**Dubuque**
Drummond, Richard Henry *religion educator*
Hanus, Jerome George *archbishop*
Pike, George Harold, Jr. *religious organization executive, clergyman*

**Grinnell**
Mitchell, Orlan E. *clergyman, former college president*

**Iowa City**
Baird, Robert Dahlen *religious educator*
Bayne, David Cowan *priest, legal scholar, law educator*
Forell, George Wolfgang *religion educator*
Holstein, Jay Allen *Judaic studies educator*

**Middle Amana**
Setzer, Kirk *religious leader*

**Orange City**
Scorza, Sylvio Joseph *religion educator*

**Sioux City**
Soens, Lawrence D. *bishop*

**Storm Lake**
Miller, Curtis Herman *bishop*

## KANSAS

**Copeland**
Birney, Walter Leroy *religious administrator*

**Dodge City**
Schlarman, Stanley Gerard *bishop*

**Goodland**
Ross, Chester Wheeler *retired clergyman, consultant*

**Kansas City**
Forst, Marion Francis *bishop*
Strecker, Ignatius J. *archbishop*

**Leavenworth**
McGilley, Sister Mary Janet *nun, educator, writer, academic administrator*

**North Newton**
Fast, Darrell Wayne *minister*
Preheim, Vern Quincy *religious organization administrator, minister*

**Salina**
Fitzsimons, George K. *bishop*

**Shawnee Mission**
Holter, Don Wendell *retired bishop*
Olsen, Stanley Severn *minister*

**Topeka**
†Gauger, Randy Jay *minister*
Mutti, Albert Frederick *minister*
Smalley, William Edward *bishop*

**Wichita**
Armstrong, Hart Reid *minister, editor, publisher*
Essey, Basil *bishop*
Gerber, Eugene J. *bishop*

## KENTUCKY

**Crestwood**
Roy, Elmon Harold *minister*

**Erlanger**
†Muench, Robert W. *bishop*

**Frankfort**
Hestand, Joel Dwight *minister, evangelist*

**Lexington**
Landon, John William *minister, social worker, educator*
Williams, James Kendrick *bishop*

**Louisville**
Dale, Judy Ries *religious organization administrator*
Goff, Jim *religious organization administrator*
Granady, Juanita H. *religious organization administrator*
Jenkins, C(arle) Frederick *religious organization executive, minister, lawyer*
Kelly, Thomas Cajetan *archbishop*
Miller, John Ulman *minister, author*
Reed, David Benson *bishop*
Wingenbach, Gregory Charles *priest, religious-ecumenical agency director*
Zimmerman, Gideon K. *minister*

**Owensboro**
McRaith, John Jeremiah *bishop*

**Pineville**
Whittaker, Bill Douglas *minister*

**Wilmore**
Kinlaw, Dennis Franklin *clergyman, society executive*

## LOUISIANA

**Alexandria**
Hargrove, Robert Jefferson, Jr. *bishop*

**Baton Rouge**
Hughes, Alfred Clifton *bishop*
Jemison, Theodore Judson *religious organization administrator*
Swaggart, Jimmy Lee *evangelist, gospel singer*
Witcher, Robert Campbell *bishop*

**Deridder**
Mackey, Jeffrey Allen *minister*

**Donaldsonville**
Watson, Stanley Ellis *clergyman, financial company executive*

**Greenwood**
Scudder, Robert *minister, youth home administrator*

**Harvey**
Romagosa, Elmo Lawrence *clergyman, retired editor*

**Houma**
Jarrell, Charles Michael *bishop*

**Lafayette**
O'Donnell, Edward Joseph *bishop, former editor*

**Lake Charles**
Speyrer, Jude *bishop*

**New Iberia**
Henton, Willis Ryan *bishop*

**New Orleans**
Brown, James Barrow *bishop*
Schulte, Francis B. *archbishop*
Stovall, Gerald Thomas *religious organization administrator*
Truehill, Marshall, Jr. *minister*

**Pineville**
Boswell, Bill Reeser *religious organization executive*

**Ragley**
Magee, Thomas Eston, Jr. *minister*

**Shreveport**
Friend, William Benedict *bishop*
Jones, Ernest Edward *minister, religious organization administrator*

Webb, Donald Arthur *minister*

**Tioga**
Tenney, Tom Fred *bishop*

## MAINE

**Bangor**
Turner, Marta Dawn *youth program specialist*

**Brunswick**
Geoghegan, William Davidson *religion educator, minister*

**Friendship**
Du Bois, Clarence Hazel, Jr. *clergy member*

**Hancock**
Truitt, Charlotte Frances *clergywoman*

**Leeds**
Lynn, Robert Wood *theologian, educator, dean*

**Lewiston**
Baxter, William MacNeil *priest*

**Portland**
Gerry, Joseph John *bishop*
O'Leary, Edward Cornelius *former bishop*

**South Bristol**
Lasher, Esther Lu *minister*

**Yarmouth**
Hopkins, Harold Anthony, Jr. *bishop*

## MARYLAND

**Baltimore**
Houck, John Roland *clergyman*
Macleod, Donald *clergyman, educator*
Mocko, George Paul *minister*
Murphy, Philip Francis *bishop*
Newman, William C. *bishop*
O'Leary, David Michael *priest, educator*
Ricard, John H. *bishop, educator*
Strickland, Marshall Hayward *bishop*
Zaiman, Joel Hirsh *rabbi*

**Bethesda**
Corbett, Jack Elliott *clergyman, retired foundation administrator, author*

**Catonsville**
Hammond, Deborah Lynn *lay worker*
Wynn, John Charles *clergyman, retired religion educator*

**Columbia**
Freeman, Joel Arthur *behavioral consultant*

**Ellicott City**
Veasel, Walter *minister, educator*

**Emmitsburg**
Obloy, Leonard Gerard *priest*

**Forestville**
Payne, Paula Marie *minister*

**Gaithersburg**
Hall, Arthur Raymond, Jr. *minister*
Rupert, (Lynn) Hoover *minister*

**Hagerstown**
Coles, Robert Nelson, Sr. *religious organization administrator*
Hamby, Jim Leon *pastor*

**Hyattsville**
Dimino, Joseph T. *archbishop*

**Landover**
Drahmann, Brother Theodore *religious order official*

**Parsonsburg**
Feeney, Edward Charles Patrick *minister, psychologist, writer, composer*

**Pikesville**
Davis, Esther Yvonne Butler *religious studies educator*

**Rockville**
Meade, Kenneth Albert *minister*

**Sandy Spring**
Moulton, Phillips Prentice *religion and philosophy educator*

**Silver Spring**
Beach, Bert Beverly *clergyman*
Beckmann, David Milton *minister, economist, social activist*
Doerr, Edd *religious liberty organization administrator*
Oliver, Wilbert Henry *religious organization administrator*
Thompson, George Ralph *church administrator*

## MASSACHUSETTS

**Amherst**
Wills, David Wood *minister, educator*

**Auburn**
Bachelder, Robert Stephen *minister*

**Boston**
Barry, William Anthony *priest, writer*
Harris, Barbara C(lementine) *bishop*
Harris, Virginia Sydness *publisher, educator*

Katz, Steven Theodore *religious studies educator*
Kessler, Diane Cooksey *religious organization administrator, minister*
Korff, Yitzchok Aharon *rabbi*
Mason, Herbert Warren, Jr. *religion and history educator, author*
Nesmith, Richard Duey *clergyman, theology educator*
Williams, Rhys *minister*
Worthley, Harold Field *minister, educator*

**Boston College**
Helmick, Raymond G. *priest, educator*

**Brewster**
Coburn, John Bowen *retired bishop*

**Brighton**
Law, Bernard Francis Cardinal *archbishop*

**Brockton**
Holland, David Vernon *minister*

**Brookfield**
Kring, Walter Donald *minister*

**Brookline**
Newman, Thomas Daniel *minister, school administrator*

**Cambridge**
Fiorenza, Francis P. *religion educator*
Gomes, Peter John *clergyman, educator*
Graham, William Albert *religion educator, history educator*
Gyger, Terrell Lee *minister*
Kaufman, Gordon Dester *theology educator*
Koester, Helmut Heinrich *theologian, educator*
Potter, Ralph Benajah, Jr. *theology and social ethics educator*
Schuessler Fiorenza, Elisabeth *theology educator*
Shaw, M. Thomas, III *bishop*
Williams, George Huntston *church historian, educator*
Williams, Preston Noah *theology educator*

**Chestnut Hill**
Mc Innes, William Charles *priest, campus ministry director*

**Dedham**
Spoolstra, Linda Carol *minister, educator, religious organization administrator*

**Fall River**
O'Malley, Sean *bishop*

**Gloucester**
Braver, Barbara Leix *religious organization communications administrator*

**Harvard**
Sutherland, Malcolm Read, Jr. *clergyman, educator*

**Hyde Park**
Riley, Lawrence Joseph *bishop*

**Lexington**
Schultz, Samuel Jacob *clergyman, educator*

**Longmeadow**
Hasty, Richard Spencer *minister*
Stewart, Alexander Doig *bishop*

**Marlborough**
Lohr, Harold Russell *bishop*

**Natick**
†Kushner, Harold Samuel *rabbi*

**Newton**
Capon, Edwin Gould *church organization administrator, clergyman*
Deats, Paul Kindred, Jr. *religion educator, clergyman*

**Northampton**
Derr, Thomas Sieger *religion educator*
Donfried, Karl Paul *minister, theology educator*
Flesher, Hubert Louis *religion educator*
Unsworth, Richard Preston *minister, school administrator*

**Pepperell**
Holmes, Reed M. *clergyman, historian, photographer*

**South Easton**
Clarke, Cornelius Wilder *religious organization administrator, minister*

**South Hamilton**
Kalland, Lloyd Austin *minister*

**Springfield**
†Dupre, Thomas L. *bishop*

**Waltham**
Delaney, Mary Anne *pastoral educator*
Johnson, William Alexander *clergyman, philosophy educator*
Murray, Pius Charles William *priest, educator*
Reisman, Bernard *theology educator*

**West Newton**
Elya, John Adel *bishop*

**West Stockbridge**
Stokes, Allison *pastor, researcher, religion educator*

**Williamstown**
Eusden, John Dykstra *theology educator, minister*

**Worcester**
Isaksen, Robert L. *bishop*
Parsons, Edwin Spencer *clergyman, educator*
Reilly, Daniel Patrick *bishop*

## MICHIGAN

**Berrien Springs**
Andreasen, Niels-Erik Albinus *religious educator*

**Detroit**
Adams, Charles Gilchrist *pastor*
Anderson, Moses B. *bishop*
Gumbleton, Thomas J. *bishop*
Hardon, John Anthony *priest, research educator*
Maida, Adam Joseph Cardinal *cardinal*
Mc Gehee, H(arry) Coleman, Jr. *bishop*
Ross, Mary O. *religious organization administrator*
Ursache, Victorin (His Eminence The Most Reverend Archbishop Victorin) *archbishop*
Vigneron, Allen Henry *theology educator, rector, auxiliary bishop*
Willingham, Edward Bacon, Jr. *ecumenical minister, administrator*
Wood, R. Stewart *bishop*

**East Lansing**
Shaw, Robert Eugene *minister, administrator*

**Eastpointe**
Andrzejewski, Darryl Lee *clergyman*

**Farmington**
Pittelko, Roger Dean *clergyman*
Wine, Sherwin Theodore *rabbi*

**Farmington Hills**
Plaut, Jonathan Victor *rabbi*

**Ferndale**
Dunn, Elwood *minister*

**Flint**
McClanahan, Connie Dea *pastoral minister*
Meissner, Suzanne Banks *pastoral associate*

**Gaylord**
Cooney, Patrick Ronald *bishop*

**Grand Rapids**
Anderson, Roger Gordon *minister*
Babcock, Wendell Keith *religion educator*
Beeke, Joel Robert *minister, theology educator, writer*
Borgdorff, Peter *church adminstrator*
Brink, William P. *clergyman*
DeHaan, John *religious organization administrator*
DeVries, Robert K. *religious book publisher*
Hofman, Leonard John *minister*
Hollies, Linda Hall *pastor, educator, author, publisher*
Rozeboom, John A. *religious organization administrator*
Schwanda, Tom *religious studies educator*

**Grass Lake**
Popp, Nathaniel *bishop*

**Grosse Pointe**
Canfield, Francis Xavier *priest, English language educator*

**Holland**
Cook, James Ivan *clergyman, religion educator*
Hesselink, I(ra) John, Jr. *theology educator*

**Jackson**
Nathaniel *bishop*

**Kalamazoo**
Lee, Edward L. *bishop*

**Livonia**
Davis, Lawrence Edward *church official*
Hess, Bartlett Leonard *clergyman*
Hess, Margaret Johnston *religious writer, educator*

**Marquette**
Burt, John Harris *bishop*
Garland, James H. *bishop*
Ray, Thomas Kreider *bishop*
Skogman, Dale R. *bishop*

**Pinckney**
Hernandez, Ramon Robert *clergyman, librarian*

**Saginaw**
Untener, Kenneth E. *bishop*
Williams, Herbert J. *bishop*

**Southfield**
Ibrahim, Ibrahim N. *bishop*
Priest, Ruth Emily *music minister, choir director, composer arranger*

**Spring Arbor**
Dillman, Charles Norman *religion educator*
Thompson, Stanley B. *church administrator*

## MINNESOTA

**Alexandria**
Hultstrand, Donald Maynard *bishop*

**Bloomington**
McDill, Thomas Allison *minister*
Thomas, Margaret Jean *clergywoman, religious research consultant*

**Chisago City**
Bergstrand, Wilton Everet *minister*

**Cottage Grove**
Hudnut, Robert Kilborne *clergyman, author*

**Crookston**
Balke, Victor H. *bishop*

**Duluth**
Aadland, Thomas Vernon *minister*
Schwietz, Roger L. *bishop*

**Edina**
Putnam, Frederick Warren, Jr. *bishop*

**Fergus Falls**
Egge, Joel *clergy member, academic administrator*
Jahr, Armin *clergy member, church administrator*
Overgaard, Robert Milton *religious organization administrator*

**Little Falls**
Zirbes, Mary Kenneth *social justice ministry coordinator*

**Mankato**
Orvick, George Myron *church denomination executive, minister*

**Minneapolis**
Brown, Laurence David *retired bishop*
Cedar, Paul Arnold *church executive, minister*
†Corts, John Ronald *minister, religious organization executive*
Ferm, Lois Roughan *religious organization administrator*
Fleischer, Daniel *minister, religious organization administrator*
Graham, William Franklin (Billy Graham) *evangelist*
Hamel, William John *church administrator, minister*
Johnson, Larry Dean *religious organization executive, minister*
Lee, Robert Lloyd *pastor, religious association executive*
Lindberg, Duane R. *minister, historian, church body administrator*
Miller, William Alvin *clergyman, author, lecturer*
Palms, Roger Curtis *religious magazine editor, clergyman*
Swatsky, Ben *church administrator*
Wang, L. Edwin *church official*

**New Ulm**
Lucker, Raymond Alphonse *bishop*

**Northfield**
Crouter, Richard Earl *religion educator*
Knutson, Gerhard I. *retired bishop*

**Preston**
Schommer, Trudy Marie *pastoral minister, religion education*

**Robbinsdale**
Be Vier, William A. *religious studies educator*

**Rochester**
Hudson, Winthrop Still *minister, history educator*
Nycklemoe, Glenn Winston *bishop*

**Saint Paul**
Flynn, Harry Joseph *bishop*
Hopper, David Henry *religion educator*
McMillan, Mary Bigelow *retired minister, volunteer*
Preus, David Walter *bishop, minister*
Roach, John Robert *retired archbishop*

**South Saint Paul**
Koenig, Robert August *clergyman, educator*

## MISSISSIPPI

**Biloxi**
Howze, Joseph Lawson Edward *bishop*

**Clinton**
Hensley, John Clark *religious organization administrator, minister*

**Gulfport**
Freret, René Joseph *minister*

**Indianola**
Matthews, David *clergyman*

**Jackson**
Allin, John Maury *bishop*
Gray, Duncan Montgomery, Jr. *retired bishop*
Houck, William Russell *bishop*
McKnight, William Edwin *minister*

**Kosciusko**
Kearley, F. Furman *minister, religious educator, magazine editor*

**Long Beach**
Horton, Jerry Smith *minister*

**Meridian**
Lindstrom, Donald Fredrick, Jr. *priest*

**Myrtle**
Pirkle, Estus Washington *minister*

**Starkville**
MacLeod, John Daniel, Jr. *religious organization administrator*

**Stringer**
Gordon, Granville Hollis *church official*

## MISSOURI

**Bridgeton**
Asma, Lawrence Francis *priest*

**Excelsior Springs**
Mitchell, Earl Wesley *clergyman*

**Fayette**
Keeling, Joe Keith *religion educator, college vice president and dean*

**Hazelwood**
Rose, Joseph Hugh *clergyman*
Urshan, Nathaniel Andrew *minister, church administrator*

**Highlandville**
Pruter, Karl Hugo *bishop*

**Independence**
Booth, Paul Wayne *retired minister*
Hansen, Francis Eugene *minister*
Lindgren, A(lan) Bruce *church administrator*
Sheehy, Howard Sherman, Jr. *minister*
Swails, Norman E. *church officer*
Tyree, Alan Dean *clergyman*

**Jefferson City**
Kelley, Patrick Michael *minister, state legislator*
King, Robert Henry *minister, church denomination executive, former educator*
Mc Auliffe, Michael F. *bishop*

**Joplin**
Gee, James David *minister*
Minor, Ronald Ray *minister*
Wilson, Aaron Martin *religious studies educator, college executive*

**Kansas City**
Boland, Raymond James *bishop*
Bowers, Curtis Ray, Jr. *chaplain*
Brannon, Wilbur *church administrator*
Cloud, Randall R. *church administrator*
†Cunningham, Paul George *minister*
†Diehl, James Harvey *church administrator*
Estep, Michael R. *church administrator*
Frank, Eugene Maxwell *bishop*
Fullerton, Fred *church administrator*
Gray, Helen Theresa Gott *religion editor*
Hall, Miriam *church administrator*
Jenkins, Orville Wesley *retired religious administrator*
Johnson, Jerald D. *religious organization administrator*
Juarez, Martin *priest*
Knight, John Allan *clergyman, philosophy and religion educator*
Owens, Donald D. *church officer*
Prince, William J. *church officer*
Stone, Jack *religious organization administrator*
Sullivan, Bill *church administrator*
Vogel, Arthur Anton *clergyman*

**Laddonia**
Scheffler, Lewis Francis *pastor, educator, research scientist*

**Neosho**
Hargis, Billy James *minister*

**Perryville**
Fischer, James Adrian *clergyman*

**Poplar Bluff**
Black, Ronnie Delane *religious organization administrator, mayor*
Carr, Charles Louis *retired religious organization administrator*
Duncan, Leland Ray *mission administrator*

**Saint Charles**
McClintock, Eugene Jerome *minister*

**Saint Louis**
Anderson, Vinton Randolph *bishop*
Barry, A. L. *church official*
Boldt, H. James *church administrator*
†Carberry, John J. Cardinal *archbishop*
Doggett, John Nelson, Jr. *clergyman*
Haake, Arthur C. *church administrator*
Krenzke, Richard L. *church administrator, clergy member, social worker*
Mahsman, David Lawrence *religious publications editor*
Merrell, James Lee *religious editor, clergyman*
Muller, Lyle Dean *religious organization administrator*
Ong, Walter Jackson *priest, English educator, author*
O'Shoney, Glenn *church administrator*
Pfautch, Roy *minister, public affairs consultant*
Prenzlow, Elmer John-Charles, Jr. *minister*
Rigali, Justin F. *archbishop*
Rockwell, Hays Hamilton *bishop*
Rosin, Walter L. *religious organization administrator*
Ward, R. J. *bishop*
Weber, Gloria Richie *minister, retired state representative*
Wilke, LeRoy *church administrator*

**Springfield**
Baird, Robert Dean *mission director*
Cunningham, Robert Cyril *clergyman, editor*
Grams, Betty Jane *minister, educator, writer*
Trask, Thomas Edward *religious organization administrator*
Triplett, Loren O. *religious organization administrator*

**Tipton**
Wazir, Tadar Jihad *chaplain, small business owner*

## MONTANA

**Great Falls**
Milone, Anthony M. *bishop*

**Helena**
Brunett, Alexander J. *bishop*
Jones, Charles Irving *bishop*

## NEBRASKA

**Grand Island**
Mc Namara, Lawrence J. *bishop*
Zichek, Melvin Eddie *retired clergyman, educator*

**Lincoln**
Bruskewitz, Fabian W. *bishop*
Wiersbe, Warren Wendell *clergyman, author, lecturer*

**Norfolk**
Stites, Ray Dean *minister, college president*

**Omaha**
Curtiss, Elden F. *bishop*
Krotz, James Edward *bishop*
McDaniels, B. T. *bishop*
Sheehan, Daniel Eugene *bishop*
Zuerlein, Damian Joseph *priest*

**Scottsbluff**
Scovil, Larry Emery *minister*

**West Point**
Paschang, John Linus *retired bishop*

**NEVADA**

**Las Vegas**
Walsh, Daniel Francis *bishop*

**Reno**
Chrystal, William George *minister*
Savoy, Douglas Eugene *bishop, religion educator, explorer, writer*
Straling, Phillip Francis *bishop*
Walrath, Harry Rienzi *minister*
Weld, Roger Bowen *clergyman*

**NEW HAMPSHIRE**

**Center Sandwich**
Booty, John Everitt *historiographer*

**Concord**
Theuner, Douglas Edwin *bishop*

**Hanover**
Green, Ronald Michael *ethics and religious studies educator*

**Hillsboro**
Gibson, Raymond Eugene *clergyman*

**Jaffrey**
Van Ness, Patricia Wood *religious studies educator, consultant*

**Keene**
Blacketor, Paul Garber *minister*

**Loudon**
Moore, Beatrice *religious organization administrator*

**Manchester**
O'Neil, Leo E. *bishop*

**West Chesterfield**
Garinger, Louis Daniel *religion educator*

**NEW JERSEY**

**Bloomfield**
Becker, Robert Clarence *clergyman*

**Browns Mills**
McNabb, Talmadge Ford *religious organization administrator, retired military chaplain*

**Camden**
McHugh, James T. *bishop*

**Cherry Hill**
Belin, Henry A., Jr. *bishop*

**Clifton**
Rodimer, Frank Joseph *bishop*

**Englewood**
Hertzberg, Arthur *rabbi, educator*
Khouri, Antoun *church administrator*
Saliba, Philip E. *archbishop*

**Lakewood**
Levovitz, Pesach Zechariah *rabbi*
Taylor, Robert M. *minister*

**Leonia**
Fjordbotten, Alf Lee *minister*

**Liberty Corner**
Rothenberger, Jack Renninger *clergyman*

**Madison**
Yrigoyen, Charles, Jr. *church denomination executive*

**Mahwah**
Padovano, Anthony Thomas *theologian, educator*

**Metuchen**
Hughes, Edward T. *bishop*

**Monmouth Junction**
Yun, Samuel *minister, educator*

**Mullica Hill**
Demola, James, Sr. *church administrator*

**New Brunswick**
Bowden, Henry Warner *religion educator*

**Newark**
Mc Carrick, Theodore Edgar *archbishop*
McKelvey, Jack M. *bishop*
Spong, John Shelby *bishop*

**Piscataway**
Stedge-Fowler, Joyce *retired clergywoman*

**Princeton**
Allen, Diogenes *clergyman, philosophy educator*
Armstrong, Richard Stoll *minister, educator, writer, poet*
Belshaw, George Phelps Mellick *bishop*

Davies, Horton Marlais *clergyman, religion educator*
Douglass, Jane Dempsey *theology educator*
Gordon, Ernest *clergyman*
Metzger, Bruce Manning *clergyman, educator*
Miller, Patrick Dwight, Jr. *religion educator, minister*
Mulder, Edwin George *minister, church official*
West, Charles Converse *theologian, educator*

**Rutherford**
Gerety, Peter Leo *archbishop*

**Short Hills**
Pilchik, Ely Emanuel *rabbi, writer*

**South Orange**
Fleming, Edward J. *priest, educator*
Goldman, Harvey S. *therapist, rabbi*

**Summit**
May, Ernest Max *charitable organization official*

**Teaneck**
Meno, John Peter *chorepiscopus*

**Tenafly**
Stowe, David Metz *clergyman*

**Tinton Falls**
Priesand, Sally Jane *rabbi*

**Toms River**
Donaldson, Marcia Jean *lay worker*

**Trenton**
Courtney, Esau *bishop*
Medley, Alex Roy *executive minister*
Old, Hughes Oliphant *research theologian, clergyman*
Reiss, John C. *bishop*

**West Milford**
Stelpstra, William John *minister*

**West New York**
Arias, David *bishop*

**Westfield**
Gutman, Sharon Weissman *Holocaust educator, poet*

**Westville**
Doughty, A. Glenn *minister*

**Wharton**
Loughlin, William Joseph *priest, religious organization administrator*

**Willingboro**
Bass, Joseph Oscar *minister*

**NEW MEXICO**

**Albuquerque**
Griffin, W. C. *bishop*
Kelshaw, Terence *bishop*
Sheehan, Michael Jarboe *archbishop*

**Farmington**
Plummer, Steven Tsosie *bishop*

**Hobbs**
Martin, Thomas Howard *pastor*

**Las Cruces**
Ramirez, Ricardo *bishop*

**Roswell**
Pretti, Bradford Joseph *lay worker, insurance company executive*

**NEW YORK**

**Adams Center**
Hood, Thomas Gregory *minister*

**Albany**
Bowen, Mary Lu *ecumenical developer, community organizer*
Hubbard, Howard James *bishop*

**Barrytown**
Tsirpanlis, Constantine N. *theology, philosophy, classic and history educator*

**Binghamton**
Fay, Rowan Hamilton *minister*

**Bronx**
Dulles, Avery *priest, theologian*
Fahey, Charles Joseph *priest, gerontology educator*
Hennessy, Thomas Christopher *clergyman, educator, retired university dean*
McShane, Joseph Michael *priest, dean, theology educator*
Parker, Everett Carlton *clergyman*

**Bronxville**
L'Huillier, Peter (Peter) *archbishop*

**Brooklyn**
Al-Hafeez, Humza *minister, editor*
Baltakis, Paul Antanas *bishop*
Breen, Vincent de Paul *vicar, school system administrator*
Daily, Thomas V. *bishop*
Grayson, D. W. *bishop*
Sullivan, Joseph M. *bishop*
Williams, Carl E., Sr. *bishop*
Youngblood, Johnny Ray *pastor*

**Buffalo**
Jerge, Marie Charlotte *minister*
Lamb, Charles F. *minister*
†Mansell, Henry J. *bishop*

†Smith, Bennett Walker *minister*

**Canton**
O'Connor, Daniel William *retired religious studies and classical languages educator*

**Cross River**
Larsen, Lawrence Bernard, Jr. *priest, pastoral psychotherapist*

**Douglaston**
Valero, René Arnold *clergyman*

**East Aurora**
Hayes, Bonaventure Francis *priest*

**Far Rockaway**
Kelly, George Anthony *clergyman, author, educator*

**Garrison**
Egan, Daniel Francis *priest*

**Hague**
Jones, Tracey Kirk, Jr. *minister, educator*

**Hamburg**
Green, Gerard Leo *priest, educator*

**Hamilton**
Carter, John Ross *philosophy and religion educator*

**Hyde Park**
Pastrana, Ronald Ray *Christian ministry counselor, theology and biblical studies educator, former school system administrator*

**Ithaca**
Little, George Daniel *clergyman*

**Jamaica**
Clemmons, Ithiel *bishop*
Taylor, Joyce *religious organization executive*

**Lawrence**
Wurzburger, Walter Samuel *rabbi, philosophy educator*

**Lily Dale**
Merrill, Joseph Hartwell *religious association executive*
Wittich, Brenda June *religious organization executive, minister*

**Lima**
Spencer, Ivan Carlton *clergyman*

**Lindenhurst**
Hamilton, Daniel Stephen *clergyman*

**Manhasset**
Fendt, John W. *minister, religious organization administrator*
Spitz, Charles Thomas, Jr. *clergyman*

**Maryknoll**
†LaVerdiere, Claudette Marie *sister, head religious order*

**Mount Vernon**
Richardson, W. Franklyn *minister*

**New Hyde Park**
Daley, John Terence *priest*

**New Rochelle**
Kelly, James Anthony *priest*

**New York**
Ashjian, Mesrob *archbishop*
Barsamian, Khajag Sarkis *primate*
Benson, Constance Louise *religious educator*
Brown, Raymond Edward *educator, priest*
Browning, Edmond Lee *bishop*
†Campbell, Joan Brown *religious organization executive*
Cato, John David *religious organization administrator*
Chinnis, Pamela P. *religion organization administrator*
Church, Frank Forrester *minister, author, columnist*
Cohen, Samuel Israel *clergyman, organization executive*
Cone, James Hal *theologian, educator, author*
Dennis, Walter Decoster *suffragan bishop*
Donohue, William Anthony *religious organization administrator*
Driver, Tom Faw *theologian, writer, justice/peace advocate*
Geer, John Farr *religious organization administrator*
Ginsberg, Hersh Meier *rabbi, religious organization executive*
Graham, Alma Eleanor *religious magazine editor, writer, educational consultant*
Grein, Richard Frank *bishop, pastoral theology educator*
Gross, Abraham *rabbi, educator*
Habecker, Eugene Brubaker *religious association executive*
Harris, Lyndon F. *priest*
Hawley, John Stratton *religious studies educator*
Howard, M(oses) William, Jr. *minister, seminary president*
Hunt, George William *priest, magazine editor*
Iakovos, (Demetrios A. Coucouzis) *archbishop*
Johnson, Douglas Wayne *church organization official, minister*
Kazanjian, Shant *religious organization administrator*
Kreitman, Benjamin Zvi *rabbi, Judaic studies educator*
Laurus, (Laurus Skurla) *archbishop*
McGeady, Sister Mary Rose *religious organization administrator, psychologist*
McNutt, Charlie Fuller, Jr. *bishop*
McWilliam, Joanne Elizabeth *religion educator*
Miller, Israel *rabbi, university administrator*
Moore, Paul, Jr. *bishop*
Morris, Clayton Leslie *priest*
†Morton, James Parks *priest*
Nadich, Judah *rabbi*

Neuhaus, Richard John *priest, research institute president*
Norgren, William Andrew *religious denomination administrator*
O'Connor, John Joseph Cardinal *archbishop, former naval officer*
O'Keefe, Vincent Thomas *clergyman, educational administrator*
Osborn, Frederick Henry, III *church foundation executive*
Perry, David *priest*
Poppen, Alvin J. *religious organization administrator*
Powers, Edward Alton *minister, educator*
Read, David Haxton Carswell *clergyman*
Riddle, Sturgis Lee *minister*
Rosenberg, Ellen Y. *religious association administrator*
Roth, Sol *rabbi*
Rusch, William Graham *religious organization administrator*
Salisbury, Nancy *convent director*
Schindler, Alexander Moshe *rabbi, organization executive*
Schorsch, Ismar *clergyman, Jewish history educator*
Sharpton, Alfred Charles *minister, political activist*
Shriver, Donald Woods, Jr. *theology educator*
Simpson, Mary Michael *priest, psychotherapist*
†Sohl, Joyce Darlene *religious organization administrator*
Solheim, James Edward *church executive, journalist*
Stolper, Pinchas Aryeh *religious organization executive, rabbi*
Tannenbaum, Bernice Salpeter *religious organization executive*
Tertzakian, Hovhannes *bishop*
Thompson, Faye Alison *minister*
†Thurman, Robert *theology, religious studies educator*
Truesdell, Walter George *minister, librarian*
Twiname, John Dean *minister, health care executive*
Weiss, David *religion educator*
Wiener, Marvin S. *rabbi, editor, executive*

**Niagara Falls**
Grove, Jeffery Lynn *minister*

**North Syracuse**
Williamson, Donna Maria *pastoral counselor*

**Nyack**
Mann, Kenneth Walker *retired minister, psychologist*
Ortiz, Angel Vicente *church administrator*

**Ogdensburg**
Loverde, Paul S. *bishop*

**Orchard Park**
Reid, Thomas Fenton *minister*

**Oyster Bay**
Prey, Jeffrey Drew *minister*

**Pawling**
Peale, Ruth Stafford (Mrs. Norman Vincent Peale) *religious leader*

**Pine City**
Searle, Robert Ferguson *minister*

**Poughkeepsie**
Glasse, John Howell *retired philosophy and theology educator*

**Rochester**
Burrill, William George *bishop*
Clark, Matthew Harvey *bishop*

**Rockville Centre**
McGann, John Raymond *bishop*

**Spencerport**
Webster, Gordon Visscher, Jr. *minister*

**Staten Island**
Zayek, Francis Mansour *bishop*

**Syosset**
Hull, Gretchen Gaebelein *lay worker, writer, lecturer*
Lazor, Theodosius (His Beatitude Metropolitan Theodosius) *archbishop*

**Syracuse**
Cole, Ned *bishop*
Costello, Thomas Joseph *bishop*
Schiess, Betty Bone *priest*
Wiggins, James Bryan *religion educator*

**Troy**
Phelan, Thomas *clergyman, academic administrator, educator*

**Trumansburg**
Billings, Peggy Marie *religious organization administrator, educator*

**Walworth**
Reynolds, Lewis Dayton *administrator, pastor*

**Watertown**
Waterston, William King *minister, educator, academic administrator*

**West Nyack**
Irwin, Ronald Gilbert *minister*

**Westbury**
De Pauw, Gommar Albert *priest, educator*

**White Plains**
Gurahian, Vincent *church official, former judge*

**Williamsville**
Jones, Robert Alfred *clergyman*

**Woodside**
Vasilachi, Gheorghe Vasile *priest, vicar*

**Yonkers**
Gunner, Murray *Jewish organization administrator*

**Yorktown Heights**
Braddock, Nonnie Clarke *religious organization administrator*

## NORTH CAROLINA

**Black Mountain**
Kennedy, William Bean *theology educator*

**Boiling Springs**
Hearne, Stephen Zachary *minister, educator*

**Brevard**
Flory, Margaret Martha *retired religious organization administrator*

**Cary**
Smith, Roy Jordan *religious organization administrator*

**Chapel Hill**
Dixon, John Wesley, Jr. *retired religion and art educator*
Van Seters, John *biblical literature educator*

**Charlotte**
Curlin, William G. *bishop*
Freeman, Sidney Lee *minister, educator*
Prosser, Bruce Reginal, Jr. (Bo Prosser) *minister, consultant*
Ross, David Edmond *church official*
Sustar, T. David *college president*
Wilson, Edward Cox *minister*

**Davidson**
McKelway, Alexander Jeffrey *religion studies educator*

**Dunn**
Blackman, Danny *religious organization administrator*
Davis, Dolly *religious organization administrator*
Heath, Preston *clergy member, religious organization administrator*
Taylor, David *clergy member, religious administrator*

**Durham**
Campbell, Dennis Marion *theology dean, educator, university administrator*
Langford, Thomas Anderson *retired theology educator, academic administrator*
Meyers, Eric Mark *religion educator*
Smith, Harmon Lee, Jr. *clergyman, moral theology educator*
Steinmetz, David Curtis *religion educator, publisher, minister*
Westbrook, Don Arlen *minister*

**Elizabethtown**
Taylor, David Wyatt Aiken *retired clergyman*

**Fairview**
Eck, David Wilson *minister*

**Gastonia**
Carson, John Little *historical theology educator, clergyman*

**Goldsboro**
Sauls, Don *clergyman*

**Greensboro**
Lolley, William Randall *minister*
Rights, Graham Henry *minister*
Willis, C. Paul *minister*

**Greenville**
Jackson, Bobby Rand *minister*
Wood, Gerald David *religious organization administrator*

**Haw River**
Poindexter, Richard Grover *minister*

**Hendersonville**
Sims, Bennett Jones *minister, educator*

**Hickory**
McDaniel, Michael Conway Dixon *bishop, theology educator*

**High Point**
Wood, Stephen Wray *educator, legislator, minister, singer, songwriter*

**Kinston**
Sanders, Brice Sidney *bishop*

**Lake Junaluska**
Bryan, Monk *retired bishop*
Goodgame, Gordon Clifton *minister*
Hale, Joseph Rice *church organization executive*
Tullis, Edward Lewis *retired bishop*

**Liberty**
Garner, Mildred Maxine *retired religious studies educator*

**Manteo**
Miller, William Lee, Jr. *minister*

**Mount Olive**
Boyd, Julia Margaret (Mrs. Shelton B. Boyd) *lay church worker*

**Raleigh**
Collins, Thomas Asa *minister*
Gossman, Francis Joseph *bishop*
Miller, John Henry *clergyman*

**Southern Pines**
Lowry, Charles Wesley *clergyman, lecturer*

**Southport**
Harrelson, Walter Joseph *minister, religion educator emeritus*

**Wake Forest**
Binkley, Olin Trivette *clergyman, seminary president emeritus*
Blackmore, James Herrall *clergyman, educator, author*

**Weaverville**
Edwards, Otis Carl, Jr. *theology educator*

**Winston Salem**
Fitzgerald, Ernest Abner *retired bishop*
Martin, James Alfred, Jr. *religious studies educator*
McElveen, William Henry *minister*
Spach, Jule Christian *church executive*
Winn, Albert Curry *clergyman*

## NORTH DAKOTA

**Bismarck**
Montz, Florence Stolte *church official*

**Fargo**
Fairfield, Andrew H. *bishop*
Foss, Richard John *bishop*
Sullivan, James Stephen *bishop*

## OHIO

**Ashland**
Waters, Ronald W. *educator, church executive, pastor*
Watson, JoAnn Ford *theology educator*

**Canton**
Boulton, Edwin Charles *retired bishop*

**Chagrin Falls**
Pickett, Arthur William, Jr. *minister*

**Cincinnati**
Crumes, William Edward *bishop*
Harrington, Jeremy Thomas *clergyman, publisher*
Hendricks, Harry *church administrator*
Huron, Roderick Eugene *religious organization administrator*
Linsey, Nathaniel L. *bishop*
Molitor, Sister Margaret Anne *nun, former college president*
Perry, Norman Robert *priest, magazine editor*
Pilarczyk, Daniel Edward *archbishop*
Sweeten, Gary Ray *religious counseling educator*
Thompson, Herbert, Jr. *bishop*

**Circleville**
Norman, Jack Lee *church administrator, consultant*
Tipton, Daniel L. *religious organization executive*

**Cleveland**
Buhrow, William Carl *religious organization administrator*
Chapman, Robert L. *bishop*
Dipko, Thomas Earl *minister, national church executive*
Epp, Eldon Jay *religion educator*
Holck, Frederick H. George *priest, educator*
Pilla, Anthony Michael *bishop*
Sherry, Paul Henry *minister, religious organization administrator*
Williams, Arthur Benjamin, Jr. *bishop*

**Columbus**
Jackson, David Gordon *religious organization administrator*
Plagenz, George Richard *minister, journalist, columnist*
Simms, Lowelle *synod executive*
Yurcisin, John *church official*

**Concord**
Nielson, William Brooks *clergyman*

**Dayton**
McCrabb, Donald Raymond *religious ministry director*

**Dublin**
Baker, Mary Evelyn *church librarian, retired academic librarian*

**Englewood**
Shearer, Velma Miller *clergywoman*

**Findlay**
Martin, Jim G. *church renewal consultant*
Rave, James A. *bishop*
Wilkin, Richard Edwin *clergyman, religious organization executive*

**London**
Hughes, Clyde Matthew *religious denomination executive*

**Lyons**
Myers, John William *minister, poet, editor, publisher*

**Mount Saint Joseph**
Roach, Sister Jeanne *nun, hospital administrator*

**Niles**
Cornell, William Harvey *clergyman*

**Oberlin**
Zinn, Grover Alfonso, Jr. *religion educator*

**Parma**
Moskal, Robert M. *bishop*

**Steubenville**
Scanlan, Michael *priest, academic administrator*
Sheldon, Gilbert Ignatius *clergyman*

**Toledo**
Hoffman, James R. *bishop*
James, William *bishop*

**Westerville**
Schultz, Arthur LeRoy *clergyman, educator*

**Wickliffe**
Pevec, Anthony Edward *bishop*

**Worthington**
Craig, Judith *bishop*

## OKLAHOMA

**Bartlesville**
Woodruff, William Jennings *theology educator*

**Bethany**
Leggett, James Daniel *church administrator*
Shelton, Muriel Moore *religious education administrator*

**Broken Arrow**
Janning, Sister Mary Bernadette *nun, retired association executive*

**Lawton**
Young, J. A. *bishop*

**Norman**
Fuerbringer, Alfred Ottomar *clergyman*

**Oklahoma City**
Andrews, Robert Frederick *religious organization administrator, retired bishop*
Beltran, Eusebius Joseph *archbishop*
Jones, Robert Lee *religion educator*
†Kuner, Charles Michael *minister*
Moody, Robert M. *bishop*
Ponder, Alonza *church administrator*
Ridley, Betty Ann *educator, church worker*
Underwood, Bernard Edward *religious organization administrator*

**Piedmont**
Clayton, Lawrence Otto *minister, writer*

**Purcell**
Lucas, Roy Edward, Jr. *minister*

**Stillwater**
Lawson, F. D. *bishop*

**Tulsa**
Ashby, John Forsythe *retired bishop*
Cox, William Jackson *bishop*
Gottschalk, Sister Mary Therese *nun, hospital administrator*
Rex, Lonnie Royce *religious organization administrator*
Roberts, (Granville) Oral *clergyman*
Slattery, Edward J. *bishop*

## OREGON

**Beaverton**
Mitchell, Bettie Phaenon *religious organization administrator*

**Bend**
Connolly, Thomas Joseph *bishop*

**Corvallis**
Steiner, Kenneth Donald *bishop*

**Dallas**
Calkins, Loren Gene *church executive, clergyman*

**Eugene**
Osborn, Ronald Edwin *minister, church history educator*
Sanders, Jack Thomas *religious studies educator*

**Lake Oswego**
Ladehoff, Robert Louis *bishop*

**Newport**
Langrock, Karl Frederick *former academic administrator*

**Portland**
Held, Jay Allen *pastor*
Huenemann, Ruben Henry *clergyman*
Richards, Herbert East *minister emeritus, commentator*
Sevetson, Donald James *retired minister, church administrator*

**West Linn**
Bohrer, Richard William *religious writer, editor, educator*

**Wilsonville**
Gross, Hal Raymond *bishop*

## PENNSYLVANIA

**Akron**
Lapp, John Allen *retired religious organization administrator*

**Allentown**
Jodock, Darrell Harland *minister, religion educator*
Welsh, Thomas J. *bishop*

**Allison Park**
Mc Dowell, John B. *bishop*

**Ambridge**
Frey, William Carl *retired bishop, academic administrator*

**Ardmore**
Shaull, Richard *theologian, educator*

**Bethlehem**
Sommers, Gordon L. *religious organization administrator*
Steffen, Lloyd Howard *minister, religion educator*

**Bradford**
Conley, Thomas Anthony *minister, counselor*

**Bryn Mawr**
Ledwith, Sister Margaret Christine *nun, counselor*

**Camp Hill**
Johnston, Thomas McElree, Jr. *church administrator*

**Clearfield**
Pride, Douglas Spencer *minister*

**Confluence**
Bower, Roy Donald *minister, counselor*

**Coopersburg**
Eckardt, Arthur Roy *religion studies educator emeritus*

**Cornwall**
Ehrhart, Carl Yarkers *retired minister, retired college administrator*

**Cranberry Township**
Bashore, George Willis *bishop*
Tiller, Olive Marie *retired church worker*

**Doylestown**
Maser, Frederick Ernest *clergyman*

**Drexel Hill**
Thompson, William David *minister, homiletics educator*

**Elizabethtown**
Brown, Dale Weaver *clergyman, theologian, educator*

**Erie**
Rowley, Robert Deane, Jr. *bishop*
Trautman, Donald W. *bishop*

**Fogelsville**
Ault, James Mase *bishop*

**Grantham**
Sider, Harvey Ray *minister, church administrator*

**Harrisburg**
Chambers, Clarice Lorraine *clergy, educational consultant*
Dattilo, Nicholas C. *bishop*
Edmiston, Guy S., Jr. *bishop*

**Haverford**
Kee, Howard Clark *religion educator*

**Huntingdon**
Durnbaugh, Donald Floyd *church history educator, researcher*

**Jim Thorpe**
Umbehocker, Kenneth Sheldon *priest*

**Johnstown**
Miloro, Protopresbter Frank *church official, religious studies educator*
Nicholas, (Richard G. Smisko) *bishop*
Smisko, Nicholas Richard *bishop, educator*

**Lancaster**
Augsburger, Aaron Donald *clergyman*
Carlisle, James Patton *clergyman*
Daugherty, Ruth Alice *religious association consultant*
Glick, Garland Wayne *retired theological seminary president*

**Lewisburg**
Jump, Chester Jackson, Jr. *clergyman, church official*
Main, A. Donald *bishop*

**Merion Station**
Littell, Franklin Hamlin *theologian, educator*

**New Holland**
West, Daniel Charles *lay worker, dentist*

**New Stanton**
Black, Cora Jean *evangelist, wedding consultant*

**Philadelphia**
Bartlett, Allen Lyman, Jr. *bishop*
Bevilacqua, Anthony Joseph Cardinal *archbishop*
Birchard, Bruce *religious organization administrator*
Butz, Geneva Mae *pastor*
Goldin, Judah *Hebrew literature educator*
Hammond, Charles Ainley *clergyman*
Harvey, William J. *religious service organization, religious publication editor*
Hickey, Gregory Joseph *priest, educational administrator*
Howard, Gerald Kenneth *minister*
Jones, O. T. *bishop*
Kraft, Robert Alan *history of religion educator*
Marple, Dorothy Jane *retired church executive*
Sulyk, Stephen *archbishop*
Turner, Franklin Delton *bishop*
Waskow, Arthur Ocean *theologian, educator*

**Pittsburgh**
Collins, Rose Ann *minister*
Koedel, Robert Craig *minister, historian, educator*
Maximos, (Maximos Demetrios Aghiorgoussis) *bishop*
McCoid, James James *bishop*
Muto, Susan Annette *religion educator, academic administrator*
Procyk, Judson M. *metropolitan archbishop*
Schaub, Marilyn McNamara *religion educator*
Wuerl, Donald W. *bishop*

**Rydal**
Black, Thomas Donald *retired religious organization administrator*
Kirkland, Bryant Mays *clergyman*

**Saint Davids**
Maahs, Kenneth Henry, Sr. *religion educator*

**Scranton**
De Celles, Charles Edouard *theologian, educator*
Shipula, Anthony James, II *church diocese administrator*
Timlin, James Clifford *bishop*

**Seneca**
Spring, Paull E. *bishop*

**Souderton**
Lapp, James Merrill *clergyman, marriage and family therapist*

**Swarthmore**
Cornelsen, Rufus *clergyman*
Frost, Jerry William *religion and history educator, library administrator*
Swearer, Donald Keeney *Asian religions educator, writer*

**Upper Darby**
Clemens, David Allen *minister*
Livingston, Margery Elsie *missionary, clinical psychologist*

**Valley Forge**
Penfield, Carole H. (Kate Penfield) *minister, church official*
Smith, G. Elaine *religious organization executive*
Smith, Gordon E. *religious organization executive*
Sundquist, John A. *religious organization executive*
Weiss, Daniel Edwin *clergyman, educator*
Wright-Riggins, Aidsand F., III *religious organization executive*

**Villanova**
Palmer, Donald Curtis *interdenominational missionary society executive*

**Wayne**
Green, Norman Marston, Jr. *minister*

**Wernersville**
Mackey, Sheldon Elias *minister*

**Williamsport**
Van Voorst, Robert E. *theology educator, minister*

**Willow Grove**
Duff, Donald James *religious organization administrator*

**Wrightsville**
Johnson, Clarence Ray *minister*

**Wyncote**
Burton, DeWitt A. *bishop*

**Wynnewood**
Russell, Horace Orlando *dean of chapel, theology educator*
Sider, Ronald J. *theology educator, author*

**RHODE ISLAND**

**Lincoln**
Barlow, August Ralph, Jr. *minister*

**Providence**
Frerichs, Ernest Sunley *religious studies educator*
Gelineau, Louis Edward *bishop*
Milhaven, John Giles *religious studies educator*
Mulvee, Robert Edward *bishop*
Pearce, George Hamilton *archbishop*

**Westerly**
Looper, George Kirk *religious society executive*

**SOUTH CAROLINA**

**Anderson**
Wisler, Darla Lee *pastor*

**Chapin**
Branham, Mack Carison, Jr. *retired theological seminary educator, minister*

**Charleston**
Donehue, John Douglas *interdenominational ministries executive*
Salmon, Edward Lloyd, Jr. *bishop*
Thompson, David B. *bishop*

**Columbia**
Adams, John Hurst *bishop*
Aull, James Stroud *retired bishop*
Blount, Evelyn *religious organization administrator*
Brubaker, Lauren Edgar *minister, educator*
Martell, Denise Mills *lay worker*

**Due West**
Ruble, Randall Tucker *theologian, educator, academic administrator*

**Gaffney**
Harrison, Richard Dean *minister, counselor*

**Georgetown**
Allison, Christopher FitzSimons *bishop*

**Goose Creek**
Johnson, Johnnie *bishop*

**Greenville**
Kowalski, Paul Randolph *minister*
McKnight, Edgar Vernon *religion educator*

Smith, Morton Howison *religious organization administrator, educator*

**Hilton Head Island**
Radest, Howard Bernard *clergyman, educator*

**Leesville**
Crumley, James Robert, Jr. *retired clergyman*

**Mauldin**
Phillips, James Oscar *minister*

**Spartanburg**
Bullard, John Moore *religion educator, church musician*

**Taylors**
Vaughn, John Carroll *minister, educator*

**SOUTH DAKOTA**

**Sioux Falls**
Carlson, Robert James *bishop*
Cowles, Ronald Eugene *church administrator*

**Watertown**
Witcher, Gary Royal *minister, educator*

**TENNESSEE**

**Antioch**
Vallance, James *church administrator, religious publication editor*
Waddell, R. Eugene *minister*
Worthington, Melvin Leroy *minister, writer*

**Brentwood**
Bennett, Harold Clark *clergyman, religious organization administrator*

**Chattanooga**
Hughes, Michael Randolph *evangelist*
Mohney, Ralph Wilson *minister*
Ragon, Robert Ronald *clergyman*

**Cleveland**
Albert, Leonard *religious organization executive*
Alford, Delton L. *religious organization executive*
Baker, Michael Lyndon *minister*
Chambers, O. Wayne *religious organization executive*
Fisher, Robert Elwood *minister, church official*
Jackson, Joseph Essard *religious organization administrator*
Murray, Billy Dwayne, Sr. *church administrator*
Rayburn, Billy J. *Church administrator*
Reyes, Jose Antonio, Sr. *minister*
Robinson, Julian B. *church administrator*
Taylor, William Al *church administrator*
Vaughan, Roland *church administrator*
Vest, R. Lamar *church administrator*

**East Ridge**
Hodge, Raymond Douglas *minister*

**Germantown**
Hamilton, David Eugene *minister, educator*

**Hermitage**
Chambers, Curtis Allen *clergyman, church communications executive*

**Jackson**
Maynard, Terrell Dennis *minister*

**Johnson City**
Shaw, Angus Robertson, III *minister*

**Knoxville**
O'Connell, Anthony J. *bishop*
Stooksbury, William Claude *minister*

**La Follette**
Eads, Ora Wilbert *clergyman, church official*

**Livingston**
Harrison, Jim Rush, Jr. *minister of music*

**Loudon**
Jones, Robert Gean *religion educator*

**Memphis**
Booker, Bruce Robert *theology educator, author, educational consultant*
Brooks, P. A., II *bishop*
Hamilton, W. W. *church administrator*
Lawson, Katherine Elaine *minister, counselor, psychologist*
Macklin, F. Douglas *bishop*
Magrill, Joe Richard, Jr. *religious organization administrator, minister*
Porter, W. L. *bishop*
Steib, James Terry *bishop*
Thomas, Nathaniel Charles *clergyman*
Todd, Virgil Holcomb *clergyman, religion educator*

**Murfreesboro**
Walker, David Ellis, Jr. *educator, minister, consultant*

**Nashville**
Abstein, William Robert, II *minister*
Atchison, David Warren *church officer*
Buttrick, David Gardner *religion educator*
Chapman, Morris Hines *denominational executive*
Draper, James Thomas, Jr. (Jimmy Draper) *clergyman*
Forlines, Franklin Leroy *minister, educator*
Forstman, Henry Jackson *theology educator, university dean*
Harrod, Howard Lee *religion educator*
Jones, Kathryn Cherie *pastor*
Kmiec, Edward Urban *bishop*
Mills, Liston Oury *theology educator*
Picirilli, Robert Eugene *clergyman, college dean, writer*

**Sewanee**
Hughes, Robert Davis, III *theological educator*
Lytle, Guy Fitch, III *priest, educator, dean*

**Signal Mountain**
Hall, Thor *religion educator*

**Springfield**
Fagan, A. Rudolph *minister*

**TEXAS**

**Aledo**
Barton, Charles David *religious studies educator, author, researcher, historian*

**Alice**
Tetlie, Harold *priest*

**Amarillo**
Klein, Jerry Lee, Sr. *religion educator, minister*
Matthiesen, Leroy Theodore *bishop*

**Arlington**
Dingwerth, Joan H. *religious organization administrator*
†Harris, Ronald Leon *minister, communications executive*
Lingerfelt, B. Eugene, Jr. *minister*
†Machle, Edward Johnstone *emeritus educator*

**Austin**
Ahlschwede, Arthur Martin *church educational official*
Denham, William Ernest, Jr. *minister*
Hale, Arnold Wayne *religious studies educator, army officer, clergyman, psychotherapist*
Mc Carthy, John Edward *bishop*
Wahlberg, Philip Lawrence *former bishop*
Worthing, Carol Marie *minister*

**Beaumont**
Galante, Joseph A. *bishop*
McGary, Betty Winstead *minister, counselor, individual, marriage, and family therapist*

**Brownsville**
Fitzpatrick, John J. *bishop*
Pena, Raymundo Joseph *bishop*

**Brownwood**
Chapman, Dan G. *minister*

**Childress**
Mayes, Ila Laverne *minister*

**Conroe**
Little, Don Barron *clergyman*

**Corpus Christi**
Doty, James Edward *pastor, psychologist*
Gracida, Rene Henry *bishop*
Kenna, John Thomas *priest*
Pivonka, Leonard Daniel *priest*

**Dallas**
Barnhouse, Ruth Tiffany *priest, psychiatrist*
Blue, J(ohn) Ronald *evangelical mission executive*
Closser, Patrick Denton *radio evangelist, artist*
Harrell, Roy Harrison, Jr. *minister*
Haynes, J. Neauell *clergyman, bishop*
Herbener, Mark Basil *bishop*
Jenkins, Chester Phillip *religious organization, church administration*
Kirby, James Edmund, Jr. *theology educator*
Morgan, Larry Ronald *minister*
Oden, William Bryant *bishop, educator*
Pinson, William Meredith, Jr. *pastor, writer*
Valentine, Foy Dan *clergyman*
Wiles, Charles Preston *minister*

**De Soto**
Jackson, Johnny W. *minister*

**Fort Worth**
Delaney, Joseph P. *bishop*
Edwards, Samuel Lee *religious organization executive*
Elliott, John Franklin *clergyman*
Gilbert, James Cayce *minister*
Gross, John Birney *retired minister*
Hendricks, William Lawrence *theology educator*
Newport, John Paul *philosophy of religion educator, former academic administrator*
Rogers, Charles Ray *minister, religious organization administrator*
Suggs, Marion Jack *minister, college dean*
Teegarden, Kenneth Leroy *clergyman*

**Galveston**
Millikan, Charles Reagan *pastor*

**Garrison**
Herrington, Dale Elizabeth *lay worker*

**Gary**
Speer, James *religious organization administrator*

**Houston**
Arnold, James Phillip *religious studies educator, history educator*
Barrett, Michael Joseph *priest*
Bui, Long Van *church custodian, translator*
Fiorenza, Joseph A. *bishop*
Henderson, Nathan H. *bishop*
Joyce, James Daniel *clergyman*
Karff, Samuel Egal *rabbi*
Meeks, Herbert Lessig, III *pastor, former school system administrator*
Nelson, John Robert *theology educator, clergyman*
Nielsen, Niels Christian, Jr. *theology educator*
Prescott, William Bruce *minister*
Sampson, Franklin Delano *minister*
Stephens, Carson Wade *minister*
Sudbury, John Dean *religious foundation executive, petroleum chemist*

**Irving**
†Evans, Michael David *clergyman, author*

**Jacksonville**
Blaylock, James Carl *clergyman, librarian*
Pruitt, William Charles, Jr. *minister, educator*

**Longview**
Brannon, Clifton Woodrow, Sr. *evangelist, lawyer*

**Lubbock**
Hulsey, Sam Byron *bishop*
Rodriguez, Placido *bishop*

**Mcallen**
Sutton, William Blaylock *pastor*

**Pecan Gap**
Williams, Jessie Willmon *lay religious worker, retired librarian*

**Plano**
Lee, Allan Wren *clergyman*

**Richardson**
Conrad, Flavius Leslie, Jr. *minister*
Williams, James Francis, Jr. *religious organization administrator*

**San Angelo**
Pfeifer, Michael David *bishop*

**San Antonio**
Caudill, Howard Edwin *bishop, educator*
Flores, Patrick F. *archbishop*
Iglehart, T. D. *bishop*
Jacobson, David *rabbi*
Langlinais, Joseph Willis *educator, chaplain*
Leies, John Alex *theology educator, clergyman*
Mc Allister, Gerald Nicholas *retired bishop, clergyman*
Nix, Robert Lynn *minister*
Walker, William Oliver, Jr. *educator, university dean*

**Spring**
Hunt, T(homas) W(ebb) *retired religion educator*

**Texarkana**
Cross, Irvie Keil *religious organization executive*
Silvey, James L. *religious publisher*

**Tyler**
Carmody, Edmond *bishop*

**Van Alstyne**
Daves, Don Michael *minister*

**Victoria**
Fellhauer, David E. *bishop*

**Waco**
Chewning, Richard Carter *religious business ethics educator*
Flanders, Henry Jackson, Jr. *religious studies educator*
Wood, James E., Jr. *religion educator, author*

**Waxahachie**
Tschoepe, Thomas *bishop*

**UTAH**

**Bountiful**
Carter, Richard Bert *retired church official, retired government official*

**Ogden**
Harrington, Mary Evelina Paulson (Polly Harrington) *religious journalist, writer, educator*

**Provo**
Beckham, Janette Hales *religious organization administrator*

**Salt Lake City**
†Eyring, Henry Bennion *bishop*
Faust, James E. *church official*
Hinckley, Gordon B. *church official*
†Holland, Jeffrey R. *religious organization administrator*
Maxwell, Neal A. *church official*
Monson, Thomas Spencer *church official, publishing company executive*
Niederauer, George H. *bishop*
Packer, Boyd K. *church official*
Scott, Richard G. *church official*
Smith, Eldred Gee *church leader*
Wirthlin, Joseph B. *church official*

**VERMONT**

**Burlington**
Angell, Kenneth Anthony *bishop*

**Middlebury**
Ferm, Robert Livingston *religion educator*

**Newport**
Guerrette, Richard Hector *priest, psychotherapist, management consultant, writer*

**Northfield**
Wick, William Shinn *clergyman, chaplain*

**Norwich**
Post, Avery Denison *retired church official*

**Pawlet**
Buechner, Carl Frederick *minister, author*

**VIRGINIA**

**Arlington**
Bailey, Amos Purnell *clergyman, syndicated columnist*
Keating, John Richard *bishop*

Moshier, David Irwin *church administrator*
Soderquist, Ronald Bruce *minister, ministry director*

**Blacksburg**
Grover, Norman LaMotte *theologian, philosopher*

**Charlottesville**
Childress, James Franklin *theology and medical educator*
Hartt, Julian Norris *religion educator*
Scharlemann, Robert Paul *religious studies educator, clergyman*
Scott, Nathan Alexander, Jr. *minister, educator, literary critic*

**Colonial Beach**
McClain, Gregory David *minister*

**Emory**
Kellogg, Frederic Richard *religious studies educator*

**Fairfax**
Anders, Camille Shephard *director of adult and family ministries*

**Falls Church**
Bankson, Marjory *religious association administrator*

**Front Royal**
Andes, Larry Dale *minister*

**Hampton**
Henderson, Salathiel James *minister, clergy*

**Harrisonburg**
†Burkholder, Owen Eugene *religious organization administrator*

**Keswick**
Massey, Donald Wayne *Episcopal minister, small business owner*

**Lexington**
Hodges, Louis Wendell *religion educator*

**Madison Heights**
Falwell, Jerry L. *clergyman*

**Manassas**
Gustavson, Brandt *religious association executive*

**Martinsville**
Shackleford, William Alton, Sr. *minister*

**Mc Lean**
Lotz, Denton *minister, church official*
Wümpelmann, Knud Aage Abildgaard *clergyman, religious organization administrator*

**Norfolk**
Agnew, Christopher Mack *minister*
Vest, Frank Harris, Jr. *bishop*

**Palmyra**
Brown, Nan Marie *clergywoman*

**Penn Laird**
Wise, Charles Conrad, Jr. *educator, past government official, author*

**Portsmouth**
Thomas, Ted, Sr. *minister*

**Reedville**
Westbrook, Walter Winfield *minister*

**Richmond**
Aigner, Emily Burke *lay worker*
Anderson, James Frederick *clergyman*
Bagby, Daniel Gordon *religious studies educator, clergyman*
Barton, Jonathan Miller *clergyman*
Brown, Aubrey Neblett, Jr. *minister, editor*
Fuller, Reginald Horace *clergyman, biblical studies educator*
Gerrish, Brian Albert *theologian, educator*
Lee, Peter James *bishop*
Leggett, Gloria Jean *minister*
Leith, John Haddon *clergyman, theology educator*
McDonough, Reginald Milton *religious organization executive*
Moore, John Sterling, Jr. *minister*
Nunn, Charles Burgess *religious organization executive*
Richerson, Stephen Wayne *minister*
Rogers, Isabel Wood *religious studies educator*
Sullivan, Walter Francis *bishop*
Swezey, Charles Mason *Christian ethics educator, administrator*
Turner, James Wesley *minister, former church administrator*

**Roanoke**
Marmion, William Henry *retired bishop*

**Rockbridge Baths**
Patteson, Roy Kinnear, Jr. *clergyman, administrator*

**Salem**
Bansemer, Richard Frederick *bishop*

**Sweet Briar**
Armstrong, Gregory Timon *religious studies educator, minister*

**Williamsburg**
Holmes, David L. *religious educator*

**Woodbridge**
Townsend, Kenneth Ross *retired priest*

**WASHINGTON**

**Belfair**
Walker, E. Jerry *retired clergyman*

**Fort Lewis**
Tille, James Eugene *army chaplain*

**Greenbank**
Tuell, Jack Marvin *retired bishop*

**Seattle**
Averill, Lloyd James, Jr. *religion educator*
Burrows, Elizabeth MacDonald *religious organization executive, educator*
Galvan, Elias Gabriel *bishop*
Galvin, Elias *bishop*
Murphy, Thomas Joseph *archbishop*
Raible, Peter Spilman *minister*
Robb, John Wesley *religion educator*
Warner, Vincent W. *bishop*
Zehr, Clyde James *church administrator*

**Spanaway**
Westbrook, T. L. *bishop*

**Spokane**
Keller, Robert M. *bishop*
Polley, Harvey Lee *retired missionary and educator*
Skylstad, William S. *bishop*
Terry, Frank Jeffrey *bishop*

**Stevenson**
Clausel, Nancy Karen *minister*

**Sunnyside**
Capener, Regner Alvin *minister, electronics engineer, author, inventor*

**Tacoma**
Wiegman, Eugene William *minister, former college administrator*
Wold, David C. *bishop*

**WEST VIRGINIA**

**Charleston**
Ives, Samuel Clifton *minister*
Scott, Olof Henderson, Jr. *priest*

**Hamlin**
Barrett, Brian Lee *minister, evangelist*

**Morgantown**
Meitzen, Manfred Otto *religious studies educator*

**Parkersburg**
Poling, Kermit William *minister*

**Wheeling**
Schmitt, Bernard W. *bishop*

**WISCONSIN**

**Amery**
Mickelson, Arnold Rust *consultant, religious denominational official*

**Cedarburg**
Clark, Harry Wilber *church administrator*

**Eau Claire**
Wantland, William Charles *bishop, lawyer*

**Green Bay**
Banks, Robert J. *bishop*
Geisendorfer, James Vernon *author*

**Kenosha**
Schultz, Clarence John *minister*

**La Crosse**
Bubar, Joseph Bedell, Jr. *church official*
Larson, April Ulring *bishop*
Paul, John Joseph *bishop*

**Madison**
Bullock, William Henry *bishop*
Enslin, Jon S. *bishop*
Fox, Michael Vass *Hebrew educator, rabbi*
†Hayner, Stephen A. *religious organization administrator*
Wirz, George O. *bishop*

**Manitowoc**
Plank, William Brandt *minister*

**Middleton**
McDermott, Molly *lay minister*

**Milwaukee**
Wagner, Diane M(argaret) *theology educator*
Weakland, Rembert G. *archbishop*

**Nashotah**
Kriss, Gary W(ayne) *Episcopal priest*

**Oak Creek**
Robertson, Michael Swing *religious association administrator*

**Oshkosh**
Barwig, Regis Norbert James *priest*

**Watertown**
Henry, Carl Ferdinand Howard *theologian*
Thompson, Richard Lloyd *pastor*

**Windsor**
Baumer, Martha Ann *minister*

**WYOMING**

**Cheyenne**
Hart, Joseph H. *bishop*

**Cody**
Grimes, Daphne Buchanan *priest, artist*

**TERRITORIES OF THE UNITED STATES**

**AMERICAN SAMOA**

**Pago Pago**
Weitzel, John Quinn *bishop*

**FEDERATED STATES OF MICRONESIA**

**Chuuk**
Neylon, Martin Joseph *retired bishop*
Samo, Amando *bishop*

**GUAM**

**Agana**
Apuron, Anthony Sablan *archbishop*

**NORTHERN MARIANA ISLANDS**

**Saipan**
Camacho, Tomas Aguon *bishop*

**PUERTO RICO**

**Carolina**
Velázquez de Cancel, Lourdes *religious organization executive, educator, interpreter, translator, poet*

**Mayaguez**
Casiano Vargas, Ulises *bishop*
Del Valle, Harry Fred Imzarry *minister, economist*

**Ponce**
Torres Oliver, Juan Fremiot *bishop*

**Santurce**
Aponte Martinez, Luis Cardinal *archbishop*

**CANADA**

**ALBERTA**

**Calgary**
Curtis, John Barry *archbishop*
O'Byrne, Paul J. *bishop*

**Camrose**
Campbell, John Douglas *minister*

**Cochrane**
Schmidt, Allen Edward *religious denomination administrator*

**Edmonton**
Mac Neil, Joseph Neil *archbishop*

**McLennan**
Légaré, Henri Francis *archbishop*

**Saint Paul**
Roy, Raymond *bishop*

**BRITISH COLUMBIA**

**Abbotsford**
Holdcroft, Leslie Thomas *clergyman, educator*

**Kamloops**
Cruickshank, James David *bishop*
Sabatini, Lawrence *bishop*

**Prince Rupert**
Hannen, John Edward *bishop*

**Richmond**
Plomp, Teunis (Tony Plomp) *minister*

**Salt Spring Island**
Shepherd, R. F. *retired bishop*

**Surrey**
Farley, Lawrence *clergyman*

**Vancouver**
Exner, Adam *archbishop*
Wakefield, Wesley Halpenny *church official*

**Victoria**
De Roo, Remi Joseph *bishop*

**MANITOBA**

**Churchill**
Rouleau, Reynald *bishop*

**Otterburne**
McKinney, Larry *religious organization administrator*

**Saint Boniface**
Hacault, Antoine Joseph Leon *archbishop*

**The Pas**
Sutton, Peter Alfred *archbishop*

**Winnipeg**
Frey, Marvin *religious organization administrator*
Gilbertson, Leon Charles *church administrator*
Harder, Helmut George *religious organization administrator*
Wall, Leonard J. *bishop*

**NEW BRUNSWICK**

**Fredericton**
Lemmon, George Colborne *bishop*

**NEWFOUNDLAND**

**Corner Brook**
Payne, Sidney Stewart *archbishop*

**Saint John's**
Harvey, Donald Frederick *bishop*
Troy, J. Edward *bishop*

**NORTHWEST TERRITORIES**

**Yellowknife**
Croteau, Denis *bishop*

**NOVA SCOTIA**

**Antigonish**
Campbell, Colin *bishop*

**Halifax**
Burke, Austin E. *archbishop*

**Parrsboro**
Hatfield, Leonard Fraser *retired bishop*

**Yarmouth**
Wingle, James Mathew *bishop*

**ONTARIO**

**Barrie**
Clune, Robert Bell *bishop*

**Brampton**
Bastian, Donald Noel *bishop, retired*

**Burlington**
Elgersma, Ray *relief and development organization executive*
Hamilton, Donald Gordon *religious association administrator*
Karsten, Albert *religious organization administrator*

**Cambridge**
Hooper, Wayne Nelson *clergy member*
MacBain, William Halley *minister, theology educator, seminary chancellor*

**Campbellville**
Georgije, Djokic *bishop*

**Cornwall**
La Rocque, Eugene Philippe *bishop*

**Etobicoke**
Coleman, K. Virginia *diaconal minister*

**Hamilton**
Asbil, Walter *bishop*
Tonnos, Anthony *bishop*

**Kingston**
Read, Allan Alexander *minister*
Spence, Francis John *archbishop*

**Kitchener**
Huras, William David *bishop*
Winger, Roger Elson *church administrator*

**Leamington**
Epp, Menno Henry *clergyman*

**London**
Peterson, Leslie Ernest *bishop*
Scott, W. Peter *bishop*
Sherlock, John Michael *bishop*

**Mississauga**
Griffin, William Arthur *clergyman, religious organization executive*

**Ottawa**
Landriault, Jacques Emile *retired bishop*
Ryan, William Francis *priest*
Squire, Anne Marguerite *religious leader*

**Peterborough**
Doyle, James Leonard *bishop*
Kristensen, John *church organization administrator*

**Saint Catharines**
Fulton, Thomas Benjamin *retired bishop*
O'Mara, John Aloysius *bishop*

**Sault Sainte Marie**
Ferris, Ronald Curry *bishop*

**Scarborough**
Mikloshazy, Attila *bishop*

**Schumacher**
Lawrence, Caleb James *bishop*

**Timmins**
Cazabon, Gilles *bishop*

PROFESSIONAL INDEX 5395 SCIENCE: LIFE SCIENCE


**Toronto**
Athanassoulas, Sotirios (Sotirios of Toronto) *bishop*
Black, Betty *religious organization leader*
Carter, Gerald Emmett *retired archbishop*
Ching, Julia *philosophy and religion educator*
Finlay, Terence Edward *bishop*
Garland, Rick D. *religious organization administrator*
Jay, Charles Douglas *religion educator, college administrator, clergyman*
MacMillin, James *religious organization administrator*
Mills, Robert Harry *church administrator*
Mowatt, E. Ann *women's voluntary leader, lawyer*
Novak, David *Judaic studies educator, rabbi*
Owens, Joseph *clergyman*
Plaut, Wolf Gunther *minister, author*
Synan, Edward Aloysius, Jr. *clergyman, former institute president*
Tindal, Douglas *religious organization administrator*
Wilson, Lois M. *minister*

**Unionville**
Rusnak, Michael *bishop*

**Waterloo**
Mills (Kutz-Harder), Helga *religious organization executive*

**Windsor**
Whitney, Barry Lyn *religious studies educator*

QUEBEC

**Amos**
Drainville, Gerard *bishop*

**Chicoutimi**
Couture, Jean Guy *bishop*

**Haute-Ville**
Fortier, Jean-Marie *retired archbishop*

**Hull**
Ebacher, Roger *archbishop*

**Joliette**
Audet, Rene *bishop*

**Mont Laurier**
Gratton, Jean *clergyman*

**Montreal**
Charron, André Joseph Charles Pierre *theologian, educator, former dean*
Hakim, Michel *religious leader*
Hall, Douglas John *minister, educator*
Hutchison, Andrew S. *bishop*
Turcotte, Jean-Claude Cardinal *archbishop*

**Outremont**
Derderian, Hovnan *church official*

**Quebec**
Stavert, Alexander Bruce *bishop*

**Rimouski**
Blanchet, Bertrand *archbishop*
Levesque, Louis *bishop*

**Rouyn**
Hamelin, Jean-Guy *bishop*

**Saint Hyacinthe**
Langevin, Louis-de-Gonzaque *bishop*

**Saint Jerome**
Valois, Charles *bishop*

**Sillery**
Couture, Maurice *archbishop*

**Succhz**
Noël, Laurent *bishop, educator*

**Valleyfield**
Lebel, Robert *bishop*

SASKATCHEWAN

**Muenster**
Novecosky, Peter Wilfred *abbot*

**Prince Albert**
Burton, Anthony John *bishop*
Morand, Blaise E. *bishop*

**Regina**
Bays, Eric *retired bishop*
Holm, Roy K. *church administrator*
Mallon, Peter *archbishop*

**Saltcoats**
Farquharson, Walter Henry *minister, church official*

**Saskatoon**
Filevich, Basil *bishop*
Jacobson, Sverre Theodore *retired minister*
Morgan, Thomas Oliver *bishop*

YUKON TERRITORY

**Whitehorse**
Lobsinger, Thomas *bishop*

MEXICO

**Chihuahua**
Almeida Merino, Adalberto *archbishop*

**Guadalajara**
Godinez Flores, Ramon *auxiliary bishop*
Sandoval Iñiguez, Juan Cardinal *archbishop*

**Matamoros**
Chavolla Ramos, Francisco Javier *bishop*

**Saltillo**
Villalobos Padilla, Francisco *bishop*

**San Nicolas de Garza**
Suarez Rivera, Adolfo Antonio *archbishop*

**Veracruz**
Ranzahuer, Guillermo Gonzalez *bishop*

BELGIUM

**Brussels**
Jadot, Jean Lambert Octave *clergyman*

BRAZIL

**Rio de Janeiro**
Sales, Eugenio de Araujo Cardinal *archbishop*

ENGLAND

**Birmingham**
Hick, John Harwood *theologian, philosopher, educator*

**London**
Gilbert, Patrick Nigel Geoffrey *organization executive*
Hornyak, Eugene Augustine *bishop*
Van Culin, Samuel *religious organization administrator*

**Oxford**
Gulbrandsen, Natalie Webber *religious association administrator*

**Tunbridge Wells**
Howden, Frank Newton *Episcopal priest, humanities educator*

**York**
Grant, Patrick Oliver *priest*

HONG KONG

**Hong Kong**
Chiang, Samuel Edward *theological educator, humanities educator*
Kwong, Peter Kong Kit *bishop*

INDIA

**Yavatmal**
Ward, Daniel Thomas *bishop*

INDONESIA

**Irian Jaya**
Sowada, Alphonse Augustus *bishop*

IRAN

**Tehran**
Dinkha, Mar, IV *church administrator*

ISRAEL

**Jerusalem**
Schindler, Pesach *rabbi, educator, author*

ITALY

**Rome**
Audet, Leonard *theologian*
Baum, William Wakefield Cardinal *archbishop*

JAPAN

**Nishinomiya**
Ogida, Mikio *history of religion educator*

**Tenri**
Miyata, Gen *history of religion educator*

JORDAN

**Amman**
O'Connell, Kevin George *priest, foreign missionary, former college president*

LATVIA

**Riga**
Varsbergs, Vilis *minister, former religious organization administrator*

NAMIBIA

**Ondangwa**
Haertel, Charles Wayne *minister*

NORWAY

**Lillestrøm**
Borgen, Ole Edvard *bishop, educator*

THE PHILIPPINES

**Pasay**
Lim, Sonia Yii *minister*

SAINT LUCIA

**Castries**
Felix, Kelvin Edward *archbishop*

UKRAINE

**Lviv**
†Lubachivsky, Myroslav Ivan Cardinal *archbishop*

VATICAN CITY

**Vatican City**
John Paul, His Holiness Pope, II (Karol Jozef Wojtyla) *bishop of Rome*
Szoka, Edmund Casimir Cardinal *archbishop*

ADDRESS UNPUBLISHED

Acker, Raymond Abijah *retired minister and army officer*
Allan, Hugh James Pearson *retired bishop*
Ambrozic, Aloysius Matthew *archbishop*
Anderson, Charles D. *former bishop*
Anderson, John Firth *church administrator, librarian*
Bell, H. Jenkins *clergyman, bishop*
Bender, Ross Thomas *minister*
Bishop, Cecil *bishop*
Blank, Richard Glenn *religious organization administrator, counselor*
Bollback, Anthony George *minister*
Borecky, Isidore *bishop*
Bosco, Anthony Gerard *bishop*
Bothwell, John Charles *archbishop*
Bryant, Roy, Sr. *bishop*
Buchanan, John Clark *bishop*
Charleston, Steve *bishop*
Charlton, Gordon Taliaferro, Jr. *retired bishop*
Chinula, Donald McLean *religious studies educator*
Christopher, Sharon A. Brown *bishop*
Chrysostomos, (González-Alexopoulos) *archbishop, clergyman, psychologist, educator*
Cliff, Judith Anita *author, biblical studies lecturer*
Clymer, Wayne Kenton *bishop*
Cobb, John Boswell, Jr. *clergyman, educator*
Cole, Clifford Adair *clergyman*
Crabtree, Davida Foy *minister*
Crudup, W. *bishop*
Davenport, L. B. *bishop*
Davis, Theodore Roosevelt *bishop, contractor*
Dirksen, Richard Wayne *canon precentor, organist, choirmaster*
Dixon, Ernest Thomas, Jr. *retired bishop*
Docker, John Thornley *religious organization administrator, minister*
Douty, Robert Watson *minister, educator*
Drobena, Thomas John *minister, educator*
Duecker, Robert Sheldon *retired bishop*
Eitrheim, Norman Duane *bishop*
Ellis, Howard Woodrow *evangelist, creative agent, clergyman, artist, author*
Emerson, R. Clark *priest, business administrator*
Erickson, James Huston *clergyman, physician*
Fricklas, Anita Alper *religious organization administrator*
Fry, Malcolm Craig *retired clergyman*
Gemignani, Michael Caesar *clergyman, retired educator*
Gervais, Marcel Andre *bishop*
†Grahmann, Charles V. *bishop*
Grant, Jacquelyn *minister, religion educator*
Gregory, Myra May *religious organization administrator, educator*
Griffin, James Anthony *bishop*
Gutmann, Reinhart Bruno *clergyman, social worker*
Hambidge, Douglas Walter *archbishop*
Handy, William Talbot, Jr. *bishop*
Hansen, Wendell Jay *clergyman, gospel broadcaster*
Hazuda, Ronald A. *church administrator*
Hendrickson, Louise *retired association executive, retired social worker*
Hilton, Clifford Thomas *clergyman*
Holle, Reginald Henry *retired bishop*
Hoops, William James *clergyman*
Hummel, Gene Maywood *retired bishop*
Hunt, George Nelson *bishop*
Hurn, Raymond Walter *minister, religious order administrator*
Isom, Dotcy Ivertus, Jr. *bishop*
John, K. K. (John Kuruvilla Kaiyalethe) *minister*
Jones, William Augustus, Jr. *retired bishop*
Joslin, David Bruce *bishop*
Kalkwarf, Leonard V. *minister*
Keeler, William Henry *cardinal*
Keyser, Charles Lovett, Jr. *bishop*
Kucera, Daniel William *retired bishop*
Landes, George Miller *biblical studies educator*
Lewis, C. A. *church administrator*
Light, Arthur Heath *bishop*
Lohmuller, Martin Nicholas *bishop*
Loppnow, Milo Alvin *clergyman, former church official*
Losten, Basil Harry *bishop*
Luetkehoelter, Gottlieb Werner (Lee) *retired bishop, clergyman*
Madera, Joseph J. *bishop*
Malone, James William *retired bishop*
Mann, Lowell D. *religious organization executive*
McBean, Sharon Elizabeth *church administrator*
McCandless, J(ane) Bardarah *retired religion educator*
McClinton, Wendell C. *religious organization administrator*
McConnell, Calvin Dale *clergyman*
McDermott, Lucinda Mary *ecumenical minister, teacher, philosopher, poet, author*
McKinley, Ellen Bacon *priest*
McQuilkin, John Robertson *religion educator, academic administrator, writer*
Melczek, Dale J. *bishop*
Melvin, Billy Alfred *clergyman*
Milhouse, Paul William *bishop*
Mischke, Carl Herbert *religious association executive, retired*
Moore, E. Harris *bishop*
Moreton, Thomas Hugh *minister*
Muckerman, Norman James *priest, writer*
Mullan, Donald William *bishop*
Newhall, Jeffrey Robert *religious organization administrator*
Norris, Dennis E. *religious organization executive*
Nottingham, William Jesse *retired church mission executive, minister*
Ochs, Carol Rebecca *theologian, philosophy and religion educator*
O'Connell, Brian James *priest, former university president*
Osborne, James Alfred *religious organization administrator*
Parsons, Elmer Earl *retired clergyman*
Patterson, Donis Dean *bishop*
Peers, Michael Geoffrey *archbishop*
Pelotte, Donald Edmond *bishop*
Pleming-Yocum, Laura Chalker *religion educator*
Poteat, James Donald *diaconal minister, retired military officer*
Povish, Kenneth Joseph *retired bishop*
Procter, John Ernest *former publishing company executive*
Quick, Norman *bishop*
Reed, Cynthia Kay *minister*
Reed, Thomas Lee, II *minister, elementary education educator*
Righter, Walter Cameron *bishop*
Rooks, Charles Shelby *minister*
Rose, Robert John *bishop*
Rose, T. T. *bishop*
Roy, Ralph Lord *clergyman*
Salatka, Charles Alexander *archbishop*
Sams, John Roland *retired mission executive, missionary*
Sayre, Francis Bowes, Jr. *clergyman*
Schmiel, David Gerhard *clergyman, religious education administrator*
Schmitt, Howard Stanley *minister*
Schuelke, John Paul *religious organization administrator*
Scott, Robert Hal *minister*
Scott, Waldron *mission executive*
Seale, James Millard *religious organization administrator, clergyman*
Sherman, Joseph Howard *clergyman*
Shotwell, Malcolm Green *retired minister*
Sloyan, Gerard Stephen *religious studies educator, priest*
Soro, Mar Bawai *bishop*
Spence, Glen Oscar *clergyman*
Stendahl, Krister *retired bishop*
Stevens, John Flournoy *priest*
Stevens, Lisa Gay *minister, choral director*
Storms, Margaret LaRue *librarian*
Strasser, Gabor *priest, management consultant*
Sullivan, James Lenox *clergyman*
Sullivan, Leon Howard *clergyman*
Swanson, Paul Rubert *minister*
Tanquary, Oliver Leo *minister*
Taylor, June Ruth *retired minister*
Taylor, Lewis Jerome, Jr. *priest*
Thompson, Eugene Mayne *retired minister*
Thottupuram, Kurian Cherian *priest, college director, educator*
Vachon, Louis-Albert Cardinal *archbishop*
van Dyck, Nicholas Booraem *minister, foundation official*
Watson, W. H. *bishop*
Weinhauer, William Gillette *retired bishop*
Weinkauf, Mary Louise Stanley *clergywoman*
Williams, Ervin Eugene *religious organization administrator*
Williams, John Christopher Richard *bishop*
Wills, Charles Francis *former church executive, retired career officer*
Wright, Earl Jerome *pastor, bishop*
Yun, Hsing *head religious order*

SCIENCE: LIFE SCIENCE

UNITED STATES

ALABAMA

**Auburn**
Bailey, Wilford Sherrill *retired parasitology educator, science administrator, university president*
Ball, Donald Maury *agronomist, consultant*
Bergen, Werner Gerhard *animal science educator, nutritionist*
Klesius, Phillip Harry *microbiologist, researcher*
Oli, Madan Kumar *wildlife ecologist*
†Thompson, Emmett Frank *forestry educator, dean*

**Birmingham**
Bradley, John M(iller), Jr. *forestry executive*
Brown, Jerry William *cell biology and anatomy educator*
Davenport, Horace Willard *physiologist*
Elgavish, Ada *molecular, cellular biologist*
Finley, Sara Crews *medical geneticist, educator*
Navia, Juan Marcelo *biologist, educator*
Oglesby, Sabert, Jr. *retired research institute administrator*
Page, John Gardner *research administrator, scientist*
Rouse, John Wilson, Jr. *research institute administrator*
Schafer, James Arthur *physiologist*
Stokes, Robert Allan *science research facility executive, physicist*

### Dauphin Island
Cowan, James Howard, Jr. *fishery scientist, biological oceanographer*

### Homewood
Haddox, Jeffrey Lynn *cell biologist, electron microscopist*

### Mobile
French, Elizabeth Irene *biology educator, violinist*
Gottlieb, Sheldon Fred *biologist, educator*
Taylor, Aubrey Elmo *physiologist, educator*

### Normal
Bishnoi, Udai Ram *agronomy and seed technology educator*
Coleman, Tommy Lee *soil science educator, researcher, laboratory director*

### Selma
Datiri, Benjamin Chumang *soil and environmental scientist*

### Tuscaloosa
Darden, William Howard, Jr. *biology educator*
Wetzel, Robert George *botany educator*

### Tuskegee
Smith, Edward Jude *biologist*

## ALASKA

### Fairbanks
Kessel, Brina *ornithologist, educator*
White, Robert Gordon *research director, biology educator*

### Juneau
Willson, Mary F. *ecology researcher, educator*

## ARIZONA

### Cortaro
Smith, Dwight Raymond *ecology and wildlife educator, writer*

### Flagstaff
Price, Peter Wilfrid *ecology educator, researcher*

### Phoenix
Adler, Eugene Victor *forensic toxicologist, consultant*
Anderson, Edward Frederick *biology educator*
Kimball, Bruce Arnold *soil scientist*
Witherspoon, James Donald *biology educator*

### Tempe
Gerking, Shelby Delos, Jr. *zoologist, educator*
Herald, Cherry Lou *research educator, research director*
Patten, Duncan Theunissen *ecologist educator*

### Tucson
Acker, Robert Flint *microbiologist*
Cortner, Hanna Joan *science administrator, research scientist, educator*
Fritts, Harold Clark *dendrochronology educator, researcher*
Gerba, Charles Peter *microbiologist, educator*
Green, Robert Scott *biotechnology company executive*
Hull, Herbert Mitchell *plant physiologist, researcher*
Jeter, Wayburn Stewart *retired microbiology educator, microbiologist*
McCormick, Floyd Guy, Jr. *agricultural educator, college administrator*
Metcalfe, Darrel Seymour *agronomist, educator*
Neuman, Shlomo P. *hydrology educator*
Osterberg, Charles Lamar *marine radioecologist, oceanographer*
Pepper, Ian L. *environmental microbiologist, research scientist, educator*
Shannon, Robert Rennie *optical sciences center administrator, educator*
Strausfeld, Nicholas James *neurobiology and evolutionary biology researcher, educator*
Sypherd, Paul Starr *microbiologist*
Winfree, Arthur Taylor *biologist, educator*
Yocum, Harrison Gerald *horticulturist, botanist, educator, researcher*

### Window Rock
Hathaway, Loline *zoo and botanic park curator*

## ARKANSAS

### Bella Vista
Musacchia, X(avier) J(oseph) *physiology and biophysics educator*

### Cherokee Village
Hollingsworth, John Alexander *retired science and mathematics educator, writer, consultant*

### Fayetteville
Brown, Connell Jean *retired animal science educator*
Clayton, Frances Elizabeth *cytologist, scientist, educator*
Evans, William Lee *biologist*
Kellogg, David Wayne *agriculture educator, researcher*
Morris, Justin Roy *food scientist, consultant, enologist, research director*
Musick, Gerald Joe *entomology educator*
Riggs, Robert Dale *plant pathology/nematology educator, researcher*
Rutledge, Elliott Moye *soil scientist, educator*
Scifres, Charles Joel *agricultural educator*
Wolf, Duane Carl *microbiologist*

### Jefferson
Casciano, Daniel Anthony *biologist*
Schwetz, Bernard Anthony *toxicologist*

### Little Rock
Barron, Almen Leo *microbiologist*
Hinson, Jack Allsbrook *research toxicologist, educator*

### State University
Bednarz, James C. *wildlife ecologist educator*

## CALIFORNIA

### Alameda
Blatt, Beverly Faye *biologist, consultant*
Koenig, Gina Lee *microbiologist*
Paustenbach, Dennis James *environmental toxicologist*

### Arcata
Barratt, Raymond William *biologist, educator*

### Atherton
Starr, Chauncey *research institute executive*

### Azusa
Kimnach, Myron William *botanist, horticulturist, consultant*

### Berkeley
Anderson, John Richard *entomologist, educator*
Baldwin, Bruce Gregg *botany educator, researcher*
Barrett, Reginald Haughton *biology educator, wildlife management educator*
Berkner, Klaus Hans *laboratory administrator, physicist*
Bern, Howard Alan *science educator, research biologist*
Burnside, Mary Beth *biology educator, researcher*
Casida, John Edward *entomology educator*
Chemsak, John Andrew *entomologist*
Collins, James Francis *toxicologist*
Dahlsten, Donald Lee *entomology educator, university dean*
Dempster, Lauramay Tinsley *botanist*
Getz, Wayne Marcus *biomathematician, researcher, educator*
Hess, Wilmot Norton *science administrator*
Johnson, Ned Keith *ornithologist, educator*
Licht, Paul *zoologist, educator*
Lidicker, William Zander, Jr. *zoologist, educator*
Ornduff, Robert *botany educator*
Pitelka, Frank Alois *zoologist, educator*
Rubin, Gerald Mayer *molecular biologist, biochemistry educator*
Schachman, Howard Kapnek *molecular biologist, educator*
†Schwimmer, Sigmund *food enzymologist*
Scott, Eugenie Carol *science foundation director, anthropologist*
Shatz, Carla J. *biology educator*
Spear, Robert Clinton *environmental health educator, consultant*
Teeguarden, Dennis Earl *forest economist*
Vedros, Neylan Anthony *microbiologist*
Wake, David Burton *biology educator*
Wake, Marvalee Hendricks *biology educator*
Willhite, Calvin Campbell *toxicologist*
Wood, David L. *entomologist, educator*

### Bodega Bay
Allard, Robert Wayne *geneticist, educator*
Clegg, James Standish *physiologist, biochemist, educator*
Hand, Cadet Hammond, Jr. *marine biologist, educator*

### Bolinas
Lerner, Michael Albers *educator*

### Cambria
Villeneuve, Donald Avila *biology educator*

### Chico
Ediger, Robert Ike *botanist, educator*
Kistner, David Harold *biology educator*

### Claremont
Purves, William Kirkwood *biologist, educator*
Taylor, Roy Lewis *botanist, educator*

### Clovis
Ensminger, Marion Eugene *animal science educator, author*

### Coalinga
Harris, John Charles *agriculturalist*

### Concord
Ivy, Edward Everett *entomologist, consultant*

### Corona Del Mar
Brokaw, Charles Jacob *educator, cellular biologist*

### Cupertino
Anderson, Charles Arthur *former research institute administrator*
Cheeseman, Douglas Taylor, Jr. *wildlife tour executive, photographer, educator*

### Davis
Addicott, Fredrick Taylor *retired botany educator*
Barbour, Michael G(eorge) *botany educator, ecological consultant*
Baskin, Ronald Joseph *cell biologist, physiologist, biophysicist educator, dean*
Bruening, George E. *virologist*
Butler, Edward Eugene *plant pathology educator*
Carman, Hoy Fred *agricultural sciences educator*
Cliver, Dean Otis *microbiologist, educator*
Colvin, Harry Walter, Jr. *physiology educator*
Crane, Julian Coburn *agriculturist,retired educator*
Epstein, Emanuel *plant physiologist*
Freedland, Richard Allan *retired biologist, educator*
Gifford, Ernest Milton *biologist, educator*
Grey, Robert Dean *biology educator*
Hess, Charles Edward *environmental horticulture educator*
Horwitz, Barbara Ann *physiologist, educator, consultant*
Hughes, John P. *equine research adminstrator*
Kado, Clarence Isao *molecular biologist*
Kester, Dale Emmert *pomologist, educator*
Klasing, Susan Allen *environmental toxicologist, consultant*
Kofranek, Anton Miles *floriculturist, educator*
Kunkee, Ralph Edward *viticulture and enology educator*
Laidlaw, Harry Hyde, Jr. *entomology educator*
Learn, Elmer Warner *agricultural economics educator, retired*
Meyer, Margaret Eleanor *microbiologist, educator*
Moyle, Peter Briggs *fisheries and biology educator*
Murphy, Terence Martin *biology educator*
Pappagianis, Demosthenes *microbiology educator, physician*
Qualset, Calvin O. *agronomy educator*
Rappaport, Lawrence *plant physiology and horticulture educator*
Rick, Charles Madeira, Jr. *geneticist, educator*
Rost, Thomas Lowell *plant biology educator*
Schoener, Thomas William *zoology educator, researcher*
Sillman, Arnold Joel *physiologist, educator*
Stewart, James Ian *agricultural water scientist, cropping system developer, consultant*
Uyemoto, Jerry Kazumitsu *plant pathologist, educator*
Watt, Kenneth Edmund Ferguson *zoology educator*
Williams, William Arnold *agronomy educator*
Wilson, Barry William *biology educator*

### Del Mar
Farquhar, Marilyn Gist *cell biology and pathology educator*

### Duarte
Lundblad, Roger Lauren *research director*
Ohno, Susumu *research scientist*
Smith, Steven Sidney *molecular biologist*
Vaughn, James English, Jr. *neurobiologist*

### El Centro
Flock, Robert Ashby *retired entomologist*

### Encinitas
†Motoyama, Hiroshi *science association administrator*

### Eureka
Roberts, Robert Chadwick *ecologist, environmental scientist, consultant*

### Flintridge
Clauser, Francis H. *applied science educator*

### Foster City
Baselt, Randall Clint *toxicologist*
Miller, Jon Philip *research and development organization executive*

### Fresno
Gump, Barry Hemphill *research institute director*

### Fullerton
Brattstrom, Bayard Holmes *biology educator*
Jones, Claris Eugene, Jr. *botanist, educator*

### Gardena
Hu, Steve Seng-Chiu *scientific research company executive, academic administrator*

### Hayward
Flora, Edward Benjamin *research and development company executive, mechanical engineer*

### Hopland
Jones, Milton Bennion *agronomist, educator*

### Irvine
Ayala, Francisco José *geneticist, educator*
Dandashi, Fayad Alexander *operations research scientist*
Demetrescu, Mihai Constantin *research scientist, educator, computer company executive*
Fan, Hung Y. *virology educator, consultant*
Fitch, Walter M(onroe) *molecular biologist, educator*
Gutman, George Andre *molecular biologist, educator*
Lambert, Robert Lowell *scientific investigator*
Larson, Kirk David *pomologist and extension specialist*
Lenhoff, Howard Maer *biological sciences educator, academic administrator, activist*
Silverman, Paul Hyman *parasitologist, former university official*

### Kelseyville
Sandmeyer, E. E. *toxicologist, consultant*

### Kensington
Stent, Gunther Siegmund *molecular biologist, educator*

### La Jolla
Alvariño De Leira, Angeles (Angeles Alvariño) *biologist, oceanographer*
Bloom, Floyd Elliott *physician, research scientist*
Brooks, Charles Lee, III *computational biophysicist, educator*
Case, Ted Joseph *biologist, educator*
Dulbecco, Renato *biologist, educator*
Fishman, William Harold *cancer research foundation executive, biochemist*
Guillemin, Roger C. L. *physiologist*
Haxo, Francis Theodore *marine biologist*
Helinski, Donald Raymond *biologist, educator*
Jones, Galen Everts *microbiologist, educator*
Lewin, Ralph Arnold *biologist*
Pollard, Thomas Dean *cell biologist, educator*
Quinton, Paul Marquis *physiology educator*
Saier, Milton H, Jr. *biology educator*
Vacquier, Victor Dimitri *biology educator*
Walker, Joseph *retired research executive*
West, John Burnard *physiologist, educator*
Wilkie, Donald Walter *biologist, aquarium museum director*
Yang, Zhen *research scientist*
Zwain, Ismail Hassan *molecular endocrinologist*

### Lake Arrowhead
Asher, James Edward *forestry consultant, engineer, arborist, forensic expert*

### Lemon Grove
Whitehead, Marvin Delbert *plant pathologist*

### Loma Linda
Longo, Lawrence Daniel *physiologist, obstetrician-gynecologist*
Taylor, Barry Llewellyn *microbiologist, educator*

### Long Beach
Iliff, Warren Jolidon *zoo administrator*
Small, Richard David *research scientist*
Swatek, Frank Edward *microbiology educator*

### Los Altos
Frey, Christian Miller *research center executive*

### Los Angeles
Baker, Robert Frank *molecular biologist, educator*
Birren, James Emmett *university research center executive*
Bok, Dean *cell biologist, educator*
Collias, Elsie Cole *zoologist*
Craft, Cheryl Mae *neurobiologist, anatomist, researcher*
Davies, Kelvin James Anthony *research scientist, educator, consultant, author*
Finch, Caleb Ellicott *neurobiologist, educator*
Finegold, Sydney Martin *microbiology and immunology educator*
Gibson, Arthur Charles *biologist, educator*
Gilman, John Joseph *research scientist*
Gordon, Malcolm Stephen *biology educator*
Haglund, Thomas Roy *research biologist, consultant, educator*
Korge, Paavo *cell physiologist*
Martin, Walter Edwin *biology educator*
McClure, William Owen *biologist*
Mockary, Peter Ernest *clinical laboratory scientist, researcher*
Mohr, John Luther *biologist, environmental consultant*
Sonnenschein, Ralph Robert *physiologist*
Szego, Clara Marian *cell biologist, educator*
†Taylor, Charles Ellett *biologist*
Wright, Ernest Marshall *physiologist, consultant*
Yang, Yang *research scientist*

### Martinez
Thomas, Walter Dill, Jr. *forest pathologist, consultant*

### Menlo Park
Crane, Hewitt David *science advisor*
Fuhrman, Frederick Alexander *physiology educator*
Jorgensen, Paul J. *research company executive*
MacGregor, James Thomas *toxicologist*
Pake, George Edward *research executive, physicist*

### Mentone
Halstead, Bruce Walter *biotoxicologist*

### Moffett Field
Greenleaf, John Edward *research physiologist*
Morrison, David *science administrator*
Munechika, Ken Kenji *research center administrator*

### Mountain View
Klein, Harold Paul *microbiologist*

### Newport Beach
Swan, Peer Alden *scientific company executive, bank director*

### Northridge
Oppenheimer, Steven Bernard *biology educator*

### Oakland
Earle, Sylvia Alice *research biologist, oceanographer*
Whitsel, Richard Harry *biologist, entomologist*

### Pacific Grove
Epel, David *biologist, educator*

### Pacific Palisades
Lewis, Frank Harlan *botanist, educator*

### Palm Desert
Sausman, Karen *zoological park administrator*

### Palo Alto
Balzhiser, Richard Earl *research and development company executive*
Briggs, Winslow Russell *plant biologist, educator*
De Smedt, Philippe *research scientist, technologist*
Eggers, Alfred John, Jr. *research corporation executive*
Garland, Harry Thomas *research administrator*
Johnson, Noble Marshall *research scientist*
Tsien, Richard Winyu *biology educator*
Zuckerkandl, Emile *molecular evolutionary biologist, scientific institute executive*

### Pasadena
Beer, Reinhard *atmospheric scientist*
Lewis, Edward B. *biology educator*
†Medina-Puerta, Antonio *scientist*
Meyerowitz, Elliot Martin *biologist, educator*
North, Wheeler James *marine ecologist, educator*
Owen, Ray David *biology educator*
Revel, Jean-Paul *biology educator*
Wayland, J(ames) Harold *biomedical scientist, educator*

### Pleasanton
Choy, Clement Kin-Man *research scientist*
Eby, Frank Shilling *retired research scientist*

### Pomona
Burrill, Melinda Jane *animal science educator*
Keating, Eugene Kneeland *animal scientist, educator*

### Redwood City
Neville, Roy Gerald *scientist, chemical management and environmental consultant*

### Richmond
Beall, Frank Carroll *science director and educator*
Zavarin, Eugene *forestry science educator*

Melnick, Vijaya Lakshmi *biology educator, research center director*
Menzer, Robert Everett *toxicologist, educator*
Meyers, Wayne Marvin *microbiologist*
Miller, Alan Stanley *ecology center administrator, law educator*
Moss, Thomas Henry *science association administrator*
Nabholz, Joseph Vincent *biologist, ecologist*
Nightingale, Elena Ottolenghi *geneticist, physician, administrator*
O'Neil, Joseph Francis *association executive*
Podgorny, Richard Joseph *biologist, science administrator*
Pyke, Thomas Nicholas, Jr. *government science and engineering administrator*
Ralls, Katherine *zoologist*
Reginato, Robert Joseph *soil scientist*
Ritter, Donald Lawrence *environmental policy institute executive*
Roberts, Howard Richard *food scientist, association administrator*
Robinson, Michael Hill *zoological park director, biologist*
Sass, Neil Leslie *toxicologist*
Schad, Theodore MacNeeve *science research administrator, consultant*
Schiff, Stefan Otto *zoologist, educator*
Schroeder, Paul Herman *entomologist*
Simpson, Michael Marcial *science specialist, consultant*
Smith, Philip Meek *science policy consultant, writer*
Steinberg, Marcia Irene *science foundation program director*
Tidball, M. Elizabeth Peters *physiologist, educator, research director*
Todhunter, John Anthony *toxicologist*
Torrey, Barbara Boyle *research council administrator*
Vandiver, Pamela Bowren *research scientist*
Wasshausen, Dieter Carl *systematic botanist*
West, Robert MacLellan *science education consultant*
Wilkinson, Ronald Sterne *science administrator, environmentalist, historian*

## FLORIDA

### Belle Glade
Waddill, Van Hulen *entomology educator*

### Boca Raton
Reid, George Kell *biology educator, researcher, author*
Samuels, William Mason *physiology association executive*

### Bonita Springs
Dacey, George Clement *retired laboratory administrator, consultant*

### Bowling Green
Klein, Philip Howard *park ranger*

### Boynton Beach
Mirman, Irving R. *scientific adviser*

### Bradenton
Maynard, Donald Nelson *horticulturist, educator*

### Chuluota
Hatton, Thurman Timbrook, Jr. *retired horticulturist, consultant*

### Clearwater
Bramante, Pietro Ottavio *physiology educator, retired pathology specialist*
Byrd, Mary Laager *animal scientist, researcher, consultant*

### Daytona Beach
Duma, Richard Joseph *microbiologist, physician, pathologist, researcher, educator*

### Delray Beach
Chavin, Walter *biological science educator and researcher*

### Fort Pierce
Calvert, David Victor *soil science educator*
Rice, Mary Esther *biologist*

### Gainesville
Agrios, George Nicholas *plant pathology educator*
Besch, Emerson Louis *physiology educator, past academic administrator*
Cantliffe, Daniel James *horticulture educator*
Childers, Norman Franklin *horticulture educator*
Christie, Richard Gary *plant pathologist*
Dilcher, David Leonard *paleobotany educator, research scholar*
Drury, Kenneth Clayton *biological scientist*
Edwardson, John Richard *agronomist*
Gelband, Craig Harris *physiologist, pharmacologist*
Gerberg, Eugene Jordan *entomologist*
Gutekunst, Richard Ralph *microbiology educator*
Hoy, Marjorie Ann *entomology educator*
Jones, Richard Lamar *entomology educator*
Locascio, Salvadore Joseph *horticulturist*
Mead, Frank Waldreth *taxonomic entomologist*
Oberlander, Herbert *insect physiologist, educator*
Otis, Arthur Brooks *physiologist, educator*
Popenoe, Hugh Llywelyn *soils educator*
Purcifull, Dan Elwood *plant virologist, educator*
Quesenberry, Kenneth Hays *agronomy educator*
Schelske, Claire L. *limnologist, educator*
Schmidt-Nielsen, Bodil Mimi (Mrs. Roger G. Chagnon) *physiologist*
†Smith, Wayne H. *forest resources and conservation educator*
Stern, William Louis *botanist, educator*
Teixeira, Arthur Alves *food engineer, educator, consultant*
Vasil, Indra Kumar *botanist*
Wilcox, Charles Julian *geneticist, educator*
Williams, Norris Hagan, Jr. *biologist, educator, curator*

### Gulf Breeze
Mayer, Foster Lee, Jr. *toxicologist*

### Homestead
Revuelta, René Sergio *marine scientist, educator*
Roberts, Larry Spurgeon *biological sciences educator, zoologist*

### Jacksonville
Bodkin, Lawrence Edward *research development company executive, gemologist, inventor*
Hartzell, Charles R. *research administrator, biochemist, cell biologist*

### Jay
Brecke, Barry John *weed scientist, researcher, educator*
Peacock, Hugh Anthony *agricultural research director*

### LaBelle
Lester, W(illiam) Bernard *agricultural economist, business executive*

### Lake Alfred
Kender, Walter John *horticulturist, educator*

### Lake Placid
Layne, James Nathaniel *vertebrate biologist*

### Lehigh Acres
Moore, John Newton *retired natural science educator*

### Longboat Key
Maha, George Edward *research facility administrator, consultant*

### Melbourne
Helmstetter, Charles Edward *microbiologist*
Storrs, Eleanor Emerett *research institute consultant*

### Miami
Colwin, Arthur Lentz *biologist, educator*
Correll, Helen Butts *botanist, researcher*
Hayashi, Teru *zoologist, educator*
Manniello, John Baptiste Louis *research scientist*
Muench, Karl H. *clinical geneticist*
Myrberg, Arthur August, Jr. *marine biological sciences educator*
Zeiller, Warren *former aquarium executive, consultant*

### Ona
Rechcigl, Jack Edward *soil and environmental sciences educator*

### Orlando
Smith, Paul Frederick *plant physiologist, consultant*

### Osprey
Cort, Winifred Mitchell *microbiologist, biochemist*

### Palm Beach
Hopper, Arthur Frederick *biological science educator*

### Pensacola
Loesch, Harold C. *retired marine biologist, consultant*
Ray, Donald Hensley *biologist*

### Punta Gorda
Beever, James William, III *biologist*

### Quincy
Teare, Iwan Dale *retired research scientist*

### Ramrod Key
Clark, John Russell *ecologist*

### Saint Augustine
Greenberg, Michael John *biologist, editor*

### Saint Petersburg
Byrd, Isaac Burlin *fishery biologist, fisheries administrator*
Mueller, O. Thomas *molecular geneticist, pediatrics educator*

### Sarasota
Borle, André Bernard *physiologist*
Gilbert, Perry Webster *emeritus educator*
Mahadevan, Kumar *marine laboratory director, researcher*
Pierce, Richard Harry *research director for laboratory*
Seibert, Russell Jacob *botanist, research associate*

### Spring Hill
Collins, Stephen Allen *environmental consultant*

### Surfside
Polley, Richard Donald *microbiologist, polymer chemist*

### Tallahassee
Friedmann, E(merich) Imre *biologist, educator*
Friedmann, Roseli Ocampo *microbiologist, educator*
Harris, Natholyn Dalton *food science educator, researcher*
James, Frances Crews *zoology educator*
Koontz, Christine Miller *research faculty*
Lipner, Harry *retired physiologist, educator*
Meredith, Michael *science educator, researcher*
Sengbusch, Howard George *biology, parasitology educator*
Taylor, J(ames) Herbert *cell biology educator*

### Tampa
Falls, William Wayne *aquaculturist*
Hickman, Hugh V. *science educator, researcher*
Hinsch, Gertrude Wilma *biology educator*
Lim, Daniel Van *microbiology educator*

### Vero Beach
Baker, Richard H. *geneticist, educator*
Grobman, Arnold Brams *retired biology educator and academic administrator*
Grobman, Hulda Gross (Mrs. Arnold B. Grobman) *retired health sciences educator*

### West Palm Beach
Sturrock, Thomas Tracy *botany educator, horticulturist*

### Winter Haven
Grierson, William *retired agricultural educator*

### Winter Park
Dawson, Ray Fields *research scientist, educator, consultant, tropical agriculturist*

## GEORGIA

### Alpharetta
Balows, Albert *microbiologist, educator*

### Athens
Agosin, Moises Kankolsky *zoology educator*
Albersheim, Peter *biology educator*
Atwater, Mary Monroe *science educator*
Baile, Clifton A. *biologist, researcher*
Boyd, Louis Jefferson *agricultural scientist, educator*
Giles, Norman Henry *educator, geneticist*
Hildebrand, Don *science foundation executive*
Langdale, George Wilfred *soil scientist, researcher*
Payne, William Jackson *microbiologist, educator*
Plummer, Gayther L(ynn) *climatologist, ecologist, researcher*
Sumner, Malcom Edward *agronomist, educator*
Van Eseltine, William Parker *microbiologist, educator*

### Atlanta
Barnard, Susan Muller *zookeeper*
Carey, Gerald John, Jr. *research institute director, former air force officer*
Circeo, Louis Joseph, Jr. *research center director, civil engineer*
Clifton, David Samuel, Jr. *research executive, economist*
Compans, Richard W. *microbiology educator*
Gunn, Robert Burns *physiology educator*
Humphrey, Charles Durham *microbiologist, biomedical researcher*
Jeffery, Geoffrey Marron *medical parasitologist*
Joiner, Ronald Luther *toxicologist*
La Farge, Timothy *plant geneticist*
Langdale, Noah Noel, Jr. *research educator, former university president*
Long, Leland Timothy *geophysics educator, seismologist*
McGowan, John Edward, Jr. *medical and public health educator, epidemiologist*
Melvin, Dorothy Mae *retired microbiologist*
Mirsky, Jeffrey *science foundation administrator*
Navalkar, Ramchandra Govindrao *microbiologist, immunologist*
Pratt, Harry Davis *retired entomologist*
Schwartz, Miriam Catherine *biology educator*
Spitznagel, John Keith *microbiologist, immunologist*
Tamin, Azaibi *molecular virologist, researcher*
Zumpe, Doris *ethologist, researcher, educator*

### Bogart
Butts, David Phillip *science educator*

### Columbus
Gore, James Arnold *biology educator, aquatic ecologist, hydrologist*
Riggsby, Ernest Duward *science educator, educational development executive*

### Duluth
Johnson, Barry Lee *public health research administrator*

### Dunwoody
La Motte, Louis Cossitt, Jr. *medical scientist, consultant*

### Evans
Little, Robert Colby *physiologist, educator*

### Griffin
Doyle, Michael Patrick *food microbiologist, educator, administrator*
Duncan, Ronny Rush *agriculturist, turf researcher*
Shuman, Larry Myers *soil chemist*
Wilkinson, Robert Eugene *plant physiologist*

### Macon
Adkison, Linda Russell *geneticist, consultant*
Volpe, Erminio Peter *biologist, educator*

### Norcross
Darst, Bobby Charles *soil chemist, administrator*
Dibb, David Walter *research association administrator*
McDonald, James *science foundation executive*
Nottay, Baldev Kaur *microbiologist*
Wagner, Robert Earl *agronomist*

### Sapelo Island
Alberts, James Joseph *scientist, researcher*

### Savannah
Eaves, George Newton *lecturer, consultant, research administrator*

### Tifton
Austin, Max Eugene *horticulture educator*
Douglas, Charles Francis *agronomist*
Miller, John David *retired agronomist*
Rogers, Charlie Ellic *entomologist*

### Tucker
O'Neil, Daniel Joseph *science research executive, university consultant*

## HAWAII

### Haleiwa
Woolliams, Keith Richard *arboretum and botanical garden director*

### Hilo
Nagao, Mike Akira *horticulturist, county administrator*

### Honolulu
Abbott, Isabella Aiona *biology educator*
Ashton, Geoffrey Cyril *geneticist, educator*
Fok, Agnes Kwan *cell biologist, educator*
Greenfield, David W. *zoology educator*
Hertlein, Fred, III *industrial hygiene laboratory executive*
Kamemoto, Fred Isamu *zoologist*
Kamemoto, Haruyuki *horticulture educator*
Kay, Elizabeth Alison *zoology educator*
Lamoureux, Charles Harrington *botanist, arboretum administrator*
Laughlin, Charles William *agriculture educator, research administrator*
Mandel, Morton *molecular biologist*
Naitoh, Yutaka *biology educator*
Sagawa, Yoneo *horticulturist, educator*
Sherman, Martin *entomologist*
Smith, Albert Charles *biologist, educator*

### Tripler Army Medical Center
Uyehara, Catherine Fay Takako (Yamauchi) *physiologist, educator, pharmacologist*

## IDAHO

### Aberdeen
Sparks, Walter Chappel *horticulturist, educator*

### Boise
Brownfield, Shelby Harold *soil scientist*

### Hayden Lake
Lehrer, William Peter, Jr. *animal scientist*

### Moscow
Crawford, Don Lee *microbiologist*
Mahler, Robert Louis *soil scientist, educator*
Roberts, Lorin Watson *botanist, educator*
Scott, James Michael *research biologist*

### Pocatello
McCune, Mary Joan Huxley *microbiology educator*
Seeley, Rod Ralph *physiology educator*

## ILLINOIS

### Abbott Park
Kim, Yung Dai *research scientist*

### Argonne
Schriesheim, Alan *research administrator*

### Brookfield
Pawley, Ray Lynn *zoological park herpetology curator*
Rabb, George Bernard *zoologist*

### Canton
Godt, Earl Wayne, II *technology education educator*

### Carbondale
Bozzola, John Joseph *botany educator, researcher*
Burr, Brooks Milo *zoology educator*
Kapusta, George *botany educator, agronomy educator*

### Champaign
Batzli, George Oliver *ecology educator*
Getz, Lowell Lee *zoology educator*
Levin, Geoffrey Arthur *botanist*
Ridlen, Samuel Franklin *agriculture educator*
Sanderson, Glen Charles *science director*
Smith, Robert Lee *agriculturalist*
Sprugel, George, Jr. *ecologist*

### Chicago
Altmann, Stuart Allen *biologist, educator*
Beattie, Ted Arthur *zoological gardens and aquarium administrator*
Beecher, William John *zoologist, museum director*
Braddock, David Lawrence *health science educator*
Buss, Daniel Frank *environmental scientist*
Chakrabarty, Ananda Mohan *microbiologist*
Cohen, Edward Philip *microbiology and immunology educator, physician*
Crane, Peter Robert *botanist, geologist, paleontologist, educator*
Davidson, Richard Laurence *geneticist, educator*
Desjardins, Claude *physiologist, dean, administrator*
Ernest, J. Terry *ocular physiologist, educator*
Fenters, James Dean *research institute administrator*
Fisher, Lester Emil *zoo administrator*
Fuchs, Elaine V. *molecular biologist, educator*
Fukui, Yoshio *biology educator*
Goldman, Robert David *cell biologist, educator*
Greenberg, Bernard *entomologist, educator*
Haselkorn, Robert *virology educator*
Helms, Byron Eldon *associate director of research, biology and physiology administrator*
Houk, James Charles *physiologist, educator*
Kass, Leon Richard *educator*
Lewert, Robert Murdoch *microbiologist, educator*
Mahowald, Anthony Peter *geneticist, cell biologist, educator*
Mateles, Richard Isaac *biotechnologist*
McCrone, Walter Cox *research institute executive*
McKinley, Vicky Lynn *biology educator*
Miller, Patrick William *research administrator, educator*
Nakajima, Yasuko *medical educator*
Overton, Jane Vincent Harper *biology educator*
Park, Thomas Joseph *biology researcher, educator*
Pick, Ruth *research scientist, physician, educator*
Pumper, Robert William *microbiologist*
Roizman, Bernard *virologist, educator*
Rothman-Denes, Lucia Beatriz *biology educator*
Rymer, William Zev *research scientist, administrator*
Scott, John Brooks *research institute executive*
Solaro, Ross John *physiologist, biophysicist*
Straus, Helen Lorna Puttkammer *biologist, educator*
Van Valen, Leigh Maiorana *biologist, educator*

### Des Plaines
Lee, Bernard Shing-Shu *research company executive*

Stewart, Doris Mae *biology educator*
Suskind, Sigmund Richard *microbiology educator*
Trpis, Milan *vector biologist, scientist, educator*

### Beltsville
Adams, Jean Ruth *entomologist, researcher*
Collins, Anita Marguerite *research geneticist*
Hoberg, Eric Paul *parasitologist*
Pachepsky, Ludmila Baudinovna *ecologist*
Palm, Mary Egdahl *mycologist*
Shands, Henry Lee *plant geneticist, administrator*
Terrill, Clair Elman *animal scientist, geneticist, consultant*
Zehner, Lee Randall *biotechnologist, research director*

### Bethesda
Ahmed, S. Basheer *research company executive, educator*
Barrick, Joan Lizbeth *genetics researcher*
Becerra, Sofia Patricia *biomedical research scientist*
Bennink, Jack Richard *microbiologist, researcher*
Brady, Roscoe Owen *neurogeneticist, educator*
Bryan, Billie Marie (Mrs. James A. Mackey) *biologist*
Bunger, Rolf *physiology educator*
Burg, Maurice Benjamin *renal physiologist, physician*
Chang, Kai *molecular biologist, geneticist*
Collins, Francis S. *medical research scientist*
Di Marzo Veronese, Fulvia *research scientist*
Di Paolo, Joseph Amedeo *geneticist*
Felsenfeld, Gary *government official, scientist*
Frank, Martin *physiology educator, health scientist, association executive*
Fraumeni, Joseph F., Jr. *scientific researcher, medical educator, physician, military officer*
Gartland, William Joseph, Jr. *research institute administrator*
Gilbert, Daniel Lee *physiologist*
Gordis, Enoch *science administrator, internist*
Gruber, Jack *medical virologist, biomedical research administrator*
Guttman, Helene Nathan *biomedical research consultant, regression therapist*
Hancock, Charles Cavanaugh, Jr. *scientific association administrator*
Harding, Fann *health scientist, administrator*
Hausman, Steven Jack *health science administrator*
Henning, Karla Ann *molecular biologist, research scientist*
Hodgdon, Harry Edward *association executive, wildlife biologist*
Horakova, Zdenka Zahutova *retired toxicologist, pharmacologist*
Jackson, Michael John *physiologist, association executive*
Jordan, Elke *molecular biologist, government medical research institute executive*
Kelly, William Clark *science administrator*
Law, Lloyd William *geneticist*
Martino, Robert Louis *computational scientist and engineer, researcher*
Miller, Louis Howard *biologist, researcher*
Monjan, Andrew Arthur *health science administrator*
Myers, Lawrence Stanley, Jr. *radiation biologist*
Petralia, Ronald Sebastian *entomologist, neurobiologist, educator*
Piatigorsky, Joram Paul *research scientist, molecular biologist*
Pospisil, George Curtis *biomedical research administrator*
Purcell, Robert Harry *virologist*
Raben, Nina *molecular biologist, biochemist*
Rosen, Saul Woolf *research scientist, health facility administrator*
Salmoiraghi, Gian Carlo *physiologist, educator*
Sanford, Katherine Koontz *cancer researcher*
Shulman, Lawrence Edward *biomedical research administrator, rheumatologist*
Slavkin, Harold Charles *biologist*
Sponsler, George Curtis, III *research administrator, lawyer*
Underwood, Brenda S. *microbiologist, grants administrator*
Vieira, Nancy Elizabeth *biologist, researcher*
Walleigh, Robert Shuler *consultant*
Woolley, George Walter *biologist, geneticist, educator*
Yamada, Kenneth Manao *cell biologist*
Zierdt, Charles Henry *microbiologist*

### Chester
Pelczar, Michael Joseph, Jr. *microbiologist, educator*

### Chevy Chase
Anderson, Owen Raymond *scientific and educational organization executive*
Choppin, Purnell Whittington *research administrator, virology researcher, educator*
Cowan, William Maxwell *neurobiologist*
Harter, Donald Harry *research administrator, medical educator*

### Claiborne
Moorhead, Paul Sidney *geneticist*

### College Park
Clark, Eugenie *zoologist, educator*
Colwell, Rita Rossi *microbiologist, molecular biologist, educator*
Diener, Theodor Otto *plant pathologist*
Fanning, Delvin Seymour *soil science educator*
Gantt, Elisabeth *botany educator and researcher*
Gouin, Francis Romeo *physiologist*
Heath, James Lee *food science educator, researcher*
Lea-Cox, John Derek *plant physiologist*
Miller, Raymond Jarvis *agronomy educator*
Patterson, Glenn Wayne *botany educator*
Popper, Arthur N. *zoology educator*
Quebedeaux, Bruno *horticulture and plant physiology educator*
Stark, Francis C., Jr. *horticulturist, educator*
Vandersall, John Henry *dairy science educator*
Weil, Raymond Richard *soil scientist*

### Columbia
Grewal, Parwinder S. *biologist, researcher*
Keeton, Morris Teuton *research institute director*

### Frederick
Aiuto, Russell *science education consultant*
Housewright, Riley Dee *microbiologist/former scientific society executive*
Knisely, Ralph Franklin *retired microbiologist*

### Gaithersburg
O'Hern, Elizabeth Moot *microbiologist, writer*
Semerjian, Hratch Gregory *research and development executive*

### Galena
Haenlein, George Friedrich Wilhelm *dairy scientist, educator*

### Garrett Park
Baldwin, Calvin Benham, Jr. *retired medical research administrator*

### Greenbelt
Krulisch, Lee *science facility administrator*
Thomas, Lindsey Kay, Jr. *biologist, educator, consultant*

### Hancock
Popenoe, John *horticultural consultant, retired botanical garden administrator*

### Kensington
Jackson, William David *research executive*

### Laurel
Kushlan, James A. *biologist, educator, research administrator*
Robbins, Chandler S(eymour) *research biologist*
Rorie, Conrad Jonathan *scientist, naval officer*

### Libertytown
Lindblad, Richard Arthur *retired health services administrator, drug abuse epidemiologist*

### Potomac
Bollum, Frederick James *biotechnology executive*

### Rockville
Adams, Mark David *molecular biologist*
Carter, Kenneth Charles *geneticist*
Cosmides, George James *medical scientist, consultant*
Garotta, Gianni *research scientist*
Ginsberg, Harold Samuel *virologist, educator*
Landon, John Campbell *medical research company executive*
Leef, James Lewis *biology educator, immunology research executive*
Lewis, Andrew Morris, Jr. *virologist*
Marsik, Frederic John *microbiologist*
Mertz, Walter *retired government research executive*
Poljak, Roberto J(uan) *research director, biotechnology educator*
Rafajko, Robert Richard *medical research company executive*
Shah, Vinod Purushottam *research scientist*

### Salisbury
Moultrie, Fred *geneticist*

### Silver Spring
Calabrese, Diane Marie *entomologist, writer*
Kohler, Max Adam *consulting hydrologist, weather service administrator*
Leedy, Daniel Loney *ecologist*

### Sykesville
Buck, John Bonner *retired biologist*

### Temple Hills
Whidden, Stanley John *physiologist, physician*

### Towson
Wubah, Daniel Asua *microbiologist*

### Wye Mills
Lednum, Florence Nash *biological sciences educator*

## MASSACHUSETTS

### Amherst
Belt, Edward Scudder *sedimentologist, educator*
Coppinger, Raymond Parke *biologist, educator*
Godfrey, Paul Joseph *science foundation director*
Holmes, Francis William *plant pathologist*
Litsky, Bertha Yanis *microbiologist, artist*
Palser, Barbara F. *botany researcher, retired educator*
Stein, Otto Ludwig *botany educator*
Tippo, Oswald *botanist, educator, university administrator*
Tirrell, David A. *research scientist, educator*

### Bedford
Griffin, Donald R(edfield) *zoology educator*

### Beverly
McReynolds, Larry Austin *molecular biologist*
Roberts, Richard John *molecular biologist, consultant, research director*

### Billerica
Kolb, Charles Eugene *research corporation executive*

### Boston
Beinfeld, Margery Cohen *neurobiology educator*
Broitman, Selwyn Arthur *microbiologist, educator*
Carradini, Lawrence *comparative biologist, science administrator*
Coffin, John Miller *molecular biologist, educator*
Cohen, Jonathan Brewer *molecular neurobiologist, biochemist*
Essex, Myron Elmer *microbiology educator*
Faller, Douglas V. *cancer research scientist, physician*
Girouard, Donald Joseph, Jr. *marine ecologist, bacteriologist*
Hornig, Donald Frederick *scientist*
Hubel, David Hunter *physiologist, educator*
Jha, Prakash Kumar *molecular biologist, researcher*
Kahn, Carl Ronald *research laboratory administrator*
Kaminer, Benjamin *physician, educator*
Kety, Seymour S(olomon) *physiologist, neuroscientist*
Kunkel, Louis Martens *research scientist, educator*
Lanner, Michael *research administrator, consultant*
Lees, Sidney *research facility administrator, bioengineering educator*
Malamy, Michael H(oward) *molecular biology and microbiology educator*
McLinden, James Hugh *molecular biologist*
Nichols, Guy Warren *retired institute executive, utilities executive*
Park, James Theodore *microbiologist, educator*
Prescott, John Hernage *aquarium executive*
Sastry, Kedarnath Nanjund *microbiologist, educator*
Schubel, Jerry Robert *marine science educator, scientist, university dean*
Slechta, Robert Frank *biologist, educator*
Sonenshein, Abraham Lincoln *microbiology educator*
Streilein, J. Wayne *research scientist*
Tosteson, Daniel Charles *physiologist, medical school dean*
Turner, Raymond Edward *science educator, researcher, administrator*

### Brookline
West, Doe *bioethicist, social justice activist*

### Cambridge
†Alters, Brian Josiah *science educator*
Ashton, Peter Shaw *tropical forest science educator*
Baltimore, David *microbiologist, educator*
Bazzaz, Fakhri A. *plant biology educator, administrator*
Berg, Howard C. *biology educator*
Bogorad, Lawrence *biologist, educator*
Cook, Robert Edward *plant ecology educator, research director*
Demain, Arnold Lester *microbiologist, educator*
Dowling, John Elliott *biology educator*
Forman, Richard T. T. *ecology educator*
Fox, Maurice Sanford *molecular biologist, educator*
Friedman, Orrie Max *biotechnology company executive*
Gage, (Leonard) Patrick *research company executive*
Gilbert, Walter *molecular biologist, educator*
Goldberg, Ray Allan *agribusiness educator*
Goldblith, Samuel Abraham *food science educator*
Goldman, Ralph Frederick *research physiologist, educator*
Hartl, Daniel Lee *genetics educator*
Hastings, John Woodland *biologist, educator*
Horvitz, Howard Robert *biology educator, researcher*
Hubbard, Ruth *biology educator*
Hynes, Richard Olding *biology researcher and educator*
Jacobson, Ralph Henry *laboratory executive, former air force officer*
Knoll, Andrew Herbert *biology educator*
Lerman, Leonard Solomon *science educator, scientist*
Levi, Herbert Walter *biologist, educator*
Levins, Richard *science educator*
Liu, Guosong *neurobiologist*
Lodish, Harvey Franklin *biologist, educator*
Lynch, Harry James *biologist*
Magee, John Francis *research company executive*
Mayr, Ernst *retired zoologist, philosopher*
McMahon, Thomas Arthur *biology and applied mechanics educator*
Pardue, Mary Lou *biology educator*
Pierce, Naomi Ellen *biology educator, researcher*
Rich, Alexander *molecular biologist, educator*
Schultes, Richard Evans *retired botanist, biology educator*
Shultz, Leila McReynolds *botanist, educator*
Tannenbaum, Steven Robert *toxicologist, chemist*
Tonegawa, Susumu *biology educator*
Torriani-Gorini, Annamaria *microbiologist*
Wilson, Edward Osborne *biologist, educator, author*
Winkler, Gunther *biotechnology executive, drug development expert*
Wogan, Gerald Norman *toxicology educator*
Wurtman, Judith Joy *research scientist*

### Canton
Lyman, Charles Peirson *comparative physiologist*

### Charlestown
Gusella, James F. *geneticist, educator*
Wong, Po Kee *research company executive, educator*

### Concord
Huxley, Hugh Esmor *molecular biologist, educator*

### Falmouth
Schlesinger, Robert Walter *microbiologist, microbiology educator emeritus*

### Grafton
Haggerty, John Edward *research center administrator, former army officer*

### Great Barrington
Stonier, Tom *theoretical biologist, educator*

### Lexington
Drouilhet, Paul Raymond, Jr. *science laboratory director, electrical engineer*
Fillios, Louis Charles *retired science educator*
Gibbs, Martin *biologist, educator*
Melngailis, Ivars *solid state research executive*

### Lowell
Coleman, Robert Marshall *biology educator*

### Medford
Harrison, Bettina Hall *retired biology educator*

### Methuen
Bonanno, A. Richard *weed management scientist, educator*

### Natick
Lachica, R(eynato) Victor *microbiologist*
Sahatjian, Ronald Alexander *science foundation executive*

### North Falmouth
Morse, Robert Warren *research administrator*

### Northampton
Anderson, Margaret Ellen (Margaret Ellen Anderson) *physiologist, educator*
Burk, Carl John *biological sciences educator*

### Norwood
Pence, Robert Dudley *biomedical research administrator, hospital administrator*

### Quincy
Hagar, William Gardner, III *photobiology educator*

### South Hadley
Townsend, Jane Kaltenbach *zoologist, educator*

### Sudbury
Richards, James Carlton *microbiologist, business executive*

### Vineyard Haven
Billingham, Rupert Everett *zoologist, educator*

### Waltham
Galinat, Walton C. *research scientist*
Levitan, Irwin Barry *neuroscience educator, academic administrator*

### Wayland
Blair, John *consulting scientist*

### Wellesley
Gerety, Robert John *microbiologist, pharmaceutical company executive, pediatrician, vaccinologist*

### West Falmouth
Vaccaro, Ralph Francis *marine biologist*

### Woburn
Gelb, Arthur *science association executive, electrical and systems engineer*

### Woods Hole
Copeland, Donald Eugene *research marine biologist*
Ebert, James David *research biologist, educator*
Grice, George Daniel *marine biologist, science administrator*
Inoué, Shinya *microscopy and cell biology scientist, educator*
Jannasch, Holger Windekilde *microbiologist*
Loewenstein, Werner Randolph *physiologist, biophysicist, educator*
Woodwell, George Masters *ecology research director, lecturer*

### Worcester
Bagshaw, Joseph Charles *molecular biologist, educator*
Camougis, George *health, safety and environmental protection consultant*
Escott, Shoolah Hope *microbiologist*

### Yarmouth Port
Stauffer, Robert Allen *former research company executive*

## MICHIGAN

### Ann Arbor
Allen, Sally Lyman *biologist*
Anderson, William R. *botanist, educator, curator, director*
Bryant, Barbara Everitt *academic researcher, market research consultant, former federal agency administrator*
Cochran, Kenneth William *toxicologist*
Dawson, William Ryan *zoology educator*
Drach, John Charles *scientist, educator*
Easter, Stephen Sherman, Jr. *biology educator*
Evans, Francis Cope *ecologist*
Faulkner, John Arthur *physiologist, educator*
Gelehrter, Thomas David *medical and genetics educator, physician*
Ginsburg, David *human genetics educator, researcher*
Hartung, Rolf *environmental toxicology educator, researcher, consultant*
Hawkins, Joseph Elmer, Jr. *retired acoustic physiologist, educator*
Horowitz, Samuel Boris *biomedical researcher, educational consultant*
Horton, William David, Jr. *scientist*
Kaufman, Peter Bishop *biological sciences educator*
Kleinsmith, Lewis Joel *cell biologist, educator*
Kostyo, Jack Lawrence *physiology educator*
Lowe, John Burton *molecular biology educator, pathologist*
Moore, Thomas E. *biology educator, museum director*
†Morton, Harrison Leon *forestry educator*
Neidhardt, Frederick Carl *microbiologist*
Richardson, Rudy James *toxicology and neurosciences educator*
Savageau, Michael Antonio *microbiology and immunology educator*
Shappirio, David Gordon *biologist, educator*
Steiner, Erich Ernst *botany educator*
Stoermer, Eugene Filmore *biology educator*
Wagner, Warren Herbert, Jr. *botanist, educator*
Williams, John Andrew *physiology educator, consultant*
Yocum, Charles Fredrick *biology educator*

### Big Rapids
Barnes, Isabel Janet *microbiology educator, college dean*

### Dearborn
Schneider, Michael Joseph *biologist*

### Detroit
Krawetz, Stephen Andrew *molecular biology and genetics educator*
Lerner, Stephen Alexander *microbiologist, physician, educator*
Miller, Dorothy Anne Smith *retired cytogenetics educator*
Novak, Raymond Francis *research institute director, pharmacology educator*
Phillis, John Whitfield *physiologist, educator*
Zaremba, Thomas Edmund Michael Barry *biology educator*

### East Lansing
Bukovac, Martin John *horticulturist, educator*

PROFESSIONAL INDEX 5401 SCIENCE: LIFE SCIENCE


Chimoskey, John Edward *physiologist, medical educator*
Dennis, Frank George, Jr. *retired horticulture educator*
Fischer, Lawrence Joseph *toxicologist, educator*
Fluck, Michele M(arguerite) *biology educator*
Fromm, Paul Oliver *physiology educator*
Gast, Robert Gale *agriculture educator, experiment station administrator*
Gerhardt, Philipp *microbiologist, educator*
Hackel, Emanuel *science educator*
Hollingworth, Robert Michael *toxicology researcher*
Hull, Jerome, Jr. *horticultural extension specialist*
Isleib, Donald R. *agricultural researcher*
Kamrin, Michael Arnold *toxicology educator*
Kende, Hans Janos *plant physiology educator*
Knobloch, Irving William *retired biology educator, author*
†Koelling, Melvin R. *forestry educator*
Lockwood, John LeBaron *plant pathologist*
Lucas, Robert Elmer *soil scientist*
Lund, Lois A. *retired food science and human nutrition educator*
McMeekin, Dorothy *botany, plant pathology educator*
Nelson, Ronald Harvey *animal science educator, researcher*
Patterson, Maria Jevitz *microbiology-pediatric infectious disease educator*
Paul, Eldor Alvin *agriculture, ecology educator*
Petrides, George Athan *ecologist, educator*
Root-Bernstein, Robert Scott *biologist, educator*
Sparks, Harvey Vise, Jr. *physiologist*
Tesar, Milo Benjamin *agricultural researcher, educator, and administrator*

**Edwardsburg**
Floyd, Alton David *cell biologist, consultant*

**Farmington Hills**
Dragun, James *soil chemist*

**Grand Rapids**
Petkus, Alan Francis *microbiologist*

**Hickory Corners**
Klug, Michael J. *microbiology educator, ecology educator*
Lauff, George Howard *biologist*

**Highland Park**
Crittenden, Mary Lynne *science educator*

**Kalamazoo**
Dietz, Alma *microbiologist*
Marshall, Vincent de Paul *industrial microbiologist, researcher*
Slatter, John Gregory *research scientist*

**Lansing**
Carlotti, Ronald John *food scientist*
Hull, Christopher Neil *state agency biologist*

**Midland**
Bus, James Stanley *toxicologist*

**Mount Pleasant**
Novitski, Charles Edward *biology educator*

**Rochester**
Unakar, Nalin Jayantilal *biological sciences educator*

**Sanford**
Wilmot, Thomas Ray *medical entomologist, educator*

**Ypsilanti**
Caswell, Herbert Hall, Jr. *retired biology educator*

## MINNESOTA

**Duluth**
Heller, Lois Jane *physiologist, educator, researcher*
Johnson, Arthur Gilbert *microbiology educator*

**Mapleton**
John, Hugo Herman *natural resources educator*

**Marcell**
Aldrich, Richard John *agronomist, educator*

**Marshall**
Rice, Stanley Arthur *biology educator*

**Minneapolis**
Danielson, James Walter *research microbiologist*
Dworkin, Martin *microbiologist, educator*
Evans, Robert Leonard *mathematical physiologist, educator*
Gorham, Eville *ecologist, biogeochemist*
Gudmundson, Barbara Rohrke *ecologist*
Haase, Ashley Thomson *microbiology educator, researcher*
Howe, Craig Walter Sandell *medical organization executive, internist*
Joo, Pilju Kim *agronomist*
Lee, Hon Cheung *physiology educator*
Meyer, Maurice Wesley *physiologist, dentist, neurologist*
Miller, Robert Francis *physiologist, educator*
Olson, Theodore Alexander *former environmental biology educator*
Rahman, Yueh-Erh *biologist*
Reynolds, David G(eorge) *physiologist, educator*
Scott, Rebecca Andrews *biology educator*
Smyrl, William Hiram *chemical engineering educator*
Symosek, Peter Frank *research scientist*
Watson, Dennis Wallace *microbiology educator, scientist*

**Moorhead**
Gee, Robert LeRoy *agriculturist, dairy farmer*

**Park Rapids**
Tonn, Robert James *entomologist*

**Prior Lake**
Tufte, Obert Norman *retired research executive*

**Rochester**
Bajzer, Željko *scientist, educator*
Maher, L. James, III *molecular biologist*
Shepherd, John Thompson *physiologist*
Wood, Earl Howard *physiologist, educator*

**Roseville**
Marten, Gordon Cornelius *research agronomist, educator, federal agency administrator*

**Saint Cloud**
Kirick, Daniel John *agronomist*
Musah, Al-Hassan Issah *reproductive physiologist*

**Saint Louis Park**
Frestedt, Joy Louise *scientist, educator, consultant*

**Saint Paul**
Baker, Donald Gardner *retired soil science educator*
Barnwell, Franklin Hershel *zoology educator*
Burnside, Orvin Charles *agronomy educator, researcher*
Caldwell, Elwood Fleming *food scientist*
Cheng, H(wei) H(sien) *soil scientist, agriculture and environmental science educator*
Chiang, Huai Chang *entomologist, educator*
Crookston, Robert Kent *agronomy educator*
Davis, Margaret Bryan *paleoecology researcher, educator*
D'Cruz, Osmond Jerome *research scientist, educator*
Ek, Alan Ryan *forestry educator*
Kommedahl, Thor *plant pathology educator*
Leonard, Kurt John *plant pathologist, university program director*
Magee, Paul Terry *geneticist and molecular biologist, college dean*
McKinnell, Robert Gilmore *zoology, genetics and cell biology educator*
Phillips, Ronald Lewis *plant geneticist, educator*
Roy, Robert Russell *toxicologist*
Stadelmann, Eduard Joseph *plant physiologist, educator*
Tordoff, Harrison Bruce *retired zoologist, educator*
Wendt, Hans W(erner) *life scientist*
Zeyen, Richard John *plant pathology educator*

## MISSISSIPPI

**Lorman**
Ezekwe, Michael Obi *reseach scientist*

**Meridian**
Blackwell, Cecil *science association executive*

**Mississippi State**
Dorough, H. Wyman *toxicologist, educator, consultant*
Hurt, Verner Gene *forestry researcher*
Jenkins, Johnie Norton *research geneticist, research administrator*
Reddy, Kambham Raja *plant physiology educator*
White, Charles H. *food science and technology educator*

**Ocean Springs**
Gunter, Gordon *zoologist*

**Oxford**
Duke, Stephen Oscar *physiologist, researcher*
Foster, George Rainey *soil erosion research scientist*

**Picayune**
Pardue, Larry G. *botanical garden administrator, educator*

**Stennis Space Center**
Baker, Robert Andrew *environmental research scientist*

**Stoneville**
Hardee, D. D. *laboratory director, research program leader*
Ranney, Carleton David *plant pathology researcher, administrator*
Wilson, Alphus Dan *plant pathologist, researcher*

**University**
Keiser, Edmund Davis, Jr. *biologist, educator*

**Vicksburg**
Mather, Bryant *research administrator*

## MISSOURI

**Bridgeton**
Hemming, Bruce Clark *microbiologist*

**Cape Girardeau**
Blackwelder, Richard E(liot) *entomologist, zoology educator, archivist*

**Columbia**
Blevins, Dale Glenn *agronomy educator*
Blount, Don H. *physiology educator*
Brown, Olen Ray *medical microbiology research educator*
Burdick, Allan Bernard *geneticist*
Darrah, Larry Lynn *plant breeder*
Davis, James O(thello) *physician, educator*
Duncan, Donald Pendleton *retired forestry educator*
Finkelstein, Richard Alan *microbiologist*
Ignoffo, Carlo Michael *insect pathologist-virologist*
Lambeth, Victor Neal *horticulturist, researcher*
Mc Ginnes, Edgar Allen, Jr. *forestry educator*
Mitchell, Roger Lowry *agronomy educator*
Morehouse, Georgia Lewis *microbiologist, researcher*
Novacky, Anton Jan *plant pathologist, educator*
Poehlmann, Carl John *agronomist, researcher*
†Vogt, Albert R. *forester, educator, program director*
Yanders, Armon Frederick *biological sciences educator, research administrator*

**Eureka**
Lindsey, Susan Lyndaker *zoologist*

**Jefferson City**
Reidinger, Russell Frederick, Jr. *fish and wildlife scientist*

**Kansas City**
Cook, Mary Rozella *psychophysiologist*
Davidson, Ian Edwards *pharmaceutical research and development director*
Hagsten, Ib *animal scientist, educator*
Mc Kelvey, John Clifford *research institute executive*

**Saint Charles**
Radke, Rodney Owen *agricultural research executive*

**Saint Louis**
Allen, Garland Edward *biology educator, science historian*
Asa, Cheryl Suzanne *biologist*
Bourne, Carol Elizabeth Mulligan *biology educator, phycologist*
Curran, Michael Walter *management scientist*
Curtiss, Roy, III *biology educator*
Feir, Dorothy Jean *entomologist, physiologist, educator*
Green, Maurice *molecular biologist, virologist, educator*
Hamburger, Viktor *retired biology educator*
Hoessle, Charles Herman *zoo director*
Laskowski, Leonard Francis, Jr. *microbiologist*
Schlesinger, Milton J. *virology educator, researcher*
Sexton, Owen James *vertebrate ecology educator, conservationist*
Templeton, Alan Robert *biology educator*
Wold, William Sydney *molecular biology educator*
Zhuo, Min *neurobiology educator*

**West Plains**
Wilcoxson, Roy Dell *plant pathology educator and researcher*

**Windyville**
Condron, Barbara O'Guinn *metaphysics educator, school administrator, publisher*

## MONTANA

**Bozeman**
Costerton, John William Fisher *microbiologist*
Hovin, Arne William *agronomist, educator*
Lavin, Matthew T. *horticultural educator*
Todd, Kenneth S., Jr. *parasitologist, educator*

**Corvallis**
Koch, Peter *wood scientist*

**Hamilton**
Garon, Claude Francis *laboratory administrator, researcher*
Munoz, John Joaquin *research microbiologist*
Rudbach, Jon Anthony *biotechnical company executive*

**Havre**
Clouse, Vickie Rae *biology and paleontology educator*

**Miles City**
Bellows, Robert Alvin *research physiologist*
Heitschmidt, Rodney Keith *rangeland ecologist*

**Missoula**
Jenni, Donald Alison *zoology educator*
Nakamura, Mitsuru James *microbiologist, educator*
Wright, Barbara Evelyn *microbiologist*

**Polson**
Flamm, Barry Russell *ecologist*
Stanford, Jack Arthur *biological station administrator*

**Red Lodge**
Kauffman, Marvin Earl *geoscience consultant*

**Sidney**
Onsager, Jerome Andrew *research entomologist*

## NEBRASKA

**Clay Center**
Laster, Danny Bruce *animal scientist*

**Gering**
Weihing, John Lawson *plant pathologist, state senator*

**Humboldt**
Rumbaugh, Melvin Dale *geneticist, agronomist*

**Lincoln**
Adams, Charles Henry *retired animal scientist, educator*
Gardner, Charles Olda *plant geneticist and breeder, design consultant, analyst*
Genoways, Hugh Howard *systematic biologist, educator*
Hanway, Donald Grant *retired agronomist, educator*
Johnson, Virgil Allen *retired agronomist*
Massengale, Martin Andrew *agronomist, university president*
McClurg, James Edward *research laboratory executive*
Mignon, Paul Killian *laboratory executive*
Morris, M(ary) Rosalind *cytogeneticist, educator*
Sander, Donald Henry *soil scientist, researcher*
Swartzendruber, Dale *soil physicist, educator*
Taylor, Stephen Lloyd *food toxicologist, educator, food scientist*

**Omaha**
Andrews, Richard Vincent *physiologist, educator*
Badeer, Henry Sarkis *physiology educator*

## NEVADA

**Boulder City**
Shrader, Thomas Henry *biologist*

**Las Vegas**
Hess, John Warren *scientific institute administrator, educator*

**Reno**
Bohmont, Dale Wendell *agricultural consultant*
Gifford, Gerald Frederic *education educator*
Johnson, Arthur William, Jr. *planetarium executive*
Wehrli, John Erich *biotechnology executive*

## NEW HAMPSHIRE

**Durham**
Aber, John David *global ecosystem research adminstrator*
Harter, Robert Duane *soil scientist, educator*
Pistole, Thomas Gordon *microbiology educator, researcher*

**Hanover**
Gilbert, John Jouett *aquatic ecologist, educator*
Lubin, Martin *cell physiologist educator*
Roos, Thomas Bloom *biological scientist, educator*
Spiegel, Evelyn Sclufer *biology educator, researcher*
Spiegel, Melvin *retired biology educator*

**Lebanon**
Mc Cann, Frances Veronica *physiologist, educator*
Munck, Allan Ulf *physiologist, educator*

**Lyme**
Swan, Henry *forester, consultant*

**Sanbornton**
Andrews, Henry Nathaniel, Jr. *botanist, scientist, educator*

**Silver Lake**
Pallone, Adrian Joseph *research scientist*

## NEW JERSEY

**Annandale**
Drakeman, Donald Lee *biotechnology company executive, lawyer*

**Camden**
Kirk, James Robert *research development and quality assurance executive*

**Cranbury**
Burke, Peter Arthur *microbiologist, chemist*

**East Hanover**
Nemecek, Georgina Marie *molecular pharmacologist*

**Florham Park**
Eidt, Clarence Martin, Jr. *research and development executive*

**Hoboken**
Abel, Robert Berger *science administrator*

**Jamesburg**
Chase, Aurin Moody, Jr. *biology educator*

**Kinnelon**
Richardson, Joseph Blancet *former biology educator, educational facilities planning consultant*

**Livingston**
Schlesinger, Stephen Lyons *horticulturist*

**Madison**
Campbell, William Cecil *biologist*
George, David J. *toxicologist, pharmacologist*

**Montclair**
Mayo, Joan Bradley *microbiologist, healthcare administrator*

**Mount Arlington**
Cohen, Irving David *science administrator*

**New Brunswick**
Ballou, Janice Marie *research director*
Day, Peter Rodney *geneticist, educator*
Day-Salvatore, Debra Lynn *medical geneticist*
Ehrenfeld, David William *biology educator, author*
Funk, Cyril Reed, Jr. *agronomist, educator*
Gupta, Ayodhya Prasad *entomologist, immunologist, cell biologist*
Hayakawa, Kan-Ichi *food science educator*
Lachance, Paul Albert *food science educator, clergyman*
Maramorosch, Karl *virologist, educator*
Psuty, Norbert Phillip *marine sciences educator*
Solberg, Myron *food scientist, educator*
Tedrow, John Charles Fremont *soils educator*

**Newark**
Chinard, Francis Pierre *physiologist, physician*
Jonakait, Gene Miller *developmental neurobiologist*
Weis, Judith Shulman *biology educator*

**Nutley**
Dennin, Robert Aloysius, Jr. *pharmaceutical research scientist*

**Piscataway**
Denhardt, David Tilton *molecular and cell biology educator*
Liu, Alice Yee-Chang *biology educator*
Passmore, Howard Clinton, Jr. *geneticist, biological sciences educator*
Pramer, David *microbiologist, educator, research administrator*
Witkin, Evelyn Maisel *geneticist*

**Pomona**
Jahangir, Z(ulfiquar) M(uhammed) G(olam) Sarwar *molecular biology educator*

**Port Norris**
Canzonier, Walter Jude *shellfish aquaculturist*

**Princeton**
Crandall, David LeRoy *research scientist*
Gould, James L. *biology educator*
Grant, Peter Raymond *biologist, researcher, educator*
Jacobs, William Paul *botanist, educator*
Merrill, Leland Gilbert, Jr. *retired environmental science educator*
Morrill, William Ashley *research executive*
Silhavy, Thomas Joseph *molecular biology educator*
Steinberg, Malcolm Saul *biologist, educator*
Swenson, Christine Erica *microbiologist*
Wieschaus, Eric F. *molecular biologist, educator*

**Rahway**
Dombrowski, Anne Wesseling *microbiologist, researcher*
Reynolds, Glenn Franklin *medicinal research scientist*
Scolnick, Edward Mark *science administrator*
Sundelof, Jon Grenville *microbiologist*

**Shrewsbury**
Gilbert, Liane Marie *research scientist executive*

**Somerville**
Grant, Robert James *animal nutritional research manager*
Palmer, Stuart Michael *microbiologist*

**Stockton**
Kent, George Cantine, Jr. *zoology educator*

**Tenafly**
Kronenwett, Frederick Rudolph *microbiologist*

**Teterboro**
Gambino, S(alvatore) Raymond *medical laboratory executive, educator*

**Toms River**
Adamo, Joseph Albert *biologist, educator, researcher*
Okusanya, Olubukanla Tejumola *ecologist*

**Wayne**
†Wallace, Edith *biology educator*
†Werth, Jean Marie *biology educator*
White, Doris Gnauck *science educator, biochemical and biophysics researcher*

## NEW MEXICO

**Albuquerque**
Henderson, Rogene Faulkner *toxicologist, researcher*
Hsi, David Ching Heng *plant pathologist and geneticist, educator*
Mauderly, Joe Lloyd *pulmonary toxicologist*
Narath, Albert *laboratory administrator*
Rosenberg, Arthur James *company executive*
Sanchez, Victoria Wagner *science educator*
Ward, Charles Richard *extension and research entomologist, educator*

**Alto**
Thrasher, Jack D. *toxicologist, researcher, consultant*

**Las Cruces**
Schemnitz, Sanford David *wildlife biology educator*

**Los Alamos**
Gregg, Charles Thornton *research company executive*
Gupta, Goutam *biologist, biophysicist*
McComas, David John *science administrator, space physicist*
Wallace, Terry Charles, Sr. *technical administrator, researcher, consultant*

**Santa Fe**
Myers, Charlotte Will *biology educator*

**Tijeras**
Van Arsdel, Eugene Parr *tree pathologist, consultant meteorologist*

## NEW YORK

**Albany**
Able, Kenneth Paul *biology educator*
Demerjian, Kenneth Leo *atmospheric science educator, research center director*
Hitchcock, Karen Ruth *biology educator, university dean, academic administrator*
Schmidt, John Thomas *neurobiologist*
Stevens, Roy White *microbiologist*
Stewart, Margaret McBride *biology educator, researcher*
Tieman, Suzannah Bliss *neurobiologist*
Toombs, Russ William *laboratory director*

**Annandale On Hudson**
Ferguson, John Barclay *biology educator*
Kiviat, Erik *ecologist, administrator, educator*

**Briarcliff Manor**
Callahan, Daniel John *biomedical researcher*

**Bronx**
Cannizzaro, Linda Ann *geneticist, researcher*
†Conway, William Gaylord *zoologist, zoo director, conservationist*
Frenz, Dorothy Ann *cell and developmental biologist*
Lattis, Richard Lynn *zoo director*
Waelsch, Salome Gluecksohn *geneticist, educator*

**Bronxville**
Hutchison, Dorris Jeannette *retired microbiologist, educator*

**Brooklyn**
Altura, Bella T. *physiologist, educator*
Altura, Burton Myron *physiologist, educator*
Carswell, Lois Malakoff *botanical gardens executive, consultant*
Gabriel, Mordecai Lionel *biologist, educator*
Garibaldi, Louis E. *aquarium administrator*
Gootman, Phyllis Myrna *physiology, biophysics, educator*
Jacobson, Leslie Sari *biologist, educator*
Kramer, Allan Franklin, II *botanical garden official, researcher*
Pagala, Murali Krishna *physiologist*
Schiffman, Gerald *microbiologist, educator*
Sultzer, Barnet Martin *microbiology and immunology researcher*
Verma, Ram Sagar *geneticist, educator, author, administrator*
Zuk, Judith *botanic garden administrator*

**Buffalo**
Bishop, Beverly Petterson *physiologist*
Duax, William Leo *biological researcher*
He, Guang Sheng *research scientist*
Kite, Joseph Hiram, Jr. *microbiologist, educator*
Tomasi, Thomas B. *cell biologist, administrator*

**Cobleskill**
Ingels, Jack Edward *horticulture educator*

**Cold Spring Harbor**
Ma, Hong *plant molecular biologist, educator*
Watson, James Dewey *molecular biologist, educator*

**Cooperstown**
Harman, Willard Nelson *malacologist, educator*

**Craryville**
Payson, Ronald Sears *biology educator*

**East Patchogue**
Metz, Donald Joseph *retired science educator*

**East Setauket**
Briggs, Philip Terry *biologist*

**Elmira**
Hall, Geraldine Cristofaro *biology educator*

**Elmsford**
Sklarew, Robert Jay *biomedical research educator, consultant*

**Flushing**
Commoner, Barry *biologist, educator*
Schnall, Edith Lea (Mrs. Herbert Schnall) *microbiologist, educator*

**Fredonia**
Benton, Allen Haydon *biology educator*

**Garden City**
Podwall, Kathryn Stanley *biology educator*

**Geneva**
Siebert, Karl Joseph *food science educator*

**Hamilton**
Kessler, Dietrich *biology educator*

**Highland**
Rosenberger, David A. *research scientist, cooperative extension specialist*

**Homer**
Gustafson, John Alfred *biology educator*

**Ithaca**
Adler, Kraig (Kerr) *biology educator*
Alexander, Martin *microbiology educator, consultant*
Arntzen, Charles Joel *bioscience educator*
Blackler, Antonie William Charles *biologist*
Calnek, Bruce Wixson *virologist, zoologist*
Davies, Peter John *plant physiology educator, researcher*
Earle, Elizabeth Deutsch *biology educator*
Eisner, Thomas *biologist, educator*
Ewing, Elmer Ellis *agricultural science educator*
Fick, Gary Warren *agronomy educator, forage crops researcher*
Foote, Robert Hutchinson *animal physiology educator*
Gillett, James Warren *toxicologist, educator*
Grunes, David Leon *research soil scientist, educator, editor*
Hairston, Nelson George, Jr. *ecologist, educator*
Jagendorf, Andre Tridon *plant physiologist*
Kennedy, Wilbert Keith, Sr. *agronomy educator, retired university official*
Kingsbury, John Merriam *botanist, educator*
Korf, Richard Paul *mycology educator*
Kramer, John Paul *entomologist, educator*
Lengemann, Frederick William *physiology educator, scientist*
Lund, Daryl Bert *food science educator*
Mai, William Frederick *plant nematologist, educator*
Mortlock, Robert Paul *microbiologist, educator*
Naylor, Harry Brooks *microbiologist*
Novak, Joseph Donald *science educator, knowlege studies specialist*
Obendorf, Sharon Kay *fiber science educator*
Pimentel, David *entomologist, educator*
Plaisted, Robert Leroy *plant breeder, educator*
Seeley, Harry Wilbur, Jr. *microbiology educator*
Seeley, John George *horticulture educator*
Vandenberg, John Donald *entomologist*
Viands, Donald Rex *plant breeder and educator*
Walcott, Charles *neurobiology and behvior educator*
Ward, William Binnington *agricultural communicator*
Wasserman, Robert Harold *biology educator*
Welch, Ross Maynard *plant physiologist, researcher, educator*
Wootton, John Francis *physiology educator*

**Manhasset**
Bialer, Martin George *geneticist*
Bukrinsky, Michael Ilya *virologist*
Lipson, Steven Mark *cliniical virologist, educator*

**Millbrook**
Likens, Gene Elden *biology and ecology educator, administrator*

**New Hyde Park**
Isenberg, Henry David *microbiology educator*

**New Rochelle**
Beardsley, Robert Eugene *microbiologist, educator*

**New York**
Allfrey, Vincent George *cell biologist*
Anderson, O(rvil) Roger *biology educator, marine biology and protozoology, researcher*
Anderson, Sydney *biologist, museum curator*
Basilico, Claudio *geneticist, educator*
Ben-Hur, Ehud *research scientist*
Binkowski, Edward Stephan *research analysis director, lawyer, educator*
Blobel, Günter *cell biologist, educator*
Bock, Walter Joseph *zoology educator*
Bucolo, Gail Ann *biotechnologist*
Calame, Kathryn Lee *microbiologist, educator*
Carlson, Marian Bille *geneticist, researcher, educator*
Catanzaro, Daniel Frank *molecular biologist, educator*
Chaganti, Raju S. *geneticist, educator, researcher*
Cherksey, Bruce David *physiology educator*
Cheung, Ambrose Lin-Yau *microbiologist, researcher*
Choi, Ye-Chin *microbial geneticist*
Chua, Nam-Hai *plant molecular biologist, educator*
Cohen, Joel Ephraim *scientist, educator*
Cronholm, Lois S. *biology educator*
Dales, Samuel *microbiologist, virologist, educator*
Darnell, James Edwin, Jr. *molecular biologist, educator*
Desnick, Robert John *human geneticist*
Despommier, Dickson Donald *microbiology educator, parasitologist, researcher*
Grafstein, Bernice *physiology and neuroscience educator, researcher*
Hanafusa, Hidesaburo *virologist*
Hirschhorn, Rochelle *genetics educator*
Hutner, Seymour Herbert *microbiologist, protozoologist*
King, Marvin *research executive*
Kramer, Fred Russell *molecular biologist*
Lederberg, Joshua *geneticist, educator*
Lee, Lillian Vanessa *microbiologist*
Li, David Wan-Cheng *cell biologist*
Luck, David Jonathan Lewis *biologist, educator*
Maas, Werner Karl *microbiology educator*
Manski, Wladyslaw Julian *microbiology educator, medical scientist*
Model, Peter *molecular biologist*
Moroz, Pavel Emanuel *research scientist*
Morse, Stephen Scott *virologist, immunologist*
Pietruski, John Michael, Jr. *biotechnology company executive, pharmaceuticals executive*
Pogo, Beatriz Teresa Garcia-Tunon *cell biologist, virologist, educator*
Pollack, Robert Elliot *biologist, educator*
Rozen, Jerome George, Jr. *research entomologist, museum curator and research administrator*
Segal, Sheldon Jerome *biologist, educator, foundation administrator*
Silverstein, Samuel Charles *cellular biology and physiology educator, researcher*
Stotzky, Guenther *microbiologist, educator*
Thomson, Keith Stewart *biologist, writer*
Tietjen, John Henry *biology and oceanography educator, consultant*
Tomasz, Alexander *cell biologist*
Trager, William *biology educator*
Underwood, Joanna DeHaven *environmental research and education organizations president*
Wharton, Danny Carroll *zoo biologist*
Windhager, Erich Ernst *physiologist, educator*
Young, Michael Warren *geneticist, educator*
Zinder, Norton David *genetics educator, university dean*

**Olean**
Rauhut, Horst Wilfried *research scientist*

**Olmstedville**
Frost, David *former biology educator, medical editor, consultant*

**Orangeburg**
Squires, Richard Felt *research scientist*

**Patchogue**
Gibbons, Edward Francis *psychobiologist*

**Pearl River**
Barik, Sudhakar *microbiologist, research scientist*

**Purchase**
Ehrman, Lee *geneticist*

**Rego Park**
Ben-Harari, Ruben Robert *research scientist, medical writer, medical communications consultant*

**Rochester**
Chang, Jack Che-man *photoscience research laboratory director*
Clarkson, Thomas William *toxicologist, educator*
Coleman, Paul David *neurobiology researcher, educator*
Morrow, Paul Edward *toxicology educator*
Muchmore, William Breuleux *zoologist, educator*
Oberdorster, Gunter *toxicologist*

**Saranac Lake**
North, Robert John *biologist*

**Schenectady**
Bedard, Donna Lee *environmental microbiologist*

**Stanley**
Jones, Gordon Edwin *horticulturist*

**Staten Island**
Wisniewski, Henryk Miroslaw *pathology and neuropathology educator, research facility administrator, research scientist*

**Stony Brook**
Erk, Frank Chris *biologist, educator*
Kim, Charles Wesley *microbiology educator*
Lennarz, William Joseph *research biologist, educator*
Levinton, Jeffrey S. *biology educator, oceanographer*
Rohlf, F. James *biometrician, educator*
Williams, George Christopher *biologist, ecology and evolution educator*
Wurster, Charles Frederick *environmental scientist, educator*

**Syracuse**
Burgess, Robert Lewis *ecologist, educator*
Collette, Alfred Thomas *biology and science education educator*
Delmar, Mario *cardiac physiology educator*
Dunham, Philip Bigelow *biology educator, physiologist*
Kriebel, Mahlon Edward *physiology educator, inventor*
Phillips, Arthur William, Jr. *biology educator*
Russell-Hunter, Gus W(illiam) D(evigne) *zoology educator, research biologist, writer*
Turner, Christopher Edward *cell biology educator*

**Tarrytown**
Kinigakis, Panagiotis *research principal scientist, engineer, author*

**Troy**
Breed, Helen Illick *ichthyologist, educator*
Ehrlich, Henry Lutz *biology educator*

**Tuxedo Park**
Heusser, Calvin John *biology educator, researcher*
Rossman, Toby Gale *genetic toxicology educator, researcher*

**Upton**
Petrakis, Leonidas *research scientist, educator, administrator*

**Utica**
Antzelevitch, Charles *research center executive*

**Valhalla**
Hommes, Frits Aukustinus *biology educator*
Kilbourne, Edwin Dennis *virologist, educator*
Wolin, Michael Stuart *physiology educator*

**Wading River**
Hall, Kimball Parker *research scientist*

**White Plains**
Peyton, Donald Leon *retired standards association executive*

**Williamsville**
Greizerstein, Hebe Beatriz *research scientist, educator*

**Woodbury**
Doering, Charles Henry *research scientist, educator, editor, publisher*

## NORTH CAROLINA

**Asheboro**
Jones, David M. *zoological park director*

**Atlantic Beach**
Barnes, James Thomas, Jr. *aquarium director*

**Beaufort**
Ramus, Joseph S. *marine biologist*

**Burlington**
Tolley, Jerry Russell *clinical laboratory executive*
Turanchik, Michael *research and development director*

**Cary**
Mochrie, Richard D. *physiology educator*

**Chapel Hill**
Andersen, Melvin Ernest *toxicologist, consultant*
Andrews, Richard Nigel Lyon *environmental policy educator, environmental studies administrator*
Farber, Rosann Alexander *geneticist, educator*
Gilbert, Lawrence Irwin *biologist, educator*
Hackenbrock, Charles R. *cell biologist, educator*
Hairston, Nelson George *retired animal ecologist*
Judd, Burke Haycock *geneticist*
Kuenzler, Edward Julian *ecologist and environmental biologist*
Manire, George Philip *bacteriologist, educator*
McBay, Arthur John *toxicologist, consultant*
Mueller, Nancy Schneider *retired biology educator*
Scott, Tom Keck *biologist, educator*
Smithies, Oliver *geneticist, educator*
Stiven, Alan Ernest *population biologist, ecologist*
Stumpf, Walter Erich *cell biology educator, researcher*
Warren, Donald William *physiology educator, dentistry educator*
Weiss, Charles Manuel *environmental biologist*
Wyrick, Priscilla Blakeney *microbiologist*

**Durham**
Blum, Jacob Joseph *physiologist, educator*
†Bolognesi, Dani Paul *virologist, educator*
Cook, Clarence Edgar *research facility scientist*
Cruze, Alvin M. *research institute executive*
Culberson, William Louis *botany educator*
Gillham, Nicholas Wright *geneticist, educator*
Keene, Jack Donald *molecular genetics and microbiology educator*
Malindzak, George Steve, Jr. *cardiovascular physiology, biomedical engineer*
Naylor, Aubrey Willard *botany educator*
Nicklas, Robert Bruce *cell biologist*
Pearsall, Samuel Haff, III *landscape ecologist, geographer, foundation administrator*
Raetz, Christian R. H. *biochemistry educator*
Richardson, Curtis John *ecology educator*
Richardson, Stephen Giles *biotechnology company executive*
Rouse, Doris Jane *physiologist, research administrator*
Schmidt-Nielsen, Knut *physiologist, educator*
Searles, Richard Brownlee *botany educator, marine biology researcher*
Sheetz, Michael Patrick *cell biology educator*

Somjen, George Gustav *physiologist*
Swaim, Mark Wendell *molecular biologist, gastroenterologist*
Sykes, Richard Brook *microbiologist*

**Franklinton**
Lange, Niels Erik Krebs *biotechnology company executive*

**Greensboro**
Ahmed, Fahim Uddin *research fellow, scientist*

**Greenville**
Maier, Robert Hawthorne *biology educator*
Thurber, Robert Eugene *physiologist, researcher*

**Hendersonville**
Brittain, James Edward *science and technology educator, researcher*
Kehr, August Ernest *geneticist, researcher*

**Kitty Hawk**
Sjoerdsma, Albert *research institute executive*

**Kure Beach**
Lanier, James Alfred, III *aquarium administrator*

**Little Switzerland**
Gross, Samson Richard *geneticist, biochemist, educator*

**New Bern**
Ash, William James *geneticist*

**Oxford**
Spurr, Harvey W., Jr. *plant pathology research administrator*

**Pinehurst**
Burris, Kenneth Wayne *biologist, educator*
Stroud, Richard Hamilton *aquatic biologist, scientist, consultant*

**Raleigh**
Atchley, William Reid *geneticist, evolutionary biologist, educator*
Benson, D(avid) Michael *plant pathologist*
Bishop, Paul Edward *microbiologist*
Clauberg, Martin *research scientist*
Cook, Maurice Gayle *soil science educator, consultant*
Cooper, Arthur Wells *ecologist, educator*
Cummings, Ralph Waldo *soil scientist, educator, researcher*
Davey, Charles Bingham *soil science educator*
De Hertogh, August Albert *horticulture educator, researcher*
Dunphy, Edward James *crop science extension specialist*
Goodman, Major Merlin *botanical sciences educator*
Gordon, Morris Aaron *medical mycologist, microbiologist*
Hardin, James W. *botanist, herbarium curator, educator*
Hodgson, Ernest *toxicology educator*
Kelman, Arthur *plant pathologist, educator*
Moore, Jeannette Aileen *animal nutrition educator*
Moreland, Donald Edwin *plant physiologist*
Perkins, Frank Overton *marine scientist, educator*
Scandalios, John George *geneticist, educator*
Shih, Jason Chia-Hsing *biotechnology educator*
Speck, Marvin Luther *microbiologist, educator*
Stuber, Charles William *genetics educator, researcher*
Timothy, David Harry *biology educator*
Triantaphyllou, H. H. *plant pathologist*
Wilson, Richard Ferrol *plant physiologist, educator*
Wollum, Arthur George, II *microbiologist, researcher, educator*
Zeng, Zhao-Bang *geneticist, educator*

**Research Triangle Park**
Butterworth, Byron E. *toxicologist*
de Serres, Frederick Joseph *genetic toxicologist*
Heck, Henry D'Arcy *toxicologist*
McClellan, Roger Orville *toxicologist*
Mumford, Stephen Douglas *population growth control research scientist*
Ross, Jeffrey Alan *research biologist*
Wooten, Frank Thomas *research facility executive*

**Southern Pines**
Towell, William Earnest *forester, former association executive*

**Wilmington**
Bolen, Eric George *biology educator*
Brauer, Ralph Werner *physiologist, educator*
Roer, Robert David *physiologist, educator*
Watanabe, Wade Osamu *marine biologist*

**Winston Salem**
de Tombe, Pieter Philippus *physiologist*
Ganz, Charles *laboratory executive*
Herndon, Claude Nash *retired geneticist, physician*
Laxminarayana, Dama *geneticist, researcher, educator*

**Winterville**
Myers, Robert Durant *biologist, research director, medical educator*

**Wrightsville Beach**
Phull, B. S. *scientist*

## NORTH DAKOTA

**Fargo**
Joppa, Leonard Robert *research geneticist, agronomist, educator*
Schmidt, Claude Henri *retired research administrator*
Williams, Norman Dale *geneticist, researcher*
Zimmerman, Don Charles *plant physiologist, biochemist*

**Grand Forks**
Fox, Carl Alan *research institute executive*

**Jamestown**
Kirby, Ronald Eugene *fish and wildlife research administrator*

**Mandan**
Halvorson, Ardell David *research leader, soil scientist*
Halvorson, Gary Alfred *soil scientist*

## OHIO

**Athens**
Cohn, Norman Stanley *botany educator, university dean*
Ungar, Irwin Allan *botany educator*

**Bowling Green**
Clark, Eloise Elizabeth *biologist, university official*
Heckman, Carol A. *biology educator*

**Cincinnati**
Etges, Frank Joseph *parasitology educator*
Maruska, Edward Joseph *zoo administrator*
Monaco, John J. *molecular genetics research educator*
Nebert, Daniel Walter *molecular geneticist, research administrator*
Rosato, Laura Marie *toxicologist, educator*
Saal, Howard Max *clinical geneticist, pediatrician, educator*
Safferman, Robert Samuel *microbiologist*
Schaefer, Frank William, III *microbiologist, researcher*
Sperelakis, Nicholas, Sr. *physiology and biophysics educator, researcher*

**Cleveland**
Caplan, Arnold I. *biology educator*
Rutishauser, Urs Stephen *cell biologist*
Steinberg, Arthur G(erald) *geneticist*
Taylor, Steve Henry *zoologist*

**Columbus**
Banwart, George Junior *food microbiology educator*
Boerner, Ralph E. J. *forest soil ecologist, plant biology educator*
Deep, Ira Washington *plant pathology educator*
Disinger, John Franklin *natural resources educator*
Fausey, Norman Ray *soil scientist*
Fawcett, Sherwood Luther *research laboratory executive*
Floyd, Gary Leon *plant cell biologist*
Fry, Donald Lewis *physiologist, educator*
Glaser, Ronald *microbiology educator, scientist*
Kapral, Frank Albert *medical microbiology and immunology educator*
Marushige-Knopp, Yuka *food scientist*
Miller, Paul Dean *breeding company consultant, geneticist*
Moore, Jay Winston *director cytogenetics laboratory*
Needham, Glen Ray *entology and acarology educator*
Olesen, Douglas Eugene *research institute executive*
Pappas, Peter William *zoology educator*
Peterle, Tony John *zoologist, educator*
Pieper, Heinz Paul *physiology educator*
Reeve, John Newton *molecular biology and microbiology educator*
Roth, Robert Earl *environmental educator*
Triplehorn, Charles A. *entomology educator, insects curator*
Warmbrod, James Robert *agriculture educator, university administrator*
Wood, Jackie Dale *physiologist, educator, researcher*
Yohn, David Stewart *virologist, science administrator*
Zartman, David Lester *animal sciences educator, researcher*

**Cumberland**
Reece, Robert William *zoological park administrator*

**Dayton**
Byczkowski, Janusz Zbigniew *toxicologist*
Isaacson, Milton Stanley *research and development company executive, engineer*

**Delaware**
Fry, Anne Evans *zoology educator*

**Findlay**
Reynolds, Robert Gregory *toxicologist, management consultant*

**Granville**
Haubrich, Robert Rice *biology educator*

**Kent**
Cooperrider, Tom Smith *botanist*

**Kirtland**
Munson, Richard Howard *horticulturist*

**Newark**
Greenstein, Julius Sidney *zoology educator*

**Oberlin**
Stinebring, Warren Richard *microbiologist, educator*

**Oxford**
Eshbaugh, W(illiam) Hardy *botanist, educator*
Haley-Oliphant, Ann Elizabeth *science educator*
Heimsch, Charles *retired botany educator*
Miller, Harvey Alfred *botanist, educator*
Williamson, Clarence Kelly *microbiologist, educator*

**Springfield**
Ryu, Kyoo-Hai Lee *physiologist*

**Toledo**
Chakraborty, Joana *physiology educator, research center administrator*

**Upper Arlington**
Snyder, Susan Leach *science educator*

**Wooster**
Ferree, David Curtis *horticultural researcher*
Lafever, Howard Nelson *plant breeder, geneticist, educator*
Madden, Laurence Vincent *plant pathology educator*

## OKLAHOMA

**Edmond**
Caire, William *biologist, educator*

**El Reno**
Phillips, William A. *research animal scientist*

**Langston**
Mallik, Muhammad Abdul-Bari *soil microbiologist*
Simpson, Ocleris C. *agricultural research administrator*

**Norman**
Carpenter, Charles Congden *zoologist, educator*
Cross, George Lynn *foundation administrator, former university president*
Hill, Loren G. *biology researcher*
Hutchison, Victor Hobbs *biologist, educator*
Mares, Michael Allen *ecologist, educator*
Schindler, Charles Alvin *microbiologist, educator*

**Ochelata**
Hitzman, Donald Oliver *microbiologist*

**Oklahoma City**
Alexander, Patrick Byron *zoological society executive*
Branch, John Curtis *biology educator, lawyer*
Scott, Lawrence Vernon *microbiology educator*

**Ponca City**
Bolene, Margaret Rosalie Steele *bacteriologist, civic worker*

**Stillwater**
Campbell, John Roy *animal scientist educator, academic administrator*
Durham, Norman Nevill *microbiologist, scientist, educator*
Grischkowsky, Daniel Richard *research scientist, educator*
Langwig, John Edward *retired wood science educator*
Ownby, Charlotte Ledbetter *anatomy educator*
Whitcomb, Carl Ervin *horticulturist, researcher*

**Tulsa**
Johnson, Gerald, III *cardiovascular physiologist, researcher*

## OREGON

**Ashland**
Christianson, Roger Gordon *biology educator*
MacMillen, Richard Edward *biological sciences educator, researcher*

**Corvallis**
Blus, Lawrence John *biologist*
Brown, George *research forester and educator*
Chambers, Kenton Lee *botany educator*
Farkas, Daniel Frederick *food science and technology educator*
Frakes, Rod Vance *plant geneticist, educator*
Ho, Iwan *research plant pathologist*
Leong, Jo-Ann Ching *microbiologist, educator*
Lubchenco, Jane *marine biologist, educator*
Moore, Thomas Carrol *botanist, educator*
Morita, Richard Yukio *microbiology and oceanography educator*
Pearson, Albert Marchant *food science and nutrition educator*
Rounds, Donald Edwin *retired cell biologist*
Rygiewicz, Paul Thaddeus *plant ecologist*
Schmidt, Bruce Randolph *science administrator, researcher*
Tarrant, Robert Frank *soil science educator, researcher*
Trappe, James Martin *mycologist*
Westwood, Melvin Neil *horticulturist, pomologist*
Young, J. Lowell *soil chemist, biologist*
Zobel, Donald Bruce *botany educator*

**Eugene**
Holzapfel, Christina Marie *biologist*
Matthews, Brian W. *molecular biology educator*
McConnaughey, Bayard Harlow *biology educator*
Sprague, George Frederick *geneticist*
Wessells, Norman Keith *biologist, educator, university administrator*

**Gresham**
Arney, James Douglas *forestry biometrics consultant*
Poulton, Charles Edgar *natural resources consultant*

**La Grande**
Fanning, Edward John *soil scientist*

**Mcminnville**
Roberts, Michael Foster *biology educator*

**Newport**
Weber, Lavern John *marine science administrator, educator*

**Pendleton**
Klepper, Elizabeth Lee *physiologist*
Smiley, Richard Wayne *research center administrator, researcher*

**Portland**
Burton, Mike *zoological park administrator*
Glass, Laurel Ellen *gerontologist, developmental biologist, physician, retired educator*
Hagenstein, William David *forester, consultant*
Wilson, Thomas Woodrow, III *research scientist, consultant*

**Yachats**
Gerdemann, James Wessel *plant pathologist, educator*

## PENNSYLVANIA

**Alcoa Center**
Lederman, Frank L. *scientist, research center administrator*

**Ambler**
Crowell, Richard Lane *microbiologist*

**Annville**
Verhoek, Susan Elizabeth *botany educator*

**Bala Cynwyd**
Corliss, John Ozro *zoology educator*

**Bryn Mawr**
Hung, Paul Porwen *biotechnologist, educator, consultant*

**Cochranton**
Baldwin, Anthony Blair *systems theoretician, agricultural executive*

**Danville**
Morgan, Howard Edwin *physiologist*

**Doylestown**
Mishler, John Milton (Yochanan Menashsheh ben Shaul) *natural sciences educator, academic administrator*

**Edinboro**
Miller, G(erson) H(arry) *research institute director, mathematician, computer scientist, chemist*

**Elizabethville**
Romberger, John Albert *scientist, historian*

**Elkins Park**
Fussell, Catharine Pugh *biological researcher*

**Erie**
Gilloteaux, Jacques Jean-Marie Anthime *cell biologist, researcher*

**Exton**
Pollock, Roy Van Horn *pharmaceutical company animal health researcher*

**Gettysburg**
Hendrix, Sherman Samuel *biology educator, researcher*

**Gladwyne**
Allen, Theresa Ohotnicky *neurobiologist, consultant*

**Grantham**
Falk, Noel Wesley *biology educator, radio and television program host, horticultural consultant*

**Greensburg**
Speedy, Eric Dawson *laboratory technician*

**Harrisburg**
Wei, I-Yuan *research and development consultant and director*

**Hershey**
Chen, Qian *cell biologist, developmental biologist*
Vary, Thomas Crispin *physiologist*

**Holland**
Umbreit, Wayne William *bacteriologist, educator*

**Indiana**
Purdy, David Lawrence *biotechnical company executive*

**Lancaster**
Bernstein, Alan *retired virologist*
Hess, Eugene Lyle *biologist, retired association executive*

**Langhorne**
Venable, Robert Ellis *crop scientist*

**Lewisburg**
Candland, Douglas Keith *educator*
Sojka, Gary Allan *biologist, educator, university official*

**Malvern**
Popp, James Alan *toxicologist, toxicology executive*

**Narberth**
Nathanson, Neal *virologist, epidemiologist, educator*

**New Bethlehem**
Fedak, John G. *biology education educator*

**Newtown**
Carpenter, Esther *biological science educator*

**Philadelphia**
Brinster, Ralph Lawrence *biologist*
Brobeck, John Raymond *physiology educator*
Chan, Marion Man-Ying *biologist*
Davis, Robert Harry *physiology educator*
DiBerardino, Marie Antoinette *developmental biologist, educator*
Eisenstein, Toby K. *microbiology educator*
Erickson, Ralph O. *botany educator*
Faber, Donald Stuart *neurobiology and anatomy educator*
Fisher, Aron Baer *physiology and medicine educator*
Furth, John Jacob *molecular biologist, pathologist, educator*
Hammond, Benjamin Franklin *microbiologist, educator*
Hand, Christopher Michael *cancer research scientist, medical consultant, educator*
Hand, Peter James *neurobiologist, educator*
Hoskins, Alexander L. (Pete Hoskins) *zoological park administrator*
Johnson, E(lmer) Marshall *biology educator, reproductive toxicologist*
Kaji, Akira *microbiology scientist, educator*

Kleinzeller, Arnost *physiologist, physician, emeritus educator*
Knudson, Alfred George, Jr. *medical geneticist*
Koprowski, Hilary *microbiologist, educator*
Krutsick, Robert Stanley *science center executive*
Lefer, Allan Mark *physiologist*
Lu, Ponzy *molecular biology educator*
McEachron, Donald Lynn *biology educator, researcher*
Meyer, Paul William *arboretum director, horticulturist*
Morahan, Page S. *microbiologist, educator*
Niewiarowski, Stefan *physiology educator, biomedical research scientist*
Patterson, Donald Floyd *human, medical and veterinary genetics educator*
Peachey, Lee DeBorde *biology educator*
Pepe, Frank A. *cell and developmental biology educator*
Perry, Robert Palese *molecular biologist, educator*
Porter, Roger John *medical research administrator, neurologist, pharmacologist*
Schneider, Adele Sandra *clinical geneticist*
Shockman, Gerald David *microbiologist, educator*
Siegman, Marion Joyce *physiology educator*
Silvers, Willys Kent *geneticist*
Stevens, Rosemary A. *public health and social history educator*
Tricoli, James Vincent *cancer genetics educator*
Xin, Li *physiologist*
Young, Robert Crabill *medical researcher, science facility administrator, internist*
Yunis, Jorge Jose *anatomy, pathology, and microbiology educator*

### Pipersville
Erickson, Edward Leonard *biotechnology company executive*

### Pittsburgh
Boyce, Alfred Warne *analytical laboratory executive*
Brunson, Kenneth Wayne *cancer biologist*
Feingold, David Sidney *microbiology educator*
Fletcher, Ronald Darling *microbiologist educator*
Gollin, Susanne Merle *cytogeneticist, cell biologist*
Henry, Susan Armstrong *biology educator, university dean*
Ho, Chien *biological sciences educator*
Jones, Elizabeth Winifred *biology educator*
Kaufman, William Morris *research institute administrator, engineer*
Keleti, Georg *retired microbiologist, researcher*
Kiger, Robert William *botanist, science historian, educator*
Kuster, Janice Elizabeth *biology educator, researcher*
McGovern, John Joseph *retired air pollution control executive*
McWilliams, Betty Jane *science administrator, communication disorders educator, researcher*
Murray, Sandra Ann *biology research scientist, educator*
Parkes, Kenneth Carroll *ornithologist*
Partanen, Carl Richard *biology educator*
Slifkin, Malcolm *microbiologist*
Taylor, D. Lansing *cell biology educator*
Tung, Frank Yao-Tsung *microbiologist educator*
Youngner, Julius Stuart *microbiologist, educator*

### Quakertown
de Limantour, Clarice Barr *food scientist*

### Schuylkill Haven
Sarno, Patricia Ann *biology educator*

### Scranton
Clymer, Jay Phaon, III *science educator*

### Spring House
Frederick, Clay Bruce *toxicologist, researcher*

### State College
Bergman, Ernest L. *retired horticulture educator*
Bittner, Carl S. *retired university educator*
Hettche, L. Raymond *research director*

### Swarthmore
Gilbert, Scott Frederick *biologist, educator, author*
Sawyers, Claire Elyce *arboretum administrator*

### Swiftwater
Melling, Jack *biotechnologist*

### Titusville
Peaslee, Margaret Mae Hermanek *zoology educator*

### University Park
Bollag, Jean-Marc *soil biochemistry educator, consultant*
Brenchley, Jean Elnora *microbiologist, researcher*
Buskirk, Elsworth Robert *physiologist, educator*
Cowen, Barrett Stickney *microbiology educator*
Dunson, William Albert *biology educator*
Fowler, H(oratio) Seymour *retired science educator*
Hagen, Daniel Russell *physiologist, educator*
Jeffery, William Richard *developmental biology educator, researcher*
Kim, Ke Chung *entomology, systematics, and biodiversity educator, researcher*
Kuhns, Larry J. *horticulturist, educator*
Manbeck, Harvey B. *agricultural and biological engineer, wood engineer, educator*
Rashid, Kamal A. *program director, researcher*
Stern, Robert Morris *gastrointestinal psychophysiology researcher, psychology educator*
Stinson, Richard Floyd *retired horticulturalist, educator*
Tammen, James F. *plant pathologist, educator*
Traverse, Alfred *palynology educator, clergyman*
Tukey, Loren Davenport *pomology educator, researcher*

### Villanova
Steg, Leo *research and development executive*

### Wallingford
Severdia, Anthony George *chemistry research investigator*

### Wayne
Thelen, Edmund *research executive*

### West Mifflin
Clayton, John Charles *scientist, researcher*

### West Point
Caskey, Charles Thomas *biology and genetics educator*
Hilleman, Maurice Ralph *virus research scientist*

### Wilkes Barre
Hayes, Wilbur Frank *biology educator*
Ogren, Robert Edward *biologist, educator*

## RHODE ISLAND

### Cranston
Mruk, Charles Karzimer *agronomist*

### Kingston
Goos, Roger Delmon *mycologist*
Harlin, Marilyn Miler *marine botany educator, researcher, consultant*
Harrison, Robert William *zoologist, educator*
Hufnagel, Linda Ann *biology educator, researcher*

### Newport
Koch, Robert Michael *research scientist, consultant, educator*

### Portsmouth
Pearson, Oscar Harris *plant breeder, geneticist*

### Providence
Gerbi, Susan Alexandra *biology educator*
Marshall, Jean McElroy *physiologist*
Miller, Kenneth Raymond *biologist, educator*
Rothman, Frank George *biology educator, biochemical genetics researcher*
Schmitt, Johanna Marie *plant population biologist, educator*
Wood, Craig Breckenridge *paleobiologist, natural science educator*

## SOUTH CAROLINA

### Charleston
Brusca, Richard Charles *zoologist, researcher, educator*
Burrell, Victor Gregory, Jr. *marine scientist*
Cheng, Thomas Clement *parasitologist, immunologist, educator, author*

### Clemson
Gangemi, J(oseph) David *microbiology educator, biomedical researcher, research administrator, hospital administrator*
Hays, Sidney Brooks *retired entomology educator*

### Columbia
Abel, Francis Lee *physiology educator*
Baker, Carleton Harold *physiology educator*
Best, Robert Glen *geneticist*
Cole, Benjamin Theodore *biologist*
Corey, David Thomas *invertebrate zoology specialist*
Dawson, Wallace Douglas, Jr. *geneticist*
Henderson, Robert Edward *research institute director*
Vernberg, Frank John *marine and biological sciences educator*
Watabe, Norimitsu *biology and marine science educator*

### Conway
Moore, Richard Harlan *biology educator, university official*

### Florence
Kittrell, Benjamin Upchurch *agronomist*

### Gaffney
Jones, Nancy Gale *retired biology educator*

### Greenville
Cureton, Claudette Hazel Chapman *biology educator*

### Hartsville
Terry, Stuart L(ee) *research manager*

### Hilton Head Island
Adams, William Hensley *ecologist, educator*
Flemister, Launcelot Johnson *physiologist, educator*
Rapp, Fred *virologist*

### Spartanburg
Leonard, Walter Raymond *retired biology educator*

## SOUTH DAKOTA

### Brookings
Hugghins, Ernest Jay *biology educator*
MacFarland, Craig George *natural resource management professional*
Morgan, Walter *retired poultry science educator*
Sword, Christopher Patrick *microbiologist, university dean*

### Vermillion
Langworthy, Thomas Allan *microbiologist, educator*

### Volga
Moldenhauer, William Calvin *soil scientist*

## TENNESSEE

### Clinton
Tyndall, Richard Lawrence *microbiologist, researcher*

### Cookeville
Forest, Herman Silva *biology educator*

### Gatlinburg
Cave, Kent R. *national park ranger*

### Johnson City
Rasch, Ellen Myrberg *cell biology educator*

### Knoxville
Anderson, Ilse Janell *clinical geneticist*
Caponetti, James Dante *botany educator*
Chen, James Pai-fun *biology educator, researcher*
Conger, Bob Vernon *plant and soil science educator*
Draughon, Frances Ann *microbiology educator*
Harris, William Franklin, III *biologist, environmental science director and educator*
Holton, Raymond William *botanist, educator*
Maxson, Linda Ellen *biologist, educator*
Mc Hargue, Carl Jack *research laboratory administrator*
Sharp, Aaron John *botanist, educator*
Swingle, Homer Dale *horticulturist, educator*
White, David Cleaveland *microbial ecologist, environmental toxicologist*

### Maryville
Hall, Marion Trufant *botany educator, arboretum director*

### Memphis
Chung, King-Thom *microbiologist, educator*
Curran, Thomas *molecular biologist, educator*
Freeman, Bob A. *retired microbiology educator, retired dean*
Hofmann, Polly A. *physiology educator*
Howe, Martha Morgan *microbiologist, educator*
Miller, Neil Austin *biology educator*
Ryan, Kevin William *research virologist, educator*
Wilson, Charles Glen *zoo administrator*

### Nashville
Altman, David Wayne *geneticist*
Orgebin-Crist, Marie-Claire *biology educator*
Phillips, John A(tlas), III *geneticist, educator*
Snyders, Dirk Johan *electrophysiologist, biophysicist, educator*
Wang, Taylor Gunjin *science administrator, astronaut, educator*

### Oak Ridge
Auerbach, Stanley Irving *ecologist, environmental scientist, educator*
Boyle, William R. *science administrator*
Hosker, Rayford Peter, Jr. *air pollution research scientist*
Luxmoore, Robert John *soil and plant scientist*
Mazur, Peter *cell physiologist, cryobiologist*
Slusher, Kimberly Goode *researcher*

### Sewanee
Croom, Henrietta Brown *biology educator*
Yeatman, Harry Clay *biologist, educator*

## TEXAS

### Amarillo
Myers, Terry Lewis *clinical geneticist, educator*

### Austin
Albin, Leslie Owens *biology educator*
Biesele, John Julius *biologist, educator*
Bronson, Franklin H. *zoology educator*
Delevoryas, Theodore *botanist, educator*
Drummond Borg, Lesley Margaret *clinical geneticist*
Fryxell, Greta Albrecht *marine botany educator, oceanographer*
Gans, Carl *zoologist, educator*
Grant, Verne Edwin *biology educator*
Hubbs, Clark *zoologist, researcher*
Jacobson, Antone Gardner *zoology educator*
Northington, David Knight, III *research center director, botanist, educator*
Poulsen, Lawrence LeRoy *research scientist*
Simpson, Beryl Brintnall *botany educator*
Starr, Richard Cawthon *botany educator*
Sutton, Harry Eldon *geneticist, educator*
Thornton, Joseph Scott *research institute executive, materials scientist*
Turner, Billie Lee *botanist, educator*
Walker, James Roy *microbiologist*
Wheeler, Marshall Ralph *zoologist, educator*

### Brooks AFB
Convertino, Victor Anthony *physiologist, educator, research scientist, civil servant*
Cox, Ann Bruger *biological scientist, editor, researcher*

### Brownsville
Farst, Don David *zoo director, veterinarian*

### Bryan
Röller, Herbert Alfred *biology and medical scientist, educator*

### Bushland
Unger, Paul Walter *soil scientist*

### Cibolo
Newsom, Melvin Max *retired research company executive*

### College Station
Armstrong, Robert Beall *physiologist*
Black, Samuel Harold *microbiology and immunology educator*
Borlaug, Norman Ernest *agricultural scientist*
Bryant, Vaughn Motley, Jr. *botany and anthropology educator*
Feagin, Clarence Elmer, Jr. *microbiologist*
Fisher, Richard Forrest *soils educator*
Hall, Timothy C. *biology educator, consultant*
Kohel, Russell James *geneticist*
Milford, Murray Hudson *soil science educator*
Neill, William Harold, Jr. *biological science educator and researcher*
Rosberg, David William *plant sciences educator*
Smith, Roberta Hawking *plant physiologist*
Summers, Max (Duanne) *entomologist, scientist, educator*
Wilding, Lawrence Paul *pedology educator, soil science consultant*
Wu, Guoyao *animal science, nutrition and physiology educator*

### Corpus Christi
Berkebile, Charles Alan *geology educator, hydrogeology researcher*
Eddleman, Bobby Ross *agriculturist, economist*

Parker, Roy Denver, Jr. *entomologist*
Schake, Lowell Martin *animal science educator*

### Dallas
Brown, Michael Stuart *geneticist, educator, administrator*
Denur, Jack Boaz *scientific researcher, scientific consultant*
Hudspeth, Albert James *biomedical researcher, educator*
Land, Geoffrey Allison *science administrator*
McKnight, Steven Lanier *molecular biologist*
Murad, John Louis *clinical microbiology educator*
Reinert, James A. *entomologist, educator*
Vanatta, John Crothers, III *physiologist, physician, educator*

### Denton
Garcia-Heras, Jaime *clinical cytogeneticist, researcher*
Schwalm, Fritz Ekkehardt *biology educator*

### El Paso
Harris, Arthur Horne *biology educator*
Johnson, Jerry Douglas *biology educator*

### Fort Worth
Sheets, John Wesley, Jr. *research scientist*
Stormdancer, Rowan Ehlenfeldt *traditional herbalist, management consultant*

### Galveston
Baskaran, Mahalingam *marine science educator*
Budelmann, Bernd Ulrich *zoologist, educator*
Giam, Choo-Seng *marine science educator*
Prakash, Satya *biology educator*
Santschi, Peter Hans *marine sciences educator*
Smith, Eric Morgan *virology educator*
Thompson, Edward Ivins Brad *biological chemistry and genetics educator, molecular endocrinologist, department chairman*
Würsig, Bernd Gerhard *marine biology educator*
Zimmerman, Roger Joseph *fishery biologist*

### Georgetown
Girvin, Eb Carl *biology educator*

### Houston
Baughn, Robert Elroy *microbiology educator*
Brown, Jack Harold Upton *physiology educator, university official, biomedical engineer*
Butel, Janet Susan *virology educator*
DeBakey, Lois *science communications educator, writer, editor*
DeBakey, Selma *science communications educator, writer, editor, lecturer*
de Hostos, Eugenio Luis *cell biologist*
Garcia, Hector David *toxicologist*
Goldstein, Margaret Ann *biologist*
Henkel, Jenny Saucier *neurovirologist*
Hung, Mien-Chie *cancer biologist*
Jurtshuk, Peter, Jr. *microbiologist*
Konisky, Jordan *microbiology educator*
Müller-Eberhard, Hans Joachim *medical research scientist, administrator*
Nelson, David Loren *geneticist, educator*
Nichols, Buford Lee, Jr. *physiologist*
O'Malley, Bert William *cell biologist, educator, physician*
Patterson, Donald Eugene *research scientist*
Sass, Ronald Lewis *biology and chemistry educator*
Schultz, Stanley George *physiologist, educator*
Seaton, Alberta Jones *biologist, consultant*

### Kerrville
Kunz, Sidney *entomologist*

### Kingsville
Perez, John Carlos *biology educator*

### Longview
Martin, Ulrike Balk *laboratory analyst*

### Lubbock
Hentges, David John *microbiology educator*
Jackson, Raymond Carl *cytogeneticist*
Skoog, Gerald Duane *science educator*
Wendt, Charles William *soil physicist, educator*

### Magnolia
Ramsey, Kathleen Sommer *toxicologist*

### Nacogdoches
Worrell, Albert Cadwallader *forest economics educator*

### Overton
Randel, Ronald Dean *physiologist, educator*

### Port Aransas
Wohlschlag, Donald Eugene *zoologist, marine ecologist, educator emeritus*

### Richardson
Gray, Donald Melvin *molecular and cell biology educator*
Rutford, Robert Hoxie *geoscience educator*

### Round Rock
Schneider, Dennis Ray *microbiology educator*

### San Antonio
Betts, Austin Wortham *retired research company executive*
Blystone, Robert Vernon *developmental cell biologist, educator, textbook consultant*
Burch, James Leo *science research institute executive*
Corrigan, Helen González *cytologist*
Donaldson, Willis Lyle *research institute administrator*
Gates, Mahlon Eugene *applied research executive, former government official, former army officer*
Goland, Martin *research institute executive*
Kalter, Seymour Sanford *virologist, educator*
†Kittle, Joseph S. *science administrator, consultant*
Masoro, Edward Joseph, Jr. *physiology educator*
Polan-Curtain, Jodie Lea *physiologist researcher*
Spannagel, Alan Wayne *physiologist*
Stone, William Harold *geneticist, educator*
Taylor, Robert Dalton *microbiologist*
Whelen, Andrew Christian *microbiologist, army officer*

## VIRGIN ISLANDS

**Kingshill**
Crossman, Stafford Mac Arthur *agronomist, researcher*

## MILITARY ADDRESSES OF THE UNITED STATES

## ATLANTIC

**APO**
Knowlton, Nancy *biologist*
Rubinoff, Ira *biologist, research administrator, conservationist*

## CANADA

## ALBERTA

**Brooks**
Krahn, Thomas Richard *horticultural research administrator*

**Calgary**
Jones, Geoffrey Melvill *physiology research educator*
Mossop, Grant Dilworth *geological institute director*
Rattner, Jerome Bernard *biologist, anatomist, educator*
Yoon, Ji-Won *virology, immunology and diabetes educator, research administrator*

**Edmonton**
Cossins, Edwin Albert *biology educator, academic administrator*
Hiruki, Chuji *plant virologist, science educator*

## BRITISH COLUMBIA

**Bamfield**
Druehl, Louis Dix *biology educator*

**Burnaby**
Borden, John Harvey *entomologist, educator*

**Nanaimo**
Ricker, William Edwin *biologist*

**Sidney**
Bigelow, Margaret Elizabeth Barr *mycologist educator*
Davis, John Christopher *zoologist, aquatic toxicologist*
Kendrick, William Bryce *biology educator, author, publisher*
Mann, Cedric Robert *retired institute administrator, oceanographer*

**Summerland**
Looney, Norman Earl *pomologist, plant physiologist*

**Vancouver**
Blair, Robert *animal science administrator, educator, researcher*
Campbell, Jack James Ramsay *microbiology educator*
Chitty, Dennis Hubert *zoology educator*
Copp, Douglas Harold *physiologist, educator*
Hoar, William Stewart *zoologist, educator*
Jones, David Robert *zoology educator*
Lindsey, Casimir Charles *zoologist*
March, Beryl Elizabeth *animal scientist, educator*
McBride, Barry Clarke *microbiology and oral biology educator, research microbiologist*
Mc Lean, Donald Millis *microbiology, pathology educator, physician*
Newman, Murray Arthur *aquarium administrator*
Phillips, Anthony George *neurobiology educator*
Phillips, John Edward *zoologist, educator*
Randall, David John *physiologist, zoologist, educator*
Rennie, Paul Steven *research scientist*
Shaw, Michael *biologist, educator*
Wellington, William George *plant science and ecology educator*

**West Vancouver**
Donaldson, Edward Mossop *research scientist, aquaculture consultant*

## MANITOBA

**Winnipeg**
Eales, John Geoffrey *zoology educator*
Findlay, Glen Marshall *agrologist*
McAlpine, Phyllis Jean *genetics educator, researcher*
Suzuki, Isamu *microbiology educator, researcher*
Tipples, Keith Howard *research director*

## NEWFOUNDLAND

**Saint John's**
Davis, Charles Carroll *aquatic biologist, educator*

## NOVA SCOTIA

**Dartmouth**
Bhartia, Prakash *defense research management executive, researcher, educator*
Mann, Kenneth Henry *marine ecologist*

**Halifax**
Hall, Brian Keith *biology educator, author*
O'Dor, Ron *physiologist, marine biology educator*

**Wolfville**
Toews, Daniel Peter *zoologist*

## ONTARIO

**Caledon**
Fallis, Albert Murray *microbiology educator*

**Deep River**
Newcombe, Howard Borden *biologist, consultant*

**Downsview**
Forer, Arthur H. *biology educator, researcher, editor*
Moens, Peter B. *biology researcher and educator*

**Guelph**
Beveridge, Terrance James *microbiology educator, researcher*
Bewley, John Derek *botany researcher, educator*
Jorgensen, Erik *forest pathologist, educator, consultant*
Kasha, Kenneth John *crop science educator*
Oaks, B. Ann *plant physiologist, educator*
Sells, Bruce Howard *biomedical sciences educator*

**Kingston**
Bisby, Mark Ainley *physiology educator*
Leggett, William C. *biology educator, academic administrator*
Turpin, David Howard *biologist, educator*
Wyatt, Gerard Robert *biology educator, researcher*

**London**
Locke, Michael *zoology educator*

**Nepean**
†Adams, Gabrielle *biologist*
Beare-Rogers, Joyce Louise *former research executive*
Bishop, Claude Titus *retired biological sciences research administrator, editor*

**North York**
Davey, Kenneth George *biologist, university official*

**Ottawa**
Batra, Tilak Raj *research scientist*
Carty, Arthur John *research council administrator*
Dence, Michael Robert *research director*
Dueck, John *agricultural researcher, plant pathologist*
Hughes, Stanley John *mycologist*
Lister, Earle Edward *animal science consultant*
Perry, Malcolm Blythe *biologist*
Sinha, Ramesh Chandra *plant pathologist*
Storey, Kenneth Bruce *biology educator*
Topp, George Clarke *soil physicist*

**Peterborough**
Hutchinson, Thomas Cuthbert *ecology and environmental educator*

**Port Rowan**
Francis, Charles MacKenzie *wildlife biologist*

**Sault Sainte Marie**
Kondo, Edward Shinichi *plant pathologist, researcher*

**Scarborough**
White, Calvin John *zoo executive, financial manager, zoological association executive*

**Stittsville**
MacLeod, Robert Angus *microbiology educator, researcher*

**Toronto**
Atwood, Harold Leslie *physiology and zoology educator*
Heath, Michele Christine *botany educator*
Kerr, David Wylie *natural resource company executive*
Kushner, Donn Jean *microbiologist, children's author*
Liversage, Richard Albert *cell biologist*
MacLennan, David Herman *research scientist, educator*
McNeill, John *botanist*
Mustard, James Fraser *research institute executive*
Pawson, Anthony J. *molecular biologist*
Sigal, Israel Michael *scientist*
Stadelman, William Ralph *chemical institution executive*
Tobe, Stephen Solomon *zoology educator*
Tsui, Lap-Chee *molecular genetics educator*

**Waterloo**
Hynes, Hugh Bernard Noel *biology educator*

**Yarker**
Smallman, Beverley N. *biology educator*

## QUEBEC

**Ile Perrot**
Tomlinson, George Herbert *retired industrial company research executive*

**Laval**
Kluepfel, Dieter *microbiologist*
Pavilanis, Vytautas *microbiology educator, physician*

**Montreal**
Carroll, Robert Lynn *biology educator, vertebrate paleontologist, museum curator*
Chang, Thomas Ming Swi *medical scientist, biotechnologist*
Dansereau, Pierre *ecologist*
Gibbs, Sarah Preble *biologist, educator*
Goldstein, Sandu *biotechnology executive, researcher*
Guindon, Yvan *science administrator, research scientist*
Hamet, Pavel *research scientist*
Jolicoeur, Paul *molecular biologist*
Maclachlan, Gordon Alistair *biology educator, researcher*
Murphy, Beverley Elaine Pearson *scientist, physician, educator*
Plaa, Gabriel Leon *toxicologist, educator*
Sattler, Rolf *plant morphologist, educator*
Stanners, Clifford Paul *molecular and cell biologist, biochemistry educator*

**Quebec**
Bourget, Edwin Robert *marine ecologist, educator*
Potvin, Pierre *physiologist, educator*
Trudel, Marc J. *botanist*
Villeneuve, Jean-Pierre *science association director, educator*

**Sainte Anne de Bellevue**
Grant, William Frederick *geneticist, educator*
Steppler, Howard Alvey *agronomist*

**Sainte Foy**
Cardinal, André *phycologist, educator*
Frisque, Gilles *forestry engineer*

## SASKATCHEWAN

**Regina**
Davis, Gordon Richard Fuerst *retired biologist, translator*
Sonntag, Bernard H. *agrologist, research executive*

**Saskatoon**
Babiuk, Lorne Alan *virologist, immunologist, research administrator*
Bell, John Milton *agricultural science educator*
Harvey, Bryan Laurence *crop science educator*
Huang, Pan Ming *soil science educator*
Shokeir, Mohamed Hassan Kamel *medical geneticist, educator*

## ARGENTINA

**Buenos Aires**
Balve, Beba Carmen *research center administrator*

## AUSTRALIA

**Randwick**
Hall, Peter Francis *physiologist*

## CUBA

**Havana**
Kouri, Gustavo Pedro *virologist*

## ENGLAND

**Cranbrook**
Hattersley-Smith, Geoffrey Francis *retired government research scientist*

**Leeds**
Phillips, Oliver *tropical biodiversity scientist*

**London**
Pecorino, Lauren Teresa *biologist*

## FINLAND

**Kuopio**
Sen, Chandan Kumar *physiologist, scientist, educator*

## FRANCE

**Orsay**
Fiszer-Szafarz, Berta (Berta Safars) *research scientist*

**Paris**
LeGoffic, Francois *biotechnology educator*
Robert, Leslie (Ladislas) *research center administrator, consultant*

## GERMANY

**Dusseldorf**
Stuhl, Oskar Paul *scientific and regulatory consultant*

**Katlenburg**
Hagfors, Tor *institute director*

**Munich**
Berg, Jan Mikael *science educator*

**Wachtberg**
Pitrella, Francis Donald *human factors professional*

**Wurzburg**
Hölldobler, Berthold Karl *zoologist, educator*

## HONG KONG

**Kowloon**
Kung, Shain-dow *molecular biologist, academic administrator*

**Sha Tin**
Chang, Shu Ting *fungal geneticist, mushroom biologist*

## ITALY

**Camerino**
Miyake, Akio *biologist, educator*

**Frascati**
Haegi, Marcel *scientist, physicist*

**Naples**
Tarro, Giulio *virologist*

## JAPAN

**Fukuoka**
Aizawa, Keio *biology educator*

**Iwate**
Kawauchi, Hiroshi *hormone science educator*

**Kanagawa**
Okui, Kazumitsu *biology educator*

**Kobe**
Tochikura, Tatsurokuro *applied microbiologist, home economics educator*

**Osaka**
Watanabe, Toshiharu *ecologist, educator*

**Tokyo**
Arai, Toshihiko *retired microbiology and immunology educator*
Ishii, Akira *medical parasitologist, malariologist, allergologist*
Takahashi, Keiichi *zoology educator*
Ueno, Tomiko F. *forestry company executive*

## KENYA

**South Nyanza**
Khan, Zeyaur Rahman *entomologist*

## PERU

**Lima**
French, Edward Ronald *plant pathologist*

## POLAND

**Warsaw**
Koscielak, Jerzy *scientist, science administrator*

## PORTUGAL

**Lisbon**
De Jesus, Fernando *science administrator*

## SAUDI ARABIA

**Riyadh**
Chaudhary, Shaukat Ali *ecologist, plant taxonomist*

## SCOTLAND

**Gullane**
Collins, Jeffrey Hamilton *research facility administrator, electrical engineering educator*

## SWITZERLAND

**Lausanne**
Stingelin, Valentin *research center director, mechanical engineer*

## TAIWAN

**Yung-Ho**
Liu, Shi-Kau *microbiologist, research scientist*

## WEST INDIES

**Roseau**
Jeffries, Charles Dean *microbiology educator, scientist*

## ADDRESS UNPUBLISHED

Ahearne, John Francis *scientific research administrator, researcher*
Ahlquist, Paul Gerald *molecular biology researcher, educator*
Allen, Lew, Jr. *laboratory executive, former air force officer*
Armstrong, Thomas Newton, III *American art and garden specialist, consultant*
Arnott, Howard Joseph *biology educator, university dean*
Baldwin, C. Andrew, Jr. *retired science educator*
Barabino, William Albert *science and technology researcher, inventor*
Barnard, Donald Roy *entomologist*
Barrett, Izadore *retired fisheries research administrator*
Berlowitz Tarrant, Laurence *biotechnologist, university administrator*
Bernard, Richard Lawson *geneticist, retired*
Bers, Donald Martin *physiology educator*
Bidwell, Roger Grafton Shelford *biologist, educator*
Birchem, Regina *cell biologist, environment consultant, educator, writer*
Bonner, John Tyler *biology educator*
Bremner, John McColl *agronomy and biochemistry educator*
Brill, Winston Jonas *microbiologist, educator, research director, publisher and management consultant*
Brock, Mary Anne *research biologist, consultant*
Brody, Edward Norman *molecular biologist, educator*
Bullock, Theodore Holmes *biologist, educator*

Burdett, Barbra Elaine biology educator
Bush, Guy Louis biology educator
Cameron, Roy Eugene scientist
Carlquist, Sherwin biology and botany educator
Carter, David LaVere soil scientist, researcher, consultant
Catlin, B. Wesley microbiologist
Chegini, Nasser cell biology educator, reproductive endocrinologist
Cole, Jerome Foster research company executive
Creech, John Lewis retired scientist, consultant
D'Alesandro, Philip Anthony parasitologist, immunologist, retired educator
De Antoni, Edward Paul cancer control research scientist
Decker, Walter Johns toxicologist
DeRoo, Sally A. biology and geology educator
Dubesa, Elaine J. biotechnology company executive
Dugan, Patrick Raymond microbiologist, university dean
Durham, Thena Monts microbiologist, researcher, management executive
Easterbrook, Kenneth Brian retired microbiologist
Eicher, George John aquatic biologist
Ellner, Paul Daniel clinical microbiologist
Erlenmeyer-Kimling, L. psychiatric and behavior genetics researcher, educator
Evans, Charles Wayne, II biologist, researcher
Farber, Neal Mark biotechnologist, molecular biologist
Finney, Essex Eugene, Jr. agricultural research administrator
Flemming, David Paul biologist
Florence, Paul Smith agronomist, business owner
Foy, Charles Daley retired soil scientist
Frizzell, Linda Diane Bane exercise physiologist
Galas, David John molecular biology educator, researcher, administrator
Gallo, Robert Charles research scientist
Gennaro, Antonio L. biology educator
Gill, William Robert soil scientist
Giordano, James Joseph neuroscientist, educator
Glick, J. Leslie biotechnology entrepreneur
Goldstein, Walter Elliott biotechnology executive
Greenman, David Lewis consultant physiologist, toxicologist
Hamilton, William Howard laboratory executive
Haraga, Liana T. biologist, researcher
Harriman, Philip Darling geneticist, science foundation executive
Harris, Elliott Stanley toxicologist
Harrises, Antonio Efthemios biology educator
Hartman, Margaret J. biologist, educator, university official
Heine, Ursula Ingrid biologist, researcher, artist
Herz, Michael Joseph marine environmental scientist
Honour, Lynda Charmaine research scientist, educator, psychotherapist
Hsiao, Kwang-Jen genetics and biochemistry educator
Inouye, David William zoology educator
Izlar, Robert Lee forester
Jackson, Victor Louis retired naturalist
Jacobs, Abigail Conway toxicologist
Jacobs, Hyde Spencer soil chemistry educator
Katz, Anne Harris biologist, educator, writer, aviator
Kearney, Patricia Michal retired natural sciences educator, poet, consultant
King, John Quill Taylor science center administrator, college administrator emeritus
Kirsteuer, Ernst Karl Eberhart biologist, curator
Kozlowski, Theodore Thomas botany educator, research director, author, editor
Kuper, George Henry research and development institute executive
Latham, James Richard research scientist
Leath, Kenneth Thomas research plant pathologist, educator, agricultural consultant
Leder, Philip geneticist, educator
Lindsay, Dale Richard research administrator
Lindstedt-Siva, (Karen) June marine biologist, environmental consultant
Machida, Curtis A. research molecular neurobiologist
Mannering, Jerry Vincent agronomist, educator
Markovitz, Alvin molecular biologist, geneticist
Maroni, Donna Farolino biologist, researcher
Martin, George Conner pomology educator
Martino, Joseph Paul research scientist
Maslansky, Carol Jeanne toxicologist
Mathew, Porunelloor Abraham molecular biologist, educator
Maunder, Addison Bruce agronomic research company executive
McShefferty, John retired research company executive, consultant
Mehta, Peshotan Rustom magnetobiologist
Melnick, Joseph L. virologist, educator
Menn, Julius Joel research scientist
Micks, Don Wilfred biologist, educator
Moscona, Aron Arthur biology educator, scientist
Myers, Jack Edgar biologist, educator
Neel, James Van Gundia geneticist, educator
Nelson, Wallace Warren retired superintendent experimental station, agronomy educator
O'Brien, Stephen James geneticist
Olson, Phillip David LeRoy agriculturist, chemist
Oswald, Robert Bernard science administrator, nuclear engineer
Paganelli, Charles Victor physiologist
Palade, George Emil biologist, educator
Parmelee, David Freeland biologist, educator
Peter, Richard Ector zoology educator
Pielou, Evelyn C. biologist
Pierce, John Thomas industrial hygienist, toxicologist
Pinter, Gabriel George physiologist
Pionke, Harry Bernhard research leader and soil scientist
Post, Boyd Wallace forester
Rabson, Robert plant physiologist, retired science administrator
Ramanarayanan, Madhava Prabhu science administrator, researcher, educator
Reetz, Harold Frank, Jr. industrial agronomist
Rogers, Jack David plant pathologist, educator
Sabatini, David Domingo cell biologist, biochemist
Santacana, Guido E. physiology educator
Schaller, George Beals zoologist
Schmidt, Jean Marie microbiology educator
Schwab, John Harris microbiology and immunology educator
Shepherd, Robert James plant pathology researcher, retired educator
Simpson, Frederick James retired research administrator
Sjostrand, Fritiof Stig biologist, educator
Skinner, James Stanford physiologist, educator
Smietana, Walter educational research director
Smith, Philip Luther patent information scientist
Sokal, Robert Reuven biology educator, author
Soper, James Herbert botanist, curator
South, Frank Edwin physiologist, educator
Southwick, Charles Henry zoologist, educator
Stark, Nellie May forest ecology educator
Stefano, George B. neurobiologist, researcher
Stickle, David Walter microbiologist
Stone, John Floyd soil physics researcher and educator
Sund, Kelly G. public health science administrator
Tenney, Stephen Marsh physiologist, educator
Tzimopoulos, Nicholas D. science and mathematics education specialist
Vaughan, John Charles, III horticultural products executive
Weinstock, Ronald Jay research and development company executive
Wiatr, Christopher L. microbiologist
Wilkinson, Stanley Ralph agronomist
Wormwood, Richard Naughton retired naturalist
Wright, Philip Lincoln zoologist, educator
Yang, Xiangzhong research scientist, administrator, educator
Zhu, Yong research scientist

## SCIENCE: MATHEMATICS AND COMPUTER SCIENCE

### UNITED STATES

#### ALABAMA

**Birmingham**
Peeples, William Dewey, Jr. mathematics educator

**Florence**
Foote, Avon Edward webmaster, communications educator
Johnson, Johnny Ray mathematics educator

**Huntsville**
Freas, George Wilson, II computer consultant
Pruitt, Alice Fay mathematician, engineer

**Mobile**
Yett, Fowler Redford mathematics educator

**Pelham**
Turner, Malcolm Elijah biomathematician, educator

**Tuscaloosa**
Davis, Anthony Michael John mathematics educator
Drake, Albert Estern retired statistics educator, farming administrator
Rice, Margaret Lucille computer technology educator

#### ALASKA

**Anchorage**
Mann, Lester Perry mathematics educator

**Tununak**
Bond, Ward Charles mathematics and computer educator

#### ARIZONA

**Chandler**
Rudibaugh, Melinda Campbell mathematics educator

**Mesa**
Stott, Brian software company executive

**Phoenix**
Friesen, Oris Dewayne software engineer, historian

**Prescott**
Anderson, Arthur George laboratory director, former computer company executive, consultant

**Sierra Vista**
Sizemore, Nicky Lee computer scientist

**Sun City**
Jackson, Randy computer networking executive

**Tempe**
Hoppensteadt, Frank Charles mathematician, university administrator
Ihrig, Edwin Charles, Jr. mathematics educator
Smith, Harvey Alvin mathematics educator, consultant
Yau, Stephen Sik-sang computer science and engineering educator, computer scientist, researcher

**Tucson**
Goodman, Seymour Evan computer science and international studies educator, researcher, consultant
Re Velle, Jack B(oyer) statistician, consultant
Smarandache, Florentin mathematics researcher, writer
Willoughby, Stephen Schuyler mathematics educator

#### ARKANSAS

**Batesville**
Carius, Robert Wilhelm mathematics and science educator, retired naval officer

**Fort Smith**
Smith-Leins, Terri L. mathematics educator

**Little Rock**
McDermott, Cecil Wade mathematics educator, educational program director
Townsend, James Willis computer scientist

**Searcy**
Oldham, Bill W. mathematics educator

#### CALIFORNIA

**Antioch**
Neimann, Albert Alexander mathematician, business owner

**Azusa**
Sambasivam, Ezhilarasan computer science and mathematics educator

**Berkeley**
Arveson, William Barnes mathematics educator
Bergman, George Mark mathematician, educator
Berlekamp, Elwyn Ralph mathematic educator, electronics company executive,
Bickel, Peter John statistician, educator
Chern, Shiing-Shen mathematics educator
Chorin, Alexandre Joel mathematician, educator
Cooper, William Secord information science educator
Freedman, David Amiel statistics educator, consultant
Harrison, Michael Alexander computer scientist, educator
Henkin, Leon Albert mathematician, educator
Henzinger, Thomas Anton computer science educator
Kaplansky, Irving mathematician, educator, research institute director
Le Cam, Lucien Marie mathematics educator
McKusick, Marshall Kirk computer scientist
Moore, Calvin C. mathematics educator, administrator
Osserman, Robert mathematician, educator
Patterson, David Andrew computer scientist, educator, consultant
Sequin, Carlo H. computer science educator
Smith, Alan Jay computer science educator, consultant
Speed, Terence Paul statistician, educator
Tarter, Michael Ernest biostatistician, educator
Thomas, Paul Emery mathematics educator
Vojta, Paul Alan mathematics educator
Wolf, Joseph Albert mathematician, educator
Xie, Ganquan mathematician, computational geophysical scientist, educator

**Carlsbad**
Halberg, Charles John August, Jr. mathematics educator

**Carmichael**
Givant, Philip Joachim mathematics educator, real estate investment executive

**Carson**
Kowalski, Kazimierz computer science educator, researcher
Suchenek, Marek Andrzej computer science educator

**Castroville**
Guglielmo, Eugene Joseph software engineer

**Chatsworth**
Koerber, John Robert computer programmer

**Claremont**
Bentley, Donald Lyon mathematics and statistics educator
Coleman, Courtney Stafford mathematician, educator
Cooke, Kenneth Lloyd mathematician, educator
Grabiner, Sandy mathematics educator
Henriksen, Melvin mathematician, educator
Mullikin, Harry Copeland mathematics educator
White, Alvin Murray mathematics educator, consultant

**Concord**
Fuld, Fred, III computer consultant, financial consultant

**Costa Mesa**
Arismendi-Pardi, Eduardo J. mathematics educator
Camacho, Dianne Lynne mathematics educator, administrator

**Culver City**
Hankins, Hesterly G., III computer systems analyst, inventor, educator

**Cupertino**
Holmes, Richard Albert software engineer, consultant
Togasaki, Shinobu computer scientist

**Davis**
Mulase, Motohico mathematics educator
Reed, Nancy Ellen computer science educator
Rocke, David Morton statistician, educator

**Elk Grove**
McDavid, Douglas Warren systems consultant

**Fountain Valley**
Berman, Steven Richard computer systems analyst, research engineer

**Fremont**
Barreto, Charlton Bodenberg software engineer
Lautzenheiser, Marvin Wendell computer software engineer

**Fresno**
Cohen, Moses Elias mathematician, educator

**Fullerton**
Natsuyama, Harriet Hatsune mathematician

**Garden Grove**
Chacon, Michael Ernest computer networking specialist

**Hayward**
Prada, Gloria Ines mathematics and Spanish language educator
Sabharwal, Ranjit Singh mathematician

**Irvine**
Bennett, Bruce Michael mathematics educator, musician
Hoffman, Donald David cognitive and computer science educator
Wan, Frederic Yui-Ming mathematician, educator

**La Jolla**
Goguen, Joseph Amadee computer science educator
Halkin, Hubert mathematics educator, research mathematician
Martin, James John, Jr. retired consulting research firm executive, systems analyst
Reissner, Eric (Max Erich Reissner) applied mechanics researcher
Rosenblatt, Murray mathematics educator
Terras, Audrey Anne mathematics educator
Wulbert, Daniel Eliot mathematician, educator
Zyroff, Ellen Slotoroff information scientist, classicist, educator

**Livermore**
Blattner, Meera McCuaig computer science educator
Haga, Enoch John computer educator, author

**Long Beach**
Palacios, Alana Sue computer programmer
Schroeder, Arnold Leon mathematics educator

**Los Angeles**
Afifi, Abdelmonem A. biostatistics educator, academic dean
Arbib, Michael Anthony neuroscientist, educator, cybernetician
Bekey, George Albert computer scientist, educator, engineer
Chacko, George Kuttickal systems science educator, consultant
Delaney, Matthew Sylvester mathematics educator, academic administrator
Estrin, Gerald computer scientist, engineering educator, academic administrator
Ginsburg, Seymour computer science educator
Gordon, Basil mathematics educator
Greenberger, Martin educator, technologist
Harris, Theodore Edward mathematician, educator
Hu, Sze-Tsen mathematics educator
Jacobsen, Laren mathematician, classical musician
Kalaba, Robert Edwin applied mathematician
Kleinrock, Leonard computer scientist
Lerner, Vladimir Semion computer scientist, educator
Lyashenko, Nikolai Nikolaevich mathematician, educator
Palmer, Roger Cain information scientist
Pearl, Judea computer scientist, educator
Petak, William John systems management educator
Port, Sidney Charles mathematician, educator
Rector, Robert Wayman mathematics and engineering educator, former association executive
Shapley, Lloyd Stowell mathematics and economics educator
Stormes, John Max instructional systems developer
Symonds, Norman Leslie computer programming specialist
Waterman, Michael Spencer mathematics educator, biology educator

**Los Gatos**
Rissanen, Jorma Johannes computer scientist

**Marina Del Rey**
Touch, Joseph Dean computer scientist, educator

**Menlo Park**
Bourne, Charles Percy information scientist, educator
Neumann, Peter Gabriel computer scientist

**Milpitas**
Hodson, Roy Goode, Jr. retired logistician

**Mission Viejo**
Stampfli, John Francis logistics consultant

**Monterey**
Gaskell, Robert Eugene mathematician, educator
Hamming, Richard Wesley computer scientist

**Moss Landing**
Lange, Lester Henry mathematics educator

**Mountain View**
Martin, Roger John computer scientist
Oki, Brian Masao software engineer
Shah, Devang Kundanlal software engineer

**Newport Beach**
Cook, Marcy Lynn mathematics educator, consultant

**Oakland**
Long, William Joseph software engineer

**Palo Alto**
Beretta, Giordano Bruno computer scientist, researcher
Lamport, Leslie B. computer scientist
Leong, Helen Vanessa systems programmer
Mahmood, Aamer computer system architect
Roberts, Charles S. software engineer
Spinrad, Robert Joseph computer scientist
Weiser, Mark David computer scientist, researcher

**Pasadena**
Franklin, Joel Nicholas mathematician, educator
Luxemburg, Wilhelmus Anthonius Josephus mathematics educator
Marsden, Jerrold Eldon mathematician, educator, engineer
Patterson, Mark Jerome computer software designer
Saffman, Philip G. mathematician
Todd, John mathematician, educator
Whitham, Gerald Beresford mathematics educator

**Pleasanton**
Petersen, Ann Nevin *computer systems administrator, consultant*

**Pomona**
Bernau, Simon John *mathematics educator*

**Portola Valley**
Kuo, Franklin F. *computer scientist, electrical engineer*

**Ramona**
Bennett, James Chester *computer consultant, real estate developer*

**Redondo Beach**
Burris, Harrison Robert *computer and software developer*

**Redwood City**
Itnyre, Jacqueline Harriet *programmer*

**Riverside**
Bhanu, Bir *computer information scientist, educator, director university program*
Ratliff, Louis Jackson, Jr. *mathematics educator*
Shapiro, Victor Lenard *mathematics educator*

**Rosemead**
Hattar, Michael Mizyed *mathematics educator*

**Sacramento**
Burger, John Barclay *systems architect, computer scientist*
Sawiris, Milad Youssef *statistician, educator*

**San Diego**
Burgin, George Hans *computer scientist, educator*
Burke, John *science technology company executive*
Campo, Catherine (Sauter) *computer programmer*
Garrison, Betty Bernhardt *retired mathematics educator*
Hales, Alfred Washington *mathematics educator, consultant*
Huang, Kun Lien *software engineer, scientist*
Willerding, Margaret Frances *mathematician*

**San Francisco**
Backus, John *computer scientist*
Cruse, Allan Baird *mathematician, computer scientist, educator*
Farrell, Edward Joseph *retired mathematics educator*
Komissarchik, Edward A. *computer scientist*
Leung, Kason Kai Ching *computer specialist*
Masuda, Yoshinori *systems analyst*

**San Jose**
Aylesworth, John Richard *software professional*
†Morgridge, John P. *computer business executive*
Schindler, Keith William *software engineer*

**San Juan Capistrano**
Botway, Lloyd Frederick *computer scientist, consultant*

**San Luis Obispo**
Grimes, Joseph Edward *computer science educator*

**San Marino**
Lashley, Virginia Stephenson Hughes *retired computer science educator*

**San Pedro**
Colman, Ronald William *computer science educator*

**San Ramon**
Rose, Joan L. *computer security specialist*
Schofield, James Roy *computer programmer*

**Santa Barbara**
Fan, Ky *mathematician, educator*
Johnsen, Eugene Carlyle *mathematician and educator*
Marcus, Marvin *mathematician, educator*
Minc, Henryk *mathematics educator*
Newman, Morris *mathematician*
Rosenberg, Alex *mathematician, educator*
Simons, Stephen *mathematics educator, researcher*
Zelmanowitz, Julius Martin *mathematics educator, university administrator*

**Santa Clara**
Alexanderson, Gerald Lee *mathematician, educator, writer*
Halmos, Paul Richard *mathematician, educator*
Jain, Jawahar *computer scientist, engineer, researcher*
Klosinski, Leonard Frank *mathematics educator*
Sproule, Betty Ann *computer industry strategic planning manager*

**Santa Cruz**
Huskey, Harry Douglas *information and computer science educator*

**Santa Monica**
Anderson, Robert Helms *information scientist*
Ware, Willis Howard *computer scientist*

**Santee**
Peters, Raymond Eugene *computer systems company executive*

**Saratoga**
Park, Joseph Chul Hui *computer scientist*

**Scotts Valley**
Janssen, James Robert *consulting software engineer*

**Simi Valley**
Stratton, Gregory Alexander *computer specialist, administrator, mayor*

**Stanford**
Anderson, Theodore Wilbur *statistics educator*
Brown, Byron William, Jr. *biostatistician, educator*
Cover, Thomas M. *statistician, electrical engineer, educator*
Dantzig, George Bernard *applied mathematics educator*
Efron, Bradley *mathematics educator*
Johnstone, Iain Murray *statistician, educator, consultant*
Karlin, Samuel *mathematics educator, researcher*
Keller, Joseph Bishop *mathematician, educator*
Knuth, Donald Ervin *computer sciences educator*
Lieberman, Gerald J. *statistics educator*
McCarthy, John *computer scientist, educator*
Moses, Lincoln E. *statistician, educator*
Olshen, Richard A. *statistician, educator*
Ornstein, Donald Samuel *mathematician, educator*
Phillips, Ralph Saul *mathematics educator*
Rubin, Karl Cooper *mathematics educator*
Switzer, Paul *statistics educator*
Ullman, Jeffrey David *computer science educator*

**Thousand Oaks**
Sladek, Lyle Virgil *mathematician, educator*

**Torrance**
Houston, Samuel Robert *statistics educator, consultant*

**Westlake Village**
Munson, John Backus *computer systems consultant, retired computer engineering company executive*

**Woodland Hills**
Fitzpatrick, Dennis Michael *information systems executive*

## COLORADO

**Aurora**
Barth, David Victor *computer systems designer, consultant*

**Boulder**
Beylkin, Gregory *mathematician*
Burleski, Joseph Anthony, Jr. *information services professional*
Crow, Edwin Louis *mathematical statistician, consultant*
Glover, Fred William *artificial intelligence and optimization research director, educator*
Mycielski, Jan *mathematician, educator*

**Colorado Springs**
Cole, Julian Wayne (Perry Cole) *computer educator, consultant, programmer, analyst*
Couger, James Daniel *computer scientist, writer*
Heffron, Michael Edward *software engineer, computer scientist*
Macon, Jerry Lyn *software company owner, software publisher*
Nowosatko, Jerome Raymond *software engineer*
Simmons, George Finlay *mathematics educator*
Thor, Paul Viets *computer science educator, software engineer, consultant*

**Denver**
Cutter, Gary Raymond *biostatistician*
Kushner, Todd Roger *computer scientist, software engineer*
Larsen, Gwynne E. *computer information systems educator*
Mendez, Celestino Galo *mathematics educator*

**Divide**
Trench, William Frederick *mathematics educator*

**Durango**
Spencer, Donald Clayton *mathematician*

**Englewood**
Leigh, Shari Greer *software consulting firm executive*

**Fort Collins**
Mielke, Paul William, Jr. *statistician*
Tweedie, Richard Lewis *statistics educator, consultant*

**Golden**
Friede, Heather Ellen *computer consultant*
Murphy, Robin Roberson *computer science educator*

**Longmont**
Ford, Byron Milton *computer consultant*

**Westminster**
Poteet, Mary Jane *computer scientist*

## CONNECTICUT

**Bloomfield**
Johnson, Linda Thelma *information specialist*

**Bridgeport**
Sobh, Tarek Mahmoud *computer science educator, researcher*

**East Hartford**
Ahlberg, John Harold *mathematician, educator*

**Fairfield**
Eigel, Edwin George, Jr. *mathematics educator, retired university president*
Shaffer, Dorothy Browne *retired mathematician, educator*

**Farmington**
Miser, Hugh Jordan *systems analyst, operations researcher, consultant*

**Hartford**
Welna, Cecilia *mathematics educator*

**Middletown**
Comfort, William Wistar *mathematics educator*
Hager, Anthony Wood *mathematics educator*
Maltese, George John *mathematics educator*
Reid, James Dolan *mathematics educator, researcher*
Rosenbaum, Robert Abraham *mathematics educator*

**New Haven**
Fischer, Michael John *computer science educator*
Holford, Theodore Richard *biostatistician, educator*
Howe, Roger Evans *mathematician, educator*
Massey, William S. *mathematician, educator*
Mostow, George Daniel *mathematics educator*
Rickart, Charles Earl *mathematician, educator*
Seligman, George Benham *mathematics educator*
Szczarba, Robert Henry *mathematics educator, mathematician*
Tufte, Edward Rolf *statistics educator, publisher*
Zhang, Heping *biostatistician*

**Stamford**
Fuller, Cassandra Miller *programmer analyst*

**Vernon Rockville**
Roden, Jon-Paul *computer science educator*

**West Haven**
Fischer, Alice Edna Waltz *computer science educator*

**Westport**
Hotaling, Brock Elliot *software development leader*

**Wilton**
Brown, James Thompson, Jr. *computer information scientist*

## DELAWARE

**Dover**
Olagunju, Amos Omotayo *computer science educator, consultant*

**Newark**
Collins, George Edwin *computer scientist, mathematician, educator*
Colton, David Lem *mathematician, educator*
Stark, Robert Martin *mathematician, civil engineer, educator*

**Wilmington**
Stakgold, Ivar *mathematics educator*

## DISTRICT OF COLUMBIA

**Washington**
Chiazze, Leonard, Jr. *biostatistician, epidemiologist, educator*
Coles, Bertha Sharon Giles *visual information specialist*
†Courtright, John R. *information management specialist*
Denning, Dorothy Elizabeth Robling *computer scientist*
Ellison, Earl Otto *computer scientist*
Flournoy, Nancy *statistician, educator*
Friestedt, Amédée Chabrisson *systems analyst*
Gastwirth, Joseph Lewis *statistician, educator*
Goldfield, Edwin David *statistician*
Goldhaber, Jacob Kopel *retired mathematician, educator*
Gray, Mary Wheat *statistician, lawyer*
Hammer, Carl *computer scientist, former computer company executive*
Hedges, Harry George *computer scientist, educator*
Kahlow, Barbara Fenvessy *statistician*
Killion, Ruth Ann *statistical researcher*
Loosbrock, Carol Marie *information management professional*
Maisel, Herbert *computer science educator*
Raphael, Louise Arakelian *mathematician, educator*
Ryan, David Alan *computer specialist*
Sandefur, James Tandy *mathematics educator*
Sanderson, Jerome Alan *survey statistician, accountant*
Saworotnow, Parfeny Pavlovich *mathematician, educator*
Shaw, William Frederick *statistician*
Stokes, Arnold Paul *mathematics educator*
Tidball, Charles Stanley *computer scientist, educator*
Viehe, Karl William *mathematics educator, lawyer, investment banker*
Wulf, William Allan *computer information scientist, educator*

## FLORIDA

**Alachua**
Neubauer, Hugo Duane, Jr. *software engineer*

**Clearwater**
Klingbiel, Paul Herman *information science consultant*
Puckett, Stanley Allen *consultant, realtor, marketing-management educator*

**Coral Gables**
Howard, Bernard Eufinger *mathematics and computer science educator*

**Delray Beach**
Hegstrom, William Jean *mathematics educator*

**Fort Lauderdale**
Gude, Nancy Carlson *computer consultant*
Kemper Littman, Marlyn *information scientist, educator*
Kontos, George *computer science educator*

**Gainesville**
Bednarek, Alexander Robert *mathematician, educator*
Dinculeanu, Nicolae *mathematician*
Emch, Gerard Gustav *mathematics and physics educator*
Keesling, James Edgar *mathematics educator*

**Highland Beach**
Schor, Stanley Sidney *mathematical sciences educator*

**Indialantic**
Carroll, Charles Lemuel, Jr. *mathematician*

**Jacksonville**
Roth, Robert Allen *systems consultant*

**Kennedy Space Center**
Evenson, Michael Donald *software engineer*

**Lakeland**
Sheppard, Albert Parker, Jr. *mathematics educator*

**Melbourne**
Arnold, Toni Lavalle *software engineer*
Lakshmikantham, Vangipuram *mathematics educator*

**Miami**
Zanakis, Steve H. *management science/information systems educator*

**Milton**
McKinney, George Harris, Jr. *training systems analyst*

**Naples**
Ciano, James Francis *computer systems analyst*

**North Lauderdale**
Hawn, Micaela (Micki Hawn) *mathematics educator*

**Orlando**
Denton, Carol Forsberg *training systems designer*
Deo, Narsingh *computer science educator*
Medin, Julia Adele *mathematics educator, researcher*
Sathre, Leroy *mathematics educator, consultant*

**Palm Bay**
Bellstedt, Olaf *senior software engineer*

**Port Charlotte**
Soben, Robert Sidney *computer scientist*

**Punta Gorda**
Smith, Charles Edwin *computer science educator, consultant*

**Saint Petersburg**
Kazor, Walter Robert *statistical process control and quality assurance consultant*
Shi, Feng Sheng *mathematician*

**Sarasota**
Eachus, Joseph J(ackson) *computer scientist, consultant*
Hagen, George Leon *computer systems consultant*
Jacobson, Melvin Joseph *applied mathematician, acoustician, educator*
Lewis, Brian Kreglow *computer consultant*

**Sebring**
Vance, Elbridge Putnam *mathematics educator*

**Tallahassee**
Gilmer, Robert *mathematics educator*
Hunter, Christopher *mathematics educator*
Leavell, Michael Ray *computer programmer, analyst*
Loper, David Eric *mathematics educator, geophysics educator*
Nichols, Eugene Douglas *mathematics educator*
Stino, Farid K.R. *biostatistician, educator, researcher, consultant*

**Tampa**
Dickinson, Wendy Buchanan *measurement and research educator, artist*
Harriman, Malcolm Bruce *software developer, healthcare consultant*
Thompson, Denisse R. *mathematics educator*
Williams, Thomas Arthur *biomedical computing consultant, psychiatrist*

**Winter Park**
Swan, Richard Gordon *retired mathematics educator*

## GEORGIA

**Athens**
Lynch, James Walter *mathematician, educator*
Neter, John *statistician*

**Atlanta**
Ames, William Francis *mathematician, educator*
Ehrlich, Margaret Isabella Gorley *systems engineer, mathematics educator, consultant*
Hale, Jack K. *mathematics educator, research center administrator*
Johnson, Ellis Lane *mathematician*
King, K(imberly) N(elson) *computer science educator*
Oliker, Vladimir *mathematician, educator*
Vaishnavi, Vijay Kumar *computer science educator, researcher*
Wilkins, J. Ernest, Jr. *mathematician*
Williams, Charles Murray *computer information systems educator, consultant*

**Augusta**
Christensen, David William *mathematician, engineer*

**East Point**
Pierre, Charles Bernard *mathematician, statistician, educator*

**Glynco**
Mihal, Sandra Powell *distance learning specialist*

**Marietta**
Kanter, Donald Richard *statistician, pharmaceutical and psychobiology researcher*
Rutherfoord, Rebecca Hudson *computer science educator*

**Savannah**
Albert, Theodore Merton *computer scientist*
Wheeler, Ed Ray *mathematics educator*

Warga, Jack *mathematician, educator*
Zelen, Marvin *statistics educator*

### Cambridge
Anderson, Donald Gordon Marcus *mathematics educator*
Bartee, Thomas Creson *computer scientist, educator*
Berwick, Robert Cregar *computer science educator*
Bott, Raoul *mathematician, educator*
Carrier, George Francis *applied mathematics educator*
Cheatham, Thomas Edward, Jr. *computer scientist, educator*
Chernoff, Herman *statistics educator*
Conrades, George Henry *information systems company executive*
Dudley, Richard Mansfield *mathematician, educator*
†Elkies, Noam D. *mathematics educator*
Foley, James David *computer science educator, consultant*
Frenkel, Edward Vladimir *mathematician, educator*
Gagliardi, Ugo Oscar *systems software architect, educator*
Gleason, Andrew Mattei *mathematician, educator*
Greenspan, Harvey Philip *applied mathematician, educator*
Grosz, Barbara Jean *computer science educator*
Helgason, Sigurdur *mathematician, educator*
Jackson, Francis Joseph *research and development company executive*
Kac, Victor G. *mathematician, educator*
Light, Richard Jay *statistician, education educator*
Lynch, Nancy Ann *computer scientist, educator*
Mack, Robert Whiting *computer consultant*
Moses, Joel *computer scientist, educator*
Mosteller, Frederick *mathematical statistician, educator*
Oettinger, Anthony Gervin *mathematician, educator*
Orlin, James Berger *mathematician, management scientist, educator*
Roberts, Edward Baer *technology management educator*
Roberts, Nancy *computer educator*
Rockart, John Fralick *information systems reseacher*
Rubin, Donald Bruce *statistician, educator, research company executive*
Schmid, Wilfried *mathematician*
Segal, Irving Ezra *mathematics educator*
Strang, William Gilbert *mathematician, educator*
Stroock, Daniel Wyler *mathematician, educator*
Toomre, Alar *applied mathematician, theoretical astronomer*
Valiant, Leslie Gabriel *computer scientist*
Welsch, Roy Elmer *statistician*

### Duxbury
Thrasher, Dianne Elizabeth *mathematics educator, computer consultant*

### Falmouth
Bonn, Theodore Hertz *computer scientist, consultant*

### Framingham
Lavin, Philip Todd *biostatistician executive*
Scherr, Allan Lee *computer scientist, executive*

### Greenfield
Robinson, John Alan *logic and computer science educator*

### Lexington
Guivens, Norman Roy, Jr. *mathematician, engineer*

### Lincoln
LeGates, John Crews Boulton *information scientist*

### Lowell
Ruskai, Mary Beth *mathematics researcher, educator*

### Medford
Nitecki, Zbigniew Henry *mathematician, educator*
Reynolds, William Francis *mathematics educator*

### Medway
Yonda, Alfred William *mathematician*

### Quincy
Hayes, Bernardine Frances *computer systems analyst*

### Stow
Champine, George A. *computer scientist*

### Tewksbury
Hantman, Barry G. *software engineer*

### Wakefield
Hatch, Mark Bruce *software engineer*

### Waltham
Brown, Edgar Henry, Jr. *mathematician, educator*
O'Donnell, Teresa Hohol *software development engineer, antennas engineer*
Paris, Steven Mark *software engineer*

### Wellesley
Hildebrand, Francis Begnaud *mathematics educator*

### Westfield
Buckmore, Alvah Clarence, Jr. *computer scientist, ballistician*

### Westford
Selesky, Donald Bryant *software developer*

### Westport Point
Fanning, William Henry, Jr. *computer scientist*

### Williamstown
Hill, Victor Ernst, IV *mathematics educator, musician*
Morgan, Frank *mathematics educator*

### Worcester
Johnston, Robert Everett *information management administrator*
Malone, Joseph James *mathematics educator, researcher*

## MICHIGAN

### Ann Arbor
Bartle, Robert Gardner *mathematics educator*
Beutler, Frederick Joseph *information scientist*
Brown, Morton B. *biostatistics educator*
Duren, Peter Larkin *mathematician, educator*
Gehring, Frederick William *mathematician, educator*
Hill, Bruce Marvin *statistician, scientist, educator*
Hochster, Melvin *mathematician, educator*
Jones, Phillip Sanford *mathematics educator emeritus*
Kister, James Milton *mathematician, educator*
Lewis, Donald John *mathematics educator*
Schriber, Thomas Jude *computer and information systems educator, researcher*

### Auburn Hills
Neumann, Charles Henry *mathematics educator*

### Bloomfield Hills
Greenwood, Frank *information scientist*
Nuss, Shirley Ann *computer coordinator, educator*

### Dearborn
Brown, James Ward *mathematician, educator, author*

### Detroit
Rajlich, Vaclav Thomas *computer science educator, researcher, consultant*
Schreiber, Bertram Manuel *mathematics educator*

### East Lansing
Hocking, John Gilbert *mathematics educator*
Moran, Daniel Austin *mathematician*
Stapleton, James Hall *statistician, educator*
Weng, John Juyang *computer science educator, researcher*
Wojcik, Anthony Stephen *computer science educator*

### Farmington
Ginsberg, Myron *computer scientist*

### Farmington Hills
Karniotis, Stephen Paul *computer scientist*

### Kalamazoo
Calloway, Jean Mitchener *mathematician, educator*
Clarke, Allen Bruce *mathematics educator, retired academic administrator*

### Marquette
Geiger, David Scott *mathematician, researcher*

### Mount Pleasant
Rubin, Stuart Harvey *computer science educator, researcher*

### Saline
Cornell, Richard Garth *biostatistics educator*

### Sterling Heights
Chang, Peter Hon-You *computer software architect and designer*

### Troy
Ibrahim, Mamdouh H. *computer scientist*
Miller, Hugh Thomas *computer consultant*

### Warren
Bley, Ann *program analyst*

### West Bloomfield
Miller, Nancy Ellen *computer consultant*

### Ypsilanti
Gledhill, Roger Clayton *statistician, engineer, mathematician, educator*
Ullman, Nelly Szabo *statistician, educator*

## MINNESOTA

### Golden Valley
Savitt, Steven Lee *computer scientist*

### Mankato
Hopkins, Layne Victor *computer science educator*

### Minneapolis
Aris, Rutherford *applied mathematician, educator*
Brasket, Curt Justin *systems analyst, chess player*
Du, Ding-Zhu *mathematician, educator*
Friedman, Avner *mathematician, educator*
Infante, Ettore Ferrari *mathematician, educator, university administrator*
Loud, Warren Simms *mathematician*
Markus, Lawrence *retired mathematics educator*
Miller, Willard, Jr. *mathematician, educator*
Nitsche, Johannes Carl Christian *mathematics educator*
Pedoe, Daniel *mathematician, writer, artist*
Pour-El, Marian Boykan *mathematician, educator*
Rosen, Judah Ben *computer scientist*
Serrin, James Burton *mathematics educator*
Slagle, James Robert *computer science educator*
Smith, Michael Lawrence *computer company executive, consultant*
Warner, William Hamer *applied mathematician*

### Moorhead
Heuer, Gerald Arthur *mathematician, educator*

### New Brighton
Shier, Gloria Bulan *mathematics educator*

### Northfield
Appleyard, David Frank *mathematics and computer science educator*
Schuster, Seymour *mathematician, educator*
Steen, Lynn Arthur *mathematician, educator*

### Rochester
Van Norman, Willis Roger *computer systems researcher*

### Saint Paul
Bingham, Christopher *statistics educator*
Christiano, Mary Helen *systems analyst*
Martin, Frank Burke *statistics consultant*

## MISSISSIPPI

### Hattiesburg
Miller, James Edward *computer scientist, educator*

### Jackson
Galloway, Patricia Kay *systems analyst, ethnohistorian*

## MISSOURI

### Columbia
Basu, Asit Prakas *statistician*
Beem, John Kelly *mathematician, educator*
Schrader, Keith William *mathematician*
Williams, Frederick *statistics educator*
Zemmer, Joseph Lawrence, Jr. *mathematics educator*

### Kansas City
Flora, Jairus Dale, Jr. *statistician*

### Lees Summit
Kahwaji, George Antoine *computer and mathematics educator*

### Nevada
Hornback, Joseph Hope *mathematics educator*

### Rolla
Grimm, Louis John *mathematician, educator*
Ingram, William Thomas, III *mathematics educator*
Zobrist, George Winston *computer scientist, educator*

### Saint Louis
Baernstein, Albert, II *mathematician*
Boothby, William Munger *mathematics educator*
Haskins, James Leslie *mathematics educator*
Ihde, Mary Katherine *mathematics educator*
Jenkins, James Allister *mathematician, educator*
Nussbaum, A(dolf) Edward *mathematician, educator*
Pollack, Seymour Victor *computer science educator*
Raeuchle, John Steven *computer analyst*
Ungacta, Malissa Sumagaysay *software engineer*
Wilson, Edward Nathan *mathematician, educator*

### Salem
Pace, Karen Yvonne *mathematics and computer science educator*

### Springfield
Robertson, Ruth Ann *systems analyst, engineer*

## MONTANA

### Big Timber
Yuzeitis, James Richard *information specialist*

## NEBRASKA

### Lincoln
Wiegand, Sylvia Margaret *mathematician, educator*

### Omaha
Chen, Zhengxin *computer scientist*
Gessaman, Margaret Palmer *mathematics educator, college dean*

## NEVADA

### Carson City
Yoder, Marianne Eloise *software developer, consultant*

### Incline Village
Diederich, J(ohn) William *internet publisher*

### Las Vegas
Bahorski, Judy Ann Wong *computer specialist, learning strategist*
Miel, George Joseph *computer scientist, mathematician, system engineer*
Snyder, John Henry *computer science educator, consultant*

## NEW HAMPSHIRE

### Durham
Appel, Kenneth I. *mathematician, educator*

### Hanover
Baumgartner, James Earl *mathematics educator*
Bogart, Kenneth Paul *mathematics educator, consultant*
Crowell, Richard Henry *mathematician, educator*
Kurtz, Thomas Eugene *mathematics educator*
Lamperti, John Williams *mathematician, educator*
Slesnick, William Ellis *mathematician, educator*
Snell, James Laurie *mathematician, educator*

### Londonderry
Nelson, Lloyd Steadman *statistics consultant*

### Nashua
Smith, Thomas Raymond, III *software engineer*

### New Hampton
Lockwood, Joanne Smith *mathematician educator*

## NEW JERSEY

### Basking Ridge
Bodden, M. David *computer professional*

### Blackwood
Sperduto, Leonard Anthony *mathematics eductor*

### Clark
Burtnick, Ronald *sales executive*

### East Hanover
Reiley, T. Phillip *systems analyst, consultant*

### Englewood
Lapidus, Arnold *mathematician*

### Flemington
Bieri, Barbara Normile *systems analyst, consultant*

### Florham Park
Sloane, Neil James Alexander *mathematician, researcher*

### Fort Monmouth
Leciston, David John *computer scientist*

### Glassboro
Stone, Don Charles *computer science educator*

### Hackensack
Nemets, Boris Lvovich *programmer*

### Holmdel
Orost, Joseph Martin *internet applications architect*

### Jersey City
Makar, Boshra Halim *mathematics educator*
Poiani, Eileen Louise *mathematics educator, college administrator, higher education planner*

### Lakewood
Houle, Joseph E. *mathematics educator*
Sloyan, Sister Stephanie *mathematics educator*

### Liberty Corner
Bergeron, Robert Francis, Jr. (Terry Bergeron) *software engineer*

### Mahwah
Korb, Miriam Meyers *computer analyst*

### Mount Laurel
Stallings, Viola Patricia Elizabeth *systems engineer, educational systems specialist*

### Neshanic Station
Muckenhoupt, Benjamin *retired mathematics educator*

### New Brunswick
Amarel, Saul *computer scientist, educator*
Kulikowski, Casimir Alexander *computer science educator*
Scanlon, Jane Cronin *mathematics educator*
Strawderman, William E. *statistics educator*

### New Providence
Fishburn, Peter Clingerman *research mathematician, economist*
Garavaglia, Susan Berger *decision systems designer*
Graham, Ronald Lewis *mathematician*
Wyner, Aaron Daniel *mathematician*

### Parsippany
Wernick, Edward Raymond *company executive, computer consultant*

### Princeton
Aizenman, Michael *mathematics and physics educator, researcher*
Borel, Armand *mathematics educator*
Deligné, Pierre R. *mathematician*
Gear, Charles William *computer scientist*
Griffiths, Phillip A. *mathematician, academic administrator*
Gunning, Robert Clifford *mathematician, educator*
Hunter, John Stuart *statistician, consultant*
Kohn, Joseph John *mathematician, educator*
Langlands, Robert Phelan *mathematician*
Lehmann, Erich Leo *statistics educator*
Levin, Simon Asher *mathematician, ecologist, educator*
MacPherson, Robert Duncan *mathematician, educator*
Nash, John Forbes, Jr. *research mathematician*
Singer, Burton Herbert *statistics educator*
†Wiles, Andrew J. *mathematician, educator*
Zierler, Neal *retired mathematician*

### Ridgefield Park
Jurasek, John Paul *mathematics educator, counselor*
Litwinowicz, Anthony *information specialist, researcher*

### South Orange
Babu, Addagatla John Gabrial *decision sciences educator*

### Summit
Slepian, David *mathematician, communications engineer*

### Teaneck
Zwass, Vladimir *computer scientist, educator*

### Trenton
Shindledecker, J. Gregory *programmer, analyst*

### Watchung
Schaefer, Jacob Wernli *military systems consultant*

### West Caldwell
Vachher, Sheila Ann *information systems analyst*

### Willingboro
Ingerman, Peter Zilahy *infosystems consultant*

## NEW MEXICO

**Albuquerque**
Bell, Stoughton *computer scientist, mathematician, educator*
Ehrhorn, Thomas Frederick *software quality assurance engineer*
Sobolewski, John Stephen *computer information scientist, consultant*

**Belen**
Gutjahr, Allan Leo *mathematics educator, researcher*

**Farmington**
Hagan, Richard Francies *computer system educator*

**Las Cruces**
Kilmer, Neal Harold *software engineer*
Reinfelds, Juris *computer science educator*
Southward, Glen Morris *statistician, educator*

**Los Alamos**
Tingley, Walter Watson *computer systems manager*

**Santa Fe**
†Allen, Ethan Edward *internet specialist, webmaster*
Price, Thomas Munro *computer consultant*

## NEW YORK

**Albany**
Murray, Neil Vincent *computer science educator*
Rosenkrantz, Daniel J. *computer science educator*

**Amherst**
Brown, Stephen Ira *mathematics educator*
Eberlein, Patricia James *mathematician, computer scientist, educator*

**Batavia**
Rigerman, Ruth Underhill *mathematics educator*

**Binghamton**
Hilton, Peter John *mathematician, educator*
Klir, George Jiri *systems science educator*

**Bronx**
Koranyi, Adam *mathematics educator*
Rose, Israel Harold *mathematics educator*
Seltzer, William *statistician, social researcher, former international organization director*
Tong, Hing *mathematician, educator*

**Brooklyn**
Bachman, George *mathematics educator*
Hochstadt, Harry *mathematician, educator*
Pennisten, John William *computer scientist, linguist, actuary*
Pustilnik, Seymour W. *mathematics educator, education educator*
Weill, Georges Gustave *mathematics educator*

**Buffalo**
Berner, Robert Frank *statistics educator*
Bross, Irwin Dudley Jackson *biostatistician*
Coburn, Lewis Alan *mathematics educator*
Goodberry, Diane Jean (Oberkircher) *mathematics educator, tax accountant*
Hauptman, Herbert Aaron *mathematician, educator, researcher*
Ho, Alex Wing-keung *statistician*
Menasco, William Wyatt *mathematics educator*
Piech, Margaret Ann *mathematics educator*
Priore, Roger L. *biostatistics educator, consultant*
Seitz, Mary Lee *mathematics educator*
Selman, Alan Louis *computer science educator*
Shapiro, Stuart Charles *computer scientist, educator*
Wiesenberg, Russel John *statistician*

**Delmar**
Houghton, Raymond Carl, Jr. *computer science educator*

**Dix Hills**
Blumstein, Reneé J. *research and statistical consultant*

**Fairport**
Nastasi, Kathleen Patricia *systems analyst*

**Flushing**
Chako, Nicholas *mathematician, physicist, educator*
Mendelson, Elliott *mathematician, educator*

**Garden City**
Zirkel, Gene *computer science and mathematics educator*

**Geneseo**
Small, William Andrew *mathematics educator*

**Hamilton**
Pownall, Malcolm Wilmor *mathematics educator*
Tucker, Thomas William *mathematics professor*

**Hawthorne**
Green, Paul Eliot, Jr. *communications scientist*
Karnaugh, Maurice *computer scientist, educator*

**Hempstead**
Lally, Laura Holloway *computer information systems educator*

**Hicksville**
Yen, Henry Chin-Yuan *computer systems programmer, engineer, consulting company executive*

**Ithaca**
Billera, Louis J(oseph) *mathematics educator*
Conway, Richard Walter *computer scientist, educator*
Earle, Clifford John, Jr. *mathematician*
Nerode, Anil *mathematician, educator*
Payne, Lawrence Edward *mathematics educator*
Shore, Richard Arnold *mathematics educator*

**Trotter**, Leslie Earl *operations research educator, consultant*

**Morrisville**
Rouse, Robert Moorefield *mathematician, educator*

**New Paltz**
Fleisher, Harold *computer scientist*
Richbart, Carolyn Mae *mathematics educator*

**New York**
Apter, Arthur William *mathematician*
Bass, Hyman *mathematician, educator*
Bauer, Frances Brand *research mathematician*
Berman, Simeon Moses *mathematician, educator*
Bloomfield, Peter *statistics educator*
Chichilnisky, Graciela *mathematician, economist, educator, consultant*
Derman, Cyrus *mathematical statistician*
Edwards, Harold Mortimer *mathematics educator*
Frankel, Martin Richard *statistician, educator, consultant*
Garabedian, Paul Roesel *mathematics educator*
Gilmore, Jennifer A. *computer systems analyst*
Gomory, Ralph Edward *mathematician, manufacturing company executive, foundation executive*
Gross, Jonathan Light *computer scientist, mathematician, educator*
Hilton, Alice Mary *cybernetics and computing systems consultant, author, mathematician, art historian*
Kavalerchik, Boris Yakovlevich *computer systems developer, researcher*
Kurnow, Ernest *statistician, educator*
Lax, Peter David *mathematics educator*
Lucas, Henry Cameron, Jr. *information systems educator, writer, consultant*
Majda, Andrew J. *mathematician, educator*
Moise, Edwin Evariste *mathematician, educator*
Morawetz, Cathleen Synge *mathematics educator*
Moyne, John Abel *computer scientist, linguist, educator*
Nirenberg, Louis *mathematician, educator*
Padberg, Manfred Wilhelm *mathematics educator*
Posamentier, Alfred Steven *mathematics educator, university administrator*
Rajkumar, Ajay *computer scientist, consultant*
Sellers, Peter Hoadley *mathematician*
Sohmer, Bernard *mathematics educator, administrator*
Traub, J(oseph) F(rederick) *computer scientist, educator*
Weitzner, Harold *mathematics educator*
Widlund, Olof Bertil *computer science educator*
Wyn-Jones, Alun (William Wyn-Jones) *software developer, mathematician*

**Northport**
Gelfand, Andrew *software developer, consultant*

**Orangeburg**
Siegel, Carole Ethel *mathematician*

**Pearl River**
Galante, Joseph Anthony, Jr. *computer programmer*

**Pittsford**
Hollingsworth, Jack Waring *mathematics and computer science educator*

**Queens Village**
Le, Dan Hoang *data administrator, consultant*

**Rochester**
Alling, Norman Larrabee *mathematics educator*
Segal, Sanford Leonard *mathematics educator*
Simon, William *biomathematician, educator*

**Rome**
Allen, Paul Christopher *computer specialist*

**Sleepy Hollow**
Maun, Mary Ellen *computer consultant*

**Staten Island**
Shullich, Robert Harlan *systems analyst*

**Stony Brook**
Anderson, Michael Thomas *mathematics researcher, educator*
Feinberg, Eugene Alexander *mathematics educator*
Glimm, James Gilbert *mathematician*
Laspina, Peter Joseph *computer resource educator*
Lawson, H(erbert) Blaine, Jr. *mathematician, educator*
Tucker, Alan Curtiss *mathematics educator*

**Syracuse**
Berra, P. Bruce *computer educator*
Church, Philip Throop *mathematician, educator*
Covillion, Jane Tanner *mathematics educator*
Dudewicz, Edward John *statistician*
Graver, Jack Edward *mathematics educator*
Hansen, Per Brinch *computer scientist*
Pardee, Otway O'Meara *computer science educator*
Peters, Christopher Allen *computer consultant*
Waterman, Daniel *mathematician, educator*

**Troy**
Berg, Daniel *science and technology educator*
Drew, Donald Allen *mathematical sciences educator*
McNaughton, Robert Forbes, Jr. *computer science educator*

**Wallkill**
Bittner, Ronald Joseph *computer systems analyst, magician*

**West Hempstead**
Guggenheimer, Heinrich Walter *mathematician, educator*

**West Point**
Barr, Donald Roy *statistics and operations research educator, statistician*
Barrett, Lida Kittrell *mathematics educator*

**Westbury**
Sandler, Gerald Howard *computer science educator, company executive*

**White Plains**
Cheng, Alexander Lihdar *computer scientist, researcher*
Machover, Carl *computer graphics consultant*
Merritt, Susan Mary *computer science educator, university dean*

**Williamsville**
Jensen, David Lynn *mathematician, infosystems specialist*

**Yonkers**
Goon, Gilbert *software consultant*

**Yorktown Heights**
Allen, Frances Elizabeth *computer scientist*
d'Heurle, François Max *research scientist, engineering educator*
Hoffman, Alan Jerome *mathematician, educator*
Mandelbrot, Benoit B. *mathematician, scientist, educator*
Rigoutsos, Isidore *computer scientist*
Winograd, Shmuel *mathematician*

## NORTH CAROLINA

**Apex**
Rawlings, John Oren *statistician, researcher*

**Cape Carteret**
Mullikin, Thomas Wilson *mathematics educator*

**Cary**
†Goodnight, James *software company executive*

**Chapel Hill**
Coulter, Elizabeth Jackson *biostatistician, educator*
Stasheff, James Dillon *mathematics educator*
Wahl, Jonathan Michael *mathematics educator*
Wogen, Warren Ronald *mathematics educator*

**Charlotte**
Johnson, Phillip Eugene *mathematics educator*
Moland, Kathryn Johnetta *computer scientist, software engineer*
Nelson, Barbara Secrest *educational developer*

**Cullowhee**
Willis, Ralph Houston *mathematics educator*

**Davidson**
Klein, Benjamin Garrett *mathematics educator*

**Durham**
Allard, William Kenneth *mathematician*
Keepler, Manuel *mathematics educator, researcher*
Loveland, Donald William *computer science educator*
Rose, Donald James *computer science educator*
Vitter, Jeffrey Scott *computer science educator, consultant*
Warner, Seth L. *mathematician, educator*
Woodbury, Max Atkin *polymath, educator*

**Greensboro**
Casterlow, Gilbert, Jr. *mathematics educator*
Posey, Eldon Eugene *mathematician, educator*

**Raleigh**
Chou, Wushow *computer scientist, educator*
Chukwu, Ethelbert Nwakuche *mathematics educator*
Kiser, Anita Hope *project team leader, technical writer*
McPherson, Samuel Dace, III *computer scientist, instructor, consultant*
Nelson, Larry A. *statistics educator, consultant*
Peterson, Elmor Lee *mathematical scientist, educator*
Wesler, Oscar *mathematician, educator*
Wetsch, John Robert *information systems specialist*

**Wilson**
Welsh, James John *computer consultant*

**Winston Salem**
Baxter, Lawrence Gerald *strategic analyst, law educator, consultant*
Espeland, Mark Andrew *biostatistics educator*
Kerr, Sandria Neidus *mathematics and computer science educator*
Lu, Dan *systems analyst, mathematician, consultant*

## OHIO

**Akron**
Hollis, William Frederick *information scientist*
Powell, Robert Eugene *computer operator*

**Ashtabula**
Taylor, Norman Floyd *computer educator, administrator, band director*

**Athens**
Wen, Shih-Liang *mathematics educator*

**Canton**
Barb, Cynthia Marie *mathematics educator*

**Cincinnati**
Flick, Thomas Michael *mathematics educator, educational administrator*
Rabe, Laura Mae *mathematician, educator*
Semon, Warren Lloyd *retired computer sciences educator*
Wilsey, Philip Arthur *computer science educator*

**Cleveland**
Clark, Robert Arthur *mathematician, educator*
de Acosta, Alejandro Daniel *mathematician, educator*
Goffman, William *mathematician, educator*
Szarek, Stanislaw Jerzy *mathematics educator*
Waren, Allan David *computer information scientist, educator*
Woyczynski, Wojbor Andrzej *mathematician, educator*

**Columbia Station**
Pingatore, Sam Robert *systems analyst, consultant, business executive*

**Columbus**
Chandrasekaran, Balakrishnan *computer and information science educator*
Dowling, Thomas Allan *mathematics educator*
Kindig, Fred Eugene *statistics educator, arbitrator*
Santner, Thomas *statistician, educator*
Zweben, Stuart Harvey *information scientist, educator*

**Dayton**
Bedell, Kenneth Berkley *computer specialist, educator*
Garcia, Oscar Nicolas *computer science educator*
Khalimsky, Efim *mathematics and computer science educator*
Stander, Joseph William *mathematics educator, former university official*

**Defiance**
Mirchandaney, Arjan Sobhraj *mathematics educator*

**Delaware**
Mendenhall, Robert Vernon *mathematics educator*

**Dublin**
Roeder, Rebecca Emily *software engineer*

**Kent**
Cummins, Kenneth Burdette *retired science and mathematics educator*
Stackelberg, Olaf Patrick Von *mathematician*
Varga, Richard Steven *mathematics educator*

**Mansfield**
Gregory, Thomas Bradford *mathematics educator*

**Milford**
Zimov, Bruce Steven *software engineer*

**Newark**
Perera, Vicumpriya Sriyantha *mathematics educator*

**Powell**
Miller, Charles *business management research and measurements consultant*

**Upper Sandusky**
Baker, Harrison Scott *computer consultant*

**West Chester**
Bahrani, Neda Jean *programmer/analyst, consultant*

**Westlake**
Whitehouse, John Harlan, Jr. *systems software consultant, diagnostician*

**Worthington**
Rowe, Lisa Dawn *computer programmer/analyst, computer consultant*

## OKLAHOMA

**Edmond**
Loman, Mary LaVerne *retired mathematics educator*

**Norman**
Lakshmivarahan, Sivaramakrishnan *computer science educator*
MacFarland, Miriam Katherine (Mimi) *computer science consultant, writer*

**Oklahoma City**
Tang, Irving Che-hong *mathematician, educator*

**Stillwater**
Jaco, William H. *mathematics educator*
Lu, Huizhu *computer scientist, educator*
Provine, Lorraine *mathematics educator*

## OREGON

**Albany**
Yu, Kitson Szewai *computer science educator*

**Bend**
Mayer, Richard Dean *mathematics educator*

**Corvallis**
Parks, Harold Raymond *mathematician, educator*
Petersen, Bent Edvard *mathematician, educator*
Wechsler, Susan Linda *software design engineer*

**Eugene**
Andrews, Fred Charles *mathematics educator*

**Florence**
Gray, Augustine Heard, Jr. *computer consultant*

**Monmouth**
Forcier, Richard Charles *information technology educator, computer applications consultant*

**Portland**
Ahuja, Jagdish Chand *mathematics educator*

**Tualatin**
Brown, Robert Wallace *mathematics educator*

## PENNSYLVANIA

**Abington**
Ayoub, Ayoub Barsoum *mathematician, educator*

**Allentown**
Russell, Alan Harold *computer specialist, educator*

**Ardmore**
Ryan, Barbara Diane *management information systems director*

**Aston**
Horvath, David B. *computer consultant, writer, educator*

**Bala Cynwyd**
Ackoff, Russell Lincoln *systems sciences educator*

**Berwyn**
Swank, Annette Marie *software designer*

**Bethlehem**
Ghosh, Bhaskar Kumar *statistics educator, researcher*
McAulay, Alastair D. *electrical and computer engineer, educator*
Rivlin, Ronald Samuel *mathematics educator emeritus*

**Blue Bell**
Young, Charles Randall *software professional*

**Bristol**
Bush, Harold Ehrig *computer consultant*

**Carlisle**
Winkler, Ira Samuel *information security consultant, educator, author*

**Chester**
Frank, Amalie Julianna *computer science, electrical engineering and mathematics educator, consultant*

**Coatesville**
Burton, Mary Louise Himes *computer specialist*

**Hershey**
King, Carolyn Marie *mathematics educator*

**Levittown**
Phillips, Edward John *computer scientist, writer*

**Meadville**
Cable, Charles Allen *mathematician*

**Media**
King, Kathleen Palombo *computer technology and adult education educator, consultant*

**Mercer**
Brady, Wray Grayson *mathematician, educator*

**Norristown**
Lafredo, Stephen Christopher *consultant*

**Philadelphia**
Altshuler, David Thomas *computer scientist*
Badler, Norman Ira *computer and information science educator*
Banerji, Ranan Bihari *mathematics and computer science educator*
Brown, Ronald Rea *software engineer, artist*
Collons, Rodger Duane *decision sciences educator*
Cowles, Roger E. *computer consultant*
de Cani, John Stapley *statistician, educator*
Freyd, Peter John *mathematician, computer scientist, educator*
Goldstine, Herman Heine *mathematician, association executive*
Harbater, David *mathematician*
Hildebrand, David Kent *statistics educator*
Iglewicz, Boris *statistician, educator*
Joshi, Aravind Krishna *computer educator, information scientist*
Kadison, Richard Vincent *mathematician, educator*
Knopp, Marvin Isadore *mathematics educator*
Mode, Charles J. *mathematician, educator*
Morrison, Donald Franklin *statistician, educator*
Porter, Gerald Joseph *mathematician, educator*
Prywes, Noah Shmarya *computer scientist, educator*
Scandura, Joseph Michael *mathematics educator, researcher, software engineer*
Shatz, Stephen Sidney *mathematician, educator*
Warner, Frank Wilson, III *mathematics educator*
Williams, Richard Charles *computer programmer, consultant*

**Pittsburgh**
Balas, Egon *applied mathematician, educator*
Berliner, Hans Jack *computer scientist*
Bryant, Randal Everitt *computer science educator, consultant*
Deskins, Wilbur Eugene *mathematician, educator*
Fienberg, Stephen Elliott *statistician*
Gurtin, Morton Edward *mathematics educator*
Hall, Charles Allan *numerical analyst, educator*
Heath, David Clay *mathematics educator, consultant*
Kadane, Joseph B. *statistics educator*
Lehoczky, John Paul *statistics educator*
Moore, Richard Allan *mathematics educator*
Rheinboldt, Werner Carl *mathematics educator, researcher*
Shaw, Mary M. *computer science educator*
Thompson, Gerald Luther *operations research and applied mathematics educator*

**Plymouth Meeting**
Schott, Jeffrey Brian *software engineer*

**Reading**
Rochowicz, John Anthony, Jr. *mathematician, mathematics and physics educator*

**Scranton**
Powell, Robert Ellis *mathematics educator, college dean*

**State College**
Arnold, Douglas Norman *mathematics educator*

**Swarthmore**
Kelemen, Charles F. *computer science educator*

**University Park**
Andrews, George Eyre *mathematics educator*
Antle, Charles Edward *statistics educator*
Lindsay, Bruce George *statistics educator*
Rao, Calyampudi Radhakrishna *statistician, educator*
Rosenberger, James Landis *statistician, educator, consultant*

**Vandergrift**
Kulick, Richard John *computer scientist, researcher*

**Villanova**
Beck, Robert Edward *computer scientist, educator*

**Wayne**
Clelland, Richard Cook *statistics educator, university administrator*

## RHODE ISLAND

**Kingston**
Driver, Rodney David *mathematics educator, former state legislator*
Roxin, Emilio Oscar *mathematics educator*

**Providence**
Banchoff, Thomas Francis *mathematics educator*
Charniak, Eugene *computer scientist, educator*
Dafermos, Constantine Michael *applied mathematics educator*
Davis, Philip J. *mathematician*
Fleming, Wendell Helms *mathematician, educator*
Freiberger, Walter Frederick *mathematics educator, actuarial science consultant, educator*
Gottschalk, Walter Helbig *mathematician, educator*
Grenander, Ulf *mathematics educator*
Kushner, Harold Joseph *mathematics educator*
Mumford, David Bryant *mathematics educator*
Savage, John Edmund *computer science educator, researcher*
Shu, Chi-Wang *mathematics educator, researcher*
Silverman, Joseph Hillel *mathematics educator*

## SOUTH CAROLINA

**Clemson**
Kenelly, John Willis, Jr. *mathematician, educator*

**Columbia**
Eastman, Caroline Merriam *computer science educator*
Watt, (Arthur) Dwight, Jr. *computer programming and microcomputer specialist*

**Florence**
Strong, Roger Lee *mathematics educator*

**Orangeburg**
Clark, Paul Buddy *management information systems educator, consultant*
Staley, Frank Marcellus, Jr. *mathematics educator*

**Spartanburg**
Hilton, Theodore Craig *computer scientist, computer executive*
Wilde, Edwin Frederick *mathematics educator*

## SOUTH DAKOTA

**Sioux Falls**
Crawford, Thomas Williams, Jr. *information scientist, soil scientist*

## TENNESSEE

**Brownsville**
Kalin, Robert *retired mathematics educator*

**Chattanooga**
Johnson, Joseph Erle *mathematician*

**Dickson**
Peterson, Bonnie Lu *mathematics educator*

**Franklin**
Huey, George Irving, Jr. *computer senior systems consultant*

**Gallatin**
Evans, Robert Byron *software engineer, educator*

**Knoxville**
Borden, Eugene Owen *software engineer*
Rosinski, Jan *mathematics educator*
Sherman, Gordon Rae *computer science educator*
Ward, Robert Cleveland *research mathematician, science administrator*

**Maryville**
Inscho, Barbara Pickel *mathematics educator*

**Memphis**
Franklin, Stanley Phillip *computer scientist, cognitive scientist, mathematician, educator*
Goldstein, Jerome Arthur *mathematics educator*

**Nashville**
Blair, Joyce Allsmiller *computer science educator*
Crooke, Philip Schuyler *mathematics educator*
Dupont, William Dudley *biostatistician, educator*
Fischer, Patrick Carl *computer scientist, educator*
Jonsson, Bjarni *mathematician, educator*
Schumaker, Larry Lee *mathematics educator*

**Oak Ridge**
Gardiner, Donald Andrew *statistician, consultant*
Kliewer, Kenneth Lee *computational scientist, research administrator*
Penniman, W. David *information scientist, educator, consultant*
Raridon, Richard Jay *computer specialist*

**Sewanee**
Puckette, Stephen Elliott *mathematics educator, mathematician*

## TEXAS

**Allen**
Wilhelm, Walter Tinkham *information systems consultant*

**Arlington**
Greenspan, Donald *mathematician, educator*
Han, Chien-Pai *statistics educator*
Kendall, Jillian D. *information systems specialist, program developer, educator, consultant*

**Austin**
Bona, Jerry Lloyd *mathematician, educator*
Clark, Charles T(aliferro) *retired business statistics educator*
Dijkstra, Edsger Wybe *computer science educator, mathematician*
Garner, Harvey Louis *computer scientist, consultant, electrical engineering educator*
Gillman, Leonard *mathematician, educator*
Huang, Yee-Wei *strategic analyst, chemical engineering educator*
Jones, William Richard *open systems product support representative*
Kozmetsky, George *computer science educator*
Lam, Simon Shin-Sing *computer science educator*
Misra, Jayadev *computer science educator*
Rentz, Tamara Holmes *software consultant*
Sager, Thomas William *statistics research administrator*
Sturdevant, Wayne Alan *computer-based training development administrator*
Taber, Patrick E. *computer programmer*
Turney, James Edward *computer scientist*
Uhlenbeck, Karen Keskulla *mathematician, educator*
Warlick, Charles Henry *mathematician/computer science educator*
Young, William David *computer scientist*

**Belton**
Bumpus, Floyd David, Jr. *microcomputer analyst*

**College Station**
Blakley, George Robert, Jr. *mathematician, computer scientist*
Chui, Charles K. *mathematics educator*
Douglas, Ronald George *mathematician*
Ewing, Richard Edward *mathematics, chemical and petroleum engineering educator*
Parzen, Emanuel *statistical scientist*
Sanchez, David Alan *mathematics educator*

**Dallas**
Aranas, Noel Bautista *systems analyst, consultant*
Browne, Richard Harold *statistician, consultant*
Burlingame, David Hartley *software development manager*
Eyerman, David John *software engineer*
Kruse, Ann Gray *computer programer*
Matelan, Mathew Nicholas *software engineer*

**De Soto**
Ball, Millicent Joan (Penny Ball) *multimedia developer*

**El Paso**
Gianelli, Victor F. *mathematics and physics educator*
Quevedo, Hector Adolf *operations research analyst, environmental scientist*

**Fort Worth**
Doran, Robert Stuart *mathematician, educator*
Sullenberger, Ara Broocks *mathematics educator*

**Grapevine**
Gibbons, Michael Lawrence *software engineer*

**Houston**
Auchmuty, Giles *applied mathematics educator*
Fenn, Sandra Ann *programmer, analyst*
Freeman, Marjorie Schaefer *mathematics educator*
Gardner, Everette Shaw, Jr. *information sciences educator*
Glowinski, Roland *mathematics educator*
Harvey, F. Reese *mathematics educator*
Hempel, John P. *mathematics educator*
Hoang, Hung Manh *information systems analyst, consultant*
Kennedy, Ken *computer science educator*
Parker, Norman Neil, Jr. *software systems analyst, mathematics educator*
Scott, David Warren *statistics educator*
Wang, Chao-Cheng *mathematician, engineer*
Ward, Jo Alice *computer consultant, educator*
Wells, Raymond O., Jr. *mathematics educator, researcher*

**Irving**
Anastasi, Richard Joseph *computer software consultant*
Anderson, Michael Curtis *computer industry analyst*

**Kingsville**
Cecil, David Rolf *mathematician, educator*
Morey, Philip Stockton, Jr. *mathematics educator*

**Lewisville**
Ferguson, R Neil *computer systems consultant*

**Lubbock**
Bobylev, Alexandre Vasiliy *mathematician, researcher*
Conover, William Jay *statistics educator*
Hennessey, Audrey Kathleen *computer researcher, educator*
Li, Hua Harry *computer scientist*

**Plano**
Conrad, Philip Jefferson *software development engineer*
Hinton, Norman Wayne *information services executive*

**Richardson**
Pervin, William Joseph *computer science educator*

**San Antonio**
Ahmad, Shair *mathematics educator*
Blaylock, Neil Wingfield, Jr. *applied statistics educator*
Estep, Myrna Lynne *systems analyst, philosophy educator*
Grubb, Robert Lynn *computer system designer*
Phinazee, Henry Charles *systems analyst, educator*
Tucker, Roy Nelson *mathematics educator, minister*

**Stockdale**
Bowden, Dorothy Jackson *mathematics, art educator, artist*

**Temple**
Rajab, Mohammad Hasan *biostatistician, educator*

**Waco**
Odell, Patrick Lowry *mathematics educator*
Rolf, Howard Leroy *mathematician, educator*

## UTAH

**Draper**
Averett, Robert Lee *educator, information system professional*

**Logan**
Cheng, Heng-Da *computer scientist*

**Orem**
Moore, Hal G. *mathematician, educator*

**Provo**
Hansen, James Vernon *computer science, information systems educator*
Lang, William Edward *mathematics educator*

**Salt Lake City**
Horn, Susan Dadakis *statistics educator*

## VERMONT

**Burlington**
Crouse, Roger Leslie *information analyst, quality consultant, facilitator*
Haugh, Larry Douglas *statistics professor*

**Norwich**
Snapper, Ernst *mathematics educator*

**West Danville**
Somers, Melvin Claude *retired mathematics educator and dean*

## VIRGINIA

**Alexandria**
Olson, Warren Kinley *operations research analyst, engineer, physicist*
Shrier, Stefan *mathematician, educator*

**Annandale**
Santi, Ellyn E. (Ellyn E. Wagner) *mathematics educator*

**Arlington**
Ciment, Melvyn *mathematician*
Golladay, Mary Jean *statistician*
Green, Judy *mathematics educator*
Hartmanis, Juris *computer scientist, educator*
Long, Madeleine J. *mathematics and science educator*
Murray, Jeanne Morris *computer scientist, educator, consultant*
Nodeen, Janey Price *government official*
Schafer, Alice Turner *retired mathematics educator*
Voigt, Robert Gary *numerical analyst*

**Blacksburg**
Fox, Edward Alan *computer science educator*
Good, Irving John *statistics educator, mathematician, philosopher of science*
Krutchkoff, Richard Gerald *statistics educator, researcher*
Olin, Robert Floyd *mathematics educator and reseacher*

**Charlottesville**
Catlin, Avery *engineering and computer science educator, writer*
Horgan, Cornelius Oliver *applied mathematics and applied mechanics educator*
Martin, Nathaniel Frizzel Grafton *mathematician, educator*
Rosenblum, Marvin *mathematics educator*
Thomas, Lawrence Eldon *mathematics educator*

**Clifton**
Hoffman, Karla Leigh *mathematician*

**Fairfax**
Croog, Roslyn Deborah *computer systems analyst*
Denning, Peter James *computer scientist, engineer*
Hungate, Joseph Irvin, III *computer scientist*
Sage, Andrew Patrick, Jr. *systems information and software engineering educator*
Santore, Carrie-Beth *computer management professional*
Schneck, Paul Bennett *computer scientist*
Tucker, Dewey Duane *systems analyst*

**Falls Church**
Okay, John Louis *telecommunications executive*

**Fort Lee**
Johnson, Harry Watkins *defense analyst*

**Fredericksburg**
Hajek, Otomar *mathematics educator*

**Hampton**
Keyes, David Elliot *scientific computing educator, researcher*

**Heathsville**
Stubbs, Susan Conklin *statistician*

**Herndon**
Gullace, Marlene Frances *information engineer, systems analyst, consultant*
Hermansen, John Christian *computational linguist*

**Lynchburg**
Moorman, Steve Thomas *systems analyst*

**Manassas**
Smith, Todd Lawrence *computer scientist*

**Mc Lean**
Gangemi, Gaetano Tommaso, Sr. *computer company executive*

**Newport News**
Summerville, Richard M. *mathematician, retired academic administrator*

**Norfolk**
Maly, Kurt John *computer science educator*
Marchello, Joseph Maurice *mathematics and physical science educator*

**Reston**
Arnberg, Robert Lewis *mathematician*
Basinger, William Daniel *computer programmer*
Fredette, Richard Chester *computer specialist*

**Richlands**
Witten, Thomas Jefferson, Jr. *mathematics educator*

**Richmond**
Charlesworth, Arthur Thomas *mathematics and computer science educator*

**Springfield**
Tomlinson, Ian *software engineer*

**Vienna**
Gardenier, John Stark, II *statistician, management scientist*
Lillard, Mark Hill, III *computer consulting executive, former air force officer*

**Virginia Beach**
Brennan, Patrick Jeremiah *computer system architect*
Cheng, Richard Tien-ren *computer scientist, educator*

**Williamsburg**
Lutzer, David John *mathematics professor*
Rodman, Leiba *mathematics educator*
Zhang, Xiaodong *computer science educator and researcher*

## WASHINGTON

**Bothell**
Jaundalderis, Julia Lee *software engineer*

**Ellensburg**
Comstock, Dale Robert *mathematics educator*

**Everett**
Labayen, Louie Anthony Lopez *information analyst, consultant*

**Federal Way**
Cunningham, John Randolph *systems analyst*

**Lacey**
Wells, Roger Stanley *software engineer*

**Lynnwood**
Vierheller, Todd *software engineering consultant*

**Orcas**
Greever, John *retired mathematics educator*

**Pullman**
Hildebrandt, Darlene Myers *information scientist*
Kallaher, Michael Joseph *mathematics educator*

**Redmond**
Kimmich, Jon Bradford *computer science program executive*
MacKenzie, Peter Sean *instructional designer*

**Richland**
Cochran, James Alan *mathematics educator*

**Seattle**
Breslow, Norman Edward *biostatistics educator, researcher*
Criminale, William Oliver, Jr. *applied mathematics educator*
Hewitt, Edwin *mathematician, educator*
Kevorkian, Jirair *applied mathematics, aeronautics and astronautics educator*
Klee, Victor La Rue *mathematician, educator*
Lee, John Marshall *mathematics educator*
Michael, Ernest Arthur *mathematics educator*
Murray, James Dickson *mathematical biology educator*
Nelson, Walter William *computer programmer, consultant*
Nijenhuis, Albert *mathematician, educator*
Noe, Jerre Donald *computer science educator*
O'Malley, Robert Edmund, Jr. *mathematics educator*
Pyke, Ronald *mathematics educator*
Segal, Jack *mathematics educator*

**Spokane**
Mayer, Herbert Carleton, Jr. *computer consultant*

**Yakima**
Jongeward, George Ronald *retired systems analyst*

## WEST VIRGINIA

**Morgantown**
Butcher, Donald Franklin *statistics educator, computer scientist*
De Vore, Paul Warren *technology educator*

Holtan, Boyd DeVere *mathematics educator*
Vest, Marvin Lewis *mathematical educator*

**Shepherdstown**
Hendricks, Ida Elizabeth *mathematics educator*

## WISCONSIN

**Altoona**
Powell, Christopher Robert *systems engineer/manager, computer scientist*

**Brookfield**
Kraut, Joanne Lenora *computer programmer, analyst*

**Delavan**
Nichols, Greg Mark *systems analyst*

**Dodgeville**
Fry, David Francis *computing educator*

**Madison**
Askey, Richard Allen *mathematician*
Beck, Anatole *mathematician, educator*
de Boor, Carl *mathematician*
Draper, Norman Richard *statistician, educator*
Harvey, John Grover *mathematics educator*
Hickman, James Charles *business and statistics educator, business school dean*
Johnson, Millard Wallace, Jr. *mathematics and engineering educator*
Johnson, Richard Arnold *statistics educator, consultant*
Levin, Jacob Joseph *mathematician, educator*
Moore, Edward Forrest *computer scientist, mathematician, former educator*
Robinson, Stephen Michael *applied mathematician, educator*
Wahba, Grace *statistician, educator*

**Mequon**
Locklair, Gary Hampton *computer science educator*

**Milwaukee**
Krieger, Robert Alan *software engineer*
Lawrence, Willard Earl *mathematics, statistics and computer science educator emeritus*
Simms, John Carson *logic, mathematics and computer science educator*
Solomon, Donald William *mathematician, educator, consultant*

## WYOMING

**Cheyenne**
Southworth, Rod Brand *computer science educator*

## TERRITORIES OF THE UNITED STATES

## PUERTO RICO

**Mayaguez**
Collins, Dennis Glenn *mathematics educator*

**San Juan**
Bangdiwala, Ishver Surchand *statistician, educator*

## CANADA

## ALBERTA

**Edmonton**
Davis, Wayne Alton *computer science educator*

## BRITISH COLUMBIA

**Burnaby**
Borwein, Peter Benjamin *mathematician*

**Vancouver**
Boyd, David William *mathematician, educator*
Clark, Colin Whitcomb *mathematics educator*
Feldman, Joel Shalom *mathematician*
Granirer, Edmond Ernest *mathematician, educator*
Miura, Robert Mitsuru *mathematician, researcher, educator*
Seymour, Brian Richard *mathematician*
Sion, Maurice *mathematics educator*
Swanson, Charles Andrew *mathematics educator*

**Victoria**
Manning, Eric *computer science and engineering educator, university dean, researcher*

## NOVA SCOTIA

**Halifax**
Fillmore, Peter Arthur *mathematics educator*

## ONTARIO

**Hamilton**
Banaschewski, Bernhard *mathematics educator*
Parnas, David Lorge *computer scientist, engineer, educator*

**Kingston**
Campbell, L(ouis) Lorne *mathematics educator*
Coleman, Albert John *mathematics educator*

**London**
Bauer, Michael Anthony *computer scientist, educator*

Borwein, David *mathematics educator*
Ehrman, Joachim Benedict *mathematics educator*

**Ottawa**
Csörgö, Miklós *statistician*
Dlab, Vlastimil *mathematics educator, researcher*
Fellegi, Ivan Peter *statistician*
Macphail, Moray St. John *mathematics educator emeritus*

**Toronto**
Arthur, James Greig *mathematics educator*
Cook, Stephen Arthur *mathematics and computer science educator*
Coxeter, Harold Scott Macdonald *mathematician*
Davis, (Horace) Chandler *mathematics educator*
Dawson, Donald Andrew *mathematics educator, researcher*
Fraser, Donald Alexander Stuart *mathematics educator*
Friedlander, John Benjamin *mathematics educator*
Gotlieb, Calvin Carl *computer scientist, educator*
Greiner, Peter Charles *mathematics educator, researcher*
Halperin, John Stephen *mathematics educator*
Murasugi, Kunio *mathematician, educator*
Rooney, Paul George *mathematics educator*
Tall, Franklin David *mathematics educator*

**Waterloo**
Aczel, Janos Dezso *mathematics educator*
Cowan, Donald Douglas *mathematician, educator, computer scientist*
Gladwell, Graham Maurice Leslie *mathematician, civil engineering educator*
Paldus, Josef *mathematics educator*
Sprott, David Arthur *statistics and psychology educator*
Stewart, Cameron Leigh *mathematics educator*

## QUEBEC

**Montreal**
Dubuc, Serge *mathematics educator*
Maag, Urs Richard *statistics educator*
Moser, William Oscar Jules *mathematics educator*
Saint-Pierre, Jacques *statistics educator, consultant*
Suen, Ching Yee *computer scientist and educator, researcher*

**Quebec**
Theodorescu, Radu Amza Serban *mathematician, educator*

## MEXICO

**Guadalajara**
Levine, Guillermo *computer scientist, educator*

## AUSTRALIA

**Canberra**
Gani, Joseph Mark *statistics educator, administrator, researcher*

## AUSTRIA

**Vienna**
Niederreiter, Harald Guenther *mathematician, researcher*

## BRAZIL

**Sao Jose dos Campos**
Berman, Marcelo Samuel *mathematics and physics educator, cosmology researcher*

## ENGLAND

**Leicester**
Harijan, Ram *computer scientist, technology transfer researcher*

**London**
Ralston, Anthony *computer scientist, mathematician, educator*

## FRANCE

**Angers**
Chauvet, Gilbert André *mathematics educator*

**Avignon**
De Mori, Renato *computer science educator, researcher*

**Paris**
Yuechiming, Roger Yue Yuen Shing *mathematics educator*

## GERMANY

**Darmstadt**
Hofmann, Karl Heinrich *mathematics educator*

**Paderborn**
Belli, Fevzi *computing science educator, consultant*

## GREECE

**Athens**
Panaretos, John *mathematics and statistics educator*

## HONG KONG

**Hong Kong**
Chen, Concordia Chao *mathematician*

**Kowloon**
Hsieh, Din-Yu *applied mathematics educator*

**Sha Tin**
†Xu, Lei *computer scientist, educator*

## ISRAEL

**Ramat Aviv**
Bernstein, Joseph N. *mathematician, researcher, educator*

## ITALY

**Padua**
Rosati, Mario *mathematician, educator*

## JAPAN

**Chiba**
Yamada, Shinichi *mathematician, computer scientist, educator*

**Ikoma**
Kasami, Tadao *information science educator*

**Nagoya**
Kimura, Miyoshi *statistics educator, researcher*

**Nakano**
Eto, Hajime *information scientist, educator*

## SAUDI ARABIA

**Dhahran**
Warne, Ronson Joseph *mathematics educator*

## SWITZERLAND

**Zurich**
Kalman, Rudolf Emil *research mathematician, system scientist*
Lanford, Oscar Erasmus, III *mathematics educator*
Nievergelt, Jurg *computer science educator*

## ADDRESS UNPUBLISHED

Ancheta, Caesar Paul *software developer*
Arden, Bruce Wesley *computer science and electrical engineering educator*
Balsamello, Joseph Vincent *information services manager*
Basch, Reva *information services company executive*
Bogdan, Victor Michael *mathematics educator, scientist*
Borwein, Jonathan Michael *mathematics educator*
Box, George Edward Pelham *statistics educator*
Bradunas, Edward Terence *data processing management and technology management consultant*
Browder, Felix Earl *mathematician, educator*
Butson, Alton Thomas *mathematics educator*
Caudill, Maureen *author and computer consultant*
Choi, Man-Duen *mathematics educator*
Colvin, Burton Houston *mathematician, government official*
Dalton, Robert Edgar *mathematician, computer scientist*
Davenport, William Harold *mathematics educator*
Doubledee, Deanna Gail *software engineer, consultant*
Downey, Deborah Ann *systems specialist*
Edwards, Elwood Gene *mathematician, educator*
Elliott, David LeRoy *mathematician, educator, engineering educator*
Fitting-Gifford, Marjorie Ann *mathematician, educator, consultant*
Fornaess, John Erik *mathematics educator*
Freitag, Harlow *retired computer scientist and corporate executive*
Frieder, Gideon *computer science and engineering educator*
Glassman, Arthur Joseph *software engineer*
Goldberg, Samuel *retired mathematician, foundation officer*
Graham, Kirsten R. *computer science educator*
Grebb, Michael D. *systems analyst*
Greever, Margaret Quarles *retired mathematics educator*
Halberstam, Heini *mathematics educator*
Hamblen, John Wesley *computer scientist, genealogist*
Heinicke, Peter Hart *computer consultant*
Hill, Shirley Ann *mathematics educator*
Horton, Wilfred Henry *mathematics educator*
House, Stephen Eugene *information systems consultant*
Hughes, Richard Gene *computer executive, consultant*
Hunte, Beryl Eleanor *mathematics educator, consultant*
Husain, Taqdir *mathematics educator*
Israel, Robert Allan *statistician*
Jaw, Andrew Chung-Shiang *software analyst*
Jones, Anita Katherine *computer scientist, educator*
Jones, Margaret Louise *supervisory production analyst*
Juister, Barbara Joyce *retired mathematics educator*
Kadota, Takashi Theodore *mathematician, electrical engineer*
Kelley, Mary Elizabeth (LaGrone) *computer specialist*
Kent, Jack Thurston *retired mathematics educator*
Knight, Thomas Jefferson, Jr. *computer consultant, trainer*
Krantz, Steven George *mathematics educator*
Lamm, Harriet A. *mathematics educator*
Lampson, Butler Wright *computer scientist*

Laning, J. Halcombe *retired computer scientist*
Larson, Janice Talley *computer science educator*
Lasry, Jean-Michel *mathematics educator*
Low, Emmet Francis, Jr. *mathematics educator*
Mahoney, Linda Kay *mathematics educator*
Main, Myrna Joan *mathematics educator*
Marchione, Sharyn Lee *computer scientist*
Maxwell, Barbara Sue *systems analyst consultant, educator*
McKinnon, Kathleen Ann *software engineer*
McLaughlin, Robert Bruce *software designer*
Merilan, Jean Elizabeth *statistics educator*
Mints, Grigori Efroim *specialist in mathematical logic*
Nicolau, Alexandru *educator*
Norman, E. Gladys *business computer educator, consultant*
Padberg, Harriet Ann *mathematics educator*
Pattison, Jon Allen *computer scientist, consultant*
Pendleton, Joan Marie *microprocessor designer*
Perko, Walter Kim *computer consultant*
Pickle, Linda Williams *biostatistician*
Pierce, Charles Earl *software engineer*
Pollock, Karen Anne *computer analyst*
Price, Griffith Baley *mathematician, educator*
Pritzker, Leon *statistician, consultant*
Purdy, Teddy George, Jr. *programmer, analyst, researcher, consultant*
Religa, James Paul *software engineer*
Roberts, Marie Dyer *computer systems specialist*
Roitman, Judith *mathematician*
Sagan, Hans *mathematician, educator, author*
Smith, Kathleen Ann *mathematics educator*
Somes, Grant William *statistician, biomedical researcher*
Spence, Dianna Jeannene *software engineer, educator*
Stern, Nancy Fortgang *mathematics and computer science, educator*
Stilman, Boris *computer science educator, researcher*
Suppes, Patrick *statistics, education, philosophy and psychology educator*
Tan, Hui Qian *computer science and civil engineering educator*
Temam, Roger M. *mathematician*
Tietjen, Scott Phillips *computer programmer, analyst*
Urban, Gary Ross *computer and information processing consultant*
Weiner, Louis Max *retired mathematics educator*
Williams, David Keith *technical trainer*
Winder, Robert Owen *retired mathematician, computer engineer executive*
Yntema, Mary Katherine *retired mathematics educator*
Zheng, Lisa Liqing *computer consultant*

## SCIENCE: PHYSICAL SCIENCE

## UNITED STATES

### ALABAMA

#### Auburn
Carr, Howard Earl *physicist, educator*

#### Birmingham
Bauman, Robert Poe *physicist*
Bugg, Charles Edward *biochemistry educator, scientist*
Longenecker, Herbert Eugene *biochemist, former university president*
Montgomery, John Atterbury *research chemist, consultant*
Robinson, Edward Lee *retired physics educator, consultant*
Shealy, David Lee *physicist, educator*
Shealy, Y. Fulmer *biochemist*
Thompson, Wynelle Doggett *chemistry educator*

#### Dauphin Island
Porter, John Finley, Jr. *physicst, conservationist, retired educator*

#### Decatur
Kuehnert, Harold Adolph *retired petroleum geologist*

#### Enterprise
†Steinhoff, Raymond O(akley) *consulting geologist*

#### Harvest
Norman, Ralph Louis *physicist, consultant*

#### Huntsville
Allan, Barry David *research chemist, government official*
Anderson, Elmer Ebert *physicist, educator*
Chappell, Charles Richard *space scientist*
Decher, Rudolf *physicist*
de Loach, Anthony Cortelyou *solar physicist*
Dimmock, John Oliver *university research center director*
Johnson, Charles Leslie *aerospace physicist, consultant*
McCollough, Michael Leon *astronomer*
McKnight, William Baldwin *physics educator*
Mc Manus, Samuel Plyler *chemist, academic administrator*
Parnell, Thomas Alfred *physicist*
Perkins, James Francis *physicist*
Roberts, Thomas George *retired physicist*
Smith, Robert Earl *space scientist*
Stuhlinger, Ernst *physicist*
Vaughan, William Walton *atmospheric scientist*
Wright, John Collins *chemistry educator*

#### Mobile
Fox, Sidney Walter *chemist, educator*
Perry, Nelson Allen *radiation safety engineer, radiological consultant*

#### Montgomery
Tan, Boen Hie *analytical biochemist, biomedical scientist*

#### Normal
Caulfield, Henry John *physics educator*

#### Selma
Collins, Eugene Boyd *chemist, molecular pathologist, consultant*

#### Sheffield
Meagher, James Francis *atmospheric research executive*

#### Tuscaloosa
Cava, Michael Patrick *chemist, educator*
Cole, George David *physicist*
Coulter, Philip Wylie *physicist, educator*
Izatt, Jerald Ray *physics educator*
LaMoreaux, Philip Elmer *geologist, hydrogeologist, consultant*
Mancini, Ernest Anthony *geologist, educator, researcher*
Van Artsdalen, Ervin Robert *physical chemist, educator*

### ALASKA

#### Anchorage
Ennis, William Lee *physics educator*

#### Fairbanks
Fathauer, Theodore Frederick *meteorologist*
Fischer, Robert Edward *meteorologist*
Helfferich, Merritt Randolph *technology transfer administrator*
Hopkins, David Moody *geologist*
Lingle, Craig Stanley *glaciologist, educator*
Roederer, Juan Gualterio *physics educator*
Weller, Gunter Ernst *geophysics educator*

### ARIZONA

#### Flagstaff
Chen, Jian Hua *medical physicist*
Colbert, Edwin Harris *paleontologist, museum curator*
Millis, Robert Lowell *astronomer*
Shoemaker, Carolyn Spellmann *planetary astronomer*
Shoemaker, Eugene Merle *geologist*
Zoellner, Robert William *chemistry educator*

#### Green Valley
Bates, Charles Carpenter *oceanographer*
Ramette, Richard Wales *chemistry educator*

#### Peoria
Bernstein, Eugene Merle *physicist, retired educator*

#### Phoenix
Allen, John Rybolt L. *chemist, biochemist*
Bolin, Vladimir Dustin *chemist*
Depies, Lisa J. *physicist*
Hudson, Laura Lyn Whitaker *scientific researcher*

#### Scottsdale
Cary, Boyd Balford, Jr. *physicist*
Hockmuth, Joseph Frank *physicist, psychotherapist*
Kinsinger, Jack Burl *chemist, educator*
McPherson, Donald J. *metallurgist*
Newman, William Louis *geologist*

#### Sedona
Otto, Klaus *physicist, physical chemist*

#### Sun City
Dapples, Edward Charles *geologist, educator*

#### Sun City West
Mariella, Raymond P. *chemistry educator, consultant*

#### Tempe
Bauer, Ernst Georg *physicist, educator*
Blankenship, Robert Eugene *chemistry educator*
Burgoyne, Edward Eynon *chemistry educator*
Buseck, Peter Robert *geochemistry educator*
Cowley, John Maxwell *physics educator*
Glick, Milton Don *chemist, university administrator*
Goronkin, Herbert *physicist*
Greeley, Ronald *geology educator*
Juvet, Richard Spalding, Jr. *chemistry educator*
Mahajan, Subhash *electronic materials educator*
Moore, Carleton Bryant *geochemistry educator*
Nigam, Bishan Perkash *physics educator*
Page, John Boyd *physics educator*
Pettit, George Robert *chemistry educator, cancer researcher*
Péwé, Troy Lewis *geologist, educator*
Quadt, Raymond Adolph *metallurgist, cement company executive*
Smith, David John *physicist, educator*
Starrfield, Sumner Grosby *astrophysics educator, researcher*
Vandenberg, Edwin James *chemist, educator*

#### Tucson
Angel, James Roger Prior *astronomer*
Barrett, Bruce Richard *physics educator*
Bartocha, Bodo *scientist, educator*
Beckers, Jacques Maurice *astrophysicist*
Broadfoot, Albert Lyle *physicist*
Buras, Nathan *hydrology and water resources educator*
Carruthers, Peter Ambler *physicist, educator*
Clarke, Robert Francis *nuclear physicist, consultant*
Crawford, David L. *astronomer*
Davies, Roger *geoscience educator*
Davis, Stanley Nelson *hydrologist, educator*
Dessler, Alexander Jack *space physics and astronomy educator, scientist*
De Young, David Spencer *astrophysicist, educator*
Dickinson, Robert Earl *atmospheric scientist, educator*
Dodd, Charles Gardner *physical chemist*
Fang, Li-Zhi *physicist, educator*
Forster, Leslie Stewart *chemistry educator*
Gruhl, James *energy scientist, artist*
Hartmann, William Kenneth *astronomy scientist*
Haynes, Caleb Vance, Jr. *geology and archaeology educator*
Hays, James Fred *geologist, educator*
Hill, Henry Allen *physicist, educator*
Hoffmann, William Frederick *astronomer*
Howard, Robert Franklin *observatory administrator, astronomer*
Hruby, Victor Joseph *chemistry educator*
Hubbard, William Bogel *planetary sciences educator*
Hunten, Donald Mount *planetary scientist, educator*
Jackson, Kenneth Arthur *physicist, researcher*
Jeffay, Henry *biochemistry educator*
Jefferies, John Trevor *astronomer, astrophysicist, observatory administrator*
Karkoschka, Erich *planetary science researcher, writer*
Kessler, John Otto *physicist, educator*
Kiersch, George Alfred *geological consultant, retired educator*
Krider, E. Philip *atmospheric scientist, educator*
Lamb, Willis Eugene, Jr. *physicist, educator*
Law, John Harold *biochemistry educator*
Lunine, Jonathan Irving *planetary scientist, educator*
Marcialis, Robert Louis *planetary astronomer*
McEwen, Alfred Sherman *planetary geologist*
Ning, Cun-Zheng *physicist*
Parmenter, Robert Haley *physics educator*
Powell, Richard C. *physicist, educator, researcher*
Roemer, Elizabeth *astronomer, educator*
Rountree, Janet Caryl *astrophysicist*
Schaefer, John Paul *chemist, corporate executive*
Scotti, James Vernon *astronomer*
Sprague, Ann Louise *space scientist*
Strittmatter, Peter Albert *astronomer, educator*
Swalin, Richard Arthur *scientist, company executive*
Tifft, William Grant *astronomer*
White, Alvin Swauger *aerospace scientist, consultant*
Willis, Clifford Leon *geologist*
Wolff, Sidney Carne *astronomer, observatory administrator*

### ARKANSAS

#### Bella Vista
Johnson, A(lyn) William *chemistry educator, writer, researcher, consultant*

#### Fayetteville
Steele, Kenneth Franklin, Jr. *hydrology educator, resource center director*

#### Little Rock
Braithwaite, Wilfred John *physics educator*
Darsey, Jerome Anthony *chemistry educator, consultant*

#### Pine Bluff
Walker, Richard Brian *chemistry educator*

### CALIFORNIA

#### Anaheim
Brigham, Gerald Allen *research physicist, consultant*
Loeblich, Helen Nina Tappan *paleontologist, educator*

#### Apple Valley
Mays, George Walter, Jr. *educational technology educator, consultant, tutor*

#### Arcata
Wayne, Lowell Grant *air pollution scientist, consultant*

#### Atascadero
Ogier, Walter Thomas *retired physics educator*

#### Atherton
Fisher, Leon Harold *physicist, emeritus educator*
Fried, John H. *chemist*

#### Auburn
Hess, Patrick Henry *chemist*

#### Bakersfield
Dorer, Fred Harold *chemistry educator*

#### Banning
Holmes, John Richard *physicist, educator*

#### Bayside
Cocks, George Gosson *retired chemical microscopy educator*

#### Bellflower
Martin, Melissa Carol *radiological physicist*

#### Berkeley
Alpen, Edward Lewis *biophysicist, educator*
Ames, Bruce N(athan) *biochemist, molecular biologist*
Attwood, David Thomas *physicist, educator*
Barker, Horace Albert *biochemist, microbiologist*
Barnett, R(alph) Michael *theoretical physicist, educational agency administrator*
Bartlett, Neil *chemist, educator*
Bartlett, Paul A. *organic chemist*
Bergman, Robert George *chemist, educator*
Berry, William Benjamin Newell *geologist, educator, former museum administrator*
Bolt, Bruce Alan *seismologist, educator*
Bragg, Robert Henry *physicist, educator*
Brewer, Leo *physical chemist, educator*
Bukowinski, Mark Stefan Tadeusz *geophysics educator*
Calvin, Melvin *chemist, educator*
Carmichael, Ian Stuart Edward *geologist, educator*
Cerny, Joseph, III *chemistry educator, scientific laboratory administrator, university dean and official*
Chamberlain, Owen *nuclear physicist*
Chamberlin, Michael John *biochemistry educator*
Chandler, David *scientist, educator*
Chew, Geoffrey Foucar *physicist*
Clarke, John *physics educator*
Cohen, Marvin Lou *physics educator*
Curtis, Garniss Hearfield *geology educator*
Diamond, Richard Martin *nuclear chemist*
Ely, Robert Pollock, Jr. *physics educator, researcher*
Fowler, Thomas Kenneth *physicist*
Fréchet, Jean Marie Joseph *chemistry educator*
Fuhs, G(eorg) Wolfgang *environmental research manager*
Gaillard, Mary Katharine *physics educator*
Glaser, Donald Arthur *physicist*
Gregory, Joseph Tracy *paleontologist, educator*
Hahn, Erwin Louis *physicist, educator*
Haller, Eugene Ernest *materials scientist, educator*
Hearst, John Eugene *chemistry educator, pharmaceutical executive*
Heathcock, Clayton Howell *chemistry educator, researcher*
Helmholz, August Carl *physicist, educator emeritus*
Hoffman, Darleane Christian *chemistry educator*
Holdren, John Paul *energy and resource educator, researcher, author, consultant*
Jackson, J(ohn) David *physicist, educator*
Jeanloz, Raymond *geophysicist, educator*
Kerth, Leroy T. *physics educator*
Kikuchi, Ryoichi *physics educator*
Kim, Sung-Hou *chemistry educator, biophysical and biological chemist*
King, Ivan Robert *astronomy educator*
Kirsch, Jack Frederick *biochemistry educator*
Kittel, Charles *physicist, educator emeritus*
Klinman, Judith Pollock *biochemist, educator*
Kurtzman, Ralph Harold *retired biochemist, researcher, consultant*
Leopold, Luna Bergere *geology educator*
Lester, William Alexander, Jr. *chemist, educator*
Linn, Stuart Michael *biochemist, educator*
Lipps, Jere Henry *paleontology educator*
Malina, Roger F. *astronomer*
Mandelstam, Stanley *physicist*
Marg, Elwin *physiological optics, optometry educator*
Markowitz, Samuel Solomon *chemistry educator*
Matson, Pamela Anne *environmental science educator*
McKee, Christopher Fulton *astrophysics and astronomy educator*
Miller, William Hughes *theoretical chemist, educator*
Moore, C. Bradley *chemistry educator*
Muller, Richard August *physicist, author*
Nero, Anthony Vincent, Jr. *physicist, environmental scientist, writer*
†Pavlath, Attila Endre *research chemist*
Perez-Mendez, Victor *physics educator*
Perry, Dale Lynn *chemist*
Pines, Alexander *chemistry educator, researcher, consultant*
Pitzer, Kenneth Sanborn *chemist, educator*
Rasmussen, John Oscar *nuclear scientist*
Raymond, Kenneth Norman *chemistry educator, research chemist*
Reynolds, John Hamilton *physicist, educator*
Ritchie, Robert Oliver *materials science educator*
Sadoulet, Bernard *astrophysicist, educator*
Saykally, Richard James *chemistry educator*
Schultz, Peter G. *chemistry educator*
Seaborg, Glenn Theodore *chemistry educator*
Searcy, Alan Winn *chemist, educator*
Sessler, Andrew Marienhoff *physicist*
Shen, Yuen-Ron *physics educator*
Shugart, Howard Alan *physicist, educator*
Smith, Neville Vincent *physicist*
Smoot, George Fitzgerald, III *astrophysicist*
Somorjai, Gabor Arpad *chemist, educator*
Spinrad, Hyron *astronomer*
Steiner, Herbert Max *physics educator*
Strauss, Herbert Leopold *chemistry educator*
Streitwieser, Andrew, Jr. *chemistry educator*
Symons, Timothy James McNeil *physicist*
Thomas, Gareth *metallurgy educator*
Thompson, Anthony Wayne *metallurgist, educator, consultant*
Tjian, Robert Tse Nan *bichemistry educator, biology rsercher, virology researcher*
Townes, Charles Hard *physics educator*
Trilling, George Henry *physicist, educator*
Tsina, Richard Vasil *chemistry educator*
Valentine, James William *paleobiology, educator, author*
Vollhardt, Kurt Peter Christian *chemistry educator*
Weber, Eicke Richard *physicist*
Yuan Tseh Lee *chemistry educator*

#### Bonita
Wood, Fergus James *geophysicist, consultant*

#### Brea
Shen, Gene Giin-Yuan *organic chemist*

#### Burbank
Ingersoll, John Gregory *physicist, energy specialist, educator*

#### Burlingame
Hotz, Henry Palmer *physicist*

#### Camarillo
Leerabhandh, Marjorie Bravo *chemist, educator*

#### Cameron Park
Buckles, Robert Edwin *chemistry educator*

#### Canyon Lake
Schilling, Frederick Augustus, Jr. *geologist, consultant*

#### Carlsbad
Smith, Warren James *optical scientist, consultant, lecturer*

#### China Lake
Bennett, Jean Louise McPherson *physicist, research scientist*

#### Claremont
Beilby, Alvin Lester *chemistry educator*
Helliwell, Thomas McCaffree *physicist, educator*
Kronenberg, Klaus J(ohannes) *physicist*
Kubota, Mitsuru *chemistry educator*
Long, Franklin Asbury *chemistry educator*
White, Kathleen Merritt *geologist*

#### Corona
Garrett, Thomas Monroe *chemist*

#### Corona Del Mar
Britten, Roy John *biophysicist*

#### Costa Mesa
Lattanzio, Stephen Paul *astronomy educator*
Lorance, Elmer Donald *organic chemistry educator*

**Crescent City**
Carter, Neville Louis *geophysicist, educator*

**Cupertino**
Nelson, Richard Burton *physicist, engineer, former patent consultant*

**Davis**
Axelrod, Daniel Isaac *geology and botany educator*
Black, Arthur Leo *biochemistry educator*
Cahill, Thomas Andrew *physicist, educator*
Conn, Eric Edward *plant biochemist*
Day, Howard Wilman *geology educator*
Feeney, Robert Earl *research biochemist*
Hedrick, Jerry Leo *biochemistry and biophysics educator*
Higgins, Charles Graham *geology educator*
Jungerman, John Albert *physics educator*
Keizer, Joel Edward *theoretical scientist, educator*
Mazelis, Mendel *plant biochemist, educator, reseacher*
Mukherjee, Amiya K *metallurgy and materials science educator*
Nash, Charles Presley *chemistry educator*
Painter, Ruth Robbins *retired environmental biochemist*
Shelton, Robert Neal *physics educator, researcher*
Stumpf, Paul Karl *biochemistry educator emeritus*
Troy, Frederic Arthur, II *medical biochemistry educator*
Volman, David Herschel *chemistry educator*
Wooten, Frederick (Oliver) *applied science educator*

**Del Mar**
Stevenson, Robert Everett *oceanography consultant*

**Duarte**
Greenstein, Jesse Leonard *astronomer, educator*

**El Cajon**
Burnett, Lowell Jay *physicist, educator*

**El Cerrito**
Amoore, John Ernest *biochemist*
Griffith, Ladd Ray *retired chemical research director*
Gwinn, William Dulaney *physical chemist, educator, executive, consultant*
Siri, William E. *physicist*

**El Granada**
Heere, Karen R. *astrophysicist*

**El Segundo**
Paulikas, George Algis *physicist*

**Emeryville**
Masri, Merle Sid *biochemist, consultant*

**Encinitas**
Goldberg, Edward Davidow *geochemist, educator*
Moe, Chesney Rudolph *physics educator*

**Encino**
Hawthorne, Marion Frederick *chemistry educator*

**Escondido**
Tomomatsu, Hideo *chemist*

**Foothill Ranch**
Testa, Stephen Michael *geologist, consultant*

**Foster City**
Zaidi, Iqbal Mehdi *biochemist, scientist*

**Fountain Valley**
Gittleman, Morris *metallurgist, consultant*

**Fremont**
Gill, Stephen Paschall *physicist, mathematician*

**Fresno**
Kauffman, George Bernard *chemistry educator*

**Fullerton**
Fearn, Heidi *physicist, educator*
Shapiro, Mark Howard *physicist, educator, academic dean, consultant*

**Glendale**
Farmer, Crofton Bernard *atmospheric physicist*

**Hayward**
Hirschfeld, Sue Ellen *geological sciences educator*
Warnke, Detlef Andreas *geologist, educator*

**Hemet**
Berger, Lev Isaac *physicist, educator*

**Inglewood**
Lewis, Roy Roosevelt *physicist*

**Irvine**
Bander, Myron *physics educator, university dean*
Bradshaw, Ralph Alden *biochemistry educator*
Bron, Walter Ernest *physics educator*
Cho, Zang Hee *physics educator*
Clark, Bruce Robert *geology consultant*
Dzyaloshinskii, Igor Ekhielievich *physicist*
Hemminger, John Charles *chemist, educator*
Knight, Patricia Marie *optics researcher*
Lanyi, Janos Karoly *biochemist, educator*
Maradudin, Alexei A. *physics educator*
McLaughlin, Calvin Sturgis *biochemistry educator*
Nalcioglu, Orhan *physics educator, radiological sciences educator*
Nomura, Masayasu *biological chemistry educator*
Overman, Larry Eugene *chemistry educator*
Phalen, Robert Franklynn *environmental scientist*
Reines, Frederick *physicist, educator*
Rentzepis, Peter M. *chemistry educator*
Rowland, Frank Sherwood *chemistry educator*
Rynn, Nathan *physics educator, consultant*
Trolinger, James Davis *laser scientist*
Wallis, Richard Fisher *physicist, educator*
White, Stephen Halley *biophysicist, educator*

**Kensington**
Connick, Robert Elwell *retired chemistry educator*

**La Canada Flintridge**
Pickering, William Hayward *physics educator, scientist*

**La Habra**
Woyski, Margaret Skillman *retired geology educator*

**La Jolla**
Andre, Michael Paul *physicist, educator*
Arnold, James Richard *chemist, educator*
Asmus, John Fredrich *physicist*
Backus, George Edward *theoretical geophysicist*
Benson, Andrew Alm *biochemistry educator*
Berger, Wolfgang H. *oceanographer, marine geologist*
Boger, Dale L. *chemistry educator*
Brand, Larry Milton *biochemist*
Buckingham, Michael John *oceanography educator*
Bukry, John David *geologist*
Burbidge, E. Margaret *astronomer, educator*
Burbidge, Geoffrey *astrophysicist, educator*
Christensen, Halvor Niels *biochemist, educator*
Continetti, Robert E. *chemistry educator*
Cox, Charles Shipley *oceanography researcher, educator*
Cunningham, Bruce Arthur *biochemist*
Doolittle, Russell Francis *biochemist, educator*
Driscoll, Charles F. *physics educator*
Edelman, Gerald Maurice *biochemist, educator*
Feher, George *physics and biophysics scientist, educator*
Geiduschek, E(rnest) Peter *biophysics and molecular biology educator*
Gilbert, James Freeman *geophysics educator*
Goodman, Murray *chemistry educator*
Grier, Herbert Earl *scientist, consultant*
Grine, Donald Reaville *retired geophysicist, research executive*
Itano, Harvey Akio *biochemistry educator*
Joyce, Gerald Francis *biochemist, educator*
Kadonaga, James Takuro *biochemist*
Keeling, Charles David *oceanography educator*
Kitada, Shinichi *biochemist*
Knox, Robert Arthur *oceanographer, academic administrator*
Lal, Devendra *nuclear geophysics educator*
Lauer, James Lothar *physicist, educator*
MacDougall, John Douglas *earth science educator*
McCammon, James Andrew *chemistry educator*
McIlwain, Carl Edwin *physicist*
Mestril, Ruben *biochemist, researcher*
Mullin, Michael Mahlon *Biology and oceanography educator*
Mullis, Kary Banks *biochemist*
Munk, Walter Heinrich *geophysics educator*
Ohkawa, Tihiro *physicist*
O'Neil, Thomas Michael *physicist, educator*
Onuchic, Jóse Nelson *biophysics educator, electrical engineer*
Patton, Stuart *biochemist, educator*
Peterson, Laurence E. *physics educator*
Rotenberg, Manuel *physics educator*
Seegmiller, Jarvis Edwin *biochemist, educator*
Sham, Lu Jeu *physics educator*
Shor, George G., Jr. *geophysicist, oceanographic administrator, engineer*
Shuler, Kurt Egon *chemist, educator*
Somerville, Richard Chapin James *atmospheric scientist, educator*
Spiess, Fred Noel *oceanographer, educator*
Suhl, Harry *physics educator*
Tietz, Norbert Wolfgang *clinical chemistry educator, administrator*
Van Lint, Victor Anton Jacobus *physicist*
Wall, Frederick Theodore *retired chemistry educator*
Watson, Kenneth Marshall *physics educator*
York, Herbert Frank *physics educator, government official*

**Laguna Beach**
Wilson, James Newman *retired laboratory executive*

**Laguna Hills**
Batdorf, Samuel B(urbridge) *physicist*
Howard, Hildegarde (Mrs. Henry Anson Wylde) *paleontologist*
Iberall, Arthur Saul *physicist, publisher*

**Livermore**
Alder, Berni Julian *physicist*
Chung, Dae Hyun *retired geophysicist*
Cook, Robert Crossland *research chemist*
Ellsaesser, Hugh Walter *retired atmospheric scientist*
Hooper, Edwin Bickford *physicist*
Hulet, Ervin Kenneth *retired nuclear chemist*
Kidder, Ray Edward *physicist, consultant*
Kirkwood, Robert Keith *applied physicist*
Lau, Albert Man-Fai *physicist*
Leith, Cecil Eldon, Jr. *retired physicist*
Max, Claire Ellen *physicist*
Nuckolls, John Hopkins *physicist, researcher*
Schock, Robert Norman *geophysicist*
Shotts, Wayne J. *nuclear scientist, federal agency administrator*
Tarter, Curtis Bruce *physicist, science administrator*
Wong, Joe *physical chemist*

**Loma Linda**
Slattery, Charles Wilbur *biochemistry educator*
Wilcox, Ronald Bruce *biochemistry educator, researcher*

**Long Beach**
Bauer, Roger Duane *chemistry educator, science consultant*
Hu, Chi Yu *physicist, educator*
McGaughey, Charles Gilbert *retired research biochemist*

**Los Altos**
Barker, William Alfred *physics educator*
Hahn, Harold Thomas *physical chemist, chemical engineer*
Hall, Charles Frederick *space scientist, government administrator*
Jones, Robert Thomas *aerospace scientist*
Twersky, Victor *mathematical physicist, educator*
van Tamelen, Eugene Earle *chemist, educator*

**Los Angeles**
Adamson, Arthur Wilson *chemistry educator*
Aki, Keiiti *seismologist, educator*
Aller, Lawrence Hugh *astronomy educator, researcher*
Allerton, Samuel Ellsworth *biochemist*
Anderson, W. French *biochemist, physician*
Benson, Sidney William *chemistry researcher*
Bhaumik, Mani Lal *physicist*
Billig, Franklin Anthony *chemist*
Bird, Peter *geology educator*
Bottjer, David John *earth sciences educator*
Braginsky, Stanislav Iosifovich *physicist, geophysicist, researcher*
Byers, Nina *physics educator*
Campbell, Kenneth Eugene, Jr. *vertebrate paleontologist*
Carter, Emily Ann *physical chemist, educator*
Chapman, Orville Lamar *chemist, educator*
Chester, Marvin *physics educator*
Coleman, Charles Clyde *physicist, educator*
Coleman, Paul Jerome, Jr. *physicist, educator*
Cornwall, John Michael *physics educator, consultant, researcher*
Coroniti, Ferdinand Vincent *physics educator, consultant*
Cram, Donald James *chemistry educator*
Dalton, Larry Raymond *chemistry educator, researcher, consultant*
Dawson, John Myrick *plasma physics educator*
Dows, David Alan *chemistry educator*
Dunn, Arnold Samuel *biochemistry educator*
Dunn, Bruce Sidney *materials science educator*
Edwards, Kenneth Neil *chemist, consultant*
Fischer, Alfred George *geology educator*
Foote, Christopher Spencer *chemist, educator*
Fried, Burton David *physicist, educator*
Fulco, Armand John *biochemist*
Ganas, Perry Spiros *physicist*
Ghez, Andrea Mia *astronomy and physics educator*
Glitz, Dohn George *biochemistry educator*
Hall, Clarence Albert, Jr. *geologist, educator*
Hellwarth, Robert Willis *physicist, educator*
Houk, Kendall Newcomb *chemistry educator*
Igo, George Jerome *physics educator*
Jaffe, Sigmund *chemist, educator*
Kaplan, Isaac Raymond *chemistry educator, corporate executive*
Kaula, William Mason *geophysicist, educator*
Kivelson, Margaret Galland *physicist*
Koga, Rokutaro *physicist*
Krupp, Edwin Charles *astronomer*
Laaly, Heshmat Ollah *chemist, roofing materials executive, consultant*
Levine, Raphael David *chemistry educator*
Logan, Joseph Granville, Jr. *physicist*
Maki, Kazumi *physicist, educator*
Markland, Francis Swaby, Jr. *biochemist, educator*
McLean, Ian Small *astronomer, physics educator*
Neufeld, Elizabeth Fondal *biochemist, educator*
Nimni, Marcel Ephraim *biochemistry educator*
Olah, George Andrew *chemist, educator*
O'Leary, Dennis Patrick *biophysicist*
Onak, Thomas Philip *chemistry educator*
Paulson, Donald Robert *chemistry educator*
Reiss, Howard *chemistry educator*
Roberts, Sidney *biological chemist*
Scott, Robert Lane *chemist, educator*
Shapiro, Isadore *materials scientist, consultant*
Smathers, James Burton *medical physicist, educator*
Smith, Emil L. *biochemist, consultant*
Smith, William Ray *retired biophysicist, engineer*
Stellwagen, Robert Harwood *biochemistry educator*
Szwarc, Michael *polymer scientist*
Thorne, Richard Mansergh *physicist*
Trimble, Stanley Wayne *hydrology and geography educator*
Trueblood, Kenneth Nyitray *retired chemist, educator*
Ufimtsev, Pyotr Yakovlevich *physicist, electrical engineer, educator*
Whitten, Charles Alexander, Jr. *physics educator*
Wittry, David Beryle *physicist, educator*
Woodruff, Fay *paleoceanographer, geological researcher*
Wurtele, Morton Gaither *meteorologist, educator*

**Magalia**
Joffre, Stephen Paul *consulting chemist*

**Malibu**
Chester, Arthur Noble *physicist*
Margerum, J(ohn) David *chemist*
Mataré, Herbert F. *physicist, consultant*
Pepper, David M. *physicist, educator, author, inventor*

**Marina**
Shane, William Whitney *astronomer*

**Menlo Park**
Boyarski, Adam Michael *physicist*
Funkhouser, Lawrence William *retired geologist*
Hodgen, Laurie Dee *geologist, editor*
Holzer, Thomas Lequear *geologist*
Kuwabara, James Shigeru *research hydrologist*
Luepke, Gretchen *geologist*
Tokheim, Robert Edward *physicist*
Vickers, Roger Spencer *physicist, program director*
Wallace, Robert Earl *geologist*

**Milpitas**
Le, Yvonne Diemvan *chemist*
Lee, Kenneth *physicist*

**Modesto**
Morrison, Robert Lee *physical scientist*

**Moffett Field**
Kittel, Peter *research scientist*
Lissauer, Jack Jonathan *astronomy educator*
Ragent, Boris *physicist*
Seiff, Alvin *planetary, atmospheric and aerodynamics scientist*

**Montecito**
Wheelon, Albert Dewell *physicist*

**Monterey**
Atchley, Anthony Armstrong *physicist, educator*
Collins, Curtis Allan *oceanographer*
Shull, Harrison *chemist, educator*

**Moraga**
Hollingsworth, Robert Edgar *nuclear consultant*

**Morgan Hill**
Kuster, Robert Kenneth *scientist*

**Moss Landing**
Brewer, Peter George *ocean geochemist*
Heath, George Ross *oceanographer*

**Mountain View**
McCormac, Billy Murray *physicist, research institution executive, former army officer*

**Northridge**
Court, Arnold *climatologist*

**Novato**
Simon, Lee Will *astronomer*

**Oak Park**
Caldwell, Stratton Franklin *kinesiologist*

**Oakland**
Brust, David *physicist*
Harpster, Robert Eugene *engineering geologist*
Jukes, Thomas Hughes *biological chemist, educator*
Kropschot, Richard H. *physicist, science laboratory administrator*
Mikalow, Alfred Alexander, II *deep sea diver, marine surveyor, marine diving consultant*

**Orinda**
Heftmann, Erich *biochemist*

**Pacific Palisades**
Abrams, Richard Lee *physicist*
Csendes, Ernest *chemist, corporate and financial executive*
Fink, Robert Morgan *biological chemistry educator*
Gregor, Eduard *laser physicist, consultant*

**Palo Alto**
Andersen, Torben Brender *optical researcher, astronomer, software engineer*
Bienenstock, Arthur Irwin *physicist, educator*
Breiner, Sheldon *geophysics educator, business executive*
Cutler, Leonard Samuel *physicist*
Datlowe, Dayton Wood *space scientist, physicist*
Eng, Lawrence Fook *biochemistry educator, neurochemist*
Ernst, Wallace Gary *geology educator*
Flory, Curt A. *research physicist*
Haisch, Bernhard Michael *astronomer*
Holmes, Richard Brooks *mathematical physicist*
Loew, Gilda Harris *research biophysicist, biology research executive*
Loewenstein, Walter Bernard *nuclear power technologist*
Panofsky, Wolfgang Kurt Hermann *physicist, educator*
Saxena, Arjun Nath *physicist*
Schreiber, Everett Charles, Jr. *chemist, educator*
Stringer, John *materials scientist*
Taimuty, Samuel Isaac *physicist*
Theeuwes, Felix *physical chemist*

**Palos Verdes Peninsula**
Reynolds, Harry Lincoln *physicist*

**Pasadena**
Ahrens, Thomas J. *geophysicist*
Albee, Arden Leroy *geologist, educator*
Anderson, Don Lynn *geophysicist, educator*
Anderson, John David *astronomer, researcher*
Anson, Fred Colvig *chemistry educator*
Babcock, Horace W. *astronomer*
Baines, Kevin Hays *planetary scientist, astronomer*
Baldeschwieler, John Dickson *chemist, educator*
Barnes, Charles Andrew *physicist, educator*
Beaudet, Robert Arthur *chemistry educator*
Bejczy, Antal Károly *research scientist, research facility administrator*
Bercaw, John Edward *chemistry educator, consultant*
Blandford, Roger David *astronomy educator*
Boehm, Felix Hans *physicist, educator*
Chahine, Moustafa Toufic *atmospheric scientist*
Chan, Sunney Ignatius *chemist*
Cohen, Marshall Harris *astronomer, educator*
Culick, Fred Ellsworth Clow *physics and engineering educator*
Dervan, Peter Brendan *chemistry educator*
Dougherty, Dennis A. *chemistry educator*
Dressler, Alan Michael *astronomer*
Duxbury, Thomas Carl *planetary scientist*
Epstein, Samuel *geologist, educator*
Frautschi, Steven Clark *physicist, educator*
Fu, Lee-Lueng *oceanographer*
Golombek, Matthew Philip *structural and planetary geologist*
Goodstein, David Louis *physics educator*
Gray, Harry Barkus *chemistry educator*
Grubbs, Robert Howard *chemistry educator*
Gurnis, Michael Christopher *geological sciences educator*
Heindl, Clifford Joseph *physicist*
Hitlin, David George *physicist, educator*
Ingersoll, Andrew Perry *planetary science educator*
Jastrow, Robert *physicist*
Kanamori, Hiroo *geophysics educator*
Kavanagh, Ralph William *physics educator*
Koonin, Steven Elliot *physicist, professor*
Leonard, Nelson Jordan *chemistry educator*
Lewis, Nathan Saul *chemistry educator*
Liepmann, Hans Wolfgang *physicist, educator*
Marcus, Rudolph Arthur *chemist, educator*
Mc Koy, Basil Vincent Charles *theoretical chemist, educator*
Mercereau, James Edgar *physicist, educator*
Neugebauer, Marcia *physicist, administrator*
Oemler, Augustus, Jr. *astronomy educator*
Politzer, Hugh David *physicist, educator*
Roberts, John D. *chemist, educator*
Sargent, Wallace Leslie William *astronomer, educator*
Schmidt, Maarten *astronomy educator*
Sekanina, Zdenek *astronomer*
Sharp, Robert Phillip *geology educator, researcher*
Stevenson, David John *planetary scientist, educator*
Stone, Edward Carroll *physicist, educator*
Tombrello, Thomas Anthony, Jr. *physics educator, consultant*
Vogt, Rochus Eugen *physicist, educator*
Wasserburg, Gerald Joseph *geology and geophysics educator*
Westphal, James Adolph *planetary science educator*
Wyllie, Peter John *geologist, educator*
Yau, Kevin Kam-ching *astronomer*
Yeomans, Donald Keith *astronomer*

Zachariasen, Fredrik *physics educator*
Zirin, Harold *astronomer, educator*

### Petaluma
Belmares, Hector *chemist*
Eck, Robert Edwin *physicist*

### Phillips Ranch
Koestel, Mark Alfred *geologist, photographer, consultant*

### Pleasant Hill
Weiss, Lionel Edward *geology educator*

### Pomona
Bidlack, Wayne Ross *nutritional biochemist, toxicologist, food scienti*

### Rancho Santa Fe
Creutz, Edward Chester *physicist, museum consultant*

### Redlands
Clopine, Gordon Alan *consulting geologist, educator, business and facilities manager*

### Redondo Beach
Ball, William Paul *physicist, engineer*
Roth, Thomas J. *physicist*

### Redwood City
Nacht, Sergio *biochemist*

### Richmond
Thomas, John Richard *chemist*
Ward, Carl Edward *research chemist*

### Ridgecrest
Bennett, Harold Earl *physicist, optics researcher*
Lepie, Albert Helmut *chemist, reseacher*
St. Amand, Pierre *geophysicist*

### Riverside
Fung, Sun-Yiu Samuel *physics educator*
Green, Harry Western, II *geology-geophysics educator, university official*
Norman, Anthony Westcott *biochemistry educator*
Orbach, Raymond Lee *physicist, educator*
Rabenstein, Dallas Leroy *chemistry educator*
White, Robert Stephen *physics educator*
Wild, Robert Lee *physics educator*
Wilkins, Charles L. *chemistry educator*

### Rohnert Park
Trowbridge, Dale Brian *educator*

### Sacramento
Nussenbaum, Siegfried Fred *chemistry educator*
Sydnor, Robert Hadley *state government geologist*

### San Diego
Cobble, James Wikle *chemistry educator*
Fisher, Frederick Hendrick *oceanographer*
Gastil, Russell Gordon *geologist, educator*
Greene, John M. *physicist*
Gu, Zu-Han *research scientist*
Hosker, Donald *materials research technician*
Kerr, Donald MacLean, Jr. *physicist*
Kraus, Pansy Daegling *gemology consultant, editor, writer*
Lao, Lang Li *nuclear fusion research physicist*
Mohan, Chandra *research biochemistry educator*
Pecsok, Robert Louis *chemist, educator*
Pincus, Howard Jonah *geologist, engineer, educator*
Roeder, Stephen Bernhard Walter *chemistry and physics educator*
Shneour, Elie Alexis *biochemist*
Wright, Jon Alan *physicist, researcher*

### San Francisco
Appelman, Evan Hugh *retired chemist*
Burlingame, Alma Lyman *chemist, educator*
Burri, Betty Jane *research chemist*
Cluff, Lloyd Sterling *earthquake geologist*
Dickinson, Wade *physicist, oil company executive, educator*
Featherstone, John Douglas Bernard *biochemistry educator*
Grodsky, Gerold Morton *biochemistry educator*
Kelly, Regis Baker *biochemistry educator, biophysics educator*
Landahl, Herbert Daniel *biophysicist, mathematical biologist, researcher, consultant*
Majumdar, Sharmila *research scientist, educator*
Mandra, York T. *geology educator*
Seibel, Erwin *oceanographer, educator*
Sussman, Brian Jay *meteorologist, weather broadcaster*

### San Jose
Berkland, James Omer *geologist*
Castellano, Joseph Anthony *chemist, management consulting firm executive*
Dafforn, Geoffrey Alan *biochemist*
Eigler, Donald Mark *physicist*
Forster, Julian *physicist, consultant*
Gruber, John Balsbaugh *physics educator, university administrator*
Houle, Frances Anne *physical chemist*
Morawitz, Hans *physicist*
Neptune, John Addison *chemistry educator, consultant*
Parkin, Stuart S. P. *materials scientist*
Winters, Harold Franklin *physicist*

### San Leandro
Stallings, Charles Henry *physicist*

### San Luis Obispo
Grismore, Roger *physics educator, researcher*
Hafemeister, David Walter *physicist*

### San Pedro
Simmons, William *physicist, aerospace research executive*

### Santa Barbara
Atwater, Tanya Maria *marine geophysicist, educator*
Byers, Horace Robert *former meteorology educator*
Christman, Arthur Castner, Jr. *scientific advisor*
Crowell, John C(hambers) *geology educator, researcher*
Dudziak, Walter Francis *physicist*
Dunne, Thomas *geology educator*
Eisberg, Robert Martin *physics educator, computer software author and executive*
Ford, Peter C. *chemistry educator*
Gossard, Arthur Charles *physicist*
Gutsche, Steven Lyle *physicist*
Heeger, Alan Jay *physicist*
Kennedy, John Harvey *chemistry educator*
Kennett, James Peter *geology and oceanography educator*
Kohn, Walter *educator, physicist*
Langer, James Stephen *physicist, educator*
Luyendyk, Bruce Peter *geophysicist, educator, institution administrator*
Macdonald, Ken Craig *geophysicist*
Meinel, Aden Baker *optics scientist*
Norris, Robert Matheson *geologist*
Peale, Stanton Jerrold *physics educator*
Pilgeram, Laurence Oscar *biochemist*
Tilton, George Robert *geochemistry educator*
Wilson, Leslie *biochemist, cell biologist, biology educator*
Witherell, Michael S. *physics educator*
Wudl, Fred *chemistry educator*

### Santa Clara
Bjorkholm, John Ernst *physicist*

### Santa Cruz
Bunnett, Joseph Frederick *chemist, educator*
Drake, Frank Donald *radio astronomer, educator*
Faber, Sandra Moore *astronomer, educator*
Flatté, Stanley Martin *physicist, educator*
Griggs, Gary Bruce *earth sciences educator, oceanographer, geologist, consultant*
Heusch, Clemens August *physicist, educator*
Hill, Terrell Leslie *chemist, biophysicist*
Kraft, Robert Paul *astronomer, educator*
Laporte, Leo Frederic *earth sciences educator*
Lay, Thorne *geosciences educator*
Millhauser, Glenn Lawrence *biochemist, educator*
Noller, Harry Francis, Jr. *biochemist, educator*
Osterbrock, Donald E(dward) *astronomy educator*
Sands, Matthew Linzee *physicist, educator*
Silver, Mary Wilcox *oceanography educator*
Williams, Quentin Christopher *geophysicist, educator*
Wipke, W. Todd *chemistry educator*
Woosley, Stanford Earl *astrophysicist*

### Santa Maria
Ellis, Emory Leon *retired biochemist*

### Santa Monica
Davies, Merton Edward *planetary scientist*
Intriligator, Devrie Shapiro *physicist*

### Santa Rosa
Mc Donald, David William *retired chemist, educator*

### Scotts Valley
Snyder, Charles Theodore *geologist*

### Solana Beach
Agnew, Harold Melvin *physicist*

### Stanford
Allen, Matthew Arnold *physicist*
Andersen, Hans Christian *chemistry educator*
Baldwin, Robert Lesh *biochemist, educator*
Ballam, Joseph *physicist, educator*
Berg, Paul *biochemist, educator*
Bonner, William Andrew *chemistry educator*
Brauman, John I. *chemist, educator*
Bube, Richard Howard *materials scientist*
Coleman, Robert Griffin *geology educator*
Collman, James Paddock *chemistry educator*
Deal, Bruce Elmer *physical chemist, educator*
Djerassi, Carl *chemist, educator, writer*
Drell, Sidney David *physicist, educator*
Fetter, Alexander Lees *theoretical physicist, educator*
Flinn, Paul Anthony *materials scientist*
Graham, Stephan Alan *earth sciences educator*
Harbaugh, John Warvelle *applied earth sciences educator*
Harrison, Walter Ashley *physicist, educator*
Herring, William Conyers *physicist, emeritus educator*
Kennedy, Donald *environmental science educator, former academic administrator*
Kornberg, Arthur *biochemist*
Kornberg, Roger David *biochemist, structural biologist*
Kovach, Robert Louis *geophysics educator*
Krauskopf, Konrad Bates *geology educator*
Lehman, (Israel) Robert *biochemistry educator, consultant*
Levinthal, Elliott Charles *physicist, educator*
Little, William Arthur *physicist, educator*
McConnell, Harden Marsden *biophysical chemistry researcher, chemistry educator*
Osheroff, Douglas Dean *physicist, researcher*
Pecora, Robert *chemistry educator*
Perl, Martin Lewis *physicist, educator*
Petrosian, Vahé *astrophysicist, educator*
Richter, Burton *physicist, educator*
Ross, John *physical chemist, educator*
Sa, Luiz Augusto Discher *physicist*
Schawlow, Arthur Leonard *physicist, educator*
Schneider, Stephen Henry *climatologist, environmental policy analyst, researcher*
Shaw, Herbert John *physics educator emeritus*
Spicer, William Edward, III *physicist, educator*
Taube, Henry *chemistry educator*
Taylor, Richard Edward *physicist, educator*
Teller, Edward *physicist*
Thompson, George Albert *geophysics educator*
Trost, Barry Martin *chemist, educator*
Wagoner, Robert Vernon *astrophysicist, educator*
Walt, Martin *physicist, consulting educator*
Wender, Paul Anthony *chemistry educator*
Wojcicki, Stanley George *physicist, educator*
Yearian, Mason Russell *physicist*
Zare, Richard Neil *chemistry educator*

### Stockton
Whiteker, Roy Archie *retired chemistry educator*

### Sunnyvale
DeMello, Austin Eastwood *astrophysicist, concert artist, poet, writer*
Thissell, James Dennis *physicist*

### Tarzana
Meyers, Robert Allen *physical chemist, publisher*

### Thousand Oaks
Sherman, Gerald *nuclear physicist, financial estate adviser, financial company executive*
Wang, I-Tung *atmospheric scientist*

### Torrance
Manasson, Vladimir Alexandrovich *physicist*
Rogers, Howard H. *chemist*

### Walnut Creek
Kieffer, William Franklinn *chemistry educator*
Speziale, A. John *organic chemist, consultant*

### Woodland Hills
Sharma, Brahama D. *chemistry educator*

### Woodside
Ashley, Holt *aerospace scientist, educator*

## COLORADO

### Arvada
Knight, William V. *geologist*

### Aspen
Pullen, Margaret I. *genetic physicist*

### Boulder
Albritton, Daniel Lee *atmospheric scientist*
Alldredge, Leroy Romney *retired geophysicist*
Bailey, Dana Kavanagh *radiophysicist, botanist*
Baker, Daniel Neil *physicist*
Bartlett, David Farnham *physics educator*
Begelman, Mitchell Craig *astrophysicist, educator*
Behrendt, John Charles *research geophysicist*
Brown, Jack D(elbert) *chemist, researcher*
Calvert, Jack George *atmospheric chemist, educator*
Cech, Thomas Robert *chemistry and biochemistry educator*
Chappell, Charles Franklin *meteorologist, consultant*
Conti, Peter Selby *astronomy educator*
Cristol, Stanley Jerome *chemistry educator*
DePuy, Charles Herbert *chemist, educator*
Dryer, Murray *physicist*
Fleming, Rex James *meteorologist*
Garstang, Roy Henry *astrophysicist, educator*
Hay, William Winn *natural history and geology educator, former museum director*
Hermann, Allen Max *physics educator*
Hildner, Ernest Gotthold, III *solar physicist, science administrator*
Hofmann, David John *atmospheric science researcher, educator*
Hogg, David Clarence *physicist*
Holzer, Thomas E. *physicist*
Joselyn, Jo Ann *space scientist*
Kellogg, William Welch *meteorologist*
King, Edward Louis *retired chemistry educator*
Kisslinger, Carl *geophysicist, educator*
Koch, Tad Harbison *chemistry educator, researcher*
Lally, Vincent Edward *atmospheric scientist*
Leone, Stephen Robert *chemical physicist, educator*
Lineberger, William Carl *chemistry educator*
Low, Boon Chye *physicist*
Mahanthappa, Kalyana Thipperudraiah *physicist, educator*
Malde, Harold Edwin *retired federal government geologist*
McCray, Richard Alan *astrophysicist, educator*
Norcross, David Warren *physicist, researcher*
Ostrovsky, Lev Aronovich *physicist, oceanographer, educator*
Pankove, Jacques Isaac *physicist*
Peterson, Roy Jerome *physics educator*
Phelps, Arthur Van Rensselaer *physicist, consultant*
Robinson, Peter *paleontology educator, consultant*
Roellig, Leonard Oscar *physics educator*
Schneider, Nicholas McCord *planetary scientist, educator*
Smythe, William Rodman *physicist, educator*
Snow, Theodore Peck *astrophysics educator*
Speiser, Theodore Wesley *astrophysics, planetary and atmospheric sciences educator*
Tatarskii, Valerian Il'Ich *physics researcher*
Tolbert, Bert Mills *biochemist, educator*
Trenberth, Kevin Edward *atmospheric scientist*
Washington, Warren Morton *meteorologist*
Whiteside, Lowell Stanley *seismologist*
Wieman, Carl E. *physics educator*

### Canon City
Fair, Annie May *geological computer specialist*

### Colorado Springs
Hoffman, John Raleigh *physicist*
Rogers, Steven Ray *physicist*
Schwartz, Donald *chemistry educator*

### Denver
Boudreau, Robert Donald *meteorology educator*
Chappell, Willard Ray *physics educator, environmental scientist*
Cobban, William Aubrey *paleontologist*
Eaton, Gareth Richard *chemistry educator, university dean*
Foster, Norman Holland *geologist*
Hetzel, Fredrick William *biophysicist, educator*
Iona, Mario *retired physics educator*
Klipping, Robert Samuel *geophysicist*
Landon, Susan Melinda *petroleum geologist*
Miller, Stanley Custer, Jr. *physicist, retired educator*
Mullineaux, Donal Ray *geologist*
Neumann, Herschel *physics educator*
Pakiser, Louis Charles, Jr. *geophysicist*
Quinn, John Michael *physicist, geophysicist*
Selbin, Joel *chemistry educator*
Smith, Dwight Morrell *chemistry educator*
Weihaupt, John George *geosciences educator, scientist, university administrator*

### Englewood
Brown, Steven Harry *corporation health physicist, consultant*
Rosich, Rayner Karl *physicist*

### Evergreen
Haun, John Daniel *petroleum geologist, educator*
Phillips, Adran Abner (Abe Phillips) *geologist, oil and gas exploration consultant*

### Fort Collins
Bamburg, James Robert *biochemistry educator*
Bernstein, Elliot Roy *chemistry educator*
Curthoys, Norman P. *biochemistry educator, consultant*
Elkind, Mortimer Murray *biophysicist, educator*
Fixman, Marshall *chemist, educator*
Johnson, Robert Britten *geology educator*
Ladanyi, Branka Maria *chemist, educator*
Meyers, Albert Irving *chemistry educator*
Mosier, Arvin Ray *chemist, researcher*
Patton, Carl Elliott *physics educator*
Runnells, Donald DeMar *geochemist, consultant*
Saysette, Janice Elaine *vertebrate paleontologist, zoo archaeologist*
Schumm, Stanley Alfred *geologist, educator*

### Golden
Grose, Thomas Lucius Trowbridge *geologist, educator*
Hamilton, Warren Bell *research geologist, educator*
Hutchinson, Richard William *geology educator, consultant*
Kennedy, George Hunt *chemistry educator*
Kotch, Alex *chemistry educator*
Krauss, George *metallurgist*
Morrison, Roger Barron *geologist*
Sims, Paul Kibler *geologist*
Tilton, John Elvin *mineral economics educator*
Weimer, Robert Jay *geology educator, energy consultant, civic leader*
White, James Edward *geophysicist*

### Grand Junction
Rutz, Richard Frederick *physicist, researcher*

### Lafayette
McNeill, William *environmental scientist*

### Lakewood
Parker, John Marchbank *consulting geologist*

### Littleton
Choquette, Philip Wheeler *geologist, educator*
Sjolander, Gary Walfred *physicist*

### Louisville
Brault, James William *physicist*

### Monument
Henrickson, Eiler Leonard *retired geologist, educator*

### Nathrop
Ebel, Marvin Emerson *physicist,educator*

### Ridgway
Lathrop, Kaye Don *nuclear scientist, educator*

### Silverthorne
Ponder, Herman *geologist*

### Snowmass
Lovins, Amory Bloch *physicist, energy consultant*

## CONNECTICUT

### Avon
Goodson, Richard Carle, Jr. *chemist, hazardous waste management consultant*

### Bridgeport
Chih, Chung-Ying *physicist, consultant*
Ettre, Leslie Stephen *chemist*
Reed, Charles Eli *retired chemist, chemical engineer*

### Brookfield
Schetky, Laurence McDonald *metallurgist, researcher*

### Danbury
Joyce, William H. *chemist*

### East Hartford
Chao, Yong-Sheng *physicist*

### Farmington
Herbette, Leo Gerard *biophysics educator*
Osborn, Mary Jane Merten *biochemist*
Spencer, Richard Paul *biochemist, educator, physician*

### Greenwich
Heath, Gloria Whitton *aerospace scientist, consultant*

### Groton
Pinson, Ellis Rex, Jr. *chemist, consultant*
Sinko, Christopher Michael *pharmaceutical scientist*
Swindell, Archie Calhoun, Jr. *research biochemist, statistician*

### Hartford
Church, William Handy *chemistry educator*
Kung, Pang-Jen *materials scientist, electrical engineer*

### Litchfield
Cox, Robert Hames *chemist, scientific consultant*

### Manchester
Galasso, Francis Salvatore *materials scientist*

### Middletown
Beveridge, David Lewis *chemistry educator*
Fry, Albert Joseph *chemistry educator*
Haake, Paul *chemistry and biochemistry educator*
Sease, John W(illiam) *chemistry educator*
Upgren, Arthur Reinhold, Jr. *astronomer, educator, outdoor lighting consultant*

### Mystic
Chiang, Albert Chinfa *polymer chemist*

PROFESSIONAL INDEX 5417 SCIENCE: PHYSICAL SCIENCE


**New Britain**
Baskerville, Charles Alexander *geologist, educator*
Dimmick, Charles William *geology educator*

**New Haven**
Aylor, Donald Earl *biophysicist, research meteorologist, plant pathology educator and reseacher*
Bennett, William Ralph, Jr. *physicist, educator*
Berner, Robert Arbuckle *geochemist, educator*
Berson, Jerome Abraham *chemistry educator*
Bromley, David Allan *physicist, engineer, educator*
Brünger, Axel Thomas *biophysicist, researcher, educator*
Casten, Richard Francis *physicist*
Chang, Richard Kounai *physics educator*
Chupka, William Andrew *chemical physicist, educator*
Coleman, Joseph Emory *biophysics and biochemistry educator*
Crothers, Donald Morris *biochemist, educator*
Gordon, Robert Boyd *geophysics educator*
Graedel, Thomas Eldon *chemist, researcher*
Handschumacher, Robert Edmund *biochemistry educator*
Herzenberg, Arvid *physicist, educator*
Hoffleit, Ellen Dorrit *astronomer*
Hohenberg, Pierre Claude *research physicist*
Jorgensen, William L. *chemistry educator*
Klein, Martin Jesse *physicist, educator, science historian*
Mac Dowell, Samuel Wallace *physics educator*
Marchesi, Vincent T. *biochemist, educator*
Moore, Peter Bartlett *biochemist, educator*
Ostrom, John H. *vertebrate paleontologist, educator, museum curator*
Reifsnyder, William Edward *meteorologist*
Richards, Frederic Middlebrook *biochemist, educator*
Rodgers, John *geologist, educator*
Saltzman, Barry *meteorologist, educator*
Shulman, Robert Gerson *biophysics educator*
Skinner, Helen Catherine Wild *biomineralogist*
Slayman, Clifford Leroy *biophysicist, educator*
Sofia, Sabatino *astronomy educator*
Steitz, Joan Argetsinger *biochemistry educator*
Tully, John Charles *research chemical physicist*
Turekian, Karl Karekin *geochemistry educator*
Wolf, Werner Paul *physicist, educator*
Zeller, Michael Edward *physicist, educator*
Zinn, Robert James *astronomer, educator*

**New Milford**
Fabricand, Burton Paul *physicist, educator*

**Newtown**
Bockelman, Charles Kincaid *physics educator*

**Plainfield**
Baranowski, Paul Joseph *instrumentation technician*

**Redding**
Foster, Edward John *engineering physicist*

**Ridgefield**
Farina, Peter R. *biochemist*

**Rocky Hill**
Chu, Hsien-Kun *chemist, researcher*
Griesé, John William, III *astronomer*

**Shelton**
Zeller, Claude *physicist, researcher*

**Southington**
Barry, Richard William *chemist, consultant*

**Stamford**
Ge, Wen-Zheng *materials scientist*
Hagner, Arthur Feodor *geologist, educator*
Porosoff, Harold *chemist, research and development director*

**Stonington**
Mantz, Arlan W. *physics educator*

**Storrs Mansfield**
Azaroff, Leonid Vladimirovitch *physics educator*
Bartram, Ralph Herbert *physicist*
Bobbitt, James McCue *chemist*
Devereux, Owen Francis *metallurgy educator*
Klemens, Paul Gustav *physicist, educator*
Schuster, Todd Mervyn *biophysics educator, biotechnology company executive*
Stwalley, William Calvin *physics and chemistry educator*

**West Hartland**
Perkins, Bob(by) F(rank) *geologist, dean*

**West Haven**
Yoshizumi, Terry Takatoshi *medical physicist*

**Wilton**
Simpson, W(ilburn) Dwain *physicist, corporate executive, computer systems, telecommunications, and advanced fueling systems consultant*

**Woodbury**
Skinner, Brian John *geologist, educator*


## DELAWARE


**Dover**
Wasfi, Sadiq Hassan *chemistry educator*

**Greenville**
Levitt, George *retired chemist*

**Hockessin**
Crippen, Raymond C. *chemist, consultant*

**New Castle**
Bellenger, George Collier, Jr. *physics educator*

**Newark**
Böer, Karl Wolfgang *physicist, educator*
Burmeister, John Luther *chemistry educator*
Daniels, William Burton *physicist, educator*
Evans, Dennis Hyde *chemist, educator*
Evenson, Paul Arthur *physics educator*
Hossain, Murshed *physicist*
Hutton, David Glenn *environmental scientist, consultant, chemical engineer*
Jordan, Robert Reed *geologist, educator*
Kasprzak, Lucian Alexander *physicist, researcher*
Mather, John Russell *climatologist, educator*
Murray, Richard Bennett *physics educator*
Ness, Norman Frederick *astrophysicist, educator, administrator*
Wetlaufer, Donald Burton *biochemist, educator*

**Newport**
Kirkland, Joseph J. *research chemist*

**Wilmington**
Crittenden, Eugene Dwight, Jr. *chemical company executive*
Jacobson, Howard W. *chemist*
Jezl, Barbara Ann *chemist, automation consultant*
Kissa, Erik *retired chemist, consultant*
Kwolek, Stephanie Louise *chemist*
Moore, Carl Gordon *chemist, educator*
Parshall, George William *research chemist*
Smook, Malcolm Andrew *chemist, chemical company executive*
Webster, Owen Wright *chemist*


## DISTRICT OF COLUMBIA


**Washington**
Abelson, Philip Hauge *physicist*
Alexander, Joseph Kunkle, Jr. *physicist*
Baldwin, Sheryl Denise *chemist, writer, editor*
Bednarek, Jana Maria *biochemist*
Bennett, Gary Lee *physicist, consultant*
Berendzen, Richard *astronomer, educator, author*
Bierly, Eugene Wendell *meteorologist, science administrator*
Boss, Alan Paul *astrophysicist*
Brown, Louis *physicist, researcher*
†Callahan, Debra Jean *environmental organization executive*
Chapman, Kenneth Maynard *chemical technology educator*
Chubb, Talbot Albert *physicist*
Coffey, Timothy *physicist, think-tank executive*
Crandall, David Hugh *physicist*
Creech, Denise Latnia *chemical educator, administrator*
Darby, Joseph Branch, Jr. *metallurgist, government official*
Davidson, Eugene Abraham *biochemist, university administrator*
Devine, Katherine *environmental consultant, educator*
Donohue, Joyce Morrissey *biochemist, toxicologist, nutritionist, educator*
Dusold, Laurence Richard *chemist, computer specialist*
Dutro, John Thomas, Jr. *geologist, paleontologist*
Eghbal, Morad *geologist, lawyer*
El Khadem, Hassan Saad *chemistry educator, researcher*
Fainberg, Anthony *physicist*
Firestone, David *chemist*
Fleischer, Michael *chemist*
Fogleman, Guy Carroll *physicist, mathematician, educator*
Galloway, Eilene Marie *space and astronautics consultant*
Garavelli, John Stephen *biochemistry research scientist*
Goldstein, Allan Leonard *biochemist, educator*
Hallgren, Richard Edwin *meteorologist*
Harrison, Edward Thomas, Jr. *retired chemist*
Harwit, Martin Otto *astrophysicist, writer, educator, museum director*
Heineman, Heinz *chemist*
Heinemann, Heinz *chemist, educator, researcher, consultant*
Holland, Christie Anna *biochemist, virologist*
Holloway, John Thomas *physicist*
Imam, M. Ashraf *materials scientist, educator*
Johnston, Kenneth John *astronomer, scientific director naval observatory*
Karle, Jerome *physicist, researcher*
Kier, Porter Martin *paleontologist*
Knopman, Debra Sara *hydrologist, policy analyst*
Kouts, Herbert John Cecil *physicist*
Krebs, Martha *physicist, federal agency administrator*
Ledley, Robert Steven *biophysicist*
Lehmberg, Robert Henry *research physicist*
Leibowitz, Jack Richard *physicist, educator*
Lintz, Paul Rodgers *physicist, engineer, patent examiner*
Lozansky, Edward Dmitry *physicist, author, consultant*
Mandula, Jeffrey Ellis *physicist*
Mason, Brian Harold *geologist, curator*
Maynard, Nancy Gray *biological oceanographer*
McDonald, Bryant Edward *physicist, oceanographer*
Mead, Gilbert D(unbar) *geophysicist, lawyer*
Meijer, Paul Herman Ernst *educator, physicist*
Mielke, James Edward *geochemist*
Nelson, George Driver *astronomy and education educator, former astronaut*
O'Connor, Thomas Edward *petroleum geologist, world bank officer*
Oertel, Goetz K. H. *physicist, professional association administrator*
Oliver, William Albert, Jr. *paleontologist*
Oran, Elaine Surick *physicist*
Perros, Theodore Peter *chemist, educator*
Pojeta, John, Jr. *geologist*
Pope, Michael Thor *chemist*
Press, Frank *geophysicist, educator*
Prewitt, Charles Thompson *geochemist*
Rittner, Edmund Sidney *physicist*
Romanowski, Thomas Andrew *physics educator*
Roscher, Nina Matheny *chemistry educator*
Rosenberg, Jerome David *physicist*
Rosenberg, Norman Jack *agricultural meteorologist, educator*
Scott, Raymond Peter William *chemistry research educator, writer*
Siegel, Frederic Richard *geology educator*
Singer, Maxine Frank *biochemist, think tank executive*
Soderberg, David Lawrence *chemist*
Solomon, Sean Carl *geophysicist, lab administrator*
†Spilhaus, Athelstan Frederick, Jr. *oceanographer, association executive*
Stanley, Daniel Jean *geological oceanographer, senior scientist*
Uberall, Herbert Michael Stefan *physicist, educator*
Villforth, John Carl *health physicist*
Wallace, Jane House *geologist*
Watters, Thomas Robert *geologist, museum administrator*
Weiler, Kurt Walter *radio astronomer*
Werntz, Carl Weber *physics educator*
Wetherill, George West *geophysicist, planetary scientist*
White, John Arnold *physics educator, research scientist*
White, Robert Mayer *meteorologist*
Whitmore, Frank Clifford, Jr. *geologist*
Wilson, William Stanley *oceanographer*
Yochelson, Ellis L(eon) *paleontologist*
Yoder, Hatten Schuyler, Jr. *petrologist*
Youtcheff, John Sheldon *physicist*


## FLORIDA


**Alachua**
Schneider, Richard T(heodore) *optics research executive, engineer*

**Boca Raton**
Carraher, Charles Eugene, Jr. *chemistry educator, university administrator*
Finkl, Charles William, II *geologist, educator*
Nanz, Robert Augustus *biochemist*
Resnick, Robert *physicist, educator*
Ross, Fred Michael *organic chemist*
Weissbach, Herbert *biochemist*
Wiesenfeld, John Richard *chemistry educator*

**Boynton Beach**
Balis, Moses Earl *biochemist, educator*
Fields, Theodore *consulting medical radiation physicist*
Zarwyn, Berthold *physical scientist*

**Cape Coral**
West, John Merle *retired physicist, nuclear consultant*

**Cocoa**
Hutton, Michael Thomas *planetarium and observatory administrator*

**Coconut Creek**
Cazes, Jack *chemist, marketing consultant, editor*

**Coral Gables**
Criss, Cecil M. *chemistry educator*
Einspruch, Norman Gerald *physicist, educator*
Leblanc, Roger Maurice *chemistry educator*

**Dade City**
Burdick, Glenn Arthur *physicist, engineering educator*

**Dania**
Dodge, Richard Eugene *oceanographer, educator, marine life administrator*

**Deerfield Beach**
Treibl, Hans George *industrial chemist*

**Deland**
Coolidge, Edwin Channing *chemistry educator*

**Delray Beach**
Shang, Charles Yulin *medical physicist*

**Fort Lauderdale**
Zikakis, John P. *consultant, educator, researcher, biochemist*

**Fort Myers**
Missimer, Thomas Michael *geologist*

**Fort Pierce**
Solon, Leonard R(aymond) *physicist, educator, consultant*

**Gainesville**
Andrew, Edward Raymond *physicist*
Bodor, Nicholas Stephen *medicinal chemistry researcher, educator, consultant*
Carr, Thomas Deaderick *astronomer/physics educator, science administrator*
Cousins, Robert John *nutritional biochemist, educator*
Davis, George Kelso *nutrition biochemist, educator*
Dewar, Michael James Steuart *chemistry educator*
Drago, Russell Stephen *chemist, educator*
Eichhorn, Heinrich Karl *astronomer, educator, consultant*
Ernsberger, Fred Martin *retired materials scientist*
Gander, John Edward *biochemistry educator*
Hanrahan, Robert Joseph *chemist, educator*
Hanson, Harold Palmer *physicist, government official, editor, academic administrator*
Harrison, Willard W. *chemist, educator*
Holloway, Paul Howard *materials science educator*
Hope, George Marion *vision scientist*
Jacobs, Alan Martin *physicist, educator*
Katritzky, Alan Roy *chemistry educator, consultant*
Klauder, John Rider *physics educator*
Merdinger, Emanuel *retired chemistry educator*
Micha, David Allan *chemistry and physics educator*
Ohrn, Nils Yngve *chemistry and physics educator*
Park, Robert McIlwraith *science and engineering educator*
Person, Willis Bagley *chemistry educator*
Sisler, Harry Hall *chemist, educator*
Smith, Alexander Goudy *physics and astronomy educator*
Stehli, Francis Greenough *geologist, educator*
Sullivan, Neil Samuel *physicist, researcher, educator*
Young, David Michael *biochemistry and molecular biology educator, physician*
Zerner, Michael Charles *chemistry and physics educator, consultant, researcher*

**Gonzalez**
Plischke, Le Moyne Wilfred *research chemist*

**Hialeah**
Stewart, Burch Byron *chemist, physicist*

**Jacksonville**
Beattie, Donald A. *energy scientist, consultant*
Enns, John Benjamin *polymer scientist*
Huebner, Jay Stanley *physicist, engineer, forensics consultant*

**Jupiter**
Jacobson, Jerry Irving *biophysicist, theoretical physicist*

**Key West**
Trammell, Herbert Eugene *physicist, laboratory executive*

**Lake Alfred**
Nagy, Steven *biochemist*

**Lakeland**
McFarlin, Richard Francis *industrial chemist, researcher*

**Longboat Key**
Stapleton, Harvey James *physics educator*

**Lutz**
Castle, Raymond Nielson *chemist, educator*

**Margate**
Chastain, David Lee, Jr. *organic chemist*

**Melbourne**
Babich, Michael Wayne *chemistry educator, educational administrator*
Button, Kenneth John *physicist*
Nelson, Gordon Leigh *chemist, educator*

**Miami**
Blanco, Luciano-Nilo *physicist*
Carter, James Harrison *chemist, research director*
Corcoran, Eugene Francis *chemist, educator*
Dammann, William Paul *oceanographer*
Donelan, Mark Anthony *physicist*
Fine, Rana Arnold *chemical, physical oceanographer*
Man, Eugene Herbert *chemist, educator, business executive*
Mooers, Christopher Northrup Kennard *physical oceanographer, educator*
Ostlund, H. Gote *atmospheric and marine scientist, educator*
Precht, William Frederick *environmental specialist*
Rosenthal, Stanley Lawrence *meteorologist*
Van Vliet, Carolyne Marina *physicist, educator*
Wells, Daniel Ruth *physics educator*

**Naples**
Ancker-Johnson, Betsy *physicist, engineer, retired automotive company executive*
Leitner, Alfred *mathematical physicist, educator, educational film producer*
Stewart, Harris Bates, Jr. *oceanographer*

**Ocala**
Forgue, Stanley Vincent *physics educator*
Fredericks, William John *chemistry educator*

**Orange Park**
Walsh, Gregory Sheehan *optical systems professional*

**Orlando**
Baker, Peter Mitchell *laser scientist and executive, educator*
Barlow, Nadine Gail *planetary geoscientist*
Blue, Joseph Edward *physicist*
Llewellyn, Ralph Alvin *physics educator*
Silfvast, William T. *laser physics educator, consultant*
Ting, Robert Yen-ying *physicist*

**Palmetto**
Compton, Charles Daniel *chemistry educator*

**Panama City Beach**
Shugart, Cecil Glenn *retired physics educator*

**Saint Petersburg**
Hallock-Muller, Pamela *oceanography educator, biogeologist, researcher*
Hansel, Paul George *physicist, consultant*
Rydstrom, Carlton Lionel *chemist, paint and coating consultant*

**Sanford**
Dickison, Alexander Kane *physical science educator*

**Sanibel**
Herriott, Donald Richard *optical physicist*
Horecker, Bernard Leonard *retired biochemistry educator*

**Sarasota**
Kerker, Milton *chemistry educator*
Myerson, Albert Leon *physical chemist*
Wysnewski, Roy Edward *physicist*

**Sun City Center**
Calviello, Joseph Anthony *research electrophysicist, consultant*

**Tallahassee**
Caspar, Donald Louis Dvorak *biophysics and structural biology educator*
Choppin, Gregory Robert *chemistry educator*
Clarke, Allan J. *oceanography educator, consultant*
Crow, Jack E. *physics administrator*
Herndon, Roy Clifford *physicist*
Johnsen, Russell Harold *chemist, educator*
Kemper, Kirby Wayne *physics educator*
Mandelkern, Leo *biophysics and chemistry educator*
Marshall, Alan George *chemistry and biochemistry educator*
Moulton, Grace Charbonnet *physics educator*
Owens, Joseph Francis, III *physics educator*
Pfeffer, Richard Lawrence *geophysics educator*
Robson, Donald *physics educator*
Schrieffer, John Robert *physics educator, science administrator*
Walborsky, Harry M. *chemistry educator, consultant*

### Tampa
Binford, Jesse Stone, Jr. *chemistry educator*
DeMontier, Paulette LaPointe *chemist*
Johnson, Anthony O'Leary (Andy Johnson) *meteorologist, consultant*
Zhou, Huanchun *chemist, administrator*

### Venice
Leidheiser, Henry, Jr. *retired chemistry educator, consultant*

### Vero Beach
Hungerford, Lugene Green *physicist*

## GEORGIA

### Albany
McManus, James William *chemist, researcher*

### Alpharetta
Barr, John Baldwin *chemist, research scientist*
Hung, William Mo-Wei *chemist*

### Alto
Mosavi, Reza Khonsari *laser physicist*

### Athens
Allinger, Norman Louis *chemistry educator*
Black, Clanton Candler, Jr. *biochemistry educator, researcher*
Darvill, Alan G. *biochemist, botanist, educator*
DerVartanian, Daniel Vartan *biochemistry educator*
Eriksson, Karl-Erik Lennart *biochemist, educator*
Johnson, Michael Kenneth *chemistry educator*
King, Robert Bruce *chemistry educator, writer*
Landau, David Paul *physics educator*
Melton, Charles Estel *retired physicist, educator*
Pelletier, S. William *chemistry educator*
Schaefer, Henry Frederick, III *chemistry educator*
Shaw, James Scott *astronomy research administrator*
Yamaguchi, Yukio *chemistry research scientist*
Yen, William Mao-Shung *physicist*

### Atlanta
Ashby, Eugene Christopher *chemistry educator*
Bosah, Francis N. *molecular biochemist, educator*
Copeland, John Alexander, III *physicist*
Cramer, Howard Ross *geologist, environmental consultant*
Dennison, Daniel Bassel *chemist*
Finkelstein, David Ritz *physicist, educator, consultant*
Fox, Ronald Forrest *physics educator*
Goldstein, Jacob Herman *retired physical chemist*
Hicks, Heraline Elaine *environmental health scientist, educator*
Iacobucci, Guillermo Arturo *chemist*
Johnson, Ronald Carl *chemistry educator*
Kahn, Bernd *radiochemist, educator*
Lin, Ming-Chang *physical chemistry educator, researcher*
Long, Maurice Wayne *physicist, electrical engineer, radar consultant*
Massey, Walter Eugene *physicist, science foundation administrator*
McCormick, Donald Bruce *biochemist, educator*
Moran, Thomas Francis *chemistry educator*
Perkowitz, Sidney *physicist, educator, author*
Stafford, Patrick Morgan *biophysicist*
Strekowski, Lucjan *chemistry educator*
Wartell, Roger Martin *biophysics educator*
Wiesenfeld, Kurt Arn *physicist, educator*
Wong, Ching-Ping *chemist, materials scientist, engineer, educator*

### Decatur
Sadun, Alberto Carlo *astrophysicist, physics educator*

### Marietta
Bridges, Alan Lynn *physicist, computer scientist, systems software engineer*

### Peachtree City
Roobol, Norman Richard *industrial painting consultant, educator*

### Riverdale
Awachie, Peter Ifeacho Anazoba *chemistry educator, research chemist*

### Roswell
Wang, Dehua *chemist*

### Savannah
Su, Helen Chien-fan *research chemist*
Walter, Paul Hermann Lawrence *chemistry educator*
Windom, Herbert Lynn *oceanographer, environmental scientist*

### Tucker
Valk, Henry Snowden *physicist, educator*

## HAWAII

### Hawaii National Park
Swanson, Donald Alan *geologist*

### Hilo
Griep, David Michael *astronomical scientist, researcher*
Schnell, Russell Clifford *atmospheric scientist, researcher*

### Honolulu
Brantley, Lee Reed *chemistry educator*
Chambers, Kenneth Carter *astronomer*
Hall, Donald Norman Blake *astronomer*
Hawke, Bernard Ray *planetary scientist*
Herbig, George Howard *astronomer, educator*
Ihrig, Judson La Moure *chemist*
Joseph, Robert David *astronomer, educator*
Keil, Klaus *geology educator, consultant*
Khan, Mohammad Asad *geophysicist, educator, former energy minister and senator of Pakistan*
Kong, Laura S. L. *geophysicist*
Learned, John Gregory *physicist*
Mader, Charles Lavern *chemist*
Meech, Karen Jean *astronomer*
Ogburn, Hugh Bell *chemical engineer, consultant*
Raleigh, Cecil Baring *geophysicist*
Scheuer, Paul Josef *chemistry educator*
Sharma, Shiv Kumar *geophysicist*
Wyrtki, Klaus *oceanography educator*
Yount, David Eugene *physicist, educator*

## IDAHO

### Idaho Falls
Reich, Charles William *nuclear physicist*

### Moscow
Bitterwolf, Thomas Edwin *chemistry educator*
LeTourneau, Duane John *biochemist, educator*
Miller, Maynard Malcolm *geologist, educator, research institute director, explorer, state legislator*
Renfrew, Malcolm MacKenzie *chemist, educator*
Shreeve, Jean'ne Marie *chemist, educator*
Stumpf, Bernhard Josef *physicist*

## ILLINOIS

### Abbott Park
Jeng, Tzyy-Wen *biochemist*

### Argonne
Berger, Edmond Louis *theoretical physicist*
Blander, Milton *chemist*
Carpenter, John Marland *engineer, physicist*
Derrick, Malcolm *physicist*
Ferraro, John Ralph *chemist*
Fields, Paul Robert *research nuclear chemist, consultant*
Green, David William *chemist, educator*
Herzenberg, Caroline Stuart Littlejohn *physicist*
Katz, Joseph Jacob *chemist, educator*
Lawson, Robert Davis *theoretical nuclear physicist*
Morss, Lester Robert *chemist*
Nolen, Jerry Aften, Jr. *physicist*
Perlow, Gilbert J(erome) *physicist, editor*
Peshkin, Murray *physicist*
Schiffer, John Paul *physicist*
Steindler, Martin Joseph *chemist*
Stock, Leon Milo *chemist, educator*

### Arlington Heights
Lewin, Seymour Zalman *chemistry educator, consultant*

### Batavia
Bardeen, William Allan *research physicist*
Chrisman, Bruce Lowell *physicist, administrator*
Jonckheere, Alan Mathew *physicist*
Lach, Joseph Theodore *physicist*
Tollestrup, Alvin Virgil *physicist*

### Brookfield
Stejskal, Joseph Frank, Jr. *carbohydrate chemist*

### Carbondale
Tao, Rongjia *physicist, educator*
Wotiz, John Henry *chemist, educator*

### Champaign
Balbach, Harold Edward *environmental scientist*
Buschbach, Thomas Charles *geologist, consultant*
Cartwright, Keros *hydrogeologist, researcher*
Gross, David Lee *geologist*
Herzog, Beverly Leah *hydrogeologist*
Simmons, Ralph Oliver *physics educator*
Slichter, Charles Pence *physicist, educator*
Wolfram, Stephen *physicist, computer company executive*

### Chicago
Anderson, Louise Eleanor *biochemistry educator*
Barany, Kate *biophysics educator*
Blumberg, Avrom Aaron *physical chemistry educator*
Bonham, Russell Aubrey *chemistry educator*
Brown, Charles Eric *biochemistry educator, analytical instrumentation consultant, petrochemical analytical researcher*
Charlier, Roger Henri *oceanographer, geographer, educator*
Clayton, Robert Norman *chemist, educator*
Coppersmith, Susan Nan *physicist*
Cronin, James Watson *physicist, educator*
Epstein, Wolfgang *biochemist, educator*
Erber, Thomas *physics educator*
Evans, Earl Alison, Jr. *biochemist*
Fano, Ugo *physicist, educator*
Fanta, Paul Edward *chemist, educator*
Fleming, Graham Richard *chemistry educator*
Freed, Karl Frederick *chemistry educator*
Fried, Josef *chemist, educator*
Frisch, Henry Jonathan *physics educator*
Fultz, Dave *meteorology educator*
Gislason, Eric Arni *chemistry educator*
Goldsmith, Julian Royce *geochemist, educator*
Goldwasser, Eugene *biochemist, educator*
Gomer, Robert *chemistry educator*
Halpern, Jack *chemist, educator*
Harvey, Ronald Gilbert *research chemist*
Hildebrand, Roger Henry *astrophysicist, physicist*
Huston, John Lewis *chemistry educator*
Iqbal, Zafar Mohd *cancer researcher, biochemist, pharmacologist, toxicologist, consultant, molecular biologist*
Jain, Nemi Chand *chemist, coating scientist, educator*
Kadanoff, Leo Philip *physicist*
Kleppa, Ole J. *chemistry educator*
Kouvel, James Spyros *physicist, educator*
Krawetz, Arthur Altshuler *chemist, science administrator*
Lanzl, Lawrence Herman *medical physicist*
Lederman, Leon Max *physicist, educator*
Lehman, Dennis Dale *chemistry educator*
†Levi-Setti, Riccardo *physicist, director*
Levy, Donald Harris *chemistry educator*
Liao, Shutsung *biochemist, oncologist*
Light, John Caldwell *chemistry educator*
Makinen, Marvin William *biophysicist, educator*
Margoliash, Emanuel *biochemist, educator*
Mintzer, David *physics educator*
Nagel, Sidney Robert *physics educator*
Nambu, Yoichiro *physics educator*
Oehme, Reinhard *physicist, educator*
Oka, Takeshi *physicist, chemist, astronomer, educator*
Olsen, Edward John *geologist, educator*
Oxtoby, David William *chemistry educator*
Palmer, Patrick Edward *radio astronomer, educator*
Platzman, George William *geophysicist, educator*
Rafelson, Max Emanuel, Jr. *biochemist, medical school administrator*
Reiffel, Leonard *physicist, scientific consultant*
Rosner, Jonathan Lincoln *physicist, educator*
Rosner, Robert *astrophysicist*
Sachs, Robert Green *physicist, educator, laboratory administrator*
Sager, William F. *retired chemistry educator*
Sawinski, Vincent John *chemistry educator*
Scherer, Norbert Franz *chemistry educator*
Schillinger, Edwin Joseph *physics educator*
Schramm, David Norman *astrophysicist, educator*
Schug, Kenneth Robert *chemistry educator*
Simpson, John Alexander *physicist*
Skilling, Thomas Ethelbert, III *meteorologist, meteorology educator*
Steck, Theodore Lyle *biochemistry and molecular biology educator, physician*
Steiner, Donald Frederick *biochemist, physician, educator*
Truran, James Wellington, Jr. *astrophysicist*
Turkevich, Anthony Leonid *chemist, educator*
Turner, Michael Stanley *physics educator*
Williams-Ashman, Howard Guy *biochemistry educator*
Winston, Roland *physicist, educator*
York, Donald Gilbert *astronomy educator, researcher*
Zhao, Meishan *chemical physics educator, researcher*

### De Kalb
Kevill, Dennis Neil *chemistry educator*
Kimball, Clyde William *physicist, educator*
Rossing, Thomas D. *physics educator*

### Downers Grove
Hubbard, Lincoln Beals *retired medical physicist, consultant*

### Evanston
Allred, Albert Louis *chemistry educator*
Basolo, Fred *chemistry educator*
Bordwell, Frederick George *chemistry educator*
Brown, Laurie Mark *physicist, educator*
Burwell, Robert Lemmon, Jr. *chemist, educator*
Cohen, Jerome Bernard *materials science educator*
Freeman, Arthur J. *physics educator*
Ibers, James Arthur *chemist, educator*
Johnson, David Lynn *materials scientist, educator*
Ketterson, John Boyd *physics educator*
Klotz, Irving Myron *chemist, educator*
Lambert, Joseph Buckley *chemistry educator*
Letsinger, Robert Lewis *chemistry educator*
Lippincott, James Andrew *biochemistry and biological sciences educator*
Meshii, Masahiro *materials science educator*
Oakes, Robert James *physics educator*
Olson, Gregory Bruce *materials science and engineering educator, academic director*
Poeppelmeier, Kenneth Reinhard *chemistry educator*
Pople, John Anthony *chemistry educator*
Ratner, Mark Alan *chemistry educator*
Sachtler, Wolfgang Max Hugo *chemistry educator*
Seidman, David N(athaniel) *materials science and engineering educator*
Shriver, Duward Felix *chemistry educator, researcher, consultant*
Silverman, Richard Bruce *chemist, biochemist, educator*
Spears, Kenneth George *chemistry educator*
Taam, Ronald Everett *physics and astronomy educator*
Ulmer, Melville Paul *physics and astronomy educator*
Van Duyne, Richard Palmer *analytical chemistry and chemical physics educator*
Vaynman, Semyon *materials scientist*
Weertman, Johannes *materials science educator*
Weertman, Julia Randall *materials science and engineering educator*
Wessels, Bruce W. *materials scientist, educator*

### Glen Ellyn
Mooring, F. Paul *physics editor*

### Glencoe
Grossweiner, Leonard Irwin *physicist, educator*

### Glenview
Rorig, Kurt Joachim *chemist, research director*
Savic, Stanley Dimitrius *physicist*

### Hinsdale
Kaminsky, Manfred Stephan *physicist*
Karplus, Henry Berthold *physicist, research engineer*

### Homewood
Parker, Eugene Newman *retired physicist, educator*

### Lake Bluff
Coutts, John Wallace *chemist, educator*

### Lake Forest
Walter, Robert Irving *chemistry educator, chemist*
Weston, Arthur Walter *chemist, scientific and business executive*

### Lemont
Tomkins, Frank Sargent *physicist*
Williams, Jack Marvin *research chemist*

### Lisle
Staab, Thomas Eugene *chemist*

### Marseilles
Van Horn, John Kenneth *health physicist, consultant*

### Mount Carmel
Fornoff, Frank J(unior) *retired chemistry educator, consultant*

### Naperville
Arzoumanidis, Gregory G. *chemist*
Copley, Stephen Michael *materials science and engineering educator*
Hensley, Albert Lloyd, Jr. *research chemist, technical consultant*
Rosenmann, Daniel *physicist, educator*
Sherren, Anne Terry *chemistry educator*

### Normal
Young, Robert Donald *physicist, educator*

### North Chicago
Loga, Sanda *physicist, educator*

### Northbrook
Colton, Frank Benjamin *retired chemist*

### Northfield
Shabica, Charles Wright *geologist, earth science educator*

### O'Fallon
Jenner, William Alexander *meteorologist, educator*

### Peoria
Chamberlain, Joseph Miles *retired astronomer, educator*
Cunningham, Raymond Leo *research chemist*
King, Jerry Wayne *research chemist*
Nielsen, Harald Christian *retired chemist*
Osborn, Terry Wayne *biochemist, executive*
†Saha, Badal Chandra *biochemist*

### Rock Island
Hammer, William Roy *paleontologist, educator*
Sundelius, Harold W. *geology educator*

### Rockford
Walhout, Justine Simon *chemistry educator*

### Round Lake
Breillatt, Julian Paul, Jr. *biochemist, biomedical engineer*

### Skokie
Filler, Robert *chemist educator*

### Springfield
Gallina, Charles Onofrio *nuclear scientist*

### Urbana
Aref, Hassan *fluid mechanics educator*
Beak, Peter Andrew *chemistry educator*
Birnbaum, Howard Kent *materials science educator*
Brown, Theodore Lawrence *chemistry educator*
Crofts, Antony Richard *biophysics educator*
Debrunner, Peter George *physics educator*
Drickamer, Harry George *retired chemistry educator*
Dunn, Floyd *biophysicist, bioengineer, educator*
Eades, J. A. *electron microscopist, physicist, consultant*
Faulkner, Larry Ray *chemistry educator, academic officer*
Forbes, Richard Mather *biochemistry educator*
Ginsberg, Donald Maurice *physicist, educator*
Goldwasser, Edwin Leo *physicist*
Govindjee *biophysics and biology educator*
Greene, Laura Helen *physicist*
Gruebele, Martin *chemistry educator*
Gutowsky, Herbert Sander *chemistry educator*
Hager, Lowell Paul *biochemistry educator*
Hay, Richard Le Roy *geology educator*
Iben, Icko, Jr. *astrophysicist, educator*
Jackson, Edwin Atlee *physicist, educator*
Kirkpatrick, R(obert) James *geology educator*
Klein, Miles Vincent *physics educator*
Kushner, Mark Jay *physicist educator*
Langenheim, Ralph Louis, Jr. *geology educator*
Lauterbur, Paul C(hristian) *chemistry educator*
Lazarus, David *physicist, educator*
Lo, Kwok-Yung *astronomer*
Makri, Nancy *chemistry educator*
Mapother, Dillon Edward *physicist, university official*
Mihalas, Dimitri Manuel *astronomer, educator*
Rowland, Theodore Justin *physicist, educator*
Salamon, Myron Ben *physicist, educator*
Satterthwaite, Cameron B. *physics educator*
Schweizer, Kenneth Steven *physics educator*
Simon, Jack Aaron *geologist, former state official*
Snyder, Lewis Emil *astrophysicist*
Suslick, Kenneth Sanders *chemistry educator*
Switzer, Robert Lee *biochemistry educator*
White, W(illiam) Arthur *geologist*
Wolynes, Peter Guy *chemistry researcher, educator*

### Wheaton
Wolfram, Thomas *physicist*

### Wilmette
Rocek, Jan *chemist, educator*

### Worth
Ammeraal, Robert Neal *biochemist*

## INDIANA

### Bloomington
Bair, Edward Jay *chemistry educator*
Bent, Robert Demo *physicist, educator*
Bundy, Wayne M. *retired geologist, consultant*
Cameron, John M. *nuclear scientist, educator, science administrator*
Campaigne, Ernest Edward *chemistry educator*
Chisholm, Malcolm Harold *chemistry educator*
Davidson, Ernest Roy *chemist, educator*
Day, Harry Gilbert *nutritional biochemist, consultant*
Edmondson, Frank Kelley *astronomer*
Goodman, Charles David *physicist, educator*
Grieco, Paul Anthony *chemistry educator*
Hattin, Donald Edward *geologist, educator*
Johnson, Hollis Ralph *astronomy educator*
Macfarlane, Malcolm Harris *physics educator*
Murray, Haydn Herbert *geology educator*
Parmenter, Charles Stedman *chemistry educator*
Peters, Dennis Gail *chemist*
Pollock, Robert Elwood *nuclear physicist*
Putnam, Frank William *biochemistry and immunology educator*
Roush, William R. *chemistry educator*
Schaich, William L. *physics educator*

Lijinsky, William *biochemist*

### Crofton
Watson, Robert Tanner *physical scientist*

### Dayton
Fischell, Robert Ellentuch *physicist*

### Derwood
Stadtman, Thressa Campbell *biochemist*

### Edgewood
Matthews, Jeffrey Alan *physicist*

### Fort Washington
Behrens, James William *physicist, administrator*

### Frederick
Carton, Robert John *environmental scientist*
Cragg, Gordon Mitchell *government chemist*
Garver, Robert Vernon *research physicist*
Ji, Xinhua *physical chemist, educator, crystallographer*
Kappe, David Syme *environmental chemist*
Press, Jeffery Bruce *chemist*
Smith, Sharron Williams *chemistry educator*

### Gaithersburg
Adams, James Michael *physicist*
Berger, Harold *physicist*
Cahn, John Werner *metallurgist, educator*
Caplin, Jerrold Leon *health physicist*
Caswell, Randall Smith *physicist*
Celotta, Robert James *physicist*
Clark, Alan Fred *physicist*
Costrell, Louis *physicist*
Danos, Michael *physicist*
Dean, Stephen Odell *physicist*
Harman, George Gibson *physicist, consultant*
Hougen, Jon Torger *physical chemist, researcher*
Hsu, Stephen M. *materials scientist, chemical engineer*
Hubbell, John Howard *radiation physicist*
Jacox, Marilyn Esther *chemist*
Kessler, Karl Gunther *physicist*
Kushner, Lawrence Maurice *physical chemist*
Kuyatt, Chris E(rnie) (Earl) *physicist, administrator*
Levelt Sengers, Johanna Maria Henrica *research physicist*
Phillips, William Daniel *physicist*
Pierce, Daniel Thornton *physicist*
Reader, Joseph *physicist*
Taylor, Barry Norman *physicist*
Verkouteren, Robert Michael *chemist*
Weber, Alfons *physicist*
Wiese, Wolfgang Lothar *physicist*

### Garrett Park
Melville, Robert Seaman *chemist*

### Germantown
Fowler, Earle Cabell *physicist, administrator*
Plano, Richard James *physicist, educator*

### Glenelg
Williams, Donald John *research physicist*

### Greenbelt
Day, John H. *physicist*
Degnan, John James, III *physicist*
Fichtel, Carl Edwin *physicist*
Fischel, David *astrophysicist, remote sensing specialist*
Holt, Stephen S. *astrophysicist*
Krueger, Arlin James *physicist*
Langel, Robert Allan, III *geophysicist*
Liu, Han-Shou *space scientist, researcher*
Maran, Stephen Paul *astronomer*
Mather, John Cromwell *astrophysicist*
Mumma, Michael Jon *physicist*
Ormes, Jonathan Fairfield *astrophysicist, science administrator, researcher*
Ramaty, Reuven Robert *physicist, researcher*
Simpson, Joanne Malkus *meteorologist*
Stief, Louis John *chemist*

### Laurel
Avery, William Hinckley *physicist, chemist*
Babin, Steven Michael *atmospheric scientist, researcher*
Fristrom, Robert Maurice *chemist*
Kossiakoff, Alexander *chemist*

### Mechanicsville
Henderson, Madeline Mary (Berry) (Berry Henderson) *chemist, researcher, consultant*

### Millersville
Kreps, Robert Wilson *research chemist*

### Olney
Terry, Glenn A. *retired nuclear chemist*

### Oxon Hill
McLean, Edgar Alexander *physicist*

### Parkton
Fitzgerald, Edwin Roger *physicist, educator*

### Parkville
Jensen, Arthur Seigfried *consulting engineering physicist*

### Pasadena
Young, Russell Dawson *physics consultant*

### Poolesville
Blush, Steven Michael *nuclear scientist, safety consultant*

### Potomac
Baer, Ledolph *oceanographer, meteorologist*
Casella, Russell Carl *physicist*
Engelmann, Rudolf Jacob *meteorologist*
Epstein, Edward S. *meteorologist*
Whang, Yun Chow *space science educator*

### Rockville
Buchanan, John Donald *health physicist, radiochemist*
Day, LeRoy Edward *aerospace scientist, consultant*
Dunn, Bonnie Brill *chemist*
Finlayson, John Sylvester *biochemist*
Grady, Lee Timothy *pharmaceutical chemist*
Jamieson, Graham A. *biochemist, organization official*
Murray, Peter *metallurgist, manufacturing company executive*
Rinkenberger, Richard Krug *physical scientist, geologist*
Schindler, Albert Isadore *physicist, educator*
Zoon, Kathryn Egloff *biochemist*

### Saint Leonard
Sanders, James Grady *biogeochemist*

### Sandy Spring
Kanarowski, Stanley Martin *chemist, chemical engineer, government official*

### Silver Spring
Douglass, Carl Dean *biochemistry consultant, former government official*
Golden, Joseph Hilary *meteorologist*
McQueen, Jeffery Thomas *meteorologist*
Rueger, Lauren John *retired physicist, consultant*
Scheer, Milton David *chemical physicist*
Tokar, John Michael *oceanographer, ocean engineer*
White, Herbert Laverne *meterologist, federal agency administrator*
Young, Jay Alfred *chemical safety and health consultant, writer, editor*

### Suitland
Rao, Desiraju Bhavanarayana *meteorologist, oceanographer, educator*

### Temple Hills
Strauss, Simon Wolf *chemist, materials scientist*

### West Bethesda
Gaunaurd, Guillermo C. *physicist, engineer, researcher*

## MASSACHUSETTS

### Amherst
Archer, Ronald Dean *chemist, educator*
Byron, Frederick William, Jr. *physicist, educator, university vice chancellor*
Carpino, Louis A. *chemist, educator*
Ehrlich, Paul *chemist, educator*
Fink, Richard David *chemist, educator*
Goldstein, Joseph Irwin *materials scientist, educator*
Kantor, Simon William *chemistry educator*
Lenz, Robert William *polymer chemistry educator*
MacKnight, William John *chemist, educator*
Peterson, Gerald Alvin *physics educator*
Porter, Roger Stephen *chemistry educator*
Rabin, Monroe Stephen Zane *physicist*
Romer, Robert Horton *physicist, educator*
Scott, David Knight *physicist, university administrator*
Slakey, Linda Louise *biochemistry educator*
Stein, Richard Stephen *chemistry educator*

### Bedford
Carr, Paul Henry *physicist*
Frederickson, Arthur Robb *physicist*
Sizer, Irwin Whiting *biochemistry educator*

### Belmont
Hauser, George *biochemist, educator*

### Beverly
Harris, Miles Fitzgerald *meteorologist*

### Boston
Anselme, Jean-Pierre Louis Marie *chemist*
Aronow, Saul *physicist*
Blout, Elkan Rogers *biological chemistry educator, university dean*
Brecher, Kenneth *astrophysicist*
Brownell, Gordon Lee *physicist, educator*
Cantor, Charles Robert *biochemistry educator*
Cohen, Robert Sonné *physicist, philosopher, educator*
Deutsch, Thomas Frederick *physicist*
Edmonds, Dean Stockett, Jr. *physicist, educator, director*
El-Baz, Farouk *research director, educator*
Hopkins, Esther Arvilla Harrison *chemist, patent lawyer*
Kaplan, Michael Daniel *physics and chemistry researcher, educator*
Karnovsky, Manfred L. *biochemistry educator*
Kennedy, Eugene Patrick *biochemist, educator*
Kolodner, Richard David *biochemist, educator*
Kornberg, Sir Hans Leo *biochemist*
Kravitz, Edward Arthur *biochemist*
Le Quesne, Philip William *chemistry educator, researcher*
Lichtin, Norman Nahum *chemistry educator*
Malenka, Bertram Julian *physicist, educator*
Miliora, Maria Teresa *chemist, psychotherapist, psychoanalyst, educator*
Pardee, Arthur Beck *biochemist, educator*
Quelle, Frederick William, Jr. *physicist*
Simmons, Jean Elizabeth Margaret (Mrs. Glen R. Simmons) *chemistry educator*
Solomon, Arthur Kaskel *biophysics educator*
Stanley, H(arry) Eugene *physicist, educator*
Stollar, Bernard David *biochemist, educator*
Villee, Claude Alvin, Jr. *biochemistry educator*
Webster, Edward William *medical physicist*
Zimmerman, George Ogurek *physicist, educator*

### Brookline
Lynton, Ernest Albert *physicist, educator, former university official*
Saini, Gulshan Rai *soil physicist, agricultural hydrologist*
Tuchman, Avraham *physicist, researcher*
Vallee, Bert Lester *biochemist, physician, educator*

### Burlington
Africk, Steven Allen *physicist*
Shaikh, Naimuddin *medical physicist*

### Cambridge
Alberty, Robert Arnold *chemistry educator*
Anderson, James Gilbert *chemistry educator*
Barger, James Edwin *physicist*
Biemann, Klaus *chemistry educator*
Birgeneau, Robert Joseph *physicist, educator*
Bloch, Konrad Emil *biochemist*
Bloembergen, Nicolaas *physicist, educator*
Boyle, Edward Allen *oceanography educator*
Bradt, Hale Van Dorn *physicist, x-ray astronomer, educator*
Branscomb, Lewis McAdory *physicist*
Burchfiel, Burrell Clark *geology educator*
Burke, Bernard Flood *physicist, educator*
Burnham, Charles Wilson *mineralogy educator*
Butler, James Newton *chemist, educator*
Cameron, Alastair Graham Walter *astrophysicist, educator*
Canizares, Claude Roger *astrophysicist, educator*
Carter, Ashton Baldwin *physicist, educator, government agency executive*
Coleman, Sidney Richard *physicist, educator*
Corey, Elias James *chemistry educator*
Covert, Eugene Edzards *aerophysics educator*
Dalgarno, Alexander *astronomy educator*
Danheiser, Rick Lane *organic chemistry educator*
Donnelly, Thomas William *physicist*
Dresselhaus, Mildred Spiewak *physics and engineering educator*
Durant, Graham John *medicinal chemist, drug researcher*
Eagar, Thomas Waddy *metallurgist, educator*
Eagleson, Peter Sturges *hydrologist, educator*
Edsall, John Tileston *biological chemistry educator*
Ehrenreich, Henry *physicist, educator*
Emanuel, Kerry Andrew *earth sciences educator*
Feld, Michael Stephen *physics educator*
Feldman, Gary Jay *physicist, educator*
Feshbach, Herman *physicist, educator*
Field, Robert Warren *chemistry educator*
Foner, Simon *research physicist*
French, Anthony Philip *physicist, educator*
Frey, Frederick August *geochemistry researcher, educator*
Garland, Carl Wesley *chemist, educator*
Geller, Margaret Joan *astrophysicist, educator*
Georgi, Howard *physics educator*
Gingerich, Owen Jay *astronomer, educator*
Glauber, Roy Jay *theoretical physics educator*
Goldstone, Jeffrey *physicist*
Gordon, Roy Gerald *chemistry educator*
Gould, Stephen Jay *paleontologist, educator*
Greene, Frederick D., II *chemistry educator*
Grindlay, Jonathan Ellis *astrophysics educator*
Grove, Timothy Lynn *geology educator*
Halperin, Bertrand Israel *physics educator*
Herschbach, Dudley Robert *chemistry educator*
Hodges, Kip Vernon *geologist, educator*
Hoffman, Paul Felix *geologist, educator*
Holton, Gerald *physicist, science historian*
Horwitz, Paul *physicist*
Houtchens, Robert Austin, Jr. *biochemist*
Huang, Kerson *physics educator*
Huchra, John Peter *astronomer, educator*
Irwin, William Edward, III *health physicist*
Jackiw, Roman *physicist, educator*
Jordan, Thomas Hillman *geophysicist, educator*
Joss, Paul Christopher *astrophysicist, atmospheric physicist, educator*
Kamentsky, Louis Aaron *biophysicist*
Keck, James Collyer *physicist, educator*
Kendall, Henry Way *physicist*
Kerman, Arthur Kent *physicist, educator*
Khorana, Har Gobind *chemist, educator*
Kim, Peter Sungbai *biochemistry educator*
King, Ronold Wyeth Percival *physics educator*
Kirby, Kate Page *physicist*
Kistiakowsky, Vera *physics researcher, educator*
Klemperer, William *chemistry educator*
Klibanov, Alexander Maxim *chemistry educator*
Knowles, Jeremy Randall *chemist, educator*
Lightman, Alan Paige *physicist, writer, educator*
Lindzen, Richard Siegmund *meteorologist, educator*
Lippard, Stephen James *chemist, educator*
Lipscomb, William Nunn, Jr. *retired physical chemistry educator*
Litster, James David *physics educator, dean*
Livingston, James Duane *physicist, educator*
Lomon, Earle Leonard *physicist, educator, consultant*
Low, Francis Eugene *physics educator*
Luu, Jane *astronomer*
Lyon, Richard Harold *physicist educator,*
Marsden, Brian Geoffrey *astronomer*
Martin, Paul Cecil *physicist, educator*
Marvin, Ursula Bailey *geologist*
Mazur, Eric *physicist, educator*
Meselson, Matthew Stanley *biochemist, educator*
Meyers, Harold Vernon *chemist*
Molina, Mario Jose *physical chemist, educator*
Moniz, Ernest Jeffrey *physics educator*
Moran, James Michael, Jr. *astronomer*
Narayan, Ramesh *astronomy educator*
Negele, John William *physics educator, consultant*
Nelson, Keith Adam *chemistry educator*
Newell, Reginald Edward *physics educator*
Oppenheim, Irwin *chemical physicist, educator*
Orme-Johnson, William Henry, III *chemist, educator*
Papaliolios, Costas Demetrios *physics educator*
Paul, William *physicist, educator*
Pershan, Peter Silas *physicist, educator*
Petersen, Ulrich *geology educator*
Pettengill, Gordon H(emenway) *physicist, educator*
Press, William Henry *astrophysicist, computer scientist*
Ptashne, Mark Steven *biochemistry educator*
Rajur, Sharanabasava Basappa *chemistry educator, researcher*
Ramsey, Norman F. *physicist, educator*
Rediker, Robert Harmon *physicist*
Redwine, Robert Page *physicist, educator*
Rice, James Robert *engineering scientist, geophysicist*
Roedder, Edwin Woods *geologist*
Rose, Robert Michael *materials science and engineering educator*
Rosenblith, Walter Alter *scientist, educator*
Rubin, Lawrence Gilbert *physicist, laboratory manager*
Sadoway, Donald Robert *materials science educator*
Schimmel, Paul Reinhard *biochemist, biophysicist, educator*
Seyferth, Dietmar *chemist, educator*
Shapiro, Irwin Ira *physicist, educator*
Silbey, Robert James *chemistry educator, researcher, consultant*
Spaepen, Frans August *applied physics researcher, educator*
Steinfeld, Jeffrey Irwin *chemistry educator, consultant, writer*
Steinmetz, Michael *biochemist*
Strandberg, Malcom Woodrow Pershing *physicist*
Strauch, Karl *physicist, educator*
Thaddeus, Patrick *physicist, educator*
Ting, Samuel Chao Chung *physicist, educator*
Tinkham, Michael *physicist, educator*
Verdine, Gregory Lawrence *chemist, educator*
Vessot, Robert Frederick Charles *physicist*
Villars, Felix Marc Hermann *physicist, educator*
Waugh, John Stewart *chemist, educator*
Westheimer, Frank Henry *chemist, educator*
Whipple, Fred Lawrence *astronomer*
Whitesides, George McClelland *chemistry educator*
Wiley, Don Craig *biochemistry and biophysics educator*
Wilson, Robert Woodrow *radio astronomer*
Wood, John Armstead *planetary scientist, geological sciences educator*
Wu, Tai Tsun *physicist, educator*
Wunsch, Carl Isaac *oceanographer, educator*

### Chelmsford
Sheldon, Eric *retired physics educator*

### Chestnut Hill
Fourkas, John T. *chemistry educator*

### Concord
Valley, George Edward, Jr. *physicist, educator*

### Cotuit
Miller, Robert Charles *retired physicist*

### East Longmeadow
Skutnik, Bolesh *optics scientist, lay worker, lawyer*

### East Walpole
Oh, Se-Kyung *immunochemist*

### Eastham
Miller, Gabriel Lorimer *physicist, researcher*

### Falmouth
Goody, Richard Mead *geophysicist*
Hollister, Charles Davis *oceanographer*

### Framingham
Dawicki, Doloretta Diane *research biochemist, educator*

### Gloucester
Socolow, Arthur Abraham *geologist*

### Hanscom AFB
Mailloux, Robert Joseph *physicist*

### Haverhill
DeSchuytner, Edward Alphonse *biochemist, educator*

### Hull
Chase, David Marion *applied physicist, mathematical modeler*

### Lexington
Buchanan, John Machlin *biochemistry educator*
Caslavska, Vera Barbara *chemist, researcher*
Cathou, Renata Egone *chemist, consultant*
Dionne, Gerald Francis *research physicist, consultant*
Garing, John Seymour *retired physicist, research executive*
Guertin, Robert Powell *physics educator, university dean*
Kanter, Irving *mathematical physicist*
Kirkpatrick, Francis H(ubbard), Jr. *biophysicist, intellectual property practitioner, consultant*
Mollo-Christensen, Erik Leonard *oceanographer*
Nash, Leonard Kollender *chemistry educator*
Samour, Carlos Miguel *chemist*
Shull, Clifford G. *physicist, educator*
Smith, Edgar Eugene *biochemist, university administrator*
Williamson, Richard Cardinal *physicist*

### Lowell
Carr, George Leroy *physicist, educator*
Reinisch, Bodo Walter *atmospheric science educator*
Salamone, Joseph Charles *polymer chemistry educator*
Tripathy, Sukant Kishore *chemistry educator*
Wakim, Fahd George *physicist, educator*

### Mashpee
LeBaron, Francis Newton *biochemistry educator*

### Medford
Cormack, Allan MacLeod *physicist, educator*
Garrelick, Joel Marc *acoustical scientist, consultant*
Gunther, Leon *physicist*
Klema, Ernest Donald *nuclear physicist, educator*
Mc Carthy, Kathryn A. *physicist*
Milburn, Richard Henry *physics educator*
Schneps, Jack *physics educator*
Sung, Nak-Ho *science educator*
Urry, Grant Wayne *chemistry educator*

### Natick
Cukor, Peter *chemical research and development executive, educator, consultant*
Milius, Richard A. *organic chemist*
Narayan, K(rishnamurthi) Ananth *biochemist*
Wang, Chia Ping *physicist, educator*

### New Bedford
Bennett, Michelle Swann *quality control chemist, scientist*

### Newton
Dunlap, William Crawford *physicist*
Heyn, Arno Harry Albert *retired chemistry educator*

### Northampton
Fleck, George Morrison *chemistry educator*

### Roxbury
Franzblau, Carl *biochemist, consultant, researcher*
MacNichol, Edward Ford, Jr. *biophysicist, educator*
Simons, Elizabeth R(eiman) *biochemist, educator*

Small, Donald MacFarland *biophysics educator, gastroenterologist*

### South Hadley
Campbell, Mary Kathryn *chemistry educator*
Harrison, Anna Jane *chemist, educator*
Williamson, Kenneth Lee *chemistry educator*

### Stow
Becherer, Richard Joseph *scientific consulting firm executive, physicist*

### Sturbridge
McMahon, Maribeth Lovette *physicist*

### Sudbury
Blackey, Edwin Arthur, Jr. *geologist*

### Waltham
Abeles, Robert Heinz *biochemistry educator*
Cohen, Saul G. *chemist, educator*
De Rosier, David John *biophysicist, educator*
Deser, Stanley *physicist, educator*
Epstein, Irving Robert *chemistry educator*
Fasman, Gerald David *biochemistry educator*
Foxman, Bruce Mayer *chemist, educator*
Jeanloz, Roger William *biochemist, educator*
Jencks, William Platt *biochemist, educator*
Kustin, Kenneth *chemist*
Lees, Marjorie Berman *biochemist, neuroscientist*
Nisonoff, Alfred *biochemist, educator*
Petsko, Gregory Anthony *chemistry and biochemistry educator*
Schweber, Silvan Samuel *physics and history educator*
Snider, Barry B. *organic chemist*
†Tamasanis, Douglas Thomas *physicist*

### Watertown
Lin, Alice Lee Lan *physicist, researcher, educator*

### Wayland
Clark, Melville, Jr. *physicist, electrical engineer, consultant*
Neumeyer, John Leopold *research company administrator, chemistry educator*

### Wellesley
Kobayashi, Yutaka *biochemist, consultant*

### Wenham
Herrmann, Robert Lawrence *biochemistry, science, religion educator*

### Westford
Salah, Joseph Elias *research scientist, educator*

### Weston
Schloemann, Ernst Fritz (Rudolf August) *physicist, engineer*
Whitehouse, David Rempfer *physicist*

### Westwood
Bernfeld, Peter Harry William *biochemist*

### Williamstown
Crampton, Stuart Jessup Bigelow *physicist, educator*
Markgraf, J(ohn) Hodge *chemist, educator*
Park, David Allen *physicist, educator*
Pasachoff, Jay Myron *astronomer, educator*
Wobus, Reinhard Arthur *geologist, educator*

### Woods Hole
Berggren, William Alfred *geologist, research micropaleontologist, educator*
Butman, Bradford *oceanographer*
Cohen, Seymour Stanley *biochemist, educator*
Emery, Kenneth Orris *marine geologist*
Fofonoff, Nicholas Paul *oceanographer, educator*
Gagosian, Robert B. *chemist, educator*
Hart, Stanley Robert *geochemist, educator*
Steele, John Hyslop *marine scientist, oceanographic institute administrator*
Uchupi, Elazar *geologist, researcher*
Von Herzen, Richard Pierre *research scientist, consultant*

### Worcester
Hohenemser, Christoph *physics educator, researcher*
Pavlik, James William *chemistry educator*

## MICHIGAN

### Ann Arbor
Agranoff, Bernard William *biochemist, educator*
Akerlof, Carl William *physics educator*
Aller, Margo Friedel *astronomer*
Ashe, Arthur James, III *chemistry educator*
Atreya, Sushil Kumar *space science educator, astrophysicist, researcher*
Banks, Peter Morgan *enviromental research business executive*
Bartell, Lawrence Sims *chemist, educator*
Bernstein, Isadore Abraham *biochemistry educator, researcher*
Blinder, Seymour Michael *chemistry educator*
Chupp, Timothy Edward *physicist, educator, nuclear scientist, academic administrator*
Clarke, John Terrel *astrophysicist*
Cordes, Eugene Harold *pharmacy and chemistry educator*
Crane, Horace Richard *physicist, educator*
Dekker, Eugene Earl *biochemistry educator*
Dixon, Jack E. *biological chemistry educator, consultant*
Donahue, Thomas Michael *physics educator*
Drake, Richard Paul *physicist, educator*
Farrand, William Richard *geology educator*
Filisko, Frank Edward *physicist, educator*
Fisk, Lennard Ayres *physicist, educator*
Freese, Katherine *physicist, educator*
Gingerich, Philip Derstine *paleontologist, evolutionary biologist, educator*
Haddock, Fred T. *astronomer, educator*
Jones, Lawrence William *educator, physicist*
Kapteyn, Henry Cornelius *physics educator*
Kesler, Stephen Edward *economic geology educator*
Krimm, Samuel *physicist, educator*
Krisch, Alan David *physics educator*
Longone, Daniel Thomas *chemistry educator*
Marletta, Michael *biochemistry educator, researcher, pharmacologist*
Massey, Vincent *biochemist, educator*
Matthews, Rowena Green *biological chemistry educator*
Neal, Homer Alfred *physics educator, researcher, university administrator*
Nordman, Christer Eric *chemistry educator*
Nriagu, Jerome Okon *environmental geochemist*
Parkinson, William Charles *physicist, educator*
Pollack, Henry Nathan *geophysics educator*
Rea, David K. *geology and oceanography educator*
Robertson, Richard Earl *physical chemist, educator*
Roe, Byron Paul *physics educator*
Samson, Perry J. *environmental scientist, educator*
Schacht, Jochen Heinrich *biochemistry educator*
Shaw, Jiajiu *chemist*
Steel, Duncan Gregory *physics educator*
Tamres, Milton *chemistry educator*
Townsend, LeRoy B. *chemistry educator, university administrator, researcher*
Van der Voo, Rob *geophysicist*
Weinreich, Gabriel *physicist, minister, educator*
Wharton, John James, Jr. *research physicist*
Wong, Victor Kenneth *physics educator, academic administrator*
Woo, Peter Wing Kee *organic chemist*
Yeh, Gregory Soh-Yu *physicist, educator*
Zhang, Youxue *geology educator*

### Big Rapids
Mathison, Ian William *chemistry educator, academic dean*

### Cross Village
Stowe, Robert Allen *catalytic and chemical technology consultant*

### Dearborn
Tai, Julia Chow *chemistry educator*

### Detroit
Bohm, Henry Victor *physicist*
Brown, Ray Kent *biochemist, physician, educator*
Frade, Peter Daniel *chemist, educator*
Gupta, Suraj Narayan *physicist, educator*
Johnson, Carl Randolph *chemist, educator*
Kirschner, Stanley *chemist*
Oliver, John Preston *chemistry educator, academic administrator*
Orton, Colin George *medical physicist*
Stewart, Melbourne George, Jr. *physicist, educator*
Wierzbicki, Jacek Gabriel *physicist, researcher*

### East Lansing
Abolins, Maris Arvids *physics researcher and educator*
Austin, Sam M. *physics educator*
Benenson, Walter *nuclear physics educator*
Blosser, Henry Gabriel *physicist*
Brown, Boyd Alex *physicist, educator*
Burnett, Jean Bullard (Mrs. James R. Burnett) *biochemist*
Cantlon, John E. *environmental scientist, consultant*
Case, Eldon Darrel *materials science educator*
Cross, Aureal Theophilus *geology and botany educator*
D'Itri, Frank Michael *environmental research chemist*
Dye, James Louis *chemistry educator*
Gelbke, Claus-Konrad *nuclear physics educator*
Harrison, Michael Jay *physicist, educator*
Kaplan, Thomas Abraham *physics educator*
Luecke, Richard William *biochemist*
Macrakis, Kristie Irene *history of science educator*
Pollack, Gerald Leslie *physicist, educator*
Preiss, Jack *biochemistry educator*
Spence, Robert Dean *physics educator*
Summitt, (William) Robert *chemist, educator*
Tien, H. Ti *biophysics and physiology educator, scientist*
Wolterink, Lester Floyd *biophysicist, educator*
Yussouff, Mohammed *physicist, educator*

### Holland
Inghram, Mark Gordon *physicist, educator*

### Houghton
McGinnis, Gary David *chemist, science educator*

### Kalamazoo
Cheney, Brigham Vernon *physical chemist*
Greenfield, John Charles *bio-organic chemist*

### Leland
Small, Hamish *chemist*

### Madison Heights
Chapman, Gilbert Bryant *physicist*

### Midland
Chao, Marshall *chemist*
Crummett, Warren Berlin *analytical chemistry consultant*
Dorman, Linneaus Cuthbert *retired chemist*
Nowak, Robert Michael *chemist*
Shastri, Ranganath Krishna *materials scientist*
Stenger, Vernon Arthur *analytical chemist, consultant*
Stull, Daniel Richard *retired research thermochemist, educator, consultant*
Weyenberg, Donald Richard *chemist*
Wright, Antony Pope *research chemist*

### Mount Pleasant
Dietrich, Richard Vincent *geologist, educator*
Thompson, Clifton C. *chemistry educator, university administrator*

### Rochester
Callewaert, Denis Marc *biochemistry educator*

### Southfield
Castain, Ralph Henri *physicist*

### Three Rivers
Boyer, Nicodemus Elijah *organic-polymer chemist, consultant*

### Troy
Fritzsche, Hellmut *physics educator*
Ovshinsky, Stanford Robert *physicist, inventor, energy and information company executive*

### Warren
Franetovic, Vjekoslav *physicist*
Herbst, Jan Francis *physicist, researcher*
Heremans, Joseph Pierre *physicist*
Schwartz, Shirley E. *chemist*
Smith, George Wolfram *physicist, educator*
Smith, John Robert *physicist*
Taylor, Kathleen (Christine) *physical chemist*

### Ypsilanti
Barnes, James Milton *physics and astronomy educator*

### Zeeland
Guarr, Thomas Frederick *research chemist*

## MINNESOTA

### Austin
Holman, Ralph Theodore *biochemistry and nutrition educator*
Schmid, Harald Heinrich Otto *biochemistry educator, academic director*

### Duluth
Rapp, George Robert, Jr. (Rip Rapp) *geology and archeology educator*

### Lakeville
Phinney, William Charles *retired geologist*

### Marshall
Skramstad, Robert Allen *retired oceanographer*

### Minneapolis
Ackerman, Eugene *biophysics educator*
Berg, Stanton Oneal *firearms and ballistics consultant*
Carr, Charles William *biochemist, emeritus educator*
Carr, Robert Wilson, Jr. *chemistry educator*
Gasiorowicz, Stephen George *physics educator*
Gentry, William Ronald *scientist, entrepreneur*
Goldman, Allen Marshall *physics educator*
Halley, James Woods *physics educator*
Hamermesh, Morton *physicist, educator*
Hobbie, Russell Klyver *physics educator*
Hogenkamp, Henricus Petrus Cornelis *biochemistry researcher, biochemistry educator*
Hooke, Roger LeBaron *geomorphology and glaciology educator*
Jones, Thomas Walter *astrophysics educator, researcher*
Kelts, Kerry R. *geology educator*
Kruse, Paul Walters, Jr. *physicist, consultant*
Kuhi, Leonard Vello *astronomer, university administrator*
Lumry, Rufus Worth, II *chemist, educator*
Majumder, Sabir Ahmed *physical and analytical chemist*
Marshak, Marvin Lloyd *physicist, educator*
Portoghese, Philip Salvatore *medicinal chemist, educator*
Prager, Stephen *chemistry educator*
Rubens, Sidney Michel *physicist, technical advisor*
Siepmann, Joern Ilja *chemistry educator*
Truhlar, Donald Gene *chemist, educator*
Wood, Wellington Gibson, III *biochemistry educator*
Wright, Herbert E(dgar), Jr. *geologist*

### Northfield
Casper, Barry Michael *physics educator*
Cederberg, James *physics educator*
Noer, Richard J. *physics educator, researcher*

### Rochester
Kao, Pai Chih *clinical chemist*

### Roseville
Berry, James Frederick *biochemistry educator*

### Saint Paul
Bloomfield, Victor Alfred *biochemistry educator*
Clapp, C(harles) Edward *research chemist, soil biochemistry educator*
Farnum, Sylvia Arlyce *physical chemist*
Nicholson, Morris Emmons, Jr. *metallurgist, educator*
Perry, James Alfred *environmental scientist, consultant, educator, administrator*
Southwick, David Leroy *geology researcher*
Thompson, Mary Eileen *chemistry educator*
Walker, Charles Thomas *physicist, educator*
Walton, Matt Savage *retired geologist, educator*

### White Bear Lake
Holmen, Reynold Emanuel *chemist*

## MISSISSIPPI

### Bay Saint Louis
Zeile, Fred Carl *oceanographer, meteorologist*

### Brandon
Read, Virginia Hall *biochemistry educator*

### Hattiesburg
Bedenbaugh, Angela Lea Owen *chemistry educator, researcher*

### Itta Bena
Thomas, William Eric *biochemistry educator*

### Jackson
Leszczynski, Jerzy Ryszard *chemistry educator, researcher*

### Mississippi State
Alley, Earl Gifford *chemist*
Howell, Everette Irl *physicist, educator*

### Pascagoula
Corben, Herbert Charles *physicist, educator*

### Starkville
Emerich, Donald Warren *retired chemistry educator*

### Stennis Space Center
Hurlburt, Harley Ernest *oceanographer*

## MISSOURI

### Columbia
Bauman, John E., Jr. *chemistry educator*
Decker, Wayne Leroy *meteorologist, educator*
Ethington, Raymond Lindsay *geology educator, researcher*
Gehrke, Charles William *biochemistry educator*
Johns, Williams Davis, Jr. *geologist, educator*
Mayer, Dennis Thomas *biochemist, educator*
Pfeifer, Peter Martin *physics educator*
Plummer, Patricia Lynne Moore *chemistry and physics educator*
Rabjohn, Norman *chemistry educator emeritus*
Rhyne, James Jennings *condensed matter physicist*
Shelton, Kevin L. *geology educator*
Unklesbay, Athel Glyde *geologist, educator*
Weisman, Gary Andrew *biochemist*

### Creve Coeur
Bockserman, Robert Julian *chemist*

### Joplin
Malzahn, Ray Andrew *chemistry educator, university dean*

### Kansas City
Gier, Audra May Calhoon *environmental chemist*
Grosskreutz, Joseph Charles *physicist, engineering researcher, educator*
Martinez-Carrion, Marino *biochemist, educator*
Parizek, Eldon Joseph *geologist, college dean*
Rodenhuis, David Roy *meteorologist, educator*
Rost, William Joseph *chemist*
Wilkinson, Ralph Russell *biochemistry educator, toxicologist*

### Rolla
Adawi, Ibrahim Hasan *physics educator*
Alexander, Ralph William, Jr. *physics educator*
Armstrong, Daniel Wayne *chemist, educator*
Hagni, Richard Davis *geology and geophysics educator*
James, William Joseph *chemistry educator*
Leventis, Nicholas *chemistry educator, consultant*
Mc Farland, Robert Harold *physicist, educator*
O'Keefe, Thomas Joseph *metallurgical engineer*
Rueppel, Melvin Leslie *environmental research director and educator*
Shrestha, Bijaya *nuclear scientist*

### Saint Louis
Ackerman, Joseph J. H. *chemistry educator*
Bender, Carl Martin *physics educator, consultant*
Burgess, James Harland *physics educator, researcher*
Callis, Clayton Fowler *research chemist*
Frieden, Carl *biochemist, educator*
Friedlander, Michael Wulf *physicist, educator*
Gibbons, Patrick Chandler *physicist, educator*
Gross, Michael Lawrence *chemistry educator*
Handel, Peter H. *physics educator*
Heinrich, Ross Raymond *geophysicist, educator*
Holtzer, Alfred Melvin *chemistry educator*
Horwitt, Max Kenneth *biochemist, educator*
Israel, Martin Henry *astrophysicist, educator, academic administrator*
Kornfeld, Rosalind Hauk *research biochemist*
Lipkin, David *chemist*
Macias, Edward S. *chemistry educator, university official and dean*
Marshall, Garland Ross *biochemist, biophysicist, medical educator*
Miller, James Gegan *research scientist, physics educator*
Murray, Robert Wallace *chemistry educator*
Norberg, Richard Edwin *physicist, educator*
Profeta, Salvatore, Jr. *chemist*
Rosenthal, Harold Leslie *biochemistry educator*
Sikorski, James Alan *research chemist*
Sly, William S. *biochemist, educator*
Stauder, William Vincent *geophysics educator*
Takano, Masaharu *physical chemist*
Taylor, Morris Anthony *chemistry educator*
Walker, Robert Mowbray *physicist, educator*
Weber, Morton M. *microbial biochemist, educator*
Welch, Michael John *chemistry educator, researcher*
Will, Clifford Martin *physicist, educator*
Wrighton, Mark Stephen *chemistry educator*

## MONTANA

### Billings
Darrow, George F. *natural resources company owner, consultant*

### Bozeman
Horner, John Robert *paleontologist, researcher*
Mertz, Edwin Theodore *biochemist, emeritus educator*

### Dayton
Volborth, Alexis von *geochemistry and geological engineering educator*

### Missoula
Jakobson, Mark John *physics educator*
Murray, Raymond Carl *forensic geologist, educator*
Osterheld, R(obert) Keith *chemistry educator*
Peterson, James Algert *geologist, educator*

## NEBRASKA

### Crete
Brakke, Myron Kendall *retired research chemist, educator*

### Lincoln
Blad, Blaine L. *agricultural meteorology educator, consultant*
Eckhardt, Craig Jon *chemistry educator*
Hubbard, Kenneth Gene *climatologist*

Jolliff, Carl R. *clinical biochemist, immunologist, laboratory administrator*
Jones, Lee Bennett *chemist, educator*
Sellmyer, David Julian *physicist, educator*
Treves, Samuel Blain *geologist, educator*
Yoder, Bruce Alan *chemist*

### Omaha
Gambal, David *biochemistry educator*
Lovas, Sándor *chemist, researcher, educator*
Watt, Dean Day *retired biochemistry educator*
Zepf, Thomas Herman *physics educator, researcher*

## NEVADA

### Carson City
Crawford, John Edward *geologist, scientist*

### Henderson
Bentley, Kenton Earl *aerospace scientist, researcher*

### Las Vegas
Levich, Robert Alan *geologist*

### Reno
Bonham, Harold Florian *research geologist, consultant*
Horton, Robert Carlton *geologist*
Leipper, Dale Frederick *physical oceanographer, educator*
Pierson, William Roy *chemist*
Pough, Frederick Harvey *mineralogist*
Price, Jonathan G. *geologist*
Sladek, Ronald John *physics educator*
Taranik, James Vladimir *geologist, educator*

## NEW HAMPSHIRE

### Alstead
Hanson, George Fulford *geologist*

### Bedford
Effenberger, John Albert *research chemist*

### Durham
Tischler, Herbert *geologist, educator*

### Glen
Zager, Ronald I. *chemist, consultant*

### Groveton
Kegeles, Gerson *chemistry educator*

### Hanover
Braun, Charles Louis *chemistry educator, researcher*
Doyle, William Thomas *physicist, educator*
Drake, Charles Lum *geology educator*
Kantrowitz, Arthur *physicist, educator*
Montgomery, David Campbell *physicist, educator*
Perrin, Noel *environmental studies educator*
Stockmayer, Walter H(ugo) *retired chemistry educator*
Sturge, Michael Dudley *physicist*
Wegner, Gary Alan *astronomer*
Wetterhahn, Karen Elizabeth *chemistry educator*

### Jaffrey
Walling, Cheves Thomson *chemistry educator*

### Lee
Blidberg, D. Richard *marine engineer*

### New London
Hurley, Patrick Mason *geology educator*

### Rumney
Smith, F(rederick) Dow(swell) *physicist, retired college president*

### Salem
Simmons, Marvin Gene *geophysics educator*

### Wolfeboro
Varnerin, Lawrence John *physicist, retired educator*

## NEW JERSEY

### Allendale
Castor, William Stuart, Jr. *chemist, consultant, laboratory executive, educator*

### Annandale
Cohen, Morrel Herman *physicist, biologist, educator*
Gorbaty, Martin Leo *chemist, researcher*
Sinfelt, John Henry *chemist*

### Belle Mead
Hansen, Ralph Holm *chemist*

### Berkeley Heights
Geusic, Joseph Edward *physicist*
Mac Rae, Alfred Urquhart *physicist, electrical engineer*

### Bogota
Condon, Francis Edward *retired chemistry educator*

### Boonton
Fuller, Ross Kennedy *chemist*

### Bound Brook
Karol, Frederick John *industrial chemist*

### Bridgewater
Albrethsen, Adrian Edysel *metallurgist, consultant*
Torrey, Henry Cutler *physicist*

### Camden
Beck, David Paul *biochemist*

### Cape May
Wilson, H(arold) Fred(erick) *chemist, research scientist*

### Chatham
Merianos, John James *medicinal chemist*

### Cherry Hill
Hayasi, Nisiki *physicist, business executive, inventor*

### Cliffside Park
Ginos, James Zissis *retired research chemist*

### East Brunswick
Wagman, Gerald Howard *retired biochemist*

### Edison
Johnson, Dewey, Jr. *biochemist*
Lo Surdo, Antonio *physical chemist, educator*

### Far Hills
McCall, David Warren *retired chemistry research director, consultant*

### Highland Park
Brudner, Harvey Jerome *physicist*
Feigenbaum, Abraham Samuel *nutritional biochemist*

### Hightstown
Di Carlo, Lawrence *analytical research chemist, manager*

### Hoboken
Bose, Ajay Kumar *chemistry educator*
Donskoy, Dimitri Michailovitch *physicist, researcher, educator*
Fajans, Jack *physics educator*
Schmidt, George *physicist*

### Holmdel
Burrus, Charles Andrew, Jr. *research physicist*
Gordon, James Power *optics scientist*
Lundgren, Carl William, Jr. *physicist*
Mollenauer, Linn Frederick *physicist*
Stolen, Rogers Hall *optics scientist*

### Jersey City
Koster, Emlyn Howard *geologist, educator*
Nakhla, Atif Mounir *scientist, biochemist*

### Kenilworth
Cayen, Mitchell Ness *biochemist*
Ganguly, Ashit Kumar *organic chemist*

### Madison
Udenfriend, Sidney *biochemist*

### Mahwah
Borowitz, Grace Burchman *chemistry educator, researcher*

### Manahawkin
Logan, Ralph Andre *physicist*

### Maplewood
Leeds, Norma S. *chemistry educator*
Newmark, Harold Leon *biochemist*
Tatyrek, Alfred Frank *consultant, materials/environmental engineer, analytical/research chemist*

### Matawan
Klein, George D. *geologist, executive*

### Mendham
Lunt, Harry Edward *metallurgist, consultant*

### Morristown
Arnow, Leslie Earle *scientist*
Baughman, Ray Henry *materials scientist*
Golecki, Ilan *physicist, researcher, educator*

### Murray Hill
Laskowski, Edward John *chemist*

### Neptune
Aguiar, Adam Martin *chemist, educator*

### New Brunswick
Eisenreich, Steven John *chemistry educator, environmental scientist*
Fisher, Hans *nutritional biochemistry educator*
Gale, Paula Jane *chemist*
Grassle, John Frederick *oceanographer, marine sciences educator*
Ho, Chi-Tang *food chemistry educator*
Lebowitz, Joel Louis *mathematical physicist, educator*
Liao, Mei-June *biopharmaceutical company executive*
Pandey, Ramesh Chandra *chemist, executive*
Rosen, Robert Thomas *analytical and food chemist*
Strauss, Ulrich Paul *chemist, educator*
Uchrin, Christopher George *environmental scientist*

### New Providence
Baker, William Oliver *research chemist, educator*
Bishop, David John *physicist*
Brinkman, William Frank *physicist, research executive*
Capasso, Federico *physicist, research administrator*
Faist, Jerome *physicist*
Gaylord, Norman Grant *chemical and polymer consultant*
Glass, Alastair Malcolm *physicist, research director*
Helfand, Eugene *chemist*
Johnson, David Wilfred, Jr. *ceramic scientist, researcher*
Lanzerotti, Louis John *physicist*
Laudise, Robert Alfred *research chemist*
Morgan, Samuel P(ope) *physicist, applied mathematician*
Murray, Cherry Ann *physicist, researcher*
Pinczuk, Aron *physicist*
Sivco, Deborah Lee *research materials scientist*
Stillinger, Frank Henry *chemist, educator*
Stormer, Horst Ludwig *physicist*
van Dover, Robert Bruce *physicist*
Wernick, Jack Harry *chemist*
White, Alice Elizabeth *physicist, researcher*

### Newark
Murnick, Daniel Ely *physicist, educator*
Waelde, Lawrence Richard *chemist*

### North Plainfield
Steiner, Ulrich Alfred *chemist*

### Paulsboro
Domingue, Raymond Pierre *chemist, consultant, educator*

### Pennington
Halasi-Kun, George Joseph *hydrologist, educator*
Widmer, Kemble *geologist*

### Piscataway
Devlin, Thomas Joseph *physicist*
Gotsch, Audrey Rose *environmental health sciences educator, researcher*
Idol, James Daniel, Jr. *chemist, educator, inventor, consultant*
Kear, Bernard Henry *materials scientist*
Lindenfeld, Peter *physics educator*
Lioy, Paul James *environmental health scientist*
Madey, Theodore Eugene *physics educator*
Manowitz, Paul *biochemist, researcher, educator*
Pond, Thomas Alexander *physics educator*
Robbins, Allen Bishop *physics educator*
Shatkin, Aaron Jeffrey *biochemistry educator*
Snitzer, Elias *physicist*
Witz, Gisela *chemist, educator*
Yacowitz, Harold *biochemist, nutritionist*
Zaleski, Jan Franciszek *biochemist*

### Pomona
Sharon, Yitzhak Yaakov *physicist, educator*

### Port Murray
Kunzler, John Eugene *physicist*

### Pottersville
Mellberg, James Richard *dental research chemist*

### Princeton
Adler, Stephen Louis *physicist*
Bahcall, John Norris *astrophysicist*
Bahcall, Neta Assaf *astrophysicist*
Bonini, William Emory *geophysics educator*
Bryan, Kirk, Jr. *research meteorologist, research oceanographer*
Chang, Clarence Dayton *chemist*
Davidson, Ronald Crosby *physicist, educator*
Denne-Hinnov, Gerd Boël *physicist*
Dyson, Freeman John *physicist*
Fisch, Nathaniel Joseph *physicist*
Fitch, Val Logsdon *physics educator*
Florey, Klaus Georg *chemist, pharmaceutical consultant*
Fresco, Jacques Robert *biochemist, educator*
Gott, J. Richard, III *astrophysicist*
Green, Joseph *chemist*
Grisham, Larry Richard *physicist*
Groves, John Taylor, III *chemist, educator*
Haldane, Frederick Duncan Michael *physics educator*
Happer, William, Jr. *physicist, educator*
Harford, James Joseph *aerospace historian*
Harris, Don Navarro *biochemist, pharmacologist*
Hawryluk, Richard Janusz *physicist*
Hopfield, John Joseph *biophysicist, educator*
Hulse, Russell Alan *physicist*
Hut, Piet *astrophysics educator*
Jenkins, Edward Beynon *research astronomer*
Judson, Sheldon *geology educator*
Kauzmann, Walter Joseph *chemistry educator*
Kyin, Saw William *chemist, consultant*
Lemonick, Aaron *physicist, educator*
Lieb, Elliott Hershel *physicist, mathematician, educator*
Long, Frank Wesley, Jr. *chemist*
Mahlman, Jerry David *research meteorologist*
Manabe, Syukuro *climatologist*
Mc Clure, Donald Stuart *physical chemist, educator*
Ondetti, Miguel Angel *chemist, consultant*
Oort, Abraham Hans *meteorologist, researcher, educator*
Ostriker, Jeremiah Paul *astrophysicist, educator*
Page, Lyman Alexander, Jr. *physicist*
Rebenfeld, Ludwig *chemist, educator*
Reynolds, George Thomas *physics educator, researcher, consultant*
Robertson, Nat Clifton *chemist*
Rodwell, John Dennis *biochemist*
Royce, Barrie Saunders Hart *physicist, educator*
Rutherford, Paul Harding *physicist*
Seman, Charles Jacob *research meteorologist*
Shoemaker, Frank Crawford *physicist, educator*
Smagorinsky, Joseph *meteorologist*
Smith, Arthur John Stewart *physicist, educator*
Spiro, Thomas George *chemistry educator*
Sterzer, Fred *research physicist*
Stix, Thomas Howard *physicist, educator*
Tang, Chao *physicist*
Taylor, Edward Curtis *chemistry educator*
Taylor, Joseph Hooton, Jr. *radio astronomer, physicist*
Treiman, Sam Bard *physics educator*
Turner, Edwin Lewis *astronomy educator, researcher*
Van Houten, Franklyn Bosworth *geologist, educator*
Villafranca, Joseph J. *pharmaceutical executive, chemistry educator*
Wightman, Arthur Strong *physicist, educator*
Wilczek, Frank Anthony *physics educator*
Wilkinson, David Todd *physics educator*
Wood, Eric Franklin *earth and environmental sciences educator*

### Rahway
Garcia, Maria Luisa *biochemist*
Kaczorowski, Gregory John *biochemist, researcher, science administrator*
Patchett, Arthur Allan *medicinal chemist, pharmaceutical executive*
Shapiro, Bennett Michaels *biochemist, educator*

### Raritan
Haller, William Paul *analytical chemist, robotics specialist*

### Red Bank
Harbison, James Prescott *research physicist*

### Ridgefield
Goldman, Arnold Ira *biophysicist, statistical analyst*

### Ringoes
Overton, Santford Vance *applications chemist*

### Somerville
Dammel, Ralph Rainer *chemist, researcher*

### Springfield
Panish, Morton B. *physicial chemist, consultant*

### Stirling
Walsh, Peter Joseph *physics educator*

### Summit
Phillips, James Charles *physicist, educator*
Rosensweig, Ronald Ellis *scientist consultant*
Wissbrun, Kurt Falke *chemist, consultant*
Ziegler, John Benjamin *chemist, lepidopterist*

### Teaneck
Kramer, Bernard *physicist, educator*
Nagy, Christa Fiedler *biochemist*
Tamir, Theodor *electrophysics researcher, educator*

### Titusville
Godly, Gordon Thomas *retired chemist, consultant*

### Trenton
Brown, Richard Alexander *chemist*
Cushman, David Wayne *research biochemist*

### Union
Zois, Constantine Nicholas Athanasios *meteorology educator*

### Upper Montclair
Kowalski, Stephen Wesley *chemistry educator*

### Westfield
Bartok, William *environmental technologies consultant*

### Westwood
Schutz, Donald Frank *geochemist, healthcare corporate executive*

### Whippany
Maggiore, Susan *geophysical oceanographer*
Nwosu, Kingsley Chukwudum *research and development scientist, educator*

## NEW MEXICO

### Albuquerque
Beckel, Charles Leroy *physics educator*
Dasgupta, Amitava *chemist, educator*
Evans, Pauline D. *physicist, educator*
Garland, James Wilson, Jr. *retired physics educator*
Harrison, Charles Wagner, Jr. *applied physicist*
Hylko, James Mark *health physicist, certified quality auditor*
Loftfield, Robert Berner *biochemistry educator*
Papike, James Joseph *geology educator, science institute director*
Picraux, Samuel Thomas *applied science and physics researcher*
Robinson, Charles Paul *nuclear physicist, diplomat, business executive*
Romig, Alton Dale, Jr. *metallurgist, educator*
Seiler, Fritz Arnold *physicist*
Sparks, Morgan *physicist*
Van Devender, J. Pace *physical scientist, management consultant*
Vianco, Paul Thomas *metallurgist*

### Kirtland AFB
Degnan, James Henry *physicist*

### Las Cruces
Coburn, Horace Hunter *retired physics educator*
Kemp, John Daniel *biochemist, educator*
Lease, Jane Etta *environmental science consultant*

### Los Alamos
Baker, George Allen, Jr. *physicist*
Becker, Stephen A. *physicist, designer*
Bell, George Irving *biophysics researcher*
Bradbury, Norris Edwin *physicist*
Campbell, Mary Stinecipher *research chemist, educator*
Colgate, Stirling Auchincloss *physicist*
Cucchiara, Alfred Louis *health physicist*
Engelhardt, Albert George *physicist*
Friar, James Lewis *physicist*
Gibson, Benjamin Franklin *physicist*
Grilly, Edward Rogers *physicist*
Jarmie, Nelson *physicist*
Johnson, Mikkel Borlaug *physicist*
Judd, O'Dean P. *physicist*
Keepin, George Robert, Jr. *physicist*
Kelly, Robert Emmett *physicist, educator*
Kubas, Gregory Joseph *research chemist*
Linford, Rulon Kesler *physicist, engineer*
Matlack, George Miller *radiochemist*
McNally, James Henry *physicist, defense consultant*
Michaudon, André Francisque *physicist*
Mitchell, Terence Edward *materials scientist*
Nix, James Rayford *nuclear physicist, consultant*
Pack, Russell T. *theoretical chemist*
Penneman, Robert Allen *retired chemist*
Petschek, Albert George *physicist, consultant*
Ramsay, John Barada *research chemist, educator*
Rosen, Louis *physicist*
Selden, Robert Wentworth *physicist, science advisor*
Simon-Gillo, Jehanne E. *physicist*
Smith, James Lawrence *research physicist*
Terrell, (Nelson) James *physicist*
Wahl, Arthur Charles *retired chemistry educator*
Whetten, John Theodore *geologist*
Williams, Joel Mann *polymer material scientist*
WoldeGabriel, Giday *research geologist*
Zweig, George *physicist, neurobiologist*

### Los Lunas
Graham, Robert Albert *research physicist*

### Mesilla
Harrison, Edward Robert *physicist, educator*

### Santa Fe
Cowan, George Arthur *chemist, bank executive, director*
Fisher, Philip Chapin *physicist*

Fisher, Robert Alan *laser physicist*
Gell-Mann, Murray *theoretical physicist, educator*
Giovanielli, Damon Vincent *physicist, consulting company executive*
Jones, Walter Harrison *chemist*
Ratliff, Floyd *biophysics educator, scientist*
White, David Hywel *physics educator*

**Socorro**
Kottlowski, Frank Edward *geologist*

**Sunspot**
Altrock, Richard Charles *astrophysicist*

## NEW YORK

**Albany**
Frost, Robert Edwin *chemistry educator*
Hof, Liselotte Bertha *biochemist*
Kim, Jai Soo *physics educator*
Reichert, Leo Edmund, Jr. *biochemist, endocrinologist*
Roth, Laura Maurer *physics educator, researcher*
Schneider, Allan Stanford *biochemistry neurosience and pharmacology educator, biomedical research scientist*

**Alfred**
Pye, Lenwood David *materials science educator, researcher, consultant*
Rossington, David Ralph *physical chemistry educator*

**Bayport**
Courant, Ernest David *physicist*

**Binghamton**
Coates, Donald Robert *geology educator, scientist*
Eisch, John Joseph *chemist, educator*
Whittingham, M(ichael) Stanley *chemist*

**Blue Point**
O'Hare, John Dignan *library director*

**Briarcliff Manor**
Bhargava, Rameshwar Nath *physicist*

**Bronx**
Moldovan, Leonard Michael *chemist*
Shamos, Morris Herbert *physicist educator*
Siddons, Sarah Mae *chemist*
Singer, Jeffrey Michael *organic analytical chemist*
Thysen, Benjamin *biochemist, health science facility administrator, researcher*
Yalow, Rosalyn Sussman *medical physicist*

**Brooklyn**
Castleman, Louis Samuel *metallurgist, educator*
Charton, Marvin *chemist, educator*
Choudhury, Deo Chand *physicist, educator*
Eirich, Frederick Roland *chemist, educator*
Franco, Victor *theoretical physics educator*
Friedman, Gerald Manfred *geologist, educator*
Friedman, Paul *chemistry educator*
Kjeldaas, Terje, Jr. *physics educator emeritus*
Morawetz, Herbert *chemistry educator*
Pearce, Eli M. *chemistry educator, administrator*
Stracher, Alfred *biochemistry educator*
Tesoro, Giuliana Cavaglieri *chemistry research educator, consultant*
Weil, Edward David *chemistry researcher, consultant, inventor*
Wolf, Edward Lincoln *physics educator*

**Buffalo**
Amborski, Leonard Edward *chemist*
Anbar, Michael *biophysics educator*
Bardos, Thomas Joseph *chemist, educator*
Basu, Rajat Subhra *physicist, researcher*
Borst, Lyle Benjamin *physicist, educator*
Coppens, Philip *chemist*
Hall, Linda McIntyre *biochemical pharmacology educator, consultant*
Jain, Piyare Lal *physics educator*
Patel, Mulchand Shambhubhai *biochemist*
Reitan, Paul Hartman *geologist, educator*
Treanor, Charles Edward *physicist*
Wang, Jui Hsin *biochemistry educator*

**Canton**
Romey, William Dowden *geologist, educator*

**Clinton**
Ring, James Walter *physics educator*

**Cooperstown**
Peters, Theodore, Jr. *research biochemist, consultant*

**Corning**
Josbeno, Larry Joseph *physics educator*
Keck, Donald Bruce *physicist*
Maurer, Robert Distler *retired industrial physicist*

**Croton On Hudson**
Adelson, Alexander Michael *physicist*

**Dobbs Ferry**
Triplett, Kelly B. *chemist*
Williams, Ross Edward *physicist*

**East Hampton**
Garrett, Charles Geoffrey Blythe *physicist*

**Fairport**
Bolt, Richard Henry *science educator, business executive, author*

**Farmingdale**
Marcuvitz, Nathan *electrophysics educator*

**Flushing**
Finks, Robert Melvin *paleontologist, educator*
Gafney, Harry D. *chemistry educator*
Goldman, Norman Lewis *chemistry educator*
Hatcher, Robert Douglas *physicist, educator*
Speidel, David Harold *geology educator*

**Fredonia**
Barnard, Walther M. *geosciences educator*

**Freeport**
Pullman, Maynard Edward *biochemist*

**Geneva**
Roelofs, Wendell Lee *biochemistry educator, consultant*

**Glen Cove**
Dehn, Joseph William, Jr. *chemist*

**Hamilton**
Holbrow, Charles Howard *physicist, educator*

**Hawthorne**
Batstone, Joanna L. *physicist*

**Hempstead**
Sparberg, Esther B. *chemist, educator*

**Irvington**
Devons, Samuel *educator, physicist*

**Islip**
DeCillis, Michael Arthur *hydrogeologist*

**Ithaca**
Ashcroft, Neil William *physics educator, researcher*
Bassett, William Akers *geologist, educator*
Batterman, Boris William *physicist, educator, academic director*
Bauer, Simon Harvey *chemistry educator*
Bauman, Dale Elton *nutritional biochemistry educator*
Berkelman, Karl *physics educator*
Bethe, Hans Albrecht *physicist, educator*
Burns, Joseph Arthur *planetary science educator*
Carpenter, Barry Keith *chemistry educator, researcher*
Clardy, Jon Christel *chemistry educator, consultant*
Clark, David Delano *physicist, educator*
Craighead, Harold G. *physics educator*
Dodd, Jack Gordon, Jr. *physicist, educator*
Fay, Robert Clinton *chemist, educator*
Fitchen, Douglas Beach *physicist, educator*
Freed, Jack Herschel *chemist, educator*
Gold, Thomas *astronomer, educator*
Goldsmith, Paul Felix *physics and astronomy educator*
Gottfried, Kurt *physicist, educator*
Greisen, Kenneth Ingvard *physicist, emeritus educator*
Hart, Edward Walter *physicist*
Hess, George Paul *biochemist, educator*
Hoffmann, Roald *chemist, educator*
Holcomb, Donald Frank *physicist, academic administrator*
Kinoshita, Toichiro *physicist*
Lee, David Morris *physics educator*
Liboff, Richard Lawrence *physicist, educator*
Lumley, John Leask *physicist, educator*
McDaniel, Boyce Dawkins *physicist, educator*
McLafferty, Fred Warren *chemist, educator*
McMurry, John Edward *chemistry educator*
Meinwald, Jerrold *chemist, educator*
Morrison, George Harold *chemist, educator*
Oliver, Jack Ertle *geophysicist*
Orear, Jay *physics educator, researcher*
Pohl, Robert Otto *physics educator*
Richardson, Robert Coleman *physics educator, researcher*
Ruoff, Arthur Louis *physicist, educator*
Salpeter, Edwin Ernest *physical sciences educator*
Scheraga, Harold Abraham *physical chemistry educator*
Sievers, Albert John, III *physics educator*
Slate, Floyd Owen *chemist, materials scientist, civil engineer, educator, researcher*
Terzian, Yervant *astronomy and astrophysics educator*
Thomas, J. Earl *physicist*
Turcotte, Donald Lawson *geophysical sciences educator*
Webb, Watt Wetmore *physicist, educator*
Widom, Benjamin *chemistry educator*
Wilson, Robert Rathbun *retired physicist*
Wu, Ray Jui *biochemistry educator*
Zilversmit, Donald Berthold *nutritional biochemist, educator*

**Jamaica**
Greenberg, Jacob *biochemist, educator, consultant*
Lengyel, István *chemist, educator*

**Lancaster**
Weinberg, Norman Louis *electrochemist*

**Larchmont**
Guttenplan, Joseph B. *biochemist*
Rosenberg, Paul *physicist, consultant*

**Lewiston**
Dexter, Theodore Henry *chemist*

**Lynbrook**
Yee, David *chemist, pharmaceutical company executive*

**Mamaroneck**
Mazzola, Claude Joseph *physicist, small business owner*

**Manhasset**
Callaway, David James Edward *physicist/ bioinformaticist, expedition mountaineer*

**Middle Village**
Farb, Edith Himel *chemist*

**New York**
Agosta, William Carleton *chemist, educator*
Allison, Michael David *space scientist, astronomy educator*
Bederson, Benjamin *physicist, educator*
Berne, Bruce J. *chemistry educator*
Birman, Joseph Leon *physics educator*
Borowitz, Sidney *retired physics educator*
Breslow, Esther May Greenberg *biochemistry educator, researcher*
Breslow, Ronald Charles *chemist, educator*
Campbell, George, Jr. *physicist, administrator*
Chargaff, Erwin *biochemistry educator emeritus, writer*
Cheng, Chuen Yan *biochemist, educator*
Chevray, Rene *physics educator*
Christman, Edward Arthur *physicist*
Cohen, Ezechiel Godert David *physicist, educator*
Colby, Frank Gerhardt *scientific consultant*
Cross, George Alan Martin *biochemistry educator, researcher*
Cummins, Herman Zachary *physicist*
Dailey, Benjamin Peter *chemistry educator*
de Duve, Christian René *chemist, educator*
Doorish, John Francis *physicist, mathematician, educator*
Eisenthal, Kenneth B. *physical chemistry educator*
Erlanger, Bernard Ferdinand *biochemist, educator*
Feigelson, Philip *biochemist, educator*
Finlay, Thomas Hiram *biochemist, researcher*
Flynn, George William *chemistry educator, researcher*
Fox, Jack Jay *chemist, educator*
Fraenkel, George Kessler *chemistry educator*
Friesner, Richard A. *chemistry educator*
Glassgold, Alfred Emanuel *physicist, educator*
Goldstein, Menek *neurochemistry educator*
Goulianos, Konstantin *physics educator*
Grunberger, Dezider *biochemist, researcher*
Gudas, Lorraine Jean *biochemist, molecular biologist, educator*
Gyulassy, Miklos *physics educator*
Hajjar, David P. *biochemist, educator*
Halpern, Alvin Michael *physicist, educator*
Harris, Cyril Manton *physicist, engineering and architecture educator, consulting acoustical engineer*
Hendrickson, Wayne A(rthur) *biochemist, educator*
Hoffert, Martin Irving *applied science educator*
Hoffman, Linda M. *chemist, educator*
Honig, Barry Hirsh *biophysics educator*
Hutter, Rudolf Gustav Emil *physics educator*
Kaku, Michio *theoretical nuclear physicist*
Katsoyannis, Panayotis George *biochemist, educator*
Katz, Thomas J. *chemistry educator*
Kellogg, Herbert Humphrey *metallurgist, educator*
Khuri, Nicola Najib *physicist, educator*
King, Edward Joseph *clinical chemist, laboratory administrator*
Krasna, Alvin Isaac *biochemist, educator*
Kuo, John Tsungfen *geophysicist, educator, researcher*
Laughlin, John Seth *physicist, educator*
Lax, Melvin *theoretical physicist*
Lee, Tsung-Dao *physicist, educator*
Lieberman, Seymour *biochemistry educator emeritus*
Low, Barbara Wharton *biochemist, biophysicist*
Machlin, Eugene Solomon *metallurgy educator, consultant*
Mader, Bryn John *vertebrate paleontologist*
Marshall, Thomas Carlisle *applied physics educator*
Mc Kenna, Malcolm Carnegie *vertebrate paleontologist, curator, educator*
Meislich, Herbert *chemistry educator emeritus*
Merrifield, Robert Bruce *biochemist, educator*
Middleton, David *physicist, applied mathematician, educator*
Nakanishi, Koji *chemistry educator, research institute administrator*
Newell, Norman Dennis *paleontologist, geologist, museum curator, educator*
Norell, Mark Allen *paleontology educator*
Novick, Robert *physicist, educator*
Nowick, Arthur Stanley *metallurgy and materials science educator*
Oppenheimer, Michael *physicist*
Oreskes, Irwin *biochemistry educator*
Oreskes, Naomi *earth sciences educator, historian*
Osgood, Richard Magee, Jr. *applied physics and electrical engineering educator, research administrator*
Pais, Abraham *physicist, educator*
Parkin, Gerard Francis Ralph *chemistry educator, researcher*
Pechukas, Philip *chemistry educator*
Percus, Jerome Kenneth *physicist, educator*
Piore, Emanuel Ruben *physicist*
Rhodes, Yorke E(dward) *chemist*
Robinson, Enders Anthony *geophysics educator, writer*
Roeder, Robert Gayle *biochemist, educator*
Rougier, Guillermo Walter *paleontologist*
Russell, Charlotte Sananes *biochemistry educator, researcher*
Sakita, Bunji *physicist, educator*
Sarachik, Myriam Paula *physics educator*
Saxena, Brij B. *biochemist, endocrinologist, educator*
Schwartz, Melvin *physics educator, laboratory administrator*
Shih, Wei *astrophysicist*
Sidran, Miriam *retired physics educator, researcher*
Simon, Eric Jacob *neurochemist, educator*
Smith, Norman Obed *physical chemist, educator*
Sonenberg, Martin *biochemistry educator, physician*
Spector, Abraham *ophthalmic biochemist, educator, laboratory administrator*
Sprinson, David Benjamin *biochemistry educator*
Stork, Gilbert *chemistry educator, investigator*
Stroke, Hinko Henry *physicist, educator*
Szer, Wlodzimierz *biochemist, educator*
Tomashefsky, Philip *biophysicis*
Turro, Nicholas John *chemistry educator*
Werthamer, N. Richard *physicist*
Zakim, David *biochemist*

**Niagara Falls**
Knowles, Richard Norris *chemist*

**Niskayuna**
Edelheit, Lewis S. *research physicist*
Katz, Samuel *geophysics educator*
Lafferty, James Martin *physicist*
Mihran, Theodore Gregory *retired physicist*

**Oneonta**
Hickey, Francis Roger *physicist, educator*
Merilan, Michael Preston *astrophysicist, dean, educator*

**Oswego**
Kumar, Alok *physics educator*
Silveira, Augustine, Jr. *chemistry educator*

**Painted Post**
Hammond, George Simms *chemist, consultant*

**Palisades**
Cane, Mark Alan *oceanography and climate researcher*
Hayes, Dennis Edward *geophysicist, educator*
Kent, Dennis Vladimir *geophysicist, researcher*
Langmuir, Charles Herbert *geology educator*
Richards, Paul Granston *geophysics educator, seismologist*
Scholz, Christopher Henry *geophysicist, writer*
Sykes, Lynn Ray *geologist, educator*

**Plattsburgh**
Heintz, Roger Lewis *biochemist, educator, researcher*

**Potsdam**
Mackay, Raymond Arthur *chemist*
Matijevic, Egon *chemistry educator,*

**Poughkeepsie**
Beck, Curt Werner *chemist, educator*
Deiters, Sister Joan Adele *chemistry educator, nun*
Lang, William Warner *physicist*
Maling, George Croswell, Jr. *physicist*
Pliskin, William Aaron *physicist*
Tavel, Morton Allen *physics educator, researcher*

**Rochester**
Abood, Leo George *biochemistry educator*
Bigelow, Nicholas Pierre *physicist, educator*
Boeckman, Robert Kenneth, Jr. *chemistry educator, organic chemistry researcher*
Cain, B(urton) Edward *chemistry educator*
Cline, Douglas *physicist, educator*
Duarte, Francisco Javier *physicist, researcher*
Eisenberg, Richard S. *chemistry educator*
Elder, Fred Kingsley, Jr. *physicist, educator*
Ferbel, Thomas *physics educator, physicist*
Garcia-Prichard, Diana *research scientist, chemical physicist*
Gates, Marshall DeMotte, Jr. *chemistry educator*
George, Nicholas *optics educator, researcher*
Goldstein, David Arthur *biophysicist, educator*
Hall, Dennis Gene *optics educator*
Hilf, Russell *biochemist*
Kampmeier, Jack August Carlos *chemist, educator*
Kende, Andrew Steven *chemistry educator*
Kingslake, Rudolf *retired optical designer*
Knauer, James Philip *physicist*
Knox, Robert Seiple *physicist, educator*
Kreilick, Robert W. *chemist, educator*
Li, James Chen Min *materials science educator*
Makous, Walter Leon *visual scientist, educator*
Mandel, Leonard *physics and optics educator*
Maniloff, Jack *biophysicist, educator*
Marinetti, Guido V. *biochemistry educator*
McCrory, Robert Lee *physicist, mechanical engineering educator*
Saunders, William Hundley, Jr. *retired chemist, educator*
Sherman, Fred *biochemist, educator*
Simon, Albert *physicist, engineer, educator*
Skupsky, Stanley *laser fusion scientist*
Thomas, John Howard *astrophysicist, engineer, educator*
Thorndike, Edward Harmon *physicist*
Whitten, David George *chemistry educator*
Wolf, Emil *physics educator*
Yin, Fang-Fang *medical physicist, educator*

**Rouses Point**
Weierstall, Richard Paul *pharmaceutical chemist*

**Saint James**
Bigeleisen, Jacob *chemist, educator*

**Scarborough**
Wittcoff, Harold Aaron *chemist*

**Scarsdale**
Josevie, Arnold Jean Phillipe *physicist, scientific consultant*

**Schenectady**
Alpher, Ralph Asher *physicist*
Billmeyer, Fred Wallace, Jr. *chemist, educator*
Bulloff, Jack John *physical chemist, consultant*
Engeler, William Ernest *physicist*
Hebb, Malcolm Hayden *physicist*
Kambour, Roger Peabody *polymer physical chemist, researcher*
Luborsky, Fred Everett *research physicist*
Philip, A. G. Davis *astronomer, editor, educator*
Rougeot, Henri Max *medical imaging engineer, physicist*
Zheng, Maggie (Xiaoci) *materials scientist, vacuum coating specialist*

**Smithtown**
Friedlander, Gerhart *nuclear chemist*

**Southold**
Bachrach, Howard L. *biochemist*

**Stony Brook**
Alexander, John Macmillan, Jr. *chemistry educator*
Bonner, Francis Truesdale *chemist, educator, university dean*
Brown, Gerald Edward *physicist, educator*
Chen Ning Yang *physicist, educator*
Hanson, Gilbert Nikolai *geochemistry educator*
Herman, Herbert *materials science educator*
Kahn, Peter B. *physics educator*
Ojima, Iwao *chemistry educator*
Solomon, Philip Myron *astronomer, atmospheric scientist*
Swanson, Robert Lawrence *oceanographer, academic program administrator*
Weidner, Donald J. *geophysicist educator*
Yang, Chen Ning *physicist, educator*

**Syracuse**
Baldwin, John Edwin *chemistry educator*
Birge, Robert Richards *chemistry educator*
Conan, Robert James, Jr. *chemistry educator, consultant*
Fendler, Janos Hugo *chemistry educator*
Fox, Geoffrey Charles *computer science and physics educator*
Gitsov, Ivan *chemist*
Honig, Arnold *physics educator, researcher*
Levy, H. Richard *biochemistry educator*
Martonosi, Anthony Nicholas *biochemistry educator, researcher*

Muller, Ernest H. *geology educator*
Nafie, Laurence Allen *chemistry educator*
Prucha, John James *geologist, educator*
Robinson, Joseph Edward *geology educator, consulting petroleum geologist*
Smith, Kenneth Judson, Jr. *chemist, theoretician, educator*
Vook, Richard Werner *physics educator*
Wellner, Marcel Nahum *physics educator, researcher*

### Tarrytown
Gross, Stanislaw *environmental sciences educator, activist*

### Troy
Bunce, Stanley Chalmers *chemist, educator*
Corelli, John Charles *physicist, educator*
Daves, Glenn Doyle, Jr. *science educator, chemist, researcher*
Ferris, James Peter *chemist, educator*
Fleischer, Robert Louis *physics educator*
Giaever, Ivar *physicist*
Krause, Sonja *chemistry educator*
Levinger, Joseph Solomon *physicist, educator*
Medicus, Heinrich Adolf *physicist, educator*
Potts, Kevin T. *emeritus chemistry educator*
Sperber, Daniel *physicist*
White, Frederick Andrew *physics educator, physicist*
Wiberley, Stephen Edward *chemistry educator, consultant*

### Tuxedo Park
Hall, Frederick Keith *chemist*

### Upton
Axe, John Donald, Jr. *physicist, researcher*
Blume, Martin *physicist*
Bond, Peter Danford *physicist*
Goldhaber, Maurice *physicist*
Hankes, Lawrence Valentine *biochemist*
Harbottle, Garman *chemist*
Hendrie, Joseph Mallam *physicist, nuclear engineer, government official*
Holroyd, Richard Allen *research scientist*
Kato, Walter Yoneo *physicist*
Lindenbaum, S(eymour) J(oseph) *physicist*
Lowenstein, Derek Irving *physicist*
Marr, Robert Bruce *physicist, educator*
McWhan, Denis Bayman *physicist*
Meinhold, Charles Boyd *health physicist*
Morris, Samuel Cary *environmental scientist, consultant, educator*
Ozaki, Satoshi *physicist*
Rau, Ralph Ronald *retired physicist*
Ruckman, Mark Warren *physicist*
Samios, Nicholas Peter *physicist*
Setlow, Jane Kellock *biophysicist*
Setlow, Richard Burton *biophysicist*
Shutt, Ralph P. *research physicist*
Souw, Bernard Eng-Kie *physicist, consultant*
Sutin, Norman *chemistry educator, scientist*
Wolf, Alfred Peter *research chemist, educator*
Zarcone, Michael Joseph *experimental physicist, consultant*

### Utica
Iodice, Arthur Alfonso *biochemist*

### Wappingers Falls
Maissel, Leon Israel *physicist, engineer*

### Webster
Conwell, Esther Marly *physicist*

### Wellsville
Taylor, Theodore Brewster *physicist, business executive*
Van Tyne, Arthur Morris *geologist*

### West Point
Leupold, Herbert August *physicist*
Oldaker, Bruce Gordon *physicist, military officer*

### White Plains
Flanigen, Edith Marie *materials scientist, consultant*

### Yorktown Heights
Fowler, Alan Bicksler *retired physicist*
Keyes, Robert William *physicist*
Kirkpatrick, Edward Scott *physicist*
Landauer, Rolf William *physicist*
Lang, Norton David *physicist*
Ning, Tak Hung *physicist, microelectronic technologist*
Sorokin, Peter Pitirimovich *physicist*
Spiller, Eberhard Adolf *physicist*

## NORTH CAROLINA

### Apex
Liu, Andrew Tze Chiu *chemical researcher and developer*

### Asheville
Deitch, D. Gregory *meteorologist*
Haggard, William Henry *meteorologist*
Smith, Norman Cutler *geologist, business executive, educator*

### Black Mountain
Lathrop, Gertrude Adams *chemist, consultant*

### Cary
Ahmadieh, Aziz *metallurgy materials science educator*

### Chapel Hill
Brookhart, Maurice S. *chemist*
Bruck, Stephen Desiderius *biochemist*
Buck, Richard Pierson *chemistry educator, researcher*
Bursey, Maurice M. *chemistry educator*
Davis, Morris Schuyler *astronomer*
Dennison, John Manley *geologist, educator*
Dolan, Louise Ann *physicist*
Eliel, Ernest Ludwig *chemist, educator*
Forman, Donald T. *biochemist*
Frampton, Paul Howard *physics researcher, educator*
Fullagar, Paul David *geology educator, geochemical consultant*
Goldman, Leonard Manuel *physicist, engineering educator*
Hubbard, Paul Stancyl, Jr. *physics educator*
Irene, Eugene Arthur *physical chemistry and materials science educator, researcher*
Lee, Kuo-Hsiung *medicinal chemistry educator*
Ligett, Waldo Buford *chemist*
Macdonald, James Ross *physicist, educator*
Markham, Jordan J. *physicist, retired educator*
McKay, Kenneth Gardiner *physicist, electronics company executive*
Merzbacher, Eugen *physicist, educator*
Meyer, Thomas J. *chemistry educator*
Miller, Daniel Newton, Jr. *geologist, consultant*
Mitchell, Earl Nelson *physicist, educator*
Murray, Royce Wilton *chemistry educator*
Neumann, Andrew Conrad *geological oceanography educator*
Parr, Robert Ghormley *chemistry educator*
Roberts, Louis Douglas *physics educator, researcher*
Rogers, John James William *geology educator*
St. Jean, Joseph, Jr. *micropaleontologist, educator*
Sancar, Aziz *research biochemist*
Slifkin, Lawrence Myer *physics educator*
Wilson, John Eric *biochemistry educator*
Wolfenden, Richard Vance *biochemistry educator*
York, James Wesley, Jr. *theoretical physicist, educator*

### Charlotte
Hall, Peter Michael *physics educator, electronics researcher*
Hayes, Peter Charles *research chemist*
Monroe, Frederick Leroy *chemist*
Mueller, Werner Heinrich *organic chemist, chemical engineering technology administrator*
Roels, Oswald Albert *oceanographer, educator, business executive*

### Davidson
Burnett, John Nicholas *chemistry educator*

### Durham
Chesnut, Donald Blair *chemistry educator*
Cocks, Franklin Hadley *materials scientist*
Evans, Ralph Aiken *physicist, consultant*
Fridovich, Irwin *biochemistry educator*
Hammes, Gordon G. *chemistry educator*
Han, Moo-Young *physicist*
Hobbs, Marcus Edwin *chemistry educator*
Jaszczak, Ronald Jack *physicist, researcher, consultant*
Joklik, Wolfgang Karl *biochemist, virologist, educator*
Kay, Richard Frederick *paleontology and biological anthropology educator*
Meyer, Horst *physics educator*
Opara, Emmanuel Chukwuemeka *biochemistry educator*
Pearsall, George Wilbur *materials scientist, mechanical engineer, educator, consultant*
Perkins, Ronald Dee *geologist, educator*
Pirrung, Michael Craig *chemistry educator, consultant*
Roberson, Nathan Russell *physicist, educator*
Smith, Peter *chemist, educator, consultant*
Stroscio, Michael Anthony *physicist, educator*
Walter, Richard Lawrence *physicist, educator*
Wilder, Pelham, Jr. *chemist, pharmacologist, educator, academic administrator*

### Fayetteville
Resnick, Paul R. *research chemist*

### Greensboro
Banegas, Estevan Brown *environmental biotechnology executive*
Clark, Clifton Bob *physicist*
Williams, Irving Laurence *physics educator*

### Greenville
Clemens, Donald Faull *chemistry educator*
Frisell, Wilhelm Richard *biochemist, educator*
Sayetta, Thomas Charles *physics educator*
Snyder, Scott William *geology educator*

### Hendersonville
Saby, John Sanford *physicist*

### Linwood
Barnes, Melver Raymond *retired chemist*

### Morrisville
Bursey, Joan Tesarek *chemist*

### Pinehurst
Huizenga, John Robert *nuclear chemist, educator*

### Pittsboro
Quinn, Jarus William *physicist, former association executive*

### Raleigh
Aspnes, David Erik *physicist, educator*
Cuomo, Jerome John *materials scientist*
Davis, William Robert *physicist*
Droessler, Earl George *geophysicist educator*
Ebisuzaki, Yukiko *chemistry educator*
Goldstein, Irving Solomon *chemistry educator, consultant*
Horton, Horace Robert *biochemistry educator*
Hugus, Z Zimmerman, Jr. *chemistry educator*
McGregor, Ralph *chemistry educator*
Mitchell, Gary Earl *physicist, educator*
Senzel, Alan Joseph *analytical chemistry consultant, music critic*
Stiles, Phillip John *physicist, educator*
Swaisgood, Harold Everett *biochemist, educator*
Sykes, Alston Leroy *analytical chemist, musician*
Whitten, Jerry Lynn *chemistry educator*

### Research Triangle Park
Chao, James Lee *chemist*
Fisher, Robert Perry *health effects scientist*
Jameson, Charles William *chemist*
Rodbell, Martin *biochemist*
Selkirk, James Kirkwood *biochemist*
Wiener, Russell Warren *environmental scientist, researcher*

### Salemburg
Baugh, Charles Milton *biochemistry educator, college dean*

### Spring Hope
Lavatelli, Leo Silvio *retired physicist, educator*

### Thomasville
Gray, Bowman *chemist*

### Wendell
Price, Howard Charles *chemist*

### Wilmington
Kelley, Patricia Hagelin *geology educator*
Martin, Ned Harold *chemistry educator*
Quin, Louis DuBose *chemist, educator*
Worzel, John Lamar *geophysicist, educator*

### Winston Salem
Mokrasch, Lewis Carl *neurochemist, educator*
Rodgman, Alan *chemist, consultant*

## NORTH DAKOTA

### Bismarck
Cornatzer, William Eugene *retired biochemistry educator*

### Grand Forks
Jacobs, Francis Albin *biochemist, educator*
Nordlie, Robert Conrad *biochemistry educator*

## OHIO

### Akron
Bohm, Georg G. A. *physicist*
Cheng, Stephen Zheng Di *chemistry educator, polymeric material researcher*
Gent, Alan Neville *physicist, educator*
Kennedy, Joseph Paul *polymer scientist, researcher*
Maximovich, Michael Joseph *chemist, consultant*
Piirma, Irja *chemist, educator*

### Alliance
Rodman, James Purcell *astrophysicist, educator*

### Athens
Eckelmann, Frank Donald *retired geology educator, dean emeritus*

### Berea
Jensen, Adolph Robert *former chemistry educator*

### Bowling Green
Brecher, Arthur Seymour *biochemistry educator*

### Burbank
Koucky, Frank Louis *geology educator, archeogeology researcher*

### Canton
Koniecko, Edward S(tanley) *biochemist*
Starchman, Dale Edward *medical radiation biophysics educator*

### Chardon
Dietrich, Joseph Jacob *retired chemist, research executive*

### Chillicothe
Johnson, Mark Alan *biochemist*

### Cincinnati
Alexander, John J. *chemistry educator*
Briskin, Madeleine *paleoceanographer, paleoclimatologist, micropaleontologist*
Devitt, John William *physicist*
Ford, Emory A. *chemist, researcher*
Francis, Marion David *consulting chemist*
Goodman, Bernard *physics educator*
Gray, John Augustus *physical chemist*
Hauck, Frederick Alexander *nuclear scientist, philosopher*
Heineman, William Richard *chemistry educator*
Hubbard, Arthur Thornton *chemistry educator, electro-surface chemist*
Kawahara, Fred Katsumi *research chemist*
Lienhart, David Arthur *geologist, consultant, laboratory director*
Martin, Daniel William *acoustical physicist*
Meal, Larie *chemistry educator, researcher, consultant*
Menyhert, Stephan *retired chemist*
Merchant, Mylon Eugene *physicist, engineer*
Pelton, John Tom *biochemist*
Rockwell, R(onald) James, Jr. *laser and electro-optics consultant*
Rudney, Harry *biochemist, educator*
Startup, William Harry *chemist*
Sullivan, James F. *physicist, educator*
Williams, James Case *metallurgist*
Witten, Louis *physics educator*

### Cleveland
Banerjee, Amiya Kumar *biochemist*
Bidelman, William Pendry *astronomer, educator*
Blackwell, John *polymers scientist, educator*
Bockhoff, Frank James *chemistry educator*
Carey, Paul Richard *biophysicist*
Deissler, Robert George *fluid dynamicist, researcher*
Dowell, Michael Brendan *chemist*
Hanson, Richard Winfield *biochemist, educator*
Jenkins, Thomas Llewellyn *physics educator*
Klopman, Gilles *chemistry educator*
Koenig, Jack L. *chemist, educator*
Kosmahl, Henry Gottfried *electron physicist*
Kowalski, Kenneth Lawrence *physicist, educator*
Krieger, Irvin Mitchell *chemistry educator, consultant*
Landau, Bernard Robert *biochemistry educator, physician*
Landis, Geoffrey Alan *physicist, writer*
Lando, Jerome Burton *macromolecular science educator*
Litt, Morton Herbert *macromolecular science educator, researcher*
Mawardi, Osman Kamel *plasma physicist*
McGervey, John Donald *physics educator, researcher*
Myers, Ronald Eugene *chemist, consultant, educator*
Ritchey, William Michael *chemistry educator*
Rogers, Charles Edwin *physical chemistry educator*
Schuele, Donald Edward *physics educator*
Uscheek, David Petrovich *chemist*
Yeager, Ernest Bill *physical chemist, electrochemist, educator*

### Columbus
Behrman, Edward Joseph *biochemistry educator*
Bergstrom, Stig Magnus *geology educator*
Brierley, Gerald P. *physiological chemistry educator*
Corbato, Charles Edward *geology educator*
Cornwell, David George *biochemist, educator*
Daehn, Glenn Steven *materials scientist*
De Lucia, Frank Charles *physicist, educator*
Elliot, David Hawksley *geologist*
Epstein, Arthur Joseph *physics and chemistry educator*
Faure, Gunter *geology educator*
Firestone, Richard Francis *chemistry educator*
Foland, Kenneth A. *geological sciences educator*
Goodridge, Alan Gardner *research biochemist, educator*
Herbst, Eric *physicist, astronomer*
Jossem, Edmund Leonard *physics educator*
Kolattukudy, Pappachan Ettoop *biochemist, educator*
Ling, Ta-Yung *physics educator*
Lowther, Frank Eugene *research physicist*
Markham, Richard Lawrence *chemist*
Marzluf, George Austin *biochemistry educator*
Mayer, Victor James *earth system science educator*
Meites, Samuel *clinical chemist, educator*
Milford, Frederick John *retired research company executive*
Miller, Terry Alan *chemistry educator*
Mills, Robert Laurence *physicist, educator*
Newsom, Gerald Higley *astronomy educator*
Pitzer, Russell Mosher *chemistry educator*
Reese, Douglas Wayne *geologist*
Reibel, Kurt *physicist, educator*
Relle, Ferenc Matyas *chemist*
Slettebak, Arne *astronomer, educator*
Snyder, Robert Lyman *materials scientist, educator*
Soloway, Albert Herman *medicinal chemist*
Sugarbaker, Evan R. *nuclear science research administrator*
Voss, Anne Coble *nutritional biochemist*
Wali, Mohan Kishen *environmental science and natural resources educator*
Webb, Thomas Evan *biochemistry educator*
Wilkins, John Warren *physics educator*
Wojcicki, Andrew Adalbert *chemist, educator*

### Dayton
Battino, Rubin *chemistry educator, retired*
Emrick, Donald Day *chemist, consultant*
Fang, Zhaoqiang *research physicist*
Gregor, Clunie Bryan *geology educator*
Janning, John Louis *research scientist, consultant*
Spicer, John Austin *physicist*

### Euclid
Parks, John Morris *metallurgist*

### Hamilton
Conditt, Margaret Karen *scientist, policy analyst*
Robertson, Jerald Lee *physicist*

### Kent
Doane, J. William *physics educator and researcher, science administrator*
Gould, Edwin Sheldon *chemist, educator*
Heimlich, Richard Allen *geologist, educator*
Tuan, Debbie Fu-Tai *chemistry educator*

### Manchester
McCluskey, Matthew Clair *physical chemist*

### Mansfield
Beiter, Thomas Albert *crystallographer, research scientist, consultant*

### Norwalk
Germann, Richard Paul *pharmaceutical company chemist, executive*

### Oberlin
Carlton, Terry Scott *chemist, educator*
Simonson, Bruce Miller *geologist, educator*

### Oxford
Baldwin, Arthur Dwight, Jr. *geology educator*
Cox, James Allan *chemistry educator*
Gordon, Gilbert *chemist, educator*
Macklin, Philip Alan *physics educator*

### Painesville
Scozzie, James Anthony *chemist*

### Piketon
Manuta, David Mark *research chemist*

### Sylvania
Kneller, William Arthur *geologist, educator*

### Toledo
Saffran, Murray *biochemist*

### Twinsburg
Mohr, Eileen Theresa *environmental geologist*

### Wickliffe
Dunn, Horton, Jr. *organic chemist*

### Wilberforce
Gupta, Vijay Kumar *chemistry educator*

### Wright Patterson AFB
Eastwood, DeLyle *chemist*
Turner, Wade Slover *biochemist, pilot*

### Yellow Springs
Spokane, Robert Bruce *biophysical chemist*

## OKLAHOMA

### Ada
Stafford, Donald Gene *chemistry educator*

### Bartlesville
Dwiggins, Claudius William, Jr. *chemist*
Hogan, J(ohn) Paul *chemistry researcher, consultant*

### Broken Arrow
Chambers, Richard Lee *geoscientist, researcher*

### Edmond
Aclin, Keith Andrew *radar meteorologist*
Troutman, George William *geologist, geological consulting firm executive*

### Fort Towson
Pike, Thomas Harrison *plant chemist*

### Muskogee
Kendrick, Thomas Rudolph *chemist*

### Norman
Atkinson, Gordon *chemistry educator*
Bluestein, Howard Bruce *meteorology educator*
Christian, Sherril D. *chemistry educator, administrator*
Ciereszko, Leon Stanley *chemistry educator*
Dryhurst, Glenn *chemistry educator*
Kessler, Edwin *meteorology educator, consultant*
Lamb, Peter James *meteorology educator, researcher, consultant*
Mankin, Charles John *geology educator*
Pigott, John Dowling *geologist, geophysicist, geochemist, educator, consultant*

### Nowata
Osborn, Ann George *retired chemist*

### Oklahoma City
Alaupovic, Petar *biochemist, educator*
Dunn, Parker Southerland *retired chemical company consultant*
England, Gary Alan *television meteorologist*
Hartsuck, Jean Ann *chemist*
Jackson, Gaines Bradford *environmental science educator*
Johnson, B(ruce) Connor *biochemist, educator, consultant*
Magarian, Robert Armen *medicinal chemist, researcher, educator*
Weigel, Paul Henry *biochemistry educator, researcher, consultant*

### Stillwater
Berlin, Kenneth Darrell *chemistry educator, consultant, researcher*
Gorin, George *retired chemistry educator*
Leach, Franklin Rollin *biochemistry educator*

### Tulsa
Anderson, David Walter *physics educator, consultant*
Blais, Roger Nathaniel *physics educator*
Horn, Myron Kay *consulting petroleum geologist, author, educator*
Rummerfield, Benjamin Franklin *geophysicist*
Smothers, William Edgar, Jr. *geophysical exploration company executive*

## OREGON

### Albany
Dooley, George Joseph, III *metallurgist*

### Ashland
Abrahams, Sidney Cyril *physicist, crystallographer*
Addicott, Warren Oliver *retired geologist, educator*
Grover, James Robb *chemist, editor*

### Chiloquin
Siemens, Richard Ernest *retired metallurgy administrator, researcher*

### Corvallis
Arp, Daniel James *biochemistry educator*
Becker, Robert Richard *biochemist, educator*
Dalrymple, Gary Brent *research geologist*
Drake, Charles Whitney *physicist*
Evans, Harold J. *plant physiologist, biochemist, educator*
Huyer, Adriana *oceanographer, educator*
Keller, George Henrik *marine geologist*
Sleight, Arthur William *chemist, educator*
Thomas, Thomas Darrah *chemistry educator*
Van Holde, Kensal Edward *biochemistry educator*
Yeats, Robert Sheppard *geologist, educator*

### Eugene
Boekelheide, Virgil Carl *chemistry educator*
Chezem, Curtis Gordon *physicist, former retail executive*
Crasemann, Bernd *physicist, educator*
Deshpande, Nilendra Ganesh *physics educator*
Donnelly, Russell James *physicist, educator*
Girardeau, Marvin Denham *physics educator*
Griffith, Osbie Hayes *chemistry educator*
He, Xianguo *chemist, consultant*
Mazo, Robert Marc *chemistry educator, retired*
Peticolas, Warner Leland *physical chemistry educator*
Retallack, Gregory John *geologist educator*
Schellman, John A. *chemistry educator*
von Hippel, Peter Hans *chemistry educator*
Youngquist, Walter Lewellyn *consulting geologist*

### Hillsboro
Carruthers, John Robert *scientist*

### Medford
Bouquet, Francis Lester *physicist*

### Monmouth
White, Donald Harvey *physics educator emeritus*

### Otter Rock
Kassner, Michael Ernest *materials science educator, researcher*

### Portland
Abel, William Edward *applied physicist, consultant*
Claycomb, Cecil Keith *biochemist, educator*
Cohen, Norm *chemist*
Cronyn, Marshall William *chemistry educator*
Dunne, Thomas Gregory *chemistry educator, researcher*
Jones, Richard Theodore *biochemistry educator*
Lincoln, Sandra Eleanor *chemistry educator*
Marsh, John Harrison *environmental planner, lawyer*
Pearson, David Petri *chemist*
Weeks, Wilford Frank *retired geophysics educator, glaciologist*
Wetzel, Karl Joseph *physics educator, university official and dean*

## PENNSYLVANIA

### Abington
Schuster, Ingeborg Ida *chemistry educator*

### Alcoa Center
Dobbs, Charles Luther *analytical chemist*

### Allentown
Goldey, James Mearns *physicist*
Pez, Guido Peter *research chemist*

### Ardmore
Stanley, Edward Alexander *geologist, forensic scientist, technical and academic administrator*

### Bethlehem
Alhadeff, Jack Abraham *biochemist, educator*
Allen, Eugene Murray *chemist*
Evenson, Edward Bernard *geologist*
Gunton, James Douglas *physics educator*
Heindel, Ned Duane *chemistry educator*
Hertzberg, Richard Warren *materials science and engineering educator, researcher*
Kanofsky, Alvin Sheldon *physicist*
Sclar, Charles Bertram *geology educator, researcher*
Smyth, Donald Morgan *chemical educator, researcher*
Watkins, George Daniels *physics educator*
Weidner, Richard Tilghman *physicist, educator*

### Bryn Mawr
Berliner, Ernst *chemistry educator*
Crawford, Maria Luisa Buse *geology educator*
Crawford, William Arthur *geologist*
Mallory, Frank Bryant *chemistry educator*

### Carlisle
Laws, Kenneth L. *physics educator, author*
Laws, Priscilla Watson *physics educator*
Long, Howard Charles *physics educator emeritus*

### Collegeville
Holder, Neville Lewis *chemist*

### Dallas
Rockensies, Kenneth Jules *physicist, educator*

### Doylestown
Brink, Frank, Jr. *biophysicist, former educator*

### Elkins Park
Prince, Morton Bronenberg *physicist*

### Erie
Karlson, Eskil Leannart *biophysicist*

### Gettysburg
Holland, Koren Alayne *chemistry educator*
Schildknecht, Calvin E(verett) *chemist, consultant, educator*

### Harrisburg
Vaughn, Stephen Anthony *biochemist, physician, educator*
Zook, Merlin Wayne *meteorologist*

### Hazleton
Miller, David Emanuel *physics educator, researcher*

### Huntingdon Valley
Leibholz, Stephen Wolfgang *physicist, engineering company executive, entrepreneur*

### Kennett Square
Lippincott, Sarah Lee *astronomer, graphologist*

### King Of Prussia
Ohnishi, Stanley Tsuyoshi *biomedical director, biophysicist*

### Lansdale
Schnable, George Luther *chemist*

### Lincoln University
Roberts, Lynn Ernest *theoretical physicist, educator*
Williams, Willie, Jr. *physicist, educator*

### Malvern
Fisher, Sallie Ann *chemist*

### Meadville
Lotze, Barbara *physicist*

### Media
Fehnel, Edward Adam *chemist, educator*

### Merion Station
Amado, Ralph David *physics educator*

### Monroeville
Parker, James Roger *chemist*

### Narberth
Fenichel, Richard Lee *retired biochemist*

### New Holland
Papadakis, Emmanuel Philippos *physicist, consultant*

### Newtown
Carlson, David Emil *physicist*

### Philadelphia
Ajzenberg-Selove, Fay *physicist, educator*
Bludman, Sidney Arnold *theoretical physicist, astrophysicist*
Burstein, Elias *physicist, educator*
Childress, Scott Julius *medicinal chemist*
Cohn, Mildred *biochemist, educator*
Creech, Hugh John *chemist*
Davis, Raymond, Jr. *physical chemistry researcher*
Devlin, Thomas McKeown *biochemist, educator*
Dutton, Peter Leslie *biochemist, educator*
Dymicky, Michael *retired chemist*
Farber, Emmanuel *pathology and biochemistry educator*
Fitts, Donald Dennis *chemist, educator*
Gamarnik, Moisey Yankelevich *solid state physicist*
Glick, Jane Mills *biochemistry educator*
Glusker, Jenny Pickworth *chemist*
Hameka, Hendrik Frederik *chemist, educator*
Havas, Peter *physicist, educator*
Hernandez, Marissa *physicist*
Hirschmann, Ralph Franz *chemist*
Intemann, Robert Louis *physics educator, researcher*
Klein, Abraham *physics educator, researcher*
Klein, Michael Lawrence *research chemist, educator*
Kritchevsky, David *biochemist, educator*
Lande, Kenneth *physicist, astronomer, educator*
Langacker, Paul George *physics educator*
Larson, Donald Clayton *physics educator, consultant*
Levitt, Israel Monroe *astronomer*
Litwack, Gerald *biochemistry researcher, educator, administrator*
Magee, Wayne Edward *biochemistry educator, researcher*
Malamud, Daniel *biochemistry educator*
Maurer, Paul Herbert *biochemist, educator*
Muzykantov, Vladimir Rurick *immunochemist, researcher*
Nixon, Eugene Ray *chemist, educator*
Noordergraaf, Abraham *biophysics educator*
Otvos, Laszlo Istvan, Jr. *organic chemist*
Pollack, Solomon Robert *bioengineering educator*
Prairie, Celia Esther Freda *biochemistry educator*
Prockop, Darwin Johnson *biochemist, physician*
Rosen, Gerald Harris *physicist, consultant, educator*
Rutman, Robert Jesse *biochemist, educator*
Shen, Benjamin Shih-Ping *scientist, engineer, educator*
Vitek, Vaclav *materials scientist*
Wales, Walter D. *physicist, educator*
Walter, James Frederic *biochemical engineer*
Weisz, Paul B(urg) *physicist, chemical engineer*

### Pittsburgh
Berry, Guy Curtis *polymer science educator, researcher*
Biondi, Manfred Anthony *physicist, educator*
Bothner-By, Aksel Arnold *chemist, horseman*
Caretto, Albert Alexander *chemist, educator*
Carr, Walter James, Jr. *research physicist, consultant*
Cassidy, William Arthur *geology and planetary science educator*
Choyke, Wolfgang Justus *physicist*
Cohen, Bernard Leonard *physicist, educator*
Coltman, John Wesley *physicist*
Emmerich, Werner Sigmund *physicist*
Feller, Robert Livingston *chemist, art conservation scientist*
Finn, Frances Mary *biochemistry researcher*
Friedberg, Simeon Adlow *physicist, educator*
Gerjuoy, Edward *physicist, lawyer*
Griffiths, Robert Budington *physics educator*
Janis, Allen Ira *retired physicist, educator*
Kisslinger, Leonard Sol *physicist, educator*
Laughlin, David Eugene *materials science educator, metallurgical consultant*
Massalski, Thaddeus Bronislaw *material scientist, educator*
Matyjaszewski, Krzysztof *chemist, educator*
Mortimer, James Winslow *analytical chemist*
Page, Lorne Albert *physicist, educator*
Pezacka, Ewa Hanna *biochemist, educator*
Plazek, Donald John *materials science educator*
Pratt, Richard Houghton *physics educator*
Rosenberg, Jerome Laib *chemist, educator*
Rosenkranz, Herbert S. *environmental toxicology educator*
Sashin, Donald *physicist, radiological physicist, educator*
Sekerka, Robert Floyd *physics educator, scientist*
Sorensen, Raymond Andrew *physics educator*
White, Robert Marshall *physicist, educator*
Wolken, Jerome Jay *biophysicist, educator*
Yates, John Thomas, Jr. *chemistry educator, research director*
Young, Hugh David *physics educator, writer, organist*

### Plymouth Meeting
Gilstein, Jacob Burrill *physicist*

### Quakertown
McDaniel, Robert Stephen *technical professional*

### Spring House
Klotz, Wendy Lynnett *analytical chemist*
Reitz, Allen Bernard *organic chemist*

### State College
Garrett, Steven Lurie *physicist*
German, Randall Michael *materials science educator, consultant*
Kenealy, Matthew H., III *hydrogeologist*

### Swarthmore
Bilaniuk, Oleksa Myron *physicist, educator*
Hammons, James Hutchinson *chemistry educator, researcher*
Oneal, Glen, Jr. *retired physicist*
Pasternack, Robert Francis *chemistry educator*

### University Park
Allcock, Harry R. *chemistry educator*
Badding, John Victor *chemistry educator*
Barnes, Hubert Lloyd *geochemistry educator*
Barron, Eric *earth scientist*
Benkovic, Stephen James *chemist*
Bernheim, Robert Allan *chemistry educator*
Blackadar, Alfred Kimball *meteorologist, educator*
Cahir, John Joseph *meteorologist, educational administrator*
Castleman, Albert Welford, Jr. *physical chemist, educator*
Coleman, Michael Murray *polymer science educator*
Dutton, John Altnow *meteorologist, educator*
Frankl, Daniel Richard *physicist, educator*
Hogg, Richard *mineral/particle process engineering educator*
Hosler, Charles Luther, Jr. *meteorologist, educator*
Howell, Benjamin Franklin, Jr. *geophysicist, educator*
Jackman, Lloyd Miles *chemistry educator*
Kasting, James Fraser *research meteorologist, physicist*
Lampe, Frederick Walter *chemistry educator, consultant*
Mészáros, Peter Istvan *astrophysicist, researcher, astronomy educator*
Pazur, John Howard *biochemist, educator*
Roy, Rustum *interdisciplinary materials researcher, educator*
Rusinko, Frank, Jr. *fuels and materials scientist*
Taylor, William Daniel *biophysics educator, university dean*
White, William Blaine *geochemist, educator*
Winograd, Nicholas *chemist*

### Valley Forge
Erb, Doretta Louise Barker *polymer applications scientist*
Erb, Robert Allan *physical scientist*
Hergert, Herbert Lawrence *chemist*

### Villanova
Edwards, John Ralph *chemist, educator*
Phares, Alain Joseph *physicist, educator*

### West Chester
Young, Franklin *biochemistry educator*

### West Mifflin
Smith, Stewart Edward *physical chemist*

### Wyncote
Baldridge, Robert Crary *retired biochemistry educator*

### Wyndmoor
Pfeffer, Philip Elliot *biophysicist*

### Wynnewood
Weinhouse, Sidney *biochemist, educator*

### Wyoming
Singer, Sandra Maria *forensic scientist*

### Wyomissing
Boyer, Robert Allen *physics educator*

## RHODE ISLAND

### Coventry
Traficante, Daniel Dominick *chemist*

### Kingston
Nixon, Scott West *oceanography science educator*

### Middletown
Mellberg, Leonard Evert *physicist*

### Narragansett
Pilson, Michael Edward Quinton *oceanography educator*

### Providence
Avery, Donald Hills *metallurgist, educator, ethnographer*
Bray, Philip James *physicist*
Briant, Clyde Leonard *metallurgist, researcher*
Carpenter, Gene Blakely *crystallography and chemistry educator*
Cooper, Leon N. *physicist, educator*
Dahlberg, Albert Edward *biochemistry educator*
Elbaum, Charles *physicist, educator, researcher*
Estrup, Peder Jan *physics and chemistry educator*
Gerritsen, Hendrik Jurjen *physics educator, researcher*
Greene, Edward Forbes *chemistry educator*
Houghton, Anthony *physics educator, research scientist*
Lanou, Robert Eugene, Jr. *physicist, educator*
Levin, Frank S. *physicist, educator*
Parmentier, E. M. (Marc) *geophysics educator*
Pieters, C.M. *geology educator, planetary scientist, researcher*
Rieger, Philip Henri *chemistry educator*
Risen, William Maurice, Jr. *chemistry educator*
Stratt, Richard Mark *chemistry researcher, educator*
Tauc, Jan *physics educator*
Webb, Thompson *geological sciences educator, researcher*
Westervelt, Peter Jocelyn *physics educator*
Widgoff, Mildred *physicist, educator*

### Wakefield
Moore, George Emerson, Jr. *geologist, educator*

### West Greenwich
Anderson, Theodore Robert *physicist*

## SOUTH CAROLINA

### Aiken
Dickson, Paul Wesley, Jr. *physicist*
Hofstetter, Kenneth John *research chemist*
Miller, Phillip Edward *environmental scientist*

### Anderson
Apinis, John *chemist*
†Elzerman, Alan William *environmental chemistry educator*

### Central
Reid, William James *retired physicist, educator*

### Charleston
Adelman, Saul Joseph *astronomy educator, researcher*
Delli Colli, Humbert Thomas *chemist, product development specialist*
Fenn, Jimmy O'Neil *physicist*
Gadsden, Richard Hamilton *clinical biochemistry educator*

**Clemson**
Clayton, Donald Delbert *astrophysicist, nuclear physicist, educator*
Griffin, Villard Stuart, Jr. *geology educator*
Krause, Lois Ruth Breur *chemistry educator*

**Columbia**
Edge, Ronald Dovaston *physics educator*
Gandy, James Thomas *meteorologist*
Schuette, Oswald Francis *physics educator*
Secor, Donald Terry, Jr. *geologist, educator*
Teague, Peyton Clark *chemist, educator*

**Conway**
Skinner, Samuel Ballou, III *physics educator, researcher*

**Greenville**
Miller, Cecelia Smith *chemist*

**Johns Island**
Failla, Patricia McClement *biomedical and environmental research adminstrator*

**Pendleton**
Spain, James Dorris, Jr. *biochemist, educator*

**Salem**
Gentry, Robert Cecil *meteorological consultant, research scientist*

## SOUTH DAKOTA

**Brookings**
Duffey, George Henry *physics educator*

**Hot Springs**
Hiller, William Clark *retired physics educator, engineering educator*

**Rapid City**
Gries, John Paul *geologist*
Smith, Paul Letton, Jr. *geophysicist*

**Spearfish**
Erickson, Richard Ames *physicist, emeritus educator*

**Vermillion**
Neuhaus, Otto Wilhelm *biochemistry educator*

## TENNESSEE

**Chattanooga**
Howe, Lyman Harold, III *chemist*
Kiser, Thelma Kay *analytical chemist*

**Cookeville**
Swartling, Daniel Joseph *chemistry educator, researcher*

**Fairfield Glade**
Gillis, Bernard Thomas *retired chemistry educator*

**Hendersonville**
Hill, William Thomas *geological consultant*

**Jefferson City**
Bahner, Carl Tabb *retired chemistry educator, researcher*

**Johnson City**
McIntosh, Cecilia Ann *biochemist, educator*
Miller, Barney E. *biochemist*

**Kingsport**
Germinario, Louis Thomas *materials scientist*
Gose, William Christopher *chemist*
Young, Howard Seth *chemist, researcher*

**Kingston**
Manly, William Donald *metallurgist*

**Knoxville**
Alexeff, Igor *physicist, electrical engineer, educator emeritus*
Blass, William Errol *physics and astronomy educator*
Borie, Bernard Simon, Jr. *physicist, educator*
Dean, John Aurie *chemist, author, chemistry educator emeritus*
Lietzke, Milton Henry *chemistry educator*
Mahan, Gerald Dennis *physics educator, researcher*
Painter, Linda Robinson *physics educator, dean*
Renshaw, Amanda Frances *retired physicist, nuclear engineer*
Schweitzer, George Keene *chemistry educator*
Wehlitz, Ralf *physicist*
Williams, Thomas Ffrancon *chemist, educator*
Wunderlich, Bernhard *physical chemistry educator*

**Memphis**
Crane, Laura Jane *research chemist*
Desiderio, Dominic Morse, Jr. *chemistry and neurochemistry educator*
Fain, John Nicholas *biochemistry educator*
Lasslo, Andrew *medicinal chemist, educator*
Wildman, Gary Cecil *chemist*

**Nashville**
Bayuzick, Robert J. *materials scientist*
Chytil, Frank *biochemist*
Cohen, Stanley *biochemistry educator*
Cunningham, Leon William *biochemist, educator*
Dettbarn, Wolf-Dietrich *neurochemist, pharmacologist, educator*
Fort, Tomlinson *chemist, chemical engineering educator*
†Hall, Douglas Scott *astronomy educator*
Hamilton, Joseph Hants, Jr. *physicist, educator*
Harris, Thomas Munson *chemistry educator, researcher*
Heiser, Arnold Melvin *astronomer*
Hercules, David Michael *chemistry educator, consultant*
Holladay, Wendell Gene *physics educator*
Inagami, Tadashi *biochemist, educator*
Kono, Tetsuro *biochemist, physiologist, educator*
Lukehart, Charles Martin *chemistry educator*
Miller, Calvin Francis *geology educator*
Panvini, Robert S. *physics researcher/educator*
Silberman, Enrique *physics researcher and administrator*
Stubbs, Gerald *biochemist, educator*
Tarbell, Dean Stanley *chemistry educator*
Tolk, Norman Henry *physics educator*
Weeks, Robet Andrew *materials science researcher, educator*
Wert, James Junior *materials scientist, educator*
Wilson, David James *chemistry researcher, educator*

**Oak Ridge**
Beasley, Cloyd Orris, Jr. *physicist, researcher*
Cawley, Charles Nash *enviromental scientist*
Dickens, Justin Kirk *nuclear physicist*
Garrett, Jerry Dale *nuclear physicist*
Gifford, Franklin Andrew, Jr. *meteorologist*
Grimes, James Gordon *geologist*
Huff, Dale Duane *hydrologist, educator*
Krause, Manfred Otto *physicist*
Larson, Bennett Charles *solid state physicist, researcher*
Maienschein, Fred C. *physicist*
Plasil, Franz *physicist*
Postma, Herman *physicist, consultant*
Satchler, George Raymond *physicist*
Totter, John Randolph *biochemist*
Trivelpiece, Alvin William *physicist, corporate executive*
Weinberg, Alvin Martin *physicist*
Wilkinson, Michael Kennerly *physicist*
Yalcintas, M. Güven *medical physicist*
Zucker, Alexander *physicist, administrator*

**Powell**
Gentry, Robert Vance *physicist, researcher, writer*

**Tullahoma**
Dahotre, Narendra Bapurao *materials scientist, researcher, educator*

## TEXAS

**Arlington**
Burkart, Burke *geology educator, researcher*
Pomerantz, Martin *chemistry educator, researcher*
Rajeshwar, Krishnan *chemist, educator*
Smith, Charles Isaac *geology educator*

**Austin**
Bard, Allen Joseph *chemist, educator*
Barker, Daniel Stephen *geology educator*
Bash, Frank Ness *astronomer, educator*
Bengtson, Roger Dean *physicist*
Boggs, James Ernest *chemistry educator*
Campion, Alan *chemistry educator*
Dalziel, Ian William Drummond *geologist, educator, researcher*
de Wette, Frederik Willem *physics educator*
DeWitt-Morette, Cécile *physicist*
Dicus, Duane A. *physicist, educator*
Duncombe, Raynor Lockwood *astronomer*
Ellison, Samuel Porter, Jr. *geologist, educator*
Erskine, James Lorenzo *physics educator*
Fisher, William Lawrence *geologist, educator*
Folk, Robert Louis *geologist, educator*
Fonken, Gerhard Joseph *retired chemistry educator, academic administrator*
Fox, Marye Anne *chemistry educator*
Gardiner, William Cecil, Jr. *chemist, educator*
Gavenda, J(ohn) David *physicist*
Gentle, Kenneth William *physicist*
Griffy, Thomas Alan *physics educator*
Hazeltine, Richard Deimel *physics educator, university institute director*
Heller, Adam *chemist, researcher*
Herman, Robert *physics educator*
Hill, David Wayne *geologist*
Ho, Paul Siu-Chung *physics educator*
Horton, Claude Wendell *physicist, educator*
Hudspeth, Emmett LeRoy *physicist, educator*
Jefferys, William Hamilton, III *astronomer*
Lagowski, J(oseph) J(ohn) *chemist*
Lundelius, Ernest Luther, Jr. *vertebrate paleontologist, educator*
Maxwell, Arthur Eugene *oceanographer, marine geophysicist, educator*
Mohrmann, Leonard Edward, Jr. *chemist, chemical engineer*
Nguyen, Truc Chinh *analytical chemist*
Reed, Lester James *biochemist, educator*
Snell, Esmond Emerson *biochemist*
Stewart, Kent Kallam *analytical biochemistry educator*
Swinney, Harry Leonard *physics educator*
Trafton, Laurence Munro *astronomer*
Tyler, Noel *geological researcher and educator*
Vishniac, Ethan Tecumseh *astronomy educator*
Wheeler, John Craig *astrophysicist, writer*
White, John Michael *chemistry educator*
Willson, C. Grant *chemistry educator, engineering educator*
Ziegler, Daniel Martin *chemistry educator*

**Baytown**
Mendelson, Robert Allen *polymer scientist, rheologist*

**Brownsville**
Tijerina, Raul Martin *physics and mathematics educator*

**Bryan**
Hoskins, Earl R., Jr. *geophysics department dean*

**Carrollton**
Ali, Odeh Said *petroleum geologist*

**College Station**
Anderson, Aubrey Lee *oceanographer, educator*
Anderson, Duwayne Marlo *earth and polar scientist, university administrator*
Arnowitt, Richard Lewis *physics educator, researcher*
Berg, Robert Raymond *geologist, educator*
Berner, Leo De Witte, Jr. *retired oceanographer*
Conway, Dwight Colbur *chemistry educator*
Cotton, Frank Albert *chemist, educator*
Duce, Robert Arthur *atmospheric chemist, university administrator*
Duff, Michael James *physicist*
Fackler, John Paul, Jr. *chemistry educator*
Goodman, David Wayne *research chemist*
Hardy, John Christopher *physicist*
Laane, Jaan *chemistry educator*
Martell, Arthur Earl *chemistry educator*
McIntyre, John Armin *physics educator*
McIntyre, Peter Mastin *physicist, educator*
Nachman, Ronald James *research chemist*
Natowitz, Joseph B. *chemistry educator, research administrator*
O'Connor, Rod *chemist, inventor*
Prescott, John Mack *biochemist, retired university administrator*
Rezak, Richard *geology and oceanography educator*
Scott, Alastair Ian *chemistry educator*
Stanton, Robert James, Jr. *geologist, educator*
Stewart, Robert Henry *oceanographer, educator*
Stipanovic, Robert Douglas *chemist, researcher*
Wild, James Robert *biochemistry and genetics educator*

**Conroe**
Westmoreland, Thomas Delbert, Jr. *chemist*

**Corpus Christi**
Berryhill, Henry Lee, Jr. *geologist*
de Wys, Egbert Christiaan *geochemist*

**Dallas**
Benge, Raymond Doyle, Jr. *astronomy educator*
Blattner, Wolfram Georg Michael *meteorologist*
Brooks, James Elwood *geologist, educator*
Esquivel, Agerico Liwag *research physicist*
Estabrook, Ronald Winfield *chemistry educator*
Gibbs, James Alanson *geologist*
Green, Cecil Howard *geophysicist, consultant, educator*
Konrad, Dusan *chemist*
Marshall, John Harris, Jr. *geologist, oil company executive*
Ries, Edward Richard *petroleum geologist, consultant*
Sharp, William Wheeler *geologist*

**Denton**
Brostow, Witold Konrad *materials scientist, educator*
Saleh, Farida Yousry *chemistry educator*

**El Paso**
Cook, Clarence Sharp *physics educator*
Groat, Charles George *geologist, science administrator*
Hardaway, Robert Morris, III *physician, educator, retired army officer*
Wang, Paul Weily *materials science and physics educator*

**Fort Worth**
Caldwell, Billy Ray *geologist*
Gutsche, Carl David *chemistry educator*
Koger, David Gordon *oil and gas exploration, analyst, consultant*
Landolt, Robert George *chemistry educator*
Mills, John James *research director*
Quarles, Carroll Adair, Jr. *physicist, educator*
Reinecke, Manfred G. *chemistry educator*
Smith, William Burton *chemist, educator*
Webb, Theodore Stratton, Jr. *aerospace scientist, consultant*
Wilson, Ronald James *geologist*

**Galveston**
Bonchev, Danail Georgiev *chemist, educator*
Gorenstein, David G. *chemistry and biochemistry educator*
Kurosky, Alexander *biochemist, educator*
Merrell, William John, Jr. *oceanography educator*
Schoenbucher, Bruce *health physicist*

**Highland Village**
Coogan, Melinda Ann Strank *chemistry educator*

**Horseshoe Bay**
Ramey, James Melton *chemist*

**Houston**
Anderson, Richard Carl *geophysical exploration company executive*
Askew, William Earl *chemist, educator*
Baker, Stephen Denio *physics educator*
Bennett, George Nelson *biochemistry educator*
Bonner, Billy Edward *physics educator*
Brandt, I. Marvin *chemist, engineer*
Brooks, Philip Russell *chemistry educator, researcher*
Brotzen, Franz Richard *materials science educator*
Burke, Kevin Charles Antony *geologist*
Cameron, William Duncan *plastics company executive*
Chaku, Pran Nath *international consulting metallurgist*
Chamberlain, Joseph Wyan *astronomer, educator*
Chu, Paul Ching-Wu *physicist*
Chu, Wei-Kan *physicist, educator*
Curl, Robert Floyd, Jr. *chemistry educator*
De Bremaecker, Jean-Claude *geophysics educator*
Estle, Thomas Leo *physicist, educator*
Gibson, Everett Kay, Jr. *space scientist, geochemist*
Gibson, Quentin Howieson *biochemist*
Gordon, William Edwin *physicist, engineer, educator, university official*
Haas, Merrill Wilber *geologist, oil company executive*
Hackerman, Norman *chemist, consultant, academic administrator*
†Haslam, Charles Linn *aerospace executive, lawyer, educator*
Hasling, Jill Freeman *meteorologist*
Haymes, Robert C. *physicist, educator*
Huang, Huey Wen *physicist, educator*
Hungerford, Ed Vernon, III *physics educator*
Ignatiev, Alex *physics researcher*
Kalmaz, Errol Ekrem *environmental scientist*
Kevan, Larry *chemistry educator*
Kinsey, James Lloyd *chemist, educator*
Kit, Saul *biochemist, educator*
Kochi, Jay Kazuo *chemist, educator*
Kouri, Donald Jack *chemist, educator*
Krakower, Terri Jan *biochemist, researcher*
Kraus-Friedmann, Naomi *biochemistry educator*
Lewis, Edward Sheldon *chemistry educator*
Liang, Edison Parktak *astrophysicist, educator, researcher*
Lucid, Shannon W. *biochemist, astronaut*
Margrave, John Lee *chemist, educator, university administrator*
Mateker, Emil Joseph, Jr. *geophysicist*
Matthews, Kathleen Shive *biochemistry educator*
May, John Andrew *petrophysicist, geologist*
McCleary, Henry Glen *geophysicist*
Mehra, Jagdish *physicist*
Meindl, Max J., III *environmental consultant, professional inspector*
Norton, Norman James *exploration geologist*
Overfield, Robert Edward *physicist*
Powell, Michael Robert *biophysicist, physicist, chemist*
Reiff, Patricia Hofer *space physicist, educator*
Reso, Anthony *geologist, earth resources economist*
Rudolph, Frederick Byron *biochemistry educator*
Schroepfer, George John, Jr. *biochemistry educator*
Scuseria, Gustavo Enrique *theoretical chemist*
Sisson, Virginia Baker *geology educator*
Skolnick, Malcolm Harris *biophysics researcher, educator, patent lawyer, mediator*
Slaugh, Lynn H. *chemist*
Smalley, Richard Errett *chemistry and physics educator, researcher*
Smith, Ken A. *physicist*
Smith, Michael Alexis *petroleum geologist*
Talwani, Manik *geophysicist, educator*
Tung, Shih-Ming Samuel *medical physicist*
Wakil, Salih Jawad *biochemistry educator*
Weinstein, Roy *physics educator, researcher*
Willcott, Mark Robert, III *chemist, educator, researcher*
Wilson, Thomas Leon *physicist*
Wold, Finn *biochemist, educator*
Yang, Chao Yuh *chemistry educator*
Zlatkis, Albert *chemistry educator*

**Humble**
Brinkley, Charles Alexander *geologist*

**Irving**
Hendrickson, Constance Marie McRight *chemist, consultant*
Holdar, Robert Martin *chemist*

**Kerrville**
Shaw, Alan Bosworth *geologist, paleontologist, retired*

**Lake Jackson**
Tasa, Kendall Sherwood *chemistry educator*

**Lubbock**
Marx, John Norbert *chemistry educator*
Murray, Grover Elmer *geologist, educator*
Robinson, G. Wilse *molecular physicist, educator*

**Missouri City**
Strier, Murray Paul *chemist, consultant*

**New Braunfels**
Wilson, James Lee *retired geology educator, consultant*

**Orange**
Adkins, John E(arl), Jr. *chemist*

**Pantego**
Schimelpfenig, C(larence) W(illiam), Jr. *retired chemistry educator*

**Pasadena**
Root, M. Belinda *chemist*

**Plano**
Broyles, Michael Lee *geophysics and physics educator*
Dahiya, Jai Bhagwan *chemist*
Moore, Christopher Robertson Kinley *petroleum geologist*

**Richardson**
Cordell, Robert James *retired geologist*
Johnson, Francis Severin *physicist*
Nevill, William Albert *chemistry educator*
Urquhart, Sally Ann *environmental scientist, chemist*

**Richmond**
Willis, David Edwin *retired geophysicist*

**Rockport**
Jones, Lawrence Ryman *retired research chemist*
Mulle, George Ernest *petroleum geologist*

**San Antonio**
Ball, M(ary) Isabel *chemistry educator, dean*
Bhandari, Basant *biochemist, molecular biologist, chemical engineer, food technologist, chemist*
Budalur, Thyagarajan Subbanarayan *chemistry educator*
Burton, Russell Rohan *aerospace scientist, researcher*
Doyle, Frank Lawrence *geologist, hydrologist, executive*
Duncan, Jo Dee *chemist, research and development specialist*
Gladstone, George Randall *planetary scientist*
Greenberg, Marvin Keith *chemist*
Hamm, William Joseph *retired physics educator*
Hanahan, Donald James *biochemist, educator*
Jones, James Ogden *geologist, educator*
Lyle, Robert Edward *chemist*
Masters, Bettie Sue Siler *biochemist, educator*
Mills, Nancy Stewart *chemistry educator*
Rodgers, Robert Aubrey *physicist*
Sablik, Martin John *research physicist*
Siler-Khodr, Theresa Marie *biochemistry educator*
Sinkin, Fay Marie *environmentalist*

**Seguin**
Scheie, Paul Olaf *physics educator*

**Southlake**
Herrmann, Debra McGuire *chemist, educator*

**Spring**
Jones, Katharine Jean *research physicist*

**Temple**
Coulter, John Breitling, III *biochemist, educator*

PROFESSIONAL INDEX 5427 SCIENCE: PHYSICAL SCIENCE


**Tyler**
Walsh, Kenneth Albert *chemist*

**Vernon**
Roberson, Mark Allen *physicist, educator*

**Waco**
Pedrotti, Leno Stephano *physics educator*

**Wimberley**
Upchurch, Garland Rudolph, Jr. *paleontologist, researcher*

## UTAH

**Draper**
Partridge, William Schaubel *retired physicist, research company executive*

**Garrison**
Beeston, Joseph Mack *metallurgist*

**Logan**
Aust, Steven Douglas *biochemistry, biotechnology and toxicology educator*
Bowles, David Stanley *engineering educator, consultant*
Schunk, Robert Walter *space physics research administrator*
Scouten, William Henry *chemistry educator, academic administrator*

**Ogden**
Buss, Walter Richard *geology educator*
Evans, Robert John *retired biochemistry educator, researcher*
Welch, Garth Larry *chemistry educator, retired*

**Provo**
Hall, Howard Tracy *chemist*

**Salt Lake City**
Anspaugh, Lynn Richard *research biophysicist*
Caldwell, Karin D. *biochemist educator*
Dick, Bertram Gale, Jr. *physics educator*
Dworzanski, Jacek Pawel *analytical biochemist, researcher*
Foltz, Rodger Lowell *chemistry educator, mass spectroscopist*
Gladysz, John Andrew *chemistry educator*
Gortatowski, Melvin Jerome *retired chemist*
Hill, George Richard *chemistry educator*
Hunt, Charles Butler *geologist*
Kanes, William Henry *geology educator, research center administrator*
Liou, Kuo-Nan *atmospheric science educator, researcher*
Loh, Eugene C. *physicist, educator*
Miller, Jan Dean *metallurgy educator*
Miller, Joel Steven *solid state scientist*
Moe, Scott Thomas *chemist*
O'Halloran, Thomas Alphonsus, Jr. *physicist, educator*
Olson, Ferron Allred *metallurgist, educator*
Parry, Robert Walter *chemistry educator*
Poulter, Charles Dale *chemist, educator, consultant*
Rashba, Emmanuel Iosif *physicist, educator*
Stang, Peter John *organic chemist*
Velick, Sidney Frederick *research biochemist, educator*

## VERMONT

**Burlington**
Chiu, Jen-Fu *biochemistry educator*
White, William North *chemistry educator*

**Killington**
Laing, David *natural science educator*

**Middlebury**
Winkler, Paul Frank, Jr. *astrophysicist, educator*

**Thetford**
Hoagland, Mahlon Bush *biochemist, educator*

## VIRGINIA

**Abingdon**
Taylor, Alfred Raleigh *geologist*

**Alexandria**
Berman, Alan *physicist*
Biberman, Lucien Morton *physicist*
Brenner, Alfred Ephraim *physicist*
Campbell, Francis James *retired chemist*
Masterson, Kleber Sanlin, Jr. *physicist*
Milling, Marcus Eugene, Sr. *geologist*
Muir, Warren Roger *chemist, toxic substances specialist*
Sayre, Edward Vale *chemist*
Shapiro, Maurice Mandel *astrophysicist*
Straus, Leon Stephan *physicist*
Toulmin, Priestley *geologist*
Wolicki, Eligius Anthony *nuclear physicist, consultant*
Yaworsky, George Myroslaw *physicist, technical and management consultant*
Zook, Theresa Fuetterer *gemologist, consultant*

**Annandale**
Matuszko, Anthony Joseph *research chemist, administrator*
Raab, Harry Frederick, Jr. *physicist*

**Arlington**
Barnhart, Beverly Jean *physicist*
Bautz, Laura Patricia *astronomer*
Berg, John Richard *chemist, former federal government executive*
Borchers, Robert Reece *physicist and administrator*
Brown, Elliott Rowe *physicist*
Cavanaugh, Margaret Anne *chemist*
Dickman, Robert Laurence *physicist, researcher*
Ensminger, Luther Glenn *chemist*
Erb, Karl Albert *physicist, government official*
Gergely, Tomas *astronomer*
Hartley, David Minor *physicist*
Johnson, Charles Nelson, Jr. *physicist*
Khosla, Rajinder Paul *physicist*
Lawrence, Ray Vance *chemist*
Mooney, John Bradford, Jr. *oceanographer, engineer, consultant*
Ordway, Frederick Ira, III *educator, consultant, researcher, author*
Reynolds, Peter James *physicist*
Romney, Carl F. *seismologist*
Sancetta, Constance Antonina *oceanographer*
Sinclair, Rolf Malcolm *physicist*
Van Horn, Hugh *physicist, astronomer*
Wayland, Russell Gibson, Jr. *retired geology consultant, government official*
Whitcomb, James Hall *geophysicist, foundation administrator*
Wodarczyk, Francis John *chemist*
Yankwich, Peter Ewald *chemistry educator*
Zirkind, Ralph *physicist, educator*

**Ashburn**
Bennett, Lawrence Herman *physicist*

**Blacksburg**
Bauer, Henry Hermann *chemistry and science educator*
Cairns, John, Jr. *environmental science educator, researcher*
Graybeal, Jack Daniel *chemist, educator*
McGrath, James Edward *chemistry educator*
Mo, Luke Wei *physicist, educator*
Ogliaruso, Michael Anthony *chemist, educator*
Terhune, Robert William *optics scientist*

**Charlottesville**
Biltonen, Rodney Lincoln *biochemistry and pharmacology educator*
Bloomfield, Louis Aub *physicist, educator*
Boring, John Wayne *physicist, educator*
Bradbeer, Clive *biochemistry and microbiology educator, research scientist*
Brill, Arthur Sylvan *biophysics educator*
Carpenter, Richard Amon *chemist*
Chevalier, Roger Alan *astronomy educator, consultant*
Du Bar, Jules Ramon *geologist, retired educator*
Duffis, Allen Jacobus *polymer chemistry extrusion specialist*
Fredrick, Laurence William *astronomer, educator*
Gallagher, Thomas Francis *physicist*
Gaskin, Felicia *biochemist, educator*
Goodell, Horace Grant *environmental sciences educator*
Grimes, Russell Newell *chemistry educator, inorganic chemist*
Grisham, Charles Milton *biochemist, educator*
Gugelot, Piet Cornelis *physics educator*
Hereford, Frank Loucks, Jr. *physicist, educator*
Hunt, Donald Frederick *chemistry educator*
Kellermann, Kenneth Irwin *astronomer*
Kerr, Anthony Robert *scientist*
Kuhlmann-Wilsdorf, Doris *physics and materials science educator*
Larson, Daniel John *physics educator*
MacDonald, Timothy Lee *chemistry educator*
Martin, Robert Bruce *chemistry educator*
Meem, James Lawrence, Jr. *nuclear scientist*
Rastinejad, Fraydoon *biophysicist, structural biologist, educator*
Roberts, Morton Spitz *astronomer*
Sarazin, Craig Leigh *astronomer, educator*
Shen, Tsung Ying *medicinal chemistry educator*
Song, Xiaotong *physicist, educator*
Sundberg, Richard Jay *chemistry educator*
Vanden Bout, Paul Adrian *astronomer, physicist, educator*

**Dahlgren**
Holt, William Henry *physicist, researcher*

**Fairfax**
Morowitz, Harold Joseph *biophysicist, educator*
Singer, S(iegfried) Fred *geophysicist, educator*

**Falls Church**
Benson, William Edward (Barnes) *geologist*
Feldmann, Edward George *pharmaceutical chemist*
Spindel, William *chemist, consultant*

**Gainesville**
Steger, Edward Herman *chemist*

**Galax**
Sense, Karl August *physicist, educator*

**Hampden Sydney**
Joyner, Weyland Thomas *physicist, educator, business consultant*
Kniffen, Donald Avery *astrophysicist, educator, researcher*
Porterfield, William Wendell *chemist, educator*

**Hampton**
Deepak, Adarsh *meteorologist, aerospace engineer, atmospheric scientist*
Houbolt, John Cornelius *physicist*

**Herndon**
Crossfield, Albert Scott *aeronautical science consultant, pilot*

**Lexington**
Spencer, Edgar Winston *geology educator*

**Lynchburg**
Morgan, Evan *chemist*

**Machipongo**
Salter, Robert Mundhenk, Jr. *physicist, consultant*

**Manassas**
Tidman, Derek Albert *physics researcher*

**Manassas Park**
Bussard, Robert William *physicist*

**Mc Lean**
Carter, William Walton *physicist*
Cotterill, Carl Hayden *mineral and metals company executive*
Doyle, Frederick Joseph *government research scientist*
Hoffman, Ronald Bruce *biophysicist, life scientist, human factors consultant*
Theon, John Speridon *meteorologist*
Watt, William Stewart *physical chemist*

**Middleburg**
Spilhaus, Athelstan *meteorologist, oceanographer*

**Newport News**
Cardman, Lawrence S. *physics educator*
Isgur, Nathan Gerald *physicist, educator*

**Norfolk**
Schellenberg, Karl Abraham *biochemist*

**Petersburg**
Stronach, Carey Elliott *physicist, educator*

**Philomont**
Conte, Joseph John, II *meteorologist, management consultant*

**Reston**
Brett, Robin *geologist*
Burton, James Samuel *physical chemist*
Clark, Sandra Helen Becker *geologist*
Cohen, Philip *retired hydrogeologist*
Eaton, Gordon Pryor *geologist, research director*
Hamilton, Robert Morrison *geophysicist*
Huebner, John Stephen *geologist*
Naeser, Nancy Dearien *geologist, researcher*
Peck, Dallas Lynn *retired geologist*
Ross, Malcolm *mineralogist, crystallographer*
Sato, Motoaki *geologist, researcher*

**Richmond**
Ham, William Taylor, Jr. *biophysics educator, researcher*
Suleymanian, Mirik *biophysicist*
Tiedemann, Albert William, Jr. *chemist*
Wakeham, Helmut Richard Rae *chemist, consulting company executive*

**Roanoke**
Al-Zubaidi, Amer Aziz *physicist, educator*
Husted, John Edwin *geologist, educator*

**Salem**
Fisher, Charles Harold *chemistry educator, researcher*

**Springfield**
Baker, George Harold, III *physicist*
Doe, Bruce Roger *geologist*
Sebastian, Richard Lee *physicist, executive*
Steele, Lendell Eugene *research scientist*

**Sweet Briar**
McClenon, John Raymond *chemistry educator*

**Vienna**
Zehl, Otis George *optical physicist*

**Warm Springs**
Orem, Henry Philip *retired chemist, chemical engineer, consultant*

**Williamsburg**
Goodwin, Bruce Kesseli *geology educator, researcher*
Mc Knight, John Lacy *physics educator*
Orwoll, Robert Arvid *chemistry educator*
Siegel, Robert Ted *physicist*
Starnes, William Herbert, Jr. *chemist, educator*

**Winchester**
Ludwig, George Harry *physicist*

## WASHINGTON

**Battle Ground**
Morris, William Joseph *paleontologist, educator*

**Bellevue**
Benveniste, Jacob *retired physicist*
Chen, Ching-Hong *medical biochemist, biotechnology company executive*
Fremouw, Edward Joseph *physicist*
Watson, Mathew D. *optical scientist*

**Bellingham**
Morse, Joseph Grant *chemistry educator*

**Bothell**
Garr, Cheryl Denise *research chemist*

**Clinton**
Forward, Robert L(ull) *physicist, writer, consultant*

**Eastsound**
Fowles, George Richard *physicist, educator*

**Edmonds**
Galster, Richard W. *engineering geologist*

**Ellensburg**
Rosell, Sharon Lynn *physics and chemistry educator, researcher*
Yu, Roger Hong *physics educator*

**Kalama**
Liang, Jason Chia *research chemist*

**Lake Forest Park**
Favorite, Felix *oceanographer*

**Lynnwood**
Olsen, Kenneth Harold *geophysicist, astrophysicist*

**Manchester**
Fearon, Lee Charles *chemist*

**Oak Harbor**
Crampton, George Harris *science educator, retired army officer*

**Olympia**
Bloomquist, Rodney Gordon *geologist*

**Pullman**
Crosby, Glenn Arthur *chemistry educator*
Dodgen, Harold Warren *chemistry and physics educator*
Lutz, Julie Haynes *astronomy and mathematics educator*
Randall, Linda Lea *biochemist, educator*
Ryan, Clarence Augustine, Jr. *biochemistry educator*

**Redmond**
Malik, Sohail *chemistry educator, researcher, consultant*

**Richland**
Bevelacqua, Joseph John *physicist, researcher*
Bush, Spencer Harrison *metallurgist*
Campbell, Milton Hugh *chemist*
Elderkin, Charles Edwin *retired meteorologist*
Jacobsen, Gerald Bernhardt *biochemist*
Moore, Emmett Burris, Jr. *physical chemist*
Ramesh, Kalahasti Subrahmanyam *materials scientist*

**Seattle**
Andersen, Niels Hjorth *chemistry educator, biophysics researcher, consultant*
Anderson, Arthur G., Jr. *chemistry educator*
Arons, Arnold Boris *physicist, educator*
Banse, Karl *retired oceanography educator*
Baum, William Alvin *astronomer, educator*
Bernard, Eddie Nolan *oceanographer*
Bichsel, Hans *physicist, consultant, researcher*
Bodansky, David *physicist, educator*
Borden, Weston Thatcher *chemistry educator*
Brown, Craig William *physical chemist*
Brown, Frederick Calvin *physicist, educator*
Brown, Lowell Severt *physicist, educator*
Brown, Robert Alan *atmospheric science educator, research scientist*
Brownlee, Donald Eugene, II *astronomer, educator*
Charlson, Robert Jay *atmospheric sciences educator, scientist*
Christian, Gary Dale *chemistry educator*
Clark, Kenneth Courtright *retired physics and geophysics educator*
Cramer, John Gleason, Jr. *physics educator, experimental physicist*
Creager, Joe Scott *geology and oceanography educator*
Dash, J. Gregory *physicist, educator*
Dehmelt, Hans Georg *physicist*
Ellis, Stephen D. *physics educator*
Engel, Thomas *chemistry educator*
Evans, Bernard William *geologist, educator*
Fischer, Edmond Henri *biochemistry educator*
Fischer, Fred Walter *physicist, engineer, educator*
Fleagle, Robert Guthrie *meteorologist, educator*
Floss, Heinz G. *chemistry educator, scientist*
Fortson, Edward Norval *physics educator*
Geballe, Ronald *physicist, university dean*
Gerhart, James Basil *physics educator*
Gordon, Milton Paul *biochemist, educator*
Gouterman, Martin Paul *chemistry educator*
Gregory, Norman Wayne *chemistry educator, researcher*
Halver, John Emil *nutritional biochemist*
Harrison, Don Edmunds *oceanographer, educator*
Hartmann, Dennis Lee *atmospheric science educator*
Henley, Ernest Mark *physics educator, university dean emeritus*
Hodge, Paul William *astronomer, educator*
Ingalls, Robert Lynn *physicist, educator*
Krebs, Edwin Gerhard *biochemistry educator*
Kwiram, Alvin L. *physical chemistry educator, university official*
Lingafelter, Edward Clay, Jr. *chemistry educator*
Lord, Jere Johns *retired physics educator*
Lubatti, Henry Joseph *physicist, educator*
Mallory, V(irgil) Standish *geologist, educator*
Margon, Bruce Henry *astrophysicist, educator*
Olmstead, Marjorie Ann *physics educator*
Pocker, Yeshayau *chemistry, biochemistry educator*
Porter, Stephen Cummings *geologist, educator*
Rabinovitch, Benton Seymour *chemist, educator emeritus*
Reed, Richard John *retired meteorology educator*
Reinhardt, William Parker *chemical physicist, educator*
Rhines, Peter Broomell *oceanographer, atmospheric scientist*
Robertson, Robert Graham Hamish *physicist*
Spinrad, Bernard Israel *physicist, educator*
Stern, Edward Abraham *physics educator*
Stuiver, Minze *geological sciences educator*
Szkody, Paula *astronomy educator, researcher*
Taketomi, Susamu *physicist, researcher*
Thouless, David James *physicist, educator*
Varanasi, Usha *environmental scientist*
Wallerstein, George *astronomy educator*
Walsh, Kenneth Andrew *biochemist*
Weitkamp, William George *retired nuclear physicist*
Wilets, Lawrence *physics educator*
Williams, Robert Walter *physics educator*

**Sequim**
Woodruff, Truman O(wen) *physicist, emeritus educator*

**Silverdale**
Walske, M(ax) Carl, Jr. *physicist*

**Spokane**
Benson, Allen B. *chemist, educator, consultant*

**Tacoma**
Ames, Kenneth Carl *hydrologist, geology educator*
Gregory, Arthur Stanley *retired chemist*
Tonn, Sheri Jeanne *chemistry educator, dean*

**Yakima**
Shuman, Mark Samuel *environmental and electroanalytical chemistry educator*

## WEST VIRGINIA

**Charleston**
Bhasin, Madan Mohan *chemical research scientist*

### Fairmont
Swiger, Elizabeth Davis *chemistry educator*

### Huntington
Hubbard, John Lewis *chemist, educator, researcher*

### Institute
DasSarma, Basudeb *chemistry educator*

### Morgantown
Beattie, Diana Scott *biochemistry educator*
Butcher, Fred R. *biochemistry educator, university administrator*
Fodor, Gábor Béla *chemistry educator, researcher*
Seehra, Mohindar Singh *physics educator, researcher*

## WISCONSIN

### Appleton
Van den Akker, Johannes Archibald *physicist*

### Kenosha
Kolb, Vera M. *chemistry educator*

### La Crosse
Rozelle, Lee Theodore *physical chemist*

### Madison
Adler, Julius *biochemist, biologist, educator*
Anderson, Louis Wilmer, Jr. *physicist, educator*
Barger, Vernon Duane *physicist, educator*
Bentley, Charles Raymond *geophysics educator*
Botez, Dan *physicist*
Bretherton, Francis P. *atmospheric and oceanic sciences educator*
Bryson, Reid Allen *earth sciences educator*
Burris, Robert Harza *biochemist, educator*
Cassinelli, Joseph Patrick *astronomy educator*
Christensen, Nikolas Ivan *geophysicist, educator*
Churchwell, Edward Bruce *astronomer, educator*
Clark, David Leigh *marine geologist, educator*
Clay, Clarence Samuel *acoustical oceanographer*
Cleland, W(illiam) Wallace *biochemistry educator*
Connors, Kenneth Antonio *retired chemistry educator*
Cornwell, Charles Daniel *physical chemist, educator*
Craddock, (John) Campbell *geologist, educator*
Curtiss, Charles Francis *chemist, educator*
Deutsch, Harold Francis *biochemist, researcher, educator*
DeWerd, Larry Albert *medical physicist, educator*
Dott, Robert Henry, Jr. *geologist, educator*
Ediger, Mark D. *chemistry educator*
Ellis, Arthur Baron *chemist, educator*
Evenson, Merle Armin *chemist, educator*
Farrar, Thomas C. *chemist, educator*
Fennema, Owen Richard *food chemistry educator*
Ferry, John Douglass *retired chemist, educator*
Fry, William Frederick *physics educator*
Gorski, Jack *biochemistry educator*
Hamers, Robert J. *chemistry educator, researcher*
Hedden, Gregory Dexter *environmental science educator, consultant*
Hokin, Lowell Edward *biochemist, educator*
Houghton, David Drew *meteorologist, educator*
Kraushaar, William Lester *physicist, educator*
Lagally, Max Gunter *physics educator*
Lardy, Henry A(rnold) *biochemistry educator*
Larsen, Edwin Merritt *retired chemist, educator*
Lawler, James Edward *physics educator*
Maher, Louis James, Jr. *geologist, educator*
Moore, John Ward *chemistry educator*
Morton, Stephen Dana *chemist*
Mukerjee, Pasupati *chemistry educator*
Perlman, D(avid) *biochemist, educator*
Pondrom, Lee Girard *physicist, educator*
Pray, Lloyd Charles *geologist, educator*
Rich, Daniel Hulbert *chemistry educator*
Richards, Hugh Taylor *physics educator*
Robertson, James Magruder *geological research administrator*
Rowe, John Westel *retired organic chemist*
Satter, Larry Dean *biochemist, scientific research administrator*
Savage, Blair deWillis *astronomer, educator*
Sih, Charles John *pharmaceutical chemistry educator*
Skinner, James Lauriston *chemist, educator*
Vaughan, Worth Edward *chemistry educator*
Wang, Herbert Fan *geophysics educator*
West, Robert Culbertson *chemistry educator*
†Young, Raymond Allen *chemist, educator*
Zimmerman, Howard Elliot *chemist, educator*

### Middleton
Ferry, James Allen *physicist, electrostatics company executive*
Ostrom, Meredith Eggers *retired geologist*

### Milwaukee
Aita, Carolyn Rubin *materials scientist*
Bader, Alfred Robert *chemist*
Baker, John Edward *cardiac biochemist, educator*
Greenler, Robert George *physics educator, researcher*
Griffith, Owen Wendell *biochemistry educator*
Haworth, Daniel Thomas *chemistry educator*
Hendee, William Richard *medical physics educator, university official*
Jache, Albert William *retired chemistry educator, scientist*
Karkheck, John Peter *physics educator, researcher*
Miller, David Hewitt *environmental scientist, writer*
Paull, Richard Allen *geologist, educator*
Walters, William LeRoy *physics educator*

### Neenah
Workman, Jerome James, Jr. *chemist*

### Racine
Coyle-Rees, Margaret Mary *chemist*
Langenegger, Armin *radiation physicist*

### Stevens Point
George, Thomas Frederick *chemistry educator*

### Stoughton
Huber, David Lawrence *physicist, educator*
Kuhn, Peter Mouat *atmospheric physicist*

### Washington Island
Raup, David Malcolm *paleontology educator*

### Williams Bay
Hobbs, Lewis Mankin *astronomer*

## WYOMING

### Casper
Seese, William Shober *chemistry educator*
Wold, John Schiller *geologist, former congressman*

### Jackson Hole
Paulson, Glenn *environmental scientist*

### Laramie
Grandy, Walter Thomas, Jr. *physicist, educator*
Meyer, Edmond Gerald *energy and natural resources educator, resources scientist, entrepreneur, former chemistry educator, university administrator*
Roark, Terry Paul *academic administrator, physicist*

## TERRITORIES OF THE UNITED STATES

## PUERTO RICO

### Manati
Silva-Ruíz, Sergio Andrés *biochemist*

### Vega Alta
Matos, Cruz Alfonso *environmental consultant*

## MILITARY ADDRESSES OF THE UNITED STATES

## EUROPE

### APO
Bikales, Norbert M. *chemist, science administrator*

## CANADA

## ALBERTA

### Calgary
Armstrong, David Anthony *physical chemist, educator*
Campbell, Finley Alexander *geologist*
Hyne, James Bissett *chemistry educator, industrial scientist, consultant*
Nigg, Benno Maurus *biomechanics educator*
Thorsteinsson, Raymond *geology research scientist*

### Drumheller
Currie, Philip John *research paleontologist, museum program director*

### Edmonton
Folinsbee, Robert Edward *retired geology educator*
Gough, Denis Ian *geophysics educator*
Harris, Walter Edgar *chemistry educator*
Jones, Richard Norman *physical chemist, researcher*
Kay, Cyril Max *biochemist*
Khanna, Faqir Chand *physics educator*
Kratochvil, Byron George *chemistry educator, researcher*
Lemieux, Raymond Urgel *chemistry educator*
Rostoker, Gordon *physicist, educator*
Rutter, Nathaniel Westlund *geologist, educator*
Stelck, Charles Richard *geology educator*
Sykes, Brian Douglas *biochemistry educator, researcher*
Vance, Dennis Edward *biochemistry educator*

## BRITISH COLUMBIA

### Maple Ridge
Wainwright, David Stanley *intellectual property professional*

### North Saanich
Weichert, Dieter Horst *seismologist, researcher*

### Sidney
Petrie, William *physicist*
van den Bergh, Sidney *astronomer*

### Vancouver
Aubke, Friedhelm *chemistry educator*
Bloom, Myer *physicist, educator*
Clarke, Garry Kenneth Connal *geophysics educator*
Hardy, Walter Newbold *physics educator, researcher*
James, Brian Robert *chemistry educator*
Ozier, Irving *physicist, educator*
Pickard, George Lawson *physics educator*
Pincock, Richard Earl *chemistry educator*
Russell, Richard Doncaster *geophysicist, educator, geoscientist*
Sinclair, Alastair James *geology educator*
Smith, Michael *biochemistry educator*
Snider, Robert F. *chemistry educator, researcher*
Stewart, Ross *chemistry educator*
Underhill, Anne Barbara *astrophysicist*
Vogt, Erich Wolfgang *physicist, academic administrator*
Warren, Harry Verney *geological sciences educator, consulting geological engineer*
Wheeler, John Oliver *geologist*

### Victoria
Barnes, Christopher Richard *geologist*
Batten, Alan Henry *astronomer*
Best, Melvyn Edward *geophysicist*
Hutchings, John Barrie *astronomer, researcher*
Israel, Werner *physics educator*
Leffek, Kenneth Thomas *chemist, educator*
MacLeod, John Munroe *radio astronomer*
Mc Carter, John Alexander *biochemistry educator*
Morton, Donald Charles *astronomer*
Oke, John Beverley *astronomy educator*
Stetson, Peter Brailey *astronomer*
Wiles, David McKeen *chemist*
Wright, Kenneth Osborne *retired astronomer*

### West Vancouver
Wynne-Edwards, Hugh Robert *entrepreneur, scientist*

### White Rock
Cooke, Herbert Basil Sutton *geologist, educator*

## MANITOBA

### Winnipeg
Barber, Robert Charles *physics educator*
Bigelow, Charles Cross *biochemist, university administrator*
Ferguson, Robert Bury *mineralogy educator*
Kanfer, Julian Norman *biochemist, educator*
Mantsch, Henry Horst *chemistry educator*
Schaefer, Theodore Peter *chemistry educator*
Smith, Ian Cormack Palmer *biophysicist*

## NEW BRUNSWICK

### Fredericton
Valenta, Zdenek *chemistry educator*
Vaníček, Petr *geodesist*

## NEWFOUNDLAND

### Saint John's
Rochester, Michael Grant *geophysics educator*
Williams, Harold *geology educator*

## NOVA SCOTIA

### Dartmouth
Elliott, James A. *oceanographer, researcher*
Keen, Charlotte Elizabeth *marine geophysicist, researcher*
Platt, Trevor Charles *oceanographer, scientist*

### Halifax
Dahn, Jeff R. *physics educator*
Geldart, Donald James Wallace *physics educator*
†Gillis, John William *geologist, provincial government legislator*
Gold, Edgar *marine affairs educator, mariner, lawyer*

### Wallace
Boyle, Willard Sterling *physicist*

### Wolfville
Bishop, Roy Lovitt *physics and astronomy educator*

## ONTARIO

### Ancaster
Brockhouse, Bertram Neville *physicist, retired educator*

### Burlington
Cragg, Laurence Harold *chemist, former university president*

### Chalk River
Milton, John Charles Douglas *nuclear physicist*
Torgerson, David Franklyn *chemist, research facility administrator*

### Deep River
Hanna, Geoffrey Chalmers *nuclear scientist*

### Downsview
Pritchard, Huw Owen *chemist, educator*
Ribner, Herbert Spencer *physicist, educator*
Tennyson, Roderick C. *aerospace scientist*

### Etobicoke
Bahadur, Birendra *display specialist, liquid crystal researcher*

### Gloucester
Marsters, Gerald Frederick *retired aerospace science and technology executive*

### Guelph
Dickinson, William Trevor *hydrologist, educator*
Karl, Gabriel *physics educator*
Simpson, John Joseph *physics educator, researcher*

### Hamilton
Basinski, Zbigniew Stanislaw *metal physicist, educator*
Childs, Ronald Frank *chemistry educator, science administrator*
Datars, William Ross *physicist, educator*
Davies, John Arthur *physics and engineering educator, scientist*
Garland, William James *engineering physics educator*
Gillespie, Ronald James *chemistry educator, researcher, writer*
MacLean, David Bailey *chemistry educator, researcher*
Schwarcz, Henry Philip *geologist, educator*
Spenser, Ian Daniel *chemist educator*
Sprung, Donald Whitfield Loyal *physics educator*
Walker, Roger Geoffrey *geology educator, consultant*
Welch, Douglas Lindsay *physics educator*

### Kingston
Ewan, George Thomson *physicist, educator*
McDonald, Arthur Bruce *physics educator*
Sayer, Michael *physics educator*
Spencer, John Hedley *biochemistry educator*
Stewart, Alec Thompson *physicist*
Szarek, Walter Anthony *chemist, educator*

### Lions Bay
Bartholomew, Gilbert Alfred *retired physicist*

### London
Bancroft, George Michael *chemical physicist, educator*
Carroll, Kenneth Kitchener *biochemist, nutritionist, educator*
Dreimanis, Aleksis *emeritus geology educator*
Fyfe, William Sefton *geochemist, educator*
Roach, Margot Ruth *biophysicist, educator*
Stewart, Harold Brown *biochemist*
Stillman, M. J. *physical science rsch. administrator, bioinorganic chemist*
Stothers, John B. *chemistry educator*
Weedon, Alan Charles *chemist, educator, university dean*

### Manotick
Hobson, George Donald *retired geophysicist*

### North York
Bohme, Diethard Kurt *chemistry educator*
Carswell, Allan Ian *physics educator*

### Ottawa
Alper, Howard *chemistry educator*
Andrew, Bryan Haydn *astronomer*
Conrad, A. B. *physical science administrator*
Fallis, Alexander Graham *chemistry educator*
Halliday, Ian *astronomer*
Harington, Charles Richard *vertebrate paleontologist*
Haworth, Richard Thomas *geophysicist, science director*
Herzberg, Gerhard *physicist*
Himms-Hagen, Jean Margaret *biochemist*
Holmes, John Leonard *chemistry educator*
Ingold, Keith Usherwood *chemist, educator*
Kates, Morris *biochemist, educator*
Lossing, Frederick Pettit *retired chemist*
Marmet, Paul *physicist*
McLaren, Digby Johns *geologist, educator*
Puddington, Ira Edwin *chemist*
Ramsay, Donald Allan *physical chemist*
Redhead, Paul Aveling *physicist*
St-Onge, Denis Alderic *geologist, research scientist*
Schneider, William George *chemist, research consultant*
Templeton, Ian Malcolm *retired physicist*
Varshni, Yatendra Pal *physicist*
Veizer, Ján *geology educator*
Whitehead, J. Rennie *science consultant*
Whitham, Kenneth *science and technology consultant*

### Owen Sound
Morley, Lawrence Whitaker *geophysicist, remote sensing consultant*

### Richmond Hill
Bolton, Charles Thomas *astronomer*
Fernie, John Donald *astronomer, educator*
Garrison, Robert Frederick *astronomer, educator*
MacRae, Donald Alexander *astronomy educator*

### Saint Catharines
Jolly, Wayne Travis *geologist, educator*
Terasmae, Jaan *geology educator*

### Toronto
Alcock, Charles Benjamin *materials science consultant*
Baines, Andrew DeWitt *medical biochemist*
Brook, Adrian Gibbs *chemistry educator*
Brumer, Paul William *chemical physicist, educator*
Dunlop, David John *geophysics educator, researcher*
Goldberg, David Meyer *biochemistry educator*
Haynes, Robert Hall *biophysicist, educator*
Hofmann, Theo *biochemist, educator*
Ivey, Donald Glenn *physics educator*
Jervis, Robert E. *chemistry educator*
Kresge, Alexander Jerry *chemistry educator*
List, Roland *physicist, educator, former UN official*
Litherland, Albert Edward *physics educator*
McNeill, K(enneth) G(ordon) *medical physicist*
Moffat, John William *physics educator*
Naldrett, Anthony James *geology educator*
Norris, Geoffrey *geology educator, consultant*
Ottaway, Terri Louise *geologist, gemologist*
Packham, Marian Aitchison *biochemistry educator*
Pilliar, Robert Mathews *metallurgy educator, materials scientist*
Polanyi, John Charles *chemist, educator*
Prugovecki, Eduard *mathematical physicist, educator, author*
Rowe, David John *physics educator*
Seaquist, Ernest Raymond *astronomy educator*
†Siminovitch, Louis *biophysics educator, scientist*
Spooner, Ed Thornton Casswell *geology educator and researcher*
Stoicheff, Boris Peter *physicist, educator*
Tidwell, Thomas Tinsley *chemistry educator*
Tremaine, Scott Duncan *astrophysicist*
Whittington, Stuart Gordon *chemistry educator*
Wicks, Frederick John *research mineralogist, museum curator*
Yip, Cecil Cheung-Ching *biochemist, educator*

### Waterloo
Morgan, Alan Vivian *geologist, educator*

### Windsor
Drake, Gordon William Frederic *physics educator*
Jones, William Ernest *chemistry educator*
Thibert, Roger Joseph *clinical chemist, educator*

## QUEBEC

### Laval
David, Michel Louis *geostatistician, consultant*

### Montreal
Chan, Tak Hang *chemist, educator*
Das Gupta, Subal *physics educator, researcher*
Derome, Jacques Florian *meteorology educator*
de Takacsy, Nicholas Benedict *physicist, educator*
Edward, John Thomas *chemist, educator*
Eisenberg, Adi *chemist*
Fontaine, Gilles *physics educator*
Gaudry, Roger *chemist, university official*
Hay, Allan Stuart *chemist, educator*
Johnstone, Rose Mamelak (Mrs. Douglas Johnstone) *biochemistry educator*
Langleben, Manuel Phillip *physics educator*
Mark, Shew-Kuey Tommy *physics educator*

Nemec, Josef organic chemist, researcher
Neumark, Gertrude Fanny materials science educator
Nobles, Laurence Hewit retired geology educator
Noyes, H(enry) Pierre physicist
Olsen, Clifford Wayne retired physical chemist, consultant
Orttung, William Herbert chemistry educator
Oster, Ludwig Friedrich physicist
Parreira, Helio Correa physical chemist
Pearson, Donald Emanual chemist, educator
Pearson, Ralph Gottfrid chemistry educator
Penzias, Arno Allan astrophysicist, research scientist, information systems specialist
Petersen, Arne Joaquin chemist
Piehl, Donald Herbert chemist, consultant
Pirkle, Earl Charnell geologist, educator
Pocock, Frederick James environmental scientist, engineer, consultant
Portis, Alan Mark physicist, educator
Posin, Daniel Q. physics educator, television lecturer
Pound, Robert Vivian physics educator
Price, Clifford Warren retired metallurgist, researcher
Price, Paul Buford physicist, educator
Proctor, Richard J. geologist, consultant
Pursey, Derek Lindsay physics educator
Qutub, Musa Yacub hydrogeologist, educator, consultant
Rabó, Jule Anthony chemical researcher, consultant
Rasmusson, Gary Henry medicinal chemist
Rast, Walter, Jr. hydrologist, water quality management
Redda, Kinfe Ken chemist, educator
Reichmanis, Elsa chemist
Rice, Stuart Alan chemist, educator
Richards, Paul Linford physics educator, researcher
Richardson, Charles Clifton biochemist, educator
Robertson, John Archibald Law nuclear scientist
Robinson, Bruce Butler physicist
Rose, Marian Henrietta physics researcher
Ross, Alberta Barkley retired chemist
Roychoudhuri, Chandrasekhar physicist
Rubin, Vera Cooper research astronomer
Rugge, Hugo Robert physicist
Salzer, Louis William chemist
Sayre, David physicist
Schachter, Harry biochemist, educator
Schmidt, Ruth A(nna) M(arie) geologist
Schmitt, George Joseph chemist
Schonhorn, Harold chemist, researcher
Schwartz, Lyle H. materials scientist, science administrator
Schwarzschild, Martin astronomer, educator
Sellin, Ivan Armand physicist, educator, researcher
Shaw, Melvin Phillip physicist, engineering educator, psychologist
Shirley, David Arthur chemistry educator, science administrator
Smith, Charles Haddon geoscientist, consultant
Speier, John Leo, Jr. retired chemist
Spejewski, Eugene Henry physicist, educator
Spitzer, Lyman, Jr. astronomer
Squibb, Samuel Dexter chemistry educator
Steinmetz, John Charles geologist, paleontologist
Stevenson, Paul Michael physics educator, researcher
Strouth, Baron Howard Steven geologist, mining engineer
Sturtevant, Julian Munson biophysical chemist, educator
Sullivan, Nicholas G. science educator, speleologist
Sundaresan, Mosur Kalyanaraman physics educator
Sunderman, Duane Neuman chemist, research institute executive
Symchowicz, Samson biochemist
Taylor, Hugh Pettingill, Jr. geologist, educator
Tedford, Charles Franklin biophysicist
Thompson, Julia Ann physicist
Thuillier, Richard Howard meteorologist
Tribble, Alan Charles physicist
Tucker, Robert Keith environmental sciences educator, researcher
Turco, Richard Peter atmospheric scientist
Ullman, Edwin Fisher research chemist
Vanderwalker, Diane Mary materials scientist
Vanier, Jacques physicist
Veronis, George geophysicist, educator
Vitaliano, Charles J(oseph) geologist, educator
Vook, Frederick Ludwig physicist, constultant
Wahl, Floyd Michael geologist
Wald, Francine Joy Weintraub (Mrs. Bernard J. Wald) physicist, academic administrator
Warshawsky, Isidore physicist, consultant
Wattenberg, Albert physicist, educator
Waymouth, John Francis physicist, consultant
Weinberg, Steven physics educator
Weisburger, Elizabeth Kreiser chemist, editor
Weiss, Michael James chemistry educator
Wells, Robert Hartley chemistry professional
Welton, Theodore Allen retired theoretical physics educator, consultant
Whistler, Roy Lester chemist, educator, industrialist
Wickman, Herbert Hollis physical chemist, condensed matter physicist
Wilson, Kenneth Geddes physics research administrator, educator
Wolff, Manfred Ernst medicinal chemist, pharmaceutical company executive
Wolff, Peter Adalbert physicist, educator
Wroblowa, Halina Stefania electrochemist
Yates, David John C. chemist, researcher
Zaffaroni, Alejandro C. biochemist, medical research company executive
Zhou, Ming De aeronautical scientist, educator
Zimm, Bruno Hasbrouck physical chemistry educator
Ziock, Klaus Otto Heinrich retired physics educator

# SOCIAL SCIENCE

## UNITED STATES

## ALABAMA

### Birmingham
Liu, Ray Ho forensic science program director, educator
McCarl, Henry N. economics and geology educator
Nunn, Grady Harrison political science educator emeritus

### Collinsville
Beasley, Mary Catherine home economics educator, administrator, researcher

### Dothan
Wright, Burton sociologist

### Florence
Butler, Michael Ward economics educator

### Huntsville
Traylor, Orba Forest economist, lawyer, educator

### Jacksonville
Dunaway, Carolyn Bennett sociology educator

### Maxwell AFB
Wendzel, Robert Leroy political science educator

### Mobile
Bobo, James Robert economics educator

### Montevallo
McChesney, Robert Michael, Sr. political science educator

### Tuscaloosa
Abdel-Ghany, Mohamed family economics educator
Baklanoff, Eric Nicholas economist, educator
Cramer, Dale Lewis economics educator
Fish, Mary Martha economics educator

## ALASKA

### Anchorage
Jones, Garth Nelson business and public administration educator

### Fairbanks
Kunz, Michael Lenney archaeologist
McBeath, Gerald Alan political science educator

## ARIZONA

### Bisbee
Eley, Lynn W. political science educator, former mayor

### Casa Grande
Davies, Harriett Marie (Lolly Davies) educator

### Phoenix
Maguire, Alan Edward economist, public policy consultant

### Scottsdale
Farris, Martin Theodore economist, educator

### Sedona
Eggert, Robert John, Sr. economist

### Tempe
Alisky, Marvin Howard political science educator
Farber, Bernard sociologist, educator
Gordon, Leonard sociology educator
Lounsbury, John Frederick geographer, educator
Metcalf, Virgil Alonzo economics educator
Miller, Warren Edward political scientist
Montero, Darrel Martin sociologist, social worker, educator
O'Neil, Michael Joseph opinion survey executive, marketing consultant
Rice, Ross R(ichard) political science educator
Schneller, Eugene S. sociology educator
Simon, Sheldon Weiss political science educator
Weigend, Guido Gustav geographer, educator

### Tucson
Block, Michael Kent economics and law educator, public policy association executive, former government official, consultant
Brewer, David L. sociologist
Clarke, James Weston political science educator, writer
Denton, Michael John research economist, electric utility expert, consultant
Goodall, Jane anthropologist
Marshall, Robert Herman economics educator
Mishler, William, II political science educator
Rodeffer, Stephanie Lynn Holschlag archaeologist, government official
Smith, Vernon Lomax economist, researcher
Soren, David archaeology educator, administrator
Stini, William Arthur anthropologist, educator
Stubblefield, Thomas Mason agricultural economist, educator
Thompson, Raymond Harris anthropologist, educator
Underwood, Jane Hainline Hammons anthropologist, educator
Volgy, Thomas John political science educator, organization official
Wahlke, John Charles political science educator
Whiting, Allen Suess political science educator, writer, consultant

### Yuma
Norton, Dunbar Sutton economic developer

## ARKANSAS

### Arkadelphia
Sandford, Juanita Dadisman sociologist, educator, writer

### Conway
Mc New, Bennie Banks economics and finance educator

### Fayetteville
Cramer, Gail Latimer economist
Green, Thomas James archaeologist
Mc Gimsey, Charles Robert, III anthropologist
Purvis, Hoyt Hughes political scientist, academic administrator, educator

### Little Rock
Ledbetter, Calvin Reville, Jr. (Cal Ledbetter) political science educator, university dean, former legislator

### Morrilton
Thompson, Robert Lee agricultural economist, nonprofit executive

### State University
Power, Mary Susan political science educator

## CALIFORNIA

### Arcata
Emenhiser, JeDon Allen political science educator, academic administrator

### Bakersfield
Glynn, James A. sociology educator, author

### Berkeley
Adelman, Irma Glicman economics educator
Alhadeff, David Albert economics educator
Auerbach, Alan Jeffrey economist
Bellah, Robert Neelly sociologist, educator
Brandes, Stanley Howard anthropology educator, writer
Breslauer, George William political science educator
Cain, Bruce Edward political science educator, consultant
Cheit, Earl Frank economist, educator
Clark, John Desmond anthropology educator
Colson, Elizabeth Florence anthropologist
Debreu, Gerard economics and mathematics educator
Duster, Troy sociology educator
Foster, George McClelland, Jr. anthropologist
Frankel, Jeffrey Alexander economics educator, consultant
Gilbert, Richard Joseph economics educator
Gilkerson, Tom Moffet economist, company executive, education consultant
Graburn, Nelson Hayes Henry anthropologist, educator
Gurgin, Vonnie Ann social scientist
Harsanyi, John Charles economics educator
Howell, Francis Clark anthropologist, educator
Johanson, Donald Carl physical anthropologist
Kallgren, Joyce Kislitzin political science educator
Landau, Martin political science educator
Lane, Sylvia economist, educator
Lee, Ronald Demos demographer, economist, educator
Letiche, John Marion economist, educator
Lipson, Leslie Michael political science educator
Luker, Kristin sociology educator
Maisel, Sherman Joseph economist, educator
Meier, Richard Louis futurist, planner, behavioral scientist
Muir, William Ker, Jr. political science educator
Quigley, John Michael economist, educator
Ranney, (Joseph) Austin political science educator
Reich, Michael economics educator
Rowe, John Howland anthropologist, educator
Shack, William Alfred anthropology educator, researcher, consultant
Shapiro, Carl economics educator and consultant
Smolensky, Eugene economics educator
Varian, Hal Ronald economics educator
Waltz, Kenneth Neal political science educator
Wilensky, Harold L. political science and industrial relations educator
Williamson, Oliver Eaton economics and law educator
Wolfinger, Raymond Edwin political science educator

### Beverly Hills
†Berton, Peter Alexander Menquez emeritus international relations educator, lecturer

### Calistoga
Spindler, George Dearborn anthropologist, educator, author, editor

### Carmichael
Hellmuth, William Frederick, Jr. economics educator

### Carpinteria
Schmidhauser, John Richard political science educator
Wheeler, John Harvey political scientist

### Chico
Farrer, Claire Anne Rafferty anthropologist, folklorist, educator
Rodrigue, Christine M(ary) geography educator, business consultant

### Claremont
Arndt, Sven William economics educator
Benson, George Charles Sumner political science educator
Bjork, Gordon Carl economist, educator
Bond, Floyd Alden economist, educator
Gold, Bela economist, educator
Hinshaw, Randall (Weston) economist, educator
†Jaffa, Harry Victor political philosophy educator emeritus
Likens, James Dean economics educator
Phelps, Orme Wheelock economics educator emeritus
Wykoff, Frank Champion economics educator

### Compton
Drew, Sharon Lee sociologist

### Corona Del Mar
Hinderaker, Ivan political science educator

### Davis
Cohen, Lawrence Edward sociology educator, criminologist
Crowley, Daniel John anthropologist
Elmendorf, William Welcome anthropology educator
Groth, Alexander Jacob political science educator
Ives, John David (Jack Ives) geography and environmental sciences educator
Jett, Stephen Clinton geography educator, researcher
Lofland, John Franklin sociologist, educator
Lofland, Lyn Hebert sociology educator

McHenry, Henry Malcolm anthropologist, educator
Musolf, Lloyd Daryl political science educator, institute administrator
Siverson, Randolph Martin political science educator
Skinner, G(eorge) William anthropologist, educator
Smith, Michael Peter social science educator, researcher
Storm, Donald John archaeologist, historian
Sumner, Daniel Alan economist, educator
Wegge, Leon Louis François economics educator

### Encinitas
Bloomberg, Warner, Jr. urban affairs educator emeritus

### Fair Oaks
Parker, Brian Prescott forensic scientist

### Foster City
Thomlinson, Ralph demographer, educator

### Fresno
Dackawich, S. John sociology educator
O'Brien, John Conway economist, educator, writer

### Glendale
Hadley, Paul Ervin international relations educator

### Hayward
Smith, J(ohn) Malcolm political science educator

### Irvine
Aigner, Dennis John economics educator, consultant
Burton, Michael Ladd anthropology educator
Cushman, Robert Fairchild political science educator, author, editor
Danziger, James Norris political science educator
Freeman, Linton Clarke sociology educator
Geis, Gilbert Lawrence sociology educator emeritus
Ingram, Helen Moyer political science educator
Lave, Charles Arthur economics educator
Margolis, Julius economist, educator
Schonfeld, William Rost political science educator, researcher
Small, Kenneth Alan economics educator
White, Douglas R. anthropology educator

### La Jolla
Attiyeh, Richard Eugene economics educator
Hoston, Germaine Annette political science educator
Jacobson, Gary Charles political science educator
Schiller, Herbert Irving social scientist, author
Spiro, Melford Elliot anthropology educator
Starr, Ross Marc economist, educator
White, Halbert Lynn, Jr. economist, educator, consultant

### Laguna Beach
Bent, Alan Edward political science educator, administrator
Dale, Leon Andrew economist, educator
Fagin, Henry public administration consultant

### Laguna Hills
Kaplan, Sidney Joseph sociologist, educator
Noble, Marion Ellen retired home economist

### Loomis
Hartmann, Frederick Howard political science educator emeritus

### Los Angeles
Alexander, Herbert E. political scientist
Allen, William Richard retired economist
Alvarez, Rodolfo sociology educator, consultant
Anawalt, Patricia Rieff anthropologist
Anderson, Austin Gilman economics research company consultant
Arnold, Jeanne Eloise anthropologist, educator
Basch, Darlene Chakin clinical social worker
Bennett, Charles Franklin, Jr. biogeographer, educator
Blakely, Edward James economics educator
Broderick, Carlfred Bartholomew sociology educator
Brubaker, William Rogers sociology educator
Champagne, Duane Willard sociology educator
Clark, Burton Robert sociologist, educator
Coombs, Robert Holman behavioral scientist, medical educator, therapist, author
Darby, Michael Rucker economist, educator
Dekmejian, Richard Hrair political science educator
Demsetz, Harold economist, educator
Ellickson, Bryan Carl economics educator
Elliott, John Ed economics educator
Glaser, Daniel sociologist
Goldschmidt, Walter Rochs anthropologist, educator
Hahn, Harlan Dean political science educator, consultant
Harberger, Arnold Carl economist, educator
Heer, David Macalpine sociology educator
Hirsch, Werner Zvi economist, educator
Hoffenberg, Marvin political science educator, consultant
Intriligator, Michael David economist, educator
Jamison, Dean Tecumseh economist
Klein, Benjamin economics educator, consultant
La Force, James Clayburn, Jr. economist, educator
Leijonhufvud, Axel Stig Bengt economics educator
Levine, Robert Arthur economist, policy analyst
Lowenthal, Abraham Frederic international relations educator
Malecki, Edward Stanley, Jr. political science educator
Maquet, Jacques Jerome Pierre anthropologist, writer
Morgner, Aurelius economist, educator
Nelson, Howard Joseph geographer, educator
Nilles, John Mathias (Jack Nilles) futurist
Nixon, John Harmon economist
Orme, Antony Ronald geography educator
Riley, John Graham economics educator
Scott, Allen John public policy and geography educator
Seeman, Melvin sociologist, educator
Sklar, Richard Lawrence political science educator
Somers, Harold Milton economist, educator
Thompson, Earl Albert economics educator
Thrower, Norman Joseph William geographer, educator
Totten, George Oakley, III political science educator
Turner, Ralph Herbert sociologist, educator
Vuckovic, Gojko Milos public administration scholar
Williams, Robert Martin economist, consultant

Gubser, Peter Anton *political scientist, writer, educator*
Gutierrez-Santos, Luis Emiliano *economist*
Halperin, Morton H. *political scientist*
Hartmann, Heidi Irmgard Victoria *economist, research organization executive*
Helms, Robert Brake *economist, research director*
Hermens, Ferdinand Aloys *political science educator*
Hess, Stephen *political scientist, author*
Hickman, R(obert) Harrison *political pollster, strategist*
Horowitz, Herbert Eugene *educator, consultant, former ambassador*
Hudson, Michael Craig *political science educator*
Hughes, Ann Hightower *economist, international trade consultant*
Hughes, Kent Higgon *economist*
James, Estelle *economics educator*
Jamme, Albert Joseph *archaeologist, educator*
Jaspersen, Frederick Zarr *economist*
Johnson, Omotunde Evan George *economist*
Johnson, Robert Henry *political science educator*
†Joyner, Christopher C. *international relations educator*
Keck, Lois T. *anthropology educator*
Kemp, Geoffrey Thomas Howard *international affairs specialist*
Kendrick, John Whitefield *economist, educator, consultant*
Khadduri, Majid *international studies educator*
Kirkpatrick, Jeane Duane Jordan *political scientist, government official*
Kitchen, John Howard *economist*
Kling, William *economist, retired foreign service officer*
Knapp, Charles Boynton *economist, educator, academic administrator*
Korologos, Tom Chris *government affairs consultant, former federal official*
Kristol, Irving *social sciences educator, editor*
Krulfeld, Ruth Marilyn *anthropologist, educator*
Kuh, Charlotte Virginia *economist*
Laden, Ben Ellis *economist*
Lardy, Nicholas Richard *economics educator*
LeoGrande, William Mark *political science educator, writer*
Liebenson, Herbert *economist, trade association executive*
Lieber, Robert James *political science educator, writer*
Lin, William Wen-Rong *economist*
Lindsey, Lawrence Benjamin *economist*
Liska, George *political science educator, author*
†Lustig, Nora Claudia *researcher*
Luttwak, Edward Nicolae *academic, writer policy and business consultant*
Malashevich, Bruce Peter *economic consultant*
Malmgren, Harald Bernard *economist*
Manatos, Andrew Emanuel *policy consultant, former government official*
Mann, Thomas Edward *political scientist*
Marcuss, Rosemary Daly *economist*
Martinez, Herminia S. *economist, banker*
Maudlin, Robert V. *economics and government affairs consultant*
McElroy, Frederick William *economics educator, consultant*
Meggers, Betty J(ane) *anthropologist*
Mellor, John Williams *economist, policy consultant firm executive*
Millar, James Robert *economist, educator, university official*
Miller, James Clifford, III *economist*
Minarik, Joseph John *economist, researcher*
Morrison, Joel Lynn *cartographer, geographer*
Nagorski, Zygmunt *political scientist*
Nakhleh, Emile A. *governmental sciences educator*
Nehmer, Stanley *economics consultant*
Nelson, Candice Jean *political science educator*
Newman, Monroe *retired economist, educator*
Niskanen, William Arthur, Jr. *economist, think tank executive*
Noland, Marcus *economist, educator*
Norwood, Janet Lippe *economist*
Offutt, Susan Elizabeth *economist*
Oh, John Kie-Chiang *political science educator, university official*
O'Neill, June Ellenoff *economist*
Ooms, Van Doorn *economist*
Ornstein, Norman Jay *political scientist*
†Orszag, Peter Richard *economist*
Ortner, Donald J. *biological anthropologist, educator*
Oweiss, Ibrahim Mohamed *economist, educator*
Perry, George Lewis *research economist, consultant*
Phillips, Karen Borlaug *economist, association executive*
Phillips, Susan Meredith *financial economist, former university administrator*
Pickenpaugh, Thomas Edward *archaeologist*
Polak, Jacques Jacobus *economist, foundation administrator*
Potvin, Raymond Herve *sociology educator, author*
Preeg, Ernest Henry *strategic and international studies center executive*
Prell, Michael Jack *economist*
Prestowitz, Clyde Vincent *economist, research administrator*
Randall, Robert L(ee) *ecological economist*
Ravenal, Earl Cedric *international relations educator, author*
Reich, Bernard *political science educator*
Reynolds, Alan Anthony *economist, speaker, consultant*
Reynolds, Mary Trackett *political scientist*
Reynolds, Robert Joel *economist, consultant*
Roberts, Markley *economist, educator*
Roberts, Walter Ronald *political science educator, former government official*
Roett, Riordan *political science educator, consultant*
Rosenau, James Nathan *political scientist, author*
Ruttenberg, Stanley Harvey *economist*
Ryn, Claes Gösta *political science educator, author, research institute administrator*
Salant, Walter S. *economist*
Salop, Steven Charles *economics educator*
Sanderson, Fred Hugo *economist*
Sawhill, Isabel Van Devanter *economist*
Scheppach, Raymond Carl, Jr. *association executive, economist*
Scheraga, Joel Dov *economist*
Schlesinger, James Rodney *economist*
Schley, Wayne Arthur *political consultant*
Schluter, Gerald Emil *economist*
Schultze, Charles Louis *economist, educator*
Shah-Jahan, M. M. *economist*
Simes, Dimitri Konstantin *international affairs expert and educator*
Smith, Bruce David *archaeologist*
Smythe-Haith, Mabel Murphy *consultant on African economic development, speaker, writer*
Soldo, Beth Jean *demography educator, researcher*
Solomon, Elinor Harris *economics educator*
Solomon, Richard Harvey *political scientist*
Stanford, Dennis Joe *archaeologist, museum curator*
Stanley, Timothy Wadsworth *economist*
Stavrou, Nikolaos Athanasios *political science educator*
Stein, Herbert *economist*
Steiner, Gilbert Yale *political scientist*
Stelzer, Irwin Mark *economist*
Sterner, Michael Edmund *international affairs consultant*
Stone, Russell A. *sociology educator*
Strauss, Elliott Bowman *economic development consultant, retired naval officer*
Sundquist, James Lloyd *political scientist*
Sunley, Emil McKee *economist*
Sweeney, Richard James *economics educator*
Taylor, William Jesse, Jr. *international studies educator, research center executive*
Teele, Thurston Ferdinand *economist*
Toder, Eric Jay *economist*
Tolchin, Susan Jane *public administration educator, writer*
Van Beek, Gus Willard *archaeologist*
Walinsky, Louis Joseph *economic consultant, writer*
Wallis, W(ilson) Allen *economist, educator, statistician*
Warne, William Robert *economist*
Weiss, David Alan *international economist*
Wilensky, Gail Roggin *economist*
Wilson, Ewen Maclellan *economist*
Yellen, John Edward *archaeologist*

## FLORIDA

### Boca Raton
Feuerlein, Willy John Arthur *economist, educator*
McNulty, James Ergler *finance educator*

### Bonita Springs
McDonald, Jacquelyn Milligan *parent and family studies educator*

### Boynton Beach
Mittel, John J. *economist, corporate executive*

### Coral Gables
Shipley, Vergil Alan *political science educator*

### Deerfield Beach
Fosback, Norman George *stock market econometrician, researcher*

### Delray Beach
Blankenheimer, Bernard *economics consultant*

### Fort Lauderdale
Bartelstone, Rona Sue *gerontologist*

### Gainesville
Barton, Allen Hoisington *sociologist*
Bernard, H. Russell *anthropology educator, scientific editor*
Carr, Glenna Dodson *economics educator*
Maples, William Ross *anthropology educator, consultant*
Milanich, Jerald Thomas *archaeologist, museum curator*
Smith, Stanley Kent *economics and demographics educator*
von Mering, Otto Oswald *anthropology educator*
Zabel, Edward *economist, educator*

### Hawthorne
Ross, James Elmer *economist, administrator*

### Jacksonville
Brady, James Joseph *economics educator*
Ejimofor, Cornelius Ogu *political scientist, educator*
Godfrey, John Munro *economics consultant*
Moore, David Graham *sociologist, educator*
Seroka, James Henry *social sciences educator, university administrator*

### Jupiter
Biebuyck, Daniel Prosper *retired anthropologist, educator*

### Maitland
Blackburn, John Oliver *economist, consultant*

### Miami
Averch, Harvey Allan *economist, educator, academic administrator*
Chirovsky, Nicholas Ludomir *economics educator, historian, author*
Salazar-Carrillo, Jorge *economics educator*

### Mount Dora
Myren, Richard Albert *criminal justice consultant*

### Ocala
Grissom, Robert Jesse, Sr. *criminal justice educator*

### Pensacola
Killian, Lewis Martin *sociology educator*
Long, H. Owen *retired economics educator, fiction writer*

### Ponte Vedra Beach
Wu, Hsiu Kwang *economist, educator*

### Saint Augustine
Armstrong, John Alexander *political scientist, educator*
Theil, Henri *economist, educator*

### Saint Petersburg
Serrie, Hendrick *anthropology and international business educator*

### Sanibel
Crown, David Allan *criminologist, educator*

### Sarasota
Fabrycy, Mark Zdzislaw *retired economist*
Gordon, Sanford Daniel *economics educator*
Hamberg, Daniel *economist, educator*
Roberts, Merrill Joseph *economist, educator*

### Sun City Center
Darling, Frank Clayton *former political science educator, educational institute administrator*

### Tallahassee
Brueckheimer, William Rogers *social science educator*
Colberg, Marshall Rudolph *economist*
Dye, Thomas Roy *political science educator*
Holcombe, Randall Gregory *economics educator*
Laird, William Everette, Jr. *economics educator, administrator*
Nam, Charles Benjamin *sociologist, demographer, educator*
Newell, Barbara Warne *economist, educator*
Paredes, James Anthony *anthropologist, educator*
Rittberg, Eric Dondaro *political consultant*
Serow, William John *economics educator*

### Tampa
MacManus, Susan Ann *political science educator, researcher*

### Tarpon Springs
Padberg, Daniel Ivan *agricultural economics educator, researcher*

### West Palm Beach
Lively, Edwin Lowe *sociology educator*

## GEORGIA

### Athens
Allsbrook, Ogden Olmstead, Jr. *economics educator*
Bullock, Charles Spencer, III *political science educator, author, consultant*
Clute, Robert Eugene *political and social science educator*
Dunn, Delmer Delano *political science educator*
Garbin, Albeno Patrick *sociology educator*
Kamerschen, David Roy *economist, educator*

### Atlanta
Bahl, Roy Winford *economist, educator, consultant*
Cameron, Rondo *economic history educator*
Curran, Christopher *economics educator*
Endicott, John Edgar *international relations educator*
Kafoglis, Milton Zachary *economics educator*
Levy, Daniel *economics educator*
Muth, Richard Ferris *economics educator*
Swanson, David H(enry) *economist, educator*
Tillman, Mary Norman *urban affairs consultant*
Wald, Michael Leonard *economist*

### Carrollton
Clark, Janet Eileen *political scientist, educator*

### Dahlonega
Friedman, Barry David *political scientist, educator*

### Lilburn
Neumann, Thomas William *archaeologist*

### Milledgeville
Bouley, Eugene Edward, Jr. *criminal justice and sociology educator*

### Norcross
Conway, Hobart McKinley, Jr. *geo-economist*

### Oxford
Cody, William Bermond *political science educator*

### Stockbridge
Grimes, Richard Allen *economics educator*

### Stone Mountain
Nelson, Larry Keith *document investigation laboratory executive*

## HAWAII

### Hilo
Wang, James Chia-Fang *political science educator*

### Honolulu
Cho, Lee-Jay *social scientist, demographer*
Gaydos, Gregory George *political scientist, educator*
Kuroda, Yasumasa *political science educator, researcher*
Laney, Leroy Olan *economist, banker*
Mark, Shelley Muin *economist, educator, government official*
Morse, Richard *social scientist*
Ogawa, Dennis Masaaki *American studies educator*
Paige, Glenn Durland *political scientist, educator*
Rambo, A. Terry *anthropologist, research program director*
Riggs, Fred Warren *political science educator*
Solheim, Wilhelm Gerhard, II *anthropologist, educator*
Suh, Dae-Sook *political science educator*

### Kaneohe
Baker, Paul Thornell *anthropology educator*

## IDAHO

### Boise
Overgaard, Willard Michele *retired political scientist, jurisprudent*

### Caldwell
Lonergan, Wallace Gunn *economics educator, management consultant*

### Moscow
Martin, Boyd Archer *political science educator emeritus*

### Sandpoint
Glock, Charles Young *sociologist*

## ILLINOIS

### Barrington
Chung, Joseph Sang-hoon *economics educator*

### Carbondale
Eynon, Thomas Grant *sociology educator*
Handler, Jerome Sidney *anthropology educator*
Harper, Robert Alexander *geography educator*
Somit, Albert *political educator*

### Champaign
Arnould, Richard Julius *economist, educator, consultant*
Brems, Hans Julius *economist, educator*
Cohen, Stephen Philip *political science and history educator*
Due, John Fitzgerald *economist, educator emeritus*
Frankel, Marvin *economist, educator*
Kanet, Roger Edward *political science educator, university administrator*
Nagel, Stuart Samuel *political science educator, lawyer*
Orr, Daniel *educator, economist*
Scott, Anna Marie Porter Wall *sociology educator*
Sprenkle, Case Middleton *economics educator*

### Charleston
Price, Dalias Adolph *geography educator*
Smith, Betty Elaine *geography educator*

### Chicago
Aliber, Robert Z. *economist, educator*
Annable, James Edward *economist*
Arditti, Fred D. *economist, educator*
Baum, Bernard Helmut *sociologist, educator*
Becker, Gary Stanley *economist, educator*
Bidwell, Charles Edward *sociologist, educator*
Boyce, David Edward *transportation and regional science educator*
Boyer, John William *history educator, dean*
Bradburn, Norman M. *behavioral science educator*
Braidwood, Linda Schreiber *archaeologist*
Braidwood, Robert John *archaeologist, educator*
Carlton, Dennis William *economics educator*
Coase, Ronald Harry *economics educator*
Cohler, Bertram Joseph *social sciences educator, clinical psychologist*
Cox, Charles C. *economist*
Cropsey, Joseph *political science educator*
Fogel, Robert William *economist, educator, historian*
Freeman, Leslie Gordon *anthropologist, educator*
Freeman, Susan Tax *anthropologist, educator*
Friedrich, Paul *anthropologist, linguist, poet*
Genetski, Robert James *economist*
Gibson, McGuire *archaeologist, educator*
Ginsburg, Norton Sydney *geography educator*
Gould, John Philip *economist, educator*
Graber, Doris Appel *political scientist, editor, author*
Hamada, Robert S(eiji) *economist, educator*
Harris, Chauncy Dennison *geographer, educator*
Hayes, William Aloysius *economics educator*
Hebel, Doris A. *astrologer*
Heckman, James Joseph *economist, econometrician, educator*
Hotz, V. Joseph *economics educator*
Johnson, Janet Helen *Egyptology educator*
Kaplan, Morton A. *political science educator*
Klarich, Nina Marie *economic development executive*
Laitin, David Dennis *political science educator*
Larson, Allan Louis *political scientist, educator, lay church worker*
Laumann, Edward Otto *sociology educator*
Levine, Donald Nathan *sociologist, educator*
Liu, Ben-chieh *economist*
Lopata, Helena Znaniecka *sociologist, researcher, educator*
Malik, Raymond Howard *economist, scientist, corporate executive, inventor, educator*
Mikesell, Marvin Wray *geography educator*
Mirza, David Brown *economist, educator*
Morris, Norval *criminologist, educator*
Nicholas, Ralph Wallace *anthropologist, educator*
Peltzman, Sam *economics educator*
Reed, Charles Allen *anthropologist*
Rosen, George *economist, educator*
Rosen, Sherwin *economist, educator*
Rosenblum, Victor Gregory *political science and law educator*
Scheinkman, José Alexandre *economics educator*
Schloss, Nathan *economist*
Schultz, Theodore William *retired economist, educator*
Smith, Raymond Thomas *anthropology educator*
Smith, Stan Vladimir *economist, financial service company executive*
Stocking, George Ward, Jr. *anthropology educator*
Stover, Leon (Eugene) *anthropology educator, writer, critic*
Sumner, William Marvin *anthropology and archaeology educator*
Sween, Joyce Ann *sociologist, psychologist, evaluation methodologist*
Taub, Richard Paul *social sciences educator*
Tsou, Tang *political science educator, researcher*
Wiser, James Louis *political science educator*
Zellner, Arnold *economics and statistics educator*
Zonis, Marvin *political scientist, educator*

### De Kalb
†Das, Man Singh *sociology educator*
McSpadden, Lettie *political science educator*

### Edwardsville
Virgo, John Michael *economist, researcher, educator*

### Evanston
Bienen, Henry Samuel *political science educator, university executive*
Braeutigam, Ronald Ray *economics educator*
Domowitz, Ian *economics educator*
Eisner, Robert *economics educator*
Gordon, Robert James *economics educator*
Handler, Douglas Perry *economist*
Hurter, Arthur Patrick *economist, educator*
Irons, William George *anthropology educator*
Moskos, Charles C. *sociology educator*
Myerson, Roger Bruce *economist, game theorist, educator*

PROFESSIONAL INDEX 5433 SOCIAL SCIENCE


Porter, Robert Hugh *economics educator*
Reiter, Stanley *economist, educator*
Schnaiberg, Allan *sociology educator*
Shanas, Ethel *sociology educator*

**Glen Ellyn**
Frateschi, Lawrence Jan *economist, statistician, educator*

**Hinsdale**
Dederick, Robert Gogan *economist*

**Joliet**
Holmgren, Myron Roger *social sciences educator*

**Macomb**
Walzer, Norman Charles *economics educator*

**Naperville**
Galvan, Mary Theresa *economics and business educator*

**Normal**
Jelks, Edward Baker *archaeologist, educator*

**Olympia Fields**
Sprinkel, Beryl Wayne *economist, consultant*

**Palatine**
Nagatoshi, Konrad R. *anthropology educator, information systems specialist*

**Park Ridge**
Tongue, William Walter *economics and business consultant, educator emeritus*

**Romeoville**
Houlihan, James William *criminal justice educator*

**Schaumburg**
Kennedy, Patrick Michael *fire analyst*

**Springfield**
Wehrle, Leroy Snyder *economist, educator*
Whitney, John Freeman, Jr. *political science educator*

**Urbana**
Baer, Werner *economist, educator*
Bruner, Edward M. *anthropology educator*
Carmen, Ira Harris *political scientist, educator*
Cunningham, Clark Edward *anthropology educator*
Dovring, Folke *land economics educator, consultant*
Due, Jean Margaret *agricultural economist, educator*
Giertz, J. Fred *economics educator*
Giles, Eugene *anthropology educator*
Gove, Samuel Kimball *political science educator*
Jakle, John Allais *geography educator*
Kolodziej, Edward Albert *political scientist, educator*
Leuthold, Raymond Martin *agricultural economics educator*
Linowes, David Francis *political economist, educator, corporate executive*
Nardulli, Peter F. *political science educator*
Nettl, Bruno *anthropology and musicology educator*
Resek, Robert William *economist*
Rich, Robert F. *political sciences educator, academic administrator*
Schmidt, Stephen Christopher *agricultural economist, educator*
Spitze, Robert George Frederick *agricultural economics educator*
Wirt, Frederick Marshall *political scientist*
Yu, George Tzuchiao *political science educator*

**Western Springs**
Zamora, Marjorie Dixon *retired political science educator*

**Wilmette**
Espenshade, Edward Bowman, Jr. *geographer, educator*

INDIANA

**Bloomington**
Adams, William Richard *archaeologist, lecturer, curator*
Bauman, Richard *anthropologist, educator*
Braden, Samuel Edward *economics educator*
Caldwell, Lynton Keith *social scientist, educator*
Conrad, Geoffrey Wentworth *archaeologist, educator*
Diamant, Alfred *political science educator*
Muth, John Fraser *economics educator*
O'Meara, Patrick O. *political science educator*
Ostrom, Vincent A(lfred) *political science educator*
Patrick, John Joseph *social sciences educator*
†Peebles, Christopher Spalding *anthropologist, dean, academic administrator*
Risinger, C. Frederick *social studies educator*
Saunders, W(arren) Phillip, Jr. *economics educator, consultant, author*
Schuessler, Karl Frederick *sociologist, educator*
Smith, Frederick Robert, Jr. *social studies educator*
Spulber, Nicolas *economics educator emeritus*
Stolnitz, George Joseph *economist, educator, demographer*
Stryker, Sheldon *sociologist, educator*
Vincent, Jeffrey Robert *labor studies educator*
von Furstenberg, George Michael *economics educator, researcher*
Wilson, John Douglas *economics educator*

**Columbus**
Hackett, John Thomas *economist*

**Franklin**
Launey, George Volney, III *economics educator*

**Greencastle**
Bonifield, William Clarence *economist, educator*

**Indianapolis**
Capehart, Harriet Jane Holmes *economics educator*
Krauss, John Landers *public policy and urban affairs consultant*

**Lafayette**
Hardin, Lowell Stewart *retired economics educator*

**Muncie**
Carmin, Robert Leighton *retired geography educator*
Cheng, Chu Yuan *economics educator*
Sargent, Thomas Andrew *political science educator, university program director*
Swartz, B(enjamin) K(insell), Jr. *archaeologist, educator*

**North Manchester**
Harshbarger, Richard B. *economics educator*

**Notre Dame**
Arnold, Peri Ethan *political scientist*
Bartell, Ernest *economist, educator*
Craypo, Charles *labor economics educator*
Despres, Leo Arthur *sociology and anthropology educator, academic administrator*
Dowty, Alan Kent *political scientist, educator*
Goulet, Denis André *political science educator, writer, development ethicist*
Kennedy, John Joseph *political science educator*
Leege, David Calhoun *political scientist, educator*
Loescher, Gilburt Damian *international relations educator*
Mirowski, Philip Edward *economics educator*
Swartz, Thomas R. *economist, educator*
Walshe, Aubrey Peter *political science educator*
Weigert, Andrew Joseph *sociology educator*

**Terre Haute**
Mausel, Paul Warner *geography educator*
Puckett, Robert Hugh *political scientist, educator*

**West Lafayette**
Anderson, James George *sociologist, educator*
Farris, Paul Leonard *agricultural economist*
Horwich, George *economist, educator*
Perrucci, Robert *sociologist, educator*
Schrader, Lee Frederick *agricultural economist*
Theen, Rolf Heinz-Wilhelm *political science educator*
Thursby, Jerry Gilbert *economics educator, consultant*
Tyner, Wallace Edward *economics educator*
Weinstein, Michael Alan *political science educator*
Wright, Gordon Pribyl *management, operations research educator*

IOWA

**Ames**
Fox, Karl August *economist, eco-behavioral scientist*
Harl, Neil Eugene *economist, lawyer, educator*
Klonglan, Gerald Edward *sociology educator*
MacDonald, Maurice Marcus *economics educator*
Meyers, William Henry *economics educator*

**Clive**
Miller, Kenneth Edward *sociologist, educator*

**Iowa City**
Albrecht, William Price *economist, educator, government official*
Barkan, Joel David *political science educator*
Forsythe, Robert Elliott *economics educator*
Fuller, John Williams *economics educator*
Green, William *archaeologist*
Kim, Chong Lim *political science educator*
Krause, Walter *retired economics educator, consultant*
Loewenberg, Gerhard *political science educator*
Ross, Russell Marion *political science educator*
Shannon, Lyle William *sociology educator*
Siebert, Calvin D. *economist, educator*

**Mount Vernon**
Ruppel, Howard James, Jr. *sociologist*

**Oskaloosa**
Porter, David Lindsey *history and political science educator, author*

KANSAS

**Lawrence**
Augelli, John Pat *geography educator, author, consultant, rancher*
Heller, Francis H(oward) *law and political science educator emeritus*
Laird, Roy Dean *political science educator*
Seibold, Ronald Lee *sociologist, writer*
Sheridan, Richard Bert *economics educator*
Willner, Ann Ruth *political scientist, educator*

**Manhattan**
Babcock, Michael Ward *economics educator*
Hoyt, Kenneth Boyd *educational psychology educator*
Nafziger, Estel Wayne *economics educator*
Parish, Thomas Scanlan *human development educator*
Thomas, Lloyd Brewster *economics educator*

**Overland Park**
Burger, Henry G. *anthropologist, vocabulary scientist, publisher*

**Pittsburg**
Behlar, Patricia Ann *political science educator*

**Shawnee Mission**
Gaar, Marilyn Audrey Wiegraffe *political science educator, property manager*

**Topeka**
Jervis, David Thompson *political science educator*

KENTUCKY

**Bowling Green**
Cravens, Raymond Lewis *retired political science educator*
Kalab, Kathleen Alice *sociology educator*

**Highland Heights**
Hopgood, James F. *anthropologist*

**Lexington**
Davis, Vincent *political science educator*
Hochstrasser, Donald Lee *cultural anthropologist, community health and public administration educator*
Hultman, Charles William *economics educator*
Schmitt, Frederick Adrian *gerontologist, neuropsychologist*
Straus, Robert *behavioral sciences educator*
Ulmer, Shirley Sidney *political science educator, researcher, consultant*

**Prestonsburg**
Mc Aninch, Robert Danford *philosophy and government affairs educator*

**Versailles**
Stober, William John, II *economics educator*

LOUISIANA

**Baton Rouge**
West, Robert Cooper *geography educator*

**Lafayette**
Dur, Philip Francis *political scientist, educator, retired foreign service officer*

**Metairie**
Falco, Maria Josephine *political scientist, academic administrator*

**New Orleans**
Balée, William L. *anthropology educator*
Boudreaux, Kenneth Justin *economics and finance educator, consultant*
Bricker, Harvey Miller *anthropology educator*
Bricker, Victoria Reifler *anthropology educator*
Freudenberger, Herman *retired economics educator*
Jacobsen, Thomas Warren *archaeologist, educator*
Lief, Thomas Parrish *sociologist, educator*
Mason, Henry Lloyd *political science educator*
Robins, Robert Sidwar *political science educator, administrator*

**New Roads**
Haag, William George *anthropologist, educator*

**Ruston**
Sale, Tom S., III *financial economist, educator*

**Shreveport**
Hall, John Whitling *geography educator*
Pederson, William David *political scientist, educator*

MAINE

**Auburn**
Phillips, Charles Franklin *economic consultant*

**Augusta**
Nickerson, John Mitchell *political science educator*

**Bath**
Stoudt, Howard Webster *biological anthropologist, human factors specialist, consultant*

**Brunswick**
Morgan, Richard Ernest *political scientist, educator*

**Camden**
Weidman, Hazel Hitson *anthropologist, educator*

**Canaan**
Walker, Willard Brewer *anthropology educator, linguist*

**Kittery Point**
Howells, William White *anthropology educator*

**Lewiston**
Murray, Michael Peter *economist, educator*

**Orono**
Cohn, Steven Frederick *sociology educator, consultant*
Devino, William Stanley *economist, educator*

**Phippsburg**
Schuman, Howard *sociologist, educator*

**Portland**
Durgin, Frank Albert *economics educator*

**Waterville**
Gemery, Henry Albert *economics educator*
Mavrinac, Albert Anthony *political scientist, educator, lawyer, international legal consultant*

MARYLAND

**Adamstown**
Ohlke, Clarence Carl *public affairs consultant*

**Baltimore**
Anderson, Gerard Fenton *economist, university program administrator*
Bright, Margaret *sociologist*
Bucher, Richard David *sociology educator*
Cooper, Joseph *political scientist, educator*
Dietze, Gottfried *political science educator*
Entwisle, Doris Roberts *sociology educator*
Ginsberg, Benjamin *political science educator*
Goedicke, Hans *archeology educator*
Grossman, Joel B(arry) *political science educator*
Henderson, Lenneal Joseph, Jr. *political science educator*
Howard, J. Woodford, Jr. *political science educator*
Karni, Edi *economics educator*
Katz, Richard Stephen *political science educator*
Klarman, Herbert Elias *economist, educator*

Kohn, Melvin L. *sociologist*
Kumar, Martha Joynt *political science educator*
Maccini, Louis John *economic educator*
Mintz, Sidney Wilfred *anthropologist*
Rose, Hugh *retired economics educator*
Salamon, Lester Milton *political science educator*
Sorkin, Alan Lowell *economist, educator*
Wolman, M. Gordon *geography educator*

**Bethesda**
Berns, Walter Fred *political scientist, educator*
Bloomfield, Arthur Irving *economics educator*
Bowles, Walter Donald *economist, educator*
de Vries, Margaret Garritsen *economist*
Dommen, Arthur John *agricultural economist*
Ernst, Roger *international studies educator, consultant*
Ferris, Frederick Joseph *gerontologist, social worker*
Gates, Theodore Ross *economic consultant*
Holland, Robert Carl *economist*
Hyson, Charles David *economist, consultant*
Kleine, Herman *economist*
Lystad, Mary Hanemann (Mrs. Robert Lystad) *sociologist, author, consultant*
Raullerson, Calvin Henry *political scientist, consultant*
Riley, Matilda White (Mrs. John W. Riley, Jr.) *sociology educator*
Sayre, E(noch) Phillip *political scientist, state official, retired*
Schwartz, Charles Frederick *retired economist, consultant*
Solomon, Robert *economist*
Spangler, Miller Brant *science and technology analyst, planner, consultant*
Striner, Herbert Edward *economics educator*
Willner, Dorothy *anthropologist, educator*
Yager, Joseph Arthur, Jr. *economist*

**Cabin John**
Gallagher, Hugh Gregory *government affairs author, consultant*

**Chestertown**
Wendel, Richard Frederick *economist, educator, consultant*

**Chevy Chase**
Emery, Robert Firestone *economist, educator*
Geber, Anthony *economist, retired foreign service officer*
Nance, William Bennett *economic development specialist*
Norwood, Bernard *economist*
Riley, John Winchell, Jr. *consulting sociologist*
Scammon, Richard Montgomery *retired political scientist, retired editor*
Teitel, Simon *economist, educator*

**College Park**
Davidson, Roger H(arry) *political scientist, educator*
Just, Richard Eugene *agricultural and resource economics educator consultant*
Lyon, Andrew Bennet *economics educator*
Nerlove, Marc Leon *economics educator*
Piper, Don Courtney *political science educator*
Presser, Harriet Betty *sociology educator*
Presser, Stanley *sociology educator*
Quester, George Herman *political science educator*
Schelling, Thomas Crombie *economist, educator*
Ulmer, Melville Jack *economist, educator*
Williams, Aubrey Willis *anthropology educator*

**Cumberland**
Heckert, Paul Charles *sociologist, educator*

**Fort Washington**
McCafferty, James Arthur *sociologist*
Schlotzhauer, Virginia Hughes *parliamentarian*

**Glen Echo**
Simpson, Robert Edward *economist, consultant*

**Lanham**
Corrothers, Helen Gladys *criminal justice official*

**Mitchellville**
Blough, Roy *retired economist*
Manvel, Allen Dailey *fiscal economist*

**Potomac**
Fischetti, Michael *public administration educator, arbitrator*
Jones, Sidney Lewis *economist, government official*
Vadus, Gloria A. *scientific document examiner*
Walker, Charls Edward *economist, consultant*

**Rockville**
Knox, C. Neal *political and governmental affairs consultant, writer*
Niewiaroski, Trudi Osmers (Gertrude Niewiaroski) *social studies educator*

**Royal Oak**
Israel, Lesley Lowe *political consultant*

**Silver Spring**
Hsueh, Chun-tu *political scientist, historian, foundation executive*
Oswald, Rudolph A. *economist*

**Temple Hills**
Day, Mary Jane Thomas *cartographer*

MASSACHUSETTS

**Amherst**
Alfange, Dean, Jr. *political science educator*
Beals, Ralph Everett *economist, educator*
Benson, Lucy Peters Wilson *political and diplomatic consultant*
Demerath, Nicholas Jay, III *sociology educator*
Goldman, Sheldon *political science educator*
Klare, Michael Thomas *social science educator, program director*
Mc Donagh, Edward Charles *sociologist, university administrator*
Mills, Patricia Jagentowicz *political philosophy educator, writer*
Rossi, Alice S. *sociology educator, author*

Taubman, William Chase *political science educator*
Woodbury, Richard Benjamin *anthropologist, educator*

### Andover
Mac Neish, Richard Stockton *archaeologist, educator*

### Babson Park
Genovese, Francis Charles (Frank Genovese) *economist, consultant, editor*

### Belmont
Bergson, Abram *economist, educator*
Washburn, Barbara Polk *cartographer, researcher, explorer*

### Boston
Adams, John Quincy *economist, educator*
Amy-Moreno de Toro, Angel Alberto *social sciences educator, writer, oral historian*
Bustin, Edouard Jean *political scientist, educator*
Crotty, William *political science educator*
Dentler, Robert Arnold *sociologist, educator*
Fieleke, Norman Siegfried *economist*
Gamst, Frederick Charles *anthropology educator*
Hammond, Norman David Curle *archaeology educator, researcher*
Kurzweil, Edith *sociology educator, editor*
Markham, Jesse William *economist*
Merton, Robert C. *economist, educator*
Newbrander, William Carl *health economist, management consultant*
Newhouse, Joseph Paul *economics educator*
Norton, Augustus Richard *political science educator*
Palmer, David Scott *political scientist, educator*
Psathas, George *sociologist, educator*
Rossell, Christine Hamilton *political science educator*
Sanders, Irwin Taylor *sociology educator*
Sinai, Allen Leo *economist, educator*
†Woerner, Frederick Frank *international relations educator*

### Boxford
Schubert, Glendon *political scientist, educator*

### Brookline
Cromwell, Adelaide M. *sociology educator*

### Burlington
Harding, Wayne Michael *sociologist, researcher*

### Cambridge
Abt, Clark C. *social scientist, executive, engineer, publisher, educator*
Alt, James Edward *political science educator*
Bator, Francis Michel *economist, educator*
Berliner, Joseph Scholom *economics educator*
Berndt, Ernst Rudolf *economist, educator*
Bishop, Robert Lyle *economist, educator*
Blackmer, Donald Laurence Morton *political scientist*
Bloomfield, Lincoln Palmer *political scientist*
Bolnick, Bruce Robert *economist, professor*
Borjas, George J(esus) *economics educator*
Brown, Edgar Cary *retired economics educator*
Champion, (Charles) Hale *political science educator, former public official*
†Collins, Susan Margaret *economics educator*
Cooper, Richard Newell *economist, educator*
Coser, Lewis Alfred *sociology educator*
Dominguez, Jorge Ignacio *government educator*
Dorfman, Robert *economics educator*
Dornbusch, Rudiger *economics educator*
Dunlop, John Thomas *economics educator, former secretary of labor*
Eckaus, Richard Samuel *economist, educator*
Ellwood, David T. *public policy educator, university administrator*
Feldstein, Martin Stuart *economist, educator*
Fisher, Franklin Marvin *economist*
†Fountain, Jane Ellen *public policy educator*
Friedman, Benjamin Morton *economics educator*
Frisch, Rose Epstein *population sciences researcher*
Galizzi, Monica *economics researcher*
Goldin, Claudia Dale *economics educator*
Goodwin, Neva R. *economist*
Griliches, Zvi *economist, educator*
Hart, Oliver D'Arcy *economics educator*
Hausman, Jerry Allen *economics educator, consultant*
†Hogan, William Walter *public policy educator, administrator, consultant*
Holbik, Karel *economics educator*
Horowitz, Morris A. *economist*
Hsiao, William C. *economist, actuary, educator*
Huntington, Samuel Phillips *political science educator*
Jacoby, Henry Donnan *economist, educator*
Jencks, Christopher Sandys *public policy educator*
Johnson, Willard Raymond *political science educator, consultant*
Jorgenson, Dale Weldeau *economist, educator*
Joskow, Paul Lewis *economist, educator*
Kaysen, Carl *economics educator*
Kennedy, Stephen Dandridge *economist, researcher*
Keyfitz, Nathan *sociologist, demographer, educator*
Khoury, Philip S. *social sciences educator, historian*
Kilson, Martin Luther, Jr. *government educator*
Lamberg-Karlovsky, Clifford Charles *anthropologist, archaeologist*
Lehner, Mark *archaeologist, educator*
Lieberson, Stanley *sociologist, educator*
Maass, Arthur *political science and environmental studies educator*
†Mansbridge, Jane Jebb *political scientist, educator*
Meyer, John Robert *economist, educator*
Mitten, David Gordon *classical archaeologist*
Montgomery, John Dickey *political science educator*
Moore, Mark Harrison *criminal justice and public policy educator*
Neustadt, Richard Elliott *political scientist, educator*
Nichols, Albert L. *economics consultant*
†Nye, Joseph S(amuel), Jr. *government studies educator, administrator*
Oye, Kenneth A. *political scientist, educator*
Patterson, Orlando *sociologist*
Peattie, Lisa Redfield *urban anthropology educator*
Perkins, Dwight Heald *economics educator*
Pfaltzgraff, Robert Louis, Jr. *political scientist, educator*
Piore, Michael Joseph *educator*
Plotkin, Irving H(erman) *economist, consultant*
Polenske, Karen Rosel *economics educator*
Poterba, James Michael *economist, educator*
Pye, Lucian Wilmot *political science educator*
Rathjens, George William *political scientist, educator*
Robinson, Marguerite Stern *anthropologist, educator, consultant*
†Rodrik, Dani *economics and international affairs educator*
Rosovsky, Henry *economist, educator*
Rotemberg, Julio Jacobo *economist, educator, consultant*
Samuels, Richard Joel *political science educator*
Samuelson, Paul Anthony *economics educator*
Sapolsky, Harvey Morton *political scientist, educator*
Scherer, Frederic Michael *economics educator*
Schmalensee, Richard Lee *economist, former government official, educator*
Siegel, Abraham J. *economics educator, academic administrator*
Skolnikoff, Eugene B. *political science educator*
Solow, Robert Merton *economist, educator*
Stager, Lawrence E. *archaeologist, educator*
Tambiah, Stanley Jeyarajah *anthropologist*
Temin, Peter *economics educator*
Thompson, Dennis Frank *political science and ethics educator, consultant*
Timmer, Charles Peter *agricultural economist*
Ulam, Adam B. *history and political science educator*
van der Merwe, Nikolaas Johannes *archaeologist*
Verba, Sidney *political scientist, educator*
Vernon, Raymond *economist, educator*
Vogel, Ezra F. *sociology educator*
Vogt, Evon Zartman, Jr. *anthropologist*
Weiner, Myron *political science educator*
Willie, Charles Vert *sociology educator*
Wilson, William Julius *sociologist, educator*
Zeckhauser, Richard Jay *economist, educator*
Zeidenstein, George *population educator*
Zinberg, Dorothy Shore *science policy educator*

### Chestnut Hill
Belsley, David Alan *economics educator, consultant*

### Cohasset
Campbell, John Coert *political scientist, author*

### Concord
Codere, Helen Frances *anthropologist, educator, university dean*

### East Orleans
Hallowell, Burton Crosby *economist, educator*

### Fitchburg
Wiegersma, Nan *economics educator*

### Harwich
Randolph, Robert Lee *economist, educator*

### Ipswich
Jennings, Frederic Beach, Jr. *economist, consultant, saltwater flyfishing guide*

### Lenox
Pierson, John Herman Groesbeck *economist, writer*

### Leverett
Barkin, Solomon *economist*

### Lexington
Baer, Michael Alan *political scientist, educator*
Bell, Carolyn Shaw *economist, educator*
Holzman, Franklyn Dunn *economics educator*
Kindleberger, Charles P., II *economist, educator*
Papanek, Gustav Fritz *economist, educator*

### Medford
Conklin, John Evan *sociology educator*

### Newton
Cleary, Paul David *sociomedical educator*
McEvoy, Michael Joseph *economist*

### Newton Center
Adams, F. Gerard *economist, educator*

### North Dartmouth
Barrow, Clyde Wayne *political scientist, educator*

### Northampton
Lehmann, Phyllis Williams *archaeologist, educator*
Robinson, Donald Leonard *social scientist, educator*
Rose, Peter Isaac *sociologist, writer*

### South Dartmouth
Stern, T. Noel *political scientist, educator*

### Waltham
Brown, Seyom *international relations educator, government consultant*
Conrad, Peter *sociology educator*
Evans, Robert, Jr. *economics educator*
McCulloch, Rachel *economics researcher, educator*
Ross, George William *social scientist, educator*

### Wayland
Boulding, Elise Marie *sociologist, educator*
Hagenstein, Perry Reginald *economist*

### Wellesley
Eilts, Hermann Frederick *international relations educator, former diplomat*
Miller, Linda B. *political scientist*

### Weston
Kraft, Gerald *economist*

### Williamstown
Bolton, Roger Edwin *economist, educator*
Burns, James MacGregor *political scientist, historian*
Sabot, Richard Henry *economics educator, researcher, consultant*
Sheahan, John Bernard *economist, educator*

### Worcester
Hanson, Susan Easton *geography educator*
Lidz, Charles Wilmanns *sociologist*
Turner, Billie Lee, II *geography educator*

## MICHIGAN

### Adrian
Weathers, Milledge Wright *retired economics educator*

### Ann Arbor
Arlinghaus, Sandra Judith Lach *mathematical geographer, educator*
Bornstein, Morris *economist, educator*
Brewer, Garry Dwight *social scientist, educator*
Campbell, John Creighton *political science educator, association administrator*
Cohen, Malcolm Stuart *economist, research institute director*
Converse, Philip Ernest *social science educator*
Courant, Paul Noah *economist, educator*
†Dominguez, Kathryn Mary *educator*
Fifield, Russell Hunt *political science educator*
Freedman, Ronald *sociology educator*
Fusfeld, Daniel Roland *economist*
Garn, Stanley Marion *physical anthropologist, educator*
Holbrook, Robert Sumner *economist, educator*
Howrey, Eugene Philip *economics educator, consultant*
Jacobson, Harold Karan *political science educator, researcher*
Johnston, Lloyd Douglas *social scientist*
Kelly, Raymond Case *anthropology educator*
Kingdon, John Wells *political science educator*
Kmenta, Jan *economics educator*
Mc Cracken, Paul Winston *retired economist, business educator*
Mitchell, Edward John *economist, retired educator*
Morgan, James Newton *research economist, educator*
Organski, Abramo Fimo Kenneth *political scientist, educator*
Paige, Jeffery Mayland *sociologist, educator*
Parsons, Jeffrey Robinson *anthropologist, educator*
Pedley, John Griffiths *archaeologist, educator*
Pierce, Roy *political science educator*
Shapiro, Matthew David *economist*
Singer, Eleanor *sociologist, editor*
Singer, Joel David *political science educator*
Smith, Dean Gordon *economist, educator*
Stafford, Frank Peter, Jr. *economics educator, consultant*
Steiner, Peter Otto *economics educator, dean*
Steiss, Alan Walter *research administrator, educator*
Stolper, Wolfgang Friedrich *retired economist, educator*
White, Michelle Jo *economics educator*
Whitman, Marina Von Neumann *economist*

### Big Rapids
Santer, Richard Arthur *geography educator*

### Buchanan
French, Robert Warren *economics educator emeritus, writer, consultant*

### Detroit
Baba, Marietta Lynn *business anthropologist*
Ferguson, Tamara *clinical sociologist*
Goodman, Allen Charles *economics educator*
Gould, Wesley Larson *political science educator*
Kaplan, Bernice Antoville *anthropologist, educator*
Lasker, Gabriel Ward *anthropologist, educator*
Marx, Thomas George *economist*
Weiss, Mark Lawrence *anthropology educator*

### East Lansing
Abramson, Paul Robert *political scientist, educator*
Allen, Bruce Templeton *economics educator*
Axinn, George Harold *rural sociology educator*
Fisher, Ronald C. *economics educator*
Kreinin, Mordechai Eliahu *economics educator*
Lang, Marvel *urban affairs educator*
Manderscheid, Lester Vincent *agricultural economics educator*
Manning, Peter Kirby *sociology educator*
Menchik, Paul Leonard *economist, educator*
Olson, Judy Mae *geography, cartography educator*
Papsidero, Joseph Anthony *social scientist, educator*
Poland, Robert Paul *business educator, consultant*
Press, Charles *retired political science educator*
Rasche, Robert Harold *economics educator*
Ricks, Donald Jay *agricultural economist*
Robbins, Lawrence Harry *anthropologist*
Schlesinger, Joseph Abraham *political scientist*
Sommers, Lawrence Melvin *geographer, educator*
Strassmann, W. Paul *economics educator*
Suits, Daniel Burbidge *economist*
Useem, John Hearld *sociologist, anthropologist*
Useem, Ruth Hill *sociology educator*
Woodbury, Stephen Abbott *economics educator*

### Hancock
Dresch, Stephen Paul *economist, state legislator*

### Lansing
Ballbach, Philip Thornton *political consultant*

### Mount Pleasant
Croll, Robert Frederick *economist, educator*
Grabinski, C. Joanne *gerontologist, educator*
Meltzer, Bernard N(athan) *sociologist, educator*

### Northport
Thomas, Philip Stanley *economics educator*

### Okemos
Solo, Robert Alexander *economist, educator*

### Rochester
Gregory, Karl Dwight *economist, educator, consultant*

### Sault Sainte Marie
Johnson, Gary Robert *political scientist, editor*

### Ypsilanti
Weinstein, Jay A. *social science educator, researcher*

## MINNESOTA

### Duluth
Lease, Martin Harry, Jr. *retired political science educator*

### Excelsior
Hoyt, Richard Comstock *economics consulting company executive*

### Forest Lake
Marchese, Ronald Thomas *ancient history and archaeology educator*

### Minneapolis
Adams, John Stephen *geography educator*
Chipman, John Somerset *economist, educator*
Erickson, W(alter) Bruce *business and economics educator, entrepreneur*
Fulton, Robert Lester *sociology educator*
Geweke, John Frederick *economics educator*
Gray, Virginia Hickman *political science educator*
Gudeman, Stephen Frederick *anthropology educator*
Holt, Robert Theodore *political scientist, dean, educator*
Johnson, Badri Nahvi *sociology educator, real estate business owner*
Knoke, David Harmon *sociology educator*
Kudrle, Robert Thomas *economist, educator*
Porter, Philip Wayland *geography educator*
Reiss, Ira Leonard *retired sociology educator, writer*
Rogers, William Cecil *political science educator*
Schreiner, John Christian *economics consultant, software publisher*
Scoville, James Griffin *economics educator*
Shively, William Phillips *political scientist, educator*
Ward, David Allen *sociology educator*

### Moorhead
Noblitt, Harding Coolidge *political scientist, educator*
Trainor, John Felix *retired economics educator*

### Morris
Kahng, Sun Myong *economics educator*

### Northfield
Clark, William Hartley *political science educator*
Lamson, George Herbert *economics educator*
Lewis, Stephen Richmond, Jr. *economist, academic administrator*
Will, Robert Erwin *economics educator*

### Saint Cloud
Frank, Stephen Ira *political science educator*
Tripp, Luke Samuel *educator*

### Saint Joseph
Bye, Lynn Ellen *social work educator*

### Saint Paul
Dahl, Reynold Paul *applied economics educator*
Jessup, Paul Frederick *financial economist, educator*
Lanegran, David Andrew *geography educator*
Peterson, Willis Lester *economics educator*
Ruttan, Vernon Wesley *agricultural economist*

### Saint Peter
Mc Rostie, Clair Neil *economics educator*
Ostrom, Don *political science educator*

### Scandia
Borchert, John Robert *geography educator*

## MISSISSIPPI

### Biloxi
Cox, Albert Harrington, Jr. *economist*

### Hattiesburg
Burrus, John N(ewell) *sociology educator*

### Mississippi State
Clynch, Edward John *political science educator, researcher*
Wall, Diane Eve *political science educator*

### Ridgeland
Lee, Daniel Kuhn *economist*

### Starkville
Loftin, Marion Theo *sociologist, educator*

### University
Bomba, Anne Killingsworth *family relations and child development educator*

## MISSOURI

### Bolivar
Jackson, James Larry *recreation educator*

### Columbia
Breimyer, Harold Frederick *agricultural economist*
Bunn, Ronald Freeze *political science educator, lawyer*
Ratti, Ronald Andrew *economics educator*
Rowlett, Ralph Morgan *archaeologist, educator*
Twaddle, Andrew Christian *sociology educator*
Yarwood, Dean Lesley *political science educator*
Yesilada, Birol Ali *political science educator*

### Half Way
Graves, Jerrell Loren *demographic studies researcher*

### Kansas City
Rethemeyer, Robert John *social studies educator*

### Saint Clair
Gullet, Leon Estle *retired cartographer*

### Saint Louis
Barnett, William Arnold *economics educator*
Beck, Lois Grant *anthropologist, educator*
Browman, David L(udvig) *archaeologist*
Etzkorn, K. Peter *sociology educator, author*
Fox, Richard Gabriel *anthropologist, educator*
Greenbaum, Stuart I. *economist, educator*
Kagan, Sioma *economics educator*
Kling, Merle *political scientist, university official*
Leguey-Feilleux, Jean-Robert *political scientist, educator*

PROFESSIONAL INDEX 5435 SOCIAL SCIENCE


Leven, Charles Louis *economics educator*
Le Vine, Victor Theodore *political science educator*
Miller, Gary J. *political economist*
Neuefeind, Wilhelm *economics educator, university administrator*
North, Douglass Cecil *economist, educator*
Pittman, David Joshua *sociologist, educator, researcher, consultant*
Rasmussen, David Tab *physical anthropology educator*
Salisbury, Robert Holt *political science educator*
Watson, Patty Jo *anthropology educator*
Weidenbaum, Murray Lew *economics educator*
Witherspoon, William *investment economist*
Worseck, Raymond Adams *economist*

**Springfield**
Stone, Allan David *economics educator*
Van Cleave, William Robert *international relations educator*

## MONTANA

**Bozeman**
Spencer, Robert C. *political science educator*
Stroup, Richard Lyndell *economics educator, writer*

**Missoula**
Lopach, James Joseph *political science educator*
Power, Thomas Michael *economist, educator*

## NEBRASKA

**Alliance**
Haefele, Edwin Theodore *political theorist, consultant*

**Kearney**
Glazier, Stephen Davey *anthropologist, theologian*

**Lincoln**
MacPhee, Craig Robert *economist, educator*
Ottoson, Howard Warren *agricultural economist, former university administrator*
Peterson, Wallace Carroll, Sr. *economics educator*

**Omaha**
Wunsch, James Stevenson *political science educator*

## NEVADA

**Incline Village**
Jones, Robert Alonzo *economist*

**Las Vegas**
Goodall, Leonard Edwin *public administration educator*
Hardbeck, George William *economics educator*
McCracken, Robert Dale *anthropologist, writer*

**Reno**
Haynes, Gary Anthony *archaeologist*
Leland, Joy Hanson *anthropologist, alcohol research specialist*
Weems, Robert Cicero *economist, educator*
Weinberg, Leonard Burton *political scientist*

**Sparks**
Chapman, Samuel Greeley *political science educator, criminologist*

## NEW HAMPSHIRE

**Durham**
Palmer, Stuart Hunter *sociology educator*
Romoser, George Kenneth *political science educator*
Rosen, Sam *economics educator emeritus*
Simos, Evangelos Otto *economist, educator*

**Hanover**
Campbell, Colin Dearborn *economist, educator*
Clement, Meredith Owen *economist, educator*
Demko, George Joseph *geographer*
Fischel, William Alan *economics educator*
Gustman, Alan Leslie *economics educator*
Hall, Raymond *sociology educator*
Logue, Dennis Emhardt *financial economics educator, consultant*
Lyons, Gene Martin *political scientist, educator*
Masters, Roger Davis *government educator*
Rutter, Jeremy Bentham *archaeologist, educator*
Starzinger, Vincent Evans *political science educator*
Young, Oran Reed *political scientist, educator*

**Henniker**
Braiterman, Thea Gilda *economics educator, state legislator*

**Laconia**
Shoup, Carl Sumner *retired economist*

**West Lebanon**
Bower, Richard Stuart *economist, educator*

**Wolfeboro**
Mancke, Richard Bell *economics writer, investor*
Murray, Roger Franklin *economist, educator*

## NEW JERSEY

**Caldwell**
Kapusinski, Albert Thomas *economist, educator*

**Camden**
Sigler, Jay Adrian *political scientist, educator*

**Cape May**
Janosik, Edward Gabriel *retired political science educator*

**Denville**
Breed, Ria *anthropologist*

**Dover**
Lichtig, Leo Kenneth *health economist*

**East Orange**
Wolff, Derish Michael *economist, company executive*

**Fairview**
Ciccone, Joseph Lee *criminal justice educator*

**Glen Ridge**
Szamek, Pierre Ervin *anthropologist, researcher*

**Hawthorne**
Cole, Leonard Aaron *political scientist, dentist*

**Hightstown**
Fitch, Lyle Craig *economist, administrator*

**Jersey City**
D'Amico, Thomas F. *economist, educator*

**Lyndhurst**
Bunda, Stephen Myron *political advisor, consultant, lawyer, classical philosopher*

**Marlboro**
Leveson, Irving Frederick *economist*

**New Brunswick**
Alexander, Robert Jackson *economist, educator*
Boocock, Sarane Spence *sociologist*
Chelius, James Robert *economics educator*
Elinson, Jack *sociology educator*
Glasser, Paul Harold *sociologist, educator, university administrator, social worker*
Glickman, Norman Jay *economist, urban policy analyst*
Jacob, Charles Elmer *political scientist, educator*
Leggett, John Carl *sociology educator*
Mechanic, David *social sciences educator*
Midlarsky, Manus Issachar *political scientist, educator*
Reock, Ernest C., Jr. *retired government services educator, academic director*
Russell, Louise Bennett *economist, educator*
Stuart, Robert Crampton *economics educator*
Tiger, Lionel *social scientist, anthropology consultant*
Toby, Jackson *sociologist, educator*

**Newark**
Hallard, Wayne Bruce *economist*
Hiltz, Starr Roxanne *sociologist, educator, computer scientist, writer, lecturer, consultant*
Holzer, Marc *public administrator educator*

**Paramus**
Aronson, Miriam Klausner *gerontologist, consultant, researcher, educator*

**Piscataway**
Riss, Richard Michael *research economist, church history educator*

**Pompton Lakes**
Wildebush, Joseph Frederick *economist*

**Princeton**
Ashenfelter, Orley Clark *economics educator*
Barlow, Walter Greenwood *public opinion analyst, management consultant*
Berry, Charles Horace *economist, educator*
Bogan, Elizabeth Chapin *economist, educator*
Bradford, David Frantz *economist*
Chow, Gregory Chi-Chong *economist, educator*
Coffey, Joseph Irving *international affairs educator*
Cook, Michael Allan *social sciences educator*
Doig, Jameson Wallace *political science educator*
Geertz, Clifford James *anthropology educator*
Geertz, Hildred Storey *anthropology educator*
Gilpin, Robert George, Jr. *political science educator*
Gordenker, Leon *political sciences educator*
Greenstein, Fred Irwin *political science educator*
Halpern, Manfred *political science educator*
Hirschman, Albert Otto *political economist, educator*
Issawi, Charles Philip *economist, educator*
Joyce, Carol Bertani *social studies educator*
Kateb, George Anthony *political science educator*
Kenen, Peter Bain *economist, educator*
Kuenne, Robert Eugene *economics educator*
Lester, Richard Allen *economist, educator*
†Lewis, John Prior *economist, educator*
Malkiel, Burton Gordon *economics educator*
Montagu, Ashley *anthropologist, social biologist*
Quandt, Richard Emeric *economics educator*
Rogoff, Kenneth S. *economics educator*
Rosenthal, Howard Lewis *political science educator*
Rozman, Gilbert Friedell *sociologist, educator*
Shear, Ione Mylonas *archaeologist*
Shear, Theodore Leslie, Jr. *archaeologist, educator*
Sigmund, Paul Eugene *political science educator*
Starr, Paul Elliot *sociologist, writer, editor, educator*
Tienda, Marta *demographer, educator*
Ullman, Richard Henry *political science educator*
Von Hippel, Frank Niels *public and international affairs educator*
Wallace, Walter L. *sociologist, educator*
Walzer, Michael Laban *political science educator*
Westoff, Charles Francis *demographer, educator*
Willig, Robert Daniel *economics educator*

**Red Bank**
McWhinney, Madeline H. (Mrs. John Denny Dale) *economist*

**Short Hills**
Parks, Robert Henry *consulting economist, educator*

**South Orange**
Green, Donald Webb *economist*

**Springfield**
Shilling, A. Gary *economic consultant, investment advisor*

**Teaneck**
Browne, Robert Span *economist*
Brudner, Helen Gross *social sciences educator*
Cassimatis, Peter John *economics educator*

**Upper Montclair**
Cordasco, Francesco *sociologist, educator, author*

## NEW MEXICO

**Albuquerque**
Basso, Keith Hamilton *cultural anthropologist, linguist, educator*
Bretton, Henry L. *political scientist, educator*
Coes, Donald Vinton *economics educator*
Condie, Carol Joy *anthropologist, research facility administrator*
Harris, Fred R. *political science educator, former senator*
Heady, Ferrel *retired political science educator*
May, Philip Alan *sociology educator*
Schwerin, Karl Henry *anthropology educator, researcher*
Sickels, Robert Judd *political science educator*
Stuart, David Edward *anthropologist, author, educator*
Wollman, Nathaniel *economist, educator*

**Aztec**
Moore, Roger Albert, Jr. *archaeologist*

**Las Cruces**
Lease, Richard Jay *police science educator, former police officer*

**Las Vegas**
Riley, Carroll Lavern *anthropology educator*

**Portales**
Agogino, George Allen *anthropologist, educator*

**Santa Fe**
Whiteford, Andrew Hunter *anthropologist*
Williams, Stephen *anthropologist, educator*

**Taos**
Young, Jon Nathan *archeologist*

## NEW YORK

**Albany**
Harris, Eric R. *policy analyst, county official*
Mehtabdin, Khalid Rauf *economist, educator*
Nathan, Richard P(erle) *political scientist, educator*
Thompson, Frank Joseph *political science educator*
Thornberry, Terence Patrick *criminologist, educator*
Wright, Theodore Paul, Jr. *political science educator*
Zimmerman, Joseph Francis *political scientist, educator*

**Annandale On Hudson**
Papadimitriou, Dimitri Basil *economist, college administrator*

**Armonk**
Grove, David Lawrence *economist*

**Averill Park**
Haines, Walter Wells *retired economics educator*

**Binghamton**
Banks, Arthur Sparrow *political scientist, educator*
Mazrui, Ali Al'Amin *political science educator, researcher*
O'Neil, Patrick Michael *political scientist, educator*

**Bronx**
Battista, Leon Joseph, Jr. *economics educator*
Fishman, Joshua Aaron *sociolinguist, educator*
Heilbrun, James *economist, educator*

**Bronxville**
Kirk, Grayson Louis *retired political science educator, retired universtiy president, trustee*

**Brooklyn**
Bowers, Patricia Eleanor Fritz *economist*
Kaplan, Mitchell Alan *sociologist, researcher*
Masterson, Charles Francis *retired social scientist*
Minkoff, Jack *economics educator*
Szenberg, Michael *economics educator, editor, consultant*

**Brookville**
Abdolali, Nasrin *political scientist, educator, consultant*

**Buffalo**
Abrahams, Athol Denis *geography researcher, educator*
Aurbach, Herbert Alexander *sociology educator*
Gort, Michael *economics educator*
Hetzner, Donald Raymund *social studies educator, forensic social scientist*
Levine, Murray *psychology educator*
Rosenthal, Donald B. *political scientist, educator*
Tedlock, Barbara Helen *anthropologist, educator*
Tedlock, Dennis *anthropology and literature educator*
Zagare, Frank Cosmo *political science educator*
Zarembka, Paul *economics educator*

**Catskill**
Markou, Peter John *economic developer*

**Chappaqua**
Brockway, George Pond *economist*

**Conesus**
Dadrian, Vahakn Norair *sociology educator*

**Dobbs Ferry**
Kraetzer, Mary C. *sociologist, educator, consultant*
Sutton, Francis Xavier *social scientist, consultant*

**Farmingdale**
Kostanoski, John Ivan *criminal justice educator*

**Flushing**
Hacker, Andrew *political science educator*
Psomiades, Harry John *political science educator*
Smith, Charles William *social sciences educator, sociologist*

**Fredonia**
Dowd, Morgan Daniel *political science educator*

**Garden City**
Ohrenstein, Roman Abraham *economics educator, economist, rabbi*

**Geneseo**
Battersby, Harold Ronald *anthropologist, archaeologist, linguist*

**Great Neck**
Christie, George Nicholas *economist, consultant*
Hamovitch, William *economist, educator, university official*
Joskow, Jules *economic research company executive*

**Hamilton**
Farnsworth, Frank Albert *retired economics educator*
Johnston, (William) Michael *political science educator, university administrator*

**Hempstead**
Turgeon, Edgar Lynn *economics educator*
Wattel, Harold Louis *economics educator*

**Henrietta**
Carmel, Simon J(acob) *anthropologist*

**Irvington**
Wolf, Eric Robert *anthropologist, educator*

**Ithaca**
Ascher, Robert *anthropologist, archaeologist, educator, filmmaker*
Beneria, Lourdes *economist, educator*
Blau, Francine Dee *economics educator*
Briggs, Vernon Mason, Jr. *economics educator*
Easley, David *economics educator*
Ehrenberg, Ronald Gordon *economist, educator*
Fireside, Harvey Francis *political scientist, educator*
Forker, Olan Dean *agricultural economics educator*
Hockett, Charles Francis *anthropology educator*
Isard, Walter *economics educator*
Jarrow, Robert Alan *economics and finance educator, consultant*
Kahin, George McTurnan *political science and history educator*
Kahn, Alfred Edward *economist, educator, government official*
Kennedy, Kenneth Adrian Raine *biological anthropologist, forensic anthropologist*
Kirsch, A(nthony) Thomas *anthropology and Asian studies educator, researcher*
Kramnick, Isaac *government educator*
Lowi, Theodore J(ay) *political science educator*
Lyons, Thomas Patrick *economics educator*
Shell, Karl *economics educator*
Smith, Robert John *anthropology educator*
Stycos, Joseph Mayone *demographer, educator*
Thorbecke, Erik *economics educator*
Tomek, William Goodrich *agricultural economist*

**Mexico**
Sade, Donald Stone *anthropology educator*

**New City**
†Wechman, Robert Joseph *economist, educator*

**New Hyde Park**
Reddan, Harold Jerome *sociologist, educator*

**New Paltz**
Schnell, George Adam *geographer, educator*

**New Rochelle**
Berlage, Gai Ingham *sociologist, educator*

**New York**
Abu-Lughod, Janet Lippman *sociologist, educator*
Adler, Freda Schaffer (Mrs. G. O. W. Mueller) *criminologist, educator*
Alford, Robert Ross *sociologist*
Angell, Wayne D. *economist, banker*
Anspach, Ernst *economist, lawyer*
Baldwin, David Allen *political science educator*
Betts, Richard Kevin *political science educator*
Bond, George Clement *anthropologist, educator*
Boodey, Cecil Webster, Jr. *political science educator*
Boorstein, Laurence *economist*
Bowen, William Gordon *economist, educator, foundation administrator*
Braham, Randolph Lewis *political science educator*
Brams, Steven John *political scientist, educator, game theorist*
Brancato, Carolyn Kay *economist, consultant*
Broisman, Emma Ray *economist, retired international official*
Brusca, Robert Andrew *economist*
Caraley, Demetrios James *political scientist, educator, author*
Cochrane, James Louis *economist*
Cohen, Stephen Frand *political scientist, historian, educator, author, broadcaster*
Comitas, Lambros *anthropologist*
Costa, Rosann *sociologist, educator*
Dalton, Dennis Gilmore *political science educator*
Denoon, David Baugh Holden *economist, educator, consultant*
Dhrymes, Phoebus James *economist, educator*
Dowling, Edward Thomas *economics educator*
Duke, Anthony Drexel *sociologist, educator, philanthropist*
Edinger, Lewis Joachim *political science educator*
Edwards, Franklin R. *economist, educator, consultant*
Elliott-Smith, Paul Henry *marketing and economics consultant*
Emerson, Alice Frey *political scientist, educator emerita*
Engler, Robert *political science educator, author*
Epstein, Cynthia Fuchs *sociology educator, writer*
Fabbri, Brian John *economist, investment strategist*
Finger, Seymour Maxwell *political science educator, former ambassador*

Franklin, Julian Harold political science educator
Freedman, Audrey Willock economist
Freund, William Curt economist
Gans, Herbert J. sociologist, educator
Ginzberg, Eli economist, emeritus educator, government consultant, author
Goss, Mary E. Weber sociology educator
Gould, Jay Martin economist, consultant
Habachy, Suzan Salwa Saba development economist, non profit administrator
Hahn, Fred retired political science and history educator
Halper, Thomas political science educator
Heal, Geoffrey Martin economics educator
Heilbroner, Robert Louis economist, author
Helmreich, William Benno sociology educator, consultant
Heydebrand, Wolf Von sociology educator
Holloway, Ralph Leslie anthropology educator
Hormats, Robert David economist, investment banker
Hormozi, Farrokh Zad economist, educator, consultant, business forecaster
Hoxter, Curtis Joseph international economic adviser, public relations and affairs counselor
Hufbauer, Gary Clyde economist, lawyer, educator
Hurewitz, J(acob) C(oleman) retired international relations educator, author, consultant
Hurwitz, Sol business policy organization executive
Ianni, Francis Anthony James anthropologist, psychoanalyst, educator
James, Gary Douglas biological anthropologist, educator, researcher
Jervis, Robert political science educator
Jones, David Milton economist, educator
Jurman, Elisabeth Antonie economist
Kamsky, Leonard economist, retired manufacturing executive, financial advisor
Kaplan, Leo Sylvan social scientist, former college administrator
Kavesh, Robert A. economist, educator
Kazemi, Farhad political science educator
Kesselman, Mark Jonathan political science educator, writer
Komarovsky, Mirra (Mrs. Marcus A. Heyman) sociology educator
Kvint, Vladimir Lev economist, educator, mining engineer
Lakah, Jacqueline Rabbat political scientist, educator
Lancaster, Kelvin John economics educator
Laurendi, Nat criminologist
Lehman, Edward William sociology educator, researcher
Leontief, Wassily economist, educator
Lewis, Hylan Garnet sociologist, educator
Lichtblau, John H. economist
Lieberman, Charles economist
Lipsey, Robert Edward economist, educator
Mac Namara, Donal Eoin Joseph criminologist
Maldonado-Bear, Rita Marinita economist, educator
Marlin, John Tepper economist, writer, consultant
McKesson, John Alexander, III international relations educator
Merton, Robert K. sociologist, educator
Mincer, Jacob economics educator
Molz, Redmond Kathleen public administration educator
Moore, Geoffrey Hoyt economist
Moskowitz, Arnold X. economist, strategist, educator
†Mroz, John Edwin political scientist
Muller, Charlotte Feldman economist, educator
Mundell, Robert Alexander economics educator
Murphy, Austin de la Salle economist, educator, banker
Murphy, Joseph Samson political science educator
Nadiri, M. Ishaq economics educator, researcher, lecturer, consultant
Nakamura, James I. economics educator
Nathan, Andrew James political science educator
Nelkin, Dorothy sociology and science policy educator
Netzer, Dick economics educator
Patrick, Hugh Talbot economist, educator
Patterson, Perry William economist, publishing company executive
Peck, Fred Neil economist, educator
Persell, Caroline Hodges sociologist, educator, author, researcher, consultant
Petchesky, Rosalind Pollack political science and women's studies educator
Phelps, Edmund Strother economics educator
Piven, Frances Fox political scientist, educator
Prewitt, Kenneth political science educator, foundation executive
Pye, Gordon Bruce economist
Quackenbush, Margery Clouser psychoanalyst, administrator
Radner, Roy economist, educator, researcher
Ramirez, Maria Fiorini economist, investment advisor
Rivlin, Benjamin political science educator
Robock, Stefan Hyman economics educator emeritus
Ross, Jeffrey Allan political scientist, educator
Rothschild, Joseph political science educator
Sartori, Giovanni political scientist
Scanlon, Rosemary economist
Scelsa, Joseph Vincent sociologist
Schachter, Barry economist
Schilling, Warner Roller political scientist, educator
Schneider, Greta Sara economist, financial consultant
Schotter, Andrew Roye economics educator, consultant
Schwab, George David social science educator
Schwartz, Anna Jacobson economic historian
Schwartzman, David economist, educator
Sennett, Richard sociologist, writer
Shapiro, Judith R. anthropology educator, academic administrator
Sheldon, Eleanor Harriet Bernert sociologist
Sherry, George Leon political science educator
Silver, Morris economist, educator
Silverman, Sydel Finfer anthropologist
Simon, Jacqueline Albert political scientist, writer
Small, George LeRoy geographer, educator
Snyder, Jack L. social sciences administrator
Sylla, Richard Eugene economics educator
Taylor, Lance Jerome economics educator
Tepper, Lynn Marsha gerontology educator
Updike, Helen Hill economist, investment manager, financial planner
Vickrey, William Spencer economist, educator
Vora, Ashok financial economist
Walter, Ingo economics educator
Watts, Harold Wesley economist, educator
Wenglowski, Gary Martin economist
Westin, Alan Furman political science educator
Wetzler, James Warren economist
White, Lawrence J. economics educator
Wojnilower, Albert Martin economist
Wrong, Dennis Hume sociologist, educator
Yorburg, Betty (Mrs. Leon Yorburg) sociology educator

### Old Westbury
Ozelli, Tunch economics educator, consultant

### Oyster Bay
Trevor, Bronson economist

### Port Washington
Kellner, Irwin L. economist

### Potsdam
Hanson, David Justin sociology educator, researcher

### Poughkeepsie
Johnson, M(aurice) Glen political science educator
Marshall, Natalie Junemann economics educator

### Purchase
Ryan, Edward W. economics educator
Siegel, Nathaniel Harold sociology educator

### Rhinebeck
†Flexner, Kurt Fisher economics educator

### Rochester
Bluhm, William Theodore political scientist, educator
D'Agostino, Anthony Carmen anthropologist, educator
Engerman, Stanley Lewis economist, educator, historian
Fenno, Richard Francis, Jr. political science educator
Hanushek, Eric Alan economics educator
Harris, Alfred social anthropologist, educator
Hopkins, Thomas Duvall economics educator
Jacobs, Bruce political science educator
Jones, Ronald Winthrop economics educator
Long, John Broaddus, Jr. economist, educator
Mc Kenzie, Lionel Wilfred economist, educator
Mueller, John Ernest political science educator, dance critic and historian
Niemi, Richard Gene political science educator
Phelps, Charles Elliott economics educator
Regenstreif, S(amuel) Peter political scientist, educator
Rosett, Richard Nathaniel economist, educator
Sangree, Walter Hinchman social anthropologist, educator
Steamer, Robert Julius political science educator

### Sag Harbor
Baer, Jon Alan political scientist

### Scarsdale
Cohen, Irwin economist

### Schenectady
Board, Joseph Breckinridge, Jr. political scientist, educator

### Slingerlands
Fenton, William Nelson anthropologist, anthropology educator emeritus

### South Salem
Saurwein, Virginia Fay international affairs specialist

### Staten Island
Meltzer, Yale Leon economist, educator

### Stony Brook
Fleagle, John Gwynn anthropology and paleontology educator
Goodman, Norman sociologist, researcher
Neuberger, Egon economics educator
Schneider, Mark political science educator
Stone, Elizabeth Caecilia anthropology educator
Tanur, Judith Mark sociologist, educator
Travis, Martin Bice political scientist, educator

### Syracuse
Birkhead, Guthrie Sweeney, Jr. political scientist, university dean
Braungart, Richard Gottfried sociology and international relations educator
Frohock, Fred Manuel political science educator
Jensen, Robert Granville geography educator, university dean
Jump, Bernard, Jr. economics educator
Kriesberg, Louis sociologist, educator
Mazur, Allan Carl sociologist, engineer, educator
Meinig, Donald William geography educator
Monmonier, Mark geographer, graphics educator, essayist
Palmer, John L. social sciences researcher, educator
Schwartz, Richard Derecktor sociologist, educator
Wadley, Susan Snow anthropologist

### Tarrytown
Marcus, Sheldon social sciences educator

### Troy
Brazil, Harold Edmund political science educator
Diwan, Romesh Kumar economics educator
Schechter, Stephen L. political scientist

### Wantagh
Dawson, George Glenn economics educator emeritus

### Yonkers
Varma, Baidya Nath sociologist, broadcaster, poet

## NORTH CAROLINA

### Cary
Goodwin, Barry Kent economics educator

### Chapel Hill
Black, Stanley Warren, III economics educator
Blau, Peter Michael sociologist, educator
Brockington, Donald Leslie anthropologist, archaeologist, educator
Brown, Frank social science educator
Crane, Julia Gorham anthropology educator
Friedman, James Winstein economist, educator
Gallman, Robert Emil economics and history educator
Gil, Federico Guillermo political science educator
Graham, George Adams political scientist, emeritus educator
Gulick, John anthropology educator
Huber, Evelyne political science educator
Ingram, James Carlton economist, educator
MacRae, Duncan, Jr. social scientist, educator
Pfouts, Ralph William economist, consultant
Richardson, Richard Judson political science educator
Rindfuss, Ronald Richard sociology educator
Schoultz, Lars political scientist, educator
Simpson, Richard Lee sociologist, educator
Steponaitis, Vincas Petras archaeologist, anthropologist, educator
Treml, Vladimir Guy economist, educator
Udry, J. Richard sociology educator
Waud, Roger Neil economics educator
Wilson, Glenn economist, educator
Wilson, Robert Neal sociologist, educator
Wright, Deil Spencer political science educator
Yarnell, Richard Asa anthropologist

### Charlotte
Neel, Richard Eugene economics educator
Pyle, Gerald Fredric medical geographer, educator
Webster, Murray Alexander, Jr. sociologist

### Dallas
Blanton, Robert D'Alden anthropology and history educator

### Davidson
Ratliff, Charles Edward, Jr. economics educator

### Dillsboro
Lefler, Lisa Jane anthropologist and social sciences educator

### Durham
Aldrich, John Herbert political science educator
Barber, James David political scientist, retired educator
Behn, Robert Dietrich public policy educator, writer
Braibanti, Ralph John political scientist, educator
Budd, Isabelle Amelia research economist
Burmeister, Edwin economics educator
Clotfelter, Charles T. economics educator
Elliot, Jeffrey M. political science educator, author
Gittler, Joseph Bertram sociology educator
Handy, Rollo Leroy economics educator, research executive
Holsti, Ole Rudolf political scientist, educator
†Hough, Jerry Fincher political science educator
Kelley, Allen Charles economist, educator
Keohane, Robert Owen political scientist, educator
†Kramer, Randall A. economist, educator
Kreps, Juanita Morris economics educator, former government official
Land, Kenneth Carl sociology educator, demographer, statistician, consultant
Leach, Richard Heald political scientist, educator
Mickiewicz, Ellen Propper political science educator
Myers, George Carleton sociology and demographics educator
Sloan, Frank Allen economics educator
Tiryakian, Edward Ashod sociology educator

### Franklin
Earhart, Eileen Magie retired child and family life educator

### Gastonia
Kiser, Clyde Vernon retired demographer

### Greensboro
Helms-VanStone, Mary Wallace anthropology educator
Hidore, John Junior geographer, educator
Shelton, David Howard economics educator
Zopf, Paul Edward, Jr. sociologist

### Greenville
Cramer, Robert Eli geography educator
Williams, Melvin John sociologist, educator

### Hendersonville
Bastedo, Ralph W(alter) social science educator

### Hillsborough
Goodwin, Craufurd David economics educator

### Pittsboro
Doenges, Byron Frederick economist, educator, former government official

## NORTH DAKOTA

### Fargo
Query, Joy Marves Neale medical sociology educator
Riley, Thomas Joseph anthropologist

## OHIO

### Akron
Byrne, Dennis Michael economist, educator
Coyne, Thomas Joseph economist, finance educator
Sam, David Fiifi political economist, educator

### Ashland
Ford, Lucille Garber economist, educator

### Athens
Gallaway, Lowell Eugene economist, educator
Wagner, Eric Armin sociology educator

### Beachwood
Wolf, Milton Albert economist, former ambassador, investor

### Berea
Miller, Dennis Dixon economics educator

### Bowling Green
McCaghy, Charles Henry sociology educator

### Brecksville
Conaway, Orrin Bryte political scientist, educator

### Cincinnati
Bishop, George Franklin political social psychologist, educator
Katz, Robert Langdon human relations educator, rabbi

### Cleveland
Beall, Cynthia anthropologist, educator
Binstock, Robert Henry public policy educator, writer, lecturer
Burke, John Francis, Jr. economist
Carlsson, Bo Axel Vilhelm economics educator
Carter, John Dale organizational development executive
Chatterjee, Pranab social sciences educator
Goldstein, Melvyn C. anthropologist, educator
Grundy, Kenneth William political science educator
Mayland, Kenneth Theodore economist
McHale, Vincent Edward political science educator
Murray, Thomas Henry bioethics educator, writer
Rosegger, Gerhard economist, educator
Sibley, Willis Elbridge anthropology educator, consultant
Stein, Herman David social sciences educator, past university provost

### Cleveland Heights
Daroff, William C. political consultant, public policy analyst

### Columbus
Alger, Chadwick Fairfax political scientist, educator
Beck, Paul Allen political science educator
Bourguignon, Erika Eichhorn anthropologist, educator
Cunnyngham, Jon economist, information systems educator
Epstein, Erwin Howard sociology and education educator
Gilliom, Morris Eugene social studies and global educator
Huber, Joan Althaus sociology educator
Huff, C(larence) Ronald criminology educator and public administration
Ichiishi, Tatsuro economics and mathematics educator
Kessel, John Howard political scientist, educator
Ladman, Jerry R. economist, educator
Lundstedt, Sven Bertil behavioral and social scientist, educator
Lynn, Arthur Dellert, Jr. economist, educator
Maddala, Gangadharrao Soundaryarao economics educator
Marble, Duane Francis geography educator, researcher
Namboodiri, Krishnan sociology educator
Patterson, Samuel Charles political science educator
Poirier, Frank Eugene physical anthropology educator
Ray, Edward John economics educator, administrator
Richardson, Laurel Walum sociology educator
Ripley, Randall Butler political scientist, educator
Taaffe, Edward James geography educator
Weisberg, Herbert Frank political science educator

### Hamilton
New, Rosetta Holbrock home economics educator, nutrition consultant

### Kent
Williams, Harold Roger economist, educator

### Oberlin
Taylor, Richard Wirth political science educator

### Oxford
Rejai, Mostafa political science educator

### Toledo
Attoh, Samuel Aryeetey geographer, educator, planner

### Waterford
Riley, Nancy Mae retired vocational home economics educator

## OKLAHOMA

### Edmond
Smock, Donald Joe governmental liaison, political consultant

### Norman
Affleck, Marilyn sociology educator
Albert, Lois Eldora Wilson archaeologist
Bell, Robert Eugene anthropologist educator
Cella, Francis Raymond economist, research consultant
Henderson, George educational sociologist, educator
Kondonassis, Alexander John economist, educator

### Stillwater
Bynum, Jack Edward, Jr. sociology educator
Moomaw, Ronald Lee economics educator
Poole, Richard William economics educator

### Tulsa
Cooke, Marvin Lee sociologist, consultant, urban planner
Nixon, James Gregory economic development consultant

## OREGON

### Ashland
Houston, John Albert political science educator

### Corvallis
Castle, Emery Neal agricultural and resource economist, educator
Harter, Lafayette George, Jr. economics educator emeritus
Towey, Richard Edward economics educator

**Eugene**
Aikens, C(lyde) Melvin *anthropology educator, archaeologist*
Davis, Richard Malone *economics educator*
Khang, Chulsoon *economics educator*
McGuire, Timothy William *economics and management educator, dean*
Mikesell, Raymond Frech *economics educator*

**Mcminnville**
Blodgett, Forrest Clinton *economics educator*

**Monmouth**
Shay, Roshani Cari *political science educator*

**Neotsu**
Archer, Stephen Hunt *economist, educator*

**Portland**
Broughton, Ray Monroe *economic consultant*
Davis, James Allan *gerontologist, educator*
Kristof, Ladis Kris Donabed *political scientist, author*

**Siletz**
Jennings, Jesse David *anthropology educator*

## PENNSYLVANIA

**Allentown**
Bannon, George *retired economics educator, department chairman*
Bednar, Charles Sokol *political scientist, educator*

**Bethlehem**
Aronson, Jay Richard *economics educator, researcher, academic administrator*
Frankel, Barbara Brown *cultural anthropologist*
Schwartz, Eli *economics educator, writer*

**Birdsboro**
Hill, Lenora Mae *astrologer*

**Bryn Mawr**
Porter, Judith Deborah Revitch *sociologist, educator*

**Carlisle**
Jacobs, Norman G(abriel) *sociologist, educator*
Jones, Oliver Hastings *consulting economist*

**East Stroudsburg**
Briggs, Philip James *political science educator, author, lecturer*

**Easton**
Kincaid, John *political science educator, editor*

**Erie**
Adovasio, J. M. *anthropologist, archeologist, educator*

**Gettysburg**
Plischke, Elmer *political science educator*

**Gwynedd**
Zumeta, Bertram William *retired economist*

**Haverford**
de Laguna, Frederica *anthropology educator emeritus, author, consultant*
Mellink, Machteld Johanna *archaeologist, educator*
Northrup, Herbert Roof *economist, business executive*

**Indiana**
Mc Cauley, R. Paul *criminologist, educator*
Miller, Vincent Paul, Jr. *geography and regional planning educator*
Walker, Donald Anthony *economist, educator*

**King Of Prussia**
Draayer, Shari Lynn *sociologist*

**Kutztown**
Dougherty, Percy H. *geographer, educator, politician, planner*

**Lancaster**
Stephenson, Donald Grier, Jr. *government studies educator*

**Meadville**
Adams, Earl William, Jr. *economics educator*

**Media**
Smith, David Gilbert *political science educator*

**Newtown**
Coale, Ansley Johnson *economics educator*

**Philadelphia**
Behrman, Jere Richard *economics educator*
Buerkle, Jack Vincent *sociologist, educator*
Cass, David *economist, educator*
Clark, John J. *economics and finance educator*
Duffy, Francis Ramon *sociology educator*
Evan, William Martin *sociologist, educator*
Fox, Renée Claire *sociology educator*
Frankel, Francine Ruth *political science educator*
Goodenough, Ward Hunt *anthropologist, educator*
Grossman, Sanford Jay *economics educator*
Klausner, Samuel Zundel *sociologist, educator*
Klein, Lawrence Robert *economist, educator*
Kopecky, Kenneth John *economics educator*
Lang, Richard Warren *economist*
Lee, Chong-Sik *political scientist, educator*
Libby, Ronald Theodore *political science educator, consultant, researcher*
Mansfield, Edwin *economist, educator*
Menken, Jane Ava *demographer, educator*
Michael, Henry N. *geographer, anthropologist*
Miller, Ronald Eugene *regional science educator*
Preston, Samuel Hulse *demographer*
Rieff, Philip *sociologist*
Rima, Ingrid Hahne *economics educator*
Ruane, Joseph William *sociologist*
Rubinstein, Alvin Zachary *political science educator, author*
Rubinstein, Robert Lawrence *anthropologist, gerontologist*
Sabloff, Jeremy Arac *archaeologist*
Segal, Geraldine Rosenbaum *sociologist*
Sigmond, Robert M. *medical economist*
Summers, Anita Arrow *public policy and management educator*
Summers, Robert *economics educator*
Van De Walle, Etienne *demographer*
Wallace, Anthony Francis Clarke *anthropologist, educator*
Weeks, Gerald *psychology educator*
Wolfbein, Seymour Louis *economist, educator*
Wolfgang, Marvin Eugene *sociologist, criminologist, educator*

**Pittsburgh**
Andrews, Shannon Kay *sociologist, educator*
Blumstein, Alfred *urban and public affairs educator*
Bobrow, Davis Bernard *public policy educator*
Carroll, Holbert Nicholson *political science educator*
Davis, Otto Anderson *economics educator*
Eaton, Joseph W. *sociology educator*
Fararo, Thomas John *sociologist, educator*
Farrow, Robert Scott *economist, educator*
Ginsburg, Mark Barry *sociology of education educator*
Hammond, Paul Young *political scientist, educator*
Holzner, Burkart *sociologist, educator*
Howard, Lawrence Cabot *international affairs educator*
Katz, Arnold *economics educator*
Keefe, William Joseph *political science educator*
Kenkel, James Lawrence *economics educator*
Lave, Judith Rice *economics educator*
Lave, Lester Bernard *economist, educator, researcher*
McCallum, Bennett Tarlton *economics educator*
Meltzer, Allan H. *economist, educator*
Mesa-Lago, Carmelo *economist, educator*
Ogul, Morris Samuel *political science educator, consultant*
Perlman, Mark *economist, educator*
Roth, Alvin Eliot *economics educator*
Simon, Herbert A(lexander) *social scientist*
Strauss, Robert Philip *economics educator*
Sussna, Edward *economist, educator*

**Saint Davids**
Heebner, Albert Gilbert *economist, banker, educator*

**Scranton**
Parente, William Joseph *political science educator*

**State College**
Gould, Peter Robin *geographer, educator*
Miller, E. Willard *geography educator*

**Swarthmore**
Hopkins, Raymond Frederick *political science educator*
Keith, Jennie *anthropology educator and administrator, writer*
Saffran, Bernard *economist, educator*

**University Park**
Durrenberger, Edward Paul *anthropologist educator*
Epp, Donald James *economist, educator*
Friedman, Robert Sidney *political science educator*
Klein, Philip Alexander *economist*
Lewis, Peirce Fee *geographer, educator*
Nelsen, Hart Michael *sociologist, educator*
Pashek, Robert Donald *economics educator emeritus*
Rose, Adam Zachary *economist, educator*
Snow, Dean Richard *anthropology educator, archaeologist*
Walden, Daniel *humanities and social sciences educator*

**Villanova**
Hadley, Judith Marie *archaeologist, educator*
Johannes, John Roland *political science educator, college dean*
Langran, Robert Williams *political scientist*
Lesch, Ann Mosely *political scientist, educator*
Malik, Hafeez *political scientist, educator*

**Wayne**
MacNeal, Edward Arthur *economic consultant*

**West Chester**
Green, Andrew Wilson *economist, lawyer, educator*

**Wynnewood**
Khouri, Fred John *political science educator*
Phillips, Almarin *economics educator, consultant*

**York**
McMillan, Wendell Marlin *agricultural economist*

## RHODE ISLAND

**Kingston**
Alexander, Lewis McElwain *geographer, educator*
Gelles, Richard James *sociology and psychology educator*
Zucker, Norman Livingston *political scientist, educator, author*

**Providence**
Anton, Thomas Julius *political science and public policy educator, consultant*
Borts, George Herbert *economist, educator*
Goldstein, Sidney *sociology educator, demographer*
Goodman, Elliot Raymond *political scientist, educator*
Grossman, Herschel I. *economics educator*
Heath, Dwight Braley *anthropologist, educator*
Hogan, Dennis Patrick *sociology educator*
Hopmann, Philip Terrence *political science educator*
Marsh, Robert Mortimer *sociologist, educator*
Perkins, Whitney Trow *political science educator emeritus*
Poole, William *economics educator, consultant*
Putterman, Louis G. *economics educator*
Rueschemeyer, Dietrich *sociology educator*
Stein, Jerome Leon *economist, educator*
Stultz, Newell Maynard *political science educator*

## SOUTH CAROLINA

**Camden**
Reich, Merrill Drury *intelligence consultant, writer*

**Charleston**
Moore, William Vincent *political science educator*

**Clemson**
Trevillian, Wallace Dabney *economics educator, retired dean*

**Columbia**
Clower, Robert Wayne *economics educator, consultant*
Cohn, Elchanan *economics educator*
Feinn, Barbara Ann *economist*
Hatch, David Lincoln *sociology educator*
Kiker, Billy Frazier *economics educator*
Morris, James Aloysius *economist, educator*
Norton, Hugh Stanton *economist, educator*
Starr, Harvey *political scientist*
Weatherbee, Donald Emery *political scientist, educator*
Wilder, Ronald Parker *economics educator*

## SOUTH DAKOTA

**Brookings**
Gilbert, Howard Alden *economics educator*
Janssen, Larry Leonard *economics educator, researcher*
Wagner, Mary Kathryn *sociology educator, former state legislator*

**Vermillion**
Carlson, Loren Merle *political science educator*
Clem, Alan Leland *political scientist*
Dahlin, Donald C(lifford) *political science educator*

## TENNESSEE

**Chattanooga**
Rabin, Alan Abraham *economics educator*

**Knoxville**
Cole, William Edward *economics educator, consultant*
Hammond, Edwin Hughes *geography educator*
Harris, Diana Koffman *sociologist, educator*
Harrison, Faye Venetia *anthropologist, educator*

**Memphis**
Daniel, Coldwell, III *economist, educator*
Depperschmidt, Thomas Orlando *economist, educator*
Mealor, William Theodore, Jr. *geography educator, university administrator, consultant*
†Tuckman, Howard Paul *economics educator, consultant*

**Nashville**
Buckles, Stephen Gary *economist, educator*
Finegan, Thomas Aldrich *economist*
Gibbs, Jack Porter *sociologist, educator*
Gove, Walter R. *sociology educator*
Graham, George J., Jr. *political scientist, educator*
Hancock, M(arion) Donald *political science educator*
Hargrove, Erwin Charles, Jr. *political science educator*
Jamison, Connie Joyce *sociology educator*
Klein, Christopher Carnahan *economist*
Russell, Clifford Springer *economics and public policy educator*
Scheffman, David Theodore *economist, management educator, consultant*
Smith, Dani Allred *sociologist, educator*
Spores, Ronald Marvin *anthropology educator, ethnohistorian*
Westfield, Fred M. *economics educator*

**Sewanee**
Mohiuddin, Yasmeen Niaz *economics educator*

## TEXAS

**Abilene**
Davis, Burl Edward *social sciences research consulting company executive, communications educator*

**Arlington**
Cole, Richard Louis *political scientist, educator*
Mullendore, Walter Edward *economist*
Nelson, Wallace Boyd *economics and business administration educator*
Ramsey, Charles Eugene *sociologist, educator*

**Austin**
Blodgett, Warren Terrell *public affairs educator*
Buchanan, Bruce, II *political science educator*
Burnham, Walter Dean *political science educator*
Davis, Edward Mott *anthropology educator and researcher*
Doolittle, William Emery, III *geography educator*
Dusansky, Richard *economist, educator*
†Eaton, David *natural resource policy studies educator*
Epstein, Jeremiah Fain *anthropologist, educator*
Glade, William Patton, Jr. *economics educator*
Glenn, Norval Dwight *sociologist, educator*
Hamermesh, Daniel Selim *economics educator*
Hester, Thomas Roy *anthropologist*
Holz, Robert Kenneth *geography educator*
Huff, David L. *geography educator*
Jannuzi, F. Tomasson *economics educator*
Jordan, Terry Gilbert *geography educator*
Kendrick, David Andrew *economist, educator*
Lariviere, Richard Wilfred *Asian studies educator, consultant*
Leiden, Carl *political scientist, educator*
Lopreato, Joseph *sociology educator, author*
Mc Donald, Stephen Lee *economics educator*
Phelps, Gerry Charlotte *economist, minister*
†Pingree, Dianne *sociologist, educator, mediator*
Roach, James Robert *retired political science educator*
Rostow, Walt Whitman *economist, educator*
Schmandt-Besserat, Denise *archaeologist, educator*
Schmitt, Karl Michael *retired political scientist*
Smith, Alfred Goud *anthropologist, educator*
Smith, Todd Malcolm *political consultant*
Weintraub, Sidney *economist, educator*

**Brooks AFB**
Wilde, James Dale *archaeologist, educator*

**Bryan**
Branson, Robert Earl *marketing economist*
Lynch, Thomas Francis *archeologist, educator*

**College Station**
Bass, George Fletcher *archaeology educator*
Bond, Jon Roy *political science educator*
Copp, James Harris *sociologist, educator*
Furubotn, Eirik Grundtvig *economics educator*
Greenhut, Melvin Leonard *economist, educator*
Knutson, Ronald Dale *economist, educator, academic adminstrator*
Solecki, R. Stefan *anthropologist, educator*
Steffy, John Richard *nautical archaeologist, educator*
Van Riper, Paul Pritchard *political science educator*

**Dallas**
Betts, Dianne Connally *economist, educator*
Cochran, Kendall Pinney *economics educator*
Free, Mary Moore *anthropologist*
Fry, Edward Irad *anthropology educator*
Kemper, Robert Van *anthropologist, educator*
Murphy, John Carter *economics educator*
Reagan, Barbara Benton *economics educator*

**Denton**
Newell, Charldean *public administration educator*

**Egypt**
Krenek, Mary Louise *political science researcher, educator*

**El Paso**
Blevins, Leon Wilford *political science educator, minister*
Melton, Melinda Wallace *archaeologist, laboratory director*
Stoddard, Ellwyn R. *sociology and anthropology educator*

**Fort Worth**
Fleshman, Linda Eilene Scalf *private investigator, writer, columnist, consultant, communications and marketing executive*

**Georgetown**
Neville, Gwen Kennedy *anthropology educator*

**Houston**
Brito, Dagobert Llanos *economics educator*
Bryant, John Bradbury *economics educator, consultant*
Condit, Linda Faulkner *economist*
Cuthbertson, Gilbert Morris *political science educator*
Davidson, Chandler *sociologist, educator*
Ebaugh, Helen Rose *sociology educator, researcher*
Ewoh, Andrew Ikeh Emmanuel *political science educator*
Foster, Dale Warren *political scientist, educator, management consultant, real estate*
Gordon, Wendell Chaffee *economics educator*
Martin, William C. *sociology educator, writer*
McIntosh, Susan Keech *anthropology educator*
Pelaez, Rolando Federico *economics educator, consultant*
Tesarek, William Paul *business consultant, writer, financial executive*
Wilson, Rick Keith *political science educator*

**Huntsville**
Flanagan, Timothy James *criminal justice educator, university official*

**Irving**
Cooper, Kathleen Bell *economist*

**Lancaster**
Wendorf, Denver Fred, Jr. *anthropology educator*

**Lubbock**
Collins, Harker *economist, manufacturing executive, publisher, marketing, financial, business and legal consultant*
Gilliam, John Charles *economist, educator*
Havens, Murray Clark *political scientist, educator*
Jonish, James Edward *economist, educator*
Stein, William Warner *anthropology educator*

**Mc Kinney**
Berry, Brian Joe Lobley *geographer, political economist, urban planner*

**Post**
Earl, Lewis Harold *economics and management consultant, lawyer*

**Prairie View**
Prestage, Jewel Limar *political science educator*
Server, Ronald Douglas *criminologist, political scientist, lawyer, educator*

**Richardson**
Andrews, Melinda Wilson *human development researcher*

**San Antonio**
Bellows, Thomas John *political scientist, educator*
Benz, George Albert *economic consultant, retired educator*
Firestone, Juanita Marlies *sociology educator*
Furino, Antonio *economist, educator*
Hazuda, Helen Pauline *sociologist, educator*
Mott, Peggy Laverne *sociologist, educator*
Spiro, Herbert John *political scientist, politician, educator, ambassador*
Whittington, Floyd Leon *economist, business consultant, retired oil company executive, foreign service officer*

**San Marcos**
Boehm, Richard Glennon *geography and planning educator, writer*
Schultz, Clarence Carven, Jr. *sociology educator*

**Waco**
Osborne, Harold Wayne *sociology educator, consultant*
Sharp, Ronald Arvell *sociology educator*

## UTAH

**Provo**
Bahr, Howard Miner *sociologist, educator*
Christiansen, John Rees *sociologist, educator*
Fry, Earl Howard *political scientist, educator*
Kunz, Phillip Ray *sociologist, educator*
Porter, Blaine Robert Milton *sociology and psychology educator*
Snow, Karl Nelson, Jr. *public management educator, university administrator, former state senator*
Wilson, Ramon B. *educator, administrator*

**Salt Lake City**
Lease, Ronald Charles *financial economics educator*
Mangum, Garth Leroy *economist, educator*

## VERMONT

**Burlington**
Cutler, Stephen Joel *sociologist*
Sampson, Samuel Franklin *sociology educator*
Smallwood, Franklin *political science educator*

**Middlebury**
Wilson, George Wilton *economics educator*
Wonnacott, (Gordon) Paul *economics educator*

**South Pomfret**
Arkin, William Morris *military and political analyst, writer*

## VIRGINIA

**Alexandria**
Corson, Walter Harris *sociologist*
Kollander, Mel *social scientist, statistician*
Mann, Seymour Zalmon *political science and public administration educator emeritus, union official*
Puscheck, Herbert Charles *social sciences educator*
Spar, Edward Joel *demographer*
Tucker, John Robert *financial executive*

**Arlington**
Brown, Robert Lyle *foreign affairs consultant*
Collins, Eileen Louise *economist*
Fuchs, Roland John *geography educator, university science official*
Funseth, Robert Lloyd Eric Martin *international consultant, lecturer, retired senior foreign service officer*
Henderson, John Brown *economist*
Henle, Peter *retired economic consultant, arbitrator*
Kerns, Wilmer Lee *social science researcher*
Marshall, Charles Burton *political science consultant*
Morgan, Bruce Ray *international consultant*
Weidemann, Celia Jean *social scientist, international business and financial development consultant*
Zakheim, Dov Solomon *economist, government official*

**Bedford**
Haymes, Harmon Hayden *economist, educator*

**Blacksburg**
Bryant, Clifton Dow *sociologist, educator*
Herndon, James Francis *retired political science educator*
Shepard, Jon Max *sociologist*

**Chantilly**
Dowdy, Dorothy Williams *political science educator*

**Charlotte Court House**
Prophett, Andrew Lee *political science educator*

**Charlottesville**
Abraham, Henry Julian *political science educator*
Bierstedt, Robert *sociologist, author*
Bovet, Eric David *economist, consultant*
Claude, Inis Lothair, Jr. *political scientist, educator*
Gottesman, Irving Isadore *psychology educator*
Henry, Laurin Luther *public affairs educator*
Holt, Charles Asbury *economics educator*
Hymes, Dell Hathaway *anthropologist, educator*
Lanham, Betty Bailey *anthropologist, educator*
Leng, Shao Chuan *political science educator*
McClain, Paula Denice *political scientist*
Meiburg, Charles Owen *business administration educator*
Perdue, Charles L., Jr. *anthropology and English educator*
Quandt, William Bauer *political scientist*
Rhoads, Steven Eric *political science educator*
Sabato, Larry Joseph *political science educator*
Sherman, Roger *economics educator*
Snavely, William Pennington *economics educator*
Sykes, Gresham M'Cready *sociologist, educator, artist*
Wagner, Roy *anthropology educator, researcher*
Whitaker, John King *economics educator*

**Earlysville**
Caplow, Theodore *sociologist*

**Eastville**
Williams, Ida Jones *consumer and home economics educator, writer*

**Emory**
Morris, Thomas Robbins *college president, political science educator*

**Fairfax**
Barth, Michael Carl *economist*
Bennett, James Thomas *economics educator*
Buchanan, James McGill *economist, educator*
Dennis, Rutledge Melvin *sociology educator, researcher*
Dobson, Allen *economist*
Goode, William Josiah *sociology educator*
Kash, Don Eldon *political science educator*
Lipset, Seymour Martin *sociologist, political scientist, educator*
Vaughn, Karen Iversen *economics educator*
Williams, Thomas Rhys *anthropologist, educator*

**Fairfax Station**
Sielicki-Korczak, Boris Zdzislaw *political educator, investigative consultant*

**Falls Church**
Calkins, Susannah Eby *retired economist*
Green, James Wyche *sociologist, anthropologist, psychotherapist*
LeBlanc, Hugh Linus *political science educator, consultant*
Waldo, (Clifford) Dwight *political science educator*
Weiss, Armand Berl *economist, association management executive*

**Farmville**
Dorrill, William Franklin *political scientist, educator*

**Harrisonburg**
Cline, Paul Charles *political science educator, state legislator*
Ivory, Ming Marie *political scientist*

**Herndon**
Altalib, Omar Hisham *sociologist*
Spragens, William Clark *public policy educator, consultant*

**Keswick**
Baratz, Morton Sachs *economic consultant, writer*

**Lexington**
Herrick, Bruce Hale *economics educator*
John, Lewis George *political science educator*
Phillips, Charles Franklin, Jr. *economist, educator*
Winfrey, John Crawford *economist, educator*

**Lynchburg**
Duff, Ernest Arthur *political scientist, educator*
Morland, John Kenneth *sociology and anthropology educator*

**Mc Lean**
Deardourff, John D. *political consultant*
Struelens, Michel Maurice Joseph Georges *political science educator, foreign affairs consultant*

**Midlothian**
Stringham, Luther Winters *economist, administrator*

**Norfolk**
Ahrari, M. Ehsan *political science educator, researcher, consultant*
Ershler, William Baldwin *biogerontologist, educator*

**Reston**
Kelly, Robert William *economist*
Payne, Roger Lee *geographer*

**Richmond**
Albanese, Jay Samuel *criminologist, educator*
Baretski, Charles Allan *political scientist, librarian, educator, historian, municipal official*
Campbell, Thomas Corwith, Jr. *economics educator*
Geary, David Patrick *criminal justice educator, consultant, author*
Hall, James Curtis *economics and business educator*

**Round Hill**
Pugh, Marion Stirling *archaeologist, author*

**Sperryville**
Armor, David J. *sociologist*

**Springfield**
Whitener, Lawrence Bruce *political consultant, consumer advocate, educator*

**Sterling**
Blum, John Curtis *agricultural economist*

**Suffolk**
Tritten, James John *national security educator*

**Sweet Briar**
Miller, Reuben George *economics educator*
Shea, Brent Mack *social science educator*

**Vienna**
Schneider, Peter Raymond *political scientist*

**Williamsburg**
Blouet, Brian Walter *geography educator*
Noël Hume, Ivor *retired archaeologist, consultant*
Price, Richard *anthropologist, author*
Smith, Roger Winston *political theorist, educator*

## WASHINGTON

**Bellingham**
Burdge, Rabel James *sociology educator*

**Friday Harbor**
de Vries, Rimmer *economist*

**Kirkland**
Goldman, Ralph Morris *political science educator*

**La Conner**
Knopf, Kenyon Alfred *economist, educator*

**Port Angeles**
Osborne, Richard Hazelet *anthropology and medical genetics educator*

**Pullman**
Catton, William Robert, Jr. *sociology educator*
Dillman, Donald Andrew *sociologist, educator*
Sheldon, Charles Harvey *political science educator*

**Seattle**
Beyers, William Bjorn *geography educator*
Borgatta, Edgar F. *social psychologist, educator*
Bourque, Philip John *business economist, educator*
Chirot, Daniel *sociology and international studies educator*
Dunnell, Robert Chester *archaeologist, educator*
Ellings, Richard James *political and economic research institution executive*
Gore, William Jay *political science educator*
Gross, Edward *retired sociologist, educator, lawyer*
Hirschman, Charles, Jr. *sociologist, educator*
Inlow, Edgar Burke *political science educator*
Lang, Kurt *sociologist, educator, writer*
Mah, Feng-hwa *economics educator*
Matthews, Donald Rowe *political scientist, educator*
Morrill, Richard Leland *geographer, educator*
Narver, John Colin *business administration educator*
Olson, David John *political science educator*
Schall, Lawrence Delano *economics educator, consultant*
Turnovsky, Stephen John *economics educator*
van den Berghe, Pierre Louis *sociologist, anthropologist*
Wolfle, Dael Lee *public affairs educator*

**Spokane**
Novak, Terry Lee *public adminstration educator*

**Tacoma**
Strege, Timothy Melvin *economic consultant*

**University Place**
Bourgaize, Robert G. *economist*

**Vancouver**
Craven, James Michael *economist, educator*

**Walla Walla**
Stevens, David *economics educator*

## WEST VIRGINIA

**Martinsburg**
Yoe, Harry Warner *retired agricultural economist*

**Morgantown**
Peterson, Sophia *international studies educator*
Witt, Tom *economics researcher, educator*

**Saint Albans**
Richards, John Dale *sociology and philosophy educator, counselor*

**Salem**
Frasure, Carl Maynard *political science educator*

## WISCONSIN

**Beloit**
Davis, Harry Rex *political science educator*

**Eau Claire**
Davidson, John Kenneth, Sr. *sociologist, educator, researcher, author, consultant*

**Madison**
Anderson, Odin Waldemar *sociologist, educator*
Andreano, Ralph Louis *economist, educator*
Baldwin, Robert Edward *economics educator*
Barrows, Richard Lee *economics educator, academic administrator*
Bennett, Kenneth Alan *biological anthropologist*
Brock, William Allen, III *economics educator, consultant*
Bromley, Daniel Wood *economics educator, consultant*
Cohen, Bernard Cecil *political scientist, educator*
Culbertson, John Mathew *economist, educator*
Downs, Donald Alexander, Jr. *political scientist, educator*
Eisinger, Peter K(endall) *political science educator*
Freudenburg, William R. *sociology educator*
Goldberger, Arthur Stanley *economics educator*
Graf, Truman Frederick *agricultural economist, educator*
Haller, Archibald Orben *sociologist, educator*
Hansen, W. Lee *economics educator, author*
Haveman, Robert Henry *economics educator*
Hester, Donald Denison *economics educator*
Levine, Solomon Bernard *business and economics educator*
Lewis, Herbert Samuel *anthropologist, educator*
Luening, Robert Adami *agricultural economics educator emeritus*
Metz, Mary Haywood *sociologist*
Mueller, Willard Fritz *economics educator*
Nichols, Donald Arthur *economist, educator*
Penniman, Clara *political scientist, educator*
Robinson, Arthur Howard *geography educator*
Schmidt, John Richard *agricultural economics educator*
Sewell, William Hamilton *sociologist*
Strasma, John Drinan *economist, educator*
Strier, Karen Barbara *anthropology educator*
Thiesenhusen, William Charles *agricultural economist*
Voos, Paula Beth *economics educator*
Waldron, Ellis Leigh *retired political science educator*
Wilson, Franklin D. *sociology educator*
Young, Merwin Crawford *political science educator*

**Milwaukee**
Baumann, Carol Edler *political science educator*
Handelman, Howard *political scientist, educator*
Hawkins, Brett William *political science educator*
Lydolph, Paul Edward *geography educator*
Moberg, David Oscar *sociology educator*
Paulson, Belden Henry *political scientist*
Perlman, Richard Wilfred *economist, educator*
Quade, Quentin Lon *political science educator*
Schur, Leon Milton *economist, educator*
Shea, Donald Richard *political science educator*

**Oregon**
Dorner, Peter Paul *retired economist, educator*

**Oshkosh**
Gruberg, Martin *political science educator*

**Whitewater**
Bhargava, Ashok *economics educator*
Refior, Everett Lee *labor economist, educator*

## WYOMING

**Laramie**
Chai, Winberg *political science educator, foundation chair*
Crocker, Thomas Dunstan *economics educator*
Gill, George Wilhelm *anthropologist*
Nelson, Elmer Kingsholm, Jr. *educator, writer, mediator, consultant*
Shaffer, Sherrill Lynn *economist*

# CANADA

## ALBERTA

**Calgary**
Forbis, Richard George *archaeologist*
Kelley, Jane Holden *archaeology educator*
Stebbins, Robert Alan *sociology educator*

**Edmonton**
Freeman, Milton Malcolm Roland *anthropology educator*
Krotki, Karol Jozef *sociology educator, demographer*
Smith, Peter John *geographer, educator*

## BRITISH COLUMBIA

**Burnaby**
Brantingham, Patricia Louise *criminology educator*
Brantingham, Paul Jeffrey *criminology educator*
Copes, Parzival *economist, researcher*

**Vancouver**
Aberle, David Friend *anthropologist, educator*
Elkins, David J. *political science educator*
Ericson, Richard Victor *social science-law educator, university official*
Feaver, George A. *political science educator*
Holsti, Kalevi Jacque *political scientist, educator*
Kesselman, Jonathan Rhys *economics educator, public policy researcher*
Langdon, Frank Corriston *political science educator, researcher*
Laponce, Jean Antoine *political scientist*
Lipsey, Richard George *economist, educator*
Marchak, Maureen Patricia *anthropology and sociology educator*
Pearson, Richard Joseph *archaeologist, educator*
Robinson, John Lewis *geography educator*
Shearer, Ronald Alexander *economics educator*
Slaymaker, H. Olav *geography educator*
Stankiewicz, Wladyslaw Jozef *political philosopher, educator*

**Victoria**
Barber, Clarence Lyle *economics educator*
Chard, Chester Stevens *archaeologist, educator*

## NEW BRUNSWICK

**Fredericton**
Kenyon, Gary Michael *gerontology educator, researcher*

## NEWFOUNDLAND

**Saint John's**
†Aylward, Kevin *economist*

## NOVA SCOTIA

**Halifax**
Borgese, Elisabeth Mann *political science educator, author*
Shaw, Timothy Milton *political science educator*
Stairs, Denis Winfield *political science educator*
Winham, Gilbert Rathbone *political science educator*

## ONTARIO

**Dundas**
Jones, Frank Edward *sociology educator*

**Hamilton**
George, Peter James *economist, educator*
King, Leslie John *geography educator*

**Kingston**
Kaliski, Stephan Felix *economics educator*
Meisel, John *political scientist*

**London**
Laidler, David Ernest William *economics educator*
Wonnacott, Ronald Johnston *economics educator*

**Nepean**
Cornell, Peter McCaul *economic consultant, former government official*

**Niagara-on-the-Lake**
Olley, Robert Edward *economist, educator*

**North York**
Richmond, Anthony Henry *sociologist, emeritus educator*

**Ottawa**
Brooks, David Barry *resource economist*
Griller, David *economics and technology consultant*
Mc Rae, Kenneth Douglas *political scientist, educator*

**Richmond Hill**
†Sharma, Marilyn I. *economist*

**Toronto**
Clark, Samuel Delbert *sociology educator*
Dean, William George *geography educator*
Goldfarb, Martin *sociologist*
Grayson, Albert Kirk *Near Eastern studies educator*
Grinspun, Ricardo *economist, educator*
Helleiner, Gerald Karl *economics educator*
Hollander, Samuel *economist, educator*
Munro, John Henry Alexander *economics educator, writer*
Pratt, Robert Cranford *political scientist, educator*
Rapoport, Anatol *peace studies educator, mathematical biologist*
Rose, Jeffrey Raymond *economist, educator, negotiator*
Ross, Murray George *social science educator, university president emeritus*
Shearing, Clifford Denning *criminology and sociology educator*
Wilson, Thomas Arthur *economics educator*

**Waterloo**
Fallding, Harold Joseph *sociology educator*
Nash, Peter Hugh John *geographer, educator, planner*
Nelson, J. Gordon *geography educator*
Warner, Barry Gregory *geographer, educator*

**QUEBEC**

**Hull**
†Cappe, Melvin Samuel *economist*
MacDonald, George Frederick *anthropologist, Canadian museum director*

**Ile des Soeurs**
Dagenais, Marcel Gilles *economist, educator*

**Montreal**
Brecher, Irving *economics educator*
Brecher, Michael *political science educator*
Chateau, John-Peter D(avid) *economics and finance educator, mining company executive*
Dufour, Jean-Marie *economics researcher, educator*
Ikawa-Smith, Fumiko *anthropologist, educator*
Jonassohn, Kurt *sociologist, educator*
Nayar, Baldev Raj *political science educator*
Normandeau, Andre Gabriel *criminologist, educator*
Orban, Edmond Henry *political science educator*
Raynauld, Andre *economist, educator*
Smith, Philip Edward Lake *anthropology educator*
Szabo, Denis *criminologist, educator*
Tremblay, Richard Ernest *psychology educator*
Tremblay, Rodrigue *economics educator*
Trigger, Bruce Graham *anthropology educator*
Vaillancourt, Jean-Guy *sociology educator*
Waller, Harold Myron *political science educator*

**Quebec**
Belanger, Gerard *economics educator*
†Lisée, Jean-François *political scientist, writer*
Migue, Jean Luc *economics educator*
Tremblay, Marc Adélard *anthropologist, educator*

**Sainte Croix**
Grenier, Fernand *geographer, consultant*

**MEXICO**

**Jalisco**
Wolf, Charlotte Elizabeth *sociologist*

**BELIZE**

**San Ignacio**
Ripinsky-Naxon, Michael *archaeologist, art historian, ethnologist*

**BRAZIL**

**Rio Claro**
Christofoletti, Antonio *geography educator*

**Salvador**
Davidson, Ralph Kirby *economist, retired foundation executive, consultant*

**ENGLAND**

**Birmingham**
Fry, Maxwell John *economist, educator*

**Claverton Down**
Buchanan, Robert Angus *archaeology educator*

**Cornwall**
Dark, Philip John Crosskey *anthropologist, educator*

**Devon**
Rossmiller, George Eddie *agricultural economist*

**London**
Batty, J. Michael *geographer, educator*
Douglas, Mary Tew *anthropology and humanities educator*
Junz, Helen B. *economist*
Kuper, Adam Jonathan *anthropologist, educator*

**Oxford**
Cairncross, Sir Alexander Kirkland *economist*

**FRANCE**

**Fontainebleu**
Ayres, Robert Underwood *environmental economics and technology educator*

**Paris**
Lubell, Harold *economic consultant*

**GERMANY**

**Luneburg**
Linde, Robert Hermann *economics educator*

**Munich**
Whetten, Lawrence Lester *international relations educator*

**GREECE**

**Athens**
Iakovidis, Spyros Eustace *archaeologist*
Kalamotousakis, George John *economist*

**ISRAEL**

**Netanya**
Ades, Maurice Raphael *economist*

**Tel Aviv**
Rubin, Barry Mitchel *foreign policy analyst, writer*

**ITALY**

**Bologna**
Alliney, Stefano Guido *economics educator, researcher, consultant*

**JAPAN**

**Tokyo**
Nishiyama, Chiaki *economist, educator*

**THE NETHERLANDS**

**Utrecht**
Ginkel, Johannes Auguste van *geographer, educator*

**PORTUGAL**

**Lisbon**
Thore, Sten Anders *economics and aerospace engineering educator*

**REPUBLIC OF KOREA**

**Seoul**
Steinberg, David Isaac *economic development consultant, educator*

**Suwon**
Lee, Tong Hun *economics educator*

**SRI LANKA**

**Colombo**
Spain, James William *political scientist, writer, investor*

**SWITZERLAND**

**Geneva**
Twarog, Sophia Nora *international association administrator*

**ADDRESS UNPUBLISHED**

Abere, Andrew Evan *economist*
Adams, Robert McCormick *anthropologist, educator*
Adelman, Richard Charles *gerontologist, educator*
Alker, Hayward R. *political science educator*
Allen, John Lyndon *social studies educator*
Anderson, Bernard E. *economist*
Axilrod, Stephen Harvey *financial markets consultant, economist*
Bambrick, James Joseph *labor economist, labor relations executive*
Barnett, Vincent MacDowell, Jr. *political science educator*
Bateson, Mary Catherine *anthropology educator*
Beckman, James Wallace Bim *economist, marketing executive*
Bohannan, Paul James *anthropologist, writer, former university administrator*
Bonnell, Victoria Eileen *sociologist*
Brandl, John Edward *public affairs educator*
Bredfeldt, John Creighton *economist, financial analyst, retired air force officer*
Calleo, David Patrick *political science educator*
Campbell, Mary Ann *social psychologist*
Chinitz, Benjamin *economics educator*
Christian, James Wayne *economist*
Clark, Caleb Morgan *political scientist, educator*
Cope, Alfred Haines *political scientist, educator*
Crampton, Esther Larson *sociology and political science educator*
Daniels, Arlene Kaplan *sociology educator*
de Blij, Harm Jan *geography educator, editor*
DeFleur, Melvin Lawrence *sociologist, communication educator*
Denevan, William Maxfield *geographer, educator, ecologist*

Dobriansky, Lev Eugene *economist, educator, diplomat*
Drummond, Dorothy Weitz *geography education consultant, educator, author*
Earle, Timothy Keese *anthropology educator*
Edmonson, Munro Sterling *anthropologist, educator*
Farah, Tawfic Elias *political scientist, educator*
Field, Julia Allen *futurist, conceptual planner*
Gabel, Creighton *retired anthropologist, educator*
Gelman, Norman Ira *public policy consultant*
Gerlach, Luther Paul *anthropologist*
Gottschalk, Charles M. *international relations consultant*
Grassmuck, George Ludwig *political science educator*
Greeley, Andrew Moran *sociologist, author*
Griffin, James Bennett *anthropologist, educator*
Grindea, Daniel *international economist*
Grow, Robert Theodore *economist, association executive*
Hall, Bernard *retired economics educator and university official*
Hare, Frederick Kenneth *geography and environmental educator, university official*
Hefferan, Colien Joan *economist*
Helfgott, Roy B. *economist, educator*
Hiler, Monica Jean *sociology and reading educator*
Hilliard, Sam Bowers *geography educator*
Holloway, Robert Ross *archaeologist, educator*
Holmes, Paul Luther *political scientist, educational consultant*
Jaquette, Peter Barnes *economist*
Johnson, Albert Wesley *consultant on governance*
Jones, Joan Megan *anthropologist*
Juviler, Peter Henry *political scientist, educator*
Kahana, Eva Frost *sociology educator*
Kenyon, Daphne Anne *economics educator*
Keyes, Margaret Naumann *home economics educator*
Klass, Morton *anthropology educator, consultant*
Kottler, Raymond George Michael *economist, researcher*
Lanzillotti, Robert Franklin *economist, educator*
Laughlin, Louis Gene *economic analyst, consultant*
Lee, Mordecai *political scientist, educator*
Leith, James Clark *economics educator*
Lejins, Peter Pierre *criminologist, sociologist, educator*
Levi, Maurice David *economics educator*
Lichtenberg, Byron K. *futurist, manufacturing executive, space flight consultant, pilot*
Liebman, Nina R. *economic developer*
Ludden, John Franklin *retired financial economist*
Maranda, Pierre Jean *anthropologist, writer*
Marini, Frank Nicholas *political science and public administration educator*
Markovich, Patricia *economist, art consultant*
Martin, Catherine Elizabeth *anthropology educator*
Mc Clellan, Catharine *anthropologist, educator*
McGough, Duane Theodore *economist, retired government official*
McHugh, Betsy Baldwin *sociologist, educator, journalist, business owner*
Mian, Ahmad Zia *economist*
Michael, Donald Nelson *social scientist, educator*
Modigliani, Franco *economics and finance educator*
Monsen, Raymond Joseph, Jr. *economist, educator, art patron*
Moore, John Runyan *agricultural and resource economics educator*
Morris, Jane Elizabeth *home economics educator*
Naylor, Thomas Herbert *economist, educator, consultant*
Newborn, Jud *anthropologist, writer, lyricist*
Obligacion, Freddie Rabelas *sociology educator, researcher*
O'Brien, John Wilfrid *economist, emeritus university president, educator*
Oksas, Joan Kay *economist, educator*
Olson, William Clinton *international affairs educator, author, lecturer*
Pedersen, Knud George *economics educator, university president*
Piore, Nora Kahn *economist, health policy analyst*
Pollack, Gerald Alexander *economist, government official*
Randall, Richard Rainier *geographer*
Roberts, John Benjamin, II *public policy consultant, television producer, writer*
Roberts, Paul Craig, III *economics educator, author, columnist*
Robinson, Marshall Alan *economics educator, foundation executive*
Rosen, Lawrence *anthropology educator*
Rossi, Peter Henry *sociology educator*
Ruderman, Armand Peter *health economics educator, consultant, volunteer*
Sebastian, Peter *international affairs consultant, former ambassador*
Shapiro, Leo J. *social researcher*
Sharpe, William Forsyth *economics educator*
Sheppard, Harold Lloyd *gerontologist, educator*
Siddayao, Corazón Morales *economist, educator, energy and environment consultant*
Sills, Richard Reynolds *scientist, educator*
Sims, Kent Otway *economist*
Smith, Edward K. *economist, consultant*
Smith, V. Kerry *economics educator*
Smith, Verna Mae Edom *sociology educator, freelance writer, photographer*
Spencer, Milton Harry *economics and finance educator*
Stalon, Charles Gary *retired economics educator, institute administrator*
Steffens, Dorothy Ruth *political economist*
Stiglitz, Joseph Eugene *economist*
Striker, Cecil Leopold *archaeologist, educator*
Sutton, Willis Anderson, Jr. *sociology educator*
Swanstrom, Thomas Evan *economist*
Swindler, Daris Ray *physical anthropologist, forensic anthropologist*
Tarr, David William *political scientist, educator*
Tarrance, Vernon Lance, Jr. *public opinion research executive*
Taylor, Norman William *economics educator*
terHorst, Jerald Franklin *public affairs counsel*
Textor, Robert Bayard *cultural anthropology writer, consultant, educator*
Theobald, H Rupert *retired political scientist*
Tonello-Stuart, Enrica Maria *political economist*
Udick, Robert Alan *political science and media educator*
Volcker, Paul A. *economist*
Weber, Mary Ellen Healy *economist*
Weil, Rolf Alfred *economist, university president emeritus*
Wengert, Norman Irving *political science educator*
Wilkinson, Doris *medical sociology educator*

Willey, Gordon Randolph *retired anthropologist, archaeologist, educator*
Wolfe, Gregory Baker *international relations educator*
Wonders, William Clare *geography educator*
Wood, Andrée Robitaille *archaeologist, researcher*
Wood, Robert Coldwell *political scientist*
Wright, James David *sociology educator, writer*
Zeigler, L(uther) Harmon *political science educator*

# Retiree Index

The index below lists the names of those individuals whose biographical sketches last appeared in the 49th, 50th, or 51st Edition of *Who's Who in America*. The latest volume containing a full sketch is indicated by *49, 50,* or *51* following each name. The listees have since retired from active participation in their respective occupations.


A

Adams, Hall, Jr. (Cap Adams), 50
Adams, James R., 50
Addicott, Warren Oliver, 49
Addison, Edward L., 50
Addy, George Arthur, 49
Adelizzi, Robert Frederick, 50
Aguilar, Robert P., 51
Ahern, Patrick V., 49
Akerson, Daniel Francis, 50
Albers, John Richard, 50
Albosta, Richard Francis, 50
Alexander, Charles Thomas, 49
Allard, James Edward, 49
Allen, Chuck, 50
Allen, Frederic W., 51
Alpern, Robert Zellman, 51
Altenstadter, Shelley G., 51
Amundson, Clyde Howard, 50
Anderluh, John Russell, 50
Anderson, Alan R., 50
Anderson, George W., 50
Andreuzzi, Denis, 50
Andrew, Gwen, 51
Andrews, James Edgar, 51
Aoki, John H., 50
Aquilina, Nick C., 50
Arimoto, Masahiko, 50
Armour, Laurance Hearne, Jr., 49
Arnot, David Sheldon, 50
Arrison, Clement R., 50
Ashton, P. J., 50
Asplundh, Robert H., 50
Asselin, Martial, 51
Atkinson, Robert Poland, 51
Atwater, Horace Brewster, Jr., 50

B

Babbitt, Milton Byron, 49
Backer, David F., 50
Backer, William Montague, 50
Badura-Skoda, Paul (Ludwig Badura), 49
Baeder, Donald Lee, 50
Bagdonas, Kathy Joann, 50
Bailey, R. W., 49
Bailey, William O., 50
Baker, Clifford Cornell, 51
Balestrero, Gregory, 50
Ballard, Claude Mark, Jr., 50
Bantle, Louis Francis, 50
Barents, Brian Edward, 50
Barker, Willie G., Jr., 50
Barnes, B. Jack, 50
Barnett, Robert James, 51
Barone, Robert Paul, 50
Barr, Kenneth John, 50
Barr, Robert Alfred, Jr., 51
Barrett, James, 50
Barry, Robert Louis, 50
Bartels, Gerald Lee, 51
Bartholomew, Byron Simpson, Jr., 49
Bartolo, Adolph Marion, 50
Bassist, Donald Herbert, 51
Batchelder, William F., 50
Bates, George Edmonds, 51
Batres, Eduardo, 50
Baughn, Juan R., 51
Baumgarten, Herbert Joseph, 50
Baxter, Elaine, 50
Begley, Michael Joseph, 51
Begley, R. T., 49
Belew, David Owen, Jr., 51
Bell, Daniel Long, Jr., 51
Bell, Edward Francis, 50
Belzer, Alan, 50
Bembridge, John Anthony, 51
Benedict, Samuel S., 49
Bennett, David Michael, 50
Benson, Robert Slater, 50
Bentsen, Lloyd, 50
Berg, W. Robert, 50
Berger, Arthur Victor, 51
Bergerson, J. Steven, 50
Bergin, John Francis, 50
Bermingham, Richard P., 50
Bernstein, Lionel M., 51
Bessey, Edward Cushing, 50
Betz, Charles W., 51
Bevis, James Wayne, 50
Binkerd, Gordon Ware, 49
Birnbaum, Robert Jack, 50
Blacker, Coit Dennis, 51
Blake, Larry Jay, 51
Bobbitt, Max E., 50
Bogomolny, Richard Joseph, 50
Bohn, John Augustus, Jr., 50
Boley, John N., 50
Boliek, Luther C., 50
Bolstad, D. D., 51
Bonaventura, Vincent E., 50
Bond, Thomas Alden, 51
Bonini, Victor, 50
Bonney, John Dennis, 50
Bonney, M. Doane, 51
Bonser, Sidney Henry, 50
Bookner, Becci Jane, 51
Booth, I(srael) MacAllister, 50
Boren, Arthur Rodney, 51
Borgelt, Burton C., 50
Boudreaux, Warren Louis, 51
Bourdo, G. F., 51
Bowe, Riddick Lamont, 51
Bowen, James, 51
Bowen, John Sheets, 50
Bower, Marvin D., 50
Bowman, Robert Gibson, 50
Boyd, William Beaty, 51
Bozone, Billie Rae, 51
Brachtenbach, Robert F., 50
Brackett, Norman E., 50
Bradley, George H., 50
Bradshaw, William David, 50
Braker, William Paul, 49
Brandt, Yale M., 50
Bratton, Ronald B., 51
Braznell, Gerald K., 50
Brengel, Fred Lenhardt, 50
Brennan, Edward A., 51
Brennan, John Edward, 50
Brewer, Warren Wesley, 51
Brice, James John, 50
Briggs, Thorley D., 50
Brill-Edwards, Harry Walter, 50
Brinkmann, Klaus Peter, 50
Brock, Harry Blackwell, Jr., 50
Brooks, Maurice Edward, 49
Brown, Corrick, 51
Brown, George J., 51
Brown, Nicholas, 51
Brown, William Ernest, 50
Brown, William Lee Lyons, Jr., 50
Browning, Robert Masters, 50
Bryant, Robert Parker, 50
Brzana, Stanislaus Joseph, 49
Budig, Gene Arthur, 49
Buesinger, Ronald Ernest, 49
Butterworth, Kenneth W., 50

C

Cabot, John G. L., 50
Cahill, Clyde S., 50
Callen, John Holmes, Jr., 50
Calloway, D. Wayne, 51
Campanella, Anton J., 50
Campbell, Robert L., 50
Canas, Jon, 50
Canfield, Earle Lloyd, 50
Cantrell, Joseph Doyle, 51
Cantu, John Maurice, 50
Capellupo, John P., 50
Carberry, John J. Cardinal, 50
Carestio, Ralph M., Jr., 50
Carpenter, Bruce H., 51
Carpenter, Charles, 50
Carpenter, David Roland, 50
Carpenter, William Levy, 51
Carson, Edward Mansfield, 50
Carson, Kent (Lovett Carson), 50
Case, Andrew J., 51
Cassidy, Robert Joseph, 50
Cavenar, Jesse Oscar, Jr., 51
Cerveny, Frank Stanley, 51
Chain, Beverly Jean, 50
Chalfant, Edward Cole, 51
Chambers, Patrick Joseph, Jr., 50
Chanen, Franklin Allen, 50
Chapin, Hugh A., 50
Chapman, Carleton Burke, 50
Chapman, James Claude, 50
Chiasson, Donat, 51
Chilstrom, Herbert Walfred, 51
Chinnery, Michael Alistair, 50
Chitwood, Harold Otis, 50
Chou, Wen-chung, 49
Christensen, George B., 50
Christopher, Glenn A., 50
Christopher, Robert Allan, 50
Chubb, Harold D., 51
Churchill, James Paul, 50
Clabby, William Robert, 51
Clapp, Joseph Mark, 50
Clarie, T. Emmet, 51
Clark, Donald Cameron, 50
Clark, Raymond Robert, 50
Clark, Worley H., Jr., 50
Clarke, Don R., 51
Clayton, Constance, 51
Clifford, Robert L., 50
Cline, Ned Aubrey, 51
Clough, Charles Elmer, 50
Cochran, Larry B., 50
Cohen, Isidore Leonard, 49
Cohen, Lester, 50
Cole, Charles W., Jr., 50
Coleman, Martin, 49
Coleman, Roger William, 50
Collins, David Edmond, 50
Collins, Jerry Allan, 51
Comey, Dale Raymond, 50
Comparin, Robert Anton, 51
Compton, Robert H., 50
Congdon, Marsha B., 50
Conlin, Alfred Thomas, 49
Connolly, Eugene B., Jr., 51
Conrad, Herbert J., 50
Constable, Elinor Greer, 50
Cooley, Edward H., 50
Corn, Jack W., 50
Correu, James M., 51
Corry, Charles Albert, 51
Cotliar, George J., 51
Cournoyea, Nellie J., 51
Cowart, Elgin Courtland, Jr., 50
Coyne, Mary Jeanne, 51
Craib, Donald Forsyth, Jr., 50
Crain, Charles Anthony, 49
Crawford, William Basil, Jr., 51
Crim, Reuben Sidney, 51
Croom, John Henry, III, 51
Crull, Timm F., 50
Cryer, Eugene Edward, 51
Cuatrecasas, Pedro Martin, 51
Curtis, James Austin, 50
Cuthill, Robert T., 51

D

Daeschner, Charles William, Jr., 49
Dahl, John Anton, 51
Dale, Charles, 50
Daly, James Joseph, 51
Dameron, William H., III, 51
Dane, Paul Nelson, 51
Danforth, Douglas Dewitt, 50
Danilova, Alexandra, 51
Darling, George Bapst, Jr., 49
Darragh, John K., 50
Daughtry, Sylvia, 51
Davis, Delmont Alvin, Jr., 50
Davis, George Alfred, 50
Davis, George Wilmot, 50
Davis, John Massey, 51
Davis, Luther, Jr., 49
Dawson, Andre Nolan, 51
Day, Castle Nason, 50
Day, Thomas Brennock, 51
Dear, Joseph A., 51
Dearman, Henry Hursell, 50
DeBruler, Roger O., 51
Deihl, Richard Harry, 50
Delaquis, Noel, 51
Delchamps, Randolph, 50
Del Santo, Lawrence A., 51
Dempsey, John Cornelius, 50
Denny, James McCahill, 50
Densmore, William Phillips, 50
Deputy, Byard Sanford, 51
DesBarres, John P., 50
Dewberry, James Terry, 50
Dicker, Marvin, 50
Dickey, Crawford Marshall, 50
Dickson, Alex Dockery, 51
Di Cosimo, Joanne Violet, 51
Dill, Donald, 50
Dolson, Franklin Robert, 51
Doms, Keith, 50
Donnahoe, Alan Stanley, 51
Donoho, Clive W., Jr., 50
Donovan, Paul V., 49
Dorius, Kermit Parrish, 51
Dornburgh, William Walter, 49
D'Ornellas, Robert W., 51
Dorsey, Peter, 50
Doyle, Francis Xavier, 51
Doyle, Wilfred Emmett, 51
Dozier, O(llin) Kemp, 50
Drennen, William Miller, 51
Dresher, James T., 50
Drew, James Vandervort, 51
Dreyfus, Daniel, 51
Droz, Henry, 50
Dudick, Michael Joseph, 51
Duffy, Kenneth J., 50
Dumbauld, Edward, 50
Duncan, John Lapsley, 50
Dunford, Edsel D., 50
Dunlap, Albert John, 50
Dutko, H.J., 51
Dyer, Alexander Patrick, 50
Dyer, Noel John, 50

E

Ealy, Robert Phillip, 50
Early, Patrick Joseph, 50
Easterling, William K., 50
Eastman, Albert Theodore, 51
Eckenhoff, James Edward, 50
Effa, Herman, 51
Eisenstat, Albert A., 50
Ekstrom, Walter F., 50
Elish, Herbert, 50
Elliott, Charles W., 50
Elliott, Robert M., Jr., 50
Ellis, William Ben, 50
Emmen, Dennis R., 50
Endries, John Michael, 50
Englander, Roman, 51
Epp, Telfer L., 51
Erburu, Robert F., 50
Erdmann, August, 51
Estill, Robert Whitridge, 51
Etheridge, James Edward, Jr., 51
Exum, James Gooden, Jr., 50

F

Feaster, Robert K., 51
Ferguson, Thomas H., 50
Ferguson, William Charles, 50
Ferraez, Leon R., 50
Ferrara, Arthur Vincent, 51
Ferrario, Joseph A., 49
Ferris, Thomas Francis, 51
Fery, John Bruce, 50
Figgie, Harry E., Jr., 50
Finesilver, Sherman Glenn, 51
Finlayson, John L., 50
Finnegan, John Robert, Sr., 51
Fischer, Newton Duchan, 50
Fisher, Bob, 50
Fisher, John Edwin, 50
Fisher, Robert Allison, 51
Fletcher, Anne Bosshard, 51
Flinn, Patrick L., 50
Flint, Myles Edward, 50
Flood, Howard L., 50
Flores, Thomas R., 51
Flower, Joseph Reynolds, 51
Flynn, Robert Emmett, 50
Foley, Patrick Martin, 50
Folley, Clyde H., 50
Fox, David Wayne, 50
Frame, John Timothy, 51
Frank, Harold Roy, 50
Frank, James Alan, 50
Frappier, Gilles, 51
Freeman, Graydon LaVerne, 50
Frelick, Linden Frederick, 50
French, Philip Franks, 50
Fricke, H. Walter, 51
Friedman, Herbert, 51
Fritsch, Robert Bruce, 50
Fuhrman, Robert Alexander, 50
Funk, Paul Edward, 50

G

Galbis, Ignacio Ricardo Maria, 51
Gallagher, Richard Hugo, 51
Galloway, Gerald Edward, Jr., 51
Ganter, Bernard J., 51
Gariepy, Corinne, 51
Garrison, Lawrence Duane, 50
Gates, Robert C., 50
Gault, Stanley Carleton, 51
Gelber, Herbert Donald, 51
Genge, Kenneth Lyle, 51
Genin, Roland, 50
Georgas, John William, 50
Georges, John A., 51
Gerstein, Hilda Kirschbaum, 50
Giannini, Margaret Joan, 51
Gibbons, Thomas Michael, 50
Gideon, Miriam, 49
Gilbert, Donald Floyd, 51
Gillespie, Gwain Homer, 50
Ginzburg, Rubin, 50
Glaser, Harold, 49
Glaskowsky, Elizabeth Pope, 51
Glasner, LeRoy A., 50
Gleason, Edward L., 50
Gleason, Norman Dale, 50
Gloth, Fred M., Jr., 50
Glotzer, Marilyn, 51
Golbus, Mitchell S., 51
Golden, Hyman, 50
Goldman, Israel David, 50
Goldsmith, Robert Holloway, 50
Gonzalez, Ruben, 51
Goodchild, Robert Marshall, 50
Goodridge, Noel Herbert Alan, 51
Gordon, Richard Joseph, 50
Gossage, Thomas Layton, 51
Grant, Walter Leroy, 50
Greeley, Walter Franklin, 50
Green, David Marvin, 50
Green, George, 51
Greendorfer, Terese Grosman, 51
Greenhouse, Bernard, 49
Griffin, Gwyn, 51
Grodus, Edward T., 51
Grossman, Everett Philip, 50
Grove, William Boyd, 51
Groves, George L., Jr., 50
Gudinas, Donald Jerome, 50
Guyette, James M., 50

H

Haake, Earle E., 49
Hagemann, Kenneth L., Sr., 50
Hagiwara, Kokichi, 50
Hahn, Thomas Marshall, Jr., 50
Haines, Milton L. (Lee Haines), 50
Haley, Clifton Edward, 50
Hall, John Richard, 51
Hall, Miles W., 50
Hall, Ronald E., 50
Halverson, Richard Christian, 51
Hambrick, Jackson Reid, 49
Hamilton, Milton Holmes, Sr., 50
Hammett, William M. H., 50
Handelsman, M. Gene, 51
Hank, Bernard J., Jr., 49
Hankinson, James Floyd, 49
Hanlon, David Patrick, 50
Hanna, Robert C., 50
Harding, Frank I., III, 50
Harding, W. M., 50
Hardy, Duane Horace, 51
Harr, Joseph, 51
Harrington, Timothy J., 49
Harris, Jean Louise, 50
Harrison, Lou Silver, 51
Harvey, Cynthia, 51
Harvey, George Burton, 51
Harvey, J. R., 50
Haslam, Robert B., 51
Hastrich, Jerome Joseph, 49
Hatch, Monroe W., Jr., 50
Hathaway, Alden Moinet, 51
Hay, Robert J., 50
Hayes, Don A., 50
Hayne, David Mackness, 49
Haynes, William Eli, 50
Haynie, Howard Edward, 50
Head, Edward Dennis, 51
Headlee, Richard Harold, 50
Healy, Sonya Ainslie, 50
Hedrick, Charles Lynnwood, 50
Hegyi, Julius, 49
Heistand, Joseph Thomas, 51
Heller, Charles Andrew, Jr., 50
Hemley, M. Rogue, 50

Henderson, Thomas James, 50
Hendricksen, Holmes G., 50
Hennessey, Joseph E., 50
Hennig, Frederick E., 50
Henry, James B., 51
Herder, Robert H., 51
Herrin, Frances Sudomier, 51
Hess, Karsten, 50
Hewes, Henry, 51
Hext, George D., 50
Hibbard, Dwight H., 50
Hickey, Robert Philip, Jr., 51
Highleyman, Samuel Locke, III, 51
Hill, Errol Gaston, 51
Himstead, Scott, 51
Hinton, Christopher Jerrod, 51
Hiscock, Boyd L., 50
Hitchings, George Herbert, 50
Holden, Gwen Adams, 51
Holland, Darrell Wendell, 51
Holm, Jeanne Marjorie, 51
Holt, Jack Wilson, Jr., 51
Holthouse, Rita J., 51
Holtz, Abel, 50
Honderich, Beland Hugh, 51
Hoover, William R(ay), 51
Hopkins, Thomas Gene, 50
Horner, Charles Albert, 50
Horner, Larry Dean, 50
Horsey, William Grant, 50
Horton, John Alden, 50
Hosmer, Bradley Clark, 50
Howard, Joseph Clemens, 51
Howard, R. L., 50
Hoyt, Stanley Charles, 49
Huang, Elsie Lee, 51
Hubbard, Randall Dee, 50
Hudgins, Michael Pharr, 50
Hughes, Author E., 51
Hughes, Donald R., 50
Hughes, Harold Hasbrouck, Jr., 51
Hughes, Thomas Joseph, 50
Hughes, William Anthony, 51
Huismans, Sipko, 50
Hulst, John B., 51
Humphrey, Howard C., 50
Hunter, Charles David, 50
Hurd, G. David, 50
Hurley, Mark Joseph, 49
Hutchcraft, Arthur Stephens, Jr., 50
Hutchinson, Frederick Edward, 51
Hytche, William Percy, 51

**I**

Iacobell, Frank Peter, 50
Ianni, Lawrence Albert, 51
Inkster, Norman David, 49
Irwin, Joe Robert, 50
Irwin, Sister Marie Cecilia, 50
Itin, James Richard, 50
Iversen, James Delano, 51

**J**

Jackson, Keith Jerome, 51
Jacobsen, Arthur, 50
Jacobsen, William Ludwig, Jr., 50
Jarrett, Anthony, 50
Jefferson, Bernard S., 51
Jelinek, Fran, 51
Jenrette, Richard Hampton, 50
Jensen, Shirley Wulff, 49
Jernigan, Bob, 50
Jobe, Edward B., 50
Johnson, Alan, 50
Johnson, Charles Christopher, Jr., 51
Johnson, Julius Frank, 50
Johnson, Lloyd Peter, 50
Johnson, Raymond A., 51
Johnson, Robert Raymond, 50
Johnston, Lynn Henry, 50
Jones, Bob Gordon, 51
Jones, Johnie H., 49
Jones, Thomas Curtis, 51
Jones, Vernon Thomas, 50
Jones, William Edward, 50
Jones-Smith, Jacqueline, 50
Jordan, David Loran, 51

**K**

Kahn, Harold, 50
Kaplan, Philip Thomas, 50
Karch, Sargent, 50
Kauffman, Robert Craig, 51
Kay, Ulysses Simpson, 49
Keesler, Allen John, Jr., 50
Keiffer, Edwin Gene, 50
Kelley, Robert C., 50
Kelly, Patrick Farrell, 51
Kenna, E. Douglas, 50
Kennedy, William Francis, 50
Kilmartin, Thomas John, III, 50
Kim, Earl, 49
King, Russell C., Jr., 49
King, William J., 50
Kirchner, Leon, 49
Kirkley, T. A., 50
Klein, Anton J., 51
Klein, Richard Dean, 50
Klein, Willie, 51
Klobuchar, James John, 51
Kluge, J. Hans, 50
Knadle, Richard D., 50
Knox, James Lloyd, 51
Kocisko, Stephen John, 49
Koester, Charles R., 51
Koile, Earl, 49
Korte, Loren A., 50
Koten, John A., 50
Kotler, Martin, 50
Krakauer, Albert Alexander, 49
Kraus, Michael, 51
Krumm, William Frederick, 50
Kundert, Alice E., 51

**L**

Lam, David C., 51
Lamore, George L., 50
Landau, Irwin, 50
Landes, Robert Nathan, 50
Langlitz, Harold N., 50
Langmead, Jeffrey P., 50
Lanzoni, Vincent, 51
Larrouilh, Michel, 50
Larson, Mel, 50
Lassen, John R., 49
Lassen, Laurence E., 49
Lauterbach, Hans, 50
Laws, Robert E., 50
Lawson, David Jerald, 51
Leader, Robert Wardell, 49
LeHane, Louis James, 49
Lehman, Edwin, 51
Lerner, Aaron Bunsen, 51
Lewis, Sydney, 50
Liebe, Hans J., 51
Lincoln, Lucian Abraham, 50
Lindley, James Gunn, 50
Ling, Dwight L., 51
Link, William P., 51
Litt, Nahum, 50
Livingston, Robert Burr, 49
Loftus, Stephen Francis, 50
Long, Tom, 50
Longnaker, John Leonard, 50
Loomis, Worth (Alfred Worthington Loomis), 51
Lorenz, Richard Theodore, Jr., 50
Loughead, Thomas A., 50
Loughlin, Martin Francis, 50
Lowden, Suzanne, 51
Lowrey, E. James, 50
Lowry, Sheldon Gaylon, 49
Lucas, Malcolm Millar, 50
Lustig, Harry, 49
Lutjeharms, Joseph Earl, 50
Lynch, Thomas C., 50

**M**

MacAulay, Colin Alexander, 51
MacBurney, Edward Harding, 51
MacCarthy, John Peters, 50
Macke, Richard Chester, 50
Mackey, Sally Schear, 51
Mackinnon, Robert, 50
Macquarrie, Heath Nelson, 50
Mahoney, Richard John, 49
Malloy, James B., 49
Mancheski, Frederick John, 51
Manera, Anthony S., 50
Manning, Donald O., 50
Maple, John E., 51
Marsh, Caryl Glenn, 51
Marshall, John Aloysius, 51
Marston, Charles, 50
Marteau, Kimberly K., 51
Martin, Bruce Douglas, 51
Martin, James Smith, 50
Massa, Paul Peter, 51
Mastro, A. F., 50
Mate, Martin, 51
Mathis, James Forrest, 50
Mattingly, Donald Arthur, 51
Mattson, Walter Edward, 50
Maw, Sam H., 50
Maxwell, Hamish, 50
McAllister, Gene Robert, 50
McAninch, Harold D., 51
Mc Bride, John Alexander, 50
McCarthy, Edward Anthony, 49
McCarthy, John Thomas, 50
McCarthy, Leo Tarcisius, 50
Mc Carthy, Patrick Edward, 50
McCaughan, John F., 50
McClain, Charles William, Jr. (Bill McClain), 50
McCollow, Thomas James, 50
McConomy, Thomas Arthur, 50
McCowan, Rodney A., 51
McCoy, James M., 50
McCrary, Douglas L., 50
Mc Dermott, Robert Francis, 50
McDowell, Marion, 51
McElroy, Charlotte Ann, 51
McFarlane, William F., 50
McGiverin, Donald Scott, 50
McGonigal, Pearl, 51
McGrath, Edward A., 50
McGuire, Raymond L., 50
McIntyre, Robert Malcolm, 50
McKay, John A., 50
McKenna, Quentin Carnegie, 50
McKenny, Jere Wesley, 50
McKibben, Gordon Charles, 49
McLaughlin, Audrey, 51
Mc Manus, Charles Anthony, Jr., 49
McNamara, John F., 51
McNeese, Jack Marvin, 50
McNeill, Alfred Thomas, Jr., 51
McPhee, Richard S., 51
Mealey, George Allan, 50
Meissner, Harold C., 50
Mendel, Perry, 50
Merlo, Harry Angelo, 50
Merritt, John C., 50
Metcalf, Jerry D., 50
Metzler, Cynthia A., 51
Meyer, John, 51
Meyer, Richard E., 50
Millard, David Ralph, Jr., 49
Miller, Donald E., 50
Miller, Gerald E., 51
Miller, James Hugh, Jr., 50
Minnick, Carlton Printess, Jr., 51
Mitchell, Douglas Farrell, 50
Mitchell, Glenn R., 50
Mitchell, John Francis, 50
Miya, Tom Saburo, 50
Miyamoto, Owen, 50
Modigliani, Lazzaro G., 50
Molloy, James B., 50
Monachino, Francis Leonard, 51
Monk, Art, 51
Monke, Edwin John, 50
Montgomery, John E., 51
Moor, Manly Eugene, Jr., 50
Moore, Ronald L., 50
Moore, Walter Bruce, 51
Moos, Eugene, 51
Moose, Richard M., 51
Morita, Akio, 49
Moritz, Charles Worthington, 50
Morr, Charles Vernon, 50
Morton, David, 49
Morton, Leland Clure, 51
Mouch, Frank Messman, 51
Moulder, James Edwin, 49
Mowatt, Wayne L., 51
Mulligan, William G(oeckel), 50
Mulvoy, Mark, 51
Murphy, Barth T., 50
Murphy, Robert C(harles), 51
Murphy, Thomas S., 50
Murray, Joseph Edward, 50
Murray, William, 50

**N**

Nasi, John Roderick, 50
Neary, Robert D., 50
Nesi, Vincent, 50
Neufeld, Edward Peter, 50
Neugarten, Bernice Levin, 51
Newton, John T., 50
Nieves, Joesphine, 51
Nokes, Mary Triplett, 50
Noland, Jon David, 50
Norris, Robert F., 50
Norris, T. H., 50
Nuchia, Samuel M., 51
Nurcombe, Barry, 51

**O**

O'Briain, Niall P., 50
O'Connor, Richard Donald, 51
Odegaard, Charles Edwin, 51
O'Hearn, John Howard, 50
Oishi, Satoshi, 51
O'Keefe, Joseph Thomas, 51
O'Keefe, Patrick, 50
O'Kelly, Bernard, 51
O'Leary, Robert W., 50
Oliver, Thomas K., Jr., 51
O'Malley, Shaun F., 50
Ondrejka, Ronald, 49
O'Neill, Arthur J., 49
Ontiveros, Steven, 51
Opitz, Joachim Ludwig, 50
Orozco, Raymond E., 51
Osborn, William C., 50
Oski, Frank Aram, 50
Owens, Lewis E., 51
Owens, William Arthur, 51
Ozanne, James Herbert, 50
Ozbun, Jim L., 51

**P**

Page, Austin P., 51
Painter, Joseph T., 49
Palmer, Lester Davis, 51
Parente, Emil J., 50
Parker, Gordon Rae, 50
Patten, John W., 51
Paul, Gabriel (Gabe Paul), 49
Pearson, Donna Sutherland, 51
Peebles, David L., 50
Penney, Alphonsus Liguori, 51
Pentland, Barbara Lally, 49
Perelman, Melvin, 50
Perkins, Donald S., 50
Peters, Frank Lewis, Jr., 51
Peterson, Esther, 51
Peterson, Lowell N., 50
Peterson, Roger Eric, 50
Petrocelli, Americo William, 50
Petry, Paul E., 50
Petterson, Donald K., 50
Pfeiffer, Carl E., 50
Philbin, Edward James, 50
Philip, Thomas Peter, 50
Phillips, Jack Carter, 51
Phillips, John F., 50
Phillips, Lawrence S., 50
Phillips, Stanley F, 50
Phillips, William George, 50
Phoenix, Paul Joseph, 50
Pinch, John G., 51
Pincus, George, 51
Pinotti, Joseph R., 50
Pirnie, Malcolm, Jr., 49
Pister, Karl Stark, 51
Plowman, R. Dean, 50
Plummer, Raymond J., 50
Porter, Donald James, 50
Poulos, Gary Peter, 51
Precourt, Lyman Arthur, 50
Prezio, Joseph Anthony, 51
Priestner, Edward Bernard, 50
Pritchard, Paul C(lement), 51
Prude, Elaine S., 51
Pye, Mort, 49

**Q**

Quinby, Charles Edward, Jr., 50

**R**

Radecki, Anthony Eugene, 50
Raff, Gilbert, 50
Rainear, Robert E., 50
Randall, William Theodore, 51
Rasco, Carol Hampton, 51
Reed, William G., Jr., 51
Reeds, Roger, 51
Reese, Errol Lynn, 51
Reichardt, Carl E., 49
Reid, Marion L., 50
Reitz, Elmer A., 50
Remington, Charles Bradford, 50
Remy, Ray, 51
Rentmeester, Lawrence Raymond, 50
Reppond, Jim D., 50
Resnik, Frank Edward, 50
Reznicek, Bernard William, 50
Ricart, Paul F., Sr., 50
Rice, Robert H., 51
Rich, Clayton, 51
Rimerman, Morton Walter, 49
Rimmereid, Arthur V., 51
Roberts, Elizabeth Porcher, 50
Robillard, Donald J., 51
Robinson, R. Larry, 50
Robinson, Sumner Martin, 51
Rodewig, John Stuart, 50
Rodman, Oliver, 51
Roeder, Myron A., 50
Roffey, Robert C., Jr., 50
Roger, Richard R., 50
Rollins, Henry Moak, 50
Rooney, John Joseph, 50
Rosen, Jerome, 49
Rosenberger, Walter Emerson, 49
Rotunno, Joseph Rocco, 50
Rowe, Richard Lloyd, 50
Rowland, Herbert Leslie, 50
Rummery, Terrance Edward, 50
Russell, Charles T., 50
Russell, George Albert, 51
Ryan, Buddy (James Ryan), 51

**S**

Sago, Paul Edward, 51
Saldich, Robert Joseph, 50
Samuels, Nathaniel, 50
Samuelson, Cecil O., 50
Sanchez, Robert Fortune, 51
Sands, Don William, 50
Sarnoff, William, 50
Sauer, Kenneth H., 51
Sauer, Robert C., 51
Sayers, Roger, 51
Sayler, J. W., Jr., 50
Schad, James L., 51
Schaeneman, Lewis G., Jr., 49
Schenk, George, 50
Schmidt, Albert Daniel, 49
Schmidt, Jack, 49
Schmidt, Peter, 50
Schnabel, Karl Ulrich, 49
Schofield, Seth Eugene, 50
Scholz, Garret Arthur, 50
Schorzman, Clarice B., 51
Schuenke, Donald John, 50
Schuiling, William E., 51
Schurman, Joseph Rathborne, 50
Schwindt, Robert F., 50
Scott, Charles R., 50
Scott, I. B., 49
Scribner, Belding Hibbard, 50
Segal, D. Robert, 50
Seidler, Norman Howard, 50
Sekely, George Frank, 50
Sella, George John, Jr., 50
Sellers, Wallace Osborne, 50
Sells, Harold E., 50
Seymour, Jon, 50
Shapero, Harold (Samuel), 51
Sharp, Edgar E., 50
Shaw, James, 51
Shea, Donald Francis, 51
Sheehan, Daniel Eugene, 49
Sheng, Jack Tse-liang, 51
Shields, Perry, 50
Shill, Victor Lamar, 51
Shirpser, Clara, 50
Shoults, Harold E., 50
Shur, Walter, 50
Siegel, Jack S., 50
Sigler, Andrew Clark, 51
Sigman, Eugene M., 49
Simmons, Samuel Lee, 50
Simon, David, 51
Simon, Richard A., 50
Sinner, George Albert, 51
Sipes, Larry L., 50
Siphron, Joseph Rider, 50
Siskind, Paul M., 50
Skeete, F. Herbert, 51
Skiles, Paul, 51
Skinner, Clifford, 50
Slater, Oliver Eugene, 51
Smilow, Michael A., 50
Smith, Charles, 51
Smith, Daniel R., 51
Smith, Donald William, 50
Smith, Hamilton Othanel, 51
Smith, James Forest, Jr., 50
Smith, Joe Mauk, 51
Smith, Karl, 50
Smith, Raymond Victor, 51
Smith, Richard D., 50
Smith, Richard D., 50
Sneider, Martin Karl, 50
Snyder, C(laude) Robert, 50
Snyder, Frank R., 50
Soren, Howard, 50
Sowers, George Frederick, 49
Speaks, Ruben Lee, 51
Speed, John Sackett, 51
Speicher, Opal, 51
Spencer, Geoffrey F., 51
Spencer, W. E., 50
Spina, Dennis J., 50
Stallings, Gene Clifton, 51
Stauffer, John H., 51
Stegemoeller, Harvey A., 51
Steinhardt, Ralph Gustav, Jr., 49
Stern, Theodore, 50
Stevens, Sinclair McKnight, 50
Stevens, William Louis, 51
Stinchcomb, Robert G., 50
Stith, Forrest Christopher, 51
Stockton, Thomas B., 51
Stofft, William A., 51
Stone, Warren R., 51
Strait, Bradley Justus, 50
Strickland, William James, 51
Strong, Warren Robert, 50
Stull, G. Alan, 51
Suckling, Robert McCleary, 51
Suggs, James C., 51
Sullivan, Donald, 51
Sullivan, John Joseph, 49
Sullivan, Patricia Clare, 50
Sullivan, Thomas John, 51
Sullivan, William James, 51
Swenson, Daniel Lee, 51
Swindells, David W., 49

**T**

Tait, John Edwin, 51
Tarnow, Robert L., 50
Tarr, Paul Cresson, III, 50
Taylor, Claude I., 50
Tcherkassky, Marianna Alexsavena, 51
Teague, Wayne, 51
Tempel, Thomas Robert, 51
Terenzio, Joseph Vincent, 50
Terranova, Paul, 50
Terrill, James E., 51
Terry, William E., 50
Thelen, Max, Jr., 51
Theodore, Nick Andrew, 51
Thomas, Dudley Breckinridge, 51
Thomas, Fred, 50
Thomas, Jack E., 50
Thomas, Lawrason Dale, 50
Thomas, Robert Dean, 51
Thomas, Roy Lee, 51
Thompson, Granville Berry, 51
Thomsen, Mark William, 51
Thurman, Ralph Holloway, 50
Timms, Leonard Joseph, Jr., 50
Tinghitella, Stephen, 50
Toller, William Robert, 51
Tomlinson, Kenneth Y., 51
Toney, Robert L., 50
Tortorella, Albert James, 50
Tourino, Ralph Gene, 50
Townsend, M. Wilbur, 50
Tracy, Philip R., 50
Tregde, Lorraine C., 50
Tretter, James Ray, 50
Triggiani, Leonard Vincent, 50
Trowbridge, Edward Kenneth, 50
Turbeville, Gus, 51
Turner, Jack Henry, 50
Turner, Stuart, 50

**U**

Utley, Edward H., 50

**V**

Valentini, Robert M., 50
Van Wagner, Bruce, 50
Verkuil, Paul Robert, 50
Vetack, Richard S., 50
Vittoria, Joseph V., 51
Voell, Richard Allen, 51

**W**

Wagoner, William Hampton, 51
Wakeman, Fred Joseph, 49
Waldman, Diane, 51
Walker, John Neal, 50
Walker, LeRoy, 51
Wallace, Robert Fergus, 50
Walmsley, Arthur Edward, 51
Walsh, Patrick J., 50
Walsh, Robert Francis, 50
Walter, James W., 50
Ward, Patrick J., 50
Warner, Homer R., 51
Warren, Gerald Lee, 51
Warshaw, Jerry, 50
Watkins, Stanley, 51
Watts, Heather, 51
Weaver, John B., 50
Webb, J. A., 50
Weber, David C(arter), 51
Weber, Fred J., 50
Weber, Ronald Gilbert, 51
Weber, Roy Edwin, 50
Weimer, Paul K(essler), 51
Weissenbuehler, Wayne, 51
Weitzel, Peter Andre, 51
Wells, Charles William, 50
Wendt, Henry, III, 50
Wenz, Richard L., 51
Werger, Paul Myron, 51
Werner, Charles George, 51
Whitaker, Meade, 50
White, Jerry Allen, 50
Whitehead, Lewis E, Jr., 50
Whitfield, Princess D., 51
Wilder, Margaret T., 50
Wilkes, Robert Edmond, 50
Wilkinson, John Burke, 51
Wilks, Ivor Gordon Hughes, 51
Willett, Robert Lee, 50
Williams, Larry Emmett, 50
Williams, Phillip L., 51
Williams, Richard David, III, 51
Williams, Walter W., 50
Williamson, Harwood Danford, 50
Willis, Carl Bertram, 51
Willis, John Randolph, 50
Wilson, James Milton, III, 50
Wilson, Marjorie Price, 51
Windle, Joseph Raymond, 51
Winslow, Robert Albert, 50
Woeste, John Theodore, 51
Woitach, Richard, 51
Wood, James Clarence, 50
Wood, Richard Donald, 50
Woodruff, Harrison D., Jr., 51
Woods, James Dudley, 51
Woodward, John Taylor, III, 50
Woodward, M. Cabell, Jr., 50
Wray, Marc Frederick, 50
Wuest, George W., 50
Wynn, William Harrison, 50

**Y**

Yamaoka, Seigen Haruo, 51
Yeakel, Joseph Hughes, 51
Young, Kenneth Laurence, 50
Youngblood, Ray Wilson, 50
Younger, Kenneth G., 50

**Z**

Zalokar, Robert H., 50
Zehfuss, Lawrence Thomas, 50
Zemke, (E.) Joseph, 50
Zerr, Emil Martin, 50
Zimmerman, Adam Hartley, 50
Zinbarg, Edward Donald, 50
Zinn, Dale W., 49
Zlatoper, Ronald Joseph, 51
Zoller, Richard Bernard, 50
Zoon, William K., 50

# Necrology

Biographees of the 51st Edition of *Who's Who in America* whose deaths have been reported to the editors prior to the close of compilation of this edition are listed below. For those individuals whose deaths were reported prior to July 1996, complete biographical information, including date of death and place of interment, can be found in Volume XI of *Who Was Who in America*.

**A**

Adamkiewicz, Vincent Witold
Agnew, Spiro Theodore
Ahlers, B. Orwin
Akers, Sheldon Buckingham, Jr.
Albrecht, Paul Abraham
Albright, Lois
Alford, John William
Alps, Glen Earl
Amerman, John Ellis
Andersen, Ernest Christopher
Anderson, Stephen Thomas
Archambault, Bennett
Arnstein, Sherry Phyllis
Aronovitz, Sidney M.
Arrol, John
Athnasios, Albert Kamel
Atteberry, William Duane
Auerback, Alfred
Austin, William Lamont
Aylward, Thomas James, Jr.

**B**

Babbage, Joan Dorothy
Backlund, Ralph Theodore
Bailar, John Christian, Jr.
Bain, Robert Addison
Baird, Russell Miller
Baker, Lillian L.
Balsley, Howard Lloyd
Baltzell, E(dward) Digby
Barkan, Philip
Barkhuus, Arne
Barringer, J(ohn) Paul
Barschall, Henry Herman
Barthelme, Donald
Barton, Evan Mansfield
Bartunek, Robert Richard
Batten, James Knox
Battin, James Franklin
Bayne, James Wilmer
Bean, Charles Palmer
Beckwith, Charles Emilio
Behrstock, Julian Robert
Bell, James Milton
Benjamin, Theodore Simon
Bernardin, Joseph Louis Cardinal
Bethea, Joseph Benjamin
Beyer, Karl Henry, Jr.
Biedenharn, Lawrence C., Jr.
Billings, Marland Pratt
Billings, William Dwight
Black, Theodore Michael, Sr.
Blackburn, John Lewis
Blackstone, Harry Bouton, Jr.
Boba, Imre
Bombeck, Erma Louise (Mrs. William Bombeck)
Bond, Calhoun
Booth, George Warren
Bowers, Grayson Hunter
Brackley, William Lowell
Brahtz, John Frederick Peel
Brantley, Oliver Wiley
Braymer, Marguerite Annetta
Bricker, Seymour (Murray)
Broccoli, Albert Romolo
Bronfman, Peter Frederick
Broughton, Carl L(ouis)
Brown, Beatrice
Brown, Frederick Harold
Brown, Louis Morris
Brown, Mary Eleanor
Browne, Millard Child
Bruno, Michael Peter
Bulbulian, Arthur H.
Bullard, Helen (Mrs. Joseph Marshall Krechniak)
Bullough, Bonnie
Bundy, Harvey Hollister
Bundy, McGeorge
Burgar, Ruby Rich
Burnham, Virginia Schroeder
Burris, Kathryn Ann
Butcher, James Walter
Butler, James Robert
Byrd, John Luther, Jr.

**C**

Cade, John A.

Caen, Herb
Callister, Marion Jones
Callmer, James Peter
Cameron, Eleanor
Capehart, Homer Earl, Jr.
Carnow, Bertram Warren
Carpenter, John Wilson, III
Carrigan, Richard Alfred
Casado, Antonio Francisco
Caverly, Gardner A.
Ceci, Anthony Thomas
Chancellor, John William
Chapman, G. Arnold
Cheng, Chung-Chieh
Cherry, Walter Lorain
Child, Arthur James Edward
Chiriaeff, Ludmilla Gorny
Cholakis, Constantine George
Christensen, Albert Sherman
Christine, Virginia Feld
Chronic, Byron John
Clark, Clayton
Clark, Roger Arthur
Clark, William Stratton
Clay, James Ray
Clayton, Preston Copeland
Cockerham, Columbus Clark
Coe, Ward Baldwin, Jr.
Cohen, Burton Jerome
Cohen, Hennig
Colbert, Claudette (Lily Chauchoin)
Colby, Jeffrey John
Coleman, Almand Rouse
Collier, Clifford Warthen, Jr.
Condit, Carl Wilbur
Conger, Kyril B.
Connelly, Donald Webb
Converti, Vincenzo
Cooke, Jack Kent
Cooper, Nelson Jess
Cooper, Paul
Cornuelle, Herbert Cumming
Cousteau, Jacques-Yves
Cox, Winston H.
Crain, Gertrude Ramsay
Crispin, Mildred Swift (Mrs. Frederick Eaton Crispin)
Crummer, Murray Thomas, Jr.
Cummins, Evelyn Freeman
Cuny, Frederick C.
Currie, Leonard James

**D**

Daciuk, Myron Michael
Dahl, Harry Waldemar
Daly, T(homas) F(rancis) Gilroy
Dart, Robert
Davidson, Dalwyn Robert
Davidson, Josephine F.
Davies, Martha Hill
Davis, Kingsley
Davis, Moshe
Davison, Roderic Hollett
Day, Eugene Davis, Sr.
Day, J(ames) Edward
Derge, David Richard
de Stwolinski, Gail Rounce Boyd
Dew, Jess Edward
Dianis, Walter Joseph
Dibble, George Smith, Jr.
Dicke, Robert Henry
Dickson, John R.
Dinger, Charlotte
Dishman, Leonard I.
Dixon, Jeane
Dobkin, Irving Bern
Dockstader, E. Stanley
Domar, Evsey David
Dorris, Michael Anthony
Dowd, Paul
Duffy, John
Dwass, Meyer

**E**

Easton, William Heyden
Efron, Samuel
Ehrensberger, Ray
Ekstrand, Bruce Rowland
El-Azghal, Hussein Ibrahim
Eliot, Robert Salim
Eliscu, Frank
Elliott, Byron Kauffman

Enfield, Franklin D.
Engelbrecht, Richard Stevens
Epley, Marion Jay
Epstein, Laura
Erickson, Frank William
Esslinger, Nell Daniel
Ewers, John Canfield

**F**

Fahim, Mostafa Safwat
Farrell, Eugene George
Farrior, Joseph Brown
Fawcett, Howard Hoy
Federici, Tony
Feist, Leonard
Fellers, James Davison
Ferguson, John Henry
Ferris, Benjamin Greeley, Jr.
Fest, Thorrel Brooks
Fey, Russell Conwell
Fialkow, Philip Jack
Fink, Eugene Richard
Finney, Ross Lee
Fleming, Russell, Jr.
Flood-Stoller, Joan Elizabeth
Foley, Daniel Edmund
Force, Roland Wynfield
Forkert, Clifford Arthur
Forkin, Thomas S.
Foss, Harlan Funston
Fowke, Edith Margaret Fulton
Fowler, Elizabeth Milton
Frame, James Sutherland
Fredricks, Anthony Theo
Freedberg, Sydney Joseph
Frost, Earle Wesley
Fuson, Wayne Edward

**G**

Gadbois, Richard A., Jr.
Gairdner, John Smith
Garner, Samuel Paul
Garver, Oliver Bailey, Jr.
Garvey, Robert Robey, Jr.
Gates, Larry
Gaull, Gerald Edward
Geis, Norman Winer
Gerber, Heinz Joseph
Gibbons, Ronald John
Giller, Robert Maynard
Gingras, Gustave
Ginsberg, Allen
Ginsberg, Edward
Gius, Julius
Glasser, Otto John
Gleason, Ralph Newton
Goff, James Albert
Goldstein, David Garson
Goodman, Miles
Gordon, Robert Edward
Gordon, Saul Wolfe
Graham, Robert Klark
Gray, Barry Sherman
Gray, Hope Diffenderfer
Green, David
Greene, David Mason
Greene, Glen Lee
Gregory, William Edgar
Gross, Paul
Grunwald, Arnold Paul

**H**

Haas, Walter J.
Hahn, Emily
Hall, Luther Egbert, Jr.
Hameister, Lavon Louetta
Hamilton, T. Earle
Hanson, Maurice Francis (Maury Hanson)
Hanson, Raymond Lester
Hardenburg, Robert Earle
Harlow, James Gindling, Jr.
Hartley, James Michaelis
Hartley, Richard Glendale
Hartmann, Hudson Thomas
Hartsough, Walter Douglas
Hay, Eloise Knapp
Hayden, Ralph Frederick
Hecker, Bruce Albert
Heckscher, August

Heintz, Jack
Helmsley, Harry B.
Hemsing, Albert E.
Hendel, Frank J(oseph)
Hendrickson, Robert Augustus
Herington, Cecil John
Hermaniuk, Maxim
Hershey, Alfred Day
Hexter, Jack H.
Heyborne, Robert Linford
Heyer, Paul Otto
Hicks, Marshall M.
Hill, John deKoven
Hoffman, Walter Edward
Hogan, Henry Leon, III
Holberg, Ralph Gans, Jr.
Holden, James Stuart
Hollywood, John Matthew
Holm, Robert Arthur
House, Charles Staver
Howrey, Edward F.
Hoyer, Harvey Conrad
Hubert, Bernard
Hudacek, George C.
Huggins, Charles Brenton
Hull, Edward Whaley Seabrook
Hungerford, Herbert Eugene
Hunt, Frank Bouldin
Hunt, Jacob Tate

**I**

Idler, David Richard
Igasaki, Masao, Jr.
Ilutovich, Leon
Irsay, Robert

**J**

Jackson, Robert John
Jacob, Herbert
Jacobs, Bernard B.
Jacobs, Helen Hull
James, Earl Eugene, Jr.
Jenkins, Lawrence Eugene
Jennings, Burgess Hill
Johnson, Charles Edgar
Johnson, Ferd
Johnson, Marvin Melrose
Johnson, Norman
Johnson, U. Alexis
Jones, Catherine Ann
Jones, Lillie Agnes
Jones, Mary Ellen
Jones, Roxanne Harper
Jordan, Ellen Rausen

**K**

Kahn, Herman Bernard
Kaitschuk, John Paul
Kalamaros, Edward Nicholas
Kalmus, Allan Henry
Karaba, Frank Andrew
Kaus, Otto Michael
Keating, Larry Grant
Keeney, Arthur Hail
Keith, Brian Michael
Kelley, Noble Henry
Kemelman, Harry
Kent, Frederick Heber
Kern, Harry Frederick
Kerr, Walter F.
Key, Kerim Kami
Kilham, Walter H., Jr.
Klehs, Henry John Wilhelm
Kloss, Gene (Alice Geneva Glasier)
Kolodner, Ignace Izaak
Koopman, Richard, J.W.
Krainik, Ardis
Kramer, Aaron
Krasner, Oscar Jay
Kresh, Paul
Krist, Peter Christopher
Krueger, Robert Blair
Krusen, Henry Stanley
Kubly, Herbert
Kugelman, Irwin Jay
Kuhner, Arlene Elizabeth
Kuralt, Charles Bishop
Kuttner, Stephan George
Kuvshinoff, Nicolai Vasily

**L**

L'abbé, Gerrit Karel
Laird, Alan Douglas Kenneth
Lang, H. Jack
Larkin, Peter Anthony
Layton, William Isaac
Leary, Timothy
Leber, Lester
Lee, William States
Lehman, Robert Nathan
LeMoyne, Irve Charles
Leonard, Sheldon
Lescaze, Lee Adrien
Leva, Marx
Levi, Julian Hirsch
Levin, Paul Joseph
Levine, Sol
Lewis, Irving James
Lewis, Welbourne Walker, Jr.
Liberman, Ira L.
Lilja, Sven Ingvar
Lillich, Richard B.
Loeb, Frances Lehman
Loeb, John Langeloth
Loew, Ralph William
Loferski, Joseph John
López-Morillas, Juan
Low, Philip Funk
Lowry, Oliver Howe
Ludwig, Patric E.
Luening, Otto
Luhring, John William
Lukas, J. Anthony

**M**

Magness, Bob John
Mahoney, J. Daniel
Maisel, Michael
Malone, James L.
Maloney, John Frederick
Mandino, Og
Manners, Robert Alan
Margolis, Leo
Markiewicz, Alfred John
Marshall, J(ulian) Howard, Jr.
Marteka, Vincent James, Jr.
Martin, Edgar Thomas
Mason, David Dickenson
Masoner, Paul Henry
Mastroianni, Marcello
Mather, Allen Frederick
Maxwell, John Raymond
McBurney, George William
McCallum, Kenneth James
Mc Clelland, James Craig
Mc Closkey, Robert James
Mc Connell, John Wilkinson
McCusker, Mary Lauretta
McGarry, Eugene L.
McGinnis, Robert Campbell
McGinty, John
McKee, Penelope Melna
McKinley, (Jennifer Carolyn) Robin
Mc Laren, Malcolm Grant, IV
McQuillen, Harry A.
Menius, Arthur Clayton, Jr.
Merrill, Charles Merton
Meyer, Charles Appleton
Miccio, Joseph V.
Michels, Eugene
Miller, Tevie
Milsten, David Randolph
Minnich, Virginia
Mitchell, Joseph (Quincy)
Mitchum, Robert Charles Durman (Charles Mitchum)
Mitford, Jessica
Mongan, Agnes
Monroe, William Smith
Montgomery, Donald Joseph
Morrell, Frank
Morrin, Virginia White
Morris, Kenneth Baker
Morris, Robert
Motherway, Joseph Edward
Mueller, Stephan
Muir, John Scott
Mulcahy, John J.
Mundel, Marvin Everett
Muth, George Edward
Myers, Al

**N**

Namias, Jerome
Nash, Bradley DeLamater
Nelson, Raymond John
Nichols, Robert E(dmund)
Nichols, Robert Lee
Nies, Helen Wilson
Nisbet, Robert A.
Nothmann, Gerhard Adolf

**O**

O'Connor, Lawrence Joseph, Jr.
Oehmler, George Courtland
Offner, Hebe Zonchello
Olney, Peter Butler, Jr.
Olson, Donald Ernest
Omori, Morio
Omura, James Matsumoto
Ornstein-Galicia, Jacob Leonard (Jack Ornstein-Galicia)
Osborn, Leslie Andrewartha
Ostenso, Ned Allen
Ostheimer, Gerard William
Oughton, James Henry, Jr.
Owen, William Harold, Jr.
Oxley, John Thurman

**P**

Packard, Vance Oakley
Parcher, James Vernon
Parker, Edna G.
Parker, Pierson
Parrish, Alvin Edward
Parsons, Frederick Ambrose
Parsons, James Jerome
Parsons, Keith I.
Patai, Raphael
Patton, Wendell Melton, Jr.
Paul, Martin Ambrose
Pearson, Louise Mary
Pearson, Willard
Perret, Maurice Edmond
Petering, Janice Faye
Pfriem, Bernard Aldine
Pickard, Franklin George Thomas
Pineda, Marianna
Pipal, George Henry
Pliskin, Marvin Robert
Pogue, Forrest Carlisle
Pollard, David Edward
Poorman, Paul Arthur
Popovich, Peter Stephen
Poppe, Fred Christoph
Potter, Hamilton Fish, Jr.
Powe, Ralph Elward
Powell, Allen Royal
Powell, Robert
Pritchett, Sir Victor Sawdon
Pritikin, Roland I.
Puchta, Charles George
Purcell, Edward Mills
Purves, Alan Carroll

**R**

Radnay, Paul Andrew
Rains, Harry Hano
Rand, Paul
Reagan, Reginald Lee
Reese, John Terence
Reeves, Robert Grier LeFevre
Reich, Jack Egan
Reistle, Carl Ernest, Jr.
Rey, Margret Elizabeth
Rhodes, Rondell Horace
Richey, Charles Robert
Ridder, Eric
Riebe, Norman John
Riley, Joseph Harry
Rodman, Harry Eugene
Roehl, Joseph E.
Rosberg, Carl Gustaf
Rose, Rubye Blevins (Patsy Montana)
Rosensweig, Stanley Harold
Rosenthal, Macha Louis
Rossberg, Robert Howard
Rownd, Robert Harvey
Royce, Mary Weller Sa'id
Royko, Mike
Royster, Vermont (Connecticut)
Rozelle, Pete (Alvin Ray Rozelle)
Rupp, John Norris
Ruppe, Loret Miller
Russell, Josiah Cox

**S**

Sagan, Carl Edward
Salisbury, Franklin Cary
Saltarelli, Eugene A.
Sament, Sidney
Samers, Bernard Norman
Sandefur, Thomas Edwin, Jr.
Sanford, Jay Philip
Saperston, Howard Truman, Sr.
Scanlan, John Joseph
Schiller, Alfred George
Schirmer, Henry William
Schlesinger, David Harvey
Schlesinger, Ruth Hirschland
Schmidt, Stephen Robert
Schomaker, Verner
Schorre, Louis Charles, Jr.
Schuknecht, Harold Frederick
Schulman, Eveline Dolin
Schwarting, Arthur Ernest
Schwebel, Andrew I.
Scott, Henry Lawrence
Scott, James White
Scudder, David Benjamin
Seager, Floyd Williams
Sedwick, (Benjamin) Frank
Sengstacke, John Herman Henry
Senkier, Robert Joseph
Serra-Badue, Daniel Francisco
Seth, Oliver
Shanker, Albert
Shea, John Martin, Jr.
Shepard, Paul Howe
Sherman, John Clinton
Short, Byron Elliott
Skelton, John Edward
Skewes-Cox, Bennet

Smith, Hallett Darius
Smith, Leon Polk
Smith, Russell L.
Solursh, Michael
Spencer, Harry Chadwick
Squier, Leslie Hamilton
Stabile, Rose K. Towne (Mrs. Fred Stabile)
Stafford, Josephine Howard
Standaert, Frank George
Stanley, Justin Armstrong
Stenehjem, Leland Manford
Stewart, James Maitland
Stiff, John Sterling
Stillman, George
Stockwell, Richard E.
Stone, James Michael
Straus, Kenneth Hollister
Suhrbier, Klaus Rudolf
Summerfield, Martin
Surwill, Benedict Joseph, Jr.
Szathmáry, Louis István, II

**T**

Takayama, Akira
Taylor, Millard Benjamin
Teichert, Curt
Tejeda, Frank
Temmer, Georges Maxime
Teschner, Richard Rewa
Thimann, Kenneth Vivian
Thompson, Edward Kramer
Thompson, Tina Lewis Chryar
Thornton, J. Edward
Thornton, William James, Jr.
Tierney, John James
Tilbury, Roger Graydon
Tobin, John Everard
Tombaugh, Clyde William
Torre, Douglas Paul
Tousey, Richard
Trilling, Diana
Trueman, Walter
Trustman, Benjamin Arthur
Tsongas, Paul Efthemios
Tull, Donald Stanley
Turnbull, Fred Gerdes
Turrell, Eugene Snow

**U**

Ullrich, John Frederick

**V**

Van Metre, Thomas Earle
Verduin, Jacob
Verity, George Luther
Versace, Gianni
Vuckovich, Dragomir Michael

**W**

Wagman, Frederick Herbert
Wald, George
Wales, Harold Webster
Wall, Fred Willard
Wallace, Jane Young (Mrs. Donald H. Wallace)
Wallingford, Dana R(io)
Walters, Everett
Ward, Wallace Dixon
Ware, Marcus John
Warren, Kenneth S.
Warren, William Gerald
Watson, Billy
Weatherford, Willis Duke, Jr.
Weiss, Ira Francis
Weiss, Jerome Paul
Westfall, Richard Samuel
Wetzel, Carroll Robbins
Wheeler, Harold Alden
White, Jesse Marc
White, Merit Penniman
Wilbur, James Benjamin, III
Wilentz, Robert Nathan
Wilhelm, Harley A(lmey)
Willcox, Frederick Preston
Williams, Tony
Williford, Richard Allen
Winokur, George
Wissner, John Karl
Wixon, Rufus
Wolf, Lewis Isidore
Wolfman Jack, Robert Weston Smith)
Wood, Evelyn Nielsen
Woodman, William E.
Woodring, Margaret Daley
Worner, Lloyd Edson

**Y**

Yamabe, Shigeru
Yerby, Alonzo Smythe
Yoder, Amos
Young, Richard Stuart
Young, Thomas Daniel
Youngblood, J. Craig

**Z**

Zerman, Maxine Loraine
Ziff, Lloyd Richard
Zimmerman, Robert Earl
Zinnemann, Fred
Zipper, Herbert